Tolley's Orange Tax Handbook 2009–10

36th Edition

The legislation relating to—

value added tax

stamp taxes

insurance premium tax

landfill tax

aggregates levy

climate change levy

CONSULTANT EDITOR

Roderick Cordara QC SC(NSW) MA(Cantab) FIIT

Barrister

Essex Court Chambers

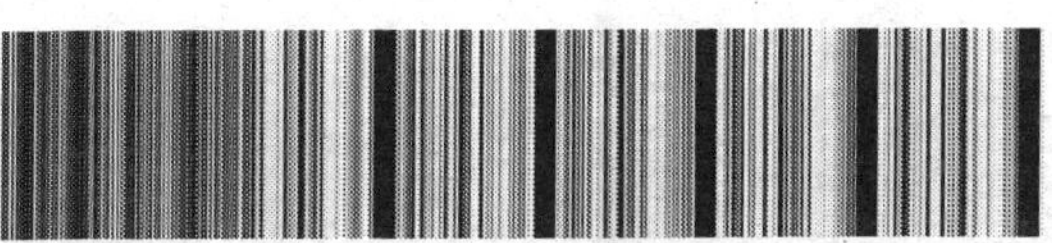

Members of the LexisNexis Group worldwide

United Kingdom	LexisNexis Butterworths, a Division of Reed Elsevier (UK) Ltd, Halsbury House, 35 Chancery Lane, London, WC2A 1EL, and London House, 20–22 East London Street, Edinburgh EH7 4BQ
Australia	LexisNexis Butterworths, CHATSWOOD, New South Wales
Austria	LexisNexis Verlag ARD Orac GmbH & Co KG, VIENNA
Canada	LexisNexis Butterworths, MARKHAM, Ontario
Czech Republic	Nakladatelství Orac sro, PRAGUE
France	LexisNexis SA, PARIS
Germany	LexisNexis Deutschland GmbH, FRANKFURT and MUNSTER
Hong Kong	LexisNexis Butterworths, HONG KONG
Hungary	HVG-Orac, BUDAPEST
India	LexisNexis Butterworths, NEW DELHI
Italy	Giuffrè Editore, MILAN
Malaysia	Malayan Law Journal Sdn Bhd, KUALA LUMPUR
New Zealand	LexisNexis Butterworths, WELLINGTON
Poland	Wydawnictwo Prawnicze LexisNexis, WARSAW
Singapore	LexisNexis Butterworths, SINGAPORE
South Africa	LexisNexis Butterworths, DURBAN
Switzerland	Stämpfli Verlag AG, BERNE
USA	LexisNexis, DAYTON, Ohio

First published in 1976

Published by LexisNexis Butterworths

A CIP Catalogue record for this book is available from the British Library.

ISBN 9781405742306

Typeset by Letterpart Ltd, Reigate, Surrey

Printed in the UK by CPI William Clowes Beccles NR34 7TL

Visit LexisNexis Butterworths at www.lexisnexis.co.uk or email the editorial department on: yellowandorange@lexisnexis.co.uk

CONTENTS

Detailed contents lists are provided at the beginning of each subject group.

Tolley's Orange Tax Handbook 2009–10

Finance Act 2009—key dates

Budget Day	22 April 2009
Finance Act 2009 passed	21 July 2009

Publishers' Note

Tax legislation

Tolley's Yellow and Orange Tax Handbooks are indispensable to the practitioner who needs to refer to the tax legislation as currently in force. Each year the legislation is augmented and amended by one or more Finance Acts and lesser amendments are made from time to time by a variety of other statutes. An increasing amount of the detailed regulation of taxes is contained in statutory instruments—orders or regulations—which are also amended frequently. The Handbooks are normally published annually. They contain the text of the relevant statutes and statutory instruments as amended together with current texts of extra-statutory concessions, statements of practice, published official interpretations and decisions and selected press releases.

The Orange Tax Handbook covers value added tax, stamp taxes, insurance premium tax, landfill tax, aggregates levy and climate change levy. Its companion volume, the Yellow Tax Handbook, covers income tax, corporation tax, capital gains tax, inheritance tax, National Insurance contributions, tax credits and petroleum revenue tax.

This edition of the Orange Tax Handbook contains texts as they applied at 21 July 2009. It does not take account of changes made after that date.

Organisation

The contents of this Handbook are arranged in separate sections for each of the taxes covered. The start of each section is marked with a grey tab on the front edge of the book. The texts in each section are arranged in the following order—UK statutes, statutory instruments, EC legislation for VAT, extra-statutory concessions, statements of practice, VAT Notices with the force of law, press releases (published by HMRC, and extracts from Hansard). Within each of those categories, items are printed in chronological order. To enable individual items to be located quickly, an item reference is printed in bold type in the outside top corner of each page.

Provisions relating to National Insurance contributions which were formerly in this Handbook have been moved into the Yellow Tax Handbook. This is due to the transfer of functions from the DSS to HMRC in relation to National Insurance contributions matters. It also reflects practitioners' needs, particularly those dealing with PAYE who want to see income tax and NICs together. Inheritance Tax and Petroleum Revenue Tax are located in the Yellow Tax Handbook as they are direct taxes and therefore more appropriately positioned there.

Amendments and modifications

Amendments to existing legislation which take effect during the calendar year are made in the text of the amended legislation. An **Amendment** note under the amended text indicates the authority for the amendment and, where appropriate, the timing of its commencement. All relevant provisions of the current Finance Act are reproduced in full but otherwise the text of provisions which merely amend other Acts is generally omitted and replaced by a note indicating the legislation amended.

Sometimes the effect of a provision is modified by a later Act or statutory instrument but the scope of the modification is limited in some way so that the original provision remains generally unaffected. In this case, the original provision is printed without modification but a **Cross reference** to the later Act or statutory instrument is provided, see below.

Prospective amendments

The Handbook sets out the text of the legislation as it applies for the current tax year. Amendments which are stated to come into effect on a specified date after the end of that year are therefore strictly outside the scope of the current edition and are not made in the text of the Act affected. However, a **Prospective amendment** note is provided to indicate the existence of the amendment and the provision making the prospective amendment is retained in full in successive editions of the Handbook until the amendment becomes effective.

Retrospective amendments

For the tax legislation as it applied in an earlier year, reference should be made to the appropriate earlier edition of the Orange Tax Handbook. Care must be taken, however, to ensure that amendments made retrospectively are not overlooked. A list of provisions affected by amendments made retrospectively by this year's Finance Act is provided at the front of this edition. Similar lists are provided for amendments made by each year's Finance Act(s) in the corresponding earlier editions.

Repealed legislation

Generally, repealed legislation is omitted. Exceptionally, where it may be necessary to refer to the repealed text in dealing with tax liabilities for the current year, the text is retained and is printed in italics.

Defined terms

Where a word or phrase used in the main Acts has been defined elsewhere, a cross-reference to the definition is provided in a **Definitions** note below the text.

Cross references

The notes under each section or Schedule paragraph include references to commentary in Butterworths Tax Services and to relevant statutory provisions, statutory instruments, published HMRC practice and other published or unpublished official and professional bodies' views. These are presented under the following headings—

Commentary—refers to paragraph numbers for commentary relating to the provision in *De Voil Indirect Tax Service* for VAT.

Concession; Statement of Practice; HMRC Interpretations and Decisions—refer to published official practice separately reproduced in the same section of this Handbook.

Press releases etc—refer to published or unpublished official and professional bodies' views reproduced in this Handbook or BDO Stoy Hayward's Orange Tax Guide.

Cross reference—refers to provisions in the same or another Act or statutory instrument.

Simon's Tax Cases—provides references to the most significant cases reported in *Simon's Tax Cases* and *Simon's Tax Cases Special Commissioners' Decisions*. Cases decided on the previous corresponding statutory provision are marked by an asterisk.

Note—introduces other references not within any of the above categories.

July 2009

LIST OF ABBREVIATIONS

art	=	article
CA 1985	=	Companies Act 1985
CAA 2001	=	Capital Allowances Act 2001
CCL	=	Climate change levy
CED(GR)A 1979	=	Customs & Excise Duties (General Relief) Act 1979
CEMA 1979	=	Customs & Excise Management Act 1979
CGTA 1979	=	Capital Gains Tax Act 1979
Ch	=	Chapter(s) of statute
col	=	column(s)
Comrs	=	Commissioners
CPA 1947	=	Crown Proceedings Act 1947
CTA 2009	=	Corporation Tax Act 2009
DLT	=	Development land tax
edn	=	edition
EEC	=	European Economic Community
ESC	=	Extra-statutory concession
FA	=	Finance Act
F(No 2)A	=	Finance (No 2) Act
Gp	=	Group (VAT legislation)
HA 1980	=	Highways Act 1980
HM	=	Her Majesty
HMRC	=	Her Majesty's Revenue & Customs
HMSO	=	Her Majesty's Stationery Office
IA	=	Interpretation Act
ICAEW	=	Institute of Chartered Accountants in England & Wales
IOM	=	Isle of Man
IoT	=	Institute of Taxation
IPT	=	Insurance Premium Tax
IR	=	Inland Revenue
LIFFE	=	London International Financial Futures and Options Exchange
LPA 1925	=	Law of Property Act 1925
NB	=	(nota bene) note well
NHA 1980	=	National Heritage Act 1980
OJ	=	Official Journal of the European Communities
para	=	paragraph(s)
PAYE	=	Pay as you earn
PCTA 1968	=	Provisional Collection of Taxes Act 1968
PEP	=	Personal equity plan
PET	=	Potentially exempt transfer
PR	=	Press releases
Pt	=	Part(s)
r	=	rule(s)
RA 1898	=	Revenue Act 1898
reg	=	regulations
RD	=	Revenue decisions
Regulations	=	EC Regulations
RI	=	Revenue interpretation
s	=	section(s)
SA 1891	=	Stamp Act 1891
Sch	=	Schedule
SDMA 1891	=	Stamp Duties Management Act 1891
SDLT	=	Stamp duty land tax
SDRT	=	Stamp duty reserve tax
SD(TP)A 1992	=	Stamp Duty (Temporary Provisions) Act 1992
SI	=	Statutory Instrument

SP	=	Statement of Practice
STC	=	Simon's Tax Cases
STI	=	Simon's Tax Intelligence
sub-para	=	sub-paragraph(s)
sub-s	=	sub-section(s)
TA	=	Income and Corporation Taxes Act
Taxes Act 1970	=	Income and Corporation Taxes Act 1970
Taxes Act 1988	=	Income and Corporation Taxes Act 1988
TMA 1970	=	Taxes Management Act 1970
VAT	=	Value added tax
VATA 1994	=	Value Added Tax Act 1994
vol	=	volume(s)

RETROSPECTIVE LEGISLATION

Subscribers are advised to retain Handbooks for earlier years to use when dealing with tax for those years. Each Handbook shows the legislation operative for the corresponding year so far as it was known at the time of the passing of the Finance Act of that year. In view of the increasing practice of passing tax legislation with retrospective effect, it is necessary when dealing with past years to consider whether the provisions have been affected or amended by subsequent legislation.

Finance Act 2009 does not make retrospective provision in relation to existing legislation in the Orange Book 2009–10.

VALUE ADDED TAX

CONTENTS

PROVISIONAL COLLECTION OF TAXES ACT 1968

(1968 Chapter 2)

An Act to consolidate the Provisional Collection of Taxes Act 1913 and certain other enactments relating to the provisional collection of taxes or matters connected therewith.

[1st February 1968]

1 Temporary statutory effect of House of Commons resolutions affecting …, [value added tax][1], …

(1) This section applies only to …, [value added tax][1], …

[(1A) …][2]

(2) Subject to that, and to the provisions of subsections (4) to (8) below, where the House of Commons passes a resolution which—

(*a*) provides for the renewal for a further period of any tax in force or imposed during the previous financial year (whether at the same or a different rate, and whether with or without modifications) or for the variation or abolition of any existing tax, and

(*b*) contains a declaration that it is expedient in the public interest that the resolution should have statutory effect under the provisions of this Act,

the resolution shall, for the period specified in the next following subsection, have statutory effect as if contained in an Act of Parliament and, where the resolution provides for the renewal of a tax, all enactments which were in force with reference to that tax as last imposed by Act of Parliament shall during that period have full force and effect with respect to the tax as renewed by the resolution.

In this section references to the renewal of a tax include references to its reimposition, and references to the abolition of a tax include references to its repeal.

(3) The said period is—

(*a*) in the case of a resolution passed in [November or December][3] in any year, one expiring with [5th May in the next calendar year][4];

[(*aa*) in the case of a resolution passed in February or March in any year, one expiring with 5th August in the same calendar year; and][7]

(*b*) in the case of any other resolution, one expiring at the end of four months after the date on which it is expressed to take effect or, if no such date is expressed, after the date on which it is passed.

(4) A resolution shall cease to have statutory effect under this section unless within the next [thirty][5] days on which the House of Commons sits after the day on which the resolution is passed—

(*a*) a Bill renewing, varying or, as the case may be, abolishing the tax is read a second time by the House, or

(*b*) a Bill is amended by the House [in Committee or on Report, or by any [Public Bill Committee][8] of the House][6] so as to include provision for the renewal, variation or, as the case may be, abolition of the tax.

(5) A resolution shall also cease to have statutory effect under this section if—

(*a*) the provisions giving effect to it are rejected during the passage of the Bill containing them through the House, or

(*b*) an Act comes into operation renewing, varying or, as the case may be, abolishing the tax, or

(*c*) Parliament is dissolved or prorogued.

(6) Where, in the case of a resolution providing for the renewal or variation of a tax, the resolution ceases to have statutory effect by virtue of subsection (4) or (5) above, or the period specified in subsection (3) above terminates, before an Act comes into operation renewing or varying the tax, any money paid in pursuance of the resolution shall be repaid or made good, and any deduction made in pursuance of the resolution shall be deemed to be an unauthorised deduction.

(7) Where any tax as renewed or varied by a resolution is modified by the Act renewing or varying the tax, any money paid in pursuance of the resolution which would not have been payable under the new conditions affecting the tax shall be repaid or made good, and any deduction made in pursuance of the resolution shall, so far as it would not have been authorised under the new conditions affecting the tax, be deemed to be an unauthorised deduction.

(8) When during any session a resolution has had statutory effect under this section, statutory effect shall not be again given under this section in the same session to the same resolution or to a resolution having the same effect.

Commentary—*De Voil Indirect Tax Service* **V1.131**.

Note—Words and any subsection not relevant for the purposes of VAT have been omitted.

Cross references—See VATA 1994 s 90(1) (VAT paid by virtue of a resolution under this Act becoming repayable under sub-ss (6) or (7) above).

Amendments—[1] Words in the heading and in sub-s (1) added by virtue of VATA 1983 Sch 9 para 1.

[2] Sub-s (1A) repealed by FA 1993 ss 205(1), (3), 213, Sch 23 Pt VI, in relation to resolutions passed after 27 July 1993.

[3] Words in sub-s (3)(*a*) substituted by FA 1993 s 205 in relation to resolutions passed after 27 July 1993.
[4] Words in sub-s (3)(*a*) substituted by FA 1993 s 205 in relation to resolutions passed after 27 July 1993.
[5] Word in sub-s (4) substituted by FA 1993 s 205 in relation to resolutions passed after 27 July 1993.
[6] Words in sub-s (4)(*b*) inserted by FA 1968 s 60.
[7] Words in sub-s (3) inserted by F(No 2)A 1997 s 50 in relation to resolutions passed after 31 July 1997.
[8] Words in sub-s (4)(*b*) substituted by FA 2007 s 112(1) with effect from 19 July 2007.

5 House of Commons resolution giving provisional effect to motions affecting taxation

(1) This section shall apply if the House of Commons resolves that provisional statutory effect shall be given to one or more motions to be moved by the Chancellor of the Exchequer, or some other Minister, and which, if agreed to by the House, would be resolutions—

(*a*) to which statutory effect could be given under section 1 of this Act, or

(*b*), (*c*) …[1]

(2) Subject to subsection (3) below, on the passing of the resolution under subsection (1) above, sections 1… of this Act, … shall apply as if each motion to which the resolution applies had then been agreed to by a resolution of the House.

(3) Subsection (2) above shall cease to apply to a motion if that motion, or a motion containing the same proposals with modifications, is not agreed to by a resolution of the House (in this section referred to as "a confirmatory resolution") within the next ten days on which the House sits after the resolution under subsection (1) above is passed, and, if it ceases to apply, all such adjustments, whether by way of discharge or repayment of tax, or discharge of security, or otherwise, shall be made as may be necessary to restore the position to what it would have been if subsection (2) above had never applied to that motion, and to make good any deductions which have become unauthorised deductions.

(4) …

Commentary—*De Voil Indirect Tax Service* **V1.131**.
Note—Sub-ss (1)(*b*), (4) and words omitted from sub-s (2) are not relevant to VAT.
Cross references—See VATA 1994 s 90(1) (VAT paid by virtue of a resolution under this Act becoming repayable under sub-s (3) above).
Amendments—[1] Sub-s (1)(*c*) and the word "or" immediately preceding it repealed by FA 1993 ss 205(6), (7), 213, Sch 23 Pt VI, in relation to resolutions passed after 27 July 1993.

6 Short title, repeals and saving as respects Northern Ireland

(1) This Act may be cited as the Provisional Collection of Taxes Act 1968.

(2) …

(3) …[1]

Note—Sub-s (2) repeals enactments specified in Schedule.
Amendments—[1] Sub-s (3) repealed by Northern Ireland Constitution Act 1973 s 41(1)(*a*), Sch 6 Pt 1, with effect from 18 July 1973.

INTERPRETATION ACT 1978

(1978 Chapter 30)

ARRANGEMENT OF SECTIONS

General provisions as to enactment and operation

Interpretation and construction

Statutory powers and duties

Repealing enactments

An Act to consolidate the Interpretation Act 1889 and certain other enactments relating to the construction and operation of Acts of Parliament and other instruments, with amendments to give effect to recommendations of the Law Commission and the Scottish Law Commission.

[20th July 1978]

Note—Only so much of this Act is printed as is likely to be required for the purposes of this Handbook.

General provisions as to enactment and operation

1 Words of enactment

Every section of an Act takes effect as a substantive enactment without introductory words.

3 Judicial notice

Every Act is a public Act to be judicially noticed as such, unless the contrary is expressly provided by the Act.

4 Time of commencement

An Act or provision of an Act comes into force—

(*a*) where provision is made for it to come into force on a particular day, at the beginning of that day;
(*b*) where no provision is made for its coming into force, at the beginning of the day on which the Act receives the Royal Assent.

Interpretation and construction

5 Definitions

In any Act, unless the contrary intention appears, words and expressions listed in Schedule 1 to this Act are to be construed according to that Schedule.

Simon's Tax Cases—*IRC v Clydebridge Properties Ltd* [1980] STC 68*; *IRC v Frampton (Trustees of the Worthing Rugby Football Club)* [1985] STC 186*; *Starke and anor (executors of Brown decd) v IRC* [1995] STC 689.

6 Gender and number

In any Act, unless the contrary intention appears,—

(*a*) words importing the masculine gender include the feminine;
(*b*) words importing the feminine gender include the masculine;
(*c*) words in the singular include the plural and words in the plural include the singular.

Simon's Tax Cases—*Floor v Davis* [1976] STC 475*.

7 References to service by post

Where an Act authorises or requires any document to be served by post (whether the expression "serve" or the expression "give" or "send" or any other expression is used) then, unless the contrary intention appears, the service is deemed to be effected by properly addressing, pre-paying and posting a letter containing the document and, unless the contrary is proved, to have been effected at the time at which the letter would be delivered in the ordinary course of post.

Simon's Tax Cases—*Wing Hung Lai v Bale* [1999] STC (SCD) 238.

10 References to the Sovereign

In any Act a reference to the Sovereign reigning at the time of the passing of the Act is to be construed, unless the contrary intention appears, as a reference to the Sovereign for the time being.

11 Construction of subordinate legislation

Where an Act confers power to make subordinate legislation, expressions used in that legislation have, unless the contrary intention appears, the meaning which they bear in the Act.

Statutory powers and duties

12 Continuity of powers and duties

(1) Where an Act confers a power or imposes a duty it is implied, unless the contrary intention appears, that the power may be exercised, or the duty is to be performed, from time to time as occasion requires.

(2) Where an Act confers a power or imposes a duty on the holder of an office as such, it is implied, unless the contrary intention appears, that the power may be exercised, or the duty is to be performed, by the holder for the time being of the office.

13 Anticipatory exercise of powers

Where an Act which (or any provision of which) does not come into force immediately on its passing confers power to make subordinate legislation, or to make appointments, give notices, prescribe forms or do any other thing for the purposes of the Act, then, unless the contrary intention appears, the power may be exercised, and any instrument made thereunder may be made so as to come into force, at any time after the passing of the Act so far as may be necessary or expedient for the purpose—

(*a*) of bringing the Act or any provision of the Act into force; or

(*b*) of giving full effect to the Act or any such provision at or after the time when it comes into force.

14 Implied power to amend

Where an Act confers power to make—

(*a*) rules, regulations or bylaws; or

(*b*) Orders in Council, orders or other subordinate legislation to be made by statutory instrument,

it implies, unless the contrary intention appears, a power, exercisable in the same manner and subject to the same conditions or limitations, to revoke, amend or re-enact any instrument made under the power.

Repealing enactments

15 Repeal of repeal

Where an Act repeals a repealing enactment, the repeal does not revive any enactment previously repealed unless words are added reviving it.

16 General savings

(1) Without prejudice to section 15, where an Act repeals an enactment, the repeal does not, unless the contrary intention appears,—

(*a*) revive anything not in force or existing at the time at which the repeal takes effect;

(*b*) affect the previous operation of the enactment repealed or anything duly done or suffered under that enactment;

(*c*) affect any right, privilege, obligation or liability acquired, accrued or incurred under that enactment;

(*d*) affect any penalty, forfeiture or punishment incurred in respect of any offence committed against that enactment;

(*e*) affect any investigation, legal proceeding or remedy in respect of any such right, privilege, obligation, liability, penalty, forfeiture or punishment;

and any such investigation, legal proceeding or remedy may be instituted, continued or enforced, and any such penalty, forfeiture or punishment may be imposed, as if the repealing Act had not been passed.

(2) This section applies to the expiry of a temporary enactment as if it were repealed by an Act.

17 Repeal and re-enactment

(1) Where an Act repeals a previous enactment and substitutes provisions for the enactment repealed, the repealed enactment remains in force until the substituted provisions come into force.

(2) Where an Act repeals and re-enacts, with or without modification, a previous enactment then, unless the contrary intention appears,—

(*a*) any reference in any other enactment to the enactment so repealed shall be construed as a reference to the provision re-enacted;

(*b*) in so far as any subordinate legislation made or other thing done under the enactment so repealed, or having effect as if so made or done, could have been made or done under the provision re-enacted, it shall have effect as if made or done under that provision.

Miscellaneous

18 Duplicated offences

Where an act or omission constitutes an offence under two or more Acts, or both under an Act and at common law, the offender shall, unless the contrary intention appears, be liable to be prosecuted and punished under either or any of those Acts or at common law, but shall not be liable to be punished more than once for the same offence.

19 Citation of other Acts

(1) Where an Act cites another Act by year, statute, session or chapter, or a section or other portion of another Act by number or letter, the reference shall, unless the contrary intention appears, be read as referring—

(*a*) in the case of Acts included in any revised edition of the statutes printed by authority, to that edition;

(*b*) in the case of Acts not so included but included in the edition prepared under the direction of the Record Commission, to that edition;

(*c*) in any other case, to the Acts printed by the Queen's Printer, or under the superintendence or authority of Her Majesty's Stationery Office.

(2) An Act may continue to be cited by the short title authorised by any enactment notwithstanding the repeal of that enactment.

20 References to other enactments

(1) Where an Act describes or cites a portion of an enactment by referring to words, sections or other parts from or to which (or from and to which) the portion extends, the portion described or cited includes the words, sections or other parts referred to unless the contrary intention appears.

(2) Where an Act refers to an enactment, the reference, unless the contrary intention appears, is a reference to that enactment as amended, and includes a reference thereto as extended or applied, by or under any other enactment, including any other provision of that Act.

[20A References to Community instruments

Where an Act passed after the commencement of this section refers to a Community instrument that has been amended, extended or applied by another such instrument, the reference, unless the contrary intention appears, is a reference to that instrument as so amended, extended or applied.][1]

Amendments—[1] This section inserted by the Legislative and Regulatory Reform Act 2006, s 25(1) with effect from 8 January 2007.

Prospective amendments—In section heading, words "EU instruments" to be substituted for words "Community instruments", and words "EU instrument" to be substituted for words "Community instrument", by the European Union (Amendment) Act 2008 s 3(3), Sch Pt 2 with effect from a date to be appointed.

Supplementary

21 Interpretation etc

(1) In this Act "Act" includes a local and personal or private Act; and "subordinate legislation" means Orders in Council, orders, rules, regulations, schemes, warrants, byelaws and other instruments made or to be made under any Act.

(2) This Act binds the Crown.

26 Commencement

This Act shall come into force on 1st January 1979.

27 Short title

This Act may be cited as the Interpretation Act 1978.

SCHEDULES

SCHEDULE 1

WORDS AND EXPRESSIONS DEFINED

Simon's Tax Cases—*IRC v Clydebridge Properties Ltd* [1980] STC 68*; *IRC v Frampton (Trustees of the Worthing Rugby Football Club)* [1985] STC 186*; *Starke (executors of Brown decd) v IRC* [1995] STC 689.

Note—The years or dates which follow certain entries in the Schedule are relevant for the purposes of paragraph 4 of Schedule 2 (application to existing enactments).

Definitions

"Associated state" means a territory maintaining a status of association with the United Kingdom in accordance with the West Indies Act 1967. [16th February 1967]

"Bank of England" means, as the context requires, the Governor and Company of the Bank of England or the bank of the Governor and Company of the Bank of England.

"Bank of Ireland" means, as the context requires, the Governor and Company of the Bank of Ireland or the bank of the Governor and Company of the Bank of Ireland.

"British Islands" means the United Kingdom, the Channel Islands and the Isle of Man. [1889]

["British overseas territory" has the same meaning as in the British Nationality Act 1981.]

"British possession" means any part of Her Majesty's dominions outside the United Kingdom; and where parts of such dominions are under both a central and a local legislature, all parts under the central legislature are deemed, for the purposes of this definition, to be one British possession. [1889]

...

"Building regulations", in relation to England and Wales, [has the meaning given by section 122 of the Building Act 1984].

"Central funds", in an enactment providing in relation to England and Wales for the payment of costs out of central funds, means money provided by Parliament.

["Charity Commission" means the Charity Commission for England and Wales established by section 1A of the Charities Act 1993.]

"Church Commissioners" means the Commissioners constituted by the Church Commissioners Measure 1947.

["Civil partnership" means a civil partnership which exists under or by virtue of the Civil Partnership Act 2004 (and any reference to a civil partner is to be read accordingly).]

"Colonial legislature", and "legislature" in relation to a British possession, mean the authority, other than the Parliament of the United Kingdom or Her Majesty in Council, competent to make laws for the possession. [1889]

"Colony" means any part of Her Majesty's dominions outside the British Islands except—

(*a*) countries having fully responsible status within the Commonwealth;

(*b*) territories for whose external relations a country other than the United Kingdom is responsible;

(*c*) associated states;

and where parts of such dominions are under both a central and a local legislature, all parts under the central legislature are deemed for the purposes of this definition to be one colony. [1889]

"Commencement", in relation to an Act or enactment, means the time when the Act or enactment comes into force.

"Committed for trial" means—

(*a*) *in relation to England and Wales, committed in custody or on bail by a magistrates' court pursuant to [section 6 of the Magistrates' Courts Act 1980], or by any judge or other authority having power to do so, with a view to trial before a judge and jury; [1889]*

(*b*) in relation to Northern Ireland, committed in custody or on bail by a magistrates' court pursuant to [Article 37 of the Magistrates' Courts (Northern Ireland) Order 1981], or by a court, judge, resident magistrate, ... or other authority having power to do so, with a view to trial on indictment. [1st January 1979]

"The Communities", "the Treaties" or "the Community Treaties" and other expressions defined by section 1 of and Schedule 1 to the European Communities Act 1972 have the meanings prescribed by that Act.

"Comptroller and Auditor General" means the Comptroller-General of the receipt and issue of Her Majesty's Exchequer and Auditor-General of Public Accounts appointed in pursuance of the Exchequer and Audit Departments Act 1866.

"Consular officer" has the meaning assigned by Article 1 of the Vienna Convention set out in Schedule 1 to the Consular Relations Act 1968.

["The Corporation Tax Acts" means the enactments relating to the taxation of the income and chargeable gains of companies and of company distributions (including provisions relating to income tax).]

"County court" means—

(*a*) in relation to England and Wales, a court held for a district under [the County Courts Act 1984]; [1846]

(*b*) in relation to Northern Ireland, a court held for a division under the County Courts [(Northern Ireland) Order 1980]. [1889]

"Court of Appeal" means—

(*a*) in relation to England and Wales, Her Majesty's Court of Appeal in England;

(*b*) in relation to Northern Ireland, Her Majesty's Court of Appeal in Northern Ireland.

"Court of summary jurisdiction", "summary conviction" and "Summary Jurisdiction Acts", in relation to Northern Ireland, have the same meanings as in Measures of the Northern Ireland Assembly and Acts of the Parliament of Northern Ireland.

"Crown Court" means—

(*a*) in relation to England and Wales, the Crown Court constituted by section 4 of the Courts Act 1971;

(*b*) in relation to Northern Ireland, the Crown Court constituted by section 4 of the Judicature (Northern Ireland) Act 1978.

"Crown Estate Commissioners" means the Commissioners referred to in section 1 of the Crown Estate Act 1961.

["EEA agreement" means the agreement on the European Economic Area signed at Oporto on 2nd May 1992, together with the Protocol adjusting that Agreement signed at Brussels on 17th March 1993, as modified or supplemented from time to time.

"EEA state", in relation to any time, means—

(*a*) a state which at that time is a member State; or

(*b*) any other state which at that time is a party to the EEA agreement.]

"England" means, subject to any alteration of boundaries under Part IV of the Local Government Act 1972 the area consisting of the countries established by section 1 of that Act, Greater London and the Isles of Scilly. [1st April 1974]

"Financial year" means, in relation to matters relating to the Consolidated Fund, the National Loans Fund, or moneys provided by Parliament, or to the Exchequer or to central taxes or finance, the twelve months ending with 31st March. [1889]

"Governor-General" includes any person who for the time being has the powers of the Governor-General, and "Governor", in relation to any British possession, includes the officer for the time being administering the government of that possession. [1889]

["Her Majesty's Revenue and Customs" has the meaning given by section 4 of the Commissioners for Revenue and Customs Act 2005.]

"High Court" means—

(*a*) in relation to England and Wales, Her Majesty's High Court of Justice in England;

(*b*) in relation to Northern Ireland, Her Majesty's High Court of Justice in Northern Ireland.

["The Immigration Acts" has the meaning given by [section 61 of the UK Borders Act 2007].]

"The Income Tax Acts" means all enactments relating to income tax, including any provisions of the Corporation Tax Acts which relate to income tax.

"Land" includes buildings and other structures, land covered with water, and any estate, interest, easement, servitude or right in or over land. [1st January 1979]

"Land Clauses Acts" means—

(*a*) in relation to England and Wales, the Land Clauses Consolidation Act 1845 and the Lands Clauses Consolidation Acts Amendment Act 1860, and any Acts for the time being in force amending those Acts; [1889]

(*b*) in relation to Scotland, the Lands Clauses Consolidation (Scotland) Act 1845 and the Lands Clauses Consolidation Acts Amendment Act 1860, and any Acts for the time being in force amending those Acts; [1889]

(*c*) in relation to Northern Ireland, the enactments defined as such by section 46(1) of the Interpretation Act (Northern Ireland) 1954. [1889]

"Local land charges register", in relation to England and Wales, means a register kept pursuant to section 3 of the Local Land Charges Act 1975 and "the appropriate local land charges register" has the meaning assigned by section 4 of that Act.

"London borough" means a borough described in Schedule 1 to the London Government Act 1963 "inner London borough" means one of the boroughs so described and numbered from 1 to 12 and "outer London borough" means one of the boroughs so described and numbered from 13 to 32, subject (in each case) to any alterations made under Part IV of the Local Government Act 1972[, Part 2 of the Local Government Act 1992 or Part 1 of the Local Government and Public Involvement in Health Act 2007].

"Lord Chancellor" means the Lord High Chancellor of Great Britain.

"Magistrates' court" has the meaning assigned to it—

(*a*) in relation to England and Wales, by [section 148 of the Magistrates' Courts Act 1980];

(*b*) in relation to Northern Ireland, by [Article 2(2) of the Magistrates' Courts (Northern Ireland) Order 1981].

"Month" means calendar month. [1850]

"National Debt Commissioners" means the Commissioners for the Reduction of the National Debt.

"Northern Ireland legislation" has the meaning assigned by section 24(5) of this Act. [1st January 1979]

"Oath" and "affidavit" include affirmation and declaration, and "swear" includes affirm and declare.

["Officer of a provider of probation services" in relation to England and Wales, has the meaning given by section 9(1) of the Offender Management Act 2007;]

["Officer of Revenue and Customs" has the meaning given by section 2(1) of the Commissioners for Revenue and Customs Act 2005.]

"Ordnance Map" means a map made under powers conferred by the Ordnance Survey Act 1841 or the Boundary Survey (Ireland) Act 1854.

"Parliamentary Election" means the election of a Member to serve in Parliament for a constituency. [1889]

["PAYE income" has the meaning given by section 683 of the Income Tax (Earnings and Pensions) Act 2003.]

["PAYE regulations" means regulations under section 684 of that Act.]

"Person" includes a body of persons corporate or unincorporate. [1889]

"Police area", "police authority" and other expressions relating to the police have the meaning or effect described—

(*a*) in relation to England and Wales, by [section 101(1) of the Police Act 1996];

(*b*) in relation to Scotland, by sections 50 and 51(4) of the Police (Scotland) Act 1967.

["Police Service of Northern Ireland" and "Police Service of Northern Ireland Reserve" have the same meaning as in the Police (Northern Ireland) Act 2000.]

"The Privy Council" means the Lords and others of Her Majesty's Most Honourable Privy Council.

["Provider of probation services", in relation to England and Wales, has the meaning given by section 3(6) of the Offender Management Act 2007;]

["Registered" in relation to nurses and midwives, means registered in the register maintained under article 5 of the [Nursing and Midwifery Order 2001] by virtue of qualifications in nursing or midwifery, as the case may be.]

"Registered medical practitioner" means a fully registered person within the meaning of [the Medical Act 1983]. [1st January 1979]

"Rules of Court" in relation to any court means rules made by the authority having power to make rules or orders regulating the practice and procedure of that court, and in Scotland includes Acts of Adjournal and Acts of Sederunt; and the power of the authority to make rules of court (as above defined) includes power to make such rules for the purpose of any Act which directs or authorises anything to be done by rules of court. [1889]

"Secretary of State" means one of Her Majesty's Principal Secretaries of State.

["Sent for trial" means, in relation to England and Wales, sent by a magistrates' court to the Crown Court for trial pursuant to section 51 or 51A of the Crime and Disorder Act 1998.]

["Sewerage undertaker, in relation to England and Wales, shall be construed in accordance with [section 6 of the Water Industry Act 1991].]

"Sheriff", in relation to Scotland, includes sheriff principal. [1889]

["The standard scale", with reference to a fine or penalty for an offence triable only summarily,—

(*a*) in relation to England and Wales, has the meaning given by section 37 of the Criminal Justice Act 1982;

(*b*) in relation to Scotland, has the meaning given by section 289G of the Criminal Procedure (Scotland) Act 1975;

(*c*) in relation to Northern Ireland, has the meaning given by Article 5 of the Fines and Penalties (Northern Ireland) Order 1984.]

"Statutory declaration" means a declaration made by virtue of the Statutory Declarations Act 1835.

["Statutory maximum", with reference to a fine or penalty on summary conviction for an offence,—

(*a*) in relation to England and Wales, means the prescribed sum within the meaning of section 32 of the Magistrates' Courts Act 1980;

(*b*) in relation to Scotland, means the prescribed sum within the meaning of section 289B(6) of the Criminal Procedure (Scotland) Act 1975; and

(*c*) in relation to Northern Ireland, means the prescribed sum within the meaning of Article 4 of the Fines and Penalties (Northern Ireland) Order 1984.]

"Supreme Court" means—

(*a*) in relation to England and Wales, the Court of Appeal and the High Court together with the Crown Court;

(*b*) in relation to Northern Ireland, the Supreme Court of Judicature of Northern Ireland.

["The Tax Acts" means the Income Tax Acts and the Corporation Tax Acts.]

["Transfer for trial" means the transfer of proceedings against an accused to the Crown Court for trial under section 7 of the Magistrates' Courts Act 1980.]

"The Treasury" means the Commissioners of Her Majesty's Treasury.

["Trust of land" and "trustees of land", in relation to England and Wales, have the same meanings as in the Trusts of Land and Appointment of Trustees Act 1996.]

"United Kingdom" means Great Britain and Northern Ireland. [12th April 1927]

["Wales" means the combined area of counties which were created by section 20 of the Local Government Act 1972, as originally enacted, but subject to any alteration made under section 73 of that Act (consequential alteration of boundary following alteration of watercourse).]

["Water undertaker", in relation to England and Wales, shall be construed in accordance with [section 6 of the Water Industry Act 1991].]

"Writing" includes typing, printing, lithography, photography and other modes of representing or reproducing words in a visible form, and expressions referring to writing are construed accordingly.

…

…

Construction of certain expressions relating to offences

In relation to England and Wales—

(*a*) "indictable offence" means an offence which, if committed by an adult, is triable on indictment, whether it is exclusively so triable or triable either way;
(*b*) "summary offence" means an offence which, if committed by an adult, is triable only summarily;
(*c*) "offence triable either way" means an offence [, other than an offence triable on indictment only by virtue of Part V of the Criminal Justice Act 1988] which, if committed by an adult, is triable either on indictment or summarily;

and the terms "indictable", "summary" and "triable either way", in their application to offences, are to be construed accordingly.

In the above definitions references to the way or ways in which an offence is triable are to be construed without regard to the effect, if any, of [section 22 of the Magistrates' Courts Act 1980] on the mode of trial in a particular case.

[Construction of certain references to relationships

In relation to England and Wales—

(*a*) references (however expressed) to any relationship between two persons;
(*b*) references to a person whose father and mother were or were not married to each other at the time of his birth; and
(*c*) references cognate with references falling within paragraph (*b*) above,

shall be construed in accordance with section 1 of the Family Law Reform Act 1987. [4th April 1988]]

Amendments—Definition of "British overseas territory" inserted by the British Overseas Territories Act 2002 s 1(3) with effect from 26 February 2002.
The definitions of "British subject" and "Commonwealth citizen" repealed by the British Nationality Act 1981 Sch 9.
Words in the definition of "Building regulations" substituted by the Building Act 1984 Sch 6 para 19.
Definition of "Charity Commission" substituted for definition "Charity Commissioners" as originally enacted, by the Charities Act 2006, Sch 8, para 61 with effect from 27 February 2007 (SI 2007/309, art 2, Schedule).
Definition of "Civil Partnership" inserted by the Civil Partnership Act 2004 s 261(1) Sch 27 para 59, with effect from 5 December 2005 (SI 2005/3175, art 2(2)).
Words in the definition of "Committed for trial" substituted by the Magistrates' Courts Act 1980 Sch 7 para 169 and the Magistrates' Courts (Northern Ireland) Order, SI 1981/1675 Sch 6 para 56. The whole of para(*a*) of this definition is repealed, as from a day to be appointed, by the Criminal Justice Act 2003 s 41 Sch 3 Pt 2 para 49(*a*).
In para (*b*) of the definition of "Committed for trial", words "justice of the peace" repealed by the Justice (Northern Ireland) Act 2002 s 86, Sch 13 with effect from 1 April 2005: see the Justice (Northern Ireland) Act 2002 (Commencement No 8) Order 2005, SR 2005/109, art 2, Schedule.
Definition of "The Corporation Tax Acts" substituted by FA 1987 s 71 Sch 15 para 12.
Words in the definition of "County court" substituted by the County Courts Act 1984 Sch 2 para 68 and the County Courts (Northern Ireland) Order, SI 1980/397 Sch 1 Pt II.
Definitions of "EEA agreement" and "EEA state" inserted by the Legislative and Regulatory Reform Act 2006, s 26(1) with effect from 8 January 2007.
Definition of "Her Majesty's Revenue and Customs" inserted by the Commissioners for Revenue and Customs Act 2005 s 4 with effect from 7 April 2005 at 1745 hours (by virtue of SI 2005/1126 art 2(1)).
Definition of "The Immigration Acts" inserted by the Immigration, Asylum and Nationality Act 2006 s 64 with effect from 30 March 2006, and words in definition substituted by the UK Borders Act 2007 s 61(4) with effect from 30 October 2007.
Words in the definition of "London borough" substituted by the Local Government and Public Involvement in Health Act 2007 s 22, Sch 1 para 14 with effect from 1 November 2007 (by virtue of SI 2007/3136, art 2(*b*)).
Words in para (*a*) of the definition of "Magistrates' court" substituted by the Magistrates' Courts Act 1980 s 154 Sch 7 para 169 and, in para (*b*), by the Magistrates' Court (Northern Ireland) Order, SI 1981/1675 art 170(2) Sch 6 Pt I para 56.
Definition "Officer of a provider of probation services" inserted by the Offender Management Act 2007 s 39, Sch 3 para 2 with effect from 1 April 2008 (by virtue of SI 2008/504, art 3(*l*)).
Definition of "Officer of Revenue and Customs" inserted by the Commissioners for Revenue and Customs Act 2005 s 2 with effect from 7 April 2005 at 1745 hours (by virtue of SI 2005/1126 art 2(1)).
Definitions of "PAYE income" and "PAYE regulations" inserted by ITEPA 2003 s 722, Sch 6 para 148 with effect, for income tax purposes, from 2003–04; and for corporation tax purposes, for accounting periods ending after 5 April 2003. For transitional provisions and savings see ITEPA 2003 s 723, Sch 7.
Words in the definition of "police area substituted by the Police Act 1996 Sch 7 para 32.
Definition of "Police Service of Northern Ireland" and "Police Service of Northern Ireland Reserve" inserted by the Police (Northern Ireland) Act 2000 s 78(1), Sch 6 para 5 with effect from 4 December 2001 (by virtue of SR 2001/396).
Definition "Provider of probation services" inserted by the Offender Management Act 2007 s 39, Sch 3 para 2 with effect from 1 April 2008 (by virtue of SI 2008/504, art 3(*l*)).
Definition of "Registered" substituted by the Nursing and Midwifery Order 2001, SI 2002/253, art 54, Sch 5 para 7 with effect from 1 August 2004.
Words in the definition of "Registered" substituted by the Health Act 1999 (Consequential Amendments) (Nursing and Midwifery) Order, 2004/1771 art 3 Sch Pt 1 para 7, with effect from 1 August 2004 (by virtue of SI 2004/1771 art 1(2)).
Words in the definition of "Registered medical practitioner" substituted by the Medical Act 1983 Sch 5 para 18.
Definition of "Sent for trial" inserted by the Criminal Justice Act 2003 s 41, Sch 3, Pt 2, para 49(*b*) with effect from 9 May 2005 (by virtue of SI 2005/1267).
Definition of "Sewerage undertaker" inserted by the Water Act 1989 s 190(1), Sch 25 para 55(1), (2), as amended by the Water Consolidation (Consequential Provisions) Act 1991 s 2(1) Sch 1 para 32.
Definition of "The standard scale" inserted by the Criminal Justice Act 1988 s 170(1) Sch 15 para 58(*a*).
Definition of "Statutory maximum" inserted by the Criminal Justice Act 1988 s 170(1) Sch 15 para 58(*b*).
Definition of "The Tax Acts" substituted by FA 1987 s 71 Sch 15 para 12.
Definition "Transfer for trial" inserted by the Criminal Justice and Public Order Act 1994 Sch 4 para 28(*b*), as from a day to be appointed.
Definitions of "Trust of land" and trustees of land" inserted by the Trusts of Land and Appointment of Trustees Act 1996 s 25(1), Sch 3 para 16, as from a day to be appointed.
Definition of "Wales" substituted by the Local Government (Wales) Act 1994 Sch 2 para 9.
Definition of "Water undertaker" substituted for the definitions "Water authority" and "Water authority area" by the Water Act 1989 s 190(1) Sch 25 para 55(1), (3), as amended by the Water Consolidation (Consequential Provisions) Act 1991 s 2(1) Sch 1 para 32.
The entry relating to the construction of certain expressions relating to children is repealed by the Children Act 1989 s 108(7) Sch 15.

In the entry relating to the construction of certain expressions relating to offences (i) the words in the definition "offence triable either way" inserted by the Criminal Justice Act 1988 s 170(1) Sch 15 para 59; (ii) the words "section 22 of the Magistrates' Courts Act 1980" substituted by the Magistrates' Courts Act 1980 s 154 Sch 7 para 169.

The entry relating to the construction of references to relationships added at the end by the Family Law Reform Act 1987 s 33(1), Sch 2 para 73.

Prospective amendments—In definition of "Committed for trial", para (*a*) to be repealed by the Criminal Justice Act 2003 ss 41, 332, Sch 3 para 49(*a*), Sch 37 Pt 4.

Definition of "Registered medical practitioner" to be substituted by the Medical Act 1983 (Amendment) Order, SI 2002/3135 art 16(1), Sch 1 para 10 with effect from a date to be appointed. The substituted definition to read as follows—

"Registered medical practitioner" means a fully registered person within the meaning of the Medical Act 1983 who holds a licence to practise under that Act.".

Definition of "Supreme Court" to be substituted by the Constitutional Reform Act 2005 s 59, Sch 11 para 24 with effect from a date to be appointed. That definition to read as follows—

" 'Supreme Court' means the Supreme Court of the United Kingdom.".

Definitions of "Court of Judicature" and "Senior Courts" to be inserted by the Constitutional Reform Act 2005 s 59, Sch 11 para 24 with effect from a date to be appointed. Those definitions to read as follows—

" 'Court of Judicature' means the Court of Judicature of Northern Ireland.".

" 'Senior Courts' means the Senior Courts of England and Wales.".

In definition ' "The Communities", "the Treaties" or "the Community Treaties" ', words ' "The EU" or "the EU Treaties" ' to be substituted for words ' "The Communities", "the Treaties" or "the Community Treaties" ' by the European Union (Amendment) Act 2008 s 3(3), Sch Pt 2 with effect from a date to be appointed.

Definition "Registered provider of social housing" to be inserted by the Housing and Regeneration Act 2008 s 277, Sch 9 para 5 with effect from a date to be appointed. That definition to read as follows—

" 'Registered provider of social housing' has the meaning given by section 80(2) of the Housing and Regeneration Act 2008 (and "non-profit" and "profit-making" in connection with a provider have the meanings given by section 115 of that Act).".

SCHEDULE 2

APPLICATION OF ACT TO EXISTING ENACTMENTS

PART I

ACTS

1 The following provisions of this Act apply to Acts whenever passed—

Section 6(*a*) and (*c*) so far as applicable to enactments relating to offences punishable on indictment or on summary conviction
Section 9
Section 10
Section 11 so far as it relates to subordinate legislation made after the year 1889
Section 18
Section 19(2)

2 The following apply to Acts passed after the year 1850—

Section 1
Section 3
Section 6(*a*) and (*c*) so far as not applicable to such Acts by virtue of paragraph 1
Section 15
Section 17(1)

3 The following apply to Acts passed after the year 1889—

Section 4
Section 7
Section 12
Section 13
Section 14 so far as it relates to rules, regulations or byelaws
Section 16(1)
Section 17(2)(*a*)
Section 19(1)
Section 20(1)

4— (1) Subject to the following provisions of this paragraph—

(*a*) paragraphs of Schedule 1 at the end of which a year or date ...[1] is specified [or described][2] apply, so far as applicable, to Acts passed on or after the date, or after the year, so specified [or described][2]; and

(*b*) paragraphs of the Schedule at the end of which no year or date is specified [or described][3] apply, so far as applicable, to Acts passed at any time.

(4) The definition of "Lord Chancellor" does not apply to Acts passed before 1st October 1921 in which that expression was used in relation to Ireland only.

(5) The definition of "person", so far as it includes bodies corporate, applies to any provision of an Act whenever passed relating to an offence punishable on indictment or on summary conviction.

Amendments—[1] Words omitted from para 4(1)(*a*) repealed by the Family Law Reform Act 1987 s 33(1), Sch 2 para 74, Sch 4.

[2] Words "or described" in that paragraph inserted in both places where they occur, by the Family Law Reform Act 1987 s 33(1), Sch 2 para 74.
[3] Words "or described" in sub-para (1)(*b*) inserted by the Family Law Reform Act 1987 s 33(1), Sch 2 para 74.

5 The following definitions shall be treated as included in Schedule 1 for the purposes specified in this paragraph—

(*a*) in any Act passed before 1st April 1974, a reference to England includes Berwick upon Tweed and Monmouthshire and, in the case of an Act passed before the Welsh Language Act 1967 Wales;
(*b*) in any Act passed before the commencement of this Act and after the year 1850, "land", includes messuages, tenements and hereditaments, houses and buildings of any tenure;
(*c*) in any Act passed before the commencement of the Criminal Procedure (Scotland) Act 1975 "the Summary Jurisdiction (Scotland) Acts" means Part II of that Act.

PART II

SUBORDINATE LEGISLATION

7 The definition in Schedule 1 of "county court", in relation to England and Wales, applies to Orders in Council made after the year 1846.

CUSTOMS AND EXCISE MANAGEMENT ACT 1979

(1979 Chapter 2)

ARRANGEMENT OF SECTIONS

PART I

PRELIMINARY

PART II

ADMINISTRATION

Appointment and duties of Commissioners, officers, etc

Offences in connection with Commissioners, officers, etc

Commissioners' receipts and expenses

PART III

CUSTOMS AND EXCISE CONTROL AREAS

PART IV

CONTROL OF IMPORTATION

Inward entry and clearance

VAT

PART XII
GENERAL AND MISCELLANEOUS

General powers, etc

An Act to consolidate the enactments relating to the collection and management of the revenues of customs and excise and in some cases to other matters in relation to which the Commissioners of Customs and Excise for the time being perform functions, with amendments to give effect to recommendations of the Law Commission and the Scottish Law Commission.

[22nd February 1979]

Construction—FA 1988 s 8 to be construed as one with this Act; see FA 1988 s 8(4).
Cross references—See VATA 1994 s 16(1) (application of this Act with certain exceptions for the purposes of value added tax).

PART I
PRELIMINARY

1 Interpretation

(1) In this Act, unless the context otherwise requires—

"aerodrome" means any area of land or water designed, equipped, set apart or commonly used for affording facilities for the landing and departure of aircraft;

...[15]

"approved wharf" has the meaning given by [section 20A][8] below;

"armed forces" means the Royal Navy, the Royal Marines, the regular army and the regular air force, and any reserve or auxiliary force of any of those services which has been called out on permanent service, [...][24] or embodied;

["assigned matter" means any matter in relation to which the Commissioners, or officers of Revenue and Customs, have a power or duty;][27]

"boarding station" means a boarding station for the time being appointed under section 19 below;

"boundary" means the land boundary of Northern Ireland;

"British ship" means a British ship within the meaning of the [Merchant Shipping Act 1995][21];

"claimant", in relation to proceedings for the condemnation of any thing as being forfeited, means a person claiming that the thing is not liable to forfeiture;

"coasting ship" has the meaning given by section 69 below;

"commander", in relation to an aircraft, includes any person having or taking the charge or command of the aircraft;

["the Commissioners" means the Commissioners for Her Majesty's Revenue and Customs;][27]

"Community transit goods"—

(*a*) in relation to imported goods, means—

(i) goods which have been imported under the internal or external Community transit procedure for transit through the United Kingdom with a view to exportation where the importation was and the transit and exportation are to be part of one Community transit operation; or

(ii) goods which have, at the port or airport at which they were imported, been placed under the internal or external Community transit procedure for transit through the United Kingdom with a view to exportation where the transit and exportation are to be part of one Community transit operation;

(*b*) in relation to goods for exportation, means—

(i) goods which have been imported as mentioned in paragraph (*a*)(i) of this definition and are to be exported as part of the Community transit operation in the course of which they were imported; or

(ii) goods which have, under the internal or external Community transit procedure, transited the United Kingdom from the port or airport at which they were imported and are to be exported as part of the Community transit operation which commenced at that port or airport;

[and for the purposes of para (*a*)(i) above the Isle of Man shall be treated as if it were part of the United Kingdom;][1]

"container" includes any bundle or package and any [baggage,][29] box, cask or other receptacle whatsoever;

"the customs and excise Acts" means the Customs and Excise Acts 1979 and any other enactment for the time being in force relating to customs or excise;

"the Customs and Excise Acts 1979" means—

this Act,
the Customs and Excise Duties (General Reliefs) Act 1979
the Alcoholic Liquor Duties Act 1979
the Hydrocarbon Oil Duties Act 1979
...[13] and
the Tobacco Products Duty Act 1979;

"customs warehouse" means a place of security approved by the Commissioners under subsection (2) (whether or not it is also approved under subsection (1)) of section 92 below;[9]

"customs and excise airport" has the meaning given by section 21(7) below;

"customs and excise station" has the meaning given by section 26 below;

["designation order" has the meaning given by section 100A(5);][4]

"drawback goods" means goods in the case of which a claim for drawback has been or is to be made;

"dutiable goods", except in the expression "dutiable or restricted goods", means goods of a class or description subject to any duty of customs or excise, whether or not those goods are in fact chargeable with that duty, and whether or not that duty has been paid thereon;

"dutiable or restricted goods" has the meaning given by section 52 below;

"examination station" has the meaning given by [section 22A][8] below;

["excise duty point" has the meaning given by section 1 of the Finance (No 2) Act 1992;][11]

"excise licence trade" means, subject to subsection (5) below, a trade or business for the carrying on of which an excise licence is required;

"excise warehouse" means a place of security approved by the Commissioners under subsection (1) (whether or not it is also approved under subsection (2)) of section 92 below, and, except in that section, also includes a distiller's warehouse;

"exporter", in relation to goods for exportation or for use as stores, includes the shipper of the goods and any person performing in relation to an aircraft functions corresponding with those of a shipper;

["free zone" has the meaning given by section 100A(2);][4]

["free zone goods" are goods which are within a free zone][18]

[10]

"goods" includes stores and baggage;

"holiday", in relation to any part of the United Kingdom, means any day that is a bank holiday in that part of the United Kingdom under the Banking and Financial Dealings Act 1971 Christmas Day, Good Friday and the day appointed for the purposes of customs and excise for the celebration of Her Majesty's birthday;

"hovercraft" means a hovercraft within the meaning of the Hovercraft Act 1968;

"importer", in relation to any goods at any time between their importation and the time when they are delivered out of charge, includes any owner or other person for the time being possessed of or beneficially interested in the goods and, in relation to goods imported by means of a pipe-line, includes the owner of the pipe-line;

"justice" and "justice of the peace" in Scotland includes a sheriff and in Northern Ireland, in relation to any powers and duties which can under any enactment for the time being in force be exercised and performed only by a resident magistrate, means a resident magistrate;

"land" and "landing", in relation to aircraft, include alighting on water;

"law officer of the Crown" means the Attorney General or [for the purpose of criminal proceedings in Scotland, the Lord Advocate or, for the purpose of civil proceedings in Scotland, the appropriate Law Officer within the meaning of section 4A of the Crown Suits (Scotland) Act 1857][25] or in Northern Ireland the Attorney General for Northern Ireland;

"licence year", in relation to an excise licence issuable annually, means the period of 12 months ending on the date on which that licence expires in any year;

"master", in relation to a ship, includes any person having or taking the charge or command of the ship;

...[6]

"night" means the period between 11 pm and 5 am;

"occupier", in relation to any bonded premises, [includes any][12] person who has given security to the Crown in respect of those premises;

"officer" means, subject to section 8(2) below, a person commissioned by the Commissioners;

"owner", in relation to an aircraft, includes the operator of the aircraft;

"owner", in relation to a pipe-line, means (except in the case of a pipe-line vested in the Crown which in pursuance of arrangements in that behalf is operated by another) the person in whom the line is vested and, in the said excepted case, means the person operating the line;

"perfect entry" means an entry made in accordance with [regulation 5 of the Customs Controls on Importation of Goods Regulations 1991][14] or warehousing regulations, as the case may require;[20]

"pipe-line" has the meaning given by section 65 of the Pipe-lines Act 1962 (that Act being taken, for the purposes of this definition, to extend to Northern Ireland);

"port" means a port appointed by the Commissioners under section 19 below;

"prescribed area" means such an area in Northern Ireland adjoining the boundary as the Commissioners may by regulations prescribe;

"prescribed sum", in relation to the penalty provided for an offence, has the meaning given by section 171(2) below;

"prohibited or restricted goods" means goods of a class or description of which the importation, exportation or carriage coastwise is for the time being prohibited or restricted under or by virtue of any enactment;

"proper", in relation to the person by, with or to whom, the place at which, anything is to be done, means the person or place appointed or authorised in that behalf by the Commissioners;

"proprietor", in relation to any goods, includes any owner, importer, exporter, shipping or other person for the time being possessed of or beneficially interested in those goods;

"Queen's warehouse" means any place provided by the Crown or appointed by the Commissioners for the deposit of goods for security thereof and of the duties chargeable thereon;

["registered excise dealer and shipper" means a revenue trader approved and registered by the Commissioners under section 100G below;

"registered excise dealers and shippers regulations" means regulations under section 100G below;][19]

"the revenue trade provisions of the customs and excise Acts" means—

(*a*) the provisions of the customs and excise Acts relating to the protection, security, collection or management of the revenues derived from the duties of excise on goods produced or manufactured in the United Kingdom;

(*b*) the provisions of the customs and excise Acts relating to any activity or facility for the carrying on or provision of which an excise licence is required; ...[16]

(*c*) the provisions of [the Betting and Gaming Duties Act 1981][3] (so far as not included in paragraph (*b*) above); ...[22]

[(*d*) the provisions of Chapter II of Part I of the Finance Act 1993;][16]

[(*e*) the provisions of section 10 to 15 of , and Schedule 1 to, the Finance Act 1997;][22]

"revenue trader" means—

[(*a*)][2] any person carrying on a trade or business subject to any of the revenue trade provisions of the customs and excise Acts, [or which consists of or includes—

(i) the buying, selling, importation, exportation, dealing in or handling of any goods of a class or description which is subject to a duty of excise (whether or not duty is chargeable on the goods);][7] ...[17]

[(ia) the buying, selling, importation, exportation, dealing in or handling of tickets or chances on the taking of which lottery duty is or will be chargeable;][17]...[23]

[(ib) being (within the meaning of sections 10 to 15 of the Finance Act 1997) the provider of any premises for gaming;][23]

[(ic) the organisation, management or promotion of [gaming within the meaning of the Betting and Gaming Duties Act 1981 (see section 33(1))][28]; or][23]

[(ii) the financing or facilitation of any such transactions or activities][7] [as are mentioned in sub-paragraph (i)[, (ia), (ib) or (ic)][23] above][17]

whether or not that trade or business is an excise licence trade[; and[2]

[(*b*) any person who is a wholesaler or an occupier of an excise warehouse (so far as not included in paragraph (*a*) above),

and includes a registered club;][2]

"ship", and "vessel" include any boat or other vessel whatsoever (and, to the extent provided in section 2 below, any hovercraft);

"shipment" includes loading into an aircraft, and "shipped" and cognate expressions shall be construed accordingly;

"stores" means, subject to subsection (4) below, goods for use in a ship or aircraft and includes fuel and spare parts and other articles of equipment, whether or not for immediate fitting;

"tons register" means the tons of a ship's net tonnage as ascertained and registered according to the tonnage regulations of the [Merchant Shipping Act 1995][21] or, in the case of a ship which is not registered under that Act, ascertained in like manner as if it were to be so registered;

"transit goods", except in the expression "Community transit goods", means imported goods entered on importation for transit or transhipment;

"transit or transhipment", in relation to the entry of goods, means transit through the United Kingdom or transhipment with a view to the re-exportation of the goods in question [or transhipment of those goods for use as stores][5];

"transit shed" has the meaning given by [section 25A][8] below;

["tribunal" means the First-tier Tribunal or, where determined by or under Tribunal Procedure Rules, the Upper Tribunal;][30]

["United Kingdom waters" means any waters (including inland waters) within the seaward limits of the Territorial sea of the United Kingdom.][6]

"vehicle" includes a railway vehicle;

["victualling warehouse" means a place of security approved by the Commissioners under subsection (2) (whether or not it is also a place approved under subsection (1) of section 92 below).][9]

"warehouse", except in the expressions "Queen's warehouse" and "distiller's warehouse", means a place of security approved by the Commissioners under subsection (1) or (2) or subsections (1) and (2) of section 92 below and, except in that section, also includes a distiller's warehouse; and "warehoused" and cognate expressions shall, subject to subsection (4) of that section [and any regulations made by virtue of section 93(2)(*da*)(i) or (*ee*) or (4) below][11], be construed accordingly;

"warehousing regulations" means regulations under section 93 below.

(2) This Act and the other Acts included in the Customs and Excise Acts 1979 shall be construed as one Act but where a provision of this Act refers to this Act that reference is not to be construed as including a reference to any of the others.

(3) Any expression used in this Act or in any instrument made under this Act to which a meaning is given by any other Act included in the Customs and Excise Acts 1979 has, except where the context otherwise requires, the same meaning in this Act or any such instrument as in that Act; ...

[(4) Goods for use in a ship or aircraft as merchandise for sale to persons carried in the ship or aircraft shall be treated for the purposes of the customs and excise Acts as stores if, and only if—

(*a*) the goods are to be sold by retail either—

(i) in the course of a relevant journey, or

(ii) for consumption on board;

and

(*b*) the goods are not treated as exported by virtue of regulations under section 12 of the Customs and Excise Duties (General Reliefs) Act 1979 (goods for use in naval ships or establishments).

(4A) For the purposes of subsection (4) above a relevant journey is any journey beginning in the United Kingdom and having an immediate destination outside the member States.

(4B) In relation to goods treated as stores by virtue of subsection (4) above, any reference in the customs and excise Acts to the consumption of stores shall be construed as referring to the sale of the goods as mentioned in paragraph (*a*) of that subsection.][26]

(5) A person who deals in or sells tobacco products in the course of a trade or business carried on by him shall be deemed for the purposes of this Act to be carrying on an excise licence trade (and to be a revenue trader) notwithstanding that no excise licence is required for carrying on that trade or business.

(6) In computing for the purposes of this Act any period expressed therein as a period of clear days no account shall be taken of the day of the event from which the period is computed or of any Sunday or holiday.

(7) The provisions of this Act in so far as they relate to customs duties apply, notwithstanding that any duties are imposed for the benefit of the Communities, as if the revenue from duties so imposed remained part of the revenues of the Crown.

Notes—Words omitted from sub-s (3) are not relevant to VAT.

Cross references—See Police and Criminal Evidence Act 1984 s 114 (application of that Act to Customs and Excise).

Amendments—[1] Words in the definition of "Community transit goods" in sub-s (1) inserted by Isle of Man Act 1979 s 13, Sch 1.

[2] "(*a*)", para (*b*) and the word "and" preceding it in the definition of "revenue trader" in sub-s (1) inserted by FA 1981 Sch 8 para 1(1).

[3] Words in para (*c*) of the definition of "the revenue trade provisions of the customs and excise Acts" in sub-s (1) substituted by Betting and Gaming Duties Act 1981 Sch 5 para 5(*a*).

[4] Definitions inserted by FA 1984 Sch 4 Pt II, para 1.

[5] Words in the definition of "transit or transhipment" added by F(No 2)A 1987 s 103(3).

[6] Definition of "United Kingdom waters" inserted, and definition of "nautical mile" repealed, by Territorial Sea Act 1987 s 3(1), (4), Sch 1 para 4(1), Sch 2 with effect from 1 October 1987; see SI 1987/1270.

[7] Words in the definition of "revenue trader" inserted by FA 1991 s 11(2).

[8] Words in the definitions of "approved wharf", "examination station", "transit shed" in sub-s (1) substituted by Customs Controls on Importation of Goods Regulations, SI 1991/2724 reg 6(1), (2).

[9] Definition of "customs warehouse" repealed and definition of "victualling warehouse" inserted by Customs Warehousing Regulations, SI 1991/2725 regs 3(1), (2), 4, except in relation to its application to VAT by virtue of VATA 1994 s 16.

[10] Definition of "free zone regulations" repealed by Free Zone Regulations, SI 1991/2727 reg 4, with effect from 1 January 1992.

[11] Definition of "excise duty point" and words in the definition of "warehouse" in sub-s (1) inserted by F(No 2)A 1992 ss 1(8), 3 and Sch 1 para 1 and Sch 2 para 1 with effect from 9 December 1992 by virtue of F(No 2)A 1992 (Commencement No 3) Order, SI 1992/3104.

[12] Words in the definition of "occupier" in sub-s (1) substituted for the words "means the" by F(No 2)A 1992 s 3 and Sch 2 para 1 with effect from 9 December 1992 by virtue of F(No 2)A 1992 (Commencement No 3) Order, SI 1992/3104.

[13] Words omitted from the definition of "the Customs and Excise Acts 1979" in sub-s (1) repealed by F(No 2)A 1992 Sch 18 Pt II with effect from 1 January 1993.

[14] Words in the definition of "perfect entry" in sub-s (1) substituted by the Customs and Excise (Single Market etc) Regulations, SI 1992/3095 Sch 1 para 2 with effect from 1 January 1993.

15 Definition of "approved route" in sub-s (1) repealed by the Customs and Excise (Single Market etc) Regulations, SI 1992/3095 regs 2, 3(1) and Sch 2 with effect from 1 January 1993.
16 Word "and" in the definition of "revenue trade provisions of the customs and excise Acts" repealed and para (*d*) added to that definition by FA 1993 ss 30(1), (2), 41, 213, Sch 23 Pt I.
17 Word "or" in the definition of "revenue trader" repealed and sub-para (*ia*) and the words in sub-para (ii) inserted in that definition by FA 1993 ss 30(1), (2)(*a*), (*b*), 41, 213, Sch 23 Pt I.
18 Definition "free zone goods" substituted by VATA 1994 s 100, Sch 14 para 6.
19 Definitions "registered excise dealer and shipper" and "registered excise dealers and shippers regulations" inserted by FA 1991 s 11(1).
20 Definition "perfect entry" in sub-s (1) is repealed with effect from a day to be appointed by C & E Commissioners by FA 1981 Sch 19 Pt I.
21 Words in the definitions of "British ship" and "tons register" substituted by Merchant Shipping Act 1995 Sch 13 para 53(1), (2) with effect from 1 January 1996.
22 Word "and" in the definition of "revenue trade provisions of the customs and excise Acts" repealed and para (*e*) added to that definition by FA 1997 s 13, Sch 2 para 2, Sch 18 Pt II with effect from 19 March 1997.
23 Word "or" in the definition of "revenue trader" repealed, sub-paras (*a*)(ib)and (*a*)(ic) inserted and words in sub-para (*a*)(ii) substituted by FA 1997 s 13, Sch 2 para 2, Sch 18 Part II with effect from 19 March 1997.
24 Words "or called into actual service" in the definition of "armed forces" repealed by The Reserved Forces Act 1996 (Consequential Provisions etc.) Regulations 1998 reg 10(3), with effect from 1 January 1999.
25 Words in the definition "law officer of the Crown" substituted by Scotland Act 1998 (Consequential Modifications) (No 1) Order, SI 1999/1042 Article 4 Sch 2 Part 1 para 6 with effect from 20 May 1999.
26 Sub-ss (4), (4A), (4B) substituted by FA 1999 s 10 with effect from 1 July 1999.
27 Definitions of "assigned matter" and "the Commissioners" substituted by Commissioners for Revenue and Customs Act 2005 s 50, Sch 4 para 22 with effect from 18 April 2005 by virtue of the Commissioners for Revenue and Customs Act 2005 (Commencement) Order, SI 2005/1126, art 2(2).
28 In sub-s (1), in para (*a*)(*ic*) of the definition of "revenue trader", words substituted for words "any gaming (within the meaning of the Gaming Act 1968 or the Betting, Gaming, Lotteries and Amusements (Northern Ireland) Order 1985)" by FA 2007 s 105, Sch 25 para 22 with effect from a date to be appointed.
29 Word in definition of "container" inserted by FA 2008 s 117(1), (2) with effect from 21 July 2008.
30 Definition of "tribunal" inserted by the Transfer of Tribunal Functions and Revenue and Customs Appeals Order, SI 2009/56 art 3, Sch 1 paras 88, 89 with effect from 1 April 2009.

Prospective amendments—In sub-s (1), definition of "nuclear material" to be inserted at the appropriate place, by the Criminal Justice and Immigration Act 2008 s 75, Sch 17 para 8(1), (2) with effect from a date to be appointed. This amendment will not extend to Scotland. That definition to read as follows—

" "nuclear material" has the same meaning as in the Nuclear Material (Offences) Act 1983 (see section 6 of that Act);".

5 Time of importation, exportation, etc

(1) The provisions of this section shall have effect for the purposes of the customs and excise Acts.

(2) Subject to subsections (3) and (6) below, the time of importation of any goods shall be deemed to be—

(*a*) where the goods are brought by sea, the time when the ship carrying them comes within the limits of a port;
(*b*) where the goods are brought by air, the time when the aircraft carrying them lands in the United Kingdom or the time when the goods are unloaded in the United Kingdom, whichever is the earlier;
(*c*) where the goods are brought by land, the time when the goods are brought across the boundary into Northern Ireland.

(3) In the case of goods brought by sea of which entry is not required under [regulation 5 of the Customs Controls on Importation of Goods Regulations 1991][1], the time of importation shall be deemed to be the time when the ship carrying them came within the limits of the port at which the goods are discharged.

(4) Subject to subsections (5) and (7) below, the time of exportation of any goods from the United Kingdom shall be deemed to be—

(*a*) where the goods are exported by sea or air, the time when the goods are shipped for exportation;
(*b*) where the goods are exported by land, the time when they are cleared by the proper officer at the last customs and excise station on their way to the boundary.

(5) In the case of goods of a class or description with respect to the exportation of which any prohibition or restriction is for the time being in force under or by virtue of any enactment which are exported by sea or air, the time of exportation shall be deemed to be the time when the exporting ship or aircraft departs from the last port or customs and excise airport at which it is cleared before departing for a destination outside the United Kingdom.

(6) Goods imported by means of a pipe-line shall be treated as imported at the time when they are brought within the limits of a port or brought across the boundary into Northern Ireland.

(7) Goods exported by means of a pipe-line shall be treated as exported at the time when they are charged into that pipe-line for exportation.

(8) A ship shall be deemed to have arrived at or departed from a port at the time when the ship comes within or, as the case may be, leaves the limits of that port.

Commentary—*De Voil Indirect Tax Service* **V3.307, V4.307.**

Cross references—See VATA 1994 Sch 13 para 19 (importation of goods around that date; determination of time of importation);

Postal Packets (Customs and Excise) Regulations, SI 1986/260 reg 5(*a*) (modification of this section in its application to goods contained in postal packets).

Amendments—[1] Words in sub-s (3) substituted by Customs and Excise (Single Market etc) Regulations, SI 1992/3095 Sch 1 para 3 with effect from 1 January 1993.

PART II
ADMINISTRATION

Appointment and duties of Commissioners, officers, etc

6 ...[1]

Commentary—*De Voil Indirect Tax Service* **V1.264, V1.265.**
Amendments—[1] Section repealed by Commissioners for Revenue and Customs Act 2005 ss 50, 52, Sch 4 para 21 and Sch 5 with effect from 18 April 2005 by virtue of the Commissioners for Revenue and Customs Act 2005 (Commencement) Order, SI 2005/1126, art 2(2).

Offences in connection with Commissioners, officers, etc

15 ...[1]

Commentary—*De Voil Indirect Tax Service* **V5.303.**
Amendments—[1] Section repealed by the Commissioners for Revenue and Customs Act 2005 s 52, Sch 5 with effect from 18 April 2005 (by virtue of SI 2005/1126, art 2(2)(i)).

16 ...[1]

Commentary—*De Voil Indirect Tax Service* **V5.303.**
Amendments—[1] Section repealed by Commissioners for Revenue and Customs Act 2005 ss 50, 52, Sch 4 para 21 and Sch 5 with effect from 18 April 2005 by virtue of the Commissioners for Revenue and Customs Act 2005 (Commencement) Order, SI 2005/1126, art 2(2).

Commissioners' receipts and expenses

17 ...[1]

Commentary—*De Voil Indirect Tax Service* **V1.264.**
Amendments—[1] Section repealed by Commissioners for Revenue and Customs Act 2005 ss 50, 52, Sch 4 para 21 and Sch 5 with effect from 18 April 2005 by virtue of the Commissioners for Revenue and Customs Act 2005 (Commencement) Order, SI 2005/1126, art 2(2).

PART III
CUSTOMS AND EXCISE CONTROL AREAS

19 Appointment of ports, etc

(1) The Commissioners may by order made by statutory instrument appoint and name as a port for the purposes of customs and excise any area in the United Kingdom specified in the order.

(2) The appointment of any port for those purposes made before 1st August 1952 may be revoked, and the name or limits of any such port may be altered, by an order under subsection (1) above as if the appointment had been made by an order under that subsection.

(3) The Commissioners may in any port from time to time appoint boarding stations for the purpose of the boarding of or disembarkation from ships by officers.

Commentary—*De Voil Indirect Tax Service* **V3.307, V4.251**

21 Control of movement of aircraft, etc into and out of the United Kingdom

(1)–(6) ...

(7) In this Act "customs and excise airport" means an aerodrome for the time being designated as a place for the landing or departure of aircraft for the purposes of the customs and excise Acts by an order made by the Secretary of State with the concurrence of the Commissioners which is in force under an Order in Council made in pursuance of [section 60 of the Civil Aviation Act 1982][1].

(8) ...

Commentary—*De Voil Indirect Tax Service* **V3.307.**
Note—Sub-ss (1)–(6), (8) are not relevant to VAT.
Amendments—[1] Words substituted by Civil Aviation Act 1982 Sch 15 para 23.

PART IV
CONTROL OF IMPORTATION

Inward entry and clearance

37 ...

Amendments—This section repealed by Customs and Excise (Single Market etc) Regulations, SI 1992/3095 regs 2, 3(5) and Sch 2 with effect from 1 January 1993.

[37A Initial and supplementary entries

[(1) The Commissioners may—

(*a*) give such directions as they think fit for enabling an entry under regulation 5 of the Customs Controls on Importation of Goods Regulations 1991 to consist of an initial entry and a supplementary entry where the importer is authorised for the purposes of this section in accordance with the directions; and

(*b*) include in the directions such supplementary provision in connection with entries consisting of initial and supplementary entries as they think fit.][5]

[(1A) Without prejudice to section 37 above, a direction under that section may—

(*a*) provide that where the importer is not authorised for the purposes of this section but a person who is so authorised is appointed as his agent for the purpose of entering the goods, the entry may consist of an initial entry made by the person so appointed and a supplementary entry so made; and

(*b*) make such supplementary provision in connection with entries consisting of initial and supplementary entries made as mentioned in paragraph (*a*) above as the Commissioners think fit.][3]

[(2) Where—

(*a*) an initial entry made under subsection (1) above has been accepted and the importer has given security by deposit of money or otherwise to the satisfaction of the Commissioners for payment of the unpaid duty, or

(*b*) an initial entry made under subsection (1A) above has been accepted and the person making the entry on the importer's behalf has given such security as is mentioned in paragraph (*a*) above,

the goods may][4] be delivered without payment of any duty chargeable in respect of the goods, but any such duty shall be paid within such time as the Commissioners may direct.

(3) An importer who makes an initial entry [under subsection (1) above][3] shall complete the entry by delivering the supplementary entry within such time as the Commissioners may direct.

[(3A) A person who makes an initial entry under subsection (1A) above on behalf of an importer shall complete the entry by delivering the supplementary entry within such time as the Commissioners may direct.][3]

(4) For the purposes of the customs and excise Acts an entry of goods shall be taken to have been delivered when an initial entry of the goods has been delivered, and accepted when an initial entry has been accepted.][1–2]

Commentary—*De Voil Indirect Tax Service* **V3.308**

Amendments—[1–2] This section inserted by FA 1984 Sch 5 para 2.

[3] Sub-ss (1A), (3A) and words in sub-s (3) inserted by FA 1990 s 7 and Sch 3 paras 1, 2(1), (3), (6), in relation to goods imported after 25 July 1990.

[4] Words in sub-s (2) substituted by FA 1990 s 7 and Sch 3 paras 1, 2(1), (4) in relation to goods imported after 25 July 1990.

[5] Sub-s (1) substituted by Customs and Excise (Single Market etc) Regulations, SI 1992/3095 Sch 1 para 5 with effect from 1 January 1993.

[37B Postponed entry

(1) The Commissioners may, if they think fit, direct that where—

(*a*) such goods as may be specified in the direction are imported by an importer authorised for the purposes of this subsection;

(*b*) the importer has delivered a document relating to the goods to the proper officer, in such form and manner, containing such particulars and accompanied by such documents as the Commissioners may direct; and

(*c*) the document has been accepted by the proper officer,

the goods may be delivered before an entry of them has been delivered or any duty chargeable in respect of them has been paid.

[(1A) The Commissioners may, if they think fit, direct that where—

(*a*) such goods as may be specified in the direction are imported by an importer who is not authorised for the purposes of this subsection;

(*b*) a person who is authorised for the purposes of this subsection is appointed as his agent for the purpose of entering the goods;

(*c*) the person so appointed has delivered a document relating to the goods to the proper officer, in such form and manner, containing such particulars and accompanied by such documents as the Commissioners may direct; and

(*d*) the document has been accepted by the proper officer,

the goods may be delivered before an entry of them has been delivered or any duty chargeable in respect of them has been paid.][2]

(2) The Commissioners may, if they think fit, direct that where—

(*a*) such goods as may be specified in the direction are imported by an importer authorised for the purposes of this subsection;

(*b*) the goods have been removed from the place of importation to a place approved by the Commissioners for the clearance out of charge of such goods; and

(*c*) the conditions mentioned in subsection (3) below have been satisfied,

the goods may be delivered before an entry of them has been delivered or any duty chargeable in respect of them has been paid.

(3) The conditions are that—

(*a*) on the arrival of the goods at the approved place the importer delivers to the proper officer a notice of the arrival of the goods in such form and containing such particulars as may be required by the directions;

(*b*) within such time as may be so required the importer enters such particulars of the goods and such other information as may be so required in a record maintained by him at such place as the proper officer may require; and

(*c*) the goods are kept secure in the approved place for such period as may be required by the directions.

[(3A) The Commissioners may, if they think fit, direct that where—

(*a*) such goods as may be specified in the direction are imported by an importer who is not authorised for the purposes of this subsection;

(*b*) a person who is authorised for the purposes of this subsection is appointed as his agent for the purpose of entering the goods;

(*c*) the goods have been removed from the place of importation to a place approved by the Commissioners for the clearance out of charge of such goods; and

(*d*) the conditions mentioned in subsection (3B) below have been satisfied,

the goods may be delivered before an entry of them has been delivered or any duty chargeable in respect of them has been paid.][2]

[(3B) the conditions are that—

(*a*) on the arrival of the goods at the approved place the person appointed as the agent of the importer for the purpose of entering the goods delivers to the proper officer a notice of the arrival of the goods in such form and containing such particulars as may be required by the directions;

(*b*) within such time as may be so required the person appointed as the agent of the importer for the purpose of entering the goods enters such particulars of the goods and such other information as may be so required in a record maintained by him at such place as the proper officer may require; and

(*c*) the goods are kept secure in the approved place for such period as may be required by the directions.][3]

(4) The Commissioners may direct that the condition mentioned in subsection (3)(*a*) [or (3B)(*a*)][3] above shall not apply in relation to any goods specified in the direction and such a direction may substitute another condition.

(5) No goods shall be delivered under [subsection (1) or (2) above][4] unless the importer gives security by deposit of money or otherwise to the satisfaction of the Commissioners for the payment of any duty chargeable in respect of the goods which is unpaid.

[(5A) No goods shall be delivered under subsection (1A) or (3A) above unless the person appointed as the agent of the importer for the purpose of entering the goods gives security by deposit of money or otherwise to the satisfaction of the Commissioners for the payment of any duty chargeable in respect of the goods which is unpaid.][2]

(6) Where goods of which no entry has been made have been delivered under [sub-section (1) or (2) above][4], the importer shall deliver an entry of the goods under [regulation 5 of the Customs Controls on Importation of Goods Regulations 1991][5] within such time as the Commissioners may direct.

[(6A) Where goods of which no entry has been made have been delivered under sub-section (1A) or (3A) above, the person appointed as the agent of the importer for the purpose of entering the goods shall deliver an entry of the goods under section 37(1) above within such time as the Commissioners may direct.][2]

(7) For the purposes of section 43(2)(*a*) below such an entry shall be taken to have been accepted—

(*a*) in the case of goods delivered by virtue of a direction under subsection (1) [or (1A)][3] above, on the date on which the document mentioned in that subsection was accepted; and

(*b*) in the case of goods delivered by virtue of a direction under subsection (2) above, on the date on which particulars of the goods were entered as mentioned in subsection (3)(*b*) above;][1] [and][2]

[(*c*) in the case of goods delivered by virtue of a direction under subsection (3A) above, on the date on which particulars of the goods were entered as mentioned in subsection (3B)(*b*) above.][2]

Commentary—*De Voil Indirect Tax Service* **V3.308, V3.313**.

Amendments—[1] This section inserted by FA 1984 Sch 5 para 2.

[2] Sub-ss (1A), (3A), (3B), (5A), (6A), (7)(*c*) inserted by FA 1990 s 7 and Sch 3 paras 1, 3(1), (2), (3), (6), (8), (9)(*b*) in relation to goods imported after 25 July 1990.

[3] Words in sub-ss (4), (7)(*a*) inserted by FA 1990 s 7 and Sch 3 paras 1, 3(1), (4), (9)(*a*).

[4] Words in sub-ss (5), (6) substituted by FA 1990 s 7 and Sch 3 paras 1, 3(1), (5), (7).

[5] Words in sub-s (6) substituted by Customs and Excise (Single Market etc) Regulations, SI 1992/3095 Sch 1 para 6 with effect from 1 January 1993.

[37C Provisions supplementary to ss 37A and 37B

(1) The Commissioners may, if they think fit—

(*a*) authorise any [person][2] for the purposes of section 37A, or 37B(1) [, (1A), (2) or (3A)][3] above; and

(*b*) suspend or cancel the authorisation of any [person][2] where it appears to them that he has failed to comply with any requirement imposed on him by or under this Part of this Act or that there is other reasonable cause for suspension or cancellation.

(2) The Commissioners may give directions—

(*a*) imposing such requirements as they think fit on any [person][2] authorised under this section; or

(*b*) varying any such requirements previously imposed.

(3) If any person without reasonable excuse contravenes any requirement imposed by or under section 37A, 37B or this section he shall be liable on summary conviction to a penalty of level 4 on the standard scale.][1]

Commentary—*De Voil Indirect Tax Service* **V3.308**.

Amendments—[1] This section inserted by FA 1984 Sch 5 para 2.

[2] Word in sub-ss (1)(*a*), (*b*), (2)(*a*) substituted by FA 1990 s 7 and Sch 3 paras 1, 4 in relation to goods imported after 25 July 1990.

[3] Words in sub-s (1)(*a*) substituted by FA 1990 s 7 and Sch 3 paras 1, 4 in relation to goods imported after 25 July 1990.

[38B Correction and cancellation of entry

(1) Where goods have been entered for home use or for free circulation the importer may correct any of the particulars contained in an entry of the goods after it has been accepted if—

(*a*) the goods have not been cleared from customs and excise charge;

(*b*) he has not been notified by an officer that the goods are to be examined; and

(*c*) the entry has not been found by an officer to be incorrect.

(2) The proper officer may permit or require any correction allowed by subsection (1) above to be made by the delivery of a substituted entry.

(3) An entry of goods may at the request of the importer be cancelled at any time before the goods are cleared from customs and excise charge if the importer proves to the satisfaction of the Commissioners that the entry was delivered by mistake or that the goods cannot be cleared for free circulation.][1]

Commentary—*De Voil Indirect Tax Service* **V3.308**.

Amendments—[1] This section inserted by FA 1981 s 10(1), Sch 6 para 4 with effect from 1 April 1982; see FA 1981 (Import Procedures) (Commencement) Order, SI 1982/205.

41 Failure to comply with provisions as to entry

Without prejudice to any liability under any other provision of the Customs and Excise Acts 1979, any person making entry of goods on their importation who fails to comply with any of the requirements of this Part of this Act in connection with that entry shall be liable on summary conviction to a penalty of [level 2 on the standard scale][2] and the goods in question shall be liable to forfeiture [but this section shall not apply to—][1]

[(*a*) any failure which has been or may be remedied by virtue of section 38B(1); or][1]

[(*b*) any failure in respect of an entry which by virtue of section 38B(3) has been or may be cancelled at his request.][1]

Amendments—[1] Paras (*a*), (*b*) and the preceding words added by FA 1981 s 10(1), Sch 6 para 6 with effect from 1 April 1982; see FA 1981 (Import Procedures) (Commencement) Order, SI 1982/205.

[2] Words substituted by virtue of Criminal Justice Act 1982 ss 37, 46.

42 Power to regulate unloading, removal, etc of imported goods

(1) The Commissioners may make regulations—

(*a*) prescribing the procedure to be followed by a ship arriving at a port, an aircraft arriving at a customs and excise airport, or a person conveying goods into Northern Ireland by land;

(*b*) regulating the unloading, landing, movement and removal of goods on their importation;

and different regulations may be made with respect to importation by sea, air or land respectively.

(2) If any person contravenes or fails to comply with any regulation made under this section or with any direction given by the Commissioners or the proper officer in pursuance of any such regulation, he shall be liable on summary conviction to a penalty of [level 3 on the standard scale][1] and any goods in respect of which the offence was committed shall be liable to forfeiture.

[(3) Subsection (1)(*b*) above shall not apply in relation to goods imported on or after 1st January 1992 from a place outside the customs territory of the Community][2] [or to any goods which are moving under the procedure specified in [Article 165 of Council Regulation (EEC) No 2913/92 and Article 311 of Commission Regulation (EEC) No 2454/93][4] (transit procedures).][3]

Cross references—See Channel Tunnel (Customs and Excise) Order, SI 1990/2167 Schedule, para 6 (modification of sub-s (1)(*a*) above to extend its application to a vehicle arriving at a Customs approved area in France or through the tunnel from France).

FA 1994 s 14(1)(*d*) and Sch 5 para 2(3) (decisions by Commissioners for the purposes of regulations under this section; Commissioners' obligation to review certain decisions if required by any person affected by them).

Amendments—[1] Words in sub-s (2) substituted by virtue of Criminal Justice Act 1982 ss 37, 38, 46.

[2] Sub-s (3) added by Customs Controls on Importation of Goods Regulations, SI 1991/2724 reg 6(1), (9).

[3] Words in sub-s (3) added by Customs and Excise (Single Market etc) Regulations, SI 1992/3095 reg 3(2) with effect from 1 January 1993.

[4] Words in sub-s (3) substituted by Community Customs Code (Consequential Amendment of References) Regulations, SI 1993/3014 reg 2(1), (2).

Provisions as to duty on imported goods

43 Duty on imported goods

(1) Save as permitted by or under the customs and excise Acts or section 2(2) of the European Communities Act 1972 or any Community regulation or other instrument having the force of law, no imported goods shall be delivered or removed on importation until the importer has paid to the proper officer any duty chargeable thereon, and that duty shall, in the case of goods of which entry is made, be paid on making the entry.

(2) [Subject to subsections (2A), (2B) [(2C) and (2D)][7] below,][3] the duties of customs or excise and the rates thereof chargeable on imported goods—

[(*a*) if entry is made thereof, except where the entry is for warehousing, or if they are declared under section 78 below, shall be those in force with respect to such goods at the time when the entry is accepted or the declaration is made;][1]

(*b*) if entry *or, in the case of goods entered by bill of sight, perfect entry* is made thereof for warehousing, shall be ascertained in accordance with warehousing regulations;

[(*c*) if no entry is made thereof and the goods are not declared under section 78 below shall be—

(i) as respects Community customs duties, those in force with respect to such goods at the time of their entry into the customs territory of the Community; and

(ii) as respects other duties, those in force with respect to such goods at the time of their importation.][4]

[(2A) Where the Commissioners require a duty of customs to be paid because of a failure to comply with a condition or other obligation imposed under section 47 or 48 below (not being a condition or obligation required to be complied with before the goods were allowed to be removed or delivered) the duty shall be charged as if entry of the goods had been accepted at the time when the non-compliance occurred.][5]

[(2B) Where any duties of customs are chargeable in respect of waste or debris resulting from the destruction of imported goods in free circulation, those duties and their rates shall be those in force at the time when the goods were destroyed.][5]

[(2C) As respects goods which have been unlawfully removed from customs charge, subsection (2)(*c*) above shall have effect with respect to any duties of customs as if they had entered the customs territory of the Community, or, as the case may be, had been imported at the time of their removal.][5]

[(2D) Nothing in the provisions of subsections (1) and (2) above or of subsection (6) below or in any exception to any of those provisions made by or under any of sections 44 to 48 below shall have effect for the purposes of any duty of excise chargeable on any goods for which—

(*a*) the excise duty point is fixed by regulations under section 1 of the Finance (No 2) Act 1992; and

(*b*) the applicable rate of duty is determined in accordance with subsection (2) of that section.][6]

(3) Any goods brought or coming into the United Kingdom by sea otherwise than as cargo, stores or baggage carried in a ship shall be chargeable with the like duty, if any, as would be applicable to those goods if they had been imported as merchandise; and if any question arises as to the origin of the goods they shall, unless that question is determined under section 120 below, section 14 of the Customs and Excise Duties (General Reliefs) Act 1979 (produce of the sea or continental shelf) or under a Community regulation or other instrument having the force of law, be deemed to be the produce of such country as the Commissioners may on investigation determine.

(4) Where, in accordance with approval given by the Commissioners, entry of goods is made by any method involving the use of a computer, subsection (2) above shall have effect as if the reference in paragraph (a) to the time of the delivery of the entry were a reference to the time when particulars contained in the entry are accepted by the computer.

(5) …

[(6) Where entry of goods is made otherwise than for warehousing and there is a reduction in the rate of duty of customs or excise chargeable on the goods between—

(*a*) the time mentioned in subsection (2)(*a*) above; and

(*b*) the time when the goods are cleared from customs and excise charge,

the rate of the duty chargeable on the goods shall, if the importer so requests, be that in force at the time mentioned in paragraph (*b*) above unless clearance of the goods has been delayed by reason of any act or omission for which the importer is responsible.][2]

[(7) Notwithstanding section 6(5) of the European Communities Act 1972 "duty of customs" in subsection (6) above does not include any agricultural levy.][2]

[(8) Where samples are taken of goods under section 38A above and the quantity of the goods covered by the entry which is subsequently delivered does not include the samples the duties of customs and the rates of those duties chargeable on the samples shall be those in force at the time when the application under subsection (1) of that section was made and shall be determined by reference to the particulars contained in the application.][2]

[(9) Where a substituted entry is delivered under section 38(2) or 38B(2) above the entry referred to in subsection (2)(*a*) above is the original entry.][2]

Commentary—*De Voil Indirect Tax Service* **V3.312**.
Notes—Sub-s (5) does not apply to VAT; see VAT Regulations, SI 1995/2518 reg 118(*c*)(i).
Cross references—See VATA 1994 s 16(1) and VAT Regulations, SI 1995/2518 reg 118(*c*)(i) (this section not to apply in relation to any tax chargeable on importation of goods from non-EEC countries with effect from 1 December 1992);
Postal Packets (Customs and Excise) Regulations, SI 1986/260 reg 5(*d*) (modification of this section in its application to goods contained in postal packets).
Amendments—[1] Sub-s (2)(*a*) substituted by FA 1981 s 10(3) and Sch 6 para 7(2) with effect from 1 April 1982; see FA 1981 (Import Procedures) (Commencement) Order, SI 1982/205.
[2] Sub-ss (6)–(9) added by FA 1981 s 10(3) and Sch 6 para 7(2) with effect from 1 April 1982; see FA 1981 (Import Procedures) (Commencement) Order, SI 1982/205.
[3] Words at the beginning of sub-s (2) substituted by Customs Duty Regulations, SI 1982/1324 reg 2(2).
[4] Sub-s (2)(*c*) substituted by Customs Duty Regulations, SI 1982/1324 reg 2(3) with effect from 15 October 1982.
[5] Sub-ss (2A)–(2C) inserted by Customs Duty Regulations, SI 1982/1324 reg 2(4) with effect from 15 October 1982.
[6] Sub-s (2D) inserted by F(No 2)A 1992 s 1(8) and Sch 1 para 2 with effect from 1 December 1992 by virtue of F(No 2)A 1992 (Commencement No 2 and Transitional Provisions) Order, SI 1992/2979 art 4 and Schedule, Pt II.
[7] Words in sub-s (2) substituted by F(No 2)A 1992 s 1(8) and Sch 1 para 2 with effect from 1 December 1992 by virtue of F(No 2)A 1992 (Commencement No 2 and Transitional Provisions) Order, SI 1992/2979 art 4 and Schedule, Pt II.
Prospective amendment—Words in italics in sub-s (2)(*b*) and whole of sub-s (4) repealed by FA 1981 Sch 19 Pt I, with effect from an appointed day.

44 Exclusion of section 43(1) for importers etc keeping standing deposits

Where the Commissioners so direct, section 43(1) above shall not apply if and so long as the importer or his agent pays to, and keeps deposited with, the Commissioners a sum by way of standing deposit sufficient in their opinion to cover any duty which may become payable in respect of goods entered by that importer or agent, and if the importer or agent complies with such other conditions as the Commissioners may impose.

Commentary—*De Voil Indirect Tax Service* **V5.117, V5.118**.

45 Deferred payment of customs duty

(1) The Commissioners may by regulations provide for the payment of customs duty to be deferred in such cases as may be specified by the regulations and subject to such conditions as may be imposed by or under the regulations; and duty of which payment is deferred under the regulations shall be treated, for such purposes as may be specified thereby, as if it had been paid.

(2) Regulations under this section may make different provision for goods of different descriptions or for goods of the same description in different circumstances.

Commentary—*De Voil Indirect Tax Service* **V5.117**.
Regulations—See Customs Duties (Deferred Payment) Regulations, SI 1976/1223.
Customs and Excise (Deferred Payment) (RAF Airfields and Offshore Installations) (No 2) Regulations, SI 1988/1898.
Excise Duties (Deferred Payment) Regulations, SI 1992/3152.

46 Goods to be warehoused without payment of duty

Any goods which are on their importation permitted to be entered for warehousing shall be allowed, subject to such conditions or restrictions as may be imposed by or under warehousing regulations, to be warehoused without payment of duty.

Commentary—*De Voil Indirect Tax Service* **V3.332**.

47 Relief from payment of duty of goods entered for transit or transhipment

Where any goods are entered for transit or transhipment, the Commissioners may allow the goods to be removed for that purpose, subject to such conditions and restrictions as they see fit, without payment of duty.

Commentary—*De Voil Indirect Tax Service* **V3.333**.
Cross references—See FA 1994 s 14(1)(*d*) and Sch 5 para 2(1)(*j*) (decisions by Commissioners for the purposes of this section; Commissioners' obligation to review any decision if required by any person affected by it).

48 Relief from payment of duty of goods temporarily imported

In such cases as the Commissioners may by regulations prescribe, where the Commissioners are satisfied that goods are imported only temporarily with a view to subsequent re-exportation, they may permit the goods to be delivered on importation, subject to such conditions as they see fit to impose, without payment of duty.

Commentary—*De Voil Indirect Tax Service* **V3.338**.
Cross references—See FA 1994 s 14(1)(*d*) and Sch 5 para 2(1)(*k*) (decisions by Commissioners for the purposes of this section; Commissioners' obligation to review any decision if required by any person affected by it).

Forfeiture, offences, etc in connection with importation

49 Forfeiture of goods improperly imported

(1) Where—

(*a*) except as provided by or under the Customs and Excise Acts 1979, any imported goods, being goods chargeable on their importation with customs or excise duty, are, without payment of that duty—

(i) unshipped in any port,

(ii) unloaded from any aircraft in the United Kingdom,

(iii) unloaded from any vehicle in, or otherwise brought across the boundary into, Northern Ireland, or

(iv) removed from their place of importation or from any approved wharf, examination station or transit shed; or

(*b*) any goods are imported, landed or unloaded contrary to any prohibition or restriction for the time being in force with respect thereto under or by virtue of any enactment; or

(*c*) any goods, being goods chargeable with any duty or goods the importation of which is for the time being prohibited or restricted by or under any enactment, are found, whether before or after the unloading thereof, to have been concealed in any manner on board any ship or aircraft or, while in Northern Ireland, in any vehicle; or

(*d*) any goods are imported concealed in a container holding goods of a different description; or

(*e*) any imported goods are found, whether before or after delivery, not to correspond with the entry made thereof; or

(*f*) any imported goods concealed or packed in any manner appearing to be intended to deceive an officer,

those goods shall, subject to subsection (2) below, be liable to forfeiture.

(2) Where any goods, the importation of which is for the time being prohibited or restricted by or under any enactment, are on their importation either—

(*a*) reported as intended for exportation in the same ship, aircraft or vehicle; or

(*b*) entered for transit or transhipment; or

(*c*) entered to be warehoused for exportation or for use as stores,

the Commissioners may, if they see fit, permit the goods to be dealt with accordingly.

Cross references—See Postal Packets (Customs and Excise) Regulations, SI 1986/260 (modification of this section in its application to postal packets).

Channel Tunnel (Customs and Excise) Order, SI 1990/2167 Schedule, para 7 (modification of sub-s (1) above to extend its application to goods unloaded from or concealed on a train or vehicle arriving through the tunnel from France or Belgium).

50 Penalty for improper importation of goods

(1) Subsection (2) below applies to goods of the following descriptions, that is to say—

(*a*) goods chargeable with a duty which has not been paid; and

(*b*) goods the importation, landing or unloading of which is for the time being prohibited or restricted by or under any enactment.

(2) If any person with intent to defraud Her Majesty of any such duty or to evade any such prohibition or restriction as is mentioned in subsection (1) above—

(*a*) unships or lands in any port or unloads from any aircraft in the United Kingdom or from any vehicle in Northern Ireland any goods to which this subsection applies, or assists or is otherwise concerned in such unshipping, landing or unloading; or

(*b*) removes from their place of importation or from any approved wharf, examination station, transit shed or customs and excise station any goods to which this subsection applies or assists or is otherwise concerned in such removal,

he shall be guilty of an offence under this subsection and may be [arrested.][3]

(3) If any person imports or is concerned in importing any goods contrary to any prohibition or restriction for the time being in force under or by virtue of any enactment with respect to those goods, whether or not the goods are unloaded, and does so with intent to evade the prohibition or restriction, he shall be guilty of an offence under this subsection and may be [arrested.][3]

(4) Subject to subsection [(5), (5A) or (5B)][1] below, a person guilty of an offence under sub-section (2) or (3) above shall be liable—

(*a*) on summary conviction, to a penalty of the prescribed sum or of three times the value of the goods, whichever is the greater, or to imprisonment for a term not exceeding 6 months, or to both; or

(*b*) on conviction on indictment, to a penalty of any amount, or to imprisonment for a term not exceeding [7 years][4], or to both.

(5) In the case of an offence under subsection (2) or (3) above in connection with a prohibition or restriction on importation having effect by virtue of section 3 of the Misuse of Drugs Act 1971 subsection (4) above shall have effect subject to the modifications specified in Schedule 1 to this Act.

[(5A) In the case of—

(*a*) an offence under subsection (2) or (3) above committed in Great Britain in connection with a prohibition or restriction on the importation of any weapon or ammunition that is of a kind mentioned in section 5(1)(*a*), (*ab*), (*aba*), (*ac*), (*ad*), (*ae*), (*af*) or (*c*) or (1A)(*a*) of the Firearms Act 1968,

(*b*) any such offence committed in Northern Ireland in connection with a prohibition or restriction on the importation of any weapon or ammunition that is of a kind mentioned in [Article 45(1)(*a*), (*b*), (*c*), (*d*), (*e*) or (*g*) or (2)(*a*)][7] of the Firearms (Northern Ireland) Order [2004][6], or

(c) any such offence committed in connection with the prohibition contained in section 20 of the Forgery and Counterfeiting Act 1981,

subsection (4)(b) above shall have effect as if for the words "7 years" there were substituted the words "10 years".][5]

[(5B) In the case of an offence under subsection (2) or (3) above in connection with the prohibition contained in regulation 2 of the Import of Seal Skins Regulations 1996, subsection (4) above shall have effect as if—

(*a*) for paragraph (*a*) there were substituted the following—

"(*a*) on summary conviction, to a fine not exceeding the statutory maximum or to imprisonment for a term not exceeding three months, or both"; and

(*b*) in paragraph (*b*) for the words "7 years" there were substituted the words "2 years".".][1]

(6) If any person—

(*a*) imports or causes to be imported any goods concealed in a container holding goods of a different description; or

(*b*) directly or indirectly imports or causes to be imported or entered any goods found, whether before or after delivery, not to correspond with the entry made thereof,

he shall be liable on summary conviction to a penalty of three times the value of the goods or [level 3 on the standard scale][2], whichever is the greater.

(7) In any case where a person would, apart from this subsection, be guilty of—

(*a*) an offence under this section in connection with the importation of goods contrary to a prohibition or restriction; and

(*b*) a corresponding offence under the enactment or other instrument imposing the prohibition or restriction, being an offence for which a fine or other penalty is expressly provided by that enactment or other instrument,

he shall not be guilty of the offence mentioned in paragraph (*a*) of this subsection.

Cross references—See Channel Tunnel (Customs and Excise) Order, SI 1990/2167 Schedule, para 8 (extension of the application of sub-ss (1), (2) above to a person who unloads etc goods brought on a vehicle arriving through the tunnel from France or is concerned with bringing goods into a control zone in France or Belgium).

Modification—Controlled Drugs (Drug Precursors) (Community External Trade) Regulations, SI 2008/296 reg 7 (modification of sub-s (4)(*a*), (*b*) in relation to breaches of Articles 20 and 12 of Council Regulation (EC) No 111/2005).

Amendments—[1] Words in sub-s (4) substituted, and sub-s (5B) inserted, by the Import of Seal Skins Regulations, SI 1996/2686 reg 4(1), with effect from 15 November 1996.

[2] Words in sub-s (6) substituted by virtue of Criminal Justice Act 1982 ss 37, 38, 46.

[3] Words in sub-ss (2), (3) substituted by Police and Criminal Evidence Act 1984 s 114(1) with effect from 1 January 1986; see Police and Criminal Evidence Act 1984 (Commencement No 3) Order, SI 1985/1934.

[4] Words in sub-s (4)(*b*) substituted by FA 1988 s 12(1)(*a*).

[5] Sub-s (5A) substituted by the Criminal Justice Act 2003 s 293(1), (2) with effect from 22 January 2004 (by virtue of SI 2004/81), except in relation to any offences committed before that date.

[6] Words and figure in sub-s (5A) substituted by the Firearms (Northern Ireland) Order, SI 2004/702 art 82(1), Sch 7 para 3 with effect from 1 February 2005 (by virtue of SR 2005/4).

Prospective amendments—In sub-s (4) words for ", (5B) or (5C)" to be substituted for words "or (5B)", and sub-a (5C) inserted, by the Criminal Justice and Immigration Act 2008 s 75, Sch 17 para 8(1), (3) with effect from a date to be appointed. This amendment will not extend to Scotland. Sub-s (5C) to read as follows—

"(5C) In the case of an offence under subsection (2) or (3) above in connection with a prohibition or restriction relating to the importation of nuclear material, subsection (4)(*b*) above shall have effect as if for the words "7 years" there were substituted the words "14 years".".

PART VII

CUSTOMS AND EXCISE CONTROL: SUPPLEMENTARY PROVISIONS

Additional provisions as to information

77 Information in relation to goods imported or exported

(1) An officer may require any person—

(*a*) concerned with the …[2] shipment for carriage coastwise of goods of which [for that purpose an entry is required by regulation 5 of the Customs Controls on Importation of Goods Regulations 1991 or an entry or specification is required by or under this Act][3]; or

(*b*) concerned in the carriage, unloading, landing or loading of goods which are being or have been imported or exported,

to furnish in such form as the officer may require any information relating to the goods and to produce and allow the officer to inspect and take extracts from or make copies of any invoice, bill of lading or other book or document whatsoever relating to the goods.

(2) If any person without reasonable cause fails to comply with a requirement imposed on him under subsection (1) above he shall be liable on summary conviction to a penalty of [level 3 on the standard scale.][1]

(3) Where any prohibition or restriction to which this subsection applies, that is to say, any prohibition or restriction under or by virtue of any enactment with respect to—

(*a*) the exportation of goods to any particular destination; or

(*b*) the exportation of goods of any particular class or description to any particular destination,

is for the time being in force, then, if any person about to ship for exportation or to export any goods or, as the case may be, any goods of that class or description, in the course of making entry thereof before shipment or exportation makes a declaration as to the ultimate destination thereof, and the Commissioners have reason to suspect that the declaration is untrue in any material particular, the goods may be detained until the Commissioners are satisfied as to the truth of the declaration, and if they are not so satisfied the goods shall be liable to forfeiture.

(4) Any person concerned in the exportation of any goods which are subject to any prohibition or restriction to which subsection (3) above applies shall, if so required by the Commissioners, satisfy the Commissioners that those goods have not reached any destination other than that mentioned in the entry delivered in respect of the goods.

(5) If any person required under subsection (4) above to satisfy the Commissioners as mentioned in that subsection fails to do so, then, unless he proves—

(*a*) that he did not consent to or connive at the goods reaching any destination other than that mentioned in the entry delivered in respect of the goods; and

(*b*) that he took all reasonable steps to secure that the ultimate destination of the goods was not other than that so mentioned,

he shall be liable on summary conviction to a penalty of three times the value of the goods or [level 3 on the standard scale][2], whichever is the greater.

Cross references—See Postal Packets (Customs and Excise) Regulations, SI 1986/260 (modification of this section in its application to postal packets).

FA 1994 s 14(1)(*d*) and Sch 5 para 2(1)(*m*) (decisions by Commissioners for the purposes of this section; Commissioners' obligation to review any decision if required by any person affected by it).

Amendments—[1] Words in sub-ss (2) and (5) substituted by virtue of Criminal Justice Act 1982 ss 37, 38, 46.

[2] Words in sub-s (1)(*a*) repealed by FA 1987 ss 10, 72(7) and Sch 16 Pt III.

[3] Words in sub-s (1) substituted by Customs and Excise (Single Market etc) Regulations, SI 1992/3095 reg 10(1), Sch 1 para 7.

[77A Information powers

(1) Every person who is concerned (in whatever capacity) in the importation or exportation of goods for which [for that purpose an entry is required by regulation 5 of the Customs Controls on Importation of Goods Regulations 1991 or an entry or specification is required by or under this Act][2] shall—

(*a*) furnish to the Commissioners, within such time and in such form as they may reasonably require, such information relating to the goods or to the importation or exportation as the Commissioners may reasonably specify; and

(*b*) if so required by an officer, produce or cause to be produced for inspection by the officer—

(i) at the principal place of business of the person upon whom the demand is made or at such other place as the officer may reasonably require, and

(ii) at such time as the officer may reasonably require,

any documents relating to the goods or to the importation or exportation.

(2) Where, by virtue of subsection (1) above, an officer has power to require the production of any documents from any such person as is referred to in that subsection, he shall have the like power to require production of the documents concerned from any other person who appears to the officer to be in possession of them; but where any such other person claims a lien on any document produced by him, the production shall be without prejudice to the lien.

(3) An officer may take copies of, or make extracts from, any document produced under subsection (1) or subsection (2) above.

(4) If it appears to him to be necessary to do so, an officer may, at a reasonable time and for a reasonable period, remove any document produced under subsection (1) or subsection (2) above and shall, on request, provide a receipt for any document so removed; and where a lien is claimed on a document produced under subsection (2) above, the removal of the document under this subsection shall not be regarded as breaking the lien.

(5) Where a document removed by an officer under subsection (4) above is reasonably required for the proper conduct of a business, the officer shall, as soon as practicable, provide a copy of the document, free of charge, to the person by whom it was produced or caused to be produced.

(6) Where any documents removed under the powers conferred by this section are lost or damaged, the Commissioners shall be liable to compensate their owner for any expenses reasonably incurred by him in replacing or repairing the documents.

(7) If any person fails to comply with a requirement under this section, he shall be liable on summary conviction to a penalty of level 3 on the standard scale.][1]

Amendments—[1] This section inserted by FA 1987 s 10.
[2] Words in sub-s (1) substituted by virtue of Customs and Excise (Single Market etc) Regulations, SI 1992/3095 reg 10(1) and Sch 1 para 7.

78 Customs and Excise control of persons entering or leaving the United Kingdom

(1) Any person entering the United Kingdom shall, at such place and in such manner as the Commissioners may direct, declare any thing contained in his baggage or carried with him which—

(*a*) he has obtained outside the United Kingdom; or

(*b*) being dutiable goods or chargeable goods, he has obtained in the United Kingdom without payment of duty or tax,

and in respect of which he is not entitled to exemption from duty and tax by virtue of any order under section 13 of the Customs and Excise Duties (General Reliefs) Act 1979 (personal reliefs).

In this subsection "chargeable goods" means goods on the importation of which value added tax is chargeable or goods obtained in the United Kingdom before 1st April 1973 which are chargeable goods within the meaning of the Purchase Tax Act 1963; and "tax" means value added tax or purchase tax.

[(1A) Subsection (1) above does not apply to a person entering the United Kingdom from the Isle of Man as respects anything obtained by him in the Island unless it is chargeable there with duty or value added tax and he has obtained it without payment of the duty or tax.][1]

[(1B) Subsection (1) above does not apply to a person entering the United Kingdom from another member State, except—

(*a*) where he arrives at a customs and excise airport in an aircraft in which he began his journey in a place outside the member States; or

(*b*) as respects such of his baggage as—

(i) is carried in the hold of the aircraft in which he arrives at a customs and excise airport, and

(ii) notwithstanding that it was transferred on one or more occasions from aircraft to aircraft at an airport in a member State, began its journey by air from a place outside the member States.][4]

(2) Any person entering or leaving the United Kingdom shall answer such questions as the proper officer may put to him with respect to his baggage and any thing contained therein or carried with him, and shall, if required by the proper officer, produce that baggage and any such thing for examination at such place as the Commissioners may direct.

[(2A) Subject to subsection (1A) above, where the journey of a person arriving by air in the United Kingdom is continued or resumed by air to a destination in the United Kingdom which is not the place where he is regarded for the purposes of this section as entering the United Kingdom, subsections (1) and (2) above shall apply in relation to that person on his arrival at that destination as they apply in relation to a person entering the United Kingdom.][3]

(3) Any person failing to declare any thing or to produce any baggage or thing as required by this section shall be liable on summary conviction to a penalty of three times the value of the thing not declared or of the baggage or thing not produced, as the case may be, or [level 3 on the standard scale][2], whichever is the greater.

(4) Any thing chargeable with any duty or tax which is found concealed, or is not declared, and any thing which is being taken into or out of the United Kingdom contrary to any prohibition or restriction for the time being in force with respect thereto under or by virtue of any enactment, shall be liable to forfeiture.

Commentary—*De Voil Indirect Tax Service* **V3.345, V3.346**.
Cross references—See F(No 2)A 1992 s 4(3)(*g*) (restriction of enforcement powers under this section with effect from 1 January 1993 in relation to movements of persons or things between member States).
Amendments—[1] Sub-s (1A) inserted by Isle of Man Act 1979 s 13, Sch 1.
[2] Words in sub-s (3) substituted by virtue of Criminal Justice Act 1982 ss 37, 38, 46.
[3] Sub-s (2A) inserted by F(No 2)A 1992 s 5 with effect from 1 January 1993.
[4] Sub-s (1B) inserted by Customs and Excise (Single Market etc) Regulations, SI 1992/3095 reg 3(10) with effect from 1 January 1993.

79 Power to require evidence in support of information

(1) The Commissioners may, if they consider it necessary, require evidence to be produced to their satisfaction in support of any information required by or under Parts III to VII of this Act to be provided in respect of goods imported or exported.

(2) Without prejudice to subsection (1) above, where any question as to the duties chargeable on any imported goods, or the operation of any prohibition or restriction on importation depends on any question as to the place from which the goods were consigned, or any question where they or other goods are to be treated as grown, manufactured or produced, or any question as to payments made or relief from duty allowed in any country or territory, then—

(*a*) the Commissioners may require the importer of the goods to furnish to them, in such form as they may prescribe, proof of—

(i) any statement made to them as to any fact necessary to determine that question, or
(ii) the accuracy of any certificate or other document furnished in connection with the importation of the goods and relating to the matter in issue,

and if such proof is not furnished to their satisfaction, the question may be determined without regard to that statement or to that certificate or document; and

(*b*) if in any proceedings relating to the goods or to the duty chargeable thereon the accuracy of any such certificate or document comes in question, it shall be for the person relying on it to furnish proof of its accuracy.

Cross references—See FA 1994 s 14(1)(*d*) and Sch 5 para 2(1)(*m*) (decisions by Commissioners for the purposes of this section; Commissioners' obligation to review any decision if required by any person affected by it).

PART VIII
WAREHOUSES AND QUEEN'S WAREHOUSES AND RELATED PROVISIONS ABOUT PIPE-LINES

92 Approval of warehouses

(1) The Commissioners may approve, for such periods and subject to such conditions as they think fit, places of security for the deposit, keeping and securing—

(*a*) of imported goods chargeable as such with excise duty (whether or not also chargeable with customs duty) without payment of the excise duty;
(*b*) of goods for exportation or for use as stores, being goods not eligible for home use;
(*c*) of goods manufactured or produced in the United Kingdom [or the Isle of Man][1] and permitted by or under the customs and excise Acts to be warehoused without payment of any duty of excise chargeable thereon;
(*d*) of goods imported into or manufactured or produced in the United Kingdom [or the Isle of Man][1] and permitted by or under the customs and excise Acts to be warehoused on drawback,

subject to and in accordance with warehousing regulations; and any place of security so approved is referred to in this Act as an "excise warehouse".

(2) The Commissioners may approve, for such periods and subject to such conditions as they think fit, places of security for the deposit, keeping and securing—

(*a*) of imported goods chargeable with customs duty or otherwise not for the time being in free circulation in member States (whether or not also chargeable with excise duty) without payment of the customs duty;
[(*b*) of such other goods as the Commissioners may allow to be warehoused—
(i) for exportation or for use as stores in cases where relief from or repayment of any customs duty or other payment is conditional on their exportation or use as stores; or
(ii) for exportation or for use for a purpose referred to in a Community regulation in cases where payment of an export refund under such a regulation is conditional on their exportation or use for such a purpose,][2]

subject to and in accordance with warehousing regulations; and any place of security so approved is referred to in this Act as a "customs warehouse".

(3) The same place may be approved under this section both as a customs and as an excise warehouse.

(4) Notwithstanding subsection (2) above and the terms of the approval of the warehouse but subject to directions under subsection (5) below, goods of the following descriptions, not being goods chargeable with excise duty which has not been paid, that is to say—

(*a*) goods originating in member States;
(*b*) goods which are in free circulation in member States; and
(*c*) goods placed on importation under a customs procedure (other than warehousing) involving the suspension of, or the giving of relief from, customs duties,

may be kept, without being warehoused, in a customs warehouse.

(5) The Commissioners may from time to time give directions—

(*a*) as to the goods which may or may not be deposited in any particular warehouse or class of warehouse;
(*b*) as to the part of any warehouse in which any class or description of goods may be kept or secured.

(6) If, after the approval of a warehouse as an excise warehouse, the occupier thereof makes without the previous consent of the Commissioners any alteration therein or addition thereto, [the making of the alteration or addition shall attract a penalty under section 9 of the Finance Act 1994 (civil penalties).][3]

(7) The Commissioners may at any time for reasonable cause revoke or vary the terms of their approval of any warehouse under this section.

[(8) Where any person contravenes or fails to comply with any condition imposed or direction given by the Commissioners under this section, his contravention or failure to comply shall attract a penalty under section 9 of the Finance Act 1994 (civil penalties).][3]

Commentary—*De Voil Indirect Tax Service* **V3.138, V3.332, V5.141**.
Notes—By virtue of Customs Warehousing Regulations, SI 1991/2725 regs 3(1), (4), 4 the following provisions of this section apply for VAT purposes only—
(i) sub-s (2)
(ii) the word "customs" in sub-s (3)
(iii) the words "customs warehouse" in sub-s (4).
Cross references—See FA 1994 s 14(1)(*d*) and Sch 5 para 2(1)(*n*) (decisions by Commissioners for the purposes of this section; Commissioners' obligation to review certain decisions if required by any person affected by them).
Amendments—[1] Words in sub-s (1)(*c*), (*d*) inserted by Isle of Man Act 1979 s 13, Sch 1 para 21.
[2] Sub-s (2)(*b*) substituted by FA 1988 s 9(1).
[3] Sub-s (8) and words in sub-s (6) substituted by FA 1994 Sch 4 paras 1, 2.

PART VIIIA
FREE ZONES

Amendments—This Part (ie ss 100A–100F) inserted by FA 1984 Sch 4 Pt I.

[100A Designation of free zones

(1) The Treasury may by order designate any area in the United Kingdom as a special area for customs purposes.

(2) An area so designated shall be known as a "free zone".

(3) An order under subsection (1) above—

(*a*) shall have effect for such period as shall be specified in the order;

(*b*) may be made so as to take effect, in relation to the area or any part of the area designated by a previous order under this section, on the expiry of the period specified in the previous order;

(*c*) shall appoint one or more persons as the responsible authority or authorities for the free zone;

(*d*) may impose on any responsible authority such conditions or restrictions as may be specified; and

(*e*) may be revoked if the Commissioners are satisfied that there has been a failure to comply with any condition or restriction.

(4) The Treasury may by order—

(*a*) from time to time vary—

(i) the conditions or restrictions imposed by a designation order, or

(ii) with the agreement of the responsible authority, the area designated; or

(*b*) appoint one or more persons as the responsible authority or authorities for a free zone either in addition to or in substitution for any person appointed as such by a designation order.

(5) In this Act "designation order" means an order made under subsection (1) above.

(6) Any order under this section shall be made by statutory instrument.][1]

Commentary—*De Voil Indirect Tax Service* **V3.331**.
Orders—See Free Zone (Birmingham Airport) Designation Order, SI 1991/1737; Free Zone (Humberside) Designation Order, SI 1994/144; Free Zone (Port of Sheerness) Designation Order, SI 1994/2898; Free Zone (Southampton) Designation Order, SI 2001/2880; Free Zone (Liverpool) Designation Order, SI 2001/2881; Free Zone (Prestwick Airport) Designation Order, SI 2001/2882; Free Zone (Port of Tilbury) Order, SI 2002/1418.
Amendments—[1] This section inserted by FA 1984 Sch 4 Pt I.

[100B Free zone regulations][1]

Commentary—*De Voil Indirect Tax Service* **V3.331**.
Amendments—[1] This section inserted by FA 1984 Sch 4 Pt I.
This section repealed by Free Zone Regulations, SI 1991/2727 reg 3(1) with effect from 1 January 1992, but subject to reg 3(2); and repealed fully by VATA 1994 s 100(2) and Sch 15, with effect from 1 September 1994.

[100C Free zone goods: customs duties, etc][1]

Commentary—*De Voil Indirect Tax Service* **V3.331**
Amendments—[1] This section inserted by FA 1984 Sch 4 Pt I.
This section repealed by VATA 1994 s 100(2), Sch 15, with effect from 1 September 1994.

[100D Free zone regulations: supplemental][1]

Commentary—*De Voil Indirect Tax Service* **V3.331**.
Amendments—[1] This section inserted by FA 1984 Sch 4 Pt I.
This section repealed by Free Zone Regulations, SI 1991/2727 reg 3(1) with effect from 1 January 1992.

[100E Control of trading in free zones][1]

Commentary—*De Voil Indirect Tax Service* **V3.331**.

Amendments—[1] This section inserted by FA 1984 Sch 4 Pt I.
This section repealed by the Free Zone Regulations, SI 1991/2727 reg 3(1) with effect from 1 January 1992.

[100F Powers of search

(1) Any person entering or leaving a free zone shall answer such questions as any officer may put to him with respect to any goods and shall, if required by the officer, produce those goods for examination at such place as the Commissioners may direct.

(2) At a time while a vehicle is entering or leaving a free zone, any officer may board the vehicle and search any part of it.

(3) Any officer may at any time enter upon and inspect a free zone and all buildings and goods within the zone.][1]

Commentary—*De Voil Indirect Tax Service* **V3.331**.
Amendments—[1] This section inserted by FA 1984 Sch 4 Pt I.

PART X

DUTIES AND DRAWBACKS—GENERAL PROVISIONS

General provisions relating to imported goods

125 Valuation of goods for purposes of *ad valorem* duties

(1), (2) …

(3) The Commissioners may make regulations for the purpose of giving effect to the *foregoing provisions of this section*, and in particular for requiring any importer or other person concerned with the importation of goods—

(*a*) to furnish to the Commissioners in such form as they may require, such information as is in their opinion necessary for a proper valuation of the goods; and

(*b*) to produce any books of account or other documents of whatever nature relating to the purchase, importation or sale of the goods by that person.

(4) If any person contravenes or fails to comply with any regulation made under sub-section (3) above he shall be liable on summary conviction to a penalty of [level 3 on the standard scale].[1]

Commentary—*De Voil Indirect Tax Service* **V3.314**.
Notes—Sub-ss (1) and (2) are excepted from the enactments which apply to value added tax by virtue of VATA 1994 s 16(1): VAT Regulations, SI 1995/2518 reg 118(*c*)(ii).
Sub-s (3) has effect in its application to value added tax by virtue of VATA 1994 s 16(1) as if the reference to the preceding subsections of s 125 (i e the italicised words) included a reference to VATA 1983 s 11: VAT Regulations, SI 1995/2518 reg 121.
Amendments—[1] Words in sub-s (4) substituted by virtue of Criminal Justice Act 1982 ss 37, 38, 46.

PART XI

[ARREST][1] OF PERSONS, FORFEITURE AND LEGAL PROCEEDINGS

[Arrest][1] of persons

Amendments—[1] Words in square brackets substituted by Police and Criminal Evidence Act 1984 s 114(1) with effect from 1 January 1986; see Police and Criminal Evidence Act 1984 (Commencement No 3) Order, SI 1985/1934.

138 Provisions as to [arrest][1] of persons

(1) Any person who has committed, or whom there are reasonable grounds to suspect of having committed, any offence for which he is liable to be [arrested][1] under the customs and excise Acts may be [arrested][1] by any officer …[2] or any member of Her Majesty's armed forces or coastguard at any time within [20 years][4] from the date of the commission of the offence.

(2) Where it was not practicable to [arrest][1] any person so liable at the time of the commission of the offence, or where any such person having been then or subsequently [arrested][1] for that offence has escaped, he may be [arrested][1] by any officer …[2] or any member of Her Majesty's armed forces or coastguard at any time and may be proceeded against in like manner as if the offence had been committed at the date when he was finally [arrested][1].

(3) Where any person who is a member of the crew of any ship in Her Majesty's employment or service is [arrested][1] by an officer for an offence under the customs and excise Acts, the commanding officer of the ship shall, if so required by the [arresting][1] officer, keep that person secured on board that ship until he can be brought before a court and shall then deliver him up to the proper officer.

[(4) Where any person has been arrested by a person who is not an officer—

(*a*) by virtue of this section; or

(*b*) by virtue of section 24 [or 24A][6] of the Police and Criminal Evidence Act 1984 in its application to offences under the customs and excise Acts, [or][5]

[(*c*) by virtue of Article 26 of the Police and Criminal Evidence (Northern Ireland) Order 1989 in its application to such offences][5] the person arresting him shall give notice of the arrest to an officer at the nearest convenient office of customs and excise.][3]

Cross reference—Nuclear Material (Offences) Act 1983 s 1D(2) (as inserted by Criminal Justice and Immigration Act 2008 s 75, Sch 17 para 3) (Offences of importing or exporting etc nuclear material: extended jurisdiction).

Amendments—[1] Words in sub-ss (1)–(3) substituted by Police and Criminal Evidence Act 1984 s 114(1) with effect from 1 January 1986; see Police and Criminal Evidence Act 1984 (Commencement No 3) Order, SI 1985/1934.

[2] Words in sub-ss (1), (2) repealed by Police and Criminal Evidence Act 1984 ss 26(1), 119(2), 120, Sch 7 with effect from 1 January 1986; see Police and Criminal Evidence Act 1984 (Commencement No 3) Order, SI 1985/1934.

[3] Sub-s (4) substituted by Police and Criminal Evidence Act 1984 s 119(1), Sch 6 Pt II, para 37 with effect from 1 January 1986; see Police and Criminal Evidence Act 1984 (Commencement No 3) Order, SI 1985/1934.

[4] Words in sub-s (1) substituted by FA 1988 s 11(1), (2).

[5] Words in sub-s (4) inserted by Police and Criminal Evidence (Northern Ireland) Order, SI 1989/1341 art 90(1), Sch 6 para 9.

[6] In sub-s (4)(*b*), words inserted by the Serious Organised Crime and Police Act 2005 s 111, Sch 7 para 54 with effect from 1 January 2006, see Serious Organised Crime and Police Act 2005 (Commencement No 4 and Transitory Provision), SI 2005/3495, art 2(1)(*m*).

Forfeiture

139 Provisions as to detention, seizure and condemnation of goods, etc

(1) Any thing liable to forfeiture under the customs and excise Acts may be seized or detained by any officer or constable or any member of Her Majesty's armed forces or coastguard.

(2) Where any thing is seized or detained as liable to forfeiture under the customs and excise Acts by a person other than an officer, that person shall, subject to subsection (3) below, either—

(*a*) deliver that thing to the nearest convenient office of customs and excise; or

(*b*) if such delivery is not practicable, give to the Commissioners at the nearest convenient office of customs and excise notice in writing of the seizure or detention with full particulars of the thing seized or detained.

(3) Where the person seizing or detaining any thing as liable to forfeiture under the customs and excise Acts is a constable and that thing is or may be required for use in connection with any proceedings to be brought otherwise than under those Acts it may, subject to subsection (4) below, be retained in the custody of the police until either those proceedings are completed or it is decided that no such proceedings shall be brought.

(4) The following provisions apply in relation to things retained in the custody of the police by virtue of subsection (3) above, that is to say—

(*a*) notice in writing of the seizure or detention and of the intention to retain the thing in question in the custody of the police, together with full particulars as to that thing, shall be given to the Commissioners at the nearest convenient office of customs and excise;

(*b*) any officer shall be permitted to examine that thing and take account thereof at any time while it remains in the custody of the police;

(*c*) nothing in the Police (Property) Act 1897 shall apply in relation to that thing.

(5) Subject to subsections (3) and (4) above and to Schedule 3 to this Act, any thing seized or detained under the customs and excise Acts shall, pending the determination as to its forfeiture or disposal, be dealt with, and, if condemned or deemed to have been condemned or forfeited, shall be disposed of in such manner as the Commissioners may direct.

(6) Schedule 3 to this Act shall have effect for the purpose of forfeitures, and of proceedings for the condemnation of any thing as being forfeited, under the customs and excise Acts.

(7) If any person, not being an officer, by whom any thing is seized or detained or who has custody thereof after its seizure or detention, fails to comply with any requirement of this section or with any direction of the Commissioners given thereunder, he shall be liable on summary conviction to a penalty of [level 2 on the standard scale][1].

(8) Subsections (2) to (7) above shall apply in relation to any dutiable goods seized or detained by any person other than an officer notwithstanding that they were not so seized as liable to forfeiture under the customs and excise Acts.

Commentary—*De Voil Indirect Tax Service* **V4.309, V4.346.**

Amendments—[1] Reference to level 2 on the standard scale substituted by virtue of Criminal Justice Act 1982 ss 37, 46.

General provisions as to legal proceedings

Cross references—See VATA 1994 s 72(12) (ss 145–155 of this Act to apply in relation to offences under the value added tax legislation);

Free Zone Regulations, SI 1991/2727 reg 7 (ss 145–155 of this Act to apply in relation to offences and penalties under reg 6 of the Regulations).

Statistics of Trade (Customs and Excise) Regulations, SI 1992/2790 (ss 145–148, 150–154 of this Act apply to these regulations).

145 Institution of proceedings

(1) Subject to the following provisions of this section, no proceedings for an offence under the customs and excise Acts or for condemnation under Schedule 3 to this Act shall be instituted [except—

(*a*) by or with the consent of the Director of Revenue and Customs Prosecutions, or

(*b*) by order of, or with the consent of, the Commissioners for Her Majesty's Revenue and Customs.][2]

(2) Subject to the following provisions of this section, any proceedings under the customs and excise Acts instituted [by order of the Commissioners][2] in a magistrates' court, and any such proceedings instituted [by order of the Commissioners][2] in a court of summary jurisdiction in Northern Ireland, shall be commenced in the name of an officer [of Revenue and Customs][2].

(3) Subsections (1) and (2) above shall not apply to proceedings on indictment in Scotland.

[(4) In the case of the death, removal, discharge or absence of the officer in whose name any proceedings were commenced under subsection (2) above, those proceedings may be continued by any officer authorised in that behalf by the Commissioners.] [2]

(5) Nothing in the foregoing provisions of this section shall prevent the institution of proceedings for an offence under the customs and excise Acts by order and in the name of a law officer of the Crown in any case in which he thinks it proper that proceedings should be so instituted.

(6) Notwithstanding anything in the foregoing provisions of this section, where any person has been [arrested][1] for any offence for which he is liable to be [arrested][1] under the customs and excise Acts, any court before which he is brought may proceed to deal with the case although the proceedings have not been instituted [in accordance with this section][2] or have not been commenced in the name of an officer.

Commentary—*De Voil Indirect Tax Service* **V5.304**.

Cross reference—Nuclear Material (Offences) Act 1983 s 1D(3) (as inserted by Criminal Justice and Immigration Act 2008 s 75, Sch 17 para 3) (Offences of importing or exporting etc nuclear material: extended jurisdiction).

Amendments—[1] Words in sub-s (6) substituted by Police and Criminal Evidence Act 1984 s 114(1) with effect from 1 January 1986; see Police and Criminal Evidence Act 1984 (Commencement No 3) Order, SI 1985/1934.

[2] Words in sub-ss (1), (6) substituted, words in sub-s (2) inserted, and words in sub-s (4) repealed, by Commissioners for Revenue and Customs Act 2005 ss 50, 52, Sch 4 para 23 and Sch 5 with effect from 18 April 2005 by virtue of the Commissioners for Revenue and Customs Act 2005 (Commencement) Order, SI 2005/1126, art 2(2).

146 Service of process

(1) Any summons or other process issued anywhere in the United Kingdom for the purpose of any proceedings under the customs and excise Acts may be served on the person to whom it is addressed in any part of the United Kingdom without any further endorsement, and shall be deemed to have been duly served—

(*a*) if delivered to him personally; or

(*b*) if left at his last known place of abode or business or, in the case of a body corporate, at their registered or principal office; or

(*c*) if left on board any vessel or aircraft to which he may belong or have lately belonged.

(2) Any summons, notice, order or other document issued for the purposes of any proceedings under the customs and excise Acts, or of any appeal from the decision of the court in any such proceedings, may be served by an officer.

In this subsection "appeal" includes an appeal by way of case stated.

(3) This section shall not apply in relation to proceedings instituted in the High Court or Court of Session.

Commentary—*De Voil Indirect Tax Service* **V5.304**.

Cross references—See Channel Tunnel (Customs and Excise) Order, SI 1990/2167 Schedule, para 22 (process deemed to have been duly served if left on the vehicle of a person using the tunnel; service in the United Kingdom includes a control zone in France within the tunnel system).

Nuclear Material (Offences) Act 1983 s 1D(3) (as inserted by Criminal Justice and Immigration Act 2008 s 75, Sch 17 para 3) (Offences of importing or exporting etc nuclear material: extended jurisdiction).

[146A Time limits for proceedings

(1) Except as otherwise provided in the customs and excise Acts, and notwithstanding anything in any other enactment, the following provisions shall apply in relation to proceedings for an offence under those Acts.

(2) Proceedings for an indictable offence shall not be commenced after the end of the period of 20 years beginning with the day on which the offence was committed.

(3) Proceedings for a summary offence shall not be commenced after the end of the period of 3 years beginning with that day but, subject to that, may be commenced at any time within 6 months from the date on which sufficient evidence to warrant the proceedings came to the knowledge of the prosecuting authority.

(4) For the purposes of subsection (3) above, a certificate of the prosecuting authority as to the date on which such evidence as is there mentioned came to that authority's knowledge shall be conclusive evidence of that fact.

(5) In the application of this section to Scotland—

(*a*) in subsection (2), "proceedings for an indictable offence" means proceedings on indictment;

(*b*) in subsection (3), "proceedings for a summary offence" means summary proceedings.

(6) In the application of this section to Northern Ireland—

(*a*) "indictable offence" means an offence which, if committed by an adult, is punishable on conviction on indictment (whether only on conviction on indictment, or either on conviction on indictment or on summary conviction);

(*b*) "summary offence" means an offence which, if committed by an adult, is punishable only on summary conviction.

(7) In this section, "prosecuting authority" means—

[(*a*) in England and Wales, means the Director of Revenue and Customs Prosecutions,
(*b*) in Scotland, means the Commissioners or the procurator fiscal, and
(*c*) in Northern Ireland, means the Commissioners.][2]][1]

Commentary—*De Voil Indirect Tax Service* **V5.304**.
Cross reference—Nuclear Material (Offences) Act 1983 s 1D(3) (as inserted by Criminal Justice and Immigration Act 2008 s 75, Sch 17 para 3) (Offences of importing or exporting etc nuclear material: extended jurisdiction).
Amendments—[1] This section inserted by FA 1989 s 16(1), (4) in relation to offences committed after 26 July 1989.
[2] Words in sub-s (7) inserted by the Commissioners for Revenue and Customs Act 2005 s 50, Sch 4 para 24 with effect from 18 April 2005 (by virtue of SI 2005/1126).

147 Proceedings for offences

(1) ...[3]

(2) *[Where, in England or Wales, on an application under section 6 of the Magistrates' Courts Act 1980 for dismissal of a charge under the customs and excise Acts, the court has begun to consider the evidence and any representations permitted under that section,][4] the court shall not proceed under [section 25(3) of the Magistrates' Courts Act 1980][1] to try the information summarily without the consent of—*

(*a*) *the Attorney General, in a case where the proceedings were instituted by his order and in his name; or*
(*b*) *the Commissioners, in any other case.*

(3) In the case of proceedings in England or Wales, without prejudice to any right to require the statement of a case for the opinion of the High Court, the prosecutor may appeal to the Crown Court against any decision of a magistrates' court in proceedings for an offence under the customs and excise Acts.

(4) In the case of proceedings in Northern Ireland, without prejudice to any right to require the statement of a case for the opinion of the High Court, the prosecutor may appeal to the county court against any decision of a court of summary jurisdiction in proceedings for an offence under the customs and excise Acts.

(5) ...[2]

Commentary—*De Voil Indirect Tax Service* **V5.304, V5.308**.
Cross reference—Nuclear Material (Offences) Act 1983 s 1D(3) (as inserted by Criminal Justice and Immigration Act 2008 s 75, Sch 17 para 3) (Offences of importing or exporting etc nuclear material: extended jurisdiction).
Amendments—[1] Words in sub-s (2) substituted by Magistrates' Courts Act 1980 Sch 7 para 176.
[2] Sub-s (5) repealed by Criminal Justice Act 1982 Sch 16.
[3] Sub-s (1) repealed by FA 1989 s 16(2), (4) and Sch 17 Pt I in relation to offences committed after 26 July 1989.
[4] Words in sub-s (2) substituted by Criminal Justice and Public Order Act 1994 s 44(3), Sch 4 Pt II, para 29(1), (2) with effect from a day to be appointed. The substituted words as originally enacted read "Where, in England or Wales, a magistrates' court has begun to inquire into an information charging a person with an offence under the customs and excise Acts as examining justices".
Prospective amendments—Sub-s (2) to be repealed (except in relation to Northern Ireland) by the Criminal Justice Act 2003 ss 41, 332, Sch 3 para 50, Sch 37 Pt 4 with effect from a date to be appointed.

148 Place of trial for offences

(1) Proceedings for an offence under the customs and excise Acts may be commenced—

(*a*) in any court having jurisdiction in the place where the person charged with the offence resides or is found; or
(*b*) if any thing was detained or seized in connection with the offence, in any court having jurisdiction in the place where that thing was so detained or seized or was found or condemned as forfeited; or
(*c*) in any court having jurisdiction anywhere in that part of the United Kingdom, namely—

(i) England and Wales,
(ii) Scotland, or
(iii) Northern Ireland,

in which the place where the offence was committed is situated.

(2) Where any such offence was committed at some place outside the area of any commission of the peace, the place of the commission of the offence shall, for the purposes of the jurisdiction of any court, be deemed to be any place in the United Kingdom where the offender is found or to which he is first brought after the commission of the offence.

(3) The jurisdiction under subsection (2) above shall be in addition to and not in derogation of any jurisdiction or power of any court under any other enactment.

Commentary—*De Voil Indirect Tax Service* **V5.304**.
Cross reference—Nuclear Material (Offences) Act 1983 s 1D(3) (as inserted by Criminal Justice and Immigration Act 2008 s 75, Sch 17 para 3) (Offences of importing or exporting etc nuclear material: extended jurisdiction).

149 Non-payment of penalties, etc: maximum terms of imprisonment

(1) Where, in any proceedings for an offence under the customs and excise Acts, a magistrates' court in England or Wales or a court of summary jurisdiction in Scotland, in addition to ordering the person convicted to pay a penalty for the offence—

(*a*) orders him to be imprisoned for a term in respect of the same offence; and

(*b*) further (whether at the same time or subsequently) orders him to be imprisoned for a term in respect of non-payment of that penalty or default of a sufficient distress to satisfy the amount of that penalty,

the aggregate of the terms for which he is so ordered to be imprisoned shall not exceed 15 months.

(2) …[1]

(3) Where, under any enactment for the time being in force in Northern Ireland, a court of summary jurisdiction has power to order a person to be imprisoned in respect of the non-payment of a penalty, or of the default of a sufficient distress to satisfy the amount of that penalty, for a term in addition and succession to a term of imprisonment imposed for the same offence as the penalty, then in relation to a sentence for an offence under the customs and excise Acts the aggregate of those terms of imprisonment may, notwithstanding anything in any such enactment, by any period not exceeding 15 months.

Commentary—*De Voil Indirect Tax Service* **V5.308**.

Amendments—[1] Sub-s (2) repealed by Criminal Justice (Scotland) Act 1980 Sch 8.

Prospective amendments—Sub-s (1A) to be inserted by the Tribunals, Courts and Enforcement Act 2007 s 50, Sch 10 paras 44 with effect from a date to be appointed. Sub-s (1A) as inserted, to read—

"(1A) In subsection (1)(*b*) as it applies to a magistrates' court in England or Wales the reference to default of sufficient distress to satisfy the amount of the penalty is a reference to want of sufficient goods to satisfy the amount, within the meaning given by section 79(4) of the Magistrates' Courts Act 1980.".

150 Incidental provisions as to legal proceedings

(1) Where liability for any offence under the customs and excise Acts is incurred by two or more persons jointly, those persons shall each be liable for the full amount of any pecuniary penalty and may be proceeded against jointly or severally as [the Director of Revenue and Customs Prosecutions (in relation to proceedings instituted in England and Wales) or the Commissioners (in relation to proceedings instituted in Scotland or Northern Ireland)][1] may see fit.

(2) In any proceedings for an offence under the customs and excise Acts instituted in England, Wales or Northern Ireland, any court by whom the matter is considered may mitigate any pecuniary penalty as they see fit.

(3) In any proceedings for an offence or for the condemnation of any thing as being forfeited under the customs and excise Acts, the fact that security has been given by bond or otherwise for the payment of any duty or for compliance with any condition in respect of the non-payment of which or non-compliance with which the proceedings are instituted shall not be a defence.

Commentary—*De Voil Indirect Tax Service* **V5.304, V5.307**.

Cross reference—Nuclear Material (Offences) Act 1983 s 1D(3) (as inserted by Criminal Justice and Immigration Act 2008 s 75, Sch 17 para 3) (Offences of importing or exporting etc nuclear material: extended jurisdiction).

Amendment—[1] Words in sub-s (1) substituted by Commissioners for Revenue and Customs Act 2005 s 50, Sch 4 para 25 with effect from 18 April 2005 by virtue of the Commissioners for Revenue and Customs Act 2005 (Commencement) Order, SI 2005/1126, art 2(2).

151 Application of penalties

The balance of any sum paid or recovered on account of any penalty imposed under the customs and excise Acts, after paying any such compensation or costs as are mentioned in [section 139 of the Magistrates' Courts Act 1980][1] to persons other than the Commissioners shall, notwithstanding any local or other special right or privilege of whatever origin, be accounted for and paid to the Commissioners or as they direct.

Cross reference—Nuclear Material (Offences) Act 1983 s 1D(3) (as inserted by Criminal Justice and Immigration Act 2008 s 75, Sch 17 para 3) (Offences of importing or exporting etc nuclear material: extended jurisdiction).

Amendments—[1] Words substituted by Magistrates' Courts Act 1980 Sch 7 para 177.

152 Power of Commissioners to mitigate penalties, etc

The Commissioners may, as they see fit—

(*a*) stay, sist or [compound an offence (whether or not proceedings have been instituted in respect of it) and compound proceedings][1] or for the condemnation of any thing as being forfeited under the customs and excise Acts; or

(*b*) restore, subject to such conditions (if any) as they think proper, any thing forfeited or seized under those Acts; or

(*c*), (*d*) …[2]

but paragraph (*a*) above shall not apply to proceedings on indictment in Scotland.

Commentary—*De Voil Indirect Tax Service* **V5.308**.

Cross references—See FA 1994 s 14(1)(*d*) and Sch 5 para 2(1)(*r*) (decisions by Commissioners under para (*b*) above; Commissioners' obligation to review any decision if required by any person affected by it).

Nuclear Material (Offences) Act 1983 s 1D(3) (as inserted by Criminal Justice and Immigration Act 2008 s 75, Sch 17 para 3) (Offences of importing or exporting etc nuclear material: extended jurisdiction).

Amendments—[1] Words substituted by Commissioners for Revenue and Customs Act 2005 s 50, Sch 4 para 26 with effect from 18 April 2005 by virtue of the Commissioners for Revenue and Customs Act 2005 (Commencement) Order, SI 2005/1126, art 2(2).

[2] Paras (*c*), (*d*) repealed by the Commissioners for Revenue and Customs Act 2005 s 52, Sch 5 with effect from 18 April 2005 by virtue of SI 2005/1126, art 2(2)(i).

153 …[1]

Amendments—[1] Section repealed by Commissioners for Revenue and Customs Act 2005 ss 50, 52, Sch 4 para 21 and Sch 5 with effect from 18 April 2005 by virtue of the Commissioners for Revenue and Customs Act 2005 (Commencement) Order, SI 2005/1126, art 2(2).

154 Proof of certain other matters

(1) An averment in any process in proceedings under the customs and excise Acts—

(*a*) that those proceedings were instituted by the order of the Commissioners; or

(*b*) that any person is or was a Commissioner, officer or constable, or a member of Her Majesty's armed forces or coastguard; or

(*c*) that any person is or was appointed or authorised by the Commissioners to discharge, or was engaged by the orders or with the concurrence of the Commissioners in the discharge of, any duty; or

(*d*) that the Commissioners have or have not been satisfied as to any matter as to which they are required by any provision of those Acts to be satisfied; or

(*e*) that any ship is a British ship; or

(*f*) that any goods thrown overboard, staved or destroyed were so dealt with in order to prevent or avoid the seizure of those goods,

shall, until the contrary is proved, be sufficient evidence of the matter in question.

(2) Where in any proceedings relating to customs or excise any question arises as to the place from which any goods have been brought or as to whether or not—

(*a*) any duty has been paid or secured in respect of any goods; or

(*b*) any goods or other things whatsoever are of the description or nature alleged in the information, writ or other process; or

(*c*) any goods have been lawfully imported or lawfully unloaded from any ship or aircraft; or

(*d*) any goods have been lawfully loaded into any ship or aircraft or lawfully exported or were lawfully waterborne; or

(*e*) any goods were lawfully brought to any place for the purpose of being loaded into any ship or aircraft or exported; or

(*f*) any goods are or were subject to any prohibition of or restriction on their importation or exportation,

then, where those proceedings are brought by or against the Commissioners, a law officer of the Crown or an officer, or against any other person in respect of anything purporting to have been done in pursuance of any power or duty conferred or imposed on him by or under the customs and excise Acts, the burden of proof shall lie upon the other party to the proceedings.

Commentary—*De Voil Indirect Tax Service* **V5.305**.

Cross references—See VATA 1994 s 72(12) (application of ss 145–155 of this Act to offences in relation to value added tax and accordingly "duty" in sub-s (2) above to include a reference to value added tax);

Channel Tunnel (Customs and Excise) Order, SI 1990/2167 Schedule, para 23 (extension of the application of sub-s (2) above to goods on a vehicle using the tunnel).

Nuclear Material (Offences) Act 1983 s 1D(3) (as inserted by Criminal Justice and Immigration Act 2008 s 75, Sch 17 para 3) (Offences of importing or exporting etc nuclear material: extended jurisdiction).

155 Persons who may conduct proceedings

[(1) An officer of Revenue and Customs or other person authorised by the Commissioners may conduct criminal proceedings relating to an assigned matter before a court of summary jurisdiction in Scotland or Northern Ireland.][1]

[(2) Any person who has been admitted as a solicitor and is employed by the Commissioners may act as a solicitor in any proceedings in England, Wales or Northern Ireland relating to any assigned matter notwithstanding that he does not hold a current practising certificate.][2]

Commentary—*De Voil Indirect Tax Service* **V5.305**.

Nuclear Material (Offences) Act 1983 s 1D(3) (as inserted by Criminal Justice and Immigration Act 2008 s 75, Sch 17 para 3) (Offences of importing or exporting etc nuclear material: extended jurisdiction).

Amendments—[1] Sub-s (1) substituted by Commissioners for Revenue and Customs Act 2005 s 50, Sch 4 para 27 with effect from 18 April 2005 by virtue of the Commissioners for Revenue and Customs Act 2005 (Commencement) Order, SI 2005/1126, art 2(2).

[2] Sub-s (2) repealed by Commissioners for Revenue and Customs Act 2005 ss 50, 52, Sch 4 para 21 and Sch 5 with effect from 18 April 2005 by virtue of the Commissioners for Revenue and Customs Act 2005 (Commencement) Order, SI 2005/1126, art 2(2).

Saving for outlying enactments of certain general provisions as to offences

156 Saving for outlying enactments of certain general provisions as to offences

(1) In subsections (2), (3) and (4) below (which reproduce certain enactments not required as general provisions for the purposes of the enactments re-enacted in the Customs and Excise Acts 1979) "the outlying provisions of the customs and excise Acts" [means the provisions][1] of the

customs and excise Acts, as for the time being amended, which were passed before the commencement of this Act and are not re-enacted in the Customs and Excise Acts 1979 [or the Betting and Gaming Duties Act 1981][1].

(2) It is hereby declared that any act or omission in respect of which a pecuniary penalty (however described) is imposed by any of the outlying provisions of the customs and excise Acts is an offence under that provision; and accordingly in this Part of this Act any reference to an offence under the customs and excise Acts includes a reference to such an act or omission.

(3) Subject to any express provision made by the enactment in question, an offence under any of the outlying provisions of the customs and excise Acts—

(*a*) where it is punishable with imprisonment for a term of 2 years, with or without a pecuniary penalty, shall be punishable either on summary conviction or on conviction on indictment;

(*b*) in any other case, shall be punishable on summary conviction.

…[2]

[(4) The maximum term of imprisonment which may be imposed on summary conviction in the sheriff court of an offence under any of the outlying provisions of the customs and excise Acts shall be 6 months.

(5) Where, in Scotland, an offence under any of the outlying provisions of the customs and excise Acts is triable only summarily by virtue of subsection (3)(b) above, the penalty for the offence shall be that to which a person was liable on summary conviction of the offence immediately before 29th July 1977 (the date of the passing of the Criminal Law Act 1977) subject to any increase by virtue of section 289C(5) of the Criminal Procedure (Scotland) Act 1975 or Part IV of the Criminal Justice Act 1982.][3]

Amendments—[1] Words sub-s (1) substituted by the Betting and Gaming Duties Act 1981, s 34(1), Sch 5, para 5.
[2] Words omitted repealed by the Criminal Justice Act 1982, ss 77, 78, Sch 14, para 43, Sch 16.
[3] Sub-ss (4), (5) substituted for original sub-s (4) by the Criminal Justice Act 1982, s 77, Sch 14, para 43.

PART XII
GENERAL AND MISCELLANEOUS

General powers, etc

157 Bonds and security

(1) Without prejudice to any express requirement as to security contained in the customs and excise Acts, the Commissioners may, if they see fit, require any person to give security [(or further security) by bond, guarantee][1] or otherwise for the observance of any condition in connection with customs or excise.

[(1A) For the purposes of this section "condition in connection with excise" includes a condition in connection with excise duty charged, under the law of a member State other than the United Kingdom, on—

(*a*) manufactured tobacco,
(*b*) alcohol or alcoholic beverages, or
(*c*) mineral oils.

The expressions used in paragraphs (*a*) to (*c*) above have the same meaning as in Council Directive 92/12/EEC.][2]

(2) Any bond[, guarantee or other security][3] taken for the purposes of any assigned matter—

(*a*) shall be taken [either on behalf of Her Majesty or on behalf of Her Majesty and the tax authorities of each member State other than the United Kingdom][4]; and

(*b*) shall be valid notwithstanding that it is entered into by a person under full age; and

(*c*) may be cancelled at any time by or by order of the Commissioners.

[In this subsection "assigned matter" includes any excise duty charged as mentioned in subsection (1A) above.][5]

Amendments—[1] Words in sub-s (1) substituted by the Finance Act 2000, s 27(1), (2) with effect from 28 July 2000.
[2] Sub-s (1A) inserted by the Finance Act 2000, s 27(1), (3) with effect from 28 July 2000.
[3] Words in sub-s (2) inserted by the Finance Act 2000, s 27(1), (4) with effect from 28 July 2000.
[4] Words in sub-s (2) inserted by the Finance Act 2000, s 27(1), (5) with effect from 28 July 2000.
[5] Words substituted by the Finance Act 2000, s 27(1), (6) with effect from 28 July 2000.

158 Power to require provision of facilities

(1) A person to whom this section applies, that is to say, a revenue trader and any person required by the Commissioners under the Customs and Excise Acts 1979 to give security in respect of any premises or place to be used for the examination of goods by an officer, shall—

(*a*) provide and maintain such appliances and afford such other facilities reasonably necessary to enable an officer to take any account or make any examination or search or to perform any other of his duties on the premises of that trader or at the bonded premises or place as the Commissioners may direct;

(*b*) keep any appliances so provided in a convenient place approved by the proper officer for that purpose; and

(*c*) allow the proper officer at any time to use anything so provided and give him any assistance necessary for the performance of his duties.

(2) Any person who contravenes or fails to comply with any provision of subsection (1) above shall be liable on summary conviction to a penalty of [level 3 on the standard scale][1].

(3) A person to whom this section applies shall provide and maintain any fitting required for the purpose of affixing any lock which the proper officer may require to affix to the premises of that person or any part thereof or to any vessel, utensil or other apparatus whatsoever kept thereon, and in default—

(*a*) the fitting may be provided or any work necessary for its maintenance may be carried out by the proper officer, and any expenses so incurred shall be paid on demand by that person; and

(*b*) if that person fails to pay those expenses on demand, he shall in addition be liable on summary conviction to a penalty of [level 3 on the standard scale][1].

(4) If any person to whom this section applies or any servant of his—

(*a*) wilfully destroys or damages any such fitting as is mentioned in subsection (3) above or any lock or key provided for use therewith, or any label or seal placed on any such lock; or

(*b*) improperly obtains access to any place or article secured by any such lock; or

(*c*) has any such fitting or any article intended to be secured by means thereof so constructed that that intention is defeated,

he shall be liable on summary conviction to a penalty of [level 5 on the standard scale][2] and may be [arrested][2].

Amendments—[1] References in sub-ss (2), (3) to level 3 on the standard scale substituted by virtue of the Criminal Justice Act 1982, ss 37, 38, 46.

[2] Reference in sub-s (4) to level 5 on the standard scale substituted by virtue of the Criminal Justice Act 1982, ss 37, 38, 46; word "arrested" substituted by the Police and Criminal Evidence Act 1984, s 114(1).

159 Power to examine and take account of goods

(1) Without prejudice to any other power conferred by the Customs and Excise Acts 1979, an officer may examine and take account of any goods—

(*a*) which are imported; or

(*b*) which are in a warehouse or Queen's warehouse; or

[(*bb*) which are in a free zone; or][2]

(*c*) which have been loaded into any ship or aircraft at any place in the United Kingdom [or the Isle of Man][1]; or

(*d*) which are entered for exportation or for use as stores; or

(*e*) which are brought to any place in the United Kingdom for exportation or for shipment for exportation or as stores; or

(*f*) in the case of which any claim for drawback, allowance, rebate, remission or repayment of duty is made;

and may for that purpose [open or unpack any container or][5] require any container to be opened or unpacked [and search it or anything in it.][5]

(2) Any examination of goods by an officer under the Customs and Excise Acts 1979 shall be made at such place as the Commissioners appoint for the purpose.

(3) In the case of such goods as the Commissioners may direct, and subject to such conditions as they see fit to impose, an officer may permit goods to be skipped on the quay or bulked, sorted, lotted, packed or repacked before account is taken thereof.

(4) Any opening, unpacking, weighing, measuring, repacking, bulking, sorting, lotting, marking, numbering, loading, unloading, carrying or landing of goods or their containers for the purposes of, or incidental to, the examination by an officer, removal or warehousing thereof shall be done, and any facilities or assistance required for any such examination shall be provided, by or at the expense of the proprietor of the goods[; but if an officer opens or unpacks any container, or searches it or anything in it, the Commissioners are to bear the expense of doing so.][5]

(5) If any imported goods which an officer has power under the Customs and Excise Acts 1979 to examine are without the authority of the proper officer removed from customs and excise charge before they have been examined, those goods shall be liable to forfeiture.

(6) If any goods falling within subsection (5) above are removed by a person with intent to defraud Her Majesty of any duty chargeable thereon or to evade any prohibition or restriction for the time being in force with respect thereto under or by virtue of any enactment, that person shall be guilty of an offence under this subsection and may be [arrested][3].

(7) A person guilty of an offence under subsection (6) above shall be liable—

(*a*) on summary conviction, to a penalty of the prescribed sum or of three times the value of the goods, whichever is the greater, or to imprisonment for a term not exceeding 6 months, or to both; or

(*b*) on conviction on indictment, to a penalty of any amount, or to imprisonment for a term not exceeding [7 years][4], or to both.

(8) Without prejudice to the foregoing provisions of this section, where by this section or by or under any other provision of the Customs and Excise Acts 1979 an account is authorised or required to be taken of any goods for any purpose by an officer, the Commissioners may, with the consent of the proprietor of the goods, accept as the account of those goods for that purpose an account taken by such other person as may be approved in that behalf by both the Commissioners and the proprietor of the goods.

Cross references—See Channel Tunnel (Customs and Excise) Order, SI 1990/2167 Schedule, para 24 (extension of the application of sub-s (1) above to goods loaded on a vehicle for exportation through the tunnel).

Amendments—[1] Words in sub-s (1)(*c*) inserted by Isle of Man Act 1979 s 13, Sch 1, para 22.

[2] Sub-s (1)(*bb*) inserted by FA 1984 Sch 4 Pt II, para 5.

[3] Word in sub-s (6) substituted by Police and Criminal Evidence Act 1984 s 114(1) with effect from 1 January 1986; see Police and Criminal Evidence Act 1984 (Commencement No 3) Order, SI 1985/1934.

[4] Words in sub-s (7)(*b*) substituted by FA 1988 s 12(1)(*a*).

[5] Words in sub-ss (1), (4) inserted by FA 2008 s 117(3)–(5) with effect from 21 July 2008.

164 Power to search persons

(1) Where there are reasonable grounds to suspect that any person to whom this section applies [(referred to in this section as "the suspect")][2] is carrying any article—

(*a*) which is chargeable with any duty which has not been paid or secured or

(*b*) with respect to the importation or exportation of which any prohibition or restriction is for the time being in force under or by virtue of any enactment,

[an officer may exercise the powers conferred by subsection (2) below and, if the suspect is not under arrest, may detain him for so long as may be necessary for the exercise of those powers and (where applicable) the exercise of the rights conferred by subsection (3) below.][3]

[(2) The officer may require the suspect—

(*a*) to permit such a search of any article which he has with him; and

(*b*) subject to subsection (3) below, to submit to such searches of his person, whether rub-down, strip or intimate,

as the officer may consider necessary or expedient; but no such requirement may be imposed under paragraph (*b*) above without the officer informing the suspect of the effect of subsection (3) below.][4]

[(3) If the suspect is required to submit to a search of his person, he may require to be taken—

(*a*) except in the case of a rub-down search, before a justice of the peace or a superior of the officer concerned; and

(*b*) in the excepted case, before such a superior;

and the justice or superior shall consider the grounds for suspicion and direct accordingly whether the suspect is to submit to the search.][4]

[(3A) A rub-down or strip search shall not be carried out except by a person of the same sex as the suspect; and an intimate search shall not be carried out except by a suitably qualified person.][4]

(4) This section applies to the following persons, namely—

(*a*) any person who is on board or has landed from any ship or aircraft;

(*b*) any person entering or about to leave the United Kingdom;

(*c*) any person within the dock area of a port;

(*d*) any person at a customs and excise airport;

(*e*) any person in, entering or leaving any approved wharf or transit shed which is not in a port;

[(*ee*) any person in, entering or leaving a free zone;][1]

(*f*) in Northern Ireland, any person travelling from or to any place which is on or beyond the boundary.

[(5) In this section—

"intimate search" means any search which involves a physical examination (that is, an examination which is more than simply a visual examination) of a person's body orifices;

"rub-down search" means any search which is neither an intimate search nor a strip search;

"strip search" means any search which is not an intimate search but which involves the removal of an article of clothing which—

(*a*) is being worn (wholly or partly) on the trunk; and

(*b*) is being so worn either next to the skin or next to an article of underwear;

"suitably qualified person" means a registered medical practitioner or a registered nurse.][5]

[(6) Notwithstanding anything in subsection (4) of section 48 of the Criminal Justice (Scotland) Act 1987 (detention and questioning by customs officers), detention of the suspect under subsection (1) above shall not prevent his subsequent detention under subsection (1) of that section.][5]

Cross references—See Channel Tunnel (Customs and Excise) Order, SI 1990/2167 Schedule, para 25 (this section to apply to any person in the tunnel system in the United Kingdom, in a through train in the United Kingdom, in, entering or leaving a customs approved area in the United Kingdom or in a control zone in France or Belgium).

F(No 2)A 1992 s 4(3)(*h*) (restriction on powers under this section with effect from 1 January 1993 in relation to movements of persons and things between member States).

Amendments—[1] Sub-s (4)(*ee*) inserted by FA 1984 Sch 4 Pt II, para 6.
[2] Words in sub-s (1) inserted by FA 1988 s 10(1)(*a*).
[3] Words in sub-s (1) substituted by FA 1988 s 10(1)(*b*).
[4] Sub-ss (2), (3), (3A) substituted for sub-ss (2), (3) by FA 1988 s 10(2).
[5] Sub-ss (5), (6) inserted by FA 1988 s 10(3).

General offences

167 Untrue declarations, etc

(1) If any person either knowingly or recklessly—

(*a*) makes or signs, or causes to be made or signed, or delivers or causes to be delivered to the Commissioners or any officer, any declaration, notice, certificate or other document whatsoever; or

(*b*) makes any statement in answer to any question put to him by an officer which he is required by or under any enactment to answer,

being a document or statement produced or made for any purpose of any assigned matter, which is untrue in any material particular, he shall be guilty of an offence under this subsection and may be [arrested][2]; and any goods in relation to which the document or statement was made shall be liable to forfeiture.

(2) Without prejudice to subsection (4) below, a person who commits an offence under subsection (1) above shall be liable—

(*a*) on summary conviction, to a penalty of the prescribed sum, or to imprisonment for a term not exceeding 6 months, or to both; or

(*b*) on conviction on indictment, to a penalty of any amount, or to imprisonment for a term not exceeding 2 years, or to both.

(3) If any person—

(*a*) makes or signs, or causes to be made or signed, or delivers or causes to be delivered to the Commissioners or an officer, any declaration, notice, certificate or other document whatsoever; or

(*b*) makes any statement in answer to any question put to him by an officer which he is required by or under any enactment to answer,

being a document or statement produced or made for any purpose of any assigned matter, which is untrue in any material particular, then, without prejudice to subsection (4) below, he shall be liable on summary conviction to a penalty of [level 4 on the standard scale.][1]

(4) Where by reason of any such document or statement as is mentioned in subsection (1) or (3) above the full amount of any duty payable is not paid or any overpayment is made in respect of any drawback, allowance, rebate of repayment of duty, the amount of the duty unpaid or of the overpayment shall be recoverable as a debt to the Crown or may be summarily recovered as a civil debt.

[(5) An amount of excise duty, or the amount of an overpayment in respect of any drawback, allowance, rebate or repayment of any excise duty, shall not be recoverable as mentioned in subsection (4) above unless the Commissioners have assessed the amount of the duty or of the overpayment as being excise duty due from the person mentioned in subsection (1) or (3) above and notified him or his representative accordingly.][3]

Commentary—*De Voil Indirect Tax Service* **V5.304**.
Note—Statistics of Trade (Customs and Excise) Regulations, SI 1992/2790 reg 12 modifies sub-s (2)(*a*) above by substituting "3 months" for "6 months" when a person is convicted under sub-s (1) above under the Intrastat System.
Cross references—See FA 1985 s 10(5), (6)(*c*) (meaning of document).
CRCA 2005 Sch 2 para 6 (this section does not apply in relation to a declaration, document or statement for a function relating to a matter to which CRCA 2005 s 7 applies).
Amendments—[1] Words in sub-s (3) substituted by virtue of Criminal Justice Act 1982 ss 37, 38, 46.
[2] Word in sub-s (1) substituted by Police and Criminal Evidence Act 1984 s 114(1) with effect from 1 January 1986; see Police and Criminal Evidence Act 1984 (Commencement No 3) Order, SI 1985/1934.
[3] Sub-s (5) inserted by FA 1997 s 50(2), Sch 6 para 5 with effect from a date to be appointed by the Commissioners.

168 Counterfeiting documents, etc

(1) If any person—

(*a*) counterfeits or falsifies any document which is required by or under any enactment relating to an assigned matter or which is used in the transaction of any business relating to an assigned matter; or

(*b*) knowingly accepts, receives or uses any such document so counterfeited or falsified; or

(*c*) alters any such document after it is officially issued; or

(*d*) counterfeits any seal, signature, initials or other mark of, or used by, any officer for the verification of such a document or for the security of goods or for any other purpose relating to an assigned matter,

he shall be guilty of an offence under this section and may be [arrested.][1]

(2) A person guilty of an offence under this section shall be liable—

(*a*) on summary conviction, to a penalty of the prescribed sum, or to imprisonment for a term not exceeding 6 months, or to both; or

(*b*) on conviction on indictment, to a penalty of any amount, or to imprisonment for a term not exceeding 2 years, or to both.

Commentary—*De Voil Indirect Tax Service* **V5.304**.
Note—Statistics of Trade (Customs and Excise) Regulations, SI 1992/2790 reg 12 modifies sub-s (2)(*a*) above by substituting "3 months" for "6 months" when a person is convicted under sub-s (1) above under the Intrastat System.
Cross references—See FA 1985 s 10(5), (6)(*d*) (meaning of document).
Amendments—[1] Word in sub-s (1) substituted by Police and Criminal Evidence Act 1984 s 114(1) with effect from 1 January 1986; see Police and Criminal Evidence Act 1984 (Commencement No 3) Order, SI 1985/1934.

171 General provisions as to offences and penalties

(1) Where—

(*a*) by any provision of any enactment relating to an assigned matter a punishment is prescribed for any offence thereunder or for any contravention of or failure to comply with any regulation, direction, condition or requirement made, given or imposed thereunder; and
(*b*) any person is convicted in the same proceedings of more than one such offence, contravention or failure,

that person shall be liable to that punishment for each such offence, contravention or failure of which he is so convicted.

(2) In this Act the "prescribed sum", in relation to the penalty provided for an offence, means—

(*a*) if the offence was committed in England [or Wales][2], the prescribed sum within the meaning of [section 32 of the Magistrates' Courts Act 1980 (£1,000 or other sum substituted by order under section 143(1) of that Act)][1];
(*b*) if the offence was committed in Scotland, the prescribed sum within the meaning of section 289B of the Criminal Procedure (Scotland) Act 1975 (£1,000 or other sum substituted by order under section 289D(1) of that Act);
[(*c*) if the offence was committed in Northern Ireland, the prescribed sum within the meaning of Article 4 of the Fines and Penalties (Northern Ireland) Order 1984 ([£5,000][3] or other sum substituted by order under Article 17 of that Order);][2]

and in subsection (1)(*a*) above, the reference to a provision by which a punishment is prescribed includes a reference to a provision which makes a person liable to a penalty of the prescribed sum within the meaning of this subsection.

[(2A) …][5]

(3) Where a penalty for an offence under any enactment relating to an assigned matter is required to be fixed by reference to the value of any goods, that value shall be taken as the price which those goods might reasonably be expected to have fetched, after payment of any duty or tax chargeable thereon, if they had been sold in the open market at or about the date of the commission of the offence for which the penalty is imposed.

(4) Where an offence under any enactment relating to an assigned matter which has been committed by a body corporate is proved to have been committed with the consent or connivance of, or to be attributable to any neglect on the part of, any director, manager, secretary or other similar officer of the body corporate or any person purporting to act in any such capacity, he as well as the body corporate shall be guilty of that offence and shall be liable to be proceeded against and punished accordingly.

In this subsection "director", in relation to any body corporate established by or under any enactment for the purpose of carrying on under national ownership any industry or part of an industry or undertaking, being a body corporate whose affairs are managed by the members thereof, means a member of that body corporate.

[(4A) Subsection (4) shall not apply to an offence which relates to a matter listed in Schedule 1 to the Commissioners for Revenue and Customs Act 2005 (former Inland Revenue matters).][6]

(5) Where in any proceedings for an offence under the customs and excise Acts any question arises as to the duty or the rate thereof chargeable on any imported goods, and it is not possible to ascertain the relevant time specified in section 43 above [or the relevant excise duty point][4], that duty or rate shall be determined as if the goods had been imported without entry at the time when the proceedings were commenced [or, as the case may be, as if the time when the proceedings were commenced was the relevant excise duty point][4].

Commentary—*De Voil Indirect Tax Service* **V5.306, V5.307**.
Simon's Tax Cases—*Chaudhry v R&C Prosecution Office* [2008] STC 2357.
Amendments—[1] Words in sub-s (2)(*a*) substituted by Magistrates' Courts Act 1980 Sch 7 para 178.
[2] Words in sub-s (2)(*a*) substituted and sub-s (2)(*c*) inserted by Fines and Penalties (Northern Ireland) Order, SI 1984/703 art 19(1), Sch 6 para 7 with effect from 19 July 1984.
[3] Figure in square brackets in sub-s (2)(*c*) substituted for the figure "£2,000" by virtue of Criminal Justice (Northern Ireland) Order, SI 1994/2795 art 3(1) with effect from a day to be appointed.
[4] Words in sub-s (5) inserted by F(No 2)A 1992 s 3 and Sch 2 para 9 with effect from 9 December 1992 by virtue of F(No 2)A 1992 (Commencement No 3) Order, SI 1992/3104.
[5] Sub-s (2A) repealed by Statute Law (Repeals) Act 1993 s 1(1), Sch 1 Pt XIV.
[6] Sub-s (4A) inserted by Commissioners for Revenue and Customs Act 2005 s 50, Sch 4 para 28 with effect from 18 April 2005 by virtue of the Commissioners for Revenue and Customs Act 2005 (Commencement) Order, SI 2005/1126, art 2(2).

SCHEDULES

SCHEDULE 3

PROVISIONS RELATING TO FORFEITURE

Sections 139, 143, 145

Notice of seizure

1— (1) The Commissioners shall, except as provided in sub-paragraph (2) below, give notice of the seizure of any thing as liable to forfeiture and of the grounds therefor to any person who to their knowledge was at the time of the seizure the owner or one of the owners thereof.

(2) Notice need not be given under this paragraph if the seizure was made in the presence of—

(*a*) the person whose offence or suspected offence occasioned the seizure; or

(*b*) the owner or any of the owners of the thing seized or any servant or agent of his; or

(*c*) in the case of any thing seized in any ship or aircraft, the master or commander.

2 Notice under paragraph 1 above shall be given in writing and shall be deemed to have been duly served on the person concerned—

(*a*) if delivered to him personally; or

(*b*) if addressed to him and left or forwarded by post to him at his usual or last known place of abode or business or, in the case of a body corporate, at their registered or principal office; or

(*c*) where he has no address within the United Kingdom [or the Isle of Man][1], or his address is unknown, by publication of notice of the seizure in the London, Edinburgh or Belfast Gazette.

Amendments—[1] Words in para 2(*c*) inserted by Isle of Man Act 1979 s 13 and Sch 1, para 23.

Notice of claim

3 Any person claiming that any thing seized as liable to forfeiture is not so liable shall, within one month of the date of the notice of seizure or, where no such notice has been served on him, within one month of the date of the seizure, give notice of his claim in writing to the Commissioners at any office of customs and excise.

4— (1) Any notice under paragraph 3 above shall specify the name and address of the claimant and, in the case of a claimant who is outside the United Kingdom [and the Isle of Man][1], shall specify the name and address of a solicitor in the United Kingdom who is authorised to accept service of process and to act on behalf of the claimant.

(2) Service of process upon a solicitor so specified shall be deemed to be proper service upon the claimant.

Amendments—[1] Words in para 4(1) inserted by Isle of Man Act 1979 s 13 and Sch 1. para 24.

Condemnation

5 If on the expiration of the relevant period under paragraph 3 above for the giving of notice of claim in respect of any thing no such notice has been given to the Commissioners, or if, in the case of any such notice given, any requirement of paragraph 4 above is not complied with, the thing in question shall be deemed to have been duly condemned as forfeited.

6 Where notice of claim in respect of any thing is duly given in accordance with paragraphs 3 and 4 above, the Commissioners shall take proceedings for the condemnation of that thing by the court, and if the court finds that the thing was at the time of seizure liable to forfeiture the court shall condemn it as forfeited.

7 Where any thing is in accordance with either of paragraphs 5 or 6 above condemned or deemed to have been condemned as forfeited, then, without prejudice to any delivery up or sale of the thing by the Commissioners under paragraph 16 below, the forfeiture shall have effect as from the date when the liability to forfeiture arose.

Proceedings for condemnation by court

8 Proceedings for condemnation shall be civil proceedings and may be instituted—

(*a*) in England or Wales either in the High Court or in a magistrates' court;

(*b*) in Scotland either in the Court of Session or in the sheriff court;

(*c*) in Northern Ireland either in the High Court or in a court of summary jurisdiction.

9 Proceedings for the condemnation of any thing instituted in a magistrates' court in England or Wales, in the sheriff court in Scotland or in a court of summary jurisdiction in Northern Ireland may be so instituted—

(*a*) in any such court having jurisdiction in the place where any offence in connection with that thing was committed or where any proceedings for such an offence are instituted; or

(*b*) in any such court having jurisdiction in the place where the claimant resides or, if the claimant has specified a solicitor under paragraph 4 above, in the place where that solicitor has his office; or (*c*) in any such court having jurisdiction in the place where that thing was found, detained or seized or to which it is first brought after being found, detained or seized.

10— (1) In any proceedings for condemnation instituted in England, Wales or Northern Ireland, the claimant or his solicitor shall make oath that the thing seized was, or was to the best of his knowledge and belief, the property of the claimant at the time of the seizure.

(2) In any such proceedings instituted in the High Court, the claimant shall give such security for the costs of the proceedings as may be determined by the Court.

(3) If any requirement of this paragraph is not complied with, the court shall give judgment for the Commissioners.

11— (1) In the case of any proceedings for condemnation instituted in a magistrates' court in England or Wales, without prejudice to any right to require the statement of a case for the opinion of the High Court, either party may appeal against the decision of that court to the Crown Court.

(2) In the case of any proceedings for condemnation instituted in a court of summary jurisdiction in Northern Ireland, without prejudice to any right to require the statement of a case for the opinion of the High Court, either party may appeal against the decision of that court to the county court.

12 Where an appeal, including an appeal by way of case stated, has been made against the decision of the court in any proceedings for the condemnation of any thing, that thing shall, pending the final determination of the matter, be left with the Commissioners or at any convenient office of customs and excise.

Provisions as to proof

13 In any proceedings arising out of the seizure of any thing, the fact, form and manner of the seizure shall be taken to have been as set forth in the process without any further evidence thereof, unless the contrary is proved.

14 In any proceedings, the condemnation by a court of any thing as forfeited may be proved by the production either of the order or certificate of condemnation or of a certified copy thereof purporting to be signed by an officer of the court by which the order or certificate was made or granted.

Special provisions as to certain claimants

15 For the purposes of any claim to, or proceedings for the condemnation of, any thing, where that thing is at the time of seizure the property of a body corporate, of two or more partners or of any number of persons exceeding five, the oath required by paragraph 10 above to be taken and any other thing required by this Schedule or by any rules of the court to be done by, or by any person authorised by, the claimant or owner may be taken or done by, or by any other person authorised by, the following persons respectively, that is to say—

(*a*) where the owner is a body corporate, the secretary or some duly authorised officer of that body;

(*b*) where the owners are in partnership, any one of those owners;

(*c*) where the owners are any number of persons exceeding five not being in partnership, any two of those persons on behalf of themselves and their co-owners.

Power to deal with seizures before condemnation, etc

16 Where any thing has been seized as liable to forfeiture the Commissioners may at any time if they see fit and notwithstanding that the thing has not yet been condemned, or is not yet deemed to have been condemned, as forfeited—

(*a*) deliver it up to any claimant upon his paying to the Commissioners such sum as they think proper, being a sum not exceeding that which in their opinion represents the value of the thing, including any duty or tax chargeable thereon which has not been paid;

(*b*) if the thing seized is a living creature or is in the opinion of the Commissioners of a perishable nature, sell or destroy it.

17— (1) If, where any thing is delivered up, sold or destroyed under paragraph 16 above, it is held in proceedings taken under this Schedule that the thing was not liable to forfeiture at the time of its seizure, the Commissioners shall, subject to any deduction allowed under sub-paragraph (2) below, on demand by the claimant tender to him—

(*a*) an amount equal to any sum paid by him under sub-paragraph (*a*) of that paragraph; or

(*b*) where they have sold the thing, an amount equal to the proceeds of sale; or

(*c*) where they have destroyed the thing, an amount equal to the market value of the thing at the time of its seizure.

(2) Where the amount to be tendered under sub-paragraph (1)(*a*), (*b*) or (*c*) above includes any sum on account of any duty or tax chargeable on the thing which had not been paid before its seizure the Commissioners may deduct so much of that amount as represents that duty or tax.

(3) If the claimant accepts any amount tendered to him under sub-paragraph (1) above, he shall not be entitled to maintain any action on account of the seizure, detention, sale or destruction of the thing.

(4) For the purposes of sub-paragraph (1)(*c*) above, the market value of any thing at the time of its seizure shall be taken to be such amount as the Commissioners and the claimant may agree or, in default of agreement, as may be determined by a referee appointed by the Lord Chancellor (not being an official of any government department [or an office-holder in, or a member of the staff of, the Scottish Administration][1]), whose decision shall be final and conclusive; and the procedure on any reference to a referee shall be such as may be determined by the referee.

[(5) The Lord Chancellor may make an appointment under sub-paragraph (4) only with the concurrence—

(*a*) where the proceedings referred to in sub-paragraph (1) were taken in England and Wales, of the Lord Chief Justice of England and Wales;

(*b*) where those proceedings were taken in Scotland, of the Lord President of the Court of Session;

(*c*) where those proceedings were taken in Northern Ireland, of the Lord Chief Justice of Northern Ireland.

(6) The Lord Chief Justice of England and Wales may nominate a judicial office holder (as defined in section 109(4) of the Constitutional Reform Act 2005) to exercise his functions under this paragraph.

(7) The Lord President of the Court of Session may nominate a judge of the Court of Session who is a member of the First or Second Division of the Inner House of that Court to exercise his functions under this paragraph.

(8) The Lord Chief Justice of Northern Ireland may nominate any of the following to exercise his functions under this paragraph—

(*a*) the holder of one of the offices listed in Schedule 1 to the Justice (Northern Ireland) Act 2002;

(*b*) a Lord Justice of Appeal (as defined in section 88 of that Act).][2]

Amendments—[1] Words in para (4) inserted by The Scotland Act 1998 (Consequential Modifications) (No 2) Order, SI 1999/1820 s 59, which comes into force on the "principle appointed day", currently 1 July 1999, by virtue of the Scotland Act 1998 (Commencement) Order 1998/3178.

[2] Sub-paras (5)–(8) inserted by the Constitutional Reform Act 2005 s 15, Sch 4 para 97 with effect from 3 April 2006 (by virtue of SI 2006/1014, art 2(*a*), Sch 1, para 11).

CUSTOMS AND EXCISE DUTIES (GENERAL RELIEFS) ACT 1979

(1979 Chapter 3)

Cross references—See VATA 1994 s 16(1), (application of the following provisions of this Act for the purposes of value added tax),

VAT Regulations, SI 1995/2518 reg 118(*d*) (this Act, except ss 8, 9(*b*), not to apply in relation to any tax chargeable on importation of goods from non-EEC countries with effect from 1 December 1992).

Miscellaneous reliefs from customs and excise duties

[7 Power to provide for reliefs from duty and value added tax in respect of imported legacies

(1) The Commissioners may by order make provision for conferring reliefs from duty and value added tax in respect of goods imported into the United Kingdom by or for any person who has become entitled to them as legatee.

(2) Any such relief may take the form either of an exemption from payment of duty and tax or of a provision whereby the sum payable by way of duty or tax is less than it would otherwise be.

(3) The Commissioners may by order make provision supplementing any Community relief, in such manner as they think necessary or expedient.

(4) An order under this section—

(*a*) may make any relief for which it provides or any Community relief subject to conditions, including conditions which are to be complied with after the importation of the goods to which the relief applies;

(*b*) may, in relation to any relief conferred by order made under this section, contain such incidental and supplementary provisions as the Commissioners think necessary or expedient; and

(*c*) may make different provision for different cases.

(5) In this section—

"Community relief " means any relief which is conferred by a Community instrument and is of a kind, or of a kind similar to that, which could otherwise be conferred by order made under this section;

"duty" means customs or excise duty chargeable on goods imported into the United Kingdom and, in the case of excise duty, includes any addition to the duty by virtue of section 1 of the Excise Duties (Surcharges or Rebates) Act 1979;

"legatee" means any person taking under a testamentary disposition or donatio mortis causa or on an intestacy; and

"value added tax" means value added tax chargeable on the importation of goods.][1]

Commentary—*De Voil Indirect Tax Service* **V3.341**.

Orders—See Customs and Excise Duties (Personal Reliefs for Goods Permanently Imported) Order, SI 1992/3193.

Amendments—[1] This section substituted by FA 1984 s 14(1), (3) with effect from 1 July 1984.

8 Relief from customs or excise duty on trade samples, labels, etc

The Commissioners may allow the delivery without payment of customs or excise duty on importation, subject to such conditions and restrictions as they see fit—

(*a*) of trade samples of such goods as they see fit, whether imported as samples or drawn from the goods on their importation;

(*b*) of labels or other articles supplied without charge for the purpose of being re-exported with goods manufactured or produced in, and to be exported from, the United Kingdom [or the Isle of Man.][1]

Commentary—*De Voil Indirect Tax Service* **V3.342, 3.343**.

Amendments—[1] Words in para (*b*) inserted by Isle of Man Act 1979 s 13, Sch 1 para 26.

9 Relief from customs or excise duty on antiques, prizes, etc

The Commissioners may allow the delivery without payment of customs or excise duty on importation—

(*a*) of any goods (other than spirits or wine) which are proved to the satisfaction of the Commissioners to have been manufactured or produced more than 100 years before the date of importation;

(*b*) of articles which are shown to the satisfaction of the Commissioners to have been awarded abroad to any person for distinction in art, literature, science or sport, or for public service, or otherwise as a record of meritorious achievement or conduct, and to be imported by or on behalf of that person.

Commentary—*De Voil Indirect Tax Service* **V3.344**.

Personal reliefs

13 Power to provide, in relation to persons entering the United Kingdom, for reliefs from duty and value added tax and for simplified computation of duty and tax

(1) The Commissioners may by order make provision for conferring on persons entering the United Kingdom reliefs from duty and value added tax; and any such relief may take the form either of an exemption from payment of duty and tax or of a provision whereby the sum payable by way of duty or tax is less than it would otherwise be.

[(1A) The Commissioners may by order make provision supplementing any Community relief, in such manner as they think necessary or expedient.][1]

(2) Without prejudice to subsection (1) above, the Commissioners may by order make provision whereby, in such cases and to such extent as may be specified in the order, a sum calculated at a rate specified in the order is treated as the aggregate amount payable by way of duty and tax in respect of goods imported by a person entering the United Kingdom; but any order making such provision shall enable the person concerned to elect that duty and tax shall be charged on the goods in question at the rate which would be applicable apart from that provision.

(3) An order under this section—

(*a*) may make any relief for which it provides [, or any Community relief,][1] subject to conditions, including conditions which are to be complied with after the importation of the goods to which the relief applies [and conditions with respect to the conduct in relation to the goods of persons other than the person on whom the relief is conferred and of persons whose identity cannot be ascertained at the time of importation][2];

(*b*) may [, in relation to any relief conferred by order made under this section,][1] contain such incidental and supplementary provisions as the Commissioners think necessary or expedient, including [provisions requiring any person to whom a condition of the relief at any time relates to notify the Commissioners of any non-compliance with the condition and][2] provisions for the forfeiture of goods in the event of non-compliance with any condition subject to which they have been relieved from duty or tax; and

(*c*) may make a different provision for different cases,

[(3A) An order under this section may provide, in relation to any relief which under such an order is made subject to a condition, for there to be a presumption that, in such cases as may be described in the order by reference—

(*a*) to the quantity of goods in question; or

(*b*) to any other factor which the Commissioners consider appropriate,

the condition is to be treated, unless the Commissioners are satisfied to the contrary, as not being complied with.][3]

[(3B) An order under this section may provide, in relation to any requirement of such an order for the Commissioners to be notified of non-compliance with a condition to which any relief from payment of any duty of excise is made subject, for goods to be exempt from forfeiture under section 124 of the Customs and Excise Management Act 1979 (forfeiture for breach of certain conditions) in respect of non-compliance with that condition if—

(*a*) the non-compliance is notified to the Commissioners in accordance with that requirement;

(*b*) any duty which becomes payable on those goods by virtue of the non-compliance is paid; and

(*c*) the circumstances are otherwise such as may be described in the order.][3]

[(3C) If any person fails to comply with any requirement of an order under this section to notify the Commissioners of any non-compliance with a condition to which any relief is made subject—

(*a*) he shall be liable, on summary conviction, to a penalty of an amount not exceeding level 5 on the standard scale; and

(*b*) the goods in respect of which the offence was committed shall be liable to forfeiture.][3]

(4) In this section—

["Community relief" means any relief which is conferred by a Community instrument and is of a kind, or of a kind similar to that, which could otherwise be conferred by order made under this section;][1]

["conduct", in relation to any person who has or may acquire possession or control of any goods, includes that person's intentions at any time in relation to those goods;][4]

"duty" means customs or excise duty chargeable on goods imported into the United Kingdom and, in the case of excise duty, includes any addition thereto by virtue of section 1 of the Excise Duties (Surcharges or Rebates) Act 1979; and

"value added tax" or "tax" means value added tax chargeable on the importation of goods [from places outside the member States or on the acquisition of goods from member States other than the United Kingdom][5].

(5) Nothing in any order under this section shall be construed as authorising any person to import any thing in contravention of any prohibition or restriction for the time being in force with respect thereto under or by virtue of any enactment.

Commentary—*De Voil Indirect Tax Service* **V3.345, 3.346**.

Orders—See Customs and Excise Duties (Personal Reliefs for Goods Permanently Imported) Order, SI 1992/3193; Travellers' Allowances Order, SI 1994/955; Travellers' Reliefs (Fuel and Lubricants) Order, SI 1995/1777.

Cross reference—See VATA 1994 Sch 8, Group 14 (tax-free shops).

Amendments—[1] Sub-s (1A) and words in sub-ss (3)(*a*), (*b*), (4) inserted by FA 1984 s 15(1)–(5), (8) with effect from 31 March 1984.

[2] Words in sub-s (3)(*a*), (*b*) inserted by F(No 2)A 1992 s 1(8), Sch 1 para 8 with effect from 1 December 1992 by virtue of F(No 2)A 1992 (Commencement No 2 and Transitional Provisions) Order, SI 1992/2979 art 4 and Schedule, Pt II.

[3] Sub-ss (3A)–(3C) inserted by F(No 2)A 1992 s 1(8), Sch 1 para 8 with effect from 1 December 1992 by virtue of F(No 2)A 1992 (Commencement No 2 and Transitional Provisions) Order, SI 1992/2979 art 4 and Schedule, Pt II.

[4] Definition of "conduct" in sub-s (4) inserted by F(No 2)A 1992 s 1(8), Sch 1 para 8 with effect from 1 December 1992 by virtue of F(No 2)A 1992 (Commencement No 2 and Transitional Provisions) Order, SI 1992/2979 art 4 and Schedule, Pt II.

[5] Words in the definition of "value added tax" in sub-s (4) added by F(No 2)A 1992 s 14(3), Sch 3 para 93 with effect from 1 January 1993 by virtue of F(No 2)A 1992 (Commencement No 4 and Transitional Provisions) Order, SI 1992/3261.

[13A Reliefs from duties and taxes for persons enjoying certain immunities and privileges

(1) The Commissioners may by order make provision for conferring in respect of any persons to whom this section applies reliefs, by way of remission or repayment, from payment by them or others of duties of customs or excise, value added tax or car tax.

(2) An order under this section may make any relief for which it provides subject to such conditions binding the person in respect of whom the relief is conferred and, if different, the person liable apart from the relief for payment of the tax or duty (including conditions which are to be complied with after the time when, apart from the relief, the duty or tax would become payable) as may be imposed by or under the order.

(3) An order under this section may include any of the provisions mentioned in subsection (4) below for cases where—

(*a*) relief from payment of any duty of customs or excise, value added tax or car tax chargeable on any goods, or on the supply of any goods or services or the importation of any goods has been conferred (whether by virtue of an order under this section or otherwise) in respect of any person to whom this section applies, and

(*b*) any condition required to be complied with in connection with the relief is not complied with.

(4) The provisions referred to in subsection (3) above are—

(*a*) provision for payment to the Commissioners of the tax or duty by—

(i) the person liable, apart from the relief, for its payment, or

(ii) any person bound by the condition, or

(iii) any person who is or has been in possession of the goods or has received the benefit of the services,

or for two or more of those persons to be jointly and severally liable for such payment, and

(*b*) in the case of goods, provision for forfeiture of the goods.

(5) An order under this section—

(*a*) may contain such incidental and supplementary provisions as the Commissioners think necessary or expedient, and
(*b*) may make different provision for different cases.

(6) In this section and section 13C of this Act—

"duty of customs" includes any agricultural levy within the meaning of section 6 of the European Communities Act 1972 chargeable on goods imported into the United Kingdom, and

"duty of excise" means any duty of excise chargeable on goods and includes any addition to excise duty by virtue of section 1 of the Excise Duties (Surcharges or Rebates) Act 1979.

(7) For the purposes of this section and section 13C of this Act, where in respect of any person to whom this section applies relief is conferred (whether by virtue of an order under this section or otherwise) in relation to the use of goods by any persons or for any purposes, the relief is to be treated as conferred subject to a condition binding on him that the goods will be used only by those persons or for those purposes.

(8) Nothing in any order under this section shall be construed as authorising a person to import any thing in contravention of any prohibition or restriction for the time being in force with respect to it under or by virtue of any enactment.][1]

Commentary—*De Voil Indirect Tax Service* **V3.347**.
Orders—See Customs and Excise (Personal Reliefs for Special Visitors) Order, SI 1992/3156.
Amendments—[1] This section inserted by FA 1989 s 28(1).

[13B Persons to whom section 13A applies

(1) The persons to whom section 13A of this Act applies are—

(*a*) any person who, for the purposes of any provision of the Visiting Forces Act 1952 or the International Headquarters and Defence Organisations Act 1964 is—

(i) a member of a visiting force or of a civilian component of such a force or a dependant of such a member, or
(ii) a headquarters, a member of a headquarters or a dependant of such a member,

(*b*) any person enjoying any privileges or immunities under or by virtue of—

(i) the Diplomatic Privileges Act 1964
(ii) the Commonwealth Secretariat Act 1966
(iii) the Consular Relations Act 1968
(iv) the International Organisations Act 1968 or
[(v) the International Development Act 2002.][2]

(*c*) any person enjoying, under or by virtue of section 2 of the European Communities Act 1972 any privileges or immunities similar to those enjoyed under or by virtue of the enactments referred to in paragraph (*b*) above.

(2) The Secretary of State may by order amend subsection (1) above to include any persons enjoying any privileges or immunities similar to those enjoyed under or by virtue of the enactments referred to in paragraph (*b*) of that subsection.

(3) No order shall be made under this section unless a draft of the order has been laid before and approved by resolution of each House of Parliament.][1]

Commentary—*De Voil Indirect Tax Service* **V3.347**.
Amendments—[1] This section inserted by FA 1989 s 28(1).
[2] In sub-s (1), para (*b*)(v) substituted by the International Development Act 2002 s 19, Sch 3 para 7 with effect from 17 June 2002 (by virtue of SI 2002/1408). Sub-s (1)(*b*)(v) previously read as follows—
"(v) the Overseas Development and Co-operation Act 1980".

[13C Offence where relieved goods used, etc, in breach of condition

(1) Subsection (2) below applies where—

(*a*) any relief from payment of any duty of customs or excise, value added tax or car tax chargeable on, or on the supply or importation of, any goods has been conferred (whether by virtue of an order under section 13A of this Act or otherwise) in respect of any person to whom that section applies subject to any condition as to the persons by whom or the purposes for which the goods may be used, and
(*b*) if the tax or duty has subsequently become payable, it has not been paid.

(2) If any person—

(*a*) acquires the goods for his own use, where he is not permitted by the condition to use them, or for use for a purpose that is not permitted by the condition or uses them for such a purpose, or
(*b*) acquires the goods for use, or causes or permits them to be used, by a person not permitted by the condition to use them or by a person for a purpose that is not permitted by the condition or disposes of them to a person not permitted by the condition to use them,

with intent to evade payment or any tax or duty that has become payable or that, by reason of the disposal, acquisition or use, becomes or will become payable, he is guilty of an offence.

(3) For the purposes of this section—

(*a*) in the case of a condition as to the persons by whom goods may be used, a person is not permitted by the condition to use them unless he is a person referred to in the condition as permitted to use them, and

(*b*) in relation to a condition as to the purposes for which goods may be used, a purpose is not permitted by the condition unless it is a purpose referred to in the condition as a permitted purpose,

and in this section "dispose" includes "lend" and "let on hire", and "acquire" shall be interpreted accordingly.

(4) A person guilty of an offence under this section may be detained and shall be liable—

(*a*) on summary conviction, to a penalty of the statutory maximum or of three times the value of the goods (whichever is the greater), or to imprisonment for a term not exceeding six months, or to both, or

(*b*) on conviction on indictment, to a penalty of any amount, or to imprisonment for a term not exceeding seven years, or to both.][1]

[(5) Where any person is guilty of an offence under this section, the goods in respect of which the offence was committed shall be liable to forfeiture.][2]

Commentary—*De Voil Indirect Tax Service* **V5.303**.
Amendments—[1] This section inserted by FA 1989 s 28(1), (2) and has effect where relief is conferred after 26 July 1989.
[2] Sub-s (5) added by F(No 2)A 1992 s 3, Sch 2 para 10 with effect from 9 December 1992 by virtue of F(No 2)A 1992 (Commencement No 3) Order, SI 1992/3104.

ISLE OF MAN ACT 1979

(1979 Chapter 58)

ARRANGEMENT OF SECTIONS

An Act to make such amendments of the law relating to customs and excise, value added tax, car tax and the importation and exportation of goods as are required for giving effect to an Agreement between the government of the United Kingdom and the government of the Isle of Man signed on 15th October 1979; to make other amendments as respects the Isle of Man in the law relating to those matters; to provide for the transfer of functions vested in the Lieutenant Governor of the Isle of Man or, as respects that Island, in the Commissioners of Customs and Excise; and for purposes connected with those matters.

[20th December 1979]

1 Common duties

(1) Subject to subsection (2) below, in this Act "common duties" means—

(*a*)–[(*ca*)] …

(*d*) value added tax chargeable under the law of the United Kingdom or the Isle of Man except tax chargeable in accordance with [section][1] [23 of the Value Added Tax Act 1994][2] (gaming machines);

(*e*) …

(2) The Treasury may by order amend subsection (1) above by adding or deleting any duty or tax which is under the care and management of the Commissioners of Customs and Excise (in this Act referred to as "the Commissioners") or any corresponding duty or tax chargeable under the law of the Isle of Man; and any such order may apply to a duty or tax generally or in such cases or subject to such restrictions as may be specified in the order.

(3) The power to make orders under subsection (2) above shall be exercisable by statutory instrument subject to annulment in pursuance of a resolution of the House of Commons.

Commentary—*De Voil Indirect Tax Service* **V1.217**.
Note—Sub-s (1)(*a*)–(*ca*), (*e*) are not relevant to this work.
Amendments—[1] Word in sub-s (1)(*d*) substituted by VATA 1983 Sch 9 para 3(*a*).
[2] Words in sub-s (1)(*d*) substituted by VATA 1994 s 100, Sch 14 para 7(1).

2 Isle of Man share of common duties

(1) Of the moneys standing to the credit of the General Account of the Commissioners an amount ascertained for each financial year in accordance with subsection (2) below shall be paid by the Commissioners, at such times and in such manner as they may determine, to the Treasurer of the Isle of Man.

(2) There shall be calculated in such manner as the Treasury may direct—

(*a*) the amount of common duties, whether collected in the United Kingdom or the Isle of Man, which is attributable to goods consumed or used in the Island, to services supplied in the Island or (as respects pool betting duty) to bets placed by persons in the Island;

(*b*) the cost incurred by the Commissioners in collecting the amount so attributable together with the amount of any drawback or repayment referable to that amount;

and the amount arrived at by deducting from the amount calculated under paragraph (*a*) above the amount calculated under paragraph (*b*) above shall be known as the net Isle of Man share of common duties; and the amount mentioned in subsection (1) above shall be the excess of the net Isle of Man share of common duties over the common duties collected in the Island.

(3) For the purposes of this section the amount of common duties collected in the Isle of Man and the United Kingdom, or in the Isle of Man, shall be calculated by reference to the amount so collected in respect of such duties after giving effect to any addition or deduction provided for under section 1 of the Excise Duties (Surcharges or Rebates) Act 1979 or any Isle of Man equivalent.

(4) The Commissioners shall for each financial year prepare, in such form and manner as the Treasury may direct, an account showing the payments made by them under this section and shall send it, not later than the end of November in the following financial year, to the Comptroller and Auditor General, who shall examine and certify the account.

(5) The Comptroller and Auditor General shall send every account examined and certified by him under this section and his report thereon to the Treasury and a copy of every such account and report to the Treasurer of the Isle of Man; and the Treasury shall lay copies of the account and report before Parliament.

Commentary—*De Voil Indirect Tax Service* **V1.262**.

3 Recovery of common duties chargeable in Isle of Man

(1) Any liability to pay an amount on account of a common duty chargeable under the law of the Isle of Man shall, to the extent to which it has not been discharged or enforced there, be enforceable in the United Kingdom as if it were a liability to pay an amount on account of the corresponding common duty chargeable under the law of the United Kingdom.

(2) Any amount recoverable by the Commissioners from any person under subsection (1) above may be set off against any amount recoverable by him from the Commissioners on account of a common duty chargeable under the law of the United Kingdom.

Commentary—*De Voil Indirect Tax Service* **V1.271**.

4 Enforcement of Isle of Man judgments for common duties

(1) Subject to subsection (2) below, the provisions of sections 2 to 5 of the Foreign Judgments (Reciprocal Enforcement) Act 1933 shall have effect in relation to any judgment or order given or made by the High Court of Justice of the Isle of Man under which an amount is payable on account of—

(*a*) a common duty chargeable under the law of the Island; or

(*b*) a fine or penalty imposed in connection with such a duty,

as if the judgment or order were a judgment to which Part I of that Act applied.

(2) Subsection (1) above does not apply to a judgment or order given or made on appeal from a lower court but, except when given or made in criminal proceedings, applies notwithstanding that it is subject to appeal or that an appeal against it is pending.

(3) In their application by virtue of subsection (1) above the provisions there mentioned shall have effect—

(*a*) with the omission of so much of section 2(1) as imposes a time-limit for applications for registration;

(*b*) with the omission of section 4(1)(*a*)(v) and (vi); and

(*c*) as if the Commissioners were the judgment creditor and any criminal proceedings in which the judgment or order was given or made were an action.

(4) The reference in subsection (1) above to sections 2 to 5 of the said Act of 1933 includes a reference to so much of sections 11 to 13 of that Act as is relevant to those sections and the definition of "appeal" in section 11 shall apply for the purposes of subsection (2) above.

(5) The reference in subsection (1) above to the High Court of Justice of the Isle of Man includes a reference to the Court of General Gaol Delivery.

Commentary—*De Voil Indirect Tax Service* **V1.271**.

5 Offences relating to common duties etc

(1) Any summons or other process requiring a person in the Isle of Man to appear before a court in the United Kingdom—

(*a*) to answer a charge that he has committed an offence relating to a common duty chargeable under the law of the United Kingdom or to the importation or exportation of anything into or from the United Kingdom; or

(*b*) to give evidence or to produce any document or thing in proceedings for any such offence,

may be served by being sent to him by registered post or the recorded delivery service.

(2) In relation to proceedings for any such offence as is mentioned in subsection (1) above—

(*a*) [section 97 of the Magistrates' Courts Act 1980][1] (summons to witness and warrant for his arrest) shall have effect as if the reference in subsection (1) of that section to a person in England and Wales included a reference to a person in the Isle of Man;

(*b*) in Scotland a warrant for the citation of accused persons and witnesses shall include a warrant to cite accused persons and witnesses in the Isle of Man.

(3) In relation to proceedings for any such offence as is mentioned in subsection (1) above—

(*a*) [section 9 of the Criminal Justice Act 1967 and section 102 of the Magistrates' Courts Act 1980][1] (admission of written statements) shall apply also to written statements made in the Isle of Man but with the omission of subsections (2)(*b*) and (3A) of [section 102][1] and subsections (2)(*b*) and (3A) of section 9;

(*b*) section 1 of the Criminal Justice (Miscellaneous Provisions) Act (Northern Ireland) 1968 and section 3 of the Criminal Procedure (Committal for Trial) Act (Northern Ireland) 1968 (which contain corresponding provisions) shall apply also to written statements made in the Isle of Man but with the omission of subsection (2)(*b*) of section 1 and subsection (2)(*c*) of section 3.

(4) Subject to subsection (5) below, a warrant issued in the Isle of Man for the arrest of—

(*a*) a person charged with an offence relating to a common duty chargeable under the law of the Isle of Man or to the importation or exportation of anything into or from the Island; or

(*b*) a person required to give evidence or to produce any document or thing in proceedings for any such offence,

may be executed in England and Wales by any constable acting within his police area, in Scotland by any officer of law as defined in [section 307(1) of the Criminal Procedure (Scotland) Act 1995][2] and in Northern Ireland by any member of the Royal Ulster Constabulary or the Royal Ulster Constabulary Reserve.

(5) A warrant, other than one for the arrest of a person charged with an offence punishable with at least two years' imprisonment, shall not be executed under subsection (4) above unless it has been endorsed for execution under that subsection by a justice of the peace in England, Wales, Scotland or Northern Ireland, as the case may be; and any warrant which purports to have been issued as mentioned in that subsection may be so endorsed without further proof.

(6) A warrant for the arrest of a person charged with an offence may be executed by a constable under subsection (4) above notwithstanding that it is not in his possession at the time but the warrant shall, on demand of that person, be shown to him as soon as practicable.

(7) Subsections (1) and (4) above are without prejudice to any other enactment enabling any process to be served or executed otherwise than as provided in those subsections.

(8) References in this section to a warrant for the arrest of any person include references to any process for that purpose available under the law of the Isle of Man; and references to an offence relating to a common duty or to importation or exportation include references to any offence which relates to any of those matters whether or not it is an offence under a provision dealing specifically with that matter.

Commentary—*De Voil Indirect Tax Service* **V1.217, 1.263.**

Amendments—[1] Words in sub-ss (2)(*a*) and (3)(*a*) substituted by Magistrates' Courts Act 1980 s 154, Sch 7 para 198.

[2] Words in sub-s (4) substituted by Criminal Procedure (Consequential Provisions)(Scotland) Act 1995 Sch 4 para 25.

6 Value added tax

(1) For the purpose of giving effect to any Agreement between the government of the United Kingdom and the government of the Isle of Man whereby both countries are to be treated as a single area for the purposes of value added tax charged under [the Value Added Tax Act [1994][2]][1] and value added tax charged under the corresponding Act of Tynwald, Her Majesty may by Order in Council make provision for securing that tax is charged under [the Act of [1994][2]][1] as if all or any of the references in it to the United Kingdom included both the United Kingdom and the Isle of Man but so that tax is not charged under both Acts in respect of the same transaction.

(2) An Order in Council under this section may make provision—

(*a*) for determining, or enabling the Commissioners to determine, under which Act a person is to be registered and for transferring a person registered under one Act to the register kept under the other;

(*b*) for treating a person who is a taxable person for the purposes of the Act of Tynwald as a taxable person for all or any of the purposes of [the Act of [1994][2]][1];

(*c*) for extending any reference in [the Act of [1994][2]][1] to tax under that Act so as to include tax under the Act of Tynwald;

(*d*) for treating any requirement imposed by or under either Act as a requirement imposed by or under the other;

(*e*) for treating any permission, direction, notice, determination or other thing given, made or done under the Act of Tynwald by the Isle of Man authority corresponding to the Commissioners as given, made or done by the Commissioners under [the Act of [1994][2]][1];

(*f*) for enabling the Commissioners to determine for the purposes of [section [43][2]][1] of [the Act of [1994][2]][1] (groups of companies) which member of a group is to be the representative member in cases where supplies are made both in the United Kingdom and the Isle of Man;

(*g*) for modifying or excluding, as respects goods removed from the Isle of Man to the United Kingdom or from the United Kingdom to the Isle of Man, any provision relating to importation or exportation contained in [the Act of [1994][2]][1] or in the customs and excise Acts as applied by that Act;

(*h*) for any supplementary, incidental or transitional matter.

(3) An Order in Council under this section may make such modifications of any provision contained in or having effect under any Act of Parliament relating to value added tax as appears to Her Majesty to be necessary or expedient for the purposes of the Order.

(4) While an Order in Council under this section is in force and without prejudice to the powers conferred by the foregoing provisions—

(*a*) [section [30(10)][2]][1] of [the Act of [1994][2]][1] (forfeiture of zero-rated goods) shall have effect as if the reference to goods zero-rated under the regulations there mentioned included a reference to goods zero-rated under any corresponding regulations made under the Act of Tynwald;

(*b*) [paragraph 10(3) of [Schedule 11][2]][1] to] [the Act of [1994][2]][1] (search of premises where offence is suspected) shall have effect as if the references to an offence in connection with the tax included references to an offence in connection with the tax charged under the Act of Tynwald;

(*c*) [section [72(8)][2]][1] of [the Act of [1994][2]][1] (course of conduct involving offences) shall have effect as if the reference to offences under the provisions there mentioned included a reference to offences under the corresponding provisions of the Act of Tynwald.

(5) Provision may be made by or under an Act of Tynwald for purposes corresponding to those of this section and of any Order in Council made under it.

Commentary—*De Voil Indirect Tax Service* **V1.236**.
Orders—See VAT (Isle of Man) Orders: SI 1982/1067; (No 2) Order, SI 1982/1068.
Cross references—See VATA 1994 Sch 13 para 23 (validity of orders made under this section prior to coming into force of VATA 1994 not affected).
Amendments—[1] Words in sub-ss (1), (2), (4) substituted by VATA 1983 Sch 9 para 3.
[2] Word and figures in sub-ss (1), (2), (4) substituted by VATA 1994 s 100, Sch 14 para 7(2).

10 Exchange of information

No obligation as to secrecy or other restriction on the disclosure of information imposed by statute or otherwise shall prevent the Commissioners or any officer of the Commissioners from disclosing information to the Isle of Man customs and excise service for the purpose of facilitating the proper administration of common duties and the enforcement of prohibitions or restrictions on importation or exportation into or from the Isle of Man or the United Kingdom.

11 Transfer of functions to Isle of Man authorities

(1) Her Majesty may by Order in Council make such modifications in any provision contained in or having effect under any Act of Parliament extending to the Isle of Man as appear to Her Majesty to be appropriate for the purpose of transferring to any authority or person constituted by or having functions under the law of the Island—

(*a*) any functions under that provision of the Lieutenant Governor of the Isle of Man (whether referred to by that title or otherwise) or of a deputy governor of the Island;

(*b*) any functions under that provision, so far as exercisable in relation to the Island, of the Commissioners or an officer of the Commissioners.

(2) Any statutory instrument made by virtue of this section shall be subject to annulment in pursuance of a resolution of either House of Parliament.

12 Proof of Acts of Tynwald etc

(1) Without prejudice to the Evidence (Colonial Statutes) Act 1907 any Act of Tynwald or other instrument forming part of the law of the Isle of Man may, in any proceedings in the United Kingdom relating to a common duty or to importation or exportation into or from the United Kingdom or the Isle of Man, be proved by producing a copy of the Act or instrument authenticated by a certificate purporting to be signed by or on behalf of the Attorney General for the Island.

(2) Any provision contained in or having effect under an Act of Tynwald which—

(*a*) prescribes the mode or burden of proof with respect to any matter in proceedings relating to a common duty chargeable under the law of the Isle of Man; and (*b*) corresponds to a provision of United Kingdom law for similar purposes,

shall apply to any proceedings in the United Kingdom relating to that duty.

(3) For the purposes of any proceedings in the United Kingdom relating to a common duty an order may be made under the Bankers' Books Evidence Act 1879 in respect of books and persons in the Isle of Man.

13 Amendments of customs and excise Acts etc

The enactments mentioned in Schedule 1 to this Act shall have effect with the amendments there specified, being amendments which—

(*a*) extend certain references to the United Kingdom in the customs and excise Acts so as to include the Isle of Man; or

(*b*) are otherwise consequential on the provisions of this Act.

14 Short title, interpretation, repeals, commencement and extent

(1) This Act may be cited as the Isle of Man Act 1979.

(2) In this Act—

"the Commissioners" means the Commissioners of Customs and Excise;

"common duties" has the meaning given in section 1 above and "common duty" shall be construed accordingly;

"customs duty" includes any levy or other charge which is treated as a customs duty by section 6 of the European Communities Act 1972.

(3) …

(4) Without prejudice to section 2(3) above,—

(*a*) …

(*b*) any sum recoverable as a debt due to the Crown under [paragraph 5(3) of Schedule 11 to the Value Added Tax Act 1994][1] (sums shown in invoices as value added tax) or any Isle of Man equivalent,

shall be treated for the purposes of this Act as an amount of excise duty or value added tax chargeable under the law of the United Kingdom or, as the case may be, the Isle of Man.

(5) The enactments mentioned in Schedule 2 to this Act (which include spent provisions) are hereby repealed to the extent specified in the third column of that Schedule.

(6) Subject to subsection (7) below, this Act shall come into force on 1st April 1980.

(7) Sections 6, 7, 10 and 11 above shall come into force on the passing of this Act but no Order in Council shall be made under section 6, 7 or 11, and no provision shall by virtue of section 6(5) or 7(5) be made by or under an Act of Tynwald, so as to come into force before 1st April 1980.

(8) Except for sections 6, 7, 11 and this section, this Act does not extend to the Isle of Man as part of the law of the Island.

Note—Sub-ss (3) and (4)(*a*) are not relevant to VAT.

Amendments—[1] Words in sub-s (4)(*b*) substituted by VATA 1994 s 100, Sch 14 para 7(3).

COMPANIES ACT 1985

(1985 Chapter 6)

PART XXVI

INTERPRETATION

[736 "Subsidiary", "holding company" and "wholly owned subsidiary"

[(1) A company is a "subsidiary" of another company, its "holding company", if that other company—

(*a*) *holds a majority of the voting rights in it, or*

(*b*) *is a member of it and has the right to appoint or remove a majority of its board of directors, or*

(*c*) *is a member of it and controls alone, pursuant to an agreement with other shareholders or members, a majority of the voting rights in it,*

or if it is a subsidiary of a company which is itself a subsidiary of that other company.

(2) A company is a "wholly-owned subsidiary" of another company if it has no members except that other and that other's wholly-owned subsidiaries or persons acting on behalf of that other or its wholly-owned subsidiaries.

(3) In this section "company" includes any body corporate.][1, 2]

Cross references—See VATA 1994 s 43A (Groups: eligibility).

Amendments—[1] Substituted, together with s 736A, for s 736 as originally enacted, by the Companies Act 1989, s 144(1).
[2] This section repealed by the Companies Act 2006 s 1295, Sch 16 with effect from 1 October 2009 (by virtue of SI 2008/2860 arts 4, 5, 8, Sch 1 Pt 1, Sch 2 para 1).

[736A Provisions supplementing s 736

[(1) The provisions of this section explain expressions used in section 736 and otherwise supplement that section.

(2) In section 736(1)(a) and (c) the references to the voting rights in a company are to the rights conferred on shareholders in respect of their shares or, in the case of a company not having a share capital, on members, to vote at general meetings of the company on all, or substantially all, matters.

(3) In section 736(1)(b) the reference to the right to appoint or remove a majority of the board of directors is to the right to appoint or remove directors holding a majority of the voting rights at meetings of the board on all, or substantially all, matters; and for the purposes of that provision—

(a) a company shall be treated as having the right to appoint to a directorship if—

(i) a person's appointment to it follows necessarily from his appointment as director of the company, or

(ii) the directorship is held by the company itself; and

(b) a right to appoint or remove which is exercisable only with the consent or concurrence of another person shall be left out of account unless no other person has a right to appoint or, as the case may be, remove in relation to that directorship.

(4) Rights which are exercisable only in certain circumstances shall be taken into account only—

(a) when the circumstances have arisen, and for so long as they continue to obtain, or

(b) when the circumstances are within the control of the person having the rights;

and rights which are normally exercisable but are temporarily incapable of exercise shall continue to be taken into account.

(5) Rights held by a person in a fiduciary capacity shall be treated as not held by him.

(6) Rights held by a person as nominee for another shall be treated as held by the other; and rights shall be regarded as held as nominee for another if they are exercisable only on his instructions or with his consent or concurrence.

(7) Rights attached to shares held by way of security shall be treated as held by the person providing the security—

(a) where apart from the right to exercise them for the purpose of preserving the value of the security, or of realising it, the rights are exercisable only in accordance with his instructions;

(b) where the shares are held in connection with the granting of loans as part of normal business activities and apart from the right to exercise them for the purpose of preserving the value of the security, or of realising it, the rights are exercisable only in his interests.

(8) Rights shall be treated as held by a company if they are held by any of its subsidiaries; and nothing in subsection (6) or (7) shall be construed as requiring rights held by a company to be treated as held by any of its subsidiaries.

(9) For the purposes of subsection (7) rights shall be treated as being exercisable in accordance with the instructions or in the interests of a company if they are exercisable in accordance with the instructions of or, as the case may be, in the interests of—

(a) any subsidiary or holding company of that company, or

(b) any subsidiary of a holding company of that company.

(10) The voting rights in a company shall be reduced by any rights held by the company itself.

(11) References in any provision of subsections (5) to (10) to rights held by a person include rights falling to be treated as held by him by virtue of any other provision of those subsections but not rights which by virtue of any such provision are to be treated as not held by him.

(12) In this section "company" includes any body corporate.][1, 2]

Cross references—See VATA 1994 s 43A (Groups: eligibility).

Amendments—[1] Substituted, together with s 736A, for s 736 as originally enacted, by the Companies Act 1989, s 144(1).
[2] This section repealed by the Companies Act 2006 s 1295, Sch 16 with effect from 1 October 2009 (by virtue of SI 2008/2860 arts 4, 5, 8, Sch 1 Pt 1, Sch 2 para 1).

Modification—Modified in relation to local authorities by the Local Government and Housing Act 1989, s 68.

INCOME AND CORPORATION TAXES ACT 1988

(1988 Chapter 1)

PART XIX

SUPPLEMENTAL

Miscellaneous

827 VAT penalties etc

(1) Where, under [Part IV of the Value Added Tax Act 1994][2] *(value added tax), a person is liable to make a payment by way of—*

(a) penalty under any of sections [60 to 70][2]; or
(b) interest under section [74][2]; or
(c) surcharge under section [59][2];

the payment shall not be allowed as a deduction in computing any income, profits or losses [for any corporation tax purposes (but see also subsection (3)(a) below)][9].

[(1A) Where a person is liable to make a payment by way of a penalty under any of sections 8 to 11 of the Finance Act 1994 (penalties relating to excise), that payment shall not be allowed as a deduction in computing any income, profits or losses [for any corporation tax purposes (but see also subsection (3)(a) below)][9].][3]

[(1B) Where a person is liable to make a payment by way of—
(a) penalty under any of paragraphs 12 to 19 of Schedule 7 to the Finance Act 1994 (insurance premium tax), or
(b) interest under paragraph 21 of that Schedule,

the payment shall not be allowed as to deduction in computing any income, profits or losses [for any corporation tax purposes (but see also subsection (3)(a) below)][9].][1]

[(1C) Where a person is liable to make a payment by way of—
(a) penalty under Part V of Schedule 5 to the Finance Act 1996 (landfill tax), or
(b) interest under paragraph 26 or 27 of that Schedule,

the payment shall not be allowed as a deduction in computing any income, profits or losses [for any corporation tax purposes (but see also subsection (3)(a) below)][9].][4]

[(1D) Where a person is liable to make a payment by way of—
(a) any penalty under any provision of Schedule 6 to the Finance Act 2000 (climate change levy),
(b) interest under paragraph 70 of that Schedule (interest on recoverable overpayments etc),
(c) interest under any of paragraphs 81 to 85 of that Schedule (interest on climate change levy due and on interest), or
(d) interest under paragraph 109 of that Schedule (interest on penalties),

the payment shall not be allowed as a deduction in computing any income, profits or losses [for any corporation tax purposes (but see also subsection (3)(a) below)][9].][5]

[(1E) Where a person is liable to make a payment by way of—
(a) any penalty under any provision of Part II of the Finance Act 2001 (aggregates levy),
(b) interest under any of paragraphs 5 to 9 of Schedule 5 to that Act (interest on aggregates levy due and on interest),
(c) interest under paragraph 6 of Schedule 8 to that Act (interest on recoverable overpayments etc), or
(d) interest under paragraph 5 of Schedule 10 to that Act (interest on penalties),

the payment shall not be allowed as a deduction in computing any income, profits or losses [for any corporation tax purposes (but see also subsection (3)(a) below)][9].][6]

[(1F) Where a person is liable to make a payment by way of a penalty under section 25 or 26 of the Finance Act 2003 (evasion of, or contravention of relevant rule relating to, certain taxes and duties under the management of the Commissioners of Customs and Excise etc) the payment shall not be allowed as a deduction in computing any income, profits or losses [for any corporation tax purposes (but see also subsection (3)(a) below)][9].][7]

[(1G) Where a person is liable to make a payment by way of—
(a) any penalty under Part 4 of the Finance Act 2003 (stamp duty land tax), or
(b) interest under any provision of that Part,

the payment shall not be allowed as a deduction in computing any income, profits or losses [for any corporation tax purposes (but see also subsection (3)(a) below)][9].][8]

[(1H) Where a person is liable to make a payment by way of penalty under Schedule 24 to the Finance Act 2007 (penalties for errors) the payment shall not be allowed as a deduction in computing any income, profits or losses for any corporation tax purposes (but see also subsection (3)(a) below).][10]

(2) A sum paid to any person by way of supplement under section [79 of that Act][2] (VAT repayment supplements) shall be disregarded for all purposes of corporation tax [(but see also subsection (3)(b) below)][9].

[(3) For income tax purposes—
(a) provision corresponding to that made by this section (other than subsection (2) above) is made by sections 54 and 869 of ITTOIA 2005, and
(b) provision corresponding to that made by subsection (2) above is made by section 777 of ITTOIA 2005 (as read with Chapter 10 of Part 6 of that Act).][9, 11]

Definitions—"Income tax", s 832(4); "interest", s 832(1); "tax", s 832(3).

Amendments—[1] Sub-s (1B) inserted by FA 1994 s 64, Sch 7 Pt VI, para 31 and applies when insurance premium tax is charged on the receipt of a premium by an insurer under a taxable insurance contract after 30 September 1994; see FA 1994 ss 48, 49.

[2] Words and figures in square brackets in sub-ss (1), (2) substituted by the Value Added Tax Act 1994 s 100(1), Sch 14 para 10(1), (2)(*a*)–(*d*).

VAT

3 Sub-s (1A) inserted by FA 1994 ss 18(7), (8), 19 in relation to any chargeable period ending after 1 November 1994 (for purposes of air passenger duty) or 1 January 1995 (remaining purposes) (by virtue of the Finance Act 1994 Part I, (Appointed Day etc) Order 1994, SI 1994/2679 arts 2, 3).
4 Sub-s (1C) inserted by FA 1996 Sch 5 para 40.
5 Sub-s (1D) inserted by FA 2000 s 30(2), Sch 7 para 4 with effect from 28 July 2000.
6 Sub-s (1E) inserted by FA 2001 s 49(3) with effect from 11 May 2001.
7 Sub-s (1F) (originally numbered (1E), inserted by FA 2003 s 40 with effect from 10 July 2003.
8 Sub-s (1G) (originally numbered 1F) inserted by FA 2003 s 123(1), Sch 18 para 3(1), (6) with effect in accordance with FA 2003 s 124, Sch 19.
9 Words in sub-ss (1A)–(1G), (2) and the whole of sub-s (3) inserted by ITTOIA 2005 s 882, Sch 1 para 332 with effect, for income tax purposes, for the tax year 2005–06 and subsequent years, and for corporation tax purposes, for accounting periods ending after 5 April 2005.
10 Sub-s (1H) inserted by the Finance Act 2008, Schedule 40 (Appointed Day, Transitional Provisions and Consequential Amendments) Order, SI 2009/571 art 8, Sch 1 paras 19, 20 with effect from 1 April 2009.
11 This section repealed by CTA 2009 ss 1322, 1326, Sch 1 paras 1, 268, Sch 3 Part 1. CTA 2009 applies for accounting periods ending on or after 1 April 2009 (for corporation tax purposes) and for tax years 2009–10 onwards (for income and capital gains tax purposes).

Interpretation

839 Connected persons

(1) For the purposes of, and subject to, the provisions of the [Corporation Tax Acts][5] which apply this section, any question whether a person is connected with another shall be determined in accordance with the following provisions of this section (any provision that one person is connected with another being taken to mean that they are connected with one another).

(2) A person is connected with an individual if that person is the individual's [spouse or civil partner][3], or is a relative, or the [spouse or civil partner][3] of a relative, of the individual or of the individual's [spouse or civil partner][3].

[(3) A person, in his capacity as trustee of a settlement, is connected with—

(*a*) any individual who in relation to the settlement is a settlor,
(*b*) any person who is connected with such an individual, …[4]
(*c*) any body corporate which is connected with that settlement.
[(*d*) if the settlement is the principal settlement in relation to one or more sub-fund settlements, the trustees of the sub-fund settlements, and
(*e*) if the settlement is a sub-fund settlement in relation to a principal settlement, the trustees of any other sub-fund settlements in relation to the principal settlement.][4]][2]

[(3A) For the purpose of subsection (3) above a body corporate is connected with a settlement if—

(*a*) it is a close company (or only not a close company because it is not resident in the United Kingdom) and the participators include the trustees of the settlement; or
(*b*) it is controlled (within the meaning of section 840) by a company falling within paragraph (*a*) above.][2]

[(3B) For the purpose of subsection (3) above—

(*a*) "settlement" has the same meaning as in section 620 of ITTOIA 2005,
(*b*) "trustee", in relation to a settlement in relation to which there would be no trustees apart from this paragraph, means any person—
[(i) in whom the property comprised in the settlement is for the time being vested, or
(ii) in whom the management of that property is for the time being vested][5], and
(*c*) "principal settlement" and "sub-fund settlement" have the meaning given by paragraph 1 of Schedule 4ZA to the 1992 Act.][4]

(4) Except in relation to acquisitions or disposals of partnership assets pursuant to bona fide commercial arrangements, a person is connected with any person with whom he is in partnership, and with the [spouse or civil partner][3] or relative of any individual with whom he is in partnership.

(5) A company is connected with another company—

(*a*) if the same person has control of both, or a person has control of one and persons connected with him, or he and persons connected with him, have control of the other; or
(*b*) if a group of two or more persons has control of each company, and the groups either consist of the same persons or could be regarded as consisting of the same persons by treating (in one or more cases) a member of either group as replaced by a person with whom he is connected.

(6) A company is connected with another person if that person has control of it or if that person and persons connected with him together have control of it.

(7) Any two or more persons acting together to secure or exercise control of a company shall be treated in relation to that company as connected with one another and with any person acting on the directions of any of them to secure or exercise control of the company.

(8) In this section—

"company" includes any body corporate or unincorporated association, but does not include a partnership, and this section shall apply in relation to any unit trust scheme as if the scheme were a company and as if the rights of the unit holders were shares in the company;
"control" shall be construed in accordance with section 416; and

"relative" means brother, sister, ancestor or lineal descendant.

. . .[1]

Commentary—*Simon's Taxes* **A1.156**.
Rewrite destinations—Sub-s (1) rewritten to ITA 2007 ss 993(1), 994(4), Sch 1 para 411.
Sub-s (2) rewritten to ITA 2007 s 993(2), Sch 1 para 411.
Sub-s (3) rewritten to ITA 2007 ss 993(3), 994(1), Sch 1 para 411.
Sub-s (3A) rewritten to ITA 2007 s 993(3).
Sub-s (3B) rewritten to ITA 2007 s 994(1), (3).
Sub-ss (4)–(7) rewritten to ITA 2007 s 993(4)–(7), Sch 1 para 411.
Sub-s (8) rewritten to ITA 2007 s 994(1), (2), Sch 1 para 411.
Note—This section continues in force for corporation tax purposes.
Concession C9—For the purposes of "small companies marginal relief", TA 1988 s 13, the Revenue will, by concession, not treat companies in certain circumstances as associated, and "relative" includes only a husband or wife or minor child where there is no substantial commercial interdependence.
Simon's Tax Cases—s 839(7), *Steele v European Vinyls Corp (Holdings) BV* [1996] STC 785.
Definitions—"Close company", s 832(1); "the Tax Acts", s 831(2); "unit holders", s 468(6), by virtue of s 832(1); "unit trust scheme", s 469, by virtue of s 832(1).
Cross references—See TA 1988 s 587B(10A) (this section applies for the purposes of TA 1988 s 587B on gifts of shares, securities and real property to charities etc).
FA 2000 Sch 14 para 71(2) (this section applies for the purposes of FA 2000 Sch 14 on enterprise management incentives).
FA 2002 s 55(5) (this section applies for the purposes of FA 2002 s 55(4) on gifts of medical supplies and equipment).
FA 2003 Sch 26 para 7(3) (this section applies for the purposes of FA 2003 Sch 26 on transactions carried out on behalf of non-resident companies by a United Kingdom broker, investment manager or a members' or managing agent at Lloyd's).
FA 2000 Sch 22 para 89A(6) (this section applies for the purposes of that paragraph: tonnage tax: quantitative restrictions not to apply to ordinary charters).
FA 2003 Sch 15 para 39 (this section has effect for the purposes of FA 2003 Sch 15 Pt 3).
FA 2004 Sch 15 para 2 (this paragraph applies for the purposes of FA 2004 Sch 15 on the charge to income tax on benefits received by a former owner of property, but as if in this section, "relative" includes uncle, aunt, nephew and niece, and "settlement", "settlor" and "trustee" has the same meanings as in IHTA 1984).
F(No 2)A 2005 Sch 3 para 12 (avoidance involving tax arbitrage: this section has effect for the purposes of F(No 2)A 2005 Sch 3 Pt 4).
Amendments—[1] Words in sub-s (8) ceased to have effect on 29 April 1988 by virtue of TA 1988 (Appointed Day) Order, SI 1988/745.
[2] Sub-ss (3), (3A) substituted for sub-s (3) as originally enacted by FA 1995 s 74, Sch 17 para 20, with effect from the year 1995–96 (and apply to every settlement wherever and whenever made or entered into).
[3] Words in sub-ss (2), (4) substituted by Tax and Civil Partnership Regulations, SI 2005/3229, regs 47, 100, with effect from 5 December 2005 (reg 1(1)).
[4] Word "and" at the end of sub-s (3)(*b*) repealed; sub-s (3)(*d*), (*e*) substituted for words after sub-s (3)(*c*), and sub-s (3B) inserted by FA 2006 ss 89, 178, Sch 13 paras 7, 25, Sch 26 Pt 3(15) with effect from 6 April 2006 (in relation to settlements whenever created).
[5] Words in sub-ss (1), (3B)(*b*) substituted by ITA 2007 s 1027, Sch 1 paras 1, 223, with effect for income tax purposes from 6 April 2007, and corporation tax purposes for accounting periods ending after 5 April 2007.

FINANCE ACT 1988

(1988 Chapter 39)

An Act to grant certain duties, to alter other duties, and to amend the law relating to the National Debt and the Public Revenue, and to make further provision in connection with Finance.

[29th July 1988]

PART I
CUSTOMS AND EXCISE

Management

8 Disclosure of information as to imports

(1) The Commissioners may, for the purpose of supplementing the information as to imported goods which may be made available to persons other than the Commissioners, disclose information to which this section applies to such persons as they think fit.

(2) Such information may be so disclosed on such terms and conditions (including terms and conditions as to the payment of fees or charges to the Commissioners and the making of the information available to other persons) as the Commissioners think fit.

(3) This section applies to information consisting of the names and addresses of persons declared as consignees in entries of imported goods, arranged by reference to such classifications of imported goods as the Commissioners think fit.

(4) This section shall be construed as if it were contained in the Customs and Excise Management Act 1979.

PART IV
MISCELLANEOUS AND GENERAL

Miscellaneous

149 Short title

This Act may be cited as the Finance Act 1988.

FINANCE ACT 1989

(1989 Chapter 26)

An Act to grant certain duties, to alter other duties, and to amend the law relating to the National Debt and the Public Revenue, and to make further provision in connection with Finance.

[27th July 1989]

PART III
MISCELLANEOUS AND GENERAL

Miscellaneous

182 Disclosure of information

(1) A person who discloses any information which he holds or has held in the exercise of tax functions … is guilty of an offence if it is information about any matter relevant, for the purposes … of those functions—

[(*a*) to tax … in the case of any identifiable person, …

[(*ab*),][4] (*b*), (*c*) …][3]

(2) In this section "tax functions" means functions relating to tax …—

(*a*) of the Commissioners, … and their officers,

(*aa*) …

(*b*) of any person carrying out the administrative work of any tribunal mentioned in subsection (3) below, and

(*c*) of any other person providing, or employed in the provision of, services to any person mentioned in paragraph (*a*) or (*b*) above.

…

(3) The tribunals referred to in subsection (2)(*b*) above are—

(*a*) …

(*b*) any value added tax tribunal,

(*c*), (*d*) …

(4) A person who discloses any information which—

(*a*) he holds or has held in the exercise of functions—

(i) of the Comptroller and Auditor General and any member of the staff of the National Audit Office,

(ii) of the Parliamentary Commissioner for Administration and his officers,

[(iii) of the Auditor General for Wales and any member of his staff, …[3]

[(iv) of the Public Services Ombudsman for Wales and any member of his staff, or][5]

(v) of the Scottish Public Services Ombudsman and any member of his staff,][3]

(*b*) is, or is derived from, information which was held by any person in the exercise of tax functions …, and

(*c*) is information about any matter relevant, for the purposes of tax functions … —

[(i) to tax … in the case of any identifiable person …,

…

is guilty of an offence.

(5) Subsections (1) and (4) above do not apply to any disclosure of information—

(*a*) with lawful authority,

(*b*) with the consent of any person in whose case the information is about a matter relevant to tax …, or

(*c*) which has been lawfully made available to the public before the disclosure is made.

(6) For the purposes of this section a disclosure of any information is made with lawful authority if, and only if, it is made—

(*a*) by a Crown servant in accordance with his official duty, (*b*) by any other person for the purposes of the function in the exercise of which he holds the information and without contravening any restriction duly imposed by the person responsible,

(*c*) to, or in accordance with an authorisation duly given by, the person responsible,

(*d*) in pursuance of any enactment or of any order of a court, or

(*e*) in connection with the institution of or otherwise for the purposes of any proceedings relating to any matter within the general responsibility of the Commissioners …,

and in this subsection "the person responsible" means the Commissioners, … the Comptroller [, the Parliamentary Commissioner, the Auditor General for Wales[, [the Public Services Ombudsman for Wales][5] or the Scottish Public Services Ombudsman][3],][2] as the case requires.

(7) It is a defence for a person charged with an offence under this section to prove that at the time of the alleged offence—

(*a*) he believed that he had lawful authority to make the disclosure in question and had no reasonable cause to believe otherwise, or

(*b*) he believed that the information in question had been lawfully made available to the public before the disclosure was made and had no reasonable cause to believe otherwise.

(8) A person guilty of an offence under this section is liable—

(*a*) on conviction on indictment, to imprisonment for a term not exceeding two years or a fine or both, and

(*b*) on summary conviction, to imprisonment for a term not exceeding six months or a fine not exceeding the statutory maximum or both.

(9) No prosecution for an offence under this section shall be instituted in England and Wales or in Northern Ireland except—

(*a*) by the Commissioners …, or

(*b*) by or with the consent of the Director of Public Prosecutions or, in Northern Ireland, the Director of Public Prosecutions for Northern Ireland.

(10) In this section—

…

"the Commissioners" means the Commissioners of Customs and Excise,

…[3]

"Crown servant" has the same meaning as in the Official Secrets Act 1989 and

"tax …" means any tax … within the general responsibility of the Commissioners …

[(10A) In this section, in relation to the disclosure of information "identifiable person" means a person whose identity is specified in the disclosure or can be deduced from it.][4]

(11) In this section—

(*a*) references to the Comptroller and Auditor General include the Comptroller and Auditor General for Northern Ireland,

(*b*) references to the National Audit Office include the Northern Ireland Audit Office, and

(*c*) references to the Parliamentary Commissioner for Administration include the Health Service Commissioner for England …[5], …[3] the [Assembly Ombudsman for Northern Ireland][1] and the Northern Ireland Commissioner for Complaints.

(12) This section shall come into force on the repeal of section 2 of the Official Secrets Act 1911.

Note—This section came into force on 1 March 1990 when the repeal of Official Secrets Act 1911 came into force by virtue of the Official Secrets Act 1989 (Commencement) Order, SI 1990/199.

Words omitted in various places are not relevant to VAT.

Amendments—[1] Words substituted by Ombudsman (Northern Ireland) Order, SI 1996/1298 (NI 8) art 21(1), Sch 5.

[2] Sub-ss (4)(*a*)(iii) and (iv) inserted and words in sub-s (6) substituted by the Government of Wales Act 1998, Sch 12 para 31 with effect from 1 February 1999 by virtue of The Government of Wales Act 1998 (Commencement No 3) Order, SI 1999/118. Words in sub-s (6) previously read "or the Parliamentary Commissioner,".

[3] Word "or" in sub-s (4)(*a*)(iii) repealed, sub-s (4)(*a*)(v) and words in sub-s (6) inserted, words in sub-s (11)(*c*) repealed by Scottish Public Services Ombudsman Act 2002 (Consequential Provisions and Modifications) Order, SI 2004/1823 with effect from 14 July 2004.

[4] Sub-s (10A) inserted by CRCA 2005 s 50, Sch 4 para 39 with effect from 18 April 2005 (by virtue of SI 2005/1126).

[5] Sub-s (4)(*a*)(iv) substituted, words in sub-s (6) substituted, and words omitted from sub-s (11)(*c*) repealed, by Public Services Ombudsman (Wales) Act 2005 s 39, Sch 6 para 22, Sch 7 with effect from 1 April 2006 (by virtue of SI 2005/2800, art 5(1)).

Prospective amendments—This section to be amended by the Work and Families Act 2006 s 11, Sch 1 para 2 with effect from a date to be appointed, as follows—

In each of the following provisions—

(a) subsection (1)(*c*),
(b) subsection (2A)(*a*),
(c) subsection (4)(*c*)(iii),
(d) subsection (5)(*b*), and
(e) subsection (11A),

for "statutory paternity pay" substitute "ordinary statutory paternity pay, additional statutory paternity pay".

General

186 Interpretation etc

(1) In this Act "the Taxes Act 1970" means the Income and Corporation Taxes Act 1970 and "the Taxes Act 1988" means the Income and Corporation Taxes Act 1988.

(2), (3) …

Note—Sub-ss (2), (3) are not relevant to VAT.

188 Short title

This Act may be cited as the Finance Act 1989.

TRIBUNALS AND INQUIRIES ACT 1992

(1992 Chapter 53)

An Act to consolidate the Tribunals and Inquiries Act 1971 and certain other enactments relating to tribunals and inquiries

[16th July 1992]

Judicial control of tribunals etc

11 Appeals from certain tribunals

(1) Subject to subsection (2), if any party to proceedings before any tribunal specified in paragraph … 44 of Schedule 1 is dissatisfied in point of law with a decision of the tribunal he may, according as rules of court may provide, either appeal from the tribunal to the High Court or require the tribunal to state and sign a case for the opinion of the High Court.

(2) …

(3) Rules of court made with respect to all or any of the tribunals referred to in subsection (1) may provide for authorising or requiring a tribunal, in the course of proceedings before it, to state, in the form of a special case for the decision of the High Court, any question of law arising in the proceedings; and a decision of the High Court on a case stated by virtue of this subsection shall be deemed to be a judgment of the Court within the meaning of section 16 of the Supreme Court Act 1981 (jurisdiction of Court of Appeal to hear and determine appeals from judgments of the High Court).

(4) In relation to proceedings in the High Court or the Court of Appeal brought by virtue of this section, the power to make rules of court shall include power to make rules prescribing the powers of the High Court or the Court of Appeal with respect to—

(*a*) the giving of any decision which might have been given by the tribunal;

(*b*) the remitting of the matter with the opinion or direction of the court for re-hearing and determination by the tribunal;

(*c*) the giving of directions to the tribunal;

and different provisions may be made for different tribunals.

(5) An appeal to the Court of Appeal shall not be brought by virtue of this section except with the leave of the High Court or the Court of Appeal.

(6) …[1]

(7) The following provisions shall have effect for the application of this section to Scotland—

(*a*) in relation to any proceedings in Scotland of any of the tribunals referred to in the preceding provisions of this section, *or on an appeal under section 41 of the Consumer Credit Act 1974 by a company registered in Scotland or by any other person whose principal or prospective principal place of business in the United Kingdom is in Scotland*[1], this section shall have effect with the following modifications—

(i) for references to the High Court or the Court of Appeal there shall be substituted references to the Court of Session,

(ii) in subsection (3) for "in the form of a special case for the decision of the High Court" there shall be substituted "a case for the opinion of the Court of Session on" and the words from "and a decision" to the end of the subsection shall be omitted, and

(iii) subsection (5) shall be omitted,

(*b*) this section shall apply, with the modifications specified in paragraph (*a*)—

(i) to proceedings before any such tribunal as is specified in paragraph 51, 56(*b*), 59 or 63 of Schedule 1, and

(ii) subject to paragraph (*c*) below, to proceedings before the Lands Tribunal for Scotland, as it applies to proceedings before the tribunals referred to in subsection (1);

(*c*) subsection (1) shall not apply in relation to proceedings before the Lands Tribunal for Scotland which arise under section 1(3A) of the Lands Tribunal Act 1949 (jurisdiction of the tribunal in valuation matters);

(*d*) an appeal shall lie, with the leave of the Court of Session or the House of Lords, from any decision of the Court of Session under this section, and such leave may be given on such terms as to costs or otherwise as the Court of Session or the House of Lords may determine.

(8) In relation to any proceedings in Northern Ireland of any of the tribunals referred to in subsection (1) …[1], this section shall have effect with the following modifications—

(*a*) in subsection (3), for the words from the beginning to "provide" there shall be substituted "Rules may be made under section 55 of the Judicature (Northern Ireland) Act 1978

providing", and for "section 16 of the Supreme Court Act 1981" there shall be substituted "section 35 of the Judicature (Northern Ireland) Act 1978";
(*b*) in subsection (4), for "the power to make rules of court shall include power to make rules" there shall be substituted "rules may be made under section 55 of the Judicature (Northern Ireland) Act 1978";
(*c*) at the beginning of subsection (5), there shall be inserted "Rules made under section 55 of the Judicature (Northern Ireland) Act 1978, relating to such proceedings as are mentioned in subsection (4), shall provide that the appeal shall be heard, or as the case may be, the decision of the High Court shall be given, by a single judge, but".

(9) …

(10) In this section "decision" includes any direction or order, and references to the giving of a decision shall be construed accordingly.

Note—Words omitted are not relevant for the purposes of VAT.
Simon's Tax Cases—*R v C&E Comrs, ex p Menzies* [1989] STC 40*; *R v London Value Added Tax and Duties Tribunal, ex p Conoco Ltd* [1995] STC 468; *Conoco Ltd v C&E Comrs* [1995] STC 1022. (VAT)
Prospective amendments—In sub-s (7)(*d*) words "Supreme Court" to be substituted for words "House of Lords" in each place by the Constitutional Reform Act 2005 s 40, Sch 9 para 59 with effect from a date to be appointed.
Amendments—[1] Sub-s (6), and words in sub-ss (7)(*a*), (8), repealed, by Consumer Credit Act 2006 s 70, Sch 4 with effect from 6 April 2008 (except in relation to determinations made by the OFT before that date): SI 2007/3300, art 3(2), Sch 2; Consumer Credit Act 2006 s 69(1), Sch 3 paras 1, 27(1), (2).

Supplementary provisions

19 Short title, commencement and extent

(1) This Act may be cited as the Tribunals and Inquiries Act 1992.

(2) This Act shall come into force on 1st October 1992.

(3) This Act extends to Northern Ireland.

SCHEDULES

SCHEDULE 1

TRIBUNALS UNDER GENERAL SUPERVISION OF COUNCIL

Section 1

PART I

TRIBUNALS UNDER DIRECT SUPERVISION OF COUNCIL

Matters with which tribunal concerned	*Tribunal and statutory authority*
…	
[[VAT and duties	*44 VAT and duties tribunals for England and Wales and for Northern Ireland, constituted in accordance with Schedule [12 to the Value Added Tax Act 1994]*[2]*.]*[1]][3]

Note—Words omitted are not relevant for the purposes of VAT
Amendments—[1] Substituted by FA 1994 s 7(6).
[2] Substituted by VATA 1994 s 100(1), Sch 14, para 12.
[3] Repealed by the Transfer of Tribunal Functions and Revenue and Customs Appeals Order, SI 2009/56 art 3, Sch 1 para 188 with effect from 1 April 2009.

CHARITIES ACT 1993

(1993 Chapter 10)

[10 Disclosure of information to Commission

(1) Any relevant public authority may disclose information to the Commission if the disclosure is made for the purpose of enabling or assisting the Commission to discharge any of its functions.

(2) But Revenue and Customs information may be disclosed under subsection (1) only if it relates to an institution, undertaking or body falling within one (or more) of the following paragraphs—
(*a*) a charity;
(*b*) an institution which is established for charitable, benevolent or philanthropic purposes;

(*c*) an institution by or in respect of which a claim for exemption has at any time been made under section 505(1) of the Income and Corporation Taxes Act 1988;
(*d*) a subsidiary undertaking of a charity;
(*e*) a body entered in the Scottish Charity Register which is managed or controlled wholly or mainly in or from England or Wales.

(3) In subsection (2)(*d*) above "subsidiary undertaking of a charity" means an undertaking (as defined by [section 1161(1) of the Companies Act 2006][2]) in relation to which—
(*a*) a charity is (or is to be treated as) a parent undertaking in accordance with the provisions of [section 1162 of, and Schedule 7 to, the Companies Act 2006][2], or
(*b*) two or more charities would, if they were a single charity, be (or be treated as) a parent undertaking in accordance with those provisions.

(4) For the purposes of the references to a parent undertaking—
(*a*) in subsection (3) above, and
(*b*) in [section 1162 of, and Schedule 7 to, the Companies Act 2006][2] as they apply for the purposes of that subsection,

"undertaking" includes a charity which is not an undertaking as defined by [section 1161(1)][2] of that Act.][1]

Amendments—[1] Sections 10–10C substituted for s 10 as originally enacted by the Charities Act 2006, s 75(1), Sch 8, paras 96, 104, with effect from—
– in so far as it confers power to make regulations, 8 November 2006 (Charities Act 2006, s 79(1)(*g*));
– for remaining purposes, 27 February 2007 (SI 2007/309, art 2, Schedule).
[2] In sub-ss (3), (4) words substituted by the Companies Act 2006 (Consequential Amendments etc) Order, SI 2008/948 arts 3(1)(*b*), 6, Sch 1 para 192(1), (2) with effect from 6 April 2008.

[10A Disclosure of information by Commission

(1) Subject to subsections (2) and (3) below, the Commission may disclose to any relevant public authority any information received by the Commission in connection with any of the Commission's functions—
(*a*) if the disclosure is made for the purpose of enabling or assisting the relevant public authority to discharge any of its functions, or
(*b*) if the information so disclosed is otherwise relevant to the discharge of any of the functions of the relevant public authority.

(2) In the case of information disclosed to the Commission under section 10(1) above, the Commission's power to disclose the information under subsection (1) above is exercisable subject to any express restriction subject to which the information was disclosed to the Commission.

(3) Subsection (2) above does not apply in relation to Revenue and Customs information disclosed to the Commission under section 10(1) above; but any such information may not be further disclosed (whether under subsection (1) above or otherwise) except with the consent of the Commissioners for Her Majesty's Revenue and Customs.

(4) Any responsible person who discloses information in contravention of subsection (3) above is guilty of an offence and liable—
(*a*) on summary conviction, to imprisonment for a term not exceeding 12 months or to a fine not exceeding the statutory maximum, or both;
(*b*) on conviction on indictment, to imprisonment for a term not exceeding two years or to a fine, or both.

(5) It is a defence for a responsible person charged with an offence under subsection (4) above of disclosing information to prove that he reasonably believed—
(*a*) that the disclosure was lawful, or
(*b*) that the information had already and lawfully been made available to the public.

(6) In the application of this section to Scotland or Northern Ireland, the reference to 12 months in subsection (4) is to be read as a reference to 6 months.

(7) In this section "responsible person" means a person who is or was—
(*a*) a member of the Commission,
(*b*) a member of the staff of the Commission,
(*c*) a person acting on behalf of the Commission or a member of the staff of the Commission, or
(*d*) a member of a committee established by the Commission.][1]

Amendments—[1] Sections 10–10C substituted for s 10 as originally enacted by the Charities Act 2006, s 75(1), Sch 8, paras 96, 104, with effect from—
– in so far as it confers power to make regulations, 8 November 2006 (Charities Act 2006, s 79(1)(*g*));
– for remaining purposes, 27 February 2007 (SI 2007/309, art 2, Schedule).

[10B Disclosure to and by principal regulators of exempt charities

(1) Sections 10 and 10A above apply with the modifications in subsections (2) to (4) below in relation to the disclosure of information to or by the principal regulator of an exempt charity.

(2) References in those sections to the Commission or to any of its functions are to be read as references to the principal regulator of an exempt charity or to any of the functions of that body or person as principal regulator in relation to the charity.

(3) Section 10 above has effect as if for subsections (2) and (3) there were substituted—

"(2) But Revenue and Customs information may be disclosed under subsection (1) only if it relates to—

(*a*) the exempt charity in relation to which the principal regulator has functions as such, or

(*b*) a subsidiary undertaking of the exempt charity.

(3) In subsection (2)(*b*) above "subsidiary undertaking of the exempt charity" means an undertaking (as defined by [section 1161(1) of the Companies Act 2006][2]) in relation to which—

(*a*) the exempt charity is (or is to be treated as) a parent undertaking in accordance with the provisions of [section 1162 of, and Schedule 7 to, the Companies Act 2006][2], or

(*b*) the exempt charity and one or more other charities would, if they were a single charity, be (or be treated as) a parent undertaking in accordance with those provisions."

(4) Section 10A above has effect as if for the definition of "responsible person" in subsection (7) there were substituted a definition specified by regulations under section 13(4)(*b*) of the Charities Act 2006 (regulations prescribing principal regulators).

(5) Regulations under section 13(4)(*b*) of that Act may also make such amendments or other modifications of any enactment as the Secretary of State considers appropriate for securing that any disclosure provisions that would otherwise apply in relation to the principal regulator of an exempt charity do not apply in relation to that body or person in its or his capacity as principal regulator.

(6) In subsection (5) above "disclosure provisions" means provisions having effect for authorising, or otherwise in connection with, the disclosure of information by or to the principal regulator concerned.][1]

Amendments—[1] Sections 10–10C substituted for s 10 as originally enacted by the Charities Act 2006, s 75(1), Sch 8, paras 96, 104, with effect from—

- in so far as it confers power to make regulations, 8 November 2006 (Charities Act 2006, s 79(1)(*g*));
- for remaining purposes, a date to be appointed.

[2] In sub-s (3), in substituted s 10(3), words substituted by the Companies Act 2006 (Consequential Amendments etc) Order SI 2008/948 arts 3(1)(*b*), 6, Sch 1 para 192(1), (3) with effect from 6 April 2008.

[10C Disclosure of information: supplementary

(1) In sections 10 and 10A above "relevant public authority" means—

(*a*) any government department (including a Northern Ireland department),

(*b*) any local authority,

(*c*) any constable, and

(*d*) any other body or person discharging functions of a public nature (including a body or person discharging regulatory functions in relation to any description of activities).

(2) In section 10A above "relevant public authority" also includes any body or person within subsection (1)(*d*) above in a country or territory outside the United Kingdom.

(3) In sections 10 to 10B above and this section—

"enactment" has the same meaning as in the Charities Act 2006;

"Revenue and Customs information" means information held as mentioned in section 18(1) of the Commissioners for Revenue and Customs Act 2005.

(4) Nothing in sections 10 and 10A above (or in those sections as applied by section 10B(1) to (4) above) authorises the making of a disclosure which—

(*a*) contravenes the Data Protection Act 1998, or

(*b*) is prohibited by Part 1 of the Regulation of Investigatory Powers Act 2000.][1]

Amendments—[1] Sections 10–10C substituted for s 10 as originally enacted by the Charities Act 2006, s 75(1), Sch 8, paras 96, 104, with effect from—

- in so far as it confers power to make regulations, 8 November 2006 (Charities Act 2006, s 79(1)(*g*));
- for remaining purposes, a date to be appointed.

FINANCE ACT 1994

(1994 Chapter 9)

CHAPTER II

APPEALS AND PENALTIES

[The meaning of tribunal

7 Meaning of tribunal

In the following provisions of this Chapter references to an appeal tribunal are references to the First-tier Tribunal or, where determined by or under Tribunal Procedure Rules, the Upper Tribunal.][1]

Amendments—[1] Section 7 substituted by the Transfer of Tribunal Functions and Revenue and Customs Appeals Order, SI 2009/56 art 3, Sch 1 paras 196, 197 with effect from 1 April 2009. This section previously read as follows—

"VAT and duties tribunals

7 VAT and duties tribunals

(1), (2) …

(3) In the following provisions of this Chapter references to an appeal tribunal are references to a VAT and duties tribunal.

(4) Sections 85 and 87 of the Value Added Tax Act 1994 (settling of appeals by agreement and enforcement of decisions of tribunal) shall have effect as if—

(a) the references to section 83 of that Act included references to this Chapter; and
(b) references to value added tax included references to any relevant duty.

(5) Without prejudice to the generality of the power conferred by paragraph 9 of Schedule 12 to the Value Added Tax Act 1994 (rules of procedure for tribunals), rules under that paragraph may provide for costs awarded against an appellant on an appeal by virtue of this Chapter to be recoverable, and for any directly applicable Community legislation relating to any relevant duty or any enactment so relating to apply, as if the amount awarded were an amount of duty which the appellant is required to pay.

(6), (7) …".

VALUE ADDED TAX ACT 1994

(1994 Chapter 23)

ARRANGEMENT OF SECTIONS

PART I
THE CHARGE TO TAX

PART IV
ADMINISTRATION, COLLECTION AND ENFORCEMENT

PART V
REVIEWS AND APPEALS

PART VI
SUPPLEMENTARY PROVISIONS

Change in rate of VAT etc and disclosure of information

88 Supplies spanning change of rate etc.
89 Adjustments of contracts on changes in VAT.
90 Failure of resolution under Provisional Collection of Taxes Act 1968.
91 Disclosure of information for statistical purposes.

Interpretative provisions

92 Taxation under the laws of other member States etc.
93 Territories included in references to other member States etc.
94 Meaning of "business" etc.
95 Meaning of "new means of transport".
96 Other interpretative provisions.

Supplementary provisions

97 Orders, rules and regulations.
97A Place of supply orders: transitional provision.
98 Service of notices.
99 Refund of VAT to Government of Northern Ireland.
100 Savings and transitional provisions, consequential amendments and repeals.
101 Commencement and extent.
102 Short title.

SCHEDULES:

Schedule A1—Charge at reduced rate. (*repealed*)
Schedule 1—Registration in respect of taxable supplies.
Schedule 2—Registration in respect of supplies from other member States.
Schedule 3—Registration in respect of acquisitions from other member States.
Schedule 3A—Registration in respect of disposals of assets for which a VAT repayment is claimed
Schedule 3B—Supply of electronic services in member States: special accounting scheme
Schedule 4—Matters to be treated as supply of goods or services.
Schedule 5—Services supplied where received.
Schedule 5A—Goods eligible to be fiscally warehoused.
Schedule 6—Valuation: special cases.
Schedule 7—Valuation of acquisitions from other member States: special cases.
Schedule 7A—Charge at reduced rate
Schedule 8—Zero-rating.
Part I—Index to zero-rated supplies of goods and services.
Part II—The Groups.
Schedule 9—Exemptions.
Part I—Index to exempt supplies of goods and services.
Part II—The Groups.
Schedule 9A—Anti-avoidance provisions: groups.
Schedule 10—Buildings and land.
Schedule 10A—Face-value vouchers.
Schedule 11—Administration, collection and enforcement.
Schedule 11A—Disclosure of avoidance schemes.
Schedule 12—Constitution and procedure of tribunals. (repealed)
Schedule 13—Transitional provisions and savings.
Schedule 14—Consequential amendments.
Schedule 15—Repeals. (not printed)

An Act to consolidate the enactments relating to value added tax, including certain enactments relating to VAT tribunals.

[5th July 1994]

PART I
THE CHARGE TO TAX

Cross reference—See Isle of Man Act 1979 s 6, VAT (Isle of Man) Orders, SI 1982/1067, SI 1982/1068 and VATA 1994 Sch 13 para 23 (treatment of UK and Isle of Man as a single area for the purposes of this Act).

Imposition and rate of VAT

1 Value added tax

(1) Value added tax shall be charged, in accordance with the provisions of this Act—

(*a*) on the supply of goods or services in the United Kingdom (including anything treated as such a supply),

(*b*) on the acquisition in the United Kingdom from other member States of any goods, and

(*c*) on the importation of goods from places outside the member States,

and references in this Act to VAT are references to value added tax.

(2) VAT on any supply of goods or services is a liability of the person making the supply and (subject to provisions about accounting and payment) becomes due at the time of supply.

(3) VAT on any acquisition of goods from another member State is a liability of the person who acquires the goods and (subject to provisions about accounting and payment) becomes due at the time of acquisition.

(4) VAT on the importation of goods from places outside the member States shall be charged and payable as if it were a duty of customs.

Commentary—*De Voil Indirect Tax Service* **V1.101**.
Simon's Tax Cases—s 1(1), *C&E Comrs v Fine Art Developments plc* [1989] STC 85*.
Definitions—"Acquisition of goods from another member State", s 11; "another member State", s 96(1); "importation of goods from places outside the member States", s 15; "other member States", s 96(1); "supply ", s 5, Sch 4; "time of acquisition", s 12; "time of supply", s 6; "United Kingdom", s 96(11); "VAT", s 96(1).

2 Rate of VAT

(1) Subject to the following provisions of this section [and to the provisions of section 29A][2]...[1], VAT shall be charged at the rate of *17.5*[4] per cent and shall be charged—

(*a*) on the supply of goods or services, by reference to the value of the supply as determined under this Act; and

(*b*) on the acquisition of goods from another member State, by reference to the value of the acquisition as determined under this Act; and

(*c*) on the importation of goods from a place outside the member States, by reference to the value of the goods as determined under this Act.

(1A)–(1C) ...[2].

(2) The Treasury may by order increase or decrease the rate of VAT for the time being in force [under this section][3] by such percentage thereof not exceeding 25 per cent as may be specified in the order, but any such order [that has not previously expired or been revoked][5] shall cease to be in force at the expiration of a period of one year from the date on which it takes effect, unless continued in force by a further order under this subsection.

(3) In relation to an order made under subsection (2) above to continue, vary or replace a previous order, the reference in that subsection to the rate for the time being in force [under this section][3] is a reference to the rate which would be in force if no order under that subsection had been made.

Commentary—*De Voil Indirect Tax Service* **V3.101, V3.102**.
Definitions—"Acquisition of goods from another member State", s 11; "another member State", s 96(1); "importation of goods from a place outside the member States", s 15; "supply", s 5, Sch 4; "VAT", ss 1, 96(1); "value of the acquisition", s 20; "value of the goods", s 21; "value of the supply", s 19, Sch 6.
Cross references—See VATA 1994 s 50A (Treasury may by order provide an option for VAT to be charged by reference to profit margin rather than value in relation to certain supplies);
VATA 1994 s 88 (supplies spanning date of change in rate of VAT);
VAT Regulations, SI 1995/2518 reg 15 (credit note to be issued by supplier following change of rate, where an election is made under s 88).
FA 2009 Sch 3 (supplementary charge to VAT).
Amendments—[1] Words omitted from sub-s (1) repealed by FA 1995 s 21(2), (6), with effect in relation to any supply made after 31 March 1995 and any acquisition or importation taking place after that date.
[2] Words in sub-s (1) inserted, and sub-s (1A), (1B) repealed by FA 2001 s 99(2), (3) with effect for supplies made, and acquisitions and importations taking place, after 31 October 2001. Sub-s (1C) repealed by FA 2001 s 99(2), (3) with effect from 1 November 2001.
[3] Words in sub-ss (2), (3) inserted by FA 2001 s 99(6), Sch 31 para 2 with effect for orders under sub-s (2) that make changes only in the rate of VAT that is in force at times after 31 October 2001.
[4] In sub-s (1), the standard rate of tax is reduced to 15%, by the VAT (Change of Rate) Order, SI 2008/3020 arts 2, 3 with effect from 1 December 2008 to 31 December 2009 (extended from 30 November 2009 by FA 2009 s 9). On 1 January 2010 the standard rate will revert to 17.5%.
[5] Words in sub-s (2) inserted by FA 2009 Sch 3 para 25(2) with effect from 21 July 2009.

3 Taxable persons and registration

(1) A person is a taxable person for the purposes of this Act while he is, or is required to be, registered under this Act.

(2) [Schedules 1 to 3A][1] shall have effect with respect to registration.

(3) Persons registered under any of those Schedules shall be registered in a single register kept by the Commissioners for the purposes of this Act; and, accordingly, references in this Act to being registered under this Act are references to being registered under any of those Schedules.

(4) The Commissioners may by regulations make provision as to the inclusion and correction of information in that register with respect to the Schedule under which any person is registered.

Commentary—*De Voil Indirect Tax Service* **V3.123**.
Regulations—See VAT Regulations, SI 1995/2518 regs 5–7.
Press releases etc—C&E News Release 22/96 4-4-96 (prohibition on disclosure of information on the VAT register continues).
Simon's Tax Cases—*R&C Comrs v Pal and others* [2008] STC 2442.

Definitions—"The Commissioners", s 96(1); "regulations", s 96(1).
Amendments—[1] Words in sub-s (2) substituted by FA 2000 s 136(1), with effect for supplies made after 20 March 2000.

[3A Supply of electronic services in member States: special accounting scheme

(1) Schedule 3B (scheme enabling persons who supply electronically supplied services in any member State, but who are not established in a member State, to account for and pay VAT in the United Kingdom on those supplies) has effect.

(2) The Treasury may by order amend Schedule 3B.

(3) The power of the Treasury by order to amend Schedule 3B includes power to make such incidental, supplemental, consequential and transitional provision in connection with any amendment of that Schedule as they think fit.][1]

Amendments—[1] This section inserted by FA 2003 s 23, Sch 2 paras 1, 2 in relation to qualifying supplies made after 30 June 2003, see FA 2003 s 23(2).

Supply of goods or services in the United Kingdom

4 Scope of VAT on taxable supplies

(1) VAT shall be charged on any supply of goods or services made in the United Kingdom, where it is a taxable supply made by a taxable person in the course or furtherance of any business carried on by him.

(2) A taxable supply is a supply of goods or services made in the United Kingdom other than an exempt supply.

Commentary—*De Voil Indirect Tax Service* **V3.101, V3.502**.
HMRC Manuals—VAT Guidance V1-3: Supply and consideration para 2.1 (scope of VAT).
Simon's Tax Cases—*C&E Comrs v Professional Footballers' Association (Enterprises) Ltd* [1993] STC 86*; *R v Ryan* [1994] STC 446*; *B J Rice & Associates v C&E Comrs* [1996] STC 581*; *ICAEW v C&E Comrs* [1999] STC 398.
Press releases etc—C&E VAT Notes 1/95 (oath fees retained personally by associate or assistant solicitor not subject to VAT generally).
Definitions—"Business", s 96(1); "exempt supply", s 31, Sch 9; "supply", s 5, Sch 4; "taxable person", s 3; "United Kingdom", s 3; "VAT", ss 1, 96(1).

5 Meaning of supply: alteration by Treasury order

(1) Schedule 4 shall apply for determining what is, or is to be treated as, a supply of goods or a supply of services.

(2) Subject to any provision made by that Schedule and to Treasury orders under subsections (3) to (6) below—

(*a*) "supply" in this Act includes all forms of supply, but not anything done otherwise than for a consideration;

(*b*) anything which is not a supply of goods but is done for a consideration (including, if so done, the granting, assignment or surrender of any right) is a supply of services.

(3) The Treasury may by order provide with respect to any description of transaction—

(*a*) that it is to be treated as a supply of goods and not as a supply of services; or
(*b*) that it is to be treated as a supply of services and not as a supply of goods; or
(*c*) that it is to be treated as neither a supply of goods nor a supply of services;

and without prejudice to the foregoing, such an order may provide that paragraph 5(4) of Schedule 4 is not to apply, in relation to goods of any prescribed description used or made available for use in prescribed circumstances, so as to make that a supply of services under that paragraph and may provide that paragraph 6 of that Schedule shall not apply, in such circumstances as may be described in the order, so as to make a removal of assets a supply of goods under that paragraph.

(4) Without prejudice to subsection (3) above, the Treasury may by order make provision for securing, with respect to services of any description specified in the order, that where—

(*a*) a person carrying on a business does anything which is not a supply of services but would, if done for a consideration, be a supply of services of a description specified in the order; and
(*b*) such other conditions as may be specified in the order are satisfied,

such services are treated for the purposes of this Act as being supplied by him in the course or furtherance of that business.

(5) The Treasury may by order make provision for securing, subject to any exceptions provided for by or under the order, that where in such circumstances as may be specified in the order goods of a description so specified are taken possession of or produced by a person in the course or furtherance of a business carried on by him and—

(*a*) are neither supplied to another person nor incorporated in other goods produced in the course or furtherance of that business; but
(*b*) are used by him for the purpose of a business carried on by him,

the goods are treated for the purposes of this Act as being both supplied to him for the purpose of that business and supplied by him in the course or furtherance of it.

(6) The Treasury may by order make provision for securing, with respect to services of any description specified in the order, that where—

(*a*) a person, in the course or furtherance of a business carried on by him, does anything for the purpose of that business which is not a supply of services but would, if done for a consideration, be a supply of services of a description specified in the order; and

(*b*) such other conditions as may be specified in the order are satisfied,

such services are treated for the purposes of this Act as being both supplied to him for the purpose of that business and supplied by him in the course or furtherance of it.

(7) For the purposes of this section, where goods are manufactured or produced from any other goods, those other goods shall be treated as incorporated in the first-mentioned goods.

(8) An order under subsection (4) or (6) above may provide for the method by which the value of any supply of services which is treated as taking place by virtue of the order is to be calculated.

Commentary—*De Voil Indirect Tax Service* **V3.111, V3.118**.
HMRC Manuals—VAT Guidance V1–3: Supply and consideration, para 2.2 (supply for consideration).
Para 2.8 (list of Orders made under this section).
Para 2.9–2.11 (definitions of supply of goods and supply of services).
Para 2.12 (self-supply).
Para 4.2 (supply of services for consideration).
Para 4.12 (sale of goodwill as taxable supply of services).
Para 15.3 (supply of services: sale of options).
Simon's Tax Cases—*C&E Comrs v Apple and Pear Development Council* [1985] STC 383*; *C&E Comrs v High Street Vouchers Ltd* [1990] STC 575*; *Phillip Drakard Trading Ltd v C&E Comrs* [1992] STC 568*; *Church of England Children's Society v Revenue and Customs Commissioners* [2005] STC 1644.
s 5(1), *Philips Exports Ltd v C&E Comrs* [1990] STC 508*.
s 5(2), *C&E Comrs v Professional Footballers' Association (Enterprises) Ltd* [1992] STC 294*; *Eastbourne Town Radio Cars Association v C&E Comrs* [2001] STC 606; *C&E Comrs v Church Schools Foundation Ltd* [2001] STC 1661.
s 5(2)(*b*), *C&E Comrs v Diners Club Ltd* [1989] STC 407*; *C&E Comrs v Battersea Leisure Ltd* [1992] STC 213*.
s 5(3), *C&E Comrs v Co-operative Wholesale Society Ltd* [1995] STC 983*; *WHA Ltd and another v C&E Comrs* [2004] STC 1081.
Orders—See VAT (Treatment of Transactions) (No 1) Order, SI 1973/325; VAT (Treatment of Transactions) Order, SI 1986/896; VAT (Tour Operators) Order, SI 1987/1806; VAT (Self-supply of Construction Services) Order, SI 1989/472; VAT (Water) Order, SI 1989/1114; VAT (Treatment of Transactions) Order, SI 1992/630; VAT (Removal of Goods) Order, SI 1992/3111; VAT (Cars) Order, SI 1992/3122; VAT (Supply of Temporarily Imported Goods) Order, SI 1992/3130; VAT (Supply of Services) Order, SI 1993/1507; VAT (Treatment of Transactions) Order, SI 1995/958; VAT (Special Provisions) Order, SI 1995/1268; VAT (Fiscal Warehousing) (Treatment of Transactions) Order , SI 1996/1255.
Press releases etc—C&E Business Brief 8/95 5-5-95 (Barter transactions subject to VAT).
Definitions—"Business", s 94; "prescribed", s 96(1).
Cross references—See VATA 1994 s 6(11) (goods treated as supplied by an order under sub-s (5) of this section: time of supply);
VATA 1994 s 43(2) (VAT groups: orders under sub-s (5) or (6) of this section may provide that certain goods or services may be treated as supplied to or by representative member of group);
VATA 1994 s 97(3), (4) (procedure for making orders under sub-s (4) of this section);
VATA 1994 Sch 6 para 6 (valuation of transactions treated as supplies of goods by virtue of an order under sub-s (5) of this section);
VATA 1994 Sch 6 para 7 (valuation of transactions treated as supplies of services by virtue of an order under sub-s (4) of this section).
VAT Regulations, SI 1995/2518 reg 81(2) (time of supply of services specified in orders made under sub-s (4) of this section).

6 Time of supply

(1) The provisions of this section shall apply, subject to [sections 18, 18B and 18C][1], for determining the time when a supply of goods or services is to be treated as taking place for the purposes of the charge to VAT.

(2) Subject to subsections (4) to (14) below, a supply of goods shall be treated as taking place—

(*a*) if the goods are to be removed, at the time of the removal;

(*b*) if the goods are not to be removed, at the time when they are made available to the person to whom they are supplied;

(*c*) if the goods (being sent or taken on approval or sale or return or similar terms) are removed before it is known whether a supply will take place, at the time when it becomes certain that the supply has taken place or, if sooner, 12 months after the removal.

(3) Subject to subsections (4) to (14) below, a supply of services shall be treated as taking place at the time when the services are performed.

(4) If, before the time applicable under subsection (2) or (3) above, the person making the supply issues a VAT invoice in respect of it or if, before the time applicable under subsection (2)(*a*) or (*b*) or (3) above, he receives a payment in respect of it, the supply shall, to the extent covered by the invoice or payment, be treated as taking place at the time the invoice is issued or the payment is received.

(5) If, within 14 days after the time applicable under subsection (2) or (3) above, the person making the supply issues a VAT invoice in respect of it, then, unless he has notified the Commissioners in writing that he elects not to avail himself of this subsection, the supply shall (to the extent that it is not treated as taking place at the time mentioned in subsection (4) above) be treated as taking place at the time the invoice is issued.

(6) The Commissioners may, at the request of a taxable person, direct that subsection (5) above shall apply in relation to supplies made by him (or such supplies made by him as may be specified in the direction) as if for the period of 14 days there were substituted such longer period as may be specified in the direction.

(7) Where any supply of goods involves both—

(*a*) the removal of the goods from the United Kingdom; and

(*b*) their acquisition in another member State by a person who is liable for VAT on the acquisition in accordance with provisions of the law of that member State corresponding, in relation to that member State, to the provisions of section 10,

subsections (2), (4) to (6) and (10) to (12) of this section shall not apply and the supply shall be treated for the purposes of this Act as taking place on whichever is the earlier of the days specified in subsection (8) below.

(8) The days mentioned in subsection (7) above are—

(*a*) the 15th day of the month following that in which the removal in question takes place; and

(*b*) the day of the issue, in respect of the supply, of a VAT invoice or of an invoice of such other description as the Commissioners may by regulations prescribe.

(9) …[3]

(10) The Commissioners may, at the request of a taxable person, by direction alter the time at which supplies made by him (or such supplies made by him as may be specified in the direction) are to be treated as taking place, either—

(*a*) by directing those supplies to be treated as taking place—

(i) at times or on dates determined by or by reference to the occurrence of some event described in the direction; or

(ii) at times or on dates determined by or by reference to the time when some event so described would in the ordinary course of events occur,

the resulting times or dates being in every case earlier than would otherwise apply; or

(*b*) by directing that, notwithstanding subsections (5) and (6) above, those supplies shall (to the extent that they are not treated as taking place at the time mentioned in subsection (4) above) be treated as taking place—

(i) at the beginning of the relevant working period (as defined in his case in and for the purposes of the direction); or

(ii) at the end of the relevant working period (as so defined).

(11) Where goods are treated as supplied by an order under section 5(5), the supply is treated as taking place when they are appropriated to the use mentioned in that section.

(12) Where there is a supply of goods by virtue only of paragraph 5(1) of Schedule 4, the supply is treated as taking place when the goods are transferred or disposed of as mentioned in that paragraph.

(13) Where there is a supply of services by virtue only of paragraph 5(4) of Schedule 4, the supply is treated as taking place when the goods are appropriated to the use mentioned in that paragraph.

(14) The Commissioners may by regulations make provision with respect to the time at which (notwithstanding subsections (2) to (8) and (11) to (13) above or section 55(4)) a supply is to be treated as taking place in cases where—

(*a*) it is a supply of goods or services for a consideration the whole or part of which is determined or payable periodically, or from time to time, or at the end of any period, or

(*b*) it is a supply of goods for a consideration the whole or part of which is determined at the time when the goods are appropriated for any purpose, or

(*c*) there is a supply to which section 55 applies, or

(*d*) there is a supply of services by virtue of paragraph 5(4) of Schedule 4 or an order under section 5(4);

and for any such case as is mentioned in this subsection the regulations may provide for goods or services to be treated as separately and successively supplied at prescribed times or intervals.

[(14A) …,[4] This section and any regulations under this section or section 8(4) shall have effect subject to section 97A.][2]

(15) In this Act "VAT invoice" means such an invoice as is required under [paragraph 2A][3] of Schedule 11, or would be so required if the person to whom the supply is made were a person to whom such an invoice should be issued.

Commentary—*De Voil Indirect Tax Service* **V3.131**.

Simon's Tax Cases—*Purshotam M Pattni & Sons v C&E Comrs* [1987] STC 1*; *BJ Rice & Associates v C&E Comrs* [1996] STC 581*; *C&E Comrs v BRS Automotive Ltd* [1997] STC 336; *C&E Comrs v Thorn Materials Supply Ltd and Thorn Resources Ltd* [1998] STC 725*.

s 6(2)(*c*), *R&C Comrs v Robertson's Electrical Ltd* [2007] STC 612.

s 6(4), *C&E Comrs v Richmond Theatre Management Ltd* [1995] STC 257*; *Higher Education Statistics Agency v C&E Comrs* [2000] STC 332; *Cumbernauld Development Corporation v C&E Comrs* [2002] STC 226.

Regulations—See VAT Regulations, SI 1995/2518 regs 81, 84–86, 88–95.

Press releases etc—ICAEW 15/94 16-8-94 (guidance notes on supplies by accountants). VAT Information Sheet 13/95 1.9.95 (tax point will be time at which supplier keys details of transaction into the system where a corporate purchasing or procurement card is used).

Definitions—"Another member State", s 96(1); "the Commissioners", s 96(1); "document", s 96(1); "invoice", s 96(1); "law of that member State", s 92; "prescribed", s 96(1); "regulations", s 96(1); "supply", s 5, Sch 4; "taxable person", s 3; "VAT", ss 1, 96(1).

Cross references—See VATA 1994 s 17(5)(*b*) (supplies of free zone goods: provision for regulations to determine time of supply);

VATA 1994 s 55(4) (disapplication of sub-ss (4)–(10) of this section in relation to certain supplies of gold and other precious metals and stones);

VATA 1994 s 88 (supplies spanning date of change in rate of VAT),

VATA 1994 Sch 11 paras 2(9), 3(3) (provisions as to deemed date of issue of an invoice described in regulations made for purposes of sub-s (8)(*b*) of this section and VAT to be accounted for by reference to that date);
VATA 1994 Sch 13 para 4 (pre-21 April 1975 arrangements as to time of supplies: treatment for purposes of this section as if a direction had been issued by the Commissioners under sub-s (10)).
VAT Regulations, SI 1995/2518 reg 14(3) (consignment or delivery note: whether treated as a VAT invoice for the purposes of sub-ss (2)(*c*), (5) of this section);
VAT Regulations, SI 1995/2518 reg 84(1) (compulsory purchase of land: consideration not known at time of purchase);
VAT Regulations, SI 1995/2518 reg 84(2) (grant or assignment of fee simple in land: total consideration not determinable at time of grant etc);
VAT Regulations, SI 1995/2518 reg 85 (grant of tenancy or lease: consideration payable periodically: time of supply);
VAT Regulations, SI 1995/2518 reg 86 (supplies of water, gas and other forms of heat, power, ventilation or refrigeration: time of supply);
VAT Regulations, SI 1995/2518 reg 88 (agreements by which supplier retains property in goods pending appropriation by buyer: time of supply);
VAT Regulations, SI 1995/2518 reg 89 (retention of part of consideration pending performance of contract: time of supply);
VAT Regulations, SI 1995/2518 reg 90 (continuous supplies of services);
VAT Regulations, SI 1995/2518 reg 91 (royalties etc: time of supply);
VAT Regulations, SI 1995/2518 reg 92 (services of barristers and advocates: time of supply);
VAT Regulations, SI 1995/2518 reg 93 (construction industry supplies: consideration payable periodically: time of supply);
VAT (Tour Operators) Order, SI 1987/1806 art 4 (disapplication of this section to supplies of designated travel services).

Amendments—[1] Words in sub-s (1) substituted by FA 1996 Sch 3 para 1 with effect in relation to any supply taking place on or after 1 June 1996; see Finance Act 1996, Section 26, (Appointed Day) Order , SI 1996/1249.
[2] Sub-s (14A) inserted by FA 1998 s 22 with effect from 17 March 1998.
[3] Sub-s (9) repealed, and in sub-s (15), words substituted by FA 2002 ss 24(1)(*a*), (4)(*a*), (5), 139, Sch 40 Pt 2(2) with effect from 1 December 2003 (by virtue of SI 2003/3043).
[4] In sub-s (14A) words "In relation to any services of a description specified in an order under section 7(11)" repealed by FA 2009 s 76, Sch 36 para 2 with effect from 1 January 2010.

7 Place of supply [of goods][2]

(1) This section shall apply (subject to [sections 14, 18 and 18B][1]) for determining, for the purposes of this Act, whether goods ...[2] are supplied in the United Kingdom.

(2) Subject to the following provisions of this section, if the supply of any goods does not involve their removal from or to the United Kingdom they shall be treated as supplied in the United Kingdom if they are in the United Kingdom and otherwise shall be treated as supplied outside the United Kingdom.

(3) Goods shall be treated—

(*a*) as supplied in the United Kingdom where their supply involves their installation or assembly at a place in the United Kingdom to which they are removed; and

(*b*) as supplied outside the United Kingdom where their supply involves their installation or assembly at a place outside the United Kingdom to which they are removed.

(4) Goods whose place of supply is not determined under any of the preceding provisions of this section shall be treated as supplied in the United Kingdom where—

(*a*) the supply involves the removal of the goods to the United Kingdom by or under the directions of the person who supplies them;

(*b*) the supply is a transaction in pursuance of which the goods are acquired in the United Kingdom from another member State by a person who is not a taxable person;

(*c*) the supplier—

(i) is liable to be registered under Schedule 2; or

(ii) would be so liable if he were not already registered under this Act or liable to be registered under Schedule 1; and

(*d*) the supply is neither a supply of goods consisting in a new means of transport nor anything which is treated as a supply for the purposes of this Act by virtue only of paragraph 5(1) or 6 of Schedule 4.

(5) Goods whose place of supply is not determined under any of the preceding provisions of this section and which do not consist in a new means of transport shall be treated as supplied outside the United Kingdom where—

(*a*) the supply involves the removal of the goods, by or under the directions of the person who supplies them, to another member State;

(*b*) the person who makes the supply is taxable in another member State; and

(*c*) provisions of the law of that member State corresponding, in relation to that member State, to the provisions made by subsection (4) above make that person liable to VAT on the supply;

but this subsection shall not apply in relation to any supply in a case where the liability mentioned in paragraph (*c*) above depends on the exercise by any person of an option in the United Kingdom corresponding to such an option as is mentioned in paragraph 1(2) of Schedule 2 unless that person has given, and has not withdrawn, a notification to the Commissioners that he wishes his supplies to be treated as taking place outside the United Kingdom where they are supplies in relation to which the other requirements of this subsection are satisfied.

(6) Goods whose place of supply is not determined under any of the preceding provisions of this section shall be treated as supplied in the United Kingdom where—

(*a*) their supply involves their being imported from a place outside the member States; and

(*b*) the person who supplies them is the person by whom, or under whose directions, they are so imported.

(7) Goods whose place of supply is not determined under any of the preceding provisions of this section but whose supply involves their removal to or from the United Kingdom shall be treated—

(*a*) as supplied in the United Kingdom where their supply involves their removal from the United Kingdom without also involving their previous removal to the United Kingdom; and

(*b*) as supplied outside the United Kingdom in any other case.

(8) For the purposes of the preceding provisions of this section, where goods, in the course of their removal from a place in the United Kingdom to another place in the United Kingdom, leave and re-enter the United Kingdom the removal shall not be treated as a removal from or to the United Kingdom.

(9) The Commissioners may by regulations provide that a notification for the purposes of subsection (5) above is not to be given or withdrawn except in such circumstances, and in such form and manner, as may be prescribed.

(10) …[2]

(11) The Treasury may by order provide, in relation to goods …[2] generally or to particular goods …[2] specified in the order, for varying the rules for determining where a supply of goods …[2] is made.

Commentary—*De Voil Indirect Tax Service* **V3.124**.

Simon's Tax Cases—s 7(1), *Purshotam M Pattni & Sons v C&E Comrs* [1987] STC 1*; *Tas-Stage Ltd v C&E Comrs* [1988] STC 436*; *Nevisbrook Ltd v C&E Comrs , Dormers Builders (London) Ltd v C&E Comrs, C&E Comrs v West Yorkshire Independent Hospital (Contract Services) Ltd C&E, Comrs v Faith Construction Ltd* [1989] STC 539*, [1992] STC 544*

Regulations—See VAT Regulations, SI 1995/2518 reg 98.

Orders—See VAT (Tour Operators) Order, SI 1987/1806; VAT (Place of Supply of Services) Order, SI 1992/3121; VAT (Place of Supply of Goods) Order, SI 1992/3283.

Press releases etc—ICAEW 15/94 16-8-94 (guidance note on supplies by accountants).

C&E Business Brief 26/96 19-12-96 (the service of carrying out of a statutory order of the accounts of a UK incorporated company trading entirely overseas is supplied in the UK and is standard-rated).

Definitions—"Acquisition of goods from another member State", s 11; "another member State", s 96(1); "belongs in the "United Kingdom"; belongs in that other country", s 9; "the Commissioners", s 96(1); "imported from a place outside the member States", s 15; "law of that member State", s 92; "new means of transport", s 95; "person …taxable in another member State", s 92; "prescribed", s 96(1); "registered", s 3(3); "regulations", s 96(1); "supply ", s 5, Sch 4; "taxable person", s 3; "United Kingdom", s 96(11); "VAT", ss 1, 96(1).

Cross references—See VAT (Isle of Man) Order, SI 1982/1067 art 1(4) (treatment of UK and Isle of Man as a single area for VAT purposes);

VAT (Tour Operators) Order, SI 1987/1806 art 7 (modification of this section in relation to supplies of designated travel services).

Amendments—[1] Words in sub-s (1) substituted by FA 1996 Sch 3 para 2, with effect in relation to any supply taking place on or after 1 June 1996; see Finance Act 1996, Section 26, (Appointed Day) Order, SI 1996/1249.

[2] Words inserted in heading, and words "or services" in sub-ss (1), (11) and whole of sub-s (10) repealed, by FA 2009 s 76, Sch 36 paras 1, 3 with effect in relation to supplies made on or after 1 January 2010. Sub-s (10) previously read as follows—

"(10) A supply of services shall be treated as made—

(*a*) in the United Kingdom if the supplier belongs in the United Kingdom; and

(*b*) in another country (and not in the United Kingdom) if the supplier belongs in that other country.".

[7A Place of supply of services

(1) This section applies for determining, for the purposes of this Act, the country in which services are supplied.

(2) A supply of services is to be treated as made—

(*a*) in a case in which the person to whom the services are supplied is a relevant business person, in the country in which the recipient belongs, and

(*b*) otherwise, in the country in which the supplier belongs.

(3) The place of supply of a right to services is the same as that in which the supply of the services would be treated as made if made by the supplier of the right to the recipient of the right (whether or not the right is exercised); and for this purpose a right to services includes any right, option or priority with respect to the supply of services and an interest deriving from a right to services.

(4) For the purposes of this Act a person is a relevant business person in relation to a supply of services if the person—

(*a*) is a taxable person within the meaning of Article 9 of Council Directive 2006/112/EC,

(*b*) is registered under this Act,

(*c*) is identified for the purposes of VAT in accordance with the law of a member State other than the United Kingdom, or

(*d*) is registered under an Act of Tynwald for the purposes of any tax imposed by or under an Act of Tynwald which corresponds to value added tax,

and the services are received by the person otherwise than wholly for private purposes.

(5) Subsection (2) has effect subject to Schedule 4A.

(6) The Treasury may by order—

(*a*) amend subsection (4),

(*b*) amend Schedule 4A, or

(*c*) otherwise make provision for exceptions from either or both of the paragraphs of subsection (2).

VAT

(7) An order under subsection (6) may include incidental, supplemental, consequential and transitional provision.][1]

Amendments—[1] Section 7A inserted by FA 2009 s 76, Sch 3 paras 1, 4 with effect in relation to supplies made on or after 1 January 2010, except the powers contained in sub-s (6) which may be exercised at any time from 21 July 2009.

8 Reverse charge on supplies received from abroad

[(1) Where services are supplied by a person who belongs in a country other than the United Kingdom in circumstances in which this subsection applies, this Act has effect as if (instead of there being a supply of the services by that person)—

(*a*) there were a supply of the services by the recipient in the United Kingdom in the course or furtherance of a business carried on by the recipient, and

(*b*) that supply were a taxable supply.

(2) Subsection (1) above applies if—

(*a*) the recipient is a relevant business person who belongs in the United Kingdom, and

(*b*) the place of supply of the services is inside the United Kingdom,

and, where the supply of the services is one to which any paragraph of Part 1 or 2 of Schedule 4A applies, the recipient is registered under this Act.][2]

(3) Supplies which are treated as made by the recipient under subsection (1) above are not to be taken into account as supplies made by him when determining any allowance of input tax in his case under section 26(1).

(4) In applying subsection (1) above, the supply of services treated as made by the recipient shall be assumed to have been made at a time to be determined in accordance with regulations prescribing rules for attributing a time of supply in cases within that subsection.

[(4A) Subsection (1) does not apply to services of any of the descriptions specified in Schedule 9.][2]

(5) The Treasury may by order [amend subsection (4A) by altering the descriptions of services specified in that subsection][2].

(6) …[2]

[(7) The power of the Treasury by order to [amend subsection (4A)][2] shall include power to make such incidental, supplemental, consequential and transitional provision in connection with any [amendment of that subsection][2] as they think fit.][1]

[(8) Without prejudice to the generality of subsection (7) above, the provision that may be made under that subsection includes—

(*a*) provision making such modifications of section 43(2A) to (2E) as the Treasury may think fit in connection with any [amendment of subsection (4A)][2]; and

(*b*) provision modifying the effect of any regulations under subsection (4) above in relation to any services added to [that subsection][2].][1]

Commentary—*De Voil Indirect Tax Service* **V3.231**.
Regulations—See VAT Regulations, SI 1995/2518 reg 82.
VAT (Reverse Charge) (Anti-avoidance) Order, SI 1997/1523.
Definitions—"Belongs in another country other than the United Kingdom", s 9; "business", s 94; "input tax", s 24; "regulations", s 96(1); "supply", s 5, Sch 4; "taxable person", s 3; "taxable supply", s 4(2); "time of supply", s 6; "United Kingdom", s 96(11); "VAT", ss 1, 96(1).
Cross references—See VATA 1994 Sch 5 para 10 (sub-s (1) of this section to apply to certain services which are supplied to registered persons and whose place of supply is determined by order to be in the UK as if the recipient belonged in the UK for the purposes of sub-s (1)(*b*));
VATA 1994 Sch 6 para 8 (valuation of supplies of services treated by virtue of this section as made by the recipient).
VAT Regulations, SI 1995/2518 reg 82 (time of deemed supplies under sub-s (1) of this section).
Press releases etc—Business Brief 6/02, 14-3-02 (VAT: clarification of the treatment of internet service packages).
Amendments—[1] Sub-s (7) and (8) inserted by FA 1997 s 42 with effect from 19 March 1997.
[2] Sub-ss (1), (2), words "add to or vary Schedule 5" in sub-ss (5), (7), "addition to or variation of that Schedule" in sub-ss (7), (8)(*a*), "the Schedule" in sub-s (8)(*b*) substituted, sub-s (4A) inserted and sub-s (6) repealed, by FA 2009 s 76, Sch 36 paras 1, 5 with effect in relation to supplies made on or after 1 January 2010. Sub-ss (1), (2), (6) previously read as follows—

"(1) Subject to subsection (3) below, where relevant services are—

(*a*) supplied by a person who belongs in a country other than the United Kingdom, and

(*b*) received by a person ("the recipient") who belongs in the United Kingdom for the purposes of any business carried on by him,

then all the same consequences shall follow under this Act (and particularly so much as charges VAT on a supply and entitles a taxable person to credit for input tax) as if the recipient had himself supplied the services in the United Kingdom in the course or furtherance of his business, and that supply were a taxable supply.

(2) In this section "relevant services" means services of any of the descriptions specified in Schedule 5, not being services within any of the descriptions specified in Schedule 9.". "(6) The power of the Treasury by order to add to or vary Schedule 5 shall include power, where any services whose place of supply is determined by an order under section 7(11) are added to that Schedule, to provide that subsection (1) above shall have effect in relation to those services as if a person belongs in the United Kingdom for the purposes of paragraph (*b*) of that subsection if, and only if, he is a taxable person.".

[9 Place where supplier or recipient of services belongs

(1) This section has effect for determining for the purposes of section 7A (or Schedule 4A) or section 8, in relation to any supply of services, whether a person who is the supplier or recipient belongs in one country or another.

(2) A person who is a relevant business person is to be treated as belonging in the relevant country.

(3) In subsection (2) "the relevant country" means—

(*a*) if the person has a business establishment, or some other fixed establishment, in a country (and none in any other country), that country,

(*b*) if the person has a business establishment, or some other fixed establishment or establishments, in more than one country, the country in which the relevant establishment is, and

(*c*) otherwise, the country in which the person's usual place of residence is.

(4) In subsection (3)(*b*) "relevant establishment" means whichever of the person's business establishment, or other fixed establishments, is most directly concerned with the supply.

(5) A person who is not a relevant business person is to be treated as belonging in the country in which the person's usual place of residence is.

(6) In this section "usual place of residence", in relation to a body corporate, means the place where it is legally constituted.][1]

Commentary—*De Voil Indirect Tax Service* **V3.124**.
Simon's Tax Cases—*C&E Comrs v Chinese Channel (Hong Kong) Ltd* [1998] STC 347.
Definitions—"Business", s 94; "supply of services", s 5, Sch 4.
Cross reference—See VAT (Tour Operators) Order, SI 1987/1806 art 7 (modification of this section in relation to supplies of designated travel services).
Press releases etc—Business Brief 12/98 21-5-98 (Overseas businesses established in the UK through agencies).
VAT Information Sheet 3/01 April 2001 (guidance on the VAT treatment of digitised publications).
Amendments—[1] Section substituted by FA 2009 s 76, Sch 36 paras 1, 6 with effect in relation to supplies made on or after 1 January 2010. Section 9 previously read as follows—

"**9 Place where supplier or recipient of services belongs**

(1) Subsection (2) below shall apply for determining, in relation to any supply of services, whether the supplier belongs in one country or another and subsections (3) and (4) below shall apply (subject to any provision made under section 8(6)) for determining, in relation to any supply of services, whether the recipient belongs in one country or another.

(2) The supplier of services shall be treated as belonging in a country if—

(*a*) he has there a business establishment or some other fixed establishment and no such establishment elsewhere; or
(*b*) he has no such establishment (there or elsewhere) but his usual place of residence is there; or
(*c*) he has such establishments both in that country and elsewhere and the establishment of his which is most directly concerned with the supply is there.

(3) If the supply of services is made to an individual and received by him otherwise than for the purposes of any business carried on by him, he shall be treated as belonging in whatever country he has his usual place of residence.

(4) Where subsection (3) above does not apply, the person to whom the supply is made shall be treated as belonging in a country if—

(*a*) either of the conditions mentioned in paragraphs (*a*) and (*b*) of subsection (2) above is satisfied; or
(*b*) he has such establishments as are mentioned in subsection (2) above both in that country and elsewhere and the establishment of his at which, or for the purposes of which, the services are most directly used or to be used is in that country.

(5) For the purposes of this section (but not for any other purposes)—

(*a*) a person carrying on a business through a branch or agency in any country shall be treated as having a business establishment there; and
(*b*) "usual place of residence", in relation to a body corporate, means the place where it is legally constituted.".

[9A Reverse charge on gas and electricity supplied by persons outside the United Kingdom

(1) This section applies if relevant goods are supplied—

(*a*) by a person who is outside the United Kingdom,

(*b*) to a person who is registered under this Act,

for the purposes of any business carried on by the recipient.

(2) The same consequences follow under this Act (and particularly so much as charges VAT on a supply and entitles a taxable person to credit for input tax) as if—

(*a*) the recipient had himself supplied the relevant goods in the course or furtherance of his business, and

(*b*) that supply were a taxable supply.

(3) But supplies which are treated as made by the recipient under subsection (2) are not to be taken into account as supplies made by him when determining any allowance of input tax in his case under section 26(1).

(4) In applying subsection (2) the supply of relevant goods treated as made by the recipient shall be assumed to have been made at a time to be determined in accordance with regulations prescribing rules for attributing a time of supply in cases to which this section applies.

(5) "Relevant goods" means gas supplied through the natural gas distribution network, and electricity.

(6) Whether a person is outside the United Kingdom is to be determined in accordance with an order made by the Treasury.][1]

Commentary—*De Voil Indirect Tax Service* **V3.178**.
Amendments—[1] This section inserted by FA 2004 s 21 with effect for supplies made after 31 December 2004.

Acquisition of goods from member States

10 Scope of VAT on acquisitions from member States

(1) VAT shall be charged on any acquisition from another member State of any goods where—

(*a*) the acquisition is a taxable acquisition and takes place in the United Kingdom;
(*b*) the acquisition is otherwise than in pursuance of a taxable supply; and
(*c*) the person who makes the acquisition is a taxable person or the goods are subject to a duty of excise or consist in a new means of transport.

(2) An acquisition of goods from another member State is a taxable acquisition if—

(*a*) it falls within subsection (3) below or the goods consist in a new means of transport; and
(*b*) it is not an exempt acquisition.

(3) An acquisition of goods from another member State falls within this subsection if—

(*a*) the goods are acquired in the course or furtherance of—

(i) any business carried on by any person; or
(ii) any activities carried on otherwise than by way of business by any body corporate or by any club, association, organisation or other unincorporated body;

(*b*) it is the person who carries on that business or, as the case may be, those activities who acquires the goods; and
(*c*) the supplier—

(i) is taxable in another member State at the time of the transaction in pursuance of which the goods are acquired; and
(ii) in participating in that transaction, acts in the course or furtherance of a business carried on by him.

Commentary—*De Voil Indirect Tax Service* **V3.366**.
Simon's Tax Cases—*C&E Comrs v Westmorland Motorway Services Ltd* [1998] STC 431.
Definitions—"Acquisition of goods from another member State", s 11; "another member State", s 96(1); "business", s 94; "exempt acquisition", s 31, Sch 9; "new means of transport", s 95; "taxable in another member State", s 92; "taxable person", s 3; "taxable supply", s 4(2); "United Kingdom", s 96(11); "VAT", ss 1, 96(1).

11 Meaning of acquisition of goods from another member State

(1) Subject to the following provisions of this section, references in this Act to the acquisition of goods from another member State shall be construed as references to any acquisition of goods in pursuance of a transaction in relation to which the following conditions are satisfied, that is to say—

(*a*) the transaction is a supply of goods (including anything treated for the purposes of this Act as a supply of goods); and
(*b*) the transaction involves the removal of the goods from another member State;

and references in this Act, in relation to such an acquisition, to the supplier shall be construed accordingly.

(2) It shall be immaterial for the purposes of subsection (1) above whether the removal of the goods from the other member State is by or under the directions of the supplier or by or under the directions of the person who acquires them or any other person.

(3) Where the person with the property in any goods does not change in consequence of anything which is treated for the purposes of this Act as a supply of goods, that supply shall be treated for the purposes of this Act as a transaction in pursuance of which there is an acquisition of goods by the person making it.

(4) The Treasury may by order provide with respect to any description of transaction that the acquisition of goods in pursuance of a transaction of that description is not to be treated for the purposes of this Act as the acquisition of goods from another member State.

Commentary—*De Voil Indirect Tax Service* **V3.367**.
Orders—See VAT (Treatment of Transactions) (No 2) Order, SI 1992/3132; VAT (Special Provisions) Order, SI 1995/1268.
Definitions—"Another (other) member State", s 96(1); "supply", s 5, Sch 4.

12 Time of acquisition

(1) Subject to [sections 18 and 18B][1] and any regulations under subsection (3) below, where goods are acquired from another member State, the acquisition shall be treated for the purposes of this Act as taking place on whichever is the earlier of—

(*a*) the 15th day of the month following that in which the event occurs which, in relation to that acquisition, is the first relevant event for the purposes of taxing the acquisition; and
(*b*) the day of the issue, in respect of the transaction in pursuance of which the goods are acquired, of an invoice of such a description as the Commissioners may by regulations prescribe.

(2) For the purposes of this Act the event which, in relation to any acquisition of goods from another member State, is the first relevant event for the purposes of taxing the acquisition is the first removal of the goods which is involved in the transaction in pursuance of which they are acquired.

(3) The Commissioners may by regulations make provision with respect to the time at which an acquisition is to be treated as taking place in prescribed cases where the whole or part of any

consideration comprised in the transaction in pursuance of which the goods are acquired is determined or payable periodically, or from time to time, or at the end of a period; and any such regulations may provide, in relation to any case to which they apply, for goods to be treated as separately and successively acquired at prescribed times or intervals.

Commentary—*De Voil Indirect Tax Service* **V3.388**.
Regulations—See VAT Regulations, SI 1995/2518 regs 83, 87.
Definitions—"Acquisition of goods from another member State", s 11; "another member State", s 96(1); "the Commissioners", s 96(1); "invoice", s 96(1); "prescribed", s 96(1); "regulations", s 96(1).
Cross references—See VATA 1994 s 14(4) (modification of sub-s (1) of this section in relation to acquisitions from persons belonging in other member states);
VATA 1994 Sch 11 paras 2(9), 3(3) (provisions as to deemed date of issue of an invoice described in regulations made for purposes of sub-s (1)(*b*) of this section and VAT to be accounted for by reference to that date).
VAT Regulations, SI 1995/2518 reg 83 (description of invoice for purposes of sub-s(1)(*b*) of this section).
VAT Regulations, SI 1995/2518 reg 87 (acquisitions of water, gas and other forms of heat, power, ventilation or refrigeration from another member state: time of acquisition).
Amendments—[1] Words in sub-s (1) substituted by FA 1996 Sch 3 para 3, with effect in relation to any acquisition of goods from another member State taking place on or after 1 June 1996; see Finance Act 1996, Section 26, (Appointed Day) Order, SI 1996/1249.

13 Place of acquisition

(1) This section shall apply (subject to [sections 18 and 18B][1]) for determining for the purposes of this Act whether goods acquired from another member State are acquired in the United Kingdom.

(2) The goods shall be treated as acquired in the United Kingdom if they are acquired in pursuance of a transaction which involves their removal to the United Kingdom and does not involve their removal from the United Kingdom, and (subject to the following provisions of this section) shall otherwise be treated as acquired outside the United Kingdom.

(3) Subject to subsection (4) below, the goods shall be treated as acquired in the United Kingdom if they are acquired by a person who, for the purposes of their acquisition, makes use of a number assigned to him for the purposes of VAT in the United Kingdom.

(4) Subsection (3) above shall not require any goods to be treated as acquired in the United Kingdom where it is established, in accordance with regulations made by the Commissioners for the purposes of this section that VAT—

(*a*) has been paid in another member State on the acquisition of those goods; and
(*b*) fell to be paid by virtue of provisions of the law of that member State corresponding, in relation to that member State, to the provision made by subsection (2) above.

(5) The Commissioners may by regulations make provision for the purposes of this section—

(*a*) for the circumstances in which a person is to be treated as having been assigned a number for the purposes of VAT in the United Kingdom;
(*b*) for the circumstances in which a person is to be treated as having made use of such a number for the purposes of the acquisition of any goods; and
(*c*) for the refund, in prescribed circumstances, of VAT paid in the United Kingdom on acquisitions of goods in relation to which the conditions specified in subsection (4)(*a*) and (*b*) above are satisfied.

Commentary—*De Voil Indirect Tax Service* **V3.376**.
Definitions—"Acquisition of goods from another member State", s 81; "another member State", s 96(1); "the Commissioners", s 96(1); "law of that member State", s 92; "prescribed", s 96(1); "regulations", s 96(1); "VAT", ss 1, 96(1).
Cross references—See VATA 1994 s 60(1), (2) (civil penalty for evading VAT by dishonestly claiming a refund under regulations made under sub-s (5) of this section);
VATA 1994 s 72(1), (2) (criminal penalty for fraudulent evasion of VAT by falsely claiming a refund under regulations made under sub-s (5) of this section);
VATA 1994 s 83 (appeal to a tribunal with respect to a claim for a refund under regulations made under sub-s (5) of this section).
Amendments—[1] Words in sub-s (1) substituted by FA 1996 Sch 3 para 4, with effect in relation to any acquisition of goods from another member State taking place on or after 1 June 1996; see Finance Act 1996, Section 26, (Appointed Day) Order, SI 1996/1249.

14 Acquisitions from persons belonging in other member States

(1) Subject to subsection (3) below, where—

(*a*) a person ("the original supplier") makes a supply of goods to a person who belongs in another member State ("the intermediate supplier");
(*b*) that supply involves the removal of the goods from another member State and their removal to the United Kingdom but does not involve the removal of the goods from the United Kingdom;
(*c*) both that supply and the removal of the goods to the United Kingdom are for the purposes of the making of a supply by the intermediate supplier to another person ("the customer") who is registered under this Act;
(*d*) neither of those supplies involves the removal of the goods from a member State in which the intermediate supplier is taxable at the time of the removal without also involving the previous removal of the goods to that member State; and
(*e*) there would be a taxable acquisition by the customer if the supply to him involved the removal of goods from another member State to the United Kingdom,

the supply by the original supplier to the intermediate supplier shall be disregarded for the purposes of this Act and the supply by the intermediate supplier to the customer shall be treated for the purposes of this Act, other than Schedule 3, as if it did involve the removal of the goods from another member State to the United Kingdom.

(2) Subject to subsection (3) below, where—

(*a*) a person belonging in another member State makes such a supply of goods to a person who is registered under this Act as involves their installation or assembly at a place in the United Kingdom to which they are removed; and

(*b*) there would be a taxable acquisition by the registered person if that supply were treated as not being a taxable supply but as involving the removal of the goods from another member State to the United Kingdom,

that supply shall be so treated except for the purposes of Schedule 3.

(3) Neither subsection (1) nor subsection (2) above shall apply in relation to any supply unless the intermediate supplier or, as the case may be, the person making the supply complies with such requirements as to the furnishing (whether before or after the supply is made) of invoices and other documents, and of information, to—

(*a*) the Commissioners, and

(*b*) the person supplied,

as the Commissioners may by regulations prescribe; and regulations under this subsection may provide for the times at which, and the form and manner in which, any document or information is to be furnished and for the particulars which it is to contain.

(4) Where this section has the effect of treating a taxable acquisition as having been made, section 12(1) shall apply in relation to that acquisition with the omission of the words from "whichever" to "acquisition; and" at the end of paragraph (*a*).

(5) For the purposes of this section a person belongs in another member State if—

(*a*) he does not have any business establishment or other fixed establishment in the United Kingdom and does not have his usual place of residence in the United Kingdom;

(*b*) he is neither registered under this Act nor required to be so registered;

(*c*) he does not have a VAT representative and is not for the time being required to appoint one; and

(*d*) he is taxable in another member State;

but, in determining for the purposes of paragraph (*b*) above whether a person is required to be registered under this Act, there shall be disregarded any supplies which, if he did belong in another member State and complied with the requirements prescribed under subsection (3) above, would fall to be disregarded by virtue of this section.

(6) Without prejudice to section 13(4), where—

(*a*) any goods are acquired from another member State in a case which corresponds, in relation to another member State, to the case specified in relation to the United Kingdom in subsection (1) above; and

(*b*) the person who acquires the goods is registered under this Act and would be the intermediate supplier in relation to that corresponding case,

the supply to him of those goods and the supply by him of those goods to the person who would be the customer in that corresponding case shall both be disregarded for the purposes of this Act, other than the purposes of the information provisions referred to in section 92(7).

(7) References in this section to a person being taxable in another member State shall not include references to a person who is so taxable by virtue only of provisions of the law of another member State corresponding to the provisions of this Act by virtue of which a person who is not registered under this Act is a taxable person if he is required to be so registered.

(8) This section does not apply in relation to any supply of goods by an intermediate supplier to whom the goods were supplied before 1st August 1993.

Commentary—*De Voil Indirect Tax Service* **V3.364**.

Regulations—See VAT Regulations, SI 1995/2518 regs 11, 12, 17–19.

Definitions—"Another member State", s 96(1); "business", s 94; "the Commissioners", s 96(1); "document", s 96(1); "invoice", s 96(1); "law of that member State", s 92; "registered", s 3(3); "regulations", s 96(1); "supply", s 5, Sch 4; "taxable acquisition", s 10(2); "taxable in another member State", s 92; "taxable person", ss 3, 96(1); "taxable supply", s 4(2); "United Kingdom", s 96(11); "VAT", ss 1, 96(1); "VAT representative", s 48.

Cross references—See VATA 1994 Sch 13 para 6 (continued application of VATA 1983 s 32B (overseas suppliers accounting through their customers) in relation to supplies to which this section does not apply by virtue of sub-s (8)).

VAT Regulations, SI 1995/2518 reg 11 (notification of intended supplies by intermediate suppliers under sub-s (1) of this section).

VAT Regulations, SI 1995/2518 reg 12 (notification of intended supplies by persons belonging in other member States under sub-s (2) of this section);

VAT Regulations, SI 1995/2518 reg 17 (tax invoices for supplies under sub-s (6) of this section to persons belonging in other member States);

VAT Regulations, SI 1995/2518 reg 18 (tax invoices for supplies under sub-s (1) of this section by intermediate suppliers);

VAT Regulations, SI 1995/2518 reg 19 (tax invoices for supplies under sub-s (2) of this section by persons belonging in other member States).

Importation of goods from outside the member States

15 General provisions relating to imported goods

(1) For the purposes of this Act goods are imported from a place outside the member States where—

(*a*) having been removed from a place outside the member States, they enter the territory of the Community;

(*b*) they enter that territory by being removed to the United Kingdom or are removed to the United Kingdom after entering that territory; and

(*c*) the circumstances are such that it is on their removal to the United Kingdom or subsequently while they are in the United Kingdom that any Community customs debt in respect of duty on their entry into the territory of the Community would be incurred.

(2) Accordingly—

(*a*) goods shall not be treated for the purposes of this Act as imported at any time before a Community customs debt in respect of duty on their entry into the territory of the Community would be incurred, and

(*b*) the person who is to be treated for the purposes of this Act as importing any goods from a place outside the member States is the person who would be liable to discharge any such Community customs debt.

(3) Subsections (1) and (2) above shall not apply, except in so far as the context otherwise requires or provision to the contrary is contained in regulations under section 16(1), for construing any references to importation or to an importer in any enactment or subordinate legislation applied for the purposes of this Act by section 16(1).

Commentary—*De Voil Indirect Tax Service* **V3.302**.
Definitions—"Regulations", s 96(1); "subordinate legislation", s 96(1); "United Kingdom, s 96(11).

16 Application of customs enactments

(1) Subject to such exceptions and adaptations as the Commissioners may by regulations prescribe and except where the contrary intention appears—

(*a*) the provision made by or under the Customs and Excise Acts 1979 and the other enactments and subordinate legislation for the time being having effect generally in relation to duties of customs and excise charged on the importation of goods into the United Kingdom; and

(*b*) the Community legislation for the time being having effect in relation to Community customs duties charged on goods entering the territory of the Community,

shall apply (so far as relevant) in relation to any VAT chargeable on the importation of goods from places outside the member States as they apply in relation to any such duty of customs or excise or, as the case may be, Community customs duties.

(2) Regulations under [section 105 of the Postal Services Act 2000][1] (which provides for the application of customs enactments to postal packets) may make special provision in relation to VAT.

Commentary—*De Voil Indirect Tax Service* **V1.262, V1.263**.
Regulations—See Postal Packets (Customs and Excise) Regulations, SI 1986/260; VAT Regulations, SI 1995/2518 regs 118–121.
Definitions—"The Commissioners", s 96(1); "goods imported form a place outside the member States", s 15; "regulations", s 96(1); "subordinate legislation", s 96(1); "United Kingdom", s 96(11); "VAT", ss 1, 96(1).
Cross references—See VAT (Isle of Man) Order, SI 1982/1067 art 7 (references to VAT in this section to include references to VAT chargeable under Isle of Man legislation);
VAT Regulations, SI 1995/2518 regs 118–120 (prescribed exceptions for the purposes of sub-s (1) of this section);
VAT Regulations, SI 1995/2518 reg 121 (prescribed adaptations for the purposes of sub-s (1) of this section).
Amendments—[1] Words in sub-s (2) substituted by the Postal Services Act 2000 s 127(4), Sch 8 para 22(1), (2) as from 26 March 2001 (by virtue of SI 2000/2957).

17 Free zone regulations

(1) This section applies in relation to VAT chargeable on the importation of goods from places outside the member States; and in this section "free zone" has the meaning given by section 100A(2) of the Management Act.

(2) Subject to any contrary provision made by any directly applicable Community provision, goods which are chargeable with VAT may be moved into a free zone and may remain as free zone goods without payment of VAT.

(3) The Commissioners may by regulations ("free zone regulations") make provision with respect to the movement of goods into, and the removal of goods from, any free zone and the keeping, securing and treatment of goods which are within a free zone, and subject to any provision of the regulations, "free zone goods" means goods which are within a free zone.

(4) Without prejudice to the generality of subsection (3), free zone regulations may make provision—

(*a*) for enabling the Commissioners to allow goods to be removed from a free zone without payment of VAT in such circumstances and subject to such conditions as they may determine;

(*b*) for determining where any VAT becomes payable in respect of goods which cease to be free zone goods—

(i) the rates of any VAT applicable; and
(ii) the time at which those goods cease to be free zone goods;

(*c*) for determining for the purpose of enabling VAT to be charged in respect of free zone goods in a case where a person wishes to pay that VAT notwithstanding that the goods will continue to be free zone goods, the rate of VAT to be applied; and

(*d*) permitting free zone goods to be destroyed without payment of VAT in such circumstances and subject to such conditions as the Commissioners may determine.

(5) The Commissioners, with respect to free zone goods or the movement of goods into any free zone, may by regulations make provision—

(*a*) for relief from the whole or part of any VAT chargeable on the importation of goods into the United Kingdom in such circumstances as they may determine;

(*b*) in place of, or in addition to, any provision made by section 6 or any other enactment, for determining the time when a supply of goods which are or have been free zone goods is to be treated as taking place for the purposes of the charge to VAT; and

(*c*) as to the treatment, for the purposes of VAT, of goods which are manufactured or produced within a free zone from other goods or which have other goods incorporated in them while they are free zone goods.

Commentary—*De Voil Indirect Tax Service* **V3.331**.
Regulations—See Free Zone Regulations, SI 1984/1177; SI 1991/2727.
Definitions—"The Commissioners", s 96(1); "goods imported from a place outside the member States", s 15; "the Management Act", s 96(1); "regulations", s 96(1); "United Kingdom", s 96(11); "VAT", ss 1, 96(1).

Goods subject to a warehousing regime

18 Place and time of acquisition or supply

(1) Where—

(*a*) any goods have been removed from a place outside the member States and have entered the territory of the Community;

(*b*) the material time for any acquisition of those goods from another member State or for any supply of those goods is while they are subject to a warehousing regime and before the duty point; and

(*c*) those goods are not mixed with any dutiable goods which were produced or manufactured in the United Kingdom or acquired from another member State,

then the acquisition or supply mentioned in paragraph (*b*) above shall be treated for the purposes of this Act as taking place outside the United Kingdom.

[(1A) The Commissioners may by regulations prescribe circumstances in which subsection (1) above shall not apply.][2]

(2) Subsection (3) below applies where—

(*a*) any dutiable goods are acquired from another member State; or
(*b*) any person makes a supply of—

(i) any dutiable goods which were produced or manufactured in the United Kingdom or acquired from another member State; or
(ii) any goods comprising a mixture of goods falling within sub-paragraph (i) above and other goods.

(3) Where this subsection applies and the material time for the acquisition or supply mentioned in subsection (2) above is while the goods in question are subject to a warehousing regime and before the duty point, that acquisition or supply shall be treated for the purposes of this Act as taking place outside the United Kingdom if the material time for any subsequent supply of those goods is also while the goods are subject to the warehousing regime and before the duty point.

(4) Where the material time for any acquisition or supply of any goods in relation to which subsection (3) above applies is while the goods are subject to a warehousing regime and before the duty point but the acquisition or supply nevertheless falls, for the purposes of this Act, to be treated as taking place in the United Kingdom—

(*a*) that acquisition or supply shall be treated for the purposes of this Act as taking place at the earlier of the following times, that is to say, the time when the goods are removed from the warehousing regime and the duty point; and

(*b*) in the case of a supply, any VAT payable on the supply shall be paid (subject to any regulations under subsection (5) below)—

(i) at the time when the supply is treated as taking place under paragraph (*a*) above; and
(ii) by the person by whom the goods are so removed or, as the case may be, together with the duty or agricultural levy, by the person who is required to pay the duty or levy.

[(5) The Commissioners may by regulations make provision for enabling a taxable person to pay the VAT he is required to pay by virtue of paragraph (*b*) of subsection (4) above at a time later than that provided for by that paragraph.][1]

[(5A) Regulations under subsection (5) above may in particular make provision for either or both of the following—

(*a*) for the taxable person to pay the VAT together with the VAT chargeable on other supplies by him of goods and services;

(*b*) for the taxable person to pay the VAT together with any duty of excise deferment of which has been granted to him under section 127A of the Customs and Excise Management Act 1979;

and they may make different provision for different descriptions of taxable person and for different descriptions of goods.][1]

(6) In this section—

"dutiable goods" means any goods which are subject—

(*a*) to a duty of excise; or

(*b*) in accordance with any provision for the time being having effect for transitional purposes in connection with the accession of any State to the European Communities, to any Community customs duty or agricultural levy of the Economic Community;

"the duty point", in relation to any goods, means—

(*a*) in the case of goods which are subject to a duty of excise, the time when the requirement to pay the duty on those goods takes effect; and

(*b*) in the case of goods which are not so subject, the time when any Community customs debt in respect of duty on the entry of the goods into the territory of the Community would be incurred or, as the case may be, the corresponding time in relation to any such duty or levy as is mentioned in paragraph (*b*) of the definition of dutiable goods;

"material time"—

(*a*) in relation to any acquisition or supply the time of which is determined in accordance with regulations under section 6(14) or 12(3), means such time as may be prescribed for the purpose of this section by those regulations;

(*b*) in relation to any other acquisition, means the time of the event which, in relation to the acquisition, is the first relevant event for the purposes of taxing it; and

(*c*) in relation to any other supply, means the time when the supply would be treated as taking place in accordance with subsection (2) of section 6 if paragraph (*c*) of that subsection were omitted;

"warehouse" means any warehouse where goods may be stored in any member State without payment of any one or more of the following, that is to say—

(*a*) Community customs duty;

(*b*) any agricultural levy of the European Community;

(*c*) VAT on the importation of the goods into any member State;

(*d*) any duty of excise or any duty which is equivalent in another member State to a duty of excise.

(7) References in this section to goods being subject to a warehousing regime is a reference to goods being kept in a warehouse or being transported between warehouses (whether in the same or different member States) without the payment in a member State of any duty, levy or VAT; and references to the removal of goods from a warehousing regime shall be construed accordingly.

Commentary—*De Voil Indirect Tax Service* **V3.138**.
Regulations—VAT Regulations, SI 1995/2518 reg 43.
Definitions—"Acquisition of goods from another member State", s 11; "another member State", s 96(1); "the Commissioners ", s 96(1); "prescribed", s 96(1); "regulations", s 96(1); "supply", s 5, Sch 4; "taxable person", ss 3, 96(1); "United Kingdom", s 96(11); "VAT", ss 1, 96(1).
Cross reference—See VATA 1994 s 73(7B) (the Commissioners may assess VAT due to the best of their judgment where goods are removed from a warehouse without payment of VAT payable under sub-s (4) above).
VAT (Isle of Man) Order, SI 1982/1067 art 8 (taxable persons for the purposes of Isle of Man VAT legislation to be treated as taxable persons for the purposes of this section).
Amendments—[1] Sub-ss (5), (5A) substituted for original sub-s (5) by FA 1995 s 29.
[2] Sub-s (1A) inserted by F(No 2)A 2005 s 1 with effect from 20 July 2005.

[18A Fiscal warehousing

(1) The Commissioners may, if it appears to them proper, upon application approve any registered person as a fiscal warehouse keeper; and such approval shall be subject to such conditions as they shall impose.

(2) Subject to those conditions and to regulations made under section 18F such a person shall be entitled to keep a fiscal warehouse.

(3) "Fiscal warehouse" means such place in the United Kingdom in the occupation or under the control of the fiscal warehouse keeper, not being retail premises, as he shall notify to the Commissioners in writing; and such a place shall become a fiscal warehouse on receipt by the Commissioners of that notification or on the date stated in it as the date from which it is to have effect, whichever is the later, and, subject to subsection (6) below, shall remain a fiscal warehouse so long as it is in the occupation or under the control of the fiscal warehouse keeper or until he shall notify the Commissioners in writing that it is to cease to be a fiscal warehouse.

(4) The Commissioners may in considering an application by a person to be a fiscal warehouse-keeper take into account any matter which they consider relevant, and may without prejudice to the generality of that provision take into account all or any one or more of the following—

(*a*) his record of compliance and ability to comply with the requirements of this Act and regulations made hereunder;

(*b*) his record of compliance and ability to comply with the requirements of the customs and excise Acts (as defined in the Management Act) and regulations made thereunder;

(*c*) his record of compliance and ability to comply with Community customs provisions;

(*d*) his record of compliance and ability to comply with the requirements of other member States relating to VAT and duties equivalent to duties of excise;

(*e*) if the applicant is a company the records of compliance and ability to comply with the matters set out at (*a*) to (*d*) above of its directors, persons connected with its directors, its managing officers, any shadow directors or any of those persons, and, if it is a close company, the records of compliance and ability to comply with the matters set out at (*a*) to (*d*) above of the beneficial owners of the shares of the company or any of them; and

(*f*) if the applicant is an individual the records of compliance and ability to comply with the matters set out at (*a*) to (*d*) above of any company of which he is or has been a director, managing officer or shadow director or, in the case of a close company, a shareholder or the beneficial owner of shares,

and for the purposes of paragraphs (*e*) and (*f*) "connected" shall have the meaning given by section 24(7), "managing officer" the meaning given by section 61(6), "shadow director" the meaning given by [section 251 of the Companies Act 2006][2] and "close company" the meaning given by the Taxes Act.

(5) Subject to subsection (6) below, a person approved under subsection (1) shall remain a fiscal warehouse keeper until he ceases to be a registered person or until he shall notify the Commissioners in writing that he is to cease to be a fiscal warehouse keeper.

(6) The Commissioners may if they consider it appropriate from time to time—

(*a*) impose conditions on a fiscal warehouse keeper in addition to those conditions, if any, which they imposed under subsection (1), and vary or revoke any conditions previously imposed;

(*b*) withdraw approval of any person as a fiscal warehouse keeper, and

(*c*) withdraw fiscal warehouse status from any premises.

(7) Any application by or on behalf of a person to be a fiscal warehousekeeper shall be in writing in such form as the Commissioners may direct and shall be accompanied by such information as they shall require.

(8) Any approval by the Commissioners under subsection (1) above, and any withdrawal of approval or other act by them under subsection (6) above, shall be notified by them to the fiscal warehousekeeper in writing and shall take effect on such notification being made or on any later date specified for the purpose in the notification.

(9) Without prejudice to the provisions of section 43 concerning liability for VAT, in subsections (1) and (2) above "registered person" includes any body corporate which under that section is for the time being treated as a member of a group.][1]

Commentary—*De Voil Indirect Tax Service* **V3.384**.

Definitions—"The Commissioners", s 96(1); "fiscal warehousekeeper", s 18F(1); "the Management Act", s 96(1); "other member States", s 96(1); "registered", s 96(2); "regulations", s 96(1); "the Taxes Act", s 96(1); "United Kingdom", s 96(11).

Cross references—See VATA 1994 s 18F (supplementary provisions).

VATA 1994 s 69(1)(*g*) (penalties for failure to comply with conditions imposed under sub-ss (1) or (6) above).

VATA 1994 ss 83, 84 (appeals relating to decisions of the Commissioners as to approval of fiscal warehousekeepers and fiscal warehouses).

Amendments—[1] This section, and ss 18B–18F, inserted by FA 1996 Sch 3 para 5, with effect from 1 June 1996; see Finance Act 1996, Section 26, (Appointed Day) Order, SI 1996/1249, and applying to any acquisition of goods from another member State and any supply taking place on or after that day, except in so far as these sections confer power to make regulations, when they come into force on 29 April 1996.

[2] Words in sub-s (4) substituted by the Companies Act 2006 (Commencement No 3, Consequential Amendments, Transitional Provisions and Savings) Order, SI 2007/2194 art 10(1), Sch 4 para 85 with effect from 1 October 2007.

[18B Fiscally warehoused goods: relief

(1) Subsections (3) and (4) below apply where—

(*a*) there is an acquisition of goods from another member State;

(*b*) those goods are eligible goods;

(*c*) either—

(i) the acquisition takes place while the goods are subject to a fiscal warehousing regime; or

(ii) after the acquisition but before the supply, if any, of those goods which next occurs, the acquirer causes the goods to be placed in a fiscal warehousing regime; and

(*d*) the acquirer, not later than the time of the acquisition, prepares and keeps a certificate that the goods are subject to a fiscal warehousing regime, or (as the case may be) that he will cause paragraph (*c*)(ii) above to be satisfied; and the certificate shall be in such form and be kept for such period as the Commissioners may by regulations specify.

(2) Subsections (3) and (4) below also apply where—

(*a*) there is a supply of goods;

(*b*) those goods are eligible goods;

(*c*) either—

(i) that supply takes place while the goods are subject to a fiscal warehousing regime; or

(ii) after that supply but before the supply, if any, of those goods which next occurs, the person to whom the former supply is made causes the goods to be placed in a fiscal warehousing regime;

(*d*) in a case falling within paragraph (*c*)(ii) above, the person to whom the supply is made gives the supplier, not later than the time of the supply, a certificate in such form as the Commissioners may by regulations specify that he will cause paragraph (*c*)(ii) to be satisfied; and

(*e*) the supply is not a retail transaction.

(3) The acquisition or supply in question shall be treated for the purposes of this Act as taking place outside the United Kingdom if any subsequent supply of those goods is while they are subject to the fiscal warehousing regime.

(4) Where subsection (3) does not apply and the acquisition or supply in question falls, for the purposes of this Act, to be treated as taking place in the United Kingdom, that acquisition or supply shall be treated for the purposes of this Act as taking place when the goods are removed from the fiscal warehousing regime.

(5) Where—

(*a*) subsection (4) above applies to an acquisition or a supply,

(*b*) the acquisition or supply is taxable and not zero-rated, and

(*c*) the acquirer or supplier is not a taxable person but would be were it not for paragraph 1(9) of Schedule 1, paragraph 1(7) of Schedule 2 and paragraph 1(6) of Schedule 3, or any of those provisions,

VAT shall be chargeable on that acquisition or supply notwithstanding that the acquirer or the supplier is not a taxable person.

(6) In this section "eligible goods" means goods—

(*a*) of a description falling within Schedule 5A;

(*b*) upon which any import duties, as defined in article 4(10) of the Community Customs Code of 12th October 1992 (Council Regulation (EEC) No 2913/92), either have been paid or have been deferred under article 224 of that Code or regulations made under section 45 of the Management Act;

(*c*) (in the case of goods imported from a place outside the member States) upon which any VAT chargeable under section 1(1)(*c*) has been either paid or deferred in accordance with Community customs provisions, and

(*d*) (in the case of goods subject to a duty of excise) upon which that duty has been either paid or deferred under section 127A of the Management Act.

(7) For the purposes of this section, apart from subsection (4), an acquisition or supply shall be treated as taking place at the material time for the acquisition or supply.

(8) The Treasury may by order vary Schedule 5A by adding to or deleting from it any goods or varying any description of any goods.][1]

Commentary—*De Voil Indirect Tax Service* **V3.384**.

Definitions—"Acquisition of goods from another member State", s 11; "another member State", s 96(1); "the Commissioners", s 96(1); "fiscal warehousing regime", s 18F(2); "the Management Act", s 96(1); "material time", s 18F(1); "regulations", s 96(1); "supply of goods", s 5, Sch 4; "taxable person", ss 3, 96(1); "taxable supply", ss 4(2), 96(1); "United Kingdom", s 96(11); "VAT", s 96(1).

Cross references—See VATA 1994 s 18D (payment of VAT on supplies within sub-s (4) and acquisitions within sub-s (5) above).

VATA 1994 s 18F (supplementary provisions).

VATA 1994 s 30(8A) (regulations may provide for the zero-rating of a supply of goods involving the removal of goods from a fiscal warehousing regime to an equivalent regime in another member State).

VATA 1994 s 62(1) (penalty for the preparation or giving of an incorrect certificate under sub-ss (1) and (2) above).

Amendments—[1] This section inserted by FA 1996 Sch 3 para 5, with effect from 1 June 1996; (see Finance Act 1996, Section 26, (Appointed Day) Order, SI 1996/1249), and applying to any acquisition of goods from another member State and any supply taking place on or after that day, except in so far as it confers power to make regulations, when it comes into force on 29 April 1996.

[18C Warehouses and fiscal warehouses: services

(1) Where—

(*a*) a taxable person makes a supply of specified services;

(*b*) those services are wholly performed on or in relation to goods while those goods are subject to a warehousing or fiscal warehousing regime;

(*c*) (except where the services are the supply by an occupier of a warehouse or a fiscal warehousekeeper of warehousing or fiscally warehousing the goods) the person to whom the supply is made gives the supplier a certificate, in such a form as the Commissioners may by regulations specify, that the services are so performed;

(*d*) the supply of services would (apart from this section) be taxable and not zero-rated; and

(*e*) the supplier issues to the person to whom the supply is made an invoice of such a description as the Commissioners may by regulations prescribe,

his supply shall be zero-rated.

(2) If a supply of services is zero-rated under subsection (1) above ("the zero-rated supply of services") then, unless there is a supply of the goods in question the material time for which is—

(*a*) while the goods are subject to a warehousing or fiscal warehousing regime, and

(*b*) after the material time for the zero-rated supply of services,

subsection (3) below shall apply.

(3) Where this subsection applies—

(*a*) a supply of services identical to the zero-rated supply of services shall be treated for the purposes of this Act as being, at the time the goods are removed from the warehousing or fiscal warehousing regime or (if earlier) at the duty point, both made (for the purposes of his business) to the person to whom the zero-rated supply of services was actually made and made by him in the course or furtherance of his business,

(*b*) that supply shall have the same value as the zero-rated supply of services,

(*c*) that supply shall be a taxable (and not a zero-rated) supply, and

(*d*) VAT shall be charged on that supply even if the person treated as making it is not a taxable person.

(4) In this section "specified services" means—

(*a*) services of an occupier of a warehouse or a fiscal warehousekeeper of keeping the goods in question in a warehousing or fiscal warehousing regime;

(*b*) in relation to goods subject to a warehousing regime, services of carrying out on the goods operations which are permitted to be carried out under Community customs provisions or warehousing regulations as the case may be; and

(*c*) in relation to goods subject to a fiscal warehousing regime, services of carrying out on the goods any physical operations (other than any prohibited by regulations made under section 18F), for example, and without prejudice to the generality of the foregoing words, preservation and repacking operations.][1]

Commentary—*De Voil Indirect Tax Service* **V3.384**.

Definitions—"The Commissioners", s 96(1); "fiscal warehousekeeper", s 18F(1); "fiscal warehousing regime", s 18F(2); "the material time", s 18F(1); "regulations", s 96(1); "supply", s 5, Sch 4; "taxable person", ss 3, 96(1); "taxable supply", ss 4(2), 96(1); "warehouse", s 18F(1); "warehousing regime", s 18F(3); "warehousing regulations", s 18F(1).

Cross references—See VATA 1994 s 18D (payment of VAT on a supply within sub-s (3) above).

VATA 1994 s 18F (supplementary provisions).

VATA 1994 s 62(1) (penalty for the giving of an incorrect certificate under sub-s (1) above).

Amendments—[1] This section inserted by FA 1996 Sch 3 para 5, with effect from 1 June 1996; (see Finance Act 1996, Section 26, (Appointed Day) Order, SI 1996/1249), and applying to any acquisition of goods from another member State and any supply taking place on or after that day, except in so far as it confers power to make regulations, when it comes into force on 29 April 1996.

[18D Removal from warehousing: accountability

(1) This section applies to any supply to which section 18B(4) or section 18C(3) applies (supply treated as taking place on removal or duty point) and any acquisition to which section 18B(5) applies (acquisition treated as taking place on removal where acquirer not a taxable person).

(2) Any VAT payable on the supply or acquisition shall (subject to any regulations under subsection (3) below) be paid—

(*a*) at the time when the supply or acquisition is treated as taking place under the section in question; and

(*b*) by the person by whom the goods are removed or, as the case may be, together with the excise duty, by the person who is required to pay that duty.

(3) The Commissioners may by regulations make provision for enabling a taxable person to pay the VAT he is required to pay by virtue of subsection (2) above at a time later than that provided by that subsection; and they may make different provisions for different descriptions of taxable persons and for different descriptions of goods and services.][1]

Commentary—*De Voil Indirect Tax Service* **V3.384**.

Definitions—"The Commissioners", s 96(1); "regulations", s 96(1); "supply", s 5, Sch 4; "taxable person", ss 3, 96(1); "VAT", s 96(1).

Cross references—See VATA 1994 s 18F (supplementary provisions).

VATA 1994 s 30(8A) (regulations may provide for the zero-rating of a supply of goods involving their removal from a fiscal warehousing regime to an equivalent regime in another member State).

VATA 1994 s 73(7B) (Commissioners may assess VAT due to the best of their judgment where it appears to them that goods have been removed from a fiscal warehouse without payment of VAT payable under this section).

Amendments—[1] This section inserted by FA 1996 Sch 3 para 5, with effect from 1 June 1996; (see Finance Act 1996, Section 26, (Appointed Day) Order, SI 1996/1249)., and applying to any acquisition of goods from another member State and any supply taking place on or after that day, except in so far as it confers power to make regulations, when it comes into force on 29 April 1996.

[18E Deficiency in fiscally warehoused goods

(1) This section applies where goods have been subject to a fiscal warehousing regime and, before being lawfully removed from the fiscal warehouse, they are found to be missing or deficient.

(2) In any case where this section applies, unless it is shown to the satisfaction of the Commissioners that the absence of or deficiency in the goods can be accounted for by natural waste or other legitimate cause, the Commissioners may require the fiscal warehousekeeper to pay immediately in respect of the missing goods or of the whole or any part of the deficiency, as they see fit, the VAT that would have been chargeable.

(3) In subsection (2) "VAT that would have been chargeable" means VAT that would have been chargeable on a supply of the missing goods, or the amount of goods by which the goods are deficient, taking place at the time immediately before the absence arose or the deficiency occurred, if the value of that supply were the open market value; but where that time cannot be ascertained to the Commissioners' satisfaction, that VAT shall be the greater of the amounts of VAT which would have been chargeable on a supply of those goods—

(*a*) if the value of that supply were the highest open market value during the period (the relevant period) commencing when the goods were placed in the fiscal warehousing regime and ending when the absence or deficiency came to the notice of the Commissioners, or

(*b*) if the rate of VAT chargeable on that supply were the highest rate chargeable on a supply of such goods during the relevant period and the value of that supply were the highest open market value while that rate prevailed.

(4) This section has effect without prejudice to any penalty incurred under any other provision of this Act or regulations made under it.]

Commentary—*De Voil Indirect Tax Service* **V3.384**.
Definitions—"The Commissioners", s 96(1); "fiscal warehouse", ss 18A(3), 18F(1); "fiscal warehousekeeper", s 18F(1); "fiscal warehousing regime", s 18F(2); "open market value", s 19(5); "regulations", s 96(1); "VAT", s 96(1).
Cross references—See VATA 1994 s 18F (supplementary provisions).
VATA 1994 s 73(7A) (Commissioners may assess VAT due to the best of their judgment where fiscal warehousekeeper fails to pay VAT required under sub-s (2) above).
Amendments—This section inserted by FA 1996 Sch 3 para 5, with effect from 1 June 1996; (see Finance Act 1996, Section 26, (Appointed Day) Order, SI 1996/1249).

[18F Sections 18A to 18E: supplementary

(1) In sections 18A to 18E and this section—

"duty point" has the meaning given by section 18(6);

"eligible goods" has the meaning given by section 18B(6);

"fiscal warehouse" means a place notified to the Commissioners under section 18A(3) and from which such status has not been withdrawn;

"fiscal warehousekeeper" means a person approved under section 18A(1);

"material time"—

(*a*) in relation to any acquisition or supply the time of which is determined in accordance with regulations under section 6(14) or 12(3), means such time as may be prescribed for the purpose of this section by those regulations;

(*b*) in relation to any other acquisition, means the time when the goods reach the destination to which they are despatched from the member State in question;

(*c*) in relation to any other supply of goods, means the time when the supply would be treated as taking place in accordance with subsection (2) of section 6 if paragraph (*c*) of that subsection were omitted; and

(*d*) in relation to any other supply of services, means the time when the services are performed;

"warehouse", except in the expression "fiscal warehouse", has the meaning given by section 18(6);

"warehousing regulations" has the same meaning as in the Management Act.

(2) Any reference in sections 18A to 18E or this section to goods being subject to a fiscal warehousing regime is, subject to any regulations made under subsection (8)(*e*) below, a reference to eligible goods being kept in a fiscal warehouse or being transferred between fiscal warehouses in accordance with such regulations; and any reference to the removal of goods from a fiscal warehousing regime shall be construed accordingly.

(3) Subject to subsection (2) above, any reference in sections 18C and 18D to goods being subject to a warehousing regime or to the removal of goods from a warehousing regime shall have the same meaning as in section 18(7).

(4) Where as a result of an operation on eligible goods subject to a fiscal warehousing regime they change their nature but the resulting goods are also eligible goods, the provisions of sections 18B to 18E and this section shall apply as if the resulting goods were the original goods.

(5) Where as a result of an operation on eligible goods subject to a fiscal warehousing regime they cease to be eligible goods, on their ceasing to be so sections 18B to 18E shall apply as if they had at that time been removed from the fiscal warehousing regime; and for that purpose the proprietor of the goods shall be treated as if he were the person removing them.

(6) Where—

(*a*) any person ceases to be a fiscal warehouse keeper; or

(*b*) any premises cease to have fiscal warehouse status,

sections 18B to 18E and this section shall apply as if the goods of which he is the fiscal warehousekeeper, or the goods in the fiscal warehouse, as the case may be, had at that time been removed from the fiscal warehousing regime; and for that purpose the proprietor of the goods shall be treated as if he were the person removing them.

(7) The Commissioners may make regulations governing the deposit, keeping, securing and treatment of goods in a fiscal warehouse, and the removal of goods from a fiscal warehouse.

(8) Regulations may, without prejudice to the generality of subsection (7) above, include provisions—

(*a*) in relation to—

(i) goods which are, have been or are to be subject to a fiscal warehousing regime,

(ii) other goods which are, have been or are to be kept in fiscal warehouses,

(iii) fiscal warehouse premises, and

(iv) fiscal warehousekeepers and their businesses,

as to the keeping, preservation and production of records and the furnishing of returns and information by fiscal warehousekeepers and any other persons;

(*b*) requiring goods deposited in a fiscal warehouse to be produced to or made available for inspection by an authorised person on request by him;

(*c*) prohibiting the carrying out on fiscally warehoused goods of such operations as they may prescribe;

(*d*) regulating the transfer of goods from one fiscal warehouse to another;

(*e*) concerning goods which, though kept in a fiscal warehouse, are not eligible goods or are not intended by a relevant person to be goods in respect of which reliefs are to be enjoyed under sections 18A to 18E and this section;

(*f*) prohibiting the fiscal warehouse keeper from allowing goods to be removed from the fiscal warehousing regime without payment of any VAT payable under section 18D on or by reference to that removal and, if in breach of that prohibition he allows goods to be so removed, making him liable for the VAT jointly and severally with the remover,

and may contain such incidental or supplementary provisions as the Commissioners think necessary or expedient.

(9) Regulations may make different provision for different cases, including different provision for different fiscal warehousekeepers or descriptions of fiscal warehousekeeper, for fiscal warehouses of different descriptions or for goods of different classes or descriptions or of the same class or description in different circumstances.][1]

Commentary—*De Voil Indirect Tax Service* **V3.384**.

Definitions—"Authorised person", s 96(1); "the Commissioners", s 96(1); "the Management Act", s 96(1); "regulations", s 96(1); "supply", s 5, Sch 4; "VAT", ss 1, 96(1).

Amendments—[1] This section inserted by FA 1996 Sch 3 para 5, with effect from 1 June 1996; (see Finance Act 1996, Section 26, (Appointed Day) Order, SI 1996/1249)., and applying to any acquisition of goods from another member State and any supply taking place on or after that day, except in so far as it confers power to make regulations, when it comes into force on 29 April 1996.

Determination of value

19 Value of supply of goods or services

(1) For the purposes of this Act the value of any supply of goods or services shall, except as otherwise provided by or under this Act, be determined in accordance with this section and Schedule 6, and for those purposes subsections (2) to (4) below have effect subject to that Schedule.

(2) If the supply is for a consideration in money its value shall be taken to be such amount as, with the addition of the VAT chargeable, is equal to the consideration.

(3) If the supply is for a consideration not consisting or not wholly consisting of money, its value shall be taken to be such amount in money as, with the addition of the VAT chargeable, is equivalent to the consideration.

(4) Where a supply of any goods or services is not the only matter to which a consideration in money relates, the supply shall be deemed to be for such part of the consideration as is properly attributable to it.

(5) For the purposes of this Act the open market value of a supply of goods or services shall be taken to be the amount that would fall to be taken as its value under subsection (2) above if the supply were for such consideration in money as would be payable by a person standing in no such relationship with any person as would affect that consideration.

Commentary—*De Voil Indirect Tax Service* **V3.152, V3.161**.

Simon's Tax Cases—s 19, *Naturally Yours Cosmetics Ltd v C&E Comrs* [1988] STC 879*; *Fine Art Developments plc v C&E Comrs* [1993] STC 29*; *C&E Comrs v Thorn Materials Supply Ltd and Thorn Resources Ltd* [1998] STC 725*; *C&E Comrs v Euphony Communications Ltd* [2004] STC 301.

s 19(2), *Trafalgar Tours Ltd v C&E Comrs* [1990] STC 127*; *C&E Comrs v Tron Theatre Ltd* [1994] STC 177*; *C&E Comrs v British Telecommunications plc* [1999] STC 758; *Total UK Ltd v R&C Comrs* [2007] STC 564.

s 19(3), *Boots Co plc v C&E Comrs* [1988] STC 138*; *C&E Comrs v Sai Jewellers* [1996] STC 269*; *C&E Comrs v Bugeja* [2000] STC 1; *Hartwell plc v C&E Comrs* [2002] STC 22.

s 19(4), *C&E Comrs v Tron Theatre Ltd* [1994] STC 177*; *C&E Comrs v Ping (Europe) Ltd* [2002] STC 1186, CA.

Press releases etc—C&E Business Brief 8/95 5-5-95 (Value of barter transactions).

C&E Business Brief 21/96 17-10-96 (a discount given by an MOT test centre to an unapproved garage is no longer treated as consideration for a taxable supply).

Definitions—"Money", s 96(1); "supply", s 5, Sch 4; "VAT", ss 1, 96(1).

Cross references—See VATA 1994 s 20(2) (valuation of acquisitions from other member states otherwise than through a taxable supply: disapplication of this section);

VATA 1994 s 52 (provision for regulations modifying this section in relation to the valuation of supplies of goods under trading stamp schemes);

VATA 1994 Sch 6 para 4 (valuation of supplies made on terms allowing discount for prompt payment);

VATA 1994 Sch 6 para 12 (treatment of money paid in respect of a supply by persons other than the person to whom the supply was made).

VAT Regulations, SI 1995/2518 reg 77 (modifications of sub-s (5) of this section in relation to goods supplied in exchange for trading stamps).

20 Valuation of acquisitions from other member States

(1) [Subject to section 18C,][1] For the purposes of this Act the value of any acquisition of goods from another member State shall be taken to be the value of the transaction in pursuance of which they are acquired.

(2) Where goods are acquired from another member State otherwise than in pursuance of a taxable supply, the value of the transaction in pursuance of which they are acquired shall be determined for the purposes of subsection (1) above in accordance with this section and Schedule 7, and for those purposes—

(*a*) subsections (3) to (5) below have effect subject to that Schedule; and

(*b*) section 19 and Schedule 6 shall not apply in relation to the transaction.

(3) If the transaction is for a consideration in money, its value shall be taken to be such amount as is equal to the consideration.

(4) If the transaction is for a consideration not consisting or not wholly consisting of money, its value shall be taken to be such amount in money as is equivalent to the consideration.

(5) Where a transaction in pursuance of which goods are acquired from another member State is not the only matter to which a consideration in money relates, the transaction shall be deemed to be for such part of the consideration as is properly attributable to it.

Commentary—*De Voil Indirect Tax Service* **V3.390**.

Definitions—"Acquisition of goods from another member State", s 11; "another member State", s 96(1); "money", s 96(1); "taxable supply", s 4(2).

Cross reference—See VATA 1994 s 52 (provision for regulations modifying this section in relation to the valuation of acquisitions of goods under trading stamp schemes).

Amendments—[1] Words in sub-s (1) inserted by FA 1996 Sch 3 para 6, with effect to any acquisition of goods from another member State taking place on or after 1 June 1996; (see Finance Act 1996, Section 26, (Appointed Day) Order, SI 1996/1249).

21 Value of imported goods

(1) For the purposes of this Act, the value of goods imported from a place outside the member States shall (subject to subsections (2) [to (4)][1] below) be determined according to the rules applicable in the case of Community customs duties, whether or not the goods' in question are subject to any such duties.

(2) For the purposes of this Act the value of any goods imported from a place outside the member States shall [(subject to subsection (2A) below)][5] be taken to include the following so far as they are not already included in that value in accordance with the rules mentioned in subsection (1) above, that is to say—

(*a*) all taxes, duties and other charges levied either outside or, by reason of importation, within the United Kingdom (except VAT); …[2]

[(*b*) all incidental expenses, such as commission, packing, transport and insurance costs, up to the goods' first destination in the United Kingdom; and

(*c*) if at the time of the importation of the goods from a place outside the member States a further destination for the goods is known, and that destination is within the United Kingdom or another member State, all such incidental expenses in so far as they result from the transport of the goods to that other destination;

and in this subsection "the goods' first destination" means the place mentioned on the consignment note or any other document by means of which the goods are imported into the United Kingdom, or in the absence of such documentation it means the place of the first transfer of cargo in the United Kingdom.][2]

[(2A) Where—

(*a*) any goods falling within subsection (5) below are sold by auction at a time when they are subject to the procedure specified in subsection (2B) below, and

(*b*) arrangements made by or on behalf of the purchaser of the goods following the sale by auction result in the importation of the goods from a place outside the member States,

the value of the goods shall not be taken for the purposes of this Act to include, in relation to that importation, any commission or premium payable to the auctioneer in connection with the sale of the goods.

(2B) That procedure is the customs procedure for temporary importation with total relief from import duties provided for in Articles 137 to 141 of Council Regulation 2913/92/EEC establishing the Community Customs Code.][5]

(3) Subject to subsection (2) above, where—

(*a*) goods are imported from a place outside the member States for a consideration which is or includes a price in money payable as on the transfer of property;

(*b*) the terms on which those goods are so imported allow a discount for prompt payment of that price;

(*c*) those terms do not include provision for payment of that price by instalments; and

(*d*) payment of that price is made in accordance with those terms so that the discount falls to be allowed, the value of the goods shall be taken for the purposes of this Act to be reduced by the amount of the discount.

[(4) [Subject to subsection (6D) below,][3] for the purposes of this Act, the value of any goods falling within subsection (5) below which are imported from a place outside the member States shall be taken to be an amount equal to [33.34][3, 6] per cent of the amount which, apart from this subsection, would be their value for those purposes.][1]

[(5) The goods that fall within this subsection are—

(*a*) any work of art;

(*b*) any antique, not falling within paragraph (*a*) above or (*c*) below, that is more than one hundred years old;

(*c*) any collection or collector's piece that is of zoological, botanical, mineralogical, anatomical, historical, archaeological, palaeontological, ethnographic, numismatic or philatelic interest.

(6) In this section "work of art" means, subject to subsections (6A) and (6B) below—

(*a*) any mounted or unmounted painting, drawing, collage, decorative plaque or similar picture that was executed by hand;

(*b*) any original engraving, lithograph or other print which—

(i) was produced from one or more plates executed by hand by an individual who executed them without using any mechanical or photomechanical process; and

(ii) either is the only one produced from the plate or plates or is comprised in a limited edition;

(*c*) any original sculpture or statuary, in any material;

(*d*) any sculpture cast which—

(i) was produced by or under the supervision of the individual who made the mould or became entitled to it by succession on the death of that individual; and

(ii) either is the only cast produced from the mould or is comprised in a limited edition;

(*e*) any tapestry or other hanging which—

(i) was made by hand from an original design; and

(ii) either is the only one made from the design or is comprised in a limited edition;

(*f*) any ceramic executed by an individual and signed by him;

(*g*) any enamel on copper which—

(i) was executed by hand;

(ii) is signed either by the person who executed it or by someone on behalf of the studio where it was executed;

(iii) either is the only one made from the design in question or is comprised in a limited edition; and

(iv) is not comprised in an article of jewellery or an article of a kind produced by goldsmiths or silversmiths;

(*h*) any mounted or unmounted photograph which—

(i) was printed by or under the supervision of the photographer;

(ii) is signed by him; and

(iii) either is the only print made from the exposure in question or is comprised in a limited edition;

(6A) The following do not fall within subsection (5) above by virtue of subsection (6)(*a*) above, that is to say—

(*a*) any technical drawing, map or plan;

(*b*) any picture comprised in a manufactured article that has been hand-decorated; or

(*c*) anything in the nature of scenery, including a backcloth.

(6B) An item comprised in a limited edition shall be taken to be so comprised for the purposes of subsection (6)(*d*) to (*h*) above only if—

(*a*) in the case of sculpture casts—

(i) the edition is limited so that the number produced from the same mould does not exceed eight; or

(ii) the edition comprises a limited edition of nine or more casts made before 1st January 1989 which the Commissioners have directed should be treated, in the exceptional circumstances of the case, as a limited edition for the purposes of subsection (6)(*d*) above;

(*b*) in the case of tapestries and hangings, the edition is limited so that the number produced from the same design does not exceed eight;

(*c*) in the case of enamels on copper—

(i) the edition is limited so that the number produced from the same design does not exceed eight; and

(ii) each of the enamels in the edition is numbered and is signed as mentioned in subsection (6)(*g*)(ii) above;

(*d*) in the case of photographs—

(i) the edition is limited so that the number produced from the same exposure does not exceed thirty; and

(ii) each of the prints in the edition is numbered and is signed as mentioned in subsection (6)(*h*)(ii) above.

(6C) For the purposes of this section a collector's piece is of philatelic interest if—

(*a*) it is a postage or revenue stamp, a postmark, a first-day cover or an item of pre-stamped stationery; and

(*b*) it is franked or (if unfranked) it is not legal tender and is not intended for use as such.

(6D) Subsection (4) above does not apply in the case of any goods imported from outside the member States if—

(*a*) the whole of the VAT chargeable on their importation falls to be relieved by virtue of an order under section 37(1); or

(*b*) they were exported from the United Kingdom during the period of twelve months ending with the date of their importation [in circumstances where the exportation and subsequent importation were effected to obtain the benefit of that subsection][7].][4]

(7) An order under section 2(2) may contain provision making such alteration of the percentage for the time being specified in subsection (4) above as the Treasury consider appropriate in consequence of any increase or decrease by that order of the rate of VAT.][1]

Commentary—*De Voil Indirect Tax Service* **V3.322–V3.324**.

Press releases etc—HC Official Report, Standing Committee D 2-2-95 (new sub-s (5)(*b*) restricts the reduced rate to first importation; glass crystal is covered by new sub-s (5)(*c*)).

C&E News Release 20/95 3-4-95 (implementation of charges to the valuation of imported works of art etc introduced by FA 1995 delayed until 1 June 1996).

VAT Information Sheet 9/95 1-5-95 (valuation of imported works of art, antiques and collectors' pieces from 1 June 1996).

C&E News Release 29/99 2-7-99 and VAT Information Sheet 9/99 July 1999 (increase in the reduced rate from 2.5% to 5% and extension of scope).

C&E News Release 15-4-02 (new concession: revocation of the rule denying the reduced rate where goods are exported from the UK within 12 months before the date of re-importation).

Definitions—"Another member State", s 96(1); "goods imported from a place outside the member States", s 15; "member States", s 15; "money", s 96(1); "United Kingdom", s 96(11); "VAT", ss 1, 96(1).

Amendments—[1] Words in sub-s (1) substituted, and sub-ss (4)–(7) added, by FA 1995 s 22 with effect in relation to goods imported at any time on or after 1 May 1995.

[2] Word omitted from sub-s (2)(*a*) repealed and sub-s (2)(*b*), (*c*) and words following substituted for sub-s (2)(*b*) by FA 1996 s 27, Sch 41 Pt IV(3) with effect in relation to goods imported after 31 December 1995.

[3] Words in sub-s (4) inserted and figures amended, by FA 1999 s 12 in relation to goods imported at any time from 27 July 1999.

[4] Sub-ss (5), (6) substituted by (5)–(6D) by FA 1999 s 12 in relation to goods imported at any time from 27 July 1999.

[5] Words '(subject to subsection (2A) below)' in sub-s (2) and sub-ss (2A) and (2B) inserted by FA 2006 s 18 with effect from 1 September 2006 (by virtue of SI 2006/2149).

[6] Figure in sub-s (4) temporarily substituted for figure "28.58" by the VAT (Change of Rate) Order, SI 2008/3020 arts 2, 4 with effect from 1 December 2008 to 31 December 2009 (extended from 30 November 2009 by FA 2009 s 9).

[7] In sub-s (6D)(*b*), words inserted by the Enactment of Extra-Statutory Concessions Order, SI 2009/730 art 17 with effect in relation to importations on or after 6 April 2009.

22 Value of certain goods

Amendments—This section repealed by FA 1996 s 28, Sch 41 Pt IV(2) with effect in relation to supplies made after 31 December 1995.

23 Gaming machines

(1) Where a person [gambles][1] by means of a gaming machine, then for the purposes of VAT (but without prejudice to subsection (2) below) the amount paid by him […][2] shall be treated as the consideration for a supply of services to him.

(2) The value to be taken as the value of supplies made in the circumstances mentioned in subsection (1) above in any period shall be determined as if the consideration for the supplies were reduced by an amount equal to the amount (if any) received in that period by persons (other than the person making the supply and persons acting on his behalf) [gambling][3] successfully.

(3) The insertion of a token into a machine shall be treated for the purposes of subsection (1) above as the payment of an amount equal to that for which the token can be obtained; and the receipt of a token by a person [gambling][4] successfully shall be treated for the purposes of subsection (2) above—

(*a*) if the token is of a kind used [to use][4] the machine, as the receipt of an amount equal to that for which such a token can be obtained;

(*b*) if the token is not of such a kind but can be exchanged for money, as the receipt of an amount equal to that for which it can be exchanged.

[(4) In this section "gaming machine" means a machine which is designed or adapted for use by individuals to gamble (whether or not it can also be used for other purposes).

(5) But—

(*a*) a machine is not a gaming machine to the extent that it is designed or adapted for use to bet on future real events,

(*b*) a machine is not a gaming machine to the extent that—

(i) it is designed or adapted for the playing of bingo, and

(ii) bingo duty is charged under section 17 of the Betting and Gaming Duties Act 1981 (c. 63) on the playing of that bingo, or would be charged but for paragraphs 1 to 5 of Schedule 3 to that Act, and (*c*) a machine is not a gaming machine to the extent that—

(i) it is designed or adapted for the playing of a real game of chance, and

(ii) the playing of the game is dutiable gaming for the purposes of section 10 of the Finance Act 1997 (c 16), or would be dutiable gaming but for subsections (3) and (4) of that section.

(6) [For the purposes of this section—][6]

(*a*) a reference to gambling is a reference to—

[(i) playing a game of chance for a prize, and

(ii) betting,][6]

(*b*) a reference to a machine is a reference to any apparatus which uses or applies mechanical power, electrical power or both,

(*c*) a reference to a machine being designed or adapted for a purpose includes a reference to a machine to which anything has been done as a result of which it can reasonably be expected to be used for that purpose,

(*d*) a reference to a machine being adapted includes a reference to computer software being installed on it,

(*e*) "real" has the meaning given by section 353(1) of [the Gambling Act 2005][6],

(*f*) "game of chance" [includes—

(i) a game that involves both an element of chance and an element of skill,

(ii) a game that involves an element of chance that can be eliminated by superlative skill, and

(iii) a game that is presented as involving an element of chance, but does not include a sport,][6],

(*g*) "bingo" means any version of that game, irrespective of by what name it is described.

[(*h*) "prize", in relation to a machine, does not include the opportunity to play the machine again,

(*i*) a person plays a game of chance if he participates in a game of chance—

(i) whether or not there are other participants in the game, and

(ii) whether or not a computer generates images or data taken to represent the actions of other participants in the game.][6]

(7) The Treasury may by order amend subsections (4) to (6).][5]

Commentary—*De Voil Indirect Tax Service* **V3.264**.
Simon's Tax Cases—*Feehan v C&E Comrs* [1995] STC 75*.
Definitions—"Money", s 96(1); "supply of services", s 5, Sch 4; "VAT", ss 1, 96(1); "value of supply of services", s 19, Sch 6.
Cross reference—See VATA 1994 Sch 11 para 9 (power to require action necessary to ascertain value of supplies relating to gaming machines).

Amendments—[1] Words in sub-s (1) substituted by FA 2006 s 16(2) in relation to anything done after 5 December 2005.
[2] Words in sub-s (1) omitted by FA 2006 ss 16(2), 178, Sch 26 Part 2 in relation to anything done after 5 December 2005.
[3] Words in sub-s (2) substituted by FA 2006 s 16(3) in relation to anything done after 5 December 2005.
[4] Words in sub-s (3) substituted by FA 2006 s 16(4) in relation to anything done after 5 December 2005.
[5] Sub-s (4) substituted by sub-ss (4)–(7) by FA 2006 s 16(5) in relation to anything done after 5 December 2005. In the application of sub-s (5)(*c*) as so substituted in relation to anything done before 1 November 2006, 'game of chance' has the same meaning as in the Gaming Act 1968.
[6] In sub-s (6), opening words, para (*a*)(i), (ii), words in paras (*e*), (*f*), substituted, and paras (*h*), (*i*) inserted, by the Value Added Tax (Gaming Machines) Order, SI 2006/2686 art 2, with effect from 1 November 2006.

Payment of VAT by taxable persons

24 Input tax and output tax

(1) Subject to the following provisions of this section, "input tax", in relation to a taxable person, means the following tax, that is to say—

(*a*) VAT on the supply to him of any goods or services;

(*b*) VAT on the acquisition by him from another member State of any goods; and

(*c*) VAT paid or payable by him on the importation of any goods from a place outside the member States,

being (in each case) goods or services used or to be used for the purpose of any business carried on or to be carried on by him.

(2) Subject to the following provisions of this section, "output tax", in relation to a taxable person, means VAT on supplies which he makes or on the acquisition by him from another member State of goods (including VAT which is also to be counted as input tax by virtue of subsection (1)(*b*) above).

(3) For the purposes of subsections (1) and (2) above, where goods or services are supplied to a company, goods are acquired by a company from another member State or goods are imported by a company from a place outside the member States and the goods or services which are so supplied, acquired or imported are used or to be used in connection with the provision of accommodation by the company, they shall not be treated as used or to be used for the purposes of any business carried on by the company to the extent that the accommodation is used or to be used for domestic purposes by—

(*a*) a director of the company, or

(*b*) a person connected with a director of the company.

(4) The Treasury may by order provide with respect to any description of goods or services that, where goods or services of that description are supplied to a person who is not a taxable person, they shall, in such circumstances as may be specified in the order, be treated for the purposes of subsections (1) and (2) above as supplied to such other person as may be determined in accordance with the order.

(5) Where goods or services supplied to a taxable person, goods acquired by a taxable person from another member State or goods imported by a taxable person from a place outside the member States are used or to be used partly for the purposes of a business carried on or to be carried on by him and partly for other purposes, VAT on supplies, acquisitions and importations shall be apportioned so that only so much as is referable to his business purposes is counted as his input tax.

(6) Regulations may provide—

(*a*) for VAT on the supply of goods or services to a taxable person, VAT on the acquisition of goods by a taxable person from other member States and VAT paid or payable by a taxable person on the importation of goods from places outside the member States to be treated as his input tax only if and to the extent that the charge to VAT is evidenced and quantified by reference to such documents [or other information][1] as may be specified in the regulations or the Commissioners may direct either generally or in particular cases or classes of cases;

(*b*) for a taxable person to count as his input tax, in such circumstances, to such extent and subject to such conditions as may be prescribed, VAT on the supply to him of goods or services or on the acquisition of goods by him from another member State or paid by him on the importation of goods from places outside the member States notwithstanding that he was not a taxable person at the time of the supply, acquisition or payment;

(*c*) for a taxable person that is a body corporate to count as its input tax, in such circumstances, to such extent and subject to such conditions as may be prescribed, VAT on the supply, acquisition or importation of goods before the company's incorporation for appropriation to the company or its business or on the supply of services before that time for its benefit or in connection with its incorporation;

(*d*) in the case of a person who has been, but is no longer, a taxable person, for him to be paid by the Commissioners the amount of any VAT on a supply of services made to him for the purposes of the business carried on by him when he was a taxable person.

(7) For the purposes of this section "director" means—

(*a*) in relation to a company whose affairs are managed by a board of directors or similar body, a member of that board or similar body;

(*b*) in relation to a company whose affairs are managed by a single director or similar person, that director or person;

(*c*) in relation to a company whose affairs are managed by the members themselves, a member of the company,

and a person is connected with a director if that person is the director's wife or husband, or is a relative, or the wife or husband of a relative, of the director or of the director's wife or husband.

Commentary—*De Voil Indirect Tax Service* **V3.402, V3.501**.

HMRC Manuals—VAT Guidance V1–3: Supply and consideration, para 5.7 (business/non-business use: *Lennartz* ruling).

Simon's Tax Cases—s 24(1), *Schemepanel Trading Ltd v C&E Comrs* [1996] STC 871; *WHA Ltd and another v C&E Comrs* [2003] STC 648, [2004] STC 1081; *BUPA Purchasing Ltd and others v C&E Comrs* [2003] STC 1203; *R&C Comrs v Jeancharm Ltd (trading as Beaver International)* [2005] STC 918; *R&C Comrs v Gracechurch Management Services Ltd* [2008] STC 795.

s 24(2), *C&E Comrs v Rosner* [1994] STC 228*.

s 24(3)(*a*), *Turner (T/A Turner Agricultural) v C&E Comrs* [1992] STC 621*.

s 24(5), *Victoria and Albert Museum Trustees v C&E Comrs* [1996] STC 1016*; *St Helen's School Northwood Ltd v R&C Comrs* [2007] STC 633.

Orders—See VAT (Input Tax) (Person Supplied) Order, SI 1991/2306.

Press releases etc—C&E Business Brief 18/96 27-8-96 (guidelines issued on the recovery of input tax incurred on repairs to farmhouses).

C&E Business Brief 19/96 16-9-96 (Customs have relaxed the requirements to recover the VAT paid by a supplier when goods have been lost through fraud; it is no longer necessary for a conviction to have been obtained).

Definitions—"Acquisition of goods from another member State", s 11; "another member State", s 96(1); "business", s 94; "the Commissioners", s 96(1); "document", s 96(1); "goods imported from a place outside the member States", s 15; "prescribed", s 96(1); "regulations", s 96(1); "supply ", s 5, Sch 4; "tax", s 96(1); "taxable person", s 3; "VAT", ss 1, 96(1).

Cross references—See VATA 1994 s 56(5) (no apportionment of VAT to be made under sub-s (5) of this section in respect of fuel for private use).

VAT (Isle of Man) Order, SI 1982/1067 art 7 (references to VAT in this section to include references to VAT chargeable under Isle of Man legislation);

VAT (Tour Operators) Order, SI 1987/1806 art 12 (disallowance of credit for input tax on goods and services acquired by a tour operator for re-supply as designated travel services);

VAT (Input Tax) (Person Supplied) Order, SI 1991/2306 art 3 (road fuel supplied to non-taxable persons where cost is reimbursed by a taxable person).

Amendments—[1] Words in sub-s (6)(*a*) inserted by FA 2003, s 17(2) with effect from 10 April 2003.

25 Payment by reference to accounting periods and credit for input tax against output tax

(1) A taxable person shall—

(*a*) in respect of supplies made by him, and

(*b*) in respect of the acquisition by him from other member States of any goods, account for and pay VAT by reference to such periods (in this Act referred to as "prescribed accounting periods") at such time and in such manner as may be determined by or under regulations and regulations may make different provision for different circumstances.

(2) Subject to the provisions of this section, he is entitled at the end of each prescribed accounting period to credit for so much of his input tax as is allowable under section 26, and then to deduct that amount from any output tax that is due from him.

(3) If either no output tax is due at the end of the period, or the amount of the credit exceeds that of the output tax then, subject to subsections (4) and (5) below, the amount of the credit or, as the case may be, the amount of the excess shall be paid to the taxable person by the Commissioners; and an amount which is due under this subsection is referred to in this Act as a "VAT credit".

(4) The whole or any part of the credit may, subject to and in accordance with regulations, be held over to be credited in and for a subsequent period; and the regulations may allow for it to be so held over either on the taxable person's own application or in accordance with general or special directions given by the Commissioners from time to time.

(5) Where at the end of any period a VAT credit is due to a taxable person who has failed to submit returns for any earlier period as required by this Act, the Commissioners may withhold payment of the credit until he has complied with that requirement.

(6) A deduction under subsection (2) above and payment of a VAT credit shall not be made or paid except on a claim made in such manner and at such time as may be determined by or under regulations; and, in the case of a person who has made no taxable supplies in the period concerned or any previous period, payment of a VAT credit shall be made subject to such conditions (if any) as the Commissioners think fit to impose, including conditions as to repayment in specified circumstances.

(7) The Treasury may by order provide, in relation to such supplies, acquisitions and importations as the order may specify, that VAT charged on them is to be excluded from any credit under this section; and—

(*a*) any such provision may be framed by reference to the description of goods or services supplied or goods acquired or imported, the person by whom they are supplied, acquired or imported or to whom they are supplied, the purposes for which they are supplied, acquired or imported, or any circumstances whatsoever; and

(*b*) such an order may contain provision for consequential relief from output tax.

Commentary—*De Voil Indirect Tax Service* **V3.402, V3.501**.

Simon's Tax Cases—*Betterware Products Ltd v C&E Comrs (No 2)* [1988] STC 6*; *C&E Comrs v Fine Art Developments plc* [1989] STC 85*; *Neuvale Ltd v C&E Comrs* [1989] STC 395*; *R v C&E Comrs, ex p Kay & Co Ltd* [1996] STC 1500.

s 25(2), (3), *R v Comrs of Customs and Excise, ex p Strangewood Ltd* [1987] STC 502*.

s 25(7), *Group Ltd v C&E Comrs* [1996] STC 898*; *R v C&E Comrs, ex p Greater Manchester Police Authority* [2000] STC 620, [2001] STC 406, CA.

Orders—See VAT (Input Tax) Order, SI 1992/3222.

Definitions—"Acquisition of goods from another member State", s 11; "another member State", s 96(1); "the Commissioners", s 96(1); "input tax", s 24; "output tax", s 24; "regulations", s 96(1); "supply", s 5, Sch 4; "taxable person", s 3; "taxable supply", s 4(2); "VAT", ss 1, 96(1).

Press releases etc—Business Brief 2/98 27-1-98 (VAT: three year time limit for refunds).

Cross references—See VATA 1994 s 27(1) (VAT payable by taxable person on importation of goods partly or wholly for private purposes is not to be treated as input tax eligible for deduction or credit under this section);

VATA 1994 s 34(1) (capital expenditure on supply of machinery or plant: relief for VAT which is not eligible for credit under this section);

VATA 1994 s 54(3) (supplies under flat rate scheme for farmers: treatment of percentage of consideration as VAT for purposes of determining entitlement to input tax credit of person supplied);

VATA 1994 s 69(1), (5) (penalty for failure to pay VAT within time limit imposed by regulations made under sub-s (1) of this section);

VATA 1994 s 80(5) (repayment supplement: treatment as credit due under sub-s (3) of this section);

VATA 1994 s 81(1) (interest payable by Commissioners: treatment as credit due under sub-s (3) of this section);

VATA 1994 s 90(3) (VAT repaid as a result of the failure of a resolution under PCTA 1968 may not be credited as input tax under this section);

VATA 1994 s 97(3), (4) (procedure for making orders for excluding any VAT from credit under this section).

VAT (Isle of Man) Order, SI 1982/1067 art 7 (references to VAT in sub-s (7) of this section to include references to VAT chargeable under Isle of Man legislation);

VAT (Tour Operators) Order, SI 1987/1806 art 12 (disallowance of credit for input tax on goods and services acquired by a tour operator for re-supply as designated travel services);

VAT (Input Tax) Order, SI 1992/3222 (disallowance of credit for input tax on specified supplies, acquisitions and importations).

VAT Regulations, SI 1995/2518 reg 6(3) (business transferred as a going concern: repayment of input tax);

VAT Regulations, SI 1995/2518 reg 29 (claims for deduction of input tax: form and documentation);

VAT Regulations, SI 1995/2518 reg 34 (correction of over- and understatements of input tax credit);

VAT Regulations, SI 1995/2518 reg 101(3) (where a supply is excluded from output tax by an order under sub-s (7), its value is to be excluded in determining proportion of input tax attributable to taxable supplies under reg 101(2)(*d*)).

FA 2008 s 121(2) (the requirement in sub-s (6) that a claim for deduction of input tax be made at such time as may be determined by or under regulations does not apply to a claim that became chargeable, and in respect of which the claimant held the required evidence, in a prescribed accounting period ending before 1 May 1997 if the claim is made before 1 April 2009).

26 Input tax allowable under section 25

(1) The amount of input tax for which a taxable person is entitled to credit at the end of any period shall be so much of the input tax for the period (that is input tax on supplies, acquisitions and importations in the period) as is allowable by or under regulations as being attributable to supplies within subsection (2) below.

(2) The supplies within this subsection are the following supplies made or to be made by the taxable person in the course or furtherance of his business—

(*a*) taxable supplies;

(*b*) supplies outside the United Kingdom which would be taxable supplies if made in the United Kingdom;

(*c*) such other supplies outside the United Kingdom and such exempt supplies as the Treasury may by order specify for the purposes of this subsection.

(3) The Commissioners shall make regulations for securing a fair and reasonable attribution of input tax to supplies within subsection (2) above, and any such regulations may provide for—

(*a*) determining a proportion by reference to which input tax for any prescribed accounting period is to be provisionally attributed to those supplies;

(*b*) adjusting, in accordance with a proportion determined in like manner for any longer period comprising two or more prescribed accounting periods or parts thereof, the provisional attribution for any of those periods;

(*c*) the making of payments in respect of input tax, by the Commissioners to a taxable person (or a person who has been a taxable person) or by a taxable person (or a person who has been a taxable person) to the Commissioners, in cases where events prove inaccurate an estimate on the basis of which an attribution was made; and

(*d*) preventing input tax on a supply which, under or by virtue of any provision of this Act, a person makes to himself from being allowable as attributable to that supply.

(4) Regulations under subsection (3) above may make different provision for different circumstances and, in particular (but without prejudice to the generality of that subsection) for different descriptions of goods or services; and may contain such incidental and supplementary provisions as appear to the Commissioners necessary or expedient.

Commentary—*De Voil Indirect Tax Service* **V3.417**.
Simon's Tax Cases—*C&E Comrs v Apple and Pear Development Council* [1985] STC 383*; *Neuvale Ltd v C&E Comrs* [1989] STC 395*; *St Helen's School Northwood Ltd v R&C Comrs* [2007] STC 633.
s 26(2), *WHA Ltd and another v C&E Comrs* [2004] STC 1081.
s 26(3), *C&E Comrs v University of Wales College, Cardiff* [1995] STC 611*; *Kwik-Fit (GB) Ltd v C&E Comrs* [1998] STC 159; *Banbury Visionplus Ltd v R&C Comrs and other appeals* [2006] STC 1568.
Orders—VAT (Input Tax) (Specified Supplies) Order, SI 1999/3121.
Regulations—See VAT Regulations, SI 1995/2518 regs 99–111.
Definitions—"Business", s 94; "the Commissioners", s 96(1); "exempt supply", s 31; "input tax", s 24; "prescribed accounting period", s 25(1); "regulations", s 96(1); "supply", s 5, Sch 4; "taxable person", s 3; "taxable supply", s 4(2); "United Kingdom", s 96(11).
Press releases etc—C&E Business Brief 6/95 28-3-95 (services of investigating accountants; rules determining the person to whom they are supplied). Business Brief 23/97, 10-10-97 (Input tax blocked goods—VAT changes on sales of input tax blocked goods).
C&E Business Brief 8/01 2-7-01 (Customs' policy on the deduction of input tax incurred on expenses relating to the transfer of part of a business as a going concern).
Cross references—See VATA 1994 s 8(3) (supplies treated as made by recipient under reverse charge provisions are not to be taken into account as supplies made by him in determining his entitlement to input tax credit under sub-s (1) of this section);
VATA 1994 s 44(6) (deemed supply to and by representative member of VAT group where a business is transferred as a going concern to a group member: deemed supply by representative member not to be taken into account in determining allowance of input tax under this section);
VATA 1994 s 54(3) (supplies under flat rate scheme for farmers: treatment of percentage of consideration as VAT for purposes of determining entitlement to input tax credit of person supplied);
VATA 1994 ss 83, 84 (appeal to a tribunal as to the proportion of input tax allowable under this section).
VAT (Tour Operators) Order, SI 1987/1806 art 12 (disallowance of credit for input tax on goods and services acquired by a tour operator for re-supply as designated travel services);
VAT (Input Tax) (Specified Supplies) Order, SI 1999/3121 (supplies specified for the purposes of sub-s (2)(*c*) of this section).
VAT Regulations, SI 1995/2518 reg 103(1) (extent to which input tax used or to be used in making supplies within sub-s (2)(*b*) or (*c*) of this section is to be attributed to taxable supplies).
FA 1999 s 11(1) (regs made under s 26(3), in respect of exempt supplies relating to gold, may provide that input tax is allowable as being attributable to the supplies only in relation to specified matters).

[26A Disallowance of input tax where consideration not paid

(1) Where—

(*a*) a person has become entitled to credit for any input tax, and

(*b*) the consideration for the supply to which that input tax relates, or any part of it, is unpaid at the end of the period of six months following the relevant date,

he shall be taken, as from the end of that period, not to have been entitled to credit for input tax in respect of the VAT that is referable to the unpaid consideration or part.

(2) For the purposes of subsection (1) above "the relevant date", in relation to any sum representing consideration for a supply, is—

(*a*) the date of the supply; or

(*b*) if later, the date on which the sum became payable.

(3) Regulations may make such supplementary, incidental, consequential or transitional provisions as appear to the Commissioners to be necessary or expedient for the purposes of this section.

(4) Regulations under this section may in particular—

(*a*) make provision for restoring the whole or any part of an entitlement to credit for input tax where there is a payment after the end of the period mentioned in subsection (1) above;

(*b*) make rules for ascertaining whether anything paid is to be taken as paid by way of consideration for a particular supply;
(*c*) make rules dealing with particular cases, such as those involving payment of part of the consideration or mutual debts.

(5) Regulations under this section may make different provision for different circumstances.

(6) Section 6 shall apply for determining the time when a supply is to be treated as taking place for the purposes of construing this section.][1]

Commentary—*De Voil Indirect Tax Service* **V3.421**.
Amendments—[1] This section inserted by FA 2002 s 22(1), (3) with effect for supplies made after 31 December 2002 (by virtue of SI 2002/3028).

[26AB Adjustment of output tax in respect of supplies under section 55A

(1) This section applies if—

(*a*) a person is, as a result of section 26A, taken not to have been entitled to any credit for input tax in respect of any supply, and
(*b*) the supply is one in respect of which the person is required under section 55A(6) to account for and pay VAT.

(2) The person is entitled to make an adjustment to the amount of VAT which he is so required to account for and pay.

(3) The amount of the adjustment is to be equal to the amount of the credit for the input tax to which the person is taken not to be entitled.

(4) Regulations may make such supplementary, incidental, consequential or transitional provisions as appear to the Commissioners to be necessary or expedient for the purposes of this section.

(5) Regulations under this section may in particular—

(*a*) make provision for the manner in which, and the period for which, the adjustment is to be given effect,
(*b*) require the adjustment to be evidenced and quantified by reference to such records and other documents as may be specified by or under the regulations,
(*c*) require the person entitled to the adjustment to keep, for such period and in such form and manner as may be so specified, those records and documents,
(*d*) make provision for readjustments if any credit for input tax is restored under section 26A.

(6) Regulations under this section may make different provision for different circumstances.][1]

Commentary—*De Voil Indirect Tax Service* **V3.231, V3.233**.
Press releases etc—HMRC Brief 24/07, 20-3-07 (Proposed reverse charge accounting for businesses trading in mobile telephones and computer chips: announcement of targeted implementation and details of how the rules will operate in practice; and exposure of draft legislation for comment).
Amendments—[1] Section inserted by FA 2006 s 19(2), (8) in relation to supplies made on or after 1 June 2007 (by virtue of the Finance Act 2006, section 19, (Appointed Day) Order, SI 2007/1419).

[26B Flat-rate scheme

(1) The Commissioners may by regulations make provision under which, where a taxable person so elects, the amount of his liability to VAT in respect of his relevant supplies in any prescribed accounting period shall be the appropriate percentage of his relevant turnover for that period.

A person whose liability to VAT is to any extent determined as mentioned above is referred to in this section as participating in the flat-rate scheme.

(2) For the purposes of this section—

(*a*) a person's "relevant supplies" are all supplies made by him except supplies made at such times or of such descriptions as may be specified in the regulations;
(*b*) the "appropriate percentage" is the percentage so specified for the category of business carried on by the person in question;
(*c*) a person's "relevant turnover" is the total of—

(i) the value of those of his relevant supplies that are taxable supplies, together with the VAT chargeable on them, and
(ii) the value of those of his relevant supplies that are exempt supplies.

(3) The regulations may designate certain categories of business as categories in relation to which the references in subsection (1) above to liability to VAT are to be read as references to entitlement to credit for VAT.

(4) The regulations may provide for persons to be eligible to participate in the flat-rate scheme only in such cases and subject to such conditions and exceptions as may be specified in, or determined by or under, the regulations.

(5) Subject to such exceptions as the regulations may provide for, a participant in the flat-rate scheme shall not be entitled to credit for input tax.

This is without prejudice to subsection (3) above.

(6) The regulations may—

(*a*) provide for the appropriate percentage to be determined by reference to the category of business that a person is expected, on reasonable grounds, to carry on in a particular period;

(*b*) provide, in such circumstances as may be prescribed, for different percentages to apply in relation to different parts of the same prescribed accounting period;

(*c*) make provision for determining the category of business to be regarded as carried on by a person carrying on businesses in more than one category.

(7) The regulations may provide for the following matters to be determined in accordance with notices published by the Commissioners—

(*a*) when supplies are to be treated as taking place for the purposes of ascertaining a person's relevant turnover for a particular period;

(*b*) the method of calculating any adjustments that fall to be made in accordance with the regulations in a case where a person begins or ceases to participate in the flat-rate scheme.

(8) The regulations may make provision enabling the Commissioners—

(*a*) to authorise a person to participate in the flat-rate scheme with effect from—

(i) a day before the date of his election to participate, or

(ii) a day that is not earlier than that date but is before the date of the authorisation;

(*b*) to direct that a person shall cease to be a participant in the scheme with effect from a day before the date of the direction.

The day mentioned in paragraph (*a*)(i) above may be a day before the date on which the regulations come into force.

(9) Regulations under this section—

(*a*) may make different provision for different circumstances;

(*b*) may make such incidental, supplemental, consequential or transitional provision as the Commissioners think fit, including provision disapplying or applying with modifications any provision contained in or made under this Act.][1]

Amendments—[1] This section inserted by FA 2002 s 23(1), (4) and deemed to have come into force on 24 April 2002.

27 Goods imported for private purposes

(1) Where goods are imported by a taxable person from a place outside the member States and—

(*a*) at the time of importation they belong wholly or partly to another person; and

(*b*) the purposes for which they are to be used include private purposes either of himself or of the other,

VAT paid or payable by the taxable person on the importation of the goods shall not be regarded as input tax to be deducted or credited under section 25; but he may make a separate claim to the Commissioners for it to be repaid.

(2) The Commissioners shall allow the claim if they are satisfied that to disallow it would result, in effect, in a double charge to VAT; and where they allow it they shall do so only to the extent necessary to avoid the double charge.

(3) In considering a claim under this section, the Commissioners shall have regard to the circumstances of the importation and, so far as appearing to them to be relevant, things done with, or occurring in relation to, the goods at any subsequent time.

(4) Any amount allowed by the Commissioners on the claim shall be paid by them to the taxable person.

(5) The reference above to a person's private purposes is to purposes which are not those of any business carried on by him.

Commentary—*De Voil Indirect Tax Service* **V5.153**.
Definitions—"Business", s 94; "the Commissioners", s 96(1); "goods imported from a place outside the member States", s 15; "input tax", s 24; "VAT", ss 1, 96(1).
Cross references—See VATA 1994 s 83 (appeal to a tribunal in respect of a claim by a taxable person under this section).
VAT (Isle of Man) Order, SI 1982/1067 art 7 (references to VAT in this section to include references to VAT chargeable under Isle of Man legislation);
VAT (Isle of Man) Order, SI 1982/1067 art 8 (taxable persons for the purposes of Isle of Man VAT legislation to be treated as taxable persons for the purposes of this section).

28 Payments on account of VAT

(1) The Treasury may make an order under this section if they consider it desirable to do so in the interests of the national economy.

(2) An order under this section may provide that a taxable person of a description specified in the order shall be under a duty—

(*a*) to pay, on account of any VAT he may become liable to pay in respect of a prescribed accounting period, amounts determined in accordance with the order, and

(*b*) to do so at such times as are so determined.

[(2AA) An order under this section may provide for the matters with respect to which an appeal under section 83 lies to a tribunal to include such decisions of the Commissioners under that or any other order under this section as may be specified in the order.][2]

[(2A) The Commissioners may give directions, to persons who are or may become liable by virtue of any order under this section to make payments on account of VAT, about the manner in which they are to make such payments; and where such a direction has been given to any person and has not subsequently been withdrawn, any duty of that person by virtue of such an order to make such a payment shall have effect as if it included a requirement for the payment to be made in the manner directed.][1]

(3) Where an order is made under this section, the Commissioners may make regulations containing such supplementary, incidental or consequential provisions as appear to the Commissioners to be necessary or expedient.

(4) A provision of an order or regulations under this section may be made in such way as the Treasury or, as the case may be, the Commissioners think fit (whether by amending provisions of or made under the enactments relating to VAT or otherwise).

(5) An order or regulations under this section may make different provision for different circumstances.

Commentary—*De Voil Indirect Tax Service* **V5.110**.
Regulations—See VAT Regulations, SI 1995/2518 regs 44–48.
Orders—See VAT (Payments on Account) Order, SI 1993/2001.
Definitions—"The Commissioners", s 96(1); "prescribed accounting period", s 25(1); "regulations", s 96(1); "taxable person", s 3; "VAT", ss 1, 96(1).
Cross reference—See VATA 1994 s 97(3), (4) (procedure for making orders under this section).
Amendments—[1] Sub-s (2A) inserted by FA 1996 s 34.
[2] Sub-s (2AA) inserted by FA 1997 s 43 with effect from 19 March 1997.

29 Invoices provided by recipients of goods or services

Where—

(*a*) a taxable person ("the recipient") provides a document to himself which purports to be an invoice in respect of a taxable supply of goods or services to him by another taxable person; and

(*b*) that document understates the VAT chargeable on the supply,

the Commissioners may, by notice served on the recipient and on the supplier, elect that the amount of VAT understated by the document shall be regarded for all purposes as VAT due from the recipient and not from the supplier.

Commentary—*De Voil Indirect Tax Service* **V3.523**.
Definitions—"The Commissioners", s 96(1); "document", s 96(1); "invoice", s 96(1); "supply", s 5, Sch 4; "taxable person", s 3; "taxable supply", s 4(2); "VAT", ss 1, 96(1).

PART II

RELIEFS, EXEMPTIONS AND REPAYMENTS

Reliefs etc generally available

[29A Reduced rate

(1) VAT charged on—

(*a*) any supply that is of a description for the time being specified in Schedule 7A, or

(*b*) any equivalent acquisition or importation,

shall be charged at the rate of 5 per cent.

(2) The reference in subsection (1) above to an equivalent acquisition or importation, in relation to any supply that is of a description for the time being specified in Schedule 7A, is a reference (as the case may be) to—

(*a*) any acquisition from another member State of goods the supply of which would be such a supply; or

(*b*) any importation from a place outside the member States of any such goods.

(3) The Treasury may by order vary Schedule 7A by adding to or deleting from it any description of supply or by varying any description of supply for the time being specified in it.

(4) The power to vary Schedule 7A conferred by subsection (3) above may be exercised so as to describe a supply of goods or services by reference to matters unrelated to the characteristics of the goods or services themselves.

In the case of a supply of goods, those matters include, in particular, the use that has been made of the goods.][1]

Amendments—[1] This section inserted by FA 2001 s 99(4), (7)(*c*) with effect for sub-ss (1), (2) in relation to supplies made, and acquisitions and importations taking place, after 31 October 2001.

30 Zero-rating

(1) Where a taxable person supplies goods or services and the supply is zero-rated, then, whether or not VAT would be chargeable on the supply apart from this section—

(*a*) no VAT shall be charged on the supply; but

(*b*) it shall in all other respects be treated as a taxable supply;

and accordingly the rate at which VAT is treated as charged on the supply shall be nil.

(2) A supply of goods or services is zero-rated by virtue of this subsection if the goods or services are of a description for the time being specified in Schedule 8 or the supply is of a description for the time being so specified.

[(2A) A supply by a person of services which consist of applying a treatment or process to another person's goods is zero-rated by virtue of this subsection if by doing so he produces goods, and either—

(*a*) those goods are of a description for the time being specified in Schedule 8; or

(*b*) a supply by him of those goods to the person to whom he supplies the services would be of a description so specified.][2]

(3) Where goods of a description for the time being specified in that Schedule, or of a description forming part of a description of supply for the time being so specified, are acquired in the United Kingdom from another member State or imported from a place outside the member States, no VAT shall be chargeable on their acquisition or importation, except as otherwise provided in that Schedule.

(4) The Treasury may by order vary Schedule 8 by adding to or deleting from it any description or by varying any description for the time being specified in it.

[(5) The export of any goods by a charity to a place outside the member States shall for the purposes of this Act be treated as a supply made by the charity—

(*a*) in the United Kingdom, and

(*b*) in the course or furtherance of a business carried on by the charity.][1]

(6) A supply of goods is zero-rated by virtue of this subsection if the Commissioners are satisfied that the person supplying the goods—

(*a*) has exported them to a place outside the member States; or

(*b*) has shipped them for use as stores on a voyage or flight to an eventual destination outside the United Kingdom, or as merchandise for sale by retail to persons carried on such a voyage or flight in a ship or aircraft,

and in either case if such other conditions, if any, as may be specified in regulations or the Commissioners may impose are fulfilled.

(7) Subsection (6)(*b*) above shall not apply in the case of goods shipped for use as stores on a voyage or flight to be made by the person to whom the goods were supplied and to be made for a purpose which is private.

(8) Regulations may provide for the zero-rating of supplies of goods, or of such goods as may be specified in the regulations, in cases where—

(*a*) the Commissioners are satisfied that the goods have been or are to be exported to a place outside the member States or that the supply in question involves both—

(i) the removal of the goods from the United Kingdom; and

(ii) their acquisition in another member State by a person who is liable for VAT on the acquisition in accordance with provisions of the law of that member State corresponding, in relation to that member State, to the provisions of section 10; and

(*b*) such other conditions, if any, as may be specified in the regulations or the Commissioners may impose are fulfilled.

[(8A) Regulations may provide for the zero-rating of supplies of goods, or of such goods as may be specified in regulations, in cases where—

(*a*) the Commissioners are satisfied that the supply in question involves both—

(i) the removal of the goods from a fiscal warehousing regime within the meaning of section 18F(2); and

(ii) their being placed in a warehousing regime in another member State, or in such member State or States as may be prescribed, where that regime is established by provisions of the law of that member State corresponding, in relation to that member State, to the provisions of sections 18A and 18B; and

(*b*) such other conditions, if any, as may be specified in the regulations or the Commissioners may impose are fulfilled.][3]

(9) Regulations may provide for the zero-rating of a supply of services which is made where goods are let on hire and the Commissioners are satisfied that the goods have been or are to be removed from the United Kingdom during the period of the letting, and such other conditions, if any, as may be specified in the regulations or the Commissioners may impose are fulfilled.

(10) Where the supply of any goods has been zero-rated by virtue of subsection (6) above or in pursuance of regulations made under [subsection (8), (8A) or (9)][2] above and—

(*a*) the goods are found in the United Kingdom after the date on which they were alleged to have been or were to be exported or shipped or otherwise removed from the United Kingdom; or

(*b*) any condition specified in the relevant regulations under [subsection (6), (8), (8A) or (9)][3] above or imposed by the Commissioners is not complied with,

and the presence of the goods in the United Kingdom after that date or the non-observance of the condition has not been authorised for the purposes of this subsection by the Commissioners, the goods shall be liable to forfeiture under the Management Act and the VAT that would have been chargeable on the supply but for the zero-rating shall become payable forthwith by the person to whom the goods were supplied or by any person in whose possession the goods are found in the United Kingdom; but the Commissioners may, if they think fit, waive payment of the whole or part of that VAT.

Commentary—*De Voil Indirect Tax Service* **V4.201, V4.202**.
Regulations—See VAT Regulations, SI 1995/2518 regs 127–135.
Orders—See VAT (Tour Operators) Order, SI 1987/1806.
Definitions—"Acquisition of goods from another member State", s 11; "another member State", s 96(1); "business", s 94; "the Commissioners", s 96(1); "goods being acquired by a person in another member State", s 92; "goods imported from a place outside the member States", s 15; "law of that member State", s 92; "the Management Act", s 96(1); "regulations", s 96(10); "ship", s 96(1); "supply", s 5, Sch 4; "taxable person", s 3; "taxable supply", s 4(2); "United Kingdom", s 96(11); "VAT", ss 1, 96(1).
Cross references—See VATA 1994 s 35(5) (extension of the power of the Treasury to vary Sch 8 to matters relating to the refund of VAT to persons constructing certain residential or charitable buildings).
VATA 1994 Sch 8 Group 5 note (13) (sub-s (3) of this section does not apply to goods forming part of a description of a supply within Sch 8 Group 5 (zero rating: construction of buildings etc));
VATA 1994 Sch 8 Group 10 note (2) (sub-s (3) of this section does not apply to goods forming part of a description of a supply within Sch 8 Group 10 (zero rating: gold));
VATA 1994 Sch 8 Group 12 note (1) (sub-s (3) of this section does not apply to goods forming part of a description of certain supplies within Sch 8 Group 12 (zero rating: drugs, medicines, aids for the handicapped etc)).
VAT Regulations, SI 1995/2518 reg 123 (temporary importations).
Amendments—[1] Sub-s (5) substituted by FA 1995 s 28 with effect in relation to transactions occurring on or after 1 May 1995.
[2] Sub-s (2A) inserted by FA 1996 s 29(2), with effect in relation to supplies made after 31 December 1995.
[3] Sub-s (8A) inserted and words in sub-s (10) substituted by FA 1996 s 26(1), (3) Sch 3 para 7, with effect from 29 April 1996.

31 Exempt supplies and acquisitions

(1) A supply of goods or services is an exempt supply if it is of a description for the time being specified in Schedule 9 and an acquisition of goods from another member State is an exempt acquisition if the goods are acquired in pursuance of an exempt supply.

(2) The Treasury may by order vary that Schedule by adding to or deleting from it any description of supply or by varying any description of supply for the time being specified in it, and the Schedule may be varied so as to describe a supply of goods by reference to the use which has been made of them or to other matters unrelated to the characteristics of the goods themselves.

Commentary—*De Voil Indirect Tax Service* **V3.368, V4.101**.
Simon's Tax Cases—*Cooper and Chapman (Builders) Ltd v C&E Comrs* [1993] STC 1*.
Definitions—"Acquisition of goods from another member State", s 11; "another member State", s 96(1); "supply", s 5, Sch 4.
Cross references—See FA 1999 s 13(2) (an order under 31(2), may provide that what would other wise be an exempt supply under the terms of the order shall be, if the supplier chooses, a taxable supplies. It may also make provision by reference to public notices).

32 Relief on supply of certain second-hand goods

...

Amendments—This section repealed by FA 1995 ss 24(2), 162, Sch 29 Pt VI(3) with effect from 1 June 1995 by virtue of SI 1995/1374.

33 Refunds of VAT in certain cases

(1) Subject to the following provisions of this section, where—

(*a*) VAT is chargeable on the supply of goods or services to a body to which this section applies, on the acquisition of any goods by such a body from another member State or on the importation of any goods by such a body from a place outside the member States, and

(*b*) the supply, acquisition or importation is not for the purpose of any business carried on by the body,

the Commissioners shall, on a claim made by the body at such time and in such form and manner as the Commissioners may determine, refund to it the amount of the VAT so chargeable.

(2) Where goods or services so supplied to or acquired or imported by the body cannot be conveniently distinguished from goods or services supplied to or acquired or imported by it for the purpose of a business carried on by it, the amount to be refunded under this section shall be such amount as remains after deducting from the whole of the VAT chargeable on any supply to or acquisition or importation by the body such proportion thereof as appears to the Commissioners to be attributable to the carrying on of the business; but where—

(*a*) the VAT so attributable is or includes VAT attributable, in accordance with regulations under section 26, to exempt supplies by the body, and

(*b*) the VAT attributable to the exempt supplies is in the opinion of the Commissioners an insignificant proportion of the VAT so chargeable,

they may include it in the VAT refunded under this section.

(3) The bodies to which this section applies are—

(*a*) a local authority;

(*b*) a river purification board established under section 135 of the Local Government (Scotland) Act 1973 and a water development board within the meaning of section 109 of the Water (Scotland) Act 1980;

(*c*) an internal drainage board;
[(*d*) an Integrated Transport Authority, Passenger Transport Authority or Passenger Transport Executive for the purposes of Part 2 of the Transport Act 1968;][3]
(*e*) a port health authority within the meaning of the Public Health (Control of Disease) Act 1984 and a port local authority and joint port local authority constituted under Part X of the Public Health (Scotland) Act 1897;
(*f*) a police authority and the Receiver for the Metropolitan Police District;
(*g*) a development corporation within the meaning of the New Towns Act 1981 or the New Towns (Scotland) Act 1968 a new town commission within the meaning of the New Towns Act (Northern Ireland) 1965 and the Commission for the New Towns;
(*h*) a general lighthouse authority within the meaning of [Part VIII of the Merchant Shipping Act 1995][1];
(*i*) the British Broadcasting Corporation;
[(*j*) the appointed news provider referred to in section 280 of the Communications Act 2003; and][2]
(*k*) any body specified for the purposes of this section by an order made by the Treasury.

(4) No VAT shall be refunded under this section to a general lighthouse authority which in the opinion of the Commissioners is attributable to activities other than those concerned with the provision, maintenance or management of lights or other navigational aids.

(5) No VAT shall be refunded under this section to [an appointed][2] news provider which in the opinion of the Commissioners is attributable to activities other than the provision of news programmes for broadcasting by holders of regional Channel 3 licences (within the meaning of Part I of the Broadcasting Act 1990).

(6) References in this section to VAT chargeable do not include any VAT which, by virtue of any order under section 25(7), is excluded from credit under that section.

Commentary—*De Voil Indirect Tax Service* **V5.162.**

Simon's Tax Cases—*R v C&E Comrs, ex p Greater Manchester Police Authority* [2000] STC 620, [2001] STC 406, CA; *Ashfield District Council v C&E Comrs* [2001] STC 1706; *R (on the application of Cardiff County Council) v C&E Comrs* [2002] STC 1318, [2004] STC 356.

s 33(1), (2), *Haringey London Borough Council v C&E Comrs* [1995] STC 830*.

s 33(3)(*f*), (*k*), *R v HM Treasury, ex p Service Authority for the National Crime Squad and others* [2000] STC 638.

Orders—See VAT (Refund of Tax) Orders, SI 1973/2121, SI 1976/2028, SI 1985/1101, SI 1986/336, SI 1986/532, SI 1989/1217, SI 1995/1978, SI 1995/2999, SI 1997/2558, SI 1999/2076, SI 2000/1046, SI 2001/3453, 2006/1793.

VAT (Refund of Tax to Charter Trustees and Conservators) Order, SI 2009/1177.

Definitions—"Acquisition of goods from another member State", s 11; "another member State", s 96(1); "the Commissioners", s 96(1); "exempt supply", s 31; "goods imported from a place outside the member States", s 15; "local authority", s 96(1), (4); "regulations", s 96(1); "supply ", s 5, Sch 4; "VAT", ss 1, 96(1).

Press releases etc—C&E Business Brief 9/95 18-5-95 (services between local authorities).

Cross references—See VATA 1994 s 80(5) (repayment supplement: treatment as refund due under this section);

VATA 1994 s 90(3) (VAT repaid as a result of the failure of a resolution under PCTA 1968 may not be refunded under this section).

VAT (Isle of Man) Order, SI 1982/1067 art 7 (references to VAT in this section to include references to VAT chargeable under Isle of Man legislation).

Amendments—[1] Words in sub-s (3)(*h*) substituted by the Merchant Shipping Act 1995 Sch 13 para 95 with effect from 1 January 1996.

[2] Sub-s (3)(*j*) substituted, and words in sub-s (5) substituted, by the Communications Act 2003 s 406, Sch 17 para 129(1), (2) with effect from 29 December 2003 (by virtue of SI 2003/3142).

[3] Sub-s (3)(*d*) substituted, in relation to England and Wales, by the Local Transport Act 2008 s 77(5), Sch 4 para 59 with effect from 9 February 2009 (by virtue of SI 2009/107 art 2(1), Sch 1 Pt 1). Sub-s (3)(*d*) previously read as follows—

"(*d*) a passenger transport authority or executive within the meaning of Part II of the Transport Act 1968;".

Prospective amendments—Sub-s (3) to be amended by the Greater London Authority Act 1999, s 325, Sch 27 para 68 with effect from a day to be appointed.

In sub-s (3)(*e*), words from "and a port" to "Public Health (Scotland) Act 1897" to be repealed by the Public Health etc (Scotland) Act 2008 s 126(1), Sch 3 Pt 1 with effect from a date to be appointed.

[33A Refunds of VAT to museums and galleries

(1) Subsections (2) to (5) below apply where—

(*a*) VAT is chargeable on—

(i) the supply of goods or services to a body to which this section applies,
(ii) the acquisition of any goods by such a body from another member State, or
(iii) the importation of any goods by such a body from a place outside the member States,

(*b*) the supply, acquisition or importation is attributable to the provision by the body of free rights of admission to a relevant museum or gallery, and

(*c*) the supply is made, or the acquisition or importation takes place, on or after 1st April 2001.

(2) The Commissioners shall, on a claim made by the body in such form and manner as the Commissioners may determine, refund to the body the amount of VAT so chargeable.

(3) The claim must be made before the end of the claim period.

(4) Subject to subsection (5) below, "the claim period" is the period of [4 years][2] beginning with the day on which the supply is made or the acquisition or importation takes place.

(5) If the Commissioners so determine, the claim period is such shorter period beginning with that day as the Commissioners may determine.

(6) Subsection (7) below applies where goods or services supplied to, or acquired or imported by, a body to which this section applies that are attributable to free admissions cannot conveniently be distinguished from goods or services supplied to, or acquired or imported by, the body that are not attributable to free admissions.

(7) The amount to be refunded on a claim by the body under this section shall be such amount as remains after deducting from the VAT related to the claim such proportion of that VAT as appears to the Commissioners to be attributable otherwise than to free admissions.

(8) For the purposes of subsections (6) and (7) above—

(*a*) goods or services are, and VAT is, attributable to free admissions if they are, or it is, attributable to the provision by the body of free rights of admission to a relevant museum or gallery;

(*b*) the VAT related to a claim is the whole of the VAT chargeable on—

(i) the supplies to the body, and

(ii) the acquisitions and importations by the body,

to which the claim relates.

(9) The Treasury may by order—

(*a*) specify a body as being a body to which this section applies;

(*b*) when specifying a body under paragraph (*a*), specify any museum or gallery that, for the purposes of this section, is a "relevant" museum or gallery in relation to the body;

(*c*) specify an additional museum or gallery as being, for the purposes of this section, a "relevant" museum or gallery in relation to a body to which this section applies;

(*d*) when specifying a museum or gallery under paragraph (*b*) or (*c*), provide that this section shall have effect in the case of the museum or gallery as if in subsection (1)(*c*) there were substituted for 1st April 2001 a later date specified in the order.

(10) References in this section to VAT do not include any VAT which, by virtue of any order under section 25(7), is excluded from credit under that section.][1]

Orders—See VAT (Refund of Tax to Museums and Galleries) Order, SI 2001/2879.

Press releases etc—Business Brief 16/01, 19-11-01, Concession for "section 33A" museums and galleries.

Amendments—[1] This section inserted by FA 2001 s 98(2), (10), (11) with effect from 11 May 2001 for the purpose only of the exercise of the power to make orders under sub-s (9). Subject to that, this section comes into force on 1 September 2001.

[2] In sub-s (4) words substituted for words "3 years" by FA 2008 s 118, Sch 39 paras 32, 33 with effect from 1 April 2009 (by virtue of SI 2009/403). FA 2008 Sch 39 para 33 is disregarded where, for the purposes of VATA 1994 s 33A, the day on which the supply was made or the acquisition or importation took place was on or before 31 March 2006 (SI 2009/403 art 3).

34 Capital goods

(1) The Treasury may by order make provision for the giving of relief, in such cases, to such extent and subject to such exceptions as may be specified in the order, from VAT paid on the supply, acquisition or importation for the purpose of a business carried on by any person of machinery or plant or any specified description of machinery or plant in cases where that VAT or part of that VAT cannot be credited under section 25 and such other conditions are satisfied as may be specified in the order.

(2) Without prejudice to the generality of subsection (1) above, an order under this section may provide for relief to be given by deduction or refunding of VAT and for aggregating or excluding the aggregation of value where goods of the same description are supplied, acquired or imported together.

Commentary—*De Voil Indirect Tax Service* **V5.166**.

35 Refund of VAT to persons constructing certain buildings

[(1) Where—

(*a*) a person carries out works to which this section applies,

(*b*) his carrying out of the works is lawful and otherwise than in the course or furtherance of any business, and

(*c*) VAT is chargeable on the supply, acquisition or importation of any goods used by him for the purposes of the works,

the Commissioners shall, on a claim made in that behalf, refund to that person the amount of VAT so chargeable.

(1A) The works to which this section applies are—

(*a*) the construction of a building designed as a dwelling or number of dwellings;

(*b*) the construction of a building for use solely for a relevant residential purpose or relevant charitable purpose; and

(*c*) a residential conversion.

(1B) For the purposes of this section goods shall be treated as used for the purposes of works to which this section applies by the person carrying out the works in so far only as they are building materials which, in the course of the works, are incorporated in the building in question or its site.

(1C) Where—

(*a*) a person ("the relevant person") carries out a residential conversion by arranging for any of the work of the conversion to be done by another ("a contractor"),

(*b*) the relevant person's carrying out of the conversion is lawful and otherwise than in the course or furtherance of any business,

(*c*) the contractor is not acting as an architect, surveyor or consultant or in a supervisory capacity, and

(*d*) VAT is chargeable on services consisting in the work done by the contractor,

the Commissioners shall, on a claim made in that behalf, refund to the relevant person the amount of VAT so chargeable.

(1D) For the purposes of this section works constitute a residential conversion to the extent that they consist in the conversion of a non-residential building, or a non-residential part of a building, into—

(*a*) a building designed as a dwelling or a number of dwellings;

(*b*) a building intended for use solely for a relevant residential purpose; or

(*c*) anything which would fall within paragraph (*a*) or (*b*) above if different parts of a building were treated as separate buildings.][1]

(2) The Commissioners shall not be required to entertain a claim for a refund of VAT under this section unless the claim—

(*a*) is made within such time and in such form and manner, and

(*b*) contains such information, and

(*c*) is accompanied by such documents, whether by way of evidence or otherwise,

as the Commissioners may by regulations prescribe [or, in the case of documents, as the Commissioners may determine in accordance with the regulations][1].

(3) This section shall have effect—

(*a*) as if the reference in subsection (1) above to the VAT chargeable on the supply of any goods included a reference to VAT chargeable on the supply in accordance with the law of another member State; and

(*b*) in relation to VAT chargeable in accordance with the law of another member State, as if references to refunding VAT to any person were references to paying that person an amount equal to the VAT chargeable in accordance with the law of that member State;

and the provisions of this Act and of any other enactment or subordinate legislation (whenever passed or made) so far as they relate to a refund under this section shall be construed accordingly.

[(4) The notes to Group 5 of Schedule 8 shall apply for construing this section as they apply for construing that Group [but this is subject to subsection (4A) below.][2]

[(4A) The meaning of "non-residential" given by Note (7A) of Group 5 of Schedule 8 (and not that given by Note (7) of that Group) applies for the purposes of this section but as if—

(*a*) references in that Note to item 3 of that Group were references to this section, and

(*b*) paragraph (*b*)(iii) of that Note were omitted.][2]

(5) The power of the Treasury by order under section 30 to vary Schedule 8 shall include—

(*a*) power to apply any variation made by the order for the purposes of this section; and

(*b*) power to make such consequential modifications of this section as they may think fit.][1]

Commentary—*De Voil Indirect Tax Service* **V5.164**.
Regulations—See VAT Regulations, SI 1995/2518 regs 200, 201.
Press releases etc—News Release 15/96, 13-3-96 (C&E will consider making refunds of VAT under the DIY scheme to certain charitable organisations, even though they are in business, which are unable to sell the converted property).
Simon's Tax Cases—*C&E Comrs v Arnold* [1996] STC 1271*; *C&E Comrs v Blom-Cooper* [2002] STC 1061, [2003] STC 669; *C&E Comrs v Jacobs* [2005] STC 1518.
Definitions—"Acquisition of goods from another member State", s 11; "another member State", s 96(1); "building designed as a dwelling or number of dwellings", Sch 8 Group 5 note (2); "building materials", Sch 8 Group 5 note (22); "business", s 94; "the Commissioners", s 96(1); "document", s 96(1); "importation of goods from a place outside the member States", s 15; "law of another member State", s 92; "non-residential building", Sch 8 Group 5 note (7); "regulations", s 96(1); "relevant charitable purpose", Sch 8 Group 5 note (6); "relevant residential purpose", Sch 8 Group 5 note (4); "subordinate legislation", s 96(10); "supply", s 5, Sch 4; "VAT", ss 1, 96(1); "zero-rating", s 30.
Cross references—See VATA 1994 s 60(1), (2) (civil penalty for evading VAT by dishonestly claiming a refund under this section);
VATA 1994 s 72(1), (2) (criminal penalty for fraudulent evasion of VAT by falsely claiming a refund under this section);
VATA 1994 s 83 (appeal to a tribunal in respect of the amount of a refund under this section);
VATA 1994 s 90(3) (VAT repaid as a result of the failure of a resolution under PCTA 1968 may not be refunded under this section).
VAT (Isle of Man) Order, SI 1982/1067 art 9 (this section does not apply to the construction of dwellings in the Isle of Man).
VAT (Conversion of Buildings) Order, SI 2001/2305 art 4 (VATA 1994 Sch 8 Group 5 note (7A)shall apply for the purposes of this section).
Amendments—[1] Sub-ss (1), (1A)–(1D) substituted for sub-s (1), words in sub-s (2) inserted and sub-ss (4), (5) added by FA 1996 s 30, with effect in relation to any case in which a claim for repayment under this section is made at any time on or after 29 April 1996.
[2] Sub-s (4) amended, and sub-s (4A) inserted, by the VAT (Conversion of Buildings) Order, SI 2001/2305 arts 1, 4 with effect for supplies made after 31 July 2001.

36 Bad debts

(1) Subsection (2) below applies where—

VAT

(*a*) a person has supplied goods or services [...][2] and has accounted for and paid VAT on the supply,

(*b*) the whole or any part of the consideration for the supply has been written off in his accounts as a bad debt, and

(*c*) a period of 6 months (beginning with the date of the supply) has elapsed.

(2) Subject to the following provisions of this section and to regulations under it the person shall be entitled, on making a claim to the Commissioners, to a refund of the amount of VAT chargeable by reference to the outstanding amount.

[(3) In subsection (2) above "the outstanding amount" means—

(*a*) if at the time of the claim no part of the consideration written off in the claimant's accounts as a bad debt has been received, an amount equal to the amount of the consideration so written off;

(*b*) if at that time any part of the consideration so written off has been received, an amount by which that part is exceeded by the amount of the consideration written off;

and in this subsection "received" means received either by the claimant or by a person to whom has been assigned a right to receive the whole or any part of the consideration written off.][5]

[(3A) For the purposes of this section, where the whole or any part of the consideration for the supply does not consist of money, the amount in money that shall be taken to represent any non-monetary part of the consideration shall be so much of the amount made up of—

(*a*) the value of the supply, and

(*b*) the VAT charged on the supply,

as is attributable to the non-monetary consideration in question.][4]

(4) A person shall not be entitled to a refund under subsection (2) above unless—

(*a*) the value of the supply is equal to or less than its open market value, ...[1]

(*b*) ...[1]

(4A) ...[7]

(5) Regulations under this section may—

(*a*) require a claim to be made at such time and in such form and manner as may be specified by or under the regulations;

(*b*) require a claim to be evidenced and quantified by reference to such records and other documents as may be so specified;

(*c*) require the claimant to keep, for such period and in such form and manner as may be so specified, those records and documents and a record of such information relating to the claim and to [anything subsequently received][3] by way of consideration as may be so specified;

(*d*) require the repayment of a refund allowed under this section where any requirement of the regulations is not complied with;

(*e*) require the repayment of the whole or, as the case may be, an appropriate part of a refund allowed under this section [where any part (or further part) of the consideration written off in the claimant's accounts as a bad debt is subsequently received either by the claimant or, except in such circumstances as may be prescribed, by a person to whom has been assigned a right to receive the whole or any part of that consideration;][6]

(*ea*) ...[7]

(*f*) include such supplementary, incidental, consequential or transitional provisions as appear to the Commissioners to be necessary or expedient for the purposes of this section;

(*g*) make different provision for different circumstances.

(6) The provisions which may be included in regulations by virtue of subsection (5)(*f*) above may include rules for ascertaining—

(*a*) whether, when and to what extent consideration is to be taken to have been written off in accounts as a bad debt;

(*b*) whether [anything received][3] is to be taken as received by way of consideration for a particular supply;

(*c*) whether, and to what extent, [anything received][3] is to be taken as received by way of consideration written off in accounts as a bad debt.

(7) The provisions which may be included in regulations by virtue of subsection (5)(*f*) above may include rules dealing with particular cases, such as those involving [receipt of part of the consideration][3] or mutual debts; and in particular such rules may vary the way in which the following amounts are to be calculated—

(*a*) the outstanding amount mentioned in subsection (2) above, and

(*b*) the amount of any repayment where a refund has been allowed under this section.

(8) Section 6 shall apply for determining the time when a supply is to be treated as taking place for the purposes of construing this section.

Commentary—*De Voil Indirect Tax Service* **V5.156.**
Regulations—VAT Regulations, SI 1995/2518 regs 156–172.
Press releases etc—Business Brief 9/97, 27-3-97 (changes to the VAT bad debt relief scheme). Business Brief 21/97, 3-10-97 (bad debt relief scheme changes for barter transactions). Business Brief 5/98 10.2.98 (VAT bad debt relief—insolvency practitioners). Business Brief 19/01, 6-12-01 (VAT—bad debt relief on goods supplied by hire purchase or conditional sale).
Simon's Tax Cases—*Goldsmiths (Jewellers) Ltd v C&E Comrs* (Case C-330/95) [1997] STC 1073*.

Definitions—"The Commissioners", s 96(1); "document", s 96(1); "money", s 96(1); "open market value of a supply of goods or services", s 19(5); "regulations", s 96(1); "supply", s 5, Sch 4; "VAT", ss 1, 96(1); "value of supply of goods or services", s 19, Sch 6.
Cross references—See VATA 1994 s 60(1), (2) (civil penalty for evading VAT by dishonestly claiming a refund under this section);
VATA 1994 s 72(1), (2) (criminal penalty for fraudulent evasion of VAT by falsely claiming a refund under this section);
VATA 1994 s 83 (appeal to a tribunal in respect of a claim for a refund under this section);
VATA 1994 Sch 13 para 9 (claims for refunds of VAT relating to supplies made between 1 April 1989 and 31 August 1994).
Value Added Tax Regulations, SI 1995/2158 reg 6(3)(*d*) (rights to claims for refunds of VAT on transfer of going concern).
FA 1999 s 15(4) (Value Added Tax Regulations, SI 1995/2518 Part XIX, other than reg 171, shall, subject to provisions made under VATA 1994 s 36, be read as if a reference to a payment being received by the claimant includes a payment received by a person to whom a right to receive it has been assigned).
Amendments—[1] Sub-s (4)(*b*), and the word "and" immediately preceding it, repealed by FA 1997 s 39(1), Sch 18 Pt IV(3) in respect of any claim made under this section in relation to a supply of goods made after 19 March 1997.
[2] In sub-s (1)(*a*) the words "for a consideration in money" repealed by FA 1998 s 23(1), Sch 27 Part II with effect from 31 July 1998.
[3] Words in sub-ss (3)(*a*), (*b*), (5)(*c*), (6)(*b*), (*c*) and (7) substituted by FA 1998 s 23 with effect from 31 July 1998.
[4] Sub-s (3A) inserted by FA 1998 s 23 with effect from 31 July 1998.
[5] Sub-s (3) substituted by FA 1999 s 15 with effect for the purposes of the making of any refund or repayment after 9 March 1999, but do not have effect in relation to anything received on or before that day.
[6] Words in sub-s (5)(*e*) substituted by FA 1999 s 15 with effect from 27 July 1999.
[7] Sub-ss (4A) and (5)(*ea*) repealed by FA 2002 ss 22(2), (3), 139, Sch 40 Pt 2(1) with effect for supplies made after 31 December 2002 (by virtue of SI 2002/3028).

[Acquisitions

36A Relief from VAT on acquisition if importation would attract relief

(1) The Treasury may by order make provision for relieving from VAT the acquisition from another member State of any goods if, or to the extent that, relief from VAT would be given by an order under section 37 if the acquisition were an importation from a place outside the member States.

(2) An order under this section may provide for relief to be subject to such conditions as appear to the Treasury to be necessary or expedient.

These may—

(*a*) include conditions prohibiting or restricting the disposal of or dealing with the goods concerned;

(*b*) be framed by reference to the conditions to which, by virtue of any order under section 37 in force at the time of the acquisition, relief under such an order would be subject in the case of an importation of the goods concerned.

(3) Where relief from VAT given by an order under this section was subject to a condition that has been breached or not complied with, the VAT shall become payable at the time of the breach or, as the case may be, at the latest time allowed for compliance.][1]

Commentary—*De Voil Indirect Tax Service* **V3.398**.
Orders—See the VAT (Acquisitions) Relief Order, SI 2002/1935.
Amendments—[1] This section inserted by FA 2002 s 25 with effect from 24 July 2002.

Imports, overseas businesses etc

37 Relief from VAT on importation of goods

(1) The Treasury may by order make provision for giving relief from the whole or part of the VAT chargeable on the importation of goods from places outside the member States, subject to such conditions (including conditions prohibiting or restricting the disposal of or dealing with the goods) as may be imposed by or under the order, if and so far as the relief appears to the Treasury to be necessary or expedient, having regard to any international agreement or arrangements.

(2) In any case where—

(*a*) it is proposed that goods which have been imported from a place outside the member States by any person ("the original importer") with the benefit of relief under subsection (1) above shall be transferred to another person ("the transferee"), and

(*b*) on an application made by the transferee, the Commissioners direct that this subsection shall apply,

this Act shall have effect as if, on the date of the transfer of the goods (and in place of the transfer), the goods were exported by the original importer and imported by the transferee and, accordingly, where appropriate, provision made under subsection (1) above shall have effect in relation to the VAT chargeable on the importation of the goods by the transferee.

(3) The Commissioners may by regulations make provision for remitting or repaying, if they think fit, the whole or part of the VAT chargeable on the importation of any goods from places outside the member States which are shown to their satisfaction to have been previously exported from the United Kingdom or removed from any member State.

(4) The Commissioners may by regulations make provision for remitting or repaying the whole or part of the VAT chargeable on the importation of any goods from places outside the member States if they are satisfied that the goods have been or are to be re-exported or otherwise removed from the United Kingdom and they think fit to do so in all the circumstances and having regard—

(*a*) to the VAT chargeable on the supply of like goods in the United Kingdom;
(*b*) to any VAT which may have become chargeable in another member State in respect of the goods

Commentary—*De Voil Indirect Tax Service* **V3.316**.
Regulations—See VAT Regulations, SI 1995/2518 regs 123–126.
Orders—See VAT (Imported Goods) Relief Order, SI 1984/746; VAT (Small Non-commercial Consignments) Relief Order, SI 1986/939; VAT (Imported Gold) Relief Order, SI 1992/3124; VAT (Importation of Investment Gold) Relief Order, SI 1999/3115.
Press releases etc—News Release 35/97, 12-12-97 (New VAT avoidance on property developments blocked).
Definitions—"Another member State", s 96(1); "the Commissioners", s 96(1); "importation of goods from places outside the member States", s 15; "regulations", s 96(1); "supply" s 5, Sch 4; "United Kingdom", s 96(11); "VAT", ss 1, 96(1).
Cross references—See FA 1999 s 13(3) (an order made under s 37(1) which gives relief from VAT on certain importations of gold may make provision by reference to public notices).

38 Importation of goods by taxable persons

The Commissioners may by regulations make provision for enabling goods imported from a place outside the member States by a taxable person in the course or furtherance of any business carried on by him to be delivered or removed, subject to such conditions or restrictions as the Commissioners may impose for the protection of the revenue, without payment of the VAT chargeable on the importation, and for that VAT to be accounted for together with the VAT chargeable on the supply of goods or services by him or on the acquisition of goods by him from other member States.

Commentary—*De Voil Indirect Tax Service* **V5.122**.
Regulations—See VAT Regulations, SI 1995/2518 reg 122.
Definitions—"Acquisition of goods from other member States", s 11; "business", s 94; "the Commissioners", s 96(1); "goods imported from a place outside the member States", s 15; "other member States", s 96(1); "regulations", s 96(1); "supply", s 5, Sch 4; "taxable person", s 3; "VAT", ss 1, 96(1).
Cross references—See VATA 1994 s 43(1) (VAT groups: goods imported by group companies to be treated as imported by representative member for purposes of this section).
VAT (Isle of Man) Order, SI 1982/1067 art 8 (taxable persons for the purposes of Isle of Man VAT legislation to be treated as taxable persons for the purposes of this section).

39 Repayment of VAT to those in business overseas

(1) The Commissioners may, by means of a scheme embodied in regulations, provide for the repayment, to persons to whom this section applies, of VAT on supplies to them in the United Kingdom or on the importation of goods by them from places outside the member States which would be input tax of theirs if they were taxable persons in the United Kingdom.

(2) This section—

(*a*) applies to persons carrying on business in another member State, and
(*b*) shall apply also to persons carrying on business in other countries, if, pursuant to any Community Directive, rules are adopted by the Council of the Communities about refunds of VAT to persons established elsewhere than in the member States,

but does not apply to persons carrying on business in the United Kingdom.

(3) Repayment shall be made in such cases [and to such extent][1] only, and subject to such conditions, as the scheme may prescribe (being conditions specified in the regulations or imposed by the Commissioners either generally or in particular cases); and the scheme may provide—

(*a*) for claims and repayments to be made only through agents in the United Kingdom;
(*b*) either generally or for specified purposes—

(i) for the agents to be treated under this Act as if they were taxable persons; and
(ii) for treating claims as if they were returns under this Act [in respect of such period as may be prescribed][1] and repayments as if they were repayments of input tax;

[(*ba*) for and in connection with the payment of interest to or by the Commissioners (including in relation to the repayment of interest wrongly paid), and][1]
(*c*) for generally regulating the [time by which and manner in which claims must be made][1] the amount of any repayment is to be determined and the repayment is to be made.

Commentary—*De Voil Indirect Tax Service* **V5.151, V5.152**.
Regulations—See VAT Regulations, SI 1995/2518 regs 173–197.
Definitions—"Another member State", s 96(1); "business", s 94; "the Commissioners", s 96(1); "importation of goods from places outside the member States", s 15; "input tax", s 24; "regulations", s 96(1); "supply", s 5, Sch 4; "taxable person", s 3; "United Kingdom", s 96(11); "VAT", ss 1, 96(1).
Cross references—See VATA 1994 s 54(5) (supplies under flat rate scheme for farmers: power to provide for repayment of percentage of consideration paid by persons carrying on business overseas as if it were VAT);
VATA 1994 s 60(1), (2) (civil penalty for evading VAT by dishonestly claiming a repayment under this section);
VATA 1994 s 72(1), (2) (criminal penalty for fraudulent evasion of VAT by falsely claiming a repayment under this section).
VAT (Isle of Man) Order, SI 1982/1067 art 7 (references to VAT in this section to include references to VAT chargeable under Isle of Man legislation).
Amendments—[1] In sub-s (3) words inserted, para (*ba*) inserted and in para (*c*) words "methods by which" substituted, by FA 2009 s 77 with effect from 21 July 2009.

[39A Applications for forwarding of VAT repayment claims to other member States

The Commissioners must make arrangements for dealing with applications made to the Commissioners by taxable persons, in accordance with Council Directive 2008/9/EC, for the forwarding to the tax authorities of another member State of claims for refunds of VAT on—

(*a*) supplies to them in that member State, or
(*b*) the importation of goods by them into that member State from places outside the member States.][1]

Amendments—[1] Section 39A inserted by FA 2009 s 77 with effect from 21 July 2009.

40 Refunds in relation to new means of transport supplied to other member States

(1) Subject to subsection (2) below, where a person who is not a taxable person makes such a supply of goods consisting in a new means of transport as involves the removal of the goods to another member State, the Commissioners shall, on a claim made in that behalf, refund to that person, as the case may be—

(*a*) the amount of any VAT on the supply of that means of transport to that person, or
(*b*) the amount of any VAT paid by that person on the acquisition of that means of transport from another member State or on its importation from a place outside the member States.

(2) The amount of VAT refunded under this section shall not exceed the amount that would have been payable on the supply involving the removal if it had been a taxable supply by a taxable person and had not been zero-rated.

(3) The Commissioners shall not be entitled to entertain a claim for refund of VAT under this section unless the claim—

(*a*) is made within such time and in such form and manner;
(*b*) contains such information; and
(*c*) is accompanied by such documents, whether by way of evidence or otherwise,

as the Commissioners may by regulations prescribe.

Commentary—*De Voil Indirect Tax Service* **V5.154**.
Regulations—See VAT Regulations, SI 1995/2518 regs 146, 149–154.
Definitions—"Acquisition from another member State", s 11; "another member State", s 96(1); "the Commissioners", s 96(1); "document", s 96(1); "importation from a place outside the member States", s 15; "means of transport", s 95; "new means of transport", s 95; "regulations", s 96(1); "supply", s 5, Sch 4; "taxable person", s 3; "taxable supply", s 4(2); "VAT", ss 1, 96(1); "zero-rated", s 30.
Cross references—See VATA 1994 s 60(1), (2) (civil penalty for evading VAT by dishonestly claiming a refund under this section);
VATA 1994 s 72(1), (2) (criminal penalty for fraudulent evasion of VAT by falsely claiming a refund under this section);
VATA 1994 s 83 (appeal to a tribunal in respect of the amount of a refund under this section);
VATA 1994 s 90(3) (VAT repaid as a result of the failure of a resolution under PCTA 1968 may not be refunded under this section).

PART III

APPLICATION OF ACT IN PARTICULAR CASES

Cross reference—See VATA 1994 Sch 13 para 6 (VATA 1983 s 32B (overseas suppliers accounting through their customers) is to continue to apply in relation to supplies to which s 14 of this Act (acquisitions from persons belonging in other member states) does not apply by virtue of s 14(8) (supplies before 1 August 1993), and for that purpose s 32B is to be treated as if it were included in this Part of this Act).

41 Application to the Crown

(1) This Act shall apply in relation to taxable supplies by the Crown as it applies in relation to taxable supplies by taxable persons.

(2) Where the supply by a Government department of any goods or services does not amount to the carrying on of a business but it appears to the Treasury that similar goods or services are or might be supplied by taxable persons in the course or furtherance of any business, then, if and to the extent that the Treasury so direct, the supply of those goods or services by that department shall be treated for the purposes of this Act as a supply in the course or furtherance of any business carried on by it.

(3) Where VAT is chargeable on the supply of goods or services to a Government department, on the acquisition of any goods by a Government department from another member State or on the importation of any goods by a Government department from a place outside the member States and the supply, acquisition or importation is not for the purpose—

(*a*) of any business carried on by the department, or
(*b*) of a supply by the department which, by virtue of a direction under subsection (2) above, is treated as a supply in the course or furtherance of a business,

then, if and to the extent that the Treasury so direct and subject to subsection (4) below, the Commissioners shall, on a claim made by the department at such time and in such form and manner as the Commissioners may determine, refund to it the amount of the VAT so chargeable.

(4) The Commissioners may make the refunding of any amount due under subsection (3) above conditional upon compliance by the claimant with requirements with respect to the keeping, preservation and production of records relating to the supply, acquisition or importation in question.

(5) For the purposes of this section goods or services obtained by one Government department from another Government department shall be treated, if and to the extent that the Treasury so direct, as supplied by that other department and similarly as regards goods or services obtained by or from the Crown Estate Commissioners.

(6) In this section "Government department" includes [the Scottish Administration][2] [, the [Welsh Assembly Government][7]][1], a Northern Ireland department, a Northern Ireland health and social services body, any body of persons exercising functions on behalf of a Minister of the Crown, including ...[4] and any part of a Government department (as defined in the foregoing) designated for the purposes of this subsection by a direction of the Treasury.

(7) For the purposes of subsection (6) above, [a health service body as defined in section 60(7) of the National Health Service and Community Care Act 1990, and a National Health Service trust established under Part I of that Act][4] or the National Health Service (Scotland) Act 1978 [an NHS foundation trust][6] [and a Primary Care Trust][3] [and a Local Health Board][5] shall be regarded as a body of persons exercising functions on behalf of a Minister of the Crown.

(8) In subsection (6) "a Northern Ireland health and social services body" means—

(*a*) a health and social services body as defined in Article 7(6) of the Health and Personal Social Services (Northern Ireland) Order 1991; and

(*b*) a Health and Social Services trust established under that Order.

Commentary—*De Voil Indirect Tax Service* **V5.161**.

Press releases etc—C&E Business Brief 18/03 (extent to which government departments and NHS bodies can recover VAT on two new types of PFI arrangement).

London Gazette 12-4-96 (Treasury direction dated 1 April 1996 under sub-ss (2), (5) and (6) above).

London Gazette 2-7-96 (amended Treasury direction dated 2 July 1996 under sub-s (3) above).

London Gazette 10-1-03 (amended Treasury direction dated 2 December 2002 under sub-s (3) above).

Definitions—"Acquisition of goods from another member State", s 11; "another member State", s 96(1); "business", s 94; "the Commissioners", s 96(1); "importation of goods from a place outside the member States", s 15; "supply", s 5, Sch 4; "taxable person", s 3; "taxable supply", s 4(2); "VAT", ss 1, 96(1).

Amendments—[1] Words in sub-s (6) inserted by the Government of Wales Act 1998 Sch 12 para 35 with effect from 1 April 1999 by virtue of the Government of Wales Act 1998 (Commencement No 4) Order, SI 1999/782.

[2] Words in sub-s (6) inserted by the Scotland Act 1998 Sch 8 para 30, with effect from 6 May 1999 by virtue of by the Scotland Act 1998 (Commencement) Order SI 1998/3178.

[3] Words in sub-s (7) inserted by the Health Act 1999 s 65 Sch 8 para 86 with effect from 1 April 2000 (by virtue of the Health Act 1999 (Commencement No 2) Order, SI 1999/2342 art 2(4)(*b*)(*iii*)).

[4] Words in sub-s (6) revoked and words in sub-s (7) substituted by the Health Act 1999 (Supplementary, Consequential etc Provisions) Order, SI 2000/90 art 3(1), Sch 1 para 29 with effect from 8 February 2000.

[5] Words inserted by the National Health Service Reform and Health Care Professions Act 2002 s 6(2), Sch 5 para 40 with effect from 10 October 2002 (by virtue of SI 2002/2532).

[6] Words in sub-s (7) inserted by the Health and Social Care (Community Health and Standards) Act 2003 s 33(3) with effect from 1 April 2004 (by virtue of SI 2004/759, art 2).

[7] Words in sub-s (6) substituted by the Government of Wales Act 2006, s 160(1), Sch 10, para 39 with effect from 25 May 2007, being the date on which the initial period ended (following the appointment of the First Minister) (Government of Wales Act 2006, ss 46, 161(4), (5)).

42 Local authorities

A local authority which makes taxable supplies is liable to be registered under this Act, whatever the value of the supplies; and accordingly Schedule 1 shall apply, in a case where the value of the taxable supplies made by a local authority in any period of one year does not exceed the sum for the time being specified in paragraph 1(1)(*a*) of that Schedule, as if that value exceeded that sum.

Commentary—*De Voil Indirect Tax Service* **V2.108**.

Press releases etc—C&E Business Brief 9/95 18-5-95 (services between local authorities).

C&E Business Brief 9/95 18-5-95 (VAT standard rated on local authority sporting services).

C&E Business Brief 23/95 24-10-95 and 26/95, 11-12-95 (building regulation fees charged by local authorities are outside the scope of VAT except where there is competition to supply building regulation services).

New release 10/96, 16-2-96 (refunds of VAT incorrectly charged by local authorities on building regulation fees).

Definitions—"Local authority", s 96(1), (4); "registered", s 3(3); "taxable supply", s 4(2); "value of supply", s 19, Sch 6.

43 Groups of companies

(1) Where under [sections 43A to 43D][10] any bodies corporate are treated as members of a group, any business carried on by a member of the group shall be treated as carried on by the representative member, and—

(*a*) any supply of goods or services by a member of the group to another member of the group shall be disregarded; and

(*b*) any [supply which is a supply to which paragraph (*a*) above does not apply and is a supply][1] of goods or services by or to a member of the group shall be treated as a supply by or to the representative member; and

(*c*) any VAT paid or payable by a member of the group on the acquisition of goods from another member State or on the importation of goods from a place outside the member States shall be treated as paid or payable by the representative member and the goods shall be treated—

(i) in the case of goods acquired from another member State, for the purposes of section 73(7); and

(ii) in the case of goods imported from a place outside the member States, for those purposes and the purposes of section 38,

as acquired or, as the case may be, imported by the representative member;

and all members of the group shall be liable jointly and severally for any VAT due from the representative member.

[(1AA) Where—

(*a*) it is material, for the purposes of any provision made by or under this Act ('the relevant provision'), whether the person by or to whom a supply is made, or the person by whom goods are acquired or imported, is a person of a particular description,

(*b*) paragraph (*b*) or (*c*) of subsection (1) above applies to any supply, acquisition or importation, and

(*c*) there is a difference that would be material for the purposes of the relevant provision between—

(i) the description applicable to the representative member, and

(ii) the description applicable to the body which (apart from this section) would be regarded for the purposes of this Act as making the supply, acquisition or importation or, as the case may be, as being the person to whom the supply is made.

the relevant provision shall have effect in relation to that supply, acquisition or importation as if the only description applicable to the representative member were the description in fact applicable to that body.][5]

[(1AB) Subsection (1AA) above does not apply to the extent that what is material for the purposes of the relevant provision is whether a person is a taxable person."][5]

[(1A) …][4]

(2) An order under section 5(5) or (6) may make provision for securing that any goods or services which, if all the members of the group were one person, would fall to be treated under that section as supplied to and by that person, are treated as supplied to and by the representative member [and may provide for that purpose that the representative member is to be treated as a person of such description as may be determined under the order][6].

[(2A) A supply made by a member of a group ('the supplier') to another member of the group ('the UK member') shall not be disregarded under subsection (*1*)(*a*) above if—

(*a*) it would (if there were no group) be a supply of services [to which section 7A(2)(*a*) applies made][11] to a person belonging in the United Kingdom;

(*b*) those services are not within any of the descriptions specified in Schedule 9;

(*c*) the supplier has been supplied (whether or not by a person belonging in the United Kingdom) with [any services …[11] which do not fall within any of the descriptions specified in Schedule 9][8] [and section 7A(2)(*a*) applied to the supply][11];

(*d*) the supplier belonged outside the United Kingdom when it was supplied with the services mentioned in paragraph (*c*) above; and

(*e*) the services so mentioned have been used by the supplier for making the supply to the UK member.][7]

[(2B) Subject to subsection (2C) below, where a supply is excluded by virtue of subsection (2A) above from the supplies that are disregarded in pursuance of subsection (1)(*a*) above, all the same consequences shall follow under this Act as if that supply—

(*a*) were a taxable supply in the United Kingdom by the representative member to itself, and

(*b*) without prejudice to that, were made by the representative member in the course or furtherance of its business.][7]

[(2C) [Except in so far as the Commissioners may be regulations otherwise provide][9] a supply which is deemed by virtue of subsection (2B) above to be a supply by the representative member to itself—

(*a*) shall not be taken into account as a supply made by the representative member when determining any allowance of input tax under section 26(1) in the case of the representative member;

(*b*) shall be deemed for the purposes of paragraph 1 of Schedule 6 to be a supply in the case of which the person making the supply and the person supplied are connected within the meaning of section 839 of the Taxes Act (connected persons); and

(*c*) subject to paragraph (*b*) above, shall be taken to be a supply the value and time of which are determined as if it were a supply of services which is treated by virtue of section 8 as made by the person by whom the services are received.][7]

[(2D) For the purposes of subsection (2A) above where—

(*a*) there has been a supply of the assets of a business of a person ('the transferor') to a person to whom the whole or any part of that business was transferred as a going concern ('the transferee'),

(*b*) that supply is either—

(i) a supply falling to be treated, in accordance with an order under section 5(3), as being neither a supply of goods nor a supply of services, or

(ii) a supply that would have fallen to be so treated if it had taken place in the United Kingdom,

and

(*c*) the transferor was supplied with services ...[11] at a time before the transfer when the transferor belonged outside the United Kingdom [and section 7A(2)(*a*) applied to the supply][11],

those services, so far as they are used by the transferee for making any supply [to which section 7A(2)(*a*) applies][11], shall be deemed to have been supplied to the transferee at a time when the transferee belonged outside the United Kingdom.][7]

[(2E) Where, in the case of a supply of assets falling within paragraphs (*a*) and (*b*) of subsection (2D) above—

(*a*) the transferor himself acquired any of the assets in question by way of a previous supply of assets falling within those paragraphs, and

(*b*) [there is a supply to which section 7A(2)(*a*) applies of services which, if used by the transferor for making such a supply][11], would be deemed by virtue of that subsection to have been supplied to the transferor at a time when he belonged outside the United Kingdom,

that subsection shall have effect, notwithstanding that the services have not been so used by the transferor, as if the transferor were a person to whom those services were supplied and as if he were a person belonging outside the United Kingdom at the time of their deemed supply to him; and this subsection shall apply accordingly through any number of successive supplies of assets falling within paragraphs (*a*) and (*b*) of that subsection.][7]

(3)–(8) ...[2]

[(9) Schedule 9A (which makes provision for ensuring that this section is not used for tax avoidance) shall have effect.][3]

Commentary—*De Voil Indirect Tax Service* **V2.190**.

Orders—See VAT (Self-supply of Construction Services) Order, SI 1989/472; VAT (Cars) Order, SI 1992/3122; VAT (Special Provisions) Order, SI 1995/1268.

Press releases etc—C&E Business Brief 31/97 22.12.97 (Refusing applications for group treatment to protect the revenue). C&E Business Brief 15/99 12/7/99 (New anti-avoidance provisions).

Simon's Tax Cases—*C&E Comrs v Kingfisher plc* [1994] STC 63*; *C&E Comrs v Thorn Materials Supply Ltd and Thorn Resources Ltd* [1998] STC 725*; *C&E Comrs v Barclays Bank plc* [2000] STC 665; *R&C Comrs v Gracechurch Management Services Ltd* [2008] STC 795.

Definitions—"Acquisition of goods from another member State", s 11; "another member State", s 96(1); "belonging", s 9(2), (3); "business", s 94; "the Commissioners", s 96(1); "importation of goods from a place outside the member States", s 15; "prescribed accounting period", s 25(1); "supply", s 5, Sch 4; "taxable person", s 3; "United Kingdom", s 96(11); "VAT", ss 1, 96(1).

Cross references—See VATA 1994 s 43(1)(*d*) (tour operators: provision for orders excluding a body corporate from the application of this section);

VATA 1994 s 83 (appeal to a tribunal in respect of the refusal of an application under this section);

VATA 1994 Sch 9A para 2(2) (assumption that supply does not fall within sub-s (1)(*a*) above to the extent that the Commissioners so direct);

VATA 1994 Sch 9A para 2(3) (assumption that a body corporate is (not) to be treated as a member of a group where the Commissioners so direct).

VAT (Isle of Man) Order, SI 1982/1067 art 10 (supplies made both in UK and in Isle of Man: determination of representative member of group);

VAT (Isle of Man) Order, SI 1982/1067 art 11(6) (group member acquiring an establishment in the Isle of Man: notification required);

VAT (Tour Operators) Order, SI 1987/1806 art 13 (tour operators: eligibility for treatment as group members);

VAT (Self-supply of Construction Services) Order, SI 1989/472 art 3(4) (construction supplies by group members otherwise than for consideration);

VAT (Cars) Order, SI 1992/3122 art 7 (deemed self-supplies of cars by group members);

VAT (Payments on Account) Order, SI 1993/2001 art 17 (payments on account by group members);

VAT (Special Provisions) Order, SI 1995/1268 art 11(4) (deemed self-supplies of printed matter by group members).

FA 1999 Sch 2 paras 6(1), (3), (4) (transitional provisions—VAT groups anti-avoidance legislation).

Amendments—[1] Words in sub-s (1)(*b*) substituted by FA 1995 s 25(2), (5), with effect in relation to any supply made on or after 1 March 1995 and any supply made before that date in the case of which both the body making the supply and the body supplied continued to be members of the group in question until at least that date.

[2] Words in sub-ss (3) to (8) repealed by FA 1999 s 16, Sch 2 para 1 with effect from 27 July 1999, subject to FA 1999 Sch 2 para 6.

[3] Sub-s (9) added by FA 1996 s 31(1) with effect from 29 April 1996.

[4] Sub-s (1A) (inserted by FA 1995 s 25(2)) repealed by FA 1996 s 31(5), Sch 41 Pt IV(5) with effect in relation to supplies on or after 29 April 1996.

[5] Sub-ss (1AA) and (1AB) inserted by FA 1997 s 40(1) in relation to any supply made after 26 November 1996 and in relation to any acquisition or importation taking place after that date.

[6] Words in sub-s (2) inserted by FA 1997 s 40(2) with effect from 19 March 1997.

[7] Sub-ss (2A)–(2E) inserted by FA 1997 s 41 in relation to supplies made on or after 26 November 1996.

[8] Words in sub-s (2A) (*c*) substituted by FA 1997 s 41(3), (4) in relation to supplies made after 19 March 1997. In relation to supplies made after 25 November 1996 and before 20 March 1997, the substituted words read 'services falling within any of paragraphs 1 to 8 of Schedule 5'.

[9] Words in sub-s (2C) inserted by FA 1997 s 41 (4)(5) in relation to supplies made after 19 March 1997.

[10] Words in sub-s (1) substituted by FA 2004 s 20(3) with effect from 22 July 2004.

[11] In sub-s (2A)(*a*) words "falling within Schedule 5", in sub-s (2D) "falling within that Schedule", in sub-s (2E)(*b*) "there are services falling within paragraphs 1 to 8 of Schedule 5 which, if used by the transferor for making supplies falling within that Schedule" substituted, in sub-ss (2A)(*c*), (2D)(*c*) words inserted and "falling within paragraphs 1 to 8 of Schedule 5" repealed, by FA 2009 s 76, Sch 36 paras 1, 7, 14, with effect from 1 January 2010. The references to a supply to which s 7A(2) applies include a supply of services falling within Sch 5 paras 1 to 8 made before that date.

[43A Groups: eligibility

(1) Two or more bodies corporate are eligible to be treated as members of a group if each is established or has a fixed establishment in the United Kingdom and—

(*a*) one of them controls each of the others,

(*b*) one person (whether a body corporate or an individual) controls all of them, or

(*c*) two or more individuals carrying on a business in partnership control all of them.

(2) For the purposes of this section a body corporate shall be taken to control another body corporate if it is empowered by statute to control that body's activities or if it is that body's holding company within the meaning of section [1159 of and Schedule 6 to][2] the Companies Act [2006][2].

(3) For the purposes of this section an individual or individuals shall be taken to control a body corporate if he or they, were he or they a company, would be that body's holding company within the meaning of [those provisions][2].][1]

Commentary—*De Voil Indirect Tax Service* **V2.190**.
Cross references—See the VAT (Groups: eligibility) Order, SI 2004/1931 (modification regarding this section).
Press releases etc—C&E Business Brief 15/99 12/7/99 (New anti-avoidance provisions).
Amendments—[1] This section inserted by FA 1999 s 16, Sch 2 para 2 with effect from 27 July 1999, subject to FA 1999 Sch 2 para 6.
[2] In sub-s (2), words substituted for words "736 of" and "1985", and in sub-s (3), words substituted for words "that section", by the Companies Act 2006 (Consequential Amendments) (Taxes and National Insurance) Order, SI 2009/1890 art 4(1)(*j*), (3) with effect from 1 October 2009.

[43AA Power to alter eligibility for grouping

(1) The Treasury may by order provide for section 43A to have effect with specified modifications in relation to a specified class of person.

(2) An order under subsection (1) may, in particular—

(*a*) make provision by reference to generally accepted accounting practice;
(*b*) define generally accepted accounting practice for that purpose by reference to a specified document or instrument (and may provide for the reference to be read as including a reference to any later document or instrument that amends or replaces the first);
(*c*) adopt any statutory or other definition of generally accepted accounting practice (with or without modification);
(*d*) make provision by reference to what would be required or permitted by generally accepted accounting practice if accounts, or accounts of a specified kind, were prepared for a person.

(3) An order under subsection (1) may also, in particular, make provision by reference to—

(*a*) the nature of a person;
(*b*) past or intended future activities of a person;
(*c*) the relationship between a number of persons;
(*d*) the effect of including a person within a group or of excluding a person from a group.

(4) An order under subsection (1) may—

(*a*) make provision which applies generally or only in specified circumstances;
(*b*) make different provision for different circumstances;
(*c*) include supplementary, incidental, consequential or transitional provision.][1]

Commentary—*De Voil Indirect Tax Service* **V2.190**.
Orders—See VAT (Groups: eligibility) Order, SI 2004/1931.
Amendments—[1] This section inserted by FA 2004 s 20(1) with effect from 22 July 2004.

[43B Groups: applications

(1) This section applies where an application is made to the Commissioners for two or more bodies corporate, which are eligible [by virtue of section 43A][2], to be treated as members of a group.

(2) This section also applies where two or more bodies corporate are treated as members of a group and an application is made to the Commissioners—

(*a*) for another body corporate, which is eligible [by virtue of section 43A][2] to be treated as a member of the group, to be treated as a member of the group,
(*b*) for a body corporate to cease to be treated as a member of the group,
(*c*) for a member to be substituted as the group's representative member, or
(*d*) for the bodies corporate no longer to be treated as members of a group.

(3) An application with respect to any bodies corporate—

(*a*) must be made by one of them or by the person controlling them, and
(*b*) in the case of an application for the bodies to be treated as a group, must appoint one of them as the representative member.

(4) Where this section applies in relation to an application it shall, subject to subsection (6) below, be taken to be granted with effect from—

(*a*) the day on which the application is received by the Commissioners, or
(*b*) such earlier or later time as the Commissioners may allow.

(5) The Commissioners may refuse an application, within the period of 90 days starting with the day on which it was received by them, if it appears to them—

(*a*) in the case of an application such as is mentioned in subsection (1) above, that the bodies corporate are not eligible [by virtue of section 43A][2] to be treated as members of a group,
(*b*) in the case of an application such as is mentioned in subsection (2)(*a*) above, that the body corporate is not eligible [by virtue of section 43A][2] to be treated as a member of the group, or
(*c*) in any case, that refusal of the application is necessary for the protection of the revenue.

(6) If the Commissioners refuse an application it shall be taken never to have been granted.][1]

Commentary—*De Voil Indirect Tax Service* **V2.190**.
Press releases etc—C&E Business Brief 15/99 12/7/99 (New anti-avoidance provisions).
Amendments—[1] This section inserted by FA 1999 s 16, Sch 2 para 2 with effect from 27 July 1999, subject to FA 1999 Sch 2 para 6.
[2] Words in sub-ss (1), (2)(*a*), (5)(*a*) and (5)(*b*) substituted by FA 2004 s 20(4) with effect from 22 July 2004.

[43C Groups: termination of membership

(1) The Commissioners may, by notice given to a body corporate, terminate its treatment as a member of a group from a date—

(*a*) which is specified in the notice, and
(*b*) which is, or falls after, the date on which the notice is given.

(2) The Commissioners may give a notice under subsection (1) above only if it appears to them to be necessary for the protection of the revenue.

(3) Where—

(*a*) a body is treated as a member of a group, and
(*b*) it appears to the Commissioners that the body is not, or is no longer, eligible [by virtue of section 43A][2] to be treated as a member of the group,

the Commissioners shall, by notice given to the body, terminate its treatment as a member of the group from a date specified in the notice.

(4) The date specified in a notice under subsection (3) above may be earlier than the date on which the notice is given but shall not be earlier than—

(*a*) the first date on which, in the opinion of the Commissioners, the body was not eligible to be treated as a member of the group, or
(*b*) the date on which, in the opinion of the Commissioners, the body ceased to be eligible to be treated as a member of the group.][1]

Commentary—*De Voil Indirect Tax Service* **V2.190**.
Press releases etc—C&E Business Brief 15/99 12/7/99 (New anti-avoidance provisions).
Amendments—[1] This section inserted by FA 1999 s 16, Sch 2 para 2 with effect from 27 July 1999 subject to FA 1999 Sch 2 para 6.
[2] Words in sub-s (3)(*b*) substituted by FA 2004 s 20(4) with effect from 22 July 2004.

[43D Groups: duplication

(1) A body corporate may not be treated as a member of more than one group at a time.

(2) A body which is a member of one group is not eligible by virtue of section 43A to be treated as a member of another group.

(3) If—

(*a*) an application under section 43B(1) would have effect from a time in accordance with section 43B(4), but
(*b*) at that time one or more of the bodies specified in the application is a member of a group (other than that to which the application relates),

the application shall have effect from that time, but with the exclusion of the body or bodies mentioned in paragraph (*b*).

(4) If—

(*a*) an application under section 43B(2)(*a*) would have effect from a time in accordance with section 43B(4), but
(*b*) at that time the body specified in the application is a member of a group (other than that to which the application relates),

the application shall have no effect.

(5) Where a body is a subject of two or more applications under section 43B(1) or (2)(*a*) that have not been granted or refused, the applications shall have no effect.][1]

Commentary—*De Voil Indirect Tax Service* **V2.190**.
Amendments—[1] This section inserted by FA 2004 s 20(2) with effect from 22 July 2004.

44 Supplies to groups

(1) Subject to subsections (2) to (4) below, subsection (5) below applies where—

(*a*) a business, or part of a business, carried on by a taxable person is transferred as a going concern to a body corporate treated as a member of a group under section 43;
(*b*) on the transfer of the business or part, chargeable assets of the business are transferred to the body corporate; and
(*c*) the transfer of the assets is treated by virtue of section 5(3)(*c*) as neither a supply of goods nor a supply of services.

(2) Subsection (5) below shall not apply if the representative member of the group is entitled to credit for the whole of the input tax on supplies to it and acquisitions and importations by it—

(*a*) during the prescribed accounting period in which the assets are transferred, and
(*b*) during any longer period to which regulations under section 26(3)(*b*) relate and in which the assets are transferred.

(3) Subsection (5) below shall not apply if the Commissioners are satisfied that the assets were assets of the taxable person transferring them more than 3 years before the day on which they are transferred.

(4) Subsection (5) below shall not apply to the extent that the chargeable assets consist of capital items in respect of which regulations made under section 26(3) and (4), and in force when the assets are transferred, provide for adjustment to the deduction of input tax.

(5) The chargeable assets shall be treated for the purposes of this Act as being, on the day on which they are transferred, both supplied to the representative member of the group for the purpose of its business and supplied by that member in the course or furtherance of its business.

(6) A supply treated under subsection (5) above as made by a representative member shall not be taken into account as a supply made by him when determining the allowance of input tax in his case under section 26.

(7) The value of a supply treated under subsection (5) above as made to or by a representative member shall be taken to be the open market value of the chargeable assets.

(8) For the purposes of this section, the open market value of any chargeable assets shall be taken to be the price that would be paid on a sale (on which no VAT is payable) between a buyer and a seller who are not in such a relationship as to affect the price.

(9) The Commissioners may reduce the VAT chargeable by virtue of subsection (5) above in a case where they are satisfied that the person by whom the chargeable assets are transferred has not received credit for the full amount of input tax arising on the supply to or acquisition or importation by him of the chargeable assets.

(10) For the purposes of this section, assets are chargeable assets if their supply in the United Kingdom by a taxable person in the course or furtherance of his business would be a taxable supply (and not a zero-rated supply).

Commentary—*De Voil Indirect Tax Service* **V3.246**.
Definitions—"Business", s 94; "the Commissioners", s 96(1); "input tax", s 24; "prescribed accounting period", s 25(1); "regulations", s 96(1); "representative member", s 43(4); "supply", s 5, Sch 4; "taxable person", s 4(2); "taxable supply", s 4(2); "United Kingdom", s 96(11); "VAT", ss 1, 96(1).
Cross references—See VATA 1994 Sch 9A para 2(3) (assumption that a body corporate is (not) to be treated as a member of a group where the Commissioners so direct).

45 Partnerships

(1) The registration under this Act of persons—

(*a*) carrying on a business in partnership, or

(*b*) carrying on in partnership any other activities in the course or furtherance of which they acquire goods from other member States,

may be in the name of the firm; and no account shall be taken, in determining for any purpose of this Act whether goods or services are supplied to or by such persons or are acquired by such persons from another member State, of any change in the partnership.

(2) Without prejudice to section 36 of the Partnership Act 1890 (rights of persons dealing with firm against apparent members of firm), until the date on which a change in the partnership is notified to the Commissioners a person who has ceased to be a member of a partnership shall be regarded as continuing to be a partner for the purposes of this Act and, in particular, for the purpose of any liability for VAT on the supply of goods or services by the partnership or on the acquisition of goods by the partnership from another member State.

(3) Where a person ceases to be a member of a partnership during a prescribed accounting period (or is treated as so doing by virtue of subsection (2) above) any notice, whether of assessment or otherwise, which is served on the partnership and relates to, or to any matter arising in, that period or any earlier period during the whole or part of which he was a member of the partnership shall be treated as served also on him.

(4) Without prejudice to section 16 of the Partnership Act 1890 (notice to acting partner to be notice to the firm) any notice, whether of assessment or otherwise, which is addressed to a partnership by the name in which it is registered by virtue of subsection (1) above and is served in accordance with this Act shall be treated for the purposes of this Act as served on the partnership and, accordingly, where subsection (3) above applies, as served also on the former partner.

(5) Subsections (1) and (3) above shall not affect the extent to which, under section 9 of the Partnership Act 1890, a partner is liable for VAT owed by the firm; but where a person is a partner in a firm during part only of a prescribed accounting period, his liability for VAT on the supply by the firm of goods or services during that accounting period or on the acquisition during that period by the firm of any goods from another member State shall be such proportion of the firm's liability as may be just.

Commentary—*De Voil Indirect Tax Service* **V2.110**.
Simon's Tax Cases—s 45(1), *Scrace v R&C Comrs* [2007] STC 269; *R&C Comrs v Pal and others* [2008] STC 2442.
s 45(2), *C&E Comrs v Jamieson* [2002] STC 1418.
Definitions—"Acquisition of goods from other member States", s 11; "another member State", s 96(1); "business", s 94; "the Commissioners", s 96(1); "other member States", s 96(1); "prescribed accounting period", s 25(1); "registered", s 3(3); "supply", s 5, Sch 4; "VAT", ss 1, 96(1).

46 Business carried on in divisions or by unincorporated bodies, personal representatives etc

(1) The registration under this Act of a body corporate carrying on a business in several divisions may, if the body corporate so requests and the Commissioners see fit, be in the names of those divisions.

(2) The Commissioners may by regulations make provision for determining by what persons anything required by or under this Act to be done by a person carrying on a business is to be done where a business is carried on in partnership or by a club, association or organisation the affairs of which are managed by its members or a committee or committees of its members.

(3) The registration under this Act of any such club, association or organisation may be in the name of the club, association or organisation; and in determining whether goods or services are supplied to or by such a club, association or organisation or whether goods are acquired by such a club, association or organisation from another member State, no account shall be taken of any change in its members.

(4) The Commissioners may by regulations make provision for persons who carry on a business of a taxable person who has died or become bankrupt or has had his estate sequestrated or has become incapacitated to be treated for a limited time as taxable persons, and for securing continuity in the application of this Act in cases where persons are so treated.

(5) In relation to a company which is a taxable person, the reference in subsection (4) above to the taxable person having become bankrupt or having had his estate sequestrated or having become incapacitated shall be construed as a reference to its being in liquidation or receivership or [administration][1].

(6) References in this section to a business include references to any other activities in the course or furtherance of which any body corporate or any club, association, organisation or other unincorporated body acquires goods from another member State.

Commentary—*De Voil Indirect Tax Service* **V2.190A**.
Regulations—See VAT Regulations, SI 1995/2518 regs 8, 9.
Definitions—"Acquisition of goods from another member State", s 11; "another member State", s 96(1); "business", s 94; "the Commissioners", s 96(1); "registered", s 3(3); "regulations", s 96(1); "supply", s 5, Sch 4; "taxable person", s 3.
Cross reference—See VAT (Payments on Account) Order, SI 1993/2001 art 16 (payments on account: businesses carried on in divisions).
Amendments—[1] Word in sub-s (5) substituted by the Enterprise Act 2002 (Insolvency) Order, SI 2003/2096 art 4, Schedule paras 24, 25 with effect from 15 September 2003. However, this amendment does not apply in any case where a petition for an administration order was presented before that date: SI 2003/2096 arts 1, 6.

47 Agents etc

(1) Where—

(*a*) goods are acquired from another member State by a person who is not a taxable person and a taxable person acts in relation to the acquisition, and then supplies the goods as agent for the person by whom they are so acquired; or

(*b*) goods are imported from a place outside the member States by a taxable person who supplies them as agent for a person who is not a taxable person,

[then, if the taxable person acts in relation to the supply in his own name, the goods shall][1] be treated for the purposes of this Act as acquired and supplied or, as the case may be, imported and supplied by the taxable person as principal.

(2) For the purposes of subsection (1) above a person who is not resident in the United Kingdom and whose place or principal place of business is outside the United Kingdom may be treated as not being a taxable person if as a result he will not be required to be registered under this Act.

[(2A) Where, in the case of any supply of goods to which subsection (1) above does not apply, goods are supplied through an agent who acts in his own name, the supply shall be treated both as a supply to the agent and as a supply by the agent.][2]

(3) Where …[3] services are supplied through an agent who acts in his own name the Commissioners may, if they think fit, treat the supply both as a supply to the agent and as a supply by the agent.

Commentary—*De Voil Indirect Tax Service* **V3.221**.
Simon's Tax Cases—s 47(3), *Metropolitan Borough of Wirral v C&E Comrs* [1995] STC 597*.
Definitions—"Acquisition of goods from another member State", s 11; "another member State", s 96(1); "business", s 94; "the Commissioners", s 96(1); "goods imported from a place outside the member States", s 15; "registered", s 3(3); "supply", s 5, Sch 4; "taxable person", s 3; "United Kingdom", s 96(11).
Press releases etc—Business Brief 28/97, 12-12-97 (VAT treatment of debt collection revised).
Amendments—[1] Words in sub-s (1) substituted by FA 1995 s 23(1), (4)(*a*) with effect in relation to goods acquired or imported on or after 1 May 1995.
[2] Sub-s (2A) inserted by FA 1995 s 23(2), (4)(*b*) with effect in relation to any supply taking place on or after 1 May 1995.
[3] Words repealed by FA 1995 s 23(3), (4)(*b*), Sch 29 Pt VI(2) with effect in relation to any supply taking place on or after 1 May 1995.

48 VAT representatives

(1) Where any person—

(*a*) is a taxable person for the purposes of this Act or, without being a taxable person, is a person who makes taxable supplies or who acquires goods in the United Kingdom from one or more other member States;

[(*b*) is not established, and does not have any fixed establishment, in the United Kingdom;][2]

[(*ba*) is established in a country or territory in respect of which it appears to the Commissioners that the condition specified in subsection (1A) below is satisfied; and][2]
(*c*) in the case of an individual, does not have his usual place of residence in the United Kingdom,

the Commissioners may direct that person to appoint another person (in this Act referred to as a "VAT representative") to act on his behalf in relation to VAT.

[(1A) The condition mentioned in subsection (1)(*ba*) above is that—

(*a*) the country or territory is neither a member State nor a part of a member State, and
(*b*) there is no provision for mutual assistance between the United Kingdom and the country or territory similar in scope to the assistance provided for between the United Kingdom and each other member State by the mutual assistance provisions.][7]

[(1B) In subsection (1A) above "the mutual assistance provisions" means—

[(*a*) section 134 of the Finance Act 2002 and Schedule 39 to that Act (recovery of taxes etc due in other member States);][3]
(*b*) section 197 of the Finance Act 2003 (exchange of information between tax authorities of member States);][3]
[(*c*) Council Regulation (EC) No 1798/2003 of 7th October 2003 (on administrative cooperation in the field of value added tax).]][4]

[(2) With the agreement of the Commissioners, a person—

(*a*) who has not been required under subsection (1) above to appoint another person to act on his behalf in relation to VAT, and
(*b*) in relation to whom the conditions specified in paragraphs (*a*), (*b*) and (*c*) of that subsection are satisfied,

may appoint another person to act on his behalf in relation to VAT.][2]

[(2A) In this Act "VAT representative" means a person appointed under subsection (1) or (2) above.][2]

(3) Where any person is appointed by virtue of this section to be the VAT representative of another ("his principal"), then, subject to subsections (4) to (6) below, the VAT representative—

(*a*) shall be entitled to act on his principal's behalf for any of the purposes of this Act, of any other enactment (whenever passed) relating to VAT or of any subordinate legislation made under this Act or any such enactment;
(*b*) shall, subject to such provisions as may be made by the Commissioners by regulations, secure (where appropriate by acting on his principal's behalf) his principal's compliance with and discharge of the obligations and liabilities to which his principal is subject by virtue of this Act, any such other enactment or any such subordinate legislation; and
(*c*) shall be personally liable in respect of—

(i) any failure to secure his principal's compliance with or discharge of any such obligation or liability; and
(ii) anything done for purposes connected with acting on his principal's behalf,

as if the obligations and liabilities imposed on his principal were imposed jointly and severally on the VAT representative and his principal.

(4) A VAT representative shall not be liable by virtue of subsection (3) above himself to be registered under this Act, but regulations made by the Commissioners may—

(*a*) require the registration of the names of VAT representatives against the names of their principals in any register kept for the purposes of this Act; and
(*b*) make it the duty of a VAT representative, for the purposes of registration, to notify the Commissioners, within such period as may be prescribed, that his appointment has taken effect or has ceased to have effect.

(5) A VAT representative shall not by virtue of subsection (3) above be guilty of any offence except in so far as—

(*a*) the VAT representative has consented to, or connived in, the commission of the offence by his principal;
(*b*) the commission of the offence by his principal is attributable to any neglect on the part of the VAT representative; or
(*c*) the offence consists in a contravention by the VAT representative of an obligation which, by virtue of that subsection, is imposed both on the VAT representative and on his principal.

(6) The Commissioners may by regulations make provision as to the manner and circumstances in which a person is to be appointed, or is to be treated as having ceased to be, another's VAT representative; and regulations under this subsection may include such provision as the Commissioners think fit for the purposes of subsection (4) above with respect to the making or deletion of entries in any register.

(7) Where a person fails to appoint a VAT representative in accordance with any direction under subsection (1) above, the Commissioners may require him to provide such security, or further security, as they may think appropriate for the payment of any VAT which is or may become due from him.

[(7A) A sum required by way of security under subsection (7) above shall be deemed for the purposes of—

(*a*) section 51 of the Finance Act 1997 (enforcement by distress) and any regulations under that section, and

(*b*) section 52 of that Act (enforcement by diligence),

to be recoverable as if it were VAT due from the person who is required to provide it.][1]

(8) For the purposes of this Act a person shall not be treated as having been directed to appoint a VAT representative, or as having been required to provide security under subsection (7) above, unless the Commissioners have either—

(*a*) served notice of the direction or requirement on him; or

(*b*) taken all such other steps as appear to them to be reasonable for bringing the direction or requirement to his attention.

[(9) The Treasury may by order amend the definition of "the mutual assistance provisions" in subsection (1B) above.][3]

Commentary—*De Voil Indirect Tax Service* **V2.106, 146.**

Regulations—See VAT Regulations, SI 1995/2518 reg 10.

Definitions—"Acquisition of goods from another member State", s 11; "business", s 94; "the Commissioners", s 96(1); "other member States", s 96(1); "prescribed", s 96(1); "registered", s 3(3); "regulations", s 96(1); "subordinate legislation", s 96(1); "taxable person", s 3; "taxable supply", s 4(2); "United Kingdom", s 96(11); "VAT", ss 1, 96(1).

Cross references—See VATA 1994 s 69(1) (penalty for breach of regulations made under this section requiring a VAT representative to notify the Commissioners of his appointment or of the cessation of his appointment);

VATA 1994 ss 83, 84 (appeal to a tribunal in respect of a requirement for security under sub-s (7) of this section);

VATA 1994 Sch 11 para 5(10) (recovery of sums required by way of security under sub-s (7) of this section).

VAT Regulations, SI 1995/2518 reg 10(1), Sch 1, form 8 (form of notification of appointment as VAT representative);

VAT Regulations, SI 1995/2518 reg 10(3) (registration of VAT representatives);

VAT Regulations, SI 1995/2518 reg 10(5) (cessation of appointment as VAT representative).

Amendments—[1] Sub-s (7A) inserted by FA 1997 s 53 (6) with effect from 1 July 1997 (see SI 1997/1432).

[2] Sub-s (1)(*b*), (*ba*) substituted for original sub-s (1)(*b*), sub-ss (1A), (1B) inserted, and sub-ss (2), (2A) substituted for original sub-s (2) by FA 2001 s 100 with effect from 31 December 2001.

[3] Sub-s (1B)(*a*), (*b*) substituted, and sub-s (9) inserted, by FA 2003 s 197(7) with effect from 10 July 2003.

[4] Sub-s (1B)(*c*) substituted by the Mutual Assistance Provisions Order, SI 2003/3092 art 2 with effect from 1 January 2004.

Prospective amendments—In sub-s (7A) words "by taking control of goods or, in Northern Ireland," to be inserted after "enforcement", by the Tribunals, Courts and Enforcement Act 2007 s 62(3), Sch 13 paras 117, 118 with effect from a date to be appointed.

49 Transfers of going concerns

(1) Where a business[, or part of a business,][1] carried on by a taxable person is transferred to another person as a going concern, then—

(*a*) for the purpose of determining whether the transferee is liable to be registered under this Act he shall be treated as having carried on the business [or part of the business][1] before as well as after the transfer and supplies by the transferor shall be treated accordingly; ...[1]

(*b*) ...[1]

(2) Without prejudice to subsection (1) above, the Commissioners may by regulations make provision for securing continuity in the application of this Act in cases where a business[, or part of a business,][1] carried on by a taxable person is transferred to another person as a going concern and the transferee is registered under this Act in substitution for the transferor.

[(2A) Regulations under subsection (2) above may, in particular, provide for the duties under this Act of the transferor to preserve records relating to the business or part of the business for any period after the transfer to become duties of the transferee unless the Commissioners, at the request of the transferor, otherwise direct.][1]

(3) Regulations under subsection (2) above may, in particular, provide—

(*a*) for liabilities and duties under this Act (excluding sections 59 to 70) of the transferor [(other than the duties mentioned in subsection (2A) above)][1] to become, to such extent as may be provided by the regulations, liabilities and duties of the transferee; and

(*b*) for any right of either of them to repayment or credit in respect of VAT to be satisfied by making a repayment or allowing a credit to the other;

but no such provision as is mentioned in paragraph (*a*) or (*b*) of this subsection shall have effect in relation to any transferor and transferee unless an application in that behalf has been made by them under the regulations.

[(4) Subsection (5) below applies where—

(*a*) a business, or part of a business, carried on by a taxable person is transferred to another person as a going concern, and

(*b*) the transferor continues to be required under this Act to preserve for any period after the transfer any records relating to the business or part of the business.

(5) So far as is necessary for the purpose of complying with the transferee's duties under this Act, the transferee ("E") may require the transferor—

(*a*) to give to E, within such time and in such form as E may reasonably require, such information contained in the records as E may reasonably specify,

(*b*) to give to E, within such time and in such form as E may reasonably require, such copies of documents forming part of the records as E may reasonably specify, and (*c*) to make the records available for E's inspection at such time and place as E may reasonably require (and permit E to take copies of, or make extracts from, them).

(6) Where a business, or part of a business, carried on by a taxable person is transferred to another person as a going concern, the Commissioners may disclose to the transferee any information relating to the business when it was carried on by the transferor for the purpose of enabling the transferee to comply with the transferee's duties under this Act.][1]

Commentary—*De Voil Indirect Tax Service* **V2.226**.
Regulations—See VAT Regulations, SI 1995/2518 reg 6.
Definitions—"Business", s 94; "the Commissioners", s 96(1); "registered", s 3(3); "regulations", s 96(1); "supply", s 5, Sch 4; "taxable person", s 3; "VAT", ss 1, 96(1).
Cross reference—See VAT (Special Provisions) Order, SI 1995/1268 art 5 (certain transfers of going concerns treated as neither a supply of goods or services).
Amendments—[1] Words in sub-s (1) inserted and repealed, words in sub-ss (2), (3) and whole of sub-ss (2A), (4)–(6) inserted, by FA 2007 ss 100(1)–(6), 114, Sch 27 Pt 6(2) with effect in relation to transfers pursuant to contracts entered into on or after 1 September 2007.

50 Terminal markets

(1) The Treasury may by order make provision for modifying the provisions of this Act in their application to dealings on terminal markets and such persons ordinarily engaged in such dealings as may be specified in the order, subject to such conditions as may be so specified.

(2) Without prejudice to the generality of subsection (1) above, an order under this section may include provision—

(*a*) for zero-rating the supply of any goods or services or for treating the supply of any goods or services as exempt;

(*b*) for the registration under this Act of any body of persons representing persons ordinarily engaged in dealing on a terminal market and for disregarding such dealings by persons so represented in determining liability to be registered under this Act, and for disregarding such dealings between persons so represented for all the purposes of this Act;

(*c*) for refunding, to such persons as may be specified by or under the order, input tax attributable to such dealings on a terminal market as may be so specified,

and may contain such incidental and supplementary provisions as appear to the Treasury to be necessary or expedient.

(3) An order under this section may make different provision with respect to different terminal markets and with respect to different commodities.

Commentary—*De Voil Indirect Tax Service* **V4.208**.
Orders—See VAT (Terminal Markets) Order, SI 1973/173.
Definitions—"Exempt supply", s 31; "input tax", s 24; "registered", s 3(3); "supply", s 5, Sch 4; "zero-rating", s 30.

[50A Margin schemes

(1) The Treasury may by order provide, in relation to any such description of supplies to which this section applies as may be specified in the order, for a taxable person to be entitled to opt that, where he makes supplies of that description, VAT is to be charged by reference to the profit margin on the supplies, instead of by reference to their value.

(2) This section applies to the following supplies, that is to say—

(*a*) supplies of works of art, antiques or collectors' items;

(*b*) supplies of motor vehicles;

(*c*) supplies of second-hand goods; and

(*d*) any supply of goods through a person who acts as an agent, but in his own name, in relation to the supply.

(3) An option for the purposes of an order under this section shall be exercisable, and may be withdrawn, in such manner as may be required by such an order.

(4) Subject to subsection (7) below, the profit margin on a supply to which this section applies shall be taken, for the purposes of an order under this section, to be equal to the amount (if any) by which the price at which the person making the supply obtained the goods in question is exceeded by the price at which he supplies them.

(5) For the purposes of this section the price at which a person has obtained any goods and the price at which he supplies them shall each be calculated in accordance with the provisions contained in an order under this section; and such an order may, in particular, make provision stipulating the extent to which any VAT charged on a supply, acquisition or importation of any goods is to be treated as included in the price at which those goods have been obtained or are supplied.

(6) An order under this section may provide that the consideration for any services supplied in connection with a supply of goods by a person who acts as an agent, but in his own name, in relation to the supply of the goods is to be treated for the purposes of any such order as an amount to be taken into account in computing the profit margin on the supply of the goods, instead of being separately chargeable to VAT as comprised in the value of the services supplied.

(7) An order under this section may provide for the total profit margin on all the goods of a particular description supplied by a person in any prescribed accounting period to be calculated by—

(*a*) aggregating all the prices at which that person obtained goods of that description in that period together with any amount carried forward to that period in pursuance of paragraph (*d*) below;

(*b*) aggregating all the prices at which he supplies goods of that description in that period;

(*c*) treating the total profit margin on goods supplied in that period as being equal to the amount (if any) by which, for that period, the aggregate calculated in pursuance of paragraph (*a*) above is exceeded by the aggregate calculated in pursuance of paragraph (*b*) above; and

(*d*) treating any amount by which, for that period, the aggregate calculated in pursuance of paragraph (*b*) above is exceeded by the aggregate calculated in pursuance of paragraph (*a*) above as an amount to be carried forward to the following prescribed accounting period so as to be included, for the period to which it is carried forward, in any aggregate falling to be calculated in pursuance of paragraph (*a*) above.

(8) An order under this section may—

(*a*) make different provision for different cases; and

(*b*) make provisions of the order subject to such general or special directions as may, in accordance with the order, be given by the Commissioners with respect to any matter to which the order relates.][1]

Commentary—*De Voil Indirect Tax Service* **V3.531–V3.536**.
Order—VAT (Special Provisions) Order, SI 1995/1268.
Press releases etc—VAT Information Sheet 6/01 (December 2001) (changes to the VAT second-hand margin scheme).
Definitions—"Acquisition of goods from another member state", s 11; "the Commissioners", s 96(1); "prescribed accounting period", s 25(1); "supply", s 5, Sch 4; "taxable person", s 3; "VAT", s 96(1).
Cross references—See Value Added Tax Regulations, SI 1995/2518 reg 172A (bad debt relief under margin schemes).
Amendments—[1] Section inserted by FA 1995 s 24(1).

51 Buildings and land

(1) Schedule 10 shall have effect with respect to buildings and land.

(2) The Treasury may by order amend Schedule 10.

Commentary—*De Voil Indirect Tax Service* **V4.111–V4.115**.
Cross reference—See VATA 1994 s 97(3), (4) (procedure for making certain orders under this section).

[51A Co-owners etc of buildings and land

(1) This section applies to a supply consisting in the grant, assignment or surrender of any interest in or right over land in a case where there is more than one person by whom the grant, assignment or surrender is made or treated as made; and for this purpose—

(a) a licence to occupy land, and

(b) in relation to land in Scotland, a personal right to call for or be granted any interest or right in or over land,

shall be taken to be a right over land.

(2) The persons who make or are treated as making a supply to which this section applies ("the grantors") shall be treated, in relation to that supply and in relation to any other such supply with respect to which the grantors are the same, as a single person ("the property-owner") who is distinct from each of the grantors individually.

(3) Registration under this Act of the property-owner shall be in the name of the grantors acting together as a property-owner.

(4) The grantors shall be jointly and severally liable in respect of the obligations falling by virtue of this section on the property-owner.

(5) Any notice, whether of assessment or otherwise, which is addressed to the property-owner by the name in which the property-owner is registered and is served on any of the grantors in accordance with this Act shall be treated for the purposes of this Act as served on the property-owner.

(6) Where there is any change in some, but not all, of the persons who are for the time being to be treated as the grantors in relation to any supply to which this section applies—

(a) that change shall be disregarded for the purposes of this section in relation to any prescribed accounting period beginning before the change is notified in the prescribed manner to the Commissioners; and

(b) any notice (whether of assessment or otherwise) which is served, at any time after such a notification, on the property-owner for the time being shall, so far as it relates to, or to any matter arising in, such a period, be treated for the purposes of this Act as served on whoever was the property-owner in that period.][1, 2]

Commentary—*De Voil Indirect Tax Service* **V2.117**.
Definitions—"Assignment", s 96(1); "the Commissioners", s 96(1); "prescribed", s 96(1); "prescribed accounting period", s 25(1); "registered", s 3(3); "supply", s 5.
Amendments—[1] Section inserted by FA 1995 s 26(1), (4) with effect from a day to be appointed by order made by the Commissioners of Customs and Excise.
[2] This section repealed by the Value Added Tax (Buildings and Land) Order, SI 2008/1146 art 5(2) with effect in relation to supplies made on or after 1 June 2008, subject to savings in Sch 2 of the Order.

[51B Face-value vouchers

Schedule 10A shall have effect with respect to face-value vouchers.][1]

Amendments—[1] Section inserted by FA 2003 s 19, Sch 1 para 1 with effect for supplies of tokens, stamps or vouchers issued after 8 April 2003.

52 Trading stamp schemes

The Commissioners may by regulations modify sections 19 and 20 and Schedules 6 and 7 for the purpose of providing (in place of the provision for the time being contained in those sections and Schedules) for the manner of determining for the purposes of this Act the value of—

(*a*) a supply of goods, or

(*b*) a transaction in pursuance of which goods are acquired from another member State,

in a case where the goods are supplied or acquired under a trading stamp scheme (within the meaning of the Trading Stamps Act 1964 or the Trading Stamps Act (Northern Ireland) 1965) or under any scheme of an equivalent description which is in operation in another member State.

Commentary—*De Voil Indirect Tax Service* **V3.116**.
Regulations—See VAT Regulations, SI 1995/2518 regs 76–80.
Definitions—"Acquisition of goods from another member State", s 11; "another member State", s 96(1); "the Commissioners", s 96(1); "regulations", s 96(1); "supply", s 5, Sch 4; "value of supply of goods", s 19, Sch 6; "value of goods acquired from another member State", s 20.

53 Tour operators

(1) The Treasury may by order modify the application of this Act in relation to supplies of goods or services by tour operators or in relation to such of those supplies as may be determined by or under the order.

(2) Without prejudice to the generality of subsection (1) above, an order under this section may make provision—

(*a*) for two or more supplies of goods or services by a tour operator to be treated as a single supply of services;

(*b*) for the value of that supply to be ascertained, in such manner as may be determined by or under the order, by reference to the difference between sums paid or payable to and sums paid or payable by the tour operator;

(*c*) for account to be taken, in determining the VAT chargeable on that supply, of the different rates of VAT that would have been applicable apart from this section;

(*d*) excluding any body corporate from the application of section 43;

(*e*) as to the time when a supply is to be treated as taking place.

(3) In this section "tour operator" includes a travel agent acting as principal and any other person providing for the benefit of travellers services of any kind commonly provided by tour operators or travel agents.

(4) Section 97(3) shall not apply to an order under this section, notwithstanding that it makes provision for excluding any VAT from credit under section 25.

Commentary—*De Voil Indirect Tax Service* **V3.519**.
Orders—See VAT (Tour Operators) Order, SI 1987/1806.
Press releases etc—VAT Information Sheet 5/95 1-4-95 (guidance on new rules from 1 January 1996).
VAT Information Sheet 2/96, 3/96, 4/96 1-7-96 (practical implementation of "trader to trader options", "airline charter option" and "agency option").
VAT Information Sheet 6/96 1-11-96 (guidance on "seat only" sales).
VAT Information Sheet 1/97 (practical implementation of the 'trader to trader (wholesale) option').
Business Brief 14/97, 30-6-97 (treatment of tour operators making supplies to other businesses).
Simon's Tax Cases—*Madgett and Baldwin (T/A Howden Court Hotel) v C&E Comrs* [1998] STC 1189*.
Definitions—"Supply", s 5, Sch 4; "value of supply of goods or services", s 19, Sch 6; "VAT", ss 1, 96(1).
Cross references—See Value Added Tax Regulations, SI 1995/2518 reg 172B (bad debt relief under tour operators margin scheme).

54 Farmers etc

(1) The Commissioners may, in accordance with such provision as may be contained in regulations made by them, certify for the purposes of this section any person who satisfies them—

(*a*) that he is carrying on a business involving one or more designated activities;

(*b*) that he is of such a description and has complied with such requirements as may be prescribed; and

(*c*) where an earlier certification of that person has been cancelled, that more than the prescribed period has elapsed since the cancellation or that such other conditions as may be prescribed are satisfied.

(2) Where a person is for the time being certified under this section, then (whether or not that person is a taxable person) so much of any supply by him of any goods or services as, in accordance with provision contained in regulations, is allocated to the relevant part of his business shall be disregarded for the purpose of determining whether he is, has become or has ceased to be liable or entitled to be registered under Schedule 1.

(3) The Commissioners may by regulations provide for an amount included in the consideration for any taxable supply which is made—

(*a*) in the course or furtherance of the relevant part of his business by a person who is for the time being certified under this section;

(*b*) at a time when that person is not a taxable person; and (*c*) to a taxable person,

to be treated, for the purpose of determining the entitlement of the person supplied to credit under sections 25 and 26, as VAT on a supply to that person.

(4) The amount which, for the purposes of any provision made under subsection (3) above, may be included in the consideration for any supply shall be an amount equal to such percentage as the Treasury may by order specify of the sum which, with the addition of that amount, is equal to the consideration for the supply.

(5) The Commissioners' power by regulations under section 39 to provide for the repayment to persons to whom that section applies of VAT which would be input tax of theirs if they were taxable persons in the United Kingdom includes power to provide for the payment to persons to whom that section applies of sums equal to the amounts which, if they were taxable persons in the United Kingdom, would be input tax of theirs by virtue of regulations under this section; and references in that section, or in any other enactment, to a repayment of VAT shall be construed accordingly.

(6) Regulations under this section may provide—

(*a*) for the form and manner in which an application for certification under this section, or for the cancellation of any such certification, is to be made;

(*b*) for the cases and manner in which the Commissioners may cancel a person's certification;

(*c*) for entitlement to a credit such as is mentioned in subsection (3) above to depend on the issue of an invoice containing such particulars as may be prescribed, or as may be notified by the Commissioners in accordance with provision contained in regulations; and

(*d*) for the imposition on certified persons of obligations with respect to the keeping, preservation and production of such records as may be prescribed and of obligations to comply with such requirements with respect to any of those matters as may be so notified;

and regulations made by virtue of paragraph (*b*) above may confer on the Commissioners power, if they think fit, to refuse to cancel a person's certification, and to refuse to give effect to any entitlement of that person to be registered, until the end of such period after the grant of certification as may be prescribed.

(7) In this section references, in relation to any person, to the relevant part of his business are references—

(*a*) where the whole of his business relates to the carrying on of one or more designated activities, to that business; and

(*b*) in any other case, to so much of his business as does so relate.

(8) In this section "designated activities" means such activities, being activities carried on by a person who, by virtue of carrying them on, falls to be treated as a farmer for the purposes of Article 25 of the directive of the Council of the European Communities dated 17th May 1977 No 77/388/EEC (common flat-rate scheme for farmers), as the Treasury may by order designate.

Commentary—*De Voil Indirect Tax Service* **V2.191**.
Regulations—See VAT Regulations, SI 1995/2518 regs 202–211.
Orders—See VAT (Flat-rate Scheme for Farmers) (Designated Activities) Order, SI 1992/3220; VAT (Flat-rate Scheme for Farmers) (Percentage Addition) Order, SI 1992/3221.
Definitions—"Business", s 94; "the Commissioners", s 96(1); "input tax", s 24; "invoice", s 96(1); "prescribed", s 96(1); "registered", s 3(3); "regulations", s 96(1); "supply", s 5, Sch 4; "taxable person", s 3; "taxable supply", s 4(2); "United Kingdom", s 96(11); "VAT", ss 1, 96(1).
Cross references—See VATA 1994 s 83 (appeal to a tribunal in respect of a refusal of, cancellation of, or refusal to cancel certification under this section);
VATA 1994 s 97(3), (4) (procedure for making orders under sub-s (4) or (8) of this section).
VAT (Flat-rate Scheme for Farmers) (Designated Activities) Order, SI 1992/3220 (designated activities for the purposes of this section).
VAT (Flat-rate Scheme for Farmers) (Percentage Addition) Order, SI 1992/3221 (the percentage specified for the purposes of sub-s (4) of this section is 4 per cent).
VAT Regulations, SI 1995/2518 reg 209(1) (treatment of amounts within sub-s (4) of this section as VAT on a supply for purposes of determining entitlement to input tax credit).

55 Customers to account for tax on supplies of gold etc

(1) Where any person makes a supply of gold to another person and that supply is a taxable supply but not a zero rated supply, the supply shall be treated for purposes of Schedule 1—

(*a*) as a taxable supply of that other person (as well as a taxable supply of the person who makes it); and

(*b*) in so far as that other person is supplied in connection with the carrying on by him of any business, as a supply made by him in the course or furtherance of that business;

but nothing in paragraph (*b*) above shall require any supply to be disregarded for the purposes of that Schedule on the grounds that it is a supply of capital assets of that other person's business.

(2) Where a taxable person makes a supply of gold to a person who—

(*a*) is himself a taxable person at the time when the supply is made; and

(*b*) is supplied in connection with the carrying on by him of any business,

it shall be for the person supplied, on the supplier's behalf, to account for and pay tax on the supply, and not for the supplier.

(3) So much of this Act and of any other enactment or any subordinate legislation as has effect for the purposes of or in connection with, the enforcement of any obligation to account for and

pay VAT shall apply for the purposes of this section in relation to any person who is required under subsection (2) above to account for and pay any VAT as if that VAT were VAT on a supply made by him.

(4) Section 6(4) to (10) shall not apply for determining when any supply of gold is to be treated as taking place.

(5) References in this section to a supply of gold are references to—

[(*a*) any supply of goods consisting in fine gold, in gold grain of any purity or in gold coins of any purity; ...[2]][1]

(*b*) any supply of goods containing gold where the consideration for the supply (apart from any VAT) is, or is equivalent to, an amount which does not exceed, or exceeds by no more than a negligible amount, the open market value of the gold contained in the goods [; or

(*c*) any supply of services consisting in the application to another person's goods of a treatment or process which produces goods a supply of which would fall within paragraph (*a*) above.][2]

(6) The Treasury may by order provide for this section to apply, as it applies to the supplies specified in subsection (5) above, to such other supplies of—

(*a*) goods consisting in or containing any precious or semi-precious metal or stones; or

(*b*) services relating to, or to anything containing, any precious or semi-precious metal or stones,

as may be specified or described in the order.

Commentary—*De Voil Indirect Tax Service* **V5.143**.

Definitions—"Business", s 94; "open market value", s 19(5); "subordinate legislation", s 96(1); "supply", s 5, Sch 4; "tax", s 96(1); "taxable person", s 3; "taxable supply", s 4(2); "VAT", ss 1, 96(1); "zero-rating", s 30.

Cross reference—See VATA 1994 s 6(14) (provision for regulations to determine the time of a supply under this section).

Amendments—[1] Sub-s (5)(*a*) substituted by FA 1996 s 32 in relation to any supply after 28 November 1995.

[2] Word omitted from sub-s (5) repealed and sub-s (5)(*c*) and word "; or" preceding it inserted by FA 1996 s 29(3), Sch 41 Pt IV(2), with effect in relation to supplies made after 31 December 1995.

[55A Customers to account for tax on supplies of goods of a kind used in missing trader intra-community fraud

(1) Subsection (3) applies if—

(*a*) a taxable (but not a zero-rated) supply of goods ("the relevant supply") is made to a person ("the recipient"),

(*b*) the relevant supply is of goods to which this section applies (see subsection (9)),

(*c*) the relevant supply is not an excepted supply (see subsection (10)), and

(*d*) the total value of the relevant supply, and of corresponding supplies made to the recipient in the month in which the relevant supply is made, exceeds £1,000 ("the disregarded amount").

(2) For this purpose a "corresponding supply" means a taxable (but not a zero-rated) supply of goods which—

(*a*) is a supply of goods to which this section applies, and

(*b*) is not an excepted supply.

(3) The relevant supply, and the corresponding supplies made to the recipient in the month in which the relevant supply is made, are to be treated for the purposes of Schedule 1—

(*a*) as taxable supplies of the recipient (as well as taxable supplies of the person making them), and

(*b*) in so far as the recipient is supplied in connection with the carrying on by him of any business, as supplies made by him in the course or furtherance of that business,

but the relevant supply, and those corresponding supplies, are to be so treated only in so far as their total value exceeds the disregarded amount.

(4) Nothing in subsection (3)(*b*) requires any supply to be disregarded for the purposes of Schedule 1 on the grounds that it is a supply of capital assets of the recipient's business.

(5) For the purposes of subsections (1) and (3), the value of a supply is determined on the basis that no VAT is chargeable on the supply.

(6) If—

(*a*) a taxable person makes a supply of goods to a person ("the recipient") at any time,

(*b*) the supply is of goods to which this section applies and is not an excepted supply, and

(*c*) the recipient is a taxable person at that time and is supplied in connection with the carrying on by him of any business,

it is for the recipient, on the supplier's behalf, to account for and pay tax on the supply and not for the supplier.

(7) The relevant enforcement provisions apply for the purposes of this section, in relation to any person required under subsection (6) to account for and pay any VAT, as if that VAT were VAT on a supply made by him.

(8) For this purpose "the relevant enforcement provisions" means so much of—

(*a*) this Act and any other enactment, and

(*b*) any subordinate legislation,

as has effect for the purposes of, or in connection with the enforcement of, any obligation to account for and pay VAT.

(9) For the purposes of this section, goods are goods to which this section applies if they are of a description specified in an order made by the Treasury.

(10) For the purposes of this section, an "excepted supply" means a supply which is of a description specified in, or determined in accordance with, provision contained in an order made by the Treasury.

(11) Any order made under subsection (10) may describe a supply of goods by reference to—

(*a*) the use which has been made of the goods, or

(*b*) other matters unrelated to the characteristics of the goods themselves.

(12) The Treasury may by order substitute for the sum for the time being specified in subsection (1)(*d*) such greater sum as they think fit.

(13) The Treasury may by order make such amendments of any provision of this Act as they consider necessary or expedient for the purposes of this section or in connection with this section.

An order under this subsection may confer power on the Commissioners to make regulations or exercise any other function, but no order may be made under this subsection on or after 22nd March 2009.

(14) Any order made under this section (other than one under subsection (12)) may—

(*a*) make different provision for different cases, and

(*b*) contain supplementary, incidental, consequential or transitional provisions.][1]

Commentary—*De Voil Indirect Tax Service* **V3.231, V3.233.**

Press releases etc—HMRC Brief 24/07, 20-3-07 (Proposed reverse charge accounting for businesses trading in mobile telephones and computer chips: announcement of targeted implementation and details of how the rules will operate in practice; and exposure of draft legislation for comment).

Amendments—[1] This section inserted by FA 2006 s 19(1), (8) in relation to supplies made on or after 1 June 2007 (by virtue of the Finance Act 2006, section 19, (Appointed Day) Order, SI 2007/1419).

56 Fuel for private use

(1) The provisions of this section apply where, in any prescribed accounting period, fuel which is or has previously been supplied to or imported or manufactured by a taxable person in the course of his business—

(*a*) is provided or to be provided by the taxable person to an individual for private use in his own vehicle or a vehicle allocated to him and is so provided by reason of that individual's employment; or

(*b*) where the taxable person is an individual, is appropriated or to be appropriated by him for private use in his own vehicle; or

(*c*) where the taxable person is a partnership, is provided or to be provided to any of the individual partners for private use in his own vehicle.

(2) For the purposes of this section fuel shall not be regarded as provided to any person for his private use if it is supplied at a price which—

(*a*) in the case of fuel supplied to or imported by the taxable person, is not less than the price at which it was so supplied or imported; and

(*b*) in the case of fuel manufactured by the taxable person, is not less than the aggregate of the cost of the raw material and of manufacturing together with any excise duty thereon.

(3) For the purposes of this section and section 57—

(*a*) "fuel for private use" means fuel which, having been supplied to or imported or manufactured by a taxable person in the course of his business, is or is to be provided or appropriated for private use as mentioned in subsection (1) above;

(*b*) any reference to fuel supplied to a taxable person shall include a reference to fuel acquired by a taxable person from another member State and any reference to fuel imported by a taxable person shall be confined to a reference to fuel imported by that person from a place outside the member States;

(*c*) any reference to an individual's own vehicle shall be construed as including any vehicle of which for the time being he has the use, other than a vehicle allocated to him;

(*d*) subject to subsection (9) below, a vehicle shall at any time be taken to be allocated to an individual if at that time it is made available (without any transfer of the property in it) either to the individual himself or to any other person, and is so made available by reason of the individual's employment and for private use; and

(*e*) fuel provided by an employer to an employee and fuel provided to any person for private use in a vehicle which, by virtue of paragraph (*d*) above, is for the time being taken to be allocated to the employee shall be taken to be provided to the employee by reason of his employment.

(4) Where under section 43 any bodies corporate are treated as members of a group, any provision of fuel by a member of the group to an individual shall be treated for the purposes of this section as provision by the representative member.

(5) In relation to the taxable person, tax on the supply, acquisition or importation of fuel for private use shall be treated for the purposes of this Act as input tax, notwithstanding that the

fuel is not used or to be used for the purposes of a business carried on by the taxable person (and, accordingly, no apportionment of VAT shall fall to be made under section 24(5) by reference to fuel for private use).

(6) At the time at which fuel for private use is put into the fuel tank of an individual's own vehicle or of a vehicle allocated to him, the fuel shall be treated for the purposes of this Act as supplied to him by the taxable person in the course or furtherance of his business for a consideration determined in accordance with subsection (7) below (and, accordingly, where the fuel is appropriated by the taxable person to his own private use, he shall be treated as supplying it to himself in his private capacity).

(7) In any prescribed accounting period of the taxable person in which, by virtue of subsection (6) above, he is treated as supplying fuel for private use to an individual, the consideration for all the supplies made to that individual in that period in respect of any one vehicle shall be that which, by virtue of section 57, is appropriate to a vehicle of that description, and that consideration shall be taken to be inclusive of VAT.

(8) In any case where—

(*a*) in any prescribed accounting period, fuel for private use is, by virtue of subsection (6) above, treated as supplied to an individual in respect of one vehicle for a part of the period and in respect of another vehicle for another part of the period; and
(*b*) at the end of that period one of those vehicles neither belongs to him nor is allocated to him,

subsection (7) above shall have effect as if the supplies made to the individual during those parts of the period were in respect of only one vehicle.

(9) In any prescribed accounting period a vehicle shall not be regarded as allocated to an individual by reason of his employment if—

(*a*) in that period it was made available to, and actually used by, more than one of the employees of one or more employers and, in the case of each of them, it was made available to him by reason of his employment but was not in that period ordinarily used by any one of them to the exclusion of the others; and
(*b*) in the case of each of the employees, any private use of the vehicle made by him in that period was merely incidental to his other use of it in that period; and
(*c*) it was in that period not normally kept overnight on or in the vicinity of any residential premises where any of the employees was residing, except while being kept overnight on premises occupied by the person making the vehicle available to them.

(10) In this section and section 57—

"employment" includes any office; and related expressions shall be construed accordingly;
"vehicle" means a mechanically propelled road vehicle other than—

(*a*) a motor cycle as defined in section 185(1) of the Road Traffic Act 1988 or, for Northern Ireland, in Article 37(1)(*f*) of the Road Traffic (Northern Ireland) Order 1981, or
(*b*) an invalid carriage as defined in that section or, for Northern Ireland, in Article 37(1)(*g*) of that Order.

Commentary—*De Voil Indirect Tax Service* **V3.266.**

Sub-ss (6)–(10): FA 1986 s 9(6)–(10), Road Traffic (Consequential Provisions) Act 1988 Sch 3 para 32.
Definitions—"acquired from another member State", s 11; "another member State", s 96(1); "business", s 94; "excise duty", s 96(5); "importation from a place outside the member States", s 15; "input tax", s 24; "prescribed accounting period", s 25(1); "representative member", s 43(4); "supply", s 5, Sch 4; "tax", s 96(1); "taxable person", s 3; "VAT", ss 1, 96(1).

57 Determination of consideration for fuel supplied for private use

(1) This section has effect to determine the consideration referred to in section 56(7) in respect of any one vehicle; and in this section—

"the prescribed accounting period" means that in respect of supplies in which the consideration is to be determined; and
"the individual" means the individual to whom those supplies are treated as made.

[(1A) Where the prescribed accounting period is a period of 12 months, the consideration appropriate to any vehicle is that specified in relation to a vehicle of the appropriate description in the second column of Table A below.][1]

(2) Where the prescribed accounting period is a period of 3 months, the consideration appropriate to any vehicle is that specified in relation to a vehicle of the appropriate description in the [third][1] column of Table A below.

(3) Where the prescribed accounting period is a period of one month, the consideration appropriate to any vehicle is that specified in relation to a vehicle of the appropriate description in the [fourth][1] column of Table A below.

[TABLE A

Description of vehicle: vehicle's CO_2 emissions figure	*12 month period* £	*3 month period* £	*1 month period* £
120 or less	505.00	126.00	42.00
125	755.00	189.00	63.00
130	755.00	189.00	63.00
135	755.00	189.00	63.00
140	805.00	201.00	67.00
145	855.00	214.00	71.00
150	905.00	226.00	75.00
155	960.00	239.00	79.00
160	1,010.00	251.00	83.00
165	1,060.00	264.00	88.00
170	1,110.00	276.00	92.00
175	1,160.00	289.00	96.00
180	1,210.00	302.00	100.00
185	1,260.00	314.00	104.00
190	1,310.00	327.00	109.00
195	1,360.00	339.00	113.00
200	1,410.00	352.00	117.00
205	1,465.00	365.00	121.00
210	1,515.00	378.00	126.00
215	1,565.00	390.00	130.00
220	1,615.00	403.00	134.00
225	1,665.00	416.00	138.00
230	1,715.00	428.00	142.00
235 or more	1,765.00	441.00	147.00][5]

[*Notes*

(1) If a CO_2 emissions figure is specified in relation to a vehicle in an EC certificate of conformity or a UK approval certificate, the vehicle's CO_2 emissions figure for the purposes of Table A is determined as follows.

(2) If only one figure is specified in the certificate, that figure is the vehicle's CO_2 emissions figure for those purposes.

(3) If more than one figure is specified in the certificate, the figure specified as the CO_2 (combined) emissions figure is the vehicle's CO_2 emissions figure for those purposes.

(4) If separate CO_2 emissions figures are specified for different fuels, the lowest figure specified or, in a case within note (3), the lowest CO_2 emissions (combined) figure specified is the vehicle's CO_2 emissions figure for those purposes.

(5) If the vehicle's CO_2 emissions figure (determined in accordance with notes (2) to (4)) is not a multiple of 5, it is rounded down to the nearest multiple of 5 for those purposes.

(6) If no EC certificate of conformity or UK approval certificate is issued in relation to a vehicle or no emissions figure is specified in relation to it in any such certificate, the vehicle's CO_2 emissions figure for those purposes is—

(*a*) 140 …[4] (if its cylinder capacity is 1,400 cubic centimetres or less),

(*b*) 175 (if its cylinder capacity exceeds 1,400 cubic centimetres but does not exceed 2,000 cubic centimetres), and

(*c*) [235][4] or more (if its cylinder capacity exceeds 2,000 cubic centimetres).][3]

(4) The Treasury may by order taking effect from the beginning of any prescribed accounting period beginning after the order is made substitute a different Table for Table A for the time being set out above.

[(4A) The power conferred by subsection (4) above includes power to substitute for Table A a Table (whether or not of the same or a similar configuration) where any description of vehicle may be by reference to any one or more of the following—

(*a*) the CO_2 emissions figure for the vehicle;
(*b*) the type or types of fuel or power by which the vehicle is, or is capable of being, propelled;
(*c*) the cylinder capacity of the engine in cubic centimetres.

(4B) The provision that may be included in any such Table includes provision for the purpose of enabling the consideration to be determined by reference to the Table—

(*a*) by applying a percentage specified in the Table to a monetary amount specified in the Table, or
(*b*) by any other method.

(4C) Table A, as from time to time substituted by virtue of subsection (4A) above, may be implemented or supplemented by either or both of the following—

(*a*) provision in Rules inserted before the Table, prescribing how the consideration is to be determined by reference to the Table;
(*b*) provision in Notes inserted after the Table in accordance with the following provisions of this section.

(4D) The provision that may be made in Notes includes provision—

(*a*) with respect to the interpretation or application of the Table or any Rules or Notes;
(*b*) with respect to the figure that is to be regarded as the CO_2 emissions figure for any vehicle or any particular description of vehicle;
(*c*) for treating a vehicle as a vehicle with a particular CO_2 emissions figure;
(*d*) for treating a vehicle with a CO_2 emissions figure as a vehicle with a different CO_2 emissions figure;
(*e*) for or in connection with determining the consideration appropriate to vehicles of any particular description (in particular, vehicles falling within any one or more of the descriptions in subsection (4E) below).

(4E) The descriptions are—

(*a*) vehicles capable of being propelled by any particular type or types of fuel or power;
(*b*) vehicles first registered before 1st January 1998;
(*c*) vehicles first registered on or after that date which satisfy the condition in subsection (4F) below (registration without a CO_2 emissions figure).

(4F) The condition is that the vehicle is not one which, when it is first registered, is so registered on the basis of—

(*a*) an EC certificate of conformity that specifies a CO_2 emissions figure, or
(*b*) a UK approval certificate that specifies such a figure.

(4G) Any Rules or Notes do not form part of the Table, but the Treasury, by order taking effect from the beginning of any prescribed accounting period beginning after the order is made, may—

(*a*) insert Rules or Notes,
(*b*) vary or remove Rules or Notes, or
(*c*) substitute any or all Rules or Notes.][2]

(5) Where, by virtue of section 56(8), subsection (7) of that section has effect as if, in the prescribed accounting period, supplies of fuel for private use made in respect of 2 or more vehicles were made in respect of only one vehicle, the consideration appropriate shall be determined as follows—

(*a*) if each of the 2 or more vehicles falls within the same description of vehicle specified in [Table A above or any Notes, that Table and those Notes][2] shall apply as if only one of the vehicles were to be considered throughout the whole period, and
(*b*) if one of those vehicles falls within a description of vehicle specified in that Table [or those Notes][2] which is different from the other or others, the consideration shall be the aggregate of the relevant fractions of the consideration appropriate for each description of vehicle under that Table [or those Notes][2].

(6) For the purposes of subsection (5)(*b*) above, the relevant fraction in relation to any vehicle is that which the part of the prescribed accounting period in which fuel for private use was supplied in respect of that vehicle bears to the whole of that period.

(7) In the case of a vehicle having an internal combustion engine with one or more reciprocating pistons, its cubic capacity for the purposes of Table A above [and any Notes][2] is the capacity of its engine as calculated for the purposes of the Vehicle Excise and Registration Act 1994.

(8) In the case of a vehicle not falling within subsection (7) above, its cubic capacity shall be such as may be determined for the purposes of Table A above [and any Notes][2] by order by the Treasury.

[(9) In this section—

"CO2 emissions figure" means a CO2 emissions figure expressed in grams per kilometre driven;

"EC certificate of conformity" means a certificate of conformity issued by a manufacturer under any provision of the law of a Member State implementing Article 6 of Council Directive 70/ 156/EEC, as from time to time amended;

"Notes" means Notes inserted by virtue of subsection (4C)(*b*) above;

"Rules" means Rules inserted by virtue of subsection (4C)(*a*) above;

"UK approval certificate" means a certificate issued under—

(*a*) section 58(1) or (4) of the Road Traffic Act 1988, or

(*b*) Article 31A(4) or (5) of the Road Traffic (Northern Ireland) Order 1981.

(10) If the Treasury consider it necessary or expedient to do so in consequence of—

(*a*) the form or content of any Table substituted or to be substituted by virtue of subsection (4A) above, or

(*b*) any provision included or to be included in Rules or Notes,

they may by order amend, repeal or replace so much of this section as for the time being follows subsection (1) and precedes Table A and relates to the use of that Table.][2]

Commentary—*De Voil Indirect Tax Service* **V3.266**.

Definitions—"Fuel for private use", s 56(3)(*a*); "supply", s 5, Sch 4; "vehicle", s 56(10).

Amendments—[1] Sub-s (1A) inserted and words in sub-ss (2), (3) substituted by FA 1995 s 30 with effect in relation to prescribed accounting periods beginning after 5 April 1995 (but not so as to be taken to prejudice any practice by which the consideration appropriate to a vehicle is arrived at where a prescribed accounting period beginning before 6 April 1995 is a period of 12 months).

[2] Sub-ss (4A)–(4G), (9), (10) inserted; in sub-s (5)(*a*) words substituted; in sub-s (5)(*b*) words inserted; and in sub-ss (7), (8) words inserted; by F(No 2)A 2005 s 2 with effect from 22 March 2007 (by virtue of SI 2007/946, art 2).

[3] Notes inserted by the Value Added Tax (Consideration for Fuel Provided for Private Use) Order 2007, SI 2007/966 art 4 with effect from the beginning of prescribed accounting periods beginning on or after 1 May 2007.

[4] In sub-s (3), in Note (6)(*a*), (*c*), words substituted by the VAT (Consideration for Fuel Provided for Private Use) Order, SI 2008/722 art 3 with effect from the beginning of prescribed accounting periods beginning on or after 1 May 2008.

[5] Table A substituted by the Value Added Tax (Consideration for Fuel Provided for Private Use) Order, SI 2009/1030 art 2 with effect from the beginning of prescribed accounting periods beginning on or after 1 May 2009.

PART IV

ADMINISTRATION, COLLECTION AND ENFORCEMENT

Cross reference—See VATA 1994 Sch 13 para 12 (this Part of this Act, except s 72, does not apply in relation to any act or omission before 25 July 1985).

General administrative provisions

58 General provisions relating to the administration and collection of VAT

Schedule 11 shall have effect, subject to section 92(6), with respect to the administration, collection and enforcement of VAT.

Definition—"VAT", ss 1, 96(1).

Disclosure of avoidance schemes

[58A Disclosure of avoidance schemes

Schedule 11A (which imposes disclosure requirements relating to the use of schemes for avoiding VAT) shall have effect.][1]

Commentary—*De Voil Indirect Tax Service* **V5.213, 358**.

Definition—"VAT", ss 1, 96(1).

Amendments—[1] This section inserted by FA 2004 s 19, Sch 2 para 1 with effect from the passing of FA 2004, so far as is necessary for enabling the making of any orders or regulations by virtue of FA 2004 Sch 2, and otherwise with effect from 1 August 2004 (by virtue of SI 2004/1934).

[58B Payment by cheque

Regulations under section 95(1) of the Finance Act 2007 (payment by cheque) may, in particular, provide for a payment which is made by cheque in contravention of regulations under section 25(1) above to be treated as made when the cheque clears, as defined in the regulations under section 95(1) of that Act.][1]

Amendments—[1] This section inserted by FA 2007 s 95(8) with effect from 19 July 2007.

Default surcharges and other penalties and criminal offences

59 The default surcharge

(1) [Subject to subsection (1A) below][1] If, by the last day on which a taxable person is required in accordance with regulations under this Act to furnish a return for a prescribed accounting period—

(*a*) the Commissioners have not received that return, or

(*b*) the Commissioners have received that return but have not received the amount of VAT shown on the return as payable by him in respect of that period, then that person shall be regarded for the purposes of this section as being in default in respect of that period.

[(1A) A person shall not be regarded for the purposes of this section as being in default in respect of any prescribed accounting period if that period is one in respect of which he is required by virtue of any order under section 28 to make any payment on account of VAT.][1]

(2) Subject to subsections (9) and (10) below, subsection (4) below applies in any case where—

(*a*) a taxable person is in default in respect of a prescribed accounting period; and

(*b*) the Commissioners serve notice on the taxable person (a "surcharge liability notice") specifying as a surcharge period for the purposes of this section a period ending on the first anniversary of the last day of the period referred to in paragraph (*a*) above and beginning, subject to subsection (3) below, on the date of the notice.

(3) If a surcharge liability notice is served by reason of a default in respect of a prescribed accounting period and that period ends at or before the expiry of an existing surcharge period already notified to the taxable person concerned, the surcharge period specified in that notice shall be expressed as a continuation of the existing surcharge period and, accordingly, for the purposes of this section, that existing period and its extension shall be regarded as a single surcharge period.

(4) Subject to subsections (7) to (10) below, if a taxable person on whom a surcharge liability notice has been served—

(*a*) is in default in respect of a prescribed accounting period ending within the surcharge period specified in (or extended by) that notice, and

(*b*) has outstanding VAT for that prescribed accounting period,

he shall be liable to a surcharge equal to whichever is the greater of the following, namely, the specified percentage of his outstanding VAT for that prescribed accounting period and £30.

(5) Subject to subsections (7) to (10) below, the specified percentage referred to in subsection (4) above shall be determined in relation to a prescribed accounting period by reference to the number of such periods in respect of which the taxable person is in default during the surcharge period and for which he has outstanding VAT, so that—

(*a*) in relation to the first such prescribed accounting period, the specified percentage is 2 per cent;

(*b*) in relation to the second such period, the specified percentage is 5 per cent;

(*c*) in relation to the third such period, the specified percentage is 10 per cent; and

(*d*) in relation to each such period after the third, the specified percentage is 15 per cent.

(6) For the purposes of subsections (4) and (5) above a person has outstanding VAT for a prescribed accounting period if some or all of the VAT for which he is liable in respect of that period has not been paid by the last day on which he is required (as mentioned in subsection (1) above) to make a return for that period; and the reference in subsection (4) above to a person's outstanding VAT for a prescribed accounting period is to so much of the VAT for which he is so liable as has not been paid by that day.

(7) If a person who, apart from this subsection, would be liable to a surcharge under subsection (4) above satisfies the Commissioners or, on appeal, a tribunal that, in the case of a default which is material to the surcharge—

(*a*) the return or, as the case may be, the VAT shown on the return was despatched at such a time and in such a manner that it was reasonable to expect that it would be received by the Commissioners within the appropriate time limit, or

(*b*) there is a reasonable excuse for the return or VAT not having been so despatched,

he shall not be liable to the surcharge and for the purposes of the preceding provisions of this section he shall be treated as not having been in default in respect of the prescribed accounting period in question (and, accordingly, any surcharge liability notice the service of which depended upon that default shall be deemed not to have been served).

(8) For the purposes of subsection (7) above, a default is material to a surcharge if—

(*a*) it is the default which, by virtue of subsection (4) above, gives rise to the surcharge; or

(*b*) it is a default which was taken into account in the service of the surcharge liability notice upon which the surcharge depends and the person concerned has not previously been liable to a surcharge in respect of a prescribed accounting period ending within the surcharge period specified in or extended by that notice.

(9) In any case where—

(*a*) the conduct by virtue of which a person is in default in respect of a prescribed accounting period is also conduct falling within section 69(1), and

(*b*) by reason of that conduct, the person concerned is assessed to a penalty under that section,

the default shall be left out of account for the purposes of subsections (2) to (5) above.

(10) If the Commissioners, after consultation with the Treasury, so direct, a default in respect of a prescribed accounting period specified in the direction shall be left out of account for the purposes of subsections (2) to (5) above.

[(11) For the purposes of this section references to a thing's being done by any day include references to its being done on that day.][1]

Commentary—*De Voil Indirect Tax Service* **V5.371–V5.376.**
Press releases etc—C&E Press Notice 23/95 10-4-95 (Customs error in imposing penalties).
Simon's Tax Cases—s 59(7), *T E Davey Photo Service Ltd v C&E Comrs* [1997] STC 889*; *CMS Peripherals Ltd v R&C Comrs* [2008] STC 985.
Definitions—"The Commissioners", s 96(1); "prescribed accounting period", s 25(1); "reasonable excuse", s 71(1); "regulations", s 96(1); "taxable person", s 3; "tribunal", s 82; "VAT", ss 1, 96(1).
Cross references—See VATA 1994 s 59B(1)(*b*), (3) (application of this section where a prescribed accounting period in respect of which a person is not liable to make a payment on account ends within a surcharge period under s 59A).
VATA 1994 s 66(7) (failure to submit EC sales statement within time limit: circumstances in which person is not to be treated as in default);
VATA 1994 s 69(4)(*a*), (9) (avoidance of double penalty for same conduct);
VATA 1994 s 71(1) (reasonable excuse for conduct within this section);
VATA 1994 s 71(2) (meaning of "credit for input tax");
VATA 1994 ss 76, 77 (assessment of surcharges under this section);
VATA 1994 ss 83, 84 (appeal to a tribunal in respect of a surcharge under this section);
VATA 1994 Sch 13 para 14 (modification of this section in its application to certain periods before the commencement of VATA 1994).
FA 2009 s 108 (suspension of penalties during currency of agreement for deferred payment).
Amendments—[1] Words in sub-s (1), and sub-ss (1A), (11), inserted by FA 1996 s 35(3), (4), with effect in relation to any prescribed accounting period ending on or after 1 June 1996, but a liability to make a payment on account of VAT shall be disregarded for the purposes of the amendments made by FA 1996 s 35 if the payment is one becoming due before that date.

[59A Default surcharge: payments on account

(1) For the purposes of this section a taxable person shall be regarded as in default in respect of any prescribed accounting period if the period is one in respect of which he is required, by virtue of an order under section 28, to make any payment on account of VAT and either—

(*a*) a payment which he is so required to make in respect of that period has not been received in full by the Commissioners by the day on which it became due; or
(*b*) he would, but for section 59(1A), be in default in respect of that period for the purposes of section 59.

(2) Subject to subsections (10) and (11) below, subsection (4) below applies in any case where—

(*a*) a taxable person is in default in respect of a prescribed accounting period; and
(*b*) the Commissioners serve notice on the taxable person (a "surcharge liability notice") specifying as a surcharge period for the purposes of this section a period which—

(i) begins, subject to subsection (3) below, on the date of the notice; and
(ii) ends on the first anniversary of the last day of the period referred to in paragraph (*a*) above.

(3) If—

(*a*) a surcharge liability notice is served by reason of a default in respect of a prescribed accounting period, and
(*b*) that period ends at or before the expiry of an existing surcharge period already notified to the taxable person concerned,

the surcharge period specified in that notice shall be expressed as a continuation of the existing surcharge period; and, accordingly, the existing period and its extension shall be regarded as a single surcharge period.

(4) Subject to subsections (7) to (11) below, if—

(*a*) a taxable person on whom a surcharge liability notice has been served is in default in respect of a prescribed accounting period,
(*b*) that prescribed accounting period is one ending within the surcharge period specified in (or extended by) that notice, and
(*c*) the aggregate value of his defaults in respect of that prescribed accounting period is more than nil,

that person shall be liable to a surcharge equal to whichever is the greater of £30 and the specified percentage of the aggregate value of his defaults in respect of that prescribed accounting period.

(5) Subject to subsections (7) to (11) below, the specified percentage referred to in subsection (4) above shall be determined in relation to a prescribed accounting period by reference to the number of such periods during the surcharge period which are periods in respect of which the taxable person is in default and in respect of which the value of his defaults is more than nil, so that—

(*a*) in relation to the first such prescribed accounting period, the specified percentage is 2 per cent;
(*b*) in relation to the second such period, the specified percentage is 5 per cent;
(*c*) in relation to the third such period, the specified percentage is 10 per cent; and
(*d*) in relation to each such period after the third, the specified percentage is 15 per cent.

(6) For the purposes of this section the aggregate value of a person's defaults in respect of a prescribed accounting period shall be calculated as follows—

(*a*) where the whole or any part of a payment in respect of that period on account of VAT was not received by the Commissioners by the day on which it became due, an amount equal to that payment or, as the case may be, to that part of it shall be taken to be the value of the default relating to that payment;

(*b*) if there is more than one default with a value given by paragraph (*a*) above, those values shall be aggregated;

(*c*) the total given by paragraph (*b*) above, or (where there is only one default) the value of the default under paragraph (*a*) above, shall be taken to be the value for that period of that person's defaults on payments on account;

(*d*) the value of any default by that person which is a default falling within subsection (1)(*b*) above shall be taken to be equal to the amount of any outstanding VAT less the amount of unpaid payments on account; and

(*e*) the aggregate value of a person's defaults in respect of that period shall be taken to be the aggregate of—

(i) the value for that period of that person's defaults (if any) on payments on account; and

(ii) the value of any default of his in respect of that period that falls within subsection (1)(*b*) above.

(7) In the application of subsection (6) above for the calculation of the aggregate value of a person's defaults in respect of a prescribed accounting period—

(*a*) the amount of outstanding VAT referred to in paragraph (*d*) of that subsection is the amount (if any) which would be the amount of that person's outstanding VAT for that period for the purposes of section 59(4); and

(*b*) the amount of unpaid payments on account referred to in that paragraph is the amount (if any) equal to so much of any payments on account of VAT (being payments in respect of that period) as has not been received by the Commissioners by the last day on which that person is required (as mentioned in section 59(1)) to make a return for that period.

(8) If a person who, apart from this subsection, would be liable to a surcharge under subsection (4) above satisfies the Commissioners or, on appeal, a tribunal—

(*a*) in the case of a default that is material for the purposes of the surcharge and falls within subsection (1)(*a*) above—

(i) that the payment on account of VAT was despatched at such a time and in such a manner that it was reasonable to expect that it would be received by the Commissioners by the day on which it became due, or

(ii) that there is a reasonable excuse for the payment not having been so despatched,

or

(*b*) in the case of a default that is material for the purposes of the surcharge and falls within subsection (1)(*b*) above, that the condition specified in section 59(7)(*a*) or (*b*) is satisfied as respects the default,

he shall not be liable to the surcharge and for the purposes of the preceding provisions of this section he shall be treated as not having been in default in respect of the prescribed accounting period in question (and, accordingly, any surcharge liability notice the service of which depended upon that default shall be deemed not to have been served).

(9) For the purposes of subsection (8) above, a default is material to a surcharge if—

(*a*) it is the default which, by virtue of subsection (4) above, gives rise to the surcharge; or

(*b*) it is a default which was taken into account in the service of the surcharge liability notice upon which the surcharge depends and the person concerned has not previously been liable to a surcharge in respect of a prescribed accounting period ending within the surcharge period specified in or extended by that notice.

(10) In any case where—

(*a*) the conduct by virtue of which a person is in default in respect of a prescribed accounting period is also conduct falling within section 69(1), and

(*b*) by reason of that conduct, the person concerned is assessed to a penalty under section 69,

the default shall be left out of account for the purposes of subsections (2) to (5) above.

(11) If the Commissioners, after consultation with the Treasury, so direct, a default in respect of a prescribed accounting period specified in the direction shall be left out of account for the purposes of subsections (2) to (5) above.

(12) For the purposes of this section the Commissioners shall be taken not to receive a payment by the day on which it becomes due unless it is made in such a manner as secures (in a case where the payment is made otherwise than in cash) that, by the last day for the payment of that amount, all the transactions can be completed that need to be completed before the whole amount of the payment becomes available to the Commissioners.

(13) In determining for the purposes of this section whether any person would, but for section 59(1A), be in default in respect of any period for the purposes of section 59, subsection (12) above shall be deemed to apply for the purposes of section 59 as it applies for the purposes of this section.

(14) For the purposes of this section references to a thing's being done by any day include references to its being done on that day.][1]

Commentary—*De Voil Indirect Tax Service* **V5.371–V5.376**.
Simon's Tax Cases—s 59A(1), *CMS Peripherals Ltd v R&C Comrs* [2008] STC 985.
Definitions—"The Commissioners", s 96(1); "prescribed accounting period", s 25(1); "reasonable excuse", s 71(1); "taxable person", ss 3, 96(1); "tribunal", ss 82, 96(1); "VAT", s 96(1).
Cross references—See VATA 1994 s 59B(1)(*a*), (2) (application of this section where a prescribed accounting period in respect of which a person is liable to make a payment on account ends within a surcharge period under s 59).
VATA 1994 s 66(7) (failure to submit EC sales statement within time limit: circumstances in which a person is not to be treated as in default).
VATA 1994 s 69(4)(*a*), (9) (avoidance of double penalty for the same conduct).
VATA 1994 ss 76, 77 (assessment of surcharges under this section).
FA 2009 s 108 (suspension of penalties during currency of agreement for deferred payment).
Amendments—[1] Section inserted by FA 1996 s 35(2), with effect in relation to any prescribed accounting period ending on or after 1 June 1996, but a liability to make a payment on account of VAT shall be disregarded for the purposes of the amendments made by FA 1996 s 35 if the payment is one becoming due before that date.

[59B Relationship between sections 59 and 59A

(1) This section applies in each of the following cases, namely—

(*a*) where a section 28 accounting period ends within a surcharge period begun or extended by the service on a taxable person (whether before or after the coming into force of section 59A) of a surcharge liability notice under section 59; and

(*b*) where a prescribed accounting period which is not a section 28 accounting period ends within a surcharge period begun or extended by the service on a taxable person of a surcharge liability notice under section 59A.

(2) In a case falling within subsection (1)(*a*) above section 59A shall have effect as if—

(*a*) subject to paragraph (*b*) below, the section 28 accounting period were deemed to be a period ending within a surcharge period begun or, as the case may be, extended by a notice served under section 59A; but

(*b*) any question—

(i) whether a surcharge period was begun or extended by the notice, or

(ii) whether the taxable person was in default in respect of any prescribed accounting period which was not a section 28 accounting period but ended within the surcharge period begun or extended by that notice,

were to be determined as it would be determined for the purposes of section 59.

(3) In a case falling within subsection (1)(*b*) above section 59 shall have effect as if—

(*a*) subject to paragraph (*b*) below, the prescribed accounting period that is not a section 28 accounting period were deemed to be a period ending within a surcharge period begun or, as the case may be, extended by a notice served under section 59;

(*b*) any question—

(i) whether a surcharge period was begun or extended by the notice, or

(ii) whether the taxable person was in default in respect of any prescribed accounting period which was a section 28 accounting period but ended within the surcharge period begun or extended by that notice,

were to be determined as it would be determined for the purposes of section 59A; and

(*c*) that person were to be treated as having had outstanding VAT for a section 28 accounting period in any case where the aggregate value of his defaults in respect of that period was, for the purposes of section 59A, more than nil.

(4) In this section "a section 28 accounting period", in relation to a taxable person, means any prescribed accounting period ending on or after the day on which the Finance Act 1996 was passed in respect of which that person is liable by virtue of an order under section 28 to make any payment on account of VAT.][1]

Commentary—*De Voil Indirect Tax Service* **V5.371–V5.376**.
Definitions—"Prescribed accounting period", s 25(1); "surcharge liability notice", s 59(2); "taxable person", ss 3, 96(1).
Amendments—[1] Section inserted by FA 1996 s 35(5), with effect in relation to any prescribed accounting period ending on or after 1 June 1996, but a liability to make a payment on account of VAT shall be disregarded for the purposes of the amendments made by FA 1996 s 35 if the payment is one becoming due before that date.

60 VAT evasion: conduct involving dishonesty

(1) In any case where—

(a) for the purpose of evading VAT, a person does any act or omits to take any action, and

(b) his conduct involves dishonesty (whether or not it is such as to give rise to criminal liability),

he shall be liable, subject to subsection (6) below, to a penalty equal to the amount of VAT evaded or, as the case may be, sought to be evaded, by his conduct.

(2) The reference in subsection (1)(a) above to evading VAT includes a reference to obtaining any of the following sums—

(a) a refund under any regulations made by virtue of section 13(5);

(b) a VAT credit;

(c) a refund under section 35, 36 or 40 of this Act or section 22 of the 1983 Act; and

(d) a repayment under section 39,

in circumstances where the person concerned is not entitled to that sum.

(3) The reference in subsection (1) above to the amount of the VAT evaded or sought to be evaded by a person's conduct shall be construed—

(a) in relation to VAT itself or a VAT credit as a reference to the aggregate of the amount (if any) falsely claimed by way of credit for input tax and the amount (if any) by which output tax was falsely understated; and

(b) in relation to the sums referred to in subsection (2)(a), (c) and (e) above, as a reference to the amount falsely claimed by way of refund or repayment.

(4) Statements made or documents produced by or on behalf of a person shall not be inadmissible in any such proceedings as are mentioned in subsection (5) below by reason only that it has been drawn to his attention—

(a) that, in relation to VAT, the Commissioners may assess an amount due by way of a civil penalty instead of instituting criminal proceedings and, though no undertaking can be given as to whether the Commissioners will make such an assessment in the case of any person, it is their practice to be influenced by the fact that a person has made a full confession of any dishonest conduct to which he has been a party and has given full facilities for investigation, and

(b) that the Commissioners or, on appeal, a tribunal have power under section 70 to reduce a penalty under this section,

and that he was or may have been induced thereby to make the statements or produce the documents.

(5) The proceedings mentioned in subsection (4) above are—

(a) any criminal proceedings against the person concerned in respect of any offence in connection with or in relation to VAT, and

(b) any proceedings against him for the recovery of any sum due from him in connection with or in relation to VAT.

(6) Where, by reason of conduct falling within subsection (1) above, a person is convicted of an offence (whether under this Act or otherwise), that conduct shall not also give rise to liability to a penalty under this section.

(7) On an appeal against an assessment to a penalty under this section, the burden of proof as to the matters specified in subsection (1)(a) and (b) above shall lie upon the Commissioners.[1]

Commentary—*De Voil Indirect Tax Service* **V5.341**.

Simon's Tax Cases—*Nidderdale Building Ltd v C&E Comrs* [1997] STC 800; *1st Indian Cavalry Club Ltd and Chowdhury v C&E Comrs* [1998] STC 293; *Ali (T/A Vakas Balti) v R&C Comrs* [2007] STC 618.

s 60(1), *Stuttarrd and anor v C&E Comrs* [2000] STC 342; *McNicholas Construction Limited v C&E Comrs* [2000] STC 553, *C&E Comrs v Han* [2001] STC 1188; *Khan (t/a Greyhound Dry Cleaners) v C&E Comrs* [2006] STC 1167.

s 60(2), *Stevenson and Telford Building & Design Ltd v C&E Comrs* [1996] STC 1096*.

s 60(3), *C&E Comrs v Stevenson* [1995] STC 667*; *Stevenson and Telford Building & Design Ltd v C&E Comrs* [1996] STC 1096*.

Definitions—"The 1983 Act", s 96(1); "the Commissioners", s 96(1); "credit for input tax", s 71(2); "document", s 96(1); "input tax", s 24; "output tax", s 24; "tribunal", s 82; "VAT", ss 1, 96(1); "VAT credit", s 25(3).

Cross references—See VATA 1994 ss 63(11), 64(6), 67(8), 69(9) (avoidance of double penalty for the same conduct);

VATA 1994 s 66(7) (failure to submit EC sales statement within time limit: circumstances in which person is not to be treated as in default);

VATA 1994 s 70(1) (mitigation of penalties imposed under this section);

VATA 1994 s 71(1) (reasonable excuse for conduct within this section);

VATA 1994 s 71(2) (meaning of "credit for input tax");

VATA 1994 ss 76, 77 (assessment of penalties under this section);

VATA 1994 ss 83, 84 (appeal to a tribunal in respect of a penalty under this section);

VATA 1994 Sch 13 para 17 (modification of this section in relation to penalties assessed before 27 July 1993).

VAT Tribunals Rules, SI 1986/590 reg 7 (statement of case, defence and reply in appeals under this section);

VAT Tribunals Rules, SI 1986/590 reg 20(2) (time limit for service of documents in appeals under this section);

VAT Tribunals Rules, SI 1986/590 reg 21(6) (time limit for witness statements in appeals under this section);

VAT Tribunals Rules, SI 1986/590 reg 27(2) (procedure for hearing of appeals under this section).

Amendments—[1] This section repealed by FA 2007 ss 97, 114, Sch 24 para 29(*d*), Sch 27 Pt 5(5) with effect as follows (by virtue of SI 2008/568 art 2, and subject to transitional provisions and savings in arts 3, 4)—

– 1 April 2008 in relation to relevant documents relating to tax periods commencing on or after that date;

– 1 April 2008 in relation to assessments falling within Sch 24 para 2 for tax periods commencing on or after that date;

– 1 July 2008 in relation to relevant documents relating to claims under the Thirteenth Council Directive (arrangements for the refund of value added tax to persons not established in Community territory) for years commencing on or after that date;

– 1 January 2009 in relation to relevant documents relating to claims under the Eighth Council Directive (arrangements for the refund of value added tax to taxable persons not established in the territory of the country) for years commencing on or after that date;

– 1 April 2009 in relation to documents relating to all other claims for repayments of relevant tax made on or after 1 April 2009 which are not related to a tax period; and

– in any other case, 1 April 2009 in relation to documents given where a person's liability to pay relevant tax arises on or after that date.

Sections 60, 61 shall continue to have effect with respect to conduct involving dishonesty which does not relate to an inaccuracy in a document or a failure to notify HMRC of an under-assessment by HMRC (SI 2008/568 art 4).

Notwithstanding FA 2007 Sch 24 para 29(*d*), ss 60 and 61 shall continue to have effect with respect to conduct involving dishonesty which does not relate to an inaccuracy in a document or a failure to notify HMRC of an under-assessment by HMRC (SI 2009/571 art 7).

61 VAT evasion: liability of directors etc

(1) Where it appears to the Commissioners—

(a) that a body corporate is liable to a penalty under section 60, and

(b) that the conduct giving rise to that penalty is, in whole or in part, attributable to the dishonesty of a person who is, or at the material time was, a director or managing officer of the body corporate (a "named officer"),

the Commissioners may serve a notice under this section on the body corporate and on the named officer.

(2) A notice under this section shall state—

(a) the amount of the penalty referred to in subsection (1)(a) above ("the basic penalty"), and
(b) that the Commissioners propose, in accordance with this section, to recover from the named officer such portion (which may be the whole) of the basic penalty as is specified in the notice.

(3) Where a notice is served under this section, the portion of the basic penalty specified in the notice shall be recoverable from the named officer as if he were personally liable under section 60 to a penalty which corresponds to that portion; and the amount of that penalty may be assessed and notified to him accordingly under section 76.

(4) Where a notice is served under this section—

(a) the amount which, under section 76, may be assessed as the amount due by way of penalty from the body corporate shall be only so much (if any) of the basic penalty as is not assessed on and notified to a named officer by virtue of subsection (3) above; and
(b) the body corporate shall be treated as discharged from liability for so much of the basic penalty as is so assessed and notified.

(5) No appeal shall lie against a notice under this section as such but—

(a) where a body corporate is assessed as mentioned in subsection (4)(a) above, the body corporate may appeal against the Commissioners' decision as to its liability to a penalty and against the amount of the basic penalty as if it were specified in the assessment; and
(b) where an assessment is made on a named officer by virtue of subsection (3) above, the named officer may appeal against the Commissioners' decision that the conduct of the body corporate referred to in subsection (1)(b) above is, in whole or part, attributable to his dishonesty and against their decision as to the portion of the penalty which the Commissioners propose to recover from him.

(6) In this section a "managing officer", in relation to a body corporate, means any manager, secretary or other similar officer of the body corporate or any person purporting to act in any such capacity or as a director; and where the affairs of a body corporate are managed by its members, this section shall apply in relation to the conduct of a member in connection with his functions of management as if he were a director of the body corporate.[1]

Commentary—*De Voil Indirect Tax Service* **V5.341**.
Simon's Tax Cases—*C&E Comrs v Bassimeh* [1997] STC 33*; *Nidderdale Building Ltd v C&E Comrs*; *Lofthouse v C&E Comrs* [1997] STC 800.
s 61(1), (6), *McNicholas Construction Limited v C&E Comrs* [2000] STC 553.
Definitions—"The Commissioners", s 96(1).
Cross references—See VATA 1994 ss 64(6), 69(9) (avoidance of double penalty for the same conduct);
VATA 1994 s 66(7) (failure to submit EC sales statement within time limit: circumstances in which person is not to be treated as in default);
VATA 1994 s 71(1) (reasonable excuse for conduct within this section);
VATA 1994 s 71(2) (meaning of "credit for input tax");
VATA 1994 ss 76, 77 (assessment of penalties under this section);
VATA 1994 ss 83, 84 (appeal to a tribunal in respect of a penalty or a decision of the Commissioners under this section);
VATA 1994 Sch 13 para 17 (modification of sub-s (6) of this section in relation to penalties assessed before 27 July 1993).
VAT Tribunals Rules, SI 1986/590 reg 7 (statement of case, defence and reply in appeals under this section);
VAT Tribunals Rules, SI 1986/590 reg 20(2) (time limit for service of documents in appeals under this section);
VAT Tribunals Rules, SI 1986/590 reg 21(6) (time limit for witness statements in appeals under this section);
VAT Tribunals Rules, SI 1986/590 reg 27(2) (procedure for hearing of appeals under this section).
Amendments—[1] This section repealed by FA 2007 ss 97, 114, Sch 24 para 29(*d*), Sch 27 Pt 5(5) with effect as follows (by virtue of SI 2008/568 art 2, and subject to transitional provisions and savings in arts 3, 4)—

- 1 April 2008 in relation to relevant documents relating to tax periods commencing on or after that date;
- 1 April 2008 in relation to assessments falling within Sch 24 para 2 for tax periods commencing on or after that date;
- 1 July 2008 in relation to relevant documents relating to claims under the Thirteenth Council Directive (arrangements for the refund of value added tax to persons not established in Community territory) for years commencing on or after that date;
- 1 January 2009 in relation to relevant documents relating to claims under the Eighth Council Directive (arrangements for the refund of value added tax to taxable persons not established in the territory of the country) for years commencing on or after that date;
- 1 April 2009 in relation to documents relating to all other claims for repayments of relevant tax made on or after 1 April 2009 which are not related to a tax period; and
- in any other case, 1 April 2009 in relation to documents given where a person's liability to pay relevant tax arises on or after that date.

Sections 60, 61 shall continue to have effect with respect to conduct involving dishonesty which does not relate to an inaccuracy in a document or a failure to notify HMRC of an under-assessment by HMRC (SI 2008/568 art 4).
Notwithstanding FA 2007 Sch 24 para 29(*d*), ss 60 and 61 shall continue to have effect with respect to conduct involving dishonesty which does not relate to an inaccuracy in a document or a failure to notify HMRC of an under-assessment by HMRC (SI 2009/571 art 7).

62 Incorrect certificates as to zero-rating etc

[(1) Subject to subsections (3) and (4) below, where—

(*a*) a person to whom one or more supplies are, or are to be, made—

(i) gives to the supplier a certificate that the supply or supplies fall, or will fall, wholly or partly within [any of the Groups of Schedule 7A][3], Group 5 or 6 of Schedule 8 or Group 1 of Schedule 9, or

(ii) gives to the supplier a certificate for the purposes of section 18B(2)(*d*) or 18C(1)(*c*), and

(*b*) the certificate is incorrect,

the person giving the certificate shall be liable to a penalty.

(1A) Subject to subsections (3) and (4) below, where—

(*a*) a person who makes, or is to make, an acquisition of goods from another member State prepares a certificate for the purposes of section 18B(1)(*d*), and

(*b*) the certificate is incorrect,

the person preparing the certificate shall be liable to a penalty.

(2) The amount of the penalty shall be equal to—

(*a*) in a case where the penalty is imposed by virtue of subsection (1) above, the difference between—

(i) the amount of the VAT which would have been chargeable on the supply or supplies if the certificate had been correct; and

(ii) the amount of VAT actually chargeable;

(*b*) in a case where it is imposed by virtue of subsection (1A) above, the amount of VAT actually chargeable on the acquisition.][2]

(3) The giving [or preparing][1] of a certificate shall not give rise to a penalty under this section if the person who gave [or prepared][1] it satisfies the Commissioners or, on appeal, a tribunal that there is a reasonable excuse for his having given [or prepared][1] it.

(4) Where by reason of giving [or preparing][1] a certificate a person is convicted of an offence (whether under this Act or otherwise), the giving [or preparing][1] of the certificate shall not also give rise to a penalty under this section.

Commentary—*De Voil Indirect Tax Service* **V5.342**.

Definitions—"The 1983 Act", s 96(1); "acquisition of goods from another member State", s 11; "the Commissioners", s 96(1); "reasonable excuse", s 71(1); "supply", s 5, Sch 4; "tribunal", s 82; "VAT", ss 1, 96(1).

Cross references—See VATA 1994 ss 64(6), 69(9) (avoidance of double penalty for the same conduct);
VATA 1994 s 66(7) (failure to submit EC sales statement within time limit: circumstances in which person is not to be treated as in default);
VATA 1994 s 71(1) (reasonable excuse for conduct within this section);
VATA 1994 s 71(2) (meaning of "credit for input tax");
VATA 1994 ss 76, 77 (assessment of penalties under this section);
VATA 1994 ss 83, 84 (appeal to a tribunal in respect of a penalty under this section).

Amendments—[1] Words in sub-ss (3) and (4) inserted and word "or" at the end of sub-para (i) and word "and" at the end of sub-para (ii) of sub-s (1)(*a*) repealed by FA 1996 Sch 3 para 8, Sch 41 Pt IV(1), with effect from 1 June 1996 (see Finance Act 1996, Section 26, (Appointed Day) Order, SI 1996/1249), and applying to any acquisition of goods from another member State and any supply taking place on or after that day.

[2] Sub-ss (1) and (2) substituted and sub-s (1A) inserted by FA 1999 s 17 with effect in relation to certificates given or, as the case may be, prepared on or after 27 July 1999.

[3] Words substituted for "paragraph 1 of Schedule A1" by FA 2001 s 99(6), Sch 31 para 3 with effect for supplies made, or to be made, after 31 October 2001.

63 Penalty for misdeclaration or neglect resulting in VAT loss for one accounting period equalling or exceeding certain amounts

(1) In any case where, for a prescribed accounting period—

(a) a return is made which understates a person's liability to VAT or overstates his entitlement to a VAT credit, or

(b) an assessment is made which understates a person's liability to VAT and, at the end of the period of 30 days beginning on the date of the assessment, he has not taken all such steps as are reasonable to draw the understatement to the attention of the Commissioners,

and the circumstances are as set out in subsection (2) below, the person concerned shall be liable, subject to subsections (10) and (11) below, to a penalty equal to 15 per cent of the VAT which would have been lost if the inaccuracy had not been discovered.

(2) The circumstances referred to in subsection (1) above are that the VAT for the period concerned which would have been lost if the inaccuracy had not been discovered equals or exceeds whichever is the lesser of £1,000,000 and 30 per cent of the relevant amount for that period.

(3) Any reference in this section to the VAT for a prescribed accounting period which would have been lost if an inaccuracy had not been discovered is a reference to the amount of the understatement of liability or, as the case may be, overstatement of entitlement referred to, in relation to that period, in subsection (1) above.

(4) In this section "the relevant amount", in relation to a prescribed accounting period, means—

(a) for the purposes of a case falling within subsection (1)(a) above, the gross amount of VAT for that period; and

(b) for the purposes of a case falling within subsection (1)(b) above, the true amount of VAT for that period.

(5) In this section "the gross amount of tax", in relation to a prescribed accounting period, means the aggregate of the following amounts, that is to say—

(*a*) *the amount of credit for input tax which* (*subject to subsection* (8) *below*) *should have been stated on the return for that period, and*

(*b*) *the amount of output tax which* (*subject to that subsection*) *should have been so stated.*

(6) *In relation to any return which, in accordance with prescribed requirements, includes a single amount as the aggregate for the prescribed accounting period to which the return relates of—*

(*a*) *the amount representing credit for input tax, and*

(*b*) *any other amounts representing refunds or repayments of VAT to which there is an entitlement,*

references in this section to the amount of credit for input tax shall have effect (*so far as they would not so have effect by virtue of subsection* (9) *below*) *as references to the amount of that aggregate.*

(7) *In this section "the true amount of VAT", in relation to a prescribed accounting period, means the amount of VAT which was due from the person concerned for that period or, as the case may be, the amount of the VAT credit* (*if any*) *to which he was entitled for that period.*

(8) *Where—*

(*a*) *a return for any prescribed accounting period overstates or understates to any extent a person's liability to VAT or his entitlement to a VAT credit, and*

(*b*) *that return is corrected, in such circumstances and in accordance with such conditions as may be prescribed, by a return for a later such period which understates or overstates, to the corresponding extent, that liability or entitlement,*

it shall be assumed for the purposes of this section that the statements made by each of those returns (*so far as they are not inaccurate in any other respect*) *are correct statements for the accounting period to which it relates.*

(9) *This section shall have effect in relation to a body which is registered and to which section 33 applies as if—*

(*a*) *any reference to a VAT credit included a reference to a refund under that section, and*

(*b*) *any reference to credit for input tax included a reference to VAT chargeable on supplies, acquisitions or importations which were not for the purposes of any business carried on by the body.*

[(9A) This section shall have effect in relation to a body which is registered and to which section 33A applies as if—

(*a*) *any reference to a VAT credit included a reference to a refund under that section, and*

(*b*) *any reference to credit for input tax included a reference to VAT chargeable on supplies, acquisitions or importations which were attributable to the provision by the body of free rights of admission to a museum or gallery that in relation to the body was a relevant museum or gallery for the purposes of section 33A.]*[1]

(10) *Conduct falling within subsection* (1) *above shall not give rise to liability to a penalty under this section if—*

(*a*) *the person concerned satisfies the Commissioners or, on appeal, a tribunal that there is a reasonable excuse for the conduct, or*

(*b*) *at a time when he had no reason to believe that enquiries were being made by the Commissioners into his affairs, so far as they relate to VAT, the person concerned furnished to the Commissioners full information with respect to the inaccuracy concerned.*

(11) *Where, by reason of conduct falling within subsection* (1) *above—*

(*a*) *a person is convicted of an offence* (*whether under this Act or otherwise*), *or*

(*b*) *a person is assessed to a penalty under section 60,*

that conduct shall not also give rise to liability to a penalty under this section.[2]

Commentary—*De Voil Indirect Tax Service* **V5.343, V5.344**.

Definitions—"Business", s 94; "the Commissioners", s 96(1); "credit for input tax", s 71(2); "input tax", s 24; "output tax", s 24; "prescribed", s 96(1); "prescribed accounting period", s 25(1); "reasonable excuse", s 71(1); "registered", s 3(3); "supply", s 5, Sch 4; "tribunal", s 82; "VAT", ss 1, 96(1); "VAT credit", s 25(3).

Cross references—See VATA 1994 ss 64(6), 69(9) (avoidance of double penalty for the same conduct);

VATA 1994 s 66(7) (failure to submit EC sales statement within time limit: circumstances in which person is not to be treated as in default);

VATA 1994 s 70(1) (mitigation of penalties imposed under this section);

VATA 1994 s 71(1) (reasonable excuse for conduct within this section);

VATA 1994 s 71(2) (meaning of "credit for input tax");

VATA 1994 ss 76, 77 (assessment of penalties under this section);

VATA 1994 ss 83, 84 (appeal to a tribunal in respect of a penalty under this section);

VATA 1994 Sch 13 para 15 (this section does not apply to returns and assessments made for prescribed accounting periods beginning before 1 April 1990 and applies with modifications in relation to periods beginning after that date but before 1 June 1994).

Amendments—[1] Sub-s (9A) inserted by FA 2001 s 98(1), (3) with effect from 1 September 2001.

[2] This section repealed by FA 2007 ss 97, 114, Sch 24 para 29(*d*), Sch 27 Pt 5(5) with effect as follows (by virtue of SI 2008/568 art 2, and subject to transitional provisions and savings in arts 3, 4)—

– 1 April 2008 in relation to relevant documents relating to tax periods commencing on or after that date;

– 1 April 2008 in relation to assessments falling within Sch 24 para 2 for tax periods commencing on or after that date;

– 1 July 2008 in relation to relevant documents relating to claims under the Thirteenth Council Directive (arrangements for the refund of value added tax to persons not established in Community territory) for years commencing on or after that date;

– 1 January 2009 in relation to relevant documents relating to claims under the Eighth Council Directive (arrangements for the refund of value added tax to taxable persons not established in the territory of the country) for years commencing on or after that date;

– 1 April 2009 in relation to documents relating to all other claims for repayments of relevant tax made on or after 1 April 2009 which are not related to a tax period; and
– in any other case, 1 April 2009 in relation to documents given where a person's liability to pay relevant tax arises on or after that date.

64 Repeated misdeclarations

(1) In any case where—

(a) for a prescribed accounting period (including one beginning before the commencement of this section), a return has been made which understates a person's liability to VAT or overstates his entitlement to a VAT credit; and

(b) the VAT for that period which would have been lost if the inaccuracy had not been discovered equals or exceeds whichever is the lesser of £500,000 and 10 per cent of the gross amount of tax for that period,

the inaccuracy shall be regarded, subject to subsections (5) and (6) below, as material for the purposes of this section.

(2) Subsection (3) below applies in any case where—

(a) there is a material inaccuracy in respect of any prescribed accounting period;

(b) the Commissioners serve notice on the person concerned (a "penalty liability notice") specifying a penalty period for the purposes of this section;

(c) that notice is served before the end of 5 consecutive prescribed accounting periods beginning with the period in respect of which there was the material inaccuracy; and

(d) the period specified in the penalty liability notice as the penalty period is the period of 8 consecutive prescribed accounting periods beginning with that in which the date of the notice falls.

(3) If, where a penalty liability notice has been served on any person, there is a material inaccuracy in respect of any of the prescribed accounting periods falling within the penalty period specified in the notice, that person shall be liable, except in relation to the first of those periods in respect of which there is a material inaccuracy, to a penalty equal to 15 per cent of the VAT for the prescribed accounting period in question which would have been lost if the inaccuracy had not been discovered.

(4) Subsections (3), (5), (8) and (9) of section 63 shall apply for the purposes of this section as they apply for the purposes of that section.

(5) An inaccuracy shall not be regarded as material for the purposes of this section if—

(a) the person concerned satisfies the Commissioners or, on appeal, a tribunal that there is a reasonable excuse for the inaccuracy; or

(b) at a time when he had no reason to believe that enquiries were being made by the Commissioners into his affairs, so far as they relate to VAT, the person concerned furnished to the Commissioners full information with respect to the inaccuracy.

[(6) Subject to subsection (6A) below, where by reason of conduct falling within subsection (1) above—

(a) a person is convicted of an offence (whether under this Act or otherwise), or

(b) a person is assessed to a penalty under section 60 or 63,

the inaccuracy concerned shall not be regarded as material for the purposes of this section.][1]

[(6A) Subsection (6) above shall not prevent an inaccuracy by reason of which a person has been assessed to a penalty under section 63—

(a) from being regarded as a material inaccuracy in respect of which the Commissioners may serve a penalty liability notice under subsection (2) above; or

(b) from being regarded for the purposes of subsection (3) above as a material inaccuracy by reference to which any prescribed accounting period falling within the penalty period is to be treated as the first prescribed accounting period so falling in respect of which there is a material inaccuracy.][1]

[(7) Where subsection (5) or (6) above requires any inaccuracy to be regarded as not material for the purposes of the serving of a penalty liability notice, any such notice served in respect of that inaccuracy shall be deemed not to have been served.][1, 2]

Commentary—*De Voil Indirect Tax Service* **V5.344**.

Definitions—"The Commissioners", s 96(1); "prescribed accounting period", s 25(1); "reasonable excuse", s 71(1); "tribunal", s 82; "VAT", ss 1, 96(1); "VAT credit", s 25(3); "VAT which would have been lost if the inaccuracy had not been discovered", s 64(3).

Cross references—See VATA 1994 s 66(7) (failure to submit EC sales statement within time limit: circumstances in which person is not to be treated as in default);
VATA 1994 s 70(1) (mitigation of penalties imposed under this section);
VATA 1994 s 71(1) (reasonable excuse for conduct within this section);
VATA 1994 s 71(2) (meaning of "credit for input tax");
VATA 1994 ss 76, 77 (assessment of penalties under this section);
VATA 1994 ss 83, 84 (appeal to a tribunal in respect of a penalty under this section);
VATA 1994 Sch 13 para 16 (this section applies with modifications in relation to prescribed accounting periods beginning before 1 December 1993; a penalty liability notice cannot be served under this section by reference to a material inaccuracy for a period beginning before that date).

Amendments—[1] Sub-ss (6), (6A), (7) substituted for sub-ss (6), (7) by FA 1996 s 36, with effect in relation to inaccuracies contained in returns made on or after 29 April 1996.

[2] This section repealed by FA 2007 ss 97, 114, Sch 24 para 29(*d*), Sch 27 Pt 5(5) with effect as follows (by virtue of SI 2008/568 art 2, and subject to transitional provisions and savings in arts 3, 4)—
– 1 April 2008 in relation to relevant documents relating to tax periods commencing on or after that date;

– 1 April 2008 in relation to assessments falling within Sch 24 para 2 for tax periods commencing on or after that date;
– 1 July 2008 in relation to relevant documents relating to claims under the Thirteenth Council Directive (arrangements for the refund of value added tax to persons not established in Community territory) for years commencing on or after that date;
– 1 January 2009 in relation to relevant documents relating to claims under the Eighth Council Directive (arrangements for the refund of value added tax to taxable persons not established in the territory of the country) for years commencing on or after that date;
– 1 April 2009 in relation to documents relating to all other claims for repayments of relevant tax made on or after 1 April 2009 which are not related to a tax period; and
– in any other case, 1 April 2009 in relation to documents given where a person's liability to pay relevant tax arises on or after that date.

65 Inaccuracies in EC sales statements [or in statements relating to section 55A][1]

(1) Where—

(*a*) an EC sales statement containing a material inaccuracy has been submitted by any person to the Commissioners;

(*b*) the Commissioners have, within 6 months of discovering the inaccuracy, issued that person with a written warning identifying that statement and stating that future inaccuracies might result in the service of a notice for the purposes of this section;

(*c*) another EC sales statement containing a material inaccuracy ("the second inaccurate statement") has been submitted by that person to the Commissioners;

(*d*) the submission date for the second inaccurate statement fell within the period of 2 years beginning with the day after the warning was issued;

(*e*) the Commissioners have, within 6 months of discovering the inaccuracy in the second inaccurate statement, served that person with a notice identifying that statement and stating that future inaccuracies will attract a penalty under this section;

(*f*) yet another EC sales statement containing a material inaccuracy is submitted by that person to the Commissioners; and

(*g*) the submission date for the statement falling within paragraph (*f*) above is not more than 2 years after the service of the notice or the date on which any previous statement attracting a penalty was submitted by that person to the Commissioners,

that person shall be liable to a penalty of £100 in respect of the statement so falling.

(2) Subject to subsections (3) and (4) below, an EC sales statement shall be regarded for the purposes of this section as containing a material inaccuracy if, having regard to the matters required to be included in the statement, the inclusion or omission of any information from the statement is misleading in any material respect.

(3) An inaccuracy contained in an EC sales statement shall not be regarded as material for the purposes of this section if—

(*a*) the person who submitted the statement satisfies the Commissioners or, on appeal, a tribunal that there is a reasonable excuse for the inaccuracy; or

(*b*) at a time when he had no reason to believe that enquiries were being made by the Commissioners into his affairs, that person furnished the Commissioners with full information with respect to the inaccuracy.

(4) Where, by reason of the submission of a statement containing a material inaccuracy by any person, that person is convicted of an offence (whether under this Act or otherwise), the inaccuracy to which the conviction relates shall be regarded for the purposes of this section as not being material.

(5) Where the only statement identified in a warning or notice served for the purposes of subsection (1)(*b*) or (*e*) above is one which (whether by virtue of either or both of subsections (3) and (4) above or otherwise) is regarded as containing no material inaccuracies, that warning or notice shall be deemed not to have been issued or served for those purposes.

(6) In this section—

"EC sales statement" means any statement which is required to be submitted to the Commissioners in accordance with regulations under paragraph 2(3) of Schedule 11; and

"submission date", in relation to such a statement, means whichever is the earlier of the last day for the submission of the statement to the Commissioners in accordance with those regulations and the day on which it was in fact submitted to the Commissioners.

[(7) This section applies in relation to a statement which is required to be submitted to the Commissioners in accordance with regulations under paragraph 2(3A) of Schedule 11 as it applies in relation to an EC sales statement.][1]

Commentary—*De Voil Indirect Tax Service* **V5.346**.
Definitions—"The Commissioners", s 96(1); "reasonable excuse", s 71(1); "tribunal", s 82.
Cross references—See VATA 1994 s 66(7) (failure to submit EC sales statement within time limit: circumstances in which person is not to be treated as in default);
VATA 1994 s 71(1) (reasonable excuse for conduct within this section);
VATA 1994 s 71(2) (meaning of "credit for input tax");
VATA 1994 ss 76, 77 (assessment of penalties under this section);
VATA 1994 ss 83, 84 (appeal to a tribunal in respect of a penalty under this section).
Amendments—[1] Heading amended and sub-s (7) inserted by FA 2006 s 19(3), (8) with effect for supplies made on or after 1 June 2007 (by virtue of the Finance Act 2006, section 19, (Appointed Day) Order, SI 2007/1419).

66 Failure to submit EC sales statement [or statement relating to section 55A][1]

(1) If, by the last day on which a person is required in accordance with regulations under this Act to submit an EC sales statement for any prescribed period to the Commissioners, the Commissioners have not received that statement, that person shall be regarded for the purposes of this section as being in default in relation to that statement until it is submitted.

(2) Where any person is in default in respect of any EC sales statement the Commissioners may serve notice on him stating—

(*a*) that he is in default in relation to the statement specified in the notice;

(*b*) that (subject to the liability mentioned in paragraph (*d*) below) no action will be taken if he remedies the default before the end of the period of 14 days beginning with the day after the service of the notice;

(*c*) that if the default is not so remedied, that person will become liable in respect of his default to penalties calculated on a daily basis from the end of that period in accordance with the following provisions of this section; and

(*d*) that that person will become liable, without any further notices being served under this section, to penalties under this section if he commits any more defaults before a period of 12 months has elapsed without his being in default.

(3) Where a person has been served with a notice under subsection (2) above, he shall become liable under this section—

(*a*) if the statement to which the notice relates is not submitted before the end of the period of 14 days beginning with the day after the service of the notice, to a penalty in respect of that statement; and

(*b*) whether or not that statement is so submitted, to a penalty in respect of any EC sales statement the last day for the submission of which is after the service and before the expiry of the notice and in relation to which he is in default.

(4) For the purposes of this section a notice served on any person under subsection (2) above shall continue in force—

(*a*) except in a case falling within paragraph (*b*) below, until the end of the period of 12 months beginning with the day after the service of the notice; and

(*b*) where at any time in that period of 12 months that person is in default in relation to any EC sales statement other than one in relation to which he was in default when the notice was served, until a period of 12 months has elapsed without that person becoming liable to a penalty under this section in respect of any EC sales statement.

(5) The amount of any penalty to which a person who has been served with a notice under subsection (2) above is liable under this section shall be whichever is the greater of £50 and—

(*a*) in the case of a liability in respect of the statement to which the notice relates, a penalty of £5 for every day for which the default continues after the end of the period of 14 days mentioned in subsection (3)(*a*) above, up to a maximum of 100 days; and

(*b*) in the case of a liability in respect of any other statement, a penalty of the relevant amount for every day for which the default continues, up to a maximum of 100 days.

(6) In subsection (5)(*b*) above "the relevant amount", in relation to a person served with a notice under subsection (2) above, means—

(*a*) £5, where (that person not having been liable to a penalty under this section in respect of the statement to which the notice relates) the statement in question is the first statement in respect of which that person has become liable to a penalty while the notice has been in force;

(*b*) £10 where the statement in question is the second statement in respect of which he has become so liable while the notice has been in force (counting the statement to which the notice relates where he has become liable in respect of that statement); and

(*c*) £15 in any other case.

(7) If a person who, apart from this subsection, would be liable to a penalty under this section satisfies the Commissioners or, on appeal a tribunal, that—

(*a*) an EC sales statement has been submitted at such a time and in such a manner that it was reasonable to expect that it would be received by the Commissioners within the appropriate time limit; or

(*b*) there is a reasonable excuse for such a statement not having been dispatched,

he shall be treated for the purposes of this section and sections 59 to 65 and 67 to 71, 73, 75 and 76 [and Schedule 24 to the Finance Act 2007][2] as not having been in default in relation to that statement and, accordingly, he shall not be liable to any penalty under this section [or that Schedule][2] in respect of that statement and any notice served under subsection (2) above exclusively in relation to the failure to submit that statement shall have no effect for the purposes of this section.

(8) If it appears to the Treasury that there has been a change in the value of money since 1st January 1993 or, as the case may be, the last occasion when the sums specified in subsections (5) and (6) above were varied, they may by order substitute for the sums for the time being specified in those subsections such other sums as appear to them to be justified by the change; but an order under this section shall not apply to any default in relation to a statement the last day for the submission of which was before the order comes into force.

(9) In this section "EC sales statement" means any statement which is required to be submitted to the Commissioners in accordance with regulations under paragraph 2(3) of Schedule 11.

[(10) This section applies in relation to a statement which is required to be submitted to the Commissioners in accordance with regulations under paragraph 2(3A) of Schedule 11 as it applies in relation to an EC sales statement.][1]

Commentary—*De Voil Indirect Tax Service* **V5.355**.
Definitions—"The Commissioners", s 96(1); "prescribed", s 96(1); "reasonable excuse", s 71(1); "regulations", s 96(1); "tribunal", s 82.
Cross references—See VATA 1994 s 71(1) (reasonable excuse for conduct within this section);
VATA 1994 s 71(2) (meaning of "credit for input tax");
VATA 1994 ss 76, 77 (assessment of penalties under this section).
Amendments—[1] Heading amended and sub-s (10) inserted by FA 2006 s 19(3), (8) with effect for supplies on or after 1 June 2007 (by virtue of the Finance Act 2006, section 19, (Appointed Day) Order, SI 2007/1419).
[2] Words in sub-s (7) inserted by the Finance Act 2008, Schedule 40 (Appointed Day, Transitional Provisions and Consequential Amendments) Order, SI 2009/571 art 8, Sch 1 paras 22, 23 with effect from 1 April 2009.

67 Failure to notify and unauthorised issue of invoices

(1) In any case where—

(*a*) a person fails to comply with any of paragraphs 5, 6[, 7][2] and 14(2) and (3) of Schedule 1 with paragraph 3 of Schedule 2[, with paragraph 3 or 8(2) of Schedule 3 or paragraph 3, 4 or 7(2) or (3) of Schedule 3A][3], or

(*b*) a person fails to comply with a requirement of regulations under paragraph 2(4) of Schedule 11, or

(*c*) an unauthorised person issues one or more invoices showing an amount as being VAT or as including an amount attributable to VAT,

he shall be liable, subject to subsections (8) and (9) below, to a penalty equal to the specified percentage of the relevant VAT or, if it is greater or the circumstances are such that there is no relevant VAT, to a penalty of £50.

(2) In subsection (1)(*c*) above, "an unauthorised person" means anyone other than—

(*a*) a person registered under this Act; or
(*b*) a body corporate treated for the purposes of section 43 as a member of a group; or
(*c*) a person treated as a taxable person under regulations made under section 46(4); or
(*d*) a person authorised to issue an invoice under regulations made under paragraph 2(12) of Schedule 11; or
(*e*) a person acting on behalf of the Crown.

(3) In subsection (1) above "relevant VAT" means (subject to subsections (5) and (6) below)—

(*a*) in relation to a person's failure to comply with paragraph 5 [, 6 or 7][2] of Schedule 1, paragraph 3 of Schedule 2[, paragraph 3 of Schedule 3 or paragraph 3 or 4 of Schedule 3A][3], the VAT (if any) for which he is liable for the period beginning on the date with effect from which he is, in accordance with that paragraph, required to be registered and ending on the date on which the Commissioners received notification of, or otherwise became fully aware of, his liability to be registered; and

(*b*) in relation to a person's failure to comply with sub-paragraph (2) or (3) of paragraph 14 of Schedule 1[, with sub-paragraph (2) of paragraph 8 of Schedule 3 or with sub-paragraph (2) or (3) of paragraph 7 of Schedule 3A][3], the VAT (if any) for which, but for any exemption from registration, he would be liable for the period beginning on the date of the change or alteration referred to in that sub-paragraph and ending on the date on which the Commissioners received notification of, or otherwise became fully aware of, that change or alteration; and

(*c*) in relation to a person's failure to comply with a requirement of regulations under paragraph 2(4) of Schedule 11, the VAT on the acquisition to which the failure relates; and

(*d*) in relation to the issue of one or more invoices as are referred to in subsection (1)(*c*) above, the amount which is, or the aggregate of the amounts which are—

(i) shown on the invoice or invoices as VAT, or
(ii) to be taken as representing VAT.

(4) For the purposes of subsection (1) above the specified percentage is—

(*a*) [5 per cent][1] where the relevant VAT is given by subsection (3)(*a*) or (*b*) above and the period referred to in that paragraph does not exceed 9 months or where the relevant VAT is given by subsection (3)(*c*) above and the failure in question did not continue for more than 3 months;

(*b*) [10 per cent][1] where that VAT is given by subsection (3)(*a*) or (*b*) above and the period so referred to exceeds 9 months but does not exceed 18 months or where that VAT is given by subsection (3)(*c*) and the failure in question continued for more than 3 months but did not continue for more than 6 months; and

(*c*) [15 per cent][1] in any other case.

(5) Where—

(*a*) the amount of VAT which (apart from this subsection) would be treated for the purposes of subsection (1) above as the relevant VAT in relation to a failure mentioned in subsection (3)(*a*) above includes VAT on an acquisition of goods from another member State; and (*b*) the Commissioners are satisfied that VAT has been paid under the law of another member State on the supply in pursuance of which those goods were acquired,

then, in the determination of the amount of the relevant VAT in relation to that failure, an allowance shall be made for the VAT paid under the law of that member State; and the amount of the allowance shall not exceed the amount of VAT due on the acquisition but shall otherwise be equal to the amount of VAT which the Commissioners are satisfied has been paid on that supply under the law of that member State.

(6) Where—

(*a*) the amount of VAT which (apart from this subsection) would be treated for the purposes of subsection (1) above as the relevant VAT in relation to a failure mentioned in subsection (3)(*a*) above includes VAT chargeable by virtue of section 7(4) on any supply; and

(*b*) the Commissioners are satisfied that VAT has been paid under the law of another member State on that supply,

then, in the determination of the amount of the relevant VAT in relation to that failure, an allowance shall be made for the VAT paid under the law of the other member State; and the amount of the allowance shall not exceed the amount of VAT chargeable by virtue of section 7(4) on that supply but shall otherwise be equal to the amount of VAT which the Commissioners are satisfied has been paid on that supply under the law of that other member State.

(7) This section shall have effect in relation to any invoice which—

(*a*) for the purposes of any provision made under section 54(3) shows an amount as included in the consideration for any supply, and

(*b*) either—

(i) fails to comply with the requirements of any regulations under that section; or

(ii) is issued by a person who is not for the time being authorised to do so for the purposes of that section,

as if the person issuing the invoice were an unauthorised person and that amount were shown on the invoice as an amount attributable to VAT.

(8) Conduct falling within subsection (1) above shall not give rise to liability to a penalty under this section if the person concerned satisfies the Commissioners or, on appeal, a tribunal that there is a reasonable excuse for his conduct.

(9) Where, by reason of conduct falling within subsection (1) above—

(*a*) a person is convicted of an offence (whether under this Act or otherwise), or

(*b*) a person is assessed to a penalty under section 60,

that conduct shall not also give rise to liability to a penalty under this section.

(10) If it appears to the Treasury that there has been a change in the value of money since 25th July 1985 or, as the case may be, the last occasion when the power conferred by this subsection was exercised, they may by order substitute for the sum for the time being specified in subsection (1) above such other sum as appears to them to be justified by the change.

(11) An order under subsection (10) above shall not apply in relation to a failure to comply which ended on or before the date on which the order comes into force.

Commentary—*De Voil Indirect Tax Service* **V5.347–V5.350**.

Press releases etc—C&E Press Notice 23/95 10-4-95 (Customs error in imposing penalties).

Simon's Tax Cases—s 67(9)(*b*), *Stevenson and Telford Building & Design Ltd v C&E Comrs* [1996] STC 1096*; *Khan (t/a Greyhound Dry Cleaners) v C&E Comrs* [2006] STC 1167.

Definitions—"Acquisition of goods from another member State", s 11; "another member State", s 96(1); "the Commissioners", s 96(1); "invoice", s 96(1); "law of another member State", s 92; "reasonable excuse", s 71(1); "registered", s 3(3); "regulations", s 96(1); "supply", s 5, Sch 4; "taxable person", s 3; "tribunal", s 82; "VAT", ss 1, 96(1).

Cross references—See VATA 1994 s 66(7) (failure to submit EC sales statement within time limit: circumstances in which person is not to be treated as in default);

VATA 1994 s 70(1) (mitigation of penalties imposed under this section);

VATA 1994 s 71(1) (reasonable excuse for conduct within this section);

VATA 1994 s 71(2) (meaning of "credit for input tax");

VATA 1994 ss 76, 77 (assessment of penalties under this section);

VATA 1994 ss 83, 84 (appeal to a tribunal in respect of a penalty under this section).

FA 2008 Sch 41 (Penalties: Failure to notify and certain VAT and Excise wrongdoing).

Amendments—[1] Words in sub-s (4) substituted by FA 1995 s 32(1), (3), (4) with effect where a penalty is assessed after 31 December 1994 (but not in the case of a supplementary assessment if the original assessment was made on or before that date).

[2] Words in sub-s (1) inserted and words in sub-s (3) substituted by FA 1996 s 37, with effect in relation to (*a*) any person becoming liable to be registered by virtue of Sch 1 para 1(2) to this Act on or after 1 January 1996; and (*b*) any person who became liable to be registered by virtue of that sub-paragraph before that date but who had not notified the Commissioners of the liability before that date. In relation to a person falling within head (*b*), this section shall have effect as if in sub-s (3)(*a*) for the words "the date with effect from which he is, in accordance with that paragraph, required to be registered" there were substituted "1st January 1996".

[3] Words in sub-s (1)(*a*), (3)(*a*), (3)(*b*) substituted by FA 2000 s 136(2), with effect for supplies made after 20 March 2000.

Prospective amendments—Section 67 to be repealed by FA 2008 Sch 41 para 25(*f*) with effect from 1 April 2010 (by virtue of SI 2009/511 art 2).

Section 67A to be inserted by the Tribunals, Courts and Enforcement Act 2007 s 62(3), Sch 13 paras 117, 119 with effect from a date to be appointed. Section 67A to be repealed by FA 2008 s 129, Sch 43 para 4 from such day as the Commissioners may by statutory instrument appoint.

That section to read—

"67A Breach of controlled goods agreement

(1) This section applies where an enforcement agent acting under the power conferred by section 51(A1) of the Finance Act 1997 (power to use the procedure in Schedule 12 to the Tribunals, Courts and Enforcement Act 2007) has entered into a controlled goods agreement with the person against whom the power is exercisable ("the person in default").
(2) In this section, "controlled goods agreement" has the meaning given by paragraph 13(4) of that Schedule.
(3) Subject to subsection (4) below, if the person in default removes or disposes of goods (or permits their removal or disposal) in breach of the controlled goods agreement, he is liable to a penalty equal to half of the VAT or other amount recoverable under section 51(A1) of the Finance Act 1997.
(4) The person in default shall not be liable to a penalty under subsection (3) above if he satisfies the Commissioners or, on appeal, a tribunal that there is a reasonable excuse for the breach in question. (5) This section extends only to England and Wales."

68 Breaches of walking possession agreements

(1) This section applies where—

(*a*) in accordance with regulations under [section 51 of the Finance Act 1997 (enforcement by distress)][1], a distress is authorised to be levied on the goods and chattels of a person (a "person in default") who has refused or neglected to pay any VAT due or any amount recoverable as if it were VAT due, and

(*b*) the person levying the distress and the person in default have entered into a walking possession agreement, as defined in subsection (2) below.

(2) In this section a "walking possession agreement" means an agreement under which, in consideration of the property distrained upon being allowed to remain in the custody of the person in default and of the delaying of its sale, the person in default—

(*a*) acknowledges that the property specified in the agreement is under distraint and held in walking possession; and

(*b*) undertakes that, except with the consent of the Commissioners and subject to such conditions as they may impose, he will not remove or allow the removal of any of the specified property from the premises named in the agreement.

(3) Subject to subsection (4) below, if the person in default is in breach of the undertaking contained in a walking possession agreement, he shall be liable to a penalty equal to half of the VAT or other amount referred to in subsection (1)(*a*) above.

(4) The person in default shall not be liable to a penalty under subsection (3) above if he satisfies the Commissioners or, on appeal, a tribunal that there is a reasonable excuse for the breach in question.

(5) This section does not extend to Scotland.

Commentary—*De Voil Indirect Tax Service* **V5.351**.
Definitions—"The Commissioners", s 96(1); "reasonable excuse", s 71(1); "regulations", s 96(1); "tribunal", s 82; "VAT", ss 1, 96(1).
Cross references—See VATA 1994 s 66(7) (failure to submit EC sales statement within time limit: circumstances in which person is not to be treated as in default);
VATA 1994 s 71(1) (reasonable excuse for conduct within this section);
VATA 1994 s 71(2) (meaning of "credit for input tax");
VATA 1994 ss 76, 77 (assessment of penalties under this section);
VATA 1994 ss 83, 84 (appeal to a tribunal in respect of a penalty under this section).
Amendments—[1] Words in sub-s (1)(*a*) substituted for the words "paragraph 5(4) of Schedule 11" by FA 1997 s 53(7) with effect from 1 July 1997 (see SI 1997/1432).
Prospective amendments—Sub-s (5) to be substituted by the Tribunals, Courts and Enforcement Act 2007 s 62(3), Sch 13 paras 117, 120 with effect from a date to be appointed. Sub-s (5) as substituted to read—
"(5) This section extends only to Northern Ireland.".

69 Breaches of regulatory provisions

(1) If any person fails to comply with a regulatory requirement, that is to say, a requirement imposed under—

(*a*) paragraph 11 or 12 of Schedule 1, paragraph 5 of Schedule 2[, paragraph 5 of Schedule 3 or paragraph 5 of Schedule 3A][3]; or

(*b*) any regulations made under section 48 requiring a VAT representative, for the purposes of registration, to notify the Commissioners that his appointment has taken effect or has ceased to have effect; or

[(*ba*) paragraph 2(3B) of Schedule 11; or][4]

(*c*) paragraph 6(1) or 7 of Schedule 11; or

(*d*) any regulations or rules made under this Act, other than rules made under paragraph 9 of Schedule 12; or

(*e*) any order made by the Treasury under this Act; or

(*f*) any regulations made under the European Communities Act 1972 and relating to VAT [; or

(*g*) section 18A in the form of a condition imposed by the Commissioners under subsection (1) or (6) of that section,][1]

he shall be liable, subject to subsections (8) and (9) below and section 76(6), to a penalty equal to the prescribed rate multiplied by the number of days on which the failure continues (up to a maximum of 100) or, if it is greater, to a penalty of £50.

(2) If any person fails to comply with a requirement to preserve records imposed under paragraph 6(3) of Schedule 11, he shall be liable, subject to the following provisions of this section, to a penalty of £500.

(3) Subject to subsection (4) below, in relation to a failure to comply with any regulatory requirement, the prescribed rate shall be determined by reference to the number of occasions in the period of 2 years preceding the beginning of the failure in question on which the person concerned has previously failed to comply with that requirement and, subject to the following provisions of this section, the prescribed rate shall be—

(*a*) if there has been no such previous occasion in that period, £5;
(*b*) if there has been only one such occasion in that period, £10; and
(*c*) in any other case, £15.

(4) For the purposes of subsection (3) above—

(*a*) a failure to comply with any regulatory requirement shall be disregarded if, as a result of the failure, the person concerned became liable for a surcharge under section 59 [or 59A][2];
(*b*) a continuing failure to comply with any such requirement shall be regarded as one occasion of failure occurring on the date on which the failure began;
(*c*) if the same omission gives rise to a failure to comply with more than one such requirement, it shall nevertheless be regarded as the occasion of only one failure; and
(*d*) in relation to a failure to comply with a requirement imposed by regulations as to the furnishing of a return or as to the payment of VAT, a previous failure to comply with such a requirement as to either of those matters shall be regarded as a previous failure to comply with the requirement in question.

(5) Where the failure referred to in subsection (1) above consists—

(*a*) in not paying the VAT due in respect of any period within the time required by regulations under section 25(1), or
(*b*) in not furnishing a return in respect of any period within the time required by regulations under paragraph 2(1) of Schedule 11,

the prescribed rate shall be whichever is the greater of that which is appropriate under subsection (3)(*a*) to (*c*) above and an amount equal to one-sixth, one-third or one-half of 1 per cent of the VAT due in respect of that period, the appropriate fraction being determined according to whether subsection (3)(*a*), (*b*) or (*c*) above is applicable.

(6) For the purposes of subsection (5) above, the VAT due—

(*a*) if the person concerned has furnished a return, shall be taken to be the VAT shown in the return as that for which he is accountable in respect of the period in question, and
(*b*) in any other case, shall be taken to be such VAT as has been assessed for that period and notified to him under section 73(1).

(7) If it appears to the Treasury that there has been a change in the value of money since 25th July 1985 or, as the case may be, the last occasion when the power conferred by this subsection was exercised, they may by order substitute for the sums for the time being specified in subsections (2) and (3)(*a*) to (*c*) above such other sums as appear to them to be justified by the change; but an order under this subsection shall not apply to a failure which began before the date on which the order comes into force.

(8) A failure by any person to comply with any regulatory requirement or the requirement referred to in subsection (2) above shall not give rise to liability to a penalty under this section if the person concerned satisfies the Commissioners or, on appeal, a tribunal that there is a reasonable excuse for the failure; and a failure in respect of which the Commissioners or tribunal have been so satisfied shall be disregarded for the purposes of subsection (3) above.

(9) Where, by reason of conduct falling within subsection (1) or (2) above—

(*a*) a person is convicted of an offence (whether under this Act or otherwise), or
(*b*) a person is assessed to a surcharge under section 59 [or 59A][2], or
(*c*) a person is assessed to a penalty under section 60 or 63 [or a penalty under Schedule 24 to the Finance Act 2007][5],

that conduct shall not also give rise to liability to a penalty under this section.

(10) This section applies in relation to failures occurring before as well as after the commencement of this Act, and for that purpose any reference to any provision of this Act includes a reference to the corresponding provision of the enactments repealed by this Act.

Commentary—*De Voil Indirect Tax Service* **V5.352, V5.354**.
Definitions—"The Commissioners", s 96(1); "prescribed", s 96(1); "reasonable excuse", s 71(1); "regulations", s 96(1); "tribunal", s 82; "VAT", ss 1, 96(1); "VAT representative", s 48.
Cross references—See VATA 1994 s 59(9) (avoidance of double penalty for same conduct);
VATA 1994 s 66(7) (failure to submit EC sales statement within time limit: circumstances in which person is not to be treated as in default);
VATA 1994 s 71(1) (reasonable excuse for conduct within this section);
VATA 1994 s 71(2) (meaning of "credit for input tax");
VATA 1994 ss 76, 77 (assessment of penalties under this section);
VATA 1994 ss 83, 84 (appeal to a tribunal in respect of a penalty under this section).
Amendments—[1] Words in sub-s (1) added by FA 1996 Sch 3 para 9, with effect from 1 June 1996 (see Finance Act 1996, Section 26, (Appointed Day) Order, SI 1996/1249), and applying to any acquisition of goods from another member State and any supply taking place on or after that day.
[2] Words in sub-ss (4), (9) inserted by FA 1996 s 35(6), with effect in relation to any prescribed accounting period ending on or after 1 June 1996, but a liability to make a payment on account of VAT shall be disregarded for the purposes of the amendments made by FA 1996 s 35 if the payment is one becoming due before that date.
[3] Words in sub-s (1)(*a*) substituted by FA 2000 s 136(3), with effect for supplies made after 20 March 2000.

[4] Sub-s (1)(*ba*) inserted by FA 2006 s 19(5), (8) with effect for supplies made on or after 1 June 2007 (by virtue of the Finance Act 2006, section 19, (Appointed Day) Order, SI 2007/1419).
[5] Words in sub-s (9)(*c*) inserted by the Finance Act 2008, Schedule 40 (Appointed Day, Transitional Provisions and Consequential Amendments) Order, SI 2009/571 art 8, Sch 1 paras 22, 24 with effect from 1 April 2009.

[69A Breach of record-keeping requirements etc in relation to transactions in gold

(1) This section applies where a person fails to comply with a requirement of regulations under section 13(5)(*a*) or (*b*) of the Finance Act 1999 (gold: duties to keep records or provide information).

Where this section applies, the provisions of section 69 do not apply.

(2) A person who fails to comply with any such requirement is liable to a penalty not exceeding 17.5% of the value of the transactions to which the failure relates.

(3) For the purposes of assessing the amount of any such penalty, the value of the transactions to which the failure relates shall be determined by the Commissioners to the best of their judgement and notified by them to the person liable.

(4) No assessment of a penalty under this section shall be made more than 2 years after evidence of facts sufficient in the opinion of the Commissioners to justify the making of the assessment comes to their knowledge.

(5) The reference in subsection (4) above to facts sufficient to justify the making of the assessment is to facts sufficient—

(*a*) to indicate that there had been a failure to comply with any such requirement as is referred to in subsection (1) above, and

(*b*) to determine the value of the transactions to which the failure relates.

(6) A failure by any person to comply with any such requirement as is mentioned in subsection (1) above shall not give rise to a liability to a penalty under this section if the person concerned satisfies the Commissioners or, on appeal, a tribunal, that there is a reasonable excuse for the failure.

(7) Where by reason of conduct falling within subsection (1) above a person—

(*a*) is assessed to a penalty under section 60 [or a penalty for a deliberate inaccuracy under Schedule 24 to the Finance Act 2007][2], or

(*b*) is convicted of an offence (whether under this Act or otherwise),

that conduct shall not also give rise to a penalty under this section.][1]

Amendments—[1] This section inserted by FA 2000 s 137(1), (2), with effect from 28 July 2000.
[2] Words in sub-s (7)(*b*) inserted by the Finance Act 2008, Schedule 40 (Appointed Day, Transitional Provisions and Consequential Amendments) Order, SI 2009/571 art 8, Sch 1 paras 22, 25 with effect from 1 April 2009.

[69B Breach of record-keeping requirements imposed by directions

(1) If any person fails to comply with a requirement imposed under paragraph 6A(1) of Schedule 11, the person is liable to a penalty.

(2) The amount of the penalty is equal to £200 multiplied by the number of days on which the failure continues (up to a maximum of 30 days).

(3) If any person fails to comply with a requirement to preserve records imposed under paragraph 6A(6) of Schedule 11, the person is liable to a penalty of £500.

(4) If it appears to the Treasury that there has been a change in the value of money since—

(*a*) the day on which the Finance Act 2006 is passed, or

(*b*) (if later) the last occasion when the power conferred by this subsection was exercised,

they may by order substitute for the sums for the time being specified in subsections (2) and (3) such other sums as appear to them to be justified by the change.

(5) But any such order does not apply to a failure which began before the date on which the order comes into force.

(6) A failure by any person to comply with any requirement mentioned in subsection (1) or (3) does not give rise to a liability to a penalty under this section if the person concerned satisfies—

(*a*) the Commissioners, or

(*b*) on appeal, a tribunal,

that there is a reasonable excuse for the failure.

(7) If by reason of conduct falling within subsection (1) or (3) a person—

(*a*) is assessed to a penalty under section 60 [or a penalty for a deliberate inaccuracy under Schedule 24 to the Finance Act 2007][2], or

(*b*) is convicted of an offence (whether under this Act or otherwise),

that conduct does not also give rise to a penalty under this section.][1]

Amendments—[1] Inserted by FA 2006 s 21(2) with effect from 19 July 2006.
[2] Words in sub-s (7)(*a*) inserted by the Finance Act 2008, Schedule 40 (Appointed Day, Transitional Provisions and Consequential Amendments) Order, SI 2009/571 art 8, Sch 1 paras 22, 26 with effect from 1 April 2009.

70 Mitigation of penalties under sections 60, 63, 64 and 67

(1) Where a person is liable to a penalty under section 60, 63, 64[, 67 or 69A][1] [or under paragraph 10 of Schedule 11A][2], the Commissioners or, on appeal, a tribunal may reduce the penalty to such amount (including nil) as they think proper.

(2) In the case of a penalty reduced by the Commissioners under subsection (1) above, a tribunal, on an appeal relating to the penalty, may cancel the whole or any part of the reduction made by the Commissioners.

(3) None of the matters specified in subsection (4) below shall be matters which the Commissioners or any tribunal shall be entitled to take into account in exercising their powers under this section.

(4) Those matters are—

(*a*) the insufficiency of the funds available to any person for paying any VAT due or for paying the amount of the penalty;

(*b*) the fact that there has, in the case in question or in that case taken with any other cases, been no or no significant loss of VAT;

(*c*) the fact that the person liable to the penalty or a person acting on his behalf has acted in good faith.

Commentary—*De Voil Indirect Tax Service* **V5.334**.
Definitions—"The Commissioners", s 96(1); "tribunal", s 82; "VAT", ss 1, 96(1).
Cross references—See VATA 1994 s 66(7) (failure to submit EC sales statement within time limit: circumstances in which person is not to be treated as in default);
VATA 1994 s 71(1) (reasonable excuse for conduct within this section);
VATA 1994 Sch 13 para 17 (this section does not apply in relation to a penalty assessed before 27 July 1993).
Amendments—[1] Words in sub-s (1) substituted for "or 67" by FA 2000 s 137(1), (3), with effect from 28 July 2000.
[2] Words in sub-s (1) inserted by FA 2004 s 19, Sch 2 para 3 with effect from the passing of FA 2004, so far as is necessary for enabling the making of any orders or regulations by virtue of FA 2004 Sch 2, and otherwise with effect from such day as the Treasury may by order made by statutory instrument appoint.

71 Construction of sections 59 to 70

(1) For the purpose of any provision of sections 59 to 70 which refers to a reasonable excuse for any conduct—

(*a*) an insufficiency of funds to pay any VAT due is not a reasonable excuse; and

(*b*) where reliance is placed on any other person to perform any task, neither the fact of that reliance nor any dilatoriness or inaccuracy on the part of the person relied upon is a reasonable excuse.

(2) In relation to a prescribed accounting period, any reference in sections 59 to 69 to credit for input tax includes a reference to any sum which, in a return for that period, is claimed as a deduction from VAT due.

Commentary—*De Voil Indirect Tax Service* **V5.335**.
Simon's Tax Cases—s 71(1), *Profile Security Services Ltd v C&E Comrs* [1996] STC 808*; *T E Davey Photo Service Ltd v C&E Comrs* [1997] STC 889*.
Definitions—"Input tax", ss 24, 96(1); "prescribed accounting period", s 25(1); "VAT", ss 1, 96(1).
Cross reference—See VATA 1994 s 66(7) (failure to submit EC sales statement within time limit: circumstances in which person is not to be treated as in default).

72 Offences

(1) If any person is knowingly concerned in, or in the taking of steps with a view to, the fraudulent evasion of VAT by him or any other person, he shall be liable—

(*a*) on summary conviction, to a penalty of the statutory maximum or of three times the amount of the VAT, whichever is the greater, or to imprisonment for a term not exceeding 6 months or to both; or

(*b*) on conviction on indictment, to a penalty of any amount or to imprisonment for a term not exceeding 7 years or to both.

(2) Any reference in subsection (1) above or subsection (8) below to the evasion of VAT includes a reference to the obtaining of—

(*a*) the payment of a VAT credit; or
(*b*) a refund under section 35, 36 or 40 of this Act or section 22 of the 1983 Act; or
(*c*) a refund under any regulations made by virtue of section 13(5); or
(*d*) a repayment under section 39;

and any reference in those subsections to the amount of the VAT shall be construed—

(i) in relation to VAT itself or a VAT credit, as a reference to the aggregate of the amount (if any) falsely claimed by way of credit for input tax and the amount (if any) by which output tax was falsely understated, and

(ii) in relation to a refund or repayment falling within paragraph (*b*), (*c*) or (*d*) above, as a reference to the amount falsely claimed by way of refund or repayment.

(3) If any person—

(*a*) with intent to deceive produces, furnishes or sends for the purposes of this Act or otherwise makes use for those purposes of any document which is false in a material particular; or (*b*) in furnishing any information for the purposes of this Act makes any statement which he knows to be false in a material particular or recklessly makes a statement which is false in a material particular,

he shall be liable—

(i) on summary conviction, to a penalty of the statutory maximum or, where subsection (4) or (5) below applies, to the alternative penalty specified in that subsection if it is greater, or to imprisonment for a term not exceeding 6 months or to both; or

(ii) on conviction on indictment, to a penalty of any amount or to imprisonment for a term not exceeding 7 years or to both.

(4) In any case where—

(*a*) the document referred to in subsection (3)(*a*) above is a return required under this Act, or

(*b*) the information referred to in subsection (3)(*b*) above is contained in or otherwise relevant to such a return,

the alternative penalty referred to in subsection (3)(i) above is a penalty equal to three times the aggregate of the amount (if any) falsely claimed by way of credit for input tax and the amount (if any) by which output tax was falsely understated.

(5) In any case where—

(*a*) the document referred to in subsection (3)(*a*) above is a claim for a refund under section 35, 36 or 40 of this Act or section 22 of the 1983 Act, for a refund under any regulations made by virtue of section 13(5) or for a repayment under section 39, or

(*b*) the information referred to in subsection (3)(*b*) above is contained in or otherwise relevant to such a claim,

the alternative penalty referred to in subsection (3)(i) above is a penalty equal to 3 times the amount falsely claimed.

(6) The reference in subsection (3)(*a*) above to furnishing, sending or otherwise making use of a document which is false in a material particular, with intent to deceive, includes a reference to furnishing, sending or otherwise making use of such a document, with intent to secure that a machine will respond to the document as if it were a true document.

(7) Any reference in subsection (3)(*a*) or (6) above to producing, furnishing or sending a document includes a reference to causing a document to be produced, furnished or sent.

(8) Where a person's conduct during any specified period must have involved the commission by him of one or more offences under the preceding provisions of this section, then, whether or not the particulars of that offence or those offences are known, he shall, by virtue of this subsection, be guilty of an offence and liable—

(*a*) on summary conviction, to a penalty of the statutory maximum or, if greater, 3 times the amount of any VAT that was or was intended to be evaded by his conduct, or to imprisonment for a term not exceeding 6 months or to both, or

(*b*) on conviction on indictment to a penalty of any amount or to imprisonment for a term not exceeding 7 years or to both.

(9) Where an authorised person has reasonable grounds for suspecting that an offence has been committed under the preceding provisions of this section, he may arrest anyone whom he has reasonable grounds for suspecting to be guilty of the offence.[2]

(10) If any person acquires possession of or deals with any goods, or accepts the supply of any services, having reason to believe that VAT on the supply of the goods or services, on the acquisition of the goods from another member State or on the importation of the goods from a place outside the member States has been or will be evaded, he shall be liable on summary conviction to a penalty of level 5 on the standard scale or three times the amount of the VAT, whichever is the greater.

(11) If any person supplies [or is supplied with][1] goods or services in contravention of paragraph 4(2) of Schedule 11, he shall be liable on summary conviction to a penalty of level 5 on the standard scale.

(12) Subject to subsection (13) below, sections 145 to 155 of the Management Act (proceedings for offences, mitigation of penalties and certain other matters) shall apply in relation to offences under this Act (which include any act or omission in respect of which a penalty is imposed) and penalties imposed under this Act as they apply in relation to offences and penalties under the customs and excise Acts as defined in that Act; and accordingly in section 154(2) as it applies by virtue of this subsection the reference to duty shall be construed as a reference to VAT.

(13) In subsection (12) above the references to penalties do not include references to penalties under sections 60 to 70.

Commentary—*De Voil Indirect Tax Service* **V5.311–V5.316**.

Simon's Tax Cases—*R v Dealy* [1995] STC 217*; *R v Ike* [1996] STC 391.

s 72(1), (3), (8), *R v Choudhury; R v Uddin* [1996] STC 1163*; *Coudrat v Revenue and Customs Commissioners* [2005] STC 1006.

s 72(11), *Chaudhry v R&C Prosecution Office* [2008] STC 2357.

Definitions—"The 1983 Act", s 96(1); "acquisition of goods from another member State", s 11; "another member State", s 96(1); "authorised person", s 96(1); "credit for input tax", s 71(2); "document", s 96(1); "importation of goods from a place outside the member States", s 15; "input tax", s 24; "the Management Act", s 96(1); "output tax", s 24; "regulations", s 96(1); "supply", s 5, Sch 4; "VAT", ss 1, 96(1); "VAT Credit", s 25(3).

Cross references—See VATA 1994 Sch 11 para 10(3), (4) (power to issue search warrants in respect of premises where an offence under sub-s (1)–(8) of this section is suspected to have taken place);
VATA 1994 Sch 13 para 13 (modification of this section in relation to offences committed or allegedly committed between 25 July 1983 and 26 July 1985).

Amendments—[1] Words in sub-s (11) inserted by FA 2003 s 17(5) with effect from 10 April 2003.
[2] Sub-s (9) repealed by FA 2007 ss 84, 114, Sch 22 paras 3, 8(a), Sch 27 Pt 5(1) with effect from 1 December 2007 (by virtue of SI 2007/3166 art 3(*a*)).

VAT

Assessments of VAT and other payments due

73 Failure to make returns etc

(1) Where a person has failed to make any returns required under this Act (or under any provision repealed by this Act) or to keep any documents and afford the facilities necessary to verify such returns or where it appears to the Commissioners that such returns are incomplete or incorrect, they may assess the amount of VAT due from him to the best of their judgment and notify it to him.

(2) In any case where, for any prescribed accounting period, there has been paid or credited to any person—

(*a*) as being a repayment or refund of VAT, or
(*b*) as being due to him as a VAT credit,

an amount which ought not to have been so paid or credited, or which would not have been so paid or credited had the facts been known or been as they later turn out to be, the Commissioners may assess that amount as being VAT due from him for that period and notify it to him accordingly.

(3) An amount—

(*a*) which has been paid to any person as being due to him as a VAT credit, and
(*b*) which, by reason of the cancellation of that person's registration under paragraph 13(2) to (6) of Schedule 1, paragraph 6(2) of Schedule 2[, paragraph 6(2) or (3) of Schedule 3 or paragraph 6(1) or (2) of Schedule 3A][2] ought not to have been so paid,

may be assessed under subsection (2) above notwithstanding that cancellation.

(4) Where a person is assessed under subsections (1) and (2) above in respect of the same prescribed accounting period the assessments may be combined and notified to him as one assessment.

(5) Where the person failing to make a return, or making a return which appears to the Commissioners to be incomplete or incorrect, was required to make the return as a personal representative, trustee in bankruptcy, interim or permanent trustee, receiver, liquidator or person otherwise acting in a representative capacity in relation to another person, subsection (1) above shall apply as if the reference to VAT due from him included a reference to VAT due from that other person.

(6) An assessment under subsection (1), (2) or (3) above of an amount of VAT due for any prescribed accounting period must be made within the time limits provided for in section 77 and shall not be made after the later of the following—

(*a*) 2 years after the end of the prescribed accounting period; or
(*b*) one year after evidence of facts, sufficient in the opinion of the Commissioners to justify the making of the assessment, comes to their knowledge,

but (subject to that section) where further such evidence comes to the Commissioners' knowledge after the making of an assessment under subsection (1), (2) or (3) above, another assessment may be made under that subsection, in addition to any earlier assessment.

[(6A) In the case of an assessment under subsection (2), the prescribed accounting period referred to in subsection (6)(*a*) and in section 77(1)(*a*) is the prescribed accounting period in which the repayment or refund of VAT, or the VAT credit, was paid or credited.][3]

(7) Where a taxable person—

(*a*) has in the course or furtherance of a business carried on by him, been supplied with any goods, acquired any goods from another member State or otherwise obtained possession or control of any goods, or
(*b*) has, in the course or furtherance of such a business, imported any goods from a place outside the member States,

the Commissioners may require him from time to time to account for the goods; and if he fails to prove that the goods have been or are available to be supplied by him or have been exported or otherwise removed from the United Kingdom without being exported or so removed by way of supply or have been lost or destroyed, they may assess to the best of their judgment and notify to him the amount of VAT that would have been chargeable in respect of the supply of the goods if they had been supplied by him.

[(7A) Where a fiscal warehousekeeper has failed to pay VAT required by the Commissioners under section 18E(2), the Commissioners may assess to the best of their judgment the amount of that VAT due from him and notify it to him.

(7B) Where it appears to the Commissioners that goods have been removed from a warehouse or fiscal warehouse without payment of the VAT payable under section 18(4) or section 18D on that removal, they may assess to the best of their judgment the amount of VAT due from the person removing the goods or other person liable and notify it to him][1].

(8) In any case where—

(*a*) as a result of a person's failure to make a return for a prescribed accounting period, the Commissioners have made an assessment under subsection (1) above for that period,

(*b*) the VAT assessed has been paid but no proper return has been made for the period to which the assessment related, and

(*c*) as a result of a failure to make a return for a later prescribed accounting period, being a failure by a person referred to in paragraph (*a*) above or a person acting in a representative capacity in relation to him, as mentioned in subsection (5) above, the Commissioners find it necessary to make another assessment under subsection (1) above,

then, if the Commissioners think fit, having regard to the failure referred to in paragraph (*a*) above, they may specify in the assessment referred to in paragraph (*c*) above an amount of VAT greater than that which they would otherwise have considered to be appropriate.

(9) Where an amount has been assessed and notified to any person under subsection (1), (2), (3) [, (7), (7A) or (7B)][1] above it shall, subject to the provisions of this Act as to appeals, be deemed to be an amount of VAT due from him and may be recovered accordingly, unless, or except to the extent that, the assessment has subsequently been withdrawn or reduced.

(10) For the purposes of this section notification to a personal representative, trustee in bankruptcy, interim or permanent trustee, receiver, liquidator or person otherwise acting as aforesaid shall be treated as notification to the person in relation to whom he so acts.

Commentary—*De Voil Indirect Tax Service* **V5.131–V5.140**.

Simon's Tax Cases—*C&E Comrs v Pegasus Birds Ltd* [2004] STC 262; *Courts plc v C&E Comrs* [2004] STC 690, [2005] STC 27; *Hossain v C&E Comrs* [2004] STC 1572; *BUPA Purchasing Ltd and others v C&E Comrs* (No 2) [2008] STC 101.

s 73(1), *Bennett v C&E Comrs (No 2)* [2001] STC 137; *Rahman (T/A Khayam Restaurant) v C&E Comrs (No 2)* [2003] STC 150, CA; *Hindle and another (trading as D J Baker Bar) v C&E Comrs* [2004] STC 412; *C&E Comrs v Pegasus Birds Ltd* [2004] STC 1509; *Westone Wholesale Ltd v R&C Comrs* [2008] STC 828; *R&C Comrs v Raj Restaurant (a firm) and others* [2009] STC 729.

s 73(2), *Mr Wishmore Ltd v Customs and Excise* [1988] STC 723*; *C&E Comrs v Croydon Hotel & Leisure Co Ltd* [1996] STC 1105*; *C&E Comrs v Laura Ashley Ltd* [2004] STC 635.

s 73(6), *Lord Advocate v Shanks (T/A Shanks & Co)* [1992] STC 928*, *C&E Comrs v Croydon Hotel & Leisure Co Ltd* [1996] STC 1105*; *Cheeseman (T/A Well in Tune) v C&E Comrs* [2000] STC 1119.

s 73(6)(*b*), *Cutts v C&E Comrs* [1989] STC 201*; *Spillane v C&E Comrs* [1990] STC 212*; *C&E Comrs v Post Office* [1995] STC 749*; *Pegasus Birds Ltd v C&E Comrs* [2000] STC 91; *McNicholas Construction Limited v C&E Comrs* [2000] STC 553.

s 73(9), *Lord Advocate v Shanks (T/A Shanks & Co)* [1992] STC 928*; *Elias Gale Racing v C&E Comrs* [1999] STC 66; *Bennett v C&E Comrs (No 2)* [2001] STC 137.

Definitions—"Acquisition of goods from another member State", s 11; "another member State", s 96(1); "business", s 94; "the Commissioners", s 96(1); "document", s 96(1); "fiscal warehouse", ss 18A(3), 18F(1); "fiscal warehouse keeper", s 18F(1); "importation of goods from a place outside the member States", s 15; "interim trustee", s 96(1); "permanent trustee", s 96(1); "prescribed accounting period", s 25(1); "registered", s 3(3); "supply", s 5, Sch 4; "taxable person", s 3; "United Kingdom", s 96(11); "VAT", ss 1, 96(1); "VAT credit", s 25(3); "warehouse", s 18(6).

Press releases etc—C&E Business Brief 5/01 13-3-01 (changes to Customs' practice of making and notifying assessments for under-declared VAT, with effect from 1 March 2001).

Cross references—See VATA 1994 s 43(1) (VAT groups: goods acquired from another member state or imported by group companies to be treated as acquired or imported by representative member for purposes of sub-s (7) of this section);

VATA 1994 s 66(7) (failure to submit EC sales statement within time limit: circumstances in which person is not to be treated as in default);

VATA 1994 s 76(5) (ability to combine assessments under s 76(3) and sub-ss (1), (2), (7), (7A) and (7B) above).

VATA 1994 ss 83, 84 (appeal to a tribunal in respect of an assessment under sub-s (1), (2), (7), (7A) or (7B) of this section);

VATA 1994 s 92(6), (7) (exercise of information powers under sub-s (7) of this section in relation to matters relevant to a charge to VAT under the law of another member state),

VATA 1994 Sch 13 para 20 (modification of this section in its application to amounts paid or credited before the commencement of VATA 1994).

VAT Regulations, SI 1995/2518 reg 181 (claim for repayment by Community trader: treatment as return required under Sch 11 para 2);

VAT Regulations, SI 1995/2518 reg 194 (claim for repayment by third country trader: treatment as return required under Sch 11 para 2);

VAT Regulations, SI 1995/2518 reg 212 (recovery of amounts due under sub-s (9) of this section: distress).

Distress for Customs and Excise Duties and Other Indirect Taxes Regulations, SI 1997/1431 reg 5 (levying distress where tax due under s 73(9) above).

Amendments—[1] Sub-ss (7A), (7B) inserted and words in sub-s (9) substituted by FA 1996 Sch 3 paras 10, 11, with effect from 1 June 1996 (see Finance Act 1996, Section 26, (Appointed Day) Order, SI 1996/1249), and applying to any acquisition of goods from another member State and any supply taking place on or after that day.

[2] Words in sub-s (3)(*b*) substituted by FA 2000 s 136(4), with effect for supplies made after 20 March 2000.

[3] Sub-s (6A) inserted by FA 2008 s 120(1). This amendment is treated as having come into force on 19 March 2008.

74 Interest on VAT recovered or recoverable by assessment

(1) Subject to section 76(8), where an assessment is made under any provision of section 73 and, in the case of an assessment under section 73(1) at least one of the following conditions is fulfilled, namely—

(*a*) the assessment relates to a prescribed accounting period in respect of which either—

(i) a return has previously been made, or

(ii) an earlier assessment has already been notified to the person concerned,

(*b*) the assessment relates to a prescribed accounting period which exceeds 3 months and begins on the date with effect from which the person concerned was, or was required to be, registered, (*c*) the assessment relates to a prescribed accounting period at the beginning of which the person concerned was, but should no longer have been, exempted from registration under paragraph 14(1) of Schedule 1[, under paragraph 8 of Schedule 3 or under paragraph 7 of Schedule 3A][2],

the whole of the amount assessed shall, subject to subsection (3) below, carry interest at [the rate applicable under section 197 of the Finance Act 1996][1] from the reckonable date until payment.

(2) In any case where—

(*a*) the circumstances are such that an assessment falling within subsection (1) above could have been made, but

(*b*) before such an assessment was made the VAT due or other amount concerned was paid (so that no such assessment was necessary),

the whole of the amount paid shall, subject to subsection (3) below, carry interest at [the rate applicable under section 197 of the Finance Act 1996][1] from the reckonable date until the date on which it was paid.

(3) Where (apart from this subsection)—

(*a*) the period before the assessment in question for which any amount would carry interest under subsection (1) above; or

(*b*) the period for which any amount would carry interest under subsection (2) above,

would exceed 3 years, the part of that period for which that amount shall carry interest under that subsection shall be confined to the last 3 years of that period.

(4) Where an unauthorised person, as defined in section 67(2), issues an invoice showing an amount as being VAT or as including an amount attributable to VAT, the amount which is shown as VAT or, as the case may be, is to be taken as representing VAT shall carry interest at [the rate applicable under section 197 of the Finance Act 1996][1] from the date of the invoice until payment.

(5) The references in subsections (1) and (2) above to the reckonable date shall be construed as follows—

(*a*) where the amount assessed or paid is such an amount as is referred to in section 73(2)(*a*) or (*b*), the reckonable date is the seventh day after the day on which a written instruction was issued by the Commissioners directing the making of the payment of the amount which ought not to have been repaid or paid to the person concerned; and

(*b*) in all other cases the reckonable date is the latest date on which (in accordance with regulations under this Act) a return is required to be made for the prescribed accounting period to which the amount assessed or paid relates; and

(*c*) in the case of an amount assessed under section 73(7) the sum assessed shall be taken for the purposes of paragraph (*b*) above to relate to the period for which the assessment was made;

and interest under this section shall run from the reckonable date even if that date is a non-business day, within the meaning of section 92 of the Bills of Exchange Act 1882.

(6) …[1]

(7) Interest under this section shall be paid without any deduction of income tax.

Commentary—*De Voil Indirect Tax Service* **V5.161–V5.163**.

Press releases etc—C&E Press Notice 34/94 7-9-94 (interest will not be assessed unless it represents commercial restitution).

C&E News Release 9/95 31-1-95 (interest no longer to be assessed on underdeclaration voluntary disclosures where the net amount of the errors is £2000 or less).

Simon's Tax Cases—*C&E Comrs v Musashi Autoparts Europe Ltd (formerly TAP Manufacturing Ltd)* [2004] STC 220.

Definitions—"The Commissioners", s 96(1); "invoice", s 96(1); "prescribed", s 96(1); "prescribed accounting period", s 25(1); "registered", s 3(3); "regulations", s 96(1); "VAT", ss 1, 96(1).

Cross references—See VATA 1994 ss 76, 77 (assessment of interest under this section);

VATA 1994 Sch 9A para 5(8) (limitation on amount of interest which may be assessed resulting from a direction under Sch 9A (anti-avoidance provisions: groups)).

VATA 1994 Sch 13 para 18 (this section does not apply to prescribed accounting periods beginning before 1 April 1990 and sub-s (3) does not apply to interest on amounts assessed or paid before 1 October 1993).

Amendments—[1] Words in sub-ss (1), (2), (4) substituted for words "the prescribed rate" and sub-s (6) repealed by FA 1996 s 197(6)(*d*), (7), Sch 41 Pt VIII(1) with effect for periods beginning on or after 1 April 1997 (see SI 1997/1015) and with effect in relation to interest running from before that day, as well as in relation to interest running from, or from after, that day.

[2] Words in sub-s (1)(*c*) substituted by FA 2000 s 136(5), with effect for supplies made after 20 March 2000.

75 Assessments in cases of acquisitions of certain goods by non-taxable persons

(1) Where a person who has, at a time when he was not a taxable person, acquired in the United Kingdom from another member State any goods subject to a duty of excise or consisting in a new means of transport and—

(*a*) notification of that acquisition has not been given to the Commissioners by the person who is required to give one by regulations under paragraph 2(4) of Schedule 11 (whether before or after the commencement of this Act);

(*b*) the Commissioners are not satisfied that the particulars relating to the acquisition in any notification given to them are accurate and complete; or

(*c*) there has been a failure to supply the Commissioners with the information necessary to verify the particulars contained in any such notification, they may assess the amount of VAT due on the acquisition to the best of their judgment and notify their assessment to that person.

(2) An assessment under this section must be made within the time limits provided for in section 77 and shall not be made after whichever is the later of the following—

(*a*) 2 years after the time when a notification of the acquisition of the goods in question is given to the Commissioners by the person who is required to give one by regulations under paragraph 2(4) of Schedule 11;

(*b*) one year after evidence of the facts, sufficient in the opinion of the Commissioners to justify the making of the assessment, comes to their knowledge,

but (subject to section 77) where further such evidence comes to the Commissioners' knowledge after the making of an assessment under this section, another assessment may be made under this section, in addition to any earlier assessment.

(3) Where an amount has been assessed and notified to any person under this section, it shall, subject to the provisions of this Act as to appeals, be deemed to be an amount of VAT due from him and may be recovered accordingly, unless, or except to the extent that, the assessment has subsequently been withdrawn or reduced.

(4) For the purposes of this section, notification to a personal representative, trustee in bankruptcy, interim or permanent trustee, receiver, liquidator or person otherwise acting in a representative capacity in relation to the person who made the acquisition in question shall be treated as notification to the person in relation to whom he so acts.

Commentary—*De Voil Indirect Tax Service* **V5.111**.

Definitions—"Acquisition of goods from another member State", s 11; "another member State", s 96(1); "the Commissioners", s 96(1); "interim trustee", s 96(1); "means of transport", s 95; "new means of transport", s 95; "permanent trustee", s 96(1); "regulations", s 96(1); "taxable person", s 3; "United Kingdom", s 96(11); "VAT", ss 1, 96(1).

Cross references—See VATA 1994 s 66(7) (failure to submit EC sales statement within time limit: circumstances in which person is not to be treated as in default);

VATA 1994 ss 83, 84 (appeal to a tribunal in respect of an assessment under this section).

76 Assessment of amounts due by way of penalty, interest or surcharge

(1) Where any person is liable—

(*a*) to a surcharge under section 59 [or 59A][1], or

(*b*) to a penalty under any of sections 60 [to [69B][5]][4], or

(*c*) for interest under section 74, [or

(*d*) a penalty under regulations made under section 135 of the Finance Act 2002 (mandatory electronic filing of returns) in connection with VAT,][6]

the Commissioners may, subject to subsection (2) below, assess the amount due by way of penalty, interest or surcharge, as the case may be, and notify it to him accordingly; and the fact that any conduct giving rise to a penalty under any of sections 60 [to [69B][5]][4] [or the regulations][6] may have ceased before an assessment is made under this section shall not affect the power of the Commissioners to make such an assessment.

(2) Where a person is liable to a penalty under section 69 for any failure to comply with such a requirement as is referred to in subsection (1)(*c*) to (*f*) of that section, no assessment shall be made under this section of the amount due from him by way of such penalty unless, within the period of 2 years preceding the assessment, the Commissioners have issued him with a written warning of the consequences of a continuing failure to comply with that requirement.

(3) In the case of the penalties, interest and surcharge referred to in the following paragraphs, the assessment under this section shall be of an amount due in respect of the prescribed accounting period which in the paragraph concerned is referred to as "the relevant period"—

(*a*) in the case of a surcharge under section 59 [or 59A][1], the relevant period is the prescribed accounting period in respect of which the taxable person is in default and in respect of which the surcharge arises;

(*b*) in the case of a penalty under section 60 relating to the evasion of VAT, the relevant period is the prescribed accounting period for which the VAT evaded was due;

(*c*) in the case of a penalty under section 60 relating to the obtaining of the payment of a VAT credit, the relevant period is the prescribed accounting period in respect of which the payment was obtained;

(*d*) in the case of a penalty under section 63, the relevant period is the prescribed accounting period for which liability to VAT was understated or, as the case may be, for which entitlement to a VAT credit was overstated; …[6]

(*e*) in the case of interest under section 74, the relevant period is the prescribed accounting period in respect of which the VAT (or amount assessed as VAT) was due[; and

(*f*) in the case of a penalty under regulations made under section 135 of the Finance Act 2002, the relevant period is the prescribed accounting period in respect of which the contravention of, or failure to comply with, the regulations occurred.][6]

(4) In any case where the amount of any penalty, interest or surcharge falls to be calculated by reference to VAT which was not paid at the time it should have been and that VAT (or the supply which gives rise to it) cannot be readily attributed to any one or more prescribed accounting

periods, it shall be treated for the purposes of this Act as VAT due for such period or periods as the Commissioners may determine to the best of their judgement and notify to the person liable for the VAT and penalty, interest or surcharge.

(5) Where a person is assessed under this section to an amount due by way of any penalty, interest or surcharge falling within subsection (3) above and is also assessed under section 73(1), (2)[, (7), (7A) or (7B)][2] for the prescribed accounting period which is the relevant period under subsection (3) above, the assessments may be combined and notified to him as one assessment, but the amount of the penalty, interest or surcharge shall be separately identified in the notice.

(6) An assessment to a penalty under section 67 by virtue of subsection (1)(*b*) of that section may be combined with an assessment under section 75 and the 2 assessments notified together but the amount of the penalty shall be separately identified in the notice.

(7) In the case of an amount due by way of penalty under section 66 or 69 or interest under section 74—

(*a*) a notice of assessment under this section shall specify a date, being not later than the date of the notice, to which the aggregate amount of the penalty which is assessed or, as the case may be, the amount of interest is calculated; and

(*b*) if the penalty or interest continues to accrue after that date, a further assessment or assessments may be made under this section in respect of amounts which so accrue.

(8) If, within such period as may be notified by the Commissioners to the person liable to a penalty under section 66 or 69 or for interest under section 74—

(*a*) a failure or default falling within section 66(1) or 69(1) is remedied, or

(*b*) the VAT or other amount referred to in section 74(1) is paid,

it shall be treated for the purposes of section 66 or 69 or, as the case may be, section 74 as paid or remedied on the date specified as mentioned in subsection (7)(*a*) above.

(9) If an amount is assessed and notified to any person under this section, then unless, or except to the extent that, the assessment is withdrawn or reduced, that amount shall be recoverable as if it were VAT due from him.

(10) For the purposes of this section, notification to a personal representative, trustee in bankruptcy, interim or permanent trustee, receiver, liquidator or person otherwise acting in a representative capacity in relation to [another][3] shall be treated as notification to the person in relation to whom he so acts.

Commentary—*De Voil Indirect Tax Service* **V5.333, V5.336, V5.379**.

Simon's Tax Cases—*Georgiou (T/A Marios Chippery) v C&E Comrs* [1996] STC 463*; *C&E Comrs v Bassimeh* [1997] STC 33*; *R&C Comrs v Raj Restaurant (a firm) and others* [2009] STC 729.

Modifications—Recovery of Duties and Taxes Etc Due on Other Member States (Corresponding UK Claims, Procedure and Supplementary) (adaptation of this section with respect to VAT interest).

Definitions—"The Commissioners", s 96(1); "interim trustee", s 96(1); "permanent trustee", s 96(1); "prescribed accounting period", s 25(1); "supply", s 5, Sch 4; "taxable person", s 3; "VAT", ss 1, 96(1); "VAT credit", s 25(3).

Cross references—See VATA 1994 s 61(3), (4) (liability of body corporate to penalty for evasion of VAT: assessment of part of penalty on director);

VATA 1994 s 66(7) (failure to submit EC sales statement within time limit: circumstances in which person is not to be treated as in default);

VATA 1994 ss 83, 84 (appeal to a tribunal in respect of the amount of any penalty, interest or surcharge specified in an assessment under this section).

VATA 1994 Sch 9A para 5(8) (modification of the application of this section to interest under s 74 resulting from a direction under Sch 9A (anti-avoidance provisions: groups)).

Recovery of Duties and Taxes Etc Due in Other Member States (Corresponding UK Claims, Procedure and Supplementary) Regulations, SI 2004/674 Sch 2 para 3 (modification of the application of this section in respect of the recovery of VAT interest).

Amendments—[1] Words in sub-ss (1), (3) inserted by FA 1996 s 35(7), with effect in relation to any prescribed accounting period ending on or after 1 June 1996, but a liability to make a payment on account of VAT shall be disregarded for the purposes of the amendments made by FA 1996 s 35 if the payment is one becoming due before that date.

[2] Words in sub-s (5) substituted by FA 1996 Sch 3 para 11, with effect from 1 June 1996 (see Finance Act 1996, Section 26, (Appointed Day) Order, SI 1996/1249), and applying to any acquisition of goods from another member State and any supply taking place on or after that day.

[3] Word "another" in sub-s(10) substituted by FA 1997 s 45(6) and deemed always to have had effect.

[4] Words in sub-s (1) substituted for "to 69" by FA 2000 s 137(1), (4), with effect from 28 July 2000.

[5] Words "69B" in both places substituted by FA 2006 s 21(3) with effect from 19 July 2006.

[6] Sub-s (1)(*d*) and preceding word "or", words in sub-s (1), and sub-s (3)(*f*) and preceding word "and", inserted, and in sub-s (3)(*d*) word "and" repealed, by FA 2007 ss 93(4)–(7), 114, Sch 27 Pt 5(4) with effect from 19 July 2007.

77 Assessments: time limits and supplementary assessments

(1) Subject to the following provisions of this section, an assessment under section 73, 75 or 76, shall not be made—

(*a*) more than [4 years][2] after the end of the prescribed accounting period or importation or acquisition concerned, or

(*b*) in the case of an assessment under section 76 of an amount due by way of a penalty which is not among those referred to in subsection (3) of that section, [4 years][2] after the event giving rise to the penalty.

[(2) Subject to subsection (5) below, an assessment under section 76 of an amount due by way of any penalty, interest or surcharge referred to in subsection (3) of that section may be made at any time before the expiry of the period of 2 years beginning with the time when the amount of VAT due for the prescribed accounting period concerned has been finally determined.][1]

[(2A) Subject to subsection (5) below, an assessment under section 76 of a penalty under section 65 or 66 may be made at any time before the expiry of the period of 2 years beginning with the time when facts sufficient in the opinion of the Commissioners to indicate, as the case may be—

(*a*) that the statement in question contained a material inaccuracy, or

(*b*) that there had been a default within the meaning of section 66(1),

came to the Commissioners' knowledge.][1]

(3) In relation to an assessment under section 76, any reference in subsection (1) or (2) above to the prescribed accounting period concerned is a reference to that period which, in the case of the penalty, interest or surcharge concerned, is the relevant period referred to in subsection (3) of that section.

[(4) In any case falling within subsection (4A), an assessment of a person ("P"), or of an amount payable by P, may be made at any time not more than 20 years after the end of the prescribed accounting period or the importation, acquisition or event giving rise to the penalty, as appropriate (subject to subsection (5)).

(4A) Those cases are—

(*a*) a case involving a loss of VAT brought about deliberately by P (or by another person acting on P's behalf),

(*b*) a case in which P has participated in a transaction knowing that it was part of arrangements of any kind (whether or not legally enforceable) intended to bring about a loss of VAT,

(*c*) a case involving a loss of VAT attributable to a failure by P to comply with a notification obligation, and

(*d*) a case involving a loss of VAT attributable to a scheme in respect of which P has failed to comply with an obligation under paragraph 6 of Schedule 11A.

(4B) In subsection (4A) the references to a loss of tax brought about deliberately by P or another person include a loss that arises as a result of a deliberate inaccuracy in a document given to Her Majesty's Revenue and Customs by that person.

(4C) In subsection (4A)(*c*) "notification obligation" means an obligation under—

(*a*) paragraph 5, 6, 7 or 14(2) or (3) of Schedule 1,

(*b*) paragraph 3 of Schedule 2,

(*c*) paragraph 3 or 8(2) of Schedule 3,

(*d*) paragraph 3, 4 or 7(2) or (3) of Schedule 3A, or

(*e*) regulations under paragraph 2(4) of Schedule 11.][2]

(5) Where, after a person's death, the Commissioners propose to assess a sum as due by reason of some conduct (howsoever described) of the deceased, including a sum due by way of penalty, interest or surcharge—

(*a*) the assessment shall not be made more than [4 years][2] after the death; *and*[2]

(*b*) *if the circumstances are as set out in subsection (4) above, the modification of subsection (1) above contained in that subsection shall not apply but any assessment which (from the point of view of time limits) could have been made immediately after the death may be made at any time within 3 years after it.*[2]

(6) If, otherwise than in circumstances falling within section 73(6)(*b*) or 75(2)(*b*), it appears to the Commissioners that the amount which ought to have been assessed in an assessment under that section or under section 76 exceeds the amount which was so assessed, then—

(*a*) under the like provision as that assessment was made, and

(*b*) on or before the last day on which that assessment could have been made,

the Commissioners may make a supplementary assessment of the amount of the excess and shall notify the person concerned accordingly.

Commentary—*De Voil Indirect Tax Service* **V5.137, V5.139**.
Simon's Tax Cases—*C&E Comrs v Post Office* [1995] STC 749*.
S 77(1)(*a*), *R&C Comrs v Dunwood Travel Ltd* [2008] STC 959.
s 77(2), *Ali (T/A Vakas Balti) v R&C Comrs* [2007] STC 618.
s 77(4), *McNicholas Construction Limited v C&E Comrs* [2000] STC 553.
Definitions—"The Commissioners", s 96(1); "prescribed accounting period", s 25(1); "VAT", ss 1, 96(1).
Cross reference—See VATA 1994 ss 83, 84 (appeal to a tribunal in respect of an assessment under sub-s (4) of this section).
VATA 1994 Sch 9A para 5(8) (this section, except sub-s (6) does not apply to an assessment for interest under s 74 resulting from a direction under Sch 9A (anti-avoidance provisions: groups)).

Amendments—[1] Sub-s (2) substituted and sub-s (2A) inserted by FA 1999 s 18 with effect in relation to any amount by way of penalty, interest or surcharge which becomes due on or after 27 July 1999.

[2] In sub-ss (1)(*a*), (*b*), (5)(*a*), words substituted for words "3 years", sub-ss (4)–(4C) substituted for previous sub-s (4), and sub-s (5)(*b*) and preceding word "and" repealed, by FA 2008 Sch 39 para 34 with effect from 1 April 2009 (by virtue of SI 2009/403 art 2(2)). FA 2008 Sch 39 para 34 is disregarded where—

– for the purposes of VATA 1994 s 77, the end of the prescribed accounting period or the importation, acquisition or event giving rise to the penalty, as appropriate, occurred on or before 31 March 2006; and

– after a person's death, a sum is assessed as due by reason of some conduct (however described) of the deceased, including a sum due by way of penalty, interest or surcharge, and the date of the death is on or before 31 March 2006 (SI 2009/403 art 4).Sub-s (4A)(*c*), (*d*) shall not apply where the end of the prescribed accounting period or the importation, acquisition or event giving rise to the penalty, as appropriate, occurred on or before 31 March 2010, except where VAT has been lost in circumstances giving rise to a penalty under VATA 1994 s 67 (SI 2009/403 art 9).

Sub-s (4) previously read as follows—

"(4) Subject to subsection (5) below, if VAT has been lost—

(*a*) as a result of conduct falling within section 60(1) or for which a person has been convicted of fraud, or
(*b*) in circumstances giving rise to liability to a penalty under section 67,

an assessment may be made as if, in subsection (1) above, each reference to [3 years][1] were a reference to 20 years.".

[Liability for unpaid VAT of another

77A Joint and several liability of traders in supply chain where tax unpaid

(1) This section applies to goods [which fall within any one or more][2] of the following descriptions—

[(*a*) any equipment made or adapted for use as a telephone and any other equipment made or adapted for use in connection with telephones or telecommunication;
(*b*) any equipment made or adapted for use as a computer and any other equipment made or adapted for use in connection with computers or computer systems (including, in particular, positional determination devices for use with satellite navigation systems);
(*c*) any other electronic equipment made or adapted for use by individuals for the purposes of leisure, amusement or entertainment and any other equipment made or adapted for use in connection with any such electronic equipment;

and in this subsection "other equipment" includes parts, accessories and software.][2]

(2) Where—

(*a*) a taxable supply of goods to which this section applies has been made to a taxable person, and
(*b*) at the time of the supply the person knew or had reasonable grounds to suspect that some or all of the VAT payable in respect of that supply, or on any previous or subsequent supply of those goods, would go unpaid,

the Commissioners may serve on him a notice specifying the amount of the VAT so payable that is unpaid, and stating the effect of the notice.

(3) The effect of a notice under this section is that—

(*a*) the person served with the notice, and
(*b*) the person liable, apart from this section, for the amount specified in the notice,

are jointly and severally liable to the Commissioners for that amount.

(4) For the purposes of subsection (2) above the amount of VAT that is payable in respect of a supply is the lesser of—

(*a*) the amount chargeable on the supply, and
(*b*) the amount shown as due on the supplier's return for the prescribed accounting period in question (if he has made one) together with any amount assessed as due from him for that period (subject to any appeal by him).

(5) The reference in subsection (4)(*b*) above to assessing an amount as due from a person includes a reference to the case where, because it is impracticable to do so, the amount is not notified to him.

(6) For the purposes of subsection (2) above, a person shall be presumed to have reasonable grounds for suspecting matters to be as mentioned in paragraph (*b*) of that subsection if the price payable by him for the goods in question—

(*a*) was less than the lowest price that might reasonably be expected to be payable for them on the open market, or
(*b*) was less than the price payable on any previous supply of those goods.

(7) The presumption provided for by subsection (6) above is rebuttable on proof that the low price payable for the goods was due to circumstances unconnected with failure to pay VAT.

(8) Subsection (6) above is without prejudice to any other way of establishing reasonable grounds for suspicion.

[(9) The Treasury may by order amend subsection (1) above.

(9A) The Treasury may by order amend this section in order to extend or otherwise alter the circumstances in which a person shall be presumed to have reasonable grounds for suspecting matters to be as mentioned in subsection (2)(*b*) above.

(9B) Any order under this section may make such incidental, supplemental, consequential or transitional provision as the Treasury think fit.][3]

(10) For the purposes of this section—

(*a*) "goods" includes services;
(*b*) an amount of VAT counts as unpaid only to the extent that it exceeds the amount of any refund due.][1]

Commentary—*De Voil Indirect Tax Service* **V1.285, V3.233**.

Simon's Tax Cases—*R (on the application of Federation of Technological Industries and others) v C&E Comrs and another* [2004] STC 1424; *C&E Comrs and another v Federation of Technological Industries and others* [2006] STC 1483.

Amendments—[1] This section inserted by FA 2003 s 18(1) with effect from 10 April 2003.
[2] In sub-s (1) words substituted, and paras (*a*)–(*c*) substituted for original paras (*a*), (*b*), by the VAT (Amendment of section 77A of the VATA 1994) Order, SI 2007/939 reg 2 with effect from 1 May 2007.
[3] Sub-ss (9)–(9B) substituted for original sub-s (9) by FA 2007 s 98(1) with effect from 19 July 2007.

VAT

Interest, repayment supplements etc payable by Commissioners

78 Interest in certain cases of official error

(1) Where, due to an error on the part of the Commissioners, a person has—

(*a*) accounted to them for an amount by way of output tax which was not output tax due from him [and, as a result, they are liable under section 80(2A) to pay (or repay) an amount to him,][5] or

(*b*) failed to claim credit under section 25 for an amount for which he was entitled so to claim credit and which they are in consequence liable to pay to him, or

(*c*) (otherwise than in a case falling within paragraph (*a*) or (*b*) above) paid to them by way of VAT an amount that was not VAT due and which they are in consequence liable to repay to him, or

(*d*) suffered delay in receiving payment of an amount due to him from them in connection with VAT,

then, if and to the extent that they would not be liable to do so apart from this section, they shall pay interest to him on that amount for the applicable period, but subject to the following provisions of this section.

[(1A) In subsection (1) above—

(*a*) references to an amount which the Commissioners are liable in consequence of any matter to pay or repay to any person are references, where a claim for the payment or repayment has to be made, to only so much of that amount as is the subject of a claim that the Commissioners are required to satisfy or have satisfied; and

(*b*) the amounts referred to in paragraph (*d*) do not include any amount payable under this section.][2]

(2) Nothing in subsection (1) above requires the Commissioners to pay interest—

(*a*) on any amount which falls to be increased by a supplement under section 79; or

(*b*) where an amount is increased under that section, on so much of the increased amount as represents the supplement.

(3) Interest under this section shall be payable at [the rate applicable under section 197 of the Finance Act 1996][1].

(4) The "applicable period" in a case falling within subsection (1)(*a*) or (*b*) above is the period—

(*a*) beginning with the appropriate commencement date, and

(*b*) ending with the date on which the Commissioners authorise payment of the amount on which the interest is payable.

(5) In subsection (4) above, the "appropriate commencement date"—

(*a*) in a case where an amount would have been due from the person by way of VAT in connection with the relevant return, had his input tax and output tax been as stated in that return, means the date on which the Commissioners received payment of that amount; and

(*b*) in a case where no such payment would have been due from him in connection with that return, means the date on which the Commissioners would, apart from the error, have authorised payment of the amount on which the interest is payable;

and in this subsection "the relevant return" means the return in which the person accounted for, or (as the case may be) ought to have claimed credit for, the amount on which the interest is payable.

(6) The "applicable period" in a case falling within subsection (1)(*c*) above is the period—

(*a*) beginning with the date on which the payment is received by the Commissioners, and

(*b*) ending with the date on which they authorise payment of the amount on which the interest is payable.

(7) The "applicable period" in a case falling within subsection (1)(*d*) above is the period—

(*a*) beginning with the date on which, apart from the error, the Commissioners might reasonably have been expected to authorise payment of the amount on which the interest is payable, and

(*b*) ending with the date on which they in fact authorise payment of that amount.

[(8) In determining in accordance with subsection (4), (6) or (7) above the applicable period for the purposes of subsection (1) above, there shall be left out of account any period by which the Commissioners' authorisation of the payment of interest is delayed by the conduct of the person who claims the interest.][4]

[(8A) The reference in subsection (8) above to a period by which the Commissioners' authorisation of the payment of interest is delayed by the conduct of the person who claims it includes, in particular, any period which is referable to—

(*a*) any unreasonable delay in the making of the claim for interest or in the making of any claim for the payment or repayment of the amount on which interest is claimed;

(*b*) any failure by that person or a person acting on his behalf or under his influence to provide the Commissioners—

(i) at or before the time of the making of a claim, or

(ii) subsequently in response to a request for information by the Commissioners, with all the information required by them to enable the existence and amount of the claimant's entitlement to a payment or repayment, and to interest on that payment or repayment, to be determined; and

(*c*) the making, as part of or in association with either—

(i) the claim for interest, or

(ii) any claim for the payment or repayment of the amount on which interest is claimed,

of a claim to anything to which the claimant was not entitled.][4]

[(9) In determining for the purposes of subsection (8A) above whether any period of delay is referable to a failure by any person to provide information in response to a request by the Commissioners, there shall be taken to be so referable, except so far as may be prescribed, any period which—

(*a*) begins with the date on which the Commissioners require that person to provide information which they reasonably consider relevant to the matter to be determined; and

(*b*) ends with the earliest date on which it would be reasonable for the Commissioners to conclude—

(i) that they have received a complete answer to their request for information;

(ii) that they have received all that they need in answer to that request; or

(iii) that it is unnecessary for them to be provided with any information in answer to that request.][4]

(10) The Commissioners shall only be liable to pay interest under this section on a claim made in writing for that purpose.

[(11) A claim under this section shall not be made more than [4 years][6] after the end of the applicable period to which it relates.][3]

(12) In this section—

(*a*) references to the authorisation by the Commissioners of the payment of any amount include references to the discharge by way of set-off (whether under section 81(3) or otherwise) of the Commissioners' liability to pay that amount; and][2]

(*b*) any reference to a return is a reference to a return required to be made in accordance with paragraph 2 of Schedule 11.

Commentary—*De Voil Indirect Tax Service* **V5.196.**

Orders—See VATA 1983 (Interest on Overpayments etc) (Prescribed Rate) Order, SI 1991/1754.

Simon's Tax Cases—s 78, *R (on the application of Elite Mobile plc) v Customs and Excise Commissioners* [2005] STC 275; *R (on the application of Mobile Export 365 Ltd and another) v R&C Comrs* [2006] STC 1069; *R&C Comrs v RSPCA and another, R&C Comrs v ToTel Ltd* [2008] STC 885.

s 78(1)(*a*), *Mathieson v C&E Comrs* [1999] STC 835.

Definitions—"Authorised person", s 96(1); "the Commissioners", s 96(1); "input tax", s 24; "output tax", s 24; "VAT", ss 1, 96(1).

Cross references—See VATA 1994 s 83 (appeal to a tribunal in respect of any liability of the Commissioners to pay interest under this section);

VATA 1994 s 101(2) (this section to have effect generally to the exclusion of VATA 1983 s 39).

FA 1997 s 44(6) (corresponding amendments in earlier enactments).

Amendments—[1] Words in sub-s (3) substituted by FA 1996 s 197(6)(*d*) with effect for periods beginning or after 1 April 1997 (see SI 1997/1015) and with effect in relation to interest running from before that day, as well as in relation to interest running from, or from after, that day.

[2] Sub-s (1A) inserted, and sub-s (12)(*a*) substituted, by FA 1997 s 44 (1), (3) and deemed always to have had effect.

[3] Sub-s (11) substituted by FA 1997 s 44 (2) in relation to claims made on or after 18 July 1996 and deemed always to have had effect in relation to such claims.

[4] Sub-s (8), (8A) and (9) substituted by FA 1997 s 44 (4), (5) for the purposes of determining whether any period beginning on or after 19 March 1997 is left out of account.

[5] In sub-s (1)(*a*), words substituted for the words "and which they are in consequence liable to repay to him" by F(No 2)A 2005 s 4(1), (2) with effect in any case where a claim under VATA 1994 s 80(2) is made on or after 26 May 2005, whenever the event occurred in respect of which the claim is made: F(No 2)A 2005 s 4(6).

[6] In sub-s (11), words substituted for words "three years" by FA 2008 Sch 39 para 35 with effect from 1 April 2009 (by virtue of SI 2009/403 art 2(2)). FA 2008 Sch 39 para 35 is disregarded where, for the purposes of a claim under VATA 1994 s 78, the end of the applicable period to which the claim relates was on or before 31 March 2006 (SI 2009/403 art 5).

[78A Assessment for interest overpayments

(1) Where—

(*a*) any amount has been paid to any person by way of interest under section 78, but

(*b*) that person was not entitled to that amount under that section,

the Commissioners may, to the best of their judgement, assess the amount so paid to which that person was not entitled and notify it to him.

(2) An assessment made under subsection (1) above shall not be made more than two years after the time when evidence of facts sufficient in the opinion of the Commissioners to justify the making of the assessment comes to the knowledge of the Commissioners.

(3) Where an amount has been assessed and notified to any person under subsection (1) above, that amount shall be deemed (subject to the provisions of this Act as to appeals) to be an amount of VAT due from him and may be recovered accordingly.

(4) Subsection (3) above does not have effect if or to the extent that the assessment in question has been withdrawn or reduced.

(5) An assessment under subsection (1) above shall be a recovery assessment for the purposes of section 84(3A).

VAT

(6) Sections 74 and 77(6) apply in relation to assessments under subsection (1) above as they apply in relation to assessments under section 73 but as if the reference in subsection (1) of section 74 to the reckonable date were a reference to the date on which the assessment is notified.

(7) Where by virtue of subsection (6) above any person is liable to interest under section 74—

(*a*) section 76 shall have effect in relation to that liability with the omission of subsections (2) to (6); and

(*b*) section 77, except subsection (6), shall not apply to an assessment of the amount due by way of interest;

and (without prejudice to the power to make assessments for interest for later periods) the interest to which any assessment made under section 76 by virtue of paragraph (*a*) above may relate shall be confined to interest for a period of no more than two years ending with the time when the assessment to interest is made.

(8) For the purposes of this section notification to a personal representative, trustee in bankruptcy, interim or permanent trustee, receiver, liquidator or person otherwise acting in a representative capacity in relation to another shall be treated as notification to the person in relation to whom he so acts.][1]

Commentary—*De Voil Indirect Tax Service* **V5.196.**
Simon's Tax Cases—*R v C&E Comrs, ex p Building Societies Ombudsman Co Ltd* [2000] STC 892; *C&E Comrs v DFS Furniture Co plc* [2004] STC 559, CA.
Definitions—"The Commissioners", s 96(1).
Amendments—[1] Inserted by FA 1997 s 45(1) and deemed to have come into force on 4 December 1996 in relation to amounts paid by way of interest on or after 18 July 1996.

79 Repayment supplement in respect of certain delayed payments or refunds

(1) In any case where—

(*a*) a person is entitled to a VAT credit, or

(*b*) a body which is registered and to which section 33 applies is entitled to a refund under that section, [or

(*c*) a body which is registered and to which section 33A applies is entitled to a refund under that section,][2]

and the conditions mentioned in subsection (2) below are satisfied, the amount which, apart from this section, would be due by way of that payment or refund shall be increased by the addition of a supplement equal to 5 per cent of that amount or £50, whichever is the greater.

(2) The said conditions are—

(*a*) that the requisite return or claim is received by the Commissioners not later than the last day on which it is required to be furnished or made, and

(*b*) that a written instruction directing the making of the payment or refund is not issued by the Commissioners within [the relevant period][1], and

(*c*) that the amount shown on that return or claim as due by way of payment or refund does not exceed the payment or refund which was in fact due by more than 5 per cent of that payment or refund or £250, whichever is the greater.

[(2A) The relevant period in relation to a return or claim is the period of 30 days beginning with the later of—

(*a*) the day after the last day of the prescribed accounting period to which the return or claim relates, and

(*b*) the date of the receipt by the Commissioners of the return or claim.][1]

(3) Regulations may provide that, in computing the period of 30 days referred to in [subsection (2A)][1] above, there shall be left out of account periods determined in accordance with the regulations and referable to—

(*a*) the raising and answering of any reasonable inquiry relating to the requisite return or claim,

(*b*) the correction by the Commissioners of any errors or omissions in that return or claim, and

(*c*) in the case of a payment, the following matters, namely—

(i) any such continuing failure to submit returns as is referred to in section 25(5), and

(ii) compliance with any such condition as is referred to in paragraph 4(1) of Schedule 11.

(4) In determining for the purposes of regulations under subsection (3) above whether any period is referable to the raising and answering of such an inquiry as is mentioned in that subsection, there shall be taken to be so referable any period which—

(*a*) begins with the date on which the Commissioners first consider it necessary to make such an inquiry, and

(*b*) ends with the date on which the Commissioners—

(i) satisfy themselves that they have received a complete answer to the inquiry, or

(ii) determine not to make the inquiry or, if they have made it, not to pursue it further,

but excluding so much of that period as may be prescribed; and it is immaterial whether any inquiry is in fact made or whether it is or might have been made of the person or body making the requisite return or claim or of an authorised person or of some other person.

(5) Except for the purpose of determining the amount of the supplement—

(*a*) a supplement paid to any person under subsection (1)(*a*) above shall be treated as an amount due to him by way of credit under section 25(3), and

(*b*) a supplement paid to any body under subsection (1)(*b*) above shall be treated as an amount due to it by way of refund under section 33[, and

(*c*) a supplement paid to any body under subsection (1)(*c*) shall be treated as an amount due to it by way of refund under section 33A.][2]

(6) In this section "requisite return or claim" means—

(*a*) in relation to a payment, the return for the prescribed accounting period concerned which is required to be furnished in accordance with regulations under this Act, and

(*b*) in relation to a refund, the claim for that refund which is required to be made in accordance with the Commissioners' determination under section 33 [or (as the case may be) the Commissioners' determination under, and the provisions of, section 33A.][2]

(7) If the Treasury by order so direct, any period specified in the order shall be disregarded for the purpose of calculating the period of 30 days referred to in [subsection (2A)][1] above.

Commentary—*De Voil Indirect Tax Service* **V5.191, V5.192.**
Regulations—See VAT Regulations, SI 1995/2518 regs 198, 199.
Simon's Tax Cases—*R&C Comrs v RSPCA and another, R&C Comrs v ToTel Ltd* [2008] STC 885.
Definitions—"Authorised person", s 96(1); "the Commissioners", s 96(1); "prescribed", s 96(1); "prescribed accounting period", s 25(1); "registered", s 3(3); "regulations", s 96(1); "VAT credit", s 25(3).
Cross reference—See VAT Regulations, SI 1995/2518 reg 198 (computation of 30-day period for purposes of sub-s (2)(*b*) of this section).
Amendments—[1] Words in sub-s (2)(*b*), (3) and (7) substituted, and sub-s (2A) inserted by FA 1999 s 19 with effect in relation to returns and claims received by the Commissioners on or after 9 March 1999.
[2] Sub-ss (1)(*c*), (5)(*c*) inserted, and words in sub-s (6)(*b*) added by FA 2001 s 98(4)–(7) with effect from 1 September 2001.

80 [Credit for, or repayment of, overstated or overpaid VAT][4]

[(1) Where a person—

(*a*) has accounted to the Commissioners for VAT for a prescribed accounting period (whenever ended), and

(*b*) in doing so, has brought into account as output tax an amount that was not output tax due,

the Commissioners shall be liable to credit the person with that amount.][4]

[(1A) Where the Commissioners—

(*a*) have assessed a person to VAT for a prescribed accounting period (whenever ended), and

(*b*) in doing so, have brought into account as output tax an amount that was not output tax due,

they shall be liable to credit the person with that amount.][4]

[(1B) Where a person has for a prescribed accounting period (whenever ended) paid to the Commissioners an amount by way of VAT that was not VAT due to them, otherwise than as a result of—

(*a*) an amount that was not output tax due being brought into account as output tax, or

(*b*) an amount of input tax allowable under section 26 not being brought into account,

the Commissioners shall be liable to repay to that person the amount so paid.][4]

(2) The Commissioners shall only be liable to [credit or][4] repay an amount under this section on a claim being made for the purpose.

[(2A) Where—

(*a*) as a result of a claim under this section by virtue of subsection (1) or (1A) above an amount falls to be credited to a person, and

(*b*) after setting any sums against it under or by virtue of this Act, some or all of that amount remains to his credit,

the Commissioners shall be liable to pay (or repay) to him so much of that amount as so remains.][4]

(3) It shall be a defence, in relation to a claim [under this section by virtue of subsection (1) or (1A) above, that the crediting][4] of an amount would unjustly enrich the claimant.

[(3A) Subsection (3B) below applies for the purposes of subsection (3) above where—

(*a*) an amount would (apart from subsection (3) above) fall to be credited under subsection (1) or (1A) above to any person ("the taxpayer"), and

(*b*) the whole or a part of the amount brought into account as mentioned in paragraph (*b*) of that subsection has, for practical purposes, been borne by a person other than the taxpayer.][4]

[(3B) Where, in a case to which this subsection applies, loss or damage has been or may be incurred by the taxpayer as a result of mistaken assumptions made in his case about the operation of any VAT provisions, that loss or damage shall be disregarded, except to the extent of the quantified amount, in the making of any determination—

(*a*) of whether or to what extent the [crediting][4] of an amount to the taxpayer would enrich him; or

(*b*) of whether or to what extent any enrichment of the taxpayer would be unjust.][1]

VAT

[(3C) In subsection (3B) above—

"the quantified amount" means the amount (if any) which is shown by the taxpayer to constitute the amount that would appropriately compensate him for loss or damage shown by him to have resulted, for any business carried on by him, from the making of the mistaken assumptions; and

"VAT provisions" means the provisions of—

(*a*) any enactment, subordinate legislation or Community legislation (whether or not still in force) which relates to VAT or to any matter connected with VAT; or

(*b*) any notice published by the Commissioners under or for the purposes of any such enactment or subordinate legislation.][1]

[(4) The Commissioners shall not be liable on a claim under this section—

(*a*) to credit an amount to a person under subsection (1) or (1A) above, or

(*b*) to repay an amount to a person under subsection (1B) above,

if the claim is made more than [4 years][6] after the relevant date.][4]

[(4ZA) The relevant date is—

(*a*) in the case of a claim by virtue of subsection (1) above, the end of the prescribed accounting period mentioned in that subsection, unless paragraph (*b*) below applies;

(*b*) in the case of a claim by virtue of subsection (1) above in respect of an erroneous voluntary disclosure, the end of the prescribed accounting period in which the disclosure was made;

(*c*) in the case of a claim by virtue of subsection (1A) above in respect of an assessment issued on the basis of an erroneous voluntary disclosure, the end of the prescribed accounting period in which the disclosure was made;

(*d*) in the case of a claim by virtue of subsection (1A) above in any other case, the end of the prescribed accounting period in which the assessment was made;

(*e*) in the case of a claim by virtue of subsection (1B) above, the date on which the payment was made.

In the case of a person who has ceased to be registered under this Act, any reference in paragraphs (*b*) to (*d*) above to a prescribed accounting period includes a reference to a period that would have been a prescribed accounting period had the person continued to be registered under this Act.][4]

[(4ZB) For the purposes of this section the cases where there is an erroneous voluntary disclosure are those cases where—

(*a*) a person discloses to the Commissioners that he has not brought into account for a prescribed accounting period (whenever ended) an amount of output tax due for the period;

(*b*) the disclosure is made in a later prescribed accounting period (whenever ended); and

(*c*) some or all of the amount is not output tax due.][4]

[(4A) Where—

(*a*) an amount has been credited under subsection (1) or (1A) above to any person at any time on or after 26th May 2005, and

(*b*) the amount so credited exceeded the amount which the Commissioners were liable at that time to credit to that person,

the Commissioners may, to the best of their judgement, assess the excess credited to that person and notify it to him.][4]

[(4AA) An assessment under subsection (4A) shall not be made more than 2 years after the later of—

(*a*) the end of the prescribed accounting period in which the amount was credited to the person, and

(*b*) the time when evidence of facts sufficient in the opinion of the Commissioners to justify the making of the assessment comes to the knowledge of the Commissioners.][5]

(4B)… [4]

[(4C) Subsections [(3)][5] to (8) of section 78A apply in the case of an assessment under subsection (4A) above as they apply in the case of an assessment under section 78A(1).][3]

(5) …[2]

(6) A claim under this section shall be made in such form and manner and shall be supported by such documentary evidence as the Commissioners prescribe by regulations; and regulations under this subsection may make different provision for different cases.

[(7) Except as provided by this section, the Commissioners shall not be liable to credit or repay any amount accounted for or paid to them by way of VAT that was not VAT due to them.][4]

Commentary—*De Voil Indirect Tax Service* **V5.159**.
Regulations—See VAT Regulations, SI 1995/2518 reg 37.
Simon's Tax Cases—*Hawthorn v Smallcorn* [1998] STC 591*; *R (on the application of Cardiff County Council) v C&E Comrs* [2002] STC 1318; *Midlands Co-operative Society Ltd v R&C Comrs* [2008] STC 1803; *Marks & Spencer plc v R&C Comrs* [2009] STC 452.
s 80(1), *Marks and Spencer plc v C&E Comrs, University of Sussex v C&E Comrs* [2004] STC 1; *R (on the application of Cardiff County Council) v C&E Comrs* [2004] STC 356.

s 80(3), *C&E Comrs v McMaster Stores (Scotland) Ltd (in receivership)* [1995] STC 846*; *C&E Comrs v National Westminster Bank plc* [2003] STC 1072; *Marks and Spencer plc v C&E Comrs, University of Sussex v C&E Comrs* [2004] STC 1; *Baines & Ernst Ltd v C&E Comrs* [2006] STC 1632.
s 80(4), (4A), (4B), *R (oao DFS Furniture Co plc) v C&E Comrs* [2003] STC 1, CA; *C&E Comrs v DFS Furniture Co plc* [2003] STC 739; *Marks and Spencer plc v C&E Comrs, University of Sussex v C&E Comrs* [2004] STC 1; *R (on the application of Cardiff County Council) v C&E Comrs* [2004] STC 356.
Definitions—"The Commissioners", s 96(1); "prescribed", s 96(1); "regulations", s 96(1); "VAT", ss 1, 96(1).
Cross reference—See VATA 1994 s 83 (appeal to a tribunal in respect of a repayment claim under this section).
VAT Regulations, SI 1995/2518 reg 37 (form of repayment claim).
FA 1997 s 47(3)–(5) (repayments after 17 July 1996 where legal proceedings previously brought).
FA 1997 s 47(12) (references to a claim in sub-s (4)).
FA 2008 s 121(1) (disapplication of requirement that a claim under this section be made within three years of the relevant date in respect of an amount brought into account or paid for a prescribed accounting period ending before 4 December 1996 if the claim is made before 1 April 2009).
Press releases etc—Business Brief 2/98, 27-1-98 (three year time limit for refunds).
Business Brief 4/02 22-2-02 (late claims to input tax submitted before 1 May 1997).
Business Brief 13/06 24-8-06 (Court of Appeal Judgment in Michael Fleming t/a Bodycraft).
Amendments—[1] Sub-ss (3A)–(3C) inserted by FA 1997 s 46(1) with effect for the purposes of making any repayment on or after 19 March 1997, even if the claim for that repayment was made before that date.
[2] Sub-s (4) substituted for sub-ss (4), (5) by FA 1997 s 47(1) with effect from 18 July 1996, subject to transitional provisions in FA 1997 s 47(3)–(5).
[3] Sub-ss (4A)–(4C) inserted by FA 1997 s 47(6) and deemed to have come into force on 4 December 1996.
[4] Sub-s (1)–(1B) substituted for sub-s (1); words inserted in sub-s (2); sub-s (2A) inserted; in sub-s (3), words substituted for the words "under this section, that repayment"; sub-ss (3A), (7) substituted; in sub-s (3B)(*a*), word substituted for the word "repayment"; sub-ss (4)–(4ZB) substituted for sub-s (4); sub-s (4A) substituted for sub-ss (4A), (4B); and Heading substituted; by F(No 2)A 2005 s 3 with effect in any case where a claim under sub-s (2) above is made on or after 26 May 2005, whenever the event occurred in respect of which the claim is made: F(No 2)A 2005 s 4(6).
Sub-s (1) previously read as follows—
"(1) Where a person has (whether before or after the commencement of this Act) paid an amount to the Commissioners by way of VAT which was not VAT due to them, they shall be liable to repay the amount to him.".
Sub-s (3A) previously read as follows—
"(3A) Subsection (3B) below applies for the purposes of subsection (3) above where—
(*a*) there is an amount paid by way of VAT which (apart from subsection (3) above) would fall to be repaid under this section to any person ('the taxpayer'), and
(*b*) the whole or a part of the cost of the payment of that amount to the Commissioners has, for practical purposes, been borne by a person other than the taxpayer.".
Sub-s (4) previously read as follows—
"(4) The Commissioners shall not be liable, on a claim made under this section, to repay any amount paid to them more than three years before the making of the claim.".
Sub-ss (4A), (4B) previously read as follows
"(4A) Where—
(*a*) any amount has been paid, at any time on or after 18th July 1996, to any person by way of a repayment under this section, and
(*b*) the amount paid exceeded the Commissioners' repayment liability to that person at that time,
the Commissioners may, to the best of their judgement, assess the excess paid to that person and notify it to him.
(4B) For the purposes of subsection (4A) above the Commissioners' repayment liability to a person at any time is—
(*a*) in a case where any provision affecting the amount which they were liable to repay to that person at that time is subsequently deemed to have been in force at that time, the amount which the Commissioners are to be treated, in accordance with that provision, as having been liable at that time to repay to that person; and
(*b*) in any other case, the amount which they were liable at that time to repay to that person.".
Sub-s (7) previously read as follows—
"(7) Except as provided by this section, the Commissioners shall not be liable to repay an amount paid to them by way of VAT by virtue of the fact that it was not VAT due to them.".
Heading previously read as follows—
"Recovery of overpaid VAT".
[5] Sub-s (4AA) inserted, and reference in sub-s (4C) substituted by FA 2008 s 120(2)–(4). These amendments are treated as having come into force on 19 March 2008.
[6] In sub-s (4) words substituted for words "3 years" by FA 2008 Sch 39 para 36 with effect from 1 April 2009 (by virtue of SI 2009/403 art 2(2)). FA 2008 Sch 39 para 36 is disregarded where, for the purposes of VATA 1994 s 80, the relevant date is on or before 31 March 2006 (SI 2009/403 art 6).

[80A Arrangements for reimbursing customers

(1) The Commissioners may by regulations make provision for reimbursement arrangements made by any person to be disregarded for the purposes of section 80(3) except where the arrangements—

(*a*) contain such provision as may be required by the regulations; and
(*b*) are supported by such undertakings to comply with the provisions of the arrangements as may be required by the regulations to be given to the Commissioners.

(2) In this section 'reimbursement arrangements' means any arrangements for the purposes of a claim under section 80 which—

(*a*) are made by any person for the purpose of securing that he is not unjustly enriched by the [crediting][2] of any amount in pursuance of the claim; and
(*b*) provide for the reimbursement of persons who have for practical purposes borne the whole or any part of [the amount brought into account as mentioned in paragraph (*b*) of subsection (1) or (1A) of that section][2].

(3) Without prejudice to the generality of subsection (1) above, the provision that may be required by regulations under this section to be contained in reimbursement arrangements includes—

(*a*) provision requiring a reimbursement for which the arrangements provide to be made within such period after the [crediting of the amount][2] to which it relates as may be specified in the regulations;
[(*b*) provision for cases where an amount is credited but an equal amount is not reimbursed in accordance with the arrangements;][2]

(*c*) provision requiring interest paid by the Commissioners on any amount [paid (or repaid)][2] by them to be treated in the same way as that amount for the purposes of any requirement under the arrangements to make reimbursement or to repay the Commissioners;

(*d*) provision requiring such records relating to the carrying out of the arrangements as may be described in the regulations to be kept and produced to the Commissioners, or to an officer of theirs.

(4) Regulations under this section may impose obligations on such persons as may be specified in the regulations—

(*a*) [to make the repayments, or give the notifications, to the Commissioners that they are required to make or give][2] in pursuance of any provisions contained in any reimbursement arrangements by virtue of subsection (3)(*b*) or (*c*) above;

(*b*) to comply with any requirements contained in any such arrangements by virtue of subsection (3)(*d*) above.

(5) Regulations under this section may make provision for the form and manner in which, and the times at which, undertakings are to be given to the Commissioners in accordance with the regulations; and any such provision may allow for those matters to be determined by the Commissioners in accordance with the regulations.

(6) Regulations under this section may—

(*a*) contain any such incidental, supplementary, consequential or transitional provision as appears to the Commissioners to be necessary or expedient; and

(*b*) make different provision for different circumstances.

(7) Regulations under this section may have effect (irrespective of when the claim for [credit][2] was made) for the purposes of [the crediting of any amount][2] by the Commissioners after the time when the regulations are made; and, accordingly, such regulations may apply to arrangements made before that time.][1]

Commentary—*De Voil Indirect Tax Service* **V5.151–V5.166**.
Definitions—"The Commissioners", s 96(1); "regulations", s 96(1).
Amendments—[1] This section inserted by FA 1997 s 46(2).
[2] In sub-s (2)(*a*), (3)(*a*), (7), words substituted for the word "repayment"; in sub-s (2)(*b*), words substituted for the words "the cost of the original payment of that amount to the Commissioners"; sub-s (3)(*b*) substituted; in sub-s (3)(*c*), words substituted for the word "repaid"; in sub-s (4)(*a*), words substituted for the words "to make the repayments to the Commissioners that they are required to make"; in sub-s (7), words substituted for the words "the making of any repayment"; by F(No 2)A 2005 s 4(1), (3) with effect in any case where a claim under VATA 1994 s 80(2) is made on or after 26 May 2005, whenever the event occurred in respect of which the claim is made: F(No 2)A 2005 s 4(6).
Sub-s (3)(*b*) previously read as follows—
"(*b*) provision for the repayment of amounts to the Commissioners where those amounts are not reimbursed in accordance with the arrangements;".

[80B Assessments of amounts due under section 80A arrangements

(1) Where any person is liable to pay any amount to the Commissioners in pursuance of an obligation imposed by virtue of section 80A(4)(*a*), the Commissioners may, to the best of their judgement, assess the amount due from that person and notify it to him.

[(1A) Where—

(*a*) an amount ("the gross credit") has been credited to any person under subsection (1) or (1A) of section 80,

(*b*) any sums were set against that amount, in accordance with subsection (2A) of that section, and

(*c*) the amount reimbursed in accordance with the reimbursement arrangements was less than the gross credit,

subsection (1B) below applies.][2]

[(1B) In any such case—

(*a*) the person shall cease to be entitled to so much of the gross credit as exceeds the amount so reimbursed, and

(*b*) the Commissioners may, to the best of their judgement, assess the amount due from that person and notify it to him,

but an amount shall not be assessed under this subsection to the extent that the person is liable to pay it to the Commissioners as mentioned in subsection (1) above.][2]

[(1C) In determining the amount that a person is liable to pay as mentioned in subsection (1) above, any amount reimbursed in accordance with the reimbursement arrangements shall be regarded as first reducing so far as possible the amount that he would have been liable so to pay, but for the reimbursement of that amount.][2]

[(1D) For the purposes of this section, nil is an amount.][2]

[(1E) Any reference in any other provision of this Act to an assessment under subsection (1) above includes, if the context so admits, a reference to an assessment under subsection (1B) above.][2]

(2) Subsections (2) to (8) of section 78A apply in the case of an assessment under subsection (1) above as they apply in the case of an assessment under section 78A(1).][1]

Commentary—*De Voil Indirect Tax Service* **V5.151–V5.166**.
Definitions—"The Commissioners", s 96(1).

Amendments—[1] This section inserted by FA 1997 s 46(2).
[2] Sub-ss (1A)–(1E) inserted by F(No 2)A 2005 s 4(1), (4) with effect in any case where a claim under VATA 1994 s 80(2) is made on or after 26 May 2005, whenever the event occurred in respect of which the claim is made: F(No 2)A 2005 s 4(6).

81 Interest given by way of credit and set-off of credits

(1) Any interest payable by the Commissioners (whether under an enactment or instrument or otherwise) to a person on a sum due to him under or by virtue of any provision of this Act shall be treated as an amount due by way of credit under section 25(3).

(2) Subsection (1) above shall be disregarded for the purpose of determining a person's entitlement to interest or the amount of interest to which he is entitled.

(3) Subject to subsection (1) above, in any case where—

(*a*) an amount is due from the Commissioners to any person under any provision of this Act, and

(*b*) that person is liable to pay a sum by way of VAT, penalty, interest or surcharge,

the amount referred to in paragraph (*a*) above shall be set against the sum referred to in paragraph (*b*) above and, accordingly, to the extent of the set-off, the obligations of the Commissioners and the person concerned shall be discharged.

[(3A) Where—

(*a*) the Commissioners are liable to pay or repay any amount to any person under this Act,

(*b*) that amount falls to be paid or repaid in consequence of a mistake previously made about whether or to what extent amounts were payable under this Act to or by that person, and

(*c*) by reason of that mistake a liability of that person to pay a sum by way of VAT, penalty, interest or surcharge was not assessed, was not enforced or was not satisfied,

any limitation on the time within which the Commissioners are entitled to take steps for recovering that sum shall be disregarded in determining whether that sum is required by subsection (3) above to be set against the amount mentioned in paragraph (*a*) above.][2]

[(4A) Subsection (3) above shall not require any such amount as is mentioned in paragraph (*a*) of that subsection ("the credit") to be set against any such sum as is mentioned in paragraph (*b*) of that subsection ("the debit") in any case where—

(*a*) an insolvency procedure has been applied to the person entitled to the credit;

(*b*) the credit became due after that procedure was so applied; and

(*c*) the liability to pay the debit either arose before that procedure was so applied or (having arisen afterwards) relates to, or to matters occurring in the course of, the carrying on of any business at times before the procedure was so applied.][1]

[(4B) Subject to subsection (4C) below, the following are the times when an insolvency procedure is to be taken, for the purposes of this section, to be applied to any person, that is to say—

[(*a*) when a bankruptcy order or winding-up order or award of sequestration is made or an administrator is appointed in relation to that person;][3]

(*b*) when that person is put into administrative receivership;

(*c*) when that person, being a corporation, passes a resolution for voluntary winding up;

(*d*) when any voluntary arrangement approved in accordance with Part I or VIII of the Insolvency Act 1986 or Part II or Chapter II of Part VIII of the Insolvency (Northern Ireland) Order 1989 comes into force in relation to that person;

(*e*) when a deed of arrangement registered in accordance with the Deeds of Arrangement Act 1914 or Chapter I of Part VIII of that Order of 1989 takes effect in relation to that person;

(*f*) when that person's estate becomes vested in any other person as that person's trustee under a trust deed.][1]

[(4C) In this section, references to the application of an insolvency procedure to a person do not include—

(*a*) the application of an insolvency procedure to a person at a time when another insolvency procedure applies to the person, or

(*b*) the application of an insolvency procedure to a person immediately upon another insolvency procedure ceasing to have effect.][4]

[(4D) For the purposes of this section a person shall be regarded as being in administrative receivership throughout any continuous period for which (disregarding any temporary vacancy in the office of receiver) there is an administrative receiver of that person, and the reference in subsection (4B) above to a person being put into administrative receivership shall be construed accordingly.][1]

(5) In [this section][1]—

(a) "administration order" means an administration order under Part II of the Insolvency Act 1986 or an administration order within the meaning of Article 5(1) of the Insolvency (Northern Ireland) Order 1989;[4]

(*b*) "administrative receiver" means an administrative receiver within the meaning of section 251 of [the Insolvency Act 1986][4] or Article 5(1) of [the Insolvency (Northern Ireland) Order 1989][4];

[(*ba*) "administrator" means a person appointed to manage the affairs, business and property of another person under Schedule B1 to that Act or to that Order;][4] and (*c*) "trust deed" has the same meaning as in the Bankruptcy (Scotland) Act 1985.

Commentary—*De Voil Indirect Tax Service* **V5.196**.
Definitions—"The Commissioners", s 96(1); "interim trustee", s 96(1); "permanent trustee", s 96(1); "VAT", ss 1, 96(1).
Cross references—See VATA 1994 Sch 13 para 21 (modification of this section in its application to amounts becoming due before 10 May 1994).
VAT Regulations, SI 1995/2518 reg 48(3) (this section cannot require overpayments on account in respect of one division of a business to be set against liabilities of another division).
Press releases etc—Business Brief 5/98 10-2-98 (VAT bad debt relief—insolvency practitioners).
Amendments—[1] Sub-ss (4A)–(4D) substituted for sub-s (4) as originally enacted, and words in sub-s (5) substituted by FA 1995 s 27 with effect in relation to amounts becoming due from the Commissioners of Customs and Excise at times on or after 1 May 1995.
[2] Sub-s (3A) inserted by FA 1997 s 48(1) and deemed to have come into force on 18 July 1996 for determining the amount of any payment or repayment by C&E on or after that date.
[3] Sub-ss (4B)(*a*) substituted, by the Enterprise Act 2002 (Insolvency) Order, SI 2003/2096 art 4, Schedule, paras 24, 26 with effect from 15 September 2003. However, this amendment does not apply in any case where a petition for an administration order was presented before that date: SI 2003/2096 arts 1, 6.
[4] Sub-s (4C) substituted, sub-s (5)(*a*) repealed, in sub-s (5)(*b*), words substituted for words "that Act of 1986", and "that Order of 1989", and sub-s (5)(*ba*) inserted, by FA 2008 s 132 with effect from 21 July 2008. Sub-s (4C) previously read as follows—

"(4C) In this section references, in relation to any person, to the application of an insolvency procedure to that person shall not include—

(*a*) the making of a bankruptcy order, winding-up order … or an award of sequestration [or the appointment of an administrator] at a time when any such arrangement or deed as is mentioned in subsection (4B)(*d*) to (*f*) above is in force in relation to that person;
(*b*) the making of a winding-up order at any of the following times, that is to say—
[(i) immediately upon the appointment of an administrator in respect of the person ceasing to have effect;]
(ii) when that person is being wound up voluntarily;
(iii) when that person is in administrative receivership;
or
(*c*) the making of an administration order in relation to that person at any time when that person is in administrative receivership."

PART V
[REVIEWS AND APPEALS]

Cross reference—See VATA 1994 Sch 13 para 22 (references in this Part to any provision of VATA 1994 include a reference to the corresponding provision of the enactments repealed by that Act).
VAT Tribunals Rules, SI 1986/590 (procedure for appeals before tribunals).
Amendments—Heading substituted for previous heading "Appeals" by the Transfer of Tribunal Functions and Revenue and Customs Appeals Order, SI 2009/56 art 3, Sch 1 para 217 with effect from 1 April 2009, subject to transitional and savings provisions in Sch 3 para 4.

[82 Meaning of "tribunal"

In this Act "tribunal" means the First-tier Tribunal or, where determined by or under Tribunal Procedure Rules, the Upper Tribunal.][2]

Commentary—*De Voil Indirect Tax Service* **V1.288**.
Definitions—"VAT", ss 1, 96(1).
Amendments—[1] Words in sub-s (3) substituted by the Courts Act 2003 s 109(1), Sch 8 para 363 with effect from 1 April 2005 (by virtue of SI 2005/910).
[2] This section substituted by the Transfer of Tribunal Functions and Revenue and Customs Appeals Order, SI 2009/56 art 3, Sch 1 para 218 with effect from 1 April 2009, subject to transitional and savings provisions in Sch 3 para 4. Section 82 previously read as follows—

82 Appeal tribunals

(1) Any reference in this Act to a tribunal is a reference to a tribunal constituted in accordance with Schedule 12, and that Schedule shall have effect generally with respect to appointments to and the procedure and administration of the tribunals.

(2) The tribunals shall continue to have jurisdiction in relation to matters relating to VAT conferred upon them by this Part of this Act and jurisdiction in relation to matters relating to customs and excise conferred by Chapter II of Part I of the Finance Act 1994.

(3) Officers and staff may be appointed under [section 2(1) of the Courts Act 2003] (court staff) for carrying out the administrative work of the tribunals in England and Wales.

(4) The Secretary of State may make available such officers and staff as he may consider necessary for carrying out the administrative work of the tribunals in Scotland.

83 Appeals

[(1)][21] Subject to [sections 83G and 84][21], an appeal shall lie to [the tribunal][21] with respect to any of the following matters—

(*a*) the registration or cancellation of registration of any person under this Act;
(*b*) the VAT chargeable on the supply of any goods or services, on the acquisition of goods from another member State or, subject to section 84(9), on the importation of goods from a place outside the member States;
(*c*) the amount of any input tax which may be credited to a person;
(*d*) any claim for a refund under any regulations made by virtue of section 13(5);
[(*da*) a decision of the Commissioners under section 18A—

(i) as to whether or not a person is to be approved as a fiscal warehouse keeper or the conditions from time to time subject to which he is so approved;
(ii) for the withdrawal of any such approval; or

(iii) for the withdrawal of fiscal warehouse status from any premises;][1]

(*e*) the proportion of input tax allowable under section 26;

(*f*) a claim by a taxable person under section 27;

[(*fza*) a decision of the Commissioners—

(i) refusing or withdrawing authorisation for a person's liability to pay VAT (or entitlement to credit for VAT) to be determined as mentioned in subsection (1) of section 26B;

(ii) as to the appropriate percentage or percentages (within the meaning of that section) applicable in a person's case.][10]

[(*fa*) a decision contained in a notification under paragraph (4) of article 12A of the Value Added Tax (Payments on Account) Order 1993 that an election under paragraph (1) of that article shall cease to have effect;][6]

(*g*) the amount of any refunds under section 35;

(*h*) a claim for a refund under section 36 or section 22 of the 1983 Act;

[(*ha*) any decision of the Commissioners to refuse to make a repayment under a scheme under section 39;][22]

(*j*) the amount of any refunds under section 40;

[(*k*) the refusal of an application such as is mentioned in section 43B(1) or (2);

(*ka*) the giving of a notice under section 43C(1) or (3);][7]

(*l*) the requirement of any security under section 48(7) or [paragraph 4(1A) or (2)][11] of Schedule 11;

(*m*) any refusal or cancellation of certification under section 54 or any refusal to cancel such certification;

(*n*) any liability to a penalty or surcharge by virtue of any of sections [59 to [69B][17]][8];

(*o*) a decision of the Commissioners under section 61 (in accordance with section 61(5));

(*p*) an assessment—

(i) under section 73(1) or (2) in respect of a period for which the appellant has made a return under this Act; or

(ii) under [subsections (7), (7A) or (7B)][1] of that section; or

(iii) under section 75;

or the amount of such an assessment;

(*q*) the amount of any penalty, interest or surcharge specified in an assessment under section 76;

(*r*) the making of an assessment on the basis set out in section 77(4);

[(*ra*) any liability arising by virtue of section 77A;][12]

(*s*) any liability of the Commissioners to pay interest under section 78 or the amount of interest so payable;

[(*sa*) an assessment under section 78A(1) or the amount of such an assessment;][3]

(*t*) a claim for the [crediting or][16] repayment of an amount under section 80[, an assessment under subsection (4A) of that section or the amount of such an assessment;][5]

[(*ta*) an assessment under section 80B(1) [or (1B)][16] or the amount of such an assessment;][4]

(*u*) any direction or supplementary direction made under paragraph 2 of Schedule 1;

(*v*) any direction under paragraph 1[, 1A][15] or 2 of Schedule 6 or under paragraph 2 of Schedule 4 to the 1983 Act;

(*w*) any direction under paragraph 1 of Schedule 7;

[(*wa*) any direction or assessment under Schedule 9A;][2]

[(*wb*) any refusal of the Commissioners to grant any permission under, or otherwise to exercise in favour of a particular person any power conferred by, any provision of Part 1 of Schedule 10;][20]

(*x*) any refusal to permit the value of supplies to be determined by a method described in a notice published under paragraph 2(6) of Schedule 11;

(*y*) any refusal of authorisation or termination of authorisation in connection with the scheme made under paragraph 2(7) of Schedule 11;

[(*z*) any conditions imposed by the Commissioners in a particular case by virtue of paragraph 2B(2)(*c*) or 3(1) of Schedule 11][13]

[(*zza*) a direction under paragraph 6A of Schedule 11;][18]

[(*za*) a direction under paragraph 8 of Schedule 11A;][14]

[(*zb*) any liability to a penalty under paragraph 10(1) of Schedule 11A, any assessment under paragraph 12(1) of that Schedule or the amount of such an assessment;][14]

[(*zc*) a decision of the Commissioners about the application of regulations under section 135 of the Finance Act 2002 (mandatory electronic filing of returns) in connection with VAT (including, in particular, a decision as to whether a requirement of the regulations applies and a decision to impose a penalty);][19]

(*zz*) …[9]

[(2) In the following provisions of this Part, a reference to a decision with respect to which an appeal under this section lies, or has been made, includes any matter listed in subsection (1) whether or not described there as a decision.][21]

Commentary—*De Voil Indirect Tax Service* **V5.404**.

Simon's Tax Cases—*Odhams Leisure Group Ltd v C&E Comrs* [1992] STC 332*; *C&E Comrs v Pegasus Birds Ltd* [2004] STC 262.

s 83(*b*), *Don Pasquale (a firm) v C&E Comrs* [1990] STC 556*.

s 83(*c*), *Touchwood Services Ltd v R&C Comrs* [2007] STC 1425; *R&C Comrs v Mobilx Ltd* [2008] STC 3071.
s 83(*e*), *Banbury Visionplus Ltd v R&C Comrs and other appeals* [2006] STC 1568.
s 83(*l*), *John Dee Ltd v C&E Comrs* [1995] STC 941*.
s 83(*n*), (*q*), *Dollar Land (Feltham) Ltd, Dollar Land (Cumbernauld) Ltd and Dollar Land (Calthorpe House) Ltd v C&E Comrs* [1995] STC 414*.
s 83(*p*), *Don Pasquale (a firm) v C&E Comrs* [1990] STC 556*; *Murat v C&E Comrs* [1998] STC 923; *Touchwood Services Ltd v R&C Comrs* [2007] STC 1425.
s 83(*t*), *C&E Comrs v National Westminster Bank plc* [2003] STC 1072.

Definitions—"The 1983 Act", s 96(1); "acquisition of goods from another member State", s 11; "another member State", s 96(1); "the Commissioners", s 96(1); "fiscal warehouse", ss 18A(3), 18F(1); "fiscal warehouse keeper", s 18F(1); "importation of goods from a place outside the member States", s 15; "input tax", s 24; "registered", s 3(3); "regulations", s 96(1); "supply", s 5, Sch 4; "taxable person", s 3; "tribunal", s 82; "VAT", ss 1, 96(1).

Cross references—See VATA 1994 Sch 13 para 22 (application of this section to acts and omissions before the coming into force of VATA 1994).

VAT (Isle of Man) Order, SI 1982/1067 art 8 (taxable persons for the purposes of Isle of Man VAT legislation to be treated as taxable persons for the purposes of sub-s(1)(*g*) of this section);

VAT Regulations, SI 1995/2518 reg 182 (repayment claimed by Community trader: treatment as an amount of input tax for the purposes of para (*c*) of this section);

VAT Regulations, SI 1995/2518 reg 195 (repayment claimed by third country trader: treatment as an amount of input tax for the purposes of para (*c*) of this section).

Amendments—[1] Para (*da*) inserted and words in para (*p*)(ii) substituted by FA 1996 Sch 3 para 12, with effect from 1 June 1996 (see Finance Act 1996, Section 26, (Appointed Day) Order SI 1996/1249), and applying to any acquisition of goods from another member State and any supply taking place on or after that day.

[2] Para (*wa*) inserted by FA 1996 s 31(3).

[3] Para (*sa*) inserted by FA 1997 s 45(2) and deemed to have come into force on 4 December 1996 in relation to assessments made on or after that date.

[4] Para (*ta*) inserted by FA 1997 s 46 (3).

[5] Words in para (*t*) inserted by FA 1997 s 47 (7) with effect from 4 December 1996.

[6] Para (*fa*) inserted by the VAT (Payments on Account) (Appeals) Order, SI 1997/2542 with effect from 1 December 1997.

[7] Para (*k*) substituted and para (*ka*) inserted by FA 1999 s 16, Sch 2 para 3 with effect from 27 July 1999 subject to FA 1999 Sch 2 para 6.

[8] Words in para (*n*) substituted for "59 to 69" by FA 2000 s 137(1), (5), with effect from 28 July 2000.

[9] Para (*zz*) (originally added by the Money Laundering Regulations 2001) repealed by the Money Laundering Regulations, SI 2007/2157 reg 51, Sch 6 para 1 with effect from 15 December 2007.

[10] Para (*fza*) inserted by FA 2002 s 23(2), (4) and deemed to have come into force on 24 April 2002.

[11] Words in para (*l*) substituted for the words "paragraph 4(2)" by FA 2003 s 17(6) with effect from 10 April 2003.

[12] Para (*ra*) inserted by FA 2003 s 18(2) with effect from 10 April 2003.

[13] Para (*z*) substituted by FA 2002 s 24(4)(*b*), (5), with effect from 1 December 2003 (by virtue of SI 2003/3043).

[14] Paras (*za*) and (*zb*) inserted by FA 2004 s 19, Sch 2 para 4 with effect from the passing of FA 2004, so far as is necessary for enabling the making of any orders or regulations by virtue of FA 2004 Sch 2, and otherwise with effect from such day as the Treasury may by order made by statutory instrument appoint.

[15] Words in para (*v*) inserted by FA 2004 s 22(3) with effect from 22 July 2004.

[16] Words in paras (*t*), (*ta*) inserted by F(No 2)A 2005 s 4(1), (5) with effect in any case where a claim under VATA 1994 s 80(2) is made on or after 26 May 2005, whenever the event occurred in respect of which the claim is made: F(No 2)A 2005 s 4(6).

[17] Words "69B" in para (*n*) substituted by FA 2006 s 21(4) with effect from 19 July 2006.

[18] Para (*zza*) inserted by FA 2006 s 21(4) with effect from 19 July 2006.

[19] Para (*zc*) inserted by FA 2007 s 93(8) with effect from 19 July 2007.

[20] Para (*wb*) inserted by the Value Added Tax (Buildings and Land) Order, SI 2008/1146, art 3(1), (2) with effect in relation to supplies made on or after 1 June 2008, subject to savings in Sch 2 of the Order.

[21] Sub-s (1) numbered as such; in new sub-s (1) words in the first place substituted for the words "section 84" and in the second place substituted for the words "a tribunal"; sub-s (2) inserted by the Transfer of Tribunal Functions and Revenue and Customs Appeals Order, SI 2009/56 art 3, Sch 1 para 219 with effect from 1 April 2009, subject to transitional and savings provisions in Sch 3 para 4.

[22] Para (*ha*) inserted by FA 2009 s 77 with effect from 21 July 2009.

[83A Offer of review

(1) HMRC must offer a person (P) a review of a decision that has been notified to P if an appeal lies under section 83 in respect of the decision.

(2) The offer of the review must be made by notice given to P at the same time as the decision is notified to P.

(3) This section does not apply to the notification of the conclusions of a review.][1]

Amendments—[1] Sections 83A–83G inserted by the Transfer of Tribunal Functions and Revenue and Customs Appeals Order, SI 2009/56 art 3, Sch 1 para 220 with effect from 1 April 2009, subject to transitional and savings provisions in Sch 3 para 4.

[83B Right to require review

(1) Any person (other than P) who has the right of appeal under section 83 against a decision may require HMRC to review that decision if that person has not appealed to the tribunal under section 83G.

(2) A notification that such a person requires a review must be made within 30 days of that person becoming aware of the decision.][1]

Amendments—[1] Sections 83A–83G inserted by the Transfer of Tribunal Functions and Revenue and Customs Appeals Order, SI 2009/56 art 3, Sch 1 para 220 with effect from 1 April 2009, subject to transitional and savings provisions in Sch 3 para 4.

[83C Review by HMRC

(1) HMRC must review a decision if—

(*a*) they have offered a review of the decision under section 83A, and

(*b*) P notifies HMRC accepting the offer within 30 days from the date of the document containing the notification of the offer.

(2) But P may not notify acceptance of the offer if P has already appealed to the tribunal under section 83G.

(3) HMRC must review a decision if a person other than P notifies them under section 83B.

(4) HMRC shall not review a decision if P, or another person, has appealed to the tribunal under section 83G in respect of the decision.][1]

Amendments—[1] Sections 83A–83G inserted by the Transfer of Tribunal Functions and Revenue and Customs Appeals Order, SI 2009/56 art 3, Sch 1 para 220 with effect from 1 April 2009, subject to transitional and savings provisions in Sch 3 para 4.

[83D Extensions of time

(1) If under section 83A HMRC have offered P a review of a decision, HMRC may within the relevant period notify P that the relevant period is extended.

(2) If under section 83B another person may require HMRC to review a matter, HMRC may within the relevant period notify the other person that the relevant period is extended.

(3) If notice is given the relevant period is extended to the end of 30 days from—

(*a*) the date of the notice, or

(*b*) any other date set out in the notice or a further notice.

(4) In this section "relevant period" means—

(*a*) the period of 30 days referred to in—

(i) section 83C(1)(*b*) (in a case falling within subsection (1)), or

(ii) section 83B(2) (in a case falling within subsection (2)), or

(*b*) if notice has been given under subsection (1) or (2), that period as extended (or as most recently extended) in accordance with subsection (3).][1]

Amendments—[1] Sections 83A–83G inserted by the Transfer of Tribunal Functions and Revenue and Customs Appeals Order, SI 2009/56 art 3, Sch 1 para 220 with effect from 1 April 2009, subject to transitional and savings provisions in Sch 3 para 4.

[83E Review out of time

(1) This section applies if—

(*a*) HMRC have offered a review of a decision under section 83A and P does not accept the offer within the time allowed under section 83C(1)(*b*) or 83D(3); or

(*b*) a person who requires a review under section 83B does not notify HMRC within the time allowed under that section or section 83D(3).

(2) HMRC must review the decision under section 83C if—

(*a*) after the time allowed, P, or the other person, notifies HMRC in writing requesting a review out of time,

(*b*) HMRC are satisfied that P, or the other person, had a reasonable excuse for not accepting the offer or requiring review within the time allowed, and

(*c*) HMRC are satisfied that P, or the other person, made the request without unreasonable delay after the excuse had ceased to apply.

(3) HMRC shall not review a decision if P, or another person, has appealed to the tribunal under section 83G in respect of the decision.][1]

Amendments—[1] Sections 83A–83G inserted by the Transfer of Tribunal Functions and Revenue and Customs Appeals Order, SI 2009/56 art 3, Sch 1 para 220 with effect from 1 April 2009, subject to transitional and savings provisions in Sch 3 para 4.

[83F Nature of review etc

(1) This section applies if HMRC are required to undertake a review under section 83C or 83E.

(2) The nature and extent of the review are to be such as appear appropriate to HMRC in the circumstances.

(3) For the purpose of subsection (2), HMRC must, in particular, have regard to steps taken before the beginning of the review—

(*a*) by HMRC in reaching the decision, and

(*b*) by any person in seeking to resolve disagreement about the decision.

(4) The review must take account of any representations made by P, or the other person, at a stage which gives HMRC a reasonable opportunity to consider them.

(5) The review may conclude that the decision is to be—

(*a*) upheld,

(*b*) varied, or

(*c*) cancelled.

(6) HMRC must give P, or the other person, notice of the conclusions of the review and their reasoning within—

(*a*) a period of 45 days beginning with the relevant date, or

(*b*) such other period as HMRC and P, or the other person, may agree.

(7) In subsection (6) "relevant date" means—

(*a*) the date HMRC received P's notification accepting the offer of a review (in a case falling within section 83A), or

(*b*) the date HMRC received notification from another person requiring review (in a case falling within section 83B), or

(*c*) the date on which HMRC decided to undertake the review (in a case falling within section 83E).

(8) Where HMRC are required to undertake a review but do not give notice of the conclusions within the time period specified in subsection (6), the review is to be treated as having concluded that the decision is upheld.

(9) If subsection (8) applies, HMRC must notify P or the other person of the conclusion which the review is treated as having reached.][1]

Amendments—[1] Sections 83A–83G inserted by the Transfer of Tribunal Functions and Revenue and Customs Appeals Order, SI 2009/56 art 3, Sch 1 para 220 with effect from 1 April 2009, subject to transitional and savings provisions in Sch 3 para 4.

[83G Bringing of appeals

(1) An appeal under section 83 is to be made to the tribunal before—

(*a*) the end of the period of 30 days beginning with—

(i) in a case where P is the appellant, the date of the document notifying the decision to which the appeal relates, or

(ii) in a case where a person other than P is the appellant, the date that person becomes aware of the decision, or

(*b*) if later, the end of the relevant period (within the meaning of section 83D).

(2) But that is subject to subsections (3) to (5).

(3) In a case where HMRC are required to undertake a review under section 83C—

(*a*) an appeal may not be made until the conclusion date, and

(*b*) any appeal is to be made within the period of 30 days beginning with the conclusion date.

(4) In a case where HMRC are requested to undertake a review in accordance with section 83E—

(*a*) an appeal may not be made—

(i) unless HMRC have decided whether or not to undertake a review, and

(ii) if HMRC decide to undertake a review, until the conclusion date; and

(*b*) any appeal is to be made within the period of 30 days beginning with—

(i) the conclusion date (if HMRC decide to undertake a review), or

(ii) the date on which HMRC decide not to undertake a review.

(5) In a case where section 83F(8) applies, an appeal may be made at any time from the end of the period specified in section 83F(6) to the date 30 days after the conclusion date.

(6) An appeal may be made after the end of the period specified in subsection (1), (3)(*b*), (4)(b) or (5) if the tribunal gives permission to do so.

(7) In this section "conclusion date" means the date of the document notifying the conclusions of the review.][1]

Amendments—[1] Sections 83A–83G inserted by the Transfer of Tribunal Functions and Revenue and Customs Appeals Order, SI 2009/56 art 3, Sch 1 para 220 with effect from 1 April 2009, subject to transitional and savings provisions in Sch 3 para 4.

84 Further provisions relating to appeals

(1) References in this section to an appeal are references to an appeal under section 83.

(2) ...[13]

[(3) Subject to subsections (3B) and (3C), where the appeal is against a decision with respect to any of the matters mentioned in section 83(1)(*b*), (*n*), (*p*), (*q*), (*ra*) or (*zb*), it shall not be entertained unless the amount which HMRC have determined to be payable as VAT has been paid or deposited with them.][13]

[(3A) Subject to subsections (3B) and (3C), where the appeal is against an assessment which is a recovery assessment for the purposes of this subsection, or against the amount of such an assessment, it shall not be entertained unless the amount notified by the assessment has been paid or deposited with HMRC.][13]

[(3B) In a case where the amount determined to be payable as VAT or the amount notified by the recovery assessment has not been paid or deposited an appeal shall be entertained if—

(*a*) HMRC are satisfied (on the application of the appellant), or

(*b*) the tribunal decides (HMRC not being so satisfied and on the application of the appellant),

that the requirement to pay or deposit the amount determined would cause the appellant to suffer hardship.

(3C) Notwithstanding the provisions of sections 11 and 13 of the Tribunals, Courts and Enforcement Act 2007, the decision of the tribunal as to the issue of hardship is final.][13]

(4) Subject to subsection (11) below, where—

(*a*) there is an appeal against a decision of [HMRC][13] with respect to, or to so much of any assessment as concerns, the amount of input tax that may be credited to any person or the proportion of input tax allowable under section 26, and

(*b*) that appeal relates, in whole or in part, to any determination by [HMRC][13]—

(i) as to the purposes for which any goods or services were or were to be used by any person, or

(ii) as to whether or to what extent the matters to which any input tax was attributable were or included matters other than the making of supplies within section 26(2), and

(*c*) VAT for which, in pursuance of that determination, there is no entitlement to a credit is VAT on the supply, acquisition or importation of something in the nature of a luxury, amusement or entertainment,

the tribunal shall not allow the appeal or, as the case may be, so much of it as relates to that determination unless it considers that the determination is one which it was unreasonable to make or which it would have been unreasonable to make if information brought to the attention of the tribunal that could not have been brought to the attention of [HMRC][13] had been available to be taken into account when the determination was made.

[(4ZA) Where an appeal is brought—

(*a*) against such a decision as is mentioned in section [83(1)][13](*fza*), or

(*b*) to the extent that it is based on such a decision, against an assessment,

the tribunal shall not allow the appeal unless it considers that [HMRC][13] could not reasonably have been satisfied that there were grounds for the decision.][6]

[(4A) Where an appeal is brought against the refusal of an application such as is mentioned in section 43B(1) or (2) on the grounds stated in section 43B(5)(*c*)—

(*a*) the tribunal shall not allow the appeal unless it considers that [HMRC][13] could not reasonably have been satisfied that there were grounds for refusing the application,

(*b*) the refusal shall have effect pending the determination of the appeal, and

(*c*) if the appeal is allowed, the refusal shall be deemed not to have occurred.

(4B) Where an appeal is brought against the giving of a notice under section 43C(1) or (3)—

(*a*) the notice shall have effect pending the determination of the appeal, and

(*b*) if the appeal is allowed, the notice shall be deemed never to have had effect.

(4C) Where an appeal is brought against the giving of a notice under section 43C(1), the tribunal shall not allow the appeal unless it considers that [HMRC][13] could not reasonably have been satisfied that there were grounds for giving the notice.

(4D) Where—

(*a*) an appeal is brought against the giving of a notice under section 43C(3), and

(*b*) the grounds of appeal relate wholly or partly to the date specified in the notice,

the tribunal shall not allow the appeal in respect of the date unless it considers that [HMRC][13] could not reasonably have been satisfied that it was appropriate.][5]

[(4E) Where an appeal is brought against a requirement imposed under paragraph 4(2)(*b*) of Schedule 11 that a person give security, the tribunal shall allow the appeal unless [HMRC satisfies][13] the tribunal that—

(*a*) there has been an evasion of, or an attempt to evade, VAT in relation to goods or services supplied to or by that person, or

(*b*) it is likely, or without the requirement for security it is likely, that VAT in relation to such goods or services will be evaded.

(4F) A reference in subsection (4E) above to evading VAT includes a reference to obtaining a VAT credit that is not due or a VAT credit in excess of what is due.][7]

(5) Where, on an appeal against a decision with respect to any of the matters mentioned in section [83(1)][13](*p*)—

(*a*) it is found that the amount specified in the assessment is less than it ought to have been, and

(*b*) the tribunal gives a direction specifying the correct amount,

the assessment shall have effect as an assessment of the amount specified in the direction, and that amount shall be deemed to have been notified to the appellant.

(6) Without prejudice to section 70, nothing in section[83(1)][13](*q*) shall be taken to confer on a tribunal any power to vary an amount assessed by way of penalty, interest or surcharge except in so far as it is necessary to reduce it to the amount which is appropriate under sections 59 to 70; and in this subsection "penalty" includes an amount assessed by virtue of section 61(3) or (4)(*a*).

[(6A) Without prejudice to section 70, nothing in section [83(1)][13](*zb*) shall be taken to confer on a tribunal any power to vary an amount assessed by way of penalty except in so far as it is necessary to reduce it to the amount which is appropriate under paragraph 11 of Schedule 11A.][9]

[(6B) Nothing in section [83(1)][13](*zc*) shall be taken to confer on a tribunal any power to vary an amount assessed by way of penalty except in so far as it is necessary to reduce it to the amount which is appropriate under regulations made under section 135 of the Finance Act 2002.][11]

(7) Where there is an appeal against a decision to make such a direction as is mentioned in section [83(1)][13](*u*), the tribunal shall not allow the appeal unless it considers that [HMRC][13] could not reasonably have been satisfied [that there were grounds for making the direction][3].

[(7A) Where there is an appeal against a decision to make such a direction as is mentioned in section [83(1)][13](*wa*), the cases in which the tribunal shall allow the appeal shall include (in addition to the case where the conditions for the making of the direction were not fulfilled) the case where the tribunal are satisfied in relation to the relevant event by reference to which the direction was given, that—

(*a*) the change in the treatment of the body corporate, or

(*b*) the transaction in question,

had as its main purpose or, as the case may be, as each of its main purposes a genuine commercial purpose unconnected with the fulfilment of the condition specified in paragraph 1(3) of Schedule 9A.][2]

[(7ZA) Where there is an appeal against such a refusal as is mentioned in section [83(1)][13](*wb*)—

(*a*) the tribunal shall not allow the appeal unless it considers that [HMRC][13] could not reasonably have been satisfied that there were grounds for the refusal, and

(*b*) the refusal shall have effect pending the determination of the appeal.][12]

[(7B) Where there is an appeal against a decision to make such a direction as is mentioned in section [83(1)][13](*zza*)—

(*a*) the tribunal shall not allow the appeal unless it considers that [HMRC][13] could not reasonably have been satisfied that there were grounds for making the direction;

(*b*) the direction shall have effect pending the determination of the appeal.][10]

(8) …[13]

(9) No appeal shall lie under this section with respect to the subject-matter of any decision which by virtue of section 16 is a decision to which section 14 [or 14A][13] of the Finance Act 1994 (decisions subject to review) applies unless the decision—

(*a*) relates exclusively to one or both of the following matters, namely whether or not section 30(3) applies in relation to the importation of the goods in question and (if it does not) the rate of tax charged on those goods; and

(*b*) is not one in respect of which notice has been given to [HMRC][13] under section 14 of that Act requiring them to review it[;. and

(*c*) a review is not being undertaken following a request under section 14A of that Act; and

(*d*) a review is not being undertaken under section 15 of that Act as a consequence of section 15B(3), 15C(3) or 15E(3) of that Act.][13]

(10) Where an appeal is against [an HMRC decision][13] which depended upon a prior decision taken …[13] in relation to the appellant, the fact that the prior decision is not within section 83 shall not prevent the tribunal from allowing the appeal on the ground that it would have allowed an appeal against the prior decision.

(11) Subsection (4) above shall not apply in relation to any appeal relating to the input tax that may be credited to any person at the end of a prescribed accounting period beginning before 27th July 1993.

Commentary—*De Voil Indirect Tax Service* **V5.401**.

Simon's Tax Cases—s 84(2), *R v Value Added Tax Tribunal, ex p Minster Associates* [1988] STC 386*; *R v C&E Comrs, ex p Menzies* [1989] STC 40*; *R v London Value Added Tax Tribunal and C&E Comrs, ex p Theodorou* [1989] STC 292*.
s 84(3), *Don Pasquale (a firm) v C&E Comrs* [1990] STC 556*.
s 84(5), *Elias Gale Racing v C&E Comrs* [1999] STC 66; *BUPA Purchasing Ltd and others v C&E Comrs* [2008] STC 101.
S 84(8), *R&C Comrs v RSPCA and another, R&C Comrs v ToTel Ltd* [2008] STC 885.
s 84(10), *C&E Comrs v Arnold* [1996] STC 1271.

Definitions—"The Commissioners", s 96(1); "input tax", s 24; "prescribed accounting period", s 25(1); "recovery assessment", s 78A(5); "supply", s 5, Sch 4; "tax", s 96(1); "tribunal", s 82; "VAT", ss 1, 96(1); "VAT credit", s 25(3).

Cross reference—See VATA 1994 Sch 13 para 22 (modification of this section in its application before the day appointed for the purposes of FA 1994 s 18(3)).

Modifications—Money Laundering Regulations, SI 2007/2157 reg 44(3), Sch 5 para 1 (repeal of this section in relation to appeals to a VAT and duties tribunal made under SI 2007/2157 reg 44).

Transfer of Funds (Information on the Payer) Regulations, SI 2007/3298 reg 13(4), Sch 2 para 2 (repeal of this section in relation to appeals to a VAT and duties tribunal made under SI 2007/3298 reg 13).

Amendments—[1] Words omitted from sub-s (2) repealed by FA 1995 s 31, Sch 29 Pt VI(4) with effect in relation to appeals brought after 1 May 1995.

[2] Sub-s (7A) inserted by FA 1996 s 31(4).

[3] Words in sub-s (7) substituted for the words 'as to the matters in sub-paragraph (2)(*a*) to (*d*) of paragraph 2 of Schedule 1 or, as the case may be, as to the matters in sub-paragraph (4) of that paragraph" by FA 1997 s 31 in relation to directions made on or after the date of passing of FA 1997.

[4] Sub-s (3A) inserted by FA 1997 s 45(3) and deemed to have come into force on 4 December 1996 in relation to assessments made on or after that date.

[5] Sub-ss (4A)–(4D) inserted by FA 1999 s 16, Sch 2 para 4 with effect from 27 July 1999 subject to FA 1999 Sch 2 para 6.

[6] Sub-s (4ZA) inserted by FA 2002 s 23(3), (4) and deemed to have come into force on 24 April 2002.

[7] Sub-ss (4E), (4F) inserted by FA 2003 s 17(7) with effect from 10 April 2003.

[8] Words in sub-s (3) substituted for "or (*q*)" by FA 2003 s 18(3) in relation to any appeal notice given after 9 July 2003.

[9] Words in sub-s (3) substituted for the words "or (*ra*)", and sub-s (6A) inserted, by FA 2004 s 19, Sch 2 para 5 with effect from the passing of FA 2004, so far as is necessary for enabling the making of any orders or regulations by virtue of FA 2004 Sch 2, and otherwise with effect from such day as the Treasury may by order made by statutory instrument appoint.

[10] Sub-ss (7B) inserted by FA 2006 s 21(5) with effect from 19 July 2006.

[11] Sub-s (6B) inserted by FA 2007 s 93(9) with effect from 19 July 2007.

[12] Sub-s (7ZA) inserted by the Value Added Tax (Buildings and Land) Order, SI 2008/1146, art 3(1), (3) with effect in relation to supplies made on or after 1 June 2008, subject to savings in Sch 2 of the Order.

[13] The following amendments made by the Transfer of Tribunal Functions and Revenue and Customs Appeals Order, SI 2009/56 art 3, Sch 1 para 221 with effect from 1 April 2009, subject to transitional and savings provisions in Sch 3 para 4—
- sub-ss (2), (8) repealed;
- sub-ss (3), (3A) substituted;
- sub-ss (3B), (3C) inserted;
- in sub-ss (4)(a), (b) and words at the end, (4ZA), (4A)(a), (4C), (4D), (7), (7ZA) and (7B), words substituted for the words "the Commissioners";
- in sub-ss (4ZA)(a), (5), (6), (6A), (6B), (7), (7A), (7ZA) and (7B) words substituted for the words "83";
- in sub-s (4E) words substituted for the words "the Commissioners satisfy";
- in sub-s (9) words at the beginning inserted; words in (9)(b) substituted for "the Commissioners"; sub-(9);
- in sub-s (10) words in the first place substituted for the words "a decision of the Commissioners" and words "by them" in the second place repealed.

Sub-ss (2), (3), (3A), (8) previously read as follows—

"(2) An appeal shall not be entertained unless the appellant has made all the returns which he was required to make under paragraph 2(1) of Schedule 11 and, …, has paid the amounts shown in those returns as payable by him.

(3) Where the appeal is against a decision with respect to any of the matters mentioned in section 83(*b*), (*n*), (*p*)[, (*q*)[, (*ra*) or (*zb*)]] it shall not be entertained unless—

(*a*) the amount which the Commissioners have determined to be payable as VAT has been paid or deposited with them; or

(*b*) on being satisfied that the appellant would otherwise suffer hardship the Commissioners agree or the tribunal decides that it should be entertained notwithstanding that that amount has not been so paid or deposited.

[(3A) An appeal against an assessment which is a recovery assessment for the purposes of this subsection, or against the amount of such an assessment, shall not be entertained unless—

(*a*) the amount notified by the assessment has been paid or deposited with the Commissioners; or

(*b*) on being satisfied that the appellant would otherwise suffer hardship, the Commissioners agree, or the tribunal decides, that the appeal should be entertained notwithstanding that that amount has not been so paid or deposited.]"

"(8) Where on an appeal it is found—

(*a*) that the whole or part of any amount paid or deposited in pursuance of subsection (3) above is not due; or

(*b*) that the whole or part of any VAT credit due to the appellant has not been paid,

so much of that amount as is found not to be due or not to have been paid shall be repaid (or, as the case may be, paid) with interest at such rate as the tribunal may determine; and where the appeal has been entertained notwithstanding that an amount determined by the Commissioners to be payable as VAT has not been paid or deposited and it is found on the appeal that that amount is due, the tribunal may, if it thinks fit, direct that that amount shall be paid with interest at such rate as may be specified in the direction."

85 Settling appeals by agreement

(1) Subject to the provisions of this section, where a person gives notice of appeal under section 83 and, before the appeal is determined by a tribunal, [HMRC][1] and the appellant come to an agreement (whether in writing or otherwise) under the terms of which the decision under appeal is to be treated—

(*a*) as upheld without variation, or

(*b*) as varied in a particular manner, or

(*c*) as discharged or cancelled,

the like consequences shall ensue for all purposes as would have ensued if, at the time when the agreement was come to, a tribunal had determined the appeal in accordance with the terms of the agreement …[1].

(2) Subsection (1) above shall not apply where, within 30 days from the date when the agreement was come to, the appellant gives notice in writing to [HMRC][1] that he desires to repudiate or resile for the agreement.

(3) Where an agreement is not in writing—

(*a*) the preceding provisions of this section shall not apply unless the fact that an agreement was come to, and the terms agreed, are confirmed by notice in writing given by [HMRC][1] to the appellant or by the appellant to [HMRC][1], and

(*b*) references in those provisions to the time when the agreement was come to shall be construed as references to the time of the giving of that notice of confirmation.

(4) Where—

(*a*) a person who has given a notice of appeal notifies [HMRC][1], whether orally or in writing, that he desires not to proceed with the appeal; and

(*b*) 30 days have elapsed since the giving of the notification without [HMRC][1] giving to the appellant notice in writing indicating that they are unwilling that the appeal should be treated as withdrawn,

the preceding provisions of this section shall have effect as if, at the date of the appellant's notification, the appellant and [HMRC][1] had come to an agreement, orally or in writing, as the case may be, that the decision under appeal should be upheld without variation.

(5) References in this section to an agreement being come to with an appellant and the giving of notice or notification to or by an appellant include references to an agreement being come to with, and the giving of notice or notification to or by, a person acting on behalf of the appellant in relation to the appeal.

Note—In sub-s (2), the word "for" after "resile" appears to be an error. In the previous enactment, FA 1985 s 25(2), the grammatically correct word "from" is used.
Commentary—*De Voil Indirect Tax Service* **V5.461**.
Simon's Tax Cases—*R (oao DFS Furniture Co plc) v C&E Comrs* [2003] STC 1, CA.
Definitions—"HMRC", s 96(1); "tribunal", s 82.

Amendments—[1] Word substituted in each place for the words "the Commissioners" and in sub-s (1) words "(including any terms as to costs)" at the end repealed by the Transfer of Tribunal Functions and Revenue and Customs Appeals Order, SI 2009/56 art 3, Sch 1 para 222 with effect from 1 April 2009, subject to transitional and savings provisions in Sch 3 para 4.

[85A Payment of tax on determination of appeal

(1) This section applies where the tribunal has determined an appeal under section 83.

(2) Where on the appeal the tribunal has determined that—

(*a*) the whole or part of any disputed amount paid or deposited is not due, or

(*b*) the whole or part of any VAT credit due to the appellant has not been paid,

so much of that amount, or of that credit, as the tribunal determines not to be due or not to have been paid shall be paid or repaid with interest at the rate applicable under section 197 of the Finance Act 1996.

(3) Where on the appeal the tribunal has determined that—

(*a*) the whole or part of any disputed amount not paid or deposited is due, or

(*b*) the whole or part of any VAT credit paid was not payable,

so much of that amount, or of that credit, as the tribunal determines to be due or not payable shall be paid or repaid to HMRC with interest at the rate applicable under section 197 of the Finance Act 1996.

(4) Interest under subsection (3) shall be paid without any deduction of income tax.

(5) Nothing in this section requires HMRC to pay interest—

(*a*) on any amount which falls to be increased by a supplement under section 79 (repayment supplement in respect of certain delayed payments or refunds); or

(*b*) where an amount is increased under that section, on so much of the increased amount as represents the supplement.][1]

Amendments—[1] Sections 85A–85B inserted by the Transfer of Tribunal Functions and Revenue and Customs Appeals Order, SI 2009/56 art 3, Sch 1 para 223 with effect from 1 April 2009, subject to transitional and savings provisions in Sch 3 para 4.

[85B Payment of tax where there is a further appeal

(1) Where a party makes a further appeal, notwithstanding that the further appeal is pending, value added tax or VAT credits, or a credit of overstated or overpaid value added tax shall be payable or repayable in accordance with the determination of the tribunal or court against which the further appeal is made.

(2) But if the amount payable or repayable is altered by the order or judgment of the tribunal or court on the further appeal—

(*a*) if too much value added tax has been paid or the whole or part of any VAT credit due to the appellant has not been paid the amount overpaid or not paid shall be refunded with such interest, if any, as the tribunal or court may allow; and

(*b*) if too little value added tax has been charged or the whole or part of any VAT credit paid was not payable so much of the amount as the tribunal or court determines to be due or not payable shall be due or repayable, as appropriate, at the expiration of a period of thirty days beginning with the date on which HMRC issue to the other party a notice of the total amount payable in accordance with the order or judgment of that tribunal or court.

(3) If, on the application of HMRC, the relevant tribunal or court considers it necessary for the protection of the revenue, subsection (1) shall not apply and the relevant tribunal or court may—

(*a*) give permission to withhold any payment or repayment; or

(*b*) require the provision of adequate security before payment or repayment is made.

(4) If, on the application of the original appellant, HMRC are satisfied that financial extremity might be reasonably expected to result if payment or repayment is required or withheld as appropriate, HMRC may do one or more of the things listed in subsection (6).

(5) If on the application of the original appellant, the relevant tribunal or court decides that—

(*a*) the original appellant has applied to HMRC under subsection (4),

(*b*) HMRC have decided that application,

(*c*) financial extremity might be reasonably expected to result from that decision by HMRC,

the relevant tribunal or court may replace, vary or supplement the decision by HMRC by doing one or more of the things listed in subsection (6).

(6) These are the things which HMRC or the relevant tribunal or court may do under subsection (4) or (5)—

(*a*) decide how much, if any, of the amount under appeal should be paid or repaid as appropriate,

(*b*) require the provision of adequate security from the original appellant,

(*c*) stay the requirement to pay or repay under subsection (1).

(7) Subsections (3) to (6) cease to have effect when the further appeal has been determined.

(8) In this section—

"adequate security" means security that is of such amount and given in such manner—

(*a*) as the tribunal or court may determine (in a case falling within subsection (3) or (5)), or
(*b*) as HMRC consider adequate to protect the revenue (in a case falling within subsection (4));

"further appeal" means an appeal against—
(*a*) the tribunal's determination of an appeal under section 83, or
(*b*) a decision of the Upper Tribunal or a court that arises (directly or indirectly) from that determination;

"original appellant" means the person who made the appeal to the tribunal under section 83;
"relevant tribunal or court" means the tribunal or court from which permission or leave to appeal is sought.][1]

Amendments—[1] Sections 85A–85B inserted by the Transfer of Tribunal Functions and Revenue and Customs Appeals Order, SI 2009/56 art 3, Sch 1 para 223 with effect from 1 April 2009, subject to transitional and savings provisions in Sch 3 para 4. If an appeal from a decision of a VAT and duties tribunal, or from a court, is made before 1 April 2009, this section does not apply in relation to that decision (SI 2009/56 Sch 3 para 10).

[86 Appeals to Court of Appeal

(1) The Lord Chancellor may by order provide that—
(a) in such classes of appeal as may be prescribed by the order, and
(b) subject to the consent of the parties and to such other conditions as may be so prescribed,

an appeal from a tribunal shall lie to the Court of Appeal.

(2) An order under this section may provide that section 11 of the Tribunals and Inquiries Act 1992 (which provides for appeals to the High Court from a tribunal) shall have effect, in relation to any appeal to which the order applies, with such modifications as may be specified in the order.

[(2A) Before making an order under this section that relates to England and Wales, the Lord Chancellor must consult the Lord Chief Justice of England and Wales.

(2B) Before making an order under this section that relates to Northern Ireland, the Lord Chancellor must consult the Lord Chief Justice of Northern Ireland.

(2C) The Lord Chief Justice of England and Wales may nominate a judicial office holder (as defined in section 109(4) of the Constitutional Reform Act 2005) to exercise his functions under this section.

(2D) The Lord Chief Justice of Northern Ireland may nominate any of the following to exercise his functions under this section—
(a) the holder of one of the offices listed in Schedule 1 to the Justice (Northern Ireland) Act 2002;
(b) a Lord Justice of Appeal (as defined in section 88 of that Act).][1]

(3) This section does not extend to Scotland.][2]

Commentary—*De Voil Indirect Tax Service* **V5.476**.
Orders—See VAT Tribunals Appeals Order, SI 1986/2288; VAT Tribunals Appeals (Northern Ireland) Order, SI 1994/1978.
Definition—"Tribunal", s 82.
Cross reference—See VATA 1994 s 97(2) (a statutory instrument containing an order under this section is subject to annulment in pursuance of a resolution of either House of Parliament).
Amendments—[1] Sub-ss (2A)–(2D) inserted by Constitutional Reform Act 2005 s 15, Sch 4 paras 235, 236 with effect from 3 April 2006 by virtue of SI 2006/1014 art 2(*a*), Sch 1 para 11.
[2] This section repealed by the Transfer of Tribunal Functions and Revenue and Customs Appeals Order, SI 2009/56 art 3, Sch 1 para 224 with effect from 1 April 2009, subject to transitional and savings provisions in Sch 3 para 4.

[87 Enforcement of registered or recorded tribunal decisions etc

(1) If the decision of a tribunal in England and Wales on an appeal under section 83 is registered by the Commissioners in accordance with rules of court, payment of—
(a) any amount which, as a result of the decision, is, or is recoverable as, VAT due from any person, and
(b) any costs awarded to the Commissioners by the decision,

may be enforced by the High Court as if that amount or, as the case may be, the amount of those costs were an amount due to the Commissioners in pursuance of a judgment or order of the High Court.

(2) If the decision of a tribunal in Scotland on an appeal under section 83—
(a) confirms or varies an amount which is, or is recoverable as, VAT due from any person, or
(b) awards costs to the Commissioners,

the decision may be recorded for execution in the Books of Council and Session and shall be enforceable accordingly.

(3) Subsection (4) below shall apply in relation to the decision of a tribunal in Northern Ireland on an appeal under section 83 where—
(a) any amount is, or is recoverable as, VAT due from any person, as a result of the decision, whether with or without an award of costs to the Commissioners; or
(b) any costs are awarded to the Commissioners by the decision.

(4) Where this subsection applies—

(*a*) *payment of the amount mentioned in paragraph* (*a*) *of subsection* (3) *above or, as the case may be, the amount of the costs mentioned in paragraph* (*b*) *of that subsection may be enforced by the Enforcement of Judgments Office; and*

(*b*) *a sum equal to any such amount shall be deemed to be payable under a money judgment within the meaning of Article 2(2) of the Judgments Enforcement (Northern Ireland) Order 1981, and the provisions of that Order shall apply accordingly.*

(5) *Any reference in this section to a decision of a tribunal includes a reference to an order (however described) made by a tribunal for giving effect to a decision.*][1]

Commentary—*De Voil Indirect Tax Service* **V5.174**.
Definitions—"The Commissioners", s 96(1); "tribunal", s 82; "VAT", ss 1, 96(1).
Modifications—Money Laundering Regulations, SI 2007/2157 reg 44(3), Sch 5 para 1 (in sub-ss (1)(*a*), (2)(*a*), (3)(*a*), words ", or is recoverable as, VAT" repealed, in relation to appeals to a VAT and duties tribunal made under SI 2007/2157 reg 44).
Amendments—[1] This section repealed by the Transfer of Tribunal Functions and Revenue and Customs Appeals Order, SI 2009/56 art 3, Sch 1 para 224 with effect from 1 April 2009, subject to transitional and savings provisions in Sch 3 para 4.

PART VI
SUPPLEMENTARY PROVISIONS

Change in rate of VAT etc and disclosure of information

88 Supplies spanning change of rate etc

(1) This section applies where there is a change in the rate of VAT in force under section 2 [or 29A][1] or in the descriptions of exempt[, zero-rated or reduced-rate][1] supplies or exempt[, zero-rated or reduced-rate][1] acquisitions.

(2) Where—

(*a*) a supply affected by the change would, apart from section 6(4), (5), (6) or (10), be treated under section 6(2) or (3) as made wholly or partly at a time when it would not have been affected by the change; or

(*b*) a supply not so affected would apart from section 6(4), (5), (6) or (10) be treated under section 6(2) or (3) as made wholly or partly at a time when it would have been so affected,

the rate at which VAT is chargeable on the supply, or any question whether it is zero-rated or exempt [or a reduced-rate supply][1], shall if the person making it so elects be determined without regard to section 6(4), (5), (6) or (10).

(3) Any power to make regulations under this Act with respect to the time when a supply is to be treated as taking place shall include power to provide for this section to apply as if the references in subsection (2) above to section 6(4), (5), (6) or (10) included references to specified provisions of the regulations.

(4) Where—

(*a*) any acquisition of goods from another member State which is affected by the change would not have been affected (in whole or in part) if it had been treated as taking place at the time of the event which, in relation to that acquisition, is the first relevant event for the purposes of taxing the acquisition; or

(*b*) any acquisition of goods from another member State which is not so affected would have been affected (in whole or in part) if it had been treated as taking place at the time of that event,

the rate at which VAT is chargeable on the acquisition, or any question whether it is zero-rated or exempt [or a reduced-rate acquisition][1], shall, if the person making the acquisition so elects, be determined as at the time of that event.

(5) Regulations under [paragraph 2A][2] of Schedule 11 may make provision for the replacement or correction of any VAT invoice which—

(*a*) relates to a supply in respect of which an election is made under this section, but

(*b*) was issued before the election was made.

(6) No election may be made under this section in respect of a supply to which [paragraph 7 of Schedule 4 or paragraph 2B(4) of Schedule 11][2] applies.

(7) References in this section to an acquisition being zero-rated are references to an acquisition of goods from another member State being one in relation to which section 30(3) provides for no VAT to be chargeable.

[(8) References in this section—

(*a*) to a supply being a reduced-rate supply, or

(*b*) to an acquisition being a reduced-rate acquisition,

are references to a supply, or (as the case may be) an acquisition, being one on which VAT is charged at the rate in force under section 29A.][1]

Commentary—*De Voil Indirect Tax Service* **V3.141**.
Regulations—See VAT Regulations, SI 1995/2518 reg 95.
Press releases etc—Business Brief 21/95 8-10-95 (operation of retail scheme spanning rate change).

Definitions—"Acquisition of goods from another member State", s 11; "another member State", s 96(1); "exempt acquisition", s 31; "exempt supply", s 31; "regulations", s 96(1); "supply", s 5, Sch 4; "VAT", ss 1, 96(1); "VAT invoice", s 6(15); "zero-rating", s 30.
Cross references—See VAT Regulations, SI 1995/2518 reg 15 (credit note to be issued by supplier following change of rate, where an election is made under this section).
VAT Regulations, SI 1995/2518 reg 95 (supplies spanning change in rate of VAT: deemed time of supply: extension of sub-s (2) of this section).
Amendments—[1] In sub-s (1), "or 29A" inserted, and words substituted for "or zero-rated"; words in sub-ss (2), (4) inserted; and sub-s (8) added, by FA 2001 s 99(6), Sch 31 para 4 with effect from 11 May 2001.
[2] Words in sub-ss (5), (6) substituted by FA 2002 s 24(4)(*c*), (5) with effect from 1 December 2003 (by virtue of SI 2003/3043).

89 Adjustments of contracts on changes in VAT

(1) Where, after the making of a contract for the supply of goods or services and before the goods or services are supplied, there is a change in the VAT charged on the supply, then, unless the contract otherwise provided, there shall be added to or deducted from the consideration for the supply an amount equal to the change.

(2) Subsection (1) above shall apply in relation to a tenancy or lease as it applies in relation to a contract except that a term of a tenancy or lease shall not be taken to provide that the rule contained in that subsection is not to apply in the case of the tenancy or lease if the term does not [refer][1] specifically to VAT or this section.

(3) References in this section to a change in the VAT charged on a supply include references to a change to or from no VAT being charged on the supply (including a change attributable to the making of an [option to tax any land under Part 1 of Schedule 10][2]).

Commentary—*De Voil Indirect Tax Service* **V3.151**.
Definitions—"Supply", s 5, Sch 4; "VAT", ss 1, 96(1).
Note—[1] The Commissioners have confirmed that the word "refer" has been accidentally omitted from s 89(2).
[2] In sub-s (3) words substituted by the Value Added Tax (Buildings and Land) Order, SI 2008/1146, art 6, Sch 1 paras 1, 2 with effect in relation to supplies made on or after 1 June 2008, subject to savings in Sch 2 of the Order.

90 Failure of resolution under Provisional Collection of Taxes Act 1968

(1) Where—

(*a*) by virtue of a resolution having effect under the Provisional Collection of Taxes Act 1968 VAT has been paid at a rate specified in the resolution on the supply of any goods or services by reference to a value determined under section 19(2) or on the acquisition of goods from another member State by reference to a value determined under section 20(3), and

(*b*) by virtue of section 1(6) or (7) or 5(3) of that Act any of that VAT is repayable in consequence of the restoration in relation to that supply or acquisition of a lower rate,

the amount repayable shall be the difference between the VAT paid by reference to that value at the rate specified in the resolution and the VAT that would have been payable by reference to that value at the lower rate.

(2) Where—

(*a*) by virtue of such a resolution VAT is chargeable at a rate specified in the resolution on the supply of any goods or services by reference to a value determined under section 19(2) or on the acquisition of goods from another member State by reference to a value determined under section 20(3), but

(*b*) before the VAT is paid it ceases to be chargeable at that rate in consequence of the restoration in relation to that supply or acquisition of a lower rate,

the VAT chargeable at the lower rate shall be charged by reference to the same value as that by reference to which VAT would have been chargeable at the rate specified in the resolution.

(3) The VAT that may be credited as input tax under section 25 or refunded under section 33, [or 33A,][1] 35 or 40 does not include VAT that has been repaid by virtue of any of the provisions mentioned in subsection (1)(*b*) above or that would be repayable by virtue of any of those provisions if it had been paid.

Commentary—*De Voil Indirect Tax Service* **V1.131**.
Definitions—"Acquisition of goods from another member State", s 11; "another member State", s 96(1); "input tax", s 24; "supply", s 5, Sch 4; "VAT", ss 1, 96(1).
Amendments—[1] Words in sub-s (3) inserted by FA 2001 s 98(8) with effect from 1 September 2001.

91 Disclosure of information for statistical purposes

(1) For the purpose of the compilation or maintenance by the Department of Trade and Industry or the [Statistics Board][1] of a central register of businesses, or for the purpose of any statistical survey conducted or to be conducted by that Department [or Board][1], the Commissioners or an authorised officer of the Commissioners may disclose to an authorised officer of that Department [or Board][1] particulars of the following descriptions obtained or recorded by them in pursuance of this Act—

(*a*) numbers allocated by the Commissioners on the registration of persons under this Act and reference numbers for members of a group;

(*b*) names, trading styles and addresses of persons so registered or of members of groups and status and trade classifications of businesses; and

(*c*) actual or estimated value of supplies.

(2) Subject to subsection (3) below, no information obtained by virtue of this section by an officer of the Department of Trade and Industry or the [Statistics Board][1] may be disclosed except to an officer of a Government department (including a Northern Ireland department [or to a member of the staff of the Scottish Administration][2]) for the purpose for which the information was obtained, or for a like purpose.

(3) Subsection (2) above does not prevent the disclosure—

(*a*) of any information in the form of a summary so framed as not to enable particulars to be identified as particulars relating to a particular person or to the business carried on by a particular person; or

(*b*) with the consent of any person, of any information enabling particulars to be identified as particulars relating only to him or to a business carried on by him.

(4) If any person who has obtained any information by virtue of this section discloses it in contravention of this section he shall be liable—

(*a*) on summary conviction to a fine not exceeding the statutory maximum; and

(*b*) on conviction on indictment to imprisonment for a term not exceeding 2 years or to a fine of any amount or to both.

(5) In this section, references to the Department of Trade and Industry or the [Statistics Board][1] include references to any Northern Ireland department [or to any part of the Scottish Administration][2] carrying out similar functions.

Commentary—*De Voil Indirect Tax Service* **V1.270**.
Definitions—"The Commissioners", s 96(1); "business", s 94; "registered", s 3(3); "supply", s 5, Sch 4.
Amendments—[1] Words in sub-ss (1), (2), (5) substituted by Statistics and Registration Service Act 2007 s 46, Sch 2 para 6 with effect from 1 April 2008, by virtue of SI 2008/839, art 2.
[2] Words in sub-ss (2), (5) inserted by The Scotland Act 1998 (Consequential Modifications) (No 2) Order, SI 1999/1820 s 114(2), which comes into force on the "principle appointed day", currently 1 July 1999, by virtue of the Scotland Act 1998 (Commencement) Order 1998/3178.

Interpretative provisions

92 Taxation under the laws of other member States etc

(1) Subject to the following provisions of this section, references in this Act, in relation to another member State, to the law of that member State shall be construed as confined to so much of the law of that member State as for the time being has effect for the purposes of any Community instrument relating to VAT.

(2) Subject to the following provisions of this section—

(*a*) references in this Act to a person being taxable in another member State are references to that person being taxable under so much of the law of that member State as makes provision for purposes corresponding, in relation to that member State, to the purposes of so much of this Act as makes provision as to whether a person is a taxable person; and

(*b*) references in this Act to goods being acquired by a person in another member State are references to goods being treated as so acquired in accordance with provisions of the law of that member State corresponding, in relation to that member State, to so much of this Act as makes provision for treating goods as acquired in the United Kingdom from another member State.

(3) Without prejudice to subsection (5) below, the Commissioners may by regulations make provision for the manner in which any of the following are to be or may be proved for any of the purposes of this Act, that is to say—

(*a*) the effect of any provisions of the law of any other member State;

(*b*) that provisions of any such law correspond or have a purpose corresponding, in relation to any member State, to or to the purpose of any provision of this Act.

(4) The Commissioners may by regulations provide—

(*a*) for a person to be treated for prescribed purposes of this Act as taxable in another member State only where he has given such notification, and furnished such other information, to the Commissioners as may be prescribed;

(*b*) for the form and manner in which any notification or information is to be given or furnished under the regulations and the particulars which it is to contain;

(*c*) for the proportion of any consideration for any transaction which is to be taken for the purposes of this Act as representing a liability, under the law of another member State, for VAT to be conclusively determined by reference to such invoices or in such other manner as may be prescribed.

(5) In any proceedings (whether civil or criminal), a certificate of the Commissioners—

(*a*) that a person was or was not, at any date, taxable in another member State; or

(*b*) that any VAT payable under the law of another member State has or has not been paid,

shall be sufficient evidence of that fact until the contrary is proved, and any document purporting to be a certificate under this subsection shall be deemed to be such a certificate until the contrary is proved.

(6) Without prejudice to the generality of any of the powers of the Commissioners under the relevant information provisions, those powers shall, for the purpose of facilitating compliance with any Community obligations, be exercisable with respect to matters that are relevant to a

charge to VAT under the law of another member State, as they are exercisable with respect to matters that are relevant for any of the purposes of this Act.

(7) The reference in subsection (6) above to the relevant information provisions is a reference to the provisions of section 73(7) and Schedule 11 relating to—

(*a*) the keeping of accounts;
(*b*) the making of returns and the submission of other documents to the Commissioners;
(*c*) the production, use and contents of invoices;
(*d*) the keeping and preservation of records; and
(*e*) the furnishing of information and the production of documents.

Commentary—*De Voil Indirect Tax Service* **V1.272**.
Definitions—"Acquisition of goods from another member State", s 11; "another member State", s 96(1); "the Commissioners", s 96(1); "document", s 96(1); "invoice", s 96(1); "prescribed", s 96(1); "regulations", s 96(1); "taxable person", s 3; "United Kingdom", s 96(11); "VAT", ss 1, 96(1).

93 Territories included in references to other member States etc

(1) The Commissioners may by regulations provide for the territory of the Community, or for the member States, to be treated for any of the purposes of this Act as including or excluding such territories as may be prescribed.

(2) Without prejudice to the generality of the powers conferred by subsection (1) and section 16, the Commissioners may, for any of the purposes of this Act, by regulations provide for prescribed provisions of any customs and excise legislation to apply in relation to cases where any territory is treated under subsection (1) above as excluded from the territory of the Community, with such exceptions and adaptations as may be prescribed.

(3) In subsection (2) above the reference to customs and excise legislation is a reference to any enactment or subordinate or Community legislation (whenever passed, made or adopted) which has effect in relation to, or to any assigned matter connected with, the importation or exportation of goods.

(4) In subsection (3) above "assigned matter" has the same meaning as in the Management Act.

Commentary—*De Voil Indirect Tax Service* **V1.213**.
Regulations—See VAT Regulations, SI 1995/2518 regs 118–121, 136–145.
Definitions—"The Commissioners", s 96(1); "subordinate legislation", s 96(1).

94 Meaning of "business" etc

(1) In this Act "business" includes any trade, profession or vocation.

(2) Without prejudice to the generality of anything else in this Act, the following are deemed to be the carrying on of a business—

(*a*) the provision by a club, association or organisation (for a subscription or other consideration) of the facilities or advantages available to its members; and
(*b*) the admission, for a consideration, of persons to any premises.

(3) ...[1]

(4) Where a person, in the course or furtherance of a trade, profession or vocation, accepts any office, services supplied by him as the holder of that office are treated as supplied in the course or furtherance of the trade, profession or vocation.

(5) Anything done in connection with the termination or intended termination of a business is treated as being done in the course or furtherance of that business.

(6) The disposition of a business[, or part of a business,][2] as a going concern, or of [the assets or liabilities of the business or part of the business][2] (whether or not in connection with its reorganisation or winding up), is a supply made in the course or furtherance of the business.

Commentary—*De Voil Indirect Tax Service* **V2.202**.
HMRC Manuals—VAT Guidance V1-3: Supply and consideration, para 4.9 (office holders: services supplied in the course of trade).
Simon's Tax Cases—*C&E Comrs v Apple and Pear Development Council* [1984] STC 296*; *Lord Advocate v Largs Golf Club* [1985] STC 226*.
s 94(2), *Eastbourne Town Radio Cars Association v C&E Comrs* [2001] STC 606.
s 94(2)(*a*), *C&E Comrs v British Field Sports Society* [1998] STC 315*.
s 94(3), *C&E Comrs v British Field Sports Society* [1997] STC 746*.
Definition—"Supply", s 5, Sch 4.
Amendments—[1] Sub-s (3) repealed by FA 1999 s 20 Sch 20 Pt II with effect from 1 December 1999 (by virtue of the Finance Act 1999, Section 20, (Appointed Day) Order, SI 1999/2769, art 2).
[2] In sub-s (6) words inserted and substituted by FA 2007 s 100(7), (10) with effect in relation to transfers pursuant to contracts entered into on or after 1 September 2007.

95 Meaning of "new means of transport"

(1) In this Act "means of transport" in the expression "new means of transport" means, subject to subsection (2) below, any of the following, that is to say—

(*a*) any ship exceeding 7.5 metres in length;
(*b*) any aircraft the take-off weight of which exceeds 1550 kilograms;
(*c*) any motorised land vehicle which—

(i) has an engine with a displacement or cylinder capacity exceeding 48 cubic centimetres; or

(ii) is constructed or adapted to be electrically propelled using more than 7.2 kilowatts.

(2) A ship, aircraft or motorised land vehicle does not fall within subsection (1) above unless it is intended for the transport of persons or goods.

[(3) For the purposes of this Act a means of transport shall be treated as new, in relation to any supply or any acquisition from another member State, at any time unless at that time—

(*a*) the period that has elapsed since its first entry into service is—

(i) in the case of a ship or aircraft, a period of more than 3 months; and

(ii) in the case of a land vehicle, a period of more than 6 months;

and][1]

(*b*) it has, since its first entry into service, travelled under its own power—

(i) in the case of a ship, for more than 100 hours;

(ii) in the case of an aircraft, for more than 40 hours; and

(iii) in the case of a land vehicle, for more than [6000 kilometres][1].

(4) The Treasury may by order vary this section—

(*a*) by adding or deleting any ship, aircraft or vehicle of a description specified in the order to or from those which are for the time being specified in subsection (1) above; and

(*b*) by altering, omitting or adding to the provisions of subsection (3) above for determining whether a means of transport is new.

(5) The Commissioners may by regulations make provision specifying the circumstances in which a means of transport is to be treated for the purposes of this section as having first entered into service.

Commentary—*De Voil Indirect Tax Service* **V1.294**.
Regulations—See VAT Regulations, SI 1995/2518 reg 147.
Definitions—"The Commissioners", s 96(1); "regulations", s 96(1); "ship", s 96(1).
Cross reference—See VAT Regulations, SI 1995/2518 reg 147 (time when a means of transport is treated as having first entered into service).
Amendments—[1] Words in sub-s (3) substituted by the Value Added Tax (Means of Transport) Order, SI 1994/3128 with effect in relation to means of transport whose first entry into service is on or after 1 January 1995.

96 Other interpretative provisions

(1) In this Act—

"the 1983 Act" means the Value Added Tax Act 1983;

"another member State" means, subject to section 93(1), any member State other than the United Kingdom, and "other member States" shall be construed accordingly;

"assignment", in relation to Scotland, means assignation;

"authorised person" means any person acting under the authority of the Commissioners;

"the Commissioners" means the Commissioners of Customs and Excise;

["document" means anything in which information of any description is recorded; and][2]

["copy", in relation to a document, means anything onto which information recorded in the document has been copied, by whatever means and whether directly or indirectly;][2]

"fee simple"—

(*a*) in relation to Scotland, means the ...[9] interest of the owner;

(*b*) in relation to Northern Ireland, includes the estate of a person who holds land under a fee farm grant;

["HMRC" means Her Majesty's Revenue and Customs;][11]

"invoice" includes any document similar to an invoice;

"input tax" has the meaning given by section 24;

"interim trustee" has the same meaning as in the Bankruptcy (Scotland) Act 1985;

"local authority" has the meaning given by subsection (4) below;

"major interest", in relation to land, means the fee simple or a tenancy for a term certain exceeding 21 years, and in relation to Scotland means [the][9] interest of the owner, or the lessee's interest under a lease for a period [of not less than 20 years][5];

"the Management Act" means the Customs and Excise Management Act 1979;

"money" includes currencies other than sterling;

"output tax" has the meaning given by section 24;

"permanent trustee" has the same meaning as in the Bankruptcy (Scotland) Act 1985;

["the Post Office company" has the same meaning as in Part IV of the Postal Services Act 2000][7]

"prescribed" means prescribed by regulations;

"prescribed accounting period" has the meaning given by section 25(1);

"quarter" means a period of 3 months ending at the end of March, June, September or December;

"regulations" means regulations made by the Commissioners under this Act;

["relevant business person" has the meaning given by section 7A(4)][12];

"ship" includes hovercraft;

"subordinate legislation" has the same meaning as in the Interpretation Act 1978;

"tax" means VAT;

"taxable acquisition" has the meaning given by section 10(2);

"taxable person" means a person who is a taxable person under section 3;

"taxable supply" has the meaning given by section 4(2);
"the Taxes Act" means the Income and Corporation Taxes Act 1988;
"tribunal" has the meaning given by section 82;
"VAT" means value added tax charged in accordance with this Act or, where the context requires, with the law of another member State;
"VAT credit" has the meaning given by section 25(3);
"VAT invoice" has the meaning given by section 6(15);
"VAT representative" has the meaning given by section 48;

and any reference to a particular section, Part or Schedule is a reference to that section or Part of, or Schedule to, this Act.

(2) Any reference in this Act to being registered shall be construed in accordance with section 3(3).

(3) Subject to section 93—

(*a*) the question whether or not goods have entered the territory of the Community;
(*b*) the time when any Community customs debt in respect of duty on the entry of any goods into the territory of the Community would be incurred; and
(*c*) the person by whom any such debt would fall to be discharged,

shall for the purposes of this Act be determined (whether or not the goods in question are themselves subject to any such duties) according to the Community legislation applicable to goods which are in fact subject to such duties.

(4) In this Act "local authority" means the council of a county, [county borough,][1] district, London borough, parish or group of parishes (or, in Wales, community or group of communities), the Common Council of the City of London, the Council of the Isles of Scilly, and any joint committee or joint board established by two or more of the foregoing and, in relation to Scotland, a regional, islands or district council within the meaning of the Local Government (Scotland) Act 1973 any combination and any joint committee or joint board established by two or more of the foregoing and any joint board to which section 226 of that Act applies.

(5) Any reference in this Act to the amount of any duty of excise on any goods shall be taken to be a reference to the amount of duty charged on those goods with any addition or deduction falling to be made under section 1 of the Excise Duties (Surcharges or Rebates) Act 1979.

(6), (7) …[3]

(8) The question whether, in relation to any supply of services, the supplier or the recipient of the supply belongs in one country or another shall be determined …[12] in accordance with section 9.

(9) Schedules [7A,][6] 8 and 9 shall be interpreted in accordance with the notes contained in those Schedules; and accordingly the powers conferred by this Act to vary those Schedules include a power to add to, delete or vary those notes.

(10) The descriptions of Groups in those Schedules are for ease of reference only and shall not affect the interpretation of the descriptions of items in those Groups.

[(10A) Where—

(*a*) the grant of any interest, right, licence or facilities gives rise for the purposes of this Act to supplies made at different times after the making of the grant, and
(*b*) a question whether any of those supplies is zero-rated or exempt falls to be determined according to whether or not the grant is a grant of a description specified in Schedule 8 or 9 or [any of paragraphs 5 to 11 of Schedule 10][10],

that question shall be determined according to whether the description is applicable as at the time of supply, rather than by reference to the time of the grant.][4]

[(10B) Notwithstanding subsection (10A) above—

(*a*) item 1 of Group 1 of Schedule 9 does not make exempt any supply that arises for the purposes of this Act from the prior grant of a fee simple falling within paragraph (*a*) of that item; and
(*b*) that paragraph does not prevent the exemption of a supply that arises for the purposes of this Act from the prior grant of a fee simple not falling within that paragraph.][8]

(11) References in this Act to the United Kingdom include the territorial sea of the United Kingdom.

Definition—"Supply", s 5, Sch 4.

Amendments—[1] Words in sub-s (4) inserted by the Local Government Reorganisation (Wales) (Consequential Amendments No 2) Order, SI 1995/1510 art 2 with effect from 16 June 1995.

[2] Definitions "document" and "copy" in sub-s (1) inserted by the Civil Evidence Act 1995 Sch 1 para 20 with effect from 31 January 1997 (see SI 1996/3217).

[3] Sub-ss (6), (7) repealed by the Civil Evidence Act 1995 Sch 2 with effect from 31 January 1997 (see SI 1996/3217).

[4] Sub-s (10A) inserted by FA 1997 s 35 and deemed always to have had effect.

[5] Words in the definition of "major interest" in para (*b*) substituted by FA 1998 s 24 with effect from 31 July 1998.

[6] In sub-s (9), "7A" inserted by FA 2001 s 99(6), Sch 31 para 5 with effect from 11 May 2001.

[7] Definition of "the Post Office company" inserted by the Postal Services Act 2000 (Consequential Modifications No 1) Order, SI 2001/1149 art 3, Sch 1 para 101 with effect from 26 March 2001.

[8] Sub-s (10B) inserted by FA 2003 s 20 with effect for any supply that arises for the purposes of VATA 1994 from the prior grant of a fee simple made after 8 April 2003.

[9] In sub-s (1), words in definition of "fee simple" repealed and words in definition of "major interest" substituted by the Abolition of Feudal Tenure etc (Scotland) Act 2000 s 76(1), (2), Sch 12 Pt I para 57, Sch 13 Pt 1 with effect from 28 November 2004 (by virtue of SI 2003/456).

[10] In sub-s (10A)(*b*), words substituted by the Value Added Tax (Buildings and Land) Order, SI 2008/1146, art 6, Sch 1 paras 1, 3 with effect in relation to supplies made on or after 1 June 2008, subject to savings in Sch 2 of the Order.
[11] In sub-s (1) definition of "HMRC" inserted by the Transfer of Tribunal Functions and Revenue and Customs Appeals Order, SI 2009/56 art 3, Sch 1 para 225 with effect from 1 April 2009, subject to transitional and savings provisions in Sch 3 para 4.
[12] In sub-s (1) words inserted, in sub-s (8) words "(subject to any provision made under section 8(6))" repealed by FA 2009 s 76, Sch 36 paras 1, 8 with effect in relation to supplies made on or after 1 January 2010.

Supplementary provisions

97 Orders, rules and regulations

(1) Any order made by the Treasury …[12] under this Act and any regulations or rules under this Act shall be made by statutory instrument.

(2) …[12]

(3) An order to which this subsection applies shall be laid before the House of Commons; and unless it is approved by that House before the expiration of a period of 28 days beginning with the date on which it was made, it shall cease to have effect on the expiration of that period, but without prejudice to anything previously done thereunder or to the making of a new order.

In reckoning any such period no account shall be taken of any time during which Parliament is dissolved or prorogued or during which the House of Commons is adjourned for more than 4 days.

(4) Subject to section 53(4), subsection (3) above applies to—

(*aa*) …[1]

(*a*) an order under section 5(4)[, 7A(6)][14] or 28;

[(*ab*) an order under paragraph 5(7) of Schedule 4 substituting a lesser sum for the sum for the time being specified in paragraph 5(2)(*a*) of that Schedule;][2]

(*b*) …[3]

(*c*) an order under this Act making provision—

(i) for increasing the rate of VAT in force [under section 2][4] at the time of the making of the order;

(ii) for excluding any VAT from credit under section 25;

[(iia) for varying Schedule 7A so as to cause VAT to be charged on a supply at the rate in force under section 2 instead of that in force under section 29A;][5]

(iii) for varying Schedule 8 or 9 so as to abolish the zero-rating of a supply or to abolish the exemption of a supply without zero-rating it;

[(*ca*) an order under section 43AA(1) if as a result of the order any bodies would cease to be eligible to be treated as members of a group;][8]

(*d*) an order under section 51, except one making only such amendments as are necessary or expedient in consequence of provisions of an order under this Act which—

(i) vary Schedule [7A,][5] 8 or 9; but

(ii) are not within paragraph (*c*) above;

(*e*) an order under section 54(4) or (8);

[(*ea*) an order under section 55A(13);][10]

[(*eb*) an order under section 77A(9) or (9A);][11]

[(*f*) an order under paragraph 1A(7) of Schedule 6;][6]

[(*fa*) an order under paragraph 3(4) of Schedule 10A);][9]

[(*g*) an order under paragraph 3 or 4 of Schedule 11A][7].

[(4A) Where an order under section 2(2) is in force, the reference in subsection (4)(*c*)(i) of this section to the rate of VAT in force under section 2 at the time of the making of an order is a reference to the rate which would be in force at that time if no such order had been made.][13]

(5) A statutory instrument made under any provision of this Act except—

(*a*) an order made under section 79, or

(*b*) an instrument as respects which any other Parliamentary procedure is expressly provided, or

(*c*) an instrument containing an order appointing a day for the purposes of any provision of this Act, being a day as from which the provision will have effect, with or without amendments, or will cease to have effect,

shall be subject to annulment in pursuance of a resolution of the House of Commons.

Commentary—*De Voil Indirect Tax Service* **V1.236**.
Definitions—"Exempt supply", s 31; "regulations", s 96(1); "supply", s 5, Sch 4; "VAT", ss 1, 96(1); "zero-rating", s 30.
Cross references—See VATA 1994 s 53(4) (sub-s (3) of this section disapplied in relation to orders under s 53 (tour operators)).
VAT (Isle of Man) Order, SI 1982/1067 art 7 (references to VAT in this section to include references to VAT chargeable under Isle of Man legislation).
Amendments—[1] Sub-s (4)(*aa*) inserted by FA 1995 s 21(4), (6), with effect in relation to any supply made after 31 March 1995 and any acquisition or importation taking place after that date, and repealed by FA 2001 s 110, Sch 33 Pt 3(1) with effect from 1 November 2001.
[2] Sub-s (4)(*ab*) inserted by FA 1996 s 33(3).
[3] Sub-s (4)(*b*) repealed by FA 1996 Sch 41 Pt IV(2).
[4] Words in sub-s (4)(*c*)(i) inserted by FA 2001 s 99(6), Sch 31 para 6(2) with effect in relation to orders under VATA 1994 s 2(2) that make changes only in the rate of VAT that is in force at times after 31 October 2001.

[5] Sub-s (4)(*c*)(iia) inserted, and words in sub-s (4)(*d*)(i) inserted, by FA 2001 s 99(6), Sch 31 para 6(3), (4) with effect from 11 May 2001.
[6] Sub-s (4)(*f*) inserted by FA 2004 s 22(4) with effect from 22 July 2004.
[7] Sub-s (4)(*g*) inserted by FA 2004 s 19, Sch 2 para 6 with effect from the passing of FA 2004, so far as is necessary for enabling the making of any orders or regulations by virtue of FA 2004 Sch 2, and otherwise with effect from such day as the Treasury may by order made by statutory instrument appoint.
[8] Sub-s (*ca*) inserted by FA 2004 s 20(5) with effect from 22 July 2004.
[9] Sub-s (4)(*fa*) inserted by FA 2006 s 22(2) with effect from 19 July 2006.
[10] Sub-s (4)(*ea*) inserted by FA 2006 s 19(6), (8) with effect for supplies made on or after 1 June 2007 (by virtue of the Finance Act 2006, Section 19, (Appointed Day) Order, SI 2007/1419).
[11] Sub-s (4)(*eb*) inserted by FA 2007 s 98(2) with effect from 19 July 2007.
[12] In sub-s (1) words "or the Lord Chancellor" repealed; sub-(2) repealed by the Transfer of Tribunal Functions and Revenue and Customs Appeals Order, SI 2009/56 art 3, Sch 1 para 226 with effect from 1 April 2009, subject to transitional and savings provisions in Sch 3 para 4.
[13] Sub-s (4A) inserted by FA 2009 Sch 3 para 25(3) with effect from 21 July 2009.
[14] Words in sub-s (4)(*a*) inserted by FA 2009 s 76, Sch 36 paras 1, 9 with effect in relation to supplies made on or after 1 January 2010.

VAT

[97A Place of supply orders: transitional provision.

(1) This section shall have effect for the purpose of giving effect to any order made [under section 7A(6)][2], if—

(*a*) the order provides for services of a description specified in the order to be treated as supplied in the United Kingdom;
(*b*) the services would not have fallen to be so treated apart from the order;
(*c*) the services are not services that would have fallen to be so treated under any provision re-enacted in the order; and
(*d*) the order is expressed to come into force in relation to services supplied on or after a date specified in the order ("the commencement date").

(2) Invoices and other documents provided to any person before the commencement date shall be disregarded in determining the time of the supply of any services which, if their time of supply were on or after the commencement date, would be treated by virtue of the order as supplied in the United Kingdom.

(3) If there is a payment in respect of any services of the specified description that was received by the supplier before the commencement date, so much (if any) of that payment as relates to times on or after that date shall be treated as if it were a payment received on the commencement date.

(4) If there is a payment in respect of services of the specified description that is or has been received by the supplier on or after the commencement date, so much (if any) of that payment as relates to times before that date shall be treated as if it were a payment received before that date.

(5) Subject to subsection (6) below, a payment in respect of any services shall be taken for the purposes of this section to relate to the time of the performance of those services.

(6) Where a payment is received in respect of any services the performance of which takes place over a period a part of which falls before the commencement date and a part of which does not—

(*a*) an apportionment shall be made, on a just and reasonable basis, of the extent to which the payment is attributable to so much of the performance of those services as took place before that date;
(*b*) the payment shall, to that extent, be taken for the purposes of this section to relate to a time before that date; and
(*c*) the remainder, if any, of the payment shall be taken for those purposes to relate to times on or after that date.][1]

Amendments—[1] This section inserted by FA 1998 s 22 with effect from 17 March 1998.
[2] In sub-s (1) words "on or after 17th March 1998 under section 7(11)" substituted by FA 2009 s 76, Sch 36 paras 1, 10 with effect in relation to supplies made on or after 1 January 2010.

98 Service of notices

Any notice, notification, requirement or demand to be served on, given to or made of any person for the purposes of this Act may be served, given or made by sending it by post in a letter addressed to that person or his VAT representative at the last or usual residence or place of business of that person or representative.

Commentary—*De Voil Indirect Tax Service* **V5.371, V5.373**
Definitions—"Business", s 94; "VAT representative", s 48.

99 Refund of VAT to Government of Northern Ireland

The Commissioners shall refund to the Government of Northern Ireland the amount of the VAT charged on the supply of goods or services to that Government, on the acquisition of any goods by that Government from another member State or on the importation of any goods by that Government from a place outside the member States, after deducting therefrom so much of that amount as may be agreed between them and the Department of Finance and Personnel for Northern Ireland as attributable to supplies, acquisitions and importations for the purpose of a business carried on by the Government of Northern Ireland.

Commentary—*De Voil Indirect Tax Service* **V1.215.**

Definitions—"Acquisition of goods from another member State", s 11; "another member State", s 96(1); "business", s 94; "the Commissioners", s 96(1); "importation of goods from a place outside the member States", s 15; "supply", s 5, Sch 4; "VAT", ss 1, 96(1).

Cross reference—See VAT (Isle of Man) Order, SI 1982/1067 art 7 (references to VAT in this section to include references to VAT chargeable under Isle of Man legislation).

100 Savings and transitional provisions, consequential amendments and repeals

(1) Schedule 13 (savings and transitional provisions) and Schedule 14 (consequential amendments) shall have effect.

(2) The enactments and Orders specified in Schedule 15 are hereby repealed to the extent mentioned in the third column of that Schedule.

(3) This section is without prejudice to the operation of sections 15 to 17 of the Interpretation Act 1978 (which relate to the effect of repeals).

101 Commencement and extent

(1) This Act shall come into force on 1st September 1994 and Part I shall have effect in relation to the charge to VAT on supplies, acquisitions and importations in prescribed accounting periods ending on or after that date.

(2) Without prejudice to section 16 of the Interpretation Act 1978 (continuation of proceedings under repealed enactments) except in so far as it enables proceedings to be continued under repealed enactments, section 72 shall have effect on the commencement of this Act to the exclusion of section 39 of the 1983 Act.

(3) This Act extends to Northern Ireland.

(4) Paragraph 23 of Schedule 13 and paragraph 7 of Schedule 14 shall extend to the Isle of Man but no other provision of this Act shall extend there.

Definitions—"Prescribed accounting period", s 25(1); "supply", s 5, Sch 4; "VAT", ss 1, 96(1).

102 Short title

This Act may be cited as the Value Added Tax Act 1994.

SCHEDULES

[SCHEDULE A1
CHARGE AT REDUCED RATE]

Section 2

Amendments—Sch A1 inserted by FA 1995 s 21(3), (6), with effect in relation to any supply made after 31 March 1995 and any acquisition or importation taking place after that date, and repealed by FA 2001 s 99(3) with effect for supplies made, and acquisitions and importations taking place, after 31 October 2001. See VATA 1994 Sch 7A for supplies, etc after 31 October 2001.

SCHEDULE 1
REGISTRATION IN RESPECT OF TAXABLE SUPPLIES

Section 3(2)

Cross references—See VATA 1994 s 54(2) (flat rate scheme for farmers: exclusion of supplies within scheme in determining liability for registration under this Schedule);

VATA 1994 s 55(1), (5) (supplies of gold and other precious metals and stones).

Liability to be registered

1— (1) Subject to sub-paragraphs (3) to (7) below, a person who makes taxable supplies but is not registered under this Act becomes liable to be registered under this Schedule—

(*a*) at the end of any month, if the value of his taxable supplies in the period of one year then ending has exceeded [£68,000][2]; or

(*b*) at any time, if there are reasonable grounds for believing that the value of his taxable supplies in the period of 30 days then beginning will exceed [£68,000][2].

(2) Where a business[, or part of a business,][4] carried on by a taxable person is transferred to another person as a going concern and the transferee is not registered under this Act at the time of the transfer, then, subject to sub-paragraphs (3) to (7) below, the transferee becomes liable to be registered under this Schedule at that time if—

(*a*) the value of his taxable supplies in the period of one year ending at the time of the transfer has exceeded [£68,000][2]; or

(*b*) there are reasonable grounds for believing that the value of his taxable supplies in the period of 30 days beginning at the time of the transfer will exceed [£68,000][2].

(3) A person does not become liable to be registered by virtue of sub-paragraph (1)(*a*) or (2)(*a*) above if the Commissioners are satisfied that the value of his taxable supplies in the period of one year beginning at the time at which, apart from this sub-paragraph, he would become liable to be registered will not exceed [£66,000][2].

(4) In determining the value of a person's supplies for the purposes of sub-paragraph (1)(*a*) or (2)(*a*) above, supplies made at a time when he was previously registered under this Act shall be disregarded if—

(*a*) his registration was cancelled otherwise than under paragraph 13(3) below, paragraph 6(2) of Schedule 2[, paragraph 6(3) of Schedule 3 or paragraph 6(2) of Schedule 3A][3], and

(*b*) the Commissioners are satisfied that before his registration was cancelled he had given them all the information they needed in order to determine whether to cancel the registration.

(5) A person shall be treated as having become liable to be registered under this Schedule at any time when he would have become so liable under the preceding provisions of this paragraph but for any registration which is subsequently cancelled under paragraph 13(3) below, paragraph 6(2) of Schedule 2[, paragraph 6(3) of Schedule 3 or paragraph 6(2) of Schedule 3A][3].

(6) A person shall not cease to be liable to be registered under this Schedule except in accordance with paragraph 2(5), 3 or 4 below.

(7) In determining the value of a person's supplies for the purposes of sub-paragraph (1) or (2) above, supplies of goods or services that are capital assets of the business in the course or furtherance of which they are supplied and any taxable supplies which would not be taxable supplies apart from section 7(4) shall be disregarded.

(8) Where, apart from this sub-paragraph, an interest in, right over or licence to occupy any land would under sub-paragraph (7) above be disregarded for the purposes of sub-paragraph (1) or (2) above, it shall not be if it is supplied on a taxable supply which is not zero-rated.

[(9) In determining the value of a person's supplies for the purposes of sub-paragraph (1) or (2) above, supplies to which section 18B(4) (last acquisition or supply of goods before removal from fiscal warehousing) applies and supplies treated as made by him under section 18C(3) (self-supply of services on removal of goods from warehousing) shall be disregarded.][1]

Commentary—*De Voil Indirect Tax Service* **V2.120–V.122, V2.135, V2.136.**
Simon's Tax Cases—*Bennett v C&E Comrs* [1999] STC 248*; *Dyer v C&E Comrs* [2005] STC 715.
Sub-para (1)(*a*)(i), *Neal v C&E Comrs* [1988] STC 131*.
Definitions—"Business", s 94; "the Commissioners", s 96(1); "registered", s 3(3); "supplies", Sch 1 para 19; "taxable person", s 3; "taxable supply", s 4(2); "zero-rating", s 30.
Amendments—[1] Sub-para (9) added by FA 1996 Sch 3 para 13, with effect from 1 June 1996 (see Finance Act 1996, Section 26, (Appointed Day) Order, SI 1996/1249), and applying to any acquisition of goods from another member State and any supply taking place on or after that day.
[2] Sums in sub-paras (1)(*a*), (*b*), (2)(*a*), (*b*), (3) substituted by the VAT (Increase of Registration Limits) Order, SI 2009/1031 arts 2, 3 with effect from 1 May 2009.
[3] Words in sub-paras (4)(*a*), (5) substituted by FA 2000 s 136(6), with effect for supplies made after 20 March 2000.
[4] Words in sub-para (2) inserted by FA 2007 s 100(8), (10) with effect in relation to transfers pursuant to contracts entered into on or after 1 September 2007.

[1A—(1) Paragraph 2 below is for the purpose of preventing the maintenance or creation of any artificial separation of business activities carried on by two or more persons from resulting in an avoidance of VAT.

(2) In determining for the purposes of sub-paragraph (1) above whether any separation of business activities is artificial, regard shall be had to the extent to which the different persons carrying on those activities are closely bound to one another by financial, economic and organisational links.][1]

Amendments—[1] This paragraph inserted by FA 1997 s 31(1) in relation to directions made on or after 19 March 1997.

2— (1) Without prejudice to paragraph 1 above, if the Commissioners make a direction under this paragraph, the persons named in the direction shall be treated as a single taxable person carrying on the activities of a business described in the direction and that taxable person shall be liable to be registered under this Schedule with effect from the date of the direction or, if the direction so provides, from such later date as may be specified therein.

(2) The Commissioners shall not make a direction under this paragraph naming any person unless they are satisfied—

(*a*) that he is making or has made taxable supplies; and

(*b*) that the activities in the course of which he makes or made those taxable supplies form only part of certain activities ...[1], the other activities being carried on concurrently or previously (or both) by one or more other persons; and

(*c*) that, if all the taxable supplies [the business described in the direction][1] were taken into account, a person carrying on that business would at the time of the direction be liable to be registered by virtue of paragraph 1 above; ...[1]

(*d*)...[1]

(3) A direction made under this paragraph shall be served on each of the persons named in it.

(4) Where, after a direction has been given under this paragraph specifying a description of business, it appears to the Commissioners that a person who was not named in that direction is making taxable supplies in the course of activities which should ...[1] be regarded as part of the

activities of that business, the Commissioners may make and serve on him a supplementary direction referring to the earlier direction and the description of business specified in it and adding that person's name to those of the persons named in the earlier direction with effect from—

(*a*) the date on which he began to make those taxable supplies, or
(*b*) if it was later, the date with effect from which the single taxable person referred to in the earlier direction became liable to be registered under this Schedule.

(5) If, immediately before a direction (including a supplementary direction) is made under this paragraph, any person named in the direction is registered in respect of the taxable supplies made by him as mentioned in sub-paragraph (2) or (4) above, he shall cease to be liable to be so registered with effect from whichever is the later of—

(*a*) the date with effect from which the single taxable person concerned became liable to be registered; and
(*b*) the date of the direction.

(6) In relation to a business specified in a direction under this paragraph, the persons named in the direction, together with any person named in a supplementary direction relating to that business (being the persons who together are to be treated as the taxable person), are in sub-paragraphs (7) and (8) below referred to as "the constituent members".

(7) Where a direction is made under this paragraph then, for the purposes of this Act—

(*a*) the taxable person carrying on the business specified in the direction shall be registrable in such name as the persons named in the direction may jointly nominate by notice in writing given to the Commissioners not later than 14 days after the date of the direction or, in default of such a nomination, in such name as may be specified in the direction;
(*b*) any supply of goods or services by or to one of the constituent members in the course of the activities of the taxable person shall be treated as a supply by or to that person;
(*c*) any acquisition of goods from another member State by one of the constituent members in the course of the activities of the taxable person shall be treated as an acquisition by that person;
(*d*) each of the constituent members shall be jointly and severally liable for any VAT due from the taxable person;
(*e*) without prejudice to paragraph (*d*) above, any failure by the taxable person to comply with any requirement imposed by or under this Act shall be treated as a failure by each of the constituent members severally; and
(*f*) subject to paragraphs (*a*) to (*e*) above, the constituent members shall be treated as a partnership carrying on the business of the taxable person and any question as to the scope of the activities of that business at any time shall be determined accordingly.

(8) If it appears to the Commissioners that any person who is one of the constituent members should no longer be regarded as such for the purposes of paragraphs (*d*) and (*e*) of sub-paragraph (7) above and they give notice to that effect, he shall not have any liability by virtue of those paragraphs for anything done after the date specified in that notice and, accordingly, on that date he shall be treated as having ceased to be a member of the partnership referred to in paragraph (*f*) of that sub-paragraph.

Commentary—*De Voil Indirect Tax Service* **V2.120**
Simon's Tax Cases—Sub-para (1), *Chamberlain v C&E Comrs* [1989] STC 505*.
Sub-para (2), *Chamberlain v C&E Comrs* [1989] STC 505*; *Osman v C&E Comrs* [1989] STC 596*.
Definitions—"Acquisition of goods from another member State", s 11; "business", s 94; "the Commissioners", s 96(1); "registrable", Sch 1 para 18; "registered", s 3(3); "supply", s 5, Sch 4; "taxable person", s 3; "taxable supply", s 4(2);
Cross reference—See VATA 1994 ss 83, 84 (appeal to a tribunal in respect of a direction under this para).
Amendments—[1] Word in sub-para (2)(*b*), (4) and whole of sub-para (2)(*d*) and the word "and " preceding it repealed, and words in sub-para (2)(*c*) substituted by FA 1997 s 31(2), (4), Sch 18 Pt IV(1) with effect in relation to directions made after 18 March 1997.

3 A person who has become liable to be registered under this Schedule shall cease to be so liable at any time if the Commissioners are satisfied in relation to that time that he—

(*a*) has ceased to make taxable supplies; or
(*b*) is not at that time a person in relation to whom any of the conditions specified in paragraphs 1(1)(*a*) and (*b*) and (2)(*a*) and (*b*) above is satisfied.

Commentary—*De Voil Indirect Tax Service* **V2.151**.
Definitions—"The Commissioners", s 96(1); "registered", s 3(3); "taxable supply", s 4(2);
Cross reference—See VATA 1994 ss 83, 84 (appeal to a tribunal in respect of a direction under this para).

4— (1) Subject to sub-paragraph (2) below, a person who has become liable to be registered under this Schedule shall cease to be so liable at any time after being registered if the Commissioners are satisfied that the value of his taxable supplies in the period of one year then beginning will not exceed [£66,000][1].

(2) A person shall not cease to be liable to be registered under this Schedule by virtue of sub-paragraph (1) above if the Commissioners are satisfied that the reason the value of his taxable supplies will not exceed [£66,000][1] is that in the period in question he will cease making taxable supplies, or will suspend making them for a period of 30 days or more.

(3) In determining the value of a person's supplies for the purposes of sub-paragraph (1) above, supplies of goods or services that are capital assets of the business in the course or furtherance of which they are supplied and any taxable supplies which would not be taxable supplies apart from section 7(4) shall be disregarded.

(4) Where, apart from this sub-paragraph, an interest in, right over or licence to occupy any land would under sub-paragraph (3) above be disregarded for the purposes of sub-paragraph (1) above, it shall not be if it is supplied on a taxable supply which is not zero-rated.

Commentary—*De Voil Indirect Tax Service* **V2.151**.
Definitions—"Business", s 94; "the Commissioners", s 96(1); "registered", s 3(3); "supplies", Sch 1 para 19; "taxable supply", s 4(2); "zero-rating", s 30.
Cross reference—See VATA 1994 ss 83, 84 (appeal to a tribunal in respect of a direction under this para).
Amendments—[1] Sums in sub-paras (1), (2) substituted by the VAT (Increase of Registration Limits) Order, SI 2009/1031 arts 2, 3 with effect from 1 May 2009.

Notification of liability and registration

5— (1) A person who becomes liable to be registered by virtue of paragraph 1(1)(*a*) above shall notify the Commissioners of the liability within 30 days of the end of the relevant month.

(2) The Commissioners shall register any such person (whether or not he so notifies them) with effect from the end of the month following the relevant month or from such earlier date as may be agreed between them and him.

(3) In this paragraph "the relevant month", in relation to a person who becomes liable to be registered by virtue of paragraph 1(1)(*a*) above, means the month at the end of which he becomes liable to be so registered.

Commentary—*De Voil Indirect Tax Service* **V2.135**.
Simon's Tax Cases—*Neal v C&E Comrs* [1988] STC 131*.
Sub-para (3), *Henderson and anor (T/A Tony's Fish and Chip Shop) v C&E Comrs* [2001] STC 47; *Dyer v C&E Comrs* [2005] STC 715.
Definitions—"The Commissioners", s 96(1); "registered", s 3(3).
Cross references—See VATA 1994 s 67(1) (penalty for failure to comply with this para).
VAT (Isle of Man) Order, SI 1982/1067 art 11(3), (4) (persons registrable under Isle of Man VAT legislation);
VAT (Isle of Man) Order, SI 1982/1067 art 11(5) (notification required from persons having an establishment in the Isle of Man);
VAT Regulations, SI 1995/2518 reg 5(1), Sch 1 forms 1, 2 (form of application for VAT registration).

6— (1) A person who becomes liable to be registered by virtue of paragraph 1(1)(*b*) above shall notify the Commissioners of the liability before the end of the period by reference to which the liability arises.

(2) The Commissioners shall register any such person (whether or not he so notifies them) with effect from the beginning of the period by reference to which the liability arises.

Commentary—*De Voil Indirect Tax Service* **V2.136**.
Definitions—"The Commissioners", s 96(1); "registered", s 3(3).
Cross references—See VATA 1994 s 67(1) (penalty for failure to comply with this para).
VAT (Isle of Man) Order, SI 1982/1067 art 11(3), (4) (persons registrable under Isle of Man VAT legislation);
VAT (Isle of Man) Order, SI 1982/1067 art 11(5) (notification required from persons having an establishment in the Isle of Man);
VAT Regulations, SI 1995/2518 reg 5(1), Sch 1 forms 1, 2 (form of application for VAT registration).

7— (1) A person who becomes liable to be registered by virtue of paragraph 1(2) above shall notify the Commissioners of the liability within 30 days of the time when the business is transferred.

(2) The Commissioners shall register any such person (whether or not he so notifies them) with effect from the time when the business is transferred.

Commentary—*De Voil Indirect Tax Service* **V2.131**.
Definitions—"Business", s 94; "the Commissioners", s 96(1); "registered", s 3(3).
Cross reference—VAT Regulations, SI 1995/2518 reg 5(4), (5), Sch 1, form 3 (form of application for VAT registration).

8 Where a person becomes liable to be registered by virtue of paragraph 1(1)(*a*) above and by virtue of paragraph 1(1)(*b*) or 1(2) above at the same time, the Commissioners shall register him in accordance with paragraph 6(2) or 7(2) above, as the case may be, rather than paragraph 5(2) above.

Definitions—"The Commissioners", s 96(1); "registered", s 3(3).

Entitlement to be registered

9 Where a person who is not liable to be registered under this Act and is not already so registered satisfies the Commissioners that he—

(*a*) makes taxable supplies; or

(*b*) is carrying on a business and intends to make such supplies in the course or furtherance of that business,

they shall, if he so requests, register him with effect from the day on which the request is made or from such earlier date as may be agreed between them and him.

Commentary—*De Voil Indirect Tax Service* **V2.144, V2.145**.
Press releases etc—Business Brief 8/97, 25 March 1997 (retrospective voluntary registration).
Simon's Tax Cases—*C&E Comrs v Eastwood Care Homes (Ilkeston) Ltd and others* [2001] STC 1629.
Definitions—"Business", s 94; "the Commissioners", s 96(1); "registered", s 3(3); "supplies", Sch 1 para 19; "taxable supply", s 4(2);

Cross references—See VATA 1994 Sch 2 para 4(3) (a person who is entitled to be registered under this para but requests registration under Sch 2 para 4 (registration in respect of supplies from other member states) must instead be registered under this para);
VATA 1994 Sch 3 para 4(4) (a person who is entitled to be registered under this para but requests registration under Sch 3 para 4 (registration in respect of acquisitions from other member states) must instead be registered under this para).

10— (1) Where a person who is not liable to be registered under this Act and is not already so registered satisfies the Commissioners that he—

(*a*) makes supplies within sub-paragraph (2) below; or

(*b*) is carrying on a business and intends to make such supplies in the course or furtherance of that business,

and (in either case) is within sub-paragraph (3) below, they shall, if he so requests, register him with effect from the day on which the request is made or from such earlier date as may be agreed between them and him.

[(2) A supply is within this sub-paragraph if—

(*a*) it is made outside the United Kingdom but would be a taxable supply if made in the United Kingdom; or

(*b*) it is specified for the purposes of subsection (2) of section 26 in an order made under paragraph (*c*) of that subsection.][1]

(3) A person is within this sub-paragraph if—

(*a*) he has a business establishment in the United Kingdom or his usual place of residence is in the United Kingdom; and

(*b*) he does not make and does not intend to make taxable supplies.

(4) For the purposes of this paragraph—

(*a*) a person carrying on a business through a branch or agency in the United Kingdom shall be treated as having a business establishment in the United Kingdom, and

(*b*) "usual place of residence", in relation to a body corporate, means the place where it is legally constituted.

Commentary—*De Voil Indirect Tax Service* **V2.146**.
Definitions—"Business", s 94; "the Commissioners", s 96(1); "registered", s 3(3); "supplies", Sch 1 para 19; "supply", s 5, Sch 4; "taxable supply", s 4(2); "United Kingdom", s 96(11).
Cross references—See VATA 1994 Sch 2 para 4(3) (a person who is entitled to be registered under this para but requests registration under Sch 2 para 4 (registration in respect of supplies from other member states) must instead be registered under this para);
VATA 1994 Sch 3 para 4(4) (a person who is entitled to be registered under this para but requests registration under Sch 3 para 4 (registration in respect of acquisitions from other member states) must instead be registered under this para).
Amendments—[1] Sub-para (2) substituted by FA 1997 s 32 with effect from 19 March 1997.

Notification of end of liability or entitlement etc

11 A person registered under paragraph 5, 6 or 9 above who ceases to make or have the intention of making taxable supplies shall notify the Commissioners of that fact within 30 days of the day on which he does so unless he would, when he so ceases, be otherwise liable or entitled to be registered under this Act if his registration and any enactment preventing a person from being liable to be registered under different provisions at the same time were disregarded.

Commentary—*De Voil Indirect Tax Service* **V2.151**.
Definitions—"The Commissioners", s 96(1); "registered", s 3(3); "taxable supplies", s 4(2).
Cross references—See VATA 1994 s 69(1) (penalty for breach of a requirement imposed under this para).
VAT Regulations, SI 1995/2518 reg 5(3) (form of notification under this para);
VAT Regulations, SI 1995/2518 reg 6(2) (notification of transfer of business as a going concern).

12 A person registered under paragraph 10 above who—

(*a*) ceases to make or have the intention of making supplies within sub-paragraph (2) of that paragraph; or

(*b*) makes or forms the intention of making taxable supplies,

shall notify the Commissioners of that fact within 30 days of the day on which he does so unless, in the case of a person ceasing as mentioned in sub-paragraph (*a*) above, he would, when he so ceases, be otherwise liable or entitled to be registered under this Act if his registration and any enactment preventing a person from being liable to be registered under different provisions at the same time were disregarded.

Commentary—*De Voil Indirect Tax Service* **V2.152**.
Definitions—"The Commissioners", s 96(1); "registered", s 3(3); "taxable supplies", s 4(2).
Cross references—See VATA 1994 s 69(1) (penalty for breach of a requirement imposed under this para).
VAT Regulations, SI 1995/2518 reg 5(3) (form of notification under this para).

Cancellation of registration

13— (1) Subject to sub-paragraph (4) below, where a registered person satisfies the Commissioners that he is not liable to be registered under this Schedule, they shall, if he so requests, cancel his registration with effect from the day on which the request is made or from such later date as may be agreed between them and him.

(2) Subject to sub-paragraph (5) below, where the Commissioners are satisfied that a registered person has ceased to be registrable, they may cancel his registration with effect from the day on which he so ceased or from such later date as may be agreed between them and him.

(3) Where the Commissioners are satisfied that on the day on which a registered person was registered he was not registrable, they may cancel his registration with effect from that day.

(4) The Commissioners shall not under sub-paragraph (1) above cancel a person's registration with effect from any time unless they are satisfied that it is not a time when that person would be subject to a requirement to be registered under this Act.

(5) The Commissioners shall not under sub-paragraph (2) above cancel a person's registration with effect from any time unless they are satisfied that it is not a time when that person would be subject to a requirement, or entitled, to be registered under this Act.

(6) In determining for the purposes of sub-paragraph (4) or (5) above whether a person would be subject to a requirement, or entitled, to be registered at any time, so much of any provision of this Act as prevents a person from becoming liable or entitled to be registered when he is already registered or when he is so liable under any other provision shall be disregarded.

(7) In this paragraph, any reference to a registered person is a reference to a person who is registered under this Schedule.

[(8) This paragraph is subject to paragraph 18 of Schedule 3B (cancellation of registration under this Schedule of persons seeking to be registered under that Schedule, etc).][1]

Commentary—*De Voil Indirect Tax Service* **V2.151, V2.152**.
Definitions—"The Commissioners", s 96(1); "registrable", Sch 1, para 18; "registered", s 3(3).
Amendments—[1] Sub-para (8) inserted by FA 2003 s 23, Sch 2 paras 1, 3 with effect for qualifying supplies made after 30 June 2003.

Exemption from registration

14— (1) Notwithstanding the preceding provisions of this Schedule, where a person who makes or intends to make taxable supplies satisfies the Commissioners that any such supply is zero-rated or would be zero-rated if he were a taxable person, they may, if he so requests and they think fit, exempt him from registration under this Schedule until it appears to them that the request should no longer be acted upon or is withdrawn.

(2) Where there is a material change in the nature of the supplies made by a person exempted under this paragraph from registration under this Schedule, he shall notify the Commissioners of the change—

(*a*) within 30 days of the date on which it occurred; or

(*b*) if no particular day is identifiable as the day on which it occurred, within 30 days of the end of the quarter in which it occurred.

(3) Where there is a material alteration in any quarter in the proportion of taxable supplies of such a person that are zero-rated, he shall notify the Commissioners of the alteration within 30 days of the end of the quarter.

Commentary—*De Voil Indirect Tax Service* **V2.139**.
Definitions—"The Commissioners", s 96(1); "quarter", s 96(1), "registered", s 3(3), "supplies", Sch 1 para 19; "supply", s 6, Sch 4; "taxable person", s 3; "taxable supply", s 4(2); "zero-rating", s 30.
Cross reference—See VATA 1994 s 67(1) (penalty for failure to comply with sub-para (2) or (3) of this para).

Power to vary specified sums by order

15 The Treasury may by order substitute for any of the sums for the time being specified in this Schedule such greater sums as they think fit.

Supplementary

16 The value of a supply of goods or services shall be determined for the purposes of this Schedule on the basis that no VAT is chargeable on the supply.

Definitions—"Supply", s 5, Sch 4; "VAT", ss 1, 96(1).

17 Any notification required under this Schedule shall be made in such form and shall contain such particulars as the Commissioners may by regulations prescribe.

Regulations—See VAT Regulations, SI 1995/2518 reg 5 Sch 1.
Definitions—"The Commissioners", s 96(1); "regulations", s 96(1).

18 In this Schedule "registrable" means liable or entitled to be registered under this Schedule.

Definitions—"Registered", s 3(3);

19 References in this Schedule to supplies are references to supplies made in the course or furtherance of a business.

Definitions—"Business", s 94.

SCHEDULE 2

REGISTRATION IN RESPECT OF SUPPLIES FROM OTHER MEMBER STATES

Section 3(2)

Liability to be registered

1— (1) A person who—

(*a*) is not registered under this Act; and

(*b*) is not liable to be registered under Schedule 1,

becomes liable to be registered under this Schedule on any day if, in the period beginning with 1st January of the year in which that day falls, that person has made relevant supplies whose value exceeds £70,000.

(2) A person who is not registered or liable to be registered as mentioned in sub-paragraph (1)(*a*) and (*b*) above becomes liable to be registered under this Schedule where—

(*a*) that person has exercised any option, in accordance with the law of any other member State where he is taxable, for treating relevant supplies made by him as taking place outside that member State;

(*b*) the supplies to which the option relates involve the removal of goods from that member State and, apart from the exercise of the option, would be treated, in accordance with the law of that member State, as taking place in that member State; and

(*c*) that person makes a relevant supply at a time when the option is in force in relation to him.

(3) A person who is not registered or liable to be registered as mentioned in sub-paragraph (1)(*a*) and (*b*) above becomes liable to be registered under this Schedule if he makes a supply in relation to which the following conditions are satisfied, that is to say—

(*a*) it is a supply of goods subject to a duty of excise;

(*b*) it involves the removal of the goods to the United Kingdom by or under the directions of the person making the supply;

(*c*) it is a transaction in pursuance of which the goods are acquired in the United Kingdom from another member State by a person who is not a taxable person;

(*d*) it is made on or after 1st January 1993 and in the course or furtherance of a business carried on by the supplier; and

(*e*) it is not anything which is treated as a supply for the purposes of this Act by virtue only of paragraph 5(1) or 6 of Schedule 4.

(4) A person shall be treated as having become liable to be registered under this Schedule at any time when he would have become so liable under the preceding provisions of this paragraph but for any registration which is subsequently cancelled under paragraph 6(2) below, paragraph 13(3) of Schedule 1[, paragraph 6(3) of Schedule 3 or paragraph 6(2) of Schedule 3A][2].

(5) A person shall not cease to be liable to be registered under this Schedule except in accordance with paragraph 2 below.

(6) In determining for the purposes of this paragraph the value of any relevant supplies, so much of the consideration for any supply as represents any liability of the supplier, under the law of another member State, for VAT on that supply shall be disregarded.

[(7) For the purposes of sub-paragraphs (1) and (2) above supplies to which section 18B(4) (last acquisition or supply of goods before removal from fiscal warehousing) applies shall be disregarded.][1]

Commentary—*De Voil Indirect Tax Service* **V2.120–V2.122**.
Definitions—"Another member State", s 96(1); "business", s 94; "other member State", s 96(1); "registered", s 3(3); "relevant supply", Sch 2 para 10; "supply", s 5, Sch 4; "United Kingdom", s 96(11); "VAT", ss 1, 96(1).
Amendments—[1] Sub-para (7) added by FA 1996 Sch 3 para 14, with effect for any supply taking place on or after 1 June 1996 (see Finance Act 1996, Section 26, (Appointed Day) Order, SI 1996/1249).
[2] Words in sub-para (4) substituted by FA 2000 s 136(6), with effect for supplies made after 20 March 2000.

2— (1) Subject to sub-paragraph (2) below, a person who has become liable to be registered under this Schedule shall cease to be so liable if at any time—

(*a*) the relevant supplies made by him in the year ending with 31st December last before that time did not have a value exceeding £70,000 and did not include any supply in relation to which the conditions mentioned in paragraph 1(3) above were satisfied; and

(*b*) the Commissioners are satisfied that the value of his relevant supplies in the year immediately following that year will not exceed £70,000 and that those supplies will not include a supply in relation to which those conditions are satisfied.

(2) A person shall not cease to be liable to be registered under this Schedule at any time when such an option as is mentioned in paragraph 1(2) above is in force in relation to him.

Commentary—*De Voil Indirect Tax Service* **V2.151**.
Definitions—"The Commissioners", s 96(1); "registered", s 3(3); "relevant supply", Sch 2 para 10; "supply", s 5, Sch 4.

Notification of liability and registration

3— (1) A person who becomes liable to be registered under this Schedule shall notify the Commissioners of the liability within the period of 30 days after the day on which the liability arises.

(2) The Commissioners shall register any such person (whether or not he so notifies them) with effect from the day on which the liability arose or from such earlier time as may be agreed between them and him.

Commentary—*De Voil Indirect Tax Service* **V2.126**.
Definitions—"The Commissioners", s 96(1); "registered", s 3(3).
Cross references—See VATA 1994 s 67(1) (penalty for failure to comply with this para).
VAT Regulations, SI 1995/2518 reg 5(1), Sch 1 forms 2, 6 (form of application for VAT registration: distance sales).

Request to be registered

4— (1) Where a person who is not liable to be registered under this Act and is not already so registered—

(*a*) satisfies the Commissioners that he intends—

(i) to exercise an option such as is mentioned in paragraph 1(2) above and, from a specified date, to make relevant supplies to which that option will relate;

(ii) from a specified date to make relevant supplies to which any such option that he has exercised will relate; or

(iii) from a specified date to make supplies in relation to which the conditions mentioned in paragraph 1(3) above will be satisfied; and

(*b*) requests to be registered under this Schedule,

the Commissioners may, subject to such conditions as they think fit to impose, register him with effect from such date as may be agreed between them and him.

(2) Conditions imposed under sub-paragraph (1) above—

(*a*) may be so imposed wholly or partly by reference to, or without reference to, any conditions prescribed for the purposes of this paragraph; and

(*b*) may, whenever imposed, be subsequently varied by the Commissioners.

(3) Where a person who is entitled to be registered under paragraph 9 or 10 of Schedule 1 requests registration under this paragraph, he shall be registered under that Schedule, and not under this Schedule.

Commentary—*De Voil Indirect Tax Service* **V2.151, V2.152.**
Press releases etc—C&E Business Brief 8/96 17-5-96 (following abolition of the self-supply charge for developers, VAT offices require detailed information before allowing intending trader registration
Definitions—"The Commissioners", s 96(1); "prescribed", s 96(1); "registered", s 3(3); "relevant supplies", Sch 2 para 10; "supply", s 5, Sch 4.

Notification of matters affecting continuance of registration

5— (1) Any person registered under this Schedule who ceases to be registrable under this Act shall notify the Commissioners of that fact within 30 days of the day on which he does so.

(2) A person registered under paragraph 4 above by reference to any intention of his to exercise any option or to make supplies of any description shall notify the Commissioners within 30 days of exercising that option or, as the case may be, of the first occasion after his registration when he makes such a supply, that he has exercised the option or made such a supply.

(3) A person who has exercised such an option as is mentioned in paragraph 1(2) above which, as a consequence of its revocation or otherwise, ceases to have effect in relation to any relevant supplies by him shall notify the Commissioners, within 30 days of the option's ceasing so to have effect, that it has done so.

(4) For the purposes of this paragraph, a person ceases to be registrable under this Act where—

(*a*) he ceases to be a person who would be liable or entitled to be registered under this Act if his registration and any enactment preventing a person from being liable to be registered under different provisions at the same time were disregarded; or

(*b*) in the case of a person who (having been registered under paragraph 4 above) has not been such a person during the period of his registration, he ceases to have any such intention as is mentioned in sub-paragraph (1)(*a*) of that paragraph.

Commentary—*De Voil Indirect Tax Service* **V2.151, V2.152**.
Definitions—"The Commissioners", s 96(1); "registered", s 3(3); "relevant supplies", Sch 2 para 10; "supply", s 5, Sch 4.
Cross reference—See VATA 1994 s 69(1) (penalty for breach of a requirement imposed under this para).
VAT Regulations, SI 1995/2518 reg 5(3) (form of notification under this para).

Cancellation of registration

6— (1) Subject to paragraph 7 below, where a person registered under this Schedule satisfies the Commissioners that he is not liable to be so registered, they shall, if he so requests, cancel his registration with effect from the day on which the request is made or from such later date as may be agreed between them and him.

(2) Where the Commissioners are satisfied that, on the day on which a person was registered under this Schedule, he—

(*a*) was not liable to be registered under this Schedule; and

(*b*) in the case of a person registered under paragraph 4 above, did not have the intention by reference to which he was registered,

they may cancel his registration with effect from that day.

(3) Subject to paragraph 7 below, where the Commissioners are satisfied that a person who has been registered under paragraph 4 above and is not for the time being liable to be registered under this Schedule—

(*a*) has not, by the date specified in his request to be registered, begun to make relevant supplies, exercised the option in question or, as the case may be, begun to make supplies in relation to which the conditions mentioned in paragraph 1(3) above are satisfied; or

(*b*) has contravened any condition of his registration,

they may cancel his registration with effect from the date so specified or, as the case may be, the date of the contravention or from such later date as may be agreed between them and him.

Commentary—*De Voil Indirect Tax Service* **V2.130**.
Definitions—"The Commissioners", s 96(1); "registered", s 3(3); "relevant supplies", Sch 2 para 10; "supply", s 5, Sch 4.

Conditions of cancellation

7— (1) The Commissioners shall not, under paragraph 6(1) above, cancel a person's registration with effect from any time unless they are satisfied that it is not a time when that person would be subject to a requirement to be registered under this Act.

(2) The Commissioners shall not, under paragraph 6(3) above, cancel a person's registration with effect from any time unless they are satisfied that it is not a time when that person would be subject to a requirement, or entitled, to be registered under this Act.

(3) The registration of a person who has exercised such an option as is mentioned in paragraph 1(2) above shall not be cancelled with effect from any time before the 1st January which is, or next follows, the second anniversary of the date on which his registration took effect.

(4) In determining for the purposes of this paragraph whether a person would be subject to a requirement, or entitled, to be registered at any time, so much of any provision of this Act as prevents a person from becoming liable or entitled to be registered when he is already registered or when he is so liable under any other provision shall be disregarded.

Commentary—*De Voil Indirect Tax Service* **V2.130**.
Definitions—"The Commissioners", s 96(1); "registered", s 3(3).

Power to vary specified sums by order

8 The Treasury may by order substitute for any of the sums for the time being specified in this Schedule such greater sums as they think fit.

Supplementary

9 Any notification required under this Schedule shall be made in such form and shall contain such particulars as the Commissioners may by regulations prescribe.

Regulations—VAT Regulations, SI 1995/2518 reg 5, Sch 1.
Definitions—"The Commissioners", s 96(1); "regulations", s 96(1);

10 For the purposes of this Schedule a supply of goods is a relevant supply where—

(*a*) the supply involves the removal of the goods to the United Kingdom by or under the directions of the person making the supply;

(*b*) the supply does not involve the installation or assembly of the goods at a place in the United Kingdom;

(*c*) the supply is a transaction in pursuance of which goods are acquired in the United Kingdom from another member State by a person who is not a taxable person;

(*d*) the supply is made on or after 1st January 1993 and in the course or furtherance of a business carried on by the supplier; and

(*e*) the supply is neither an exempt supply nor a supply of goods which are subject to a duty of excise or consist in a new means of transport and is not anything which is treated as a supply for the purposes of this Act by virtue only of paragraph 5(1) or 6 of Schedule 4.

Commentary—*De Voil Indirect Tax Service* **V3.173**.
Definitions—"Another member State", s 96(1); "business", s 94; "exempt supply", s 31; "new means of transport", s 95; "supply", s 5, Sch 4; "United Kingdom", s 96(11).

SCHEDULE 3

REGISTRATION IN RESPECT OF ACQUISITIONS FROM OTHER MEMBER STATES

Section 3(2)

Liability to be registered

1— (1) A person who—

(*a*) is not registered under this Act; and

(*b*) is not liable to be registered under Schedule 1 or 2,

becomes liable to be registered under this Schedule at the end of any month if, in the period beginning with 1st January of the year in which that month falls, that person had made relevant acquisitions whose value exceeds [£68,000][2].

(2) A person who is not registered or liable to be registered as mentioned in sub-paragraph (1)(*a*) and (*b*) above becomes liable to be registered under this Schedule at any time if there are reasonable grounds for believing that the value of his relevant acquisitions in the period of 30 days then beginning will exceed [£68,000][2].

(3) A person shall be treated as having become liable to be registered under this Schedule at any time when he would have become so liable under the preceding provisions of this paragraph but

for any registration which is subsequently cancelled under paragraph 6(3) below, paragraph 13(3) of Schedule 1[, paragraph 6(2) of Schedule 2 or paragraph 6(2) of Schedule 3A][3].

(4) A person shall not cease to be liable to be registered under this Schedule except in accordance with paragraph 2 below.

(5) In determining the value of any person's relevant acquisitions for the purposes of this paragraph, so much of the consideration for any acquisition as represents any liability of the supplier, under the law of another member State, for VAT on the transaction in pursuance of which the acquisition is made, shall be disregarded.

[(6) In determining the value of a person's acquisitions for the purposes of sub-paragraph (1) or (2) above, acquisitions to which section 18B(4) (last acquisition or supply of goods before removal from fiscal warehousing) applies shall be disregarded.][1]

Commentary—*De Voil Indirect Tax Service* **V3.213**.
Definitions—"Another member State", s 96(1); "registered", s 3(3); "relevant acquisition", Sch 3 para 11; "VAT", ss 1, 96(1).
Amendments—[1] Sub-para (6) inserted by FA 1996 Sch 3 para 15, with effect for any acquisition of goods from another member State taking place on or after 1 June 1996 (see Finance Act 1996, Section 26, (Appointed Day) Order, SI 1996/1249).
[2] Sums in sub-paras (1), (2) substituted by the VAT (Increase of Registration Limits) Order, SI 2009/1031 arts 2, 4 with effect from 1 May 2009.
[3] Words in sub-para (3) substituted by FA 2000 s 136(7), with effect for supplies made after 20 March 2000.

2— (1) Subject to sub-paragraph (2) below, a person who has become liable to be registered under this Schedule shall cease to be so liable if at any time—

(*a*) his relevant acquisitions in the year ending with 31st December last before that time did not have a value exceeding [£68,000][1]; and

(*b*) the Commissioners are satisfied that the value of his relevant acquisitions in the year immediately following that year will not exceed [£68,000][1].

(2) A person shall not cease to be liable to be registered under this Schedule at any time if there are reasonable grounds for believing that the value of that person's relevant acquisitions in the period of 30 days then beginning will exceed [£68,000][1].

Commentary—*De Voil Indirect Tax Service* **V3.213**.
Definitions—"The Commissioners", s 96(1); "registered", s 3(3); "relevant acquisition", Sch 3 para 11.
Amendments—[1] Sums substituted by the VAT (Increase of Registration Limits) Order, SI 2009/1031 arts 2, 4 with effect from 1 May 2009.

Notification of liability and registration

3— (1) A person who becomes liable to be registered under this Schedule shall notify the Commissioners of the liability—

(*a*) in the case of a liability under sub-paragraph (1) of paragraph 1 above, within 30 days of the end of the month when he becomes so liable; and

(*b*) in the case of a liability under sub-paragraph (2) of that paragraph, before the end of the period by reference to which the liability arises.

(2) The Commissioners shall register any such person (whether or not he so notifies them) with effect from the relevant time or from such earlier time as may be agreed between them and him.

(3) In this paragraph "the relevant time"—

(*a*) in a case falling within sub-paragraph (1)(*a*) above, means the end of the month following the month at the end of which the liability arose; and

(*b*) in a case falling within sub-paragraph (1)(*b*), means the beginning of the period by reference to which the liability arose.

Commentary—*De Voil Indirect Tax Service* **V3.213**.
Definitions—"The Commissioners", s 96(1); "registered", s 3(3);
Cross references—See VATA 1994 s 67(1) (penalty for failure to comply with this para).
VAT Regulations, SI 1995/2518 reg 5(1), Sch 1 forms 2, 7 (form of application for VAT registration: acquisitions).

Entitlement to be registered etc

4— (1) Where a person who is not liable to be registered under this Act and is not already so registered satisfies the Commissioners that he makes relevant acquisitions, they shall, if he so requests, register him with effect from the day on which the request is made or from such earlier date as may be agreed between them and him.

(2) Where a person who is not liable to be registered under this Act and is not already so registered—

(*a*) satisfies the Commissioners that he intends to make relevant acquisitions from a specified date; and

(*b*) requests to be registered under this Schedule,

the Commissioners may, subject to such conditions as they think fit to impose, register him with effect from such date as may be agreed between them and him.

(3) Conditions imposed under sub-paragraph (2) above—

(*a*) may be so imposed wholly or partly by reference to, or without reference to, any conditions prescribed for the purposes of this paragraph, and

(*b*) may, whenever imposed, be subsequently varied by the Commissioners.

(4) Where a person who is entitled to be registered under paragraph 9 or 10 of Schedule 1 requests registration under this paragraph, he shall be registered under that Schedule, and not under this Schedule.

Commentary—*De Voil Indirect Tax Service* **V3.213**.
Definitions—"The Commissioners", s 96(1); "registered", s 3(3); "relevant acquisition", Sch 3 para 11.

Notification of matters affecting continuance of registration

5— (1) Any person registered under this Schedule who ceases to be registrable under this Act shall notify the Commissioners of that fact within 30 days of the day on which he does so.

(2) A person registered under paragraph 4(2) above shall notify the Commissioners, within 30 days of the first occasion after his registration when he makes a relevant acquisition, that he has done so.

(3) For the purposes of this paragraph a person ceases to be registrable under this Act where—

(*a*) he ceases to be a person who would be liable or entitled to be registered under this Act if his registration and any enactment preventing a person from being liable to be registered under different provisions at the same time were disregarded; or

(*b*) in the case of a person who (having been registered under paragraph 4(2) above) has not been such a person during the period of his registration, he ceases to have any intention of making relevant acquisitions.

Commentary—*De Voil Indirect Tax Service* **V3.213**.
Definitions—"The Commissioners", s 96(1); "registered", s 3(3); "relevant acquisition", Sch 3 para 11.
Cross references—See VATA 1994 s 69(1) (penalty for breach of a requirement imposed under this para).
VAT Regulations, SI 1995/2518 reg 5(3) (form of notification under this para).

Cancellation of registration

6—(1) Subject to paragraph 7 below, where a person registered under this Schedule satisfies the Commissioners that he is not liable to be so registered, they shall, if he so requests, cancel his registration with effect from the day on which the request is made or from such later date as may be agreed between them and him.

(2) Subject to paragraph 7 below, where the Commissioners are satisfied that a person registered under this Schedule has ceased since his registration to be registrable under this Schedule, they may cancel his registration with effect from the day on which he so ceased or from such later date as may be agreed between them and him.

(3) Where the Commissioners are satisfied that, on the day on which a person was registered under this Schedule, he—

(*a*) was not registrable under this Schedule; and

(*b*) in the case of a person registered under paragraph 4(2) above, did not have the intention by reference to which he was registered,

they may cancel his registration with effect from that day.

(4) Subject to paragraph 7 below, where the Commissioners are satisfied that a person who has been registered under paragraph 4(2) above and is not for the time being liable to be registered under this Schedule—

(*a*) has not begun, by the date specified in his request to be registered, to make relevant acquisitions; or

(*b*) has contravened any condition of his registration,

they may cancel his registration with effect from the date so specified or, as the case may be, the date of the contravention or from such later date as may be agreed between them and him.

(5) For the purposes of this paragraph a person is registrable under this Schedule at any time when he is liable to be registered under this Schedule or is a person who makes relevant acquisitions.

Commentary—*De Voil Indirect Tax Service* **V3.213**.
Definitions—"The Commissioners", s 96(1); "registered", s 3(3); "relevant acquisition", Sch 3 para 11.

Conditions of cancellation

7— (1) The Commissioners shall not, under paragraph 6(1) above, cancel a person's registration with effect from any time unless they are satisfied that it is not a time when that person would be subject to a requirement to be registered under this Act.

(2) The Commissioners shall not, under paragraph 6(2) or (4) above, cancel a person's registration with effect from any time unless they are satisfied that it is not a time when that person would be subject to a requirement, or entitled, to be registered under this Act.

(3) Subject to sub-paragraph (4) below, the registration of a person who—

(*a*) is registered under paragraph 4 above; or

(*b*) would not, if he were not registered, be liable or entitled to be registered under any provision of this Act except paragraph 4 above,

shall not be cancelled with effect from any time before the 1st January which is, or next follows, the second anniversary of the date on which his registration took effect.

(4) Sub-paragraph (3) above does not apply to cancellation under paragraph 6(3) or (4) above.

(5) In determining for the purposes of this paragraph whether a person would be subject to a requirement, or entitled, to be registered at any time, so much of any provision of this Act as prevents a person from becoming liable or entitled to be registered when he is already registered or when he is so liable under any other provision shall be disregarded.

Commentary—*De Voil Indirect Tax Service* **V3.213**.
Definitions—"The Commissioners", s 96(1); "registered", s 3(3).

Exemption from registration

8— (1) Notwithstanding the preceding provisions of this Schedule, where a person who makes or intends to make relevant acquisitions satisfies the Commissioners that any such acquisition would be an acquisition in pursuance of a transaction which would be zero-rated if it were a taxable supply by a taxable person, they may, if he so requests and they think fit, exempt him from registration under this Schedule until it appears to them that the request should no longer be acted upon or is withdrawn.

(2) Where a person who is exempted under this paragraph from registration under this Schedule makes any relevant acquisition in pursuance of any transaction which would, if it were a taxable supply by a taxable person, be chargeable to VAT otherwise than as a zero-rated supply, he shall notify the Commissioners of the change within 30 days of the date on which he made the acquisition.

Commentary—*De Voil Indirect Tax Service* **V3.213**.
Definitions—"The Commissioners", s 96(1); "registration", s 3(3); "relevant acquisition", Sch 3 para 11; "taxable person", s 3; "taxable supply", s 4(2); "VAT", ss 1, 96(1); "zero-rated", s 30.
Cross reference—See VATA 1994 s 67(1) (penalty for failure to comply with sub-para (2) of this para).

Power to vary specified sums by order

9 The Treasury may by order substitute for any of the sums for the time being specified in this Schedule such greater sums as they think fit.

Supplementary

10 Any notification required under this Schedule shall be made in such form and shall contain such particulars as the Commissioners may by regulations prescribe.

Regulations—See VAT Regulations, SI 1995/2518 reg 5, Sch 1.
Definitions—"The Commissioners", s 96(1); "prescribe", s 96(1); "regulations", s 96(1);

11 For the purposes of this Schedule an acquisition of goods from another member State is a relevant acquisition where—

(*a*) it is a taxable acquisition of goods other than goods which are subject to a duty of excise or consist in a new means of transport;

(*b*) it is an acquisition otherwise than in pursuance of a taxable supply and is treated, for the purposes of this Act, as taking place in the United Kingdom; and

(*c*) the event which, in relation to that acquisition, is the first relevant event for the purposes of taxing that acquisition occurs on or after 1st January 1993.

Definitions—"Acquisition of goods from another member State", s 11; "new means of transport", s 95; "taxable acquisition", s 10(2); "taxable supply", s 4(2); "United Kingdom", s 96(11).

[SCHEDULE 3A

REGISTRATION IN RESPECT OF DISPOSALS OF ASSETS FOR WHICH A VAT REPAYMENT IS CLAIMED][1]

Section 3(2)

Amendments—[1] Sch 3A inserted by FA 2000 s 136(8), Sch 36, with effect for relevant supplies (within the meaning of this Schedule) made after 20 March 2000.

Liability to be registered

[1— (1) A person who is not registered under this Act, and is not liable to be registered under Schedule 1, 2 or 3, becomes liable to be registered under this Schedule at any time—

(*a*) if he makes relevant supplies; or

(*b*) if there are reasonable grounds for believing that he will make such supplies in the period of 30 days then beginning.

(2) A person shall be treated as having become liable to be registered under this Schedule at any time when he would have become so liable under sub-paragraph (1) above but for any registration which is subsequently cancelled under paragraph 6(2) below, paragraph 13(3) of Schedule 1, paragraph 6(2) of Schedule 2 or paragraph 6(3) of Schedule 3.

(3) A person shall not cease to be liable to be registered under this Schedule except in accordance with paragraph 2 below.][1]

Amendments—[1] Sch 3A inserted by FA 2000 s 136(8), Sch 36, with effect for relevant supplies (within the meaning of this Schedule) made after 20 March 2000.

[2 A person who has become liable to be registered under this Schedule shall cease to be so liable at any time if the Commissioners are satisfied that he has ceased to make relevant supplies.][1]

Amendments—[1] Sch 3A inserted by FA 2000 s 136(8), Sch 36, with effect for relevant supplies (within the meaning of this Schedule) made after 20 March 2000.

Notification of liability and registration

[3— (1) A person who becomes liable to be registered by virtue of paragraph 1(1)(*a*) above shall notify the Commissioners of the liability before the end of the period of 30 days beginning with the day on which the liability arises.

(2) The Commissioners shall register any such person (whether or not he so notifies them) with effect from the beginning of the day on which the liability arises.][1]

Amendments—[1] Sch 3A inserted by FA 2000 s 136(8), Sch 36, with effect for relevant supplies (within the meaning of this Schedule) made after 20 March 2000.

[4— (1) A person who becomes liable to be registered by virtue of paragraph 1(1)(*b*) above shall notify the Commissioners of the liability before the end of the period by reference to which the liability arises.

(2) The Commissioners shall register any such person (whether or not he so notifies them) with effect from the beginning of the period by reference to which the liability arises.][1]

Amendments—[1] Sch 3A inserted by FA 2000 s 136(8), Sch 36, with effect for relevant supplies (within the meaning of this Schedule) made after 20 March 2000.

Notification of end of liability

[5— (1) Subject to sub-paragraph (2) below, a person registered under paragraph 3 or 4 above who ceases to make or have the intention of making relevant supplies shall notify the Commissioners of that fact within 30 days of the day on which he does so.

(2) Sub-paragraph (1) above does not apply if the person would, when he so ceases, be otherwise liable or entitled to be registered under this Act if his registration and any enactment preventing a person from being liable to be registered under different provisions at the same time were disregarded.][1]

Amendments—[1] Sch 3A inserted by FA 2000 s 136(8), Sch 36, with effect for relevant supplies (within the meaning of this Schedule) made after 20 March 2000.

Cancellation of registration

[6— (1) Subject to sub-paragraph (3) below, where the Commissioners are satisfied that a registered person has ceased to be liable to be registered under this Schedule, they may cancel his registration with effect from the day on which he so ceased or from such later date as may be agreed between them and him.

(2) Where the Commissioners are satisfied that on the day on which a registered person was registered he was not registrable, they may cancel his registration with effect from that day.

(3) The Commissioners shall not under sub-paragraph (1) above cancel a person's registration with effect from any time unless they are satisfied that it is not a time when that person would be subject to a requirement, or entitled, to be registered under this Act.

(4) In determining for the purposes of sub-paragraph (3) above whether a person would be subject to a requirement, or entitled, to be registered at any time, so much of any provision of this Act as prevents a person from becoming liable or entitled to be registered when he is already registered or when he is so liable under any other provision shall be disregarded.][1]

Amendments—[1] Sch 3A inserted by FA 2000 s 136(8), Sch 36, with effect for relevant supplies (within the meaning of this Schedule) made after 20 March 2000.

Exemption from registration

[7— (1) Notwithstanding the preceding provisions of this Schedule, where a person who makes or intends to make relevant supplies satisfies the Commissioners that any such supply is zero-rated or would be zero-rated if he were a taxable person, they may, if he so requests and they think fit, exempt him from registration under this Schedule.

(2) Where there is a material change in the nature of the supplies made by a person exempted under this paragraph from registration under this Schedule, he shall notify the Commissioners of the change—

(*a*) within 30 days of the date on which the change occurred; or

(*b*) if no particular date is identifiable as the day on which it occurred, within 30 days of the end of the quarter in which it occurred.

(3) Where there is a material alteration in any quarter in the proportion of relevant supplies of such a person that are zero-rated, he shall notify the Commissioners of the alteration within 30 days of the end of the quarter.

(4) If it appears to the Commissioners that a request under sub-paragraph (1) above should no longer have been acted upon on or after any day, or has been withdrawn on any day, they shall register the person who made the request with effect from that day.][1]

Amendments—[1] Sch 3A inserted by FA 2000 s 136(8), Sch 36, with effect for relevant supplies (within the meaning of this Schedule) made after 20 March 2000.

Supplementary

[**8** Any notification required under this Schedule shall be made in such form and shall contain such particulars as the Commissioners may by regulations prescribe.][1]

Amendments—[1] Sch 3A inserted by FA 2000 s 136(8), Sch 36, with effect for relevant supplies (within the meaning of this Schedule) made after 20 March 2000.

[**9**— (1) For the purposes of this Schedule a supply of goods is a relevant supply where—

(*a*) the supply is a taxable supply;

(*b*) the goods are assets of the business in the course or furtherance of which they are supplied; and

(*c*) the person by whom they are supplied, or a predecessor of his, has received or claimed, or is intending to claim, a repayment of VAT on the supply to him, or the importation by him, of the goods or of anything comprised in them.

(2) In relation to any goods, a person is the predecessor of another for the purposes of this paragraph if—

(*a*) that other person is a person to whom he has transferred assets of his business by a transfer of that business, or part of it, as a going concern;

(*b*) those assets consisted of or included those goods; and

(*c*) the transfer of the assets is one falling by virtue of an order under section 5(3) (or under an enactment re-enacted in section 5(3)) to be treated as neither a supply of goods nor a supply of services;

and the reference in this paragraph to a person's predecessor includes references to the predecessors of his predecessor through any number of transfers.

(3) The reference in this paragraph to a repayment of VAT is a reference to such a repayment under a scheme embodied in regulations made under section 39.][1]

Amendments—[1] Sch 3A inserted by FA 2000 s 136(8), Sch 36, with effect for relevant supplies (within the meaning of this Schedule) made after 20 March 2000.

[SCHEDULE 3B
SUPPLY OF ELECTRONIC SERVICES IN MEMBER STATES: SPECIAL ACCOUNTING SCHEME][1]

Section 3A

Amendments—[1] Sch 3B inserted by FA 2003 s 23, Sch 2 paras 1, 4 with effect for qualifying supplies made after 30 June 2003, see FA 2003 s 23(2).

PART 1
REGISTRATION

The register

[**1** Persons registered under this Schedule are to be registered in a single register kept by the Commissioners for the purposes of this Schedule.][1]

Amendments—[1] Sch 3B inserted by FA 2003 Sch 2 para 4 with effect in relation to qualifying supplies made after 30 June 2003, see FA 2003 s 23(2).

Persons who may be registered

[**2**— (1) A person may be registered under this Schedule if he satisfies the following conditions.

(2) Condition 1 is that the person makes or intends to make qualifying supplies in the course of a business carried on by him.

(3) Condition 2 is that the person has neither his business establishment nor a fixed establishment in the United Kingdom or in another member State in relation to any supply of goods or services.

(4) Condition 3 is that the person is not—

(*a*) registered under this Act,

(*b*) identified for the purposes of VAT in accordance with the law of another member State, or

(*c*) registered under an Act of Tynwald for the purposes of any tax imposed by or under an Act of Tynwald which corresponds to VAT.

(5) Condition 4 is that the person—

(*a*) is not required to be registered or identified as mentioned in condition 3, or

(*b*) is required to be so registered or identified, but solely by virtue of the fact that he makes or intends to make qualifying supplies.

(6) Condition 5 is that the person is not identified under any provision of the law of another member State which implements Article 26c.

(7) In this Schedule, "Article 26c" means Article 26c of the 1977 VAT Directive (which is inserted by Article 1(3) of the 2002 VAT Directive).

(8) References in this Schedule to a person's being registered under this Act do not include a reference to that person's being registered under this Schedule.][1]

Amendments—[1] Sch 3B inserted by FA 2003 Sch 2 para 4 with effect in relation to qualifying supplies made after 30 June 2003, see FA 2003 s 23(2).

Qualifying supplies

[3 In this Schedule, "qualifying supply" means a supply of electronically supplied services (within the meaning of paragraph 7C of Schedule 5) to a person who—

(*a*) belongs in the United Kingdom or another member State, and

(*b*) receives those services otherwise than for the purposes of a business carried on by him.][1]

Amendments—[1] Sch 3B inserted by FA 2003 Sch 2 para 4 with effect in relation to qualifying supplies made after 30 June 2003, see FA 2003 s 23(2).

Registration request

[4— (1) If a person—

(*a*) satisfies the Commissioners that the conditions in paragraph 2 above are satisfied in his case, and

(*b*) makes a request in accordance with this paragraph (a "registration request"),

the Commissioners must register him under this Schedule.

(2) Sub-paragraph (1) above is subject to paragraph 9 below.

(3) A registration request must contain the following particulars—

(*a*) the name of the person making the request;

(*b*) his postal address;

(*c*) his electronic addresses (including any websites);

(*d*) where he has been allocated a number by the tax authorities in the country in which he belongs, that number;

(*e*) the date on which he began, or intends to begin, making qualifying supplies.

(4) A registration request must include a statement that the person making the request is not—

(*a*) registered under this Act,

(*b*) identified for the purposes of VAT in accordance with the law of another member State, or

(*c*) registered under an Act of Tynwald for the purposes of any tax imposed by or under an Act of Tynwald which corresponds to VAT.

(5) A registration request must be made by such electronic means, and in such manner, as the Commissioners may direct or may by regulations prescribe.][1]

Amendments—[1] Sch 3B inserted by FA 2003 Sch 2 para 4 with effect in relation to qualifying supplies made after 30 June 2003, see FA 2003 s 23(2).

Date on which registration takes effect

[5— (1) Where a person is registered under this Schedule, his registration takes effect—

(*a*) on the date on which his registration request is made, or

(*b*) on such earlier or later date as may be agreed between him and the Commissioners.

(2) For the purposes of sub-paragraph (1) above—

(*a*) no registration is to take effect before 1st July 2003, and

(*b*) registration requests made before that date are to be treated as if they were made on that date.][1]

Amendments—[1] Sch 3B inserted by FA 2003 Sch 2 para 4 with effect in relation to qualifying supplies made after 30 June 2003, see FA 2003 s 23(2).

Registration number

[6 On registering a person under this Schedule, the Commissioners must—

(*a*) allocate a registration number to him, and

(*b*) notify him electronically of the number.][1]

Amendments—[1] Sch 3B inserted by FA 2003 Sch 2 para 4 with effect in relation to qualifying supplies made after 30 June 2003, see FA 2003 s 23(2).

Obligation to notify changes

[7— (1) A person who has made a registration request must notify the Commissioners if subsequently—

(*a*) there is a change in any of the particulars contained in his request in accordance with paragraph 4(3) above,

(*b*) he ceases to make, or to have the intention of making, qualifying supplies, or (*c*) he ceases to satisfy the conditions in any of sub-paragraphs (3) to (6) of paragraph 2 above.

(2) A notification under this paragraph must be given within the period of 30 days beginning with the date of the change of particulars or of the cessation.

(3) A notification under this paragraph must be given by such electronic means, and in such manner, as the Commissioners may direct or may by regulations prescribe.][1]

Amendments—[1] Sch 3B inserted by FA 2003 Sch 2 para 4 with effect in relation to qualifying supplies made after 30 June 2003, see FA 2003 s 23(2).

Cancellation of registration

[8— (1) The Commissioners must cancel a person's registration under this Schedule if—

(*a*) he notifies them that he has ceased to make, or to have the intention of making, qualifying supplies,

(*b*) they otherwise determine that he has ceased to make, or to have the intention of making, qualifying supplies,

(*c*) he notifies them that he has ceased to satisfy the conditions in any of sub-paragraphs (3) to (6) of paragraph 2 above,

(*d*) they otherwise determine that he has ceased to satisfy any of those conditions, or

(*e*) they determine that he has persistently failed to comply with his obligations under this Schedule.

(2) In a case falling within sub-paragraph (1)(*a*) or (*c*) above, cancellation of a person's registration under this paragraph takes effect—

(*a*) on the date on which the notification is received, or

(*b*) on such earlier or later date as may be agreed between him and the Commissioners.

(3) In a case falling within sub-paragraph (1)(*b*), (*d*) or (*e*) above, cancellation of a person's registration under this paragraph takes effect—

(*a*) on the date on which the determination is made, or

(*b*) on such earlier or later date as the Commissioners may in his particular case direct.][1]

Amendments—[1] Sch 3B inserted by FA 2003 Sch 2 para 4 with effect in relation to qualifying supplies made after 30 June 2003, see FA 2003 s 23(2).

Registration after cancellation for persistent default

[9— (1) The Commissioners—

(*a*) are not required by paragraph 4(1) above to register a person under this Schedule if he is a persistent defaulter, but

(*b*) shall have the power to do so.

(2) In this paragraph, "persistent defaulter" means a person—

(*a*) whose previous registration under this Schedule has been cancelled under paragraph 8(1)(*e*) above (persistent failure to comply with obligations under this Schedule), or

(*b*) who has been excluded from the identification register under any provision of the law of another member State which implements Article 26c(*B*)(4)(*d*) of the 1977 VAT Directive (persistent failure to comply with rules concerning the special scheme).][1]

Amendments—[1] Sch 3B inserted by FA 2003 Sch 2 para 4 with effect in relation to qualifying supplies made after 30 June 2003, see FA 2003 s 23(2).

PART 2

OBLIGATIONS FOLLOWING REGISTRATION, ETC

Liability for VAT

[10— (1) A person is liable to pay VAT under and in accordance with this Schedule if—

(*a*) he makes a qualifying supply, and

(*b*) he is registered under this Schedule when he makes the supply.

(2) The amount of VAT which a person is liable to pay by virtue of this Schedule on any qualifying supply is to be determined in accordance with sub-paragraphs (3) and (4) below.

(3) If the qualifying supply is treated as made in the United Kingdom, the amount is the amount of VAT that would have been charged on the supply under this Act if the person had been registered under this Act when he made the supply.

(4) If the qualifying supply is treated as made in another member State, the amount is the amount of VAT that would have been charged on the supply in accordance with the law of that member State if the person had been identified for the purposes of VAT in that member State when he made the supply.

(5) Where a person is liable to pay VAT by virtue of this Schedule—

(*a*) any amount falling to be determined in accordance with sub-paragraph (3) above is to be regarded for the purposes of this Act as VAT charged in accordance with this Act, and (*b*) any amount falling to be determined in accordance with sub-paragraph (4) above in relation to another member State is to be regarded for those purposes as VAT charged in accordance with the law of that member State.][1]

Amendments—[1] Sch 3B inserted by FA 2003 Sch 2 para 4 with effect in relation to qualifying supplies made after 30 June 2003, see FA 2003 s 23(2).

Obligation to submit special accounting returns

[11— (1) A person who is, or has been, registered under this Schedule must submit a return (a "special accounting return") to the Controller for each reporting period.

(2) Each quarter for the whole or any part of which a person is registered under this Schedule is a "reporting period" in the case of that person.

(3) The special accounting return must state the person's registration number.

(4) For each member State in which the person is treated as having made qualifying supplies for the reporting period, the special accounting return must specify—

(*a*) the total value of his qualifying supplies treated as made in that member State in that period, apart from the VAT which he is liable to pay by virtue of this Schedule in respect of those supplies,

(*b*) the rate of VAT applicable to those supplies by virtue of sub-paragraph (3) or (4) (as the case may be) of paragraph 10 above, and

(*c*) the total amount of VAT payable by him by virtue of this Schedule in respect of those supplies in that period.

(5) The special accounting return must state the total amount of VAT which the person is liable to pay by virtue of this Schedule in respect of all qualifying supplies treated as made by him in all member States in the reporting period.

(6) If a person is registered under this Schedule for part only of a reporting period, references in this paragraph to his qualifying supplies in that period are references to his qualifying supplies in that part of that period.

(7) In this Schedule, "the Controller" means the Controller, Customs and Excise Value Added Tax Central Unit.][1]

Amendments—[1] Sch 3B inserted by FA 2003 Sch 2 para 4 with effect in relation to qualifying supplies made after 30 June 2003, see FA 2003 s 23(2).

Further obligations with respect to special accounting returns

[12— (1) A special accounting return must set out in sterling the amounts referred to in paragraph 11 above.

(2) Any conversion from one currency into another for the purposes of sub-paragraph (1) above shall be made by using the exchange rates published by the European Central Bank—

(*a*) for the last day of the reporting period to which the special accounting return relates, or

(*b*) if no such rate is published for that day, for the next day for which such a rate is published.

(3) A special accounting return must be submitted to the Controller within the period of 20 days after the last day of the reporting period to which it relates.

(4) A special accounting return must be submitted by such electronic means, and in such manner, as the Commissioners may direct or may by regulations prescribe.][1]

Amendments—[1] Sch 3B inserted by FA 2003 Sch 2 para 4 with effect in relation to qualifying supplies made after 30 June 2003, see FA 2003 s 23(2).

Payment of VAT

[13— (1) A person who is required to submit a special accounting return must, at the same time as he submits the return, pay to the Controller in sterling the amount referred to in paragraph 11(5) above in respect of the reporting period to which the return relates.

(2) A payment under this paragraph must be made in such manner as the Commissioners may direct or may by regulations prescribe.][1]

Amendments—[1] Sch 3B inserted by FA 2003 Sch 2 para 4 with effect in relation to qualifying supplies made after 30 June 2003, see FA 2003 s 23(2).

Obligations to keep and produce records

[14— (1) A person must keep records of the transactions which he enters into for the purposes of, or in connection with, qualifying supplies made by him at any time when he is registered under this Schedule.

(2) The records to be kept must be such as will enable the tax authorities for the member State in which a qualifying supply is treated as made to determine whether any special accounting return which is submitted in respect of that supply is correct.

(3) Any records required to be kept must be made available—

(*a*) to the tax authorities for the member State in which the qualifying supply to which the records relate was treated as made, if they so request, or

(*b*) to the Commissioners, if they so request.

(4) Records must be made available electronically under sub-paragraph (3) above.

(5) The records relating to a transaction must be maintained for a period of ten years beginning with the 1st January following the date on which the transaction was entered into.][1]

Amendments—[1] Sch 3B inserted by FA 2003 Sch 2 para 4 with effect in relation to qualifying supplies made after 30 June 2003, see FA 2003 s 23(2).

Commissioners' power to request production of records

[15— (1) The Commissioners may request a person to make available to them electronically records of the transactions entered into by him for the purposes of, or in connection with, qualifying supplies to which this paragraph applies.

(2) This paragraph applies to qualifying supplies which—

(*a*) are treated as made in the United Kingdom, and

(*b*) are made by the person while he is identified under any provision of the law of another member State which implements Article 26c.][1]

Amendments—[1] Sch 3B inserted by FA 2003 Sch 2 para 4 with effect in relation to qualifying supplies made after 30 June 2003, see FA 2003 s 23(2).

PART 3

UNDERSTATEMENTS AND OVERSTATEMENTS OF UK VAT

Understatement or overstatement of UK VAT in special scheme return

[16— (1) If the Commissioners consider that a person who is or has been a participant in the special scheme has submitted a special scheme return which understates his liability to UK VAT, they may give him a notice—

(*a*) identifying the return in which they consider that the understatement was made,

(*b*) specifying the amount by which they consider that the person's liability to UK VAT has been understated, and

(*c*) requesting him to pay that amount to the Controller within the period of 30 days beginning with the date on which the notice is given.

(2) If the Commissioners consider that a person who is or has been a participant in the special scheme has submitted a special scheme return which overstates his liability to UK VAT, they may give him a notice—

(*a*) identifying the return in which they consider that the overstatement was made, and

(*b*) specifying the amount by which they consider that the person's liability to UK VAT has been overstated.

(3) Where the Commissioners give a person a notice under sub-paragraph (2) above, they are liable to pay him the amount specified in the notice.

(4) No notice under this paragraph may be given more than 3 years after the end of the period for which the special scheme return in question was made.

(5) In this Schedule, "participant in the special scheme" means a person who—

(*a*) is registered under this Schedule, or

(*b*) is identified under any provision of the law of another member State which implements Article 26c.

(6) In this paragraph—

"special scheme return" means—

(*a*) a special accounting return; or

(*b*) a value added tax return submitted to the tax authorities of another member State;

"UK VAT" means VAT which a person is liable to pay (whether in the United Kingdom or another member State) in respect of qualifying supplies treated as made in the United Kingdom at a time when he is or was a participant in the special scheme;

"value added tax return", in relation to another member State, means any value added tax return required to be submitted under any provision of the law of that member State which implements Article 26c(*B*)(5) of the 1977 VAT Directive.][1]

Amendments—[1] Sch 3B inserted by FA 2003 Sch 2 para 4 with effect in relation to qualifying supplies made after 30 June 2003, see FA 2003 s 23(2).

PART 4

APPLICATION OF PROVISIONS RELATING TO VAT

Registration under this Act

[17 Notwithstanding any provision in this Act to the contrary, a participant in the special scheme is not required to be registered under this Act by virtue of making qualifying supplies.][1]

Amendments—[1] Sch 3B inserted by FA 2003 Sch 2 para 4 with effect in relation to qualifying supplies made after 30 June 2003, see FA 2003 s 23(2).

De-registration

[18 Where a person who is registered under Schedule 1 satisfies the Commissioners that he intends to apply for—

(*a*) registration under this Schedule, or

(*b*) identification under any provision of the law of another member State which implements Article 26c,

they may, if he so requests, cancel his registration under Schedule 1 with effect from the day on which the request is made or from such later date as may be agreed between him and the Commissioners.][1]

Amendments—[1] Sch 3B inserted by FA 2003 Sch 2 para 4 with effect in relation to qualifying supplies made after 30 June 2003, see FA 2003 s 23(2).

VAT representatives

[19 Section 48(1) (VAT representatives) does not permit the Commissioners to direct a participant in the special scheme to appoint a VAT representative.][1]

Amendments—[1] Sch 3B inserted by FA 2003 Sch 2 para 4 with effect in relation to qualifying supplies made after 30 June 2003, see FA 2003 s 23(2).

Appeals

[20— (1) An appeal shall lie to a tribunal with respect to any of the following—

(*a*) the registration or cancellation of the registration of any person under this Schedule;

(*b*) a decision of the Commissioners to give a notice under sub-paragraph (1) of paragraph 16 above;

(*c*) the amount specified in any such notice or in a notice under sub-paragraph (2) of that paragraph.

[(2) Part 5 (appeals), and any order or regulations under that Part, have effect as if an appeal under this paragraph were an appeal which lies to the tribunal under section 83(1) (but not under any particular paragraph of that subsection).][2]][1]

Amendments—[1] Sch 3B inserted by FA 2003 Sch 2 para 4 with effect in relation to qualifying supplies made after 30 June 2003, see FA 2003 s 23(2).

[2] Sub-para (2) substituted by the Transfer of Tribunal Functions and Revenue and Customs Appeals Order, SI 2009/56 art 3, Sch 1 para 227 with effect from 1 April 2009, subject to transitional and savings provisions in Sch 3 para 4. Sub-para (2) previously read as follows—

"(2) Part 5 (appeals), and any orders or regulations under that Part, have effect in relation to an appeal under this paragraph as if it were an appeal under section 83 (but not under any particular paragraph of that section)."

Payments on account of non-UK VAT to other member States

[21— (1) Neither—

(*a*) paragraph 1(2) of Schedule 11, nor

[(*b*) section 44 of the Commissioners for Revenue and Customs Act 2005,][2]

applies to money or securities for money collected or received for or on account of VAT if required to be paid to another member State by virtue of the VAT Co-operation Regulation.

(2) In sub-paragraph (1) above, "the VAT Co-operation Regulation" means the Council Regulation of 27 January 1992 on administrative co-operation in the field of indirect taxation (*VAT*) (218/92/EEC), as amended by the Council Regulation of 7 May 2002 (792/2002/EC) (which temporarily amends the VAT Co-operation Regulation as regards additional measures regarding electronic commerce).][1]

Amendments—[1] Sch 3B inserted by FA 2003 Sch 2 para 4 with effect in relation to qualifying supplies made after 30 June 2003, see FA 2003 s 23(2).

[2] Sub-para (1)(*b*) substituted by Commissioners for Revenue and Customs Act 2005 s 50, Sch 4 para 55 with effect from 18 April 2005 by virtue of the Commissioners for Revenue and Customs Act 2005 (Commencement) Order, SI 2005/1126, art 2(2).

Refund of UK VAT

[22— (1) The provisions which give effect to the 1986 VAT Refund Directive in the United Kingdom have effect in relation to a participant in the special scheme, but with the following modifications.

(2) The provision which gives effect to Article 2(1) of the 1986 VAT Refund Directive (as at 9th April 2003, see regulation 186 of the Value Added Tax Regulations 1995) shall apply in relation to a participant in the special scheme, but only so as to entitle him to a refund of VAT charged on—

(*a*) goods imported by him into the United Kingdom, and

(*b*) supplies made to him in the United Kingdom,

in connection with the making by him of qualifying supplies while he is a participant in the special scheme.

(3) The following provisions shall be omitted.

(4) The first provision is that which gives effect to Article 1(1) of the 1986 VAT Refund Directive, so far as it requires a member State to prevent a person who is deemed to have supplied services

in that member State during a period from being granted a refund of VAT for that period (as at 9th April 2003, see regulation 188(2)(*b*) of the Value Added Tax Regulations 1995).

(5) The second provision is that which gives effect to Article 2(2) of the 1986 VAT Refund Directive (which permits member States to make refunds conditional upon the granting by third States of comparable advantages regarding turnover taxes: as at 9th April 2003, see regulation 188(1) of the Value Added Tax Regulations 1995).

(6) The third provision is that which gives effect to Article 2(3) of the 1986 VAT Refund Directive (which permits member States to require the appointment of a tax representative: as at 9th April 2003, see regulation 187 of the Value Added Tax Regulations 1995).

(7) The fourth provision is that which gives effect to Article 4(2) of the 1986 VAT Refund Directive (which permits member States to provide for the exclusion of certain expenditure and to make refunds subject to additional conditions).

(8) In this paragraph "the 1986 VAT Refund Directive" means the Thirteenth Council Directive of 17th November 1986 on the harmonisation of the laws of the member States relating to turnover taxes—arrangements for the refund of value added tax to taxable persons not established in Community territory (86/560/EEC).][1]

Amendments—[1] Sch 3B inserted by FA 2003 Sch 2 para 4 with effect in relation to qualifying supplies made after 30 June 2003, see FA 2003 s 23(2).

PART 5
SUPPLEMENTARY

Interpretation

[23— (1) In this Schedule—

"the 1977 VAT Directive" means the Sixth Council Directive of 17 May 1977 on the harmonisation of the laws of the member States relating to turnover taxes—common system of value added tax: uniform basis of assessment (77/388/EEC);

"the 2002 VAT Directive" means the Council Directive of 7 May 2002 amending and amending temporarily the 1977 VAT Directive as regards the value added tax arrangements applicable to radio and television broadcasting services and certain electronically supplied services (2002/38/EC);

"Article 26c" has the meaning given by paragraph 2(7) above;

"the Controller" has the meaning given by paragraph 11(7) above;

"participant in the special scheme" has the meaning given by paragraph 16(5) above;

"qualifying supply" has the meaning given by paragraph 3 above;

"registration number" means the number allocated to a person on his registration under this Schedule in accordance with paragraph 6(*a*) above;

"registration request" is to be construed in accordance with paragraph 4(1)(*b*) above;

"reporting period" is to be construed in accordance with paragraph 11(2) above;

"special accounting return" is to be construed in accordance with paragraph 11(1) above.

(2) References in this Schedule to a qualifying supply being "treated as made" in a member State are references to its being treated as made—

(*a*) in the United Kingdom, by virtue of any provision which gives effect in the United Kingdom to Article 9(2)(*f*) of the 1977 VAT Directive (which is inserted by Article 1(1)(*b*) of the 2002 VAT Directive), or

(*b*) in another member State, by virtue of any provision of the law of that member State which gives effect to that Article.

(3) The provision which, as at 9th April 2003, is to give effect in the United Kingdom to Article 9(2)(*f*) of the 1977 VAT Directive (as mentioned in sub-paragraph (2)(*a*) above) is article 16A of the Value Added Tax (Place of Supply of Services) Order 1992 (which is prospectively inserted by article 3 of the Value Added Tax (Place of Supply of Services) (Amendment) Order 2003).][1]

Amendments—[1] Sch 3B inserted by FA 2003 Sch 2 para 4 with effect in relation to qualifying supplies made after 30 June 2003, see FA 2003 s 23(2).

SCHEDULE 4
MATTERS TO BE TREATED AS SUPPLY OF GOODS OR SERVICES

Section 5

HMRC Manuals—VAT Guidance V1-3: Supply and consideration, para 2.7 (supplies of goods or services).
Simon's Tax Cases—*Philips Exports Ltd v C&E Comrs* [1990] STC 508*.

1— (1) Any transfer of the whole property in goods is a supply of goods; but, subject to sub-paragraph (2) below, the transfer—

(*a*) of any undivided share of the property, or

(*b*) of the possession of goods,

is a supply of services.

(2) If the possession of goods is transferred—

(*a*) under an agreement for the sale of the goods, or

(*b*) under agreements which expressly contemplate that the property also will pass at some time in the future (determined by, or ascertainable from, the agreements but in any case not later than when the goods are fully paid for),

it is then in either case a supply of the goods.

Commentary—*De Voil Indirect Tax Service* **V3.112, V3.113**.
HMRC Manuals—VAT Guidance V1-3: Supply and consideration, para 2.9 (definition of supply of goods).
Paras 2.11, 4.2 (supply of services).
Para 15.7 (distinguishing between an outright supply of goods or a lease hire (supply of services).
Press releases etc—C&E Business Brief 17/94 12-9-94 (transfer of milk quota without land is a supply of services).
Simon's Tax Cases—*Phillip Drakard Trading Ltd v C&E Comrs* [1992] STC 568*; *British Airways plc v C&E Comrs* [1996] STC 1127*, *Stewart (tla GT Shooting) v C&E Comrs* [2002] STC 255.
Definitions—"Supply", s 5, Sch 4.

2 …[1]

Amendments—[1] Paragraph repealed by FA 1996 s 29(4), Sch 41 Pt IV(2), with effect in relation to supplies made after 31 December 1995.

3 The supply of any form of power, heat, refrigeration or ventilation is a supply of goods.

Commentary—*De Voil Indirect Tax Service* **V3.112**.
Definitions—"Supply", s 5, Sch 4.

4 The grant, assignment or surrender of a major interest in land is a supply of goods.

Commentary—*De Voil Indirect Tax Service* **V3.112**.
Definitions—"Assignment", s 96(1); "major interest", s 96(1); "supply", s 5, Sch 4;
Cross reference—See VAT Regulations, SI 1995/2518 reg 85 (grant of tenancy or lease: consideration payable periodically: time of supply).

5— (1) Subject to sub-paragraph (2) below, where goods forming part of the assets of a business are transferred or disposed of by or under the directions of the person carrying on the business so as no longer to form part of those assets, whether or not for a consideration, that is a supply by him of goods.

(2) Sub-paragraph (1) above does not apply where the transfer or disposal is—

[(*a*) a business gift the cost of which, together with the cost of any other business gifts made to the same person in the same year, was not more than £50;][6]

(*b*) subject to sub-paragraph (3) below, a gift to any person of a sample of any goods.

[(2ZA) In sub-paragraph (2) above—

"business gift" means a gift of goods that is made in the course or furtherance of the business in question;

"cost", in relation to a gift of goods, means the cost to the donor of acquiring or, as the case may be, producing the goods;

"the same year", in relation to a gift, means any period of twelve months that includes the day on which the gift is made.][7]

[(2A) For the purposes of determining the cost to the donor of acquiring or producing goods of which he has made a gift, where—

(*a*) the acquisition by the donor of the goods, or anything comprised in the goods, was by means of a transfer of a business, or a part of a business, as a going concern,

(*b*) the assets transferred by that transfer included those goods or that thing, and

(*c*) the transfer of those assets is one falling by virtue of an order under section 5(3) (or under an enactment re-enacted in section 5(3)) to be treated as neither a supply of goods nor a supply of services,

the donor and his predecessor or, as the case may be, all of his predecessors shall be treated as if they were the same person.][4]

(3) Where—

(*a*) a person is given a number of samples by the same person (whether all on one occasion or on different occasions), and

(*b*) those samples are identical or do not differ in any material respect from each other,

sub-paragraph (1) above shall apply to all except one of those samples or, as the case may be, to all except the first to be given.

(4) Where by or under the directions of a person carrying on a business goods held or used for the purposes of the business are put to any private use or are used, or made available to any person for use, for any purpose other than a purpose of the business, whether or not for a consideration, that is a supply of services.

(4A) …[8]

(5) Neither sub-paragraph (1) nor [sub-paragraph (4) above][1] shall require anything which a person carrying on a business does otherwise than for a consideration in relation to any goods to be treated as a supply except in a case where that person [or any of his predecessors is a person who (disregarding this paragraph) has or will become][3] entitled—

[(*a*) under sections 25 and 26, to credit for the whole or any part of the VAT on the supply, acquisition or importation of those goods or of anything comprised in them; or (*b*) under a scheme embodied in regulations made under section 39, to a repayment of VAT on the supply or importation of those goods or of anything comprised in them.][5]

[(5A) In relation to any goods or anything comprised in any goods, a person is the predecessor of another for the purposes of this paragraph if—

(*a*) that other person is a person to whom he has transferred assets of his business by a transfer of that business, or a part of it, as a going concern;

(*b*) those assets consisted of or included those goods or that thing; and

(*c*) the transfer of the assets is one falling by virtue of an order under section 5(3) (or under an enactment re-enacted in section 5(3)) to be treated as neither a supply of goods nor a supply of services;

and references in this paragraph to a person's predecessors include references to the predecessors of his predecessors through any number of transfers.][4]

(6) Anything which is a supply of goods or services by virtue of sub-paragraph (1) or (4) above is to be treated as made in the course or furtherance of the business (if it would not otherwise be so treated); and in the case of a business carried on by an individual—

(*a*) sub-paragraph (1) above applies to any transfer or disposition of goods in favour of himself personally; and

(*b*) [sub-paragraph (4) above][1] applies to goods used, or made available for use, by himself personally.

[(7) The Treasury may by order substitute for the sum for the time being specified in sub-paragraph (2)(*a*) above such sum, not being less than £10, as they think fit.][2]

Commentary—*De Voil Indirect Tax Service* **V3.211, V3.212.**

HMRC Manuals—VAT Guidance V1-3: Supply and consideration, para 2.4 (supply for no consideration).

Para 4.2 (supply of services for consideration).

Para 5.1 (assets used for business purposes).

Para 5.5 (supply of samples: first sample exempt).

Para 6.2 (free loan of business assets).

Simon's Tax Cases—Sub-para (1), *C&E Comrs v Professional Footballers' Association (Enterprises) Ltd* [1993] STC 86*; *Church of England Children's Society v Revenue and Customs Commissioners* [2005] STC 1644.

Definitions—"Supply", s 5, Sch 4; "VAT", ss 1, 96(1).

Cross references—See VATA 1994 s 5(3) (orders providing that sub-para (4) of this para is not to apply to make the use of prescribed goods in prescribed circumstances a supply of services);

VATA 1994 s 6(12) (supplies treated as taking place by virtue of sub-para (1) of this para: time of supply);

VATA 1994 s 6(13), (14) (supplies treated as taking place by virtue of sub-para (4) of this para: time of supply);

VATA 1994 s 97(3), (4) (procedure for making an order under sub-s (7) above specifying a lesser sum than in sub-s (2)(*a*)).

VATA 1994 Sch 6 para 6 (valuation of supplies made otherwise than for consideration which are treated as supplies of goods by virtue of sub-para (1) of this para);

VATA 1994 Sch 6 para 7 (valuation of supplies made otherwise than for consideration which are treated as supplies of services by virtue of sub-para (3) of this para);

VATA 1994 Sch 7 para 3 (valuation of transactions involving the acquisition of goods from another member state otherwise than for consideration which are treated as supplies by virtue of sub-para (1) of this para).

VAT Regulations, SI 1995/2518 reg 81(1) (supplies treated as taking place by virtue of sub-para (4) of this para: time of supply).

Amendments—[1] Words in sub-paras (5), (6)(*b*) substituted by FA 1995 s 33(1), (3)(*a*) and are deemed to have always had effect.

[2] Sub-para (7) added by FA 1996 s 33(2).

[3] Words in sub-paras (2)(*a*), (5) inserted by FA 1998 s 21 with effect for goods transferred or disposed of, or put to use, used or made available for use after 16 March 1998.

[4] Sub-paras (2A), (5A) inserted by FA 1998 s 21 with effect for goods transferred or disposed of, or put to use, used or made available for use after 16 March 1998.

[5] Words in sub-para (5) substituted by FA 2000 s 136(9), with effect for supplies made after 20 March 2000.

[6] Words in sub-para (2)(*a*) substituted by FA 2003 s 21(2) with effect for gifts made after 30 September 2003. Sub-para (2)(*a*) previously read:

"a gift of goods made in the course or furtherance of the business (otherwise than as one forming part of a series or succession of gifts made to the same person from time to time) where the cost to the donor of acquiring or, as the case may be, producing the goods was not more than £50;".

[7] Sub-para (2ZA) inserted by FA 2003 s 21(3) with effect for gifts made after 30 September 2003.

[8] Sub-para (4A) repealed by FA 2007 ss 99(1), (2), (6), 114, Sch 27 Pt 6(1) with effect from 1 September 2007.

6— (1) Where, in a case not falling within paragraph 5(1) above, goods forming part of the assets of any business—

(*a*) are removed from any member State by or under the directions of the person carrying on the business; and

(*b*) are so removed in the course or furtherance of that business for the purpose of being taken to a place in a member State other than that from which they are removed,

then, whether or not the removal is or is connected with a transaction for a consideration, that is a supply of goods by that person.

(2) Sub-paragraph (1) above does not apply—

(*a*) to the removal of goods from any member State in the course of their removal from one part of that member State to another part of the same member State; or

(*b*) to goods which have been removed from a place outside the member States for entry into the territory of the Community and are removed from a member State before the time when any Community customs debt in respect of any Community customs duty on their entry into that territory would be incurred.

Commentary—*De Voil Indirect Tax Service* **V3.213.**

Definitions—"Business", s 94.

VAT

Cross references—See VATA 1994 s 5(3) (orders providing that this para is not to apply to make a removal of assets a supply of goods in prescribed circumstances);
VATA 1994 Sch 6 para 6 (valuation of supplies made otherwise than for consideration which are treated as supplies of goods by virtue of this para);
VATA 1994 Sch 7 para 3 (valuation of transactions involving the acquisition of goods from another member state otherwise than for consideration which are treated as supplies by virtue of this para).
VAT (Removal of Goods) Order, SI 1992/3111 (this paragraph not to apply to removals of goods between member states in specified circumstances).
VAT (Removal of Gas and Electricity) Order, SI 2004/3150 (sub-para (1) not to apply to the removal of gas through the natural gas distribution network, or electricity, from a Member State to a place in any other Member State. This Order has effect in relation to supplies made on or after 1 January 2005).

7 Where in the case of a business carried on by a taxable person goods forming part of the assets of the business are, under any power exercisable by another person, sold by the other in or towards satisfaction of a debt owed by the taxable person, they shall be deemed to be supplied by the taxable person in the course or furtherance of his business.

Commentary—*De Voil Indirect Tax Service* **V3.226**.
Definitions—"Business", s 94; "taxable person", s 3;
Cross references—See VATA 1994 Sch 11 para 2(12) (provision for regulations as to payment of VAT chargeable on deemed supply under this para).
VAT Regulations, SI 1995/2518 reg 13(2), (5) (VAT invoices in respect of deemed supplies under this para);
VAT Regulations, SI 1995/2518 reg 27 (returns in respect of deemed supplies under this para).

8— (1) Where a person ceases to be a taxable person, any goods then forming part of the assets of a business carried on by him shall be deemed to be supplied by him in the course or furtherance of his business immediately before he ceases to be a taxable person, unless—

(*a*) the business is transferred as a going concern to another taxable person; or
(*b*) the business is carried on by another person who, under regulations made under section 46(4), is treated as a taxable person; or
(*c*) the VAT on the deemed supply would not be more than [£1,000][1].

(2) This paragraph does not apply to any goods in the case of which the taxable person can show to the satisfaction of the Commissioners—

(*a*) that no credit for input tax has been allowed to him in respect of the supply of the goods, their acquisition from another member State or their importation from a place outside the member States;
(*b*) that the goods did not become his as part of the assets of a business[, or part of a business,][2] which was transferred to him as a going concern by another taxable person; and
(*c*) that he has not obtained relief in respect of the goods under section 4 of the Finance Act 1973.

(3) This paragraph does not apply where a person ceases to be a taxable person in consequence of having been certified under section 54.

(4) The Treasury may by order increase or further increase the sum specified in sub-paragraph (1)(*c*) above.

Commentary—*De Voil Indirect Tax Service* **V3.261**.
HMRC Manuals—VAT Guidance V1-3: Supply and consideration, para 5.6 (deemed supply of goods where a person ceases to be a taxable person, with business assets on hand).
Definitions—"Acquisition of goods from another member State", s 11; "another member State", s 96(1); "business", s 94; "the Commissioners", s 96(1); "importation of goods from a place outside the member States", s 15; "input tax", s 24; "regulations", s 96(1); "taxable person", s 3; "VAT", ss 1, 96(1).
Cross references—See VATA 1994 Sch 6 para 6 (valuation of supplies which are treated as supplies of goods by virtue of this para).
VAT (Isle of Man) Order, SI 1982/1067 art 11(8) (persons who become registered under Isle of Man VAT legislation remain taxable persons for the purposes of this para).
Amendments—[1] Figure in para (1)(*c*) substituted by the VAT (Deemed Supply of Goods) Order, SI 2000/266, art 2 with effect from 1 April 2000.
[2] Words in sub-para (2)(*b*) inserted by FA 2007 s 100(9), (10) with effect in relation to transfers pursuant to contracts entered into on or after 1 September 2007.

9— (1) Subject to sub-paragraphs (2) and (3) below, paragraphs 5 to 8 above have effect in relation to land forming part of the assets of, or held or used for the purposes of, a business as if it were goods forming part of the assets of, or held or used for the purposes of, a business.

(2) In the application of those paragraphs by virtue of sub-paragraph (1) above, references to transfer, disposition or sale shall have effect as references to the grant or assignment of any interest in, right over or licence to occupy the land concerned.

(3) Except in relation to—

(*a*) the grant or assignment of a major interest; or
(*b*) a grant or assignment otherwise than for a consideration,

in the application of paragraph 5(1) above by virtue of sub-paragraph (1) above the reference to a supply of goods shall have effect as a reference to a supply of services.

[(4) In this paragraph "grant" includes surrender.][1]

Commentary—*De Voil Indirect Tax Service* **V3.211**.
Definitions—"Assignment", s 96(1); "business", s 94; "major interest", s 96(1); "supply", s 5, Sch 4.
Amendments—[1] Sub-para (4) inserted by FA 2007 s 99(1), (3), (7) with effect for surrenders on or after 21 March 2007.

[SCHEDULE 4A
PLACE OF SUPPLY OF SERVICES: SPECIAL RULES][1]

Section 7A

Amendments—[1] Sch 4A inserted by FA 2009 s 76, Sch 36 paras 1, 11 with effect in relation to supplies made on or after 1 January 2010.

[PART 1
GENERAL EXCEPTIONS

Services relating to land

1— (1) A supply of services to which this paragraph applies is to be treated as made in the country in which the land in connection with which the supply is made is situated.

(2) This paragraph applies to—

(*a*) the grant, assignment or surrender of any interest in or right over land,

(*b*) the grant, assignment or surrender of a personal right to call for or be granted any interest in or right over land,

(*c*) the grant, assignment or surrender of a licence to occupy land or any other contractual right exercisable over or in relation to land (including the provision of holiday accommodation, seasonal pitches for caravans and facilities at caravan parks for persons for whom such pitches are provided and pitches for tents and camping facilities),

(*d*) the provision in an hotel, inn, boarding house or similar establishment of sleeping accommodation or of accommodation in rooms which are provided in conjunction with sleeping accommodation or for the purpose of a supply of catering,

(*e*) any works of construction, demolition, conversion, reconstruction, alteration, enlargement, repair or maintenance of a building or civil engineering work, and

(*f*) services such as are supplied by estate agents, auctioneers, architects, surveyors, engineers and others involved in matters relating to land.

(3) In sub-paragraph (2)(*c*) "holiday accommodation" includes any accommodation in a building, hut (including a beach hut or chalet), caravan, houseboat or tent which is advertised or held out as holiday accommodation or as suitable for holiday or leisure use.

(4) In sub-paragraph (2)(*d*) "similar establishment" includes premises in which there is provided furnished sleeping accommodation, whether with or without the provision of board or facilities for the preparation of food, which are used by, or held out as being suitable for use by, visitors or travellers.][1]

Amendments—[1] Sch 4A inserted by FA 2009 s 76, Sch 36 paras 1, 11 with effect in relation to supplies made on or after 1 January 2010.

[Passenger transport

2— (1) A supply of services consisting of the transportation of passengers (or of any luggage or motor vehicles accompanying passengers) is to be treated as made in the country in which the transportation takes place, and (in a case where it takes place in more than one country) in proportion to the distances covered in each.

(2) For the purposes of sub-paragraph (1) transportation which takes place partly outside the territorial jurisdiction of a country is to be treated as taking place wholly in the country if—

(*a*) it takes place in the course of a journey between two points in the country (whether or not as part of a longer journey involving travel to or from another country), and

(*b*) the means of transport used does not (except in an emergency or involuntarily) stop, put in or land in another country in the course of the journey between those two points.

(3) For the purposes of sub-paragraph (1) a pleasure cruise is to be regarded as the transportation of passengers (so that services provided as part of a pleasure cruise are to be treated as supplied in the same place as the transportation of the passengers).

(4) In sub-paragraph (3) "pleasure cruise" includes a cruise wholly or partly for education or training.][1]

Amendments—[1] Sch 4A inserted by FA 2009 s 76, Sch 36 paras 1, 11 with effect in relation to supplies made on or after 1 January 2010.

[Hiring of means of transport

3— (1) A supply of services consisting of the short-term hiring of a means of transport is to be treated as made in the country in which the means of transport is actually put at the disposal of the person by whom it is hired.

But this is subject to sub-paragraphs (3) and (4).

(2) For the purposes of this Schedule the hiring of a means of transport is "short-term" if it is hired for a continuous period not exceeding—

(*a*) if the means of transport is a vessel, 90 days, and

(*b*) otherwise, 30 days.

(3) Where—

(*a*) a supply of services consisting of the hiring of a means of transport would otherwise be treated as made in the United Kingdom, and

(*b*) the services are to any extent effectively used and enjoyed in a country which is not a member State,

the supply is to be treated to that extent as made in that country.

(4) Where—

(*a*) a supply of services consisting of the hiring of a means of transport would otherwise be treated as made in a country which is not a member State, and

(*b*) the services are to any extent effectively used and enjoyed in the United Kingdom,

the supply is to be treated to that extent as made in the United Kingdom.][1]

Amendments—[1] Sch 4A inserted by FA 2009 s 76, Sch 36 paras 1, 11 with effect in relation to supplies made on or after 1 January 2010.

[Cultural, educational and entertainment services etc

4— (1) A supply of services to which this paragraph applies is to be treated as made in the country in which the services are physically carried out.

(2) This paragraph applies to the provision of—

(*a*) services relating to cultural, artistic, sporting, scientific, educational, entertainment or similar activities (including fairs and exhibitions), and

(*b*) ancillary services relating to such activities, including services of organisers of such activities.][1]

Amendments—[1] Sch 4A inserted by FA 2009 s 76, Sch 36 paras 1, 11 with effect in relation to supplies made on or after 1 January 2010.

Prospective amendments—Para 4 to be repealed by FA 2009 s 76, Sch 36 paras 1, 15(2) with effect in relation to supplies made on or after 1 January 2011.

[Restaurant and catering services: general

5— (1) A supply of services to which this paragraph applies is to be treated as made in the country in which the services are physically carried out.

(2) This paragraph applies to the provision of restaurant services and the provision of catering services, other than the provision of services to which paragraph 6 applies.][1]

Amendments—[1] Sch 4A inserted by FA 2009 s 76, Sch 36 paras 1, 11 with effect in relation to supplies made on or after 1 January 2010.

[EC on-board restaurant and catering services

6— (1) A supply of services consisting of

(*a*) the provision of restaurant services, or

(*b*) the provision of catering services,

on board a ship, aircraft or train in connection with the transportation of passengers during an intra-EC passenger transport operation is to be treated as made in the country in which the relevant point of departure is located.

(2) An intra-EC passenger transport operation is a passenger transport operation which, or so much of a passenger transport operation as,—

(*a*) has as the first place at which passengers can embark a place which is within the EC,

(*b*) has as the last place at which passengers who embarked in a member State can disembark a place which is within the EC, and

(*c*) does not include a stop at a place which is not within the EC and at which passengers can embark or passengers who embarked in a member State can disembark.

(3) "Relevant point of departure", in relation to an intra-EC passenger transport operation, is the first place in the intra-EC passenger transport operation at which passengers can embark.

(4) A place is within the EC if it is within any member State.

(5) For the purposes of this paragraph the return stage of a return passenger transport operation is to be regarded as a separate passenger transport operation; and for this purpose—

(*a*) a return passenger transport operation is one which takes place in more than one country but is expected to end in the country in which it begins, and

(*b*) the return stage of a return passenger transport operation is the part of it which ends in the country in which it began and begins with the last stop at a place at which there has not been a previous stop during it.][1]

Amendments—[1] Sch 4A inserted by FA 2009 s 76, Sch 36 paras 1, 11 with effect in relation to supplies made on or after 1 January 2010.

[Hiring of goods

7— (1) Where—

(*a*) a supply of services consisting of the hiring of any goods other than a means of transport would otherwise be treated as made in the United Kingdom, and (*b*) the services are to any extent effectively used and enjoyed in a country which is not a member State,

the supply is to be treated to that extent as made in that country.

(2) Where—

(*a*) a supply of services consisting of the hiring of any goods other than a means of transport would otherwise be treated as made in a country which is not a member State, and

(*b*) the services are to any extent effectively used and enjoyed in the United Kingdom,

the supply is to be treated to that extent as made in the United Kingdom.][1]

Amendments—[1] Sch 4A inserted by FA 2009 s 76, Sch 36 paras 1, 11 with effect in relation to supplies made on or after 1 January 2010.

[Telecommunication and broadcasting services

8— (1) This paragraph applies to a supply of services consisting of the provision of—

(*a*) telecommunication services, or

(*b*) radio or television broadcasting services.

(2) In this Schedule "telecommunication services" means services relating to the transmission, emission or reception of signals, writing, images and sounds or information of any nature by wire, radio, optical or other electromagnetic systems, including—

(*a*) the related transfer or assignment of the right to use capacity for such transmission, emission or reception, and

(*b*) the provision of access to global information networks.

(3) Where—

(*a*) a supply of services to which this paragraph applies would otherwise be treated as made in the United Kingdom, and

(*b*) the services are to any extent effectively used and enjoyed in a country which is not a member State,

the supply is to be treated to that extent as made in that country.

(4) Where—

(*a*) a supply of services to which this paragraph applies would otherwise be treated as made in a country which is not a member State, and

(*b*) the services are to any extent effectively used and enjoyed in the United Kingdom,

the supply is to be treated to that extent as made in the United Kingdom.][1]

Amendments—[1] Sch 4A inserted by FA 2009 s 76, Sch 36 paras 1, 11 with effect in relation to supplies made on or after 1 January 2010.

[PART 2

EXCEPTIONS RELATING TO SUPPLIES MADE TO RELEVANT BUSINESS PERSON

Electronically-supplied services

9— (1) Where—

(*a*) a supply of services consisting of the provision of electronically supplied services to a relevant business person would otherwise be treated as made in the United Kingdom, and

(*b*) the services are to any extent effectively used and enjoyed in a country which is not a member State,

the supply is to be treated to that extent as made in that country.

(2) Where—

(*a*) a supply of services consisting of the provision of electronically supplied services to a relevant business person would otherwise be treated as made in a country which is not a member State, and

(*b*) the services are to any extent effectively used and enjoyed in the United Kingdom,

the supply is to be treated to that extent as made in the United Kingdom.

(3) Examples of what are electronically supplied services for the purposes of this Schedule include—

(*a*) website supply, web-hosting and distance maintenance of programmes and equipment,

(*b*) the supply of software and the updating of software,

(*c*) the supply of images, text and information, and the making available of databases,

(*d*) the supply of music, films and games (including games of chance and gambling games),

(*e*) the supply of political, cultural, artistic, sporting, scientific, educational or entertainment broadcasts (including broadcasts of events), and

(*f*) the supply of distance teaching.

(4) But where the supplier of a service and the supplier's customer communicate via electronic mail, this does not of itself mean that the service provided is an electronically supplied service for the purposes of this Schedule.][1]

Amendments—[1] Sch 4A inserted by FA 2009 s 76, Sch 36 paras 1, 11 with effect in relation to supplies made on or after 1 January 2010.

Prospective amendments—Para 9A to be inserted by FA 2009 s 76, Sch 36 paras 1, 15(3) with effect in relation to supplies made on or after 1 January 2011. Para 9A to read as follows—

"Admission to cultural, educational and entertainment activities etc

9A— (1) A supply to a relevant business person of services to which this paragraph applies is to be treated as made in the country in which the events in question actually take place.

(2) This paragraph applies to the provision of—

(*a*) services in respect of admission to cultural, artistic, sporting, scientific, educational, entertainment or similar events (including fairs and exhibitions), and

(*b*) ancillary services relating to admission to such events.".

[PART 3
EXCEPTIONS RELATING TO SUPPLIES NOT MADE TO RELEVANT BUSINESS PERSON

Intermediaries

10— (1) A supply of services to which this paragraph applies is to be treated as made in the same country as the supply to which it relates.

(2) This paragraph applies to a supply to a person who is not a relevant business person consisting of the making of arrangements for a supply by or to another person or of any other activity intended to facilitate the making of such a supply.][1]

Amendments—[1] Sch 4A inserted by FA 2009 s 76, Sch 36 paras 1, 11 with effect in relation to supplies made on or after 1 January 2010.][1]

[Transport of goods: general

11— (1) A supply of services to a person who is not a relevant business person consisting of the transportation of goods is to be treated as made in the country in which the transportation takes place, and (in a case where it takes place in more than one country) in proportion to the distances covered in each.

(2) For the purposes of sub-paragraph (1) transportation which takes place partly outside the territorial jurisdiction of a country is to be treated as taking place wholly in the country if—

(*a*) it takes place in the course of a journey between two points in the country (whether or not as part of a longer journey involving travel to or from another country), and

(*b*) the means of transport used does not (except in an emergency or involuntarily) stop, put in or land in another country in the course of the journey between those two points.

(3) This paragraph does not apply to a transportation of goods beginning in one member State and ending in another (see paragraph 12).][1]

Amendments—[1] Sch 4A inserted by FA 2009 s 76, Sch 36 paras 1, 11 with effect in relation to supplies made on or after 1 January 2010.

[Intra-Community transport of goods

12— A supply of services to a person who is not a relevant business person consisting of the transportation of goods which begins in one member State and ends in another is to be treated as made in the member State in which the transportation begins.][1]

Amendments—[1] Sch 4A inserted by FA 2009 s 76, Sch 36 paras 1, 11 with effect in relation to supplies made on or after 1 January 2010.

[Ancillary transport services

13— (1) A supply to a person who is not a relevant business person of ancillary transport services is to be treated as made where the services are physically performed.

(2) "Ancillary transport services" means loading, unloading handling and similar activities.][1]

Amendments—[1] Sch 4A inserted by FA 2009 s 76, Sch 36 paras 1, 11 with effect in relation to supplies made on or after 1 January 2010.

Prospective amendments—Para 13A to be inserted by FA 2009 s 76, Sch 36 paras 1, 17 with effect in relation to supplies made on or after 1 January 2013. Para 13A to read as follows—

"Long-term hiring of means of transport

13A— (1) A supply to a person who is not a relevant business person ("the recipient") of services consisting of the long-term hiring of a means of transport is to be treated as made in the country in which the recipient belongs.

But this is subject to sub-paragraph (2) and paragraph 3(3) and (4).

(2) A supply to a person who is not a relevant business person ("the recipient") of services consisting of the long-term hiring of a pleasure boat which is actually put at the disposal of the recipient at the supplier's business establishment, or some other fixed establishment of the supplier, is to be treated as made in the country where the pleasure boat is actually put at the disposal of the recipient.

(3) For the purposes of this Schedule, the hiring of a means of transport is "long-term" if it is not short-term (as to the meaning of which see paragraph 3(2)).".

[Valuation services etc

14 A supply to a person who is not a relevant business person of services consisting of the valuation of, or carrying out of work on, goods is to be treated as made where the services are physically performed.][1]

Amendments—[1] Sch 4A inserted by FA 2009 s 76, Sch 36 paras 1, 11 with effect in relation to supplies made on or after 1 January 2010.

Prospective amendments—Para 14A to be inserted by FA 2009 s 76, Sch 36 paras 1, 15(4) with effect in relation to supplies made on or after 1 January 2011. Para 14A to read as follows—

"Cultural, educational and entertainment services etc

14A— (1) A supply to a person who is not a relevant business person of services to which this paragraph applies is to be treated as made in the country in which the activities concerned actually take place.

(2) This paragraph applies to the provision of—

(*a*) services relating to cultural, artistic, sporting, scientific, educational, entertainment or similar activities (including fairs and exhibitions), and

(*b*) ancillary services relating to such activities, including services of organisers of such activities.".

[Electronic services

15 A supply consisting of the provision by a person who belongs in a country which is not a member State (other than the Isle of Man) of electronically supplied services (as to the meaning of which see paragraph 9(3) and (4)) to a person ("the recipient") who—

(*a*) is not a relevant business person, and

(*b*) belongs in a member State,

is to be treated as made in the country in which the recipient belongs.][1]

Amendments—[1] Sch 4A inserted by FA 2009 s 76, Sch 36 paras 1, 11 with effect in relation to supplies made on or after 1 January 2010.

[Other services provided to recipient belonging outside EC

16— (1) A supply consisting of the provision to a person ("the recipient") who—

(*a*) is not a relevant business person, and

(*b*) belongs in a country which is not a member State (other than the Isle of Man),

of services to which this paragraph applies is to be treated as made in the country in which the recipient belongs.

(2) This paragraph applies to—

(*a*) transfers and assignments of copyright, patents, licences, trademarks and similar rights,

(*b*) the acceptance of any obligation to refrain from pursuing or exercising (in whole or in part) any business activity or any rights within paragraph (*a*),

(*c*) advertising services,

(*d*) services of consultants, engineers, consultancy bureaux, lawyers, accountants, and similar services, data processing and provision of information, other than any services relating to land,

(*e*) banking, financial and insurance services (including reinsurance), other than the provision of safe deposit facilities,

(*f*) the provision of access to, and of transport or transmission through, natural gas and electricity distribution systems and the provision of other directly linked services,

(*g*) the supply of staff,

(*h*) the letting on hire of goods other than means of transport,

(*i*) telecommunication services (as to the meaning of which see paragraph 8(2)),

(*j*) radio and television broadcasting services, and

(*k*) electronically supplied services (as to the meaning of which see paragraph 9(3) and (4)).][1]

Amendments—[1] Sch 4A inserted by FA 2009 s 76, Sch 36 paras 1, 11 with effect in relation to supplies made on or after 1 January 2010.

SCHEDULE 5

SERVICES SUPPLIED WHERE RECEIVED[1]

Section 8

Commentary—*De Voil Indirect Tax Service* **V3.193**.

Cross references—VAT (Place of Supply of Services) Order, SI 1992/3121 art 16 (services within paragraphs 1–8 below supplied where the recipient belongs either (i) outside the EC or (ii) in another member state and carries on business).

Amendments—[1] Sch 5 repealed by FA 2009 s 76, Sch 36 paras 1, 12 with effect in relation to supplies made on or after 1 January 2010.

1 *Transfers and assignments of copyright, patents, licences, trademarks and similar rights.*[1]

Definitions—"Assignment", s 96(1).

Amendments—[1] Sch 5 repealed by FA 2009 s 76, Sch 36 paras 1, 12 with effect in relation to supplies made on or after 1 January 2010.

2 *Advertising services.*[1]

Simon's Tax Cases—*Bophuthatswana National Commercial Corp Ltd v C&E Comrs* [1992] STC 741*.

Amendments—[1] Sch 5 repealed by FA 2009 s 76, Sch 36 paras 1, 12 with effect in relation to supplies made on or after 1 January 2010.

3 Services of consultants, engineers, consultancy bureaux, lawyers, accountants and other similar services; data processing and provision of information (but excluding from this head any services relating to land).[1]

Simon's Tax Cases—*Bophuthatswana National Commercial Corp Ltd v C&E Comrs* [1992] STC 741*.

Amendments—[1] Sch 5 repealed by FA 2009 s 76, Sch 36 paras 1, 12 with effect in relation to supplies made on or after 1 January 2010.

4 Acceptance of any obligation to refrain from pursuing or exercising, in whole or part, any business activity or any such rights as are referred to in paragraph 1 above.[1]

Amendments—[1] Sch 5 repealed by FA 2009 s 76, Sch 36 paras 1, 12 with effect in relation to supplies made on or after 1 January 2010.

5 Banking, financial and insurance services (including reinsurance, but not including the provision of safe deposit facilities).[1]

Amendments—[1] Sch 5 repealed by FA 2009 s 76, Sch 36 paras 1, 12 with effect in relation to supplies made on or after 1 January 2010.

[5A The provision of access to, and of transport or transmission through, natural gas and electricity distribution systems and the provision of other directly linked services.][1 2]

Amendments—[1] This paragraph inserted by the VAT (Reverse Charge) (Gas and Electricity) Order, SI 2004/3149 with effect from 1 January 2005, in relation to supplies made on or after that date.

[2] Sch 5 repealed by FA 2009 s 76, Sch 36 paras 1, 12 with effect in relation to supplies made on or after 1 January 2010.

6 The supply of staff.[1]

Amendments—[1] Sch 5 repealed by FA 2009 s 76, Sch 36 paras 1, 12 with effect in relation to supplies made on or after 1 January 2010.

7 The letting on hire of goods other than means of transport.[1]

Amendments—[1] Sch 5 repealed by FA 2009 s 76, Sch 36 paras 1, 12 with effect in relation to supplies made on or after 1 January 2010.

[7A Telecommunications services, that is to say services relating to the transmission, emission or reception of signals, writing, images and sounds or information of any nature by wire, radio, optical or other electromagnetic systems, including—

(a) the related transfer or assignment of the right to use capacity for such transmission, emission or reception, and

(b) the provision of access to global information networks.][1, 2]

Amendments—[1] This paragraph which was inserted by Value Added Tax (Reverse Charge) (Anti-avoidance) Order, SI 1997/1523 art 3 in relation to any services performed on or after 1 July 1997, has been substituted by the VAT (Reverse Charge) (Amendment) Order, SI 2003/863 art 2(1), (2) with effect for any services performed after 30 June 2003.

[2] Sch 5 repealed by FA 2009 s 76, Sch 36 paras 1, 12 with effect in relation to supplies made on or after 1 January 2010.

[7B Radio and television broadcasting services.][1, 2]

Amendments—[1] This paragraph inserted by the VAT (Reverse Charge) (Amendment) Order, SI 2003/863 art 2(1), (3) with effect for any services performed after 30 June 2003.

[2] Sch 5 repealed by FA 2009 s 76, Sch 36 paras 1, 12 with effect in relation to supplies made on or after 1 January 2010.

[7C Electronically supplied services, for example—

(a) website supply, web-hosting and distance maintenance of programmes and equipment;

(b) the supply of software and the updating of software;

(c) the supply of images, text and information, and the making available of databases;

(d) the supply of music, films and games (including games of chance and gambling games);

(e) the supply of political, cultural, artistic, sporting, scientific and entertainment broadcasts (including broadcasts of events);

(f) the supply of distance teaching.

But where the supplier of a service and his customer communicate via electronic mail, this shall not of itself mean that the service performed is an electronically supplied service.][1, 2]

Amendments—[1] This paragraph inserted by the VAT (Reverse Charge) (Amendment) Order, SI 2003/863 art 2(1), (3) with effect for any services performed after 30 June 2003.

[2] Sch 5 repealed by FA 2009 s 76, Sch 36 paras 1, 12 with effect in relation to supplies made on or after 1 January 2010.

8 The services rendered by one person to another in procuring for the other any of the services mentioned in [paragraphs 1 to 7C][1] *above.*[2]

Amendments—[1] Words substituted for "paragraphs 1 to 7A" by the VAT (Reverse Charge) (Amendment) Order, SI 2003/863 art 2(1), (4) with effect for any services performed after 30 June 2003.

[2] Sch 5 repealed by FA 2009 s 76, Sch 36 paras 1, 12 with effect in relation to supplies made on or after 1 January 2010.

9 Any services not of a description specified in [paragraphs 1 to 7 and 8][1] above when supplied to a recipient who is registered under this Act.[2]

Amendments—[1] Words substituted for "paragraphs 1 to 8' by Value Added Tax (Reverse Charge) (Anti-avoidance) Order, SI 1997 1523 reg 3 in relation to any services performed on or after 1 July 1997.
[2] Sch 5 repealed by FA 2009 s 76, Sch 36 paras 1, 12 with effect in relation to supplies made on or after 1 January 2010.

10 Section 8(1) shall have effect in relation to any service—

(a) which are of a description specified in paragraph 9 above; and

(b) whose place of supply is determined by an order under section 7(11) to be in the United Kingdom,

as if the recipient belonged in the United Kingdom for the purposes of section 8(1)(b).[1]

Definitions—"Supply", s 5, Sch 4; "United Kingdom", s 96(11).
Amendments—[1] Sch 5 repealed by FA 2009 s 76, Sch 36 paras 1, 12 with effect in relation to supplies made on or after 1 January 2010.

VAT

[SCHEDULE 5A
GOODS ELIGIBLE TO BE FISCALLY WAREHOUSED

Section 18B

Description of goods	*Combined nomenclature code of the European Communities*
Tin	8001
Copper	7402
	7403
	7405
	7408
Zinc	7901
Nickel	7502
Aluminium	7601
Lead	7801
Indium	ex 811291
	ex 811299
Cereals	1001 to 1005
	1006: unprocessed rice only
	1007 to 1008
Oil seeds and oleaginous fruit	1201 to 1207
Coconuts, Brazil nuts and cashew nuts	0801
Other nuts	0502
Olives	071120
Grains and seeds (including soya beans)	1201 to 1207
Coffee, not roasted	0901 11 00
	0901 12 00
Tea	0902
Cocoa beans, whole or broken, raw or roasted	1801
Raw sugar	1701 11
	1701 12
Rubber, in primary forms or in plates, sheets or strip	4001
	4002
Wool	5101
Chemicals in bulk	Chapters 28 and 29
Mineral oils (including propane and butane; also including crude petroleum oils)	2709
	2710
	2711 12
	2711 13
Silver	7106
Platinum (palladium, rhodium)	7110 11 00
	7110 21 00
	7110 31 00
Potatoes	0701
Vegetable oils and fats and their fractions, whether or not refined, but not chemically modified	1507 to 1515][1]

Cross reference—VATA 1994 s 18B(8) (Treasury may by order vary this Schedule).
Amendments—[1] Schedule inserted by FA 1996 Sch 3 para 18, with effect from 1 June 1996 (see Finance Act 1996, Section 26, (Appointed Day) Order, SI 1996/1249).

SCHEDULE 6

VALUATION: SPECIAL CASES

Section 19

Cross references—See VATA 1994 s 20(2) (valuation of acquisitions from other member states otherwise than through a taxable supply: disapplication of this Schedule);
VATA 1994 s 52 (provision for regulations modifying this Schedule in relation to the valuation of supplies of goods under trading stamp schemes).

1— (1) Where—

(*a*) the value of a supply made by a taxable person for a consideration in money is (apart from this paragraph) less than its open market value, and
(*b*) the person making the supply and the person to whom it is made are connected, and
(*c*) if the supply is a taxable supply, the person to whom the supply is made is not entitled under sections 25 and 26 to credit for all the VAT on the supply,

the Commissioners may direct that the value of the supply shall be taken to be its open market value.

(2) A direction under this paragraph shall be given by notice in writing to the person making the supply, but no direction may be given more than 3 years after the time of the supply.

(3) A direction given to a person under this paragraph in respect of a supply made by him may include a direction that the value of any supply—

(*a*) which is made by him after the giving of the notice, or after such later date as may be specified in the notice, and
(*b*) as to which the conditions in paragraphs (*a*) to (*c*) of sub-paragraph (1) above are satisfied,

shall be taken to be its open market value.

(4) For the purposes of this paragraph any question whether a person is connected with another shall be determined in accordance with section 839 of the Taxes Act.

(5) This paragraph does not apply to a supply to which paragraph 10 below applies.

Commentary—*De Voil Indirect Tax Service* **V3.162**.
Definitions—"The Commissioners", s 96(10); "money", s 96(1); "open market value", s 19(5); "prescribed", s 96(1); "supply", s 5, Sch 4; "taxable person", s 3; "taxable supply", s 4(2); "the Taxes Act", s 96(1); "VAT", ss 1, 96(1).
Cross reference—See VATA 1994 s 83 (appeal to a tribunal in respect of a direction under this para).

[1A— (1) Where—

(*a*) the value of a supply made by a taxable person for a consideration is (apart from this sub-paragraph) less than its open market value,
(*b*) the taxable person is a motor manufacturer or motor dealer,
(*c*) the person to whom the supply is made is—

(i) an employee of the taxable person,
(ii) a person who, under the terms of his employment, provides services to the taxable person, or
(iii) a relative of a person falling within sub-paragraph (i) or (ii) above,

(*d*) the supply is a supply of services by virtue of sub-paragraph (4) of paragraph 5 of Schedule 4 (business goods put to private use etc),
(*e*) the goods mentioned in that sub-paragraph consist of a motor car (whether or not any particular motor car) that forms part of the stock in trade of the taxable person, and
(*f*) the supply is not one to which paragraph 1 above applies,

the Commissioners may direct that the value of the supply shall be taken to be its open market value.

(2) A direction under this paragraph shall be given by notice in writing to the person making the supply, but no direction may be given more than 3 years after the time of the supply.

(3) A direction given to a person under this paragraph in respect of a supply made by him may include a direction that the value of any supply—

(*a*) which is made by him after the giving of the notice, or after such later date as may be specified in the notice, and
(*b*) as to which the conditions in paragraphs (*a*) to (*f*) of sub-paragraph (1) above are satisfied,

shall be taken to be its open market value.

(4) In this paragraph—

"motor car" means any motor vehicle of a kind normally used on public roads which has three or more wheels and either—

(*a*) is constructed or adapted solely or mainly for the carriage of passengers, or (*b*) has to the rear of the driver's seat roofed accommodation which is fitted with side windows or which is constructed or adapted for the fitting of side windows,

but does not include any vehicle excluded by sub-paragraph (5) below;

"motor dealer" means a person whose business consists in whole or in part of obtaining supplies of, or acquiring from another member State or importing, new or second-hand motor cars for resale with a view to making an overall profit on the sale of them (whether or not a profit is made on each sale);

"motor manufacturer" means a person whose business consists in whole or part of producing motor cars including producing motor cars by conversion of a vehicle (whether a motor car or not);

"relative" means husband, wife, brother, sister, ancestor or lineal descendant;

"stock in trade" means new or second-hand motor cars (other than second-hand motor cars which are not qualifying motor cars within sub-paragraph (6) below) which are—

(*a*) produced by a motor manufacturer or, as the case may require, supplied to or acquired from another member State or imported by a motor dealer, for the purpose of resale, and

(*b*) intended to be sold—

(i) by a motor manufacturer within 12 months of their production, or

(ii) by a motor dealer within 12 months of their supply, acquisition from another member State or importation, as the case may require,

and such motor cars shall not cease to be stock in trade where they are temporarily put to a use in the motor manufacturer's or, as the case may be, the motor dealer's business which involves making them available for private use.

(5) The vehicles excluded by this sub-paragraph are—

(*a*) vehicles capable of accommodating only one person;

(*b*) vehicles which meet the requirements of Schedule 6 to the Road Vehicles (Construction and Use) Regulations 1986 and are capable of carrying twelve or more seated persons;

(*c*) vehicles of not less than three tonnes unladen weight (as defined in the Table to regulation 3(2) of the Road Vehicles (Construction and Use) Regulations 1986);

(*d*) vehicles constructed to carry a payload (the difference between—

(i) a vehicle's kerb weight (as defined in the Table to regulation 3(2) of the Road Vehicles (Construction and Use) Regulations 1986), and

(ii) its maximum gross weight (as defined in that Table)),

of one tonne or more;

(*e*) caravans, ambulances and prison vans;

(*f*) vehicles constructed for a special purpose other than the carriage of persons and having no other accommodation for carrying persons than such as is incidental to that purpose.

(6) For the purposes of this paragraph a motor car is a "qualifying motor car" if—

(*a*) it has never been supplied, acquired from another member State, or imported in circumstances in which the VAT on that supply, acquisition or importation was wholly excluded from credit as input tax by virtue of an order under section 25(7) (as at 17th March 2004 see article 7 of the Value Added Tax (Input Tax) Order 1992); or

(*b*) a taxable person has elected under such an order for it to be treated as such.

(7) The Treasury may by order amend any of the definitions in this paragraph.][1]

Commentary—*De Voil Indirect Tax Service* **V3.242**.

Amendments—[1] This paragraph inserted by FA 2004 s 22(1), (2), (5), (6) in relation to any use or availability for use on or after such day as the Treasury may by order made by statutory instrument appoint, whatever the date of the directions mentioned in VATA 1994 Sch 4 para 5(4). The appointed date is 1 January 2005 (by virtue of SI 2004/3104).

2 Where—

(*a*) the whole or part of a business carried on by a taxable person consists in supplying to a number of persons goods to be sold, whether by them or others, by retail, and

(*b*) those persons are not taxable persons,

the Commissioners may by notice in writing to the taxable person direct that the value of any such supply by him after the giving of the notice or after such later date as may be specified in the notice shall be taken to be its open market value on a sale by retail.

Commentary—*De Voil Indirect Tax Service* **V3.163**.

Simon's Tax Cases—*Direct Cosmetics Ltd and Laughtons Photographs Ltd v C&E Comrs* [1988] STC 540*; *Gold Star Publications Ltd v C&E Comrs* [1992] STC 365*; *Fine Art Developments plc v C&E Comrs* [1996] STC 246*.

Definitions—"Business", s 94; "the Commissioners", s 96(10); "open market value", s 19(5);

Cross reference—See VATA 1994 s 83 (appeal to a tribunal in respect of a direction under this para).

3— (1) Where—

(*a*) any goods whose supply involves their removal to the United Kingdom—

(i) are charged in connection with their removal to the United Kingdom with a duty of excise; or

(ii) on that removal are subject, in accordance with any provision for the time being having effect for transitional purposes in connection with the accession of any State to the European Communities, to any Community customs duty or agricultural levy of the Economic Community; or (*b*) the time of supply of any dutiable goods, or of any goods which comprise a mixture of dutiable goods and other goods, is determined under section 18(4) to be the duty point,

then the value of the supply shall be taken for the purposes of this Act to be the sum of its value apart from this paragraph and the amount, so far as not already included in that value, of the duty or, as the case may be, agricultural levy which has been or is to be paid in respect of the goods.

(2) In this paragraph "dutiable goods" and "duty point" have the same meanings as in section 18.

Commentary—*De Voil Indirect Tax Service* **V5.141**.
Definitions—"Supply", s 5, Sch 4; "United Kingdom", s 96(11).

4— (1) Where goods or services are supplied for a consideration in money and on terms allowing a discount for prompt payment, the consideration shall be taken for the purposes of section 19 as reduced by the discount, whether or not payment is made in accordance with those terms.

(2) This paragraph does not apply where the terms include any provision for payment by instalments.

Commentary—*De Voil Indirect Tax Service* **V3.157**.
Simon's Tax Cases—*Gold Star Publications Ltd v C&E Comrs* [1992] STC 365*.
Definitions—"Money", s 96(1).

5 ...

Amendments—Paragraph repealed by FA 2003 ss 19, 216, Sch 1 para 3, Sch 43 Pt 2 with effect for supplies of tokens, stamps or vouchers issued after 8 April 2003.

6— (1) Where there is a supply of goods by virtue of—

(*a*) a Treasury order under section 5(5); or
(*b*) paragraph 5(1) or 6 of Schedule 4 but otherwise than for a consideration); or
(*c*) paragraph 8 of that Schedule,

then, except where paragraph 10 below applies, the value of the supply shall be determined as follows.

(2) The value of the supply shall be taken to be—

(*a*) such consideration in money as would be payable by the person making the supply if he were, at the time of the supply, to purchase goods identical in every respect (including age and condition) to the goods concerned; or
(*b*) where the value cannot be ascertained in accordance with paragraph (*a*) above, such consideration in money as would be payable by that person if he were, at that time, to purchase goods similar to, and of the same age and condition as, the goods concerned; or
(*c*) where the value can be ascertained in accordance with neither paragraph (*a*) nor paragraph (*b*) above, the cost of producing the goods concerned if they were produced at that time.

(3) For the purposes of sub-paragraph (2) above the amount of consideration in money that would be payable by any person if he were to purchase any goods shall be taken to be the amount that would be so payable after the deduction of any amount included in the purchase price in respect of VAT on the supply of the goods to that person.

Commentary—*De Voil Indirect Tax Service* **V3.211, V3.213, V3.242, V3.243**.
Simon's Tax Cases—*C&E Comrs v Telemed Ltd* [1992] STC 89*; *C&E Comrs v Professional Footballers' Association (Enterprises) Ltd* [1993] STC 86*; *Church of England Children's Society v Revenue and Customs Commissioners* [2005] STC 1644.
Definitions—"Supply", s 5, Sch 4; "VAT", ss 1, 96(1).

7— [(1)][2] Where there is a supply of services by virtue of—

(*a*) a Treasury order under section 5(4); or
(*b*) [paragraph 5(4)][1] of Schedule 4 (but otherwise than for a consideration),

the value of the supply shall be taken to be the full cost to the taxable person of providing the services except where paragraph 10 below applies.

[(2) Regulations may, in relation to a supply of services by virtue of paragraph 5(4) of Schedule 4 (but otherwise than for a consideration), make provision for determining how the full cost to the taxable person of providing the services is to be calculated.

(3) The regulations may, in particular, make provision for the calculation to be made by reference to any prescribed period.

(4) The regulations may make—

(*a*) different provision for different circumstances;
(*b*) such incidental, supplementary, consequential or transitional provision as the Commissioners think fit.][2]

Commentary—*De Voil Indirect Tax Service* **V3.212**.
Simon's Tax Cases—*Comrs of Customs and Excise v Teknequip Ltd* [1987] STC 664*.
Definitions—"Supply", s 5, Sch 4; "taxable person", s 3;
Amendments—[1] Words in sub-para (*b*) substituted by FA 1995 s 33(1), (3)(*b*) and are deemed to have always had effect.
[2] Sub-s (1) numbered as such, and sub-ss (2)–(4) inserted by FA 2007 s 99(4), (5) with effect from 19 July 2007.

8 Where any supply of services is treated by virtue of section 8[, or any supply of goods is treated by virtue of section 9A,][1] as made by the person by whom they are received, the value of the supply shall be taken—

(*a*) in a case where the consideration for which the services [or goods][1] were in fact supplied to him was a consideration in money, to be such amount as is equal to that consideration; and

(*b*) in a case where that consideration did not consist or not wholly consist of money, to be such amount in money as is equivalent to that consideration.

Commentary—*De Voil Indirect Tax Service* **V3.231**.
Definitions—"Money", s 96(1); "supply", s 5, Sch 4.
Cross reference—See VAT (Reverse Charge) (Anti-avoidance) Order, SI 1997/1523 arts 7, 8 (modification of Sch 6 para 8 in relation to telecommunication services).
Amendments—[1] Words inserted by F(No 2)A 2005 s 5 with effect in relation to supplies made on or after 17 March 2005.

9— (1) This paragraph applies where a supply of services consists in the provision of accommodation falling within paragraph (*d*) of Item 1 of Group 1 in Schedule 9 and—

(*a*) that provision is made to an individual for a period exceeding 4 weeks; and

(*b*) throughout that period the accommodation is provided for the use of the individual either alone or together with one or more other persons who occupy the accommodation with him otherwise than at their own expense (whether incurred directly or indirectly).

(2) Where this paragraph applies—

(*a*) the value of so much of the supply as is in excess of 4 weeks shall be taken to be reduced to such part thereof as is attributable to facilities other than the right to occupy the accommodation; and

(*b*) that part shall be taken to be not less than 20 per cent.

Commentary—*De Voil Indirect Tax Service* **V3.166**.
Definitions—"Supply", s 5, Sch 4.

10— (1) This paragraph applies to a supply of goods or services, whether or not for consideration, which is made by an employer and consists of—

(*a*) the provision in the course of catering of food or beverages to his employees, or

(*b*) the provision of accommodation for his employees in a hotel, inn, boarding house or similar establishment.

(2) The value of a supply to which this paragraph applies shall be taken to be nil unless the supply is for a consideration consisting wholly or partly of money, and in that case its value shall be determined without regard to any consideration other than money.

Commentary—*De Voil Indirect Tax Service* **V3.166**.
HMRC Manuals—VAT Guidance V1-3; Supply and consideration, para 5.3 (supplies by employer to employees).
Definitions—"Money", s 96(1); "supply", s 5, Sch 4.

11— (1) Subject to the following provisions of this paragraph, where—

(*a*) there is a supply of goods or services; and

(*b*) any sum relevant for determining the value of the supply is expressed in a currency other than sterling,

then, for the purpose of valuing the supply, that sum is to be converted into sterling at the market rate which, on the relevant day, would apply in the United Kingdom to a purchase with sterling by the person to whom they are supplied of that sum in the currency in question.

(2) Where the Commissioners have published a notice which, for the purposes of this paragraph, specifies—

(*a*) rates of exchange; or

(*b*) methods of determining rates of exchange,

a rate specified in or determined in accordance with the notice, as for the time being in force, shall apply (instead of the rate for which sub-paragraph (1) above provides) in the case of any supply by a person who opts, in such manner as may be allowed by the Commissioners, for the use of that rate in relation to that supply.

(3) An option for the purposes of sub-paragraph (2) above for the use of a particular rate or method of determining a rate—

(*a*) shall not be exercised by any person except in relation to all such supplies by him as are of a particular description or after a particular date; and

(*b*) shall not be withdrawn or varied except with the consent of the Commissioners and in such manner as they may require.

(4) In specifying a method of determining a rate of exchange a notice published by the Commissioners under sub-paragraph (2) above may allow a person to apply to the Commissioners for the use, for the purpose of valuing some or all of his supplies, of a rate of exchange which is different from any which would otherwise apply.

(5) On an application made in accordance with provision contained in a notice under sub-paragraph (4) above, the Commissioners may authorise the use with respect to the applicant of such a rate of exchange, in such circumstances, in relation to such supplies and subject to such conditions as they think fit.

(6) A notice published by the Commissioners for the purposes of this paragraph may be withdrawn or varied by a subsequent notice published by the Commissioners.

(7) The time by reference to which the appropriate rate of exchange is to be determined for the purpose of valuing any supply is the time when the supply takes place; and, accordingly, the day on which it takes place is the relevant day for the purposes of sub-paragraph (1) above.

Commentary—*De Voil Indirect Tax Service* **V3.166, V3.393**.
Customs and Excise Notices—Notice 700: The VAT Guide, para 7.7 (values expressed in foreign currency).
Definitions—"The Commissioners", s 96(10); "supply", s 5, Sch 4; "United Kingdom", s 96(11).

12 Regulations may require that in prescribed circumstances there is to be taken into account, as constituting part of the consideration for the purposes of section 19(2) (where it would not otherwise be so taken into account), money paid in respect of the supply by persons other than those to whom the supply is made.

Commentary—*De Voil Indirect Tax Service* **V3.154**.
Definitions—"Supply", s 5, Sch 4.

13 A direction under paragraph 1 or 2 above may be varied or withdrawn by the Commissioners by a further direction given by notice in writing.

Commentary—*De Voil Indirect Tax Service* **V3.162, V3.163**.
Definitions—"The Commissioners", s 96(10).

SCHEDULE 7
VALUATION OF ACQUISITIONS FROM OTHER MEMBER STATES: SPECIAL CASES

Section 20

Cross reference—See VATA 1994 s 52 (provision for regulations modifying this Schedule in relation to the valuation of acquisitions of goods under trading stamp schemes).

1— (1) Where, in the case of the acquisition of any goods from another member State—

(*a*) the relevant transaction is for a consideration in money;

(*b*) the value of the relevant transaction is (apart from this paragraph) less than the transaction's open market value;

(*c*) the supplier and the person who acquires the goods are connected; and

(*d*) that person is not entitled under sections 25 and 26 to credit for all the VAT on the acquisition,

the Commissioners may direct that the value of the relevant transaction shall be taken to be its open market value.

(2) A direction under this paragraph shall be given by notice in writing to the person by whom the acquisition in question is made; but no direction may be given more than 3 years after the relevant time.

(3) A direction given to a person under this paragraph in respect of a transaction may include a direction that the value of any transaction—

(*a*) in pursuance of which goods are acquired by him from another member State after the giving of the notice, or after such later date as may be specified in the notice; and

(*b*) as to which the conditions in paragraphs (*a*) to (*d*) of sub-paragraph (1) above are satisfied,

shall be taken to be its open market value.

(4) For the purposes of this paragraph the open market value of a transaction in pursuance of which goods are acquired from another member State shall be taken to be the amount which would fall to be taken as its value under section 20(3) if it were for such consideration in money as would be payable by a person standing in no such relationship with any person as would affect that consideration.

(5) For the purposes of this paragraph any question whether a person is connected with another shall be determined in accordance with section 839 of the Taxes Act.

(6) A direction under this paragraph may be varied or withdrawn by the Commissioners by a further direction given by notice in writing.

Commentary—*De Voil Indirect Tax Service* **V3.390, V3.391**.
Definitions—"Acquisition of goods from another member State", s 11; "another member State", s 96(1); "the Commissioners", s 96(1); "money", s 96(1); "open market value", s 19(5); "prescribed", s 96(1); "the Taxes Act", s 96(1); "VAT", ss 1, 96(1).
Cross reference—See VATA 1994 s 83 (appeal to a tribunal in respect of a direction under this para).

2— (1) Where, in such cases as the Commissioners may by regulations prescribe, goods acquired in the United Kingdom from another member State—

(*a*) are charged in connection with their removal to the United Kingdom with a duty of excise; or

(*b*) on that removal are subject, in accordance with any provision for the time being having effect for transitional purposes in connection with the accession of any State to the European Communities, to any Community customs duty or agricultural levy of the Economic Community, then the value of the relevant transaction shall be taken for the purposes of this Act to be the sum of its value apart from this paragraph and the amount, so far as not already included in that value, of the duty or, as the case may be, agricultural levy which has been or is to be paid in respect of those goods.

(2) Sub-paragraph (1) above shall not require the inclusion of any amount of duty or agricultural levy in the value of a transaction in pursuance of which there is an acquisition of goods which, under subsection (4) of section 18, is treated as taking place before the time which is the duty point within the meaning of that section.

Commentary—*De Voil Indirect Tax Service* **V3.392**.
Regulations—See VAT Regulations, SI 1995/2518 regs 96, 97.
Definitions—"Amount of any duty of excise", s 96(5); "the Commissioners", s 96(1).
Cross reference—See VAT Regulations, SI 1995/2518 reg 97 (cases to which this para applies).

3— (1) Where goods are acquired from another member State in pursuance of anything which is treated as a supply for the purposes of this Act by virtue of paragraph 5(1) or 6 of Schedule 4, the value of the relevant transaction shall be determined, in a case where there is no consideration, as follows.

(2) The value of the transaction shall be taken to be—

(*a*) such consideration in money as would be payable by the supplier if he were, at the time of the acquisition, to purchase goods identical in every respect (including age and condition) to the goods concerned; or
(*b*) where the value cannot be ascertained in accordance with paragraph (*a*) above, such consideration in money as would be payable by the supplier if he were, at that time, to purchase goods similar to, and of the same age and condition as, the goods concerned; or
(*c*) where the value can be ascertained in accordance with neither paragraph (*a*) nor paragraph (*b*) above, the cost of producing the goods concerned if they were produced at that time.

(3) For the purposes of sub-paragraph (2) above the amount of consideration in money that would be payable by any person if he were to purchase any goods shall be taken to be the amount that would be so payable after the deduction of any amount included in the purchase price in respect of VAT on the supply of the goods to that person.

Commentary—*De Voil Indirect Tax Service* **V3.390**.
Definitions—"Acquisition of goods from another member State", s 11; "another member State", s 11; "VAT", ss 1, 96(1).

4— (1) Subject to the following provisions of this paragraph, where—

(*a*) goods are acquired from another member State; and
(*b*) any sum relevant for determining the value of the relevant transaction is expressed in a currency other than sterling,

then, for the purpose of valuing the relevant transaction, that sum is to be converted into sterling at the market rate which, on the relevant day, would apply in the United Kingdom to a purchase with sterling by the person making the acquisition of that sum in the currency in question.

(2) Where the Commissioners have published a notice which, for the purposes of this paragraph, specifies—

(*a*) rates of exchange; or
(*b*) methods of determining rates of exchange,

a rate specified in or determined in accordance with the notice, as for the time being in force, shall apply (instead of the rate for which sub-paragraph (1) above provides) in the case of any transaction in pursuance of which goods are acquired by a person who opts, in such manner as may be allowed by the Commissioners, for the use of that rate in relation to that transaction.

(3) An option for the purposes of sub-paragraph (2) above for the use of a particular rate or method of determining a rate—

(*a*) shall not be exercised by any person except in relation to all such transactions in pursuance of which goods are acquired by him from another member State as are of a particular description or after a particular date; and
(*b*) shall not be withdrawn or varied except with the consent of the Commissioners and in such manner as they may require.

(4) In specifying a method of determining a rate of exchange a notice published by the Commissioners under sub-paragraph (2) above may allow a person to apply to the Commissioners for the use, for the purpose of valuing some or all of the transactions in pursuance of which goods are acquired by him from another member State, of a rate of exchange which is different from any which would otherwise apply.

(5) On an application made in accordance with provision contained in a notice under sub-paragraph (4) above, the Commissioners may authorise the use with respect to the applicant of such a rate of exchange, in such circumstances, in relation to such transactions and subject to such conditions as they think fit.

(6) A notice published by the Commissioners for the purposes of this paragraph may be withdrawn or varied by a subsequent notice published by the Commissioners.

(7) Where goods are acquired from another member State, the appropriate rate of exchange is to be determined for the purpose of valuing the relevant transaction by reference to the relevant time; and, accordingly, the day on which that time falls is the relevant day for the purposes of sub-paragraph (1) above.

Commentary—*De Voil Indirect Tax Service* **V3.166, V3.393.**
Definitions—"Acquisition of goods from another member State", s 11; "amount of any duty of excise", s 96(5); "another member State", s 96(1); "the Commissioners", s 96(1); "United Kingdom", s 96(11).

5 In this Schedule—

"relevant transaction", in relation to any acquisition of goods from another member State, means the transaction in pursuance of which the goods are acquired;

"the relevant time", in relation to any such acquisition, means—

(*a*) if the person by whom the goods are acquired is not a taxable person and the time of acquisition does not fall to be determined in accordance with regulations made under section 12(3), the time of the event which, in relation to that acquisition, is the first relevant event for the purposes of taxing the acquisition; and

(*b*) in any other case, the time of acquisition.

[SCHEDULE 7A

CHARGE AT REDUCED RATE][1]

Section 29A

Amendments—[1] This Schedule inserted by FA 2001 s 99(5), Sch 31 with effect for supplies made, and acquisitions and importations taking place, after 31 October 2001.

[PART I

INDEX TO REDUCED-RATE SUPPLIES OF GOODS AND SERVICES

Children's car seats	Group 5
[Contraceptive products	Group 8][2]
Domestic fuel or power	Group 1
Energy-saving materials: installation	Group 2
Heating equipment, security goods and gas supplies: grant-funded installation or connection	Group 3
[Installation of mobility aids for the elderly	Group 10][3]
Residential renovations and alterations	Group 7
Residential conversions	Group 6
[Smoking cessation products	Group 11][3]
[Welfare advice or information	Group 9][2]
Women's sanitary products][1]	Group 4

Amendments—[1] This Schedule inserted by FA 2001 s 99(5), Sch 31 with effect for supplies made, and acquisitions and importations taking place, after 31 October 2001.
[2] Entries inserted by the Value Added Tax (Reduced Rate) Order, SI 2006/1472 arts 2, 3 with effect from 1 July 2006.
[3] Entries inserted by the Value Added Tax (Reduced Rate) Order, SI 2007/1601 arts 2, 3. Entry "Installation of mobility aids for the elderly" has effect in relation to supplies made on or after 1 July 2007. Entry "Smoking cessation products" has effect in relation to supplies made on or after 1 July 2007 but before 1 July 2008.

[PART II

THE GROUPS

GROUP 1

SUPPLIES OF DOMESTIC FUEL OR POWER

Item No.

1 Supplies for qualifying use of—

(*a*) coal, coke or other solid substances held out for sale solely as fuel;
(*b*) coal gas, water gas, producer gases or similar gases;
(*c*) petroleum gases, or other gaseous hydrocarbons, whether in a gaseous or liquid state;
(*d*) fuel oil, gas oil or kerosene; or
(*e*) electricity, heat or air-conditioning.

NOTES:

Matters included or not included in the supplies

1—(1) Item 1(*a*) shall be deemed to include combustible materials put up for sale for kindling fires but shall not include matches.

(2) Item 1(*b*) and (*c*) shall not include any road fuel gas (within the meaning of the Hydrocarbon Oil Duties Act 1979) on which a duty of excise has been charged or is chargeable.

(3) Item 1(*d*) shall not include hydrocarbon oil on which a duty of excise has been or is to be charged without relief from, or rebate of, such duty by virtue of the provisions of the Hydrocarbon Oil Duties Act 1979[, unless the oil is—

(*a*) kerosene in respect of which a relevant declaration has been made under section 13AC(3) of that Act (use of rebated kerosene for private pleasure-flying); or

(*b*) oil in respect of which a relevant declaration has been made under section 14E(3) of that Act (use of rebated heavy oil for private pleasure craft)][2].

Meaning of "fuel oil", "gas oil" and "kerosene"

2—(1) In this Group "fuel oil" means heavy oil which contains in solution an amount of asphaltenes of not less than 0.5 per cent. or which contains less than 0.5 per cent. but not less than 0.1 per cent. of asphaltenes and has a closed flash point not exceeding 150°C.

(2) In this Group "gas oil" means heavy oil of which not more than 50 per cent. by volume distils at a temperature not exceeding 240°C and of which more than 50 per cent. by volume distils at a temperature not exceeding 340°C.

(3) In this Group "kerosene" means heavy oil of which more than 50 per cent. by volume distils at a temperature not exceeding 240°C.

(4) In this paragraph "heavy oil" has the same meaning as in the Hydrocarbon Oil Duties Act 1979.

Meaning of "qualifying use"

3 In this Group "qualifying use" means—

(*a*) domestic use; or

(*b*) use by a charity otherwise than in the course or furtherance of a business.

Supplies only partly for qualifying use

4 For the purposes of this Group, where there is a supply of goods partly for qualifying use and partly not—

(*a*) if at least 60 per cent. of the goods are supplied for qualifying use, the whole supply shall be treated as a supply for qualifying use; and

(*b*) in any other case, an apportionment shall be made to determine the extent to which the supply is a supply for qualifying use.

Supplies deemed to be for domestic use

5 For the purposes of this Group the following supplies are always for domestic use—

(*a*) a supply of not more than one tonne of coal or coke held out for sale as domestic fuel;

(*b* a supply of wood, peat or charcoal not intended for sale by the recipient;

(*c*) a supply to a person at any premises of piped gas (that is, gas within item 1(*b*), or petroleum gas in a gaseous state, provided through pipes) where the gas (together with any other piped gas provided to him at the premises by the same supplier) was not provided at a rate exceeding 150 therms a month or, if the supplier charges for the gas by reference to the number of kilowatt hours supplied, 4397 kilowatt hours a month;

(*d*) a supply of petroleum gas in a liquid state where the gas is supplied in cylinders the net weight of each of which is less than 50 kilogrammes and either the number of cylinders supplied is 20 or fewer or the gas is not intended for sale by the recipient;

(*e*) a supply of petroleum gas in a liquid state, otherwise than in cylinders, to a person at any premises at which he is not able to store more than two tonnes of such gas;

(*f*) a supply of not more than 2,300 litres of fuel oil, gas oil or kerosene;

(*g*) a supply of electricity to a person at any premises where the electricity (together with any other electricity provided to him at the premises by the same supplier) was not provided at a rate exceeding 1000 kilowatt hours a month.

Other supplies that are for domestic use

6 For the purposes of this Group supplies not within paragraph 5 are for domestic use if and only if the goods supplied are for use in—

(*a*) a building, or part of a building, that consists of a dwelling or number of dwellings;

(*b*) a building, or part of a building, used for a relevant residential purpose;

(*c*) self-catering holiday accommodation;

(*d*) a caravan; or

(*e*) a houseboat.

Interpretation of paragraph 6

7—(1) For the purposes of this Group, "use for a relevant residential purpose" means use as—

(*a*) a home or other institution providing residential accommodation for children, (*b*) a home or other institution providing residential accommodation with personal care for persons in need of personal care by reason of old age, disablement, past or present dependence on alcohol or drugs or past or present mental disorder,

(*c*) a hospice,

(*d*) residential accommodation for students or school pupils,

(*e*) residential accommodation for members of any of the armed forces,

(*f*) a monastery, nunnery or similar establishment, or

(*g*) an institution which is the sole or main residence of at least 90 per cent. of its residents,

except use as a hospital, a prison or similar institution or an hotel or inn or similar establishment.

(2) For the purposes of this Group "self-catering holiday accommodation" includes any accommodation advertised or held out as such.

(3) In paragraph 6 "houseboat" means a boat or other floating decked structure designed or adapted for use solely as a place of permanent habitation and not having means of, or capable of being readily adapted for, self-propulsion.][1]

Amendments—[1] This Schedule inserted by FA 2001 s 99(5), Sch 31 with effect for supplies made, and acquisitions and importations taking place, after 31 October 2001.

[2] In Note 1 para (3), words inserted at end by the Value Added Tax (Reduced Rate) (Supplies of Domestic Fuel or Power) Order, SI 2008/2676 art 2 with effect from 1 November 2008.

[GROUP 2
INSTALLATION OF ENERGY-SAVING MATERIALS

Item No.

1 Supplies of services of installing energy-saving materials in—

(*a*) residential accommodation, or

(*b*) a building intended for use solely for a relevant charitable purpose.

2 Supplies of energy-saving materials by a person who installs those materials in—

(*a*) residential accommodation, or

(*b*) a building intended for use solely for a relevant charitable purpose.

NOTES:

Meaning of "energy-saving materials"

1 For the purposes of this Group "energy-saving materials" means any of the following—

(*a*) insulation for walls, floors, ceilings, roofs or lofts or for water tanks, pipes or other plumbing fittings;

(*b*) draught stripping for windows and doors;

(*c*) central heating system controls (including thermostatic radiator valves);

(*d*) hot water system controls;

(*e*) solar panels;

(*f*) wind turbines;

(*g*) water turbines;

[(*h*) ground source heat pumps][2].

[(*i*) air source heat pumps;

(*j*) micro combined heat and power units;][3]

[(*k*) boilers designed to be fuelled solely by wood, straw or similar vegetal matter.][4]

Meaning of "residential accommodation"

2—(1) For the purposes of this Group "residential accommodation" means—

(*a*) a building, or part of a building, that consists of a dwelling or a number of dwellings;

(*b*) a building, or part of a building, used for a relevant residential purpose;

(*c*) a caravan used as a place of permanent habitation; or

(*d*) a houseboat.

(2) For the purposes of this Group "use for a relevant residential purpose" has the same meaning as it has for the purposes of Group 1 (see paragraph 7(1) of the Notes to that Group).

(3) In sub-paragraph (1)(*d*) "houseboat" has the meaning given by paragraph 7(3) of the Notes to Group 1.

Meaning of "use for a relevant charitable purpose"

3 For the purposes of this Group "use for a relevant charitable purpose" means use by a charity in either or both of the following ways, namely—

(*a*) otherwise than in the course or furtherance of a business;

(*b*) as a village hall or similarly in providing social or recreational facilities for a local community.][1]

Amendments—[1] This Schedule inserted by FA 2001 s 99(5), Sch 31 with effect for supplies made, and acquisitions and importations taking place, after 31 October 2001.

[2] Note (1)(*h*) inserted by the VAT (Reduced Rate) Order, SI 2004/777 with effect from 1 June 2004.

[3] Note (1)(*i*), (*j*) inserted by the VAT (Reduced Rate) Order, SI 2005/726 with effect from 7 April 2005.
[4] Note (1)(*k*) inserted by the VAT (Reduced Rate) (No 2) Order, SI 2005/3329 with effect from 1 January 2006.

[GROUP 3

GRANT-FUNDED INSTALLATION OF HEATING EQUIPMENT OR SECURITY GOODS OR CONNECTION OF GAS SUPPLY

Item No.

1 Supplies to a qualifying person of any services of installing heating appliances in the qualifying person's sole or main residence.

2 Supplies of heating appliances made to a qualifying person by a person who installs those appliances in the qualifying person's sole or main residence.

3 Supplies to a qualifying person of services of connecting, or reconnecting, a mains gas supply to the qualifying person's sole or main residence.

4 Supplies of goods made to a qualifying person by a person connecting, or reconnecting, a mains gas supply to the qualifying person's sole or main residence, being goods whose installation is necessary for the connection, or reconnection, of the mains gas supply.

5 Supplies to a qualifying person of services of installing, maintaining or repairing a central heating system in the qualifying person's sole or main residence.

6 Supplies of goods made to a qualifying person by a person installing, maintaining or repairing a central heating system in the qualifying person's sole or main residence, being goods whose installation is necessary for the installation, maintenance or repair of the central heating system.

7 Supplies consisting in the leasing of goods that form the whole or part of a central heating system installed in the sole or main residence of a qualifying person.

8 Supplies of goods that form the whole or part of a central heating system installed in a qualifying person's sole or main residence and that, immediately before being supplied, were goods leased under arrangements such that the consideration for the supplies consisting in the leasing of the goods was, in whole or in part, funded by a grant made under a relevant scheme.

[8A Supplies to a qualifying person of services of installing, maintaining or repairing a renewable source heating system in the qualifying person's sole or main residence.][2]

[8B Supplies of goods made to a qualifying person by a person installing, maintaining or repairing a renewable source heating system in the qualifying person's sole or main residence, being goods whose installation is necessary for the installation, maintenance or repair of the system.][2]

9 Supplies to a qualifying person of services of installing qualifying security goods in the qualifying person's sole or main residence.

10 Supplies of qualifying security goods made to a qualifying person by a person who installs those goods in the qualifying person's sole or main residence.

NOTES:

Supply only included so far as grant-funded

1—(1) Each of [items 1 to 7 and 8A to 10][2] applies to a supply only to the extent that the consideration for the supply is, or is to be, funded by a grant made under a relevant scheme.

(2) Item 8 applies to a supply only to the extent that the consideration for the supply—

(*a*) is, or is to be, funded by a grant made under a relevant scheme; or

(*b*) is a payment becoming due only by reason of the termination (whether by the passage of time or otherwise) of the leasing of the goods in question.

Meaning of "relevant scheme"

2—(1) For the purposes of this Group a scheme is a "relevant scheme" if it is one which satisfies the conditions specified in this paragraph.

(2) The first condition is that the scheme has as one of its objectives the funding of the installation of energy-saving materials in the homes of any persons who are qualifying persons.

(3) The second condition is that the scheme disburses, whether directly or indirectly, its grants in whole or in part out of funds made available to it in order to achieve that objective—

(*a*) by the Secretary of State,

(*b*) by the Scottish Ministers,

(*c*) by the National Assembly for Wales,

(*d*) by a Minister (within the meaning given by section 7(3) of the Northern Ireland Act 1998) or a Northern Ireland department,

(*e*) by the European Community,

(*f*) under an arrangement approved by the Gas and Electricity Markets Authority,

(*g*) under an arrangement approved by the Director General of Electricity Supply for Northern Ireland, or

(*h*) by a local authority.

(4) The reference in sub-paragraph (3)(*f*) to an arrangement approved by the Gas and Electricity Markets Authority includes a reference to an arrangement approved by the Director General of Electricity Supply, or the Director General of Gas Supply, before the transfer (under the Utilities Act 2000) of his functions to the Authority.

Apportionment of grants that also cover other supplies

3 Where a grant is made under a relevant scheme in order—

(*a*) to fund a supply of a description to which any of items 1 to 10 applies ("the relevant supply"), and

(*b*) also to fund a supply to which none of those items applies ("the non-relevant supply"),

the proportion of the grant that is to be attributed, for the purposes of paragraph 1, to the relevant supply shall be the same proportion as the consideration reasonably attributable to that supply bears to the consideration for that supply and for the non-relevant supply.

Meaning of "heating appliances"

4 For the purposes of items 1 and 2 "heating appliances" means any of the following—

(*a*) gas-fired room heaters that are fitted with thermostatic controls;
(*b*) electric storage heaters;
(*c*) closed solid fuel fire cassettes;
(*d*) electric dual immersion water heaters with [factory-insulated][2] hot water tanks;
(*e*) gas-fired boilers;
(*f*) oil-fired boilers;
(*g*) radiators.

[Meaning of "central heating system"

4A For the purposes of items 5 to 8 "central heating system" includes a system which generates electricity.][2]

[Meaning of "renewable source heating system"

4B For the purposes of items 8A and 8B "renewable source heating system" means a space or water heating system which uses energy from—

(*a*) renewable sources, including solar, wind and hydroelectric power; or
(*b*) near renewable resources, including ground and air heat.][2]

Meaning of "qualifying security goods"

5 For the purposes of items 9 and 10 "qualifying security goods" means any of the following—

(*a*) locks or bolts for windows;
(*b*) locks, bolts or security chains for doors;
(*c*) spy holes;
(*d*) smoke alarms.

Meaning of "qualifying person"

6—(1) For the purposes of this Group, a person to whom a supply is made is "a qualifying person" if at the time of the supply he—

(*a*) is aged 60 or over; or
(*b*) is in receipt of one or more of the benefits mentioned in sub-paragraph (2).

(2) Those benefits are—

(*a*) council tax benefit under Part VII of the Contributions and Benefits Act;

(*b*) disability living allowance under Part III of the Contributions and Benefits Act or Part III of the Northern Ireland Act;

(*c*) [any element of child tax credit other than the family element, working tax credit,][3] housing benefit or income support under Part VII of the Contributions and Benefits Act or Part VII of the Northern Ireland Act;

(*d*) an income-based jobseeker's allowance within the meaning of section 1(4) of the Jobseekers Act 1995 or Article 3(4) of the Jobseekers (Northern Ireland) Order 1995;

(*e*) disablement pension under Part V of the Contributions and Benefits Act, or Part V of the Northern Ireland Act, that is payable at the increased rate provided for under section 104 (constant attendance allowance) of the Act concerned;

(*f*) war disablement pension under the Naval, Military and Air Forces Etc. (Disablement and Death) Service Pensions Order 1983 that is payable at the increased rate provided for under article 14 (constant attendance allowance) or article 26A (mobility supplement) of that Order.

(3) In sub-paragraph (2)—

(*a*) "the Contributions and Benefits Act" means the Social Security Contributions and Benefits Act 1992; and

(*b*) "the Northern Ireland Act" means the Social Security Contributions and Benefits (Northern Ireland) Act 1992.][1]

Amendments—[1] This Schedule inserted by FA 2001 s 99(5), Sch 31 with effect for supplies made, and acquisitions and importations taking place, after 31 October 2001.

[2] Items 8A, 8B inserted, words in Notes (1), (4) substituted, and Notes (4A), (4B) inserted, by the VAT (Reduced Rate) Order, SI 2002/1100 arts 2, 3 with effect from 1 June 2002.

[3] Words substituted by TCA 2002 s 47, Sch 3 paras 47, 48 with effect from 6 April 2003 (by virtue of SI 2003/962).

[GROUP 4
WOMEN'S SANITARY PRODUCTS

Item No.

1 Supplies of women's sanitary products.

NOTES:

Meaning of "women's sanitary products"

1—(1) In this Group "women's sanitary products" means women's sanitary products of any of the following descriptions—

(*a*) subject to sub-paragraph (2), products that are designed, and marketed, as being solely for use for absorbing, or otherwise collecting, lochia or menstrual flow;

(*b*) panty liners, other than panty liners that are designed as being primarily for use as incontinence products;

(*c*) sanitary belts.

(2) Sub-paragraph (1)(*a*) does not include protective briefs or any other form of clothing.][1]

Amendments—[1] This Schedule inserted by FA 2001 s 99(5), Sch 31 with effect for supplies made, and acquisitions and importations taking place, after 31 October 2001.

[GROUP 5
CHILDREN'S CAR SEATS

Item No.

1 Supplies of children's car seats.

NOTES:

Meaning of "children's car seats"

1—(1) For the purposes of this Group, the following are "children's car seats"—

(*a*) a safety seat;

[(*aa*) a related base unit for a safety seat;][2]

(*b*) the combination of a safety seat and a related wheeled framework;

(*c*) a booster seat;

(*d*) a booster cushion.

(2) In this Group "child" means a person aged under 14 years.

Meaning of "safety seat"

2 In this Group "safety seat" means a seat—

(*a*) designed to be sat in by a child in a road vehicle,

[(*b*) designed so that, when in use in a road vehicle, it can be restrained in one or more of the following ways—

(i) by a seat belt fitted in the vehicle, or

(ii) by belts, or anchorages, that form part of the seat being attached to the vehicle, or

(iii) by a related base unit, and][2]

(*c*) incorporating an integral harness, or integral impact shield, for restraining a child seated in it.

[Meaning of "related base unit"

2A In this Group "related base unit" means a base unit which is designed solely for the purpose of attaching a safety seat securely in a road vehicle by means of anchorages that form part of the base unit and which, when in use in a road vehicle, can be restrained in one or more of the following ways—

(*a*) by a seat belt fitted in the vehicle, or

(*b*) by permanent anchorage points in the vehicle, or

(*c*) by belts attached to permanent anchorage points in the vehicle.][2]

Meaning of "related wheeled framework"

3 For the purposes of this Group, a wheeled framework is "related" to a safety seat if the framework and the seat are each designed so that—

(*a*) when the seat is not in use in a road vehicle it can be attached to the framework, and

(*b*) when the seat is so attached, the combination of the seat and the framework can be used as a child's pushchair.

Meaning of "booster seat"

4 In this Group "booster seat" means a seat designed—

(*a*) to be sat in by a child in a road vehicle, and

(*b*) so that, when in use in a road vehicle, it and a child seated in it can be restrained by a seat belt fitted in the vehicle.

Meaning of "booster cushion"

5 In this Group "booster cushion" means a cushion designed—

(*a*) to be sat on by a child in a road vehicle, and

(*b*) so that a child seated on it can be restrained by a seat belt fitted in the vehicle.][1]

Amendments—[1] This Schedule inserted by FA 2001 s 99(5), Sch 31 with effect for supplies made, and acquisitions and importations taking place, after 31 October 2001.

[2] In Note 1, para (1)(*aa*) inserted, Note 2 para (*b*) substituted, and Note 2A inserted, by the Value Added Tax (Reduced Rate) (Children's Car Seats) Order, SI 2009/1359 arts 2, 3 with effect in relation to supplies made, and acquisitions and importations taking place, on or after 1 July 2009.

[GROUP 6
RESIDENTIAL CONVERSIONS

Item No.

1 The supply, in the course of a qualifying conversion, of qualifying services related to the conversion.

2 The supply of building materials if—

(*a*) the materials are supplied by a person who, in the course of a qualifying conversion, is supplying qualifying services related to the conversion, and

(*b*) those services include the incorporation of the materials in the building concerned or its immediate site.

NOTES:

Supplies only partly within item 1

1—(1) Sub-paragraph (2) applies where a supply of services is only in part a supply to which item 1 applies.

(2) The supply, to the extent that it is one to which item 1 applies, is to be taken to be a supply to which item 1 applies.

(3) An apportionment may be made to determine that extent.

Meaning of "qualifying conversion"

2—(1) A "qualifying conversion" means—

(*a*) a changed number of dwellings conversion (see paragraph 3);

(*b*) a house in multiple occupation conversion (see paragraph 5); or

(*c*) a special residential conversion (see paragraph 7).

(2) Sub-paragraph (1) is subject to paragraphs 9 and 10.

Meaning of "changed number of dwellings conversion"

3—(1) A "changed number of dwellings conversion" is—

(*a*) a conversion of premises consisting of a building where the conditions specified in this paragraph are satisfied, or

(*b*) a conversion of premises consisting of a part of a building where those conditions are satisfied.

(2) The first condition is that after the conversion the premises being converted contain a number of single household dwellings that is—

(*a*) different from the number (if any) that the premises contain before the conversion, and

(*b*) greater than, or equal to, one.

(3) The second condition is that there is no part of the premises being converted that is a part that after the conversion contains the same number of single household dwellings (whether zero, one or two or more) as before the conversion.

Meaning of "single household dwelling" and "multiple occupancy dwelling"

4—(1) For the purposes of this Group "single household dwelling" means a dwelling—

(*a*) that is designed for occupation by a single household, and

(*b*) in relation to which the conditions set out in sub-paragraph (3) are satisfied.

(2) For the purposes of this Group "multiple occupancy dwelling" means a dwelling—

(*a*) that is designed for occupation by persons not forming a single household, ...[2]

[(*aa*) that is not to any extent used for a relevant residential purpose, and][2]

(*b*) in relation to which the conditions set out in sub-paragraph (3) are satisfied.

(3) The conditions are—

(*a*) that the dwelling consists of self-contained living accommodation,
(*b*) that there is no provision for direct internal access from the dwelling to any other dwelling or part of a dwelling,
(*c*) that the separate use of the dwelling is not prohibited by the terms of any covenant, statutory planning consent or similar provision, and
(*d*) that the separate disposal of the dwelling is not prohibited by any such terms.

(4) For the purposes of this paragraph, a dwelling "is designed" for occupation of a particular kind if it is so designed—

(*a*) as a result of having been originally constructed for occupation of that kind and not having been subsequently adapted for occupation of any other kind, or
(*b*) as a result of adaptation.

Meaning of "house in multiple occupation conversion"

5—(1) A "house in multiple occupation conversion" is—

(*a*) a conversion of premises consisting of a building where the condition specified in sub-paragraph (2) below is satisfied, or
(*b*) a conversion of premises consisting of a part of a building where that condition is satisfied.

(2) The condition is that—

[(*a*) before the conversion the premises being converted do not contain any multiple occupancy dwellings,][2]
(*b*) after the conversion those premises contain only a multiple occupancy dwelling or two or more such dwellings, and
(*c*) the use to which those premises are intended to be put after the conversion is not to any extent use for a relevant residential purpose.

Meaning of "use for a relevant residential purpose"

6 For the purposes of this Group "use for a relevant residential purpose" means use as—

(*a*) a home or other institution providing residential accommodation for children,
(*b*) a home or other institution providing residential accommodation with personal care for persons in need of personal care by reason of old age, disablement, past or present dependence on alcohol or drugs or past or present mental disorder,
(*c*) a hospice,
(*d*) residential accommodation for students or school pupils,
(*e*) residential accommodation for members of any of the armed forces,
(*f*) a monastery, nunnery or similar establishment, or
(*g*) an institution which is the sole or main residence of at least 90 per cent. of its residents,

except use as a hospital, prison or similar institution or an hotel, inn or similar establishment.

Meaning of "special residential conversion"

7—(1) A "special residential conversion" is a conversion of premises consisting of—

(*a*) a building or two or more buildings,
(*b*) a part of a building or two or more parts of buildings, or
(*c*) a combination of—
  (i) a building or two or more buildings, and
  (ii) a part of a building or two or more parts of buildings,

where the conditions specified in this paragraph are satisfied.

[(2) The first condition is that—

(*a*) the use to which the premises being converted were last put before the conversion was not to any extent use for a relevant residential purpose, and
(*b*) those premises are intended to be used solely for a relevant residential purpose after the conversion.][2]

(3)–(5) …[2]

(6) The [second][2] condition is that, where the relevant residential purpose [for which the premises are intended to be used][2] is an institutional purpose, the premises being converted must be intended to form after the conversion the entirety of an institution used for that purpose.

(7) In sub-paragraph (6) "institutional purpose" means a purpose within paragraph 6(*a*) to (*c*), (*f*) or (*g*).

Special residential conversions: reduced rate only for supplies made to intended user of converted accommodation

8—(1) This paragraph applies where the qualifying conversion concerned is a special residential conversion.

(2) Item 1 or 2 does not apply to a supply unless—

(*a*) it is made to a person who intends to use the premises being converted for the relevant residential purpose, and (*b*) before it is made, the person to whom it is made has given to the person making it a certificate that satisfies the requirements in sub-paragraph (3).

(3) Those requirements are that the certificate—

(*a*) is in such form as may be specified in a notice published by the Commissioners, and

(*b*) states that the conversion is a special residential conversion.

(4) In sub-paragraph (2)(*a*) "the relevant residential purpose" means the purpose within paragraph 6 for which the premises being converted are intended to be used after the conversion.

"Qualifying conversion" includes related garage works

9—(1) A qualifying conversion includes any garage works related to the—

(*a*) changed number of dwellings conversion,

(*b*) house in multiple occupation conversion, or

(*c*) special residential conversion,

concerned.

(2) In this paragraph "garage works" means—

(*a*) the construction of a garage, or

(*b*) a conversion of a non-residential building, or of a non-residential part of a building, that results in a garage.

(3) For the purposes of sub-paragraph (1), garage works are "related" to a conversion if—

(*a*) they are carried out at the same time as the conversion, and

(*b*) the resulting garage is intended to be occupied with—

(i) where the conversion concerned is a changed number of dwellings conversion, a single household dwelling that will after the conversion be contained in the building, or part of a building, being converted,

(ii) where the conversion concerned is a house in multiple occupation conversion, a multiple occupancy dwelling that will after the conversion be contained in the building, or part of a building, being converted, or

(iii) where the conversion concerned is a special residential conversion, the institution or other accommodation resulting from the conversion.

(4) In sub-paragraph (2) "non-residential" means neither designed, nor adapted, for use—

(*a*) as a dwelling or two or more dwellings, or

(*b*) for a relevant residential purpose.

Conversion not "qualifying" if planning consent and building control approval not obtained

10—(1) A conversion is not a qualifying conversion if any statutory planning consent needed for the conversion has not been granted.

(2) A conversion is not a qualifying conversion if any statutory building control approval needed for the conversion has not been granted.

Meaning of "supply of qualifying services"

11—(1) In the case of a conversion of a building, "supply of qualifying services" means a supply of services that consists in—

(*a*) the carrying out of works to the fabric of the building, or

(*b*) the carrying out of works within the immediate site of the building that are in connection with—

(i) the means of providing water, power, heat or access to the building,

(ii) the means of providing drainage or security for the building, or

(iii) the provision of means of waste disposal for the building.

(2) In the case of a conversion of part of a building, "supply of qualifying services" means a supply of services that consists in—

(*a*) the carrying out of works to the fabric of the part, or

(*b*) the carrying out of works to the fabric of the building, or within the immediate site of the building, that are in connection with—

(i) the means of providing water, power, heat or access to the part,

(ii) the means of providing drainage or security for the part, or

(iii) the provision of means of waste disposal for the part.

(3) In this paragraph—

(*a*) references to the carrying out of works to the fabric of a building do not include the incorporation, or installation as fittings, in the building of any goods that are not building materials;

(*b*) references to the carrying out of works to the fabric of a part of a building do not include the incorporation, or installation as fittings, in the part of any goods that are not building materials.

Meaning of "building materials"

12 In this Group "building materials" has the meaning given by Notes (22) and (23) of Group 5 to Schedule 8 (zero-rating of construction and conversion of buildings).][1]

Amendments—[1] This Schedule inserted by FA 2001 s 99(5), Sch 31 with effect for supplies made, and acquisitions and importations taking place, after 31 October 2001.

[2] Note (4)(2)(*aa*) inserted, Notes 5(2)(*a*), 7(2) and words in Note 7(6) substituted, Notes 7(3)–(5) repealed, by the VAT (Reduced Rate) Order, SI 2002/1100 arts 2, 4 with effect from 1 June 2002.

[GROUP 7

[RESIDENTIAL RENOVATIONS AND ALTERATIONS][2]

Item No.

1 The supply, in the course of the renovation or alteration of [qualifying residential premises][2], of qualifying services related to the renovation or alteration.

2 The supply of building materials if—

(*a*) the materials are supplied by a person who, in the course of the renovation or alteration of a [qualifying residential premises][2], is supplying qualifying services related to the renovation or alteration, and

(*b*) those services include the incorporation of the materials in [the premises concerned or their immediate site][2].

NOTES:

Supplies only partly within item 1

1—(1) Sub-paragraph (2) applies where a supply of services is only in part a supply to which item 1 applies.

(2) The supply, to the extent that it is one to which item 1 applies, is to be taken to be a supply to which item 1 applies.

(3) An apportionment may be made to determine that extent.

Meaning of "alteration" and "single household dwelling"

2—(1) For the purposes of this Group—

"alteration" includes extension;

"qualifying residential premises" means—

(*a*) a single household dwelling,

(*b*) a multiple occupancy dwelling, or

(*c*) a building, or part of a building, which, when it was last lived in, was used for a relevant residential purpose.

(2) Where a building, when it was last lived in, formed part of a relevant residential unit then, to the extent that it would not be so regarded otherwise, the building shall be treated as having been used for a relevant residential purpose.

(3) A building forms part of a relevant residential unit at any time when—

(*a*) it is one of a number of buildings on the same site, and

(*b*) the buildings are used together as a unit for a relevant residential purpose.

(4) The following expressions have the same meaning in this Group as they have in Group 6—

"multiple occupancy dwelling" (paragraph 4(2) of the Notes to that Group);

"single household dwelling" (paragraph 4(1) of the Notes);

"use for a relevant residential purpose" (paragraph 6 of the Notes).][2]

Items 1 and 2 only apply where [premises have][2] been empty for at least [2 years][3]

3—[(1) Item 1 or 2 does not apply to a supply unless—

(*a*) the first empty home condition is satisfied, or

(*b*) if the premises are a single household dwelling, either of the empty home conditions is satisfied.][2]

[(2) The first "empty home condition" is that neither—

(*a*) the premises concerned, nor

(*b*) where those premises are a building, or part of a building, which, when it was last lived in, formed part of a relevant residential unit, any of the other buildings that formed part of the unit,

have been lived in during the period of [2 years][3] ending with the commencement of the relevant works.][2]

(3) The second "empty home condition" is that—

(*a*) the dwelling was not lived in during a period of at least [2 years][3] ;

(*b*) the person, or one the persons, whose beginning to live in the dwelling brought that period to an end was a person who (whether alone or jointly with another or others) acquired the dwelling at a time—

(i) no later than the end of that period, and

(ii) when the dwelling had been not lived in for at least [2 years][3];

(*c*) no works by way of renovation or alteration were carried out to the dwelling during the period of [2 years][3] ending with the acquisition;

(*d*) the supply is made to a person who is—

(i) the person, or one of the persons, whose beginning to live in the property brought to an end the period mentioned in paragraph (*a*), and

(ii) the person, or one of the persons, who acquired the dwelling as mentioned in paragraph (*b*); and

(*e*) the relevant works are carried out during the period of one year beginning with the day of the acquisition.

(4) In this paragraph "the relevant works" means—

(*a*) where the supply is of the description set out in item 1, the works that constitute the services supplied;

(*b*) where the supply is of the description set out in item 2, the works by which the materials concerned are incorporated in [the premises concerned or their immediate site].[2]

(5) In sub-paragraph (3), references to a person acquiring a dwelling are to that person having a major interest in the dwelling granted, or assigned, to him for a consideration.

[Items 1 and 2 apply to related garage works

3A—(1) For the purposes of this Group a renovation or alteration of any premises includes any garage works related to the renovation or alteration.

(2) In this paragraph "garage works" means—

(*a*) the construction of a garage,

(*b*) the conversion of a building, or of a part of a building, that results in a garage, or

(*c*) the renovation or alteration of a garage.

(3) For the purposes of sub-paragraph (1), garage works are "related" to a renovation or alteration if—

(*a*) they are carried out at the same time as the renovation or alteration of the premises concerned, and

(*b*) the garage is intended to be occupied with the premises.][2]

Items 1 and 2 only apply if planning consent and building control approval obtained

4—(1) Item 1 or 2 does not apply to a supply unless any statutory planning consent needed for the renovation or alteration has been granted.

(2) Item 1 or 2 does not apply to a supply unless any statutory building control approval needed for the renovation or alteration has been granted.

[Items 1 and 2 only apply if building used for relevant residential purpose is subsequently used solely for that purpose

4A—(1) Item 1 or 2 does not apply to a supply if the premises in question are a building, or part of a building, which, when it was last lived in, was used for a relevant residential purpose unless—

(*a*) the building or part is intended to be used solely for such a purpose after the renovation or alteration, and

(*b*) before the supply is made the person to whom it is made has given to the person making it a certificate stating that intention.

(2) Where a number of buildings on the same site are—

(*a*) renovated or altered at the same time, and

(*b*) intended to be used together as a unit solely for a relevant residential purpose,

then each of those buildings, to the extent that it would not be so regarded otherwise, shall be treated as intended for use solely for a relevant residential purpose.][2]

Meaning of "supply of qualifying services"

5—(1) "Supply of qualifying services" means a supply of services that consists in—

(*a*) the carrying out of works to the fabric of the [premises][2], or

(*b*) the carrying out of works within the immediate site of the [premises][2] that are in connection with—

(i) the means of providing water, power, heat or access to the [premises][2],

(ii) the means of providing drainage or security for the [premises][2], or

(iii) the provision of means of waste disposal for the [premises][2].

(2) In sub-paragraph (1)(*a*), the reference to the carrying out of works to the fabric of the [premises][2] does not include the incorporation, or installation as fittings, in the [premises][2] of any goods that are not building materials.

Meaning of "building materials"

6 In this Group "building materials" has the meaning given by Notes (22) and (23) of Group 5 to Schedule 8 (zero-rating of construction and conversion of buildings).][1]

Commentary—*De Voil Indirect Tax Service* **V4.413**.

Amendments—[1] This Schedule inserted by FA 2001 s 99(5), Sch 31 with effect for supplies made, and acquisitions and importations taking place, after 31 October 2001.

[2] Title substituted, words in Items 1 and 2, Note (2) substituted, Notes (3) and (5) amended, and Notes (3A), (4A) inserted, by the VAT (Reduced Rate) Order, SI 2002/1100 arts 2, 5 with effect from 1 June 2002.

[3] Words in Note (3), and in heading to Note (3), substituted by the VAT (Reduced Rate) (No 2) Order, SI 2007/3448 regs 2–4 with effect from 1 January 2008: SI 2007/3448 reg 1.

[GROUP 8
CONTRACEPTIVE PRODUCTS

Item No

1 Supplies of contraceptive products, other than relevant exempt supplies.

NOTES:

Meaning of "contraceptive products"

1 In this Group "contraceptive product" means any product designed for the purposes of human contraception, but does not include any product designed for the purpose of monitoring fertility.

Meaning of "relevant exempt supplies"

2 In this Group "relevant exempt supplies" means supplies which fall within item 4 of Group 7 of Schedule 9 (exempt supplies of goods in any hospital etc in connection with medical or surgical treatment etc).][1]

Amendments—[1] This Group inserted by the Value Added Tax (Reduced Rate) Order, SI 2006/1472 arts 2, 4, Schedule with effect from 1 July 2006.

[GROUP 9
WELFARE ADVICE OR INFORMATION

Item No

1 Supplies of welfare advice or information by—

(*a*) a charity, or

(*b*) a state-regulated private welfare institution or agency.

NOTES:

Meaning of "welfare advice or information"

1 In this Group "welfare advice or information" means advice or information which directly relates to—

(*a*) the physical or mental welfare of elderly, sick, distressed or disabled persons, or

(*b*) the care or protection of children and young persons.

Meaning of "state-regulated"

2 For the purposes of this Group "state-regulated" has the same meaning as in Group 7 (health and welfare) of Schedule 9 (see Note (8) of that Group).

Supplies not included in item 1

3 Item 1 does not include—

(*a*) supplies that would be exempt by virtue of Group 6 of Schedule 9 (education) if they were made by an eligible body within the meaning of that Group,

(*b*) supplies of goods, unless the goods are supplied wholly or almost wholly for the purpose of conveying the advice or information, or

(*c*) supplies of advice or information provided solely for the benefit of a particular individual or according to his personal circumstances.][1]

Amendments—[1] This Group inserted by the Value Added Tax (Reduced Rate) Order, SI 2006/1472 arts 2, 4, Schedule with effect from 1 July 2006.

[GROUP 10
INSTALLATION OF MOBILITY AIDS FOR THE ELDERLY

Item No

1 The supply of services of installing mobility aids for use in domestic accommodation by a person who, at the time of the supply, is aged 60 or over.

2 The supply of mobility aids by a person installing them for use in domestic accommodation by a person who, at the time of the supply, is aged 60 or over.

NOTES:

Meaning of "mobility aids"

1 For the purposes of this Group "mobility aids" means any of the following—
(*a*) grab rails;
(*b*) ramps;
(*c*) stair lifts;
(*d*) bath lifts;
(*e*) built-in shower seats or showers containing built-in shower seats;
(*f*) walk-in baths fitted with sealable doors.

Meaning of "domestic accommodation"

2 For the purposes of this Group "domestic accommodation" means a building, or part of a building, that consists of a dwelling or a number of dwellings.][1]

Amendments—[1] This Group inserted by the Value Added Tax (Reduced Rate) Order, SI 2007/1601 arts 2, 4, with effect in relation to supplies made on or after 1 July 2007.

[GROUP 11
SMOKING CESSATION PRODUCTS

Item No.

1 Supplies of pharmaceutical products designed to help people to stop smoking tobacco.][1]

Order—The Value Added Tax (Reduced Rate) (Smoking Cessation Products) Order, SI 2008/1410 arts 2, 3 (the reduced rate provided for in Group 11 shall have effect in relation to supplies made on or after 1 July 2008).
Amendments—[1] This Group inserted by the Value Added Tax (Reduced Rate) Order, SI 2007/1601 arts 2, 5, with effect in relation to supplies made on or after 1 July 2007 but before 1 July 2008. The reduced rate for smoking cessation products continues in relation to supplies made on or after 1 July 2008: see note above.

SCHEDULE 8
ZERO-RATING

Section 30

Simon's Tax Cases—*Home Protection Co v C&E Comrs* [1984] STC 278*; *C&E Comrs v Sutton Housing Trust* [1984] STC 352*.
Cross references—See VATA 1994 s 97(3), (4) (procedure for making orders for varying this Schedule so as to abolish the zero rating of a supply);
VATA 1994 Sch 13 para 8 (preservation of zero rating for certain supplies in the course of an approved alteration of a protected building made pursuant to an obligation incurred before 21 June 1988).

PART I
INDEX TO ZERO-RATED SUPPLIES OF GOODS AND SERVICES

Subject matter	*Group Number*
Bank notes	Group 11
Books etc	Group 3
Caravans and houseboats	Group 9
Charities etc	Group 15
Clothing and footwear	Group 16
Construction of buildings etc	Group 5
Drugs, medicines, aids for the handicapped etc	Group 12
Food	Group 1
Gold	Group 10
Imports, exports etc	Group 13
International services	Group 7
Protected buildings	Group 6
Sewerage services and water	Group 2
Talking books for the blind and handicapped and wireless sets for the blind	Group 4
[…][1]	
Transport	Group 8

Amendments—[1] Group 14 deleted by the Value Added Tax (Abolition of Zero-Rating for Tax Free Shops) Order, SI 1999/1642, with effect from 1 July 1999.

PART II
THE GROUPS

GROUP 1 — FOOD

The supply of anything comprised in the general items set out below, except—

(*a*) a supply in the course of catering; and

(*b*) a supply of anything comprised in any of the excepted items set out below, unless it is also comprised in any of the items overriding the exceptions set out below which relates to that excepted item.

General items

Item No

1 Food of a kind used for human consumption.

2 Animal feeding stuffs.

3 Seeds or other means of propagation of plants comprised in item 1 or 2.

4 Live animals of a kind generally used as, or yielding or producing, food for human consumption.

Excepted items

Item No

1 Ice cream, ice lollies, frozen yoghurt, water ices and similar frozen products, and prepared mixes and powders for making such products.

2 Confectionery, not including cakes or biscuits other than biscuits wholly or partly covered with chocolate or some product similar in taste and appearance.

3 Beverages chargeable with any duty of excise specifically charged on spirits, beer, wine or made-wine and preparations thereof.

4 Other beverages (including fruit juices and bottled waters) and syrups, concentrates, essences, powders, crystals or other products for the preparation of beverages.

5 Any of the following when packaged for human consumption without further preparation, namely, potato crisps, potato sticks, potato puffs, and similar products made from the potato, or from potato flour, or from potato starch, and savoury food products obtained by the swelling of cereals or cereal products; and salted or roasted nuts other than nuts in shell.

6 Pet foods, canned, packaged or prepared; packaged foods (not being pet foods) for birds other than poultry or game; and biscuits and meal for cats and dogs.

7 Goods described in items 1, 2 and 3 of the general items which are canned, bottled, packaged or prepared for use—

(*a*) in the domestic brewing of any beer;

(*b*) in the domestic making of any cider or perry;

(*c*) in the domestic production of any wine or made-wine.

Items overriding the exceptions

Item No

1 Yoghurt unsuitable for immediate consumption when frozen.

2 Drained cherries.

3 Candied peels.

4 Tea, maté, herbal teas and similar products, and preparations and extracts thereof.

5 Cocoa, coffee and chicory and other roasted coffee substitutes, and preparations and extracts thereof.

6 Milk and preparations and extracts thereof.

7 Preparations and extracts of meat, yeast or egg.

NOTES:

(1) "Food" includes drink.

(2) "Animal" includes bird, fish, crustacean and mollusc.

(3) A supply of anything in the course of catering includes—

(*a*) any supply of it for consumption on the premises on which it is supplied; and

(*b*) any supply of hot food for consumption off those premises;

and for the purposes of paragraph (*b*) above "hot food" means food which, or any part of which—

(i) has been heated for the purposes of enabling it to be consumed at a temperature above the ambient air temperature; and

[(ii) is above that temperature at the time it is provided to the customer.][1]

(4) Item 1 of the items overriding the exceptions relates to item 1 of the excepted items.

(5) Items 2 and 3 of the items overriding the exceptions relate to item 2 of the excepted items; and for the purposes of item 2 of the excepted items "confectionery" includes chocolates, sweets and biscuits; drained, glacé or crystallised fruits; and any item of sweetened prepared food which is normally eaten with the fingers.

(6) Items 4 to 6 of the items overriding the exceptions relate to item 4 of the excepted items.

(7) Any supply described in this Group shall include a supply of services described in paragraph 1(1) of Schedule 4.

Commentary—*De Voil Indirect Tax Service* **V4.221, V4.226, V4.227**.
Press releases etc—C&E Business Brief 18/94 6-10-94 (scope of item 4 overriding the exceptions).
C&E Business Brief 6/95 28-3-95 (ostriches and fertilised ostrich eggs zero-rated from 1-4-95).
C&E Business Brief 12/95 19-6-95 (pre-germinated grass seed standard rated with effect from 1 October 1995).
Simon's Tax Cases—*R v C&E Comrs, ex p Sims (T/A Supersonic Snacks)* [1988] STC 210*; *C&E Comrs v Lawson Tancred* [1988] STC 326*; *John Pimblett & Sons Ltd v C&E Comrs* [1988] STC 358*, *EC Commission v United Kingdom* [1988] STC 456*; *R&C Comrs v Compass Contract Services UK Ltd* [2006] STC 1999.
Sub-para (*a*), *British Airways plc v C&E Comrs* [1990] STC 643*; *C&E Comrs v Safeway Stores plc* [1997] STC 163.
Item 1, Note (3)(*b*)(i), *British Airways plc v C&E Comrs* [1990] STC 643*; *C&E Comrs v Safeway Stores plc* [1997] STC 163; *Malik (T/A Hotline Foods) v C&E Comrs* [1998] STC 537.
Item 1, *C&E Comrs v Macphie & Co (Glenbervie) Ltd* [1992] STC 886*.
Item 2, *Fluff Ltd (T/A Mag-it) v C&E Comrs* [2001] STC 674.
Excepted item 1, *Meschia's Frozen Foods v C&E Comrs* [2001] STC 1.
Excepted item 2, *C&E Comrs v Ferrero UK Ltd* [1997] STC 881*; *R&C Comrs v Premier Foods Ltd* [2008] STC 176.
Excepted item 4, *Kalron Foods Ltd v R&C Comrs* [2007] STC 1100.
Definitions—"Supply", s 5, Sch 4.
Cross reference—See VAT Regulations, SI 1995/2518 reg 73 (retailers making both zero-rated supplies of food and supplies in course of catering: method of accounting).
Note—VATA 1994 Sch 8 Group 1 shall, in respect of preparations of meat, yeast or egg, shall be deemed to have and to always have had effect as if for Items "4 to 6" in Note (6) there were substituted "Items 4 to 7", FA 1999 s 14.
Amendments—[1] In Note (3), para (ii) substituted by the VAT (Food) Order, SI 2004/3343 with effect from 1 January 2005.

GROUP 2 — SEWERAGE SERVICES AND WATER

Item No

1 Services of—

(*a*) reception, disposal or treatment of foul water or sewage in bulk, and
(*b*) emptying of cesspools, septic tanks or similar receptacles which are used otherwise than in connection with the carrying on in the course of a business of a relevant industrial activity.

2 The supply, for use otherwise than in connection with the carrying on in the course of a business of a relevant industrial activity, of water other than—

(*a*) distilled water, deionised water and water of similar purity,…[1]
(*b*) water comprised in any of the excepted items set out in Group 1 [and
(*c*) water which has been heated so that it is supplied at a temperature higher than that at which it was before it was heated][1].

Note: "Relevant industrial activity" means any activity described in any of Divisions 1 to 5 of the 1980 edition of the publication prepared by the Central Statistical Office and known as the Standard Industrial Classification.

Commentary—*De Voil Indirect Tax Service* **V4.271**.
Press releases etc—C&E Business Brief 15/94 19-7-94 (VAT treatment of connection charges to caravans and mobile homes by caravan park owner to follow treatment of rent).
Simon's Tax Cases—*EC Commission v United Kingdom* [1988] STC 456*.
Definitions—"Business", s 94; "Supply", s 5, Sch 4.
Amendments—[1] Word revoked from para (*a*) of item 2 and para (*c*) added to item 2 by the Value Added Tax (Anti-avoidance (Heating)) Order, SI 1996/1661 with effect from 27 June 1996.

GROUP 3 — BOOKS, ETC

Item No

1 Books, booklets, brochures, pamphlets and leaflets.

2 Newspapers, journals and periodicals.

3 Children's picture books and painting books.

4 Music (printed, duplicated or manuscript).

5 Maps, charts and topographical plans.

6 Covers, cases and other articles supplied with items 1 to 5 and not separately accounted for.

Note: Items 1 to 6—

(*a*) do not include plans or drawings for industrial, architectural, engineering, commercial or similar purposes; but
(*b*) include the supply of the services described in paragraph 1(1) of Schedule 4 in respect of goods comprised in the items.

Commentary—*De Voil Indirect Tax Service* **V4.237**.
Simon's Tax Cases—*Odhams Leisure Group Ltd v C&E Comrs* [1992] STC 332*.
Item 1, *C&E Comrs v Colour Offset Ltd* [1995] STC 85*; *R&C Comrs v Weight Watchers (UK) Ltd* [2008] STC 301.
Item 2, *Telewest Communications v C&E Comrs* [2004] STC 517; *R&C Comrs v Weight Watchers (UK) Ltd* [2008] STC 301.
Definition—"Supply", s 5, Sch 4.

GROUP 4 — TALKING BOOKS FOR THE BLIND AND HANDICAPPED AND WIRELESS SETS FOR THE BLIND

Item No

1 The supply to the Royal National Institute for the Blind, the National Listening Library or other similar charities of—

(*a*) magnetic tape specially adapted for the recording and reproduction of speech for the blind or severely handicapped;

(*b*) apparatus designed or specially adapted for the making on a magnetic tape, by way of the transfer of recorded speech from another magnetic tape, of a recording described in paragraph (*f*) below;

(*c*) apparatus designed or specially adapted for transfer to magnetic tapes of a recording made by apparatus described in paragraph (*b*) above;

(*d*) apparatus for re-winding magnetic tape described in paragraph (*f*) below;

(*e*) apparatus designed or specially adapted for the reproduction from recorded magnetic tape of speech for the blind or severely handicapped which is not available for use otherwise than by the blind or severely handicapped;

(*f*) magnetic tape upon which has been recorded speech for the blind or severely handicapped, such recording being suitable for reproduction only in the apparatus mentioned in paragraph (*e*) above;

(*g*) apparatus solely for the making on a magnetic tape of a sound recording which is for use by the blind or severely handicapped;

(*h*) parts and accessories (other than a magnetic tape for use with apparatus described in paragraph (*g*) above) for goods comprised in paragraphs (*a*) to (*g*) above;

(*i*) the supply of a service of repair or maintenance of any goods comprised in paragraphs (*a*) to (*h*) above.

2 The supply to a charity of—

(*a*) wireless receiving sets; or

(*b*) apparatus solely for the making and reproduction of a sound recording on a magnetic tape permanently contained in a cassette,

being goods solely for gratuitous loan to the blind.

Note: The supply mentioned in items 1 and 2 includes the letting on hire of goods comprised in the items.

Commentary—*De Voil Indirect Tax Service* **V4.262**.
Definition—"Supply", s 5, Sch 4.

[GROUP 5—CONSTRUCTION OF BUILDINGS, ETC

Item No

1 The first grant by a person—

(*a*) constructing a building—

(i) designed as a dwelling or number of dwellings; or

(ii) intended for use solely for a relevant residential or a relevant charitable purpose; or

(*b*) converting a non-residential building or a non-residential part of a building into a building designed as a dwelling or number of dwellings or a building intended for use solely for a relevant residential purpose,

of a major interest in, or in any part of, the building, dwelling or its site.

2 The supply in the course of the construction of—

(*a*) a building designed as a dwelling or number of dwellings or intended for use solely for a relevant residential purpose or a relevant charitable purpose; or

(*b*) any civil engineering work necessary for the development of a permanent park for residential caravans,

of any services related to the construction other than the services of an architect, surveyor or any person acting as a consultant or in a supervisory capacity.

3 The supply to a [relevant housing association][2] in the course of conversion of a non-residential building or a non-residential part of a building into—

(*a*) a building or part of a building designed as a dwelling or number of dwellings; or

(*b*) a building or part of a building intended for use solely for a relevant residential purpose,

of any services related to the conversion other than the services of an architect, surveyor or any person acting as a consultant or in a supervisory capacity.

4 The supply of building materials to a person to whom the supplier is supplying services within item 2 or 3 of this Group which include the incorporation of the materials into the building (or its site) in question.

NOTES

(1) "Grant" includes an assignment or surrender.

(2) A building is designed as a dwelling or a number of dwellings where in relation to each dwelling the following conditions are satisfied—

(*a*) the dwelling consists of self-contained living accommodation;
(*b*) there is no provision for direct internal access from the dwelling to any other dwelling or part of a dwelling;
(*c*) the separate use, or disposal of the dwelling is not prohibited by the term of any covenant, statutory planning consent or similar provision; and
(*d*) statutory planning consent has been granted in respect of that dwelling and its construction or conversion has been carried out in accordance with that consent.

(3) The construction of, or conversion of a non-residential building to, a building designed as a dwelling or a number of dwellings includes the construction of, or conversion of a non-residential building to, a garage provided that—
(*a*) the dwelling and the garage are constructed or converted at the same time; and
(*b*) the garage is intended to be occupied with the dwelling or one of the dwellings.

(4) Use for a relevant residential purpose means use as—
(*a*) a home or other institution providing residential accommodation for children;
(*b*) a home or other institution providing residential accommodation with personal care for persons in need of personal care by reason of old age, disablement, past or present dependence on alcohol or drugs or past or present mental disorder;
(*c*) a hospice;
(*d*) residential accommodation for students or school pupils;
(*e*) residential accommodation for members of any of the armed forces;
(*f*) a monastery, nunnery or similar establishment; or
(*g*) an institution which is the sole or main residence of at least 90 per cent of its residents,
except use as a hospital, prison or similar institution or an hotel, inn or similar establishment.

(5) Where a number of buildings are—
(*a*) constructed at the same time and on the same site; and
(*b*) are intended to be used together as a unit solely for a relevant residential purpose;
then each of those buildings, to the extent that they would not be so regarded but for this Note, are to be treated as intended for use solely for a relevant residential purpose.

(6) Use for a relevant charitable purpose means use by a charity in either or both the following ways, namely—
(*a*) otherwise than in the course or furtherance of a business;
(*b*) as a village hall or similarly in providing social or recreational facilities for a local community.

[(7) For the purposes of item 1(*b*), and for the purposes of these Notes so far as having effect for the purposes of item 1(*b*), a building or part of a building is "non-residential" if—
(*a*) it is neither designed, nor adapted, for use—
(i) as a dwelling or number of dwellings, or
(ii) for a relevant residential purpose; or
(*b*) it is designed, or adapted, for such use but—
(i) it was constructed more than 10 years before the grant of the major interest; and
(ii) no part of it has, in the period of 10 years immediately preceding the grant, been used as a dwelling or for a relevant residential purpose.][3]

[(7A) For the purposes of item 3, and for the purposes of these Notes so far as having effect for the purposes of item 3, a building or part of a building is "non-residential" if—
(*a*) it is neither designed, nor adapted, for use—
(i) as a dwelling or number of dwellings, or
(ii) for a relevant residential purpose; or
(*b*) it is designed, or adapted, for such use but—
(i) it was constructed more than 10 years before the commencement of the works of conversion, and
(ii) no part of it has, in the period of 10 years immediately preceding the commencement of those works, been used as a dwelling or for a relevant residential purpose, and
(iii) no part of it is being so used.][3]

(8) References to a non-residential building or a non-residential part of a building do not include a reference to a garage occupied together with a dwelling.

(9) The conversion, other than to a building designed for a relevant residential purpose, of a non-residential part of a building which already contains a residential part is not included within items 1(*b*) or 3 unless the result of that conversion is to create an additional dwelling or dwellings.

(10) Where—
(*a*) part of a building that is constructed is designed as a dwelling or number of dwellings or is intended for use solely for a relevant residential purpose or relevant charitable purpose (and part is not); or

(*b*) part of a building that is converted is designed as a dwelling or number of dwellings or is used solely for a relevant residential purpose (and part is not)—

then in the case of—

(i) a grant or other supply relating only to the part so designed or intended for that use (or its site) shall be treated as relating to a building so designed or intended for such use;

(ii) a grant or other supply relating only to the part neither so designed nor intended for such use (or its site) shall not be so treated; and

(iii) any other grant or other supply relating to, or to any part of, the building (or its site), an apportionment shall be made to determine the extent to which it is to be so treated.

(11) Where, a service falling within the description in items 2 or 3 is supplied in part in relation to the construction or conversion of a building and in part for other purposes, an apportionment may be made to determine the extent to which the supply is to be treated as falling within items 2 or 3.

(12) Where all or part of a building is intended for use solely for a relevant residential purpose or a relevant charitable purpose—

(*a*) a supply relating to the building (or any part of it) shall not be taken for the purposes of items 2 and 4 as relating to a building intended for such use unless it is made to a person who intends to use the building (or part) for such a purpose; and

(*b*) a grant or other supply relating to the building (or any part of it) shall not be taken as relating to a building intended for such use unless before it is made the person to whom it is made has given to the person making it a certificate in such form as may be specified in a notice published by the Commissioners stating that the grant or other supply (or a specified part of it) so relates.

(13) The grant of an interest in, or in any part of—

(*a*) a building designed as a dwelling or number of dwellings; or

(*b*) the site of such a building,

is not within item 1 if—

(i) the interest granted is such that the grantee is not entitled to reside in the building or part, throughout the year; or

(ii) residence there throughout the year, or the use of the building or part as the grantee's principal private residence, is prevented by the terms of a covenant, statutory planning consent or similar permission.

(14) Where the major interest referred to in item l is a tenancy or lease—

(*a*) if a premium is payable, the grant falls within that item-only to the extent that it is made for consideration in the form of the premium; and

(*b*) if a premium is not payable, the grant falls within that item only to the extent that it is made for consideration in the form of the first payment of rent due under the tenancy or lease.

(15) The reference in item 2(*b*) of this Group to the construction of a civil engineering work does not include a reference to the conversion, reconstruction, alteration or enlargement of a work.

(16) For the purpose of this Group, the construction of a building does not include—

(*a*) the conversion, reconstruction or alteration of an existing building; or

(*b*) any enlargement of, or extension to, an existing building except to the extent the enlargement or extension creates an additional dwelling or dwellings; or

(*c*) subject to Note (17) below, the construction of an annexe to an existing building.

(17) Note 16(*c*) above shall not apply [where the whole or a part of an annexe is intended for use solely for a relevant charitable purpose and][4]—

(*a*) [the annexe][4] is capable of functioning independently from the existing building; and

(*b*) the only access or where there is more than one means of access, the main access to:

(i) the annexe is not via the existing building; and

(ii) the existing building is not via the annexe.

(18) A building only ceases to be an existing building when:

(*a*) demolished completely to ground level; or

(*b*) the part remaining above ground level consists of no more than a single facade or where a corner site, a double facade, the retention of which is a condition or requirement of statutory planning consent or similar permission.

(19) A caravan is not a residential caravan if residence in it throughout the year is prevented by the terms of a covenant, statutory planning consent or similar permission.

(20) Item 2 and Item 3 do not include the supply of services described in paragraph 1(1) or 5(4) of Schedule 4.

[(21) In Item 3 "relevant housing association" means—

(*a*) a registered social landlord within the meaning of Part 1 of the Housing Act 1996,

(*b*) a registered housing association within the meaning of the Housing Associations Act 1985 (Scottish registered housing associations), or

(*c*) a registered housing association within the meaning of Part II of the Housing (Northern Ireland) Order 1992 (Northern Irish registered housing association).][2]

(22) "Building materials", in relation to any description of building, means goods of a description ordinarily incorporated by builders in a building of that description, (or its site), but does not include—

(*a*) finished or prefabricated furniture, other than furniture designed to be fitted in kitchens;
(*b*) materials for the construction of fitted furniture, other than kitchen furniture;
(*c*) electrical or gas appliances, unless the appliance is an appliance which is—

(i) designed to heat space or water (or both) or to provide ventilation, air cooling, air purification, or dust extraction; or
(ii) intended for use in a building designed as a number of dwellings and is a door-entry system, a waste disposal unit or a machine for compacting waste; or
(iii) a burglar alarm, a fire alarm, or fire safety equipment or designed solely for the purpose of enabling aid to be summoned in an emergency; or
(iv) a lift or hoist;

(*d*) carpets or carpeting material.

(23) For the purposes of Note (22) above the incorporation of goods in a building includes their installation as fittings.

(24) Section 30(3) does not apply to goods forming part of a description of supply in this Group.][1]

Commentary—*De Voil Indirect Tax Service* **V4.233, V4.237, V4.238, V4.242**.
Press releases etc—VAT Information Sheet 10/95 11-4-95 (guidance on the changes to the liability of supplies in connection with buildings with effect from 1 March 1995).
Business Brief 12/97, 5 June 1997 (Fitted Furniture in new buildings).
VAT Information Sheet 5/01 July 2001 (guidance on the adjustment to the zero rate for the sale of houses that are renovated after having been empty for at least 10 years).
HMRC Brief 66/07, 5-11-07 (treatment of the construction of houses or flats in the grounds of existing care homes, nursing homes or similar buildings).
Simon's Tax Cases—*EC Commission v United Kingdom* [1988] STC 456*.
Item 1, *C&E Comrs v Link Housing Association Ltd* [1992] STC 718*.
Item 1(*a*)(ii), note (4), *R (on the application of Greenwich Property Ltd) v C&E Comrs* [2001] STC 618.
Item 2, *C&E Comrs v Rannoch School Ltd* [1993] STC 389*; *C&E Comrs v Lewis* [1994] STC 739*; *C&E Comrs v Marchday Holdings Ltd* [1995] STC 898*; *C&E Comrs v St Mary's RC High School* [1996] STC 1091*; *C&E Comrs v St Paul's Community Project Ltd* [2005] STC 95; *Riverside Housing Association Ltd v R&C Comrs* [2006] STC 2072.
Item 2(*a*), Notes 4(*b*), (6)(*a*), (*b*), *Jubilee Hall Recreation Centre Ltd v C&E Comrs* [1999] STC 381; *C&E Comrs v Yarburgh Children's Trust* [2002] STC 207.
Item 3, *C&E Comrs v John Willmott Housing Ltd* [1987] STC 692*; *C&E Comrs v Arbib* [1995] STC 490*; *C&E Comrs v Jeffs (T/A J & J Joinery)* [1995] STC 759*.
Note (4)(*b*), *R&C Comrs v Fenwood Developments Ltd* [2006] STC 644.
Note (9), *C&E Comrs v Lewis* [1994] STC 739*; *C&E Comrs v Marchday Holdings Ltd* [1997] STC 272*; *C&E Comrs v Jacobs* [2005] STC 1518.
Note (16) *Cantrell v C&E Comrs* [2000] STC 100.
Definitions—"Assignment", s 96(1); "business", s 94; "the Commissioners", s 96(1); "major interest", s 96(1); "supply", s 5, Sch 4.
Cross references—See VATA 1994 s 62(1) (penalty for incorrect certificate that a supply is eligible for zero rating within this Group);
VATA 1994 Sch 9 Group 1 note (11) (any grant of a major interest which is excluded from item 1 of this Group by note (7) is included in Sch 9 Group 1 item 1(*e*) (exemption: land);
VAT Regulations, SI 1995/2518 reg 101(3) (exclusion of supplies within item 1 of this Group in determining proportion of input tax attributable to taxable supplies under reg 101(2)(*d*)).
VATA 1994 s 35 (note (7A) above shall apply for the purposes of that section).
Amendments—[1] Group 5 substituted by the Value Added Tax (Construction of Buildings) Order, SI 1995/280 with effect from 1 March 1995.
[2] Words in Item No 3 and Note (21) substituted by the VAT (Registered Social Landlords)(No 1) Order, SI 1997/50 with effect from 1 March 1997.
[3] Notes (7), (7A) substituted for Note (7) by the VAT (Conversion of Buildings) Order, SI 2001/2305 arts 1–3 with effect for supplies made after 31 July 2001.
[4] Words in Note (17) substituted and inserted by the VAT (Construction of Buildings) Order, SI 2002/1101 art 2 with effect from 1 June 2002.

[GROUP 6—PROTECTED BUILDINGS

Item No

1 The first grant by a person substantially reconstructing a protected building, of a major interest in, or in any part of, the building or its site.

2 The supply, in the course of an approved alteration of a protected building, of any services other than the services of an architect, surveyor or any person acting as consultant or in a supervisory capacity.

3 The supply of building materials to a person to whom the supplier is supplying services within item 2 of this Group which include the incorporation of the materials into the building (or its site) in question.

NOTES

(1) "Protected building" means a building which is designed to remain as or become a dwelling or number of dwellings (as defined in Note (2) below) or is intended for use solely for a relevant residential purpose or a relevant charitable purpose after the reconstruction or alteration and which, in either case, is—

(*a*) a listed building, within the meaning of—

(i) the Planning (Listed Buildings and Conservation Areas) Act 1990; or
(ii) [the Planning (Listed Buildings and Conservation Areas) (Scotland) Act 1997][3]; or

(iii) the Planning (Northern Ireland) Order 1991; or

(*b*) a scheduled monument, within the meaning of—

(i) the Ancient Monuments and Archaeological Areas Act 1979; or

(ii) [the Historic Monuments and Archaeological Objects (Northern Ireland) Order 1995.][2]

(2) A building is designed to remain as or become a dwelling or number of dwellings where in relation to each dwelling the following conditions are satisfied—

(*a*) the dwelling consists of self-contained living accommodation;

(*b*) there is no provision for direct internal access from the dwelling to any other dwelling or part of a dwelling;

(*c*) the separate use, or disposal of the dwelling is not prohibited by the terms of any covenant, statutory planning consent or similar provision,

and includes a garage (occupied together with a dwelling) either constructed at the same time as the building or where the building has been substantially reconstructed at the same time as that reconstruction.

(3) Notes (1), (4), (6), (12) to (14) and (22) to (24) of Group 5 apply in relation to this Group as they apply in relation to that Group but subject to any appropriate modifications.

(4) For the purposes of item 1, a protected building shall not be regarded as substantially reconstructed unless the reconstruction is such that at least one of the following conditions is fulfilled when the reconstruction is completed—

(*a*) that, of the works carried out to effect the reconstruction, at least three-fifths, measured by reference to cost, are of such a nature that the supply of services (other than excluded services), materials and other items to carry out the works, would, if supplied by a taxable person, be within either item 2 or item 3 of this Group; and

(*b*) that the reconstructed building incorporates no more of the original building (that is to say, the building as it was before the reconstruction began) than the external walls, together with other external features of architectural or historic interest;

and in paragraph (*a*) above "excluded services" means the services of an architect, surveyor or other person acting as consultant or in a supervisory capacity.

(5) Where part of a protected building that is substantially reconstructed is designed to remain as or become a dwelling or a number of dwellings or is intended for use solely for a relevant residential or relevant charitable purpose (and part is not)—

(*a*) a grant or other supply relating only to the part so designed or intended for such use (or its site) shall be treated as relating to a building so designed or intended for such use;

(*b*) a grant or other supply relating only to the part neither so designed nor intended for such use (or its site) shall not be so treated; and

(*c*) in the case of any other grant or other supply relating to, or to any part of, the building (or its site), an apportionment shall be made to determine the extent to which it is to be so treated.

(6) "Approved alteration" means—

(*a*) in the case of a protected building which is an ecclesiastical building to which section 60 of the Planning (Listed Buildings and Conservation Areas) Act 1990 applies, any works of alteration; and

(*b*) in the case of a protected building which is a scheduled monument within the meaning of the Historic Monuments Act (Northern Ireland) 1971 and in respect of which a protection order, within the meaning of that Act, is in force, works of alteration for which consent has been given under section 10 of that Act; and

(*c*) in any other case, works of alteration which may not, or but for the existence of a Crown interest or Duchy interest could not, be carried out unless authorised under, or under any provision of—

(i) Part I of the Planning (Listed Buildings and Conservation Areas) Act 1990,

(ii) [Part I of the Planning (Listed Buildings and Conservation Areas) (Scotland) Act 1997][3],

(iii) Part V of the Planning (Northern Ireland) Order 1991,

(iv) Part I of the Ancient Monuments and Archaeological Areas Act 1979,

and for which, except in the case of a Crown interest or Duchy interest, consent has been obtained under any provision of that Part,

but does not include any works of repair or maintenance, or any incidental alteration to the fabric of a building which results from the carrying out of repairs, or maintenance work.

(7) For the purposes of paragraph (*a*) of Note (6), a building used or available for use by a minister of religion wholly or mainly as a residence from which to perform the duties of his office shall be treated as not being an ecclesiastical building.

(8) For the purposes of paragraph (*c*) of Note (6) "Crown interest" and "Duchy interest" have the same meaning as in section 50 of the Ancient Monuments and Archaeological Areas Act 1979.

(9) Where a service is supplied in part in relation to an approved alteration of a building, and in part for other purposes, an apportionment may be made to determine the extent to which the supply is to be treated as falling within item 2.

(10) For the purposes of item 2 the construction of a building separate from, but in the curtilage of, a protected building does not constitute an alteration of the protected building.

(11) Item 2 does not include the supply of services described in paragraph 1(1) or 5(4) of Schedule 4.][1]

Commentary—*De Voil Indirect Tax Service* **V4.235, V4.239**.

Simon's Tax Cases—Item 2, *C&E Comrs v Arbib* [1995] STC 490*; *C&E Comrs v Windflower Housing Association* [1995] STC 860*; *Jubilee Hall Recreation Centre Ltd v C&E Comrs* [1998] STC 954*.

Item 2, note (1), *Jubilee Hall Recreation Centre Ltd v C&E Comrs* [1999] STC 381; *C&E Comrs v Zielinski Baker & Partners Ltd* [2004] STC 456, UKHL; *C&E Comrs v Tinsley* [2005] STC 1612.

Item 2, note (2), *C&E Comrs v Zielinski Baker & Partners Ltd* [2002] STC 829.

Notes (1), (2), *Jubilee Hall Recreation Centre Ltd v C&E Comrs* [1997] STC 414.

Note (6), *C&E Comrs v Windflower Housing Association* [1995] STC 860*; *C&E Comrs v Morrish* [1998] 954.

Note (10), *C&E Comrs v Arbib* [1995] STC 490*.

Definitions—"Building materials", Sch 8 Group 5 note (22); "grant", Sch 8 Group 5 note (1); "major interest", s 96(1); "use for a relevant charitable purpose", Sch 8 Group 5 note (6); "use for a relevant residential purpose", Sch 8 Group 5 note (4); "supply", s 5, Sch 4; "taxable person", s 3.

Cross reference—See VATA 1994 s 62(1) (penalty for incorrect certificate that a supply is eligible for zero rating within this Group).

VAT Regulations, SI 1995/2518 reg 101(3) (exclusion of supplies within item 1 of this Group in determining proportion of input tax attributable to taxable supplies under reg 101(2)(*d*)).

Amendments—[1] Group 6 substituted by the Value Added Tax (Protected Buildings) Order, SI 1995/283 with effect from 1 March 1995.

[2] Words in Note (1)(*b*)(ii) substituted by the Historic Monuments and Archaeological Objects (Northern Ireland) Order, SI 1995/1625 (NI 9) Sch 3 para 4 with effect from 29 August 1995.

[3] Words in notes (1)(*a*)(ii) and (6)(*c*)(ii) substituted by the Planning (Consequential Provisions) (Scotland) Act 1997, s 4, Sch 2, para 57(*a*).

Purported amendments—The following amendments were purportedly made to Note (4): para (*b*) and the word "or" at the end of para (*c*)(iii) are repealed, and in para (*c*), sub-para (*v*) and the word "or" immediately preceding it are inserted as follows by the Historic Objects (Northern Ireland) Order, SI 1995/1625 (NI 9) Sch 3 para 4, Sch 4, with effect from 29 August 1995:

"(*v*) Part II of the Historic Monuments and Archaeological Objects (Northern Ireland) Order 1995,".

This amendment relates to the text of this Group prior to its substitution by SI 1995/283 (see note [1] above) and it is submitted that Note (6), as so substituted, should be considered in the light of these amendments.

GROUP 7 — INTERNATIONAL SERVICES

Item No

1 The supply of services of work carried out on goods which, for that purpose, have been obtained or acquired in, or imported into, any of the member States and which are intended to be, and in fact are, subsequently exported to a place outside the member States—

(*a*) by or on behalf of the supplier; or

(*b*) where the recipient of the services belongs in a place outside the member States, by or on behalf of the recipient.

2 The supply of services consisting of the making of arrangements for—

(*a*) the export of any goods to a place outside the member States;

(*b*) a supply of services of the description specified in item 1 of this Group; or

(*c*) any supply of services which is made outside the member States.

NOTE

This Group does not include any services of a description specified in Group 2 or Group 5 of Schedule 9.

Commentary—*De Voil Indirect Tax Service* **V4.246**.

Simon's Tax Cases—*Bophuthatswana National Commercial Corp Ltd v C&E Comrs* [1992] STC 741*.

Definition—"Supply", s 5, Sch 4.

GROUP 8 — TRANSPORT

Item No

[1 The supply, repair or maintenance of a qualifying ship or the modification or conversion of any such ship provided that when so modified or converted it will remain a qualifying ship.][3]

[2 The supply, repair or maintenance of a qualifying aircraft or the modification or conversion of any such aircraft provided that when so modified or converted it will remain a qualifying aircraft.][3]

[2A The supply of parts and equipment, of a kind ordinarily installed or incorporated in, and to be installed, or incorporated in,—

(*a*) the propulsion, navigation or communication systems; or

(*b*) the general structure,

of a qualifying ship or, as the case may be, aircraft.][3]

[2B The supply of life jackets, life rafts, smoke hoods and similar safety equipment for use in a qualifying ship or, as the case may be, aircraft.][3]

3

(*a*) The supply to and repair or maintenance for a charity providing rescue or assistance at sea of—

(i) any lifeboat;

(ii) carriage equipment designed solely for the launching and recovery of lifeboats;

(iii) tractors for the sole use of the launching and recovery of lifeboats;

(iv) winches and hauling equipment for the sole use of the recovery of lifeboats.

(*b*) The construction, modification, repair or maintenance for a charity providing rescue or assistance at sea of slipways used solely for the launching and recovery of lifeboats.

(*c*) The supply of spare parts or accessories to a charity providing rescue or assistance at sea for use in or with goods comprised in paragraph (*a*) above or slipways comprised in paragraph (*b*) above.

[(*d*) The supply to a charity providing rescue or assistance at sea of equipment that is to be installed, incorporated or used in a lifeboat and is of a kind ordinarily installed, incorporated or used in a lifeboat.][7]

[(*e*) The supply of fuel to a charity providing rescue or assistance at sea where the fuel is for use in a lifeboat.][9]

4 Transport of passengers—

(*a*) in any vehicle, ship or aircraft designed or adapted to carry not less than [10][6] passengers;

(*b*) by [the Post Office company][5];

(*c*) on any scheduled flight; or

(*d*) from a place within to a place outside the United Kingdom or vice versa, to the extent that those services are supplied in the United Kingdom.

5 The transport of goods from a place within to a place outside the member States or vice versa, to the extent that those services are supplied within the United Kingdom.

6 Any services provided for—

(*a*) the handling of ships or aircraft in a port, customs and excise airport or outside the United Kingdom; or

[(*b*) the handling or storage—

(i) in a port,

(ii) on land adjacent to a port,

(iii) in a customs and excise airport, or

(iv) in a transit shed,

of goods carried in a ship or aircraft.][8]

[**6A** Air navigation services.][2]

7 Pilotage services.

8 Salvage or towage services.

9 Any services supplied for or in connection with the surveying of any ship or aircraft or the classification of any ship or aircraft for the purposes of any register.

10 The making of arrangements for—

(*a*) the supply of, or of space in, any ship or aircraft;…

(*b*) the supply of any service included in [items 1 and 2, 3 to 9 and 11; or][3]

[(*c*) the supply of any goods of a description falling within items 2A or 2B][3][, or paragraph (*d*) of item 3.][7]

11 The supply—

(*a*) of services consisting of

(i) the handling or storage of goods at, or their transport to or from, a place at which they are to be exported to or have been imported from a place outside the member States; or

(ii) the handling or storage of such goods in connection with such transport; or

(*b*) to a person who receives the supply for the purpose of a business carried on by him and who belongs outside the United Kingdom, of services of a description specified in paragraph (*a*) of item 6, [item 6A,][2] item 9 or paragraph (*a*) of item 10 of this Group.

12 The supply of a designated travel service to be enjoyed outside the European Community, to the extent to which the supply is so enjoyed.

13 Intra-Community transport services supplied in connection with the transport of goods to or from the Azores or Madeira or between those places, to the extent that the services are treated as supplied in the United Kingdom.

NOTES

[(A1) In this Group—

(*a*) a "qualifying ship" is any ship of a gross tonnage of not less than 15 tons which is neither designed nor adapted for use for recreation or pleasure; and

(*b*) a "qualifying aircraft" is any aircraft of a weight of not less than 8,000 kilograms which is neither designed nor adapted for use for recreation or pleasure.][3]

(1) In items 1 and 2 the supply of a [qualifying][3] ship or, as the case may be, aircraft includes the supply of services under a charter of that ship or aircraft except where the services supplied under such a charter consist wholly of any one or more of the following—

(*a*) transport of passengers;

(*b*) accommodation;

(*c*) entertainment;

(*d*) education;

being services wholly performed in the United Kingdom.

(2) Items 1, 2 [, 2A, 2B][3] and 3 include the letting on hire of the goods specified in the items.

[(2A) Items 2A and 2B do not include the supply of parts and equipment to a Government department [or any part of the Scottish Administration][4] unless—

(*a*) they are installed or incorporated in the course of a supply which is treated as being made in the course of furtherance of a business carried on by the department; or

(*b*) the parts and equipment are to be installed or incorporated in ships or aircraft used for the purpose of providing rescue or assistance at sea.][3]

(3) Item 3 shall not apply unless, before the supply is made, the recipient of the supply gives to the person making the supply a certificate stating—

(*a*) the name and address of the recipient;

(*b*) that the supply is of a description specified in item 3 of this Group.

(4) "Lifeboat" means any vessel used or to be used solely for rescue or assistance at sea.

[(4A) Item 4 does not include the transport of passengers—

(*a*) in any vehicle to, from or within—

(i) a place of entertainment, recreation or amusement; or

(ii) a place of cultural, scientific, historical or similar interest,

by the person, or a person connected with him, who supplies a right of admission to, or a right to use facilities at, such a place;

(*b*) in any motor vehicle between a car park (or land adjacent thereto) and an airport passenger terminal (or land adjacent thereto) by the person, or a person connected with him, who supplies facilities for the parking of vehicles in that car park; or

(*c*) in an aircraft where the flight is advertised or held out to be for the purpose of—

(i) providing entertainment, recreation or amusement; or

(ii) the experience of flying, or the experience of flying in that particular aircraft,

and not primarily for the purpose of transporting passengers from one place to another.][1]

[(4B) For the purposes of Note (4A) any question whether a person is connected with another shall be determined in accordance with section 839 of the Taxes Act.][1]

[(4C) In Note (4A)(*b*) "motor vehicle" means a mechanically propelled vehicle intended or adapted for use on the roads.][1]

[(4D) Item 4(*a*) includes the transport of passengers in a vehicle—

(*a*) which is designed, or substantially and permanently adapted, for the safe carriage of a person in a wheelchair or two or more such persons, and

(*b*) which, if it were not so designed or adapted, would be capable of carrying no less than 10 persons.][6]

(5) Item 6 does not include the letting on hire of goods.

(6) "Port"[,"customs and excise airport" and "transit shed"][8] have the same meanings as in the Management Act.

[(6A) "Air navigation services" has the same meaning as in the Civil Aviation Act 1982.][2]

(7) Except for the purposes of item 11, paragraph (*a*) of item 6, [item 6A,][2] item 9 and paragraph (*a*) of item 10 [only include supplies of services where the ships or aircraft referred to in those paragraphs are qualifying ships or, as the case may be, aircraft.][3]

(8) "Designated travel service" has the same meaning as in the Value Added Tax Tour Operators) Order 1987.

(9) "Intra-Community transport services" means—

(*a*) the intra-Community transport of goods within the meaning of the Value Added Tax (Place of Supply of Services) Order 1992;

(*b*) ancillary transport services within the meaning of the Value Added Tax (Place of Supply of Services) Order 1992 which are provided in connection with the intra-Community transport of goods; or

(*c*) the making of arrangements for the supply by or to another person of a supply within (*a*) or (*b*) above or any other activity which is intended to facilitate the making of such a supply,

and, for the purpose of this Note only, the Azores and Madeira shall each be treated as a separate member State.

Commentary—*De Voil Indirect Tax Service* **V4.251**.

Press releases etc—C&E Business Brief 27/95 18-12-95 (a holiday cruise is a single supply of passenger transport zero-rated under item 4; C&E to appeal decision).

C&E Business Brief 2/96 9-2-96 (guidance on the VAT treatment of commission for transport only sales by travel agents).

C&E Business Brief 4/96 13-3-96 (conditions for treatment of airline passenger perks as part of air passenger transport).

C&E Business Brief 14/96 15-7-96 (VAT treatment of holiday and other cruises).

Simon's Tax Cases—Item 1, *R&C Comrs v Stone; The Kei* [2008] STC 2501.

Item 4, *Virgin Atlantic Airways v C&E Comrs* [1995] STC 341*.

Item 4(*a*), *British Airways plc v C&E Comrs* [1990] STC 643*; *C&E Comrs v Peninsular and Oriental Steam Navigation Co Ltd* [1996] STC 698; *Cirdan Sailing Trust v C&E Comrs* [2006] STC 185.

Item 4(*c*), *British Airways plc v C&E Comrs* [1990] STC 643*.

Item 6, *R&C Comrs v EB Central Services Ltd and another* [2008] STC 2209.

Item 10, *Société Internationale de Télécommunications Aéronautiques v C&E Comrs* [2004] STC 950.

Item 11(*a*), *R&C Comrs v EB Central Services Ltd and another* [2008] STC 2209.

Definitions—"Business", s 94; "the Management Act", s 96(1); "ship", s 96(1); "supply", s 5, Sch 4; "United Kingdom", s 96(11).

Amendments—[1] Notes (4A)–(4C) inserted by the Value Added Tax (Transport) Order, SI 1994/3014 with effect from 1 April 1995.

[2] Item 6A and Note (6A) inserted, and words in item 11(*b*) and Note (7) inserted, by the Value Added Tax (Transport) Order, SI 1995/653 with effect from 1 April 1995.

[3] Items 1 and 2 substituted, items 2A, 2B inserted, words in item 10 substituted, Notes (A1), (2A) and words in Notes (1), (2) inserted and words in Note (7) substituted by the Value Added Tax (Ships and Aircraft) Order, SI 1995/3039 with effect from 1 January 1996.

[4] Words in sub-ss (2A) inserted by The Scotland Act 1998 (Consequential Modifications) (No 2) Order, SI 1999/1820 s 114(2), which comes into force on the "principle appointed day", currently 1 July 1999, by virtue of the Scotland Act 1998 (Commencement) Order 1998/3178.

[5] Words in item 4 substituted by the Postal Services Act 2000 s 127(4), Sch 8 para 22(1), (3) as from 26 March 2001 (by virtue of SI 2000/2957).

[6] Figure in item 4 substituted, and Note (4D) inserted by the Value Added Tax (Passenger Vehicles) Order, SI 2001/753 arts 2, 3 with effect for supplies made after 31 March 2001.

[7] Para (*d*) in item 3 added, and words in item 10 added, by the VAT (Equipment in Lifeboats) Order, SI 2002/456 with effect from 1 April 2002.

[8] Para (*b*) of item 6, and words in Note (6) substituted by the Value Added Tax (Transport) Order, SI 2002/1173 art 2 with effect from 1 June 2002.

[9] Para (*e*) of item 3 inserted by the Value Added Tax (Lifeboats) Order, SI 2006/1750 arts 1, 2 with effect from 1 August 2006.

GROUP 9 — CARAVANS AND HOUSEBOATS

Item No

1 Caravans exceeding the limits of size for the time being permitted for the use on roads of a trailer drawn by a motor vehicle having an unladen weight of less than 2,030 kilogrammes.

2 Houseboats being boats or other floating decked structures designed or adapted for use solely as places of permanent habitation and not having means of, or capable of being readily adapted for, self-propulsion.

3 The supply of such services as are described in paragraph 1(1) or 5(3) of Schedule 4 in respect of a caravan comprised in item 1 or a houseboat comprised in item 2.

Note: This Group does not include—

(*a*) removable contents other than goods of a kind mentioned in item 3 of Group 5; or
(*b*) the supply of accommodation in a caravan or houseboat.

Commentary—*De Voil Indirect Tax Service* **V4.275**.
Simon's Tax Cases—*Talacre Beach Caravan Sales Ltd v C&E Comrs* [2006] STC 1671.
Definition—"Supply", s 5, Sch 4.
Note—The Commissioners have confirmed that the cross reference in item 3 should refer to 5(4) of Schedule 4 and not 5(3) of Schedule 4 as stated in the Act. Likewise, Note (*a*) should cross refer to item 4 of Group 5 and not item 3 of Group 5.

GROUP 10 — GOLD

Item No

1 The supply, by a Central Bank to another Central Bank or a member of the London Gold Market, of gold held in the United Kingdom.

2 The supply, by a member of the London Gold Market to a Central Bank, of gold held in the United Kingdom.

NOTES

(1) "Gold" includes gold coins.

(2) Section 30(3) does not apply to goods forming part of a description of supply in this Group.

(3) Items 1 and 2 include—

(*a*) the granting of a right to acquire a quantity of gold; and
(*b*) any supply described in those items which by virtue of paragraph 1 of Schedule 4 is a supply of services.

Commentary—*De Voil Indirect Tax Service* **V4.277**.
Definitions—"Supply", s 5, Sch 4; "United Kingdom", s 96(11).

GROUP 11 — BANK NOTES

Item No

1 The issue by a bank of a note payable to bearer on demand.

Simon's Tax Cases—Item 1 *Royal Bank of Scotland Group plc v C & E Comrs* [2002] STC 575.
Commentary—*De Voil Indirect Tax Service* **V4.279**.

GROUP 12 — DRUGS, MEDICINES, AIDS FOR THE HANDICAPPED, ETC

Item No

1 The [supply of any qualifying goods dispensed to an individual for his personal use where the dispensing is][2] by a person registered in [the Register of Pharmacists maintained under the Pharmacists and Pharmacy Technicians Order 2007 or in the register of pharmaceutical chemists kept under][12] the Pharmacy (Northern Ireland) Order 1976, on the prescription of a person registered in the register of medical practitioners, the register of medical practitioners with limited registration or the dentists' register.

[1A The supply of any [qualifying][2] goods in accordance with a requirement or authorisation under—

(*a*) regulation 20 of the National Health Service (Pharmaceutical Services) Regulations 1992;
(*b*) regulation 34 of the National Health Service (General Medical Services) (Scotland) Regulations 1995; or
(*c*) [regulation 12 of the Pharmaceutical Services Regulations (Northern Ireland) 1997][2],

by a person registered in the register of medical practitioners or the register of medical practitioners with limited registration.][1]

2 The supply to a handicapped person for domestic or his personal use, or to a charity for making available to handicapped persons by sale or otherwise, for domestic or their personal use, of—

(*a*) medical or surgical appliances designed solely for the relief of a severe abnormality or severe injury;
(*b*) electrically or mechanically adjustable beds designed for invalids;
(*c*) commode chairs, commode stools, devices incorporating a bidet jet and warm air drier and frames or other devices for sitting over or rising from a sanitary appliance;
(*d*) chair lifts or stair lifts designed for use in connection with invalid wheelchairs;
(*e*) hoists and lifters designed for use by invalids;
(*f*) motor vehicles designed or substantially and permanently adapted for the carriage of a person in a wheelchair or on a stretcher and of no more than [11][8] other persons;
(*g*) equipment and appliances not included in paragraphs (*a*) to (*f*) above designed solely for use by a handicapped person;
(*h*) parts and accessories designed solely for use in or with goods described in paragraphs (*a*) to (*g*) above;
(*i*) boats designed or substantially and permanently adapted for use by handicapped persons.

[2A The supply of a qualifying motor vehicle—

(*a*) to a handicapped person—
 (i) who usually uses a wheelchair, or
 (ii) who is usually carried on a stretcher, for domestic or his personal use; or
(*b*) to a charity for making available to such a handicapped person by sale or otherwise, for domestic or his personal use.][7]

3 The supply to a handicapped person of services of adapting goods to suit his condition.

4 The supply to a charity of services of adapting goods to suit the condition of a handicapped person to whom the goods are to be made available, by sale or otherwise, by the charity.

5 The supply to a handicapped person or to a charity of a service of repair or maintenance of any goods specified in item 2, [2A,][8] 6, 18 or 19 and supplied as described in that item.

6 The supply of goods in connection with a supply described in item 3, 4 or 5.

7 The supply to a handicapped person or to a charity of services necessarily performed in the installation of equipment or appliances (including parts and accessories therefor) specified in item 2 and supplied as described in that item.

8 The supply to a handicapped person of a service of constructing ramps or widening doorways or passages for the purpose of facilitating his entry to or movement within his private residence.

9 The supply to a charity of a service described in item 8 for the purpose of facilitating a handicapped person's entry to or movement within any building.

10 The supply to a handicapped person of a service of providing, extending or adapting a bathroom, washroom or lavatory in his private residence where such provision, extension or adaptation is necessary by reason of his condition.

[11 The supply to a charity of a service of providing, extending or adapting a bathroom, washroom or lavatory for use by handicapped persons—

(*a*) in residential accommodation, or
(*b*) in a day-centre where at least 20 per cent of the individuals using the centre are handicapped persons,

where such provision, extension or adaptation is necessary by reason of the condition of the handicapped persons.][6]

12 The supply to a charity of a service of providing, extending or adapting a washroom or lavatory for use by handicapped persons in a building, or any part of a building, used principally by a charity for charitable purposes where such provision, extension or adaptation is necessary to facilitate the use of the washroom or lavatory by handicapped persons.

13 The supply of goods in connection with a supply described in items 8, 9, 10 or 11.

14 The letting on hire of a motor vehicle for a period of not less than 3 years to a handicapped person in receipt of a disability living allowance by virtue of entitlement to the mobility component or of mobility supplement where the lessor's business consists predominantly of the provision of motor vehicles to such persons.

15 The sale of a motor vehicle which had been let on hire in the circumstances described in item 14, where such sale constitutes the first supply of the vehicle after the end of the period of such letting.

16 The supply to a handicapped person of services necessarily performed in the installation of a lift for the purpose of facilitating his movement between floors within his private residence.

17 The supply to a charity providing a permanent or temporary residence or day-centre for handicapped persons of services necessarily performed in the installation of a lift for the purpose of facilitating the movement of handicapped persons between floors within that building.

18 The supply of goods in connection with a supply described in item 16 or 17.

19 The supply to a handicapped person for domestic or his personal use, or to a charity for making available to handicapped persons by sale or otherwise for domestic or their personal use, of an alarm system designed to be capable of operation by a handicapped person, and to enable him to alert directly a specified person or a control centre.

20 The supply of services necessarily performed by a control centre in receiving and responding to calls from an alarm system specified in item 19.

NOTES

(1) Section 30(3) does not apply to goods forming part of a description of supply in item 1 [or item 1A][1], nor to other goods forming part of a description of supply in this Group, except where those other goods are acquired from another member State or imported from a place outside the member States by a handicapped person for domestic or his personal use, or by a charity for making available to handicapped persons, by sale or otherwise, for domestic or their personal use.

(2) …[13]

[(2A) In items 1 and 1A, 'qualifying goods' means any goods designed or adapted for use in connection with any medical or surgical treatment except—

(*a*) hearing aids;
(*b*) dentures; and
(*c*) spectacles and contact lenses.][3]

(3) "Handicapped" means chronically sick or disabled.

(4) Item 2 shall not include hearing aids (except hearing aids designed for the auditory training of deaf children), dentures, spectacles and contact lenses but shall be deemed to include—

(*a*) clothing, footwear and wigs;
(*b*) invalid wheelchairs, and invalid carriages […][4]; and
(*c*) renal haemodialysis units, oxygen concentrators, artificial respirators and other similar apparatus.

(5) The supplies described in Items 1[, 1A][1] [, 2 and 2A][8] include supplies of services of letting on hire of the goods respectively comprised in those items.

[(5A) In item 1 the reference to personal use does not include any use which is, or involves, a use by or in relation to an individual while that individual, for the purposes of being provided (whether or not by the person making the supply) with medical or surgical treatment, or with any form of care—

(*a*) is an in-patient or resident in a relevant institution which is a hospital or nursing home; or
(*b*) is attending at the premises of a relevant institution which is a hospital or nursing home.

(5B) Subject to Notes (5C) and (5D), in item 2 the reference to domestic or personal use does not include any use which is, or involves, a use by or in relation to a handicapped person while that person, for the purposes of being provided (whether or not by the person making the supply) with medical or surgical treatment, or with any form of care—

(*a*) is an in-patient or resident in a relevant institution; or
(*b*) is attending at the premises of a relevant institution.

(5C) Note (5B) does not apply for the purpose of determining whether any of the following supplies falls within item 2, that is to say—

(*a*) a supply to a charity;
(*b*) a supply by a person mentioned in any of paragraphs (*a*) to (*g*) of Note (5H) of an invalid wheelchair or invalid carriage;
(*c*) a supply by a person so mentioned of any parts or accessories designed solely for use in or with an invalid wheelchair or invalid carriage.

(5D) Note (5B) applies for the purpose of determining whether a supply of goods by a person not mentioned in any of paragraphs (*a*) to (*g*) of Note (5H) falls within item 2 only if those goods are—

(*a*) goods falling within paragraph (*a*) of that item;
(*b*) incontinence products and wound dressings; or
(*c*) parts and accessories designed solely for use in or with goods falling within paragraph (*a*) of this Note.

(5E) Subject to Note (5F), item 2 does not include—

(*a*) a supply made in accordance with any agreement, arrangement or understanding (whether or not legally enforceable) to which any of the persons mentioned in paragraphs (*a*) to (*g*) of Note (5H) is or has been a party otherwise than as the supplier; or (*b*) any supply the whole or any part of the consideration for which is provided (whether directly or indirectly) by a person so mentioned.

(5F) A supply to a handicapped person of an invalid wheelchair or invalid carriage is excluded from item 2 by Note (5E) only if—

(*a*) that Note applies in relation to that supply by reference to a person falling within paragraph (*g*) of Note (5H); or

(*b*) the whole of the consideration for the supply is provided (whether directly or indirectly) by a person falling within any of paragraphs (*a*) to (*f*) of Note (5H).

(5G) In Notes (4), (5C) and (5F), the references to an invalid wheelchair and to an invalid carriage do not include references to any mechanically propelled vehicle which is intended or adapted for use on roads.

(5H) The persons referred to in Notes (5C) to (5F) are—

[(*a*) a Strategic Health Authority or Special Health Authority in England;][10]

[(*aa*) a Health Authority, Special Health Authority or Local Health Board in Wales;][10]

(*b*) a Health Board or Special Health Board in Scotland;

(*c*) a Health and Social Services Board in Northern Ireland;

(*d*) the Common Services Agency for the Scottish Health Service, the Northern Ireland Central Services Agency for Health and Social Services and the Isle of Man Health Services Board;

(*e*) a National Health Service trust established under Part I of the National Health Service and Community Care Act 1990 or the National Health Service (Scotland) Act 1978;

[(*eaa*) an NHS foundation trust;][11]

[(*ea*) a Primary Care Trust established under section 16A of the National Health Service Act 1977;][5]

(*f*) a Health and Social Services trust established under Article 10 of the Health and Personal Social Services (Northern Ireland) Order 1991; or

(*g*) any person not falling within any of paragraphs (*a*) to (*f*) above who is engaged in the carrying on of any activity in respect of which a relevant institution is required to be approved, licensed or registered or as the case may be, would be so required if not exempt.

(5I) In Notes (5A), (5B) and (5H), 'relevant institution' means any institution (whether a hospital, nursing home or other institution) which provides care or medical or surgical treatment and is either—

(*a*) approved, licensed or registered in accordance with the provisions of any enactment or Northern Ireland legislation; or

(*b*) exempted by or under the provisions of any enactment or Northern Ireland legislation from any requirement to be approved, licensed or registered;

and in this Note the references to the provisions of any enactment or Northern Ireland legislation include references only to provisions which, so far as relating to England, Wales, Scotland or Northern Ireland, have the same effect in every locality within that part of the United Kingdom.][3]

[(5J) For the purposes of item 11 "residential accommodation" means—

(*a*) a residential home, or

(*b*) self-contained living accommodation,

provided as a residence (whether on a permanent or temporary basis or both) for handicapped persons, but does not include an inn, hotel, boarding house or similar establishment or accommodation in any such type of establishment.

(5K) In this Group "washroom" means a room that contains a lavatory or washbasin (or both) but does not contain a bath or a shower or cooking, sleeping or laundry facilities.][6]

[(5L) A "qualifying motor vehicle" for the purposes of item 2A is a motor vehicle (other than a motor vehicle capable of carrying more than 12 persons including the driver)—

(*a*) that is designed or substantially and permanently adapted to enable a handicapped person—

(i) who usually uses a wheelchair, or

(ii) who is usually carried on a stretcher,

to enter, and drive or be otherwise carried in, the motor vehicle; or

(*b*) that by reason of its design, or being substantially and permanently adapted, includes features whose design is such that their sole purpose is to allow a wheelchair used by a handicapped person to be carried in or on the motor vehicle.][7]

(6) Item 14 applies only—

(*a*) where the vehicle is unused at the commencement of the period of letting; and

(*b*) where the consideration for the letting consists wholly or partly of sums paid to the lessor by [the Department for Work and Pensions][9] or the Ministry of Defence on behalf of the lessee in respect of the mobility component of the disability living allowance or mobility supplement to which he is entitled.

(7) In item 14—

(*a*) "disability living allowance" is a disability living allowance within the meaning of section 71 of the Social Security Contributions and Benefits Act 1992 or section 71 of the Social Security Contributions and Benefits (Northern Ireland) Act 1992; and

(*b*) "mobility supplement" is a mobility supplement within the meaning of Article 26A of the Naval, Military and Air Forces etc (Disablement and Death Service Pensions Order 1983, Article 25A of the Personal Injuries (Civilians) Scheme 1983, Article 3 of the Motor Vehicles (Exemption from Vehicles Excise Duty) Order 1985 or Article 3 of the Motor Vehicles (Exemption from Vehicles Excise Duty) (Northern Ireland) Order 1985.

(8) Where in item 3 or 4 the goods are adapted in accordance with that item prior to their supply to the handicapped person or the charity, an apportionment shall be made to determine the supply of services which falls within item 3 or 4.

(9) In item 19 or 20, a specified person or control centre is a person or centre who or which—

(*a*) is appointed to receive directly calls activated by an alarm system described in that item, and

(*b*) retains information about the handicapped person to assist him in the event of illness, injury or similar emergency.

Commentary—*De Voil Indirect Tax Service* **V4.281**.

Press releases etc—C&E Business Brief 12/95 19-6-95 (supplies of drugs, prostheses etc by hospitals as part of an exempt supply of hospital services under Sch 9 Group 7 cannot be separately zero-rated).

C&E Business Brief 18/95 6-9-95 (end of concessionary treatment for supplies of dispensed medicines on prescription by doctors).

C&E Business Brief 23/95 24-10-95 (supplies of incontinence products to commercial nursing homes and NHS Trusts).

C&E Business Brief 16/96 30-7-96 (allergy relief products will be liable to VAT at the standard rate irrespective of to whom supplied).

C&E Business Brief 16/96 30-7-96 (zero rated supplies of incontinence products can no longer be made by NHS or non-charitable nursing homes).

C&E Business Brief 5/97 5-3-97 (supplies of incontinence products to patients residing at home are zero rated).

VAT Information Sheet 7/01 June 2001 (guidance on when a supplier is entitled to zero rate the supply of an eligible adapted motor vehicle to a disabled person, a charitable institution and certain other eligible bodies. Also details the necessary documentation with regard to the relief).

Simon's Tax Cases—Item 1, *British United Provident Association Ltd v C&E Comrs* [1995] STC 628*; *Provident Association Ltd* [1997] STC 445*.

Items 2, 7, *British United Provident Association Ltd v C&E Comrs* [1995] STC 628*; Provident Association Ltd [1997] STC 445*; *Dr Beynon and Partners v C&E Comrs* [2003] STC 169, CA.

Definitions—"Acquisition of goods from another member State", s 11; "another member State", s 96(1); "business", s 94; "importation of goods from a place outside the member States", s 15; "supply", s 5, Sch 4.

Cross reference—See VAT Regulations, SI 1995/2518 reg 74 (retail schemes: adjustment of calculations for supplies within this Group).

Amendments—[1] Item 1A, and words in Notes (1), (5), inserted by the VAT (Supply of Pharmaceutical Goods) Order, SI 1995/652 with effect from 1 April 1995.

[2] Words in Items 1, 1A substituted and inserted by the VAT (Drugs, Medicines and Aids for the Handicapped) Order, SI 1997/2744 with effect from 1 January 1998.

[3] Notes (2A), (5A), (5B), (5C), (5D), (5E), (5F), (5G), (5H), (5I), inserted by the VAT (Drugs, Medicines and Aids for the Handicapped) Order, SI 1997/2744 with effect from 1 January 1998.

[4] Words in Note (4)(*b*) deleted by the VAT (Drugs, Medicines and Aids for the Handicapped) Order, SI 1997/2744 with effect from 1 January 1998.

[5] Para (*ea*) in Note (5H) inserted by the VAT (Drugs, Medicines, Aids for the Handicapped and Charities Etc) Order, SI 2000/503 arts 2, 3 with effect from 1 April 2000.

[6] Item 11 substituted and Notes (5J), (5K) inserted by the VAT (Charities and Aids for the Handicapped) Order, SI 2000/805 arts 2, 3 with effect from 1 April 2000.

[7] Item 2A and Note (5L) inserted by the Value Added Tax (Vehicles Designed or Adapted for Handicapped Persons) Order, SI 2001/754 arts 3, 6 with effect for supplies, acquisitions or importations made after 31 March 2001.

[8] Figure substituted in Item 2(*f*); "2A" added in Item 5, and words substituted in Note (5) by SI 2001/754 arts 2, 4 and 5 with effect for supplies, acquisitions or importations made after 31 March 2001.

[9] Words in Note (6)(*b*) substituted by the Secretaries of State for Education and Skills and for Work and Pensions Order, SI 2002/1397 art 12, Schedule para 11 with effect from 27 June 2002.

[10] Note (5H)(*a*), (*aa*) substituted for Note (5H)(*a*) as originally enacted, by the VAT (Drugs, Medicines, Aids for the Handicapped and Charities Etc) Order, SI 2002/2813 arts 2, 3 with effect from 5 December 2002.

[11] In Note (5H), para (*eaa*) inserted by the Health and Social Care (Community Health and Standards) Act 2003 s 34, Sch 4 paras 97, 98 with effect, in relation to England and Wales, from 1 April 2004 (by virtue of SI 2004/759) and in relation to Scotland, from a date to be appointed.

[12] Words in Item 1 substituted by the Pharmacists and Pharmacy Technicians Order, SI 2007/289, art 67, Sch 1, Pt 1, para 5(1), (2) with effect from 30 March 2007.

[13] Note 2 repealed by the European Qualifications (Health and Social Care Professions) Regulations, SI 2007/3101 reg 65(a) with effect from 3 December 2007.

GROUP 13 — IMPORTS, EXPORTS ETC

Item No

1 The supply before the delivery of an entry (within the meaning of regulation 5 of the Customs Controls on Importation of Goods Regulations 1991)) under an agreement requiring the purchaser to make such entry of goods imported from a place outside the member States.

2 The supply to or by an overseas authority, overseas body or overseas trader, charged with the management of any defence project which is the subject of an international collaboration arrangement or under direct contract with any government or government-sponsored international body participating in a defence project under such an arrangement, of goods or services in the course of giving effect to that arrangement.

3 The supply to an overseas authority, overseas body or overseas trader of jigs, patterns, templates, dies, punches and similar machine tools used in the United Kingdom solely for the manufacture of goods for export to places outside the member States.

Notes

(1) An "international collaboration arrangement" means any arrangement which—

(*a*) is made between the United Kingdom Government and the government of one or more other countries, or any government-sponsored international body for collaboration in a joint project of research, development or production; and

(*b*) includes provision for participating governments to relieve the cost of the project from taxation.

(2) "Overseas authority" means any country other than the United Kingdom or any part of or place in such a country or the government of any such country, part or place.

(3) "Overseas body" means a body established outside the United Kingdom.

(4) "Overseas trader" means a person who carries on a business and has his principal place of business outside the United Kingdom.

(5) Item 3 does not apply where the overseas authority, overseas body or overseas trader is a taxable person, another member State, any part of or place in another member State, the government of any such member State, part or place, a body established in another member State or a person who carries on business, or has a place of business, in another member State.

Commentary—*De Voil Indirect Tax Service* **V.283**.
Definitions—"Another member State", s 96(1); "business", s 94; "importation of goods from a place outside the member States", s 15; "supply", s 5, Sch 4; "taxable person", s 3; "United Kingdom", s 96(11).

GROUP 14 — TAX-FREE SHOPS

…

Commentary—*De Voil Indirect Tax Service* **V4.285**.
Amendments—Group 14 deleted by the Value Added Tax (Abolition of Zero-Rating for Tax Free Shops) Order, SI 1999/1642, with effect from 1 July 1999.

GROUP 15 — CHARITIES ETC

Item No

[**1** The sale, or letting on hire, by a charity of any goods donated to it for—

(*a*) sale,
(*b*) letting,
(*c*) sale or letting,
(*d*) sale or export,
(*e*) letting or export, or
(*f*) sale, letting or export.

1A The sale, or letting on hire, by a taxable person of any goods donated to him for—

(*a*) sale,
(*b*) letting,
(*c*) sale or letting,
(*d*) sale or export,
(*e*) letting or export, or
(*f*) sale, letting or export,

if he is a profits-to-charity person in respect of the goods.

2 The donation of any goods for any one or more of the following purposes—

(*a*) sale by a charity or a taxable person who is a profits-to-charity person in respect of the goods;
(*b*) export by a charity or such a taxable person;
(*c*) letting by a charity or such a taxable person.][3]

3 The export of any goods by a charity to a place outside the member States.

4 The supply of any relevant goods for donation to a nominated eligible body where the goods are purchased with funds provided by a charity or from voluntary contributions.

5 The supply of any relevant goods to an eligible body which pays for them with funds provided by a charity or from voluntary contributions or to an eligible body which is a charitable institution providing care or medical or surgical treatment for handicapped persons.

6 Repair and maintenance of relevant goods owned by an eligible body.

7 The supply of goods in connection with the supply described in item 6.

[**8** The supply to a charity of a right to promulgate an advertisement by means of a medium of communication with the public.

8A A supply to a charity that consists in the promulgation of an advertisement by means of such a medium.

8B The supply to a charity of services of design or production of an advertisement that is, or was intended to be, promulgated by means of such a medium.

8C The supply to a charity of goods closely related to a supply within item 8B.][3]

9 The supply to a charity, providing care or medical or surgical treatment for human beings or animals, or engaging in medical or veterinary research, of a medicinal product [or veterinary medicinal product][6] where the supply is solely for use by the charity in such care, treatment or research.

10 The supply to a charity of a substance directly used for synthesis or testing in the course of medical or veterinary research.

NOTES

[(1) Item 1 or 1A does not apply unless the sale or letting—

(*a*) takes place as a result of the goods having been made available—

(i) to two or more specified persons, or

(ii) to the general public,

for purchase or hire (whether so made available in a shop or elsewhere), and

(*b*) does not take place as a result of any arrangements (whether legally binding or not) relating to the goods and entered into, before the goods were made so available, by—

(i) each of the parties to the sale or letting, or

(ii) the donor of the goods and either or both of those parties.

(1A) For the purposes of items 1, 1A and 2, goods are donated for letting only if they are donated for—

(*a*) letting, and

(*b*) re-letting after the end of any first or subsequent letting, and

(*c*) all or any of—

(i) sale,

(ii) export, or

(iii) disposal as waste,

if not, or when no longer, used for letting.

(1B) Items 1 and 1A do not include (and shall be treated as having not included) any sale, or letting on hire, of particular donated goods if the goods, at any time after they are donated but before they are sold, exported or disposed of as waste, are whilst unlet used for any purpose other than, or in addition to, that of being available for purchase, hire or export.

(1C) In Note (1) "specified person" means a person who—

(*a*) is handicapped, or

(*b*) is entitled to any one or more of the specified benefits, or

(*c*) is both handicapped and so entitled.

(1D) For the purposes of Note (1C) the specified benefits are—

(*a*) income support under Part VII of the Social Security Contributions and Benefits Act 1992 or Part VII of the Social Security Contributions and Benefits (Northern Ireland) Act 1992;

(*b*) housing benefit under Part VII of the Social Security Contributions and Benefits Act 1992 or Part VII of the Social Security Contributions and Benefits (Northern Ireland) Act 1992;

(*c*) council tax benefit under Part VII of the Social Security Contributions and Benefits Act 1992;

(*d*) an income-based jobseeker's allowance within the meaning of section 1(4) of the Jobseekers Act 1995 or article 3(4) of the Jobseekers (Northern Ireland) Order 1995;

[(*e*) any element of child tax credit other than the family element; and][5]

[(*f*) working tax credit.][5]

(1E) For the purposes of items 1A and 2 a taxable person is a "profits-to-charity" person in respect of any goods if—

(*a*) he has agreed in writing (whether or not contained in a deed) to transfer to a charity his profits from supplies and lettings of the goods, or

(*b*) his profits from supplies and lettings of the goods are otherwise payable to a charity.

(1F) In items 1, 1A and 2, and any Notes relating to any of those items, "goods" means goods (and, in particular, does not include anything that is not goods even though provision made by or under an enactment provides for a supply of that thing to be, or be treated as, a supply of goods).][3]

(2) "Animals" includes any species of the animal kingdom.

(3) "Relevant goods" means—

(*a*) medical, scientific, computer, video, sterilising, laboratory or refrigeration equipment for use in medical or veterinary research, training, diagnosis or treatment;

(*b*) ambulances;

(*c*) parts or accessories for use in or with goods described in paragraph (*a*) or (*b*) above;

(*d*) goods of a kind described in item 2 of Group 12 of this Schedule;

(*e*) motor vehicles (other than vehicles with more than 50 seats) designed or substantially and permanently adapted for the safe carriage of a handicapped person in a wheelchair provided that—

(i) in the case of vehicles with more than 16 but fewer than 27 seats, the number of persons for which such provision shall exist shall be at least 2;
(ii) in the case of vehicles with more than 26 but fewer than 37 seats, the number of persons for which such provision shall exist shall be at least 3;
(iii) in the case of vehicles with more than 36 but fewer than 47 seats, the number of persons for which such provision shall exist shall be at least 4;
(iv) in the case of vehicles with more than 46 seats, the number of persons for which such provision shall exist shall be at least 5;
(v) there is either a fitted electrically or hydraulically operated lift or, in the case of vehicles with fewer than 17 seats, a fitted ramp to provide access for a passenger in a wheelchair;

(*f*) motor vehicles (with more than 6 but fewer than 51 seats) for use by an eligible body providing care for blind, deaf, mentally handicapped or terminally sick persons mainly to transport such persons;
(*g*) telecommunication, aural, visual, light enhancing or heat detecting equipment (not being equipment ordinarily supplied for private or recreational use) solely for use for the purpose of rescue or first aid services undertaken by a charitable institution providing such services.

(4) "Eligible body" means—

[(*a*) a Strategic Health Authority or Special Health Authority in England;][4]
[(*aa*) a Health Authority, Special Health Authority or Local Health Board in Wales;][4]
(*b*) a Health Board in Scotland;
(*c*) a Health and Social Services Board in Northern Ireland;
(*d*) a hospital whose activities are not carried on for profit;
(*e*) a research institution whose activities are not carried on for profit;
(*f*) a charitable institution providing care or medical or surgical treatment for handicapped persons;
(*g*) the Common Services Agency for the Scottish Health Service, the Northern Ireland Central Services Agency for Health and Social Services or the Isle of Man Health Services Board;
(*h*) a charitable institution providing rescue or first-aid services;
(*i*) a National Health Service trust established under Part I of the National Health Service and Community Care Act 1990 or the National Health Service (Scotland) Act 1978;
[(*j*) a Primary Care Trust established under section 16A of the National Health Service Act 1977][2].

[(4A) Subject to Note (5B), a charitable institution shall not be regarded as providing care or medical or surgical treatment for handicapped persons unless—

(*a*) it provides care or medical or surgical treatment in a relevant establishment; and
(*b*) the majority of the persons who receive care or medical or surgical treatment in that establishment are handicapped persons.][1]

[(4B) "Relevant establishment" means—

(*a*) a day-centre, other than a day-centre which exists primarily as a place for activities that are social or recreational or both; or
(*b*) an institution which is—

(i) approved, licensed or registered in accordance with the provisions of any enactment or Northern Ireland legislation; or
(ii) exempted by or under the provisions of any enactment or Northern Ireland legislation from any requirement to be approved, licensed or registered;

and in paragraph (*b*) above the references to the provisions of any enactment or Northern Ireland legislation are references only to provisions which, so far as relating to England, Wales, Scotland or Northern Ireland, have the same effect in every locality within that part of the United Kingdom.][1]

(5) "Handicapped" means chronically sick or disabled.

[(5A) Subject to Note (5B), items 4 to 7 do not apply where the eligible body falls within Note (4)(*f*) unless the relevant goods are or are to be used in a relevant establishment in which that body provides care or medical or surgical treatment to persons the majority of whom are handicapped.][1]

[(5B) Nothing in Note (4A) or (5A) shall prevent a supply from falling within items 4 to 7 where—

(*a*) the eligible body provides medical care to handicapped persons in their own homes;
(*b*) the relevant goods fall within Note (3)(*a*) or are parts or accessories for use in or with goods described in Note (3)(*a*); and
(*c*) those goods are or are to be used in or in connection with the provision of that care.][1]

(6) Item 4 does not apply where the donee of the goods is not a charity and has contributed in whole or in part to the funds for the purchase of the goods.

(7) Item 5 does not apply where the body to whom the goods are supplied is not a charity and has contributed in whole or in part to the funds for the purchase of the goods.

(8) Items 6 and 7 do not apply unless—

(*a*) the supply is paid for with funds which have been provided by a charity or from voluntary contributions, and

(*b*) in a case where the owner of the goods repaired or maintained is not a charity, it has not contributed in whole or in part to those funds.

(9) Items 4 and 5 include the letting on hire of relevant goods; accordingly in items 4, 5 and 6 and the notes relating thereto, references to the purchase or ownership of goods shall be deemed to include references respectively to their hiring and possession.

(10) Item 5 includes computer services by way of the provision of computer software solely for use in medical research, diagnosis or treatment.

[(10A) Neither of items 8 and 8A includes a supply where any of the members of the public (whether individuals or other persons) who are reached through the medium are selected by or on behalf of the charity.

For this purpose "selected" includes selected by address (whether postal address or telephone number, e-mail address or other address for electronic communications purposes) or at random.

(10B) None of items 8 to 8C includes a supply used to create, or contribute to, a website that is the charity's own.

For this purpose a website is a charity's own even though hosted by another person.

(10C) Neither of items 8B and 8C includes a supply to a charity that is used directly by the charity to design or produce an advertisement.][3]

(11) In item 9—

(*a*) a "medicinal product" means any substance or article (not being an instrument, apparatus or appliance) which is for use wholly or mainly in either or both of the following ways—

(i) by being administered to one or more human beings …[6] for a medicinal purpose;

(ii) as an ingredient in the preparation of a substance or article which is to be administered to one or more human beings …[6] for a medicinal purpose;

(*b*) a "medicinal purpose" has the meaning assigned to it by section 130(2) of the Medicines Act 1968;

(*c*) "administer" has the meaning assigned to it by section 130(9) of the Medicines Act 1968;

[(*d*) "veterinary medicinal product" has the meaning assigned to it by regulation 2 of the Veterinary Medicines Regulations 2006.][6]

(12) In items 9 and 10 "substance" and "ingredient" have the meanings assigned to them by section 132 of the Medicines Act 1968.

Commentary—*De Voil Indirect Tax Service* **V4.266**.
Concession ESC 3.22—Charities: sale of poor quality donated goods. Supplies of 'relevant goods' to charities.
Press releases etc—C&E Business Brief 9/96 24-5-96 (zero-rating of job recruitment advertising by charities).
C&E Business Brief 18/96 27-8-96 ("eligible body" in relation to supplies of community transport vehicles for the disabled is defined).
C&E Business Brief 18/96 27-8-96 (zero-rating no longer applies to certain supplies of stationery to charities).
C&E Business Brief 21/96 17-10-96 (confirmation that share dealing by charities is outside the scope of VAT).
Simon's Tax Cases—Item 5, *C&E Comrs v David Lewis Centre* [1995] STC 485*; *C&E Comrs v Help The Aged* [1997] STC 406.
Item 5, note (3)(*c*), *Royal Midland Counties Home for Disabled People v C&E Comrs* [2002] STC 395.
Item 8(*c*), *C&E Comrs v Royal Society for the Encouragement of Arts Manufacture and Commerce* [1997] STC 437.
Note (3), *C&E Comrs v David Lewis Centre* [1995] STC 485*.
Notes (3)(*e*), (4)(*f*), *C&E Comrs v Help The Aged* [1997] STC 406.
Definitions—"Computer", s 96(1); "supply", s 5, Sch 4; "taxable person", s 3.
Amendments—[1] Notes (4A), (4B), (5A) and (5B) inserted by FA 1997 s 34 in relation to supplies made on or after 26 November 1996.
[2] Para (*j*) in Note (4) added by the VAT (Drugs, Medicines, Aids for the Handicapped and Charities Etc) Order, SI 2000/503 arts 2, 4 with effect from 1 April 2000.
[3] Items 1, 1A and 2 substituted for original items 1, 2 and items 8, 8A, 8B, 8C substituted for original item 8, Notes (1)–(1F) substituted for original Note (1) and Notes (10A)–(10C) inserted by the VAT (Charities and Aids for the Handicapped) Order, SI 2000/805 arts 5–9 with effect from 1 April 2000.
[4] Note (4)(*a*), (*aa*) substituted for Note (4)(*a*) by the VAT (Drugs, Medicines, Aids for the Handicapped and Charities Etc) Order, SI 2002/2813 arts 2, 4 with effect from 5 December 2002.
[5] Note (1D)(*e*), (*f*) substituted by TCA 2002 s 47, Sch 3 paras 47, 49 with effect from 6 April 2003 (by virtue of SI 2003/962).
[6] Words in item 9 and Note (11)(*a*), and Note (11)(*d*) inserted by the Veterinary Medicines Regulations, SI 2006/2407, reg 44(3), Sch 9 para 10(*a*), (*b*) with effect from 1 October 2006.

GROUP 16 — CLOTHING AND FOOTWEAR

Item No

1 Articles designed as clothing or footwear for young children and not suitable for older persons.

2 The supply to a person for use otherwise than by employees of his of protective boots and helmets for industrial use.

3 Protective helmets for wear by a person driving or riding a motor bicycle [or riding a pedal cycle][2].

NOTES

(1) "Clothing" includes hats and other headgear.

(2) Item 1 does not include articles of clothing made wholly or partly of fur skin, except—

(*a*) headgear;

(*b*) gloves;

(*c*) buttons, belts and buckles;

(*d*) any garment merely trimmed with fur skin unless the trimming has an area greater than one-fifth of the area of the outside material or, in the case of a new garment, represents a cost to the manufacturer greater than the cost to him of the other components.

(3) "Fur skin" means any skin with fur, hair or wool attached except—

(*a*) rabbit skin;

(*b*) woolled sheep or lamb skin; and

(*c*) the skin, if neither tanned nor dressed, of bovine cattle (including buffalo), equine animals, goats or kids (other than Yemen, Mongolian and Tibetan goats or kids), swine (including peccary), chamois, gazelles, deer or dogs.

(4) [Item 2 applies only where the goods to which it refers are—][1]

(*a*) goods which—

(i) are manufactured to standards approved by the British Standards Institution; and

(ii) bear a marking indicating compliance with the specification relating to such goods; or

(*b*) goods which—

(i) are manufactured to standards which satisfy requirements imposed (whether under the law of the United Kingdom or the law of any other member State) for giving effect to the directive of the Council of the European Communities dated 21st December 1989 No 89/686/EEC [or to that directive as amended by Council Directives 93/68/EEC of 22nd July 1993, 93/95/EEC of 29th October 1993 and 96/58/EC of 3rd September 1996][3]; and

(ii) bear any mark of conformity provided for by virtue of that directive[, or (as the case may be) that directive as so amended,][3] in relation to those goods.

[(4A) Item 3 does not apply to a protective helmet unless—

(*a*) it is of a type that on 30th June 2000 is prescribed by regulations made under section 17 of the Road Traffic Act 1988 (types of helmet recommended as affording protection to persons on or in motor cycles from injury in the event of accident); or

(*b*) it is of a type that—

(i) is manufactured to a standard which satisfies requirements imposed (whether under the law of the United Kingdom or the law of any other member State) for giving effect to Council Directive 89/686/EEC of 21st December 1989 as amended by Council Directives 93/68/EEC of 22nd July 1993, 93/95/EEC of 29th October 1993 and 96/58/EC of 3rd September 1996; and

(ii) bears any mark of conformity required by virtue of those directives.][3]

(5) Items 1, 2 and 3 include the supply of the services described in paragraphs 1(1) and [5(4)][1] of Schedule 4 in respect of goods comprised in the items, but, in the case of goods comprised in item 2, only if the goods are for use otherwise than by employees of the person to whom the services are supplied.

Commentary—*De Voil Indirect Tax Service* **V4.287**.

Press releases etc—C&E Business Brief 8/96 17-5-96 (maximum size for zero-rating boys' footwear is UK size 6½, equivalent to continental size 40).

Simon's Tax Cases—*EC Commission v United Kingdom* [1988] STC 456*.

Item 1, *C&E Comrs v Ali Baba Tex Ltd* [1992] STC 590*; *H&M Hennes Ltd v C&E Comrs* [2005] STC 1749.

Definitions—"Law of any member State", s 92; "other member States", s 96(1); "supply", s 5, Sch 4; "United Kingdom", s 96(11).

Amendments—[1] Words in Note (4), (5) substituted by the VAT (Protective Helmets) Order, SI 2000/1517 arts 2–5 with effect in relation to supplies made after 29 June 2000.

[2] Words in Item 3 inserted by the Value Added Tax (Protective Helmets) Order, SI 2001/732 art 3 with effect for supplies made after 31 March 2001

[3] Words in Notes (4)(*b*)(i) and (4)(*b*)(ii) inserted; and Note (4A) substituted by SI 2001/732 arts 4–6 with effect for supplies made after 31 March 2001.

SCHEDULE 9

EXEMPTIONS

Sections 8 and 31

PART I

INDEX TO EXEMPT SUPPLIES OF GOODS AND SERVICES

Cross reference—See VATA 1994 s 97(3), (4) (procedure for making orders for varying this Schedule so as to abolish the exemption of a supply without zero rating it).

Betting, gaming and lotteries	Group 4
Burial and cremation	Group 8
[Cultural services etc	Group 13][1]
Education	Group 6
Finance	Group 5

Fund raising events by charities and other qualifying bodies	Group 12
Health and welfare	Group 7
Insurance	Group 2
[Investment gold	Group 15][2]
Land	Group 1
Postal services	Group 3
Sport, sports competitions and physical education	Group 10
[Supplies of goods where input tax cannot be recovered	Group 14][3]
[Subscriptions to trade unions, professional and other public interest bodies	Group 9][1]
Works of art etc	Group 11

Amendments—[1] Entry inserted and words substituted by the Value Added Tax (Subscriptions to Trade Unions, Professional and Other Public Interest Bodies) Order, SI 1999/2834, arts 2, 3, with effect from 1 December 1999.
[2] Entry inserted by the Value Added Tax (Investment Gold) Order, SI 1999/3116, art 2(1), (2), with effect from 1 January 2000.
[3] Entry inserted by the Value Added Tax (Supplies of Goods where Input Tax cannot be recovered) Order, SI 1999/2833, art 2(1), (2), with effect from 1 March 2000.

PART II
THE GROUPS

GROUP 1 — LAND

Item No

1 The grant of any interest in or right over land or of any licence to occupy land, or, in relation to land in Scotland, any personal right to call for or be granted any such interest or right, other than—

(*a*) the grant of the fee simple in—

(i) a building which has not been completed and which is neither designed as a dwelling or number of dwellings nor intended for use solely for a relevant residential purpose or a relevant charitable purpose;

(ii) a new building which is neither designed as a dwelling or number of dwellings nor intended for use solely for a relevant residential purpose or a relevant charitable purpose after the grant;

(iii) a civil engineering work which has not been completed;

(iv) a new civil engineering work;

(*b*) a supply made pursuant to a developmental tenancy, developmental lease or developmental licence;

(*c*) the grant of any interest, right or licence consisting of a right to take game or fish unless at the time of the grant the grantor grants to the grantee the fee simple of the land over which the right to take game or fish is exercisable;

(*d*) the provision in an hotel, inn, boarding house or similar establishment of sleeping accommodation or of accommodation in rooms which are provided in conjunction with sleeping accommodation or for the purpose of a supply of catering;

(*e*) the grant of any interest in, right over or licence to occupy holiday accommodation;

(*f*) the provision of seasonal pitches for caravans, and the grant of facilities at caravan parks to persons for whom such pitches are provided;

(*g*) the provision of pitches for tents or of camping facilities;

(*h*) the grant of facilities for parking a vehicle;

(*j*) the grant of any right to fell and remove standing timber;

(*k*) the grant of facilities for housing, or storage of, an aircraft or for mooring, or storage of, a ship, boat or other vessel;

(*l*) the grant of any right to occupy a box, seat or other accommodation at a sports ground, theatre, concert hall or other place of entertainment;

(*m*) the grant of facilities for playing any sport or participating in any physical recreation; and

(*n*) the grant of any right, including—

(i) an equitable right,

(ii) a right under an option or right of pre-emption, or

(iii) in relation to land in Scotland, a personal right,

to call for or be granted an interest or right which would fall within any of paragraphs (*a*) or (*c*) to (*m*) above.

NOTES

[(1) "Grant" includes an assignment or surrender and the supply made by the person to whom an interest is surrendered when there is a reverse surrender.][1]

[(1A) A "reverse surrender" is one in which the person to whom the interest is surrendered is paid by the person by whom the interest is being surrendered to accept the surrender.][1]

(2) A building shall be taken to be completed when an architect issues a certificate of practical completion in relation to it or it is first fully occupied, whichever happens first; and a civil engineering work shall be taken to be completed when an engineer issues a certificate of completion in relation to it or it is first fully used, whichever happens first.

(3) [Notes (2) to (10) and (12)][1] to Group 5 of Schedule 8 apply in relation to this Group as they apply in relation to that Group.

(4) A building or civil engineering work is new if it was completed less than three years before the grant.

(5) Subject to Note (6), the grant of the fee simple in a building or work completed before 1st April 1989 is not excluded from this Group by paragraph (*a*) (ii) or (iv).

(6) Note (5) does not apply where the grant is the first grant of the fee simple made on or after 1st April 1989 and the building was not fully occupied, or the work not fully used, before that date.

(7) A tenancy of, lease of or licence to occupy a building or work is treated as becoming a developmental tenancy, developmental lease or developmental licence (as the case may be) when a tenancy of, lease of or licence to occupy a building or work, whose construction, reconstruction, enlargement or extension commenced on or after 1st January 1992, is treated as being supplied to and by the developer under paragraph 6(1) of Schedule 10 [(except where that paragraph applies by virtue of paragraph 5(1)(*b*) of that Schedule)][1].

(8) Where a grant of an interest in, right over or licence to occupy land includes a valuable right to take game or fish, an apportionment shall be made to determine the supply falling outside this Group by virtue of paragraph (*c*).

(9) "Similar establishment" includes premises in which there is provided furnished sleeping accommodation, whether with or without the provision of board or facilities for the preparation of food, which are used by or held out as being suitable for use by visitors or travellers.

(10) "Houseboat" includes a houseboat within the meaning of Group 9 of Schedule 8.

(11) Paragraph (*e*) includes—

(*a*) any grant excluded from item 1 of Group 5 of Schedule 8 by [Note (13)][1] in that Group;

(*b*) any supply made pursuant to a tenancy, lease or licence under which the grantee is or has been permitted to erect and occupy holiday accommodation.

(12) Paragraph (*e*) does not include a grant in respect of a building or part which is not a new building of—

(*a*) the fee simple, or

(*b*) a tenancy, lease or licence to the extent that the grant is made for a consideration in the form of a premium.

(13) "Holiday accommodation" includes any accommodation in a building, hut (including a beach hut or chalet), caravan, houseboat or tent which is advertised or held out as holiday accommodation or as suitable for holiday or leisure use, but excludes any accommodation within paragraph (*d*).

(14) A seasonal pitch is a pitch—

(*a*) which is provided for a period of less than a year, or

(*b*) which is provided for a year or a period longer than a year but which the person to whom it is provided is prevented by the terms of any covenant, statutory planning consent or similar permission from occupying by living in a caravan at all times throughout the period for which the pitch is provided.

(15) "Mooring" includes anchoring or berthing.

(16) Paragraph (*m*) shall not apply where the grant of the facilities is for—

(*a*) a continuous period of use exceeding 24 hours; or

(*b*) a series of 10 or more periods, whether or not exceeding 24 hours in total, where the following conditions are satisfied—

(i) each period is in respect of the same activity carried on at the same place;

(ii) the interval between each period is not less than one day and not more than 14 days;

(iii) consideration is payable by reference to the whole series and is evidenced by written agreement;

(iv) the grantee has exclusive use of the facilities; and

(v) the grantee is a school, a club, an association or an organisation representing affiliated clubs or constituent associations.

Commentary—*De Voil Indirect Tax Service* **V4.111–V4.113**.

Press releases etc—C&E Business Brief 17/94 12-9-94 (supply of milk quota with land follows VAT liability of the land). C&E Business Brief 4/03 27-5-03 (VAT on property – clarification of recent judgments).

Simon's Tax Cases—*C & E Comrs v Mirror Group plc* (Case C-409/98) [2001] STC 1453), ECJ.

C&E Comrs v Sinclair Collis Ltd [2001] STC 989.

Item 1, *Billingham v Myers* [1994] STC 101*; *Nell Gwynn House Maintenance Fund Trustees v C&E Comrs* [1999] STC 79*; *C&E Comrs v Latchmere Properties Ltd* [2005] STC 731; *Byrom and others (t/a Salon 24) v R&C Comrs* [2006] STC 992; *R&C Comrs v Denyer* [2008] STC 633; *Holland (t/a The Studio Hair Company) v R&C Comrs, Vigdor Ltd v R&C Comrs* [2009] STC 150.

Item 1(*b*), *Cooper and Chapman (Builders) Ltd v C&E Comrs* [1993] STC 1*.

Item 1(*e*), *C&E Comrs v Parkinson* [1989] STC 51*.

Item 1(*f*), *Colaingrove Ltd v C&E Comrs* [2003] STC 680; [2004] STC 712; *R&C Comrs v Tallington Lakes Ltd* [2008] STC 2734.
Item 1(*h*), *C&E Comrs v Trinity Factoring Services Ltd* [1994] STC 504*.
Note (1), *Cooper and Chapman (Builders) Ltd v C&E Comrs* [1993] STC 1*; *Lubbock Fine & Co v C&E Comrs* (Case C-63/92) [1994] STC 101*.
Definitions—"Assignment", s 96(1); "building designed as a dwelling or number of dwellings", Sch 8 Group 5 note (2); "dwelling", Sch 8 Group 5 note (2); "fee simple", s 96(1); "ship", s 96(1); "supply", s 5, Sch 4; "use for a relevant charitable purpose", Sch 8 Group 5 note (6); "use for a relevant residential purpose", Sch 8 Group 5 note (4).
Cross references—See VATA 1994 s 62(1) (penalty for incorrect certificate that a supply is eligible for exemption within this Group);
VATA 1994 Sch 6 para 9 (valuation of certain supplies of accommodation within item 1 para (*d*) of this Group);
VAT Regulations, SI 1995/2518 reg 101(3) (exclusion of grants within item 1 or 1(*a*) of this Group in determining proportion of input tax attributable to taxable supplies under reg 101(2)(*d*)).
Amendments—[1] Note (1) and words in Notes (3), (11) substituted, Note (1A) inserted, and words in Note (7) added, by the Value Added Tax (Land) Order, SI 1995/282 with effect from 1 March 1995.
Prospective amendments—Item 1(*b*), and Note (7), to be repealed by the Value Added Tax (Buildings and Land) Order, SI 2008/1146 art 4 with effect in relation to supplies made on or after 1 June 2020. The fact that former VATA 1994 Sch 10 paras 5–7 are not rewritten by SI 2008/1146 art 2 is not to affect the continued operation of Sch 9 Group 1 item 1(*b*), as read with Note (7), in relation to supplies made before 1 June 2020.

[GROUP 2 — INSURANCE

Item No.

[1 Insurance transactions and reinsurance transactions.][3]

4 The provision by an insurance broker or insurance agent of any of the services of an insurance intermediary in a case in which those services—

(*a*) are related (whether or not [a contract of insurance][2] [or reinsurance][3] is finally concluded) to [an insurance transaction or a reinsurance transaction][3]; and

(*b*) are provided by that broker or agent in the course of his acting in an intermediary capacity.

NOTES

(A1)–(C1) …[3]

(1) For the purposes of item 4 services are services of an insurance intermediary if they fall within any of the following paragraphs—

(*a*) the bringing together, with a view to the insurance or reinsurance of risks, of—

(i) persons who are or may be seeking insurance or reinsurance, and

(ii) persons who provide insurance or reinsurance;

(*b*) the carrying out of work preparatory to the conclusion of contracts of insurance or reinsurance;

(*c*) the provision of assistance in the administration and performance of such contracts, including the handling of claims;

(*d*) the collection of premiums.

(2) For the purposes of item 4 an insurance broker or insurance agent is acting 'in an intermediary capacity' wherever he is acting as an intermediary, or one of the intermediaries, between—

(*a*) a person who provides [insurance or reinsurance][3], and

(*b*) a person who is or may be seeking insurance or reinsurance or is an insured person.

(3) Where—

(*a*) a person ('the supplier') makes a supply of goods or services to another ('the customer'),

(*b*) the supply of the goods or services is a taxable supply and is not a zero-rated supply,

(*c*) a transaction under which insurance is to be or may be arranged for the customer is entered into in connection with the supply of the goods or services,

(*d*) a supply of services which are related (whether or not a contract of insurance is finally concluded) to the provision of insurance in pursuance of that transaction is made by—

(i) the person by whom the supply of the goods or services is made, or

(ii) a person who is connected with that person and, in connection with the provision of that insurance, deals directly with the customer,

and

(*e*) the related services do not consist in the handling of claims under the contract for that insurance,

those related services do not fall within item 4 unless the relevant requirements are fulfilled.

(4) For the purposes of Note (3) the relevant requirements are—

(*a*) that a document containing the statements specified in Note (5) is prepared;

(*b*) that the matters that must be stated in the document have been disclosed to the customer at or before the time when the transaction mentioned in Note (3)(*c*) is entered into; and

(*c*) that there is compliance with all such requirements (if any) as to—

(i) the preparation and form of the document,

(ii) the manner of disclosing to the customer the matters that must be stated in the document, and

(iii) the delivery of a copy of the document to the customer, as may be set out in a notice that has been published by the Commissioners and has not been withdrawn.

(5) The statements referred to in Note (4) are—

(*a*) a statement setting out the amount of the premium under any contract of insurance that is to be or may be entered into in pursuance of the transaction in question; and

(*b*) a statement setting out every amount that the customer is, is to be or has been required to pay, otherwise than by way of such a premium, in connection with that transaction or anything that is to be, may be or has been done in pursuance of that transaction.

(6) For the purposes of Note (3) any question whether a person is connected with another shall be determined in accordance with section 839 of the Taxes Act.

(7) Item 4 does not include—

(*a*) the supply of any market research, product design, advertising, promotional or similar services; or

(*b*) the collection, collation and provision of information for use in connection with market research, product design, advertising, promotional or similar activities.

(8) Item 4 does not include the supply of any valuation or inspection services.

(9) Item 4 does not include the supply of any services by loss adjusters, average adjusters, motor assessors, surveyors or other experts except where—

(*a*) the services consist in the handling of a claim under a contract of insurance or reinsurance;

(*b*) the person handling the claim is authorised when doing so to act on behalf of the insurer or reinsurer; and

(*c*) that person's authority so to act includes written authority to determine whether to accept or reject the claim and, where accepting it in whole or in part, to settle the amount to be paid on the claim.

(10) Item 4 does not include the supply of any services which—

(*a*) are supplied in pursuance of a contract of insurance or reinsurance or of any arrangements made in connection with such a contract; and

(*b*) are so supplied either—

(i) instead of the payment of the whole or any part of any indemnity for which the contract provides, or

(ii) for the purpose, in any other manner, of satisfying any claim under that contract, whether in whole or in part.][1]

Commentary—*De Voil Indirect Tax Service* **V4.121–V4.124**.

Press releases etc—C&E Business Brief 6/95 28-3-95 (VAT on costs of settling insurance claims should be attributed to the supply which gives rise to the item).

Simon's Tax Cases—Item 1, *Card Protection Plan Ltd v C&E Comrs* [1999] STC 270*; *Ford Motor Co Ltd v R&C Comrs* [2007] STC 1783.

Item 3, *Card Protection Plan Ltd v C&E Comrs* [1999] STC 270*; *Peugeot Motor Company plc and another v C&E Comrs* [2003] STC 1438.

Item 4, *Century Life plc v C&E Comrs* [2001] STC 38, CA; *WHA Ltd and another v C&E Comrs* [2004] STC 1081; *Ford Motor Co Ltd v R&C Comrs* [2007] STC 1783.

Note 5(*b*), *C R Smith Glaziers (Dunfermline) Ltd v C&E Comrs* [2001] STC 770, [2203] STC 419.

Definitions—"Belongs", s 9(2)(3); "supply", s 5, Sch 4; "United Kingdom", s 96(11).

Cross reference—See VAT Regulations, SI 1995/2518 reg 105(1) (treatment of certain exempt input tax attributable to a supply within item 3 of this Group as attributable to taxable supplies).

Amendments—[1] This Group substituted by FA 1997 s 38 with effect in relation to supplies made on or after 19 March 1997.

[2] Items 1, 2 substituted, words in Item 4 substituted, and Notes (A1), (B1) and (C1) inserted, by the Financial Services and Markets Act 2000 (Consequential Amendments and Repeals) Order, SI 2001/3649 art 347 with effect from 1 December 2001.

[3] Item 1 substituted for Items 1–3, words in Item 4(*a*) substituted and inserted, Notes (A1)–(C1) repealed, and words in Note (2)(*a*) substituted, by the VAT (Insurance) Order, SI 2004/3083 with effect from 1 January 2005.

GROUP 3 — POSTAL SERVICES

Item No

1 The conveyance of postal packets by [the Post Office company][1].

2 The supply by [the Post Office company][1] of any services in connection with the conveyance of postal packets.

NOTES

(1) "Postal packet" has the same meaning as in [the Postal Services Act 2000][1].

(2) Item 2 does not include the letting on hire of goods.

Commentary—*De Voil Indirect Tax Service* **V4.126**.

Definition—"Supply", s 5, Sch 4.

Amendments—[1] Words substituted in Items 1 and 2, and Note (1) by the Postal Services Act 2000 s 127(4), Sch 8 para 22(1), (4) as from 26 March 2001 (by virtue of SI 2000/2957).

GROUP 4 — BETTING, GAMING AND LOTTERIES

Item No

1 The provision of any facilities for the placing of bets [or for the playing of any games of chance for a prize][1].

2 The granting of a right to take part in a lottery.

NOTES

(1) Item 1 does not include—

(*a*) admission to any premises; or

(*b*) ...[2]

(*c*) the provision by a club of such facilities to its members as are available to them on payment of their subscription but without further charge; or

(*d*) the provision of [anything which is a gaming machine for the purposes of section 23][1].

[(2) "Game of chance"—

(*a*) includes—

(i) a game that involves both an element of chance and an element of skill,

(ii) a game that involves an element of chance that can be eliminated by superlative skill, and

(iii) a game that is presented as involving an element of chance, but

(*b*) does not include a sport.

(3) A person plays a game of chance if he participates in a game of chance—

(*a*) whether or not there are other participants in the game, and

(*b*) whether or not a computer generates images or data taken to represent the actions of other participants in the game.

(4) "Prize" does not include the opportunity to play the game again.][1]

(5)–(11) ...[2]

Commentary—*De Voil Indirect Tax Service* **V4.131**.

Press releases etc—Business Brief 16/06, 13-10-06 (new definitions of "gambling" and "game of chance").

Simon's Tax Cases—Item 1, *C&E Comrs v Annabel's Casino Ltd* [1995] STC 225*; *United Utilities plc v C&E Comrs*, [2003] STC 223.

Note (1)(*d*), *R v Ryan* [1994] STC 446*; *C&E Comrs v Feehan* [1995] STC 75*.

Amendments—[1] Words in item 1 and words in Note (1)(*d*) substituted, and Notes (2)–(4) substituted for Notes (2)–(8) as previously enacted, by the Value Added Tax (Betting, Gaming and Lotteries) Order, SI 2006/2685 art 2, with effect from 1 November 2006.

[2] Note (1)(*b*) and Notes (5)–(11) repealed by FA 2009 s 113 with effect from 27 April 2009.

GROUP 5 — FINANCE

Item No

1 The issue, transfer or receipt of, or any dealing with, money, any security for money or any note or order for the payment of money.

2 The making of any advance or the granting of any credit.

[2A The management of credit by the person granting it.][7]

3 The provision of the facility of instalment credit finance in a hire-purchase, conditional sale or credit sale agreement for which facility a separate charge is made and disclosed to the recipient of the supply of goods.

4 The provision of administrative arrangements and documentation and the transfer of title to the goods in connection with the supply described in item 3 if the total consideration therefor is specified in the agreement and does not exceed £10.

5 [The provision of intermediary services in relation to any transaction comprised in item 1, 2, 3, 4 or 6 (whether or not any such transaction is finally concluded) by a person acting in an intermediary capacity.][2]

[5A— The underwriting of an issue within item 1 or any transaction within item 6.][2]

6 The issue, transfer or receipt of, or any dealing with, any security or secondary security being—

(*a*) shares, stocks, bonds, notes (other than promissory notes), debentures, debenture stock or shares in an oil royalty; or

(*b*) any document relating to money, in any currency, which has been deposited with the issuer or some other person, being a document which recognises an obligation to pay a stated amount to bearer or to order, with or without interest, and being a document by the delivery of which, with or without endorsement, the right to receive that stated amount, with or without interest, is transferable; or

(*c*) any bill, note or other obligation of the Treasury or of a Government in any part of the world, being a document by the delivery of which, with or without endorsement, title is transferable, and not being an obligation which is or has been legal tender in any part of the world; or

(*d*) any letter of allotment or rights, any warrant conferring an option to acquire a security included in this item, any renounceable or scrip certificates, rights coupons, coupons representing dividends or interest on such a security, bond mandates or other documents conferring or containing evidence of title to or rights in respect of such a security; or

(*e*) units or other documents conferring rights under any trust established for the purpose, or having the effect of providing, for persons having funds available for investment, facilities for the participation by them as beneficiaries under the trust, in any profits or income arising from the acquisition, holding, management or disposal of any property whatsoever.

7 [...][3]

8 The operation of any current, deposit or savings account.

[**9** The management of—

(*a*) an authorised open-ended investment company; or

(*b*) an authorised unit trust scheme; or

(*c*) a Gibraltar collective investment scheme that is not an umbrella scheme; or

(*d*) a sub-fund of any other Gibraltar collective investment scheme; or

(*e*) an individually recognised overseas scheme that is not an umbrella scheme; or

(*f*) a sub-fund of any other individually recognised overseas scheme; or

(*g*) a recognised collective investment scheme authorised in a designated country or territory that is not an umbrella scheme; or

(*h*) a sub-fund of any other recognised collective investment scheme authorised in a designated country or territory; or

(*i*) a recognised collective investment scheme constituted in another EEA state that is not an umbrella scheme; or

(*j*) a sub-fund of any other recognised collective investment scheme constituted in another EEA state.][8]

[**10** The management of a closed-ended collective investment undertaking.][8]

NOTES

(1) Item 1 does not include anything included in item 6.

[(1A) Item 1 does not include a supply of services which is preparatory to the carrying out of a transaction falling within that item.][3]

(2) This Group does not include the supply of a coin or a banknote as a collectors' piece or as an investment article.

(2A) ...[7]

(2B) ... [6]

(3) Item 2 includes the supply of credit by a person, in connection with a supply of goods or services by him, for which a separate charge is made and disclosed to the recipient of the supply of goods or services.

(4) This Group includes any supply by a person carrying on a credit card, charge card or similar payment card operation made in connection with that operation to a person who accepts the card used in the operation when presented to him in payment for goods or services.

[(5) For the purposes of item 5 "intermediary services" consist of bringing together, with a view to the provision of financial services—

(*a*) persons who are or may be seeking to receive financial services, and

(*b*) persons who provide financial services,

together with (in the case of financial services falling within item 1, 2, 3 or 4) the performance of work preparatory to the conclusion of contracts for the provision of those financial services, but do not include the supply of any market research, product design, advertising, promotional or similar services or the collection, collation and provision of information in connection with such activities.

(5A) For the purposes of item 5 a person is "acting in an intermediary capacity" wherever he is acting as an intermediary, or one of the intermediaries, between—

(*a*) a person who provides financial services, and

(*b*) a person who is or may be seeking to receive financial services ...[7]

(5B) For the purposes of notes 5 and 5A "financial services" means the carrying out of any transaction falling within item 1, 2, 3, 4 or 6.][4]

[(6) For the purposes of this Group—

"authorised open-ended investment company" and "authorised unit trust scheme" have the meaning given in section 237(3) of the Financial Services and Markets Act 2000;

"closed-ended collective investment undertaking" means an undertaking in relation to which the following conditions are satisfied—

(*a*) its sole object is the investment of capital, raised from the public, wholly or mainly in securities; and

(*b*) it manages its assets on the principle of spreading investment risk; and

(*c*) all of its ordinary shares (of each class if there is more than one) or equivalent units are included in the official list maintained by the Financial Services Authority pursuant to section 74(1) of the Financial Services and Markets Act 2000; and

(*d*) all of its ordinary shares (of each class if there is more than one) or equivalent units are admitted to trading on a regulated market situated or operating in the United Kingdom;

"collective investment scheme" has the meaning given in section 235 of the Financial Services and Markets Act 2000;

"Gibraltar collective investment scheme" means—

(*a*) a collective investment scheme to which section 264 of the Financial Services and Markets Act 2000 applies pursuant to an order made under section 409(1)(*d*) of that Act; or

(*b*) a collective investment scheme to which the Financial Services and Markets Act 2000 applies pursuant to an order made under section 409(1)(*f*) of that Act;

"individually recognised overseas scheme" means a collective investment scheme declared by the Financial Services Authority to be a recognised scheme pursuant to section 272 of the Financial Services and Markets Act 2000;

"recognised collective investment scheme authorised in a designated country or territory" means a collective investment scheme recognised pursuant to section 270 of the Financial Services and Markets Act 2000;

"recognised collective investment scheme constituted in another EEA state" means a collective investment scheme which is recognised pursuant to section 264 of the Financial Services and Markets Act 2000;

"regulated market" has the meaning given in section 103(1) of the Financial Services and Markets Act 2000;

"sub-fund" means a separate part of the property of an umbrella scheme that is pooled separately;

"umbrella scheme" means a collective investment scheme under which the contributions of the participants in the scheme and the profits or income out of which payments are to be made to them are pooled separately in relation to separate parts of the scheme property.][8]

[(6A) A collective investment scheme, or sub-fund, that is not for the time being marketed in the United Kingdom is to be treated as not falling within item 9(*c*) to (*j*) if—

(*a*) it has never been marketed in the United Kingdom, or

(*b*) less than 5% of its shares or units are held by, or on behalf of, investors who are in the United Kingdom.][8]

(7) …[7]

(8) For the purposes of item 10 …[7], an open-ended investment company's scheme property is the property subject to the collective investment scheme constituted by that company.[8]

(9) …[7]

[(10) For the purposes of this Group—

"collective investment scheme" has the meaning given in section 235 of the Financial Services and Markets Act 2000; and

"open-ended investment company" has the meaning given in section 236 of that Act.][5]*]*[1, 8]

Commentary—*De Voil Indirect Tax Service* **V4.136–V4.136J**.

HMRC Manuals—VAT Guidance V1-3: Supply and consideration, para 4.11 (agreements with finance companies at non-standard rates of interest).

Press releases etc—C&E Business Brief 10/03 25-7-03 (VAT – changes to finance exemptions)

C&E Business Brief 25/94 16-12-94 (restocking of cash point machines by supermarket does not fall within this group).

C&E Business Brief 25/95 20-11-95 (all issues of, or dealings in, securities falling within item 1 will be treated as a supply of services.)

C&E Business Brief 15/96 22-7-96 (VAT treatment of goods sold on interest-free credit).

C&E News Releases 12/97 13-3-97 (the investment management of open-ended investment companies by their authorised corporate directors is VAT exempt from 24 March 1997).

VAT Information Sheet 10/99 August 1999 (notes on changes introduced by SI 1999/594).

Simon's Tax Cases—Item 1, *Kingfisher plc v C&E Comrs* [2000] STC 992; *R&C Comrs v Axa UK plc* [2008] STC 2091.

Item 2, *C&E Comrs v BAA plc* [2002] STC 327; *HBOS plc v R&C Comrs* [2009] STC 486.

Item 5, *Primback Ltd v C&E Comrs* [1996] STC 757*; *C&E Comrs v Civil Service Motoring Association Ltd* [1998] STC 111*; *C&E Comrs v BAA plc; Institute of Directors v C&E Comrs* [2003] STC 35, CA; *Bookit Ltd v R&C Comrs* [2006] STC 1367; *HBOS plc v R&C Comrs* [2009] STC 486.

Items 6(*a*), 7, *Ivory & Sime Trustlink Ltd v C&E Comrs* [1998] STC 597.

Note (3), *Primback Ltd v C&E Comrs* [1996] STC 757*

Definitions—"Document", s 96(1); "money", s 96(1); "supply", s 5, Sch 4.

Cross references—See VAT Regulations, SI 1995/2518 reg 101(3) (exclusion of supplies within this Group in determining proportion of input tax attributable to taxable supplies under reg 101(2)(*d*));

VAT Regulations, SI 1995/2518 reg 103(2) (attribution of certain input tax used in making both supplies within item 1 or 6 of this Group and any other supply).

Amendments—[1] Item 10 and Notes (7)–(10) inserted by the VAT (Finance) Order, SI 1997/510 art 2 with effect from 24 March 1997.

[2] Item 5 substituted and Item 5A inserted by the VAT (Finance) Order, SI 1999/594 art 3, with effect from 10 March 1999.

[3] Item 7 repealed, and Notes (1A), (2A), (2B) inserted by the VAT (Finance) Order, SI 1999/594 arts 4, 5 and 6 respectively, with effect from 10 March 1999.

[4] Note (5) substituted and Notes (5A), (5B) inserted by the VAT (Finance) Order, SI 1999/594 art 7, with effect from 10 March 1999.

[5] Note (10) substituted by the Financial Services and Markets Act 2000 (Consequential Amendments and Repeals) Order, SI 2001/3649 art 348 with effect from 1 December 2001.

[6] Note (2B) (inserted by SI 1999/594) repealed by the VAT (Finance) Order, SI 2003/1568 with effect for any services performed after 31 July 2003.

[7] Item 2A inserted, Notes (2A), (7) and (9), words in Note (5A), and words in Note (8) repealed, by the VAT (Finance) (No 2) Order, SI 2003/1569 with effect for any services performed after 31 July 2003.

[8] Items 9, 10 and Note (6) substituted, Note (6A) inserted, and Notes (8), (9) repealed, by the Value Added Tax (Finance) (No 2) Order, SI 2008/2547 art 3 with effect from 1 October 2008.

Note that the intention appears to have been to repeal Note (10) rather than Note (9) which was already repealed as per footnote 7 above.

Items 9 and 10 previously read as follows—

"**9** The management of an authorised unit trust scheme or of a trust based scheme.

10 The management of the scheme property of an open-ended investment company.".

Note (6) previously read as follows—

"(6) In item 9—
"authorised unit trust scheme" has the meaning given in section 23 7(3) of the Financial Services and Markets Act 2000;
"trust based scheme" means a scheme the purpose or effect of which is to enable persons taking part in the scheme, by becoming beneficiaries under a trust, to participate in or receive profits or income arising from the acquisition, holding, management or disposal of property of a kind described in section 239(3)(*a*) of the Financial Services and Markets Act 2000 or sums paid out of such profits or income.".

Note that Items 9, 10, and Note (6) were to be substituted, and Notes (8), (10) were to be repealed, by the Value Added Tax (Finance) Order, SI 2008/1892 art 2(1), (2) with effect from 1 October 2008. However, this Order was revoked, following further consultation, by the Value Added Tax (Finance) (No 2) Order, SI 2008/2547 art 2 with effect from 30 September 2008 and was therefore revoked before it was due to take effect.

GROUP 6 — EDUCATION

Item No

1 The provision by an eligible body of—

(*a*) education;

(*b*) research, where supplied to an eligible body; or

(*c*) vocational training.

2 The supply of private tuition, in a subject ordinarily taught in a school or university, by an individual teacher acting independently of an employer.

3 The provision of examination services—

(*a*) by or to an eligible body; or

(*b*) to a person receiving education or vocational training which is—

(i) exempt by virtue of items 1, 2[, 5 or 5A][4]; or

(ii) provided otherwise than in the course or furtherance of a business.

4 The supply of any goods or services (other than examination services) which are closely related to a supply of a description falling within item 1 (the principal supply) by or to the eligible body making the principal supply provided—

(*a*) the goods or services are for the direct use of the pupil, student or trainee (as the case may be) receiving the principal supply; and

(*b*) where the supply is to the eligible body making the principal supply, it is made by another eligible body.

5 The provision of vocational training, and the supply of any goods or services essential thereto by the person providing the vocational training, to the extent that the consideration payable is ultimately a charge to funds provided pursuant to arrangements made under section 2 of the Employment and Training Act 1973, section 1A of the Employment and Training Act (Northern Ireland) 1950 or section 2 of the Enterprise and New Towns (Scotland) Act 1990.

[**5A** The provision of education or vocational training and the supply, by the person providing that education or training, of any goods or services essential to that provision, to the extent that the consideration payable is ultimately a charge to funds provided by the Learning and Skills Council for England or the National Council for Education and Training for Wales under Part I or Part II of the Learning and Skills Act 2000.][4]

6 The provision of facilities by—

(*a*) a youth club or an association of youth clubs to its members; or

(*b*) an association of youth clubs to members of a youth club which is a member of that association.

NOTES

(1) For the purposes of this Group an "eligible body" is—

(*a*) a school within the meaning of [The Education Act 1996][2], the Education (Scotland) Act 1980 the Education and Libraries (Northern Ireland) Order 1986 or the Education Reform (Northern Ireland) Order 1989, which is—

(i) provisionally or finally registered or deemed to be registered as a school within the meaning of the aforesaid legislation in a register of independent schools; or

(ii) a school in respect of which grants are made by the Secretary of State to the proprietor or managers; or

(iii) [[a community, foundation or voluntary school within the meaning of the School Standards and Framework Act 1998, a special school within the meaning of section 337 of the Education Act 1996][3] or a maintained school within the meaning of][2] the Education and Libraries (Northern Ireland) Order 1986; or

(iv) a public school within the meaning of section 135(1) of the Education (Scotland) Act 1980; or

(v) …[3]; or

(vi) …[5]

(vii) …[3]; or

(viii) a grant-maintained integrated school within the meaning of Article 65 of the Education Reform (Northern Ireland) Order 1989;

(*b*) a United Kingdom university, and any college, institution, school or hall of such a university;

(*c*) an institution—

(i) falling within section 91(3)(*a*) or (*b*) or section 91(5)(*b*) or (*c*) of the Further and Higher Education Act 1992; or
(ii) which is a designated institution as defined in section 44(2) of the Further and Higher Education (Scotland) Act 1992; or
(iii) managed by a board of management as defined in section 36(1) of the Further and Higher Education (Scotland) Act 1992; or
(iv) to which grants are paid by the Department of Education for Northern Ireland under Article 66(2) of the Education and Libraries (Northern Ireland) Order 1986;

(*d*) a public body of a description in Note (5) to Group 7 below;
[(*e*) a body which—
(i) is precluded from distributing and does not distribute any profit it makes; and
(ii) applies any profits made from supplies of a description within this Group to the continuance or improvement of such supplies;][1]
[(*f*) a body not falling within paragraphs (*a*) to (*e*) above which provides the teaching of English as a foreign language.][1]

(2) A supply by a body, which is an eligible body only by virtue of falling within Note [(1)(*f*)][1], shall not fall within this Group insofar as it consists of the provision of anything other than the teaching of English as a foreign language.

[(3) "Vocational training" means—
training, re-training or the provision of work experience for—
(*a*) any trade, profession or employment; or
(*b*) any voluntary work connected with—
(i) education, health, safety, or welfare; or
(ii) the carrying out of activities of a charitable nature.][1]

(4) "Examination services" include the setting and marking of examinations, the setting of educational or training standards, the making of assessments and other services provided with a view to ensuring educational and training standards are maintained.

(5) For the purposes of item 5 a supply of any goods or services shall not be taken to be essential to the provision of vocational training unless the goods or services in question are provided directly to the trainee.

[(5A) For the purposes of item 5A a supply of any goods or services shall not be taken to be essential to the provision of education or vocational training unless—
(*a*) in the case of the provision of education, the goods or services are provided directly to the person receiving the education;
(*b*) in the case of the provision of vocational training, the goods or services are provided directly to the person receiving the training.][4]

(6) For the purposes of item 6 a club is a "youth club" if—
(*a*) it is established to promote the social, physical, educational or spiritual development of its members;
(*b*) its members are mainly under 21 years of age; and
(*c*) it satisfies the requirements of Note (1)(*f*)(i) and (ii).

Note—The reference in Note (6)(*c*) to "Note 1(*f*)(i) and (ii)" appears to be an error. It appears that the reference should instead be to "Note 1(*e*)(i) and (ii)".
Commentary—*De Voil Indirect Tax Service* **V4.141**.
Press releases etc—VAT Information Sheet 5/94 (1-12-94 as amended 1-1-95) (school photographers).
C&E Business Brief 13/96 1-7-96 (supplies of training, re-training or work experience paid for using Further Education Funding Council funds is exempt under item 5 of this Group).
C&E Business Brief 18/99 18-8-99 (extent of exemption for providers of the teaching of English as a foreign language).
Simon's Tax Cases—*C&E Comrs v Zinn* [1988] STC 57*; *C&E Comrs v Bell Concord Educational Trust Ltd* [1988] STC 143*.
Item 1, *C&E Comrs v Bell Concord Educational Trust Ltd* [1999] STC 1027; *R&C Comrs v Board of Governors of the Robert Gordon University* [2008] STC 1890; *Birkdale School, Sheffield v R&C Comrs* [2008] STC 2002.
Item 1, note (1), *C&E Comrs v School of Finance and Management (London) Ltd* [2002] STC 1690.
Items 1, 4, notes (1)(*f*), (2), *Pilgrims Language Courses Ltd v C&E Comrs* [1999] STC 874
Item 2(*a*), *C&E Comrs v Bell Concord Educational Trust Ltd* [1989] STC 264*.
Item 4, notes (1)(*b*), (*e*), *C&E Comrs v University of Leicester Student's Union, CA* [2002] STC 147; *College of Estate Management v C&E Comrs* [2004] STC 235; [2004] STC 1471; *College of Estate Management v C&E Comrs* [2005] STC 1597.
Definitions—"Business ", s 94; "supply", s 5, Sch 4; "United Kingdom", s 96(11).
Amendments—[1] Notes (1)(*e*), (*f*), (3) and the figure in note (2) substituted by the Value Added Tax (Education) (No 2) Order, SI 1994/2969 with effect from 1 January 1995.
[2] Words in Note (1)(*a*) substituted by Education Act 1996 s 582(1), Sch 37 Part I para 125.
[3] Words in Note (1)(*a*)(iii) substituted and sub-paras (v) and (vii) omitted by School Standards and Framework Act 1998 Sch 30 para 51, with effect from 1 September 1999, by the School Standards and Framework Act 1998 (Commencement No 7 and Saving and Transitional Provisions) Order SI 1999/2323 para 2(1), Sch 1.
[4] Words in Item 3 substituted, Item 5A and Note (5A) inserted by the Learning and Skills Act 2000 Sch 9 para 47 with effect from 1 April 2001 (by virtue of SI 2001/654).
[5] Note (1)(*a*)(vi) repealed by the Standards in Scotland's Schools etc Act 2000 s 60(2), Sch 3 with effect from 31 December 2004 (by virtue of SSI 2004/528).

GROUP 7 — HEALTH AND WELFARE

Item No

1 The supply of services [consisting in the provision of medical care][9] by a person registered or enrolled in any of the following—

(*a*) the register of medical practitioners or the register of medical practitioners with limited registration;

(*b*) either of the registers of ophthalmic opticians or the register of dispensing opticians kept under the Opticians Act 1989 or either of the lists kept under section 9 of that Act of bodies corporate carrying on business as ophthalmic opticians or as dispensing opticians;

[(*c*) the register kept under the Health Professions Order 2001;][7]

[(*ca*) the register of osteopaths maintained in accordance with the provisions of the Osteopaths Act 1993;][3]

[(*cb*) the register of chiropractors maintained in accordance with the provisions of the Chiropractors Act 1994;][4]

[(*d*) the register of qualified nurses and midwives maintained under article 5 of the Nursing and Midwifery Order 2001][2]

(*e*) the register of dispensers of hearing aids or the register of persons employing such dispensers maintained under section 2 of the Hearing Aid Council Act 1968.

2 [The supply of any services consisting in the provision of medical care, or the supply of dental prostheses, by][9] —

(*a*) a person registered in the dentists' register;

[(*b*) a person registered in the dental care professionals register established under section 36B of the Dentists Act 1984;][8]…[9]

[2A The supply of any services or dental prostheses by a dental technician.][9]

3 The supply of any services [consisting in the provision of medical care][9] by a person registered in the register of pharmaceutical chemists kept under the Pharmacy Act 1954 or the Pharmacy (Northern Ireland) Order 1976.

4 The provision of care or medical or surgical treatment and, in connection with it, the supply of any goods, in any hospital [or state regulated institution][5].

5 The provision of a deputy for a person registered in the register of medical practitioners or the register of medical practitioners with limited registration.

6 Human blood.

7 Products for therapeutic purposes, derived from human blood.

8 Human (including foetal) organs or tissue for diagnostic or therapeutic purposes or medical research.

[9 The supply by—

(*a*) a charity,

(*b*) a state-regulated private welfare institution [or agency][6], or

(*c*) a public body,

of welfare services and of goods supplied in connection with those welfare services.][5]

10 The supply, otherwise than for profit, of goods and services incidental to the provision of spiritual welfare by a religious community to a resident member of that community in return for a subscription or other consideration paid as a condition of membership.

11 The supply of transport services for sick or injured persons in vehicles specially designed for that purpose.

NOTES

(1) Item 1 does not include the letting on hire of goods except where the letting is in connection with a supply of other services comprised in the item.

(2) Paragraphs (*a*) to (*d*) of item 1 and paragraphs (*a*) and (*b*) of item 2 include supplies of services made by a person who is not registered or enrolled in any of the registers or rolls specified in those paragraphs where the services are wholly performed or directly supervised by a person who is so registered or enrolled.

[(2A Item 3 includes supplies of services made by a person who is not registered in either of the registers specified in that item where the services are wholly performed by a person who is so registered.][1]

(3) Item 3 does not include the letting on hire of goods.

(4) …[10]

(5) In item 9 "public body" means—

(*a*) a Government department within the meaning of section 41(6);

(*b*) a local authority;

(*c*) a body which acts under any enactment or instrument for public purposes and not for its own profit and which performs functions similar to those of a Government department or local authority.

[(6) In item 9 "welfare services" means services which are directly connected with—

(*a*) the provision of care, treatment or instruction designed to promote the physical or mental welfare of elderly, sick, distressed or disabled persons,

(*b*) the care or protection of children and young persons, or (*c*) the provision of spiritual welfare by a religious institution as part of a course of instruction or a retreat, not being a course or a retreat designed primarily to provide recreation or a holiday,

and, in the case of services supplied by a state-regulated private welfare institution, includes only those services in respect of which the institution is so regulated.][5]

(7) Item 9 does not include the supply of accommodation or catering except where it is ancillary to the provision of care, treatment or instruction.

[(8) In this Group "state-regulated" means approved, licensed, registered or exempted from registration by any Minister or other authority pursuant to a provision of a public general Act, other than a provision that is capable of being brought into effect at different times in relation to different local authority areas.

Here "Act" means—

(*a*) an Act of Parliament;
(*b*) an Act of the Scottish Parliament;
(*c*) an Act of the Northern Ireland Assembly;
(*d*) an Order in Council under Schedule 1 to the Northern Ireland Act 1974;
(*e*) a Measure of the Northern Ireland Assembly established under section 1 of the Northern Ireland Assembly Act 1973;
(*f*) an Order in Council under section 1(3) of the Northern Ireland (Temporary Provisions) Act 1972;
(*g*) an Act of the Parliament of Northern Ireland.][5]

Commentary—*De Voil Indirect Tax Service* **V4.146**.

Press releases etc—C&E Business Brief 8/95 5-5-95 (clarification for opticians on VAT treatment of corrective spectacles).
C&E Business Brief 12/95 19-6-95 (drugs and prostheses provided in course of hospital care are an exempt supply).
C&E Business Brief 19/95 13-9-95 (procedures for opticians claiming overpaid VAT).
C&E Press Notice 48/95 9-10-95 (commercial agencies providing homecare services without charging VAT).
C&E News Release 23/96, 11-4-96 (item 1, note 2: healthcare services of unqualified staff "directly supervised" by qualified professionals: guidance on when services are "directly supervised" when the qualified professional is not physically present).
C&E Business Brief 8/96 (Customs now accept that General Practitioners and General Dental Practitioners were in business for their supplies to the NHS prior to 19 March 1993).
C&E VAT Information sheet 5/96 1-5-96 (clarification of the VAT treatment of supplies by dentists).
C&E Business Brief 26/96 19-12-96 (Customs have changed the liability of certain medico-legal services provided by doctors from exempt to taxable when made to third parties).
C&E Business Brief 1/97 24-1-97 (item above limited to activities of 'legal' persons).
C&E Business Brief 2/97 7-2-97 (medico-legal services clarified).
C&E Business Brief 3/02 12-2-02 (single and multiple supplies—sale of spectacles and contact lenses—Customs' policy clarified).
C&E Business Brief 7/02 21-3-02 (while commercially provided residential care (other than nursing or medical care) does not qualify for exemption as care in a hospital or similar establishment, it qualifies for the exemption that applies to residential accommodation).

Simon's Tax Cases—*EC Commission v United Kingdom* [1988] STC 251*; *Barkworth v C&E Comrs* [1988] STC 771*.
Item 1(*a*), *Dr Beynon and Partners v C&E Comrs* [2003] STC 169, CA, [2005] STC 55, HL.
Item 1(*b*), *C&E Comrs v Leightons Ltd* [1995] STC 458*.
Item 2, *d'Ambrumenil and another v C&E Comrs* (Case C-307/01) [2005] STC 650.
Item 4, *C&E Comrs v St Martins Hospital Ltd* [1995] STC 628*; *Gregg v Comrs of Customs and Excise* (Case C-216/97) [1999] STC 934; *C&E Comrs v Kingscrest Associates Ltd (t/a Kingscrest Residential Care Homes)* [2002] STC 490.
Item 9, *Kingscrest Associates Ltd and another v C&E Comrs* [2005] STC 1547; *Revenue and Customs Commissioners v K & L Childcare Service Ltd* [2006] STC 18.

Definitions—"Local authority", s 96(4); "supply", s 5, Sch 4.

Amendments—[1] Note (2A) inserted by the VAT (Pharmaceutical Chemists) Order, SI 1996/2949 with effect from 1 January 1997.
[2] Words in Item 1(*d*) substituted by the Nursing and Midwifery Order, SI 2002/253 art 54, Sch 5 para 12 with effect from 1 August 2004 (see the London Gazette, 21 July 2004).
[3] Item 1(*ca*) inserted by Value Added Tax (Osteopaths) Order, SI 1998/1294 with effect from 12 June 1998.
[4] Item 1 (*cb*) inserted by Value Added Tax (Chiropractors) Order, SI 1999/1575 with effect from 29 June 1999 (implements art 13A(1)(*c*) of the Sixth Council Directive, 77/388/EEC (OJ L145, 17.05.1977, p1)).
[5] Words in Item 4 substituted, Item 9 and Note (6) substituted, and Note (8) added, by the Value Added Tax (Health and Welfare) Order, SI 2002/762 with effect from 21 March 2002.
[6] Words in Item 9(*b*) inserted by the VAT (Health and Welfare) Order, SI 2003/24 with effect from 31 January 2003.
[7] Item 1(*c*) substituted by the Health Professions Order, SI 2002/254 art 48, Sch 4 para 6 with effect from 9 July 2003 (see the London Gazette, 27 June 2003).
[8] Item 2(*b*) substituted by the Dentists Act 1984 (Amendment) Order, SI 2005/2011 art 49, Sch 6 para 3 with effect from 31 July 2006.
[9] Words in items 1, 3 inserted, words in item 2 substituted, item 2(*c*) and preceding word "or" repealed, and item 2A inserted, by the VAT (Health and Welfare) Order, SI 2007/206 arts 2–6 with effect from 1 May 2007.
[10] Note 4 repealed by the European Qualifications (Health and Social Care Professions) Regulations, SI 2007/3101 reg 65(*b*) with effect from 3 December 2007.

GROUP 8 — BURIAL AND CREMATION

Item No

1 The disposal of the remains of the dead.

2 The making of arrangements for or in connection with the disposal of the remains of the dead.

Commentary—*De Voil Indirect Tax Service* **V4.151**.

Simon's Tax Cases—Item 2, *Network Insurance Brokers Ltd v C&E Comrs* [1998] STC 742; *Co-operative Wholesale Society Ltd v C&E Comrs* [1999] STC 1096; *Co-operative Wholesale Society Ltd v C&E Comrs* [2000] STC 727.

VAT

[GROUP 9 — SUBSCRIPTIONS TO TRADE UNIONS, PROFESSIONAL AND OTHER PUBLIC INTEREST BODIES][1]

Item No

1 The supply to its members of such services and, in connection with those services, of such goods as are both referable only to its aims and available without payment other than a membership subscription by any of the following non-profit-making organisations—

(*a*) a trade union or other organisation of persons having as its main object the negotiation on behalf of its members of the terms and conditions of their employment;

(*b*) a professional association, membership of which is wholly or mainly restricted to individuals who have or are seeking a qualification appropriate to the practice of the profession concerned;

(*c*) an association, the primary purpose of which is the advancement of a particular branch of knowledge, or the fostering of professional expertise, connected with the past or present professions or employments of its members;

(*d*) an association, the primary purpose of which is to make representations to the Government on legislation and other public matters which affect the business or professional interests of its members.

[(*e*) a body which has objects which are in the public domain and are of a political, religious, patriotic, philosophical, philanthropic or civic nature.][1]

NOTES

(1) Item 1 does not include any right of admission to any premises, event or performance, to which non-members are admitted for a consideration.

(2) "Trade union" has the meaning assigned to it by section 1 of the Trade Union and Labour Relations (Consolidation) Act 1992.

(3) Item 1 shall include organisations and associations the membership of which consists wholly or mainly of constituent or affiliated associations which as individual associations would be comprised in the item; and "member" shall be construed as including such an association and "membership subscription" shall include an affiliation fee or similar levy.

(4) Paragraph (*c*) does not apply unless the association restricts its membership wholly or mainly to individuals whose present or previous professions or employments are directly connected with the purposes of the association.

(5) Paragraph (*d*) does not apply unless the association restricts its membership wholly or mainly to individuals or corporate bodies whose business or professional interests are directly connected with the purposes of the association.

Commentary—*De Voil Indirect Tax Service* **V4.156**.
Simon's Tax Cases—*Institute of Leisure and Amenity Management v C&E Comrs* [1988] STC 602*.
Item 1(*b*), (*c*), *Committee of Directors of Polytechnics v C&E Comrs* [1992] STC 873*.
Item 1(*e*), *Expert Witness Institute v C&E Comrs, CA* [2002] STC 42.
Definitions—"Business", s 94; "supply", s 5, Sch 4.
Amendments—[1] Group title substituted, and Item 1, para (*e*) inserted by the Value Added Tax (Subscriptions to Trade Unions, Professional and Other Public Interest Bodies) Order, SI 1999/2834, arts 2, 4.

GROUP 10 — SPORT, SPORTS COMPETITIONS AND PHYSICAL EDUCATION

Item No

1 The grant of a right to enter a competition in sport or physical recreation where the consideration for the grant consists in money which is to be allocated wholly towards the provision of a prize or prizes awarded in that competition.

2 The grant, by a [an eligible body][1] established for the purposes of sport or physical recreation, of a right to enter a competition in such an activity.

3 The supply by a [an eligible body][1] to an individual, except, where the body operates a membership scheme, an individual who is not a member, of services closely linked with and essential to sport or physical education in which the individual is taking part.

NOTES

(1) Item 3 does not include the supply of any services by a [an eligible body][1] of residential accommodation, catering or transport.

(2) An individual shall only be considered to be a member of a [an eligible body][1] for the purpose of Item 3 where he is granted membership for a period of three months or more.

[(2A) Subject to Notes (2C) and (3), in this Group "eligible body" means a non-profit making body which—

(*a*) is precluded from distributing any profit it makes, or is allowed to distribute any such profit by means only of distributions to a non-profit making body;

(*b*) applies in accordance with Note (2B) any profits it makes from supplies of a description within Item 2 or 3; and

(*c*) is not subject to commercial influence.

(2B) For the purposes of Note (2A)(*b*) the application of profits made by any body from supplies of a description within Item 2 or 3 is in accordance with this Note only if those profits are applied for one or more of the following purposes, namely—

(*a*) the continuance or improvement of any facilities made available in or in connection with the making of the supplies of those descriptions made by that body;

(*b*) the purposes of a non-profit making body.

(2C) In determining whether the requirements of Note (2A) for being an eligible body are satisfied in the case of any body, there shall be disregarded any distribution of amounts representing unapplied or undistributed profits that falls to be made to the body's members on its winding-up or dissolution.][1]

(3) In Item 3 a "[an eligible body][1]" does not include—

(*a*) a local authority;

(*b*) a Government department within the meaning of section 41(6); or

(*c*) a non-departmental public body which is listed in the 1993 edition of the publication prepared by the Office of Public Service and Science and known as Public Bodies.

[(4) For the purposes of this Group a body shall be taken, in relation to a sports supply, to be subject to commercial influence if, and only if, there is a time in the relevant period when—

(*a*) a relevant supply was made to that body by a person associated with it at that time;

(*b*) an emolument was paid by that body to such a person;

(*c*) an agreement existed for either or both of the following to take place after the end of that period, namely—

(i) the making of a relevant supply to that body by such a person; or

(ii) the payment by that body to such a person of any emoluments.

(5) In this Group "the relevant period", in relation to a sports supply, means—

(*a*) where that supply is one made before 1st January 2003, the period beginning with 14th January 1999 and ending with the making of that sports supply; and

(*b*) where that supply is one made on or after 1st January 2003, the period of three years ending with the making of that sports supply.

(6) Subject to Note (7), in this Group "relevant supply", in relation to any body, means a supply falling within any of the following paragraphs—

(*a*) the grant of any interest in or right over land which at any time in the relevant period was or was expected to become sports land;

(*b*) the grant of any licence to occupy any land which at any such time was or was expected to become sports land;

(*c*) the grant, in the case of land in Scotland, of any personal right to call for or be granted any such interest or right as is mentioned in paragraph (*a*) above;

(*d*) a supply arising from a grant falling within paragraph (*a*), (*b*) or (*c*) above, other than a grant made before 1st April 1996;

(*e*) the supply of any services consisting in the management or administration of any facilities provided by that body;

(*f*) the supply of any goods or services for a consideration in excess of what would have been agreed between parties entering into a commercial transaction at arm's length.

(7) A supply which has been, or is to be or may be, made by any person shall not be taken, in relation to a sports supply made by any body, to be a relevant supply for the purposes of this Group if—

(*a*) the principal purpose of that body is confined, at the time when the sports supply is made, to the provision for employees of that person of facilities for use for or in connection with sport or physical recreation, or both;

(*b*) the supply in question is one made by a charity or local authority or one which (if it is made) will be made by a person who is a charity or local authority at the time when the sports supply is made;

(*c*) the supply in question is a grant falling within Note (6)(*a*) to (*c*) which has been made, or (if it is made) will be made, for a nominal consideration;

(*d*) the supply in question is one arising from such a grant as is mentioned in paragraph (*c*) above and is not itself a supply the consideration for which was, or will or may be, more than a nominal consideration; or

(*e*) the supply in question—

(i) is a grant falling within Note (6)(*a*) to (*c*) which is made for no consideration; but

(ii) falls to be treated as a supply of goods or services, or (if it is made) will fall to be so treated, by reason only of the application, in accordance with paragraph 9 of Schedule 4, of paragraph 5 of that Schedule.

(8) Subject to Note (10), a person shall be taken, for the purposes of this Group, to have been associated with a body at any of the following times, that is to say—

(*a*) the time when a supply was made to that body by that person;

(*b*) the time when an emolument was paid by that body to that person; or

(*c*) the time when an agreement was in existence for the making of a relevant supply or the payment of emoluments,

if, at that time, or at another time (whether before or after that time) in the relevant period, that person was an officer or shadow officer of that body or an intermediary for supplies to that body.

(9) Subject to Note (10), a person shall also be taken, for the purposes of this Group, to have been associated with a body at a time mentioned in paragraph (*a*), (*b*) or (*c*) of Note (8) if, at that time, he was connected with another person who in accordance with that Note—

(*a*) is to be taken to have been so associated at that time; or

(*b*) would be taken to have been so associated were that time the time of a supply by the other person to that body.

(10) Subject to Note (11), a person shall not be taken for the purposes of this Group to have been associated with a body at a time mentioned in paragraph (*a*), (*b*) or (*c*) of Note (8) if the only times in the relevant period when that person or the person connected with him was an officer or shadow officer of the body are times before 1st January 2000.

(11) Note (10) does not apply where (but for that Note) the body would be treated as subject to commercial influence at any time in the relevant period by virtue of—

(*a*) the existence of any agreement entered into on or after 14th January 1999 and before 1st January 2000; or

(*b*) anything done in pursuance of any such agreement.

(12) For the purposes of this Group a person shall be taken, in relation to a sports supply, to have been at all times in the relevant period an intermediary for supplies to the body making that supply if—

(*a*) at any time in that period either a supply was made to him by another person or an agreement for the making of a supply to him by another was in existence; and

(*b*) the circumstances were such that, if—

(i) that body had been the person to whom the supply was made or (in the case of an agreement) the person to whom it was to be or might be made; and

(ii) Note (7) above were to be disregarded to the extent (if at all) that it would prevent the supply from being a relevant supply, the body would have fallen to be regarded in relation to the sports supply as subject to commercial influence.

(13) In determining for the purposes of Note (12) or this Note whether there are such circumstances as are mentioned in paragraph (*b*) of that Note in the case of any supply, that Note and this Note shall be applied first for determining whether the person by whom the supply was made, or was to be or might be made, was himself an intermediary for supplies to the body in question, and so on through any number of other supplies or agreements.

(14) In determining for the purposes of this Group whether a supply made by any person was made by an intermediary for supplies to a body, it shall be immaterial that the supply by that person was made before the making of the supply or agreement by reference to which that person falls to be regarded as such an intermediary.

(15) Without prejudice to the generality of subsection (1AA) of section 43, for the purpose of determining—

(*a*) whether a relevant supply has at any time been made to any person;

(*b*) whether there has at any time been an agreement for the making of a relevant supply to any person; and

(*c*) whether a person falls to be treated as an intermediary for the supplies to any body by reference to supplies that have been, were to be or might have been made to him,

references in the preceding Notes to a supply shall be deemed to include references to a supply falling for other purposes to be disregarded in accordance with section 43(1)(*a*).

(16) In this Group—

"agreement" includes any arrangement or understanding (whether or not legally enforceable);

"emolument" means any emolument (within the meaning of the Income Tax Acts) the amount of which falls or may fall, in accordance with the agreement under which it is payable, to be determined or varied wholly or partly by reference—

(i) to the profits from some or all of the activities of the body paying the emolument; or

(ii) to the level of that body's gross income from some or all of its activities;

"employees", in relation to a person, includes retired employees of that person;

"grant" includes an assignment or surrender;

"officer", in relation to a body, includes—

(i) a director of a body corporate; and

(ii) any committee member or trustee concerned in the general control and management of the administration of the body;

"shadow officer", in relation to a body, means a person in accordance with whose directions or instructions the members or officers of the body are accustomed to act;

"sports land", in relation to any body, means any land used or held for use for or in connection with the provision by that body of facilities for use for or in connection with sport or physical recreation, or both;

"sports supply" means a supply which, if made by an eligible body, would fall within Item 2 or 3.

(17) For the purposes of this Group any question whether a person is connected with another shall be determined in accordance with section 839 of the Taxes Act (connected persons).][1]

Commentary—*De Voil Indirect Tax Service* **V4.161**.
Definitions—"Local authority", s 96(4); "money", s 96(1); "supply", s 5, Sch 4.
Simon's Tax Cases—*Messenger Leisure Developments Ltd v Revenue and Customs Commissioners* [2005] STC 1078.
Cross references—Council Directive (EEC) 77/388, Article 13A(1)(*m*).
Amendments—[1] Words in Items 2 and 3 substituted and notes (2A)–(2C) and (4)–(17) inserted by the VAT (Sport, Sports Competitions and Physical Education) Order, SI 1999/1994, arts 2–5, with effect from 1 January 2000.

GROUP 11 — WORKS OF ART ETC

Item No

1 The disposal of an object with respect to which estate duty is not chargeable by virtue of section 30(3) of the Finance Act 1953, section 34(1) of the Finance Act 1956 or the proviso to section 40(2) of the Finance Act 1930.

2 The disposal of an object with respect to which inheritance tax is not chargeable by virtue of paragraph 1(3)(*a*) or (4), paragraph 3(4)(*a*), or the words following paragraph 3(4), of Schedule 5 to the Inheritance Tax Act 1984.

3 The disposal of property with respect to which inheritance tax is not chargeable by virtue of section 32(4) or 32A(5) or (7) of the Inheritance Tax Act 1984.

4 The disposal of an asset in a case in which any gain accruing on that disposal is not a chargeable gain by virtue of section 258(2) of the Taxation of Chargeable Gains Act 1992.

Commentary—*De Voil Indirect Tax Service* **V4.166**.

[GROUP 12—FUND-RAISING EVENTS BY CHARITIES AND OTHER QUALIFYING BODIES

Item No.

1 The supply of goods and services by a charity in connection with an event—

(*a*) that is organised for charitable purposes by a charity or jointly by more than one charity,
(*b*) whose primary purpose is the raising of money, and
(*c*) that is promoted as being primarily for the raising of money.

2 The supply of goods and services by a qualifying body in connection with an event—

(*a*) that is organised exclusively for the body's own benefit,
(*b*) whose primary purpose is the raising of money, and
(*c*) that is promoted as being primarily for the raising of money.

3 The supply of goods and services by a charity or a qualifying body in connection with an event—

(*a*) that is organised jointly by a charity, or two or more charities, and the qualifying body,
(*b*) that is so organised exclusively for charitable purposes or exclusively for the body's own benefit or exclusively for a combination of those purposes and that benefit,
(*c*) whose primary purpose is the raising of money, and
(*d*) that is promoted as being primarily for the raising of money.

NOTES

(1) For the purposes of this Group "event" includes an event accessed (wholly or partly) by means of electronic communications.

For this purpose "electronic communications" includes any communications by means of [an electronic communications network][2].

(2) For the purposes of this Group "charity" includes a body corporate that is wholly owned by a charity if—

(*a*) the body has agreed in writing (whether or not contained in a deed) to transfer its profits (from whatever source) to a charity, or
(*b*) the body's profits (from whatever source) are otherwise payable to a charity.

(3) For the purposes of this Group "qualifying body means—

(*a*) any non-profit making organisation mentioned in item 1 of Group 9;
(*b*) any body that is an eligible body for the purposes of Group 10 and whose principal purpose is the provision of facilities for persons to take part in sport or physical education; or
(*c*) any body that is an eligible body for the purposes of item 2 of Group 13.

(4) Where in a financial year of a charity or qualifying body there are held at the same location more than 15 events involving the charity or body that are of the same kind, items 1 to 3 do not apply (or shall be treated as having not applied) to a supply in connection with any event involving the charity or body that is of that kind and is held in that financial year at that location.

(5) In determining whether the limit of 15 events mentioned in Note (4) has been exceeded in the case of events of any one kind held at the same location, disregard any event of that kind held at that location in a week during which the aggregate gross takings from events involving the charity or body that are of that kind and are held in that location do not exceed £1,000.

(6) In the case of a financial year that is longer or shorter than a year, Notes (4) and (5) have effect as if for "15" there were substituted the whole number nearest to the number obtained by—

(*a*) first multiplying the number of days in the financial year by 15, and (*b*) then dividing the result by 365.

(7) For the purposes of Notes (4) and (5)—

(*a*) an event involves a charity if the event is organised by the charity or a connected charity;

(*b*) an event involves a qualifying body if the event is organised by the body.

In this Note "organised" means organised alone or jointly in any combination, and "organising" in Note (8) shall be construed accordingly.

(8) Items 1 to 3 do not include any supply in connection with an event if—

(*a*) accommodation in connection with the event is provided to a person by means of a supply, or in pursuance of arrangements, made by—

(i) the charity or any of the charities, or the qualifying body, organising the event, or

(ii) a charity connected with any charity organising the event,

and

(*b*) the provision of the accommodation is not incidental to the event.

(9) For the purposes of Note (8) the provision of accommodation is incidental to the event only if accommodation provided to the person by such means, or in pursuance of such arrangements, as are mentioned in paragraph (*a*) of that Note—

(*a*) does not exceed two nights in total (whether or not consecutive), and

(*b*) is not to any extent provided by means of a supply to which an order under section 53 applies.

(10) For the purposes of Notes (7)(*a*) and (8), two charities are connected if—

(*a*) one is a charity for the purposes of this Group only by virtue of Note (2) and the other is the charity that owns it, or

(*b*) each is a charity for the purposes of this Group only by virtue of Note (2) and the two of them are owned by the same charity.

(11) Items 1 to 3 do not include any supply the exemption of which would be likely to create distortions of competition such as to place a commercial enterprise carried on by a taxable person at a disadvantage.][1]

Commentary—*De Voil Indirect Tax Service* **V4.171**.
Definition—"Supply", s 5, Sch 4.
Amendments—[1] Group substituted by the Value Added Tax (Fund-Raising Events by Charities and Other Qualifying Bodies) Order, SI 2000/802 arts 2, 3 with effect in the case of supplies made from 1 April 2000.
[2] Words in Note (1) substituted by the Communications Act 2003 s 406, Sch 17 para 129(1), (3) with effect from 25 July 2003 to 29 December 2003 for certain purposes (see SI 2003/1900), 29 December 2003 for other purposes (see SI 2003/3142), and from a date to be appointed for remaining purposes.

[GROUP 13 —CULTURAL SERVICES ETC

Item No

1 The supply by a public body of a right of admission to—

(*a*) a museum, gallery, art exhibition or zoo; or

(*b*) a theatrical, musical or choreographic performance of a cultural nature.

2 The supply by an eligible body of a right of admission to—

(*a*) a museum, gallery, art exhibition or zoo; or

(*b*) a theatrical, musical or choreographic performance of a cultural nature.

NOTES

(1) For the purposes of this Group "public body" means—

(*a*) a local authority;

(*b*) a government department within the meaning of section 41(6); or

(*c*) a non-departmental public body which is listed in the 1995 edition of the publication prepared by the Office of Public Service and known as "Public Bodies".

(2) For the purposes of item 2 "eligible body" means any body (other than a public body) which—

(*a*) is precluded from distributing, and does not distribute, any profit it makes;

(*b*) applies any profits made from supplies of a description falling within item 2 to the continuance or improvement of the facilities made available by means of the supplies; and

(*c*) is managed and administered on a voluntary basis by persons who have no direct or indirect financial interest in its activities.

(3) Item 1 does not include any supply the exemption of which would be likely to create distortions of competition such as to place a commercial enterprise carried on by a taxable person at a disadvantage

(4) Item 1(*b*) includes the supply of a right of admission to a performance only if the performance is provided exclusively by one or more public bodies, one or more eligible bodies or any combination of public bodies and eligible bodies.][1]

Commentary—*De Voil Indirect Tax Service* **V4.176**.
Simon's Tax Cases—*Bournemouth Symphony Orchestra v C&E Comrs, Longborough Festival Opera v R&C Comrs* [2007] STC 198.
Definitions—"Supply", s 5, Sch 4.

Press releases etc—HMRC Brief 27/07, 22-3-07 (Cultural exemption – clarification of "direct or indirect financial interest" following recent CA Judgments in *Bournemouth Symphony Orchestra* (C3/2005/1681) and *Longborough Festival Opera* (C3/2006/0369)).

Amendments—[1] This group inserted by the VAT (Cultural Services) Order, SI 1996/1256, with effect from 1 June 1996.

[GROUP 14—SUPPLIES OF GOODS WHERE INPUT TAX CANNOT BE RECOVERED

Item No

1 A supply of goods in relation to which each of the following conditions is satisfied, that is to say—

(*a*) there is input tax of the person making the supply ('the relevant supplier'), or of any predecessor of his, that has arisen or will arise on the supply to, or acquisition or importation by, the relevant supplier or any such predecessor of goods used for the supply made by the relevant supplier;

(*b*) the only such input tax is non-deductible input tax; and

(*c*) the supply made by the relevant supplier is not a supply which would be exempt under Item 1 of Group 1 of Schedule 9 but for an [option to tax any land under Part 1 of Schedule 10][3].

NOTES

(1) Subject to Note (2) below, in relation to any supply of goods by the relevant supplier, the goods used for that supply are—

(*a*) the goods supplied, and

(*b*) any goods used in the process of producing the supplied goods so as to be comprised in them.

(2) In relation to a supply by any person consisting in or arising from the grant of a major interest in land ('the relevant supply')—

(*a*) any supply consisting in or arising from a previous grant of a major interest in the land is a supply of goods used for the relevant supply, and

(*b*) subject to paragraph (*a*) above, the goods used for the relevant supply are any goods used in the construction of a building or civil engineering work so as to become part of the land.

(3) Subject to Notes (7) to (10) below, non-deductible input tax is input tax to which Note (4) or (5) below applies.

(4) This Note applies to input tax which (disregarding this Group and regulation 106 of the Value Added Tax Regulations 1995 (*de minimis* rule)) is not, and will not become, attributable to supplies to which section 26(2) applies.

(5) This Note applies to input tax if—

(*a*) disregarding this Group and the provisions mentioned in Note (6) below, the relevant supplier or a predecessor of his has or will become entitled to credit for the whole or a part of the amount of that input tax; and

(*b*) the effect (disregarding this Group) of one or more of those provisions is that neither the relevant supplier nor any predecessor of his has or will become entitled to credit for any part of that amount.

(6) The provisions mentioned in Note (5) above are—

(*a*) Article 5 of the Value Added Tax (Input Tax) Order 1992 (no credit for input tax on goods or services used for business entertainment);

(*b*) Article 6 of that Order (no credit for input tax on non-building materials incorporated in building or site);

(*c*) Article 7 of that Order (no credit for input tax on motor cars);

(*d*) any provision directly or indirectly re-enacted (with or without modification) in a provision mentioned in paragraphs (*a*) to (*c*) above.

(7) For the purposes of this Group the input tax of a person shall be deemed to include any VAT which—

(*a*) has arisen or will arise on a supply to, or acquisition or importation by, that person; and

(*b*) would fall to be treated as input tax of that person but for its arising when that person is not a taxable person.

(8) Subject to Note (9) below, the input tax that is taken to be non-deductible input tax shall include any VAT which—

(*a*) is deemed to be input tax of any person by virtue of Note (7) above; and

(*b*) would be input tax to which Note (4) or (5) above would apply if it were input tax of that person and, in the case of a person to whom section 39 applies, if his business were carried on in the United Kingdom.

(9) Non-deductible input tax does not include any VAT that has arisen or will arise on a supply to, or acquisition or importation by, any person of any goods used for a supply of goods ('the relevant supply') if—

(*a*) that VAT; or

(*b*) any other VAT arising on the supply to, or acquisition or importation by, that person or any predecessor of his of any goods used for the relevant supply,

has been or will be refunded under section 33, [33A,][2] 39 or 41.

(10) Input tax arising on a supply, acquisition or importation of goods shall be disregarded for the purposes of determining whether the conditions in Item No 1(*a*) and (*b*) are satisfied if, at a time after that supply, acquisition or importation but before the supply by the relevant supplier, a supply of the goods or of anything in which they are comprised is treated under or by virtue of any provision of this Act as having been made by the relevant supplier or any predecessor of his to himself.

(11) In relation to any goods or anything comprised in any goods, a person is a predecessor of another ('the putative successor') only if Note (12) or (13) below applies to him in relation to those goods or that thing; and references in this Group to a person's predecessors include references to the predecessors of his predecessors through any number of transfers and events such as are mentioned in Notes (12) and (13).

(12) This Note applies to a person in relation to any goods or thing if—

(*a*) the putative successor is a person to whom he has transferred assets of his business by a transfer of that business, or a part of it, as a going concern;

(*b*) those assets consisted of or included those goods or that thing; and

(*c*) the transfer of the assets is one falling by virtue of an Order under section 5(3) (or under an enactment re-enacted in section 5(3)) to be treated as neither a supply of goods nor a supply of services.

(13) This Note applies to a body corporate in relation to any goods or thing if—

(*a*) those goods or that thing formed part of the assets of the business of that body at a time when it became a member of a group of which the putative successor was at that time the representative member;

(*b*) those goods or that thing formed part of the assets of the business of that body corporate, or of any other body corporate which was a member of the same group as that body, at a time when that body was succeeded as the representative member of the group by the putative successor; or

(*c*) those goods or that thing formed part of the assets of the putative successor at a time when it ceased to be a member of a group of which the body corporate in question was at the time the representative member.

(14) References in Note (13) above to a body corporate's being or becoming or ceasing to be a member of a group or the representative member of a group are references to its falling to be so treated for the purposes of section 43.

(15) In Notes (11) to (13) above the references to anything comprised in other goods shall be taken, in relation to any supply consisting in or arising from the grant of a major interest in land, to include anything the supply, acquisition or importation of which is, by virtue of Note (2) above, taken to be a supply, acquisition or importation of goods used for making the supply so consisting or arising.

(16) Notes (1) and (1A) to Group 1 shall apply for the purposes of this Group as they apply for the purposes of that Group.][1]

Commentary—*De Voil Indirect Tax Service* **V4.181**.

Amendments—[1] This group inserted by the Value Added Tax (Supplies of Goods where Input Tax cannot be recovered) Order, SI 1999/2833, art 2(1), (3), with effect from 1 March 2000.

[2] In Note (9), "33A," inserted after "33" by FA 2001 s 98(9) with effect from 1 September 2001.

[3] In Item 1(*c*) words substituted by the Value Added Tax (Buildings and Land) Order, SI 2008/1146, art 6, Sch 1 paras 1, 4 with effect in relation to supplies made on or after 1 June 2008, subject to savings in Sch 2 of the Order.

[GROUP 15—INVESTMENT GOLD

Item no:

1 The supply of investment gold.

2 The grant, assignment or surrender of any right, interest, or claim in, over or to investment gold if the right, interest or claim is or confers a right to the transfer of the possession of investment gold.

3 The supply, by a person acting as agent for a disclosed principal, of services consisting of—

(*a*) the effecting of a supply falling within item 1 or 2 that is made by or to his principal, or

(*b*) attempting to effect a supply falling within item 1 or 2 that is intended to be made by or to his principal but is not in fact made.

NOTES:

(1) For the purposes of this Group "investment gold" means—

(*a*) gold of a purity not less than 995 thousandths that is in the form of a bar, or a wafer, of a weight accepted by the bullion markets;

(*b*) a gold coin minted after 1800 that—

(i) is of a purity of not less than 900 thousandths,

(ii) is, or has been, legal tender in its country of origin, and

(iii) is of a description of coin that is normally sold at a price that does not exceed 180% of the open market value of the gold contained in the coin; or

(*c*) a gold coin of a description specified in a notice that has been published by the Commissioners for the purposes of this Group and has not been withdrawn.

(2) A notice under Note (1)(*c*) may provide that a description specified in the notice has effect only for the purposes of supplies made at times falling within a period specified in the notice.

(3) Item 2 does not include—

(*a*) the grant of an option, or

(*b*) the assignment or surrender of a right under an option at a time before the option is exercised.

(4) This Group does not include a supply—

(*a*) between members of the London Bullion Market Association, or

(*b*) by a member of that Association to a taxable person who is not a member or by such a person to a member.][1]

Commentary—*De Voil Indirect Tax Service* **V4.186.**

Amendments—[1] This group inserted by the Value Added Tax (Investment Gold) Order, SI 1999/3116, art 2(1), (3), with effect from 1 January 2000.

[SCHEDULE 9A
ANTI-AVOIDANCE PROVISIONS: GROUPS]

Section 43(9)

Commentary—*De Voil Indirect Tax Service* **V2.104.**

Cross references—See VATA 1994 ss 83, 84 (appeals against directions or assessments under this Schedule).

Amendments—This Schedule inserted by FA 1996 s 31(2), Sch 4.

Power to give directions

[1— (1) Subject to paragraph 2 below, the Commissioners may give a direction under this Schedule if, in any case—

(*a*) a relevant event has occurred;

(*b*) the condition specified in sub-paragraph (3) below is fulfilled;

(*c*) that condition would not be fulfilled apart from the occurrence of that event; and

(*d*) in the case of an event falling within sub-paragraph (2)(*b*) below, the transaction in question is not a supply which is the only supply by reference to which the case falls within paragraphs (*a*) to (*c*) above.

(2) For the purposes of this Schedule, a relevant event occurs when a body corporate—

(*a*) begins to be, or ceases to be, treated as a member of a group; or

(*b*) enters into any transaction.

(3) The condition mentioned in sub-paragraph (1) above is that—

(*a*) there has been, or will or may be, a taxable supply on which VAT has been, or will or may be, charged otherwise than by reference to the supply's full value;

(*b*) there is at least a part of the supply which is not or, as the case may be, would not be zero-rated; and

(*c*) the charging of VAT on the supply otherwise than by reference to its full value gives rise or, as the case may be, would give rise to a tax advantage.

(4) For the purposes of this paragraph the charging of VAT on a supply ("the undercharged supply") otherwise than by reference to its full value shall be taken to give rise to a tax advantage if, and only if, a person has become entitled—

(*a*) to credit for input tax allowable as attributable to that supply or any part of it, or

(*b*) in accordance with regulations under section 39, to any repayment in respect of that supply or any part of it.

(5) The case where a person shall be taken for the purposes of sub-paragraph (4) above to have become entitled to a credit for input tax allowable as attributable to the undercharged supply, or to a part of it, shall include any case where—

(*a*) a person has become entitled to a credit for any input tax on the supply to him, or the acquisition or importation by him, of any goods or services; and

(*b*) whatever the supplies to which the credit was treated as attributable when the entitlement to it arose, those goods or services are used by him in making the undercharged supply, or a part of it.

(6) For the purposes of sub-paragraphs (4) and (5) above where—

(*a*) there is a supply of any of the assets of a business of a person ("the transferor") to a person to whom the whole or any part of that business is transferred as a going concern ("the transferee"), and

(*b*) that supply is treated, in accordance with an order under section 5(3), as being neither a supply of goods nor a supply of services,

the question, so far as it falls to be determined by reference to those assets, whether a credit for input tax to which any person has become entitled is one allowable as attributable to the whole or any part of a supply shall be determined as if the transferor and the transferee were the same person.

(7) Where, in a case to which sub-paragraph (6) above applies, the transferor himself acquired any of the assets in question by way of a supply falling within paragraphs (*a*) and (*b*) of that sub-paragraph, that sub-paragraph shall have the effect, as respects the assets so acquired, of requiring the person from whom those assets were acquired to be treated for the purposes of sub-paragraphs (4) and (5) above as the same person as the transferor and the transferee, and so on in the case of any number of successive supplies falling within those paragraphs.

(8) For the purposes of this paragraph any question—

(*a*) whether any credit for input tax to which a person has become entitled was, or is to be taken to have been, a credit allowable as attributable to the whole or any part of a supply, or

(*b*) whether any repayment is a repayment in respect of the whole or any part of a supply,

shall be determined, in relation to a supply of a right to goods or services or to a supply of goods or services by virtue of such a right, as if the supply of the right and supplies made by virtue of the right were a single supply of which the supply of the right and each of those supplies constituted different parts.

(9) References in this paragraph to the full value of a supply are references to the amount which (having regard to any direction under paragraph 1 of Schedule 6) would be the full value of that supply for the purposes of the charge to VAT if that supply were not a supply falling to be disregarded, to any extent, in pursuance of section 43(1)(*a*).

(10) References in this paragraph to the supply of a right to goods or services include references to the supply of any right, option or priority with respect to the supply of goods or services, and to the supply of an interest deriving from any right to goods or services.][1]

Definitions—"The Commissioners", s 96(1); "input tax", ss 24, 96(1); "supply", s 5, Sch 4; "taxable supply", ss 4(2), 96(1); "VAT", ss 1, 96(1).

Amendments—[1] This Schedule inserted by FA 1996 s 31(2), Sch 4.

Restrictions on giving directions

[2— [(1)][2] The Commissioners shall not give a direction under this Schedule by reference to a relevant event if they are satisfied that—

(*a*) the change in the treatment of the body corporate, or

(*b*) the transaction in question,

had as its main purpose or, as the case may be, as each of its main purposes a genuine commercial purpose unconnected with the fulfilment of the condition specified in paragraph 1(3) above.][1]

[(2) This paragraph shall not apply where the relevant event is the termination of a body corporate's treatment as a member of a group by a notice under section 43C(1) or (3).][2]

Definitions—"The Commissioners", s 96(1); "relevant event", Sch 9A para 1(2).

Amendments—[1] This Schedule inserted by FA 1996 s 31(2), Sch 4.

[2] Para 2 amended to renumber existing text as sub-para (1), and sub-para (2) inserted by FA 1999 s 16, Sch 2 para 5 with effect from 27 July 1999 subject to FA 1999 Sch 2 para 6.

Form of directions under Schedule

[3— (1) The directions that may be given by the Commissioners under this Schedule are either—

(*a*) a direction relating to any supply of goods or services that has been made, in whole or in part, by one body corporate to another; or

(*b*) a direction relating to a particular body corporate.

(2) A direction under this Schedule relating to a supply shall require it to be assumed (where it would not otherwise be the case) that, to the extent described in the direction, the supply was not a supply falling to be disregarded in pursuance of section 43(1)(*a*).

(3) A direction under this Schedule relating to a body corporate shall require it to be assumed (where it would not otherwise be the case) that, for such period (comprising times before the giving of the direction or times afterwards or both) as may be described in the direction, the body corporate—

(*a*) did not fall to be treated, or is not to be treated, as a member of a group, or of a particular group so described; or

(*b*) fell to be treated, or is to be treated, as a member of any group so described of which, for that period, it was or is eligible to be a member.

(4) Where a direction under this Schedule requires any assumptions to be made, then—

(*a*) so far as the assumptions relate to times on or after the day on which the direction is given, this Act shall have effect in relation to such times in accordance with those assumptions; and

(*b*) paragraph 6 below shall apply for giving effect to those assumptions in so far as they relate to earlier times.

(5) A direction falling within sub-paragraph (3)(*b*) above may identify in relation to any times or period the body corporate which is to be assumed to have been, or to be, the representative member of the group at those times or for that period.

(6) A direction under this Schedule may vary the effect of a previous direction under this Schedule.

(7) The Commissioners may at any time, by notice in writing to the person to whom it was given, withdraw a direction under this Schedule.

(8) The refusal or non-refusal by the Commissioners of an application [such as is mentioned in section 43B][2] shall not prejudice the power of the Commissioners to give a direction under this Schedule requiring any case to be assumed to be what it would have been had the application not been refused or, as the case may be, had it been refused.][1]

Definitions—"The Commissioners", s 96(1); "representative member", s 43(4); "supply", s 5, Sch 4.
Amendments—[1] This Schedule inserted by FA 1996 s 31(2), Sch 4.
[2] Words in sub-para (8) substituted by FA 1999 s 16, Sch 2 para 5 with effect from 27 July 1999 subject to FA 1999 Sch 2 para 6.

Time limit on directions

[4— (1) A direction under this Schedule shall not be given more than six years after whichever is the later of—

(*a*) the occurrence of the relevant event by reference to which it is given; and
(*b*) the time when the relevant entitlement arose.

(2) A direction under this Schedule shall not be given by reference to a relevant event occurring on or before 28th November 1995.

(3) Subject to sub-paragraphs (1) and (2) above, a direction under this Schedule—

(*a*) may be given by reference to a relevant event occurring before the coming into force of this Schedule; and
(*b*) may require assumptions to be made in relation to times (including times before 29th November 1995) falling before the occurrence of the relevant event by reference to which the direction is given, or before the relevant entitlement arose.

(4) For the purposes of this paragraph the reference, in relation to the giving of a direction, to the relevant entitlement is a reference to the entitlement by reference to which the requirements of paragraph 1(4) above are taken to be satisfied for the purposes of that direction.][1]

Press releases etc—Hansard 6-2-96 (scope for retrospective directions under this paragraph).
Definitions—"Input tax", ss 24, 96(1); "prescribed accounting period", s 25(1).
Amendments—[1] This Schedule inserted by FA 1996 s 31(2), Sch 4.

Manner of giving directions

[5— (1) A direction under this Schedule relating to a supply may be given to—

(*a*) the person who made the supply to which the direction relates; or
(*b*) any body corporate which, at the time when the direction is given, is the representative member of a group of which that person was treated as being a member at the time of the supply.

(2) A direction under this Schedule relating to a body corporate ("the relevant body") may be given to that body or to any body corporate which at the time when the direction is given is, or in pursuance of the direction is to be treated as, the representative member of a group of which the relevant body—

(*a*) is treated as being a member;
(*b*) was treated as being a member at a time to which the direction relates; or
(*c*) is to be treated as being, or having been, a member at any such time.

(3) A direction given to any person under this Schedule shall be given to him by notice in writing.

(4) A direction under this Schedule must specify the relevant event by reference to which it is given.][1]

Definitions—"The Commissioners", s 96(1); "representative member", s 43(4).
Amendments—[1] This Schedule inserted by FA 1996 s 31(2), Sch 4.

Assessment in consequence of a direction

[6— (1) Subject to sub-paragraph (3) below, where—

(*a*) a direction is given under this Schedule, and
(*b*) there is an amount of VAT ("the unpaid tax") for which a relevant person would have been liable before the giving of the direction if the facts had accorded with the assumptions specified in the direction,

the Commissioners may, to the best of their judgment, assess the amount of unpaid tax as tax due from the person to whom the direction was given or another relevant person and notify their assessment to that person.

(2) In sub-paragraph (1) above the reference to an amount of VAT for which a person would, on particular assumptions, have been liable before the giving of a direction under this Schedule is a reference to the aggregate of the following—

(*a*) any amount of output tax which, on those assumptions but not otherwise, would have been due from a relevant person at the end of a prescribed accounting period ending before the giving of the direction;

(*b*) the amount of any credit for input tax to which a relevant person is treated as having been entitled at the end of such an accounting period but to which he would not have been entitled on those assumptions; and

(*c*) the amount of any repayment of tax made to a relevant person in accordance with regulations under section 39 but to which he would not have been entitled on those assumptions.

(3) Where any assessment falls to be made under this paragraph in a case in which the Commissioners are satisfied that the actual revenue loss is less than the unpaid tax, the total amount to be assessed under this paragraph shall not exceed what appears to them, to the best of their judgement, to be the amount of that loss.

(4) For the purposes of the making of an assessment under this paragraph in relation to any direction, the actual revenue loss shall be taken to be equal to the amount of the unpaid tax less the amount given by aggregating the amounts of every entitlement—

(*a*) to credit for input tax, or

(*b*) to a repayment in accordance with regulations under section 39,

which (whether as an entitlement of the person in relation to whom the assessment is made or as an entitlement of any other person) would have arisen on the assumptions contained in the direction, but not otherwise.

(5) An assessment under this paragraph relating to a direction may be notified to the person to whom that direction is given by being incorporated in the same notice as that direction.

(6) An assessment under this paragraph shall not be made—

(*a*) more than one year after the day on which the direction to which it relates was given, or

(*b*) in the case of any direction that has been withdrawn.

(7) Where an amount has been assessed on any person under this paragraph and notified to him—

(*a*) that amount shall be deemed (subject to the provisions of this Act as to appeals) to be an amount of VAT due from him;

(*b*) that amount may be recovered accordingly, either from that person or, in the case of a body corporate that is for the time being treated as a member of a group, from the representative member of that group; and

(*c*) to the extent that more than one person is liable by virtue of any assessment under this paragraph in respect of the same amount of unpaid tax, those persons shall be treated as jointly and severally liable for that amount.

(8) Sub-paragraph (7) above does not have effect if or to the extent that the assessment in question has been withdrawn or reduced.

(9) Sections 74 and 77(6) apply in relation to assessments under this paragraph as they apply in relation to assessments under section 73 but as if the reference in subsection (1) of section 74 to the reckonable date were a reference to the date on which the assessment is notified.

(10) Where by virtue of sub-paragraph (9) above any person is liable to interest under section 74—

(*a*) section 76 shall have effect in relation to that liability with the omission of subsections (2) to (6); and

(*b*) section 77, except subsection (6), shall not apply to an assessment of the amount due by way of interest;

and (without prejudice to the power to make assessments for interest for later periods) the interest to which any assessment made under section 76 by virtue of paragraph (*a*) above may relate shall be confined to interest for a period of no more than two years ending with the time when the assessment to interest is made.

(11) In this paragraph "a relevant person", in relation to a direction, means—

(*a*) the person to whom the direction is given;

(*b*) the body corporate which was the representative member of any group of which that person was treated as being, or in pursuance of the direction is to be treated as having been, a member at a time to which the assumption specified in the direction relates; or

(*c*) any body corporate which, in pursuance of the direction, is to be treated as having been the representative member of such a group.][1]

Definitions—"The Commissioners", s 96(1); "input tax", ss 24, 96(1); "prescribed accounting period", s 25(1); "VAT", ss 1, 96(1).

Amendments—[1] This Schedule inserted by FA 1996 s 31(2), Sch 4.

Interpretation of Schedule etc

[7— (1) References in this Schedule to being treated as a member of a group and to being eligible to be treated as a member of a group shall be construed in accordance with [sections 43 to 43C][2].

(2) For the purposes of this Schedule the giving of any notice or notification to any receiver, liquidator or person otherwise acting in a representative capacity in relation to another shall be treated as the giving of a notice or, as the case may be, notification to the person in relation to whom he so acts.][1]

Amendments—[1] This Schedule inserted by FA 1996 s 31(2), Sch 4.
[2] Words in sub-para (1) substituted by FA 1999 s 16, Sch 2 para 5 with effect from 27 July 1999 subject to FA 1999 Sch 2 para 6.

VAT

[SCHEDULE 10
BUILDINGS AND LAND

Section 51][1]

Press releases etc—HMRC Brief 28/08, 30-5-08 (Land & buildings – announcing a new revised Notice 742A "Opting to tax land and buildings and associated forms and certificates" (see *VAT Notices* section ante.))
Amendments—[1] Schedule 10 substituted by the Value Added Tax (Buildings and Land) Order, SI 2008/1146, art 2 with effect in relation to supplies made on or after 1 June 2008, subject to savings in Sch 2 of the Order.

[PART 1
THE OPTION TO TAX LAND

INTRODUCTION

Overview of the option to tax

1— (1) This Part of the Schedule makes provision for a person to opt to tax any land.

(2) The effect of the option to tax is dealt with in paragraph 2 (exempt supplies become taxable), as read with paragraph 3.

(3) Grants are excluded from the effect of paragraph 2 by—

(*a*) paragraph 5 (dwellings designed or adapted, and intended for use, as dwelling etc),
(*b*) paragraph 6 (conversion of buildings for use as dwelling etc),
(*c*) paragraph 7 (charities),
(*d*) paragraph 8 (residential caravans),
(*e*) paragraph 9 (residential houseboats),
(*f*) paragraph 10 (relevant housing associations), and
(*g*) paragraph 11 (grant to individual for construction of dwelling).

(4) Paragraphs 12 to 17 (anti-avoidance: developers of land etc) provide for certain supplies to which any grant gives rise to be excluded from the effect of paragraph 2.

(5) Paragraphs 18 to 30 deal with—

(*a*) the scope of the option to tax,
(*b*) the day from which the option to tax has effect,
(*c*) notification requirements,
(*d*) elections to opt to tax land subsequently acquired,
(*e*) the revocation of the option,
(*f*) the effect of the option to tax in relation to new buildings, and
(*g*) requirements for prior permission in the case of exempt grants made before the exercise of an option to tax.

(6) Paragraphs 31 to 34 deal with definitions which apply for the purposes of this Part, as well as other supplemental matters.][1]

Commentary—*De Voil Indirect Tax Service* **V3.248, V4.113.**
Cross reference—See VATA 1994 Sch 13 para 8 (preservation of zero rating for certain supplies in the course of an approved alteration of a protected building made pursuant to an obligation incurred before 21 June 1988: such supplies are not "relevant zero rated supplies" for the purposes of this para).
Amendments—[1] Schedule 10 substituted by the Value Added Tax (Buildings and Land) Order, SI 2008/1146, art 2 with effect in relation to supplies made on or after 1 June 2008, subject to savings in Sch 2 of the Order.

[THE OPTION TO TAX

Effect of the option to tax: exempt supplies become taxable

2— (1) This paragraph applies if—

(*a*) a person exercises the option to tax any land under this Part of this Schedule, and
(*b*) a grant is made in relation to the land at any time when the option to tax it has effect.

(2) If the grant is made—

(*a*) by the person exercising that option, or
(*b*) by a relevant associate (if that person is a body corporate),

the grant does not fall within Group 1 of Schedule 9 (exemptions for land).

(3) For the meaning of "relevant associate", see paragraph 3.][1]

Commentary—*De Voil Indirect Tax Service* **V4.115.**
Simon's Tax Cases—*Marlow Gardner & Cooke Ltd Directors' Pension Scheme v R&C Comrs* [2006] STC 2014*; *R&C Comrs v Principal and Fellows of Newnham College in the University of Cambridge* [2008] STC 1225*, *Mason v Boscawen* [2009] STC 624.
Press releases etc—C&E Business Brief 8/01 2-7-01 (from 1 August 2001, where vendor of building has opted to tax, and immediate purchaser does not intend to use building himself as a dwelling, nor to convert it into dwellings for sale or rent, the vendor must account for the VAT on the sale).

Amendments—[1] Schedule 10 substituted by the Value Added Tax (Buildings and Land) Order, SI 2008/1146, art 2 with effect in relation to supplies made on or after 1 June 2008, subject to savings in Sch 2 of the Order.

[Meaning of "relevant associate"

3— (1) This paragraph explains for the purposes of this Part of this Schedule what is meant by a "relevant associate" in a case where a body corporate ("the opter") exercises an option to tax in relation to any building or land.

(2) A body corporate is a relevant associate of the opter if under sections 43A to 43D (groups of companies) the body corporate—

(*a*) was treated as a member of the same group as the opter at the time when the option first had effect,

(*b*) has been so treated at any later time when the opter had a relevant interest in the building or land, or

(*c*) has been treated as a member of the same group as a body corporate within paragraph (*a*) or (*b*) or this paragraph at a time when that body had a relevant interest in the building or land.

(3) But a body corporate ceases to be a relevant associate of the opter in relation to the building or land in the following circumstances.

(4) The body corporate ceases to be a relevant associate of the opter in relation to the building or land at the time when all of the following conditions are first met—

(*a*) the body corporate has no relevant interest in the building or land [,

(*aa*) where the body corporate has disposed of such an interest, it is not the case that a supply for the purposes of the charge to VAT in respect of the disposal—

(i) is yet to take place, or

(ii) would be yet to take place if one or more conditions (such as the happening of an event or the doing of an act) were to be met,][2]

(*b*) the body corporate or the opter is not treated under sections 43A to 43D as a member of the group mentioned above, and

(*c*) the body corporate is not connected with any person who has a relevant interest in the building or land where that person is the opter or another relevant associate of the opter.

(5) The body corporate also ceases to be a relevant associate of the opter in relation to the building or land if the body corporate—

(*a*) meets conditions specified in a public notice (see paragraph 4), or

(*b*) gets the prior permission of the Commissioners (also, see that paragraph).

The time when the body corporate ceases to be a relevant associate of the opter is determined in accordance with that paragraph.

(6) In this paragraph "relevant interest in the building or land" means an interest in, right over or licence to occupy the building or land (or any part of it).][1]

Commentary—*De Voil Indirect Tax Service* **V4.115**.

Simon's Tax Cases—Sub-para (9), *C&E Comrs v R & R Pension Fund Trustees* [1996] STC 889*; *Marlow Gardner & Cooke Ltd Directors' Pension Scheme v R&C Comrs* [2006] STC 2014*.

Amendments—[1] Schedule 10 substituted by the Value Added Tax (Buildings and Land) Order, SI 2008/1146, art 2 with effect in relation to supplies made on or after 1 June 2008, subject to savings in Sch 2 of the Order.

[2] In sub-para (4), words substituted for words "and no part of any consideration payable in respect of any disposal by the body corporate of such a interest is unpaid,", by the Value Added Tax (Buildings and Land) Order, SI 2009/1966 arts 2, 3 with effect in relation to supplies made on or after 1 August 2009.

[Permission for a body corporate to cease to be a relevant associate of the opter

4— (1) This paragraph applies for the purposes of paragraph 3(5) in relation to a body corporate which has been a relevant associate of the opter.

(2) If the conditions specified in the public notice under paragraph 3(5)(*a*) are met in relation to the body corporate, it ceases to be a relevant associate of the opter only if notification of those conditions being met is given to the Commissioners.

(3) The notification must—

(*a*) be made in a form specified in a public notice,

(*b*) state the day from which the body corporate is to cease to be a relevant associate of the opter (which may not be before the day on which the notification is given),

(*c*) contain a statement by the body corporate certifying that, on that day, the conditions specified in the public notice under paragraph 3(5)(*a*) are met in relation to it, and

(*d*) contain other information specified in a public notice.

(4) An application for the prior permission of the Commissioners must—

(*a*) be made in a form specified in a public notice,

(*b*) contain a statement by the body corporate certifying which (if any) of the conditions specified in the public notice under paragraph 3(5)(*a*) are met in relation to it, and

(*c*) contain other information specified in a public notice.

(5) If the body corporate gets the prior permission of the Commissioners, it ceases to be a relevant associate of the opter from—

(*a*) the day on which the Commissioners give their permission, or (*b*) such earlier or later day as they specify in their permission.

(6) The Commissioners may specify an earlier day only if—

(*a*) the body corporate has purported to give a notification of its ceasing to be a relevant associate of the opter,

(*b*) the conditions specified in the public notice are not, in the event, met in relation to the body corporate, and

(*c*) the Commissioners consider that the grounds on which those conditions are not so met are insignificant.

(7) The day specified may be the day from which the body corporate would have ceased to be a relevant associate of the opter if those conditions had been so met.

(8) The Commissioners may specify conditions subject to which their permission is given and, if any of those conditions are broken, they may treat the application as if it had not been made.][1]

Commentary—*De Voil Indirect Tax Service* **V4.115**.

Simon's Tax Cases—Sub-para (9), *C&E Comrs v R & R Pension Fund Trustees* [1996] STC 889*; *Marlow Gardner & Cooke Ltd Directors' Pension Scheme v R&C Comrs* [2006] STC 2014*.

Amendments—[1] Schedule 10 substituted by the Value Added Tax (Buildings and Land) Order, SI 2008/1146, art 2 with effect in relation to supplies made on or after 1 June 2008, subject to savings in Sch 2 of the Order.

[EXCLUSIONS FROM EFFECT OF OPTION TO TAX

Dwellings designed or adapted, and intended for use, as dwelling etc

5— (1) An option to tax has no effect in relation to any grant in relation to a building or part of a building if the building or part of the building is designed or adapted, and is intended, for use—

(*a*) as a dwelling or number of dwellings, or

(*b*) solely for a relevant residential purpose.

(2) In relation to the expression "relevant residential purpose", see the certification requirement imposed as a result of the application of Note (12) of Group 5 of Schedule 8 by paragraph 33 of this Schedule.][1]

Commentary—*De Voil Indirect Tax Service* **V4.115**.

Simon's Tax Cases—*Principal and Fellows of Newnham College in the University of Cambridge v R&C Comrs* [2006] STC 1010*; *Marlow Gardner & Cooke Ltd Directors' Pension Scheme v R&C Comrs* [2006] STC 2014*.

Amendments—[1] Schedule 10 substituted by the Value Added Tax (Buildings and Land) Order, SI 2008/1146, art 2 with effect in relation to supplies made on or after 1 June 2008, subject to savings in Sch 2 of the Order.

[Conversion of buildings for use as dwelling etc

6— (1) An option to tax has no effect in relation to any grant made to a person ("the recipient") in relation to a building or part of a building if the recipient certifies that the building or part of the building is intended for use—

(*a*) as a dwelling or number of dwellings, or

(*b*) solely for a relevant residential purpose.

(2) The recipient must give the certificate to the person making the grant ("the seller")—

(*a*) within the period specified in a public notice, or

(*b*) if the seller agrees, at any later time before the seller makes a supply to which the grant gives rise.

(3) The recipient may give the certificate to the seller only if the recipient—

(*a*) intends to use the building or part of the building as mentioned above,

(*b*) has the relevant conversion intention, or

(*c*) is a relevant intermediary.

(4) The recipient is a relevant intermediary if—

(*a*) the recipient intends to dispose of the relevant interest to another person, and

(*b*) that other person gives the recipient a certificate stating that the other person has the relevant conversion intention or the relevant disposal intention.

(5) For this purpose a person has the relevant disposal intention if—

(*a*) the person intends to dispose of the relevant interest to a third person, and

(*b*) the third person gives a qualifying certificate to the person.

(6) A person (P) gives a qualifying certificate to another if P gives a certificate to that other person stating that P has the relevant conversion intention or intends to dispose of the relevant interest to another person (Q) who has given a certificate to P stating—

(*a*) that Q has the relevant conversion intention, or

(*b*) that Q intends to dispose of the relevant interest to another person who has given a qualifying certificate to Q,

and so on (in the case of further disposals of the relevant interest).

(7) In this paragraph—

"the relevant conversion intention", in relation to a person, means an intention of the person to convert the building or part of the building with a view to its being used as mentioned above, and "the relevant interest", in relation to any interest in the building or part of the building to which the grant gives rise, means the whole of that interest.

(8) For the purposes of this paragraph a building or part of a building is not to be regarded as intended for use as a dwelling or number of dwellings at any time if there is intended to be a period before that time during which it will not be so used (but disregarding use for incidental or other minor purposes).

(9) For the purposes of this paragraph the reference to use solely for a relevant residential purpose is to be read without regard to Note (12) of Group 5 of Schedule 8 (which would otherwise apply as a result of paragraph 33 of this Schedule).

(10) The Commissioners may publish a notice for the purposes of this paragraph—

(*a*) preventing a person from giving any certificate under this paragraph unless the person meets conditions specified in the notice,

(*b*) specifying the form in which any certificate under this paragraph must be made, and

(*c*) specifying any information which any certificate under this paragraph must contain.][1]

Commentary—*De Voil Indirect Tax Service* **V4.115**.

Simon's Tax Cases—*Principal and Fellows of Newnham College in the University of Cambridge v R&C Comrs* [2006] STC 1010*; *Marlow Gardner & Cooke Ltd Directors' Pension Scheme v R&C Comrs* [2006] STC 2014*.

Amendments—[1] Schedule 10 substituted by the Value Added Tax (Buildings and Land) Order, SI 2008/1146, art 2 with effect in relation to supplies made on or after 1 June 2008, subject to savings in Sch 2 of the Order.

[Charities

7—(1) An option to tax has no effect in relation to any grant made to a person in relation to a building or part of a building intended by the person for use—

(*a*) solely for a relevant charitable purpose, but

(*b*) not as an office.

(2) In relation to the expression "relevant charitable purpose", see the certification requirement imposed as a result of the application of Note (12) of Group 5 of Schedule 8 by paragraph 33 of this Schedule.][1]

Commentary—*De Voil Indirect Tax Service* **V4.115**.

Simon's Tax Cases—*Principal and Fellows of Newnham College in the University of Cambridge v R&C Comrs* [2006] STC 1010*; *Marlow Gardner & Cooke Ltd Directors' Pension Scheme v R&C Comrs* [2006] STC 2014*.

Amendments—[1] Schedule 10 substituted by the Value Added Tax (Buildings and Land) Order, SI 2008/1146, art 2 with effect in relation to supplies made on or after 1 June 2008, subject to savings in Sch 2 of the Order.

Residential caravans

8— (1) An option to tax has no effect in relation to any grant made in relation to a pitch for a residential caravan.

(2) A caravan is not a residential caravan if residence in it throughout the year is prevented by the terms of a covenant, statutory planning consent or similar permission.][1]

Commentary—*De Voil Indirect Tax Service* **V4.115**.

Simon's Tax Cases—*Principal and Fellows of Newnham College in the University of Cambridge v R&C Comrs* [2006] STC 1010*; *Marlow Gardner & Cooke Ltd Directors' Pension Scheme v R&C Comrs* [2006] STC 2014*.

Amendments—[1] Schedule 10 substituted by the Value Added Tax (Buildings and Land) Order, SI 2008/1146, art 2 with effect in relation to supplies made on or after 1 June 2008, subject to savings in Sch 2 of the Order.

[Residential houseboats

9—(1) An option to tax has no effect in relation to any grant made in relation to facilities for the mooring of a residential houseboat.

"Mooring" includes anchoring or berthing.

(2) In this paragraph—

(*a*) "houseboat" means a houseboat within the meaning of Group 9 of Schedule 8, and

(*b*) a houseboat is not a residential houseboat if residence in it throughout the year is prevented by the terms of a covenant, statutory planning consent or similar permission.][1]

Commentary—*De Voil Indirect Tax Service* **V4.115**.

Simon's Tax Cases—*Principal and Fellows of Newnham College in the University of Cambridge v R&C Comrs* [2006] STC 1010*; *Marlow Gardner & Cooke Ltd Directors' Pension Scheme v R&C Comrs* [2006] STC 2014*.

Amendments—[1] Schedule 10 substituted by the Value Added Tax (Buildings and Land) Order, SI 2008/1146, art 2 with effect in relation to supplies made on or after 1 June 2008, subject to savings in Sch 2 of the Order.

[Relevant housing associations

10— (1) An option to tax has no effect in relation to any grant made to a relevant housing association in relation to any land if the association certifies that the land is to be used (after any necessary demolition work) for the construction of a building or buildings intended for use—

(*a*) as a dwelling or number of dwellings, or

(*b*) solely for a relevant residential purpose.

(2) The association must give the certificate to the person making the grant ("the seller")—

(*a*) within the period specified in a public notice, or

(*b*) if the seller agrees, at any later time before the seller makes a supply to which the grant gives rise.

(3) In this paragraph "relevant housing association" means—

(*a*) a registered social landlord within the meaning of Part 1 of the Housing Act 1996 (English or Welsh registered social landlords),

(*b*) a registered social landlord within the meaning of the Housing (Scotland) Act 2001 (Scottish registered social landlords), or

(*c*) a registered housing association within the meaning of Part 2 of the Housing (Northern Ireland) Order 1992 (Northern Irish registered housing associations).

(4) For the purposes of this paragraph the reference to use solely for a relevant residential purpose is to be read without regard to Note (12) of Group 5 of Schedule 8 (which would otherwise apply as a result of paragraph 33 of this Schedule).

(5) The Commissioners may publish a notice for the purposes of this paragraph—

(*a*) specifying the form in which any certificate under this paragraph must be made, and

(*b*) specifying any information which any certificate under this paragraph must contain.][1]

Commentary—*De Voil Indirect Tax Service* **V4.115**.
Simon's Tax Cases—*Principal and Fellows of Newnham College in the University of Cambridge v R&C Comrs* [2006] STC 1010*; *Marlow Gardner & Cooke Ltd Directors' Pension Scheme v R&C Comrs* [2006] STC 2014*.
Amendments—[1] Schedule 10 substituted by the Value Added Tax (Buildings and Land) Order, SI 2008/1146, art 2 with effect in relation to supplies made on or after 1 June 2008, subject to savings in Sch 2 of the Order.

[Grant to individual for construction of dwelling

11 An option to tax has no effect in relation to any grant made to an individual if—

(*a*) the land is to be used for the construction of a building intended for use by the individual as a dwelling, and

(*b*) the construction is not carried out in the course or furtherance of a business carried on by the individual.][1]

Commentary—*De Voil Indirect Tax Service* **V4.115**.
Simon's Tax Cases—*Principal and Fellows of Newnham College in the University of Cambridge v R&C Comrs* [2006] STC 1010*; *Marlow Gardner & Cooke Ltd Directors' Pension Scheme v R&C Comrs* [2006] STC 2014*.
Amendments—[1] Schedule 10 substituted by the Value Added Tax (Buildings and Land) Order, SI 2008/1146, art 2 with effect in relation to supplies made on or after 1 June 2008, subject to savings in Sch 2 of the Order.

[ANTI-AVOIDANCE

Developers of exempt land

12— (1) A supply is not, as a result of an option to tax, a taxable supply if—

(*a*) the grant giving rise to the supply was made by a person ("the grantor") who was a developer of the land, and

(*b*) the exempt land test is met.

(2) The exempt land test is met if, at the time when the grant was made (or treated for the purposes of this paragraph as made), the relevant person intended or expected that the land—

(*a*) would become exempt land (whether immediately or eventually and whether or not as a result of the grant), or

(*b*) would continue, for a period at least, to be exempt land.

(3) "The relevant person" means—

(*a*) the grantor, or

(*b*) a development financier.

(4) For the meaning of a development financier, see paragraph 14.

(5) For the meaning of "exempt land", see paragraphs 15 and 16.

(6) If a supply is made by a person other than the person who made the grant giving rise to it—

(*a*) the person making the supply is treated for the purposes of this paragraph as the person who made the grant giving rise to it, and

(*b*) the grant is treated for the purposes of this paragraph as made at the time when that person made the first supply arising from the grant.

(7) For a special rule in the case of a grant made on or after 19th March 1997 and before 10th March 1999, see paragraph 17.

(8) Nothing in this paragraph applies in relation to a supply arising from—

(*a*) a grant made before 26th November 1996, or

(*b*) a grant made on or after that date but before 30th November 1999, in pursuance of a written agreement entered into before 26th November 1996, on terms which (as terms for which provision was made by that agreement) were fixed before 26th November 1996.][1]

Commentary—*De Voil Indirect Tax Service* **V4.115**.
Amendments—[1] Schedule 10 substituted by the Value Added Tax (Buildings and Land) Order, SI 2008/1146, art 2 with effect in relation to supplies made on or after 1 June 2008, subject to savings in Sch 2 of the Order.

[Meaning of grants made by a developer

13— (1) This paragraph applies for the purposes of paragraph 12.

(2) A grant made by any person ("the grantor") in relation to any land is made by a developer of the land if—

(*a*) the land is, or was intended or expected to be, a relevant capital item (see sub-paragraphs (3) to (5)), and

(*b*) the grant is made at an eligible time as respects that capital item (see sub-paragraph (6)).

(3) The land is a relevant capital item if—

(*a*) the land, or

(*b*) the building or part of a building on the land,

is a capital item in relation to the grantor.

(4) The land was intended or expected to be a relevant capital item if the grantor, or a development financier, intended or expected that—

(*a*) the land, or

(*b*) a building or part of a building on, or to be constructed on, the land,

would become a capital item in relation to the grantor or any relevant transferee.

(5) A person is a relevant transferee if the person is someone to whom the land, building or part of a building was to be transferred—

(*a*) in the course of a supply, or

(*b*) in the course of a transfer of a business or part of a business as a going concern.

(6) A grant is made at an eligible time as respects a capital item if it is made before the end of the period provided in the relevant regulations for the making of adjustments relating to the deduction of input tax as respects the capital item.

(7) But if—

(*a*) a person other than the grantor is treated by paragraph 12(6) as making the grant of the land, and

(*b*) the grant is consequently treated as made at what would otherwise be an ineligible time,

the grant is treated instead as if were not made at an ineligible time.

(8) In this paragraph a "capital item", in relation to any person, means an asset falling, in relation to the person, to be treated as a capital item for the purposes of the relevant regulations.

(9) In this paragraph "the relevant regulations", as respects any item, means regulations under section 26(3) and (4) providing for adjustments relating to the deduction of input tax to be made as respects that item.][1]

Amendments—[1] Schedule 10 substituted by the Value Added Tax (Buildings and Land) Order, SI 2008/1146, art 2 with effect in relation to supplies made on or after 1 June 2008, subject to savings in Sch 2 of the Order.

[Meaning of "development financier"

14— (1) This paragraph explains for the purposes of paragraphs 12 to 17 what is meant, in relation to the grantor of any land, by a development financier.

(2) A "development financier" means a person who—

(*a*) has provided finance for the grantor's development of the land, or

(*b*) has entered into any arrangement to provide finance for the grantor's development of the land,

with the intention or in the expectation that the land will become exempt land or continue (for a period at least) to be exempt land.

(3) For the purposes of this paragraph references to finance being provided for the grantor's development of the land are to doing (directly or indirectly) any one or more of the following—

(*a*) providing funds for meeting the whole or any part of the cost of the grantor's development of the land,

(*b*) procuring the provision of such funds by another,

(*c*) providing funds for discharging (in whole or in part) any liability that has been or may be incurred by any person for or in connection with the raising of funds to meet the cost of the grantor's development of the land, and

(*d*) procuring that any such liability is or will be discharged (in whole or in part) by another.

(4) For the purposes of this paragraph references to providing funds for a particular purpose are to—

(*a*) the making of a loan of funds that are or are to be used for that purpose,

(*b*) the provision of any guarantee or other security in relation to such a loan,

(*c*) the provision of any of the consideration for the issue of any shares or other securities issued wholly or partly for raising those funds,

(*d*) the provision of any consideration for the acquisition by any person of any shares or other securities issued wholly or partly for raising those funds, or

(*e*) any other transfer of assets or value as a consequence of which any of those funds are made available for that purpose.

(5) For the purposes of this paragraph references to the grantor's development of the land are to the acquisition by the grantor of the asset which—

(*a*) consists in the land or a building or part of a building on the land, and (*b*) is, or (as the case may be) was intended or expected to be, a relevant capital item in relation to the grantor (within the meaning of paragraph 13).

(6) For this purpose the reference to the acquisition of the asset includes—

(*a*) its construction or reconstruction, and

(*b*) the carrying out in relation to it of any other works by reference to which it is, or was intended or expected to be, a relevant capital item (within the meaning of paragraph 13).

(7) In this paragraph "arrangement" means any agreement, arrangement or understanding (whether or not legally enforceable).][1]

Amendments—[1] Schedule 10 substituted by the Value Added Tax (Buildings and Land) Order, SI 2008/1146, art 2 with effect in relation to supplies made on or after 1 June 2008, subject to savings in Sch 2 of the Order.

[Meaning of "exempt land": basic definition

15— (1) This paragraph explains for the purposes of paragraphs 12 to 17 what is meant by exempt land.

(2) Land is exempt land if, at any time before the end of the relevant adjustment period as respects that land—

(*a*) a relevant person is in occupation of the land, and

(*b*) that occupation is not wholly, or substantially wholly, for eligible purposes.

(3) Each of the following is a relevant person—

(*a*) the grantor,

(*b*) a person connected with the grantor,

(*c*) a development financier, and

(*d*) a person connected with a development financier.

(4) The relevant adjustment period as respects any land is the period provided in the relevant regulations (within the meaning of paragraph 13) for the making of adjustments relating to the deduction of input tax as respects the land.

(5) For the purposes of this paragraph any question whether a person's occupation of any land is "wholly, or substantially wholly," for eligible purposes is to be decided by reference to criteria specified in a public notice.][1]

Commentary—*De Voil Indirect Tax Service* **V4.115**.

Amendments—[1] Schedule 10 substituted by the Value Added Tax (Buildings and Land) Order, SI 2008/1146, art 2 with effect in relation to supplies made on or after 1 June 2008, subject to savings in Sch 2 of the Order.

[Meaning of "exempt land": eligible purposes

16— (1) This paragraph explains what is meant for the purposes of paragraph 15 by a person occupying land for eligible purposes.

(2) A person cannot occupy land at any time for eligible purposes unless the person is a taxable person at that time (but this rule is qualified by sub-paragraphs (5) and (6)).

(3) A taxable person occupies land for eligible purposes so far as the occupation is for the purpose of making creditable supplies (but this rule is qualified by sub-paragraphs (5) to (7)).

(4) "Creditable supplies" means supplies which—

(*a*) are or are to be made in the course or furtherance of a business carried on by the person, and

(*b*) are supplies of such a description that the person would be entitled to a credit for any input tax wholly attributable to those supplies.

(5) Any occupation of land by a body to which section 33 applies (local authorities etc) is occupation of the land for eligible purposes so far as the occupation is for purposes other than those of a business carried on by the body.

(6) Any occupation of land by a Government department (within the meaning of section 41) is occupation of the land for eligible purposes.

(7) Any occupation of land by a person is occupation of the land for eligible purposes in so far as the occupation arises merely by reference to any automatic teller machine of the person which is fixed to the land.

(8) If a person occupying land—

(*a*) holds the land in order to put it to use for particular purposes, and

(*b*) does not occupy it for any other purpose,

the person is treated for the purposes of this paragraph, for so long as the conditions in paragraphs (*a*) and (*b*) continue to be met, as occupying the land for the purposes for which the person proposes to use it.

(9) If land is in the occupation of a person ("A") who—

(*a*) is not a taxable person, but

(*b*) is a person whose supplies are treated for the purposes of this Act as made by another person ("B") who is a taxable person,

the land is treated for the purposes of this paragraph as if A and B were a single taxable person.

(10) For the purposes of this paragraph a person occupies land—

(*a*) whether the person occupies it alone or together with one or more other persons, and
(*b*) whether the person occupies all of the land or only part of it.][1]

Commentary—*De Voil Indirect Tax Service* **V4.115**.
Amendments—[1] Schedule 10 substituted by the Value Added Tax (Buildings and Land) Order, SI 2008/1146, art 2 with effect in relation to supplies made on or after 1 June 2008, subject to savings in Sch 2 of the Order.

[Paragraph 12: grants made on or after 19th March 1997 and before 10th March 1999

17— (1) A grant in relation to land which was made—

(*a*) on or after 19th March 1997, and
(*b*) before 10th March 1999,

is treated for the purposes of paragraph 12 as made on 10th March 1999 if, at the time of the grant, the capital item test was met.

(2) The capital item test was met if the person making the grant, or a development financier, intended or expected that—

(*a*) the land, or
(*b*) a building or part of a building on, or to be constructed on, the land,

would become a capital item in relation to the grantor or any relevant transferee but it had not become such an item.

(3) For the purposes of that test "capital item" and "relevant transferee" have the meaning given by paragraph 13.][1]

Commentary—*De Voil Indirect Tax Service* **V4.115**.
Simon's Tax Cases—*Principal and Fellows of Newnham College in the University of Cambridge v R&C Comrs* [2006] STC 1010*; *Marlow Gardner & Cooke Ltd Directors' Pension Scheme v R&C Comrs* [2006] STC 2014*.
Amendments—[1] Schedule 10 substituted by the Value Added Tax (Buildings and Land) Order, SI 2008/1146, art 2 with effect in relation to supplies made on or after 1 June 2008, subject to savings in Sch 2 of the Order.

[SCOPE OF THE OPTION, ITS DURATION, NOTIFICATION ETC

Scope of the option

18— (1) An option to tax has effect in relation to the particular land specified in the option.

(2) If an option to tax is exercised in relation to—

(*a*) a building, or
(*b*) part of a building,

the option has effect in relation to the whole of the building and all the land within its curtilage.

(3) If an option to tax—

(*a*) is exercised in relation to any land, but
(*b*) is not exercised by reference to a building or part of a building,

the option is nonetheless taken to have effect in relation to any building which is (or is to be) constructed on the land (as well as in relation to land on which no building is constructed).

(4) For the purposes of this paragraph—

(*a*) buildings linked internally or by a covered walkway, and
(*b*) complexes consisting of a number of units grouped around a fully enclosed concourse,

are treated as a single building.

(5) But for those purposes—

(*a*) buildings which are linked internally are not treated as a single building if the internal link is created after the buildings are completed, and
(*b*) buildings which are linked by a covered walkway are not treated as a single building if the walkway starts to be constructed after the buildings are completed.

(6) In this paragraph a "building" includes—

(*a*) an enlarged or extended building,
(*b*) an annexe to a building, and
(*c*) a planned building.

(7) In this paragraph "covered walkway" does not include a covered walkway to which the general public has reasonable access.][1]

Commentary—*De Voil Indirect Tax Service* **V4.115**.
Amendments—[1] Schedule 10 substituted by the Value Added Tax (Buildings and Land) Order, SI 2008/1146, art 2 with effect in relation to supplies made on or after 1 June 2008, subject to savings in Sch 2 of the Order.

[The day from which the option has effect

19— (1) An option to tax has effect from—

(*a*) the start of the day on which it is exercised, or
(*b*) the start of any later day specified in the option.

(2) But if, when an option to tax is exercised, the person exercising the option intends to revoke it in accordance with paragraph 23 (revocation of option: the "cooling off" period), the option is treated for the purposes of this Act as if it had never been exercised.

(3) An option to tax may be revoked in accordance with paragraph 22(2) or (3) and any of paragraphs 23 to 25, but not otherwise.

(4) This paragraph needs to be read with—

(*a*) paragraph 20 (requirement to notify the option), and

(*b*) paragraph 29(3) (application for prior permission in the case of an exempt grant before the exercise of an option to tax).][1]

Amendments—[1] Schedule 10 substituted by the Value Added Tax (Buildings and Land) Order, SI 2008/1146, art 2 with effect in relation to supplies made on or after 1 June 2008, subject to savings in Sch 2 of the Order.

[Requirement to notify the option

20— (1) An option to tax has effect only if—

(*a*) notification of the option is given to the Commissioners within the allowed time, and

(*b*) that notification is given together with such information as the Commissioners may require.

(2) Notification of an option is given within the allowed time if (and only if) it is given—

(*a*) before the end of the period of 30 days beginning with the day on which the option was exercised, or

(*b*) before the end of such longer period beginning with that day as the Commissioners may in any particular case allow.

(3) The Commissioners may publish a notice for the purposes of this paragraph specifying—

(*a*) the form in which a notification under this paragraph must be made, and

(*b*) the information which a notification under this paragraph must contain.

(4) Notification of an option to tax does not need to be given under this paragraph if the option is treated as exercised in accordance with paragraph 29(3).][1]

Commentary—*De Voil Indirect Tax Service* **V4.115**.

Amendments—[1] Schedule 10 substituted by the Value Added Tax (Buildings and Land) Order, SI 2008/1146, art 2 with effect in relation to supplies made on or after 1 June 2008, subject to savings in Sch 2 of the Order.

[Real estate elections: elections to opt to tax land subsequently acquired

21— (1) A person (E) may make an election (a "real estate election") for this paragraph to have effect in relation to—

(*a*) relevant interests in any building or land which E acquires after the election is made, and

(*b*) relevant interests in any building or land which a body corporate acquires after the election is made at a time when the body is a relevant group member.

(2) If E makes a real estate election—

(*a*) E is treated for the purposes of this Part of this Schedule as if E had exercised an option to tax in relation to the building or land in which the relevant interest is acquired,

(*b*) that option is treated for those purposes as if it had been exercised on the day on which the acquisition was made and as if it had effect from the start of that day, and

(*c*) paragraph 20 does not apply in relation to that option,

but this sub-paragraph is subject to sub-paragraphs (3) to (5).

(3) A person (P) is not to be treated as a result of this paragraph as exercising an option to tax in relation to any building or land where at any time—

(*a*) P, or any body corporate which was a relevant group member at that time, exercises an option to tax in relation to the building (or part of the building) or land apart from this paragraph, and

(*b*) that option has effect from a time earlier than the time from which an option to tax exercised by P in relation to the building or land would otherwise have been treated as having effect as a result of this paragraph.

(4) A person (P) is not to be treated as a result of this paragraph as exercising an option to tax in relation to any building or land in which a relevant interest is acquired ("the later interest") if—

(*a*) the person making the acquisition in question held another relevant interest in that building or land before P makes a real estate election, and

(*b*) the person making the acquisition in question continues to hold that other relevant interest at the time when the later interest is acquired.

(5) A person is not to be treated as a result of this paragraph as exercising an option to tax in relation to any building or land if—

(*a*) a relevant interest in the building or land is acquired as mentioned in sub-paragraph (1), and

(*b*) on the relevant assumptions the case would fall within paragraph 28 (pre-option exempt grants: requirement for prior permission before exercise of option to tax).

(6) The relevant assumptions are that—

(*a*) the effect of this paragraph is disregarded, and

(*b*) the day from which the person would want the option to tax to have effect for the purposes of paragraphs 28 or 29(3) is the day on which the relevant interest is acquired.

(7) A real estate election has effect only if—

(*a*) notification of the election is given to the Commissioners before the end of the period of 30 days beginning with the day on which it was made or such longer period as the Commissioners may in any particular case allow,

(*b*) the notification is made in a form specified in a public notice, and

(*c*) the notification contains information so specified.

(8) The Commissioners may at any time require a person who has made a real estate election to give to the Commissioners information specified in a public notice before the end of—

(*a*) the period of 30 days beginning with that time, or

(*b*) such longer period as the Commissioners may in any particular case allow.

(9) If a person (P) does not comply with that requirement—

(*a*) the Commissioners may revoke the election, and

(*b*) that revocation has effect in relation to relevant interests in any building or land acquired after the notified time by P or a body corporate which is a relevant group member at the time of acquisition.

"The notified time" means the time specified in a notification given by the Commissioners to P (which may not be before the notification is given).

(10) A real estate election may not be revoked except in accordance with sub-paragraph (9).

(11) If a real estate election made by a person (P) is revoked in accordance with that sub-paragraph, another real estate election may be made at any subsequent time by—

(*a*) P, or

(*b*) any body corporate which is a relevant group member at that subsequent time,

but only with the prior permission of the Commissioners.

(12) In this paragraph—

"relevant group member", in relation to any person making a real estate election and any time, means a body corporate which is treated under sections 43A to 43D as a member of the same group as that person at that time, and

"relevant interest", in relation to any building or land, means any interest in, right over or licence to occupy the building or land (or any part of it).][1]

[(13) For the purposes of this paragraph, the time at which a relevant interest in any building or land is acquired is—

(*a*) the time at which a supply is treated as taking place for the purposes of the charge to VAT in respect of the acquisition, or

(*b*) if there is more than one such time, the earliest of them.

(14) For the purposes of sub-paragraph (13)(*a*), any order under section 5(3)(*c*) that would otherwise have the effect that the acquisition in question is to be treated as neither a supply of goods nor a supply of services is to be disregarded.][2]

Amendments—[1] Schedule 10 substituted by the Value Added Tax (Buildings and Land) Order, SI 2008/1146, art 2 with effect in relation to supplies made on or after 1 June 2008, subject to savings in Sch 2 of the Order.

[2] Sub-paras (13), (14) inserted by the Value Added Tax (Buildings and Land) Order, SI 2009/1966 arts 2, 4 with effect in relation to supplies made on or after 1 August 2009.

[Real estate elections: supplementary

22— (1) This paragraph applies if, at any time ("the relevant time"), a person (*e*) makes a real estate election under paragraph 21.

(2) An option to tax exercised in relation to any building or part of any building before the relevant time by—

(*a*) E, or

(*b*) any relevant group member,

is treated for the purposes of this Part of this Schedule as if it had been revoked from the relevant time if, at that time, neither E nor any relevant group member has a relevant interest in that building.

(3) An option to tax exercised in relation to any land (otherwise than by reference to any building or part of a building) before the relevant time by—

(*a*) E, or

(*b*) any relevant group member,

is treated for the purposes of this Part of this Schedule as if it had been revoked in accordance with sub-paragraph (4) from the relevant time if, at that time, neither E nor any relevant group member has a relevant interest in that land, or E or any relevant group member has a relevant interest in only some of it.

(4) The option is treated for the purposes of this Part of this Schedule as if it had been revoked in relation to—

(*a*) that land, or

(*b*) the parts of that land in which neither E nor any relevant group member has a relevant interest at the relevant time,

as the case may be.

(5) Sub-paragraphs (2) and (3) are subject to paragraph 26 (anti-avoidance).

(6) An option to tax ("the original option") exercised in relation to any land (otherwise than by reference to any building or part of a building) before the relevant time by—

(*a*) E, or

(*b*) any relevant group member,

may, in circumstances specified in a public notice, be converted by E into separate options to tax if, at the relevant time, E or any relevant group member has a relevant interest in the land or any part of it.

(7) The original option is converted into separate options to tax different parcels of land comprised in that land or part.

(8) Those separate options to tax are treated for the purposes of this Part of this Schedule—

(*a*) as if they had been exercised by E, and

(*b*) as if they had effect from the time from which the original option had effect.

(9) But—

(*a*) those separate options to tax are treated for the purposes of paragraph 3(2) as if they had effect from the relevant time, and

(*b*) paragraph 23 (revocation of an option: the "cooling off" period) does not apply to those separate options to tax.

(10) The notification of the election given by E must identify—

(*a*) the separate options to tax treated as exercised by E as a result of sub-paragraphs (6) to (8), and

(*b*) the different parcels of land in relation to which those separate options to tax are treated as having effect.

(11) In this paragraph—

(*a*) any reference to any relevant group member is to a body corporate which is a relevant group member at the relevant time, and

(*b*) any reference to any relevant group member, in relation to any relevant interest in any building or land (or any part of it), is to any relevant group member regardless of whether it has exercised an option to tax the building or land (or any part of it).

(12) In this paragraph "relevant group member" and "relevant interest", have the meaning given by paragraph 21.

(13) In this paragraph any reference to a real estate election under paragraph 21 does not include an election which is made under sub-paragraph (11) of that paragraph.][1]

Amendments—[1] Schedule 10 substituted by the Value Added Tax (Buildings and Land) Order, SI 2008/1146, art 2 with effect in relation to supplies made on or after 1 June 2008, subject to savings in Sch 2 of the Order.

[Revocation of option: the "cooling off" period

23— (1) An option to tax any land exercised by any person ("the taxpayer") may be revoked with effect from the day on which it was exercised if—

(*a*) the time that has lapsed since the day on which the option had effect is less than 6 months,

(*b*) the taxpayer has not used the land since the option had effect,

(*c*) no tax has become chargeable as a result of the option,

(*d*) there is no relevant transfer of a business as a going concern (see sub-paragraph (2)), and

(*e*) notification of the revocation is given to the Commissioners (see sub-paragraph (3)).

(2) There is no relevant transfer of a business as a going concern if, since the option had effect, no grant in relation to the land has been made which is treated as neither a supply of goods nor a supply of services because—

(*a*) the supply is a supply of the assets of a business by the taxpayer to a person to whom the business (or part of it) is transferred as a going concern, or

(*b*) the supply is a supply of assets of a business by a person to the taxpayer to whom the business (or part of it) is so transferred.

(3) The notification of the revocation must—

(*a*) be made in a form specified in a public notice, and

(*b*) contain information so specified.

(4) The Commissioners may publish a notice for the purposes of this paragraph providing that a revocation under this paragraph is effective only if—

(*a*) the conditions specified in the notice are met in relation to the option, or

(*b*) the taxpayer gets the prior permission of the Commissioners on an application made to them before the end of the 6 month period mentioned above.

(5) A notice under sub-paragraph (4) may—

(*a*) provide that, in a case falling with paragraph (*a*) of that sub-paragraph, the taxpayer must certify that the conditions specified under that paragraph are met in relation to the option,

(*b*) specify the form in which an application under paragraph (*b*) of that sub-paragraph must be made,

(*c*) provide that an application under that paragraph must contain a statement by the taxpayer certifying which (if any) of the conditions specified under sub-paragraph (4)(*a*) are met in relation to the option, (*d*) specify other information which an application under sub-paragraph (4)(*a*) must contain, and

(*e*) provide that the Commissioners may specify conditions subject to which their permission is given and, if any of those conditions are broken, the Commissioners may treat the revocation as if it had not been made.][1]

Amendments—[1] Schedule 10 substituted by the Value Added Tax (Buildings and Land) Order, SI 2008/1146, art 2 with effect in relation to supplies made on or after 1 June 2008, subject to savings in Sch 2 of the Order.

[Revocation of option: lapse of 6 years since having a relevant interest

24— (1) An option to tax exercised by any person in relation to any building or land is treated for the purposes of this Part of this Schedule as revoked if the person does not have a relevant interest in the building or land throughout any continuous period of 6 years beginning at any time after the option has effect.

(2) The option to tax is treated for the purposes of this Part of this Schedule as revoked from the end of that period.

(3) In this paragraph "a relevant interest in the building or land" means an interest in, right over or licence to occupy the building or land (or any part of it).

(4) This paragraph is subject to paragraph 26 (anti-avoidance).][1]

Amendments—[1] Schedule 10 substituted by the Value Added Tax (Buildings and Land) Order, SI 2008/1146, art 2 with effect in relation to supplies made on or after 1 June 2008, subject to savings in Sch 2 of the Order.

[Revocation of option: lapse of more than 20 years since option had effect

25— (1) An option to tax any land exercised by any person ("the taxpayer") may be revoked if the time that has lapsed since the day on which the option had effect is more than 20 years and—

(*a*) at the time when the option is to be revoked the conditions specified in a public notice are met in relation to the option (in which case, see sub-paragraphs (2) to (4)), or

(*b*) the taxpayer gets the prior permission of the Commissioners (in which case, see the remaining sub-paragraphs).

(2) If the conditions specified in the public notice are met in relation to the option, the revocation has effect only if notification of the revocation is given to the Commissioners.

(3) The notification must—

(*a*) be made in the specified form,

(*b*) state the day from which the option is to be revoked (which may not be before the day on which the notification is given),

(*c*) contain a statement by the taxpayer certifying that, on that day, the conditions specified in the public notice are met in relation to the option, and

(*d*) contain other information specified in a public notice.

(4) If—

(*a*) notification of the revocation of an option is given to the Commissioners on the basis that the conditions specified in the public notice were met in relation to the option, but

(*b*) it is subsequently discovered that those conditions were not met in relation to the option,

the Commissioners may nonetheless treat the option as if it had been validly revoked in accordance with this paragraph.

(5) An application for the prior permission of the Commissioners must—

(*a*) be made in a form specified in a public notice,

(*b*) contain a statement by the taxpayer certifying which (if any) of the conditions specified in the public notice under sub-paragraph (1)(*a*) are met in relation to the option, and

(*c*) contain other information specified in a public notice.

(6) If the taxpayer gets the prior permission of the Commissioners for the revocation of an option, the option is revoked from—

(*a*) the day on which the Commissioners give their permission, or

(*b*) such earlier or later day [or time as they may][2] specify in their permission.

(7) The Commissioners may specify an earlier day [or time][2] only if—

(*a*) the taxpayer has purported to give a notification of the revocation of the option,

(*b*) the conditions specified in the public notice are not, in the event, met in relation to the option, and

(*c*) the Commissioners consider that the grounds on which those conditions are not so met are insignificant.

[(8) The Commissioners may specify a day or time under sub-paragraph (6)(*b*) by reference to the happening of an event or the meeting of a condition.][2]

(9) The Commissioners may specify conditions subject to which their permission is given and, if any of those conditions are broken, they may treat the revocation as if it had not been made.][1]

Amendments—[1] Schedule 10 substituted by the Value Added Tax (Buildings and Land) Order, SI 2008/1146, art 2 with effect in relation to supplies made on or after 1 June 2008, subject to savings in Sch 2 of the Order.

[2] In sub-para (6)(*b*), words substituted for words "as they", in sub-para (7), words inserted, and sub-para (8) substituted, by the Value Added Tax (Buildings and Land) Order, SI 2009/1966 arts 2, 4 with effect in relation to supplies made on or after 1 August 2009. Sub-para (8) previously read as follows—

"(8) The day specified may be the day from which the option would have been revoked if those conditions had been so met.".

[26— (1) Sub-paragraphs (2) and (3) of paragraph 22 (revocation of option to tax where a real estate election is made) do not apply if condition A or B is met.

(2) Paragraph 24 (lapse of option to tax) does not apply if condition A, B or C is met.

(3) Condition A is that—

(*a*) the opter, or a relevant associate of the opter, disposes of a relevant interest in the building or land before the relevant time, and

(*b*) at the relevant time, a supply for the purposes of the charge to VAT in respect of the disposal—

(i) is yet to take place, or

(ii) would be yet to take place if one or more conditions (such as the happening of an event or the doing of an act) were to be met.

(4) Condition B is that—

(*a*) the opter is a body corporate that was, at any time before the relevant time, treated under sections 43A to 43D as a member of a group ("the group"), and

(*b*) before the relevant time, a relevant associate of the opter in relation to the building or land ceased to be treated under those sections as a member of the group without at the same time meeting the conditions in sub-paragraph (5).

(5) A person ("A") meets the conditions in this sub-paragraph if—

(*a*) A has no relevant interest in the building or land,

(*b*) where A has disposed of such an interest, it is not the case that a supply for the purposes of the charge to VAT in respect of the disposal—

(i) is yet to take place, or

(ii) would be yet to take place if one or more conditions (such as the happening of an event or the doing of an act) were to be met, and

(*c*) A is not connected with any person who has a relevant interest in the building or land where that person is the opter or another relevant associate of the opter.

(6) Condition C is that the opter is a body corporate and, at the relevant time, a relevant associate of the opter in relation to the building or land—

(*a*) is treated under sections 43A to 43D as a member of the same group as the opter, and

(*b*) holds a relevant interest in the building or land or has held such an interest at any time within the previous 6 years.

(7) In this paragraph—

"relevant interest in the building or land" means an interest in, right over or license to occupy the building or land (or any part of it);

"the relevant time", in relation to any option to tax, means the time from which the option would (but for this paragraph) have been treated as revoked as a result of paragraph 22(2) or (3) or 24;

"opter" means the person who exercised the option to tax in question.][1]

Amendments—[1] This para substituted, by the Value Added Tax (Buildings and Land) Order, SI 2009/1966 arts 2, 6 with effect in relation to supplies made on or after 1 August 2009. This para previously read as follows—

"Revocation of option under paragraph 22(2) or (3) or 24: anti-avoidance

26 Paragraphs 22(2) and (3) and 24 (which in particular circumstances treat an option to tax exercised in relation to any building or land as revoked) do not apply if—

(*a*) the person exercising the option mentioned in paragraph 22(2) or (3) or 24 ("the opter") is a body corporate,

(*b*) the opter has been treated under sections 43A to 43D as a member of a group at any time in the relevant 6 year period, and

(*c*) any relevant associate of the opter in relation to the building or land ceases to be treated under those sections as a member of the same group as the opter without at the same time ceasing to be a relevant associate of the opter in relation to the building or land in accordance with paragraph 3(4).

(2) In sub-paragraph (1)(*c*) the reference to a relevant associate of the opter in relation to any building or land includes a body corporate which has been a relevant associate of the opter in relation to the building or land at any time before the start of the relevant 6 year period.

(3) In this paragraph "the relevant 6 year period", in relation to any option to tax, means the period of 6 years ending with the time from which the option would (but for this paragraph) have been treated as revoked as a result of paragraph 22(2) or (3) or 24."

[Exclusion of new building from effect of an option

27— (1) This paragraph applies if—

(*a*) a person ("the taxpayer") has at any time opted to tax any land,

(*b*) at any subsequent time the construction of a building ("the new building") on the land begins, and

(*c*) no land within the curtilage of the new building is within the curtilage of an existing building.

(2) The taxpayer may exclude—

(*a*) the whole of the new building, and

(*b*) all the land within its curtilage,

from the effect of the option if notification of that exclusion is given to the Commissioners.

(3) The exclusion has effect from the earliest of the following times—

(*a*) the time when a grant of an interest in, or in any part of, the new building is first made,
(*b*) the time when the new building, or any part of it, is first used,
(*c*) the time when the new building is completed.

(4) The notification of the exclusion must—

[(*za*) be given before the end of the period of 30 days beginning with the day on which it is to have effect or such longer period as the Commissioners may in any case allow,][2]
(*a*) be made in a form specified in a public notice,
[(*b*) state the time from which it is to have effect, and][2]
(*c*) contain other information so specified.

(5) Sub-paragraphs (4) to (6) of paragraph 18 (meaning of "building") apply for the purposes of this paragraph as they apply for the purposes of that paragraph.

(6) For the purposes of this paragraph the reference to the construction of a building is to be read without regard to Note (17) or (18)(*b*) of Group 5 of Schedule 8 (which would otherwise apply as a result of paragraph 33 of this Schedule).

(7) The Commissioners may publish a notice for determining the time at which the construction of a building on any land is to be taken to begin for the purposes of this paragraph.][1]

Amendments—[1] Schedule 10 substituted by the Value Added Tax (Buildings and Land) Order, SI 2008/1146, art 2 with effect in relation to supplies made on or after 1 June 2008, subject to savings in Sch 2 of the Order.
[2] In sub-para (4), para (*za*) inserted and para (*b*) substituted, by the Value Added Tax (Buildings and Land) Order, SI 2009/1966 arts 2, 7 with effect in relation to supplies made on or after 1 August 2009. Sub-para (4)(*b*) previously read as follows—
"(*b*) be given before the time from which it is to have effect and state that time, and".

[Pre-option exempt grants: requirement for prior permission before exercise of option to tax

28— (1) This paragraph applies if—

(*a*) a person wants to exercise an option to tax any land with effect from a particular day,
(*b*) at any time ("the relevant time") before that day the person has made, makes or intends to make an exempt supply to which any grant in relation to the land gives rise, and
(*c*) the relevant time is within the period of 10 years ending with that day.

(2) The person may exercise the option to tax the land only if—

(*a*) the conditions specified in a public notice are met in relation to the land, or
(*b*) the person gets the prior permission of the Commissioners (but see also paragraph 30).

(3) The Commissioners must refuse their permission if they are not satisfied that there would be a fair and reasonable attribution of relevant input tax to relevant supplies.

(4) For this purpose—

"relevant input tax" means input tax incurred, or likely to be incurred, in relation to the land, and
"relevant supplies" means supplies to which any grant in relation to the land gives rise which would be taxable (if the option has effect).

(5) In deciding whether there would be a fair and reasonable attribution of relevant input tax to relevant supplies, the Commissioners must have regard to all the circumstances of the case.

(6) But they must have regard in particular to—

(*a*) the total value of any exempt supply to which any grant in relation to the land gives rise and which is made or to be made before the day from which the person wants the option to have effect,
(*b*) the expected total value of any supply to which any grant in relation to the land gives rise that would be taxable (if the option has effect), and
(*c*) the total amount of input tax incurred, or likely to be incurred, in relation to the land.][1]

Amendments—[1] Schedule 10 substituted by the Value Added Tax (Buildings and Land) Order, SI 2008/1146, art 2 with effect in relation to supplies made on or after 1 June 2008, subject to savings in Sch 2 of the Order.

[Paragraph 28: application for prior permission

29— (1) An application for the prior permission of the Commissioners under paragraph 28 must—

(*a*) be made in a form specified in a public notice,
(*b*) contain a statement by the applicant certifying which (if any) of the conditions specified in the public notice under paragraph 28(2)(*a*) are met in relation to the land, and
(*c*) contain other information specified in a public notice.

(2) The Commissioners may specify conditions subject to which their permission is given and, if any of those conditions are broken, they may treat the application as if it had not been made.

(3) If the applicant (*a*) gets the prior permission of the Commissioners, A is, as a result of this sub-paragraph, treated for the purposes of this Part of this Schedule as if A had exercised the option to tax the land with effect from—

(*a*) the start of the day on which the application was made, or (*b*) the start of any later day specified in the application.][1]

Amendments—[1] Schedule 10 substituted by the Value Added Tax (Buildings and Land) Order, SI 2008/1146, art 2 with effect in relation to supplies made on or after 1 June 2008, subject to savings in Sch 2 of the Order.

[Paragraph 28: purported exercise where prior permission not obtained

30— (1) This paragraph applies if—

(*a*) an option to tax was purportedly exercised in a case where, before the option could be exercised, the prior permission of the Commissioners was required under paragraph 28, and

(*b*) notification of the purported option was purportedly given to the Commissioners in accordance with paragraph 20.

(2) The Commissioners may, in the case of any such option, subsequently dispense with the requirement for their prior permission to be given under paragraph 28.

(3) If the Commissioners dispense with that requirement, a purported option—

(*a*) is treated for the purposes of this Part of this Schedule as if it had instead been validly exercised, and

(*b*) has effect in accordance with paragraph 19.][1]

Amendments—[1] Schedule 10 substituted by the Value Added Tax (Buildings and Land) Order, SI 2008/1146, art 2 with effect in relation to supplies made on or after 1 June 2008, subject to savings in Sch 2 of the Order.

[SUPPLEMENTARY PROVISIONS

Timing of grant and supplies

31— (1) This paragraph applies if—

(*a*) an option to tax is exercised in relation to any land,

(*b*) a grant in relation to the land would otherwise be taken to have been made (whether in whole or in part) before the time when the option has effect, and

(*c*) the grant gives rise to supplies which are treated for the purposes of this Act as taking place after that time.

(2) For the purposes of this Part of this Schedule, the option to tax has effect, in relation to those supplies, as if the grant had been made after that time.][1]

Amendments—[1] Schedule 10 substituted by the Value Added Tax (Buildings and Land) Order, SI 2008/1146, art 2 with effect in relation to supplies made on or after 1 June 2008, subject to savings in Sch 2 of the Order.

[Supplies in relation to a building where part designed or intended for residential or charitable use and part designed or intended for other uses

32 Note (10) of Group 5 of Schedule 8 applies for the purposes of this Part of this Schedule.][1]

Amendments—[1] Schedule 10 substituted by the Value Added Tax (Buildings and Land) Order, SI 2008/1146, art 2 with effect in relation to supplies made on or after 1 June 2008, subject to savings in Sch 2 of the Order.

[Definitions in Schedules 8 or 9 that are applied for the purposes of this Schedule

33 In this Part of this Schedule, references to the expressions listed in the first column are to be read in accordance with the provisions listed in the second column—

Expression	*Provision*
building designed or adapted for use as a dwelling or a number of dwellings	Note (2) to Group 5 of Schedule 8
completion of a building	Note (2) to Group 1 of Schedule 9
construction of a building	Notes (16) to (18) to Group 5 of Schedule 8 (but see paragraph 27(6) of this Schedule)
construction of a building intended for use as a dwelling or a number of dwellings	Note (3) to Group 5 of Schedule 8
Grant	Note (1) to Group 5 of Schedule 8/ Notes (1) and (1A) to Group 1 of Schedule 9
use for a relevant charitable purpose	Notes (6) and (12) to Group 5 of Schedule 8
use for a relevant residential purpose	Notes (4), (5) and (12) to Group 5 of Schedule 8 (but see paragraphs 6(9) and 10(4) of this Schedule)][1]

Amendments—[1] Schedule 10 substituted by the Value Added Tax (Buildings and Land) Order, SI 2008/1146, art 2 with effect in relation to supplies made on or after 1 June 2008, subject to savings in Sch 2 of the Order.

[Other definitions etc

34— (1) In this Part of this Schedule—

"notification" means written notification, and

"permission" means written permission.

(2) For the purposes of this Part of this Schedule any question whether a person is connected with another person is to be decided in accordance with section 839 of the Taxes Act[; but this is subject to sub-paragraph (2A)][2].

[(2A) For the purposes of this Part of this Schedule, a company is not connected with another company only because both are under the control of—

(*a*) the Crown,

(*b*) a Minister of the Crown,

(*c*) a government department, or

(*d*) a Northern Ireland department.

(2B) In sub-paragraph (2A) "company" and "control" have the same meaning as in section 839 of the Taxes Act.][2]

(3) Any reference in any provision of this Part of this Schedule to a public notice is to a notice published by the Commissioners for the purposes of that provision.][1]

Amendments—[1] Schedule 10 substituted by the Value Added Tax (Buildings and Land) Order, SI 2008/1146, art 2 with effect in relation to supplies made on or after 1 June 2008, subject to savings in Sch 2 of the Order.

[2] In sub-para (2), words inserted and sub-paras (2A), (2B) inserted, by the Value Added Tax (Buildings and Land) Order, SI 2009/1966 arts 2, 8 with effect in relation to supplies made on or after 1 August 2009.

[PART 2
RESIDENTIAL AND CHARITABLE BUILDINGS: CHANGE OF USE ETC

Meaning of "relevant zero-rated supply"

35 For the purposes of this Part of this Schedule a "relevant zero-rated supply" means a grant or other supply which—

(*a*) relates to a building (or part of a building) intended for use solely for a relevant residential purpose, or

(*b*) relates to a building (or part of a building) intended for use solely for a relevant charitable purpose,

and which, as a result of Group 5 of Schedule 8, is zero-rated (in whole or in part).][1]

Commentary—*De Voil Indirect Tax Service* **V3.248, V4.113**.

Amendments—[1] Schedule 10 substituted by the Value Added Tax (Buildings and Land) Order, SI 2008/1146, art 2 with effect in relation to supplies made on or after 1 June 2008, subject to savings in Sch 2 of the Order.

[Person to whom supply made grants interest etc in building and building not intended solely for relevant residential or charitable purpose

36— (1) This paragraph applies if—

(*a*) one or more relevant zero-rated supplies relating to a building (or part of a building) have been made to a person, and

(*b*) conditions A and B are met.

(2) Condition A is that, within the period of 10 years beginning with the day on which the building is completed, the person grants an interest in, right over or licence to occupy—

(*a*) the building or any part of it, or

(*b*) the building or any part of it including, consisting of or forming part of the part to which the relevant zero-rated supply or supplies related.

(3) Condition B is that after the grant—

(*a*) the whole or any part of the building or of the part to which the grant relates, or

(*b*) the whole of the building or of the part to which the grant relates, or any part of it including, consisting of or forming part of the part to which the relevant zero-rated supply or supplies related,

is not intended for use solely for a relevant residential purpose or a relevant charitable purpose.

(4) So far as the grant relates to so much of the building as—

(*a*) by reason of its intended use gave rise to the relevant zero-rated supply or supplies, and

(*b*) is not intended for use solely for a relevant residential purpose or a relevant charitable purpose after the grant,

it is taken to be a taxable supply in the course or furtherance of a business which is not zero-rated as a result of Group 5 of Schedule 8.][1]

Commentary—*De Voil Indirect Tax Service* **V3.248, V4.113**.

Amendments—[1] Schedule 10 substituted by the Value Added Tax (Buildings and Land) Order, SI 2008/1146, art 2 with effect in relation to supplies made on or after 1 June 2008, subject to savings in Sch 2 of the Order.

VAT

[Person to whom supply made uses building otherwise than for relevant residential or charitable purpose

37— (1) This paragraph applies if one or more relevant zero-rated supplies relating to a building (or part of a building) have been made to a person and, within the period of 10 years beginning with the day on which the building is completed, the person uses—

(*a*) the building or any part of it, or

(*b*) the building or any part of it including, consisting of or forming part of the part to which the relevant zero-rated supply or supplies related,

for a purpose which is neither a relevant residential purpose nor a relevant charitable purpose.

(2) The person's interest in, right over or licence to occupy so much of the building as—

(*a*) by reason of its intended use gave rise to the relevant zero-rated supply or supplies, and

(*b*) is used otherwise than for a relevant residential purpose or a relevant charitable purpose,

is treated as follows.

(3) The interest, right or licence is treated for the purposes of this Act as—

(*a*) supplied to the person for the purposes of a business which the person carries on, and

(*b*) supplied by the person in the course or furtherance of the business when the person first uses it for a purpose which is neither a relevant residential purpose nor a relevant charitable purpose.

(4) The supply is taken to be a taxable supply which is not zero-rated as a result of Group 5 of Schedule 8.

(5) The value of the supply is taken to be the amount obtained by the formula—

$$A \times \left(\frac{10 - B}{10}\right)$$

(6) For the purposes of the formula, A is the amount that yields an amount of VAT chargeable on it equal to—

(*a*) the VAT which would have been chargeable on the relevant zero-rated supply, or

(*b*) if there was more than one supply, the aggregate amount of the VAT which would have been chargeable on the supplies,

had so much of the building not been intended for use solely for a relevant residential purpose or a relevant charitable purpose.

(7) For the purposes of the formula, B is the number of whole years since the day the building was completed for which the building or part concerned has been used for—

(*a*) a relevant residential purpose, or

(*b*) a relevant charitable purpose.][1]

Commentary—*De Voil Indirect Tax Service* **V3.248, V4.113.**

Amendments—[1] Schedule 10 substituted by the Value Added Tax (Buildings and Land) Order, SI 2008/1146, art 2 with effect in relation to supplies made on or after 1 June 2008, subject to savings in Sch 2 of the Order.

[Supplies in relation to a building where part designed for residential or charitable use and part designed for other uses

38 Note (10) of Group 5 of Schedule 8 applies for the purposes of this Part of this Schedule.][1]

Amendments—[1] Schedule 10 substituted by the Value Added Tax (Buildings and Land) Order, SI 2008/1146, art 2 with effect in relation to supplies made on or after 1 June 2008, subject to savings in Sch 2 of the Order.

[Definitions

39 In this Part of this Schedule, references to the expressions listed in the first column are to be read in accordance with the provisions listed in the second column—

Expression	*Provision*
completion of a building	Note (2) to Group 1 of Schedule 9
grant	Note (1) to Group 5 of Schedule 8/ Notes (1) and (1A) to Group 1 of Schedule 9
use for a relevant charitable purpose	Notes (6) and (12) to Group 5 of Schedule 8
use for a relevant residential purpose	Notes (4), (5) and (12) to Group 5 of Schedule 8][1]

[PART 3

GENERAL

Benefit of consideration for grant accruing to a person other than the grantor

40— (1) This paragraph applies if the benefit of the consideration for the grant of an interest in, right over or licence to occupy land accrues to a person ("the beneficiary") other than the person making the grant.

(2) The beneficiary is to be treated for the purposes of this Act as the person making the grant.

(3) So far as any input tax of the person actually making the grant is attributable to the grant, it is to be treated for the purposes of this Act as input tax of the beneficiary.][1]

Commentary—*De Voil Indirect Tax Service* **V4.111**.

Amendments—[1] Schedule 10 substituted by the Value Added Tax (Buildings and Land) Order, SI 2008/1146, art 2 with effect in relation to supplies made on or after 1 June 2008, subject to savings in Sch 2 of the Order.

Former enactment—Before substitution by the Value Added Tax (Buildings and Land) Order, SI 2008/1146, art 2, Sch 10 previously read as follows—

"SCHEDULE 10 – BUILDINGS AND LAND

Section 51

Residential and charitable buildings: change of use etc

1—(1) In this paragraph "relevant zero-rated supply" means a grant or other supply taking place on or after 1st April 1989 which—

(*a*) relates to a building intended for use solely for a relevant residential purpose or a relevant charitable purpose or part of such a building; and

(*b*) is zero-rated, in whole or in part, by virtue of Group 5 of Schedule 8.

(2) Sub-paragraph (3) below applies where—

(*a*) one or more relevant zero-rated supplies relating to a building (or part of a building) have been made to any person,

(*b*) within the period of 10 years beginning with the day on which the building is completed, the person grants an interest in, right over or licence to occupy the building or any part of it (or the building or any part of it including, consisting of or forming part of the part to which the relevant zero-rated supply or supplies related), and

(*c*) after the grant the whole or any part of the building, or of the part to which the grant relates, (or the whole of the building or of the part to which the grant relates, or any part of it including, consisting of or forming part of the part to which the relevant zero-rated supply or supplies related) is not intended for use solely for a relevant residential purpose or a relevant charitable purpose.

(3) Where this sub-paragraph applies, to the extent that the grant relates to so much of the building as—

(*a*) by reason of its intended use gave rise to the relevant zero-rated supply or supplies; and

(*b*) is not intended for use solely for a relevant residential purpose or a relevant charitable purpose after the grant,

it shall be taken to be a taxable supply in the course or furtherance of a business which is not zero-rated by virtue of Group 5 of Schedule 8 (if it would not otherwise be such a supply).

(4) Sub-paragraph (5) below applies where—

(*a*) one or more relevant zero-rated supplies relating to a building (or part of a building) have been made to any person; and

(*b*) within the period of 10 years beginning with the day on which the building is completed, the person uses the building or any part of it (or the building or any part of it including, consisting of or forming part of the part to which the relevant zero-rated supply or supplies related) for a purpose which is neither a relevant residential purpose nor a relevant charitable purpose.

(5) Where this sub-paragraph applies, his interest in, right over or licence to occupy so much of the building as—

(*a*) by reason of its intended use gave rise to the relevant zero-rated supply or supplies, and

(*b*) is used otherwise than for a relevant residential purpose or a relevant charitable purpose,

shall be treated for the purposes of this Act as supplied to him for the purpose of a business carried on by him and supplied by him in the course or furtherance of the business when he first uses it for a purpose which is neither a relevant residential purpose nor a relevant charitable purpose.

(6) Where sub-paragraph (5) applies—

(*a*) the supply shall be taken to be a taxable supply which is not zero-rated by virtue of Group 5 of Schedule 8 (if it would not otherwise be such a supply); and

(*b*) the value of the supply shall be taken to be such amount as is obtained by using the formula—

$A \times (10 - B/10)$

where—

A is the amount that yields an amount of VAT chargeable on it equal to the VAT which would have been chargeable on the relevant zero-rated supply (or, where there was more than one supply, the aggregate amount which would have been chargeable on them) had so much of the building as is mentioned in sub-paragraph (5) above not been intended for use solely for a relevant residential purpose or a relevant charitable purpose; and

B is the number of whole years since the day the building was completed for which the building or part concerned has been used for a relevant residential purpose or a relevant charitable purpose.

Election to waive exemption

2—(1) Subject to sub-paragraphs (2), (3) and (3A) and paragraph 3 below, where an election under this paragraph has effect in relation to any land, if and to the extent that any grant made in relation to it at a time when the election has effect by the person who made the election, or where that person is a body corporate by that person or a relevant associate, would (apart from this sub-paragraph) fall within Group 1 of Schedule 9, the grant shall not fall within that Group.

(2) Sub-paragraph (1) above shall not apply in relation to a grant if the grant is made in relation to—

(*a*) a building or part of a building intended for use as a dwelling or number of dwellings or solely for a relevant residential purpose; or

(*b*) a building or part of a building intended for use solely for a relevant charitable purpose, other than as an office.

(*c*) a pitch for a residential caravan;

(*d*) facilities for the mooring of a residential houseboat.

(2A) Subject to the following provisions of this paragraph, where—

(*a*) an election has been made for the purposes of this paragraph in relation to any land, and

(*b*) a supply is made that would fall, but for sub-paragraph (2)(*a*) above, to be treated as excluded by virtue of that election from Group 1 of Schedule 9,

then, notwithstanding sub-paragraph (2)(*a*) above, that supply shall be treated as so excluded if the conditions in sub-paragraph (2B) below are satisfied.

(2B) The conditions mentioned in sub-paragraph (2A) above are—

(*a*) that an agreement in writing made, at or before the time of the grant, between—

(i) the person making the grant, and

(ii) the person to whom it is made,

declares that the election is to apply in relation to the grant; and

(*b*) that the person to whom the supply is made intends, at the time when it is made, to use the land for the purpose only of making a supply which is zero-rated by virtue of paragraph (*b*) of item 1 of Group 5 of Schedule 8.

(3) Sub-paragraph (1) above shall not apply in relation to a grant if—

(*a*) the grant is made to a relevant housing association and the association has given to the grantor a certificate stating that the land is to be used (after any necessary demolition work) for the construction of a building or buildings intended for use as a dwelling or number of dwellings or solely for a relevant residential purpose; or

(*b*) the grant is made to an individual and the land is to be used for the construction, otherwise than in the course or furtherance of a business carried on by him, of a building intended for use by him as a dwelling.

(3AA) Where an election has been made under this paragraph in relation to any land, a supply shall not be taken by virtue of that election to be a taxable supply if—

(*a*) the grant giving rise to the supply was made by a person ("the grantor") who was a developer of the land; and
(*b*) at the time of the grant, or at the time it was treated as made by virtue of sub-paragraphs (3AAA) or (3B) below, it was the intention or expectation of—
(i) the grantor, or
(ii) a person responsible for financing the grantor's development of the land for exempt use,
that the land would become exempt land (whether immediately or eventually and whether or not by virtue of the grant) or, as the case may be, would continue, for a period at least, to be such land.

(3AAA) For the purposes of sub-paragraph (3AA) above a grant (the original grant) in relation to land made on or after 19th March 1997 and before 10th March 1999 shall be treated as being made on 10th March 1999 if at the time of the original grant —
(*a*) the grantor or a person responsible for financing the grantor's development of the land for exempt use, intended or expected that the land or a building or part of a building on, or to be constructed on, that land would become an asset falling in relation to—
(i) the grantor, or
(ii) any person to whom that land, building or part of a building was to be transferred either in the course of a supply or in the course of a transfer of a business or part of a business as a going concern,
to be treated as a capital item for the purposes of any regulations made under section 26(3) and (4) providing for adjustments relating to the deduction of input tax to be made as respects that item, and
(*b*) the land or a building or part of a building on, or to be constructed on, that land had not become such an asset.

(3A) …

(3B) Where a supply is made by a person other than the person who made the grant giving rise to it, then for the purposes of sub-paragraph (3AA) above—
(*a*) the person making the supply shall be treated as the person who made the grant that gave rise to that supply; and
(*b*) the grant shall be treated as made at the time when that person made his first supply arising from the grant.

(4) Subject to the following provisions of this paragraph, no input tax on any supply or importation which, apart from this sub-paragraph, would be allowable by virtue of the operation of this paragraph shall be allowed if the supply or importation took place before the first day for which the election in question has effect.

(5) Subject to sub-paragraph (6) below, sub-paragraph (4) above shall not apply where the person by whom the election was made—
(*a*) has not, before the first day for which the election has effect, made in relation to the land in relation to which the election has effect any grant falling within Group 1 of Schedule 9; or
(*b*) has before that day made in relation to that land a grant or grants so falling but the grant, or all the grants—
(i) were made in the period beginning with 1st April 1989 and ending with 31st July 1989; and
(ii) would have been taxable supplies but for the amendments made by Schedule 3 to the Finance Act 1989.

(6) Sub-paragraph (5) above does not make allowable any input tax on supplies or importations taking place before 1st August 1989 unless—
(*a*) it is attributable by or under regulations to grants made by the person on or after 1st April 1989 which would have been taxable supplies but for the amendments made by Schedule 3 to the Finance Act 1989 and
(*b*) the election has effect from 1st August 1989.

(7) Sub-paragraph (4) above shall not apply in relation to input tax on grants or other supplies which are made in the period beginning with 1st April 1989 and ending with 31st July 1989 if—
(*a*) they would have been zero-rated by virtue of item 1 or 2 of Group 5 of Schedule 8 or exempt by virtue of item 1 of Group 1 of Schedule 9 but for the amendments made by Schedule 3 to the Finance Act 1989; and
(*b*) the election has effect from 1st August 1989.

(8) Sub-paragraph (4) above shall not apply in relation to any election having effect from any day on or after 1st January 1992, except in respect of the input tax on a supply or importation which took place before 1st August 1989.

(9) Where a person has made an exempt grant in relation to any land and has made an election in relation to that land which has effect from any day before 1st January 1992, he may apply to the Commissioners for sub-paragraph (4) above to be disapplied in respect of any input tax on a supply or importation which took place on or after 1st August 1989, but the Commissioners shall only permit the disapplication of that sub-paragraph if they are satisfied, having regard to all the circumstances of the case, and in particular to—
(*a*) the total value of—
(i) exempt grants made;
(ii) taxable grants made or expected to be made, in relation to the land; and
(*b*) the total amount of input tax in relation to the land which had been incurred before the day from which the election had effect,
that a fair and reasonable attribution of the input tax mentioned in paragraph (*b*) above will be secured.

3—(1) An election under paragraph 2 above shall have effect—
(*a*) subject to the following provisions of this paragraph, from the beginning of the day on which the election is made or of any later day specified in the election; or
(*b*) where the election was made before 1st November 1989, from the beginning of 1st August 1989 or of any later day so specified.

(2) An election under paragraph 2 above shall have effect in relation to any land specified, or of a description specified, in the election.

(3) Where such an election is made in relation to, or to part of, a building (or planned building), it shall have effect in relation to the whole of the building and all the land within its curtilage and for the purposes of this sub-paragraph buildings linked internally or by a covered walkway, and complexes consisting of a number of units grouped around a fully enclosed concourse, shall be taken to be a single building (if they otherwise would not be).

(4) Subject to sub-paragraph (5) below, an election under paragraph 2 above shall be irrevocable.

(5) Where—
(*a*) the time that has elapsed since the day on which an election had effect is—
(i) less than 3 months; or
(ii) more than 20 years;
(*b*) in a case to which paragraph (*a*)(i) above applies—
(i) no tax has become chargeable and no credit for input tax has been claimed by virtue of the election; and
(ii) no grant in relation to the land which is the subject of the election has been made which, by virtue of being a supply of the assets of a business to a person to whom the business (or part of it) is being transferred as a going concern, has been treated as neither a supply of goods nor a supply of services; and
(*c*) the person making the election obtains the written consent of the Commissioners;
the election shall be revoked, in a case to which paragraph (*a*)(i) above applies, from the date on which it was made, and in a case to which paragraph (*a*)(ii) above applies, from the date on which the written consent of the Commissioners is given or such later date as they may specify in their written consent.

(5A) Where—
(*a*) an election under paragraph 2 above is made in relation to any land, and
(*b*) apart from this sub-paragraph, a grant in relation to that land would be taken to have been made (whether in whole or in part) before the time when the election takes effect,
that paragraph shall have effect, in relation to any supplies to which the grant gives rise which are treated for the purposes of this Act as taking place after that time, as if the grant had been made after that time.

(5B) Accordingly, the references in paragraph 2(9) above and sub-paragraph (9) below to grants being exempt or taxable shall be construed as references to supplies to which a grant gives rise being exempt or, as the case may be, taxable.

(6) An election under paragraph 2 above shall have effect after 1st March 1995 only if—

(*a*) in the case of an election made before that date—

(i) it also had effect before that date; or

(ii) written notification of the election is given to the Commissioners not later than the end of the period of 30 days beginning with the day on which the election was made, or not later than the end of such longer period beginning with that day as the Commissioners may in any particular case allow, together with such information as the Commissioners may require;

(*b*) in the case of an election made on or after that date—

(i) written notification of the election is given to the Commissioners not later than the end of the period of 30 days beginning with the day on which the election is made, or not later than the end of such longer period beginning with that day as the Commissioners may in any particular case allow, together with such information as the Commissioners may require; and

(ii) in a case in which sub-paragraph (9) below requires the prior written permission of the Commissioners to be obtained, that permission has been given.

(7) In paragraph 2 above and this paragraph "relevant associate", in relation to a body corporate by which an election under paragraph 2 above has been made in relation to any building or land, means a body corporate which under section 43—

(*a*) was treated as a member of the same group as the body corporate by which the election was made at the time when the election first had effect;

(*b*) has been so treated at any later time when the body corporate by which the election was made had an interest in, right over or licence to occupy the building or land (or any part of it); or

(*c*) has been treated as a member of the same group as a body corporate within paragraph (*a*) or (*b*) above or this paragraph at a time when that body corporate had an interest in, right over or licence to occupy the building or land (or any part of it).

(7A) In paragraph 2 above—

(*a*) "houseboat" means a houseboat within the meaning of Group 9 of Schedule 8; and

(*b*) a houseboat is not a residential houseboat if residence in it throughout the year is prevented by the terms of a covenant, statutory planning consent or similar permission.

(8) In paragraph 2 above "relevant housing association" means—

(*a*) a registered social landlord within the meaning of Part 1 of the Housing Act 1996,

(*b*) a registered housing association within the meaning of the Housing Associations Act 1985 (Scottish registered housing associations), or

(*c*) a registered housing association within the meaning of Part II of the Housing (Northern Ireland) Order 1992 (Northern Irish registered housing associations).

(8A) ...

(9) Where a person who wishes to make an election in relation to any land (the relevant land) to have effect on or after 1st January 1992, has made, makes or intends to make, an exempt grant in relation to the relevant land at any time between 1st August 1989 and before the beginning of the day from which he wishes an election in relation to the relevant land to have effect, he shall not make an election in relation to the relevant land unless [the conditions for automatic permission specified in a notice published by the Commissioners are met or] he obtains the prior written permission of the Commissioners, who shall only give such permission if they are satisfied having regard to all the circumstances of the case and in particular to—

(*a*) the total value of exempt grants in relation to the relevant land made or to be made before the day from which the person wishes his election to have effect;

(*b*) the expected total value of grants relating to the relevant land that would be taxable if the election were to have effect; and

(*c*) the total amount of input tax which has been incurred on or after 1st August 1989 or is likely to be incurred in relation to the relevant land,

that there would be secured a fair and reasonable attribution of the input tax mentioned in paragraph (*c*) above to grants in relation to the relevant land which, if the election were to have effect, would be taxable.

3A—(1) This paragraph shall have effect for the construction of paragraph 2(3AA), (3AAA) and (3B) above.

(2) For the purposes of paragraph 2(3AA), (3AAA) and (3B) above, a grant made by any person in relation to any land is a grant made by a developer of that land if—

(*a*) the land or building or part of a building on that land is an asset falling in relation to that person to be treated as a capital item for the purposes of any regulations under section 26(3) and (4) providing for adjustments relating to the deduction of input tax; or

(*b*) that person or a person financing his development of the land for exempt use intended or expected that the land or a building or part of a building on, or to be constructed on, that land would become an asset falling in relation to—

(i) the grantor, or

(ii) any person to whom it was to be transferred either in the course of a supply or in the course of a transfer of a business or part of a business as a going concern,

to be treated as a capital item for the purposes of the regulations referred to in sub-paragraph (*a*) above,

unless the grant was made at a time falling after the expiry of the period over which such regulations require or allow adjustments relating to the deduction of input tax to be made as respects that item.

(2A) For the purposes of paragraph 2(3AA) where—

(*a*) by virtue of paragraph 2(3B), a person is treated as making the grant of the land giving rise to a supply made by him; and

(*b*) the grant is not a grant made by a developer of that land within sub-paragraph (2) above only because it is treated as made at a time falling after the expiry of the period for adjustments of input tax by virtue of regulations made under section 26(3) and (4),

the grant shall be treated as having been made by a developer of the land to which the grant relates.

(3) In paragraph 2(3AA), (3AAA) and (3B) above and this paragraph the references to a person's being responsible for financing the grantor's development of the land for exempt use are references to his being a person who, with the intention or in the expectation that the land will become, or continue (for a period at least) to be, exempt land—

(*a*) has provided finance for the grantor's development of the land; or

(*b*) has entered into any agreement, arrangement or understanding (whether or not legally enforceable) to provide finance for the grantor's development of the land.

(4) In sub-paragraph (3)(*a*) and (*b*) above the references to providing finance for the grantor's development of the land are references to doing any one or more of the following, that is to say—

(*a*) directly or indirectly providing funds for meeting the whole or any part of the cost of the grantor's development of the land;

(*b*) directly or indirectly procuring the provision of such funds by another;

(*c*) directly or indirectly providing funds for discharging, in whole or in part, any liability that has been or may be incurred by any person for or in connection with the raising of funds to meet the cost of the grantor's development of the land;

(*d*) directly or indirectly procuring that any such liability is or will be discharged, in whole or in part, by another.

(5) The references in sub-paragraph (4) above to the provision of funds for a purpose referred to in that sub-paragraph include references to—

(*a*) the making of a loan of funds that are or are to be used for that purpose;

(*b*) the provision of any guarantee or other security in relation to such a loan;

(*c*) the provision of any of the consideration for the issue of any shares or other securities issued wholly or partly for raising those funds; …

(*cc*) the provision of any consideration for the acquisition by any person of any shares or other securities described in paragraph (*c*) above; or

(*d*) any other transfer of assets or value as a consequence of which any of those funds are made available for that purpose.

(6) In sub-paragraph (4) above the references to the grantor's development of the land are references to the acquisition by the grantor of the asset which—

(*a*) consists in the land or a building or part of a building on the land, and

(*b*) in relation to the grantor falls or, as the case may be, is intended or expected to fall to be treated for the purposes mentioned in sub-paragraph (2)(*a*) or (*b*) above as a capital item;

and for the purposes of this sub-paragraph the acquisition of an asset shall be taken to include its construction or reconstruction and the carrying out in relation to that asset of any other works by reference to which it falls or, as the case may be, is intended or expected to fall, to be treated for the purposes mentioned in sub-paragraph (2)(*a*) or (*b*) above as a capital item.

(7) For the purposes of paragraph 2(3AA), (3AAA) and (3B) above and this paragraph land is exempt land if, at a time falling before the expiry of the period provided in regulations made under section 26(3) and (4) for the making of adjustments relating to the deduction of input tax as respects that land—

(*a*) the grantor,

(*b*) a person responsible for financing the grantor's development of the land for exempt use, or

(*c*) a person connected with the grantor or with a person responsible for financing the grantor's development of the land for exempt use,

is in occupation of the land without being in occupation of it wholly or mainly for eligible purposes.

(8) For the purposes of this paragraph, but subject to sub-paragraphs (10) and (12) below, a person's occupation at any time of any land is not capable of being occupation for eligible purposes unless he is a taxable person at that time.

(9) Subject to sub-paragraphs (10) to (12) below, a taxable person in occupation of any land shall be taken for the purposes of this paragraph to be in occupation of that land for eligible purposes to the extent only that his occupation of that land is for the purpose of making supplies which—

(*a*) are or are to be made in the course or furtherance of a business carried on by him; and

(*b*) are supplies of such a description that any input tax of his which was wholly attributable to those supplies would be input tax for which he would be entitled to a credit.

(10) For the purposes of this paragraph—

(*a*) occupation of land by a body to which section 33 applies is occupation of the land for eligible purposes to the extent that the body occupies the land for purposes other than those of a business carried on by that body; and

(*b*) any occupation of land by a Government department (within the meaning of section 41) is occupation of the land for eligible purposes.

(11) For the purposes of this paragraph, where land of which any person is in occupation—

(*a*) is being held by that person in order to be put to use by him for particular purposes, and

(*b*) is not land of which he is in occupation for any other purpose,

that person shall be deemed, for so long as the conditions in paragraphs (*a*) and (*b*) above are satisfied, to be in occupation of that land for the purposes for which he proposes to use it.

(12) Sub-paragraphs (8) to (11) above shall have effect where land is in the occupation of a person who—

(*a*) is not a taxable person, but

(*b*) is a person whose supplies are treated for the purposes of this Act as supplies made by another person who is a taxable person,

as if the person in occupation of the land and that other person were a single taxable person.

(13) For the purposes of this paragraph a person shall be taken to be in occupation of any land whether he occupies it alone or together with one or more other persons and whether he occupies all of that land or only part of it.

(14) Any question for the purposes of this paragraph whether one person is connected with another shall be determined in accordance with section 839 of the Taxes Act.

4

…

Developers of certain non-residential buildings etc

5—(1) Paragraph 6 below shall apply—

(*a*) on the first occasion during the period beginning with the day when the construction of a building or work within sub-paragraph (2) below is first planned and ending 10 years after the completion of the building or work on which a person who is a developer in relation to the building or work—

(i) grants an interest in, right over or licence to occupy the building or work (or any part of it) which is an exempt supply; or

(ii) is in occupation of the building, or uses the work (or any part of it) when not a fully taxable person (or, if a person treated under section 43 as a member of a group when the representative member is not a fully taxable person); or

(*b*) if construction commenced before 1st March 1995 and the period referred to in paragraph (*a*) above has not then expired, on 1st March 1997;

whichever is the earlier.

(2) Subject to sub-paragraph (3) [and (3A)] below, the buildings and works within this sub-paragraph are—

(*a*) any building neither designed as a dwelling or number of dwellings nor intended for use solely for a relevant residential purpose or a relevant charitable purpose; and

(*b*) any civil engineering work, other than a work necessary for the development of a permanent park for residential caravans.

(3) A building or work is not within sub-paragraph (2) above if—

(*a*) construction of it was commenced before 1st August 1989 or after 28th February 1995; or

(*b*) a grant of the fee simple in it which falls within paragraph (*a*)(ii) or (iv) of item 1 of Group 1 of Schedule 9 has been made before the occasion concerned.

(3A) A building or work which would, apart from this sub-paragraph, fall within sub-paragraph (2) above is not within that sub-paragraph if—

(*a*) construction of it was commenced before 1st March 1995 but had not been completed by that date; and

(*b*) the developer—

(i) makes no claim after that date to credit for input tax, entitlement to which is dependent upon his being treated in due course as having made a supply by virtue of paragraph 6 below; and

(ii) has made no such claim prior to that date; or

(iii) accounts to the Commissioners for a sum equal to any such credit that has previously been claimed.

(4) For the purposes of this paragraph a taxable person is, in relation to any building or work, a fully taxable person throughout a prescribed accounting period if—

(*a*) at the end of that period he is entitled to credit for input tax on all supplies to, and acquisitions and importations by, him in the period (apart from any on which input tax is excluded from credit by virtue of section 25(7); or

(*b*) the building or work is not used by him at any time during the period in, or in connection with, making any exempt supplies of goods or services.

(5) Subject to sub-paragraph (6) below, in this paragraph and paragraph 6 below "developer", in relation to a building or work, means any person who—

(*a*) constructs it;

(*b*) order it to be constructed; or

(*c*) finances its construction,

with a view to granting an interest in, right over or licence to occupy it (or any part of it) or to occupying or using it (or any part of it) for his own purposes.

(6) Where—

(*a*) a body corporate treated under section 43 as a member of a group is a developer in relation to a building or work, and

(*b*) it grants an interest in, right over or licence to occupy the building or work (or any part of it) to another body corporate which is treated under that section as a member of the group,

then, for the purposes of this paragraph and paragraph 6 below, as from the time of the grant any body corporate such as is mentioned in sub-paragraph (7) below shall be treated as also being a developer in relation to the building or work.

(7) The bodies corporate referred to in sub-paragraph (6) above are any which under section 43—

(*a*) was treated as a member of the same group as the body corporate making the grant at the time of the grant; or

(*b*) has been so treated at any later time when the body corporate by which the grant was made had an interest in, right over or licence to occupy the building or work (or any part of it); or

(*c*) has been treated as a member of the same group as a body corporate within paragraph (*a*) or (*b*) above or this paragraph at a time when that body corporate had an interest in, right over or licence to occupy the building or work (or any part of it).

(8) Subject to sub-paragraph (10) below, sub-paragraphs (1), (2) and (3A) to (7) above shall apply in relation to any of the following reconstructions, enlargements or extensions—

(*a*) a reconstruction, enlargement or extension of an existing building which is commenced on or after 1st January 1992 and before 1st March 1995 and—

(i) which is carried out wholly or partly on land (hereafter referred to as new building land) adjoining the curtilage of the existing building, or

(ii) as a result of which the gross external floor area of the reconstructed, enlarged or extended building (excluding any floor area on new building land) exceeds the gross external floor area of the existing building by not less than 20 per cent of the gross external floor area of the existing building;

(*b*) a reconstruction of an existing building which is commenced on or after 1st January 1992 and before 1st March 1995 and in the course of which at least 80 per cent of the area of the floor structures of the existing building are removed;

(*c*) a reconstruction, enlargement or extension of a civil engineering work which is commenced on or after 1st January 1992 and before 1st March 1995 and which is carried out wholly or partly on land (hereafter referred to as new land) adjoining the land on or in which the existing work is situated,

as if references to the building or work were references to the reconstructed, enlarged or extended building or work and as if references to construction were references to reconstruction, enlargement or extension.

(9) For the purposes of sub-paragraph (8)(*a*) above, extensions to an existing building shall include the provision of any annex having internal access to the existing building.

(10) Sub-paragraphs (1) and (2) and sub-paragraphs (3A) to (7) above shall not apply to a reconstruction, enlargement or extension—

(*a*) falling within sub-paragraph (8)(*a*)(i) or (ii) or (*c*) above where the developer has held an interest in at least 75 per cent of all of the land on which the reconstructed, enlarged or extended building or work stands, or is constructed, throughout the period of 10 years ending with the last day of the prescribed accounting period during which the reconstructed, enlarged or extended building or work becomes substantially ready for occupation or use; or

(*b*) to the extent that it falls within sub-paragraph (8)(*a*)(ii) above or falling within sub-paragraph (8)(*b*) above, where the interest in, right over or licence to occupy the building concerned (or any part of it) has already been treated as supplied to and by the developer under paragraph 6(1) below.

6—(1) Where this paragraph applies the interest in, right over or licence to occupy the buildings or work (or any part of it) held by the developer shall be treated for the purposes of this Act as supplied to the developer for the purpose of a business carried on by him and supplied by him in the course or furtherance of the business on the last day of the prescribed accounting period during which it applies, or, if later, of the prescribed accounting period during which the building or work becomes substantially ready for occupation or use.

(2) The supply treated as made by sub-paragraph (1) above shall be taken to be a taxable supply and the value of the supply shall be the aggregate of—

(*a*) the value of grants relating to the land on which the building or work is constructed made or to be made to the developer, but excluding, in a case where construction of the building or work in question commenced before 1st January 1992, the value of any grants to be made for consideration in the form of rent the amount of which cannot be ascertained by the developer when the supply is treated as made, and in any other case excluding the value of any—

(i) grants made before the relevant day to the extent that consideration for such grants was in the form of rent, and to the extent that such rent was properly attributable to a building which has been demolished,

(ii) grants made before the relevant day in respect of a building which has been reconstructed, enlarged or extended so that the reconstruction, enlargement or extension falls within paragraph 5(8)(*a*)(ii) above, and does not fall also within paragraph 5(8)(*b*) above, to the extent that consideration for such grants was in the form of rent, and to the extent that such rent was properly attributable to the building as it existed before the commencement of the reconstruction, enlargement or extension,

(iii) grants made before the relevant day in respect of a building which has been so reconstructed that the reconstruction falls within paragraph 5(8)(*b*) above, to the extent that consideration for such grants was in the form of rent, and to the extent that such rent was properly attributable to the building before the reconstruction commenced,

(iv) grants falling within paragraph (*b*) of item 1 of Group 1 of Schedule 9, and

(*b*) the value of all the taxable supplies of goods and services, other than any that are zero-rated, made or to be made for or in connection with the construction of the building or work.

(3) Where the rate of VAT (the lower rate) chargeable on a supply (the construction supply) falling within sub-paragraph (2)(*b*) above, the value of which is included in the value of a supply (the self-supply) treated as made by sub-paragraph (1) above, is lower than the rate of VAT (the current rate) chargeable on that self-supply, then VAT on the self-supply shall be charged—

(*a*) on so much of its value as is comprised of the relevant part of the value of the construction supply, at the lower rate; and

(*b*) on the remainder of its value at the current rate.

(4) For the purposes of sub-paragraph (3)(*a*) above, the relevant part of the value of the construction supply means—

(*a*) where the construction supply is a supply of goods, the value of such of those goods as have actually been delivered by the supplier;

(*b*) where the construction supply is a supply of services, the value of such of those services as have actually been performed by the supplier,

on or before the last day upon which the lower rate is in force.

(5) Where the value of a supply which, apart from this sub-paragraph, would be treated as made by sub-paragraph (1) above would be less than £100,000, no supply shall be treated as made by that sub-paragraph.

(6) For the purposes of sub-paragraph (2)(*a*)(i) above, the relevant day is the day on which the demolition of the building in question commenced and, for the purposes of sub-paragraph (2)(*a*)(ii) and (iii) above, the relevant day is the day on which the reconstruction, enlargement or extension in question commenced.

(7) In the application of sub-paragraphs (1) to (6) above to a reconstruction, enlargement or extension to which sub-paragraphs (1) and (2) and sub-paragraphs (3A) to (7) of paragraph 5 above apply by virtue of paragraph 5(8) above—

(*a*) references to the building or work shall be construed as references to the reconstructed enlarged or extended building or work, and references to construction shall be construed as references to reconstruction, enlargement or extension;

(*b*) the reference in paragraph (*a*) of sub-paragraph (2) to the value of grants relating to the land on which the building or work is constructed shall be construed as a reference—

(i) in relation to a reconstruction, enlargement or extension of an existing building to the extent that it falls within paragraph 5(8)(*a*)(i) above and does not fall also within paragraph 5(8)(*b*) above, to the value of grants relating to the new building land;

(ii) in relation to a reconstruction, enlargement or extension of an existing building, to the extent that it falls within paragraph 5(8)(*a*)(ii) above and does not fall also within paragraph 5(8)(*b*) above, to the value of grants relating to the land on which the existing building stands multiplied by the appropriate fraction;

(iii) in relation to a reconstruction, enlargement or extension to a work falling within paragraph 5(8)(*c*) above, to the value of grants relating to the new land.

(8) For the purposes of sub-paragraph (7)(*b*)(ii) above the appropriate fraction shall be calculated by dividing the additional gross external floor area resulting from the reconstruction, enlargement or extension (excluding any floor area on new building land) by the gross external floor area of the reconstructed, enlarged or extended building (excluding any floor area on new building land).

(9) Where this paragraph applies by virtue of paragraph 5(1)(*b*) above it shall have effect as if—

(*a*) in sub-paragraph (1)—

(i) the words "(or any part of it)" were omitted; and

(ii) for the words "the last day" to "ready for occupation or use" there were substituted "1st March 1997";

(*b*) in sub-paragraph (2)(*a*) the words "or to be made" and the words "to be made" were omitted;

(*c*) in sub-paragraph (2)(*b*) the words "or to be made" were omitted; and

(*d*) sub-paragraph (5) were omitted.

7—(1) Where a developer is a tenant, lessee or licensee and becomes liable to a charge to VAT under paragraph 6(1) above (except where that paragraph applies by virtue of paragraph 5(1)(*b*)) in respect of his tenancy, lease or licence he shall notify forthwith in writing his landlord, lessor or licensor (as the case may be)—

(*a*) of the date from which the tenancy, lease or licence becomes a developmental tenancy, developmental lease or developmental licence for the purposes of paragraph (*b*) of item 1 of Group 1 of Schedule 9;

(*b*) in a case falling within paragraph 5(8)(*a*)(ii) above, of the appropriate fraction determined in accordance with paragraph 6(8) above.

(2) Where the appropriate fraction has been notified in accordance with sub-paragraph (1)(*b*) above, any supply made pursuant to the tenancy, lease or licence in question shall be treated as made pursuant to a developmental tenancy, developmental lease or developmental licence (a developmental supply) as if, and only to the extent that, the consideration for the developmental supply is for an amount equal to the whole of the consideration for the supply made pursuant to the tenancy, lease or licence, multiplied by the appropriate fraction.

General

8—(1) Where the benefit of the consideration for the grant of an interest in, right over or licence to occupy land accrues to a person but that person is not the person making the grant—

(*a*) the person to whom the benefit accrues shall for the purposes of this Act be treated as the person making the grant; and

(*b*) to the extent that any input tax of the person actually making the grant is attributable to the grant it shall be treated as input tax of the person to whom the benefit accrues.

(2) Where the consideration for the grant of an interest in, right over or licence to occupy land is such that its provision is enforceable primarily—

(*a*) by the person who, as owner of an interest or right in or over that land, actually made the grant, or

(*b*) by another person in his capacity as the owner for the time being of that interest or right or of any other interest or right in or over that land,

that person, and not any person (other than that person) to whom a benefit accrues by virtue of his being a beneficiary under a trust relating to the land, or the proceeds of sale of any land, shall be taken for the purposes of this paragraph to be the person to whom the benefit of the consideration accrues.

(3) Sub-paragraph (2) above shall not apply to the extent that the Commissioners, on an application made in the prescribed manner jointly by—

(*a*) the person who (apart from this sub-paragraph) would be taken under that sub-paragraph to be the person to whom the benefit of the consideration accrues, and

(*b*) all the persons for the time being in existence who, as beneficiaries under such a trust as is mentioned in that sub-paragraph, are persons who have or may become entitled to or to a share of the consideration, or for whose benefit any of it is to be or may be applied,

may direct that the benefit of the consideration is to be treated for the purposes of this paragraph as a benefit accruing to the persons falling within paragraph (*b*) above, and not (unless he also falls within paragraph (*b*) above) to the person falling within paragraph (*a*) above.

9 Notes (1) to (6), (10), (12) and (19) to Group 5 of Schedule 8 and Notes (1), (1A), (2) and (15) to Group 1 of Schedule 9 apply in relation to this Schedule as they apply in relation to their respective Groups but subject to any appropriate modifications.".

Notes—Former para 8(2), (3) repealed without being rewritten in new Sch 10: SI 2008/1146 art 5(2).

An election under former Sch 10 para 2 which was made before 1 November 1989 continues to have effect in accordance with former Sch 10 para 3(1)(*b*): SI 2008/1146 art 7, Sch 2 para 8.

An election under former Sch 10 para 2 which was made before 1 March 1995 continues to have effect in accordance with former Sch 10 para 3(6)(*a*): SI 2008/1146 art 7, Sch 2 para 9.

The fact that former Sch 10 paras 5–7 are not rewritten by SI 2008/1146 art 2 is not to affect—

(*a*) the continued operation of Part 15 of the Value Added Tax Regulations, SI 1995/2518 (adjustments to the deduction of input tax on capital items) in relation to supplies treated as made on or before 1 March 1997, or

(*b*) the continued operation of VATA 1994 Sch 9, Group 1, item 1, para (*b*), as read with Note (7), in relation to supplies made before 1 June 2020: SI 2008/1146 art 7, Sch 2 para 10.

The fact that the words ", or of a description specified," in former Sch 10 para 3(2) are not rewritten by SI 2008/1146 art 2 is not to affect the continued operation of an option to tax any land—

(*a*) which was made before 1 June 2008, and

(*b*) which specified a description of land.

[SCHEDULE 10A

FACE-VALUE VOUCHERS]

Section 51B

Amendments—This Schedule inserted by FA 2003 s 19, Sch 1 para 2 with effect for supplies of tokens, stamps or vouchers issued after 8 April 2003.

Meaning of "face-value voucher" etc

[1— (1) In this Schedule "face-value voucher" means a token, stamp or voucher (whether in physical or electronic form) that represents a right to receive goods or services to the value of an amount stated on it or recorded in it.

(2) References in this Schedule to the "face value" of a voucher are to the amount referred to in sub-paragraph (1) above.][1]

Simon's Tax Cases—*Leisure Pass Group Ltd v R&C Comrs* [2008] STC 3340.

Amendments—[1] Schedule inserted by FA 2003 Sch 1 para 2 in relation to supplies of tokens, stamps or vouchers issued after 8 April 2003.

Nature of supply

[2 The issue of a face-value voucher, or any subsequent supply of it, is a supply of services for the purposes of this Act.][1]

Amendments—[1] Schedule inserted by FA 2003 Sch 1 para 2 in relation to supplies of tokens, stamps or vouchers issued after 8 April 2003.

Treatment of credit vouchers

[3— (1) This paragraph applies to a face-value voucher issued by a person who—

(*a*) is not a person from whom goods or services may be obtained by the use of the voucher, and

(*b*) undertakes to give complete or partial reimbursement to any such person from whom goods or services are so obtained.

Such a voucher is referred to in this Schedule as a "credit voucher".

(2) The consideration for any supply of a credit voucher shall be disregarded for the purposes of this Act except to the extent (if any) that it exceeds the face value of the voucher.

(3) Sub-paragraph (2) above does not apply if any of the persons from whom goods or services are obtained by the use of the voucher fails to account for any of the VAT due on the supply of those goods or services to the person using the voucher to obtain them.][1]

[(4) The Treasury may by order specify other circumstances in which sub-paragraph (2) above does not apply.][2]

Simon's Tax Cases—para 3, *R (on the application of IDT Card Services Ireland Ltd) v Customs and Excise Commissioners* [2005] STC 314; *R&C Comrs v IDT Card Service Ireland Ltd* [2006] STC 1252.

Amendments—[1] Schedule inserted by FA 2003 Sch 1 para 2 in relation to supplies of tokens, stamps or vouchers issued after 8 April 2003.

[2] Sub-para (4) inserted by FA 2006 s 22(3) with effect from 19 July 2006.

Treatment of retailer vouchers

[4— (1) This paragraph applies to a face-value voucher issued by a person who—

(*a*) is a person from whom goods or services may be obtained by the use of the voucher, and

(*b*) if there are other such persons, undertakes to give complete or partial reimbursement to those from whom goods or services are so obtained.

Such a voucher is referred to in this Schedule as a "retailer voucher".

(2) The consideration for the issue of a retailer voucher shall be disregarded for the purposes of this Act except to the extent (if any) that it exceeds the face value of the voucher.

(3) Sub-paragraph (2) above does not apply if—

(*a*) the voucher is used to obtain goods or services from a person other than the issuer, and

(*b*) that person fails to account for any of the VAT due on the supply of those goods or services to the person using the voucher to obtain them.

(4) Any supply of a retailer voucher subsequent to the issue of it shall be treated in the same way as the supply of a voucher to which paragraph 6 applies.][1]

Amendments—[1] Schedule inserted by FA 2003 Sch 1 para 2 in relation to supplies of tokens, stamps or vouchers issued after 8 April 2003.

Treatment of postage stamps

[5 The consideration for the supply of a face-value voucher that is a postage stamp shall be disregarded for the purposes of this Act except to the extent (if any) that it exceeds the face value of the stamp.][1]

Amendments—[1] Schedule inserted by FA 2003 Sch 1 para 2 in relation to supplies of tokens, stamps or vouchers issued after 8 April 2003.

Treatment of other kinds of face-value voucher

[6— (1) This paragraph applies to a face-value voucher that is not a credit voucher, a retailer voucher or a postage stamp.

(2) A supply of such a voucher is chargeable at the rate in force under section 2(1) (standard rate) except where sub-paragraph (3), (4) or (5) below applies.

(3) Where the voucher is one that can only be used to obtain goods or services in one particular non-standard rate category, the supply of the voucher falls in that category.

(4) Where the voucher is used to obtain goods or services all of which fall in one particular non-standard rate category, the supply of the voucher falls in that category.

(5) Where the voucher is used to obtain goods or services in a number of different rate categories—

(*a*) the supply of the voucher shall be treated as that many different supplies, each falling in the category in question, and

(*b*) the value of each of those supplies shall be determined on a just and reasonable basis.][1]

Amendments—[1] Schedule inserted by FA 2003 Sch 1 para 2 in relation to supplies of tokens, stamps or vouchers issued after 8 April 2003.

Vouchers supplied free with other goods or services

[7 Where—

(*a*) a face-value voucher (other than a postage stamp) and other goods or services are supplied to the same person in a composite transaction, and

(*b*) the total consideration for the supplies is no different, or not significantly different, from what it would be if the voucher were not supplied, the supply of the voucher shall be treated as being made for no consideration.][1]

Amendments—[1] Schedule inserted by FA 2003 Sch 1 para 2 in relation to supplies of tokens, stamps or vouchers issued after 8 April 2003.

Interpretation

[8— (1) In this Schedule—

"credit voucher" has the meaning given by paragraph 3(1) above;

"face value" has the meaning given by paragraph 1(2) above;

"face value voucher" has the meaning given by paragraph 1(1) above;

"retailer voucher" has the meaning given by paragraph 4(1) above.

(2) For the purposes of this Schedule—

(*a*) the "rate categories" of supplies are—

(i) supplies chargeable at the rate in force under section 2(1) (standard rate),

(ii) supplies chargeable at the rate in force under section 29A (reduced rate),

(iii) zero-rated supplies, and

(iv) exempt supplies;

(*b*) the "non-standard rate categories" of supplies are those in sub-paragraphs (ii), (iii) and (iv) of paragraph (*a*) above;

(*c*) goods or services are in a particular rate category if a supply of those goods or services falls in that category.

(3) A reference in this Schedule to a voucher being used to obtain goods or services includes a reference to the case where it is used as part-payment for those goods or services.][1]

Amendments—[1] Schedule inserted by FA 2003 Sch 1 para 2 in relation to supplies of tokens, stamps or vouchers issued after 8 April 2003.

SCHEDULE 11

ADMINISTRATION, COLLECTION AND ENFORCEMENT

Section 58

Cross reference—See VATA 1994 s 92(6), (7) (exercise of certain information powers under this Schedule in relation to matters relevant to a charge to VAT under the law of another member state).
See FA 2008 s 127 (Enforcement by taking control of goods: England and Wales).
See FA 2008 s 128 (Summary warrant: Scotland).

General

[1— The Commissioners for Her Majesty's Revenue and Customs shall be responsible for the collection and management of VAT.][1]

Commentary—*De Voil Indirect Tax Service* **V1.262, V1.264.**
Definitions—"The Commissioners", s 96(1); "VAT", ss 1, 96(1).
Amendments—[1] Para substituted by the Commissioners for Revenue and Customs Act 2005 s 50, Sch 4 para 56 with effect from 18 April 2005 by virtue of the Commissioners for Revenue and Customs Act 2005 (Commencement) Order, SI 2005/1126, art 2(2).

Accounting for VAT ...[2] and payment of VAT

2— (1) Regulations under this paragraph may require the keeping of accounts and the making of returns in such form and manner as may be specified in the regulations ...[2]

(2), (2A) ...[2]

(3) Regulations under this paragraph may require the submission to the Commissioners by taxable persons, at such times and intervals, in such cases and in such form and manner as may be—

(*a*) specified in the regulations; or

(*b*) determined by the Commissioners in accordance with powers conferred by the regulations,

of statements containing such particulars of transactions in which the taxable persons are concerned and [to which this sub-paragraph applies][5], and of the persons concerned in those transactions, as may be prescribed.

[(3ZA) Sub-paragraph (3) above applies to—

(*a*) transactions involving the movement of goods between member States, and

(*b*) transactions involving the supply of services to a person in a member State other than the United Kingdom who is required to pay VAT on the supply in accordance with provisions of the law of that other member State giving effect to Article 196 of Council Directive 2006/112/EC.][5]

[(3A) Regulations under this paragraph may require the submission to the Commissioners by taxable persons, at such times and intervals, in such cases and in such form and manner as may be—

(*a*) specified in the regulations, or

(*b*) determined by the Commissioners in accordance with powers conferred by the regulations,

of statements containing such particulars of supplies to which section 55A(6) applies in which the taxable persons are concerned, and of the persons concerned in those supplies, as may be prescribed.

[(3B) Regulations under this paragraph may make provision for requiring—

(*a*) a person who first makes a supply of goods to which section 55A(6) applies (a "reverse charge supply"),

(*b*) a person who ceases making reverse charge supplies without intending subsequently to make such supplies, or

(*c*) a person who has fallen within paragraph (*b*) above but who nonetheless starts to make reverse charge supplies again,

to give to the Commissioners such notification of that fact at such time and in such form and manner as may be specified in the regulations or determined by the Commissioners in accordance with powers conferred by the regulations.][4].][3]

(4) Regulations under this paragraph may make provision in relation to cases where—

(*a*) any goods which are subject to a duty of excise or consist in a new means of transport are acquired in the United Kingdom from another member State by any person;

(*b*) the acquisition of the goods is a taxable acquisition and is not in pursuance of a taxable supply; and

(*c*) that person is not a taxable person at the time of the acquisition,

for requiring the person who acquires the goods to give to the Commissioners such notification of the acquisition, and for requiring any VAT on the acquisition to be paid, at such time and in such form or manner as may be specified in the regulations.

(5) Regulations under this paragraph may provide for a notification required by virtue of sub-paragraph (4) above—

(*a*) to contain such particulars relating to the notified acquisition and any VAT chargeable thereon as may be specified in the regulations; and

(*b*) to be given, in prescribed cases, by the personal representative, trustee in bankruptcy, interim or permanent trustee, receiver, liquidator or person otherwise acting in a representative capacity in relation to the person who makes that acquisition.

(6) Regulations under this paragraph may make special provision for such taxable supplies by retailers of any goods or of any description of goods or of services or any description of services as may be determined by or under the regulations and, in particular—

(*a*) for permitting the value which is to be taken as the value of the supplies in any prescribed accounting period or part thereof to be determined, subject to any limitations or restrictions, by such method or one of such methods as may have been described in any notice published by the Commissioners in pursuance of the regulations and not withdrawn by a further notice or as may be agreed with the Commissioners; and

(*b*) for determining the proportion of the value of the supplies which is to be attributed to any description of supplies; and

(*c*) for adjusting that value and proportion for periods comprising two or more prescribed accounting periods or parts thereof.

(7) Regulations under this paragraph may make provision whereby, in such cases and subject to such conditions as may be determined by or under the regulations, VAT in respect of a supply may be accounted for and paid by reference to the time when consideration for the supply is received; and any such regulations may make such modifications of the provisions of this Act (including in particular, but without prejudice to the generality of the power, the provisions as to the time when, and the circumstances in which, credit for input tax is to be allowed) as appear to the Commissioners necessary or expedient.

(8) Regulations under this paragraph may make provision whereby, in such cases and subject to such conditions as may be determined by or under the regulations—

(*a*) VAT in respect of any supply by a taxable person of dutiable goods, or

(*b*) VAT in respect of an acquisition by any person from another member State of dutiable goods,

may be accounted for and paid, and any question as to the inclusion of any duty or agricultural levy in the value of the supply or acquisition determined, by reference to the duty point or by reference to such later time as the Commissioners may allow.

In this sub-paragraph "dutiable goods" and "duty point" have the same meanings as in section 18.

(9) Regulations under this paragraph may provide for the time when any invoice described in regulations made for the purposes of section 6(8)(*b*) or 12(1)(*b*) is to be treated as having been issued and provide for VAT accounted for and paid by reference to the date of issue of such an invoice to be confined to VAT on so much of the value of the supply or acquisition as is shown on the invoice.

(10) Regulations under this paragraph may make provision—

(*a*) for treating VAT chargeable in one prescribed accounting period as chargeable in another such period; and

(*b*) with respect to the making of entries in accounts for the purpose of making adjustments, whether for the correction of errors or otherwise; and

(*c*) for the making of financial adjustments in connection with the making of entries in accounts for the purpose mentioned in paragraph (*b*) above [and

(*d*) for a person, for purposes connected with the making of any such entry or financial adjustment, to be required to provide to any prescribed person, or to retain, a document in the prescribed form containing prescribed particulars of the matters to which the entry or adjustment relates; and

(*e*) for enabling the Commissioners, in such cases as they may think fit, to dispense with or relax a requirement imposed by regulations made by virtue of paragraph (*d*) above.][1]

(11) Regulations under this paragraph may make different provision for different circumstances and may provide for different dates as the commencement of prescribed accounting periods applicable to different persons.

(12) The provisions made by regulations under this paragraph for cases where goods are treated as supplied by a taxable person by virtue of paragraph 7 of Schedule 4 may require VAT chargeable on the supply to be accounted for and paid, and particulars thereof to be provided, by such other person and in such manner as may be specified by the regulations.

(13) Where, at the end of a prescribed accounting period, the amount of VAT due from any person or the amount of any VAT credit would be less than £1, that amount shall be treated as nil.

Commentary—*De Voil Indirect Tax Service* **V5.109**.
Simon's Tax Cases—Sub-para (6), *C&E Comrs v Kingfisher plc* [1994] STC 63*.
Definitions—"Acquisition of goods from another member State", s 11; "another member State", s 96(1); "the Commissioners", s 96(1); "document", s 96(1); "input tax", s 24; "interim trustee", s 96(1); "invoice", s 96(1); "law of another member State", s 92; "new means of transport", s 95; "permanent trustee", s 96(1); "place of supply", s 7; "prescribed", s 96(1); "prescribed accounting period", s 25(1); "regulations", s 96(1); "supply", s 5, Sch 4; "taxable acquisition", s 10(2); "taxable person", s 3; "taxable supply", s 4(2); "time of acquisition", s 12; "time of supply", s 6; "United Kingdom", s 96(11); "VAT", ss 1, 96(1); "VAT credit", s 25(3); "VAT invoice", s 6(15); "value of acquisition", s 20; "value of supply", s 19, Sch 6.
Regulations—See VAT Regulations, SI 1995/2518 regs 13–20 (VAT and other invoices); regs 21–23 (EC sales statements); regs 24–42 (accounting and records); regs 49–55 (annual accounting scheme); regs 56–65 (cash accounting scheme); regs 66–75 (retail schemes); regs 146–155 (new means of transport).
Cross references—See VATA 1994 s 67(1) (penalty for failure to comply with regulations under sub-para (4) of this para);
VATA 1994 s 69(1), (5) (penalty for failure to comply with time limit for submission of return imposed by regulations under sub-para (1) of this para);
VATA 1994 s 75 (assessment of VAT where notification of an acquisition has not been given as required by regulations under sub-para (4) of this para);
VATA 1994 s 83 (appeals to a tribunal against a refusal to allow the use of a retail scheme under sub-para (6) of this para and against a refusal of authorisation to use a cash accounting scheme under sub-para (7) of this para);
VATA 1994 s 88(5) (supplies spanning date of change in rate of VAT: power to make regulations under this para providing for replacement or correction of VAT invoices).
VAT (Isle of Man) Order, SI 1982/1067 art 8 (taxable persons for the purposes of Isle of Man VAT legislation to be treated as taxable persons for the purposes of this para).
Amendments—[1] Sub-para (2A) and sub-para (10)(*d*), (*e*) inserted by FA 1996 s 38.
[2] Words in Heading and sub-para (1) repealed, and sub-paras (2), (2A) repealed by FA 2002 ss 24(1)(*b*), (5), 139, Sch 40 Pt 2(2) with effect 1 December 2003 (by virtue of SI 2003/3043).
[3] Sub-paras (3A), (3B) inserted by FA 2006 s 19(7), (8) with effect for supplies made on or after 1 June 2007 (by virtue of the Finance Act 2006, Section 19, (Appointed Day) Order, SI 2007/1419).
[4] Sub-para (3B) substituted by the VAT (Administration, Collection and Enforcement) Order, SI 2007/1421 art 2 with effect from 1 June 2007.
[5] Words "which involve the movement of goods between member States" in sub-para (3) substituted, and sub-para (3ZA) inserted, by FA 2009 s 78 with effect from 21 July 2009.

[VAT invoices

2A— (1) Regulations may require a taxable person supplying goods or services to provide an invoice (a "VAT invoice") to the person supplied.

(2) A VAT invoice must give—

(*a*) such particulars as may be prescribed of the supply, the supplier and the person supplied;

(*b*) such an indication as may be prescribed of whether VAT is chargeable on the supply under this Act or the law of another member State;

(*c*) such particulars of any VAT that is so chargeable as may be prescribed.

(3) Regulations may confer power on the Commissioners to allow the requirements of any regulations as to the information to be given in a VAT invoice to be relaxed or dispensed with.

(4) Regulations may—

(*a*) provide that the VAT invoice that is required to be provided in connection with a particular description of supply must be provided within a prescribed time after the supply is treated as taking place, or at such time before the supply is treated as taking place as may be prescribed;

(*b*) allow for the invoice to be issued later than required by the regulations where it is issued in accordance with general or special directions given by the Commissioners.

(5) Regulations may—

(*a*) make provision about the manner in which a VAT invoice may be provided, including provision prescribing conditions that must be complied with in the case of an invoice issued by a third party on behalf of the supplier;

(*b*) prescribe conditions that must be complied with in the case of a VAT invoice that relates to more than one supply;

(*c*) make, in relation to a document that refers to a VAT invoice and is intended to amend it, such provision corresponding to that which may be made in relation to a VAT invoice as appears to the Commissioners to be appropriate.

(6) Regulations may confer power on the Commissioners to require a person who has received in the United Kingdom a VAT invoice that is (or part of which is) in a language other than English to provide them with an English translation of the invoice (or part).

(7) Regulations under this paragraph—

(*a*) may be framed so as to apply only in prescribed cases or only in relation to supplies made to persons of prescribed descriptions;

(*b*) may make different provision for different circumstances.][1]

Amendments—[1] Para 2A inserted by FA 2002 s 24(2), (5) with effect from 1 December 2003 (by virtue of SI 2003/3043).

[Self-billed invoices

2B— (1) This paragraph applies where a taxable person provides to himself a document (a "self-billed invoice") that purports to be a VAT invoice in respect of a supply of goods or services to him by another taxable person.

(2) Subject to compliance with such conditions as may be—

(*a*) prescribed,

(*b*) specified in a notice published by the Commissioners, or

(*c*) imposed in a particular case in accordance with regulations,

a self-billed invoice shall be treated as the VAT invoice required by regulations under paragraph 2A above to be provided by the supplier.

(3) For the purposes of section 6(4) (under which the time of supply can be determined by the prior issue of an invoice) a self-billed invoice shall not be treated as issued by the supplier.

(4) For the purposes of section 6(5) and (6) (under which the time of supply can be determined by the subsequent issue of an invoice) a self-billed invoice in relation to which the conditions mentioned in sub-paragraph (2) are complied with shall, subject to compliance with such further conditions as may be prescribed, be treated as issued by the supplier.

In such a case, any notice of election given or request made for the purposes of section 6(5) or (6) by the person providing the self-billed invoice shall be treated for those purposes as given or made by the supplier.

(5) Regulations under this paragraph—

(*a*) may be framed so as to apply only in prescribed cases or only in relation to supplies made to persons of prescribed descriptions;

(*b*) may make different provision for different circumstances.][1]

Amendments—[1] Para 2B inserted by FA 2002 s 24(2), (5) with effect 1 December 2003 (by virtue of SI 2003/3043).

[Electronic communication and storage of VAT invoices etc

3— (1) Regulations may prescribe, or provide for the Commissioners to impose in a particular case, conditions that must be complied with in relation to—

(*a*) the provision by electronic means of any item to which this paragraph applies;

(*b*) the preservation by electronic means of any such item or of information contained in any such item.

(2) The items to which this paragraph applies are—

(*a*) any VAT invoice;

(*b*) any document that refers to a VAT invoice and is intended to amend it;

(*c*) any invoice described in regulations made for the purposes of section 6(8)(*b*) or 12(1)(*b*).

(3) Regulations under this paragraph may make different provision for different circumstances.][1]

Amendments—[1] This paragraph substituted by FA 2002 s 24(3), (5) with effect from 1 December 2003 (by virtue of SI 2003/3043).

Power to require security and production of evidence

4— [(1) The Commissioners may, as a condition of allowing or repaying input tax to any person, require the production of such evidence relating to VAT as they may specify.

(1A) If they think it necessary for the protection of the revenue, the Commissioners may require, as a condition of making any VAT credit, the giving of such security for the amount of the payment as appears to them appropriate.][1]

[(2) If they think it necessary for the protection of the revenue, the Commissioners may require a taxable person, as a condition of his supplying or being supplied with goods or services under a taxable supply, to give security, or further security, for the payment of any VAT that is or may become due from—

(*a*) the taxable person, or

(*b*) any person by or to whom relevant goods or services are supplied.

(3) In sub-paragraph (2) above "relevant goods or services" means goods or services supplied by or to the taxable person.

(4) Security under sub-paragraph (2) above shall be of such amount, and shall be given in such manner, as the Commissioners may determine.

(5) The powers conferred on the Commissioners by sub-paragraph (2) above are without prejudice to their powers under section 48(7).][2]

Commentary—*De Voil Indirect Tax Service* **V5.186**.

Simon's Tax Cases—Sub-para (1), *Garage Molenheide BVBA and ors v Belgian State* (Joined cases C-286/94, C-340/95, C-401/95 and C-47/96) [1998] STC 126, ECJ.

Sub-para (2), *C&E Comrs v Peachtree Enterprises Ltd* [1994] STC 747; *C&E Comrs and another v Federation of Technological Industries and others* [2006] STC 1483, *Chaudhry v R&C Prosecution Office* [2008] STC 2357.

Definitions—"The Commissioners", s 96(1); "document", s 96(1); "input tax", s 24; "supply", s 5, Sch 4; "taxable person", s 3; "taxable supply", s 4(2); "VAT", ss 1, 96(1); "VAT credit", s 25(3).

Cross references—See VATA 1994 s 72(11) (penalty for making supplies in contravention of sub-para (2) of this para); VATA 1994 ss 83, 84 (appeal to a tribunal in respect of a requirement for security under sub-para (2) of this para).

VAT (Isle of Man) Order, SI 1982/1067 art 7 (references to VAT in this para to include references to VAT chargeable under Isle of Man legislation).

Amendments—[1] Sub-paras (1), (1A) substituted for sub-para (1) by FA 2003 s 17(3) with effect from 10 April 2003.

[2] Sub-paras (2)–(5) substituted for sub-s (2) by FA 2003 s 17(4) with effect from 10 April 2003.

Recovery of VAT, etc

5— (1) VAT due from any person shall be recoverable as a debt due to the Crown.

(2) Where an invoice shows a supply of goods or services as taking place with VAT chargeable on it, there shall be recoverable from the person who issued the invoice an amount equal to that which is shown on the invoice as VAT or, if VAT is not separately shown, to so much of the total amount shown as payable as is to be taken as representing VAT on the supply.

(3) Sub-paragraph (2) above applies whether or not—

(*a*) the invoice is a VAT invoice issued in pursuance of paragraph 2(1) above; or

(*b*) the supply shown on the invoice actually takes or has taken place, or the amount shown as VAT, or any amount of VAT, is or was chargeable on the supply; or

(*c*) the person issuing the invoice is a taxable person;

and any sum recoverable from a person under the sub-paragraph shall, if it is in any case VAT be recoverable as such and shall otherwise be recoverable as a debt due to the Crown.

(4)–(10) …[1]

Commentary—*De Voil Indirect Tax Service* **V5.171, V5.173**.

Regulations—See VAT Regulations, SI 1995/2518 regs 212, 213.

Simon's Tax Cases—*C&E Comrs v International Language Centres Ltd* [1986] STC 279*.

Definitions—"The Commissioners", s 96(1); "invoice", s 96(1); "regulations", s 96(1); "supply", s 5, Sch 4; "taxable person", s 3; "VAT", ss 1, 96(1); "VAT invoice", s 6(15).

Cross reference—See VAT (Isle of Man) Order, SI 1982/1067 art 7 (references to VAT in this para to include references to VAT chargeable under Isle of Man legislation).

Amendments—[1] Sub-paras (4)–(10) repealed by FA 1997 Sch 18(2) Part V(2) with effect from 1 July 1997 (see SI 1997/1433).

Duty to keep records

6— (1) Every taxable person shall keep such records as the Commissioners may by regulations require, and every person who, at a time when he is not a taxable person, acquires in the United Kingdom from another member State any goods which are subject to a duty of excise or consist in a new means of transport shall keep such records with respect to the acquisition (if it is a taxable acquisition and is not in pursuance of a taxable supply) as the Commissioners may so require.

(2) Regulations under sub-paragraph (1) above may make different provision for different cases and may be framed by reference to such records as may be specified in any notice published by the Commissioners in pursuance of the regulations and not withdrawn by a further notice.

(3) The Commissioners may require any records kept in pursuance of this paragraph to be preserved for such period not exceeding 6 years as they may [specify in writing (and different periods may be specified for different cases)][1].

[(4) The duty under this paragraph to preserve records may be discharged—

(*a*) by preserving them in any form and by any means, or

(*b*) by preserving the information contained in them in any form and by any means,

subject to any conditions or exceptions specified in writing by the Commissioners for Her Majesty's Revenue and Customs.][1]

Commentary—*De Voil Indirect Tax Service* **V5.201**.
Regulations—See VAT Regulations, SI 1995/2518 regs 31, 33.
Definitions—"Acquisition of goods from another member State", s 11; "another member State", s 96(1); "the Commissioners", s 96(1); "copy", s 96(1); "document", s 96(1); "new means of transport", s 95; "regulations", s 96(1); "taxable acquisition", s 10(2); "taxable person", s 3; "taxable supply", s 4(2); "United Kingdom", s 96(11).
Cross references—See VATA 1994 s 49(1) (transfer of going concerns: preservation of records by transferee);
VATA 1994 s 69(1) (penalty for breach of a requirement imposed under sub-para (1) of this para);
VATA 1994 s 69(2) (penalty for breach of a requirement to keep records imposed under sub-para (3) of this para).
VAT (Isle of Man) Order, SI 1982/1067 art 8 (taxable persons for the purposes of Isle of Man VAT legislation to be treated as taxable persons for the purposes of this para).
Amendments—[1] In sub-para (3), words substituted for word "require", and sub-para (4) substituted for previous sub-para (4), by FA 2008 s 115, Sch 37 paras 4, 5 with effect from 1 April 2009 (by virtue of SI 2009/402). Sub-paras (4)–(6) previously read as follows—

"(4) The duty under this paragraph to preserve records may be discharged by the preservation of the information contained therein by such means as the Commissioners may approve; and where that information is so preserved a copy of any document forming part of the records shall, subject to the following provisions of this paragraph, be admissible in evidence in any proceedings, whether civil or criminal, to the same extent as the records themselves.

(5) The Commissioners may, as a condition of approving under sub-paragraph (4) above any means of preserving information contained in any records, impose such reasonable requirements as appear to them necessary for securing that the information will be as readily available to them as if the records themselves had been preserved.

(6) A statement contained in a document produced by a computer shall not by virtue of sub-paragraph (4) above be admissible in evidence—

(*a*) …
(*b*) …
(*c*) …; and
(*d*) …

This sub-paragraph does not apply in relation to Scotland.".

[6A— (1) The Commissioners may direct any taxable person named in the direction to keep such records as they specify in the direction in relation to such goods as they so specify.

(2) A direction under this paragraph may require the records to be compiled by reference to VAT invoices or any other matter.

(3) The Commissioners may not make a direction under this paragraph unless they have reasonable grounds for believing that the records specified in the direction might assist in identifying taxable supplies in respect of which the VAT chargeable might not be paid.

(4) The taxable supplies in question may be supplies made by—

(*a*) the person named in the direction, or

(*b*) any other person.

(5) A direction under this paragraph—

(*a*) must be given by notice in writing to the person named in it,

(*b*) must warn that person of the consequences under section 69B of failing to comply with it, and

(*c*) remains in force until it is revoked or replaced by a further direction.

(6) The Commissioners may require any records kept in pursuance of this paragraph to be preserved for such period not exceeding 6 years as they may require.

(7) [Sub-paragraph (4) of paragraph 6 (preservation of information) applies][2] for the purposes of this paragraph as [it applies][2] for the purposes of that paragraph.

(8) This paragraph is without prejudice to the power conferred by paragraph 6(1) to make regulations requiring records to be kept.

(9) Any records required to be kept by virtue of this paragraph are in addition to any records required to be kept by virtue of paragraph 6.][1]

Amendments—[1] Para 6A inserted by FA 2006 s 21(6) with effect from 19 July 2006.
[2] Words in sub-para (7) substituted by FA 2008 Sch 37 paras 4, 6 with effect from 1 April 2009 (by virtue of SI 2009/402). Sub-para (7) previously read as follows—

"(7) Sub-paragraphs (4) to (6) of paragraph 6 (preservation of information by means approved by the Commissioners) apply for the purposes of this paragraph as they apply for the purposes of that paragraph.".

Furnishing of information and production of documents

7— (1) The Commissioners may by regulations make provision for requiring taxable persons to notify to the Commissioners such particulars of changes in circumstances relating to those persons or any business carried on by them as appear to the Commissioners required for the purpose of keeping the register kept under this Act up to date.

(2) *Every person who is concerned (in whatever capacity) in the supply of goods or services in the course or furtherance of a business or to whom such a supply is made, every person who is concerned*

(in whatever capacity) in the acquisition of goods from another member State and every person who is concerned (in whatever capacity) in the importation of goods from a place outside the member States in the course or furtherance of a business shall—

(a) furnish to the Commissioners, within such time and in such form as they may reasonably require, such information relating to the goods or services or to the supply, acquisition or importation as the Commissioners may reasonably specify; and

(b) upon demand made by an authorised person, produce or cause to be produced for inspection by that person—

(i) at the principal place of business of the person upon whom the demand is made or at such other place as the authorised person may reasonably require, and

(ii) at such time as the authorised person may reasonably require,

any documents relating to the goods or services or to the supply, acquisition or importation.

(3) Where, by virtue of sub-paragraph (2) above, an authorised person has power to require the production of any documents from any such person as is referred to in that sub-paragraph, he shall have the like power to require production of the documents concerned from any other person who appears to the authorised person to be in possession of them; but where any such other person claims a lien on any document produced by him, the production shall be without prejudice to the lien.

(4) For the purposes of this paragraph, the documents relating to the supply of goods or services, to the acquisition of goods from another member State or to the importation of goods from a place outside the member States shall be taken to include any profit and loss account and balance sheet relating to the business in the course of which the goods or services are supplied or the goods are imported or (in the case of an acquisition from another member State) relating to any business or other activities of the person by whom the goods are acquired.

(5) An authorised person may take copies of, or make extracts from, any document produced under sub-paragraph (2) or (3) above.

(6) If it appears to him to be necessary to do so, an authorised person may, at a reasonable time and for a reasonable period, remove any document produced under sub-paragraph (2) or (3) above and shall, on request, provide a receipt for any document so removed; and where a lien is claimed on a document produced under sub-paragraph (3) above the removal of the document under this sub-paragraph shall not be regarded as breaking the lien.

(7) Where a document removed by an authorised person under sub-paragraph (6) above is reasonably required for the proper conduct of a business he shall, as soon as practicable, provide a copy of the document, free of charge, to the person by whom it was produced or caused to be produced.

(8) Where any documents removed under the powers conferred by this paragraph are lost or damaged the Commissioners shall be liable to compensate their owner for any expenses reasonably incurred by him in replacing or repairing the documents.

[(9) For the purposes of this paragraph a person to whom has been assigned a right to receive the whole or any part of the consideration for a supply of goods or services shall be treated as a person concerned in the supply.][1, 2]

Commentary—*De Voil Indirect Tax Service* **V5.234, V5.235.**
Regulations—See VAT Regulations, SI 1995/2518 regs 31, 33.
Simon's Tax Cases—*EMI Records Ltd v Spillane* [1986] STC 374*, *Singh v HM Advocate* [2001] STC 790*.
Definitions—"Acquisition of goods from another member State", s 11; "another member State", s 96(1); "authorised person", s 96(1); "business", s 94; "the Commissioners", s 96(1); "copy", s 96(1); "document", s 96(1); "importation of goods from a place outside the member States" s 15; "regulations", s 96(1); "supply", s 5, Sch 4; "taxable person", s 3.
Cross reference—See VATA 1994 s 69(1) (penalty for breach of a requirement imposed under this para).
Amendments—[1] Sub-para (9) inserted by FA 1999 s 15 with effect from 27 July 1999.
[2] Sub-paras (2)–(9) repealed by FA 2008 s 113, Sch 36 para 87 with effect from 1 April 2009 (by virtue of SI 2009/404 art 2).

Power to take samples

8— (1) An authorised person, if it appears to him necessary for the protection of the revenue against mistake or fraud, may at any time take, from the goods in the possession of any person who supplies goods or acquires goods from another member State [, or in the possession of a fiscal warehouse keeper,][1] such samples as the authorised person may require with a view to determining how the goods or the materials of which they are made ought to be or to have been treated for the purposes of VAT.

(2) Any sample taken under this paragraph shall be disposed of and accounted for in such manner as the Commissioners may direct.

(3) Where a sample is taken under this paragraph from the goods in any person's possession and is not returned to him within a reasonable time and in good condition the Commissioners shall pay him by way of compensation a sum equal to the cost of the sample to him or such larger sum as they may determine.

Commentary—*De Voil Indirect Tax Service* **V5.240.**
Definitions—"Acquires goods from another member State", s 11; "another member State", s 96(1); "authorised person", s 96(1); "the Commissioners", s 96(1); "fiscal warehouse keeper", s 18F(1); "supply", s 5, Sch 4; "VAT", ss 1, 96(1).
Cross reference—See VAT (Isle of Man) Order, SI 1982/1067 art 7 (references to VAT in this para to include references to VAT chargeable under Isle of Man legislation).

Amendments—[1] Words in sub-para (1) inserted by FA 1996 Sch 3 para 16, with effect from 1 June 1996 (see Finance Act 1996, Section 26, (Appointed Day) Order, SI 1996/1249).

Power to require opening of gaming machines

9 An authorised person may at any reasonable time require a person making such a supply as is referred to in section 23(1) or any person acting on his behalf—

(*a*) to open any gaming machine, within the meaning of that section; and

(*b*) to carry out any other operation which may be necessary to enable the authorised person to ascertain the amount which, in accordance with subsection (2) of that section, is to be taken as the value of supplies made in the circumstances mentioned in subsection (1) of that section in any period.

Commentary—*De Voil Indirect Tax Service* **V5.238**.
Definitions—"Authorised person", s 96(1); "supply", s 5, Sch 4; "value of supply", s 19, Sch 6.

Entry and search of premises and persons

10— *(1) For the purpose of exercising any powers under this Act an authorised person may at any reasonable time enter premises used in connection with the carrying on of a business.*

(2) Where an authorised person has reasonable cause to believe that any premises are used in connection with the supply of goods under taxable supplies or with the acquisition of goods under taxable acquisitions from other member States and that goods to be so supplied or acquired are on those premises [, or that any premises are used as a fiscal warehouse,][1] he may at any reasonable time enter and inspect those premises and inspect any goods found on them.

[(2A) The power under sub-paragraph (2) above to inspect any goods includes, in particular,—

(a) power to mark the goods, or anything containing the goods, for the purpose of indicating that they have been inspected, and

(b) power to record any information (which may be obtained by electronic or any other means) relating to the goods that have been inspected.][3, 5]

(3) If a justice of the peace or in Scotland a justice (within the meaning of [section 308 of the Criminal Procedure (Scotland) Act 1995][2]) is satisfied on information on oath that there is reasonable ground for suspecting that a fraud offence which appears to be of a serious nature is being, has been or is about to be committed on any premises or that evidence of the commission of such an offence is to be found there, he may issue a warrant in writing authorising, subject to sub-paragraphs (5) and (6) below, any authorised person to enter those premises, if necessary by force, at any time within one month from the time of the issue of the warrant and search them; and any person who enters the premises under the authority of the warrant may—

(a) take with him such other persons as appear to him to be necessary;

(b) seize and remove any documents or other things whatsoever found on the premises which he has reasonable cause to believe may be required as evidence for the purposes of proceedings in respect of a fraud offence which appears to him to be of a serious nature; and

(c) search or cause to be searched any person found on the premises whom he has reasonable cause to believe to be in possession of any such documents or other things;

but no woman or girl shall be searched except by a woman.

(4) In sub-paragraph (3) above "a fraud offence" means an offence under any provision of section 72(1) to (8).

(5) The powers conferred by a warrant under this paragraph shall not be exercisable—

(a) by more than such number of authorised persons as may be specified in the warrant; nor

(b) outside such times of day as may be so specified; nor

(c) if the warrant so provides, otherwise than in the presence of a constable in uniform.

(6) An authorised person seeking to exercise the powers conferred by a warrant under this paragraph or, if there is more than one such authorised person, that one of them who is in charge of the search shall provide a copy of the warrant endorsed with his name as follows—

(a) if the occupier of the premises concerned is present at the time the search is to begin, the copy shall be supplied to the occupier;

(b) if at that time the occupier is not present but a person who appears to the authorised person to be in charge of the premises is present, the copy shall be supplied to that person; and

(c) if neither paragraph (a) nor paragraph (b) above applies, the copy shall be left in a prominent place on the premises.[4]

Commentary—*De Voil Indirect Tax Service* **V5.231, V5.233**.
Simon's Tax Cases—*R v C&E Comrs and IRC, ex p X Ltd* [1997] STC 1197.
Sub-para (5)(*a*), *Singh v HM Advocate* [2001] STC 790*.
R (oao Paul Da Costa & Co (a firm) v Thames Magistrates Court [2002] STC 267.
Cross references—Criminal Justice and Police Act 2001 s 50, Sch 1 Pt 1 (s 50 of that Act which provides additional powers of seizure from premises applies to the power of seizure conferred under sub-para (3) above).
Definitions—"Acquisition of goods from other member States", s 11; "authorised person", s 96(1); "business", s 94; "copy", s 96(1); "document", s 96(1); "fiscal warehouse", ss 18A(3), 18F(1); "other member State", s 96(1); "supply", s 5, Sch 4; "taxable acquisition", s 10(2); "taxable supply", s 4(2).
Amendments—[1] Words in sub-para (2) inserted by FA 1996 Sch 3 para 17, with effect from 1 June 1996 (see Finance Act 1996, Section 26, (Appointed Day) Order, SI 1996/1249).
[2] Words in sub-para (3) substituted, subject to transitional provisions and savings, by Criminal Procedure (Consequential Provisions)(Scotland) Act 1995 Sch 3, Sch 4 para 91(*a*).

[3] Sub-para (2A) inserted by FA 2006 s 20 with effect from 19 July 2006.
[4] Sub-paras (3)–(6) repealed by FA 2007 ss 84, 114, Sch 22 paras 3, 8(b), Sch 27 Pt 5(1) with effect from 1 December 2007 (by virtue of SI 2007/3166 art 3(*a*)).
[5] Sub-paras (1)–(2A) repealed by FA 2008 s 113, Sch 36 para 87 with effect from 1 April 2009 (by virtue of SI 2009/404 art 2).

Order for access to recorded information etc

11— (1) Where, on an application by an authorised person, a justice of the peace or, in Scotland, a justice (within the meaning of [section 308 of the Criminal Procedure (Scotland) Act 1975][1]) is satisfied that there are reasonable grounds for believing—

(*a*) that an offence in connection with VAT is being, has been or is about to be committed, and

(*b*) that any recorded information (including any document of any nature whatsoever) which may be required as evidence for the purpose of any proceedings in respect of such an offence is in the possession of any person,

he may make an order under this paragraph.

(2) An order under this paragraph is an order that the person who appears to the justice to be in possession of the recorded information to which the application relates shall—

(*a*) give an authorised person access to it, and

(*b*) permit an authorised person to remove and take away any of it which he reasonably considers necessary,

not later than the end of the period of 7 days beginning on the date of the order or the end of such longer period as the order may specify.

(3) The reference in sub-paragraph (2)(*a*) above to giving an authorised person access to the recorded information to which the application relates includes a reference to permitting the authorised person to take copies of it or to make extracts from it.

(4) Where the recorded information consists of information [stored in any electronic form][2], an order under this paragraph shall have effect as an order to produce the information in a form in which it is visible and legible [or from which it can readily be produced in a visible and legible form][2] and, if the authorised person wishes to remove it, in a form in which it can be removed.

(5) This paragraph is without prejudice to paragraphs 7 and 10 above.

Commentary—*De Voil Indirect Tax Service* **V5.236**.
Simon's Tax Cases—*R v Epsom Justices, ex p Bell* [1989] STC 169*; *R v City of London Magistrates, ex p Asif* [1997] STC 141; *C&E Comrs v City of London Magistrates' Court* [2000] STC 447.
Sub-para (1)(*a*), *Singh v HM Advocate* [2001] STC 790*.
Definitions—"Authorised person", s 96(1); "copy", s 96(1); "document", s 96(1); "VAT", ss 1, 96(1).
Amendments—[1] Words in sub-para (1) substituted, subject to transitional provisions and savings by Criminal Procedure (Consequential Provisions) (Scotland) Act 1995 Sch 3, Sch 4 para 91(*b*).
[2] Words in sub-para (4) substituted and inserted by Criminal Justice and Police Act 2001 ss 70, 138, Sch 2 Pt 2 para 13 with effect from 1 April 2003 (by virtue of SI 2003/708).

Procedure where documents etc are removed

12— (1) An authorised person who removes anything in the exercise of a power conferred by or under paragraph 10 or 11 above shall, if so requested by a person showing himself—

(*a*) to be the occupier of premises from which it was removed, or

(*b*) to have had custody or control of it immediately before the removal,

provide that person with a record of what he removed.

(2) The authorised person shall provide the record within a reasonable time from the making of the request for it.

(3) Subject to sub-paragraph (7) below, if a request for permission to be granted access to anything which—

(*a*) has been removed by an authorised person, and

(*b*) is retained by the Commissioners for the purposes of investigating an offence,

is made to the officer in overall charge of the investigation by a person who had custody or control of the thing immediately before it was so removed or by someone acting on behalf of such a person, the officer shall allow the person who made the request access to it under the supervision of an authorised person.

(4) Subject to sub-paragraph (7) below, if a request for a photograph or copy of any such thing is made to the officer in overall charge of the investigation by a person who had custody or control of the thing immediately before it was so removed, or by someone acting on behalf of such a person, the officer shall—

(*a*) allow the person who made the request access to it under the supervision of an authorised person for the purpose of photographing it or copying it, or

(*b*) photograph or copy it, or cause it to be photographed or copied.

(5) Where anything is photographed or copied under sub-paragraph (4)(*b*) above the photograph or copy shall be supplied to the person who made the request.

(6) The photograph or copy shall be supplied within a reasonable time from the making of the request.

(7) There is no duty under this paragraph to grant access to, or to supply a photograph or copy of, anything if the officer in overall charge of the investigation for the purposes of which it was removed has reasonable grounds for believing that to do so would prejudice—

(*a*) that investigation;

(*b*) the investigation of an offence other than the offence for the purposes of the investigation of which the thing was removed; or

(*c*) any criminal proceedings which may be brought as a result of—

(i) the investigation of which he is in charge, or

(ii) any such investigation as is mentioned in paragraph (*b*) above.

(8) Any reference in this paragraph to the officer in overall charge of the investigation is a reference to the person whose name and address are endorsed on the warrant or order concerned as being the officer so in charge.

Commentary—*De Voil Indirect Tax Service* **V5.233, V5.236.**

Definitions—"Authorised person", s 96(1); "the Commissioners", s 96(1); "copy", s 96(1).

13— (1) Where, on an application made as mentioned in sub-paragraph (2) below, the appropriate judicial authority is satisfied that a person has failed to comply with a requirement imposed by paragraph 12 above, the authority may order that person to comply with the requirement within such time and in such manner as may be specified in the order.

(2) An application under sub-paragraph (1) above shall be made—

(*a*) in the case of a failure to comply with any of the requirements imposed by paragraph 12(1) and (2) above, by the occupier of the premises from which the thing in question was removed or by the person who had custody or control of it immediately before it was so removed, and

(*b*) in any other case, by the person who had such custody or control.

(3) In this paragraph "the appropriate judicial authority" means—

(*a*) in England and Wales, a magistrates' court;

(*b*) in Scotland, the sheriff; and

(*c*) in Northern Ireland, a court of summary jurisdiction.

(4) In England and Wales and Northern Ireland, an application for an order under this paragraph shall be made by way of complaint; and sections 21 and 42(2) of the Interpretation Act (Northern Ireland) 1954 shall apply as if any reference in those provisions to any enactment included a reference to this paragraph.

Commentary—*De Voil Indirect Tax Service* **V5.233, V5.236.**

Evidence by certificate, etc

14— (1) A certificate of the Commissioners—

(*a*) that a person was or was not, at any date, registered under this Act; or

(*b*) that any return required by or under this Act has not been made or had not been made at any date; or

(*c*) that any statement or notification required to be submitted or given to the Commissioners in accordance with any regulations under paragraph 2(3) or (4) above has not been submitted or given or had not been submitted or given at any date; [...][1]

(*d*) ...[1]

shall be sufficient evidence of that fact until the contrary is proved.

(2) A photograph of any document furnished to the Commissioners for the purposes of this Act and certified by them to be such a photograph shall be admissible in any proceedings, whether civil or criminal, to the same extent as the document itself.

(3) Any document purporting to be a certificate under sub-paragraph (1) or (2) above shall be deemed to be such a certificate until the contrary is proved.

Commentary—*De Voil Indirect Tax Service* **V5.457.**

Definitions—"The Commissioners", s 96(1); "document", s 96(1); "registered", s 3(3); "regulations", s 96(1); "VAT", ss 1, 96(1).

Amendments—[1] Sub-para (1)(*d*) and preceding word "or" repealed by FA 2008 s 138, Sch 44 para 6 with effect from 21 July 2008. Sub-para (1)(*d*) previously read as follows

"(*d*) that any VAT shown as due in any return or assessment made in pursuance of this Act has not been paid;".

[SCHEDULE 11A
DISCLOSURE OF AVOIDANCE SCHEMES][1]

Section 51B

Commentary—*De Voil Indirect Tax Service* **V5.213, 358.**

Amendments—[1] Schedule inserted by FA 2004 s 19, Sch 2 para 2 with effect from the passing of FA 2004 so far as is necessary for enabling the making of any orders or regulations by virtue of FA 2004 Sch 2, and otherwise with effect from 1 August 2004 (by virtue of SI 2004/1934).

VAT

[Interpretation

1 In this Schedule—

"designated scheme" has the meaning given by paragraph 3(4);

["non-deductible tax", in relation to a taxable person, has the meaning given by paragraph 2A;][2]

"notifiable scheme" has the meaning given by paragraph 5(1);

"scheme" includes any arrangements, transaction or series of transactions;

"tax advantage" is to be read in accordance with paragraph 2.][1]

Amendments—[1] Schedule inserted by FA 2004 s 19, Sch 2 para 2 with effect from the passing of FA 2004, so far as is necessary for enabling the making of any orders or regulations by virtue of FA 2004 Sch 2, and otherwise with effect from 1 August 2004 (by virtue of SI 2004/1934).

[2] Definition of "non-deductible tax" inserted by F(No 2)A 2005 s 6, Sch 1 paras 1, 2 with effect from 1 August 2005, by virtue of SI 2005/2010 art 2, subject to savings in arts 3, 4.

[Obtaining a tax advantage

[2— (1) For the purposes of this Schedule, a taxable person obtains a tax advantage if—

(*a*) in any prescribed accounting period, the amount by which the output tax accounted for by him exceeds the input tax deducted by him is less than it would otherwise be,

(*b*) he obtains a VAT credit when he would not otherwise do so, or obtains a larger VAT credit or obtains a VAT credit earlier than would otherwise be the case,

(*c*) in a case where he recovers input tax as a recipient of a supply before the supplier accounts for the output tax, the period between the time when the input tax is recovered and the time when the output tax is accounted for is greater than would otherwise be the case, or

(*d*) in any prescribed accounting period, the amount of his non-deductible tax is less than it would otherwise be.

(2) For the purposes of this Schedule, a person who is not a taxable person obtains a tax advantage if his non-refundable tax is less than it would otherwise be.

(3) In sub-paragraph (2), "non-refundable tax", in relation to a person who is not a taxable person, means—

(*a*) VAT on the supply to him of any goods or services,

(*b*) VAT on the acquisition by him from another member State of any goods, and

(*c*) VAT paid or payable by him on the importation of any goods from a place outside the member States,

but excluding (in each case) any VAT in respect of which he is entitled to a refund from the Commissioners by virtue of any provision of this Act.][2]][1]

Amendments—[1] Schedule inserted by FA 2004 s 19, Sch 2 para 2 with effect from the passing of FA 2004, so far as is necessary for enabling the making of any orders or regulations by virtue of FA 2004 Sch 2, and otherwise with effect from 1 August 2004 (by virtue of SI 2004/1934).

[2] This paragraph substituted by F(No 2)A 2005 s 6, Sch 1 paras 1, 3 with effect from 1 August 2005 (by virtue of SI 2005/2010 art 2, subject to savings in arts 3, 4).

[Meaning of "non-deductible tax"

2A— (1) In this Schedule "non-deductible tax", in relation to a taxable person, means—

(*a*) input tax for which he is not entitled to credit under section 25, and

(*b*) any VAT incurred by him which is not input tax and in respect of which he is not entitled to a refund from the Commissioners by virtue of any provision of this Act.

(2) For the purposes of sub-paragraph (1)(*b*), the VAT "incurred" by a taxable person is—

(*a*) VAT on the supply to him of any goods or services,

(*b*) VAT on the acquisition by him from another member State of any goods, and

(*c*) VAT paid or payable by him on the importation of any goods from a place outside the member States.][1]

Amendments—[1] Paragraph 2A inserted by F(No 2)A 2005 s 6, Sch 1 paras 1, 4 with effect from 1 August 2005 (by virtue of SI 2005/2010 art 2, subject to savings in arts 3, 4).

[Designation by order of avoidance schemes

3— (1) If it appears to the Treasury—

(*a*) that a scheme of a particular description has been, or might be, entered into for the purpose of enabling any person to obtain a tax advantage, and

(*b*) that it is unlikely that persons would enter into a scheme of that description unless the main purpose, or one of the main purposes, of doing so was the obtaining by any person of a tax advantage,

the Treasury may by order designate that scheme for the purposes of this paragraph.

(2) A scheme may be designated for the purposes of this paragraph even though the Treasury are of the opinion that no scheme of that description could as a matter of law result in the obtaining by any person of a tax advantage.

(3) The order must allocate a reference number to each scheme.

(4) In this Schedule "designated scheme" means a scheme of a description designated for the purposes of this paragraph.][1]

Orders—See VAT (Disclosure of Avoidance Schemes) (Designations) Order, SI 2004/1933.

Amendments—[1] Schedule inserted by FA 2004 s 19, Sch 2 para 2 with effect from the passing of FA 2004, so far as is necessary for enabling the making of any orders or regulations by virtue of FA 2004 Sch 2, and otherwise with effect from 1 August 2004 (by virtue of SI 2004/1934).

[Designation by order of provisions included in or associated with avoidance schemes

4— (1) If it appears to the Treasury that a provision of a particular description is, or is likely to be, included in or associated with schemes that are entered into for the purpose of enabling any person to obtain a tax advantage, the Treasury may by order designate that provision for the purposes of this paragraph.

(2) A provision may be designated under this paragraph even though it also appears to the Treasury that the provision is, or is likely to be, included in or associated with schemes that are not entered into for the purpose of obtaining a tax advantage.

(3) In this paragraph "provision" includes any agreement, transaction, act or course of conduct.][1]

Orders—

See VAT (Disclosure of Avoidance Schemes) (Designations) Order, SI 2004/1933.

Amendments—[1] Schedule inserted by FA 2004 s 19, Sch 2 para 2 with effect from the passing of FA 2004, so far as is necessary for enabling the making of any orders or regulations by virtue of FA 2004 Sch 2, and otherwise with effect from 1 August 2004 (by virtue of SI 2004/1934).

[Meaning of "notifiable scheme"

5— (1) For the purposes of this Schedule, a scheme is a "notifiable scheme" if—

(*a*) it is a designated scheme, or

(*b*) although it is not a designated scheme, conditions A and B below are met in relation to it.

(2) Condition A is that the scheme includes, or is associated with, a provision of a description designated under paragraph 4.

(3) Condition B is that the scheme has as its main purpose, or one of its main purposes, the obtaining of a tax advantage by any person.][1]

Amendments—[1] Schedule inserted by FA 2004 s 19, Sch 2 para 2 with effect from the passing of FA 2004, so far as is necessary for enabling the making of any orders or regulations by virtue of FA 2004 Sch 2, and otherwise with effect from 1 August 2004 (by virtue of SI 2004/1934).

[Duty to notify Commissioners

6— (1) This paragraph applies in relation to a taxable person where—

(*a*) the amount of VAT shown in a return in respect of a prescribed accounting period as payable by or to him is less than or greater than it would be but for any notifiable scheme to which he is party, ...[2]

(*b*) he makes a claim for the repayment of output tax or an increase in credit for input tax in respect of any prescribed accounting period in respect of which he has previously delivered a return and the amount claimed is greater than it would be but for such a scheme[, or

(*c*) the amount of his non-deductible tax in respect of any prescribed accounting period is less than it would be but for such a scheme.][2]

(2) Where the scheme is a designated scheme, the taxable person must notify the Commissioners within the prescribed time, and in such form and manner as may be required by or under regulations, of the reference number allocated to the scheme under paragraph 3(3).

[(2A) Sub-paragraph (2) does not apply to a taxable person in relation to any scheme if he has on a previous occasion—

(*a*) notified the Commissioners under that sub-paragraph in relation to the scheme, or

(*b*) provided the Commissioners with prescribed information under sub-paragraph (3) (as it applied before the scheme became a designated scheme) in relation to the scheme.][2]

(3) Where the scheme is not a designated scheme, the taxable person must, subject to sub-paragraph (4), provide the Commissioners within the prescribed time, and in such form and manner as may be required by or under regulations, with prescribed information relating to the scheme.

(4) Sub-paragraph (3) does not apply where the scheme is one in respect of which any person has previously—

(*a*) provided the Commissioners with prescribed information under paragraph 9, and

(*b*) provided the taxable person with a reference number notified to him by the Commissioners under paragraph 9(2)(*b*).

[(5) Sub-paragraph (3) also does not apply where the scheme is one in respect of which the taxable person has on a previous occasion provided the Commissioners with prescribed information under that sub-paragraph.][2]

(6) This paragraph has effect subject to paragraph 7.][1]

Orders—See VAT (Disclosure of Avoidance Schemes) Regulations, SI 2004/1929.

Amendments—[1] Schedule inserted by FA 2004 s 19, Sch 2 para 2 with effect from the passing of FA 2004, so far as is necessary for enabling the making of any orders or regulations by virtue of FA 2004 Sch 2, and otherwise with effect from 1 August 2004 (by virtue of SI 2004/1934).

[2] Word "or" in sub-para (1)(*a*) repealed; sub-paras (1)(*c*), (2A) inserted; and sub-para (5) substituted; by F(No 2)A 2005 ss 6, 70, Sch 1 paras 1, 5, Sch 11 Pt 1 with effect from 1 August 2005 (by virtue of SI 2005/2010 art 2, subject to savings in arts 3, 4). Paragraph 6(1)(*c*) shall not apply in relation to any prescribed accounting period beginning before 1 August 2005.

[Exemptions from duty to notify under paragraph 6

7— (1) Paragraph 6 does not apply to a taxable person in relation to a scheme—

(*a*) where the taxable person is not a group undertaking in relation to any other undertaking and conditions A and B below, as they have effect in relation to the scheme, are met in relation to the taxable person, or

(*b*) where the taxable person is a group undertaking in relation to any other undertaking and conditions A and B below, as they have effect in relation to the scheme, are met in relation to the taxable person and every other group undertaking.

(2) Condition A is that the total value of the person's taxable supplies and exempt supplies in the period of twelve months ending immediately before the beginning of the relevant period is less than the minimum turnover.

(3) Condition B is that the total value of the person's taxable supplies and exempt supplies in the prescribed accounting period immediately preceding the relevant period is less than the appropriate proportion of the minimum turnover.

(4) In sub-paragraphs (2) and (3) "the minimum turnover" means—

(*a*) in relation to a designated scheme, £600,000, and

(*b*) in relation to any other notifiable scheme, £10,000,000.

(5) In sub-paragraph (3) "the appropriate proportion" means the proportion which the length of the prescribed accounting period bears to twelve months.

(6) The value of a supply of goods or services shall be determined for the purposes of this paragraph on the basis that no VAT is chargeable on the supply.

(7) The Treasury may by order substitute for the sum for the time being specified in sub-paragraph (4)(*a*) or (*b*) such other sum as they think fit.

(8) This paragraph has effect subject to paragraph 8.

(9) In this paragraph—

"relevant period" means the prescribed accounting period referred to in paragraph [6(1)(*a*), (*b*) or (*c*)][2];

"undertaking" and "group undertaking" have the same meanings as in [section 1161 of the Companies Act 2006][3].][1]

Amendments—[1] Schedule inserted by FA 2004 s 19, Sch 2 para 2 with effect from the passing of FA 2004, so far as is necessary for enabling the making of any orders or regulations by virtue of FA 2004 Sch 2, and otherwise with effect from 1 August 2004 (by virtue of SI 2004/1934).

[2] In the definition of "relevant period", words substituted for the words "6(1)(*a*) or (*b*)" by F(No 2)A 2005 s 6, Sch 1 paras 1, 6 with effect from 1 August 2005 (by virtue of SI 2005/2010 art 2, subject to savings in arts 3, 4).

[3] Words in sub-para (9) substituted by the Companies Act 2006 (Consequential Amendments) (Taxes and National Insurance) Order, SI 2008/954 art 20 with effect from 6 April 2008.

[Power to exclude exemption

8— (1) The purpose of this paragraph is to prevent the maintenance or creation of any artificial separation of business activities carried on by two or more persons from resulting in an avoidance of the obligations imposed by paragraph 6.

(2) In determining for the purposes of sub-paragraph (1) whether any separation of business activities is artificial, regard shall be had to the extent to which the different persons carrying on those activities are closely bound to one another by financial, economic and organisational links.

(3) If the Commissioners make a direction under this section—

(*a*) the persons named in the direction shall be treated for the purposes of paragraph 7 as a single taxable person carrying on the activities of a business described in the direction with effect from the date of the direction or, if the direction so provides, from such later date as may be specified in the direction, and

(*b*) if paragraph 7 would not exclude the application of paragraph 6, in respect of any notifiable scheme, to that single taxable person, it shall not exclude the application of paragraph 6, in respect of that scheme, to the persons named in the direction.

(4) The Commissioners shall not make a direction under this section naming any person unless they are satisfied—

(*a*) that he is making or has made taxable or exempt supplies,

(*b*) that the activities in the course of which he makes those supplies form only part of certain activities, the other activities being carried on concurrently or previously (or both) by one or more other persons, and

(*c*) that, if all the taxable and exempt supplies of the business described in the direction were taken into account, conditions A and B in paragraph 7(2) and (3), as those conditions have effect in relation to designated schemes, would not be met in relation to that business.

(5) A direction under this paragraph shall be served on each of the persons named in it.

(6) A direction under this paragraph remains in force until it is revoked or replaced by a further direction.][1]

Amendments—[1] Schedule inserted by FA 2004 s 19, Sch 2 para 2 with effect from the passing of FA 2004, so far as is necessary for enabling the making of any orders or regulations by virtue of FA 2004 Sch 2, and otherwise with effect from 1 August 2004 (by virtue of SI 2004/1934).

[Voluntary notification of avoidance scheme that is not designated scheme

9— (1) Any person may, at any time, provide the Commissioners with prescribed information relating to a scheme or proposed scheme of a particular description which is (or, if implemented, would be) a notifiable scheme by virtue of paragraph 5(1)(*b*).

(2) On receiving the prescribed information, the Commissioners may—

(*a*) allocate a reference number to the scheme (if they have not previously done so under this paragraph), and

(*b*) notify the person who provided the information of the number allocated.][1]

Orders—

See VAT (Disclosure of Avoidance Schemes) Regulations, SI 2004/1929.

Amendments—[1] Schedule inserted by FA 2004 s 19, Sch 2 para 2 with effect from the passing of FA 2004, so far as is necessary for enabling the making of any orders or regulations by virtue of FA 2004 Sch 2, and otherwise with effect from 1 August 2004 (by virtue of SI 2004/1934).

[Penalty for failure to notify use of notifiable scheme

10— (1) A person who fails to comply with paragraph 6 shall be liable, subject to sub-paragraphs (2) and (3), to a penalty of an amount determined under paragraph 11.

(2) Conduct falling within sub-paragraph (1) shall not give rise to liability to a penalty under this paragraph if the person concerned satisfies the Commissioners or, on appeal, a tribunal that there is a reasonable excuse for the failure.

(3) Where, by reason of conduct falling within sub-paragraph (1)—

(*a*) a person is convicted of an offence (whether under this Act or otherwise), or

(*b*) a person is assessed to a penalty under section 60 [or a penalty for a deliberate inaccuracy under Schedule 24 to the Finance Act 2007][2],

that conduct shall not give rise to a penalty under this paragraph.][1]

Amendments—[1] Schedule inserted by FA 2004 s 19, Sch 2 para 2 with effect from the passing of FA 2004, so far as is necessary for enabling the making of any orders or regulations by virtue of FA 2004 Sch 2, and otherwise with effect from 1 August 2004 (by virtue of SI 2004/1934).

[2] Words in sub-para (3)(*b*) inserted by the Finance Act 2008, Schedule 40 (Appointed Day, Transitional Provisions and Consequential Amendments) Order, SI 2009/571 art 8, Sch 1 paras 22, 27 with effect from 1 April 2009.

[Amount of penalty

11— (1) Where the failure mentioned in paragraph 10(1) relates to a notifiable scheme that is not a designated scheme, the amount of the penalty is £5,000.

(2) Where the failure mentioned in paragraph 10(1) relates to a designated scheme, the amount of the penalty is 15 per cent. of the VAT saving (as determined under sub-paragraph (3)).

(3) For this purpose the VAT saving is—

(*a*) to the extent that the case falls within paragraph 6(1)(*a*), the aggregate of—

(i) the amount by which the amount of VAT that would, but for the scheme, have been shown in returns in respect of the relevant periods as payable by the taxable person exceeds the amount of VAT that was shown in those returns as payable by him, and

(ii) the amount by which the amount of VAT that was shown in such returns as payable to the taxable person exceeds the amount of VAT that would, but for the scheme, have been shown in those returns as payable to him, . . .[2]

(*b*) to the extent that the case falls within paragraph 6(1)(*b*), the amount by which the amount claimed exceeds the amount which the taxable person would, but for the scheme, have claimed[, and

(*c*) to the extent that—

(i) the case falls within paragraph 6(1)(*c*), and

(ii) the excess of the notional non-deductible tax of the taxable person for the relevant periods over his non-deductible tax for those periods is not represented by a corresponding amount which by virtue of paragraph (*a*) or (*b*) is part of the VAT saving,

the amount of the excess.][2]

(4) In sub-paragraph (3)(*a*) [and (*c*)][2] "the relevant periods" means the prescribed accounting periods beginning with that in respect of which the duty to comply with paragraph 6 first arose and ending with the earlier of the following—

(*a*) the prescribed accounting period in which the taxable person complied with that paragraph, and

(*b*) the prescribed accounting period immediately preceding the notification by the Commissioners of the penalty assessment.][1]

[(5) In sub-paragraph (3)(*c*), "notional non-deductible tax", in relation to a taxable person, means the amount that would, but for the scheme, have been the amount of his non-deductible tax.][2]

Amendments—[1] Schedule inserted by FA 2004 s 19, Sch 2 para 2 with effect from the passing of FA 2004, so far as is necessary for enabling the making of any orders or regulations by virtue of FA 2004 Sch 2, and otherwise with effect from 1 August 2004 (by virtue of SI 2004/1934).

[2] Word "and" in sub-para (3)(*a*) repealed; sub-para (3)(*c*) inserted; words in sub-para (4) inserted; and sub-para (5) inserted; by F(No 2)A 2005 ss 6, 70, Sch 1 paras 1, 7, Sch 11 Pt 1 with effect from 1 August 2005 (by virtue of SI 2005/2010 art 2, subject to savings in arts 3, 4).

[Penalty assessments

12— (1) Where any person is liable under paragraph 10 to a penalty of an amount determined under paragraph 11, the Commissioners may, subject to sub-paragraph (3), assess the amount due by way of penalty and notify it to him accordingly.

(2) The fact that any conduct giving rise to a penalty under paragraph 10 may have ceased before an assessment is made under this paragraph shall not affect the power of the Commissioners to make such an assessment.

[(3) In a case where—

(*a*) the penalty falls to be calculated by reference to the VAT saving as determined under paragraph 11(3), and

(*b*) the notional tax cannot readily be attributed to any one or more prescribed accounting periods,

the notional tax shall be treated for the purposes of this Schedule as attributable to such period or periods as the Commissioners may determine to the best of their judgment and notify to the person liable for the penalty.][2]

[(3A) In sub-paragraph (3) "the notional tax" means—

(*a*) the VAT that would, but for the scheme, have been shown in returns as payable by or to the taxable person, or

(*b*) any amount that would, but for the scheme, have been the amount of the non-deductible tax of the taxable person.][2]

(4) No assessment to a penalty under this paragraph shall be made more than two years from the time when facts sufficient, in the opinion of the Commissioners, to indicate that there has been a failure to comply with paragraph 6 in relation to a notifiable scheme came to the Commissioners' knowledge.

(5) Where the Commissioners notify a person of a penalty in accordance with sub-paragraph (1), the notice of assessment shall specify—

(*a*) the amount of the penalty,

(*b*) the reasons for the imposition of the penalty,

(*c*) how the penalty has been calculated, and

(*d*) any reduction of the penalty in accordance with section 70.

(6) Where a person is assessed under this paragraph to an amount due by way of penalty and is also assessed under section 73(1), (2), (7), (7A) or (7B) for any of the prescribed accounting periods to which the assessment under this paragraph relates, the assessments may be combined and notified to him as one assessment, but the amount of the penalty shall be separately identified in the notice.

(7) If an amount is assessed and notified to any person under this paragraph, then unless, or except to the extent that, the assessment is withdrawn or reduced, that amount shall be recoverable as if it were VAT due from him.

(8) Subsection (10) of section 76 (notification to certain persons acting for others) applies for the purposes of this paragraph as it applies for the purposes of that section.][1]

Amendments—[1] Schedule inserted by FA 2004 s 19, Sch 2 para 2 with effect from the passing of FA 2004, so far as is necessary for enabling the making of any orders or regulations by virtue of FA 2004 Sch 2, and otherwise with effect from 1 August 2004 (by virtue of SI 2004/1934).

[2] Sub-paras (3), (3A) substituted for sub-para (3) by F(No 2)A 2005 s 6, Sch 1 paras 1, 8 with effect from 1 August 2005 (by virtue of SI 2005/2010 art 2, subject to savings in arts 3, 4).

[**13** Regulations under this Schedule—

(*a*) may make different provision for different circumstances, and

(*b*) may include transitional provisions or savings.] [1]

Orders—See VAT (Disclosure of Avoidance Schemes) Regulations, SI 2004/1929.

Amendments—[1] Schedule inserted by FA 2004 s 19, Sch 2 para 2 with effect from the passing of FA 2004, so far as is necessary for enabling the making of any orders or regulations by virtue of FA 2004 Sch 2, and otherwise with effect from 1 August 2004 (by virtue of SI 2004/1934).

SCHEDULE 12

CONSTITUTION AND PROCEDURE OF TRIBUNALS[1]

Section 61

Note—The term "VAT and duties tribunals" substituted for "VAT tribunals" throughout Schedule 12, from 1 September 1994, by virtue of Sch 12 para 1(2).

Amendments—[1] This schedule repealed by the Transfer of Tribunal Functions and Revenue and Customs Appeals Order, SI 2009/56 art 3, Sch 1 para 228 with effect from 1 April 2009, subject to transitional and savings provisions in Sch 3 para 4.

Establishment of tribunals

1— *(1) There shall continue to be tribunals for England and Wales, Scotland and Northern Ireland respectively known as [VAT and duties tribunals].*

(2) If section 7(1) and (2) of the Finance Act 1994 have come into force before this Schedule comes into force then for any reference in this Schedule to VAT tribunals there shall, as from the commencement of this Schedule, be substituted a reference to VAT and duties tribunals.

(3) If sub-paragraph (2) above does not apply, then, as from a day to be appointed by order made by the Commissioners by statutory instrument for the purposes of this paragraph, for any reference in this Schedule to VAT tribunals there shall be substituted a reference to VAT and duties tribunals.

(4) Any reference in any enactment or any subordinate legislation to a value added tax tribunal (or to a [VAT and duties tribunal]) shall be construed in accordance with paragraphs (1) to (3) above, and cognate expressions shall be construed similarly.[1]

Commentary—*De Voil Indirect Tax Service* **V1.288**.
Definitions—"The Commissioners", s 96(1); "subordinate legislation", s 96(1); "tribunal", s 82; "VAT", ss 1, 96(1).
Amendment—[1] This schedule repealed by the Transfer of Tribunal Functions and Revenue and Customs Appeals Order, SI 2009/56 art 3, Sch 1 para 228 with effect from 1 April 2009, subject to transitional and savings provisions in Sch 3 para 4.

The President

2— *(1) There shall continue to be a President of [VAT and duties tribunals], who shall perform the functions conferred on him by the following provisions of this Schedule in relation to [VAT and duties tribunals] in any part of the United Kingdom.*

(2) The President shall be appointed by the Lord Chancellor after consultation with the [Secretary of State][1] *and shall be—*

[(a) a person who satisfies the judicial-appointment eligibility condition on a 7-year basis;][2]
(b) an advocate or solicitor in Scotland of at least [7][2] *years' standing; or*
(c) a member of the Bar of Northern Ireland or solicitor of the Supreme Court of Northern Ireland of at least [7][2] *years' standing.*

(3) Subject to paragraph 3 below, the appointment of the President shall be for such term and subject to such conditions as may be determined by the Lord Chancellor, after consultation with the [Secretary of State][1]*, and a person who ceases to hold the office of President shall be eligible for re-appointment thereto.*[3]

Commentary—*De Voil Indirect Tax Service* **V1.241**.
Definitions—"Tribunal", s 82; "United Kingdom", s 96(11); "VAT", ss 1, 96(1).
Amendments—[1] Words substituted by the Transfer of Functions (Lord Advocate and Secretary of State) Order, SI 1999/678 with effect from 19 May 1999.
[2] Sub-para (2)(*a*) substituted, and in sub-para (2)(*b*), (*c*) figure "7" substituted for figure "10", by the Tribunals, Courts and Enforcement Act 2007 s 50, Sch 10 para 24 with effect from 21 July 2008 (by virtue of SI 2008/1653 art 2(*d*)). Sub-s (2)(*a*) previously read as follows—
"(*a*) a person who has a 10 year general qualification, within the meaning of section 71 of the Courts and Legal Services Act 1990;"
[3] This schedule repealed by the Transfer of Tribunal Functions and Revenue and Customs Appeals Order, SI 2009/56 art 3, Sch 1 para 228 with effect from 1 April 2009, subject to transitional and savings provisions in Sch 3 para 4.

3— *(1) The President may resign his office at any time and shall vacate his office—*

(a) at the end of the completed year of service in which he attains the age of 72, or
(b) if sub-paragraph (2) below applies, on the date on which he attains the age of 75.

This sub-paragraph shall cease to have effect on the day appointed under section 31 of the Judicial Pensions and Retirement Act 1993 ("the 1993 Act") for the coming into force of section 26 of that Act.

(2) If the Lord Chancellor, after consultation with the [Secretary of State][1]*, considers it desirable in the public interest to do so he may authorise the President to continue in office after the end of the completed year of service mentioned in sub-paragraph (1)(a) above.*

(3) The President—

(a) may resign his office at any time; and
(b) shall vacate his office on the day on which he attains the age of 70;

but sub-paragraph (b) above is subject to section 26(4) to (6) of the 1993 Act (power to authorise continuance in office up to the age of 75).

This sub-paragraph shall come into force on the day appointed under section 31 of the 1993 Act for the coming into force of section 26 of that Act.

(4) The Lord Chancellor may, if he thinks fit and after consultation with the [Secretary of State][1]*, remove the President from office on the ground of incapacity or misbehaviour.*

(5) The functions of the President may, if he is for any reason unable to act or his office is vacant, be discharged by a person nominated for the purpose by the Lord Chancellor after consultation with the [Secretary of State][1]*.*

[(5A) The Lord Chancellor may remove a person from office under sub-paragraph (4), or nominate a person under sub-paragraph (5), only with the concurrence of all of the following—

(a) the Lord Chief Justice of England and Wales;

(b) the Lord President of the Court of Session;

(c) the Lord Chief Justice of Northern Ireland.][2]

(6) There shall be paid to the President such salary or fees and there may be paid to or in respect of a former President such pension, allowance or gratuity as the Lord Chancellor may with the approval of the Treasury determine.

(7) Sub-paragraph (6) above, so far as relating to pensions allowances and gratuities, shall not have effect in relation to a person to whom Part I of the 1993 Act applies, except to the extent provided under or by that Act.

(8) If a person ceases to be President of [VAT and duties tribunals] and it appears to the Lord Chancellor that there are special circumstances which make it right that he should receive compensation, there may be paid to that person a sum of such amount as the Lord Chancellor may with the approval of the Treasury determine.

[(9) The Lord Chief Justice of England and Wales may nominate a judicial office holder (as defined in section 109(4) of the Constitutional Reform Act 2005) to exercise his functions under sub-paragraph (5A) in relation to the nomination of a person under sub-paragraph (5).

(10) The Lord President of the Court of Session may nominate a judge of the Court of Session who is a member of the First or Second Division of the Inner House of that Court to exercise his functions under sub-paragraph (5A) in relation to the nomination of a person under sub-paragraph (5).

(11) The Lord Chief Justice of Northern Ireland may nominate any of the following to exercise his functions under sub-paragraph (5A) in relation to the nomination of a person under sub-paragraph (5)—

(a) the holder of one of the offices listed in Schedule 1 to the Justice (Northern Ireland) Act 2002;

(b) a Lord Justice of Appeal (as defined in section 88 of that Act)][2].[3]

Commentary—*De Voil Indirect Tax Service* **V1.241**.
Definitions—"Tribunal", s 82; "VAT", ss 1, 96(1).
Amendments—[1] Words substituted by the Transfer of Functions (Lord Advocate and Secretary of State) Order, SI 1999/678 with effect from 19 May 1999.
[2] Sub-paras (5A), (9)–(11) inserted by the Constitutional Reform Act 2005 s 15, Sch 4 paras 235, 237(1), (2) with effect from 3 April 2006 by virtue of SI 2006/1014 art 2(*a*), Sch 1 para 11.
[3] This schedule repealed by the Transfer of Tribunal Functions and Revenue and Customs Appeals Order, SI 2009/56 art 3, Sch 1 para 228 with effect from 1 April 2009, subject to transitional and savings provisions in Sch 3 para 4.

Sittings of tribunals

4— [*(1)] Such number of [VAT and duties tribunals] shall be established as the Lord Chancellor or, in relation to Scotland, the Secretary of State may from time to time determine, and they shall sit at such times and at such places as the Lord Chancellor or, as the case may be, the Secretary of State may from time to time determine.*

[(2) The powers of the Lord Chancellor under sub-paragraph (1) may be exercised—

(a) in relation to England and Wales only after consulting the Lord Chief Justice of England and Wales;

(b) in relation to Northern Ireland only after consulting the Lord Chief Justice of Northern Ireland.

(3) The Lord Chief Justice of England and Wales may nominate a judicial office holder (as defined in section 109(4) of the Constitutional Reform Act 2005) to exercise his functions under this paragraph.

(4) The Lord Chief Justice of Northern Ireland may nominate any of the following to exercise his functions under this paragraph—

(a) the holder of one of the offices listed in Schedule 1 to the Justice (Northern Ireland) Act 2002;

(b) a Lord Justice of Appeal (as defined in section 88 of that Act).][1], [2]

Commentary—*De Voil Indirect Tax Service* **V1.241**.
Definitions—"Tribunal", s 82; "VAT", ss 1, 96(1).
Amendments—[1] Paragraph renumbered as sub-para (1), and sub-paras (2)–(4) inserted, by the Constitutional Reform Act 2005 s 15, Sch 4 paras 235, 237(1), (3) with effect from 3 April 2006, by virtue of SI 2006/1014 art 2(*a*), Sch 1 para 11.
[2] This schedule repealed by the Transfer of Tribunal Functions and Revenue and Customs Appeals Order, SI 2009/56 art 3, Sch 1 para 228 with effect from 1 April 2009, subject to transitional and savings provisions in Sch 3 para 4.

Composition of tribunals

5— *(1) A [VAT and duties tribunal] shall consist of a chairman sitting either with two other members or with one other member or alone.*

(2) If the tribunal does not consist of the chairman sitting alone, its decisions may be taken by a majority of votes and the chairman, if sitting with one other member, shall have a casting vote.[1]

Commentary—*De Voil Indirect Tax Service* **V1.241**.
Simon's Tax Cases—Sub-para (2), *Rahman (T/A Khayam Restaurant) v C&E Comrs* [1998] STC 826.

Definitions—"Tribunal", s 82; "VAT", ss 1, 96(1).

Amendment—[1] This schedule repealed by the Transfer of Tribunal Functions and Revenue and Customs Appeals Order, SI 2009/56 art 3, Sch 1 para 228 with effect from 1 April 2009, subject to transitional and savings provisions in Sch 3 para 4.

Membership of tribunals

6 *For each sitting of a [VAT and duties tribunal] the chairman shall be either the President or if so authorised by the President, a member of the appropriate panel of chairmen constituted in accordance with paragraph 7 below; and any other member of the tribunal shall be a person selected from the appropriate panel of other members so constituted, the selection being made either by the President or by a member of the panel of chairmen, authorised by the President to make it.*[1]

Commentary—*De Voil Indirect Tax Service* **V1.241**.

Definitions—"Document", s 96(1); "subordinate legislation", s 96(1); "tribunal", s 82; "VAT", ss 1, 96(1).

Amendment—[1] This schedule repealed by the Transfer of Tribunal Functions and Revenue and Customs Appeals Order, SI 2009/56 art 3, Sch 1 para 228 with effect from 1 April 2009, subject to transitional and savings provisions in Sch 3 para 4.

7— *(1) There shall be a panel of chairmen and a panel of other members of [VAT and duties tribunals] for England and Wales, Scotland and Northern Ireland respectively.*

(2) One member of each panel of chairmen shall be known as Vice-President of [VAT and duties tribunals].

(3) Appointments to a panel of chairmen shall be made by the appropriate authority, that is to say—

(a) for England and Wales, the Lord Chancellor;
(b) for Scotland, the Lord President of the Court of Session; and
(c) for Northern Ireland, the [Lord Chancellor][1]*;*

and appointments to a panel of other members shall be made by the Treasury.

(4) No person may be appointed to a panel of chairmen of tribunals for England and Wales or Northern Ireland unless he is—

[(a) a person who satisfies the judicial-appointment eligibility condition on a 5-year basis; or][2]
(b) a member of the Bar of Northern Ireland or solicitor of the Supreme Court of Northern Ireland of at least [5][2] *years' standing,*

and no person may be appointed to a panel of chairmen of tribunals for Scotland unless he is an advocate or solicitor of not less than [5][2] *years' standing.*

(5) Subject to the following provisions of this paragraph, the appointment of a chairman of [VAT and duties tribunals] shall be for such term and subject to such conditions as may be determined by the appropriate authority, and a person who ceases to hold the office of chairman shall be eligible for re-appointment thereto.

(6) A chairman of [VAT and duties tribunals]—

(a) may resign his office at any time; and
(b) shall vacate his office on the day on which he attains the age of 70 years;

but paragraph (b) above is subject to section 26(4) to (6) of the Judicial Pensions and Retirement Act 1993 (power to authorise continuance in office up to the age of 75).

(7) The appropriate authority may, if he thinks fit, remove a chairman of [VAT and duties tribunals] from office on the ground of incapacity or misbehaviour.

[(7A) The Lord Chancellor may, with the concurrence of the Lord Chief Justice of England and Wales, remove from office on the ground of incapacity or misbehaviour a chairman of VAT Tribunals appointed under sub-paragraph (3)(a).

(7B) The Lord President of the Court of Session may remove from office on the ground of incapacity or misbehaviour a chairman of VAT Tribunals appointed under sub-paragraph (3)(b).][1]

(8) There shall be paid to a chairman of [VAT and duties tribunals] such salary or fees, and to other members such fees, as the Lord Chancellor may with the approval of the Treasury determine; and there may be paid to or in respect of a former chairman of [VAT and duties tribunals] such pension, allowance or gratuity as the Lord Chancellor may with the approval of the Treasury determine.

(9) Sub-paragraph (8) above, so far as relating to pensions allowances and gratuities, shall not have effect in relation to a person to whom Part I of the Judicial Pensions and Retirement Act 1993 applies, except to the extent provided under or by that Act.

(10) If a person ceases to be a chairman of [VAT and duties tribunals] and it appears to the Lord Chancellor that there are special circumstances which make it right that he should receive compensation, there may be paid to that person a sum of such amount as the Lord Chancellor may with the approval of the Treasury determine.[3]

Commentary—*De Voil Indirect Tax Service* **V1.241**.

Definitions—"Tribunal", s 82; "VAT", ss 1, 96(1).

Amendments—[1] In sub-para (3)(*c*), words substituted for words "Lord Chief Justice of Northern Ireland"; and sub-paras (7A), (7B) substituted for former sub-para (7); by the Constitutional Reform Act 2005 s 15, Sch 4 paras 235, 237(1), (4) with from 3 April 2006, by virtue of SI 2006/1014 art 2(*a*), Sch 1 para 11.

[2] Sub-para (4)(*a*) substituted, and in sub-para (4)(*b*) and in the words following that para, figure "5" substituted for figure "7", by the Tribunals, Courts and Enforcement Act 2007 s 50, Sch 10 para 24(1), (3) with effect from 21 July 2008 (by virtue of SI 2008/1653 art 2(*d*)). Sub-s (4)(*a*) previously read as follows—

"(*a*) a person who has a 7 year general qualification, within the meaning of section 71 of the Courts and Legal Services Act 1990; or".

[3] This schedule repealed by the Transfer of Tribunal Functions and Revenue and Customs Appeals Order, SI 2009/56 art 3, Sch 1 para 228 with effect from 1 April 2009, subject to transitional and savings provisions in Sch 3 para 4.

Exemption from jury service

8 *No member of a [VAT and duties tribunal] shall be compelled to serve on any jury in Scotland or Northern Ireland.*[1]

Commentary—*De Voil Indirect Tax Service* **V1.241.**
Definitions—"Tribunal", s 82; "VAT", ss 1, 96(1).
Amendment—[1] This schedule repealed by the Transfer of Tribunal Functions and Revenue and Customs Appeals Order, SI 2009/56 art 3, Sch 1 para 228 with effect from 1 April 2009, subject to transitional and savings provisions in Sch 3 para 4.

Rules of procedure

9 *The Lord Chancellor after consultation with the [Secretary of State]*[1] *may make rules with respect to the procedure to be followed on appeals to and in other proceedings before [VAT and duties tribunals] and such rules may include provisions—*

(*a*) *for limiting the time within which appeals may be brought;*
(*b*) *for enabling hearings to be held in private in such circumstances as may be determined by or under the rules;*
(*c*) *for parties to proceedings to be represented by such persons as may be determined by or under the rules;*
(*d*) *for requiring persons to attend to give evidence;*
(*e*) *for discovery and for requiring persons to produce documents;*
(*f*) *for the payment of expenses and allowances to persons attending as witnesses or producing documents;*
(*g*) *for the award and recovery of costs;*
(*h*) *for authorising the administration of oaths to witnesses; and*
(*j*) *with respect to the joinder of appeals brought by different persons where a notice is served under section 61 and the appeals relate to, or to different portions of, the basic penalty referred to in the notice.*[2]

Commentary—*De Voil Indirect Tax Service* **V1.241, V5.401**.
Rules—See VAT Tribunals Rules, SI 1986/590.
Definitions—"Document", s 96(1); "tribunal", s 82; "VAT", ss 1, 96(1).
Cross reference—See VATA 1994 s 97(2) (a statutory instrument containing rules under this para is subject to annulment in pursuance of a resolution of either House of Parliament).
Amendments—[1] Words substituted by the Transfer of Functions (Lord Advocate and Secretary of State) Order, SI 1999/678 with effect from 19 May 1999.
[2] This schedule repealed by the Transfer of Tribunal Functions and Revenue and Customs Appeals Order, SI 2009/56 art 3, Sch 1 para 228 with effect from 1 April 2009, subject to transitional and savings provisions in Sch 3 para 4.

10— *(1) A person who fails to comply with a direction or summons issued by a [VAT and duties tribunal] under rules made under paragraph 9 above shall be liable to a penalty not exceeding £1,000.*

(2) A penalty for which a person is liable by virtue of sub-paragraph (1) above may be awarded summarily by a tribunal notwithstanding that no proceedings for its recovery have been commenced.

(3) An appeal shall lie to the High Court or, in Scotland, the Court of Session as the Court of Exchequer in Scotland, from the award of a penalty under this paragraph, and on such an appeal the court may either confirm or reverse the decision of the tribunal or reduce or increase the sum awarded.

(4) A penalty awarded by virtue of this paragraph shall be recoverable as if it were VAT due from the person liable for the penalty.[1]

Commentary—*De Voil Indirect Tax Service* **V5.391**.
Definitions—"Tribunal", s 82; "VAT", ss 1, 96(1).
Amendments—[1] This schedule repealed by the Transfer of Tribunal Functions and Revenue and Customs Appeals Order, SI 2009/56 art 3, Sch 1 para 228 with effect from 1 April 2009, subject to transitional and savings provisions in Sch 3 para 4.

SCHEDULE 13

TRANSITIONAL PROVISIONS AND SAVINGS

Section 100

General provisions

1— (1) The continuity of the law relating to VAT shall not be affected by the substitution of this Act for the enactments repealed by this Act and earlier enactments repealed by and corresponding to any of those enactments ("the repealed enactments").

(2) Any reference, whether express or implied, in any enactment, instrument or document (including this Act or any Act amended by this Act) to, or to things done falling to be done under or for the purposes of, any provision of this Act shall, if and so far as the nature of the reference permits, be construed as including, in relation to the times, years or periods, circumstances or purposes in relation to which the corresponding provision in the repealed enactments has or had effect, a reference to, or as the case may be, to things done or falling to be done under or for the purposes of, that corresponding provision.

(3) Any reference, whether express or implied, in any enactment, instrument or document (including the repealed enactments and enactments, instruments and documents passed or made or otherwise coming into existence after the commencement of this Act) to, or to things done or falling to be done under or for the purposes of, any of the repealed enactments shall, if and so far as the nature of the reference permits, be construed as including, in relation to the times, years or periods, circumstances or purposes in relation to which the corresponding provision of this Act has effect, a reference to, or as the case may be to things done or falling to be done under or for the purposes of, that corresponding provision.

(4) Without prejudice to paragraphs (1) to (3) above, in any case where as respects the charge to VAT on any supply, acquisition or importation made at a time before 1st September 1994 but falling in a prescribed accounting period to which Part I applies

(*a*) an enactment applicable to that charge to VAT is not re-enacted in this Act or is re-enacted with amendments which came into force after that time, or

(*b*) a repealed enactment corresponding to an enactment in this Act did not apply to that charge to VAT,

any question arising under Part I and relating to that charge to VAT shall continue to be determined in accordance with the law in force at that time.

Definitions—"Document", s 96(1); "supply", s 5, Sch 4; "VAT", ss 1, 96(1).

Validity of subordinate legislation

2 So far as this Act re-enacts any provision contained in a statutory instrument made in exercise of powers conferred by any Act, it shall be without prejudice to the validity of that provision, and any question as to its validity shall be determined as if the re-enacted provision were contained in a statutory instrument made under those powers.

Provisions related to the introduction of VAT

3 Where a vehicle in respect of which purchase tax was remitted under section 23 of the Purchase Tax Act 1963 (vehicles for use outside the United Kingdom) is brought back to the United Kingdom the vehicle shall not, when brought back, be treated as imported for the purpose of VAT chargeable on the importation of goods.

Definitions—"United Kingdom", s 96(11); "VAT", ss 1, 96(1).

Supply in accordance with pre-21.4.75 arrangements

4 Where there were in force immediately before 21st April 1975 arrangements between the Commissioners and any taxable person for supplies made by him (or such supplies made by him as were specified in the arrangements) to be treated as taking place at times or on dates which, had section 6(10) been in force when the arrangements were made, could have been provided for by a direction under that section, he shall be treated for the purposes of that section as having requested the Commissioners to give a direction thereunder to the like effect, and the Commissioners may give a direction (or a general direction applying to cases of any class or description specified in the direction) accordingly.

Definitions—"The Commissioners", s 96(1); "supply", s 5, Sch 4; "taxable person", s 82.

President, chairmen etc of tribunals

5— (1) Any appointment to a panel of chairmen of the tribunals current at the commencement of this Act and made by the Treasury before the passing of the 1983 Act shall not be affected by the repeal by this Act of paragraph 8 of Schedule 10 to that Act.

(2) The terms of appointment of any person who was appointed to the office of President of the tribunal or chairman or other member of the tribunals before 1st April 1986 and holds that office on the coming into force of this Act shall continue to have effect notwithstanding the re-enactment, as Schedule 12 to this Act, of Schedule 8 to the 1983 Act as amended by Schedule 8 to the Finance Act 1985.

Overseas suppliers accounting through their customers

6 Notwithstanding the repeal by this Act of section 32B of the 1983 Act, that section shall continue to apply in relation to any supply in relation to which section 14 does not apply by virtue of section 14(8), and for the purposes to this paragraph section 32B shall have effect as if it were included in Part III of this Act, any reference in section 32B to any enactment repealed by this Act being read as a reference to the corresponding provision of this Act.

Supplies of fuel and power for domestic or charity use

7 ...[1]

Amendments—[1] Para 7 repealed by FA 1995 s 21(5), (6), Sch 29 Pt VI(1), with effect in relation to any supply made after 31 March 1995 and any acquisition or importation taking place after that date.

Zero-rated supplies of goods and services

8— (1) A supply of services made after the commencement of this Act in pursuance of a legally binding obligation incurred before 21st June 1988 shall if—

(*a*) the supply fell within item 2 of Group 8A of Schedule 5 to the 1983 Act immediately before 1st April 1989, and

(*b*) it was by virtue of paragraph 13(1) of Schedule 3 to the Finance Act 1989 a zero-rated supply,

be a zero-rated supply for the purposes of this Act.

(2) Where a grant, assignment or other supply is zero-rated by virtue of this paragraph, it is not a relevant zero-rated supply for the purposes of [Part 2 of Schedule 10][1].

Commentary—*De Voil Indirect Tax Service* **V4.206**.
Definitions—"Supply", s 5, Sch 4.
Amendments—[1] In sub-para (2), words substituted by the Value Added Tax (Buildings and Land) Order, SI 2008/1146, art 6, Sch 1 paras 1, 5(*a*) with effect in relation to supplies made on or after 1 June 2008, subject to savings in Sch 2 of the Order.

Bad debt relief

9— (1) ...[2]

[(2) Claims for refunds of VAT shall not be made in accordance with section 36 of this Act in relation to—

(*a*) any supply made before 1st April 1989; or

(*b*) any supply as respects which a claim is or has been made under section 22 of the 1983 Act.][1]

Commentary—*De Voil Indirect Tax Service* **V5.156**.
Definitions—"Supply", s 5, Sch 4; "VAT", ss 1, 96(1);
Amendments—[1] Sub-para (2) substituted by FA 1995 s 33(1), (4) and is deemed to have always had effect.
[2] Sub-para (1) repealed by FA 1997 Sch 18 Part IV(3) in relation to claims made after 19 March 1997.

Supplies during construction of buildings and works

10— (1) Nothing in paragraphs 5 and 6 of Schedule 10 shall apply—

(a) in relation to a person who has constructed a building if he incurred before 21st June 1988 a legally binding obligation to make a grant or assignment of a major interest in, or in any part of, the building or its site;

(b) in relation to a building or work if there was incurred before that date a legally binding obligation to make in relation to the building or work a supply within item 2 of Group 8 of Schedule 5 to the 1983 Act;

(c) in relation to a person who has constructed a building if—

(i) he incurred before that date a legally binding obligation to construct the building or any development of which it forms part, and

(ii) planning permission for the construction of the building was granted before that date, and

(iii) he has made a grant or assignment of a major interest in, or in any part of, the building or its site before 21st June 1993.

(2) Sub-paragraph (1) above shall not apply in any case where the Commissioners required proof of any of the matters specified in paragraph (a), (b) or (c)(i) above to be given to their satisfaction by the production of documents made before 21st June 1988 and that requirement was not complied with.[1]

Commentary—*De Voil Indirect Tax Service* **V4.231–V4.242**.
Definitions—"Assignment", s 96(1); "the Commissioners", s 96(1).
Amendments—[1] Para 10 repealed by the Value Added Tax (Buildings and Land) Order, SI 2008/1146, art 6, Sch 1 paras 1, 5(*b*) with effect in relation to supplies made on or after 1 June 2008, subject to savings in Sch 2 of the Order.

Offences and Penalties

11 Where an offence for the continuation of which a penalty was provided has been committed under an enactment repealed by this Act, proceedings may be taken under this Act in respect of the continuance of the offence after the commencement of this Act in the same manner as if the offence had been committed under the corresponding provision of this Act.

12 Part IV of this Act, except section 72, shall not apply in relation to any act done or omitted to be done before 25th July 1985, and the following provision of this Schedule shall have effect accordingly.

13— (1) Section 72 shall have effect in relation to any offence committed or alleged to have been committed at any time ("the relevant time") before the commencement of this Act subject to the following provisions of this paragraph.

(2) Where the relevant time falls between 25th July 1983 and 26th July 1985 (the dates of passing of the 1983 and 1985 Finance Acts respectively), section 72 shall apply—

(*a*) with the substitution in subsection (1)(*b*), (3)(ii) and (8)(*b*) of "2 years" for "7 years";
(*b*) with the omission of subsections (2) and (4) to (7).

14— (1) The provisions of this paragraph have effect in relation to section 59.

(2) Section 59 shall apply in any case where a person is in default in respect of a prescribed accounting period which has ended before the commencement of this Act, but shall have effect in any case where the last day referred to in subsection (1) of that section falls before 1st October 1993 subject to the following modifications—

(*a*) for the words "a prescribed accounting period" in subsection (2)(*a*) there shall be substituted "any two prescribed accounting periods";
(*b*) with the addition of the following paragraph in subsection (2)—
"(*aa*) the last day of the later one of those periods falls on or before the first anniversary of the last day of the earlier one; and";
(*c*) for the words "period referred to in paragraph (*a*)" in subsection (2)(*b*) there shall be substituted "later period referred to in paragraph (aa)"; and
(*d*) for the words "a default in respect of a prescribed accounting period and that period" in subsection (3) there shall be substituted "defaults in respect of two prescribed accounting periods and the second of those periods".

(3) Section 59 shall have effect, in any case where a person has been served with a surcharge liability notice and that person is in default in respect of a prescribed accounting period because of a failure of the Commissioners to receive a return or an amount of VAT on or before a day falling before 30th September 1993 with the omission of—

(*a*) subsection (4)(*b*);
(*b*) the words in subsection (5) "and for which he has outstanding VAT"; and
(*c*) subsection (6).

15— (1) Section 63 does not apply in relation to returns and assessments made for prescribed accounting periods beginning before 1st April 1990 but subject to that shall have effect in relation to the cases referred to in the following sub-paragraphs subject to the modifications there specified.

(2) Subsection (1) shall have effect in a case falling within paragraph (*b*) of that subsection where the assessment was made on or before 10th March 1992 with the substitution of "20 per cent" for "15 per cent".

(3) In relation to any prescribed accounting period beginning before 1st December 1993 section 63 shall have effect with the substitution—

(*a*) for the words in subsection (2) following "exceeds" of "either 30 per cent of the true amount of the VAT for that period or whichever is the greater of £10,000 and 5 per cent of the true amount of VAT for that period." and with the omission of subsections (4) to (6); and
(*b*) for the words in subsection (8) from "subsections" to "statements" of "subsection (7) that the statement by each of those returns is a correct statement".

(4) In relation to any prescribed accounting period beginning before 1st June 1994 section 63 shall have effect with the substitution for subsection (3) of the following subsection—

"(3) Any reference in this section to the VAT for a prescribed accounting period which would have been lost if an inaccuracy had not been discovered is a reference to the aggregate of—

(*a*) the amount (if any) by which credit for input tax for that period was overstated; and
(*b*) the amount (if any) by which output tax for that period was understated;

but if for any period there is an understatement of credit for input tax or an overstatement of output tax, allowance shall be made for that error in determining the VAT for that period which would have been so lost."

and in subsection (8) for "this section" there shall be substituted "subsections (5) and (7) above".

Commentary—*De Voil Indirect Tax Service* **V5.344.**
Definitions—"Input tax", s 24; "output tax", s 24; "VAT", ss 1, 96(1).

16— (1) In relation to any prescribed accounting period beginning before 1st December 1993 section 64 shall have effect subject to the following modifications—

(*a*) in subsection (1)(*b*) for the words from "whichever" to "period" there shall be substituted "whichever is the greater of £100 and 1 per cent of the true amount of VAT for that period";
(*b*) for subsections (2) and (3) there shall be substituted—

"(2) Subsection (3) below applies in any case where—

(*a*) there is a material inaccuracy in respect of any two prescribed accounting periods, and
(*b*) the last day of the later one of those periods falls on or before the second anniversary of the last day of the earlier one, and
(*c*) after 29th July 1988 the Commissioners serve notice on the person concerned ("a penalty liability notice") specifying as a penalty period for the purposes of this section a period beginning on the date of the notice and ending on the second anniversary of that date.

(3) If there is a material inaccuracy in respect of a prescribed accounting period ending within the penalty period specified in a penalty liability notice served on the person concerned that person shall be liable to a penalty equal to 15 per cent of the VAT for that period which would have been lost if the inaccuracy had not been discovered.";

(*c*) in subsection (4) for "(5)" there shall be substituted "(7)"; and

(*d*) in subsection (6) the words from "except" to the end shall be omitted.

(2) A penalty liability notice shall not be served under section 64 by reference to any material inaccuracy in respect of a prescribed accounting period beginning before 1st December 1993, and the penalty period specified in any penalty liability notice served before that day shall be deemed to end with the day before that day.

Commentary—*De Voil Indirect Tax Service* **V5.344**.
Definitions—"The Commissioners", s 96(1); "prescribed accounting period", s 25(1); "VAT", ss 1, 96(1).

17 Section 70 shall not apply in relation to any penalty to which a person has been assessed before 27th July 1993 and in the case of any penalty in relation to which that section does not apply by virtue of this paragraph, section 60 shall have effect subject to the following modifications—

(*a*) in subsection (1) for "subsection (6)" there shall be substituted "subsections (3A) and (6)";

(*b*) after subsection (3) there shall be inserted—

"(3A) If a person liable to a penalty under this section has co-operated with the Commissioners in the investigation of his true liability to tax or, as the case may be, of his true entitlement to any payment, refund or repayment, the Commissioners or, on appeal, a tribunal may reduce the penalty to an amount which is not less than half what it would have been apart from this subsection; and in determining the extent of any reduction under this subsection, the Commissioners or tribunal shall have regard to the extent of the co-operation which the person concerned has given to the Commissioners in their investigation.";

(*c*) in subsection (4)(*b*) for the words from "under" to "this section" there shall be substituted "to reduce a penalty under this section, as provided in subsection (4) above, and, in determining the extent of such a reduction in the case of any person, the Commissioners or tribunal will have regard to the extent of the co-operation which he has given to the Commissioners in their investigation";

and in section 61(6) for "70" there shall be substituted "60(3A)".

Commentary—*De Voil Indirect Tax Service* **V5.334**.
Definitions—"The Commissioners", s 96(1); "tribunal", s 82.

18 Section 74 shall not apply in relation to prescribed accounting periods beginning before 1st April 1990 and subsection (3) of that section shall not apply in relation to interest on amounts assessed or, as the case may be, paid before 1st October 1993.

Importation of goods

19 Nothing in this Act shall prejudice the effect of the Finance (No 2) Act 1992 (Commencement No 4 and Transitional Provisions) Order 1992 and accordingly—

(*a*) where Article 4 of that Order applies immediately before the commencement of this Act in relation to any importation of goods, that Article and the legislation repealed by this Act shall continue to apply in relation to that importation as if this Act had not been enacted, and

(*b*) where Article 5 of that Order applies in relation to any goods, this Act shall apply in relation to those goods in accordance with that Article and Article 6 of that Order.

Assessments

20 An assessment may be made under section 73 in relation to amounts paid or credited before the commencement of this Act but—

(*a*) in relation to an amount paid or credited before 30th July 1990 section 73(2) shall have effect with the omission of the words from "or which" to "out to be", and

(*b*) in relation to amounts repaid or paid to any person before the passing of the Finance Act 1982 section 73 shall have effect with the omission of subsection (2).

Set-off of credits

21 Section 81 shall have effect in relation to amounts becoming due before 10th May 1994 with the omission of subsections (4) and (5).

VAT tribunals

22— (1) Without prejudice to paragraph 1 above, section 83 applies to things done or omitted to be done before the coming into force of this Act and accordingly references in Part V to any provision of this Act includes a reference to the corresponding provision of the enactments repealed by this Act or by any enactment repealed by such an enactment.

(2) Section 84 shall have effect before such day as may be appointed for the purposes of section 18(3) of the Finance Act 1994 with the substitution for subsection (5) of the following subsection—

"(5) No appeal shall lie with respect to any matter that has been or could have been referred to arbitration under section 127 of the Management Act as applied by section 16."

Isle of Man

23 Nothing in paragraph 7 of Schedule 14 shall affect the validity of any Order made under section 6 of the Isle of Man Act 1979 and, without prejudice to section 17 of the Interpretation Act 1978 for any reference in any such Order to any enactment repealed by this Act there shall be substituted a reference to the corresponding provision of this Act.

SCHEDULE 14

CONSEQUENTIAL AMENDMENTS

1–5 (*amend* provisions outside the scope of this Publication).

Customs and Excise Management Act 1979 c 2

6 (*amends* CEMA 1979 s 1(1)).

Isle of Man Act 1979 c 58

7 (*amends* IOM 1979 ss 1(1), 6(1), 14(4)).

Cross references—See VATA 1994 s 101(4) (this para to extend to the Isle of Man);
VATA 1994 Sch 13 para 23 (this para does not affect the validity of any order made under Isle of Man Act 1979 s 6).

Insolvency Act 1986 c 45

8 (*amended* Sch 6, *repealed by* the Enterprise Act 2002 s 278, Sch 26).

Bankruptcy (Scotland) Act 1985 c 66

9 (*amends* Sch 3 para 8).

Income and Corporation Taxes Act 1988 c 1

10 (*amends* TA 1988 s 827).

Capital Allowances Act 1990 c 1

11 (*amended* s 159A, *repealed by* CAA 2001 s 580, Sch 4 with effect in accordance with CAA 2001 s 579).

Tribunals and Inquiries Act 1992 c 53

[12 (*amends Sch 1*).]¹

Amendments—[1] This para repealed by the Transfer of Tribunal Functions and Revenue and Customs Appeals Order, SI 2009/56 art 3, Sch 1 para 229 with effect from 1 April 2009, subject to transitional and savings provisions in Sch 3 para 4.

Finance Act 1994 c 9

13 (*amends* s 7(4), (5) (and is *amended* by FA 1995 s 33(1), (5), this amendment being deemed to have always had effect)).

Vehicle Excise and Registration Act 1994 c 22

14 (*amends* Sch 2 para 23).

VATA 1994: DESTINATION TABLE

This table shows in column (1) the enactments and instruments repealed or revoked by VATA 1994 and in column (2) the provisions of that Act corresponding thereto.

In certain cases the enactment or instrument in column (1), though having a corresponding provision in column (2), is not, or not wholly, repealed or revoked as it is still required, or partly required, for the purposes of other legislation.

A "dash" adjacent to a repealed or revoked provision indicates that that provision is spent, unnecessary or for some other reason not specifically reproduced.

Subsequent amendments to VATA 1994 after its date of Royal Assent are not accounted for in the table below.

(1)	(2)
Customs and Excise Management Act 1979 (c 2)	Value Added Tax Act 1994 (c 23)
s 100B	s 17(3)
s 100C(1)	s 17(2)
s 100C(2)	Rep SI 1991/2727, reg 3(1)
s 100C(3)	s 17(4)
s 100C(4)(*a*)–(*c*)	s 17(5)
s 100C(4)(*d*)	s 17(3)
Value Added Tax Act 1983 (c 55)	Value Added Tax Act 1994 (c 23)
s 1	s 1(1)
s 2(1)	s 4(1)
s 2(2)	s 4(2)
s 2(3)	s 1(2)
s 2(4), (5)	Rep 1992 c 48, s 82, Sch 18 Pt V(1)
s 2A(1)–(3)	s 10(1)–(3)
s 2A(4)	s 1(3)
s 2B(1)	s 1(4)
s 2B(2)–(4)	s 15(1)–(3)
s 2C	s 3
s 3	s 5
s 4	s 6(1)–(3)
s 5(1)–(3)	s 6(4)–(6)
s 5(3A), (3B)	s 6(7), (8)
s 5(4)–(10)	s 6(9)–(15)
s 6(1), (2)	s 7(1), (2)
s 6(2A)–(2D)	s 7(3)–(6)
s 6(3), (4)	s 7(7), (8)
s 6(4A)	s 7(9)
s 6(5), (6)	s 7(10), (11)
s 7	s 8
s 8	s 9
s 8A	s 11
s 8B	s 12
s 8C	s 13
s 8D	s 14(1)–(7)
s 9	s 2
s 10(1)–(5)	s 19(1)–(5)
s 10(6)	Rep 1992 c 48, s 82, Sch 18 Pt V(1)
s 10A	s 20
s 11(1), (2)	s 21(1), (2)
s 11(2A)	s 21(3)
s 11(3), (4)	Rep 1992 c 48, s 82, Sch 18 Pt V(1)
s 12	s 22
s 13	s 23
s 14(1), (2)	s 25(1), (2)
s 14(3)	s 24(1), (2)
s 14(3A), (3B)	s 24(3), (4)
s 14(4)	s 24(5)
s 14(5)–(8)	s 25(3)–(6)
s 14(9)	s 24(6)

(1)	(2)
Value Added Tax Act 1983 (c 55)	Value Added Tax Act 1994 (c 23)
s 14(10)	s 25(7)
s 14(11)	s 24(7)
s 15	s 26
s 16(1)–(6)	s 30(1)–(6)
s 16(6A)	s 30(7)
s 16(7)–(9)	s 30(8)–(10)
s 17	s 31
s 18	s 32
s 19(1)	s 37(1)
s 19(1A)	s 37(2)
s 19(2), (3)	s 37(3), (4)
s 20(1)–(4)	s 33(1)–(4)
s 20(4A)	s 33(5)
s 20(5)	s 33(6)
s 20(6)	s 96(4)
s 20A	s 40
s 21(1), (2)	s 35(1), (2)
s 21(2A)	s 35(3)
s 22	Rep 1990 c 29, ss 11(9), 132, Sch 19 Pt III
s 23	s 39
s 24(1)	s 16(1)
s 24(2), (3)	—
s 24(4)	s 16(2)
s 25	s 38
s 26	s 27
s 27(1), (2)	s 41(1), (2)
s 27(2A), (2B)	s 41(3), (4)
s 27(3)–(6)	s 41(5)–(8)
s 28(1)	s 42
s 28(2)	—
s 29(1), (2)	s 43(1), (2)
s 29(3), (3A)	s 43(3)
s 29(4)–(8)	s 43(4)–(8)
s 29A(1)–(3)	s 44(1)–(3)
s 29A(3A)	s 44(4)
s 29A(4)–(9)	s 44(5)–(10)
s 30	s 45
s 31	s 46
s 32(1)	Rep 1992 c 48, s 82, Sch 18 Pt V(1)
s 32(2)–(4)	s 47
s 32A	s 48
s 32B	Rep 1993 c 34, ss 44(2), 213, Sch 23 Pt II(3)
s 33(1)	s 49(1)
s 33(1A)	Rep 1990 c 29, ss 10(7), 132, Sch 19 Pt III
s 33(2), (3)	s 49(2), (3)
s 34	s 50
s 35	s 18
s 35A	s 51

† Not repealed
* Repealed in part

(1) Value Added Tax Act 1983 (c 55)	(2) Value Added Tax Act 1994 (c 23)
s 36(1), (2)	s 34(1), (2)
s 36(3)	Rep 1992 c 48, s 82, Sch 18 Pt V(1)
s 37	s 52
s 37A	s 53
s 37B	s 54
s 37C	s 55
s 38	s 58
s 38A(1)–(8)	s 78(1)–(8)
s 38A(8A)	s 78(9)
s 38A(9)–(11)	s 78(10)–(12)
s 38A(12)	—
s 38B	s 81(1), (2)
s 38C	s 28
s 39(1)	s 72(1)
s 39(1A)	s 72(2)
s 39(2)	s 72(3)
s 39(2A)–(2D)	s 72(4)–(7)
s 39(3)	s 72(8)
s 39(3A)	s 72(9)
s 39(4), (5)	s 72(10), (11)
s 39(6)–(8)	Rep 1985 c 54, ss 12(7), 98(6), Sch 27 Pt IV
s 39(9)	s 72(12)
s 40(1)	s 83
s 40(1A)	s 84(6)
s 40(2), (3)	s 84(2), (3)
s 40(3A)	s 84(7)
s 40(3ZA)	s 84(4)
s 40(3B)	s 84(5)
s 40(4)–(6)	s 84(8)–(10)
s 41(1)–(3)	s 88(1)–(3)
s 41(3A)	s 88(4)
s 41(4)–(6)	s 88(5)–(7)
s 42(1)	s 89(1)
s 42(1A)	s 89(2)
s 42(2)	s 89(3)
s 43	s 90
s 44	s 91
s 45(1)	s 97(1)
s 45(2)	s 97(5)
s 45(3), (4)	s 97(3), (4)
s 46	s 98
s 46A	s 92
s 46B	s 93
s 47	s 94
s 47A(1)	s 95(1)
s 47A(1A)	s 95(2)
s 47A(2)–(4)	s 95(3)–(5)
s 48(1)	s 96(1)
s 48(1A), (1B)	s 96(3), (5)
s 48(2), (3)	Rep 1993 c 50, s 1(1), Sch 1 Pt XIV
s 48(4)	s 96(6)
s 48(5)–(8)	s 96(8)–(11)
s 48(9)	s 96(2)
s 49	s 99
ss 50, 51	—
Sch 1, para 1(1)–(4)	Sch 1, para 1(1)–(4)
para 1(4A), (4B)	Sch 1, para 1(5),(6)
para 1(5), (6)	Sch 1, para 1(7),(8)
para 1A	Sch 1, para 2

(1) Value Added Tax Act 1983 (c 55)	(2) Value Added Tax Act 1994 (c 23)
para 1B	Sch 1, para 3
para 2	Sch 1, para 4
paras 3, 4	Sch 1, paras 5, 6
paras 4A, 4B	Sch 1, paras 7, 8
para 5	Sch 1, para 9
para 5A	Sch 1, para 10
para 6	Rep 1987 c 16, ss 14(6), 72, Sch 16 Pt IV
para 7	Sch 1, para 11
para 7A	Sch 1, para 12
para 8	Rep 1987 c 16, s 72, Sch 16 Pt IV
para 8A(1)	Sch 1, para 13(1)
para 8A(1A)	Sch 1, para 13(4)
para 8A(1B)	Sch 1, para 13(6)
para 8A(2)	Sch 1, para 13(7)
para 9(1)	Sch 1, para 13(2)
para 9(1A)	Sch 1, para 13(5)
para 9(1B)	Sch 1, para 13(6)
para 9(2)	Sch 1, para 18
para 10	Sch 1, para 13(3)
paras 11, 12	Sch 1, paras 14, 15
para 13	Sch 1, para 16
para 14	Sch 1, para 17
para 15	Sch 1, para 19
Sch 1A	Sch 2
Sch 1B	Sch 3
Sch 2, paras 1–4	Sch 4, paras 1–4
para 5(1), (2)	Sch 4, para 5(1),(2)
para 5(2A)	Sch 4, para 5(3)
para 5(3)	Sch 4, para 5(4)
para 5(3A)	Sch 4, para 5(5)
para 5(4)	Sch 4, para 5(6)
para 5A	Sch 4, para 6
para 6	Sch 4, para 7
para 7(1), (2)	Sch 4, para 8(1),(2)
para 7(2A)	Sch 4, para 8(3)
para 7(3)	Sch 4, para 8(4)
para 8	Sch 4, para 9
Sch 3, paras 1–6	Sch 5, paras 1–6
para 6A	Sch 5, para 7
paras 7, 8	Sch 5, paras 8, 9
Sch 4, para 1	Sch 6, para 1
para 2	Rep 1992 c 48, ss 14, 82, Sch 3 Pt I para 61(1), Sch 18, Pt V(1)
para 3	Sch 6, para 2
para 3A	Sch 6, para 3
para 4	Sch 6, para 4
para 5	Rep 1992 c 48, ss 14, 82, Sch 3 Pt I para 61(1), Sch 18, Pt V(1)
paras 6–8	Sch 6, paras 5–7
para 8A	Sch 6, para 8
paras 9–13	Sch 6, paras 9–13
Sch 4A	Sch 7
Sch 5, Groups 1–4	Sch 8, Pt II, Groups 1–4
Group 5	Rep 1985 c 54, ss 11, 98(6), Sch 27 Pt IV
Group 6	Rep 1989 c 26, ss 20, 187(1), Sch 17 Pt III
Group 7	Rep 1993 c 34, s 213, Sch 23 Pt II(1)
Group 8	Sch 8, Pt II, Group 5
Group 8A	Sch 8, Pt II, Group 6
Groups 9–15	Sch 8, Pt II, Groups 7–13
Group 15A	Sch 8, Pt II, Group 14
Groups 16, 17	Sch 8, Pt II, Groups 15, 16

† Not repealed
* Repealed in part

(1)	(2)
Value Added Tax Act 1983 (c 55)	Value Added Tax Act 1994 (c 23)
Sch 6, Groups 1–12	Sch 9, Pt II, Groups 1–12
Sch 6A, paras 1, 2	Sch 10, paras 1, 2
para 3(1)–(6)	Sch 10, para 3(1)–(6)
para 3(7)	Rep SI 1991/2569, art 4(*c*)
para 3(8)–(10)	Sch 10, para 3(7)–(9)
paras 4, 5	Sch 10, paras 4, 5
para 6(1), (2)	Sch 10, para 6(1),(2)
para 6(2A), (2B)	Sch 10, para 6(3),(4)
para 6(3)–(6)	Sch 10, para 6(5)–(8)
para 6A	Sch 10, para 7
paras 7, 8	Sch 10, paras 8, 9
Sch 7, para 1	Sch 11, para 1
para 2(1), (2)	Sch 11, para 2(1),(2)
para 2(2A)–(2C)	Sch 11, para 2(3)–(5)
para 2(3)	Sch 11, para 2(6)
para 2(3A)	Sch 11, para 2(7)
para 2(3B), (3C)	Sch 11, para 2(8),(9)
para 2(4)–(7)	Sch 11, para 2(10)–(13)
para 3(1), (2)	Sch 11, para 3(1),(2)
para 3(2A)	Sch 11, para 3(3)
para 3(3), (4)	Rep 1985 c 54, s 98(6), Sch 27 Pt IV
para 4(1), (2)	s 73(1), (2)
para 4(2A)	s 73(3)
para 4(3)–(6)	s 73(4)–(7)
para 4(6A)	s 73(8)
para 4(7), (8)	Rep 1985 c 54, ss 22(6), 98(6), Sch 27 Pt IV
para 4(9), (10)	s 73(9), (10)
para 4A	s 75
para 5	Sch 11, para 4
para 6(1)–(3)	Sch 11, para 5(1)–(3)
para 6(4)(*a*)	Sch 11, para 5(4)
para 6(4)(*b*)	Applies to Scotland
para 6(5)–(9)	Apply to Scotland
para 6(10)	Sch 11, para 5(10)
para 7(1)	Sch 11, para 6(1)
para 7(1A)	Sch 11, para 6(2)
para 7(2)–(5)	Sch 11, para 6(3)–(6)
para 7(6)–(8)	Rep 1984 c 60, s 119(2), Sch 7 Pt III
para 8(1)–(4)	Sch 11, para 7(1)–(4)
para 8(4A)–(4C)	Sch 11, para 7(5)–(7)
para 8(5)	Sch 11, para 7(8)
para 9	Sch 11, para 8
para 9A	Sch 11, para 9
para 10	Sch 11, para 10
paras 10A–10C	Sch 11, paras 11–13
para 11	Sch 11, para 14
para 12	Rep 1985 c 65, s 235(3), Sch 10 Pt IV
Sch 8, paras 1, 2	Sch 12, paras 1, 2
para 3(1)	Sch 12, para 3(1),(3)
para 3(1A)	Sch 12, para 3(2)
para 3(2)–(4)	Sch 12, para 3(4)–(6)
para 3(4A)	Sch 12, para 3(7)
para 3(5)	Sch 12, para 3(8)
paras 4–6	Sch 12, paras 4–6

(1)	(2)
Value Added Tax Act 1983 (c 55)	Value Added Tax Act 1994 (c 23)
para 7(1)–(3)	Sch 12, para 7(1)–(3)
para 7(3A), (3B)	Sch 12, para 7(4),(5)
para 7(3C)	Sch 12, para 7(6)
para 7(3D)	—
para 7(3E)	Sch 12, para 7(7)
para 7(4)	Sch 12, para 7(8)
para 7(4A)	Sch 12, para 7(9)
para 7(5)	Sch 12, para 7(10)
paras 8–10	Sch 12, paras 8–10
Sch 10	Cf Sch 13
Sch 11	—

Finance Act 1984 (c 43)	Value Added Tax Act 1994 (c 23)
s 10	—
s 11	s 41(3), (4)
s 12	Rep 1989 c 39, s 148, Sch 14 Pt III
s 13	—
Sch 6, Pt I	Sch 8, Pt II, Group I
Pt II	Rep 1989 c 26, s 187(1), Sch 17 Pt III
Pt III	Sch 8, Pt II, Group 6

Inheritance Act 1984 (c 51)	Value Added Tax Act 1994 (c 23)
Sch 8, para 24	Sch 9, Pt II, Group 11

Finance Act 1985 (c 54)	Value Added Tax Act 1994 (c 23)
s 11	—
s 12(1)	—
s 12(2)	s 72(1), (3), (8)
s 12(3)	s 72(2)
s 12(4)	s 73(3)
s 12(5)	s 72(4)–(7)
s 12(6)	s 72(9)
s 12(7)	—
s 12(8)	—
s 12(9)	—
s 13(1)–(3)	s 60(1)–(3)
s 13(4)	Rep 1993 c 34, ss 49, 213, Sch 2 para 3(2), Sch 23, Pt II(4)
s 13(5)–(7)	s 60(4)–(6)
s 13A	s 62
s 14(1), (2)	s 63(1), (2)
s 14(3)	—
s 14(4)	s 63(3)
s 14(4A)–(4C)	s 63(4)–(6)
s 14(5)	s 63(7)
s 14(5A), (5B)	s 63(8), (9)
s 14(6), (7)	s 63(10), (11)
s 14(8)	—
s 14A	s 64
s 14B	s 65
s 15(1)–(3)	s 67(1)–(3)
s 15(3A)–(3D)	s 67(4)–(7)
s 15(4)–(7)	s 67(8)–(11)
s 15(8)	s 97(5)
s 15A	s 70
s 16	s 68
s 17(1)–(3)	s 69(1)–(3)
s 17(4)(*a*), (*c*)–(*e*)	s 69(4)

† Not repealed
* Repealed in part

(1)	(2)
Finance Act 1985 (c 54)	Value Added Tax Act 1994 (c 23)
s 17(4)(*b*)	—
s 17(5)	s 69(5)
s 17(6), (7)	s 69(6), (7)
s 17(8)	s 97(5)
s 17(9), (10)	s 69(8), (9)
s 17A(1)–(8)	s 66(1)–(8)
s 17A(9)	s 97(5)
s 17A(10)	s 66(9)
s 18(1)	s 74(1)
s 18(2)	Rep 1988 c 39, ss 18(4), 148, Sch 14 Pt III
s 18(3)	s 74(2)
s 18(3A)	s 74(3)
s 18(4), (5)	Rep 1990 c 29, ss 16(4), 132, Sch 19 Pt III
s 18(6), (7)	s 74(4), (5)
s 18(8)(*a*), (*b*)	s 74(6)
s 18(8)(*c*)	s 97(1), (5)
s 18(9)	s 74(7)
s 18(10)	—
s 19(1)–(5)	s 59(1)–(5)
s 19(5A)	s 59(6)
s 19(6)–(9)	s 59(7)–(10)
s 19(10)	—
s 20(1)–(3)	s 79(1)–(3)
s 20(3A)	s 79(4)
s 20(4), (5)	s 79(5), (6)
s 20(6)	—
s 20(7)	s 79(7)
s 21(1)	s 76(1)
s 21(1A)	s 76(2)
s 21(2)–(4)	s 76(3)–(5)
s 21(4A)	s 76(6)
s 21(5)–(8)	s 76(7)–(10)
s 22(1)–(5)	s 77(1)–(5)
s 22(6)	—
s 22(7)	s 77(6)
s 23	—
s 24(1)	s 83(*n*), (*q*), (*r*)
s 24(2)	s 84(6)
s 24(3)	s 84(2)
s 24(4)	s 84(3)
s 24(5)	s 84(5)
s 25	s 85
s 26(1)	s 86(1)
s 26(2)(*a*)	s 86(2)
s 26(2)(*b*)	s 97(1), (2)
s 26(3)	s 86(3)
s 27(1)	s 60(7)
s 27(2), (3)(*a*)	Sch 12, para 9
s 27(3)(*b*)	—
s 27(3)(*c*)	s 97(1), (2)
s 27(4)	s 97(5)
s 28	Sch 12, para 10
s 29	s 84
s 30(1)	s 82(1)
s 30(2), (3)	—
s 31	s 46(5)
s 32	Rep 1990 c 29, s 132, Sch 19 Pt III
s 33(1)	—
s 33(2), (3)	s 71(1), (2)
s 33(4)	Rep 1988 c 39, s 148, Sch 14 Pt III
s 33(5)(*a*)	s 72(13)
s 33(5)(*b*)	—
s 75(11)†	s 73(10)
Sch 6	—
Sch 7, para 1(1)	Rep 1988 c 39, s 148, Sch 14 Pt III
para 1(2)	s 73(7)
para 1(3)	s 73(8)
para 2	Sch 11, para 6(3)
para 3(1)	Sch 11, para 7(2),(3)
para 3(2)	Sch 11, para 7(4)
para 3(3)	Sch 11, para 7(5)–(7)
para 4	Sch 11, para 9
para 5(1)	Sch 11, para 10(3)
para 5(2)	Sch 11, para 10(4)–(6)
para 6	Sch 11, paras 11–13
Sch 8, para 1	—
para 2(1)	Sch 12, para 2(2)
para 2(2)	Sch 12, para 2(3)
para 3(1)	Sch 12, para 3(1)
para 3(2)	Sch 12, para 3(2)
para 3(3)	Sch 12, para 3(4)
para 3(4)	Sch 12, para 3(5)
para 3(5)	Sch 12, para 3(6)
para 3(6)	Sch 12, para 3(8)
para 4	Sch 12, para 4
para 5(1)	Sch 12, para 7(3)
para 5(2)	Sch 12, para 7(4),(5), (7)
para 5(3)	Sch 12, para 7(8)
para 5(4)	Sch 12, para 7(10)
para 6	—
Sch 26, para 14	Sch 9, Pt II, Group 11

(1)	(2)
Finance Act 1986 (c 41)	Value Added Tax Act 1994 (c 23)
s 9(1), (2)	s 56(1), (2)
s 9(3)(*a*)	s 56(3)(*a*)
s 9(3)(aa)	s 56(3)(*b*)
s 9(3)(*b*)–(*d*)	s 56(3)(*c*)–(*e*)
s 9(4)–(9)	s 56(4)–(9)
s 9(10)	s 56(10)
s 9(11)	—
s 10(1)	Sch 1, para 2
s 10(2)	s 83(4)
s 10(3)	s 84(5), (7)
s 11(1)	Sch 6, para 9
s 11(2)	—
s 12(1)	s 30(6)
s 12(2)	s 30(10)
s 13	s 37(2)
s 14(1)–(5)	s 61(1)–(5)
s 14(6)	ss 83(*o*), 84(6)
s 14(7)	Sch 12, para 9
s 14(8)	s 61(6)
s 14(9)	—
s 15(1)	s 69(1)
s 15(2)	—
Sch 6, para 1	s 57(1)
para 2	s 57(2), (3)
para 3	Rep 1993 c 34, ss 43(1), 213, Sch 23 Pt II(2)
para 4	s 57(4)
para 5(1)	s 57(5)
para 5(2)	s 57(6)
para 6(1)	s 57(7)
para 6(2)	s 57(8)

† Not repealed
* Repealed in part

(1)	(2)
Finance Act 1987 (c 16)	Value Added Tax Act 1994 (c 23)
s 11(1)	s 25(1)
s 11(2)	Sch 11, para 2(7)
s 12(1)	s 26(1)–(3)
s 12(2)	s 7(1)
s 12(3)	Rep 1992 c 48, s 82, Sch 18 Pt V(1)
s 12(4)	—
s 13(1)	—
s 13(2), (3)	Rep 1992 c 48, s 82, Sch 18 Pt V(1)
s 13(4)	Rep 1988 c 39, s 148, Sch 14 Pt III
s 13(5)	—
s 14(1)	—
s 14(2)	Sch 1, para 1(4),(7)
s 14(3)	Sch 1, para 4(1)–(3)
s 14(4), (5)	Rep 1990 c 29, s 132, Sch 19 Pt III
s 14(7)–(9)	Rep 1988 c 39, s 148, Sch 14 Pt III
s 14(10)	Sch 1, paras 16, 17, 19
s 15(1)	s 44(1)–(3), (5)–(10)
s 15(2)	—
s 16(1)	s 53
s 16(2)	s 97(4)
s 17(1)	Sch 6, para 1(1)
s 17(2)	—
s 18(1)	Sch 9, Pt II, Group 5
s 18(2)	—
s 19	—
Sch 2, para 1	s 8(1), (3), (4)
para 2	s 39(1)
para 3	Rep 1990 c 29, s 132, Sch 19 Pt III
para 4	s 80(*e*)

Debtors (Scotland) Act 1987 (c 18)	Value Added Tax Act 1994 (c 23)
Sch 4, para 4	Applies to Scotland

Finance Act 1988 (c 39)	Value Added Tax Act 1994 (c 23)
s 13(1)	—
s 13(2), (3)	Sch 9, Pt II, Group 7
s 13(4)	—
s 14(1)	—
s 14(2)	Sch 1, paras 1(7), 4(3)
s 14(3)	—
s 14(4)	Sch 1, paras 9, 10
s 14(5)	Sch 1, paras 11, 12
s 14(6)	Sch 1, paras 13, 18
s 14(7)	Sch 1, paras 14, 15
s 14(8)(*a*)	Rep 1992 c 48, s 82, Sch 18 Pt V(1)
s 14(8)(*b*)	s 74(1)
s 15(1)	—
s 15(2)	s 73(2), (3)
s 15(3)	s 73(6)
s 15(4)	s 73(9)
s 16(1)	—
s 16(2)	s 63(2)
s 16(3)	s 63(3)
s 16(4)	s 63(7)
s 16(5)	s 63(8), (9)

(1)	(2)
Finance Act 1988 (c 39)	Value Added Tax Act 1994 (c 23)
s 17	s 64
s 18(1)	s 67(1)
s 18(2)	s 67(3)
s 18(3)	s 67(4)
s 18(4)(*a*)	—
s 18(4)(*b*)	s 74(2)
s 18(5)*	
s 18(6)	—
s 19(1)	s 69(1)
s 19(2)	s 69(3)
s 19(3)	s 76(1), (2)
s 19(4)	—
s 19(5)	—
s 20	s 79(1)–(3), (5)–(7)
s 21(1)	s 81(3)
s 21(2)	s 81(4)
s 21(3)	s 81(5)
s 22	s 29

Road Traffic (Consequential Provisions) Act 1988 (c 54)	Value Added Tax Act 1994 (c 23)
Sch 3, para 32	s 56(10)

Finance Act 1989 (c 26)	Value Added Tax Act 1994 (c 23)
s 18	—
s 19(1)–(4)	Sch 8, Pt II, Group 2
s 19(5)	—
ss 20, 21	—
s 22(1), (2)	Sch 8, Pt II, Group 16
s 22(3)	—
s 23(1)	s 62
s 23(2)	—
s 24(1)–(7)	s 80(1)–(7)
s 24(8)	s 80(1)
s 24(9)	s 83(*t*)
s 24(10), (11)	—
s 25(1)	—
s 25(2)	Sch 11, para 2(10)(*b*), (*c*)
s 25(3)	Sch 11, para 6(1)
s 25(4)	Sch 11, para 6(2)
s 25(5), (6)	—
s 26	s 26(3)(*d*)
Sch 3, para 1	Sch 8, Pt II, Group 5
para 2	Sch 8, Pt II, Group 6
para 3	Sch 8, Pt II, Group 9
para 4(1)	Sch 9, Pt II, Group 1
para 4(2)	Sch 6, para 9
para 5	s 35(1), (2)
para 6(1)	s 51
para 6(2)	Sch 10
para 7(*a*)	s 89(2)
para 7(*b*)	s 89(3)
para 8	s 97(4)(*d*)
para 9	s 96(1)
para 10(*a*)	Sch 1, para 1(8)
para 10(*b*)	Sch 1, para 4(4)

† Not repealed
* Repealed in part

(1)	(2)
Finance Act 1989 (c 26)	Value Added Tax Act 1994 (c 23)
para 11(*a*)	Sch 4, para 4
para 11(*b*)	Sch 4, para 5(1)
para 11(*c*)	Sch 4, para 9
paras 12, 13	—
Companies Act 1989 (c 40)	Value Added Tax Act 1994 (c 23)
Sch 18, para 27	s 43(8)
Opticians Act 1989 (c 44)	Value Added Tax Act 1994 (c 23)
s 37(3)	Sch 9, Pt II, Group 7
Planning (Consequential Provisions) Act 1990 (c 11)	Value Added Tax Act 1994 (c 23)
Sch 2, para 61	Sch 8, Pt II, Group 6
National Health Service and Community Care Act 1990 (c 19)	Value Added Tax Act 1994 (c 23)
s 61(4)	s 41(7)
Sch 8, para 9	s 41(6)
Finance Act 1990 (c 29)	Value Added Tax Act 1994 (c 23)
s 10(1)	—
s 10(2)	Sch 1, para 1(1)–(3)
s 10(3)	Sch 1, para 1(4)
s 10(4)	Sch 1, para 1(7)
s 10(5)	Sch 1, para 1(8)
s 10(6)	Sch 1, paras 5–8
s 10(7)	—
s 10(8)	s 42
s 10(9), (10)	—
s 11(1)–(7)	s 36(1)–(7)
s 11(8)	—
s 11(9)	—
s 11(10)	s 36(8)
s 11(11)(*a*)	s 72(2)(*b*)
s 11(11)(*b*)	s 83(*h*)
s 11(12)	s 60(2)(*c*)
s 12(1)	—
s 12(2)	s 24(3)
s 12(3)	s 24(7)
s 12(4)	—
s 13(1)	s 30(7)
s 13(2)	—
s 14(1)	—
s 14(2)	s 44(1)
s 14(3)	s 44(4)

(1)	(2)
Finance Act 1990 (c 29)	Value Added Tax Act 1994 (c 23)
s 14(4)	—
s 15(1)	s 73(2)
s 15(2)	—
s 16(1)	—
s 16(2)	s 74(1)
s 16(3)	s 74(2)
s 16(4)	—
s 16(5)	s 74(5)
s 16(6)	—
Courts and Legal Services Act 1990 (c 41)	Value Added Tax Act 1994 (c 23)
Sch 10, para 52(1)	Sch 12, para 2(2)
para 52(2)	Sch 12, para 7(4)
Broadcasting Act 1990 (c 42)	Value Added Tax Act 1994 (c 23)
Sch 20, para 37(*a*)	s 33(3)
para 37(*b*)	s 33(5)
Disability Living Allowance and Disability Working Allowance Act 1991 (c 21)	Value Added Tax Act 1994 (c 23)
Sch 2, para 13	Sch 8, Pt II, Group 12
Finance Act 1991 (c 31)	Value Added Tax Act 1994 (c 23)
s 13(1)	s 2(1)
s 13(2)	—
s 14	s 24(4)
s 15	—
s 16(1)	—
s 16(2), (3)	s 43(3)
s 17(1)	ss 78(1)–(8), (10)–(12), 81(1), (2)
s 17(2)	s 83(*s*)
s 18	—
Taxation of Chargeable Gains Act 1992 (c 12)	Value Added Tax Act 1994 (c 23)
Sch 10, para 6	Sch 9, Pt II, Group 11
Finance Act 1992 (c 20)	Value Added Tax Act 1994 (c 23)
s 6(1)	s 28
s 6(2)	s 97(4)(*a*)
s 7(1)	s 63(1)
s 7(2)–(5)	—
Finance (No 2) Act 1992 (c 48)	Value Added Tax Act 1994 (c 23)
s 14	—
s 15(1)	s 79(4)
s 15(2)	s 78(9)
s 15(3), (4)	—

† Not repealed
* Repealed in part

(1) Finance (No 2) Act 1992 (c 48)	(2) Value Added Tax Act 1994 (c 23)
s 16(1)	s 54
s 16(2)	s 83(*m*)
s 16(3)	s 97(4)(*e*)
s 16(4)	Sch 4, para 8(3)
s 16(5)	s 67(7)
s 16(6)	—
s 17	—
Sch 3, Pt I	
para 1	—
para 2	s 1(1)
para 3	ss 1(3), (4), 3, 10, 15
para 4(1)	s 5(3)
para 4(2)	s 5(5)
para 5	s 6(1)
para 6(1)	s 6(7), (8)
para 6(2)(*a*)	s 6(14)
para 6(2)(*b*)	Rep 1993 c 34, s 213, Sch 23 Pt II(3)
para 6(3)	s 6(15)
para 7(1)	s 7(1)
para 7(2)	s 7(2)
para 7(3)	s 7(3)–(7)
para 7(4)	s 7(8)
para 7(5)	s 7(9)
para 7(6)	s 7(11)
para 8	s 8(6)
para 9	s 9(1)
para 10	ss 11, 12, 13
para 11	s 2(1)
para 12(1)	s 19(1)
para 12(2)	s 19(3)
para 13	s 20
para 14(1)	s 21(1)
para 14(2)	s 21(2)
para 14(3)	s 21(3)
para 15(1)	s 25(1)
para 15(2)	s 24(1), (2)
para 15(3)	s 24(3)
para 15(4)	s 24(5)
para 15(5)	s 24(6)
para 15(6)	s 25(7)
para 16(1)	s 26(1)
para 16(2)	s 26(2)(*c*)
para 17(1)	s 30(3)
para 17(2)	s 30(6)
para 17(3)	s 30(8)
para 17(4)	s 30(9)
para 17(5)	s 30(10)
para 18	s 31(1)
para 19(1)	s 32(3)
para 19(2)	s 32(4)
para 20(1)	s 37(1)
para 20(2)	s 37(2)
para 20(3)	s 37(3)
para 20(4)	s 37(4)
para 21(1)	s 33(1)
para 21(2)	s 33(2)
para 22	s 40
para 23(1)	s 35(1)
para 23(2)	s 35(3)
para 24(1)	s 39(1)
para 24(2)	s 39(2)
para 25	s 16(1)
para 26	s 38
para 27	s 27(1)

(1) Finance (No 2) Act 1992 (c 48)	(2) Value Added Tax Act 1994 (c 23)
para 28(1)	s 41(3)
para 28(2)	s 41(4)
para 29	s 43(1)
para 30(1)	s 44(2)
para 30(2)	s 44(3)
para 30(3)	s 44(8)
para 31(1)	s 45(1)
para 31(2)	s 45(2)
para 31(3)	s 45(5)
para 32(1)	s 46(3)
para 32(2)	s 46(6)
para 33	s 47(1)
para 34	s 48
para 35	s 18
para 36(1)	s 34(1)
para 36(2)	s 34(2)
para 37	s 52
para 38	s 58
para 39(1)	s 72(2)
para 39(2)	s 72(5)(*a*)
para 39(3)	s 72(10)
para 40(*a*)	s 83(*b*)
para 40(*b*)	s 83(*j*)
para 40(*c*)	s 83(*d*)
para 40(*d*)	s 83(*w*)
para 40(*e*)	s 83(*p*)
para 40(*f*)	s 83(*l*)
para 40(*g*)	s 83(*n*)
para 41(1)	s 88(1)
para 41(2)	s 88(4)
para 41(3)	s 88(7)
para 42(1)	s 90(1)
para 42(2)	s 90(2)
para 42(3)	s 90(3)
para 43	s 98
para 44	ss 92, 93
para 45	s 95(1), (3)–(5)
para 46(1)	s 96(1)
para 46(2)	s 96(3), (5)
para 46(3)	s 96(8)
para 46(4)	s 96(2)
para 47	s 99
para 48(1)	Sch 1, para 1(1)
para 48(2)	Sch 1, para 1(2)
para 48(3)	Sch 1, para 1(4)
para 48(4)	Sch 1, para 1(5),(6)
para 48(5)	Sch 1, para 1(7)
para 49(1)	Sch 1, para 2(1),(4)(*b*)
para 49(2)	Sch 1, para 2(7)(*c*)
para 50	Sch 1, para 3
para 51(1)	Sch 1, para 4(1)
para 51(2)	Sch 1, para 4(2)
para 51(3)	Sch 1, para 4(3)
para 52	Sch 1, para 5(3)
para 53	Sch 1, paras 9, 10(1)
para 54	Sch 1, para 11
para 55	Sch 1, para 12
para 56(1)	Sch 1, para 13(1)
para 56(2)	Sch 1, para 13(4)
para 56(3)	Sch 1, para 13(7)
para 57(1)	Sch 1, para 13(2)
para 57(2)	Sch 1, para 13(5)
para 57(3)	Sch 1, para 18
para 58(1)	Sch 1, para 14(1)

† Not repealed
* Repealed in part

(1)	(2)
Finance (No 2) Act 1992 (c 48)	Value Added Tax Act 1994 (c 23)
para 58(2)	Sch 1, para 14(2)
para 59	Schs 2, 3
para 60(1)	Sch 4, para 6
para 60(2)	Sch 4, para 8(2)
para 61(1)	—
para 61(2)	Sch 6, para 3
para 61(3)	Sch 6, para 6
para 61(4)	Sch 6, para 8
para 61(5)	Sch 6, para 11
para 62	Sch 7
para 63(1)	Sch 8, Pt II, Group 12
para 63(2), (3)	Sch 8, Pt II, Group 13
para 63(4)	Sch 8, Pt II, Group 15
para 64(1)	Sch 11, para 2(1)
para 64(2)	Sch 11, para 2(2)
para 64(3)	Sch 11, para 2(3)–(5)
para 64(4)	Sch 11, para 2(8),(9)
para 65	Sch 11, para 3(3)
para 66(1)	s 73(3)
para 66(2)	s 73(6)
para 66(3)	s 73(7)
para 67	s 75
para 68	Sch 11, para 4(2)
para 69	Sch 11, para 5(10)
para 70	Sch 11, para 6(1)
para 71(1)	Sch 11, para 7(2)
para 71(2)	Sch 11, para 7(4)
para 72	Sch 11, para 8(1)
para 73	Sch 11, para 10(2)
para 74	Sch 11, para 14(1)(*c*)
para 75	—
Pt II	
para 76	—
para 77(1)	s 60(2)(*a*), (*c*)
para 77(2)	s 60(3)
para 78	s 63(9)
para 79	s 65
para 80(1)	s 67(1)(*a*), (*b*)
para 80(2)	s 67(3)(*a*)–(*c*)
para 80(3)	s 67(4)
para 80(4)	s 67(5), (6)
para 81	s 69(1)(*a*), (*b*)
para 82	ss 66, 97(5)
para 83	s 74(1)(*c*)
para 84(1)	s 76(1)
para 84(2)	s 76(6)
para 84(3)	s 76(7)
para 84(4)	s 76(8)
para 85(1)	s 77(1)
para 85(2)	s 77(2)
para 85(3)	s 77(6)
para 86	s 72(13)
Pt III	
para 87	Cf Sch 14, para 1
para 88	Cf Sch 14, para 2
para 89	Cf Sch 14, para 3
para 90	Cf Sch 14, para 4
para 91	Rep 1994 c 22, s 65, Sch 5 Pt I

(1)	(2)
Finance (No 2) Act 1992 (c 48)	Value Added Tax Act 1994 (c 23)
para 92	Cf Sch 14, para 5
para 93	—
para 94(*a*)	s 56(3)(*b*)
para 94(*b*)	s 56(5)
para 95	Cf Sch 14, para 10
Trade Union and Labour Relations (Consolidation) Act 1992 (c 52)	**Value Added Tax Act 1994 (c 23)**
Sch 2, para 32	Sch 9, Pt II, Group 9
Tribunals and Inquiries Act 1992 (c 53)	**Value Added Tax Act 1994 (c 23)**
Sch 3, para 17	s 86(2)
Judicial Pensions and Retirement Act 1993 (c 8)	**Value Added Tax Act 1994 (c 23)**
Sch 6, para 35(1)	Sch 12, para 3(3)
para 35(2)	Sch 12, para 7(6)
Sch 8, para 16(1)	Sch 12, para 3(7)
para 16(2)	Sch 12, para 7(9)
Finance Act 1993 (c 34)	**Value Added Tax Act 1994 (c 23)**
s 42	—
s 43(1)	—
s 43(2)(*a*)	s 57(5)(*a*)
s 43(2)(*b*)	s 57(5)(*b*)
s 43(2)(*c*)	s 57(7)
s 43(2)(*d*)	s 57(8)
s 43(3)	s 57(4)
s 44(1)	s 14(1)–(7)
s 44(2)	—
s 44(3)(*a*)	s 7(1)
s 44(3)(*b*)	s 13(1)
s 44(4)	s 14(8)
s 45(1)	s 55
s 45(2)	s 6(14)
s 45(3)	—
s 46(1)	s 84(4)
s 46(2)	s 84(11)
s 47(1)	—
s 47(2)	Sch 4, para 5(2)
s 47(3)	Sch 4, para 5(3)
s 47(4)	Sch 4, para 5(5)
s 48(1)	s 36(1)(*c*)
s 48(2)	—
s 49	—
s 50(1)–(3)	—
s 50(4)	Sch 11, para 2(8)
Sch 2, para 1(1)	s 63(2)
para 1(2)	s 63(4)–(6)
para 1(3)	s 63(8)
para 1(4)	—
para 2(1)	s 64(1)
para 2(2)	s 64(2), (3)
para 2(3)	s 64(4)
para 2(4)	s 64(6)
para 2(5), (6)	—
para 3(1)	s 70
para 3(2)(*a*)	s 60(1)
para 3(2)(*b*)	s 60(4)
para 3(2)(*c*)	s 84(6)
para 3(3)	—
para 4(1)	s 74(1), (2)
para 4(2)	s 74(3)
para 4(3)	—

† Not repealed
* Repealed in part

(1)	(2)	(1)	(2)

Finance Act 1993 (c 34)	Value Added Tax Act 1994 (c 23)
para 5(1)	s 59(2)
para 5(2)	s 59(3)
para 5(3)	—
para 6(1)	s 59(4)
para 6(2)	s 59(5)
para 6(3)	s 59(6)
para 6(4)	—
para 7(1), (2)	—
para 7(3)	s 59(5)
para 7(4)	—
para 8	—

Finance Act 1994 (c 9)	Value Added Tax Act 1994 (c 23)
s 7(1), (2)	s 82(1), (2), Sch 12, para 1
s 18(3)*	s 84(9)
s 45(1)	—
s 45(2)	s 63(3)
s 45(3)	s 63(8)
s 45(4)	—
s 46(1)	—
s 46(2)	s 79(1)
s 46(3)	s 79(2)
s 46(4)	—
s 47(1)	s 81(4), (5)
s 47(2)	—

Vehicle Excise and Registration Act 1994 (c 22)	Value Added Tax Act 1994 (c 23)
Sch 3, para 21	s 57(7)

Value Added Tax (Fuel and Power) Order 1980 (SI 1980/440)	Value Added Tax Act 1994 (c 23)
...	—

Value Added Tax (Charities, Etc) Order 1983 (SI 1983/1717)	Value Added Tax Act 1994 (c 23)
...	Sch 8, Pt II, Group 15

Value Added Tax (Handicapped Persons) Order 1984 (SI 1984/489)	Value Added Tax Act 1994 (c 23)
...	Sch 8, Pt II, Group 12

Value Added Tax (Lifeboats) Order 1984 (SI 1984/631)	Value Added Tax Act 1994 (c 23)
...	Sch 8, Pt II, Group 8

Value Added Tax (Charities, Etc) Order 1984 (SI 1984/766)	Value Added Tax Act 1994 (c 23)
...	Sch 8, Pt II, Group 15

Value Added Tax (Marine etc Insurance) Order 1984 (SI 1984/767)	Value Added Tax Act 1994 (c 23)
...	—

Value Added Tax (Handicapped Persons) (No 2) Order 1984 (SI 1984/959)	Value Added Tax Act 1994 (c 23)
...	Sch 8, Pt II, Group 12

Value Added Tax (Optical Appliances) Order 1984 (SI 1984/1784)	Value Added Tax Act 1994 (c 23)
...	—

Value Added Tax (Protected Buildings) Order 1985 (SI 1985/18)	Value Added Tax Act 1994 (c 23)
...	Sch 8, Pt II, Group 6

Value Added Tax (Charities, Etc) Order 1985 (SI 1985/431)	Value Added Tax Act 1994 (c 23)
...	—

Value Added Tax (Finance) Order 1985 (SI 1985/432)	Value Added Tax Act 1994 (c 23)
...	Sch 9, Pt II, Group 5

† Not repealed
* Repealed in part

(1)	(2)
Value Added Tax (Hiring of Goods) Order 1985 (SI 1985/799)	Value Added Tax Act 1994 (c 23)
arts 1, 2	—
art 3	Sch 5, paras 7, 8
art 4	—
Value Added Tax (Handicapped Persons) Order 1985 (SI 1985/919)	Value Added Tax Act 1994 (c 23)
art 3	Sch 8, Pt II, Group 12
Value Added Tax (Welfare) Order 1985 (SI 1985/1900)	Value Added Tax Act 1994 (c 23)
...	Sch 9, Pt II, Group 7
Value Added Tax (Handicapped Persons and Charities) Order 1986 (SI 1986/530)	Value Added Tax Act 1994 (c 23)
art 1	—
art 2	Sch 8, Pt II, Group 4
art 3	Sch 8, Pt II, Group 12
art 4	Sch 8, Pt II, Group 15
Value Added Tax (Charities) Order 1987 (SI 1987/437)	Value Added Tax Act 1994 (c 23)
art 1	—
art 2	Sch 8, Pt II, Group 12
art 3	Sch 8, Pt II, Group 15
Value Added Tax (Betting, Gaming and Lotteries) Order 1987 (SI 1987/517)	Value Added Tax Act 1994 (c 23)
...	Sch 9, Pt II, Group 4
Value Added Tax (International Services) Order 1987 (SI 1987/518)	Value Added Tax Act 1994 (c 23)
...	—
Value Added Tax (Construction of Buildings) (No 2) Order 1987 (SI 1987/1072)	Value Added Tax Act 1994 (c 23)
art 2	—
Value Added Tax (Finance) Order 1987 (SI 1987/860)	Value Added Tax Act 1994 (c 23)
...	Sch 9, Pt II, Group 5
Value Added Tax (Education) Order 1987 (SI 1987/1259)	Value Added Tax Act 1994 (c 23)
...	—
Value Added Tax (Tour Operators) Order 1987 (SI 1987/1806)	Value Added Tax Act 1994 (c 23)
art 11	Sch 8, Pt II, Group 8
Value Added Tax (Cash Accounting) Regulations 1987 (SI 1987/1427)	Value Added Tax Act 1994 (c 23)
reg 11†	s 83(*y*)
Value Added Tax (Confectionery) Order 1988 (SI 1988/507)	Value Added Tax Act 1994 (c 23)
...	Sch 8, Pt II, Group 1
Value Added Tax (Training) Order 1988 (SI 1988/1282)	Value Added Tax Act 1994 (c 23)
...	—
Value Added Tax (Education) Order 1989 (SI 1989/267)	Value Added Tax Act 1994 (c 23)
...	—
Value Added Tax (Fund-Raising Events and Charities) Order 1989 (SI 1989/470)	Value Added Tax Act 1994 (c 23)
art 1	—
art 2	Sch 8, Pt II, Group 15
art 3	Sch 9, Pt II, Group 12
Value Added Tax (Finance, Health and Welfare) Order 1989 (SI 1989/2272)	Value Added Tax Act 1994 (c 23)
art 1	—
art 2	Sch 9, Pt II, Group 5
art 3	Sch 9, Pt II, Group 7

† Not repealed
* Repealed in part

(1)	(2)
Value Added Tax (Increase of Registration Limits) Order 1990 (SI 1990/682)	Value Added Tax Act 1994 (c 23)
....	—
Value Added Tax (Charities) Order 1990 (SI 1990/750)	Value Added Tax Act 1994 (c 23)
....	Sch 8, Pt II, Group 15
Value Added Tax (Transport) Order 1990 (SI 1990/752)	Value Added Tax Act 1994 (c 23)
....	Sch 8, Pt II, Group 8
Value Added Tax (Insurance) Order 1990 (SI 1990/2037)	Value Added Tax Act 1994 (c 23)
....	Sch 9, Pt II, Group 2
Value Added Tax (Charities) (No 2) Order 1990 (SI 1990/2129)	Value Added Tax Act 1994 (c 23)
....	Sch 8, Pt II, Group 15
Value Added Tax (Construction of Dwellings and Land) Order 1990 (SI 1990/2553)	Value Added Tax Act 1994 (c 23)
art 1	—
art 2	Sch 8, Pt II, Group 5
art 3	Sch 9, Pt II, Group 1
Value Added Tax (Charities) Order 1991 (SI 1991/737)	Value Added Tax Act 1994 (c 23)
arts 1, 2	—
arts 3–6	Sch 8, Pt II, Group 15
art 7	—
art 8	Sch 8, Pt II, Group 15
art 9	Sch 9, Pt II, Group 12
Value Added Tax (Increase of Registration Limits) Order 1991 (SI 1991/738)	Value Added Tax Act 1994 (c 23)
....	—

(1)	(2)
Value Added Tax (Piped Gas) (Metrication) Order 1991 (SI 1991/2534)	Value Added Tax Act 1994 (c 23)
....	—
Value Added Tax (Buildings and Land) Order 1991 (SI 1991/2569)	Value Added Tax Act 1994 (c 23)
art 1	—
art 2	Sch 9, Pt II, Group 1
art 3	Sch 10, para 2(8),(9)
art 4	Sch 10, para 3(1),(6), (9)
art 5	Sch 10, para 5(8)–(10)
art 6	Sch 10, para 6(2)–(4), (6)–(8)
art 7	Sch 10, para 7
art 8	Sch 10, para 9
Value Added Tax (Charities and Aids for Handicapped Persons) Order 1992 (SI 1992/628)	Value Added Tax Act 1994 (c 23)
art 1	—
art 2	Sch 8, Pt II, Group 4
art 3	Sch 8, Pt II, Group 8
art 4	Sch 8, Pt II, Group 12
Value Added Tax (Increase of Registration Limits) Order 1992 (SI 1992/629)	Value Added Tax Act 1994 (c 23)
....	—
Value Added Tax (Increase of Consideration for Fuel) Order 1992 (SI 1992/733)	Value Added Tax Act 1994 (c 23)
....	—
Value Added Tax (Motor Vehicles for the Handicapped) Order 1992 (SI 1992/3065)	Value Added Tax Act 1994 (c 23)
....	Sch 8, Pt II, Group 12
Customs and Excise (Single Market etc) Regulations 1992 (SI 1992/3095)	Value Added Tax Act 1994 (c 23)
Sch 1, para 8†	Sch 8, Pt II, Group 13

† Not repealed
* Repealed in part

(1)	(2)
Value Added Tax (Transport) Order 1992 (SI 1992/3126)	Value Added Tax Act 1994 (c 23)
....	Sch 8, Pt II, Group 8
Value Added Tax (Means of Transport) Order 1992 (SI 1992/3127)	Value Added Tax Act 1994 (c 23)
....	s 95(1), (2)
Value Added Tax (Tax Free Shops) Order 1992 (SI 1992/3131)	Value Added Tax Act 1994 (c 23)
....	Sch 8, Pt II, Group 14
Value Added Tax (International Services and Transport) Order 1992 (SI 1992/3223)	Value Added Tax Act 1994 (c 23)
art 1..	—
art 2..	Sch 8, Pt II, Group 7
art 3..	Sch 8, Pt II, Group 8
art 4..	—
Value Added Tax (Increase of Consideration for Fuel) Order 1993 (SI 1993/765)	Value Added Tax Act 1994 (c 23)
....	—
Value Added Tax (Increase of Registration Limits) Order 1993 (SI 1993/766)	Value Added Tax Act 1994 (c 23)
....	—
Value Added Tax (Protective Boots and Helmets) Order 1993 (SI 1993/767)	Value Added Tax Act 1994 (c 23)
....	Sch 8, Pt II, Group 16
Value Added Tax (Education) (No 2) Order 1993 (SI 1993/1124)	Value Added Tax Act 1994 (c 23)
....	—
Finance Act 1993 (Appointed Day) Order 1993 (SI 1993/2214)	Value Added Tax Act 1994 (c 23)
....	—
Value Added Tax (Revenue Charge) Order 1993 (SI 1993/2328)	Value Added Tax Act 1994 (c 23)
arts 1, 2..............................	—
art 3..................................	Sch 5, para 9
art 4..................................	Sch 5, para 10
art 5..................................	—
Value Added Tax (Beverages) Order 1993 (SI 1993/2498)	Value Added Tax Act 1994 (c 23)
....	Sch 8, Pt II, Group I
Value Added Tax (Increase of Consideration for Fuel) (No 2) Order 1993 (SI 1993/2952)	Value Added Tax Act 1994 (c 23)
....	s 57(3), Table A
Value Added Tax (Increase of Registration Limits) (No 2) Order 1993 (SI 1993/2953)	Value Added Tax Act 1994 (c 23)
art 1..................................	—
art 2..................................	Sch 1, paras 1(1)–(3), 4(1), (2)
art 3..................................	Sch 3, paras 1(1), (2), 2
Value Added Tax (Tax Free Shops) Order 1994 (SI 1994/686)	Value Added Tax Act 1994 (c 23)
....	Sch 8, Pt II, Group 14
Value Added Tax (Sport, Physical Education and Fund-Raising Events) Order 1994 (SI 1994/687)	Value Added Tax Act 1994 (c 23)
art 1..................................	—
art 2..................................	Sch 9, Pt II, Group 10
art 3..................................	Sch 9, Pt II, Group 12
Value Added Tax (Education) Order 1994 (SI 1994/1188)	Value Added Tax Act 1994 (c 23)
....	Sch 9, Pt II, Group 6

† Not repealed
* Repealed in part

FINANCE ACT 1995

(1995 Chapter 4)

An Act to grant certain duties, to alter other duties, and to amend the law relating to the National Debt and the Public Revenue, and to make further provision in connection with Finance.

[1 May 1995]

PART II

VALUE ADDED TAX AND INSURANCE PREMIUM TAX

Value added tax

21 Fuel and power for domestic or charity use

Amendments—This section repealed by FA 2001 s 110, Sch 33 Pt 3(1) with effect for supplies made, and acquisitions and importations taking place, after 31 October 2001 (by virtue of FA 2001 s 99(7)(*b*)).

22 Imported works of art, antiques, etc

(1) (*amends* VATA 1994 s 21).

(2) This section shall have effect in relation to goods imported at any time on or after the day on which this Act is passed.

Commentary—*De Voil Indirect Tax Service* **V3.355**.

23 Agent acting in their own names

(1)–(3) (*amend* VATA 1994 s 47).

(4) This section shall have effect—

(*a*) so far as it amends section 47(1) of that Act, in relation to goods acquired or imported on or after the day on which this Act is passed; and

(*b*) for other purposes, in relation to any supply taking place on or after that day.

24 Margin schemes

(1) (*inserts* VATA 1994 s 50A).

(2) Section 32 of that Act (relief on supply of certain second-hand goods) shall cease to have effect on such day as the Commissioners of Customs and Excise may by order made by statutory instrument appoint.

Commentary—*De Voil Indirect Tax Service* **V3.351**.
Notes—"That Act" in sub-s (2) is VATA 1994.

25 Groups of companies

(1) Section 43 of the Value Added Tax Act 1994 (groups of companies) shall be amended as follows.

(*2*) (*amends* VATA 1994 s 43).

(*3*), (4) …[1]

(5) Subsection (2) above has effect in relation to—

(*a*) any supply made on or after 1st March 1995, and

(*b*) any supply made before that date in the case of which both the body making the supply and the body supplied continued to be members of the group in question until at least that date,

and subsections (3) and (4) above have effect in relation to applications made on or after the day on which this Act is passed.

Commentary—*De Voil Indirect Tax Service* **V2.113**.
Amendments—[1] Sub-ss (3), (4) repealed by FA 1999 Sch 20 Pt II with effect from 27 July 1999 subject to FA 1999 s 16, Sch 2 para 6.

26 Co-owners etc of buildings and land

Repeal—This section repealed by the Value Added Tax (Buildings and Land) Order, SI 2008/1146 art 5(1) with effect in relation to supplies in relation to supplies made on or after 1 June 2008, subject to savings in Sch 2 of the Order.

27 Set-off of credits

(1) Section 81 of the Value Added Tax Act 1994 (which includes provision as to the setting off of credits) shall be amended as follows.

(2) (3) (*amends* VATA 1994 s 81).

(4) This section shall have effect in relation to amounts becoming due from the Commissioners of Customs and Excise at times on or after the day on which this Act is passed.

28 Transactions treated as supplies for purposes of zero-rating etc

(1) (*amends* VATA 1994 s 30).

(2) This section shall have effect in relation to transactions occurring on or after the day on which this Act is passed.

Commentary—*De Voil Indirect Tax Service* **V4.266**.

29 Goods removed from warehousing regime

(*amends* VATA 1994 s 18).

Commentary—*De Voil Indirect Tax Service* **V3.138**.

30 Fuel supplied for private use

(1) Section 57 of the Value Added Tax Act 1994 (determination of consideration for fuel supplied for private use) shall be amended as follows.

(2)–(5) (*amends* VATA 1994 s 57).

(6) This section shall apply in relation to prescribed accounting periods beginning on or after 6th April 1995.

(7) Nothing in this section shall be taken to prejudice any practice by which the consideration appropriate to a vehicle is arrived at where a prescribed accounting period beginning before 6th April 1995 is a period of 12 months.

Commentary—*De Voil Indirect Tax Service* **V3.176**.

31 Appeals: payment of amounts shown in returns

(1) (*amends* VATA 1994 s 84).

(2) This section shall apply in relation to appeals brought after the day on which this Act is passed.

32 Penalties for failure to notify etc

(1) (*amends* VATA 1994 s 67).

(2) Section 15(3A) of the Finance Act 1985 (provision which is repealed by the 1994 Act and which corresponds to section 67(4)) shall have effect subject to the amendments made by subsection (1) above.

(3) Subject to subsection (4) below, subsections (1) and (2) above shall apply where a penalty is assessed on or after 1st January 1995.

(4) Subsections (1) and (2) above shall not apply in the case of a supplementary assessment if the original assessment was made before 1st January 1995.

Commentary—*De Voil Indirect Tax Service* **V5.347–5.350**.

Prospective amendments—This section to be repealed by FA 2008 s 123, Sch 41 para 25(*g*) with effect from 1 April 2010 (by virtue of SI 2009/511 art 2).

33 Correction of consolidation errors

(1) The Value Added Tax Act 1994 shall have effect, and be deemed always to have had effect, as if it had been enacted as follows.

(2)–(5) (*amends* VATA 1994 s 35, Sch 4 para 5, Sch 6 para 7, Sch 13 para 9, Sch 14 para 13).

PART VI
MISCELLANEOUS AND GENERAL

General

163 Short title

This Act may be cited as the Finance Act 1995.

FINANCE ACT 1996

(1996 Chapter 8)

ARRANGEMENT OF SECTIONS

PART II
VALUE ADDED TAX

EC Second VAT Simplification Directive

An Act to grant certain duties, to alter other duties, and to amend the law relating to the National Debt and the Public Revenue, and to make further provision in connection with Finance.

29th April 1996

PART II

VALUE ADDED TAX

EC Second VAT Simplification Directive

25 EC Second VAT Simplification Directive

Sections 26 to 29 of and Schedule 3 to this Act are for the purpose of giving effect to requirements of the directive of the Council of the European Communities dated 17th May 1977 No 77/388/EEC and the amendments of that directive by the directive of that Council dated 10th April 1995 No 95/7/EC (amendments with a view to introducing new simplification measures with regard to value added tax).

Commentary—*De Voil Indirect Tax Service* **V1.227**.

26 Fiscal and other warehousing

(1) The provisions of Schedule 3 to this Act shall have effect.

(2) Subject to subsection (3) below, this section and Schedule 3 to this Act shall come into force on such day as the Commissioners of Customs and Excise may by order made by statutory instrument appoint, and shall apply to any acquisition of goods from another member State and any supply taking place on or after that day.

(3) In so far as the provisions inserted by Schedule 3 to this Act confer power to make regulations they shall come into force on the day this Act is passed.

Commentary—*De Voil Indirect Tax Service* **V3.176, V3.332**.

27 Value of imported goods

(1) Section 21 of the Value Added Tax Act 1994 (value of imported goods) shall be amended as follows.

(2), (3) (*amends* VATA 1994 s 21(2)(*a*), (*b*)).

(4) This section shall have effect in relation to goods imported on or after 1st January 1996.

Commentary—*De Voil Indirect Tax Service* **V3.323**.

28 Adaptation of aircraft and hovercraft

(1) Section 22 of the Value Added Tax Act 1994 shall be omitted.

(2) This section shall apply to supplies made on or after 1st January 1996.

29 Work on materials

(1) The Value Added Tax Act 1994 shall be amended as follows.

(2), (3) (*insert* VATA 1994 ss 30(2A), 55(5)(*c*)).

(4) Paragraph 2 of Schedule 4 (which provides that the treatment or processing of another person's goods shall in certain circumstances be a supply of goods) shall be omitted.

(5) This section shall apply to supplies made on or after 1st January 1996.

Commentary—*De Voil Indirect Tax Service* **V3.112; V4.206; V5.143.**

Other provisions relating to charges to VAT

30 Refunds in connection with construction and conversion

(1)–(3) (*substitute* VATA 1994 s 35(1), (1A)–(1D), *amend* s 35(2) and *insert* s 34(4), (5)).

(4) This section applies in relation to any case in which a claim for repayment under section 35 of the Value Added Tax Act 1994 is made at any time on or after the day on which this Act is passed.

Commentary—*De Voil Indirect Tax Service* **V5.164**.

31 Groups: anti-avoidance

(1) (*inserts* VATA 1994 s 43(9)).

(2) After Schedule 9 to that Act there shall be inserted the Schedule set out in Schedule 4 to this Act.

(3), (4) (*amend* VATA 1994 s 83(*ab*) and *insert* VATA 1994 s 84(7A)).

(5) Subsection (1A) of section 43 of that Act shall not have effect in relation to supplies on or after the day on which this Act is passed.

Commentary—*De Voil Indirect Tax Service* **V2.104, V2.113**.

32 Supplies of gold etc

(1) (*substitutes* VATA 1994 s 55(5) (*a*)).

(2) This section applies in relation to any supply after 28th November 1995.

Commentary—*De Voil Indirect Tax Service* **V3.502, V5.143**.

33 Small gifts

(1)–(3) (*amend* VATA 1994 Sch 4 para 5(2)(*a*) and *insert* s 97(4)(*ab*), Sch 4, para 5(7)).

(4) Subsection (1) above shall apply where a gift is made after 28th November 1995.

Commentary—*De Voil Indirect Tax Service* **V3.211**.

Payment and enforcement

34 Method of making payments on account

(*inserts* VATA 1994 s 28(2A)).

Commentary—*De Voil Indirect Tax Service* **V3.211**.

35 Default surcharges

(1) The Value Added Tax Act 1994 shall be amended as follows.

(2)–(7) (*insert* VATA 1994 s 59(11), 59A, 59B and *amend* ss 59(1), 69(4)(*a*), (9)(*b*), 76(1), (3)(*a*)).

(8) This section applies in relation to any prescribed accounting period ending on or after 1st June 1996, but a liability to make a payment on account of VAT shall be disregarded for the purposes of the amendments made by this section if the payment is one becoming due before that date.

Commentary—*De Voil Indirect Tax Service* **V5.371–5.380**.

36 Repeated misdeclaration penalty

(1) (*substitutes* VATA 1994 s 64(6), (6A), (7) *for* s 64(6), (7)).

(2) This section has effect in relation to inaccuracies contained in returns made on or after the day on which this Act is passed.

Commentary—*De Voil Indirect Tax Service* **V5.344**.
Prospective amendment—This section to be repealed by FA 2007 ss 97, 114, Sch 27 Pt 5(5) with effect from a date to be appointed.

37 Penalties for failure to notify

(1) (amends VATA 1994 s 67(1), (a), 3(a)).

(2) Subject to subsection (3) below, subsection (1) above shall apply in relation to—

(a) any person becoming liable to be registered by virtue of sub-paragraph (2) of paragraph 1 of Schedule 1 to the Value Added Tax Act 1994 on or after 1st January 1996; and

(b) any person who became liable to be registered by virtue of that sub-paragraph before that date but who had not notified the Commissioners of the liability before that date.

(3) In relation to a person falling within subsection (2)(b) above, section 67 of the Value Added Tax Act 1994 shall have effect as if in subsection (3)(a) for the words "the date with effect from which he is, in accordance with that paragraph, required to be registered" there were substituted "1st January 1996".

Commentary—*De Voil Indirect Tax Service* **V2.129, V2.137; V5.347.**

Prospective amendments—This section to be repealed by FA 2008 s 123, Sch 41 para 25 from 1 April 2010 (by virtue of SI 2009/511 art 2).

38 VAT invoices and accounting

(1) Paragraph 2 of Schedule 11 to the Value Added Tax Act 1994 (regulations about accounting for VAT, VAT invoices etc) shall be amended as follows.

(2), (3) (*insert* VATA 1994 Sch 11, para 2(2A), 10(*d*), (*e*)); *repealed in part* by FA 2002 s 139(2), Sch 40 Pt 2(2) with effect from 1 December 2003 (by virtue of SI 2003/3043)).

Commentary—*De Voil Indirect Tax Service* **V3.514, V3.518–3.520.**

PART VII

MISCELLANEOUS AND SUPPLEMENTAL

Miscellaneous: indirect taxation

197 Setting of rates of interest

(1) The rate of interest applicable for the purposes of an enactment to which this section applies shall be the rate which for the purposes of that enactment is provided for by regulations made by the Treasury under this section.

(2) This section applies to—

(*a*), (*b*) …

(*c*) sections 74 and 78 of the Value Added Tax Act 1994 (interest on VAT recovered or recoverable by assessment and interest payable in cases of official error); …

(*d*)–(*h*) …

(3) Regulations under this section may—

(*a*) make different provision for different enactments or for different purposes of the same enactment,

(*b*) either themselves specify a rate of interest for the purposes of an enactment or make provision for any such rate to be determined, and to change from time to time, by reference to such rate or the average of such rates as may be referred to in the regulations,

(*c*) provide for rates to be reduced below, or increased above, what they otherwise would be by specified amounts or by reference to specified formulae,

(*d*) provide for rates arrived at by reference to averages or formulae to be rounded up or down,

(*e*) provide for circumstances in which changes of rates of interest are or are not to take place, and

(*f*) provide that changes of rates are to have effect for periods beginning on or after a day determined in accordance with the regulations in relation to interest running from before that day, as well as in relation to interest running from, or from after, that day.

(4) The power to make regulations under this section shall be exercisable by statutory instrument subject to annulment in pursuance of a resolution of the House of Commons.

(5) *Where—*

(*a*) *regulations under this section provide, without specifying the rate determined in accordance with the regulations, for a new method of determining the rate applicable for the purposes of any enactment, or*

(*b*) *the rate which, in accordance with regulations under this section, is the rate applicable for the purposes of any enactment changes otherwise than by virtue of the making of regulations specifying a new rate,*

the Commissioners of Customs and Excise shall make an order specifying the new rate and the day from which, in accordance with the regulations, it has effect.[1]

(6) The words "the rate applicable under section 197 of the Finance Act 1996" shall be substituted—

(*a*)–(*c*) …

(*d*) in the Value Added Tax Act 1994—

(i), (ii) (*amends* VATA 1994 s 74(1), (2), (4), 78(3)).

(7) Subsections (1) and (6) above shall have effect for periods beginning on or after such day as the Treasury may by order made by statutory instrument appoint and shall have effect in relation to interest running from before that day, as well as in relation to interest running from, or from after, that day; and different days may be appointed under this subsection for different purposes.

Commentary—*De Voil Indirect Tax Service* **V5.196, V5.361–5.365**.

Note—Sub-ss (2)(*a*), (*b*), (*d*)–(*h*), (6)(*a*)–(*c*) are not relevant to VAT.

Sub-ss (1), (6) have effect for periods beginning on or after 1 April 1997 (see FA 1996 s 197 (Appointed Day) Order, SI 1997/1015).

Amendment—[1] Sub-s (5) repealed by FA 2009 s 105(6)(*b*) with effect from 21 July 2009.

Supplemental

205 Repeals

(1) The enactments mentioned in Schedule 41 to this Act (which include spent provisions) are hereby repealed to the extent specified in the third column of that Schedule.

(2) The repeals specified in that Schedule have effect subject to the commencement provisions and savings contained in, or referred to, in the notes set out in that Schedule.

206 Short title

This Act may be cited as the Finance Act 1996.

SCHEDULES

SCHEDULE 3

VALUE ADDED TAX: FISCAL AND OTHER WAREHOUSING

Section 26

1–18 (*amend* VATA 1994 ss 6(1), 7(1), 12(1), 13(1), 20(1), 30(10), 62(1), (3), (4), 73(9), 76(5), 83(*p*)(ii), Sch 11 para 8(1), 10(2), and *insert* ss 18A–18F, 30(8A), 69(1)(*g*), 73(7A), (7B), 83(*da*), Sch 2 para 1(7), Sch 3, para 1(6), Sch 5A).

Commentary—*De Voil Indirect Tax Service* **V3.176, V3.332**.

Amendment—Para 17 repealed by FA 2008 s 113, Sch 36 para 92(*e*), (*f*) with effect from 1 April 2009 (by virtue of SI 2009/404 art 2).

In consequence of SI 2009/404 arts 1–11, the amendments made by FA 2008 Sch 36 para 92 shall be disregarded so far as they affect any notice referred to in those provisions, given on or before 31 March 2009.

SCHEDULE 4

VALUE ADDED TAX: ANTI-AVOIDANCE PROVISIONS

Section 31

(*Inserts VATA 1994 Sch 9A.*)

Commentary—*De Voil Indirect Tax Service* **V2.104, V2.113**.

SCHEDULE 41

REPEALS

Section 205

Note—All repeals relevant to VAT are already in effect and have therefore been omitted.

FINANCE ACT 1997

(1997 Chapter 16)

ARRANGEMENT OF SECTIONS

PART I

EXCISE DUTIES

Gaming duty

PART III
VALUE ADDED TAX

PART IV
PAYMENTS AND OVERPAYMENTS IN RESPECT OF INDIRECT TAXES

An Act to grant certain duties, to alter other duties, and to amend the law relating to the National Debt and the Public Revenue, and to make further provision in connection with Finance.

[19th March 1997]

PART I

EXCISE DUTIES

Gaming duty

13 Supplemental provisions relating to gaming duty

(2) Schedule 2 to this Act (which amends the Customs and Excise Management Act 1979 and contains other amendments) shall have effect.

PART III

VALUE ADDED TAX

Registration

31 Aggregation of businesses

(1) (*inserts* VATA 1994 Sch 1 para 1A).

(2), (3) (*amend* VATA 1994 s 84(7) Sch 1 para 2(2)(4)).

(4) This section has effect in relation to the making of directions on or after the day on which this Act is passed.

Commentary—*De Voil Indirect Tax Service* **V2.223**.

32 Voluntary registration

(*substitutes* VATA 1994 Sch 1 para 10(2)).

Commentary—*De Voil Indirect Tax Service* **V4.136**.

Zero-rating

33 Sale of goods donated to charity

(1) (*substitutes* VATA 1994 Sch 8 Group 15 Note (1)).

(2) This section has effect in relation to supplies made on or after 26th November 1996.

Commentary—*De Voil Indirect Tax Service* **V4.266**.

34 Charitable institutions providing care etc

(1), (2) (*inserts* VATA 1994 Sch 8 Group 15 Notes (4A) and (4B), (5A) and (5B)).

(3) This section has effect in relation to supplies made on or after 26th November 1996.

Commentary—*De Voil Indirect Tax Service* **V4.266**.

Buildings and land

35 References to grants

(1), (2) (*insert* VATA 1994 s 96(10A), Sch 10 para 3(5A) and (5B); sub-s (2) *repealed* by SI 2008/1146 with effect in relation to supplies made on or after 1 June 2008).

(3) Amendments corresponding to those made by subsections (1) and (2) above shall be deemed to have had effect, for the purposes of the cases to which it applied, in relation to the Value Added Tax Act 1983; and any provisions about the coming into force of any amendment of that Act shall be deemed to have had effect accordingly.

(4) Nothing in this section shall be taken to affect the operation, in relation to times before its repeal took effect, of paragraph 4 of Schedule 10 to the Value Added Tax Act 1994 or of any enactment re-enacted in that paragraph.

Commentary—*De Voil Indirect Tax Service* **V4.115**.

36 Buildings intended to be used as dwellings

Repeal—Section 36 repealed by the Value Added Tax (Buildings and Land) Order, SI 2008/1146, art 6, Sch 1 paras 6, 8 with effect in relation to supplies made on or after 1 June 2008, subject to savings in Sch 2 of the Order.

37 Supplies to non-taxable persons etc

(1) Paragraphs 2(3A) and 3(8A) of Schedule 10 to the Value Added Tax Act 1994 (which relate to grants of land made to connected persons where they are not fully taxable) shall not have effect in relation to any supply made after 26th November 1996.

(2)–(6) …[1]

Commentary—*De Voil Indirect Tax Service* **V4.115**.

Amendments—[1] Sub-ss (2)–(6) repealed by the Value Added Tax (Buildings and Land) Order, SI 2008/1146, art 6, Sch 1 paras 6, 9 with effect in relation to supplies made on or after 1 June 2008, subject to savings in Sch 2 of the Order.

Exempt insurance supplies

38 Exempt insurance supplies

(1) (*substitutes* VATA 1994 Sch 9 Group 2).

(2) This section has effect in relation to supplies made on or after the day on which this Act is passed.

Commentary—*De Voil Indirect Tax Service* **V4.121**.

Bad debt relief

39 Bad debt relief

(1) In section 36 of the Value Added Tax Act 1994, paragraph (*b*) of subsection (4) (condition of bad debt relief that property in goods supplied has passed) shall not apply in the case of any claim made under that section in relation to a supply of goods made after the day on which this Act is passed.

(2) (*inserts* VATA 1994 s 36(4A)).

(3) Subsection (2) above has effect in relation to any entitlement under section 36 of that Act of 1994 to a refund of VAT charged on a supply made after 26th November 1996.

(4) (*inserts* VATA 1994 s 36(5)(*ea*)).

(5) No claim for a refund may be made in accordance with section 22 of the Value Added Tax Act 1983 (old scheme for bad debt relief) at any time after the day on which this Act is passed.

Commentary—*De Voil Indirect Tax Service* **V5.156**.

Prospective amendments—Sub-s (2)–(4) to be repealed by FA 2002 s 139, Sch 40 Pt 2(1) with effect for supplies made on or after such day as the Commissioners appoint by statutory instrument.

Groups of companies

40 Groups containing bodies of different descriptions

(1), (2) (*inserts* VATA 1994 s 43(1AA) and (1AB) and amends s 43(2)).

(3) Subsection (1) above has effect in relation to any supply made after 26th November 1996 and in relation to any acquisition or importation taking place after that date.

Commentary—*De Voil Indirect Tax Service* **V2.104**.

41 Group supplies using an overseas member

(1) (*inserts* VATA 1994 s 43(2A), (2B), (2C), ((2D) and (2E)).

(2) Subject to subsection (3) below, subsection (1) above has effect in relation to supplies made on or after 26th November 1996.

(3) Section 43 of the Value Added Tax Act 1994 shall have effect in relation to supplies made after the day on which this Act is passed with the provisions inserted by subsection (1) above modified in accordance with subsections (4) and (5) below.

(4) In subsection (2A), in paragraph (*c*) for the words from "services" to the end of the paragraph there shall be substituted "any services falling within paragraphs 1 to 8 of Schedule 5 which do not fall within any of the descriptions specified in Schedule 9;".

(5) In subsection (2C), at the beginning there shall be inserted "Except in so far as the Commissioners may by regulations otherwise provide,".

Commentary—*De Voil Indirect Tax Service* **V2.104**.

Incidental and supplemental provisions etc

42 Services subject to the reverse charge

(*inserts* VATA 1994 s 8(7) and (8)).

Commentary—*De Voil Indirect Tax Service* **V3.181–V3.183**.

43 Payments on account: appeals

(*inserts* VATA 1994 s 28(2AA)).

Commentary—*De Voil Indirect Tax Service* **V5.110**.

PART IV

PAYMENTS AND OVERPAYMENTS IN RESPECT OF INDIRECT TAXES

Value added tax

44 Liability of Commissioners to interest

(1) (*inserts* VATA 1994 s 78(1A)).

(2)–(4) (*substitute* VATA 1994 ss 74(8), (9), (12)(*a*), 78(11)).

(5) Subsection (4) above shall have effect for the purposes of determining whether any period beginning on or after the day on which this Act is passed is left out of account.

(6) Amendments corresponding to those made by subsections (1) and (3) above shall be deemed to have had effect, for the purposes of the cases to which the enactments applied, in relation to the enactments directly or indirectly re-enacted in section 78 of the Value Added Tax Act 1994.

Commentary—*De Voil Indirect Tax Service* **V5.151–V5.166**.

45 Assessment for overpayments of interest

(1)–(3) (*insert* VATA 1994 s 78A, 83(*sa*), 84(3A).)

(4) Subsection (1) above shall be deemed to have come into force on 4th December 1996 in relation to amounts paid by way of interest at any time on or after 18th July 1996.

(5) Subsections (2) and (3) above shall be deemed to have come into force on 4th December 1996 in relation to assessments made on or after that date.

(6) (*amends* VATA 1994 s 76(10)).

Commentary—*De Voil Indirect Tax Service* **V5.151–V5.166**.

46 Repayments of overpayments: unjust enrichment

(1)–(3) (*insert* VATA 1994 ss 80(3A), (3B), (3C), 80A, 80B, 83(*ta*)).

(4) Subsection (1) above has effect for the purposes of making any repayment on or after the day on which this Act is passed, even if the claim for that repayment was made before that day.

Commentary—*De Voil Indirect Tax Service* **V5.151–V5.166**.

47 Repayments and assessments: time limits

(1) (*substitutes* VATA 1994 s 80(4) and (5)).

(2) Subject to subsections (3) and (4) below, subsection (1) above shall be deemed to have come into force on 18th July 1996 as a provision applying, for the purposes of the making of any repayment on or after that date, to all claims under section 80 of the Value Added Tax Act 1994, including claims made before that date and claims relating to payments made before that date.

(3) Subsection (4) below applies as respects the making of any repayment on or after 18th July 1996 on a claim under section 80 of the Value Added Tax Act 1994 if—

(*a*) legal proceedings for questioning any decision ("the disputed decision") of the Commissioners, or of an officer of the Commissioners, were brought by any person at any time before that date,

(*b*) a determination has been or is made in those proceedings that the disputed decision was wrong or should be set aside,

(*c*) the claim is one made by that person at a time after the proceedings were brought (whether before or after the making of the determination), and

(*d*) the claim relates to—

(i) an amount paid by that person to the Commissioners on the basis of the disputed decision, or

(ii) an amount paid by that person to the Commissioners before the relevant date (including an amount paid before the making of the disputed decision) on grounds which, in all material respects, correspond to those on which that decision was made.

(4) Where this subsection applies in the case of any claim—

(*a*) subsection (4) of section 80 of the Value Added Tax Act 1994 (as inserted by this section) shall not apply, and shall be taken never to have applied, in relation to so much of that claim as relates to an amount falling within subsection (3)(*d*)(i) or (ii) above, but

(*b*) the Commissioners shall not be liable on that claim, and shall be taken never to have been liable on that claim, to repay any amount so falling which was paid to them more than three years before the proceedings mentioned in subsection (3)(*a*) above were brought.

(5) In subsection (3)(*d*) above—

(*a*) the reference to the relevant date is a reference to whichever is the earlier of 18th July 1996 and the date of the making of the determination in question; and

(*b*) the reference to an amount paid on the basis of a decision, or on any grounds, includes an amount so paid on terms (however expressed) which questioned the correctness of the decision or, as the case may be, of those grounds.

(6), (7) (*insert* VATA 1994 s 80(4A), (4B) and (4C), and *amend* s 83(*t*)).

(8) Nothing contained in—

(*a*) any regulations under section 25(1) of, or paragraph 2 of Schedule 11 to, that Act relating to the correction of errors or the making of adjustments, or

(*b*) any requirement imposed under any such regulations,

shall be taken, in relation to any time on or after 18th July 1996, to have conferred an entitlement on any person to receive, by way of repayment, any amount to which he would not have had any entitlement on a claim under section 80 of that Act.

(9) Subsections (6) to (8) above shall be deemed to have come into force on 4th December 1996.

(10) (*amends* VATA 1994 s 77(1) and (4)).

(11) In this section—

"the Commissioners" means the Commissioners of Customs and Excise; and

"legal proceedings" means any proceedings before a court or tribunal.

(12) Without prejudice to the generality of paragraph 1(2) of Schedule 13 to the Value Added Tax Act 1994 (transitional provisions), the references in this section, and in subsection (4) of section 80 of that Act (as inserted by this section), to a claim under that section include references to a claim first made under section 24 of the Finance Act 1989 which was re-enacted in section 80.

Commentary—*De Voil Indirect Tax Service* **V5.151–V5.166**.

Prospective amendments—In sub-s (10) to be repealed by FA 2008 Sch 39 para 65(*c*) with effect from 1 April 2010 (by virtue of SI 2009/403 art 2(2)), subject to transitional provisions in SI 2009/403 art 10(2) (where art 10 applies the appointed day is 1 April 2012).

48 Set-off of credits and debits

(1) (*inserts* VATA 1994 s 81(3A)).

(2) Subsection (1) above shall be deemed to have come into force on 18th July 1996 as a provision applying for determining the amount of any payment or repayment by the Commissioners on or after that date, including a payment or repayment in respect of a liability arising before that date.

Commentary—*De Voil Indirect Tax Service* **V5.151–V5.166**.

49 Transitional provision for set-offs etc

(1) Where—

(*a*) at any time before 4th December 1996, any person ("the taxpayer") became liable to pay any sum ("the relevant sum") to the Commissioners by way of VAT, penalty, interest or surcharge,

(*b*) at any time on or after 18th July 1996 and before 4th December 1996 an amount was set against the whole or any part of the relevant sum,

(*c*) the amount set against that sum was an amount which is treated under section 47 above as not having been due from the Commissioners at the time when it was set against that sum, and

(*d*) as a consequence, the taxpayer's liability to pay the whole or a part of the relevant sum falls to be treated as not having been discharged in accordance with section 81(3) of the 1994 Act,

the Commissioners may, to the best of their judgement, assess the amount of the continuing liability of the taxpayer and notify it to him.

(2) In subsection (1) above the reference to the continuing liability of the taxpayer is a reference to so much of the liability to pay the relevant sum as—

(*a*) would have been discharged if the amount mentioned in subsection (1)(*b*) above had been required to be set against the relevant sum in accordance with section 81(3) of the 1994 Act, but

(*b*) falls, by virtue of section 47 above, to be treated as not having been discharged in accordance with section 81(3) of that Act.

(3) The taxpayer's only liabilities under the 1994 Act in respect of his failure, on or after the time mentioned in subsection (1)(*b*) above, to pay an amount assessable under this section shall be—

(*a*) his liability to be assessed for that amount under this section; and

(*b*) liabilities arising under the following provisions of this section.

(4) Subsections (2) to (8) of section 78A of the 1994 Act apply in the case of an assessment under subsection (1) above as they apply in the case of an assessment under section 78A(1) of that Act.

(5) The 1994 Act shall have effect as if the matters specified in section 83 of that Act (matters subject to appeal) included an assessment under this section and the amount of such an assessment.

(6) Nothing contained in—

(*a*) any regulations under section 25(1) of, or paragraph 2 of Schedule 11 to, the 1994 Act relating to the correction of errors or the making of adjustments, or

(*b*) any requirement imposed under any such regulations,

shall be taken, in relation to any time on or after 18th July 1996, to have conferred on any person any entitlement, otherwise than in accordance with section 81(3) of that Act, to set any amount, as an amount due from the Commissioners, against any sum which that person was liable to pay to the Commissioners by way of VAT, penalty, interest or surcharge.

(7) In this section—

"the 1994 Act" means the Value Added Tax Act 1994; and

"the Commissioners" means the Commissioners of Customs and Excise.

(8) This section shall be deemed to have come into force on 4th December 1996.

(9) Where at any time on or after 4th December 1996 and before the day on which this Act is passed any assessment corresponding to an assessment under this section was made under a resolution of the House of Commons having effect in accordance with the provisions of the Provisional Collection of Taxes Act 1968, this section has effect, on and after the day on which this Act is passed, as if that assessment were an assessment under this section and as if any appeal brought under that resolution had been brought under this section.

Commentary—*De Voil Indirect Tax Service* **V5.151–V5.166**

Excise duties and other indirect taxes

50 Overpayments, interest, assessments, etc

…

(2) Schedule 6 to this Act (which makes further provision for the assessment of amounts payable under enactments relating to excise duty) shall also have effect.

Notes—Words omitted are not relevant for the purposes of VAT.

Enforcement of payment

51 Enforcement by distress

(1) The Commissioners may by regulations make provision—

(*a*) for authorising distress to be levied on the goods and chattels of any person refusing or neglecting to pay—

(i) any amount of relevant tax due from him, or

(ii) any amount recoverable as if it were relevant tax due from him;

(*b*) for the disposal of any goods or chattels on which distress is levied in pursuance of the regulations; and

(*c*) for the imposition and recovery of costs, charges, expenses and fees in connection with anything done under the regulations.

(2) The provision that may be contained in regulations under this section shall include, in particular—

(*a*) provision for the levying of distress, by any person authorised to do so under the regulations, on goods or chattels located at any place whatever (including on a public highway); and

(*b*) provision authorising distress to be levied at any such time of the day or night, and on any such day of the week, as may be specified or described in the regulations.

(3) Regulations under this section may—

(*a*) make different provision for different cases, and

(*b*) contain any such incidental, supplemental, consequential or transitional provision as the Commissioners think fit;

and the transitional provision that may be contained in regulations under this section shall include transitional provision in connection with the coming into force of the repeal by this Act of any other power by regulations to make provision for or in connection with the levying of distress.

(4) The power to make regulations under this section shall be exercisable by statutory instrument subject to annulment in pursuance of a resolution of the House of Commons.

(5) The following are relevant taxes for the purposes of this section, that is to say—

(*a*) …

(*b*) value added tax;

(*c*)–(*f*) …

(6) In this section "the Commissioners" means the Commissioners of Customs and Excise.

(7) Regulations made under this section shall not have effect in Scotland.

Commentary—*De Voil Indirect Tax Service* **V5.173**.

Note—Sub-ss (5)(*a*), (*c*)–(*f*) are not relevant to VAT.

Regulations—See Distress for Customs and Excise Duties and other Indirect Taxes Regulations, SI 1997/1431.

Prospective amendments—Sub-s (A1) to be inserted by the Tribunals, Courts and Enforcement Act 2007 ss 62(3), 146, Sch 13 para 126 with effect from a date to be appointed.

Sub-s (A1) as inserted, to read—

"(A1) The Commissioners may, in England and Wales, use the procedure in Schedule 12 to the Tribunals, Courts and Enforcement Act 2007 (taking control of goods) to recover any of these that a person refuses or neglects to pay—

(*a*) any amount of relevant tax due from him;

(*b*) any amount recoverable as if it were relevant tax due from him.".

Sub-s (A1) also to be repealed by FA 2008 s 129, Sch 43 para 6 (as part of the proposed reform of HMRC powers) from such day as the Commissioners may by statutory instrument appoint.

In sub-s (1) words "not having effect in England and Wales or Scotland" to be inserted after words "by regulations", and sub-s (7) to be repealed, by the Tribunals, Courts and Enforcement Act 2007 ss 62(3), 146, Sch 13 para 126, Sch 23 Pt 3 with effect from a date to be appointed.

52 Enforcement by diligence

(1) Where any amount of relevant tax or any amount recoverable as if it were relevant tax is due and has not been paid, the sheriff, on an application by the Commissioners accompanied by a certificate by them—

(*a*) stating that none of the persons specified in the application has paid the amount due from him;

(*b*) stating that payment of the amount due from each such person has been demanded from him; and

(*c*) specifying the amount due from and unpaid by each such person,

shall grant a summary warrant in a form prescribed by Act of Sederunt authorising the recovery, by any of the diligences mentioned in subsection (2) below, of the amount remaining due and unpaid.

(2) The diligences referred to in subsection (1) above are—

[(*a*) an attachment;][1]

(*b*) an earnings arrestment;

(*c*) an arrestment and action of furthcoming or sale.

(3) Subject to subsection (4) below and without prejudice to [section 39(1) of the Debt Arrangement and Attachment (Scotland) Act 2002 (asp 17) (expenses of attachment)][1] the sheriff officer's fees, together with the outlays necessarily incurred by him, in connection with the execution of a summary warrant shall be chargeable against the debtor.

(4) No fees shall be chargeable by the sheriff officer against the debtor for collecting, and accounting to the Commissioners for, sums paid to him by the debtor in respect of the amount owing.

(5) The following are relevant taxes for the purposes of this section, that is to say—

(*a*) …

(*b*) value added tax;

(*c*)–(*f*) …

(6) In this section "the Commissioners" means the Commissioners of Customs and Excise.

(7) This section shall come into force on such day as the Commissioners of Customs and Excise may by order made by statutory instrument appoint, and different days may be appointed under this subsection for different purposes.

(8) This section extends only to Scotland.

Commentary—*De Voil Indirect Tax Service* **V5.173**.
Notes—Sub-ss (5)(*a*), (*c*)–(*f*) are not relevant to VAT.
The appointed day under sub-s (7) above is 1 July 1997 (see SI 1997/1432).
Prospective amendments—Sub-s (2)(*aa*) to be inserted by the Bankruptcy and Diligence etc (Scotland) Act 2007 s 226(1), Sch 5 para 24 with effect from a date to be appointed. That para to read as follows—
"(*aa*) a money attachment;"
In sub-s (3), words to be inserted by the Bankruptcy and Diligence etc (Scotland) Act 2007 s 226(1), Sch 5 para 24 with effect from a date to be appointed. Those words to read as follows—
"and section 196(1) of the Bankruptcy and Diligence etc (Scotland) Act 2007 (asp 3) (expenses of money attachment)"
Section 52 to be repealed by FA 2008 s 129, Sch 43 para 15 with effect from such day as the Commissioners may by statutory instrument appoint. See also FA 2008 ss 127,128.
Amendments—[1] Sub-s (2)(*a*) and words in sub-s (3) substituted by the Debt Arrangement and Attachment (Scotland) Act 2002, s 61, Sch 3, Pt 1, para 26 with effect from 30 December 2002.

53 Amendments consequential on sections 51 and 52

…

(6) (*inserts* VATA 1994 s 48(7A)).

(7) (*amends* VATA 1994 s 68(1)(*a*)).

…

(9) This section shall come into force on such day as the Commissioners of Customs and Excise may by order made by statutory instrument appoint, and different days may be appointed under this subsection for different purposes.

Commentary—*De Voil Indirect Tax Service* **V5.171**.
Notes—Words omitted are not relevant for the purposes of VAT.
The appointed day under sub-s (9) above is 1 July 1997 (see SI 1997/1432).

Miscellaneous

110 Obtaining information from social security authorities

(1) This section applies to—

(*a*) any information held by the Secretary of State or the Department of Health and Social Services for Northern Ireland for the purposes of any of his or its functions relating to social security; and

(*b*) any information held by a person in connection with the provision by him to the Secretary of State or that Department of any services which that person is providing for purposes connected with any of those functions.

(2) Subject to the following provisions of this section, the person holding any information to which this section applies shall be entitled to supply it to—

(*a*) the Commissioners of Customs and Excise or any person by whom services are being provided to those Commissioners for purposes connected with any of their functions; or

(*b*) the Commissioners of Inland Revenue or any person by whom services are being provided to those Commissioners for purposes connected with any of their functions.

(3) Information shall not be supplied to any person under this section except for one or more of the following uses—

(*a*) use in the prevention, detection, investigation or prosecution of criminal offences which it is a function of the Commissioners of Customs and Excise, or of the Commissioners of Inland Revenue, to prevent, detect, investigate or prosecute;

(*b*) use in the prevention, detection or investigation of conduct in respect of which penalties which are not criminal penalties are provided for by or under any enactment;

(*c*) use in connection with the assessment or determination of penalties which are not criminal penalties;

(*d*) use in checking the accuracy of information relating to, or provided for purposes connected with, any matter under the care and management of the Commissioners of Customs and Excise or the Commissioners of Inland Revenue;

(*e*) use (where appropriate) for amending or supplementing any such information; and

(*f*) use in connection with any legal or other proceedings relating to anything mentioned in paragraphs (*a*) to (*e*) above.

(4) An enactment authorising the disclosure of information by a person mentioned in subsection (2)(*a*) or (*b*) above shall not authorise the disclosure by such a person of information supplied to him under this section except to the extent that the disclosure is also authorised by a general or specific permission granted by the Secretary of State or by the Department of Health and Social Services for Northern Ireland.

(5) In this section references to functions relating to social security include references to—

(*a*) functions in relation to …[1] social security benefits (whether contributory or not) or national insurance numbers; and

(*b*) functions under the Jobseekers Act 1995 or the Jobseekers (Northern Ireland) Order 1995.

[(5AA) The reference to social security benefits in subsection (5)(*a*) above does not include a reference to working families' tax credit or disabled person's tax credit.][2]

[(5A) …][1]

(6) In this section "conduct" includes acts, omissions and statements.

(7) This section shall come into force on such day as the Treasury may by order made by statutory instrument appoint, and different days may be appointed under this subsection for different purposes.

Commentary—*De Voil Indirect Tax Service* **V1.270**.
Notes—The appointed day under sub-s (7) above was 2 July 1997 (see SI 1997/1603).
Amendments—[1] Words in sub-ss (5)(*a*) repealed and sub-section (5A) inserted by the Social Security Contributions (Transfer of Functions, etc) Act 1999 Sch 6 para 10, with effect from 1 April 1999 (by virtue of SI 1999/527). Wording omitted not relevant to VAT.
[2] Sub-s (5AA) inserted by the Tax Credit Act 1999 s 7(2) with effect from 5 October 1999.
Prospective amendment—Words "statutory paternity pay" in sub-s (5A) to be substituted by the Work and Families Act 2006 s 11, Sch 1 para 45 with effect from a date to be appointed.
Words as substituted to read as follows—
"ordinary statutory paternity pay, additional statutory paternity pay".

111 Report on VAT on energy saving materials

…

Amendments—This section repealed by Statute Law (Repeals) Act 1998 Sch 1 Group 5, with effect from 19 November 1998.

Supplemental

113 Repeals

(1) The enactments mentioned in Schedule 18 to this Act (which include spent provisions) are hereby repealed to the extent specified in the third column of that Schedule.

(2) The repeals specified in that Schedule have effect subject to the commencement provisions and savings contained or referred to in the notes set out in that Schedule.

114 Short title

This Act may be cited as the Finance Act 1997.

SCHEDULES

SCHEDULE 2

GAMING DUTY: CONSEQUENTIAL AND INCIDENTAL AMENDMENTS

Section 13

PART I

AMENDMENTS OF THE CUSTOMS AND EXCISE MANAGEMENT ACT 1979

Introductory

1 The Customs and Excise Management Act 1979 shall be amended in accordance with the provisions of this Part of this Schedule.

Meaning of "revenue trade provisions" and "revenue trader"

2— (1) This paragraph amends section 1(1) (interpretation).
(2)–(4) (*amends* CEMA 1979 s 1(1)).

SCHEDULE 6

ASSESSMENTS FOR EXCISE DUTY PURPOSES

Section 50

Assessments in cases of untrue declarations etc

5 (*inserts* CEMA 1979 s 167(5)).

SCHEDULE 18

REPEALS

Section 113

Note—All repeals relevant to VAT are already in effect and have therefore been omitted.

FINANCE ACT 1998

(1998 Chapter 36)

An Act to grant certain duties, to alter other duties, and to amend the law relating to the National Debt and the Public Revenue, and to make further provision in connection with Finance.

[31 July 1998]

PART II

VALUE ADDED TAX

21 Deemed supplies.

(1) Paragraph 5 of Schedule 4 to the Value Added Tax Act 1994 (disposal of business assets) shall be amended as follows.
(2) (*amends* VATA 1994 Sch 4 para 5(2)(*a*)).
(3) (*inserts* VATA 1994 Sch 4 para 5(2A)).
(4) (*amends* VATA 1994 Sch 4 para 5(5)).
(5) (*inserts* VATA 1994 Sch 4 para 5(5A)).
(6) The preceding provisions of this section apply to any case where the time when the goods are transferred or disposed of or, as the case may be, put to use, used or made available for use is on or after 17th March 1998.

22 Changes of place of supply: transitional.

(1) (*inserts* VATA 1994 s 97A).
(2) (*inserts* VATA 1994 s 6(14A)).
(3) This section shall be deemed to have come into force on 17th March 1998.

23 Bad debt relief.

(1) (*amends* VATA 1994 s 36(1)(*a*)).

(2) (*amends* VATA 1994 s 36(3)).

(3) (*inserts* VATA 1994 s 36(3A)).

(4) In subsection (5) of that section—

(*a*) (*amends* VATA 1994 s 36(5)(*c*)).
(*b*) (*amends* VATA 1994 s 36(5)(*e*)).

(5) (*amends* VATA 1994 s 36(6)(*b*), (*c*)).

(6) (*amends* VATA 1994 s 36(7)).

(7) Subsections (1) to (3) above have effect in relation to claims made on or after the day on which this Act is passed.

24 Long leases in Scotland.

(*amends* VATA 1994 s 96(1) definition of "major interest").

PART VI
MISCELLANEOUS AND SUPPLEMENTAL

Supplemental

165 Repeals.

(1) The enactments mentioned in Schedule 27 to this Act (which include spent provisions) are hereby repealed to the extent specified in the third column of that Schedule.

(2) The repeals specified in that Schedule have effect subject to the commencement provisions and savings contained or referred to in the notes set out in that Schedule.

166 Short title.

This Act may be cited as the Finance Act 1998.

SCHEDULES

SCHEDULE 27
REPEALS

Section 165

Note—All repeals relevant to VAT are already in effect and have therefore been omitted.

HUMAN RIGHTS ACT 1998

(1998 Chapter 42)

An Act to give further effect to rights and freedoms guaranteed under the European Convention on Human Rights; to make provision with respect to holders of certain judicial offices who become judges of the European Court of Human Rights; and for connected purposes.

[9th November 1998]

Note—This Act was brought into force as follows—
ss 1–17 on 2 October 2000 (by the Human Rights Act 1998 (Commencement No 2) Order, SI 2000/1851 art 2).
s 19 on 24 November 1998 (by the Human Rights Act 1998 (Commencement) Order, SI 1998/2882 art 2).
s 20 on 9 November 1998 (RA).
s 21(1)–(4) (by the Human Rights Act 1998 (Commencement) Order, SI 1998/2882 art 2).
s 21(5) on 9 November 1998 (RA).
s 22 on 9 November 1998 (RA).
Schs 1, 2 (by the Human Rights Act 1998 (Commencement) Order, SI 1998/2882 art 2).

ARRANGEMENT OF SECTIONS

Introduction

1 The Convention Rights

(1) In this Act "the Convention rights" means the rights and fundamental freedoms set out in—

(*a*) Articles 2 to 12 and 14 of the Convention,
(*b*) Articles 1 to 3 of the First Protocol, and
(*c*) [Article 1 of the Thirteenth Protocol][2],

as read with Articles 16 to 18 of the Convention.

(2) Those Articles are to have effect for the purposes of this Act subject to any designated derogation or reservation (as to which see sections 14 and 15).

(3) The Articles are set out in Schedule 1.

(4) The [Secretary of State][1] may by order make such amendments to this Act as he considers appropriate to reflect the effect, in relation to the United Kingdom, of a protocol.

(5) In subsection (4) "protocol" means a protocol to the Convention—

(*a*) which the United Kingdom has ratified; or
(*b*) which the United Kingdom has signed with a view to ratification.

(6) No amendment may be made by an order under subsection (4) so as to come into force before the protocol concerned is in force in relation to the United Kingdom.

Simon's Tax Cases—*Holland (executor of Holland, dec'd) v IRC* [2003] STC (SCD) 43.

Amendments—[1] Words in square brackets substituted by the Secretary of State for Constitutional Affairs Order, SI 2003/1887 art 9, Sch 2 para 10(1) with effect from 19 August 2003.

[2] Sub-s (1)(*c*) substituted by Human Rights Act 1998 (Amendment) Order, SI 2004/1574, art 1, 2(1) with effect from 22 June 2004.

2 Interpretation of Convention rights

(1) A court or tribunal determining a question which has arisen in connection with a Convention right must take into account any—

(*a*) judgment, decision, declaration or advisory opinion of the European Court of Human Rights,
(*b*) opinion of the Commission given in a report adopted under Article 31 of the Convention,
(*c*) decision of the Commission in connection with Article 26 or 27(2) of the Convention, or
(*d*) decision of the Committee of Ministers taken under Article 46 of the Convention,

whenever made or given, so far as, in the opinion of the court or tribunal, it is relevant to the proceedings in which that question has arisen.

(2) Evidence of any judgment, decision, declaration or opinion of which account may have to be taken under this section is to be given in proceedings before any court or tribunal in such manner as may be provided by rules.

(3) In this section "rules" means rules of court or, in the case of proceedings before a tribunal, rules made for the purposes of this section—

(*a*) by ...[1] [the Lord Chancellor or][2] the Secretary of State, in relation to any proceedings outside Scotland;
(*b*) by the Secretary of State, in relation to proceedings in Scotland; or
(*c*) by a Northern Ireland department, in relation to proceedings before a tribunal in Northern Ireland—
(i) which deals with transferred matters; and
(ii) for which no rules made under paragraph (*a*) are in force.

Amendments—[1] Words revoked by the Secretary of State for Constitutional Affairs Order, SI 2003/1887 art 9, Sch 2 para 10(2) with effect from 19 August 2003.
[2] Words in sub-s (3)(*a*) inserted by Transfer of Functions (Lord Chancellor and Secretary of State) Order, SI 2005/3429 art 8, Schedule para 3 with effect from 12 January 2006.

Legislation

3 Interpretation of legislation

(1) So far as it is possible to do so, primary legislation and subordinate legislation must be read and given effect in a way which is compatible with the Convention rights.

(2) This section—

(*a*) applies to primary legislation and subordinate legislation whenever enacted;
(*b*) does not affect the validity, continuing operation or enforcement of any incompatible primary legislation; and
(*c*) does not affect the validity, continuing operation or enforcement of any incompatible subordinate legislation if (disregarding any possibility of revocation) primary legislation prevents removal of the incompatibility.

Simon's Tax Cases—*Bancroft and anor v Crutchfield* (Insp of Taxes) [2002] STC 347; *Carney v Nathan (Insp of Taxes)* [2003] STC (SCD) 28; *Holland (executor of Holland, dec'd) v IRC* [2003] STC (SCD) 43.

4 Declaration of incompatibility

(1) Subsection (2) applies in any proceedings in which a court determines whether a provision of primary legislation is compatible with a Convention right.

(2) If the court is satisfied that the provision is incompatible with a Convention right, it may make a declaration of that incompatibility.

(3) Subsection (4) applies in any proceedings in which a court determines whether a provision of subordinate legislation, made in the exercise of a power conferred by primary legislation, is compatible with a Convention right.

(4) If the court is satisfied—

(*a*) that the provision is incompatible with a Convention right, and
(*b*) that (disregarding any possibility of revocation) the primary legislation concerned prevents removal of the incompatibility,

it may make a declaration of that incompatibility.

(5) In this section "court" means—

(*a*) the House of Lords;
(*b*) the Judicial Committee of the Privy Council;
(*c*) the [Court Martial Appeal Court][2];
(*d*) in Scotland, the High Court of Justiciary sitting otherwise than as a trial court or the Court of Session;
(*e*) in England and Wales or Northern Ireland, the High Court or the Court of Appeal.
[(*f*) the Court of Protection, in any matter being dealt with by the President of the Family Division, the Vice-Chancellor or a puisne judge of the High Court.][1]

(6) A declaration under this section ("a declaration of incompatibility")—

(*a*) does not affect the validity, continuing operation or enforcement of the provision in respect of which it is given; and
(*b*) is not binding on the parties to the proceedings in which it is made.

Simon's Tax Cases—*Holland (executor of Holland, dec'd) v IRC* [2003] STC (SCD) 43.
Amendments—[1] Sub-s (5)(*f*) inserted by the Mental Capacity Act 2005 s 67(1), Sch 6 para 43 with effect from 1 October 2007 (by virtue of SI 2007/1897 art 2).

[2] In sub-s (5)(*c*), words substituted for words "Courts-Martial Appeal Court" by the Armed Forces Act 2006 s 378(1), Sch 16 para 156 with effect, for certain purposes from 28 March 2009 (by virtue of SI 2009/812 art 3(*a*), (*b*)) and for remaining purposes from a date to be appointed.

Prospective amendments—Sub-s (5)(*a*) to be substituted by the Constitutional Reform Act 2005 s 40, Sch 9 para 66(1), (2) with effect from a date to be appointed. Sub-s (5)(*a*) as substituted will read as follows—
"(*a*) the Supreme Court;".

5 Right of Crown to intervene

(1) Where a court is considering whether to make a declaration of incompatibility, the Crown is entitled to notice in accordance with rules of court.

(2) In any case to which subsection (1) applies—

(*a*) a Minister of the Crown (or a person nominated by him),
(*b*) a member of the Scottish Executive,
(*c*) a Northern Ireland Minister,
(*d*) a Northern Ireland department,

is entitled, on giving notice in accordance with rules of court, to be joined as a party to the proceedings.

(3) Notice under subsection (2) may be given at any time during the proceedings.

(4) A person who has been made a party to criminal proceedings (other than in Scotland) as the result of a notice under subsection (2) may, with leave, appeal to the House of Lords against any declaration of incompatibility made in the proceedings.

(5) In subsection (4)—

"criminal proceedings" includes all proceedings before the [Court Martial Appeal Court][1]; and

"leave" means leave granted by the court making the declaration of incompatibility or by the House of Lords.

Amendments—[1] In sub-s (5) words in definition of "criminal proceedings" substituted for words "Courts-Martial Appeal Court" by the Armed Forces Act 2006, s 378(1), Sch 16, para 157 with effect for certain purposes from 28 March 2009 (by virtue of SI 2009/812 art 3(*a*), (*b*)) and for remaining purposes from a date to be appointed.

Prospective amendment—In sub-ss (4), (5), words "Supreme Court" to be substituted for the words "House of Lords" by the Constitutional Reform Act 2005 s 40, Sch 9 para 66(1)–(3) with effect from a date to be appointed.

Public authorities

6 Acts of public authorities

(1) It is unlawful for a public authority to act in a way which is incompatible with a Convention right.

(2) Subsection (1) does not apply to an act if—

(*a*) as the result of one or more provisions of primary legislation, the authority could not have acted differently; or

(*b*) in the case of one or more provisions of, or made under, primary legislation which cannot be read or given effect in a way which is compatible with the Convention rights, the authority was acting so as to give effect to or enforce those provisions.

(3) In this section "public authority" includes—

(*a*) a court or tribunal, and
(*b*) any person certain of whose functions are functions of a public nature,

but does not include either House of Parliament or a person exercising functions in connection with proceedings in Parliament.

(4) In subsection (3) "Parliament" does not include the House of Lords in its judicial capacity.

(5) In relation to a particular act, a person is not a public authority by virtue only of subsection (3)(*b*) if the nature of the act is private.

(6) "An act" includes a failure to act but does not include a failure to—

(*a*) introduce in, or lay before, Parliament a proposal for legislation; or
(*b*) make any primary legislation or remedial order.

Simon's Tax Cases—*R (oao Wilkinson) v IRC* [2002] STC 347; *Holland (executor of Holland, decd) v IRC* [2003] STC (SCD) 43; *R (on the application of Wilkinson) v IRC* [2003] STC 1113, [2006] STC 270.

Prospective amendment—Sub-s (4) to be repealed by the Constitutional Reform Act 2005 ss 40, 146, Sch 9 para 66(1), (4), Sch 18 with effect from a date to be appointed.

7 Proceedings

(1) A person who claims that a public authority has acted (or proposes to act) in a way which is made unlawful by section 6(1) may—

(*a*) bring proceedings against the authority under this Act in the appropriate court or tribunal, or

(*b*) rely on the Convention right or rights concerned in any legal proceedings,

but only if he is (or would be) a victim of the unlawful act.

(2) In subsection (1)(*a*) "appropriate court or tribunal" means such court or tribunal as may be determined in accordance with rules; and proceedings against an authority include a counter-claim or similar proceeding.

(3) If the proceedings are brought on an application for judicial review, the applicant is to be taken to have a sufficient interest in relation to the unlawful act only if he is, or would be, a victim of that act.

(4) If the proceedings are made by way of a petition for judicial review in Scotland, the applicant shall be taken to have title and interest to sue in relation to the unlawful act only if he is, or would be, a victim of that act.

(5) Proceedings under subsection (1)(*a*) must be brought before the end of—

(*a*) the period of one year beginning with the date on which the act complained of took place; or

(*b*) such longer period as the court or tribunal considers equitable having regard to all the circumstances,

but that is subject to any rule imposing a stricter time limit in relation to the procedure in question.

(6) In subsection (1)(*b*) "legal proceedings" includes—

(*a*) proceedings brought by or at the instigation of a public authority; and

(*b*) an appeal against the decision of a court or tribunal.

(7) For the purposes of this section, a person is a victim of an unlawful act only if he would be a victim for the purposes of Article 34 of the Convention if proceedings were brought in the European Court of Human Rights in respect of that act.

(8) Nothing in this Act creates a criminal offence.

(9) In this section "rules" means—

(*a*) in relation to proceedings before a court or tribunal outside Scotland, rules made by …[1] [the Lord Chancellor or][2] the Secretary of State for the purposes of this section or rules of court,

(*b*) in relation to proceedings before a court or tribunal in Scotland, rules made by the Secretary of State for those purposes,

(*c*) in relation to proceedings before a tribunal in Northern Ireland—

(i) which deals with transferred matters; and

(ii) for which no rules made under paragraph (*a*) are in force,

rules made by a Northern Ireland department for those purposes,

and includes provision made by order under section 1 of the Courts and Legal Services Act 1990.

(10) In making rules, regard must be had to section 9.

(11) The Minister who has power to make rules in relation to a particular tribunal may, to the extent he considers it necessary to ensure that the tribunal can provide an appropriate remedy in relation to an act (or proposed act) of a public authority which is (or would be) unlawful as a result of section 6(1), by order add to—

(*a*) the relief or remedies which the tribunal may grant; or

(*b*) the grounds on which it may grant any of them.

(12) An order made under subsection (11) may contain such incidental, supplemental, consequential or transitional provision as the Minister making it considers appropriate.

(13) "The Minister" includes the Northern Ireland department concerned.

Simon's Tax Cases—*Holland (executor of Holland, decd) v IRC* [2003] STC (SCD) 43.

Amendments—[1] Words revoked by the Secretary of State for Constitutional Affairs Order, SI 2003/1887 art 9, Sch 2 para 10(2) with effect from 19 August 2003.

[2] Words in sub-s (9)(*a*) inserted by Transfer of Functions (Lord Chancellor and Secretary of State) Order, SI 2005/3429 art 8, Schedule para 3 with effect from 12 January 2006.

8 Judicial remedies

(1) In relation to any act (or proposed act) of a public authority which the court finds is (or would be) unlawful, it may grant such relief or remedy, or make such order, within its powers as it considers just and appropriate.

(2) But damages may be awarded only by a court which has power to award damages, or to order the payment of compensation, in civil proceedings.

(3) No award of damages is to be made unless, taking account of all the circumstances of the case, including—

(*a*) any other relief or remedy granted, or order made, in relation to the act in question (by that or any other court), and

(*b*) the consequences of any decision (of that or any other court) in respect of that act,

the court is satisfied that the award is necessary to afford just satisfaction to the person in whose favour it is made.

(4) In determining—

(*a*) whether to award damages, or

(*b*) the amount of an award,

the court must take into account the principles applied by the European Court of Human Rights in relation to the award of compensation under Article 41 of the Convention.

(5) A public authority against which damages are awarded is to be treated—

(*a*) in Scotland, for the purposes of section 3 of the Law Reform (Miscellaneous Provisions) (Scotland) Act 1940 as if the award were made in an action of damages in which the authority has been found liable in respect of loss or damage to the person to whom the award is made;

(*b*) for the purposes of the Civil Liability (Contribution) Act 1978 as liable in respect of damage suffered by the person to whom the award is made.

(6) In this section—

"court" includes a tribunal;

"damages" means damages for an unlawful act of a public authority; and

"unlawful" means unlawful under section 6(1).

Simon's Tax Cases—*R (on the application of Wilkinson) v IRC* [2003] STC 1113.

9 Judicial acts

(1) Proceedings under section 7(1)(*a*) in respect of a judicial act may be brought only—

(*a*) by exercising a right of appeal;

(*b*) on an application (in Scotland a petition) for judicial review; or

(*c*) in such other forum as may be prescribed by rules.

(2) That does not affect any rule of law which prevents a court from being the subject of judicial review.

(3) In proceedings under this Act in respect of a judicial act done in good faith, damages may not be awarded otherwise than to compensate a person to the extent required by Article 5(5) of the Convention.

(4) An award of damages permitted by subsection (3) is to be made against the Crown; but no award may be made unless the appropriate person, if not a party to the proceedings, is joined.

(5) In this section—

"appropriate person" means the Minister responsible for the court concerned, or a person or government department nominated by him;

"court" includes a tribunal;

"judge" includes a member of a tribunal, a justice of the peace [(or, in Northern Ireland, a lay magistrate)][1] and a clerk or other officer entitled to exercise the jurisdiction of a court;

"judicial act" means a judicial act of a court and includes an act done on the instructions, or on behalf, of a judge; and

"rules" has the same meaning as in section 7(9).

Amendments—[1] In sub-s (5), words inserted in the definition of "judge" by the Justice (Northern Ireland) Act 2002 s 10, Sch 4 para 39 with effect 1 April 2005 (by virtue of the Justice (Northern Ireland) Act 2002 (Commencement No 8) Order 2005, SR 2005/109 art 2, Schedule).

Remedial action

10 Power to take remedial action

(1) This section applies if—

(*a*) a provision of legislation has been declared under section 4 to be incompatible with a Convention right and, if an appeal lies—

(i) all persons who may appeal have stated in writing that they do not intend to do so;

(ii) the time for bringing an appeal has expired and no appeal has been brought within that time; or

(iii) an appeal brought within that time has been determined or abandoned; or

(*b*) it appears to a Minister of the Crown or Her Majesty in Council that, having regard to a finding of the European Court of Human Rights made after the coming into force of this section in proceedings against the United Kingdom, a provision of legislation is incompatible with an obligation of the United Kingdom arising from the Convention.

(2) If a Minister of the Crown considers that there are compelling reasons for proceeding under this section, he may by order make such amendments to the legislation as he considers necessary to remove the incompatibility.

(3) If, in the case of subordinate legislation, a Minister of the Crown considers—

(*a*) that it is necessary to amend the primary legislation under which the subordinate legislation in question was made, in order to enable the incompatibility to be removed, and

(*b*) that there are compelling reasons for proceeding under this section,

he may by order make such amendments to the primary legislation as he considers necessary.

(4) This section also applies where the provision in question is in subordinate legislation and has been quashed, or declared invalid, by reason of incompatibility with a Convention right and the Minister proposes to proceed under paragraph 2(*b*) of Schedule 2.

(5) If the legislation is an Order in Council, the power conferred by subsection (2) or (3) is exercisable by Her Majesty in Council.

(6) In this section "legislation" does not include a Measure of the Church Assembly or of the General Synod of the Church of England.

(7) Schedule 2 makes further provision about remedial orders.

Other rights and proceedings

11 Safeguard for existing human rights

A person's reliance on a Convention right does not restrict—

(*a*) any other right or freedom conferred on him by or under any law having effect in any part of the United Kingdom; or

(*b*) his right to make any claim or bring any proceedings which he could make or bring apart from sections 7 to 9.

12 Freedom of expression

(1) This section applies if a court is considering whether to grant any relief which, if granted, might affect the exercise of the Convention right to freedom of expression.

(2) If the person against whom the application for relief is made ("the respondent") is neither present nor represented, no such relief is to be granted unless the court is satisfied—

(*a*) that the applicant has taken all practicable steps to notify the respondent; or

(*b*) that there are compelling reasons why the respondent should not be notified.

(3) No such relief is to be granted so as to restrain publication before trial unless the court is satisfied that the applicant is likely to establish that publication should not be allowed.

(4) The court must have particular regard to the importance of the Convention right to freedom of expression and, where the proceedings relate to material which the respondent claims, or which appears to the court, to be journalistic, literary or artistic material (or to conduct connected with such material), to—

(*a*) the extent to which—

(i) the material has, or is about to, become available to the public; or

(ii) it is, or would be, in the public interest for the material to be published;

(*b*) any relevant privacy code.

(5) In this section—

"court" includes a tribunal; and

"relief" includes any remedy or order (other than in criminal proceedings).

13 Freedom of thought, conscience and religion

(1) If a court's determination of any question arising under this Act might affect the exercise by a religious organisation (itself or its members collectively) of the Convention right to freedom of thought, conscience and religion, it must have particular regard to the importance of that right.

(2) In this section "court" includes a tribunal.

Derogations and reservations

14 Derogations

(1) In this Act "designated derogation" means—

...[1] any derogation by the United Kingdom from an Article of the Convention, or of any protocol to the Convention, which is designated for the purposes of this Act in an order made by the [Secretary of State][2].

(2) ...[1].

(3) If a designated derogation is amended or replaced it ceases to be a designated derogation.

(4) But subsection (3) does not prevent the [Secretary of State][2] from exercising his power under subsection (1) ...[1] to make a fresh designation order in respect of the Article concerned.

(5) The [Secretary of State][2] must by order make such amendments to Schedule 3 as he considers appropriate to reflect—

(*a*) any designation order; or

(*b*) the effect of subsection (3).

(6) A designation order may be made in anticipation of the making by the United Kingdom of a proposed derogation.

Amendments—[1] In sub-s (1), para (*a*), and letter "(*b*)" revoked, sub-s (2) revoked, and letter "(*b*)" in sub-s (4) revoked, by the Human Rights Act (Amendment) Order, SI 2001/1216 art 2 with effect from 1 April 2001.

[2] Words in square brackets substituted by the Secretary of State for Constitutional Affairs Order, SI 2003/1887 art 9, Sch 2 para 10(1) with effect from 19 August 2003.

15 Reservations

(1) In this Act "designated reservation" means—

(*a*) the United Kingdom's reservation to Article 2 of the First Protocol to the Convention; and (*b*) any other reservation by the United Kingdom to an Article of the Convention, or of any protocol to the Convention, which is designated for the purposes of this Act in an order made by the [Secretary of State][1].

(2) The text of the reservation referred to in subsection (1)(*a*) is set out in Part II of Schedule 3.

(3) If a designated reservation is withdrawn wholly or in part it ceases to be a designated reservation.

(4) But subsection (3) does not prevent the [Secretary of State][1] from exercising his power under subsection (1)(*b*) to make a fresh designation order in respect of the Article concerned.

(5) The [Secretary of State][1] must by order make such amendments to this Act as he considers appropriate to reflect—

(*a*) any designation order; or
(*b*) the effect of subsection (3).

Amendments—[1] Words in square brackets substituted by the Secretary of State for Constitutional Affairs Order, SI 2003/1887 art 9, Sch 2 para 10(1) with effect from 19 August 2003.

16 Period for which designated derogations have effect

(1) If it has not already been withdrawn by the United Kingdom, a designated derogation ceases to have effect for the purposes of this Act—

…[1] at the end of the period of five years beginning with the date on which the order designating it was made.

(2) At any time before the period—

(*a*) fixed by subsection (1) …[1], or
(*b*) extended by an order under this subsection,

comes to an end, the [Secretary of State][2] may by order extend it by a further period of five years.

(3) An order under section 14(1) …[1] ceases to have effect at the end of the period for consideration, unless a resolution has been passed by each House approving the order.

(4) Subsection (3) does not affect—

(*a*) anything done in reliance on the order; or
(*b*) the power to make a fresh order under section 14(1) …[1].

(5) In subsection (3) "period for consideration" means the period of forty days beginning with the day on which the order was made.

(6) In calculating the period for consideration, no account is to be taken of any time during which—

(*a*) Parliament is dissolved or prorogued; or
(*b*) both Houses are adjourned for more than four days.

(7) If a designated derogation is withdrawn by the United Kingdom, the [Secretary of State][2] must by order make such amendments to this Act as he considers are required to reflect that withdrawal.

Amendments—[1] Words in sub-ss (1), (2)(*a*) revoked, and the letter "(*b*)" in sub-ss (3), (4) revoked, by the Human Rights Act (Amendment) Order, SI 2001/1216 art 3 with effect from 1 April 2001.
[2] Words in square brackets substituted by the Secretary of State for Constitutional Affairs Order, SI 2003/1887 art 9, Sch 2 para 10(1) with effect from 19 August 2003.

17 Periodic review of designated reservations

(1) The appropriate Minister must review the designated reservation referred to in section 15(1)(*a*)—

(*a*) before the end of the period of five years beginning with the date on which section 1(2) came into force; and
(*b*) if that designation is still in force, before the end of the period of five years beginning with the date on which the last report relating to it was laid under subsection (3).

(2) The appropriate Minister must review each of the other designated reservations (if any)—

(*a*) before the end of the period of five years beginning with the date on which the order designating the reservation first came into force; and
(*b*) if the designation is still in force, before the end of the period of five years beginning with the date on which the last report relating to it was laid under subsection (3).

(3) The Minister conducting a review under this section must prepare a report on the result of the review and lay a copy of it before each House of Parliament.

Judges of the European Court of Human Rights

18 Appointment to European Court of Human Rights

[not reproduced: see *Halsbury's Statutes* (4th edn) CIVIL RIGHTS and LIBERTIES].

Parliamentary procedure

19 Statements of compatibility

(1) A Minister of the Crown in charge of a Bill in either House of Parliament must, before Second Reading of the Bill—

(*a*) make a statement to the effect that in his view the provisions of the Bill are compatible with the Convention rights ("a statement of compatibility"); or

(*b*) make a statement to the effect that although he is unable to make a statement of compatibility the government nevertheless wishes the House to proceed with the Bill.

(2) The statement must be in writing and be published in such manner as the Minister making it considers appropriate.

Note—This section was brought into force on 24 November 1998 by the Human Rights Act 1998 (Commencement) Order, SI 1998/2882 art 2.

Supplemental

20 Orders etc under this Act

(1) Any power of a Minister of the Crown to make an order under this Act is exercisable by statutory instrument.

(2) The power of …[1] [the Lord Chancellor or][2] the Secretary of State to make rules (other than rules of court) under section 2(3) or 7(9) is exercisable by statutory instrument.

(3) Any statutory instrument made under section 14, 15 or 16(7) must be laid before Parliament.

(4) No order may be made by …[1] [the Lord Chancellor or][2] the Secretary of State under section 1(4), 7(11) or 16(2) unless a draft of the order has been laid before, and approved by, each House of Parliament.

(5) Any statutory instrument made under section 18(7) or Schedule 4, or to which subsection (2) applies, shall be subject to annulment in pursuance of a resolution of either House of Parliament.

(6) The power of a Northern Ireland department to make—

(*a*) rules under section 2(3)(*c*) or 7(9)(*c*), or

(*b*) an order under section 7(11),

is exercisable by statutory rule for the purposes of the Statutory Rules (Northern Ireland) Order 1979.

(7) Any rules made under section 2(3)(*c*) or 7(9)(*c*) shall be subject to negative resolution; and section 41(6) of the Interpretation Act (Northern Ireland) 1954 (meaning of "subject to negative resolution") shall apply as if the power to make the rules were conferred by an Act of the Northern Ireland Assembly.

(8) No order may be made by a Northern Ireland department under section 7(11) unless a draft of the order has been laid before, and approved by, the Northern Ireland Assembly.

Amendments—[1] Words revoked by the Secretary of State for Constitutional Affairs Order, SI 2003/1887 art 9, Sch 2 para 10(2) with effect from 19 August 2003.

[2] Words in sub-ss (2), (4) inserted by Transfer of Functions (Lord Chancellor and Secretary of State) Order, SI 2005/3429 art 8, Schedule para 3 with effect from 12 January 2006.

21 Interpretation, etc

(1) In this Act—

"amend" includes repeal and apply (with or without modifications);

"the appropriate Minister" means the Minister of the Crown having charge of the appropriate authorised government department (within the meaning of the Crown Proceedings Act 1947);

"the Commission" means the European Commission of Human Rights;

"the Convention" means the Convention for the Protection of Human Rights and Fundamental Freedoms, agreed by the Council of Europe at Rome on 4th November 1950 as it has effect for the time being in relation to the United Kingdom;

"declaration of incompatibility" means a declaration under section 4;

"Minister of the Crown" has the same meaning as in the Ministers of the Crown Act 1975;

"Northern Ireland Minister" includes the First Minister and the deputy First Minister in Northern Ireland;

"primary legislation" means any—

(*a*) public general Act;

(*b*) local and personal Act;

(*c*) private Act;

(*d*) Measure of the Church Assembly;

(*e*) Measure of the General Synod of the Church of England;

(*f*) Order in Council—

(i) made in exercise of Her Majesty's Royal Prerogative;

(ii) made under section 38(1)(*a*) of the Northern Ireland Constitution Act 1973 or the corresponding provision of the Northern Ireland Act 1998; or

(iii) amending an Act of a kind mentioned in paragraph (*a*), (*b*) or (*c*);

and includes an order or other instrument made under primary legislation (otherwise than by the [Welsh Ministers, the First Minister for Wales, the Counsel General to the Welsh Assembly Government][2], a member of the Scottish Executive, a Northern Ireland Minister or a Northern Ireland department) to the extent to which it operates to bring one or more provisions of that legislation into force or amends any primary legislation;

"the First Protocol" means the protocol to the Convention agreed at Paris on 20th March 1952;

...[1]

"the Eleventh Protocol" means the protocol to the Convention (restructuring the control machinery established by the Convention) agreed at Strasbourg on 11th May 1994;

["the Thirteenth Protocol" means the protocol to the Convention (concerning the abolition of the death penalty in all circumstances) agreed at Vilnius on 3rd May 2002;][1]

"remedial order" means an order under section 10;

"subordinate legislation" means any—

(*a*) Order in Council other than one—

(i) made in exercise of Her Majesty's Royal Prerogative;

(ii) made under section 38(1)(*a*) of the Northern Ireland Constitution Act 1973 or the corresponding provision of the Northern Ireland Act 1998; or

(iii) amending an Act of a kind mentioned in the definition of primary legislation;

(*b*) Act of the Scottish Parliament;

[(*ba*) Measure of the National Assembly for Wales;

(*bb*) Act of the National Assembly for Wales;][2]

(*c*) Act of the Parliament of Northern Ireland;

(*d*) Measure of the Assembly established under section 1 of the Northern Ireland Assembly Act 1973;

(*e*) Act of the Northern Ireland Assembly;

(*f*) order, rules, regulations, scheme, warrant, byelaw or other instrument made under primary legislation (except to the extent to which it operates to bring one or more provisions of that legislation into force or amends any primary legislation);

(*g*) order, rules, regulations, scheme, warrant, byelaw or other instrument made under legislation mentioned in paragraph (*b*), (*c*), (*d*) or (*e*) or made under an Order in Council applying only to Northern Ireland;

(*h*) order, rules, regulations, scheme, warrant, byelaw or other instrument made by a member of the Scottish Executive[, Welsh Ministers, the First Minister for Wales, the Counsel General to the Welsh Assembly Government][2], a Northern Ireland Minister or a Northern Ireland department in exercise of prerogative or other executive functions of Her Majesty which are exercisable by such a person on behalf of Her Majesty;

"transferred matters" has the same meaning as in the Northern Ireland Act 1998; and

"tribunal" means any tribunal in which legal proceedings may be brought.

(2) The references in paragraphs (*b*) and (*c*) of section 2(1) to Articles are to Articles of the Convention as they had effect immediately before the coming into force of the Eleventh Protocol.

(3) The reference in paragraph (*d*) of section 2(1) to Article 46 includes a reference to Articles 32 and 54 of the Convention as they had effect immediately before the coming into force of the Eleventh Protocol.

(4) The references in section 2(1) to a report or decision of the Commission or a decision of the Committee of Ministers include references to a report or decision made as provided by paragraphs 3, 4 and 6 of Article 5 of the Eleventh Protocol (transitional provisions).

(5) Any liability under the Army Act 1955, the Air Force Act 1955 or the Naval Discipline Act 1957 to suffer death for an offence is replaced by a liability to imprisonment for life or any less punishment authorised by those Acts; and those Acts shall accordingly have effect with the necessary modifications.[3]

Amendments—[1] Definition of "the Sixth Protocol" revoked, and definition of "the Thirteenth Protocol" inserted by Human Rights Act 1998 (Amendment) Order, SI 2004/1574, art 1, 2(2) with effect from 22 June 2004.

[2] In sub-s (1), in definition of "primary legislation", words substituted; and in definition of "subordinate legislation" paras (*ba*), (*bb*) and words in para (*h*) inserted; by the Government of Wales Act 2006 s 160(1), Sch 10 para 56(1)–(3) with effect from 25 May 2007, being the date on which the initial period ended (following the appointment of the First Minister).

[3] Sub-s (5) repealed by the Armed Forces Act 2006 s 378(2), Sch 17 with effect for certain purposes from 28 March 2009 (by virtue of SI 2009/812, art 3(*a*), (*b*)) and for remaining purposes from a date to be appointed.

22 Short title, commencement, application and extent

(1) This Act may be cited as the Human Rights Act 1998.

(2) Sections 18, 20 and 21(5) and this section come into force on the passing of this Act.

(3) The other provisions of this Act come into force on such day as the Secretary of State may by order appoint; and different days may be appointed for different purposes.

(4) Paragraph (*b*) of subsection (1) of section 7 applies to proceedings brought by or at the instigation of a public authority whenever the act in question took place; but otherwise that subsection does not apply to an act taking place before the coming into force of that section.

(5) This Act binds the Crown.

(6) This Act extends to Northern Ireland.

(7) Section 21(5), so far as it relates to any provision contained in the Army Act 1955, the Air Force Act 1955 or the Naval Discipline Act 1957, extends to any place to which that provision extends.[1]

Amendments—[1] Sub-s (7) repealed by the Armed Forces Act 2006 s 378(2), Sch 17 with effect for certain purposes from 28 March 2009 (by virtue of SI 2009/812, art 3(*a*), (*b*)) and for remaining purposes from a date to be appointed.

SCHEDULES

SCHEDULE 1
THE ARTICLES

Section 1(3)

PART I
THE CONVENTION

RIGHTS AND FREEDOMS

[Article 2 (Right to life), Article 3 (Prohibition of torture), Article 4 and Article 5 (Right to liberty and security) (Prohibition of slavery and forced labour) are not reproduced here: see *Halsbury's Statutes* (4th edn) CIVIL RIGHTS and LIBERTIES].

Article 6
Right to a fair trial

1 In the determination of his civil rights and obligations or of any criminal charge against him, everyone is entitled to a fair and public hearing within a reasonable time by an independent and impartial tribunal established by law. Judgment shall be pronounced publicly but the press and public may be excluded from all or part of the trial in the interest of morals, public order or national security in a democratic society, where the interests of juveniles or the protection of the private life of the parties so require, or to the extent strictly necessary in the opinion of the court in special circumstances where publicity would prejudice the interests of justice.

2 Everyone charged with a criminal offence shall be presumed innocent until proved guilty according to law.

3 Everyone charged with a criminal offence has the following minimum rights:

(*a*) to be informed promptly, in a language which he understands and in detail, of the nature and cause of the accusation against him;

(*b*) to have adequate time and facilities for the preparation of his defence;

(*c*) to defend himself in person or through legal assistance of his own choosing or, if he has not sufficient means to pay for legal assistance, to be given it free when the interests of justice so require;

(*d*) to examine or have examined witnesses against him and to obtain the attendance and examination of witnesses on his behalf under the same conditions as witnesses against him;

(*e*) to have the free assistance of an interpreter if he cannot understand or speak the language used in court.

Simon's Tax Cases—*Bancroft and anor v Crutchfield* (Insp of Taxes) [2002] STC 347; *Khan (trading as Greyhound Dry Cleaners) v C&E Comrs* [2005] STC 1271; *Significant Ltd v Farrel (Insp of Taxes)* [2006] STC 1626; *Sharkey v R&C Comrs* [2006] STC 2026.

Article 7
No punishment without law

[not reproduced: see *Halsbury's Statutes* (4th edn) CIVIL RIGHTS and LIBERTIES].

Article 8
Right to respect for private and family life

1 Everyone has the right to respect for his private and family life, his home and his correspondence.

2 There shall be no interference by a public authority with the exercise of this right except such as is in accordance with the law and is necessary in a democratic society in the interests of national security, public safety or the economic well-being of the country, for the prevention of disorder or crime, for the protection of health or morals, or for the protection of the rights and freedoms of others.

[Article 9 (Freedom of thought, conscience and religion), Article 10 (Freedom of expression), Article 11 (Freedom of assembly and association) and Article 12 (Right to marry) not reproduced here: see *Halsbury's Statutes* (4th edn) CIVIL RIGHTS and LIBERTIES].

Article 14
Prohibition of discrimination

The enjoyment of the rights and freedoms set forth in this Convention shall be secured without discrimination on any ground such as sex, race, colour, language, religion, political or other opinion, national or social origin, association with a national minority, property, birth or other status.

Simon's Tax Cases—*Aston Cantlow and Wilmcote with Billesley Parochial Church Council v Wallbank* [2002] STC 313; *R (oao Wilkinson) v IRC* [2002] STC 347; *Burden and another v UK* [2007] STC 252; *Walker v United Kingdom* [2008] STC 786; *Burden and another v UK* [2008] STC 1305; *Hobbs and others v UK* [2008] STC 1469.

[Article 16 (Restrictions on political activity of aliens) not reproduced here: see *Halsbury's Statutes* (4th edn) CIVIL RIGHTS and LIBERTIES].

Article 17
Prohibition of abuse of rights

Nothing in this Convention may be interpreted as implying for any State, group or person any right to engage in any activity or perform any act aimed at the destruction of any of the rights and freedoms set forth herein or at their limitation to a greater extent than is provided for in the Convention.

Article 18
Limitation on use of restrictions on rights

The restrictions permitted under this Convention to the said rights and freedoms shall not be applied for any purpose other than those for which they have been prescribed.

PART II

THE FIRST PROTOCOL

Article 1
Protection of property

Every natural or legal person is entitled to the peaceful enjoyment of his possessions. No one shall be deprived of his possessions except in the public interest and subject to the conditions provided for by law and by the general principles of international law.

The preceding provisions shall not, however, in any way impair the right of a State to enforce such laws as it deems necessary to control the use of property in accordance with the general interest or to secure the payment of taxes or other contributions or penalties.

[Article 2 (Right to education) and Article 3 (Right to free elections) not reproduced.]

Simon's Tax Cases—*R (oao Wilkinson) v IRC* [2002] STC 347; *R (on the application of Carvill) v IRC (No 2)* [2003] STC 1539; *C&E Comrs v Pegasus Birds Ltd* [2004] STC 262; *Burden and another v UK* [2007] STC 252; *R (on the application of the Federation of Tour Operators and others) v HM Treasury* [2008] STC 547; *Walker v UK* [2008] STC 786; *Hobbs and others v UK* [2008] STC 1469.

[PART III

ARTICLE 1 OF THE THIRTEENTH PROTOCOL]

(not reproduced)

SCHEDULE 2

REMEDIAL ORDERS

Section 10

Orders

1— (1) A remedial order may—

(*a*) contain such incidental, supplemental, consequential or transitional provision as the person making it considers appropriate;

(*b*) be made so as to have effect from a date earlier than that on which it is made;

(*c*) make provision for the delegation of specific functions;

(*d*) make different provision for different cases.

(2) The power conferred by sub-paragraph (1)(*a*) includes—

(*a*) power to amend primary legislation (including primary legislation other than that which contains the incompatible provision); and

(*b*) power to amend or revoke subordinate legislation (including subordinate legislation other than that which contains the incompatible provision).

(3) A remedial order may be made so as to have the same extent as the legislation which it affects.

(4) No person is to be guilty of an offence solely as a result of the retrospective effect of a remedial order.

Procedure

2 No remedial order may be made unless—

(*a*) a draft of the order has been approved by a resolution of each House of Parliament made after the end of the period of 60 days beginning with the day on which the draft was laid; or

(*b*) it is declared in the order that it appears to the person making it that, because of the urgency of the matter, it is necessary to make the order without a draft being so approved.

Orders laid in draft

3— (1) No draft may be laid under paragraph 2(*a*) unless—

(*a*) the person proposing to make the order has laid before Parliament a document which contains a draft of the proposed order and the required information; and

(*b*) the period of 60 days, beginning with the day on which the document required by this sub-paragraph was laid, has ended.

(2) If representations have been made during that period, the draft laid under paragraph 2(*a*) must be accompanied by a statement containing—

(*a*) a summary of the representations; and

(*b*) if, as a result of the representations, the proposed order has been changed, details of the changes.

Urgent cases

4— (1) If a remedial order ("the original order") is made without being approved in draft, the person making it must lay it before Parliament, accompanied by the required information, after it is made.

(2) If representations have been made during the period of 60 days beginning with the day on which the original order was made, the person making it must (after the end of that period) lay before Parliament a statement containing—

(*a*) a summary of the representations; and

(*b*) if, as a result of the representations, he considers it appropriate to make changes to the original order, details of the changes.

(3) If sub-paragraph (2)(*b*) applies, the person making the statement must—

(*a*) make a further remedial order replacing the original order; and

(*b*) lay the replacement order before Parliament.

(4) If, at the end of the period of 120 days beginning with the day on which the original order was made, a resolution has not been passed by each House approving the original or replacement order, the order ceases to have effect (but without that affecting anything previously done under either order or the power to make a fresh remedial order).

Definitions

5 In this Schedule—

"representations" means representations about a remedial order (or proposed remedial order) made to the person making (or proposing to make) it and includes any relevant Parliamentary report or resolution; and

"required information" means—

(*a*) an explanation of the incompatibility which the order (or proposed order) seeks to remove, including particulars of the relevant declaration, finding or order; and

(*b*) a statement of the reasons for proceeding under section 10 and for making an order in those terms.

Calculating periods

6 In calculating any period for the purposes of this Schedule, no account is to be taken of any time during which—

(*a*) Parliament is dissolved or prorogued; or

(*b*) both Houses are adjourned for more than four days.

[**7**— (1) This paragraph applies in relation to—

(*a*) any remedial order made, and any draft of such an order proposed to be made—

(i) by the Scottish Ministers; or

(ii) within devolved competence (within the meaning of the Scotland Act 1998) by Her Majesty in Council; and

(*b*) any document or statement to be laid in connection with such an order (or proposed order).

(2) This Schedule has effect in relation to any such order (or proposed order), document or statement subject to the following modifications.

(3) Any reference to Parliament, each House of Parliament or both Houses of Parliament shall be construed as a reference to the Scottish Parliament.

(4) Paragraph 6 does not apply and instead, in calculating any period for the purposes of this Schedule, no account is to be taken of any time during which the Scottish Parliament is dissolved or is in recess for more than four days.]

Amendments—Para 7 inserted by the Scotland Act 1998 (Consequential Modifications) Order, SI 2000/2040 art 2, Schedule para 21 with effect from 27 July 2000.

SCHEDULE 3

DEROGATION AND RESERVATION

(not reproduced)

SCHEDULE 4

JUDICIAL PENSIONS

(not reproduced)

FINANCE ACT 1999

(1999 Chapter 16)

An Act to grant certain duties, to alter other duties, and to amend the law relating to the National Debt and the Public Revenue, and to make further provision in connection with Finance.

[27 July 1999]

PART II

VALUE ADDED TAX

12 Works of art, antiques, etc

(1), (2) (*Amend* VATA 1994 s 21(4) and *substitute* s 21(5), (6)).

(3) This section has effect in relation to goods imported at any time on or after the day on which this Act is passed.

Commentary—*De Voil Indirect Tax Service* **V3.325**.

13 Gold

(1) Notwithstanding the words preceding paragraph (*a*) in section 26(3) of the Value Added Tax Act 1994 (input tax allowable against output tax), regulations which—

(*a*) are made under section 26(3), and

(*b*) have effect in respect of exempt supplies which relate to gold,

may provide that input tax is allowable, as being attributable to the supplies, only in relation to specified matters.

(2) An order under section 31(2) of that Act (exempt supplies and acquisitions) which provides for certain supplies which relate to gold to be exempt supplies may—

(*a*) provide that a supply which would be an exempt supply by virtue of the order shall, if the supplier so chooses, be a taxable supply;

(*b*) make provision by reference to notices to be published by the Commissioners.

(3) An order under section 37(1) of that Act (relief on importation of goods) which gives relief from VAT on certain importations of gold may make provision by reference to notices to be published by the Commissioners.

(4) Provision made by virtue of subsection (2) or (3) above may be expressed—

(*a*) to apply only in specified circumstances;

(*b*) to apply subject to compliance with specified conditions (which may include conditions relating to general or specific approval of the Commissioners).

(5) Regulations may—

(*a*) require specified persons to keep specified records in relation to specified transactions concerning gold;

(*b*) require specified persons to give specified information to the Commissioners about specified transactions concerning gold;

(*c*) *provide for paragraph 10(2) of Schedule 11 to that Act (entry and inspection of premises) to apply in relation to specified transactions concerning gold as it applies in relation to the supply of goods under taxable supplies.*[2]

(6) The provisions of that Act (including, in particular, section 97 and paragraph 6(2) to [(4)][1] of Schedule 11) shall apply in relation to regulations under subsection (5) above[, and to records kept in pursuance of such regulations,][1] as they apply in relation to regulations under paragraph 6(1) of Schedule 11 to that Act [and to records kept in pursuance of that paragraph][1].

(7) In this section "the Commissioners" means the Commissioners of Customs and Excise.

Commentary—*De Voil Indirect Tax Service* **V5.143, V6.151**.

Amendments—[1] In sub-s (6), figure substituted for figure "(6)", and words inserted, by FA 2008 s 115, Sch 37 para 10 with effect from 1 April 2009 (by virtue of SI 2009/402).

[2] Sub-s (5)(*c*) repealed by FA 2008 Sch 36 para 89 with effect from 1 April 2009 (by virtue of SI 2009/404 art 2).

14 Preparations etc of meat, yeast or egg

(*Amends* VATA 1994 Sch 8).

15 Assignment of debts

(1)–(3)[2] (*Substitute* VATA 1994 s 36(3) and *amend* (5)(*e*), Sch 11, para 7).

(4) …[1]

(5) Subsections (1) and (4) above have effect for the purposes of the making of any refund or repayment after 9th March 1999, but do not have effect in relation to anything received on or before that day.

Commentary—*De Voil Indirect Tax Service* **V3.140, V5.156**.

Amendments—[1] Sub-s (4) repealed by the Value Added Tax Regulations, SI 1999/3029, regs 2, 5 with effect from 1 December 1999.

[2] Sub-s (3) repealed by FA 2008 s 113, Sch 36 para 92(*h*) with effect from 1 April 2009 (by virtue of SI 2009/404 art 2). In consequence of SI 2009/404 arts 1–11, the amendments made by FA 2008 Sch 36 para 92 shall be disregarded so far as they affect any notice referred to in those provisions, given on or before 31 March 2009.

16 Groups of companies

Schedule 2 to this Act (which makes changes to provisions about the treatment of bodies corporate as members of a group) shall have effect.

Commentary—*De Voil Indirect Tax Service* **V2.104**.

17 Penalties for incorrect certificates

(1) (*Substitutes* VATA 1994 s 62(1), (2)).

(2) Subsection (1) above has effect in relation to certificates given or, as the case may be, prepared on or after the day on which this Act is passed.

Commentary—*De Voil Indirect Tax Service* **V5.342**.

18 EC sales statements: time limits for assessments to penalties

(1) (*Substitutes* VATA 1994 s 77(2)).

(2) Subsection (1) above has effect in relation to any amount by way of penalty, interest or surcharge which becomes due on or after the day on which this Act is passed.

Commentary—*De Voil Indirect Tax Service* **V5.346, 355**.

19 Period before repayment supplement payable

(1)–(4) (*Amend* VATA 1994 s 79(2)(*b*), (3), (7) and *insert* s 79(2A)).

(5) This section has effect in relation to returns and claims received by the Commissioners on or after 9th March 1999.

Commentary—*De Voil Indirect Tax Service* **V5.191, 192**.

20 Meaning of "business"

(1) (*Repeals* VATA 1994 s 94(3)).

(2) This section shall come into force in accordance with such provision as the Commissioners of Customs and Excise may make by order made by statutory instrument.

Commentary—*De Voil Indirect Tax Service* **V2.241, V4.156**.

21 Accounting for VAT by Government departments

Commentary—*De Voil Indirect Tax Service* **V3.501, V6.156**.

Amendment—This section repealed by the Government Resources and Accounts Act 2000 ss 21, 29(2), Sch 2 with effect from 1 April 2001 (by virtue of SI 2000/3349 art 3).

PART VIII
MISCELLANEOUS AND SUPPLEMENTAL

General administration of tax

132 Power to provide for use of electronic communications

(1) Regulations may be made, in accordance with this section, for facilitating the use of electronic communications for—

(*a*) the delivery of information the delivery of which is authorised or required by or under any legislation relating to a taxation matter;

(*b*) the making of payments under any such legislation.

(2) The power to make regulations under this section is conferred—

(*a*) on the Commissioners of Inland Revenue in relation to matters which are under their care and management; and

(*b*) on the Commissioners of Customs and Excise in relation to matters which are under their care and management.

(3) For the purposes of this section provision for facilitating the use of electronic communications includes any of the following—

(*a*) provision authorising persons to use electronic communications for the delivery of information to tax authorities, or for the making of payments to tax authorities;

(*b*) provision requiring electronic communications to be used for the making to tax authorities of payments due from persons using such communications for the delivery of information to those authorities;

(*c*) provision authorising tax authorities to use electronic communications for the delivery of information to other persons or for the making of any payments;

(*d*) provision as to the electronic form to be taken by any information that is delivered to any tax authorities using electronic communications;

(*e*) provision requiring persons to prepare and keep records of information delivered to tax authorities by means of electronic communications, and of payments made to any such authorities by any such means;

(*f*) provision for the production of the contents of records kept in accordance with any regulations under this section;

(*g*) provision imposing conditions that must be complied with in connection with any use of electronic communications for the delivery of information or the making of any payment;

(*h*) provision, in relation to cases where use is made of electronic communications, for treating information as not having been delivered, or a payment as not having been made, unless conditions imposed by any such regulations are satisfied;

(*i*) provision, in relation to such cases, for determining the time when information is delivered or a payment is made;

(*j*) provision, in relation to such cases, for determining the person by whom information is to be taken to have been delivered or by whom a payment is to be taken to have been made;

(*k*) provision, in relation to cases where information is delivered by means of electronic communications, for authenticating whatever is delivered.

(4) The power to make provision under this section for facilitating the use of electronic communications shall also include power to make such provision as the persons exercising the power think fit (including provision for the application of conclusive or other presumptions) as to the manner of proving for any purpose—

(*a*) whether any use of electronic communications is to be taken as having resulted in the delivery of information or the making of a payment;

(*b*) the time of delivery of any information for the delivery of which electronic communications have been used;

(*c*) the time of the making of any payment for the making of which electronic communications have been used;

(*d*) the person by whom information delivered by means of electronic communications was delivered;

(*e*) the contents of anything so delivered;

(*f*) the contents of any records;

(*g*) any other matter for which provision may be made by regulations under this section.

(5) Regulations under this section may—

(*a*) allow any authorisation or requirement for which such regulations may provide to be given or imposed by means of a specific or general direction given by the Commissioners of Inland Revenue or the Commissioners of Customs and Excise;

(*b*) provide that the conditions of any such authorisation or requirement are to be taken to be satisfied only where such tax authorities as may be determined under the regulations are satisfied as to specified matters;

(*c*) allow a person to refuse to accept delivery of information in an electronic form or by means of electronic communications except in such circumstances as may be specified in or determined under the regulations;

(*d*) allow or require use to be made of intermediaries in connection with—

(i) the delivery of information, or the making of payments, by means of electronic communications; or

(ii) the authentication or security of anything transmitted by any such means.

(6) Power to make provision by regulations under this section shall include power—

(*a*) to provide for a contravention of, or any failure to comply with, a specified provision of any such regulations to attract a penalty of a specified amount not exceeding £1,000;

(*b*) to provide that specified enactments relating to penalties imposed for the purposes of any taxation matter (including enactments relating to assessments, review and appeal) are to apply, with or without modifications, in relation to penalties under such regulations;

(*c*) to make different provision for different cases;

(*d*) to make such incidental, supplemental, consequential and transitional provision in connection with any provision contained in any such regulations as the persons exercising the power think fit.

(7) The power to make regulations under this section shall be exercisable by statutory instrument subject to annulment in pursuance of a resolution of the House of Commons.

(8) References in this section to the delivery of information include references to any of the following (however referred to)—

(*a*) the production or furnishing to a person of any information, account, record or document;

(*b*) the giving, making, issue or surrender to, or service on, any person of any notice, notification, statement, declaration, certificate or direction;

(*c*) the imposition on any person of any requirement or the issue to any person of any request;

(*d*) the making of any return, claim, election or application;

(*e*) the amendment or withdrawal of anything mentioned in paragraphs (*a*) to (*d*) above.

(9) References in this section to a taxation matter are references to any of the matters which are under the care and management of the Commissioners of Inland Revenue or of the Commissioners of Customs and Excise.

(10) In this section—

"electronic communications" includes any communications by means of [an electronic communications service][1];

"legislation" means any enactment, Community legislation or subordinate legislation;

"payment" includes a repayment;

"records" includes records in electronic form;

"subordinate legislation" has the same meaning as in the Interpretation Act 1978;

"tax authorities" means—

(*a*) the Commissioners of Inland Revenue or the Commissioners of Customs and Excise,

(*b*) any officer of either body of Commissioners; or

(*c*) any other person who for the purposes of electronic communications is acting under the authority of either body of Commissioners.

Cross references—See Income Tax (Electronic Communications) Regulations, SI 2000/945 (delivery by electronic means of information in respect of income tax assessments).

FA 2000 Sch 38 para 1(1) (regulations may be made in accordance with FA 2000 Sch 38 for providing incentives to use electronic communications the purposes of mention in sub-s (1) above).

Amendments—[1] In sub-s (10), words in definition of "electronic communications" substituted by the Communications Act 2003 s 406, Sch 17 para 156 with effect from 25 July 2003 to 29 December 2003 for certain purposes (see SI 2003/1900), 29 December 2003 for other purposes (see SI 2003/3142), and from a date to be appointed for remaining purposes.

133 Use of electronic communications under other provisions

(1) Without prejudice to section 132 above, where any power to make subordinate legislation for or in connection with the delivery of information or the making of payments is conferred in relation to any taxation matter on—

(*a*) the Commissioners of Inland Revenue,

(*b*) the Commissioners of Customs and Excise, or

(*c*) the Treasury,

that power shall be taken (to the extent that it would not otherwise be so taken) to include power to make any such provision in relation to the delivery of that information or the making of those payments as could be made by any person by regulations in exercise of a power conferred by that section.

(2) Provision made in exercise of the powers conferred by section 132 above or subsection (1) above shall have effect notwithstanding so much of any enactment or subordinate legislation as (apart from the provision so made) would require—

(*a*) any information to be delivered, or

(*b*) any amount to be paid,

in a form or manner that would preclude the use of electronic communications for its delivery or payment, or the use in connection with its delivery or payment of an intermediary.

(3) Schedule 3A to the Taxes Management Act 1970 (electronic lodgement of tax returns etc) shall cease to have effect.

(4) Subsection (3) above shall come into force on such day as the Treasury may by order made by statutory instrument appoint; and different days may be appointed under this subsection for different purposes.

(5) Expressions used in this section and section 132 above have the same meanings in this section as in that section.

Cross references—See Income Tax (Electronic Communications) Regulations, SI 2000/945 (delivery by electronic means of information in respect of income tax assessments).

Supplemental

139 Repeals

(1) The enactments mentioned in Schedule 20 to this Act (which include provisions that are spent or of no practical utility) are hereby repealed to the extent specified in the third column of that Schedule.

(2) The repeals specified in that Schedule have effect subject to the commencement provisions and savings contained or referred to in the notes set out in that Schedule.

140 Short title

This Act may be cited as the Finance Act 1999.

SCHEDULES

SCHEDULE 2

VAT: GROUPS OF COMPANIES

Section 16

Commentary—*De Voil Indirect Tax Service* **V2.104**.

Amendment of Value Added Tax Act 1994

1, 2 (*amend* VATA 1994 s 43(1), *repeal* s 43(3)–(8) and *insert* ss 43A–43C).

3 (*amends* VATA 1994 s 83(*k*)).

4 (*inserts* VATA 1994 s 84(4A)–(4D)).

5 (*amends* VATA 1994 Sch 9A).

Transitional provisions

6— (1) In this paragraph—

"the old law" means sections 43, 83 and 84 of, and Schedule 9A to, the Value Added Tax Act 1994 as they have effect without the amendments in paragraphs 1 to 5 of this Schedule, and

"the new law" means sections 43 to 43C, 83 and 84 of, and Schedule 9A to, that Act as they have effect by virtue of paragraphs 1 to 5 of this Schedule.

(2) Where, immediately before this Schedule comes into force, two or more bodies corporate are treated as members of a group by virtue of the old law—

(*a*) they shall continue to be treated as members of a group, and

(*b*) in their treatment as members of a group after this Schedule comes into force, they shall be treated as if any application under the old law by virtue of which they are treated as members of a group had been an equivalent application under the new law.

(3) Where an application under section 43 of the Value Added Tax Act 1994 is received by the Commissioners, and has neither taken effect nor been refused before the day on which this Act is passed, the old law shall apply to determine whether the application is to take effect; but where it is determined under this sub-paragraph that an application is to take effect—

(*a*) it shall be treated as if it were an equivalent application under the new law, and

(*b*) it shall be taken to have been granted under the new law at the time when it would have taken effect in accordance with the old law.

(4) In a case to which sub-paragraph (2) or (3) above applies, the power under section 43C(3) shall not be used to terminate the treatment of a body corporate as a member of a group—

(*a*) on the ground that the body corporate is not established, and does not have a fixed establishment, in the United Kingdom, and

(*b*) from a date before 1st January 2000.

(5) Where an application which purports to be an application under the old law is received by the Commissioners after the day on which this Act is passed—

(*a*) it shall be treated as if it were an application under the new law, and (*b*) section 43B of the new law shall apply notwithstanding any provision in the application for a date from which it is to take effect.

SCHEDULE 20

REPEALS

Section 139

PART II

VALUE ADDED TAX

Note—All repeals relevant to VAT are already in effect and have therefore been omitted.

FINANCE ACT 2000

(2000 Chapter 17)

An act to grant certain duties, to alter other duties, and to amend the law relating to the National Debt and the Public Revenue, and to make further provision in connection with finance.

[28 July 2000]

PART V

OTHER TAXES

Value added tax

135 Supplies to which reduced rate applies

Amendments—This section repealed by FA 2001 s 110, Sch 33 Pt 3(1) with effect for supplies made, and acquisitions and importations taking place, after 31 October 2001 (by virtue of FA 2001 s 99(7)(*b*)).

136 Disposals of assets for which a VAT repayment is claimed

(1) (*amends* VATA 1994 s 3(2)).

(2) (*amends* VATA 1994 s 67).

(3) (*amends* VATA 1994 s 69(1)).

(4) (*amends* VATA 199A s 73(3)).

(5) (*amends* VATA 1994 s 74(1)).

(6) (*amends* VATA 1994 Sch 1 para 1, Sch 2 para 1).

(7) (*amends* VATA 1994 Sch 3 para 1).

(8) (*inserts* VATA 1994 Sch 3A).

(9) (*amends* VATA 1994 Sch 4 para 5).

(10) Subsections (1) to (7) and (9) above have effect in relation to supplies made on or after 21st March 2000; and subsection (8) above and Schedule 36 to this Act have effect in relation to relevant supplies (within the meaning of Schedule 3A to that Act) made on or after that date.

Commentary—*De Voil Indirect Tax Service* **V2.171, V5.151, V5.152**.

Prospective amendments—Sub-s (2) to be repealed by FA 2008 s 123, Sch 41 para 25(*k*) with effect from 1 April 2010 (by virtue of SI 2009/511 art 2).

137 Gold: penalty for failure to comply with record-keeping requirements etc

(1) Part IV of the Value Added Tax Act 1994 (administration, collection and enforcement) is amended as follows.

(2) (*inserts* VATA 1994 s 69A).

(3) (*amends* VATA 1994 s 70(1)).

(4) (*amends* VATA 1994 s 76(1)).

(5) (*amends* VATA 1994 s 83).

Commentary—*De Voil Indirect Tax Service* **V5.143**.

PART VI
MISCELLANEOUS AND SUPPLEMENTARY PROVISIONS

Incentives for electronic communications

143 Power to provide incentives to use electronic communications

(1) Regulations may be made in accordance with Schedule 38 to this Act for providing incentives to use electronic communications.

(2) …[1]

Commentary—*Simon's Taxes* **A4.101**.

Amendments—[1] Sub-s (2) repealed by CTA 2009 ss 1322, 1326, Sch 1 paras 462, 466. CTA 2009 applies for accounting periods ending on or after 1 April 2009 (for corporation tax purposes) and for tax years 2009–10 onwards (for income and capital gains tax purposes). Sub-s (2) previously read as follows—

"(2) Anything received by way of incentive under any such regulations shall not be regarded as income for any corporation tax purposes.".

Supplementary provisions

156 Repeals

(1) The enactments mentioned in Schedule 40 to this Act (which include provisions that are spent or of no practical utility) are repealed to the extent specified in the third column of that Schedule.

(2) The repeals specified in that Schedule have effect subject to the commencement provisions and savings contained or referred to in the notes set out in that Schedule.

157 Short title

This Act may be cited as the Finance Act 2000.

SCHEDULES

SCHEDULE 35
VALUE ADDED TAX: CHARGE AT REDUCED RATE

Section 135

Amendment—This Schedule repealed by FA 2001 s 110, Sch 33 Pt III(1) with effect for supplies made, and acquisitions and importations taking place, after 31 October 2001 (by virtue of FA 2001 s 99(7)(*b*)).

SCHEDULE 36
NEW SCHEDULE 3A TO THE VALUE ADDED TAX ACT 1994

Section 136(8)

Note—This Schedule sets out VATA 1994 Sch 3A as inserted by FA 2000 s 136(8).
Commentary—*De Voil Indirect Tax Service* **V2.171, V5.151, 152**.

SCHEDULE 38
REGULATIONS FOR PROVIDING INCENTIVES FOR ELECTRONIC COMMUNICATIONS

Section 143(1)

Regulations—See the Value Added Tax (Electronic Communications) (Incentives) Regulations, SI 2001/759.
Commentary—*Simon's Taxes* **A4.101**.

Introduction

1— (1) Regulations may be made in accordance with this Schedule for providing incentives to use electronic communications—

(*a*) for the purposes mentioned in section 132(1) of the Finance Act 1999 (power to provide for use of electronic communications for delivery of information and making of payments), or

(*b*) for any other communications with the tax authorities or in connection with taxation matters.

(2) The power to make regulations under this Schedule is conferred—

(*a*) on the Commissioners of Inland Revenue in relation to matters which are under their care and management, and

(*b*) on the Commissioners of Customs and Excise in relation to matters which are under their care and management.

Kinds of incentive

2— (1) The incentives shall be of such description as may be provided for in the regulations.

(2) They may, in particular, take the form of—

(*a*) discounts;

(*b*) the allowing of additional time to comply with any obligations under tax legislation (including obligations relating to the payment of tax or other amounts); or

(*c*) the facility to deliver information or make payments at more convenient intervals.

Conditions of entitlement

3— (1) The regulations may make provision as to the conditions of entitlement to an incentive.

(2) They may, in particular, make entitlement conditional—

(*a*) on the use of electronic communications for all communications or payments (or all communications and payments of a specified description) with, to or from the tax authority concerned, and

(*b*) on the use of specified means of electronic communication or payment acceptable to the tax authority concerned.

(3) The regulations may make provision for an appeal against a decision that the conditions of entitlement are not met.

Withdrawal of entitlement

4— (1) The regulations may make provision for the withdrawal of an incentive in specified circumstances.

(2) If they do, they may make provision—

(*a*) for giving notice of the withdrawal,

(*b*) for an appeal, and

(*c*) for the recovery of an amount not exceeding the value of the incentive.

(3) The regulations may provide that specified enactments relating to assessments, [reviews,][1] appeals and recovery of tax are to apply, with such adaptations as may be specified, in relation to the withdrawal of an incentive.

Amendment—[1] In sub-para (3), word inserted by the Transfer of Tribunal Functions and Revenue and Customs Appeals Order, SI 2009/56 art 3, Sch 1 para 295 with effect from 1 April 2009.

Power to authorise provision by directions

5 The regulations may authorise the making of any such provision as is mentioned in paragraph 3 or 4 by means of a specific or general direction given by the Commissioners of Inland Revenue or the Commissioners of Customs and Excise.

Power to provide for penalties

6— (1) The regulations may provide for contravention of, or failure to comply with, a specified provision of any such regulations to attract a penalty of a specified amount not exceeding £1,000.

(2) If they do, they may provide that specified enactments relating to penalties imposed in relation to any taxation matter (including enactments relating to assessments, review and appeals) are to apply, with or without modifications, in relation to penalties under the regulations.

General supplementary provisions

7— (1) Power to make provision by regulations under this Schedule includes power—

(*a*) to make different provision for different cases; and

(*b*) to make such incidental, supplemental, consequential and transitional provision in connection with any provision contained in any such regulations as the persons exercising the power think fit.

(2) The power to make regulations under this Schedule is exercisable by statutory instrument subject to annulment in pursuance of a resolution of the House of Commons.

Interpretation

8— (1) In this Schedule—

"discount" includes payment;

"electronic communications" includes any communications by means of [an electronic communications service][1];

"legislation" means any enactment, Community legislation or subordinate legislation;

"payment" includes a repayment;

"subordinate legislation" has the same meaning as in the Interpretation Act 1978;

"taxation matter" means any of the matters under the care and management of the Commissioners of Inland Revenue or the Commissioners of Customs and Excise;

"tax authorities" means—

(*a*) the Commissioners of Inland Revenue or the Commissioners of Customs and Excise,

(*b*) any officer of either body of Commissioners; or

(*c*) any other person who for the purposes of electronic communications is acting under the authority of either body of Commissioners;

"tax legislation" means legislation relating to any taxation matter.

(2) References in this Schedule to the delivery of information have the same meaning as in section 132 of the Finance Act 1999.

Amendments—[1] Words in definition of "electronic communications" substituted by the Communications Act 2003 s 406, Sch 17 para 160 with effect from 25 July 2003 to 29 December 2003 for certain purposes (see SI 2003/1900), 29 December 2003 for other purposes (see SI 2003/3142), and from a date to be appointed for remaining purposes.

SCHEDULE 40
REPEALS

Section 156

Note—All repeals relevant to VAT are already in effect and have therefore been omitted.

GOVERNMENT RESOURCES AND ACCOUNTS ACT 2000

(2000 Chapter 20)

Value Added Tax

21 Supplies by government departments

(1) This section applies where a government department makes supplies of goods or services which are taxable supplies for the purposes of the Value Added Tax Act 1994.

(2) The Treasury may make arrangements—

(*a*) about the treatment of receipts and payments in respect of value added tax in accounts under section 5 or 7;

(*b*) for the exemption of receipts in respect of value added tax, to such extent and on such conditions as may be specified, from any requirement for payment into the Consolidated Fund.

(3) For the purposes of this section "government department" has the same meaning as it has for the purposes of section 41 of the Value Added Tax Act 1994 (application to the Crown).

(4) …[1]

Amendment—[1] Sub-s (4) repealed by Statute Law (Repeals) Act 2004 s 1(1), Sch 1 Part 9 Group 6.

POSTAL SERVICES ACT 2000

(2000 Chapter 26)

[28 July 2000]

PART VII
MISCELLANEOUS AND SUPPLEMENTARY

Inviolability of mails etc

105 Application of customs and excise enactments to certain postal packets

(1) Subject as follows, the enactments for the time being in force in relation to customs or excise shall apply in relation to goods contained in postal packets to which this section applies which are brought into or sent out of the United Kingdom by post from or to any place outside the United Kingdom as they apply in relation to goods otherwise imported, exported or removed into or out of the United Kingdom from or to any such place.

(2) The Treasury, on the recommendation of the Commissioners of Customs and Excise and the Secretary of State, may make regulations for—

(*a*) specifying the postal packets to which this section applies,

(*b*) making modifications or exceptions in the application of the enactments mentioned in subsection (1) to such packets, (*c*) enabling persons engaged in the business of a postal operator to perform for the purposes of those enactments and otherwise all or any of the duties of the importer, exporter or person removing the goods,

(*d*) carrying into effect any arrangement with the government or postal administration of any country or territory outside the United Kingdom with respect to foreign postal packets,

(*e*) securing the observance of the enactments mentioned in subsection (1),

(*f*) without prejudice to any liability of any person under those enactments, punishing any contravention of the regulations.

(3) Duties (whether of customs or excise) charged on imported goods or other charges payable in respect of postal packets to which this section applies (whether payable to a postal operator or to a foreign administration) may be recovered by the postal operator concerned and in England and Wales and Northern Ireland may be so recovered as a civil debt due to him.

(4) In any proceedings for the recovery of any charges payable as mentioned in subsection (3), a certificate of the postal operator concerned of the amount of the charges shall be evidence (and, in Scotland, sufficient evidence) of that fact.

(5) In this section "foreign postal packet" means any postal packet either posted in the United Kingdom and sent to a place outside the United Kingdom, or posted in a place outside the United Kingdom and sent to a place within the United Kingdom, or in transit through the United Kingdom to a place outside the United Kingdom.

FINANCE ACT 2001

(2001 Chapter 9)

An Act to grant certain duties, to alter other duties, and to amend the law relating to the National Debt and the Public Revenue, and to make further provision in connection with Finance.

[11 May 2001]

PART 4
OTHER TAXES

Value added tax

96 VAT: children's car seats

(1) (*inserts* VATA 1994 Sch A1 para 1(5)).

(2) (*inserts* VATA 1994 Sch A1 para 7).

(3) The amendments made by this section have effect in relation to supplies made after the day on which this Act is passed.

Commentary—*De Voil Indirect Tax Service* **V4.4**.

97 VAT: residential conversions and renovations

(1) (*inserts* VATA 1994 Sch A1 para 1(6)–(9)).

(2) (*inserts* VATA 1994 Sch A1 paras 8–22).

(3) The amendments made by this section have effect in relation to supplies made after the day on which this Act is passed.

Commentary—*De Voil Indirect Tax Service* **V4.4**.

98 VAT: museums and galleries

(1) The Value Added Tax Act 1994 is amended as follows.

(2) (*inserts* VATA 1994 s 33A).

(3) (*inserts* VATA 1994 s 63(9A)).

(4)–(7) (*amend* VATA 1994 s 79).

(8) (*amends* VATA 1994 s 90(3)).

(9) (*amends* VATA 1994 Sch 9 Group 14 Note (9))

(10) Subject to subsection (11), this section comes into force on 1st September 2001.

(11) For the purpose only of the exercise of the power to make orders under the section 33A(9) inserted by this section, this section comes into force on the day on which this Act is passed.

Commentary—*De Voil Indirect Tax Service* **V5.162**.

Prospective amendments—Sub-s (3) to be repealed by FA 2007 ss 97, 114, Sch 27 Pt 5(5) with effect from a date to be appointed.

99 VAT: re-enactment of reduced-rate provisions

(1) For the purpose of re-enacting the provisions of the Value Added Tax Act 1994 that provide for VAT on certain supplies, acquisitions and importations to be charged at a reduced rate of 5 per cent, that Act is amended as follows.

(2) (*amends* VATA 1994 s 2(1)).

(3) (*repeals* VATA 1994 s 2(1A)–(1C)).

(4) (*inserts* VATA 1994 s 29A).

(5) (*inserts* VATA 1994 Sch 7A).

(6) The consequential amendments in Part II of Schedule 31 to this Act have effect.

(7) The following provisions have effect in relation to supplies made, and acquisitions and importations taking place, on or after 1st November 2001—

(*a*) subsections (2) and (5),

(*b*) subsection (3) so far as providing for section 2(1A) and (1B), and Schedule A1, to cease to have effect, and

(*c*) subsection (4) so far as inserting subsections (1) and (2) of the new section 29A.

(8) Subsection (3), so far as providing for section 2(1C) to cease to have effect, comes into force on 1st November 2001.

(9) Subsection (6)—

(*a*) so far as relating to the amendments made by paragraphs 2 and 6(2) of Schedule 31 to this Act, has effect in relation to orders under section 2(2) of the Value Added Tax Act 1994 that make changes only in the rate of VAT that is in force at times on or after 1st November 2001;

(*b*) so far as relating to the amendment made by paragraph 3 of Schedule 31 to this Act, has effect in relation to supplies made, or to be made, on or after 1st November 2001.

Commentary—*De Voil Indirect Tax Service* **V4.4**.

100 VAT representatives

(1)–(3) (*substitutes* VATA 1994 s 48(1)(*b*), (*ba*) for sub-s (1)(*b*), *inserts* sub-ss (1A), (1B), and *substitutes* sub-ss (2), (2)(A) for sub-s (2)).

(4) The amendments made by this section come into force on 31st December 2001.

Commentary—*De Voil Indirect Tax Service* **V2.106**.

PART 5

MISCELLANEOUS AND SUPPLEMENTARY PROVISIONS

Supplementary

...

110 Repeals and revocations

(1) The enactments mentioned in Schedule 33 to this Act (which include provisions that are spent or of no practical utility) are repealed or revoked to the extent specified.

(2) The repeals and revocations specified in that Schedule have effect subject to the commencement provisions and savings contained or referred to in the notes set out in that Schedule.

111 Short title

This Act may be cited as the Finance Act 2001.

SCHEDULES

SCHEDULE 31

VALUE ADDED TAX: RE-ENACTMENT OF REDUCED RATE PROVISIONS

Section 99

Commentary—*De Voil Indirect Tax Service* **V4.4**.

PART 1

NEW SCHEDULE 7A TO THE VALUE ADDED TAX ACT 1994

1 (*sets out* VATA 1994 Sch 7A *as inserted by* FA 2001 s 99(5)).

PART 2

CONSEQUENTIAL AMENDMENTS

Value Added Tax Act 1994 (*c 23*)

2–6 (*amend* VATA 1994 ss 2, 62, 88, 96, and 97).

Finance Act 2000 (*c 17*)

7 (*inserts* FA 2000 Sch 6 para 9(5)).

SCHEDULE 33

REPEALS

Section 101

PART 3

OTHER TAXES

(1) VALUE ADDED TAX: REDUCED RATE

Note—All repeals relevant to VAT are already in effect and have therefore been omitted.

CRIMINAL JUSTICE AND POLICE ACT 2001

(2001 Chapter 16)

ARRANGEMENT OF SECTIONS

PART 2

POWERS OF SEIZURE

Additional powers of seizure

PART 6
MISCELLANEOUS AND SUPPLEMENTAL

Supplemental

An Act to make provision for combatting crime and disorder; to make provision about the disclosure of information relating to criminal matters and about powers of search and seizure; to amend the Police and Criminal Evidence Act 1984, the Police and Criminal Evidence (Northern Ireland) Order 1989 and the Terrorism Act 2000; to make provision about the police, the National Criminal Intelligence Service and the National Crime Squad; to make provision about the powers of the courts in relation to criminal matters; and for connected purposes.

[11 May 2001]

PART 2
POWERS OF SEIZURE

Additional powers of seizure

50 Additional powers of seizure from premises

(1) Where—

(*a*) a person who is lawfully on any premises finds anything on those premises that he has reasonable grounds for believing may be or may contain something for which he is authorised to search on those premises,

(*b*) a power of seizure to which this section applies or the power conferred by subsection (2) would entitle him, if he found it, to seize whatever it is that he has grounds for believing that thing to be or to contain, and

(*c*) in all the circumstances, it is not reasonably practicable for it to be determined, on those premises—

(i) whether what he has found is something that he is entitled to seize, or

(ii) the extent to which what he has found contains something that he is entitled to seize,

that person's powers of seizure shall include power under this section to seize so much of what he has found as it is necessary to remove from the premises to enable that to be determined.

(2) Where—

(*a*) a person who is lawfully on any premises finds anything on those premises ("the seizable property") which he would be entitled to seize but for its being comprised in something else that he has (apart from this subsection) no power to seize,

(*b*) the power under which that person would have power to seize the seizable property is a power to which this section applies, and

(*c*) in all the circumstances it is not reasonably practicable for the seizable property to be separated, on those premises, from that in which it is comprised,

that person's powers of seizure shall include power under this section to seize both the seizable property and that from which it is not reasonably practicable to separate it.

(3) The factors to be taken into account in considering, for the purposes of this section, whether or not it is reasonably practicable on particular premises for something to be determined, or for something to be separated from something else, shall be confined to the following—

(*a*) how long it would take to carry out the determination or separation on those premises;

(*b*) the number of persons that would be required to carry out that determination or separation on those premises within a reasonable period;

(*c*) whether the determination or separation would (or would if carried out on those premises) involve damage to property;

(*d*) the apparatus or equipment that it would be necessary or appropriate to use for the carrying out of the determination or separation; and

(*e*) in the case of separation, whether the separation—

(i) would be likely, or

(ii) if carried out by the only means that are reasonably practicable on those premises, would be likely,

to prejudice the use of some or all of the separated seizable property for a purpose for which something seized under the power in question is capable of being used.

(4) Section 19(6) of the 1984 Act and Article 21(6) of the Police and Criminal Evidence (Northern Ireland) Order 1989 (SI 1989/1341 (NI 12)) (powers of seizure not to include power to seize anything that a person has reasonable grounds for believing is legally privileged) shall not apply to the power of seizure conferred by subsection (2).

(5) This section applies to each of the powers of seizure specified in Part 1 of Schedule 1.

(6) Without prejudice to any power conferred by this section to take a copy of any document, nothing in this section, so far as it has effect by reference to the power to take copies of documents under section 28(2)(*b*) of the Competition Act 1998 (c 41), shall be taken to confer any power to seize any document.

51 Additional powers of seizure from the person

(1) Where—

(*a*) a person carrying out a lawful search of any person finds something that he has reasonable grounds for believing may be or may contain something for which he is authorised to search,

(*b*) a power of seizure to which this section applies or the power conferred by subsection (2) would entitle him, if he found it, to seize whatever it is that he has grounds for believing that thing to be or to contain, and

(*c*) in all the circumstances it is not reasonably practicable for it to be determined, at the time and place of the search—

(i) whether what he has found is something that he is entitled to seize, or

(ii) the extent to which what he has found contains something that he is entitled to seize,

that person's powers of seizure shall include power under this section to seize so much of what he has found as it is necessary to remove from that place to enable that to be determined.

(2) Where—

(*a*) a person carrying out a lawful search of any person finds something ("the seizable property") which he would be entitled to seize but for its being comprised in something else that he has (apart from this subsection) no power to seize,

(*b*) the power under which that person would have power to seize the seizable property is a power to which this section applies, and

(*c*) in all the circumstances it is not reasonably practicable for the seizable property to be separated, at the time and place of the search, from that in which it is comprised,

that person's powers of seizure shall include power under this section to seize both the seizable property and that from which it is not reasonably practicable to separate it.

(3) The factors to be taken into account in considering, for the purposes of this section, whether or not it is reasonably practicable, at the time and place of a search, for something to be determined, or for something to be separated from something else, shall be confined to the following—

(*a*) how long it would take to carry out the determination or separation at that time and place;

(*b*) the number of persons that would be required to carry out that determination or separation at that time and place within a reasonable period;

(*c*) whether the determination or separation would (or would if carried out at that time and place) involve damage to property;

(*d*) the apparatus or equipment that it would be necessary or appropriate to use for the carrying out of the determination or separation; and

(*e*) in the case of separation, whether the separation—

(i) would be likely, or

(ii) if carried out by the only means that are reasonably practicable at that time and place, would be likely,

to prejudice the use of some or all of the separated seizable property for a purpose for which something seized under the power in question is capable of being used.

(4) Section 19(6) of the 1984 Act and Article 21(6) of the Police and Criminal Evidence (Northern Ireland) Order 1989 (SI 1989/1341 (NI 12)) (powers of seizure not to include power to seize anything a person has reasonable grounds for believing is legally privileged) shall not apply to the power of seizure conferred by subsection (2).

(5) This section applies to each of the powers of seizure specified in Part 2 of Schedule 1.

52 Notice of exercise of power under s. 50 or 51

(1) Where a person exercises a power of seizure conferred by section 50, it shall (subject to subsections (2) and (3)) be his duty, on doing so, to give to the occupier of the premises a written notice—

(*a*) specifying what has been seized in reliance on the powers conferred by that section;

(*b*) specifying the grounds on which those powers have been exercised;

(*c*) setting out the effect of sections 59 to 61;

(*d*) specifying the name and address of the person to whom notice of an application under section 59(2) to the appropriate judicial authority in respect of any of the seized property must be given; and

(*e*) specifying the name and address of the person to whom an application may be made to be allowed to attend the initial examination required by any arrangements made for the purposes of section 53(2).

(2) Where it appears to the person exercising on any premises a power of seizure conferred by section 50—

(*a*) that the occupier of the premises is not present on the premises at the time of the exercise of the power, but

(*b*) that there is some other person present on the premises who is in charge of the premises,

subsection (1) of this section shall have effect as if it required the notice under that subsection to be given to that other person.

(3) Where it appears to the person exercising a power of seizure conferred by section 50 that there is no one present on the premises to whom he may give a notice for the purposes of complying with subsection (1) of this section, he shall, before leaving the premises, instead of complying with that subsection, attach a notice such as is mentioned in that subsection in a prominent place to the premises.

(4) Where a person exercises a power of seizure conferred by section 51 it shall be his duty, on doing so, to give a written notice to the person from whom the seizure is made—

(*a*) specifying what has been seized in reliance on the powers conferred by that section;

(*b*) specifying the grounds on which those powers have been exercised;

(*c*) setting out the effect of sections 59 to 61;

(*d*) specifying the name and address of the person to whom notice of any application under section 59(2) to the appropriate judicial authority in respect of any of the seized property must be given; and

(*e*) specifying the name and address of the person to whom an application may be made to be allowed to attend the initial examination required by any arrangements made for the purposes of section 53(2).

(5) The Secretary of State may by regulations made by statutory instrument, after consultation with the Scottish Ministers, provide that a person who exercises a power of seizure conferred by section 50 shall be required to give a notice such as is mentioned in subsection (1) of this section to any person, or send it to any place, described in the regulations.

(6) Regulations under subsection (5) may make different provision for different cases.

(7) A statutory instrument containing regulations under subsection (5) shall be subject to annulment in pursuance of a resolution of either House of Parliament.

Return or retention of seized property

53 Examination and return of property seized under s. 50 or 51

(1) This section applies where anything has been seized under a power conferred by section 50 or 51.

(2) It shall be the duty of the person for the time being in possession of the seized property in consequence of the exercise of that power to secure that there are arrangements in force which (subject to section 61) ensure—

(*a*) that an initial examination of the property is carried out as soon as reasonably practicable after the seizure;

(*b*) that that examination is confined to whatever is necessary for determining how much of the property falls within subsection (3);

(*c*) that anything which is found, on that examination, not to fall within subsection (3) is separated from the rest of the seized property and is returned as soon as reasonably practicable after the examination of an the seized property has been completed; and

(*d*) that, until the initial examination of all the seized property has been completed and anything which does not fall within subsection (3) has been returned, the seized property is kept separate from anything seized under any other power.

(3) The seized property falls within this subsection to the extent only—

(*a*) that it is property for which the person seizing it had power to search when he made the seizure but is not property the return of which is required by section 54;

(*b*) that it is property the retention of which is authorised by section 56; or

(*c*) that it is something which, in all the circumstances, it will not be reasonably practicable, following the examination, to separate from property falling within paragraph (*a*) or (*b*).

(4) In determining for the purposes of this section the earliest practicable time for the carrying out of an initial examination of the seized property, due regard shall be had to the desirability of allowing the person from whom it was seized, or a person with an interest in that property, an opportunity of being present or (if he chooses) of being represented at the examination.

(5) In this section, references to whether or not it is reasonably practicable to separate part of the seized property from the rest of it are references to whether or not it is reasonably practicable to

do so without prejudicing the use of the rest of that property, or a part of it, for purposes for which (disregarding the part to be separated) the use of the whole or of a part of the rest of the property, if retained, would be lawful.

54 Obligation to return items subject to legal privilege

(1) If, at any time after a seizure of anything has been made in exercise of a power of seizure to which this section applies—

(*a*) it appears to the person for the time being having possession of the seized property in consequence of the seizure that the property—

(i) is an item subject to legal privilege, or

(ii) has such an item comprised in it,

and

(*b*) in a case where the item is comprised in something else which has been lawfully seized, it is not comprised in property falling within subsection (2),

it shall be the duty of that person to secure that the item is returned as soon as reasonably practicable after the seizure.

(2) Property in which an item subject to legal privilege is comprised falls within this subsection if—

(*a*) the whole or a part of the rest of the property is property falling within subsection (3) or property the retention of which is authorised by section 56; and

(*b*) in all the circumstances, it is not reasonably practicable for that item to be separated from the rest of that property (or, as the case may be, from that part of it) without prejudicing the use of the rest of that property, or that part of it, for purposes for which (disregarding that item) its use, if retained, would be lawful.

(3) Property falls within this subsection to the extent that it is property for which the person seizing it had power to search when he made the seizure, but is not property which is required to be returned under this section or section 55.

(4) This section applies—

(*a*) to the powers of seizure conferred by sections 50 and 51;

(*b*) to each of the powers of seizure specified in Parts 1 and 2 of Schedule 1; and

(*c*) to any power of seizure (not falling within paragraph (*a*) or (*b*)) conferred on a constable by or under any enactment, including an enactment passed after this Act.

55 Obligation to return excluded and special procedure material

(1) If, at any time after a seizure of anything has been made in exercise of a power to which this section applies—

(*a*) it appears to the person for the time being having possession of the seized property in consequence of the seizure that the property—

(i) is excluded material or special procedure material, or

(ii) has any excluded material or any special procedure material comprised in it,

(*b*) its retention is not authorised by section 56, and

(*c*) in a case where the material is comprised in something else which has been lawfully seized, it is not comprised in property falling within subsection (2) or (3),

it shall be the duty of that person to secure that the item is returned as soon as reasonably practicable after the seizure.

(2) Property in which any excluded material or special procedure material is comprised falls within this subsection if—

(*a*) the whole or a part of the rest of the property is property for which the person seizing it had power to search when he made the seizure but is not property the return of which is required by this section or section 54; and

(*b*) in all the circumstances, it is not reasonably practicable for that material to be separated from the rest of that property (or, as the case may be, from that part of it) without prejudicing the use of the rest of that property, or that part of it, for purposes for which (disregarding that material) its use, if retained, would be lawful.

(3) Property in which any excluded material or special procedure material is comprised falls within this subsection if—

(*a*) the whole or a part of the rest of the property is property the retention of which is authorised by section 56; and

(*b*) in all the circumstances, it is not reasonably practicable for that material to be separated from the rest of that property (or, as the case may be, from that part of it) without prejudicing the use of the rest of that property, or that part of it, for purposes for which (disregarding that material) its use, if retained, would be lawful.

(4) This section applies (subject to subsection (5)) to each of the powers of seizure specified in Part 3 of Schedule 1.

(5) In its application to the powers of seizure conferred by—

(*a*) ...[2]

(*b*) section 56(5) of the Drug Trafficking Act 1994 (c 37), …[1]
(*c*) Article 51(5) of the Proceeds of Crime (Northern Ireland) Order 1996 (SI 1996/1299 (NI 6)), [and
(*d*) section 352(4) of the Proceeds of Crime Act 2002,][1]

this section shall have effect with the omission of every reference to special procedure material.

(6) In this section, except in its application to—

(*a*) the power of seizure conferred by section 8(2) of the 1984 Act,
(*b*) the power of seizure conferred by Article 10(2) of the Police and Criminal Evidence (Northern Ireland) Order 1989 (SI 1989/1341 (NI 12)),
(*c*) each of the powers of seizure conferred by the provisions of paragraphs 1 and 3 of Schedule 5 to the Terrorism Act 2000 (c 11), and
(*d*) the power of seizure conferred by paragraphs 15 and 19 of Schedule 5 to that Act of 2000, so far only as the power in question is conferred by reference to paragraph 1 of that Schedule,

"special procedure material" means special procedure material consisting of documents or records other than documents.

Amendments—[1] Word in sub-s (5)(*b*) repealed, and sub-s (5)(*d*) and word preceding it inserted, by the Proceeds of Crime Act 2002 ss 456, 457, Sch 11 paras 1, 40(1), (2), Sch 12 with effect from 24 February 2003 (by virtue of SI 2003/120).
[2] Sub-s (5)(*a*) repealed by the Proceeds of Crime Act 2002 s 457, Sch 12 with effect from 24 March 2003 (by virtue of SI 2003/333).

56 Property seized by constables etc

(1) The retention of—

(*a*) property seized on any premises by a constable who was lawfully on the premises,
(*b*) property seized on any premises by a relevant person who was on the premises accompanied by a constable, and
(*c*) property seized by a constable carrying out a lawful search of any person,

is authorised by this section if the property falls within subsection (2) or (3).

(2) Property falls within this subsection to the extent that there are reasonable grounds for believing—

(*a*) that it is property obtained in consequence of the commission of an offence; and
(*b*) that it is necessary for it to be retained in order to prevent its being concealed, lost, damaged, altered or destroyed.

(3) Property falls within this subsection to the extent that there are reasonable grounds for believing—

(*a*) that it is evidence in relation to any offence; and
(*b*) that it is necessary for it to be retained in order to prevent its being concealed, lost, altered or destroyed.

(4) Nothing in this section authorises the retention (except in pursuance of section 54(2)) of anything at any time when its return is required by section 54.

[(4A) Subsection (1)(*a*) includes property seized on any premises—

(*a*) by a person authorised under section 16(2) of the 1984 Act to accompany a constable executing a warrant, or
(*b*) by a person accompanying a constable under section 2(6) of the Criminal Justice Act 1987 in the execution of a warrant under section 2(4) of that Act.][2]

(5) In subsection (1)(*b*) the reference to a relevant person's being on any premises accompanied by a constable is a reference only to a person who was so on the premises under the authority of—

(*a*) a warrant under section 448 of the Companies Act 1985 (c 6) authorising him to exercise together with a constable the powers conferred by subsection (3) of that section;
(*b*) a warrant under Article 441 of the Companies (Northern Ireland) Order 1986 (SI 1986/1032 (NI 6)) authorising him to exercise together with a constable the powers conferred by paragraph (3) of that Article;
(*c*)–(*e*) …[1]

Amendments—[1] Sub-s (5)(*c*)–(*e*) repealed by the Financial Services and Markets Act 2000 (Consequential Amendments and Repeals) Order, SI 2001/3649 art 364(*a*) with effect from 1 December 2001.
[2] Sub-s (4A) inserted by the Criminal Justice Act 2003 s 12, Sch 1 para 14 with effect from 20 January 2004 (by virtue of SI 2004/81).

57 Retention of seized items

(1) This section has effect in relation to the following provisions (which are about the retention of items which have been seized and are referred to in this section as "the relevant provisions")—

(*a*) section 22 of the 1984 Act;
(*b*) Article 24 of the Police and Criminal Evidence (Northern Ireland) Order 1989 (SI 1989/1341 (NI 12));
(*c*) *section 20CC(3) of the Taxes Management Act 1970 (c 9);*[6]
(*d*) paragraph 4 of Schedule 9 to the Weights and Measures (Northern Ireland) Order 1981 (SI 1981/231 (NI 10));
(*e*) …[1];

(*f*) section 448(6) of the Companies Act 1985 (c 6);
(*g*) paragraph 4 of [Schedule 7 to the Weights and Measures (Packaged Goods) Regulations 2006][3];
(*h*) …[1];
(*i*) Article 441(6) of the Companies (Northern Ireland) Order 1986;
(*j*) …[1];
(*k*) section 40(4) of the Human Fertilisation and Embryology Act 1990 (c 37);
(*l*) section 5(4) of the Knives Act 1997 (c 21);
(*m*) paragraph 7(2) of Schedule 9 to the Data Protection Act 1998 (c 29);
(*n*) section 28(7) of the Competition Act 1998 (c 41);
(*o*) section 176(8) of the Financial Services and Markets Act 2000 (c 8);
(*p*) paragraph 7(2) of Schedule 3 to the Freedom of Information Act 2000 (c 36).
[(*pa*) section 227F of the Enterprise Act 2002;][4]
[(*q*) paragraph 5(4) of Schedule 5 to the Human Tissue Act 2004.][2]
[(*r*) paragraph 12(3) of Schedule 2 to the Animal Welfare Act 2006.][5]

(2) The relevant provisions shall apply in relation to any property seized in exercise of a power conferred by section 50 or 51 as if the property had been seized under the power of seizure by reference to which the power under that section was exercised in relation to that property.

(3) Nothing in any of sections 53 to 56 authorises the retention of any property at any time when its retention would not (apart from the provisions of this Part) be authorised by the relevant provisions.

(4) Nothing in any of the relevant provisions authorises the retention of anything after an obligation to return it has arisen under this Part.

Amendments—[1] Sub-s (1)(*e*), (*h*), (*j*) repealed by the Financial Services and Markets Act 2000 (Consequential Amendments and Repeals) Order, SI 2001/3649 art 364(*b*) with effect from 1 December 2001.
[2] Sub-s (1)(*q*) inserted by the Human Tissue Act 2004 s 56, Sch 56 para 5(1), (2) with effect, for certain purposes, from 1 March 2006, and for other purposes from 6 April 2006. For commencement provisions, see the Human Tissue Act 2004 (Commencement No 4 and Transitional Provisions) Order, SI 2006/404 arts 2–4.
[3] Words in sub-s (1)(*g*) substituted by Weights and Measures (Packaged Goods) Regulations, SI 2006/659 reg 1(2), Sch 1 Pt2(24), (25) with effect from 6 April 2006.
[4] Sub-s (1)(*pa*) inserted by the Enterprise Act 2002 (Amendment) Regulations, SI 2006/3363 regs 24, 25 with effect from 8 January 2007.
[5] Sub-s (1)(*r*) inserted by the Animal Welfare Act 2006 s 64, Sch 3 para 14(1) with effect as follows—
– in relation to Wales, from 27 March 2007 (by virtue of SI 2007/1030 art 2(1)(*j*), (*l*));
– in relation to England, from 6 April 2007 (by virtue of SI 2007/499 art 2(2)(*l*));
– in relation to Scotland and Northern Ireland, from a date to be appointed.
[6] Sub-s (1)(*c*) repealed by FA 2007 ss 84, 114, Sch 22 para 13(1)(*a*), Sch 27 Pt 5(1) with effect from 1 December 2007 (by virtue of SI 2007/3166 art 3(*a*)).

Prospective amendment—In sub-s (1)(*k*), words "paragraph 7(4) of Schedule 3B to" to be substituted for words "section 40(4) of" by the Human Fertilisation and Embryology Act 2008 s 65, Sch 7 para 19 with effect from a date to be appointed.

58 Person to whom seized property is to be returned

(1) Where—
(*a*) anything has been seized in exercise of any power of seizure, and
(*b*) there is an obligation under this Part for the whole or any part of the seized property to be returned,

the obligation to return it shall (subject to the following provisions of this section) be an obligation to return it to the person from whom it was seized.

(2) Where—
(*a*) any person is obliged under this Part to return anything that has been seized to the person from whom it was seized, and
(*b*) the person under that obligation is satisfied that some other person has a better right to that thing than the person from whom it was seized,

his duty to return it shall, instead, be a duty to return it to that other person or, as the case may be, to the person appearing to him to have the best right to the thing in question.

(3) Where different persons claim to be entitled to the return of anything that is required to be returned under this Part, that thing may be retained for as long as is reasonably necessary for the determination in accordance with subsection (2) of the person to whom it must be returned.

(4) References in this Part to the person from whom something has been seized, in relation to a case in which the power of seizure was exercisable by reason of that thing's having been found on any premises, are references to the occupier of the premises at the time of the seizure.

(5) References in this section to the occupier of any premises at the time of a seizure, in relation to a case in which—
(*a*) a notice in connection with the entry or search of the premises in question, or with the seizure, was given to a person appearing in the occupier's absence to be in charge of the premises, and
(*b*) it is practicable, for the purpose of returning something that has been seized, to identify that person but not to identify the occupier of the premises,

are references to that person.

Remedies and safeguards

59 Application to the appropriate judicial authority

(1) This section applies where anything has been seized in exercise, or purported exercise, of a relevant power of seizure.

(2) Any person with a relevant interest in the seized property may apply to the appropriate judicial authority, on one or more of the grounds mentioned in subsection (3), for the return of the whole or a part of the seized property.

(3) Those grounds are—

(*a*) that there was no power to make the seizure;
(*b*) that the seized property is or contains an item subject to legal privilege that is not comprised in property falling within section 54(2);
(*c*) that the seized property is or contains any excluded material or special procedure material which—

(i) has been seized under a power to which section 55 applies;
(ii) is not comprised in property falling within section 55(2) or (3); and
(iii) is not property the retention of which is authorised by section 56;

(*d*) that the seized property is or contains something seized under section 50 or 51 which does not fall within section 53(3);

and subsections (5) and (6) of section 55 shall apply for the purposes of paragraph (*c*) as they apply for the purposes of that section.

(4) Subject to subsection (6), the appropriate judicial authority, on an application under subsection (2), shall—

(*a*) if satisfied as to any of the matters mentioned in subsection (3), order the return of so much of the seized property as is property in relation to which the authority is so satisfied; and
(*b*) to the extent that that authority is not so satisfied, dismiss the application.

(5) The appropriate judicial authority—

(*a*) on an application under subsection (2),
(*b*) on an application made by the person for the time being having possession of anything in consequence of its seizure under a relevant power of seizure, or
(*c*) on an application made—

(i) by a person with a relevant interest in anything seized under section 50 or 51, and
(ii) on the grounds that the requirements of section 53(2) have not been or are not being complied with,

may give such directions as the authority thinks fit as to the examination, retention, separation or return of the whole or any part of the seized property.

(6) On any application under this section, the appropriate judicial authority may authorise the retention of any property which—

(*a*) has been seized in exercise, or purported exercise, of a relevant power of seizure, and
(*b*) would otherwise fall to be returned,

if that authority is satisfied that the retention of the property is justified on grounds falling within subsection (7).

(7) Those grounds are that (if the property were returned) it would immediately become appropriate—

(*a*) to issue, on the application of the person who is in possession of the property at the time of the application under this section, a warrant in pursuance of which, or of the exercise of which, it would be lawful to seize the property; or
(*b*) to make an order under—

(i) paragraph 4 of Schedule 1 to the 1984 Act,
(ii) paragraph 4 of Schedule 1 to the Police and Criminal Evidence (Northern Ireland) Order 1989 (SI 1989/1341 (NI 12)),
(iii) section 20BA of the Taxes Management Act 1970 (c 9), or
(iv) paragraph 5 of Schedule 5 to the Terrorism Act 2000 (c 11), under which the property would fall to be delivered up or produced to the person mentioned in paragraph (*a*).

(8) Where any property which has been seized in exercise, or purported exercise, of a relevant power of seizure has parts ("part A" and "part B") comprised in it such that—

(*a*) it would be inappropriate, if the property were returned, to take any action such as is mentioned in subsection (7) in relation to part A,
(*b*) it would (or would but for the facts mentioned in paragraph (*a*)) be appropriate, if the property were returned, to take such action in relation to part B, and
(*c*) in all the circumstances, it is not reasonably practicable to separate part A from part B without prejudicing the use of part B for purposes for which it is lawful to use property seized under the power in question,

the facts mentioned in paragraph (*a*) shall not be taken into account by the appropriate judicial authority in deciding whether the retention of the property is justified on grounds falling within subsection (7).

(9) If a person fails to comply with any order or direction made or given by a judge of the Crown Court in exercise of any jurisdiction under this section—

(*a*) the authority may deal with him as if he had committed a contempt of the Crown Court; and

(*b*) any enactment relating to contempt of the Crown Court shall have effect in relation to the failure as if it were such a contempt.

(10) The relevant powers of seizure for the purposes of this section are—

(*a*) the powers of seizure conferred by sections 50 and 51;

(*b*) each of the powers of seizure specified in Parts 1 and 2 of Schedule 1; and

(*c*) any power of seizure (not falling within paragraph (*a*) or (*b*)) conferred on a constable by or under any enactment, including an enactment passed after this Act.

(11) References in this section to a person with a relevant interest in seized property are references to—

(*a*) the person from whom it was seized;

(*b*) any person with an interest in the property; or

(*c*) any person, not falling within paragraph (*a*) or (*b*), who had custody or control of the property immediately before the seizure.

(12) For the purposes of subsection (11)(*b*), the persons who have an interest in seized property shall, in the case of property which is or contains an item subject to legal privilege, be taken to include the person in whose favour that privilege is conferred.

60 Cases where duty to secure arises

(1) Where property has been seized in exercise, or purported exercise, of any power of seizure conferred by section 50 or 51, a duty to secure arises under section 61 in relation to the seized property if—

(*a*) a person entitled to do so makes an application under section 59 for the return of the property;

(*b*) in relation to England, Wales and Northern Ireland, at least one of the conditions set out in subsections (2) and (3) is satisfied;

(*c*) in relation to Scotland, the condition set out in subsection (2) is satisfied; and

(*d*) notice of the application is given to a relevant person.

(2) The first condition is that the application is made on the grounds that the seized property is or contains an item subject to legal privilege that is not comprised in property falling within section 54(2).

(3) The second condition is that—

(*a*) the seized property was seized by a person who had, or purported to have, power under this Part to seize it by virtue only of one or more of the powers specified in subsection (6); and

(*b*) the application—

(i) is made on the ground that the seized property is or contains something which does not fall within section 53(3); and

(ii) states that the seized property is or contains special procedure material or excluded material.

(4) In relation to property seized by a person who had. or purported to have, power under this Part to seize it by virtue only of one or more of the powers of seizure conferred by—

(*a*) …[1]

(*b*) section 56(5) of the Drug Trafficking Act 1994 (c 37), …[2]

(*c*) Article 51(5) of the Proceeds of Crime (Northern Ireland) Order 1996 (SI 1996/1299 (NI 6)), [or

(*d*) section 352(4) of the Proceeds of Crime Act 2002,][2]

the second condition is satisfied only if the application states that the seized property is or contains excluded material.

(5) In relation to property seized by a person who had, or purported to have, power under this Part to seize it by virtue only of one or more of the powers of seizure specified in Part 3 of Schedule 1 but not by virtue of—

(*a*) the power of seizure conferred by section 8(2) of the 1984 Act,

(*b*) the power of seizure conferred by Article 10(2) of the Police and Criminal Evidence (Northern Ireland) Order 1989 (SI 1989/1341 (NI 12)),

(*c*) either of the powers of seizure conferred by paragraphs 1 and 3 of Schedule 5 to the Terrorism Act 2000 (c 11), or

(*d*) either of the powers of seizure conferred by paragraphs 15 and 19 of Schedule 5 to that Act of 2000 so far as they are conferred by reference to paragraph 1 of that Schedule,

the second condition is satisfied only if the application states that the seized property is or contains excluded material or special procedure material consisting of documents or records other than documents.

(6) The powers mentioned in subsection (3) are—

(*a*) the powers of seizure specified in Part 3 of Schedule 1;

(*b*) the powers of seizure conferred by the provisions of Parts 2 and 3 of the 1984 Act (except section 8(2) of that Act);

(*c*) the powers of seizure conferred by the provisions of Parts 3 and 4 of the Police and Criminal Evidence (Northern Ireland) Order 1989 (except Article 10(2) of that Order);

(*d*) the powers of seizure conferred by the provisions of paragraph 11 of Schedule 5 to the Terrorism Act 2000; and

(*e*) the powers of seizure conferred by the provisions of paragraphs 15 and 19 of that Schedule so far as they are conferred by reference to paragraph 11 of that Schedule.

(7) In this section "a relevant person" means any one of the following—

(*a*) the person who made the seizure;

(*b*) the person for the time being having possession, in consequence of the seizure, of the seized property;

(*c*) the person named for the purposes of subsection (1)(*d*) or (4)(*d*) of section 52 in any notice given under that section with respect to the seizure.

Amendments—[1] Sub-s (4)(*a*) repealed by the Proceeds of Crime Act 2002 s 457, Sch 12 with effect from 24 March 2003 (by virtue of SI 2003/333).

[2] Word in sub-s (4)(*b*) repealed, and sub-s (4)(*d*) and word preceding it inserted, by the Proceeds of Crime Act 2002 ss 456, 457, Sch 11 paras 1, 40(1), (3), Sch 12 with effect from 24 February 2003 (by virtue of SI 2003/120).

61 The duty to secure

(1) The duty to secure that arises under this section is a duty of the person for the time being having possession, in consequence of the seizure, of the seized property to secure that arrangements are in force that ensure that the seized property (without being returned) is not, at any time after the giving of the notice of the application under section 60(1), either—

(*a*) examined or copied, or

(*b*) put to any use to which its seizure would, apart from this subsection, entitle it to be put,

except with the consent of the applicant or in accordance with the directions of the appropriate judicial authority.

(2) Subsection (1) shall not have effect in relation to any time after the withdrawal of the application to which the notice relates.

(3) Nothing in any arrangements for the purposes of this section shall be taken to prevent the giving of a notice under section 49 of the Regulation of Investigatory Powers Act 2000 (c 23) (notices for the disclosure of material protected by encryption etc) in respect of any information contained in the seized material; but subsection (1) of this section shall apply to anything disclosed for the purpose of complying with such a notice as it applies to the seized material in which the information in question is contained.

(4) Subsection (9) of section 59 shall apply in relation to any jurisdiction conferred on the appropriate judicial authority by this section as it applies in relation to the jurisdiction conferred by that section.

62 Use of inextricably linked property

(1) This section applies to property, other than property which is for the time being required to be secured in pursuance of section 61, if—

(*a*) it has been seized under any power conferred by section 50 or 51 or specified in Part 1 or 2 of Schedule 1, and

(*b*) it is inextricably linked property.

(2) Subject to subsection (3), it shall be the duty of the person for the time being having possession, in consequence of the seizure, of the inextricably linked property to ensure that arrangements are in force which secure that that property (without being returned) is not at any time, except with the consent of the person from whom it was seized, either—

(*a*) examined or copied, or

(*b*) put to any other use.

(3) Subsection (2) does not require that arrangements under that subsection should prevent inextricably linked property from being put to any use falling within subsection (4).

(4) A use falls within this subsection to the extent that it is use which is necessary for facilitating the use, in any investigation or proceedings, of property in which the inextricably linked property is comprised.

(5) Property is inextricably linked property for the purposes of this section if it falls within any of subsections (6) to (8).

(6) Property falls within this subsection if—

(*a*) it has been seized under a power conferred by section 50 or 51; and

(*b*) but for subsection (3)(*c*) of section 53, arrangements under subsection (2) of that section in relation to the property would be required to ensure the return of the property as mentioned in subsection (2)(*c*) of that section.

(7) Property falls within this subsection if—

(*a*) it has been seized under a power to which section 54 applies; and
(*b*) but for paragraph (*b*) of subsection (1) of that section, the person for the time being having possession of the property would be under a duty to secure its return as mentioned in that subsection.

(8) Property falls within this subsection if—

(*a*) it has been seized under a power of seizure to which section 55 applies; and
(*b*) but for paragraph (*c*) of subsection (1) of that section, the person for the time being having possession of the property would be under a duty to secure its return as mentioned in that subsection.

Construction of Part 2

63 Copies

(1) Subject to subsection (3)—

(*a*) in this Part, "seize" includes "take a copy of", and cognate expressions shall be construed accordingly;
(*b*) this Part shall apply as if any copy taken under any power to which any provision of this Part applies were the original of that of which it is a copy; and
(*c*) for the purposes of this Part, except sections 50 and 51, the powers mentioned in subsection (2) (which are powers to obtain hard copies etc of information which is stored in electronic form) shall be treated as powers of seizure, and references to seizure and to seized property shall be construed accordingly.

(2) The powers mentioned in subsection (1)(*c*) are any powers which are conferred by—

(*a*) section 19(4) or 20 of the 1984 Act;
(*b*) Article 21(4) or 22 of the Police and Criminal Evidence (Northern Ireland) Order 1989 (SI 1989/1341 (NI 12));
(*c*) section 46(3) of the Firearms Act 1968 (c 27);
[(*d*) *section 43(5)(aa) of the Gaming Act 1968 (c 65)*;] [1]
(*e*) *section 20C(3A) of the Taxes Management Act 1970 (c 9)*;[2]
(*f*) section 32(6)(*b*) of the Food Safety Act 1990 (c 16);
(*g*) Article 34(6)(*b*) of the Food Safety (Northern Ireland) Order 1991 (SI 1991/762 (NI 7));
[(*ga*) section 23E(5)(*b*) (as read with section 23K(2)) of the Criminal Law (Consolidation) (Scotland) Act 1995;][3]
(*h*) section 28(2)(*f*) of the Competition Act 1998 (c 41); or
(*i*) section 8(2)(*c*) of the Nuclear Safeguards Act 2000 (c 5).

(3) Subsection (1) does not apply to section 50(6) or 57.

Amendments—[1] Sub-s (2)(*d*) repealed by the Gambling Act 2005 s 356(4), Sch 17 with effect from 1 September 2007 (by virtue of SI 2006/3272, art 2(4)).
[2] Sub-s (2)(*e*) repealed by FA 2007 ss 84, 114, Sch 22 para 13(1)(*b*), Sch 27 Pt 5(1) with effect from 1 December 2007 (by virtue of SI 2007/3166 art 3(*a*)).
[3] Sub-s (2)(*ga*) inserted by FA 2007 s 85, Sch 23 paras 11, 12, 14 with effect from 1 December 2007 (by virtue of SI 2007/3166 art 3(*b*)).

64 Meaning of "appropriate judicial authority"

(1) Subject to subsection (2), in this Part "appropriate judicial authority" means—

(*a*) in relation to England and Wales and Northern Ireland, a judge of the Crown Court;
(*b*) in relation to Scotland, a sheriff.

(2) In this Part "appropriate judicial authority", in relation to the seizure of items under any power mentioned in subsection (3) and in relation to items seized under any such power, means—

(*a*) in relation to England and Wales and Northern Ireland, the High Court;
(*b*) in relation to Scotland, the Court of Session.

(3) Those powers are—

(*a*) the powers of seizure conferred by—
(i) section 448(3) of the Companies Act 1985 (c 6);
(ii) Article 441(3) of the Companies (Northern Ireland) Order 1986 (SI 1986/1032 (NI 6)); and
(iii) section 28(2) of the Competition Act 1998; …[1]

[(*aa*) the power of seizure conferred by section 352(4) of the Proceeds of Crime Act 2002, if the power is exercisable for the purposes of a civil recovery investigation [or a detained cash investigation][2] (within the meaning of Part 8 of that Act);][1]
(*b*) any power of seizure conferred by section 50, so far as that power is exercisable by reference to any power mentioned in paragraph (*a*).

Amendments—[1] Word in sub-s (3)(*a*)(iii) repealed, and sub-s (3)(*aa*) and word preceding it inserted, by the Proceeds of Crime Act 2002 ss 456, 457, Sch 11 paras 1, 40(1), (4), Sch 12 with effect from 24 February 2003 (by virtue of SI 2003/120).
[2] Words in sub-s (3)(*aa*) inserted by the Serious Crime Act 2007 s 77, Sch 10 para 27 with effect from 6 April 2008 (by virtue of SI 2008/755 art 17(1)(*d*)(iv)).

65 Meaning of "legal privilege"

(1) Subject to the following provisions of this section, references in this Part to an item subject to legal privilege shall be construed—

(*a*) for the purposes of the application of this Part to England and Wales, in accordance with section 10 of the 1984 Act (meaning of 1egal privilege");

(*b*) for the purposes of the application of this Part to Scotland, in accordance with section [412 of the Proceeds of Crime Act 2002][1] (interpretation); and

(*c*) for the purposes of the application of this Part to Northern Ireland, in accordance with Article 12 of the Police and Criminal Evidence (Northern Ireland) Order 1989 (meaning of "1egal privilege").

(2) In relation to property which has been seized in exercise, or purported exercise, of—

(*a*) the power of seizure conferred by section 28(2) of the Competition Act 1998, or

(*b*) so much of any power of seizure conferred by section 50 as is exercisable by reference to that power,

references in this Part to an item subject to legal privilege shall be read as references to a privileged communication within the meaning of section 30 of that Act.

(3) In relation to property which has been seized in exercise, or purported exercise, of—

(a) the power of seizure conferred by section 20C of the Taxes Management Act 1970 (c 9), or

(b) so much of any power of seizure conferred by section 50 as is exercisable by reference to that power,

references in this Part to an item subject to legal privilege shall be construed in accordance with section 20C(4A) of that Act.[3]

[(3A) In relation to property which has been seized in exercise, or purported exercise, of—

(*a*) the power of seizure conferred by section 352(4) of the Proceeds of Crime Act 2002, or

(*b*) so much of any power of seizure conferred by section 50 as is exercisable by reference to that power,

references in this Part to an item subject to legal privilege shall be read as references to privileged material within the meaning of section 354(2) of that Act.][1]

(4) An item which is, or is comprised in, property which has been seized in exercise, or purported exercise, of the power of seizure conferred by section 448(3) of the Companies Act 1985 (c 6) shall be taken for the purposes of this Part to be an item subject to legal privilege if, and only if, the seizure of that item was in contravention of section 452(2) of that Act (privileged information).

(5) An item which is, or is comprised in, property which has been seized in exercise, or purported exercise, of the power of seizure conferred by Article 441(3) of the Companies (Northern Ireland) Order 1986 (SI 1986/1032 (NI 6)) shall be taken for the purposes of this Part to be an item subject to legal privilege if, and only if, the seizure of that item was in contravention of Article 445(2) of that Order (privileged information).

(6) An item which is, or is comprised in, property which has been seized in exercise, or purported exercise, of the power of seizure conferred by sub-paragraph (2) of paragraph 3 of Schedule 2 to the Timeshare Act 1992 (c 35) shall be taken for the purposes of this Part to be an item subject to legal privilege if, and only if, the seizure of that item was in contravention of sub-paragraph (4) of that paragraph (privileged documents).

(7) An item which is, or is comprised in, property which has been seized in exercise, or purported exercise, of the power of seizure conferred by paragraph 1 of Schedule 9 to the Data Protection Act 1998 (c 29) shall be taken for the purposes of this Part to be an item subject to legal privilege if, and only if, the seizure of that item was in contravention of paragraph 9 of that Schedule (privileged communications).

(8) An item which is, or is comprised in, property which has been seized in exercise, or purported exercise, of the power of seizure conferred by paragraph 1 of Schedule 3 to the Freedom of Information Act 2000 (c 36) shall be taken for the purposes of this Part to be an item subject to legal privilege if, and only if, the seizure of that item was in contravention of paragraph 9 of that Schedule (privileged communications).

[(8A) An item which is, or is comprised in, property which has been seized in exercise, or purported exercise, of the power of seizure conferred by section 227C of the Enterprise Act 2002 (c 40) shall be taken for the purposes of this Part to be an item subject to legal privilege if, and only if, the seizure of that item was in contravention of section 227B(4) of that Act (privileged items).][2]

(9) An item which is, or is comprised in, property which has been seized in exercise, or purported exercise, of so much of any power of seizure conferred by section 50 as is exercisable by reference to a power of seizure conferred by—

(*a*) section 448(3) of the Companies Act 1985,

(*b*) Article 441(3) of the Companies (Northern Ireland) Order 1986,

(*c*) paragraph 3(2) of Schedule 2 to the Timeshare Act 1992,

(*d*) paragraph 1 of Schedule 9 to the Data Protection Act 1998, …[2]

(*e*) paragraph 1 of Schedule 3 to the Freedom of Information Act 2000, [or (*f*) section 227C of the Enterprise Act 2002,][2]

shall be taken for the purposes of this Part to be an item subject to legal privilege if, and only if, the item would have been taken for the purposes of this Part to be an item subject to legal privilege had it been seized under the power of seizure by reference to which the power conferred by section 50 was exercised.

Amendments—[1] Words in sub-s (1)(*b*) substituted, and sub-s (3A) inserted, by the Proceeds of Crime Act 2002 ss 456, Sch 11 paras 1, 40(1), (5) with effect from 24 February 2003 (by virtue of SI 2003/120).

[2] Sub-ss (8A), (9)(*f*) and preceding word "or", inserted; and word in sub-s (9)(*d*) repealed, by the Enterprise Act 2002 (Amendment) Regulations, SI 2006/3363 regs 24, 26(1)–(3) with effect from 8 January 2007.

[3] Sub-s (3) repealed by FA 2007 ss 84, 114, Sch 22 para 13(1)(*c*), Sch 27 Pt 5(1) with effect from 1 December 2007 (by virtue of SI 2007/3166 art 3(*a*)).

66 General interpretation of Part 2

(1) In this Part—

"appropriate judicial authority" has the meaning given by section 64;

"documents" includes information recorded in any form;

"item subject to legal privilege" shall be construed in accordance with section 65;

"premises" includes any vehicle, stall or moveable structure (including an offshore installation) and any other place whatever, whether or not occupied as land;

"offshore installation" has the same meaning as in the Mineral Workings (Offshore Installations) Act 1971 (c 61);

"return", in relation to seized property, shall be construed in accordance with section 58, and cognate expressions shall be construed accordingly;

"seize", and cognate expressions, shall be construed in accordance with section 63(1) and subsection (5) below;

"seized property" in relation to any exercise of a power of seizure, means (subject to subsection (5)) anything seized in exercise of that power; and

"vehicle" includes any vessel, aircraft or hovercraft.

(2) In this Part references, in relation to a time when seized property is in any person's possession in consequence of a seizure ("the relevant time"), to something for which the person making the seizure had power to search shall be construed—

(*a*) where the seizure was made on the occasion of a search carried out on the authority of a warrant, as including anything of the description of things the presence or suspected presence of which provided grounds for the issue of the warrant;

(*b*) where the property was seized in the course of a search on the occasion of which it would have been lawful for the person carrying out the search to seize anything which on that occasion was believed by him to be, or appeared to him to be, of a particular description, as including—

(i) anything which at the relevant time is believed by the person in possession of the seized property, or (as the case may be) appears to him, to be of that description; and

(ii) anything which is in fact of that description;

(*c*) where the property was seized in the course of a search on the occasion of which it would have been lawful for the person carrying out the search to seize anything which there were on that occasion reasonable grounds for believing was of a particular description, as including—

(i) anything which there are at the relevant time reasonable grounds for believing is of that description; and

(ii) anything which is in fact of that description;

(*d*) where the property was seized in the course of a search to which neither paragraph (*b*) nor paragraph (*c*) applies, as including anything which is of a description of things which, on the occasion of the search, it would have been lawful for the person carrying it out to seize otherwise than under section 50 and 51; and

(*e*) where the property was seized on the occasion of a search authorised under section 82 of the Terrorism Act 2000 (c 11) (seizure of items suspected to have been, or to be intended to be, used in commission of certain offences), as including anything—

(i) which is or has been, or is or was intended to be, used in the commission of an offence such as is mentioned in subsection (3)(*a*) or (*b*) of that section; or

(ii) which at the relevant time the person who is in possession of the seized property reasonably suspects is something falling within sub-paragraph (*i*).

(3) For the purpose of determining in accordance with subsection (2), in relation to any time, whether or to what extent property seized on the occasion of a search authorised under section 9 of the Official Secrets Act 1911 (c 28) (seizure of evidence of offences under that Act having been or being about to be committed) is something for which the person making the seizure had power to search, subsection (1) of that section shall be construed—

(*a*) as if the reference in that subsection to evidence of an offence under that Act being about to be committed were a reference to evidence of such an offence having been, at the time of the seizure, about to be committed; and

(*b*) as if the reference in that subsection to reasonable ground for suspecting that such an offence is about to be committed were a reference to reasonable ground for suspecting that at the time of the seizure such an offence was about to be committed.

(4) References in subsection (2) to a search include references to any activities authorised by virtue of any of the following—

(*a*) section 28(1) of the Trade Descriptions Act 1968 (c 29) (power to enter premises and to inspect and seize goods and documents);
(*b*) section 29(1) of the Fair Trading Act 1973 (c 41) (power to enter premises and to inspect and seize goods and documents);
(*c*) paragraph 9 of the Schedule to the Prices Act 1974 (c 24) (powers of entry and inspection);
(*d*) section 162(1) of the Consumer Credit Act 1974 (c 39) (powers of entry and inspection);
(*e*) [section 11(1) to (1C) of the Estate Agents Act 1979][8] (c 38) (powers of entry and inspection);
(*f*) Schedule 9 to the Weights and Measures (Northern Ireland) Order 1981 (SI 1981/231 (NI 10));
[(*g*) section 79 of the Weights and Measures Act 1985 (c 72) or Schedule 7 to the Weights and Measures (Packaged Goods) Regulations 2006 (powers of entry and inspection etc);][4];
(*h*) section 29 of the Consumer Protection Act 1987 (c 43) (powers of search etc);
(*i*) …[7]
(*j*) section 32(5) of the Food Safety Act 1990 (c 16) (power to inspect records relating to a food business);
(*k*) paragraph 3 of the Schedule to the Property Misdescriptions Act 1991 (c 29) (powers of seizure etc);
(*l*) Article 33(6) of the Food Safety (Northern Ireland) Order 1991 (SI 1991/762 (NI 7));
(*m*) paragraph 3 of Schedule 2 to the Timeshare Act 1992 (c 35) (powers of officers of enforcement authority).
[(*ma*) section 227C of the Enterprise Act 2002 (power to enter premises with warrant)][5]
[(*n*) paragraph 2 of Schedule 5 to the Human Tissue Act 2004 (entry and inspection of licensed premises).][2]
[(*o*) regulation 22 of the General Product Safety Regulations 2005 (powers of entry and search etc)][3]
[(*p*) sections 26(1), 27(1), 28(1) and 29(1) of the Animal Welfare Act 2006 (inspection in connection with licences, inspection in connection with registration, inspection of farm premises and inspection relating to Community obligations)][6]
[(*q*) regulation 23 of the Business Protection from Misleading Marketing Regulations 2008 (power of entry and investigation, etc);
(*r*) regulation 21 of the Consumer Protection from Unfair Trading Regulations 2008 (power of entry and investigation, etc).][7]

(5) References in this Part to a power of seizure include references to each of the powers to take possession of items under—

(*a*) …[1];
(*b*) section 448(3) of the Companies Act 1985 (c 6);
(*c*) …[1];
(*d*) Article 441(3) of the Companies (Northern Ireland) Order 1986 (SI 1986/1032 (NI 6));
(*e*) …[1];
(*f*) section 2(5) of the Criminal Justice Act 1987 (c 38);
(*g*) section 40(2) of the Human Fertilisation and Embryology Act 1990 (c 37);
(*h*) section 28(2)(*c*) of the Competition Act 1998 (c 41); and
(*i*) section 176(5) of the Financial Services and Markets Act 2000 (c 8);

and references in this Part to seizure and to seized property shall be construed accordingly.

(6) In this Part, so far as it applies to England and Wales—

(*a*) references to excluded material shall be construed in accordance with section 11 of the 1984 Act (meaning of "excluded material"); and
(*b*) references to special procedure material shall be construed in accordance with section 14 of that Act (meaning of "special procedure material").

(7) In this Part, so far as it applies to Northern Ireland—

(*a*) references to excluded material shall be construed in accordance with Article 13 of the Police and Criminal Evidence (Northern Ireland) Order 1989 (SI 1989/1341 (NI 12)) (meaning of "excluded material"); and
(*b*) references to special procedure material shall be construed in accordance with Article 16 of that Order (meaning of "special procedure material").

(8) References in this Part to any item or material being comprised in other property include references to its being mixed with that other property.

(9) In this Part "enactment" includes an enactment contained in Northern Ireland legislation.

Amendments—[1] Sub-s (5)(*a*), (*c*), (*e*) repealed by the Financial Services and Markets Act 2000 (Consequential Amendments and Repeals) Order, SI 2001/3649 art 364(*c*) with effect from 1 December 2001.

[2] Sub-s (4)(*n*) inserted by the Human Tissue Act 2004 s 56, Sch 6 para 5(1), (3) with effect, for certain purposes, from 1 March 2006, for certain purposes, from 7 April 2006, and for other purposes from 1 September 2006. For commencement provisions, see the Human Tissue Act 2004 (Commencement No 4 and Transitional Provisions) Order, SI 2006/404 arts 2–4.

[3] Sub-s (4)(*n*) inserted by the General Product Safety Regulations, SI 2005/1803 reg 47 with effect from 1 October 2005 (reg 1(1)).

[4] Sub-s (4)(*g*) substituted by Weights and Measures (Packaged Goods) Regulations, SI 2006/659 reg 1(2), Sch 1 Pt2(24), (26) with effect from 6 April 2006.
[5] Sub-s (4)(*ma*) inserted by the Enterprise Act 2002 (Amendment) Regulations, SI 2006/3363 regs 24, 27 with effect from 8 January 2007.
[6] Sub-s (4)(*p*) inserted by the Animal Welfare Act 2006 s 64, Sch 3 para 14(2) with effect as follows—
– in relation to Wales, from 27 March 2007 (by virtue of SI 2007/1030 art 2(1)(*j*), (*l*));
– in relation to England, from 6 April 2007 (by virtue of SI 2007/499 art 2(2)(*l*));
– in relation to Scotland and Northern Ireland, from a date to be appointed.
[7] Sub-s (4)(*q*), (*r*) inserted, and sub-s (4)(*i*) repealed, by the Consumer Protection from Unfair Trading Regulations, SI 2008/1277 reg 30(1), (3), Sch 2 para 63, Sch 4 Pt 1 with effect from 26 May 2008.
[8] In sub-s (4)(*e*), words substituted for words "section 11(1) of the Estate Agents Act 1979", by the Consumers, Estate Agents and Redress Act 2007 s 63, Sch 7 para 22 with effect from 1 October 2008 (by virtue of SI 2008/2550 art 2, Schedule).

Prospective amendments—Sub-s (4)(*ja*) to be inserted by the Human Fertilisation and Embryology Act 2008 s 65, Sch 7 para 20(*a*) with effect from a date to be appointed. Sub-s (4)(*ja*) to read as follows—
"(*ja*) paragraph 5 of Schedule 3B to the Human Fertilisation and Embryology Act 1990;".

Sub-s (5)(*g*) to be repealed by the Human Fertilisation and Embryology Act 2008 s 65, Sch 7 para 20(*b*) with effect from a date to be appointed.

Supplemental provisions of Part 2

67 Application to [officers of Revenue and Customs][1]

The powers conferred by section 114(2) of the 1984 Act and Article 85(1) of the Police and Criminal Evidence (Northern Ireland) Order 1989 (application of provisions relating to police officers to [officers of Revenue and Customs][1]) shall have effect in relation to the provisions of this Part as they have effect in relation to the provisions of that Act or, as the case may be, that Order.

Amendments—[1] In s 67 and heading to s 67, words substituted for words "customs officers" by FA 2007 s 84, Sch 22 para 2 with effect from 1 December 2007 (by virtue of SI 2007/3166 art 3(*a*)).

68 Application to Scotland

(1) In the application of this Part to Scotland—

(*a*) subsection (4) of section 54 and subsection (10) of section 59 shall each have effect with the omission of paragraph (*c*) of that subsection;
(*b*) section 55 and subsection (3)(*c*) of section 59 shall be omitted; and
(*c*) Schedule 1 shall have effect as if the powers specified in that Schedule did not include any power of seizure under any enactment mentioned in that Schedule, so far as it is exercisable in Scotland by a constable, except a power conferred by an enactment mentioned in subsection (2).

(2) Those enactments are—

(*a*) section 43(5) of the Gaming Act 1968 (c 65);
(*b*) …[1]
(*c*) section 448(3) of the Companies Act 1985 (c 6);
(*d*) …[1]
(*e*) …[1] and
(*f*) section 176(5) of the Financial Services and Markets Act 2000 (c 8).
[(*g*) regulation 39(6) of the Money Laundering Regulations 2007; and
(*h*) regulation 9(6) of the Transfer of Funds (Information on the Payer) Regulations 2007.][2]

Amendments—[1] Sub-s (2)(*b*), (*d*), (*e*) repealed by the Financial Services and Markets Act 2000 (Consequential Amendments and Repeals) Order, SI 2001/3649 art 364(*d*) with effect from 1 December 2001.
[2] Sub-s (2)(*g*), (*h*) inserted by the Transfer of Funds (Information on the Payer) Regulations, SI 2007/3298 reg 19, Sch 3 para 2 with effect from 15 December 2007.

69 Application to powers designated by order

(1) The Secretary of State may by order—

(*a*) provide for any power designated by the order to be added to those specified in Schedule 1 or section 63(2);
(*b*) make any modification of the provisions of this Part which the Secretary of State considers appropriate in consequence of any provision made by virtue of paragraph (*a*);
(*c*) make any modification of any enactment making provision in relation to seizures, or things seized, under a power designated by an order under this subsection which the Secretary of State considers appropriate in consequence of any provision made by virtue of that paragraph.

(2) Where the power designated by the order made under subsection (1) is a power conferred in relation to Scotland, the Secretary of State shall consult the Scottish Ministers before making the order.

(3) The power to make an order under subsection (1) shall be exercisable by statutory instrument; and no such order shall be made unless a draft of it has been laid before Parliament and approved by a resolution of each House.

(4) In this section "modification" includes any exclusion, extension or application.

Orders—Criminal Justice and Police Act 2001 (Powers of Seizure) Order, SI 2003/934.

70 Consequential applications and amendments of enactments

Schedule 2 (which applies enactments in relation to provision made by this Part and contains minor and consequential amendments) shall have effect.

PART 6

MISCELLANEOUS AND SUPPLEMENTAL

Supplemental

136 General interpretation

In this Act—

"the 1984 Act" means the Police and Criminal Evidence Act 1984 (c 60);
"the 1996 Act" means the Police Act 1996 (c 16); and
"the 1997 Act" means the Police Act 1997 (c 50).

137 Repeals

The enactments and instruments mentioned in Schedule 7 (which include spent provisions) are hereby repealed or (as the case may be) revoked to the extent specified in the third column of that Schedule.

138 Short title, commencement and extent

(1) This Act may be cited as the Criminal Justice and Police Act 2001.

(2) The provisions of this Act, other than this section and sections 42 and 43, 81 to 85, 109, 116(7) and 119(7), shall come into force on such day as the Secretary of State may by order made by statutory instrument appoint; and different days may be appointed under this subsection for different purposes.

(3) An order under subsection (2) may contain such savings as the Secretary of State thinks fit.

(4) Section 85 comes into force at the end of the period of two months beginning with the day on which this Act is passed.

(5) Subject to subsections (6) to (12), this Act extends to England and Wales only.

(6) The following provisions of this Act extend to the United Kingdom—

(*a*) sections 33 to 38;
(*b*) Part 2;
(*c*) section 86(1) and (2);
(*d*) …[1]
(*e*) section 127; and
(*f*) section 136 and this section.

(7) Except in so far as it contains provision relating to the matters mentioned in section 745(1) of the Companies Act 1985 (c 6) (companies registered or incorporated in Northern Ireland or outside Great Britain), section 45 extends to Great Britain only.

(8) Section 126 extends to Great Britain only.

(9) Sections 29, 39 to 41, 72, 75, 84 and 134 extend to England and Wales and Northern Ireland only.

(10) Section 83 extends to Northern Ireland only.

(11) Section 86(3) has the same extent as section 27 of the Petty Sessions (Ireland) Act 1851 (c 93).

(12) An amendment, repeal or revocation contained in Schedule 4, 6 or 7 has the same extent as the enactment or instrument to which it relates.

Amendments—[1] Sub-s (6)(*d*) repealed by the Serious Organised Crime and Police Act 2005 ss 59, 174(2), Sch 4 paras 162, 167, Sch 17 Pt 2 with effect from 1 April 2006 (by virtue of SI 2006/378 art 4(1), Schedule para 10).

SCHEDULES

SCHEDULE 2

APPLICATIONS AND MINOR AND CONSEQUENTIAL AMENDMENTS

PART 1

APPLICATION OF ENACTMENTS

…

Disclosure of information

11 Any provision which—

(*a*) restricts the disclosure, or permits the disclosure only for limited purposes or in limited circumstances, of information obtained through the exercise of a power of seizure specified in Part 1 or 2 of Schedule 1, or

(*b*) confers power to make provision which does either or both of those things,

shall apply in relation to information obtained under section 50 or 51 in reliance on the power in question as it applies in relation to information obtained through the exercise of that power.

Interpretation

12 For the purposes of this Part of this Schedule, an item is seized, or information is obtained, under section 50 or 51 in reliance on a power of seizure if the item is seized, or the information obtained, in exercise of so much of any power conferred by that section as is exercisable by reference to that power of seizure.

PART 2

MINOR AND CONSEQUENTIAL AMENDMENTS

13— (1) In each of the provisions mentioned in sub-paragraph (2) (which confer powers to require the production of information contained in a computer in a visible and legible form)—

(*a*) for "contained in a computer" there shall be substituted "stored in any electronic form"; and

(*b*) after "in which it is visible and legible" there shall be inserted "or from which it can readily be produced in a visible and legible form".

(2) Those provisions are—

. . .

(*f*) paragraph 11(4) of Schedule 11 to the Value Added Tax Act 1994 (c. 23);

(*g*) paragraph 4A(4) of Schedule 7 to the Finance Act 1994 (c. 9);

(*h*) paragraph 7(4) of Schedule 5 to the Finance Act 1996 (c. 8);

(*i*) paragraph 131(4) of Schedule 6 to the Finance Act 2000 (c. 17).

Note—Words omitted from this Schedule are not relevant to this publication.

ANTI-TERRORISM, CRIME AND SECURITY ACT 2001

(2001 Chapter 24)

An Act to amend the Terrorism Act 2000; to make further provision about terrorism and security; . . .; and for connected purposes.

[14 December 2001]

PART 3

DISCLOSURE OF INFORMATION

17 Extension of existing disclosure powers

(1) This section applies to the provisions listed in Schedule 4, so far as they authorise the disclosure of information.

(2) Each of the provisions to which this section applies shall have effect, in relation to the disclosure of information by or on behalf of a public authority, as if the purposes for which the disclosure of information is authorised by that provision included each of the following—

(*a*) the purposes of any criminal investigation whatever which is being or may be carried out, whether in the United Kingdom or elsewhere;

(*b*) the purposes of any criminal proceedings whatever which have been or may be initiated, whether in the United Kingdom or elsewhere;

(*c*) the purposes of the initiation or bringing to an end of any such investigation or proceedings;

(*d*) the purpose of facilitating a determination of whether any such investigation or proceedings should be initiated or brought to an end.

(3) The Treasury may by order made by statutory instrument add any provision contained in any subordinate legislation to the provisions to which this section applies.

(4) The Treasury shall not make an order under subsection (3) unless a draft of it has been laid before Parliament and approved by a resolution of each House.

(5) No disclosure of information shall be made by virtue of this section unless the public authority by which the disclosure is made is satisfied that the making of the disclosure is proportionate to what is sought to be achieved by it.

(6) Nothing in this section shall be taken to prejudice any power to disclose information which exists apart from this section.

(7) The information that may be disclosed by virtue of this section includes information obtained before the commencement of this section.

18 Restriction on disclosure of information for overseas purposes

(1) Subject to subsections (2) and (3), the Secretary of State may give a direction which—

(*a*) specifies any overseas proceedings or any description of overseas proceedings; and

(*b*) prohibits the making of any relevant disclosure for the purposes of those proceedings or, as the case may be, of proceedings of that description.

(2) In subsection (1) the reference, in relation to a direction, to a relevant disclosure is a reference to a disclosure authorised by any of the provisions to which section 17 applies which—

(*a*) is made for a purpose mentioned in subsection (2)(*a*) to (*d*) of that section; and

(*b*) is a disclosure of any such information as is described in the direction.

(3) The Secretary of State shall not give a direction under this section unless it appears to him that the overseas proceedings in question, or that overseas proceedings of the description in question, relate or would relate—

(*a*) to a matter in respect of which it would be more appropriate for any jurisdiction or investigation to be exercised or carried out by a court or other authority of the United Kingdom, or of a particular part of the United Kingdom;

(*b*) to a matter in respect of which it would be more appropriate for any jurisdiction or investigation to be exercised or carried out by a court or other authority of a third country; or

(*c*) to a matter that would fall within paragraph (*a*) or (*b*)—

(i) if it were appropriate for there to be any exercise of jurisdiction or investigation at all; and

(ii) if (where one does not exist) a court or other authority with the necessary jurisdiction or functions existed in the United Kingdom, in the part of the United Kingdom in question or, as the case may be, in the third country in question.

(4) A direction under this section shall not have the effect of prohibiting—

(*a*) the making of any disclosure by a Minister of the Crown or by the Treasury; or

(*b*) the making of any disclosure in pursuance of a Community obligation.

(5) A direction under this section—

(*a*) may prohibit the making of disclosures absolutely or in such cases, or subject to such conditions as to consent or otherwise, as may be specified in it; and

(*b*) must be published or otherwise issued by the Secretary of State in such manner as he considers appropriate for bringing it to the attention of persons likely to be affected by it.

(6) A person who, knowing of any direction under this section, discloses any information in contravention of that direction shall be guilty of an offence and liable—

(*a*) on conviction on indictment, to imprisonment for a term not exceeding two years or to a fine or to both;

(*b*) on summary conviction, to imprisonment for a term not exceeding three months or to a fine not exceeding the statutory maximum or to both.

(7) The following are overseas proceedings for the purposes of this section—

(*a*) criminal proceedings which are taking place, or will or may take place, in a country or territory outside the United Kingdom;

(*b*) a criminal investigation which is being, or will or may be, conducted by an authority of any such country or territory.

(8) References in this section, in relation to any proceedings or investigation, to a third country are references to any country or territory outside the United Kingdom which is not the country or territory where the proceedings are taking place, or will or may take place or, as the case may be, is not the country or territory of the authority which is conducting the investigation, or which will or may conduct it.

(9) In this section "court" includes a tribunal of any description.

19 Disclosure of information held by revenue departments

(1) This section applies to information which is held by or on behalf of the Commissioners of Inland Revenue or by or on behalf of the Commissioners of Customs and Excise, including information obtained before the coming into force of this section.

(2) No obligation of secrecy imposed by statute or otherwise prevents the disclosure, in accordance with the following provisions of this section, of information to which this section applies if the disclosure is made—

(*a*) …[1]

(*b*) for the purposes of any criminal investigation whatever which is being or may be carried out, whether in the United Kingdom or elsewhere;

(*c*) for the purposes of any criminal proceedings whatever which have been or may be initiated, whether in the United Kingdom or elsewhere;

VAT

(*d*) for the purposes of the initiation or bringing to an end of any such investigation or proceedings; or

(*e*) for the purpose of facilitating a determination of whether any such investigation or proceedings should be initiated or brought to an end.

(3) No disclosure of information to which this section applies shall be made by virtue of this section unless the person by whom the disclosure is made is satisfied that the making of the disclosure is proportionate to what is sought to be achieved by it.

(4) Information to which this section applies shall not be disclosed by virtue of this section except by the Commissioners by or on whose behalf it is held or with their authority.

(5) Information obtained by means of a disclosure authorised by subsection (2) shall not be further disclosed except—

(*a*) for a purpose mentioned in that subsection; and

(*b*) with the consent of the Commissioners by whom or with whose authority it was initially disclosed;

and information so obtained otherwise than by or on behalf of any of the intelligence services shall not be further disclosed (with or without such consent) to any of those services, or to any person acting on behalf of any of those services, except for a purpose mentioned in paragraphs (*b*) to (*e*) of that subsection.

(6) A consent for the purposes of subsection (5) may be given either in relation to a particular disclosure or in relation to disclosures made in such circumstances as may be specified or described in the consent.

(7) Nothing in this section authorises the making of any disclosure which is prohibited by any provision of the Data Protection Act 1998.

(8) References in this section to information which is held on behalf of the Commissioners of Inland Revenue or of the Commissioners of Customs & Excise include references to information which—

(*a*) is held by a person who provides services to the Commissioners of Inland Revenue or, as the case may be, to the Commissioners of Customs and Excise; and

(*b*) is held by that person in connection with the provision of those services.

(9) In this section "intelligence service" has the same meaning as in the Regulation of Investigatory Powers Act 2000.

(10) Nothing in this section shall be taken to prejudice any power to disclose information which exists apart from this section.

Amendments—[1] Sub-s (2)(*a*) repealed by the Counter-Terrorism Act 2008 ss 20(4), 99, Sch 1 para 1, Sch 9 Pt 2 with effect from 24 December 2008 (by virtue of SI 2008/3296 art 2).

20 Interpretation of Part 3

(1) In this Part—

"criminal investigation" means an investigation of any criminal conduct, including an investigation of alleged or suspected criminal conduct and an investigation of whether criminal conduct has taken place;

"information" includes—

(*a*) documents; and

(*b*) in relation to a disclosure authorised by a provision to which section 17 applies, anything that falls to be treated as information for the purposes of that provision;

"public authority" has the same meaning as in section 6 of the Human Rights Act 1998; and

"subordinate legislation" has the same meaning as in the Interpretation Act 1978.

(2) Proceedings outside the United Kingdom shall not be taken to be criminal proceedings for the purposes of this Part unless the conduct with which the defendant in those proceedings is charged is criminal conduct or conduct which, to a substantial extent, consists of criminal conduct.

(3) In this section—

"conduct" includes acts, omissions and statements; and

"criminal conduct" means any conduct which—

(*a*) constitutes one or more criminal offences under the law of a part of the United Kingdom; or

(*b*) is, or corresponds to, conduct which, if it all took place in a particular part of the United Kingdom, would constitute one or more offences under the law of that part of the United Kingdom.

PART 14

SUPPLEMENTAL

127 Commencement

(1) Except as provided in subsections (2) to (4), this Act comes into force on such day as the Secretary of State may appoint by order.

(2) The following provisions come into force on the day on which this Act is passed—

(*a*) Parts 2 to 6,

(*b*)–(*h*) …

(*i*) this Part, except section 125 and Schedule 8 so far as they relate to the entries—

(i) in Part 1 of Schedule 8,

(ii) in Part 5 of Schedule 8, in respect of the Nuclear Installations Act 1965,

(iii) in Part 6 of Schedule 8, in respect of the British Transport Commission Act 1962 and the Ministry of Defence Police Act 1987, so far as those entries extend to Scotland,

(iv) in Part 7 of Schedule 8, in respect of Schedule 5 to the Terrorism Act 2000.

(3), (4) …

(5) Different days may be appointed for different provisions and for different purposes.

(6) An order under this section—

(*a*) must be made by statutory instrument, and

(*b*) may contain incidental, supplemental, consequential or transitional provision.

Note—Sub-ss (2)(*b*)–(*h*), (3), (4) are outside the scope of this work.

129 Short title

This Act may be cited as the Anti-terrorism, Crime and Security Act 2001.

FINANCE ACT 2002

(2002 Chapter 23)

An Act to grant certain duties, to alter other duties, and to amend the law relating to the National Debt and the Public Revenue, and to make further provision in connection with Finance.

[24 July 2002]

PART 2

VALUE ADDED TAX

22 Disallowance of input tax where consideration not paid

(1) (*inserts* VATA 1994 s 26A).

(2) (*repeals* VATA 1994 s 36(4A), (5)(*ea*)).

(3) This section has effect in relation to supplies made on or after such day as the Commissioners of Customs and Excise may appoint by order made by statutory instrument.

Commentary—*De Voil Indirect Tax Service* **V5.157.**
Orders—Finance Act 2002, section 22, (Appointed Day) Order, SI 2002/3028 (the appointed day is 1 January 2003).

23 Flat-rate scheme

(1) (*inserts* VATA 1994 s 26B).

(2) (*inserts* VATA 1994 s 83(*fza*)).

(3) (*inserts* VATA 1994 s 84(4ZA)).

(4) This section shall be deemed to have come into force on 24th April 2002.

Commentary—*De Voil Indirect Tax Service* **V2.199B.**

24 Invoices

(1) (*repeals* VATA 1994 s 6(9) and *amends* VATA 1994 Sch 11 para 2).

(2) (*inserts* VATA 1994 Sch 11 paras 2A, 2B)

(3) (*substitutes* VATA 1994 Sch 11 para 3)

(4) The following amendments to the Value Added Tax Act 1994 (c 23) are consequential on other amendments made by this section—

(*a*) (*amends* VATA 1994 s 6(15))

(*b*) (*substitutes* VATA 1994 s 83(*z*))

(*c*) (*amends* VATA 1994 s 88(5), (6))

(5) This section comes into force on such day as the Treasury may by order made by statutory instrument appoint, and different days may be appointed for different provisions or different purposes.

(6) An order under subsection (5) may contain such transitional provisions and savings as appear to the Treasury necessary or expedient in connection with the provisions brought into force.

Commentary—*De Voil Indirect Tax Service* **V3.513–516, V3.523.**
Orders—Finance Act 2002, section 24, (Appointed Day) Order 2003, SI 2003/3043 (the appointed day is 1 December 2003).

25 Relief from VAT on acquisition if importation would attract relief
(*inserts* VATA 1994 s 36A).

PART 6
MISCELLANEOUS AND SUPPLEMENTARY PROVISIONS

Recovery of taxes etc due in other member States

134 Recovery of taxes etc due in other member States

(1) Schedule 39 to this Act has effect with respect to the recovery in the United Kingdom of amounts in respect of which a request for enforcement has been made in accordance with the Mutual Assistance Recovery Directive by an authority in another member State.

[(2) The "Mutual Assistance Recovery Directive" means Council Directive 2008/55/EC.][2]

(2A) ...[1]

(3) No obligation of secrecy imposed by statute or otherwise precludes a tax authority in the United Kingdom—

(*a*) from disclosing information to another tax authority in the United Kingdom in connection with a request for enforcement made by the competent authority of another member State;

(*b*) from disclosing information that is required to be disclosed to the competent authority of another member State by virtue of the Mutual Assistance Recovery Directive;

(*c*) from disclosing information for the purposes of a request made by the tax authority under that Directive for the enforcement in another member State of an amount claimed by the authority in the United Kingdom.

(4) In subsection (3) "tax authority in the United Kingdom" means—

(*a*) the Commissioners of Customs and Excise,

(*b*) the Commissioners of Inland Revenue, or

(*c*) in relation to agricultural levies of the European Community within the meaning of section 6 of the European Communities Act 1972 (c 72), any relevant Minister within the meaning of that section.

(5) Subsection (3)(*a*) does not apply in relation to disclosure by the Commissioners of Inland Revenue to a relevant Minister.

(6) The Treasury may by regulations make such provision as appears to them appropriate for the purpose of giving effect to any future amendments of the Mutual Assistance Recovery Directive.

The regulations may amend, replace or repeal any of the provisions of subsections (1) to (4) above or of Schedule 39.

(7) Regulations under subsection (6) shall be made by statutory instrument which shall be subject to annulment in pursuance of a resolution of the House of Commons.

Cross references—FA 2004 s 322(4) (the powers in sub-s (6) above may be exercised so as to make provision for the purposes of giving effect to the EC–Andorra Mutual Assistance Recovery Decision).
Modifications—FA 2004 s 322 (modification of this section for the purposes of giving effect to the EC–Andorra Mutual Assistance Recovery Decision).
Amendments—[1] Sub-s (2) substituted and sub-s (2A) repealed, by the Recovery of Taxes etc Due in Other Member States (Amendment of Section 134 of the Finance Act 2002) Regulations, SI 2008/2871 reg 3(*a*), (*b*) with effect from 28 November 2008.

Mandatory e-filing

135 Mandatory e-filing

(1) [The Commissioners for Her Majesty's Revenue and Customs][2] ("the Commissioners") may make regulations requiring the use of electronic communications for the delivery by specified persons of specified information required or authorised to be delivered by or under legislation relating to a taxation matter.

(2) Regulations under this section may make provision—

(*a*) as to the electronic form to be taken by information delivered to the [Revenue and Customs][1] using electronic communications;

(*b*) requiring persons to prepare and keep records of information delivered to [Revenue and Customs][1] by means of electronic communications;

(*c*) for the production of the contents of records kept in accordance with the regulations;

(*d*) as to conditions that must be complied with in connection with the use of electronic communications for the delivery of information;

(*e*) for treating information as not having been delivered unless conditions imposed by any of the regulations are satisfied;

(*f*) for determining the time at which and person by whom information is to be taken to have been delivered;

(*g*) for authenticating whatever is delivered.

(3) Regulations under this section may also make provision (which may include provision for the application of conclusive or other presumptions) as to the manner of proving for any purpose—

(*a*) whether any use of electronic communications is to be taken as having resulted in the delivery of information;

(*b*) the time of delivery of any information for the delivery of which electronic communications have been used;

(*c*) the person by whom information delivered by means of electronic communications was delivered;

(*d*) the contents of anything so delivered;

(*e*) the contents of any records;

(*f*) any other matter for which provision may be made by regulations under this section.

(4) Regulations under this section may—

(*a*) allow any authorisation or requirement for which the regulations may provide to be given or imposed by means of a specific or general direction given by the Commissioners;

(*b*) provide that the conditions of any such authorisation or requirement are to be taken to be satisfied only where the [Revenue and Customs][1] are satisfied as to specified matters;

(*c*) allow a person to refuse to accept delivery of information in an electronic form or by means of electronic communications except in such circumstances as may be specified in or determined under the regulations;

(*d*) allow or require use to be made of intermediaries in connection with—

(i) the delivery of information by means of electronic communications; or

(ii) the authentication or security of anything transmitted by any such means.

(5) Regulations under this section may contain provision—

(*a*) requiring the [Revenue and Customs][1] to notify persons appearing to them to be, or to have become, a person of a specified description and accordingly required to use electronic communications for any purpose in accordance with the regulations,

(*b*) enabling a person so notified to have the question whether he is a person of such a description determined in the same way as an appeal.

(6) Regulations under this section may provide—

(*a*) that information delivered by means of electronic communications must meet standards of accuracy and completeness set by specific or general directions given by the Commissioners, and

(*b*) that failure to meet those standards may be treated—

(i) as a failure to deliver the information, or

(ii) as a failure to comply with the requirements of the regulations.

(7) The power to make provision by regulations under this section includes power—

(*a*) to provide for a contravention of, or any failure to comply with, the regulations to attract a penalty of a specified amount not exceeding £3,000;

(*b*) to provide that specified enactments relating to penalties imposed for the purposes of any taxation matter (including enactments relating to assessments, review and appeal) apply, with or without modifications, in relation to penalties under the regulations;

[(*ba*) to specify other consequences of contravention of, or failure to comply with, the regulations (which may include disregarding a return delivered otherwise than by the use of electronic communications);][2]

(*c*) to make different provision for different cases;

(*d*) to make such incidental, supplemental, consequential and transitional provision in connection with any provision contained in any of the regulations as the Commissioners think fit.

(8) References in this section to the delivery of information include references to any of the following (however referred to)—

(*a*) the production or furnishing to a person of any information, account, record or document;

(*b*) the giving, making, issue or surrender to, or service on, any person of any notice, notification, statement, declaration, certificate or direction;

(*c*) the imposition on any person of any requirement or the issue to any person of any request;

(*d*) the making of any return, claim, election or application;

(*e*) the amendment or withdrawal of anything mentioned in paragraphs (*a*) to (*d*) above.

(9) Regulations under this section shall be made by statutory instrument subject to annulment in pursuance of a resolution of the House of Commons.

(10) In this section—

["the Revenue and Customs" means—

(*a*) the Commissioners,

(*b*) any officer of Revenue and Customs, and

(*c*) any other person who for the purposes of electronic communications is acting under the authority of the Commissioners;][1]

"legislation" means any enactment, Community legislation or subordinate legislation;
"specified" means specified by or under regulations under this section;
"subordinate legislation" has the same meaning as in the Interpretation Act 1978 (c 30);
["taxation matter" means any matter relating to a tax (or duty) for which the Commissioners are responsible.][2]

Regulations—Tax Avoidance Schemes (Information) Regulations, SI 2004/1864.
Registered Pension Schemes and Overseas Pension Schemes (Electronic Communication of Returns and Information) Regulations, SI 2006/570.

Amendments—[1] Words substituted and definition in sub-s (10) substituted by CRCA 2005 s 50, Sch 4 paras 94, 95 with effect from 18 April 2005 (by virtue of SI 2005/1126).
[2] Sub-s (7)(*ba*) inserted, and in sub-s (10), definition of "taxation matter" substituted, by FA 2007 s 93(1)–(3) with effect from 19 July 2007.

136 Use of electronic communications under other provisions

(1) Any power to make subordinate legislation for or in connection with the delivery of information conferred in relation to a taxation matter on—

(*a*) the Commissioners of Inland Revenue, or
(*b*) the Treasury,

includes power to make any such provision in relation to the delivery of that information as could be made in exercise of the power conferred by section 135.

(2) Provision made in exercise of the powers conferred by section 135 or subsection (1) above has effect notwithstanding so much of any enactment or subordinate legislation as would otherwise—

(*a*) allow information to be delivered otherwise than by means of electronic communications, or
(*b*) preclude the use of an intermediary in connection with its delivery.

(3) Expressions used in this section and section 135 have the same meaning in this section as in that section.

(4) Nothing in this section shall be read as restricting the generality of the power conferred by section 135.

Supplementary

141 Repeals

(1) The enactments mentioned in Schedule 40 to this Act (which include provisions that are spent or of no practical utility) are repealed to the extent specified.

(2) The repeals specified in that Schedule have effect subject to the commencement provisions and savings contained or referred to in the notes set out in that Schedule.

143 Short title

This Act may be cited as the Finance Act 2002.

SCHEDULES

SCHEDULE 39

RECOVERY OF TAXES ETC DUE IN OTHER MEMBER STATES

Section 134(1)

Introduction

1— (1) This Schedule applies where in accordance with the Mutual Assistance Recovery Directive an authority in another member State makes a request for the recovery in the United Kingdom of a sum claimed by that authority in that State.

(2) In this Schedule—

(*a*) the "Mutual Assistance Recovery Directive" has the meaning given by section 134; and
(*b*) the "foreign claim" means the claim in relation to which a request under that Directive is made as mentioned in sub-paragraph (1).

Enforcement of claims in the United Kingdom

2— (1) Subject to the following provisions of this Schedule—

(*a*) such proceedings may be taken by or on behalf of the relevant UK authority to enforce the foreign claim, by way of legal proceedings, distress, diligence or otherwise, as might be taken to enforce a corresponding UK claim, and
(*b*) any enactment or rule of law relating to a corresponding UK claim shall apply, with any necessary adaptations, in relation to the foreign claim.

(2) "The relevant UK authority" means—

(*a*) in relation to matters corresponding to those within the care and management of the Commissioners of Customs and Excise, those Commissioners;
(*b*) in relation to matters corresponding to those within the care and management of the Commissioners of Inland Revenue, those Commissioners;
(*c*) in relation to agricultural levies of the European Community, the relevant Minister, that is—
(i) in England, the Secretary of State,
(ii) in Scotland, the Scottish Ministers,
(iii) in Wales, the National Assembly for Wales, and
(iv) in Northern Ireland, the Department of Agriculture and Rural Development.

(3) A "corresponding UK claim" means a claim in the United Kingdom corresponding to the foreign claim.

(4) The enactments referred to in sub-paragraph (1)(*b*) include, in particular, those relating to the recovery of penalties and of interest on unpaid amounts.

Modifications—FA 2004 s 322 (modification of this paragraph for the purposes of giving effect to the EC–Andorra Mutual Assistance Recovery Decision).

Power to make supplementary provision by regulations

3— (1) The Treasury may make provision by regulations—
(*a*) as to what is a corresponding UK claim in relation to any description of foreign claim, and
(*b*) as to such other procedural and other supplementary matters as appear to them appropriate for implementing the Mutual Assistance Recovery Directive.

(2) In relation to a case where there is no claim in the United Kingdom that is directly equivalent to a particular description of foreign claim, regulations under sub-paragraph (1)(*a*) may prescribe as the corresponding UK claim one that appears to the Treasury to be closest to an equivalent.

(3) The power conferred by sub-paragraph (1)(*b*) includes power to make any provision appearing to the Treasury to be appropriate to give effect to any Commission Directive laying down detailed rules for implementing the Mutual Assistance Recovery Directive.

(4) The relevant UK authority may make provision by regulations as to the application, non-application or adaptation in relation to foreign claims of any enactment or rule of law applicable to corresponding UK claims.

This is without prejudice to the application of any such enactment or rule in relation to foreign claims in circumstances not dealt with by regulations under this sub-paragraph.

(5) Regulations under this paragraph shall be made by statutory instrument which shall be subject to annulment in pursuance of a resolution of the House of Commons.

Cross references—FA 2004 s 322(4) (the powers in this paragraph may be exercised so as to make provision for the purposes of giving effect to the EC–Andorra Mutual Assistance Recovery Decision).
Modifications—FA 2004 s 322 (modification of this paragraph for the purposes of giving effect to the EC–Andorra Mutual Assistance Recovery Decision).
Regulations—Recovery of Duties and Taxes etc Due in Other Member States (Corresponding UK Claims, Procedure and Supplementary) Regulations, SI 2004/674.

Proceedings on contested claims

4— (1) Except where permitted by virtue of regulations under paragraph 3(4) applying an enactment that permit such proceedings in the case of a corresponding UK claim, no proceedings under this Schedule shall be taken against a person if he shows that proceedings relevant to his liability on the foreign claim are pending, or are about to be instituted, before a court, tribunal or other competent body in the member State in question.

(2) For this purpose proceedings are pending so long as an appeal may be brought against any decision in the proceedings.

(3) Proceedings under this Schedule may be taken if the proceedings in the member State are not prosecuted or instituted with reasonable expedition.

Claims determined in taxpayer's favour

5— (1) No proceedings under this Schedule shall be taken against a person if a final decision on the foreign claim has been given in his favour by a court, tribunal or other competent body in the member State in question.

(2) For this purpose a final decision is one against which no appeal lies or against which an appeal lies within a period that has expired without an appeal having been brought.

(3) If he shows that such a decision has been given in respect of part of the claim no proceedings under this Schedule shall be taken in relation to that part.

Other supplementary provisions

6 For the purposes of proceedings under this Schedule—

(*a*) a request made by an authority in another member State shall be taken to be duly made in accordance with the Mutual Assistance Recovery Directive unless the contrary is proved, and
(*b*) except as mentioned in paragraph 5, no question may be raised as to a person's liability on the foreign claim.

Commentary—*De Voil Indirect Tax Service* **V1.271, 5.175.**

SCHEDULE 40
REPEALS
Section 141

PART 2
VALUE ADDED TAX

Note—The repeals made under this Part are already in effect and have therefore been omitted.

POLICE REFORM ACT 2002

(2002 c 30)

An Act to make new provision about the supervision, administration, functions and conduct of police forces, police officers and other persons serving with, or carrying out functions in relation to, the police; to amend police powers and to provide for the exercise of police powers by persons who are not police officers; to amend the law relating to anti-social behaviour orders; to amend the law relating to sex offender orders; and for connected purposes.

[24 July 2002]

Note—For the text of this legislation as modified to apply to Her Majesty's Revenue and Customs, please refer to Part 1 of *Tolley's Yellow Tax Handbook*.

FINANCE ACT 2003

(2003 Chapter 14)

ARRANGEMENT OF SECTIONS

PART 2

VALUE ADDED TAX

PART 3

TAXES AND DUTIES ON IMPORTATION AND EXPORTATION: PENALTIES

Preliminary

The penalties

Reduction of amount of penalty

An Act to grant certain duties, to alter other duties, and to amend the law relating to the National Debt and the Public Revenue, and to make further provision in connection with finance.

[10 July 2003]

PART 2

VALUE ADDED TAX

17 Requirement of evidence or security

(1) The Value Added Tax Act 1994 (c 23) is amended as follows.

(2)–(7) (*amend* ss 24(6), 72(11), 83(*l*), 84, Sch 11 para 4)

(8) This section shall be deemed to have come into force on 10th April 2003.

Commentary—*De Voil Indirect Tax Service* **V3.415, V5.186.**

18 Joint and several liability for unpaid VAT of another trader

(1)–(3) (*insert* VATA 1994 ss 77A(1), 83(*ra*), *amend* s 84(3))

(4) This section shall be deemed to have come into force on 10th April 2003 except subsection (3) which applies in relation to any appeal notice of which is given on or after the day on which this Act is passed.

Commentary—*De Voil Indirect Tax Service* **V5.171**.

19 Face-value vouchers

Schedule 1 to this Act (VAT: face-value vouchers) has effect.

Commentary—*De Voil Indirect Tax Service* **V3.166**.

20 Supplies arising from prior grant of fee simple

(1) (*inserts* VATA 1994 s 96(10B))

(2) This section applies in relation to any supply that arises for the purposes of the Value Added Tax Act 1994 (c 23) from the prior grant of a fee simple made on or after 9th April 2003.

Commentary—*De Voil Indirect Tax Service* **V3.140, V4.113**.

21 Business gifts

(1) In Schedule 4 to the Value Added Tax Act 1994 (matters to be treated as supply of goods or services), paragraph 5 (business gifts etc) is amended as follows.

(2), (3) (*amend* sub-paras (2), *insert* sub-para 2ZA)

(4) This section applies in relation to gifts made on or after 1st October 2003.

Commentary—*De Voil Indirect Tax Service* **V3.211, V6.120A**.

22 Non-business use of business property

(*inserted* VATA 1994 Sch 4 para 5(4A); *repealed by* FA 2007 s 114, Sch 27 Pt 6(1) in accordance with FA 2007 s 99)

23 Supply of electronic services in member States: special accounting scheme

(1) Schedule 2 to this Act (scheme enabling persons who supply certain electronic services in any member State, but who are not established in a member State, to account for and pay VAT in the United Kingdom on those supplies) has effect.

(2) The amendments made by that Schedule have effect in relation to qualifying supplies made on or after 1st July 2003.

Commentary—*De Voil Indirect Tax Service* **V3.196, V2.106**.

PART 3

TAXES AND DUTIES ON IMPORTATION AND EXPORTATION: PENALTIES

Commentary—*De Voil Indirect Tax Service* **V3.311, V5.301, V5.331**.
Note—The appointed day for the purposes of this Part is 27 November 2003 (by virtue of SI 2003/2985).

Preliminary

24 Introductory

(1) This Part makes provision for and in connection with the imposition of liability to a penalty where a person—

(*a*) engages in any conduct for the purpose of evading any relevant tax or duty, or

(*b*) engages in any conduct by which he contravenes a duty, obligation, requirement or condition imposed by or under legislation relating to any relevant tax or duty.

(2) For the purposes of this Part "relevant tax or duty" means any of the following—

(*a*) customs duty;
(*b*) Community export duty;
(*c*) Community import duty;
(*d*) import VAT;
(*e*) customs duty of a preferential tariff country.

(3) In this Part—

"appeal tribunal" means [the First-tier Tribunal or, where determined by or under Tribunal Procedure Rules, the Upper Tribunal][1];

"the Commissioners" means the Commissioners of Customs and Excise;

"the Community Customs Code" means Council Regulation 2913/92/EEC establishing the Community Customs Code;

"Community export duty" means any of the duties, charges or levies which are export duties within the meaning of the Community Customs Code (as at 9th April 2003, see the definition of "export duties" in Article 4(11) of that Code);

"Community import duty" means any of the duties, charges or levies which are import duties within the meaning of the Community Customs Code (as at 9th April 2003, see the definition of "import duties" in Article 4(10) of that Code);

"contravene" includes fail to comply with;

"customs duty of a preferential tariff country" includes a reference to any charge imposed by a preferential tariff country and having an equivalent effect to customs duty payable on the importation of goods into the territory of that country;

"demand notice" means a demand notice within the meaning of section 30;

["HMRC" means "Her Majesty's Revenue and Customs.][1]

"import VAT" means value added tax chargeable by virtue of section 1(1)(*c*) of the Value Added Tax Act 1994 (c 23) (importation of goods from places outside the member States);

"notice" means notice in writing;

"preferential tariff country" means a country outside the European Community which is, or is a member of a group of countries which is, party to an agreement falling within Article 20(3)(*d*) of the Community Customs Code (preferential tariff agreements with the Community);

"prescribed" means specified in, or determined in accordance with, regulations made by the Treasury;

"relevant rule", in relation to any relevant tax or duty, has the meaning given by subsection (8) of section 26 (as read with subsection (9) of that section);

"representative", in relation to any person, means—

(*a*) his personal representative,

(*b*) his trustee in bankruptcy or interim or permanent trustee,

(*c*) any receiver or liquidator appointed in relation to that person or any of his property,

or any other person acting in a representative capacity in relation to that person.

(4) References in this Part to the Community Customs Code are references to that Code as from time to time amended, whether before or after the coming into force of this Part.

(5) The Treasury may by order amend this Part for the purpose of replacing any reference to, or to a provision of,—

(*a*) the Community Customs Code, or

(*b*) any instrument referred to in this Part by virtue of an order under this subsection,

with a reference to, or (as the case may be) to a provision of, a different instrument.

(6) A statutory instrument containing an order under subsection (5) may not be made unless a draft of the instrument has been laid before, and approved by a resolution of, the House of Commons.

(7) Except for this subsection and section 41 (which accordingly come into force on the passing of this Act), this Part comes into force on such day as the Treasury may by order appoint.

Regulations—Finance Act 2003, Part 3, (Appointed Day) Order 2003, SI 2003/2985 (appoints 27 November 2003 as the date for Part 3 to come into force).

Amendments—[1] In sub-s (3) words in the definition of "appeal tribunal" substituted for the words "VAT and duties tribunal"; definition of "HMRC" inserted by the Transfer of Tribunal Functions and Revenue and Customs Appeals Order, SI 2009/56 art 3, Sch 1 para 360 with effect from 1 April 2009.

The penalties

25 Penalty for evasion

(1) In any case where—

(*a*) a person engages in any conduct for the purpose of evading any relevant tax or duty, and

(*b*) his conduct involves dishonesty (whether or not such as to give rise to any criminal liability),

that person is liable to a penalty of an amount equal to the amount of the tax or duty evaded or, as the case may be, sought to be evaded.

(2) Subsection (1) is subject to the following provisions of this Part.

(3) Nothing in this section applies in relation to any customs duty of a preferential tariff country.

(4) Any reference in this section to a person's "evading" any relevant tax or duty includes a reference to his obtaining or securing, without his being entitled to it,—

(*a*) any repayment, rebate or drawback of any relevant tax or duty,

(*b*) any relief or exemption from, or any allowance against, any relevant tax or duty, or

(*c*) any deferral or other postponement of his liability to pay any relevant tax or duty or of the discharge by payment of any such liability,

and also includes a reference to his evading the cancellation of any entitlement to, or the withdrawal of, any such repayment, rebate, drawback, relief, exemption or allowance.

(5) In relation to any such evasion of any relevant tax or duty as is mentioned in subsection (4), the reference in subsection (1) to the amount of the tax or duty evaded or sought to be evaded is a reference to the amount of—

(*a*) the repayment, rebate or drawback,

(*b*) the relief, exemption or allowance, or

(*c*) the payment which, or the liability to make which, is deferred or otherwise postponed,

as the case may be.

(6) Where, by reason of conduct falling within subsection (1) in the case of any relevant tax or duty, a person—

(*a*) is convicted of an offence,

(*b*) is given, and has not had withdrawn, a demand notice in respect of a penalty to which he is liable under section 26, or

(*c*) is liable to a penalty imposed upon him under any other provision of the law relating to that relevant tax or duty,

that conduct does not also give rise to liability to a penalty under this section in respect of that relevant tax or duty.

26 Penalty for contravention of relevant rule

(1) If, in the case of any relevant tax or duty, a person of a prescribed description engages in any conduct by which he contravenes—

(*a*) a prescribed relevant rule, or

(*b*) a relevant rule of a prescribed description,

he is liable to a penalty under this section of a prescribed amount.

(2) Subsection (1) is subject to the following provisions of this Part.

(3) The power conferred by subsection (1) to prescribe a description of person includes power to prescribe any person (without further qualification) as such a description.

(4) Different penalties may be prescribed under subsection (1) for different cases or different circumstances.

(5) Any amount prescribed under subsection (1) as the amount of a penalty must not be more than £2,500.

(6) The Treasury may by order amend subsection (5) by substituting a different amount for the amount for the time being specified in that subsection.

(7) A statutory instrument containing an order under subsection (6) may not be made unless a draft of the instrument has been laid before, and approved by a resolution of, the House of Commons.

(8) In this Part "relevant rule", in relation to any relevant tax or duty, means any duty, obligation, requirement or condition imposed by or under any of the following—

(*a*) the Customs and Excise Management Act 1979 (c 2), as it applies in relation to the relevant tax or duty;

(*b*) any other Act, or any statutory instrument, as it applies in relation to the relevant tax or duty;

(*c*) in the case of customs duty, Community export duty or Community import duty, Community customs rules;

(*d*) in the case of import VAT, Community customs rules as they apply in relation to import VAT;

(*e*) any directly applicable Community legislation relating to the relevant tax or duty;

(*f*) any relevant international rules applying in relation to the relevant tax or duty.

(9) In subsection (8)—

"Community customs rules" means customs rules, as defined in Article 1 of the Community Customs Code;

"relevant international rules" means international agreements so far as applying in relation to a relevant tax or duty and having effect as part of the law of any part of the United Kingdom by virtue of—

(*a*) any Act or statutory instrument, or

(*b*) any directly applicable Community legislation.

Regulations—Customs (Contravention of a Relevant Rule) Regulations, SI 2003/3113.

27 Exceptions from section 26

(1) A person is not liable to a penalty under section 26 if he satisfies—

(*a*) the Commissioners, or

(*b*) on appeal, an appeal tribunal,

that there is a reasonable excuse for his conduct.

(2) For the purposes of subsection (1) none of the following is a reasonable excuse—

(*a*) an insufficiency of funds available to any person for paying any relevant tax or duty or any penalty due;

(*b*) that reliance was placed by any person on another to perform any task;

(*c*) that the contravention is attributable, in whole or in part, to the conduct of a person on whom reliance to perform any task was so placed.

(3) Where, by reason of conduct falling within subsection (1) of section 26 in the case of any relevant tax or duty, a person—

(*a*) is prosecuted for an offence,

(*b*) is given, and has not had withdrawn, a demand notice in respect of a penalty to which he is liable under section 25, or
(*c*) is liable to a penalty imposed upon him under any other provision of the law relating to that relevant tax or duty,

that conduct does not also give rise to liability to a penalty under section 26 in respect of that relevant tax or duty.

(4) A person is not liable to a penalty under section 26 in respect of any conduct, so far as relating to import VAT, if in respect of that conduct—
(*a*) he is liable to a penalty under any of sections 62 to 69A of the Value Added Tax Act 1994 (c 23) (penalty for contravention of statutory requirements as to VAT), or
(*b*) he would be so liable but for section 62(4), 63(11), 64(6), 67(9), 69(9) or 69A(7) of that Act (conduct resulting in conviction, different penalty etc).

28 Liability of directors etc where body corporate liable to penalty for evasion

(1) Where it appears to the Commissioners—
(*a*) that a body corporate is liable to a penalty under section 25, and
(*b*) that the conduct giving rise to the penalty is, in whole or in part, attributable to the dishonesty of a person who is, or at the material time was, a director or managing officer of the body corporate (a "relevant officer"),

the Commissioners may give a notice under this section to the body corporate (or its representative) and to the relevant officer (or his representative).

(2) A notice under this section must state—
(*a*) the amount of the penalty referred to in subsection (1)(*a*) (the "basic penalty"), and
(*b*) that the Commissioners propose, in accordance with this section, to recover from the relevant officer such portion (which may be the whole) of the basic penalty as is specified in the notice.

(3) If a notice is given under this section, this Part shall apply in relation to the relevant officer as if he were personally liable under section 25 to a penalty which corresponds to that portion of the basic penalty specified in the notice.

(4) If a notice is given under this section—
(*a*) the amount which may be recovered from the body corporate under this Part is limited to so much (if any) of the basic penalty as is not recoverable from the relevant officer by virtue of subsection (3), and
(*b*) the body corporate is to be treated as discharged from liability for so much of the basic penalty as is so recoverable from the relevant officer.

(5) In this section "managing officer", in relation to a body corporate, means—
(*a*) a manager, secretary or other similar officer of the body corporate, or
(*b*) a person purporting to act in any such capacity or as a director.

(6) Where the affairs of a body corporate are managed by its members, this section applies in relation to the conduct of a member in connection with his functions of management as if he were a director of the body corporate.

Reduction of amount of penalty

29 Reduction of penalty under section 25 or 26

(1) Where a person is liable to a penalty under section 25 or 26—
(*a*) the Commissioners (whether originally or on review) or, on appeal, an appeal tribunal may reduce the penalty to such amount (including nil) as they think proper; and
(*b*) the Commissioners on a review, or an appeal tribunal on an appeal, relating to a penalty reduced by the Commissioners under this subsection may cancel the whole or any part of the reduction previously made by the Commissioners.

(2) In exercising their powers under subsection (1), neither the Commissioners nor an appeal tribunal are entitled to take into account any of the matters specified in subsection (3).

(3) Those matters are—
(*a*) the insufficiency of the funds available to any person for paying any relevant tax or duty or the amount of the penalty,
(*b*) the fact that there has, in the case in question or in that case taken with any other cases, been no or no significant loss of any relevant tax or duty,
(*c*) the fact that the person liable to the penalty, or a person acting on his behalf, has acted in good faith.

Demand notices

30 Demands for penalties

(1) Where a person is liable to a penalty under this Part, the Commissioners may give to that person or his representative a notice in writing (a "demand notice") demanding payment of the amount due by way of penalty.

(2) An amount demanded as due from a person or his representative in accordance with subsection (1) is recoverable as if it were an amount due from the person or, as the case may be, the representative as an amount of customs duty.

This subsection is subject to—

(*a*) any appeal under section [33][1] (appeals to tribunal); and

(*b*) subsection (3).

(3) An amount so demanded is not recoverable if or to the extent that—

(*a*) the demand has subsequently been withdrawn; or

(*b*) the amount has been reduced under section 29.

Amendments—[1] In sub-s (2) figure substituted for the figure "36"; definition of "HMRC" inserted by the Transfer of Tribunal Functions and Revenue and Customs Appeals Order, SI 2009/56 art 3, Sch 1 para 361 with effect from 1 April 2009.

31 Time limits for demands for penalties

(1) A demand notice may not be given—

(*a*) in the case of a penalty under section 25, more than 20 years after the conduct giving rise to the liability to the penalty ceased, or

(*b*) in the case of a penalty under section 26, more than 3 years after the conduct giving rise to the liability to the penalty ceased.

(2) A demand notice may not be given more than 2 years after there has come to the knowledge of the Commissioners evidence of facts sufficient in the opinion of the Commissioners to justify the giving of the demand notice.

(3) A demand notice—

(*a*) may be given in respect of a penalty to which a person was liable under section 25 or 26 immediately before his death, but

(*b*) in the case of a penalty to which the deceased was so liable under section 25, may not be given more than 3 years after his death.

32 No prosecution after demand notice for penalty under section 26

Where a demand notice is given demanding payment of an amount due by way of penalty under section 26 in respect of any conduct of a person, no proceedings may be brought against that person for any offence constituted by that conduct (whether or not the demand notice is subsequently withdrawn).

[Appeals and reviews][1]

33 [Right to appeal against certain decisions][1]

(1) If, in the case of any relevant tax or duty, [HMRC][1] give a person or his representative a notice informing him—

(*a*) that they have decided that the person has engaged in conduct by which he contravenes a relevant rule, and

(*b*) that the person is, in consequence, liable to a penalty under section 26, but

(*c*) that they do not propose to give a demand notice in respect of the penalty,

the person or his representative may [make an appeal to an appeal tribunal in respect of][1] the decision mentioned in paragraph (*a*).

(2) Where [HMRC][1] give a demand notice to a person or his representative, the person or his representative may [make an appeal to an appeal tribunal in respect of][1]—

(*a*) their decision that the person is liable to a penalty under section 25 or 26, or

(*b*) their decision as to the amount of the liability.

(3) Where [HMRC][1] give a notice under section 28 to a body corporate and to a relevant officer—

(*a*) subsection (2) does not apply to any demand notice given in respect of the liability of either of them to a penalty under this Part in respect of the conduct in question, but

(*b*) subsections (4) and (5) have effect instead in relation to any such demand notice.

(4) Where [HMRC][1] give a demand notice to the relevant officer or his representative for a penalty which corresponds to the portion of the basic penalty specified in the notice under section 28, the relevant officer or his representative may make an appeal to an appeal tribunal in respect of][1]—

(*a*) their decision that the conduct of the body corporate referred to in section 28(1)(*b*) is, in whole or in part, attributable to the relevant officer's dishonesty, or

(*b*) their decision as to the portion of the basic penalty which [HMRC][1] are seeking to recover from the relevant officer or his representative.

(5) Where [HMRC][1] give a demand notice to the body corporate or its representative for so much of the basic penalty as is not recoverable from the relevant officer by virtue of section 28(3), the body corporate or its representative may make an appeal to an appeal tribunal in respect of][1]—

(*a*) their decision that the body corporate is liable to a penalty under section 25, or

VAT

(*b*) their decision as to amount of the basic penalty as if it were the amount specified in the demand notice.

[(6) The powers of an appeal tribunal on an appeal under this section include—

(*a*) power to quash or vary a decision; and

(*b*) power to substitute the tribunal's own decision for any decision so quashed.

(7) On an appeal under this section—

(*a*) the burden of proof as to the matters mentioned in section 25(1) or 26(1) lies on HMRC; but

(*b*) it is otherwise for the appellant to show that the grounds on which any such appeal is brought have been established.][1]

Amendments—[1] The following amendments made by the Transfer of Tribunal Functions and Revenue and Customs Appeals Order, SI 2009/56 art 3, Sch 1 para 363 with effect from 1 April 2009, subject to transitional and savings provisions in Sch 3 paras 2, 3—

– crosshead substituted for the former crosshead "Reviews";

– heading substituted for the former heading "Right to review of certain decisions";

– in sub-ss (1)–(5) words in the first place and in sub-s (4)(*b*) words substituted for the words "the Commissioners";

– in sub-s (1) words in the second place substituted for the words "give a notice to the Commissioners requiring them to review";

– in sub-ss (2), (4), (5) words in the second place substituted for the words "by notice require the Commissioners to review";

– sub-ss (6), (7) substituted for former sub-s (6). Sub-s (6) previously read as follows—

"(6) A person may not under this section require a review of a decision under section 35 (decision on review).".

[33A Offer of review

(1) HMRC must offer a person (P) a review of a decision that has been notified to P if an appeal lies under section 33 in respect of the decision.

(2) The offer of the review must be made by notice given to P at the same time as the decision is notified to P.

(3) This section does not apply to the notification of the conclusions of a review.][1]

Amendments—[1] Sections 33A–33F inserted by the Transfer of Tribunal Functions and Revenue and Customs Appeals Order, SI 2009/56 art 3, Sch 1 para 364 with effect from 1 April 2009.

[33B Review by HMRC

(1) HMRC must review a decision if—

(*a*) they have offered a review of the decision under section 33A, and

(*b*) P notifies HMRC accepting the offer within 30 days from the date of the document containing the notification of the offer.

(2) But P may not notify acceptance of the offer if P has already appealed to the appeal tribunal under section 33F.

(3) HMRC shall not review a decision if P has appealed to the appeal tribunal under section 33F in respect of the decision.[1]

Amendments—[1] Sections 33A–33F inserted by the Transfer of Tribunal Functions and Revenue and Customs Appeals Order, SI 2009/56 art 3, Sch 1 para 364 with effect from 1 April 2009.

[33C Extensions of time

(1) If under section 33A, HMRC have offered P a review of a decision, HMRC may within the relevant period notify P that the relevant period is extended.

(2) If notice is given the relevant period is extended to the end of 30 days from—

(*a*) the date of the notice, or

(*b*) any other date set out in the notice or a further notice.

(3) In this section "relevant period" means—

(*a*) the period of 30 days referred to in section 33B(1)(*b*), or

(*b*) if notice has been given under subsection (1) that period as extended (or as most recently extended) in accordance with subsection (2).][1]

Amendments—[1] Sections 33A–33F inserted by the Transfer of Tribunal Functions and Revenue and Customs Appeals Order, SI 2009/56 art 3, Sch 1 para 364 with effect from 1 April 2009.

[33D Review out of time

(1) This section applies if—

(*a*) HMRC have offered a review of a decision under section 33A, and

(*b*) P does not accept the offer within the time allowed under section 33B(1)(*b*) or 33C(2).

(2) HMRC must review the decision under section 33B if—

(*a*) after the time allowed, P notifies HMRC in writing requesting a review out of time,

(*b*) HMRC are satisfied that P had a reasonable excuse for not accepting the offer or requiring review within the time allowed, and

(*c*) HMRC are satisfied that P made the request without unreasonable delay after the excuse had ceased to apply.

(3) HMRC shall not review a decision if P has appealed to the appeal tribunal under section 33F in respect of the decision.][1]

Amendments—[1] Sections 33A–33F inserted by the Transfer of Tribunal Functions and Revenue and Customs Appeals Order, SI 2009/56 art 3, Sch 1 para 364 with effect from 1 April 2009.

[33E Nature of review etc

(1) This section applies if HMRC are required to undertake a review under section 33B or 33D.

(2) The nature and extent of the review are to be such as appear appropriate to HMRC in the circumstances.

(3) For the purpose of subsection (2), HMRC must, in particular, have regard to steps taken before the beginning of the review—

(*a*) by HMRC in reaching the decision, and

(*b*) by any person in seeking to resolve disagreement about the decision.

(4) The review must take account of any representations made by P at a stage which gives HMRC a reasonable opportunity to consider them.

(5) The review may conclude that the decision is to be—

(*a*) upheld,

(*b*) varied, or

(*c*) cancelled.

(6) HMRC must give P notice of the conclusions of the review and their reasoning within—

(*a*) a period of 45 days beginning with the relevant date, or

(*b*) such other period as HMRC and P may agree.

(7) In subsection (6) "relevant date" means—

(*a*) the date HMRC received P's notification accepting the offer of a review (in a case falling within section 33A), or

(*b*) the date on which HMRC decided to undertake the review (in a case falling within section 33D).

(8) Where HMRC are required to undertake a review but do not give notice of the conclusions within the period specified in subsection (6), the review is to be treated as having concluded that the decision is upheld.

(9) If subsection (8) applies, HMRC must notify P of the conclusions which the review is treated as having reached.][1]

Amendments—[1] Sections 33A–33F inserted by the Transfer of Tribunal Functions and Revenue and Customs Appeals Order, SI 2009/56 art 3, Sch 1 para 364 with effect from 1 April 2009.

[33F Bringing of appeals

(1) An appeal under section 33 is to be made to the appeal tribunal before—

(*a*) the end of the period of 30 days beginning with the date of the document notifying the decision to which the appeal relates, or

(*b*) if later, the end of the relevant period (within the meaning of section 33C).

(2) But that is subject to subsections (3) to (5).

(3) In a case where HMRC are required to undertake a review under section 33C—

(*a*) an appeal may not be made until the conclusion date, and

(*b*) any appeal is to be made within the period of 30 days beginning with the conclusion date.

(4) In a case where HMRC are requested to undertake a review in accordance with section 33D—

(*a*) an appeal may not be made—

(i) unless HMRC have decided whether or not to undertake a review, and

(ii) if HMRC decide to undertake a review, until the conclusion date; and

(*b*) any appeal is to be made within the period of 30 days beginning with—

(i) the conclusion date (if HMRC decide to undertake a review), or

(ii) the date on which HMRC decide not to undertake a review.

(5) In a case where section 33E(8) applies, an appeal may be made at any time from the end of the period specified in section 33E(6) to the date 30 days after the conclusion date.

(6) An appeal may be made after the end of the period specified in subsection (1), (3)(*b*), (4)(*b*) or (5) if an appeal tribunal gives permission to do so.

(7) In this section "conclusion date" means the date of the document notifying the conclusions of the review.][1]

Amendments—[1] Sections 33A–33F inserted by the Transfer of Tribunal Functions and Revenue and Customs Appeals Order, SI 2009/56 art 3, Sch 1 para 364 with effect from 1 April 2009.

34 Time limit and right to further review

(1) The Commissioners are not required under section 33 to review any decision unless the notice requiring the review is given before the end of the permitted period.

(2) For the purposes of this section the "permitted period" is the period of 45 days beginning with the day on which the relevant notice is given.

(3) For the purposes of subsection (2) the "relevant notice" is—

(a) in the case of a review by virtue of subsection (1) of section 33, the notice mentioned in that subsection; or

(b) in any other case, the demand notice in question.

(4) Nothing in subsection (1) prevents the Commissioners from agreeing on request to review a decision in a case where the notice required by that subsection is not given within the permitted period.

(5) A person may give notice under section 33 requiring a decision to be reviewed a second or subsequent time only if—

(a) the grounds on which he requires the further review are that the Commissioners did not, on any previous review, have the opportunity to consider any particular facts or matters; and

(b) he does not, on the further review, require the Commissioners to consider any facts or matters which were considered on a previous review of the decision, except in so far as they are relevant to any issue to which the facts or matters not previously considered relate.[1]

Amendments—[1] Sections 34–36 and the crosshead before s 36 repealed by the Transfer of Tribunal Functions and Revenue and Customs Appeals Order, SI 2009/56 art 3, Sch 1 para 365 with effect from 1 April 2009, subject to transitional and savings provisions in Sch 3 paras 2, 3.

35 Powers of Commissioners on a review

(1) Where the Commissioners—

(a) are required in accordance with section 33 to review a decision, or

(b) agree to do so on such a request as is mentioned in section 34(4),

the following provisions of this section apply.

(2) On any such review, the Commissioners may—

(a) confirm the decision,

(b) withdraw the decision, or

(c) vary the decision.

(3) Where the Commissioners withdraw or vary the decision, they may also take such further steps (if any) in consequence of the withdrawal or variation as they may consider appropriate.

(4) If the Commissioners do not within the permitted period give notice of their determination on the review to the person who required the review or his representative, they shall be taken for the purposes of this Part to have confirmed the decision.

(5) For the purposes of subsection (4), the "permitted period" is the period of 45 days beginning with the day on which the review—

(a) is required by the person or his representative in accordance with section 33, or

(b) is agreed to by the Commissioners as mentioned in section 34(4).[1]

Amendments—[1] Sections 34–36 and the crosshead before s 36 repealed by the Transfer of Tribunal Functions and Revenue and Customs Appeals Order, SI 2009/56 art 3, Sch 1 para 365 with effect from 1 April 2009, subject to transitional and savings provisions in Sch 3 paras 2, 3.

Appeals

36 Appeals to a tribunal

(1) Where the Commissioners—

(a) are required in accordance with section 33 to review a decision, or

(b) agree to do so on such a request as is mentioned in section 34(4),

an appeal lies to an appeal tribunal against any decision by the Commissioners on the review (including any confirmation under section 35(4)).

(2) An appeal lies under this section only if the appellant is one of the following persons—

(a) the person who required the review in question,

(b) where the person who required the review in question did so as representative of another person, that other person, or

(c) a representative of a person falling within paragraph (a) or (b).

(3) The powers of an appeal tribunal on an appeal under this section include—

(a) power to quash or vary a decision; and

(b) power to substitute the tribunal's own decision for any decision so quashed.

(4) On an appeal under this section—

(a) the burden of proof as to the matters mentioned in section 25(1) or 26(1) lies on the Commissioners; but

(b) it is otherwise for the appellant to show that the grounds on which any such appeal is brought have been established.[1]

Amendments—[1] Sections 34–36 and the crosshead before s 36 repealed by the Transfer of Tribunal Functions and Revenue and Customs Appeals Order, SI 2009/56 art 3, Sch 1 para 365 with effect from 1 April 2009, subject to transitional and savings provisions in Sch 3 paras 2, 3.

[37 Appeal tribunals

Section 85 of the Value Added Tax Act 1994 (settling appeals by agreement) has effect as if the reference to section 83 of that Act included a reference to section 33 above.][1]

Amendments—[1] Sections 37 substituted by the Transfer of Tribunal Functions and Revenue and Customs Appeals Order, SI 2009/56 art 3, Sch 1 para 366 with effect from 1 April 2009, subject to transitional and savings provisions in Sch 3 paras 2, 3. Text previously read as follows—

"**37 Appeal tribunals**

(1) Sections 85 and 87 of the Value Added Tax Act 1994 (c 23) (settling of appeals by agreement and enforcement of decisions of tribunal) have effect as if—

(*a*) any reference to section 83 of that Act included a reference to section 36 above, and

(*b*) any reference to VAT included a reference to any relevant tax or duty.

(2) The provision that may be made by rules under paragraph 9 of Schedule 12 to the Value Added Tax Act 1994 (rules of procedure for tribunals) includes provision for costs awarded against an appellant on an appeal by virtue of this Part to be recoverable as if the amount awarded were an amount of customs duty which the appellant is required to pay.".

Evidence

38 Admissibility of certain statements and documents

(1) Statements made or documents produced by or on behalf of a person are not inadmissible in—

(*a*) any criminal proceedings against that person in respect of any offence in connection with or in relation to any relevant tax or duty, or

(*b*) any proceedings against that person for the recovery of any sum due from him in connection with or in relation to any relevant tax or duty,

by reason only that any of the matters specified in subsection (2) has been drawn to his attention and that he was, or may have been, induced by that matter having been brought to his attention to make the statements or produce the documents.

(2) The matters mentioned in subsection (1) are—

(*a*) that the Commissioners have power, in relation to any relevant tax or duty, to demand by means of a written notice an amount by way of a civil penalty, instead of instituting criminal proceedings;

(*b*) that it is the Commissioners' practice, without being able to give an undertaking as to whether they will make such a demand in any case, to be influenced in determining whether to make such a demand by the fact (where it is the case) that a person has made a full confession of any dishonest conduct to which he has been a party and has given full facilities for an investigation;

(*c*) that the Commissioners or, on appeal, an appeal tribunal have power to reduce a penalty under section 25, as provided in subsection (1) of section 29; and

(*d*) that, in determining the extent of such a reduction in the case of any person, the Commissioners or tribunal will have regard to the extent of the co-operation which he has given to the Commissioners in their investigation.

(3) References in this section to a relevant tax or duty do not include a reference to customs duty of a preferential tariff country.

Miscellaneous and supplementary

39 Service of notices

Any notice to be given to any person for the purposes of this Part may be given by sending it by post in a letter addressed to that person or his representative at the last or usual residence or place of business of that person or representative.

40 Penalties not to be deducted for income tax or corporation tax purposes

(*inserts* TA 1988 s 827(1E); *repealed* by CTA 2009 s 1326, Sch 3 Pt 1).

41 Regulations and orders

(1) Any power conferred on the Treasury by this Part to make regulations or an order includes power—

(*a*) to make different provision for different cases, and

(*b*) to make incidental, consequential, supplemental or transitional provision or savings.

(2) Any power conferred on the Treasury by this Part to make regulations or an order shall be exercisable by statutory instrument.

(3) Any statutory instrument containing regulations under this Part shall be subject to annulment in pursuance of a resolution of the House of Commons.

Regulations—Customs (Contravention of a Relevant Rule) Regulations, SI 2003/3113.
Order—Finance Act 2003, Part 3 (Appointed Day) Order, SI 2003/2985.

PART 9
MISCELLANEOUS AND SUPPLEMENTARY PROVISIONS

International matters

197 Exchange of information between tax authorities of member States

(1) No obligation as to secrecy imposed by statute or otherwise precludes the Commissioners or an authorised officer of the Commissioners from disclosing to the competent authorities of another member State any information required to be so disclosed by virtue of the Mutual Assistance Directive.

(2) Neither the Commissioners nor an authorised officer shall disclose any information in pursuance of the Mutual Assistance Directive unless satisfied that the competent authorities of the other State are bound by, or have undertaken to observe, rules of confidentiality with respect to the information that are not less strict than those applying to it in the United Kingdom.

(3) Nothing in this section permits the Commissioners or an authorised officer of the Commissioners to authorise the use of information disclosed by virtue of the Mutual Assistance Directive otherwise than for the purposes of taxation or to facilitate legal proceedings for failure to observe the tax laws of the receiving State.

(4) In this section—

"the Commissioners" means the Commissioners of Inland Revenue or the Commissioners of Customs and Excise;

the "Mutual Assistance Directive" means Council Directive 77/799/EEC, [as amended by Council Directives 92/12/EEC[, 2003/93/EC[, 2004/56/EC, 2004/106/EC and 2006/98/EC][3]][2]][1].

(5) The Treasury may by order make such provision amending the definition of the "Mutual Assurance Directive" in subsection (4) as appears to them appropriate for the purpose of giving effect to any Council Directive adopted after 16th April 2003 amending or replacing the Mutual Assistance Directive.

(6) An order under subsection (5) shall be made by statutory instrument which shall be subject to annulment in pursuance of a resolution of the House of Commons.

(7) (*amends* VATA 1994 s 48)

Commentary—*De Voil Indirect Tax Service* **V1.270, V5.234**.

Amendments—[1] In sub-s (4), words in the definition of the "Mutual Assistance Directive" substituted by the Mutual Assistance Provisions Order, SI 2003/3092 art 3 with effect from 1 January 2004.

[2] In sub-s (4), words in the definition of "the Mutual Assistance Directive" substituted by the Mutual Assistance Provisions Order, SI 2004/3207 with effect from 1 January 2005.

[3] In sub-s (4), words in definition of the "Mutual Assistance Directive" substituted by the Mutual Assistance Provisions Order, SI 2006/3283 art 2 with effect from 1 January 2007.

Administrative matters

204 Mandatory electronic payment ...[1]

[(1) The Commissioners for Her Majesty's Revenue and Customs may make regulations requiring a person to use electronic means in making specified payments under legislation relating to a tax (or duty) for which the Commissioners are responsible.

(2) The regulations may provide for exceptions.][1]

(3) Regulations under this section may make provision—

(*a*) as to conditions that must be complied with in connection with the use of electronic means for the making of any payment;

(*b*) for treating a payment as not having been made unless conditions imposed by any of the regulations are satisfied;

(*c*) for determining the time when payment is to be taken to have been made.

(4) Regulations under this section may also make provision (which may include provision for the application of conclusive or other presumptions) as to the manner of proving for any purpose—

(*a*) whether any use of electronic means for making a payment is to be taken as having resulted in the payment being made;

(*b*) the time of the making of any payment for the making of which electronic means have been used;

(*c*) any other matter for which provision may be made by regulations under this section.

(5) Regulations under this section may—

(*a*) allow any authorisation or requirement for which the regulations may provide to be given or imposed by means of a specific or general direction given by the Commissioners;

(*b*) provide that the conditions of any such authorisation or requirement are to be taken to be satisfied only where [Her Majesty's Revenue and Customs][1] are satisfied as to specified matters.

(6) Regulations under this section may contain provision—

(*a*) requiring [Her Majesty's Revenue and Customs][1] to notify persons appearing to them to be, or to have become, a person required to use electronic means for the making of any payments in accordance with the regulations;

(*b*) enabling a person so notified to have the question whether he is such a person determined in the same way as an appeal.

(7) Regulations under this section may confer power on the Commissioners to give specific or general directions—

(*a*) suspending, for any period during which the use of electronic means for the making of payments is impossible or impractical, any requirements imposed by the regulations relating to the use of such means;

(*b*) substituting alternative requirements for the suspended ones;

(*c*) making any provision that is necessary in consequence of the imposition of the substituted requirements.

(8) The power to make provision by regulations under this section includes power—

(*a*) to provide for [a contravention by a large employer of, or any failure by a large employer to comply with,][1] the regulations (a "default") to attract a surcharge of a specified amount;

(*b*) to provide that specified enactments relating to penalties imposed for the purposes of any [matter relating to a tax (or duty) for which the Commissioners are responsible][1] (including enactments relating to assessments, review and appeal) apply, with or without modifications, in relation to surcharges under the regulations.

(9) The regulations may specify the surcharge for each default as—

(*a*) a specified percentage, depending on the circumstances but not exceeding 10%, of the amount of the payment to which the default relates, or

(*b*) a specified percentage, depending on the circumstances but not exceeding 0.83%, of the total amount of tax due for the accounting period, year of assessment or other specified period of twelve months during which the default occurred;

but, in either case, they may specify £30 if it is more.

(10) Regulations under this section may—

(*a*) make different provision for different cases;

(*b*) make such incidental, supplemental, consequential and transitional provision in connection with any provision contained in any of the regulations as the Commissioners think fit.

(11) Regulations under this section shall be made by statutory instrument subject to annulment in pursuance of a resolution of the House of Commons.

(12) In this section—

["Her Majesty's Revenue and Customs" includes a person acting under the authority of the Commissioners in relation to payment by electronic means;][1]

["large employer" means a person paying PAYE income to 250 or more recipients (and regulations under this section may make provision as to the date or period by reference to which this is to be determined and the circumstances in which a person is to be treated as paying PAYE income to a recipient);][1]

"legislation" means any enactment, Community legislation or subordinate legislation;

"specified" means specified by or under regulations under this section;

"subordinate legislation" has the same meaning as in the Interpretation Act 1978 (c 30).

[(13) Regulations under section 95(1) of the Finance Act 2007 (payment by cheque) may, in particular, provide for a payment which is made by cheque in contravention of regulations under this section to be treated as made when the cheque clears, as defined in the regulations under that section.][2]

Amendments—[1] Sub-ss (1), (2), words in sub-ss (5)(*b*), (6)(*a*), (8)(*a*), (*b*), substituted; in sub-s (12) definition of "Her Majesty's Revenue and Customs" substituted for definition of "the Inland Revenue", and definition of "large employer" inserted; and words in heading repealed; by FA 2007 s 94(1)–(7) with effect from 19 July 2007.

[2] Sub-s (13) inserted by FA 2007 s 95(6) with effect from 19 July 2007.

205 Use of electronic means of payment under other provisions

(1) Any power to make subordinate legislation for or in connection with the making of payments conferred in relation to a taxation [(or duty)][1] matter on—

(*a*) [the Commissioners for Her Majesty's Revenue and Customs][1], or

(*b*) the Treasury,

includes power to make any such provision in relation to the making of those payments as could be made in exercise of the power conferred by section 204.

(2) Provision as to means of payment made in exercise of the powers conferred by section 204 or subsection (1) above has effect notwithstanding so much of any enactment or subordinate legislation as would otherwise allow payment to be made by any other means.

(3) Expressions used in this section and section 204 have the same meaning in this section as in that section.

(4) Nothing in this section shall be read as restricting the generality of the power conferred by section 204.

Amendments—[1] Words in sub-s (1) inserted and substituted by FA 2007 s 94(8) with effect from 19 July 2007.

Supplementary

215 Interpretation

In this Act "the Taxes Act 1988" means the Income and Corporation Taxes Act 1988.

216 Repeals

(1) The enactments mentioned in Schedule 43 to this Act (which include provisions that are spent or of no practical utility) are repealed to the extent specified.

(2) The repeals specified in that Schedule have effect subject to the commencement provisions and savings contained or referred to in the notes set out in that Schedule.

217 Short title

This Act may be cited as the Finance Act 2003.

SCHEDULES

SCHEDULE 1

VAT: FACE-VALUE VOUCHERS

Section 19

Commentary—*De Voil Indirect Tax Service* **V3.166**.

1–3 (*insert* VATA 1994 s 51B, Sch 10A and Sch 6 para 5)

4 The amendments made by this Schedule apply to supplies of tokens, stamps or vouchers issued on or after 9th April 2003.

SCHEDULE 2

SUPPLY OF ELECTRONIC SERVICES IN MEMBER STATES: VAT SPECIAL ACCOUNTING SCHEME

Section 23

Commentary—*De Voil Indirect Tax Service* **V3.196**, **V2.106**.

Introductory

1 The Value Added Tax Act 1994 is amended as follows.

Insertion of new section 3A

2 (*inserts* VATA 1994 s 3A)

Persons registered under Schedule 1

3 (*inserts* VATA 1994 Sch 1 para 13(8))

The special accounting scheme

4 (*inserts* VATA 1994 Sch 3B)

SCHEDULE 43

REPEALS

Section 216

The repeals set out in this Schedule, so far as relevant to VAT, have been noted in the affected legislation.

FINANCE ACT 2004

(2004 Chapter 12)

An Act to Grant certain duties, to alter other duties, and to amend the law relating to the National Debt and the Public Revenue, and to make further provision in connection with finance.

[22 July 2004]

PART 2

VALUE ADDED TAX

19 Disclosure of VAT avoidance schemes

(1) Schedule 2 (which relates to the disclosure of schemes for the avoidance of value added tax) has effect.

(2) Subsection (1) and that Schedule—

(*a*) come into force on the passing of this Act, so far as is necessary for enabling the making of any orders or regulations by virtue of that Schedule, and

(*b*) otherwise, come into force on such day as the Treasury may by order made by statutory instrument appoint.

Orders—See Finance Act 2004, section 19(1) and Schedule 2, (Appointed Day) Order, SI 2004/1934 (the appointed day under sub-s (2)(*b*) above, insofar as this section and FA 2004 Sch 2 are not already in force, is 1 August 2004).

20 Groups

(1) (*inserts* VATA 1994 s 43AA)

(2) (*inserts* VATA 1994 s 43D)

(3) (*amends* VATA 1994 s 43(1))

(4) (*amends* VATA 1994 s 43B)

(5) (*inserts* VATA 1994 s 97(4)(*ca*))

21 Reverse charge on gas and electricity supplied by persons outside UK

(1) (*inserts* VATA 1994 s 9A)

(2) This section has effect in relation to supplies made on or after 1st January 2005.

22 Use of stock in trade cars for consideration less than market value

(1) The Value Added Tax Act 1994 (c. 23) is amended as follows.

(2) (*inserts* VATA 1994 Sch 6 para 1A)

(3) (*amends* VATA 1994 s 83(v))

(4) (*inserts* VATA 1994 s 97(4)(*f*))

(5) The amendment made by subsection (2) applies in relation to any use or availability for use on or after the appointed day (whatever the date of the directions mentioned in paragraph 5(4) of Schedule 4 to the Value Added Tax Act 1994 (c. 23)).

(6) In subsection (5) "the appointed day" means such day as the Treasury may by order made by statutory instrument appoint.

Note—Section 22(2) has effect in relation to any use or availability for use on or after 1 January 2005, by virtue of Finance Act 2004, section 22(2), (Appointed Day) Order, SI 2004/3104, art 2.

PART 8

MISCELLANEOUS MATTERS

322 Mutual assistance: customs union with the Principality of Andorra

(1) The UK mutual assistance provisions have effect for the purposes of giving effect to the EC-Andorra Mutual Assistance Recovery Decision as they have effect for the purposes of giving effect to the Mutual Assistance Recovery Directive.

(2) In this section—

"the EC-Andorra Mutual Assistance Recovery Decision" means Chapter 2 of Title 1 of, and Annex 1 to, Decision No 1/2003 of the EC-Andorra Joint Committee of 3 September 2003 (on the laws, regulations and administrative provisions necessary for the proper functioning of the Customs Union between the European Community and the Principality of Andorra);

"the Mutual Assistance Recovery Directive" has the same meaning as in the UK mutual assistance provisions;

"the UK mutual assistance provisions" means the provisions of section 134 of the Finance Act 2002 (c. 23) (recovery of taxes etc due in other member States) and Schedule 39 to that Act.

(3) In the UK mutual assistance provisions as they have effect in accordance with subsection (1)—

(*a*) references (except those in section 134(2) and paragraph 1(2)(*a*) of Schedule 39) to the Mutual Assistance Recovery Directive shall be read as references to the EC-Andorra Mutual Assistance Recovery Decision,

(*b*) references to another member State shall be read as references to the Principality of Andorra,

(*c*) references to the competent authority of another member State shall be read as references to the competent authority of the Principality of Andorra,

(*d*) references to a tax authority in the United Kingdom, or to the relevant UK authority, shall be read as references to the Commissioners of Customs and Excise,

(*e*) the following provisions shall be treated as omitted—

(i) in section 134, subsections (3)(*a*), (4) and (5), and

(ii) in Schedule 39, paragraphs 2(2) and 3(3).

(4) The powers in section 134(6) of the Finance Act 2002 and paragraph 3 of Schedule 39 to that Act may be exercised so as to make provision for the purposes of giving effect to the EC-Andorra Mutual Assistance Recovery Decision (or amendments of the Decision) which is different to that made for the purposes of giving effect to the Mutual Assistance Recovery Directive (or amendments of the Directive).

PART 9
SUPPLEMENTARY PROVISIONS

328 Short title
This Act may be cited as the Finance Act 2004.

SCHEDULES

SCHEDULE 2
DISCLOSURE OF VALUE ADDED TAX AVOIDANCE SCHEMES

Section 19

PART 1
PRINCIPAL AMENDMENTS OF VALUE ADDED TAX ACT 1994

1 (*inserts* VATA 1994 s 58A)
2 (*inserts* VATA 1994 Sch 11A)

PART 2
CONSEQUENTIAL AMENDMENTS

3 (*amends* VATA 1994 s 70(1))
4 (*inserts* VATA 1994 s 83(*za*), (*zb*))
5 (*amends* VATA 1994 s 83)
6 (*inserts* VATA 1994 s 97(4)(*g*))

COMMISSIONERS FOR REVENUE AND CUSTOMS ACT 2005

(2005 Chapter 11)

ARRANGEMENT OF SECTIONS

Commissioners and officers

Functions

Exercise of functions

An Act to make provision for the appointment of Commissioners to exercise functions presently vested in the Commissioners of Inland Revenue and the Commissioners of Customs and Excise; for the establishment of a Revenue and Customs Prosecutions Office; and for connected purposes.

[7th April 2005]

Commissioners and officers

1 The Commissioners

(1) Her Majesty may by Letters Patent appoint Commissioners for Her Majesty's Revenue and Customs.

(2) The Welsh title of the Commissioners shall be Comisynwyr Cyllid a Thollau Ei Mawrhydi.

(3) A Commissioner—

(*a*) may resign by notice in writing to the Treasury, and

(*b*) otherwise, shall hold office in accordance with the terms and conditions of his appointment (which may include provision for dismissal).

(4) In exercising their functions, the Commissioners act on behalf of the Crown.

(5) Service as a Commissioner is service in the civil service of the State.

2 Officers of Revenue and Customs

(1) The Commissioners may appoint staff, to be known as officers of Revenue and Customs.

(2) A person shall hold and vacate office as an officer of Revenue and Customs in accordance with the terms of his appointment (which may include provision for dismissal).

(3) An officer of Revenue and Customs shall comply with directions of the Commissioners (whether he is exercising a function conferred on officers of Revenue and Customs or exercising a function on behalf of the Commissioners).

(4) Anything (including anything in relation to legal proceedings) begun by or in relation to one officer of Revenue and Customs may be continued by or in relation to another.

(5) Appointments under subsection (1) may be made only with the approval of the Minister for the Civil Service as to terms and conditions of service.

(6) Service in the employment of the Commissioners is service in the civil service of the State.

(7) In Schedule 1 to the Interpretation Act 1978 (c 30) (defined expressions) at the appropriate place insert—

" "Officer of Revenue and Customs" has the meaning given by section 2(1) of the Commissioners for Revenue and Customs Act 2005."

HMRC Manuals—Special Civil Investigations Guidance Manual SCIG 11140 (officers of Revenue and Customs must only exercise appropriate powers which are relevant to their job).

3 Declaration of confidentiality

(1) Each person who is appointed under this Act as a Commissioner or officer of Revenue and Customs shall make a declaration acknowledging his obligation of confidentiality under section 18.

(2) A declaration under subsection (1) shall be made—

(*a*) as soon as is reasonably practicable following the person's appointment, and

(*b*) in such form, and before such a person, as the Commissioners may direct.

(3) For the purposes of this section, the renewal of a fixed term appointment shall not be treated as an appointment.

4 "Her Majesty's Revenue and Customs"

(1) The Commissioners and the officers of Revenue and Customs may together be referred to as Her Majesty's Revenue and Customs.

(2) The Welsh title of the Commissioners and the officers of Revenue and Customs together shall be Cyllid a Thollau Ei Mawrhydi.

(3) (*amends* Interpretation Act 1978 Sch 1).

Functions

5 Commissioners' initial functions

(1) The Commissioners shall be responsible for—

(*a*) the collection and management of revenue for which the Commissioners of Inland Revenue were responsible before the commencement of this section,

(*b*) the collection and management of revenue for which the Commissioners of Customs and Excise were responsible before the commencement of this section, and

(*c*) the payment and management of tax credits for which the Commissioners of Inland Revenue were responsible before the commencement of this section.

(2) The Commissioners shall also have all the other functions which before the commencement of this section vested in—

(*a*) the Commissioners of Inland Revenue (or in a Commissioner), or
(*b*) the Commissioners of Customs and Excise (or in a Commissioner).

(3) This section is subject to section 35.

(4) In this Act "revenue" includes taxes, duties and national insurance contributions.

Order—See the Commissioners for Revenue and Customs Act 2005 (Commencement) Order, SI 2005/1126, art 2(2) (this section came into force on 18 April 2005).

6 Officers' initial functions

(1) A function conferred by an enactment (in whatever terms) on any of the persons listed in subsection (2) shall by virtue of this subsection vest in an officer of Revenue and Customs.

(2) Those persons are—

(*a*) an officer as defined by section 1(1) of the Customs and Excise Management Act 1979 (c 2),
(*b*) a person acting under the authority of the Commissioners of Customs and Excise,
(*c*) an officer of the Commissioners of Customs and Excise,
(*d*) a customs officer,
(*e*) an officer of customs,
(*f*) a customs and excise officer,
(*g*) an officer of customs and excise, and
(*h*) a collector of customs and excise.

(3) This section is subject to sections 7 and 35.

Order—See the Commissioners for Revenue and Customs Act 2005 (Commencement) Order, SI 2005/1126, art 2(2) (this section came into force on 18 April 2005).

Cross reference—FA 2007 s 84(2) (nothing in this section restricts the functions in connection with which officers of Revenue and Customs may exercise a power under PACE 1984 s 114 (as amended by FA 2007 s 83)).

Serious Crime Act 2007 s 88, Sch 12 para 31 (nothing in this section restricts the functions in connection with which HMRC may exercise a power under an enactment amended by SCA 2007 Sch 12).

7 Former Inland Revenue matters

(1) This section applies to the matters listed in Schedule 1.

(2) A function conferred by an enactment (in whatever terms) on any of the persons specified in subsection (3) shall by virtue of this subsection vest in an officer of Revenue and Customs—

(*a*) if or in so far as it relates to a matter to which this section applies, and
(*b*) in so far as the officer is exercising a function (whether or not by virtue of paragraph (*a*)) which relates to a matter to which this section applies.

(3) Those persons are—

(*a*) an officer of the Commissioners of Inland Revenue,
(*b*) an officer of the Board of Inland Revenue,
(*c*) an officer of inland revenue,
(*d*) a collector of Inland Revenue,
(*e*) an inspector of taxes,
(*f*) a collector of taxes,
(*g*) a person authorised to act as an inspector of taxes or collector of taxes for specific purposes,
(*h*) an officer having powers in relation to tax,
(*i*) a revenue official,
(*j*) a person employed in relation to Inland Revenue (or "the Inland Revenue"), and
(*k*) an Inland Revenue official.

(4) In so far as an officer of Revenue and Customs is exercising a function which relates to a matter to which this section applies, section 6(1) shall not apply.

(5) This section is subject to section 35.

Order—See the Commissioners for Revenue and Customs Act 2005 (Commencement) Order, SI 2005/1126, art 2(2) (this section and Sch 1 came into force on 18 April 2005).

Cross reference—FA 2007 s 84(2) (nothing in this section restricts the functions in connection with which officers of Revenue and Customs may exercise a power under PACE 1984 s 114 (as amended by FA 2007 s 83)).

Serious Crime Act 2007 s 88, Sch 12 para 31 (nothing in this section restricts the functions in connection with which HMRC may exercise a power under an enactment amended by SCA 2007 Sch 12).

8 Power to transfer functions

(1) (*inserts* Ministers of the Crown Act 1975 s 5A).

(2) For the purposes of sections 63 and 108 of the Scotland Act 1998 (c 46) (transfer of functions)—

(*a*) the Commissioners shall be treated as a Minister of the Crown, and
(*b*) the officers of Revenue and Customs shall be treated as a Minister of the Crown.

(3) An Order in Council under section 63 or 108 of that Act—

(*a*) may not make provision about a function specified in section 5(1) of this Act, and (*b*) if it transfers a function to the Commissioners or to officers of Revenue and Customs—

(i) may restrict or prohibit the exercise of specified powers in relation to that function, and

(ii) may provide that the function may be exercised only with the consent of a specified member of the Scottish Executive.

(4) For the purposes of section 22 of and Schedule 3 to the Government of Wales Act 1998 (c 38) (transfer of functions)—

(*a*) the Commissioners shall be treated as a Minister of the Crown, and

(*b*) the officers of Revenue and Customs shall be treated as a Minister of the Crown.

(5) An Order in Council under section 22 of that Act may not make provision about a function specified in section 5(1) of this Act.

Order—See the Commissioners for Revenue and Customs Act 2005 (Commencement) Order, SI 2005/1126, art 2(2) (this section came into force on 18 April 2005).

9 Ancillary powers

(1) The Commissioners may do anything which they think—

(*a*) necessary or expedient in connection with the exercise of their functions, or

(*b*) incidental or conducive to the exercise of their functions.

(2) This section is subject to section 35.

10 The Valuation Office

(1) An officer of Revenue and Customs may provide a valuation of property—

(*a*) for a purpose relating to the functions of Her Majesty's Revenue and Customs, or

(*b*) at the request of any person who appears to the officer to be a public authority, or

(*c*) at the request of any other person if the officer is satisfied that the valuation is necessary or expedient in connection with—

(i) the exercise of a function of a public nature, or

(ii) the management of money or assets received from a person exercising functions of a public nature.

(2) The Commissioners may charge a fee for the provision of a valuation under subsection (1)(*b*) or (*c*).

(3) In this section a reference to providing valuations of property includes a reference to advising about matters appearing to an officer of Revenue and Customs to be connected to the valuation of property.

Exercise of functions

11 Treasury directions

In the exercise of their functions the Commissioners shall comply with any directions of a general nature given to them by the Treasury.

12 Commissioners' arrangements

(1) The Commissioners shall make arrangements for—

(*a*) the conduct of their proceedings, and

(*b*) the conduct of the proceedings of any committee established by them.

(2) Arrangements under subsection (1) may, in particular—

(*a*) make provision for a quorum at meetings;

(*b*) provide that a function of the Commissioners—

(i) may be exercised by two Commissioners, or

(ii) may be exercised by a specified number of Commissioners (greater than two).

(3) A decision to make arrangements under subsection (1) must be taken with the agreement of more than half of the Commissioners holding office at the time.

13 Exercise of Commissioners' functions by officers

(1) An officer of Revenue and Customs may exercise any function of the Commissioners.

(2) But subsection (1)—

(*a*) does not apply to the functions specified in subsection (3), and

(*b*) is subject to directions under section 2(3) and arrangements under section 12.

(3) The non-delegable functions mentioned in subsection (2)(*a*) are—

(*a*) making, by statutory instrument, regulations, rules or an order,

(*b*) *approving an application for a warrant to search premises under section 20C of the Taxes Management Act 1970 (c 9),*

(*c*) *approving an application for a warrant to enter premises under Part 7 of Schedule 13 to the Finance Act 2003 (c 14), and*[1] (*d*) giving instructions for the disclosure of information under section 20(1)(*a*), except that an officer of Revenue and Customs may give an instruction under section 20(1)(*a*) authorising disclosure of specified information relating to—

(i) one or more specified persons,

(ii) one or more specified transactions, or

(iii) specified goods.

Amendments—[1] Sub-s (3)(*b*), (*c*) repealed by FA 2007 ss 84, 114, Sch 22 paras 3, 17(*a*), Sch 27 Pt 5(1) with effect from 1 December 2007 (by virtue of SI 2007/3166 art 3(*a*)).

14 Delegation

(1) Arrangements under section 12 may, in particular, enable the Commissioners, or a number of Commissioners acting in accordance with arrangements by virtue of section 12(2)(*b*), to delegate a function of the Commissioners, other than a function specified in subsection (2) below—

(*a*) to a single Commissioner,

(*b*) to a committee established by the Commissioners (which may include persons who are neither Commissioners nor staff of the Commissioners nor officers of Revenue and Customs), or

(*c*) to any other person.

(2) The non-delegable functions mentioned in subsection (1) are—

(*a*) making, by statutory instrument, regulations, rules or an order,

(*b*) *approving an application for a warrant to search premises under section 20C of the Taxes Management Act 1970 (c 9), and*

(*c*) *approving an application for a warrant to enter premises under Part 7 of Schedule 13 to the Finance Act 2003 (c 14).*[1]

(3) The Commissioners may not delegate the function under section 20(1)(*a*) except to a single Commissioner.

(4) The delegation of a function by virtue of subsection (1) by the Commissioners or a number of Commissioners—

(*a*) shall not prevent the exercise of the function by the Commissioners or those Commissioners, and

(*b*) shall not, subject to express provision to the contrary in directions under section 2(3) or arrangements under section 12, prevent the exercise of the function by an officer of Revenue and Customs.

(5) Where the Commissioners or a number of Commissioners delegate a function to a person by virtue of subsection (1)(*c*)—

(*a*) the Commissioners or those Commissioners shall monitor the exercise of the function by that person, and

(*b*) in the exercise of the function the delegate shall comply with any directions of the Commissioners or of those Commissioners.

Amendments—[1] Sub-s (2)(*b*), (*c*) repealed by FA 2007 ss 84, 114, Sch 22 paras 3, 17(*b*), Sch 27 Pt 5(1) with effect from 1 December 2007 (by virtue of SI 2007/3166 art 3(*a*)).

15 Agency: Scotland and Northern Ireland

(1) For the purposes of section 93 of the Scotland Act 1998 (c 46) (agency)—

(*a*) the Commissioners shall be treated as a Minister of the Crown, and

(*b*) the officers of Revenue and Customs shall be treated as a Minister of the Crown.

(2) For the purposes of section 28 of the Northern Ireland Act 1998 (c 47) (agency)—

(*a*) the Commissioners shall be treated as a Minister of the Crown, and

(*b*) the officers of Revenue and Customs shall be treated as a Minister of the Crown.

16 Restrictions, &c

Part 1 of Schedule 2 (which restricts, or makes other provision in connection with, the exercise of certain functions) shall have effect.

Order—See the Commissioners for Revenue and Customs Act 2005 (Commencement) Order, SI 2005/1126, art 2(2) (this section and Sch 2 Pt 1 came into force on 18 April 2005).

[16A Charter of standards and values

(1) The Commissioners must prepare a Charter.

(2) The Charter must include standards of behaviour and values to which Her Majesty's Revenue and Customs will aspire when dealing with people in the exercise of their functions.

(3) The Commissioners must—

(*a*) regularly review the Charter, and

(*b*) publish revisions, or revised versions, of it when they consider it appropriate to do so.

(4) The Commissioners must, at least once every year, make a report reviewing the extent to which Her Majesty's Revenue and Customs have demonstrated the standards of behaviour and values included in the Charter.][1]

Amendments—[1] This section inserted by FA 2009 s 92(1) with effect from 21 July 2009.

Information

17 Use of information

(1) Information acquired by the Revenue and Customs in connection with a function may be used by them in connection with any other function.

(2) Subsection (1) is subject to any provision which restricts or prohibits the use of information and which is contained in—

(*a*) this Act,

(*b*) any other enactment, or

(*c*) an international or other agreement to which the United Kingdom or Her Majesty's Government is party.

(3) In subsection (1) "the Revenue and Customs" means—

(*a*) the Commissioners,

(*b*) an officer of Revenue and Customs,

(*c*) a person acting on behalf of the Commissioners or an officer of Revenue and Customs,

(*d*) a committee established by the Commissioners,

(*e*) a member of a committee established by the Commissioners,

(*f*) the Commissioners of Inland Revenue (or any committee or staff of theirs or anyone acting on their behalf),

(*g*) the Commissioners of Customs and Excise (or any committee or staff of theirs or anyone acting on their behalf), and

(*h*) a person specified in section 6(2) or 7(3).

(4) In subsection (1) "function" means a function of any of the persons listed in subsection (3).

(5) In subsection (2) the reference to an enactment does not include—

(*a*) an Act of the Scottish Parliament or an instrument made under such an Act, or

(*b*) an Act of the Northern Ireland Assembly or an instrument made under such an Act.

(6) Part 2 of Schedule 2 (which makes provision about the supply and other use of information in specified circumstances) shall have effect.

18 Confidentiality

(1) Revenue and Customs officials may not disclose information which is held by the Revenue and Customs in connection with a function of the Revenue and Customs.

(2) But subsection (1) does not apply to a disclosure—

(*a*) which—

(i) is made for the purposes of a function of the Revenue and Customs, and

(ii) does not contravene any restriction imposed by the Commissioners,

(*b*) which is made in accordance with section 20 or 21,

(*c*) which is made for the purposes of civil proceedings (whether or not within the United Kingdom) relating to a matter in respect of which the Revenue and Customs have functions,

(*d*) which is made for the purposes of a criminal investigation or criminal proceedings (whether or not within the United Kingdom) relating to a matter in respect of which the Revenue and Customs have functions,

(*e*) which is made in pursuance of an order of a court,

(*f*) which is made to Her Majesty's Inspectors of Constabulary, the Scottish inspectors or the Northern Ireland inspectors for the purpose of an inspection by virtue of section 27,

(*g*) which is made to the Independent Police Complaints Commission, or a person acting on its behalf, for the purpose of the exercise of a function by virtue of section 28, or

(*h*) which is made with the consent of each person to whom the information relates.

(3) Subsection (1) is subject to any other enactment permitting disclosure.

(4) In this section—

(*a*) a reference to Revenue and Customs officials is a reference to any person who is or was—

(i) a Commissioner,

(ii) an officer of Revenue and Customs,

(iii) a person acting on behalf of the Commissioners or an officer of Revenue and Customs, or

(iv) a member of a committee established by the Commissioners,

(*b*) a reference to the Revenue and Customs has the same meaning as in section 17,

(*c*) a reference to a function of the Revenue and Customs is a reference to a function of—

(i) the Commissioners, or

(ii) an officer of Revenue and Customs,

(*d*) a reference to the Scottish inspectors or the Northern Ireland inspectors has the same meaning as in section 27, and

(*e*) a reference to an enactment does not include—

(i) an Act of the Scottish Parliament or an instrument made under such an Act, or

(ii) an Act of the Northern Ireland Assembly or an instrument made under such an Act.

Cross references—FA 2006 Sch 5 para 24 (sub-s (1) above does not prevent disclosure to the Secretary of State for the purposes of his functions under FiA 1985 Sch 1; other provisions relating to disclosure of confidential information).
Serious Crime Act 2007 s 85 (disclosure of information by HMRC).

19 Wrongful disclosure

(1) A person commits an offence if he contravenes section 18(1) or 20(9) by disclosing revenue and customs information relating to a person whose identity—

(*a*) is specified in the disclosure, or
(*b*) can be deduced from it.

(2) In subsection (1) "revenue and customs information relating to a person" means information about, acquired as a result of, or held in connection with the exercise of a function of the Revenue and Customs (within the meaning given by section 18(4)(*c*)) in respect of the person; but it does not include information about internal administrative arrangements of Her Majesty's Revenue and Customs (whether relating to Commissioners, officers or others).

(3) It is a defence for a person charged with an offence under this section of disclosing information to prove that he reasonably believed—

(*a*) that the disclosure was lawful, or
(*b*) that the information had already and lawfully been made available to the public.

(4) A person guilty of an offence under this section shall be liable—

(*a*) on conviction on indictment, to imprisonment for a term not exceeding two years, to a fine or to both, or
(*b*) on summary conviction, to imprisonment for a term not exceeding 12 months, to a fine not exceeding the statutory maximum or to both.

(5) A prosecution for an offence under this section may be instituted in England and Wales only—

(*a*) by the Director of Revenue and Customs Prosecutions, or
(*b*) with the consent of the Director of Public Prosecutions.

(6) A prosecution for an offence under this section may be instituted in Northern Ireland only—

(*a*) by the Commissioners, or
(*b*) with the consent of the Director of Public Prosecutions for Northern Ireland.

(7) In the application of this section to Scotland or Northern Ireland the reference in subsection (4)(*b*) to 12 months shall be taken as a reference to six months.

(8) This section is without prejudice to the pursuit of any remedy or the taking of any action in relation to a contravention of section 18(1) or 20(9) (whether or not this section applies to the contravention).

20 Public interest disclosure

(1) Disclosure is in accordance with this section (as mentioned in section 18(2)(*b*)) if—

(*a*) it is made on the instructions of the Commissioners (which may be general or specific),
(*b*) it is of a kind—
  (i) to which any of subsections (2) to (7) applies, or
  (ii) specified in regulations made by the Treasury, and
(*c*) the Commissioners are satisfied that it is in the public interest.

(2) This subsection applies to a disclosure made—

(*a*) to a person exercising public functions (whether or not within the United Kingdom),
(*b*) for the purposes of the prevention or detection of crime, and
(*c*) in order to comply with an obligation of the United Kingdom, or Her Majesty's Government, under an international or other agreement relating to the movement of persons, goods or services.

(3) This subsection applies to a disclosure if—

(*a*) it is made to a body which has responsibility for the regulation of a profession,
(*b*) it relates to misconduct on the part of a member of the profession, and
(*c*) the misconduct relates to a function of the Revenue and Customs.

(4) This subsection applies to a disclosure if—

(*a*) it is made to a constable, and
(*b*) either—
  (i) the constable is exercising functions which relate to the movement of persons or goods into or out of the United Kingdom, or
  (ii) the disclosure is made for the purposes of the prevention or detection of crime.

(5) This subsection applies to a disclosure if it is made—

(*a*) to the National Criminal Intelligence Service, and
(*b*) for a purpose connected with its functions under section 2(2) of the Police Act 1997 (c 50) (criminal intelligence).

(6) This subsection applies to a disclosure if it is made—

(*a*) to a person exercising public functions in relation to public safety or public health, and (*b*) for the purposes of those functions.

(7) This subsection applies to a disclosure if it—

(*a*) is made to the [National Policing Improvement Agency][1] for the purpose of enabling information to be entered in a computerised database, and

(*b*) relates to—

(i) a person suspected of an offence,
(ii) a person arrested for an offence,
(iii) the results of an investigation, or
(iv) anything seized.

(8) Regulations under subsection (1)(*b*)(ii)—

(*a*) may specify a kind of disclosure only if the Treasury are satisfied that it relates to—

(i) national security,
(ii) public safety,
(iii) public health, or
(iv) the prevention or detection of crime;

(*b*) may make provision limiting or restricting the disclosures that may be made in reliance on the regulations; and that provision may, in particular, operate by reference to—

(i) the nature of information,
(ii) the person or class of person to whom the disclosure is made,
(iii) the person or class of person by whom the disclosure is made,
(iv) any other factor, or
(v) a combination of factors;

(*c*) shall be made by statutory instrument;

(*d*) may not be made unless a draft has been laid before and approved by resolution of each House of Parliament.

(9) Information disclosed in reliance on this section may not be further disclosed without the consent of the Commissioners (which may be general or specific); (but the Commissioners shall be taken to have consented to further disclosure by use of the computerised database of information disclosed by virtue of subsection (7)).

Amendments—[1] Words in sub-s (7)(*a*) substituted by the Police and Justice Act 2006 s 1(3), Sch 1 para 91 with effect from 1 April 2007 (by virtue of SI 2007/709 art 3(*a*)).

21 Disclosure to prosecuting authority

(1) Disclosure is in accordance with this section (as mentioned in section 18(2)(*b*)) if made—

(*a*) to a prosecuting authority, and

(*b*) for the purpose of enabling the authority—

(i) to consider whether to institute criminal proceedings in respect of a matter considered in the course of an investigation conducted by or on behalf of Her Majesty's Revenue and Customs, …

(ii) to give advice in connection with a criminal investigation (within the meaning of section 35(5)(*b*)) or criminal proceedings [or

(iii) in the case of the Director of Revenue and Customs Prosecutions, to exercise his functions under, or in relation to, Part 5 or 8 of the Proceeds of Crime Act 2002 (c 29)][1].

(2) In subsection (1) "prosecuting authority" means—

(*a*) the Director of Revenue and Customs Prosecutions,

(*b*) in Scotland, the Lord Advocate or a procurator fiscal, and

(*c*) in Northern Ireland, the Director of Public Prosecutions for Northern Ireland.

(3) Information disclosed to a prosecuting authority in accordance with this section may not be further disclosed except—

(*a*) for a purpose connected with the exercise of the prosecuting authority's functions, or

(*b*) with the consent of the Commissioners (which may be general or specific).

(4) A person commits an offence if he contravenes subsection (3).

(5) It is a defence for a person charged with an offence under this section to prove that he reasonably believed—

(*a*) that the disclosure was lawful, or

(*b*) that the information had already and lawfully been made available to the public.

(6) A person guilty of an offence under this section shall be liable—

(*a*) on conviction on indictment, to imprisonment for a term not exceeding two years, to a fine or to both, or

(*b*) on summary conviction, to imprisonment for a term not exceeding 12 months, to a fine not exceeding the statutory maximum or to both.

(7) A prosecution for an offence under this section may be instituted in England and Wales only—

(*a*) by the Director of Revenue and Customs Prosecutions, or

(*b*) with the consent of the Director of Public Prosecutions.

(8) A prosecution for an offence under this section may be instituted in Northern Ireland only—

(*a*) by the Commissioners, or

(*b*) with the consent of the Director of Public Prosecutions for Northern Ireland.

(9) In the application of this section to Scotland or Northern Ireland the reference in subsection (6)(*b*) to 12 months shall be taken as a reference to six months.

Cross reference—Serious Crime Act 2007 s 37, Sch 2 para 10 (this section has effect as if the purpose mentioned in sub-s (1)(*b*) included the purpose of enabling the Director to exercise his functions under this Part).

Amendments—[1] In sub-s (1)(*b*)(i), word "or" repealed, and sub-s (1)(*b*)(iii) and preceding word "or" inserted, by the Serious Crime Act 2007 ss 74(2), 92, Sch 8 para 164, Sch 14 with effect from 1 April 2008: SI 2008/755 art 2(1)(*a*), subject to transitional provisions and savings in art 3.

22 Data protection, &c

Nothing in sections 17 to 21 authorises the making of a disclosure which—

(*a*) contravenes the Data Protection Act 1998 (c 29), or

(*b*) is prohibited by Part 1 of the Regulation of Investigatory Powers Act 2000 (c 23).

23 Freedom of information

(1) Revenue and customs information relating to a person, the disclosure of which is prohibited by section 18(1), is exempt information by virtue of section 44(1)(*a*) of the Freedom of Information Act 2000 (c 36) (prohibitions on disclosure) if its disclosure—

(*a*) would specify the identity of the person to whom the information relates, or

(*b*) would enable the identity of such a person to be deduced.

(2) Except as specified in subsection (1), information the disclosure of which is prohibited by section 18(1) is not exempt information for the purposes of section 44(1)(*a*) of the Freedom of Information Act 2000.

(3) In subsection (1) "revenue and customs information relating to a person" has the same meaning as in section 19.

Proceedings

24 Evidence

(1) A document that purports to have been issued or signed by or with the authority of the Commissioners—

(*a*) shall be treated as having been so issued or signed unless the contrary is proved, and

(*b*) shall be admissible in any legal proceedings.

(2) A document that purports to have been issued by the Commissioners and which certifies any of the matters specified in subsection (3) shall (in addition to the matters provided for by subsection (1)(*a*) and (*b*)) be treated as accurate unless the contrary is proved.

(3) The matters mentioned in subsection (2) are—

(*a*) that a specified person was appointed as a commissioner on a specified date,

(*b*) that a specified person was appointed as an officer of Revenue and Customs on a specified date,

(*c*) that at a specified time or for a specified purpose (or both) a function was delegated to a specified Commissioner,

(*d*) that at a specified time or for a specified purpose (or both) a function was delegated to a specified committee, and

(*e*) that at a specified time or for a specified purpose (or both) a function was delegated to another specified person.

(4) A photographic or other copy of a document acquired by the Commissioners shall, if certified by them to be an accurate copy, be admissible in any legal proceedings to the same extent as the document itself.

(5) Section 2 of the Documentary Evidence Act 1868 (c 37) (proof of documents) shall apply to a Revenue and Customs document as it applies in relation to the documents mentioned in that section.

(6) In the application of that section to a Revenue and Customs document the Schedule to that Act shall be treated as if—

(*a*) the first column contained a reference to the Commissioners, and

(*b*) the second column contained a reference to a Commissioner or a person acting on his authority.

(7) In this section—

(*a*) "Revenue and Customs document" means a document issued by or on behalf of the Commissioners, and

(*b*) a reference to the Commissioners includes a reference to the Commissioners of Inland Revenue and to the Commissioners of Customs and Excise.

25 Conduct of civil proceedings

(1) An officer of Revenue and Customs or a person authorised by the Commissioners may conduct civil proceedings, in a magistrates' court or in the sheriff court, relating to a function of the Revenue and Customs.

[(1A) An officer of Revenue and Customs or a person authorised by the Commissioners may conduct county court proceedings for the recovery of an amount payable to the Commissioners under or by virtue of an enactment or under a contract settlement.][1]

(2) A solicitor member of the Commissioners' staff may act as a solicitor in connection with civil proceedings relating to a function of the Revenue and Customs.

(3) A legally qualified member of the Commissioners' staff may conduct county court proceedings relating to a matter specified in section 7.

(4) A court shall grant any rights of audience necessary to enable a person to exercise a function under this section.

(5) In this section—

(*a*) a reference to a function of the Revenue and Customs is a reference to a function of—

(i) the Commissioners, or

(ii) an officer of Revenue and Customs,

(*b*) a reference to civil proceedings is a reference to proceedings other than proceedings in respect of an offence,

(*c*) a reference to county court proceedings is a reference to civil proceedings in a county court,

(*d*) the reference to a legally qualified member of the Commissioners' staff is a reference to a member of staff who has been admitted as a solicitor, or called to the Bar, whether or not he holds a practising certificate, and

(*e*) the reference to a solicitor member of the Commissioners' staff—

(i) except in relation to Scotland, is a reference to a member of staff who has been admitted as a solicitor, whether or not he holds a practising certificate,

(ii) in relation to Scotland, is a reference to a member of staff who has been admitted as a solicitor and who holds a practising certificate.

[(6) In this section "contract settlement" means an agreement made in connection with any person's liability to make a payment to the Commissioners under or by virtue of an enactment.][1]

Amendments—[1] Sub-ss (1A), (6) inserted by FA 2008 s 137(1) with effect from 21 July 2008.

[25A Certificates of debt

(1) A certificate of an officer of Revenue and Customs that, to the best of that officer's knowledge and belief, a relevant sum has not been paid is sufficient evidence that the sum mentioned in the certificate is unpaid.

(2) In subsection (1) "relevant sum" means a sum payable to the Commissioners under or by virtue of an enactment or under a contract settlement (within the meaning of section 25).

(3) Any document purporting to be such a certificate shall be treated as if it were such a certificate until the contrary is proved.

(4) Subsection (1) has effect subject to any provision treating the certificate as conclusive evidence.][1]

Amendments—[1] This section inserted by FA 2008 s 138(1) with effect from 21 July 2008.

26 Rewards

The Commissioners may pay a reward to a person in return for a service which relates to a function of—

(*a*) the Commissioners, or

(*b*) an officer of Revenue and Customs.

Inspection and complaints

27 Inspection

(1) The Treasury may make regulations conferring functions on Her Majesty's Inspectors of Constabulary, the Scottish inspectors or the Northern Ireland inspectors in relation to—

(*a*) the Commissioners for Her Majesty's Revenue and Customs, and

(*b*) officers of Revenue and Customs.

(2) Regulations under subsection (1)—

(*a*) may—

(i) in relation to Her Majesty's Inspectors of Constabulary, apply (with or without modification) or make provision similar to any provision of sections 54 to 56 of the Police Act 1996 (c 16) (inspection);

(ii) in relation to the Scottish inspectors, apply (with or without modification) or make provision similar to any provision of section 33 or 34 of the Police (Scotland) Act 1967 (c 77) (inspection);

(iii) in relation to the Northern Ireland inspectors, apply (with or without modification) or make provision similar to any provision of section 41 or 42 of the Police (Northern Ireland) Act 1998 (c 32) (inspection);

(*b*) may enable a Minister of the Crown or the Commissioners to require an inspection to be carried out;

(*c*) shall provide for a report of an inspection to be made and, subject to any exceptions required or permitted by the regulations, published;

(*d*) shall provide for an annual report by Her Majesty's Inspectors of Constabulary;

(*e*) may make provision for payment by the Commissioners to or in respect of Her Majesty's Inspectors of Constabulary, the Scottish inspectors or the Northern Ireland inspectors.

(3) An inspection carried out by virtue of this section may not address a matter of a kind which the Comptroller and Auditor General may examine under section 6 of the National Audit Act 1983 (c 44).

(4) An inspection carried out by virtue of this section shall be carried out jointly by Her Majesty's Inspectors of Constabulary and the Scottish inspectors—

(*a*) if it is carried out wholly in Scotland, or

(*b*) in a case where it is carried out partly in Scotland, to the extent that it is carried out there.

(5) Regulations under subsection (1)—

(*a*) shall be made by statutory instrument, and

(*b*) shall be subject to annulment in pursuance of a resolution of either House of Parliament.

(6) In this section—

(*a*) "the Scottish inspectors" means the inspectors of constabulary appointed under section 33(1) of the Police (Scotland) Act 1967, and

(*b*) "the Northern Ireland inspectors" means the inspectors of constabulary appointed under section 41(1) of the Police (Northern Ireland) Act 1998.

Regulations—See the Revenue and Customs (Inspections) Regulations, SI 2005/1133.

28 Complaints and misconduct: England and Wales

(1) The Treasury may make regulations conferring functions on the Independent Police Complaints Commission in relation to—

(*a*) the Commissioners for Her Majesty's Revenue and Customs, and

(*b*) officers of Revenue and Customs.

(2) Regulations under subsection (1)—

(*a*) may apply (with or without modification) or make provision similar to any provision of or made under Part 2 of the Police Reform Act 2002 (c 30) (complaints);

(*b*) may confer on the Independent Police Complaints Commission, or on a person acting on its behalf, a power of a kind conferred by this Act or another enactment on an officer of Revenue and Customs;

(*c*) may make provision for payment by the Commissioners to or in respect of the Independent Police Complaints Commission.

(3) The Independent Police Complaints Commission and the Parliamentary Commissioner for Administration may disclose information to each other for the purposes of the exercise of a function—

(*a*) by virtue of this section, or

(*b*) under the Parliamentary Commissioner Act 1967 (c 13).

(4) The Independent Police Complaints Commission and the Parliamentary Commissioner for Administration may jointly investigate a matter in relation to which—

(*a*) the Independent Police Complaints Commission has functions by virtue of this section, and

(*b*) the Parliamentary Commissioner for Administration has functions by virtue of the Parliamentary Commissioner Act 1967.

(5) Regulations under subsection (1)—

(*a*) shall be made by statutory instrument, and

(*b*) shall be subject to annulment in pursuance of a resolution of either House of Parliament.

(6) Regulations under subsection (1) shall relate to the Commissioners or officers of Revenue and Customs only in so far as their functions are exercised in or in relation to England and Wales.

Commentary—*Simon's Taxes* **A5.403**.

29 Confidentiality, &c

(1) Where Her Majesty's Inspectors of Constabulary, the Scottish inspectors or the Northern Ireland inspectors obtain information in the course of exercising a function by virtue of section 27—

(*a*) they may not disclose it without the consent of the Commissioners, and (*b*) they may not use it for any purpose other than the exercise of the function by virtue of section 27.

(2) A report of an inspection by virtue of section 27 may not include information relating to a specified person without his consent.

(3) Where the Independent Police Complaints Commission or a person acting on its behalf obtains information from the Commissioners or an officer of Revenue and Customs, or from the Parliamentary Commissioner for Administration, in the course of exercising a function by virtue of section 28—

(*a*) the Commission or person shall comply with any restriction on disclosure imposed by regulations under that section (and those regulations may, in particular, prohibit disclosure generally or only in specified circumstances or only without the consent of the Commissioners), and
(*b*) the Commission or person may not use the information for any purpose other than the exercise of the function by virtue of that section.

(4) A person commits an offence if he contravenes a provision of this section.

(5) It is a defence for a person charged with an offence under this section of disclosing or using information to prove that he reasonably believed—

(*a*) that the disclosure or use was lawful, or
(*b*) that the information had already and lawfully been made available to the public.

(6) A person guilty of an offence under this section shall be liable—

(*a*) on conviction on indictment, to imprisonment for a term not exceeding two years, to a fine or to both, or
(*b*) on summary conviction, to imprisonment for a term not exceeding 12 months, to a fine not exceeding the statutory maximum or to both.

(7) A prosecution for an offence under this section may be instituted in England and Wales only—

(*a*) by the Director of Revenue and Customs Prosecutions, or
(*b*) with the consent of the Director of Public Prosecutions.

(8) A prosecution for an offence under this section may be instituted in Northern Ireland only—

(*a*) by the Commissioners, or
(*b*) with the consent of the Director of Public Prosecutions for Northern Ireland.

(9) In the application of this section to Scotland or Northern Ireland the reference in subsection (6)(*b*) to 12 months shall be taken as a reference to six months.

(10) In this section a reference to the Scottish inspectors or the Northern Ireland inspectors has the same meaning as in section 27.

Offences

30 Impersonation

(1) A person commits an offence if he pretends to be a Commissioner or an officer of Revenue and Customs with a view to obtaining—

(*a*) admission to premises,
(*b*) information, or
(*c*) any other benefit.

(2) A person guilty of an offence under this section shall be liable on summary conviction to—

(*a*) imprisonment for a period not exceeding 51 weeks,
(*b*) a fine not exceeding level 5 on the standard scale, or
(*c*) both.

(3) In the application of this section to Scotland or Northern Ireland the reference in subsection (2)(*a*) to 51 weeks shall be taken as a reference to six months.

31 Obstruction

(1) A person commits an offence if without reasonable excuse he obstructs—

(*a*) an officer of Revenue and Customs,
(*b*) a person acting on behalf of the Commissioners or an officer of Revenue and Customs, or
(*c*) a person assisting an officer of Revenue and Customs.

(2) A person guilty of an offence under this section shall be liable on summary conviction to—

(*a*) imprisonment for a period not exceeding 51 weeks,
(*b*) a fine not exceeding level 3 on the standard scale, or
(*c*) both.

(3) In the application of this section to Scotland or Northern Ireland the reference in subsection (2)(*a*) to 51 weeks shall be taken as a reference to six months.

32 Assault

(1) A person commits an offence if he assaults an officer of Revenue and Customs.

(2) A person guilty of an offence under this section shall be liable on summary conviction to—

(*a*) imprisonment for a period not exceeding 51 weeks,
(*b*) a fine not exceeding level 5 on the standard scale, or
(*c*) both.

(3) In the application of this section to Scotland or Northern Ireland the reference in subsection (2)(*a*) to 51 weeks shall be taken as a reference to six months.

33 Power of arrest

(1) An authorised officer of Revenue and Customs may arrest a person without warrant if the officer reasonably suspects that the person—

(*a*) has committed an offence under section 30, 31 or 32,
(*b*) is committing an offence under any of those sections, or
(*c*) is about to commit an offence under any of those sections.

(2) In subsection (1) "authorised" means authorised by the Commissioners.

(3) Authorisation for the purposes of this section may be specific or general.

(4) In Scotland or Northern Ireland, a constable may arrest a person without warrant if the constable reasonably suspects that the person—

(*a*) has committed an offence under this Act,
(*b*) is committing an offence under this Act, or
(*c*) is about to commit an offence under this Act.

Prosecutions

34 The Revenue and Customs Prosecutions Office

(1) The Attorney General shall appoint an individual as Director of Revenue and Customs Prosecutions.

(2) The Director may, with the approval of the Minister for the Civil Service as to terms and conditions of service, appoint staff.

(3) The Director and his staff may together be referred to as the Revenue and Customs Prosecutions Office.

(4) Schedule 3 (which makes provision about the Office) shall have effect.

35 Functions

(1) The Director—

(*a*) may institute and conduct criminal proceedings in England and Wales relating to a criminal investigation by the Revenue and Customs, and
(*b*) shall take over the conduct of criminal proceedings instituted in England and Wales by the Revenue and Customs.

(2) The Director shall provide such advice as he thinks appropriate, to such persons as he thinks appropriate, in relation to—

(*a*) a criminal investigation by the Revenue and Customs, or
(*b*) criminal proceedings instituted in England and Wales relating to a criminal investigation by the Revenue and Customs.

(3) In this section a reference to the Revenue and Customs is a reference to—

(*a*) the Commissioners,
(*b*) an officer of Revenue and Customs, and
(*c*) a person acting on behalf of the Commissioners or an officer of Revenue and Customs.

(4) The Attorney General may by order assign to the Director a function of—

(*a*) instituting criminal proceedings,
(*b*) assuming the conduct of criminal proceedings, or
(*c*) providing legal advice.

[(4A) The Director has the functions conferred on him by, or in relation to, Part 5 or 8 of the Proceeds of Crime Act 2002 (c 29) (civil recovery of the proceeds etc of unlawful conduct, civil recovery investigations and disclosure orders in relation to confiscation investigations).][1]

(5) In this section—

(*a*) a reference to the institution of criminal proceedings shall be construed in accordance with section 15(2) of the Prosecution of Offences Act 1985 (c 23), and
(*b*) "criminal investigation" means any process—

(i) for considering whether an offence has been committed,
(ii) for discovering by whom an offence has been committed, or
(iii) as a result of which an offence is alleged to have been committed.

Order—See the Commissioners for Revenue and Customs Act 2005 (Commencement) Order, SI 2005/1126, art 2(2) (this section came into force on 18 April 2005).

Amendment—[1] Sub-s (4A) inserted by the Serious Crime Act 2007 s 74(2), Sch 8 para 165 with effect from 1 April 2008: SI 2008/755 art 2(1)(*a*), subject to transitional provisions and savings in art 3.

36 Functions: supplemental

(1) The Director shall discharge his functions under the superintendence of the Attorney General.

(2) The Director or an individual designated under section 37 or 39 or appointed under section 38 must have regard to the Code for Crown Prosecutors issued by the Director of Public Prosecutions under section 10 of the Prosecution of Offences Act 1985 (c 23)—

(*a*) in determining whether proceedings for an offence should be instituted,
(*b*) in determining what charges should be preferred,
(*c*) in considering what representations to make to a magistrates' court about mode of trial, and
(*d*) in determining whether to discontinue proceedings.

(3) Sections 23 and 23A of the Prosecution of Offences Act 1985 (power to discontinue proceedings) shall apply (with any necessary modifications) to proceedings conducted by the Director under this Act as they apply to proceedings conducted by the Director of Public Prosecutions.

(4) A power of the Director under an enactment to institute proceedings may be exercised to institute proceedings in England and Wales only.

Order—See the Commissioners for Revenue and Customs Act 2005 (Commencement) Order, SI 2005/1126, art 2(2) (this section came into force on 18 April 2005).

37 Prosecutors

(1) The Director may designate a member of the Office (to be known as a "Revenue and Customs Prosecutor") to exercise any function of the Director under or by virtue of section 35 [(excluding any function mentioned in subsection (4A) of that section)][1].

(2) An individual may be designated as a Prosecutor only if he has a general qualification within the meaning of section 71 of the Courts and Legal Services Act 1990 (c 41) (qualification for judicial appointments).

(3) A Prosecutor shall act in accordance with any instructions of the Director.

Amendments—[1] Words in sub-s (1) inserted by the Serious Crime Act 2007 s 74(2), Sch 8 para 166 with effect from 1 April 2008: SI 2008/755 art 2(1)(*a*), subject to transitional provisions and savings in art 3.

38 Conduct of prosecutions on behalf of the Office

(1) An individual who is not a member of the Office may be appointed by the Director to exercise any function of the Director under or by virtue of section 35 in relation to—

(*a*) specified criminal proceedings, or
(*b*) a specified class or description of criminal proceedings.

[(1A) An individual who is not a member of the Office may be appointed by the Director to appear in—

(*a*) specified proceedings, or
(*b*) a specified class or description of proceedings,

in which the Director or a Prosecutor would otherwise appear by virtue of section 302A of the Proceeds of Crime Act 2002 (cash recovery proceedings).][1]

(2) An individual may be appointed under this section only if he has a general qualification within the meaning of section 71 of the Courts and Legal Services Act 1990 (qualifications for judicial appointments).

(3) An individual appointed under this section shall act in accordance with any instructions of—

(*a*) the Director, or
(*b*) a Prosecutor.

Amendments—[1] Sub-s (1A) inserted by the Serious Crime Act 2007 s 84(3) with effect from 6 April 2008: SI 2008/755, art 17(1)(*h*) subject to transitional provisions and savings in SI 2008/755 art 3.

39 Designation of non-legal staff

(1) The Director may designate a member of the Office—

(*a*) to conduct summary bail applications, and
(*b*) to conduct other ancillary magistrates' criminal proceedings.

[(1A) The Director may designate a member of the Office to appear in—

(*a*) specified proceedings, or
(*b*) a specified class or description of proceedings,

in which the Director or a Prosecutor would otherwise appear by virtue of section 302A of the Proceeds of Crime Act 2002 (cash recovery proceedings).][1]

(2) In carrying out a function for which he is designated under this section an individual shall have the same powers and rights of audience as a Prosecutor.

(3) In subsection (1)—

(*a*) "summary bail application" means an application for bail made in connection with an offence—

(i) which is not triable only on indictment, and

(ii) in respect of which the accused has not been sent to the Crown Court for trial, and

(*b*) "ancillary magistrates' criminal proceedings" means criminal proceedings other than trials in a magistrates' court.

(4) An individual designated under this section shall act in accordance with any instructions of—

(*a*) the Director, or

(*b*) a Prosecutor.

Amendments—[1] Sub-s (1A) inserted by the Serious Crime Act 2007 s 84(4) with effect from 6 April 2008: SI 2008/755, art 17(1)(*h*) subject to transitional provisions and savings in SI 2008/755 art 3.

40 Confidentiality

(1) The Revenue and Customs Prosecutions Office may not disclose information which—

(*a*) is held by the Prosecutions Office in connection with any of its functions, and

(*b*) relates to a person whose identity is specified in the disclosure or can be deduced from it.

(2) But subsection (1)—

(*a*) does not apply to a disclosure which—

(i) is made for the purposes of a function of the Prosecutions Office, and

(ii) does not contravene any restriction imposed by the Director,

(*b*) does not apply to a disclosure made to Her Majesty's Revenue and Customs in connection with a function of the Revenue and Customs (within the meaning of section 25),

(*c*) does not apply to a disclosure made for the purposes of a criminal investigation or criminal proceedings (whether or not within the United Kingdom),

[(*ca*) does not apply to a disclosure made for the purposes of—

(i) the exercise of any functions of the prosecutor under Parts 2, 3 and 4 of the Proceeds of Crime Act 2002 (c 29),

(ii) the exercise of any functions of the Serious Organised Crime Agency under that Act,

(iii) the exercise of any functions of the Director of Public Prosecutions, the Director of the Serious Fraud Office, the Director of Public Prosecutions for Northern Ireland or the Scottish Ministers under, or in relation to, Part 5 or 8 of that Act,

(iv) the exercise of any functions of an officer of Revenue and Customs[, an accredited financial investigator][2] or a constable under Chapter 3 of Part 5 of that Act, or

(v) investigations or proceedings outside the United Kingdom which have led or may lead to the making of an external order within the meaning of section 447 of that Act,

(*cb*) does not apply to a disclosure of information obtained in the exercise of functions under the Proceeds of Crime Act 2002 (c 29) if the disclosure is made for the purposes of the exercise of a function which the Secretary of State thinks is a public function and which he designates by order,][1]

(*d*) does not apply to a disclosure which in the opinion of the Director is desirable for the purpose of safeguarding national security,

(*e*) does not apply to a disclosure made in pursuance of an order of a court,

(*f*) does not apply to a disclosure made with the consent of each person to whom the information relates, and

(*g*) is subject to any other enactment.

(3) A person commits an offence if he contravenes subsection (1).

(4) Subsection (3) does not apply to the disclosure of information about internal administrative arrangements of the Revenue and Customs Prosecutions Office (whether relating to a member of the Office or to another person).

(5) It is a defence for a person charged with an offence under this section of disclosing information to prove that he reasonably believed—

(*a*) that the disclosure was lawful, or

(*b*) that the information had already and lawfully been made available to the public.

(6) In this section a reference to the Revenue and Customs Prosecutions Office includes a reference to—

(*a*) former members of the Office, and

(*b*) persons who hold or have held appointment under section 38.

(7) A person guilty of an offence under this section shall be liable—

(*a*) on conviction on indictment, to imprisonment for a term not exceeding two years, to a fine or to both, or

(*b*) on summary conviction, to imprisonment for a term not exceeding 12 months, to a fine not exceeding the statutory maximum or to both.

(8) A prosecution for an offence under this section may be instituted in England and Wales only—

(*a*) by the Director of Revenue and Customs Prosecutions, or

(*b*) with the consent of the Director of Public Prosecutions.

(9) A prosecution for an offence under this section may be instituted in Northern Ireland only—

(*a*) by the Commissioners, or

(*b*) with the consent of the Director of Public Prosecutions for Northern Ireland.

(10) In the application of this section to Scotland or Northern Ireland the reference in subsection (7)(*b*) to 12 months shall be taken as a reference to six months.

[(10A) An order under subsection (2)(*cb*)—

(*a*) may include transitional or incidental provision,

(*b*) shall be made by statutory instrument, and

(*c*) shall not be made unless a draft has been laid before, and approved by a resolution of, each House of Parliament.][1]

(11) In subsection (2) the reference to an enactment does not include—

(*a*) an Act of the Scottish Parliament or an instrument made under such an Act, or

(*b*) an Act of the Northern Ireland Assembly or an instrument made under such an Act.

Amendments—[1] Sub-ss (2)(*ca*), (*cb*), (10A) inserted by the Serious Crime Act 2007 s 74(2), Sch 8 para 167 with effect from 1 April 2008: SI 2008/755 art 2(1)(*a*), subject to transitional provisions and savings in art 3.

[2] Words in sub-s (2)(*ca*)(iv) inserted by the Serious Crime Act 2007 s 79, Sch 11 para 16 with effect from 6 April 2008: SI 2008/755 art 17(1)(*f*) subject to transitional provisions and savings in SI 2008/755 art 3.

41 Disclosure of information to Director of Revenue and Customs Prosecutions

(1) A person specified in subsection (2) may disclose information held by him to the Director for a purpose connected with a specified investigation or prosecution [or for the purpose of the exercise by the Director of his functions under the Proceeds of Crime Act 2002 (c 29)][1].

(2) Those persons are—

(*a*) a constable,

(*b*) the Director General of the National Criminal Intelligence Service,

(*c*) the Director General of the National Crime Squad,

(*d*) the Director of the Serious Fraud Office,

(*e*) the Director General of the Serious Organised Crime Agency,

(*f*) the Director of Public Prosecutions,

(*g*) the Director of Public Prosecutions for Northern Ireland, and

(*h*) such other persons as the Attorney General may specify by order.

(3) An order under subsection (2)(*h*)—

(*a*) may specify a person only if, or in so far as, he appears to the Attorney General to be exercising public functions,

(*b*) may include transitional or incidental provision,

(*c*) shall be made by statutory instrument, and

(*d*) shall not be made unless a draft has been laid before, and approved by resolution of, each House of Parliament.

(4) In relation to a person if or in so far as he exercises functions in respect of Northern Ireland subsections (2)(*h*) and (3)(*a*) shall have effect as if a reference to the Attorney General were a reference to—

(*a*) the Advocate General for Northern Ireland, or

(*b*) before the commencement of section 27(1) of the Justice (Northern Ireland) Act 2002 (c 26), the Attorney General for Northern Ireland.

(5) In the application of this section to Scotland, references to the Attorney General are to be read as references to a Minister of the Crown (including the Treasury).

(6) Nothing in this section authorises the making of a disclosure which—

(*a*) contravenes the Data Protection Act 1998 (c 29), or

(*b*) is prohibited by Part 1 of the Regulation of Investigatory Powers Act 2000 (c 23).

Amendments—[1] Words in sub-s (1) inserted by the Serious Crime Act 2007 s 74(2), Sch 8 para 168 with effect from 1 April 2008: SI 2008/755 art 2(1)(*a*), subject to transitional provisions and savings in art 3.

42 Inspection

Section 2 of the Crown Prosecution Service Inspectorate Act 2000 (c 10) shall apply to the Revenue and Customs Prosecutions Office as it applies to the Crown Prosecution Service.

Money and property

43 Expenditure

Expenditure of the Commissioners in connection with the exercise of their functions shall be paid out of money provided by Parliament.

44 Payment into Consolidated Fund

(1) The Commissioners shall pay money received in the exercise of their functions into the Consolidated Fund—

(*a*) at such times and in such manner as the Treasury directs,

(*b*) with the exception of receipts specified in subsection (2), and (*c*) after deduction of the disbursements specified in subsection (3).

(2) The exceptions mentioned in subsection (1)(*b*) are—

(*a*) contributions under Part I of the Social Security Contributions and Benefits Act 1992 (c 4),

(*b*) contributions under Part I of the Social Security Contributions and Benefits (Northern Ireland) Act 1992 (c 7),

(*c*) any other sums payable, under or by virtue of an enactment, into the National Insurance Fund or the Northern Ireland National Insurance Fund,

(*d*) sums required under or by virtue of an enactment to be paid into the National Loans Fund,

(*e*) sums required to be paid to a Minister of the Crown [or other person][1] by virtue of an enactment relating to financial support for students,

(*f*) *penalties under section 21 of the National Minimum Wage Act 1998 (c 39) (non-compliance), and*[2]

(*g*) sums required under or by virtue of an enactment to be paid into the Scottish Consolidated Fund.

(3) The disbursements mentioned in subsection (1)(*c*) are—

(*a*) payments in connection with drawback, repayments and discounts,

(*b*) payments under section 77 of the Scotland Act 1998 (c 46) (additional tax),

(*c*) payments under section 2 of the Isle of Man Act 1979 (c 58) (Isle of Man share of common duties), and

(*d*) tax credits.

(4) In subsection (3)(*a*) "repayments" includes—

(*a*) payments in respect of actual or deemed credits relating to any tax or duty, and

(*b*) payments of interest (or repayment supplement) on—

(i) repayments, or

(ii) payments treated as repayments.

Amendments—[1] In sub-s (2)(*e*), words inserted, in relation to England and Wales, by the Sale of Student Loans Act 2008 s 6(5) with effect from 21 July 2008 (by virtue of the Sale of Student Loans Act 2008 s 14).

[2] Sub-s (2)(*f*) repealed by the Employment Act 2008, ss 9(5), 20, Schedule Pt 2 with effect from 6 April 2009 (by virtue of SI 2009/603 arts 2, 3 and subject to savings in relation to the enforcement of the agricultural minimum wage in Scotland and Northern Ireland in s 9(7) thereof).

45 Remuneration, &c

(1) The Commissioners shall be paid, out of money provided by Parliament, such remuneration, expenses and other allowances as may be determined by the Minister for the Civil Service.

(2) The Commissioners may incur expenditure in respect of staff (whether in respect of remuneration, allowances, pensions, gratuities or otherwise).

(3) The Commissioners shall pay to the Minister for the Civil Service, at such times as the Minister may direct, such sums as the Minister may determine in respect of any increase attributable to this Act in the sums payable under the Superannuation Act 1972 (c 11) out of money provided by Parliament.

46 Accounts

(1) The Commissioners shall provide to the Comptroller and Auditor General, in such form as the Treasury shall direct, a daily account of—

(*a*) the amount of revenue received, and

(*b*) the disposal of revenue received.

(2) The Commissioners shall provide to the Comptroller and Auditor General, in such form and at such times as the Treasury shall direct, an account of liabilities satisfied by the acceptance of property in satisfaction of tax under—

(*a*) section 230 of the Inheritance Tax Act 1984 (c 51), or

(*b*) any other enactment.

47 Payment out of Consolidated Fund

(1) This section applies if the Treasury think that the funds available to the Commissioners may be insufficient to make, under or by virtue of an enactment—

(*a*) a payment into the National Insurance Fund,

(*b*) a payment into the Northern Ireland National Insurance Fund,

(*c*) a payment of a kind specified in section 44(2)(*c*) to (*g*), or

(*d*) a disbursement of a kind specified in section 44(3).

(2) Where this section applies the Treasury may pay money to the Commissioners out of the Consolidated Fund to enable them to make a payment or disbursement.

(3) This section applies whether or not the reason for a deficiency is or may be that an amount has been paid or retained on the basis of an estimate that has proved or may prove to be inaccurate.

48 Transfer of property, &c: general

(1) Upon commencement the property, rights and liabilities of any of the old commissioners shall by virtue of this section vest in the new commissioners.

(2) Anything done by, on behalf of or in relation to any of the old commissioners which has effect immediately before commencement shall continue to have effect as if done by, on behalf of or in relation to the new commissioners.

(3) Anything (including any legal proceedings) which immediately before commencement is in the process of being done by, on behalf of or in relation to any of the old commissioners may be continued by, on behalf of or in relation to the new commissioners.

(4) Upon commencement the property, rights and liabilities of any of the old officers shall by virtue of this section vest in the officers of Revenue and Customs.

(5) Anything done by, on behalf of or in relation to any of the old officers which has effect immediately before commencement shall continue to have effect as if done by, on behalf of or in relation to an officer of Revenue and Customs.

(6) Anything (including any legal proceedings) which immediately before commencement is in the process of being done by, on behalf of or in relation to any of the old officers may be continued by, on behalf of or in relation to an officer of Revenue and Customs.

(7) So far as is necessary or appropriate in consequence of section 5 or the preceding provisions of this section, on and after commencement—

(*a*) a reference to any of the old commissioners in an agreement (whether written or not), instrument or other document shall be treated as a reference to the new commissioners, and

(*b*) a reference in an agreement (whether written or not), instrument or other document to any of the old officers shall be treated as a reference to an officer of Revenue and Customs.

(8) This section shall operate in relation to property, rights or liabilities—

(*a*) whether or not they would otherwise be capable of being transferred,

(*b*) without any instrument or other formality being required, and

(*c*) irrespective of any requirement for consent that would otherwise apply.

(9) In this section—

"commencement" means the time appointed under section 53 for the commencement of section 5,

"rights and liabilities" includes rights and liabilities relating to employment,

"the old commissioners" means—

(*a*) the Commissioners of Inland Revenue, and

(*b*) the Commissioners of Customs and Excise,

"the old officers" means any of the persons listed in section 6(2) or 7(3), and

"the new commissioners" means the Commissioners for Her Majesty's Revenue and Customs.

(10) This section is subject to section 49.

49 Transfer of property, &c: Prosecutions Office

(1) The Treasury may make a scheme identifying property, rights and liabilities of the old commissioners which shall on commencement vest not in the new commissioners but in the Director of Revenue and Customs Prosecutions.

(2) A scheme shall have effect—

(*a*) in so far as it excludes anything from the operation of section 48, on the coming into force of that section, and

(*b*) in so far as it vests anything in the Director of Revenue and Customs Prosecutions, upon the coming into force of section 35.

(3) A scheme may include consequential and incidental provision and may, in particular—

(*a*) apply (with or without modification) or make provision similar to any provision of section 48;

(*b*) modify the effect of section 48(2), (3), (5), (6) or (7);

(*c*) make provision for shared ownership, use or access.

(4) The Treasury may require the new commissioners to transfer specified property, rights and liabilities to the Director of Revenue and Customs Prosecutions (and the commissioners shall comply).

(5) In relation to any matter that becomes a function of the Director of Revenue and Customs Prosecutions under section 35, section 48(2), (3), (5), (6) and (7) shall have effect with—

(*a*) the substitution of a reference to the Director for any reference to the new commissioners or to an officer of Revenue and Customs (or officers of Revenue and Customs), and

(*b*) the substitution of a reference to this section and anything done under it for a reference to section 48.

(6) In this section the following expressions have the same meaning as in section 48—

(*a*) "commencement",

(*b*) "the old commissioners", and

(*c*) "the new commissioners".

General

50 Consequential amendments, &c

(1) In so far as is appropriate in consequence of section 5 a reference in an enactment, instrument or other document to the Commissioners of Customs and Excise, to customs and excise or to the Commissioners of Inland Revenue (however expressed) shall be taken as a reference to the Commissioners for Her Majesty's Revenue and Customs.

(2) In so far as is appropriate in consequence of sections 6 and 7 a reference in an enactment, instrument or other document to any of the persons specified in section 6(2) or 7(3) (however expressed) shall be taken as a reference to an officer of Revenue and Customs.

(3) In so far as is appropriate in consequence of this Act a reference in an enactment, instrument or other document to the Valuation Office of the Inland Revenue (however expressed) shall be taken as a reference to the Valuation Office of Her Majesty's Revenue and Customs.

(4) The Treasury may by regulations make such provision as they think appropriate in consequence of section 5, 6 or 7 in respect of a reference in an enactment (however expressed) to—

(*a*) the Commissioners of Inland Revenue (or to a Commissioner),
(*b*) the Commissioners of Customs and Excise (or to a Commissioner),
(*c*) customs,
(*d*) customs and excise,
(*e*) Inland Revenue, or
(*f*) any of the persons specified in section 6(2) or 7(3).

(5) Regulations under subsection (4) in respect of a reference in an enactment—

(*a*) may amend an enactment,
(*b*) may make incidental and consequential provision,
(*c*) shall be made by statutory instrument, and
(*d*) shall not be made unless a draft has first been laid before, and approved by resolution of, each House of Parliament.

(6) Schedule 4 (consequential amendments, &c) shall have effect (and is without prejudice to the generality of subsections (1) to (4)).

(7) Subsections (1) to (4) shall, subject to any express provision to the contrary, have effect in relation to enactments passed or made, and instruments and documents issued, whether before or after the passing of this Act.

Order—See the Commissioners for Revenue and Customs Act 2005 (Commencement) Order, SI 2005/1126, art 2(2) (this section and Sch 4 came into force on 18 April 2005).

51 Interpretation

(1) In this Act—

except where otherwise expressly provided, "enactment" includes—

(*a*) an Act of the Scottish Parliament,
(*b*) an instrument made under an Act of the Scottish Parliament,
(*c*) Northern Ireland legislation, and
(*d*) an instrument made under Northern Ireland legislation,

"officer of Revenue and Customs" means a person appointed under section 2, and
"revenue" has the meaning given by section 5(4).

(2) In this Act—

(*a*) "function" means any power or duty (including a power or duty that is ancillary to another power or duty), and
(*b*) a reference to the functions of the Commissioners or of officers of Revenue and Customs is a reference to the functions conferred—

(i) by or by virtue of this Act, or
(ii) by or by virtue of any enactment passed or made after the commencement of this Act.

(3) A reference in this Act, in an enactment amended by this Act or, subject to express provision to the contrary, in any future enactment, to responsibility for collection and management of revenue has the same meaning as references to responsibility for care and management of revenue in enactments passed before this Act.

(4) In this Act a reference to information acquired in connection with a matter includes a reference to information held in connection with that matter.

52 Repeals

(1) The following shall cease to have effect—

(*a*) (*repeals* CEMA 1979 ss 12, 15, 32, 84, 86, 152(*c*), (*d*), 169).
(*b*) (*repeals* TMA 1970 s 111(2)).

(2) The enactments specified in Schedule 5 are hereby repealed to the extent specified.

Order—See the Commissioners for Revenue and Customs Act 2005 (Commencement) Order, SI 2005/1126, art 2(2) (this section and Sch 5 came into force on 18 April 2005).

53 Commencement

(1) This Act shall come into force in accordance with provision made by order of the Treasury.

(2) An order under subsection (1)—

(*a*) may make provision generally or only in relation to specified provisions or purposes,
(*b*) may include transitional, consequential or incidental provision or savings, and
(*c*) shall be made by statutory instrument.

Orders—See the Commissioners for Revenue and Customs Act 2005 (Commencement) Order, SI 2005/1126 (the Act came into force on 7 April 2005 at 5.45pm, subject to the provisions specified in SI 2005/1126 art 2(2) which came into force on 18 April 2005).

54 Transitional: general

(1) In the application of section 5—

(*a*) a reference to responsibility before commencement of that section includes a reference to responsibility under an enactment passed or made, but not yet in force, before commencement, and
(*b*) a reference to a function vesting includes a reference to a function which is to vest under an enactment passed or made, but not yet in force, before commencement of that section.

(2) In the application of section 6 or 7 a reference to a function conferred by an enactment includes a reference to a function conferred by an enactment passed or made, but not yet in force, before commencement of that section.

(3) Where immediately before the commencement of section 6 a person holds appointment as a member of the staff of the Commissioners of Inland Revenue or of the Commissioners of Customs and Excise, his appointment shall have effect on commencement as if made by the Commissioners for Her Majesty's Revenue and Customs under section 2.

(4) The following shall be treated as being included in the list in Schedule 1—

(*a*) development land tax,
(*b*) disabled person's tax credit,
(*c*) estate duty,
(*d*) the national defence contribution under Part III of the Finance Act 1937 (c 54),
(*e*) the special tax on banking deposits under section 134 of the Finance Act 1981 (c 35), and
(*f*) working families tax credit.

(5) The Treasury may by order made by statutory instrument add to the list in subsection (4) an item relating to a matter for which the Commissioners of Inland Revenue or a person listed in section 7(3) had responsibility before the commencement of section 5, if it appears to the Treasury that the law relating to that matter has lapsed or ceased to have effect but that transitional matters may continue to arise in respect of it.

(6) An order under subsection (5)—

(*a*) may include consequential, transitional or incidental provision,
(*b*) shall be made by statutory instrument, and
(*c*) shall be subject to annulment in pursuance of a resolution of either House of Parliament

(7) A reference in this Act to anything done by, on behalf of or in relation to a specified person or class of person includes a reference to anything treated as if done by, on behalf of or in relation to that person by virtue of transitional provision of an enactment passed or made before this Act.

Order—See the Commissioners for Revenue and Customs Act 2005 (Commencement) Order, SI 2005/1126, art 2(2) (this section came into force on 18 April 2005).

55 Transitional: penalties

(1) In relation to an offence under section 19 committed before the commencement of section 282 of the Criminal Justice Act 2003 (c 44) (short sentences) the reference in section 19(4)(*b*) to 12 months shall have effect as if it were a reference to six months.

(2) In relation to an offence under section 21 committed before the commencement of section 282 of the Criminal Justice Act (short sentences), the reference in section 21(6)(*b*) to 12 months shall have effect as if it were a reference to six months.

(3) In relation to an offence under section 29 committed before the commencement of section 282 of the Criminal Justice Act 2003 (c 44) (short sentences) the reference in section 29(6)(*b*) to 12 months shall have effect as if it were a reference to six months.

(4) In relation to an offence under section 30 committed before the commencement of section 281(4) and (5) of the Criminal Justice Act 2003 (51 week maximum term of sentences) the reference in section 30(2)(*a*) to 51 weeks shall have effect as if it were a reference to six months.

(5) In relation to an offence under section 31 committed before the commencement of section 281(4) and (5) of the Criminal Justice Act 2003 (51 week maximum term of sentences) the reference in section 31(2)(*a*) to 51 weeks shall have effect as if it were a reference to one month.

(6) In relation to an offence under section 32 committed before the commencement of section 281(4) and (5) of the Criminal Justice Act 2003 (51 week maximum term of sentences) the reference in section 32(2)(*a*) to 51 weeks shall have effect as if it were a reference to six months.

(7) In relation to an offence under section 40 committed before the commencement of section 282 of the Criminal Justice Act 2003 (short sentences) the reference in section 40(7)(*b*) to 12 months shall have effect as if it were a reference to six months.

56 Extent

(1) This Act extends to the United Kingdom.

(2) But an amendment, modification or repeal effected by this Act has the same extent as the enactment (or the relevant part of the enactment) to which it relates.

57 Short title

This Act may be cited as the Commissioners for Revenue and Customs Act 2005.

SCHEDULES

SCHEDULE 1

FORMER INLAND REVENUE MATTERS

Section 7

Order—See the Commissioners for Revenue and Customs Act 2005 (Commencement) Order, SI 2005/1126, art 2(2) (this Schedule and s 7 came into force on 18 April 2005).

1 Capital gains tax.

2 Charities.

3 Child benefit.

4 Child tax credit.

5 Child trust funds.

6 Corporation tax (and amounts assessable or chargeable as if they were corporation tax).

7 Guardian's allowance.

8 Income tax.

9 Inheritance tax.

10 The issue of bank notes.

11 National insurance contributions.

12 The National Insurance Fund.

13 The national minimum wage.

14 Oil and gas royalties.

15 Payment of or in lieu of rates.

16 Payment in lieu of tax reliefs, in so far as the Commissioners of Inland Revenue were responsible before the commencement of section 5.

17 Pension schemes.

18 Petroleum revenue tax.

19 Rating lists.

20 Recovery of taxes due in other member States, in relation to matters corresponding to those for which the Commissioners of Inland Revenue were responsible before the commencement of section 5.

21 Stamp duty.

22 Stamp duty land tax.

23 Stamp duty reserve tax.

24 Statutory adoption pay.

25 Statutory maternity pay.

26 Statutory paternity pay.

Prospective amendments—Paragraphs 26, 26A to be substituted for paragraph 26 by the Work and Families Act 2006 s 11(1), Sch 1 para 61 with effect from a date to be appointed.

Paragraphs 26, 26A as substituted to read as follows—

"**26** Ordinary statutory paternity pay.

26A Additional statutory paternity pay.".

27 Statutory sick pay.

28 Student loans.

29 Valuation lists in relation to council tax.

30 Valuation of property.

VAT

31 Working tax credit.

SCHEDULE 2

FUNCTIONS OF COMMISSIONERS AND OFFICERS: RESTRICTIONS, &C

Sections 16 and 17

PART 1

GENERAL

Order—See the Commissioners for Revenue and Customs Act 2005 (Commencement) Order, SI 2005/1126, art 2(2) (Part 1 of this Schedule and s 16 came into force on 18 April 2005).

[Wireless Telegraphy Act 2006 (c 36)][1]

1 The Commissioners may not give [an authority for the purposes of section 48 of the Wireless Telegraphy Act 2006 (interception, &c)][1] *in connection with a function relating to a matter to which section 7 above applies.*[2]

Amendments—[1] Heading and words substituted by the Wireless Telegraphy Act 2006, s 123, Sch 7, para 38(*a*), (*b*) with effect from 8 February 2007.

[2] Para 1 repealed by the Serious Crime Act 2007 ss 88, 92, Sch 12 para 30, Sch 14 with effect from 15 February 2008: SI 2008/219 art 2(*b*).

Taxes Management Act 1970 (c 9)

2 A power under any of the following provisions of the Taxes Management Act 1970 may be exercised only in connection with functions relating to matters to which section 6 above applies—

(*a*) section 21 (stock jobbers' transactions),
(*b*) section 23 (copies of registers of securities), and
(*c*) section 24 (information about income from securities).

3 Section 113(3) of that Act (form of documents) shall have effect only in connection with functions relating to matters to which section 7 above applies.

Customs and Excise Management Act 1979 (c 2)

4 Section 8(2) and (3) of the Customs and Excise Management Act 1979 (person acting deemed to be proper officer) shall not apply to a person engaged in connection with a function relating to a matter to which section 7 above applies.

5— (1) Section 11 of that Act (assistance to be rendered by police, &c) shall not apply in connection with a function relating to a matter to which section 7 above applies.

(2) A person may rely for the purposes of section 11 of that Act on a statement (written or oral) of an officer of Revenue and Customs that a function does not relate to a matter to which section 7 above applies.

6 Sections 167 (untrue declarations, &c) and 168 (counterfeiting documents, &c) of that Act shall not apply in relation to a declaration, document or statement in respect of a function relating to a matter to which section 7 above applies.

Police and Criminal Evidence Act 1984 (c 60)

7— (1) Section 114 of the Police and Criminal Evidence Act 1984 (application of Act to customs and excise) shall not apply to investigations in connection with a matter to which section 7 above applies.

(2) Section 7(4) above shall not have effect in relation to a function conferred by order under section 114 of that Act.[1]

Amendments—[1] This paragraph repealed by FA 2007 ss 84(1)(*a*), (5), 114, Sch 27 Pt 5(1) with effect from 8 November 2007: SI 2007/3166 art 2(*c*).

Finance Act 1985 (c 54)

8 Section 10 of the Finance Act 1985 (computer records &c) shall not apply in connection with a function relating to a matter to which section 7 above applies.

Police and Criminal Evidence (Northern Ireland) Order 1989 (SI 1989/1341 (NI 12))

9— *(1) Article 85 of the Police and Criminal Evidence (Northern Ireland) Order 1989 (application to customs and excise) shall not apply to investigations in connection with a matter to which section 7 above applies.*

(2) Section 7(4) above shall not have effect in relation to a function conferred by order under Article 85 of that Order.[1]

Amendments—[1] This paragraph repealed by FA 2007 ss 84(1)(*b*), (5), 114, Sch 27 Pt 5(1) with effect from 8 November 2007: SI 2007/3166 art 2(*c*).

Finance Act 1998 (c 36)

10 (*amends* FA 1998 s 163(1)).

Regulation of Investigatory Powers Act 2000 (c 23)

11— (1) Action may not be taken by or on behalf of the Commissioners under or by virtue of the following provisions of the Regulation of Investigatory Powers Act 2000 in connection with a function relating to a matter to which section 7 above applies.

(2) Those provisions are—

(a) section 6(2)(h) (application for issue of an interception warrant),
(b) section 32(6)(m) (designation of officers in relation to intrusive surveillance),
(c) section 49(1)(e) and paragraphs 2(3) and 4(2) of Schedule 2 (disclosure: permission), and
(d) section 54 (secrecy).[1]

Amendments—[1] Para 11 repealed by the Serious Crime Act 2007 ss 88, 92, Sch 12 para 30, Sch 14 with effect from 15 February 2008: SI 2008/219 art 2(*b*).

Finance Act 2002 (c 23)

12— (*amended* FA 2002 s 135(10); *repealed by* FA 2007 s 14, Sch 7 Pt 5(4)).

Proceeds of Crime Act 2002 (c 29)

13 The power in section 294 of the Proceeds of Crime Act 2002 (to seize cash)—

(*a*) shall vest in an officer of Revenue and Customs only in so far as he is exercising a function relating to a matter to which section 7 above does not apply, but
(*b*) may be exercised by the officer in reliance on a suspicion that relates to a matter to which section 7 above applies.

[**13A** The powers conferred on an officer of Revenue and Customs by virtue of section 352(5)(*c*), 353(10)(*c*), 356(11)(*b*) or 378(3A)(*b*) of the Act of 2002 (powers in relation to search and seizure warrants and production orders) are exercisable only in relation to cash seized in accordance with paragraph 13 above by an officer of Revenue and Customs under section 294 of that Act.][1]

Amendments—[1] Para 13A inserted by the Serious Crime Act 2007 s 77, Sch 10 para 28 with effect from 6 April 2008: SI 2008/755 art 17(1)(*d*)(iv) subject to transitional provisions and savings in SI 2008/755 art 3.

Crime (International Co-operation) Act 2003 (c 32)

14 *An order under section 27 of the Crime (International Co-operation) Act 2003 (exercise of Secretary of State's powers by others) shall not permit the exercise of a power by the Commissioners in relation to a matter—*

(a) to which section 7 above applies, or
(b) which corresponds, in relation to a country other than the United Kingdom, to a matter to which section 7 above applies.[1]

Amendments—[1] This para repealed by the Criminal Justice and Immigration Act 2008 ss 97(2), 149, Sch 28 Pt 6 with effect from 14 July 2008 (by virtue of SI 2008/1586 art 2(1), Sch 1 paras 41, 50(1), (6)).

PART 2

USE OF INFORMATION

Teaching and Higher Education Act 1998 (c 30)

15 The Commissioners may supply information in accordance with section 24 of the Teaching and Higher Education Act 1998 (supply of information in connection with the student loan scheme) only if the information was obtained or is held in the exercise of a function relating to matters to which section 7 above applies.

Employment Relations Act 1999 (c 26)

16 The Commissioners may supply information in accordance with section 39 of the Employment Relations Act 1999 (supply of information in connection with the national minimum wage and agricultural wages) only if the information was obtained or is held in the exercise of a function relating to matters to which section 7 above applies.

Immigration and Asylum Act 1999 (c 33)

17 *The Commissioners may supply information under section 20 of the Immigration and Asylum Act 1999 (supply of information to the Secretary of State) if the information has not been held solely in the exercise of its functions relating to matters to which section 7 above applies.*[1]

Amendments—[1] Para 17 repealed by the UK Borders Act 2007 ss 40(6)(*c*), 58, Schedule, with effect from 31 January 2008 (by virtue of SI 2008/99 art 2(*m*)).

Financial Services and Markets Act 2000 (c 8)

18 The Commissioners may supply information in accordance with section 350 of the Financial Services and Markets Act 2000 (supply of information to assist with an investigation under section 168 of that Act) only if the information was obtained or is held in the exercise of a function relating to matters to which section 7 above applies.

Terrorism Act 2000 (c 11)

19 Information may be supplied in accordance with paragraph 4(2) of Schedule 14 to the Terrorism Act 2000 (exercise of officers' powers) only if the information has not been held solely in the exercise of functions relating to matters to which section 7 above applies.

Nationality, Immigration and Asylum Act 2002 (c 41)

20 *The Commissioners may supply information to the Secretary of State under section 130 of the Nationality, Immigration and Asylum Act 2002 (power to supply the Secretary of State with information) only if the information was obtained or is held in connection with a function relating to matters to which section 7 above applies.*[1]

Amendments—[1] Para 20 repealed by the UK Borders Act 2007 ss 40(6)(*c*), 58, Schedule, with effect from 31 January 2008 (by virtue of SI 2008/99 art 2(*m*)).

SCHEDULE 3

REVENUE AND CUSTOMS PROSECUTIONS OFFICE

Section 34

Appointment of Director

1 The Director must have a ten year general qualification within the meaning of section 71 of the Courts and Legal Services Act 1990 (c 41) (qualification for judicial appointments).

2 The Director shall hold and vacate office in accordance with the terms of his appointment (which may include provision for dismissal).

Money

3 The Director shall be paid such remuneration, expenses and other allowances as the Attorney General shall determine with the approval of the Minister for the Civil Service.

4 In incurring expenditure the Director shall comply with any directions given to him by the Attorney General with the consent of the Treasury.

5 Expenditure of the Director shall be paid out of money provided by Parliament.

Annual report

6— (1) As soon as is reasonably practicable after the end of each financial year the Director shall send to the Attorney General a report on the exercise of the Director's functions during that year.

(2) A report shall, in particular, give details of—

(*a*) the nature and outcomes of prosecutions undertaken,

(*b*) the criteria used to determine whether to designate individuals under section 39, and

(*c*) the arrangements for training individuals designated under that section.

(3) Where the Attorney General receives a report under sub-paragraph (1) he shall—

(*a*) lay a copy before Parliament, and

(*b*) arrange for it to be published.

Financial year

7— (1) The financial year of the Office shall begin with 1st April and end with 31st March.

(2) But the first financial year of the Office shall—

(*a*) begin with the date on which section 34 comes into force, and

(*b*) end with the following 31st March.

Status

8 Service as the Director or a member of the Office is service in the civil service of the State.

SCHEDULE 4

CONSEQUENTIAL AMENDMENTS, &C

Section 50

Order—See the Commissioners for Revenue and Customs Act 2005 (Commencement) Order, SI 2005/1126, art 2(2) (this Schedule and s 50 came into force on 18 April 2005).

Harbours, Docks, and Piers Clauses Act 1847 (c 27)

1 (*amends* Harbours, Docks and Piers Clauses Act 1847 s 14).

Public Revenue and Consolidated Fund Charges Act 1854 (c 94)

2 (*amends* Public Revenue and Consolidated Fund Charges Act Sch (*b*)).

Exchequer and Audit Departments Act 1866 (c 39)

3 (*amends* Exchequer and Audit Departments Act 1866 s 10).

Game Laws Amendment (Scotland) Act 1877 (c 28)

4 (*amends* Game Laws Amendment (Scotland) Act 1877 s 11).

Inland Revenue Regulation Act 1890 (c 21)

5 (*repeals* Inland Revenue Regulation Act 1890).

Public Accounts and Charges Act 1891 (c 24)

6 (*repeals* Public Accounts and Charges Act 1891)

Judicial Pensions Act (Northern Ireland) 1951 (c 20 (N.I))

7 (*amends* Judicial Pensions Act (Northern Ireland) 1951 Sch 2Apara 6(3) (as inserted by Judicial Pensions (Northern Ireland) Order, SI 1991/2631, Sch 2)).

County Courts Act (Northern Ireland) 1959 (c 25 (NI))

8 (*amends* County Courts Act (Northern Ireland) 1959 Sch 2A para 6(3) (as inserted by Judicial Pensions (Northern Ireland) Order, SI 1991/2631, Sch 2)).

Resident Magistrates' Pensions Act (Northern Ireland) 1960 (c 2 (NI))

9 (*amends* Resident Magistrates' Pensions Act (Northern Ireland) 1960 Sch 3 para 6(3) (as inserted by Judicial Pensions (Northern Ireland) Order, SI 1991/2631, Sch 2)).

Parliamentary Commissioner Act 1967 (c 13)

10 (*amends* Parliamentary Commissioner Act 1967 Sch 2).

Taxes Management Act 1970 (c 9)

11 The Taxes Management Act 1970 shall be amended as follows.

12 (*substitutes* TMA 1970 s 1).

13 (*repeals* TMA 1970 s 6(3), (4)).

14 (*repeals* TMA 1970 s 111(2)).

15 (*amends* TMA 1970 Sch 1 Part 1).

Finance Act 1972 (c 41)

16 (*repeals* FA 1972 s 127).

Biological Weapons Act 1974 (c 6)

17 (*amends* Biological Weapons Act 1974 s 1B).

Health and Safety at Work etc Act 1974 (c 37)

18— (1) Section 27A of the Health and Safety at Work etc Act 1974 (disclosure by Commissioners of Customs and Excise) shall be amended as follows.

(2) (*amends* Health and Safety at Work etc Act 1974 s 27A(1)).

(3) (*amends* Health and Safety at Work etc Act 1974 s 27A(3)).

(4) (*amends* heading to Health and Safety at Work etc Act 1974 s 27A).

Health and Safety at Work (Northern Ireland) Order 1978 (SI 1978/1039 (NI 9))

19— (1) Article 29A of the Health and Safety at Work (Northern Ireland) Order 1978 (disclosure by Commissioners of Customs and Excise) shall be amended as follows.

(2) (*amends* Health and Safety at Work (Northern Ireland) Order 1978 art 29A(1)).

(3) (*amends* Health and Safety at Work (Northern Ireland) Order 1978 art 29A(3)).

(4) (*amends* heading to Health and Safety at Work (Northern Ireland) Order 1978 art 29A).

Customs and Excise Management Act 1979 (c 2)

20 The Customs and Excise Management Act 1979 shall be amended as follows.

21 (*repeals* CEMA 1979 ss 6, 7, 8(1), 13, 14, 16, 17, 18, 153, 155(2), 165).

22 (*amends* CEMA 1979 s 1(1)).

23 (*amends* CEMA 1979 s 145(1), (2), (4), (6)).

24 (*amends* CEMA 1979 s 146A(7)).

25 (*amends* CEMA 1979 s 150(1)).

26 (*amends* CEMA 1979 s 152(*a*)).
27 (*substitutes* CEMA 1979 s 155(1)).
28 (*inserts* CEMA 1979 s 171(4A)).

Judicial Pensions Act 1981 (*c 20*)

29 (*amends* Judicial Pensions Act 1981 Sch 1A para 6(3)).

Police and Criminal Evidence Act 1984 (*c 60*)

30 Sections 37 to 37B of the Police and Criminal Evidence Act 1984 (guidance, &c) shall have effect, in relation to a person arrested following a criminal investigation by the Revenue and Customs, as if references to the Director of Public Prosecutions were references to the Director of Revenue and Customs Prosecutions.
31 (*repeals* PACE 1984 s114(4)).

Debtors (*Scotland*) *Act 1987* (*c 18*)

32 The Debtors (Scotland) Act 1987 shall be amended as follows.
33 (*amends* Debtors (Scotland) Act 1987 s 1(5)(*d*)).
34 (*amends* Debtors (Scotland) Act 1987 s 5(4)(*d*)).

Criminal Justice Act 1987 (*c 38*)

35— (1) (*amends* CJA 1987 s 3(1), (2)).
(2) (*inserts* CJA 1987 s 3(8)).

Consumer Protection Act 1987 (*c 43*)

36— (1) Section 37 of the Consumer Protection Act 1987 (disclosure by Commissioners of Customs and Excise) shall be amended as follows.
(2) (*amends* Consumer Protection Act 1987 s 37(1)).
(3) (*amends* Consumer Protection Act 1987 s 37(3)).
(4) (*amends* heading to Consumer Protection Act 1987 s 37).

Income and Corporation Taxes Act 1988 (*c 1*)

37 (*amends* TA 1988 s 816 and *is repealed* in part by FA 2006 s 178, Sch 26 Pt 8(2)).

Copyright, Designs and Patents Act 1988 (*c 48*)

38 (*repeals* Copyright, Designs and Patents Act 1988 s 112(5)).

Finance Act 1989 (*c 26*)

39 (*inserts* FA 1989 s 182(10A)).

Police and Criminal Evidence (*Northern Ireland*) *Order 1989* (*SI 1989/1341* (*NI 12*))

40 (*repeals* Police and Criminal Evidence (Northern Ireland) Order 1989 art 85(3)).

Criminal Justice (*International Co-operation*) *Act 1990* (*c 5*)

41 (*amends* Criminal Justice (International Co-operation) Act 1990 s 21(2)(*a*)).

Child Support Act 1991 (*c 48*)

42 (*amends* Child Support Act 1991 Sch 2).

Social Security Contributions and Benefits Act 1992 (*c 4*)

43 (*amends* Social Security Contributions and Benefits Act 1992 s 171).

Social Security Administration Act 1992 (*c 5*)

44 The Social Security Administration Act 1992 shall be amended as follows.
45 (*amends* Social Security Administration Act 1992 s 122ZA).
46 (*amends* Social Security Administration Act 1992 s 122AA).
47 (*substitutes* Social Security Administration Act 1992 s 161(1)).

Social Security Contributions and Benefits (*Northern Ireland*) *Act 1992* (*c 7*)

48 (*amends* Social Security Contributions and Benefits (Northern Ireland) Act 1992 s 167(1)).

Social Security Administration (*Northern Ireland*) *Act 1992* (*c 8*)

49 (*amends* Social Security Administration (Northern Ireland) Act 1992 s 116ZA).
50 (*amends* Social Security Administration (Northern Ireland) Act 1992 s 116AA).

Pension Schemes Act 1993 (c 48)

51 (*amends* Pension Schemes Act 1993 s 158).

Pension Schemes (Northern Ireland) Act 1993 (c 49)

52 (*amends* Pension Schemes (Northern Ireland) Act 1993 s 154).

Finance Act 1994 (c 9)

53 (*repeals* FA 1994 Sch 7 para 32).

Value Added Tax Act 1994 (c 23)

54 The Value Added Tax Act 1994 shall be amended as follows.

55 (*substitutes* VATA 1994 Sch 3B para 21(1)(*b*)).

56 (*substitutes* VATA 1994 Sch 11 para 1).

Trade Marks Act 1994 (c 26)

57 (*repeals* Trade Marks Act 1994 s 90(5)).

58— (1) (*amends* Trade Marks Act 1994 s 91).

(2) (*amends* heading to Trade Marks Act 1994 s 91).

Drug Trafficking Act 1994 (c 37)

59 (*amends* Drug Trafficking Act 1994 s 60).

Finance Act 1995 (c 4)

60 (*repeals* FA 1995 s 158).

Merchant Shipping Act 1995 (c 21)

61 (*repeals* Merchant Shipping Act 1995 s 303).

Criminal Appeal Act 1995 (c 35)

62 (*substitutes* Criminal Appeal Act 1995 s 22(4)(*e*), (*f*)).

Criminal Law (Consolidation) (Scotland) Act 1995 (c 39)

63— (1) Section 30 of the Criminal Law (Consolidation) (Scotland) Act 1995 (disclosure of information) shall be amended as follows.

(2) (*amends* Criminal Law (Consolidation) (Scotland) Act 1995 s 30(1)).

(3) (*amends* Criminal Law (Consolidation) (Scotland) Act 1995 s 30(2)).

(4) (*inserts* Criminal Law (Consolidation) (Scotland) Act 1995 s 30(7)).

Chemical Weapons Act 1996 (c 6)

64 (*amends* Chemical Weapons Act 1996 s 30A).

Finance Act 1996 (c 8)

65 (*repeals* FA 1996 Sch 5 para 41).

Landmines Act 1998 (c 33)

66 (*amends* Landmines Act 1998 s 21).

Finance Act 1998 (c 36)

67 (*repeals* FA 1998 s 145).

68 Schedule 18 to that Act (company tax returns &c) shall have effect—

(*a*) with the substitution for "the Inland Revenue", in each place, of "an officer of Revenue and Customs",

(*b*) with the omission of paragraph 95 (meaning of references to Inland Revenue), and

(*c*) with any other necessary consequential modifications.

Crime and Disorder Act 1998 (c 37)

69 (*substitutes* Crime and Disorder Act 1998 s 51B(9)(*c*)).

Scotland Act 1998 (c 46)

70 The Scotland Act 1998 shall be amended as follows.

71 (*amends* Scotland Act 1988 s 77).

72 (*repeals* Scotland Act 1998 s 78(8)).

Social Security Contributions (Transfer of Functions, etc) Act 1999 (c 2)

73 The Social Security Contributions (Transfer of Functions etc) Act 1999 shall be amended as follows.

74 (*substitutes* Social Security Contributions (Transfer of Functions etc) Act 1999 s 3(1)).

75 (*repeals* Social Security Contributions (Transfer of Functions etc) Act 1999 s 7).

Finance Act 1999 (c 16)

76 (*amends* FA 1999 s 135(2)).

Crown Prosecution Service Inspectorate Act 2000 (c 10)

77 (*inserts* Crown Prosecution Service Inspectorate Act 2000 s 2(4)).

Terrorism Act 2000 (c 11)

78 (*amends* Terrorism Act 2000 s 121).

Finance Act 2000 (c 17)

79 The Finance Act 2000 shall be amended as follows.

80 (*repeals* FA 2000 s 148(2)).

81 (*repeals* FA 2000 Sch 6 para 140).

Capital Allowances Act 2001 (c 2)

82 The Capital Allowances Act 2001 shall be amended as follows.

83— (1) For "the Inland Revenue", wherever that expression appears, substitute "an officer of Revenue and Customs" (except as provided in paragraph 84).

(2) For "the Board of Inland Revenue", wherever that expression appears, substitute "the Commissioners for Her Majesty's Revenue and Customs".

84 (amends CAA 2001 s 51).

Amendments—This para repealed by FA 2008 s 76(6) with effect from 21 July 2008.

85 (*repeals* CAA 2001 s 576).

86 (*amends* CAA 2001 Sch 1 Part 2).

Anti-terrorism, Crime and Security Act 2001 (c 24)

87 (*amends* Anti-terrorism, Crime and Security Act s 53).

Tax Credits Act 2002 (c 21)

88 (*substitutes* TCA 2002 s 2).

89 (*repeals* TCA 2002 s 40(1)(*a*)).

90 (*substitutes* TCA 2002 s 53).

91 (*repeals* TCA 2002 Sch 5 para 2).

92 To the extent that the Tax Credits Act 1999 (c 10) is saved by the Tax Credits Act 2002 (Commencement No 4, Transitional and Savings) Order 2003 (SI 2003/962), the modifications made by paragraphs 88 to 91 shall have effect in relation to the relevant provisions of that Act as they have effect in relation to the Tax Credits Act 2002 (c 21).

Employment Act 2002 (c 22)

93 (*repeals* Employment Act 2002 s 5).

Finance Act 2002 (c 23)

94 The Finance Act 2002 shall be amended as follows.

95— (1) (*amends* FA 2002 s 135).

(2) (*repealed by* FA 2007 s 114, Sch 27 Pt 5(4)).

96 (*repeals* FA 2002 Sch 13 para 26).

Proceeds of Crime Act 2002 (c 29)

97 (*substitutes* Proceeds of Crime Act 2002 s 72(9)).

98 (*inserted* Proceeds of Crime Act 2002 s 436(5)(*ga*); repealed by the Serious Crime Act 2007 Sch 14 with effect from 1 April 2008: SI 2008/755 art 2(1)(*d*)).

99 (*amends* Proceeds of Crime Act 2002 s 451).

100 In Schedule 8 to that Act (declarations) for "an offence relating to inland revenue,", in each place, substitute "an offence relating to a former Inland Revenue matter (being a matter listed in Schedule 1 to the Commissioners for Revenue and Customs Act 2005 except for paragraphs 2, 10, 13, 14, 15, 17, 19, 28, 29 and 30),".

Income Tax (Earnings and Pensions) Act 2003 (c 1)

101 The Income Tax (Earnings and Pensions) Act 2003 shall be amended as follows.

102— (1) For the expression "the Inland Revenue", wherever it appears, substitute "an officer of Revenue and Customs" (except as provided in paragraphs 109, 117 and 118).

(2) For the expression "the Board of Inland Revenue", wherever it appears, substitute "the Commissioners for Her Majesty's Revenue and Customs".

(3) In the following provisions for "Board" substitute "Commissioners" and for "Board's" substitute "Commissioners'"—

(*a*) section 28(6),
(*b*)–(*d*) …
(*e*) section 343,
(*f*) section 355,
(*g*) section 594,
(*h*) section 647,
(*i*) section 691,
(*j*) section 703,
(*k*) section 704, and
(*l*) the title of section 717.

Amendments—Sub-para (3)(*b*)–(*d*) repealed by FA 2008 s 25, Sch 7 para 79(*c*) with effect for the tax year 2008–09 and subsequent tax years.

103— (1) In the following provisions for "they" or "them" in each place substitute "the officer"—

(*a*) section 58(3),
(*b*) section 65(3),
(*c*) section 79(2),
(*d*) section 96(2),
(*e*) section 179(3),
(*f*) section 312(5),
(*g*) section 344(3),
(*h*) section 392(4) and (5),
(*i*) section 421J(4),
(*j*) paragraph 81(1) and (3) of Schedule 2,
(*k*) paragraph 84(2) of Schedule 2,
(*l*) paragraph 85(1) of Schedule 2,
(*m*) paragraph 93(1) of Schedule 2,
(*n*) paragraph 40(1) and (3) of Schedule 3,
(*o*) paragraph 42(2A) of Schedule 3,
(*p*) paragraph 43 of Schedule 3,
(*q*) paragraph 44(1) of Schedule 3,
(*r*) paragraph 45(1) of Schedule 3,
(*s*) paragraph 28(1) and (3) of Schedule 4,
(*t*) paragraph 30(3) of Schedule 4,
(*u*) paragraph 31 of Schedule 4,
(*v*) paragraph 32(1) of Schedule 4,
(*w*) paragraph 33(1) of Schedule 4,
(*x*) paragraph 46(2) of Schedule 5,
(*y*) paragraph 46(3) of Schedule 5,
(*z*) paragraph 47 of Schedule 5, and
(*aa*) paragraph 51(1) of Schedule 5.

(2) In the following provisions for "their" in each place substitute "the officer's"—

(*a*) section 715(3)(*b*),
(*b*) paragraph 85(3) of Schedule 2,
(*c*) paragraph 93(1)(*a*) of Schedule 2,
(*d*) paragraph 41(2) of Schedule 3,
(*e*) paragraph 44(3) of Schedule 3,
(*f*) paragraph 45(1) of Schedule 3,
(*g*) paragraph 29(2) of Schedule 4,
(*h*) paragraph 32(3) of Schedule 4,
(*i*) paragraph 33(1) of Schedule 4,
(*j*) paragraph 46(2) and (3) of Schedule 5,
(*k*) paragraph 47(1)(*b*) and (3)(*b*) of Schedule 5,
(*l*) paragraph 49(2) and (3) of Schedule 5, and
(*m*) paragraph 51(1) of Schedule 5.

(3) In the following provisions in each place for "their" substitute "the"—

(*a*) paragraph 81(3) of Schedule 2,
(*b*) paragraph 82(2) of Schedule 2,
(*c*) paragraph 85(3) of Schedule 2,
(*d*) paragraph 40(3) of Schedule 3,

(*e*) paragraph 43 of Schedule 3,
(*f*) paragraph 28(3) of Schedule 4,
(*g*) paragraph 31 of Schedule 4, and
(*h*) paragraph 47(1)(*a*) and (3)(*a*) of Schedule 5.

(4) In the following provisions omit "their"—

(*a*) paragraph 84(2) of Schedule 2,
(*b*) paragraph 42(2A) of Schedule 3, and
(*c*) paragraph 30(3) of Schedule 4.

104 …

Amendments—Para 104 repealed by FA 2008 s 25, Sch 7 para 79(*c*) with effect for the tax year 2008–09 and subsequent tax years.

105 In section 58(3) for "are" substitute "is".

106 In section 65—

(*a*) in subsection (3) for "are" substitute "is", and
(*b*) in subsection (4) for "agree" substitute "agrees".

107 In section 79(2) for "are" substitute "is".

108 In section 96—

(*a*) in subsection (2) for "are" substitute "is", and
(*b*) in subsection (3) for "agree" substitute "agrees".

109 In section 179(3) for "the Inland Revenue are" substitute "an officer of Revenue and Customs is".

110 In section 183(1)(*a*) for "require" substitute "requires".

111 In section 312(5) for "have" substitute "has".

112 In section 344(3) for "are satisfied" substitute "is satisfied".

113 In section 392(4) and (5) for "are satisfied" substitute "is satisfied".

114 In section 511(2)—

(*a*) in paragraph (*a*) for "are" substitute "is", and
(*b*) in paragraph (*b*) for "direct" substitute "directs".

115 In section 514(2)—

(*a*) in paragraph (*a*) for "are" substitute "is", and
(*b*) in paragraph (*b*) for "direct" substitute "directs".

116 In section 647(3)(*b*) for "is" substitute "are".

117 In section 684, in paragraph 8 of the list of provisions for "the Board or the Inland Revenue" substitute "Her Majesty's Revenue and Customs".

118 In section 715(3)(*b*) for "Inland Revenue's refusal to approve" substitute "a refusal by an officer of Revenue and Customs to approve".

119 Section 720 (meaning of "Inland Revenue", &c) shall cease to have effect.

120 In Part 2 of Schedule 1, omit the entries for "the Board of Inland Revenue" and "the Inland Revenue".

121 In Schedule 2—

(*a*) in paragraph 81—
  (i) in sub-paragraph (1), for "are" substitute "is", and
  (ii) in sub-paragraph (3), for "have" substitute "has",
(*b*) in paragraph 82(1) for "refuse" substitute "refuses",
(*c*) in paragraph 85(1) for "decide" substitute "decides",
(*d*) in paragraph 93(1)(*a*) for "require" substitute "requires", and
(*e*) in paragraph 100, omit the entries for "the Board of Inland Revenue" and "the Inland Revenue".

122 In Schedule 3—

(*a*) in paragraph 40—
  (i) in sub-paragraph (1) for "are" substitute "is", and
  (ii) in sub-paragraph (3) for "have" substitute "has",
(*b*) in paragraph 41(1) for "refuse" substitute "refuses",
(*c*) in paragraph 43 for "have" in each place substitute "has",
(*d*) in paragraph 44(1) for "decide" in each place substitute "decides",
(*e*) in paragraph 45(1) for "require" substitute "requires", and
(*f*) in paragraph 49 of Schedule 3, omit the entry for "the Inland Revenue".

123 In Schedule 4—

(*a*) in paragraph 28—
  (i) in sub-paragraph (1) for "are" substitute "is", and
  (ii) in sub-paragraph (3) for "have" substitute "has",
(*b*) in paragraph 29(1) for "refuse" substitute "refuses",
(*c*) in paragraph 31 for "have" in each place substitute "has",

(*d*) in paragraph 32(1) for "decide" in each place substitute "decides",
(*e*) in paragraph 33(1)(*a*) for "require" substitute "requires", and
(*f*) in paragraph 37 omit the entry for "the Inland Revenue".

124 In Schedule 5—

(*a*) in paragraph 46—
(i) in sub-paragraphs (2) and (3) for "give" substitute "gives", and
(ii) in sub-paragraph (6) for "discover" substitute "discovers",
(*b*) in paragraph 47—
(i) in sub-paragraph (1) for "give" substitute "gives" and for "have" substitute "has",
(ii) in sub-paragraph (2) for "conclude" substitute "concludes", and
(iii) in sub-paragraph (3) for "give" substitute "gives" and for "have" substitute "has",
(*c*) in paragraph 48(5) for "have" substitute "has",
(*d*) in paragraph 49(1) and (2) for "do" substitute "does",
(*e*) in paragraph 51(1)(*a*) for "require" substitute "requires", and
(*f*) in paragraph 59 omit the entry for "the Inland Revenue".

Finance Act 2003 (*c 14*)

125 The Finance Act 2003 shall be amended as follows.

126 (*amends* FA 2003 s 129(6)).

127 (*amends* FA 2003 s 130(6)).

Dealing in Cultural Objects (*Offences*) *Act 2003* (*c 27*)

128 (*amends* Dealing in Cultural Objects (Offences) Act 2003 s 4).

Criminal Justice Act 2003 (*c 44*)

129 (*amends* Criminal Justice Act 2003 s 27).

130 (*inserts* Criminal Justice Act 2003 s 29(5)(*ca*)).

Income Tax (*Trading and Other Income*) *Act 2005* (*c 5*)

131 The Income Tax (Trading and Other Income) Act 2005 shall be amended as follows.

132— (1) For the expression "the Inland Revenue", wherever it appears, substitute "an officer of Revenue and Customs" (except as provided by paragraph 133(2)(*b*) and (5)).

(2) For the expression "the Board of Inland Revenue", wherever it appears, substitute "the Commissioners for Her Majesty's Revenue and Customs".

(3) In the following provisions, for "Board" substitute "Commissioners" and for "Board's" substitute "Commissioners'"—

(*a*) the title of section 343,
(*b*) section 695(4),
(*c*) section 698(3) and (4),
(*d*) section 699(2),
(*e*) section 700(1)(*b*), (2) and (5),
(*f*) section 757(3),
(*g*) section 762(2),
(*h*) the title of section 873, and
(*i*) section 883(3).

133— (1) In section 75(5)—

(*a*) for "have" substitute "has", and
(*b*) in each place for "they" substitute "the officer".

(2) In section 218—

(*a*) in subsections (1) and (2) for "do" substitute "does", and
(*b*) in subsection (3)(*a*) for "the Inland Revenue are not" substitute "the officer is not".

(3) In section 305(1) for "have" substitute "has".

(4) In section 647(1)

(*a*) for "them" substitute "the officer",
(*b*) for "they" in each place substitute "the officer", and
(*c*) for "consider" substitute "considers".

[(5) In section 723(2) for "the Inland Revenue's determination" substitute "the officer's determination".][1]

(6) In section 758(5) for "has" substitute "have" '.

Amendments—[1] Sub-para (5) repealed by FA 2007 s 114, Sch 27 Pt 2(13) with effect from 6 April 2008 (by virtue of FA 2007, ss 46(9), 114, Sch 27, Pt 2(13), SI 2008/561 art 2).

134— (1) In section 878(1), omit the definitions of "the Board of Inland Revenue" and "the Inland Revenue".

(2) In Part 2 of Schedule 4, omit the entries for "the Board of Inland Revenue" and "the Inland Revenue".

SCHEDULE 5
REPEALS

Section 52

Order—See the Commissioners for Revenue and Customs Act 2005 (Commencement) Order, SI 2005/1126, art 2(2) (this Schedule and s 52 came into force on 18 April 2005).

Short title and chapter	*Extent of repeal*
Public Revenue and Consolidated Fund Charges Act 1854 (c 94)	In Schedule (b), the entry relating to the Inland Revenue.
Exchequer and Audit Departments Act 1866 (c 39)	In section 10, the words from the beginning to "at the Bank of England" and the proviso.
Inland Revenue Regulation Act 1890 (c 21)	The whole Act.
Public Accounts and Charges Act 1891 (c 24)	The whole Act.
Parliamentary Commissioner Act 1967 (c 13)	In Schedule 2, the entries relating to the Inland Revenue and Customs and Excise.
Taxes Management Act 1970 (c 9)	Section 6(3) and (4).
	Section 111(2).
	Parts II and III of Schedule 1.
Finance Act 1972 (c 41)	Section 127.
Biological Weapons Act 1974 (c 6)	Section 1B(6).
Customs and Excise Management Act 1979 (c 2)	Sections 6 and 7.
	Section 8(1).
	Sections 12 to 18.
	Section 32.
	Section 84.
	Section 86.
	Section 145(4).
	In section 152(*a*), the words "stay, sist or".
	Paragraphs (*c*) and (*d*) of section 152.
	Section 153.
	Section 155(2).
	Section 165.
	Section 169.
Police and Criminal Evidence Act 1984 (c 60)	Section 114(4).
Copyright, Designs and Patents Act 1988 (c 48)	Section 112(5).
Police and Criminal Evidence (Northern Ireland) Order 1989 (SI 1989/1341 (NI 12))	Article 85(3).
Finance Act 1994 (c 9)	Paragraph 32 of Schedule 7.
Trade Marks Act 1994 (c 26)	Section 90(5).
Drug Trafficking Act 1994 (c 37)	In section 60—
	(a) subsection (3), and
	(b) in subsection (6), the definition of "officer".
Finance Act 1995 (c 4)	Section 158.
Merchant Shipping Act 1995 (c 21)	Section 303.
Chemical Weapons Act 1996 (c 6)	Section 30A(6).
Finance Act 1996 (c 8)	Paragraph 41 of Schedule 5.
Landmines Act 1998 (c 33)	Section 21(3) and (6).
Finance Act 1998 (c 36)	Section 145.
	Paragraph 95 of Schedule 18.
Scotland Act 1998 (c 46)	Section 77(8).
	Section 78(8).

Short title and chapter	*Extent of repeal*
Social Security Contributions (Transfer of Functions, etc) Act 1999 (c 2)	Section 7.
Finance Act 2000 (c 17)	Section 148(2). Paragraph 140 of Schedule 6.
Capital Allowances Act 2001 (c 2)	Section 576. In Part 2 of Schedule 1, the entries for "the Board of Inland Revenue" and "the Inland Revenue".
Anti-terrorism, Crime and Security Act 2001 (c 24)	Section 53(6).
Tax Credits Act 2002 (c 21)	Section 40(1)(*a*). Paragraph 2 of Schedule 5.
Employment Act 2002 (c 22)	Section 5.
Finance Act 2002 (c 23)	Paragraph 26 of Schedule 13.
Proceeds of Crime Act 2002 (c 29)	Section 451(3).
Income Tax (Earnings and Pensions) Act 2003 (c 1)	Section 720. In Part 2 of Schedule 1, the entries for "the Board of Inland Revenue" and "the Inland Revenue". In paragraph 84(2) of Schedule 2, the word "their". In paragraph 100 of Schedule 2, the entries for "the Board of Inland Revenue" and "the Inland Revenue". In paragraph 42(2A) of Schedule 3, the word "their". In paragraph 49 of Schedule 3, the entry for "the Inland Revenue". In paragraph 30(3) of Schedule 4, the word "their". In paragraph 37 of Schedule 4, the entry for "the Inland Revenue". In paragraph 59 of Schedule 5, the entry for "the Inland Revenue".
Dealing in Cultural Objects (Offences) Act 2003 (c 27)	Section 4(6).
Criminal Justice Act 2003 (c 44)	In section 27, in the definition of "relevant prosecutor", items (e) and (f).
Income Tax (Trading and Other Income) Act 2005 (c 5)	In section 878(1), the definitions of "the Board of Inland Revenue" and "the Inland Revenue". In Part 2 of Schedule 4, the entries for "the Board of Inland Revenue" and "the Inland Revenue".

FINANCE (NO 2) ACT 2005

(2005 Chapter 22)

An Act to Grant certain duties, to alter other duties, and to amend the law relating to the National Debt and the Public Revenue, and to make further provision in connection with finance.

[20 July 2005]

PART 1
VALUE ADDED TAX

1 Goods subject to warehousing regime: place of acquisition or supply

(*inserts* VATA 1994 s 18(1A)).

2 Cars: determination of consideration for fuel supplied for private use

(1) Section 57 of VATA 1994 (determination of consideration for fuel supplied for private use) is amended as follows.

(2) (*inserts* VATA 1994 s 57(4A)–(4G)).

(3)–(5) (*amend* VATA 1994 s 57(5), (7), (8)).

(6) (*inserts* VATA 1994 s 57(9), (10)).

(7) The amendments made by this section come into force on such day or days as the Treasury may appoint by order made by statutory instrument; and different days may be so appointed for different purposes.

Orders—Finance (No 2) Act 2005, Section 2(7), (Appointed Day) Order, SI 2007/946 art 2 (appointed day is 22 March 2007).

3 Credit for, or repayment of, overstated or overpaid VAT

(1) Section 80 of VATA 1994 (recovery of overpaid VAT) is amended as follows.

(2) (*substitutes* VATA 1994 s 80(1)–(1B)).

(3) (*amends* VATA 1994 s 80(2)).

(4) (*inserts* VATA 1994 s 80(2A)).

(5) (*amends* VATA 1994 s 80(3)).

(6) (*substitutes* VATA 1994 s 80(3A)).

(7) (*amends* VATA 1994 s 80(3B)).

(8) (*substitutes* VATA 1994 s 80(4)–(4ZB)).

(9) (*substitutes* VATA 1994 s 80(4A)).

(10) (*substitutes* VATA 1994 s 80(7)).

(11) The side-note to the section accordingly becomes "Credit for, or repayment of, overstated or overpaid VAT".

(12) Section 4 contains consequential and supplementary provision.

4 Section 3: consequential and supplementary provision

(1) In consequence of the amendments made by section 3, VATA 1994 is amended as follows.

(2) (*amends* VATA 1994 s 78(1)(*a*)).

(3) (*amends* VATA 1994 s 80A).

(4) (*inserts* VATA 1994 s 80B(1A)–(1E)).

(5) (*amends* VATA 1994 s 83).

(6) The amendments made by section 3 and this section have effect in any case where a claim under section 80(2) of VATA 1994 is made on or after 26th May 2005, whenever the event occurred in respect of which the claim is made.

5 Reverse charge: gas and electricity valuation

(1) (*amends* VATA 1994 Sch 6 para 8).

(2) This section has effect in relation to supplies made on or after 17th March 2005.

6 Disclosure of value added tax avoidance schemes

(1) Schedule 1 (which contains amendments of Schedule 11A to VATA 1994) has effect.

(2) Subsection (1) and Schedule 1 shall come into force on such day as the Treasury may by order made by statutory instrument appoint.

(3) An order under subsection (2) may—

(*a*) appoint different days for different purposes, and

(*b*) contain transitional provisions and savings.

Orders—See the Finance (No 2) Act 2005, section 6, (Appointed Day and Savings Provisions) Order, SI 2005/2010.

PART 6
SUPPLEMENTARY PROVISIONS

70 Repeals

(1) The enactments mentioned in Schedule 11 (which include provisions that are spent or of no practical utility) are repealed to the extent specified.

(2) The repeals specified in that Schedule have effect subject to the commencement provisions and savings contained or referred to in the notes set out in that Schedule.

71 Interpretation

In this Act—

"CAA 2001" means the Capital Allowances Act 2001 (c. 2);
"FA", followed by a year, means the Finance Act of that year;
"ICTA" means the Income and Corporation Taxes Act 1988 (c. 1);
"ITEPA 2003" means the Income Tax (Earnings and Pensions) Act 2003 (c. 1);
"ITTOIA 2005" means the Income Tax (Trading and Other Income) Act 2005 (c. 5);
"TCGA 1992" means the Taxation of Chargeable Gains Act 1992 (c. 12);
"VATA 1994" means the Value Added Tax Act 1994 (c. 23);

"VERA 1994" means the Vehicle Excise and Registration Act 1994 (c. 22).

72 Short title

This Act may be cited as the Finance (No 2) Act 2005.

SCHEDULES

SCHEDULE 1
DISCLOSURE OF VALUE ADDED TAX AVOIDANCE SCHEMES

Section 6

Orders—Finance (No 2) Act 2005, section 6, (Appointed Day and Savings Provisions) Order 2005, SI 2005/2010.

Introduction

1 Schedule 11A to VATA 1994 (disclosure of avoidance schemes) is amended in accordance with this Schedule.

Interpretative provisions

2 (*amends* VATA 1994 Sch 11A para 1).
3 (*substitutes* VATA 1994 Sch 11A para 2).
4 (*inserts* VATA 1994 Sch 11A para 2A).

Duty to notify Commissioners

5— (1) Paragraph 6 (duty to notify Commissioners) is amended as follows.
(2) (*amends* VATA 1994 Sch 11A para 6(1)).
(3) (*inserts* VATA 1994 Sch 11A para 6(2A)).
(4) (*substitutes* VATA 1994 Sch 11A para 6(5)).
6 (*amends* VATA 1994 Sch 11A para 7(9)).

Amount of penalty

7— (1) Paragraph 11 (amount of penalty) is amended as follows.
(2) (*amends* VATA 1994 Sch 11A para 11(3)).
(3) (*amends* VATA 1994 Sch 11A para 11(4)).
(4) (*inserts* VATA 1994 Sch 11A para 11(5)).

Penalty assessments

8 (*substitutes* VATA 1994 Sch 11A para 12(3), (3A)).

SCHEDULE 11
REPEALS

Section 70

PART 1
VALUE ADDED TAX

Note—The repeals made under this Part are already in force and are therefore omitted.

FINANCE ACT 2006

(2006 Chapter 25)

An Act to Grant certain duties, to alter other duties, and to amend the law relating to the National Debt and the Public Revenue, and to make further provision in connection with finance.

[19 July 2006]

PART 2
VALUE ADDED TAX

Gaming machines

16 Gaming machines

(1) Section 23 of VATA 1994 (gaming machines) shall be amended as follows.
(2) (*amends* VATA 1994 s 23(1))

(3) (*amends* VATA 1994 s 23(2))

(4) (*amends* VATA 1994 s 23(3))

(5) (*substitutes* VATA 1994 s 23(4)–(7))

(6) This section shall have effect in relation to anything done on or after 6th December 2005.

(7) In the application of section 23(5)(*c*) of VATA 1994 as substituted by this section in relation to anything done before 1st November 2006, "game of chance" shall have the same meaning as in the Gaming Act 1968 (c 65).

Land

17 Buildings and land

(1) The Treasury may by order—

(*a*) make provision for substituting Schedule 10 to VATA 1994 (buildings and land) for the purpose of rewriting that Schedule with amendments;

(*b*) make provision amending sections 83 and 84 of that Act (appeals) in connection with any provision of that Schedule as so rewritten.

(2) The Treasury may by order make provision repealing—

(*a*) paragraph (*b*) of item 1 in Group 1 of Schedule 9 to VATA 1994 (exempt supplies of land not to include supplies made pursuant to a developmental tenancy, developmental lease or developmental licence), and

(*b*) Note (7) in that Group (meaning of developmental tenancy, developmental lease or developmental licence).

The power conferred by this subsection is not to be regarded as affecting in any way the power to vary Schedule 9 to that Act conferred by section 31(2) of that Act.

(3) The Treasury may by order make provision repealing—

(*a*) section 26 of FA 1995 (co-owners etc of buildings and land), and

(*b*) the enactments inserted by that section (section 51A of VATA 1994 and paragraph 8(2) and (3) of Schedule 10 to that Act).

(4) Any power to make an order under this section includes power—

(*a*) to make any provision that might be made by an Act, and

(*b*) to make incidental, consequential, supplemental, or transitional provision or savings.

(5) The consequential provision that may be made under subsection (4)(*b*) includes provision amending any Act or any instrument made under any Act.

(6) Any order under this section—

(*a*) is to be made by statutory instrument,

(*b*) must be laid before the House of Commons, and

(*c*) unless approved by that House before the end of the period of 28 days beginning with the date on which it is made, ceases to have effect at the end of that period.

(7) But, if an order so ceases to have effect, this does not affect—

(*a*) anything previously done under the order, or

(*b*) the making of a new order.

(8) In reckoning the period of 28 days no account is to be taken of any time—

(*a*) during which Parliament is dissolved or prorogued, or

(*b*) during which the House of Commons is adjourned for more than 4 days.

Orders—VAT (Buildings and Land) Order, SI 2008/1146 (made under sub-ss (1)–(5)).

Imported works of art etc

18 Value of imported works of art etc: auctioneer's commission

(1) Section 21 of VATA 1994 (value of imported goods) is amended as follows.

(2) (*amends* VATA 1994 s 21(2))

(3) (*inserts* VATA 1994 s 21(2A), (2B))

(4) Subsections (1) to (3) come into force on such day as the Treasury may by order made by statutory instrument appoint.

Notes—The appointed day for the purposes of sub-ss (1)–(3) above is 1 September 2006 by virtue of the Finance Act 2006, Section 18, (Appointed Day) Order, SI 2006/2149, art 2.

Avoidance and fraud

19 Missing trader intra-community fraud

(1) (*inserts* VATA 1994 s 55A)

(2) (*inserts* VATA 1994 s 26A)

(3) In section 65 of VATA 1994 (inaccuracies in EC sales statements)—

(*a*) (*inserts* VATA 1994 s 65(7))

(*b*) (*amends* VATA 1994 s 65 heading)

(4) In section 66 of VATA 1994 (failure to submit EC sales statements)—

(*a*) (*inserts* VATA 1994 s 66(10))

(*b*) (*amends* VATA 1994 s 66 heading)

(5) (*inserts* VATA 1994 s 69(1)(*ba*))

(6) (*inserts* VATA 1994 s 97(4)(*ea*))

(7) (*inserts* VATA 1994 Sch 11 para 2(3A), (3B))

(8) The amendments made by this section have effect in relation to supplies made on or after such day as the Treasury may by order made by statutory instrument appoint.

But no order may be made under this subsection on or after 22nd March 2009.

(9) An order under subsection (8) may contain transitional provision and savings.

Order—Finance Act 2006, section 19, (Appointed Day) Order, SI 2007/1419 (appointed day for amendments made by s 19 is 1 June 2007).

20 Power to inspect goods

(*1*) *In Schedule 11 to VATA 1994* (*administration, collection and enforcement*), *paragraph 10* (*entry and search of premises and persons*) *is amended as follows.*

(*2*) (*inserts VATA 1994 Sch 11 para 10(2A)*)

Amendments—This section repealed by FA 2008 s 113, Sch 36 para 92(*i*) with effect from 1 April 2009 (by virtue of SI 2009/404 art 2).

In consequence of SI 2009/404 arts 1–11, the amendments made by FA 2008 Sch 36 para 92 shall be disregarded so far as they affect any notice referred to in those provisions, given on or before 31 March 2009.

21 Directions to keep records where belief VAT might not be paid

(1) VATA 1994 is amended as follows.

(2) (*inserts* VATA 1994 s 69B)

(3) (*amends* VATA 1994 s 76(1))

(4) In section 83 (appeals)—

(*a*) (*amends* VATA 1994 s 83(*n*))

(*b*) (*inserts* VATA 1994 s 83(*zza*))

(5) (*inserts* VATA 1994 s 84(7B))

(6) (*inserts* VATA 1994 Sch 11 para 6A)

22 Treatment of credit vouchers

(1) VATA 1994 is amended as follows.

(2) (*inserts* VATA 1994 s 97(4)(*fa*))

(3) (*inserts* VATA 1994 Sch 10A para 3(4))

PART 9
MISCELLANEOUS PROVISIONS

Disclosure of information

177 Disclosure of information

(1) (*inserts* Gambling Act 2005 s 352A)

(2) Section 352A of the Gambling Act 2005 as inserted by subsection (1) above shall come into force on the passing of this Act.

PART 10
SUPPLEMENTARY PROVISIONS

178 Repeals

(1) The enactments mentioned in Schedule 26 (which include provisions that are spent or of no practical utility) are repealed to the extent specified.

(2) The repeals specified in that Schedule have effect subject to the commencement provisions and savings contained or referred to in the notes set out in that Schedule.

179 Interpretation

In this Act—

…

"FA", followed by a year, means the Finance Act of that year;

…

"VATA 1994" means the Value Added Tax Act 1994 (c 23);

…

SCHEDULES

SCHEDULE 26
REPEALS

Section 178

PART 2
VALUE ADDED TAX

Note—The repeals made under this Part are already in force and are therefore omitted.

FINANCE ACT 2007

(2007 Chapter 11)

CONTENTS

PART 1
CHARGES, RATES, THRESHOLDS ETC

Environment

PART 6
INVESTIGATION, ADMINISTRATION ETC

Investigation etc

Other administration

PART 7
MISCELLANEOUS

Value added tax and insurance premium tax

Other miscellaneous measures

PART 8
FINAL PROVISIONS

An Act to Grant certain duties, to alter other duties, and to amend the law relating to the National Debt and the Public Revenue, and to make further provision in connection with finance.

[19 July 2007]

PART 1

CHARGES, RATES, THRESHOLDS ETC

Environment

16 Emissions trading: charges for allocations

(1) The Treasury may impose charges by providing for Community tradeable emissions allowances to be allocated in return for payment.

(2) The Treasury must by regulations make provision for and in connection with allocations of allowances in return for payment.

(3) The regulations must provide for allocations to be overseen by an independent person appointed by the Treasury.

(4) The regulations may make any other provision about allocations which the Treasury consider appropriate, including (in particular)—

(*a*) provision as to the imposition of fees, and as to the making and forfeiting of deposits, in connection with participation in allocations,

(*b*) provision as to the persons by whom allocations are to be conducted,

(*c*) provision for the [creation of criminal offences, or for the imposition and recovery of civil penalties,][1] for failure to comply with the terms of a scheme made under subsection (5),

(*d*) provision for and in connection with the recovery of payments due in respect of allowances allocated (including provision as to the imposition and recovery of interest and penalties), and

(*e*) provision conferring rights of appeal against decisions made in allocations, the forfeiting of deposits and the imposition of penalties (including provision specifying the person, court or tribunal to hear and determine appeals).

(5) The Treasury may make schemes about the conduct and terms of allocations (to have effect subject to any regulations under this section); and schemes may in particular include provision about—

(*a*) who may participate in allocations,

(*b*) the allowances to be allocated, and

(*c*) where and when allocations are to take place.

(6) "Community tradeable emissions allowances" are transferable allowances which—

(*a*) relate to the making of emissions of greenhouse gases, and

(*b*) are allocated as part of a system made for the purpose of implementing any Community obligation of the United Kingdom relating to such emissions;

and "greenhouse gases" means carbon dioxide, methane, nitrous oxide, hydrofluorocarbons, perfluorocarbons and sulphur hexafluoride.

[(6A) Subsection (4)(*c*) does not permit the creation of a criminal offence with maximum penalties in excess of the maximum penalties which an instrument under section 2(2) of the European Communities Act 1972 may provide in respect of an offence created by such an instrument.][1]

(7) Regulations under this section are to be made by statutory instrument.

(8) A statutory instrument containing regulations under this section is subject to annulment in pursuance of a resolution of the House of Commons unless a draft of the regulations has been laid before, and approved by a resolution of, that House.

Amendments—[1] Sub-s (6A) inserted, and in sub-s (4)(*c*) words substituted for words "imposition and recovery of penalties", by FA 2008 s 164 with effect from 21 July 2008.

PART 6

INVESTIGATION, ADMINISTRATION ETC

Investigation etc

82 Criminal investigations: powers of Revenue and Customs

(1) Section 114 of the Police and Criminal Evidence Act 1984 (c 60) (application of Act to customs and excise) is amended as follows.

(2) In paragraph (*a*) of subsection (2)—

(*a*) for "investigations conducted by officers of Customs and Excise of offences which relate to assigned matters, as defined in section 1 of the Customs and Excise Management Act 1979," substitute "investigations conducted by officers of Revenue and Customs", and

(*b*) for "persons detained by officers of Customs and Excise;" substitute "persons detained by officers of Revenue and Customs;".

(3) In the opening words of paragraph (*b*) of that subsection, for "investigations of offences conducted by officers of Customs and Excise" substitute "investigations of offences conducted by officers of Revenue and Customs".

(4) In sub-paragraph (i) of that paragraph, for "section" substitute "sections".

(5) In the section 14A deemed to be inserted by that sub-paragraph—

(*a*) for "and which relates to an assigned matter, as defined in section 1 of the Customs and Excise Management Act 1979," substitute "and which relates to a matter in relation to which Her Majesty's Revenue and Customs have functions," and

(*b*) in the heading, for "**Customs and Excise**" substitute "**Revenue and Customs**".

(6) After that section insert—

"14B Revenue and Customs: restriction on other powers to apply for production of documents

(1) An officer of Revenue and Customs may make an application for the delivery of, or access to, documents under a provision specified in subsection (3) only if the condition in subsection (2) is satisfied.

(2) The condition is that the officer thinks that an application under Schedule 1 would not succeed because the material required does not consist of or include special procedure material.

(3) The provisions are—

(*a*) section 20BA of, and Schedule 1AA to, the Taxes Management Act 1970 (serious tax fraud);

(*b*) paragraph 11 of Schedule 11 to the Value Added Tax Act 1994 (VAT);

(*c*) paragraph 4A of Schedule 7 to the Finance Act 1994 (insurance premium tax);

(*d*) paragraph 7 of Schedule 5 to the Finance Act 1996 (landfill tax);

(*e*) paragraph 131 of Schedule 6 to the Finance Act 2000 (climate change levy);

(*f*) paragraph 8 of Schedule 7 to the Finance Act 2001 (aggregates levy);

(*g*) Part 6 of Schedule 13 to the Finance Act 2003 (stamp duty land tax)."

(7) In paragraph (*c*) of subsection (2)—

(*a*) for "customs detention" substitute "Revenue and Customs detention", and

(*b*) for "an officer of Customs and Excise" substitute "an officer of Revenue and Customs".

(8) After that paragraph (*c*) insert—

"(*d*) that where an officer of Revenue and Customs searches premises in reliance on a warrant under section 8 of, or paragraph 12 of Schedule 1 to, this Act (as applied by an order under this subsection) the officer shall have the power to search persons found on the premises—

(i) in such cases and circumstances as are specified in the order, and

(ii) subject to any conditions specified in the order; and

(*e*) that powers and functions conferred by a provision of this Act (as applied by an order under this subsection) may be exercised only by officers of Revenue and Customs acting with the authority (which may be general or specific) of the Commissioners for Her Majesty's Revenue and Customs."

(9) After that subsection insert—

"(2A) A certificate of the Commissioners that an officer of Revenue and Customs had authority under subsection (2)(*e*) to exercise a power or function conferred by a provision of this Act shall be conclusive evidence of that fact."

(10) For subsection (3) substitute—

"(3) An order under subsection (2)—

(*a*) may make provision that applies generally or only in specified cases or circumstances,

(*b*) may make different provision for different cases or circumstances,

(*c*) may, in modifying a provision, in particular impose conditions on the exercise of a function, and

(*d*) shall not be taken to limit a power under section 164 of the Customs and Excise Management Act 1979."

(11) The heading of section 114 accordingly becomes "**Application of Act to Revenue and Customs**".

Orders—Finance Act 2007 (Sections 82 to 84 and Schedule 23) (Commencement) Order 2007, SI 2007/3166 (this section comes into force on 8 November 2007).

83 Northern Ireland criminal investigations

(1) Article 85 of the Police and Criminal Evidence (Northern Ireland) Order 1989 (SI 1989/1341 (NI 12)) (application of Order to customs and excise) is amended as follows.

(2) In sub-paragraph (*a*) of paragraph (1)—

(*a*) for "investigations conducted by officers of Customs and Excise of offences which relate to assigned matters, as defined in section 1 of the Customs and Excise Management Act 1979," substitute "investigations conducted by officers of Revenue and Customs", and

(*b*) for "persons detained by officers of Customs and Excise;" substitute "persons detained by officers of Revenue and Customs;".

(3) In the opening words of sub-paragraph (*b*) of that paragraph, for "investigations of offences conducted by officers of Customs and Excise" substitute "investigations of offences conducted by officers of Revenue and Customs".

(4) In paragraph (i) of that sub-paragraph, for "Article" substitute "Articles".

(5) In the Article 16A deemed to be inserted by that paragraph—

(*a*) for "and which relates to an assigned matter, as defined in section 1 of the Customs and Excise Management Act 1979," substitute "and which relates to a matter in relation to which Her Majesty's Revenue and Customs have functions," and

(*b*) in the heading, for "**Customs and Excise**" substitute "**Revenue and Customs**".

(6) After that Article insert—

"16B Revenue and Customs: restriction on other powers to apply for production of documents

(1) An officer of Revenue and Customs may make an application for the delivery of, or access to, documents under a provision specified in paragraph (3) only if the condition in paragraph (2) is satisfied.

(2) The condition is that the officer thinks that an application under Schedule 1 would not succeed because the material required does not consist of or include special procedure material.

(3) The provisions are—

(*a*) section 20BA of, and Schedule 1AA to, the Taxes Management Act 1970 (serious tax fraud);

(*b*) paragraph 11 of Schedule 11 to the Value Added Tax Act 1994 (VAT);

(*c*) paragraph 4A of Schedule 7 to the Finance Act 1994 (insurance premium tax);

(*d*) paragraph 7 of Schedule 5 to the Finance Act 1996 (landfill tax);

(*e*) paragraph 131 of Schedule 6 to the Finance Act 2000 (climate change levy);

(*f*) paragraph 8 of Schedule 7 to the Finance Act 2001 (aggregates levy);

(*g*) Part 6 of Schedule 13 to the Finance Act 2003 (stamp duty land tax)."

(7) After sub-paragraph (*b*) of paragraph (1) insert—

"(*c*) that where an officer of Revenue and Customs searches premises in reliance on a warrant under Article 10 of, or paragraph 9 of Schedule 1 to, this Order (as applied by an order under this paragraph) the officer shall have the power to search persons found on the premises—

(i) in such cases and circumstances as are specified in the order, and

(ii) subject to any conditions specified in the order; and

(*d*) that powers and functions conferred by a provision of this Order (as applied by an order under this paragraph) may be exercised only by officers of Revenue and Customs acting with the authority (which may be general or specific) of the Commissioners for Her Majesty's Revenue and Customs."

(8) After that paragraph insert—

"(1A) A certificate of the Commissioners that an officer of Revenue and Customs had authority under paragraph (1)(*d*) to exercise a power or function conferred by a provision of this Order shall be conclusive evidence of that fact."

(9) For paragraph (2) substitute—

"(2) An order under paragraph (1)—

(*a*) may, in modifying a provision, in particular impose conditions on the exercise of a function, and

(*b*) shall not be taken to limit a power under section 164 of the Customs and Excise Management Act 1979."

(10) The heading of Article 85 accordingly becomes "**Application of Order to Revenue and Customs**".

Orders—Finance Act 2007 (Sections 82 to 84 and Schedule 23) (Commencement) Order 2007, SI 2007/3166 (this section comes into force on 8 November 2007).

84 Sections 82 and 83: supplementary

(1) In Schedule 2 to CRCA 2005 (restrictions on the exercise of functions), omit—

(*a*) (*repeals* CRCA 2005 Sch 2 para 7)

(*b*) paragraph 9 (Police and Criminal Evidence (Northern Ireland) Order 1989 (SI 1989/1341 (NI 12))).

(2) Nothing in section 6 or 7 of CRCA 2005 (initial functions) restricts the functions in connection with which officers of Revenue and Customs may exercise a power under—

(*a*) the Police and Criminal Evidence Act 1984 by virtue of section 114 of that Act (as amended by section 82 above), or

(*b*) the Police and Criminal Evidence (Northern Ireland) Order 1989 by virtue of Article 85 of that Order (as amended by section 83 above).

(3) But neither an order under section 114 of the Police and Criminal Evidence Act 1984 nor an order under Article 85 of the Police and Criminal Evidence (Northern Ireland) Order 1989 has effect in relation to a matter specified in section 54(4)(*b*) or (*f*) of, or in paragraphs 3, 7, 10, [14,][1] 19 or 24 to 29 of Schedule 1 to, CRCA 2005 (former Inland Revenue matters).

(4) Schedule 22 contains amendments and repeals consequential on extension of police powers to Revenue and Customs.

(5) Sections 82 and 83 and this section come into force in accordance with provision made by the Treasury by order.

(6) The power to make an order under subsection (5) is exercisable by statutory instrument.

Orders—Finance Act 2007 (Sections 82 to 84 and Schedule 23) (Commencement) Order 2007, SI 2007/3166 (this section comes into force on 8 November 2007, except for sub-s (4), which comes into force on 1 December 2007).

Amendments—[1] In sub-s (3), reference substituted by the Employment Act 2008 s 12(1) with effect from 6 April 2009 (by virtue of SI 2009/603 arts 2, 3).

85 Criminal investigations: Scotland

Schedule 23 contains provision for Scotland about the investigation of offences by Her Majesty's Revenue and Customs.

Orders—Finance Act 2007 (Sections 82 to 84 and Schedule 23) (Commencement) Order 2007, SI 2007/3166 (Schedule 23 comes into force on 1 December 2007).

86 Search warrants

In section 8 of the Police and Criminal Evidence Act 1984, after subsection (6) insert—

"(7) Section 4 of the Summary Jurisdiction (Process) Act 1881 (execution of process of English courts in Scotland) shall apply to a warrant issued on the application of an officer of Revenue and Customs under this section by virtue of section 114 below."

87 Cross-border exercise of powers

(1) This section relates to the Criminal Justice and Public Order Act 1994 (c 33).

(2) Sections 136 to 139 (execution of warrants and powers of arrest and search) shall apply to an officer of Revenue and Customs as they apply to a constable; and for that purpose—

(*a*) a reference to a constable (including a reference to a constable of a police force in England and Wales, a constable of a police force in Scotland or a constable of a police force in Northern Ireland) shall be treated as a reference to an officer of Revenue and Customs, and

(*b*) a reference to a police station, or a designated police station, includes a reference to an office of Revenue and Customs or (in England and Wales and Northern Ireland) a designated office of Revenue and Customs.

(3) In the application of section 138 to an officer of Revenue and Customs—

(*a*) in subsection (2)—

(i) the reference to subsections (2) to (8) of section 14 of the Criminal Procedure (Scotland) Act 1995 (c 46) ("the 1995 Procedure Act") shall be treated as a reference to subsections (2) to (7) of section 24 of the Criminal Law (Consolidation) (Scotland) Act 1995 (c 39) ("the 1995 Consolidation Act"), and

(ii) the reference to subsections (1), (2) and (4) to (6) of section 15 of the 1995 Procedure Act shall be treated as a reference to subsections (1) to (4) of section 25 of the 1995 Consolidation Act, and

(*b*) in subsection (6)—

(i) the references to section 14 of the 1995 Procedure Act shall be treated as references to section 24 of the 1995 Consolidation Act,

(ii) the references to section 15 of the 1995 Procedure Act shall be treated as references to section 25 of the 1995 Consolidation Act,

(iii) in paragraph (*a*), sub-paragraph (ii) shall not apply, and

(iv) paragraph (*b*) shall not apply.

(4) An officer of Revenue and Customs may exercise a power under sections 136 to 139 only in the exercise of a function relating to tax (including duties and tax credits).

(5) In subsection (2)—

"office of Revenue and Customs" means premises wholly or partly occupied by Her Majesty's Revenue and Customs, and "designated office of Revenue and Customs" has the meaning given by an order under section 114 of the Police and Criminal Evidence Act 1984 (c 60) (power to extend provisions to HMRC) or, in Northern Ireland, by an order under Article 85 of the Police and Criminal Evidence (Northern Ireland) Order 1989 (SI 1989/1341 (NI 12)) (power to extend Order to HMRC).

(6) In section 136, after subsection (8) insert—

"(9) Powers under this section and sections 137 to 139 may be exercised by an officer of Revenue and Customs in accordance with section 87 of the Finance Act 2007."

Other administration

93 Mandatory electronic filing of returns

(1) Section 135 of FA 2002 (mandatory electronic filing) is amended as follows.

(2) (*inserts* FA 2002 s 135(7)(*ba*))

(3) (*amends* FA 2002 s 135(10))

(4) Section 76 of VATA 1994 (assessment) is amended as follows.

(5) (*inserts* VATA 1994 s 76(1)(*d*))

(6) (*amends* VATA 1994 s 76(1))

(7) (*inserts* VATA 1994 s 76(3)(*f*))

(8) (*inserts* VATA 1994 s 83(*zc*))

(9) (*inserts* VATA 1994 s 84(6B))

94 Mandatory electronic payment

(1) Section 204 of FA 2003 (mandatory electronic payment by large employers) is amended as follows.

(2) (*substitutes* FA 2003 s 204(1), (2))

(3) (*amends* FA 2003 s 204(5)(*b*))

(4) (*amends* FA 2003 s 204(6)(*a*))

(5) (*amends* FA 2003 s 204(8)(*a*), (*b*))

(6) (*amends* FA 2003 s 204(12))

(7) (*amends* FA 2003 s 204 heading)

(8) (*amends* FA 2003 s 205(1))

95 Payment by cheque

(1) The Commissioners may make regulations providing for a payment to HMRC made by cheque to be treated as made when the cheque clears, as defined in the regulations.

(2) Section 70A of TMA 1970 (payment by cheque treated as made on receipt by HMRC) is subject to regulations under subsection (1).

(3) Regulations under subsection (1)—

(*a*) may make provision generally or only for specified purposes,
(*b*) may make different provision for different purposes, and
(*c*) may include incidental, consequential or transitional provision.

(4) Regulations under subsection (1)—

(*a*) shall be made by statutory instrument, and
(*b*) shall be subject to annulment in pursuance of a resolution of the House of Commons.

(5) In this section—

(*a*) "the Commissioners" means the Commissioners for Her Majesty's Revenue and Customs, and
(*b*) "HMRC" means Her Majesty's Revenue and Customs.

(6) (*inserts* FA 2003 s 204(13))

(7) (*inserts* TMA 1970 s 70A(3))

(8) (*inserts* VATA 1994 s 58B)

97 Penalties for errors

(1) Schedule 24 contains provisions imposing penalties on taxpayers who—

(*a*) make errors in certain documents sent to HMRC, or
(*b*) unreasonably fail to report errors in assessments by HMRC.

(2) That Schedule comes into force in accordance with provision made by the Treasury by order.

(3) An order—

(*a*) may commence a provision generally or only for specified purposes,
(*b*) may make different provision for different purposes, and
(*c*) may include incidental, consequential or transitional provision.

(4) The power to make an order is exercisable by statutory instrument.

Orders—Finance Act 2007, Schedule 24 (Commencement and Transitional Provisions) Order 2008, SI 2008/568.

PART 7
MISCELLANEOUS

Value added tax and insurance premium tax

98 VAT: joint and several liability of traders in supply chain where tax unpaid

(1) (*substitutes* VATA 1994 s 77A(9)–(9B))

(2) (*inserts* VATA 1994 s 97(4)(*eb*))

99 VAT: non-business use etc of business goods

(1) Schedule 4 to VATA 1994 (matters to be treated as supply of goods or services) is amended as follows.

(2) (*repeals* VATA 1994 Sch 4 para 5(4A))

(3) (*inserts* VATA 1994 Sch 4 para 9(4))

(4) Paragraph 7 of Schedule 6 to VATA 1994 (valuation of supply of services otherwise than for consideration by virtue of paragraph 5(4) of Schedule 4 etc) is amended as follows.

(5) (*inserts* VATA 1994 Sch 6 para 7(2)–(4))

(6) The amendment made by subsection (2) comes into force on 1st September 2007.

(7) The amendment made by subsection (3) has effect in relation to surrenders on or after 21st March 2007.

100 VAT: transfers of going concerns

(1) Section 49 of VATA 1994 (transfers of going concern) is amended as follows.

(2) (*amends* VATA 1994 s 49(1))

(3) (*amends* VATA 1994 s 49(2))

(4) (*inserts* VATA 1994 s 49(2A))

(5) (*amends* VATA 1994 s 49(3))

(6) (*inserts* VATA 1994 s 49(4)–(6))

(7) (*amends* VATA 1994 s 94(6))

(8) (*amends* VATA 1994 Sch 1 para 1(2))

(9) (*amends* VATA 1994 Sch 4 para 8(2)(*b*))

(10) The amendments made by this section have effect in relation to transfers pursuant to contracts entered into on or after 1st September 2007.

112 Updating references to Standing Committees

(1) (*amends* PCTA 1968 s 1(4)(*b*))

(2) (*amends* FA 1973 s 50(2)(*a*))

PART 8
FINAL PROVISIONS

113 Interpretation

(1) In this Act—

"BGDA 1981" means the Betting and Gaming Duties Act 1981 (c 63),
"CAA 2001" means the Capital Allowances Act 2001 (c 2),
"CEMA 1979" means the Customs and Excise Management Act 1979 (c 2),
"CRCA 2005" means the Commissioners for Revenue and Customs Act 2005 (c 11),
"ICTA" means the Income and Corporation Taxes Act 1988 (c 1),
"IHTA 1984" means the Inheritance Tax Act 1984 (c 51),
"ITA 2007" means the Income Tax Act 2007 (c 3),
"ITEPA 2003" means the Income Tax (Earnings and Pensions) Act 2003 (c 1),
"ITTOIA 2005" means the Income Tax (Trading and Other Income) Act 2005 (c 5),
"TCGA 1992" means the Taxation of Chargeable Gains Act 1992 (c 12),
"TMA 1970" means the Taxes Management Act 1970 (c 9),
"VATA 1994" means the Value Added Tax Act 1994 (c 23), and
"VERA 1994" means the Vehicle Excise and Registration Act 1994 (c 22).

(2) In this Act—

"FA", followed by a year, means the Finance Act of that year, and
"F(No 2)A", followed by a year, means the Finance (No 2) Act of that year.

114 Repeals
Schedule 27 contains repeals.

115 Short title
This Act may be cited as the Finance Act 2007.

SCHEDULES

SCHEDULE 22

AMENDMENTS AND REPEALS CONSEQUENTIAL ON EXTENSION OF HMRC POWERS

Section 84

Order—Finance Act 2007 (Sections 82 to 84 and Schedule 23) (Commencement) Order, SI 2007/3166 art 3(*a*) (FA 2007 s 84(4) comes into force on 1 December 2007).

PART 1

AMENDMENTS

1 (*amends* TMA 1970 s 20D(1))
2 (*amends* CJPA 2001 s 67)

PART 2

REPEALS

3 The provisions listed below are omitted.
4 (*repeals* TMA 1970 ss 20C, 20CC, and *amends* TMA 1970 s 118)
5 (*repeals* CEMA 1979 118C(3)(*c*), and *amends* CEMA 1979 s 118C(4)(*b*) and (5))
6 (*repeals* BGDA 1981 Sch 1 para 16, Sch 3 para 17, Sch 4 para 17)
7 (*repeals* FA 1989 s 148(4))
8 (*repeals* VATA 1994 s 72(9), Sch 11 para 10(3)–(6))
9 (*repeals* FA 1994 Sch 7 para 4(2)–(7))
10 (*repeals* FA 1996 Sch 5 paras 5, 6)
11 (*repeals* FA 2000 Sch 6 paras 97, 130)
12 (*repeals* FA 2001 Sch 6 para 6, Sch 7 para 7)
13— (1) (*repeals* CJPA 2001 ss 57(1)(*c*), 63(2)(*e*), 65(3))
(2) (*repeals* CJPA 2001 Sch 1 paras 13, 28, 29, 57, 58, 61, 72)
14 (*repeals* TCA 2002 s 36(2), (3))
15 (*repeals* PCA 2002 s 323(3)(*e*), (*f*))
16 (*repeals* FA 2003 Sch 13 Pt 7)
17 (*repeals* CRCA 2005 13(3)(*b*), (*c*), 14(2)(*b*), (*c*))

SCHEDULE 23

EXTENSION OF HMRC POWERS: SCOTLAND

Section 85

Orders—Finance Act 2007 (Sections 82 to 84 and Schedule 23) (Commencement) Order 2007, SI 2007/3166 (this Schedule comes into force on 1 December 2007).

Criminal Law (Consolidation) (Scotland) Act 1995 (c 39)

1–7 (amend provisions outside the scope of this publication)

Criminal Procedure (Scotland) Act 1995 (c 46)

8–10 (amend provisions outside the scope of this publication)

Criminal Justice and Police Act 2001 (c 16)

11 The Criminal Justice and Police Act 2001 is amended as follows.
12 (*inserts* CJPA 2001 s 63(2)(*ga*))
13 (amends provisions outside the scope of this publication)

14— (1) The amendments made by this Schedule come into force in accordance with provision made by the Treasury by order.

(2) The power to make an order under this paragraph is exercisable by statutory instrument.

SCHEDULE 24

PENALTIES FOR ERRORS

Section 97

Orders—The Finance Act 2007, Schedule 24 (Commencement And Transitional Provisions) Order, SI 2008/568: this Schedule has effect as follows—

(a) 1 April 2008 in relation to relevant documents relating to tax periods commencing on or after that date;

(b) 1 April 2008 in relation to assessments falling within Sch 24 para 2 for tax periods commencing on or after that date;

(c) 1 July 2008 in relation to relevant documents relating to claims under the Thirteenth Council Directive (arrangements for the refund of value added tax to persons not established in Community territory) for years commencing on or after that date;

(d) 1 January 2009 in relation to relevant documents relating to claims under the Eighth Council Directive (arrangements for the refund of value added tax to taxable persons not established in the territory of the country) for years commencing on or after that date;

(e) 1 April 2009 in relation to documents relating to all other claims for repayments of relevant tax made on or after 1 April 2009 which are not related to a tax period; and

(f) in any other case, 1 April 2009 in relation to documents given where a person's liability to pay relevant tax arises on or after that date.

PART 1

LIABILITY FOR PENALTY

Error in taxpayer's document

1— (1) A penalty is payable by a person (P) where—

(*a*) P gives HMRC a document of a kind listed in the Table below, and

(*b*) Conditions 1 and 2 are satisfied.

(2) Condition 1 is that the document contains an inaccuracy which amounts to, or leads to—

(*a*) an understatement of [a][1] liability to tax,

(*b*) a false or inflated statement of a loss ...[1], or

(*c*) a false or inflated claim to repayment of tax.

(3) Condition 2 is that the inaccuracy was [careless (within the meaning of paragraph 3) or deliberate on P's part][1].

(4) Where a document contains more than one inaccuracy, a penalty is payable for each inaccuracy.

Tax	*Document*
Income tax or capital gains tax	Return under section 8 of TMA 1970 (personal return).
Income tax or capital gains tax	Return under section 8A of TMA 1970 (trustee's return).
Income tax or capital gains tax	Return, statement or declaration in connection with a claim for an allowance, deduction or relief.
Income tax or capital gains tax	Accounts in connection with ascertaining liability to tax.
Income tax or capital gains tax	Partnership return.
Income tax or capital gains tax	Statement or declaration in connection with a partnership return.
Income tax or capital gains tax	Accounts in connection with a partnership return.
[Income tax	Return under section 254 of FA 2004.][1]
Income tax	Return for the purposes of PAYE regulations.
Construction industry deductions	Return for the purposes of regulations under section 70(1)(a) of FA 2004 in connection with deductions on account of tax under the Construction Industry Scheme.
Corporation tax	Company tax return under paragraph 3 of Schedule 18 to FA 1998.
Corporation tax	Return, statement or declaration in connection with a claim for an allowance, deduction or relief.
Corporation tax	Accounts in connection with ascertaining liability to tax.
VAT	VAT return under regulations made under paragraph 2 of Schedule 11 to VATA 1994.

Tax	*Document*
VAT	Return, statement or declaration in connection with a claim.
[Insurance premium tax	Return under regulations under section 54 of FA 1994.
Insurance premium tax	Return, statement or declaration in connection with a claim.
Inheritance tax	Account under section 216 or 217 of IHTA 1984.
Inheritance tax	Information or document under regulations under section 256 of IHTA 1984.
Inheritance tax	Statement or declaration in connection with a deduction, exemption or relief.
Stamp duty land tax	Return under section 76 of FA 2003.
Stamp duty reserve tax	Return under regulations under section 98 of FA 1986.
Petroleum revenue tax	Return under paragraph 2 of Schedule 2 to the Oil Taxation Act 1975.
Petroleum revenue tax	Statement or declaration in connection with a claim under Schedule 5, 6, 7 or 8 to the Oil Taxation Act 1975.
Petroleum revenue tax	Statement under section 1(1)(*a*) of the Petroleum Revenue Tax Act 1980.
Aggregates levy	Return under regulations under section 25 of FA 2001.
Climate change levy	Return under regulations under paragraph 41 of Schedule 6 to FA 2000.
Landfill tax	Return under regulations under section 49 of FA 1996.
Air passenger duty	Return under section 38 of FA 1994.
Alcoholic liquor duties	Return under regulations under section 13, 49, 56 or 62 of the Alcoholic Liquor Duties Act 1979.
Alcoholic liquor duties	Statement or declaration in connection with a claim for repayment of duty under section 4(4) of FA 1995.
Tobacco products duty	Return under regulations under section 7 of the Tobacco Products Duties Act 1979.
Hydrocarbon oil duties	Return under regulations under section 21 of the Hydrocarbon Oil Duties Act 1979.
Excise duties	Return under regulations under section 93 of CEMA 1979.
Excise duties	Return under regulations under section 100G or 100H of CEMA 1979.
Excise duties	Statement or declaration in connection with a claim.
General betting duty	Return under regulations under paragraph 2 of Schedule 1 to BGDA 1981.
Pool betting duty	Return under regulations under paragraph 2A of Schedule 1 to BGDA 1981.
Bingo duty	Return under regulations under paragraph 9 of Schedule 3 to BGDA 1981.
Lottery duty	Return under regulations under section 28(2) of FA 1993.
Gaming duty	Return under directions under paragraph 10 of Schedule 1 to FA 1997.
Remote gaming duty	Return under regulations under section 26K of BGDA 1981.][1]
[Any of the taxes mentioned above][1]	Any document which is likely to be relied upon by HMRC to determine, without further inquiry, a question about— (a) P's liability to tax, (b) payments by P by way of or in connection with tax, (c) any other payment by P (including penalties), or

Tax	*Document*
	(d) repayments, or any other kind of payment or credit, to P.

(5) In relation to a return under paragraph 2 of Schedule 2 to the Oil Taxation Act 1975, references in this Schedule to P include any person who, after the giving of the return for a taxable field (within the meaning of that Act), becomes the responsible person for the field (within the meaning of that Act).][1]

Cross reference—FA 2009 s 94 (Publishing details of deliberate tax defaulters).

Amendments—[1] In sub-para (2), word substituted for word "P's" and words "by P" repealed, in sub-para (3), words substituted for words "careless or deliberate (within the meaning of paragraph 3)", in the table, entries inserted, in the last entry in column 1 words substituted for words "Income tax, capital gains tax, corporation tax or VAT", and sub-para (5) inserted, by FA 2008 s 122, Sch 40 paras 1, 2 with effect from 1 April 2009 (by virtue of SI 2009/571 art 2). In their application in relation to penalties payable under paras 1, 1A of this Schedule, the entries inserted in the table (by FA 2008 Sch 40 para 2(4), (5)) shall have effect in relation to—

(a) relevant documents—

(i) which relate to tax periods commencing on or after 1 April 2009, and

(ii) for which the filing date is on or after 1 April 2010;

(b) relevant documents relating to all claims for repayments of relevant tax made on or after 1 April 2010 which are not related to a tax period;

(c) relevant documents produced under regulations under IHTA 1984 s 256 where the date of death is on or after 1 April 2009; and

(d) in any other case, relevant documents given where a person's liability to pay relevant tax arises on or after 1 April 2010 (SI 2009/571 arts 3, 4).

In their application in relation to assessments falling within para 2 of this Schedule, the entries inserted in the table (by FA 2008 Sch 40 para 2(4), (5)) shall have effect in relation to tax periods commencing on or after 1 April 2009, where the filing date for the relevant document is on or after 1 April 2010 (SI 2009/571 art 5).

[Error in taxpayer's document attributable to another person

1A— (1) A penalty is payable by a person (T) where—

(*a*) another person (P) gives HMRC a document of a kind listed in the Table in paragraph 1,

(*b*) the document contains a relevant inaccuracy, and

(*c*) the inaccuracy was attributable to T deliberately supplying false information to P (whether directly or indirectly), or to T deliberately withholding information from P, with the intention of the document containing the inaccuracy.

(2) A "relevant inaccuracy" is an inaccuracy which amounts to, or leads to—

(*a*) an understatement of a liability to tax,

(*b*) a false or inflated statement of a loss, or

(*c*) a false or inflated claim to repayment of tax.

(3) A penalty is payable under this paragraph in respect of an inaccuracy whether or not P is liable to a penalty under paragraph 1 in respect of the same inaccuracy.][1]

Cross reference—FA 2009 s 94 (Publishing details of deliberate tax defaulters).

Amendment—[1] Paragraph 1A inserted by FA 2008 s 122, Sch 40 paras 1, 3 with effect from 1 April 2009 (by virtue of SI 2009/571 art 2).

Under-assessment by HMRC

2— (1) A penalty is payable by a person (P) where—

(*a*) an assessment issued to P by HMRC understates P's liability to [a relevant tax][1], and

(*b*) P has failed to take reasonable steps to notify HMRC, within the period of 30 days beginning with the date of the assessment, that it is an under-assessment.

(2) In deciding what steps (if any) were reasonable HMRC must consider—

(*a*) whether P knew, or should have known, about the under-assessment, and

(*b*) what steps would have been reasonable to take to notify HMRC.

[(3) In sub-paragraph (1) "relevant tax" means any tax mentioned in the Table in paragraph 1.][1]

[(4) In this paragraph (and in Part 2 of this Schedule so far as relating to this paragraph)—

(*a*) "assessment" includes determination, and

(*b*) accordingly, references to an under-assessment include an under-determination.][2]

HMRC Manuals—Compliance Handbook Manual, CH81011–81013 (penalties for inaccuracies: commencement date for penalties).

CH81090 (penalties for inaccuracies: under assessment by HMRC).

CH81170–81181190 (under assessment by HMRC and onus and level of proof).

CH410100–410200 (penalties for inaccuracies: under assessments and the 30 day limit).

CH410300 (additional assessments).

Amendments—[1] In sub-para (1), words substituted for word "tax", and sub-para (3) substituted, by FA 2008 s 122, Sch 40 paras 1, 4 with effect from 1 April 2009 (by virtue of SI 2009/571 art 2). Sub-para (3) previously read as follows—

"(3) In sub-paragraph (1) "tax" means—

(*a*) income tax,

(*b*) capital gains tax,

(*c*) corporation tax, and

(*d*) VAT.".

[2] Sub-para (4) inserted by FA 2009 s 109, Sch 57 para 2 with effect from 21 July 2009.

Degrees of culpability

3— (1) [For the purposes of a penalty under paragraph 1, inaccuracy in][1] a document given by P to HMRC is—

(*a*) "careless" if the inaccuracy is due to failure by P to take reasonable care,

(*b*) "deliberate but not concealed" if the inaccuracy is deliberate [on P's part][1] but P does not make arrangements to conceal it, and

(*c*) "deliberate and concealed" if the inaccuracy is deliberate [on P's part][1] and P makes arrangements to conceal it (for example, by submitting false evidence in support of an inaccurate figure).

(2) An inaccuracy in a document given by P to HMRC, which was neither careless nor deliberate [on P's part][1] when the document was given, is to be treated as careless if P—

(*a*) discovered the inaccuracy at some later time, and

(*b*) did not take reasonable steps to inform HMRC.

HMRC Manuals—Compliance Handbook Manual, CH81080 (penalties for inaccuracies: inaccuracy discovered after document sent to HMRC).
CH81120–81140 (what is reasonable care, with examples at CH81131).
CH81141–81142 (correction of errors for indirect taxes).
CH81145 (examples of careless inaccuracy).
CH81150–81151 (deliberate but not concealed inaccuracy, with examples).
CH81160–81161 (deliberate and concealed inaccuracy, with examples).
CH81110 (penalties for inaccuracies: the four types of inaccuracy).
CH420100–420200 (penalties for inaccuracies: establishing penalty cases).
CH420300 (reliance on agent).
CH420400 (looking at each inaccuracy separately).
CH420500 (evidence needed).
CH420600 (examples of questions to establish behaviour).
CH420700 (evidence from employees)
CH420800 (evidence from agents and advisers).
CH420900 (use of evidence based on compliance history).
CH430500 (mistakes despite taking reasonable care).
CH431010 (failure to take reasonable care).
CH431020 (inaccuracy in a document subsequently discovered).
CH431030 (what records were kept).
CH431040 (repetition of errors).
CH432010–432030 (direct and indirect evidence of deliberate behaviour).
CH432500 (deliberate behaviour – when to raise the question of penalties).
CH433000–433060 (human rights advice).
CH433060 (*Delay and King v UK*).
CH433000 (approval of decisions on behaviour).
CH434000 (agreement with the person).

Amendments—[1] In sub-para (1), words substituted for words "Inaccuracy in", and in sub-paras (1), (2), words inserted, by FA 2008 s 122, Sch 40 paras 1, 5 with effect from 1 April 2009 (by virtue of SI 2009/571 art 2).

PART 2

AMOUNT OF PENALTY

Standard amount

4— (1) The penalty payable under paragraph 1 is—

(*a*) for careless action, 30% of the potential lost revenue,

(*b*) for deliberate but not concealed action, 70% of the potential lost revenue, and

(*c*) for deliberate and concealed action, 100% of the potential lost revenue.

[(1A) The penalty payable under paragraph 1A is 100% of the potential lost revenue.][1]

(2) The penalty payable under paragraph 2 is 30% of the potential lost revenue.

(3) Paragraphs 5 to 8 define "potential lost revenue".

HMRC Manuals—Compliance Handbook Manual, CH82120 (penalties for inaccuracies: introduction to amount of penalty).

Amendments—[1] Sub-para (1A) inserted by FA 2008 s 122, Sch 40 paras 1, 6 with effect from 1 April 2009 (by virtue of SI 2009/571 art 2).

Potential lost revenue: normal rule

5— (1) "The potential lost revenue" in respect of an inaccuracy in a document [(including an inaccuracy attributable to a supply of false information or withholding of information)][1] or a failure to notify an under-assessment is the additional amount due or payable in respect of tax as a result of correcting the inaccuracy or assessment.

(2) The reference in sub-paragraph (1) to the additional amount due or payable includes a reference to—

(*a*) an amount payable to HMRC having been erroneously paid by way of repayment of tax, and

(*b*) an amount which would have been repayable by HMRC had the inaccuracy or assessment not been corrected.

(3) In sub-paragraph (1) "tax" includes national insurance contributions.

(4) The following shall be ignored in calculating potential lost revenue under this paragraph—

(*a*) group relief, and
[(*b*) any relief under subsection (4) of section 419 of ICTA (relief in respect of repayment etc of loan) which is deferred under subsection (4A) of that section;][2]

(but this sub-paragraph does not prevent a penalty being charged in respect of an inaccurate claim for relief).

HMRC Manuals—Compliance Handbook Manual, CH82160–82161 (penalties for inaccuracies: single inaccuracy with examples of potential lost revenue).
CH82162 (examples of potential lost revenue for an under assessment).
Cross reference—FA 2009 s 94 (Publishing details of deliberate tax defaulters).
Amendments—[1] In sub-para (1), words inserted by FA 2008 s 122, Sch 40 paras 1, 7 with effect from 1 April 2009 (by virtue of SI 2009/571 art 2).
[2] Sub-para (4)(*b*) substituted by FA 2009 s 109, Sch 57 para 3 with effect from 21 July 2009. Sub-para (4)(*b*) previously read as follows—
"(*b*) section 419(4) of ICTA (close company: relief for loans);".

Potential lost revenue: multiple errors

6— (1) Where P is liable to a penalty [under paragraph 1][1] in respect of more than one inaccuracy, and the calculation of potential lost revenue under paragraph 5 in respect of each inaccuracy depends on the order in which they are corrected—

(*a*) careless inaccuracies shall be taken to be corrected before deliberate inaccuracies, and
(*b*) deliberate but not concealed inaccuracies shall be taken to be corrected before deliberate and concealed inaccuracies.

(2) In calculating potential lost revenue where P is liable to a penalty [under paragraph 1][1] in respect of one or more understatements in one or more documents relating to a tax period, account shall be taken of any overstatement in any document given by P which relates to the same tax period.

(3) In sub-paragraph (2)—

(*a*) "understatement" means an inaccuracy that satisfies Condition 1 of paragraph 1, and
(*b*) "overstatement" means an inaccuracy that does not satisfy that condition.

(4) For the purposes of sub-paragraph (2) overstatements shall be set against understatements in the following order—

(*a*) understatements in respect of which P is not liable to a penalty,
(*b*) careless understatements,
(*c*) deliberate but not concealed understatements, and
(*d*) deliberate and concealed understatements.

(5) In calculating [for the purposes of a penalty under paragraph 1][1] potential lost revenue in respect of a document given by or on behalf of P no account shall be taken of the fact that a potential loss of revenue from P is or may be balanced by a potential over-payment by another person (except to the extent that an enactment requires or permits a person's tax liability to be adjusted by reference to P's).

HMRC Manuals—Compliance Handbook Manual, CH82180–82250 (penalties for inaccuracies: more than one inaccuracy and when inaccuracies should or should not be grouped).
CH82260 (overstatements, with a worked example).
CH82270 (calculating potential lost revenue for multiple inaccuracies).
CH82271 (calculating potential lost revenue for multiple inaccuracies – employer and contractor issues).
CH82272 (example of allocating overstatements to potential lost revenue).
Cross reference—FA 2009 s 94 (Publishing details of deliberate tax defaulters).
Amendments—[1] In sub-paras (1), (2), (5) words inserted, by FA 2008 s 122, Sch 40 paras 1, 8 with effect from 1 April 2009 (by virtue of SI 2009/571 art 2).

Potential lost revenue: losses

7— (1) Where an inaccuracy has the result that a loss is wrongly recorded for purposes of direct tax and the loss has been wholly used to reduce the amount due or payable in respect of tax, the potential lost revenue is calculated in accordance with paragraph 5.

(2) Where an inaccuracy has the result that a loss is wrongly recorded for purposes of direct tax and the loss has not been wholly used to reduce the amount due or payable in respect of tax, the potential lost revenue is—

(*a*) the potential lost revenue calculated in accordance with paragraph 5 in respect of any part of the loss that has been used to reduce the amount due or payable in respect of tax, plus
(*b*) 10% of any part that has not.

(3) Sub-paragraphs (1) and (2) apply both—

(*a*) to a case where no loss would have been recorded but for the inaccuracy, and
(*b*) to a case where a loss of a different amount would have been recorded (but in that case sub-paragraphs (1) and (2) apply only to the difference between the amount recorded and the true amount).

(4) Where an inaccuracy has the effect of creating or increasing an aggregate loss recorded for a group of companies—

(*a*) the potential lost revenue shall be calculated in accordance with this paragraph, and
(*b*) in applying paragraph 5 in accordance with sub-paragraphs (1) and (2) above, group relief may be taken into account (despite paragraph 5(4)(*a*)).

(5) The potential lost revenue in respect of a loss is nil where, because of the nature of the loss or P's circumstances, there is no reasonable prospect of the loss being used to support a claim to reduce a tax liability (of any person).

HMRC Manuals—Compliance Handbook Manual, CH82310–82320 (calculating the penalty: losses used and not used).
CH82330 (losses available for potential lost revenue calculation).
CH82331 (losses available – income tax example).
CH82332 (losses available – capital gains tax example).
CH82333 (losses available – corporation tax example).
CH82340–82341 (aggregate group profits).
CH82342–82345 (worked examples of understatements and overstatements of profits creating or increasing and aggregate loss).
CH82350 (losses and when to assess a penalty).
CH82370–82371 (losses where there is no reasonable prospect of use, with example).
Cross reference—FA 2009 s 94 (Publishing details of deliberate tax defaulters).

Potential lost revenue: delayed tax

8— (1) Where an inaccuracy resulted in an amount of tax being declared later than it should have been ("the delayed tax"), the potential lost revenue is—

(*a*) 5% of the delayed tax for each year of the delay, or

(*b*) a percentage of the delayed tax, for each separate period of delay of less than a year, equating to 5% per year.

(2) This paragraph does not apply to a case to which paragraph 7 applies.

HMRC Manuals—Compliance Handbook Manual, CH82390 (calculating the penalty: delayed tax and potential lost revenue).
CH82395 and 82396 (examples of tax declared late).
CH82397 (capital allowances example of delayed tax).
Cross reference—FA 2009 s 94 (Publishing details of deliberate tax defaulters).

Reductions for disclosure

9— [(A1) Paragraph 10 provides for reductions in penalties under paragraphs 1, 1A and 2 where a person discloses an inaccuracy, a supply of false information or withholding of information, or a failure to disclose an under-assessment.][1]

(1) A person discloses an inaccuracy[, a supply of false information or withholding of information,][1] or a failure to disclose an under-assessment by—

(*a*) telling HMRC about it,

(*b*) giving HMRC reasonable help in quantifying the inaccuracy[, the inaccuracy attributable to the [supply of false information][2] or withholding of information, or the][1] under-assessment, and

(*c*) allowing HMRC access to records for the purpose of ensuring that the inaccuracy[, the inaccuracy attributable to the [supply of false information][2] or withholding of information, or the][1] under-assessment is fully corrected.

(2) Disclosure—

(*a*) is "unprompted" if made at a time when the person making it has no reason to believe that HMRC have discovered or are about to discover the inaccuracy[, the supply of false information or withholding of information, or the under-assessment][1], and

(*b*) otherwise, is "prompted".

(3) In relation to disclosure "quality" includes timing, nature and extent.

HMRC Manuals—Compliance Handbook Manual, CH82410 (calculating the penalty: penalty reductions for disclosure).
CH82420–82422 (unprompted and prompted disclosure, with examples).
CH82430–82431 (quality of disclosure).
CH82432 (calculating the reduction for disclosure example).
CH82440–82460 (quality of disclosure: telling, helping and giving access),
CH82470 (maximum and minimum penalties for each type of behaviour).
CH450510 (calculating penalties for inaccuracies: deciding whether disclosure will reduce the penalty).
CH450520 (prompted or unprompted disclosure).
CH450530 (quality of disclosure).
CH450540 (evidence of disclosure).

Amendments—[1] Sub-para (A1) to be inserted, and in sub-para (1), words inserted, in paras (*b*), (*c*), words substituted for word "or", and in sub-para (2)(*a*), words substituted for words "or under-assessment", by FA 2008 s 122, Sch 40 paras 1, 9 with effect from 1 April 2009 (by virtue of SI 2009/571 art 2).
[2] In sub-para (1)(*b*), (*c*), words "supply of false information" substituted for words "supply or false information" by FA 2009 s 109, Sch 57 para 4 with effect from 21 July 2009.

10— (1) Where a person who would otherwise be liable to a 30% penalty has made an unprompted disclosure, HMRC shall reduce the 30% to a percentage (which may be 0%) which reflects the quality of the disclosure.

(2) Where a person who would otherwise be liable to a 30% penalty has made a prompted disclosure, HMRC shall reduce the 30% to a percentage, not below 15%, which reflects the quality of the disclosure.

(3) Where a person who would otherwise be liable to a 70% penalty has made an unprompted disclosure, HMRC shall reduce the 70% to a percentage, not below 20%, which reflects the quality of the disclosure.

(4) Where a person who would otherwise be liable to a 70% penalty has made a prompted disclosure, HMRC shall reduce the 70% to a percentage, not below 35%, which reflects the quality of the disclosure.

(5) Where a person who would otherwise be liable to a 100% penalty has made an unprompted disclosure, HMRC shall reduce the 100% to a percentage, not below 30%, which reflects the quality of the disclosure.

(6) Where a person who would otherwise be liable to a 100% penalty has made a prompted disclosure, HMRC shall reduce the 100% to a percentage, not below 50%, which reflects the quality of the disclosure.

HMRC Manuals—Compliance Handbook Manual, CH82500–82512 (calculating the penalty: how to calculate the penalty with examples).

Cross reference—FA 2009 s 94 (Publishing details of deliberate tax defaulters).

Special reduction

11— (1) If they think it right because of special circumstances, HMRC may reduce a penalty under paragraph 1[, 1A][1] or 2.

(2) In sub-paragraph (1) "special circumstances" does not include—

(*a*) ability to pay, or

(*b*) the fact that a potential loss of revenue from one taxpayer is balanced by a potential over-payment by another.

(3) In sub-paragraph (1) the reference to reducing a penalty includes a reference to—

(*a*) staying a penalty, and

(*b*) agreeing a compromise in relation to proceedings for a penalty.

HMRC Manuals—Compliance Handbook Manual, CH82490 (calculating the penalty: guidance regarding special reduction).

CH451000 (calculating penalties for inaccuracies: special reduction).

Amendments—[1] In sub-para (1) reference inserted, by FA 2008 s 122, Sch 40 paras 1, 10 with effect from 1 April 2009 (by virtue of SI 2009/571 art 2).

Interaction with other penalties [and late payment surcharges][1]

12— (1) The final entry in the Table in paragraph 1 excludes a document in respect of which a penalty is payable under section 98 of TMA 1970 (special returns).

(2) The amount of a penalty for which P is liable under paragraph 1 or 2 in respect of a document relating to a tax period shall be reduced by the amount of any other penalty [incurred by P, or any surcharge for late payment of tax imposed on P, if the amount of the penalty or surcharge is determined by reference to the same tax liability.][1]

(3) In the application of section 97A of TMA 1970 (multiple penalties) no account shall be taken of a penalty under paragraph 1 or 2.

[(4) Where penalties are imposed under paragraphs 1 and 1A in respect of the same inaccuracy, the aggregate of the amounts of the penalties must not exceed 100% of the potential lost revenue.][1]

HMRC Manuals—Compliance Handbook Manual, CH84960 (interaction with other penalties: penalties for inaccurate documents other than returns).

CH84970–84972 (more than one penalty/surcharge on the same tax with examples).

CH84973 (examples of penalty and VAT default surcharge on the same tax).

CH87974 (penalties not to exceed 100% of the potential lost revenue).

Amendments—[1] In sub-para (2), words substituted for words "which P has incurred and the amount of which is determined by reference to P's tax liability for that period.", sub-para (4) inserted, and words inserted at end of heading, by FA 2008 s 122, Sch 40 paras 1, 11 with effect from 1 April 2009 (by virtue of SI 2009/571 art 2).

PART 3

PROCEDURE

Assessment

13— (1) [Where a person][1] becomes liable for a penalty under paragraph 1[, 1A][1] or 2 HMRC shall—

(*a*) assess the penalty,

(*b*) [notify the person][1], and

(*c*) state in the notice a tax period in respect of which the penalty is assessed.

[(1A) A penalty under paragraph 1, 1A or 2 must be paid before the end of the period of 30 days beginning with the day on which notification of the penalty is issued.][1]

(2) An assessment—

(*a*) shall be treated for procedural purposes in the same way as an assessment to tax (except in respect of a matter expressly provided for by this Act),

(*b*) may be enforced as if it were an assessment to tax, and

(*c*) may be combined with an assessment to tax.

(3) An assessment of a penalty under paragraph 1[or 1A][1] must be made [before the end of the][1] period of 12 months beginning with—

(*a*) the end of the appeal period for the decision correcting the inaccuracy, or

(*b*) if there is no assessment [to the tax concerned][1] within paragraph (*a*), the date on which the inaccuracy is corrected.

(4) An assessment of a penalty under paragraph 2 must be made [before the end of the period of 12 months beginning with—

(*a*) the end of the appeal period for the assessment of tax which corrected the understatement, or

(*b*) if there is no assessment within paragraph (*a*), the date on which the understatement is corrected.][1]

(5) For the purpose of sub-paragraphs (3) and (4) a reference to an appeal period is a reference to the period during which—

(*a*) an appeal could be brought, or

(*b*) an appeal that has been brought has not been determined or withdrawn.

(6) Subject to sub-paragraphs (3) and (4), a supplementary assessment may be made in respect of a penalty if an earlier assessment operated by reference to an underestimate of potential lost revenue.

[(7) In this Part of this Schedule references to an assessment to tax, in relation to inheritance tax and stamp duty reserve tax, are to a determination.][2]

HMRC Manuals—Compliance Handbook Manual, CH83020–83030 (processing the penalty: penalty assessments and what they must include).
CH83040 (when you should assess a penalty).
CH83050 (supplementary penalties).
CH83060 (enforcement of penalties).
CH402100–402140 (penalties for inaccuracies: who makes penalty decisions).
CH402160 (criminal investigation).
CH402200–402220 (communicating about penalties).
CH402300 (general framework of guidance on penalties for inaccuracies).
CH450100 (when to calculate penalties).
CH450200 (what has to be calculated).
CH450300 (separate penalty calculations).
CH451500–451530 (agreeing penalty calculations with the person).
CH451540 (agreement not reached).

Amendments—[1] In sub-para (1), words substituted for words "Where P" and "notify P" respectively, and words inserted, sub-para (1A) inserted, in sub-para (3), words inserted and words substituted for words "within the", and in sub-para (4), words substituted for words "within the period of 12 months beginning with the end of the appeal period for the assessment of tax which corrected the understatement.", by FA 2008 s 122, Sch 40 paras 1, 12 with effect from 1 April 2009 (by virtue of SI 2009/571 art 2).

[2] Sub-s (7) inserted by FA 2009 s 109, Sch 57 para 5 with effect from 21 July 2009.

Suspension

14— (1) HMRC may suspend all or part of a penalty for a careless inaccuracy under paragraph 1 by notice in writing to P.

(2) A notice must specify—

(*a*) what part of the penalty is to be suspended,

(*b*) a period of suspension not exceeding two years, and

(*c*) conditions of suspension to be complied with by P.

(3) HMRC may suspend all or part of a penalty only if compliance with a condition of suspension would help P to avoid becoming liable to further penalties under paragraph 1 for careless inaccuracy.

(4) A condition of suspension may specify—

(*a*) action to be taken, and

(*b*) a period within which it must be taken.

(5) On the expiry of the period of suspension—

(*a*) if P satisfies HMRC that the conditions of suspension have been complied with, the suspended penalty or part is cancelled, and

(*b*) otherwise, the suspended penalty or part becomes payable.

(6) If, during the period of suspension of all or part of a penalty under paragraph 1, P becomes liable for another penalty under that paragraph, the suspended penalty or part becomes payable.

HMRC Manuals—Compliance Handbook Manual, CH83110–83120 (suspension of a penalty: need for penalties to be assessed).
CH83130–83150 (circumstances in which you might or will not suspend a penalty).
CH83160 (conditions for suspension cannot be set).
CH83170 (penalties arising from using avoidance schemes will not be suspended).
CH83180 (suspension unlikely where history of non-compliance, with example).
CH83190 (remedial action for inaccuracies, with example).
CH83210–83211 (notice to suspend a penalty and example of what to include on notice).
CH83220 (partial suspension).
CH83230 and 83290 (period of suspension and expiry of period of suspension).
CH83250–83270 (conditions of suspension, with direct and indirect tax examples).
CH83280 (when a suspended penalty might become payable).
CH450650 (calculating penalties for inaccuracies: suspensions.
CH450660 (decisions required before any suspension is proposed).
CH450670 (records and business accounting systems).
CH450680 (proposed conditions met before issue of Notice of Suspension).

CH450690 (specific conditions for suspension).
CH450700–450730 (measurable achievable, realistic and generic conditions).
CH450740 (period of suspension).
CH451000 (special reduction).
CH451100–451200 (penalty calculator and penalty calculation summary).
CH451300 (settlement method proposed).
CH451400 (managers approval of decisions made).

Appeal

15— (1) [A person may][1] appeal against a decision of HMRC that a penalty is payable [by the person][1].

(2) [A person may][1] appeal against a decision of HMRC as to the amount of a penalty payable [by the person][1].

(3) [A person may][1] appeal against a decision of HMRC not to suspend a penalty payable [by the person][1].

(4) [A person may][1] appeal against a decision of HMRC setting conditions of suspension of a penalty payable [by the person][1].

HMRC Manuals—Compliance Handbook Manual, CH83300 (suspension of a penalty: appeal against a decision not to suspend a penalty).
CH84010–84020 (appeals against a penalty: types of appeal and entitlement to appeal).
CH433000–433060 (penalties for inaccuracies: human rights advice).
CH433060 (*Delay and King v UK*).

Amendments—[1] Words substituted for words "P may" and words "by P", in each place, by FA 2008 s 122, Sch 40 paras 1, 13 with effect from 1 April 2009 (by virtue of SI 2009/571 art 2).

[16— (1) An appeal under this Part of this Schedule shall be treated in the same way as an appeal against an assessment to the tax concerned (including by the application of any provision about bringing the appeal by notice to HMRC, about HMRC review of the decision or about determination of the appeal by the First-tier Tribunal or Upper Tribunal).

[(2) Sub-paragraph (1) does not apply—

(*a*) so as to require P to pay a penalty before an appeal against the assessment of the penalty is determined, or

(*b*) in respect of any other matter expressly provided for by this Act.][2]

(2) Sub-paragraph (1) does not apply in respect of a matter expressly provided for by this Act.][1]

HMRC Manuals—Compliance Handbook Manual, CH84070 (appeals against a penalty: which Tribunal will hear the appeal and procedures).

Amendments—[1] Paragraph 16 substituted by the Transfer of Tribunal Functions and Revenue and Customs Appeals Order, SI 2009/56 art 3, Sch 1 para 466 with effect from 1 April 2009. The previous substitution made by FA 2008 therefore effectively never took place. Para 16 as substituted by FA 2008 previously read as follows—

"**16**— An appeal may be brought to—

(*a*) the General Commissioners, in so far as the penalty relates to direct tax, or

(*b*) a VAT and duties tribunal, in so far as the penalty relates to VAT.".

[2] Sub-para (2) substituted by FA 2009 s 109, Sch 57 para 6 with effect from 21 July 2009. Sub-para (2) previously read as follows—

"(2) Sub-paragraph (1) does not apply in respect of a matter expressly provided for by this Act.".

17— (1) On an appeal under paragraph 15(1) the …[1] tribunal may affirm or cancel HMRC's decision.

(2) On an appeal under paragraph 15(2) the …[1] tribunal may—

(*a*) affirm HMRC's decision, or

(*b*) substitute for HMRC's decision another decision that HMRC had power to make.

(3) If the …[1] tribunal substitutes its decision for HMRC's, the …[1] tribunal may rely on paragraph 11—

(*a*) to the same extent as HMRC (which may mean applying the same percentage reduction as HMRC to a different starting point), or

(*b*) to a different extent, but only if the …[1] tribunal thinks that HMRC's decision in respect of the application of paragraph 11 was flawed.

(4) On an appeal under paragraph 15(3)—

(*a*) the …[1] tribunal may order HMRC to suspend the penalty only if it thinks that HMRC's decision not to suspend was flawed, and

(*b*) if the …[1] tribunal orders HMRC to suspend the penalty—

(i) P may appeal [1] against a provision of the notice of suspension, and

(ii) the …[1] tribunal may order HMRC to amend the notice.

(5) On an appeal under paragraph 15(4) the …[1] tribunal—

(*a*) may affirm the conditions of suspension, or

(*b*) may vary the conditions of suspension, but only if the …[1] tribunal thinks that HMRC's decision in respect of the conditions was flawed.

[(5A) In this paragraph "tribunal" means the First-tier Tribunal or Upper Tribunal (as appropriate by virtue of paragraph 16(1)).][1]

(6) In sub-paragraphs (3)(*b*), (4)(*a*) and (5)(*b*) "flawed" means flawed when considered in the light of the principles applicable in proceedings for judicial review.

(7) Paragraph 14 (see in particular paragraph 14(3)) is subject to the possibility of an order under this paragraph.

HMRC Manuals—Compliance Handbook Manual, CH84030–84040 (appeals against a penalty: appeals against the imposition or amount of a penalty).
CH84050 (appeals against the decision not to suspend a penalty).
CH84060 (appeals against the conditions set for penalty suspension).
CH84080 (flawed decision).

Amendment—[1] In sub-paras (1), (2), (3), (4)(*a*), (4)(*b*) in the first place, (4)(*b*)(ii), (5) in each place, word "appellate" repealed, in para (4)(*b*) (i) words "to the appellate tribunal" repealed; sub-para (5A) inserted by the Transfer of Tribunal Functions and Revenue and Customs Appeals Order, SI 2009/56 art 3, Sch 1 para 467 with effect from 1 April 2009.

PART 4

MISCELLANEOUS

Agency

18— (1) P is liable under paragraph 1(1)(*a*) where a document which contains a careless inaccuracy (within the meaning of paragraph 3) is given to HMRC on P's behalf.

(2) In paragraph 2(1)(*b*) and (2)(*a*) a reference to P includes a reference to a person who acts on P's behalf in relation to tax.

(3) Despite sub-paragraphs (1) and (2), P is not liable to a penalty [under paragraph 1 or 2][1] in respect of anything done or omitted by P's agent where P satisfies HMRC that P took reasonable care to avoid inaccuracy (in relation to paragraph 1) or unreasonable failure (in relation to paragraph 2).

(4) In paragraph 3(1)(*a*) (whether in its application to a document given by P or, by virtue of sub-paragraph (1) above, in its application to a document given on P's behalf) a reference to P includes a reference to a person who acts on P's behalf in relation to tax.

(5) In paragraph 3(2) a reference to P includes a reference to a person who acts on P's behalf in relation to tax.

HMRC Manuals—Compliance Handbook Manual, CH84520–84530 (other penalty issues: agent acting).
CH84540 (reliance on use of an agent to avoid an inaccuracy).
CH84545 (agent acting – inaccuracy attributable to another person).
CH420300 (penalties for inaccuracies: reliance on agent).
CH420800 (evidence from agents and advisers).

Amendments—[1] In sub-para (3), words inserted by FA 2008 s 122, Sch 40 paras 1, 15 with effect from 1 April 2009 (by virtue of SI 2009/571 art 2).

Companies: officers' liability

19— (1) Where a penalty under paragraph 1 is payable by a company for a deliberate inaccuracy which was attributable to [of the company, the officer is liable to pay such portion of the penalty (which may be 100%) as HMRC][1] may specify by written notice to the officer.

(2) Sub-paragraph (1) does not allow HMRC to recover more than 100% of a penalty.

(3) In the application of sub-paragraph (1) to a body corporate [other than a limited liability partnership][2] "officer" means—

(*a*) a director (including a shadow director within the meaning of section 251 of the Companies Act 2006 (c 46)), …[2]
[(*aa*) a manager, and][2]
(*b*) a secretary.

[(3A) In the application of sub-paragraph (1) to a limited liability partnership, "officer" means a member.][2]

(4) In the application of sub-paragraph (1) in any other case "officer" means—

(*a*) a director,
(*b*) a manager,
(*c*) a secretary, and
(*d*) any other person managing or purporting to manage any of the company's affairs.

[(5) Where HMRC have specified a portion of a penalty in a notice given to an officer under sub-paragraph (1)—

(*a*) paragraph 11 applies to the specified portion as to a penalty,
(*b*) the officer must pay the specified portion before the end of the period of 30 days beginning with the day on which the notice is given,
(*c*) paragraph 13(2), (3) and (5) apply as if the notice were an assessment of a penalty,
(*d*) a further notice may be given in respect of a portion of any additional amount assessed in a supplementary assessment in respect of the penalty under paragraph 13(6),
(*e*) paragraphs 15(1) and (2), 16 and 17(1) to (3) and (6) apply as if HMRC had decided that a penalty of the amount of the specified portion is payable by the officer, and
(*f*) paragraph 21 applies as if the officer were liable to a penalty.][1]

[(6) In this paragraph "company" means any body corporate or unincorporated association, but does not include a partnership, a local authority or a local authority association.][2]

HMRC Manuals—Compliance Handbook Manual, CH84610 (company penalties: officer of a company liable to a penalty).
CH84611 (deliberate action by officer of the company).
CH84620 (what is a company).
CH84625 (who is an officer of the company).
CH84630 (notice of liability).
CH84640 (amount of officer's liability).
CH84650 (personal gain),
CH84660 (insolvency or imminent insolvency).

Amendments—[1] In sub-para (1), words substituted , and sub-para (5) substituted, by FA 2008 s 122, Sch 40 paras 1, 16 with effect from 1 April 2009 (by virtue of SI 2009/571 art 2). Sub-paras (1), (5) previously read as follows—

"(1) Where a penalty under paragraph 1 is payable by a company for a deliberate inaccuracy which was attributable to an officer of the company—

(*a*) the officer as well as the company shall be liable to pay the penalty, and

(*b*) HMRC may pursue the officer for such portion of the penalty (which may be 100%) as they may specify by written notice to the officer.".

"(5) A reference to P in this Schedule (including paragraph 15) includes a reference to an officer of the company who is liable for a portion of the penalty in accordance with this paragraph.".

[2] In sub-para (3) words inserted, word "or" repealed and para (*aa*) inserted, sub-paras (3A), (6) inserted, by FA 2009 s 109, Sch 57 para 7 with effect from 21 July 2009.

Partnerships

20— (1) This paragraph applies where P is liable to a penalty under paragraph 1 for an inaccuracy in or in connection with a partnership return.

(2) Where the inaccuracy affects the amount of tax due or payable by a partner of P, the partner is also liable to a penalty ("a partner's penalty").

(3) Paragraphs 4 to 13 and 19 shall apply in relation to a partner's penalty (for which purpose a reference to P shall be taken as a reference to the partner).

(4) Potential lost revenue shall be calculated separately for the purpose of P's penalty and any partner's penalty, by reference to the proportions of any tax liability that would be borne by each partner.

(5) Paragraph 14 shall apply jointly to P's penalty and any partner's penalties.

(6) P may bring an appeal under paragraph 15 in respect of a partner's penalty (in addition to any appeal that P may bring in connection with the penalty for which P is liable).

HMRC Manuals—Compliance Handbook Manual, CH84720 (partnership penalties: partnerships and self assessment).
CH84730 (liable partners).
CH84740–84741 (calculating potential lost revenue, with example for partnerships).
CH84750–84760 (suspended penalties and appeals against penalties).

Double jeopardy

21 [A person is][1] not liable to a penalty under paragraph 1[, 1A][1] or 2 in respect of an inaccuracy or failure in respect of which [the person has][1] been convicted of an offence.

HMRC Manuals—Compliance Handbook Manual, CH84900 (partnership penalties: double jeopardy).

Amendments—[1] Words substituted for words "P is" and "the person has" respectively, and reference inserted, by FA 2008 s 122, Sch 40 paras 1, 17 with effect from 1 April 2009 (by virtue of SI 2009/571 art 2).

PART 5

GENERAL

Interpretation

22 Paragraphs 23 to [27][1] apply for the construction of this Schedule.

Amendments—[1] Reference substituted for reference "26", by FA 2008 s 122, Sch 40 paras 1, 18 with effect from 1 April 2009 (by virtue of SI 2009/571 art 2).

23 HMRC means Her Majesty's Revenue and Customs.

[**23A** "Tax", without more, includes duty.][1]

Amendments—[1] Paragraph 23A inserted by FA 2008 s 122, Sch 40 paras 1, 19 with effect from 1 April 2009 (by virtue of SI 2009/571 art 2).

24 An expression used in relation to income tax has the same meaning as in the Income Tax Acts.

25 An expression used in relation to corporation tax has the same meaning as in the Corporation Tax Acts.

26 An expression used in relation to capital gains tax has the same meaning as in the enactments relating to that tax.

27 An expression used in relation to VAT has the same meaning as in VATA 1994.

28 In this Schedule—

(*a*) a reference to corporation tax includes a reference to tax or duty which by virtue of an enactment is assessable or chargeable as if it were corporation tax, (*b*) a reference to tax includes a reference to construction industry deductions under Chapter 3 of Part 3 of FA 2004,

(*c*) "direct tax" means—

(i) income tax,
(ii) capital gains tax, ...[1]
(iii) corporation tax, [and
(iv) petroleum revenue tax,][1]

(*d*) a reference to understating liability to VAT includes a reference to overstating entitlement to a VAT credit,

[(*da*) *references to an assessment to tax, in relation to inheritance tax, means a determination,*][1, 3]

(*e*) a reference to a loss includes a reference to a charge, expense, deficit and any other amount which may be available for, or relied on to claim, a deduction or relief,

(*f*) a reference to repayment of tax includes a reference to allowing a credit [against tax or to a payment of a corporation tax credit][1],

[(*fa*) "corporation tax credit" means—

(i) an R&D tax credit under [Chapter 2 or 7 of Part 13 of CTA 2009][2],
(ii) a land remediation tax credit or life assurance company tax credit under [Chapter 3 or 4 respectively of Part 14 of CTA 2009][2],
(iii) *a tax credit under Schedule 13 to FA 2002 (vaccine research etc),*[2]
(iv) a film tax credit under [Chapter 3 of Part 15 of CTA 2009][2], or
(v) a first-year tax credit under Schedule A1 to CAA 2001,][1]

(*g*) "tax period" means a tax year, accounting period or other period in respect of which tax is charged,

(*h*) a reference to giving a document to HMRC includes a reference to communicating information to HMRC in any form and by any method (whether by post, fax, email, telephone or otherwise),

(*i*) a reference to giving a document to HMRC includes a reference to making a statement or declaration in a document,

(*j*) a reference to making a return or doing anything in relation to a return includes a reference to amending a return or doing anything in relation to an amended return, and

(*k*) a reference to action includes a reference to omission.

HMRC Manuals—Compliance Handbook Manual, CH81050 (penalties for inaccuracies: what is meant by "giving a document").

CH81071 (what is a "repayment of tax").

Amendments—[1] In sub-para (*c*), word "and" after para (ii) repealed, after para (iii) word "and" inserted, and para (iv) inserted, sub-paras (*da*), (*fa*) inserted, and in sub-para (*f*), words inserted, by FA 2008 s 122, Sch 40 para 20 with effect from 1 April 2009 (by virtue of SI 2009/571 art 2).

[2] In sub-para (*fa*)(i) words substituted for words "Schedule 20 to FA 2000"; in sub-para (*fa*)(ii) words substituted for words "Schedule 22 to FA 2001"; sub-para (*fa*)(iii) repealed; and in sub-para (*fa*)(iv) words substituted for words "Schedule 5 to FA 2006"; by CTA 2009 ss 1322, 1326, Sch 1 paras 722, 727, Sch 3 Part 1. CTA 2009 applies for accounting periods ending on or after 1 April 2009 (for corporation tax purposes) and for tax years 2009–10 onwards (for income and capital gains tax purposes).

[3] Sub-para (*da*) repealed by FA 2009 s 109, Sch 57 para 8 with effect from 21 July 2009.

Consequential amendments

29 The following provisions are omitted—

(*a*) sections 95, 95A, 97 and 98A(4) of TMA 1970 (incorrect returns and accounts),
(*b*) sections 100A(1) and 103(2) of TMA 1970 (deceased persons),
(*c*) in Schedule 18 to FA 1998 (company tax returns), paragraphs 20 and 89 (company tax returns), and
(*d*) sections 60, 61, 63 and 64 of VATA 1994 (evasion).

Note—Notwithstanding sub-para (*d*), VATA 1994 ss 60, 61 shall continue to have effect with respect to conduct involving dishonesty which does not relate to an inaccuracy in a document or a failure to notify HMRC of an under-assessment by HMRC (SI 2009/571 art 7).

30 In [paragraphs 7 and 7B][1] of Schedule 1 to the Social Security Contributions and Benefits Act 1992 (c 4) (penalties) a reference to a provision of TMA 1970 shall be construed as a reference to this Schedule so far as is necessary to preserve its effect.

Amendments—[1] Words substituted for words "paragraph 7" by FA 2009 s 109, Sch 57 para 9 with effect from 21 July 2009.

31 In [paragraphs 7 and 7B][1] of Schedule 1 to the Social Security Contributions and Benefits (Northern Ireland) Act 1992 (c 7) (penalties) a reference to a provision of TMA 1970 shall be construed as a reference to this Schedule so far as is necessary to preserve its effect.

Amendments—[1] Words substituted for words "paragraph 7" by FA 2009 s 109, Sch 57 para 9 with effect from 21 July 2009.

SCHEDULE 27
REPEALS

Section 114

PART 5
INVESTIGATION, ADMINISTRATION ETC

Note—The repeals made under this Part are already in force and are therefore omitted.

PART 6
MISCELLANEOUS

Note—The repeals made under this Part are already in force and are therefore omitted.

TRIBUNALS, COURTS AND ENFORCEMENT ACT 2007

(2007 Chapter 15)

ARRANGEMENT OF SECTIONS

PART 1
TRIBUNALS AND INQUIRIES

CHAPTER 1
TRIBUNAL JUDICIARY: INDEPENDENCE AND SENIOR PRESIDENT

CHAPTER 2
FIRST-TIER TRIBUNAL AND UPPER TRIBUNAL

Establishment

Members and composition of tribunals

Review of decisions and appeals

"Judicial review"

Miscellaneous

CHAPTER 3

TRANSFER OF TRIBUNAL FUNCTIONS

CHAPTER 4

ADMINISTRATIVE MATTERS IN RESPECT OF CERTAIN TRIBUNALS

CHAPTER 5

OVERSIGHT OF ADMINISTRATIVE JUSTICE SYSTEM, TRIBUNALS AND INQUIRIES

CHAPTER 6

SUPPLEMENTARY

PART 3

ENFORCEMENT BY TAKING CONTROL OF GOODS

CHAPTER 1

PROCEDURE

CHAPTER 3

GENERAL

PART 4

ENFORCEMENT OF JUDGMENTS AND ORDERS

Attachment of earnings orders

An Act to make provision about tribunals and inquiries; to establish an Administrative Justice and Tribunals Council; to amend the law relating to judicial appointments and appointments to the Law Commission; to amend the law relating to the enforcement of judgments and debts; to make further provision about the management and relief of debt; to make provision protecting cultural objects from seizure or forfeiture in certain circumstances; to amend the law relating to the taking of possession of land affected by compulsory purchase; to alter the powers of the High Court in judicial review applications; and for connected purposes.

[19th July 2007]

PART 1

TRIBUNALS AND INQUIRIES

CHAPTER 1

TRIBUNAL JUDICIARY: INDEPENDENCE AND SENIOR PRESIDENT

1 Independence of tribunal judiciary

(*Inserts* Constitutional Reform Act 2005 s 3(7A), (7B) with effect from 19 September 2007: SI 2007/2709 art 2)

2 Senior President of Tribunals

(1) Her Majesty may, on the recommendation of the Lord Chancellor, appoint a person to the office of Senior President of Tribunals.

(2) Schedule 1 makes further provision about the Senior President of Tribunals and about recommendations for appointment under subsection (1).

(3) A holder of the office of Senior President of Tribunals must, in carrying out the functions of that office, have regard to—

(*a*) the need for tribunals to be accessible,

(*b*) the need for proceedings before tribunals—

(i) to be fair, and

(ii) to be handled quickly and efficiently,

(*c*) the need for members of tribunals to be experts in the subject-matter of, or the law to be applied in, cases in which they decide matters, and
(*d*) the need to develop innovative methods of resolving disputes that are of a type that may be brought before tribunals.

(4) In subsection (3) "tribunals" means—

(*a*) the First-tier Tribunal,
(*b*) the Upper Tribunal,
(*c*) employment tribunals,
(*d*) the Employment Appeal Tribunal, and
(*e*) the Asylum and Immigration Tribunal.

Commencement—Tribunals, Courts and Enforcement Act 2007 (Commencement No 1) Order, SI 2007/2709 art 2(a) (this section comes into force on 19 September 2007).

CHAPTER 2

FIRST-TIER TRIBUNAL AND UPPER TRIBUNAL

Establishment

3 The First-tier Tribunal and the Upper Tribunal

(1) There is to be a tribunal, known as the First-tier Tribunal, for the purpose of exercising the functions conferred on it under or by virtue of this Act or any other Act.

(2) There is to be a tribunal, known as the Upper Tribunal, for the purpose of exercising the functions conferred on it under or by virtue of this Act or any other Act.

(3) Each of the First-tier Tribunal, and the Upper Tribunal, is to consist of its judges and other members.

(4) The Senior President of Tribunals is to preside over both of the First-tier Tribunal and the Upper Tribunal.

(5) The Upper Tribunal is to be a superior court of record.

Commencement—Tribunals, Courts and Enforcement Act 2007 (Commencement No 6 and Transitional Provisions) Order, SI 2008/2696 art 5(a) (this section comes into force on 3 November 2008).

Members and composition of tribunals

4 Judges and other members of the First-tier Tribunal

(1) A person is a judge of the First-tier Tribunal if the person—

(*a*) is a judge of the First-tier Tribunal by virtue of appointment under paragraph 1(1) of Schedule 2,
(*b*) is a transferred-in judge of the First-tier Tribunal (see section 31(2)),
(*c*) is a judge of the Upper Tribunal,
(*d*) is a member of the Asylum and Immigration Tribunal appointed under paragraph 2(1)(*a*) to (*d*) of Schedule 4 to the Nationality, Immigration and Asylum Act 2002 (c 41) (legally qualified members) and is not a judge of the Upper Tribunal, or
(*e*) is a member of a panel of chairmen of employment tribunals.

(2) A person is also a judge of the First-tier Tribunal, but only as regards functions of the tribunal in relation to appeals such as are mentioned in subsection (1) of section 5 of the Criminal Injuries Compensation Act 1995 (c 53), if the person is an adjudicator appointed under that section by the Scottish Ministers.

(3) A person is one of the other members of the First-tier Tribunal if the person—

(*a*) is a member of the First-tier Tribunal by virtue of appointment under paragraph 2(1) of Schedule 2,
(*b*) is a transferred-in other member of the First-tier Tribunal (see section 31(2)),
(*c*) is one of the other members of the Upper Tribunal, or
(*d*) is a member of a panel of members of employment tribunals that is not a panel of chairmen of employment tribunals.

(4) Schedule 2—

contains provision for the appointment of persons to be judges or other members of the First-tier Tribunal, and
makes further provision in connection with judges and other members of the First-tier Tribunal.

Commencement—Tribunals, Courts and Enforcement Act 2007 (Commencement No 6 and Transitional Provisions) Order, SI 2008/2696 art 5(a) (this section comes into force on 3 November 2008).

5 Judges and other members of the Upper Tribunal

(1) A person is a judge of the Upper Tribunal if the person—

(*a*) is the Senior President of Tribunals,
(*b*) is a judge of the Upper Tribunal by virtue of appointment under paragraph 1(1) of Schedule 3,

(*c*) is a transferred-in judge of the Upper Tribunal (see section 31(2)),
(*d*) is a member of the Asylum and Immigration Tribunal appointed under paragraph 2(1)(*a*) to (*d*) of Schedule 4 to the Nationality, Immigration and Asylum Act 2002 (c 41) (legally qualified members) who—
(i) is the President or a Deputy President of that tribunal, or
(ii) has the title Senior Immigration Judge but is neither the President nor a Deputy President of that tribunal,
(*e*) is the Chief Social Security Commissioner, or any other Social Security Commissioner, appointed under section 50(1) of the Social Security Administration (Northern Ireland) Act 1992 (c 8),
(*f*) is a Social Security Commissioner appointed under section 50(2) of that Act (deputy Commissioners),
(*g*) is within section 6(1),
(*h*) is a deputy judge of the Upper Tribunal (whether under paragraph 7 of Schedule 3 or under section 31(2)), or
(*i*) is a Chamber President or a Deputy Chamber President, whether of a chamber of the Upper Tribunal or of a chamber of the First-tier Tribunal, and does not fall within any of paragraphs (*a*) to (*h*).

(2) A person is one of the other members of the Upper Tribunal if the person—
(*a*) is a member of the Upper Tribunal by virtue of appointment under paragraph 2(1) of Schedule 3,
(*b*) is a transferred-in other member of the Upper Tribunal (see section 31(2)),
(*c*) is a member of the Employment Appeal Tribunal appointed under section 22(1)(*c*) of the Employment Tribunals Act 1996 (c 17), or
(*d*) is a member of the Asylum and Immigration Tribunal appointed under paragraph 2(1)(*e*) of Schedule 4 to the Nationality, Immigration and Asylum Act 2002 (members other than "legally qualified members").

(3) Schedule 3—
contains provision for the appointment of persons to be judges (including deputy judges), or other members, of the Upper Tribunal, and
makes further provision in connection with judges and other members of the Upper Tribunal.

Commencement—Tribunals, Courts and Enforcement Act 2007 (Commencement No 6 and Transitional Provisions) Order, SI 2008/2696 art 5(a) (this section comes into force on 3 November 2008).

6 Certain judges who are also judges of First-tier Tribunal and Upper Tribunal

(1) A person is within this subsection (and so, by virtue of sections 4(1)(*c*) and 5(1)(*g*), is a judge of the First-tier Tribunal and of the Upper Tribunal) if the person—
(*a*) is an ordinary judge of the Court of Appeal in England and Wales (including the vice-president, if any, of either division of that Court),
(*b*) is a Lord Justice of Appeal in Northern Ireland,
(*c*) is a judge of the Court of Session,
(*d*) is a puisne judge of the High Court in England and Wales or Northern Ireland,
(*e*) is a circuit judge,
(*f*) is a sheriff in Scotland,
(*g*) is a county court judge in Northern Ireland,
(*h*) is a district judge in England and Wales or Northern Ireland, or
(*i*) is a District Judge (Magistrates' Courts).

(2) References in subsection (1)(*c*) to (*i*) to office-holders do not include deputies or temporary office-holders.

Commencement—Tribunals, Courts and Enforcement Act 2007 (Commencement No 6 and Transitional Provisions) Order, SI 2008/2696 art 5(a) (this section comes into force on 3 November 2008).

7 Chambers: jurisdiction and Presidents

(1) The Lord Chancellor may, with the concurrence of the Senior President of Tribunals, by order make provision for the organisation of each of the First-tier Tribunal and the Upper Tribunal into a number of chambers.

(2) There is—
(*a*) for each chamber of the First-tier Tribunal, and
(*b*) for each chamber of the Upper Tribunal,
to be a person, or two persons, to preside over that chamber.

(3) A person may not at any particular time preside over more than one chamber of the First-tier Tribunal and may not at any particular time preside over more than one chamber of the Upper Tribunal (but may at the same time preside over one chamber of the First-tier Tribunal and over one chamber of the Upper Tribunal).

(4) A person appointed under this section to preside over a chamber is to be known as a Chamber President.

(5) Where two persons are appointed under this section to preside over the same chamber, any reference in an enactment to the Chamber President of the chamber is a reference to a person appointed under this section to preside over the chamber.

(6) The Senior President of Tribunals may (consistently with subsections (2) and (3)) appoint a person who is the Chamber President of a chamber to preside instead, or to preside also, over another chamber.

(7) The Lord Chancellor may (consistently with subsections (2) and (3)) appoint a person who is not a Chamber President to preside over a chamber.

(8) Schedule 4 (eligibility for appointment under subsection (7), appointment of Deputy Chamber Presidents and Acting Chamber Presidents, assignment of judges and other members of the First-tier Tribunal and Upper Tribunal, and further provision about Chamber Presidents and chambers) has effect.

(9) Each of the Lord Chancellor and the Senior President of Tribunals may, with the concurrence of the other, by order—

(*a*) make provision for the allocation of the First-tier Tribunal's functions between its chambers;

(*b*) make provision for the allocation of the Upper Tribunal's functions between its chambers;

(*c*) amend or revoke any order made under this subsection.

Commencement—Tribunals, Courts and Enforcement Act 2007 (Commencement No 1) Order, SI 2007/2709 art 2(a) (sub-ss (1), (9) come into force on 19 September 2007).

Tribunals, Courts and Enforcement Act 2007 (Commencement No 6 and Transitional Provisions) Order, SI 2008/2696 art 5(a) (sub-ss (2)–(8) come into force on 3 November 2008).

Orders—First-tier Tribunal and Upper Tribunal (Chambers) Order, SI 2008/2684 (made under sub-ss (1), (9)).

First-tier Tribunal and Upper Tribunal (Chambers) (Amendment) Order, SI 2009/196 (made under sub-ss (1), (9)).

8 Senior President of Tribunals: power to delegate

(1) The Senior President of Tribunals may delegate any function he has in his capacity as Senior President of Tribunals—

(*a*) to any judge, or other member, of the Upper Tribunal or First-tier Tribunal;

(*b*) to staff appointed under section 40(1).

(2) Subsection (1) does not apply to functions of the Senior President of Tribunals under section 7(9).

(3) A delegation under subsection (1) is not revoked by the delegator's becoming incapacitated.

(4) Any delegation under subsection (1) that is in force immediately before a person ceases to be Senior President of Tribunals continues in force until varied or revoked by a subsequent holder of the office of Senior President of Tribunals.

(5) The delegation under this section of a function shall not prevent the exercise of the function by the Senior President of Tribunals.

Commencement—Tribunals, Courts and Enforcement Act 2007 (Commencement No 6 and Transitional Provisions) Order, SI 2008/2696 art 5(a) (this section comes into force on 3 November 2008).

Review of decisions and appeals

9 Review of decision of First-tier Tribunal

(1) The First-tier Tribunal may review a decision made by it on a matter in a case, other than a decision that is an excluded decision for the purposes of section 11(1) (but see subsection (9)).

(2) The First-tier Tribunal's power under subsection (1) in relation to a decision is exercisable—

(*a*) of its own initiative, or

(*b*) on application by a person who for the purposes of section 11(2) has a right of appeal in respect of the decision.

(3) Tribunal Procedure Rules may—

(*a*) provide that the First-tier Tribunal may not under subsection (1) review (whether of its own initiative or on application under subsection (2)(*b*)) a decision of a description specified for the purposes of this paragraph in Tribunal Procedure Rules;

(*b*) provide that the First-tier Tribunal's power under subsection (1) to review a decision of a description specified for the purposes of this paragraph in Tribunal Procedure Rules is exercisable only of the tribunal's own initiative;

(*c*) provide that an application under subsection (2)(*b*) that is of a description specified for the purposes of this paragraph in Tribunal Procedure Rules may be made only on grounds specified for the purposes of this paragraph in Tribunal Procedure Rules;

(*d*) provide, in relation to a decision of a description specified for the purposes of this paragraph in Tribunal Procedure Rules, that the First-tier Tribunal's power under subsection (1) to review the decision of its own initiative is exercisable only on grounds specified for the purposes of this paragraph in Tribunal Procedure Rules.

(4) Where the First-tier Tribunal has under subsection (1) reviewed a decision, the First-tier Tribunal may in the light of the review do any of the following—

(*a*) correct accidental errors in the decision or in a record of the decision;

(*b*) amend reasons given for the decision;

(*c*) set the decision aside.

(5) Where under subsection (4)(*c*) the First-tier Tribunal sets a decision aside, the First-tier Tribunal must either—

(*a*) re-decide the matter concerned, or
(*b*) refer that matter to the Upper Tribunal.

(6) Where a matter is referred to the Upper Tribunal under subsection (5)(*b*), the Upper Tribunal must re-decide the matter.

(7) Where the Upper Tribunal is under subsection (6) re-deciding a matter, it may make any decision which the First-tier Tribunal could make if the First-tier Tribunal were re-deciding the matter.

(8) Where a tribunal is acting under subsection (5)(*a*) or (6), it may make such findings of fact as it considers appropriate.

(9) This section has effect as if a decision under subsection (4)(*c*) to set aside an earlier decision were not an excluded decision for the purposes of section 11(1), but the First-tier Tribunal's only power in the light of a review under subsection (1) of a decision under subsection (4)(*c*) is the power under subsection (4)(*a*).

(10) A decision of the First-tier Tribunal may not be reviewed under subsection (1) more than once, and once the First-tier Tribunal has decided that an earlier decision should not be reviewed under subsection (1) it may not then decide to review that earlier decision under that subsection.

(11) Where under this section a decision is set aside and the matter concerned is then re-decided, the decision set aside and the decision made in re-deciding the matter are for the purposes of subsection (10) to be taken to be different decisions.

Commencement—Tribunals, Courts and Enforcement Act 2007 (Commencement No 1) Order, SI 2007/2709 art 2(*a*) (sub-s (3) comes into force on 19 September 2007).
Tribunals, Courts and Enforcement Act 2007 (Commencement No 6 and Transitional Provisions) Order, SI 2008/2696 art 5(a) (sub-ss (1), (2), (4)–(11) come into force on 3 November 2008).
Orders—Tribunal Procedure (First-tier Tribunal) (Social Entitlement Chamber) Rules, SI 2008/2685 (made under sub-s (3)).
Tribunal Procedure (First-tier Tribunal) (War Pensions and Armed Forces Compensation Chamber) Rules, SI 2008/2686 (made under sub-para (3)).
Tribunal Procedure (First-tier Tribunal) (Health, Education and Social Care Chamber) Rules, SI 2008/2699 (made under sub-s (3)).
Tribunal Procedure (First-tier Tribunal) (Tax Chamber) Rules, SI 2009/273 (made under sub-s (3)).

10 Review of decision of Upper Tribunal

(1) The Upper Tribunal may review a decision made by it on a matter in a case, other than a decision that is an excluded decision for the purposes of section 13(1) (but see subsection (7)).

(2) The Upper Tribunal's power under subsection (1) in relation to a decision is exercisable—

(*a*) of its own initiative, or
(*b*) on application by a person who for the purposes of section 13(2) has a right of appeal in respect of the decision.

(3) Tribunal Procedure Rules may—

(*a*) provide that the Upper Tribunal may not under subsection (1) review (whether of its own initiative or on application under subsection (2)(*b*)) a decision of a description specified for the purposes of this paragraph in Tribunal Procedure Rules;
(*b*) provide that the Upper Tribunal's power under subsection (1) to review a decision of a description specified for the purposes of this paragraph in Tribunal Procedure Rules is exercisable only of the tribunal's own initiative;
(*c*) provide that an application under subsection (2)(*b*) that is of a description specified for the purposes of this paragraph in Tribunal Procedure Rules may be made only on grounds specified for the purposes of this paragraph in Tribunal Procedure Rules;
(*d*) provide, in relation to a decision of a description specified for the purposes of this paragraph in Tribunal Procedure Rules, that the Upper Tribunal's power under subsection (1) to review the decision of its own initiative is exercisable only on grounds specified for the purposes of this paragraph in Tribunal Procedure Rules.

(4) Where the Upper Tribunal has under subsection (1) reviewed a decision, the Upper Tribunal may in the light of the review do any of the following—

(*a*) correct accidental errors in the decision or in a record of the decision;
(*b*) amend reasons given for the decision;
(*c*) set the decision aside.

(5) Where under subsection (4)(*c*) the Upper Tribunal sets a decision aside, the Upper Tribunal must re-decide the matter concerned.

(6) Where the Upper Tribunal is acting under subsection (5), it may make such findings of fact as it considers appropriate.

(7) This section has effect as if a decision under subsection (4)(*c*) to set aside an earlier decision were not an excluded decision for the purposes of section 13(1), but the Upper Tribunal's only power in the light of a review under subsection (1) of a decision under subsection (4)(*c*) is the power under subsection (4)(*a*).

(8) A decision of the Upper Tribunal may not be reviewed under subsection (1) more than once, and once the Upper Tribunal has decided that an earlier decision should not be reviewed under subsection (1) it may not then decide to review that earlier decision under that subsection.

(9) Where under this section a decision is set aside and the matter concerned is then re-decided, the decision set aside and the decision made in re-deciding the matter are for the purposes of subsection (8) to be taken to be different decisions.

Commencement—Tribunals, Courts and Enforcement Act 2007 (Commencement No 1) Order, SI 2007/2709 art 2(*a*) (sub-s (3) comes into force on 19 September 2007).

Tribunals, Courts and Enforcement Act 2007 (Commencement No 6 and Transitional Provisions) Order, SI 2008/2696 art 5(a) (sub-ss (1), (2), (4)–(9) come into force on 3 November 2008).

11 Right to appeal to Upper Tribunal

(1) For the purposes of subsection (2), the reference to a right of appeal is to a right to appeal to the Upper Tribunal on any point of law arising from a decision made by the First-tier Tribunal other than an excluded decision.

(2) Any party to a case has a right of appeal, subject to subsection (8).

(3) That right may be exercised only with permission (or, in Northern Ireland, leave).

(4) Permission (or leave) may be given by—

(*a*) the First-tier Tribunal, or

(*b*) the Upper Tribunal,

on an application by the party.

(5) For the purposes of subsection (1), an "excluded decision" is—

(*a*) any decision of the First-tier Tribunal on an appeal made in exercise of a right conferred by the Criminal Injuries Compensation Scheme in compliance with section 5(1)(*a*) of the Criminal Injuries Compensation Act 1995 (c 53) (appeals against decisions on reviews),

(*b*) any decision of the First-tier Tribunal on an appeal under section 28(4) or (6) of the Data Protection Act 1998 (c 29) (appeals against national security certificate),

(*c*) any decision of the First-tier Tribunal on an appeal under section 60(1) or (4) of the Freedom of Information Act 2000 (c 36) (appeals against national security certificate),

(*d*) a decision of the First-tier Tribunal under section 9—

(i) to review, or not to review, an earlier decision of the tribunal,

(ii) to take no action, or not to take any particular action, in the light of a review of an earlier decision of the tribunal,

(iii) to set aside an earlier decision of the tribunal, or

(iv) to refer, or not to refer, a matter to the Upper Tribunal,

(*e*) a decision of the First-tier Tribunal that is set aside under section 9 (including a decision set aside after proceedings on an appeal under this section have been begun), or

(*f*) any decision of the First-tier Tribunal that is of a description specified in an order made by the Lord Chancellor.

(6) A description may be specified under subsection (5)(*f*) only if—

(*a*) in the case of a decision of that description, there is a right to appeal to a court, the Upper Tribunal or any other tribunal from the decision and that right is, or includes, something other than a right (however expressed) to appeal on any point of law arising from the decision, or

(*b*) decisions of that description are made in carrying out a function transferred under section 30 and prior to the transfer of the function under section 30(1) there was no right to appeal from decisions of that description.

(7) Where—

(*a*) an order under subsection (5)(*f*) specifies a description of decisions, and

(*b*) decisions of that description are made in carrying out a function transferred under section 30,

the order must be framed so as to come into force no later than the time when the transfer under section 30 of the function takes effect (but power to revoke the order continues to be exercisable after that time, and power to amend the order continues to be exercisable after that time for the purpose of narrowing the description for the time being specified).

(8) The Lord Chancellor may by order make provision for a person to be treated as being, or to be treated as not being, a party to a case for the purposes of subsection (2).

Commencement—Tribunals, Courts and Enforcement Act 2007 (Commencement No 1) Order, SI 2007/2709 art 2(*a*) (sub-ss (5)(*f*), (6)–(8) come into force on 19 September 2007).

Tribunals, Courts and Enforcement Act 2007 (Commencement No 6 and Transitional Provisions) Order, SI 2008/2696 art 5(*a*) (sub-ss (1)–(4), (5)(*a*)–(*e*) come into force on 3 November 2008).

Cross references—See Tribunals, Courts and Enforcement Act 2007 (Transitional and Consequential Provisions) Order, SI 2008/2683, art 5 (transitional provisions).

Orders—Appeals (Excluded Decisions) Order, SI 2009/275 (made under sub-s (5)(*f*)).

12 Proceedings on appeal to Upper Tribunal

(1) Subsection (2) applies if the Upper Tribunal, in deciding an appeal under section 11, finds that the making of the decision concerned involved the making of an error on a point of law.

(2) The Upper Tribunal—

(*a*) may (but need not) set aside the decision of the First-tier Tribunal, and
(*b*) if it does, must either—
(i) remit the case to the First-tier Tribunal with directions for its reconsideration, or
(ii) re-make the decision.

(3) In acting under subsection (2)(*b*)(i), the Upper Tribunal may also—
(*a*) direct that the members of the First-tier Tribunal who are chosen to reconsider the case are not to be the same as those who made the decision that has been set aside;
(*b*) give procedural directions in connection with the reconsideration of the case by the First-tier Tribunal.

(4) In acting under subsection (2)(*b*)(ii), the Upper Tribunal—
(*a*) may make any decision which the First-tier Tribunal could make if the First-tier Tribunal were re-making the decision, and
(*b*) may make such findings of fact as it considers appropriate.

Commencement—Tribunals, Courts and Enforcement Act 2007 (Commencement No 6 and Transitional Provisions) Order, SI 2008/2696 art 5(*a*) (this section comes into force on 3 November 2008).
Modification—See the Mental Health Act 1983, s 78A (as inserted by SI 2008/2833, art 9(1), Sch 3, paras 39, 60) (in relation to the application with modifications of this section to appeals from the Mental Health Review Tribunal for Wales).

13 Right to appeal to Court of Appeal etc

(1) For the purposes of subsection (2), the reference to a right of appeal is to a right to appeal to the relevant appellate court on any point of law arising from a decision made by the Upper Tribunal other than an excluded decision.

(2) Any party to a case has a right of appeal, subject to subsection (14).

(3) That right may be exercised only with permission (or, in Northern Ireland, leave).

(4) Permission (or leave) may be given by—
(*a*) the Upper Tribunal, or
(*b*) the relevant appellate court,
on an application by the party.

(5) An application may be made under subsection (4) to the relevant appellate court only if permission (or leave) has been refused by the Upper Tribunal.

(6) The Lord Chancellor may, as respects an application under subsection (4) that falls within subsection (7) and for which the relevant appellate court is the Court of Appeal in England and Wales or the Court of Appeal in Northern Ireland, by order make provision for permission (or leave) not to be granted on the application unless the Upper Tribunal or (as the case may be) the relevant appellate court considers—
(*a*) that the proposed appeal would raise some important point of principle or practice, or
(*b*) that there is some other compelling reason for the relevant appellate court to hear the appeal.

(7) An application falls within this subsection if the application is for permission (or leave) to appeal from any decision of the Upper Tribunal on an appeal under section 11.

(8) For the purposes of subsection (1), an "excluded decision" is—
(*a*) any decision of the Upper Tribunal on an appeal under section 28(4) or (6) of the Data Protection Act 1998 (c 29) (appeals against national security certificate),
(*b*) any decision of the Upper Tribunal on an appeal under section 60(1) or (4) of the Freedom of Information Act 2000 (c 36) (appeals against national security certificate),
(*c*) any decision of the Upper Tribunal on an application under section 11(4)(*b*) (application for permission or leave to appeal),
(*d*) a decision of the Upper Tribunal under section 10—
(i) to review, or not to review, an earlier decision of the tribunal,
(ii) to take no action, or not to take any particular action, in the light of a review of an earlier decision of the tribunal, or
(iii) to set aside an earlier decision of the tribunal,
(*e*) a decision of the Upper Tribunal that is set aside under section 10 (including a decision set aside after proceedings on an appeal under this section have been begun), or
(*f*) any decision of the Upper Tribunal that is of a description specified in an order made by the Lord Chancellor.

(9) A description may be specified under subsection (8)(*f*) only if—
(*a*) in the case of a decision of that description, there is a right to appeal to a court from the decision and that right is, or includes, something other than a right (however expressed) to appeal on any point of law arising from the decision, or
(*b*) decisions of that description are made in carrying out a function transferred under section 30 and prior to the transfer of the function under section 30(1) there was no right to appeal from decisions of that description.

(10) Where—
(*a*) an order under subsection (8)(*f*) specifies a description of decisions, and

VAT

(*b*) decisions of that description are made in carrying out a function transferred under section 30,

the order must be framed so as to come into force no later than the time when the transfer under section 30 of the function takes effect (but power to revoke the order continues to be exercisable after that time, and power to amend the order continues to be exercisable after that time for the purpose of narrowing the description for the time being specified).

(11) Before the Upper Tribunal decides an application made to it under subsection (4), the Upper Tribunal must specify the court that is to be the relevant appellate court as respects the proposed appeal.

(12) The court to be specified under subsection (11) in relation to a proposed appeal is whichever of the following courts appears to the Upper Tribunal to be the most appropriate—

(*a*) the Court of Appeal in England and Wales;
(*b*) the Court of Session;
(*c*) the Court of Appeal in Northern Ireland.

(13) In this section except subsection (11), "the relevant appellate court", as respects an appeal, means the court specified as respects that appeal by the Upper Tribunal under subsection (11).

(14) The Lord Chancellor may by order make provision for a person to be treated as being, or to be treated as not being, a party to a case for the purposes of subsection (2).

(15) Rules of court may make provision as to the time within which an application under subsection (4) to the relevant appellate court must be made.

Commencement—Tribunals, Courts and Enforcement Act 2007 (Commencement No 1) Order, SI 2007/2709 art 2(*a*) (sub-ss (6), (8)(*f*), (9), (10), (14), (15) come into force on 19 September 2007).
Tribunals, Courts and Enforcement Act 2007 (Commencement No 6 and Transitional Provisions) Order, SI 2008/2696 art 5(*a*) (sub-ss (1)–(5), (7), (8)(*a*)–(*e*), (11)–(13) come into force on 3 November 2008).
Orders—Appeals from the Upper Tribunal to the Court of Appeal Order, SI 2008/2834 (made under sub-s (6)).
Appeals (Excluded Decisions) Order, SI 2009/275 (made under sub-s (8)(*f*)).

14 Proceedings on appeal to Court of Appeal etc

(1) Subsection (2) applies if the relevant appellate court, in deciding an appeal under section 13, finds that the making of the decision concerned involved the making of an error on a point of law.

(2) The relevant appellate court—

(*a*) may (but need not) set aside the decision of the Upper Tribunal, and
(*b*) if it does, must either—

(i) remit the case to the Upper Tribunal or, where the decision of the Upper Tribunal was on an appeal or reference from another tribunal or some other person, to the Upper Tribunal or that other tribunal or person, with directions for its reconsideration, or
(ii) re-make the decision.

(3) In acting under subsection (2)(*b*)(i), the relevant appellate court may also—

(*a*) direct that the persons who are chosen to reconsider the case are not to be the same as those who—

(i) where the case is remitted to the Upper Tribunal, made the decision of the Upper Tribunal that has been set aside, or
(ii) where the case is remitted to another tribunal or person, made the decision in respect of which the appeal or reference to the Upper Tribunal was made;

(*b*) give procedural directions in connection with the reconsideration of the case by the Upper Tribunal or other tribunal or person.

(4) In acting under subsection (2)(*b*)(ii), the relevant appellate court—

(*a*) may make any decision which the Upper Tribunal could make if the Upper Tribunal were re-making the decision or (as the case may be) which the other tribunal or person could make if that other tribunal or person were re-making the decision, and
(*b*) may make such findings of fact as it considers appropriate.

(5) Where—

(*a*) under subsection (2)(*b*)(i) the relevant appellate court remits a case to the Upper Tribunal, and
(*b*) the decision set aside under subsection (2)(*a*) was made by the Upper Tribunal on an appeal or reference from another tribunal or some other person,

the Upper Tribunal may (instead of reconsidering the case itself) remit the case to that other tribunal or person, with the directions given by the relevant appellate court for its reconsideration.

(6) In acting under subsection (5), the Upper Tribunal may also—

(*a*) direct that the persons who are chosen to reconsider the case are not to be the same as those who made the decision in respect of which the appeal or reference to the Upper Tribunal was made;
(*b*) give procedural directions in connection with the reconsideration of the case by the other tribunal or person.

(7) In this section "the relevant appellate court", as respects an appeal under section 13, means the court specified as respects that appeal by the Upper Tribunal under section 13(11).

Commencement—Tribunals, Courts and Enforcement Act 2007 (Commencement No 6 and Transitional Provisions) Order, SI 2008/2696 art 5(*a*) (this section comes into force on 3 November 2008).

"Judicial review"

15 Upper Tribunal's "judicial review" jurisdiction

(1) The Upper Tribunal has power, in cases arising under the law of England and Wales or under the law of Northern Ireland, to grant the following kinds of relief—

(*a*) a mandatory order;
(*b*) a prohibiting order;
(*c*) a quashing order;
(*d*) a declaration;
(*e*) an injunction.

(2) The power under subsection (1) may be exercised by the Upper Tribunal if—

(*a*) certain conditions are met (see section 18), or
(*b*) the tribunal is authorised to proceed even though not all of those conditions are met (see section 19(3) and (4)).

(3) Relief under subsection (1) granted by the Upper Tribunal—

(*a*) has the same effect as the corresponding relief granted by the High Court on an application for judicial review, and
(*b*) is enforceable as if it were relief granted by the High Court on an application for judicial review.

(4) In deciding whether to grant relief under subsection (1)(*a*), (*b*) or (*c*), the Upper Tribunal must apply the principles that the High Court would apply in deciding whether to grant that relief on an application for judicial review.

(5) In deciding whether to grant relief under subsection (1)(*d*) or (*e*), the Upper Tribunal must—

(*a*) in cases arising under the law of England and Wales apply the principles that the High Court would apply in deciding whether to grant that relief under section 31(2) of the Supreme Court Act 1981 (c 54) on an application for judicial review, and
(*b*) in cases arising under the law of Northern Ireland apply the principles that the High Court would apply in deciding whether to grant that relief on an application for judicial review.

(6) For the purposes of the application of subsection (3)(*a*) in relation to cases arising under the law of Northern Ireland—

(*a*) a mandatory order under subsection (1)(*a*) shall be taken to correspond to an order of mandamus,
(*b*) a prohibiting order under subsection (1)(*b*) shall be taken to correspond to an order of prohibition, and
(*c*) a quashing order under subsection (1)(*c*) shall be taken to correspond to an order of certiorari.

Commencement—Tribunals, Courts and Enforcement Act 2007 (Commencement No 6 and Transitional Provisions) Order, SI 2008/2696 art 5(*a*) (this section comes into force on 3 November 2008).

16 Application for relief under section 15(1)

(1) This section applies in relation to an application to the Upper Tribunal for relief under section 15(1).

(2) The application may be made only if permission (or, in a case arising under the law of Northern Ireland, leave) to make it has been obtained from the tribunal.

(3) The tribunal may not grant permission (or leave) to make the application unless it considers that the applicant has a sufficient interest in the matter to which the application relates.

(4) Subsection (5) applies where the tribunal considers—

(*a*) that there has been undue delay in making the application, and
(*b*) that granting the relief sought on the application would be likely to cause substantial hardship to, or substantially prejudice the rights of, any person or would be detrimental to good administration.

(5) The tribunal may—

(*a*) refuse to grant permission (or leave) for the making of the application;
(*b*) refuse to grant any relief sought on the application.

(6) The tribunal may award to the applicant damages, restitution or the recovery of a sum due if—

(*a*) the application includes a claim for such an award arising from any matter to which the application relates, and
(*b*) the tribunal is satisfied that such an award would have been made by the High Court if the claim had been made in an action begun in the High Court by the applicant at the time of making the application.

(7) An award under subsection (6) may be enforced as if it were an award of the High Court.

(8) Where—

(*a*) the tribunal refuses to grant permission (or leave) to apply for relief under section 15(1),
(*b*) the applicant appeals against that refusal, and
(*c*) the Court of Appeal grants the permission (or leave),

the Court of Appeal may go on to decide the application for relief under section 15(1).

(9) Subsections (4) and (5) do not prevent Tribunal Procedure Rules from limiting the time within which applications may be made.

Commencement—Tribunals, Courts and Enforcement Act 2007 (Commencement No 6 and Transitional Provisions) Order, SI 2008/2696 art 5(a) (this section comes into force on 3 November 2008).
Orders—Tribunal Procedure (Upper Tribunal) Rules, SI 2008/2698 (made under sub-s (9)).
Tribunal Procedure (Amendment) Rules, SI 2009/274 (made under sub-s (9)).

17 Quashing orders under section 15(1): supplementary provision

(1) If the Upper Tribunal makes a quashing order under section 15(1)(*c*) in respect of a decision, it may in addition—

(*a*) remit the matter concerned to the court, tribunal or authority that made the decision, with a direction to reconsider the matter and reach a decision in accordance with the findings of the Upper Tribunal, or
(*b*) substitute its own decision for the decision in question.

(2) The power conferred by subsection (1)(*b*) is exercisable only if—

(*a*) the decision in question was made by a court or tribunal,
(*b*) the decision is quashed on the ground that there has been an error of law, and
(*c*) without the error, there would have been only one decision that the court or tribunal could have reached.

(3) Unless the Upper Tribunal otherwise directs, a decision substituted by it under subsection (1)(*b*) has effect as if it were a decision of the relevant court or tribunal.

Commencement—Tribunals, Courts and Enforcement Act 2007 (Commencement No 6 and Transitional Provisions) Order, SI 2008/2696 art 5(*a*) (this section comes into force on 3 November 2008).

18 Limits of jurisdiction under section 15(1)

(1) This section applies where an application made to the Upper Tribunal seeks (whether or not alone)—

(*a*) relief under section 15(1), or
(*b*) permission (or, in a case arising under the law of Northern Ireland, leave) to apply for relief under section 15(1).

(2) If Conditions 1 to 4 are met, the tribunal has the function of deciding the application.

(3) If the tribunal does not have the function of deciding the application, it must by order transfer the application to the High Court.

(4) Condition 1 is that the application does not seek anything other than—

(*a*) relief under section 15(1);
(*b*) permission (or, in a case arising under the law of Northern Ireland, leave) to apply for relief under section 15(1);
(*c*) an award under section 16(6);
(*d*) interest;
(*e*) costs.

(5) Condition 2 is that the application does not call into question anything done by the Crown Court.

(6) Condition 3 is that the application falls within a class specified for the purposes of this subsection in a direction given in accordance with Part 1 of Schedule 2 to the Constitutional Reform Act 2005 (c 4).

(7) The power to give directions under subsection (6) includes—

(*a*) power to vary or revoke directions made in exercise of the power, and
(*b*) power to make different provision for different purposes.

(8) Condition 4 is that the judge presiding at the hearing of the application is either—

(*a*) a judge of the High Court or the Court of Appeal in England and Wales or Northern Ireland, or a judge of the Court of Session, or
(*b*) such other persons as may be agreed from time to time between the Lord Chief Justice, the Lord President, or the Lord Chief Justice of Northern Ireland, as the case may be, and the Senior President of Tribunals.

(9) Where the application is transferred to the High Court under subsection (3)—

(*a*) the application is to be treated for all purposes as if it—
(i) had been made to the High Court, and
(ii) sought things corresponding to those sought from the tribunal, and

(*b*) any steps taken, permission (or leave) given or orders made by the tribunal in relation to the application are to be treated as taken, given or made by the High Court.

(10) Rules of court may make provision for the purpose of supplementing subsection (9).

(11) The provision that may be made by Tribunal Procedure Rules about amendment of an application for relief under section 15(1) includes, in particular, provision about amendments that would cause the application to become transferable under subsection (3).

(12) For the purposes of subsection (9)(*a*)(ii), in relation to an application transferred to the High Court in Northern Ireland—

(*a*) an order of mandamus shall be taken to correspond to a mandatory order under section 15(1)(*a*),

(*b*) an order of prohibition shall be taken to correspond to a prohibiting order under section 15(1)(*b*), and

(*c*) an order of certiorari shall be taken to correspond to a quashing order under section 15(1)(*c*).

Commencement—Tribunals, Courts and Enforcement Act 2007 (Commencement No 1) Order, SI 2007/2709 art 2(*a*) (sub-ss (10), (11) come into force on 19 September 2007).

Tribunals, Courts and Enforcement Act 2007 (Commencement No 6 and Transitional Provisions) Order, SI 2008/2696 art 5(*a*) (this section comes into force on 3 November 2008).

19 Transfer of judicial review applications from High Court

(1) In the Supreme Court Act 1981 (c 54), after section 31 insert—

"31A Transfer of judicial review applications to Upper Tribunal

(1) This section applies where an application is made to the High Court—

(*a*) for judicial review, or

(*b*) for permission to apply for judicial review.

(2) If Conditions 1, 2, 3 and 4 are met, the High Court must by order transfer the application to the Upper Tribunal.

(3) If Conditions 1, 2 and 4 are met, but Condition 3 is not, the High Court may by order transfer the application to the Upper Tribunal if it appears to the High Court to be just and convenient to do so.

(4) Condition 1 is that the application does not seek anything other than—

(*a*) relief under section 31(1)(*a*) and (*b*);

(*b*) permission to apply for relief under section 31(1)(*a*) and (*b*);

(*c*) an award under section 31(4);

(*d*) interest;

(*e*) costs.

(5) Condition 2 is that the application does not call into question anything done by the Crown Court.

(6) Condition 3 is that the application falls within a class specified under section 18(6) of the Tribunals, Courts and Enforcement Act 2007.

(7) Condition 4 is that the application does not call into question any decision made under—

(*a*) the Immigration Acts,

(*b*) the British Nationality Act 1981 (c 61),

(*c*) any instrument having effect under an enactment within paragraph (*a*) or (*b*), or

(*d*) any other provision of law for the time being in force which determines British citizenship, British overseas territories citizenship, the status of a British National (Overseas) or British Overseas citizenship."

(2) In the Judicature (Northern Ireland) Act 1978 (c 23), after section 25 insert—

"25A Transfer of judicial review applications to Upper Tribunal

(1) This section applies where an application is made to the High Court—

(*a*) for judicial review, or

(*b*) for leave to apply for judicial review.

(2) If Conditions 1, 2, 3 and 4 are met, the High Court must by order transfer the application to the Upper Tribunal.

(3) If Conditions 1, 2 and 4 are met, but Condition 3 is not, the High Court may by order transfer the application to the Upper Tribunal if it appears to the High Court to be just and convenient to do so.

(4) Condition 1 is that the application does not seek anything other than—

(*a*) relief under section 18(1)(*a*) to (*e*);

(*b*) leave to apply for relief under section 18(1)(*a*) to (*e*);

(*c*) an award under section 20;

(*d*) interest;

(*e*) costs.

(5) Condition 2 is that the application does not call into question anything done by the Crown Court.

(6) Condition 3 is that the application falls within a class specified under section 18(6) of the Tribunals, Courts and Enforcement Act 2007.

(7) Condition 4 is that the application does not call into question any decision made under—

(*a*) the Immigration Acts,

(*b*) the British Nationality Act 1981,

(*c*) any instrument having effect under an enactment within paragraph (*a*) or (*b*), or

(*d*) any other provision of law for the time being in force which determines British citizenship, British overseas territories citizenship, the status of a British National (Overseas) or British Overseas citizenship."

(3) Where an application is transferred to the Upper Tribunal under 31A of the Supreme Court Act 1981 (c 54) or section 25A of the Judicature (Northern Ireland) Act 1978 (transfer from the High Court of judicial review applications)—

(*a*) the application is to be treated for all purposes as if it—

(i) had been made to the tribunal, and

(ii) sought things corresponding to those sought from the High Court,

(*b*) the tribunal has the function of deciding the application, even if it does not fall within a class specified under section 18(6), and

(*c*) any steps taken, permission given, leave given or orders made by the High Court in relation to the application are to be treated as taken, given or made by the tribunal.

(4) Where—

(*a*) an application for permission is transferred to the Upper Tribunal under section 31A of the Supreme Court Act 1981 (c 54) and the tribunal grants permission, or

(*b*) an application for leave is transferred to the Upper Tribunal under section 25A of the Judicature (Northern Ireland) Act 1978 (c 23) and the tribunal grants leave,

the tribunal has the function of deciding any subsequent application brought under the permission or leave, even if the subsequent application does not fall within a class specified under section 18(6).

(5) Tribunal Procedure Rules may make further provision for the purposes of supplementing subsections (3) and (4).

(6) For the purposes of subsection (3)(*a*)(ii), in relation to an application transferred to the Upper Tribunal under section 25A of the Judicature (Northern Ireland) Act 1978—

(*a*) a mandatory order under section 15(1)(*a*) shall be taken to correspond to an order of mandamus,

(*b*) a prohibiting order under section 15(1)(*b*) shall be taken to correspond to an order of prohibition, and

(*c*) a quashing order under section 15(1)(*c*) shall be taken to correspond to an order of certiorari.

Commencement—Tribunals, Courts and Enforcement Act 2007 (Commencement No 6 and Transitional Provisions) Order, SI 2008/2696 art 5(*a*) (this section comes into force on 3 November 2008).

20 Transfer of judicial review applications from the Court of Session

(1) Where an application is made to the supervisory jurisdiction of the Court of Session, the Court—

(*a*) must, if Conditions 1, 2 and 4 are met, and

(*b*) may, if Conditions 1, 3 and 4 are met, but Condition 2 is not,

by order transfer the application to the Upper Tribunal.

(2) Condition 1 is that the application does not seek anything other than an exercise of the supervisory jurisdiction of the Court of Session.

(3) Condition 2 is that the application falls within a class specified for the purposes of this subsection by act of sederunt made with the consent of the Lord Chancellor.

(4) Condition 3 is that the subject matter of the application is not a devolved Scottish matter.

(5) Condition 4 is that the application does not call into question any decision made under—

(*a*) the Immigration Acts,

(*b*) the British Nationality Act 1981 (c 61),

(*c*) any instrument having effect under an enactment within paragraph (*a*) or (*b*), or

(*d*) any other provision of law for the time being in force which determines British citizenship, British overseas territories citizenship, the status of a British National (Overseas) or British Overseas citizenship.

(6) There may not be specified under subsection (3) any class of application which includes an application the subject matter of which is a devolved Scottish matter.

(7) For the purposes of this section, the subject matter of an application is a devolved Scottish matter if it—

(*a*) concerns the exercise of functions in or as regards Scotland, and (*b*) does not relate to a reserved matter within the meaning of the Scotland Act 1998 (c 46).

(8) In subsection (2), the reference to the exercise of the supervisory jurisdiction of the Court of Session includes a reference to the making of any order in connection with or in consequence of the exercise of that jurisdiction.

Commencement—Tribunals, Courts and Enforcement Act 2007 (Commencement No 1) Order, SI 2007/2709 art 2(*a*) (sub-ss (3), (6), (7) come into force on 19 September 2007).
Tribunals, Courts and Enforcement Act 2007 (Commencement No 6 and Transitional Provisions) Order, SI 2008/2696 art 5(*a*) (this section comes into force on 3 November 2008).

21 Upper Tribunal's "judicial review" jurisdiction: Scotland

(1) The Upper Tribunal has the function of deciding applications transferred to it from the Court of Session under section 20(1).

(2) The powers of review of the Upper Tribunal in relation to such applications are the same as the powers of review of the Court of Session in an application to the supervisory jurisdiction of that Court.

(3) In deciding an application by virtue of subsection (1), the Upper Tribunal must apply principles that the Court of Session would apply in deciding an application to the supervisory jurisdiction of that Court.

(4) An order of the Upper Tribunal by virtue of subsection (1)—

(*a*) has the same effect as the corresponding order granted by the Court of Session on an application to the supervisory jurisdiction of that Court, and
(*b*) is enforceable as if it were an order so granted by that Court.

(5) Where an application is transferred to the Upper Tribunal by virtue of section 20(1), any steps taken or orders made by the Court of Session in relation to the application (other than the order to transfer the application under section 20(1)) are to be treated as taken or made by the tribunal.

(6) Tribunal Procedure Rules may make further provision for the purposes of supplementing subsection (5).

Commencement—Tribunals, Courts and Enforcement Act 2007 (Commencement No 1) Order, SI 2007/2709 art 2(*a*) (sub-s (6) comes into force on 19 September 2007).
Tribunals, Courts and Enforcement Act 2007 (Commencement No 6 and Transitional Provisions) Order, SI 2008/2696 art 5(*a*) (sub-ss (1)–(5) come into force on 3 November 2008).

Miscellaneous

22 Tribunal Procedure Rules

(1) There are to be rules, to be called "Tribunal Procedure Rules", governing—

(*a*) the practice and procedure to be followed in the First-tier Tribunal, and
(*b*) the practice and procedure to be followed in the Upper Tribunal.

(2) Tribunal Procedure Rules are to be made by the Tribunal Procedure Committee.

(3) In Schedule 5—

Part 1 makes further provision about the content of Tribunal Procedure Rules,
Part 2 makes provision about the membership of the Tribunal Procedure Committee,
Part 3 makes provision about the making of Tribunal Procedure Rules by the Committee, and
Part 4 confers power to amend legislation in connection with Tribunal Procedure Rules.

(4) Power to make Tribunal Procedure Rules is to be exercised with a view to securing—

(*a*) that, in proceedings before the First-tier Tribunal and Upper Tribunal, justice is done,
(*b*) that the tribunal system is accessible and fair,
(*c*) that proceedings before the First-tier Tribunal or Upper Tribunal are handled quickly and efficiently,
(*d*) that the rules are both simple and simply expressed, and
(*e*) that the rules where appropriate confer on members of the First-tier Tribunal, or Upper Tribunal, responsibility for ensuring that proceedings before the tribunal are handled quickly and efficiently.

(5) In subsection (4)(*b*) "the tribunal system" means the system for deciding matters within the jurisdiction of the First-tier Tribunal or the Upper Tribunal.

Commencement—Tribunals, Courts and Enforcement Act 2007 (Commencement No 1) Order, SI 2007/2709 art 2(*a*) (this section comes into force on 19 September 2007).
Orders—Tribunal Procedure (First-tier Tribunal) (Social Entitlement Chamber) Rules, SI 2008/2685.
Tribunal Procedure (First-tier Tribunal) (War Pensions and Armed Forces Compensation Chamber) Rules, SI 2008/2686.
Tribunal Procedure (Upper Tribunal) Rules, SI 2008/2698.
Tribunal Procedure (First-tier Tribunal) (Tax Chamber) Rules, SI 2009/273.
Tribunal Procedure (Amendment) Rules, SI 2009/274.

23 Practice directions

(1) The Senior President of Tribunals may give directions—

(*a*) as to the practice and procedure of the First-tier Tribunal;
(*b*) as to the practice and procedure of the Upper Tribunal.

(2) A Chamber President may give directions as to the practice and procedure of the chamber over which he presides.

(3) A power under this section to give directions includes—

(*a*) power to vary or revoke directions made in exercise of the power, and
(*b*) power to make different provision for different purposes (including different provision for different areas).

(4) Directions under subsection (1) may not be given without the approval of the Lord Chancellor.

(5) Directions under subsection (2) may not be given without the approval of—

(*a*) the Senior President of Tribunals, and
(*b*) the Lord Chancellor.

(6) Subsections (4) and (5)(*b*) do not apply to directions to the extent that they consist of guidance about any of the following—

(*a*) the application or interpretation of the law;
(*b*) the making of decisions by members of the First-tier Tribunal or Upper Tribunal.

(7) Subsections (4) and (5)(*b*) do not apply to directions to the extent that they consist of criteria for determining which members of the First-tier Tribunal or Upper Tribunal may be chosen to decide particular categories of matter; but the directions may, to that extent, be given only after consulting the Lord Chancellor.

Commencement—Tribunals, Courts and Enforcement Act 2007 (Commencement No 6 and Transitional Provisions) Order, SI 2008/2696 art 5(*a*) (this section comes into force on 3 November 2008).

24 Mediation

(1) A person exercising power to make Tribunal Procedure Rules or give practice directions must, when making provision in relation to mediation, have regard to the following principles—

(*a*) mediation of matters in dispute between parties to proceedings is to take place only by agreement between those parties;
(*b*) where parties to proceedings fail to mediate, or where mediation between parties to proceedings fails to resolve disputed matters, the failure is not to affect the outcome of the proceedings.

(2) Practice directions may provide for members to act as mediators in relation to disputed matters in a case that is the subject of proceedings.

(3) The provision that may be made by virtue of subsection (2) includes provision for a member to act as a mediator in relation to disputed matters in a case even though the member has been chosen to decide matters in the case.

(4) Once a member has begun to act as a mediator in relation to a disputed matter in a case that is the subject of proceedings, the member may decide matters in the case only with the consent of the parties.

(5) Staff appointed under section 40(1) may, subject to their terms of appointment, act as mediators in relation to disputed matters in a case that is the subject of proceedings.

(6) In this section—

"member" means a judge or other member of the First-tier Tribunal or a judge or other member of the Upper Tribunal;
"practice direction" means a direction under section 23(1) or (2);
"proceedings" means proceedings before the First-tier Tribunal or proceedings before the Upper Tribunal.

Commencement—Tribunals, Courts and Enforcement Act 2007 (Commencement No 6 and Transitional Provisions) Order, SI 2008/2696 art 5(*a*) (this section comes into force on 3 November 2008).

25 Supplementary powers of Upper Tribunal

(1) In relation to the matters mentioned in subsection (2), the Upper Tribunal—

(*a*) has, in England and Wales or in Northern Ireland, the same powers, rights, privileges and authority as the High Court, and
(*b*) has, in Scotland, the same powers, rights, privileges and authority as the Court of Session.

(2) The matters are—

(*a*) the attendance and examination of witnesses,
(*b*) the production and inspection of documents, and
(*c*) all other matters incidental to the Upper Tribunal's functions.

(3) Subsection (1) shall not be taken—

(*a*) to limit any power to make Tribunal Procedure Rules;
(*b*) to be limited by anything in Tribunal Procedure Rules other than an express limitation.

(4) A power, right, privilege or authority conferred in a territory by subsection (1) is available for purposes of proceedings in the Upper Tribunal that take place outside that territory (as well as for purposes of proceedings in the tribunal that take place within that territory).

Commencement—Tribunals, Courts and Enforcement Act 2007 (Commencement No 6 and Transitional Provisions) Order, SI 2008/2696 art 5(*a*) (this section comes into force on 3 November 2008).
Cross-references—Tribunal Procedure (First-tier Tribunal) (Tax Chamber) Rules, SI 2009/273 rule 7 (reference to Upper Tribunal in case of failure to comply with Rules).

26 First-tier Tribunal and Upper Tribunal: sitting places

Each of the First-tier Tribunal and the Upper Tribunal may decide a case—

(*a*) in England and Wales,
(*b*) in Scotland, or
(*c*) in Northern Ireland,

even though the case arises under the law of a territory other than the one in which the case is decided.

Commencement—Tribunals, Courts and Enforcement Act 2007 (Commencement No 6 and Transitional Provisions) Order, SI 2008/2696 art 5(*a*) (this section comes into force on 3 November 2008).

27 Enforcement

(1) A sum payable in pursuance of a decision of the First-tier Tribunal or Upper Tribunal made in England and Wales—

(*a*) shall be recoverable as if it were payable under an order of a county court in England and Wales;
(*b*) shall be recoverable as if it were payable under an order of the High Court in England and Wales.

(2) An order for the payment of a sum payable in pursuance of a decision of the First-tier Tribunal or Upper Tribunal made in Scotland (or a copy of such an order certified in accordance with Tribunal Procedure Rules) may be enforced as if it were an extract registered decree arbitral bearing a warrant for execution issued by the sheriff court of any sheriffdom in Scotland.

(3) A sum payable in pursuance of a decision of the First-tier Tribunal or Upper Tribunal made in Northern Ireland—

(*a*) shall be recoverable as if it were payable under an order of a county court in Northern Ireland;
(*b*) shall be recoverable as if it were payable under an order of the High Court in Northern Ireland.

(4) This section does not apply to a sum payable in pursuance of—

(*a*) an award under section 16(6), or
(*b*) an order by virtue of section 21(1).

(5) The Lord Chancellor may by order make provision for subsection (1) or (3) to apply in relation to a sum of a description specified in the order with the omission of one (but not both) of paragraphs (*a*) and (*b*).

(6) Tribunal Procedure Rules—

(*a*) may make provision as to where, for purposes of this section, a decision is to be taken to be made;
(*b*) may provide for all or any of subsections (1) to (3) to apply only, or not to apply except, in relation to sums of a description specified in Tribunal Procedure Rules.

Commencement—Tribunals, Courts and Enforcement Act 2007 (Commencement No 1) Order, SI 2007/2709 art 2(*a*) (sub-ss (5), (6) come into force on 19 September 2007).
Tribunals, Courts and Enforcement Act 2007 (Commencement No 6 and Transitional Provisions) Order, SI 2008/2696 art 6(*a*) (sub-ss (1)–(4) come into force on 1 April 2009).

28 Assessors

(1) If it appears to the First-tier Tribunal or the Upper Tribunal that a matter before it requires special expertise not otherwise available to it, it may direct that in dealing with that matter it shall have the assistance of a person or persons appearing to it to have relevant knowledge or experience.

(2) The remuneration of a person who gives assistance to either tribunal as mentioned in subsection (1) shall be determined and paid by the Lord Chancellor.

(3) The Lord Chancellor may—

(*a*) establish panels of persons from which either tribunal may (but need not) select persons to give it assistance as mentioned in subsection (1);
(*b*) under paragraph (*a*) establish different panels for different purposes;
(*c*) after carrying out such consultation as he considers appropriate, appoint persons to a panel established under paragraph (*a*);
(*d*) remove a person from such a panel.

Commencement—Tribunals, Courts and Enforcement Act 2007 (Commencement No 6 and Transitional Provisions) Order, SI 2008/2696 art 5(*a*) (this section comes into force on 3 November 2008).

29 Costs or expenses

(1) The costs of and incidental to—

(*a*) all proceedings in the First-tier Tribunal, and
(*b*) all proceedings in the Upper Tribunal,

shall be in the discretion of the Tribunal in which the proceedings take place.

(2) The relevant Tribunal shall have full power to determine by whom and to what extent the costs are to be paid.

(3) Subsections (1) and (2) have effect subject to Tribunal Procedure Rules.

(4) In any proceedings mentioned in subsection (1), the relevant Tribunal may—

(*a*) disallow, or
(*b*) (as the case may be) order the legal or other representative concerned to meet,

the whole of any wasted costs or such part of them as may be determined in accordance with Tribunal Procedure Rules.

(5) In subsection (4) "wasted costs" means any costs incurred by a party—

(*a*) as a result of any improper, unreasonable or negligent act or omission on the part of any legal or other representative or any employee of such a representative, or
(*b*) which, in the light of any such act or omission occurring after they were incurred, the relevant Tribunal considers it is unreasonable to expect that party to pay.

(6) In this section "legal or other representative", in relation to a party to proceedings, means any person exercising a right of audience or right to conduct the proceedings on his behalf.

(7) In the application of this section in relation to Scotland, any reference in this section to costs is to be read as a reference to expenses.

Commencement—Tribunals, Courts and Enforcement Act 2007 (Commencement No 6 and Transitional Provisions) Order, SI 2008/2696 art 5(*a*) (this section comes into force on 3 November 2008).
Orders—Tribunal Procedure (First-tier Tribunal) (Social Entitlement Chamber) Rules, SI 2008/2685 (made under sub-s (3)).
Tribunal Procedure (First-tier Tribunal) (War Pensions and Armed Forces Compensation Chamber) Rules, SI 2008/2686 (made under sub-para (3)).
Tribunal Procedure (Upper Tribunal) Rules, SI 2008/2698 (made under sub-ss (3), (4)).
Tribunal Procedure (First-tier Tribunal) (Health, Education and Social Care Chamber) Rules, SI 2008/2699 (made under sub-ss (2), (3)).
Tribunal Procedure (First-tier Tribunal) (Tax Chamber) Rules, SI 2009/273 (made under sub-s (3)).
Tribunal Procedure (Amendment) Rules, SI 2009/274 (made under sub-ss (3), (4)).
Cross-references—Tribunal Procedure (First-tier Tribunal) (Tax Chamber) Rules, SI 2009/273 rule 10 (order for costs).

CHAPTER 3

TRANSFER OF TRIBUNAL FUNCTIONS

30 Transfer of functions of certain tribunals

(1) The Lord Chancellor may by order provide for a function of a scheduled tribunal to be transferred—

(*a*) to the First-tier Tribunal,
(*b*) to the Upper Tribunal,
(*c*) to the First-tier Tribunal and the Upper Tribunal with the question as to which of them is to exercise the function in a particular case being determined by a person under provisions of the order,
(*d*) to the First-tier Tribunal to the extent specified in the order and to the Upper Tribunal to the extent so specified,
(*e*) to the First-tier Tribunal and the Upper Tribunal with the question as to which of them is to exercise the function in a particular case being determined by, or under, Tribunal Procedure Rules,
(*f*) to an employment tribunal,
(*g*) to the Employment Appeal Tribunal,
(*h*) to an employment tribunal and the Employment Appeal Tribunal with the question as to which of them is to exercise the function in a particular case being determined by a person under provisions of the order, or
(*i*) to an employment tribunal to the extent specified in the order and to the Employment Appeal Tribunal to the extent so specified.

(2) In subsection (1) "scheduled tribunal" means a tribunal in a list in Schedule 6 that has effect for the purposes of this section.

(3) The Lord Chancellor may, as respects a function transferred under subsection (1) or this subsection, by order provide for the function to be further transferred as mentioned in any of paragraphs (*a*) to (*i*) of subsection (1).

(4) An order under subsection (1) or (3) may include provision for the purposes of or in consequence of, or for giving full effect to, a transfer under that subsection.

(5) A function of a tribunal may not be transferred under subsection (1) or (3) if, or to the extent that, the provision conferring the function—

(*a*) would be within the legislative competence of the Scottish Parliament if it were included in an Act of that Parliament, or (*b*) would be within the legislative competence of the Northern Ireland Assembly if it were included in an Act of that Assembly.

(6) Subsection (5) does not apply to—

(*a*) the Secretary of State's function of deciding appeals under section 41 of the Consumer Credit Act 1974 (c 39),
(*b*) functions of the Consumer Credit Appeals Tribunal,
(*c*) the Secretary of State's function of deciding appeals under section 7(1) of the Estate Agents Act 1979 (c 38), or
(*d*) functions of an adjudicator under section 5 of the Criminal Injuries Compensation Act 1995 (c 53) (but see subsection (7)).

(7) Functions of an adjudicator under section 5 of the Criminal Injuries Compensation Act 1995 (c 53), so far as they relate to Scotland, may be transferred under subsection (1) or (3) only with the consent of the Scottish Ministers.

(8) A function of a tribunal may be transferred under subsection (1) or (3) only with the consent of the Welsh Ministers if any relevant function is exercisable in relation to the tribunal by the Welsh Ministers (whether by the Welsh Ministers alone, or by the Welsh Ministers jointly or concurrently with any other person).

(9) In subsection (8) "relevant function", in relation to a tribunal, means a function which relates—

(*a*) to the operation of the tribunal (including, in particular, its membership, administration, staff, accommodation and funding, and payments to its members or staff), or
(*b*) to the provision of expenses and allowances to persons attending the tribunal or attending elsewhere in connection with proceedings before the tribunal.

Commencement—Tribunals, Courts and Enforcement Act 2007 (Commencement No 1) Order, SI 2007/2709 art 2(*a*) (this section comes into force on 19 September 2007).
Orders—Transfer of Tribunal Functions Order, SI 2008/2833 (made under sub-ss (1), (4)).
Transfer of Tribunal Functions and Revenue and Customs Appeals Order, SI 2009/56 (made under sub-ss (1), (4)).

31 Transfers under section 30: supplementary powers

(1) The Lord Chancellor may by order make provision for abolishing the tribunal by whom a function transferred under section 30(1) is exercisable immediately before its transfer.

(2) The Lord Chancellor may by order make provision, where functions of a tribunal are transferred under section 30(1), for a person—

(*a*) who is the tribunal (but is not the Secretary of State), or
(*b*) who is a member of the tribunal, or
(*c*) who is an authorised decision-maker for the tribunal,

to (instead or in addition) be the holder of an office specified in subsection (3).

(3) Those offices are—

(*a*) transferred-in judge of the First-tier Tribunal,
(*b*) transferred-in other member of the First-tier Tribunal,
(*c*) transferred-in judge of the Upper Tribunal,
(*d*) transferred-in other member of the Upper Tribunal, and
(*e*) deputy judge of the Upper Tribunal.

(4) Where functions of a tribunal are transferred under section 30(1), the Lord Chancellor must exercise the power under subsection (2) so as to secure that each person who immediately before the end of the tribunal's life—

(*a*) is the tribunal,
(*b*) is a member of the tribunal, or
(*c*) is an authorised decision-maker for the tribunal,

becomes the holder of an office specified in subsection (3) with effect from the end of the tribunal's life (if the person is not then already the holder of such an office).

(5) Subsection (4) does not apply in relation to a person—

(*a*) by virtue of the person's being the Secretary of State, or
(*b*) by virtue of the person's being a Commissioner for the general purposes of the income tax;

and a reference in subsection (4) to the end of a tribunal's life is to when the tribunal is abolished or (without being abolished) comes to have no functions.

(6) For the purposes of this section, a person is an "authorised decision-maker" for a tribunal if—

(*a*) the tribunal is listed in column 1 of an entry in the following Table, and
(*b*) the person is of the description specified in column 2 of that entry.

(1) *Tribunal*	*(2)* *Authorised decision-maker*
Adjudicator to Her Majesty's Land Registry	Member of the Adjudicator's staff who is authorised by the Adjudicator to carry out functions of the Adjudicator which are not of an administrative character
The Secretary of State as respects his function of deciding appeals under section 41 of the Consumer Credit Act 1974 (c 39)	Person who is a member of a panel under regulation 24 of the Consumer Credit Licensing (Appeals) Regulations 1998 (SI 1998/1203)
The Secretary of State as respects his function of deciding appeals under section 7(1) of the Estate Agents Act 1979 (c 38)	Person appointed, at any time after 2005, under regulation 19(1) of the Estate Agents (Appeals) Regulations 1981 (SI 1981/1518) to hear an appeal on behalf of the Secretary of State

(7) Where a function of a tribunal is transferred under section 30(1), the Lord Chancellor may by order provide for procedural rules in force immediately before the transfer to have effect, or to have effect with appropriate modifications, after the transfer (and, accordingly, to be capable of being varied or revoked) as if they were—

(*a*) Tribunal Procedure Rules, or

(*b*) employment tribunal procedure regulations, or Appeal Tribunal procedure rules, within the meaning given by section 42(1) of the Employment Tribunals Act 1996 (c 17).

(8) In subsection (7)—

"procedural rules" means provision (whether called rules or not)—

(*a*) regulating practice or procedure before the tribunal, and

(*b*) applying for purposes connected with the exercise of the function;

"appropriate modifications" means modifications (including additions and omissions) that appear to the Lord Chancellor to be necessary to secure, or expedient in connection with securing, that the procedural rules apply in relation to the exercise of the function after the transfer.

(9) The Lord Chancellor may, in connection with provision made by order under section 30 or the preceding provisions of this section, make by order such incidental, supplemental, transitional or consequential provision, or provision for savings, as the Lord Chancellor thinks fit, including provision applying only in relation to cases selected by a member—

(*a*) of the First-tier Tribunal,

(*b*) of the Upper Tribunal,

(*c*) of the Employment Appeal Tribunal, or

(*d*) of a panel of members of employment tribunals.

(10) Subsections (1), (2) and (7) are not to be taken as prejudicing the generality of subsection (9).

Commencement—Tribunals, Courts and Enforcement Act 2007 (Commencement No 1) Order, SI 2007/2709 art 2(*a*) (this section comes into force on 19 September 2007).

Orders—Tribunals, Courts and Enforcement Act 2007 (Transitional and Consequential Provisions) Order, SI 2008/2683 (made under sub-s (9)).

Tribunals, Courts and Enforcement Act 2007 (Commencement No 6 and Transitional Provisions) Order, SI 2008/2696 (made under sub-s (9)).

Transfer of Tribunal Functions Order, SI 2008/2833 (made under sub-ss (1), (2), (9)).

Transfer of Tribunal Functions and Revenue and Customs Appeals Order, SI 2009/56 (made under sub-ss (1), (2), (9)).

32 Power to provide for appeal to Upper Tribunal from tribunals in Wales

(1) Subsection (2) applies if—

(*a*) a function is transferred under section 30(1)(*a*), (*c*), (*d*) or (*e*) in relation to England but is not transferred under section 30(1) in relation to Wales, or

(*b*) a function that is not exercisable in relation to Wales is transferred under section 30(1)(*a*), (*c*), (*d*) or (*e*) in relation to England and, although there is a corresponding function that is exercisable in relation to Wales, that corresponding function is not transferred under section 30(1) in relation to Wales.

(2) The Lord Chancellor may by order—

(*a*) provide for an appeal against a decision to be made to the Upper Tribunal instead of to the court to which an appeal would otherwise fall to be made where the decision is made in exercising, in relation to Wales, the function mentioned in subsection (1)(*a*) or (as the case may be) the corresponding function mentioned in subsection (1)(*b*);

(*b*) provide for a reference of any matter to be made to the Upper Tribunal instead of to the court to which a reference would otherwise fall to be made where the matter arises in exercising, in relation to Wales, the function mentioned in subsection (1)(*a*) or (as the case may be) the corresponding function mentioned in subsection (1)(*b*).

(3) The Lord Chancellor may by order provide for an appeal against a decision of a scheduled tribunal to be made to the Upper Tribunal, instead of to the court to which an appeal would otherwise fall to be made, where the decision is made by the tribunal in exercising a function in relation to Wales.

(4) In subsection (3) "scheduled tribunal" means a tribunal in a list in Schedule 6 that has effect for the purposes of that subsection.

(5) An order under subsection (2) or (3)—

(*a*) may include provision for the purposes of or in consequence of, or for giving full effect to, provision made by the order;

(*b*) may include such incidental, supplemental, transitional or consequential provision or savings as the Lord Chancellor thinks fit.

Commencement—Tribunals, Courts and Enforcement Act 2007 (Commencement No 1) Order, SI 2007/2709 art 2(*a*) (this section comes into force on 19 September 2007).

Orders—Transfer of Tribunal Functions Order, SI 2008/2833 (made under sub-ss (3), (5)).

33 Power to provide for appeal to Upper Tribunal from tribunals in Scotland

(1) Subsection (2) applies if—

(*a*) a function is transferred under section 30(1)(*a*), (*c*), (*d*) or (*e*) in relation to England (whether or not also in relation to Wales) but is not transferred under section 30(1) in relation to Scotland,

(*b*) an appeal may be made to the Upper Tribunal against any decision, or any decision of a particular description, made in exercising the transferred function in relation to England, and

(*c*) no appeal may be made against a corresponding decision made in exercising the function in relation to Scotland.

(2) The Lord Chancellor may by order provide for an appeal against any such corresponding decision to be made to the Upper Tribunal.

(3) An order under subsection (2)—

(*a*) may include provision for the purposes of or in consequence of, or for giving full effect to, provision made by the order;

(*b*) may include such incidental, supplemental, transitional or consequential provision or savings as the Lord Chancellor thinks fit.

(4) An order under subsection (2) does not cease to have effect, and power to vary or revoke the order does not cease to be exercisable, just because either or each of the conditions in subsection (1)(*b*) and (*c*) ceases to be satisfied in relation to the function and decisions concerned.

Commencement—Tribunals, Courts and Enforcement Act 2007 (Commencement No 1) Order, SI 2007/2709 art 2(*a*) (this section comes into force on 19 September 2007).

Orders—Transfer of Tribunal Functions Order, SI 2008/2833 (made under sub-ss (2), (3)).

34 Power to provide for appeal to Upper Tribunal from tribunals in Northern Ireland

(1) Subsection (2) applies if—

(*a*) a function is transferred under section 30(1)(*a*), (*c*), (*d*) or (*e*) in relation to England (whether or not also in relation to Wales) but is not transferred under section 30(1) in relation to Northern Ireland,

(*b*) an appeal may be made to the Upper Tribunal against any decision, or any decision of a particular description, made in exercising the transferred function in relation to England, and

(*c*) no appeal may be made against a corresponding decision made in exercising the function in relation to Northern Ireland.

(2) The Lord Chancellor may by order provide for an appeal against any such corresponding decision to be made to the Upper Tribunal.

(3) An order under subsection (2)—

(*a*) may include provision for the purposes of or in consequence of, or for giving full effect to, provision made by the order;

(*b*) may include such incidental, supplemental, transitional or consequential provision or savings as the Lord Chancellor thinks fit.

(4) An order under subsection (2) does not cease to have effect, and power to vary or revoke the order does not cease to be exercisable, just because either or each of the conditions in subsection (1)(*b*) and (*c*) ceases to be satisfied in relation to the function and decisions concerned.

Commencement—Tribunals, Courts and Enforcement Act 2007 (Commencement No 1) Order, SI 2007/2709 art 2(*a*) (this section comes into force on 19 September 2007).

Orders—Transfer of Tribunal Functions Order, SI 2008/2833 (made under sub-ss (2), (3)).

35 Transfer of Ministerial responsibilities for certain tribunals

(1) The Lord Chancellor may by order—

(*a*) transfer any relevant function, so far as that function is exercisable by a Minister of the Crown—

(i) to the Lord Chancellor, or

(ii) to two (or more) Ministers of the Crown of whom one is the Lord Chancellor;

(*b*) provide for any relevant function that is exercisable by a Minister of the Crown other than the Lord Chancellor to be exercisable by the other Minister of the Crown concurrently with the Lord Chancellor;

(*c*) provide for any relevant function that is exercisable by the Lord Chancellor concurrently with another Minister of the Crown to cease to be exercisable by the other Minister of the Crown.

(2) In this section "relevant function" means a function, in relation to a scheduled tribunal, which relates—

(*a*) to the operation of the tribunal (including, in particular, its membership, administration, staff, accommodation and funding, and payments to its members or staff), or

(*b*) to the provision of expenses and allowances to persons attending the tribunal or attending elsewhere in connection with proceedings before the tribunal.

(3) In subsection (2) "scheduled tribunal" means a tribunal in a list in Schedule 6 that has effect for the purposes of this section.

(4) A relevant function may not be transferred under subsection (1) if, or to the extent that, the provision conferring the function—

(*a*) would be within the legislative competence of the Scottish Parliament if it were included in an Act of that Parliament, or

(*b*) would be within the legislative competence of the Northern Ireland Assembly if it were included in an Act of that Assembly.

(5) Subsection (4) does not apply to any relevant function of the Secretary of State—

(*a*) under section 41 of the Consumer Credit Act 1974 (c 39) (appeals), or

(*b*) under section 7 of the Estate Agents Act 1979 (c 38) (appeals).

(6) Any reference in subsection (1) to a Minister of the Crown includes a reference to a Minister of the Crown acting jointly.

(7) An order under subsection (1)—

(*a*) may relate to a function either wholly or in cases (including cases framed by reference to areas) specified in the order;

(*b*) may include provision for the purposes of, or in consequence of, or for giving full effect to, the transfer or (as the case may be) other change as regards exercise;

(*c*) may include such incidental, supplementary, transitional or consequential provision or savings as the Lord Chancellor thinks fit;

(*d*) may include provision for the transfer of any property, rights or liabilities of the person who loses functions or whose functions become shared with the Lord Chancellor.

(8) An order under subsection (1), so far as it—

(*a*) provides under paragraph (*a*) for the transfer of a function, or

(*b*) provides under paragraph (*b*) for a function to become exercisable by the Lord Chancellor, or

(*c*) provides under paragraph (*c*) for a function to cease to be exercisable by a Minister of the Crown other than the Lord Chancellor,

may not, after that transfer or other change has taken place, be revoked by another order under that subsection.

(9) Section 1 of the 1975 Act (power to transfer Ministerial functions) does not apply to a function of the Lord Chancellor—

(*a*) so far as it is a function transferred to the Lord Chancellor under subsection (1)(*a*),

(*b*) so far as it is a function exercisable by the Lord Chancellor as a result of provision under subsection (1)(*b*), or

(*c*) so far as it is a function that has become exercisable by the Lord Chancellor alone as a result of provision under subsection (1)(*c*).

(10) In this section—

"Minister of the Crown" has the meaning given by section 8(1) of the 1975 Act but includes the Commissioners for Her Majesty's Revenue and Customs;

"the 1975 Act" means the Ministers of the Crown Act 1975 (c 26).

Commencement—Tribunals, Courts and Enforcement Act 2007 (Commencement No 1) Order, SI 2007/2709 art 2(*a*) (this section comes into force on 19 September 2007).

36 Transfer of powers to make procedural rules for certain tribunals

(1) The Lord Chancellor may by order transfer any power to make procedural rules for a scheduled tribunal to—

(*a*) himself, or

(*b*) the Tribunal Procedure Committee.

(2) A power may not be transferred under subsection (1) if, or to the extent that, the provision conferring the power—

(*a*) would be within the legislative competence of the Scottish Parliament if it were included in an Act of that Parliament, or

(*b*) would be within the legislative competence of the Northern Ireland Assembly if it were included in an Act of that Assembly.

(3) Subsection (2) does not apply to—

(*a*) power conferred by section 40A(3) …[1] of the Consumer Credit Act 1974 (c 39) (power to make provision with respect to appeals), or

(*b*) power conferred by section 7(3) of the Estate Agents Act 1979 (c 38) (duty of Secretary of State to make regulations with respect to appeals under section 7(1) of that Act).

(4) An order under subsection (1)(*b*)—

(*a*) may not alter any parliamentary procedure relating to the making of the procedural rules concerned, but

(*b*) may otherwise include provision for the purpose of assimilating the procedure for making them to the procedure for making Tribunal Procedure Rules.

(5) An order under subsection (1)(*b*) may include provision requiring the Tribunal Procedure Committee to make procedural rules for purposes notified to it by the Lord Chancellor.

(6) An order under this section—

(*a*) may relate to a power either wholly or in cases (including cases framed by reference to areas) specified in the order;

(*b*) may include provision for the purposes of or in consequence of, or for giving full effect to, the transfer;

(*c*) may include such incidental, supplementary, transitional or consequential provision or savings as the Lord Chancellor thinks fit.

(7) A power to make procedural rules for a tribunal that is exercisable by the Tribunal Procedure Committee by virtue of an order under this section must be exercised by the committee with a view to securing—

(*a*) that the system for deciding matters within the jurisdiction of that tribunal is accessible and fair,

(*b*) that proceedings before that tribunal are handled quickly and efficiently,

(*c*) that the rules are both simple and simply expressed, and

(*d*) that the rules where appropriate confer on persons who are, or who are members of, that tribunal responsibility for ensuring that proceedings before that tribunal are handled quickly and efficiently.

(8) In this section—

"procedural rules", in relation to a tribunal, means provision (whether called rules or not) regulating practice or procedure before the tribunal;

"scheduled tribunal" means a tribunal in a list in Schedule 6 that has effect for the purposes of this section.

Commencement—Tribunals, Courts and Enforcement Act 2007 (Commencement No 1) Order, SI 2007/2709 art 2(*a*) (this section comes into force on 19 September 2007).

Amendments—[1] Words "or 41(2)" repealed by TCEA 2007 s 146, Sch 23 Pt 1 with effect from 3 November 2008 (by virtue of SI 2008/2696 art 5(i), (vii)).

37 Power to amend lists of tribunals in Schedule 6

(1) The Lord Chancellor may by order amend Schedule 6—

(*a*) for the purpose of adding a tribunal to a list in the Schedule;

(*b*) for the purpose of removing a tribunal from a list in the Schedule;

(*c*) for the purpose of removing a list from the Schedule;

(*d*) for the purpose of adding to the Schedule a list of tribunals that has effect for the purposes of any one or more of sections 30, 32(3), 35 and 36.

(2) The following rules apply to the exercise of power under subsection (1)—

(*a*) a tribunal may not be added to a list, or be in an added list, if the tribunal is established otherwise than by or under an enactment;

(*b*) a tribunal established by an enactment passed or made after the last day of the Session in which this Act is passed must not be added to a list, or be in an added list, that has effect for the purposes of section 30;

(*c*) if any relevant function is exercisable in relation to a tribunal by the Welsh Ministers (whether by the Welsh Ministers alone, or by the Welsh Ministers jointly or concurrently with any other person), the tribunal may be added to a list, or be in an added list, only with the consent of the Welsh Ministers;

(*d*) a tribunal may be in more than one list.

(3) In subsection (2)(*c*) "relevant function", in relation to a tribunal, means a function which relates—

(*a*) to the operation of the tribunal (including, in particular, its membership, administration, staff, accommodation and funding, and payments to its members or staff), or (*b*) to the provision of expenses and allowances to persons attending the tribunal or attending elsewhere in connection with proceedings before the tribunal.

(4) In subsection (1) "tribunal" does not include an ordinary court of law.

(5) In this section "enactment" means any enactment whenever passed or made, including an enactment comprised in subordinate legislation (within the meaning of the Interpretation Act 1978 (c 30)).

Commencement—Tribunals, Courts and Enforcement Act 2007 (Commencement No 1) Order, SI 2007/2709 art 2(*a*) (this section comes into force on 19 September 2007).
Orders—Transfer of Tribunal Functions Order, SI 2008/2833 (made under sub-s (1)).

38 Orders under sections 30 to 36: supplementary

(1) Provision in an order under any of sections 30 to 36 may take the form of amendments, repeals or revocations of enactments.

(2) In this section "enactment" means any enactment whenever passed or made, including an enactment comprised in subordinate legislation (within the meaning of the Interpretation Act 1978).

(3) Any power to extend enactments to a territory outside the United Kingdom shall have effect as if it included—

(*a*) power to extend those enactments as they have effect with any amendments and repeals made in them by orders under any of sections 30 to 36, and

(*b*) power to extend those enactments as if any amendments and repeals made in them under those sections had not been made.

Commencement—Tribunals, Courts and Enforcement Act 2007 (Commencement No 1) Order, SI 2007/2709 art 2(*a*) (this section comes into force on 19 September 2007).

CHAPTER 4
ADMINISTRATIVE MATTERS IN RESPECT OF CERTAIN TRIBUNALS

39 The general duty

(1) The Lord Chancellor is under a duty to ensure that there is an efficient and effective system to support the carrying on of the business of—

(*a*) the First-tier Tribunal,
(*b*) the Upper Tribunal,
(*c*) employment tribunals,
(*d*) the Employment Appeal Tribunal, and
(*e*) the Asylum and Immigration Tribunal,

and that appropriate services are provided for those tribunals (referred to in this section and in sections 40 and 41 as "the tribunals").

(2) Any reference in this section, or in section 40 or 41, to the Lord Chancellor's general duty in relation to the tribunals is to his duty under subsection (1).

(3) The Lord Chancellor must annually prepare and lay before each House of Parliament a report as to the way in which he has discharged his general duty in relation to the tribunals.

Commencement—Tribunals, Courts and Enforcement Act 2007 (Commencement No 1) Order, SI 2007/2709 art 2(*a*) (this section comes into force on 19 September 2007).

40 Tribunal staff and services

(1) The Lord Chancellor may appoint such staff as appear to him appropriate for the purpose of discharging his general duty in relation to the tribunals.

(2) Subject to subsections (3) and (4), the Lord Chancellor may enter into such contracts with other persons for the provision, by them or their sub-contractors, of staff or services as appear to him appropriate for the purpose of discharging his general duty in relation to the tribunals.

(3) The Lord Chancellor may not enter into contracts for the provision of staff to discharge functions which involve making judicial decisions or exercising any judicial discretion.

(4) The Lord Chancellor may not enter into contracts for the provision of staff to carry out the administrative work of the tribunals unless an order made by the Lord Chancellor authorises him to do so.

(5) Before making an order under subsection (4) the Lord Chancellor must consult the Senior President of Tribunals as to what effect (if any) the order might have on the proper and efficient administration of justice.

(6) An order under subsection (4) may authorise the Lord Chancellor to enter into contracts for the provision of staff to discharge functions—

(*a*) wholly or to the extent specified in the order,
(*b*) generally or in cases or areas specified in the order, and
(*c*) unconditionally or subject to the fulfilment of conditions specified in the order.

Commencement—Tribunals, Courts and Enforcement Act 2007 (Commencement No 1) Order, SI 2007/2709 art 2(*a*) (this section comes into force on 19 September 2007).
Orders—Contracting Out (Administrative Work of Tribunals) Order, SI 2009/121 (made under sub-s (4)).

Cross-references—Tribunal Procedure (First-tier Tribunal) (Tax Chamber) Rules, SI 2009/273 rule 4 (delegation to staff). Transfer of Tribunal Functions and Revenue and Customs Appeals Order, SI 2009/56 art 6, Sch 3 para 12 (staff appointed to existing tribunals before 1 April 2009 are, from that date, to be treated as if they had been appointed under sub-s (1)).

41 Provision of accommodation

(1) The Lord Chancellor may provide, equip, maintain and manage such tribunal buildings, offices and other accommodation as appear to him appropriate for the purpose of discharging his general duty in relation to the tribunals.

(2) The Lord Chancellor may enter into such arrangements for the provision, equipment, maintenance or management of tribunal buildings, offices or other accommodation as appear to him appropriate for the purpose of discharging his general duty in relation to the tribunals.

(3) The powers under—

(*a*) section 2 of the Commissioners of Works Act 1852 (c 28) (acquisition by agreement), and
(*b*) section 228(1) of the Town and Country Planning Act 1990 (c 8) (compulsory acquisition),

to acquire land necessary for the public service are to be treated as including power to acquire land for the purpose of its provision under arrangements entered into under subsection (2).

(4) In this section "tribunal building" means any place where any of the tribunals sits, including the precincts of any building in which it sits.

Commencement—Tribunals, Courts and Enforcement Act 2007 (Commencement No 1) Order, SI 2007/2709 art 2(*a*) (this section comes into force on 19 September 2007).

42 Fees

(1) The Lord Chancellor may by order prescribe fees payable in respect of—

(*a*) anything dealt with by the First-tier Tribunal,
(*b*) anything dealt with by the Upper Tribunal,
(*c*) anything dealt with by the Asylum and Immigration Tribunal,
(*d*) anything dealt with by an added tribunal, and
(*e*) mediation conducted by staff appointed under section 40(1).

(2) An order under subsection (1) may, in particular, contain provision as to—

(*a*) scales or rates of fees;
(*b*) exemptions from or reductions in fees;
(*c*) remission of fees in whole or in part.

(3) In subsection (1)(*d*) "added tribunal" means a tribunal specified in an order made by the Lord Chancellor.

(4) A tribunal may be specified in an order under subsection (3) only if—

(*a*) it is established by or under an enactment, whenever passed or made, and
(*b*) is not an ordinary court of law.

(5) Before making an order under this section, the Lord Chancellor must consult—

(*a*) the Senior President of Tribunals, and
(*b*) the Administrative Justice and Tribunals Council.

(6) The making of an order under subsection (1) requires the consent of the Treasury except where the order contains provision only for the purpose of altering amounts payable by way of fees already prescribed under that subsection.

(7) The Lord Chancellor must take such steps as are reasonably practicable to bring information about fees under subsection (1) to the attention of persons likely to have to pay them.

(8) Fees payable under subsection (1) are recoverable summarily as a civil debt.

(9) Subsection (8) does not apply to the recovery in Scotland of fees payable under this section.

(10) Until the Administrative Justice and Tribunals Council first has ten members appointed under paragraph 1(2) of Schedule 7, the reference to that council in subsection (5) is to be read as a reference to the Council on Tribunals.

Commencement—Tribunals, Courts and Enforcement Act 2007 (Commencement No 1) Order, SI 2007/2709 art 2(*a*) (this section comes into force on 19 September 2007).

43 Report by Senior President of Tribunals

(1) Each year the Senior President of Tribunals must give the Lord Chancellor a report covering, in relation to relevant tribunal cases—

(*a*) matters that the Senior President of Tribunals wishes to bring to the attention of the Lord Chancellor, and
(*b*) matters that the Lord Chancellor has asked the Senior President of Tribunals to cover in the report.

(2) The Lord Chancellor must publish each report given to him under subsection (1).

(3) In this section "relevant tribunal cases" means—

(*a*) cases coming before the First-tier Tribunal,
(*b*) cases coming before the Upper Tribunal,
(*c*) cases coming before the Employment Appeal Tribunal, …[1]

(*d*) cases coming before employment tribunals[, and
(*e*) cases coming before the Asylum and Immigration Tribunal.][1]

Commencement—Tribunals, Courts and Enforcement Act 2007 (Commencement No 6 and Transitional Provisions) Order, SI 2008/2696 art 5(*a*) (this section comes into force on 3 November 2008).

Amendments—[1] Word "and" in sub-s (3)(*c*) repealed, and sub-s (3)(*e*) and preceding word "and" inserted, by the UK Borders Act 2007 ss 56, 58, Schedule, with effect from 1 April 2008: SI 2008/309, art 4(*g*).

CHAPTER 5
OVERSIGHT OF ADMINISTRATIVE JUSTICE SYSTEM, TRIBUNALS AND INQUIRIES

44 The Administrative Justice and Tribunals Council

(1) There is to be a council to be known as the Administrative Justice and Tribunals Council.

(2) In Schedule 7—

Part 1 makes provision about membership and committees of the Council,
Part 2 makes provision about functions of the Council,
Part 3 requires the Council to be consulted before procedural rules for certain tribunals are made, confirmed etc, and
Part 4 contains interpretative provisions.

Commencement—Tribunals, Courts and Enforcement Act 2007 (Commencement No 1) Order, SI 2007/2709 art 3(*a*) (this section comes into force on 1 November 2007).

45 Abolition of the Council on Tribunals

(1) The following are abolished—

(*a*) the Council on Tribunals, and
(*b*) the Scottish Committee of the Council on Tribunals.

(2) In consequence of subsection (1), sections 1 to 4 of the Tribunals and Inquiries Act 1992 (c 53) cease to have effect.

(3) The Lord Chancellor may by order transfer to the Administrative Justice and Tribunals Council the property, rights and liabilities of—

(*a*) the Council on Tribunals;
(*b*) the Scottish Committee of the Council on Tribunals.

Commencement—Tribunals, Courts and Enforcement Act 2007 (Commencement No 1) Order, SI 2007/2709 art 2(*a*) (sub-s (3) comes into force on 19 September 2007).
Tribunals, Courts and Enforcement Act 2007 (Commencement No 1) Order, SI 2007/2709 art 3(*a*) (sub-ss (1), (2) come into force on 1 November 2007).

CHAPTER 6
SUPPLEMENTARY

46 Delegation of functions by Lord Chief Justice etc

(1) The Lord Chief Justice of England and Wales may nominate a judicial office holder (as defined in section 109(4) of the Constitutional Reform Act 2005) to exercise any of his functions under the provisions listed in subsection (2).

(2) The provisions are—

paragraphs 3(4) and 6(3)(*a*) of Schedule 2;
paragraphs 3(4) and 6(3)(*a*) of Schedule 3;
paragraphs 2(2) and 5(5) of Schedule 4;
paragraphs 21(2), 22, 24 and 25(2)(*a*) of Schedule 5.

(3) The Lord President of the Court of Session may nominate any of the following to exercise any of his functions under the provisions listed in subsection (4)—

(*a*) a judge who is a member of the First or Second Division of the Inner House of the Court of Session;
(*b*) the Senior President of Tribunals.

(4) The provisions are—

paragraphs 3(2) and 6(3)(*b*) of Schedule 2;
paragraphs 3(2) and 6(3)(*b*) of Schedule 3;
paragraphs 2(3) and 5(6) of Schedule 4;
paragraphs 23, 24, 25(2)(*b*) and (*c*) and 28(1)(*b*) of Schedule 5.

(5) The Lord Chief Justice of Northern Ireland may nominate any of the following to exercise any of his functions under the provisions listed in subsection (6)—

(*a*) the holder of one of the offices listed in Schedule 1 to the Justice (Northern Ireland) Act 2002 (c 26);
(*b*) a Lord Justice of Appeal (as defined in section 88 of that Act);
(*c*) the Senior President of Tribunals.

(6) The provisions are—

paragraphs 3(3) and 6(3)(*c*) of Schedule 2;

paragraphs 3(3) and 6(3)(*c*) of Schedule 3;
paragraphs 2(4) and 5(7) of Schedule 4;
paragraphs 24 and 25(2)(*c*) of Schedule 5.

Commencement—Tribunals, Courts and Enforcement Act 2007 (Commencement No 1) Order, SI 2007/2709 art 2(*b*) (this section, to the extent that it relates to Sch 5, comes into force on 19 September 2007).
Tribunals, Courts and Enforcement Act 2007 (Commencement No 6 and Transitional Provisions) Order, SI 2008/2696 art 5(*a*) (for remaining purposes, this section comes into force on 3 November 2008).

47 Co-operation in relation to judicial training, guidance and welfare

(1) Persons with responsibilities in connection with a courts-related activity, and persons with responsibilities in connection with the corresponding tribunals activity, must co-operate with each other in relation to the carrying-on of those activities.

(2) In this section "courts-related activity" and "corresponding tribunals activity" are to be read as follows—

(*a*) making arrangements for training of judiciary of a territory is a courts-related activity, and the corresponding tribunals activity is making arrangements for training of tribunal members;

(*b*) making arrangements for guidance of judiciary of a territory is a courts-related activity, and the corresponding tribunals activity is making arrangements for guidance of tribunal members;

(*c*) making arrangements for the welfare of judiciary of a territory is a courts-related activity, and the corresponding tribunals activity is making arrangements for the welfare of tribunal members.

(3) Subsection (1) applies to a person who has responsibilities in connection with a courts-related activity only if—

(*a*) the person is the chief justice of the territory concerned, or

(*b*) what the person does in discharging those responsibilities is done (directly or indirectly) on behalf of the chief justice of that territory.

(4) Subsection (1) applies to a person who has responsibilities in connection with a corresponding tribunals activity only if—

(*a*) the person is the Senior President of Tribunals, or

(*b*) what the person does in discharging those responsibilities is done (directly or indirectly) on behalf of the Senior President of Tribunals.

(5) For the purposes of this section—

(*a*) "territory" means—

(i) England and Wales,
(ii) Scotland, or
(iii) Northern Ireland;

(*b*) the "chief justice"—

(i) of England and Wales is the Lord Chief Justice of England and Wales,
(ii) of Scotland is the Lord President of the Court of Session, and
(iii) of Northern Ireland is the Lord Chief Justice of Northern Ireland;

(*c*) a person is a "tribunal member" if the person is—

(i) a judge, or other member, of the First-tier Tribunal or Upper Tribunal,
(ii) a judge, or other member, of the Employment Appeal Tribunal,
(iii) a member of a panel of members of employment tribunals (whether or not a panel of chairmen), or
(iv) any member of the Asylum and Immigration Tribunal.

Commencement—Tribunals, Courts and Enforcement Act 2007 (Commencement No 6 and Transitional Provisions) Order, SI 2008/2696 art 5(*a*) (this section comes into force on 3 November 2008).

48 Consequential and other amendments, and transitional provisions

(1) Schedule 8, which makes—

amendments consequential on provisions of this Part, and
other amendments in connection with tribunals and inquiries,

has effect.

(2) Schedule 9, which contains transitional provisions, has effect.

Commencement—Tribunals, Courts and Enforcement Act 2007 (Commencement No 1) Order, SI 2007/2709 art 2(*c*), (*d*) (sub-s (1) comes into force on 19 September 2007, to the extent that it relates to Sch 8 paras 31(1)–(3), 62, 63, 65(1), (2) and para 65(3) to the extent that it relates to the Senior President of Tribunals; sub-s (2) comes into force on 19 September 2007 to the extent that it relates to Sch 9 paras 1, 2, 12(2)).
Tribunals, Courts and Enforcement Act 2007 (Commencement No 1) Order, SI 2007/2709 art 3(*b*) (sub-s (1) comes into force on 1 November 2007, to the extent that it relates to the following paras of Sch 8—
(i) paras 2, 3, 8–12, 14, 15, 17, 19–23, 30(*a*)–(*c*), 32, 33(1), (2), 49–52, 56–61;
(ii) paras 4, 5, 7, 53 to the extent that the relate to the Administrative Justice and Tribunals Council and to the Scottish Committee of the Administrative Justice and Tribunals Council; and
(iii) para 18 to the extent that it relates to the Administrative Justice and Tribunals Council.).
Tribunals, Courts and Enforcement Act 2007 (Commencement No 1) Order, SI 2007/2709 art 4 (sub-s (1) comes into force on 1 December 2007, to the extent that it relates to Sch 8 paras 35–39).

Tribunals, Courts and Enforcement Act 2007 (Commencement No 1) Order, SI 2007/2709 art 6(*a*) (sub-s (1) comes into force on 1 June 2008, to the extent that it relates to the following paras of Sch 8—
(i) paras 4, 5 to the extent that they relate to the Welsh Committee of the Administrative Justice and Tribunals Council;
(ii) paras 7, 18, 53 to the extent that they are not already in force; and
(iii) para 30(*d*).).
Tribunals, Courts and Enforcement Act 2007 (Commencement No 5 and Transitional Provisions) Order, SI 2008/1653 art 2(*a*) (sub-s (1) comes into force on 21 July 2008 in relation to the repeal made by Sch 8 para 27 in so far as it applies to the powers of a minister).
Tribunals, Courts and Enforcement Act 2007 (Commencement No 6 and Transitional Provisions) Order, SI 2008/2696—
(i) art 5(*c*) (sub-s (1) comes into force on 3 November 2008 to the extent that it relates to the following provisions of Sch 8—
- paras 6, 16, 28, 31(4)–(6), 33(3), 40–42, 44–48, 54, 64(*b*), and 66;
- para 25 to the extent that it relates to the Tribunals and Inquiries Act 1992 Sch 1 para 7(*b*);
- paras 4 and 5 to the extent that they are not already in force; and
- para 65(3) to the extent that it is not already in force);
(ii) art 5(*d*) (sub-s (2) comes into force on 3 November 2008 to the extent that it relates to Sch 9 paras 3–11, 12(1), (3)–(7), 13–19); and
(iii) art 6(*b*) (sub-s (1) comes into force on 1 April 2009 to the extent that it related to Sch 8 paras 1, 43, 45).

49 Orders and regulations under Part 1: supplemental and procedural provisions

(1) Power—

(*a*) of the Lord Chancellor to make an order, or regulations, under this Part,
(*b*) of the Senior President of Tribunals to make an order under section 7(9), or
(*c*) of the Scottish Ministers, or the Welsh Ministers, to make an order under paragraph 25(2) of Schedule 7,

is exercisable by statutory instrument.

(2) The Statutory Instruments Act 1946 (c 36) shall apply in relation to the power to make orders conferred on the Senior President of Tribunals by section 7(9) as if the Senior President of Tribunals were a Minister of the Crown.

(3) Any power mentioned in subsection (1) includes power to make different provision for different purposes.

(4) Without prejudice to the generality of subsection (3), power to make an order under section 30 or 31 includes power to make different provision in relation to England, Scotland, Wales and Northern Ireland respectively.

(5) No order mentioned in subsection (6) is to be made unless a draft of the statutory instrument containing it (whether alone or with other provision) has been laid before, and approved by a resolution of, each House of Parliament.

(6) Those orders are—

(*a*) an order under section 11(8), 13(6) or (14), 30, 31(1), 32, 33, 34, 35, 36, 37 or 42(3);
(*b*) an order under paragraph 15 of Schedule 4;
(*c*) an order under section 42(1)(*a*) to (*d*) that provides for fees to be payable in respect of things for which fees have never been payable;
(*d*) an order under section 31(2), (7) or (9), or paragraph 30(1) of Schedule 5, that contains provision taking the form of an amendment or repeal of an enactment comprised in an Act.

(7) A statutory instrument that—

(*a*) contains—
(i) an order mentioned in subsection (8), or
(ii) regulations under Part 3 of Schedule 9, and
(*b*) is not subject to any requirement that a draft of the instrument be laid before, and approved by a resolution of, each House of Parliament,

is subject to annulment in pursuance of a resolution of either House of Parliament.

(8) Those orders are—

(*a*) an order made by the Lord Chancellor under this Part;
(*b*) an order made by the Senior President of Tribunals under section 7(9).

(9) A statutory instrument that contains an order made by the Scottish Ministers under paragraph 25(2) of Schedule 7 is subject to annulment in pursuance of a resolution of the Scottish Parliament.

(10) A statutory instrument that contains an order made by the Welsh Ministers under paragraph 25(2) of Schedule 7 is subject to annulment in pursuance of a resolution of the National Assembly for Wales.

Commencement—Tribunals, Courts and Enforcement Act 2007 (Commencement No 1) Order, SI 2007/2709 art 2(*a*) (this section comes into force on 19 September 2007).

PART 3

ENFORCEMENT BY TAKING CONTROL OF GOODS

CHAPTER 1

PROCEDURE

62 Enforcement by taking control of goods

(1) Schedule 12 applies where an enactment, writ or warrant confers power to use the procedure in that Schedule (taking control of goods and selling them to recover a sum of money).

(2) The power conferred by a writ or warrant of control to recover a sum of money, and any power conferred by a writ or warrant of possession or delivery to take control of goods and sell them to recover a sum of money, is exercisable only by using that procedure.

(3) Schedule 13—

(*a*) amends some powers previously called powers to distrain, so that they become powers to use that procedure;

(*b*) makes other amendments relating to Schedule 12 and to distress or execution.

(4) The following are renamed—

(*a*) writs of fieri facias, except writs of fieri facias de bonis ecclesiasticis, are renamed writs of control;

(*b*) warrants of execution are renamed warrants of control;

(*c*) warrants of distress, unless the power they confer is exercisable only against specific goods, are renamed warrants of control.

Note—This section does not extend to Scotland (s 147(2)).

63 Enforcement agents

(1) This section and section 64 apply for the purposes of Schedule 12.

(2) An individual may act as an enforcement agent only if one of these applies—

(*a*) he acts under a certificate under section 64;

(*b*) he is exempt;

(*c*) he acts in the presence and under the direction of a person to whom paragraph (*a*) or (*b*) applies.

(3) An individual is exempt if he acts in the course of his duty as one of these—

(*a*) a constable;

(*b*) an officer of Revenue and Customs;

(*c*) a person appointed under section 2(1) of the Courts Act 2003 (c 39) (court officers and staff).

(4) An individual is exempt if he acts in the course of his duty as an officer of a government department.

(5) For the purposes of an enforcement power conferred by a warrant, an individual is exempt if in relation to the warrant he is a civilian enforcement officer, as defined in section 125A of the Magistrates' Courts Act 1980 (c 43).

(6) A person is guilty of an offence if, knowingly or recklessly, he purports to act as an enforcement agent without being authorised to do so by subsection (2).

(7) A person guilty of an offence under this section is liable on summary conviction to a fine not exceeding level 5 on the standard scale.

Note—This section does not extend to Scotland (s 147(2)).

64 Certificates to act as an enforcement agent

(1) A certificate may be issued under this section—

(*a*) by a judge assigned to a county court district;

(*b*) in prescribed circumstances, by a district judge.

(2) The Lord Chancellor must make regulations about certificates under this section.

(3) The regulations may in particular include provision—

(*a*) for fees to be charged for applications;

(*b*) for certificates to be issued subject to conditions, including the giving of security;

(*c*) for certificates to be limited to purposes specified by or under the regulations;

(*d*) about complaints against holders of certificates;

(*e*) about suspension and cancellation of certificates;

(*f*) to modify or supplement Schedule 12 for cases where a certificate is suspended or cancelled or expires;

(*g*) requiring courts to make information available relating to certificates.

(4) A certificate under section 7 of the Law of Distress Amendment Act 1888 (c 21) which is in force on the coming into force of this section has effect as a certificate under this section, subject to any provision made by regulations.

Note—This section does not extend to Scotland (s 147(2)).

65 Common law rules replaced

(1) This Chapter replaces the common law rules about the exercise of the powers which under it become powers to use the procedure in Schedule 12.

(2) The rules replaced include—

(*a*) rules distinguishing between an illegal, an irregular and an excessive exercise of a power;

(*b*) rules that would entitle a person to bring proceedings of a kind for which paragraph 66 of Schedule 12 provides (remedies available to the debtor);

(*c*) rules of replevin;

(*d*) rules about rescuing goods.

Note—This section does not extend to Scotland (s 147(2)).

66 Pre-commencement enforcement not affected

Where—

(*a*) by any provision of this Part a power becomes a power to use the procedure in Schedule 12, and

(*b*) before the commencement of that provision, goods have been distrained or executed against, or made subject to a walking possession agreement, under the power,

this Part does not affect the continuing exercise of the power in relation to those goods.

Note—This section does not extend to Scotland (s 147(2)).

67 Transfer of county court enforcement

In section 85(2) of the County Courts Act 1984 (c 28) (under which writs of control give the district judge, formerly called the registrar, power to execute judgments or orders for payment of money) for "the registrar shall be" substitute "any person authorised by or on behalf of the Lord Chancellor is".

Note—This section does not extend to Scotland (s 147(2)).

68 Magistrates' courts warrants of control

In the Magistrates' Courts Act 1980 (c 43) after section 125 insert—

"125ZA Warrants of control

(1) This section applies to a warrant of control issued by a justice of the peace.

(2) The person to whom it is directed must endorse the warrant as soon as possible after receiving it.

(3) For the purposes of this section a person endorses a warrant by inserting on the back the date and time when he received it.

(4) No fee may be charged for endorsing a warrant under this section."

Note—This section does not extend to Scotland (s 147(2)).

69 County court warrants of control etc

For section 99 of the County Courts Act 1984 substitute—

"99 Endorsement of warrants of control etc

(1) This section applies to—

(*a*) a warrant of control issued under section 85(2);

(*b*) a warrant of delivery or of possession, but only if it includes a power to take control of and sell goods to recover a sum of money and only for the purposes of exercising that power.

(2) The person to whom the warrant is directed must, as soon as possible after receiving it, endorse it by inserting on the back the date and time when he received it.

(3) No fee may be charged for endorsing a warrant under this section."

Note—This section does not extend to Scotland (s 147(2)).

70 Power of High Court to stay execution

(1) If, at any time, the High Court is satisfied that a party to proceedings is unable to pay—

(*a*) a sum recovered against him (by way of satisfaction of the claim or counterclaim in the proceedings or by way of costs or otherwise), or

(*b*) any instalment of such a sum,

the court may stay the execution of any writ of control issued in the proceedings, for whatever period and on whatever terms it thinks fit.

(2) The court may act under subsection (1) from time to time until it appears that the cause of the inability to pay has ceased.

(3) In this section a party to proceedings includes every person, whether or not named as a party, who is served with notice of the proceedings or attends them.

Note—This section does not extend to Scotland (s 147(2)).

CHAPTER 2
RENT ARREARS RECOVERY

(not reproduced)

CHAPTER 3
GENERAL

88 Abolition of Crown preference

Crown preference for the purposes of execution against goods is abolished.

Note—This section does not extend to Scotland (s 147(2)).

89 Application to the Crown

(1) This Part binds the Crown.

(2) But the procedure in Schedule 12 may not be used—

(*a*) to recover debts due from the Crown,

(*b*) to take control of or sell goods of the Crown (including goods owned by the Crown jointly or in common with another person), or

(*c*) to enter premises occupied by the Crown.

Note—This section does not extend to Scotland (s 147(2)).

90 Regulations

(1) In this Part—

"prescribed" means prescribed by regulations;

"regulations" means regulations made by the Lord Chancellor.

(2) The following apply to regulations under this Part.

(3) Any power to make regulations is exercisable by statutory instrument.

(4) A statutory instrument containing regulations under paragraph 24(2) or 31(5) of Schedule 12 may not be made unless a draft of the instrument has been laid before, and approved by a resolution of, each House of Parliament.

(5) In any other case a statutory instrument containing regulations is subject to annulment in pursuance of a resolution of either House of Parliament.

(6) Regulations may include any of these that the Lord Chancellor considers necessary or expedient—

(*a*) supplementary, incidental or consequential provision;

(*b*) transitory, transitional or saving provision.

(7) Regulations may make different provision for different cases.

Note—This section does not extend to Scotland (s 147(2)).

PART 4
ENFORCEMENT OF JUDGMENTS AND ORDERS

Attachment of earnings orders

91 Attachment of earnings orders: deductions at fixed rates

(1) Schedule 15 makes amendments to the Attachment of Earnings Act 1971 (c 32).

(2) Those amendments are about the basis on which periodical deductions are to be made under an attachment of earnings order.

(3) In particular, they provide that deductions under certain orders are to be made in accordance with a fixed deductions scheme made by the Lord Chancellor (rather than in accordance with Part I of Schedule 3 to the 1971 Act).

92 Attachment of earnings orders: finding the debtor's current employer

(1) After section 15 of the Attachment of Earnings Act 1971 insert—

> **"15A Finding the debtor's current employer**
>
> (1) If an attachment of earnings order lapses under section 9(4), the proper authority may request the Commissioners—
>
> (*a*) to disclose whether it appears to the Commissioners that the debtor has a current employer, and
>
> (*b*) if it appears to the Commissioners that the debtor has a current employer, to disclose the name and address of that employer.
>
> (2) The proper authority may make a request under subsection (1) only for the purpose of enabling the lapsed order to be directed to the debtor's current employer.
>
> (3) The proper authority may not make a request under subsection (1) unless regulations under section 15B(5) and (8) are in force.
>
> (4) The proper authority may disclose such information (including information identifying the debtor) as it considers necessary to assist the Commissioners to comply with a request under subsection (1).

(5) The Commissioners may disclose to the proper authority any information (whether held by the Commissioners or on their behalf) that the Commissioners consider is necessary to comply with a request under subsection (1).

(6) A disclosure under subsection (4) or (5) is not to be taken to breach any restriction on the disclosure of information (however imposed).

(7) Nothing in this section is to be taken to prejudice any power to request or disclose information that exists apart from this section.

(8) The reference in subsection (5) to information held on behalf of the Commissioners includes a reference to any information which—

(*a*) is held by a person who provides services to the Commissioners, and
(*b*) is held by that person in connection with the provision of those services.

15B Offence of unauthorised use or disclosure

(1) This section applies if the Commissioners make a disclosure of information ("debtor information") under section 15A(5).

(2) A person to whom the debtor information is disclosed commits an offence if—

(*a*) he uses or discloses the debtor information, and
(*b*) the use or disclosure is not authorised by subsection (3), (5), (6) or (7).

(3) The use or disclosure of the debtor information is authorised if it is—

(*a*) for a purpose connected with the enforcement of the lapsed order (including the direction of the order to the debtor's current employer), and
(*b*) with the consent of the Commissioners.

(4) Consent for the purposes of subsection (3) may be given—

(*a*) in relation to particular use or a particular disclosure, or
(*b*) in relation to use, or a disclosure made, in such circumstances as may be specified or described in the consent.

(5) The use or disclosure of the debtor information is authorised if it is—

(*a*) in accordance with an enactment or an order of court, or
(*b*) for the purposes of any proceedings before a court,

and it is in accordance with regulations.

(6) The use or disclosure of the debtor information is authorised if the information has previously been lawfully disclosed to the public.

(7) The use or disclosure of the debtor information is authorised if it is in accordance with rules of court that comply with regulations under subsection (8).

(8) Regulations may make provision about the circumstances, if any, in which rules of court may allow any of the following—

(*a*) access to, or the supply of, debtor information;
(*b*) access to, or the supply of copies of, any attachment of earnings order which has been directed to an employer using debtor information.

(9) It is a defence for a person charged with an offence under subsection (2) to prove that he reasonably believed that the disclosure was lawful.

(10) A person guilty of an offence under subsection (2) is liable—

(*a*) on conviction on indictment, to imprisonment for a term not exceeding two years, to a fine, or to both;
(*b*) on summary conviction, to imprisonment for a term not exceeding twelve months, to a fine not exceeding the statutory maximum, or to both.

15C Regulations

(1) It is for the Lord Chancellor to make regulations under section 15B.

(2) But the Lord Chancellor may make regulations under section 15B only with the agreement of the Commissioners.

(3) Regulations under section 15B are to be made by statutory instrument.

(4) A statutory instrument containing regulations under section 15B may not be made unless a draft of the instrument has been laid before and approved by a resolution of each House of Parliament.

15D Interpretation

(1) For the purposes of sections 15A to 15C (and this section)—

"the Commissioners" means the Commissioners for Her Majesty's Revenue and Customs;
"information" means information held in any form;
"the lapsed order" means the attachment of earnings order referred to in section 15A(1);
"the proper authority" is determined in accordance with subsections (2) to (5).

(2) If the lapsed order was made by the High Court, the proper authority is the High Court.

(3) If the lapsed order was made by a county court, the proper authority is a county court.

(4) If the lapsed order was made by a magistrates' court under this Act, the proper authority is—

(*a*) a magistrates' court, or
(*b*) the designated officer for a magistrates' court.

(5) If the lapsed order was made by a magistrates' court or a fines officer under Schedule 5 to the Courts Act 2003, the proper authority is—

(*a*) a magistrates' court, or
(*b*) a fines officer."

(2) This section applies in relation to any attachment of earnings order, whether made before or after the commencement of this section.

(3) In relation to an offence committed before the commencement of section 154(1) of the Criminal Justice Act 2003 (c 44), the reference in section 15B(10)(*b*) of the Attachment of Earnings Act 1971 (c 32) to 12 months is to be read as a reference to 6 months.

Note—This section does not extend to Scotland (s 147(2)).

Charging orders

93 Payment by instalments: making and enforcing charging orders

(1) Subsections (2), (3) and (4) make amendments to the Charging Orders Act 1979 (c 53).

(2) In section 1 (charging orders), after subsection (5) insert—

"(6) Subsections (7) and (8) apply where, under a judgment or order of the High Court or a county court, a debtor is required to pay a sum of money by instalments.

(7) The fact that there has been no default in payment of the instalments does not prevent a charging order from being made in respect of that sum.

(8) But if there has been no default, the court must take that into account when considering the circumstances of the case under subsection (5)."

(3) In section 3 (provisions supplementing sections 1 and 2), after subsection (4) insert—

"(4A) Subsections (4C) to (4E) apply where—

(*a*) a debtor is required to pay a sum of money in instalments under a judgment or order of the High Court or a county court (an "instalments order"), and
(*b*) a charge has been imposed by a charging order in respect of that sum.

(4B) In subsections (4C) to (4E) references to the enforcement of a charge are to the making of an order for the enforcement of the charge.

(4C) The charge may not be enforced unless there has been default in payment of an instalment under the instalments order.

(4D) Rules of court may—

(*a*) provide that, if there has been default in payment of an instalment, the charge may be enforced only in prescribed cases, and
(*b*) limit the amounts for which, and the times at which, the charge may be enforced.

(4E) Except so far as otherwise provided by rules of court under subsection (4D)

(*a*) the charge may be enforced, if there has been default in payment of an instalment, for the whole of the sum of money secured by the charge and the costs then remaining unpaid, or for such part as the court may order, but
(*b*) the charge may not be enforced unless, at the time of enforcement, the whole or part of an instalment which has become due under the instalments order remains unpaid."

(4) In section 6(2) (meaning of references to judgment or order of High Court or county court), for "section 1" substitute "sections 1 and 3".

(5) In section 313(4) of the Insolvency Act 1986 (c 45) (charge on bankrupt's home: certain provisions of section 3 of Charging Orders Act 1979 to apply), for the words before "section 3" substitute "Subsection (1), (2), (4), (5) and (6) of".

(6) This section does not apply in a case where a judgment or order of the High Court or a county court under which a debtor is required to pay a sum of money by instalments was made, or applied for, before the coming into force of this section.

Note—This section does not extend to Scotland (s 147(2)).

94 Charging orders: power to set financial thresholds

In the Charging Orders Act 1979 (c 53), after section 3 there is inserted—

"3A Power to set financial thresholds

(1) The Lord Chancellor may by regulations provide that a charge may not be imposed by a charging order for securing the payment of money of an amount below that determined in accordance with the regulations.

(2) The Lord Chancellor may by regulations provide that a charge imposed by a charging order may not be enforced by way of order for sale to recover money of an amount below that determined in accordance with the regulations.

(3) Regulations under this section may—

(*a*) make different provision for different cases;

(*b*) include such transitional provision as the Lord Chancellor thinks fit.

(4) The power to make regulations under this section is exercisable by statutory instrument.

(5) The Lord Chancellor may not make the first regulations under subsection (1) or (2) unless (in each case) a draft of the statutory instrument containing the regulations has been laid before, and approved by a resolution of, each House of Parliament.

(6) A statutory instrument containing any subsequent regulations under those subsections is subject to annulment in pursuance of a resolution of either House of Parliament."

Note—This section does not extend to Scotland (s 147(2)).

Information requests and orders

95 Application for information about action to recover judgment debt

(1) A person who is the creditor in relation to a judgment debt may apply to the High Court or a county court for information about what kind of action it would be appropriate to take in court to recover that particular debt.

(2) An application under subsection (1) must comply with any provision made in regulations about the making of such applications.

Note—This section does not extend to Scotland (s 147(2)).

96 Action by the court

(1) This section applies if the creditor in relation to a judgment debt makes an application for information under section 95.

(2) The relevant court may make one or more of the following in relation to the debtor—

(*a*) a departmental information request;

(*b*) an information order.

(3) The relevant court may exercise its powers under subsection (2) only if it is satisfied that to do so will help it to deal with the creditor's application.

(4) Before exercising its powers under subsection (2), the relevant court must give notice to the debtor that the court intends to make a request or order.

(5) The relevant court may not make a departmental information request to the Commissioners unless regulations are in force that have been made under section 102(4) and (7) and relate to the use or disclosure of debtor information disclosed by the Commissioners.

(6) The relevant court may disclose such information (including information identifying the debtor) as it considers necessary to assist the recipient of a request or order to comply with the request or order.

(7) A disclosure under subsection (6) is not to be taken to breach any restriction on the disclosure of information (however imposed).

(8) Nothing in this section is to be taken to prejudice any power that exists apart from this section to request or order the disclosure of information.

Note—This section does not extend to Scotland (s 147(2)).

97 Departmental information requests

(1) A departmental information request is a request for the disclosure of information held by, or on behalf of, a government department.

(2) The request is to be made to the Minister of the Crown, or other person, who is in charge of the department.

(3) In the case of a request made to the designated Secretary of State, the disclosure of some or all of the following information may be requested—

(*a*) the full name of the debtor;

(*b*) the address of the debtor;

(*c*) the date of birth of the debtor;

(*d*) the national insurance number of the debtor;

(*e*) prescribed information.

(4) In the case of a request made to the Commissioners, the disclosure of some or all of the following information may be requested—

(*a*) whether or not the debtor is employed;

(*b*) the name and address of the employer (if the debtor is employed);

(*c*) the national insurance number of the debtor;

(*d*) prescribed information.

(5) In the case of any other request, the disclosure of prescribed information may be requested.

(6) In this section—

"designated Secretary of State" means the Secretary of State designated for the purpose of this section by regulations;

"government department" does not include the following—

(*a*) any part of the Scottish Administration;

(*b*) a Northern Ireland department;

(*c*) the Welsh Assembly Government or any member of staff appointed under section 52 of the Government of Wales Act 2006 (c 32);

"prescribed information", in relation to a departmental information request, means information that falls within the category or categories of information (if any) prescribed by regulations in relation to the department to which the request relates.

Note—This section does not extend to Scotland (s 147(2)).

98 Information orders

(1) An information order is an order of the relevant court which—

(*a*) specifies a prescribed person ("the information discloser"),

(*b*) specifies prescribed information relating to the debtor ("the required information"), and

(*c*) orders the information discloser to disclose the required information to the relevant court.

(2) In subsection (1) "prescribed" means prescribed in regulations.

(3) Regulations under this section may be made by reference to—

(*a*) particular persons or particular descriptions of person (or both);

(*b*) particular information or particular descriptions of information (or both).

(4) Regulations may, in particular, be made under this section so as to ensure that—

(*a*) an information order made against a particular person, or a person of a particular description, may order that person to disclose only particular information, or information of a particular description;

(*b*) an information order that orders the disclosure of particular information, or information of a particular description, may only be made against a particular person, or a person of a particular description.

(5) Regulations under this section must not make provision that would allow the relevant court to order—

(*a*) the disclosure of information by the debtor, or

(*b*) the disclosure of information held by, or on behalf of, a government department.

Note—This section does not extend to Scotland (s 147(2)).

99 Responding to a departmental information request

(1) This section applies if the relevant court makes a departmental information request.

(2) The recipient of the request may disclose to the relevant court any information (whether held by the department or on its behalf) that the recipient considers is necessary to comply with the request.

(3) A disclosure under subsection (2) is not to be taken to breach any restriction on the disclosure of information (however imposed).

(4) Nothing in this section is to be taken to prejudice any power that exists apart from this section to disclose information.

Note—This section does not extend to Scotland (s 147(2)).

100 Information order: required information not held etc

(1) An information discloser is not to be regarded as having breached an information order because of a failure to disclose some or all of the required information, if that failure is for one of the permitted reasons.

(2) These are the permitted reasons—

(*a*) the information provider does not hold the information;

(*b*) the information provider is unable to ascertain whether the information is held, because of the way in which the information order identifies the debtor;

(*c*) the disclosure of the information would involve the information discloser in unreasonable effort or expense.

(3) It is to be presumed that a failure to disclose required information is for a permitted reason if—

(*a*) the information discloser gives the relevant court a certificate that complies with subsection (4), and

(*b*) there is no evidence that the failure is not for a permitted reason.

(4) The certificate must state—

(*a*) which of the required information is not being disclosed;

(*b*) what the permitted reason is, or permitted reasons are, for the failure to disclose that information.

(5) Any reference in this section to the information discloser holding, or not holding, information includes a reference to the information being held, or not being held, on the information discloser's behalf.

Note—This section does not extend to Scotland (s 147(2)).

101 Using the information about the debtor

(1) This section applies if—

(*a*) the creditor in relation to a judgment debt makes an application for information under section 95, and

(*b*) information ("debtor information") is disclosed to the relevant court in compliance with a request or order made under section 96.

(2) The relevant court may use the debtor information for the purpose of making another request or order under section 96 in relation to the debtor.

(3) The relevant court may use the debtor information for the purpose of providing the creditor with information about what kind of action (if any) it would be appropriate to take in court (whether the relevant court or another court) to recover the judgment debt.

(4) If the creditor takes any action in the relevant court to recover the judgment debt, the relevant court may use the debtor information in carrying out functions in relation to that action.

(5) If the creditor takes any action in another court to recover the judgment debt—

(*a*) the relevant court may disclose the debtor information to the other court, and

(*b*) the other court may use that information in carrying out functions in relation to that action.

(6) Debtor information may be used or disclosed under any of subsections (3) to (5) only if—

(*a*) regulations about such use or disclosure of information are in force, and

(*b*) the use or disclosure complies with those regulations.

(7) In addition, if the debtor information was disclosed by the Commissioners, the information may be used or disclosed under any of subsections (3) to (5) only with the consent of the Commissioners.

(8) Consent for the purposes of subsection (7) may be given—

(*a*) in relation to particular use or a particular disclosure, or

(*b*) in relation to use, or a disclosure made, in such circumstances as may be specified or described in the consent.

(9) The use or disclosure of information in accordance with this section is not to be taken to breach any restriction on the use or disclosure of information (however imposed).

(10) Nothing in this section is to be taken to prejudice any power that exists apart from this section to use or disclose information.

Note—This section does not extend to Scotland (s 147(2)).

102 Offence of unauthorised use or disclosure

(1) This section applies if—

(*a*) an application is made under section 95 in relation to recovery of a judgment debt ("the relevant judgment debt"),

(*b*) a departmental information request or an information order is made in consequence of that application, and

(*c*) information ("debtor information") is disclosed in accordance with the request or order.

(2) A person to whom the debtor information is disclosed commits an offence if he—

(*a*) uses or discloses the debtor information, and

(*b*) the use or disclosure is not authorised by any of subsections (3) to (6).

(3) The use or disclosure of the debtor information is authorised if it is in accordance with section 101.

(4) The use or disclosure of the debtor information is authorised if it is—

(*a*) in accordance with an enactment or order of court, or

(*b*) for the purposes of any proceedings before a court,

and it is in accordance with regulations.

(5) The use or disclosure of the debtor information is authorised if the information has previously been lawfully disclosed to the public.

(6) The use or disclosure of the debtor information is authorised if it is in accordance with rules of court that comply with regulations under subsection (7).

(7) Regulations may make provision about the circumstances, if any, in which rules of court may allow access to, or the supply of, information disclosed in accordance with a department information request or an information order.

(8) It is a defence for a person charged with an offence under subsection (2) to prove that he reasonably believed that the use or disclosure was lawful.

(9) A person guilty of an offence under subsection (2) is liable—

(*a*) on conviction on indictment, to imprisonment for a term not exceeding two years, to a fine or to both;

(*b*) on summary conviction, to imprisonment for a term not exceeding twelve months, to a fine not exceeding the statutory maximum, or to both.

Note—This section does not extend to Scotland (s 147(2)).

103 Regulations

(1) It is for the Lord Chancellor to make information regulations.

(2) But the Lord Chancellor may make the following regulations only with the agreement of the Commissioners—

(*a*) regulations under section 97(4)(*d*);

(*b*) regulations under section 102(4) or (7) so far as the regulations relate to the use or disclosure of debtor information disclosed by the Commissioners.

(3) Information regulations are to be made by statutory instrument.

(4) A statutory instrument containing information regulations may not be made unless a draft of the instrument has been laid before and approved by a resolution of each House of Parliament.

(5) But subsection (4) does not apply in the case of a statutory instrument that contains only—

(*a*) regulations under section 95, or

(*b*) regulations under section 97 which designate a Secretary of State for the purpose of that section.

(6) In such a case, the statutory instrument is subject to annulment in pursuance of a resolution of either House of Parliament.

(7) In this section "information regulations" means regulations under any of sections 95 to 102.

Note—This section does not extend to Scotland (s 147(2)).

104 Interpretation

(1) This section applies for the purposes of sections 95 to 103.

(2) In those provisions—

"Commissioners" means the Commissioners for Her Majesty's Revenue and Customs;

"creditor", in relation to a judgment debt, means—

(*a*) the person to whom the debt is payable (whether directly or through an officer of any court or another person);

(*b*) where the debt is payable under an administration order (within the meaning of Part 6 of the County Courts Act 1984 (c 28)), any one of the creditors scheduled to the order;

"debtor", in relation to a judgment debt, means the person by whom the debt is payable;

"departmental information request" has the meaning given by section 97;

"information" means information held in any form;

"information discloser", in relation to an information order, has the meaning given by section 98(1)(*a*);

"information order" has the meaning given by section 98;

"judgment debt" means either of the following—

(*a*) a sum which is payable under a judgment or order enforceable by the High Court or a county court;

(*b*) a sum which, by virtue of an enactment, is recoverable as if it were payable under a judgment or order of the High Court or of a county court (including a sum which is so recoverable because a court so orders);

"required information", in relation to an information order, has the meaning given by section 98(1)(*b*);

"relevant court", in relation to an application under section 95, means the court to which the application is made.

(3) Any reference to information held on behalf of a government department, or on behalf of an information discloser, includes a reference to any information which—

(*a*) is held by a person who provides services to the department or to the information discloser, and

(*b*) is held by that person in connection with the provision of those services.

Note—This section does not extend to Scotland (s 147(2)).

105 Application and transitional provision

(1) Sections 95 to 104 apply in relation to any judgment debt, whether it became payable, or recoverable, before or after the commencement of those sections.

(2) In relation to an offence committed before the commencement of section 154(1) of the Criminal Justice Act 2003 (c 44), the reference in section 102(9)(*b*) to 12 months is to be read as a reference to 6 months.

Note—This section does not extend to Scotland (s 147(2)).

PART 8
GENERAL

. . .

146 Repeals

Schedule 23 contains repeals.

Commencement—Tribunals, Courts and Enforcement Act 2007 (Commencement No 1) Order, SI 2007/2709 art 3(*a*) (this section comes into force on 1 November 2007).

147 Extent

(1) Parts 1, 2 and 6 and this Part extend to England and Wales, Scotland and Northern Ireland.

(2) The other provisions of this Act extend only to England and Wales.

(3) Subsections (1) and (2) are subject to subsections (4) and (5).

(4) Unless provided otherwise, amendments, repeals and revocations in this Act extend to any part of the United Kingdom to which the provisions amended, repealed or revoked extend.

(5) The following extend also to the Isle of Man—

(*a*) section 143(1) and (2),

(*b*) the repeal by this Act of any provision specified in Part 6 of Schedule 23 that extends to the Isle of Man,

(*c*) sections 145 and 148(5) to (7) so far as relating to—

(i) section 143(1) and (2), and

(ii) the provisions of this Act by which the repeals mentioned in paragraph (*b*) are effected, and

(*d*) this section and section 149.

148 Commencement

(1) Section 60 comes into force at the end of the period of two months beginning with the day on which this Act is passed.

(2) The provisions of Chapter 3 of Part 5 come into force in accordance with provision made by the Lord Chancellor or the Secretary of State by order.

(3) The provisions of Part 6 come into force, except as provided by subsection (4), in accordance with provision made by the Secretary of State by order.

(4) The provisions of Part 6 come into force, in so far as they extend to Scotland, in accordance with provision made by the Scottish Ministers by order.

(5) The remaining provisions of this Act, except sections 53, 55, 56, 57, 145, 147, 149, this section and Schedule 11, come into force in accordance with provision made by the Lord Chancellor by order.

(6) An order under this section may make different provision for different purposes.

(7) The power to make an order under this section is exercisable by statutory instrument.

Orders—Tribunals, Courts and Enforcement Act 2007 (Commencement No 1) Order, SI 2007/2709.
Tribunals, Courts and Enforcement Act 2007 (Commencement No 2) Order, SI 2007/3613.
Tribunals, Courts and Enforcement Act 2007 (Commencement) (Scotland) Order, SSI 2008/150 (in relation to Scotland only).
Tribunals, Courts and Enforcement Act 2007 (Commencement No 3) Order, SI 2008/749.
Tribunals, Courts and Enforcement Act 2007 (Commencement No 4) Order, SI 2008/1158.
Tribunals, Courts and Enforcement Act 2007 (Commencement No 5 and Transitional Provisions) Order, SI 2008/1653.
Tribunals, Courts and Enforcement Act 2007 (Commencement No 6 and Transitional Provisions) Order, SI 2008/2696.

149 Short title

This Act may be cited as the Tribunals, Courts and Enforcement Act 2007.

SCHEDULES

SCHEDULE 1
SENIOR PRESIDENT OF TRIBUNALS

Section 2

PART 1
RECOMMENDATIONS FOR APPOINTMENT

Duty to fill vacancies

1— (1) If there is a vacancy in the office of Senior President of Tribunals, the Lord Chancellor must recommend a person for appointment to that office.

(2) Sub-paragraph (1) does not apply to a vacancy while the Lord Chief Justice of England and Wales agrees that it may remain unfilled.

Commencement—Tribunals, Courts and Enforcement Act 2007 (Commencement No 1) Order, SI 2007/2709 art 2(*g*) (paras 1–11 come into force on 19 September 2007).

The two routes to a recommendation: agreement under this paragraph or selection under Part 2

2— (1) Before the Lord Chancellor may recommend a person for appointment to the office of Senior President of Tribunals, the Lord Chancellor must consult—

(*a*) the Lord Chief Justice of England and Wales,
(*b*) the Lord President of the Court of Session, and
(*c*) the Lord Chief Justice of Northern Ireland.

(2) Sub-paragraphs (3) and (4) apply if—

(*a*) the outcome of consultation under sub-paragraph (1) is agreement between—
(i) the Lord Chancellor,
(ii) the Lord Chief Justice of England and Wales,
(iii) the Lord President of the Court of Session, and
(iv) the Lord Chief Justice of Northern Ireland,

as to the person to be recommended, and

(*b*) the person is—
(i) an ordinary judge of the Court of Appeal in England and Wales,
(ii) a judge of the Court of Session who is a member of the First or Second Division of the Inner House of that Court, or
(iii) a Lord Justice of Appeal in Northern Ireland.

(3) The Lord Chancellor must recommend the person for appointment to the office of Senior President of Tribunals, subject to sub-paragraph (4).

(4) Where the person—

(*a*) declines to be recommended, or does not agree within a time specified to him for that purpose, or
(*b*) is otherwise not available within a reasonable time to be recommended,

the Lord Chancellor must, instead of recommending the person for appointment, consult afresh under sub-paragraph (1).

(5) If the Lord Chancellor has consulted under sub-paragraph (1) but sub-paragraphs (3) and (4) do not apply following that consultation, the Lord Chancellor must make a request to the Judicial Appointments Commission for a person to be selected for recommendation for appointment to the office of Senior President of Tribunals.

Commencement—Tribunals, Courts and Enforcement Act 2007 (Commencement No 1) Order, SI 2007/2709 art 2(*g*) (paras 1–11 come into force on 19 September 2007).

PART 2
SELECTION BY THE JUDICIAL APPOINTMENTS COMMISSION

Eligibility for selection

3 A person is eligible for selection in pursuance of a request under paragraph 2(5) only if—

(*a*) he satisfies the judicial-appointment eligibility condition on a 7-year basis,
(*b*) he is an advocate or solicitor in Scotland of at least seven years' standing, or
(*c*) he is a barrister or solicitor in Northern Ireland of at least seven years' standing.

Commencement—Tribunals, Courts and Enforcement Act 2007 (Commencement No 1) Order, SI 2007/2709 art 2(*g*) (paras 1–11 come into force on 19 September 2007).

The selection process

4 In Chapter 2 of Part 4 of the Constitutional Reform Act 2005 (c 4) (appointments), after section 75 insert—

"*Senior President of Tribunals*

"75A Sections 75B to 75G apply where request made for selection

(1) Sections 75B to 75G apply where the Lord Chancellor makes a request to the Commission under paragraph 2(5) of Schedule 1 to the Tribunals, Courts and Enforcement Act 2007 (request for person to be selected for recommendation for appointment to the office of Senior President of Tribunals).

(2) Those sections are subject to section 95 (withdrawal and modification of requests).

75B Selection process

(1) On receiving a request the Commission must appoint a selection panel.

(2) The panel must—

(*a*) determine the selection process to be applied,
(*b*) apply the selection process, and
(*c*) make a selection accordingly.

(3) As part of the selection process the panel must consult—

(*a*) the Lord Chief Justice, if not a member of the panel,
(*b*) the Lord President of the Court of Session, if not a member of the panel, and
(*c*) the Lord Chief Justice of Northern Ireland, if not a member of the panel.

(4) One person only must be selected for the recommendation to which a request relates.

(5) Subsection (4) applies to selection under this section and to selection under section 75G.

(6) A selection panel is a committee of the Commission.

75C Selection panel

(1) The selection panel must consist of four members.

(2) The first member is the Lord Chief Justice, or his nominee.

(3) The second member is a person designated by the Lord Chief Justice.

(4) Unless subsection (7) applies, the third member is the chairman of the Commission or his nominee.

(5) The fourth member is a lay member of the Commission designated by the third member.

(6) Subsection (7) applies if—

(*a*) there is no chairman of the Commission, or
(*b*) the chairman of the Commission is unavailable and has not nominated a person under subsection (4).

(7) In those cases the third member is a lay member of the Commission selected by the lay members of the Commission other than the chairman.

(8) A nominee of the Lord Chief Justice must be a Head of Division or a Lord Justice of Appeal.

(9) The person designated under subsection (3) must be—

(*a*) a person who holds, or has held, the office of Senior President of Tribunals,
(*b*) a person who holds, or has held, office as a Chamber President of a chamber of the First-tier Tribunal or of a chamber of the Upper Tribunal, or
(*c*) a person who holds, or has held, an office that, in the opinion of the Lord Chief Justice, is such that a holder of it would acquire knowledge or experience of tribunals broadly similar to that which would be acquired by—

(i) a person who holds the office of Senior President of Tribunals, or
(ii) a person who holds office as a Chamber President of a chamber of the First-tier Tribunal, or
(iii) a person who holds office as a Chamber President of a chamber of the Upper Tribunal.

(10) Before designating a person under subsection (3), the Lord Chief Justice must consult—

(*a*) the Lord President of the Court of Session, and
(*b*) the Lord Chief Justice of Northern Ireland.

(11) A person may not be appointed to the panel if he is willing to be considered for selection.

(12) A person may not be appointed to the panel as the nominee of more than one person.

(13) A person appointed to the panel otherwise than as a nominee may not be a nominee.

(14) The first member is the chairman of the panel.

(15) On any vote by the panel the chairman of the panel has an additional, casting vote in the event of a tie.

75D Report

(1) After complying with section 75B(2) the selection panel must submit a report to the Lord Chancellor.

(2) The report must—

(*a*) state who has been selected;
(*b*) contain any other information required by the Lord Chancellor.

(3) The report must be in a form approved by the Lord Chancellor.

(4) After submitting the report the panel must provide any further information the Lord Chancellor may require.

75E The Lord Chancellor's options

(1) This section refers to the following stages—

Stage 1:	where a person has been selected under section 75B
Stage 2:	where a person has been selected following a rejection or reconsideration at stage 1

Stage 3: where a person has been selected following a rejection or reconsideration at stage 2

(2) At stage 1 the Lord Chancellor must do one of the following—

(*a*) accept the selection;
(*b*) reject the selection;
(*c*) require the selection panel to reconsider the selection.

(3) At stage 2 the Lord Chancellor must do one of the following—

(*a*) accept the selection;
(*b*) reject the selection, but only if it was made following a reconsideration at stage 1;
(*c*) require the selection panel to reconsider the selection, but only if it was made following a rejection at stage 1.

(4) At stage 3 the Lord Chancellor must accept the selection, unless subsection (5) applies and he accepts a selection under it.

(5) If a person whose selection the Lord Chancellor required to be reconsidered at stage 1 or 2 was not selected again at the next stage, the Lord Chancellor may, at stage 3, accept the selection made at that earlier stage.

75F Exercise of powers to reject or require reconsideration

(1) The power of the Lord Chancellor under section 75E to reject a selection at stage 1 or 2 is exercisable only on the grounds that, in the Lord Chancellor's opinion, the person selected is not suitable for the office of Senior President of Tribunals.

(2) The power of the Lord Chancellor under section 75E to require the selection panel to reconsider a selection at stage 1 or 2 is exercisable only on the grounds that, in the Lord Chancellor's opinion—

(*a*) there is not enough evidence that the person is suitable for the office of Senior President of Tribunals, or
(*b*) there is evidence that the person is not the best candidate on merit.

(3) The Lord Chancellor must give the selection panel reasons in writing for rejecting or requiring reconsideration of a selection.

75G Selection following rejection or requirement to reconsider

(1) If under section 75F the Lord Chancellor rejects or requires reconsideration of a selection at stage 1 or 2, the selection panel must select a person in accordance with this section.

(2) If the Lord Chancellor rejects a selection, the selection panel—

(*a*) may not select the person rejected, and
(*b*) where the rejection is following reconsideration of a selection, may not select the person (if different) whose selection it reconsidered.

(3) If the Lord Chancellor requires a selection to be reconsidered, the selection panel—

(*a*) may select the same person or a different person, but
(*b*) where the requirement is following a rejection, may not select the person rejected.

(4) The selection panel must inform the Lord Chancellor of the person selected following a rejection or a requirement to reconsider.

(5) Subsections (2) and (3) do not prevent a person being selected on a subsequent request under paragraph 2(5) of Schedule 1 to the Tribunals, Courts and Enforcement Act 2007."

Commencement—Tribunals, Courts and Enforcement Act 2007 (Commencement No 1) Order, SI 2007/2709 art 2(*g*) (paras 1–11 come into force on 19 September 2007).

Withdrawal and modification of requests under paragraph 2(5)

5— (1) Section 95 of the Constitutional Reform Act 2005 (c 4) (withdrawal and modification of requests) is amended as follows.

(2) In subsection (1) (application of section), after "87" insert "or paragraph 2(5) of Schedule 1 to the Tribunals, Courts and Enforcement Act 2007".

(3) In subsection (4) (limitation on withdrawal of request under subsection (2)(*c*)), after "73(2)," insert "75E(2),".

Commencement—Tribunals, Courts and Enforcement Act 2007 (Commencement No 1) Order, SI 2007/2709 art 2(*g*) (paras 1–11 come into force on 19 September 2007).

PART 3

TERMS OF OFFICE

Tenure, removal, resignation etc

6— (1) If—

(*a*) a person appointed to the office of Senior President of Tribunals is appointed on terms that provide for him to retire from the office at a particular time specified in those terms ("the end of the fixed-term"), and

(*b*) the end of the fixed-term is earlier than the time at which the person is required by the 1993 Act to retire from the office,

the person shall, if still holding the office at the end of the fixed-term, vacate the office at the end of the fixed-term.

(2) Subject to sub-paragraph (1) (and to the 1993 Act), a person appointed to the office of Senior President of Tribunals shall hold that office during good behaviour, subject to a power of removal by Her Majesty on an address presented to Her by both Houses of Parliament.

(3) It is for the Lord Chancellor to recommend to Her Majesty the exercise of the power of removal under sub-paragraph (2).

(4) In this paragraph "the 1993 Act" means the Judicial Pensions and Retirement Act 1993 (c 8).

Commencement—Tribunals, Courts and Enforcement Act 2007 (Commencement No 1) Order, SI 2007/2709 art 2(*g*) (paras 1–11 come into force on 19 September 2007).

7— (1) Sub-paragraph (2) applies to a person appointed to the office of Senior President of Tribunals on a recommendation made under paragraph 2(3).

(2) The person ceases to be Senior President of Tribunals if he ceases to fall within paragraph 2(2)(*b*).

Commencement—Tribunals, Courts and Enforcement Act 2007 (Commencement No 1) Order, SI 2007/2709 art 2(*g*) (paras 1–11 come into force on 19 September 2007).

8 A person who holds the office of Senior President of Tribunals may at any time resign that office by giving the Lord Chancellor notice in writing to that effect.

Commencement—Tribunals, Courts and Enforcement Act 2007 (Commencement No 1) Order, SI 2007/2709 art 2(*g*) (paras 1–11 come into force on 19 September 2007).

9— (1) The Lord Chancellor, if satisfied by means of a medical certificate that a person holding the office of Senior President of Tribunals—

(*a*) is disabled by permanent infirmity from the performance of the duties of the office, and

(*b*) is for the time being incapacitated from resigning the office,

may, subject to sub-paragraph (2), by instrument under his hand declare the person to have vacated the office; and the instrument shall have the like effect for all purposes as if the person had on the date of the instrument resigned the office.

(2) A declaration under sub-paragraph (1) with respect to a person shall be of no effect unless it is made with the concurrence of—

(*a*) the Lord Chief Justice of England and Wales,

(*b*) the Lord President of the Court of Session, and

(*c*) the Lord Chief Justice of Northern Ireland.

Commencement—Tribunals, Courts and Enforcement Act 2007 (Commencement No 1) Order, SI 2007/2709 art 2(*g*) (paras 1–11 come into force on 19 September 2007).

Remuneration, allowances and expenses

10 The Lord Chancellor may pay to the Senior President of Tribunals such amounts (if any) as the Lord Chancellor may determine by way of—

(*a*) remuneration;

(*b*) allowances;

(*c*) expenses.

Commencement—Tribunals, Courts and Enforcement Act 2007 (Commencement No 1) Order, SI 2007/2709 art 2(*g*) (paras 1–11 come into force on 19 September 2007).

Oaths

11— (1) A person appointed to the office of Senior President of Tribunals must take the required oaths in the presence of—

(*a*) the Lord Chief Justice of England and Wales, or

(*b*) another holder of high judicial office (as defined in section 60(2) of the Constitutional Reform Act 2005 (c 4)) who is nominated by the Lord Chief Justice of England and Wales for the purpose of taking the oaths from the person.

(2) Sub-paragraph (1) applies whether or not the person has previously taken the required oaths after accepting another office.

(3) In this paragraph "the required oaths" means—

(*a*) the oath of allegiance, and

(*b*) the judicial oath,

as set out in the Promissory Oaths Act 1868 (c 72).

Commencement—Tribunals, Courts and Enforcement Act 2007 (Commencement No 1) Order, SI 2007/2709 art 2(*g*) (paras 1–11 come into force on 19 September 2007).

PART 4
CERTAIN FUNCTIONS OF THE SENIOR PRESIDENT

Meaning of "tribunal member"

12— (1) For the purposes of this Part of this Schedule, each of the following is a "tribunal member"—

(*a*) a judge, or other member, of the First-tier Tribunal or Upper Tribunal,
(*b*) any member of the Asylum and Immigration Tribunal,
(*c*) a member of a panel of members of employment tribunals (whether or not a panel of chairmen),
(*d*) a judge, or other member, of the Employment Appeal Tribunal, and
(*e*) a person who is, or is a member of, a tribunal in a list in Schedule 6 that has effect for the purposes of section 30.

(2) In this Part of this Schedule "tribunals" means—

(*a*) the First-tier Tribunal,
(*b*) the Upper Tribunal,
(*c*) the Asylum and Immigration Tribunal,
(*d*) employment tribunals,
(*e*) the Employment Appeal Tribunal, and
(*f*) any tribunal in a list in Schedule 6 that has effect for the purposes of section 30.

Commencement—Tribunals, Courts and Enforcement Act 2007 (Commencement No 6 and Transitional Provisions) Order, SI 2008/2696 art 5(*e*) (paras 12–14 come into force on 3 November 2008).

Representations to Parliament

13 The Senior President of Tribunals may lay before Parliament written representations on matters that appear to him to be matters of importance relating—

(*a*) to tribunal members, or
(*b*) otherwise to the administration of justice by tribunals.

Commencement—Tribunals, Courts and Enforcement Act 2007 (Commencement No 6 and Transitional Provisions) Order, SI 2008/2696 art 5(*e*) (paras 12–14 come into force on 3 November 2008).

Representation of views of tribunal members

14 The Senior President of Tribunals is responsible for representing the views of tribunal members to Parliament, to the Lord Chancellor and to Ministers of the Crown generally.

Commencement—Tribunals, Courts and Enforcement Act 2007 (Commencement No 6 and Transitional Provisions) Order, SI 2008/2696 art 5(*e*) (paras 12–14 come into force on 3 November 2008).

SCHEDULE 2
JUDGES AND OTHER MEMBERS OF THE FIRST-TIER TRIBUNAL

Section 4

Power to appoint judges of First-tier Tribunal

1— (1) The Lord Chancellor may appoint a person to be one of the judges of the First-tier Tribunal.

(2) A person is eligible for appointment under sub-paragraph (1) only if the person—

(*a*) satisfies the judicial-appointment eligibility condition on a 5-year basis,
(*b*) is an advocate or solicitor in Scotland of at least five years' standing,
(*c*) is a barrister or solicitor in Northern Ireland of at least five years' standing, or
(*d*) in the Lord Chancellor's opinion, has gained experience in law which makes the person as suitable for appointment as if the person satisfied any of paragraphs (*a*) to (*c*).

(3) Section 52(2) to (5) (meaning of "gain experience in law") apply for the purposes of sub-paragraph (2)(*d*), but as if section 52(4)(*i*) referred to the Lord Chancellor instead of to the relevant decision-maker.

Commencement—Tribunals, Courts and Enforcement Act 2007 (Commencement No 6 and Transitional Provisions) Order, SI 2008/2696 art 5(*f*) (Sch 2 comes into force on 3 November 2008).

Power to appoint other members of First-tier Tribunal

2— (1) The Lord Chancellor may appoint a person to be one of the members of the First-tier Tribunal who are not judges of the tribunal.

(2) A person is eligible for appointment under sub-paragraph (1) only if the person has qualifications prescribed in an order made by the Lord Chancellor with the concurrence of the Senior President of Tribunals.

Commencement—Tribunals, Courts and Enforcement Act 2007 (Commencement No 6 and Transitional Provisions) Order, SI 2008/2696 art 5(*f*) (Sch 2 comes into force on 3 November 2008).

Orders—Qualifications for Appointment of Members to the First-tier Tribunal and Upper Tribunal Order, SI 2008/2692 (made under para 2(2)).

Appointed and transferred-in judges and other members: removal from office

3— (1) This paragraph applies to any power by which—

(*a*) a person appointed under paragraph 1(1) or 2(1),
(*b*) a transferred-in judge of the First-tier Tribunal, or
(*c*) a transferred-in other member of the First-tier Tribunal,

may be removed from office.

(2) If the person exercises functions wholly or mainly in Scotland, the power may be exercised only with the concurrence of the Lord President of the Court of Session.

(3) If the person exercises functions wholly or mainly in Northern Ireland, the power may be exercised only with the concurrence of the Lord Chief Justice of Northern Ireland.

(4) If neither of sub-paragraphs (2) and (3) applies, the power may be exercised only with the concurrence of the Lord Chief Justice of England and Wales.

Commencement—Tribunals, Courts and Enforcement Act 2007 (Commencement No 6 and Transitional Provisions) Order, SI 2008/2696 art 5(*f*) (Sch 2 comes into force on 3 November 2008).

Terms of appointment

4— (1) This paragraph applies—

(*a*) to a person appointed under paragraph 1(1) or 2(1),
(*b*) to a transferred-in judge of the First-tier Tribunal, and
(*c*) to a transferred-in other member of the First-tier Tribunal.

(2) If the terms of the person's appointment provide that he is appointed on a salaried (as opposed to fee-paid) basis, the person may be removed from office—

(*a*) only by the Lord Chancellor (and in accordance with paragraph 3), and
(*b*) only on the ground of inability or misbehaviour.

(3) Subject to sub-paragraph (2) (and to the Judicial Pensions and Retirement Act 1993 (c 8)), the person is to hold and vacate office in accordance with the terms of his appointment.

Commencement—Tribunals, Courts and Enforcement Act 2007 (Commencement No 6 and Transitional Provisions) Order, SI 2008/2696 art 5(*f*) (Sch 2 comes into force on 3 November 2008).

Remuneration, allowances and expenses

5— (1) Sub-paragraph (2) applies—

(*a*) to a person appointed under paragraph 1(1) or 2(1),
(*b*) to a transferred-in judge of the First-tier Tribunal, and
(*c*) to a transferred-in other member of the First-tier Tribunal.

(2) The Lord Chancellor may pay to a person to whom this sub-paragraph applies such amounts (if any) as the Lord Chancellor may determine by way of—

(*a*) remuneration;
(*b*) allowances;
(*c*) expenses.

Commencement—Tribunals, Courts and Enforcement Act 2007 (Commencement No 6 and Transitional Provisions) Order, SI 2008/2696 art 5(*f*) (Sch 2 comes into force on 3 November 2008).

Certain judges neither appointed under paragraph 1(1) nor transferred in

6— (1) In this paragraph "judge by request of the First-tier Tribunal" means a person who is a judge of the First-tier Tribunal but who—

(*a*) is not the Senior President of Tribunals,
(*b*) is not a judge of the First-tier Tribunal appointed under paragraph 1(1),
(*c*) is not a transferred-in judge of the First-tier Tribunal,
(*d*) is not a Chamber President, or Acting Chamber President or Deputy Chamber President, of a chamber of the First-tier Tribunal,
(*e*) is not a judge of the First-tier Tribunal by virtue of section 4(1)(*e*) (chairman of employment tribunal),
(*f*) is not a judge of the First-tier Tribunal by virtue of section 4(1)(*d*) or by virtue of the combination of sections 4(1)(*c*) and 5(1)(*d*) (legally qualified member of Asylum and Immigration Tribunal), and
(*g*) is not a judge of the First-tier tribunal by virtue of section 4(2) (criminal injuries compensation adjudicator appointed by the Scottish Ministers).

(2) A judge by request of the First-tier Tribunal may act as a judge of the First-tier Tribunal only if requested to do so by the Senior President of Tribunals.

(3) Such a request made to a person who is a judge of the First-tier Tribunal by virtue of the combination of sections 4(1)(*c*) and 5(1)(*g*) may be made only with—

(*a*) the concurrence of the Lord Chief Justice of England and Wales where the person is—
(i) an ordinary judge of the Court of Appeal in England and Wales,

(ii) a puisne judge of the High Court in England and Wales,
(iii) a circuit judge,
(iv) a district judge in England and Wales, or
(v) a District Judge (Magistrates' Courts);

(*b*) the concurrence of the Lord President of the Court of Session where the person is—
(i) a judge of the Court of Session, or
(ii) a sheriff;

(*c*) the concurrence of the Lord Chief Justice of Northern Ireland where the person is—
(i) a Lord Justice of Appeal in Northern Ireland,
(ii) a puisne judge of the High Court in Northern Ireland,
(iii) a county court judge in Northern Ireland, or
(iv) a district judge in Northern Ireland.

(4) Sub-paragraph (5) applies—

(*a*) to a judge by request of the First-tier Tribunal,

(*b*) to a person who is a judge of the First-tier Tribunal by virtue of section 4(1)(*e*) (chairman of employment tribunal), and

(*c*) to a person who is a judge of the First-tier Tribunal by virtue of section 4(1)(*d*) or by virtue of the combination of sections 4(1)(*c*) and 5(1)(*d*) (legally qualified member of Asylum and Immigration Tribunal).

(5) The Lord Chancellor may pay to a person to whom this sub-paragraph applies such amounts (if any) as the Lord Chancellor may determine by way of—

(*a*) remuneration;
(*b*) allowances;
(*c*) expenses.

Commencement—Tribunals, Courts and Enforcement Act 2007 (Commencement No 6 and Transitional Provisions) Order, SI 2008/2696 art 5(*f*) (Sch 2 comes into force on 3 November 2008).

Other members neither appointed under paragraph 2(1) nor transferred in

7— (1) In this paragraph "ex officio member of the First-tier Tribunal" means a person who is a member of the First-tier Tribunal by virtue of—

(*a*) section 4(3)(*d*) (members of employment tribunals who are not chairmen),

(*b*) the combination of sections 4(3)(*c*) and 5(2)(*c*) (members of Employment Appeal Tribunal appointed under section 22(1)(*c*) of the Employment Tribunals Act 1996), or

(*c*) the combination of sections 4(3)(*c*) and 5(2)(*d*) (members of Asylum and Immigration Tribunal who are not legally qualified members).

(2) The Lord Chancellor may pay to an ex officio member of the First-tier Tribunal such amounts (if any) as the Lord Chancellor may determine by way of—

(*a*) remuneration;
(*b*) allowances;
(*c*) expenses.

Commencement—Tribunals, Courts and Enforcement Act 2007 (Commencement No 6 and Transitional Provisions) Order, SI 2008/2696 art 5(*f*) (Sch 2 comes into force on 3 November 2008).

Training etc

8 The Senior President of Tribunals is responsible, within the resources made available by the Lord Chancellor, for the maintenance of appropriate arrangements for the training, guidance and welfare of judges and other members of the First-tier Tribunal (in their capacities as such judges and other members).

Commencement—Tribunals, Courts and Enforcement Act 2007 (Commencement No 6 and Transitional Provisions) Order, SI 2008/2696 art 5(*f*) (Sch 2 comes into force on 3 November 2008).

Oaths

9— (1) Sub-paragraph (2) applies to a person ("J")—

(*a*) who is appointed under paragraph 1(1) or 2(1), or

(*b*) who becomes a transferred-in judge, or a transferred-in other member, of the First-tier Tribunal and has not previously taken the required oaths after accepting another office.

(2) J must take the required oaths before—

(*a*) the Senior President of Tribunals, or

(*b*) an eligible person who is nominated by the Senior President of Tribunals for the purpose of taking the oaths from J.

(3) A person is eligible for the purposes of sub-paragraph (2)(*b*) if any one or more of the following paragraphs applies to him—

(*a*) he holds high judicial office (as defined in section 60(2) of the Constitutional Reform Act 2005 (c 4));

(*b*) he holds judicial office (as defined in section 109(4) of that Act);

(*c*) he holds (in Scotland) the office of sheriff.

(4) In this paragraph "the required oaths" means (subject to sub-paragraph (5))—

(*a*) the oath of allegiance, and

(*b*) the judicial oath,

as set out in the Promissory Oaths Act 1868 (c 72).

(5) Where it appears to the Lord Chancellor that J will carry out functions as a judge or other member of the First-tier Tribunal wholly or mainly in Northern Ireland, the Lord Chancellor may direct that in relation to J "the required oaths" means—

(*a*) the oath as set out in section 19(2) of the Justice (Northern Ireland) Act 2002 (c 26), or

(*b*) the affirmation and declaration as set out in section 19(3) of that Act.

Commencement—Tribunals, Courts and Enforcement Act 2007 (Commencement No 6 and Transitional Provisions) Order, SI 2008/2696 art 5(*f*) (Sch 2 comes into force on 3 November 2008).

SCHEDULE 3

JUDGES AND OTHER MEMBERS OF THE UPPER TRIBUNAL

Section 5

Power to appoint judges of Upper Tribunal

1— (1) Her Majesty, on the recommendation of the Lord Chancellor, may appoint a person to be one of the judges of the Upper Tribunal.

(2) A person is eligible for appointment under sub-paragraph (1) only if the person—

(*a*) satisfies the judicial-appointment eligibility condition on a 7-year basis,

(*b*) is an advocate or solicitor in Scotland of at least seven years' standing,

(*c*) is a barrister or solicitor in Northern Ireland of at least seven years' standing, or

(*d*) in the Lord Chancellor's opinion, has gained experience in law which makes the person as suitable for appointment as if the person satisfied any of paragraphs (*a*) to (*c*).

(3) Section 52(2) to (5) (meaning of "gain experience in law") apply for the purposes of sub-paragraph (2)(*d*), but as if section 52(4)(*i*) referred to the Lord Chancellor instead of to the relevant decision-maker.

Commencement—Tribunals, Courts and Enforcement Act 2007 (Commencement No 6 and Transitional Provisions) Order, SI 2008/2696 art 5(*f*) (Sch 3 comes into force on 3 November 2008).

Power to appoint other members of Upper Tribunal

2— (1) The Lord Chancellor may appoint a person to be one of the members of the Upper Tribunal who are not judges of the tribunal.

(2) A person is eligible for appointment under sub-paragraph (1) only if the person has qualifications prescribed in an order made by the Lord Chancellor with the concurrence of the Senior President of Tribunals.

Commencement—Tribunals, Courts and Enforcement Act 2007 (Commencement No 6 and Transitional Provisions) Order, SI 2008/2696 art 5(*f*) (Sch 3 comes into force on 3 November 2008).

Orders—Qualifications for Appointment of Members to the First-tier Tribunal and Upper Tribunal Order, SI 2008/2692 (made under para 2(2)).

Appointed and transferred-in judges and other members: removal from office

3— (1) This paragraph applies to any power by which—

(*a*) a person appointed under paragraph 1(1) or 2(1),

(*b*) a transferred-in judge of the Upper Tribunal, or

(*c*) a transferred-in other member of the Upper Tribunal,

may be removed from office.

(2) If the person exercises functions wholly or mainly in Scotland, the power may be exercised only with the concurrence of the Lord President of the Court of Session.

(3) If the person exercises functions wholly or mainly in Northern Ireland, the power may be exercised only with the concurrence of the Lord Chief Justice of Northern Ireland.

(4) If neither of sub-paragraphs (2) and (3) applies, the power may be exercised only with the concurrence of the Lord Chief Justice of England and Wales.

Commencement—Tribunals, Courts and Enforcement Act 2007 (Commencement No 6 and Transitional Provisions) Order, SI 2008/2696 art 5(*f*) (Sch 3 comes into force on 3 November 2008).

Terms of appointment

4— (1) This paragraph applies—

(*a*) to a person appointed under paragraph 1(1) or 2(1),

(*b*) to a transferred-in judge of the Upper Tribunal, and

(*c*) to a transferred-in other member of the Upper Tribunal.

(2) If the terms of the person's appointment provide that he is appointed on a salaried (as opposed to fee-paid) basis, the person may be removed from office—

(*a*) only by the Lord Chancellor (and in accordance with paragraph 3), and
(*b*) only on the ground of inability or misbehaviour.

(3) Subject to sub-paragraph (2) (and to the Judicial Pensions and Retirement Act 1993 (c 8)), the person is to hold and vacate office as a judge, or other member, of the Upper Tribunal in accordance with the terms of his appointment.

Commencement—Tribunals, Courts and Enforcement Act 2007 (Commencement No 6 and Transitional Provisions) Order, SI 2008/2696 art 5(*f*) (Sch 3 comes into force on 3 November 2008).

Remuneration, allowances and expenses

5— (1) Sub-paragraph (2) applies—

(*a*) to a person appointed under paragraph 1(1) or 2(1),
(*b*) to a transferred-in judge of the Upper Tribunal, and
(*c*) to a transferred-in other member of the Upper Tribunal.

(2) The Lord Chancellor may pay to a person to whom this sub-paragraph applies such amounts (if any) as the Lord Chancellor may determine by way of—

(*a*) remuneration;
(*b*) allowances;
(*c*) expenses.

Commencement—Tribunals, Courts and Enforcement Act 2007 (Commencement No 6 and Transitional Provisions) Order, SI 2008/2696 art 5(*f*) (Sch 3 comes into force on 3 November 2008).

Certain judges neither appointed under paragraph 1(1) nor transferred in

6— (1) In this paragraph "judge by request of the Upper Tribunal" means a person who is a judge of the Upper Tribunal but—

(*a*) is not the Senior President of Tribunals,
(*b*) is not a judge of the Upper Tribunal appointed under paragraph 1(1),
(*c*) is not a transferred-in judge of the Upper Tribunal,
(*d*) is not a judge of the Upper Tribunal by virtue of section 5(1)(*d*) (legally qualified member of Asylum and Immigration Tribunal),
(*e*) is not a deputy judge of the Upper Tribunal, and
(*f*) is not a Chamber President, or Acting Chamber President or Deputy Chamber President, of a chamber of the Upper Tribunal.

(2) A judge by request of the Upper Tribunal may act as a judge of the Upper Tribunal only if requested to do so by the Senior President of Tribunals.

(3) Such a request made to a person who is a judge of the Upper Tribunal by virtue of section 5(1)(*g*) may be made only with—

(*a*) the concurrence of the Lord Chief Justice of England and Wales where the person is—
  (i) an ordinary judge of the Court of Appeal in England and Wales,
  (ii) a puisne judge of the High Court in England and Wales,
  (iii) a circuit judge,
  (iv) a district judge in England and Wales, or
  (v) a District Judge (Magistrates' Courts);
(*b*) the concurrence of the Lord President of the Court of Session where the person is—
  (i) a judge of the Court of Session, or
  (ii) a sheriff;
(*c*) the concurrence of the Lord Chief Justice of Northern Ireland where the person is—
  (i) a Lord Justice of Appeal in Northern Ireland,
  (ii) a puisne judge of the High Court in Northern Ireland,
  (iii) a county court judge in Northern Ireland, or
  (iv) a district judge in Northern Ireland.

(4) The Lord Chancellor may pay to a judge by request of the Upper Tribunal, or a person who is a judge of the Upper Tribunal by virtue of section 5(1)(*d*), such amounts (if any) as the Lord Chancellor may determine by way of—

(*a*) remuneration;
(*b*) allowances;
(*c*) expenses.

Commencement—Tribunals, Courts and Enforcement Act 2007 (Commencement No 6 and Transitional Provisions) Order, SI 2008/2696 art 5(*f*) (Sch 3 comes into force on 3 November 2008).

Deputy judges of the Upper Tribunal

7— (1) The Lord Chancellor may appoint a person to be a deputy judge of the Upper Tribunal for such period as the Lord Chancellor considers appropriate.

(2) A person is eligible for appointment under sub-paragraph (1) only if he is eligible to be appointed under paragraph 1(1) (see paragraph 1(2)).

(3) Sub-paragraphs (4) and (5) apply—

(*a*) to a person appointed under sub-paragraph (1), and

(*b*) to a person who becomes a deputy judge of the Upper Tribunal as a result of provision under section 31(2).

(4) A person to whom this sub-paragraph applies is to hold and vacate office as a deputy judge of the Upper Tribunal in accordance with the terms of his appointment (subject to the Judicial Pensions and Retirement Act 1993 (c 8)).

(5) The Lord Chancellor may pay to a person to whom this sub-paragraph applies such amounts (if any) as the Lord Chancellor may determine by way of—

(*a*) remuneration;
(*b*) allowances;
(*c*) expenses.

Commencement—Tribunals, Courts and Enforcement Act 2007 (Commencement No 6 and Transitional Provisions) Order, SI 2008/2696 art 5(*f*) (Sch 3 comes into force on 3 November 2008).

Other members neither appointed under paragraph 2(1) nor transferred in

8— (1) In this paragraph "ex officio member of the Upper Tribunal" means—

(*a*) a person who is a member of the Upper Tribunal by virtue of section 5(2)(*c*) (member of Employment Appeal Tribunal appointed under section 22(1)(*c*) of the Employment Tribunals Act 1996 (c 17)), or

(*b*) a person who is a member of the Upper Tribunal by virtue of section 5(2)(*d*) (member of the Asylum and Immigration Tribunal who is not a legally qualified member).

(2) The Lord Chancellor may pay to an ex officio member of the Upper Tribunal such amounts (if any) as the Lord Chancellor may determine by way of—

(*a*) remuneration;
(*b*) allowances;
(*c*) expenses.

Commencement—Tribunals, Courts and Enforcement Act 2007 (Commencement No 6 and Transitional Provisions) Order, SI 2008/2696 art 5(*f*) (Sch 3 comes into force on 3 November 2008).

Training etc

9 The Senior President of Tribunals is responsible, within the resources made available by the Lord Chancellor, for the maintenance of appropriate arrangements for the training, guidance and welfare of judges and other members of the Upper Tribunal (in their capacities as such judges and other members).

Commencement—Tribunals, Courts and Enforcement Act 2007 (Commencement No 6 and Transitional Provisions) Order, SI 2008/2696 art 5(*f*) (Sch 3 comes into force on 3 November 2008).

Oaths

10— (1) Sub-paragraph (2) applies to a person ("J")—

(*a*) who is appointed under paragraph 1(1), 2(1) or 7(1), or

(*b*) who—

(i) becomes a transferred-in judge, or a transferred-in other member, of the Upper Tribunal, or

(ii) becomes a deputy judge of the Upper Tribunal as a result of provision under section 31(2),

and has not previously taken the required oaths after accepting another office.

(2) J must take the required oaths before—

(*a*) the Senior President of Tribunals, or

(*b*) an eligible person who is nominated by the Senior President of Tribunals for the purpose of taking the oaths from J.

(3) A person is eligible for the purposes of sub-paragraph (2)(*b*) if any one or more of the following paragraphs applies to him—

(*a*) he holds high judicial office (as defined in section 60(2) of the Constitutional Reform Act 2005 (c 4));

(*b*) he holds judicial office (as defined in section 109(4) of that Act);

(*c*) he holds (in Scotland) the office of sheriff.

(4) In this paragraph "the required oaths" means (subject to sub-paragraph (5))—

(*a*) the oath of allegiance, and
(*b*) the judicial oath,

as set out in the Promissory Oaths Act 1868 (c 72).

(5) Where it appears to the Lord Chancellor that J will carry out functions as a judge or other member of the Upper Tribunal wholly or mainly in Northern Ireland, the Lord Chancellor may direct that in relation to J "the required oaths" means—

(*a*) the oath as set out in section 19(2) of the Justice (Northern Ireland) Act 2002 (c 26), or

(*b*) the affirmation and declaration as set out in section 19(3) of that Act.

Commencement—Tribunals, Courts and Enforcement Act 2007 (Commencement No 6 and Transitional Provisions) Order, SI 2008/2696 art 5(*f*) (Sch 3 comes into force on 3 November 2008).

SCHEDULE 4
CHAMBERS AND CHAMBER PRESIDENTS: FURTHER PROVISION

Section 7

PART 1
CHAMBER PRESIDENTS: APPOINTMENT, DELEGATION, DEPUTIES AND FURTHER PROVISION

Eligibility for appointment as Chamber President by Lord Chancellor

1 A person is eligible for appointment under section 7(7) only if—

(*a*) he is a judge of the Upper Tribunal, or
(*b*) he does not fall within paragraph (*a*) but is eligible to be appointed under paragraph 1(1) of Schedule 3 as a judge of the Upper Tribunal (see paragraph 1(2) of that Schedule).

Commencement—Tribunals, Courts and Enforcement Act 2007 (Commencement No 6 and Transitional Provisions) Order, SI 2008/2696 art 5(*h*) (paras 1–8 come into force on 3 November 2008).

Appointment as Chamber President by Lord Chancellor: consultation and nomination

2— (1) The Lord Chancellor must consult the Senior President of Tribunals before the Lord Chancellor appoints under section 7(7) a person within—

section 6(1)(*a*) (ordinary judge of Court of Appeal in England and Wales),
section 6(1)(*b*) (Lord Justice of Appeal in Northern Ireland),
section 6(1)(*c*) (judge of the Court of Session), or
section 6(1)(*d*) (puisne judge of the High Court in England and Wales or Northern Ireland).

(2) If the Lord Chancellor, in exercise of his power under section 7(7) in a particular case, wishes that the person appointed should be drawn from among the ordinary judges of the Court of Appeal in England and Wales or the puisne judges of the High Court in England and Wales, the Lord Chancellor must first ask the Lord Chief Justice of England and Wales to nominate one of those judges for the purpose.

(3) If the Lord Chancellor, in exercise of his power under section 7(7) in a particular case, wishes that the person appointed should be drawn from among the judges of the Court of Session, the Lord Chancellor must first ask the Lord President of the Court of Session to nominate one of those judges for the purpose.

(4) If the Lord Chancellor, in exercise of his power under section 7(7) in a particular case, wishes that the person appointed should be drawn from among the Lords Justices of Appeal in Northern Ireland or the puisne judges of the High Court in Northern Ireland, the Lord Chancellor must first ask the Lord Chief Justice of Northern Ireland to nominate one of those judges for the purpose.

(5) If a judge is nominated under sub-paragraph (2), (3) or (4) in response to a request under that sub-paragraph, the Lord Chancellor must appoint the nominated judge as Chamber President of the chamber concerned.

Commencement—Tribunals, Courts and Enforcement Act 2007 (Commencement No 6 and Transitional Provisions) Order, SI 2008/2696 art 5(*h*) (paras 1–8 come into force on 3 November 2008).

Chamber Presidents: duration of appointment, remuneration etc

3— (1) A Chamber President is to hold and vacate office as a Chamber President in accordance with the terms of his appointment as a Chamber President (subject to the Judicial Pensions and Retirement Act 1993 (c 8)).

(2) The Lord Chancellor may pay to a Chamber President such amounts (if any) as the Lord Chancellor may determine by way of—

(*a*) remuneration;
(*b*) allowances;
(*c*) expenses.

Commencement—Tribunals, Courts and Enforcement Act 2007 (Commencement No 6 and Transitional Provisions) Order, SI 2008/2696 art 5(*h*) (paras 1–8 come into force on 3 November 2008).

Delegation of functions by Chamber Presidents

4— (1) The Chamber President of a chamber of the First-tier Tribunal or Upper Tribunal may delegate any function he has in his capacity as the Chamber President of the chamber—

(*a*) to any judge, or other member, of either of those tribunals;
(*b*) to staff appointed under section 40(1).

(2) A delegation under sub-paragraph (1) is not revoked by the delegator's becoming incapacitated.

(3) Any delegation made by a person under sub-paragraph (1) that is in force immediately before the person ceases to be the Chamber President of a chamber continues in force until subsequently varied or revoked by another holder of the office of Chamber President of that chamber.

(4) The delegation under sub-paragraph (1) of a function shall not prevent the exercise of the function by the Chamber President of the chamber concerned.

(5) In this paragraph "delegate" includes further delegate.

Commencement—Tribunals, Courts and Enforcement Act 2007 (Commencement No 6 and Transitional Provisions) Order, SI 2008/2696 art 5(*h*) (paras 1–8 come into force on 3 November 2008).

Deputy Chamber Presidents

5— (1) The Lord Chancellor may appoint a person who is not a Deputy Chamber President of a chamber to be a Deputy Chamber President of a chamber.

(2) The Senior President of Tribunals may appoint a person who is a Deputy Chamber President of a chamber to be instead, or to be also, a Deputy Chamber President of another chamber.

(3) The power under sub-paragraph (1) is exercisable in any particular case only if the Lord Chancellor—

(*a*) has consulted the Senior President of Tribunals about whether a Deputy Chamber President should be appointed for the chamber concerned, and
(*b*) considers, in the light of the consultation, that a Deputy Chamber President of the chamber should be appointed.

(4) A person is eligible for appointment under sub-paragraph (1) only if—

(*a*) he is a judge of the Upper Tribunal by virtue of appointment under paragraph 1(1) of Schedule 3,
(*b*) he is a transferred-in judge of the Upper Tribunal (see section 31(2)),
(*c*) he is a judge of the Upper Tribunal by virtue of—
section 5(1)(*d*) (legally qualified member of Asylum and Immigration Tribunal),
section 5(1)(*e*) (Social Security Commissioner for Northern Ireland),
section 5(1)(*g*) (certain judges of courts in the United Kingdom), or
section 5(1)(*h*) (deputy judge of the Upper Tribunal), or
(*d*) he falls within none of paragraphs (*a*) to (*c*) but is eligible to be appointed under paragraph 1(1) of Schedule 3 as a judge of the Upper Tribunal (see paragraph 1(2) of that Schedule).

(5) If the Lord Chancellor, in exercise of his power under sub-paragraph (1) in a particular case, wishes that the person appointed should be drawn from among the ordinary judges of the Court of Appeal in England and Wales or the puisne judges of the High Court in England and Wales, the Lord Chancellor must first ask the Lord Chief Justice of England and Wales to nominate one of those judges for the purpose.

(6) If the Lord Chancellor, in exercise of his power under sub-paragraph (1) in a particular case, wishes that the person appointed should be drawn from among the judges of the Court of Session, the Lord Chancellor must first ask the Lord President of the Court of Session to nominate one of those judges for the purpose.

(7) If the Lord Chancellor, in exercise of his power under sub-paragraph (1) in a particular case, wishes that the person appointed should be drawn from among the Lords Justices of Appeal in Northern Ireland or the puisne judges of the High Court in Northern Ireland, the Lord Chancellor must first ask the Lord Chief Justice of Northern Ireland to nominate one of those judges for the purpose.

(8) If a judge is nominated under sub-paragraph (5), (6) or (7) in response to a request under that sub-paragraph, the Lord Chancellor must appoint the nominated judge as a Deputy Chamber President of the chamber concerned.

(9) A Deputy Chamber President is to hold and vacate office as a Deputy Chamber President in accordance with the terms of his appointment (subject to the Judicial Pensions and Retirement Act 1993 (c 8)).

(10) The Lord Chancellor may pay to a Deputy Chamber President such amounts (if any) as the Lord Chancellor may determine by way of—

(*a*) remuneration;
(*b*) allowances;
(*c*) expenses.

(11) In sub-paragraphs (1) and (2) "chamber" means chamber of the First-tier Tribunal or chamber of the Upper Tribunal.

Commencement—Tribunals, Courts and Enforcement Act 2007 (Commencement No 6 and Transitional Provisions) Order, SI 2008/2696 art 5(*h*) (paras 1–8 come into force on 3 November 2008).

Acting Chamber Presidents

6— (1) If in the case of a particular chamber of the First-tier Tribunal or Upper Tribunal there is no-one appointed under section 7 to preside over the chamber, the Senior President of Tribunals may appoint a person to preside over the chamber during the vacancy.

(2) A person appointed under sub-paragraph (1) is to be known as an Acting Chamber President.

(3) A person who is the Acting Chamber President of a chamber is to be treated as the Chamber President of the chamber for all purposes other than—

(*a*) the purposes of this paragraph of this Schedule, and
(*b*) the purposes of the Judicial Pensions and Retirement Act 1993 (c 8).

(4) A person is eligible for appointment under sub-paragraph (1) only if he is eligible for appointment as a Chamber President.

(5) An Acting Chamber President is to hold and vacate office as an Acting Chamber President in accordance with the terms of his appointment.

(6) The Lord Chancellor may pay to an Acting Chamber President such amounts (if any) as the Lord Chancellor may determine by way of—

(*a*) remuneration;
(*b*) allowances;
(*c*) expenses.

Commencement—Tribunals, Courts and Enforcement Act 2007 (Commencement No 6 and Transitional Provisions) Order, SI 2008/2696 art 5(*h*) (paras 1–8 come into force on 3 November 2008).

Guidance

7 The Chamber President of a chamber of the First-tier Tribunal or the Upper Tribunal is to make arrangements for the issuing of guidance on changes in the law and practice as they relate to the functions allocated to the chamber.

Commencement—Tribunals, Courts and Enforcement Act 2007 (Commencement No 6 and Transitional Provisions) Order, SI 2008/2696 art 5(*h*) (paras 1–8 come into force on 3 November 2008).

Oaths

8— (1) Sub-paragraph (2) applies to a person ("the appointee")—

(*a*) appointed under section 7(7) as a Chamber President,
(*b*) appointed under paragraph 5(1) as a Deputy Chamber President of a chamber, or
(*c*) appointed as an Acting Chamber President.

(2) The appointee must take the required oaths before—

(*a*) the Senior President of Tribunals, or
(*b*) an eligible person who is nominated by the Senior President of Tribunals for the purpose of taking the oaths from the appointee.

(3) A person is eligible for the purposes of sub-paragraph (2)(*b*) if any one or more of the following paragraphs applies to him—

(*a*) he holds high judicial office (as defined in section 60(2) of the Constitutional Reform Act 2005 (c 4));
(*b*) he holds judicial office (as defined in section 109(4) of that Act);
(*c*) he holds (in Scotland) the office of sheriff.

(4) Sub-paragraph (2) does not apply to the appointee if he has previously taken the required oaths in compliance with a requirement imposed on him under paragraph 9 of Schedule 2 or paragraph 10 of Schedule 3.

(5) In this paragraph "the required oaths" means (subject to sub-paragraph (6))—

(*a*) the oath of allegiance, and
(*b*) the judicial oath,

as set out in the Promissory Oaths Act 1868 (c 72).

(6) Where it appears to the Lord Chancellor that the appointee will carry out functions under his appointment wholly or mainly in Northern Ireland, the Lord Chancellor may direct that in relation to the appointee "the required oaths" means—

(*a*) the oath as set out in section 19(2) of the Justice (Northern Ireland) Act 2002 (c 26), or
(*b*) the affirmation and declaration as set out in section 19(3) of that Act.

Commencement—Tribunals, Courts and Enforcement Act 2007 (Commencement No 6 and Transitional Provisions) Order, SI 2008/2696 art 5(*h*) (paras 1–8 come into force on 3 November 2008).

PART 2

JUDGES AND OTHER MEMBERS OF CHAMBERS: ASSIGNMENT AND JURISDICTION

Assignment is function of Senior President of Tribunals

9— (1) The Senior President of Tribunals has—

(*a*) the function of assigning judges and other members of the First-tier Tribunal (including himself) to chambers of the First-tier Tribunal, and

(*b*) the function of assigning judges and other members of the Upper Tribunal (including himself) to chambers of the Upper Tribunal.

(2) The functions under sub-paragraph (1) are to be exercised in accordance with the following provisions of this Part of this Schedule.

Commencement—Tribunals, Courts and Enforcement Act 2007 (Commencement No 6 and Transitional Provisions) Order, SI 2008/2696 art 5(*h*) (paras 9–14 come into force on 3 November 2008).

Deemed assignment of Chamber Presidents and Deputy Chamber Presidents

10— (1) The Chamber President, or a Deputy Chamber President, of a chamber—

(*a*) is to be taken to be assigned to that chamber;

(*b*) may be assigned additionally to one or more of the other chambers;

(*c*) may be assigned under paragraph (*b*) to different chambers at different times.

(2) Paragraphs 11(1) and (2) and 12(2) and (3) do not apply to assignment of a person who is a Chamber President or a Deputy Chamber President.

(3) In sub-paragraph (1) "chamber" means chamber of the First-tier Tribunal or the Upper Tribunal.

Commencement—Tribunals, Courts and Enforcement Act 2007 (Commencement No 6 and Transitional Provisions) Order, SI 2008/2696 art 5(*h*) (paras 9–14 come into force on 3 November 2008).

Assigning members of First-tier Tribunal to its chambers

11— (1) Each person who is a judge or other member of the First-tier Tribunal by virtue of appointment under paragraph 1(1) or 2(1) of Schedule 2 or who is a transferred-in judge, or transferred-in other member, of the First-tier Tribunal—

(*a*) is to be assigned to at least one of the chambers of the First-tier Tribunal, and

(*b*) may be assigned to different chambers of the First-tier Tribunal at different times.

(2) A judge or other member of the First-tier Tribunal to whom sub-paragraph (1) does not apply—

(*a*) may be assigned to one or more of the chambers of the First-tier Tribunal, and

(*b*) may be assigned to different chambers of the First-tier Tribunal at different times.

(3) The Senior President of Tribunals may assign a judge or other member of the First-tier Tribunal to a particular chamber of the First-tier Tribunal only with the concurrence—

(*a*) of the Chamber President of the chamber, and

(*b*) of the judge or other member.

(4) The Senior President of Tribunals may end the assignment of a judge or other member of the First-tier Tribunal to a particular chamber of the First-tier Tribunal only with the concurrence of the Chamber President of the chamber.

(5) Sub-paragraph (3)(*a*) does not apply where the judge, or other member, concerned is not assigned to any of the chambers of the First-tier Tribunal.

(6) Sub-paragraphs (3)(*a*) and (4) do not apply where the judge concerned is within section 6(1)(*a*) to (*d*) (judges of Courts of Appeal, Court of Session and High Courts).

(7) Sub-paragraphs (3) and (4) do not apply where the judge concerned is the Senior President of Tribunals himself.

Commencement—Tribunals, Courts and Enforcement Act 2007 (Commencement No 6 and Transitional Provisions) Order, SI 2008/2696 art 5(*h*) (paras 9–14 come into force on 3 November 2008).

Assigning members of Upper Tribunal to its chambers

12— (1) Sub-paragraph (2) applies to a person if—

(*a*) he is a judge of the Upper Tribunal by virtue of appointment under paragraph 1(1) of Schedule 3, or

(*b*) he is a transferred-in judge of the Upper Tribunal, or

(*c*) he is a deputy judge of the Upper Tribunal, or

(*d*) he is a member of the Upper Tribunal by virtue of appointment under paragraph 2(1) of Schedule 3, or

(*e*) he is a transferred-in other member of the Upper Tribunal.

(2) Each person to whom this sub-paragraph applies—

(*a*) is to be assigned to at least one of the chambers of the Upper Tribunal, and

(*b*) may be assigned to different chambers of the Upper Tribunal at different times.

(3) A judge or other member of the Upper Tribunal to whom sub-paragraph (2) does not apply—

(*a*) may be assigned to one or more of the chambers of the Upper Tribunal, and

(*b*) may be assigned to different chambers of the Upper Tribunal at different times.

(4) The Senior President of Tribunals may assign a judge or other member of the Upper Tribunal to a particular chamber of the Upper Tribunal only with the concurrence—

(*a*) of the Chamber President of the chamber, and
(*b*) of the judge or other member.

(5) The Senior President of Tribunals may end the assignment of a judge or other member of the Upper Tribunal to a particular chamber of the Upper Tribunal only with the concurrence of the Chamber President of the chamber.

(6) Sub-paragraph (4)(*a*) does not apply where the judge, or other member, concerned is not assigned to any of the chambers of the Upper Tribunal.

(7) Sub-paragraphs (4)(*a*) and (5) do not apply where the judge concerned is within section 6(1)(*a*) to (*d*) (judges of Courts of Appeal, Court of Session and High Courts).

(8) Sub-paragraphs (4) and (5) do not apply where the judge concerned is the Senior President of Tribunals himself.

Commencement—Tribunals, Courts and Enforcement Act 2007 (Commencement No 6 and Transitional Provisions) Order, SI 2008/2696 art 5(*h*) (paras 9–14 come into force on 3 November 2008).

Policy of Senior President of Tribunals as respects assigning members to chambers etc

13— (1) The Senior President of Tribunals must publish a document recording the policy adopted by him in relation to—

(*a*) the assigning of persons to chambers in exercise of his functions under paragraph 9,
(*b*) the assigning of persons to act as members of the Asylum and Immigration Tribunal in exercise of his functions under paragraphs 5A and 5B of Schedule 4 to the Nationality, Immigration and Asylum Act 2002 (c 41), and
(*c*) the nominating of persons to act as members of panels of members of employment tribunals in exercise of his functions under any such provision as is mentioned in section 5D(1) of the Employment Tribunals Act 1996 (c 17).

(2) That policy must be such as to secure—

(*a*) that appropriate use is made of the knowledge and experience of the judges and other members of the First-tier Tribunal and Upper Tribunal, and
(*b*) that, in the case of a chamber (of the First-tier Tribunal or Upper Tribunal) whose business consists of, or includes, cases likely to involve the application of the law of Scotland or Northern Ireland, sufficient knowledge and experience of that law is to be found among persons assigned to the chamber.

(3) No policy may be adopted by the Senior President of Tribunals for the purposes of sub-paragraph (1) unless the Lord Chancellor concurs in the policy.

(4) The Senior President of Tribunals must keep any policy adopted for the purposes of sub-paragraph (1) under review.

Commencement—Tribunals, Courts and Enforcement Act 2007 (Commencement No 6 and Transitional Provisions) Order, SI 2008/2696 art 5(*h*) (paras 9–14 come into force on 3 November 2008).

Choosing members to decide cases

14— (1) The First-tier Tribunal's function, or the Upper Tribunal's function, of deciding any matter in a case before the tribunal is to be exercised by a member or members of the chamber of the tribunal to which the case is allocated.

(2) The member or members must be chosen by the Senior President of Tribunals.

(3) A person choosing under sub-paragraph (2)—

(*a*) must act in accordance with any provision under paragraph 15;
(*b*) may choose himself.

(4) In this paragraph "member", in relation to a chamber of a tribunal, means a judge or other member of the tribunal who is assigned to the chamber.

Commencement—Tribunals, Courts and Enforcement Act 2007 (Commencement No 6 and Transitional Provisions) Order, SI 2008/2696 art 5(*h*) (paras 9–14 come into force on 3 November 2008).

Composition of tribunals

15— (1) The Lord Chancellor must by order make provision, in relation to every matter that may fall to be decided by the First-tier Tribunal or the Upper Tribunal, for determining the number of members of the tribunal who are to decide the matter.

(2) Where an order under sub-paragraph (1) provides for a matter to be decided by a single member of a tribunal, the order—

(*a*) must make provision for determining whether the matter is to be decided by one of the judges, or by one of the other members, of the tribunal, and
(*b*) may make provision for determining, if the matter is to be decided by one of the other members of the tribunal, what qualifications (if any) that other member must have.

(3) Where an order under sub-paragraph (1) provides for a matter to be decided by two or more members of a tribunal, the order—

(*a*) must make provision for determining how many (if any) of those members are to be judges of the tribunal and how many (if any) are to be other members of the tribunal, and
(*b*) may make provision for determining—

(i) if the matter is to be decided by persons who include one or more of the other members of the tribunal, or

(ii) if the matter is to be decided by two or more of the other members of the tribunal, what qualifications (if any) that other member or any of those other members must have.

(4) A duty under sub-paragraph (1), (2) or (3) to provide for the determination of anything may be discharged by providing for the thing to be determined by the Senior President of Tribunals, or a Chamber President, in accordance with any provision made under that sub-paragraph.

(5) Power under paragraph (*b*) of sub-paragraph (2) or (3) to provide for the determination of anything may be exercised by giving, to the Senior President of Tribunals or a Chamber President, power to determine that thing in accordance with any provision made under that paragraph.

(6) Where under sub-paragraphs (1) to (4) a matter is to be decided by two or more members of a tribunal, the matter may, if the parties to the case agree, be decided in the absence of one or more (but not all) of the members chosen to decide the matter.

(7) Where the member, or any of the members, of a tribunal chosen to decide a matter does not have any qualification that he is required to have under sub-paragraphs (2)(*b*), or (3)(*b*), and (5), the matter may despite that, if the parties to the case agree, be decided by the chosen member or members.

(8) Before making an order under this paragraph, the Lord Chancellor must consult the Senior President of Tribunals.

(9) In this paragraph "qualification" includes experience.

Commencement—Tribunals, Courts and Enforcement Act 2007 (Commencement No 1) Order, SI 2007/2709 art 2(*h*) (para 15 comes into force on 19 September 2007).
Orders—First-tier Tribunal and Upper Tribunal (Composition of Tribunal) Order, SI 2008/2835.

SCHEDULE 5

PROCEDURE IN FIRST-TIER TRIBUNAL AND UPPER TRIBUNAL

Section 22

Commencement—Tribunals, Courts and Enforcement Act 2007 (Commencement No 1) Order, SI 2007/2709 art 2(*i*) (Sch 5 comes into force on 19 September 2007).
Rules—Tribunals, Courts and Enforcement Act 2007 (Transitional and Consequential Provisions) Order, SI 2008/2683.
Tribunal Procedure (First-tier Tribunal) (Social Entitlement Chamber) Rules, SI 2008/2685.
Tribunal Procedure (First-tier Tribunal) (War Pensions and Armed Forces Compensation Chamber) Rules, SI 2008/2686.
Tribunal Procedure (Upper Tribunal) Rules, SI 2008/2698.
Tribunal Procedure (First-tier Tribunal) (Health, Education and Social Care Chamber) Rules, SI 2008/2699.
Transfer of Tribunal Functions Order, SI 2008/2833.
Transfer of Tribunal Functions and Revenue and Customs Appeals Order, SI 2009/56.
Tribunal Procedure (First-tier Tribunal) (Tax Chamber) Rules, SI 2009/273.
Tribunal Procedure (Amendment) Rules, SI 2009/274.

PART 1
TRIBUNAL PROCEDURE RULES

Introductory

1— (1) This Part of this Schedule makes further provision about the content of Tribunal Procedure Rules.

(2) The generality of section 22(1) is not to be taken to be prejudiced by—

(*a*) the following paragraphs of this Part of this Schedule, or

(*b*) any other provision (including future provision) authorising or requiring the making of provision by Tribunal Procedure Rules.

(3) In the following paragraphs of this Part of this Schedule "Rules" means Tribunal Procedure Rules.

Commencement—Tribunals, Courts and Enforcement Act 2007 (Commencement No 1) Order, SI 2007/2709 art 2(*i*) (Sch 5 comes into force on 19 September 2007).

Concurrent functions

2 Rules may make provision as to who is to decide, or as to how to decide, which of the First-tier Tribunal and Upper Tribunal is to exercise, in relation to any particular matter, a function that is exercisable by the two tribunals on the basis that the question as to which of them is to exercise the function is to be determined by, or under, Rules.

Commencement—Tribunals, Courts and Enforcement Act 2007 (Commencement No 1) Order, SI 2007/2709 art 2(*i*) (Sch 5 comes into force on 19 September 2007).

Delegation of functions to staff

3— (1) Rules may provide for functions—

(*a*) of the First-tier Tribunal, or

(*b*) of the Upper Tribunal,

to be exercised by staff appointed under section 40(1).

(2) In making provision of the kind mentioned in sub-paragraph (1) in relation to a function, Rules may (in particular)—

(*a*) provide for the function to be exercisable by a member of staff only if the member of staff is, or is of a description, specified in exercise of a discretion conferred by Rules;

(*b*) provide for the function to be exercisable by a member of staff only if the member of staff is approved, or is of a description approved, for the purpose by a person specified in Rules.

Commencement—Tribunals, Courts and Enforcement Act 2007 (Commencement No 1) Order, SI 2007/2709 art 2(*i*) (Sch 5 comes into force on 19 September 2007).

Time limits

4 Rules may make provision for time limits as respects initiating, or taking any step in, proceedings before the First-tier Tribunal or the Upper Tribunal.

Commencement—Tribunals, Courts and Enforcement Act 2007 (Commencement No 1) Order, SI 2007/2709 art 2(*i*) (Sch 5 comes into force on 19 September 2007).

Repeat applications

5 Rules may make provision restricting the making of fresh applications where a previous application in relation to the same matter has been made.

Commencement—Tribunals, Courts and Enforcement Act 2007 (Commencement No 1) Order, SI 2007/2709 art 2(*i*) (Sch 5 comes into force on 19 September 2007).

Tribunal acting of its own initiative

6 Rules may make provision about the circumstances in which the First-tier Tribunal, or the Upper Tribunal, may exercise its powers of its own initiative.

Commencement—Tribunals, Courts and Enforcement Act 2007 (Commencement No 1) Order, SI 2007/2709 art 2(*i*) (Sch 5 comes into force on 19 September 2007).

Hearings

7 Rules may—

(*a*) make provision for dealing with matters without a hearing;

(*b*) make provision as respects allowing or requiring a hearing to be in private or as respects allowing or requiring a hearing to be in public.

Commencement—Tribunals, Courts and Enforcement Act 2007 (Commencement No 1) Order, SI 2007/2709 art 2(*i*) (Sch 5 comes into force on 19 September 2007).

Proceedings without notice

8 Rules may make provision for proceedings to take place, in circumstances described in Rules, at the request of one party even though the other, or another, party has had no notice.

Commencement—Tribunals, Courts and Enforcement Act 2007 (Commencement No 1) Order, SI 2007/2709 art 2(*i*) (Sch 5 comes into force on 19 September 2007).

Representation

9 Rules may make provision conferring additional rights of audience before the First-tier Tribunal or the Upper Tribunal.

Commencement—Tribunals, Courts and Enforcement Act 2007 (Commencement No 1) Order, SI 2007/2709 art 2(*i*) (Sch 5 comes into force on 19 September 2007).

Evidence, witnesses and attendance

10— (1) Rules may make provision about evidence (including evidence on oath and administration of oaths).

(2) Rules may modify any rules of evidence provided for elsewhere, so far as they would apply to proceedings before the First-tier Tribunal or Upper Tribunal.

(3) Rules may make provision, where the First-tier Tribunal has required a person—

(*a*) to attend at any place for the purpose of giving evidence,

(*b*) otherwise to make himself available to give evidence,

(*c*) to swear an oath in connection with the giving of evidence,

(*d*) to give evidence as a witness,

(*e*) to produce a document, or

(*f*) to facilitate the inspection of a document or any other thing (including any premises),

for the Upper Tribunal to deal with non-compliance with the requirement as though the requirement had been imposed by the Upper Tribunal.

(4) Rules may make provision for the payment of expenses and allowances to persons giving evidence, producing documents, attending proceedings or required to attend proceedings.

Commencement—Tribunals, Courts and Enforcement Act 2007 (Commencement No 1) Order, SI 2007/2709 art 2(*i*) (Sch 5 comes into force on 19 September 2007).

Use of information

11— (1) Rules may make provision for the disclosure or non-disclosure of information received during the course of proceedings before the First-tier Tribunal or Upper Tribunal.

(2) Rules may make provision for imposing reporting restrictions in circumstances described in Rules.

Commencement—Tribunals, Courts and Enforcement Act 2007 (Commencement No 1) Order, SI 2007/2709 art 2(*i*) (Sch 5 comes into force on 19 September 2007).

Costs and expenses

12— (1) Rules may make provision for regulating matters relating to costs, or (in Scotland) expenses, of proceedings before the First-tier Tribunal or Upper Tribunal.

(2) The provision mentioned in sub-paragraph (1) includes (in particular)—

(*a*) provision prescribing scales of costs or expenses;

(*b*) provision for enabling costs to undergo detailed assessment in England and Wales by a county court or the High Court;

(*c*) provision for taxation in Scotland of accounts of expenses by an Auditor of Court;

(*d*) provision for enabling costs to be taxed in Northern Ireland in a county court or the High Court;

(*e*) provision for costs or expenses—

(i) not to be allowed in respect of items of a description specified in Rules;

(ii) not to be allowed in proceedings of a description so specified;

(*f*) provision for other exceptions to either or both of subsections (1) and (2) of section 29.

Commencement—Tribunals, Courts and Enforcement Act 2007 (Commencement No 1) Order, SI 2007/2709 art 2(*i*) (Sch 5 comes into force on 19 September 2007).

Set-off and interest

13— (1) Rules may make provision for a party to proceedings to deduct, from amounts payable by him, amounts payable to him.

(2) Rules may make provision for interest on sums awarded (including provision conferring a discretion or provision in accordance with which interest is to be calculated).

Commencement—Tribunals, Courts and Enforcement Act 2007 (Commencement No 1) Order, SI 2007/2709 art 2(*i*) (Sch 5 comes into force on 19 September 2007).

Arbitration

14 Rules may provide for Part 1 of the Arbitration Act 1996 (c 23) (which extends to England and Wales, and Northern Ireland, but not Scotland) not to apply, or not to apply except so far as is specified in Rules, where the First-tier Tribunal, or Upper Tribunal, acts as arbitrator.

Commencement—Tribunals, Courts and Enforcement Act 2007 (Commencement No 1) Order, SI 2007/2709 art 2(*i*) (Sch 5 comes into force on 19 September 2007).

Correction of errors and setting-aside of decisions on procedural grounds

15— (1) Rules may make provision for the correction of accidental errors in a decision or record of a decision.

(2) Rules may make provision for the setting aside of a decision in proceedings before the First-tier Tribunal or Upper Tribunal—

(*a*) where a document relating to the proceedings was not sent to, or was not received at an appropriate time by, a party to the proceedings or a party's representative,

(*b*) where a document relating to the proceedings was not sent to the First-tier Tribunal or Upper Tribunal at an appropriate time,

(*c*) where a party to the proceedings, or a party's representative, was not present at a hearing related to the proceedings, or

(*d*) where there has been any other procedural irregularity in the proceedings.

(3) Sub-paragraphs (1) and (2) shall not be taken to prejudice, or to be prejudiced by, any power to correct errors or set aside decisions that is exercisable apart from rules made by virtue of those sub-paragraphs.

Commencement—Tribunals, Courts and Enforcement Act 2007 (Commencement No 1) Order, SI 2007/2709 art 2(*i*) (Sch 5 comes into force on 19 September 2007).

Ancillary powers

16 Rules may confer on the First-tier Tribunal, or the Upper Tribunal, such ancillary powers as are necessary for the proper discharge of its functions.

Commencement—Tribunals, Courts and Enforcement Act 2007 (Commencement No 1) Order, SI 2007/2709 art 2(*i*) (Sch 5 comes into force on 19 September 2007).

Rules may refer to practice directions

17 Rules may, instead of providing for any matter, refer to provision made or to be made about that matter by directions under section 23.

Commencement—Tribunals, Courts and Enforcement Act 2007 (Commencement No 1) Order, SI 2007/2709 art 2(*i*) (Sch 5 comes into force on 19 September 2007).

Presumptions

18 Rules may make provision in the form of presumptions (including, in particular, presumptions as to service or notification).

Commencement—Tribunals, Courts and Enforcement Act 2007 (Commencement No 1) Order, SI 2007/2709 art 2(*i*) (Sch 5 comes into force on 19 September 2007).

Differential provision

19 Rules may make different provision for different purposes or different areas.

Commencement—Tribunals, Courts and Enforcement Act 2007 (Commencement No 1) Order, SI 2007/2709 art 2(*i*) (Sch 5 comes into force on 19 September 2007).

PART 2
TRIBUNAL PROCEDURE COMMITTEE

Membership

20 The Tribunal Procedure Committee is to consist of—

(*a*) the Senior President of Tribunals or a person nominated by him,
(*b*) the persons currently appointed by the Lord Chancellor under paragraph 21,
(*c*) the persons currently appointed by the Lord Chief Justice of England and Wales under paragraph 22,
(*d*) the person currently appointed by the Lord President of the Court of Session under paragraph 23, and
(*e*) any person currently appointed under paragraph 24 at the request of the Senior President of Tribunals.

Commencement—Tribunals, Courts and Enforcement Act 2007 (Commencement No 1) Order, SI 2007/2709 art 2(*i*) (Sch 5 comes into force on 19 September 2007).

Lord Chancellor's appointees

21— (1) The Lord Chancellor must appoint—

(*a*) three persons each of whom must be a person with experience of—
  (i) practice in tribunals, or
  (ii) advising persons involved in tribunal proceedings, and
(*b*) one person nominated by the Administrative Justice and Tribunals Council.

(2) Before making an appointment under sub-paragraph (1), the Lord Chancellor must consult the Lord Chief Justice of England and Wales.

(3) Until the Administrative Justice and Tribunals Council first has ten members appointed under paragraph 1(2) of Schedule 7, the reference to that council in sub-paragraph (1)(*b*) is to be read as a reference to the Council on Tribunals; and if, when the Administrative Justice and Tribunals Council first has ten members so appointed, the person appointed under sub-paragraph (1)(*b*) is a nominee of the Council on Tribunals, that person ceases to be a member of the Tribunal Procedure Committee at that time.

Commencement—Tribunals, Courts and Enforcement Act 2007 (Commencement No 1) Order, SI 2007/2709 art 2(*i*) (Sch 5 comes into force on 19 September 2007).

Lord Chief Justice's appointees

22— (1) The Lord Chief Justice of England and Wales must appoint—

(*a*) one of the judges of the First-tier Tribunal,
(*b*) one of the judges of the Upper Tribunal, and
(*c*) one person who is a member of the First-tier Tribunal, or is a member of the Upper Tribunal, but is not a judge of the First-tier Tribunal and is not a judge of the Upper Tribunal.

(2) Before making an appointment under sub-paragraph (1), the Lord Chief Justice of England and Wales must consult the Lord Chancellor.

Commencement—Tribunals, Courts and Enforcement Act 2007 (Commencement No 1) Order, SI 2007/2709 art 2(*i*) (Sch 5 comes into force on 19 September 2007).

Lord President's appointee

23— (1) The Lord President of the Court of Session must appoint one person with experience in and knowledge of the Scottish legal system.

(2) Before making an appointment under sub-paragraph (1), the Lord President of the Court of Session must consult the Lord Chancellor.

Commencement—Tribunals, Courts and Enforcement Act 2007 (Commencement No 1) Order, SI 2007/2709 art 2(*i*) (Sch 5 comes into force on 19 September 2007).

Persons appointed at request of Senior President of Tribunals

24— (1) At the request of the Senior President of Tribunals, an appropriate senior judge may appoint a person or persons with experience in and knowledge of—

(*a*) a particular issue, or

(*b*) a particular subject area in relation to which the First-tier Tribunal or the Upper Tribunal has, or is likely to have, jurisdiction,

for the purpose of assisting the Committee with regard to that issue or subject area.

(2) In sub-paragraph (1) "an appropriate senior judge" means any of—

(*a*) the Lord Chief Justice of England and Wales,

(*b*) the Lord President of the Court of Session, and

(*c*) the Lord Chief Justice of Northern Ireland.

(3) The total number of persons appointed at any time under sub-paragraph (1) must not exceed four.

(4) Before making an appointment under sub-paragraph (1), the person making the appointment must consult the Lord Chancellor.

(5) The terms of appointment of a person appointed under sub-paragraph (1) may (in particular) authorise him to act as a member of the Committee only in relation to matters specified by those terms.

Commencement—Tribunals, Courts and Enforcement Act 2007 (Commencement No 1) Order, SI 2007/2709 art 2(*i*) (Sch 5 comes into force on 19 September 2007).

Power to amend paragraphs 20 to 24

25— (1) The Lord Chancellor may by order—

(*a*) amend any of paragraphs 20, 21(1), 22(1), 23(1) and 24(1), and

(*b*) make consequential amendments in any other provision of paragraphs 21 to 24 or in paragraph 28(7).

(2) The making of an order under this paragraph—

(*a*) requires the concurrence of the Lord Chief Justice of England and Wales,

(*b*) if the order amends paragraph 23(1), requires also the concurrence of the Lord President of the Court of Session, and

(*c*) if the order amends paragraph 24(1), requires also the concurrence of the Lord President of the Court of Session and the Lord Chief Justice of Northern Ireland.

Commencement—Tribunals, Courts and Enforcement Act 2007 (Commencement No 1) Order, SI 2007/2709 art 2(*i*) (Sch 5 comes into force on 19 September 2007).

Committee members' expenses

26 The Lord Chancellor may reimburse members of the Tribunal Procedure Committee their travelling and out-of-pocket expenses.

Commencement—Tribunals, Courts and Enforcement Act 2007 (Commencement No 1) Order, SI 2007/2709 art 2(*i*) (Sch 5 comes into force on 19 September 2007).

PART 3

MAKING OF TRIBUNAL PROCEDURE RULES BY TRIBUNAL PROCEDURE COMMITTEE

Meaning of "Rules" and "the Committee"

27 In the following provisions of this Part of this Schedule—

"the Committee" means the Tribunal Procedure Committee;

"Rules" means Tribunal Procedure Rules.

Commencement—Tribunals, Courts and Enforcement Act 2007 (Commencement No 1) Order, SI 2007/2709 art 2(*i*) (Sch 5 comes into force on 19 September 2007).

Process for making Rules

28— (1) Before the Committee makes Rules, the Committee must—

(*a*) consult such persons (including such of the Chamber Presidents) as it considers appropriate,

(*b*) consult the Lord President of the Court of Session if the Rules contain provision relating to proceedings in Scotland, and

(*c*) meet (unless it is inexpedient to do so).

(2) Rules made by the Committee must be—

(*a*) signed by a majority of the members of the Committee, and
(*b*) submitted to the Lord Chancellor.

(3) The Lord Chancellor may allow or disallow Rules so made.

(4) If the Lord Chancellor disallows Rules so made, he must give the Committee written reasons for doing so.

(5) Rules so made and allowed—

(*a*) come into force on such day as the Lord Chancellor directs, and
(*b*) are to be contained in a statutory instrument to which the Statutory Instruments Act 1946 (c 36) applies as if the instrument contained rules made by a Minister of the Crown.

(6) A statutory instrument containing Rules made by the Committee is subject to annulment in pursuance of a resolution of either House of Parliament.

(7) In the case of a member of the Committee appointed under paragraph 24, the terms of his appointment may (in particular) provide that, for the purposes of sub-paragraph (2)(*a*), he is to count as a member of the Committee only in relation to matters specified in those terms.

Commencement—Tribunals, Courts and Enforcement Act 2007 (Commencement No 1) Order, SI 2007/2709 art 2(*i*) (Sch 5 comes into force on 19 September 2007).

Power of Lord Chancellor to require Rules to be made

29— (1) This paragraph applies if the Lord Chancellor gives the Committee written notice that he thinks it is expedient for Rules to include provision that would achieve a purpose specified in the notice.

(2) The Committee must make such Rules, in accordance with paragraph 28, as it considers necessary to achieve the specified purpose.

(3) Those Rules must be made—

(*a*) within such period as may be specified by the Lord Chancellor in the notice, or
(*b*) if no period is so specified, within a reasonable period after the Lord Chancellor gives the notice to the Committee.

Commencement—Tribunals, Courts and Enforcement Act 2007 (Commencement No 1) Order, SI 2007/2709 art 2(*i*) (Sch 5 comes into force on 19 September 2007).

PART 4

POWER TO AMEND LEGISLATION IN CONNECTION WITH TRIBUNAL PROCEDURE RULES

Lord Chancellor's power

30— (1) The Lord Chancellor may by order amend, repeal or revoke any enactment to the extent he considers necessary or desirable—

(*a*) in order to facilitate the making of Tribunal Procedure Rules, or
(*b*) in consequence of—

(i) section 22,
(ii) Part 1 or 3 of this Schedule, or
(iii) Tribunal Procedure Rules.

(2) In this paragraph "enactment" means any enactment whenever passed or made, including an enactment comprised in subordinate legislation (within the meaning of the Interpretation Act 1978 (c 30)).

Commencement—Tribunals, Courts and Enforcement Act 2007 (Commencement No 1) Order, SI 2007/2709 art 2(*i*) (Sch 5 comes into force on 19 September 2007).
Orders—Tribunals, Courts and Enforcement Act 2007 (Transitional and Consequential Provisions) Order, SI 2008/2683.
Transfer of Tribunal Functions Order, SI 2008/2833.
Transfer of Tribunal Functions and Revenue and Customs Appeals Order, SI 2009/56.

SCHEDULE 6

TRIBUNALS FOR THE PURPOSES OF SECTIONS 30 TO 36

Sections 30 to 37

Commencement—Tribunals, Courts and Enforcement Act 2007 (Commencement No 1) Order, SI 2007/2709 art 2(*j*) (Sch 6 comes into force on 19 September 2007).

PART 1

TRIBUNALS FOR THE PURPOSES OF SECTIONS 30, 35 AND 36

Tribunal	*Enactment*
Appeal tribunal	Chapter 1 of Part 1 of the Social Security Act 1998 (c 14)
Child Support Commissioner	Section 22 of the Child Support Act 1991 (c 48)
[Claims Management Services Tribunal	Section 12 of the Compensation Act 2006 (c 29)][1]
The Secretary of State as respects his function of deciding appeals under:	Section 41 of the Consumer Credit Act 1974 (c 39)
The Secretary of State as respects his function of deciding appeals under:	Section 7(1) of the Estate Agents Act 1979 (c 38)
Foreign Compensation Commission	Section 1 of the Foreign Compensation Act 1950 (c 12)
[Gender Recognition Panel	Section 1(3) of the Gender Recognition Act 2004 (c 7)][1]
Commissioner for the general purposes of the income tax	Section 2 of the Taxes Management Act 1970 (c 9)
Information Tribunal	Section 6 of the Data Protection Act 1998 (c 29)
Meat Hygiene Appeals Tribunal	Regulation 6 of the Fresh Meat (Hygiene and Inspection) Regulations 1995 (SI 1995/539)
Meat Hygiene Appeals Tribunal	Regulation 6 of the Poultry Meat, Farmed Game Bird Meat and Rabbit Meat (Hygiene and Inspection) Regulations 1995 (SI 1995/540)
Meat Hygiene Appeals Tribunal	Regulation 5 of the Wild Game Meat (Hygiene and Inspection) Regulations 1995 (SI 1995/2148)
Mental Health Review Tribunal for a region of England	Section 65(1) and (1A)(a) of the Mental Health Act 1983 (c 20)
Reinstatement Committee	Paragraph 1 of Schedule 2 to the Reserve Forces (Safeguard of Employment) Act 1985 (c 17)
Reserve forces appeal tribunal	Section 88 of the Reserve Forces Act 1996 (c 14)
Sea Fish Licence Tribunal	Section 4AA of the Sea Fish (Conservation) Act 1967 (c 84)
Social Security Commissioner	Schedule 4 to the Social Security Act 1998 (c 14)
Special Educational Needs and Disability Tribunal	Section 333 of the Education Act 1996 (c 56)
Transport Tribunal	Schedule 4 to the Transport Act 1985 (c 67)
[Tribunal	Section 704 of the Income Tax Act 2007 (c 3)][1]
Umpire or deputy umpire	Paragraph 5 of Schedule 2 to the Reserve Forces (Safeguard of Employment) Act 1985
VAT and duties tribunal	Schedule 12 to the Value Added Tax Act 1994 (c 23)

Commencement—Tribunals, Courts and Enforcement Act 2007 (Commencement No 1) Order, SI 2007/2709 art 2(*j*) (Sch 6 comes into force on 19 September 2007).

Amendments—[1] Entries inserted by the Transfer of Tribunal Functions Order, SI 2008/2833 art 2 with effect from 3 November 2008.

PART 2
TRIBUNALS FOR THE PURPOSES OF SECTIONS 30 AND 35

Tribunal	*Enactment*
Adjudicator	Section 5 of the Criminal Injuries Compensation Act 1995 (c 53)

Commencement—Tribunals, Courts and Enforcement Act 2007 (Commencement No 1) Order, SI 2007/2709 art 2(*j*) (Sch 6 comes into force on 19 September 2007).

PART 3
TRIBUNALS FOR THE PURPOSES OF SECTIONS 30 AND 36

Tribunal	*Enactment*
Adjudicator to Her Majesty's Land Registry	Section 107 of the Land Registration Act 2002 (c 9)
Charity Tribunal	Section 2A of the Charities Act 1993 (c 10)
Consumer Credit Appeals Tribunal	Section 40A of the Consumer Credit Act 1974 (c 39)
Financial Services and Markets Tribunal	Section 132 of the Financial Services and Markets Act 2000 (c 8)
Gambling Appeals Tribunal	Section 140 of the Gambling Act 2005 (c 19)
Immigration Services Tribunal	Section 87 of the Immigration and Asylum Act 1999 (c 33)
Lands Tribunal	Section 1(1)(b) of the Lands Tribunal Act 1949 (c 42)
Pensions Appeal Tribunal in England and Wales	Paragraph 1(1) of the Schedule to the Pensions Appeal Tribunals Act 1943 (c 39)
Pensions Regulator Tribunal	Section 102 of the Pensions Act 2004 (c 35)
Commissioner for the special purposes of the Income Tax Acts	Section 4 of the Taxes Management Act 1970 (c 9)

Commencement—Tribunals, Courts and Enforcement Act 2007 (Commencement No 1) Order, SI 2007/2709 art 2(*j*) (Sch 6 comes into force on 19 September 2007).

PART 4
TRIBUNALS FOR THE PURPOSES OF SECTION 30

Tribunal	*Enactment*
Agricultural Land Tribunal	Section 73 of the Agriculture Act 1947 (c 48)
Aircraft and Shipbuilding Industries Arbitration Tribunal	Section 42 of the Aircraft and Shipbuilding Industries Act 1977 (c 3)
Antarctic Act Tribunal	Regulation 11 of the Antarctic Regulations 1995 (SI 1995/490)

Tribunal	*Enactment*
Appeal tribunal	Part 2 of Schedule 9 to the Scheme set out in Schedule 2 to the Firefighters' Pension Scheme Order 1992 (SI 1992/129)
Asylum Support Adjudicator	Section 102 of the Immigration and Asylum Act 1999
Case tribunal, or interim case tribunal, drawn from the Adjudication Panel for England	Section 76 of the Local Government Act 2000 (c 22)
Family Health Services Appeal Authority	Section 49S of the National Health Service Act 1977 (c 49)
Insolvency Practitioners Tribunal	Section 396(1) of the Insolvency Act 1986 (c 45)
Appeals Tribunal	Part 3 of the Local Authorities (Code of Conduct) (Local Determination) Regulations 2003 (SI 2003/1483)
[Panel	Section 189(6) of the Greater London Authority Act 1999][1]
Plant Varieties and Seeds Tribunal	Section 42 of the Plant Varieties Act 1997 (c 66)
Tribunal	Rule 6 of the model provisions with respect to appeals as applied with modifications by the Chemical Weapons (Licence Appeal Provisions) Order 1996 (SI 1996/3030)
Tribunal	Health Service Medicines (Price Control Appeals) Regulations 2000 (SI 2000/124)
Tribunal	Section 706 of the Income and Corporation Taxes Act 1988 (c 1)
Tribunal	Section 150 of the Mines and Quarries Act 1954 (c 70)
Tribunal	Part 1 of Schedule 3 to the Misuse of Drugs Act 1971 (c 38)
Tribunal	Regulation H6(3) of the Police Pensions Regulations 1987 (SI 1987/257)
Tribunal	Section 9 of the Protection of Children Act 1999 (c 14)

Commencement—Tribunals, Courts and Enforcement Act 2007 (Commencement No 1) Order, SI 2007/2709 art 2(*j*) (Sch 6 comes into force on 19 September 2007).

Amendments—[1] Entry for "panel" inserted by the Transfer of Functions (Estate Agents Appeals and Additional Scheduled Tribunal) Order, SI 2009/1836 art 4 with effect from 8 July 2009.

PART 5

TRIBUNALS FOR THE PURPOSES OF SECTIONS 35 AND 36

Tribunal	*Enactment*
Employment Appeal Tribunal	Section 20 of the Employment Tribunals Act 1996 (c 17)

Commencement—Tribunals, Courts and Enforcement Act 2007 (Commencement No 1) Order, SI 2007/2709 art 2(*j*) (Sch 6 comes into force on 19 September 2007).

PART 6

TRIBUNALS FOR THE PURPOSES OF SECTION 35

Tribunal	*Enactment*
Employment tribunal	Section 1 of the Employment Tribunals Act 1996

Commencement—Tribunals, Courts and Enforcement Act 2007 (Commencement No 1) Order, SI 2007/2709 art 2(*j*) (Sch 6 comes into force on 19 September 2007).

PART 7

TRIBUNALS FOR THE PURPOSES OF SECTION 32(3)

Tribunal	*Enactment*
Case tribunal, or interim case tribunal, drawn from the Adjudication Panel for Wales	Section 76 of the Local Government Act 2000 (c 22)
Appeals Tribunal	Local Government Investigations (Functions of Monitoring Officers and Standards Committees) (Wales) Regulations 2001 (SI 2001/2281)
Mental Health Review Tribunal for Wales	Section 65(1) and (1A)(b) of the Mental Health Act 1983 (c 20)
Special Educational Needs Tribunal for Wales	Section 336ZA of the Education Act 1996 (c 56)
Tribunal	Section 27 of, and Schedule 3 to, the Education Act 2005 (c 18)

Commencement—Tribunals, Courts and Enforcement Act 2007 (Commencement No 1) Order, SI 2007/2709 art 2(*j*) (Sch 6 comes into force on 19 September 2007).

SCHEDULE 10

AMENDMENTS RELATING TO JUDICIAL APPOINTMENTS

Section 50

Note—Provisions omitted are not relevant to this work.
Commencement—Tribunals, Courts and Enforcement Act 2007 (Commencement No 5 and Transitional Provisions) Order, SI 2008/1653 art 2(*d*) (Sch 10 comes into force on 21 July 2008).

PART 1

AMENDMENTS

…

8— (1) Section 4(2) of the Taxes Management Act 1970 (c 9) (Special Commissioners) is amended as follows.

(2) For paragraph (*a*) substitute—

"(*a*) he satisfies the judicial-appointment eligibility condition on a 7-year basis;".

(3) In paragraphs (*b*) and (*c*), for "10" substitute "7".

…

19— (1) Paragraph 1(1)(*a*) of Schedule 7 to the Insolvency Act 1986 (c 45) (members of Insolvency Practitioners Tribunal) is amended as follows.

(2) For sub-paragraph (i) substitute—

"(i) satisfy the judicial-appointment eligibility condition on a 5-year basis;".

(3) In sub-paragraph (ii), for "7" substitute "5".

…

23 *In Schedule 1B to the Charities Act 1993 (c 10) (which is inserted by Schedule 3 to the Charities Act 2006 (c 50)), in paragraph 1(3) (President or legal member of Charity Tribunal), for the words from "he has" to the end substitute "he satisfies the judicial-appointment eligibility condition on a 5-year basis."*

Amendments—This para repealed by the Transfer of Functions of the Charity Tribunal Order, SI 2009/1834 art 4(1), Sch 3 with effect from 1 September 2009.

24— (1) Schedule 12 to the Value Added Tax Act 1994 (c 23) is amended as follows.

(2) In paragraph 2(2) (President of VAT and duties tribunals)—

(*a*) for paragraph (*a*) substitute—

"(*a*) a person who satisfies the judicial-appointment eligibility condition on a 7-year basis;", and

(*b*) in paragraphs (*b*) and (*c*), for "10" substitute "7".

(3) In paragraph 7(4) (panel of chairmen)—

(*a*) for paragraph (*a*) substitute—

"(*a*) a person who satisfies the judicial-appointment eligibility condition on a 5-year basis; or", and

(*b*) in paragraph (*b*) and in the words after that paragraph, for "7" substitute "5".

…

29 …

Amendments—Para 29 repealed by the Transfer of Tribunal Functions Order, SI 2008/2833 art 6, Sch 3 para 228(*r*) with effect from 3 November 2008.

…

34— (1) Schedule 13 to the Financial Services and Markets Act 2000 (c 8) is amended as follows.

(2) In paragraph 2(5) (President of Financial Services and Markets Tribunal)—

(*a*) for paragraph (*a*) substitute—

"(*a*) satisfies the judicial-appointment eligibility condition on a 7-year basis;", and

(*b*) in paragraphs (*b*) and (*c*)(i) and (ii), for "ten" substitute "7".

(3) In paragraph 3(2) (panel of chairmen)—

(*a*) for paragraph (*a*) substitute—

"(*a*) he satisfies the judicial-appointment eligibility condition on a 5-year basis;", and

(*b*) in paragraphs (*b*) and (*c*)(i) and (ii), for "seven" substitute "5".

35— (1) The Land Registration Act 2002 (c 9) is amended as follows.

(2) In section 107(2) (Adjudicator to Her Majesty's Land Registry), for the words from "have" to the end substitute "satisfy the judicial-appointment eligibility condition on a 7-year basis."

(3) In paragraph 4(2) of Schedule 9 (delegation by adjudicator of non-administrative functions to staff), for the words from "has" to the end substitute "satisfies the judicial-appointment eligibility condition on a 7-year basis."

36— (1) Paragraph 1 of Schedule 2 to the Enterprise Act 2002 (c 40) is amended as follows.

(2) In sub-paragraph (1) (President of Competition Appeal Tribunal)—

(*a*) for paragraph (*a*) substitute—

"(*a*) he satisfies the judicial-appointment eligibility condition on a 7-year basis;", and

(*b*) in paragraphs (*b*) and (*c*), for "10" substitute "7".

(3) In sub-paragraph (2) (chairmen)—

(*a*) for paragraph (*a*) substitute—

"(*a*) he satisfies the judicial-appointment eligibility condition on a 5-year basis;", and

(*b*) in paragraphs (*b*) and (*c*), for "7" substitute "5".

…

40— (1) Schedule 4 to the Pensions Act 2004 (c 35) is amended as follows.

(2) In paragraph 1(2) (panel of chairmen of Pensions Regulator Tribunal)—

(*a*) for paragraph (*a*) substitute—

"(*a*) he satisfies the judicial-appointment eligibility condition on a 5-year basis," and

(*b*) in paragraphs (*b*), (*c*) and (*d*), for "7" substitute "5".

(3) In paragraph 2(5) (President or Deputy President)—

(*a*) for paragraph (*a*) substitute—

"(*a*) satisfies the judicial-appointment eligibility condition on a 7-year basis," and

(*b*) in paragraphs (*b*), (*c*) and (*d*), for "10" substitute "7".

41— (1) Section 25 of the Constitutional Reform Act 2005 (c 4) (judges of the Supreme Court) is amended as follows.

(2) In subsection (1), for paragraph (*b*) and the word "or" immediately preceding it substitute—

"(*b*) satisfied the judicial-appointment eligibility condition on a 15-year basis, or

(*c*) been a qualifying practitioner for a period of at least 15 years."

(3) In subsection (2), omit paragraph (*a*).

42 In paragraph 1(2) of Schedule 3 to the Education Act 2005 (c 18) (Chairman of tribunal hearing appeals under section 27 of that Act), for the words from "have a" to the end substitute "satisfy the judicial-appointment eligibility condition on a 5-year basis."

43— (1) Paragraph 2 of Schedule 8 to the Gambling Act 2005 (c 19) (President and members of Gambling Appeals Tribunal) is amended as follows.

(2) For paragraph (*a*) substitute—

"(*a*) he satisfies the judicial-appointment eligibility condition on a 5-year basis,".

(3) In paragraphs (*b*) and (*c*), for "seven" substitute "5".

…

SCHEDULE 12

TAKING CONTROL OF GOODS

Section 62(1)

Note—This Schedule does not extend to Scotland (s 147(2)).

PART 1

INTRODUCTORY

The procedure

1— (1) Using the procedure in this Schedule to recover a sum means taking control of goods and selling them to recover that sum in accordance with this Schedule and regulations under it.

(2) In this Schedule a power to use the procedure to recover a particular sum is called an "enforcement power".

(3) The following apply in relation to an enforcement power.

(4) "Debt" means the sum recoverable.

(5) "Debtor" means the person liable to pay the debt or, if two or more persons are jointly or jointly and severally liable, any one or more of them.

(6) "Creditor" means the person for whom the debt is recoverable.

Enforcement agents

2— (1) In this Schedule "enforcement agent" means an individual authorised by section 63(2) to act as an enforcement agent.

(2) Only an enforcement agent may take control of goods and sell them under an enforcement power.

(3) An enforcement agent, if he is not the person on whom an enforcement power is conferred, may act under the power only if authorised by that person.

(4) In relation to goods taken control of by an enforcement agent under an enforcement power, references to the enforcement agent are references to any person for the time being acting as an enforcement agent under the power.

General interpretation

3— (1) In this Schedule—

"amount outstanding" is defined in paragraph 50(3);

"control" (except in paragraph 5(4)(*a*)) means control under an enforcement power;

"controlled goods" means goods taken control of that—

(*a*) have not been sold or abandoned,

(*b*) if they have been removed, have not been returned to the debtor (unless subject to a controlled goods agreement), and

(*c*) if they are goods of another person, have not been returned to that person;

"controlled goods agreement" has the meaning given by paragraph 13(4);

"co-owner" in relation to goods of the debtor means a person other than the debtor who has an interest in the goods, but only if the enforcement agent—

(*a*) knows that the person has an interest in the particular goods, or

(*b*) would know, if he made reasonable enquiries;

"the court", unless otherwise stated, and subject to rules of court, means—

(*a*) the High Court, in relation to an enforcement power under a writ of the High Court;

(*b*) a county court, in relation to an enforcement power under a warrant issued by a county court;

(*c*) in any other case, a magistrates' court;

"disposal" and related expressions, in relation to securities, are to be read in accordance with paragraph 48(2);

"exempt goods" means goods that regulations exempt by description or circumstances or both;
"goods" means property of any description, other than land;
"interest" means a beneficial interest;
"money" means money in sterling or another currency;
"premises" means any place, and in particular includes—

(*a*) a vehicle, vessel, aircraft or hovercraft;
(*b*) a tent or movable structure;

"securities" includes bills of exchange, promissory notes, bonds, specialties and securities for money.

(2) In this Schedule—

(*a*) references to goods of the debtor or another person are references to goods in which the debtor or that person has an interest, but
(*b*) references to goods of the debtor do not include references to trust property in which either the debtor or a co-owner has an interest not vested in possession.

PART 2

THE PROCEDURE

Binding property in the debtor's goods

4— (1) For the purposes of any enforcement power, the property in all goods of the debtor, except goods that are exempt goods for the purposes of this Schedule or are protected under any other enactment, becomes bound in accordance with this paragraph.

(2) Where the power is conferred by a writ issued from the High Court the writ binds the property in the goods from the time when it is received by the person who is under a duty to endorse it.

(3) Where the power is conferred by a warrant to which section 99 of the County Courts Act 1984 (c 28) or section 125ZA of the Magistrates' Courts Act 1980 (c 43) applies, the warrant binds the property in the goods from the time when it is received by the person who is under a duty to endorse it under that section.

(4) Where sub-paragraphs (2) and (3) do not apply but notice is given to the debtor under paragraph 7(1), the notice binds the property in the goods from the time when the notice is given.

Effect of property in goods being bound

5— (1) An assignment or transfer of any interest of the debtor's in goods while the property in them is bound for the purposes of an enforcement power—

(*a*) is subject to that power, and
(*b*) does not affect the operation of this Schedule in relation to the goods, except as provided by paragraph 61 (application to assignee or transferee).

(2) Sub-paragraph (1) does not prejudice the title to any of the debtor's goods that a person acquires—

(*a*) in good faith,
(*b*) for valuable consideration, and
(*c*) without notice.

(3) For the purposes of sub-paragraph (2)(*a*), a thing is to be treated as done in good faith if it is in fact done honestly (whether it is done negligently or not).

(4) In sub-paragraph (2)(*c*) "notice" means—

(*a*) where the property in the goods is bound by a writ or warrant, notice that the writ or warrant, or any other writ or warrant by virtue of which the goods of the debtor might be seized or otherwise taken control of, had been received by the person who was under a duty to endorse it and that goods remained bound under it;
(*b*) where the property in the goods is bound by notice under paragraph 7(1), notice that that notice had been given and that goods remained bound under it.

(5) In sub-paragraph (4)(*a*) "endorse" in relation to a warrant to which section 99 of the County Courts Act 1984 (c 28) or section 125ZA of the Magistrates' Courts Act 1980 (c 43) applies, means endorse under that section.

Time when property ceases to be bound

6— (1) For the purposes of any enforcement power the property in goods of the debtor ceases to be bound in accordance with this paragraph.

(2) The property in any goods ceases to be bound—

(*a*) when the goods are sold;
(*b*) in the case of money used to pay any of the amount outstanding, when it is used.

(3) The property in all goods ceases to be bound when any of these happens—

(*a*) the amount outstanding is paid, out of the proceeds of sale or otherwise;
(*b*) the instrument under which the power is exercisable ceases to have effect;
(*c*) the power ceases to be exercisable for any other reason.

Notice of enforcement

7— (1) An enforcement agent may not take control of goods unless the debtor has been given notice.

(2) Regulations must state—
(*a*) the minimum period of notice;
(*b*) the form of the notice;
(*c*) what it must contain;
(*d*) how it must be given;
(*e*) who must give it.

(3) The enforcement agent must keep a record of the time when the notice is given.

(4) If regulations authorise it, the court may order in prescribed circumstances that the notice given may be less than the minimum period.

(5) The order may be subject to conditions.

Time limit for taking control

8— (1) An enforcement agent may not take control of goods after the prescribed period.

(2) The period may be prescribed by reference to the date of notice of enforcement or of any writ or warrant conferring the enforcement power or any other date.

(3) Regulations may provide for the period to be extended or further extended by the court in accordance with the regulations.

Goods which may be taken

9 An enforcement agent may take control of goods only if they are—
(*a*) on premises that he has power to enter under this Schedule, or
(*b*) on a highway.

10 An enforcement agent may take control of goods only if they are goods of the debtor.

11— (1) Subject to paragraphs 9 and 10 and to any other enactment under which goods are protected, an enforcement agent—
(*a*) may take control of goods anywhere in England and Wales;
(*b*) may take control of any goods that are not exempt.

(2) Regulations may authorise him to take control of exempt goods in prescribed circumstances, if he provides the debtor with replacements in accordance with the regulations.

Value of goods taken

12— (1) Unless sub-paragraph (2) applies, an enforcement agent may not take control of goods whose aggregate value is more than—
(*a*) the amount outstanding, and
(*b*) an amount in respect of future costs, calculated in accordance with regulations.

(2) An enforcement agent may take control of goods of higher value on premises or on a highway, only to the extent necessary, if there are not enough goods of a lower value within a reasonable distance—
(*a*) on a highway, or
(*b*) on premises that he has power to enter under this Schedule, either under paragraph 14 or under an existing warrant.

(3) For the purposes of this paragraph goods are above a given value only if it is or ought to be clear to the enforcement agent that they are.

(4) Sub-paragraph (1) does not affect the power to keep control of goods if they rise in value once they have been taken.

Ways of taking control

13— (1) To take control of goods an enforcement agent must do one of the following—
(*a*) secure the goods on the premises on which he finds them;
(*b*) if he finds them on a highway, secure them on a highway, where he finds them or within a reasonable distance;
(*c*) remove them and secure them elsewhere;
(*d*) enter into a controlled goods agreement with the debtor.

(2) Any liability of an enforcement agent (including criminal liability) arising out of his securing goods on a highway under this paragraph is excluded to the extent that he acted with reasonable care.

(3) Regulations may make further provision about taking control in any of the ways listed in sub-paragraph (1), including provision—

(*a*) determining the time when control is taken;

(*b*) prohibiting use of any of those ways for goods by description or circumstances or both.

(4) A controlled goods agreement is an agreement under which the debtor—

(*a*) is permitted to retain custody of the goods,

(*b*) acknowledges that the enforcement agent is taking control of them, and

(*c*) agrees not to remove or dispose of them, nor to permit anyone else to, before the debt is paid.

Entry without warrant

14— (1) An enforcement agent may enter relevant premises to search for and take control of goods.

(2) Where there are different relevant premises this paragraph authorises entry to each of them.

(3) This paragraph authorises repeated entry to the same premises, subject to any restriction in regulations.

(4) If the enforcement agent is acting under section 72(1) (CRAR), the only relevant premises are the demised premises.

(5) If he is acting under section 121A of the Social Security Administration Act 1992 (c 5), premises are relevant if they are the place, or one of the places, where the debtor carries on a trade or business.

(6) Otherwise premises are relevant if the enforcement agent reasonably believes that they are the place, or one of the places, where the debtor—

(*a*) usually lives, or

(*b*) carries on a trade or business.

Prospective amendments—As part of the ongoing reform of the penalty regime, para 14(5) to be repealed by FA 2008 s 129, Sch 43 para 10(2) with effect from such day as the Commissioners may by statutory instrument appoint.

Entry under warrant

15— (1) If an enforcement agent applies to the court it may issue a warrant authorising him to enter specified premises to search for and take control of goods.

(2) Before issuing the warrant the court must be satisfied that all these conditions are met—

(*a*) an enforcement power has become exercisable;

(*b*) there is reason to believe that there are goods on the premises that the enforcement power will be exercisable to take control of if the warrant is issued;

(*c*) it is reasonable in all the circumstances to issue the warrant.

(3) The warrant authorises repeated entry to the same premises, subject to any restriction in regulations.

Re-entry

16— (1) This paragraph applies where goods on any premises have been taken control of and have not been removed by the enforcement agent.

(2) The enforcement agent may enter the premises to inspect the goods or to remove them for storage or sale.

(3) This paragraph authorises repeated entry to the same premises.

General powers to use reasonable force

17 Where paragraph 18 or 19 applies, an enforcement agent may if necessary use reasonable force to enter premises or to do anything for which the entry is authorised.

18 This paragraph applies if these conditions are met—

(*a*) the enforcement agent has power to enter the premises under paragraph 14 or 16 or under a warrant under paragraph 15;

(*b*) he is acting under an enforcement power conferred by a warrant of control under section 76(1) of the Magistrates' Courts Act 1980 (c 43) for the recovery of a sum adjudged to be paid by a conviction;

(*c*) he is entitled to execute the warrant by virtue of section 125A (civilian enforcement officers) or 125B (approved enforcement agencies) of that Act.

19— (1) This paragraph applies if these conditions are met—

(*a*) the enforcement agent has power to enter the premises under paragraph 16;

(*b*) he reasonably believes that the debtor carries on a trade or business on the premises;

(*c*) he is acting under an enforcement power within sub-paragraph (2).

(2) The enforcement powers are those under any of the following—

(*a*) a writ or warrant of control issued for the purpose of recovering a sum payable under a High Court or county court judgment;

(*b*) section 61(1) of the Taxes Management Act 1970 (c 9);

(*c*) section 121A(1) of the Social Security Administration Act 1992 (c 5);

(*d*) section 51(A1) of the Finance Act 1997 (c 16);

(*e*) paragraph 1A of Schedule 12 to the Finance Act 2003 (c 14).

Prospective amendments—As part of the ongoing reform of the penalty regime, sub-para (2)(*b*) to be substituted for current sub-para (2)(*b*)–(*e*), by FA 2008 s 129, Sch 43 para 10(3) as follows, (from such day as the Commissioners may by statutory instrument appoint)—

"(*b*) section 127 of the Finance Act 2008."

Application for power to use reasonable force

20— (1) This paragraph applies if an enforcement agent has power to enter premises under paragraph 14 or 16 or under a warrant under paragraph 15.

(2) If the enforcement agent applies to the court it may issue a warrant which authorises him to use, if necessary, reasonable force to enter the premises or to do anything for which entry is authorised.

21— (1) This paragraph applies if an enforcement agent is applying for power to enter premises under a warrant under paragraph 15.

(2) If the enforcement agent applies to the court it may include in the warrant provision authorising him to use, if necessary, reasonable force to enter the premises or to do anything for which entry is authorised.

22— (1) The court may not issue a warrant under paragraph 20 or include provision under paragraph 21 unless it is satisfied that prescribed conditions are met.

(2) A warrant under paragraph 20 or provision included under paragraph 21 may require any constable to assist the enforcement agent to execute the warrant.

Other provisions about powers of entry

23 Paragraphs 24 to 30 apply where an enforcement agent has power to enter premises under paragraph 14 or 16 or under a warrant under paragraph 15.

24— (1) The power to enter and any power to use force are subject to any restriction imposed by or under regulations.

(2) A power to use force does not include power to use force against persons, except to the extent that regulations provide that it does.

25— (1) The enforcement agent may enter and remain on the premises only within prescribed times of day.

(2) Regulations may give the court power in prescribed circumstances to authorise him to enter or remain on the premises at other times.

(3) The authorisation—

(*a*) may be by order or in a warrant under paragraph 15;

(*b*) may be subject to conditions.

26— (1) The enforcement agent must on request show the debtor and any person who appears to him to be in charge of the premises evidence of—

(*a*) his identity, and

(*b*) his authority to enter the premises.

(2) The request may be made before the enforcement agent enters the premises or while he is there.

27— (1) The enforcement agent may take other people onto the premises.

(2) They may assist him in exercising any power, including a power to use force.

(3) They must not remain on the premises without the enforcement agent.

(4) The enforcement agent may take any equipment onto the premises.

(5) He may leave equipment on the premises if he leaves controlled goods there.

28— (1) After entering the premises the enforcement agent must provide a notice for the debtor giving information about what the enforcement agent is doing.

(2) Regulations must state—

(*a*) the form of the notice;

(*b*) what information it must give.

(3) Regulations may prescribe circumstances in which a notice need not be provided after re-entry to premises.

(4) If the debtor is on the premises when the enforcement agent is there, the enforcement agent must give him the notice then.

(5) If the debtor is not there, the enforcement agent must leave the notice in a conspicuous place on the premises.

(6) If the enforcement agent knows that there is someone else there or that there are other occupiers, a notice he leaves under sub-paragraph (5) must be in a sealed envelope addressed to the debtor.

29 If the premises are occupied by any person apart from the debtor, the enforcement agent must leave at the premises a list of any goods he takes away.

30 The enforcement agent must leave the premises as effectively secured as he finds them.

Goods on a highway

31— (1) If the enforcement agent applies to the court it may issue a warrant which authorises him to use, if necessary, reasonable force to take control of goods on a highway.

(2) The court may not issue a warrant unless it is satisfied that prescribed conditions are met.

(3) The warrant may require any constable to assist the enforcement agent to execute it.

(4) The power to use force is subject to any restriction imposed by or under regulations.

(5) The power to use force does not include power to use force against persons, except to the extent that regulations provide that it does.

32— (1) The enforcement agent may not exercise any power under this Schedule on a highway except within prescribed times of day.

(2) Regulations may give the court power in prescribed circumstances to authorise him to exercise a power at other times.

(3) The authorisation may be subject to conditions.

33— (1) If the enforcement agent takes control of goods on a highway or enters a vehicle on a highway with the intention of taking control of goods, he must provide a notice for the debtor giving information about what he is doing.

(2) Regulations must state—

(*a*) the form of the notice;
(*b*) what information it must give.

(3) If the debtor is present when the enforcement agent is there, the enforcement agent must give him the notice then.

(4) Otherwise the enforcement agent must deliver the notice to any relevant premises (as defined by paragraph 14) in a sealed envelope addressed to the debtor.

Inventory

34— (1) If an enforcement agent takes control of goods he must provide the debtor with an inventory of them as soon as reasonably practicable.

(2) But if there are co-owners of any of the goods, the enforcement agent must instead provide the debtor as soon as reasonably practicable with separate inventories of goods owned by the debtor and each co-owner and an inventory of the goods without a co-owner.

(3) The enforcement agent must as soon as reasonably practicable provide the co-owner of any of the goods with—

(*a*) the inventory of those goods, and
(*b*) a copy of the notice under paragraph 28.

(4) Regulations must state—

(*a*) the form of an inventory, and
(*b*) what it must contain.

Care of goods removed

35— (1) An enforcement agent must take reasonable care of controlled goods that he removes from the premises or highway where he finds them.

(2) He must comply with any provision of regulations about their care while they remain controlled goods.

Valuation

36— (1) Before the end of the minimum period, the enforcement agent must—

(*a*) make or obtain a valuation of the controlled goods in accordance with regulations;
(*b*) give the debtor, and separately any co-owner, an opportunity to obtain an independent valuation of the goods.

(2) In this paragraph "minimum period" means the period specified by regulations under—

(*a*) paragraph 49, in the case of securities;
(*b*) paragraph 39, in any other case.

Best price

37— (1) An enforcement agent must sell or dispose of controlled goods for the best price that can reasonably be obtained in accordance with this Schedule.

(2) That does not apply to money that can be used for paying any of the outstanding amount, unless the best price is more than its value if used in that way.

Sale

38 Paragraphs 39 to 42 apply to the sale of controlled goods, except where—

(*a*) the controlled goods are securities, or
(*b*) the sale is by exchange of one currency for another.

39— (1) The sale must not be before the end of the minimum period except with the agreement of the debtor and any co-owner.

(2) Regulations must specify the minimum period.

40— (1) Before the sale, the enforcement agent must give notice of the date, time and place of the sale to the debtor and any co-owner.

(2) Regulations must state—

(*a*) the minimum period of notice;
(*b*) the form of the notice;
(*c*) what it must contain (besides the date, time and place of sale);
(*d*) how it must be given.

(3) The enforcement agent may replace a notice with a new notice, subject to any restriction in regulations.

(4) Any notice must be given within the permitted period.

(5) Unless extended the permitted period is 12 months beginning with the day on which the enforcement agent takes control of the goods.

(6) Any extension must be by agreement in writing between the creditor and debtor before the end of the period.

(7) They may extend the period more than once.

41— (1) The sale must be by public auction unless the court orders otherwise.

(2) The court may make an order only on an application by the enforcement agent.

(3) Regulations may make provision about the types of sale the court may order.

(4) In an application for an order under sub-paragraph (2) the enforcement agent must state whether he has reason to believe that an enforcement power has become exercisable by another creditor against the debtor or a co-owner.

(5) If the enforcement agent states that he does, the court may not consider the application until notice of it has been given to the other creditor in accordance with regulations (or until the court is satisfied that an enforcement power is not exercisable by the other creditor against the debtor or a co-owner).

42 Regulations may make further provision about the sale of controlled goods, including in particular—

(*a*) requirements for advertising;
(*b*) provision about the conduct of a sale.

Place of sale

43— (1) Regulations may make provision about the place of sale of controlled goods.

(2) They may prescribe circumstances in which the sale may be held on premises where goods were found by the enforcement agent.

(3) Except where the regulations provide otherwise, the sale may not be held on those premises without the consent of the occupier.

(4) Paragraphs 44 to 46 apply if the sale may be held on those premises.

44— (1) The enforcement agent and any person permitted by him—

(*a*) may enter the premises to conduct or attend the sale;
(*b*) may bring equipment onto the premises for the purposes of the sale.

(2) This paragraph authorises repeated entry to the premises.

(3) If necessary the enforcement agent may use reasonable force to enable the sale to be conducted and any person to enter under this paragraph.

45— (1) The enforcement agent must on request show the debtor and any person who appears to him to be in charge of the premises evidence of—

(*a*) his identity, and
(*b*) his authority to enter and hold the sale on the premises.

(2) The request may be made before the enforcement agent enters the premises or while he is there.

46 The enforcement agent must leave the premises as effectively secured as he finds them.

Holding and disposal of securities

47 Paragraphs 48 and 49 apply to securities as controlled goods.

48— (1) Regulations may make provision about how securities are to be held and disposed of.

(2) In this Schedule, references to disposal include, in relation to securities, realising the sums secured or made payable by them, suing for the recovery of those sums or assigning the right to sue for their recovery.

(3) Regulations may in particular make provision for purposes corresponding to those for which provision is made in this Schedule in relation to the disposal of other controlled goods.

(4) The power to make regulations under this paragraph is subject to paragraph 49.

49— (1) The creditor may sue in the name of the debtor, or in the name of any person in whose name the debtor might have sued, for the recovery of any sum secured or made payable by securities, when the time of payment arrives.

(2) Before any proceedings under sub-paragraph (1) are commenced or the securities are otherwise disposed of, the enforcement agent must give notice of the disposal to the debtor and any co-owner.

(3) Regulations must state—

(*a*) the minimum period of notice;
(*b*) the form of the notice;
(*c*) what it must contain;
(*d*) how it must be given.

(4) The enforcement agent may replace a notice with a new notice, subject to any restriction in regulations.

(5) Any notice must be given within the permitted period.

(6) Unless extended the permitted period is 12 months beginning with the time of payment.

(7) Any extension must be by agreement in writing between the creditor and debtor before the end of the period.

(8) They may extend the period more than once.

Application of proceeds

50— (1) Proceeds from the exercise of an enforcement power must be used to pay the amount outstanding.

(2) Proceeds are any of these—

(*a*) proceeds of sale or disposal of controlled goods;
(*b*) money taken in exercise of the power, if paragraph 37(1) does not apply to it.

(3) The amount outstanding is the sum of these—

(*a*) the amount of the debt which remains unpaid (or an amount that the creditor agrees to accept in full satisfaction of the debt);
(*b*) any amounts recoverable out of proceeds in accordance with regulations under paragraph 62 (costs).

(4) If the proceeds are less than the amount outstanding, which amounts in sub-paragraph (3)(*a*) and (*b*) must be paid, and how much of any amount, is to be determined in accordance with regulations.

(5) If the proceeds are more than the amount outstanding, the surplus must be paid to the debtor.

(6) If there is a co-owner of any of the goods, the enforcement agent must—

(*a*) first pay the co-owner a share of the proceeds of those goods proportionate to his interest;
(*b*) then deal with the rest of the proceeds under sub-paragraphs (1) to (5).

(7) Regulations may make provision for resolving disputes about what share is due under sub-paragraph (6)(*a*).

Passing of title

51— (1) A purchaser of controlled goods acquires good title, with two exceptions.

(2) The exceptions apply only if the goods are not the debtor's at the time of sale.

(3) The first exception is where the purchaser, the creditor, the enforcement agent or a related party has notice that the goods are not the debtor's.

(4) The second exception is where a lawful claimant has already made an application to the court claiming an interest in the goods.

(5) A lawful claimant in relation to goods is a person who has an interest in them at the time of sale, other than an interest that was assigned or transferred to him while the property in the goods was bound for the purposes of the enforcement power.

(6) A related party is any person who acts in exercise of an enforcement power, other than the creditor or enforcement agent.

(7) "The court" has the same meaning as in paragraph 60.

Abandonment of goods other than securities

52 Paragraphs 53 and 54 apply to controlled goods other than—

(*a*) securities;
(*b*) money to which paragraph 37(1) does not apply.

53— (1) Controlled goods are abandoned if the enforcement agent does not give the debtor or any co-owner notice under paragraph 40 (notice of sale) within the permitted period.

(2) Controlled goods are abandoned if they are unsold after a sale of which notice has been given in accordance with that paragraph.

(3) Regulations may prescribe other circumstances in which controlled goods are abandoned.

54— (1) If controlled goods are abandoned then, in relation to the enforcement power concerned, the following apply—

(*a*) the enforcement power ceases to be exercisable;

(*b*) as soon as reasonably practicable the enforcement agent must make the goods available for collection by the debtor, if he removed them from where he found them.

(2) Regulations may make further provision about arrangements under sub-paragraph (1)(*b*), including in particular provision about the disposal of goods uncollected after a prescribed period.

(3) Where the enforcement power was under a writ or warrant, sub-paragraph (1) does not affect any power to issue another writ or warrant.

Abandonment of securities

55 Paragraphs 56 and 57 apply to securities as controlled goods.

56— (1) Securities are abandoned if the enforcement agent does not give the debtor or any co-owner notice under paragraph 49 (notice of disposal) within the permitted period.

(2) Securities are abandoned if they are not disposed of in accordance with a notice of disposal under that paragraph.

(3) Regulations may prescribe other circumstances in which securities are abandoned.

57— (1) If securities are abandoned then, in relation to the enforcement power concerned, the following apply—

(*a*) the enforcement power ceases to be exercisable;

(*b*) as soon as reasonably practicable the enforcement agent must make the securities available for collection by the debtor, if he removed them from where he found them.

(2) Where the enforcement power was under a writ or warrant, sub-paragraph (1) does not affect any power to issue another writ or warrant.

Payment of amount outstanding

58— (1) This paragraph applies where the debtor pays the amount outstanding in full—

(*a*) after the enforcement agent has taken control of goods, and

(*b*) before they are sold or abandoned.

(2) If the enforcement agent has removed the goods he must as soon as reasonably practicable make them available for collection by the debtor.

(3) No further step may be taken under the enforcement power concerned.

(4) For the purposes of this paragraph the amount outstanding is reduced by the value of any controlled goods consisting of money required to be used to pay that amount, and sub-paragraph (2) does not apply to that money.

59— (1) This paragraph applies if a further step is taken despite paragraph 58(3).

(2) The enforcement agent is not liable unless he had notice, when the step was taken, that the amount outstanding had been paid in full.

(3) Sub-paragraph (2) applies to a related party as to the enforcement agent.

(4) If the step taken is sale of any of the goods the purchaser acquires good title unless, at the time of sale, he or the enforcement agent had notice that the amount outstanding had been paid in full.

(5) A person has notice that the amount outstanding has been paid in full if he would have found it out if he had made reasonable enquiries.

(6) Sub-paragraphs (2) to (4) do not affect any right of the debtor or a co-owner to a remedy against any person other than the enforcement agent or a related party.

(7) In this paragraph, "related party" has the meaning given by paragraph 65(4).

Third party claiming goods

60— (1) This paragraph applies where a person makes an application to the court claiming that goods taken control of are his and not the debtor's.

(2) After receiving notice of the application the enforcement agent must not sell the goods, or dispose of them (in the case of securities), unless directed by the court under this paragraph.

(3) The court may direct the enforcement agent to sell or dispose of the goods if the applicant fails to make, or to continue to make, the required payments into court.

(4) The required payments are—

(*a*) payment on making the application (subject to sub-paragraph (5)) of an amount equal to the value of the goods, or to a proportion of it directed by the court;

(*b*) payment, at prescribed times (on making the application or later), of any amounts prescribed in respect of the enforcement agent's costs of retaining the goods.

(5) If the applicant makes a payment under sub-paragraph (4)(*a*) but the enforcement agent disputes the value of the goods, any underpayment is to be—

(*a*) determined by reference to an independent valuation carried out in accordance with regulations, and

(*b*) paid at the prescribed time.

(6) If sub-paragraph (3) does not apply the court may still direct the enforcement agent to sell or dispose of the goods before the court determines the applicant's claim, if it considers it appropriate.

(7) If the court makes a direction under sub-paragraph (3) or (6)—

(*a*) paragraphs 38 to 49, and regulations under them, apply subject to any modification directed by the court;

(*b*) the enforcement agent must pay the proceeds of sale or disposal into court.

(8) In this paragraph "the court", subject to rules of court, means—

(*a*) the High Court, in relation to an enforcement power under a writ of the High Court;

(*b*) a county court, in relation to an enforcement power under a warrant issued by a county court;

(*c*) in any other case, the High Court or a county court.

Application to assignee or transferee

61— (1) This Schedule applies as follows where an interest of the debtor's in goods is assigned or transferred while the property in the goods is bound for the purposes of an enforcement power, and the enforcement agent—

(*a*) knows that the assignee or transferee has an interest in the particular goods, or

(*b*) would know, if he made reasonable enquiries.

(2) These apply as if the assignee or transferee were a co-owner of the goods with the debtor—

(*a*) paragraph 34 (inventory);

(*b*) paragraph 36 (valuation);

(*c*) paragraphs 39 to 41 (sale);

(*d*) paragraph 59(6) (remedies after payment of amount outstanding).

(3) If the interest of the assignee or transferee was acquired in good faith, for valuable consideration and without notice, paragraph 50(6) applies as if "co-owner" included the assignee or transferee.

(4) If the interest of the assignee or transferee was not acquired in good faith, for valuable consideration and without notice, the enforcement agent must pay any surplus under paragraph 50(5) to the assignee or transferee and to the debtor (if he retains an interest).

(5) If the surplus is payable to two or more persons it must be paid in shares proportionate to their interests.

(6) Paragraph 5(3) and (4) ("good faith" and "notice") apply for the purposes of this paragraph.

Costs

62— (1) Regulations may make provision for the recovery by any person from the debtor of amounts in respect of costs of enforcement-related services.

(2) The regulations may provide for recovery to be out of proceeds or otherwise.

(3) The amount recoverable under the regulations in any case is to be determined by or under the regulations.

(4) The regulations may in particular provide for the amount, if disputed, to be assessed in accordance with rules of court.

(5) "Enforcement-related services" means anything done under or in connection with an enforcement power, or in connection with obtaining an enforcement power, or any services used for the purposes of a provision of this Schedule or regulations under it.

Limitation of liability for sale or payment of proceeds

63— (1) Any liability of an enforcement agent or related party to a lawful claimant for the sale of controlled goods is excluded except in two cases.

(2) The first exception is where at the time of the sale the enforcement agent had notice that the goods were not the debtor's, or not his alone.

(3) The second exception is where before sale the lawful claimant had made an application to the court claiming an interest in the goods.

(4) A lawful claimant in relation to goods is a person who has an interest in them at the time of sale, other than an interest that was assigned or transferred to him while the property in the goods was bound for the purposes of the enforcement power.

64— (1) Any liability of an enforcement agent or related party to a lawful claimant for paying over proceeds is excluded except in two cases.

(2) The first exception is where at the time of the payment he had notice that the goods were not the debtor's, or not his alone.

(3) The second exception is where before that time the lawful claimant had made an application to the court claiming an interest in the goods.

(4) A lawful claimant in relation to goods is a person who has an interest in them at the time of sale.

65— (1) Paragraphs 63 and 64—

(*a*) do not affect the liability of a person other than the enforcement agent or a related party;
(*b*) do not apply to the creditor if he is the enforcement agent.

(2) The following apply for the purposes of those paragraphs.

(3) The enforcement agent or a related party has notice of something if he would have found it out if he had made reasonable enquiries.

(4) A related party is any person who acts in exercise of an enforcement power, other than the creditor or enforcement agent.

(5) "The court" has the same meaning as in paragraph 60.

Remedies available to the debtor

66— (1) This paragraph applies where an enforcement agent—

(*a*) breaches a provision of this Schedule, or
(*b*) acts under an enforcement power under a writ, warrant, liability order or other instrument that is defective.

(2) The breach or defect does not make the enforcement agent, or a person he is acting for, a trespasser.

(3) But the debtor may bring proceedings under this paragraph.

(4) Subject to rules of court, the proceedings may be brought—

(*a*) in the High Court, in relation to an enforcement power under a writ of the High Court;
(*b*) in a county court, in relation to an enforcement power under a warrant issued by a county court;
(*c*) in any other case, in the High Court or a county court.

(5) In the proceedings the court may—

(*a*) order goods to be returned to the debtor;
(*b*) order the enforcement agent or a related party to pay damages in respect of loss suffered by the debtor as a result of the breach or of anything done under the defective instrument.

(6) A related party is either of the following (if different from the enforcement agent)—

(*a*) the person on whom the enforcement power is conferred,
(*b*) the creditor.

(7) Sub-paragraph (5) is without prejudice to any other powers of the court.

(8) Sub-paragraph (5)(*b*) does not apply where the enforcement agent acted in the reasonable belief—

(*a*) that he was not breaching a provision of this Schedule, or
(*b*) (as the case may be) that the instrument was not defective.

(9) This paragraph is subject to paragraph 59 in the case of a breach of paragraph 58(3).

Remedies available to the creditor

67 If a debtor wrongfully interferes with controlled goods and the creditor suffers loss as a result, the creditor may bring a claim against the debtor in respect of the loss.

Offences

68— (1) A person is guilty of an offence if he intentionally obstructs a person lawfully acting as an enforcement agent.

(2) A person is guilty of an offence if he intentionally interferes with controlled goods without lawful excuse.

(3) A person guilty of an offence under this paragraph is liable on summary conviction to—

(*a*) imprisonment for a term not exceeding 51 weeks, or
(*b*) a fine not exceeding level 4 on the standard scale, or
(*c*) both.

(4) In relation to an offence committed before the commencement of section 281(5) of the Criminal Justice Act 2003 (c 44), the reference in sub-paragraph (3)(*a*) to 51 weeks is to be read as a reference to 6 months.

Relation to insolvency provisions

69 This Schedule is subject to sections 183, 184 and 346 of the Insolvency Act 1986 (c 45).

SCHEDULE 13

TAKING CONTROL OF GOODS: AMENDMENTS

Section 62(3)

…

Taxes Management Act 1970 (c 9)

32 The Taxes Management Act 1970 is amended as follows.

33— (1) Section 61 (distraint by collectors) is amended as follows.

(2) In subsection (1), after "the collector may" insert

"—

(*a*) in England and Wales, use the procedure in Schedule 12 to the Tribunals, Courts and Enforcement Act 2007 (taking control of goods) to recover that sum;
(*b*) in Northern Ireland,".

(3) After subsection (1) insert—

"(1A) Subsections (2) to (6) apply to distraint under subsection (1)(*b*)."

Prospective amendments—As part of the ongoing reform of the penalty regime, para 33 to be repealed by FA 2008 s 129, Sch 43 para 11(*d*) with effect from such day as the Commissioners may by statutory instrument appoint.

34 In section 62 (priority of claim for tax) at the end insert—

"(4) This section does not extend to England and Wales."

…

Customs and Excise Management Act 1979 (c 2)

44 In section 149 of the Customs and Excise Management Act 1979 (non-payment of penalties etc: maximum terms of imprisonment) after subsection (1) insert—

"(1A) In subsection (1)(*b*) as it applies to a magistrates' court in England or Wales the reference to default of sufficient distress to satisfy the amount of the penalty is a reference to want of sufficient goods to satisfy the amount, within the meaning given by section 79(4) of the Magistrates' Courts Act 1980."

…

Supreme Court Act 1981 (c 54)

66— (1) Section 43ZA of the Supreme Court Act 1981 (power of High Court to vary committal in default) is amended as follows.

(2) In subsection (1) for "distress" in both places substitute "goods".

(3) After subsection (2) insert—

"(3) In subsection (1) references to want of sufficient goods to satisfy a sum are references to circumstances where—

(*a*) there is power to use the procedure in Schedule 12 to the Tribunals, Courts and Enforcement Act 2007 to recover the sum from a person, but
(*b*) it appears, after an attempt has been made to exercise the power, that the person's goods are insufficient to pay the amount outstanding (as defined by paragraph 50(3) of that Schedule)."

…

Finance Act 1984 (c 43)

83 In the Finance Act 1984 omit section 16 (unpaid car tax and VAT: distress).

…

Insolvency Act 1986 (c 45)

85 In section 436 of the Insolvency Act 1986 (expressions used generally) insert in the appropriate place—

"“distress” includes use of the procedure in Schedule 12 to the Tribunals, Courts and Enforcement Act 2007, and references to levying distress, seizing goods and related expressions shall be construed accordingly;".

…

Social Security Administration Act 1992 (c 5)

101 The Social Security Administration Act 1992 is amended as follows.

102 In section 71 (overpayments: general), in subsection (10)(*a*) for "by execution issued from the county court" substitute "under section 85 of the County Courts Act 1984".

103 In section 75 (overpayments of housing benefit), in subsection (7)(*a*) for "by execution issued from the county court" substitute "under section 85 of the County Courts Act 1984".

104— (1) Section 121A (recovery of contributions etc in England and Wales) is amended as follows.

(2) In subsection (1)—

(*a*) in paragraph (*b*) after "relates" insert "("the sums due")";
(*b*) for the words from "distrain" to the end substitute "use the procedure in Schedule 12 to the Tribunals, Courts and Enforcement Act 2007 (taking control of goods) to recover the sums due".

(3) Omit subsections (2) to (8) and (10).

...

Prospective amendments—As part of the ongoing reform of the penalty regime, para 104(2) to be repealed by FA 2008 s 129, Sch 43 para 11(*d*) with effect from such day as the Commissioners may by statutory instrument appoint.

Finance Act 1994 (*c 9*)

113— (1) The Finance Act 1994 is amended as follows.

114 After section 10 insert—

"10A Breaches of controlled goods agreements

(1) This section applies where an enforcement agent acting under the power conferred by section 51(A1) of the Finance Act 1997 (power to use the procedure in Schedule 12 to the Tribunals, Courts and Enforcement Act 2007) has entered into a controlled goods agreement with the person against whom the power is exercisable ("the person in default").

(2) In this section, "controlled goods agreement" has the meaning given by paragraph 13(4) of that Schedule.

(3) Subject to subsection (4) below, if the person in default removes or disposes of goods (or permits their removal or disposal) in breach of the controlled goods agreement, he is liable to a penalty equal to half of the unpaid duty or other amount recoverable under section 51(A1) of the Finance Act 1997.

(4) The person in default shall not be liable to a penalty under subsection (3) above if he satisfies the Commissioners or, on appeal, an appeal tribunal that there is a reasonable excuse for the breach in question.

(5) This section extends only to England and Wales."

Prospective amendments—As part of the ongoing reform of the penalty regime, para 114 to be repealed by FA 2008 s 129, Sch 43 para 11(*d*) with effect from such day as the Commissioners may by statutory instrument appoint.

115 In section 11 (breaches of walking possession agreements), for subsection (5) substitute—

"(5) This section extends only to Northern Ireland."

116— (1) Schedule 7 (insurance premium tax) is amended as follows.

(2) After paragraph 18 insert—

"18A— (1) This paragraph applies where an enforcement agent acting under the power conferred by section 51(A1) of the Finance Act 1997 (power to use the procedure in Schedule 12 to the Tribunals, Courts and Enforcement Act 2007) has entered into a controlled goods agreement with the person against whom the power is exercisable ("the person in default").

(2) In this paragraph, "controlled goods agreement" has the meaning given by paragraph 13(4) of that Schedule.

(3) Subject to sub-paragraph (4) below, if the person in default removes or disposes of goods (or permits their removal or disposal) in breach of the controlled goods agreement, he is liable to a penalty equal to half of the tax or other amount recoverable under section 51(A1) of the Finance Act 1997.

(4) The person in default shall not be liable to a penalty under sub-paragraph (3) above if he satisfies the Commissioners or, on appeal, an appeal tribunal, that there is a reasonable excuse for the breach in question.

(5) This paragraph extends only to England and Wales."

(3) In paragraph 19, for sub-paragraph (5) substitute—

"(5) This paragraph extends only to Northern Ireland."

Prospective amendments—As part of the ongoing reform of the penalty regime, para 116(2) to be repealed by FA 2008 s 129, Sch 43 para 11(*d*) with effect from such day as the Commissioners may by statutory instrument appoint.

Value Added Tax Act 1994 (*c 23*)

117 The Value Added Tax Act 1994 is amended as follows.

118 In section 48 (VAT representatives), in subsection (7A) after "enforcement" insert "by taking control of goods or, in Northern Ireland,".

119 After section 67 (failure to notify and unauthorised invoices) insert—

"67A Breach of controlled goods agreement

(1) This section applies where an enforcement agent acting under the power conferred by section 51(A1) of the Finance Act 1997 (power to use the procedure in Schedule 12 to the Tribunals, Courts and Enforcement Act 2007) has entered into a controlled goods agreement with the person against whom the power is exercisable ("the person in default").

(2) In this section, "controlled goods agreement" has the meaning given by paragraph 13(4) of that Schedule.

(3) Subject to subsection (4) below, if the person in default removes or disposes of goods (or permits their removal or disposal) in breach of the controlled goods agreement, he is liable to a penalty equal to half of the VAT or other amount recoverable under section 51(A1) of the Finance Act 1997.

(4) The person in default shall not be liable to a penalty under subsection (3) above if he satisfies the Commissioners or, on appeal, a tribunal that there is a reasonable excuse for the breach in question.

(5) This section extends only to England and Wales."

Prospective amendments—As part of the ongoing reform of the penalty regime, para 119 to be repealed by FA 2008 s 129, Sch 43 para 11(*d*) with effect from such day as the Commissioners may by statutory instrument appoint.

120 In section 68 (breach of walking possession agreements) for subsection (5) substitute—

"(5) This section extends only to Northern Ireland."

Pensions Act 1995 (c 26)

121 In section 10 of the Pensions Act 1995 (civil penalties), in subsection (8A)(*a*) for "by execution issued from the county court" substitute "under section 85 of the County Courts Act 1984".

Finance Act 1996 (c 8)

122 Schedule 5 to the Finance Act 1996 (landfill tax) is amended as follows.

123 After paragraph 23 insert—

"23A Controlled Goods Agreements

(1) This paragraph applies where an enforcement agent acting under the power conferred by section 51(A1) of the Finance Act 1997 (power to use the procedure in Schedule 12 to the Tribunals, Courts and Enforcement Act 2007) has entered into a controlled goods agreement with the person against whom the power is exercisable ("the person in default").

(2) In this paragraph, "controlled goods agreement" has the meaning given by paragraph 13(4) of that Schedule.

(3) If the person in default removes or disposes of goods (or permits their removal or disposal) in breach of the controlled goods agreement, he is liable to a penalty equal to half of the tax or other amount recoverable under section 51(A1) of the Finance Act 1997.

(4) The person in default shall not be liable to a penalty under sub-paragraph (3) above if he satisfies the Commissioners or, on appeal, an appeal tribunal, that there is a reasonable excuse for the breach in question.

(5) This paragraph extends only to England and Wales."

Prospective amendments—As part of the ongoing reform of the penalty regime, para 123 to be repealed by FA 2008 s 129, Sch 43 para 11(*d*) with effect from such day as the Commissioners may by statutory instrument appoint.

124 In paragraph 24, for sub-paragraph (4) substitute—

"(4) This paragraph extends only to Northern Ireland."

Employment Tribunals Act 1996 (c 17)

125 In section 15 of the Employment Tribunals Act 1996 (enforcement), in subsection (1) for "by execution issued from the county court" substitute "under section 85 of the County Courts Act 1984".

Finance Act 1997 (c 16)

126— (1) Section 51 of the Finance Act 1997 (enforcement by distress) is amended as follows.

(2) Before subsection (1) insert—

"(A1) The Commissioners may, in England and Wales, use the procedure in Schedule 12 to the Tribunals, Courts and Enforcement Act 2007 (taking control of goods) to recover any of these that a person refuses or neglects to pay—

(*a*) any amount of relevant tax due from him;

(*b*) any amount recoverable as if it were relevant tax due from him."

(3) In subsection (1) after "by regulations" insert "not having effect in England and Wales or Scotland".

(4) Omit subsection (7).

Prospective amendments—As part of the ongoing reform of the penalty regime, para 126(2) to be repealed by FA 2008 s 129, Sch 43 para 11(*d*) with effect from such day as the Commissioners may by statutory instrument appoint.

Social Security (Recovery of Benefits) Act 1997 (c 27)

127 In section 7 of the Social Security (Recovery of Benefits) Act 1997 (recovery of payments due under section 6), in subsection (4) for "by execution issued from the county court" substitute "under section 85 of the County Courts Act 1984".

National Minimum Wage Act 1998 (c 39)

128 *In section 21 of the National Minimum Wage Act 1998 (financial penalty for non-compliance), in subsection (5)(a) for "by execution issued from the county court" substitute "under section 85 of the County Courts Act 1984".*

Amendments—Para 128 repealed by the Employment Act 2008 s 20, Schedule Pt 2 with effect from 6 April 2009 (by virtue of SI 2009/603 arts 2, 3).

...

Financial Services and Markets Act 2000 (c 8)

134 In Schedule 17 to the Financial Services and Markets Act 2000 (the ombudsman scheme), in paragraph 16(*a*) for "by execution issued from the county court" substitute "under section 85 of the County Courts Act 1984".

Finance Act 2000 (c 17)

135 Schedule 6 to the Finance Act 2000 (climate change levy) is amended as follows.

136 After paragraph 89 insert—

"89A Controlled goods agreements

(1) This paragraph applies where an enforcement agent acting under the power conferred by section 51(A1) of the Finance Act 1997 (power to use the procedure in Schedule 12 to the Tribunals, Courts and Enforcement Act 2007) has entered into a controlled goods agreement with the person against whom the power is exercisable ("the person in default").

(2) In this paragraph, "controlled goods agreement" has the meaning given by paragraph 13(4) of that Schedule.

(3) Subject to sub-paragraph (4), if the person in default removes or disposes of goods (or permits their removal or disposal) in breach of the controlled goods agreement, he is liable to a penalty equal to half of the levy or other amount recoverable under section 51(A1) of the Finance Act 1997.

(4) The person in default shall not be liable to a penalty under sub-paragraph (3) above if he satisfies the Commissioners or, on appeal, an appeal tribunal, that there is a reasonable excuse for the breach in question.

(5) This paragraph extends only to England and Wales."

Prospective amendments—As part of the ongoing reform of the penalty regime, para 136 to be repealed by FA 2008 s 129, Sch 43 para 11(*d*) with effect from such day as the Commissioners may by statutory instrument appoint.

137 In paragraph 90 for sub-paragraph (5) substitute—

"(5) This paragraph extends only to Northern Ireland."

Postal Services Act 2000 (c 26)

138 In section 104 of the Postal Services Act 2000 (inviolability of mails), in subsection (2) after paragraph (*b*) insert—

"(*ba*) in England and Wales, being taken control of under Schedule 12 to the Tribunals, Courts and Enforcement Act 2007,".

Finance Act 2001 (c 9)

139 Schedule 5 to the Finance Act 2001 (aggregates levy: recovery and interest) is amended as follows.

140 After paragraph 14 insert—

"14A Controlled goods agreements

(1) This paragraph applies where an enforcement agent acting under the power conferred, by virtue of paragraph 14 above, by section 51(A1) of the Finance Act 1997 (power to use the procedure in Schedule 12 to the Tribunals, Courts and Enforcement Act 2007) has entered into a controlled goods agreement with the person against whom the power is exercisable ("the person in default").

(2) In this paragraph, "controlled goods agreement" has the meaning given by paragraph 13(4) of that Schedule.

(3) Subject to sub-paragraph (4), if the person in default removes or disposes of goods (or permits their removal or disposal) in breach of the controlled goods agreement, he is liable to a penalty equal to half of the levy or other amount recoverable under section 51(A1) of the Finance Act 1997.

(4) The person in default shall not be liable to a penalty under sub-paragraph (3) above if he satisfies the Commissioners or, on appeal, an appeal tribunal, that there is a reasonable excuse for the breach in question.

(5) This paragraph extends only to England and Wales."

Prospective amendments—As part of the ongoing reform of the penalty regime, para 140 to be repealed by FA 2008 s 129, Sch 43 para 11(*d*) with effect from such day as the Commissioners may by statutory instrument appoint.

141 In paragraph 15 for sub-paragraph (5) substitute—

"(5) This paragraph extends only to Northern Ireland."

Proceeds of Crime Act 2002 (*c 29*)

142 The Proceeds of Crime Act 2002 is amended as follows.

143 In section 58 (restraint orders: restrictions), in subsection (2) after "levied" insert ", and no power to use the procedure in Schedule 12 to the Tribunals, Courts and Enforcement Act 2007 (taking control of goods) may be exercised,".

144 In section 59 (enforcement receivers: restrictions), in subsection (2) after "levied" insert ", and no power to use the procedure in Schedule 12 to the Tribunals, Courts and Enforcement Act 2007 (taking control of goods) may be exercised,".

145 ...[1]

Amendments—[1] Para 145 repealed by the Serious Crime Act 2007 s 92, Sch 14 with effect from 1 April 2008: SI 2008/755 art 2(1)(*d*).

146 In section 253 (interim receiving orders: restriction on proceedings and remedies) in subsection (1)(*b*) after "levied" insert ", and no power to use the procedure in Schedule 12 to the Tribunals, Courts and Enforcement Act 2007 (taking control of goods) may be exercised,".

Finance Act 2003 (*c 14*)

147— (1) Schedule 12 to the Finance Act 2003 (stamp duty land tax: collection and recovery of tax) is amended as follows.

(2) After paragraph 1 insert—

"1A Recovery of tax by taking control of goods

In England and Wales, if a person neglects or refuses to pay the sum charged, the collector may use the procedure in Schedule 12 to the Tribunals, Courts and Enforcement Act 2007 (taking control of goods) to recover the sum."

(3) In paragraph 2(1) omit "England and Wales or".

...

Prospective amendments—As part of the ongoing reform of the penalty regime, para 147(2) to be repealed by FA 2008 s 129, Sch 43 para 11(*d*) with effect from such day as the Commissioners may by statutory instrument appoint.

Income Tax Act 2007 (*c 3*)

157 In section 955(4) of the Income Tax Act 2007 (proceedings before set-off claim is made) after "attachment" insert "or under Schedule 12 to the Tribunals, Courts and Enforcement Act 2007 (taking control of goods)".

SCHEDULE 23
REPEALS

Section 146

PART 1
TRIBUNALS AND INQUIRIES

Reference	*Extent of repeal or revocation*
Taxes Management Act 1970 (c 9)	Sections 2 to 3A. In section 5(1), the words "General Commissioner or". In section 6— (a) in subsection (1), the words "a General Commissioner or" and the words ", or before a General Commissioner", and (b) subsection (2). In section 56(3), the words "the clerk to". Section 115(4).
Superannuation Act 1972 (c 11)	In Schedule 6, paragraph 77.
Finance Act 1972 (c 41)	Section 130.
Consumer Credit Act 1974 (c 39)	In Schedule A1, paragraph 11.
House of Commons Disqualification Act 1975 (c 24)	In Schedule 1, in Part 2—

Reference	*Extent of repeal or revocation*
	(a) the entry relating to the Council on Tribunals, and (b) the entry relating to the Scottish Committee of the Council on Tribunals.
Northern Ireland Assembly Disqualification Act 1975 (c 25)	In Schedule 1, in Part 2— (a) the entry relating to the Council on Tribunals, and (b) the entry relating to the Scottish Committee of the Council on Tribunals.
Race Relations Act 1976 (c 74)	In Schedule 1A, in Part 2, the entry relating to the Council on Tribunals.
Estate Agents Act 1979 (c 38)	Section 24(2).
Finance Act 1988 (c 39)	Section 134(1).
Food Safety Act 1990 (c 16)	In section 26(2)— (a) in paragraph (e), the words "or to a tribunal constituted in accordance with the regulations," and (b) paragraph (f). Section 37(2)(a). Section 47.
Finance (No 2) Act 1992 (c 48)	In section 75(1), paragraph (a). In Schedule 16, paragraph 2.
Tribunals and Inquiries Act 1992 (c 53)	Sections 1 to 5, 6(1) to (3), (6) and (7) and 8. In section 13— (a) subsection (2), and (b) in subsection (5)(c), the words "the reference in section 8(1) to the Foreign Compensation Commission and". Section 14(1A). In section 16(1), in the definition of "decision", "procedural rules" and "working", the words ", "procedural rules" and "working"". In Schedule 1, paragraph 19.
Judicial Pensions and Retirement Act 1993 (c 8)	In section 1(1), the word "and" at the end of paragraph (c). Section 12(1)(b).
Employment Tribunals Act 1996 (c 17)	Section 26. In section 27(1)— (a) in paragraph (b), the word "and" at the end, (b) paragraph (c), and (c) the words after "persons within paragraph (a) or (b)".
Social Security Act 1998 (c 14)	In Schedule 7, in paragraph 118(1), "subsection (3) of" and the words after "1992".
Social Security Contributions (Transfer of Functions, Etc.) Act 1999 (c 2)	In Schedule 7, paragraph 1.
Access to Justice Act 1999 (c 22)	Sections 101 to 103.
Social Security Contributions (Transfer of Functions, etc) (Northern Ireland) Order 1999 (SI 1999/671)	In Schedule 6, in paragraph 1, the words "section 2(1) (appointment of General Commissioners),".
Scotland Act 1998 (Cross-Border Public Authorities) (Adaptation of Functions etc) Order 1999 (SI 1999/1747)	Schedule 9.
Scotland Act 1998 (Transfer of Functions to the Scottish Ministers etc) Order 1999 (SI 1999/1750)	In Schedule 1, the entry in respect of sections 2(3), 2(6) and 3(4) of the Taxes Management Act 1970.
Freedom of Information Act 2000 (c 36)	In Schedule 1, in Part 6, the entry relating to the Council on Tribunals and the entry relating to the Scottish Committee of the Council on Tribunals.

Reference	*Extent of repeal or revocation*
Financial Services and Markets Act 2000 (Consequential Amendments and Repeals) Order 2001 (SI 2001/3649)	Article 335(3).
Justice (Northern Ireland) Act 2002 (c 26)	In each of Schedules 1 and 6, the entry relating to the panel of persons appointed under section 6(1) of the Tribunals and Inquiries Act 1992 to act as chairmen of tribunals that sit in Northern Ireland.
Nationality, Immigration and Asylum Act 2002 (c 41)	In Schedule 4, paragraphs 9 and 10(b) and (c).
Scottish Public Services Ombudsman Act 2002 (Consequential Provisions and Modifications) Order 2004 (SI 2004/1823)	Article 14.
Constitutional Reform Act 2005 (c 4)	In Schedule 4, paragraph 64. In Schedule 5, in the amendment made by paragraph 122(5), and in the amendment made by paragraph 126(5), the entry relating to the panel of persons appointed under section 6(1) of the Tribunals and Inquiries Act 1992 to act as chairmen of tribunals that sit in Northern Ireland. In Schedule 7, in Part A of the list in paragraph 4— (a) the entry for section 6(2), (8) and (9) of the Tribunals and Inquiries Act 1992, and (b) the entry for paragraph 7(4) of Schedule 5 to that Act. In Schedule 12, in paragraph 4(4)(a), the words "or no other except that of General Commissioner,". In Schedule 14, in Part 2, the entry relating to General Commissioner for a division in England and Wales. In Schedule 14, in Part 3, the entry relating to members of panels appointed under section 6(1) of the Tribunals and Inquiries Act 1992.
Tribunals, Courts and Enforcement Act 2007 (c 15)	In section 36(3)(a), the words "or 41(2)". In Schedule 8, paragraph 26.

Commencement—Tribunals, Courts and Enforcement Act 2007 (Commencement No 1) Order, SI 2007/2709 art 3(*d*) (entries relating to the following, come into force on 1 November 2007—

(i) House of Commons Disqualification Act 1975;
(ii) Northern Ireland Assembly Disqualification Act 1975;
(iii) Race Relations Act 1976;
(iv) Estate Agents Act 1979;
(v) Tribunals and Inquiries Act 1992 ss 1, 2, 3, 4 and 13(5)(*c*);
(vi) Scotland Act 1998 (Cross-Border Public Authorities) (Adaptation of Functions etc) Order 1999 to the extent that Schedule 9 applies to Tribunals and Inquiries Act 1992 ss 2, 4;
(vii) Freedom of Information Act 2000; and
(viii) Scottish Public Services Ombudsman Act 2002 (Consequential Provisions and Modifications) Order 2004.).

Tribunals, Courts and Enforcement Act 2007 (Commencement No 6 and Transitional Provisions) Order, SI 2008/2696 art 5(*j*) (entries relating to the following come into force on 3 November 2008—

(i) Consumer Credit Act 1974;
(ii) Judicial Pensions and Retirement Act 1993;
(iii) Employment Tribunals Act 1996;
(iv) Justice (Northern Ireland) Act 2002;
(v) Nationality, Immigration and Asylum Act 2002;
(vi) Constitutional Reform Act 2005 Sch 4; and
(vii) Tribunals, Courts and Enforcement Act 2007.).

Tribunals, Courts and Enforcement Act 2007 (Commencement No 6 and Transitional Provisions) Order, SI 2008/2696 art 6(*c*) (entries relating to the following come into force on 1 April 2009—

(i) Taxes Management Act 1970;
(ii) Superannuation Act 1972;
(iii) Finance Act 1972;
(iv) Finance Act 1988;
(v) Finance (No 2) Act 1992;
(vi) Social Security Contributions (Transfer of Functions, etc) Act 1999;
(vii) Access to Justice Act 1999;
(viii) Social Security Contributions (Transfer of Functions, etc) (Northern Ireland) Order, SI 1999/671;
(ix) Scotland Act 1998 (Transfer of Functions to the Scottish Ministers etc) Order, SI 1999/1750; and

(x) Constitutional Reform Act 2005 Sch 12, Sch 14 Pt 2.).

PART 2
JUDICIAL APPOINTMENTS

Reference	*Extent of repeal*
Courts and Legal Services Act 1990 (c 41)	In Schedule 10— (a) paragraph 4, (b) in paragraph 6(1), the words "paragraph 13(1) of" and the words after "1947", and (c) paragraphs 24, 26, 32, 49, 50(2)(b) and 57.
Judicial Pensions and Retirement Act 1993 (c 8)	In Schedule 5— (a) in the entry for a deputy district judge appointed under section 102 of the Supreme Court Act 1981, the words "for a district registry", and (b) in the entry for a deputy district judge appointed under section 8 of the County Courts Act 1984, the words "for a county court district".
Child Support Act 1991 (c 48)	In section 54, the definition of "general qualification".
Social Security Act 1998 (c 14)	In Schedule 4, paragraph 1(3).
Enterprise Act 2002 (c 40)	In Schedule 2, paragraph 1(4).
Constitutional Reform Act 2005 (c 4)	Section 25(2)(a). In Schedule 3, paragraph 2(3). In Schedule 14, in Part 2— (a) in the entry relating to a deputy district judge in a district registry of the High Court, the words "in a district registry of the High Court", and (b) in the entry relating to a deputy district judge for a county court district, the words "for a county court district". In Schedule 14, in Part 3, the entries relating to— (a) Member of the Special Immigration Appeals Commission; (b) Chairman of the Special Immigration Appeals Commission; (c) Member of the Proscribed Organisations Appeal Commission; (d) Chairman of the Proscribed Organisations Appeal Commission; (e) Member of the Pathogens Access Appeal Commission; and (f) Chairman of the Pathogens Access Appeal Commission.

Commencement—Tribunals, Courts and Enforcement Act 2007 (Commencement No 6 and Transitional Provisions) Order, SI 2008/2696 art 5(*j*) (Part 2 comes into force on 3 November 2008).

PART 3
ENFORCEMENT BY TAKING CONTROL OF GOODS

Reference	*Extent of repeal*
Inclosure Act 1773 (c 81)	In section 4, the words from "rendering" to the end. In section 16, the words from "rendering" to the end.

Reference	*Extent of repeal*
Sale of Farming Stock Act 1816 (c 50)	The whole Act.
Judgments Act 1838 (c 110)	Section 12.
Compulsory Purchase Act 1965 (c 56)	Section 13(5). Section 29.
Sea Fisheries Act 1968 (c 77)	In section 12(3), the words from "as they apply" to the end.
Criminal Justice Act 1972 (c 71)	In section 66(2), the words from ""sentence of imprisonment"" to the end.
Magistrates' Courts Act 1980 (c 43)	In section 125(2), the words from "This subsection" to the end. Section 125D(3)(c). Section 151. In Schedule 4A, paragraph 3.
British Fishing Boats Act 1983 (c 8)	In section 5(3), the words from "as they apply" to the end.
County Courts Act 1984 (c 28)	Section 85(3). Section 87(2). Sections 89 to 91. Sections 93 to 100. Sections 102 and 103. Section 123. In section 126— (a) in subsection (3) the words from "but" to the end; (b) in subsection (4) ""bailiff"". In section 147(1) the definition of "bailiff".
Finance Act 1984 (c 43)	Section 16.
Local Government Finance Act 1988 (c 41)	In Schedule 9, paragraph 3(2)(b).
Child Support Act 1991 (c 48)	Section 35(2) to (8).
Social Security Administration Act 1992 (c 5)	Section 121A(2) to (8) and (10).
Local Government Finance Act 1992 (c 14)	In Schedule 4— (a) paragraph 7; (b) in paragraph 8(1)(a) the words from "an authority" to "paragraph 7 above"; (c) paragraph 12(1)(c); (d) paragraph 19(3).
Finance Act 1997 (c 16)	Section 51(7).
Courts Act 2003 (c 39)	In Schedule 7, paragraph 8(5).
Traffic Management Act 2004 (c 18)	Section 82(3)(a). Section 83.

FINANCE ACT 2008

(2008 Chapter 9)

CONTENTS

PART 7

ADMINISTRATION

CHAPTER 1

INFORMATION ETC

New information etc powers

Other measures

CHAPTER 2

TIME LIMITS FOR CLAIMS AND ASSESSMENTS ETC

General

Income tax and corporation tax

VAT

CHAPTER 3

PENALTIES

CHAPTER 4

APPEALS ETC

Reviews and appeals etc: general

Customs and excise decisions subject to review and appeal

CHAPTER 5

PAYMENT AND ENFORCEMENT

Taking control of goods etc

Set off

Other measures

Supplementary

PART 8

MISCELLANEOUS

Payments from Exchequer accounts

Other matters

An Act to Grant certain duties, to alter other duties, and to amend the law relating to the National Debt and the Public Revenue, and to make further provision in connection with finance.

[21 July 2008]

PART 7

ADMINISTRATION

Press releases—HMRC Guidance Note, 18 July 2008 (HMRC set-off across taxes following Finance Bill 2008).

CHAPTER 1

INFORMATION ETC

New information etc powers

113 Information and inspection powers

(1) Schedule 36 contains provision about the powers of officers of Revenue and Customs to obtain information and to inspect businesses.

(2) That Schedule comes into force on such day as the Treasury may by order made by statutory instrument appoint.

(3) An order under subsection (2) may contain transitional provision and savings.

Orders—Finance Act 2008, Schedule 36 (Appointed Day and Savings) Order, SI 2009/404 (made under sub-ss (2), (3)).

114 Computer records etc

(1) This section applies to any enactment that, in connection with an HMRC matter—

(*a*) requires a person to produce a document or cause a document to be produced,

(*b*) requires a person to permit the Commissioners or an officer of Revenue and Customs—

(i) to inspect a document, or

(ii) to make or take copies of or extracts from or remove a document,

(*c*) makes provision about penalties or offences in connection with the production or inspection of documents, including in connection with the falsification of or failure to produce or permit the inspection of documents, or

(*d*) makes any other provision in connection with a requirement mentioned in paragraph (*a*) or (*b*).

(2) An enactment to which this section applies has effect as if—

(*a*) any reference in the enactment to a document were a reference to anything in which information of any description is recorded, and

(*b*) any reference in the enactment to a copy of a document were a reference to anything onto which information recorded in the document has been copied, by whatever means and whether directly or indirectly.

(3) An authorised person may, at any reasonable time, obtain access to, and inspect and check the operation of, any computer and any associated apparatus or material which is or has been used in connection with a relevant document.

(4) In subsection (3) "relevant document" means a document that a person has been, or may be, required pursuant to an enactment to which this section applies—

(*a*) to produce or cause to be produced, or

(*b*) to permit the Commissioners or an officer of Revenue and Customs to inspect, to make or take copies of or extracts from or to remove.

(5) An authorised person may require—

(*a*) the person by whom or on whose behalf the computer is or has been so used, or

(*b*) any person having charge of, or otherwise concerned with the operation of, the computer, apparatus or material,

to provide the authorised person with such reasonable assistance as may be required for the purposes of subsection (3).

(6) Any person who—

(*a*) obstructs the exercise of a power conferred by this section, or

(*b*) fails to comply within a reasonable time with a requirement under subsection (5),

is liable to a penalty of £300.

(7) Paragraphs 45 to 49 and 52 of Schedule 36 (assessment of and appeals against penalties) apply in relation to a penalty under this section as they apply in relation to a penalty under paragraph 39 of that Schedule.

(8) Omit the following—

(*a*) (*repeals* FA 1985 s 10)

(*b*) (*repeals* FA 1988 s 127)

(*c*) (*repeals* Civil Evidence Act 1995 Sch 1 paras 11(2)–(4), 13(2), (3))

(9) In this section—

"authorised person" means a person who is, or is a member of a class of persons who are, authorised by the Commissioners to exercise the powers under subsection (3),

"the Commissioners" means the Commissioners for Her Majesty's Revenue and Customs,

"enactment" includes an enactment contained in subordinate legislation (within the meaning of the Interpretation Act 1978 (c 30)),

"HMRC matter" means a matter in relation to which the Commissioners, or officers of Revenue and Customs, have a power or duty, and

"produce", in relation to a document, includes furnish, deliver and any other equivalent expression.

Other measures

115 Record-keeping

(1) Schedule 37 contains provision about the obligations to keep records for the purposes of income tax, capital gains tax, corporation tax and value added tax.

(2) The amendments made by that Schedule come into force on such day as the Treasury may by order made by statutory instrument appoint.

Orders—Finance Act 2008, Schedule 37 (Appointed Day) Order, SI 2009/402 (made under sub-s (2)).

116 Disclosure of tax avoidance schemes

(1) Schedule 38 contains amendments relating to the disclosure of tax avoidance schemes.

(2) The amendments made by that Schedule come into force on such day as the Treasury may by order made by statutory instrument appoint; and different days may be appointed for different purposes.

Orders—Finance Act 2008, Schedule 38, (Appointed Day) Order, SI 2008/1935 (made under sub-s (2)).

117 Power to open or unpack containers

(1) CEMA 1979 is amended as follows.

(2) (*amends* CEMA 1979 s 1(1))

(3) Section 159 (power to examine and take account of goods) is amended as follows.

(4) (*amends* CEMA 1979 s 159(1))

(5) (*amends* CEMA 1979 s 159(4))

CHAPTER 2
TIME LIMITS FOR CLAIMS AND ASSESSMENTS ETC

General

118 Time limits for assessments, claims etc

(1) Schedule 39 contains provision about time limits for assessments, claims etc

(2) The amendments and saving made by that Schedule come into force on such day as the Treasury may by order made by statutory instrument appoint.

(3) An order under subsection (2)—

(*a*) may make different provision for different purposes, and

(*b*) may include transitional provision and further savings.

Orders—Finance Act 2008, Schedule 39 (Appointed Day, Transitional Provision and Savings) Order, SI 2009/403 (made under sub-ss (2), (3)).

Income tax and corporation tax

119 Correction and amendment of tax returns

(1) (*amends* TMA 1970 s 9ZB(1))

(2) (*amends* TMA 1970 s 12ABB(1))

(3)–(11) (*amend* FA 1998 Sch 18)

(12) (*amends* TMA 1970 ss 46B–46D, 55; TA 1988 s 754)

(13) The amendments made by this section come into force on such day as the Treasury may by order appoint.

Orders—Finance Act 2008, Section 119 (Appointed Day) Order, SI 2009/405 (made under sub-s (13)).
Amendments—Sub-s (12)(*a*)(i), (ii) repealed by the Transfer of Tribunal Functions and Revenue and Customs Appeals Order, SI 2009/56 art 3(1), Sch 1 paras 468, 469 with effect from 1 April 2009.

VAT

120 VAT: time limits for assessments of excess credits etc

(1) (*inserts* VATA 1994 s 73(6A))

(2) Section 80 of that Act (credit for, or repayment of, overstated or overpaid VAT) is amended as follows.

(3) (*inserts* VATA 1994 s 80(4AA))

(4) (*amends* VATA 1994 s 80(4C))

(5) The amendments made by this section are treated as having come into force on 19 March 2008.

121 Old VAT claims: extended time limits

(1) The requirement in section 80(4) of VATA 1994 that a claim under that section be made within 3 years of the relevant date does not apply to a claim in respect of an amount brought into account, or paid, for a prescribed accounting period ending before 4 December 1996 if the claim is made before 1 April 2009.

(2) The requirement in section 25(6) of VATA 1994 that a claim for deduction of input tax be made at such time as may be determined by or under regulations does not apply to a claim for deduction of input tax that became chargeable, and in respect of which the claimant held the required evidence, in a prescribed accounting period ending before 1 May 1997 if the claim is made before 1 April 2009.

(3) In this section—

"input tax" and "prescribed accounting period" have the same meaning as in VATA 1994 (see section 96 of that Act), and

"the required evidence" means the evidence of the charge to value added tax specified in or under regulation 29(2) of the Value Added Tax Regulations 1995 (SI 1995/2518).

(4) This section is treated as having come into force on 19 March 2008.

CHAPTER 3

PENALTIES

122 Penalties for errors

(1) Schedule 40 contains provisions amending Schedule 24 to FA 2007 (penalties for errors in returns etc).

(2) That Schedule comes into force on such day as the Treasury may by order appoint.

(3) An order under subsection (2)—

(*a*) may commence a provision generally or only for specified purposes, and

(*b*) may appoint different days for different provisions or for different purposes.

(4) The Treasury may by order make any incidental, supplemental, consequential, transitional, transitory or saving provision which may appear appropriate in consequence of, or otherwise in connection with, Schedule 24 to FA 2007 or Schedule 40.

(5) An order under subsection (4) may include provision amending, repealing or revoking any provision of any Act or subordinate legislation whenever passed or made (including this Act and any Act amended by it).

(6) An order under subsection (4) may make different provision for different purposes.

(7) The power to make an order under this section is exercisable by statutory instrument.

(8) A statutory instrument containing an order under subsection (4) which includes provision amending or repealing any provision of an Act is subject to annulment in pursuance of a resolution of the House of Commons.

Orders—Finance Act 2008, Schedule 41 (Appointed Day and Transitional Provisions) Order, SI 2009/511.
Finance Act 2008, Schedule 40 (Appointed Day, Transitional Provisions and Consequential Amendments) Order, SI 2009/571.

123 Penalties for failure to notify etc

(1) Schedule 41 contains provisions for imposing penalties on persons in respect of failures to notify HMRC that they are chargeable to tax etc and certain wrongdoings relating to invoices showing VAT and excise duties.

(2) That Schedule comes into force on such day as the Treasury may by order appoint.

(3) An order under subsection (2)—

(*a*) may commence a provision generally or only for specified purposes, and
(*b*) may appoint different days for different provisions or for different purposes.

(4) The Treasury may by order make any incidental, supplemental, consequential, transitional, transitory or saving provision which may appear appropriate in consequence of, or otherwise in connection with, Schedule 41.

(5) An order under subsection (4) may include provision amending, repealing or revoking any provision of any Act or subordinate legislation whenever passed or made (including this Act and any Act amended by it).

(6) An order under subsection (4) may make different provision for different purposes.

(7) The power to make an order under this section is exercisable by statutory instrument.

(8) A statutory instrument containing an order under subsection (4) which includes provision amending or repealing any provision of an Act is subject to annulment in pursuance of a resolution of the House of Commons.

Orders—Finance Act 2008, Schedule 41 (Appointed Day and Transitional Provisions) Order, SI 2009/511.

CHAPTER 4

APPEALS ETC

Reviews and appeals etc: general

124 HMRC decisions etc: reviews and appeals

(1) The Treasury may by order made by statutory instrument make provision—

(*a*) for and in connection with reviews by the Commissioners, or by an officer of Revenue and Customs, of HMRC decisions, and
(*b*) in connection with appeals against HMRC decisions.

(2) An order under subsection (1) may, in particular, contain provision about—

(*a*) the circumstances in which, or the time within which—

(i) a right to a review may be exercised, or
(ii) an appeal may be made, and

(*b*) the circumstances in which, or the time at which, an appeal or review is, or may be treated as, concluded.

(3) An order under subsection (1) may, in particular, contain provision about the payment of sums by, or to, the Commissioners in cases where—

(*a*) a right to a review is exercised, or
(*b*) an appeal is made or determined.

(4) That includes provision about payment of sums where an appeal has been determined, but a further appeal may be or has been made, including provision—

(*a*) requiring payments to be made,
(*b*) enabling payments to be postponed, or
(*c*) imposing conditions in connection with the making or postponement of payments.

(5) An order under subsection (1) may, in particular, contain provision about interest on any sum that is payable by, or to, the Commissioners in accordance with a decision made on the determination of an appeal.

(6) Provision under subsection (1) may be made by amending, repealing or revoking any provision of any Act or subordinate legislation (whenever passed or made, including this Act and any Act amended by it).

(7) An order under subsection (1) may—

(*a*) provide that any provision contained in the order comes into force on a day appointed by an order of the Treasury made by statutory instrument (and may provide that different days may be appointed for different purposes), (*b*) contain incidental, supplemental, consequential, transitional, transitory and saving provision, and

(*c*) make different provision for different purposes.

(8) A statutory instrument containing an order under subsection (1) may not be made unless a draft of it has been laid before and approved by resolution of the House of Commons.

(9) But if the order, or any other order under subsection (1) contained in the statutory instrument, is made in connection with a transfer of functions carried out under the Tribunals, Courts and Enforcement Act 2007 (c 15), the statutory instrument may only be made if a draft of it has been laid before and approved by resolution of each House of Parliament.

(10) In this section—

(*a*) references to appeals against HMRC decisions include any other kind of proceedings relating to an HMRC matter, and

(*b*) references to the making, determination or conclusion of appeals are to be read accordingly.

(11) In this section—

"the Commissioners" means the Commissioners for Her Majesty's Revenue and Customs;

"HMRC decision" means—

(*a*) any decision of the Commissioners relating to an HMRC matter, or

(*b*) any decision of an officer of Revenue and Customs relating to an HMRC matter,

and references to an HMRC decision include references to anything done by such a person in connection with making such a decision or in consequence of such a decision;

"HMRC matter" means any matter connected with a function of the Commissioners or an officer of Revenue and Customs.

Orders—Transfer of Tribunal Functions and Revenue and Customs Appeals Order, SI 2009/56 (made under sub-ss (1)–(7)). Revenue and Customs Appeals Order, SI 2009/777 (made under sub-ss (1)–(7)).

Customs and excise decisions subject to review and appeal

126 Security under CEMA 1979

(1) (*amends* FA 1994 Sch 5 para 2(1)(*s*))

(2) The amendments made by subsection (1) have effect in relation to decisions made on or after the day on which this Act is passed.

CHAPTER 5

PAYMENT AND ENFORCEMENT

Taking control of goods etc

127 Enforcement by taking control of goods: England and Wales

(1) This section applies if a person does not pay a sum that is payable by that person to the Commissioners under or by virtue of an enactment or under a contract settlement.

(2) The Commissioners may use the procedure in Schedule 12 to the Tribunals, Courts and Enforcement Act 2007 (c 15) (taking control of goods) to recover that sum.

(3) This section extends to England and Wales only.

128 Summary warrant: Scotland

(1) This section applies if a person does not pay a sum that is payable by that person to the Commissioners under or by virtue of any enactment or under a contract settlement.

(2) An officer of Revenue and Customs may apply to the sheriff for a summary warrant.

(3) An application under subsection (2) must be accompanied by a certificate which—

(*a*) complies with subsection (4), and

(*b*) is signed by the officer.

(4) A certificate complies with this subsection if—

(*a*) it states that—

(i) none of the persons specified in the application has paid the sum payable by that person,

(ii) the officer has demanded payment from each such person of the sum payable by that person, and

(iii) the period of 14 days beginning with the day on which the demand is made has expired without payment being made, and

(*b*) it specifies the sum payable by each person specified in the application.

(5) Subsection (4)(*a*)(iii) does not apply to an application under subsection (2) insofar as it relates to—

(*a*) sums payable in respect of value added tax,

(*b*) sums payable in respect of deductions required to be made under section 61 of FA 2004 (sub-contractors in the construction industry), and (*c*) sums payable by a person in that person's capacity as an employer.

(6) The sheriff must, on an application by an officer of Revenue and Customs under subsection (2), grant a summary warrant in, or as nearly as may be in, the form prescribed by Act of Sederunt.

(7) A summary warrant granted under subsection (6) authorises the recovery of the sum payable by—

(*a*) attachment,
(*b*) money attachment,
(*c*) earnings arrestment,
(*d*) arrestment and action of furthcoming or sale.

(8) Subject to subsection (9) and without prejudice to section 39(1) of the Debt Arrangement and Attachment (Scotland) Act 2002 (asp 17) (expenses of attachment)—

(*a*) the sheriff officer's fees, and
(*b*) any outlays necessarily incurred by that officer,

in connection with the execution of a summary warrant are to be chargeable against the person in relation to whom the warrant was granted.

(9) No fees are to be chargeable by the sheriff officer against the person in relation to whom the summary warrant was granted for collecting, and accounting to the Commissioners for, sums paid to that officer by that person in respect of the sum payable.

(10) This section extends to Scotland only.

129 Consequential provision and commencement

(1) Part 1 of Schedule 43 contains provision consequential on section 127.

(2) Part 2 of that Schedule contains provision consequential on section 128.

(3) The extent of the amendments and repeals in Schedule 43 is the same as the provision amended or repealed.

(4) Sections 127 and 128 and Schedule 43 come into force on such day as the Commissioners may by order made by statutory instrument appoint.

(5) An order under subsection (4) may—

(*a*) make different provision for different purposes, and
(*b*) contain transitional provision and savings.

Set off

130 Set-off: England and Wales and Northern Ireland

(1) This section applies where there is both a credit and a debit in relation to a person.

(2) The Commissioners may set the credit against the debit (subject to section 131 and any obligation of the Commissioners to set the credit against another sum).

(3) The obligations of the Commissioners and the person concerned are discharged to the extent of any set-off under subsection (2).

(4) "Credit", in relation to a person, means—

(*a*) a sum that is payable by the Commissioners to the person under or by virtue of an enactment, or
(*b*) a relevant sum that may be repaid to the person by the Commissioners.

(5) For the purposes of subsection (4), in relation to a person, "relevant sum" means a sum that was paid in connection with any liability (including any purported or anticipated liability) of that person to make a payment to the Commissioners under or by virtue of an enactment or under a contract settlement.

(6) "Debit", in relation to a person, means a sum that is payable by the person to the Commissioners under or by virtue of an enactment or under a contract settlement.

(7) In this section references to sums paid, repaid or payable by or to a person (however expressed) include sums that have been or are to be credited by or to a person.

(8) This section has effect without prejudice to any other power of the Commissioners to set off amounts.

(9) (*amends* ITA 2007 s 429(5))

(10) Subsections (1) to (8) extend to England and Wales and Northern Ireland only.

131 No set-off where insolvency procedure has been applied

(1) This section applies where—

(*a*) an insolvency procedure has been applied to a person, and
(*b*) there is a post-insolvency credit in relation to that person.

(2) The Commissioners may not use the power under section 130 to set that post-insolvency credit against a pre-insolvency debit in relation to the person.

(3) "Post-insolvency credit" means a credit that—

(*a*) became due after the insolvency procedure was applied to the person, and (*b*) relates to, or to matters occurring at, times after it was so applied.

(4) "Pre-insolvency debit" means a debit that—

(*a*) arose before the insolvency procedure was applied to the person, or

(*b*) arose after that procedure was so applied but relates to, or to matters occurring at, times before it was so applied.

(5) Subject to subsection (6), an insolvency procedure is to be taken, for the purposes of this section, to be applied to a person when—

(*a*) a bankruptcy order or winding up order is made or an administrator is appointed in relation to that person,

(*b*) that person is put into administrative receivership,

(*c*) if the person is a corporation, that person passes a resolution for voluntary winding up,

(*d*) a voluntary arrangement comes into force in relation to that person, or

(*e*) a deed of arrangement takes effect in relation to that person.

(6) In this section references to the application of an insolvency procedure to a person do not include—

(*a*) the application of an insolvency procedure to a person at a time when another insolvency procedure applies to the person, or

(*b*) the application of an insolvency procedure to a person immediately upon another insolvency procedure ceasing to have effect.

(7) For the purposes of this section—

(*a*) a person shall be treated as being in administrative receivership throughout any continuous period for which there is an administrative receiver of that person (disregarding any temporary vacancy in the office of receiver), and

(*b*) the reference in subsection (5) to a person being put into administrative receivership shall be interpreted accordingly.

(8) In this section—

"administrative receiver" means an administrative receiver within the meaning of section 251 of the Insolvency Act 1986 (c 45) or Article 5(1) of the Insolvency (Northern Ireland) Order 1989 (SI 1989/2405 (NI 19)),

"administrator" means a person appointed to manage the affairs, business and property of another person under Schedule B1 to that Act or to that Order,

"credit" and "debit" have the same meaning as in section 130,

"deed of arrangement" means a deed of arrangement registered in accordance with the Deeds of Arrangement Act 1914 (c 47) or Chapter 1 of Part 8 the Insolvency (Northern Ireland) Order 1989 (SI 1989/2405 (NI 19)), and

"voluntary arrangement" means a voluntary arrangement approved in accordance with Part 1 or Part 8 of the Insolvency Act 1986 (c 45) or Part 2 or Chapter 2 of Part 8 of the Insolvency (Northern Ireland) Order 1989.

(9) This section extends to England and Wales and Northern Ireland only.

132 VAT: requirement to set-off

(1) Section 81 of VATA 1994 (set-off of credits etc) is amended as follows.

(2) (*substitutes* VATA 1994 s 81(4C))

(3) In subsection (5)—

(*a*) (*repeals* VATA 1994 s 81(5)(*a*))

(*b*) (*amends* VATA 1994 s 81(5)(*b*))

(*c*) (*inserts* VATA 1994 s 81(5)(*ba*))

133 Set-off etc where right to be paid a sum has been transferred

(1) This section applies where there has been a transfer from one person ("the original creditor") to another person ("the current creditor") of a right to be paid a sum ("the transferred sum") by the Commissioners.

(2) The Commissioners—

(*a*) must set the transferred sum against a sum payable to them by the original creditor if they would have had an obligation to do so under or by virtue of an enactment had the original creditor retained the right, and

(*b*) may do so if they would have had a power to do so under or by virtue of an enactment or under a rule of law had the original creditor retained the right.

(3) Subsection (2) applies whether the sum payable by the original creditor to the Commissioners first became payable before or after the transfer (but not if it only became payable after the Commissioners discharged their obligation to pay the transferred sum to the current creditor).

(4) The following are discharged to the extent of any set-off under this section—

(*a*) the obligations of the Commissioners in relation to the current creditor, and

(*b*) the obligations of the original creditor.

(5) An obligation under or by virtue of an enactment (other than this section) to set the transferred sum against a sum payable to the Commissioners by a person other than the original creditor has effect subject to the obligation under subsection (2)(*a*) and to any exercise of the power under subsection (2)(*b*).

(6) A power under or by virtue of an enactment (other than this section) or under a rule of law to set the transferred sum against a sum payable to the Commissioners by a person other than the original creditor has effect subject to the obligation under subsection (2)(*a*).

(7) In determining the sum (if any) to be paid, the Commissioners may make any reduction that they could have made if the original creditor had retained the right to be paid the transferred sum (in addition to any other reduction that they are entitled to make), including a reduction arising from any defence to a claim for the sum.

(8) In this section—

(*a*) references to the transfer of a right are to its transfer by assignment, assignation or any other means, except that they do not include its transfer by means of a direction under section 429 of ITA 2007 (giving through self-assessment returns),

(*b*) references to a sum that is payable by or to a person are to a sum that is to be paid, repaid or credited by or to that person and references to the payment of the sum (however expressed) are to be interpreted accordingly, and

(*c*) where a right in relation to a sum has been transferred more than once, references to the original creditor are to the person from whom the right was first transferred (except in subsection (1)).

(9) Where the right to be paid the transferred sum is dependent on the making of a claim—

(*a*) subsection (2) does not apply unless a claim in respect of the transferred sum has been made, and

(*b*) the references in subsections (2) and (7) to the obligations or powers that the Commissioners would have had if the original creditor had retained the right are references to those that they would have had if the original creditor had also made the claim in respect of the transferred sum.

(10) This section has effect where the right to be paid the transferred sum was transferred from the original creditor on or after 25 June 2008.

134 Retained funding bonds: tender by Commissioners

(1)–(4) (*amend* ITA 2007 s 939)

(5) The amendments made by this section have effect in relation to funding bonds issued on or after 12 March 2008.

Other measures

135 Interest on unpaid tax in case of disaster etc of national significance

(1) This section applies in any case where the Commissioners agree that the payment of a relevant sum may be deferred by reason of circumstances arising as a result of a disaster or emergency specified in an order under this section (an "agreement for deferred payment").

(2) In subsection (1) "relevant sum" means a sum to meet any liability to the Commissioners arising under or by virtue of an enactment or a contract settlement.

(3) No interest on the amount deferred is chargeable in respect of the relief period and no liability to a surcharge on the deferred amount arises during that period.

(4) The relief period is the period—

(*a*) beginning with a date specified in the order or, if the Commissioners so direct, a later date from which the agreement for deferred payment has effect, and

(*b*) ending with the date on which the agreement for deferred payment ceases to have effect or, if earlier, the date on which the order is revoked.

(5) The agreement for deferred payment ceases to have effect at the end of the period of deferment specified in the agreement or, if the Commissioners agree to extend (or further extend) that period by reason of circumstances arising as a result of the disaster or emergency, with the end of that extended (or further extended) period.

(6) If the agreement for deferred payment is an agreement for payment by instalments, the period of deferment in relation to each instalment ends with the date on or before which that instalment is to be paid; but if an instalment is not paid by the agreed date and the Commissioners do not agree to extend the period of deferment, the whole of the agreement for deferred payment is to be treated as ceasing to have effect on that date.

(7) This section applies whether the agreement for deferred payment was made—

(*a*) before or after the amount to which it relates becomes due and payable, or

(*b*) before or after the making of the order concerned.

(8) If in any case the Commissioners are satisfied that, although no agreement for deferred payment was made, one could have been made, this section applies as if one had been made; and the terms of the notional agreement for deferred payment are to be assumed to be such as the Commissioners are satisfied would have been agreed in the circumstances.

(9) An order under this section may be made only in relation to a disaster or emergency which the Treasury consider to be of national significance.

(10) Such an order—

(*a*) may specify a disaster or emergency which has begun (or both begun and ended) before it is made (including one which has begun, or both begun and ended, before the passing of this Act), and

(*b*) may specify a date before the date on which it is made (including a date before the passing of this Act).

(11) The power to make an order under this section is exercisable by the Treasury by statutory instrument.

(12) A statutory instrument containing such an order is subject to annulment in pursuance of a resolution of the House of Commons.

(13) In FA 2001, omit section 107 (interest on unpaid tax etc: foot and mouth disease); but the repeal of that section does not affect any agreement for deferred payment made before this Act is passed.

136 Fee for payment

(1) The Commissioners may by regulations provide that, where a person makes a payment to the Commissioners or a person authorised by the Commissioners using a method of payment specified in the regulations, the person must also pay a fee specified in, or determined in accordance with, the regulations.

(2) A method of payment may only be specified in regulations made under this section if the Commissioners expect that they, or the person authorised by them, will be required to pay a fee or charge (however described) in connection with amounts paid using that method of payment.

(3) Regulations under this section—

(*a*) may make provision about the time and manner in which the fee must or may be paid,

(*b*) may make provision generally or only for specified purposes, and

(*c*) may make different provision for different purposes.

(4) Regulations under this section are to be made by statutory instrument.

(5) A statutory instrument containing regulations under this section is subject to annulment in pursuance of a resolution of the House of Commons.

Orders—Taxes (Fees for Payment by Telephone) Regulations, SI 2008/1948 (made under sub-ss (1), (3)).
Taxes (Fees for Payment by Internet) Regulations, SI 2008/2991 (made under sub-ss (1), (3)).

137 County court proceedings

(1) (*inserts* CRCA 2005 s 25(1A), (6))

(2) (*amends* TMA 1970 s 66)

(3) (*repeals* FA 1984 s 57(2))

(4) (*amends* IHTA 1984 s 244)

(5) (*amends* Social Security Contributions (Transfer of Functions, etc) Act 1999)

(6) (*amends* FA 2003 Sch 12 para 5)

(7) Nothing in subsections (2) to (6) affects proceedings commenced or brought in the name of a collector or authorised officer before this Act is passed.

138 Certificates of debt

(1) (*inserts* CRCA 2005 s 25A)

(2) Schedule 44 contains provisions consequential on this section.

Supplementary

139 Interpretation of Chapter

In this Chapter—

"the Commissioners" means the Commissioners for Her Majesty's Revenue and Customs, and "contract settlement" means an agreement made in connection with any person's liability to make a payment to the Commissioners under or by virtue of an enactment.

PART 8

MISCELLANEOUS

Payments from Exchequer accounts

158 Power of Treasury to make payments

(1) This section applies if a person makes a claim which, in the Treasury's opinion, is a financial claim that concerns an Exchequer account.

(2) The Treasury may pay money from any Exchequer account—

(*a*) to satisfy the claim (in whole or in part), or
(*b*) to enable the claim to be satisfied (in whole or in part) from another government account.

(3) The reference in this section to a financial claim that concerns an Exchequer account includes, in particular, either of the following cases.

(4) The first case is where a financial claim relates to—

(*a*) a case where money is paid into a government account, but the money should not have, or need not have, been paid into that account, or
(*b*) a case where money should have been, or needed to be, paid out of a government account, but the money—

(i) was not paid out of that account, or
(ii) was paid out of that account, but not as it should have been, or needed to be, paid.

(5) The second case is where a financial claim relates to the exercise of functions that relate to an Exchequer account (whether the functions are exercisable by the Treasury or another person).

(6) In this section—

"Exchequer account" means—

(*a*) the Consolidated Fund,
(*b*) the Debt Management Account,
(*c*) the Exchange Equalisation Account, or
(*d*) the National Loans Fund;

and a reference to an Exchequer account includes a reference to the assets or liabilities of the account;

"financial claim" means a claim (whether or not legally enforceable) for the payment of an amount of money, including a claim in respect of—

(*a*) money paid or not paid by any person,
(*b*) interest earned or not earned by any person, or
(*c*) loss, costs or expenses incurred by any person;

"government account" means—

(*a*) an Exchequer account, or
(*b*) any other account in which money is held by or on behalf of Her Majesty's Government in the United Kingdom.

159 Payments from certain Exchequer accounts: mechanism

(1) This section applies to money to be paid under section 158 from—

(*a*) the Consolidated Fund, or
(*b*) the National Loans Fund.

(2) In the case of the Consolidated Fund—

(*a*) the Comptroller and Auditor General shall on receipt of a requisition from the Treasury grant a credit on the Exchequer Account at the Bank of England (or on its growing balance), and
(*b*) an issue shall be made on orders given to the Bank by the Treasury in accordance with a credit granted under paragraph (*a*).

(3) An issue made under subsection (2) shall be recorded in the daily account under section 15(5) of the Exchequer and Audit Departments Act 1866 (c 39).

(4) In the case of the National Loans Fund—

(*a*) the Comptroller and Auditor General shall at the request of the Treasury grant a credit on the National Loans Fund, and
(*b*) a payment out of the Fund shall be made by the Treasury in accordance with a credit granted under paragraph (*a*).

(5) A payment made under subsection (4) shall be recorded in the daily account under section 1(2) of the National Loans Act 1968 (c 13).

Other matters

160 Power to give statutory effect to concessions

(1) The Treasury may by order make provision for and in connection with giving effect to any existing HMRC concession.

(2) "Existing HMRC concession" means a statement made by the Commissioners for Her Majesty's Revenue and Customs before the passing of this Act, and having effect at that time, that they will treat persons as if they were entitled to—

(*a*) a reduction in a liability to a tax or duty, or
(*b*) any other concession relating to a tax or duty,

to which they are not, or may not be, entitled in accordance with the law.

(3) For this purpose "statement" means a statement of any sort, whether it was described as an extra-statutory concession, a statement of practice, an interpretation, a decision or a press release or in any other way.

(4) The reference in subsection (2) to the Commissioners for Her Majesty's Revenue and Customs includes the Commissioners of Inland Revenue and the Commissioners of Customs and Excise.

(5) An order under this section—

(*a*) may give effect to an existing HMRC concession with or without modification,
(*b*) may include supplementary, incidental, consequential or transitional provision, and
(*c*) may include provisions amending (or repealing or revoking) any enactment or instrument (whenever passed or made).

(6) The power to make an order under this section is exercisable by statutory instrument.

(7) No order is to be made under this section unless a draft of the order has been laid before, and approved by a resolution of, the House of Commons.

PART 9

FINAL PROVISIONS

165 Interpretation

(1) In this Act—

"ALDA 1979" means the Alcoholic Liquor Duties Act 1979 (c 4),
"BGDA 1981" means the Betting and Gaming Duties Act 1981 (c 63),
"CAA 2001" means the Capital Allowances Act 2001 (c 2),
"CEMA 1979" means the Customs and Excise Management Act 1979 (c 2),
"CRCA 2005" means the Commissioners for Revenue and Customs Act 2005 (c 11),
"CTTA 1984" means the Capital Transfer Tax Act 1984 (c 51),
"HODA 1979" means the Hydrocarbon Oil Duties Act 1979 (c 5),
"ICTA" means the Income and Corporation Taxes Act 1988 (c 1),
"IHTA 1984" means the Inheritance Tax Act 1984 (c 51),
"ITA 2007" means the Income Tax Act 2007 (c 3),
"ITEPA 2003" means the Income Tax (Earnings and Pensions) Act 2003 (c 1),
"ITTOIA 2005" means the Income Tax (Trading and Other Income) Act 2005 (c 5),
"OTA 1975" means the Oil Taxation Act 1975 (c 22),
"TCGA 1992" means the Taxation of Chargeable Gains Act 1992 (c 12),
"TMA 1970" means the Taxes Management Act 1970 (c 9),
"TPDA 1979" means the Tobacco Products Duty Act 1979 (c 7),
"VATA 1994" means the Value Added Tax Act 1994 (c 23), and
"VERA 1994" means the Vehicle Excise and Registration Act 1994 (c 22).

(2) In this Act—

"FA", followed by a year, means the Finance Act of that year, and
"F(No 2)A", followed by a year, means the Finance (No 2) Act of that year.

166 Short title

This Act may be cited as the Finance Act 2008.

SCHEDULES

SCHEDULE 36

INFORMATION AND INSPECTION POWERS

Section 113

Commencement—Finance Act 2008, Schedule 36 (Appointed Day and Savings) Order, SI 2009/404 art 2 (appointed day for the coming into force of Sch 36 is 1 April 2009).

PART 1

POWERS TO OBTAIN INFORMATION AND DOCUMENTS

Power to obtain information and documents from taxpayer

1— (1) An officer of Revenue and Customs may by notice in writing require a person ("the taxpayer")—

(*a*) to provide information, or
(*b*) to produce a document,

if the information or document is reasonably required by the officer for the purpose of checking the taxpayer's tax position.

(2) In this Schedule, "taxpayer notice" means a notice under this paragraph.

Commencement—Finance Act 2008, Schedule 36 (Appointed Day and Savings) Order, SI 2009/404 art 2 (appointed day for the coming into force of Sch 36 is 1 April 2009).

Power to obtain information and documents from third party

2— (1) An officer of Revenue and Customs may by notice in writing require a person—

(*a*) to provide information, or
(*b*) to produce a document,

if the information or document is reasonably required by the officer for the purpose of checking the tax position of another person whose identity is known to the officer ("the taxpayer").

(2) A third party notice must name the taxpayer to whom it relates, unless the [tribunal][1] has approved the giving of the notice and disapplied this requirement under paragraph 3.

(3) In this Schedule, "third party notice" means a notice under this paragraph.

Commentary—*Simon's Taxes* **A6.301A**.
Commencement—Finance Act 2008, Schedule 36 (Appointed Day and Savings) Order, SI 2009/404 art 2 (appointed day for the coming into force of Sch 36 is 1 April 2009).
HMRC Manuals—Compliance Handbook Manual, CH23060 and 23080 (HMRC inspection powers: three types of information notice and approval thereof).
CH23620 (HMRC inspection powers: specific rules regarding third party notice).
CH225050 (HMRC inspection powers – how to do a compliance check: what is a third party notice).
CH225100 (persons on whom a third party notice can be served).
CH225150 (considerations prior to issue).
CH225200 (restrictions on third party notices).
CH225610–225620 (notices sent to "relevant lawyers" and communications service providers).
CH225630 (taxpayer's spouse or partner lawyer).
CH225700–225770 (taxpayer's spouse or partner Accountant's working papers).
CH225800–225865 (bank mandates).
Amendments—[1] In sub-para (2) word substituted for the words "First-tier Tribunal" by the Transfer of Tribunal Functions and Revenue and Customs Appeals Order, SI 2009/56 art 3, Sch 1 para 471 with effect from 1 April 2009.

Approval etc of taxpayer notices and third party notices

3— (1) An officer of Revenue and Customs may not give a third party notice without—

(*a*) the agreement of the taxpayer, or
(*b*) the approval of the [tribunal][1].

(2) An officer of Revenue and Customs may ask for the approval of the [tribunal][1] to the giving of any taxpayer notice or third party notice (and for the effect of obtaining such approval see paragraphs 29, 30 and 53 (appeals against notices and offence)).

[(2A) An application for approval under this paragraph may be made without notice (except as required under sub-paragraph (3)).][2]

(3) The [tribunal][1] may not approve the giving of a taxpayer notice or third party notice unless—

(*a*) an application for approval is made by, or with the agreement of, an authorised officer of Revenue and Customs,
(*b*) the [tribunal][1] is satisfied that, in the circumstances, the officer giving the notice is justified in doing so,
(*c*) the person to whom the notice is [to be][2] addressed has been told that the information or documents referred to in the notice are required and given a reasonable opportunity to make representations to an officer of Revenue and Customs,
(*d*) the [tribunal][1] has been given a summary of any representations made by that person, and
(*e*) in the case of a third party notice, the taxpayer has been given a summary of the reasons why an officer of Revenue and Customs requires the information and documents.

(4) Paragraphs (*c*) to (*e*) of sub-paragraph (3) do not apply to the extent that the [tribunal][1] is satisfied that taking the action specified in those paragraphs might prejudice the assessment or collection of tax.

(5) Where the [tribunal][1] approves the giving of a third party notice under this paragraph, it may also disapply the requirement to name the taxpayer in the notice if it is satisfied that the officer has reasonable grounds for believing that naming the taxpayer might seriously prejudice the assessment or collection of tax.

Commentary—*Simon's Taxes* **A6.301A**.
Commencement—Finance Act 2008, Schedule 36 (Appointed Day and Savings) Order, SI 2009/404 art 2 (appointed day for the coming into force of Sch 36 is 1 April 2009).
HMRC Manuals—Compliance Handbook Manual, CH23060 and 23080 (HMRC inspection powers: three types of information notice and approval thereof).
CH23520 (HMRC inspection powers: specific rules regarding taxpayer notice).
CH23620 (HMRC inspection powers: specific rules regarding third party notice).
CH24100 (HMRC inspection powers: the Tribunal).
CH24120–24180 (taxpayer and third party notices).
CH223300 (HMRC inspection powers – how to do a compliance check: who can approve a taxpayer notice).
CH223870 and 225450 (Tribunal approval).
CH225310–225320 (where no approval is required).
CH225410 (where approval is required).
CH225420 (taxpayer agreement).
CH225430–225440 (summary of reasons and reasons not be given).
CH225460 (opportunity letter requirements).

Amendments—[1] Word substituted for the words "First-tier Tribunal" in each place; in sub-para (4) word substituted for the word "Tribunal" by the Transfer of Tribunal Functions and Revenue and Customs Appeals Order, SI 2009/56 art 3, Sch 1 para 471 with effect from 1 April 2009.

[2] Sub-para (2A), and words in sub-para (3)(*c*), inserted, by FA 2009 s 95, Sch 47 para 2 with effect from 21 July 2009.

Copying third party notice to taxpayer

4— (1) An officer of Revenue and Customs who gives a third party notice must give a copy of the notice to the taxpayer to whom it relates, unless the [tribunal][1] has disapplied this requirement.

(2) The [tribunal][1] may not disapply that requirement unless—

(*a*) an application for approval is made by, or with the agreement of, an authorised officer of Revenue and Customs, and

(*b*) the [tribunal][1] is satisfied that the officer has reasonable grounds for believing that giving a copy of the notice to the taxpayer might prejudice the assessment or collection of tax.

Commentary—*Simon's Taxes* **A6.301A**.

Commencement—Finance Act 2008, Schedule 36 (Appointed Day and Savings) Order, SI 2009/404 art 2 (appointed day for the coming into force of Sch 36 is 1 April 2009).

HMRC Manuals—Compliance Handbook Manual, CH23620 (HMRC inspection powers: specific rules regarding third party notice).

CH23640–23660 (HMRC inspection powers: copy of the notice to the named person).

CH225250 (HMRC inspection powers – how to do a compliance check: copying notice to taxpayer).

Amendments—[1] Word substituted for the words "First-tier Tribunal" in each place; in sub-para (2)(*b*) word substituted for the word "Tribunal" by the Transfer of Tribunal Functions and Revenue and Customs Appeals Order, SI 2009/56 art 3, Sch 1 para 471 with effect from 1 April 2009.

Power to obtain information and documents about persons whose identity is not known

5— (1) An authorised officer of Revenue and Customs may by notice in writing require a person—

(*a*) to provide information, or

(*b*) to produce a document,

if the condition in sub-paragraph (2) is met.

(2) That condition is that the information or document is reasonably required by the officer for the purpose of checking the UK tax position of—

(*a*) a person whose identity is not known to the officer, or

(*b*) a class of persons whose individual identities are not known to the officer.

(3) An officer of Revenue and Customs may not give a notice under this paragraph without the approval of the [tribunal][1].

[(3A) An application for approval under this paragraph may be made without notice.][2]

(4) The [tribunal][1] may not [approve the giving of a notice under][2] this paragraph unless it is satisfied that—

(*a*) the notice would meet the condition in sub-paragraph (2),

(*b*) there are reasonable grounds for believing that the person or any of the class of persons to whom the notice relates may have failed or may fail to comply with any provision of the Taxes Acts, VATA 1994 or any other enactment relating to value added tax charged in accordance with that Act,

(*c*) any such failure is likely to have led or to lead to serious prejudice to the assessment or collection of UK tax, and

(*d*) the information or document to which the notice relates is not readily available from another source.

(5) In this paragraph "UK tax" means any tax other than relevant foreign tax and value added tax charged in accordance with the law of another member State.

Commentary—*Simon's Taxes* **A6.301A**.

Commencement—Finance Act 2008, Schedule 36 (Appointed Day and Savings) Order, SI 2009/404 art 2 (appointed day for the coming into force of Sch 36 is 1 April 2009).

HMRC Manuals—Compliance Handbook Manual, CH23900 (HMRC inspection powers: identity unknown notice).

CH24200 (HMRC inspection powers: Tribunal approval of identity unknown notice).

CH227100–227200 (HMRC inspection powers – how to do a compliance check: identity unknown notice).

Amendments—[1] In sub-paras (3), (4) word substituted for the words "First-tier Tribunal" by the Transfer of Tribunal Functions and Revenue and Customs Appeals Order, SI 2009/56 art 3, Sch 1 para 471 with effect from 1 April 2009.

[2] Sub-para (3A) inserted, in sub-para (4) words substituted for words "give its approval for the purpose of", by FA 2009 s 95, Sch 47 para 3 with effect from 21 July 2009.

Prospective amendments—In sub-para (4)(*b*) words "or any other enactment relating to UK tax" to be substituted for the words ", VATA 1994 or any other enactment relating to value added tax charged in accordance with that Act", by FA 2009 s 96, Sch 48 para 2 with effect from a date to be appointed.

Notices

6— (1) In this Schedule, "information notice" means a notice under paragraph 1, 2 or 5.

(2) An information notice may specify or describe the information or documents to be provided or produced.

(3) If an information notice is given with the approval of the [tribunal][1], it must state that it is given with that approval.

[(4) A decision of the tribunal under paragraph 3, 4 or 5 is final (despite the provisions of sections 11 and 13 of the Tribunals, Courts and Enforcement Act 2007).][2]

Commentary—*Simon's Taxes* **A6.301A**.
Commencement—Finance Act 2008, Schedule 36 (Appointed Day and Savings) Order, SI 2009/404 art 2 (appointed day for the coming into force of Sch 36 is 1 April 2009).
HMRC Manuals—Compliance Handbook Manual, CH229300–229900 (HMRC inspection powers – how to do a compliance check: rules that apply to all notices).
Amendments—[1] In sub-para (3) word substituted for the words "First-tier Tribunal" by the Transfer of Tribunal Functions and Revenue and Customs Appeals Order, SI 2009/56 art 3, Sch 1 para 471 with effect from 1 April 2009.
[2] Sub-para (4) inserted by FA 2009 s 95, Sch 47 para 4 with effect from 21 July 2009.

Complying with notices

7— (1) Where a person is required by an information notice to provide information or produce a document, the person must do so—

(*a*) within such period, and
(*b*) at such time, by such means and in such form (if any),

as is reasonably specified or described in the notice.

(2) Where an information notice requires a person to produce a document, it must be produced for inspection—

(*a*) at a place agreed to by that person and an officer of Revenue and Customs, or
(*b*) at such place as an officer of Revenue and Customs may reasonably specify.

(3) An officer of Revenue and Customs must not specify a place that is used solely as a dwelling.

(4) The production of a document in compliance with an information notice is not to be regarded as breaking any lien claimed on the document.

Commencement—Finance Act 2008, Schedule 36 (Appointed Day and Savings) Order, SI 2009/404 art 2 (appointed day for the coming into force of Sch 36 is 1 April 2009).
HMRC Manuals—Compliance Handbook Manual, CH23220 (HMRC inspection powers: meaning or "provide information", with example).
CH23260 (meaning of "produce documents").
CH23420 (date by which information required).
CH23480 (complying with a notice).
CH223810 (HMRC inspection powers – how to do a compliance check: complying with the notice).
CH223820 (professional records).
CH223830–223840 (professional medical records with definitions).
CH223850 (legal professional privilege).
CH223860 (failure to comply with the notice).

Producing copies of documents

8— (1) Where an information notice requires a person to produce a document, the person may comply with the notice by producing a copy of the document, subject to any conditions or exceptions set out in regulations made by the Commissioners.

(2) Sub-paragraph (1) does not apply where—

(*a*) the notice requires the person to produce the original document, or
(*b*) an officer of Revenue and Customs subsequently makes a request in writing to the person for the original document.

(3) Where an officer of Revenue and Customs requests a document under sub-paragraph (2)(*b*), the person to whom the request is made must produce the document—

(*a*) within such period, and
(*b*) at such time and by such means (if any),

as is reasonably requested by the officer.

Commencement—Finance Act 2008, Schedule 36 (Appointed Day and Savings) Order, SI 2009/404 art 2 (appointed day for the coming into force of Sch 36 is 1 April 2009).

Restrictions and special cases

9 This Part of this Schedule has effect subject to Parts 4 and 6 of this Schedule.

Commencement—Finance Act 2008, Schedule 36 (Appointed Day and Savings) Order, SI 2009/404 art 2 (appointed day for the coming into force of Sch 36 is 1 April 2009).

PART 2

POWERS TO INSPECT BUSINESSES ETC

Power to inspect business premises etc

10— (1) An officer of Revenue and Customs may enter a person's business premises and inspect—

(*a*) the premises,
(*b*) business assets that are on the premises, and
(*c*) business documents that are on the premises,

if the inspection is reasonably required for the purpose of checking that person's tax position.

(2) The powers under this paragraph do not include power to enter or inspect any part of the premises that is used solely as a dwelling.

(3) In this Schedule—

"business assets" means assets that an officer of Revenue and Customs has reason to believe are owned, leased or used in connection with the carrying on of a business by any person [(but see sub-paragraph (4))][1],

"business documents" means documents (or copies of documents)—

(*a*) that relate to the carrying on of a business by any person, and

(*b*) that form part of any person's statutory records, and

"business premises", in relation to a person, means premises (or any part of premises) that an officer of Revenue and Customs has reason to believe are (or is) used in connection with the carrying on of a business by or on behalf of the person.

[(4) For the purposes of this Schedule, "business assets" does not include documents, other than—

(*a*) documents that are trading stock for the purposes of Chapter 11A of Part 2 of ITTOIA 2005 (see section 172A of that Act), and

(*b*) documents that are plant for the purposes of Part 2 of CAA 2001.][1]

Commentary—*Simon's Taxes* **A6.301A**.

Commencement—Finance Act 2008, Schedule 36 (Appointed Day and Savings) Order, SI 2009/404 art 2 (appointed day for the coming into force of Sch 36 is 1 April 2009).

HMRC Manuals—Compliance Handbook Manual, CH25120 (HMRC inspection powers: meaning of "enter").
CH25140–25160 (meaning of "inspect" with examples).
CH25180 (meaning of "business premises").
CH25220–25240 (inspecting business premises that are a home).
CH25260 and 25280 (meaning of "business assets" and "business documents").
CH25420 (HMRC inspection powers: start and end of an inspection).
CH25460 (when to carry out an inspection).
CH25480 (HMRC inspection powers: announced and unannounced inspection).
CH25540 (Tribunal approval).
CH25560 (wording of inspection notices).

Amendments—[1] In sub-para (3) in the definition of "business assets" words substituted for words ", excluding documents", and sub-para (4) inserted by FA 2009 s 95, Sch 47 para 5 with effect from 21 July 2009.

[Power to inspect business premises etc of involved third parties

10A— (1) An officer of Revenue and Customs may enter business premises of an involved third party (see paragraph 61A) and inspect—

(*a*) the premises,

(*b*) business assets that are on the premises, and

(*c*) relevant documents that are on the premises,

if the inspection is reasonably required by the officer for the purpose of checking the position of any person or class of persons as regards a relevant tax.

(2) The powers under this paragraph may be exercised whether or not the identity of that person is, or the individual identities of those persons are, known to the officer.

(3) The powers under this paragraph do not include power to enter or inspect any part of the premises that is used solely as a dwelling.

(4) In relation to an involved third party, "relevant documents" and "relevant tax" are defined in paragraph 61A.]

Prospective amendments—Para 10A to be inserted by FA 2009 s 96, Sch 48 para 3 with effect from a date to be appointed.

Power to inspect premises used in connection with taxable supplies etc

11— (1) This paragraph applies where an officer of Revenue and Customs has reason to believe that—

(*a*) premises are used in connection with the supply of goods under taxable supplies and goods to be so supplied [or documents relating to such goods][1] are on those premises,

(*b*) premises are used in connection with the acquisition of goods from other member States under taxable acquisitions and goods to be so acquired [or documents relating to such goods][1] are on those premises, or

(*c*) premises are used as [or in connection with][1] a fiscal warehouse.

(2) An officer of Revenue and Customs may enter the premises and inspect—

(*a*) the premises,

(*b*) any goods that are on the premises, and

(*c*) any documents on the premises that appear to the officer to relate to [the supply of goods under taxable supplies, the acquisition of goods from other member States under taxable acquisitions or fiscal warehousing][1].

(3) The powers under this paragraph do not include power to enter or inspect any part of the premises that is used solely as a dwelling.

(4) Terms used both in [this paragraph][1] and in VATA 1994 have the same meaning [here][1] as they have in that Act.

Commentary—*Simon's Taxes* **A6.301A**.

Commencement—Finance Act 2008, Schedule 36 (Appointed Day and Savings) Order, SI 2009/404 art 2 (appointed day for the coming into force of Sch 36 is 1 April 2009).
HMRC Manuals—Compliance Handbook Manual, CH25420 (HMRC inspection powers: start and end of an inspection).
CH25460 (when to carry out an inspection).
CH25480 (HMRC inspection powers: announced and unannounced inspection).
CH25540 (Tribunal approval).
CH25560 (wording of inspection notices).
Amendments—[1] In sub-para (1)(*a*), (*b*), (*c*) words inserted, in sub-para (2)(*c*) words substituted for words "such goods", in sub-para (4) words substituted in the first place for words "sub-paragraph (1)" and in the second place for words "in that sub-paragraph", by FA 2009 s 95, Sch 47 para 6 with effect from 21 July 2009.

Carrying out inspections

12— (1) An inspection under this Part of this Schedule may be carried out only—

(*a*) at a time agreed to by the occupier of the premises, or
(*b*) if sub-paragraph (2) is satisfied, at any reasonable time.

(2) This sub-paragraph is satisfied if—

(*a*) the occupier of the premises has been given at least 7 days' notice of the time of the inspection (whether in writing or otherwise), or
(*b*) the inspection is carried out by, or with the agreement of, an authorised officer of Revenue and Customs.

(3) An officer of Revenue and Customs seeking to carry out an inspection under sub-paragraph (2)(*b*) must provide a notice in writing as follows—

(*a*) if the occupier of the premises is present at the time the inspection is to begin, the notice must be provided to the occupier,
(*b*) if the occupier of the premises is not present but a person who appears to the officer to be in charge of the premises is present, the notice must be provided to that person, and
(*c*) in any other case, the notice must be left in a prominent place on the premises.

(4) The notice referred to in sub-paragraph (3) must state the possible consequences of obstructing the officer in the exercise of the power.

(5) If a notice referred to in sub-paragraph (3) is given [in respect of an inspection approved by][2] the [tribunal][1] (see paragraph 13), it must state that [the inspection has been so approved][2].

Commencement—Finance Act 2008, Schedule 36 (Appointed Day and Savings) Order, SI 2009/404 art 2 (appointed day for the coming into force of Sch 36 is 1 April 2009).
HMRC Manuals—Compliance Handbook Manual, CH25480 (HMRC inspection powers: announced and unannounced inspection).
CH25540 (Tribunal approval).
CH25560 (wording of inspection notices).
CH250000–255960 (HMRC inspection powers – how to do a compliance check: visits to business premises).
CH254000–254040 (how to do a compliance check: unannounced visits).
CH255000–255060 (how to do a compliance check: visits to private residences).
CH255500–255960 (how to do a compliance check: during a visit).
CH255520 (how to do a compliance check: what to do if entry is refused).
Amendments—[1] In sub-para (5) word substituted for the words "First-tier Tribunal" by the Transfer of Tribunal Functions and Revenue and Customs Appeals Order, SI 2009/56 art 3, Sch 1 para 471 with effect from 1 April 2009.
[2] In sub-para (5) words substituted in the first place for the words "with the approval of" and in the second place for the words "it is given with that approval", by FA 2009 s 95, Sch 47 para 7 with effect from 21 July 2009.
Prospective amendments—In heading words "*under paragraph 10, 10A or 11*" to be inserted at the end, in sub-para (1) words "paragraph 10, 10A or 11" to be substituted for the words "this Part of this Schedule", by FA 2009 s 96, Sch 48 para 4 with effect from a date to be appointed.

[Powers to inspect property for valuation etc

12A— (1) An officer of Revenue and Customs may enter and inspect premises for the purpose of valuing the premises if the valuation is reasonably required for the purpose of checking any person's position as regards income tax or corporation tax.

(2) An officer of Revenue and Customs may enter premises and inspect—

(*a*) the premises, and
(*b*) any other property on the premises,

for the purpose of valuing, measuring or determining the character of the premises or property.

(3) Sub-paragraph (2) only applies if the valuation, measurement or determination is reasonably required for the purpose of checking any person's position as regards—

(*a*) capital gains tax,
(*b*) corporation tax in respect of chargeable gains,
(*c*) inheritance tax,
(*d*) stamp duty land tax, or
(*e*) stamp duty reserve tax.

(4) A person who the officer considers is needed to assist with the valuation, measurement or determination may enter and inspect the premises or property with the officer.]

Prospective amendments—Paras 12A, 12B to be inserted by FA 2009 s 96, Sch 48 para 5 with effect from a date to be appointed.

[Carrying out inspections under paragraph 12A

12B— (1) An inspection under paragraph 12A may be carried out only if condition A or B is satisfied.

(2) Condition A is that—

(*a*) the inspection is carried out at a time agreed to by a relevant person, and

(*b*) the relevant person has been given notice in writing of the agreed time of the inspection.

(3) "Relevant person" means—

(*a*) the occupier of the premises, or

(*b*) if the occupier cannot be identified or the premises are vacant, a person who controls the premises.

(4) Condition B is that—

(*a*) the inspection has been approved by the tribunal, and

(*b*) any relevant person specified by the tribunal has been given at least 7 days' notice in writing of the time of the inspection.

(5) A notice under sub-paragraph (4)(*b*) must state the possible consequences of obstructing the officer in the exercise of the power.

(6) If a notice is given under this paragraph in respect of an inspection approved by the tribunal (see paragraph 13), it must state that the inspection has been so approved.

(7) An officer of Revenue and Customs seeking to carry out an inspection under paragraph 12A must produce evidence of authority to carry out the inspection if asked to do so by—

(*a*) the occupier of the premises, or

(*b*) any other person who appears to the officer to be in charge of the premises or property.]

Prospective amendments—Paras 12A, 12B to be inserted by FA 2009 s 96, Sch 48 para 5 with effect from a date to be appointed.

Approval of [tribunal]

13— (1) An officer of Revenue and Customs may ask the [tribunal][1] to approve an inspection under this Part of this Schedule.

[(1A) An application for approval under this paragraph may be made without notice.][2]

(2) The [tribunal][1] may not approve an inspection unless—

(*a*) an application for approval is made by, or with the agreement of, an authorised officer of Revenue and Customs, and

(*b*) the [tribunal][1] is satisfied that, in the circumstances, the inspection is justified.

[(3) A decision of the tribunal under this paragraph is final (despite the provisions of sections 11 and 13 of the Tribunals, Courts and Enforcement Act 2007).][2]

Commencement—Finance Act 2008, Schedule 36 (Appointed Day and Savings) Order, SI 2009/404 art 2 (appointed day for the coming into force of Sch 36 is 1 April 2009).

Amendments—[1] Word substituted for the words "First-tier Tribunal" in the heading and in each place; in sub-para (2)(*b*) word substituted for the word "Tribunal" by the Transfer of Tribunal Functions and Revenue and Customs Appeals Order, SI 2009/56 art 3, Sch 1 para 471 with effect from 1 April 2009.

[2] Sub-paras (1A), (3) inserted by FA 2009 s 95, Sch 47 para 8 with effect from 21 July 2009.

Prospective amendments—In sub-para (1) words "(and for the effect of obtaining such approval see paragraph 39 (penalties))" to be inserted at the end, in sub-para (1A) words "(except as required under sub-paragraph (2A))" to be inserted at the end, in sub-para (2) words "under paragraph 10, 10A or 11" to be inserted after words "an inspection", and sub-paras (2A), (2B) to be inserted, by FA 2009 s 96, Sch 48 para 6 with effect from a date to be appointed. New sub-paras (2A), (2B) to read as follows—

"(2A) The tribunal may not approve an inspection under paragraph 12A unless—

(*a*) an application for approval is made by, or with the agreement of, an authorised officer of Revenue and Customs,

(*b*) the person whose tax position is the subject of the proposed inspection has been given a reasonable opportunity to make representations to the officer of Revenue and Customs about that inspection,

(*c*) the occupier of the premises has been given a reasonable opportunity to make such representations,

(*d*) the tribunal has been given a summary of any representations made, and

(*e*) the tribunal is satisfied that, in the circumstances, the inspection is justified.

(2B) Paragraph (c) of sub-paragraph 2A does not apply if the tribunal is satisfied that the occupier of the premises cannot be identified.".

Restrictions and special cases

14 This Part of this Schedule has effect subject to Parts 4 and 6 of this Schedule.

Commencement—Finance Act 2008, Schedule 36 (Appointed Day and Savings) Order, SI 2009/404 art 2 (appointed day for the coming into force of Sch 36 is 1 April 2009).

HMRC Manuals—Compliance Handbook Manual, CH25300 (HMRC inspection powers: documents you cannot inspect).

PART 3

FURTHER POWERS

Power to copy documents

15 Where a document (or a copy of a document) is produced to, or inspected by, an officer of Revenue and Customs, such an officer may take copies of, or make extracts from, the document.

Commencement—Finance Act 2008, Schedule 36 (Appointed Day and Savings) Order, SI 2009/404 art 2 (appointed day for the coming into force of Sch 36 is 1 April 2009).
HMRC Manuals—Compliance Handbook Manual, CH23300 (HMRC inspection powers: copying or removing documents).
CH25320 (HMRC inspection powers: obtaining and recording information and copying documents).
CH255540 (HMRC inspection powers – how to do a compliance check: copying records).

Power to remove documents

16— (1) Where a document is produced to, or inspected by, an officer of Revenue and Customs, such an officer may—

(*a*) remove the document at a reasonable time, and
(*b*) retain it for a reasonable period,

if it appears to the officer to be necessary to do so.

(2) Where a document is removed in accordance with sub-paragraph (1), the person who produced the document may request—

(*a*) a receipt for the document, and
(*b*) if the document is reasonably required for any purpose, a copy of the document,

and an officer of Revenue and Customs must comply with such a request without charge.

(3) The removal of a document under this paragraph is not to be regarded as breaking any lien claimed on the document.

(4) Where a document removed under this paragraph is lost or damaged, the Commissioners are liable to compensate the owner of the document for any expenses reasonably incurred in replacing or repairing the document.

(5) In this paragraph references to a document include a copy of a document.

Commencement—Finance Act 2008, Schedule 36 (Appointed Day and Savings) Order, SI 2009/404 art 2 (appointed day for the coming into force of Sch 36 is 1 April 2009).
HMRC Manuals—Compliance Handbook Manual, CH23300 (HMRC inspection powers: copying or removing documents).
CH25320 (HMRC inspection powers: obtaining and recording information and copying documents).
CH255545–255555 (inspection powers – how to do a compliance check: removing, storing and returning records).

Power to mark assets and to record information

17 The powers under Part 2 of this Schedule include—

(*a*) power to mark business assets, and anything containing business assets, for the purpose of indicating that they have been inspected, and
(*b*) power to obtain and record information (whether electronically or otherwise) relating to the premises, assets and documents that have been inspected.

Commencement—Finance Act 2008, Schedule 36 (Appointed Day and Savings) Order, SI 2009/404 art 2 (appointed day for the coming into force of Sch 36 is 1 April 2009).
HMRC Manuals—Compliance Handbook Manual, CH25320 (HMRC inspection powers: obtaining and recording information and copying documents).
CH25340 (HMRC inspection powers: marking goods or assets).
CH255960 (HMRC inspection powers – how to do a compliance check: marking goods or assets).

Prospective amendments—In para (*b*) words "property, goods," to be inserted after the word "premises," by FA 2009 s 96, Sch 48 para 7 with effect from a date to be appointed.

PART 4
RESTRICTIONS ON POWERS

Documents not in person's possession or power

18 An information notice only requires a person to produce a document if it is in the person's possession or power.

Commentary—*Simon's Taxes* **A6.301A**.
Commencement—Finance Act 2008, Schedule 36 (Appointed Day and Savings) Order, SI 2009/404 art 2 (appointed day for the coming into force of Sch 36 is 1 April 2009).
HMRC Manuals—Compliance Handbook Manual, CH22120 (HMRC inspection powers: meaning of possession and power).

Types of information

19— (1) An information notice does not require a person to provide or produce—

(*a*) information that relates to the conduct of a pending appeal relating to tax or any part of a document containing such information, or
(*b*) journalistic material (as defined in section 13 of the Police and Criminal Evidence Act 1984 (c 60)) or information contained in such material.

(2) An information notice does not require a person to provide or produce personal records (as defined in section 12 of the Police and Criminal Evidence Act 1984) or information contained in such records, subject to sub-paragraph (3).

(3) An information notice may require a person—

(*a*) to produce documents, or copies of documents, that are personal records, omitting any information whose inclusion (whether alone or with other information) makes the original documents personal records ("personal information"), and

(*b*) to provide any information contained in such records that is not personal information.

Commentary—*Simon's Taxes* **A6.301A**.

Commencement—Finance Act 2008, Schedule 36 (Appointed Day and Savings) Order, SI 2009/404 art 2 (appointed day for the coming into force of Sch 36 is 1 April 2009).

HMRC Manuals—Compliance Handbook Manual, CH22160 (HMRC inspection powers: appeal material, with example). CH22180 and 22200 (personal records, with example).

Old documents

20 An information notice may not require a person to produce a document if the whole of the document originates more than 6 years before the date of the notice, unless the notice is given by, or with the agreement of, an authorised officer.

Commentary—*Simon's Taxes* **A6.301A**.

Commencement—Finance Act 2008, Schedule 36 (Appointed Day and Savings) Order, SI 2009/404 art 2 (appointed day for the coming into force of Sch 36 is 1 April 2009).

HMRC Manuals—Compliance Handbook Manual, CH22140 (HMRC inspection powers: old documents).

Taxpayer notices

21— (1) Where a person has made a tax return in respect of a chargeable period under section 8, 8A or 12AA of TMA 1970 (returns for purpose of income tax and capital gains tax), a taxpayer notice may not be given for the purpose of checking that person's income tax position or capital gains tax position in relation to the chargeable period.

(2) Where a person has made a tax return in respect of a chargeable period under paragraph 3 of Schedule 18 to FA 1998 (company tax returns), a taxpayer notice may not be given for the purpose of checking that person's corporation tax position in relation to the chargeable period.

(3) Sub-paragraphs (1) and (2) do not apply where, or to the extent that, any of conditions A to D is met.

(4) Condition A is that a notice of enquiry has been given in respect of—

(*a*) the return, or

(*b*) a claim or election (or an amendment of a claim or election) made by the person in relation to the chargeable period in respect of the tax (or one of the taxes) to which the return relates ("relevant tax"),

and the enquiry has not been completed.

(5) In sub-paragraph (4), "notice of enquiry" means a notice under—

(*a*) section 9A or 12AC of, or paragraph 5 of Schedule 1A to, TMA 1970, or

(*b*) paragraph 24 of Schedule 18 to FA 1998.

(6) Condition B is that an officer of Revenue and Customs has reason to suspect that[, as regards the person,][1]—

(*a*) an amount that ought to have been assessed to relevant tax for the chargeable period may not have been assessed,

(*b*) an assessment to relevant tax for the chargeable period may be or have become insufficient, or

(*c*) relief from relevant tax given for the chargeable period may be or have become excessive.

(7) Condition C is that the notice is given for the purpose of obtaining any information or document that is also required for the purpose of checking [the][1] person's VAT position.

(8) Condition D is that the notice is given for the purpose of obtaining any information or document that is required (or also required) for the purpose of checking the person's position as regards any deductions or repayments [of tax or withholding of income][1]referred to in paragraph 64(2) [or (2A)][1] (PAYE etc).

[(9) In this paragraph, references to the person who made the return are only to that person in the capacity in which the return was made.][1]

Commencement—Finance Act 2008, Schedule 36 (Appointed Day and Savings) Order, SI 2009/404 art 2 (appointed day for the coming into force of Sch 36 is 1 April 2009).

HMRC Manuals—Compliance Handbook Manual, CH23520 (HMRC inspection powers: specific rules regarding taxpayer notice).

CH23540 (HMRC inspection powers: where self assessment return made).

CH23560 (meaning of "reason to suspect").

CH223500–223700 (HMRC inspection powers – how to do a compliance check: restrictions on a taxpayer notice).

Amendments—[1] In sub-paras (6), (8) in both places, words inserted, in sub-para (7) word substituted for the word "that", and sub-para (9) inserted, by FA 2009 s 95, Sch 47 para 9 with effect from 21 July 2009.

Prospective amendments—In the heading words "*following tax return*" to be inserted at the end, in sub-para (7) words "position as regards any tax other than income tax, capital gains tax or corporation tax" to be substituted for the words "VAT position" by FA 2009 s 95, Sch 48 para 8 with effect from a date to be appointed.

[Taxpayer notices following land transaction return

21A— (1) Where a person has delivered a land transaction return under section 76 of FA 2003 (returns for purposes of stamp duty land tax) in respect of a transaction, a taxpayer notice may not be given for the purpose of checking that person's stamp duty land tax position in relation to that transaction.

(2) Sub-paragraph (1) does not apply where, or to the extent that, any of conditions A to C is met.

(3) Condition A is that a notice of enquiry has been given in respect of—

(*a*) the return, or

(*b*) a claim (or an amendment of a claim) made by the person in connection with the transaction,

and the enquiry has not been completed.

(4) In sub-paragraph (3) "notice of enquiry" means a notice under paragraph 12 of Schedule 10, or paragraph 7 of Schedule 11A, to FA 2003.

(5) Condition B is that, as regards the person, an officer of Revenue and Customs has reason to suspect that—

(*a*) an amount that ought to have been assessed to stamp duty land tax in respect of the transaction may not have been assessed,

(*b*) an assessment to stamp duty land tax in respect of the transaction may be or have become insufficient, or

(*c*) relief from stamp duty land tax in respect of the transaction may be or have become excessive.

(6) Condition C is that the notice is given for the purpose of obtaining any information or document that is also required for the purpose of checking that person's position as regards a tax other than stamp duty land tax.]

Prospective amendments—Para 21A to be inserted by FA 2009 s 96, Sch 48 para 9 with effect from a date to be appointed.

Deceased persons

22 An information notice given for the purpose of checking the tax position of a person who has died may not be given more than 4 years after the person's death.

Commencement—Finance Act 2008, Schedule 36 (Appointed Day and Savings) Order, SI 2009/404 art 2 (appointed day for the coming into force of Sch 36 is 1 April 2009).

HMRC Manuals—Compliance Handbook Manual, CH23620 (HMRC inspection powers: specific rules regarding third party notice).

Privileged communications between professional legal advisers and clients

23— (1) An information notice does not require a person—

(*a*) to provide privileged information, or

(*b*) to produce any part of a document that is privileged.

(2) For the purpose of this Schedule, information or a document is privileged if it is information or a document in respect of which a claim to legal professional privilege, or (in Scotland) to confidentiality of communications as between client and professional legal adviser, could be maintained in legal proceedings.

(3) The Commissioners may by regulations make provision for the resolution by the [tribunal][1] of disputes as to whether any information or document is privileged.

(4) The regulations may, in particular, make provision as to—

(*a*) the custody of a document while its status is being decided, …[1]

(*b*) …[1]

Commentary—*Simon's Taxes* **A6.301A**.

Commencement—Finance Act 2008, Schedule 36 (Appointed Day and Savings) Order, SI 2009/404 art 2 (appointed day for the coming into force of Sch 36 is 1 April 2009).

HMRC Manuals—Compliance Handbook Manual, CH22240 (HMRC restrictions on inspection powers: legal professional privilege).

CH223850 (HMRC information and inspection powers – how to do a compliance check: legal professional privilege).

Regulations—Information Notice: Resolution of Disputes as to Privileged Communications Regulations, SI 2009/1916.

Amendments—[1] In sub-para (3) word substituted for the words "First-tier Tribunal"; sub-para (4)(*b*) and the word "and" immediately preceding it repealed by the Transfer of Tribunal Functions and Revenue and Customs Appeals Order, SI 2009/56 art 3, Sch 1 para 471 with effect from 1 April 2009. Sub-para (4)(*b*) previously read as follows—

"(*b*) the procedures to be followed.".

Auditors

24— (1) An information notice does not require a person who has been appointed as an auditor for the purpose of an enactment—

(*a*) to provide information held in connection with the performance of the person's functions under that enactment, or

(*b*) to produce documents which are that person's property and which were created by that person or on that person's behalf for or in connection with the performance of those functions.

(2) Sub-paragraph (1) has effect subject to paragraph 26.

Commentary—*Simon's Taxes* **A6.301A, A6.310.**
Commencement—Finance Act 2008, Schedule 36 (Appointed Day and Savings) Order, SI 2009/404 art 2 (appointed day for the coming into force of Sch 36 is 1 April 2009).
HMRC Manuals—Compliance Handbook Manual, CH22240 (HMRC restrictions on inspection powers: auditors' papers).

Tax advisers

25— (1) An information notice does not require a tax adviser—

(*a*) to provide information about relevant communications, or

(*b*) to produce documents which are the tax adviser's property and consist of relevant communications.

(2) Sub-paragraph (1) has effect subject to paragraph 26.

(3) In this paragraph—

"relevant communications" means communications between the tax adviser and—

(*a*) a person in relation to whose tax affairs he has been appointed, or

(*b*) any other tax adviser of such a person,

the purpose of which is the giving or obtaining of advice about any of those tax affairs, and

"tax adviser" means a person appointed to give advice about the tax affairs of another person (whether appointed directly by that person or by another tax adviser of that person).

Commentary—*Simon's Taxes* **A6.301A, A6.310.**
Commencement—Finance Act 2008, Schedule 36 (Appointed Day and Savings) Order, SI 2009/404 art 2 (appointed day for the coming into force of Sch 36 is 1 April 2009).
HMRC Manuals—Compliance Handbook Manual, CH22240 and 22320 (HMRC restrictions on inspection powers: tax advisers' papers).

Auditors and tax advisers: supplementary

26— (1) Paragraphs 24(1) and 25(1) do not have effect in relation to—

(*a*) information explaining any information or document which the person to whom the notice is given has, as tax accountant, assisted any client in preparing for, or delivering to, HMRC, or

(*b*) a document which contains such information.

(2) In the case of a notice given under paragraph 5, paragraphs 24(1) and 25(1) do not have effect in relation to—

(*a*) any information giving the identity or address of a person to whom the notice relates or of a person who has acted on behalf of such a person, or

(*b*) a document which contains such information.

(3) Paragraphs 24(1) and 25(1) are not disapplied by sub-paragraph (1) or (2) if the information in question has already been provided, or a document containing the information in question has already been produced, to an officer of Revenue and Customs.

Commentary—*Simon's Taxes* **A6.301A, A6.310.**
Commencement—Finance Act 2008, Schedule 36 (Appointed Day and Savings) Order, SI 2009/404 art 2 (appointed day for the coming into force of Sch 36 is 1 April 2009).
HMRC Manuals—Compliance Handbook Manual, CH22340 (HMRC restrictions on inspection powers: exceptions for auditors' and tax advisers' papers).

27— (1) This paragraph applies where paragraph 24(1) or 25(1) is disapplied in relation to a document by paragraph 26(1) or (2).

(2) An information notice that requires the document to be produced has effect as if it required any part or parts of the document containing the information mentioned in paragraph 26(1) or (2) to be produced.

Commencement—Finance Act 2008, Schedule 36 (Appointed Day and Savings) Order, SI 2009/404 art 2 (appointed day for the coming into force of Sch 36 is 1 April 2009).
HMRC Manuals—Compliance Handbook Manual, CH22340 (HMRC restrictions on inspection powers: exceptions for auditors' and tax advisers' papers).

Corresponding restrictions on inspection of business documents

28 An officer of Revenue and Customs may not inspect a business document under Part 2 of this Schedule if or to the extent that, by virtue of this Part of this Schedule, an information notice given at the time of the inspection to the occupier of the premises could not require the occupier to produce the document.

Commencement—Finance Act 2008, Schedule 36 (Appointed Day and Savings) Order, SI 2009/404 art 2 (appointed day for the coming into force of Sch 36 is 1 April 2009).
Prospective amendments—In the heading, word "business" to be repealed by FA 2009 s 96, Sch 48 para 10 with effect from a date to be appointed.

PART 5

APPEALS AGAINST INFORMATION NOTICES

Right to appeal against taxpayer notice

29— (1) Where a taxpayer is given a taxpayer notice, the taxpayer may appeal …[1] against the notice or any requirement in the notice.

(2) Sub-paragraph (1) does not apply to a requirement in a taxpayer notice to provide any information, or produce any document, that forms part of the taxpayer's statutory records.

(3) Sub-paragraph (1) does not apply if the [tribunal][1] approved the giving of the notice in accordance with paragraph 3.

Commentary—*Simon's Taxes* **A6.301A**.
Commencement—Finance Act 2008, Schedule 36 (Appointed Day and Savings) Order, SI 2009/404 art 2 (appointed day for the coming into force of Sch 36 is 1 April 2009).
HMRC Manuals—Compliance Handbook Manual, CH23520 (HMRC inspection powers: specific rules regarding taxpayer notice).
CH24100 (HMRC inspection powers: appealing against a taxpayer notice).
Amendments—[1] In sub-para (1) words "to the First-tier Tribunal" repealed; in sub-para (3) word substituted for the words "First-tier Tribunal" by the Transfer of Tribunal Functions and Revenue and Customs Appeals Order, SI 2009/56 art 3, Sch 1 para 471 with effect from 1 April 2009.

Right to appeal against third party notice

30— (1) Where a person is given a third party notice, the person may appeal …[1] against the notice or any requirement in the notice on the ground that it would be unduly onerous to comply with the notice or requirement.

(2) Sub-paragraph (1) does not apply to a requirement in a third party notice to provide any information, or produce any document, that forms part of the taxpayer's statutory records.

(3) Sub-paragraph (1) does not apply if the [tribunal][1] approved the giving of the notice in accordance with paragraph 3.

Commentary—*Simon's Taxes* **A6.301A**.
Commencement—Finance Act 2008, Schedule 36 (Appointed Day and Savings) Order, SI 2009/404 art 2 (appointed day for the coming into force of Sch 36 is 1 April 2009).
HMRC Manuals—Compliance Handbook Manual, CH23620 (HMRC inspection powers: specific rules regarding third party notice).
CH24100 (HMRC inspection powers: appealing against a third party notice).
CH24420 (meaning of "unduly onerous").
Amendments—[1] In sub-para (1) words "to the First-tier Tribunal" repealed; in sub-para (3) word substituted for the words "First-tier Tribunal" by the Transfer of Tribunal Functions and Revenue and Customs Appeals Order, SI 2009/56 art 3, Sch 1 para 471 with effect from 1 April 2009.

Right to appeal against notice given under paragraph 5

31 Where a person is given a notice under paragraph 5, the person may appeal …[1] against the notice or any requirement in the notice on the ground that it would be unduly onerous to comply with the notice or requirement.

Commencement—Finance Act 2008, Schedule 36 (Appointed Day and Savings) Order, SI 2009/404 art 2 (appointed day for the coming into force of Sch 36 is 1 April 2009).
HMRC Manuals—Compliance Handbook Manual, CH23900 (HMRC inspection powers: identity unknown notice).
CH24100 (HMRC inspection powers: appealing against an identity unknown notice).
Amendments—[1] In sub-para (1) words "to the First-tier Tribunal" repealed by the Transfer of Tribunal Functions and Revenue and Customs Appeals Order, SI 2009/56 art 3, Sch 1 para 471 with effect from 1 April 2009.

Procedure

32— (1) Notice of an appeal under this Part of this Schedule must be given—

(*a*) in writing,
(*b*) before the end of the period of 30 days beginning with the date on which the information notice is given, and
(*c*) to the officer of Revenue and Customs by whom the information notice was given.

(2) Notice of an appeal under this Part of this Schedule must state the grounds of appeal.

(3) On an appeal the [that is notified to the tribunal, the tribunal][1] may—

(*a*) confirm the information notice or a requirement in the information notice,
(*b*) vary the information notice or such a requirement, or
(*c*) set aside the information notice or such a requirement.

(4) Where the [tribunal][1] confirms or varies the information notice or a requirement, the person to whom the information notice was given must comply with the notice or requirement—

(*a*) within such period as is specified by the [tribunal][1], or
(*b*) if the [tribunal][1] does not specify a period, within such period as is reasonably specified in writing by an officer of Revenue and Customs following the [tribunal's][1] decision.

[(5) Notwithstanding the provisions of sections 11 and 13 of the Tribunals, Courts and Enforcement Act 2007 a decision of the tribunal on an appeal under this Part of this Schedule is final.][1]

(6) Subject to this paragraph, the provisions of Part 5 of TMA 1970 relating to appeals have effect in relation to appeals under this Part of this Schedule as they have effect in relation to an appeal against an assessment to income tax.

Commentary—*Simon's Taxes* **A6.301A**.
Commencement—Finance Act 2008, Schedule 36 (Appointed Day and Savings) Order, SI 2009/404 art 2 (appointed day for the coming into force of Sch 36 is 1 April 2009).
HMRC Manuals—Compliance Handbook Manual, CH24340 (HMRC inspection powers: appeal procedures).
CH24440 (what the first-tier Tribunal can decide).

Amendments—[1] In sub-paras (3), (4) word substituted for the words "First-tier Tribunal"; in sub-para (4)(*a*), (*b*) word substituted for word "Tribunal" and "Tribunal's"; sub-para (5) substituted by the Transfer of Tribunal Functions and Revenue and Customs Appeals Order, SI 2009/56 art 3, Sch 1 para 471 with effect from 1 April 2009. Sub-para (5) previously read as follows—

"(5) A decision by the First-tier Tribunal on an appeal under this Part of this Schedule is final.".

Special cases

33 This Part of this Schedule has effect subject to Part 6 of this Schedule.

Commencement—Finance Act 2008, Schedule 36 (Appointed Day and Savings) Order, SI 2009/404 art 2 (appointed day for the coming into force of Sch 36 is 1 April 2009).

PART 6

SPECIAL CASES

Supply of goods or services etc

34— (1) This paragraph applies to a taxpayer notice or third party notice that refers only to information or documents that form part of any person's statutory records and relate to—

(*a*) the supply of goods or services,
(*b*) the acquisition of goods from another member State, or
(*c*) the importation of goods from a place outside the member States in the course of carrying on a business.

(2) Paragraph 3(1) (requirement for consent to, or approval of, third party notice) does not apply to such a notice.

(3) Where a person is given such a notice, the person may not appeal …[1] against the notice or any requirement in the notice.

(4) Sections 5, 11 and 15 of, and Schedule 4 to, VATA 1994, and any orders made under those provisions, apply for the purposes of this paragraph as if it were part of that Act.

Commencement—Finance Act 2008, Schedule 36 (Appointed Day and Savings) Order, SI 2009/404 art 2 (appointed day for the coming into force of Sch 36 is 1 April 2009).

HMRC Manuals—Compliance Handbook Manual, CH23520 (HMRC inspection powers: specific rules regarding taxpayer notice).

CH23620 (HMRC inspection powers: specific rules regarding third party notice).

Amendments—[1] In sub-para (3) words "to the First-tier Tribunal" repealed by the Transfer of Tribunal Functions and Revenue and Customs Appeals Order, SI 2009/56 art 3, Sch 1 para 471 with effect from 1 April 2009.

[Involved third parties

34A— (1) This paragraph applies to a third party notice or a notice under paragraph 5 if—

(*a*) it is given to an involved third party (see paragraph 61A),
(*b*) it is given for the purpose of checking the position of a person, or a class of persons, as regards the relevant tax, and
(*c*) it refers only to relevant information or relevant documents.

(2) In relation to such a third party notice—

(*a*) paragraph 3(1) (approval etc of third party notices) does not apply,
(*b*) paragraph 4(1) (copying third party notices to taxpayer) does not apply, and
(*c*) paragraph 30(1) (appeal) has effect as if it permitted an appeal on any grounds.

(3) In relation to such a notice under paragraph 5—

(*a*) sub-paragraphs (3) and (4) of that paragraph (approval of tribunal) have effect as if they permitted, but did not require, an authorised officer of Revenue and Customs to obtain the approval of the tribunal, and
(*b*) paragraph 31 (appeal) has effect as if it permitted an appeal on any grounds.

(4) The involved third party may not appeal against a requirement in the notice to provide any information, or produce any document, that forms part of the involved third party's statutory records.

(5) In relation to an involved third party, "relevant documents", "relevant information" and "relevant tax" are defined in paragraph 61A.]

Prospective amendments—Paras 34A–34C to be inserted by FA 2009 s 96, Sch 48 para 11 with effect from a date to be appointed.

[Registered pension schemes etc

34B— (1) This paragraph applies to a third party notice or a notice under paragraph 5 if it refers only to information or documents that relate to any pensions matter.

(2) "Pensions matter" means any matter relating to—

(*a*) a registered pension scheme,
(*b*) an annuity purchased with sums or assets held for the purposes of a registered pension scheme or a pre-2006 pension scheme, or
(*c*) an employer-financed retirement benefits scheme.

(3) In relation to such a third party notice—

(*a*) paragraph 3(1) (approval etc of third party notices) does not apply,
(*b*) paragraph 4(1) (copying third party notices to taxpayer) does not apply, and
(*c*) paragraph 30(1) (appeal) has effect as if it permitted an appeal on any grounds.

(4) In relation to such a notice under paragraph 5—

(*a*) sub-paragraphs (3) and (4) of that paragraph (approval of tribunal) have effect as if they permitted, but did not require, an authorised officer of Revenue and Customs to obtain the approval of the tribunal, and
(*b*) paragraph 31 (appeal) has effect as if it permitted an appeal on any grounds.

(5) A person may not appeal against a requirement in the notice to provide any information, or produce any document, that forms part of any person's statutory records.

(6) Where the notice relates to a matter within sub-paragraph (2)(*a*) or (*b*), the officer of Revenue and Customs who gives the notice must give a copy of the notice to the scheme administrator in relation to the pension scheme.

(7) Where the notice relates to a matter within sub-paragraph (2)(*c*), the officer of Revenue and Customs who gives the notice must give a copy of the notice to the responsible person in relation to the employer-financed retirement benefits scheme.

(8) Sub-paragraphs (6) and (7) do not apply if the notice is given to a person who, in relation to the scheme or annuity to which the notice relates, is a prescribed description of person.]

Prospective amendments—Paras 34A–34C to be inserted by FA 2009 s 96, Sch 48 para 11 with effect from a date to be appointed.

[Registered pension schemes etc: interpretation

34C In paragraph 34B—

"employer-financed retirement benefits scheme" has the same meaning as in Chapter 2 of Part 6 of ITEPA 2003 (see sections 393A and 393B of that Act);

"pension scheme" has the same meaning as in Part 4 of FA 2004;

"pre-2006 pension scheme" means a scheme that, at or in respect of any time before 6 April 2006, was—

(*a*) a retirement benefits scheme approved for the purposes of Chapter 1 of Part 14 of ICTA,
(*b*) a former approved superannuation fund (as defined in paragraph 1(3) of Schedule 36 to FA 2004),
(*c*) a relevant statutory scheme (as defined in section 611A of ICTA) or a pension scheme treated as if it were such a scheme, or
(*d*) a personal pension scheme approved under Chapter 4 of Part 14 of ICTA;

"prescribed" means prescribed by regulations made by the Commissioners;

"registered pension scheme" means a pension scheme that is or has been a registered pension scheme within the meaning of Part 4 of FA 2004 or in relation to which an application for registration under that Part of that Act has been made;

"responsible person", in relation to an employer-financed retirement benefits scheme, has the same meaning as in Chapter 2 of Part 6 of ITEPA 2003 (see section 399A of that Act);

"scheme administrator", in relation to a pension scheme, has the same meaning as in Part 4 of FA 2004 (see section 270 of that Act).]

Prospective amendments—Paras 34A–34C to be inserted by FA 2009 s 96, Sch 48 para 11 with effect from a date to be appointed.

Groups of undertakings

35— (1) This paragraph applies where an undertaking is a parent undertaking in relation to another undertaking (a subsidiary undertaking).

(2) Where a third party notice is given to any person for the purpose of checking the tax position of the parent undertaking and any of its subsidiary undertakings, [—

(*a*) paragraph 2(2)][1] only requires the notice to state this and name the parent undertaking[, and
(*b*) the references in paragraph 3(5) to naming the taxpayer are to making that statement and naming the parent undertaking][1].

(3) In relation to such a notice—

(*a*) in paragraphs 3 and 4 (approval etc of notices and copying third party notices to taxpayer), the references to the taxpayer have effect as if they were references to the parent undertaking, but
(*b*) in paragraph 30(2) (no appeal in relation to taxpayer's statutory records), the reference to the taxpayer has effect as if it were a reference to the parent undertaking and each of its subsidiary undertakings.

[(4) Where a third party notice is given to the parent undertaking for the purpose of checking the tax position of more than one subsidiary undertaking—

(*a*) paragraph 2(2) only requires the notice to state this, and
(*b*) the references in paragraph 3(5) to naming the taxpayer are to making that statement.

VAT

(4A) In relation to such a notice—

(*a*) in paragraph 3 (approval etc of notices), sub-paragraphs (1) and (3)(*e*) do not apply,

(*b*) paragraph 4(1) (copying third party notices to taxpayer) does not apply,

(*c*) paragraph 21 (restrictions on giving taxpayer notice where taxpayer has made return) applies as if the notice was a taxpayer notice or taxpayer notices given to each subsidiary undertaking (or, if the notice names the subsidiary undertakings to which it relates, to each of those undertakings),

(*d*) paragraph 30(1) (appeal) has effect as if it permitted an appeal on any grounds, and

(*e*) in paragraph 30(2) (no appeal in relation to taxpayer's statutory records), the reference to the taxpayer has effect as if it were a reference to the parent undertaking or any of its subsidiary undertakings.][1]

(5) Where a notice is given under paragraph 5 to the parent undertaking for the purpose of checking the tax position of one or more subsidiary undertakings whose identities are not known to the officer giving the notice[—

(*a*) sub-paragraphs (3) and (4) of that paragraph (approval of tribunal) have effect as if they permitted, but did not require, the officer to obtain the approval of the tribunal, and

(*b*) paragraph 31 (appeal) has effect as if it permitted an appeal on any grounds, but the parent undertaking may not appeal against a requirement in the notice to produce any document that forms part of the statutory records of the parent undertaking or any of its subsidiary undertakings][1].

(6) Where a third party notice or a notice under paragraph 5 is given to the parent undertaking for the purpose of checking the tax position of one or more subsidiary undertakings, the parent undertaking may not appeal against a requirement in the notice to produce any document that forms part of the statutory records of the parent undertaking or any of its subsidiary undertakings.[2]

(7) In this paragraph "parent undertaking", "subsidiary undertaking" and "undertaking" have the same meaning as in the Companies Acts (see sections 1161 and 1162 of, and Schedule 7 to, the Companies Act 2006 (c 46)).

Commencement—Finance Act 2008, Schedule 36 (Appointed Day and Savings) Order, SI 2009/404 art 2 (appointed day for the coming into force of Sch 36 is 1 April 2009).

HMRC Manuals—Compliance Handbook Manual, CH23740 (HMRC inspection powers: groups of undertakings).
CH23760–23780 (notice about the parent and its subsidiaries).
CH23900 (HMRC inspection powers: identity unknown notice).
CH225510–225530 (HMRC inspection powers – how to do a compliance check: guidance on groups of undertakings).

Amendments—[1] In sub-para (2), words substituted for the words "paragraph 2" and words at the end inserted, sub-paras (4), (4A) substituted for previous sub-para (4), words in sub-para (5) substituted for the words ", sub-paragraph (3) of that paragraph (approval of tribunal) does not apply", and sub-para (6) repealed, by FA 2009 s 95, Sch 47 para 10 with effect from 21 July 2009. Sub-para (4) previously read as follows—

"(4) Where a third party notice is given to the parent undertaking for the purpose of checking the tax position of one or more subsidiary undertakings—

(*a*) paragraphs 3(1) and 4(1) (approval etc of notices and copying third party notices to taxpayer) do not apply to the notice, but

(*b*) paragraph 21 (restrictions on giving taxpayer notice where taxpayer has made tax return) applies as if the notice was a taxpayer notice or taxpayer notices given to the subsidiary undertaking or each of the subsidiary undertakings.".

Prospective amendments—In sub-para (4A)(*c*), words "paragraphs 21 and 21A" to be substituted for the words "paragraph 21" and word "apply" to be substituted for the word "applies" by FA 2009 s 96, Sch 48 para 12 with effect from a date to be appointed.

Change of ownership of companies

36— (1) Sub-paragraph (2) applies where it appears to the Commissioners that—

(*a*) there has been a change in the ownership of a company, and

(*b*) in connection with that change a person ("the seller") may be or become liable to be assessed and charged to corporation tax under section 767A or 767AA of ICTA.

(2) Paragraph 21 (restrictions on giving taxpayer notice where taxpayer has made tax return) does not apply in relation to a taxpayer notice given to the seller.

(3) Section 769 of ICTA applies for the purposes of determining when there has been a change in the ownership of a company.

HMRC Manuals—Compliance Handbook Manual, CH23520 (HMRC inspection powers: specific rules regarding taxpayer notice).

Partnerships

37— (1) This paragraph applies where a business is carried on by two or more persons in partnership.

[(2) Where, in respect of a chargeable period, any of the partners has—

(*a*) made a tax return under section 12AA of TMA 1970 (partnership returns), or

(*b*) made a claim or election in accordance with section 42(6)(*b*) of TMA 1970 (partnership claims and elections),

paragraph 21 (restrictions where taxpayer has made tax return) has effect as if that return, claim or election had been made by each of the partners.][1]

(3) Where a third party notice is given …[1] for the purpose of checking the tax position of more than one of the partners (in their capacity as such), [—

(*a*) paragraph 2(2)][1] only requires the notice to state this and give a name in which the partnership is registered for any purpose[, and

(*b*) the references in paragraph 3(5) to naming the taxpayer are to making that statement and naming the partnership][1].

(4) In relation to such a notice [given to a person other than one of the partners][1]—

(*a*) in paragraphs 3 and 4 (approval etc of notices and copying third party notices to taxpayer), the references to the taxpayer have effect as if they were references to at least one of the partners, and

(*b*) in paragraph 30(2) (no appeal in relation to taxpayer's statutory records), the reference to the taxpayer has effect as if it were a reference to [any of the partners in the partnership][1].

[(5) In relation to a third party notice given to one of the partners for the purpose of checking the tax position of one or more of the other partners (in their capacity as such)—

(*a*) in paragraph 3 (approval etc of notices), sub-paragraphs (1) and (3)(*e*) do not apply,

(*b*) paragraph 4(1) (copying third party notices to taxpayer) does not apply,

(*c*) paragraph 30(1) (appeal) has effect as if it permitted an appeal on any grounds, and

(*d*) in paragraph 30(2) (no appeal in relation to taxpayer's statutory records), the reference to the taxpayer has effect as if it were a reference to any of the partners in the partnership.][1]

(6) Where a notice is given under paragraph 5 to one of the partners for the purpose of checking the tax position of one or more of the other partners whose identities are not known to the officer giving the notice[—

(*a*) sub-paragraphs (3) and (4) of that paragraph (approval of tribunal) have effect as if they permitted, but did not require, the officer to obtain the approval of the tribunal, and

(*b*) paragraph 31 (appeal) has effect as if it permitted an appeal on any grounds, but the partner to whom the notice is given may not appeal against a requirement in the notice to produce any document that forms part of that partner's statutory records.][1]

(7) Where a third party notice or a notice under paragraph 5 is given to one of the partners for the purpose of checking the tax position of one or more of the other partners, that partner may not appeal against a requirement in the notice to produce any document that forms part of that partner's statutory records.[1]

Commencement—Finance Act 2008, Schedule 36 (Appointed Day and Savings) Order, SI 2009/404 art 2 (appointed day for the coming into force of Sch 36 is 1 April 2009).

HMRC Manuals—Compliance Handbook Manual, CH23520 (HMRC inspection powers: specific rules regarding taxpayer notice).
CH23620 (HMRC inspection powers: specific rules regarding third party notice).
CH23680–23720 (HMRC inspection powers: notices given to partners).
CH23900 (HMRC inspection powers: identity unknown notice).
CH225540–225570 (HMRC inspection powers – how to do a compliance check: guidance on partnerships).

Amendments—[1] The following amendments made by FA 2009 s 95, Sch 47 para 11 with effect from 21 July 2009—

- sub-paras (2), (5) substituted;
- in sub-para (3) words "to any person (other than one of the partners)" repealed, words substituted for the words "paragraph 2", and para (*b*) and the preceding word "and" inserted;
- in sub-para (4) words inserted, and words substituted for the words "each of the partners";
- in sub-para (6) words substituted for the words ", sub-paragraph (3) of that paragraph (approval of tribunal) does not apply";
- sub-para (7) repealed.

Sub-paras (2), (5), previously read as follows—

"(2) If a tax return has been made by any of the partners under section 12AA of TMA 1970 (partnership returns) in respect of a chargeable period—

(*a*) paragraph 21 (restrictions where taxpayer has made tax return) has effect as if that return had been made by each of the partners in respect of that chargeable period, and

(*b*) for the purpose of that paragraph, Condition A is met in relation to a partner if a notice of enquiry has been given, and an enquiry has not been completed, in respect of that return or any other return mentioned in paragraph 21(1) or (2) made by the partner in respect of the chargeable period in question.".

"(5) Where a third party notice is given to one of the partners for the purpose of checking the tax position of one or more of the other partners (in their capacity as such), paragraphs 3(1) and 4(1) (approval etc of notices and copying third party notices to taxpayer) do not apply.".

Prospective amendments—Sub-para (2A) to be inserted by FA 2009 s 96, Sch 48 para 13 with effect from a date to be appointed. New sub-para (2A) to read as follows—

"(2A) Where, in respect of a transaction entered into as purchaser by or on behalf of the members of the partnership, any of the partners has—

(*a*) delivered a land transaction return under Part 4 of FA 2003 (stamp duty land tax), or

(*b*) made a claim under that Part of that Act,

paragraph 21A (restrictions where taxpayer has delivered land transaction return) has effect as if that return had been delivered, or that claim had been made, by each of the partners.".

[Information in connection with herd basis election

37A— (1) This paragraph applies to a taxpayer notice given to a person carrying on a trade in relation to which a herd basis election is made if the notice refers only to information or documents that relate to—

(*a*) the animals kept for the purposes of the trade, or

(*b*) the products of those animals.

(2) Paragraph 21 (restrictions on giving taxpayer notice where taxpayer has made tax return) does not apply in relation to the notice.

(3) "Herd basis election" means an election under Chapter 8 of Part 2 of ITTOIA 2005 or Chapter 8 of Part 3 of CTA 2009.][1]

Amendments—[1] Paras 37A, 37B inserted by FA 2009 s 95, Sch 47 para 12 with effect from 21 July 2009.

[Information from persons liable to counteraction of tax advantage

37B— (1) This paragraph applies to a taxpayer notice given to a person if—

(*a*) it appears to an officer of Revenue and Customs that a counteraction provision may apply to the person by reason of one or more transactions, and

(*b*) the notice refers only to information or documents relating to the transaction (or, if there are two or more transactions, any of them).

(2) Paragraph 21 (restrictions on giving taxpayer notice where taxpayer has made tax return) does not apply in relation to the notice.

(3) "Counteraction provision" means—

(*a*) section 703 of ICTA (company liable to counteraction of corporation tax advantage), or

(*b*) section 684 of ITA 2007 (person liable to counteraction of income tax advantage).][1]

Amendments—[1] Paras 37A, 37B inserted by FA 2009 s 94, Sch 47 para 12 with effect from 21 July 2009.

Application to the Crown

38 This Schedule (other than Part 8) applies to the Crown, but not to Her Majesty in Her private capacity (within the meaning of the Crown Proceedings Act 1947 (c 44)).

Commencement—Finance Act 2008, Schedule 36 (Appointed Day and Savings) Order, SI 2009/404 art 2 (appointed day for the coming into force of Sch 36 is 1 April 2009).

HMRC Manuals—Compliance Handbook Manual, CH21580 (HMRC inspection powers: meaning of "person").

PART 7
PENALTIES

...[2]Penalties [for failure to comply or obstruction][2]

39— (1) This paragraph applies to a person who—

(*a*) fails to comply with an information notice, or

(*b*) deliberately obstructs an officer of Revenue and Customs in the course of an inspection under Part 2 of this Schedule that has been approved by the [tribunal][1].

(2) [The person][2] is liable to a penalty of £300.

(3) The reference in this paragraph to a person who fails to comply with an information notice includes a person who conceals, destroys or otherwise disposes of, or arranges for the concealment, destruction or disposal of, a document in breach of paragraph 42 or 43.

Commentary—*Simon's Taxes* **A6.301A**.

Commencement—Finance Act 2008, Schedule 36 (Appointed Day and Savings) Order, SI 2009/404 art 2 (appointed day for the coming into force of Sch 36 is 1 April 2009).

HMRC Manuals—Compliance Handbook Manual, CH25700 (HMRC inspection powers: information and deliberate obstruction of an inspection).
CH26220 (penalties: failure to comply with an information notice).
CH26240 (deliberate obstruction of a Tribunal approved inspection).
CH26260 (concealing, destroying or disposing of a document).
CH26640 (details of standard penalty).
CH26760 (HMRC inspection powers: two examples relating to penalties).

Amendments—[1] In sub-para (1)(*b*) word substituted for the words "First-tier Tribunal" by the Transfer of Tribunal Functions and Revenue and Customs Appeals Order, SI 2009/56 art 3, Sch 1 para 471 with effect from 1 April 2009.
[2] In heading, word "Standard" repealed and words at the end inserted, and in sub-para (2) words substituted for the words "A person to whom this paragraph applies", by FA 2009 s 95, Sch 47 para 13 with effect from 21 July 2009.

Daily default penalties [for failure to comply or obstruction][1]

40— (1) This paragraph applies if the failure or obstruction mentioned in paragraph 39(1) continues after the date on which a penalty is imposed under that paragraph in respect of the failure or obstruction.

(2) The person is liable to a further penalty or penalties not exceeding £60 for each subsequent day on which the failure or obstruction continues.

Commentary—*Simon's Taxes* **A6.301A**.

Commencement—Finance Act 2008, Schedule 36 (Appointed Day and Savings) Order, SI 2009/404 art 2 (appointed day for the coming into force of Sch 36 is 1 April 2009).

HMRC Manuals—Compliance Handbook Manual, CH26660–26680 (HMRC inspection powers: details regarding daily penalties).
CH26760 (HMRC inspection powers: two examples relating to penalties).

Amendments—[1] In heading words at the end inserted by FA 2009 s 95, Sch 47 para 14 with effect from 21 July 2009.

[Penalties for inaccurate information and documents

40A— (1) This paragraph applies if—

(*a*) in complying with an information notice, a person provides inaccurate information or produces a document that contains an inaccuracy, and

(*b*) condition A or B is met.

(2) Condition A is that the inaccuracy is careless or deliberate.

(3) An inaccuracy is careless if it is due to a failure by the person to take reasonable care.

(4) Condition B is that the person—

(*a*) discovers the inaccuracy some time later, and

(*b*) fails to take reasonable steps to inform HMRC.

(5) The person is liable to a penalty not exceeding £3,000.

(6) Where the information or document contains more than one inaccuracy, a penalty is payable for each inaccuracy.][1]

Amendments—[1] Para 40A inserted by FA 2009 s 95, Sch 47 para 15 with effect from 21 July 2009.

Power to change amount of …[1] penalties

41— (1) If it appears to the Treasury that there has been a change in the value of money since the last relevant date, they may by regulations substitute for the sums for the time being specified in paragraphs 39(2)[, 40(2) and 40A(5)][1] such other sums as appear to them to be justified by the change.

(2) In sub-paragraph (1)[, in relation to a specified sum,][1] "relevant date" means—

(*a*) the date on which this Act is passed, and

(*b*) each date on which the power conferred by that sub-paragraph has been exercised [in relation to that sum][1].

(3) Regulations under this paragraph do not apply to[—

(*a*)][1] any failure or obstruction which began before the date on which they come into force[, or

(*b*) an inaccuracy in any information or document provided to HMRC before that date.][1]

Commencement—Finance Act 2008, Schedule 36 (Appointed Day and Savings) Order, SI 2009/404 art 2 (appointed day for the coming into force of Sch 36 is 1 April 2009).

Amendments—[1] In heading words "standard and daily default" repealed, in sub-para (1) words substituted for the words "and 40(2)", in sub-para (2) words inserted in both places, in sub-para (3) words inserted, para (*b*) and the preceding word "or" inserted, by FA 2009 s 95, Sch 47 para 16 with effect from 21 July 2009.

Concealing, destroying etc documents following information notice

42— (1) A person must not conceal, destroy or otherwise dispose of, or arrange for the concealment, destruction or disposal of, a document that is the subject of an information notice addressed to the person (subject to sub-paragraphs (2) and (3)).

(2) Sub-paragraph (1) does not apply if the person acts after the document has been produced to an officer of Revenue and Customs in accordance with the information notice, unless an officer of Revenue and Customs has notified the person in writing that the document must continue to be available for inspection (and has not withdrawn the notification).

(3) Sub-paragraph (1) does not apply, in a case to which paragraph 8(1) applies, if the person acts after the expiry of the period of 6 months beginning with the day on which a copy of the document was produced in accordance with that paragraph unless, before the expiry of that period, an officer of Revenue and Customs made a request for the original document under paragraph 8(2)(*b*).

Commencement—Finance Act 2008, Schedule 36 (Appointed Day and Savings) Order, SI 2009/404 art 2 (appointed day for the coming into force of Sch 36 is 1 April 2009).

Concealing, destroying etc documents following informal notification

43— (1) A person must not conceal, destroy or otherwise dispose of, or arrange for the concealment, destruction or disposal of, a document if an officer of Revenue and Customs has informed the person that the document is, or is likely, to be the subject of an information notice addressed to that person (subject to sub-paragraph (2)).

(2) Sub-paragraph (1) does not apply if the person acts after—

(*a*) at least 6 months has expired since the person was, or was last, so informed, or

(*b*) an information notice has been given to the person requiring the document to be produced.

Commencement—Finance Act 2008, Schedule 36 (Appointed Day and Savings) Order, SI 2009/404 art 2 (appointed day for the coming into force of Sch 36 is 1 April 2009).

Failure to comply with time limit

44 A failure by a person to do anything required to be done within a limited period of time does not give rise to liability to a penalty under paragraph 39 or 40 if the person did it within such further time, if any, as an officer of Revenue and Customs may have allowed.

Commentary—*Simon's Taxes* **A6.301A**.

Commencement—Finance Act 2008, Schedule 36 (Appointed Day and Savings) Order, SI 2009/404 art 2 (appointed day for the coming into force of Sch 36 is 1 April 2009).

Reasonable excuse

45— (1) Liability to a penalty under paragraph 39 or 40 does not arise if the person satisfies HMRC or [(on an appeal notified to the tribunal) the tribunal][1] that there is a reasonable excuse for the failure or the obstruction of an officer of Revenue and Customs.

(2) For the purposes of this paragraph—

(*a*) an insufficiency of funds is not a reasonable excuse unless attributable to events outside the person's control,

(*b*) where the person relies on any other person to do anything, that is not a reasonable excuse unless the first person took reasonable care to avoid the failure or obstruction, and

(*c*) where the person had a reasonable excuse for the failure or obstruction but the excuse has ceased, the person is to be treated as having continued to have the excuse if the failure is remedied, or the obstruction stops, without unreasonable delay after the excuse ceased.

Commentary—*Simon's Taxes* **A6.301A**.

Commencement—Finance Act 2008, Schedule 36 (Appointed Day and Savings) Order, SI 2009/404 art 2 (appointed day for the coming into force of Sch 36 is 1 April 2009).

HMRC Manuals—Compliance Handbook Manual, CH26320–26440 (HMRC inspection powers: what is and is not a reasonable excuse, with example at CH26420).

Amendments—[1] In sub-para (1) words substituted for the words "(on appeal) the First-tier Tribunal" by the Transfer of Tribunal Functions and Revenue and Customs Appeals Order, SI 2009/56 art 3, Sch 1 para 471 with effect from 1 April 2009.

Assessment of …[1] penalty

46— (1) Where a person becomes liable for a penalty under paragraph 39[, 40 or 40A][1], …[1]—

(*a*) [HMRC may][1] assess the penalty, and

(*b*) [if they do so, they must][1] notify the person.

(2) An assessment of a penalty under paragraph 39 or 40 must be made [within the period of 12 months beginning with the date on which the person became liable to the penalty, subject to sub-paragraph (3)][1].

[(3) In a case involving an information notice against which a person may appeal, an assessment of a penalty under paragraph 39 or 40 must be made within the period of 12 months beginning with the latest of the following—

(*a*) the date on which the person became liable to the penalty,

(*b*) the end of the period in which notice of an appeal against the information notice could have been given, and

(*c*) if notice of such an appeal is given, the date on which the appeal is determined or withdrawn.

(4) An assessment of a penalty under paragraph 40A must be made—

(*a*) within the period of 12 months beginning with the date on which the inaccuracy first came to the attention of an officer of Revenue and Customs, and

(*b*) within the period of 6 years beginning with the date on which the person became liable to the penalty.][1]

Commencement—Finance Act 2008, Schedule 36 (Appointed Day and Savings) Order, SI 2009/404 art 2 (appointed day for the coming into force of Sch 36 is 1 April 2009).

HMRC Manuals—Compliance Handbook Manual, CH26840 (HMRC inspection powers: what the penalty assessment must include).

CH26860 (when to issue a penalty assessment).

Amendments—[1] In the heading, words "standard penalty or daily default" repealed, in sub-para (1) words substituted for the words "or 40", words "HMRC may" repealed and words at the beginning of paras (*a*), (*b*) inserted, in sub-para (2), words substituted for the words "within 12 months of the relevant date", sub-paras (3), (4) substituted for previous sub-para (3), by FA 2009 s 95, Sch 47 para 17 with effect from 21 July 2009. Sub-para (3) previously read as follows—

"(3) In sub-paragraph (2) "the relevant date" means—

(*a*) in a case involving an information notice against which a person may appeal, the later of—

(i) the end of the period in which notice of an appeal against the information notice could have been given, and

(ii) if notice of an appeal against the information notice is given, the date on which the appeal is determined or withdrawn, and

(*b*) in any other case, the date on which the person became liable to the penalty.".

Right to appeal against …[2] penalty

47 A person may appeal …[1] against any of the following decisions of an officer of Revenue and Customs—

(*a*) a decision that a penalty is payable by that person under paragraph 39[, 40 or 40A][2], or

(*b*) a decision as to the amount of such a penalty.

Commentary—*Simon's Taxes* **A6.301A**.

Commencement—Finance Act 2008, Schedule 36 (Appointed Day and Savings) Order, SI 2009/404 art 2 (appointed day for the coming into force of Sch 36 is 1 April 2009).

HMRC Manuals—Compliance Handbook Manual, CH26900 (HMRC inspection powers (penalties): types of appeal and procedures).

Amendments—[1] Words "to the First-tier Tribunal" repealed by the Transfer of Tribunal Functions and Revenue and Customs Appeals Order, SI 2009/56 art 3, Sch 1 para 471 with effect from 1 April 2009.

[2] In the heading, words "standard penalty or daily default" repealed, in sub-para (*a*) words substituted for the words "or 40", by FA 2009 s 95, Sch 47 para 18 with effect from 21 July 2009.

Procedure on appeal against …[2] penalty

48— (1) Notice of an appeal under paragraph 47 must be given—

(*a*) in writing,

(*b*) before the end of the period of 30 days beginning with the date on which the notification under paragraph 46 was issued, and

(*c*) to HMRC.

(2) Notice of an appeal under paragraph 47 must state the grounds of appeal.

(3) On an appeal under paragraph 47(*a*), [that is notified to the tribunal, the tribunal][1] may confirm or cancel the decision.

(4) On an appeal under paragraph 47(*b*), [that is notified to the tribunal, the tribunal][1] may—

(*a*) confirm the decision, or

(*b*) substitute for the decision another decision that the officer of Revenue and Customs had power to make.

(5) Subject to this paragraph and paragraph 49, the provisions of Part 5 of TMA 1970 relating to appeals have effect in relation to appeals under this Part of this Schedule as they have effect in relation to an appeal against an assessment to income tax.

Commencement—Finance Act 2008, Schedule 36 (Appointed Day and Savings) Order, SI 2009/404 art 2 (appointed day for the coming into force of Sch 36 is 1 April 2009).

HMRC Manuals—Compliance Handbook Manual, CH26900 (HMRC inspection powers (penalties): types of appeal and procedures).

Amendments—[1] In sub-paras (3), 4) words substituted for the words "First-tier Tribunal" by the Transfer of Tribunal Functions and Revenue and Customs Appeals Order, SI 2009/56 art 3, Sch 1 para 471 with effect from 1 April 2009.

[2] In the heading, words "standard penalty or daily default" repealed by FA 2009 s 95, Sch 47 para 19 with effect from 21 July 2009.

Enforcement of …[1] penalty

49— (1) A penalty under paragraph 39[, 40 or 40A][1] must be paid—

(*a*) before the end of the period of 30 days beginning with the date on which the notification under paragraph 46 was issued, or

(*b*) if a notice of an appeal against the penalty is given, before the end of the period of 30 days beginning with the date on which the appeal is determined or withdrawn.

(2) A penalty under paragraph 39[, 40 or 40A][1] may be enforced as if it were income tax charged in an assessment and due and payable.

Commentary—*Simon's Taxes* **A6.301A**.

Commencement—Finance Act 2008, Schedule 36 (Appointed Day and Savings) Order, SI 2009/404 art 2 (appointed day for the coming into force of Sch 36 is 1 April 2009).

HMRC Manuals—Compliance Handbook Manual, CH26880 (HMRC inspection powers: when is the penalty payable).

Amendments—[1] In the heading, words "standard penalty or daily default" repealed, in sub-paras (1), (2) words substituted for the words "or 40", by FA 2009 s 95, Sch 47 para 20 with effect from 21 July 2009.

Tax-related penalty

50— (1) This paragraph applies where—

(*a*) a person becomes liable to a penalty under paragraph 39,

(*b*) the failure or obstruction continues after a penalty is imposed under that paragraph,

(*c*) an officer of Revenue and Customs has reason to believe that, as a result of the failure or obstruction, the amount of tax that the person has paid, or is likely to pay, is significantly less than it would otherwise have been,

(*d*) before the end of the period of 12 months beginning with the relevant date (within the meaning of paragraph 46), an officer of Revenue and Customs makes an application to the Upper Tribunal for an additional penalty to be imposed on the person, and

(*e*) the Upper Tribunal decides that it is appropriate for an additional penalty to be imposed.

(2) The person is liable to a penalty of an amount decided by the Upper Tribunal.

(3) In deciding the amount of the penalty, the Upper Tribunal must have regard to the amount of tax which has not been, or is not likely to be, paid by the person.

(4) Where a person becomes liable to a penalty under this paragraph, HMRC must notify the person.

(5) Any penalty under this paragraph is in addition to the penalty or penalties under paragraph 39 or 40.

(6) In the application of the following provisions, no account shall be taken of a penalty under this paragraph—

(*a*) section 97A of TMA 1970 (multiple penalties),

(*b*) paragraph 12(2) of Schedule 24 to FA 2007 (interaction with other penalties), and

(*c*) paragraph 15(1) of Schedule 41 (interaction with other penalties).

Commentary—*Simon's Taxes* **A6.301A**.

Commencement—Finance Act 2008, Schedule 36 (Appointed Day and Savings) Order, SI 2009/404 art 2 (appointed day for the coming into force of Sch 36 is 1 April 2009).

HMRC Manuals—Compliance Handbook Manual, CH26720 (HMRC inspection powers: details regarding tax related penalty).

CH26760 (HMRC inspection powers: two examples relating to penalties).

Enforcement of tax-related penalty

51— (1) A penalty under paragraph 50 must be paid before the end of the period of 30 days beginning with the date on which the notification of the penalty is issued.

(2) A penalty under paragraph 50 may be enforced as if it were income tax charged in an assessment and due and payable.

Commentary—*Simon's Taxes* **A6.301A**.

Commencement—Finance Act 2008, Schedule 36 (Appointed Day and Savings) Order, SI 2009/404 art 2 (appointed day for the coming into force of Sch 36 is 1 April 2009).

Double jeopardy

52 A person is not liable to a penalty under this Schedule in respect of anything in respect of which the person has been convicted of an offence.

Commentary—*Simon's Taxes* **A6.301A**.

Commencement—Finance Act 2008, Schedule 36 (Appointed Day and Savings) Order, SI 2009/404 art 2 (appointed day for the coming into force of Sch 36 is 1 April 2009).

HMRC Manuals—Compliance Handbook Manual, CH26880 (HMRC inspection powers (penalties): details regarding double jeopardy).

PART 8
OFFENCE

Concealing etc documents following information notice

53— (1) A person is guilty of an offence (subject to sub-paragraphs (2) and (3)) if—

(*a*) the person is required to produce a document by an information notice,

(*b*) the [tribunal][1] approved the giving of the notice in accordance with paragraph 3 or 5, and

(*c*) the person conceals, destroys or otherwise disposes of, or arranges for the concealment, destruction or disposal of, that document.

(2) Sub-paragraph (1) does not apply if the person acts after the document has been produced to an officer of Revenue and Customs in accordance with the information notice, unless an officer of Revenue and Customs has notified the person in writing that the document must continue to be available for inspection (and has not withdrawn the notification).

(3) Sub-paragraph (1) does not apply, in a case to which paragraph 8(1) applies, if the person acts after the expiry of the period of 6 months beginning with the day on which a copy of the document was so produced unless, before the expiry of that period, an officer of Revenue and Customs made a request for the original document under paragraph 8(2)(*b*).

Commencement—Finance Act 2008, Schedule 36 (Appointed Day and Savings) Order, SI 2009/404 art 2 (appointed day for the coming into force of Sch 36 is 1 April 2009).

HMRC Manuals—Compliance Handbook Manual, CH27200 (HMRC inspection powers (penalties): criminal proceedings for concealing, destroying or disposing of a document).

CH217000–217400 (HMRC inspection powers – how to do a compliance check: what to do if something is wrong).

Amendments—[1] In sub-para (1)(*b*) word substituted for the words "First-tier Tribunal" by the Transfer of Tribunal Functions and Revenue and Customs Appeals Order, SI 2009/56 art 3, Sch 1 para 471 with effect from 1 April 2009.

Concealing etc documents following informal notification

54— (1) A person is also guilty of an offence (subject to sub-paragraph (2)) if the person conceals, destroys or otherwise disposes of, or arranges for the concealment, destruction or disposal of a document after the person has been informed by an officer of Revenue and Customs in writing that—

(*a*) the document is, or is likely, to be the subject of an information notice addressed to that person, and

(*b*) an officer of Revenue and Customs intends to seek the approval of the [tribunal][1] to the giving of the notice under paragraph 3 or 5 in respect of the document.

(2) A person is not guilty of an offence under this paragraph if the person acts after—

(*a*) at least 6 months has expired since the person was, or was last, so informed, or

(*b*) an information notice has been given to the person requiring the document to be produced.

Commencement—Finance Act 2008, Schedule 36 (Appointed Day and Savings) Order, SI 2009/404 art 2 (appointed day for the coming into force of Sch 36 is 1 April 2009).

Amendments—[1] In sub-para (1)(*b*) word substituted for the words "First-tier Tribunal" by the Transfer of Tribunal Functions and Revenue and Customs Appeals Order, SI 2009/56 art 3, Sch 1 para 471 with effect from 1 April 2009.

Fine or imprisonment

55 A person who is guilty of an offence under this Part of this Schedule is liable—

(*a*) on summary conviction, to a fine not exceeding the statutory maximum, and

(*b*) on conviction on indictment, to imprisonment for a term not exceeding 2 years or to a fine, or both.

Commencement—Finance Act 2008, Schedule 36 (Appointed Day and Savings) Order, SI 2009/404 art 2 (appointed day for the coming into force of Sch 36 is 1 April 2009).

PART 9
MISCELLANEOUS PROVISIONS AND INTERPRETATION

Application of provisions of TMA 1970

56 Subject to the provisions of this Schedule, the following provisions of TMA 1970 apply for the purposes of this Schedule as they apply for the purposes of the Taxes Acts—

(*a*) section 108 (responsibility of company officers),

(*b*) section 114 (want of form), and

(*c*) section 115 (delivery and service of documents).

Commencement—Finance Act 2008, Schedule 36 (Appointed Day and Savings) Order, SI 2009/404 art 2 (appointed day for the coming into force of Sch 36 is 1 April 2009).

HMRC Manuals—Compliance Handbook Manual, CH23440 (HMRC inspection powers: serving notices).
CH23460 (mistakes in a notice).

Regulations under this Schedule

57— (1) Regulations made by the Commissioners or the Treasury under this Schedule are to be made by statutory instrument.

(2) A statutory instrument containing regulations under this Schedule is subject to annulment in pursuance of a resolution of the House of Commons.

Commencement—Finance Act 2008, Schedule 36 (Appointed Day and Savings) Order, SI 2009/404 art 2 (appointed day for the coming into force of Sch 36 is 1 April 2009).

General interpretation

58 In this Schedule—

"checking" includes carrying out an investigation or enquiry of any kind,

"the Commissioners" means the Commissioners for Her Majesty's Revenue and Customs,

"document" includes a part of a document (except where the context otherwise requires),

"enactment" includes subordinate legislation (within the meaning of the Interpretation Act 1978 (c 30)),

"HMRC" means Her Majesty's Revenue and Customs,

"premises" includes—

(*a*) any building or structure,

(*b*) any land, and

(*c*) any means of transport,

"the Taxes Acts" means—

(*a*) TMA 1970,

(*b*) the Tax Acts, and

(*c*) TCGA 1992 and all other enactments relating to capital gains tax, …[1]

"taxpayer", in relation to a taxpayer notice or a third party notice, has the meaning given in paragraph 1(1) or 2(1) (as appropriate) [and][1]

["tribunal" means the First-tier Tribunal or, where determined by or under Tribunal Procedure Rules, the Upper Tribunal.][1]

Commencement—Finance Act 2008, Schedule 36 (Appointed Day and Savings) Order, SI 2009/404 art 2 (appointed day for the coming into force of Sch 36 is 1 April 2009).

HMRC Manuals—Compliance Handbook Manual, CH21660 (HMRC inspection powers: checks).
CH23320–23360 (HMRC inspection powers: what is a "document", part of a document or electronic document).

Amendments—[1] In sub-para (*c*) in the definition of "the Taxes Acts" word "and" at the end repealed; definition of "tribunal" and the preceding word "and" inserted by the Transfer of Tribunal Functions and Revenue and Customs Appeals Order, SI 2009/56 art 3, Sch 1 para 471 with effect from 1 April 2009.

Authorised officer of Revenue and Customs

59 A reference in a provision of this Schedule to an authorised officer of Revenue and Customs is a reference to an officer of Revenue and Customs who is, or is a member of a class of officers who are, authorised by the Commissioners for the purpose of that provision.

Commencement—Finance Act 2008, Schedule 36 (Appointed Day and Savings) Order, SI 2009/404 art 2 (appointed day for the coming into force of Sch 36 is 1 April 2009).

HMRC Manuals—Compliance Handbook Manual, CH260000–262700 (HMRC inspection powers – how to do a compliance check: guidance relating to an authorised officer).
CH21720 (HMRC inspection powers: authorised officer).

Business

60— (1) In this Schedule (subject to regulations under this paragraph), references to carrying on a business include—

(*a*) the letting of property,

(*b*) the activities of a charity, and

(*c*) the activities of a government department, a local authority, a local authority association and any other public authority.

(2) In sub-paragraph (1)—

"charity" means a body of persons or trust established for charitable purposes only,
"local authority" has the meaning given in section 999 of ITA 2007, and
"local authority association" has the meaning given in section 1000 of that Act.

(3) The Commissioners may by regulations provide that for the purposes of this Schedule—

(*a*) the carrying on of an activity specified in the regulations, or

(*b*) the carrying on of such an activity (or any activity) by a person specified in the regulations,

is or is not to be treated as the carrying on of a business.

Commencement—Finance Act 2008, Schedule 36 (Appointed Day and Savings) Order, SI 2009/404 art 2 (appointed day for the coming into force of Sch 36 is 1 April 2009).

HMRC Manuals—Compliance Handbook Manual, CH25200 (HMRC inspection powers: meaning of "carrying on a business").

Chargeable period

61 In this Schedule "chargeable period" means—

(*a*) in relation to income tax or capital gains tax, a tax year, and

(*b*) in relation to corporation tax, an accounting period.

Commencement—Finance Act 2008, Schedule 36 (Appointed Day and Savings) Order, SI 2009/404 art 2 (appointed day for the coming into force of Sch 36 is 1 April 2009).

[Involved third parties

61A— (1) In this Schedule, "involved third party" means a person described in the first column of the Table below.

(2) In this Schedule, in relation to an involved third party, "relevant information", "relevant document" and "relevant tax" have the meaning given in the corresponding entries in that Table.

	Involved third party	*Relevant information and relevant documents*	*Relevant tax*
1	A body approved by an officer of Revenue and Customs for the purpose of paying donations within the meaning of Part 12 of ITEPA 2003 (donations to charity: payroll giving) (see section 714 of that Act)	Information and documents relating to the donations	Income tax
2	A plan manager (see section 696 of ITTOIA 2005 (managers of individual investment plans))	Information and documents relating to the plan, including investments which are or have been held under the plan	Income tax
3	An account provider in relation to a child trust fund (as defined in section 3 of the Child Trust Funds Act 2004)	Information and documents relating to the fund, including investments which are or have been held under the fund	Income tax
4	A person who is or has been registered as a managing agent at Lloyd's in relation to a syndicate of underwriting members of Lloyd's	Information and documents relating to, and to the activities of, the syndicate	Income tax Capital gains tax Corporation tax
5	A person involved (in any capacity) in an insurance business (as defined for the purposes of Part 3 of FA 1994)	Information and documents relating to contracts of insurance entered into in the course of the business	Insurance premium tax
6	A person who makes arrangements for persons to enter into contracts of insurance	Information and documents relating to the contracts	Insurance premium tax

7	A person who— (*a*)is concerned in a business that is not an insurance business (as defined for the purposes of Part 3 of FA 1994), and (*b*)has been involved in the entry into a contract of insurance providing cover for any matter associated with that business	Information and documents relating to the contracts	Insurance premium tax
8	A person who, in relation to a charge to stamp duty reserve tax on an agreement, transfer, issue, appropriation or surrender, is an accountable person (as defined in regulation 2 of the Stamp Duty Reserve Tax Regulations SI 1986/1711 (as amended from time to time))	Information and documents relating to the agreement, transfer, issue, appropriation or surrender	Stamp duty reserve tax
9	A responsible person in relation to an oil field (as defined for the purposes of Part 1 of OTA 1975)	Information and documents relating to the oil field	Petroleum revenue tax
10	A person involved (in any capacity) in subjecting aggregate to exploitation in the United Kingdom (as defined for the purposes of Part 2 of FA 2001) or in connected activities	Information and documents relating to matters in which the person is or has been involved	Aggregates levy
11	A person involved (in any capacity) in making or receiving taxable commodities (as defined for the purposes of Schedule 6 to FA 2000) or in connected activities	Information and documents relating to matters in which the person is or has been involved	Climate change levy
12	A person involved (in any capacity) with any landfill disposal (as defined for the purposes of Part 3 of FA 1996)	Information and documents relating to the disposal	Landfill tax]

Prospective amendments—Para 61A to be inserted by FA 2009 s 96, Sch 48 para 14 with effect from a date to be appointed.

Statutory records

62— (1) For the purposes of this Schedule, information or a document forms part of a person's statutory records if it is information or a document which the person is required to keep and preserve under or by virtue of—

(*a*) the Taxes Acts, or

(*b*) VATA 1994 or any other enactment relating to value added tax charged in accordance with that Act,

subject to the following provisions of this paragraph.

(2) To the extent that any information or document that is required to be kept and preserved under or by virtue of the Taxes Acts—

(*a*) does not relate to the carrying on of a business, and

(*b*) is not also required to be kept or preserved under or by virtue of VATA 1994 or any other enactment relating to value added tax,

it only forms part of a person's statutory records to the extent that the chargeable period or periods to which it relates has or have ended.

(3) Information and documents cease to form part of a person's statutory records when the period for which they are required to be preserved by the enactments mentioned in sub-paragraph (1) has expired.

Commencement—Finance Act 2008, Schedule 36 (Appointed Day and Savings) Order, SI 2009/404 art 2 (appointed day for the coming into force of Sch 36 is 1 April 2009).

HMRC Manuals—Compliance Handbook Manual, CH21700 (HMRC inspection powers: statutory records).

Prospective amendments—Sub-para (1)(*b*) to be substituted, and in sub-para (2) words "any other enactment relating to a tax" to be substituted for the words "VATA 1994 or any other enactment relating to value added tax", by FA 2009 s 95, Sch 48 para 15 with effect from a date to be appointed. Sub-para (1)(*b*), as substituted, to read as follows—

"(*b*) any other enactment relating to a tax,".

Tax

63— (1) In this Schedule, except where the context otherwise requires, "tax" means all or any of the following—

(*a*) income tax,
(*b*) capital gains tax,
(*c*) corporation tax,
(*d*) VAT, and
(*e*) relevant foreign tax,

and references to "a tax" are to be interpreted accordingly.

(2) In this Schedule "corporation tax" includes any amount assessable or chargeable as if it were corporation tax.

(3) In this Schedule "VAT" means—

(*a*) value added tax charged in accordance with VATA 1994,...[1]
(*b*) value added tax charged in accordance with the law of another member State, [and
(*c*) amounts listed in sub-paragraph (3A).][1]

[(3A) Those amounts are—

(*a*) any amount that is recoverable under paragraph 5(2) of Schedule 11 to VATA 1994 (amounts shown on invoices as VAT), and
(*b*) any amount that is treated as VAT by virtue of regulations under section 54 of VATA 1994 (farmers etc).][1]

(4) In this Schedule "relevant foreign tax" means—

(*a*) a tax of a member State, other than the United Kingdom, which is covered by the provisions for the exchange of information under the Directive of the Council of the European Communities dated 19 December 1977 No. 77/799/EEC (as amended from time to time), and
(*b*) any tax or duty which is imposed under the law of a territory in relation to which arrangements having effect by virtue of section 173 of FA 2006 (international tax enforcement arrangements) have been made and which is covered by the arrangements.

Commencement—Finance Act 2008, Schedule 36 (Appointed Day and Savings) Order, SI 2009/404 art 2 (appointed day for the coming into force of Sch 36 is 1 April 2009).

HMRC Manuals—Compliance Handbook Manual, CH275000–275700 (HMRC inspection powers – how to do a compliance check: transitional arrangements for time limits and claims for assessment).
CH280000–283600 (HMRC inspection powers – how to do a compliance check: VAT transition).
CH21540 (HMRC inspection powers: tax position).
CH21560 (meaning of relevant foreign tax).

Amendments—[1] In sub-para (3)(*a*) word "and" repealed, sub-para (3)(*c*) and the preceding word "and" substituted for the words "and includes any amount that is recoverable under paragraph 5(2) of Schedule 11 to VATA 1994 (amounts shown on invoices as VAT)", and sub-para (3A) inserted, by FA 2009 s 95, Sch 47 para 21 with effect from 21 July 2009.

Prospective amendment—In sub-para (1), the following words to be substituted for the words "and (*e*) relevant foreign tax" by FA 2009 s 96(1) with effect from a date to be appointed—

"(*e*) insurance premium tax,
(*f*) inheritance tax,
(*g*) stamp duty land tax,
(*h*) stamp duty reserve tax,
(*i*) petroleum revenue tax,
(*j*) aggregates levy,
(*k*) climate change levy,
(*l*) landfill tax, and
(*m*) relevant foreign tax,".

Tax position

64— (1) In this Schedule, except as otherwise provided, "tax position", in relation to a person, means the person's position as regards any tax, including the person's position as regards—

(*a*) past, present and future liability to pay any tax,
(*b*) penalties and other amounts that have been paid, or are or may be payable, by or to the person in connection with any tax, and
(*c*) claims, elections, applications and notices that have been or may be made or given in connection with [the person's liability to pay][1] any tax,

and references to a person's position as regards a particular tax (however expressed) are to be interpreted accordingly.

(2) References in this Schedule to a person's tax position include, where appropriate, a reference to the person's position as regards any deductions or repayments of tax, or of sums representing tax, that the person is required to make—

(*a*) under PAYE regulations,

(*b*) under Chapter 3 of Part 3 of FA 2004 or regulations made under that Chapter (construction industry scheme), or
(*c*) by or under any other provision of the Taxes Acts.

[(2A) References in this Schedule to a person's tax position also include, where appropriate, a reference to the person's position as regards the withholding by the person of another person's PAYE income (as defined in section 683 of ITEPA 2003).][1]

(3) References in this Schedule to the tax position of a person include the tax position of—
(*a*) a company that has ceased to exist, and
(*b*) an individual who has died.

(4) References in this Schedule to a person's tax position are to the person's tax position at any time or in relation to any period, unless otherwise stated.

Commencement—Finance Act 2008, Schedule 36 (Appointed Day and Savings) Order, SI 2009/404 art 2 (appointed day for the coming into force of Sch 36 is 1 April 2009).

Amendments—[1] In sub-para (1)(*c*) words inserted, and sub-para (2A) inserted, by FA 2009 s 95, Sch 47 para 22 with effect from 21 July 2009.

PART 10

CONSEQUENTIAL PROVISIONS

Commencement—Finance Act 2008, Schedule 36 (Appointed Day and Savings) Order, SI 2009/404 art 2 (appointed day for the coming into force of Sch 36 is 1 April 2009).

TMA 1970

65 TMA 1970 is amended as follows.

66 Omit section 19A (power to call for documents for purposes of enquiries).

67 Omit section 20 (power to call for documents of taxpayer and others).

68— (1) Section 20B (restrictions on powers to call for documents under ss 20 and 20A) is amended as follows.

(2) In the heading, for "**ss 20 and**" substitute "**section**".

(3) In subsection (1)—
(*a*) omit "under section 20(1), (3) or (8A), or",
(*b*) omit "(or, in the case of section 20(3), to deliver or make available)",
(*c*) omit ", or to furnish the particulars in question", and
(*d*) omit "section 20(7) or (8A) or, as the case may be,".

(4) Omit subsections (1A) and (1B).

(5) In subsection (2), omit from the beginning to "taxpayer; and".

(6) In subsection (3)—
(*a*) omit "under section 20(1) or (3) or", and
(*b*) omit "section 20(3) and (4) and".

(7) In subsection (4)—
(*a*) omit "section 20(1) or", and
(*b*) omit ", and as an alternative to delivering documents to comply with a notice under section 20(3) or (8A)".

(8) Omit subsections (5), (6) and (7).

(9) In subsection (8), omit "section 20(3) or (8A) or".

(10) Omit subsections (9) to (14).

69— (1) Section 20BB (falsification etc of documents) is amended as follows.

(2) In subsection (1)(*a*), omit "20 or".

(3) In subsection (2)(*b*), omit "or, in a case within section 20(3) or (8A) above, inspected".

70— (1) Section 20D (interpretation) is amended as follows.

(2) In subsection (2), for "sections 20 and" substitute "section".

(3) Omit subsection (3).

71 In section 29(6)(*c*) (assessment where loss of tax discovered), omit ", whether in pursuance of a notice under section 19A of this Act or otherwise".

72 Omit section 97AA (failure to produce documents under section 19A).

73 In section 98 (penalties), in the Table—
(*a*) in the first column, omit the entry for section 767C of ICTA, and
(*b*) in the second column, omit the entry for section 28(2) of F(No 2)A 1992.

74 *In section 100(2) (exclusions from provisions relating to determination of penalties under the Taxes Acts), insert at the end "or*
(*g*) *Schedule 36 to the Finance Act 2008."*

Annotations—Para 74 repealed by FA 2009 s 109, Sch 57 para 14(*a*) with effect from 21 July 2009.

VAT

75 (1) Section 107A (relevant trustees) is amended as follows.

(2) In subsection (2)(*a*), for ", 95 or 97AA" substitute 'or 95'.

(3) In subsection (3)(*a*), omit "or 97AA(1)(*b*)".

76 In section 118 (interpretation), in the definition of "tax", omit "20,".

77 In Schedule 1A (claims etc not included in returns), omit paragraphs 6 and 6A (power to call for documents for purposes of enquiries and power to appeal against notice to produce documents).

National Savings Bank Act 1971 (c 29)

78 In section 12(3) (secrecy), for the words from "and of section 20(3)" to the end substitute "and of Schedule 36 to the Finance Act 2008 (powers of officers of Revenue and Customs to obtain information and documents and inspect business premises)".

ICTA

79 ICTA is amended as follows.

80 In section 767B (change of company ownership: supplementary), in subsection (4), for "767AA and 767C" substitute "and 767AA".

81 Omit section 767C (change in company ownership: information).

82 In section 769 (rules for ascertaining change in ownership of company)—

(*a*) in subsections (1) and (5), omit ", 767C", and

(*b*) in subsections (2A) and (9), for "767AA or 767C" substitute "or 767AA".

FA 1990

83 In section 125 of FA 1990 (information for tax authorities in other member States)—

(*a*) omit subsections (1) and (2),

(b) in subsection (3), for "the Directive mentioned in subsection (1) above" substitute "the Directive of the Council of the European Communities dated 19 December 1977 No. 77/799/EEC (the "1977 Directive")",

(c) in subsection (4), for "such as is mentioned in subsection (1) above" substitute "which is covered by the provisions for the exchange of information under the 1977 Directive", and

(d) in subsection (6), omit the words from the beginning to "passed,".[1]

Amendments—[1] Sub-paras (*b*)–(*d*) repealed by the Finance Act 2009, Schedule 47 (Consequential Amendments) Order, SI 2009/2035 art 2, Schedule para 60 with effect from 13 August 2009.

Social Security Administration Act 1992 (c 5)

84 In section 110ZA of the Social Security Administration Act 1992 (Class 1, 1A, 1B or 2 contributions: powers to call for documents etc), for subsections (1) and (2) substitute—

"(1) Schedule 36 to the Finance Act 2008 (information and inspection powers) applies for the purpose of checking a person's position as regards relevant contributions as it applies for the purpose of checking a person's tax position, subject to the modifications in subsection (2).

(2) That Schedule applies as if—

(*a*) references to any provision of the Taxes Acts were to any provision of this Act or the Contributions and Benefits Act relating to relevant contributions,

(*b*) references to prejudice to the assessment or collection of tax were to prejudice to the assessment of liability for, and payment of, relevant contributions,

(*c*) the reference to information relating to the conduct of a pending appeal relating to tax were a reference to information relating to the conduct of a pending appeal relating to relevant contributions, and

(*d*) paragraphs 21, 35(4)(*b*), 36 and 37(2) of that Schedule (restrictions on giving taxpayer notice where taxpayer has made tax return) were omitted."

Social Security Administration (Northern Ireland) Act 1992 (c 8)

85 In section 104ZA of the Social Security Administration (Northern Ireland) Act 1992 (Class 1, 1A, 1B or 2 contributions: powers to call for documents etc), for subsections (1) and (2) substitute—

"(1) Schedule 36 to the Finance Act 2008 (information and inspection powers) applies for the purpose of checking a person's position as regards relevant contributions as it applies for the purpose of checking a person's tax position, subject to the modifications in subsection (2).

(2) That Schedule applies as if—

(*a*) references to any provision of the Taxes Acts were to any provision of this Act or the Contributions and Benefits Act relating to relevant contributions,

(*b*) references to prejudice to the assessment or collection of tax were to prejudice to the assessment of liability for, and payment of, relevant contributions,

(*c*) the reference to information relating to the conduct of a pending appeal relating to tax were a reference to information relating to the conduct of a pending appeal relating to relevant contributions, and (*d*) paragraphs 21, 35(4)(*b*), 36 and 37(2) of that Schedule (restrictions on giving taxpayer notice where taxpayer has made tax return) were omitted."

F(No 2)A 1992

86 Omit section 28(1) to (3) (powers of inspection).

VATA 1994

87 (*amends* VATA 1994 Sch 11)

FA 1998

88 In Schedule 18 to FA 1998 (company tax returns), omit paragraphs 27, 28 and 29 (notice to produce documents etc for purposes of enquiry into company tax return, power to appeal against such notices and penalty for failure to produce documents etc).

FA 1999

89 In section 13(5) (gold), omit paragraph (*c*).

Tax Credits Act 2002 (c 21)

90 In section 25 of the Tax Credits Act 2002 (payments of working tax credit by employers), omit subsections (3) and (4).

FA 2006

91 Omit section 174 of FA 2006 (international tax enforcement arrangements: information powers).

Other repeals

92 In consequence of the preceding provisions of this Part of this Schedule, omit the following—

(*a*) section 126 of FA 1988,
(*b*) sections 142(2), (3), (4), (6)(*a*), (7), (8) and (9) and 144(3), (5) and (7) of FA 1989,
(*c*) sections 187 and 255 of, and paragraph 29 of Schedule 19 to, FA 1994,
(*d*) paragraph 6 of Schedule 1 to the Civil Evidence Act 1995 (c 38),
(*e*) paragraph 17 of Schedule 3, paragraph 3 of Schedule 19 and paragraph 2 of Schedule 22 to FA 1996,
(*f*) paragraph 17 of Schedule 3, paragraph 3 of Schedule 19 and paragraph 2 of Schedule 22 to FA 1996,
(*g*) section 115 of, and paragraphs 36 and 42(6) and (7) of Schedule 19 to, FA 1998,
(*h*) section 15(3) of FA 1999,
(*i*) paragraphs 21 and 38(4) of Schedule 29 to FA 2001,
(*j*) section 20 of FA 2006, and
(*k*) paragraph 350 of Schedule 1 to ITA 2007.

SCHEDULE 37

RECORD-KEEPING

Section 115

Commencement—Finance Act 2008, Schedule 37 (Appointed Day) Order, SI 2009/402 (Sch 37 comes into force on 1 April 2009).

TMA 1970

1–3 (See the *Yellow Tax Handbook* for amendments made to TMA 1970)

Commencement—Finance Act 2008, Schedule 37 (Appointed Day) Order, SI 2009/402 (Sch 37 comes into force on 1 April 2009).

VATA 1994

4 Schedule 11 to VATA 1994 (administration, collection and enforcement) is amended as follows.

Commencement—Finance Act 2008, Schedule 37 (Appointed Day) Order, SI 2009/402 (Sch 37 comes into force on 1 April 2009).

5— (1) Paragraph 6 (duty to keep records) is amended as follows.

(2) (*amends* VATA 1994 Sch 11 para 6(3))

(3) (*substitutes* VATA 1994 Sch 11 para 6(4))

Commencement—Finance Act 2008, Schedule 37 (Appointed Day) Order, SI 2009/402 (Sch 37 comes into force on 1 April 2009).

6 (*amends* VATA 1994 Sch 11 para 6A(7))

Commencement—Finance Act 2008, Schedule 37 (Appointed Day) Order, SI 2009/402 (Sch 37 comes into force on 1 April 2009).

FA 1998

7–9 (See the *Yellow Tax Handbook* for amendments made to FA 1998)

Consequential provisions

10 (*amends* FA 1999 s 13(6))

Commencement—Finance Act 2008, Schedule 37 (Appointed Day) Order, SI 2009/402 (Sch 37 comes into force on 1 April 2009).

11 (See the *Yellow Tax Handbook* for amendments made to FA 1995, FA 1996)

SCHEDULE 39

TIME LIMITS FOR ASSESSMENTS, CLAIMS ETC

Section 118

Commencement—Finance Act 2008, Schedule 39 (Appointed Day, Transitional Provision and Savings) Order, SI 2009/403 art 2(2). The appointed day for the coming into force of paras 1–31, 37–66 is 1 April 2010, subject to transitional provisions in SI 2009/403 art 10(2): where art 10 applies the appointed day is 1 April 2012.

TMA 1970

1–15 (See the *Yellow Tax Handbook* for amendments made to TMA 1970)

ICTA

16–26 (See the *Yellow Tax Handbook* for amendments made to TA 1988)

FA 1991

27 (See the *Yellow Tax Handbook* for amendments made to FA 1991)

TCGA 1992

28–31 (See the *Yellow Tax Handbook* for amendments made to TCGA 1992)

VATA 1994

32 VATA 1994 is amended as follows.

Commencement—Finance Act 2008, Schedule 39 (Appointed Day, Transitional Provision and Savings) Order, SI 2009/403 art 2(2). The appointed day for the coming into force of paras 32–36 is 1 April 2009.

33 (*amends* VATA 1994 s 33A(4))

Commencement—Finance Act 2008, Schedule 39 (Appointed Day, Transitional Provision and Savings) Order, SI 2009/403 art 2(2). The appointed day for the coming into force of paras 32–36 is 1 April 2009.
Paragraph 33 is disregarded where, for the purposes of VATA 1994 s 33A, the day on which the supply was made or the acquisition or importation took place was on or before 31 March 2006.

34— (1) Section 77 (assessments: time limits and supplementary assessments) is amended as follows.

(2) (*amends* VATA 1994 s 77(1)(*a*), (*b*))

(3) (*substitutes* VATA 1994 s 77(4)–(4C))

(4) (*amends* VATA 1994 s 77(5))

Commencement—Finance Act 2008, Schedule 39 (Appointed Day, Transitional Provision and Savings) Order, SI 2009/403 art 2(2). The appointed day for the coming into force of paras 32–36 is 1 April 2009.
Paragraph 34 is disregarded where—
– for the purposes of VATA 1994 s 77, the end of the prescribed accounting period or the importation, acquisition or event giving rise to the penalty, as appropriate, occurred on or before 31 March 2006; and
– after a person's death, a sum is assessed as due by reason of some conduct (however described) of the deceased, including a sum due by way of penalty, interest or surcharge, and the date of the death is on or before 31 March 2006 (SI 2009/403 art 4).

35 (*amends* VATA 1994 s 78(11))

Commencement—Finance Act 2008, Schedule 39 (Appointed Day, Transitional Provision and Savings) Order, SI 2009/403 art 2(2). The appointed day for the coming into force of paras 32–36 is 1 April 2009.
Paragraph 35 is disregarded where, for the purposes of a claim under VATA 1994 s 78, the end of the applicable period to which the claim relates was on or before 31 March 2006 (SI 2009/403 art 5).

36 (*amends* VATA 1994 s 80(4))

Commencement—Finance Act 2008, Schedule 39 (Appointed Day, Transitional Provision and Savings) Order, SI 2009/403 art 2(2). The appointed day for the coming into force of paras 32–36 is 1 April 2009.
Paragraph 36 is disregarded where, for the purposes of VATA 1994 s 80, the relevant date is on or before 31 March 2006 (SI 2009/403 art 6).

FA 1998

37–47 (See the *Yellow Tax Handbook* for amendments made to FA 1998)

FA 2002

48 (See the *Yellow Tax Handbook* for amendments made to FA 2002)

ITEPA 2003

49 (See the *Yellow Tax Handbook* for amendments made to ITEPA 2003)

ITTOIA 2005

50–53 (See the *Yellow Tax Handbook* for amendments made to ITTOIA 2005)

ITA 2007

54–62 (See the *Yellow Tax Handbook* for amendments made to ITA 2007)

Consequential amendments

63 (See the *Yellow Tax Handbook* for amendments made to FA 1993 s 178(3))

64 (See the *Yellow Tax Handbook* for amendments made to FA 1994 s 225(3)(*b*))

65 In consequence of the preceding provisions of this Schedule, omit—

(*a*) section 149(4)(*a*)(i) and (ii) of FA 1989,
(*b*) paragraphs 4 and 6 of Schedule 21 to FA 1996,
(*c*) section 47(10) of FA 1997,
(*d*) paragraph 18 of Schedule 19 to FA 1998, and
(*e*) section 91(6)(*b*) of FA 2007.

Saving

66 (See the *Yellow Tax Handbook*)

SCHEDULE 40

PENALTIES: AMENDMENTS OF SCHEDULE 24 TO FA 2007

Section 122

Commencement—Finance Act 2008, Schedule 40 (Appointed Day, Transitional Provisions and Consequential Amendments) Order, SI 2009/571 art 2 (the appointed day for the purposes of this Schedule is 1 April 2009).

1 Schedule 24 to FA 2007 (penalties for errors) is amended as follows.

Commencement—Finance Act 2008, Schedule 40 (Appointed Day, Transitional Provisions and Consequential Amendments) Order, SI 2009/571 art 2 (the appointed day for the purposes of this Schedule is 1 April 2009).

2— (1) Paragraph 1 (error in taxpayer's document) is amended as follows.

(2) (*amends* FA 2007 Sch 24 para 1(2))

(3) (*amends* FA 2007 Sch 24 para 1(3))

(4)–(6) (*amend* FA 2007 Sch 24 para 1 Table)

(7) (*inserts* FA 2007 Sch 24 para 1(5))

Commencement—Finance Act 2008, Schedule 40 (Appointed Day, Transitional Provisions and Consequential Amendments) Order, SI 2009/571 art 2 (the appointed day for the purposes of this Schedule is 1 April 2009).

3 (*inserts* FA 2007 Sch 24 para 1A)

Commencement—Finance Act 2008, Schedule 40 (Appointed Day, Transitional Provisions and Consequential Amendments) Order, SI 2009/571 art 2 (the appointed day for the purposes of this Schedule is 1 April 2009).

4— (1) Paragraph 2 (under-assessment by HMRC) is amended as follows.

(2) (*amends* FA 2007 Sch 24 para 2(1))

(3) (*substitutes* FA 2007 Sch 24 para 2(3))

Commencement—Finance Act 2008, Schedule 40 (Appointed Day, Transitional Provisions and Consequential Amendments) Order, SI 2009/571 art 2 (the appointed day for the purposes of this Schedule is 1 April 2009).

5— (1) Paragraph 3 (degrees of culpability) is amended as follows

(2) (*amends* FA 2007 Sch 24 para 3(1))

(3) (*amends* FA 2007 Sch 24 para 3(2))

Commencement—Finance Act 2008, Schedule 40 (Appointed Day, Transitional Provisions and Consequential Amendments) Order, SI 2009/571 art 2 (the appointed day for the purposes of this Schedule is 1 April 2009).

6 (*inserts* FA 2007 Sch 24 para 4(1A))

Commencement—Finance Act 2008, Schedule 40 (Appointed Day, Transitional Provisions and Consequential Amendments) Order, SI 2009/571 art 2 (the appointed day for the purposes of this Schedule is 1 April 2009).

7 (*amends* FA 2007 Sch 24 para 5(1))

Commencement—Finance Act 2008, Schedule 40 (Appointed Day, Transitional Provisions and Consequential Amendments) Order, SI 2009/571 art 2 (the appointed day for the purposes of this Schedule is 1 April 2009).

8— (1) Paragraph 6 (potential lost revenue: multiple errors) is amended as follows.

(2) (*amends* FA 2007 Sch 24 para 6(1), (2))

(3) (*amends* FA 2007 Sch 24 para 6(5))

Commencement—Finance Act 2008, Schedule 40 (Appointed Day, Transitional Provisions and Consequential Amendments) Order, SI 2009/571 art 2 (the appointed day for the purposes of this Schedule is 1 April 2009).

9— (1) Paragraph 9 (reductions for disclosure) is amended as follows.

(2) (*inserts* FA 2007 Sch 24 para 9(A1))

(3) (*amends* FA 2007 Sch 24 para 9(1))

(4) (*amends* FA 2007 Sch 24 para 9(2)(*a*))

Commencement—Finance Act 2008, Schedule 40 (Appointed Day, Transitional Provisions and Consequential Amendments) Order, SI 2009/571 art 2 (the appointed day for the purposes of this Schedule is 1 April 2009).

10 (*amends* FA 2007 Sch 24 para 11(1))

Commencement—Finance Act 2008, Schedule 40 (Appointed Day, Transitional Provisions and Consequential Amendments) Order, SI 2009/571 art 2 (the appointed day for the purposes of this Schedule is 1 April 2009).

11— (1) Paragraph 12 (interaction with other penalties) is amended as follows.

(2) (*amends* FA 2007 Sch 24 para 12(2))

(3) (*inserts* FA 2007 Sch 24 para 12(4))

(4) (*amends* FA 2007 Sch 24 para 12 heading)

Commencement—Finance Act 2008, Schedule 40 (Appointed Day, Transitional Provisions and Consequential Amendments) Order, SI 2009/571 art 2 (the appointed day for the purposes of this Schedule is 1 April 2009).

12— (1) Paragraph 13 (assessment) is amended as follows.

(2) (*amends* FA 2007 Sch 24 para 13(1))

(3) (*inserts* FA 2007 Sch 24 para 13(1A))

(4) (*amends* FA 2007 Sch 24 para 13(3))

(5) (*amends* FA 2007 Sch 24 para 13(4))

Commencement—Finance Act 2008, Schedule 40 (Appointed Day, Transitional Provisions and Consequential Amendments) Order, SI 2009/571 art 2 (the appointed day for the purposes of this Schedule is 1 April 2009).

13 (*amends* FA 2007 Sch 24 para 15)

Commencement—Finance Act 2008, Schedule 40 (Appointed Day, Transitional Provisions and Consequential Amendments) Order, SI 2009/571 art 2 (the appointed day for the purposes of this Schedule is 1 April 2009).

14 (*substitutes* FA 2007 Sch 24 para 16)

Commencement—Finance Act 2008, Schedule 40 (Appointed Day, Transitional Provisions and Consequential Amendments) Order, SI 2009/571 art 2 (the appointed day for the purposes of this Schedule is 1 April 2009).

15 (*amends* FA 2007 Sch 24 para 18(3))

Commencement—Finance Act 2008, Schedule 40 (Appointed Day, Transitional Provisions and Consequential Amendments) Order, SI 2009/571 art 2 (the appointed day for the purposes of this Schedule is 1 April 2009).

16— (1) Paragraph 19 (companies: officers' liability) is amended as follows.

(2) (*amends* FA 2007 Sch 24 para 19(1))

(3) (*substitutes* FA 2007 Sch 24 para 19(5))

Commencement—Finance Act 2008, Schedule 40 (Appointed Day, Transitional Provisions and Consequential Amendments) Order, SI 2009/571 art 2 (the appointed day for the purposes of this Schedule is 1 April 2009).

17 (*amends* FA 2007 Sch 24 para 21)

Commencement—Finance Act 2008, Schedule 40 (Appointed Day, Transitional Provisions and Consequential Amendments) Order, SI 2009/571 art 2 (the appointed day for the purposes of this Schedule is 1 April 2009).

18 (*amends* FA 2007 Sch 24 para 22)

Commencement—Finance Act 2008, Schedule 40 (Appointed Day, Transitional Provisions and Consequential Amendments) Order, SI 2009/571 art 2 (the appointed day for the purposes of this Schedule is 1 April 2009).

19 (*inserts* FA 2007 Sch 24 para 23A)

Commencement—Finance Act 2008, Schedule 40 (Appointed Day, Transitional Provisions and Consequential Amendments) Order, SI 2009/571 art 2 (the appointed day for the purposes of this Schedule is 1 April 2009).

20— (1) Paragraph 28 (interpretation) is amended as follows.

(2) (*inserts* FA 2007 Sch 24 para 28(*c*)(iv))

(3) (*inserted* FA 2007 Sch 24 para 28(*da*); repealed by FA 2009 s 109, Sch 57 para 14(*b*).)

(4) (*amends* FA 2007 Sch 24 para 28(*f*))

(5) (*inserts* FA 2007 Sch 24 para 28(*fa*))

Commencement—Finance Act 2008, Schedule 40 (Appointed Day, Transitional Provisions and Consequential Amendments) Order, SI 2009/571 art 2 (the appointed day for the purposes of this Schedule is 1 April 2009).

21 In consequence of this Schedule the following provisions are omitted—

(*a*)–(*g*) …

(*h*) paragraphs 98 to 100 of Schedule 6 to FA 2000,

(*i*) in Schedule 6 to FA 2001, paragraphs 7 to 9, and in paragraph 9A(5), paragraph (*b*) and the "or" before it,

(*j*) section 133(2) to (4) of FA 2002,

(*k*) in FA 2003—

(i) section 192(8), and

(ii) paragraph 8 of Schedule 10 to FA 2003, and

(*l*) section 295(4)(*a*) of FA 2004.

Note—Omitted paras not relevant to this work.

Commencement—Finance Act 2008, Schedule 40 (Appointed Day, Transitional Provisions and Consequential Amendments) Order, SI 2009/571 art 2 (the appointed day for the purposes of this Schedule is 1 April 2009).

This para repeals the provisions listed below only in so far as those provisions relate to conduct involving dishonesty which relates to—

(a) an inaccuracy in a document, or

(b) a failure to notify HMRC of an under-assessment by HMRC.

Those provisions referred to above are—

(a) in FA 1994—
  (i) section 8; and
  (ii) Sch 7 paras 12, 13;

(b) FA 1996 Sch 5 paras 18, 19;

(c) FA 2000 Sch 6 paras 98, 99;

(d) in FA 2001 Sch 6—
  (i) paras 7, 8; and
  (ii) para 9A(5)(*b*);

(e) FA 2002 s 133(2)–(4).

SCHEDULE 41

PENALTIES: FAILURE TO NOTIFY AND CERTAIN VAT AND EXCISE WRONGDOING

Section 123

Failure to notify etc

1 A penalty is payable by a person (P) where P fails to comply with an obligation specified in the Table below (a "relevant obligation").

Tax to which obligation relates	*Obligation*
Income tax and capital gains tax	Obligation under section 7 of TMA 1970 (obligation to give notice of liability to income tax or capital gains tax).
Corporation tax	Obligation under paragraph 2 of Schedule 18 to FA 1998 (obligation to give notice of chargeability to corporation tax).
Value added tax	Obligations under paragraphs 5, 6, 7 and 14(2) and (3) of Schedule 1 to VATA 1994 (obligations to notify liability to register and notify material change in nature of supplies made by person exempted from registration).
Value added tax	Obligation under paragraph 3 of Schedule 2 to VATA 1994 (obligation to notify liability to register).
Value added tax	Obligations under paragraphs 3 and 8(2) of Schedule 3 to VATA 1994 (obligations to notify liability to register and notify acquisition affecting exemption from registration).
Value added tax	Obligations under paragraphs 3, 4 and 7(2) and (3) of Schedule 3A to VATA 1994 (obligations to notify liability to register and notify relevant change in supplies made by person exempted from registration).
Value added tax	Obligation under regulations under paragraph 2(4) of Schedule 11 to VATA 1994 (obligation to give notification of acquisition of goods from another member State).
Insurance premium tax	Obligations under section 53(1) and (2) of FA 1994 (obligations to register in respect of receipt of premiums in course of taxable business and notify intended receipt of premiums in course of taxable business).
Insurance premium tax	Obligations under section 53AA(1) and (3) of FA 1994 (obligations to register as taxable intermediary and notify intention to charge taxable intermediary's fees).

Tax to which obligation relates	*Obligation*
Aggregates levy	Obligations under section 24(2) of, and paragraph 1 of Schedule 4 to, FA 2001 (obligations to register in respect of carrying out of taxable activities and notify intention of carrying out such activities).
Climate change levy	Obligations under paragraphs 53 and 55 of Schedule 6 to FA 2000 (obligations to register in respect of taxable supplies and notify intention to make, or have made, taxable supply).
Landfill tax	Obligations under section 47(2) and (3) of FA 1996 (obligations to register in respect of carrying out of taxable activities and notify intention of carrying out such activities).
Air passenger duty	Obligation under section 33(4) of FA 1994 (obligation to give notice of liability to register to operate chargeable aircraft).
[Alcohol liquor duties	Obligation to be authorised and registered to obtain and use duty stamps under regulations under paragraph 4 of Schedule 2A to ALDA 1979 (duty stamps).
Alcohol liquor duties	Obligations under sections 12(1), 47(1), 54(2), 55(2) and 62(2) of ALDA 1979 (obligations to hold licence to manufacture spirits, register to brew beer, hold licence to produce wine or made-wine and register to make cider).
Alcohol liquor duties	Obligation to have plant and processes approved for the manufacture of spirits under regulations under section 15(6) of ALDA 1979 (distillers' warehouses).
Tobacco products duty	Obligation to manufacture tobacco products only on premises registered under regulations under section 7 of TPDA 1979 (management of tobacco products duty).
Hydrocarbon oil duties	Obligation to make entry of premises intended to be used for production of oil under regulations under section 21 of HODA 1979 (administration and enforcement).
Excise duties	Obligation to receive, deposit or hold duty suspended excise goods only in premises approved under regulations under section 92 of CEMA 1979 (approval of warehouses).
Excise duties	Obligation to receive duty suspended excise goods only if approved or registered (or approved and registered) as a REDS or an Occasional Importer under regulations under section 100G or 100H of CEMA 1979 (registered excise dealers and shippers etc).
Excise duties	Obligation to receive, deposit or hold duty suspended excise goods only if approved or registered (or approved and registered) as a registered owner, a duty representative, a registered mobile operator or a fiscal representative of a registered mobile operator or an authorised warehousekeeper under regulations under section 100G or 100H of CEMA 1979 (registered excise dealers and shippers etc).
General betting duty	Obligations under paragraph 4(1) to (3) of Schedule 1 to BGDA 1981 (obligation to notify intention to carry on general betting business and make entry of, or notify, premises).

Tax to which obligation relates	*Obligation*
Pool betting duty	Obligations under paragraphs 4(2) and 5(1) of Schedule 1 to BGDA 1981 (obligation to make entry and hold permit for carrying on pool betting business).
Bingo duty	Obligations under paragraph 10(1) and (1A) of Schedule 3 to BGDA 1981 (obligation to notify and register in respect of bingo-promotion).
Lottery duty	Obligation under section 29(1) of FA 1993 (obligation to register in respect of promotion of lotteries).
Gaming duty	Obligations under paragraphs 3 and 6 of Schedule 1 to FA 1997 (obligations to register in respect of gaming and to notify premises).
Remote gaming duty	Obligation to register under regulations under section 26J of BGDA 1981 (facilities for remote gaming).
Amusement machine licence duty	Obligation under section 21 of BGDA 1981 (obligation to licence amusement machine or premises on which amusement machine is provided for play).

Commencement—Finance Act 2008, Schedule 41 (Appointed Day and Transitional Provisions) Order, SI 2009/511 art 2 (the appointed day for the purposes of this Schedule is 1 April 2010).
Cross reference—FA 2009 s 94 (Publishing details of deliberate tax defaulters).

Issue of invoice showing VAT by unauthorised person

2— (1) A penalty is payable by a person (P) where P makes an unauthorised issue of an invoice showing VAT.

(2) P makes an unauthorised issue of an invoice showing VAT if P—

(*a*) is an unauthorised person, and

(*b*) issues an invoice showing an amount as being value added tax or as including an amount attributable to value added tax.

(3) In sub-paragraph (2)(*a*) "an unauthorised person" means anyone other than—

(*a*) a person registered under VATA 1994,

(*b*) a body corporate treated for the purposes of section 43 of that Act as a member of a group,

(*c*) a person treated as a taxable person under regulations under section 46(4) of that Act,

(*d*) a person authorised to issue an invoice under regulations under paragraph 2(12) of Schedule 11 to that Act, or

(*e*) a person acting on behalf of the Crown.

(4) This paragraph has effect in relation to any invoice which—

(*a*) for the purposes of any provision made under subsection (3) of section 54 of VATA 1994 shows an amount as included in the consideration for any supply, and

(*b*) either fails to comply with the requirements of any regulations under that section or is issued by a person who is not for the time being authorised to do so for the purposes of that section,

as if the person issuing the invoice were an unauthorised person and that amount were shown on the invoice as an amount attributable to value added tax.

Commencement—Finance Act 2008, Schedule 41 (Appointed Day and Transitional Provisions) Order, SI 2009/511 art 2 (the appointed day for the purposes of this Schedule is 1 April 2010).
Cross reference—FA 2009 s 94 (Publishing details of deliberate tax defaulters).
FA 2009 Sch 53 Part 2 (late payment interest start date).

Putting product to use that attracts higher duty

3— (1) A penalty is payable by a person ("P") where P does an act which enables HMRC to assess an amount as duty due from P under any of the provisions in the Table below (a "relevant excise provision").

Provision under which assessment may be made	*Subject-matter of provision*
ALDA 1979 section 8(4)	Spirits for use for medical or scientific purposes.
ALDA 1979 section 10(4)	Spirits for use in art or manufacture.

Provision under which assessment may be made	*Subject-matter of provision*
ALDA 1979 section 11(3)	Imported goods not for human consumption containing spirits.
HODA 1979 section 10(3)	Duty-free oil.
HODA 1979 section 13(1A)	Rebated heavy oil.
HODA 1979 section 13AB(1)(a) or (2)(a)	Kerosene.
HODA 1979 section 13AD(2)	Kerosene.
HODA 1979 section 13ZB(1)	Heating oil etc
HODA 1979 section 14(4)	Light oil for use as furnace oil.
HODA 1979 section 14D(1)	Rebated biodiesel or bioblend.
HODA 1979 section 14F(2)	Rebated heavy oil or bioblend.
HODA 1979 section 23(1B)	Road fuel gas on which no duty paid.
HODA 1979 section 24(4A)	Duty-free and rebated oil.

(2) A penalty is payable by a person ("P") where P supplies a product knowing that it will be used in a way which enables HMRC to assess an amount as duty due from another person under a relevant excise provision.

Commencement—Finance Act 2008, Schedule 41 (Appointed Day and Transitional Provisions) Order, SI 2009/511 art 2 (the appointed day for the purposes of this Schedule is 1 April 2010).
Cross reference—FA 2009 s 94 (Publishing details of deliberate tax defaulters).

Handling goods subject to unpaid excise duty

4— (1) A penalty is payable by a person (P) where—

(*a*) after the excise duty point for any goods which are chargeable with a duty of excise, P acquires possession of the goods or is concerned in carrying, removing, depositing, keeping or otherwise dealing with the goods, and

(*b*) at the time when P acquires possession of the goods or is so concerned, a payment of duty on the goods is outstanding and has not been deferred.

(2) In sub-paragraph (1)—

"excise duty point" has the meaning given by section 1 of F(No 2)A 1992, and
"goods" has the meaning given by section 1(1) of CEMA 1979.

Commencement—Finance Act 2008, Schedule 41 (Appointed Day and Transitional Provisions) Order, SI 2009/511 art 2 (the appointed day for the purposes of this Schedule is 1 April 2010).
Cross reference—FA 2009 s 94 (Publishing details of deliberate tax defaulters).

Degrees of culpability

5— (1) A failure by P to comply with a relevant obligation is—

(*a*) "deliberate and concealed" if the failure is deliberate and P makes arrangements to conceal the situation giving rise to the obligation, and

(*b*) "deliberate but not concealed" if the failure is deliberate but P does not make arrangements to conceal the situation giving rise to the obligation.

(2) The making by P of an unauthorised issue of an invoice showing VAT is—

(*a*) "deliberate and concealed" if it is done deliberately and P makes arrangements to conceal it, and

(*b*) "deliberate but not concealed" if it is done deliberately but P does not make arrangements to conceal it.

(3) The doing by P of an act which enables HMRC to assess an amount of duty as due from P under a relevant excise provision is—

(*a*) "deliberate and concealed" if it is done deliberately and P makes arrangements to conceal it, and

(*b*) "deliberate but not concealed" if it is done deliberately but P does not make arrangements to conceal it.

(4) P's acquiring possession of, or being concerned in dealing with, goods on which a payment of duty is outstanding and has not been deferred is—

(*a*) "deliberate and concealed" if it is done deliberately and P makes arrangements to conceal it, and (*b*) "deliberate but not concealed" if it is done deliberately but P does not make arrangements to conceal it.

Commencement—Finance Act 2008, Schedule 41 (Appointed Day and Transitional Provisions) Order, SI 2009/511 art 2 (the appointed day for the purposes of this Schedule is 1 April 2010).

Amount of penalty: standard amount

6— (1) The penalty payable under any of paragraphs 1, 2, 3(1) and 4 is—

(*a*) for a deliberate and concealed act or failure, 100% of the potential lost revenue,
(*b*) for a deliberate but not concealed act or failure, 70% of the potential lost revenue, and
(*c*) for any other case, 30% of the potential lost revenue.

(2) The penalty payable under paragraph 3(2) is 100% of the potential lost revenue.

(3) Paragraphs 7 to 11 define "the potential lost revenue".

Commencement—Finance Act 2008, Schedule 41 (Appointed Day and Transitional Provisions) Order, SI 2009/511 art 2 (the appointed day for the purposes of this Schedule is 1 April 2010).

Potential lost revenue

7— (1) "The potential lost revenue" in respect of a failure to comply with a relevant obligation is as follows.

(2) In the case of a relevant obligation relating to income tax or capital gains tax and a tax year, the potential lost revenue is so much of any income tax or capital gains tax to which P is liable in respect of the tax year as by reason of the failure is unpaid on 31 January following the tax year.

(3) In the case of a relevant obligation relating to corporation tax and an accounting period, the potential lost revenue is (subject to sub-paragraph (4)) so much of any corporation tax to which P is liable in respect of the accounting period as by reason of the failure is unpaid 12 months after the end of the accounting period.

(4) In computing the amount of that tax no account shall be taken of any relief under subsection (4) of section 419 of ICTA (relief in respect of repayment etc of loan) which is deferred under subsection (4A) of that section.

(5) In any case where the failure is a failure to comply with the obligation under paragraph 2(4) of Schedule 11 to VATA 1994, the potential lost revenue is the value added tax on the acquisition to which the failure relates.

(6) In the case of any other relevant obligation relating to value added tax, the potential lost revenue is the amount of the value added tax (if any) for which P is, or but for any exemption from registration would be, liable for the relevant period (see sub-paragraph (7)), but subject to sub-paragraph (8).

(7) "The relevant period" is—

(*a*) in relation to a failure to comply with paragraph 14(2) or (3) of Schedule 1 to VATA 1994, paragraph 8(2) of Schedule 3 to that Act or paragraph 7(2) or (3) of Schedule 3A to that Act, the period beginning on the date of the change or alteration concerned and ending on the date on which HMRC received notification of, or otherwise became fully aware of, that change or alteration, and
(*b*) in relation to a failure to comply with an obligation under any other provision, the period beginning on the date with effect from which P is required in accordance with that provision to be registered and ending on the date on which HMRC received notification of, or otherwise became fully aware of, P's liability to be registered.

(8) But the amount mentioned in sub-paragraph (6) is reduced—

(*a*) if the amount of the tax mentioned in that sub-paragraph includes tax on an acquisition of goods from another member State, by the amount of any VAT which HMRC are satisfied has been paid on the supply in pursuance of which the goods were acquired under the law of that member State, and
(*b*) if the amount of that tax includes tax chargeable by virtue of section 7(4) of VATA 1994 on a supply, by the amount of any VAT which HMRC are satisfied has been paid on that supply under the law of another member State.

(9) In the case of a relevant obligation under any provision relating to insurance premium tax, aggregates levy, climate change levy, landfill tax or air passenger duty, the potential lost revenue is the amount of the tax (if any) for which P is liable for the period—

(*a*) beginning on the date with effect from which P is required in accordance with that provision to be registered, and
(*b*) ending on the date on which HMRC received notification of, or otherwise became fully aware of, P's liability to be registered.

(10) In the case of a failure to comply with a relevant obligation relating to any other tax, the potential lost revenue is the amount of any tax which is unpaid by reason of the failure.

Commencement—Finance Act 2008, Schedule 41 (Appointed Day and Transitional Provisions) Order, SI 2009/511 art 2 (the appointed day for the purposes of this Schedule is 1 April 2010).
Cross reference—FA 2009 s 94 (Publishing details of deliberate tax defaulters).

8 In the case of the making of an unauthorised issue of an invoice showing VAT, the potential lost revenue is the amount shown on the invoice as value added tax or the amount to be taken as representing value added tax.

Commencement—Finance Act 2008, Schedule 41 (Appointed Day and Transitional Provisions) Order, SI 2009/511 art 2 (the appointed day for the purposes of this Schedule is 1 April 2010).
Cross reference—FA 2009 s 94 (Publishing details of deliberate tax defaulters).

9 In the case of—

(*a*) the doing of an act which enables HMRC to assess an amount of duty as due under a relevant excise provision, or

(*b*) supplying a product knowing that it will be used in a way which enables HMRC to assess an amount as duty due from another person under a relevant excise provision,

the potential lost revenue is the amount of the duty which may be assessed as due.

Commencement—Finance Act 2008, Schedule 41 (Appointed Day and Transitional Provisions) Order, SI 2009/511 art 2 (the appointed day for the purposes of this Schedule is 1 April 2010).
Cross reference—FA 2009 s 94 (Publishing details of deliberate tax defaulters).

10 In the case of acquiring possession of, or being concerned in dealing with, goods the payment of duty on which is outstanding and has not been deferred, the potential lost revenue is an amount equal to the amount of duty due on the goods.

Commencement—Finance Act 2008, Schedule 41 (Appointed Day and Transitional Provisions) Order, SI 2009/511 art 2 (the appointed day for the purposes of this Schedule is 1 April 2010).
Cross reference—FA 2009 s 94 (Publishing details of deliberate tax defaulters).

11— (1) In calculating potential lost revenue in respect of a relevant act or failure on the part of P no account is to be taken of the fact that a potential loss of revenue from P is or may be balanced by a potential over-payment by another person (except to the extent that an enactment requires or permits a person's tax liability to be adjusted by reference to P's).

(2) In this Schedule "a relevant act or failure" means—

(*a*) a failure to comply with a relevant obligation,

(*b*) the making of an unauthorised issue of an invoice showing VAT,

(*c*) the doing of an act which enables HMRC to assess an amount of duty as due under a relevant excise provision or supplying a product knowing that it will be used in a way which enables HMRC to assess an amount as duty due from another person under a relevant excise provision, or

(*d*) acquiring possession of, or being concerned in dealing with, goods the payment of duty on which is outstanding and has not been deferred.

Commencement—Finance Act 2008, Schedule 41 (Appointed Day and Transitional Provisions) Order, SI 2009/511 art 2 (the appointed day for the purposes of this Schedule is 1 April 2010).
Cross reference—FA 2009 s 94 (Publishing details of deliberate tax defaulters).

Reductions for disclosure

12— (1) Paragraph 13 provides for reductions in penalties under paragraphs 1 to 4 where P discloses a relevant act or failure

(2) P discloses a relevant act or failure by—

(*a*) telling HMRC about it,

(*b*) giving HMRC reasonable help in quantifying the tax unpaid by reason of it, and

(*c*) allowing HMRC access to records for the purpose of checking how much tax is so unpaid.

(3) Disclosure of a relevant act or failure—

(*a*) is "unprompted" if made at a time when the person making it has no reason to believe that HMRC have discovered or are about to discover the relevant act or failure, and

(*b*) otherwise, is "prompted".

(4) In relation to disclosure "quality" includes timing, nature and extent.

Commencement—Finance Act 2008, Schedule 41 (Appointed Day and Transitional Provisions) Order, SI 2009/511 art 2 (the appointed day for the purposes of this Schedule is 1 April 2010).

13— (1) Where a person who would otherwise be liable to a 100% penalty has made an unprompted disclosure, HMRC shall reduce the 100% to a percentage, not below 30%, which reflects the quality of the disclosure.

(2) Where a person who would otherwise be liable to a 100% penalty has made a prompted disclosure, HMRC shall reduce the 100% to a percentage, not below 50%, which reflects the quality of the disclosure.

(3) Where a person who would otherwise be liable to a 70% penalty has made an unprompted disclosure, HMRC shall reduce the 70% to a percentage, not below 20%, which reflects the quality of the disclosure.

(4) Where a person who would otherwise be liable to a 70% penalty has made a prompted disclosure, HMRC shall reduce the 70% to a percentage, not below 35%, which reflects the quality of the disclosure.

(5) Where a person who would otherwise be liable to a 30% penalty has made an unprompted disclosure, HMRC shall reduce the 30%—

(*a*) if the penalty is under paragraph 1 and HMRC become aware of the failure less than 12 months after the time when tax first becomes unpaid by reason of the failure, to a percentage (which may be 0%), or

(*b*) in any other case, to a percentage not below 10%,

which reflects the quality of the disclosure.

(6) Where a person who would otherwise be liable to a 30% penalty has made a prompted disclosure, HMRC shall reduce the 30%—

(*a*) if the penalty is under paragraph 1 and HMRC become aware of the failure less than 12 months after the time when tax first becomes unpaid by reason of the failure, to a percentage not below 10%, or

(*b*) in any other case, to a percentage not below 20%,

which reflects the quality of the disclosure.

Commencement—Finance Act 2008, Schedule 41 (Appointed Day and Transitional Provisions) Order, SI 2009/511 art 2 (the appointed day for the purposes of this Schedule is 1 April 2010).
Cross reference—FA 2009 s 94 (Publishing details of deliberate tax defaulters).

Special reduction

14— *(1) If HMRC think it right because of special circumstances, they may reduce a penalty under any of paragraphs 1 to 4.*

(2) In sub-paragraph (1) "special circumstances" does not include—

(a) ability to pay, or

(b) the fact that a potential loss of revenue from one taxpayer is balanced by a potential over-payment by another.

(3) In sub-paragraph (1) the reference to reducing a penalty includes a reference to—

(a) staying a penalty, and

(b) agreeing a compromise in relation to proceedings for a penalty.[1]

Commencement—Finance Act 2008, Schedule 41 (Appointed Day and Transitional Provisions) Order, SI 2009/511 art 2 (the appointed day for the purposes of this Schedule is 1 April 2010).
Cross reference—FA 2009 s 94 (Publishing details of deliberate tax defaulters).
Amendments—[1] This para repealed by the Transfer of Tribunal Functions and Revenue and Customs Appeals Order, SI 2009/56 art 3, Sch 1 para 472 with effect from 1 April 2009.

Interaction with other penalties and late payment surcharges

15— (1) The amount of a penalty for which P is liable under any of paragraphs 1 to 4 shall be reduced by the amount of any other penalty incurred by P, or any surcharge for late payment of tax imposed on P, if the amount of the penalty or surcharge is determined by reference to the same tax liability.

(2) If P is liable to a penalty under section 9 of FA 1994 in respect of a failure to comply with a relevant obligation, the amount of any penalty payable under paragraph 1 in respect of the failure is to be reduced by the amount of the penalty under that section.

(3) Where penalties are imposed under paragraph 3(1) and (2) in respect of the same act or use, the aggregate of the amounts of the penalties must not exceed 100% of the potential lost revenue.

Commencement—Finance Act 2008, Schedule 41 (Appointed Day and Transitional Provisions) Order, SI 2009/511 art 2 (the appointed day for the purposes of this Schedule is 1 April 2010).
Cross reference—FA 2009 s 94 (Publishing details of deliberate tax defaulters).

Assessment

16— (1) Where P becomes liable for a penalty under any of paragraphs 1 to 4 HMRC shall—

(*a*) assess the penalty,

(*b*) notify P, and

(*c*) state in the notice the period in respect of which the penalty is assessed.

(2) A penalty under any of paragraphs 1 to 4 must be paid before the end of the period of 30 days beginning with the day on which notification of the penalty is issued.

(3) An assessment—

(*a*) shall be treated for procedural purposes in the same way as an assessment to tax (except in respect of a matter expressly provided for by this Act),

(*b*) may be enforced as if it were an assessment to tax, and

(*c*) may be combined with an assessment to tax.

(4) An assessment of a penalty under any of paragraphs 1 to 4 must be made before the end of the period of 12 months beginning with—

(*a*) the end of the appeal period for the assessment of tax unpaid by reason of the relevant act or failure in respect of which the penalty is imposed, or

(*b*) if there is no such assessment, the date on which the amount of tax unpaid by reason of the relevant act or failure is ascertained.

(5) In sub-paragraph (4)(*a*) "appeal period" means the period during which—

(*a*) an appeal could be brought, or

VAT

(*b*) an appeal that has been brought has not been determined or withdrawn.

(6) Subject to sub-paragraph (4), a supplementary assessment may be made in respect of a penalty if an earlier assessment operated by reference to an underestimate of potential lost revenue.

(7) The references in this paragraph to "an assessment to tax" are, in relation to a penalty under paragraph 2, a demand for recovery.

Commencement—Finance Act 2008, Schedule 41 (Appointed Day and Transitional Provisions) Order, SI 2009/511 art 2 (the appointed day for the purposes of this Schedule is 1 April 2010).
Cross reference—FA 2009 s 94 (Publishing details of deliberate tax defaulters).

Appeal

17— (1) P may appeal against a decision of HMRC that a penalty is payable by P.

(2) P may appeal against a decision of HMRC as to the amount of a penalty payable by P.

Commencement—Finance Act 2008, Schedule 41 (Appointed Day and Transitional Provisions) Order, SI 2009/511 art 2 (the appointed day for the purposes of this Schedule is 1 April 2010).
Cross reference—FA 2009 s 94 (Publishing details of deliberate tax defaulters).

[**18**— (1) An appeal shall be treated in the same way as an appeal against an assessment to the tax concerned (including by the application of any provision about bringing the appeal by notice to HMRC, about HMRC review of the decision or about determination of the appeal by the First-tier Tribunal or the Upper Tribunal).

[(2) Sub-paragraph (1) does not apply—

(*a*) so as to require P to pay a penalty before an appeal against the assessment of the penalty is determined, or

(*b*) in respect of any other matter expressly provided for by this Act.][2]][1]

Commencement—Finance Act 2008, Schedule 41 (Appointed Day and Transitional Provisions) Order, SI 2009/511 art 2 (the appointed day for the purposes of this Schedule is 1 April 2010).
Amendments—[1] This para substituted by the Transfer of Tribunal Functions and Revenue and Customs Appeals Order, SI 2009/56 art 3, Sch 1 para 473 with effect from 1 April 2009. Text previously read as follows—

"**18**— (1) An appeal is to be brought to the First-tier Tribunal.

(2) An appeal shall be treated for procedural purposes in the same way as an appeal against an assessment to the tax concerned (except in respect of a matter expressly provided for by this Act).".

[2] Sub-para (2) substituted by FA 2009 s 109, Sch 57 para 11 with effect from 21 July 2009. Sub-para (2) previously read as follows—

"(2) Sub-paragraph (1) does not apply in respect of a matter expressly provided for by this Act.".

19— (1) On an appeal under paragraph 17(1) the [tribunal][1] may affirm or cancel HMRC's decision.

(2) On an appeal under paragraph 17(2) the [tribunal][1] may—

(*a*) affirm HMRC's decision, or

(*b*) substitute for HMRC's decision another decision that HMRC had power to make.

(3) If the First-tier [tribunal][1] substitutes its decision for HMRC's, the [tribunal][1] may rely on paragraph 14—

(*a*) to the same extent as HMRC (which may mean applying the same percentage reduction as HMRC to a different starting point), or

(*b*) to a different extent, but only if the [tribunal][1] thinks that HMRC's decision in respect of the application of paragraph 14 was flawed.

(4) In sub-paragraph (3)(*b*) "flawed" means flawed when considered in the light of the principles applicable in proceedings for judicial review.

[(5) In this paragraph, "tribunal" means the First-tier Tribunal or Upper Tribunal (as appropriate by virtue of paragraph 18(1)).][1]

Commencement—Finance Act 2008, Schedule 41 (Appointed Day and Transitional Provisions) Order, SI 2009/511 art 2 (the appointed day for the purposes of this Schedule is 1 April 2010).
Amendments—[1] In sub-paras (1), (2) word substituted for the words "First-tier Tribunal"; in sub-para (3) word substituted for the word "Tribunal" in each place; sub-para (5) inserted by the Transfer of Tribunal Functions and Revenue and Customs Appeals Order, SI 2009/56 art 3, Sch 1 para 473 with effect from 1 April 2009.

Reasonable excuse

20— (1) Liability to a penalty under any of paragraphs 1, 2, 3(1) and 4 does not arise in relation to an act or failure which is not deliberate if P satisfies HMRC or [(on an appeal notified to the tribunal) the tribunal][1] that there is a reasonable excuse for the act or failure.

(2) For the purposes of sub-paragraph (1)—

(*a*) an insufficiency of funds is not a reasonable excuse unless attributable to events outside P's control,

(*b*) where P relies on any other person to do anything, that is not a reasonable excuse unless P took reasonable care to avoid the relevant act or failure, and

(*c*) where P had a reasonable excuse for the relevant act or failure but the excuse has ceased, P is to be treated as having continued to have the excuse if the relevant act or failure is remedied without unreasonable delay after the excuse ceased.

Commencement—Finance Act 2008, Schedule 41 (Appointed Day and Transitional Provisions) Order, SI 2009/511 art 2 (the appointed day for the purposes of this Schedule is 1 April 2010).

Amendments—[1] In sub-para (1) words substituted for the words "(on appeal) the First-tier Tribunal" by the Transfer of Tribunal Functions and Revenue and Customs Appeals Order, SI 2009/56 art 3, Sch 1 para 473 with effect from 1 April 2009.

Agency

21— (1) In paragraph 1 the reference to a failure by P includes a failure by a person who acts on P's behalf; but P is not liable to a penalty in respect of any failure by P's agent where P satisfies HMRC or [(on an appeal notified to the tribunal) the tribunal][1] that P took reasonable care to avoid the failure.

(2) In paragraph 2 the reference to the making by P of an unauthorised issue of an invoice showing VAT includes the making of such an unauthorised issue by a person who acts on P's behalf; but P is not liable to a penalty in respect of any action by P's agent where P satisfies HMRC or (on appeal) the First-tier Tribunal that P took reasonable care to avoid it.

(3) In paragraph 3(1) the reference to the doing by P of an act which enables HMRC to assess an amount as duty due from P under a relevant excise provision includes the doing of such an act by a person who acts on P's behalf; but P is not liable to a penalty in respect of any action by P's agent where P satisfies HMRC or (on appeal) the First-tier Tribunal that P took reasonable care to avoid it.

(4) In paragraph 4 the reference to P acquiring possession of, or being concerned in dealing with, goods the payment of duty on which is outstanding and has not been deferred includes a person who acts on P's behalf doing so; but P is not liable to a penalty in respect of any action by P's agent where P satisfies HMRC or (on appeal) the First-tier Tribunal that P took reasonable care to avoid it.

Commencement—Finance Act 2008, Schedule 41 (Appointed Day and Transitional Provisions) Order, SI 2009/511 art 2 (the appointed day for the purposes of this Schedule is 1 April 2010).

Amendments—[1] In sub-para (1) words substituted for the words "(on appeal) the First-tier Tribunal" by the Transfer of Tribunal Functions and Revenue and Customs Appeals Order, SI 2009/56 art 3, Sch 1 para 473 with effect from 1 April 2009.

Companies: officers' liability

22— (1) Where a penalty under any of paragraphs 1, 2, 3(1) and 4 is payable by a company for a deliberate act or failure which was attributable to an officer of the company, the officer is liable to pay such portion of the penalty (which may be 100%) as HMRC may specify by written notice to the officer.

(2) Sub-paragraph (1) does not allow HMRC to recover more than 100% of a penalty.

(3) In the application of sub-paragraph (1) to a body corporate [other than a limited liability partnership][1] "officer" means—

(*a*) a director (including a shadow director within the meaning of section 251 of the Companies Act 2006 (c 46)), …[1]

[(*aa*) a manager, and][1]

(*b*) a secretary.

[(3A) In the application of sub-paragraph (1) to a limited liability partnership, "officer" means a member.][1]

(4) In the application of sub-paragraph (1) in any other case "officer" means—

(*a*) a director,

(*b*) a manager,

(*c*) a secretary, and

(*d*) any other person managing or purporting to manage any of the company's affairs.

(5) Where HMRC have specified a portion of a penalty in a notice given to an officer under sub-paragraph (1)—

(*a*) paragraph 14 applies to the specified portion as to a penalty,

(*b*) the officer must pay the specified portion before the end of the period of 30 days beginning with the day on which the notice is given,

(*c*) paragraph 16(3) to (5) and (7) apply as if the notice were an assessment of a penalty,

(*d*) a further notice may be given in respect of a portion of any additional amount assessed in a supplementary assessment in respect of the penalty under paragraph 16(6),

(*e*) paragraphs 17 to 19 apply as if HMRC had decided that a penalty of the amount of the specified portion is payable by the officer, and

(*f*) paragraph 23 applies as if the officer were liable to a penalty.

[(6) In this paragraph "company" means any body corporate or unincorporated association, but does not include a partnership, a local authority or a local authority association.][1]

Commencement—Finance Act 2008, Schedule 41 (Appointed Day and Transitional Provisions) Order, SI 2009/511 art 2 (the appointed day for the purposes of this Schedule is 1 April 2010).

Amendments—[1] In sub-para (3) words inserted, word "or" repealed and para (*aa*) inserted, sub-paras (3A), (6) inserted, by FA 2009 s 109, Sch 57 para 12 with effect from 21 July 2009.

Double jeopardy

23 P is not liable to a penalty under any of paragraphs 1 to 4 in respect of a failure or action in respect of which P has been convicted of an offence.

Commencement—Finance Act 2008, Schedule 41 (Appointed Day and Transitional Provisions) Order, SI 2009/511 art 2 (the appointed day for the purposes of this Schedule is 1 April 2010).

Interpretation

24— (1) This paragraph applies for the construction of this Schedule

(2) "HMRC" means Her Majesty's Revenue and Customs.

(3) "Tax", without more, includes duty.

(4) An expression used in relation to value added tax has the same meaning as in VATA 1994.

Commencement—Finance Act 2008, Schedule 41 (Appointed Day and Transitional Provisions) Order, SI 2009/511 art 2 (the appointed day for the purposes of this Schedule is 1 April 2010).

Consequential repeals

25 In consequence of this Schedule the following provisions are omitted—

(*a*)–(*e*) …

(*f*) section 67 of VATA 1994,

(*g*) section 32 of FA 1995,

(*h*) in FA 1996—

(i) section 37, and

(ii) paragraph 21(1), (2) and (4) of Schedule 5,

(*i*) section 27(11) of FA 1997,

(*j*) …

(*k*) in FA 2000—

(i) section 136(2), and

(ii) paragraph 55(2) to (6) of Schedule 6, and

(*l*) paragraph 1(2) to (6) of Schedule 4 to FA 2001.

Commencement—Finance Act 2008, Schedule 41 (Appointed Day and Transitional Provisions) Order, SI 2009/511 art 2 (the appointed day for the purposes of this Schedule is 1 April 2010).
Note—Omitted paras not relevant to this work.

SCHEDULE 43

TAKING CONTROL OF GOODS ETC: CONSEQUENTIAL PROVISION

Section 129

PART 1

CONSEQUENTIAL PROVISION: TAKING CONTROL OF GOODS

TMA 1970

(see *Yellow Tax Handbook* for amendments to TMA 1970)

Social Security Administration Act 1992 (*c 5*)

2 (see *Yellow Tax Handbook* for amendments to SSAA 1992)

FA 1994

3— (1) FA 1994 is amended as follows.

(2) Omit section 10A (breaches of controlled goods agreements).

(3) In Schedule 7 (insurance premium tax), omit paragraph 18A (breaches of controlled goods agreements).

VATA 1994

4 In VATA 1994, omit section 67A (breach of controlled goods agreement).

FA 1996

5 In Schedule 5 to FA 1996 (landfill tax), omit paragraph 23A (controlled goods agreements).

FA 1997

6 In section 51 of FA 1997 (enforcement by distress), omit subsection (A1).

FA 2000

7 In Schedule 6 to FA 2000 (climate change levy), omit paragraph 89A (controlled goods agreements).

FA 2001

8 In Schedule 5 to FA 2001 (aggregates levy: recovery and interest), omit paragraph 14A (controlled goods agreements).

FA 2003

9 In Schedule 12 to FA 2003 (stamp duty land tax: collection and recovery), omit paragraph 1A (recovery of tax in England and Wales).

Tribunals, Courts and Enforcement Act 2007 (*c 15*)

10— (1) Schedule 12 of the Tribunals, Courts and Enforcement Act 2007 (taking control of goods) is amended as follows.

(2) Omit paragraph 14(5) (relevant premises where enforcement agent acting under section 121A of Social Security Administration Act 1992).

(3) In paragraph 19(2) (powers to use reasonable force), for paragraphs (*b*) to (*e*) substitute—

"(*b*) section 127 of the Finance Act 2008."

Other repeals

11 In consequence of the preceding provisions of this Schedule, omit—

(*a*) paragraph 8 of Schedule 5 to the Social Security Contributions (Transfer of Functions, etc) Act 1999 (c 2),

(*b*) paragraph 6 of Schedule 11 to the Welfare Reform and Pensions Act 1999 (c 30),

(*c*) section 5(1) of the National Insurance Contributions and Statutory Payments Act 2004 (c 3), and

(*d*) paragraphs 33, 104(2), 114, 116(2), 119, 123, 126(2), 136, 140 and 147(2) of Schedule 13 to the Tribunals, Courts and Enforcement Act 2007 (c 15).

PART 2

CONSEQUENTIAL PROVISION: SUMMARY WARRANT

TMA 1970

12 (see *Yellow Tax Handbook* for amendments to TMA 1970)

Debtors (*Scotland*) *Act 1987* (*c 18*)

13— (1) In section 1 (time to pay directions)—

(*a*) in subsection (5)(*d*), for "in respect of tax or as if it were tax" substitute "under or by virtue of any enactment or under a contract settlement",

(*b*) in subsection (5)(*f*), omit sub-paragraphs (i), (iii) and (iv), and

(*c*) after subsection (8) insert—

"(8A) In paragraph (*d*) of subsection (5) above, "contract settlement" means an agreement made in connection with any person's liability to make a payment to the Commissioners for Her Majesty's Revenue and Customs under or by virtue of any enactment."

(2) In section 5 (time to pay orders)—

(*a*) in subsection (4)(*d*), for "in respect of tax or as if it were tax" substitute "under or by virtue of any enactment or under a contract settlement",

(*b*) in subsection (4)(*f*), omit sub-paragraphs (i), (iii) and (iv), and

(*c*) after subsection (8) insert—

"(8A) In paragraph (*d*) of subsection (4) above, "contract settlement" means an agreement made in connection with any person's liability to make a payment to the Commissioners for Her Majesty's Revenue and Customs under or by virtue of any enactment."

(3) In section 106 (interpretation), in the definition of "summary warrant"—

(*a*) omit paragraph (cc),

(*b*) in paragraph (*d*), for "any of the enactments" substitute "the enactments (other than the Taxes Management Act 1970)", and

(*c*) after that paragraph insert—

"(*e*) section 128 of the Finance Act 2008."

Social Security Administration Act 1992 (*c 5*)

14 (see *Yellow Tax Handbook* for amendments to SSAA 1992)

FA 1997

15 In FA 1997, omit section 52 (recovery of relevant tax in Scotland).

FA 2003

16 In Schedule 12 to FA 2003 (stamp duty land tax: collection and recovery), omit paragraph 3 (recovery of tax in Scotland).

SCHEDULE 44

CERTIFICATES OF DEBT: CONSEQUENTIAL PROVISION

Section 138

TMA 1970

1 (see *Yellow Tax Handbook* for amendments to TMA 1970)

OTA 1975

2 (see *Yellow Tax Handbook* for amendments to OTA 1975)

IHTA 1984

3 (see *Yellow Tax Handbook* for amendments to IHTA 1984)

Social Security Administration Act 1992 (c 5)

4 (see *Yellow Tax Handbook* for amendments to SSAA 1992)

FA 1994

5 In Schedule 7 to FA 1994 (insurance premium tax), in paragraph 29(1) (evidence by certificate)—

(*a*) in paragraph (*a*), after "Act," insert "or", and
(*b*) omit paragraph (*c*) (and the "or" before it).

VATA 1994

6 In Schedule 11 to VATA 1994 (administration, collection and enforcement of VAT), in paragraph 14(1) (evidence by certificate), omit paragraph (*d*) (and the "or" before it).

FA 1996

7 In Schedule 5 to FA 1996 (landfill tax), in paragraph 37(1) (evidence by certificate)—

(*a*) in paragraph (*a*), after "Act," insert "or", and
(*b*) omit paragraph (*c*) (and the "or" before it).

FA 2000

8 In Schedule 6 to FA 2000 (climate change levy), in paragraph 135(1) (evidence by certificate)—

(*a*) in paragraph (*a*), after "levy," insert "or", and
(*b*) omit paragraphs (*c*) and (*d*).

FA 2001

9 In Schedule 7 to FA 2001 (aggregates levy: information and evidence etc), in paragraph 12(1)—

(*a*) in paragraph (*a*), after "registered," insert "or", and
(*b*) omit paragraphs (*c*) and (*d*).

FA 2003

10 In Schedule 12 to FA 2003 (stamp duty land tax: collection and recovery of tax), omit paragraph 7 (evidence of unpaid debt) and the heading before it.

Other repeals

11 In consequence of the preceding provisions of this Schedule, omit—

(*a*) paragraph 21 of Schedule 19 to FA 1994,
(*b*) section 62(1) of the Social Security Act 1998 (c 14),
(*c*) paragraph 32 of Schedule 19 to FA 1998,
(*d*) paragraph 7(2) and (6) of Schedule 5 to the Social Security (Transfer of Functions, etc) Act 1999 (c 2),
(*e*) section 89(3) of FA 2001, and
(*f*) paragraph 135(2) of Schedule 6 to ITEPA 2003.

VAT

FINANCE ACT 2009

(2009 Chapter 10)

An Act to Grant certain duties, to alter other duties, and to amend the law relating to the National Debt and the Public Revenue, and to make further provision in connection with finance.

[21 July 2009]

PART 1

CHARGES, RATES, ALLOWANCES, ETC

Value added tax

9 Extension of reduced standard rate and anti-avoidance provision

(1) The Value Added Tax (Change of Rate) Order 2008 (SI 2008/3020) (reducing standard rate of value added tax to 15 per cent) is to cease to be in force on 1 January 2010 (rather than ceasing to be in force on 1 December 2009 in accordance with section 2(2) of VATA 1994).

(2) Schedule 3 contains—

(*a*) provision for a supplementary charge to value added tax on supplies spanning the date of the VAT change (see Parts 1 to 5), and

(*b*) minor amendments of provisions about orders changing the standard rate of value added tax (see Part 6).

PART 7

ADMINISTRATION

Standards and values

92 HMRC Charter

(1) In CRCA 2005, after section 16 insert—

"16A Charter of standards and values

(1) The Commissioners must prepare a Charter.

(2) The Charter must include standards of behaviour and values to which Her Majesty's Revenue and Customs will aspire when dealing with people in the exercise of their functions.

(3) The Commissioners must—

(*a*) regularly review the Charter, and

(*b*) publish revisions, or revised versions, of it when they consider it appropriate to do so.

(4) The Commissioners must, at least once every year, make a report reviewing the extent to which Her Majesty's Revenue and Customs have demonstrated the standards of behaviour and values included in the Charter."

(2) The duty imposed by section 16A(1) of CRCA 2005 must be complied with before the end of 2009.

93 Duties of senior accounting officers of qualifying companies

(1) Schedule 46 contains provision about the duties of senior accounting officers of qualifying companies.

(2) That Schedule has effect in relation to financial years (within the meaning of the Companies Act 2006) beginning on or after the day on which this Act is passed.

94 Publishing details of deliberate tax defaulters

(1) The Commissioners may publish information about any person if—

(*a*) in consequence of an investigation conducted by the Commissioners, one or more relevant tax penalties is found to have been incurred by the person, and

(*b*) the potential lost revenue in relation to the penalty (or the aggregate of the potential lost revenue in relation to each of the penalties) exceeds £25,000.

(2) A "relevant tax penalty" is—

(*a*) a penalty under paragraph 1 of Schedule 24 to FA 2007 (inaccuracy in taxpayer's document) in respect of a deliberate inaccuracy on the part of the person,

(*b*) a penalty under paragraph 1A of that Schedule (inaccuracy in taxpayer's document attributable to deliberate supply of false information or deliberate withholding of information by person),

(*c*) a penalty under paragraph 1 of Schedule 41 to FA 2008 (failure to notify) in respect of a deliberate failure on the part of the person, or

(*d*) a penalty under paragraph 2 (unauthorised VAT invoice), 3 (putting product to use attracting higher duty etc) or 4 (handling goods subject to unpaid excise duty) of that Schedule in respect of deliberate action by the person.

(3) "Potential lost revenue", in relation to a penalty, has the meaning given by—

(*a*) paragraphs 5 to 8 of Schedule 24 to FA 2007, or

(*b*) paragraphs 7 to 11 of Schedule 41 to FA 2008,

in relation to the inaccuracy, failure or action to which the penalty relates.

(4) The information that may be published is—

(*a*) the person's name (including any trading name, previous name or pseudonym),

(*b*) the person's address (or registered office),

(*c*) the nature of any business carried on by the person,

(*d*) the amount of the penalty or penalties and the potential lost revenue in relation to the penalty (or the aggregate of the potential lost revenue in relation to each of the penalties),

(*e*) the periods or times to which the inaccuracy, failure or action giving rise to the penalty (or any of the penalties) relates, and

(*f*) any such other information as the Commissioners consider it appropriate to publish in order to make clear the person's identity.

(5) The information may be published in any manner that the Commissioners consider appropriate.

(6) Before publishing any information the Commissioners—

(*a*) must inform the person that they are considering doing so, and

(*b*) afford the person reasonable opportunity to make representations about whether it should be published.

(7) No information may be published before the day when the penalty becomes final (or the latest day when any of the penalties becomes final).

(8) No information may be published for the first time after the end of the period of one year beginning with that day (or that latest day).

(9) No information may be published (or continue to be published) after the end of the period of one year beginning with the day on which it is first published.

(10) No information may be published if the amount of the penalty is reduced under—

(*a*) paragraph 10 of Schedule 24 to FA 2007, or

(*b*) paragraph 13 of Schedule 41 to FA 2008, (reductions for disclosure) to the full extent permitted.

(11) For the purposes of this section, a penalty becomes final—

(*a*) if it has been assessed, when the time for any appeal or further appeal relating to it expires or, if later, any appeal or final appeal relating to it is finally determined, or

(*b*) if a contract is made between the Commissioners and the person under which the Commissioners undertake not to assess the penalty or (if it has been assessed) not to take proceedings to recover it, at the time when the contract is made.

(12) The Treasury may by order vary the amount for the time being specified in subsection (1).

(13) This section comes into force on a day appointed by order made by the Treasury.

(14) Orders under this section are to be made by statutory instrument.

(15) A statutory instrument containing an order under subsection (12) is subject to annulment in pursuance of a resolution of the House of Commons.

(16) In this section "the Commissioners" means the Commissioners for Her Majesty's Revenue and Customs.

Information etc

95 Amendment of information and inspection powers

(1) Schedule 47 contains amendments of Schedule 36 to FA 2008 (information and inspection powers).

(2) The Treasury may by order make any incidental, supplemental, consequential, transitional or transitory provision or saving which appears appropriate in consequence of, or otherwise in connection with, Schedule 36 to FA 2008 or Schedule 47.

(3) An order under this section may—

(*a*) make different provision for different purposes, and

(*b*) make provision amending, repealing or revoking an enactment or instrument (whenever passed or made).

(4) An order under this section is to be made by statutory instrument.

(5) A statutory instrument containing an order under this section is subject to annulment in pursuance of a resolution of the House of Commons.

96 Extension of information and inspection powers to further taxes

(1) In paragraph 63(1) of Schedule 36 to FA 2008 (information and inspection powers: meaning of "tax"), for paragraph (*e*) (and the "and" before it) substitute—

"(*e*) insurance premium tax,

(*f*) inheritance tax,

(*g*) stamp duty land tax,

(*h*) stamp duty reserve tax,

(*i*) petroleum revenue tax,
(*j*) aggregates levy,
(*k*) climate change levy,
(*l*) landfill tax, and
(*m*) relevant foreign tax,".

(2) Schedule 48 contains further amendments of that Schedule.

(3) The amendments made by this section and Schedule 48 come into force on such day as the Treasury may by order appoint.

(4) An order under subsection (3) may—

(*a*) appoint different days for different purposes, and
(*b*) contain transitional provision and savings.

(5) The Treasury may by order make any incidental, supplemental, consequential, transitional or transitory provision or saving which appears appropriate in consequence of, or otherwise in connection with, this section and Schedule 48.

(6) An order under subsection (5) may—

(*a*) make different provision for different purposes, and
(*b*) make provision amending, repealing or revoking an enactment or instrument (whenever passed or made).

(7) An order under this section is to be made by statutory instrument.

(8) A statutory instrument containing an order under subsection (5) is subject to annulment in pursuance of a resolution of the House of Commons.

97 Powers to obtain contact details for debtors

Schedule 49 contains provision about the powers of officers of Revenue and Customs to obtain contact details of debtors.

Interest

101 Late payment interest on sums due to HMRC

(1) This section applies to any amount that is payable by a person to HMRC under or by virtue of an enactment.

(2) But this section does not apply to—

(*a*) an amount of corporation tax,
(*b*) an amount of petroleum revenue tax, or
(*c*) an amount of any description specified in an order made by the Treasury.

(3) An amount to which this section applies carries interest at the late payment interest rate from the late payment interest start date until the date of payment.

(4) The late payment interest start date in respect of any amount is the date on which that amount becomes due and payable.

(5) In Schedule 53—

(*a*) Part 1 makes special provision as to the amount on which late payment interest is calculated,
(*b*) Part 2 makes special provision as to the late payment interest start date,
(*c*) Part 3 makes special provision as to the date to which late payment interest runs, and
(*d*) Part 4 makes provision about the effect that the giving of a relief has on late payment interest.

(6) Subsection (3) applies even if the late payment interest start date is a non-business day within the meaning of section 92 of the Bills of Exchange Act 1882.

(7) Late payment interest is to be paid without any deduction of income tax.

(8) Late payment interest is not payable on late payment interest.

(9) For the purposes of this section any reference to the payment of an amount to HMRC includes a reference to its being set off against an amount payable by HMRC (and, accordingly, the reference to the date on which an amount is paid includes a reference to the date from which the set-off takes effect).

102 Repayment interest on sums to be paid by HMRC

(1) This section applies to—

(*a*) any amount that is payable by HMRC to any person under or by virtue of an enactment, and
(*b*) a relevant amount paid by a person to HMRC that is repaid by HMRC to that person or to another person.

(2) But this section does not apply to—

(*a*) an amount constituting a repayment of corporation tax,
(*b*) an amount constituting a repayment of petroleum revenue tax, or
(*c*) an amount of any description specified in an order made by the Treasury.

(3) An amount to which this section applies carries interest at the repayment interest rate from the repayment interest start date until the date on which the payment or repayment is made.

(4) In Schedule 54—

(*a*) Parts 1 and 2 define the repayment interest start date, and

(*b*) Part 3 makes supplementary provision.

(5) Subsection (3) applies even if the repayment interest start date is a non-business day within the meaning of section 92 of the Bills of Exchange Act 1882.

(6) Repayment interest is not payable on an amount payable in consequence of an order or judgment of a court having power to allow interest on the amount.

(7) Repayment interest is not payable on repayment interest.

(8) For the purposes of this section—

(*a*) "relevant amount" means any sum that was paid in connection with any liability (including any purported or anticipated liability) to make a payment to HMRC under or by virtue of an enactment, and

(*b*) any reference to the payment or repayment of an amount by HMRC includes a reference to its being set off against an amount owed to HMRC (and, accordingly, the reference to the date on which an amount is paid or repaid by HMRC includes a reference to the date from which the set-off takes effect).

Penalties

108 Suspension of penalties during currency of agreement for deferred payment

(1) This section applies if—

(*a*) a person ("P") fails to pay an amount of tax falling within the Table in subsection (5) when it becomes due and payable,

(*b*) P makes a request to an officer of Revenue and Customs that payment of the amount of tax be deferred, and

(*c*) an officer of Revenue and Customs agrees that payment of that amount may be deferred for a period ("the deferral period").

(2) P is not liable to a penalty for failing to pay the amount mentioned in subsection (1) if—

(*a*) the penalty falls within the Table, and

(*b*) P would (apart from this subsection) become liable to it between the date on which P makes the request and the end of the deferral period.

(3) But if—

(*a*) P breaks the agreement (see subsection (4)), and

(*b*) an officer of Revenue and Customs serves on P a notice specifying any penalty to which P would become liable apart from subsection (2),

P becomes liable, at the date of the notice, to that penalty.

(4) P breaks an agreement if—

(*a*) P fails to pay the amount of tax in question when the deferral period ends, or

(*b*) the deferral is subject to P complying with a condition (including a condition that part of the amount be paid during the deferral period) and P fails to comply with it.

(5) The taxes and penalties referred to in subsections (1) and (2) are—

Tax	*Penalty*
Income tax or capital gains tax	Surcharge under section 59C(2) or (3) of TMA 1970
Value added tax	Surcharge under section 59(4) or 59A(4) of VATA 1994
Aggregates levy	Penalty interest under paragraph 5 of Schedule 5 to FA 2001
Climate change levy	Penalty interest under paragraph 82 of Schedule 6 to FA 2000
Landfill tax	Penalty interest under paragraph 27(2) of Schedule 5 to FA 1996
Insurance premium tax	Penalty under paragraph 15(2) or (3) of Schedule 7 to FA 1994 which is payable by virtue of paragraph 15(1)(a) of that Schedule.
Any duty of excise	Penalty under section 9(2) or (3) of FA 1994 which is imposed for a failure to pay an amount of any duty of excise or an amount payable on account of any such duty.

(6) If the agreement mentioned in subsection (1)(*c*) is varied at any time by a further agreement between P and an officer of Revenue and Customs, this section applies from that time to the agreement as varied.

(7) The Treasury may by order amend the Table by adding or removing a tax or a penalty.

(8) An order under subsection (7) is to be made by statutory instrument.

(9) A statutory instrument containing an order under subsection (7) is subject to annulment in pursuance of a resolution of the House of Commons.

(10) In this section, except in the entries in the Table, "penalty" includes surcharge and penalty interest.

(11) This section has effect where the agreement mentioned in subsection (1)(*c*) is made on or after 24 November 2008.

109 Miscellaneous amendments

Schedule 57 contains amendments of Schedule 24 to FA 2007 (penalties for errors), Schedule 41 to FA 2008 (penalties for failure to notify and certain other wrongdoing) and certain other enactments relating to penalties.

PART 9

FINAL PROVISIONS

126 Interpretation

(1) In this Act—

"ALDA 1979" means the Alcoholic Liquor Duties Act 1979,
"BGDA 1981" means the Betting and Gaming Duties Act 1981,
"CAA 2001" means the Capital Allowances Act 2001,
"CRCA 2005" means the Commissioners for Revenue and Customs Act 2005,
"CTA 2009" means the Corporation Tax Act 2009,
"FISMA 2000" means the Financial Services and Markets Act 2000,
"HODA 1979" means the Hydrocarbon Oil Duties Act 1979,
"ICTA" means the Income and Corporation Taxes Act 1988,
"IHTA 1984" means the Inheritance Tax Act 1984,
"ITA 2007" means the Income Tax Act 2007,
"ITEPA 2003" means the Income Tax (Earnings and Pensions) Act 2003,
"ITTOIA 2005" means the Income Tax (Trading and Other Income) Act 2005,
"OTA 1975" means the Oil Taxation Act 1975,
"OTA 1983" means the Oil Taxation Act 1983,
"PRTA 1980" means the Petroleum Revenue Tax Act 1980,
"TCGA 1992" means the Taxation of Chargeable Gains Act 1992,
"TMA 1970" means the Taxes Management Act 1970,
"TPDA 1979" means the Tobacco Products Duty Act 1979,
"VATA 1994" means the Value Added Tax Act 1994, and
"VERA 1994" means the Vehicle Excise and Registration Act 1994.

(2) In this Act—

"FA", followed by a year, means the Finance Act of that year, and "F(No 2)A", followed by a year, means the Finance (No 2) Act of that year.

(3)–(5) (*amend* CAA 2001, ITEPA 2003, ITTOIA 2005)

(6) Accordingly, omit—

(*a*) in FA 2004, in Schedule 35, paragraphs 49 and 65(2),
(*b*) in F(No 2)A 2005, section 10(7),
(*c*) in FA 2006, section 84(4), and
(*d*) in FA 2008, in Schedule 25, paragraph 6.

127 Short title

This Act may be cited as the Finance Act 2009.

SCHEDULES

SCHEDULE 3

VAT: SUPPLEMENTARY CHARGE AND ORDERS CHANGING RATE

Section 9

PART 1

SUPPLEMENTARY CHARGE TO VAT

The charge

1—(1) There is a supplementary charge on a supply of goods or services that is treated as taking place on or after 25 November 2008 if—

(*a*) the supply spans the date of the VAT change,
(*b*) it is subject to VAT at the rate in force under section 2 of VATA 1994,
(*c*) the person to whom the supply is made is not entitled under VATA 1994 to credit for, or the repayment or refund of, all of the VAT on the supply, and
(*d*) a relevant condition is met.

(2) In this Schedule "the date of the VAT change" means 1 January 2010.

(3) For the cases in which a supply, other than the grant of a right to goods or services, spans the date of the VAT change and the relevant conditions in relation to such a supply, see paragraph 2.

(4) For the cases in which a supply consisting of the grant of a right to goods or services spans the date of the VAT change and the relevant conditions in relation to such a supply, see paragraph 3.

(5) Sub-paragraph (1) has effect subject to the exceptions made by or under Part 2 of this Schedule.

(6) In this Schedule—

Part 3 contains provision about liability for, and the amount of, a supplementary charge under this Schedule,
Part 4 contains special provision about listed supplies, and
Part 5 contains provision about administration and interpretation.

(7) A supplementary charge under this Schedule is to be treated for all purposes as if it were value added tax charged in accordance with VATA 1994.

Supply spanning the date of the VAT change

2— (1) For the purposes of this Schedule, a supply of goods or services spans the date of the VAT change where—

(*a*) by virtue of the issue of a VAT invoice or the receipt of a payment by the person making the supply ("the supplier"), the supply is treated as taking place before the date of the VAT change, but
(*b*) the basic time of supply (see paragraph 4) is on or after the date of the VAT change.

(2) The relevant conditions are—

(*a*) in relation to a supply that is within sub-paragraph (1)(*a*) by virtue of the issue of a VAT invoice, conditions A to D, and
(*b*) in relation to a supply that is within sub-paragraph (1)(*a*) by virtue of the receipt of a payment, conditions A to C.

(3) Condition A is that the supplier and the person to whom the supply is made are connected with each other at any time in the period—

(*a*) beginning with the day on which the supply is treated as taking place, and
(*b*) ending on the date of the VAT change.

(4) Paragraph 5 modifies condition A in cases involving a series of supplies.

(5) Condition B is that the aggregate of the following is more than £100,000—

(*a*) the relevant consideration for the supply, and
(*b*) the relevant consideration for every related supply of goods or services (including every related grant of a right to goods or services) that spans the date of the VAT change (see paragraph 6).

(6) Condition C is that a prepayment in respect of the supply is financed by the supplier or a person connected with the supplier (see paragraph 7).

(7) In sub-paragraph (6) "prepayment", in respect of a supply, means a payment that is received by the supplier before the basic time of supply.

(8) Condition D is that full payment of the amount shown on the VAT invoice referred to in sub-paragraph (1)(*a*) is not due before the end of the period of 6 months beginning with the date on which the invoice is issued.

(9) This paragraph does not apply in relation to a supply consisting of the grant of a right to goods or services (see paragraph 3).

Grant of right spanning the date of the VAT change

3— (1) For the purposes of this Schedule, a supply consisting of the grant by a person ("the grantor") of a right to goods or services spans the date of the VAT change where—

(*a*) that supply is treated as taking place before the date of the VAT change,
(*b*) the goods or services are to be supplied at a discount or free of charge, and
(*c*) the basic time of supply for the supply of some or all of the goods or services (see paragraph 4) is on or after the date of the VAT change.

(2) In relation to the grant of the right, the relevant conditions are conditions A to C.

(3) Condition A is that the grantor and the person to whom the right is granted are connected with each other at any time in the period—

(*a*) beginning with the day on which the supply consisting of the grant of the right is treated as taking place, and (*b*) ending on the date of the VAT change or, if the right is exercised (entirely or partly) on a later date, that date (or, if more than one, the first of those dates).

(4) Paragraph 5 modifies condition A in cases involving a series of supplies.

(5) Condition B is that the aggregate of the following is more than £100,000—

(*a*) the relevant consideration for the grant of the right, and

(*b*) the relevant consideration for every related supply of goods or services (including every related grant of a right to goods or services) that spans the date of the VAT change (see paragraph 6).

(6) Condition C is that the payment made in respect of the grant of the right is financed by the grantor or a person connected with the grantor (see paragraph 7).

(7) In this Schedule references to a right to goods or services include—

(*a*) any right or option with respect to such goods or services, and

(*b*) any interest deriving from such a right or option.

"Basic time of supply"

4— (1) In this Schedule the "basic time of supply" is the time given by subsection (2) or (3) of section 6 of VATA 1994 (disregarding subsections (4) to (14) of that section).

(2) Sub-paragraph (1) does not apply in relation to listed supplies (see Part 4 of this Schedule).

Series of supplies

5— (1) This paragraph applies where—

(*a*) the supply or grant of a right referred to in paragraph 2 or 3 ("the affected supply or grant") is one of a series of supplies of, or grants of a right to, the same or substantially the same goods or services, and

(*b*) each of the supplies, and the grants of a right, in the series was or will be made in the expectation that the affected supply or grant would or will take place.

(2) In condition A in paragraphs 2 and 3, the references to the supplier and the grantor include any person who makes one of the supplies or grants one of the rights in the series.

"Relevant consideration" and "related" supplies

6— (1) This paragraph applies for the purposes of condition B in paragraphs 2 and 3.

(2) "Relevant consideration" means—

(*a*) in relation to a supply that is within paragraph 2(1) by virtue of the issue of a VAT invoice, the amount shown on that invoice,

(*b*) in relation to a supply that is within paragraph 2(1) by virtue of the receipt of a payment, the amount of that payment, and

(*c*) in relation to a grant of a right to goods or services within paragraph 3(1), the consideration for the grant of the right,

but does not include any amount in respect of VAT.

(3) A supply within paragraph 2(1), or a grant of a right within paragraph 3(1), is related to another such supply or grant if they are both made as part of the same scheme.

(4) "Scheme" includes any arrangements, transaction or series of transactions.

Financing

7— (1) This paragraph applies for the purposes of condition C in paragraphs 2 and 3.

(2) A payment is financed by a person if, directly or indirectly, the person—

(*a*) provides funds to enable the person to whom the supply is made to make the whole or part of the payment (whether the funds are provided before or after the payment is made),

(*b*) procures the provision of such funds by another person,

(*c*) provides funds for discharging (in whole or in part) any liability that has been or may be incurred by any person for or in connection with raising funds to enable the person to whom the supply is made to make the payment, or

(*d*) procures that any such liability is or will be discharged (in whole or in part) by another person.

(3) In sub-paragraph (2) the references to providing funds for a purpose are to—

(*a*) making a loan of funds that are or are to be used for that purpose,

(*b*) providing a guarantee or other security in relation to such a loan,

(*c*) providing consideration for the issue of shares or other securities issued wholly or partly for raising those funds,

(*d*) providing consideration for the acquisition by any person of any such shares or securities, or

(*e*) any other transfer of assets or value as a consequence of which any of those funds are made available for that purpose.

Connected persons

8 Section 839 of ICTA (connected persons) applies for the purposes of this Schedule.

Receipt of payments

9 In this Schedule a reference to receipt of a payment by the person making a supply or granting a right (however expressed) includes a reference to receipt by a person to whom a right to receive it has been assigned.

Power to change relevant conditions

10— (1) The Treasury may by order amend this Part of this Schedule by adding, modifying or omitting relevant conditions.

(2) An order under this paragraph—

(*a*) may make different provision for different cases, and

(*b*) may make incidental or consequential amendments of this Schedule.

Supplies treated as taking place before 31 March 2009

11 In relation to supplies treated as taking place before 31 March 2009, this Schedule has effect as if—

(*a*) paragraphs 2(5), 3(5) and 6 (condition B) and all references to condition B were omitted,

(*b*) in paragraph 2(6) (condition C), the words "or a person connected with the supplier" were omitted, and

(*c*) in paragraph 3(6) (condition C), the words "or a person connected with the grantor" were omitted.

PART 2

EXCEPTIONS

Letting etc of assets

12— (1) This paragraph applies in relation to a supply within paragraph 2 which arises from the letting, hiring or rental of assets.

(2) There is no supplementary charge under this Schedule if—

(*a*) the period to which the VAT invoice or payment referred to in paragraph 2(1) relates does not exceed 12 months, and

(*b*) the VAT invoice is issued, or the payment is received, in accordance with normal commercial practice in relation to the letting, hiring or rental of such assets.

Condition B cases involving normal commercial practice

13 There is no supplementary charge under this Schedule on a supply of goods or services within paragraph 2 or a grant of a right to goods or services within paragraph 3 if—

(*a*) the only relevant condition met is condition B, and

(*b*) the supply is made, or the right is granted, in accordance with normal commercial practice in relation to the supply of, or the grant of a right to, such goods or services.

Normal commercial practice

14 In this Part of this Schedule "normal commercial practice" means normal commercial practice at a time when an increase in the rate of VAT in force under section 2 of VATA 1994 is not expected.

Further exceptions

15— (1) The Treasury may by order provide that there is no supplementary charge under this Schedule on supplies (including grants of rights to goods or services) of a description specified in the order.

(2) An order under this paragraph may make provision having effect in relation to supplies of goods or services that are treated as taking place on or after 25 November 2008 or a later date.

PART 3

LIABILITY AND AMOUNT

Liability

16— (1) A supplementary charge under this Schedule on a supply within paragraph 2—

(*a*) is a liability of the supplier (subject to sub-paragraph (3)), and

(*b*) becomes due on the date of the VAT change (rather than at the time of supply).

(2) A supplementary charge under this Schedule on a supply consisting of the grant of a right to goods or services within paragraph 3—

(*a*) is a liability of the grantor (subject to sub-paragraph (3)), and

(*b*) becomes due on the first occasion on or after the date of the VAT change on which the right is exercised (rather than at the time the right is granted).

(3) If, on the date on which the supplementary charge becomes due, the person who would be liable to pay the charge under sub-paragraph (1) or (2)—

(*a*) is not a taxable person, but

(*b*) is treated as a member of a group under sections 43A to 43D of VATA 1994,

the supplementary charge is a liability of the representative member of the group.

Amount

17— (1) The amount of the supplementary charge on a supply within paragraph 2 is equal to the difference between—

(*a*) the amount of VAT chargeable on the supply apart from this Schedule, and

(*b*) the amount of VAT that would be chargeable on the supply if it were subject to VAT at the rate of 17.5%.

(2) The amount of the supplementary charge on a grant of a right to goods or services within paragraph 3 is equal to the difference between—

(*a*) the amount of VAT chargeable on the grant of the right apart from this Schedule, and

(*b*) the amount of VAT that would be chargeable on the grant of the right if it were subject to VAT at the rate of 17.5%,

(but see sub-paragraph (3)).

(3) If the basic time of supply for some of those goods and services is before the date of the VAT change, sub-paragraph (2) has effect as if the references to the amount of VAT chargeable and to the amount of VAT that would be chargeable were references to the relevant proportion of each of those amounts.

(4) "The relevant proportion" is—

P / W

where—

P is so much of the consideration for the grant of the right as is attributable on a just and reasonable basis to a right to the goods and services for which the basic time of supply is on or after the date of the VAT change, and

W is the whole of the consideration for the grant of the right.

PART 4
LISTED SUPPLIES

"Listed supply"

18— (1) In this Schedule "listed supply" means a supply falling within sub-paragraph (2)—

(*a*) which is made for a consideration the whole or part of which is determined or payable periodically or from time to time, and

(*b*) which is treated as taking place by virtue of the issue of a VAT invoice or the receipt of a payment by the person making the supply.

(2) The following supplies fall within this sub-paragraph—

(*a*) a supply of services,

(*b*) a supply arising from the grant of a major interest in land,

(*c*) a supply of water other than—

(i) distilled water, deionised water or water of similar purity, or

(ii) bottled water,

(*d*) a supply of—

(i) coal gas, water gas, producer gases or similar gases, or

(ii) petroleum gases, or other gaseous hydrocarbons, in a gaseous state,

(*e*) a supply of power, heat, refrigeration or ventilation, and

(*f*) a supply of goods together with services in the course of the construction, alteration, demolition, repair or maintenance of a building or civil engineering work.

(3) The Treasury may by order amend sub-paragraph (2) by—

(*a*) adding or omitting any description of supply, or

(*b*) varying any description of supply for the time being listed in that sub-paragraph.

"Basic time of supply": listed supplies

19— (1) For the purposes of this Schedule, in relation to a listed supply, "the basic time of supply" is the end of the period to which the VAT invoice or payment mentioned in paragraph 18(1) relates, except as provided in sub-paragraphs (2) and (4).

(2) Where the person making the supply issues an invoice—

(*a*) in respect of part of the listed supply to which the VAT invoice or payment mentioned in paragraph 18(1) relates, and

(*b*) for a period (a "billing period") ending before the end of the period to which that VAT invoice or payment relates, "the basic time of supply", in relation to that part of the supply, is the end of the billing period.

(3) For the purposes of sub-paragraph (2), the listed supply (and the consideration for the supply) must be apportioned between periods on a just and reasonable basis.

(4) Where a listed supply is treated as taking place by virtue of—

(*a*) the issue by the person making the supply of a VAT invoice relating to a premium for the grant of a tenancy or lease, or

(*b*) the receipt by the person making the supply of such a premium, "the basic time of supply" is the date of the grant of the tenancy or lease.

PART 5

ADMINISTRATION AND INTERPRETATION

Person ceasing to be taxable person before supplementary charge due

20— (1) This paragraph applies if, on the date on which a supplementary charge under this Schedule becomes due ("the due date"), the person who is liable to pay the charge under paragraph 16 is not a taxable person.

(2) The supplementary charge must be accounted for by that person in accordance with VATA 1994 (and regulations made under that Act) as if it were VAT due in the last period for which the person was required to make a return by or under VATA 1994.

(3) If an amount assessed as due by way of supplementary charge under this Schedule would (in the absence of this sub-paragraph) carry interest from a date earlier than the due date, it is to be treated as only carrying interest from the due date.

Adjustment of contracts following the VAT change

21— (1) This paragraph applies where—

(*a*) a contract for the supply of goods or services is made before the date of the VAT change, and

(*b*) there is a supplementary charge under this Schedule on the supply.

(2) The consideration for the supply is to be increased by an amount equal to the supplementary charge, unless the contract provides otherwise.

Invoices

22 Regulations under paragraph 2A of Schedule 11 to VATA 1994 (VAT invoices) may make provision about the provision, replacement or correction of invoices in connection with a supplementary charge under this Schedule.

Orders under this Schedule

23— (1) An order under this Schedule is to be made by statutory instrument.

(2) A statutory instrument containing an order under this Schedule is subject to annulment in pursuance of a resolution of the House of Commons, unless it is an instrument to which sub-paragraph (4) applies.

(3) Sub-paragraph (4) applies to a statutory instrument containing an order made under paragraph 10 (or under that paragraph and under other provisions) which extends the supplies that are subject to a supplementary charge under this Schedule.

(4) An instrument to which this sub-paragraph applies—

(*a*) must be laid before the House of Commons, and

(*b*) ceases to have effect at the end of the period of 28 days beginning with the day on which it was made unless it is approved during that period by a resolution of the House of Commons.

(5) In reckoning the period of 28 days no account is to be taken of any time during which Parliament is dissolved or prorogued or during which the House of Commons is adjourned for more than 4 days.

(6) The order ceasing to have effect does not affect—

(*a*) anything previously done under it, or

(*b*) the making of a new order.

Interpretation: general

24— (1) Expressions used in this Schedule and in VATA 1994 have the same meaning in this Schedule as in that Act.

(2) In this Schedule—

(*a*) "treated as taking place" means treated as taking place for the purposes of the charge to VAT, and

(*b*) references to the person by or to whom a supply is made (however expressed) are to the person by or to whom the supply is treated as being made for the purposes of VATA 1994.

PART 6
AMENDMENTS OF VATA 1994

25— (1) VATA 1994 is amended as follows.

(2) In section 2(2) (orders increasing or decreasing rate of VAT), after "such order" insert "that has not previously expired or been revoked".

(3) In section 97 (orders, rules and regulations), after subsection (4) insert—

"(4A) Where an order under section 2(2) is in force, the reference in subsection (4)(*c*)(i) of this section to the rate of VAT in force under section 2 at the time of the making of an order is a reference to the rate which would be in force at that time if no such order had been made."

SCHEDULE 36
VAT: PLACE OF SUPPLY OF SERVICES ETC

Section 76

PART 1
AMENDMENTS COMING INTO FORCE IN 2010

1 VATA 1994 is amended as follows.

2 In section 6(14A) (time of supply), omit "In relation to any services of a description specified in an order under section 7(11),".

3— (1) Section 7 (place of supply) is amended as follows.

(2) In subsection (1), omit "or services".

(3) Omit subsection (10).

(4) In subsection (11), omit "or services" (in each place).

(5) In the heading, insert at the end "of goods".

4 After that section insert—

"7A Place of supply of services

(1) This section applies for determining, for the purposes of this Act, the country in which services are supplied.

(2) A supply of services is to be treated as made—

(*a*) in a case in which the person to whom the services are supplied is a relevant business person, in the country in which the recipient belongs, and

(*b*) otherwise, in the country in which the supplier belongs.

(3) The place of supply of a right to services is the same as that in which the supply of the services would be treated as made if made by the supplier of the right to the recipient of the right (whether or not the right is exercised); and for this purpose a right to services includes any right, option or priority with respect to the supply of services and an interest deriving from a right to services.

(4) For the purposes of this Act a person is a relevant business person in relation to a supply of services if the person—

(*a*) is a taxable person within the meaning of Article 9 of Council Directive 2006/112/EC,

(*b*) is registered under this Act,

(*c*) is identified for the purposes of VAT in accordance with the law of a member State other than the United Kingdom, or

(*d*) is registered under an Act of Tynwald for the purposes of any tax imposed by or under an Act of Tynwald which corresponds to value added tax,

and the services are received by the person otherwise than wholly for private purposes.

(5) Subsection (2) has effect subject to Schedule 4A.

(6) The Treasury may by order—

(*a*) amend subsection (4),

(*b*) amend Schedule 4A, or

(*c*) otherwise make provision for exceptions from either or both of the paragraphs of subsection (2).

(7) An order under subsection (6) may include incidental, supplemental, consequential and transitional provision."

5— (1) Section 8 (reverse charge on supplies received from abroad) is amended as follows.

(2) For subsections (1) and (2) substitute—

"(1) Where services are supplied by a person who belongs in a country other than the United Kingdom in circumstances in which this subsection applies, this Act has effect as if (instead of there being a supply of the services by that person)—

(*a*) there were a supply of the services by the recipient in the United Kingdom in the course or furtherance of a business carried on by the recipient, and
(*b*) that supply were a taxable supply.

(2) Subsection (1) above applies if—

(*a*) the recipient is a relevant business person who belongs in the United Kingdom, and
(*b*) the place of supply of the services is inside the United Kingdom, and, where the supply of the services is one to which any paragraph of Part 1 or 2 of Schedule 4A applies, the recipient is registered under this Act."

(3) After subsection (4) insert—

"(4A) Subsection (1) does not apply to services of any of the descriptions specified in Schedule 9."

(4) In subsection (5), for "add to, or vary, Schedule 5" substitute "amend subsection (4A) by altering the descriptions of services specified in that subsection".

(5) Omit subsection (6).

(6) In subsection (7)—

(*a*) for "add to or vary Schedule 5" substitute "amend subsection (4A)", and
(*b*) for "addition to or variation of that Schedule" substitute "amendment of that subsection".

(7) In subsection (8)—

(*a*) for "addition to or variation of that Schedule" substitute "amendment of subsection (4A)", and
(*b*) for "the Schedule" substitute "that subsection".

6 For section 9 substitute—

"9 Place where supplier or recipient of services belongs

(1) This section has effect for determining for the purposes of section 7A (or Schedule 4A) or section 8, in relation to any supply of services, whether a person who is the supplier or recipient belongs in one country or another.

(2) A person who is a relevant business person is to be treated as belonging in the relevant country.

(3) In subsection (2) "the relevant country" means—

(*a*) if the person has a business establishment, or some other fixed establishment, in a country (and none in any other country), that country,
(*b*) if the person has a business establishment, or some other fixed establishment or establishments, in more than one country, the country in which the relevant establishment is, and
(*c*) otherwise, the country in which the person's usual place of residence is.

(4) In subsection (3)(*b*) "relevant establishment" means whichever of the person's business establishment, or other fixed establishments, is most directly concerned with the supply.

(5) A person who is not a relevant business person is to be treated as belonging in the country in which the person's usual place of residence is.

(6) In this section "usual place of residence", in relation to a body corporate, means the place where it is legally constituted."

7— (1) Section 43 (groups of companies) is amended as follows.

(2) In subsection (2A)—

(*a*) in paragraph (*a*), for "falling within Schedule 5" substitute "to which section 7A(2)(*a*) applies made", and
(*b*) in paragraph (*c*)—

(i) omit "falling within paragraphs 1 to 8 of Schedule 5", and
(ii) insert at the end "and section 7A(2)(*a*) applied to the supply".

(3) In subsection (2D)—

(*a*) in paragraph (*c*)—

(i) omit "falling within paragraphs 1 to 8 of Schedule 5", and
(ii) insert at the end "and section 7A(2)(*a*) applied to the supply", and

(*b*) in the words after the paragraphs, for "falling within that Schedule," substitute "to which section 7A(2)(*a*) applies,".

(4) In subsection (2E)(*b*), for "there are services falling within paragraphs 1 to 8 of Schedule 5 which, if used by the transferor for making supplies falling within that Schedule," substitute "there is a supply to which section 7A(2)(*a*) applies of services which, if used by the transferor for making such a supply,".

8— (1) Section 96 (interpretation) is amended as follows.

(2) In subsection (1), after the definition of "regulations" insert—

""relevant business person" has the meaning given by section 7A(4);".

(3) In subsection (8), omit "(subject to any provision made under section 8(6))".

9 Section 97(4)(*a*) (orders subject to requirement of Parliamentary approval after making), after "5(4)" insert ", 7A(6)".

10 Section 97A(1) (place of supply orders: transitional provision), for "on or after 17th March 1998 under section 7(11)" substitute "under section 7A(6)".

11 After Schedule 4 insert—

"SCHEDULE 4A

PLACE OF SUPPLY OF SERVICES: SPECIAL RULES

Section 7A

PART 1

GENERAL EXCEPTIONS

Services relating to land

1— (1) A supply of services to which this paragraph applies is to be treated as made in the country in which the land in connection with which the supply is made is situated.

(2) This paragraph applies to—

(*a*) the grant, assignment or surrender of any interest in or right over land,

(*b*) the grant, assignment or surrender of a personal right to call for or be granted any interest in or right over land,

(*c*) the grant, assignment or surrender of a licence to occupy land or any other contractual right exercisable over or in relation to land (including the provision of holiday accommodation, seasonal pitches for caravans and facilities at caravan parks for persons for whom such pitches are provided and pitches for tents and camping facilities),

(*d*) the provision in an hotel, inn, boarding house or similar establishment of sleeping accommodation or of accommodation in rooms which are provided in conjunction with sleeping accommodation or for the purpose of a supply of catering,

(*e*) any works of construction, demolition, conversion, reconstruction, alteration, enlargement, repair or maintenance of a building or civil engineering work, and

(*f*) services such as are supplied by estate agents, auctioneers, architects, surveyors, engineers and others involved in matters relating to land.

(3) In sub-paragraph (2)(*c*) "holiday accommodation" includes any accommodation in a building, hut (including a beach hut or chalet), caravan, houseboat or tent which is advertised or held out as holiday accommodation or as suitable for holiday or leisure use.

(4) In sub-paragraph (2)(*d*) "similar establishment" includes premises in which there is provided furnished sleeping accommodation, whether with or without the provision of board or facilities for the preparation of food, which are used by, or held out as being suitable for use by, visitors or travellers.

Passenger transport

2— (1) A supply of services consisting of the transportation of passengers (or of any luggage or motor vehicles accompanying passengers) is to be treated as made in the country in which the transportation takes place, and (in a case where it takes place in more than one country) in proportion to the distances covered in each.

(2) For the purposes of sub-paragraph (1) transportation which takes place partly outside the territorial jurisdiction of a country is to be treated as taking place wholly in the country if—

(*a*) it takes place in the course of a journey between two points in the country (whether or not as part of a longer journey involving travel to or from another country), and

(*b*) the means of transport used does not (except in an emergency or involuntarily) stop, put in or land in another country in the course of the journey between those two points.

(3) For the purposes of sub-paragraph (1) a pleasure cruise is to be regarded as the transportation of passengers (so that services provided as part of a pleasure cruise are to be treated as supplied in the same place as the transportation of the passengers).

(4) In sub-paragraph (3) "pleasure cruise" includes a cruise wholly or partly for education or training.

Hiring of means of transport

3— (1) A supply of services consisting of the short-term hiring of a means of transport is to be treated as made in the country in which the means of transport is actually put at the disposal of the person by whom it is hired.

But this is subject to sub-paragraphs (3) and (4).

(2) For the purposes of this Schedule the hiring of a means of transport is "short-term" if it is hired for a continuous period not exceeding—

(*a*) if the means of transport is a vessel, 90 days, and

(*b*) otherwise, 30 days.

(3) Where—

(*a*) a supply of services consisting of the hiring of a means of transport would otherwise be treated as made in the United Kingdom, and

(*b*) the services are to any extent effectively used and enjoyed in a country which is not a member State,

the supply is to be treated to that extent as made in that country.

(4) Where—

(*a*) a supply of services consisting of the hiring of a means of transport would otherwise be treated as made in a country which is not a member State, and

(*b*) the services are to any extent effectively used and enjoyed in the United Kingdom,

the supply is to be treated to that extent as made in the United Kingdom.

Cultural, educational and entertainment services etc

4— (1) A supply of services to which this paragraph applies is to be treated as made in the country in which the services are physically carried out.

(2) This paragraph applies to the provision of—

(*a*) services relating to cultural, artistic, sporting, scientific, educational, entertainment or similar activities (including fairs and exhibitions), and

(*b*) ancillary services relating to such activities, including services of organisers of such activities.

Restaurant and catering services: general

5— (1) A supply of services to which this paragraph applies is to be treated as made in the country in which the services are physically carried out.

(2) This paragraph applies to the provision of restaurant services and the provision of catering services, other than the provision of services to which paragraph 6 applies.

EC on-board restaurant and catering services

6— (1) A supply of services consisting of

(*a*) the provision of restaurant services, or

(*b*) the provision of catering services,

on board a ship, aircraft or train in connection with the transportation of passengers during an intra-EC passenger transport operation is to be treated as made in the country in which the relevant point of departure is located.

(2) An intra-EC passenger transport operation is a passenger transport operation which, or so much of a passenger transport operation as,—

(*a*) has as the first place at which passengers can embark a place which is within the EC,

(*b*) has as the last place at which passengers who embarked in a member State can disembark a place which is within the EC, and

(*c*) does not include a stop at a place which is not within the EC and at which passengers can embark or passengers who embarked in a member State can disembark.

(3) "Relevant point of departure", in relation to an intra-EC passenger transport operation, is the first place in the intra-EC passenger transport operation at which passengers can embark.

(4) A place is within the EC if it is within any member State.

(5) For the purposes of this paragraph the return stage of a return passenger transport operation is to be regarded as a separate passenger transport operation; and for this purpose—

(*a*) a return passenger transport operation is one which takes place in more than one country but is expected to end in the country in which it begins, and

(*b*) the return stage of a return passenger transport operation is the part of it which ends in the country in which it began and begins with the last stop at a place at which there has not been a previous stop during it.

Hiring of goods

7— (1) Where—

(*a*) a supply of services consisting of the hiring of any goods other than a means of transport would otherwise be treated as made in the United Kingdom, and

(*b*) the services are to any extent effectively used and enjoyed in a country which is not a member State,

the supply is to be treated to that extent as made in that country.

(2) Where—

(*a*) a supply of services consisting of the hiring of any goods other than a means of transport would otherwise be treated as made in a country which is not a member State, and

(*b*) the services are to any extent effectively used and enjoyed in the United Kingdom,

the supply is to be treated to that extent as made in the United Kingdom.

Telecommunication and broadcasting services

8— (1) This paragraph applies to a supply of services consisting of the provision of—

(*a*) telecommunication services, or

(*b*) radio or television broadcasting services.

(2) In this Schedule "telecommunication services" means services relating to the transmission, emission or reception of signals, writing, images and sounds or information of any nature by wire, radio, optical or other electromagnetic systems, including—

(*a*) the related transfer or assignment of the right to use capacity for such transmission, emission or reception, and

(*b*) the provision of access to global information networks.

(3) Where—

(*a*) a supply of services to which this paragraph applies would otherwise be treated as made in the United Kingdom, and

(*b*) the services are to any extent effectively used and enjoyed in a country which is not a member State,

the supply is to be treated to that extent as made in that country.

(4) Where—

(*a*) a supply of services to which this paragraph applies would otherwise be treated as made in a country which is not a member State, and

(*b*) the services are to any extent effectively used and enjoyed in the United Kingdom,

the supply is to be treated to that extent as made in the United Kingdom.

PART 2

EXCEPTIONS RELATING TO SUPPLIES MADE TO RELEVANT BUSINESS PERSON

Electronically-supplied services

9— (1) Where—

(*a*) a supply of services consisting of the provision of electronically supplied services to a relevant business person would otherwise be treated as made in the United Kingdom, and

(*b*) the services are to any extent effectively used and enjoyed in a country which is not a member State,

the supply is to be treated to that extent as made in that country.

(2) Where—

(*a*) a supply of services consisting of the provision of electronically supplied services to a relevant business person would otherwise be treated as made in a country which is not a member State, and

(*b*) the services are to any extent effectively used and enjoyed in the United Kingdom,

the supply is to be treated to that extent as made in the United Kingdom.

(3) Examples of what are electronically supplied services for the purposes of this Schedule include—

(*a*) website supply, web-hosting and distance maintenance of programmes and equipment,

(*b*) the supply of software and the updating of software,

(*c*) the supply of images, text and information, and the making available of databases,

(*d*) the supply of music, films and games (including games of chance and gambling games),

(*e*) the supply of political, cultural, artistic, sporting, scientific, educational or entertainment broadcasts (including broadcasts of events), and

(*f*) the supply of distance teaching.

(4) But where the supplier of a service and the supplier's customer communicate via electronic mail, this does not of itself mean that the service provided is an electronically supplied service for the purposes of this Schedule.

PART 3

EXCEPTIONS RELATING TO SUPPLIES NOT MADE TO RELEVANT BUSINESS PERSON

Intermediaries

10— (1) A supply of services to which this paragraph applies is to be treated as made in the same country as the supply to which it relates.

(2) This paragraph applies to a supply to a person who is not a relevant business person consisting of the making of arrangements for a supply by or to another person or of any other activity intended to facilitate the making of such a supply.

Transport of goods: general

11— (1) A supply of services to a person who is not a relevant business person consisting of the transportation of goods is to be treated as made in the country in which the transportation takes place, and (in a case where it takes place in more than one country) in proportion to the distances covered in each.

(2) For the purposes of sub-paragraph (1) transportation which takes place partly outside the territorial jurisdiction of a country is to be treated as taking place wholly in the country if—

(*a*) it takes place in the course of a journey between two points in the country (whether or not as part of a longer journey involving travel to or from another country), and

(*b*) the means of transport used does not (except in an emergency or involuntarily) stop, put in or land in another country in the course of the journey between those two points.

(3) This paragraph does not apply to a transportation of goods beginning in one member State and ending in another (see paragraph 12).

Intra-Community transport of goods

12 A supply of services to a person who is not a relevant business person consisting of the transportation of goods which begins in one member State and ends in another is to be treated as made in the member State in which the transportation begins.

Ancillary transport services

13— (1) A supply to a person who is not a relevant business person of ancillary transport services is to be treated as made where the services are physically performed.

(2) "Ancillary transport services" means loading, unloading handling and similar activities.

Valuation services etc

14 A supply to a person who is not a relevant business person of services consisting of the valuation of, or carrying out of work on, goods is to be treated as made where the services are physically performed.

Electronic services

15 A supply consisting of the provision by a person who belongs in a country which is not a member State (other than the Isle of Man) of electronically supplied services (as to the meaning of which see paragraph 9(3) and (4)) to a person ("the recipient") who—

(*a*) is not a relevant business person, and

(*b*) belongs in a member State, is to be treated as made in the country in which the recipient belongs.

Other services provided to recipient belonging outside EC

16— (1) A supply consisting of the provision to a person ("the recipient") who—

(*a*) is not a relevant business person, and

(*b*) belongs in a country which is not a member State (other than the Isle of Man),

of services to which this paragraph applies is to be treated as made in the country in which the recipient belongs.

(2) This paragraph applies to—

(*a*) transfers and assignments of copyright, patents, licences, trademarks and similar rights,

(*b*) the acceptance of any obligation to refrain from pursuing or exercising (in whole or in part) any business activity or any rights within paragraph (*a*),

(*c*) advertising services,

(*d*) services of consultants, engineers, consultancy bureaux, lawyers, accountants, and similar services, data processing and provision of information, other than any services relating to land,

(*e*) banking, financial and insurance services (including reinsurance), other than the provision of safe deposit facilities,

(*f*) the provision of access to, and of transport or transmission through, natural gas and electricity distribution systems and the provision of other directly linked services,

(*g*) the supply of staff,

(*h*) the letting on hire of goods other than means of transport,

(*i*) telecommunication services (as to the meaning of which see paragraph 8(2)),

(*j*) radio and television broadcasting services, and

(*k*) electronically supplied services (as to the meaning of which see paragraph 9(3) and (4))."

12 Omit Schedule 5 (services supplied where received).

13 In Article 5 of the Value Added Tax (Tour Operators) Order 1987 (SI 1987/1806)—

(*a*) omit paragraph (1), and

(*b*) in paragraph (2) after "treated" insert "for the purposes of this Act", and treat that article as made under section 7A(6)(*c*) of VATA 1994 (inserted by paragraph 4).

14— (1) The powers contained in section 7A(6) of VATA 1994 (inserted by paragraph 4) may be exercised at any time on or after the day on which this Act is passed.

(2) The amendments made by paragraph 7 come into force on 1 January 2010; but the references in section 43 of VATA 1994 (as amended by that paragraph) to a supply to which section 7A(2) of that Act applies includes a supply of services falling within paragraphs 1 to 8 of Schedule 5 made before that date.

(3) Subject to that, the amendments made by this Part have effect in relation to supplies made on or after 1 January 2010.

PART 2
AMENDMENTS COMING INTO FORCE IN 2011

Admission to cultural, educational and entertainment activities etc

15— (1) Schedule 4A to VATA 1994 (inserted by paragraph 11) is amended as follows.

(2) Omit paragraph 4.

(3) After paragraph 9 insert—

"Admission to cultural, educational and entertainment activities etc

9A— (1) A supply to a relevant business person of services to which this paragraph applies is to be treated as made in the country in which the events in question actually take place.

(2) This paragraph applies to the provision of—

(*a*) services in respect of admission to cultural, artistic, sporting, scientific, educational, entertainment or similar events (including fairs and exhibitions), and

(*b*) ancillary services relating to admission to such events."

(4) After paragraph 14 insert—

"Cultural, educational and entertainment services etc

14A— (1) A supply to a person who is not a relevant business person of services to which this paragraph applies is to be treated as made in the country in which the activities concerned actually take place.

(2) This paragraph applies to the provision of—

(*a*) services relating to cultural, artistic, sporting, scientific, educational, entertainment or similar activities (including fairs and exhibitions), and

(*b*) ancillary services relating to such activities, including services of organisers of such activities."

16 The amendments made by this Part have effect in relation to supplies made on or after 1 January 2011.

PART 3
AMENDMENTS COMING INTO FORCE IN 2013

17 In Schedule 4A to VATA 1994 (inserted by paragraph 11), after paragraph 13 insert—

"Long-term hiring of means of transport

13A— (1) A supply to a person who is not a relevant business person ("the recipient") of services consisting of the long-term hiring of a means of transport is to be treated as made in the country in which the recipient belongs.

But this is subject to sub-paragraph (2) and paragraph 3(3) and (4).

(2) A supply to a person who is not a relevant business person ("the recipient") of services consisting of the long-term hiring of a pleasure boat which is actually put at the disposal of the recipient at the supplier's business establishment, or some other fixed establishment of the supplier, is to be treated as made in the country where the pleasure boat is actually put at the disposal of the recipient.

(3) For the purposes of this Schedule, the hiring of a means of transport is "long-term" if it is not short-term (as to the meaning of which see paragraph 3(2))."

18 The amendment made by this Part has effect in relation to supplies made on or after 1 January 2013.

PART 4
TRANSITIONAL PROVISIONS

19— (1) This paragraph applies where—

(*a*) amendments made by this Schedule provide for a supply of services to be treated as made in the United Kingdom,

(*b*) the supply would not have fallen to be so treated apart from the amendments, and

(*c*) the services are treated under the law of a member State other than the United Kingdom as supplied in that member State before the commencement date.

(2) The supply is not to be treated as made in the United Kingdom.

(3) "The commencement date" means the date specified by this Schedule as that on or after which a supply must be made if it is to be treated as made in the United Kingdom by virtue of the amendments.

SCHEDULE 46
DUTIES OF SENIOR ACCOUNTING OFFICERS OF QUALIFYING COMPANIES

Section 93

Main duty of senior accounting officer

1— (1) The senior accounting officer of a qualifying company must take reasonable steps to ensure that the company establishes and maintains appropriate tax accounting arrangements.

(2) The senior accounting officer of a qualifying company must, in particular, take reasonable steps—

(*a*) to monitor the accounting arrangements of the company, and

(*b*) to identify any respects in which those arrangements are not appropriate tax accounting arrangements.

Certificate for Commissioners

2— (1) The senior accounting officer of a qualifying company must provide the Commissioners with a certificate for each financial year of the company.

(2) The certificate must—

(*a*) state whether the company had appropriate tax accounting arrangements throughout the financial year, and

(*b*) if it did not, give an explanation of the respects in which the accounting arrangements of the company were not appropriate tax accounting arrangements.

(3) The certificate must be provided—

(*a*) by such means and in such form as is reasonably specified by an officer of Revenue and Customs, and

(*b*) not later than the end of the period for filing the company's accounts for the financial year (or such later time as an officer of Revenue and Customs may have allowed).

(4) A certificate may relate to more than one qualifying company.

Notifying Commissioners of name of senior accounting officer

3— (1) For each financial year a qualifying company must ensure that the Commissioners are notified of the name of each person who was its senior accounting officer at any time during the year.

(2) The notification must be given—

(*a*) by such means and in such form as is reasonably specified by an officer of Revenue and Customs, and

(*b*) not later than the end of the period for filing the company's accounts for the financial year (or such later time as an officer of Revenue and Customs may have allowed for providing the certificate for the financial year under paragraph 2).

(3) A notification may relate to more than one qualifying company.

Penalty for failure to comply with main duty

4— (1) This paragraph applies if a senior accounting officer fails to comply with paragraph 1 at any time in a financial year.

(2) The senior accounting officer is liable to a penalty of £5,000.

(3) A person is not liable to more than one penalty under this paragraph in respect of the same company and the same financial year.

Penalties for failure to provide certificate etc

5— (1) This paragraph applies if a senior accounting officer—

(*a*) fails to provide a certificate in accordance with paragraph 2, or

(*b*) provides a certificate in accordance with that paragraph that contains a careless or deliberate inaccuracy.

(2) The senior accounting officer is liable to a penalty of £5,000.

(3) For the purposes of this Schedule, an inaccuracy is careless if the inaccuracy is due to a failure by the senior accounting officer to take reasonable care.

(4) An inaccuracy in a certificate that was neither careless nor deliberate when the certificate was given is to be treated as careless if the senior accounting officer—

(*a*) discovered the inaccuracy some time later, and

(*b*) did not take reasonable steps to inform HMRC.

More than one senior accounting officer

6— (1) This paragraph applies if the identity of the senior accounting officer of a company changes.

(2) If (but for this sub-paragraph) more than one person would be liable to a penalty under paragraph 4 in respect of a financial year of the company, only the one who became the senior accounting officer latest in the year is liable to such a penalty.

(3) If a person who is or has been the senior accounting officer of the company complies, or purports to comply, with paragraph 2 in respect of a financial year, no other person is liable to a penalty under paragraph 5 in respect of that company and that financial year.

(4) A person who is replaced as the senior accounting officer of the company before the last day for compliance with paragraph 2 in respect of a financial year is not liable to a penalty under paragraph 5(1)(*a*) for failing to comply with that paragraph in respect of that company and that financial year.

Penalty for failure to notify Commissioners of name of senior accounting officer

7 A qualifying company is liable to a penalty of £5,000 if, for a financial year, the Commissioners are not notified of the name or names of its senior accounting officer or officers in accordance with paragraph 3.

Reasonable excuse

8— (1) Liability to a penalty for a failure to comply with this Schedule does not arise if the senior accounting officer or qualifying company satisfies HMRC or (on an appeal notified to the tribunal) the tribunal that there is a reasonable excuse for the failure.

(2) For the purposes of this paragraph—

(*a*) an insufficiency of funds is not a reasonable excuse unless attributable to events outside the person's control,

(*b*) where the person relies on any other person to do anything, that is not a reasonable excuse unless the first person took reasonable care to avoid the failure, and

(*c*) where the person had a reasonable excuse for the failure but the excuse has ceased, the person is to be treated as having continued to have the excuse if the failure is remedied without unreasonable delay after the excuse ceased.

Assessment of penalties

9— (1) Where a senior accounting officer or a qualifying company becomes liable for a penalty under this Schedule—

(*a*) HMRC may assess the penalty, and

(*b*) if they do so, they must notify the officer or company liable for the penalty.

(2) An assessment of a penalty under this Schedule for a failure in respect of a financial year, or an inaccuracy in a certificate for a financial year, may not be made—

(*a*) more than 6 months after the failure or inaccuracy first comes to the attention of an officer of Revenue and Customs, or

(*b*) more than 6 years after the end of the period for filing the company's accounts for the financial year.

(3) HMRC may not assess a person who is the senior accounting officer of a company ("C") as liable to a penalty under paragraph 4 or 5 for a financial year ("the relevant financial year") if—

(*a*) at any time in the relevant financial year the person was the senior accounting officer of another company that was a member of the same group as C, and

(*b*) HMRC has assessed the person as liable, as the senior accounting officer of the other company, to a penalty under that paragraph for a financial year that ends on a day in the relevant financial year.

(4) HMRC may not assess a company ("C") as liable to a penalty under paragraph 7 for a financial year ("the relevant financial year") if—

(*a*) C was a member of a group at the end of that year, and (*b*) HMRC has assessed another company that was a member of the same group as C at that time as liable to a penalty under that paragraph—

(i) for its financial year ending on the same day as the relevant financial year, or

(ii) if its financial year does not end on that day, for its financial year ending last before that day.

Appeal

10— (1) A person may appeal against a decision of HMRC that a penalty is payable by that person.

(2) Notice of an appeal must be given—

(*a*) in writing,

(*b*) before the end of the period of 30 days beginning with the date on which the notification under paragraph 9 was issued, and

(*c*) to HMRC.

(3) Notice of an appeal must state the grounds of appeal.

(4) On an appeal that is notified to the tribunal, the tribunal may confirm or cancel the decision.

(5) Subject to this paragraph and paragraph 11, the provisions of Part 5 of TMA 1970 relating to appeals have effect in relation to appeals under this Schedule as they have effect in relation to an appeal against an assessment to income tax.

Enforcement of penalties

11— (1) A penalty under this Schedule must be paid—

(*a*) before the end of the period of 30 days beginning with the date on which the notification under paragraph 9 was issued, or

(*b*) if a notice of appeal against the penalty is given, before the end of the period of 30 days beginning with the date on which the appeal is determined or withdrawn.

(2) A penalty under this Schedule may be enforced as if it were income tax charged in an assessment and due and payable.

Power to change amount of penalties

12— (1) If it appears to the Treasury that there has been a change in the value of money since the last relevant date, they may by regulations substitute for the sums for the time being specified in paragraphs 4, 5 and 7 such other sums as appear to them to be justified by the change.

(2) In sub-paragraph (1), in relation to a specified sum, "relevant date" means—

(*a*) the date on which this Act is passed, and

(*b*) in relation to that sum, each date on which the power conferred by that sub-paragraph has been exercised.

(3) Regulations under this paragraph do not apply to—

(*a*) a failure that occurs in respect of a financial year of a company that begins before the date on which they come into force, or

(*b*) an inaccuracy in a certificate that was provided to HMRC in respect of such a financial year.

Application of provisions of TMA 1970

13 Subject to the provisions of this Schedule, the following provisions of TMA 1970 apply for the purposes of this Schedule as they apply for the purposes of the Taxes Acts—

(*a*) section 108 (responsibility of company officers),

(*b*) section 114 (want of form), and

(*c*) section 115 (delivery and service of documents).

Meaning of "appropriate tax accounting arrangements"

14— (1) "Appropriate tax accounting arrangements" means accounting arrangements that enable the company's relevant liabilities to be calculated accurately in all material respects.

(2) "Accounting arrangements" includes arrangements for keeping accounting records.

(3) "Relevant liabilities", in relation to a company, means liabilities in respect of—

(*a*) corporation tax (including any amount assessable or chargeable as if it were corporation tax),

(*b*) value added tax,

(*c*) amounts for which the company is accountable under PAYE regulations,

(*d*) insurance premium tax,

(*e*) stamp duty land tax,

(*f*) stamp duty reserve tax,

(*g*) petroleum revenue tax,

(*h*) customs duties, and

(*i*) excise duties.

Meaning of "qualifying company"

15— (1) A company is a qualifying company in relation to a financial year if the qualification test was satisfied in the previous financial year (subject to any regulations under sub-paragraph (8)).

(2) The qualification test is that the company satisfied either or both of the following requirements—

1 Relevant turnover	More than £200 million
2 Relevant balance sheet total	More than £2 billion.

(3) If the company was not a member of a group at the end of the previous financial year—

(*a*) "relevant turnover" means the company's turnover, and

(*b*) "relevant balance sheet total" means the company's balance sheet total.

(4) If the company was a member of a group at the end of the previous financial year—

(*a*) "relevant turnover" means the aggregate turnover of the company ("C") and any other company that was a member of the same group as C at the end of C's previous financial year, and

(*b*) "relevant balance sheet total" means the aggregate balance sheet totals of C and any such company.

(5) If the financial year of a company that was a member of the same group as C does not end on the same day as C's previous financial year, the figures for that company that are to be included in the aggregate figures are the figures for that company's financial year ending last before the end of C's previous financial year.

(6) "Turnover", in relation to a company, has the same meaning as in Part 15 of the Companies Act 2006 (see section 474 of that Act).

(7) "Balance sheet total", in relation to a company and a financial year, means the aggregate of the amounts shown as assets in the company's balance sheet as at the end of the financial year.

(8) The Treasury may by regulations provide that a company of a description specified in the regulations is not a qualifying company for the purposes of this Schedule.

Meaning of "senior accounting officer"

16— (1) "Senior accounting officer", in relation to a company that is not a member of a group, means the director or officer who, in the company's reasonable opinion, has overall responsibility for the company's financial accounting arrangements.

(2) "Senior accounting officer", in relation to a company that is a member of a group, means the group director or officer who, in the company's reasonable opinion, has overall responsibility for the company's financial accounting arrangements.

(3) "Group director or officer", in relation to a company, means a director or officer of the company or of a relevant body that is a member of the same group as the company.

(4) A person may be the senior accounting officer of more than one company.

Regulations

17— (1) Regulations under this Schedule are to be made by statutory instrument.

(2) A statutory instrument containing regulations under this Schedule is subject to annulment in pursuance of a resolution of the House of Commons.

Other definitions

18— (1) In this Schedule—

"the Commissioners" means the Commissioners for Her Majesty's Revenue and Customs;

"company" has the same meaning as in the Companies Acts (see section 1(1) of the Companies Act 2006) but does not include a company that is an open-ended investment company (within the meaning of section 468A of ICTA) or an investment trust (within the meaning of section 842 of ICTA);

"financial year", in relation to a company, has the same meaning as in the Companies Act 2006 (see section 390 of that Act);

"HMRC" means Her Majesty's Revenue and Customs;

"period for filing", in relation to accounts, has the same meaning as in the Companies Acts (see section 442 of the Companies Act 2006);

"relevant body" means a company or other body corporate but does not include a limited liability partnership;

"tribunal" means the First-tier Tribunal or, where determined by or under Tribunal Procedure Rules, the Upper Tribunal.

(2) For the purposes of this Schedule—

(*a*) a relevant body is a member of a group if—

(i) another relevant body is its 51 per cent subsidiary, or

(ii) it is a 51 per cent subsidiary of another relevant body, and

(*b*) two relevant bodies are members of the same group if—

(i) one is a 51 per cent subsidiary of the other, or
(ii) both are 51 per cent subsidiaries of a third relevant body.

(3) Section 838 of ICTA (meaning of "51 per cent subsidiary") applies for the purposes of this Schedule as it applies for the purposes of the Corporation Tax Acts (subject to the modification in sub-paragraph (4)).

(4) It applies as if references in that section to a body corporate were to a relevant body.

SCHEDULE 47

AMENDMENT OF INFORMATION AND INSPECTION POWERS

Section 95

1 Schedule 36 to FA 2008 (information and inspection powers) is amended as follows.

2— (1) Paragraph 3 (approval etc of taxpayer notices and third party notices) is amended as follows.

(2) After sub-paragraph (2) insert—

"(2A) An application for approval under this paragraph may be made without notice (except as required under sub-paragraph (3))."

(3) In sub-paragraph (3)(*c*), after "is" insert "to be".

3— (1) Paragraph 5 (power to obtain information and documents about persons whose identity is not known) is amended as follows.

(2) After sub-paragraph (3) insert—

"(3A) An application for approval under this paragraph may be made without notice."

(3) In sub-paragraph (4), for "give its approval for the purpose of" substitute "approve the giving of a notice under".

4 In paragraph 6 (notices), insert at the end—

"(4) A decision of the tribunal under paragraph 3, 4 or 5 is final (despite the provisions of sections 11 and 13 of the Tribunals, Courts and Enforcement Act 2007)."

5— (1) Paragraph 10 (power to inspect business premises etc) is amended as follows.

(2) In sub-paragraph (3), in the definition of "business assets", for ", excluding documents" substitute "(but see sub-paragraph (4))".

(3) After that sub-paragraph insert—

"(4) For the purposes of this Schedule, "business assets" does not include documents, other than—

(*a*) documents that are trading stock for the purposes of Chapter 11A of Part 2 of ITTOIA 2005 (see section 172A of that Act), and
(*b*) documents that are plant for the purposes of Part 2 of CAA 2001."

6— (1) Paragraph 11 (power to inspect premises used in connection with taxable supplies etc) is amended as follows.

(2) In sub-paragraph (1)—

(*a*) in paragraph (*a*), after "supplied" insert "or documents relating to such goods",
(*b*) in paragraph (*b*), after "acquired" insert "or documents relating to such goods", and
(*c*) in paragraph (*c*), after "as" insert "or in connection with".

(3) In sub-paragraph (2)(*c*), for "such goods" substitute "the supply of goods under taxable supplies, the acquisition of goods from other member States under taxable acquisitions or fiscal warehousing".

(4) In sub-paragraph (4)—

(*a*) for "sub-paragraph (1)" substitute "this paragraph", and
(*b*) for "in that sub-paragraph" substitute "here".

7 In paragraph 12(5) (carrying out inspections)—

(*a*) for "with the approval of" substitute "in respect of an inspection approved by", and
(*b*) for "it is given with that approval" substitute "the inspection has been so approved".

8— (1) Paragraph 13 (approval of inspections) is amended as follows.

(2) After sub-paragraph (1) insert—

"(1A) An application for approval under this paragraph may be made without notice."

(3) Insert at the end—

"(3) A decision of the tribunal under this paragraph is final (despite the provisions of sections 11 and 13 of the Tribunals, Courts and Enforcement Act 2007)."

9— (1) Paragraph 21 (taxpayer notices) is amended as follows.

(2) In sub-paragraph (6), after "that" (in the first place) insert ", as regards the person,".

(3) In sub-paragraph (7), for "that" (in the third place) substitute "the".

(4) In sub-paragraph (8)—

(*a*) after "repayments" insert "of tax or withholding of income", and (*b*) after "64(2)" insert "or (2A)".

(5) After sub-paragraph (8) insert—

"(9) In this paragraph, references to the person who made the return are only to that person in the capacity in which the return was made."

10— (1) Paragraph 35 (special cases: groups of undertakings) is amended as follows.

(2) In sub-paragraph (2)—

(*a*) for "paragraph 2" substitute "—

(*a*) paragraph 2(2)", and

(*b*) insert at the end ", and

(*b*) the references in paragraph 3(5) to naming the taxpayer are to making that statement and naming the parent undertaking."

(3) For sub-paragraph (4) substitute—

"(4) Where a third party notice is given to the parent undertaking for the purpose of checking the tax position of more than one subsidiary undertaking—

(*a*) paragraph 2(2) only requires the notice to state this, and

(*b*) the references in paragraph 3(5) to naming the taxpayer are to making that statement.

(4A) In relation to such a notice—

(*a*) in paragraph 3 (approval etc of notices), sub-paragraphs (1) and (3)(*e*) do not apply,

(*b*) paragraph 4(1) (copying third party notices to taxpayer) does not apply,

(*c*) paragraph 21 (restrictions on giving taxpayer notice where taxpayer has made return) applies as if the notice was a taxpayer notice or taxpayer notices given to each subsidiary undertaking (or, if the notice names the subsidiary undertakings to which it relates, to each of those undertakings),

(*d*) paragraph 30(1) (appeal) has effect as if it permitted an appeal on any grounds, and

(*e*) in paragraph 30(2) (no appeal in relation to taxpayer's statutory records), the reference to the taxpayer has effect as if it were a reference to the parent undertaking or any of its subsidiary undertakings."

(4) In sub-paragraph (5), for the words after "the notice" substitute

"—

(*a*) sub-paragraphs (3) and (4) of that paragraph (approval of tribunal) have effect as if they permitted, but did not require, the officer to obtain the approval of the tribunal, and

(*b*) paragraph 31 (appeal) has effect as if it permitted an appeal on any grounds, but the parent undertaking may not appeal against a requirement in the notice to produce any document that forms part of the statutory records of the parent undertaking or any of its subsidiary undertakings."

(5) Omit sub-paragraph (6).

11— (1) Paragraph 37 (special cases: partnerships) is amended as follows.

(2) For sub-paragraph (2) substitute—

"(2) Where, in respect of a chargeable period, any of the partners has—

(*a*) made a tax return under section 12AA of TMA 1970 (partnership returns), or

(*b*) made a claim or election in accordance with section 42(6)(*b*) of TMA 1970 (partnership claims and elections),

paragraph 21 (restrictions where taxpayer has made tax return) has effect as if that return, claim or election had been made by each of the partners."

(3) In sub-paragraph (3)—

(*a*) omit "to any person (other than one of the partners)",

(*b*) for "paragraph 2" substitute

"—

(*a*) paragraph 2(2)", and

(*c*) insert at the end

", and

(*b*) the references in paragraph 3(5) to naming the taxpayer are to making that statement and naming the partnership."

(4) In sub-paragraph (4)—

(*a*) after "notice" insert "given to a person other than one of the partners", and

(*b*) in paragraph (*b*), for "each of the partners" substitute "any of the partners in the partnership".

(5) For sub-paragraph (5) substitute—

"(5) In relation to a third party notice given to one of the partners for the purpose of checking the tax position of one or more of the other partners (in their capacity as such)—

(*a*) in paragraph 3 (approval etc of notices), sub-paragraphs (1) and (3)(*e*) do not apply,

(*b*) paragraph 4(1) (copying third party notices to taxpayer) does not apply,

(*c*) paragraph 30(1) (appeal) has effect as if it permitted an appeal on any grounds, and (*d*) in paragraph 30(2) (no appeal in relation to taxpayer's statutory records), the reference to the taxpayer has effect as if it were a reference to any of the partners in the partnership."

(6) In sub-paragraph (6) for the words after "the notice" substitute

"—

(*a*) sub-paragraphs (3) and (4) of that paragraph (approval of tribunal) have effect as if they permitted, but did not require, the officer to obtain the approval of the tribunal, and

(*b*) paragraph 31 (appeal) has effect as if it permitted an appeal on any grounds, but the partner to whom the notice is given may not appeal against a requirement in the notice to produce any document that forms part of that partner's statutory records."

(7) Omit sub-paragraph (7).

12 After paragraph 37 insert—

"*Information in connection with herd basis election*

37A— (1) This paragraph applies to a taxpayer notice given to a person carrying on a trade in relation to which a herd basis election is made if the notice refers only to information or documents that relate to—

(*a*) the animals kept for the purposes of the trade, or

(*b*) the products of those animals.

(2) Paragraph 21 (restrictions on giving taxpayer notice where taxpayer has made tax return) does not apply in relation to the notice.

(3) "Herd basis election" means an election under Chapter 8 of Part 2 of ITTOIA 2005 or Chapter 8 of Part 3 of CTA 2009.

Information from persons liable to counteraction of tax advantage

37B— (1) This paragraph applies to a taxpayer notice given to a person if—

(*a*) it appears to an officer of Revenue and Customs that a counteraction provision may apply to the person by reason of one or more transactions, and

(*b*) the notice refers only to information or documents relating to the transaction (or, if there are two or more transactions, any of them).

(2) Paragraph 21 (restrictions on giving taxpayer notice where taxpayer has made tax return) does not apply in relation to the notice.

(3) "Counteraction provision" means—

(*a*) section 703 of ICTA (company liable to counteraction of corporation tax advantage), or

(*b*) section 684 of ITA 2007 (person liable to counteraction of income tax advantage)."

13— (1) Paragraph 39 (standard penalties) is amended as follows.

(2) In sub-paragraph (2), for "A person to whom this paragraph applies" substitute "The person".

(3) In the heading—

(*a*) omit "*Standard*", and

(*b*) insert at the end "*for failure to comply or obstruction*".

14 In the heading before paragraph 40 (daily default penalties), insert at the end "*for failure to comply or obstruction*".

15 After that paragraph insert—

"*Penalties for inaccurate information and documents*

40A— (1) This paragraph applies if—

(*a*) in complying with an information notice, a person provides inaccurate information or produces a document that contains an inaccuracy, and

(*b*) condition A or B is met.

(2) Condition A is that the inaccuracy is careless or deliberate.

(3) An inaccuracy is careless if it is due to a failure by the person to take reasonable care.

(4) Condition B is that the person—

(*a*) discovers the inaccuracy some time later, and

(*b*) fails to take reasonable steps to inform HMRC.

(5) The person is liable to a penalty not exceeding £3,000.

(6) Where the information or document contains more than one inaccuracy, a penalty is payable for each inaccuracy."

16— (1) Paragraph 41 (power to change amount of penalties) is amended as follows.

(2) In sub-paragraph (1), for "and 40(2)" substitute ", 40(2) and 40A(5)".

(3) In sub-paragraph (2)—

(*a*) after "(1)" insert ", in relation to a specified sum,", and

(*b*) in paragraph (*b*), insert at the end "in relation to that sum".

(4) In sub-paragraph (3)—

(*a*) after "to" insert

"—

(*a*) ", and

(*b*) insert at the end

", or

(*b*) an inaccuracy in any information or document provided to HMRC before that date."

(5) Accordingly, in the heading omit "*standard and daily default*".

17— (1) Paragraph 46 (assessment of penalty) is amended as follows.

(2) In sub-paragraph (1)—

(*a*) for "or 40" substitute ", 40 or 40A",

(*b*) omit "HMRC may",

(*c*) at the beginning of paragraph (*a*), insert "HMRC may", and

(*d*) at the beginning of paragraph (*b*), insert "if they do so, they must".

(3) In sub-paragraph (2), for "within 12 months of the relevant date" substitute "within the period of 12 months beginning with the date on which the person became liable to the penalty, subject to sub-paragraph (3)".

(4) For sub-paragraph (3) substitute—

"(3) In a case involving an information notice against which a person may appeal, an assessment of a penalty under paragraph 39 or 40 must be made within the period of 12 months beginning with the latest of the following—

(*a*) the date on which the person became liable to the penalty,

(*b*) the end of the period in which notice of an appeal against the information notice could have been given, and

(*c*) if notice of such an appeal is given, the date on which the appeal is determined or withdrawn.

(4) An assessment of a penalty under paragraph 40A must be made—

(*a*) within the period of 12 months beginning with the date on which the inaccuracy first came to the attention of an officer of Revenue and Customs, and

(*b*) within the period of 6 years beginning with the date on which the person became liable to the penalty."

(5) Accordingly, in the heading omit "*standard penalty or daily default*".

18— (1) Paragraph 47 (right to appeal) is amended as follows.

(2) In paragraph (*a*), for "or 40" substitute ", 40 or 40A".

(3) Accordingly, in the heading, omit "*standard penalty or daily default*".

19 In the heading before paragraph 48 (procedure on appeal), omit "*standard or daily default*".

20— (1) Paragraph 49 (enforcement) is amended as follows.

(2) In sub-paragraph (1), for "or 40" substitute ", 40 or 40A".

(3) In sub-paragraph (2), for "or 40" substitute ", 40 or 40A".

(4) Accordingly, in the heading, omit "*standard penalty or daily default*".

21— (1) Paragraph 63 (tax) is amended as follows.

(2) In sub-paragraph (3)—

(*a*) omit the "and" at the end of paragraph (*a*), and

(*b*) for the words following paragraph (*b*) substitute ", and

(*c*) amounts listed in sub-paragraph (3A)."

(3) After that sub-paragraph insert—

"(3A) Those amounts are—

(*a*) any amount that is recoverable under paragraph 5(2) of Schedule 11 to VATA 1994 (amounts shown on invoices as VAT), and

(*b*) any amount that is treated as VAT by virtue of regulations under section 54 of VATA 1994 (farmers etc)."

22— (1) Paragraph 64 (tax position) is amended as follows.

(2) In sub-paragraph (1)(*c*), after "with" insert "the person's liability to pay".

(3) After sub-paragraph (2) insert—

"(2A) References in this Schedule to a person's tax position also include, where appropriate, a reference to the person's position as regards the withholding by the person of another person's PAYE income (as defined in section 683 of ITEPA 2003)."

SCHEDULE 48

EXTENSION OF INFORMATION AND INSPECTION POWERS

Section 96

1 Schedule 36 to FA 2008 (information and inspection powers) is amended as follows.

2 In paragraph 5(4)(*b*) (power to obtain information and documents about persons whose identity is not known), for the words from ", VATA 1994" to the end substitute "or any other enactment relating to UK tax".

3 After paragraph 10 insert—

"Power to inspect business premises etc of involved third parties

10A— (1) An officer of Revenue and Customs may enter business premises of an involved third party (see paragraph 61A) and inspect—

(*a*) the premises,
(*b*) business assets that are on the premises, and
(*c*) relevant documents that are on the premises,

if the inspection is reasonably required by the officer for the purpose of checking the position of any person or class of persons as regards a relevant tax.

(2) The powers under this paragraph may be exercised whether or not the identity of that person is, or the individual identities of those persons are, known to the officer.

(3) The powers under this paragraph do not include power to enter or inspect any part of the premises that is used solely as a dwelling.

(4) In relation to an involved third party, "relevant documents" and "relevant tax" are defined in paragraph 61A."

4— (1) Paragraph 12 (carrying out inspections) is amended as follows.

(2) In sub-paragraph (1), for "this Part of this Schedule" substitute "paragraph 10, 10A or 11".

(3) Accordingly, in the heading, insert at the end "*under paragraph 10, 10A or 11*".

5 After that paragraph insert—

"Powers to inspect property for valuation etc

12A— (1) An officer of Revenue and Customs may enter and inspect premises for the purpose of valuing the premises if the valuation is reasonably required for the purpose of checking any person's position as regards income tax or corporation tax.

(2) An officer of Revenue and Customs may enter premises and inspect—

(*a*) the premises, and
(*b*) any other property on the premises,

for the purpose of valuing, measuring or determining the character of the premises or property.

(3) Sub-paragraph (2) only applies if the valuation, measurement or determination is reasonably required for the purpose of checking any person's position as regards—

(*a*) capital gains tax,
(*b*) corporation tax in respect of chargeable gains,
(*c*) inheritance tax,
(*d*) stamp duty land tax, or
(*e*) stamp duty reserve tax.

(4) A person who the officer considers is needed to assist with the valuation, measurement or determination may enter and inspect the premises or property with the officer.

Carrying out inspections under paragraph 12A

12B— (1) An inspection under paragraph 12A may be carried out only if condition A or B is satisfied.

(2) Condition A is that—

(*a*) the inspection is carried out at a time agreed to by a relevant person, and
(*b*) the relevant person has been given notice in writing of the agreed time of the inspection.

(3) "Relevant person" means—

(*a*) the occupier of the premises, or
(*b*) if the occupier cannot be identified or the premises are vacant, a person who controls the premises.

(4) Condition B is that—

(*a*) the inspection has been approved by the tribunal, and
(*b*) any relevant person specified by the tribunal has been given at least 7 days' notice in writing of the time of the inspection.

(5) A notice under sub-paragraph (4)(*b*) must state the possible consequences of obstructing the officer in the exercise of the power.

(6) If a notice is given under this paragraph in respect of an inspection approved by the tribunal (see paragraph 13), it must state that the inspection has been so approved.

(7) An officer of Revenue and Customs seeking to carry out an inspection under paragraph 12A must produce evidence of authority to carry out the inspection if asked to do so by—

(*a*) the occupier of the premises, or

(*b*) any other person who appears to the officer to be in charge of the premises or property."

6— (1) Paragraph 13 (approval of tribunal) is amended as follows.

(2) In sub-paragraph (1), insert at the end "(and for the effect of obtaining such approval see paragraph 39 (penalties))".

(3) In sub-paragraph (1A) (inserted by Schedule 47), insert at the end "(except as required under sub-paragraph (2A))".

(4) In sub-paragraph (2), after "an inspection" insert "under paragraph 10, 10A or 11".

(5) After that sub-paragraph insert—

"(2A) The tribunal may not approve an inspection under paragraph 12A unless—

(*a*) an application for approval is made by, or with the agreement of, an authorised officer of Revenue and Customs,

(*b*) the person whose tax position is the subject of the proposed inspection has been given a reasonable opportunity to make representations to the officer of Revenue and Customs about that inspection,

(*c*) the occupier of the premises has been given a reasonable opportunity to make such representations,

(*d*) the tribunal has been given a summary of any representations made, and

(*e*) the tribunal is satisfied that, in the circumstances, the inspection is justified.

(2B) Paragraph (*c*) of sub-paragraph (2A) does not apply if the tribunal is satisfied that the occupier of the premises cannot be identified."

7 In paragraph 17(*b*) (power to record information), after "premises," insert "property, goods,".

8— (1) Paragraph 21 (restrictions on giving taxpayer notices) is amended as follows.

(2) In sub-paragraph (7), for "VAT position" substitute "position as regards any tax other than income tax, capital gains tax or corporation tax".

(3) In the heading, insert at the end "*following tax return*".

9 After that paragraph insert—

"Taxpayer notices following land transaction return

21A— (1) Where a person has delivered a land transaction return under section 76 of FA 2003 (returns for purposes of stamp duty land tax) in respect of a transaction, a taxpayer notice may not be given for the purpose of checking that person's stamp duty land tax position in relation to that transaction.

(2) Sub-paragraph (1) does not apply where, or to the extent that, any of conditions A to C is met.

(3) Condition A is that a notice of enquiry has been given in respect of—

(*a*) the return, or

(*b*) a claim (or an amendment of a claim) made by the person in connection with the transaction,

and the enquiry has not been completed.

(4) In sub-paragraph (3) "notice of enquiry" means a notice under paragraph 12 of Schedule 10, or paragraph 7 of Schedule 11A, to FA 2003.

(5) Condition B is that, as regards the person, an officer of Revenue and Customs has reason to suspect that—

(*a*) an amount that ought to have been assessed to stamp duty land tax in respect of the transaction may not have been assessed,

(*b*) an assessment to stamp duty land tax in respect of the transaction may be or have become insufficient, or

(*c*) relief from stamp duty land tax in respect of the transaction may be or have become excessive.

(6) Condition C is that the notice is given for the purpose of obtaining any information or document that is also required for the purpose of checking that person's position as regards a tax other than stamp duty land tax."

10 In paragraph 28 (restrictions on inspection of business documents), and in the heading before that paragraph, omit "*business*".

11 After paragraph 34 insert—

"Involved third parties

34A— (1) This paragraph applies to a third party notice or a notice under paragraph 5 if—

(*a*) it is given to an involved third party (see paragraph 61A), (*b*) it is given for the purpose of checking the position of a person, or a class of persons, as regards the relevant tax, and

(*c*) it refers only to relevant information or relevant documents.

(2) In relation to such a third party notice—

(*a*) paragraph 3(1) (approval etc of third party notices) does not apply,

(*b*) paragraph 4(1) (copying third party notices to taxpayer) does not apply, and

(*c*) paragraph 30(1) (appeal) has effect as if it permitted an appeal on any grounds.

(3) In relation to such a notice under paragraph 5—

(*a*) sub-paragraphs (3) and (4) of that paragraph (approval of tribunal) have effect as if they permitted, but did not require, an authorised officer of Revenue and Customs to obtain the approval of the tribunal, and

(*b*) paragraph 31 (appeal) has effect as if it permitted an appeal on any grounds.

(4) The involved third party may not appeal against a requirement in the notice to provide any information, or produce any document, that forms part of the involved third party's statutory records.

(5) In relation to an involved third party, "relevant documents", "relevant information" and "relevant tax" are defined in paragraph 61A.

Registered pension schemes etc

34B— (1) This paragraph applies to a third party notice or a notice under paragraph 5 if it refers only to information or documents that relate to any pensions matter.

(2) "Pensions matter" means any matter relating to—

(*a*) a registered pension scheme,

(*b*) an annuity purchased with sums or assets held for the purposes of a registered pension scheme or a pre-2006 pension scheme, or

(*c*) an employer-financed retirement benefits scheme.

(3) In relation to such a third party notice—

(*a*) paragraph 3(1) (approval etc of third party notices) does not apply,

(*b*) paragraph 4(1) (copying third party notices to taxpayer) does not apply, and

(*c*) paragraph 30(1) (appeal) has effect as if it permitted an appeal on any grounds.

(4) In relation to such a notice under paragraph 5—

(*a*) sub-paragraphs (3) and (4) of that paragraph (approval of tribunal) have effect as if they permitted, but did not require, an authorised officer of Revenue and Customs to obtain the approval of the tribunal, and

(*b*) paragraph 31 (appeal) has effect as if it permitted an appeal on any grounds.

(5) A person may not appeal against a requirement in the notice to provide any information, or produce any document, that forms part of any person's statutory records.

(6) Where the notice relates to a matter within sub-paragraph (2)(*a*) or (*b*), the officer of Revenue and Customs who gives the notice must give a copy of the notice to the scheme administrator in relation to the pension scheme.

(7) Where the notice relates to a matter within sub-paragraph (2)(*c*), the officer of Revenue and Customs who gives the notice must give a copy of the notice to the responsible person in relation to the employer-financed retirement benefits scheme.

(8) Sub-paragraphs (6) and (7) do not apply if the notice is given to a person who, in relation to the scheme or annuity to which the notice relates, is a prescribed description of person.

Registered pension schemes etc: interpretation

34C In paragraph 34B—

"employer-financed retirement benefits scheme" has the same meaning as in Chapter 2 of Part 6 of ITEPA 2003 (see sections 393A and 393B of that Act);

"pension scheme" has the same meaning as in Part 4 of FA 2004;

"pre-2006 pension scheme" means a scheme that, at or in respect of any time before 6 April 2006, was—

(*a*) a retirement benefits scheme approved for the purposes of Chapter 1 of Part 14 of ICTA,

(*b*) a former approved superannuation fund (as defined in paragraph 1(3) of Schedule 36 to FA 2004),

(*c*) a relevant statutory scheme (as defined in section 611A of ICTA) or a pension scheme treated as if it were such a scheme, or

(*d*) a personal pension scheme approved under Chapter 4 of Part 14 of ICTA;

"prescribed" means prescribed by regulations made by the Commissioners;

"registered pension scheme" means a pension scheme that is or has been a registered pension scheme within the meaning of Part 4 of FA 2004 or in relation to which an application for registration under that Part of that Act has been made;

"responsible person", in relation to an employer-financed retirement benefits scheme, has the same meaning as in Chapter 2 of Part 6 of ITEPA 2003 (see section 399A of that Act);

"scheme administrator", in relation to a pension scheme, has the same meaning as in Part 4 of FA 2004 (see section 270 of that Act)."

12 In paragraph 35 (special cases: groups of undertakings), in sub-paragraph (4A)(*c*) (inserted by Schedule 47)—

(*a*) for "paragraph 21" substitute "paragraphs 21 and 21A", and
(*b*) for "applies" substitute "apply".

13 In paragraph 37 (special cases: partnerships), after sub-paragraph (2) insert—

"(2A) Where, in respect of a transaction entered into as purchaser by or on behalf of the members of the partnership, any of the partners has—

(*a*) delivered a land transaction return under Part 4 of FA 2003 (stamp duty land tax), or
(*b*) made a claim under that Part of that Act, paragraph 21A (restrictions where taxpayer has delivered land transaction return) has effect as if that return had been delivered, or that claim had been made, by each of the partners."

14 After paragraph 61 insert—

"Involved third parties

61A— (1) In this Schedule, "involved third party" means a person described in the first column of the Table below.

(2) In this Schedule, in relation to an involved third party, "relevant information", "relevant document" and "relevant tax" have the meaning given in the corresponding entries in that Table.

	Involved third party	*Relevant information and relevant documents*	*Relevant tax*
1	A body approved by an officer of Revenue and Customs for the purpose of paying donations within the meaning of Part 12 of ITEPA 2003 (donations to charity: payroll giving) (see section 714 of that Act)	Information and documents relating to the donations	Income tax
2	A plan manager (see section 696 of ITTOIA 2005 (managers of individual investment plans))	Information and documents relating to the plan, including investments which are or have been held under the plan	Income tax
3	An account provider in relation to a child trust fund (as defined in section 3 of the Child Trust Funds Act 2004)	Information and documents relating to the fund, including investments which are or have been held under the fund	Income tax
4	A person who is or has been registered as a managing agent at Lloyd's in relation to a syndicate of underwriting members of Lloyd's	Information and documents relating to, and to the activities of, the syndicate	Income tax Capital gains tax Corporation tax
5	A person involved (in any capacity) in an insurance business (as defined for the purposes of Part 3 of FA 1994)	Information and documents relating to contracts of insurance entered into in the course of the business	Insurance premium tax
6	A person who makes arrangements for persons to enter into contracts of insurance	Information and documents relating to the contracts	Insurance premium tax

	Involved third party	*Relevant information and relevant documents*	*Relevant tax*
7	A person who— (*a*) is concerned in a business that is not an insurance business (as defined for the purposes of Part 3 of FA 1994), and (*b*) has been involved in the entry into a contract of insurance providing cover for any matter associated with that business	Information and documents relating to the contracts	Insurance premium tax
8	A person who, in relation to a charge to stamp duty reserve tax on an agreement, transfer, issue, appropriation or surrender, is an accountable person (as defined in regulation 2 of the Stamp Duty Reserve Tax Regulations SI 1986/1711 (as amended from time to time))	Information and documents relating to the agreement, transfer, issue, appropriation or surrender	Stamp duty reserve tax
9	A responsible person in relation to an oil field (as defined for the purposes of Part 1 of OTA 1975)	Information and documents relating to the oil field	Petroleum revenue tax
10	A person involved (in any capacity) in subjecting aggregate to exploitation in the United Kingdom (as defined for the purposes of Part 2 of FA 2001) or in connected activities	Information and documents relating to matters in which the person is or has been involved	Aggregates levy
11	A person involved (in any capacity) in making or receiving taxable commodities (as defined for the purposes of Schedule 6 to FA 2000) or in connected activities	Information and documents relating to matters in which the person is or has been involved	Climate change levy
12	A person involved (in any capacity) with any landfill disposal (as defined for the purposes of Part 3 of FA 1996)	Information and documents relating to the disposal	Landfill tax".

15— (1) Paragraph 62 (meaning of "statutory records") is amended as follows.

(2) In sub-paragraph (1), for paragraph (*b*) substitute—

"(*b*) any other enactment relating to a tax,".

(3) In sub-paragraph (2)(*b*), for "VATA 1994 or any other enactment relating to value added tax" substitute "any other enactment relating to a tax".

SCHEDULE 49

POWERS TO OBTAIN CONTACT DETAILS FOR DEBTORS

Section 97

Requirement for contact details for debtor

1— (1) This Schedule applies where—

(*a*) a sum is payable by a person ("the debtor") to the Commissioners under or by virtue of an enactment or under a contract settlement,

(*b*) an officer of Revenue and Customs reasonably requires contact details for the debtor for the purpose of collecting that sum,

(*c*) the officer has reasonable grounds to believe that a person ("the third party") has any such details, and

(*d*) the condition in sub-paragraph (2) is met.

(2) That condition is that—

(*a*) the third party is a company, a local authority or a local authority association, or

(*b*) the officer has reasonable grounds to believe that the third party obtained the details in the course of carrying on a business.

(3) This Schedule does not apply if—

(*a*) the third party is a charity and obtained the details in the course of providing services free of charge, or

(*b*) the third party is not a charity but obtained the details in the course of providing services on behalf of a charity that are free of charge to the recipient of the service.

Power to obtain details

2— (1) An officer of Revenue and Customs may by notice in writing require the third party to provide the details.

(2) The notice must name the debtor.

Complying with notices

3 If a notice is given to the third party under this Schedule, the third party must provide the details—

(*a*) within such period, and

(*b*) at such time, by such means and in such form (if any), as is reasonably specified or described in the notice.

Right to appeal

4— (1) The third party may appeal against the notice or any requirement in the notice on the ground that it would be unduly onerous to comply with the notice or requirement.

(2) Paragraph 32 of Schedule 36 to FA 2008 (procedure on appeal to tribunal) applies to an appeal under this paragraph as it applies to an appeal relating to a notice under that Schedule.

Penalty

5— (1) This paragraph applies if the third party fails to comply with the notice.

(2) The third party is liable to a penalty of £300.

(3) Paragraphs 44 to 49 and 52 of Schedule 36 to FA 2008 (assessment and enforcement of penalties etc) apply in relation to a penalty under this paragraph as they apply in relation to a penalty under paragraph 39(1)(*a*) of that Schedule (and references in those provisions to an information notice include a notice under this Schedule).

Power to change amount of penalty

6— (1) If it appears to the Treasury that there has been a change in the value of money since the last relevant date, they may by regulations substitute for the sum for the time being specified in paragraph 5 such other sum as appears to them to be justified by the change.

(2) In sub-paragraph (1), "relevant date" means—

(*a*) the date on which this Act is passed, and

(*b*) each date on which the power conferred by that sub-paragraph has been exercised.

(3) Regulations under this paragraph do not apply to any failure which began before the date on which they come into force.

(4) Regulations made by the Treasury under this paragraph are to be made by statutory instrument.

(5) A statutory instrument containing regulations under this paragraph is subject to annulment in pursuance of a resolution of the House of Commons.

Application of provisions of TMA 1970

7 Subject to the provisions of this Schedule, the following provisions of TMA 1970 apply for the purposes of this Schedule as they apply for the purposes of the Taxes Acts—

(*a*) section 108 (responsibility of company officers),

(*b*) section 114 (want of form), and

(*c*) section 115 (delivery and service of documents).

General interpretation

8 In this Schedule—

"business" includes—

(*a*) a profession, and

(*b*) a property business;

"charity" means a company, body of persons or trust established for charitable purposes only;
"the Commissioners" means the Commissioners for Her Majesty's Revenue and Customs;
"contact details", in relation to a person, means the person's address and any other information about how the person may be contacted;
"contract settlement" means an agreement made in connection with any person's liability to make a payment to the Commissioners under or by virtue of an enactment;
"enactment" includes subordinate legislation (within the meaning of the Interpretation Act 1978);
"local authority" has the meaning given in section 999 of ITA 2007;
"local authority association" has the meaning given in section 1000 of that Act;
"property business" has the same meaning as in ITTOIA 2005 (see section 263(6) of that Act).

SCHEDULE 53

LATE PAYMENT INTEREST

Section 101

PART 2

SPECIAL PROVISION: LATE PAYMENT INTEREST START DATE

Amendments and discovery assessments etc

3— (1) This paragraph applies to any amount which is due and payable as a result of—

(*a*) an amendment or correction to an assessment or self-assessment ("assessment A"),

(*b*) an assessment made by HMRC in place of or in addition to an assessment ("assessment A") which was made by a taxpayer, or

(*c*) an assessment made by HMRC in place of an assessment ("assessment A") which ought to have been made by a taxpayer.

(2) The late payment interest start date in respect of that amount is the date which would have been the late payment interest start date if—

(*a*) assessment A had been complete and accurate and had been made on the date (if any) by which it was required to be made, and

(*b*) accordingly, the amount had been due and payable as a result of assessment A.

(3) In the case of a person ("P") who failed to give notice as required under section 7 of TMA 1970 (notice of liability to tax), the reference in sub-paragraph (1)(*c*) to an assessment which ought to have been made by P is a reference to the assessment which P would have been required to make if an officer of Revenue and Customs had given notice under section 8 of that Act.

(4) In this paragraph "assessment" means any assessment or determination (however described) of any amount due and payable to HMRC.

VAT due from persons not registered as required

10— (1) This paragraph applies where an amount of value added tax is due from a person ("P") in respect of a period during which P was liable to be registered under VATA 1994 but was not registered.

(2) The late payment interest start date in respect of the amount is the date which would have been the late payment interest date in respect of that amount if P had become registered when P had first become liable to be so.

Unauthorised VAT invoices

11— (1) This paragraph applies where an unauthorised person issues an invoice showing an amount as being value added tax or as including an amount attributable to value added tax.

(2) The late payment interest start date in respect of the amount which is shown as being value added tax, or which is to be taken as representing value added tax, is the date of the invoice.

(3) In this paragraph "unauthorised person" has the meaning given in paragraph 2 of Schedule 41 to FA 2008.

Death of taxpayer

12— (1) This paragraph applies if—

(*a*) a person chargeable to an amount of revenue dies before the amount becomes due and payable, and (*b*) the executor or administrator is unable to pay the amount before obtaining probate or letters of administration or (in Scotland) the executor is unable to pay the amount before obtaining confirmation.

(2) The late payment interest start date in respect of that amount is the later of the following—

(*a*) the date which would be the late payment interest start date apart from this paragraph, and

(*b*) the day after the end of the period of 30 days beginning with the grant of probate or letters of administration or (in Scotland) the grant of confirmation.

SCHEDULE 57

AMENDMENTS RELATING TO PENALTIES

Section 109

PART 1

AMENDMENTS OF SCHEDULE 24 TO FA 2007

1 Schedule 24 to FA 2007 (penalties for errors) is amended as follows.

2 In paragraph 2 (under-assessment by HMRC), insert at the end—

"(4) In this paragraph (and in Part 2 of this Schedule so far as relating to this paragraph)—

(*a*) "assessment" includes determination, and

(*b*) accordingly, references to an under-assessment include an under-determination."

3 In paragraph 5 (normal rule for calculating potential lost revenue), for sub-paragraph (4)(*b*) substitute—

"(*b*) any relief under subsection (4) of section 419 of ICTA (relief in respect of repayment etc of loan) which is deferred under subsection (4A) of that section;".

4 In paragraph 9(1)(*b*) and (*c*) (reductions for disclosure), for "supply or false information" substitute "supply of false information".

5 In paragraph 13 (assessment), insert at the end—

"(7) In this Part of this Schedule references to an assessment to tax, in relation to inheritance tax and stamp duty reserve tax, are to a determination."

6 For paragraph 16(2) (appeals) substitute—

"(2) Sub-paragraph (1) does not apply—

(*a*) so as to require P to pay a penalty before an appeal against the assessment of the penalty is determined, or

(*b*) in respect of any other matter expressly provided for by this Act."

7— (1) Paragraph 19 (companies: officers' liability) is amended as follows.

(2) In sub-paragraph (3)—

(*a*) after "a body corporate" insert "other than a limited liability partnership",

(*b*) in paragraph (*a*), omit the "or" at the end, and

(*c*) after that paragraph insert—

"(*aa*) a manager, and".

(3) After sub-paragraph (3) insert—

"(3A) In the application of sub-paragraph (1) to a limited liability partnership, "officer" means a member."

(4) Insert at the end—

"(6) In this paragraph "company" means any body corporate or unincorporated association, but does not include a partnership, a local authority or a local authority association."

8 Omit paragraph 28(da) (interpretation of references to assessment).

9 In paragraphs 30 and 31 (consequential amendments) for "paragraph 7" substitute "paragraphs 7 and 7B".

PART 2

AMENDMENTS OF SCHEDULE 41 TO FA 2008

10 Schedule 41 to FA 2008 (penalties for failure to notify and certain other wrongdoing) is amended as follows.

11 For paragraph 18(2) (appeals) substitute—

"(2) Sub-paragraph (1) does not apply—

(*a*) so as to require P to pay a penalty before an appeal against the assessment of the penalty is determined, or

(*b*) in respect of any other matter expressly provided for by this Act."

12— (1) Paragraph 22 (companies: officers' liability) is amended as follows.

(2) In sub-paragraph (3)—

(*a*) after "a body corporate" insert "other than a limited liability partnership",
(*b*) in paragraph (*a*), omit the "or" at the end,
(*c*) after that paragraph insert—
"(*aa*) a manager, and".

(3) After sub-paragraph (3) insert—

"(3A) In the application of sub-paragraph (1) to a limited liability partnership, "officer" means a member."

(4) Insert at the end—

"(6) In this paragraph "company" means any body corporate or unincorporated association, but does not include a partnership, a local authority or a local authority association."

PART 3

OTHER AMENDMENTS

13— (1) TMA 1970 is amended as follows.

(2) In section 100(2) (determination of penalties by officer), omit paragraph (*g*) and the "or" before it.

(3) After section 103 insert—

"103ZA Disapplication of sections 100 to 103 in the case of certain penalties

Sections 100 to 103 do not apply to a penalty under—

(*a*) Schedule 24 to FA 2007 (penalties for errors),
(*b*) Schedule 36 to FA 2008 (information and inspection powers),
(*c*) Schedule 41 to that Act (penalties for failure to notify and certain other wrongdoing),
(*d*) Schedule 55 to FA 2009 (penalties for failure to make returns etc), or
(*e*) Schedule 56 to that Act (penalties for failure to make payments on time)."

14 In FA 2008 omit—

(*a*) paragraph 74 of Schedule 36 (information and inspection powers);
(*b*) paragraph 20(3) of Schedule 40 (amendment of Schedule 24 to FA 2007).

VALUE ADDED TAX STATUTORY INSTRUMENTS

CHRONOLOGICAL LIST OF PRINTED STATUTORY INSTRUMENTS

Note—For list of current, revoked, amending, etc statutory instruments, *see post*.

SI YEAR/NO	TITLE
SI 1961/1523	Temporary Importation (Commercial Vehicles and Aircraft) Regulations 1961
SI 1973/173	VAT (Terminal Markets) Order 1973
SI 1976/1223	Customs Duties (Deferred Payment) Regulations 1976
SI 1976/2028	VAT (Refund of Tax) Order 1976
SI 1982/1067	VAT (Isle of Man) Order 1982
SI 1982/1068	VAT (Isle of Man) (No 2) Order 1982
SI 1984/746	VAT (Imported Goods) Relief Order 1984
SI 1984/1176	Control of Movement of Goods Regulations 1984
SI 1984/1177	Free Zone Regulations 1984
SI 1985/1101	VAT (Refund of Tax) Order 1985
SI 1986/260	Postal Packets (Customs and Excise) Regulations 1986
SI 1986/336	VAT (Refund of Tax) Order 1986
SI 1986/532	VAT (Refund of Tax) (No 2) Order 1986
SI 1986/590	VAT Tribunals Rules 1986
SI 1986/896	VAT (Treatment of Transactions) Order 1986
SI 1986/939	VAT (Small Non-Commercial Consignments) Relief Order 1986
SI 1986/2288	VAT Tribunals Appeals Order 1986
SI 1987/1806	VAT (Tour Operators) Order 1987
SI 1988/809	Excise Warehousing (Etc) Regulations 1988
SI 1989/472	VAT (Self-supply of Construction Services) Order 1989
SI 1989/1114	VAT (Water) Order 1989
SI 1990/2167	Channel Tunnel (Customs and Excise) Order 1990
SI 1991/2306	*VAT (Input Tax) (Person Supplied) Order 1991 (revoked)*
SI 1991/2724	Customs Controls on Importation of Goods Regulations 1991
SI 1991/2727	Free Zone Regulations 1991
SI 1992/630	VAT (Treatment of Transactions) Order 1992
SI 1992/2790	Statistics of Trade (Customs and Excise) Regulations 1992
SI 1992/3111	VAT (Removal of Goods) Order 1992
SI 1992/3121	VAT (Place of Supply of Services) Order 1992
SI 1992/3122	VAT (Cars) Order 1992
SI 1992/3124	VAT (Imported Gold) Relief Order 1992
SI 1992/3130	VAT (Supply of Temporarily Imported Goods) Order 1992
SI 1992/3132	VAT (Treatment of Transactions) (No 2) Order 1992
SI 1992/3135	Excise Goods (Holding, Movement, Warehousing and REDS) Regulations 1992
SI 1992/3152	Excise Duties (Deferred Payment) Regulations 1992
SI 1992/3156	Customs and Excise (Personal Reliefs for Special Visitors) Order 1992
SI 1992/3193	Customs and Excise Duties (Personal Reliefs for Goods Permanently Imported) Order 1992
SI 1992/3220	VAT (Flat-rate Scheme for Farmers) (Designated Activities) Order 1992
SI 1992/3221	VAT (Flat-rate Scheme for Farmers) (Percentage Addition) Order 1992
SI 1992/3222	VAT (Input Tax) Order 1992
SI 1992/3283	*VAT (Place of Supply of Goods) Order 1992 (revoked)*
SI 1993/1507	VAT (Supply of Services) Order 1993
SI 1993/2001	VAT (Payments on Account) Order 1993
SI 1994/143	*Free Zone (Prestwick Airport) Designation (Variation) Order 1994* (revoked)
SI 1994/144	Free Zone (Humberside) Designation Order 1994
SI 1994/955	Travellers' Allowances Order 1994
SI 1994/1978	VAT Tribunals Appeals (Northern Ireland) Order 1994
SI 1995/958	VAT (Treatment of Transactions) Order 1995
SI 1995/1067	Free Zone (Humberside) Designation (Variation) Order 1995
SI 1995/1268	VAT (Special Provisions) Order 1995
SI 1995/1978	VAT (Refund of Tax) Order 1995
SI 1995/2518	VAT Regulations 1995
SI 1995/2999	VAT (Refund of Tax) (No 2) Order 1995
SI 1996/1255	VAT (Fiscal Warehousing)(Treatment of Transactions) Order 1996

SI 1997/994	Free Zone (Port of Sheerness) (Substitution of Responsible Authority) Order 1997
SI 1997/1431	Distress for Customs and Excise Duties and Other Indirect Taxes Regulations 1997
SI 1997/1523	VAT (Reverse Charge) (Anti-avoidance) Order 1997
SI 1997/2558	VAT (Refund of Tax) Order 1997
SI 1998/1461	Air Passenger Duty and Other Indirect Taxes (Interest Rate) Regulations 1998
SI 1999/2076	VAT (Refund of Tax) Order 1999
SI 1999/3115	VAT (Importation of Investment Gold) Relief Order 1999
SI 1999/3116	VAT (Investment Gold) Order 1999
SI 1999/3121	VAT (Input Tax) (Specified Supplies) Order 1999
SI 2000/1046	VAT (Refund of Tax) Order 2000
SI 2000/1515	VAT (Refund of Tax) (No 2) Order 2000
SI 2000/1672	VAT (Refund of Tax) (No 3) Order 2000
SI 2001/759	VAT (Electronic Communications) (Incentives) Regulations 2001
SI 2001/2879	VAT (Refund of Tax to Museums and Galleries) Order 2001
SI 2001/2880	Free Zone (Southampton) Designation Order 2001
SI 2001/2881	Free Zone (Liverpool) Designation Order 2001
SI 2001/2882	Free Zone (Prestwick Airport) Designation Order 2001
SI 2001/3453	VAT (Refund of Tax) Order 2001
SI 2002/1280	VAT (Special Provisions) (Amendment) Order 2002
SI 2002/1418	Free Zone (Port of Tilbury) Designation Order 2002
SI 2002/1502	VAT (Cars) (Amendment) Order 2002
SI 2002/1503	VAT (Special Provisions) (Amendment) (No 2) Order
SI 2002/1935	VAT (Acquisitions) Relief Order 2002
SI 2003/3113	Customs (Contravention of a Relevant Rule) Regulations 2003
SI 2004/674	Recovery of Duties and Taxes etc Due in Other Member States (Corresponding UK Claims, Procedure and Supplementary) Regulations 2004
SI 2004/1929	VAT (Disclosure of Avoidance Schemes) Regulations 2004
SI 2004/1931	VAT (Groups: eligibility) Order 2004
SI 2004/1933	VAT (Disclosure of Avoidance Schemes) (Designations) Order 2004
SI 2004/3147	VAT (Imported Gas and Electricity) Relief Order 2004
SI 2004/3148	VAT (Place of Supply of Goods) Order 2004
SI 2005/1133	Revenue and Customs (Inspections) Regulations 2005
SI 2005/3290	VAT (Input Tax) (Reimbursement by Employers of Employees' Business Use of Road Fuel) Regulations 2005
SI 2005/3311	Revenue and Customs (Complaints and Misconduct) Regulations 2005
SI 2007/1417	VAT (Section 55A) (Specified Goods and Excepted Supplies) Order 2007
SI 2007/1509	Control of Cash (Penalties) Regulations 2007
SI 2007/2709	Tribunals, Courts and Enforcement Act 2007 (Commencement No 1) Order 2007
SI 2008/568	Finance Act 2007, Schedule 24 (Commencement and Transitional Provisions) Order 2008
SI 2008/1146	Value Added Tax (Buildings and Land) Order 2008
SI 2008/1948	Taxes (Fees for Payment by Telephone) Regulations 2008
SI 2009/403	Finance Act 2008, Schedule 39 (Appointed Day, Transitional Provision and Savings) Order 2009
SI 2009/571	Finance Act 2008, Schedule 40 (Appointed Day, Transitional Provisions and Consequential Amendments) Order 2009

CHRONOLOGICAL LIST OF STATUTORY INSTRUMENTS

Note—For list of printed statutory instruments, see above.

SI YEAR/NO	**TITLE**
SI 1961/1523	Temporary Importation (Commercial Vehicles and Aircraft) Regulations 1961
SI 1965/1776	*Rules of the Supreme Court (Revision) 1965 (superseded by SI 1998/3132)*
SI 1973/173	VAT (Terminal Markets) Order 1973
SI 1976/1223	Customs Duties (Deferred Payment) Regulations 1976

SI 1976/2028	VAT (Refund of Tax) Order 1976
SI 1977/1017	*VAT Tribunals (Amendment) Rules 1977 (revoked)*
SI 1977/1760	*VAT Tribunals (Amendment) (No 2) Rules 1977 (revoked)*
SI 1977/1790	*VAT (Imported Goods) Relief Order 1977 (revoked)*
SI 1977/1796	*VAT (Special Provisions) Order 1977 (revoked)*
SI 1978/1064	*VAT (Consolidation) Order 1978 (spent)*
SI 1978/1129	*VAT (Bad Debt Relief) Regulations 1978 (revoked)*
SI 1978/1725	*Customs Duties (Deferred Payment) (Amendment) Regulations 1978*
SI 1978/1883	*Customs Duties (Personal Reliefs) (No 1) Order 1968 (Amendment) Order 1978 (revoked)*
SI 1979/224	*VAT (Supplies by Retailers) (Amendment) Regulations 1979 (revoked)*
SI 1979/243	*VAT (Finance) Order 1979 (spent)*
SI 1979/244	*VAT (International Services) Order 1979 (spent)*
SI 1979/246	*VAT (Medical Goods and Services) Order 1979 (spent)*
SI 1979/657	*VAT (General) Order 1979 (spent)*
SI 1979/1551	*Customs Duty (Personal Reliefs) (No 1) Order 1968 (Amendment) Order 1979 (revoked)*
SI 1979/1554	*VAT (International Services) (No 2) Order 1979 (spent)*
SI 1979/1646	*VAT (Fuel and Power) (Metrication) Order 1979 (spent)*
SI 1980/303	*VAT (Gold) Order 1980 (spent)*
SI 1980/304	*VAT (Terminal Markets) (Amendment) Order 1980*
SI 1980/305	*VAT (Transport) Order 1980 (spent)*
SI 1980/440	*VAT (Fuel and Power) Order 1980 (revoked)*
SI 1980/442	*VAT (Cars) Order 1980 (revoked)*
SI 1980/1009	*VAT (Imported Goods) Relief Order 1980 (revoked)*
SI 1980/1536	*VAT (General) Regulations 1980 (revoked)*
SI 1980/1537	*VAT (Repayment to Community Traders) Regulations 1980 (revoked)*
SI 1980/1602	*VAT (Health) Order 1980 (spent)*
SI 1980/1603	*VAT (Special Provisions) (Amending) Order 1980 (revoked)*
SI 1980/1604	*VAT (Education) Order 1980 (spent)*
SI 1980/1909	*VAT (Competitions) Order 1980 (spent)*
SI 1981/338	*VAT (Terminal Markets) (Amendment) Order 1981*
SI 1981/365	*VAT (Handicapped Persons and Charities) Order 1981 (spent)*
SI 1981/663	*VAT (General) (Amendment) Regulations 1981 (revoked)*
SI 1981/955	*VAT (Terminal Markets) (Amendment) (No 2) Order 1981 (revoked)*
SI 1981/1080	*VAT (General and Bad Debt Relief) (Amendment) Regulations 1981 (revoked)*
SI 1981/1530	*VAT (General) (Amendment) (No 2) Regulations 1981 (revoked)*
SI 1981/1740	*VAT (Insurance) Order 1981 (spent)*
SI 1981/1741	*VAT (Special Provisions) Order 1981 (revoked)*
SI 1982/321	*VAT (Handicapped Persons and Charities) Order 1982 (spent)*
SI 1982/476	*VAT (Finance) Order 1982 (spent)*
SI 1982/1007	*VAT (Double-Glazing) Order 1982 (spent)*
SI 1982/1067	VAT (Isle of Man) Order 1982
SI 1982/1068	VAT (Isle of Man) (No 2) Order 1982
SI 1982/1088	*VAT (General) (Amendment) Regulations 1982 (revoked)*
SI 1982/1471	*VAT (General) (Amendment) (No 2) Regulations 1982 (revoked)*
SI 1982/1591	*Customs Duty (Personal Reliefs) (No 1) Order 1968 (Amendment) Order 1982 (revoked)*
SI 1983/295	*VAT (General) (Amendment) Regulations 1983 (revoked)*
SI 1983/401	*VAT (Increase of Registration Limits) Order 1983 (spent)*
SI 1983/475	*VAT (General) (Amendment) (No 2) Regulations 1983 (revoked)*
SI 1983/499	*VAT (Health) Order 1983 (spent)*
SI 1983/809	*VAT (Works of Art, etc) Order 1983 (spent)*
SI 1983/1099	*VAT (Horses and Ponies) Order 1983 (revoked)*
SI 1983/1717	*VAT (Charities, Etc) 1983 (revoked)*
SI 1983/1828	*Customs and Excise Duties (Personal Reliefs for Goods Permanently Imported) Order 1983 (revoked)*
SI 1983/1829	*Customs and Excise Duties (Personal Reliefs for Goods Temporarily Imported) Order 1983 (revoked)*
SI 1984/33	*VAT (Cars) (Amendment) Order 1984 (revoked)*
SI 1984/155	*VAT (General) (Amendment) Regulations 1984 (revoked)*
SI 1984/202	*VAT (Terminal Markets) (Amendment) Order 1984*

SI 1984/342	*VAT (Increase of Registration Limits) Order 1984 (spent)*
SI 1984/489	*VAT (Handicapped Persons) Order 1984 (revoked)*
SI 1984/631	*VAT (Lifeboats) Order 1984 (revoked)*
SI 1984/718	*Customs Duty (Personal Reliefs) (No 1) Order 1968 (Amendment) Order 1984 (revoked)*
SI 1984/736	*VAT (Special Provisions) (Amendment) (No 2) Order 1984 (revoked)*
SI 1984/746	VAT (Imported Goods) Relief Order 1984
SI 1984/766	*VAT (Charities, etc) Order 1984 (revoked)*
SI 1984/767	*VAT (Marine etc Insurance) Order 1984 (revoked)*
SI 1984/895	*C&E Duties (Relief for Imported Legacies) Order 1984 (revoked)*
SI 1984/929	*VAT (General) (Amendment) (No 2) Regulations 1984 (revoked)*
SI 1984/959	*VAT (Handicapped Persons) (No 2) Order 1984 (revoked)*
SI 1984/1176	Control of Movement of Goods Regulations 1984
SI 1984/1177	Free Zone Regulations 1984
SI 1984/1206	*Free Zone (Belfast Airport) Designation Order 1984 (spent)*
SI 1984/1207	*Free Zone (Birmingham Airport) Designation Order 1984 (revoked)*
SI 1984/1208	*Free Zone (Cardiff) Designation Order 1984 (spent)*
SI 1984/1209	*Free Zone (Liverpool) Designation Order 1984 (revoked)*
SI 1984/1210	*Free Zone (Prestwick Airport) Designation Order 1984 (revoked)*
SI 1984/1211	*Free Zone (Southampton) Designation Order 1984 (revoked)*
SI 1984/1376	*VAT (General Amendment) (No 2) Regulations 1984 (revoked)*
SI 1984/1685	*VAT (Place of Supply) Order 1984 (revoked)*
SI 1984/1784	*VAT (Optical Appliances) Order 1984 (revoked)*
SI 1985/18	*VAT (Protected Buildings) Order 1985 (revoked)*
SI 1985/105	*VAT (General) (Amendment) Regulations 1985 (revoked)*
SI 1985/431	*VAT (Charities) Order 1985 (revoked)*
SI 1985/432	*VAT (Finance) Order 1985 (revoked)*
SI 1985/433	*VAT (Increase of Registration Limits) Order 1985 (spent)*
SI 1985/693	*VAT (General) (Amendment) (No 2) Regulations 1985 (revoked)*
SI 1985/799	*VAT (Hiring of Goods) Order 1985 (revoked)*
SI 1985/886	*VAT (General) Regulations 1985 (revoked)*
SI 1985/919	*VAT (Handicapped Persons) Order 1985 (revoked)*
SI 1985/1046	*VAT (Terminal Markets) (Amendment) Order 1985*
SI 1985/1101	VAT (Refund of Tax) Order 1985
SI 1985/1375	*Customs Duty (Personal Reliefs) (No 1) Order 1968 (Amendment) Order 1985 (revoked)*
SI 1985/1376	*C&E Duties (Personal Reliefs for Goods Permanently Imported) Order 1983 (Amendment) Order 1985 (spent)*
SI 1985/1378	*C&E Duties (Relief for Imported Legacies) Order 1984 (Amendment) Order 1985 (revoked)*
SI 1985/1384	*VAT (Imported Goods) Relief (Amendment) Order 1985 (revoked)*
SI 1985/1646	*VAT (Temporarily Imported Goods) Relief Order 1985 (revoked)*
SI 1985/1650	*VAT (General) Regulations 1985 (Amendment) Regulations 1985 (revoked)*
SI 1985/1784	*The Companies (Department of Trade and Industry) Fees Order 1985 (lapsed)*
SI 1985/1900	*VAT (Welfare) Order 1985 (revoked)*
SI 1986/71	*VAT (General) (Amendment) Regulations 1986 (revoked)*
SI 1986/260	Postal Packets (Customs and Excise) Regulations 1986
SI 1986/305	*VAT (General) (Amendment) (No 2) Regulations 1986 (revoked)*
SI 1986/335	*VAT (Bad Debt Relief) Regulations 1986 (revoked)*
SI 1986/336	VAT (Refund of Tax) Order 1986
SI 1986/337	*Finance Act 1985 (Bad Debt Relief) (Commencement) Order 1986 (lapsed)*
SI 1986/385	*Administrative Receivers (VAT Certificates) Rules 1986 (spent)*
SI 1986/530	*VAT (Handicapped Persons and Charities) Order 1986 (revoked)*
SI 1986/531	*VAT (Increase of Registration Limits) Order 1986 (spent)*
SI 1986/532	VAT (Refund of Tax) (No 2) Order 1986
SI 1986/590	VAT Tribunals Rules 1986
SI 1986/704	*VAT (Land) Order 1986 (revoked)*
SI 1986/716	*VAT (Land) (No 2) Order 1986 (revoked)*
SI 1986/896	VAT (Treatment of Transactions) Order 1986
SI 1986/909	*VAT (Repayment Supplement) Regulations 1986 (revoked)*

SI 1986/934	*Finance Act 1985 (VAT Tribunals Rules) (Appointed Day) Order 1986 (lapsed)*
SI 1986/939	VAT (Small Non-Commercial Consignments) Relief Order 1986
SI 1986/968	*Finance Act 1985 (Default Surcharge) (Commencement) Order 1986 (lapsed)*
SI 1986/969	*Finance Act 1985 (Breaches of Regulations) (Appointed Day) Order 1986 (lapsed)*
SI 1986/970	*Finance Act 1985 (Repayment Supplement) (Appointed Day) Order 1986 (spent)*
SI 1986/1019	*Postal Packets (Customs and Excise) (Amendment) Regulations 1986*
SI 1986/1279	*VAT (Repayment Supplement) (No 2) Regulations 1986 (revoked)*
SI 1986/1989	*VAT (Temporarily Imported Goods) Relief Order 1986 (revoked)*
SI 1986/2105	*Customs Duty (Personal Reliefs) (No 1) Order 1968 (Amendment) Order 1986 (revoked)*
SI 1986/2288	VAT Tribunals Appeals Order 1986
SI 1986/2290	*VAT Tribunals (Amendment) Rules 1986*
SI 1987/150	*VAT (General) (Amendment) Regulations 1987 (revoked)*
SI 1987/154	*VAT (Small Non-Commercial Consignments) Relief (Amendment) Order 1987 (superseded)*
SI 1987/155	*VAT (Imported Goods) Relief (Amendment) Order 1987 (superseded)*
SI 1987/437	*VAT (Charities) Order 1987 (revoked)*
SI 1987/438	*VAT (Increase of Registration Limits) Order 1987 (spent)*
SI 1987/510	*VAT (General) (Amendment) (No 2) Regulations 1987 (revoked)*
SI 1987/517	*VAT (Betting, Gaming and Lotteries) Order 1987 (revoked)*
SI 1987/518	*VAT (International Services) Order 1987 (revoked)*
SI 1987/781	*VAT (Construction of Buildings) Order 1987 (spent)*
SI 1987/806	*VAT (Terminal Markets) (Amendment) Order 1987*
SI 1987/860	*VAT (Finance) Order 1987 (revoked)*
SI 1987/1072	*VAT (Construction of Buildings) (No 2) Order 1987 (revoked)*
SI 1987/1259	*VAT (Education) Order 1987 (revoked)*
SI 1987/1427	*VAT (Cash Accounting) Regulations 1987 (revoked)*
SI 1987/1712	*VAT (Supplies by Retailers) (Amendment) Regulations 1987 (revoked)*
SI 1987/1806	VAT (Tour Operators) Order 1987
SI 1987/1916	*VAT (General) (Amendment) (No 3) Regulations 1987 (revoked)*
SI 1987/1919	*Insolvency (Amendment) Rules 1987*
SI 1987/2015	*VAT (Repayments to Third Country Traders) Regulations 1987 (revoked)*
SI 1987/2108	*VAT (Imported Goods) Relief (Amendment) (No 2) Order 1987*
SI 1988/507	*VAT (Confectionery) Order 1988 (revoked)*
SI 1988/508	*VAT (Increase of Registration Limits) Order 1988 (spent)*
SI 1988/533	*Free Zone (Liverpool) Designation (Variation) Order 1988 (spent)*
SI 1988/710	*Free Zone (Amendment) Regulations 1988*
SI 1988/809	Excise Warehousing (Etc) Regulations 1988
SI 1988/886	*VAT (Annual Accounting) Regulations 1988 (revoked)*
SI 1988/1124	*VAT (Special Provisions) (Amendment) Order 1988 (revoked)*
SI 1988/1174	*VAT (Goods Imported for Private Purposes) Relief Order 1988 (revoked)*
SI 1988/1193	*VAT (Imported Goods) Relief (Amendment) Order 1988*
SI 1988/1282	*VAT (Training) Order 1988 (revoked)*
SI 1988/1343	*VAT (Repayment Supplement) Regulations 1988 (revoked)*
SI 1988/2083	*VAT (General) (Amendment) Regulations 1988 (revoked)*
SI 1988/2108	*VAT (General) (Amendment) (No 2) Regulations 1988 (revoked)*
SI 1988/2212	*VAT (Imported Goods Relief) (Amendment) (No 2) Order (amending)*
SI 1988/2217	*VAT (Repayment to Community Traders) (Amendment) Regulations 1988 (revoked)*
SI 1989/267	*VAT (Educational) Order (revoked)*
SI 1989/470	*VAT (Fund-Raising Events and Charities Order) 1989 (revoked)*
SI 1989/471	*VAT (Increase of Registration Limits) Order 1989 (superseded)*
SI 1989/472	VAT (Self-supply of Construction Services) Order 1989
SI 1989/959	*VAT (Cars) (Amendment) Order 1989 (revoked)*
SI 1989/1114	VAT (Water) Order 1989
SI 1989/1132	*VAT (General) (Amendment) Regulations 1989 (revoked)*
SI 1989/1217	*VAT (Refund of Tax) Order 1989 (spent)*
SI 1989/1302	*VAT (General) (Amendment) (No 2) Regulations 1989 (revoked)*
SI 1989/2248	*VAT (Accounting and Records) Regulations 1989 (revoked)*

SI 1989/2252	*Customs Duty (Personal Reliefs) (No 1) Order 1968 (Amendment) Order 1989 (revoked)*
SI 1989/2255	*VAT (Bad Debt Relief) (Amendment) Regulations 1989 (revoked)*
SI 1989/2256	*VAT (General) (Amendment) (No 3) Regulations 1989 (revoked)*
SI 1989/2259	*VAT (Do-It-Yourself Builders) (Refund of Tax) Regulations 1989 (revoked)*
SI 1989/2270	*Finance Act 1985 (Serious Misdeclaration and Interest on Tax) (Appointed Days) Order 1989 (lapsed)*
SI 1989/2271	*Finance Act 1989 (Recovery of Overpaid Tax and Administration) (Appointed Days) Order 1989 (lapsed)*
SI 1989/2272	*VAT (Finance, Health and Welfare) Order 1989 (revoked)*
SI 1989/2273	*VAT (Small Non-Commercial Consignments Relief) (Amendment) Order 1989 (superseded)*
SI 1989/2355	*VAT (General) (Amendment) (No 4) Regulations 1989 (revoked)*
SI 1990/139	*Free Zone (Liverpool) Designation (Variation) Order 1990 (spent)*
SI 1990/315	*VAT (Cars) (Amendment) Order 1990 (revoked)*
SI 1990/420	*VAT (Cash Accounting) (Amendment) Regulations 1990 (revoked)*
SI 1990/682	*VAT (Increase of Registration Limits) Order 1990 (revoked)*
SI 1990/750	*VAT (Charities) Order 1990 (revoked)*
SI 1990/751	*VAT (Tour Operators) (Amendment) Order 1990 (revoked in part; otherwise spent)*
SI 1990/752	*VAT (Transport) Order 1990 (revoked)*
SI 1990/1188	*VAT (Refund of Tax) (Revocation) Order 1990 (spent)*
SI 1990/1943	*VAT (Cash Accounting) (Amendment) (No 2) Regulations 1990 (revoked)*
SI 1990/2037	*VAT (Insurance) Order 1990 (revoked)*
SI 1990/2129	*VAT (Charities) (No 2) Order 1990 (revoked)*
SI 1990/2167	Channel Tunnel (Customs and Excise) Order 1990
SI 1990/2548	*VAT (Imported Goods) Relief (Amendment) Order 1990 (superseded)*
SI 1990/2553	*VAT (Construction of Dwellings and Land) Order 1990 (revoked)*
SI 1991/186	*VAT Tribunals (Amendment) Rules 1991 (amending)*
SI 1991/195	*Health and Personal Social Services (Northern Ireland Consequential Amendments) Order 1991*
SI 1991/371	*VAT (Refunds for Bad Debts) Regulations 1991 (revoked)*
SI 1991/532	*VAT (Annual Accounting) (Amendment) Regulations 1991 (spent)*
SI 1991/691	*VAT (General) (Amendment) Regulations 1991 (revoked)*
SI 1991/737	*VAT (Charities) Order 1991 (revoked)*
SI 1991/738	*VAT (Increase of Registration Limits) Order 1991 (revoked)*
SI 1991/1286	*Customs Duty (Personal Reliefs) (Amendment) Order 1991 (revoked)*
SI 1991/1287	*C&E Duties (Personal Reliefs for Goods Permanently Imported) (Amendment) Order 1991 (revoked)*
SI 1991/1293	*C&E Duties (Personal Reliefs for Goods Temporarily Imported) (Amendment) Order 1991 (revoked)*
SI 1991/1332	*VAT (General) (Amendment) (No 2) Regulations 1991 (revoked)*
SI 1991/1737	*Free Zone (Birmingham Airport) Designation Order 1991* (spent)
SI 1991/1738	*Free Zone (Liverpool) Designation Order 1991 (superseded)*
SI 1991/1739	*Free Zone (Prestwick Airport) Designation Order 1991 (superseded)*
SI 1991/1740	*Free Zone (Southampton) Designation Order 1991 (superseded)*
SI 1991/1754	*VAT (Interest on Overpayments etc) (Prescribed Rate) Order 1991 (superseded)*
SI 1991/2282	*VAT Act 1983 (Interest on Overpayments etc) (Prescribed Rate) (No 2) Order 1991 (superseded)*
SI 1991/2306	*VAT (Input Tax) (Person Supplied) Order 1991 (revoked)*
SI 1991/2312	*VAT (General) (Amendment) (No 3) Regulations 1991 (superseded)*
SI 1991/2503	*VAT (Special Provisions) (Amendment) Order 1991 (revoked)*
SI 1991/2534	*VAT (Piped Gas) (Metrication) Order 1991 (revoked)*
SI 1991/2535	*VAT (Small Non-Commercial Consignments) Relief (Amendment) Order 1991*
SI 1991/2569	*VAT (Buildings and Land) Order 1991 (revoked)*
SI 1991/2724	Customs Controls on Importation of Goods Regulations 1991
SI 1991/2727	Free Zone Regulations 1991
SI 1992/627	*VAT (Cars) (Amendment) Order 1992 (revoked)*
SI 1992/628	*VAT (Charities and Aids for Handicapped Persons) Order 1992 (revoked)*
SI 1992/629	*VAT (Increase of Registration Limits) Order 1992 (revoked)*
SI 1992/630	VAT (Treatment of Transactions) Order 1992

SI 1992/644	*VAT (Cash Accounting) (Amendment) Regulations 1992 (revoked)*
SI 1992/645	*VAT (General) (Amendment) Regulations 1992 (revoked)*
SI 1992/733	*VAT (Increase of Consideration for Fuel) Order 1992 (revoked)*
SI 1992/1510	*VAT (Payments on Account) Order 1992 (revoked)*
SI 1992/1536	*VAT (Payments on Account) Regulations 1992 (revoked)*
SI 1992/1617	*VAT (General) (Amendment) (No 2) Regulations 1992 (superseded)*
SI 1992/1654	*VAT (Cars) (Amendment) (No 2) Order 1992 (revoked)*
SI 1992/1668	*VAT (Payments on Account) (No 2) Order 1992 (revoked)*
SI 1992/1844	*VAT (Payments on Account) (No 2) Regulations 1992 (revoked)*
SI 1992/1867	Finance (No 2) Act 1992 (Commencement) Order 1992
SI 1992/2790	Statistics of Trade (Customs and Excise) Regulations 1992
SI 1992/2868	*VAT (General) (Amendment) (No 3) Regulations 1992 (superseded)*
SI 1992/2979	Finance (No 2) Act 1992 (Commencement No 2 and Transitional Provisions) Order 1992
SI 1992/3065	*VAT (Motor Vehicles for the Handicapped) Order 1992 (revoked)*
SI 1992/3095	*Customs and Excise (Single Market etc) Regulations 1992 (amending)*
SI 1992/3096	*VAT (EC Sales Statements) Regulations 1992 (revoked)*
SI 1992/3097	*VAT (Accounting and Records) (Amendment) Regulations 1992 (revoked)*
SI 1992/3098	*VAT (Repayment to Community Traders) (Amendment) Regulations 1992 (spent)*
SI 1992/3099	*VAT (Valuation of Acquisitions) Regulations 1992 (revoked)*
SI 1992/3100	*VAT (Refunds in relation to New Means of Transport) Regulations 1992 (revoked)*
SI 1992/3101	*VAT (Removal of Goods) (Accounting) Regulations 1992 (revoked)*
SI 1992/3102	*VAT (General) (Amendment No 4) Regulations 1992 (revoked)*
SI 1992/3103	*VAT (Flat-rate Scheme for Farmers) Regulations 1992 (revoked)*
SI 1992/3111	VAT (Removal of Goods) Order 1992
SI 1992/3118	*VAT (Small Non-Commercial Consignments) Relief (Amendment) Order 1992*
SI 1992/3119	*VAT (Temporarily Imported Goods and Goods Imported for Private Purposes) Reliefs (Revocation) Order 1992 (spent)*
SI 1992/3120	*VAT (Imported Goods) Relief (Amendment) Order 1992*
SI 1992/3121	VAT (Place of Supply of Services) Order 1992
SI 1992/3122	VAT (Cars) Order 1992
SI 1992/3123	*VAT (Input Tax) (Specified Supplies) Order 1992 (revoked)*
SI 1992/3124	VAT (Imported Gold) Relief Order 1992
SI 1992/3125	*VAT (Tour Operators) (Amendment) Order 1992*
SI 1992/3126	*VAT (Transport) Order 1992 (revoked)*
SI 1992/3127	*VAT (Means of Transport) Order 1992 (revoked)*
SI 1992/3128	*VAT (Reverse Charge) Order 1992 (revoked)*
SI 1992/3129	*VAT (Special Provisions) Order 1992 (revoked)*
SI 1992/3130	VAT (Supply of Temporarily Imported Goods) Order 1992
SI 1992/3131	*VAT (Tax Free Shops) Order 1992 (revoked)*
SI 1992/3132	VAT (Treatment of Transactions) (No 2) Order 1992
SI 1992/3135	Excise Goods (Holding, Movement, Warehousing and REDS) Regulations 1992
SI 1992/3152	Excise Duties (Deferred Payment) Regulations 1992
SI 1992/3153	*VAT (Repayments to Third Country Traders) (Amendment) Regulations 1992 (revoked)*
SI 1992/3156	Customs and Excise (Personal Reliefs for Special Visitors) Order 1992
SI 1992/3192	*Customs Duty (Personal Reliefs) (Amendment) Order 1992 (revoked)*
SI 1992/3193	Customs and Excise Duties (Personal Reliefs for Goods Permanently Imported) Order 1992
SI 1992/3220	VAT (Flat-rate Scheme for Farmers) (Designated Activities) Order 1992
SI 1992/3221	VAT (Flat-rate Scheme for Farmers) (Percentage Addition) Order 1992
SI 1992/3222	VAT (Input Tax) Order 1992
SI 1992/3223	*VAT (International Services and Transport) Order 1992 (revoked)*
SI 1992/3224	*Postal Packets (Customs and Excise) (Amendment) Regulations 1992*
SI 1992/3283	*VAT (Place of Supply of Goods) Order 1992 (revoked)*
SI 1993/119	*VAT (General) (Amendment) Regulations 1993 (revoked)*
SI 1993/192	*VAT Act 1983 (Interest on Overpayments etc) (Prescribed Rate) Order 1993 (lapsed)*

SI 1993/541	*Statistics of Trade (Customs and Excise) (Amendment) Regulations 1993 (revoked)*
SI 1993/761	*VAT (Accounting and Records) (Amendment) Regulations 1993 (revoked)*
SI 1993/762	*VAT (Cash Accounting) (Amendment) Regulations 1993 (revoked)*
SI 1993/763	*VAT (Education) Order 1993 (revoked)*
SI 1993/764	*VAT (General) (Amendment) (No 2) Regulations 1993 (revoked)*
SI 1993/765	*VAT (Increase of Consideration for Fuel) Order 1993 (revoked)*
SI 1993/766	*VAT (Increase of Registration Limits) Order 1993 (revoked)*
SI 1993/767	*VAT (Protective Boots and Helmets) Order 1993 (revoked)*
SI 1993/856	*VAT (General) (Amendment) (No 3) Regulations 1993 (revoked)*
SI 1993/1124	*VAT (Education) (No 2) Order 1993 (revoked)*
SI 1993/1222	*VAT (Repayments to Third Country Traders) (Amendment) Regulations 1993 (revoked)*
SI 1993/1223	*VAT (Repayments to Community Traders) (Amendment) Regulations 1993 (revoked)*
SI 1993/1224	*VAT (General) (Amendment) (No 4) Regulations 1993 (revoked)*
SI 1993/1228	*Beer Regulations 1993 (amending)*
SI 1993/1507	VAT (Supply of Services) Order 1993
SI 1993/1639	*VAT (General) (Amendment) (No 5) Regulations 1993 (revoked)*
SI 1993/1813	*Channel Tunnel (International Agreements) Order 1993 (amending)*
SI 1993/1941	*VAT (General) (Amendment) (No 6) Regulations 1993 (revoked)*
SI 1993/2001	VAT (Payments on Account) Order 1993
SI 1993/2214	*Finance Act 1993 (Appointed Day) Order 1993 (revoked)*
SI 1993/2328	*VAT (Reverse Charge) Order 1993 (revoked)*
SI 1993/2498	*VAT (Beverages) Order 1993 (revoked)*
SI 1993/2951	*VAT (Cars) (Amendment) Order 1993 (revoked)*
SI 1993/2952	*VAT (Increase of Consideration for Fuel) (No 2) Order 1993 (revoked)*
SI 1993/2953	*VAT (Increase of Registration Limits) (No 2) Order 1993 (revoked)*
SI 1993/2954	*VAT (Input Tax) (Amendment) Order 1993 (revoked)*
SI 1993/3014	*Community Customs Code (Consequential Amendment of References) Regulations 1993*
SI 1993/3015	*Statistics of Trade (Customs and Excise) (Amendment No 2) Regulations 1993*
SI 1993/3027	*VAT (General) (Amendment) (No 7) Regulations 1993 (revoked)*
SI 1993/3028	*VAT (Cash Accounting) (Amendment) (No 2) Regulations 1993 (revoked)*
SI 1994/143	*Free Zone (Prestwick Airport) Designation (Variation) Order 1994 (superseded)*
SI 1994/144	Free Zone (Humberside) Designation Order 1994
SI 1994/686	*VAT (Tax Free Shops) Order 1994 (revoked)*
SI 1994/687	*VAT (Sport, Physical Education and Fund-Raising Events) Order 1994 (revoked)*
SI 1994/803	*VAT (Accounting and Records) (Amendment) Regulations 1994 (revoked)*
SI 1994/955	Travellers' Allowances Order 1994
SI 1994/1188	*VAT (Education) Order 1994 (revoked)*
SI 1994/1234	*Finance Act 1994 Section 47, (Appointed Day) Order 1994 (revoked)*
SI 1994/1253	*Finance Act 1994 Section 47, (Appointed Day) (No 2) Order 1994 (lapsed)*
SI 1994/1257	*Finance Act 1994 section 45, (Appointed Day) Order 1994 (lapsed)*
SI 1994/1405	*Channel Tunnel (Miscellaneous Provisions) Order 1994 (amending)*
SI 1994/1410	*Free Zone (Southampton) Designation (Variation) Order 1994 (amending)*
SI 1994/1978	VAT Tribunals Appeals (Northern Ireland) Order 1994
SI 1994/2509	*Free Zone (Birmingham Airport) (Substitution of Responsible Authority) Order 1994* (spent)
SI 1994/2542	*VAT Act 1994 (Interest on Tax) (Prescribed Rate) Order 1994 (superseded)*
SI 1994/2617	*VAT Tribunals (Amendment) Rules 1994*
SI 1994/2898	*Free Zone (Port of Sheerness) Designation Order 1994 (spent)*
SI 1994/2905	*VAT (Increase of Registration Limits) Order 1994 (superseded)*
SI 1994/2914	*Statistics of Trade (Customs and Excise) (Amendment) Regulations 1994 (revoked)*
SI 1994/2969	*VAT (Education) (No 2) Order 1994 (amending)*
SI 1994/3013	*VAT (Buildings and Land) Order 1994 (revoked)*
SI 1994/3014	*VAT (Transport) Order 1994 (amending)*

SI 1994/3015	*VAT (General) (Amendment) Regulations 1994 (revoked)*
SI 1994/3128	*VAT (Means of Transport) Order 1994 (revoked)*
SI 1995/152	*VAT (General) (Amendment) Regulations 1995 (revoked)*
SI 1995/195	*VAT (General) (Amendment) Regulations 1995 (revoked)*
SI 1995/279	*VAT (Buildings and Land) Order 1995 (revoked)*
SI 1995/280	*VAT (Construction of Buildings) Order 1995 (amending)*
SI 1995/281	*VAT (Input Tax) (Amendment) Order 1995*
SI 1995/282	*VAT (Land) Order 1995 (amending)*
SI 1995/283	*VAT (Protected Buildings) Order 1995 (amending)*
SI 1995/291	*VAT (Payments on Account) (Amendment) Order 1995*
SI 1995/521	*VAT Act 1994 (Interest on Tax) (Prescribed Rate) Order 1995 (superseded)*
SI 1995/652	*VAT (Supply of Pharmaceutical Goods) Order 1995 (amending)*
SI 1995/653	*VAT (Transport) Order 1995 (amending)*
SI 1995/913	*VAT (General) (Amendment) (No 2) Regulations 1995 (revoked)*
SI 1995/957	*VAT (Special Provisions) (Amendment) Order 1995 (revoked)*
SI 1995/958	VAT (Treatment of Transactions) Order 1995
SI 1995/1046	*Excise Goods (Drawback) Regulations 1995 (amending)*
SI 1995/1067	Free Zone (Humberside) Designation (Variation) Order 1995
SI 1995/1069	*VAT (General) (Amendment) (No 3) Regulations 1995 (revoked)*
SI 1995/1267	*VAT (Input Tax) (Amendment) (No 2) Order 1995*
SI 1995/1268	VAT (Special Provisions) Order 1995
SI 1995/1269	*VAT (Cars) (Amendment) Order 1995*
SI 1995/1280	*VAT (General) (Amendment) (No 4) Regulations 1995 (revoked)*
SI 1995/1374	Finance Act 1995 section 24 (Appointed Day) Order 1995 (see VATA 1994 s 32)
SI 1995/1385	*VAT (Special Provisions) Order 1995 (Amendment) Order 1995*
SI 1995/1495	*VAT (Tour Operators) (Amendment) Order 1995*
SI 1995/1666	*VAT (Input Tax) (Amendment) (No 3) Order 1995*
SI 1995/1667	*VAT (Cars) (Amendment) (No 2) Order 1995*
SI 1995/1668	*VAT (Supply of Services) (Amendment) Order 1995*
SI 1995/1978	VAT (Refund of Tax) Order 1995
SI 1995/2518	VAT Regulations 1995
SI 1995/2946	*Statistics of Trade (Customs and Excise) (Amendment) Regulations 1995 (revoked)*
SI 1995/2999	VAT (Refund of Tax) (No 2) Order 1995
SI 1995/3037	*VAT (Increase of Registration Limits) Order 1995 (superseded)*
SI 1995/3038	*VAT (Place of Supply of Services) (Amendment) Order 1995*
SI 1995/3039	*VAT (Ships and Aircraft) Order 1995 (amending)*
SI 1995/3040	*VAT (Increase of Consideration for Fuel) Order 1995 (amending)*
SI 1995/3041	*VAT (Tax Free Shops) Order 1995 (revoked)*
SI 1995/3042	*VAT (Treatment of Transactions) (Trading Stamps) Order 1995 (amending)*
SI 1995/3043	*VAT (Trading Stamps) Regulations 1995 (amending)*
SI 1995/3044	*Travellers' Allowances Amendment Order 1995*
SI 1995/3147	*VAT (Amendment) Regulations 1995*
SI 1995/3222	*VAT (Imported Goods) Relief (Amendment) Order 1995*
SI 1996/165	*VAT Act 1994 (Interest on Tax) (Prescribed Rate) Order 1996 (lapsed)*
SI 1996/210	*VAT (Amendment) Regulations 1996*
SI 1996/542	*VAT (Annual Accounting) Regulations 1996 (amending)*
SI 1996/1196	*VAT (Payments on Account) (Amendments) Order 1996*
SI 1996/1198	*VAT (Amendment) (No 2) Regulations 1996*
SI 1996/1249	Finance Act 1996 section 26 (Appointed Day) Order 1996
SI 1996/1250	*VAT (Amendment) (No 3) Regulations 1996*
SI 1996/1255	VAT (Fiscal Warehousing) (Treatment of Transactions) Order 1996
SI 1996/1256	*VAT (Cultural Services) Order 1996 (amending)*
SI 1996/1661	*VAT (Anti-avoidance (Heating)) Order 1996 (amending)*
SI 1996/2098	*VAT (Amendment) (No 4) Regulations 1996 (lapsed)*
SI 1996/2615	*Free Zone (Southampton) Designation (Variation of Area) Order 1996 (superseded)*
SI 1996/2948	*VAT (Increase of Consideration for Fuel) Order 1996 (superseded)*
SI 1996/2949	*VAT (Pharmaceutical Chemists) Order 1996 (amending)*
SI 1996/2950	*VAT (Increase in Registration Limits) Order 1996 (superseded)*

SI 1996/2960	*VAT (Amendment) (No 5) Regulations 1996*
SI 1996/2968	*Statistics of Trade (Customs & Excise) (Amendment) Regulations 1996 (revoked)*
SI 1996/2992	*VAT (Place of Supply of Services) (Amendment) Order 1996*
SI 1997/50	*VAT (Registered Social Landlords) (No 1) Order 1997 (amending)*
SI 1997/51	*VAT (Registered Social Landlords) (No 2) Order 1997 (revoked)*
SI 1997/255	*VAT Tribunals (Amendment) Rules 1997*
SI 1997/510	*VAT (Finance) Order 1997 (amending)*
SI 1997/534	*Customs Reviews and Appeals (Tariff and Origin) Regulations 1997 (amending)*
SI 1997/994	Free Zone (Port of Sheerness) (Substitution of Responsible Authority) Order 1997
SI 1997/1015	*Finance Act 1996 s 197 (Appointed Day) Order 1997 (see FA 1996 s 197)*
SI 1997/1016	*Air Passenger Duty and Other Indirect Taxes (Interest Rate) Regulations 1997 (revoked)*
SI 1997/1086	*VAT (Amendment) Regulations 1997*
SI 1997/1431	Distress for Customs And Excise Duties and Other Indirect Taxes Regulations 1997
SI 1997/1432	*Finance Act 1997, sections 52 and 53, (Appointed Day) Order 1997 (see FA 1997 ss 52 and 53)*
SI 1997/1433	*Finance Act 1997 (Repeal of Distress and Diligence enactments) (Appointed Day) Order 1997 (see VATA 1994 Sch 11 para 5(4)–(10))*
SI 1997/1523	VAT (Reverse Charge) (Anti-avoidance) Order 1997
SI 1997/1524	*VAT (Place of Supply of Services) (Amendment) Order 1997*
SI 1997/1525	*VAT (Amendment) (No 2) Regulations 1997*
SI 1997/1603	*The Finance Act 1997, section 110 (Appointed Day) Order 1997 (see FA 1997 s 110)*
SI 1997/1614	*VAT (Amendment) (No 3) Regulations 1997*
SI 1997/1615	*VAT (Cars) (Amendment) Order 1997*
SI 1997/1616	*VAT (Special Provisions) (Amendment) Order 1997*
SI 1997/1628	*VAT (Increase of Registration Limits) Order 1997 (superseded)*
SI 1997/1836	*VAT (Terminal Markets) (Amendment) Order 1997*
SI 1997/2437	*VAT (Amendment) (No 4) Regulations 1997*
SI 1997/2542	*VAT (Payments on Account) (Appeals) Order 1997 (amending)*
SI 1997/2558	VAT (Refund of Tax) Order 1997
SI 1997/2744	*VAT (Drugs, Medicines and Aids for the Handicapped) Order 1997 (amending)*
SI 1997/2864	*Statistics of Trade (Customs and Excise) (Amendment) Order 1997*
SI 1997/2887	*VAT (Amendment) (No 5) Regulations 1997*
SI 1998/59	*VAT (Amendment) Regulations 1998*
SI 1998/759	*VAT (Cars) (Amendment) Order 1998*
SI 1998/760	*VAT (Special Provisions) (Amendment) Order 1998*
SI 1998/761	*VAT (Increase of Registration Limits) Order 1998 (superseded)*
SI 1998/762	*VAT (Supply of Services) (Amendment) Order 1998*
SI 1998/763	*VAT (Place of Supply of Services) (Amendment) Order*
SI 1998/765	*VAT (Amendment) (No 2) Regulations 1998*
SI 1998/1294	*VAT (Osteopaths) Order 1998 (amending)*
SI 1998/1375	*VAT (Reduced Rate) Order 1998 (revoked)*
SI 1998/1461	Air Passenger Duty and Other Indirect Taxes (Interest Rate) Regulations 1998
SI 1998/1898	*Rules of the Supreme Court (Amendment) 1998*
SI 1998/2767	*The VAT (Input Tax) (Amendment) Order 1998*
SI 1998/2973	*The Statistics of Trade (Customs and Excise) (Amendment) Regulations 1998 (revoked)*
SI 1998/3086	*The Reserve Forces Act 1996 (Consequential Provisions etc) Regulations 1998 (amending)*
SI 1999/438	*VAT (Amendment) Regulations 1999*
SI 1999/593	*VAT (Buildings and Land) Order 1999 (revoked)*
SI 1999/594	*VAT (Finance) Order 1999 (amending)*
SI 1999/595	*VAT (Increase of Registration Limits) Order 1999 (superseded)*
SI 1999/599	*VAT (Amendment) (No 2) Regulations 1999*
SI 1999/1374	*VAT (Amendment) (No 3) Regulations 1999*
SI 1999/1575	*VAT (Chiropractors) Order 1999 (amending)*

SI 1999/1642	*VAT (Abolition of Zero-Rating for Tax-Free Shops) Order 1999 (amending)*
SI 1999/1994	*VAT (Sport, Sports Competitions and Physical Education) Order 1999 (amending)*
SI 1999/2076	VAT (Refund of Tax) Order 1999
SI 1999/2831	*VAT (Special Provisions) (Amendment) Order 1999*
SI 1999/2832	*VAT (Cars) (Amendment) Order 1999*
SI 1999/2833	*VAT (Supplies of Goods where Input Tax cannot be recovered) Order 1999 (amending)*
SI 1999/2834	*VAT (Subscriptions to Trade Unions, Professional and Other Public Interest Bodies) Order 1999 (amending)*
SI 1999/2930	*VAT (Input Tax) (Amendment) Order 1999*
SI 1999/3029	*VAT Regulations 1999 (amending)*
SI 1999/3114	*VAT (Amendment) (No 4) Regulations 1999*
SI 1999/3115	VAT (Importation of Investment Gold) Relief Order 1999
SI 1999/3116	VAT (Investment Gold) Order 1999
SI 1999/3117	*VAT (Terminal Markets) Order 1999 (amending)*
SI 1999/3118	*VAT (Input Tax) (Amendment) (No 2) Order 1999*
SI 1999/3119	*VAT (Treatment of Transactions) (Amendment) Order 1999*
SI 1999/3120	*VAT (Special Provisions) (Amendment) (No 2) Order 1999*
SI 1999/3121	VAT (Input Tax) (Specified Supplies) Order 1999
SI 1999/3122	*Free Zone (Liverpool) Designation (Variation) Order 1999 (superseded)*
SI 1999/3269	*Statistics of Trade (Customs and Excise) (Amendment) Regulations 1999 (revoked)*
SI 2000/221	*Civil Procedure (Amendment) Rules 2000*
SI 2000/258	*VAT (Amendment) Regulations 2000*
SI 2000/266	*VAT (Deemed Supply of Goods) Order 2000 (amending)*
SI 2000/503	*VAT (Drugs, Medicines, Aids for the Handicapped and Charities Etc) Order 2000 (amending)*
SI 2000/631	*Air Passenger Duty and Other Indirect Taxes (Interest Rate) (Amendment) Regulations 2000*
SI 2000/634	*VAT (Amendment) (No 2) Regulations 2000*
SI 2000/794	*VAT (Amendment) (No 3) Regulations 2000*
SI 2000/802	*VAT (Fund-Raising Events by Charities and Other Qualifying Bodies) Order 2000 (amending)*
SI 2000/804	*VAT (Increase of Registration Limits) Order 2000 (spent)*
SI 2000/805	*VAT (Charities and Aids for the Handicapped) Order 2000 (amending)*
SI 2000/811	*VAT (Increase of Consideration for Fuel) Order 2000 (amending)*
SI 2000/1046	VAT (Refund of Tax) Order 2000
SI 2000/1515	VAT (Refund of Tax) (No 2) Order 2000
SI 2000/1517	*VAT (Protective Helmets) Order 2000 (amending)*
SI 2000/1672	VAT (Refund of Tax) (No 3) Order 2000
SI 2000/2954	*VAT (Reduced Rate) Order 2000 (revoked)*
SI 2000/3227	*Statistics of Trade (Customs and Excise) (Amendment) Regulations 2000*
SI 2001/630	*VAT (Amendment) Regulations 2001*
SI 2001/640	*VAT (Increase of Registration Limits) Order 2001 (spent)*
SI 2001/677	*VAT (Amendment) (No 2) Regulations 2001*
SI 2001/732	*VAT (Protective Helmets) Order 2001 (amending)*
SI 2001/735	*VAT (Business Gifts of Small Value) Order 2001 (amending)*
SI 2001/736	*VAT (Consideration for Fuel Provided for Private Use) Order 2001 (amending)*
SI 2001/753	*VAT (Passenger Vehicles) Order 2001 (amending)*
SI 2001/754	*VAT (Vehicles Designed or Adapted for Handicapped Persons) Order 2001 (amending)*
SI 2001/1149	*Postal Services Act 2000 (Consequential Modifications No 1) Order 2001 (amending)*
SI 2001/2305	*VAT (Conversion of Buildings) Order 2001 (amending)*
SI 2001/759	VAT (Electronic Communications) (Incentives) Regulations 2001
SI 2001/2879	VAT (Refund of Tax to Museums and Galleries) Order 2001
SI 2001/2880	Free Zone (Southampton) Designation Order 2001
SI 2001/2881	Free Zone (Liverpool) Designation Order 2001
SI 2001/2882	Free Zone (Prestwick Airport) Designation Order 2001
SI 2001/3073	VAT Tribunals (Amendment) Rules 2001

SI 2001/3337	*Air Passenger Duty and Other Indirect Taxes (Interest Rate) (Amendment) Regulations 2001*
SI 2001/3453	VAT (Refund of Tax) Order 2001
SI 2001/3500	*Transfer of Functions (Miscellaneous) Order 2001 (amending)*
SI 2001/3753	*VAT (Special Provisions) (Amendment) Order 2001*
SI 2001/3754	*VAT (Cars) (Amendment) Order 2001*
SI 2001/3828	*VAT (Amendment)(No 3) Regulations 2001*
SI 2001/3887	*Statistics of Trade (Customs and Excise) (Amendment) Regulations 2001 (revoked)*
SI 2002/1074	*VAT (Amendment) Regulations 2002*
SI 2002/1098	*VAT (Increase of Registration Limits) Order 2002 (spent)*
SI 2002/1099	*VAT (Consideration for Fuel Provided for Private Use) Order 2002 (amending)*
SI 2002/1100	*VAT (Reduced Rate) Order 2002 (amending)*
SI 2002/1101	*VAT (Construction of Buildings) Order 2002 (amending)*
SI 2002/1102	*VAT (Buildings and Land) Order 2002 (revoked)*
SI 2002/1142	*VAT (Amendment) (No 2) Regulations 2002*
SI 2002/1173	*VAT (Transport) Order 2002 (amending)*
SI 2002/1280	*VAT (Special Provisions) (Amendment) Order 2002*
SI 2002/1418	Free Zone (Port of Tilbury) Order 2002
SI 2002/1502	*VAT (Cars) (Amendment) Order 2002*
SI 2002/1503	*VAT (Special Provisions) (Amendment No 2) Order 2002*
SI 2002/1935	VAT (Acquisitions) Relief Order 2002
SI 2002/2498	*Statistics of Trade (Customs and Excise) (Amendment) Regulations 2002 (revoked)*
SI 2002/2813	*VAT (Drugs, Medicines, Aids for the Handicapped and Charities Etc) Order 2002 (amends VATA 1994)*
SI 2002/2851	*VAT Tribunals (Amendment) Rules 2002*
SI 2002/2918	*VAT (Amendment) (No 3) Regulations 2002*
SI 2002/3027	*VAT (Amendment) (No 4) Regulations 2002*
SI 2003/230	*Air Passenger Duty and Other Indirect Taxes (Interest Rate) (Amendment) Regulations 2003*
SI 2003/532	*VAT (Amendment) Regulations 2003*
SI 2003/862	*VAT (Place of Supply of Services) (Amendment) Order 2003*
SI 2003/863	*VAT (Reverse Charge) (Amendment) Order 2003*
SI 2003/1055	*VAT (Supply of Services) (Amendment) Order 2003*
SI 2003/1057	*VAT (Consideration for Fuel Provided for Private Use) Order 2003 (amending)*
SI 2003/1058	*VAT (Increase of Registration Limits) Order 2003 (amending)*
SI 2003/1069	*VAT (Amendment) (No 2) Regulations 2003*
SI 2003/1114	*VAT (Amendment) (No 3) Regulations 2003*
SI 2003/1485	*VAT (Amendment) (No 4) Regulations 2003*
SI 2003/2318	*VAT (Amendment) (No 5) Regulations 2003*
SI 2003/2757	*VAT Tribunals (Amendment) Rules 2003*
SI 2003/3092	*Mutual Assistance Provisions Order 2003 (amending)*
SI 2003/3220	*VAT (Amendment) (No 6) Regulations 2003*
SI 2003/3113	Customs (Contravention of a Relevant Rule) Regulations 2003
SI 2004/674	Recovery of Duties and Taxes etc Due in Other Member States (Corresponding UK Claims, Procedure and Supplementary) Regulations 2004
SI 2004/776	*VAT (Consideration for Fuel Provided for Private Use) Order 2004 (amending)*
SI 2004/1032	*VAT Tribunals (Amendment) Rules 2004*
SI 2004/1082	*VAT (Amendment) (No 2) Regulations 2004*
SI 2004/1501	*Criminal Justice (Evidence) (Northern Ireland) Order* (amending)
SI 2004/1929	VAT (Disclosure of Avoidance Schemes) Regulations 2004
SI 2004/1931	VAT (Groups: eligibility) Order 2004
SI 2004/1933	VAT (Disclosure of Avoidance Schemes) (Designations) Order 2004
SI 2004/3083	*VAT (Insurance) Order 2004 (amending)*
SI 2004/3084	*VAT (Cars) (Amendment) Order 2004*
SI 2004/3085	*VAT (Special Provisions) (Amendment) (No 2) Order 2004*
SI 2004/3140	*VAT (Amendment) (No 4) Regulations 2004*
SI 2004/3147	VAT (Imported Gas and Electricity) Relief Order 2004

SI 2004/3148	VAT (Place of Supply of Goods) Order 2004
SI 2004/3284	*Statistics of Trade (Customs and Excise) (Amendment) Regulations 2004*
SI 2004/3343	*VAT (Food) Order 2004 (amending)*
SI 2005/722	*VAT (Fuel Provided for Private Use) Order 2005 (amending)*
SI 2005/726	*VAT (Reduced Rate) Order 2005 (amending)*
SI 2005/727	*VAT (Increase of Registration Limits) Order 2005 (amending)*
SI 2005/762	*VAT (Amendment) Regulations 2005*
SI 2005/1133	Revenue and Customs (Inspections) Regulations 2005
SI 2005/1479	Recovery of Taxes etc Due in Other Member States (Amendment of Section 134 of the Finance Act 2002) Regulations 2005
SI 2005/1709	*Recovery of Duties and Taxes Etc Due in Other Member States (Corresponding UK Claims, Procedure and Supplementary) (Amendment) Regulations 2005 (amend SI 2004/674)*
SI 2005/1724	*VAT (Disclosure of Avoidance Schemes) (Designations) (Amendment) Order 2005 (amends SI 2004/1933)*
SI 2005/1993	*VAT (Refund of Tax to Museums and Galleries) (Amendment) Order 2005 (amends SI 2001/2879)*
SI 2005/2231	*VAT (Amendment) (No 2) Regulations 2005 (amend SI 1995/2518)*
SI 2005/3290	VAT (Input Tax) (Reimbursement by Employers of Employees' Business Use of Road Fuel) Regulations 2005
SI 2005/3291	*VAT (Input Tax) (Person Supplied) Order 2005 (revokes SI 1991/2306)*
SI 2005/3311	Revenue and Customs (Complaints and Misconduct) Regulations 2005
SI 2005/3328	*VAT (Betting, Gaming and Lotteries) Order 2005 (amends VATA 1994)*
SI 2005/3329	*VAT (Reduced Rate) (No 2) Order 2005 (amends VATA 1994)*
SI 2006/587	*VAT (Amendment) Regulations 2006 (amend SI 1995/2518)*
SI 2006/868	*VAT (Consideration for Fuel Provided for Private Use) Order 2006 (amends VATA 1994)*
SI 2006/869	*VAT (Special Provisions) (Amendment) (No 2) Order 2006 (amends SI 1995/1268)*
SI 2006/874	*VAT (Cars) (Amendment) Order 2006 (amends SI 1992/3122)*
SI 2006/876	*VAT (Increase of Registration Limits) Order 2006 (amends VATA 1994)*
SI 2006/2685	*VAT (Betting, Gaming and Lotteries) Order 2006*
SI 2006/2686	*VAT (Gaming Machines) Order (amends VATA 1994)*
SI 2006/2902	*VAT (Amendment) (No 2) Regulations 2006*
SI 2006/3216	*Statistics of Trade (Customs and Excise) (Amendment) Regulations (amend SI 1992/2790)*
SI 2006/3283	*Mutual Assistance Provisions Order 2006* (amends FA 2003)
SI 2006/3292	*VAT (Amendment) (No 3) Regulations 2006*
SI 2007/5	*C&E (Personal Reliefs for Special Visitors) (Amendment) Order*
SI 2007/206	*VAT (Health and Welfare) Order* (amending)
SI 2007/313	*VAT (Amendment) Regulations 2007*
SI 2007/768	*VAT (Amendment) (No 2) Regulations 2007*
SI 2007/939	*VAT (Amendment of section 77A of the VATA 1994) Order 2007*
SI 2007/941	*VAT (Increase of Registration Limits) Order 2007*
SI 2007/946	*Finance (No 2) Act 2005, Section 2(7), (Appointed Day) Order 2007*
SI 2007/966	*Value Added Tax (Consideration for Fuel Provided for Private Use) Order 2007*
SI 2007/1417	Value Added Tax (Section 55A) (Specified Goods and Excepted Supplies) Order 2007
SI 2007/1418	*VAT (Amendment) (No 3) Regulations 2007*
SI 2007/1419	*Finance Act 2006, Section 19, (Appointed Day) Order 2007*
SI 2007/1420	*VAT (Payments on Account) (Amendment) Order 2007*
SI 2007/1421	*VAT (Administration, Collection and Enforcement) Order 2007*
SI 2007/1509	Control of Cash (Penalties) Regulations 2007
SI 2007/1599	*VAT (Amendment) (No 4) Regulations 2007*
SI 2007/1601	*Value Added Tax (Reduced Rate) Order 2007*
SI 2007/2085	*Value Added Tax (Amendment) (No 5) Regulations 2007*
SI 2007/2163	*VAT (Betting, Gaming and Lotteries) Order 2007 (revoked)*
SI 2007/2173	*VAT (Supply of Services) (Amendment) Order 2007*
SI 2007/2351	*VAT Tribunals (Amendment) Rules 2007*
SI 2007/2709	Tribunals, Courts and Enforcement Act 2007 (Commencement No 1) Order 2007
SI 2007/2923	*VAT (Special Provisions) (Amendment) Order 2007*
SI 2007/3099	*VAT (Amendment) (No 7) Regulations 2007*

SI 2007/3166	*Finance Act 2007 (Sections 82 to 84 and Schedule 23) (Commencement) Order 2007*
SI 2007/3448	*VAT (Reduced Rate) (No 2) Order 2007*
SI 2007/3508	*Recovery of Duties and Taxes etc Due in Other Member States (Corresponding UK Claims, Procedure and Supplementary) (Amendment) Regulations 2007*
SI 2008/556	*VAT (Amendment) Regulations 2008*
SI 2008/557	*Statistics of Trade (Customs and Excise) (Amendment) Regulations 2008*
SI 2008/568	Finance Act 2007, Schedule 24 (Commencement and Transitional Provisions) Order 2008
SI 2008/722	*Value Added Tax (Consideration for Fuel Provided for Private Use) Order 2008*
SI 2008/954	*Companies Act 2006 (Consequential Amendments) (Taxes and National Insurance) Order 2008*
SI 2008/1146	Value Added Tax (Buildings and Land) Order 2008
SI 2008/1339	*VAT (Refund of Tax to Museums and Galleries) (Amendment) Order 2008*
SI 2008/1892	*Value Added Tax (Finance) Order 2008 (revoked)*
SI 2008/1948	Taxes (Fees for Payment by Telephone) Regulations 2008
SI 2008/2547	*Value Added Tax (Finance) (No 2) Order 2008*
SI 2008/2676	*Value Added Tax (Reduced Rate) (Supplies of Domestic Fuel or Power) Order*
SI 2008/2832	*Excise Warehousing (Etc) (Amendment) Regulations 2008*
SI 2008/2847	*Statistics of Trade (Customs and Excise) (Amendment) (No 2) Regulations 2008*
SI 2008/3234	*Taxes and Duties (Interest Rate) (Amendment) Regulations 2008*
SI 2009/56	*Transfer of Tribunal Functions and Revenue and Customs Appeals Order 2009*
SI 2009/215	*VAT (Place of Supply of Goods) Order 2009*
SI 2009/217	*VAT (Input Tax) (Amendment) Order 2009*
SI 2009/403	Finance Act 2008, Schedule 39 (Appointed Day, Transitional Provision and Savings) Order 2009
SI 2009/571	Finance Act 2008, Schedule 40 (Appointed Day, Transitional Provisions and Consequential Amendments) Order 2009
SI 2009/1966	*Value Added Tax (Buildings and Land) Order 2009*

STATUTORY INSTRUMENTS

1961/1523
Temporary Importation (Commercial Vehicles and Aircraft) Regulations 1961

Made by the Commissioners of Customs and Excise under the Customs and Excise Act 1952 s 40

Made	*3 August 1961*
Laid before Parliament	*10 August 1961*
Coming into Operation	*14 August 1961*

PART I

1 If any vehicle or aircraft is imported into any part of the United Kingdom other than the Isle of Man and the importer satisfies the Commissioners that—

(*a*) his principal place of business is outside the United Kingdom,

(*b*) the vehicle or aircraft is registered outside the United Kingdom,

(*c*) the vehicle or aircraft is owned and operated by a person whose principal place of business is outside the United Kingdom,

(*d*) the importation is taking place in the course of a journey which has begun and will end outside the United Kingdom,

(*e*) the purpose of the journey is to use the vehicle or aircraft either—

(i) for the transport of passengers for remuneration or for the industrial or commercial transport of goods from or to a place outside the United Kingdom, or

(ii) for such other purpose as the Commissioners may in special circumstances allow, and

(*f*) the following provisions of this Part of these Regulations, and such other conditions as may be imposed by the Commissioners, are and will be complied with,

such vehicle or aircraft may be delivered without payment of duty, and duty shall not be payable so long as the Commissioners continue to be so satisfied:

Provided that no vehicle or aircraft may be so delivered without payment of duty if the vehicle or aircraft is principally kept in the United Kingdom or if the importer principally keeps in the United Kingdom any vehicle or aircraft so delivered.

2 The importer shall at the time of importation—

(*a*) produce the vehicle or aircraft to the officer for examination,

(*b*) produce to the officer all documents in his possession which relate to the ownership or foreign registration of the vehicle or aircraft or which in the opinion of the officer might affect the entitlement to delivery of the vehicle or aircraft without payment of duty,

(*c*) if, and as, the Commissioners require, give security for payment of the duty and for compliance with these regulations either—

(i) by producing a carnet for the vehicle or aircraft issued either to the importer by name, or to another person whose principal place of business is outside the United Kingdom, or

(ii) by entering into a bond with sureties acceptable to the officer, or

(iii) by depositing such sum of money or giving such other security as the officer may require,

(*d*) furnish to the officer such documents in such form and containing such particulars as the officer may require.

3 Save as the Commissioners may allow, the vehicle or aircraft while in the United Kingdom—

(*a*) shall not be (or be offered to be) lent, sold, pledged, hired, given away, exchanged or otherwise disposed of, and shall not be used for the purpose of picking up passengers or goods at any place within the United Kingdom for conveyance to another place within the United Kingdom,

(*b*) shall be operated and used only by or on behalf of the owner or operator of the vehicle or aircraft or other person in charge thereof at the time of its importation or by other persons whose principal place of business is outside the United Kingdom who are expressly authorised in writing by the owner or operator of the vehicle or aircraft to operate and use the vehicle or aircraft,

(*c*) shall not be operated or used by, or in the service of, any other person and in particular any person whose principal place of business is in the United Kingdom.

4 The vehicle or aircraft shall be re-exported from the United Kingdom either—

(*a*) in the case of a vehicle or aircraft delivered on importation on production of a carnet, before the expiration of the period of validity of the carnet, or

(*b*) before the expiration of three months from the date of importation, or

(*c*) as soon as the purpose referred to in paragraph (*e*) of Regulation 1 of these Regulations has been served,

whichever is the earliest date, or, in any case,

(*d*) within such period as the Commissioners may allow.

5 The importer shall at the time of re-exportation—

(*a*) produce the vehicle or aircraft and any relevant import documents to the officer, and

(*b*) give such additional information and make such declaration relating to the vehicle or aircraft and the circumstances of its use in the United Kingdom as the officer may require.

PART II

6 If any spare parts or accessories of a vehicle are imported into any part of the United Kingdom other than the Isle of Man by or on behalf of a person whose principal place of business is outside the United Kingdom, and the importer satisfies the Commissioners that—

(*a*) the spare parts or accessories—

(i) are imported solely for the purpose of being incorporated in, or used with, a vehicle which has been delivered without payment of duty under the provisions of Part I of these Regulations or under Part I of the Commercial Vehicles (Temporary Importation) Regulations 1952, and

(ii) will be re-exported in, or with, the vehicle before the expiration of the period specified in Regulation 4 of these Regulations which is applicable to that vehicle, and

(*b*) the following provisions of this Part of these Regulations and such other conditions as may be imposed by the Commissioners are and will be complied with,

such spare parts or accessories may be delivered without payment of duty, and duty shall not be payable so long as the Commissioners continue to be so satisfied.

7 The importer shall—

(*a*) at the time of importation of such parts or accessories, if the Commissioners so require, deposit in accordance with the officer's directions such sum of money for securing the duty and compliance with these Regulations, and produce such documents and give such information, as the officer may require,

(*b*) use the spare parts or accessories solely for incorporation in, or with, the vehicle,

(*c*) re-export the spare parts or accessories in, or with, the vehicle before the expiration of the period specified in Regulation 4 of these Regulations which is applicable to that vehicle, and

(*d*) at the time of re-exportation, unless the Commissioners otherwise permit, produce to the officer all used or defective parts or accessories as have been displaced during the incorporation in, or use with, the vehicle by the imported spare parts or accessories, and—

(i) re-export such displaced parts or accessories, or

(ii) destroy them under such conditions as the Commissioners may specify, or

(iii) if the Commissioners so permit, abandon them to the Crown.

PART III

8 If any goods of the following descriptions are imported into any part of the United Kingdom other than the Isle of Man for the purposes hereinafter mentioned—

(*a*) spare parts or equipment imported solely for the purpose of being incorporated in, or used with, any aircraft which is—

(i) registered outside the United Kingdom,

(ii) owned and operated by a person whose principal place of business is outside the United Kingdom, and

(iii) used in international air transport services and in compliance with the provisions of Regulation 3 of these Regulations;

(*b*) aircraft, special tools, spare parts and equipment imported solely for the purpose of being used in the search for, or in the rescue, examination, repair or salvage of, an aircraft which is of the kind referred to in paragraph (*a*) of this Regulation and which has been accidentally lost or damaged;

and if the importer satisfies the Commissioners that the goods will be re-exported as soon as the purpose for which they were imported has been served or before the expiration of such period as may be allowed by the Commissioners, whichever is the earlier, and that the provisions of this Part of these Regulations and such other conditions as may be imposed by the Commissioners are and will be complied with, the goods may be delivered without payment of duty, and duty shall not be payable so long as the Commissioners continue to be so satisfied.

PART IV

9 For the purposes of these Regulations—

(*a*) the principal place of business of a person shall be deemed to be the place from which in the opinion of the Commissioners the control of the business is exercised;

(*b*) a vehicle or aircraft shall be deemed to be not principally kept in the United Kingdom if during the two years immediately preceding the date of importation of the vehicle or aircraft it has been present in the United Kingdom for less than either—

(i) a total of 365 days, or

(ii) such greater number of days as the Commissioners may in special circumstances allow;

(*c*) an importer shall be deemed not to keep a vehicle or aircraft principally in the United Kingdom if he has kept in the United Kingdom during the two years immediately preceding the date of importation of the vehicle or aircraft in question any other vehicle or aircraft which has been delivered without payment of duty under these Regulations or under the Commercial Vehicles (Temporary Importation) Regulations 1952, for an aggregate period of less than either—

(i) a total of 365 days, or
(ii) such greater number of days as the Commissioners may in special circumstances allow.

10 In these Regulations unless the context otherwise requires—

"aircraft" means any aeroplane, airship, balloon, flying machine or glider which is designed for the transport of persons for remuneration or the industrial or commercial transport of goods and also includes any accessories or component parts of any aircraft required for and imported in, or forming part of, such aircraft but does not include any accessories or component parts imported separately;

"carnet" means a carnet de passages en douane or a triptyque which is issued by an association belonging to the Federation Internationale de l'Automobile, the Alliance Internationale de Tourisme or the Federation Aeronautique Internationale, and which is covered by a guarantee given to the Commissioners by an approved association established in the United Kingdom;

"officer" means the proper officer of Customs and Excise;

"United Kingdom" means the United Kingdom including the Isle of Man;

"vehicle" means any motor road vehicle (including a trailer) which is designed for the transport of persons for remuneration or for the industrial or commercial transport of goods and also includes any accessories or component parts of such vehicle required for and imported in, or forming part of, such vehicle, but does not include any accessories or component parts imported separately.

11 The Interpretation Act 1889 shall apply for the interpretation of these Regulations as it applies for the interpretation of an Act of Parliament.

12 The Commercial Vehicles (Temporary Importation) Regulations 1952, are hereby revoked.

13 These Regulations may be cited as the Temporary Importation (Commercial Vehicles and Aircraft) Regulations 1961, and shall come into operation on the 14th day of August 1961.

1973/173
Value Added Tax (Terminal Markets) Order 1973

Made by the Treasury under FA 1972 s 26, see now VATA 1994, s 50

Made . . . . 6 February 1973
Laid before the House of Commons . . . . 13 February 1973
Coming into Operation . . . . 1 April 1973

Customs and Excise Notices—Notice 701/21: Gold; Notice 701/21A Investment Gold Coins, para 3 (list of investment gold coins).

1 This Order may be cited as the Value Added Tax (Terminal Markets) Order 1973 and shall come into operation on 1st April 1973.

2— (1) The Interpretation Act 1889[a] shall apply for the interpretation of this Order as it applies for the interpretation of an Act of Parliament.

(2) This Order applies to the following terminal markets—

the London Metal Exchange,
the London Rubber Market,
the London Cocoa Terminal Market,
the London Coffee Terminal Market,
the London Sugar Terminal Market,
the London Vegetable Oil Terminal Market,
the London Wool Terminal Market,
[[the London Bullion Market][8],][2]
[*the London Gold Futures Market,*][4]
…[8],
[the London Meat Futures Market,][5]
the London Grain Futures Market, *and*
[the London Soya Bean Meal Futures Market,][1]
the Liverpool Barley Futures Market,
[the International Petroleum Exchange of London,][3]
[the London Potato Futures Market][3] …[7]
[the London Platinum and Palladium Market][6] [and the London Securities and Derivatives Exchange Limited (OMLX).][7]

(3) References in this Order to a member of a market include any person ordinarily engaged in dealings on the market.

[(4) Notwithstanding paragraph 3 above, for the purposes of this Order a person is to be regarded as being a member of the London Bullion Market only if that person is a member of the London Bullion Market Association.] [8]

[(5) In this Order—

"investment gold" has the same meaning as that expression has for the purposes of Group 15 of Schedule 9 to the Value Added Tax Act 1994;

"the Act" means the Value Added Tax Act 1994.] [8]

Notes—[a] IA 1978.

Amendments—[1] Words in para (2) inserted and the word "and" preceding them deleted, with effect from 8 April 1975, by the VAT (Terminal Markets) (Amendment) Order, SI 1975/385 arts 1, 3.

[2] Words in para (2) inserted by the VAT (Terminal Markets) (Amendment) Order, SI 1980/304 art 2, with effect from 1 April 1980.

[3] Words in para (2) inserted by the VAT (Terminal Markets) (Amendment) Order, SI 1981/338 art 2, with effect from 6 April 1981.

[4] Words in para (2) inserted by the VAT (Terminal Markets) (Amendment) (No 2) Order, SI 1981/955 art 2, with effect from 7 September 1981, and revoked by the VAT (Terminal Markets) (Amendment) Order, SI 1985/1046 with effect from 1 August 1985 following the closure of the London Gold Futures Market on 26 June 1985.

[5] Words in para (2) inserted by the VAT (Terminal Markets) (Amendment) Order, SI 1984/202 art 2, with effect from 16 March 1984.

[6] Words in para (2) inserted by the VAT (Terminal Markets) (Amendment) Order, SI 1987/806 art 2 with effect from 1 June 1987.

[7] Words in para (2) inserted and the word "and" preceding them deleted by the VAT (Terminal Markets) (Amendment) Order, SI 1997/1836 art 2 with effect from 1 September 1997.

[8] Words in para (2) substituted and revoked, and paras (4), (5) added by the VAT (Terminal Markets) Order, SI 1999/3117, arts 2–5 with effect from 1 January 2000.

3— (1) The following supplies of goods or services in the course of dealings on a terminal market to which this Order applies are hereby zero-rated, subject to the conditions specified in this Article—

(*a*) the sale by or to a member of the market of any goods[, other than investment gold,][5] ordinarily dealt with on the market,

(*b*) the grant by or to a member of the market of a right to acquire such goods,

(*c*) where a sale of goods or the grant of a right zero-rated under sub-paragraph (*a*) or (*b*) above is made[,or where a supply of a description falling within article 4 or 5 below is made,][5] in dealings between members of the market acting as agents, the supply by those members to their principals of their services in so acting.

(2) The zero-rating of a sale by virtue of paragraph (1)(*a*) above is subject to the condition that the sale is either—

(*a*) a sale which, as a result of other dealings on the market, does not lead to a delivery of the goods by the seller to the buyer, or

(*b*) a sale by and to a member of the market which—

(i) if the market is the London Metal Exchange, is a sale between members entitled to deal in the ring,

(ii) if the market is the London Cocoa Terminal Market, the London Coffee Terminal Market, [the London Meat Futures Market,][4] [the International Petroleum Exchange of London, the London Potato Futures Market,][3] [the London Soya Bean Meal Futures Market,][1] the London Sugar Terminal Market, the London Vegetable Oil Terminal Market or the London Wool Terminal Market, is a sale registered with [the International Commodities Clearing House Limited,][2]

(iii) if the market is the London Grain Futures Market, is a sale registered in the Clearing House of the Grain and Feed Trade Association Limited, and

(iv) if the market is the Liverpool Barley Futures Market, is a sale registered at the Clearing House of the Liverpool Corn Trade Association Limited.

(3) The zero-rating of the grant of a right by virtue of paragraph (1)(*b*) above is subject to the condition that either—

(*a*) the right is exercisable at a date later than that on which it is granted, or

(*b*) any sale resulting from the exercise of the right would be a sale with respect to which the condition specified in paragraph (2) above is satisfied.

Amendments—[1] Words in para (2)(*b*)(ii) inserted by the VAT (Terminal Markets) (Amendment) Order, SI 1975/385 arts 1, 4, with effect from 8 April 1975.

[2] Words in para (2)(*b*)(ii) substituted by the VAT (Terminal Markets) (Amendment) Order, SI 1975/385 arts 1, 4, with effect from 8 April 1975.

[3] Words in para (2)(*b*)(ii) inserted by the VAT (Terminal Markets) (Amendment) Order, SI 1981/338, art 3, with effect from 6 April 1981.

[4] Words in para (2)(*b*)(ii) inserted by the VAT (Terminal Markets) (Amendment) Order, SI 1984/202, art 3, with effect from 16 March 1984.

[5] Words in para (1)(*a*), (*c*) inserted by the VAT (Terminal Markets) Order, SI 1999/3117, arts 2, 6, 7, with effect from 1 January 2000.

[**4** Supplies between taxable persons which but for Note 4(*a*) to Group 15 of Schedule 9 to the Act (exemption for investment gold) would have fallen within that Group are hereby zero-rated.][1]

Amendments—[1] This article inserted by the VAT (Terminal Markets) Order, SI 1999/3117, arts 2, 8, with effect from 1 January 2000.

[**5** Subject to articles 6 and 7 below, section 55(1) to (4) of the Act (customers to account for tax on supplies of gold) shall apply to any supply between taxable persons which but for Note 4(*b*) to Group 15 of Schedule 9 to the Act would have fallen within that Group.][1]

Amendments—[1] This article inserted by the VAT (Terminal Markets) Order, SI 1999/3117, arts 2, 8, with effect from 1 January 2000.

[**6** Subject to article 7 below, where a taxable person who is not a member of the London Bullion Market Association makes or receives a supply falling within the description in article 5 is liable to be registered under Schedule 1 or under Schedule 3 to the Act solely by virtue of that supply or acquisition, paragraphs 5 to 8 of Schedule 1 or paragraph 3 of Schedule 3 to the Act (notification of liability and registration) shall not apply.][1]

Amendments—[1] This article inserted by the VAT (Terminal Markets) Order, SI 1999/3117, arts 2, 8, with effect from 1 January 2000.

[**7** Notwithstanding section 55(2) of the Act, where articles 5 and 6 above apply, it shall be for the London Bullion Market Association member, on the non-member's behalf, to keep a record of the supplies and to pay to the Commissioners of Customs and Excise the net amount of VAT, and not for the person who is not a member.][1]

Amendments—[1] This article inserted by the VAT (Terminal Markets) Order, SI 1999/3117, arts 2, 8, with effect from 1 January 2000.

1976/1223
Customs Duties (Deferred Payment) Regulations 1976

Made by the Commissioners of Customs and Excise under F(No 2)A 1975 s 16(2) and FA 1976 s 15

Made . . . . *2 August 1976*
Laid before Parliament . . . . *10 August 1976*
Coming into Operation . . . . *1 September 1976*

Citation and commencement

1 These Regulations may be cited as the Customs Duties (Deferred Payment) Regulations 1976 and shall come into operation on 1st September 1976.

Interpretation

2— (1) In these Regulations—

"approved" means approved by the Commissioners [to apply for deferment of payment of duty on behalf of himself or another and "approve" and "approval" shall be construed accordingly][1];

"deferment" means deferment of payment of customs duty granted under these Regulations and "deferred" shall be construed accordingly;

["payment day" means the 15th day of the month next following that in which the amount of duty deferred is entered into the Commissioners' accounts, or in the case of import entries scheduled periodically, the 15th day of the period following that in which deferment is granted (save that where that day in either case falls on a non-working day it shall be the next working day thereafter);][1]

["period" means a period commencing on the 16th day of any month and ending on the 15th day of the month next following.][1]

(2) The Interpretation Act 1889[a] shall apply for the interpretation of these Regulations as it applies for the interpretation of an Act of Parliament.

(3) Where any document used or required for the purpose of deferment refers to a provision of the Customs Duties (Deferred Payment) Regulations 1972 such reference shall, unless the contrary intention appears, be construed as referring to the corresponding provision of these Regulations.

(4) Any approval granted by a Collector under the Customs Duties (Deferred Payments) Regulations 1972 and in force immediately before the commencement of these Regulations shall have effect as if granted under these Regulations.

Note—[a] IA 1978.
Amendments—[1] Words in para (1) added and definition of "payment day" in that para substituted by Customs Duties (Deferred Payment) (Amendment) Regulations, SI 1978/1725 reg 4.

Application

3 These Regulations apply in the case of customs duty ...[1] payable, apart from these Regulations, on the making of entry of goods chargeable therewith.

Amendments—[1] Words revoked by Customs Duties (Deferred Payment) (Amendment) Regulations, SI 1978/1725 reg 5.

VAT

Approval

4—(1) A person who wishes to be approved for the purposes of these Regulations shall apply to the Commissioners [in such form and manner as they shall determine][1], furnish security for payment on payment day of the amount of customs duty in respect of which he seeks deferment, and make arrangements with the Commissioners for the payment of that duty on payment day.

(2) If satisfied with the security and arrangements as aforesaid, the Commissioners shall in writing approve the applicant with respect to an amount of customs duty not exceeding that for which he has furnished security;

Provided that such approval may be limited to the deferment of customs duty payable, apart from these Regulations, on the making of entry within any named Collection.

(3) The Commissioners may, for reasonable cause, at any time vary or revoke any approval granted under this Regulation.

(4) A person to whom approval has been granted under this Regulation shall forthwith notify the Commissioners of any change in the particulars furnished, the security given, or the arrangements for payment provided for in paragraph (1) above.

Modifications—VAT Regulations, SI 1995/2518 reg 121A(1)–(4) (modification of this regulation in relation to any VAT chargeable on the importation of goods from places outside the member states).

Amendments—[1] Words in para (1) substituted by Customs Duties (Deferred Payment) (Amendment) Regulations, SI 1978/1725 reg 6.

Grant of deferment

5 Subject to Regulations 3, 4, 6 and 7, the Commissioners shall, upon application by an approved person [in such form and manner as they shall determine][1], grant deferment of customs duty until payment day.

Amendments—[1] Words substituted by Customs Duties (Deferred Payment) (Amendment) Regulations, SI 1978/1725 reg 7.

Payment

6 On each payment day an approved person shall pay to the Commissioners in accordance with the arrangements referred to in Regulation 4(1) the total amount of customs duty of which he has been granted deferment until that payment day.

7 If at any time after entry has been made the Commissioners are satisfied that—

(*a*) the full amount of customs duty payable has not been shown on the entry [or periodic schedule][1] then, save as the Commissioners otherwise allow, the balance shall forthwith be paid by the person making entry of the goods and no deferment in respect thereof shall be permitted;

(*b*) customs duty in excess of the amount payable has been shown on the entry [or periodic schedule][1], the Commissioners shall repay the excess, but the total amount shown shall nevertheless be paid on payment day.

Amendments—[1] Words in paras (*a*), (*b*) added by Customs Duties (Deferred Payment) (Amendment) Regulations, SI 1978/1725 reg 8.

[**8** Without prejudice to Regulation 6, for the purposes of—

(*a*) sections 34(1) and 260(1) of the Customs and Excise Act 1952 and the Warehousing Regulations 1975; and

(*b*) any relief by way of repayment or suspension of customs duty, or agricultural levy falling to be treated as such, under—

(i) the Inward Processing Relief Regulations 1977,

(ii) the Customs Duties and Agricultural Levies (Goods for Free Circulation) Regulations 1977,

(iii) Regulation 4 of the Import Duties (Outward Processing Relief) Regulations 1976, and

(iv) Article 4 of the Agricultural Levies (Outward Processing Relief) Order 1976

duty shall be deemed to have been paid at the time when deferment thereof was granted.][1]

Modifications—VAT Regulations, SI 1995/2518 reg 121A(3) (modification of this regulation in relation to any VAT chargeable on the importation of goods from places outside the member states).

Amendments—[1] This regulation substituted by Customs Duties (Deferred Payment) (Amendment) Regulations, SI 1978/1725 reg 9.

1976/2028

Value Added Tax (Refund of Tax) Order 1976

Made by the Treasury under FA 1972 s 15(3); see now VATA 1994 s 33(3)

Made . . . . 29 November 1976
Laid before the House of Commons . . . . 6 December 1976
Coming into Operation . . . . 1 April 1977

1 This Order may be cited as the Value Added Tax (Refund of Tax) Order 1976 and shall come into operation on 1st April 1977.

2 The Interpretation Act 1889[a] shall apply for the interpretation of this Order as it applies for the interpretation of an Act of Parliament.

3 The following bodies are hereby specified for the purposes of section 15 of the Finance Act 1972[b]—

the Commission for Local Administration in England
the Commission for Local Administration in Wales
the Commissioner for Local Administration in Scotland
the Commission for Local Authority Accounts in Scotland.

Notes—[a] IA 1978.
[b] VATA 1994 s 33.

1982/1067
Value Added Tax (Isle of Man) Order 1982

Made under the Isle of Man Act 1979 s 6

Made . . . . *30 July 1982*
Coming into Operation . . . . *1 October 1982*

1— (1) This Order may be cited as the Value Added Tax (Isle of Man) Order 1982 and shall come into operation on 1st October 1982.

(2) In this Order—

"the United Kingdom Act" means the Finance Act 1972[a];
"the Manx Act" means the Value Added Tax and Other Taxes Act 1973; and
"the Finance Board" means the Finance Board of the Isle of Man,

and any other word or expression used in this Order to which meaning is given in or under Part I of the United Kingdom Act shall have, except where the context otherwise requires, the same meaning in this Order as in or under that Part of that Act.

(3) For the purposes of this Order, the Interpretation Act 1978 shall apply to the Manx Act and to any instrument of a legislative character made thereunder as if the Manx Act were an Act of Parliament.

(4) For the purposes of this Order—

(*a*) a supply shall be treated as made in the United Kingdom if it would be so treated under section 8 or 8A of the United Kingdom Act[b] if Article 2 below were disregarded; and

(*b*) a supply shall be treated as made in the Isle of Man if it would be so treated under one or other of those sections if they were amended by substituting for the words "United Kingdom" wherever they occur the words "Isle of Man".

Notes—[a] VATA 1994.
[b] VATA 1994 s 7.

2 Subject to the provisions of this Order Part I of the United Kingdom Act shall have effect as if the Isle of Man were part of the United Kingdom.

3— (1) Notwithstanding Article 2 above, the removal of goods to the United Kingdom from the Isle of Man shall be treated for the purposes of Part I of the United Kingdom Act as the importation of those goods into the United Kingdom if they are goods which have previously been imported into or supplied in the United Kingdom or the Isle of Man and either—

(*a*) value added tax was chargeable on that previous importation or supply under Part I of the Manx Act but was not accounted for or paid at the rate which would have applied under Part I of the United Kingdom Act if the importation had been made into, or the supply had been made in, the United Kingdom; or

(*b*) that previous importation or supply was wholly or partly relieved from tax chargeable under Part I of the United Kingdom Act or value added tax chargeable under Part I of the Manx Act subject to a condition and that condition has not been complied with.

(2) The amount of tax chargeable under Part I of the United Kingdom Act on the removal into the United Kingdom from the Isle of Man of such goods as are mentioned in paragraph (1) above shall be reduced by an amount equal to any value added tax chargeable under Part I of the Manx Act which has been accounted for or paid on any earlier importation of those goods into, or supply of those goods in, the United Kingdom or the Isle of Man.

4 Tax shall not be charged under the United Kingdom Act—

(*a*) on the importation of goods into the Isle of Man except where the importation is by a taxable person otherwise than in the course or furtherance of a business carried on by him; or

(*b*) on the importation of goods into the United Kingdom by a person who is a taxable person for the purposes of the Manx Act where the importation is in the course or furtherance of a business carried on by him.

5 Any requirement imposed by or under the Manx Act shall be treated as a requirement imposed by or under the United Kingdom Act.

6 Any permission, direction, notice, determination or other thing given, made or done under the Manx Act by the Finance Board shall be treated as given, made or done by the Commissioners under the United Kingdom Act.

7 Sections 3(3)(*a*), (4), (8) and (9), 5, 14(3), 15, 15A, 17(1), 32(1), 33, 36(1), 43(4)(*b*) and 51 of the United Kingdom Act,[a] section 16 of the Finance Act 1977[b] and section 12(1) of the Finance Act 1978[c] shall have effect as if the references to tax in those sections included references to value added tax chargeable under Part I of the Manx Act.

Notes—[a] VATA 1994 ss 16(1), 24, 32, 33, 35, 39, 97(4)(*b*), 99 and Sch 11 paras 4, 5 and 8.
[b] VATA 1994 s 27.
[c] VATA 1994 s 36.

8 A person who is a taxable person for the purposes of the Manx Act shall be treated as a taxable person for the purposes of sections 18, 27(3), 30(2), 34(1) and 40(1)(*k*) of, and Note (6) to Item 4 of Group 15 of Schedule 4 to, the United Kingdom Act[a] and of section 16 of the Finance Act 1977[b].

Notes—[a] VATA 1994 ss 38, 18(3), 83(*f*), Sch 8, Group 13, item 3 and Note 5 and Sch 11 paras 2(2) and 6.
[b] VATA 1994 s 27.

9 Section 15A of the United Kingdom Act[a] shall not apply to the construction of dwellings within the Isle of Man.

Note—[a] VATA 1994 s 35.

10— (1) This Article shall have effect for enabling the Commissioners to determine for the purposes of section 21 of the United Kingdom Act[a] which member of a group is to be the representative member in cases where supplies are made both in the United Kingdom and in the Isle of Man.

(2) Where bodies corporate, which are treated as members of a group under the said section 21 have establishments both in the United Kingdom and in the Isle of Man, or do not have an establishment in either country, the Commissioners may at any time determine that another member of the group shall be substituted as the representative member from such date as they may determine.

Notes—[a] VATA 1994 s 43.

11— (1) This Article shall have effect, where a person would, apart from this Article, be liable to be registered both under Part I of the United Kingdom Act and under Part I of the Manx Act, for determining, or enabling the Commissioners to determine whether that person is to be registered under the United Kingdom Act or the Manx Act and for transferring a person registered under one Act to the register kept under the other.

(2) A person, who by virtue of paragraph 1(*a*) or (*b*) of Schedule 1 to the United Kingdom Act[a] is liable to be registered shall, if he has an establishment both in the United Kingdom and in the Isle of Man or does not have an establishment in either country, be registered either under Part I of the United Kingdom Act or under Part I of the Manx Act, as the Commissioners shall determine, but unless or until the Commissioners determine that such a person shall be registered under Part I of the Manx Act, he shall be required to be registered under Part I of the United Kingdom Act.

(3) Paragraphs 3, 5 and 6 of Schedule 1 to the United Kingdom Act[b] shall not apply to a person registered or required to be registered under Part I of the Manx Act.

(4) The Commissioners may determine that any person to whom paragraph 3, 5 or 6 of Schedule 1 to the United Kingdom Act[b] applies shall be registered under Part I of the Manx Act.

(5) Where a person, who is or was required to notify the Commissioners under paragraph 3, 5 or 6 of Schedule 1 to the United Kingdom Act,[b] has an establishment in the Isle of Man, he may notify the Isle of Man Finance Board and such notification shall be deemed for the purposes of that paragraph to be notification to the Commissioners.

(6) Any person, registered under Part I of the United Kingdom Act on or after 1st April 1980, who—

(*a*) has no establishment in the Isle of Man, or

(*b*) is the representative member of a group of bodies corporate, within the meaning of section 21 of the United Kingdom Act,[c] no member of which has an establishment in the Isle of Man,

shall notify the Commissioners if, at any later time, he or any member of the group has such an establishment and such notification shall be treated for the purposes of Schedule 1 to the United Kingdom Act and any regulations made thereunder as an event which could necessitate the cancellation of that person's, or that group of bodies corporate's, registration.

(7) Where a person, who is registered under Part I of the United Kingdom Act, has establishments both in the United Kingdom and in the Isle of Man, or does not have an establishment in either country, the Commissioners may, at any time, determine that he shall be registered under Part I of the Manx Act.

(8) Where the Commissioners determine that a person, who is registered under Part I of the United Kingdom Act, shall be registered under Part I of the Manx Act, he shall cease to be, or

required to be, registered under Part I of the United Kingdom Act from such date as they may determine, but, for the purposes of paragraph 7 of Schedule 2 to the United Kingdom Act,[d] he shall not cease to be a taxable person.

(9) Where a person, who is registered under Part I of the Manx Act, has establishments both in the United Kingdom and in the Isle of Man or does not have an establishment in either country, the Commissioners may, at any time, determine that he shall be registered under Part I of the United Kingdom Act and, if they so determine, they shall register him with effect from such date as they may determine.

(10) Where a person who was registered under Part I of the Manx Act is, pursuant to a determination of the Commissioners to that effect, registered under Part I of the United Kingdom Act, any amount of value added tax required to be paid under Part I of the Manx Act shall be deemed to have been an amount of tax due under Part I of the United Kingdom Act.

(11) Section 18(1) of the Finance (No 2) Act 1975[e] shall not apply where the person to whom the supply is made is registered under Part I of the Manx Act.

Notes—[a] VATA 1994 Sch 1 para 1.
[b] VATA 1994 Sch 1 paras 5–8.
[c] VATA 1994 s 43.
[d] VATA 1994 Sch 4 para 8.
[e] VATA s 22.

12— (1) For the purposes of Articles 10 and 11 above a person shall be deemed to have an establishment in a country if—

(*a*) there is a place in that country from which he carries on a business; or
(*b*) he carries on business through a branch or agent in that country.

(2) For the purposes of paragraph (1) above an agent is a person who has the authority or capacity to create legal relations between his principal and a third party.

13 In section 8(8)(*bb*) of the United Kingdom Act the words "under either of those Parts" are hereby repealed.

14 This Order revokes—

(*a*) the Value Added Tax (Isle of Man) Order 1980, except so much of it as relates to the Rules, Regulations and Orders specified in Schedule 2 to that Order; and
(*b*) so much of the Value Added Tax (Isle of Man) (No 2) Order 1980 as relates to the amendment of the Finance Act 1972

and accordingly the Finance Acts amended by those Orders shall have effect as if the Orders had not been made.

1982/1068
Value Added Tax (Isle of Man) (No 2) Order 1982

Made under the Isle of Man Act 1979 s 6

Made . . . . *30 July 1982*
Coming into Operation . . . . *1 October 1982*

1— (1) This Order may be cited as the Value Added Tax (Isle of Man) (No 2) Order 1982 and shall come into operation on 1st October 1982.

(2) In this Order—

"the United Kingdom Act" means the Finance Act 1972[a] and "the Manx Act" means the Value Added Tax and Other Taxes Act 1973

and any other word or expression used in this Order to which meaning is given in or under Part I of the United Kingdom Act shall have, except where the context otherwise requires, the same meaning in this Order as in or under that Part of that Act.

(3) For the purposes of this Order, the Interpretation Act 1978 shall apply to the Manx Act and to any instrument of a legislative character made thereunder as if the Manx Act were an Act of Parliament.

Notes—[a] VATA 1994.

2 In statutory instruments made under Part I of the United Kingdom Act references to the United Kingdom shall be construed as including references to the Isle of Man.

3 In the statutory instruments referred to in column 1 of the Schedule to this Order, the word or expression appearing in column 2 thereof shall, to the extent prescribed therein, be construed as including references to their equivalents specified in column 3, whether or not the same word or expression is used in their equivalents in the Manx Act or regulations made thereunder.

4 Regulation 51(4) of the Value Added Tax (General) Regulations 1980 shall not apply to a person determined by the Commissioners under paragraph (7) or (8) of Article 11 of the Value Added Tax (Isle of Man) Order 1982 to be required to be registered under Part I of the Manx Act.

5 Article 2(*a*) of the Tribunals and Inquiries (Value Added Tax Tribunals) Order 1972 and Rule 30(2) of the Value Added Tax Tribunals Rules 1972 shall have effect as if the words "England and Wales" included the Isle of Man.

6 This Order revokes—

(*a*) so much of the Value Added Tax (Isle of Man) Order 1980 as relates to the Rules, Regulations and Orders specified in Schedule 2 to that Order;
(*b*) so much of the Value Added Tax (Isle of Man) (No 2) Order 1980 as relates to the Order specified in the Schedule to that Order; and
(*c*) the Value Added Tax (Isle of Man) (No 3) Order 1980,

and accordingly the instruments amended by those Orders shall have effect as if the Orders had not been made.

SCHEDULE

Article 3

Column 1 STATUTORY INSTRUMENT	Column 2 WORDS	Column 3 MANX EQUIVALENT
The Value Added Tax (Treatment of Transactions) (No 1) Order 1973		
In Article 3(*a*)	"taxable person"	a person defined as such in section 2(2) of the Manx Act
The Value Added Tax (Do-it-yourself Builders) (Relief) Regulations 1975		
In Regulation 1(2)	"value added tax"	value added tax chargeable under Part I of the Manx Act
The Value Added Tax (Bad Debt Relief) Regulations 1978		
In Regulation 4(*b*)(i)	"invoice"	a document defined as such in section 30(2) of the Manx Act
	"Regulations"	the corresponding provisions made under the Manx Act
The Value Added Tax (Cars) Order 1980		
In Article 4(1)	"Tax"	value added tax chargeable under Part I of the Manx Act
	"taxable person", where secondly occurring	a person defined as such in section 2(2) of the Manx Act
In Article 5(2)(*b*)	"tax",	value added tax chargeable under Part I of the Manx Act
In Article 6(1)(*b*) In Article 6(1)(*c*) In Article 6(2)(*c*)	"tax", where secondly occurring "tax", where first occurring "tax", wherever occurring	value added tax chargeable under Part I of the Manx Act
The Value Added Tax (General) Regulations 1980		
In Regulation 8(1)	"taxable person", where secondly occurring	a person defined as such in section 2(2) of the Manx Act
In Regulation 8(3)	"taxable person", where secondly occurring	a person defined as such in section 2(2) of the Manx Act
	"regulation"	the corresponding provision made under the Manx Act
In Regulation 10(1)	"taxable person", where secondly occurring	a person defined as such in section 2(2) of the Manx Act
In Regulations 14 and 15	"the Act"	the corresponding provision of the Manx Act
	"invoice"	a document defined as such in section 30(2) of the Manx Act

Column 1 STATUTORY INSTRUMENT	Column 2 WORDS	Column 3 MANX EQUIVALENT
In Regulations 16(1)(*b*) and 17	"invoice"	a document defined as such in section 30(2) of the Manx Act
In Regulation 18(1)	"invoice"	a document defined as such in section 30(2) of the Manx Act
In Regulation 18(2)	"invoice", wherever occurring	a document defined as such in section 30(2) of the Manx Act
In Regulation 18(2)(*b*)	"tax"	value added tax chargeable under Part I of the Manx Act
In Regulation 18(2)(*c*)	"tax", where first occurring	
In Regulations 19, 20, 21 and 22	"invoice"	a document defined as such in section 30(2) of the Manx Act
In Regulation 29(1) In Regulation 29(2) In Regulation 29(4)	"tax", where secondly occurring "tax", where first occurring "tax"	value added tax chargeable under Part I of the Manx Act
In Regulation 30(5)	"registered person"	a person defined as such in regulations made under the Manx Act
In Regulation 33	"taxable person", wherever occurring	a person defined as such in section 2(2) of the Manx Act
	"tax"	value added tax chargeable under Part I of the Manx Act
In Regulation 33(*a*)	"the Act"	the corresponding provisions of the Manx Act
In Regulation 33(*b*)	"registration number", wherever occurring	a number defined as such in regulations made under the Manx Act
In Regulation 33(*a*) and 33(*b*)	"Commissioners"	the Isle of Man Finance Board
In Regulation 34	"tax"	value added tax chargeable under Part I of the Manx Act
	"taxable person"	a person defined as such in section 2(2) of the Manx Act
	"registration number"	a number defined as such in regulations made under the Manx Act
In Regulation 39(*a*)	"taxable person"	a person defined as such in section 2(2) of the Manx Act
In Regulation 39(*c*)(i)	"tax", where secondly occurring "tax", where first occurring	value added tax chargeable under Part I of the Manx Act
	"the Act"	the Manx Act
In Regulation 40(1)(*a*)	"tax", where secondly occurring	value added tax chargeable under Part I of the Manx Act
In Regulation 42	"port", "airport" or "depot", wherever occurring	a place in the Isle of Man corresponding to such a port, airport or depot
In Regulation 55(1)	"proper officer", wherever occurring	a person defined as such in regulations made under the Manx Act
	"tax", where secondly occurring	value added tax chargeable under Part I of the Manx Act
In Regulation 55(1)(*a*)	"registered person"	a person defined as such in regulations made under the Manx Act
	"regulation 8"	the corresponding provision made under the Manx Act

Column 1 STATUTORY INSTRUMENT	Column 2 WORDS	Column 3 MANX EQUIVALENT
In Regulation 55(1)(*c*) and 55(1)(*d*)	"tax", wherever occurring	value added tax chargeable under Part I of the Manx Act
In Regulation 58(1)	"tax", wherever occurring	value added tax chargeable under Part I of the Manx Act
	"the Act", where first occurring	the Manx Act
	"the Act", where secondly occurring	the corresponding provision of the Manx Act
In Regulation 59(*a*)	"tax", wherever occurring	value added tax chargeable under Part I of the Manx Act
	"Act"	the Manx Act
In Regulation 59(*c*), 59(*e*), 59(*f*) and 59(*g*)	"tax", wherever occurring	value added tax chargeable under Part I of the Manx Act
The Value Added Tax (Repayment to Community Traders) Regulations 1980		
In Regulation 3	"tax", where firstly and secondly occurring	value added tax chargeable under Part I of the Manx Act
In Regulation 4(*b*)(ii)	"tax"	
	"section 8B of the Act"	Section 8B of the Manx Act
In Regulation 6(1)	"tax", wherever occurring	value added tax chargeable under Part I of the Manx Act
In Regulation 7(1)	"tax", where firstly and secondly occurring	value added tax chargeable under Part I of the Manx Act
In Regulation 7(1)(*b*)(ii)	"section 3 of the Act"	Section 3 of the Manx Act
In Regulations 8 and 12	"tax", wherever occurring	value added tax chargeable under Part I of the Manx Act

1984/746
Value Added Tax (Imported Goods) Relief Order 1984

Made by the Treasury under VATA 1983 ss 19(1) and 45(1) and (2) (see now VATA 1994 ss 37(1), 97(1), (5))

Made . . . . 23 May 1984
Laid before the House of Commons . . . . 5 June 1984
Coming into Operation . . . . 1 July 1984

Citation and commencement

1 This Order may be cited as the Value Added Tax (Imported Goods) Relief Order 1984 and shall come into operation on 1st July 1984.

Interpretation

2— (1) In this Order—

["abroad" means a place outside the member States;][3]
"alcoholic beverages" means beverages falling within headings 22.03 to [22.08][2];
"approved" means approved by the Secretary of State;
["exported" means exported to a place outside the member States and "exportation" shall be construed accordingly;][3]
["sent" means sent from a place outside the member States;][3]
["third country" means a place outside the member States;][3]
"tobacco products" has the same meaning as in section 1 of the Tobacco Products Duty Act 1979.

(2) In this Order, references to a heading or sub-heading are references to a heading or sub-heading of the [Combined Nomenclature][1] of the European Economic Community.

(3) Section 48(4) of the Value Added Tax Act 1983[a] (definition of "document" etc) shall not apply for the purposes of this Order.

[(4) Except where it appears in Article 3(2) "import" means import from a place outside the member States and "importation" and "imported" shall be construed accordingly.

(5) Except where it appears in Note (3) to Group 7 of Schedule 2, for "United Kingdom" there shall be substituted "member States".][3]

Note—[a] VATA 1994 s 96(6), (7).

Amendments—[1] Words in para (2) substituted by the VAT (Imported Goods) Relief (Amendment) (No 2) Order, SI 1987/2108 art 3 with effect from 1 January 1988.

[2] Figure substituted for the figure "22.09" by the VAT (Imported Goods) Relief (Amendment) Order, SI 1988/1193 with effect from 1 August 1988.

[3] Definition of "abroad" in para (1) substituted and definitions of "exported", "exportation", "sent" and "third country" and paras (4), (5) inserted by the VAT (Imported Goods) Relief (Amendment) Order, SI 1992/3120 arts 1–3 with effect from 1 January 1993.

Application

3— (1) This Order shall apply without prejudice to relief from tax on the importation of goods afforded under or by virtue of any other enactment.

[(2) Nothing in this Order shall be construed as authorising a person to import anything from a place outside or within the member States in contravention of any prohibition or restriction for the time being in force with respect thereto under or by virtue of any enactment.][1]

Amendments—[1] Para (2) substituted by the VAT (Imported Goods) Relief (Amendment) Order, SI 1992/3120 arts 1, 2, 4 with effect from 1 January 1993.

Relief for United Nations goods

4 No tax shall be payable on the importation, for whatever purpose, of goods produced by the United Nations or by a United Nations organisation, being goods—

(*a*) of a description specified in Part I of Schedule 1 to this Order, or

(*b*) classified under any heading or sub-heading specified in column 1 of Part II of Schedule 1 to this Order and within the limits of relief specified in column 2 thereof in relation to such heading or sub-heading.

Relief for goods of other descriptions

5— (1) Subject to the provisions of this Order, no tax shall be payable on the importation of goods of a description specified in any item in Schedule 2 to this Order.

(2) Schedule 2 shall be interpreted in accordance with the notes therein contained, except that the descriptions of Groups in that Schedule are for ease of reference only and shall not affect the interpretation of the descriptions of items in those Groups.

Condition as to use or purpose of goods in Schedule 2

6— (1) Where relief has been afforded in respect of any goods by virtue of an item comprised in Schedule 2 which describes the goods by reference to a use or purpose, it shall be a condition of the relief that the goods are put to such use or the purpose fulfilled in the United Kingdom.

(2) Without prejudice to paragraph (1) above, where relief has been afforded by virtue of item 5, 6 or 7 of Group 3 of Schedule 2 in respect of goods for demonstration or use, it shall be a condition of the relief that, in the course of, or as a result of, such demonstration or use, the goods are consumed or destroyed or rendered incapable of being used again for the same purpose.

(3) Without prejudice to paragraph (1) above, where relief has been afforded by virtue of item 1 of Group 4 of Schedule 2 in respect of goods for examination, analysis or testing, the relief shall be subject to the following conditions:

(*a*) the examination, analysis or testing shall be completed within such time as the Commissioners may require; and

(*b*) any goods not completely used up or destroyed in the course of, or as a result of, such examination, analysis or testing, and any products resulting therefrom, shall forthwith be destroyed or rendered commercially worthless, or exported.

Note—The words "member States" substituted by the words "United Kingdom" with effect from 1 January 1993 by art 2(5) above.

Restriction on disposal of goods in Schedule 2, Group 6

7— (1) Without prejudice to article 6(1) above and subject to paragraph (2) below, where relief is afforded in respect of any goods by virtue of Group 6 of Schedule 2, it shall be a condition of the relief that the goods are not lent, hired-out or transferred, except in accordance with the provisions of that Group relating to those goods.

(2) Paragraph (1) above shall not apply and relief shall continue to be afforded where goods are lent, hired-out or transferred to an organisation which would be entitled to relief by virtue of Group 6 of Schedule 2, if importing the goods on that date, on condition that—

(*a*) prior notification in writing is received by the Commissioners; and

(*b*) the goods are used solely in accordance with the provisions of Group 6 relating thereto.

Supplementary provisions as to goods in Schedule 2, Group 6

8 Where any goods in respect of which relief has been afforded by virtue of Group 6 of Schedule 2—

(*a*) are to be lent, hired-out, transferred or used except in accordance with the provisions of this Order relating to those goods; or (*b*) remain in the possession of an organisation which has ceased to fulfil any condition subject to which it is approved,

and written notification thereof is given to the Commissioners, the tax payable on the goods shall be determined as if the goods had been imported on the date when the tax becomes due, provided that where the amount of the tax first relieved is less, such lesser amount shall become payable.

Revocation

9 The Value Added Tax (Imported Goods) Relief (No 1) Order 1973 and the Value Added Tax (Health) Order 1983 are hereby revoked.

SCHEDULE 1

RELIEF FOR GOODS PRODUCED BY THE UNITED NATIONS OR A UNITED NATIONS ORGANISATION

Article 4

PART I

1 Holograms for laser projection.
2 Multi-media kits.
3 Materials for programmed instruction, including materials in kit form, with the corresponding printed materials.

[PART II

Column 1 Heading or sub-heading	Column 2 Limits of Relief
370400 10	Limited to films of an educational, scientific or cultural character.
37 05	Limited to films of an educational, scientific or cultural character.
370690 51	Limited to newsreels (with or without soundtrack) depicting events of current news value at the time of importation and, in the case of each importer, not exceeding two copies of each subject for copying.
370610 99	
370690 91	Limited to—
370690 99	(i) archival film material (with our without soundtrack) intended for use in connection with newsreel films; (ii) recreational film particularly suited for children and young people, and (iii) other films of an educational, scientific or cultural character.
49 11	Limited to— (i) microcards or other information storage media required in computerised information and documentation services of an educational, scientific or cultural character; and (ii) wall charts designed solely for demonstration and education.
85 24	Limited to those of an educational, scientific or cultural character.
90 23	Limited to— (i) patterns, models and wall charts of an educational, scientific or cultural character, designed solely for demonstration and education; and (ii) mock-ups or visualisations of abstract concepts such as molecular structures or mathematical formulae.][1]

Amendments—[1] Pt II substituted by the VAT (Imported Goods) Relief (Amendment) (No 2) Order, SI 1987/2108 art 4 with effect from 1 January 1988.

SCHEDULE 2

RELIEF FOR GOODS OF OTHER DESCRIPTIONS

Article 5

GROUP 1

CAPITAL GOODS AND EQUIPMENT ON TRANSFER OF ACTIVITIES

Item No

1 Capital goods and equipment imported by a person for the purposes of a business he has ceased to carry on abroad and which he has notified the Commissions is to be carried on by him in the United Kingdom and concerned exclusively with making taxable supplies.

2 …[1]

Notes:

(1) "Capital goods and equipment" includes livestock other than livestock in the possession of dealers, but does not include—

(*a*) food of a kind used for human consumption or animal feeding stuffs;
(*b*) fuel;
(*c*) stocks of raw materials and finished or semi-finished products; or
(*d*) any motor vehicle in respect of which deduction of input tax is disallowed by article 4 of the Value Added Tax (Cars) Order 1980.

(2) For the purposes of item 1, a person is not to be treated as intending to carry on a business in the United Kingdom if such business is to be merged with, or absorbed by, another business already carried on there.

(3) Item 1 applies only where the goods—

(*a*) have been used in the course of the business for at least twelve months before it ceased to be carried on abroad;
(*b*) are imported within twelve months of the date on which such business ceased to be carried on abroad, or within such longer period as the Commissioners allow; and
(*c*) are appropriate both to the nature and size of the business to be carried on in the United Kingdom.

(4) …[1]

Note—The words "member states" substituted by the words "United Kingdom" with effect from 1 January 1993 by art 2(5) above.

Amendments—[1] Item 2 and Note (4) revoked by the VAT (Imported Goods) Relief (Amendment) Order, SI 1992/3120 arts 1, 2, 5(*a*) with effect from 1 January 1993.

GROUP 2
AGRICULTURE AND ANIMALS

Amendments—Group 2 revoked by the VAT (Imported Goods) Relief (Amendment) Order, SI 1992/3120 arts 1, 2, 5(*a*) with effect from 1 January 1993.

GROUP 3
PROMOTION OF TRADE

Item No

1 Articles of no intrinsic commercial value sent free of charge by suppliers of goods and services for the sole purpose of advertising.

2 Samples of negligible value of a kind and in quantities capable of being used solely for soliciting orders for goods of the same kind.

[3 Printed advertising matter, including catalogues, price lists, directions for use or brochures, which relates to goods for sale or hire by a person established outside the United Kingdom, …[2], or to transport, commercial insurance or banking services offered by a person established in a third country, and which clearly displays the name of the person by whom such goods or services are offered.][1]

4 Goods to be distributed free of charge at an event, as small representative samples, for use or consumption by the public.

5 Goods imported solely for the purpose of being demonstrated at an event.

6 Goods imported solely for the purpose of being used in the demonstration of any machine or apparatus displayed at an event.

7 Paints, varnishes, wallpaper and other materials of low value to be used in the building, fitting-out and decoration of a temporary stand at an event.

8 Catalogues, prospectuses, price lists, advertising posters, calendars (whether or not illustrated) unframed photographs and other printed matter or articles advertising goods displayed at an event, supplied without charge for the purpose of distribution free of charge to the public at such event.

Notes:

(1) Where the Commissioners so require, item 2 applies only to goods which are rendered permanently unusable, except as samples, by being torn, perforated, clearly and indelibly marked, or by any other process.

(2) [Save in the case of imported printed matter intended for distribution free of charge and relating to either goods for sale or hire …[2], item 3 does not apply to—][1]

(*a*) any consignment containing two or more copies of different documents;

(*b*) any consignment containing two or more copies of the same document, unless the total gross weight of such consignment does not exceed one kilogram; or

(*c*) any goods which are the subject of grouped consignments from the same consignor to the same consignee.

(3) "Event" means any of the following—

(*a*) any trade, industrial, agricultural or craft exhibition, fair or similar show or display, not being an exhibition, fair, show or display organised for private purposes in a shop or on business premises with a view to the sale of the goods displayed;

(*b*) any exhibition or meeting which is primarily organised—

(i) for a charitable purpose, or

(ii) to promote any branch of learning, art, craft, sport or scientific, technical, educational, cultural or trade union activity, or tourism, or

(iii) to promote friendship between peoples, or

(iv) to promote religious knowledge or worship;

(*c*) any meeting of representatives of any international organisation or international group of organisations; and

(*d*) any representative meeting or ceremony of an official or commemorative character.

(4) In item 4, "representative samples" means goods which are—

(*a*) imported free of charge or obtained at such event from goods imported in bulk;

(*b*) identifiable as advertising samples of low value;

(*c*) not easily marketable and, where appropriate, packaged in quantities which are less than the lowest quantity of the same goods as marketed; and

(*d*) intended to be consumed at such event, where the goods comprise foodstuffs or beverages not packaged as described in paragraph (*c*) above.

(5) Items 4, 5 and 6 do not apply to fuels, alcoholic beverages or tobacco products.

(6) Items 4 to 8 apply only where the aggregate value and quantity thereof is appropriate to the nature of the event, the number of visitors and the extent of the exhibitor's participation in it.

Note—The words "member States" substituted by the words "United Kingdom" with effect from 1 January 1993 by art 2(5) above.

Amendments—[1] Item 3 and words at the beginning of Note (2) substituted by the VAT (Imported Goods) Relief (Amendment) (No 2) Order, SI 1988/2212 art 4 with effect from 1 January 1989.

[2] Words in item 3 and Note (2) deleted by the VAT (Imported Goods) Relief (Amendment) Order, SI 1992/3120 arts, 1, 2, 5 with effect from 1 January 1993.

GROUP 4
GOODS FOR TESTING, ETC

Item No

1 Goods imported for the purpose of examination, analysis or testing to determine their composition, quality or other technical characteristics, to provide information or for industrial or commercial research.

Note:

Item 1 does not apply to goods exceeding the quantities necessary for such purposes or where the examination, analysis or testing, itself constitutes a sales promotion.

GROUP 5
HEALTH

Item No

1 Animals specially prepared for laboratory use and sent free of charge to a relevant establishment.

2 …[2]

3 Biological or chemical substances sent to a relevant establishment from [a place outside the member States][2].

4 Human blood.

5 Products for therapeutic purposes, derived from human blood.

6 Human (including foetal) organs or tissue for diagnostic or therapeutic purposes or medical research.

7 Reagents for use in blood type grouping or for the detection of blood grouping incompatibilities, by approved institutions or laboratories, exclusively for non-commercial medical or scientific purposes.

8 Reagents for use in the determination of human tissue types by approved institutions or laboratories, exclusively for non-commercial medical or scientific purposes.

9 Pharmaceutical products imported by or on behalf of persons or animals for their use while visiting the United Kingdom to participate in an international sporting event.

[10 Samples of reference substances approved by the World Health Organisation for the quality control of materials used in the manufacture of medicinal products.][1]

Notes:

(1) In items 1, ...[2] and 3, "relevant establishment" means—

(*a*) a public establishment, or a department of such establishment, principally engaged in education or scientific research; or

(*b*) a private establishment so engaged, which is approved.

(2) Item 3 applies only where the goods fulfil the conditions laid down under or by virtue of [Article 60][1] of Council Regulation (EEC) No 918/83.

(3) Items 4, 5, 6, 7 and 8 include special packaging essential for transport of the goods and any solvents or accessories necessary for their use.

(4) In items 7 and 8, "reagents" means all reagents, whether of human, animal, plant, or other, origin.

[(5) Item 10 applies only to samples addressed to consignees authorised to receive them free of tax.][2]

Note—The words "member States" substituted by the words "United Kingdom" with effect from 1 January 1993 by art 2(5) above.

Amendments—[1] Item 10 and Note (5) added and words in Note (2) substituted by the VAT (Imported Goods) Relief (Amendment) (No 2) Order, SI 1988/2212 art 5 with effect from 1 January 1989.

[2] Words in item 3 substituted and Item 2 and figure in Note (1) revoked by the VAT (Imported Goods) Relief (Amendment) Order SI 1992/3120 arts 1, 2, 5 with effect from 1 January 1993.

GROUP 6
CHARITIES, ETC

Item No

1 Basic necessities obtained without charge for distribution free of charge to the needy by a relevant organisation.

2 Goods donated by a person established abroad to a relevant organisation for use to raise funds at occasional charity events for the benefit of the needy.

3 Equipment and office materials donated by a person established abroad to a relevant organisation for meeting its operating needs or carrying out its charitable aims.

4 Goods imported by a relevant organisation for distribution or loan, free of charge, to victims of a disaster affecting the territory of one or more member States.

5 Goods imported by a relevant organisation for meeting its operating needs in the relief of a disaster affecting the territory of one or more member States.

6 Articles donated to and imported by a relevant organisation for supply to blind or other physically or mentally handicapped persons and which are specially designed for the education, employment or social advancement of such persons.

7 Spare parts, components or accessories for any article of a kind mentioned in item 6, including tools for its maintenance, checking, calibration or repair.

Notes:

(1) In items 1 to 5, "relevant organisation" means a State organisation or other approved charitable or philanthropic organisation.

(2) In item 1, "basic necessities" means food, medicines, clothing, blankets, orthopaedic equipment and crutches, required to meet a person's immediate needs.

(3) Items 1, 2 and 3 do not include alcoholic beverages, tobacco products, coffee, tea or motor vehicles other than ambulances.

(4) Items 2, 3 and 6 do not apply where there is any commercial intent on the part of the donor.

(5) Items 4 and 5 apply only where the Commission of the European Communities has made a Decision authorising importation of the goods.

(6) In item 6, "relevant organisation" means an approved organisation principally engaged in the education of, or the provision of assistance to, blind or other physically or mentally handicapped persons.

(7) In item 6, "supply" means any loan, hiring-out or transfer, for consideration or free of charge, other than on a profit-making basis.

(8) Item 7 applies only where the goods are imported with an article of a kind mentioned in item 6 to which they relate, or, if imported subsequently, are identifiable as being intended for that article, where relief from tax on that article has been afforded by virtue of item 6, or would have been so afforded if such article were imported with the goods which relate to it.

GROUP 7
Printed Matter, Etc

Item No

1 Documents sent free of charge to public services in the United Kingdom.

2 Foreign government publications and publications of official international bodies intended for free distribution.

3 Ballot papers for elections organised by bodies abroad.

4 Specimen signatures and printed circulars concerning signatures, forming part of exchanges of information between bankers or public services.

5 Official printed matter sent to a Central Bank in the United Kingdom.

6 Documents sent by companies incorporated abroad to bearers of, or subscribers to, securities issued by such companies.

7 Files, archives and other documents for use at international meetings, conferences or congresses and reports of such gatherings.

8 Plans, technical drawings, traced designs and other documents sent by any person for the purpose of participating in a competition in the United Kingdom or to obtain or fulfil an order executed abroad.

9 Documents to be used in examinations held in the United Kingdom on behalf of institutions established abroad.

10 Printed forms to be used as official documents in the international movement of vehicles or goods pursuant to international conventions.

11 Printed forms, labels, tickets and similar documents sent to travel agents in the United Kingdom by transport and tourist undertakings abroad.

12 Used commercial documents.

13 Official printed forms from national or international authorities.

14 Printed matter conforming to international standards, for distribution by an association in the United Kingdom and sent by a corresponding association abroad.

15 Documents sent for the purpose of free distribution to encourage persons to visit foreign countries, in particular to attend cultural, tourist, sporting, religious, trade or professional meetings or events.

16 Foreign hotel lists and yearbooks published by or on behalf of official tourist agencies and timetables for foreign transport services, for free distribution.

17 Yearbooks, lists of telephone and telex numbers, hotel lists, catalogues for fairs, specimens of craft goods of negligible value and literature on museums, universities, spas or other similar establishments, supplied as reference material to accredited representatives or correspondents appointed by official national tourist agencies and not intended for distribution.

[18 Official publications issued under the authority of the country of exportation, international institutions, regional or local authorities and bodies governed by public law established in the country of exportation.][1]

[19 Printed matter distributed by foreign political organisations on the occasion of elections to the European Parliament or national elections in the country in which the printed matter originates.][1]

Notes:

[(1) Items 15 and 16 do not apply where the goods contain more than 25 per cent of private commercial advertising.][1]

[(2) Items 18 and 19 apply only to publications or printed matter on which value added tax or any other tax has been paid in the third country from which they have been exported and which have not benefited, by virtue of their exportation, from any relief from payment thereof.][2]

[(3) In Item 19, "foreign political organisations" means those which are officially recognised as such in the United Kingdom.][1]

[(4) In Item 11 "travel agent" includes airlines, national railway undertakings, ferry operators and similar organisations.

(5) In Items 2, 15, 16 and 19 "foreign" means from a country other than the United Kingdom.][2]

Note—Except where it appears in Note (3) above, the words "member States" substituted by the words "United Kingdom" with effect from 1 January 1993 by art 2(5) above.

Amendments—[1] Items 18 and 19 added and Notes (1)–(3) substituted for the original Note by the VAT (Imported Goods) Relief (Amendment) (No 2) Order, SI 1988/2212 art 6 with effect from 1 January 1989.

[2] Note (2) substituted and Notes (4), (5) inserted by the VAT (Imported Goods) Relief (Amendment) Order, SI 1992/3120 arts 1, 2, 5 with effect from 1 January 1993.

GROUP 8
Articles Sent For Miscellaneous Purposes

Item No

1 Material relating to trademarks, patterns or designs and supporting documents and applications for patents, imported for the purpose of being submitted to bodies competent to deal with protection of copyright or industrial or commercial patent rights.

2 Objects imported for the purpose of being submitted as evidence, or for a like purpose, to a court or other official body in the United Kingdom.

3 Photographs, slides and stereotype mats for photographs, whether or not captioned, sent to press agencies and publishers of newspapers or magazines.

4 Recorded media, including punched cards, sound recordings and microfilm, sent free of charge for the transmission of information.

5 Any honorary decoration conferred by a government or Head of State abroad on a person resident in the United Kingdom and imported on his behalf.

6 Any cup, medal or similar article of an essentially symbolic nature, intended as a tribute to activities in the arts, sciences, sport, or the public service, or in recognition of merit at a particular event, which is either—

(*a*) donated by an authority or person established abroad for the purpose of being presented in the United Kingdom, or

(*b*) awarded abroad to a person resident in the United Kingdom and imported on his behalf.

7 Goods (other than alcoholic beverages or tobacco products) sent on an occasional basis as gifts in token of friendship or goodwill between bodies, public authorities or groups carrying on an activity in the public interest.

8 Any consignment of goods (other than alcoholic beverages, tobacco products, perfumes or toilet waters) not exceeding [£18][2] in value, …[1]

[9 Awards, trophies and souvenirs of a symbolic nature and of limited value intended for distribution free of charge at business conferences or similar events to persons normally resident in a country other than the United Kingdom.][1]

[*Note*: Items 5, 6, 7 and 9 do not apply to any importation of a commercial character.][1]

Note—The words "member States" substituted by the words "United Kingdom" with effect from 1 January 1993 by art 2(5) above.

Amendments—[1] Words in item 8 repealed, item 9 added and Note substituted by the VAT (Imported Goods) Relief (Amendment) (No 2) Order, SI 1988/2212 art 7 with effect from 1 January 1989.

[2] Amount in item 8 substituted by the VAT (Imported Goods) Relief (Amendment) Order, SI 1995/3222 with effect from 1 January 1996.

GROUP 9
WORKS OF ART AND COLLECTORS' PIECES

Item No

1 Works of art and collectors' pieces imported by approved museums, galleries or other institutions for a purpose other than sale.

Note: Item 1 applies only where the goods are—

(*a*) of an educational, scientific or cultural character; and

(*b*) imported free of charge or, if for a consideration, are not supplied to the importer in the course or furtherance of any business.

[GROUP 10
TRANSPORT][1]

[Item No

1 Fuel contained in the standard tanks of a vehicle or of a special container, for use exclusively by such vehicle or such special container.

2 Fuel, not exceeding 10 litres for each vehicle, contained in portable tanks carried by a vehicle, for use exclusively by such vehicle.

3 Lubricants contained in a vehicle, for use exclusively by such vehicle.

4 Litter, fodder and feeding stuffs contained in any means of transport carrying animals, for the use of such animals during their journey.

5 Disposable packings for the stowage and protection of goods during their transportation to the United Kingdom.

Notes:

(1) "Standard tanks" means any of the following—

(*a*) tanks permanently fitted to a vehicle and which are fitted to all vehicles of that type by the manufacturer, to supply directly fuel for the purpose of propulsion and, where appropriate, for the operation, during transport, of refrigeration systems and other systems;

(*b*) gas tanks fitted to vehicles designed for the direct use of gas as a fuel;

(*c*) tanks fitted to ancillary systems with which a vehicle is equipped; and

(*d*) tanks permanently fitted to a special container and which are fitted to all special containers of that type by the manufacturer, to supply directly fuel for the operation, during transport, of refrigeration systems and other systems with which special containers are equipped.

(2) "Vehicle" means any motor road vehicle.

(3) "Special container" means any container fitted with specially designed apparatus for refrigeration systems, oxygenation systems, thermal insulation systems and other systems.

(4) Item 2 does not apply in the case of any special purpose vehicle or a vehicle which, by its type of construction and equipment, is designed for and capable of transporting goods or more than nine persons including the driver.

(5) Item 3 applies only to lubricants necessary for the normal operation of the vehicle during its journey.

(6) Item 5 applies only where the cost of the packings is included in the consideration for the goods transported.][1]

Note—The words "member States" substituted by the words "United Kingdom" with effect from 1 January 1993 by art 2(5) above.

Amendments—[1] This group substituted by the VAT (Imported Goods) Relief (Amendment) (No 2) Order, SI 1988/2212 art 8 with effect from 1 January 1989.

GROUP 11
War Graves, Funerals, Etc

Item No

1 Goods imported by an approved organisation for use in the construction, upkeep or ornamentation of cemeteries, tombs and memorials in the United Kingdom which commemorate war victims of other countries.

2 Coffins containing human remains.

3 Urns containing human ashes.

4 Flowers, wreaths and other ornamental objects accompanying goods described in items 2 or 3.

5 Flowers, wreaths and other ornamental objects, imported without any commercial intent by a person resident abroad, for use at a funeral or to decorate a grave.

Note—The words "member States" substituted by the words "United Kingdom" with effect from 1 January 1993 by art 2(5).
Concession ESC 2.6—American war graves.

1984/1176
Control of Movement of Goods Regulations 1984

Made by the Commissioners of Customs and Excise under the Customs and Excise Management Act 1979 s 31 and all other enabling powers

Made . . . . *1 August 1984*
Laid before Parliament . . . . *3 August 1984*
Coming into Operation . . . . *6 August 1984*

Citation and commencement

1 These Regulations may be cited as the Control of Movement of Goods Regulations 1984 and shall come into operation on 6th August 1984.

Revocation

2 The Control of Movement of Goods Regulations 1981 are hereby revoked.

Interpretation

3 In these Regulations—

"the Act" means the Customs and Excise Management Act 1979;

"approved place"—

(*a*) in relation to imported goods means a place approved by the Commissioners under section 20 or 25 of the Act for the clearance out of charge of such goods, and

(*b*) in relation to goods intended for export means a place appointed under section 159 of the Act for the examination of goods which is approved by the Commissioners under section 31 of the Act for the examination of such goods before their movement to a place of exportation;

"the loader" shall have the same meaning as in section 57 of the Act; that is to say the owner of the ship or aircraft in which the goods are to be exported or a person appointed by him;

"place of importation" and "place of exportation" shall, where appropriate, include a free zone;

"removal" means a movement of goods which is authorised under these Regulations and "remove" and "removed" shall be construed accordingly;

"removal document" means a document to be obtained from or approved by the Commissioners made in such form and containing such particulars as the Commissioners may direct under section 31(2A) of the Act and for the purpose of regulation 16 shall include a copy of the application referred to in regulations 5, 6 and 7 stamped by the proper officer.

4— (1) These Regulations shall not apply where any goods are moved under the internal or external Community transit procedure.

(2) The application of regulations 11 and 13 of these Regulations to goods carried under the provisions of an international convention having effect in the United Kingdom shall be without prejudice to any such provisions.

Restrictions on the movement of goods

5 Subject to regulation 10, no imported goods not yet cleared from customs and excise charge shall be moved between their place of importation and either an approved place or a free zone and, in the case of transit goods, between their place of importation and a place of exportation unless the movement is authorised by the proper officer upon application made to him.

6 Subject to regulation 10, no goods shall be moved between—

(*a*) a free zone and a place approved for the clearance out of charge of such goods,
(*b*) such a place and a free zone, and
(*c*) a free zone and another free zone,

unless the movement is authorised by the proper officer upon application made to him.

7 Subject to regulations 9 and 10, no goods intended for export and made available at an approved place or a place designated by the proper officer under sections 53(4) or 58(3) of the Act for the purposes of examination shall be moved between any such place and a place of exportation unless the movement is authorised by the proper officer upon application made to him.

8 Save as the Commissioners may otherwise allow, the applications referred to in regulations 5, 6 and 7 above shall be made in writing on a document obtained from or approved by the Commissioners for that purpose and shall be made—

(*a*) in the case of imported goods, by the importer or the person in charge of the goods,
(*b*) in the case of goods intended for export, by the exporter or the person in charge of the goods, and
(*c*) in any other case, by the proprietor of the goods or the person in charge of the goods.

Local export control

9— (1) Where a notice under section 58A(3)(*a*)(i) of the Act is delivered by the exporter such notice shall replace the application required under regulation 7.

(2) Where the notice is for a single movement of goods, if the authority of the proper officer, required under regulation 7, is neither given nor refused by the date and time for the movement specified in that notice, it shall be deemed to be given on the date and immediately before the time so specified.

(3) Where the notice is for more than one movement of goods, if the authority of the proper officer, required under regulation 7, is neither given nor refused, it shall be deemed to be given immediately before each movement commences.

Standing permission to remove

10 Where the Commissioners so permit, during a period specified by them, goods may be moved as contemplated in regulations 5, 6 and 7 without an application to the proper officer; and, unless the proper officer previously gives or refuses his authority, it shall be deemed to be given immediately before the movement commences.

Requirement for removal document

11 Before any removal commences the person by whom, or on whose behalf, the goods are being moved shall be in possession of a removal document.

Specification of vehicles etc

12— (1) The Commissioners may, in respect of any class or description of goods, require that vehicles or containers in which goods of a particular class or description are removed shall be of a type specified by them for the removal of such goods.

(2) Save as provided by paragraph (3) below, no person shall remove any goods in respect of which a requirement under paragraph (1) above has been imposed unless the vehicle or container in which they are carried conforms to such requirement.

(3) The proper officer, upon application made to him by the person in charge of goods to be removed, may for the purposes of the removal in question relax any requirement imposed under paragraph (1) above.

Specification of routes

13 Vehicles and containers proceeding under a removal shall be moved by such routes as the Commissioners may specify.

Security of goods, vehicles and containers

14— (1) Before any goods are removed they or the vehicle or container carrying them shall be secured or identified by any such seals, locks or marks as the Commissioners may specify.

(2) Where in the United Kingdom, seals, locks or marks are affixed for any customs or excise purpose in order to secure or identify the goods to be removed or the vehicles or containers carrying the goods, they shall be so affixed by the proper officer or by such other person as the Commissioners may authorise.

15— (1) Save in the circumstances hereunder mentioned, no person shall at any time during a removal—

(*a*) wilfully break, open or remove any seal, lock or mark affixed for any customs or excise purpose on any goods or to a vehicle or container; or

(*b*) load or unload or assist in the loading or unloading of a vehicle or container.

(2) The circumstances referred to in paragraph (1) above are—

(*a*) where authorisation has been given by the proper officer; or

(*b*) in accordance with any general or special permission given by the Commissioners; or

(*c*) in an emergency in order to safeguard the goods or to protect life or property.

Completion of removals, time limits and accidents

16— (1) Save as the Commissioners otherwise allow, the person in charge of goods proceeding under a removal shall complete the removal by producing the goods, together with the vehicle or container in which they are carried if such vehicle or container has been secured or identified, and delivering a removal document to the proper officer at the approved place or, in the case of goods intended for export, at the place of exportation.

(2) The Commissioners may allow the removal of goods intended for export to be completed by the person in charge of the goods placing them, together with any container in which they are carried if such container has been secured or identified, under the control of the loader and delivering the removal document to him.

17 The person in charge of goods proceeding under a removal shall complete the removal within such period as the Commissioners may specify.

18 Where as a result of an accident or other occurrence arising during a removal a vehicle or container is delayed or diverted from a specified route the person in charge of the goods shall as soon as practicable give sufficient notification of the accident or occurrence as required by the Commissioners to the local office of customs and excise.

1984/1177
Free Zone Regulations 1984

Made by the Commissioners of Customs and Excise under CEMA 1979 ss 100B(1), 100C(3) and (4), 100D(1), (2), 125(3) and VATA 1983 s 24 (see now VATA 1994 s 16)

Made . . . . *1 August 1984*
Laid before Parliament . . . . *3 August 1984*
Coming into Operation . . . . *6 August 1984*

PART I
PRELIMINARY

Citation and commencement

1 These Regulations may be cited as the Free Zone Regulations 1984 and shall come into operation on 6th August 1984.

Interpretation

2 In these Regulations—

"chargeable operation" means any operation carried out on Community goods which are free zone goods where, because of Commission Regulation (EEC) 1371/81 and the nature of the operation, agricultural levy becomes chargeable or a negative monetary compensatory amount payable;

"Community goods" means goods which fulfil the conditions of Article 9(2) of the EEC Treaty, and goods covered by the Treaty establishing the European Coal and Steel Community which are in free circulation in the Community in accordance with that Treaty;

"tax" means value added tax;

"transfer to another customs procedure providing for suspension of, or relief from, customs duty or agricultural levy" in regulation 11 (requirement for entry) shall not be taken to include the removal of free zone goods from one free zone to another or from a free zone to a place for the clearance out of charge of imported goods.

PART II
SECURITY OF FREE ZONES

Security and recovery of expenditure by Commissioners

3 The Commissioners may by direction impose obligations on the responsible authority for a free zone to ensure the security of that free zone; and where the responsible authority fails to comply with such direction and the Commissioners thereby incur any expenditure, such expenditure shall be recoverable on demand by the Commissioners as a civil debt from that responsible authority.

Residence in free zones not permitted

4 The responsible authority shall not permit any person to take up residence within a free zone.

PART III
GOODS CHARGEABLE WITH EXCISE DUTY

Excise goods which may become free zone goods without payment of excise duty

5 Goods chargeable with excise duty may be moved into a free zone in accordance with these Regulations without payment of that duty and remain as free zone goods; provided that they are goods which, by or under the customs and excise Acts, the Commissioners may allow to be removed or delivered without payment of excise duty and which have been allowed to be so removed or delivered.

PART IV
MOVEMENT OF GOODS INTO FREE ZONE

Goods to become free zone goods

6— (1) Goods moved into a free zone shall not be free zone goods unless, within [such time as the Commissioners may direct][1], such particulars the Commissioners may direct have been entered in a record to be kept by the occupier of the premises at which the goods are received or, if the Commissioners so direct, by the responsible authority.

(2) …[1]

Amendments—[1] Words in para (1) substituted and para (2) revoked by the Free Zone (Amendment) Regulations, SI 1988/710 reg 3 with effect from 10 May 1988.

Acknowledgment of Community status of free zone goods

7— (1) Where the proprietor of free zone goods wishes to obtain an acknowledgment that the goods are Community goods he shall deliver to the proper officer, within the relevant period, a document in such form and containing such particulars as the Commissioners may direct together with such supporting evidence as will enable the officer to establish to his satisfaction that they are Community goods, and, if so satisfied, the proper officer shall provide a written acknowledgment of such Community status.

(2) The written acknowledgment referred to in paragraph (1) above shall consist of a copy of the document containing particulars of the goods, endorsed by the proper officer.

(3) In this regulation "relevant period" shall mean a period not exceeding 7 days from the time the goods become free zone goods or from the time an entry for free circulation under regulation 17(2) is accepted.

Goods from another customs procedure

8 Goods moved into a free zone which are subject to another customs procedure shall not be free zone goods until the proprietor of the goods has presented them to the proper officer and that procedure has been discharged.

PART V
OPERATIONS

Operations on free zone goods

9— (1) Operations on free zone goods shall only be permitted in accordance with this regulation and subject to any prohibition or restriction imposed by or under any enactment for the time being in force.

(2) Any operation is prohibited in which goods that are not free zone goods are mixed with or incorporated into free zone goods.

(3) The Commissioners shall allow, subject to such conditions as they may impose, operations to be carried out on free zone goods as follows—

(*a*) where only Community goods are involved, any operation;

(*b*) where any other goods are involved—

(i) the usual forms of handling listed in Article 1.1 of Council Directive 71/235/EEC,

(ii) processing under customs control for free circulation in accordance with Council Regulation (EEC) 2763/83, or

(iii) any operation carried out in accordance with the Inward Processing Relief Regulations 1977.

(4) A person intending to carry out any operation shall—

(*a*) before commencing an operation referred to in paragraph (3)(*a*) above, inform the proper officer of his intention and, in addition, where the operation is a chargeable operation enter such particulars as the Commissioners may require in a record to be kept by him, (*b*) before commencing an operation referred to in paragraph (3)(*b*)(i) above, notify the proper officer of his intention, and

(*c*) before commencing any other operation, make a declaration by entering such particulars as the Commissioners may require in a record to be kept by him.

(5) A person intending to carry out an operation referred to in paragraph (3)(*b*)(i) above may, at the time he notifies the proper officer of his intention to carry out the operation, apply for a written acknowledgment that the operation is to commence and the application shall be in such form as the Commissioners may direct and contain such particulars as the Commissioners may require to enable them to apply regulation 25(4).

(6) The written acknowledgment referred to in paragraph (5) above, shall consist of a copy of the application endorsed by the proper officer.

(7) Save as provided by this regulation, free zone goods shall not be used or consumed in a free zone unless they are entered in accordance with regulation 17(1).

(8) Notwithstanding paragraph (3) above, free zone goods chargeable with excise duty which have been removed or delivered without payment of that duty by or under the customs and excise Acts before becoming free zone goods may only be used or consumed in the free zone without payment of that duty where such use or consumption does not affect the relief from excise duty under the requirements of those Acts applicable to the relief; and paragraph (7) above shall only apply to such goods if they are also chargeable with a duty of customs or agricultural levy which has not been paid.

(9) Where an operation is carried out on free zone goods otherwise than in accordance with this regulation, they shall cease to be free zone goods, and shall be liable to forfeiture.

PART VI
ENTRY, REMOVAL AND PAYMENT OF DUTY ETC

Procedure for entering free zone goods

10— (1) Free zone goods, required by these Regulations to be entered, shall be entered by the proprietor of the goods delivering to the proper officer an entry thereof in such form and manner, containing such particulars and accompanied by such documents as the Commissioners may direct.

(2) Acceptance of an entry by the proper officer shall be signified in such manner as the Commissioners may direct.

(3) Where free zone goods are required to be entered under regulation 17, the Commissioners may direct that if the proprietor of the goods—

(*a*) enters such particulars as the Commissioners may direct in a record to be kept by him, and

(*b*) furnishes a schedule to the proper officer at such place and at such intervals as the Commissioners may direct,

an entry of the goods shall be taken to have been delivered and accepted when the particulars are entered in the record.

Entry required before removal for home use etc

11 Subject to regulation 12, before any free zone goods are removed from a free zone for—

(*a*) home use, or

(*b*) transfer to another customs procedure providing for suspension of, or relief from, customs duty or agricultural levy,

the goods shall be entered for such purpose.

Removal without entry

12— (1) Upon application by the proprietor of free zone goods, the Commissioners may allow the goods to be removed from the free zone for the purposes set out in regulation 11 without the goods being entered, if such particulars as the Commissioners may direct are entered in a record to be kept by the proprietor of the goods.

(2) Where goods are allowed to be removed from the free zone in accordance with para-graph (1) above, the proprietor of the goods shall comply with such conditions as the Commissioners may impose.

Goods to be removed after entry etc

13 Subject to regulations 15 and 16, free zone goods which have been entered under regulation 11 or in respect of which the particulars required under regulation 12 have been entered in the record, shall be removed, forthwith, from the free zone.

Removal of goods for export etc

14 Part V of the Customs and Excise Management Act 1979 (procedures for the export of goods) and any prohibition or restriction on the export of goods or their shipment as stores, imposed by or under any enactment for the time being in force, shall apply to goods removed from a free zone for export or shipment as stores.

Restriction on removal of goods

15 No goods shall be removed from a free zone except with the authority of and in accordance with any requirement made by the proper officer.

Payment of duty before removal of goods

16 Save as the Commissioners may otherwise allow and subject to such conditions as they may impose, no goods shall be removed from a free zone until any customs duty and agricultural levy chargeable thereon has been paid; and where the goods have been entered under regulation 11(*a*), such duty and levy shall be paid at the time the entry is delivered.

Entry of goods which are to remain in free zone

17— (1) Free zone goods to be used or consumed in a free zone, as provided in regulation 9(7), shall be entered for home use.

(2) Where the proprietor of free zone goods wishes to pay any customs duty or agricultural levy chargeable on the goods and for the goods to remain as free zone goods, the goods shall be entered for free circulation.

Payment of duty etc on goods to remain in free zone after entry

18— (1) Where goods are entered under regulation 17, any customs duty and agricultural levy chargeable thereon shall be paid at the time the entry is delivered.

(2) As an exception of paragraph (1) above, where the goods are entered for free circulation, tax on importation shall not be paid at the time customs duty is paid.

Agricultural levy chargeable because of chargeable operation

19 Where agricultural levy becomes chargeable or a negative monetary compensatory amount payable, because of a chargeable operation, a schedule in such form and containing such particulars of the goods and the operation as the Commissioners may direct shall be furnished by the proprietor of the goods to the proper officer at such place and at such intervals as the Commissioners may direct, and any agricultural levy so chargeable shall be paid at the time the schedule is furnished.

Customs duty etc deemed to have been paid

20 For the purposes of these Regulations, customs duty and agricultural levy shall be deemed to have been paid if payment thereof has been deferred under the Customs Duties (Deferred Payment) Regulations 1976, secured to the satisfaction of the Commissioners or otherwise accounted for.

Destruction of free zone goods

21 Subject to such conditions as the Commissioners may impose, free zone goods may be destroyed and no customs duty or agricultural levy shall be payable on them: Provided that where any scrap or waste resulting from their destruction is entered for removal for home use, duty and levy shall be chargeable thereon in accordance with regulation 25.

PART VII
CONTROLS

Production of goods

22 Goods in a free zone shall be produced to the proper officer for examination on request.

Segregation etc of goods

23 The proper officer may require any goods in a free zone to be segregated and marked or otherwise identified.

Keeping of records and provision of information

24— (1) In addition to any requirement in that regard imposed by or under these Regulations, the Value Added Tax Act 1983[a] or the Inward Processing Relief Regulations 1977, the occupier of any premises upon which free zone goods are kept or, where the Commissioners so direct, the responsible authority on his behalf, shall keep such records relating to the goods as the Commissioners may direct.

(2) Any records required to be kept under these Regulations shall be kept in the free zone or such other place as the Commissioners may allow and be kept in such form and be preserved for such time, not exceeding three years from the date the goods are removed from the free zone, as the Commissioners may direct.

(3) The person keeping the record shall—

(*a*) furnish to the Commissioners, within such time and in such form as they may require, such information relating to the goods as the Commissioners may direct, and

(*b*) upon demand made by the proper officer produce to him any records and any document relating to the goods for inspection by the proper officer and permit him to take copies of or to make extracts from them or remove them at a reasonable time and for a reasonable purpose: Provided that if the information that would otherwise be contained in any record or document is not made or preserved in a form which is easily readable or which is not readable without the aid of equipment, the person keeping the record or document, shall, at the request of the proper officer produce the information contained in the record or document in the form of a transcript or other permanent legible reproduction.

Note—[a] VATA 1994.

PART VIII
CUSTOMS DUTY ETC CHARGEABLE ON FREE ZONE GOODS

Customs duty chargeable on free zone goods

25— (1) Except as provided in paragraph (5) of this regulation (compensating products from inward processing), the customs duty and agricultural levy and the rate thereof chargeable, or the negative monetary compensatory amount and the rate thereof payable, on free zone goods—

(*a*) removed from a free zone for home use, or

(*b*) remaining in a free zone after being entered for home use or free circulation;

shall be those in force for goods of that class or description at the time of acceptance of the entry or, where the goods are allowed to be removed without entry, those in force at the time the particulars required under regulation 12 are entered in the record.

(2) The agricultural levy and the rate thereof chargeable or the negative monetary compensatory amount and the rate thereof payable on free zone goods because of a chargeable operation thereon shall be those in force for goods of that class or description at the time the operation commenced.

(3) Except as provided in paragraph (4) below, the value for customs purposes of free zone goods of any class or description shall be that ascertained or accepted by the Commissioners at the time of the acceptance of the entry for home use or free circulation.

(4) Where goods which are removed from a free zone have undergone any of the usual forms of handling referred to in regulation 9(3)(*b*)(i), provided that the proprietor of the goods—

(*a*) if the goods are entered, produces with the entry, or

(*b*) in any other case, produces to the proper officer at such time as the Commissioners may direct,

the written acknowledgment referred to in regulation 9(5), the quantity of goods, their class or description and value shall, at his option, be those accepted or ascertained at the date of the acknowledgment.

(5) Notwithstanding any other provision of this regulation, where any goods imported into the United Kingdom are granted an authorisation, or have been granted in another Member State an authorisation, for inward processing relief and the Commissioners have allowed compensating products, derived from such goods which have become free zone goods, to be entered for home use or free circulation, the customs duty and agricultural levy chargeable shall be either—

(*a*) the amount calculated in accordance with the Inward Processing Relief Regulations 1977, or

(*b*) at the option of the proprietor of the goods and provided that the Commissioners are satisfied that the amount is at least equal to the amount ascertainable under sub-paragraph (*a*) above, the amount calculated in accordance with paragraph (1) above.

(6) In this regulation, "compensating products" shall have the same meaning as in the Inwards Processing Relief Regulations 1977.

PART IX
VALUE ADDED TAX

Tax charge on removal from free zone of manufactured goods

26 ...

Amendments—This regulation revoked by the Free Zone (Amendment) Regulations, SI 1988/710 reg 4 with effect from 10 May 1988.

Relief from import tax following supply to non-registered person

27 Where free zone goods have been supplied whilst in the free zone to a person who is neither registered or liable to be registered for tax and he enters the goods for home use, the amount of tax payable shall be reduced by the amount of tax paid on the supply.

1985/1101
Value Added Tax (Refund of Tax) Order 1985

Made by the Treasury under VATA 1983 s 20(3) (see now VATA 1994 s 33(3))

Made . . . . *17 July 1985*
Laid before the House of Commons . . . . . . *18 July 1985*
Coming into Operation . . . . *1 August 1985*

1 This Order may be cited as the Value Added Tax (Refund of Tax) Order 1985 and shall come into operation on 1st August 1985.

2 The following bodies established under the Local Government Act 1985 are hereby specified for the purposes of section 20 of the Value Added Tax Act 1983[a]—

The Inner London Education Authority
The Inner London Interim Education Authority
The Northumbria Interim Police Authority
The London Fire and Civil Defence Authority
The London Residuary Body
A metropolitan county Police Authority
A metropolitan county Fire and Civil Defence Authority
A metropolitan county Passenger Transport Authority
A metropolitan county Residuary Body.

Note—[a] VATA 1994 s 33(3).

1986/260
Postal Packets (Customs and Excise) Regulations 1986

Made by the Treasury under the Post Office Act 1953 s 16(2)

Made . . . . *14 February 1986*
Coming into Operation . . . . *1 March 1986*

1 These Regulations may be cited as the Postal Packets (Customs and Excise) Regulations 1986 and shall come into force on 1st March 1986.

2— (1) In these Regulations—

"Act of 1979" means the Customs and Excise Management Act 1979;
"Commissioners" means Commissioners of Customs and Excise;
"the customs and excise Acts" has the meaning given by section 1(1) of the Act of 1979;
...[2]
"dutiable goods" has the meaning given by section 1(1) of the Act of 1979 but includes goods chargeable with value added tax and goods subject to any other charge on importation;
"duty" and "duty of customs or excise" include value added tax and any other charge on imported goods;
"exporter" and "importer" have the meanings assigned to them by section 1(1) of the Act of 1979;
["post office", "postal operator" and "registered post service" have the same meaning as in the Postal Services Act 2000;][1]
["postal packet" means a letter, parcel, packet or other article transmissible by post, conveyed by a universal service provider (within the meaning of the Postal Services Act 2000) in connection with the provision of a universal postal service (within the meaning of that Act);][1]
...[2]
"prescribed" means prescribed by the provisions of the Universal Postal Convention and Detailed Regulations made thereunder which are for the time being in force;
"proper" in relation to an officer means appointed or authorised by the Commissioners or the [postal operator][1] to perform any duty in relation to a postal packet.

(2), (3) ...[2]

Amendments—[1] In para (1), definitions of "post office", "postal operator" and "registered post service"; and "postal packet" inserted; and words substituted in the definition of "proper"; by the Postal Services Act 2000 (Consequential Modifications No 1) Order, SI 2001/1149 art 3(1), Sch 1 para 66(1), (2) with effect from 26 March 2001.
[2] In para (1), definitions of "datapost packet", "inland post", "letter packet" revoked; and paras (2), (3) revoked by SI 2001/1149 art 3(2), Sch 2 with effect from 26 March 2001.

3 The Postal Packets (Customs and Excise) Regulations 1975 are hereby revoked.

4 Section 16 of the Post Office Act 1953 shall apply to all postal packets, other than postcards, which are posted in the United Kingdom for transmission to any place outside it or which are brought by post into the United Kingdom.

5 In their application to goods contained in such postal packets, the following provisions of the Act of 1979 shall be subject to the following modifications and exceptions—

(*a*) In the application of section 5, subsection (3) shall be omitted and subsection (4) shall apply with the modification that the time of exportation of goods shall be the time when they are posted (or redirected) in the United Kingdom for transmission to a place outside it.

(*b*) ...[2]

(*c*) Section 40 shall apply only where the Commissioners have required entry to be made, and, where they have so required, shall apply only to the extent, and with the modification, set out in Regulation 14 of these Regulations.

[(*d*) In the application of section 43, subsection (1) shall not apply, and paragraph (*c*) of subsection (2) shall apply with the substitution for sub-paragraphs (i) and (ii) of the words "those in force at the time when, the packet containing the goods having been presented to the proper officer of customs and excise, the amount of duty appearing to be due is assessed by him.][1]

(*e*) In the application of section 49 subsection (1)(*a*) shall be omitted.

(*f*) For references in—

(i) section 53 to "exported", "shipped for exportation", and "exported or shipped for exportation";

(ii) section 56 to "shipped or exported by land", "exported", and "shipped";

(iii) section 58 to "shipped for exportation", and "shipped";

(iv) section 58A to "shipped for exportation or exported by land", and "shipped",

there shall be substituted references to "posted in the United Kingdom for transmission to any place outside it".

(*g*) Section 58B shall apply only in any cases, or class of cases, in which the Commissioners require a specification to be delivered.

(*h*) Section 77(1) shall apply to goods brought by post into the United Kingdom or posted in the United Kingdom for transmission to any place outside it, if an entry or specification is required of such goods when they are imported or exported otherwise than by post.

(*ij*) Section 99 shall apply to any goods deposited in a Queen's Warehouse under Regulation 14 of these Regulations as it applies to goods so deposited under or by virtue of any provision of the Act of 1979.

(*k*) Paragraph 1 of Schedule 3 shall, in the case of a thing brought by post into the United Kingdom, apply with the substitution, for the words "to any person who to their knowledge was at the time of seizure the owner or one of the owners thereof", of the following—

"to any person:

(*a*) who to their knowledge was at the time of the seizure the owner or one of the owners of the postal packet containing the thing; or

(*b*) who appears to them to be the sender of the postal packet containing the thing; or

(*c*) to whom the postal packet containing the thing was addressed"

and paragraph 10(1) shall not apply.

Amendments—[1] Para (*d*) substituted by Postal Packets (Customs and Excise) (Amendment) Regulations, SI 1986/1019 reg 2 with effect from 1 July 1986.

[2] Para (*b*) revoked by Postal Packets (Customs and Excise) (Amendment) Regulations, SI 1992/3224 reg 3(*a*) with effect from 1 January 1993.

[5A In its application to goods contained in postal packets brought into the United Kingdom, Regulation 5 of the Customs Controls on Importation of Goods Regulations 1991 shall apply only in any case, or class of cases, in which the Commissioners require an entry to be made in accordance with that Regulation.][1]

Amendments—[1] This regulation inserted by Postal Packets (Customs and Excise) (Amendment) Regulations, SI 1992/3224 reg 3(*b*) with effect from 1 January 1993.

6 Dutiable goods shall not be brought by post into the United Kingdom from a place situated outside the United Kingdom and the Isle of Man for delivery in the United Kingdom or the Isle of Man except [in a postal packet][1]—

(*a*), (*b*) ...[2]

Amendments—[1] Words inserted by the Postal Services Act 2000 (Consequential Modifications No 1) Order, SI 2001/1149 art 3(1), Sch 1 para 66(1), (3) with effect from 26 March 2001.

[2] Paras (*a*), (*b*) revoked by SI 2001/1149 art 3(2), Sch 2 with effect from 26 March 2001.

[7— (1) Subject to paragraphs (2) to (6) below, every postal packet brought into the United Kingdom containing dutiable goods shall have affixed to it, or be accompanied by, a customs declaration fully stating the nature, quantity and value of the goods which it contains or of which it consists, and such other particulars as the Commissioners or the postal operator may require.

(2) The Commissioners may, at the request of the postal operator, relax the requirements of paragraph (1) above by allowing the bringing in by post into the United Kingdom of any number of postal packets accompanied by a single customs declaration containing the particulars described in paragraph (1) above if they are brought in together, sent by or on behalf of the same person and addressed to a single addressee.

(3) Subject to paragraph (5) below, every postal packet brought into the United Kingdom the value of which exceeds £270, shall in additional to the requirements contained in paragraph (1) above, bear on the outside the top portion of a green label in the prescribed form.

VAT

(4) Subject to paragraph (6) below, every postal packet brought into the United Kingdom the value of which does not exceed £270, shall either—

(*a*) bear on the outside a green label in the prescribed form, in which the declaration as to the description, net weight and value of the contents shall be fully and correctly completed; or

(*b*) bear on the outside the top portion of a green label in the prescribed form and, in addition, have attached to it a full and correct customs declaration of the kind prescribed in paragraph (1) above.

(5) Any postal packet falling within paragraph (3) above which contains any article of value and is brought into the United Kingdom by a registered post service, may have the customs declaration referred to in paragraph (3) above enclosed in it.

(6) Any postal packet falling within paragraph (4) above which contains any article of value and is brought into the United Kingdom by registered post service, may have the customs declaration referred to in paragraph (4)(b) above enclosed in it.][1]

Amendments—[1] Substituted by the Postal Services Act 2000 (Consequential Modifications No 1) Order, SI 2001/1149 art 3(1), Sch 1 para 66(1), (4) with effect from 26 March 2001.

[**8**— (1) Subject to paragraphs (2) to (6) below, every postal packet posted into the United Kingdom for transmission to any place outside it containing dutiable goods shall have affixed to it, or be accompanied by, a customs declaration fully stating the nature, quantity and value of the goods which it contains or of which it consists, and such other particulars as the Commissioners or the postal operator may require.

(2) The Commissioners may, at the request of the postal operator, relax the requirements of paragraph (1) above by allowing the exportation by post of any number of postal packets accompanied by a single customs declaration containing the particulars described in paragraph (1) above if they are brought in together, sent by or on behalf of the same person and addressed to a single addressee.

(3) Subject to paragraph (5) below every postal packet posted in the United Kingdom for transmission to any place outside it the value of which exceeds £270, shall bear on the outside the top portion of a green label in the prescribed form and, in addition, shall have attached to it, or, if the postal administration of the country of destination so requires, enclosed in it, a full and correct customs declaration of the kind described in paragraph (1) above.

(4) Subject to paragraph (6) below, every postal packet posted in the United Kingdom for transmission to any place outside it the value of which does not exceed £270, shall either—

(*a*) bear on the outside on the outside a green label in the prescribed form, in which the declaration as to the description, net weight and value of the contents shall be fully and correctly completed; or, if the sender so prefers,

(*b*) bear on the outside the top portion of a green label in the prescribed form and, in addition, have attached to it or, if the postal administration of the country of destination so requires, enclosed in it, a full and correct customs declaration of the kind prescribed in paragraph (1) above.

(5) Any postal packet falling within paragraph (3) above which contains any article of value and is exported by registered post service, may have the customs declaration referred to in paragraph (3) above enclosed in it if the sender so prefers.

(6) Any postal packet falling within paragraph (4) above which contains any article of value and is exported by registered post service may have the customs declaration referred to in paragraph (4)(*b*) above enclosed in it if the sender so prefers.][1]

Amendments—[1] Substituted by the Postal Services Act 2000 (Consequential Modifications No 1) Order, SI 2001/1149 art 3(1), Sch 1 para 66(1), (5) with effect from 26 March 2001.

[**9**— (1) Every mail bag containing postal packets containing or consisting of goods which are dutiable in the country of destination, brought by post into the United Kingdom or posted in the United Kingdom for transmission to any place outside it by a universal service provider (within the meaning of the Postal Services Act 2000) in connection with the provision of a universal postal service (within the meaning of that Act), shall have affixed to the bag label a green label in the prescribed form][2].

[(2) Regulations 7 and 8 of these regulations and paragraph (1) of this Regulation shall not apply to a postal packet or mail bag which—

(*a*) contains only Community goods, and

(i) having been posted elsewhere in the territory of the Community, is brought by post to the United Kingdom for delivery there, or

(ii) is posted in the United Kingdom for delivery elsewhere in the territory of the Community; or

(*b*) is posted in a place situated outside the United Kingdom for delivery in another place so situated.][1]

Amendments—[1] Para (2) substituted by Postal Packets (Customs and Excise) (Amendment) Regulations, SI 1992/3224 reg 3(*c*) with effect from 1 January 1993.

[2] Para (1) substituted by the Postal Services Act 2000 (Consequential Modifications No 1) Order, SI 2001/1149 art 3(1), Sch 1 para 66(1), (6) with effect from 26 March 2001.

10 Without prejudice to the provisions of Regulations 7, 8 and 9 of these Regulations, every postal packet containing goods to be exported by post without payment of any duty of customs or excise to which they are subject, or on drawback or repayment of such duty, shall on its removal to the post office—

(*a*) be accompanied by such shipping bill, declaration or other document containing such particulars as the Commissioners may require; and

(*b*) have affixed to its outer cover in the form and manner so required a label having printed thereon the words "Exported by Post under Customs and Excise Control", or be distinguished in such other manner as may be so required.

11 The proper officer of the [postal operator][1] is hereby authorised to perform in relation to any postal packet or the goods which it contains such of the duties required by virtue of the customs and excise Acts to be performed by the importer or exporter of goods as the Commissioners may require.

Amendments—[1] Words substituted by the Postal Services Act 2000 (Consequential Modifications No 1) Order, SI 2001/1149 art 3(1), Sch 1 para 66(1), (7) with effect from 26 March 2001.

12 In such cases or classes of case as the Commissioners may so require, the proper officer of the [postal operator][1] shall produce to the proper officer of customs and excise postal packets arriving in the United Kingdom or about to be despatched from the United Kingdom and, if the proper officer of customs and excise so requires, shall open for customs examination any packets so produced.

Amendments—[1] Words substituted by the Postal Services Act 2000 (Consequential Modifications No 1) Order, SI 2001/1149 art 3(1), Sch 1 para 66(1), (7) with effect from 26 March 2001.

13 The proper officer of the [postal operator][1] accepting any outgoing packet in respect of which the requirements of paragraph (*b*) of Regulation 10 of these Regulations have been duly complied with shall endorse a certificate of the posting of the packet on the appropriate document and shall give it to the sender.

Amendments—[1] Words substituted by the Postal Services Act 2000 (Consequential Modifications No 1) Order, SI 2001/1149 art 3(1), Sch 1 para 66(1), (7) with effect from 26 March 2001.

14— (1) If goods are brought by post into the United Kingdom, and an officer of customs and excise sends to the addressee of the packet in which they are contained, or to any other person who is for the time being the importer of the goods, a notice requiring entry to be made of them or requiring a full and accurate account of them to be delivered to the proper officer of customs and excise but entry is not made or such account is not delivered within 28 days of the date of such notice or within such longer period as the Commissioners may allow, then unless the Commissioners have required the packet to be delivered to them under Regulation 17 of these Regulations the [postal operator][1] shall—

(*a*) return the goods to the sender of the packet in which they were contained, or otherwise export them from the United Kingdom in accordance with any request or indication appearing on the packet; or

(*b*) deliver the goods to the proper officer of customs and excise; or

(*c*) with the permission of the Commissioners, and under the supervision of the proper officer of customs and excise, destroy them.

(2) Where goods have been delivered to him in accordance with paragraph 1(*b*) of this Regulation, the proper officer of customs and excise may cause the goods to be deposited in a Queen's Warehouse and section 40(3) of the Act of 1979 shall apply to the goods as it applies to goods so deposited under the said Section 40.

Amendments—[1] Words substituted by the Postal Services Act 2000 (Consequential Modifications No 1) Order, SI 2001/1149 art 3(1), Sch 1 para 66(1), (8) with effect from 26 March 2001.

15— (1) On delivering a postal packet the proper officer of the [postal operator][1] may demand payment of any duty or other sum due to the Commissioners in respect of it, and any sum so received shall be paid over to the Commissioners by the [postal operator][1].

(2) If payment is not made of any duty so demanded, then, subject to paragraph (3) of this Regulation, the [postal operator][1] may, with the agreement of the Commissioners, dispose of the goods contained in the packet as it sees fit.

(3) If any amount demanded in accordance with paragraph (1) of this Regulation, but not paid, is an amount other than duty, the [postal operator][1] shall deliver the packet to the proper officer of customs and excise.

Amendments—[1] Words substituted by the Postal Services Act 2000 (Consequential Modifications No 1) Order, SI 2001/1149 art 3(1), Sch 1 para 66(1), (9) with effect from 26 March 2001.

16 If dutiable goods are brought by post into the United Kingdom in any postal packet contrary to Regulation 6 of these Regulations, or if any postal packet or mail bag to which Regulations 7, 8 and 9 of these Regulations or any of them apply does not contain, does not have affixed or attached to it, or is not accompanied by, the declaration, or does not bear the green label, required by those Regulations or any of them, or if the contents of any postal packet do not agree with the green label or customs declaration affixed or attached to the packet, or by which it is accompanied, or if the other requirements of these Regulations or any of them are not complied with in every material respect, then in every such case the postal packet or mail bag and all its contents shall be liable to forfeiture.

17 If the Commissioners require any postal packet to be delivered to them on the ground that any goods contained in it are liable to forfeiture under the customs and excise Acts (including these Regulations) the proper officer of the [postal operator][1] shall deliver the packet to the proper officer of Customs and Excise.

Amendments—[1] Words substituted by the Postal Services Act 2000 (Consequential Modifications No 1) Order, SI 2001/1149 art 3(1), Sch 1 para 66(1), (10) with effect from 26 March 2001.

18 Nothing in these Regulations shall authorise the sending or bringing of any article out of or into the United Kingdom by post contrary to any provisions of [the Postal Services Act 2000][1].

Amendments—[1] Words substituted by the Postal Services Act 2000 (Consequential Modifications No 1) Order, SI 2001/1149 art 3(1), Sch 1 para 66(1), (11) with effect from 26 March 2001.

1986/336
Value Added Tax (Refund of Tax) Order 1986

Made by the Treasury under VATA 1983 s 20(3) (see now VATA 1994 s 33(3))

Made . . . . *25 February 1986*
Laid before the House of Commons . . . . *27 February 1986*
Coming into Operation . . . . *1 April 1986*

1 This Order may be cited as the Value Added Tax (Refund of Tax) Order 1986 and shall come into operation on 1st April 1986.

2 The following bodies are hereby specified for the purposes of section 20 of the Value Added Tax Act 1983[a]:

A probation committee constituted by section 47(*a*) of, and paragraph 2 of Schedule 3 to, the Powers of Criminal Courts Act 1973

A magistrates' courts committee established under section 19 of the Justices of the Peace Act 1979

The charter trustees constituted by section 246(4) or (5) of the Local Government Act 1972.

Note—[a] VATA 1994 s 33.

1986/532
Value Added Tax (Refund of Tax) (No 2) Order 1986

Made by the Treasury under VATA 1983 s 20(3) (see now VATA 1994 s 33(3))

Made . . . . *18 March 1986*
Laid before the House of Commons . . . . *18 March 1986*
Coming into Operation . . . . *1 April 1986*

1 This Order may be cited as the Value Added Tax (Refund of Tax) (No 2) Order 1986 and shall come into operation on 1st April 1986.

2 The following bodies are hereby specified for the purposes of section 20 of the Value Added Tax Act 1983[a]—

Authorities established under section 10 of the Local Government Act 1985.

Note—[a] VATA 1994 s 33.

1986/590
Value Added Tax Tribunals Rules 1986

Made by the Commissioners of Customs and Excise, under VATA 1983 Sch 8 para 9 (see now VATA 1994 Sch 12 para 9)

Made . . . . *26 March 1986*
Laid before the House of Commons . . . . *9 April 1986*
Coming into Operation . . . . *1 May 1986*

Revocation—These Regulations revoked by the Transfer of Tribunal Functions and Revenue and Customs Appeals Order, SI 2009/56 art 3, Sch 2 para 187(*c*) with effect from 1 April 2009.

Citation, commencement, revocation and savings

1— *(1) These rules may be cited as the Value Added Tax Tribunals Rules 1986 and shall come into operation on 1st May 1986.*

(2) The Value Added Tax Tribunals Rules 1972, the Value Added Tax Tribunals (Amendment) Rules 1974, the Value Added Tax Tribunals (Amendment) Rules 1977, and the Value Added Tax Tribunals (Amendment) (No 2) Rules 1977 are hereby revoked.

(3) Anything begun under or for the purpose of any rules revoked by these rules may be continued under or, as the case may be, for the purpose of the corresponding provision of these rules.

(4) Where any document in any appeal to, or other proceedings before, a tribunal refers to a provision of any rules revoked by these rules, such reference shall, unless a contrary intention appears, be construed as referring to the corresponding provision of these rules.

Revocation—These Regulations revoked by the Transfer of Tribunal Functions and Revenue and Customs Appeals Order, SI 2009/56 art 3, Sch 2 para 187(*c*) with effect from 1 April 2009.

Interpretation

2 *In these rules, unless the context otherwise requires,—*

"the Act" means the Value Added Tax Act [1994][2]*;*

["the 1985 Act" means the Finance Act 1985][2]*;*

["the 1994 Act" means the Finance Act 1994;][3]

["the 1996 Act" means the Finance Act 1996;][3]

["the 2000 Act" means the Finance Act 2000;][4]

["the 2001 Act" means the Finance Act 2001;][5]

["the 2003 Act" means the Finance Act 2003;][6]

["appellant" means a person who, being entitled to do so under any enactment for the time being in force, brings an appeal to a VAT and duties tribunal;][8]

"the appropriate tribunal centre" means the tribunal centre for the time being appointed by the President for the area in which is situated the address to which the disputed decision was sent by the Commissioners or the tribunal centre to which the appeal against the disputed decision may be transferred under these rules;

"chairman" has the same meaning as in Schedule [12][3] *to the Act, and includes the President and any Vice-President;*

"the Commissioners" means the Commissioners [for Revenue and Customs][8]*;*

"costs" includes fees, charges, disbursements, expenses and remuneration;

["date of notification", in relation to any document, means the date on which a proper officer sends that document, or [a][3] *copy of that document, to any person under these rules;]*[1]

"disputed decision" means the decision of the Commissioners against which an appellant or intending appellant appeals or desires to appeal to a tribunal;

["evasion penalty appeal" means an appeal against an assessment to a penalty under section 60 or section 61 of the Act, or section 8 of or paragraph 12 of Schedule 7 to, [the 1994 Act or paragraph 18 or 19 of Schedule 5 to the 1996 Act][3] *[or paragraph 98 [or 99]*[5] *of Schedule 6 to the 2000 Act]*[4] *[or paragraph 7 or 8 of Schedule 6 to the 2001 Act]*[5]*[, or section 25 or 28 of the 2003 Act,] which is not solely a mitigation appeal and any accompanying appeal by the appellant against an assessment for the amount of tax alleged to have been evaded by the same conduct as that in the appeal against the assessment to a penalty;]*[2]

["the Export (Penalty) Regulations" means the Export (Penalty) Regulations 2003;][7]

["hardship direction" means a direction that an appeal or an intended appeal should be entertained notwithstanding that the amount which the Commissioners have determined to be payable as tax has not been paid or deposited with them;][1]

"mitigation appeal" means an appeal which, according to the notice of appeal or other document received from the appellant at the appropriate tribunal centre, is against a decision of the Commissioners with respect to the amount of a penalty [on grounds confined to those set out in section 13(4) of the 1985 Act (in respect of penalties imposed before 27th July 1993), or with respect to the amount of a penalty or (as the case may be) interest solely under section 70 of the Act, section 8(4) of or paragraph 13 of Schedule 7 to the 1994 Act or paragraph 25 or 28 of Schedule 5 to the 1996 Act][3] *[or paragraph 104 of Schedule 6 to the 2000 Act]*[4] *[or section 46(1) of the 2001 Act]*[5] *[or section 29 of the 2003 Act]*[6] *[or regulation 5 of the Export (Penalty) Regulations]*[7]*;*

"the President" means the President of [the VAT and [Duties][3] *Tribunals]*[2] *or the person nominated by the Lord Chancellor to discharge for the time being the functions of the President;*

"proper officer" means a member of the administrative staff of the [VAT and duties tribunals][3] *appointed by a chairman to perform the duties of a proper officer under these rules;*

["reasonable excuse appeal" means an appeal which, according to the notice of appeal or other document received from the appellant at the appropriate tribunal centre, is against a decision of the Commissioners with respect to [any liability to or the amount of any][3] *penalty or surcharge on grounds confined to those set out in sections 59(7), 62(3), 63(10), 64(5), [65(3)]*[3]*, [66(7)]*[3]*, 67(8), 68(4), or 69(8) of the Act or [[section 10(1)]*[6] *or 11(4) of or any of paragraphs 14(3), 15(5), 16(4), 17(3), 18(2) or 19(4) of Schedule 7 to the 1994 Act; [or any of paragraphs 41(4), 55(5), 90(4), 100(4), 101(4), 114(4), 124(4), 125(7), 127(5) of Schedule 6 to the 2000 Act]*[4]*]*[3]*;]*[2] *[or section 25(4) or 33(4) of or any of paragraphs 1(5) of Schedule 4, 15(4) of Schedule 5, 9(4) of Schedule 6, 1(4)(a) or (b), 2(7) or 4(5)(a) or (b) of Schedule 7 to the 2001 Act [or section 27 of the 2003 Act]*[6] *[or regulation 4 of the Export (Penalty) Regulations]*[7]*.]*[5]

"the Registrar" means the Registrar of the [VAT and duties tribunals][2] *or any member of the administrative staff of the [VAT and duties tribunals]*[2] *authorised by the [President]*[2] *to perform for the time being all or any of the duties of a Registrar under these rules;*

["tax" in relation to an appeal or application, means any tax, duty, levy or security to which that appeal or application relates;][2]

... [2]

"tribunal centre" means an administrative office of the [VAT and duties tribunals][3];

"Vice-President" means a Vice-President of [the VAT and Duties tribunals][3].

Revocation—These Regulations revoked by the Transfer of Tribunal Functions and Revenue and Customs Appeals Order, SI 2009/56 art 3, Sch 2 para 187(*c*) with effect from 1 April 2009.

Amendments—[1] Definitions of "date of notification" and "hardship direction" inserted by the VAT Tribunals (Amendment) Rules, SI 1991/186 reg 3 with effect from 1 March 1991.

[2] Figure in the definition of "the Act", definition "reasonable excuse appeal" and words in definitions of "appellant", "the President" and "the Registrar" substituted, definition of "the 1985 Act", "evasion penalty appeal" and "tax" inserted and definition of "section 13 penalty appeal" revoked by the VAT Tribunals (Amendment) Rules, SI 1994/2617 reg 4 with effect from 1 November 1994.

[3] Definitions of "the 1994 Act" and "the 1996 Act" and words in definitions "date of notification" inserted, words in the definitions of "appellant", "evasion penalty appeal", "mitigation appeal", "proper officer", "the President", "tribunal centre" and "Vice-President", figure in the definition of "chairman" and words and figures in the definition of "reasonable excuse appeal" substituted by the VAT Tribunals (Amendment) Rules, SI 1997/255 reg 4 with effect from 1 March 1997.

[4] Definition of "the 2000 Act" inserted; words in the definitions of "appellant", "evasion penalty appeal", "mitigation appeal" and "reasonable excuse appeal" inserted by the VAT Tribunals (Amendment) Rules, SI 2001/3073 regs 1, 3 with effect from 1 October 2001.

[5] Definition of "the 2001 Act" inserted, and words inserted in the definitions of "appellant", "evasion penalty appeal", "mitigation appeal", and "reasonable excuse appeal", by the VAT Tribunals (Amendment) Rules, SI 2002/2851 r 3 with effect from 9 December 2002.

[6] Definition of "the 2003 Act" inserted; words inserted in definitions of "appellant", "evasion penalty appeal", "mitigation appeal", and "reasonable excuse appeal"; and words in definition of "reasonable excuse appeal" substituted, by the VAT Tribunal Rules, SI 2003/2757 r 2 with effect from 1 December 2003.

[7] Words inserted in definitions of "mitigation appeal" and "reasonable excuse appeal", and definition of "the Export (Penalty) Regulations" inserted, by the VAT Tribunals (Amendment) Rules, SI 2004/1032 r 2 with effect from 4 May 2004.

[8] Definition of "appellant", and words in definition of "the Commissioners", substituted by the VAT Tribunals (Amendment) Rules, SI 2007/2351 rule 2(2) with effect from 17 September 2007.

Method of appealing

3— *(1) An appeal to a tribunal shall be brought by a notice of appeal served at the appropriate tribunal centre.*

(2) A notice of appeal shall be signed by or on behalf of the appellant and shall—

(a) state the name and address of the appellant;

[(aa) state the date (if any) with effect from which the appellant was registered for tax and the nature of his business;][1]

(b) state the address of the office of the Commissioners from which the disputed decision was sent;

(c) state the date of the document containing the disputed decision and the address to which it was sent;

(d) ...[1] have attached thereto a copy of the document containing the disputed decision; and

(e) set out, or have attached thereto a document containing, the grounds of the appeal, including in a reasonable excuse appeal, particulars of the excuse relied upon.

(3) A notice of appeal shall have attached thereto a copy of any letter from the Commissioners extending the appellant's time to appeal against the disputed decision and of any further letter from the Commissioners notifying him of a date from which his time to appeal against the disputed decision shall run.

(4) Subject to any direction made under rule 13, the parties to an appeal shall be the appellant and the Commissioners.

Revocation—These Regulations revoked by the Transfer of Tribunal Functions and Revenue and Customs Appeals Order, SI 2009/56 art 3, Sch 2 para 187(*c*) with effect from 1 April 2009.

Amendments—[1] Para (2)(*aa*) inserted and words in para (2)(*d*) revoked by the VAT Tribunals (Amendment) Rules, SI 1994/2617 reg 5 with effect from 1 November 1994.

Time for appealing

4— *(1) Subject to [paragraphs (2) and (3)][1] of this rule ...[1], a notice of appeal shall be served at the appropriate tribunal centre before the expiration of 30 days after the date of the document containing the disputed decision of the Commissioners.*

(2) If, during the period of 30 days after the date of the document containing the disputed decision, the Commissioners shall have notified the appellant by letter that his time to appeal against the disputed decision is extended until the expiration of 21 days after a date set out in such letter, or to be set out in a further letter to him, a notice of appeal against that disputed decision may be served at the appropriate tribunal centre at any time before the expiration of the period of 21 days set out in such letter or further letter.

[(3) Where a decision is deemed to have been confirmed by the Commissioners under [section 7C(3)(d) of the Tobacco Products Duty Act 1979,] section 15(2) of the 1994 Act, section 54(8) of the 1996 Act, paragraph 121(8) of Schedule 6 to the 2000 Act[, section 40(8) of the 2001 Act[, section 35(4) of the 2003 Act [regulation 11(4) of the Export (Penalty) Regulations, or regulation 4(5) of the Control of Cash (Penalties) Regulations 2007][4]][3]][2], a notice of appeal shall be served at the appropriate tribunal centre before the expiration of 75 days after the day on which the review was required.][1]

Revocation—These Regulations revoked by the Transfer of Tribunal Functions and Revenue and Customs Appeals Order, SI 2009/56 art 3, Sch 2 para 187(*c*) with effect from 1 April 2009, subject to transitional and savings provisions in Sch 3 paras 2–4.

Amendments—[1] Words in para (1) substituted, words "and any direction made under rule 19" revoked, and para (3) inserted, by the VAT Tribunals (Amendment) Rules, SI 2002/2851 r 4 with effect from 9 December 2002.

[2] Words in para (3) substituted by the VAT Tribunals (Amendment) Rules, SI 2003/2757 r 3 with effect from 1 December 2003.

[3] Words in para (3) substituted by the VAT Tribunals (Amendment) Rules, SI 2004/1032 r 3 with effect from 4 May 2004.

[4] In para (3) words inserted and substituted by the VAT Tribunals (Amendment) Rules, SI 2007/2351 rule 2(3) with effect from 17 September 2007.

Acknowledgment and notification of an appeal

5 *A proper officer shall send—*

(a) an acknowledgment of the service of a notice of appeal at the appropriate tribunal centre to the appellant; and

(b) a copy of the notice of appeal and of any accompanying document or documents to the Commissioners;

and the acknowledgment and such copy of the notice of appeal shall state the date of service [and the date of notification][1] *of the notice of appeal.*

Revocation—These Regulations revoked by the Transfer of Tribunal Functions and Revenue and Customs Appeals Order, SI 2009/56 art 3, Sch 2 para 187(*c*) with effect from 1 April 2009.

Amendments—[1] Words inserted by the VAT Tribunals (Amendment) Rules, SI 1991/186 reg 4 with effect from 1 March 1991.

Notice that an appeal does not lie or cannot be entertained

6— *(1) Where the Commissioners contend that an appeal does not lie to, or cannot be entertained by, a tribunal they shall serve a notice to that effect at the appropriate tribunal centre containing the grounds for such contention and applying for the appeal to be struck out or dismissed, as the case may be, as soon as practicable after the receipt by them of the notice of appeal.*

(2) Any notice served by the Commissioners under this rule shall be accompanied by a copy of the disputed decision unless a copy thereof has been served previously at the appropriate tribunal centre by either party to the appeal.

(3) In a reasonable excuse or a mitigation appeal the hearing of any application made by the Commissioners under the provisions of this rule may immediately precede the hearing of the substantive appeal.

(4) A proper officer shall send a copy of any notice or certificate served under this rule and of any document or documents accompanying the same to the appellant.

Revocation—These Regulations revoked by the Transfer of Tribunal Functions and Revenue and Customs Appeals Order, SI 2009/56 art 3, Sch 2 para 187(*c*) with effect from 1 April 2009.

Simon's Tax Cases—r 6(1), (4), *C&E Comrs v Hubbard Foundation Scotland* [1981] STC 593*; *Touchwood Services Ltd v R&C Comrs* [2007] STC 1425.

Statement of case, defence and reply in [an evasion][3] *penalty appeal*

7— *(1) Unless a tribunal shall otherwise direct, in [an evasion penalty appeal]*[2]*—*

(a) the Commissioners shall within 42 days of the date of [notification][1] *of the notice of appeal or the withdrawal or dismissal of any application made by them under rule 6 hereof (whichever shall be the later) serve at the appropriate tribunal centre a statement of case in the appeal setting out the matters and facts on which they rely for the making of the penalty assessment [or, as the case may be, the ascertainment of the penalty]*[4] *and (where also disputed) the making of the assessment for[, or, as the case may be, the ascertainment of,]*[4] *the tax alleged to have been evaded by the same conduct;*

[(aa) a statement of case served by the Commissioners in accordance with (a) above shall include full particulars of the alleged dishonesty and shall state the statutory provision under which the penalty or tax is assessed or the decision is made][2]*;*

(b) the appellant shall within 42 days of the date of [notification][1] *of such statement of case serve at the appropriate tribunal centre a defence thereto setting out the matters and facts on which he relies for his defence; and*

(c) the Commissioners may within 21 days of the date of [notification][1] *of such defence serve at the appropriate tribunal centre a reply to a defence and shall do so if it is necessary thereby to set out specifically any matter or any fact showing illegality, or*

(i) which they allege makes the defence not maintainable; or

(ii) which, if not specifically set out, might take the appellant by surprise; or

(iii) which raises any issue of fact not arising out of the statement of case.

(2) At any hearing of [an evasion penalty appeal][2] *the Commissioners shall not be required to prove, or to bring evidence relating to, any matter or fact which is admitted by the appellant in his defence.*

(3) Every statement of case, defence and reply hereunder shall be divided into paragraphs numbered consecutively, each allegation being so far as convenient contained in a separate paragraph.

(4) Each such document shall contain in summary form a brief statement of the matters and facts on which the party relies but not the evidence by which those facts are to be proved.

(5) A party may raise a point of law in such documents.

Revocation—These Regulations revoked by the Transfer of Tribunal Functions and Revenue and Customs Appeals Order, SI 2009/56 art 3, Sch 2 para 187(*c*) with effect from 1 April 2009.

Amendments—[1] Word in para (1)(*a*), (*b*), (*c*) substituted by the VAT Tribunals (Amendment) Rules, SI 1991/186 reg 5 with effect from 1 March 1991.

[2] Words in paras (1), (2) substituted and para (1)(*aa*) inserted by the VAT Tribunals (Amendment) Rules, SI 1994/2617 reg 6(*b*), (*g*) with effect from 1 November 1994.

[3] Words in heading substituted by the VAT Tribunals (Amendment) Rules, SI 1997/255 reg 5 with effect from 1 March 1997.

[4] Words in para (1)(*a*) inserted by the VAT Tribunals (Amendment) Rules, SI 2003/2757 r 4 with effect from 1 December 2003.

Statement of case in an appeal, other than [an evasion][4] penalty appeal and reasonable excuse and mitigation appeals

8 *Unless a tribunal otherwise directs, in appeals other than reasonable excuse and mitigation appeals and [evasion penalty appeals][2] the Commissioners shall [within the period of 30 days after—*

(a) the date of notification of the notice of appeal; or

(b) the date of notification of the notice of withdrawal of an application under rule 6 in the appeal; or

(c) the date on which a direction dismissing any application under rule 6 in the appeal is released in accordance with rule 30;

whichever shall be the latest][1] serve at the appropriate tribunal centre a statement of case in the appeal setting out the matters and facts on which they rely to support the disputed decision [and the statutory provision under which the tax or penalty is assessed [or, as the case may be, demanded][5] or the decision is made].[3]

Revocation—These Regulations revoked by the Transfer of Tribunal Functions and Revenue and Customs Appeals Order, SI 2009/56 art 3, Sch 2 para 187(*c*) with effect from 1 April 2009.

Simon's Tax Cases—*Elias Gale Racing v C&E Comrs* [1999] STC 66.

Amendments—[1] Words substituted by the VAT Tribunals (Amendment) Rules, SI 1991/186 reg 6 with effect from 1 March 1991.

[2] Words substituted by the VAT Tribunals (Amendment) Rules, SI 1994/2617 reg 7(*a*) with effect from 1 November 1994.

[3] Words added by the VAT Tribunals (Amendment) Rules, SI 1994/2617 reg 7(*b*) with effect from 1 November 1994.

[4] Words in heading substituted by the VAT Tribunals (Amendment) Rules, SI 1997/255 reg 5 with effect from 1 March 1997.

[5] Words inserted by the VAT Tribunals (Amendment) Rules, SI 2003/2757 r 5 with effect from 1 December 2003.

[Further provisions about statements of case][1]

[8A— *Where on an appeal against a decision with respect to an assessment [or a demand notice (as defined by section 30(1) of the 2003 Act)[2] [or regulation 6(1) of the Export (Penalty) Regulations][3] or the amount of an assessment the Commissioners wish to contend that an amount specified in the assessment [or, as the case may be, demand notice][2] is less than it ought to have been, they shall so state in their statement of case in that appeal, indicating the amount of the alleged deficiency and the manner in which it has been calculated.][1]*

Revocation—These Regulations revoked by the Transfer of Tribunal Functions and Revenue and Customs Appeals Order, SI 2009/56 art 3, Sch 2 para 187(*c*) with effect from 1 April 2009.

Simon's Tax Cases—*Elias Gale Racing v C&E Comrs* [1999] STC 66.

Amendments—[1] This rule inserted by the VAT Tribunals (Amendment) Rules, SI 1997/255 reg 6 with effect from 1 March 1997.

[2] Words inserted by the VAT Tribunals (Amendment) Rules, SI 2003/2757 r 6 with effect from 1 December 2003.

[3] Words inserted by the VAT Tribunals (Amendment) Rules, SI 2004/1032 r 4 with effect from 4 May 2004.

Further and better particulars

9 *…[1] A tribunal may at any time direct a party to an appeal to serve further particulars of his case at the appropriate tribunal centre for the appeal within such period from the date of such direction (not being less than 14 days from the date thereof) as it may specify therein.*

(2) …[1]

Revocation—These Regulations revoked by the Transfer of Tribunal Functions and Revenue and Customs Appeals Order, SI 2009/56 art 3, Sch 2 para 187(*c*) with effect from 1 April 2009.

Amendments—[1] Number "(1)" at the beginning and para (2) revoked by the VAT Tribunals (Amendment) Rules, SI 1997/255 reg 7 with effect from 1 March 1997.

Acknowledgment of and notification of service of formal documents served in an appeal

10— *(1) Any statement of case served by the Commissioners under rule 7 or rule 8 of these rules shall be accompanied by a copy of the disputed decision unless a copy of the disputed decision has been served previously at the appropriate tribunal centre by either party to the appeal.*

(2) In a reasonable excuse or a mitigation appeal the Commissioners shall serve a copy of the disputed decision at the appropriate tribunal centre as soon as practicable after the receipt by them of the copy of the notice of appeal unless a copy of the disputed decision has been so served previously by the appellant.

(3) A proper officer shall send—

(a) an acknowledgment of the service at the appropriate tribunal centre of any statement of case, defence, reply or particulars in any appeal to the party serving the same; and

(b) a copy of such document or particulars and any other document accompanying the same to the other party to the appeal.

Revocation—These Regulations revoked by the Transfer of Tribunal Functions and Revenue and Customs Appeals Order, SI 2009/56 art 3, Sch 2 para 187(*c*) with effect from 1 April 2009.

Method of applying for a direction

11— *(1) An application to a tribunal, made otherwise than at a hearing, for—*

[(a) the issue of a witness summons; or

(b) a direction (including a hardship direction or a direction for the setting aside of a witness summons)

shall be made by notice served at the appropriate tribunal centre.][1]

(2) A notice under this rule shall—

(a) state the name and address of the applicant;

(b) state the direction sought or details of the witness summons sought to be issued or set aside; and

(c) set out, or have attached thereto a document containing, the grounds of the application.

(3) In addition to the requirement of paragraph (2) hereof, any notice of application by an intending appellant shall—

(a) state the address of the office of the Commissioners from which the disputed decision was sent;

(b) state the date of the disputed decision and the address to which it was sent;

(c) set out shortly the disputed decision or have attached thereto a copy of the document containing the same; and

(d) have attached thereto a copy of any letter from the Commissioners extending the applicant's time to appeal against the disputed decision and of any letter from the Commissioners notifying him of a date from which his time of appeal against the disputed decision shall run.

(4) A notice of application for [a hardship direction][1] *shall be served at the appropriate tribunal centre within the period for the service of a notice of appeal.*

(5) Except as provided by rule 22, the parties to an application shall be the parties to the appeal or intended appeal.

(6) Except as provided by rule 22, a proper officer shall send—

(a) an acknowledgment of the service of a notice of application at the appropriate tribunal centre to the applicant; and

(b) a copy of such notice of application and of accompanying document or documents to the other party to the application (if any);

and the acknowledgment and copy of the notice of application shall state the date of service [and the date of notification][1] *of the notice of application.*

(7) Within 14 days of the date of [notification][1] *of a notice of application the other party to the application (if any) shall indicate whether or not he consents thereto and, if he does not consent thereto, the reason therefor.*

Revocation—These Regulations revoked by the Transfer of Tribunal Functions and Revenue and Customs Appeals Order, SI 2009/56 art 3, Sch 2 para 187(*c*) with effect from 1 April 2009.

Simon's Tax Cases—*C&E Comrs v Hubbard Foundation Scotland* [1981] STC 593*.

Amendments—[1] Words in paras (1), (4), (7) substituted and words in para (6) inserted by the VAT Tribunals (Amendment) Rules, SI 1991/186 regs 7–10 with effect from 1 March 1991.

Partners

12 *[One or more partners]*[1] *in a firm which is not a legal person distinct from the partners of whom it is composed may appeal against a decision of the Commissioners relating to the firm or its business, or apply to a tribunal in an appeal or intended appeal, in the name of the firm and, unless a tribunal shall otherwise direct, the proceedings shall be carried on in the name of the firm, but with the same consequences as would have ensued if the appeal or application had been brought in the names of the partners.*

Revocation—These Regulations revoked by the Transfer of Tribunal Functions and Revenue and Customs Appeals Order, SI 2009/56 art 3, Sch 2 para 187(*c*) with effect from 1 April 2009.

Amendments—Words substituted by the VAT Tribunals (Amendment) Rules, SI 1994/2617 reg 8 with effect from 1 November 1994.

Death or bankruptcy of an appellant or applicant

[13— *(1) This rule applies where, in the course of proceedings, the liability or interest of the applicant or appellant passes to another person ("the successor") by reason of death insolvency or otherwise.*

(2) The tribunal may direct, on the application of the Commissioners or the successor, and with the written consent of the successor, that the successor shall be substituted for the applicant or appellant in the proceedings.

(3) Where the tribunal is satisfied that there is no person interested in the application or appeal, or the successor fails to give written consent for his substitution in the proceedings within a period of

two months after being requested to do so by the tribunal it may, of its own motion or on application by the Commissioners and after giving prior written notice to the successor, dismiss the application or appeal.][1]

Revocation—These Regulations revoked by the Transfer of Tribunal Functions and Revenue and Customs Appeals Order, SI 2009/56 art 3, Sch 2 para 187(*c*) with effect from 1 April 2009.
Simon's Tax Cases—*Schwarcz v Aeresta Ltd and C&E Comrs* [1989] STC 230.
Amendments—[1] This rule substituted by the VAT Tribunals (Amendment) Rules, SI 1994/2617 reg 9 with effect from 1 November 1994.

Amendments

14— *(1) For the purposes of determining the issues in dispute or of correcting an error or defect in an appeal or application or intended appeal, a tribunal may at any time, either of its own motion or on the application of any party to the appeal or application, or any other person interested, direct that a notice of appeal, notice of application, statement of case, defence, reply, particulars or other document in the proceedings be amended in such manner as may be specified in such direction on such terms as it may think fit.*

(2) This rule shall not apply to a decision or direction of a tribunal.

Revocation—These Regulations revoked by the Transfer of Tribunal Functions and Revenue and Customs Appeals Order, SI 2009/56 art 3, Sch 2 para 187(*c*) with effect from 1 April 2009.
Simon's Tax Cases—*Schwarcz v Aeresta Ltd and C&E Comrs* [1989] STC 230.

Transfers between tribunal centres

15 *A tribunal on the application of a party to an appeal may direct that the appeal and all proceedings in the appeal be transferred to such tribunal centre as may be specified in such direction whereupon, for the purposes of these rules, the tribunal centre specified in such direction shall become the appropriate tribunal centre for such appeal and all proceedings therein, without prejudice to the power of a tribunal to give a further direction relating thereto under this rule.*

Revocation—These Regulations revoked by the Transfer of Tribunal Functions and Revenue and Customs Appeals Order, SI 2009/56 art 3, Sch 2 para 187(*c*) with effect from 1 April 2009.

Withdrawal of an appeal or application

16— *(1) An appellant or applicant may at any time withdraw his appeal or application by serving at the appropriate tribunal centre a notice of withdrawal signed by him or on his behalf, and a proper officer shall send a copy thereof to [the other parties to the appeal]*[1].

(2) The withdrawal of an appeal or application under this rule shall not prevent a party to such appeal or application from applying under rule 29 for an award or direction as to his or their costs or under [section 84(8)][1] *of the Act [or under section 56(3), (4) or (5) of the 1996 Act]*[2] *[or under paragraph 123(4)[, (5) or (6)]*[4] *of Schedule 6 to the 2000 Act]*[3] *[or under section 42(4), (5) or (6) of the 2001 Act]*[4] *for a direction for the payment or repayment of a sum of money with interest or prevent a tribunal from making such an award or direction if it thinks fit so to do.*

Revocation—These Regulations revoked by the Transfer of Tribunal Functions and Revenue and Customs Appeals Order, SI 2009/56 art 3, Sch 2 para 187(*c*) with effect from 1 April 2009.
Amendments—[1] Words substituted by the VAT Tribunals (Amendment) Rules, SI 1994/2617 reg 10(*a*), (*b*) with effect from 1 November 1994.
[2] Words inserted by the VAT Tribunals (Amendment) Rules, SI 1997/255 reg 8 with effect from 1 March 1997.
[3] Words inserted by the VAT Tribunals (Amendment) Rules, SI 2001/3073 regs 1, 4 with effect from 1 October 2001.
[4] Words in para (2) inserted by the VAT Tribunals (Amendment) Rules, SI 2002/2851 r 5 with effect from 9 December 2002.

Appeal or application allowed by consent

17 *Where the parties to an appeal or application have agreed upon the terms of any decision or direction to be given by a tribunal, a tribunal may give a decision or make a direction in accordance with those terms without a hearing.*

Revocation—These Regulations revoked by the Transfer of Tribunal Functions and Revenue and Customs Appeals Order, SI 2009/56 art 3, Sch 2 para 187(*c*) with effect from 1 April 2009.

Power of a tribunal to strike out or dismiss an appeal

18— *(1) A tribunal shall—*

(a) strike out an appeal where no appeal against the disputed decision lies to a tribunal; and
(b) dismiss an appeal where the appeal cannot be entertained by a tribunal.

(2) A tribunal may dismiss an appeal for want of prosecution where the appellant or the person to whom the interest or liability of the appellant has been assigned or transmitted, or upon whom such interest or liability has devolved, has been guilty of inordinate and inexcusable delay.

(3) Except in accordance with rule 17, no appeal shall be struck out or dismissed under this rule without a hearing.

Commentary—*De Voil Indirect Tax Service* **V5.453**.
Revocation—These Regulations revoked by the Transfer of Tribunal Functions and Revenue and Customs Appeals Order, SI 2009/56 art 3, Sch 2 para 187(*c*) with effect from 1 April 2009.
Simon's Tax Cases—*C&E Comrs v Gil Insurance* [2000] STC 204; *Touchwood Services Ltd v R&C Comrs* [2007] STC 1425.

Power of a tribunal to extend time and to give directions

19— *(1) A tribunal may of its own motion or on the application of any party to an appeal or application extend the time within which a party to the appeal or application or any other person is required or authorised by these rules or any decision or direction of a tribunal to do anything in relation to the appeal or application (including the time for service for a notice of application) upon such terms as it may think fit.*

(2) A tribunal may make a direction under paragraph (1) of this rule of its own motion without prior notice or reference to any party or other person and without a hearing.

(3) Without prejudice to the preceding provisions of this rule a tribunal may [of its own motion or][2] *on the application of a party to an appeal or application or other person interested give or make any direction as to the conduct of or as to any matter or thing in connection with the appeal or application which it may think necessary or expedient to ensure the speedy and just determination of the appeal [including the joining of other persons as parties to the appeal]*[2]*.*

[(3A) Where a notice is served under section 61 of the Act [or paragraph 19 of Schedule 5 to the 1996 Act][3] *[or paragraph 99 of Schedule 6 to the 2000 Act]*[4] *[or paragraph 8 of Schedule 6 to the 2001 Act]*[5] *[or section 28 of the 2003 Act]*[6] *and appeals are brought by different persons which relate to, or to different portions of, the basic penalty referred to in the notice, the tribunal may, of its own motion or on the application of any party to any such appeal, give any direction it thinks fit as to the joinder of the appeals.]*[2]

(4) If any party to an appeal or application or other person fails to comply with any direction of a tribunal, a tribunal may allow or dismiss the appeal or [application][1]*.*

(5) A tribunal may, of its own motion or on the application of any party to an appeal or application, waive any breach or non-observance of any provision of these rules or of any decision or direction of a tribunal upon such terms as it may think just.

Revocation—These Regulations revoked by the Transfer of Tribunal Functions and Revenue and Customs Appeals Order, SI 2009/56 art 3, Sch 2 para 187(*c*) with effect from 1 April 2009.

Commentary—*De Voil Indirect Tax Service* **V5.453**.

Simon's Tax Cases—r 19, *Schwarcz v Aeresta Ltd and C&E Comrs* [1989] STC 230; *C&E Comrs v Gil Insurance* [2000] STC 204; *Bennett v C&E Comrs* [2001] STC 137; *Jackson v C&E Comrs* [2004] STC 164.

Rule 19(3), *Maharani Restaurant v C&E Comrs* [1999] STC 295.

Rule 19(4), *C&E Comrs v Young* [1993] STC 394; *C&E Comrs v Neways International (UK) Ltd* [2003] STC 795; *Mobile Export 365 Ltd and another v R&C Comrs* [2007] STC 1794.

Amendments—[1] Word in para (4) substituted by the VAT Tribunals (Amendment) Rules, SI 1991/186 reg 11 with effect from 1 March 1991.

[2] Words in para (3) and whole of para (3A) inserted by the VAT Tribunals (Amendment) Rules, SI 1994/2617 regs 11, 12 with effect from 1 November 1994.

[3] Words in para (3A) inserted by the VAT Tribunals (Amendment) Rules, SI 1997/255 reg 9 with effect from 1 March 1997.

[4] Words in para (3A) inserted by the VAT Tribunals (Amendment) Rules, SI 2001/3073 regs 1, 5 with effect from 1 October 2001.

[5] Words in para (3A) inserted by the VAT Tribunals (Amendment) Rules, SI 2002/2851 r 6 with effect from 9 December 2002.

[6] Words in para (3A) inserted by the VAT Tribunals (Amendment) Rules, SI 2003/2757 r 7 with effect from 1 December 2003.

Disclosure, inspection and production of documents

20— *(1) [Each of the parties]*[1] *to an appeal other than a reasonable excuse or a mitigation appeal and [each of the parties]*[1] *to an application for [a hardship direction]*[1] *shall, before the expiration of the time set out in paragraph (2) of this rule, serve at the appropriate tribunal centre a list of the documents in his possession, custody or power which he proposes to produce at the hearing of the appeal or application.*

[(1A) The list of documents to be served by the Commissioners in accordance with paragraph (1) shall contain a reference to the documents relied upon in reaching a decision on a review under section 15 or 59 of [the 1994 Act or section 54 of the 1996 Act][3] *[or paragraph 121 of Schedule 6 to the 2000 Act]*[4] *[or section 40 of the 2001 Act]*[5] *[or section 33 of the 2003 Act]*[6] *[or regulation 9 of the Export (Penalty) Regulations]*[7] *[or regulation 4(5) of the Control of Cash (Penalties) Regulations 2007]*[8]*.]*[2]

(2) The time within which a list of documents shall be served under paragraph (1) of this rule shall be—

(a) in [an evasion penalty appeal][2]*, a period of 15 days after the last day for the service by the Commissioners of any reply pursuant to rule 7(1)(c) hereof;*

[(b) in any other appeal except a reasonable excuse appeal or a mitigation appeal, a period of 30 days after—

(i) the date of notification of the notice of appeal; or

(ii) the date of notification of the notice of withdrawal of any application under rule 6 in the appeal; or

(iii) the date on which a direction dismissing any application under rule 6 in the appeal is released in accordance with rule 30;

whichever shall be the latest;

(c) in an application for a hardship direction, a period of 30 days after the date of notification of the application.][2]

(3) In addition, and without prejudice to the foregoing provisions of this rule, a tribunal may, where it appears necessary for disposing fairly of the proceedings, on the application of a party to an appeal direct that the other party to the appeal shall serve at the appropriate tribunal centre for the appeal within such period as it may specify a list of the documents or any class of documents which are or have been in his possession, custody or power relating to any question in issue in the appeal, and may at the same time or subsequently order him to make and serve an affidavit verifying such list.

(4) If a party desires to claim that any document included in a list of documents served by him in pursuance of a direction made under paragraph (3) of this rule is privileged from production in the appeal, that claim must be made in the list of documents with a sufficient statement of the grounds of privilege.

(5) A proper officer shall send a copy of any list of documents and affidavit served under paragraph (1) or paragraph (3) of this rule to the other party to the appeal or application and such other party shall be entitled to inspect and take copies of the documents set out in such list which are in the possession, custody or power of the party who made the list and are not privileged from production in the appeal at such time and place as he and the party who served such list of documents may agree or a tribunal may direct.

(6) At the hearing of an appeal or application a party shall produce any document included in a list of documents served by him in relation to such appeal or application under paragraph (1) or paragraph (3) of this rule which is in his possession, custody or power and is not privileged from production when called upon so to do by the other party to the appeal or application.

Revocation—These Regulations revoked by the Transfer of Tribunal Functions and Revenue and Customs Appeals Order, SI 2009/56 art 3, Sch 2 para 187(*c*) with effect from 1 April 2009.
Simon's Tax Cases—*Koca v C&E Comrs* [1996] STC 58.
Amendments—[1] Words in para (1) and para (2)(*b*), (*c*) substituted by the VAT Tribunals (Amendment) Rules, SI 1991/186 regs 12, 13.
[2] Para (1A) inserted and words in para (2)(*a*) substituted by the VAT Tribunals (Amendment) Rules, SI 1994/2617 regs 13, 14 with effect from 1 November 1994.
[3] Words in para (1A) substituted by the VAT Tribunals (Amendment) Rules, SI 1997/255 reg 10 with effect from 1 March 1997.
[4] Words inserted by the VAT Tribunals (Amendment) Rules, SI 2001/3073 regs 1, 6 with effect from 1 October 2001.
[5] Words in para (1A) inserted by the VAT Tribunals (Amendment) Rules, SI 2002/2851 r 7 with effect from 9 December 2002.
[6] Words in para (1A) inserted by the VAT Tribunals (Amendment) Rules, SI 2003/2757 r 8 with effect from 1 December 2003.
[7] Words in para (1A) inserted by the VAT Tribunals (Amendment) Rules, SI 2004/1032 r 5 with effect from 4 May 2004.
[8] Words in para (1A) inserted by the VAT Tribunals (Amendment) Rules, SI 2007/2351 rule 2(4) with effect from 17 September 2007.

Witness statements

21— *(1) A party to an appeal may, within the time specified in paragraph (6) of this rule, serve at the appropriate tribunal centre a statement in writing (in these rules called "a witness statement") containing evidence proposed to be given by any person at the hearing of the appeal.*

(2) A witness statement shall contain the name, address and description of the person proposing to give the evidence contained therein and shall be signed by him.

(3) A proper officer shall send a copy of a witness statement served at the appropriate tribunal centre to the other party to the appeal and such copy shall state the date of service [and the date of notification of the witness statement][1] and shall contain or be accompanied by a note to the effect that unless a notice of objection thereto is served in accordance with paragraph (4) of this rule, the witness statement may be read at the hearing of the appeal as evidence of the facts stated therein without the person who made the witness statement giving oral evidence thereat.

(4) If a party objects to a witness statement being read at the hearing of the appeal as evidence of any fact stated therein he shall serve a notice of objection to such witness statement at the appropriate tribunal centre not later than 14 days after the date of [notification][1] of such witness statement …[3] whereupon a proper officer shall send a copy of the notice of objection to the other party and the witness statement shall not be read or admitted in evidence at such hearing but the person who signed such witness statement may give evidence orally at the hearing.

(5) Subject to paragraph (4) of this rule, unless a tribunal shall otherwise direct, a witness statement signed by any person and duly served under this rule shall be admissible in evidence at the hearing of the appeal as evidence of any fact stated therein of which oral evidence by him at that hearing would be admissible.

(6) The time within which a witness statement may be served under this rule shall be—

(a) in the case of [an evasion penalty appeal][2], before the expiration of 21 days after the last day for the service by the Commissioners of a reply pursuant to paragraph (1)(c) of rule 7;
(b) in the case of a mitigation appeal or a reasonable excuse appeal, before the expiration of 21 days after the date of [notification][1] of the Notice of Appeal; and
(c) in the case of any other appeal, before the expiration of 21 days after the date of [notification of the Commissioners' statement of case.][1]

Revocation—These Regulations revoked by the Transfer of Tribunal Functions and Revenue and Customs Appeals Order, SI 2009/56 art 3, Sch 2 para 187(*c*) with effect from 1 April 2009.
Simon's Tax Cases—*Wayne Farley Ltd v C&E Comrs* [1986] STC 487*.

Amendments—[1] Words in para (3) inserted and words in paras (4), (6)(*b*), (*c*) substituted by the VAT Tribunals (Amendment) Rules, SI 1991/186 reg 14 with effect from 1 March 1991.
[2] Words in para (6)(*a*) substituted by the VAT Tribunals (Amendment) Rules, SI 1994/2617 reg 15 with effect from 1 November 1994.
[3] Words in para (4) revoked by the VAT Tribunals (Amendment) Rules, SI 1997/255 reg 11 with effect from 1 March 1997.

[Affidavits and depositions made in other legal proceedings][1]

[21A— *(1) If—*

(a) an affidavit or deposition made in other legal proceedings (whether civil or criminal) is specified as such in a list of documents served under rule 20(1) by a party to an appeal or application or (in the case of an appeal or application to which rule 20(1) does not apply) in a notice served by such a party at the appropriate tribunal centre, and

(b) it is stated in that list or notice that the party serving the list or notice proposes to give that affidavit or deposition in evidence at the hearing of the appeal or application and that the person who made that affidavit or deposition is dead, or outside the United Kingdom or unfit by reason of his bodily or mental condition to attend as a witness or (as the case may be) that despite the exercise of reasonable diligence it has not been possible to find him,

then, subject to the following paragraphs of this rule, the affidavit or deposition shall be admissible at the hearing of the appeal or application as evidence of any fact stated therein of which oral evidence by the person who made the affidavit or deposition would be admissible.

(2) The time within which a notice may be served under paragraph (1) of this rule shall be before the expiration of 21 days after the date of notification of the notice of appeal or notice of application.

(3) When a proper officer sends a copy of any such list or notice as is mentioned in paragraph (1) of this rule to any person pursuant to rule 20(5) or rule 11(6)(b), he shall also send to that person a copy of this rule.

(4) If a party objects to an affidavit or deposition being read and admitted as evidence under paragraph (1) of this rule, he shall serve a notice of application for directions with regard to that affidavit or deposition at the appropriate tribunal centre not later than 21 days after the date of notification of the list of documents or notice (as the case may be).

(5) At the hearing of an application under paragraph (4) of this rule a tribunal may give directions as to whether, and if so how and on what conditions, the affidavit or deposition may be admitted as evidence and (where applicable) as to the manner in which the affidavit or deposition is to be proved, and the affidavit or deposition shall be admissible as evidence to the extent and on the conditions (if any) specified in the direction but not further or otherwise.

(6) The members of the tribunal hearing an application under paragraph (4) of this rule shall not sit on the hearing of the appeal or application to which the first-mentioned application relates.][1]

Revocation—These Regulations revoked by the Transfer of Tribunal Functions and Revenue and Customs Appeals Order, SI 2009/56 art 3, Sch 2 para 187(*c*) with effect from 1 April 2009.

Amendments—[1] This rule inserted by the VAT Tribunals (Amendment) Rules, SI 1991/186 reg 15 with effect from 1 March 1991.

Witness summonses and summonses to third parties

22— *(1) Where a witness is required by a party to an appeal or application to attend the hearing of an appeal or application to give oral evidence or to produce any document in his possession, custody or power necessary for the purpose of that hearing, a chairman or the Registrar shall, upon the application of such party, issue a summons requiring the attendance of such witness at such hearing or the production of the document, wherever such witness may be in the United Kingdom or the Isle of Man.*

(2) Where a party to an appeal or application desires to inspect any document necessary for the purpose of the hearing thereof which is in the possession, custody or power of any other person in the United Kingdom or the Isle of Man (whether or not such other person is a party to that appeal or application) a chairman or the Registrar shall, upon the application of such party, issue a summons requiring either—

(a) the attendance of such other person at such date, time and place as the chairman or the Registrar may direct and then and there to produce such document for inspection by such party or his representative and to allow such party or his representative then and there to peruse such document and to take a copy thereof; or

(b) such other person to post the document by ordinary post to an address in the United Kingdom or Isle of Man by First Class Mail in an envelope duly prepaid and properly addressed to the party requiring to inspect the same.

(3) A chairman or the Registrar may issue a summons under this rule without prior notice or reference to the applicant or any other person and without a hearing and the only party to the application shall be the applicant.

(4) [A summons issued under this rule shall be signed by a chairman or the Registrar and must be served—

(a) where the witness or third party is an individual, by leaving a copy of the summons with him and showing him the original thereof,

(b) where the witness or third party is a body corporate, by sending a copy of the summons by post to, or leaving it at, the registered or principal office [in the United Kingdom or the Isle of Man][2] *of the body to be served,*

not less than 4 days before the day on which the attendance of the witness or third party or the posting of the document is thereby required.][1] *A summons issued under this rule shall contain a statement, or be accompanied by a note, to the effect that the witness or third party may apply, by a notice served at the tribunal centre from which the summons was issued, for a direction that the summons be set aside.*

(5) A witness summons issued under this rule for the purpose of a hearing and duly served shall have effect until the conclusion of the hearing at which the attendance of the witness is thereby required.

(6) No person shall be required to attend to give evidence or to produce any document at any hearing or otherwise under paragraph (2) of this rule which he could not be required to give or produce on the trial of an action in a court of law.

(7) No person shall be bound to attend any hearing or to produce or post any document for the purpose of a hearing or for inspection and perusal in accordance with a summons issued under this rule unless a reasonable and sufficient sum of money to defray the expenses of coming to, attending at and returning from such hearing or place of inspection and perusal was tendered to him at the time when the summons was served on him.

(8) A tribunal may, upon the application of any person served at the appropriate tribunal centre, set aside a summons served upon him under this rule.

(9) The parties to an application to set aside a summons issued under this rule shall be the applicant and the party who obtained the issue of the summons.

Revocation—These Regulations revoked by the Transfer of Tribunal Functions and Revenue and Customs Appeals Order, SI 2009/56 art 3, Sch 2 para 187(*c*) with effect from 1 April 2009.

Amendments—[1] Words in para (4) substituted by the VAT Tribunals (Amendment) Rules, SI 1991/186 reg 16 with effect from 1 March 1991.

[2] Words in para (4)(*b*) inserted by the VAT Tribunals (Amendment) Rules, SI 1994/2617 reg 16 with effect from 1 November 1994.

Notice of hearings

23— *(1) A proper officer shall send a notice stating the date and time when, and [the]*[1] *place where, an appeal will be heard to the parties to the appeal which, unless the parties otherwise agree, shall be not earlier than 14 days after the date on which the notice is sent.*

(2) Unless a tribunal otherwise directs, an application made at a hearing shall be heard forthwith, and no notice thereof shall be sent to the parties thereto.

(3) Subject to paragraph (2) of this rule, a proper officer shall send a notice stating the date and time when, and the place where, an application will be heard which, unless the parties shall otherwise agree, shall not be earlier than 14 days after the date on which the notice is sent—

(a) in the case of an application for the issue of a witness summons, to the applicant;

(b) in the case of an application to set aside the issue of a witness summons, to the applicant and the party who obtained the issue of the witness summons;

(c) in the case of any other application, to the parties to the application.

[(4) A proper officer shall send a notice stating the date and time when, and the place where, a hearing for the purpose of giving directions relating to an appeal will take place to the parties to the appeal which, unless the parties otherwise agree, shall not be earlier than 14 days after the date on which the notice is sent.][1]

Revocation—These Regulations revoked by the Transfer of Tribunal Functions and Revenue and Customs Appeals Order, SI 2009/56 art 3, Sch 2 para 187(*c*) with effect from 1 April 2009.

Amendments—[1] Word in para (1), and para (4), inserted by the VAT Tribunals (Amendment) Rules, SI 1997/255 reg 12 with effect from 1 March 1997.

Hearings in public or in private

24— *(1) The hearing of an appeal shall be in public unless a tribunal, on the application of a party thereto, directs that the hearing or any part of the hearing shall take place in private.*

(2) Unless a tribunal otherwise directs, the hearing of any application made otherwise than at or subsequent to the hearing of an appeal shall take place in private.

(3) Any member of the Council on Tribunals or the Scottish Committee of the Council on Tribunals in his capacity as such a member may attend the hearing of any appeal or application notwithstanding that the appeal or application takes place in private.

Revocation—These Regulations revoked by the Transfer of Tribunal Functions and Revenue and Customs Appeals Order, SI 2009/56 art 3, Sch 2 para 187(*c*) with effect from 1 April 2009.

Representation at a hearing

25 *At the hearing of an appeal or application—*

(a) any party to the appeal or application (other than the Commissioners) may conduct his case himself or may be represented by any person whom he may appoint for the purpose; and

(b) the Commissioners may be represented at any hearing at which they are entitled to attend by any person whom they may appoint for the purpose.

Revocation—These Regulations revoked by the Transfer of Tribunal Functions and Revenue and Customs Appeals Order, SI 2009/56 art 3, Sch 2 para 187(*c*) with effect from 1 April 2009.

Failure to appear at a hearing

26— *(1) If, when an appeal or application is called on for hearing no party thereto appears in person or by his representative, a tribunal may dismiss or strike out the appeal or application, but a tribunal may, on the application of any such party or of any person interested served at the appropriate tribunal centre within 14 days after the date when the decision [or direction]*[1] *of the tribunal was released in accordance with rule 30, reinstate such appeal or application on such terms as it may think just.*

(2) If, when an appeal or application is called on for hearing, a party does not appear in person or by his representative, the tribunal may proceed to consider the appeal or application in the absence of that party …[2]

[(3) Subject to paragraph (4) below, the tribunal may set aside any decision or direction given in the absence of a party on such terms as it thinks just, on the application of that party or of any other person interested served at the appropriate tribunal centre within 14 days after the date when the decision or direction of the tribunal was released.

(4) Where a party makes an application under paragraph (3) above and does not attend the hearing of that application, he shall not be entitled to apply to have a decision or direction of the tribunal on the hearing of that application set aside.][2]

Revocation—These Regulations revoked by the Transfer of Tribunal Functions and Revenue and Customs Appeals Order, SI 2009/56 art 3, Sch 2 para 187(*c*) with effect from 1 April 2009.

Amendments—[1] Words in para (1) inserted by the VAT Tribunals (Amendments) Rules, SI 1991/186 reg 17.

[2] Words in para (2) revoked and paras (3), (4) added by the VAT Tribunals (Amendment) Rules, SI 1994/2617 reg 17 with effect from 1 November 1994.

Procedure at a hearing

27— *(1) At the hearing of an appeal or application other than [an evasion penalty appeal]*[1] *the tribunal shall allow—*

(a) the appellant or applicant or his representative to open his case;

(b) the appellant or applicant to give evidence in support of the appeal or application and to produce documentary evidence;

(c) the appellant or applicant or his representative to call other witnesses to give evidence in support of the appeal [or application][1] *or to produce documentary evidence, and to re-examine any such witness following his cross-examination;*

(d) the other party to the appeal or application or his representative to cross-examine any witness called to give evidence in support of the appeal or application (including the appellant or applicant if he gives evidence);

(e) the other party to the appeal or application or his representative to open his case;

(f) the other party to the appeal or application to give evidence in opposition to the appeal or application and to produce documentary evidence;

(g) the other party to the appeal or application or his representative to call other witnesses to give evidence in opposition to the appeal or application or to produce documentary evidence and to re-examine any such witness following his cross-examination;

(h) the appellant or applicant or his representative to cross-examine any witness called to give evidence in opposition to the appeal or application (including the other party to the appeal or application if he gives evidence);

(i) the other party to the appeal or application or his representative to make a second address closing his case; and

(j) the appellant or applicant or his representative to make a final address closing his case.

[(2) At the hearing of an evasion penalty appeal, or an appeal against a penalty imposed under section 114(2) of the Customs and Excise Management Act 1979 or section 22 or section 23 of the Hydrocarbon Oil Duties Act 1979 the tribunal shall follow the same procedure as is set out in paragraph(1) of this rule for the hearing of an appeal or application, but as if there were substituted—

(a) "the Commissioners" for "the appellant or applicant";

(b) "their" for "his" in sub-paragraphs (a), (c), (h) and (j);

(c) "in opposition to" for "in support of" in sub-paragraphs (b), (c) and (d); and

(d) "in support of" for "in opposition to" in sub-paragraphs (f), (g) and (h).][1]

(3) At the hearing of an appeal or application the chairman and any other member of the tribunal may put any question to any witness called to give evidence thereat (including a party to the appeal or application if he gives evidence).

(4) Subject to the foregoing provisions of this rule, a tribunal may regulate its own procedure as it may think fit [and in particular may determine the order in which the matters mentioned in paragraphs (1) and (2) are to take place.][1]

(5) A chairman or the Registrar may postpone the hearing of any appeal or application.

(6) A tribunal may adjourn the hearing of any appeal or application on such terms as it may think just.

Revocation—These Regulations revoked by the Transfer of Tribunal Functions and Revenue and Customs Appeals Order, SI 2009/56 art 3, Sch 2 para 187(*c*) with effect from 1 April 2009.
Simon's Tax Cases—*Kwik-Fit (GB) Ltd v C&E Comrs* [1998] STC 159.
Rule 27(6), *Abedin v C&E Comrs* [1979] STC 426*.
Amendments—[1] Words in para (1) and whole of para (2) substituted and words in para (1)(*c*), (4) inserted by the VAT Tribunals (Amendment) Rules, SI 1994/2617 regs 18–20 with effect from 1 November 1994.

Evidence at a hearing

28— *(1) Subject to paragraph (4) and (5) of rule 21 [and to rule 21A][1] a tribunal may direct or allow evidence of any fact to be given in any manner it may think fit and shall not refuse evidence tendered to it on the grounds only that such evidence would be inadmissible in a court of law.*

(2) A tribunal may require oral evidence of a witness (including a party to an appeal or application) to be given on oath or affirmation and for that purpose a chairman and any member of the administrative staff of the tribunals on the direction of a chairman shall have power to administer oaths or take affirmations.

(3) At the hearing of an appeal or application the tribunal shall allow a party to produce any document set out in his list of documents served under rule 20 and unless a tribunal otherwise directs—

(a) any document contained in such a list of documents which appears to be an original document shall be deemed to be an original document printed, written, signed or executed as it respectively appears to have been; and

(b) any document contained in such list of documents which appears to be a copy shall be deemed to be a true copy.

Revocation—These Regulations revoked by the Transfer of Tribunal Functions and Revenue and Customs Appeals Order, SI 2009/56 art 3, Sch 2 para 187(*c*) with effect from 1 April 2009.
Amendments—[1] Words in para (1) inserted by the VAT Tribunals (Amendments) Rules, SI 1991/186 reg 15(2).

Awards and directions as to costs

29— *(1) A tribunal may direct that a party or applicant shall pay to the other party to the appeal or application—*

(a) within such period as it may specify such sum as it may determine on account of the costs of such other party of and incidental to and consequent upon the appeal or application; or

(b) the costs of such other party of and incidental to and consequent upon the appeal or application to be [assessed by a Taxing Master of the Supreme Court or a district judge of the High Court of Justice in England and Wales by way of detailed assessment or taxed][2] [by] the Auditor of the Court of Session in Scotland or by the Taxing Master of the Supreme Court of Northern Ireland or by the Taxing Master of the High Court of Justice of the Isle of Man on such basis as it shall specify.

(2) Where a tribunal gives a direction under paragraph 1(b) of this rule in proceedings in England and Wales the provisions of [Part 47 of the Civil Procedure Rules 1998 and any practice directions supplementing that Part][2] shall apply, with the necessary modifications, to the taxation of the costs as if the proceedings in the tribunal were a cause or matter in the Supreme Court of Judicature in England.

(3) Where a tribunal gives a direction under paragraph 1(b) of this rule in proceedings in Scotland the provisions of [Chapter 42 of the Act of Sederunt (Rules of the Court of Session 1994)][1] shall apply, with the necessary modifications, to the taxation of the costs as if those proceedings were a cause or matter in the Court of Session in Scotland.

(4) Where a tribunal gives a direction under paragraph 1(b) of this rule in proceedings in Northern Ireland [provisions][1] of Order 62 of the Rules of the Supreme Court (Northern Ireland) 1980 shall apply, with the necessary modifications, to the taxation of the costs as if those proceedings were a cause or matter in the High Court of Northern Ireland.

(5) Any costs awarded under this rule shall be recoverable as a civil debt.

Revocation—These Regulations revoked by the Transfer of Tribunal Functions and Revenue and Customs Appeals Order, SI 2009/56 art 3, Sch 2 para 187(*c*) with effect from 1 April 2009.
Note—In para (1)(*b*) above, it would appear that the word "by" (in square brackets) is needed in order to give meaning to the sentence.
Simon's Tax Cases—r 29(1), *C&E Comrs v Dave* [2002] STC 900.
C&E Comrs v Ross [1990] STC 353; *Nader (T/A Try Us) v Customs and Excise* [1993] STC 806; *C&E Comrs v Vaz, Portcullis (VAT Consultancy) Ltd intervening* [1995] STC 14.
Amendments—[1] Words in paras (3), (4) substituted by the VAT Tribunals (Amendment) Rules, SI 1994/2617 regs 21, 22 with effect from 1 November 1994.
[2] Words in paras (1)(*b*), (2) substituted by the VAT Tribunals (Amendment) Rules, SI 2003/2757 r 9 with effect from 1 December 2003.

Decisions and directions

30— *(1) At the conclusion of the hearing of an appeal the chairman may give or announce the decision of the tribunal but [subject to paragraph (8) of this rule][1] the decision shall be recorded in a written document containing the findings of fact by the tribunal and its reasons for the decision which shall be signed by a chairman; provided that if a party to the appeal shall so request by notice in writing served at the appropriate tribunal centre within one year of the [date on which the decision is released in accordance with this rule][1] the outcome of the appeal and any award and* *direction as to costs or for the payment or repayment of any sum of money with or without interest given or made by the tribunal during or at the conclusion of the hearing of the appeal shall be recorded in a written direction which shall be signed by a chairman or the Registrar.*

(2) At the conclusion of the hearing of an application the chairman may give or announce the decision of the tribunal but in any event the outcome of the application and any award or direction given or made by the tribunal during or at the conclusion of the hearing shall be recorded in a written direction which shall be signed by a chairman or the Registrar; provided that if a party to the application shall so request by notice in writing served at the appropriate tribunal centre within 14 days of the [date on which the direction is released in accordance with this rule][1] *the decision of the tribunal on the application shall be recorded in a written document containing the findings of fact by the tribunal and its reasons for the decision which shall be signed by a chairman.*

(3) A proper officer shall send a copy of the decision and of any direction in an appeal to each party to the appeal and a duplicate of the direction and of any decision in an application to each party to the application.

(4) Every decision in an appeal shall bear the date when the copies thereof are released to be sent to the parties and such copies and any direction, and all copies of any direction, recording the outcome of the appeal shall state that date.

(5) Every direction on an application shall bear the date when the copies thereof are released to be sent to the parties and such copies and any decision on that application given or made under the proviso to paragraph (2) of this rule and all copies thereof shall state that date.

(6) A chairman of the Registrar may correct any clerical mistake or other error in expressing his manifest intention in a decision or direction signed by him but if a chairman or the Registrar corrects any such document after a copy thereof has been sent to a party, a proper officer shall as soon as practicable thereafter send a copy of the corrected document, or the page or pages which have been corrected, to that party.

(7) Where a copy of a decision or a direction dismissing an appeal or application or containing a decision or direction given or made in the absence of a party is sent to a party or other person entitled to apply under rule 26 to apply to have the appeal or application reinstated [or the decision or direction set aside][1]*, the copy shall contain or be accompanied by a note to that effect.*

[(8) If, at the conclusion of the hearing of a mitigation appeal or a reasonable excuse appeal the chairman gives or announces the decision of the tribunal, he may ask the parties present at the hearing whether they require the decision to be recorded in a written document in accordance with paragraph (1) of this rule, and if none of the parties present requires this the provisions of this rule shall apply as if the appeal had been an application.][2]

Revocation—These Regulations revoked by the Transfer of Tribunal Functions and Revenue and Customs Appeals Order, SI 2009/56 art 3, Sch 2 para 187(*c*) with effect from 1 April 2009.

Simon's Tax Cases—r 30(1), *Rahman (T/A Khayam Restaurant) v C&E Comrs* [1998] STC 826.

Amendments—[1] Words in paras (1), (2) substituted and words in para (7) inserted by the VAT Tribunals (Amendment) Rules, SI 1991/186 regs 19–21 with effect from 1 March 1991.

[2] Para (8) substituted by the VAT Tribunals (Amendment) Rules, SI 1994/2617 reg 23 with effect from 1 November 1994 (previously added by SI 1991/186 reg 22).

[Appeals from tribunal

30A *A party who wishes to appeal from a decision of the tribunal direct to the Court of Appeal shall apply to the tribunal in accordance with rule 11 for a certificate under Article 2(b) of the Value Added Tax Tribunals Appeals Order 1986 [or article 2(b) of the Value Added Tax Tribunals Appeals (Northern Ireland) Order 1994, as appropriate,]*[2] *at the conclusion of the hearing or within 21 days after the date when the decision of the tribunal was released in accordance with rule 30.]*[1]

Revocation—These Regulations revoked by the Transfer of Tribunal Functions and Revenue and Customs Appeals Order, SI 2009/56 art 3, Sch 2 para 187(*c*) with effect from 1 April 2009.

Amendments—[1] This rule inserted by the VAT Tribunals (Amendment) Rules, SI 1986/2290 r 2 with effect from 12 January 1987.

[2] Words added by the VAT Tribunals (Amendment) Rules, SI 1994/2617 r 24 with effect from 1 November 1994.

Service at a tribunal centre

31— *(1) Service of a notice of appeal, notice of application or other document shall be effected by the same being handed to a proper officer at the appropriate tribunal centre or by the same being received by post at the appropriate tribunal [centre or by a facsimile of the same being received at the appropriate tribunal centre by facsimile transmission process [or telex or other means of electronic communication which produces a text of the document, in which event the document shall be regarded as sent when the text of it is received in legible form]*[2]*.]*[1]

[(2) Any notice of appeal, notice of application or other document (including a facsimile of a document received by facsimile transmission process or telex or other means of electronic communication which produces a text of the document) [handed in or received at a tribunal centre other than the appropriate tribunal centre][3] *may be—*

(a) sent by post in a letter addressed to a proper officer at the appropriate tribunal centre; or

(b) handed back to the person from whom it was received; or

(c) sent by post in a letter addressed to the person from whom it appears to have been received or by whom it appears to have been sent; or

(d) if a facsimile of a document is received by facsimile transmission process or telex or other means of electronic communication which produces a text of the document, sent by the means by which it was received, either to a proper officer at the appropriate tribunal centre or to the person from whom it appears to have been received or by whom it appears to have been sent.][2]

Revocation—These Regulations revoked by the Transfer of Tribunal Functions and Revenue and Customs Appeals Order, SI 2009/56 art 3, Sch 2 para 187(*c*) with effect from 1 April 2009.

Amendments—[1] Words in para (1) substituted and words in para (2) inserted by the VAT Tribunals (Amendment) Rules, SI 1991/186 r 23 with effect from 1 March 1991.

[2] Words in para (1) inserted, and para (2) substituted, by the VAT Tribunals (Amendment) Rules, SI 2003/2757 r 10 with effect from 1 December 2003.

[3] Words in para (2) inserted by the VAT Tribunals (Amendment) Rules, SI 2004/1032 r 6 with effect from 4 May 2004.

Sending of documents to the parties

32— *(1) Any document authorised or required to be sent to the Commissioners may be sent to them by post in a letter addressed to them at the address of their office from which the disputed decision appears to have been sent, or handed or sent to them by post or in such manner and at such address as the Commissioners may from time to time request by a general notice served at the appropriate tribunal centre.*

(2) Any document authorised or required to be sent to any party to an appeal or application other than the Commissioners may be sent by post in a letter addressed to him at his address stated in his notice of appeal or application, or sent by post in a letter addressed to any person named in his notice of appeal or application as having been instructed to act for him in connection therewith at the address therein stated, or sent by post in a letter addressed to such person and at such address as he may specify from time to time by notice served at the appropriate tribunal centre; provided that where partners appeal or apply to a tribunal in the name of their firm, any document sent by post in a letter addressed to the firm at the address of the firm stated in the notice of appeal or notice of application or to any person named in the notice of appeal or application as having been instructed to act for the firm at the address therein stated or to such other address as such partners may from time to time specify by notice served at the appropriate tribunal centre, shall be deemed to have been duly sent to all such partners.

(3) Subject to the foregoing provisions of this rule any document authorised or required to be sent to any party to an appeal or application or other person may be sent by post in a letter addressed to him at his usual or last known address or addressed to him or to such other person at such address as he may from time to time specify by notice served at the appropriate tribunal centre.

[(4) Any reference in this rule to the sending of any document to any party to an appeal or application or to any other person by post shall be construed as including a reference to the transmission of a facsimile of such document by facsimile transmission process [or telex or other means of electronic communication which produces a text of the document, in which event the document shall be regarded as sent when the text of it is received in legible form][2]*.]*[1]

Revocation—These Regulations revoked by the Transfer of Tribunal Functions and Revenue and Customs Appeals Order, SI 2009/56 art 3, Sch 2 para 187(*c*) with effect from 1 April 2009.

Amendments—[1] Para (4) inserted by the VAT Tribunals (Amendment) Rules, SI 1991/186 r 24 with effect from 1 March 1991.

[2] Words in para (4) inserted by the VAT Tribunals (Amendment) Rules, SI 2003/2757 r 11 with effect from 1 December 2003.

Delegation of powers to the Registrar

33— *(1) All or any of the following powers of a tribunal or a chairman under these rules shall be exercisable by the Registrar, that is to say—*

(a) power to give or make any direction by consent of the parties to the appeal or application;
(b) power to give or make any direction on the application of one party which is not opposed by the other party to the application;
(c) power to issue a witness summons;
(d) power to postpone any hearing; and
(e) power to extend the time for the service of any notice of appeal, notice of application or other document at the appropriate tribunal centre for a period not exceeding one month without prior notice or reference to any party or other person and without a hearing.

(2) The Registrar shall have power to sign a direction recording the outcome of an appeal and any award or direction given or made by the tribunal during or at the conclusion of the hearing of an appeal as provided by rule 30(1) and to sign any document recording any direction given or made by him under this rule.

Revocation—These Regulations revoked by the Transfer of Tribunal Functions and Revenue and Customs Appeals Order, SI 2009/56 art 3, Sch 2 para 187(*c*) with effect from 1 April 2009.

1986/896
Value Added Tax (Treatment of Transactions) Order 1986

Made by the Treasury under VATA 1983 s 3(3) (see now VATA 1994 s 5(3)(*c*))

Made . . . . *22 May 1986*
Laid before the House of Commons . . . . *3 June 1986*
Coming into Operation . . . . *1 July 1986*

Citation and commencement

1 This Order may be cited as the Value Added Tax (Treatment of Transactions) Order 1986 and shall come into operation on 1st July 1986.

Interpretation

2 In this Order—

"articles in pawn" means articles subject to a pledge;

"pawnee", "pawnor" and "pledge" have the same meaning as in section 189 of the Consumer Credit Act 1974.

Treatment of Transaction

3 The following description of a transaction shall be treated as neither a supply of goods nor a supply of services:

the supply by a taxable person of goods the property in which passed to him as a pawnee by virtue of section 120(1)(*a*) of the Consumer Credit Act 1974–

(*a*) where the supply is to a person who was pawnor of those goods, and

(*b*) where the supply is made not later than three months from the date when the taxable person acquired the property in the goods.

1986/939
Value Added Tax (Small Non-Commercial Consignments) Relief Order 1986

Made by the Treasury under VATA 1983 s 19(1) (see now VATA 1994 s 37(1))

Made . . . . *3 June 1986*
Laid before the House of Commons . . . . *9 June 1986*
Coming into Operation . . . . *1 July 1986*

Citation and commencement

1 This Order may be cited as the Value Added Tax (Small Non-Commercial Consignments) Relief Order 1986 and shall come into operation on 1st July 1986.

Revocation

2 The Value Added Tax (Imported Goods) Relief Order 1980 and the Value Added Tax (Imported Goods) Relief (Amendment) Order 1985 are hereby revoked.

Relief from value added tax

3— (1) Subject to the provisions of this Order, no tax is payable on the importation [from a place outside the member States][1] of goods forming part of a small consignment of a non-commercial character.

(2) In this Order "small consignment" means a consignment (not forming part of a larger consignment) containing goods with a value for customs purposes not exceeding [£36][1].

(3) For the purposes of this Order a consignment is of a non-commercial character only if the following requirements are met, namely—

(*a*) it is consigned by one private individual to another;

(*b*) it is not imported for any consideration in money or money's worth;

(*c*) it is intended solely for the personal use of the consignee or that of his family and not for any commercial purpose.

Amendments—[1] Words in para (1) inserted and "£36" in para (2) substituted by the VAT (Small Non-Commercial Consignments) Relief (Amendment) Order, SI 1992/3118 with effect from 1 January 1993.

Conditions of relief

[**4** No relief shall be given under this Order unless the consignment is of an occasional nature.][1]

Amendments—[1] This article substituted by the VAT (Small Non-Commercial Consignments) Relief (Amendment) Order, SI 1992/3118 with effect from 1 January 1993.

Quantitative restriction on relief for certain goods

5 Where a small consignment of a non-commercial character contains goods of any of the following descriptions, namely—

(*a*) tobacco products (being cigarettes, cigars or smoking tobacco);

(*b*) alcohol and alcoholic beverages (being spirits or wine), tafia and saké; or
(*c*) perfumes or toilet waters,

in excess of the quantity shown in relation to goods of that description in the Schedule to this Order, no relief under this Order shall be given in respect of any goods of that description contained in that consignment.

Relief not applicable to travellers' baggage

6 This Order does not apply to goods contained in the baggage of a person entering the United Kingdom or carried with such a person.

SCHEDULE

Article 5

(1) Tobacco products—	
Cigarettes	50
Or	
cigarillos (cigars with a maximum weight each of 3 grammes)	25
Or	
Cigars	10
Or	
smoking tobacco	50 grammes
(2) Alcohol and alcoholic beverages—	
distilled beverages and spirits of an alcoholic strength exceeding 22% by volume; undenatured ethyl alcohol of 80% by volume and over	1 litre
Or	
distilled beverages and spirits, and aperitifs with a wine or alcohol base, tafia, saké or similar beverages of an alcoholic strength of 22% by volume or less; sparkling wines and fortified wines	1 litre
Or	
still wines	2 litres
(3) Perfumes	50 grammes
Or	
toilet waters	[250 millilitres][1]

Amendments—[1] Words in para (3) substituted by the VAT (Small Non-Commercial Consignments) Relief (Amendment) Order, SI 1991/2535 arts 1, 2 with effect from 30 November 1991.

1986/2288
Value Added Tax Tribunals Appeals Order 1986

Made by the Lord Chancellor under FA 1985 s 26 (see now VATA 1994 s 86)

Made . . . . *18 December 1986*
Laid before Parliament . . . . *22 December 1986*
Coming into Operation . . . . *12 January 1987*

Revocation—These Regulations revoked by the Transfer of Tribunal Functions and Revenue and Customs Appeals Order, SI 2009/56 art 3, Sch 2 para 187(*d*) with effect from 1 April 2009.

1 *This Order may be cited as the Value Added Tax Tribunals Appeals Order 1986 and shall come into operation on 12th January 1987.*

Revocation—These Regulations revoked by the Transfer of Tribunal Functions and Revenue and Customs Appeals Order, SI 2009/56 art 3, Sch 2 para 187(*d*) with effect from 1 April 2009.

2 *If any party to proceedings before a value added tax tribunal is dissatisfied in point of law with a decision of the tribunal he may, notwithstanding section 13 of the Tribunals and Inquiries Act 1971*[a] *appeal from the tribunal direct to the Court of Appeal if—*

(*a*) *the parties consent;*
(*b*) *the tribunal endorses its decision with a certificate that the decision involves a point of law relating wholly or mainly to the construction of an enactment, or of a statutory instrument, or of any of the Community Treaties or of any Community Instruments, which has been fully argued before it and fully considered by it; and*
(*c*) *the leave of a single judge of the Court of Appeal has been obtained pursuant to section 54(6) of the Supreme Court Act 1981.*

Revocation—These Regulations revoked by the Transfer of Tribunal Functions and Revenue and Customs Appeals Order, SI 2009/56 art 3, Sch 2 para 187(*d*) with effect from 1 April 2009.
Note—[a] TIA 1992 s 11.

1987/1806
Value Added Tax (Tour Operators) Order 1987

Made by the Treasury under VATA 1983 ss 3(3), 6(6), 16(4), 37A(1)–(2), 48(6) (see now VATA 1994 ss 5(3), 7(11), 30(4), 53(1), (2), 96(9))

Made . . . . *14 October 1987*
Laid before the House of Commons . . . . *21 October 1987*
Coming into force . . . . *1 April 1988*

Citation and Commencement

1 This Order may be cited as the Value Added Tax (Tour Operators) Order 1987 and shall come into force on 1st April 1988.

Supplies to which this Order applies

2 This Order shall apply to any supply of goods or services by a tour operator where the supply is for the benefit of travellers.

Meaning of "designated travel service"

3— (1) Subject to paragraphs (2), (3) and (4) of this article, a "designated travel service" is a supply of goods or services—

(*a*) acquired for the purposes of his business; and
(*b*) supplied for the benefit of a traveller without material alteration or further processing;

by a tour operator in a member State of the European Community in which he has established his business or has a fixed establishment.

(2) The supply of one or more designated travel services, as part of a single transaction, shall be treated as a single supply of services.

(3) The Commissioners of Customs and Excise may on being given notice by a tour operator that he is a person who to the order of a taxable person—

(*a*) acquires goods or services from another taxable person; and
(*b*) supplies those goods or services, without material alteration or further processing, to the taxable person who ordered the supply for use in the United Kingdom by that person for the purpose of that person's business other than by way of re-supply

treat supplies within sub-paragraph (*b*) as not being designated travel services.

(4) The supply of goods and services of such description as the Commissioners of Customs and Excise may specify shall be deemed not to be a designated travel service.

Press releases etc—C&E News Release 50/95 24-10-95 (guidance for tour operators on in-house supplies of transport, supplies as agent and supplies to businesses).
Business Brief 2/96 9-2-96 (guidance on the VAT treatment of commission for transport only sales by travel agents).

Time of supply

4— (1) Sections 4 and 5 of the Value Added Tax Act 1983[a] shall not apply to any supply comprising in whole or in part a designated travel service.

(2) Subject to paragraphs (3) and (4) of this article, all supplies comprising in whole or in part a designated travel service shall, at the election of the tour operator making the supplies, be treated as taking place either—

(*a*) when the traveller commences a journey or occupies any accommodation supplied, whichever is the earlier; or
(*b*) when any payment is received by the tour operator in respect of that supply which, when aggregated with any earlier such payment, exceeds 20 per cent of the total consideration, to the extent covered by that and any earlier such payment, save in so far as any earlier such payment has already been treated as determining the time of part of that supply.

(3) Save as the Commissioners of Customs and Excise may otherwise allow, all supplies comprising in whole or in part a designated travel service made by the same tour operator shall, subject to paragraph (4) of this article, be treated as taking place at the time determined under one only of the methods specified in paragraph (2) of this article.

(4) Where—

(*a*) a tour operator uses the method specified in paragraph (2)(*b*) to determine the time of a supply; and
(*b*) payment is not received in respect of all or part of the supply;

notwithstanding paragraph (3), the time of any part of that supply, which has not already been determined under paragraph (2)(*b*), shall be determined in accordance with paragraph (2)(*a*).

Note—[a] VATA 1994 s 6.

Place of supply

[**5**— (1) …[2]

(2) A designated travel service shall be treated [for the purposes of this Act][2] as supplied in the member State in which the tour operator has established his business or, if the supply was made from a fixed establishment, in the member State in which the fixed establishment is situated.][1]

Amendments—[1] This article substituted by the VAT (Tour Operators) (Amendment) Order, SI 1992/3125 with effect from 1 January 1993.
[2] In para (2) words inserted, para (1) repealed and article treated as made under VATA 19994 s 7A(6)(*c*), by FA 2009 s 76, Sch 36 para 13 with effect in relation to supplies made on or after 1 January 2010. Para (1) previously read as follows—
"(1) The application of sections 6 and 8 of the Value Added Tax Act 1983 shall be modified in accordance with paragraph (2) below."

6 …

Note—This article amended VAT (Place of Supply) Order, SI 1984/1685 arts 4, 5 (revoked).

Value of a designated travel service

7 Subject to articles 8 and 9 of this Order, the value of a designated travel service shall be determined by reference to the difference between sums paid or payable to and sums paid or payable by the tour operator in respect of that service, calculated in such manner as the Commissioners of Customs and Excise shall specify.

Simon's Tax Cases—*C&E Comrs v First Choice Holidays* [2000] STC 609, [2004] STC 1407.

8— (1) Where—

(*a*) a supply of goods or services is acquired for a consideration in money by a tour operator, for the purpose of supplying a designated travel service, and
(*b*) the value of the supply is (apart from this article) greater than its open market value, and
(*c*) the person making the supply and the tour operator to whom it is made are connected,

the Commissioners of Customs and Excise may direct that the value of the supply shall be deemed to be its open market value for the purpose of calculating the value of the designated travel service.

(2) A direction under this article shall be given by notice in writing to the tour operator acquiring the supply, but no direction may be given more than three years after the time of the supply.

(3) A direction given to a tour operator under this paragraph, in respect of a supply acquired by him, may include a direction that the value of any supply—

(*a*) which is acquired by him after the giving of the notice, or after such later date as may be specified in the notice, and
(*b*) as to which the conditions in sub-paragraph (*a*) to (*c*) of paragraph (1) above are satisfied,

shall be deemed to be its open market value for the purpose of calculating the value of the designated travel service.

(4) For the purposes of this article any question whether a person is connected with another shall be determined in accordance with section 533 of the Income and Corporation Taxes Act 1970[a].

Note—[a] TA 1988 s 839.

9— (1) Where—

(*a*) goods and services have been acquired prior to the commencement of this Order; and
(*b*) input tax credit has been claimed in respect of those goods and services; and
(*c*) the goods and services are supplied as a designated travel service or as part of a designated travel service after the commencement of this Order;

article 7 of this Order shall not apply in determining the value of that part of a designated travel service referable to goods and services on which input tax has been claimed.

(2) The value of that part of the designated travel service to which, by virtue of paragraph (1) of this article, article 7 of this Order does not apply shall be calculated in accordance with section 10 of the Value Added Tax Act 1983[a].

Note—[a] VATA 1994 s 19.

10 …

Amendments—This article revoked by the VAT (Tour Operators) (Amendment) Order, SI 1995/1495 art 2 with effect from 1 January 1996.

11 …

Amendments—This article revoked by the VATA 1994 s 100(2), Sch 15.

Disallowance of input tax

12 Input tax on goods or services acquired by a tour operator for re-supply as a designated travel service shall be excluded from credit under sections 14 and 15 of the Value Added Tax Act 1983[a].

Note—[a] VATA 1994 ss 24–26.

Disqualification from membership of group of companies

13 A tour operator shall not be eligible to be treated as a member of a group for the purposes of section 29 of the Value Added Tax Act 1983[a] if any other member of the proposed or existing group—

(*a*) has an overseas establishment;

(*b*) makes supplies outside the United Kingdom which would be taxable supplies if made within the United Kingdom; and

(*c*) supplies goods or services which will become, or are intended to become, a designated travel service.

Note—[a] VATA 1994 s 43.

Option not to treat supply as designated travel service

14— (1) Where a tour operator supplies a designated travel service he may treat that supply as not being a designated travel service if:

(*a*) there are reasonable grounds for believing that the value of all such supplies in the period of one year then beginning will not exceed one per cent of all supplies made by him during that period; and

(*b*) he makes no supplies of designated travel services consisting of accommodation or transport.

(2) For the purposes of this article the value of any supplies shall be calculated in accordance with section 10 of the Value Added Tax Act 1983[a].

Note—[a] VATA 1994 s 19.

1988/809

Excise Warehousing (Etc) Regulations 1988

Made by the Commissioners of Customs and Excise under CEMA 1979 s 93 and ALDA 1979 ss 2(3A), 15 and 56(1)

Made . . . . *29 April 1988*
Laid before Parliament . . . . *9 May 1988*
Coming into force . . . . *1 June 1988*

ARRANGEMENT OF REGULATIONS

PART II

PROCEDURES FOR EXCISE WAREHOUSES AND WAREHOUSED GOODS

PART III

RETURNS AND RECORDS

PART I
PRELIMINARY

Citation and commencement

1 These Regulations may be cited as the Excise Warehousing (Etc) Regulations 1988 and shall come into force on 1st June 1988, but the Commissioners may give consent and agree conditions, restrictions or requirements under regulation 5 (variation of provisions at request of occupier or proprietor) before that date.

Interpretation

2 In these Regulations, unless the context otherwise requires—

"duty" means excise duty;

"occupier" means the occupier of an excise warehouse, and in the case of a distiller's warehouse means the distiller;

"package" includes any bundle, case, carton, cask, or other container whatsoever;

"proprietor" means the proprietor of goods in an excise warehouse or of goods which have been in, or are to be deposited in, or are treated as being in, an excise warehouse, and "proprietorship" shall be construed accordingly;

"warehoused" means warehoused or rewarehoused in an excise warehouse, and "warehousing" and "rewarehousing" shall be construed accordingly.

Application

3— (1) Except as provided by or under the Hydrocarbon Oil Duties Act 1979 Parts I to IV of these Regulations apply to all goods chargeable with a duty of excise.

(2) Part V of these Regulations applies for all purposes of the Alcoholic Liquor Duties Act 1979.

Designated file

4— (1) For the purposes of these Regulations delivery to the proper officer of anything in writing—

(*a*) shall be effected by placing it in the relevant designated file; and

(*b*) the time of such delivery shall be when it is placed in that designated file,

but the proper officer may direct that delivery shall be effected in another manner.

(2) Nothing in a designated file shall be removed without the permission of the proper officer.

(3) Nothing in a designated file shall be altered in any way, and an amendment to anything in it shall be made by depositing a notice of amendment in the designated file.

(4) The designated file shall be kept at such place as the Commissioners direct and, if kept at the excise warehouse, shall be provided by the occupier.

(5) The designated file shall be a receptacle approved by the Commissioners for the secure keeping of written material, and different files may be approved for different purposes.

(6) For the purposes of these Regulations delivery to the proper officer of anything not in writing shall be effected in such manner, and be subject to such conditions, as the Commissioners direct.

Variation of provisions at request of occupier or proprietor

5— (1) The Commissioners may, if they see fit, consent in writing to an application by an occupier or proprietor for variation of any condition, restriction or requirement contained in or arising under regulations 11 to 24 below, and may make that consent subject to compliance with such other condition, restriction or requirement (as the case may be) as may be agreed by them and the applicant in writing.

(2) Where under paragraph (1) above any condition or restriction is varied or another is substituted for it, then, if the varied or substituted condition or restriction is one—

(*a*) subject to which goods may be deposited in, secured in, kept in or removed from an excise warehouse or made available there to their owner for any prescribed purpose; or

(*b*) subject to which an operation may be carried out on goods in an excise warehouse,

breach of the varied or substituted condition or restriction shall give rise to forfeiture of those goods, provided that breach of the original condition or restriction would have given rise to forfeiture.

6 …

Amendments—This regulation revoked by Excise Goods (Drawback) Regulations, SI 1995/1046, Pt V, reg 15(*a*) with effect from 1 June 1995.

Manner of Commissioners' directions etc

7— (1) Where, by or under these Regulations, it is provided that the Commissioners may—

(*a*) make a direction or requirement;

(*b*) give their permission or consent;

(*c*) grant approval; or

(*d*) impose a condition or restriction,

then they may do so only in writing; and they may make a direction or requirement or impose a condition or restriction by means of a public notice.

(2) Any request for the proper officer to give his permission or grant approval under these Regulations shall, if he or the Commissioners direct, be made in writing.

(3) Any right granted to the Commissioners or the proper officer by these Regulations to—

(*a*) make a direction or requirement;

(*b*) give permission or consent;

(*c*) grant approval; or

(*d*) impose a condition or restriction,

shall include a right to revoke, vary or replace any such direction, requirement, permission, consent, approval, condition or restriction.

Form of entries etc

8— (1) Except as the Commissioners otherwise allow, and subject to paragraph (2) below, any entry, account, notice, specification, record or return required by or under these Regulations shall be in writing.

(2) This regulation does not apply to the records referred to in regulation 22(3) and (4) below (records kept for the purposes of any relevant business or activity).

Revocation

9 The Excise Warehousing (Etc) Regulations 1982 and the Excise Warehousing (Etc) (Amendment) Regulations 1986 are hereby revoked.

PART II
PROCEDURES FOR EXCISE WAREHOUSES AND WAREHOUSED GOODS

Time of warehousing

10 Goods brought to an excise warehouse for warehousing shall be deemed to be warehoused when they are put in the excise warehouse.

[Goods to which section 46 of the Customs and Excise Management Act 1979 applies

10A— (1) This regulation applies to goods other than hydrocarbon oil that have been imported from a place outside the Communities ("section 46 goods").

(2) Section 46 goods may be entered for warehousing and moved from their place of importation to an excise warehouse without payment of excise duty if, but only if, the following conditions are complied with—

(*a*) any customs duty charged on the goods is paid or otherwise accounted for to the satisfaction of the Commissioners, and

(*b*) …[2]

(3) …[2]][1]

Amendments—[1] Regulation inserted by the Excise Goods (Accompanying Documents) Regulations, SI 2002/501 reg 27(1), (2) with effect from 1 April 2002.

[2] Paras (2)(*b*), (3) revoked by the Excise Warehousing (Etc) (Amendment) Regulations, SI 2008/2832 regs 2, 3(1) with effect from 1 December 2008.

Receipt of goods into warehouse

11— (1) Subject to paragraph (6) below, when goods are warehoused the occupier shall immediately deliver to the proper officer an entry of the goods in such form and containing such particulars as the Commissioners direct.

(2) When goods are warehoused the occupier shall take account of the goods and deliver a copy of that account to the proper officer by the start of business on the next day after warehousing that the warehouse is open.

(3) The occupier shall, if there is any indication that the goods may have been subject to loss or tampering in the course of removal to the excise warehouse, immediately inform the proper officer and retain the goods intact for his examination.

(4) Except as the proper officer may otherwise allow, the occupier shall, within 5 days of goods being warehoused, send a certificate of receipt for the goods to the person from whom they were received identifying the goods and stating the quantity which has been warehoused.

[(4A) Where goods are warehoused in circumstances where duty may be drawn back the certificate of receipt mentioned in paragraph (4) above shall—

(*a*) be in such form and contain such particulars as the Commissioners may require, and

(*b*) be endorsed on one of the copies of the warehousing advice note that accompanied the goods,

and in this paragraph "warehousing advice note" means a document (in such form and containing such particulars as the Commissioners may require) drawn up by the person to whom the certificate of receipt will be sent.][1]

(5) Except as the proper officer otherwise allows the occupier shall give only one receipt required by paragraph (4) above for each lot or parcel of goods warehoused.

(6) In the case of spirits warehoused at the distillery where they were produced satisfaction of the requirements of regulation 21 of the Spirits Regulations 1982 shall be deemed to be compliance with the requirements of entry and account in paragraphs (1) and (2) above.

(7) Should the occupier fail to comply with any condition or restriction imposed by or under paragraphs (1), (2), (3) or (6) above any goods in respect of which the failure occurred shall be liable to forfeiture.

Amendments—[1] Para (4A) inserted by Excise Goods (Drawback) Regulations, SI 1995/1046, Pt V, reg 15(*b*) with effect from 1 June 1995.

Securing, marking and taking stock of warehoused goods

12— (1) The occupier shall take all necessary steps to ensure that no access is had to warehoused goods other than as allowed by or under these Regulations.

(2) Goods shall be warehoused in the packages and lots in which they were first entered for warehousing.

(3) The occupier shall—

(*a*) legibly and uniquely mark and keep marked warehoused goods so that at any time they can be identified in the stock records; and

(*b*) stow warehoused goods so that safe and easy access may be had to each package or lot.

(4) The occupier shall, when required by the proper officer to do so, promptly produce to him any warehoused goods which have not lawfully been removed from the warehouse.

(5) The occupier shall take stock of all goods in the warehouse—

(*a*) monthly in the case of bulk goods in vats or in storage tanks; and

(*b*) annually in the case of all other goods,

and shall take stock at such other times and to such extent as the Commissioners may for reasonable cause require.

(6) In accordance with the Commissioners' directions the occupier shall—

(*a*) balance his stock accounts and reconcile the quantities of those balances with his Excise Warehouse Returns; and

(*b*) balance his stock accounts so that they can be compared with the result of any stock-taking.

(7) The occupier shall notify the proper officer immediately in writing of any deficiency, surplus or other discrepancy concerning stocks or records of stocks whenever or however discovered.

(8) Any goods—

(*a*) found not to be marked in accordance with paragraph (3) above; or

(*b*) found to be in excess of the relevant stock account and not immediately notified to the proper officer,

shall be liable to forfeiture.

Proprietor's examination of goods

13 The proprietor of warehoused goods may, provided that the occupier has first given his consent and has given at least 6 hours' notice to the proper officer—

(*a*) examine the goods and their packaging;

(*b*) take any steps necessary to prevent any loss therefrom; or
(*c*) display them for sale.

Operations

14— (1) Except as provided by or under this regulation or by or under sections 57 and 58 of the Alcoholic Liquor Duties Act 1979 (mixing of spirits with made-wine or wine), no operation shall be carried out on warehoused goods.

(2) The Commissioners may allow the operations described in Schedule 1 to these Regulations to be carried out on warehoused goods, and may allow other operations if they are satisfied that the control of the goods and the security and collection of the revenue will not be prejudiced.

(3) Save as the proper officer may allow in cases of emergency for the preservation of the goods, no operation shall be commenced unless the occupier has delivered to the proper officer a notice of the proposed operation with a specification of the goods involved, and 24 hours have elapsed following the delivery of that notice.

(4) Before commencing any operation on goods the occupier shall ensure that an account is taken of those goods and that immediately after completion of the operation an account is taken of the out-turn quantities.

(5) The occupier shall deliver to the proper officer a notice containing such detail of the accounts required by paragraph (4) above as the proper officer requires.

(6) The occupier shall ensure that—

(*a*) any operation is carried out in part of the warehouse approved by the Commissioners for that purpose, or in such other part as the proper officer allows; and
(*b*) such other requirements as the proper officer may impose in any particular circumstances are observed.

(7) Any goods in respect of which this regulation is not observed shall be liable to forfeiture.

(8) Nothing in paragraph (2) above shall permit the mixing of spirits with wine or made-wine while that operation is excluded from the provisions of section 93(2)(*c*) of the Customs and Excise Management Act 1979.

Removal from warehouse—occupier's responsibilities

15 The occupier shall ensure that—

(*a*) notice of intention to remove the goods is given to the proper officer in accordance with any directions made by the Commissioners;
(*b*) an entry of the goods is delivered to the proper officer in such form and containing such particulars as the Commissioners may direct;
(*c*) no goods are removed until any duty chargeable has been paid, secured, or otherwise accounted for;
(*d*) no goods are removed contrary to any condition or restriction imposed by the proper officer;
(*e*) an account of the goods is taken in such manner and to such extent as the proper officer requires and a copy of the account is delivered to the proper officer; and
(*f*) when goods are removed other than for home use, a certificate of receipt is obtained showing that all the goods arrived at the place to which they were entered on removal and, if no such receipt is obtained within 21 days of the removal, notice of that fact is given to the proper officer for the excise warehouse from which the goods were removed.

Removal from warehouse—entry

16— (1) Goods may be entered for removal from warehouse for—

(*a*) home use, if so eligible;
(*b*) exportation;
(*c*) shipment as stores; or
(*d*) removal to the Isle of Man [;

provided that, where goods are warehoused in circumstances where duty may be drawn back they may not, under this paragraph, be entered for removal from warehouse for any purpose that may result in their being consumed in the United Kingdom or the Isle of Man].

(2) The Commissioners may allow goods to be entered for removal from warehouse for—

(*a*) rewarehousing in another excise warehouse;
(*b*) temporary removal for such purposes and such periods as they may allow;
(*c*) scientific research and testing;
(*d*) removal to premises where goods of the same class or description may, by or under the customs and excise Acts, be kept without payment of excise duty;
(*e*) denaturing or destruction; or
(*f*) such other purpose as they permit,

and may by direction impose conditions and restrictions on the entry of goods or classes of goods for any of the above purposes.

(3) Save as the Commissioners direct no goods may be removed from warehouse unless they have been entered in accordance with this regulation.

(4), (5) ...

Note—Paras (4), (5) excepted from subordinate legislation (applied by the VATA 1994 s 16(1)) by the VAT Regulations, SI 1995/2518 reg 119.

Amendments—Words in para (1) added by Excise Goods (Drawback) Regulations, SI 1995/1046, Pt V, reg 15(*c*) with effect from 1 June 1995.

Removal from warehouse—general

17— (1) Any goods removed from an excise warehouse without payment of duty as samples or for scientific research and testing and which are no longer required for the purpose for which they were removed shall be—

(*a*) destroyed to the satisfaction of the proper officer;
(*b*) rewarehoused in an excise warehouse; or
(*c*) diverted to home use on payment of the duty chargeable thereon.

(2) The proper officer may require any goods entered for removal from an excise warehouse for any purpose, other than home use, to be secured or identified by the use of a seal, lock or mark, and any such requirement may continue after the goods have been removed.

(3) In such cases as the Commissioners may direct the proper officer may impose conditions and restrictions on the removal of goods from an excise warehouse in addition to those imposed elsewhere in these Regulations.

(4) Any goods in respect of which any of the provisions of these Regulations relating to removal of goods from an excise warehouse (other than regulation 15(*f*)) is contravened shall be liable to forfeiture.

(5) The Commissioners may direct that any provision of these Regulations relating to removal of goods from an excise warehouse shall not apply in the case of hydrocarbon oils.

[(6) Subject to paragraph (7) below, goods entered for removal from an excise warehouse for any of the purposes set out in regulation 16 above shall be accompanied by an accompanying document that has been completed and is used in accordance with the instructions for completion and use set out on the reverse of copy 1 of that document.

(7) Paragraph (6) above does not apply to—

(*a*) goods entered for removal for home use, shipment as stores or denaturing;
(*b*) goods entered for removal for use by a person to whom section 13A of the Customs and Excise Duties (General Reliefs) Act 1979 (reliefs from duties and taxes for persons enjoying certain immunities and privileges) applies;
(*c*) goods entered for removal that are, in accordance with regulations made under section 12(1) of the Customs and Excise Duties (General Reliefs) Act 1979 (supply of duty-free goods to Her Majesty's ships), to be treated as exported;
(*d*) spirits entered for removal for use by a person authorised to receive them in accordance with section 8 of the Alcoholic Liquor Duties Act 1979 (remission of duty in respect of spirits used for medical or scientific purposes);
(*e*) goods entered for removal for exportation in circumstances to which Part II of the Excise Goods (Accompanying Documents) Regulations 2002 apply;
(*f*) goods that are being lawfully moved under the cover of a single administrative document; or
(*g*) any goods that are entered for removal from an excise warehouse for any of the purposes set out in regulation 16 above before 1st October 2002 if those goods are accompanied by a document that has been approved by the Commissioners for that purpose.

(8) If there is a contravention of, or failure to comply with, paragraph (6) above, the excise duty point for excise goods that are required by this regulation to be accompanied by an accompanying document is the time those goods were removed from the excise warehouse.

(9) The person liable to pay the excise duty at the excise duty point is—

(*a*) the person who arranged for the security required by regulation 16(5) above, or
(*b*) if regulation 16(5) above was not complied with, the authorized warehousekeeper.

(10) Any person whose conduct caused a contravention of, or failure to comply with, paragraph (6) above is jointly and severally liable to pay the excise duty with the person specified in paragraph (9) above.

(11) Any excise duty that any person is liable to pay by virtue of this regulation must be paid immediately.

(12) In this regulation—

"single administrative document" has the same meaning as in Commission Regulation (EEC) No 2454/93;
"accompanying document" means the document set out in Schedule 4 below.][1]

Amendments—[1] Paras (6)–(12) added by the Excise Goods (Accompanying Documents) Regulations, SI 2002/501 reg 27(1), (3) with effect from 1 April 2002.

Entry of goods not in warehouse

18 Except in such cases as the Commissioners direct, goods which are to be warehoused and goods which have been lawfully removed from an excise warehouse without payment of duty may, with the permission of the proper officer, be entered or further entered by their proprietor for any of the purposes referred to in paragraphs (1) and (2) of regulation 16 above as if they were to be removed from the excise warehouse:

Provided that where any such goods are packaged and part only is to be further entered, that part shall consist of one or more complete packages.

Samples

19— (1) The Commissioners may make directions—

(*a*) allowing the proprietor of warehoused goods to draw samples thereof for such purposes and subject to such conditions as they specify; and

(*b*) …

and no sample shall be drawn or removed except as allowed by, and in accordance with directions and conditions under, this regulation.

(2) Any samples drawn or removed in breach of this regulation shall be liable to forfeiture.

Note—Para (1)(*b*) excepted from subordinate legislation (applied by the VATA 1994 s 16(1)) by the VAT Regulations, SI 1995/2518 reg 119.

PART III
RETURNS AND RECORDS

Returns

20— (1) The occupier shall complete and sign an Excise Warehouse Return and shall deliver such return to the proper officer within 14 days of the end of the stock period to which it relates.

(2) A return shall be in such form and contain such particulars of goods received into, stored in and delivered from an excise warehouse as the Commissioners direct, and different provisions may be made for goods of different classes or descriptions.

(3) The Commissioners may direct that separate returns be made in respect of goods of different classes or descriptions.

(4) The occupier shall support each return with such schedules and further information relating to the goods as the Commissioners may require.

(5) "Stock period" means one calendar month or such other period, not exceeding 5 weeks, as the proper officer, at the request of the occupier, allows.

Records to be kept

21— (1) The occupier shall, in relation to goods in an excise warehouse, keep the records prescribed by Schedule 2 to these Regulations.

(2) The proprietor of goods in an excise warehouse, or of goods which have been removed from an excise warehouse without payment of duty, or which are to be warehoused, may be required by the proper officer to keep the records prescribed by Schedule 3 to these Regulations in so far as they relate to his proprietorship of the goods.

(3) In addition to the other records required by this regulation the occupier shall, in relation to his occupation of the warehouse, keep such records of the receipt and use of goods received into the excise warehouse other than for warehousing therein as the proper officer requires.

(4) Records required by or under this regulation shall—

(*a*) be entered up promptly;

(*b*) identify the goods to which they relate;

(*c*) in the case of an occupier be kept at the warehouse;

(*d*) in the case of a proprietor be kept at his principal place of business in the United Kingdom, or at such other place as the proper officer allows; and

(*e*) be kept in such form and manner and contain such information as the Commissioners direct.

Preservation of records

22— (1) The occupier shall preserve, for not less than 3 years from the lawful removal of the goods or such shorter period as the Commissioners direct, all records which he is required to keep by virtue of regulation 21(1) above, but no record shall be destroyed until the relevant stock accounts have been balanced and any discrepancy reconciled.

(2) The proprietor shall preserve, for not less than 3 years from when he ceased to be the proprietor of the goods, or for such shorter period as the Commissioners direct, all records which he is required to keep by virtue of regulation 21(2) above.

(3) Each occupier and proprietor shall preserve all records (other than those referred to in paragraphs (1) and (2) above) kept by him for the purposes of any relevant business or activity for not less than 3 years from the events recorded in them, except that such records need not be preserved if they are records which (or records of a class which) the Commissioners have directed as not needing preservation.

(4) The requirements to preserve records imposed by paragraph (3) above may be discharged by the preservation in a form approved by the Commissioners of the information contained in those records.

Production of records

23— (1) The occupier or the proprietor shall, when required by the Commissioners, produce or cause to be produced to the proper officer any records, copy records or information which he was required by these Regulations to preserve.

(2) Production under paragraph (1) above shall—

(*a*) take place at such reasonable time as the proper officer requires; and

(*b*) take place at the excise warehouse or at such other place as the proper officer may reasonably require.

(3) The proper officer may inspect, copy or take extracts from and may remove at a reasonable time and for a reasonable period any record produced or required to be produced to him under this regulation, and the occupier and proprietor shall permit such inspection, copying, extraction and removal.

(4) Where the records required to be produced by this regulation are preserved in a form which is not readily legible, or which is legible only with the aid of equipment, the occupier or proprietor shall, if the proper officer so requires, produce a transcript or other permanently legible reproduction of the records and shall permit the proper officer to retain that reproduction.

Information for the protection of the revenue

24— (1) The occupier or the proprietor shall furnish the Commissioners with any information relating to any relevant business or activity of his which they specify as information which they think it is necessary or expedient for them to be given for the protection of the revenue.

(2) Such information shall be furnished to the Commissioners within such time, and at such place and in such form as they may reasonably require.

Further provision as to records

25 For the purposes of regulations 21 to 24 above, in relation to a proprietor—

(*a*) goods which are to be warehoused shall be treated as if they were warehoused in the warehouse to which they are being removed; and

(*b*) goods which have been removed from warehouse without payment of duty shall be treated as if they were warehoused in the warehouse from which they have been removed.

PART IV
DUTY CHARGEABLE ON WAREHOUSED GOODS

Duty chargeable on goods removed for home use

26 The duty and the rate thereof chargeable on any warehoused goods removed from an excise warehouse for home use shall be those in force for goods of that class or description at the time of their removal.

Duty chargeable on goods diverted to home use after removal without payment of duty

27— (1) The duty and the rate thereof chargeable on any goods removed from an excise warehouse without payment of duty and in respect of which duty is payable under regulation 17(1)(*c*) above shall be those in force for goods of that class or description at the time of payment of the duty.

(2) The duty and the rate thereof chargeable on any goods which have been entered for home use under regulation 18 above shall be those in force for goods of that class or description—

(*a*) where removal for home use is allowed under section 119 of the Customs and Excise Management Act 1979 on the giving of security for the duty chargeable thereon, at the time of giving of the security, or

(*b*) in any other case, at the time of payment.

Duty chargeable on missing or deficient goods

28 The duty and the rate thereof chargeable on any goods found to be missing or deficient and upon which duty is payable under section 94 of the Customs and Excise Management Act 1979 shall be those in force for goods of that class or description at the time the loss or deficiency occurred:

Provided that where that time cannot be ascertained to the proper officer's satisfaction, the rate of duty chargeable on such goods shall be the highest rate applicable thereto from the time of their deposit in the excise warehouse, or, where appropriate, from the time that the last account of them was taken, until the loss or deficiency came to the notice of the proper officer.

Calculation of duty

29— (1) Where duty is charged on any such goods as are referred to in regulation 26 above, the quantity of those goods shall be ascertained by reference to any account taken in accordance with these Regulations at the time of their removal from the excise warehouse or, if no account is taken, the quantity declared to and accepted by the proper officer as the quantity of goods being removed or, if greater, the actual quantity of goods being removed.

(2) Where duty is charged on any such goods as are referred to in regulations 27 or 28 above the quantity of such goods shall be ascertained by reference to the last account taken in accordance with these Regulations, or, if no account has been taken, the quantity declared to and accepted by the proper officer as the quantity of goods on which duty is to be charged, or, if greater, the actual quantity of goods.

Ascertainment of quantity by taking an account

30— (1) Where the quantity of warehoused goods is to be ascertained by taking an account thereof, it shall be ascertained for the purposes of these Regulations by reference to weight, measure, strength, original gravity or number as the case may require.

(2) Where under these Regulations an occupier is required to deliver a copy of an account of goods he shall deliver to the proper officer a notice giving such details of the account as the proper officer requires, and the taking of the account shall not be complete until that notice has been delivered.

PART V
ASCERTAINMENT OF DUTY BY REFERENCE TO LABELS ETC

Ascertainment of duty by reference to labels etc

31— (1) Subject to paragraph (2) of this regulation, for the purpose of charging duty on any spirits, wine or made-wine contained in any bottle or other container the strength, weight and volume of the spirits, wine or made-wine shall be ascertained conclusively by reference to any information given on the bottle or other container by means of a label, or otherwise, or by reference to any documents relating to the bottle or other container, notwithstanding any other legal provision.

(2) The method of ascertaining the strength, weight or volume, or any of them, referred to in paragraph (1) above shall not be used if another method would produce a result upon which a greater amount of duty would be charged than would be the case if the method in paragraph (1) above were used.

SCHEDULE 1
OPERATIONS WHICH MAY BE PERMITTED ON WAREHOUSED GOODS

(Regulation 14(2))

1 Sorting, separating, packing or repacking and such other operations as are necessary for the preservation, sale, shipment or disposal of the goods.

2 The rectifying and compounding of spirits.

3 The rendering sparkling of wine and made-wine.

4 The mixing of a fermented liquor or a liquor derived from a fermented liquor with any other liquor or substance so as to produce made-wine.

5 The mixing of lime or lemon juice with spirits for shipment as stores or for exportation.

6 Denaturing.

7 Reducing.

8 Marrying.

9 Blending.

SCHEDULE 2
RECORDS TO BE KEPT BY THE OCCUPIER

(Regulation 21(1))

Records of

(*a*) goods deposited in the excise warehouse, from where and from whom received, and date of warehousing;

[(*aa*) any certificate or other document that accompanied beer that contained a statement of the amount of beer produced in the brewery where the beer was produced;][1]

Amendments—[1] This paragraph inserted by the Beer and Excise Warehousing (Amendment) Regulations, SI 2002/1265 reg 3(1), (2) with effect from 1 June 2002.

(*b*) goods removed from the excise warehouse, the purpose of the removal, date of removal and (if the purpose of the removal is other than for home use) the place to which the goods are removed;
(*c*) stock of warehoused goods;
(*d*) deficiencies and increases in stock;
(*e*) operations performed;
(*f*) deficiencies and increases in operation;
(*g*) accounts taken of goods deposited in the excise warehouse, removed from the excise warehouse, put into operation, received from operation, and of stocks in the excise warehouse;
(*h*) samples drawn from warehoused goods, samples removed from warehouse, and the person to whom samples are delivered;
(*i*) the manner in which duty is paid or accounted for when goods chargeable with duty are removed for home use;
(*j*) the manner in which security is given when goods chargeable with duty are removed for purposes other than home use, and the dates when certificates of receipt or shipment are received;
(*k*) notices delivered to the proper officer and of the manner and time of delivery;
(*l*) times when the excise warehouse is opened and closed;
(*m*) names and titles of keyholders to the excise warehouse;
(*n*) the name and address of the proprietor of each lot or parcel of goods, and of changes of proprietorship.

SCHEDULE 3

RECORDS WHICH THE PROPRIETOR MAY BE REQUIRED TO KEEP

(Regulation 21(2))

Records of

(*a*) goods which are to be warehoused in an excise warehouse;
(*b*) goods which have been warehoused in an excise warehouse;
(*c*) goods which have been removed from an excise warehouse otherwise than for home use on payment of the duty chargeable, and all movements of such goods;
(*d*) his stock of goods in each excise warehouse;
(*e*) operations performed;
(*f*) samples drawn, removed from warehouse and, where that removal is other than on payment of the duty chargeable, their use, location and disposal;
(*g*) the time and manner in which the duty chargeable on goods to which regulation 21(2) relates is paid, secured or accounted for.

Note—Sch 4, as inserted by SI 2002/501 reg 27(1), (4), has not been reproduced.

[SCHEDULE 5

PARTICULARS WHICH MUST BE CONTAINED IN A DOCUMENT

Regulation 10A

1 Date of entry of the goods and their entry number.

2 Importer's name and address.

3 The name, address and approval number of the excise warehouse to which the goods are to be moved.

4 A description of the goods and their quantity.]

Amendments—This Schedule inserted by the Excise Warehousing (Etc) (Amendment) Regulations, SI 2008/2832 regs 2, 3(2) with effect from 1 December 2008.

1989/472

Value Added Tax (Self-supply of Construction Services) Order 1989

Made by the Treasury under VATA 1983 ss 3(6), (8) and 29(2) (see now VATA 1994 ss 5(6), (8) and 43(2))

Made	*14 March 1989*
Laid before the House of Commons	*14 March 1989*
Coming into force	*1 April 1989*

1 This Order may be cited as the Value Added Tax (Self-supply of Construction Services) Order 1989 and shall come into force on 1st April 1989.

2 In this Order "the Act" means the Value Added Tax Act 1983 [VATA 1994].

3— (1) Where a person, in the course or furtherance of a business carried on by him, for the purpose of that business and otherwise than for a consideration, performs any of the following services, that is to say—

(*a*) the construction of a building; or

(*b*) the extension or other alteration of, or the construction of an annexe to, any building such that additional floor area of not less than 10 per cent of the floor area of the original building is created; or

(*c*) the construction of any civil engineering work; or

(*d*) in connection with any such services as are described in sub-paragraph (*a*), (*b*) or (*c*) above, the carrying out of any demolition work contemporaneously with or preparatory thereto,

then, subject to each of the conditions specified in paragraph (2) below being satisfied, those services shall be treated for the purposes of the Act as both supplied to him for the purpose of that business and supplied by him in the course or furtherance of it.

(2) The conditions mentioned in paragraph (1) above are that—

(*a*) the value of such services is not less than £100,000; and

(*b*) such services would, if supplied for a consideration in the course or furtherance of a business carried on by a taxable person, be chargeable to tax at a rate other than nil.

(3) The preceding provisions of this article shall apply in relation to any bodies corporate which are treated for the purposes of section 29 of the Act[a] as members of a group as if those bodies were one person, but anything done which would fall to be treated by virtue of this Order as services supplied to and by that person shall be treated as supplied to and by the representative member.

Note—[a] VATA 1994 s 43.

4— (1) The value of any supply of services which is to be treated as taking place by virtue of this Order is the open market value of such services.

(2) Where any services of a description specified in article 3(1) above are in the process of being performed on the day this Order comes into force, the value of such services for the purposes of this Order shall be the value of such part of those services as are performed on or after that day.

1989/1114
Value Added Tax (Water) Order 1989

Made by the Treasury under VATA 1983 s 3(3) (see now VATA 1994 s 5(3)) and all other enabling powers

Made . . . . *3 July 1989*
Laid before the House of Commons . . . . . *11 July 1989*
Coming into force . . . . *1 August 1989*

1 This Order may be cited as the Value Added Tax (Water) Order 1989 and shall come into force on 1st August 1989.

2 The supply of water insofar as it is not otherwise a supply of goods shall be treated as a supply of goods and not as a supply of services.

1990/2167
Channel Tunnel (Customs and Excise) Order 1990

Made by the Commissioners of Customs and Excise under the Channel Tunnel Act 1987 ss 11(1)(*a*), (*c*), (*d*), (*g*), (*h*), 11(2), 11(3)(*a*), (*d*), 13(1) and (2) and all other enabling powers

Made . . . . *1 November 1990*
Laid before Parliament . . . . *9 November 1990*
Coming into force . . . . *1 December 1990*

Citation and commencement

1 This Order may be cited as the Channel Tunnel (Customs and Excise) Order 1990 and shall come into force on 1st December 1990.

Interpretation

2— (1) In this Order—

"the Act of 1979" means the Customs and Excise Management Act 1979;

"the Act of 1987" means the Channel Tunnel Act 1987;

"customs approved area" has the meaning given by article 3(1) below;

"the tunnel" except in the expression "tunnel system" means that part of the tunnel system comprising the tunnels specified in section 1(7)(*a*) of the Act 1987 or any of those tunnels.

(2) In this Order the following expressions have the meanings assigned to them by section 1 of the Act of 1979:

"approved wharf";

"the boundary";

"commander";

"the Commissioners";

"the customs and excise Acts";

"customs and excise airport";
"goods";
"officer";
"owner";
"port";
["proper";][1]
"ship";
"shipped" and cognate expressions.

(3)–(5) …

Amendments—[1] Words in para (2) inserted by Channel Tunnel (International Arrangements) Order, SI 1993/1813 art 8 Sch 5 Pt II paras 7, 8(*a*) with effect from 2 August 1993.
Note—Paras (3)–(5) outside the scope of the coverage of legislation in this handbook.

Channel tunnel customs approved areas

3 …

Note—This article is outside the scope of the coverage of legislation in this handbook.

Modification of the Act of 1979

4 The Act of 1979 shall be modified in accordance with the provisions of the Schedule to this Order.

Time of importation, exportation etc

5 …

Note—This article is outside the scope of the coverage of legislation in this handbook.

SCHEDULE
MODIFICATIONS OF THE ACT OF 1979

Article 4

[Part II of the Act of 1979: Administration

A1 In section 17(1) (disposal of duties, etc) the reference to Great Britain shall be construed as including a reference to a control zone in France [or Belgium][1].]

Part III of the Act of 1979: Customs and Excise Control Areas

[A2— (1) For the purposes of section 21 (control of movement of aircraft, etc, into and out of the United Kingdom) references to an aircraft shall be treated as including references to a through train, and in relation to such trains section 21 shall be construed in accordance with sub-paragraphs (2) to (5).

(2) References to a customs and excise airport shall be construed as references to a terminal control point or a place which is a customs approved area.

(3) References to a flight shall be construed as references to a journey, and the reference in section 21(4) to flying shall be construed accordingly.

(4) References to landing shall be construed as references to stopping for the purpose of enabling passengers or crew to board or leave the train or goods to be loaded onto or unloaded from it.

(5) References to the commander of an aircraft shall be construed as references to the train manager of a train.][2]

Amendments—[1] Paras A1, A2 inserted by Channel Tunnel (International Agreements) Order, SI 1993/1813 art 8 Sch 5 Pt II para 11 with effect from 2 August 1993.
[2] Words in para A1 inserted by Channel Tunnel (Miscellaneous Provisions) Order, SI 1994/1405 art 8 Sch 4 para 7 as from a day to be appointed.

Part IV of the Act of 1979: Control of Importation

6 In section 42(1)(*a*) (power to regulate the unloading, removal, etc of imported goods) the reference to a ship arriving at a port shall be construed as including a reference to a vehicle arriving [at a place which is a customs approved area either in France or through the tunnel from France][1] at a customs approved area through the tunnel from France.

[7 In section 49(1) (forfeiture of goods improperly imported)—

(*a*) the reference in paragraph (*a*)(ii) to goods unloaded from any aircraft in the United Kingdom shall be construed as including a reference to goods unloaded from a through train or shuttle train which has brought them into the United Kingdom and a reference to goods otherwise brought through the tunnel into the United Kingdom; and

(*b*) the reference in paragraph (*c*) to goods found to have been concealed on board any aircraft shall be construed as including references to goods found concealed—

(i) on a through train or shuttle train has brought them into the United Kingdom,
(ii) on a through train while it constitutes a control zone in France [or Belgium][2], or
(iii) in a road vehicle in a control zone in France within the tunnel system.][1]

8 Section 50(2) (penalty for improper importation of goods) shall have effect as if—

(*a*) any person who unloads or assists or is otherwise concerned in the unloading of those goods mentioned in section 50(1) from any vehicle which has arrived from France through the tunnel [or Belgium][2][, or who brings or assists or is otherwise concerned in the bringing of such goods into a control zone in France [or Belgium][2],][1] were a person who unships such goods in a port; and

(*b*) any person who removes or assists or is otherwise concerned in the removal of such goods from any customs approved area were a person who removes such goods from an approved wharf.

Part XI of the Act of 1979: Detention of Persons, Forfeiture and Legal Proceedings

22 In section 146(1) (service of process) the reference in paragraph (*c*) to an aircraft shall be construed as including a reference to a vehicle which has arrived from or is departing to France through the tunnel[, and in relation to such a vehicle the second reference to the United Kingdom shall be construed as including a reference to a control zone in France within the tunnel system][1].

23 In section 154(2) (proof of certain other matters) any reference to goods loaded or to be loaded into or unloaded from an aircraft shall be construed respectively as including references to goods loaded or to be loaded onto or unloaded from a vehicle which is departing to or has arrived from France through the tunnel.

24 In section 159(1) (power to examine and take account of goods) the reference in paragraph (*c*) to goods which have been loaded into a ship shall be construed as including a reference to goods which have been loaded onto a vehicle for exportation through the tunnel.

[25 The persons to whom section 164 (search of persons) applies shall be taken to include any person who is—

(*a*) in the tunnel system in the United Kingdom;
(*b*) in a through train in the United Kingdom;
(*c*) in, entering or leaving a customs approved area in the United Kingdom; or
(*d*) in a control zone in France [or Belgium][2]].[1]

Amendments—[1] Words in paras 6, 8(*a*), 22 inserted, and paras 7, 25 substituted, by Channel Tunnel (International Arrangements) Order, SI 1993/1813 arts 1, 8 Sch 5 Pt II paras 19–21, 32, 33, with effect from 2 August 1993.
[2] Words in paras 7(*b*)(ii); 8(*a*), 25(*d*) inserted by Channel Tunnel (Miscellaneous Provisions) Order, SI 1994/1405 arts 1, 8 Sch 4 para 7 as from a day to be appointed.

1991/2306

Value Added Tax (Input Tax) (Person Supplied) Order 1991

Amendment—This Order revoked by the VAT (Input Tax) (Person Supplied) Order, SI 2005/3291 with effect from 1 January 2006.

1991/2724

Customs Controls on Importation of Goods Regulations 1991

Made by the Commissioners of Customs and Excise under the European Communities Act 1972 s 2(2) and all other enabling powers

Made . . . . *4 December 1991*
Laid before the House of Commons . . . . . *11 December 1991*
Coming into force . . . . *1 January 1992*

Note—Amending provisions and provisions outside the scope of this Handbook have not been reproduced.

Citation and commencement

1 These Regulations may be cited as the Customs Controls on Importation of Goods Regulations 1991 and shall come into force on 1st January 1992.

Interpretation

2 In these Regulations—

"the Act" means the Customs and Excise Management Act 1979;
"the Commissioners" means the Commissioners of Customs and Excise;
"the Council Regulation" means [Council Regulation (EEC) No 2913/92][1];
["the Commission Regulation" means the Commission Regulation (EEC) No 2454/93][1]
"the customs and excise Acts" has the same meaning as in section 1(1) of the Act.

Amendments—[1] Words substituted and definition "the Commission Regulation" inserted by Community Customs Code (Consequential Amendment of References) Regulations, SI 1993/3014 reg 4(1), (2) with effect from 1 January 1994.

Presentation

3— (1) Notification to the Commissioners of the arrival of goods as required by [Article 40][1], of the Council Regulation shall be made in the form prescribed in Schedule 1 or a form to the like effect approved by the Commissioners.

(2) Where a computerised inventory system has been approved by the Commissioners presentation may consist in a computerised record capable of being printed out.

(3) Within three hours of its arrival at the wharf or airport at which a ship or aircraft carrying the goods is to unload them, notification of such arrival, as required by [Article 40][1], of the Council Regulation shall be made at the customs office for the wharf or airport; should such notification be impossible due to the office being closed during that period, the period shall end at the expiration of one hour following the re-opening of the office.

Amendments—[1] Words in paras (1), (3) substituted by Community Customs Code (Consequential Amendment of References) Regulations, SI 1993/3014 reg 4(1), (3), (4) with effect from 1 January 1994.

Summary declaration

4 The summary declaration required under [Article 43][1] of the Council Regulation shall be in the form prescribed in Schedule 2 or a form to the like effect approved by the Commissioners.

Amendments—[1] Words substituted by Community Customs Code (Consequential Amendment of References) Regulations, SI 1993/3014 reg 4(1), (5) with effect from 1 January 1994.

Entry

5— (1) For the purposes of [Article 49][2] of the Council Regulation the goods shall be entered not later than—

(*a*) [forty-five][1] days from the date on which the summary declaration is lodged in the case of goods carried by sea; or

(*b*) [twenty][1] days from the date on which the summary declaration is lodged in the case of goods carried otherwise than by sea.

(2) The entry shall be delivered by the importer to the proper officer …[1]

(3) Except with the permission of the Commissioners no entry shall be delivered before the goods have been presented at the proper office of customs and excise.

(4) Where the Commissioners permit an entry to be delivered before presentation of the goods, the goods must be presented to the proper office of customs and excise within such time as the Commissioners may allow; and if the goods are not so presented the entry shall be treated as not having been delivered.

(5) Acceptance of an entry by the proper officer shall be signified in such manner as the Commissioners may direct.

Amendments—[1] Word in paras (1)(*a*), (*b*) substituted and words in para (2) revoked by Customs and Excise (Single Market etc) Regulations, SI 1992/3095 reg 7(*a*) with effect from 1 January 1993.

[2] Words in para (1) substituted by Community Customs Code (Consequential Amendment of References) Regulations, SI 1993/3014 reg 4(1), (6) with effect from 1 January 1994.

1991/2727
Free Zone Regulations 1991

Made by the Commissioners of Customs and Excise under the European Communities Act 1972 s 2(2) and all other enabling powers

Made . . . . *4 December 1991*
Laid before Parliament . . . . *11 December 1991*
Coming into force . . . . *1 January 1992*

Citation and commencement

1 These Regulations may be cited as the Free Zone Regulations 1991 and shall come into force on 1st January 1992.

Interpretation

2 In these Regulations—

"the Act" means the Customs and Excise Management Act 1979;

"the customs and excise Acts" has the same meaning as in section 1(1) of the Act;

"relevant Community provision" means any provision of a Community Regulation specified in the first and second columns of the Schedule.

Repeals

3— (1) Subject to paragraph (2) below, the following sections of the Act are hereby repealed—

section 100B (free zone regulations),
section 100C (free zone goods: customs duties, etc), except for subsection (4),
section 100D (free zone regulations: supplemental), and
section 100E (control of trading in free zones).

(2) This regulation shall not have effect in relation to the application of the following provisions of the Act by virtue of section 24(1) of the Value Added Tax Act 1983—

section 100B (free zone regulations),

section 100C(1) (free zone goods) insofar as the subsection purports to apply to goods chargeable with customs duty, and
section 100C(3) (scope of free zone regulations).

Amendments

4, 5 (*amend* CEMA 1979 ss 1(1), 100C(4)).

Offences, penalty and forfeiture

6 In the event of any contravention or failure to comply with—

(*a*) any relevant Community provision; or
(*b*) any requirement or condition imposed by or under any such provision; or
(*c*) any undertaking given pursuant to any such provision or requirement; or
(*d*) any regulation made under section 100B of the Act in its continued application by virtue of regulation 3(2) above; or
(*e*) any regulation made under section 100C(4) of the Act,

the person responsible for the contravention or failure shall be liable on summary conviction to a penalty of level 3 on the standard scale together with a penalty of £40 for each day on which the contravention or failure continues and any goods in respect of which the offence was committed shall be liable to forfeiture.

Supplementary

7— (1) Section 139 of and Schedule 3 to the Act (detention, seizure and condemnation of goods) shall apply to any goods where liable to forfeiture under regulation 6 above as if the goods were liable to forfeiture under the customs and excise Acts.

(2) Sections 144 to 148 and 150 to 155 of the Act (proceedings for offences, mitigation of penalties, proof and other matters) shall apply in relation to offences and penalties under regulation 6 above and proceedings for such offences or for condemnation of any thing as being forfeited under that regulation as they apply in relation to offences and penalties and proceedings for offences or for condemnation under the customs and excise Acts.

[SCHEDULE

RELEVANT COMMUNITY PROVISIONS

Regulation 2

(1) *Community Regulation*	(2) *Relevant Provision*	(3) *Subject Matter of Provision*
Council Regulation (EEC) No 2913/92	Article 59	All goods intended to be placed under a customs procedure shall be covered by a declaration for that customs procedure
	Article 101(*a*)	Warehousekeeper to ensure that goods in warehouse are not removed from customs supervision
	Article 101(*b*)	Warehousekeeper to fulfil obligations arising from storage of goods
	Article 101(*c*)	Warehousekeeper to comply with conditions of authorisation
	Article 105	Designated person to keep stock records in approved form
	Article 110	Temporary removal requires authorisation
	Article 111	Transfer requires authorisation
Commission Regulation (EEC) No 2454/93	Article 513	Failure to make presentation of goods and lodge declaration
	Article 269	Authorised use of simplified procedures
	Article 517	Stock records to be made available to the supervising office
	Articles 522, 523 and 532	Authorisation for usual forms of handling
	Article 527	Inventory to be furnished when required

(1) *Community Regulation*	(2) *Relevant Provision*	(3) *Subject Matter of Provision*
	Articles 223, 528 and 864	Treatment without customs approved formalities
	Articles 529–534	Requirement for export declaration
	Article 536	Customs status and identification of Community goods.][1]

Amendments—[1] This Schedule substituted by Community Customs Code (Consequential Amendment of References) Regulations, SI 1993/3014 Sch 1 with effect from 1 January 1994.

1992/630
Value Added Tax (Treatment of Transactions) Order 1992

Made by the Treasury, under VATA 1983 s 3(3) (see now VATA 1994 s 5(3)) and all other enabling powers

Made . . . . *10 March 1992*
Laid before the House of Commons . . . . *10 March 1992*
Coming into force . . . . *1 April 1992*

1 This Order may be cited as the Value Added Tax (Treatment of Transactions) Order 1992 and shall come into force on 1st April 1992.

2 Where an employer gives an employee a choice between—

(*a*) a particular rate of wages, salary or emoluments, or

(*b*) in the alternative a lower rate of wages, salary or emoluments and, in addition, the right to the private use of a motor car provided by the employer,

and the employee chooses the alternative described in paragraph (*b*) above, then the provision to the employee of the right to use the motor car privately shall be treated as neither a supply of goods nor a supply of services (if it otherwise would be) to the extent only that the consideration for the provision of the motor car for the employee's private use is the difference between the wages, salary or emoluments available to him under paragraphs (*a*) and (*b*) of this article.

1992/2790
Statistics of Trade (Customs and Excise) Regulations 1992

Made by the Commissioners of Customs and Excise under the European Communities Act 1972 s 2(2) and all other enabling powers

Made . . . . *6 November 1992*
Laid before parliament . . . . *10 November 1992*
Coming into force . . . . *1 December 1992*

Commentary—*De Voil Indirect Tax Service* **V5.276**.
Cross references—See Commission Regulation 3046/92/EEC of 22 October 1992.

Citation, commencement and interpretation

1— (1) These Regulations may be cited as the Statistics of Trade (Customs and Excise) Regulations 1992 and shall come into force on 1st December 1992.

(2) In these Regulations—

"the Act" means the Customs and Excise Management Act 1979;

. . .[1]

. . .[3]

"authorised person" means any person acting under the authority of the Commissioners;

. . .[1]

. . .[3]

"document" includes in addition to a document in writing—

(*a*) any photograph;

(*b*) any disc, tape, sound track or other device in which sounds or other data (not being visual images) are recorded so as to be capable (with or without the aid of some other equipment) of being reproduced therefrom; and

(*c*) any film, negative, tape or other device in which one or more visual images are recorded so as to be capable (as aforesaid) of being reproduced therefrom;

"film" includes a microfilm;

. . .[3]

["Intrastat" refers to the data collection system established and implemented by—

(*a*) Council and European Parliament Regulation (EC) No 638/2004 ("establishing Regulation"); and (*b*) Commission Regulation (EC) No 1982/2004 ("implementing Regulation");][2]

. . .[4]

["periodic declaration" refers to the means of providing the simplified information in regulations 3(1) and 3(2) (VAT return) or to a supplementary declaration in regulation 4;][2]

. . .[3]

. . .[1]

. . .[3]

(3) In these Regulations, unless defined above, words and expressions shall have the meanings assigned to them by section 1 of the Act [or have the same meaning as in the establishing or implementing Regulation][2].

Amendments—[1] Definitions in para (2) revoked by Statistics of Trade (Customs and Excise) (Amendment) Regulations, SI 1997/2864 with effect from 1 January 1998 (previously inserted by Statistics of Trade (Customs and Excise) (Amendment) Regulations, SI 1993/541 reg 3).

[2] In para (2), definition of "Intrastat" substituted for that of "Intrastat system", and definition of "periodic declaration" substituted; and words in para (3) inserted; by the Statistics of Trade (Customs and Excise) (Amendment) Regulations, SI 2004/3284 regs 1(3), 2 with effect from 1 January 2005.

[3] Definitions revoked by SI 2004/3284 regs 1(3), 5, Schedule with effect from 1 January 2005. The revoked definitions are those of "arrival stage", "assimilation threshold", "dispatch stage", "goods", "Member State", "Principal Regulation", "reference period", "register of intra-Community operators", "supplementary declaration" and "Threshold Regulation".

[Application of Intrastat

2— (1) For the purposes of the United Kingdom's statistical territory (see Article 4(1) of the establishing Regulation), Intrastat is under the care and management of the Commissioners of Customs and Excise (the "Commissioners").

(2) For the purposes mentioned in paragraph (1), the Commissioners are—

(*a*) "customs" within Article 5(2) of the establishing Regulation (provision to national authority of statistical information on other goods at least once a month);

(*b*) the "national authority" within—

(i) Articles 5(2), 8(1), 8(2), 9(1) and 11 of the establishing Regulation (other goods, etc; register of intra-Community operators; identification of parties responsible for providing information; information that must be collected; statistical confidentiality); and

(ii) Articles 5, 13(4), 17(4), 21(4), 22(4) and 23(2) of the implementing Regulation (identification of persons who have declared goods for fiscal purposes; simplification for certain individual transactions; access to additional data sources in the case of vessels and aircraft, sea products, spacecraft and electricity);

(*c*) the "tax administration" within—

(i) Articles 8(2) and 8(3) of the establishing Regulation (duty to furnish lists of persons who have declared that they have supplied goods to or acquired goods from other Member States; duty to furnish information provided for fiscal purposes which could improve quality of statistics; duty to bring the Intrastat obligations to the attention of VAT-registered traders); and

(ii) Article 5 of the implementing Regulation (duty to provide specified information to identify persons who have declared goods for fiscal purposes).

(3) Also, for the purposes mentioned in paragraph (1), the duties or discretions expressed in the following Articles as those of the "Member States" must be performed or exercised by the Commissioners—

(*a*) Articles 10(6), 12 and 13 of the establishing Regulation (sending information on thresholds to Commission; transmission of that data; quality of that data and yearly quality report to Commission); and

(*b*) Articles 10, 16(2), 18, 19(3), 20(3), 23(3), 24(2), 25(2), 25(4) to 25(7) and 26(1) of the implementing Regulation (reporting nature of transaction; application of specific rules for staggered consignments, motor vehicle and aircraft parts, goods delivered to vessels and aircraft, offshore installations, electricity, military goods; transmission of data to Commission; yearly quality report to Commission).

(4) The Commissioners may do anything necessary for and reasonably incidental to any Article mentioned in paragraphs (2) and (3).

This paragraph is additional to any other basis for their doing so.

(5) For the purposes of Article 9 of the establishing Regulation (information that must or may be collected), the Commissioners must only collect information in accordance with Regulations 3, 4 and 4A (simplified information and supplementary declaration).][1]

Amendments—[1] Regulations 2–4A substituted for regulations 2–4 by the Statistics of Trade (Customs and Excise) (Amendment) Regulations, SI 2004/3284 regs 1(3), 3 with effect from 1 January 2005.

[Information collected on the value added tax return][2]

[3— (1) The Commissioners may treat the following information collected in accordance with regulations made under section 58 of, and Schedule 11 paragraphs 2(1) and 2(11) to, the Value Added Tax Act 1994 (information collected on the VAT return) for Intrastat purposes (see Article 10(1) of the establishing Regulation)—

(*a*) information about the value of supplies of goods and related costs to other Member States;

(*b*) information about the value of acquisitions of goods and related costs from other Member States.

(2) If a party's annual value of intra-Community trade is at or below [£270,000][3], that party may be treated as exempt from providing Intrastat information and is not subject to regulation 4 (supplementary declarations) (and see Article 10(1) of the establishing Regulation).][2]

(3) The threshold in paragraph (2) separately applies to a party's responsibilities for providing information about "dispatches" and "arrivals" (see Articles 3, 7 and 10(2) of the establishing Regulation).][1]

Amendments—[1] Regulations 2–4A substituted for regulations 2–4 by the Statistics of Trade (Customs and Excise) (Amendment) Regulations, SI 2004/3284 regs 1(3), 3 with effect from 1 January 2005.

[2] Heading, and paras (1), (2) substituted by the Statistics of Trade (Customs and Excise) (Amendment) Regulations, SI 2006/3216 regs 2, 3 with effect from 1 January 2007.

[3] In para (2) figure substituted by the Statistics of Trade (Customs and Excise) (Amendment) (No 2) Regulations, SI 2008/2847 reg 2(1), (2) with effect from 1 January 2009.

[Supplementary declarations

[4— (1) A party that in relation to the United Kingdom is responsible for providing the information (see Article 7 of the establishing Regulation) must, save as otherwise directed by the Commissioners under paragraph (6A), provide it to the Commissioners in the appropriate form set out in the Schedule to these Regulations ("supplementary declaration" for "arrivals" or "dispatches").

That party must provide all the information sought by the appropriate form, in accordance with the establishing and implementing Regulations.][2]

(2) But that party need provide the "delivery terms" information sought by the appropriate form only if that party's annual value of intra-Community trade relevant to that form (namely, value of "arrivals" or value of "dispatches") exceeds [£16,000,000][3].

That party must use the coding mentioned in Article 11 of the implementing Regulation in providing any "delivery terms" information pursuant to paragraph (1) and this paragraph (and see also Article 9(2)(d) of the establishing Regulation).

(3) That party must deliver the completed supplementary declaration to the Commissioners no later than the final day of the month following the end of the reference period to which it relates.

Only the reference period in Article 6(1) of the establishing Regulation applies in relation to the supplementary declaration ("calendar month of dispatch or arrival of the goods").

But the reference periods in Article 3 of the implementing Regulation may be used instead if a current Commissioners' direction so permits in the interests of better administration ("calendar month" of "chargeable event" or in which "declaration is accepted").

(4) That party must deliver that supplementary declaration—

(*a*) to a place specified in a current Commissioners' direction, or

(*b*) by means of electronic communication.

(5) A supplementary declaration sent by post is not presumed to have been delivered without proof of its posting.

(6) That party may only deliver the supplementary declaration by means of electronic communication—

(*a*) if the party applies to do so and the Commissioners approve the application, or

(*b*) in accordance with any current Commissioners' direction permitting that party to do so in such circumstances as the direction may specify.

[(6A) A party that delivers the supplementary declaration by means of electronic communication must do so in the appropriate form as directed from time to time by the Commissioners.][2]

(7) The Commissioners may at any time for reasonable cause revoke or vary any approval under paragraph (6)(*a*).

(8) A direction under paragraph (6)(*b*) may include any conditions the Commissioners deem necessary or expedient for the purpose.

(9) A direction under paragraph (3), (4)(*a*)[, (6)(*b*) or (6A)][2] is not current for the purposes of the relevant paragraph to the extent that it is varied, replaced or revoked by another Commissioners' direction.][1]

Amendments—[1] Regulations 2–4A substituted for regulations 2–4 by the Statistics of Trade (Customs and Excise) (Amendment) Regulations, SI 2004/3284 regs 1(3), 3 with effect from 1 January 2005.

[2] Para (1), and words in para (9), substituted, and para (6A) inserted, by the Statistics of Trade (Customs and Excise) (Amendment) Regulations, SI 2006/3216 regs 2, 4–7 with effect from 1 January 2007.

[3] In para (2) figure substituted by the Statistics of Trade (Customs and Excise) (Amendment) (No 2) Regulations, SI 2008/2847 reg 2(1), (3) with effect from 1 January 2009.

[Administration of rules concerning specific goods and movements

4A— (1) The Commissioners must give directions as to matters of administration for the proper application of these Regulations in the case of the rules set out in Articles 16, 17, 19, 20, 21, 22, 23 and 24 of the implementing Regulation (rules concerning specific goods and movements –

staggered consignments, vessels and aircraft, goods delivered to vessels and aircraft, offshore installations, sea products, spacecraft, electricity, military goods).

(2) The Commissioners may give such a direction in the case of the rules set out in Articles 15 and 18 of that Regulation (industrial plant, motor vehicle and aircraft parts).

(3) Regulation 4 (supplementary declarations) is subject to every current direction under this regulation.

(4) A direction is not current for the purposes of paragraph (3) to the extent that it is varied, replaced or revoked by another such direction.][1]

Amendments—[1] Regulations 2–4A substituted for regulations 2–4 by the Statistics of Trade (Customs and Excise) (Amendment) Regulations, SI 2004/3284 regs 1(3), 3 with effect from 1 January 2005.

Duty to keep and retain records

5— (1) Every person who is mentioned in the register of intra-Community operators, shall—

(*a*) keep a copy of every periodic declaration …[1] he makes [or delivers or which is made or delivered][2] on his behalf;

(*b*) keep copies of all documents which he or anyone acting on his behalf used for the purpose of compiling [his periodic declarations][1];

(*c*) produce or cause to be produced [periodic declarations and documents][1] mentioned in paragraphs (*a*) and (*b*) above when required to do so by an authorised person;

(*d*) permit an authorised person exercising the powers mentioned in paragraph (*c*) above to make [copies or extracts of those periodic declarations and documents][1] or to remove them for a reasonable period.

(2) The Commissioners may require [periodic declarations and documents][1] mentioned in paragraph (1) above to be preserved for such period not exceeding six years as they may require.

(3) For the purpose of exercising any powers granted by this regulation an authorised person may at any reasonable time enter premises used in connection with the carrying on of a business by a person mentioned in the register of intra-Community operators or another person compiling periodic declarations on his behalf.

Amendments—[1] Words in para (1)(*a*) revoked and words in paras (1)(*b*), (*c*), (*d*), (2) substituted by Statistics of Trade (Customs and Excise) (Amendment) Regulations, SI 1997/2864 reg 6 with effect from 1 January 1998.
[2] Words in para (1)(*a*) substituted by the Statistics of Trade (Customs and Excise) (Amendment) Regulations, SI 2004/3284 regs 1(3), 4(1) with effect from 1 January 2005.

Offences and evidence

6— (1) If any person required to [deliver][2] a supplementary declaration in accordance with [these Regulations][2] fails to do so he shall be liable on summary conviction to a penalty not exceeding level 4 on the standard scale.

(2) Any failure to [deliver][2] a supplementary declaration includes a failure to [provide][2] such supplementary declaration in the form and manner required by these Regulations …[3].

(3) Subject to paragraph (4) below, for the purpose of the rules against charging more than one offence in the same information—

(*a*) failure to [deliver][2] one or more supplementary declarations of trade in goods dispatched to other Member States for any given reference period shall constitute one offence; and

(*b*) failure to [deliver][2] one or more supplementary declarations of trade in goods [arriving][2] from other Member States for any given reference period shall constitute one offence.

(4) If the failure in respect of which a person is convicted under paragraph (1) above is continued after the conviction he shall be guilty of a further offence and may on summary conviction thereof be punished accordingly.

(5) …[3]

(5A) …[1]

(6) …[3]

(7) In any proceedings for an offence mentioned in this regulation it shall be a defence for the accused to prove that he took all reasonable precautions and exercised all due diligence to avoid the commission of such an offence by himself, any person under his control or any person to whom he transferred the task of providing information in accordance with [and subject to Article 7(2) of the establishing Regulation][2].

Amendments—[1] Para (5A) and words in para (6) revoked by Statistics of Trade (Customs and Excise) (Amendment) Regulations, SI 1997/2864 reg 7 with effect from 1 January 1998.
[2] Words in paras (1), (2), (3), (7) substituted by the Statistics of Trade (Customs and Excise) (Amendment) Regulations, SI 2004/3284 regs 1(3), 4(2)–(6) with effect in relation to acts, or omissions, occurring after 31 December 2004.
[3] Words in para (2) revoked, and paras (5), (6) revoked, by SI 2004/3284 regs 1(3), 5, Schedule with effect from 1 January 2005.

7— (1) In any legal proceedings, whether civil or criminal, where any question arises concerning a document furnished[, provided, delivered][2] or created for the purposes of the Intrastat system this regulation shall apply.

(2) Where any document does not consist of legible visual images its …[1] content may be proved in any proceedings by production of a copy of the information in the form of legible visual images.

Amendments—[1] Words in para (2) revoked by Statistics of Trade (Customs and Excise) (Amendment) Regulations, SI 1993/541 reg 7 with effect from 1 April 1993.

[2] Words in para (1) inserted by the Statistics of Trade (Customs and Excise) (Amendment) Regulations, SI 2004/3284 regs 1(3), 4(7) with effect in relation to acts, or omissions, occurring after 31 December 2004.

8— (1) A certificate of the Commissioners—

(*a*) that a person was or was not a party responsible for providing information in accordance with the Intrastat system;

(*b*) that a person was or was not mentioned in the register of intra-Community operators;

(*c*) that any information required for purposes connected with the Intrastat system has not been given or had not been given at any date;

(*d*) that a copy produced in accordance with paragraph (2) of regulation 7 above is, both as to form and content, identical to that received by electronic means in accordance with [regulations 4(4)(*b*) and 4(6)][1] above

shall be sufficient evidence of that fact until the contrary is proved.

(2) A photograph of any document furnished[, provided or delivered][1] to the Commissioners for the purposes of these Regulations and certified by them to be such a photograph shall be admissible in any proceedings, whether civil or criminal, to the same extent as the document itself.

(3) Any document purporting to be a certificate under paragraph (1) or (2) above shall be deemed to be such a certificate until the contrary is proved.

Amendments—[1] Words in para (1)(*d*) substituted, and words in para (2) inserted, by the Statistics of Trade (Customs and Excise) (Amendment) Regulations, SI 2004/3284 regs 1(3), 4(8), (9) with effect in relation to acts, or omissions, occurring after 31 December 2004.

Access to recorded information

9— (1) Where, on an application by an authorised person, a justice of the peace or, in Scotland, a justice (within the meaning of section 462 of the Criminal Procedure (Scotland) Act 1975) is satisfied that there are reasonable grounds for believing—

(*a*) that an offence in connection with the Intrastat system is being, has been or is about to be committed, and

(*b*) that any recorded information (including any document of any nature whatsoever) which may be required as evidence for the purpose of any proceedings in respect of such an offence is in the possession of any person,

he may make an order in accordance with this regulation.

(2) An order made in accordance with this regulation is an order that the person who appears to the justice to be in possession of the recorded information to which the application relates shall—

(*a*) give an authorised person access to it, and

(*b*) permit an authorised person to remove and take away any of it which he reasonably considers necessary,

not later than the end of the period of seven days beginning on the date of the order or the end of such longer period as the order may specify.

(3) The reference in sub-paragraph (2)(*a*) above to giving an authorised person access to the recorded information to which the application relates includes a reference to permitting the authorised person to take copies of it or to make extracts from it.

(4) Where the recorded information consists of information contained in a computer, an order made in accordance with this regulation shall have effect as an order to produce the information in a form in which it is visible and legible and, if the authorised person wishes to remove it, in a form in which it can be removed.

10— (1) An authorised person who removes anything in the exercise of a power conferred by or under regulation 9 above shall, if so requested by a person showing himself—

(*a*) to be the occupier of premises from which it was removed, or

(*b*) to have had custody or control of it immediately before the removal,

provide that person with a record of what he removed.

(2) The authorised person shall provide the record within a reasonable time from the making of the request for it.

(3) Subject to paragraph (7) below, if a request for permission to be granted access to anything which—

(*a*) has been removed by an authorised person, and

(*b*) is retained by the Commissioners for the purpose of investigating an offence, is made to the officer in overall charge of the investigation by a person who had custody or control of the thing immediately before it was so removed or by someone acting on behalf of such a person, the officer shall allow the person who made the request access to it under the supervision of an authorised person.

(4) Subject to paragraph (7) below, if a request for a photograph or copy of any such thing is made to the officer in overall charge of the investigation by a person who had custody or control of the thing immediately before it was so removed, or by someone acting on behalf of such a person, the officer shall—

(*a*) allow the person who made the request access to it under the supervision of an authorised person for the purpose of photographing it or copying it; or
(*b*) photograph or copy it, or cause it to be photographed or copied.

(5) Where anything is photographed or copied under sub-paragraph (4)(*b*) above the photograph or copy shall be supplied to the person who made the request.

(6) The photograph or copy shall be supplied within a reasonable time from the making of the request.

(7) There is no duty under this regulation to grant access to, or to supply a photograph or copy of, anything if the officer in overall charge of the investigation for the purposes of which it was removed has reasonable grounds for believing that to do so would prejudice—

(*a*) that investigation;
(*b*) the investigation of an offence other than the offence for the purposes of the investigation of which the thing was removed; or
(*c*) any criminal proceedings which may be brought as a result of—
  (i) the investigation of which he is in charge, or
  (ii) any such investigation as is mentioned in sub-paragraph (*b*) above.

(8) Any reference in this regulation to the officer in overall charge of the investigation is a reference to the person whose name and address are endorsed on the order concerned as being the officer so in charge.

11— (1) Where, on an application made as mentioned in paragraph (2) below, the appropriate judicial authority is satisfied that a person has failed to comply with a requirement imposed by regulation 10 above, the authority may order that person to comply with the requirement within such time and in such manner as may be specified in the order.

(2) An application under paragraph (1) above shall be made—

(*a*) in the case of a failure to comply with any of the requirements imposed by paragraphs (1) and (2) of regulation 10 above, by the occupier of the premises from which the thing in question was removed or by the person who had custody or control of it immediately before it was so removed, and
(*b*) in any other case, by the person who has such custody or control.

(3) In this regulation "the appropriate judicial authority" means—

(*a*) in England and Wales, a magistrates' court;
(*b*) in Scotland, the sheriff; and
(*c*) in Northern Ireland, a court of summary jurisdiction, as defined in Article 2 (2) (*a*) of the Magistrates' Court (Northern Ireland) Order 1981.

(4) In England and Wales and Northern Ireland, an application for an order under this regulation shall be made by way of complaint; and sections 21 and 42(2) of the Interpretation Act (Northern Ireland) 1954 shall apply as if any reference in those provisions to any enactment included a reference to this regulation.

Supplementary

12 Where in connection with the operation of the Intrastat system a person is convicted of an offence contrary to section 167(1) or section 168(1) of the Act, section 167(2)(*a*) and section 168(2)(*a*) of the Act shall have effect as if, in each case, for the words "6 months" there were substituted the words "3 months".

[**13** The following provisions of the Act shall apply to these Regulations as they apply to the customs and excise Acts—

Sections 145 to 148 (proceedings for offences, etc);
Sections 150 to 154 (incidental provisions as to legal proceedings, mitigation of penalties, proof and other matters).][1]

Amendments—[1] This regulation added by Statistics of Trade (Customs and Excise) (Amendment No 2) Regulations, SI 1993/3015 regs 2, 4 with effect from 1 January 1994.

SCHEDULE

Regulation 4

Note—The forms of Supplementary Declaration set out in this Schedule are not reproduced in this Handbook.
Supplementary Declaration forms substituted by the Statistics of Trade (Customs and Excise) (Amendment) Regulations, SI 2008/557 reg 2, Schedule with effect from 1 April 2008.

1992/3111
Value Added Tax (Removal of Goods) Order 1992

Made by the Treasury under VATA 1983 s 3(3) (see now VATA 1994 s 5(3)) and all other enabling powers

Made . . . . *9 December 1992*
Laid before the House of Commons . . . . *11 December 1992*
Coming into force . . . . *1 January 1993*

1 This Order may be cited as the Value Added Tax (Removal of Goods) Order 1992 and shall come into force on 1st January 1993.

2 In this Order—

"the Act" means the Value Added Tax Act 1983[a];
"the member State of arrival" means the member State to which the goods are removed;
"the member State of dispatch" means the member State from which the goods are removed;
"the owner" means the person who is carrying on the business of which the goods form part of the assets;
"registered" means either registered under the Act or registered under the provisions of the law of another member State corresponding thereto;
"temporary importation relief" means relief, other than partial relief, from payment of any duty incurred on the entry of goods into the territory of the Community which is afforded by virtue of any of the Community Regulations specified in the Schedule to this Order.

Note—[a] VATA 1994.

3 For the purposes of this Order, a person is treated as being established in a member State if he has there a business establishment or some other fixed establishment or carries on a business there through a branch or agency.

4 Subject to article 5 below, paragraph 5A of Schedule 2 to the Act[a] shall not apply to the following removals of goods from a member State to a place in any other member State—

(*a*) where the supply of the goods would be treated as having been made in a Member State other than the member State of dispatch by virtue of section 6(2A), (2B) or (2C) of the Act;[b]
(*b*) where the supply of the goods would be treated as having been made in the member State of dispatch by virtue of the Value Added Tax (Place of Supply of Goods) Order 1992;
(*c*) where the goods have been removed by or under the directions of the owner for the purpose of—
(i) his delivering them to a person to whom he is supplying those goods; or
(ii) his taking possession of them from a person who is supplying those goods to him,
and that supply is or will be zero rated by virtue of section 16(6) or (7) of the Act;[c]
(*d*) where—
(i) the owner is registered in the member State of dispatch and is not registered in the member State of arrival;
(ii) the goods have been removed for the purpose of delivering them to a person other than the owner who is to produce goods by applying a treatment or process to the goods removed; and
(iii) the owner intends that the goods produced will be returned to him by their removal to the member State of dispatch upon completion of the treatment or process;
(*e*) where—
(i) the goods have been removed for the purpose of delivering them to a person other than the owner who is to value or carry out any work on the goods; and
(ii) the supply made by the person to whom the goods have been delivered is or will be a supply of services treated as having been made in the member State of arrival;
(*f*) where—
(i) the owner is established in the member State of dispatch and is not established in the member State of arrival;
(ii) they are removed for the sole purpose of their being used by the owner in the course of a supply of services to be made by him;
(iii) at the time of their removal there exists a legally binding obligation to make that supply of services; and
(iv) the owner intends to remove them to the member State of dispatch upon his ceasing to use them in the course of making the supply;
(*g*) where—
(i) temporary importation relief would have been afforded had the goods been imported from a place outside the member States; and
(ii) the owner intends to export the goods to a place outside the member States or remove them to a member State other than the member State of arrival, in either case, not later than 2 years after the day upon which the goods were removed;
(*h*) where the goods are removed in accordance with an intention described in paragraph (*d*)(iii), (*f*)(iv) or (*g*)(ii) above;

(*i*) where goods which have been removed under the conditions described in paragraph (*e*) above are removed to the member State of dispatch when the valuation or work has been completed.

Notes—[a] VATA 1994 Sch 4 para 6.
[b] VATA 1994 s 7(3)–(5).
[c] VATA 1994 s 30(6), (8).

Cross references—See VAT (Removal of Goods) (Accounting) Regulations, SI 1992/3101 reg 3 (goods removed from a member State to a place in any other member State; removal falling within paras (*d*)–(*g*) above).

5 In the case of a removal falling within paragraph (*d*), (*f*) or (*g*) above, it shall be a condition of paragraph 5A of Schedule 2 to the Act[a] not applying that the relevant intention of the owner is fulfilled.

Note—[a] VATA 1994 Sch 4 para 6.
Cross references—See VAT (Removal of Goods) (Accounting) Regulations, SI 1992/3101 reg 3 (owner's obligation to make entry on VAT account where condition in this article is not complied with and tax has become payable).

SCHEDULE

COMMUNITY LEGISLATION RELATING TO TEMPORARY IMPORTATION RELIEF

Article 2

Council Regulation (EEC) No 3599/82
Council Regulation (EEC) No 1855/89
Council Regulation (EEC) No 3312/89
Commission Regulation (EEC) No 2249/91.

1992/3121
Value Added Tax (Place of Supply of Services) Order 1992

Made by the Treasury under VATA 1983 s 6(6) (see now VATA 1994 s 7(11)) and all other enabling powers

Made . . . . *9 December 1992*
Laid before the House of Commons . . . . . . *11 December 1992*
Coming into force . . . . *1 January 1993*

PART I
PRELIMINARY

Citation and commencement

1 This Order may be cited as the Value Added Tax (Place of Supply of Services) Order 1992 and shall come into force on 1st January 1993.

Interpretation

2 In this Order—

"the Act" means the [Value Added Tax Act 1994][1];
"ancillary transport services" means loading, unloading, handling and similar activities;
"intra-Community transport of goods" means the transportation of goods which begins in one member State and ends in a different member State;
"pleasure cruise" includes a cruise wholly or partly for the purposes of education or training;
"registration number" means an identifying number assigned to a person by a member State for the purposes of value added tax in that member State.

Amendments—[1] Words substituted by the VAT (Place of Supply of Services) (Amendment) Order, SI 1995/3038 art 3, with effect from 1 January 1996.

Revocation

3 The Value Added Tax (Place of Supply) Order 1984 is hereby revoked.

PART II
RULES FOR DETERMINING PLACE OF SUPPLY OF SERVICES

4 The rules for determining where a supply of goods or of services is made shall be varied in accordance with the following provisions of this Order.

Services relating to land

5 Where a supply of services consists of—

(*a*) the grant, assignment or surrender of—

(i) any interest in or right over land;

(ii) a personal right to call for or be granted any interest in or right over land; or

(iii) a licence to occupy land or any other contractual right exercisable over or in relation to land;

(*b*) any works of construction, demolition, conversion, reconstruction, alteration, enlargement, repair or maintenance of a building or civil engineering work;

(*c*) services such as are supplied by estate agents, auctioneers, architects, surveyors, engineers and others involved in matters relating to land,

it shall be treated as made where the land in connection with which the supply is made is situated.

Transport

6 Subject to articles 7 and 10 below, services consisting of the transportation of passengers or goods shall be treated as supplied in the country in which the transportation takes place, and only to the extent that it takes place in that country.

7 For the purposes of article 6 above, there shall be treated as taking place wholly in a country any transportation which takes place partly outside the territorial jurisdiction of that country where—

(*a*) it takes place in the course of a journey between two points in that country, whether or not as part of a longer journey involving travel to or from another country; and

(*b*) the means of transport used does not put in or land in another country in the course of the journey between those two points.

8 Any—

(*a*) goods or services provided as part of a pleasure cruise; or

(*b*) services consisting of the transportation of any luggage or motor vehicle accompanying (in either case) a passenger,

shall be treated as supplied in the same place as the transportation of the passenger is treated as supplied (whether or not they would otherwise be treated as supplied separately); and, for the purpose of this article, a pleasure cruise shall be treated as the transportation of passengers.

Simon's Tax Cases—*C&E Comrs v Peninsular and Oriental Steam Navigation Co Ltd* [1996] STC 698.

9 Subject to article 14 below, where a supply consists of ancillary transport services, it shall be treated as made where those services are physically performed.

10 Subject to article 14 below, where a supply of services consists of the intra-Community transport of goods, it shall be treated as made in the member State in which the transportation of the goods begins.

Services of intermediaries

11 Subject to article 14 below, where services consist of the making of arrangements for the intra-Community transport of goods or of any other activity intended to facilitate the making of such a supply, they shall be treated as supplied in the member State where the transportation of the goods begins.

12 Subject to article 14 below, where services consist of the making of arrangements for the supply by or to another person of ancillary transport services in connection with the intra-Community transport of goods or of any other activity intended to facilitate the making of such a supply, they shall be treated as supplied in the member State where the ancillary transport services are physically performed.

13 Subject to article 14 below, where services consist of the making of arrangements for a supply by or to another person or of any other activity intended to facilitate the making of such a supply, being a supply which is not of a description within articles 9 or 10 above or 16 below, those services shall be treated as supplied in the same place as the supply by or to that other person is treated as made.

Use of customer's registration number

14 Where a supply of services—

(*a*) falls within articles 10 to 13 above; …[1]

[(*aa*) consists of the valuation of, or work carried out on, any goods [which are then dispatched or transported out of the member state where those services were physically carried out][2]; or][1]

(*b*) consists of ancillary transport services provided in connection with the intra-Community transport of goods,

and the recipient of those services makes use, for the purpose of the supply, of a registration number, then, notwithstanding any provision of this Order to the contrary, the supply shall be treated as made in the member State which issued the registration number if, and only if, the supply would otherwise be treated as taking place in a different member State.

Amendments—[1] Words revoked, and sub-para (*aa*) inserted, by the VAT (Place of Supply of Services) (Amendment) Order, SI 1995/3038 art 4, with effect from 1 January 1996.

[2] Words in sub-para (*aa*) substituted by the VAT (Place of Supply of Services)(Amendment) Order, SI 1996/2992 with effect from 1 January 1997.

Services supplied where performed

15 Where a supply of services consists of—

(*a*) cultural, artistic, sporting, scientific, educational or entertainment services;

(*b*) services relating to exhibitions, conferences or meetings;

(*c*) services ancillary to, including those of organising, any supply of a description within paragraph (*a*) or (*b*) above; [or][2]

(*d*) the valuation of, or work carried out on, any goods, [save as provided by Article 14 above,][1]

it shall be treated as made where the services are physically carried out.

Amendments—[1] Words in sub-para (*d*) added by the VAT (Place of Supply of Services) (Amendment) Order, SI 1995/3038 art 5, with effect from 1 January 1996.

[2] Word "or" at end of sub-para (*c*) inserted by the VAT (Place of Supply of Services) (Amendment) Order, SI 1996/2992 with effect from 1 January 1997.

Services supplied where received

16 Where a supply consists of any services of a description specified in any of [paragraphs 1 to 8 of Schedule 5][1] to the Act, and the recipient of that supply—

(*a*) belongs in a country, other than the Isle of Man, which is not a member State; or

[(*b*) is a person who belongs in a member State, but in a country other than that in which the supplier belongs, and who—

(i) receives the supply for the purpose of a business carried on by him; and

(ii) is not treated as having himself supplied the services by virtue of section 8 of the Act,

it shall be treated as made where the recipient belongs.][1]

Simon's Tax Cases—*Diversified Agency Services Ltd v C&E Comrs* [1996] STC 398.

Amendments—[1] Words in square brackets substituted by the VAT (Place of Supply of Services) (Amendment) Order, SI 1995/3038 art 6, with effect from 1 January 1996.

[16A Where a supply consists of any services of a description specified in paragraph 7C of Schedule 5 to the Act and—

(*a*) the recipient of the supply is a person who belongs in a member State;

(*b*) he does not receive it for the purposes of a business carried on by him;

(*c*) it is received from a person who belongs in a country, other than the Isle of Man, which is not a member State,

it shall be treated as made where the recipient belongs.][1]

Amendments—[1] Article 16A inserted by the VAT (Place of Supply of Services) (Amendment) Order, SI 2003/862 arts 2, 3 with effect for any services supplied after 30 June 2003.

[Services supplied where enjoyed][2]

[17 Where a supply of services consists of—

(*a*) the letting on hire of any means of transport; or

[(*b*) services described in paragraph 7, 7A or 7B of Schedule 5 to the Act; or][3]

[(*c*) services described in paragraph 7C of that Schedule, when received by a person for the purposes of a business carried on by him,][3]

and those services would be treated, apart from this article, as supplied in the United Kingdom, they shall not be treated as supplied in the United Kingdom to the extent that the effective use and enjoyment of the services takes place outside the member States.][1]

Amendments—[1] Substituted by the VAT (Place of Supply of Services) (Amendment) Order, SI 1998/763 in relation to any services supplied on or after 18 March 1998.

[2] Heading substituted by the VAT (Place of Supply of Services) (Amendment) Order, SI 2003/862 arts 2, 4 with effect for any services supplied after 30 June 2003.

[3] Paras (*b*), (*c*) substituted for para (*b*), by SI 2003/862 arts 2, 5 with effect for any services supplied after 30 June 2003.

[18 Where a supply of services consists of—

(*a*) the letting on hire of any means of transport; or

[(*b*) services described in paragraph 7, 7A or 7B of Schedule 5 to the Act; or][2]

[(*c*) services described in paragraph 7C of that Schedule, when received by a person for the purposes of a business carried on by him,][2]

and those services would be treated, apart from this article, as supplied in a place outside the member States, they shall be treated as supplied in the United Kingdom to the extent that the effective use and enjoyment of the services takes place in the United Kingdom.][1]

Amendments—[1] Substituted by the VAT (Place of Supply of Services) (Amendment) Order, SI 1998/763 in relation to any services supplied on or after 18 March 1998.

[2] Paras (*b*), (*c*) substituted for para (*b*), by SI 2003/862 arts 2, 5 with effect for any services supplied after 30 June 2003.

19 …

Amendments—This paragraph revoked by the VAT (Place of Supply of Services) (Amendment) Order, SI 1998/763 in relation to any services supplied on or after 18 March 1998.

20 …

Amendments—This paragraph revoked by the VAT (Place of Supply of Services) (Amendment) Order, SI 1998/763 in relation to any services supplied on or after 18 March 1998.

[21— (1) The place of supply of a right to services shall be the same as [the place in which the supply of the services to which the right relates would be treated as made if made by the supplier of the right to the recipient of the right][2] (whether or not the right is exercised).

(2) The reference to a right to services in paragraph (1) above shall include a reference to any right, option or priority with respect to the supply of services and to the supply of an interest deriving from any right to services.][1]

Amendments—[1] This paragraph inserted by the VAT (Place of Supply of Services) (Amendment) Order, SI 1997/1524 in relation to any services performed on or after 1 July 1997.

[2] Words in para (1) substituted by the Value Added Tax (Place of Supply of Services) (Amendment) Order, SI 2006/1683 arts 2, 3 with effect from 1 August 2006.

1992/3122
Value Added Tax (Cars) Order 1992

Made by the Treasury under VATA 1983 ss 3(3), 3(5), 18(1), 18(2), 18(3), 18(4), 18(5), 18(6) and 29(2) (see now VATA 1994 ss 5(3), (5), 32(1)–(6), 43(2)) and all other enabling powers

Made . . . . *9 December 1992*
Laid before the House of Commons . . . . . . *11 December 1992*
Coming into force . . . . *1 January 1993*

Citation and commencement

1 This Order may be cited as the Value Added Tax (Cars) Order 1992 and shall come into force on 1st January 1993.

Interpretation

2[— (1)][4] In this Order—

"the Act" means the Value Added Tax Act [1994][1];

["the Manx Act" means [the Value Added Tax Act 1996][2]][1]

…[3]

"finance agreement" means an agreement for the sale of goods whereby the property in those goods is not to be transferred until the whole of the price has been paid and the seller retains the right to repossess the goods;

…[5]

["Motor car" means any motor vehicle of a kind normally used on public roads which has three or more wheels and either—

(*a*) is constructed or adapted solely or mainly for the carriage of passengers; or

(*b*) has to the rear of the driver's seat roofed accommodation which is fitted with side windows or which is constructed or adapted for the fitting of side windows;

but does not include—

(i) vehicles capable of accommodating only one person;

(ii) vehicles which meet the requirements of Schedule 6 to the Road Vehicles (Construction and Use) Regulations 1986 and are capable of carrying twelve or more seated persons;

(iii) vehicles of not less than three tonnes unladen weight (as defined in the Table to regulation 3(2) of the Road Vehicles (Construction and Use) Regulations 1986);

(iv) vehicles constructed to carry a payload (the difference between a vehicle's kerb weight (as defined in the Table to regulation 3(2) of the Road Vehicles (Construction and Use) Regulations 1986) and its maximum gross weight (as defined in that Table)) of one tonne or more;

(v) caravans, ambulances and prison vans;

(vi) vehicles constructed for a special purpose other than the carriage of persons and having no other accommodation for carrying persons than such as is incidental to that purpose;][3]

["auctioneer" means a person who sells or offers for sale goods at any public sale where persons become purchasers by competition, being the highest bidders.][1]

(2) …[5]

Press releases etc—Business Brief 16/04, 9-6-2004, clarifying HMRC's interpretation of the definition of a motor car; see also notice posted on HMRC website on 27 October 2006 concerning car derived vans and combi vans.

Simon's Tax Cases—*C&E Comrs v Jeynes (T/A Midland International (Hire) Caterers)* [1984] STC 30*; *Withers of Winsford Ltd v C&E Comrs* [1988] STC 431*.

Amendments—[1] Figure in the definition of "the Act" substituted for the figure "1983", and definitions "the Manx Act" and "auctioneer" inserted by the VAT (Cars) (Amendment) Order, SI 1995/1269 arts 2, 3 with effect from 1 June 1995.

[2] Words in the definition of "the Manx Act" substituted by the VAT (Cars) (Amendment) Order, SI 1998/759 with effect from 17 March 1998.

[3] Definition of "car dealer" revoked, and definition of "Motor car" substituted, by the VAT (Cars) (Amendment) Order, SI 1999/2832, arts 2, 3, with effect from 1 December 1999.

[4] Para (1) numbered as such, definition of "insurer" substituted, and para (2) inserted, by the Financial Services and Markets Act 2000 (Consequential Amendments and Repeals) Order, SI 2001/3649 art 432 with effect from 1 December 2001.

[5] In para (1), definition of "insurer" repealed, and para (2) repealed, by the VAT (Cars) (Amendment) Order, SI 2004/3084 with effect from 1 January 2005.

Revocations

3 The provisions specified in the first column of the Schedule to this Order are hereby revoked to the extent specified in the second column of that Schedule.

Treatment of transactions

4— (1) [Subject to paragraphs (1A) to (2) below,][2] each of the following descriptions of transactions shall be treated as neither a supply of goods nor a supply of services—

(*a*) the disposal of a used motor car by a person who repossessed it under the terms of a finance agreement, where the motor car is in the same condition as it was in when it was repossessed;

(*b*) the disposal of a used motor car by an insurer who has taken it in the settlement of a claim under a policy of insurance, where the motor car is disposed of in the same condition as it was in when it was so taken;

(*c*) the disposal of a motor car for no consideration ...[2]

[(*d*) services in connection with a supply of a used motor car provided by an agent acting in his own name to the purchaser of the motor car the consideration for which is taken into account by virtue of article 8(8) below in calculating the price at which the agent sold the motor car.][1]

[(*e*) services in connection with the sale of a used motor car provided by an auctioneer acting in his own name to the vendor or the purchaser of the motor car the consideration for which is taken into account by virtue of article 8(9) below in calculating the price at which the auctioneer obtained (or as the case may be) sold the motor car.][1]

[(*f*) a relevant supply of services by a taxable person to whom a motor car has been let on hire or supplied or by whom a motor car has been acquired from another member State or imported.][2]

[(1A) Paragraph (1) above shall not apply in relation to a case falling within paragraph (1)(*a*) to (*c*) above unless the tax on any previous supply, acquisition or importation was wholly excluded from credit under section 25 of the Act.][2]

[(1AA) Paragraph (1)(*a*) above shall not apply where adjustment, whether or not made under regulation 38 of the Value Added Regulations 1995, has taken account, or may later take account, of VAT on the initial supply under the finance agreement as a result of repossession and the motor car delivered under that agreement was delivered on or after 1st September 2006.][3]

[(1B) Paragraph (1) above shall not apply in relation to a case falling within paragraph (1)(*f*) above unless the tax on any previous letting on hire, supply, acquisition or importation was wholly or partly excluded from credit under section 25 of the Act.][2]

[(1C) For the purposes of paragraph (1)(*f*) above a relevant supply of service is—

(*a*) the letting on hire of a motor car to any person for no consideration or for a consideration which is less than that which would be payable in money if it were a commercial transaction conducted at arms length; or

(*b*) the making available of a motor car (otherwise than by letting it on hire) to any person (including, where the taxable person is an individual, himself, and where the taxable person is a partnership, a partner) for private use, whether or not for a consideration.][2]

(2) Nothing in paragraph (1)(*a*) or (*b*) above shall be construed as meaning that a transaction is not a supply for the purposes of section [11(1)(*a*)][1] of the Act.

Simon's Tax Cases—*C & E Comrs v General Motors Acceptance Corporation (UK) plc* [2004] STC 577.

Amendments—[1] Figures in para (2) substituted, and paras (1)(*d*), (*e*) added, by the VAT (Cars) (Amendment) Order, SI 1995/1269 art 4 with effect from 1 June 1995.

[2] Words in para (1) sub-para (*f*) and paras (1A)–(1C) inserted, and words in para (1)(*c*) revoked by the VAT (Cars) (Amendment) (No 2) Order, SI 1995/1667 art 3 with effect from 1 August 1995.

[3] Para (1AA) inserted by the VAT (Cars) (Amendment) Order, SI 2006/874 with effect from 13 April 2006 in relation to finance agreements entered into on or after that date. For these purposes, "finance agreement" has the meaning given in SI 1992/3122 art 2(1).

[**4A** Paragraph 5(4) of Schedule 4 to the Act shall not apply in relation to a motor car to which [article 5][2]below applies which is used or made available in circumstances where, but for the operation of that paragraph, it would be treated by virtue of [that article][2]as supplied to and by a taxable person.][1]

Amendments—[1] This article inserted by the VAT (Cars) (Amendment) (No 2) Order, SI 1995/1667 art 4 with effect from 1 August 1995.

[2] Words substituted by the VAT (Cars) (Amendment) Order, SI 1999/2832, arts 2, 4, with effect from 1 December 1999.

Self-supplies

[**5**— (1) This article applies to any motor car—

(*a*) which has been produced by a taxable person otherwise than by the conversion of a vehicle obtained by him;

(*b*) which has been produced by the taxable person by the conversion of another vehicle (whether a motor car or not) and in relation to which the condition in paragraph (2) below is satisfied; ...[2]

(*c*) which was supplied to, or acquired from another member State or imported by, a taxable person and in relation to which the condition in paragraph (2) below is satisfied[;

(*d*) which was transferred to a taxable person as an asset of a business or part of a business in the course of the transfer of that business or part of a business as a going concern—

(i) in circumstances where the transfer was treated as neither a supply of goods nor a supply of services by virtue of an Order made or having effect as if made under section 5(3) of the Act;

(ii) in the hands of the transferor or any predecessor of his the motor car was one to which this article applied by virtue of sub-paragraph (*a*), (*b*) or (*c*) above; and

(iii) the motor car has not been treated as supplied by virtue of this article to and by the transferor or any of his predecessors.][2].

(2) The condition referred to in paragraph (1)(*b*) and (*c*) above is that the tax on the supply to, or acquisition or importation by, the taxable person of the motor car or the vehicle from which it was converted, as the case may be, was not wholly excluded from credit under section 25 of the Act.

[(2A) For the purposes of paragraph (1)(*d*) above a person is a predecessor of a transferor if—

(*a*) he transferred the motor car as an asset of a business or part of a business which he transferred as a going concern—

(i) to the transferor, or

(ii) where the motor car has been the subject of more than one such transfer, to a person who made one of those transfers; and

(*b*) the transfer of the motor car was treated as neither a supply of goods nor a supply of services by virtue of any Order made or having effect as if made under section 5(3) of the Act.][2]

[(3) Where a motor car to which this article applies—

(*a*) has not been supplied by the taxable person in the course or furtherance of a business carried on by him; and

(*b*) is used by him such that had it been supplied to, or imported or acquired from another member State by, him at that time his entitlement to credit under section 25 of the Act in respect of the VAT chargeable on such a supply, importation or acquisition from another member State would have been wholly excluded by virtue of article 7 of the Value Added Tax (Input Tax) Order 1992,

it shall be treated for the purposes of the Act as both supplied to him for the purposes of a business carried on by him and supplied by him for the purposes of that business.][2]][1]

Press releases etc—C&E Business Briefs 10/95 23-5-95 and 15/95 31-7-95 and VAT Information Sheet 12/95 1-6-95 (detailed guidance on rules governing supplies of business cars).

Note—It is believed that the comma after the word "time" in para (3)(*b*) should actually appear after the word "him".

Amendments—[1] This article substituted by the VAT (Cars) (Amendment) (No 2) Order, SI 1995/1667 arts 2, 5 with effect from 1 August 1995.

[2] Word "or" at end of para (1)(*b*) revoked, words at end of para (1), and para (3), substituted, and para (2A) inserted, by the VAT (Cars) (Amendment) Order, SI 1999/2832, arts 2, 5, 6, 7, with effect from 1 December 1999.

6, 6A …

Amendments—These articles revoked by the VAT (Cars) (Amendment) Order, SI 1999/2832, arts 2, 8, with effect from 1 December 1999.

7 [Article 5][2] above shall apply in relation to any bodies corporate which are treated for the purposes of section [43][1] of the Act as members of a group as if those bodies were one person, but any motor car which would fall to be treated as supplied to and by that person shall be treated as supplied to and by the representative member.

Amendments—[1] Figure substituted for the figure "29" by the VAT (Cars) (Amendment) Order, SI 1995/1269 art 6 with effect from 1 June 1995.

[2] Words substituted by the VAT (Cars) (Amendment) Order, SI 1999/2832, arts 2, 9, with effect from 1 December 1999.

Relief for second-hand motor cars

[8— (1) Subject to complying with such conditions (including the keeping of such records and accounts) as the Commissioners may direct in a notice published by them for the purposes of this Order or may otherwise direct, and subject to paragraph (3) below, where a person supplies a used motor car which he took possession of in any of the circumstances set out in paragraph (2) below, he may opt to account for the VAT chargeable on the supply on the profit margin on the supply instead of by reference to its value.

(2) The circumstances referred to in paragraph (1) above are that the taxable person took possession of the motor car pursuant to—

(*a*) a supply in respect of which no VAT was chargeable under the Act or under Part I of the Manx Act;

(*b*) a supply on which VAT was chargeable on the profit margin in accordance with paragraph (1) above, or a corresponding provision made under the Manx Act or a corresponding provision of the law of another member State;

[(*bb*) a supply [received before 1 March 2000][3] to which the provisions of article 7(4) of the Value Added Tax (Input Tax) Order 1992 applied;][2]

[(*c*) a de-supplied transaction, other than an article 5 transaction;
(*d*) subject to paragraph (2A) below, an article 5 transaction.][5]

[(2A) An article 5 transaction does not fall within sub-paragraph (*d*) of paragraph (2) above unless the taxable person has a relevant predecessor in title.][5]

(3) This article does not apply to—

(*a*) a supply which is a letting on hire;

(*b*) the supply by any person of a motor car which was produced by him, if it was neither previously supplied by him in the course or furtherance of any business carried on by him nor treated as so supplied by virtue of article 5 above;

(*c*) any supply if an invoice or similar document showing an amount as being VAT or as being attributable to VAT is issued in respect of the supply;

(*d*) …[2]

(4) …[2]

(5) Subject to paragraph (6) below, for the purposes of determining the profit margin—

(*a*) the price at which the motor car was obtained shall be calculated as follows—

(i) (where the taxable person took possession of the used motor car pursuant to a supply) in the same way as the consideration for the supply would be calculated for the purposes of the Act;

(ii) (where the taxable person is a sole proprietor and the used motor car was supplied to him in his private capacity) in the same way as the consideration for the supply to him as a private individual would be calculated for the purposes of the Act;

[(iii) (where the taxable person took possession of the motor car pursuant to a de-supplied transaction, other than an article 5 transaction) by taking the price he paid pursuant to the transaction;

(iv) (where the taxable person took possession of the motor car pursuant to an article 5 transaction) by taking the price at which his relevant predecessor in title obtained the motor car;][5]

(*b*) the price at which the motor car is sold shall be calculated in the same way as the consideration for the supply would be calculated for the purposes of the Act;

(*c*) …[5]

(6) Subject to paragraph (7) below, where the taxable person is an agent acting in his own name the price at which the motor car was obtained shall be calculated in accordance with paragraph 5(*a*) above but the selling price calculated in accordance with paragraph 5(*b*) above shall be increased by the amount of any consideration payable to the taxable person in respect of services supplied by him to the purchaser in connection with the supply of the motor car.

(7) Instead of calculating the price at which the motor car was obtained or supplied in accordance with paragraph (6) above, an auctioneer acting in his own name may—

[(*a*) calculate the price at which the motor car was obtained by deducting from the successful bid the amount of the commission payable to him under his contract with the vendor for the sale of the motor car;][4]

(*b*) calculate the price at which the motor car was supplied by adding to the successful bid the consideration for any supply of services by him to the purchaser in connection with the sale of the motor car,

in either (or both) cases excluding the consideration for supplies of services that are not chargeable to VAT.][1].

[(8) For the purposes of this article—

"article 5 transaction" means a transaction which is a de-supplied transaction by virtue of a provision of article 5 of the Value Added Tax (Special Provisions) Order 1995 or a corresponding provision made under the Manx Act;

"de-supplied transaction" means a transaction which was treated by virtue of any Order made or having effect as if made under section 5(3) of the Act or under the corresponding provisions of the Manx Act as being neither a supply or goods nor a supply of services.][5]

[(9) For the purposes of this article a person is a relevant predecessor in title of a taxable person if—

(*a*) he is the person from whom the taxable person took possession of the motor car and himself took possession of it pursuant to a transaction within any of sub-paragraphs (*a*) to (*c*) of sub-paragraph (2) above; or

(*b*) where the motor car has been the subject of a succession of two or more article 5 transactions (culminating in the article 5 transaction to which the taxable person was a party), he was a party to one of those transactions and himself took possession of the motor car pursuant to a transaction within any of sub-paragraphs (*a*) to (*c*) of sub-paragraph (2) above.][5]

Press releases etc—C&E Press Notice 25-6-82 ("Premium and Nearly New" cars with value higher than list price sold by non-franchised dealers are unused for VAT purposes; "Personal import" cars acquired by the VAT registered dealers are also unused for VAT purposes when sold).

C&E Business Briefs 10/95 23-5-95 and 15/95 31-7-95 and VAT Information Sheet 12/95 1-6-95 (detailed guidance on rules governing supplies of business cars).

Amendments—[1] This article substituted by the VAT (Cars) (Amendment) Order, SI 1995/1269 art 7 with effect from 1 June 1995.

[2] Para (2)(*bb*) inserted and paras (3)(*d*), (4) revoked by the VAT (Cars) (Amendment) (No 2) Order, SI 1995/1667 art 8 with effect from 1 August 1995.

[3] In para 8(2)(*bb*) words inserted by the VAT (Cars) (Amendment) Order, SI 1999/2832, arts 2, 10, with effect from 1 March 2000.

[4] Para (7)(*a*) substituted by the VAT (Cars) (Amendment) Order, SI 2001/3754 art 3 with effect from 2 January 2002.

[5] Sub-paras (2)(*c*), (*d*) substituted, sub-paras (5)(*a*)(iii), (iv) substituted for sub-para (5)(*a*)(iii), sub-para (5)(*c*) revoked, and paras (8), (9) added, by the VAT (Cars) (Amendment) Order, SI 2002/1502 with effect from 1 July 2002. For further provisions as to the effect of that Order see SI 2002/1502 art 1(2).

Note—The Commissioners have confirmed that the cross reference in art 8(6) should refer to paras (5)(*a*) and (5)(*b*) above and not paras 5(*a*) and 5(*b*), as stated in the amending order SI 1995/1269 art 7.

1992/3124
Value Added Tax (Imported Gold) Relief Order 1992

Made by the Treasury under VATA 1983 s 19(1) (see now VATA 1994 s 37(1)) and all other enabling powers

Made . . . . *9 December 1992*
Laid before the House of Commons . . . . *11 December 1992*
Coming into force . . . . *1 January 1993*

1 This Order may be cited as the Value Added Tax (Imported Gold) Relief Order 1992 and shall come into force on 1st January 1993.

2 The tax chargeable upon the importation of gold (including gold coins) from a place outside the Member States shall not be payable where the importation is by a Central Bank.

3 The Value Added Tax (Imported Goods) Relief Order 1977 is hereby revoked.

1992/3130
Value Added Tax (Supply of Temporarily Imported Goods) Order 1992

Made by the Treasury under VATA 1983 s 3(3) (see now VATA 1994 s 5(3)) and all other enabling powers

Made . . . . *9 December 1992*
Laid before the House of Commons . . . . . . *11 December 1992*
Coming into force . . . . *1 January 1993*

1 This Order may be cited as the Value Added Tax (Supply of Temporarily Imported Goods) Order 1992 and shall come into force on 1st January 1993.

2— (1) Where goods held under temporary importation arrangements are supplied, that supply shall be treated as neither a supply of goods nor a supply of services provided that—

(*a*) the goods remain eligible for temporary importation arrangements; and
(*b*) the supply is to a person established outside the member States.

(2) "Goods held under temporary importation arrangements" means goods placed under customs arrangements with total relief from customs duty within the meaning of Council Regulation (EEC) No 3599/82, whether or not the goods are subject to customs duty.

1992/3132
Value Added Tax (Treatment of Transactions) (No 2) Order 1992

Made by the Treasury under VATA 1983 s 8A(4) (see now VATA 1994 s 11(4)) and all other enabling powers

Made . . . . *9 December 1992*
Laid before the House of Commons . . . . . . *11 December 1992*
Coming into force . . . . *1 January 1993*

1 This Order may be cited as the Value Added Tax (Treatment of Transactions) (No 2) Order 1992, and shall come into force on 1st January 1993.

2— (1) Where gold is supplied to a Central Bank by a supplier in another member State, and the transaction involves the removal of the gold from that or some other member State to the United Kingdom, the taking possession of the gold by the Central Bank concerned is not to be treated for the purposes of the Value Added Tax Act 1983[a] as the acquisition of goods from another member State.

(2) For the purposes of this article, gold includes gold coins.

Note—[a] VATA 1994.

1992/3135
Excise Goods (Holding, Movement, Warehousing and REDS) Regulations 1992

Made by the Commissioners of Customs and Excise under CEMA 1979 ss 93, 100G, 100H and 127A and F(No 2)A 1992 ss 1, 2

Made . . . . 10 December 1992
Laid before Parliament . . . . 14 December 1992
Coming into force . . . . 1 January 1993

PART I
PRELIMINARY

Citation and commencement

1 These Regulations may be cited as the Excise Goods (Holding, Movement, Warehousing and REDS) Regulations 1992 and shall come into force on 1st January 1993.

Interpretation

2— (1) In these Regulations except where the context requires—

"the Management Act" means the Customs and Excise Management Act 1979;

"the 1992 Act" means the Finance (No 2) Act 1992;

["accompanying document" means the accompanying administrative document set out in the Annex to Commission Regulation (EEC) No 2719/92 or, as the case may require, the simplified accompanying document set out in the Annex to Commission Regulation (EEC) No 3649/92;][3]

"approved" means approved by the Commissioners;

["authorised warehousekeeper" means the occupier of an excise warehouse or a person who is registered under section 41A of the Alcoholic Liquor Duties Act 1979][2];

["certificate of receipt" means the certificate of receipt set out on the reverse of one or more of the copies of the accompanying document;][3]

...[6]

"Community excise goods" means excise goods imported into the United Kingdom from another member State and which have been produced or are in free circulation in the European Community at that importation;

"duty"[, except in regulation 4(1B)(*d*) below,][4] means a duty of excise which becomes chargeable on excise goods by virtue of the enactments specified below in the definition of excise goods;

"excise duty point" (the time when the duty is payable by a person, whether or not payment may be deferred) has the meaning given by section 1 of the 1992 Act;

"excise goods" means a good ...[6], that is chargeable with a duty of excise by or under the Alcoholic Liquor Duties Act 1979 the Hydrocarbon Oil Duties Act 1979 or the Tobacco Products Duty Act 1979;

"excise warehouse" has the meaning given by section 1(1) of the Management Act;

"occasional importer" means a person approved under regulation 15 below;

[REDS means a registered excise dealer and shipper who is authorized, in the course of his business, to import without payment of excise duty excise goods from other member States, but who is not authorized to hold or consign those goods without first paying that duty;][5]

"tax representative" means a person who is a REDS and who agrees to be appointed, or accepts the appointment, and is appointed by a vendor pursuant to the requirements of regulation 13 below;

"tax warehouse" means an excise warehouse [and any premises registered under section 41A of the Alcoholic Liquor Duties Act 1979][1]; and

"vendor" means the person referred to as the vendor in subparagraph (*a*) of paragraph (3) below.

(2) References in these Regulations to suspension arrangements are references to the provisions made by Part IV of these Regulations or to any provision made by or under the customs and excise Acts for enabling goods to be held or moved without payment of duty or any provisions made by or under those Acts in connection with any provision enabling goods to be so held or moved.

(3) For the purposes of these Regulations there is a distance selling arrangement where:

(*a*) a person ("the vendor"), in another member State, sells or agrees to sell goods, in that State, to a person ("the purchaser") in the United Kingdom;

(*b*) those goods are dispatched by or to the order of the vendor to the purchaser or a person nominated by the purchaser and consigned to an address in the United Kingdom;

(*c*) those goods will be excise goods on their importation into the United Kingdom;

(*d*) the purchaser is not a revenue trader;

and "distance selling arrangements" in these Regulations shall be construed accordingly.

(4) "UK distance selling arrangements" means a distance selling arrangement except that the vendor is in the United Kingdom (and is referred to in these Regulations as the "UK vendor"),

the purchaser is in another member State, and the address to which the goods are consigned is in a member State other than the United Kingdom; and the goods that are the subject of that UK distance selling arrangement are excise goods, and will be charged with the equivalent of a duty in the member State to which they are consigned by the law of that State (and in these Regulations those goods are referred to as "excise products" and that duty is referred to as "the other member State's charge").

(5) In these Regulations the expression "European Community" means the European Communities and the expressions "member State" and "European Communities" respectively have the meaning given to those expressions in the European Communities Act 1972; and "another member State" means a member State other than the United Kingdom, and cognate expressions shall be construed accordingly.

(6) For the purposes of these Regulations—

(*a*) excise goods being imported into the United Kingdom shall be deemed to be moved under the instructions of—

(i) the authorised warehousekeeper who arranged the importation or to whose tax warehouse the excise goods are consigned;

(ii) the REDS who arranged the importation;

(iii) the occasional importer who arranged the importation; or

(iv) the consignee if there was no such arrangement; and

(*b*) in any other case excise goods shall be deemed to be moved under the instructions of the consignor.

Modifications—This regulation is modified in relation to shuttle train goods by the Channel Tunnel (Alcoholic Liquor and Tobacco Products) Order, SI 2000/426 art 3 Sch 1 paras 1, 2.

Amendments—[1] Words in square brackets inserted by Beer Regulations, SI 1993/1228 reg 34(*a*) with effect from 1 June 1993.

[2] Definition of "authorised warehousekeeper" in reg 2(1) substituted by the Warehousekeepers and Owners of Warehoused Goods Regulations, SI 1999/1278 with effect from 1 October 1999.

[3] Definitions of "accompanying document" and "certificate of receipt" in para (1) substituted by the Excise Goods (Accompanying Documents) Regulations, SI 2002/501 reg 28(1), (2) with effect from 1 April 2002.

[4] In para (1), words in the definition of "duty" inserted by the Excise Goods, Beer and Tobacco Products (Amendment) Regulations, SI 2002/2692 reg 2(1), (2) with effect from 1 December 2002.

[5] Definition of "REDS" in reg 2(1) substituted by Hydrocarbon Oil (Registered Remote Markers) Regulations, SI 2005/3472 reg 14 with effect from 10 January 2006.

[6] Definition of "chewing tobacco", and words omitted from definition of "excise goods", repealed by the Tobacco Products and Excise Goods (Amendment) Regulations, SI 2006/1787 with effect from 1 August 2006.

Particular application of regulations and transitional arrangements for Community excise goods

3— (1) With regard to Community excise goods imported into the United Kingdom ("those goods") these Regulations apply as follows.

(2) These Regulations apply in respect of those goods imported into the United Kingdom after 31st December 1992.

(3) Save as the Commissioners may otherwise allow, these Regulations apply in respect of those goods which are imported before 1st January 1993 and which, being required to be entered, were not entered before that date.

PART II
DETERMINATION OF THE DUTY

Excise duty point

4— (1) Except in the cases specified in paragraphs [(1A)][2] to (6) below, the excise duty point in relation to any Community excise goods shall be the time when the goods are charged with duty at importation.

[(1A) In the case of excise goods acquired by a person in another member State for his own use and transported by him to the United Kingdom, the excise duty point is the time when those goods are held or used for a commercial purpose by any person.][2]

[(1B) For the purposes of paragraph (1A) above—

(*a*) "member State" includes the Principality of Monaco[, San Marino and the United Kingdom Sovereign Base Areas of Akrotiri and Dhekelia][3], but does not include the Island of Heligoland and the territory of Büsingen in the Federal Republic of Germany, Livigno, Campione d'Italia and the waters of Lake Lugano in the Italian Republic, Ceuta, Melilla and the Canary Islands in the Kingdom of Spain, or the overseas departments of the French Republic,

(*b*) "own use" includes use as a personal gift,

(*c*) if the goods in question are—

(i) transferred to another person for money or money's worth (including any reimbursement of expenses incurred in connection with obtaining them), or

(ii) the person holding them intends to make such a transfer,

those goods are to be regarded as being held for a commercial purpose, (*d*) if the goods are not duty and tax paid in the member State at the time of acquisition, or the duty and tax that was paid will be or has been reimbursed, refunded or otherwise dispensed with, those goods are to be regarded as being held for a commercial purpose,

(*e*) without prejudice to sub-paragraphs (*c*) and (*d*) above, in determining whether excise goods are held or used for a commercial purpose by any person regard shall be taken of—

(i) that person's reasons for having possession or control of those goods,

(ii) whether or not that person is a revenue trader (as defined in section 1(1) of the Customs and Excise Management Act 1979),

(iii) that person's conduct, including his intended use of those goods or any refusal to disclose his intended use of those goods,

(iv) the location of those goods,

(v) the mode of transport used to convey those goods,

(vi) any document or other information whatsoever relating to those goods,

(vii) the nature of those goods including the nature and condition of any package or container,

(viii) the quantity of those goods, and in particular, whether the quantity exceeds any of the following quantities—

10 litres of spirits,

20 litres of intermediate products (as defined in Article 17(1) of Council Directive 92/83/EEC),

90 litres of wine,

(ix) whether that person personally financed the purchase of those goods,

(x) any other circumstance that appears to be relevant,

(*f*) "excise goods" do not include any goods chargeable with excise duty by virtue of any provision of the Hydrocarbon Oil Duties Act 1979 or of any order made under section 10 of the Finance Act 1993.][2]

(2) If any duty suspension arrangements apply to any excise goods, the excise duty point shall be the earlier of—

(*a*) the time when the excise goods are delivered for home use from a tax warehouse or are otherwise made available for consumption, including consumption in a warehouse;

(*b*) the time when the excise goods are consumed;

(*c*) the time when the excise goods are received by a REDS or by an occasional importer or by an importer for whom REDS is acting, or when the duty ceases to be suspended in accordance with those duty suspension arrangements;

(*d*) the time when the premises on which the excise goods are deposited cease to be a tax warehouse;

(*e*) the time when the person with whom the excise goods are deposited, ceases to be an authorised warehousekeeper;

(*f*) the time when the excise goods leave any tax warehouse unless—

(i) the goods are consigned to another tax warehouse in respect of which the authorised warehousekeeper has been approved in relation to the deposit and keeping of those goods, and the goods are moved in accordance with requirements prescribed in regulations 9 and 10 below;

(ii) the goods are delivered for export, shipment as stores, removal to the Isle of Man; or

(iii) any relief is conferred in relation to the goods by or under the customs and excise Acts.

(3) If duty suspension arrangements do not apply in respect of Community excise goods consigned, in accordance with these Regulations, to a REDS or to an occasional importer or to an importer for whom a REDS is acting, the excise duty point shall be the time when those goods are received by that person.

(4) If chewing tobacco or perfumed spirits are imported into the United Kingdom having been consigned from another member State and are charged with duty at that importation the excise duty point shall, unless those goods are deposited in a tax warehouse approved for the purpose, be the time when they are received by the importer, owner or person beneficially interested in the goods.

(5) [Where duty suspension arrangements do not apply in respect of Community excise goods consigned to a REDS or to an occasional importer or to an importer for whom a REDS is acting and, after importation, those goods do not arrive so that the excise duty point provided by paragraph (3) above does not occur, the excise duty point provided by paragraph (1) above shall apply.][1]

(6) If excise goods have been relieved from payment of duty and there is a contravention of any condition subject to which the relief was conferred, the excise duty point shall be the time of that contravention.

(7) In this regulation "contravention" includes a failure to comply.

(8) . . .[1]

(9) This regulation—

(*a*) shall apply to fix an excise duty point with respect to any Community excise goods imported into the United Kingdom from another member State; and (*b*) shall not apply to fix an excise duty point with respect to any other excise goods unless and until those goods are deposited in a tax warehouse under duty suspension arrangements.

Modifications—This regulation is modified in relation to shuttle train goods by the Channel Tunnel (Alcoholic Liquor and Tobacco Products) Order, SI 2000/426 art 3 Sch 1 paras 1, 3.

Amendments—[1] Para (5) substituted, and para (8) revoked, by the Excise Duty Points (Duty Suspended Movements of Excise Goods) Regulations, SI 2001/3022 regs 10, 11 with effect from 28 September 2001.

[2] Reference in para (1) substituted, and paras (1A), (1B) inserted, by the Excise Goods, Beer and Tobacco Products (Amendments) Regulations, SI 2002/2692 reg 2(1), (3) with effect from 1 December 2002.

[3] Words in para (1B)(*a*) substituted by the Excise Duty Points (Etc) (New Member States) Regulations, SI 2004/1003 reg 8 with effect from 1 May 2004.

PART III—PART VII

Note—Parts III–VII are outside the scope of this Handbook.

1992/3152
Excise Duties (Deferred Payment) Regulations 1992

Made by the Commissioners of Customs and Excise under CEMA 1979 ss 93, 127A; ALDA 1979 ss 13, 15, 56, 62(5); HODA 1979 ss 21, 24 and the ECA 1972 s 2(2)

Made . . . . *10 December 1992*
Laid before Parliament . . . . *11 December 1992*
Coming into force . . . . *1 January 1993*

PART I
PRELIMINARY

Citation, commencement and revocation

1— (1) These Regulations may be cited as the Excise Duties (Deferred Payment) Regulations 1992 and shall come into force on 1st January 1993.

(2) The Excise Duties (Deferred Payment) Regulations 1983, the Excise Duties (Hydrocarbon Oils) (Deferred Payment) Regulations 1985; the Excise Duties (Deferred Payment) (Amendment) Regulations 1986 and the Excise Duties (Deferred Payment) (Amendment) Regulations 1989 are hereby revoked.

Interpretation

2 In these Regulations—

"approved person" means a person approved by the Commissioners under regulation 4 below;

"business day" means a day which is a business day within the meaning of section 92 of the Bills of Exchange Act 1882;

"hydrocarbon oils" means goods (except petrol substitutes, power methylated spirits and road fuel gas) chargeable with excise duty by virtue of the Hydrocarbon Oil Duties Act 1979 and includes composite goods containing hydrocarbon oils on which goods excise duty is chargeable;

"imported by a registered excise dealer and shipper" includes any importation where goods are moved under the instructions of a registered excise dealer and shipper or are, in accordance with registered excise dealers and shippers regulations, deemed to be so moved;

"made-wine" includes composite goods containing made-wine on which goods excise duty is chargeable;

"spirits" includes composite goods containing spirits on which good excise duty is chargeable;

"payment day" has the meaning given by regulation 5 below;

"wine" includes composite goods containing wine on which goods excise duty is chargeable.

Application

3 These Regulations shall apply to goods on which excise duty would, but for deferment granted by these Regulations, be payable on or after 1st January 1993; being goods of any of the following descriptions—

(*a*) wine, made-wine, cider, spirits, hydrocarbon oils; and

(*b*) beer imported by a registered excise dealer and shipper.

PART II
DEFERMENT OF EXCISE DUTY

Approved persons

4— (1) A person who wishes to be granted excise duty deferment under these Regulations shall apply to be approved for excise duty deferment purposes.

(2) When approving a person under this regulation the Commissioners may specify the maximum amount of excise duty which may be deferred by that person at any time under that approval.

(3) When approving a person under this regulation the Commissioners may limit the approval to deferment in respect of goods which are at specified places.

(4) A person may be approved separately under this regulation in respect of different places.

(5) The Commissioners may, for reasonable cause, at any time vary or revoke any approval granted under this regulation.

Deferment

5— (1) Deferment shall be granted upon the giving of notice by an approved person that he wishes excise duty in respect of any goods to be deferred until a day, to be known as "payment day", provided that the notice is given in such form and manner and contains such particulars as the Commissioners may require and provided that the provisions of these Regulations are complied with.

(2) Subject to regulation 6 below, on each payment day an approved person shall pay to the Commissioners the total amount of excise duty of which he has been granted deferment until that payment day.

(3) Payment day shall be—

(*a*) in the case of beer imported by a registered excise dealer and shipper, the 25th day of the month following the month in which the duty would, but for deferment granted by these Regulations, be payable;

(*b*) in the case of any goods other than beer imported by a registered excise dealer and shipper, the 15th day of the month following the month in which the duty on those goods would, but for deferment granted by these Regulations, be payable;

(*c*) in the case of hydrocarbon oils delivered for home use from a refinery or other premises used for the production of hydrocarbon oil or from an excise warehouse on or after the 15th day of one month and not later than the 14th day of the next month, the last business day of that next month; and

(*d*) in any other case, where the duty on those goods would, but for deferment granted by these Regulations, be payable on or after the 15th day of one month and not later than the 14th day of the next month, either—

(i) the 29th day of that next month; or

(ii) where that next month has only 28 days, the 28th day of that month;

provided that where the payment day would, if determined in accordance with the foregoing provisions of this paragraph, fall on a day upon which the Bank of England is closed, the payment day shall be, in the case mentioned in sub-paragraph (*b*) above the next business day following that day and, in any other case, the last business day preceding that day.

Set-offs

6— (1) Subject to paragraph (2) below an approved person shall set-off all sums to which he is entitled as rebate under section 11 of the Hydrocarbon Oil Duties Act 1979 all sums to which he is entitled to repayment under section 15 of that Act[, regulation 3(1)(*b*) of the Hydrocarbon Oil Duties (Marine Voyages Reliefs) Regulations 1996][1] and such other sums as the Commissioners may allow against excise duty required to be paid by him on payment day under regulation 5 above.

(2) An approved person shall not set-off those sums referred to in paragraph (1) above unless on or before the said payment day he submits to the Commissioners a claim for set-off in such form and manner and containing such particulars as they may require.

(3) Rebate shall not be set-off under paragraph (1) above at a payment day earlier than that on which duty deferred under these Regulations, in respect of which the rebate exists, would have been due.

Amendments—[1] Words in para (1) inserted by Hydrocarbon Oil Duties (Marine Voyages Reliefs) Regulations, SI 1996/2537 reg 15 with effect from 1 November 1996.

Adjustments

7— (1) If a notice has been given under regulation 5 above or any other document has been submitted to the Commissioners in respect of excise duty deferment and the Commissioners are satisfied that the full amount of excise duty payable has not been shown then, save as the Commissioners may otherwise allow, the balance of excise duty shall be paid forthwith.

(2) If a notice has been given under regulation 5 above or any other document has been submitted to the Commissioners in respect of excise duty deferment and the Commissioners are satisfied that excise duty in excess of the amount payable has been shown other than by reason of a set-off under regulation 6 above, the Commissioners shall repay or give credit for that excess, but the total amount shown shall nonetheless be paid on payment day.

PART III
REQUIREMENTS TO BE OBSERVED

Security

8 A person who is approved for the purpose of applying for deferment of excise duty shall provide such security for that duty in such form and manner and in such amount as the Commissioners may require.

Conditions

9 The Commissioners may make any approval of a person or any grant of deferment of duty subject to any condition or requirement and conditions or requirements may be added to or varied at any time by the Commissioners.

Change of Circumstances

10 Any person who has applied to be approved or has been approved under regulation 4 above shall notify the Commissioners immediately of any change in circumstances which materially affects any application for approval or for deferment of duty or any security given by him under these Regulations.

PART IV
RELATIONSHIP TO OTHER ENACTMENTS

Purposes for which excise duty is treated as paid

11 Without prejudice to regulation 5 above for the purposes of the following enactments excise duty shall be deemed to have been paid at the time when deferment was granted—

(*a*) sections 24(2)(*b*), [43(1), 49(1)(*a*)][1] , 51, 67(1)(*b*), 96(1)(*a*), 127 and 162 of the Customs and Excise Management Act 1979;
(*b*) sections 10(2)(*a*) and 11(1)(*a*) of the Customs and Excise Duties (General Reliefs) Act 1979;
(*c*) sections 16, 21, 22(1), 22(3A), 22(5), 42 and 43 of the Alcoholic Liquor Duties Act 1979;
(*d*) sections 9(4), 15(1), 17(1), …[1], 19(3), 19A(1) and 20(1) of the Hydrocarbon Oils Duties Act 1979.
[(*e*) regulation 3(1)(*b*) of the Hydrocarbon Oil Duties (Marine Voyages Reliefs) Regulations 1996][1]

Amendments—[1] Words in (*a*) substituted by, words in (*d*) deleted by, and (*e*) above inserted by Hydrocarbon Oil Duties (Marine Voyages Reliefs) Regulations, SI 1996/2537 reg 15 with effect from 1 November 1996.

Savings for requirements of other Regulations

12 Nothing in these Regulations shall be taken to remove any obligation placed upon any person to comply with the requirements or conditions imposed by or under any other Regulations relating to the goods in respect of which payment of duty is deferred under these Regulations, except in so far as those other Regulations relate to the date for payment of duty and deferment of that payment is granted under these Regulations.

1992/3156
Customs and Excise (Personal Reliefs for Special Visitors) Order 1992

Made by the Commissioners of Customs and Excise under the Customs and Excise Duties (General Reliefs) Act 1979 s 13A and all other enabling powers

Made . . . . *10 December 1992*
Laid before the House of Commons . . . . *11 December 1992*
Coming into force . . . . *1 January 1993*

PART I
PRELIMINARY

1 This Order may be cited as the Customs and Excise (Personal Reliefs for Special Visitors) Order 1992 and shall come into force on 1st January 1993.

PART II
INTERPRETATION

2 In this Order—

"acquisition" means an acquisition of goods from another member State within the meaning of section 2A of the Value Added Tax Act 1983[a] and "acquired" shall be construed accordingly;
"duty" means any duty of customs or duty of excise;
"importation" means an importation from a place outside the member States, and "imported" shall be construed accordingly;
"relief" means the remission of any duty or tax which is chargeable and which a person, whether the person upon whom the relief is conferred or some other person, would be liable to pay were it not for the relief conferred;
"supply" means a supply within the meaning of section 3 of the Value Added Tax Act 1983[b] and "supplied" shall be construed accordingly;
"tax" means value added tax;

"United Kingdom national" means a British citizen, a British Dependent Territories citizen, a British National (Overseas) or a British Overseas citizen;

"used", in relation to a person's use of consumable property, includes having the property at his disposal;

"warehouse" means a warehouse within the meaning of section 1(1) of the Customs and Excise Management Act 1979 [the premises in respect of which a person is registered under section 41A, 47, or 62(2) of the Alcoholic Liquor Duties Act 1979, the premises in respect of which a person holds an excise licence under section 54(2) or 55(2) of that Act, or premises registered for the safe storage of tobacco products in accordance with regulations made under section 7(1)(b) of the Tobacco Products Duty Act 1979;][1] and "removal from warehouse" shall be construed accordingly.

Note—[a] VATA 1994 s 10.
[b] VATA 1994 s 5.

Amendments—[1] Words in definition of "warehouse" inserted by the Customs and Excise (Personal Reliefs for Special Visitors) (Amendment) Order, SI 2007/5 arts 1, 2 with effect from 1 February 2007.

PART III
CONDITIONS ATTACHING TO PART VI RELIEFS

3 In this Part—

"entitled person" means an entitled person for the purposes of Part VI.

4 It shall be a condition of the relief conferred under article 16 below that the entitled person deliver or cause to be delivered to the supplier of the motor vehicle a certificate in the form numbered 1 in the Schedule to this Order—

(*a*) containing full information in respect of the matters specified therein; and
(*b*) signed—
  (i) as to Part A, by the entitled person upon whom the relief is conferred;
  (ii) as to Part B, by the head of the mission or other body or organisation of which the entitled person is a member;
  (iii) as to Part C, by the Secretary of State or a person authorised to sign on his behalf; and
  (iv) as to Part D, by the supplier,

before the supply is made.

PART IV
CONDITIONS ATTACHING TO PART VII RELIEFS

5— (1) In this Part—

"entitled person" means an entitled person for the purposes of Part VII.

(2) For the purposes of articles 6 and 7 below, any reference to a certificate shall be construed as including a reference to a copy of such a certificate.

6— (1) It shall be a condition of relief conferred under article 19 below that the entitled person deliver or cause to be delivered in accordance with paragraph (2) below five certificates in the form numbered 2 in the Schedule to this Order—

(*a*) containing full information in respect of the matters specified therein; and
(*b*) signed—
  (i) as to Part A, by the entitled person upon whom the relief is conferred; and
  (ii) as to Part B, by the officer commanding the visiting force or other body or organisation of which the entitled person is a member or by a person authorised to sign on his behalf.

(2) The certificates referred to in paragraph (1) above shall be delivered before the supply is made as follows:

(*a*) two certificates shall be delivered to the visiting force or other body or organisation of which the entitled person is a member;
(*b*) two certificates shall be delivered to the proper officer; and
(*c*) one certificate shall be delivered to the supplier of the motor vehicle.

7— (1) It shall be a condition of relief conferred under article 20 below in respect of a motor vehicle that the entitled person deliver or cause to be delivered in accordance with paragraph (2) below four certificates in the form numbered 3 in the Schedule to this Order—

(*a*) containing full information in respect of the matters specified therein; and
(*b*) signed—
  (i) as to Part A, by the entitled person upon whom the relief is conferred; and
  (ii) as to Part B, by the officer commanding the visiting force or other body or organisation of which the entitled person is a member or by a person authorised to sign on his behalf.

(2) The certificates referred to in paragraph (1) above shall be delivered before the goods are removed by or on behalf of the entitled person as follows:

(*a*) one certificate shall be delivered to the visiting force or other body or organisation of which the entitled person is a member; and
(*b*) three certificates shall be delivered to the proper officer.

PART V
CONDITIONS ATTACHING TO ALL RELIEFS

8 In this Part—

"entitled person" means an entitled person for the purposes of either Part VI or Part VII of this Order.

9 An entitled person upon whom any relief is conferred under any Part of this Order shall be bound by the conditions described in the following provisions of this Part and in Part III or IV above, as the case may be.

10— (1) It shall be a condition of the relief that the goods shall not be lent, hired-out, given as security or transferred by the entitled person or any other person without the prior authorisation in writing of the Commissioners.

(2) Where the Commissioners authorise such disposal as is mentioned in paragraph (1) above, they may discharge the relief and the entitled person to whom the relief was afforded shall forthwith pay the duty or tax at the rate then in force, provided that where a lower rate was in force when relief was afforded the amount payable shall be determined by reference to the lower rate.

11 It shall be a condition of the relief that the goods are used exclusively by the entitled person or members of his family forming part of his household.

12 Where relief has been afforded and subsequently the Commissioners are not satisfied that any condition attaching to such relief, whether by virtue of a provision of this Order or otherwise, has been complied with, then, unless the Commissioners sanction the non-compliance in writing, the duty or tax shall become payable forthwith and the goods shall be liable to forfeiture.

13 Where relief has been afforded, but any duty or tax subsequently becomes payable by virtue of article 12 above, the following persons shall be jointly and severally liable to pay it—

(*a*) the entitled person upon whom the relief was conferred;

(*b*) any person who, at or after the time of the non-compliance with the condition which has caused the duty or tax to become payable, has been in possession of the goods.

PART VI
DIPLOMATS ETC

14 In this Part—

"entitled person" means:

(*a*) any person enjoying any privilege or immunity by virtue of his being—

(i) a diplomatic agent for the purposes of the Diplomatic Privileges Act 1964

(ii) a senior officer of the Commonwealth Secretariat for the purposes of the Commonwealth Secretariat Act 1966

(iii) a consular officer for the purposes of the Consular Relations Act 1968

(iv) a representative or a person recognised as holding a rank equivalent to a diplomatic agent for the purposes of the International Organisations Act 1968 or

(*b*) any person enjoying, under or by virtue of section 2 of the European Communities Act 1972 any privilege or immunity similar to those enjoyed under or by virtue of the enactments referred to in paragraph (*a*) above by the persons therein specified,

who is neither a United Kingdom national nor a permanent resident of the United Kingdom.

15 Where any tobacco product or beverage containing alcohol is removed from warehouse in the course of its being supplied to an entitled person, payment of any duty or tax chargeable in respect of the removal from warehouse or supply shall not be required.

16— (1) Subject to the following provisions of this article, where an entitled person purchases a motor vehicle which has been manufactured in a country, other than the United Kingdom, which is—

(*a*) a member State; or

(*b*) a member of the European Free Trade Association,

payment of any tax chargeable in respect of the supply shall not be required.

(2) No relief shall be afforded under paragraph (1) above if the entitled person has previously been afforded relief in respect of any other motor vehicle, whether under paragraph (1) above or otherwise, unless he has disposed of all previous motor vehicles in respect of which relief has been so afforded and paid any duty or tax which was required to be paid under article 10(2) above.

(3) Where the spouse [or civil partner][1] of the entitled person is present in the United Kingdom, paragraph (2) above shall apply as if the words "(or all but one)" were inserted after the words "motor vehicles".

Amendment—[1] Words in para (3) inserted by the Civil Partnership Act 2004 (Amendments to Subordinate Legislation) Order, SI 2005/2114 art 2(1), Sch 1 para 5 with effect from 5 December 2005.

17 Nothing in this Part of this Order shall be taken as conferring relief in respect of any duty or tax which is subject to remission or refund by or under any of the enactments referred to in article 14 above.

PART VII
VISITING FORCES AND HEADQUARTERS

18 In this Part—

"entitled person" means a person who is—

(*a*) for the purposes of any provision of the Visiting Forces Act 1952 a serving member of a visiting force of a country, other than the United Kingdom, which is a party to the North Atlantic Treaty, or a person recognised by the Secretary of State as a member of a civilian component of such a force, or

(*b*) a person who is a military or civilian member of a headquarters or organisation designated for the purposes of any provision of the International Headquarters and Defence Organisations Act 1964

who is neither a United Kingdom national nor a permanent resident of the United Kingdom.

19 Subject to article 22 below, where an entitled person purchases a motor vehicle which has been manufactured in a country which is—

(*a*) a member State; or

(*b*) a member of the European Free Trade Association,

payment of any tax in respect of the supply shall not be required.

20 Subject to article 22 below, where an entitled person imports, acquires or removes from warehouse any goods, payment of any duty or tax chargeable in respect of the importation, acquisition or removal from warehouse shall not be required.

21 Subject to article 22 below, where a gift of goods, other than tobacco products or beverages containing alcohol, is made to an entitled person by dispatching them to him from a place outside the United Kingdom, payment of any duty or tax chargeable in respect of their acquisition or importation shall not be required.

22— (1) No relief shall be afforded under this Part of this Order in respect of a motor vehicle if the entitled person has previously been afforded relief under this Order in respect of any other motor vehicle, unless he has disposed of all previous motor vehicles in respect of which relief has been so afforded and paid any duty or tax which was required to be paid under article 10(2) above.

(2) Where the spouse [or civil partner][1] of the entitled person is present in the United Kingdom, paragraph (1) above shall apply as if the words "(or all but one)" were inserted after the words "motor vehicles".

Amendment—[1] Words in para (2) inserted by the Civil Partnership Act 2004 (Amendments to Subordinate Legislation) Order, SI 2005/2114 art 2(1), Sch 1 para 5 with effect from 5 December 2005.

SCHEDULE

Form No 1—Certificate for use in Connection with the Purchase of an EC (not UK) or EFTA Origin Vehicle free of Value Added Tax (C 428) (Article 4).

Form No 2—Visiting Forces' Certificate of Entitlement to Relief from Duty and VAT on the purchase of a Motor Vehicle (C&E 941A) (Article 6(1)).

Form No 3—Visiting Forces' Certificate of Entitlement to Relief from Duty and VAT on the Import/Withdrawal from Warehouse of a Motor Vehicle (C 941) (Article 7(1)).

Note—See Forms C428, C&E 941A, C941 set out on the following pages.

Article 4

FORM 1

Certificate for use in Connection with the Purchase of an EC (not UK) or EFTA Origin Vehicle free of Value Added Tax

Part A: To be completed by entitled person

Surname	Forenames	Rank or status
Embassy/High Commission/International Organisation		

Signature of entitled person. .... Date ....

Part B: Certificate by Head of Mission

Official Stamp

Signature ....

Name ....
(BLOCK LETTERS)

Part C: Certificate by Foreign & Commonwealth Office

This is to certify that the above named is entitled to purchase an EC or EFTA origin vehicle at a VAT exclusive price.

Signature .... Department .... Date ....

Part D: Particular of Vehicle (to be completed by supplier)

Make and model	Engine number	Chassis number
Vehicle registration mark	Year of manufacture	

Name of supplier ....

Signature of supplier .... Date ....

SPECIMEN

C 428 CD 3433/N3(12/92) F 8660( )

Article 6(1)

FORM 2

Visiting Forces' Certificate of Entitlement to Relief from Duty and Value Added Tax on the purchase of a Motor Vehicle

Please complete all five copies.

Part A: To be completed by entitled person

Surname	Forenames	Grade and Service No.
Base in the UK to which assigned		
Private address in the UK		
Particulars of vehicle		Engine number
Make & Model		Chassis number
Vehicle registration mark		Year of manufacture

Name of Supplier ....

Declaration

I declare that:-

I am a member of/the civilian component of/the .... visiting forces and that the details given above are true and complete.

Signature of entitled person. .... Date ....

SPECIMEN

Part B: Certificate by Visiting Force

I certify that .... is a member of/the civillan component of/the Visiting Force serving in the United Kingdom.

Signature .... Date ....

Part C: For Official use

Date stamp

C&E 941A CD 24357N3(12/92) F 2379 ( )

Article 7(1)

FORM 3

Visiting Forces' Certificate of Entitlement to Relief from Duty and Value Added Tax on the Import/Withdrawal from Warehouse of a Motor Vehicle

Please complete all four copies.

Part A: To be completed by entitled person

Surname	Forenames	Grade and Service No.

Base in the UK to which assigned

Private address in the UK

Particulars of vehicle

Make and model	Engine number	Chassis number
Vehicle registration mark		Year of manufacture

Declaration

I declare that:-

I am a member of/ the civilian component of/the .... visiting forces and that the details given above are true and complete.

Signature of entitled person .... Date ....

Part B Certificate by Visiting Force

I certify that .... is a member of/the civilian component of/the Visiting Forces serving in the United Kingdom.

Signature .... Date ....

For Official Use	Date stamp

C 941 CD 3422/N3(12/92) F 8656 (

1992/3193
Customs and Excise Duties (Personal Reliefs for Goods Permanently Imported) Order 1992

Made by the Commissioners of Customs and Excise under CED(GR)A 1979 ss 7, 13.

Made . . . . *16 December 1992*
Laid before the House of Commons . . . . *17 December 1992*
Coming into force . . . . *1 January 1993*

PART I
PRELIMINARY

Citation and commencement

1 This order may be cited as the Customs and Excise Duties (Personal Reliefs for Goods Permanently Imported) Order 1992 and shall come into force on 1st January 1993.

Interpretation

2 In this Order—

"declared for relief" has the meaning assigned to it by article 8 below;
"household effects" means furnishing and equipment for personal household use;
"motor vehicle" shall include a trailer;
"normal residence" means a person's principal place of abode situated in the country where he is normally resident;
"normally resident" has the meaning assigned to it by article 3 below;
"occupational ties" shall not include attendance by a pupil or student at a school, college or university;
"personal ties" shall mean family or social ties to which a person devotes most of his time not devoted to occupational ties;
"property" means any personal property intended for personal use or for meeting household needs and shall include household effects, household provisions, household pets and riding animals, cycles, motor vehicles, caravans, pleasure boats and private aircraft, provided that there shall be excluded any goods which, by their nature or quantity, indicate that they are being imported for a commercial purpose;
"third country", shall have the meaning given by Article 3.1 of Council Directive 77/388/EEC;
"used", in relation to a person's use of consumable property, shall include having the property at his disposal.

Rules for determining where a person is normally resident

3— (1) This article shall apply for the purpose of determining, in relation to this Order, where a person is normally resident.

(2) A person shall be treated as being normally resident in the country where he usually lives—

(*a*) for a period of, or periods together amounting to, at least 185 days in a period of twelve months;
(*b*) because of his occupational ties; and
(*c*) because of his personal ties.

(3) In the case of a person with no occupational ties, paragraph (2) above shall apply with the omission of sub-paragraph (*b*), provided his personal ties show close links with that country.

(4) Where a person has his occupational ties in one country and his personal ties in another country, he shall be treated as being normally resident in the latter country provided that either—

(*a*) his stay in the former country is in order to carry out a task of a definite duration, or
(*b*) he returns regularly to the country where he has his personal ties.

(5) Notwithstanding paragraph (4) above, a United Kingdom citizen whose personal ties are in the United Kingdom but whose occupational ties are in a third country may for the purposes of relief under this Order be treated as normally resident in the country of his occupational ties, provided he has lived there for a period of, or periods together amounting to, at least 185 days in a period of twelve months.

Supplementary

4 For the purposes of this Order—

(*a*) any reference to a person who has been normally resident in a third country and who intends to become normally resident in the United Kingdom shall be taken as a reference to a person who intends to comply with the requirements of paragraphs (2), (3) or (4) of article 3 above, as the case may be, for being treated as normally resident in the United Kingdom;
(*b*) the date on which a person becomes normally resident in the United Kingdom shall be the date when having given up his normal residence in a third country he is in the United Kingdom for the purpose of fulfilling such intention as is mentioned in paragraph (*a*) above.

PART II
PROVISIONS COMMON TO CERTAIN RELIEFS

Property may be in separate consignments

5 Except as otherwise provided by this Order, where property in respect of which relief is afforded is permitted to be imported over a period it may be imported in more than one consignment during such period.

Condition as to security for certain importations

6 Where any goods are declared for relief under this Order—

(*a*) before the date on which a person becomes normally resident in the United Kingdom, or

(*b*) if he intends to become so resident on the occasion of his marriage before such marriage has taken place,

the relief shall be subject to the condition that there is furnished to the Commissioners such security as they may require.

Restriction on disposal without authorisation

7— (1) Except as provided by or under this Order, where relief is afforded under any Part of this Order, it shall be a condition of the relief that the goods are not lent, hired-out, given as security or transferred in the United Kingdom within a period of twelve months from the date on which relief was afforded, unless such disposal is authorised by the Commissioners.

(2) Where the Commissioners authorise any such disposal as is mentioned in paragraph (1) above, they may discharge the relief and the person to whom the relief was afforded shall forthwith pay tax at the rate then in force, provided that where a lower rate was in force when relief was afforded the amount payable shall be determined by reference to the lower rate.

PART III
PROVISIONS COMMON TO ALL RELIEFS

Goods to be declared for relief

8— (1) A person shall not be entitled to relief from payment of duty or tax in respect of any goods under any Part of this Order unless the goods are declared for relief to the proper officer.

(2) For the purposes of this Order, the expression "declared for relief" shall refer to the act by which a person applies for relief on importation of the goods or on their removal from another customs procedure and includes, as the case may be, any declaration under section 78 of the Customs and Excise Management Act 1979 or any entry under the Postal Packets (Customs and Excise) Regulations 1986, the Excise Warehousing (Etc) Regulations 1988, or regulation 5 of the Customs Controls on Importation of Goods Regulations 1991, or any entry required by Article 40 of Commission Regulation (EEC) No 2561/90.

Fulfilment of intention to be a condition

9 Where relief from payment of duty or tax is afforded under any Part of this Order subject to a specified intention on the part of a person in relation to his becoming normally resident in the United Kingdom, or the use of the goods in respect of which relief is afforded, it shall be a condition of the relief that such intention be fulfilled.

Enforcement

10 Where relief from payment of duty or tax has been afforded under any Part of this Order and subsequently the Commissioners are not satisfied that any condition subject to which such relief was afforded has been complied with, then, unless the Commissioners sanction the non-compliance, the duty or tax shall become payable forthwith by the person to whom relief was afforded (except to the extent that the Commissioners may see fit to waive payment of the whole or any part thereof) and the goods shall be liable to forfeiture.

PART IV
PERSONS TRANSFERRING THEIR NORMAL RESIDENCE FROM A THIRD COUNTRY

11— (1) Subject to the provisions of this Part, a person entering the United Kingdom shall not be required to pay any duty or tax chargeable in respect of property imported into the United Kingdom on condition that—

(*a*) he has been normally resident in a third country for a continuous period of at least twelve months;

(*b*) he intends to become normally resident in the United Kingdom;

(*c*) the property has been in his possession and used by him in the country where he has been normally resident, for a period of at least six months before its importation;

(*d*) the property is intended for his personal or household use in the United Kingdom; and

(*e*) the property is declared for relief—

(i) not earlier than six months before the date on which he becomes normally resident in the United Kingdom, and
(ii) not later than twelve months following that date.

(2) A person shall not be afforded relief under this Part unless the Commissioners are satisfied that the goods have borne, in their country of origin or exportation, the customs or other duties and taxes to which goods of that class or description are normally liable and that such goods have not, by reason of their exportation, been subject to any exemption from, or refund of, such duties and taxes as aforesaid, or any turnover tax, excise duty or other consumption tax.

(3) For the purposes of this Part, "property" shall not include—

(*a*) beverages containing alcohol;
(*b*) tobacco products;
(*c*) any motor road vehicle which by its type of construction and equipment is designed for and capable of transporting more than nine persons including the driver, or goods, or any special purpose vehicle or mobile workshop; and
(*d*) articles for use in the exercise of a trade or profession, other than portable instruments of the applied or liberal arts.

Supplementary

12 Where the Commissioners are satisfied that a person has given up his normal residence in a third country but is prevented by occupational ties from becoming normally resident in the United Kingdom immediately, they may allow property to be declared for relief earlier than as prescribed in article 11(1)(*e*)(i) above, subject to such conditions and restrictions as they think fit.

PART V
ADDITIONAL RELIEF FOR PROPERTY IMPORTED ON MARRIAGE FROM A THIRD COUNTRY

Relief

13— (1) Subject to the provisions of this article, in addition to the relief afforded by Part IV, a person entering the United Kingdom shall not be required to pay any duty or tax chargeable in respect of property imported into the United Kingdom on condition that—

(*a*) he has been normally resident in a third country for a continuous period of at least twelve months;
(*b*) he intends to become normally resident in the United Kingdom on the occasion of his marriage; and
(*c*) the property is declared for relief within the period provided by article 15 below.

(2) In this article "property" shall be limited to household effects and trousseaux, other than tobacco products and beverages containing alcohol.

Wedding gifts

14— (1) Subject to the provisions of this article, a person to whom article 13(1) above applies shall not be required to pay any duty or tax chargeable in respect of any wedding gift imported into the United Kingdom by him or on his behalf on condition that such wedding gift is—

(*a*) given or intended to be given to him on the occasion of his marriage by a person who is normally resident in a third country;
(*b*) declared for relief within the period provided by article 15 below.

(2) Relief shall not be afforded under this article in respect of any wedding gift the value of which exceeds £800.

(3) For the purpose of affording relief from any duty or tax under this article, a wedding gift shall be treated as if it were liable to Community customs duty and valued in accordance with the rules applicable to such duty.

(4) In this article "wedding gift" means any property customarily given on the occasion of a marriage, other than tobacco products or beverages containing alcohol.

Time limit for relief

15 The property to which this Part applies shall be declared for relief—

(*a*) not earlier than two months before the date fixed for the solemnisation of the marriage; and
(*b*) not later than four months following the date of the marriage.

PART VI
PUPILS AND STUDENTS

Relief for scholastic equipment

16— (1) Without prejudice to relief afforded under any other Part of this Order and subject to the provisions of this article, a person entering the United Kingdom shall not be required to pay any duty or tax chargeable in respect of scholastic equipment imported into the United Kingdom on condition that—

(*a*) he is a pupil or student normally resident in a third country who has been accepted to attend a full-time course at a school, college or university in the United Kingdom; and

(*b*) such equipment belongs to him and is intended for his personal use during the period of his studies.

(2) For the purposes of this article, "scholastic equipment" shall mean household effects which represent the normal furnishings for the room of a pupil or student, clothing, uniforms, and articles or instruments normally used by pupils or students for the purpose of their studies, including calculators or typewriters.

(3) The provisions of article 7 above shall not apply to relief afforded under this Part.

PART VII
HONORARY DECORATIONS, AWARDS AND GOODWILL GIFTS

Relief for honorary decorations and awards

17 Subject to article 20 below, a person entering the United Kingdom shall not be required to pay any duty or tax chargeable on the importation into the United Kingdom of any goods on condition that—

(*a*) he is normally resident in the United Kingdom; and

(*b*) such goods comprise—

(i) any honorary decoration which has been conferred on him by a government in a third country or

(ii) any cup, medal or similar article of an essentially symbolic nature which has been awarded to him in a third country as a tribute to his activities in the arts, sciences, sport, or the public service, or in recognition of merit at a particular event.

Relief for gifts received by official visitors in a third country

18 Subject to article 20 below, a person entering the United Kingdom shall not be required to pay any duty or tax chargeable on the importation into the United Kingdom of any goods on condition that—

(*a*) he is normally resident in the United Kingdom;

(*b*) he is returning from an official visit to a third country;

(*c*) the goods were given to him by the host authorities of such country on the occasion of his visit; and

(*d*) the goods are not intended for a commercial purpose.

Relief for gifts brought by official visitors

19 Subject to article 20 below, a person entering the United Kingdom shall not be required to pay any duty or tax chargeable on the importation into the United Kingdom of any goods on condition that—

(*a*) he is normally resident in a third country;

(*b*) he is paying an official visit to the United Kingdom;

(*c*) the goods are in the nature of an occasional gift which he intends to offer to the host authorities during his visit; and

(*d*) the goods are not intended for a commercial purpose.

Supplementary

20— (1) Part II shall not apply to relief afforded under this Part.

(2) No relief shall be afforded under this Part in respect of beverages containing alcohol, tobacco products or importations having a commercial character.

PART VIII
PERSONAL PROPERTY ACQUIRED BY INHERITANCE

Relief for legacies imported from a third country

21— (1) Without prejudice to relief afforded under any other Part of this Order and subject to the provisions of this article, a person who has become entitled as a legatee to property situated in a third country shall not be required to pay any duty or tax chargeable on the importation thereof into the United Kingdom, on condition that—

(*a*) he is either—

(i) normally resident in the United Kingdom or the Isle of Man; or
(ii) a secondary resident who is not normally resident in a third country; or
(iii) an eligible body;

(*b*) he furnishes proof to the officer of his entitlement as legatee to the property; and
(*c*) save as the Commissioners otherwise allow, the property is imported by or for such person not later than two years from the date on which his entitlement as legatee is finally determined.

(2) No relief shall be afforded under paragraph (1) above in respect of goods specified in the Schedule to this Order.

(3) For the purposes of this Part—

"eligible body" means a body solely concerned with carrying on a non-profit making activity and which is incorporated in the United Kingdom or the Isle of Man;

"secondary resident" means a person who, without being normally resident in the United Kingdom or the Isle of Man has a home situated in the United Kingdom which he owns or is renting for at least twelve months.

PART IX
REVOCATION

22 …

Note—Effect has been given for the revocations made by this article.

SCHEDULE

Article 21(2)

1 Beverages contain alcohol.

2 Tobacco products.

3 Any motor road vehicle which, by its type of construction and equipment, is designed for and capable of transporting more than nine persons including the driver, or goods, or any special purpose vehicle or mobile workshop.

4 Articles, other than portable instruments of the applied or liberal arts, used in the exercise of a trade or profession before his death by the person from whom the legatee has acquired them.

5 Stocks of new materials and finished or semi-finished products.

6 Livestock and stocks of agricultural products exceeding the quantities appropriate to normal family requirements.

1992/3220
Value Added Tax (Flat-rate Scheme for Farmers) (Designated Activities) Order 1992

Made by the Treasury under VATA 1983 s 37B(8) (see now VATA 1994 s 54(8)) and all other enabling powers

Made . . . . 16 December 1992
Laid before the House of Commons . . . . . 17 December 1992
Coming into force . . . . 1 January 1993

1 This Order may be cited as the Value Added Tax (Flat-rate Scheme for Farmers) (Designated Activities) Order 1992, and shall come into force on 1st January 1993.

2— (1) Subject to paragraph (2) below, the activities described in any part of the Schedule to this order are designated activities for the purposes of section 37B of the Value Added Tax Act 1983[a].

(2) The activities described in Part VI of the Schedule are not designated activities for the purposes of section 37B of the Act, unless:

(*a*) the person performing them also carries out designated activities falling within one or more of Parts I to V of the Schedule (other designated activities), and
(*b*) in carrying out the activities described in Part VI—

(i) he performs them himself, or they are performed by his employees (or both), and
(ii) any equipment he uses in carrying them out, or hires to another, for agricultural purposes is equipment which he also uses for carrying out his other designated activities.

Note—[a] VATA 1994 s 54.

SCHEDULE

Article 2

PART I
CROP PRODUCTION

1 General agriculture, including viticulture.

2 Growing of fruit and of vegetables, flowers and ornamental plants, whether in the open or under glass.

3 Production of mushrooms, spices, seeds and propagating materials; nurseries.

PART II
STOCK FARMING

1 General stock farming.

2 Poultry farming.

3 Rabbit farming.

4 Beekeeping.

5 Silkworm farming.

6 Snail farming.

PART III
FORESTRY

1 Growing, felling and general husbandry of trees in a forest, wood or copse.

PART IV
FISHERIES

1 Fresh-water fishing.

2 Fish farming.

3 Breeding of mussels, oysters and other molluscs and crustaceans.

4 Frog farming.

PART V
PROCESSING

1 The processing by a person of products deriving from his activities falling within Parts I to IV above, using only such means as are normally employed in the course of such activities.

PART VI
SERVICES

1 Field work, reaping and mowing, threshing, bailing, collecting, harvesting, sowing and planting.

2 Packing and preparing for market (including drying, cleaning, grinding, disinfecting and ensilaging) of agricultural products for market.

3 Storage of agricultural products.

4 Stock minding, rearing and fattening.

5 Hiring out of equipment for use in any of the activities described in this Schedule.

6 Technical assistance in relation to any of the activities described in this Schedule.

7 Destruction of weeds and pests, dusting and spraying of crops and land.

8 Operation of irrigation and drainage equipment.

9 Lopping, tree felling and other forestry services.

1992/3221
Value Added Tax (Flat-rate Scheme for Farmers) (Percentage Addition) Order 1992

Made by the Treasury under VATA 1983 s 37B(4) (see now VATA 1994 s 54(4)) and all other enabling powers

Made . . . . *16 December 1992*
Laid before the House of Commons . . . . . . *17 December 1992*
Coming into force . . . . *1 January 1993*

1 This Order may be cited as the Value Added Tax (Flat-rate Scheme for Farmers) (Percentage Addition) Order 1992, and shall come into force on 1st January 1993.

2 The percentage referred to in section 37B(4) of the Value Added Tax Act 1983[a] shall be 4 per cent.

Note—[a] VATA 1994 s 54(5).

1992/3222
Value Added Tax (Input Tax) Order 1992

Made by the Treasury under VATA 1983 s 14(10) (see now VATA 1994 s 25(7)) and all other enabling powers

Made . . . . *16 December 1992*
Laid before the House of Commons . . . . . . *17 December 1992*
Coming into force . . . . *1 January 1993*

Citation and commencement

1 This Order may be cited as the Value Added Tax (Input Tax) Order 1992, and shall come into force on 1st January 1993.

Interpretation

2 In this Order—

"the Act" means the Value Added Tax Act [1994][1];

"the Manx Act" means the Value Added Tax and Other Taxes Act 1973;

["antiques" means objects other than works of art or collectors' items, which are more than 100 years old;][2]

["collectors' items" means any collection or collector's piece falling within section 21(5) of the Act but excluding investment gold coins within the meaning of Note 1(*b*) and (*c*) to Group 15 of Schedule 9 to the Act;][4]

["building materials" means any goods the supply of which would be zero-rated if supplied by a taxable person to a person to whom he is also making a supply of a description within either item 2 or item 3 of Group 5, or item 2 of Group 6, of Schedule 8 to the Act][1]

...[2]

["Motor car" means any motor vehicle of a kind normally used on public roads which has three or more wheels and either—

(*a*) is constructed or adapted solely or mainly for the carriage of passengers; or

(*b*) has to the rear of the driver's seat roofed accommodation which is fitted with side windows or which is constructed or adapted for the fitting of side windows;

but does not include—

(i) vehicles capable of accommodating only one person;

(ii) vehicles which meet the requirements of Schedule 6 to the Road Vehicles (Construction and Use) Regulations 1986 and are capable of carrying [12][5] or more seated persons;

[(ii*a*) vehicles which would otherwise meet the requirements of sub-paragraph (ii) but which can carry fewer than 12 seated persons solely because they have been adapted for wheelchair users;][5]

(iii) vehicles of not less than three tonnes unladen weight (as defined in the Table to regulation 3(2) of the Road Vehicles (Construction and Use) Regulations 1986);

(iv) vehicles constructed to carry a payload (the difference between a vehicle's kerb weight (as defined in the Table to regulation 3(2) of the Road Vehicles (Construction and Use) Regulations 1986) and its maximum gross weight (as defined in that Table) of one tonne or more;

(v) caravans, ambulances and prison vans;

(vi) vehicles constructed for a special purpose other than the carriage of persons and having no other accommodation for carrying persons than such as is incidental to that purpose;][3]

["motor dealer" means a person whose business consists in whole or in part of obtaining supplies of, or acquiring from another member State or importing, new or second-hand motor cars for resale with a view to making an overall profit on the sale of them (whether or not a profit is made on each sale);

"motor manufacturer" means a person whose business consists in whole or part of producing motor cars including producing motors cars by conversion of a vehicle (whether a motor car or not);][3]

...[2]

...[3]

...[2]

["Second-hand goods" means tangible moveable property (including motor cars) that is suitable for further use as it is or after repair other than works of art, collectors' items or antiques and other than precious metals and precious stones;][2]

["stock in trade" means new or second-hand motor cars (other than second-hand motor cars which are not qualifying motor cars within the meaning of article 7(2A) below) which are—

(*a*) produced by a motor manufacturer or, as the case may require, supplied to or acquired from another member State or imported by a motor dealer, for the purpose of resale, and

(*b*) are intended to be sold by—

(i) a motor manufacturer within 12 months of their production, or

(ii) by a motor dealer within 12 months of their supply, acquisition from another member State or importation, as the case may require, and such motor cars shall not cease to be stock in trade where they are temporarily put to a use in the motor manufacturer's or, as the case may be, the motor dealer's business which involves making them available for private use;][3]

["work of art" has the same meaning as in section 21 of the Act.][4]

Amendments—[1] Word in the definition "the Act" substituted, and the definition "building materials" inserted, by the VAT (Input Tax) (Amendment) Order, SI 1995/281 art 3 with effect from 1 March 1995.

[2] Definitions of "caravan", "firearms", "motorcycle", "works of art", "antiques" and "collectors' pieces" revoked and the definitions of "antiques", and "Second-hand goods" inserted by the VAT (Input Tax) (Amendment) (No 2) Order, SI 1995/1267 art 3 with effect from 1 June 1995.

[3] Definition of "motor car" substituted, definitions of "motor dealer", "motor manufacturer" and "stock in trade" inserted, and definition of "printed matter" revoked, by the VAT (Input Tax) (Amendment) Order, SI 1999/2930, arts 2, 3 with effect from 1 December 1999.

[4] Definitions of "collectors' items" and "work of art" substituted (both definitions originally inserted by SI 1995/1267) by the VAT (Input Tax) (Amendment) (No 2) Order, SI 1999/3118, arts 2, 3, with effect from 1 January 2000.

[5] In definition of "motor car", figure "12" substituted for word "twelve" and sub-para (*b*)(ii*a*) inserted, by the VAT (Input Tax) (Amendment) Order, SI 2009/217 art 2 with effect from 6 April 2009.

Revocations

3 The provisions specified in the first column of the Schedule to this Order are hereby revoked to the extent specified in the second column of that Schedule.

Disallowance of input tax

[**4**— (1) Subject to paragraph (4) below, tax charged on the—

(*a*) supply;

(*b*) acquisition from another member State; or

(*c*) importation,

of any goods such as are described in paragraph (2) below which are supplied to, or acquired from another member State or imported by, a taxable person in the circumstances described in paragraph (3) below shall be excluded from any credit under section 25 of the Act.

(2) The goods referred to in paragraph (1) above are—

(*a*) works of art, antiques and collectors' items;

(*b*) second-hand goods.

(3) The circumstances of the supply, acquisition from another member State or importation referred to in paragraph (1) above are—

(*a*) a supply on which, by virtue of an Order made under Section 50A of the Act or a corresponding provision of the Manx Act or by virtue of a corresponding provision of the law of another member State, VAT was chargeable on the profit margin;

[(*aa*) …][2]

(*b*) (if the goods are a work of art, an antique or a collectors' item) the taxable person imported it himself;

(*c*) (if the goods are a work of art) it was supplied to the taxable person by, or acquired from another member State by him from its creator or his successor in title;

(4) Paragraph (1) above shall only apply to exclude from credit, tax chargeable on a supply of goods to or an acquisition or importation of goods by a taxable person in the circumstances set out in paragraph (3)(*b*) and (*c*) above if the taxable person—

(*a*) has opted to account for VAT chargeable on his supplies of such goods on the profit margin and

(*b*) has not elected to account for VAT chargeable on his supply of the goods by reference to its value, in accordance with the provisions of an Order made under section 50A of the Act.][1]

Amendments—[1] This article substituted by the VAT (Input Tax) (Amendment) (No 2) Order, SI 1995/1267 art 4 with effect from 1 June 1995.

[2] Para (3)(*aa*) revoked by the VAT (Input Tax) (Amendment) Order, SI 1999/2930, arts 2, 4, with effect from 1 March 2000 (previously inserted by the VAT (Input Tax) (Amendment) (No 3) Order, SI 1995/1666 art 3).

5— (1) Tax charged on any goods or services supplied to a taxable person, or on any goods acquired by a taxable person, or on any goods imported by a taxable person, is to be excluded from any credit under section [25][1] of the Act, where the goods or services in question are used or to be used by the taxable person for the purposes of business entertainment.

(2) Where, by reason of the operation of paragraph (1) above, a taxable person has claimed no input tax on …[2]a supply of any services, tax shall be charged on a supply by him of the goods in question not being a letting on hire or on a supply by him of the services in question, as if that supply were for a consideration equal to the excess of—

[(*a*) the consideration for which the services are supplied by him, over

(*b*) the consideration for which the services were supplied to him,][2]

and accordingly shall not be charged unless there is such an excess.

(3) For the purposes of this article, "business entertainment" means entertainment including hospitality of any kind provided by a taxable person in connection with a business carried on by him, but does not include the provision of any such entertainment for either or both—

(*a*) employees of the taxable person;

(*b*) if the taxable person is a body corporate, its directors or persons otherwise engaged in its management,

unless the provision of entertainment for persons such as are mentioned in sub-paragraph (*a*) and (*b*) above is incidental to its provisions for others.

(4) …[2]

Press releases etc—C&E Business Brief 21/95 8-10-95 (entertaining of guests at staff parties constitutes "business entertainment").

Simon's Tax Cases—Art 5(1), *C&E Comrs v Plant* [1994] STC 232*; *Thorn EMI plc v C&E Comrs* [1995] STC 674*; *BMW (GB) Ltd v Comrs of Customs and Excise* [1997] STC 824; *C&E Comrs v Kilroy Television Co Ltd* [1997] STC 901.
Art 5(3), [1997] STC 824, *C&E Comrs v Kilroy Television Co Ltd* [1997] STC 901.

Amendments—[1] Figure in para (1) substituted by the VAT (Input Tax) (Amendment) Order, SI 1995/281 art 5 with effect from 1 March 1995.

[2] Words in para (2), and whole of para (4) revoked, and paras (2)(*a*), (*b*) substituted, by the VAT (Input Tax) (Amendment) Order, SI 1999/2930, arts 2, 5, with effect from 1 March 2000.

[6 Where a taxable person constructing, or effecting any works to a building, in either case for the purpose of making a grant of a major interest in it or any part of it or its site which is of a description in Schedule 8 to the Act, incorporates goods other than building materials in any part of the building or its site, input tax on the supply, acquisition or importation of the goods shall be excluded from credit under section 25 of the Act.][1]

Simon's Tax Cases—*C&E Comrs v Westbury Developments (Worthing) Ltd* [1981] STC 72*; *C&E Comrs v McLean Homes Midland Ltd* [1993] STC 335*.

Amendments—[1] Substituted by the VAT (Input Tax) (Amendment) Order, SI 1995/281 art 6 with effect from 1 March 1995.

7— (1) Subject to paragraph (2) [to (2H)][2] below tax charged on—

(*a*) the supply [(including a letting on hire)][2] to a taxable person;

(*b*) the acquisition by a taxable person from another member State; or

(*c*) the importation by a taxable person,

of a motor car shall be excluded from any credit under section [25][1] of the Act.

[(2) Paragraph (1) above does not apply where—

(*a*) the motor car is—

(i) a qualifying motor car;

(ii) [supplied (including on a letting on hire) to][3] , or acquired from another member State or imported by, a taxable person; and

(iii) the relevant condition is satisfied;

[(*aa*) the motor car forms part of the stock in trade of a motor manufacturer or a motor dealer;][4]

(*b*) the supply is a letting on hire of a motor car which is not a qualifying motor car [(other than a supply on a letting on hire of a motor car which is not a qualifying motor car by virtue only of the application of paragraph (2C) below, to a person whose supply on a letting on hire prior to 1st August 1995 resulted in the application of that paragraph)][3];

(*c*) the motor car is unused and is supplied to a taxable person whose only taxable supplies are concerned with the letting of motor cars on hire to another taxable person whose business consists predominantly of making supplies of a description falling within item 14 of Group 12 of Schedule 8 to the Act; or

(*d*) the motor car is unused and is supplied on a letting on hire to a taxable person whose business consists predominantly of making supplies of a description falling within item 14 of Group 12 of Schedule 8 to the Act, by a taxable person whose only taxable supplies are concerned with the letting on hire of motor cars to such a taxable person.][2]

[(2A) Subject to paragraph (2B) and (2C) below, for the purposes of paragraph (2)(*a*) [and (*b*)][4] above a motor car is a qualifying motor car if—

(*a*) it has never been supplied, acquired from another member State, or imported in circumstances in which the VAT on that supply, acquisition or importation was wholly excluded from credit as input tax by virtue of paragraph (1) above; or

(*b*) a taxable person has elected for it to be treated as such.

(2B) A taxable person may only elect for a motor car to be treated as a qualifying motor car if it—

(*a*) is first registered on or after 1st August 1995;

(*b*) was supplied to, or acquired from another member State or imported by, him prior to that date in circumstances in which the VAT on that supply, acquisition or importation was wholly excluded from credit as input tax by virtue of paragraph (1) above; and

(*c*) had not been supplied on a letting on hire by him prior to 1st August 1995.

(2C) A motor car that is supplied, acquired from another member State or imported on or after 1st August 1995 and which would, apart from this paragraph, be a qualifying motor car by virtue of sub-paragraph (*a*) of paragraph (2A) above shall not be such a car if it was supplied on a letting on hire prior to that date by the person to whom it is supplied or by whom it is acquired or imported (as the case may be).

(2D) References in this article to registration of a motor car mean registration in accordance with section 21 of the Vehicle Excise and Registration Act 1994.

(2E) For the purposes of paragraph (2)(*a*) above the relevant condition is that the letting on hire, supply, acquisition or importation (as the case may be) is to a taxable person who intends to use the motor car either—

(*a*) exclusively for the purposes of a business carried on by him, but this is subject to paragraph (2G) below; or

(*b*) primarily for a relevant purpose.

(2F) For the purposes of paragraph (2E) above a relevant purpose, in relation to a motor car which is let on hire or supplied to, or acquired or imported by, a taxable person (as the case may be), is any of the following purposes—

(*a*) to provide it on hire with the services of a driver for the purpose of carrying passengers;

(*b*) to provide it for self-drive hire; or

(*c*) to use it as a vehicle in which instruction in the driving of a motor car is to be given by him.

(2G) A taxable person shall not be taken to intend to use a motor car exclusively for the purposes of a business carried on by him if he intends to—

(*a*) let it on hire to any person either for no consideration or for a consideration which is less than that which would be payable in money if it were a commercial transaction conducted at arms length; or

(*b*) make it available (otherwise than by letting it on hire) to any person (including, where the taxable person is an individual, himself, or where the taxable person is a partnership, a partner) for private use, whether or not for a consideration.

(2H) Where paragraph (1) above applies to a supply of a motor car on a letting on hire it shall apply to the tax charged on that supply as if for the word "tax" there were substituted "one half of the tax".][2]

(3) In this article—

(*a*) …[2]

(*b*) "self-drive hire" means hire where the hirer is the person normally expected to drive the motor car and the period of hire to each hirer, together with the period of hire of any other motor car expected to be hired to him by the taxable person—

(i) will normally be less than 30 consecutive days; and

(ii) will normally be less than 90 days in any period of 12 months.

(4), (5) …[5]

Commentary—*De Voil Indirect Tax Service* **V3.449**.

Press releases etc—C&E Business Brief 15/95 31-7-95 (Further developments or treatment of business cars).

Simon's Tax Cases—*C&E Comrs v Jeynes (T/A Midland International (Hire) Caterers)* [1984] STC 30*.

Art 7(1), *Group Ltd v C&E Comrs* [1996] STC 898.

Art 7(2), *C&E Comrs v Elm Milk Ltd* [2005] STC 776.

Art 7(2C), *C&E Comrs v BRS Automotive Ltd* [1998] STC 1210.

Art 7(2E), *C&E Comrs v Skellett (t/a Vidcom Computer Services)* [2004] STC 201; *C&E Comrs v Robbins* [2005] STC 1103; *Thompson (trading as Thompson (HAS) & Co) v C&E Comrs* [2005] STC 1777; *R&C Comrs v Shaw* [2007] STC 1525.

Art 7(2G), *C&E Comrs v Skellett (t/a Vidcom Computer Services)* [2004] STC 201; *C&E Comrs v Elm Milk Ltd* [2005] STC 776; *C&E Comrs v Robbins* [2005] STC 1103; *Thompson (trading as Thompson (HAS) & Co) v C&E Comrs* [2005] STC 1777; *R&C Comrs v Shaw* [2007] STC 1525.

Cross reference—See VAT Regulations, SI 1995/2518 (requirement to state on VAT invoice for a supply of a letting of a car, other than for self-drive hire, whether it is a qualifying vehicle under para (2A) above).

See EC Council Decision 98/198/EC of 9 March 1998 (authorisation for UK to restrict to 50% the input tax recoverable by hirers or lessees of cars used partly for private purposes).

Amendments—[1] Words in paras (1), (2)(*d*), (*f*), (4), (5)(*b*) substituted by the VAT (Input Tax) (Amendment) Order, SI 1995/281 art 7 with effect from 1 March 1995.

[2] Words in para (1), and paras (2A)–(2H) inserted, words in para (1), para (2) and the words in para (4) substituted, and para (3)(*a*) revoked by the VAT (Input Tax) (Amendment) (No 3) Order, SI 1995/1666 arts 4–8 with effect from 1 August 1995.

[3] Words in paras (2)(*a*)(ii) substituted and (2)(*b*) inserted by the VAT (Input Tax) (Amendment) Order, SI 1998/2767 with effect from 13 November 1998.

[4] Para (2)(*aa*), and words in para (2A), inserted, by the VAT (Input Tax) (Amendment) Order, SI 1999/2930, arts 2, 6(*a*), (*b*), with effect from 1 December 1999.

[5] Paras (4), (5) revoked by the VAT (Input Tax) (Amendment) Order, SI 1999/2930, arts 2, 6(*c*), with effect from 1 March 2000.

SCHEDULE

REVOCATIONS

Article 3

Note—Effect has been given to the revocations made by this Schedule.

1992/3283

Value Added Tax (Place of Supply of Goods) Order 1992

Amendment—This Order revoked by the VAT (Place of Supply of Goods) Order, SI 2004/3148 reg 3 with effect from 1 January 2005.

1993/1507
Value Added Tax (Supply of Services) Order 1993

Made by the Treasury under VATA 1983 s 3(4), (8) (see now VATA 1994 s 5(4), (8)) and all other enabling powers

Made . . . . *15 June 1993*
Laid before the House of Commons . . . . *16 June 1993*
Coming into force . . . . *1 August 1993*

1 This Order may be cited as the Value Added Tax (Supply of Services) Order 1993 and shall come into force on 1st August 1993.

HMRC Manuals—VAT Guidance V1–3: Supply and consideration, para 6.1 (private or non-business use of services).

2 In this Order—

"the Act" means the Value Added Tax Act [1994][1].

Amendments—[1] Year substituted by the VAT (Supply of Services) (Amendment) Order, SI 1995/1668 art 3 with effect from 1 August 1995.

3 Subject to articles [6, 6A and 7][1] below, where a person carrying on a business puts services which have been supplied to him to any private use or uses them, or makes them available to any person for use, for a purpose other than a purpose of the business he shall be treated for the purposes of the Act as supplying those services in the course or furtherance of the business [except for the purposes of determining whether tax on the supply of the services to him is input tax of his under section 24 of the Act][2].

Press releases etc—C&E Business Brief 17/94 12-9-94 (minor and occasional changes of use to private or non-business use should be ignored).

Amendments—[1] Words substituted by the VAT (Supply of Services) (Amendment) Order, SI 1995/1668 art 4 with effect from 1 August 1995.
[2] Words inserted by the VAT (Supply of Services) (Amendment) Order, SI 2003/1055 art 3. SI 2003/1055 comes into force on 10 April 2003, with effect for supplies made to a taxable person after 9 April 2003.

[3A For the purposes of this Order, references to services supplied to a person include references to supplies of—

(a) a major interest in land,
(b) any building or part of a building,
(c) any civil engineering work or part of such a work, or
(d) any goods incorporated or to be incorporated in a building or civil engineering work (whether by being installed as fixtures or fittings or otherwise).][1, 2]

Note—Articles 3A, 3B revoked following the ECJ decision in *P Charles and T S Charles-Tijmens v Staatssecretaris van Financiën* (Case C-434/03).

Amendments—[1] Articles 3A, 3B inserted by the VAT (Supply of Services) (Amendment) Order, SI 2003/1055 art 4. SI 2003/1055 comes into force on 10 April 2003, with effect for supplies made to a taxable person after 9 April 2003.
[2] Articles 3A, 3B revoked by the VAT (Supply of Services) (Amendment) Order, SI 2007/2173 art 2 with effect from 1 September 2007.

***3B** Where article 3 above applies in relation to supplies of goods falling within any of paragraphs (a) to (d) of article 3A above, the person shall be treated as supplying a service of making the goods available, and the other articles of this Order shall apply with appropriate modifications.]*[1, 2]

Note—Articles 3A, 3B revoked following the ECJ decision in *P Charles and T S Charles-Tijmens v Staatssecretaris van Financiën* (Case C-434/03).

Amendments—[1] Articles 3A, 3B inserted by the VAT (Supply of Services) (Amendment) Order, SI 2003/1055 art 4. SI 2003/1055 comes into force on 10 April 2003, with effect for supplies made by a taxable person after 9 April 2003.
[2] Articles 3A, 3B revoked by the VAT (Supply of Services) (Amendment) Order, SI 2007/2173 art 2 with effect from 1 September 2007.

4 In the case of a business carried on by an individual, this Order shall apply to services used, or made available for use, by himself personally.

5 The value of a supply which a person is treated as making by virtue of this Order shall be taken to be that part of the value of the supply of the services to him as fairly and reasonably represents the cost to him of providing the services.

Press releases etc—C&E Business Brief 17/94 12-9-94 (in calculating the cost of private or non-business use, a taxpayer can use his normal accounting convention for depreciating comparable business assets or any other fair and reasonable basis).

6 This Order shall not apply in respect of any services—

(*a*) which are used, or made available for use, for a consideration;
(*b*) except those in respect of which the person carrying on the business [has or will become][2] entitled under sections [25 and 26][1] of the Act to credit for the whole or any part of the tax on their supply to him;
(*c*) in respect of which any part of the tax on their supply to the person carrying on the business was not counted as being input tax of his by virtue of an apportionment made under section [24(5)][1] of the Act; or
(*d*) of a description within paragraph 10(1) of Schedule [6][1] to the Act.

Amendments—[1] Words substituted by the VAT (Supply of Services) (Amendment) Order, SI 1995/1668 art 5 with effect from 1 August 1995.

[2] Words substituted by the VAT (Supply of Services) (Amendment) Order, SI 1998/762 with effect from 18 March 1998.

[6A— (1) This Order shall not apply to any supply of services consisting of the letting on hire of a motor car where one half of the tax on that letting on hire was excluded from credit under section 25 of the Act by virtue of article 7 of the Value Added Tax (Input Tax) Order 1992.

(2) In paragraph (1) above, "motor car" has the same meaning as in article 2 of the Value Added Tax (Input Tax) Order 1992.][1]

Amendments—[1] This article inserted by the VAT (Supply of Services) (Amendment) Order, SI 1995/1668 art 6 with effect from 1 August 1995.

7 Nothing in this Order shall be construed as making any person liable for any tax which, taken together with any tax for which he was liable as a result of a previous supply of the same services which he was treated as making by virtue of this Order, would exceed the amount of input tax for which he [has or will become entitled][1] to [credit under sections 25 and 26 of the Act][1] in respect of the services used, or made available for use, by him; and, where the tax chargeable would otherwise exceed the amount of that credit—

(*a*) he shall not be treated as making a supply of the services where the amount of that credit has already been equalled or exceeded; and

(*b*) in any other case, the value of the supply shall be reduced accordingly.

Amendments—[1] Words substituted by the VAT (Supply of Services) (Amendment) Order, SI 1998/762 with effect from 18 March 1998.

[8 Where—

(*a*) there is a supply of any of the assets of a business of a person ('the transferor') to a person to whom the whole or any part of that business is transferred as a going concern ('the transferee'), and

(*b*) that supply is treated in accordance with an Order made under section 5(3) of the Act (or under an enactment re-enacted in section 5(3) of the Act) as being neither a supply of goods nor a supply of services,

the liability of the transferee to tax in accordance with articles 5, 6(*b*) and 7 above, shall be determined as if the transferor and the transferee were the same person.][1]

Amendments—[1] Inserted by the VAT (Supply of Services) (Amendment) Order, SI 1998/762 with effect from 18 March 1998.

[9 Where a transferor has himself acquired any assets by way of a supply falling within paragraphs (*a*) and (*b*) of article 8 above, that article shall have the effect of requiring the person from whom those assets were acquired to be treated for the purposes of determining the liability of the transferee to tax in accordance with articles 5, 6(*b*) and 7 above as the same person as the transferor and the transferee, and so on in the case of any number of successive supplies falling within those paragraphs.][1]

Amendments—[1] Inserted by the VAT (Supply of Services) (Amendment) Order, SI 1998/762 with effect from 18 March 1998.

1993/2001
Value Added Tax (Payments on Account) Order 1993

Made by the Treasury under VATA 1983 s 38C(1)–(2), (4), (5) (see now VATA 1994 s 28(1), (2), (4), (5)) and all other enabling powers

Made . . . . *9 August 1993*
Laid before the House of Commons . . . . *9 August 1993*
Coming into force . . . . *2 September 1993*

Citation and commencement

1 This Order may be cited as the Value Added Tax (Payments on Account) Order 1993 and shall come into force on 2nd September 1993.

Interpretation

2— (1) In this Order—

"the Act" means the Value Added Tax Act [1994][1];

"the basic period" means, in relation to a taxable person falling within article 5 or 6 below, the period of one year in which there ended the prescribed accounting periods in respect of which his liability to pay a total amount of tax exceeding £2,000,000 caused him to become such a taxable person;

"Controller" means the Controller, Customs and Excise, Value Added Tax Central Unit;

...[2]

"reference period" has the meaning ascribed to it in article 11(1) below.

(2) Any reference in articles 13 to 15 below to the total amount of tax by reference to which a taxable person's payments on account fall to be calculated being "reduced accordingly" or "increased accordingly" is in each case a reference to a reduction or increase of the same proportion as the difference between the total amount of tax by reference to which his payments on account are currently calculated and the total amount of tax, excluding the tax on goods imported from countries other than member States, which he was, or (as the case may be) which the Commissioners are satisfied that he will be, liable to pay in respect of the prescribed accounting periods the ends of which fall within the year referred to in the relevant provision of the article in question.

Amendments—[1] Substituted by SI 1996/1196 art 3 with effect from 1 June 1996.
[2] Definition of "credit transfer" repealed by SI 1996/1196 with effect from 1 June 1996.

[Supplies to which section 55A(6) of the Act applies (customers to account for tax on supplies of a kind used in missing trader intra-community fraud)

2A Where, on application, a taxable person satisfies the Commissioners that, by reason solely of any amount that he is liable to pay by virtue of section 55A(6) of the Act—

(*a*) he falls within article 5 or 6 below, or

(*b*) the amount of each of his payments on account is increased,

then, with effect from the date of the approval by the Commissioners of the application, any amount that he is so liable to pay by virtue of that section shall be disregarded for the purposes of those articles or, as the case may be, the calculation of the amount of each of his payments on account.][1]

Amendments—[1] Article 2A inserted by the VAT (Payments on Account) (Amendment) Order, SI 2007/1420 art 2 with effect from 1 June 2007.

Revocation

3— (1) Subject to paragraph (2) below, the Value Added Tax (Payments on Account) (No 2) Order 1992 is hereby revoked.

(2) The duty under the Value Added Tax (Payments on Account) (No 2) Order 1992 of any taxable person to make a payment on account in respect of a prescribed accounting period beginning before 2nd September 1993 shall not be affected by the revocation of that Order which shall continue to have effect in relation to any such payment on account.

Payments on account

4— (1) A taxable person falling within article 5 or 6 below shall be under a duty to pay, on account of any tax he may become liable to pay in respect of each prescribed accounting period exceeding one month beginning on or after [1st April each year][1] amounts (in this Order referred to as "payments on account") determined in accordance with this Order at times so determined, provided that in the case of a taxable person falling within article 6 below there shall be no duty to pay such amounts in respect of a prescribed accounting period other than one beginning after the basic period.

[(2) Where such a taxable person has a prescribed accounting period exceeding one month which begins on or after 2nd March each year and ends on or before 30th June each year, he shall be under a like duty to make payments on account also in respect of that prescribed accounting period.][1]

Amendments—[1] Words in para (1) and whole of para (2) substituted by the VAT (Payments on Account) (Amendment) Order, SI 1995/291 arts 3, 4 with effect from 2 March 1995.

Persons to whom this Order applies

[**5**— (1) Subject to paragraph (2) below and article 16 below, a taxable person falls within this article in any year if the total amount of tax which he was liable to pay in respect of the prescribed accounting periods the ends of which fell within the period of one year ending on the last day of his last prescribed accounting period ending before the previous 1st December exceeded £2,000,000.

(2) Where in any year ending 30th November a prescribed accounting period of the taxable person did not begin on the first day or did not end on the last day of a month, the period of one year shall, for the purpose of this article, be regarded as having comprised those prescribed account periods which related to the tax periods ending within the year ending 30th November of that year to which references are shown in the certificate of registration issued to him][1].

Amendments—[1] Substituted by the VAT (Payments on Account) (Amendment) Order, SI 1995/291 art 5 with effect from 2 March 1995.

6— (1) Subject to paragraph (2) below and article 16 below, a taxable person who does not fall within article 5 above shall fall within this article if the total amount of tax which he was liable to pay in respect of the prescribed accounting periods the ends of which fell within any one period of one year ending on the last day of a prescribed accounting period of his ending after [30th November of the previous year][1] exceeded £2,000,000.

(2) Where in the period of the year referred to in paragraph (1) above a prescribed accounting period of the taxable person did not begin on the first day or did not end on the last day of a month, that period of one year shall, for the purpose of this article, be regarded as having comprised those prescribed accounting periods which related to the tax periods ending within that period of one year to which references are shown in the certificate of registration issued to him.

Amendments—[1] Words in para (1) substituted by the VAT (Payments on Account) (Amendment) Order, SI 1995/291 art 6 with effect from 2 March 1995.

Cessation of duty to make payments on account

7 If the total amount of tax which a taxable person who is under a duty to make payments on account was liable to pay in respect of the prescribed accounting periods the ends of which fell within any one period of one year ending after the end of the basic period was less than £1,600,000, then, with effect from the date of the written approval by the Commissioners of a written application by the taxable person to that effect, he shall not be under a duty to make payments on account.

Time for payment

8 [Subject to article 9 below][1], in respect of each prescribed accounting period a payment on account shall be made to the Controller not later than—

(*a*) the last day of the month next following the end of the first complete month included therein, and

(*b*) the last day of the month next following the end of the second complete month included therein.

Amendments—[1] Words substituted by the VAT (Payments on Account) (Amendment) Order, SI 1996/1196 art 4 with effect from 1 June 1996.

9 …[1] where a prescribed accounting period does not begin on the first day or does not end on the last day of a month—

(*a*) the first payment on account shall be made not later than the last day of the month next following the end of the first complete month included therein, and

(*b*) the second payment on account shall be made not later than the last day of the month next following the end of the second complete month included therein.

except that where—

(i) a prescribed accounting period does not comprise more complete months than one, the first payment on account shall be made not later than the last day of that month and the second payment on account shall be made not later than the end of the prescribed accounting period, or

(ii) a prescribed accounting period comprises an incomplete month followed by two complete months, the first payment on account shall be made not later than the end of the first complete month and the second payment on account shall be made not later than the end of the second complete month, or

(iii) a prescribed accounting period comprises an incomplete month followed by two complete months and an incomplete month, the first payment on account shall be made not later than the end of the first complete month and the second payment on account shall be made not later than the end of the second complete month.

Amendments—[1] Words deleted by the VAT (Payments on Account) (Amendment) Order, SI 1996/1196 art 5 with effect from 1 June 1996.

10 …

Amendments—This article deleted by the VAT (Payments on Account) (Amendment) Order, SI 1996/1196 art 6 with effect from 1 June 1996.

Calculation of the payments on account

11—(1) Subject to paragraph (2) below and articles [12A,][2], 13, 14 and 15 below, the amount of each payment on account to be made by a taxable person who falls within article 5 above shall equal [one twenty-fourth][3] of the total amount of tax, excluding the tax on goods imported from countries other than member States, which he was liable to pay in respect of the prescribed accounting periods the ends of which fell within the period (in this Order referred to as "the reference period")—

[(*a*) 1st October to 30th September in the basic period where he has a prescribed accounting period beginning in April in any year in which he is under a duty to make payments on account,][1]

[(*b*) 1st November to 31st October in the basic period where he has a prescribed accounting period beginning in May in any year in which he is under a duty to make payments on account, and][1]

[(*c*) 1st December to 30th November in the basic period where he has a prescribed accounting period beginning in June in any year in which he is under a duty to make payments on account.][1]

(2) Where in the period of the year mentioned in sub-paragraph (*a*), (*b*) or (*c*) of paragraph (1) above a prescribed accounting period of the taxable person did not begin on the first day or did not end on the last day of a month, the reference period shall, for the purpose of paragraph (1), be regarded as having comprised those prescribed accounting periods which related to the tax periods ending within the period of the year mentioned in sub-paragraph (*a*), (*b*) or (*c*) of paragraph (1) as appropriate to which references are shown in the certificate of registration issued to him.

Amendments—[1] Para (1) (*a*)–(*c*) substituted by the VAT (Payments on Account) (Amendment) Order, SI 1995/291 arts 7–9 with effect from 2 March 1995.

[2] Words inserted by the VAT (Payments on Account) (Amendment) Order, SI 1996/1196 art 7 with effect from 1 June 1996.

[3] Words substituted by the VAT (Payments on Account) (Amendment) Order, SI 1996/1196 art 7 with effect from 1 June 1996.

12 Subject to articles [12A][1], 13, 14 and 15 below, the amount of each payment on account to be made by a taxable person who falls within article 6 above shall equal [one twenty-fourth][2] of the total amount of tax, excluding the tax on goods imported from countries other than member States, which he was liable to pay in respect of the prescribed accounting periods the ends of which fell within the basic period.

Amendments—[1] Words inserted by the VAT (Payments on Account) (Amendment) Order, SI 1996/1196 art 8 with effect from 1 June 1996.

[2] Words substituted by the VAT (Payments on Account) (Amendment) Order, SI 1996/1196 art 8 with effect from 1 June 1996.

[12A— (1) Subject to paragraph (5) below a taxable person who is under a duty to make payments on account may instead of paying the amount calculated in accordance with paragraphs 11 or 12 above elect to pay an amount equal to his liability to VAT (excluding the tax on goods imported from countries other than member States) for the preceding month.

(2) A person making an election under paragraph (1) above shall notify the Commissioners in writing of—

(*a*) the election, and

(*b*) the date (being a date not less than 30 days after the date of the notification) on which it is to take effect.

(3) Subject to paragraph (4) below, an election under paragraph (1) above shall continue to have effect until a date notified by the taxable person in writing to the Commissioners, which date shall not be earlier than the first anniversary of the date on which the election took effect.

(4) Where the Commissioners are satisfied that an amount paid by a person who has elected in accordance with paragraph (1) above is less than the amount required to be paid by virtue of that paragraph the Commissioners may notify the taxable person in writing that his election shall cease to have effect from a date specified in the notification.

(5) A person may not make an election under paragraph (1) above within 12 months of the date on which any previous election made by him ceased to have effect by virtue of paragraph (4) above.][1]

Amendments—[1] This article inserted by the VAT (Payments on Account) (Amendment) Order, SI 1996/1196 art 10 with effect from 1 June 1996.

13 If—

(*a*) the total amount of tax, excluding the tax on goods imported from countries other than member States, which the taxable person was liable to pay in respect of the prescribed accounting periods the ends of which fell within any one period of one year—

(i) in the case of a taxable person who falls within article 5 above, ending after the end of his reference period was less than 80 per cent of the total amount of tax relevant in his case under article 11 above, or

(ii) in the case of a taxable person who falls within article 6 above, ending after the end of the basic period was less than 80 per cent of the total amount of tax referred to in article 12, or

(*b*) where such a period of one year has not ended, the Commissioners are satisfied that the total amount of tax, excluding the tax on goods imported from countries other than member States, which the taxable person will be liable to pay in respect of the prescribed accounting periods the ends of which fall within that year will be less than 80 per cent of the total amount of tax referred to in sub-paragraph (i) or (ii) (as the case may be) of paragraph (*a*) above,

then, with effect from the date of the written approval by the Commissioners of a written application by the taxable person to that effect, but subject to article 14 below, the total amount of tax by reference to which his payments on account fall to be calculated shall be reduced accordingly and the amount of each payment on account beginning with the first payment on account which falls to be made after the date of that approval shall equal [one twenty-fourth][1] of the reduced amount.

Amendments—[1] Words substituted by the VAT (Payments on Account) (Amendment) Order, SI 1996/1196 art 9 with effect from 1 June 1996.

14 If the total amount of tax, excluding the tax on goods imported from countries other than member States, which the taxable person was liable to pay in respect of the prescribed accounting periods the ends of which fell within any one period of one year—

(*a*) in the case of a taxable person who falls within article 5 above, ending after the end of his reference period exceeded by 20 per cent. or more the total amount of tax by reference to which his payments on account are currently calculated, or

(*b*) in the case of a taxable person who falls within article 6 above, ending after the end of the basic period exceeded by 20 per cent. or more the total amount of tax by reference to which his payments on account are currently calculated,

then, with effect from the end of the period of one year first mentioned, but subject to article 15 below, the total amount of tax by reference to which his payments on account fall to be calculated shall be increased accordingly and the amount of each payment on account beginning with the first payment on account which falls to be made after the end of that period of one year shall equal [one twenty-fourth][1] of the increased amount.

Amendments—[1] Words substituted by the VAT (Payments on Account) (Amendment) Order, SI 1996/1196 art 9 with effect from 1 June 1996.

15 Where the payments on account payable by a taxable person have been increased by virtue of article 14 above and—

(*a*) the total amount of tax, excluding the tax on goods imported from countries other than member States, which he was liable to pay in respect of the prescribed accounting periods the ends of which fell within any one period of one year ending after such increase has taken effect was less than 80 per cent of the total amount of tax by reference to which his payments on account are currently calculated, or

(*b*) where such a period of one year has not ended, the Commissioners are satisfied that the total amount of tax, excluding the tax on goods imported from countries other than member States, which he will be liable to pay in respect of the prescribed accounting periods the ends of which fall within that year will be less than 80 per cent of the total amount of tax by reference to which his payments on account are currently calculated,

then, with effect from the date of the written approval by the Commissioners of a written application by the taxable person to that effect, the total amount of tax by reference to which his payments on account fall to be calculated shall be reduced accordingly and the amount of each payment on account beginning with the first payment on account which falls to be made after the date of that approval shall equal [one twenty-fourth][1] of the reduced amount.

Amendments—[1] Words substituted by the VAT (Payments on Account) (Amendment) Order, SI 1996/1196 art 9 with effect from 1 June 1996.

Business carried on in divisions

16— (1) Subject to paragraph (3) below, where the registration under the Act of a body corporate is and was throughout the prescribed accounting periods mentioned in article 5(1) or 6(1) above in the names of divisions under section 31(1) of the Act[a] and those divisions are the same divisions, that body corporate shall not be under a duty to make payments on account by virtue of falling within article 5 or 6 above but shall be under a duty to make payments on account by reference to the business of any division if the total amount of tax which it was liable to pay in respect of the prescribed accounting periods of that division the ends of which fell within the period of one year ending on the last day of—

(*a*) that division's last prescribed accounting period ending before [1st December of the previous year][1], or

(*b*) a prescribed accounting period of that division ending after [30th November of the previous year][1],

and which was referable to the business of that division exceeded £2,000,000.

[(2) Where a relevant division has a prescribed accounting period exceeding one month which begins on or after 2nd March each year and ends on or before 30th June each year, the body corporate shall be under a like duty to make payments on account also in respect of that prescribed accounting period.][1]

(3) Articles 5(2) and 6(2) above shall apply for the purposes of this article as if for the references therein to the taxable person there were substituted references to a relevant division.

(4) Where payments on account fall to be made under this article, they shall be calculated and made separately in the case of each relevant division as if it were a taxable person and shall be remitted to the Controller through that division.

(5) In relation to a body corporate to which this article applies, references in articles 7, 13, 14 and 15 above to—

(*a*) the total amount of tax which a taxable person was or will be liable to pay shall be construed as references to the total amount of such tax referable to the business of a relevant division; and

(*b*) an application by the taxable person shall be construed as references to an application by the division in respect of which the application is made.

(6) In this article "relevant division" means a division by reference to the business of which a body corporate is under a duty to make payments on account by virtue of paragraph (1) above.

Note—[a] VATA 1994 s 46(1).

Amendments—[1] Words in para (1) and whole of para (2) substituted by the VAT (Payments on Account) (Amendment) Order, SI 1995/291 arts 11, 12 with effect from 2 March 1995.

Groups of companies

17 This Order shall apply in relation to any bodies corporate which are treated as members of a group under [section 43][1] of the Act as if those bodies were one taxable person; and where there is a duty to make a payment on account it shall be the responsibility of the representative member, except that in default of payment by the representative member it shall be the joint and several responsibility of each member of the group.

Amendments—[1] Words substituted by the VAT (Payments on Account) (Amendment) Order, SI 1996/1196 art 11 with effect from 1 June 1996.

1994/144

Free Zone (Humberside) Designation Order 1994

Made by the Treasury under CEMA 1979 s 100A

Made . . . . 26 *January* 1994
Coming into force . . . . 1 *February* 1994

Citation and commencement

1 This Order may be cited as the Free Zone (Humberside) Designation Order 1994 and shall come into force on 1st February 1994.

Designation of area as free zone

2—(1) An area of 10.322 acres, in the parish of Stoneferry in the County of Humberside, shown enclosed by a red line on a map (in this article referred to as "the map"), being of a scale of 1:500, and signed by a Collector of Customs and Excise, shall be a free zone.

(2) The map shall be kept by the Commissioners at their Headquarters, New King's Beam House, 22 Upper Ground, London SE1 9PJ and a copy thereof at the offices of the responsible authority.

(3) The map or a copy thereof may, on application, be inspected by members of the public at reasonable hours without charge.

Cross reference—See Free Zone (Humberside) Designation (Variation) Order, SI 1995/1067.

Appointment of responsible authority

3 The responsible authority for the free zone shall be Transport Development Group Limited whose Registered Office is at Windsor House, 50 Victoria Street, London SW1H 0NR.

Period of validity of Order

4 This Order shall have effect for a period of 10 years from the date of coming into force.

Conditions imposed on responsible authority

5 The responsible authority shall—

(*a*) maintain an office in the free zone or such other place as the Commissioners may allow at which shall be kept any records, for which the responsible authority is responsible, relating to the free zone and the business carried on therein;

(*b*) keep separate accounts in connection with the free zone;

(*c*) provide such information in connection with the free zone and the operation thereof to any person authorised by the Treasury, as that person may reasonably require;

(*d*) provide, free of expense to the Crown, such accommodation and facilities including furniture, fittings and equipment as the Commissioners may reasonably require and such accommodation and facilities shall be properly maintained, heated, lighted, ventilated and kept clean by the responsible authority;

(*e*) provide, free of expense to the Crown, such area of land within the free zone as the Commissioners may reasonably require for the examination of goods and vehicles and shall provide and maintain such appliances and afford such other facilities which are reasonably necessary to enable an account to be taken of any goods or make any examination or search.

Health and safety

6 Without prejudice to the responsibilities of persons occupying premises within the free zone, the responsible authority shall ensure that the working conditions within the free zone are safe and without risk to the health and safety of persons employed by the Commissioners and shall comply with any requirements concerning health and safety imposed by any competent authority.

1994/955
Travellers' Allowances Order 1994

Made by the Commissioners of Customs and Excise under CED(GR)A 1979 s 13(1) and (3)

Made . . . . *28 March 1994*
Laid before the House of Commons . . . . *29 March 1994*
Coming into force . . . . *1 April 1994*

1 This Order may be cited as the Travellers' Allowances Order 1994 and shall come into force on 1st April 1994.

2— (1) Subject to the following provisions of this Order a person who has travelled from a third country shall on entering the United Kingdom be relieved from payment of value added tax and excise duty on goods of the descriptions and in the quantities shown in the Schedule to this Order …[1] contained in his personal luggage.

(2) For the purposes of this article—

(*a*) goods shall be treated as contained in a person's personal luggage where they are carried with or accompanied by the person or, if intended to accompany him, were at the time of his departure for the United Kingdom consigned by him as personal luggage to the transport operator with whom he travelled;

(*b*) a person shall not be treated as having travelled from a third country by reason only of his having arrived from its territorial waters or air space;

[(*c*) "third country"—

(i) shares the definition that applies to that expression for the purposes of Council Directive 2007/74/EC (this is termed "outside country" below) (see both indents of Article 3(1) of the Directive) (value added tax and excise duty exemptions for travellers from outside the Member States of the European Union, etc); but

(ii) it incorporates the definition that applies for the purposes of that Directive to "territory where the Community provisions on VAT or excise duty, or both do not apply" (this is termed "outside territory" below) (see both indents of Article 3(2) of that Directive); but

(iii) any outside territory where those "Community provisions on VAT" do apply (or where that Directive regards them as applying) is not a third country for value added tax purposes; and

(iv) any outside territory where those "Community provisions on … excise duty" do apply (or where that Directive regards them as applying) is not a third country for excise duty purposes.][1]

[(3) Where the person's journey involved transit through an outside country, or began in outside territory, this Order applies if that person is unable to establish to an officer of Revenue and Customs that the goods contained in that person's personal luggage were acquired subject to the general conditions governing taxation on the domestic market of a member State and do not qualify for any refunding of value added tax or excise duty.

(See Article 2 of Council Directive 2007/74/EC (transit, etc).)][1]

Amendments—[1] Words in para (1) revoked, para (2)(*c*) substituted, and para (3) inserted, by the Travellers' Allowances (Amendment) Order, SI 2008/3058 art 2, Sch paras 1–3 with effect from 1 December 2008.

3 The reliefs afforded under this Order are subject to the condition that the goods in question, as indicated by their nature or quantity or otherwise, are not imported for a commercial purpose nor are used for such purpose; and if that condition is not complied with in relation to any goods, those goods shall, unless the non-compliance was sanctioned by the Commissioners, be liable to forfeiture.

[That condition is complied with, for example, where an occasional importation consists exclusively of goods intended as presents, or of goods for the personal or family use of the person in question.

(See Article 6 of Council Directive 2007/74/EC (non-commercial imports).)][1]

Amendments—[1] Words inserted, by the Travellers' Allowances (Amendment) Order, SI 2008/3058 art 2, Sch para 4 with effect from 1 December 2008.

4 No relief shall be afforded under this Order to any person under the age of 17 in respect of tobacco products[, alcoholic beverages and alcohol][1].

Amendments—[1] Words substituted, by the Travellers' Allowances (Amendment) Order, SI 2008/3058 art 2, Sch para 5 with effect from 1 December 2008.

5 …

Note—Effect has been given to the revocations made by this article.

SCHEDULE …[1]

Article 2

[*Description*	*Quantity*
Goods other than fuel and those described below	Total value £340 or less, if the person travelled by air or sea. Total value £240 or less, if the person did not travel by air or sea. Notes: (a) If the person enters the United Kingdom before 1st January 2009, the respective total values are £300 or less (travel by air or sea) and £210 or less (travel not by air or sea). (b) Private pleasure-flying or private pleasure-sea-navigation does not constitute travel by air or sea for these purposes. This refers to the use of an aircraft or a sea-going vessel by its owner or the person who enjoys its use either through hire or through any other means, for purposes other than commercial and in particular other than for the carriage of passengers or goods or for the supply of services for consideration or for the purposes of public authorities. (c) The value of an individual item must not be split up. (d) The value of the person's personal luggage if imported temporarily or re-imported following its temporary export, and of medicinal products required to meet the person's personal needs, is excluded from consideration. (e) This relief corresponds to Articles 3(3), 3(4), 5 (the exclusion of fuel), 7(1), 7(3), 7(4) and 15 of Council Directive 2007/74/EC.
Alcoholic beverages and alcohol, other than beer and still wine	1 litre of alcohol and alcoholic beverages of an alcoholic strength exceeding 22% by volume, or undenatured ethyl alcohol of 80% by volume and over; or 2 litres of alcohol and alcoholic beverages of an alcoholic strength not exceeding 22% by volume. Notes: (f) Each respective amount represents 100% of the total relief afforded for alcohol and alcoholic beverages. (g) For any one person, the relief applies to any combination of the types of alcohol and alcoholic beverage described, provided that the aggregate of the percentages used up from the relief the person is afforded for such alcohol and alcoholic beverage does not exceed 100%. (h) This relief corresponds to Articles 9(1) and 9(2) of that Directive.
Beer	16 litres or less Notes: (i) This relief corresponds to Article 9(3) of that Directive (beer).
Still wine	4 litres or less Notes: (j) This relief corresponds to Article 9(3) of that Directive (still wine).

[Description	Quantity
Tobacco products	200 cigarettes, or 100 cigarillos, or 50 cigars, or 250 grams of smoking tobacco. Notes: (k) Each respective amount represents 100% of the total relief afforded for tobacco products. (l) For any one person, the relief applies to any combination of tobacco products provided that the aggregate of the percentages used up from the relief the person is afforded for such products does not exceed 100%. (m) A cigarillo is a cigar of maximum weight 3 grams. (n) This relief corresponds to Articles 8(1) and 8(4) of that Directive.][1]

Amendments—[1] Table substituted, and words in previous table heading revoked, by the Travellers' Allowances (Amendment) Order, SI 2008/3058 art 2, Sch para 6 with effect from 1 December 2008.

1994/1978
Value Added Tax Tribunals Appeals (Northern Ireland) Order 1994

Revocation—These Regulations revoked by the Transfer of Tribunal Functions and Revenue and Customs Appeals Order, SI 2009/56 art 3, Sch 2 para 187(*g*) with effect from 1 April 2009.

1995/958
Value Added Tax (Treatment of Transactions) Order 1995

Made by the Treasury under VATA 1994 s 5(3)

Made . . . . *30 March 1995*
Laid before the House of Commons . . . . . . *31 March 1995*
Coming into force in accordance with article 1 . . . . . *1 May 1995*

1 This Order may be cited as the Value Added Tax (Treatment of Transactions) Order 1995 and shall come into force on the day that the Finance Bill 1995 is passed.

[2 In this Order "work of art" has the same meaning as in section 21 of the Value Added Tax Act 1994.][1]

Amendments—[1] This article substituted by the VAT (Treatment of Transactions) (Amendment) Order, SI 1999/3119, arts 2, 3, with effect from 1 January 2000.

3— (1) Subject to paragraph (3) below, the transfer of ownership in—

(*a*) second-hand goods imported from a place outside the member States with a view to their sale by auction;

(*b*) works of art imported from a place outside the member States for the purposes of exhibition, with a view to possible sale,

at a time when the second-hand goods or works of art, as the case may be, are still subject to arrangements for temporary importation with total exemption from import duty in accordance with Articles 137 to 141 and paragraph 1 of Article 144 of Council Regulation (EEC) No 2913/92 …[1], shall be treated as neither a supply of goods nor a supply of services.

(2) Subject to paragraph (3) [and article 4][1] below, the provision of any services relating to a transfer of ownership falling within paragraph (1)(*a*) or (*b*) above shall be treated as neither a supply of goods nor a supply of services.

(3) Paragraphs (1) and (2) above shall not apply in relation to any transfer of ownership in second-hand goods which is effected otherwise than by sale by auction.

[4— (1) Article 3(1) does not apply where—

(*a*) any goods falling within paragraph (2) are sold by auction at a time when they are subject to the procedure specified in paragraph (3), and

(*b*) arrangements made by or on behalf of the purchaser of the goods following the sale by auction result in the importation of the goods from a place outside the member States.

(See section 21(2A) of the Value Added Tax Act 1994.)

(2) The goods that fall within this paragraph are—

(*a*) any work of art;

(*b*) any antique, not falling within sub-paragraph (a) or (c), that is more than one hundred years old;

(*c*) any collection or collector's piece that is of zoological, botanical, mineralogical, anatomical, historical, archaeological, palaeontological, ethnographic, numismatic or philatelic interest.

(See sections 21(5) to 21(6C) of the Value Added Tax Act 1994.)

(3) That procedure is the customs procedure for temporary importation with total relief from import duties provided for in Articles 137 to 141 of Council Regulation (EEC) No 2913/92 establishing the Community Customs Code.

(See section 21(2B) of the Value Added Tax Act 1994.)][1]

Amendments—[1] Words in art 3(1) revoked, words in 3(2), and whole of new art 4 inserted, by the Value Added Tax (Treatment of Transactions and Special Provisions) (Amendment) Order, SI 2006/2187, art 2(1)–(3), with effect from 1 September 2006.

1995/1067

Free Zone (Humberside) Designation (Variation) Order 1995

Made by the Treasury under CEMA 1979 s 100A(4)(*a*)(ii)

Made . . . . *11 April 1995*
Coming into force . . . . *12 April 1995*

1 This Order may be cited as the Free Zone (Humberside) Designation (Variation) Order 1995 and shall come into force on 12th April 1995.

2 The area designated a free zone by the Free Zone (Humberside) Designation Order 1994 shall be varied so as to consist of the area of 4.479 hectares in the parish of Stoneferry in the County of Humberside, shown enclosed by a red line on a map (being of a scale of 1:500), marked "Map referred to in article 2 of the Free Zone (Humberside) Designation (Variation) Order 1995", signed by a Collector of Customs and Excise and dated 2nd February 1995.

3 The map referred to in article 2 above shall be kept by the Commissioners at their Headquarters, New King's Beam House, 22 Upper Ground, London SE1 9PJ (and a copy thereof at the offices of Transport Development Group Limited) in substitution for the map referred to in article 2 of the Free Zone (Humberside) Designation Order 1994.

Cross references—See Free Zone (Humberside) Designation Order, SI 1994/144.

1995/1268

Value Added Tax (Special Provisions) Order 1995

Made by the Treasury under VATA 1994 ss 5(3), (5), 11(4), 43(2), 50A

Made . . . . *10 May 1995*
Laid before the House of Commons . . . . *10 May 1995*
Coming into force . . . . *1 June 1995*

Citation and commencement

1 This Order may be cited as the Value Added Tax (Special provisions) Order 1995, and shall come into force on 1st June 1995.

Interpretation

2[— (1)][4] In this Order—

"finance agreement" means an agreement for the sale of goods whereby the property in those goods is not to be transferred until the whole of the price has been paid and the seller retains the right to repossess the goods;

…[6]

"marine mortgage" means a mortgage which is registered in accordance with the [Merchant Shipping Act 1995][7] and by virtue of which a boat (but not any share thereof) is made a security for a loan;

"aircraft mortgage" means a mortgage which is registered in accordance with the Mortgaging of Aircraft Order 1972 and by virtue of which an aircraft is made security for a loan;

"the Act" means the Value Added Tax Act 1994;

"the Manx Act" means [the Value Added Tax Act 1996][1];

["work of art" has the same meaning as in section 21 of the Act.][3]

"antiques" means objects other than works of art or collectors' items, which are more than 100 years old;

["collectors' items" means any collection or collector's piece falling within section 21(5) of the Act but excluding investment gold coins within the meaning of Note 1(*b*) and (*c*) to Group 15 of Schedule 9 to the Act;][3]

["Motor car" means any motor vehicle of a kind normally used on public roads which has three or more wheels and either—

(*a*) is constructed or adapted solely or mainly for the carriage of passengers; or

(*b*) has to the rear of the driver's seat roofed accommodation which is fitted with side windows or which is constructed or adapted for the fitting of side windows;

but does not include—

(i) vehicles capable of accommodating only one person;

(ii) vehicles which meet the requirements of Schedule 6 to the Road Vehicles (Construction and Use) Regulations 1986 and are capable of carrying twelve or more seated persons;

(iii) vehicles of not less than three tonnes unladen weight (as defined in the Table to regulation 3(2) of the Road Vehicles (Construction and Use) Regulations 1986);

(iv) vehicles constructed to carry a payload (the difference between a vehicle's kerb weight (as defined in the Table to regulation 3(2) of the Road Vehicles (Construction and Use) Regulations 1986) and its maximum gross weight (as defined in that Table)) of one tonne or more;

(v) caravans, ambulances and prison vans;

(vi) vehicles constructed for a special purpose other than the carriage of persons and having no other accommodation for carrying persons than such as is incidental to that purpose;][2]

"second-hand goods" means tangible movable property that is suitable for further use as it is or after repair, other than motor cars, works of art, collectors' items or antiques and other than precious metals and precious stones;

"printed matter" includes printed stationery but does not include anything produced by typing, duplicating or photo-copying;[5]

"auctioneer" means a person who sells or offers for sale goods at any public sale where persons become purchasers by competition, being the highest bidders.

(2) …[6]

Amendments—[1] Words substituted by the VAT (Special Provisions) (Amendment) Order, SI 1998/760 with effect from 18 March 1998.

[2] Definition of "Motor car" substituted by the VAT (Special Provisions) (Amendment) Order, SI 1999/2831, art 2, with effect from 1 December 1999.

[3] Definitions of "collectors' items" and "work of art" substituted by the VAT (Special Provisions) (Amendment) (No 2) Order, SI 1999/3120, arts 2, 3, with effect from 1 January 2000.

[4] Para (1) numbered as such, definition of "insurer" substituted, and para (2) inserted, by the Financial Services and Markets Act 2000 (Consequential Amendments and Repeals) Order, SI 2001/3649 art 500 with effect from 1 December 2001.

[5] Definition of "printed matter" revoked by the VAT (Special Provisions) (Amendment) Order, SI 2002/1280 arts 2, 3 with effect from 1 June 2002. See SI 2002/1280 art 1(2) for circumstances in which this amendment shall not have effect.

[6] In para (1), definition of "insurer" repealed, and para (2) repealed, by the VAT (Special Provisions) (Amendment) (No 2) Order, SI 2004/3085 with effect from 1 January 2005.

[7] In definition of "marine mortgage", words substituted by the Value Added Tax (Treatment of Transactions and Special Provisions) (Amendment) Order, SI 2006/2187, art 3(1), with effect from 1 September 2006.

3 …

Note—Effect has been given to the revocations made by this article.

Treatment of transactions

4— (1) Each of the following descriptions of transactions shall be treated as neither a supply of goods nor a supply of services—

(*a*) the disposal of any of the goods described in paragraph (3) below by a person who repossessed them under the terms of a finance agreement;

(*b*) the disposal of any of the goods described in paragraph (3) below by an insurer who has taken possession of them in settlement of a claim under a policy of insurance;

(*c*) the disposal of a boat by a mortgagee after he has taken possession thereof under the terms of a marine mortgage;

(*d*) the disposal of an aircraft by a mortgagee after he has taken possession thereof under the terms of an aircraft mortgage;

if, in each case, the goods so disposed of are in the same condition at the time of disposal as they were when they were repossessed or taken into possession, as the case may be, and if a supply of them in the United Kingdom by the person from whom in each case they were obtained would not have been chargeable with VAT, or would have been chargeable with VAT on less than the full value of such supply.

[(1A) Paragraph (1)(*a*) above shall not apply where adjustment, whether or not made under regulation 38 of the Value Added Tax Regulations 1995, has taken account, or may later take account, of VAT on the initial supply under the finance agreement as a result of repossession and the goods delivered under that agreement were delivered on or after 1st September 2006.][2]

(2) Paragraph (1) of this article shall not apply to reimported goods which were previously exported from the United Kingdom or the Isle of Man free of VAT chargeable under the Act or VAT chargeable under Part I of the Manx Act by reason of the zero-rating provisions of either [Act, or][1] regulations made under either Act, or to imported goods which have not borne VAT chargeable under either of those Acts in the United Kingdom or the Isle of Man.

(3) The goods referred to in subparagraphs (*a*) and (*b*) of paragraph (1) above are as follows:

(*a*) works of art, antiques and collectors' items;

(*b*) second-hand goods.

Amendments—[1] Words in para (2) inserted by the VAT (Special Provisions) Order 1995 (Amendment) Order, SI 1995/1385 art 2 with effect from 1 June 1995.

[2] Para (1A) inserted by the VAT (Special Provisions) (Amendment) (No 2) Order, SI 2006/869 with effect from 13 April 2006 in relation to finance agreements entered into on or after that date. For these purposes, "finance agreement" has the meaning given in SI 1995/1268 art 2(1).

5— (1) Subject to paragraph (2) below, there shall be treated as neither a supply of goods nor a supply of services the following supplies by a person of assets of his business—

(*a*) their supply to a person to whom he transfers his business as a going concern where—

(i) the assets are to be used by the transferee in carrying on the same kind of business, whether or not as part of any existing business, as that carried on by the transferor, and

(ii) in a case where the transferor is a taxable person, the transferee is already, or immediately becomes as a result of the transfer, a taxable person or a person defined as such in [section 3(1)][1] of the Manx Act;

(*b*) their supply to a person to whom he transfers part of his business as a going concern where—

(i) that part is capable of separate operation,

(ii) the assets are to be used by the transferee in carrying on the same kind of business, whether or not as part of any existing business, as that carried on by the transferor in relation to that part, and

(iii) in a case where the transferor is a taxable person, the transferee is already, or immediately becomes as a result of the transfer, a taxable person or a person defined as such in [section 3(1)][1] of the Manx Act.

(2) A supply of assets shall not be treated as neither a supply of goods nor a supply of services by virtue of paragraph (1) above to the extent that it consists of—

(*a*) a grant which would, but for an [option which the transferor has exercised][3], fall within item 1 of Group 1 of Schedule 9 to the Act; or

(*b*) a grant of a fee simple which falls within paragraph (*a*) of item 1 of Group 1 of Schedule 9 to the Act,

unless [the conditions contained in paragraph (2A) below are satisfied][2].

[(2A) The conditions referred to in paragraph (2) above are that the transferee has, no later than the relevant date—

(*a*) [exercised an option][3] in relation to the land which has effect on the relevant date and has given any written notification of the [option required by paragraph 20 of Schedule 10][3] to the Act; and

(*b*) notified the transferor that paragraph (2B) below does not apply to him.][2]

[(2B) This paragraph applies to a transferee where—

(*a*) the supply of the asset that is to be transferred to him would become, in relation to him, a capital item as described in regulation 113 of the Value Added Tax Regulations 1995 if the supply of that asset to him—

(i) were to be treated as neither a supply of goods nor a supply of services; or

(ii) were not so treated; and

(*b*) his supplies of that asset will, or would fall, to be exempt supplies by virtue of [paragraph 12 of Schedule 10][3] to the Act.][2]

(3) In paragraph (2) of this article—

…[3]

["option" means an option to tax any land having effect under Part 1 of Schedule 10 to the Act;][3]

"relevant date" means the date upon which the grant would have been treated as having been made or, if there is more than one such date, the earliest of them;

"transferor" and "transferee" include a relevant associate of either respectively as defined in [paragraph 3 of Schedule 10][3] to the Act.

(4) There shall be treated as neither a supply of goods nor a supply of services the assignment by an owner of goods comprised in a hire-purchase or conditional sale agreement of his rights and interest thereunder, and the goods comprised therein, to a bank or other financial institution.

Press releases etc—C&E Business Brief 16/99 20-7-99 (timing of an election to tax on property forming part of the assets of a TOGC).

Simon's Tax Cases—*Higher Education Statistics Agency v C&E Comrs* [2000] STC 332.

Art 5(1), *Abbey National plc v C&E Comrs* [2001] STC 297.

Amendments—[1] Words substituted by the VAT (Special Provisions) (Amendment) Order, SI 1998/760 with effect from 18 March 1998.

[2] Words in para (2) substituted, and paras (2A), (2B) inserted, by the VAT (Special Provisions) (Amendment) Order, SI 2004/779 with effect from 18 March 2004.

[3] Words in paras (2)(*a*), (2A)(*a*), (2B)(*b*), (3) substituted, in para (3) definition of "election" revoked, and definition of "option" inserted, by the Value Added Tax (Buildings and Land) Order, SI 2008/1146, art 6, Sch 1 para 15 with effect in relation to supplies made on or after 1 June 2008, subject to savings in Sch 2 of the Order.

6 The following description of transaction shall be treated as a supply of services and not as a supply of goods—

the exchange of a reconditioned article for an unserviceable article of a similar kind by a person who regularly offers in the course of his business to provide a reconditioning facility by that means.

7 The following description of transaction shall not be treated as the acquisition of goods from another member State—

the removal of goods to the United Kingdom in pursuance of a supply to a taxable person, made by a person in another member State, where VAT on that supply is to be accounted for and paid in another member State by reference to the profit margin on the supply by virtue of the law of that member State corresponding to section 50A of the Act and any Orders made thereunder.

8 The following description of transaction shall be treated as neither a supply of goods nor a supply of services—

the removal of goods to the United Kingdom in pursuance of a supply to a person, made by a person in another member State where VAT on that supply is to be accounted for and paid in another member State by reference to the profit margin on the supply by virtue of the law of that member State corresponding to section 50A of the Act and any Orders made thereunder.

9 The following description of transaction shall be treated as neither a supply of goods nor a supply of services—

services in connection with a supply of goods provided by an agent acting in his own name to the purchaser of the goods the consideration for which is taken into account by virtue of article 12(6) below in calculating the price at which the agent obtained the goods.

10 The following description of transaction shall be treated as neither a supply of goods nor a supply of services—

services in connection with the sale of goods provided by an auctioneer acting in his own name to the vendor or the purchaser of the goods the consideration for which is taken into account by virtue of article 12(7) below in calculating the price at which the auctioneer obtained (or as the case may be) sold the goods.

[Goods put to private use or used, or made available for use, for non-business purposes

10A Paragraph 5(4) of Schedule 4 to the Act shall not apply to goods (including land treated as goods for the purposes of that paragraph by virtue of paragraph 9 of that Schedule) which have no economic life for the purposes of Part 15A of the Value Added Tax Regulations 1995 at the time when they are used or made available for use.][1]

Amendments—[1] Para 10A inserted by the VAT (Special Provisions) (Amendment) Order, SI 2007/2923 arts 2, 3 with effect from 1 November 2007 in relation to the use, on or after that date, of goods or land held or used for the purposes of a business: SI 2007/2923 art 1.

Self-supply

11— *(1) Where a person in the course or furtherance of any business carried on by him produces printed matter and the printed matter—*

(a) is not supplied to another person or incorporated in other goods produced in the course or furtherance of that business; but

(b) is used by him for the purpose of a business carried on by him,

then, subject to paragraph (2) below, the printed matter shall be treated for the purposes of the Act as both supplied to him for the purpose of that business and supplied by him in the course or furtherance of that business.

(2) Paragraph (1) of this article does not apply if—

(a) the person is a fully taxable person;

(b) the value of the supplies falling to be treated as made by and to that person would not, if those were the only supplies made or to be made by that person, make him liable to be registered for VAT pursuant to the provisions of Schedule 1 to the Act; or

(c) the Commissioners, being satisfied that the VAT (if any) which would be attributable to the supplies after allowing for any credit under sections 25 and 26 of the Act would be negligible, have given, and have not withdrawn, a direction that the paragraph is not to apply.

(3) For the purposes of paragraph (2)(a) above, a person is a fully taxable person if the only input tax of his to which he is not entitled to credit at the end of any prescribed accounting period or longer period is input tax which is excluded from any credit under section 25 of the Act by virtue of any Order made under sub-section (7) of that section.

(4) The preceding provisions of this article shall apply in relation to any bodies corporate which are treated for the purposes of section 43 of the Act as members of a group as if those bodies were one person, but any printed matter which would fall to be treated as supplied to and by that person shall be treated as supplied to and by the representative member.

Amendment—Revoked by the VAT (Special Provisions) (Amendment) Order, SI 2002/1280 arts 2, 3 with effect from 1 June 2002. See SI 2002/1280 art 1(2) for circumstances in which this amendment shall not have effect.

Relief for certain goods

12— (1) Without prejudice to article 13 below and subject to complying with such conditions as the Commissioners may direct in a notice published by them for the purposes of this Order or may otherwise direct and subject to paragraph (4) below, where a person supplies goods of a description in paragraph (2) below, of which he took possession in any of the circumstances set out in paragraph (3) below, he may opt to account for the VAT chargeable on the supply on the profit margin on the supply instead of by reference to its value.

(2) The supplies referred to in paragraph (1) above are supplies of—

(*a*) works of art, antiques and collectors' items;

(*b*) second-hand goods.

(3) The circumstances mentioned in paragraph (1) above are—

[(*a*) that the taxable person took possession of the goods pursuant to—

(i) a supply in respect of which no VAT was chargeable under the Act or under Part I of the Manx Act;

(ii) a supply on which VAT was chargeable on the profit margin in accordance with paragraph (1) above or a corresponding provision made under the Manx Act or a corresponding provision of the law of another member State;

[(iii) a de-supplied transaction, other than an article 5 transaction;

(iv) subject to paragraph (3A) below, an article 5 transaction;][4]

(v) (if the goods are a work of art) a supply to the taxable person by, or an acquisition from another member State by him from its creator or his successor in title;][1]

(*b*) (if the goods are a work of art, an antique or a collectors' item) that they were imported by the taxable person himself[, which includes – if the taxable person is an auctioneer – the auctioneer having placed them in the customs procedure for temporary importation with total relief from import duties provided for in Articles 137 to 141 of Council Regulation (EEC) No 2913/92 establishing the Community Customs Code][5].

[(3A) An article 5 transaction does not fall within paragraph (iv) of paragraph (3)(*a*) above unless the taxable person has a relevant predecessor in title.][4]

(4) A taxable person—

(*a*) may not opt under paragraph (1) above where—

(i) the supply is a letting on hire;

(ii) an invoice or similar document showing an amount as being VAT or as being attributable to VAT is issued in respect of the supply;

(iii) the supply is of an air gun unless the taxable person is registered for the purposes of the Firearms Act 1968; or

(iv) the supply is of goods which are being disposed of in the circumstances mentioned in article 4(1)(*a*)(*b*)(*c*) or (*d*) above but which is not disregarded by virtue of that article;

(*b*) may only exercise the option under paragraph (1) above in relation to supplies of—

(i) works of art of which he took possession in the circumstances mentioned in paragraph [(3)(*a*)(v)][2] above, or

(ii) works of art, antiques or collectors' items of which he took possession in circumstances set out in paragraph (3)(*b*) above,

if at the same time he exercises the option in relation to the other.

(5) Subject to paragraph (6) below, for the purposes of determining the profit margin—

(*a*) the price at which goods were obtained shall be calculated as follows—

(i) (where the taxable person took possession of the goods pursuant to a supply) in the same way as the consideration for the supply would be calculated for the purposes of the Act;

(ii) (where the taxable person is a sole proprietor and the goods were supplied to him in his private capacity) in the same way as the consideration for the supply to him as a private individual would be calculated for the purposes of the Act;

(iii) (where the goods are a work of art which was acquired from another member State by the taxable person pursuant to a supply to him by the creator of the item or his successor in title) in the same way as the value of the acquisition would be calculated for the purposes of the Act plus the VAT chargeable on the acquisition;

(iv) (where the goods are a work of art, an antique or a collectors' item which the taxable person has imported himself[, which includes – if the taxable person is an auctioneer – the auctioneer having placed them in the customs procedure for temporary importation with total relief from import duties mentioned in article 12(3)(*b*)][5]) in the same way as the value of the goods for the purpose of charging VAT on their importation would be calculated for the purposes of the Act plus any VAT chargeable on their importation;

[(v) (where the taxable person took possession of the goods pursuant to a de-supplied transaction, other than an article 5 transaction) by taking the price he paid pursuant to the transaction;

(vi) (where the taxable person took possession of the goods pursuant to an article 5 transaction) by taking the price at which his relevant predecessor in title obtained the goods;][4]

(*b*) the price at which goods are sold shall be calculated in the same way as the consideration for the supply would be calculated for the purposes of the Act[;

(*c*) ...[4]

(6) Subject to paragraph (7) below, where the taxable person is an agent acting in his own name the price at which the goods were obtained shall be calculated in accordance with paragraph (5)(*a*) above, but the selling price calculated in accordance with paragraph (5)(*b*) above shall be increased by the amount of any consideration payable to the taxable person in respect of services supplied by him to the purchaser in connection with the supply of the goods.

(7) Instead of calculating the price at which goods were obtained or supplied in accordance with paragraph (6) above an auctioneer acting in his own name may—

[(*a*) calculate the price at which they were obtained by deducting from the successful bid the amount of the commission payable to him under his contract with the vendor for the sale of the goods;][3]

(*b*) calculate the price at which they were supplied by adding to the successful bid the consideration for any supply of services by him to the purchaser in connection with the sale of the goods,

in either (or both) cases excluding the consideration for supplies of services that are not chargeable to VAT.

(8) Where a taxable person opts under paragraph (1) above in respect of goods of which he took possession in the circumstances set out in paragraph [(3)(*a*)(v)][2] and (*b*) above, the exercise of the option shall—

(*a*) be notified by him to the Commissioners in writing;

(*b*) have effect from the date of that notification or such later date as may be specified therein;

(*c*) subject to paragraph (9) below, apply to all supplies of such goods made by the taxable person in the period ending 2 years after the date on which it first had effect or the date on which written notification of its revocation is given to the Commissioners, whichever is the later.

(9) Notwithstanding paragraph (8)(*c*) above a taxable person may elect to account for VAT chargeable on any particular supply of such goods by reference to the value of that supply.

[(10) For the purposes of this article—

"article 5 transaction" means a transaction which is a de-supplied transaction by virtue of a provision of article 5 above or a corresponding provision made under the Manx Act;

"de-supplied transaction" means a transaction which was treated by virtue of any Order made or having effect as if made under section 5(3) of the Act or under the corresponding provisions of the Manx Act as being neither a supply of goods nor a supply of services.

(11) For the purposes of this article a person is a relevant predecessor in title of a taxable person if—

(*a*) he is the person from whom the taxable person took possession of the goods and himself took possession of them in any of the circumstances described in paragraph (3) above, but not pursuant to an article 5 transaction; or

(*b*) where the goods have been the subject of a succession of two or more article 5 transactions (culminating in the article 5 transaction to which the taxable person was a party), he was a party to one of those transactions and himself took possession of the goods in any of the circumstances described in paragraph (3) above, but not pursuant to an article 5 transaction.][4]

Amendments—[1] Para (3)(*a*) substituted by the VAT (Special Provisions) (Amendment) Order SI 1997/1616 with effect from 3 July 1997.

[2] Words in paras (4)(*b*)(i), (8) substituted, by the VAT (Special Provisions) (Amendment) Order, SI 1998/760 with effect from 18 March 1998.

[3] Para (7)(*a*) substituted by the VAT (Special Provisions) (Amendment) Order, SI 2001/3753 art 3 with effect from 2 January 2002.

[4] Sub-paras (3)(*a*)(iii), (iv) substituted, para (3A) inserted, sub-paras (5)(*a*)(v), (vi) substituted for sub-para (5)(*a*)(v), sub-para (5)(*c*) revoked, and paras (10), (11) added, by the VAT (Special Provisions) (Amendment) (No 2) Order, SI 2002/1503 with effect from 1 July 2002. For further provisions as to the effect of that Order see SI 2002/1503 art 1(2).

[5] Words in paras (3)(*b*) and (5)(*a*)(iv) inserted by the Value Added Tax (Tax Treatment of Transactions and Special Provisions) (Amendment) Order, SI 2006/2187, art 3(2), (3), with effect from 1 September 2006.

Global Accounting

13— (1) Subject to complying with such conditions as the Commissioners may direct in a notice published by them for the purposes of this Order or may otherwise direct, and subject to paragraph (2) below, a taxable person who has opted under article 12(1) above may account for VAT on the total profit margin on goods supplied by him during a prescribed accounting period, calculated in accordance with paragraph (3) below, instead of the profit margin on each supply.

(2) Paragraph (1) above does not apply to supplies of—

(*a*) motor vehicles;

(*b*) aircraft;

(*c*) boats and outboard motors;

(*d*) caravans and motor caravans;

(*e*) horses and ponies;

(*f*) any other individual items whose value calculated in accordance with article 12(5)(*a*) above, exceeds £500.

[(3) The total profit margin for a prescribed accounting period shall be the amount (if any) by which the total selling price calculated in accordance with paragraph (4) below, exceeds the total purchase price calculated in accordance with paragraph (5) below.][1]

(4) For the purposes of paragraph (3) above the total selling price shall be calculated by aggregating for all goods sold during the period the prices (calculated in accordance with article 12(5) or (6) above as appropriate) for which they were sold.

(5) For the purposes of paragraph (3) above the total purchase price shall be calculated by aggregating for all goods obtained during the period the prices (calculated in accordance with article 12(5) above) at which they were obtained and adding to that total the amount (if any) carried forward from the previous period in accordance with paragraph (6) below.

(6) If in any prescribed accounting period the total purchase price calculated in accordance with paragraph (5) above exceeds the total selling price, the excess amount shall be carried forward to the following prescribed accounting period for inclusion in the calculation of the total purchase price for that period.

Amendments—[1] Para (3) substituted by the VAT (Special Provisions) (Amendment) (No 2) Order, SI 1999/3120, arts 2, 4, with effect from 1 January 2000.

1995/1978
Value Added Tax (Refund of Tax) Order 1995

Made by the Treasury under VATA 1994 s 33(3)

Made . . . . *26 July 1995*
Laid before the House of Commons . . . . *26 July 1995*
Coming into force . . . . *18 August 1995*

1 This Order may be cited as the Value Added Tax (Refund of Tax) Order 1995 and shall come into force on 18th August 1995.

2 The Environment Agency (a body corporate established by section 1 of the Environment Act 1995) is hereby specified for the purposes of section 33 of the Value Added Tax Act 1994.

1995/2518
Value Added Tax Regulations 1995

Made by the Commissioners of Customs and Excise under VATA 1994 ss 3(4), 6(14), 7(9), 8(4), 12(3), 14(3), 16(1) and (2), 18(5), (5A), 24(3), (4), (6), 25(1), (4), (6), 26(1), (3), (4), 28(3), (4) and (5), 30(8), 35(2), 36(5), 37(3) and (4), 38, 39(1), 40(3), 46(2), (4), 48(3)(*b*), (4), (6), 49(2), (3), 52, 54(1), (2), (3), (6), 58, 79(3), 80(6), 88(3), (5), 92(4), 93(1), (2), 95(5), 97(1) and Sch 1 para 17, Sch 2 para 9, Sch 3 para 10, Sch 7 paras 2(1)–(2), and Sch 11 paras 2(1)–(12), 5(4), (9), 6(1)–(2) and 7(1)

Made . . . . *27 September 1995*
Laid before the House of Commons . . . . . . *28 September 1995*
Coming into force . . . . *20 October 1995*

ARRANGEMENT OF REGULATIONS

PART I
PRELIMINARY

PART II
REGISTRATION AND PROVISIONS FOR SPECIAL CASES

PART III

VAT INVOICES AND OTHER INVOICING REQUIREMENTS

PART IV

EC SALES STATEMENTS

PART IVA

REVERSE CHARGE SALES STATEMENTS

PART 4B

PROVISION OF INFORMATION RELATING TO ARRIVALS AND DISPATCHES

PART V

ACCOUNTING, PAYMENT AND RECORDS

PART VA

REIMBURSEMENT ARRANGEMENTS

Note—Part VA inserted after Part V by the VAT (Amendment) (No 5) Regulations, SI 1998/59 with effect from 11 February 1998. Regulations 37A to 37H within Part VA were originally incorrectly numbered. Regs 43A to 43H were renumbered as such by the VAT (Amendment) Regulations, SI 1999/438 regs 2, 3.

PART VI

PAYMENTS ON ACCOUNT

PART VII

ANNUAL ACCOUNTING

PART VIIA

FLAT-RATE SCHEME FOR SMALL BUSINESSES

PART VIII

CASH ACCOUNTING

PART IX

SUPPLIES BY RETAILERS

PART X

TRADING STAMPS

PART XI

TIME OF SUPPLY AND TIME OF ACQUISITION

PART XII

VALUATION OF ACQUISITIONS

PART XIII

PLACE OF SUPPLY

PART XIV

INPUT TAX AND PARTIAL EXEMPTION

PART XV

ADJUSTMENTS TO THE DEDUCTION OF INPUT TAX ON CAPITAL ITEMS

PART 15A

GOODS USED FOR NON-BUSINESS PURPOSES DURING THEIR ECONOMIC LIFE

PART XVI

IMPORTATIONS, EXPORTATIONS AND REMOVALS

PART XVI(A)

FISCAL AND OTHER WAREHOUSING REGIMES

PART XVII

NEW MEANS OF TRANSPORT

PART XVIII

BAD DEBT RELIEF (THE OLD SCHEME)

PART XIX

BAD DEBT RELIEF (THE NEW SCHEME)

PART XIXA

REPAYMENT OF INPUT TAX WHERE CLAIM MADE UNDER PART XIX

PART XIXB

REPAYMENT OF INPUT TAX WHERE CONSIDERATION NOT PAID

PART XIXC

ADJUSTMENT OF OUTPUT TAX IN RESPECT OF SUPPLIES TO WHICH SECTION 55A(6) OF THE ACT APPLIES

PART XX

REPAYMENTS TO COMMUNITY TRADERS

PART XXI

REPAYMENTS TO THIRD COUNTRY TRADERS

PART XXII

REPAYMENT OF SUPPLEMENT

Cross reference—See VAT (Isle of Man) (No 2) Order, SI 1982/1068 reg 3, Sch; VATA 1994, Sch 13 para 23 (modifications consequential on treatment of UK and Isle of Man as a single area for VAT purposes).

PART I
PRELIMINARY

Citation and commencement

1 These Regulations may be cited as the Value Added Tax Regulations 1995 and shall come into force on 20th October 1995.

Former regulation—VAT (General) Regulations, SI 1985/886 reg 1.

Interpretation—general

2— (1) In these Regulations unless the context otherwise requires—

"the Act" means the Value Added Tax Act 1994 and any reference to a Schedule to the Act includes a reference to a Schedule as amended from time to time by Order of the Treasury;

["alphabetical code" means the alphabetical prefix as set out below which shall be used to identify the member State—

Austria—AT
Belgium—BE
[Bulgaria—BG][6]
Cyprus—CY
Czech Republic—CZ
Denmark—DK
Estonia—EE
Finland—FI
France—FR
Germany—DE
Greece—EL
Hungary—HU
Ireland—IE
Italy—IT
Latvia—LV
Lithuania—LT
Luxembourg—LU
Malta—MT
Netherlands—NL
Poland—PL
Portugal—PT

[Romania—RO][6]
Slovakia—SK
Slovenia—SI
Spain—ES
Sweden—SE
United Kingdom—GB][5]

"Collector" includes Deputy Collector and Assistant Collector;

"the Community" means the European Community;

"continental shelf" means a designated area within the meaning of the Continental Shelf Act 1964;

"Controller" means the Controller, Customs and Excise Value Added Tax Central Unit;

"datapost packet" means a postal packet containing goods which is posted in the United Kingdom as a datapost packet for transmission to a place outside the United Kingdom in accordance with the terms of a contract entered into between [the Post Office company][3] and the sender of the packet; or which is received at a post office [of the Post Office company][3] in the United Kingdom from a place outside the United Kingdom for transmission and delivery in the United Kingdom [by that company][3] as if it were a datapost packet;

["fiscal or other warehousing regime" means "fiscal warehousing regime or warehousing regime";][1]

["the Post Office company" has the same meaning as in Part IV of the Postal Services Act 2000;][4]

"prescribed accounting period", subject to regulation 99(I), means a period such as is referred to in regulation 25;

"proper officer" means the person appointed or authorised by the Commissioners to act in respect of any matter in the course of his duties;

"registered person" means a person registered by the Commissioners under [Schedule 1, 2, 3 or 3A][2] to the Act;

"registration number" means the number allocated by the Commissioners to a taxable person in the certificate of registration issued to him;

"return" means a return which is required to be made in accordance with regulation 25;

"specified date" means the date specified in a person's application for registration for the purpose of VAT as that on which he expects to make his first taxable supply.

(2) A reference in these Regulations to "this Part" is a reference to the Part of these Regulations in which that reference is made.

(3) In these Regulations any reference to a form prescribed in Schedule 1 to these Regulations shall include a reference to a form which the Commissioners are satisfied is a form to the like effect.

Former regulations—Para (1): VAT (General) Regulations, SI 1985/886 reg 2(1); VAT (General) (Amendment) Regulations, SI 1992/3102 regs 1, 3, SI 1993/1941 regs 2, 3, SI 1995/152 reg 3.
Para (2): None.
Para (3): VAT (General) Regulations, SI 1985/886 reg 2(2).

Amendments—[1] Definition of "fiscal or other warehousing regime" inserted by the VAT (Amendment) (No 3) Regulations, SI 1996/1250 reg 4 with effect from 1 June 1996.

[2] Words in definition of "registered person" substituted by the VAT (Amendment) (No 3) Regulations, SI 2000/794 regs 2, 3 with effect from 22 March 2000.

[3] Words in the definition of "datapost packet" substituted and inserted by the Postal Services Act 2000 s 127(4), Sch 8 para 23 with effect from 26 March 2001 (by virtue of SI 2000/2957).

[4] Definition of "the Post Office company" inserted by the Postal Services Act 2000 (Consequential Modifications No 1) Order, SI 2001/1149 art 3, Sch 1 para 108 with effect from 26 March 2001.

[5] Definition of "alphabetical code" substituted by the VAT (Amendment) (No 2) Regulations, SI 2004/1082 regs 2, 3 with effect from 1 May 2004

[6] In para (1) entries inserted by the VAT (Amendment) (No 3) Regulations, SI 2006/3292 regs 2, 3 with effect from 1 January 2007.

Revocations and savings

3— (1) The Regulations described in Schedule 2 to these Regulations are hereby revoked.

(2) Anything begun under or for the purpose of any Regulations revoked by these Regulations shall be continued under or, as the case may be, for the purpose of the corresponding provision of these Regulations.

(3) Where any document used or required for the purpose of VAT refers to a provision of a regulation revoked by these Regulations, such reference shall, unless the context otherwise requires, be construed as a reference to the corresponding provision of these Regulations.

Former regulation—VAT (General) Regulations, SI 1985/886 reg 3.

Requirement, direction, demand or permission

4 Any requirement, direction, demand or permission by the Commissioners, under or for the purposes of these Regulations, may be made or given by a notice in writing, or otherwise.

Former regulation—VAT (General) Regulations, SI 1985/886 reg 67.

PART II
REGISTRATION AND PROVISIONS FOR SPECIAL CASES

Registration and notification

[5— (1) Where any person is required under paragraph 5(1)[, 6(1) or 7(1)][2] of Schedule 1, paragraph 3(1) of Schedule 2, paragraph 3(1) of Schedule 3 or paragraph 3(1) or 4(1) of Schedule 3A to the Act to notify the Commissioners of his liability to be registered, the notification shall contain the particulars (including the declaration) set out in forms numbered 1, 6, 7 and 7A respectively in Schedule 1 to these Regulations and shall be made in those forms; provided that, where the notification is made by a partnership, the notification shall also contain the particulars set out in the form numbered 2 in that Schedule.

(2) Every registered person except one to whom paragraph 11, 12, 13(1), (2) or (3) of Schedule 1, paragraph 5 of Schedule 2, paragraph 5 of Schedule 3 or paragraph 5 of Schedule 3A of the Act applies, shall, within 30 days of any changes being made in the name, constitution or ownership of his business, or of any other event occurring which may necessitate the variation of the register or cancellation of his registration, notify the Commissioners in writing of such change or event and furnish them with full particulars thereof.

(3) Every notification by a registered person under paragraph 11 or 12 of Schedule 1, paragraph 5 of Schedule 2, paragraph 5 of Schedule 3 or paragraph 5 of Schedule 3A to the Act shall be made in writing to the Commissioners and shall state—

(*a*) the date on which he ceased to make, or have the intention of making, taxable supplies; or

(*b*) where paragraph 12(*a*) of Schedule 1 to the Act applies, the date on which he ceased to make, or have the intention of making, supplies within paragraph 10(2) of that Schedule; or

(*c*) where paragraph 12(*b*) of Schedule 1 to the Act applies, the date on which he made, or formed the intention of making, taxable supplies; or

(*d*) where paragraph 5(1) of Schedule 2 to the Act applies, the date on which he ceased to be registrable by virtue of paragraph 5(4) of that Schedule; or

(*e*) where paragraph 5(1) of Schedule 3 to the Act applies, the date on which he ceased to be registrable by virtue of paragraph 5(3) of that Schedule; or

(*f*) where paragraph 5(1) of Schedule 3A to the Act applies, the date on which he ceased to make, or have the intention of making, relevant supplies within the meaning of paragraph 9 of that Schedule.][1]

(4) A notification subject to or required by paragraph (1), (2) or (3) may be made instead using an electronic communications system that remains specified for the purpose in a current general direction given by the Commissioners.

A system specified for a purpose of paragraph (1) may modify or dispense with any particular required for that purpose by that paragraph.

(5) The time a notification is made using such a system corresponds to when a fully mechanised feature of that system generates a relevant acknowledgement.

(6) If such a feature does not generate an acknowledgement, but would do so in the circumstances alleged, a relevant notification is not made using that system in those alleged circumstances.

(7) Paragraphs (5) and (6) apply as conclusive presumptions.

(8) Paragraph (4) only applies to a notification that is envisaged by a current direction.

(9) Paragraph (4) does not apply at a notification's deadline if the system specified for that notification is not then functioning.

A notification's deadline is the latest time by which it is required to be made.

(10) The Commissioners need not give a general direction pursuant to paragraph (4).

(11) Any general direction under paragraph (4) must specify both the form of an electronic communications system and the sole circumstances in which it may be used, and may specify different forms or circumstances for different cases.

(12) A system need not include a feature of the type envisaged by paragraph (5) or (6).

(13) A direction is not current for the purposes of paragraphs (4) and (8) to the extent that it is varied, replaced or revoked by another Commissioners' direction.

(14) A notification made under paragraph (4) carries the same consequences as a notification under paragraph (1), (2) or (3) (as appropriate), except in relation to any matter for which alternative or additional provision is made by or under paragraphs (4) to (7).

Former regulations—VAT (General) Regulations, SI 1985/886 reg 4(1)–(3); VAT (General) (Amendment) Regulations, SI 1992/3102 regs 2, 4.

Amendments—[1] This regulation substituted by the VAT (Amendment) (No 3) Regulations, SI 2000/794 regs 2, 4 with effect from 22 March 2000.

[2] Words in para (1) substituted for the words "or 6(1)", and paras (4)–(14) inserted, by the VAT (Amendment) (No 3) Regulations, SI 2004/1675 regs 1, 2 with effect from 22 July 2004.

Transfer of a going concern

6— (1) Where—

(*a*) a business [or part of a business][3] is transferred as a going concern, (*b*) the registration under Schedule 1 to the Act of the transferor has not already been cancelled,

(*c*) on the transfer of the business [or part of it][3] the registration of the transferor under that Schedule is to be cancelled and either the transferee becomes liable to be registered under that Schedule or the Commissioners agree to register him under paragraph 9 of that Schedule, and

(*d*) an application is made in the form numbered 3 in Schedule 1 to these Regulations by or on behalf of both the transferor and the transferee of that business [or the part transferred][3],

the Commissioners may as from the date of the said transfer cancel the registration under Schedule 1 to the Act of the transferor and register the transferee under that Schedule with the registration number previously allocated to the transferor.

(2) An application under paragraph (1) above shall constitute notification for the purposes of paragraph 11 of Schedule 1 to the Act.

(3) Where the transferee of a business [or part of a business][3] has under paragraph (1) above been registered under Schedule 1 to the Act in substitution for the [transferor of it][3], and with the transferor's registration number—

(*a*) any liability of the transferor existing at the date of the transfer to make a return or to account for or pay VAT under regulation 25 or [40][2] shall become the liability of the transferee,

(*b*) any right of the transferor, whether or not existing at the date of the transfer, to credit for, or to repayment of, input tax shall become the right of the transferee,...[1]

(*c*) any right of either the transferor, whether or not existing at the date of the transfer, or the transferee to payment by the Commissioners under section 25(3) of the Act shall be satisfied by payment to either of them.

[(*d*) any right of the transferor, whether or not existing at the date of the transfer, to claim a refund under section 36 of the Act shall become the right of the transferee, ...[3]

(*e*) any liability of the transferor, whether or not existing at the date of the transfer, to account for an amount under Part XIXA of these Regulations, shall become that of the transferee][1][, and

(*f*) any records relating to the business which, by virtue of these Regulations or a direction made by the Commissioners, are required to be preserved for any period after the transfer shall be preserved by the transferee unless the Commissioners, at the request of the transferor, otherwise direct.][3]

(4) In addition to the provisions set out in paragraph (3) above, where the transferee of a business [or part of a business][3] has been registered in substitution for, and with the registration number of, the transferor during a prescribed accounting period [subsequent to that in which the transfer took place][3] but with effect from [the date of the transfer][3], and any—

(*a*) return has been made,

(*b*) VAT has been accounted for and paid, or

(*c*) right to credit for input tax has been claimed,

either by or in the name of the transferee or the transferor, it shall be treated as having been done by the transferee.

Former regulations—VAT (General) Regulations, SI 1985/886 reg 4(4), (5), (7), (8); VAT (General) (Amendment) Regulations, SI 1992/3102 regs 2, 4.

Amendments—[1] Word "and" in para (3)(*b*) deleted and paras (3)(*d*), (*e*) inserted by the VAT (Amendment) Regulations, SI 1997/1086 reg 3 with effect from 1 May 1997.

[2] In para (3)(*a*), figure substituted for "41" by the VAT (Amendment) (No 3) Regulations, SI 2004/1675 regs 1(1), (3), 3 with effect from 22 July 2004.

[3] Words in sub-s (1) inserted, words in sub-ss (3), (4) inserted and substituted, and sub-s (3)(*f*) and preceding word "and" inserted, by the Value Added Tax (Amendment) (No 5) Regulations, SI 2007/2085 regs 2–5 with effect from 1 September 2007, in relation to transfers of going concerns pursuant to contracts entered into on or after that date.

Notice by partnership

7— (1) Where any notice is required to be given for the purposes of the Act or these Regulations by a partnership, it shall be the joint and several liability of all the partners to give such notice, provided that a notice given by one partner shall be a sufficient compliance with any such requirement.

(2) Where, in Scotland, a body of persons carrying on a business which includes the making of taxable supplies is a partnership required to be registered, any notice shall be given and signed in the manner indicated in section 6 of the Partnership Act 1890.

Former regulation—VAT (General) Regulations, SI 1985/886 reg 9.

Representation of club, association or organisation

8 Anything required to be done by or under the Act, these regulations or otherwise by or on behalf of a club, association or organisation, the affairs of which are managed by its members or a committee or committees of its members, shall be the joint and several responsibility of—

(*a*) every member holding office as president, chairman, treasurer, secretary or any similar office; or in default of any thereof,

(*b*) every member holding office as a member of a committee; or in default of any thereof,

(*c*) every member,

provided that if it is done by any official, committee member or member referred to above, that shall be sufficient compliance with any such requirement.

Former regulation—VAT (General) Regulations, SI 1985/886 reg 10.

Death, bankruptcy or incapacity of taxable person

9— (1) If a taxable person dies or becomes bankrupt or incapacitated, the Commissioners may, from the date on which he died or became bankrupt or incapacitated treat as a taxable person any person carrying on that business until some other person is registered in respect of the taxable supplies made or intended to be made by that taxable person in the course or furtherance of his business or the incapacity ceases, as the case may be; and the provisions of the Act and of any Regulations made thereunder shall apply to any person so treated as though he were a registered person.

(2) Any person carrying on such business shall, within 21 days of commencing to do so, inform the Commissioners in writing of that fact and of the date of the death, [the date of the bankruptcy order][1] or of the nature of the incapacity and the date on which it began.

(3) In relation to a company which is a taxable person, the references in paragraph (1) above to the taxable person becoming bankrupt or incapacitated shall be construed as references to the company going into liquidation or receivership or [entering administration][2].

Former regulations—VAT (General) Regulations, SI 1985/886 reg 11; VAT (General) (Amendment) Regulations, SI 1985/1650 reg 7.

Simon's Tax Cases—*Sargent v C&E Comrs* [1995] STC 398*.

Amendments—[1] Words in square brackets inserted by the VAT (Amendment) (No 3) Regulations, SI 1996/1250 reg 5 with effect from 1 June 1996.

[2] Words in para (3) substituted by the Enterprise Act 2002 (Insolvency) Order, SI 2003/2096 art 5, Schedule paras 55, 56 with effect from 15 September 2003. However, this amendment does not apply in any case where a petition for an administration order was presented before that date: SI 2003/2096 arts 1, 6.

VAT representatives

10— (1) Where any person is appointed by virtue of section 48 of the Act to be the VAT representative of another (in this regulation referred to as "his principal"), the VAT representative shall notify the Commissioners of his appointment on the form numbered 8 in Schedule 1 to these Regulations within 30 days of the date on which his appointment became effective and the notification shall contain the particulars (including the declaration) set out in that form.

(2) The notification referred to in this regulation shall be accompanied by evidence of the VAT representative's appointment.

(3) Where a person is appointed by virtue of section 48 of the Act to be a VAT representative, the Commissioners shall register the name of that VAT representative against the name of his principal in the register kept for the purposes of the Act.

(4) Every VAT representative who is registered in accordance with this regulation shall, within 30 days of any changes being made in the name, constitution or ownership of his business or of his ceasing to be a person's VAT representative, or of any other event occurring which may necessitate the variation of the register, notify the Commissioners in writing of such change, cessation or event and furnish them with full particulars thereof.

(5) For the purposes of this regulation the date upon which the appointment of a VAT representative ("the first VAT representative") shall be regarded as having ceased shall be treated as being whichever is the earliest of the following times—

(*a*) when the Commissioners receive any notification in accordance with regulation 5(2), or

(*b*) when the Commissioners receive a notification of appointment in accordance with paragraph (1) above of a person other than the first VAT representative, or

(*c*) when the Commissioners receive a notification of cessation in accordance with regulation 5(2), or

(*d*) when the Commissioners receive a notification of cessation in accordance with paragraph (4) above, or

(*e*) when a VAT representative dies, becomes insolvent or becomes incapacitated,

provided that if the Commissioners have not received a notification such as is mentioned in all or any of sub-paragraphs (*a*), (*c*) or (*d*) above and another person has been appointed as a VAT representative by virtue of section 48 of the Act, the Commissioners may treat the date of cessation as the date of appointment of that other person.

(6) In relation to a company which is a VAT representative, the references in paragraph (5)(*e*) above to the VAT representative becoming insolvent or incapacitated shall be construed as references to its going into liquidation or receivership or [entering administration][1].

Former regulations—VAT (General) Regulations, SI 1985/886 reg 10A; VAT (General) (Amendment) Regulations, SI 1992/3102.

Amendments—[1] Words in para (6) substituted by the Enterprise Act 2002 (Insolvency) Order, SI 2003/2096 art 5, Schedule paras 55, 57 with effect from 15 September 2003. However, this amendment does not apply in any case where a petition for an administration order was presented before that date: SI 2003/2096 arts 1, 6.

Notification of intended section 14(1) supplies by intermediate suppliers

11— (1) An intermediate supplier who has made or intends to make a supply to which he wishes section 14(1) of the Act to apply shall notify the Commissioners and the customer in writing of his intention to do so.

(2) A notification under this regulation shall contain the following particulars—

(*a*) the name and address of the intermediate supplier,

(*b*) the number including the alphabetical code, by which the intermediate supplier is identified for VAT purposes, which was used or is to be used for the purpose of the supply to him by the original supplier,

(*c*) the date upon which the goods were first delivered or are intended to be first delivered, and

(*d*) the name, address and registration number of the customer to whom the goods have been supplied or are to be supplied.

(3) A notification under this regulation shall be made no later than the provision, in accordance with regulation 18, of the first invoice in relation to the supply to which it relates, and sent to—

(*a*) the office designated by the Commissioners for the receipt of such notifications, and

(*b*) the customer.

(4) Notifications under this regulation shall be made separately in relation to each customer to whom it is intended to make supplies to which the intermediate supplier wishes section 14(1) of the Act to apply.

(5) Where an intermediate supplier has complied with the requirements of this regulation in relation to the first supply to a customer to which section 14(1) of the Act applies, those requirements shall be deemed to have been satisfied in relation to all subsequent supplies to that customer while the intermediate supplier continues to belong in another member State.

Former regulations—VAT (General) Regulations, SI 1985/886 reg 10B; VAT (General) (Amendment) Regulations, SI 1993/1941 regs 2, 4.

Notification of intended section 14(2) supplies by persons belonging in other member States

12— (1) A person belonging in another member State who has made or who intends to make a supply to which he wishes section 14(2) of the Act to apply shall notify the Commissioners and the registered person in writing of his intention to do so.

(2) A notification under this regulation shall contain the following particulars—

(*a*) the name and address of the person belonging in another member State,

(*b*) the number including the alphabetical code by which the person belonging in another member State is identified for VAT purposes in the member State in which he belongs,

(*c*) the date upon which the installation or assembly of the goods was commenced or is intended to commence, and

(*d*) the name, address and registration number of the registered person to whom the goods have been supplied or are to be supplied.

(3) A notification under this regulation shall be made no later than the provision, in accordance with regulation 19, of the first invoice in relation to the supply to which it relates, and sent to—

(*a*) the office designated by the Commissioners for the receipt of such notifications, and

(*b*) the registered person to whom the goods are to be supplied.

(4) Notifications under this regulation shall be made separately in relation to each registered person to whom it is intended to make supplies to which the person belonging in another member State wishes section 14(2) of the Act to apply.

(5) Where a person belonging in another member State has complied with the requirements of this regulation in relation to the first supply to a registered person to which section 14(2) of the Act applies, those requirements shall be deemed to have been satisfied in relation to all subsequent supplies to that registered person while the person making the supply continues to belong in another member State.

Former regulations—VAT (General) Regulations, SI 1985/886 reg 10C; VAT (General) (Amendment) Regulations, SI 1993/1941 regs 2, 5.

PART III
VAT INVOICES AND OTHER INVOICING REQUIREMENTS

[Interpretation of Part 3

A13 In this Part—

(*a*) "advanced electronic signature" means an electronic signature which meets the following requirements—

(i) it is uniquely linked to the signatory;

(ii) it is capable of identifying the signatory;

(iii) it is created using means that the signatory can maintain under his sole control; and

(iv) it is linked to the data to which it relates in such a manner that any subsequent change of the data is detectable;

(*b*) "electronic data interchange" or "EDI" means the electronic transfer, from computer to computer, of commercial and administrative data using an agreed standard to structure an EDI message;

(*c*) "EDI message" means a set of segments, structured using an agreed standard, prepared in a computer readable format and capable of being automatically and unambiguously processed;

(*d*) "electronic signature" means data in electronic form which are attached to or logically associated with other electronic data and which serve as a method of authentication;

(*e*) "electronic storage of invoices" means storage using electronic equipment for processing (including digital compression) and storage of data employing wires, radio transmission, optical technologies or other electromagnetic means;

(*f*) "electronic transmission" in relation to invoices means transmission or making available to the recipient using electronic equipment employing wires, radio transmission, optical technologies or other electromagnetic means;

(*g*) "signatory" means a person who holds a signature-creation device and acts either on his own behalf or on behalf of the natural or legal person or entity he represents.][1]

Amendments—[1] Inserted by the VAT (Amendment) (No 6) Regulations, SI 2003/3220 regs 1(*b*), 2, 3 with effect from 1 January 2004.

Obligation to provide a VAT invoice

13— (1) Save as otherwise provided in these Regulations, where a registered person—

(*a*) makes a taxable supply in the United Kingdom to a taxable person, or

(*b*) makes a supply of goods or services …[3] to a person in another member State [for the purpose of any business activity carried out by that person][3], or

(*c*) receives a payment on account in respect of a supply he has made or intends to make from a person in another member State,

he shall provide such persons as are mentioned above with a VAT invoice [(unless, in the case of that supply, he is entitled to issue and issues a VAT invoice pursuant to section 18C(1)(*e*) of the Act and regulation 145D(1) below in relation to the supply by him of specified services performed on or in relation to goods while those goods are subject to a fiscal or other warehousing regime)][1]

[(1A) Paragraph (1)(*b*) above shall not apply where the supply is an exempt supply which is made to a person in a member State which does not require an invoice to be issued for the supply.][3]

(2) The particulars of the VAT chargeable on a supply of goods described in paragraph 7 of Schedule 4 to the Act shall be provided, on a sale by auction, by the auctioneer, and, where the sale is otherwise than by auction, by the person selling the goods, on a document containing the particulars prescribed in regulation 14(1); and such a document issued to the buyer shall be treated for the purposes of paragraph (1)(*a*) above as a VAT invoice provided by the person by whom the goods are deemed to be supplied in accordance with the said paragraph 7.

[(3) Where a registered person provides a document to himself ("a self-billed invoice") that purports to be a VAT invoice in respect of a supply of goods or services to him by another registered person, that document shall be treated as the VAT invoice required to be provided by the supplier under paragraph (1)(*a*) if it complies with the conditions set out in paragraph (3A) and with any further conditions that may be contained in a notice published by the Commissioners or may be imposed in a particular case.][2]

[(3A) The following conditions must be complied with if a self-billed invoice is to be treated as a VAT invoice—

(*a*) it must have been provided pursuant to a prior agreement ("a self-billing agreement") entered into between the supplier of the goods or services to which it relates and the recipient of the goods or services ("the customer") and which satisfies the requirements in paragraph (3B);

(*b*) it must contain the particulars required under regulation 14(1) or (2);

(*c*) it must relate to a supply or supplies made by a supplier who is a taxable person.][1]

[(3B) A self-billing agreement must—

(*a*) authorise the customer to produce self-billed invoices in respect of supplies made by the supplier for a specified period which shall end not later than either—

(i) the expiry of a period of 12 months, or

(ii) the expiry of the period of any contract between the customer and the supplier for the supply of the particular goods or services to which the self-billing agreement relates;

(*b*) specify that the supplier will not issue VAT invoices in respect of supplies covered by the agreement;

(*c*) specify that the supplier will accept each self-billed invoice created by the customer in respect of supplies made to him by the supplier;

(*d*) specify that the supplier will notify the customer if he ceases to be a taxable person or if he changes his registration number.][1]

[(3C) Without prejudice to any term of a self-billing agreement, it shall be treated as having expired when—

(*a*) the business of the supplier is transferred as a going concern;

(*b*) the business of the customer is transferred as a going concern;
(*c*) the supplier ceases to be registered for VAT.][1]

[(3D) In addition to the matters set out in paragraph (3B)—

(*a*) conditions that must be complied with may be set out in a notice published by the Commissioners;
(*b*) the Commissioners may impose further conditions in particular cases.][1]

[(3E) Where a customer in another member State provides a document to himself in respect of a supply of goods or services to him by a registered person, that document shall be treated as the VAT invoice required to be provided by the supplier under paragraph 1(*b*) or (*c*) if it complies with the conditions set out in paragraph (3A).][1]

[(3F) For the purposes of the following, a self-billed invoice will not be treated as issued by the supplier (however the supplier may be described in the provision concerned)—

(*a*) regulation 84(2)(*b*)(ii);
(*b*) regulation 85(1)(*b*);
(*c*) regulation 85(2);
(*d*) regulation 86(1);
(*e*) regulation 86(2)(*b*);
(*f*) regulation 86(3);
(*g*) regulation 88(1)(*b*);
(*h*) regulation 89(*b*)(ii);
(*i*) regulation 90(1)(*b*);
(*j*) regulation 90(2);
(*k*) regulation 91;
(*l*) regulation 92(*b*);
(*m*) regulation 93(1)(*b*);
(*n*) regulation 94B(6)(*a*).][2]

(4) Where the person who makes a supply to which regulation 93 relates gives an authenticated receipt containing the particulars required under regulation 14(1) to be specified in a VAT invoice in respect of that supply, that document shall be treated as the VAT invoice required to be provided under paragraph (1)(*a*) above on condition that no VAT invoice or similar document which was intended to be or could be construed as being a VAT invoice for the supply to which the receipt relates is issued.

(5) The documents specified in paragraphs (1), (2), (3) and (4) above shall be provided within 30 days of the time when the supply is treated as taking place under section 6 of the Act, or within such longer period as the Commissioners may allow in general or special directions.

Former regulations—VAT (General) Regulations, SI 1985/886 reg 12; VAT (General) (Amendment) Regulations, SI 1992/3102 reg 8.
Cross reference—See VAT Regulations, SI 1995/2518 reg 20 (disapplication of this regulation to certain supplies made in UK).
Customs and Excise Notices—Notice 701/48 Corporate purchasing cards, para 3.3 (the line item detail VAT invoice).
Amendments—[1] Words in para (1) inserted by the VAT (Amendment) (No 3) Regulations, SI 1996/1250 reg 6 with effect from 1 June 1996.
[2] Para (3) substituted, paras (3A)–(3F) inserted, by the VAT (Amendment) (No 6) Regulations, SI 2003/3220 regs 1(1)(*b*), 2, 4 with effect from 1 January 2004.
[3] Words in para (1) revoked and inserted, and para (1A) inserted, by the Value Added Tax (Amendment) (No 5) Regulations, SI 2007/2085 regs 2, 6 with effect from 1 October 2007.

[Electronic invoicing

13A— (1) This regulation applies where a document is provided by a registered person by electronic transmission that purports to be a VAT invoice in respect of a supply of goods or services.

(2) The document is not to be treated as the VAT invoice required to be provided by the supplier under regulation 13(1) unless—

(*a*) both the supplier and the customer are able to guarantee the authenticity of the origin and integrity of the contents by one of the following means—

(i) an advanced electronic signature;
(ii) EDI;
(iii) where the document relates to supplies of goods or services made in the United Kingdom, such other electronic means as may be approved by the Commissioners in any particular case;

(*b*) the supplier has complied with any conditions imposed by the Commissioners.

(3) When the document is a self-billed invoice that purports to be a VAT invoice, paragraph (2)(*b*) applies as if the reference to the supplier is to the customer.

(4) Where an invoice has been provided or received that meets the conditions in paragraph (2) the supplier and the customer must preserve the means adopted for guaranteeing the authenticity of the origin and integrity of the contents under paragraph 2(*a*) for such time as the invoice is preserved.][1]

Amendments—[1] Inserted by the VAT (Amendment No 6) Regulations, SI 2003/3220 regs 1(1)(*b*), 2, 5 with effect from 1 January 2004.

[13B Where a VAT invoice or part of a VAT invoice is in a language other than English the Commissioners may, by notice in writing, require that an English translation of the invoice is provided to them by a person who has received such an invoice in the United Kingdom within 30 days of the date of the notice.][1]

Amendments—[1] Inserted by the VAT (Amendment) (No 6) Regulations, SI 2003/3220 regs 1(1)(*b*), 2, 6 with effect from 1 January 2004.

Contents of VAT invoice

14— (1) Subject to paragraph (2) below and regulation 16 [and save as the Commissioners may otherwise allow][2], a registered person providing a VAT invoice in accordance with regulation 13 shall state thereon the following particulars—

(*a*) [a sequential number based on one or more series which uniquely identifies the document][6],

(*b*) the time of the supply,

(*c*) the date of the issue of the document,

(*d*) the name, address and registration number of the supplier,

(*e*) the name and address of the person to whom the goods or services are supplied,

(*f*) …[3]

(*g*) a description sufficient to identify the goods or services supplied,

(*h*) for each description, the quantity of the goods or the extent of the services, and the rate of VAT and the amount payable, excluding VAT, expressed in [any currency][3],

(*i*) the gross total amount payable, excluding VAT, expressed in [any currency][3],

(*j*) the rate of any cash discount offered,

(*k*) …[3]

(*l*) the total amount of VAT chargeable, expressed in sterling,

[(*m*) the unit price.][3]

[(*n*) where a margin scheme is applied under section 50A or section 53 of the Act, a relevant reference or any indication that a margin scheme has been applied,

(*o*) where a VAT invoice relates in whole or part to a supply where the person supplied is liable to pay the tax, a relevant reference or any indication that the supply is one where the customer is liable to pay the tax.][6]

(2) [Save as the Commissioners may otherwise allow, where a registered person provides a person in another member State with a VAT invoice or any document that refers to a VAT invoice and is intended to amend it, he must ensure that it states thereon the following particulars—][4]

(*a*) the information specified in sub-paragraphs [(*a*) to (*e*), (*g*), [(*j*), (*m*), (*n*) and (*o*)][6]][4] of paragraph (1) above,

(*b*) the letters "GB" as a prefix to his registration number,

(*c*) the registration number, if any, of the recipient of the supply of goods or services and which registration number, if any, shall contain the alphabetical code of the member State in which that recipient is registered,

(*d*) the gross amount payable, excluding VAT,

(*e*) where the supply is of a new means of transport (as defined in section 95 of the Act) a description sufficient to identify it as such,

(*f*) for each description, the quantity of the goods or the extent of the services, and where a positive rate of VAT is chargeable, the rate of VAT and the amount payable, excluding VAT, expressed in sterling, …[6]

(*g*) where the supply of goods is a taxable supply, the information as specified in [sub-paragraph (*l*)][4] of paragraph (1) above[, and

(*h*) where the supply is an exempt or zero-rated supply, a relevant reference or any indication that the supply is exempt or zero-rated as appropriate][6].

(3) Where a taxable supply takes place as described in section 6(2)(*c*) or section 6(5) of the Act, any consignment or delivery note or similar document or any copy thereof issued by the supplier before the time of supply shall not, notwithstanding that it may contain all the particulars set out in paragraph (1) above, be treated as a VAT invoice provided it is endorsed "This is not a VAT invoice".

(4) Where a registered person provides an invoice containing the particulars specified in paragraphs (1) and (3) above, and specifies thereon any goods or services which are the subject of an exempt or zero-rated supply, he shall distinguish on the invoice between the goods or services which are the subject of an exempt, zero-rated or other supply and state separately the gross total amount payable in respect of each supply and rate.

(5) …[6]

[(6) Where a registered person provides a VAT invoice relating in whole or in part to a supply of the letting on hire of a motor car other than for self-drive hire, he shall state on the invoice whether that motor car is a qualifying vehicle under article 7(2A) of the Value Added Tax (Input Tax) Order 1992.][1]

[(7) Where a registered person provides documents in batches to the same recipient by electronic transmission that purport to be VAT invoices in respect of supplies of goods or services made to, or received by, him, as an exception to the requirements in regulation 14(1) and 14(2), details common to each such document need only be stated once for each batch file.][5]

[(8) In this regulation, a "relevant reference" is—

(*a*) a reference to the appropriate provision of Council Directive 2006/112/EC, or

(*b*) a reference to the corresponding provision of the Act.][6]

Former regulations—VAT (General) Regulations, SI 1985/886 reg 13; VAT (General) (Amendment) Regulations, SI 1992/3102 reg 9, SI 1993/856 reg 3.
VAT Notices—Notice 701/48 Corporate purchasing cards, para 3.3 (the line item detail VAT invoice).
Press releases etc—VAT Information Sheet 13/95 1-9-95 (contents of a VAT invoice from supplier to card company in respect of purchases using a corporate purchasing card).
HMRC Brief 36/07, 10-4-07 (Input tax deduction without a valid VAT invoice: revised Statement of Practice).
HMRC Brief 51/07, 24-7-07 (modifications made to the format of invoices with effect from 1 October 2007).
Cross reference—See VAT Regulations, SI 1995/2518 reg 20 (disapplication of this regulation to certain supplies made in UK).
Amendments—[1] Para (6) inserted by the VAT (Amendment) Regulations, SI 1995/3147 reg 3, with effect from 1 January 1996.
[2] Words in paras (1) and (2) inserted by the VAT (Amendment) (No 3) Regulations, SI 1996/1250 reg 7 with effect from 1 June 1996.
[3] In para (1), sub-paras (*f*) and (*k*) revoked, words in sub-paras (*h*) and (*i*) substituted, and sub-para (*m*) inserted, by the VAT (Amendment) (No 6) Regulations, SI 2003/3220 regs 1(1)(*b*), 2, 7 with effect from 1 January 2004.
[4] Words at beginning of sub-para (2), and in sub-paras (2)(*a*), (*g*) substituted by SI 2003/3220 regs 1(1)(*b*), 2, 8 with effect from 1 January 2004.
[5] Sub-para (7) inserted by SI 2003/3220 regs 1(1)(*b*), 2, 9 with effect from 1 January 2004.
[6] Words in paras (1), (2) substituted and inserted, para (5) revoked, and para (8) inserted, by the Value Added Tax (Amendment) (No 5) Regulations, SI 2007/2085 regs 2, 7 with effect from 1 October 2007.

Change of rate, credit notes

15 Where there is a change in the rate of VAT in force under section 2 [or 29A][1] of the Act or in the descriptions of exempt[, zero-rated or reduced-rate][1] supplies, and a VAT invoice which relates to a supply in respect of which an election is made under section 88 of the Act was issued before the election was made, the person making the supply shall, within [45 days][2] after any such change, [or within such longer period as the Commissioners may allow in general or special directions,][2] provide the person to whom the supply was made with a credit note headed "Credit note-change of VAT rate" and containing the following particulars—

(*a*) the identifying number and date of issue of the credit note,

(*b*) the name, address and registration number of the supplier,

(*c*) the name and address of the person to whom the supply is made,

(*d*) the identifying number and date of issue of the VAT invoice,

(*e*) a description sufficient to identify the goods or services supplied, and

(*f*) the amount being credited in respect of VAT.

Former regulation—VAT (General) Regulations, SI 1985/886 reg 14.
Cross reference—See VAT Regulations, SI 1995/2518 reg 20 (disapplication of this regulation to certain supplies made in UK).
Amendments—[1] Words inserted, and words substituted for the words "or zero-rated", by the VAT (Amendment) (No 4) Regulations, SI 2003/1485 regs 2, 3 with effect from 1 July 2003.
[2] Figure substituted and words inserted, by the VAT (Amendment) (No 2) Regulations, SI 2008/3021 regs 2, 3 with effect from 1 December 2008.

Retailers' invoices

16— (1) Subject to paragraph (2) below, a registered person who is a retailer shall not be required to provide a VAT invoice, except that he shall provide such an invoice at the request of a customer who is a taxable person in respect of any supply to him; but, in that event, if, but only if, the consideration for the supply does not exceed [£250][1] and the supply is other than to a person in another member State, the VAT invoice need contain only the following particulars—

(*a*) the name, address and registration number of the retailer,

(*b*) the time of the supply,

(*c*) a description sufficient to identify the goods or services supplied,

(*d*) the total amount payable including VAT, and

(*e*) for each rate of VAT chargeable, the gross amount payable including VAT, and the VAT rate applicable.

(2) Where a registered person provides an invoice in accordance with this regulation, the invoice shall not contain any reference to any exempt supply.

Former regulations—VAT (General) Regulations, SI 1985/886 reg 15; VAT (General) (Amendment) Regulations, SI 1992/3102 reg 10.
Cross reference—See VAT Regulations, SI 1995/2518 reg 20 (disapplication of this regulation to certain supplies made in UK).
Amendments—[1] Figure substituted by the VAT (Amendment) (No 6) Regulations, SI 2003/3220 regs 1(1)(*b*), 2, 10 with effect from 1 January 2004.

Section 14(6) supplies to persons belonging in other member States

17— (1) Where a registered person makes a supply such as is mentioned in section 14(6) of the Act he shall provide the person supplied with an invoice in respect of that supply.

[(2) An invoice provided under this regulation shall comply with the requirements of regulations 13 and 14.][1]

Former regulations—VAT (General) Regulations, SI 1985/886 reg 15A; VAT (General) (Amendment) Regulations, SI 1993/1941 regs 2, 8.

Cross reference—See VAT Regulations, SI 1995/2518 reg 20 (disapplication of this regulation to certain supplies made in UK).

Amendments—[1] Para (2) substituted by the Value Added Tax (Amendment) (No 5) Regulations, SI 2007/2085 regs 2, 8 with effect from 1 October 2007.

Section 14(1) supplies by intermediate suppliers

18— (1) On each occasion that an intermediate supplier makes or intends to make a supply to which he wishes section 14(1) of the Act to apply he shall, subject to paragraph (3) below, provide the customer with an invoice.

(2) An invoice provided under this regulation by an intermediate supplier shall—

(*a*) comply with the provisions of the law corresponding, in relation to the member State which provided the intermediate supplier with the identification number for VAT purposes used or to be used by him for the purpose of the supply to him by the original supplier of the goods which were subsequently removed to the United Kingdom, to regulation 17,

(*b*) be provided no later than 15 days after the time that the supply of the goods would, but for section 14(1) of the Act, have been treated as having taken place by or under section 6 of the Act,

(*c*) cover no less than the extent of the supply which would, but for section 14(1) of the Act, have been treated as having taken place by or under section 6 of the Act at the time that such an invoice is provided, …[1]

(*d*) …[1]

(3) Where an intermediate supplier makes a supply such as is mentioned in paragraph (1) above, and he has already provided the customer with an invoice that complies with the requirements of sub-paragraphs (*a*), (*c*) and (*d*) of paragraph (2) above, he shall not be required to provide the customer with a further invoice in relation to that supply.

(4) Where an intermediate supplier makes a supply such as is mentioned in paragraph (1) above and he provides the customer with an invoice such as is described in paragraphs (2) and (3) above, that invoice shall be treated as if it were an invoice for the purpose of regulation 83.

(5) Where an intermediate supplier makes a supply such as is mentioned in paragraph (1) above and he provides the customer with an invoice that complies only with the requirements of paragraph (2)(*a*) above, that invoice shall, for the purposes of this regulation only, be treated as if it were a VAT invoice.

Former regulations—VAT (General) Regulations, SI 1985/886 reg 15B; VAT (General) (Amendment) Regulations, SI 1993/1941 regs 2, 8.

Cross reference—See VAT Regulations, SI 1995/2518 reg 20 (disapplication of this regulation to certain supplies made in UK).

Amendments—[1] Para (2)(*d*) and preceding word "and" revoked by the Value Added Tax (Amendment) (No 5) Regulations, SI 2007/2085 regs 2, 9 with effect from 1 October 2007.

Section 14(2) supplies by persons belonging in other member States

19— (1) On each occasion that a person belonging in another member State makes or intends to make a supply to which he wishes section 14(2) of the Act to apply he shall, subject to paragraph (3) below, provide the registered person with an invoice.

(2) An invoice provided under this regulation by a person belonging in another member State shall—

(*a*) comply with the provisions of the law of the member State in which he belongs corresponding in relation to that member State to the provisions of regulation 14,

(*b*) be provided no later than 15 days after the time that the supply of the goods would, but for section 14(2) of the Act, have been treated as having taken place by or under section 6 of the Act,

(*c*) cover no less than the extent of the supply which would, but for section 14(2) of the Act, have been treated as having taken place by or under section 6 of the Act at the time that such an invoice is provided, …[1]

(*d*) …[1]

(3) Where a person belonging in another member State makes a supply such as is mentioned in paragraph (1) above, and he has already provided the registered person with an invoice that complies with the requirements of sub-paragraphs (*a*), (*c*) and (*d*) of paragraph (2) above, he shall not be required to provide the registered person with a further invoice in relation to that supply.

(4) Where a person belonging in another member State makes a supply such as is mentioned in paragraph (1) above and he provides the registered person with an invoice such as is described in paragraphs (2) and (3) above, that invoice shall be treated as if it were an invoice for the purpose of regulation 83.

(5) Where a person belonging in another member State makes a supply such as is mentioned in paragraph (1) above, and he provides the registered person with an invoice that complies only with the requirements of paragraph (2)(*a*) above, that invoice shall, for the purposes of this regulation only, be treated as if it were a VAT invoice.

Former regulations—VAT (General) Regulations, SI 1985/886 reg 15C; VAT (General) (Amendment) Regulations, SI 1993/1941 regs 2, 8.

Cross reference—See VAT Regulations, SI 1995/2518 reg 20 (disapplication of this regulation to certain supplies made in UK).

Amendments—[1] Para (2)(*d*) and preceding word "and" revoked by the Value Added Tax (Amendment) (No 5) Regulations, SI 2007/2085 regs 2, 10 with effect from 1 October 2007.

General

20 Regulations 13, 14, 15, 16, 17, 18 and 19 shall not apply to the following supplies made in the United Kingdom—

(*a*) any zero-rated supply other than a supply for the purposes of an acquisition in another member State,

(*b*) any supply to which an order made under section 25(7) of the Act applies,

(*c*) any supply on which VAT is charged although it is not made for consideration, or

(*d*) any supply to which an order made under section 32 of the Act applies.

Former regulations—VAT (General) Regulations, SI 1985/886 reg 16; VAT (General) (Amendment) Regulations, SI 1992/3102 reg 11, SI 1993/1941 regs 2, 9.

PART IV
EC SALES STATEMENTS

Interpretation of Part IV

21 In this Part—

...[1]

"form" means the form numbered 12 in Schedule 1 to these Regulations;

...[1]

"registered in another member State" means registered in accordance with the measures adopted by the competent authority in another member State for the purposes of the common system of VAT and "registered" shall be construed accordingly;

"relevant figure" means the sum of the amount mentioned in paragraph 1(1)(*a*) of Schedule 1 to the Act and £25,500;

"statement" means the statement which a taxable person is required to submit in accordance with this Part of these Regulations;

"total value" means the consideration for the supply including the costs of any freight transport services and services ancillary to the transport of goods charged by the supplier of the goods to the customer.

Former regulation—VAT (EC Sales Statements) Regulations, SI 1992/3096 reg 1(2).

Amendments—[1] Definitions "contract work" and "processing work" revoked by the VAT (Amendment) Regulations, SI 1996/210, reg 3 with effect from 1 March 1996.

Submission of statements

22— (1) Subject to paragraph (6) below and save as the Commissioners may otherwise allow or direct, every taxable person who in any period of a quarter has made a supply of, or has dispatched, or has transported, or has transferred, goods to a person who is or was registered in another member State shall in relation to that period submit to the Commissioners, no later than 42 days after the end of that period, a statement in the form numbered 12 in Schedule 1 to these Regulations containing full information as specified in paragraph [(3) or (5)][1] below, as the case may require and a declaration signed by him that the statement is true and complete; provided that—

(*a*) the Commissioners may allow a taxable person to submit those statements in respect of periods of one month;

(*b*) where a taxable person satisfies the Commissioners either that—

(i) at the end of any month, the value of his taxable supplies in the period of one year then ending is less than the relevant figure, or

(ii) at any time, there are reasonable grounds for believing that the value of his taxable supplies in the period of one year beginning at that or any later time will not exceed the relevant figure,

and either that—

(iii) at the end of any month, the value of his supplies to persons registered in other member States in the period of one year then ending is less than £11,000, or

(iv) at any time, there are reasonable grounds for believing that the value of his supplies to persons registered in other member States in the period of one year beginning at that or any later time will not exceed £11,000,

the Commissioners may allow that person to submit a statement which relates to the period of the year mentioned in sub-paragraphs (i) to (iv) above and which contains full information as specified in paragraph (3)(*a*) to (*d*) below and a declaration signed by him that the statement is true and complete;

(*c*) where the Commissioners have allowed a taxable person under regulation 25 to make returns; in respect of periods longer than 3 months and that person satisfies the Commissioners either that—

(i) at the end of any month, the value of his taxable supplies in the period of one year then ending is less than £145,000, or

(ii) at any time, there are reasonable grounds for believing that the value of his taxable supplies in the period of one year beginning at that or any later time will not exceed £145,000,

and either that—

(iii) at the end of any month, the value of his supplies to persons registered in other member States in the period of one year then ending is less than £11,000, or

(iv) at any time, there are reasonable grounds for believing that the value of his supplies to persons registered in other member States in the period of one year beginning at that or any later time will not exceed £11,000,

the Commissioners may allow that person to submit statements in respect of periods identical to those that have been allowed for the making of his returns and each statement shall contain full information as specified in paragraphs [(3) or (5)][1] below, as the case may require, and a declaration signed by him that the statement is true and complete; and

(*d*) where the Commissioners consider it necessary in a particular case, they may allow or direct a taxable person to submit statements to a specified address.

(2) Where the Commissioners allow a statement to be submitted as is mentioned in the proviso to paragraph (1) above, that statement shall be submitted—

(*a*) where sub-paragraph (*a*) of the proviso applies, no later than 42 days after the end of the quarter in which the month in question occurs;

(*b*) where sub-paragraph (*b*) of the proviso applies, no later than 42 days after the end of the period of the year to which the statement relates; and

(*c*) where sub-paragraph (*c*) of the proviso applies, no later than 42 days after the end of the period in respect of which the Commissioners have allowed a return to be furnished.

(3) Save as the Commissioners may otherwise allow or direct, a taxable person shall in any statement such as is mentioned in paragraph (1) above specify—

(*a*) his name, address and registration number which number shall include the prefix GB,

(*b*) the date of the submission of the statement,

(*c*) the date of the last day of the period to which the statement refers,

(*d*) the registration number of each person acquiring or deemed to have acquired goods in the period, including the alphabetical code of the member State in which each such person is registered, and

(*e*) the total value of the goods supplied in the period to each person mentioned in sub-paragraph (*d*) above ...[1].

(4) ...[1]

(5) Where a taxable person makes a supply such as is mentioned in regulation 18(1), he shall specify in the statement required under paragraph (1) above the following—

(*a*) the information mentioned in paragraph (3) above,

(*b*) the figure "2" in the box marked "indicator" on the form numbered 12 in Schedule 1 to these Regulations, and

(*c*) the total value of the goods supplied by him.

(6) Every taxable person who in any period of a quarter has made a supply of a new means of transport to a person for the purpose of acquisition by him in another member State shall in relation to that period submit to the Commissioners no later than 42 days after the end of that period a statement containing the particulars (including the declaration made by him) set out in the form numbered 13 in Schedule 1 to these Regulations,

provided that where the Commissioners consider it necessary in a particular case, they may allow or direct a taxable person to submit the statement to a specified address.

Former regulation—Paras (1)–(4) (as originally enacted): VAT (EC Sales Statements) Regulations, SI 1992/3096 reg 2(1)–(4). Para (5): None.
Para (6): VAT (EC Sales Statements) Regulations, SI 1992/3096 reg 2(5).

Amendments—[1] Words in para (1) substituted, and words in paras 3(*e*), (4) revoked, by the VAT (Amendment) Regulations, SI 1996/210 regs 4–6, with effect from 1 March 1996.

Final statements

23 Any taxable person who ceases to be registered under Schedule 1 to the Act shall, unless another person has been registered with the registration number of and in substitution for him under regulation 6(3), submit to the Commissioners a final statement on either of the forms in Schedule 1 to these Regulations numbered 12 or 13 or both, as the case may require, and unless the Commissioners in any case otherwise allow or direct, any such statement shall contain—

(*a*) the information specified in paragraphs [(3) and (5)][1] of regulation 22, or the full information required by the form numbered 13 in Schedule 1 to these Regulations or both, as the case may require, and

(*b*) a declaration signed by him that the statement is true and complete,

and the statement shall be submitted no later than 42 days after the date with effect from which his registration has been cancelled.

Former regulation—VAT (EC Sales Statements) Regulations, SI 1992/3096 reg 3.

Amendments—[1] Words in para (*a*) substituted by the VAT (Amendment) Regulations, SI 1996/210 reg 7, with effect from 1 March 1996.

[PART 4A
REVERSE CHARGE SALES STATEMENTS

Interpretation of Part 4A

23A In this Part—

"relevant supply" means a supply of goods to which section 55A(6) of the Act applies (customers to account for tax on supplies of goods of a kind used in missing trader intra-community fraud);

"statement" means the statement which a taxable person is required to submit in accordance with this Part of these Regulations.][1]

Amendments—[1] Regs 23A–23C inserted by the VAT (Amendment) (No 3) Regulations, SI 2007/1418 regs 2, 3 with effect from 1 June 2007.

Notification of first relevant supply

[23B— (1) On the first occasion on which a person makes a relevant supply, he must notify the Commissioners of that fact within 30 days of the day on which the supply is made.

(2) The notification referred to in paragraph (1) must be made on-line by using a portal provided by the Commissioners.

(3) If the portal referred to in paragraph (2) is unavailable for any reason, the Commissioners may allow the notification to be made by email.][1]

Amendments—[1] Regs 23A–23C inserted by the VAT (Amendment) (No 3) Regulations, SI 2007/1418 regs 2, 3 with effect from 1 June 2007.

Submission of Statements

[23C— (1) Every taxable person who, in any prescribed accounting period, has made a relevant supply must, in relation to that period, submit to the Commissioners, no later than the day by which he is required to make a return for that period and in such a form and manner as may be determined by the Commissioners in a notice published by them (or otherwise), a statement containing the following prescribed particulars—

(*a*) his registration number;

(*b*) the registration number of each person to whom he has made a relevant supply; and

(*c*) for each month falling within the prescribed accounting period, the total value of the relevant supplies made to each person mentioned in sub paragraph (*b*).

(2) If, in any prescribed accounting period, no relevant supplies are made, a statement to that effect must be submitted to the Commissioners in such form and manner as may be determined by them in a notice published by them (or otherwise).

(3) Sub-paragraph (2) does not apply where a taxable person has notified the Commissioners that he has ceased making relevant supplies without intending subsequently to make such supplies.

(4) A statement must contain a declaration made by the taxable person that it is true and complete.][1]

Amendments—[1] Regs 23A–23C inserted by the VAT (Amendment) (No 3) Regulations, SI 2007/1418 regs 2, 3 with effect from 1 June 2007.

[Notification of cessation and recommencement of relevant supplies

23D Where a person—

(*a*) ceases making relevant supplies without intending subsequently to make such supplies, or

(*b*) has fallen within paragraph (*a*) above but nonetheless starts to make relevant supplies again,

he shall, within 30 days of so ceasing or, as the case may be, of so recommencing, notify the Commissioners of that fact in such form and manner as may be determined in a notice published by them (or otherwise).][1]

Amendments—[1] Regulation inserted by the VAT (Amendment) (No 4) Regulations, SI 2007/1599 regs 2, 3 with effect from 1 July 2007.

[PART 4B
PROVISION OF INFORMATION RELATING TO ARRIVALS AND DISPATCHES

Interpretation of Part 4B

23E— (1) In this Part—

"establishing Regulation" means the Council and European Parliament Regulation (EC) No 638/2004;

"implementing Regulation" means the Commission Regulation (EC) N. 1982/2004;
"statistics Regulations" means the Statistics of Trade (Customs and Excise) Regulations 1992;

(2) In this Part—

"arrivals and dispatches" means those arrivals and dispatches for which a responsible party is required to provide information under the establishing Regulation, implementing Regulation and the statistics Regulations;

"for Intrastat purposes" means for any purpose under the establishing Regulation, implementing Regulation or the statistics Regulations;

"reference period" means the period applicable under Article 6(1) of the establishing Regulation or such other period directed by the Commissioners pursuant to regulation 4(3) of the statistics Regulations;

"responsible party" means a taxable person who is required by Article 7 of the establishing Regulation and regulation 3 of the statistics Regulations to provide information in relation to arrivals and dispatches;

"supplementary declaration" means the relevant form set out in the Schedule to the statistics Regulations;

"delivery terms", "nature of the transaction", "partner Member State", "quantity of the goods" and "value of the goods" shall have the same meaning as in the establishing Regulation and implementing Regulation.][1]

Amendments—[1] This regulation inserted by the VAT (Amendment) Regulations 2008, SI 2008/556 reg 2 with effect from 1 April 2008: SI 2008/556 reg 1.

23F— (1) A responsible party shall provide the information in paragraph (2) relating to arrivals and dispatches to the Commissioners.

(2) The information is—

(*a*) the registration number of the responsible party,
(*b*) the reference period,
(*c*) whether the information relates to arrival or dispatch,
(*d*) the commodity, identified by the eight digit code of the Combined Nomenclature as defined in Council Regulation (EEC) No 2658/87 of 23 July 1987 as amended on the tariff and statistical nomenclature and the Common Customs Tariff,
(*e*) the partner Member State,
(*f*) the value of the goods,
(*g*) the quantity of the goods,
(*h*) the nature of the transaction.

(3) A responsible party to whom regulation 4(2) of the statistics Regulations applies shall also provide the delivery terms relating to arrivals and dispatches to the Commissioners.

(4) The information required by paragraphs (2) and (3) shall be provided in the supplementary declaration in which, and for the same reference period as, information is provided relating to those arrivals and dispatches for Intrastat purposes.][1]

Amendments—[1] This regulation inserted by the VAT (Amendment) Regulations, SI 2008/556 reg 2 with effect from 1 April 2008: SI 2008/556 reg 1.

PART V
ACCOUNTING, PAYMENT AND RECORDS

Interpretation of Part V

24 In this Part—

"increase in consideration" means an increase in the consideration due on a supply made by a taxable person which is evidenced by a credit or debit note or any other document having the same effect and "decrease in consideration" is to be interpreted accordingly;

"insolvent person" means—

(*a*) an individual who has been adjudged bankrupt;
(*b*) a company in relation to which—
  (i) a voluntary arrangement under Part I of the Insolvency Act 1986 has been approved,
  (ii) [an administrator has been appointed][3],
  (iii) an administrative receiver has been appointed,
  (iv) a resolution for voluntary winding up has been passed, or
  (v) an order for its winding-up has been made by the court at a time when it had not already gone into liquidation by passing a resolution for voluntary winding-up;

["investment gold" has the same meaning as that expression has for the purposes of Group 15 of Schedule 9 to the Act;][1]

"negative entry" means an amount entered into the VAT account as a negative amount;

"positive entry" means an amount entered into the VAT account as a positive amount;

"VAT allowable portion", "VAT payable portion" and "VAT account" have the meanings given in regulation [32][2];

"the Removal Order" means the Value Added Tax (Removal of Goods) Order 1992;
"the owner" has the same meaning as in article 2 of the Removal Order.

Former regulations—VAT (Accounting and Records) Regulations, SI 1989/2248 reg 1(2); VAT (Removal of Goods) (Accounting) Regulations, SI 1992/3101 reg 2.
Simon's Tax Cases—*C&E Comrs v General Motors Acceptance Corp (UK) plc* [2004] STC 577.
Amendments—[1] Definition of "investment gold" inserted by the VAT (Amendment) (No 4) Regulations, SI 1999/3114, regs 2, 3, with effect from 1 January 2000.
[2] In the definition of "VAT allowable portion", "VAT payable portion" and "VAT account", figure "32" substituted for "33" by the VAT (Amendment) (No 4) Regulations, SI 2003/1485 regs 2,4 with effect from 1 July 2003.
[3] Words in definition of "insolvent person" substituted by the Enterprise Act 2002 (Insolvency) Order, SI 2003/2096 art 5, Schedule paras 55, 58 with effect from 15 September 2003. However, this amendment does not apply in any case where a petition for an administration order was presented before that date: SI 2003/2096 arts 1, 6.

VAT

Making of returns

25— (1) Every person who is registered or was or is required to be registered shall, in respect of every period of a quarter or in the case of a person who is registered, every period of 3 months ending on the dates notified either in the certificate of registration issued to him or otherwise, not later than the last day of the month next following the end of the period to which it relates, make to the Controller a return on the form numbered 4 in Schedule 1 to these Regulations [("Form 4")][1] showing the amount of VAT payable by or to him and containing full information in respect of the other matters specified in the form and a declaration, signed by him, that the return is true and complete;

provided that—

(*a*) the Commissioners may allow or direct a person to make returns in respect of periods of one month and to make those returns within one month of the periods to which they relate;

(*b*) the first return shall be for the period which includes the effective date determined in accordance with [Schedules 1, 2, 3 and 3A][2] to the Act upon which the person was or should have been registered, and the said period shall begin on that date;

(*c*) where the Commissioners consider it necessary in any particular case to vary the length of any period or the date on which any period begins or ends or by which any return shall be made, they may allow or direct any person to make returns accordingly, whether or not the period so varied has ended;

(*d*) where the Commissioners consider it necessary in any particular case, they may allow or direct a person to make returns to a specified address.

(2) Any person to whom the Commissioners give any direction in pursuance of the proviso to paragraph (1) above shall comply therewith.

(3) Where for the purposes of this Part the Commissioners have made a requirement of any person pursuant to regulation 30—

(*a*) the period in respect of which taxable supplies were being made by the person who died or became incapacitated shall end on the day previous to the date when death or incapacity took place; and

(*b*) subject to sub-paragraph (1)(*c*) above, a return made on his behalf shall be made in respect of that period no later than the last day of the month next following the end of that period; and

(*c*) the next period shall start on the day following the aforesaid period and it shall end, and all subsequent periods shall begin and end, on the dates previously determined under paragraph (1) above.

(4) Any person who—

(*a*) ceases to be liable to be registered, or

(*b*) ceases to be entitled to be registered under either or both of paragraphs 9 and 10 of Schedule 1 to the Act,

shall, unless another person has been registered with his registration number in substitution for him under regulation 6, make to the Controller a final return on the form numbered 5 in Schedule 1 to these Regulations [("Form 5")][1] and any such return shall contain full information in respect of the matters specified in the form and a declaration, signed by him, that the return is true and complete and shall be made, in the case of a person who was or is registered, within one month of the effective date for cancellation of his registration, and in the case of any other person, within one month of the date upon which he ceases to be liable to be registered, and in either case shall be in respect of the final period ending on the date aforementioned and be in substitution for the return for the period in which such date occurs.

[(4A) A person may make a return required by this regulation ...[3] using electronic communications.

(4B) Such a method of making a return shall be referred to in this Part as an "electronic return system".

(4C) A person may only make a return by way of an electronic return system on condition that—

(*a*) the electronic return system in question takes a form approved by the Commissioners in a specific or general direction; and (*b*) that person remains authorised by the Commissioners in accordance with paragraph (4G) below.

[(4D) A direction under paragraph (4C)(*a*) may in particular—

(*a*) modify or dispense with any requirement of Form 4 or Form 5 (as appropriate);

(*b*) specify circumstances in which the electronic return system may be used, or not used, by or on behalf of the person required to make the return.

For the purposes of sub-paragraph (*b*), the direction may specify different circumstances for different cases.][3]

(4E) An electronic return system shall incorporate an electronic validation process.

(4F) Subject to paragraph [(4J) below][3]—

(*a*) the use of an electronic return system shall be proved to have resulted in the making of the return to the Controller only if this has been successfully recorded as such by the relevant electronic validation process;

(*b*) the time of making the return to the Controller using an electronic return system shall be conclusively presumed to be the time recorded as such by the relevant electronic validation process; and

(*c*) the person [delivering][3] the return to the Controller shall be presumed to be the person identified as such by any relevant feature of the electronic return system.

(4G) The Commissioners may on application authorise a person to make returns using an electronic return system and may revoke any such authorisation.

(4H) The Commissioners shall pay proper regard to the following factors before authorising a person or revoking an authorisation under paragraph (4G) above—

(*a*) the state of development of any relevant electronic return system;

(*b*) the protection of the revenue;

(*c*) the degree of compliance of the person concerned with this Part; and

(*d*) any other relevant factor.

(4I) A person shall not be authorised to make returns using an electronic return system only by reason of being—

(*a*) registered under regulation 6 above in substitution for a person who has been so authorised (transfer of a going concern); or

(*b*) required by the Commissioners under regulation 30 below to comply with the requirements of this Part (person acting in a representative capacity).

[(4J) No return shall be treated as having been made using an electronic return system unless the conditions imposed by paragraph (4C) are satisfied.

The condition in paragraph (4C)(*a*) incorporates the matters mentioned in paragraph (4D).

(4K) A return made using an electronic return system carries the same consequences as a return made on Form 4 or Form 5 (as appropriate), except in relation to any matter for which alternative or additional provision is made by or under paragraphs (4C) to (4F).

(4L) Additional time is allowed to make a return for which any related payment is made solely by means of electronic communications (see paragraph (1) – time for making return, and regulations 40(2) to 40(4) – payment of VAT).

That additional time is only as the Commissioners may allow in a specific or general direction, and such a direction may allow different times for different means of payment.

The Commissioners need not give a direction pursuant to this paragraph.

(4M) In paragraphs (4C) and (4L) "direction" refers only to a current direction, and a direction is not current to the extent that it is varied, replaced or revoked by another Commissioners' direction.][3]

(5) The Commissioners may allow VAT chargeable in any period to be treated as being chargeable in such later period as they may specify.

Former regulations—VAT (General) Regulations, SI 1985/886 reg 58; VAT (General) (Amendment) Regulations, SI 1986/1900 reg 3, SI 1987/1916 reg 9, SI 1988/2108 reg 7.

Cross reference—See VAT Regulations, SI 1995/2518 reg 6(3) (transfer of a going concern: transferee assuming liabilities of transferor).

Press releases etc—Business Brief 27/97, 21-11-97 (VAT treatment of compensation payments).

Simon's Tax Cases—*Hindle and another (trading as D J Baker Bar) v C&E Comrs* [2004] STC 412; *R&C Comrs v Raj Restaurant (a firm) and others* [2009] STC 729; *R (oao BMW AG and anor) v R&C Comrs* [2009] STC 963.

Amendments—[1] Words in paras (1), (4), and paras (4A)–(4L) inserted by the VAT (Amendment) Regulations, SI 2000/258 regs 2, 3 with effect from 1 March 2000.

[2] Words in para (1)(*b*) substituted by the VAT (Amendment) (No 3) Regulations, SI 2000/794 regs 2, 5 with effect from 22 March 2000.

[3] In para (4A), words "on an electronic version of Form 4 or Form 5 (as appropriate)" revoked, para (4D) substituted, in para (4F), words substituted for the words "(4D) above", and "making", and paras (4J)–(4M) substituted for paras (4J)–(4L), by the VAT (Amendment) (No 3) Regulations, SI 2004/1675 regs 1(1), (3), 4 with effect from 22 July 2004.

Para (4D) previously read as follows—

"(4D) No return shall be treated as having been made under paragraph (4A) above unless the conditions imposed by paragraph (4C) above are satisfied.".

Paras (4J)–(4L) previously read as follows—

"(4J) The electronic versions of Forms 4 and 5 shall not differ in any material respect from those in Schedule 1 to these Regulations but may include relevant modifications.

(4K) Paragraphs (1) and (4) above shall have effect in relation to a return made by way of an electronic return system as if the expression ", signed by him," were omitted.

(4L) Paragraphs (4A) to (4K) above shall not be taken as affecting any provision except in relation to the means of making a return to the Controller.".

Accounting for VAT on an acquisition by reference to the value shown on an invoice

26 Where the time of the acquisition of any goods from another member State is determined by reference to the issue of an invoice such as is described in regulation 83, VAT shall be accounted for and paid in respect of the acquisition only on so much of its value as is shown on that invoice.

Former regulations—VAT (General) Regulations, SI 1985/886 reg 58A; VAT (General) (Amendment) Regulations, SI 1992/3102 reg 45.
Simon's Tax Cases—reg 26(1)(c), *Bjellica (T/A Eddy's Domestic Appliances) v C&E Comrs* [1995] STC 329*.

Supplies under Schedule 4, paragraph 7

27 Where goods are deemed to be supplied by a taxable person by virtue of paragraph 7 of Schedule 4 to the Act, the auctioneer on a sale by auction or, where the sale is otherwise than by auction, the person selling the goods, shall, whether or not registered under the Act, within 21 days of the sale—

(*a*) furnish to the Controller a statement showing—
(i) his name and address and, if registered, his registration number,
(ii) the name, address and registration number of the person whose goods were sold,
(iii) the date of the sale,
(iv) the description and quantity of goods sold at each rate of VAT, and
(v) the amount for which they were sold and the amount of VAT charged at each rate,

(*b*) pay the amount of VAT due, and

(*c*) send to the person whose goods were sold a copy of the statement referred to in sub-paragraph (*a*) above, and the auctioneer or person selling the goods, as the case may be, and the person whose goods were sold shall exclude the VAT chargeable on that supply of those goods from any return made under these Regulations.

Former regulation—VAT (General) Regulations, SI 1985/886 reg 59.

Estimation of output tax

28 Where the Commissioners are satisfied that a person is not able to account for the exact amount of output tax chargeable in any period, he may estimate a part of his output tax for that period, provided that any such estimated amount shall be adjusted and exactly accounted for as VAT chargeable in the next prescribed accounting period or, if the exact amount is still not known and the Commissioners are satisfied that it could not with due diligence be ascertained, in the next but one prescribed accounting period.

Former regulation—VAT (General) Regulations, SI 1985/886 reg 61.

Claims for input tax

29—(1) [Subject to paragraph (1A) below][2], and save as the Commissioners may otherwise allow or direct either generally or specially, a person claiming deduction of input tax under section 25(2) of the Act shall do so on a return made by him for the prescribed accounting period in which the VAT became chargeable [save that, where he does not at that time hold the document or invoice required by paragraph (2) below, he shall make his claim on the return for the first prescribed accounting period in which he holds that document or invoice][2].

[(1A) [Subject to paragraph (1B)][2] the Commissioners shall not allow or direct a person to make any claim for deduction of input tax in terms such that the deduction would fall to be claimed more than [4 years][2] after the date by which the return for [the first prescribed accounting period in which he was entitled to claim that input tax in accordance with paragraph (1) above][2] is required to be made.][1]

[(1B) The Commissioners shall not allow or direct a person to make any claim for deduction of input tax where the return for the first prescribed accounting period in which the person was entitled to claim that input tax in accordance with paragraph (1) above was required to be made on or before 31st March 2006.][2]

(2) At the time of claiming deduction of input tax in accordance with paragraph (1) above, a person shall, if the claim is in respect of—

(*a*) a supply from another taxable person, hold the document which is required to be provided under regulation 13;

(*b*) a supply under section 8(1) of the Act, hold the relative invoice from the supplier;

(*c*) an importation of goods, hold a document authenticated or issued by the proper officer, showing the claimant as importer, consignee or owner and showing the amount of VAT charged on the goods;

(*d*) goods which have been removed from warehouse, hold a document authenticated or issued by the proper officer showing the claimant's particulars and the amount of VAT charged on the goods;

(*e*) an acquisition by him from another member State of any goods other than a new means of transport, hold a document required by the authority in that other member State to be issued showing his registration number including the prefix "GB", the registration number of the supplier including the alphabetical code of the member State in which the supplier is registered, the consideration for the supply exclusive of VAT, the date of issue of the document and description sufficient to identify the goods supplied; or

(*f*) an acquisition by him from another member State of a new means of transport, hold a document required by the authority in that other member State to be issued showing his registration number including the prefix "GB", the registration number of the supplier including the alphabetical code of the member State in which the supplier is registered, the consideration for the supply exclusive of VAT, the date of issue of the document and description sufficient to identify the acquisition as a new means of transport as specified in section 95 of the Act;

provided that where the Commissioners so direct, either generally or in relation to particular cases or classes of cases, a claimant shall hold [or provide][1] such other ...[1] evidence of the charge to VAT as the Commissioners may direct.

(3) Where the Commissioners are satisfied that a person is not able to claim the exact amount of input tax to be deducted by him in any period, he may estimate a part of his input tax for that period, provided that any such estimated amount shall be adjusted and exactly accounted for as VAT deductible in the next prescribed accounting period or, if the exact amount is still not known and the Commissioners are satisfied that it could not with due diligence be ascertained, in the next but one prescribed accounting period.

[(4) Nothing in this regulation shall entitle a taxable person to deduct more than once input tax incurred on goods imported or acquired by him or on goods or services supplied to him.][2]

Commentary—*De Voil Indirect Tax Service* **V3.415**, **V5.415**.
Former regulations—Para (1): VAT (General) Regulations, SI 1985/886 reg 62(1); VAT (General) (Amendment) Regulations, SI 1987/1916 reg 10.
Para (2): VAT (General) Regulations, SI 1985/886 reg 62(1A); VAT (General) (Amendment) Regulations, SI 1992/3102 reg 47.
Para (3): VAT (General) Regulations, SI 1985/886 reg 62(2).
Press releases etc—Business Brief 4/02 22-2-02 (Late claims to input tax submitted before 1 May 1997).
Business Brief 13/06 24-8-06 (Court of Appeal Judgment in Michael Fleming t/a Bodycraft).
Simon's Tax Cases—Para (1A), *Local Authorities Mutual Investment Trust v C&E Comrs* [2004] STC 246; *Fleming (t/a Bodycraft) v R&C Comrs, Condé Nast Publications Ltd v R&C Comrs* [2008] STC 324.
Amendments—[1] Words in para (2) substituted, and word revoked, by the VAT (Amendment) (No 3) Regulations, SI 2003/1114 with effect from 16 April 2003.
[2] In paras (1), words substituted for words "Subject to paragraphs (1A) and (2) below", and words inserted, in para (1A), words inserted and words substituted for words "3 years" and "the prescribed accounting period in which the VAT became chargeable" respectively, and paras (1B), (4) inserted, by the VAT (Amendment) Regulations, SI 2009/586 regs 2, 3 with effect from 1 April 2009.

Persons acting in a representative capacity

30 Where any person subject to any requirements under this Part dies or becomes incapacitated and control of his assets passes to another person, being a personal representative, trustee in bankruptcy, receiver, liquidator or person otherwise acting in a representative capacity, that other person shall, if the Commissioners so require and so long as he has such control, comply with these requirements, provided that any requirement to pay VAT shall only apply to that other person to the extent of the assets of the deceased or incapacitated person over which he has control; and save to the extent aforesaid this Part shall apply to such a person, so acting, in the same way as it would have applied to the deceased or incapacitated person had that person not been deceased or incapacitated.

Former regulation—VAT (General) Regulations, SI 1985/886 reg 63.

Records

31— (1) Every taxable person shall, for the purpose of accounting for VAT, keep the following records—

(*a*) his business and accounting records,

(*b*) his VAT account,

(*c*) copies of all VAT invoices issued by him,

(*d*) all VAT invoices received by him,

[(*da*) all certificates—

(i) prepared by him relating to acquisitions by him of goods from other member States, or

(ii) given to him relating to supplies by him of goods or services,][1]

provided that, owing to provisions in force which concern fiscal or other warehousing regimes, those acquisitions or supplies are either zero-rated or treated for the purposes of the Act as taking place outside the United Kingdom,

(*e*) documentation received by him relating to acquisitions by him of any goods from other member States,

(*f*) copy documentation issued by him relating to the transfer, dispatch or transportation of goods by him to other member States, (*g*) documentation received by him relating to the transfer, dispatch or transportation of goods by him to other member States,

(*h*) documentation relating to importations and exportations by him, and

(*i*) all credit notes, debit notes, or other documents which evidence an increase or decrease in consideration that are received, and copies of all such documents that are issued by him.

[(*j*) a copy of any self-billing agreement within regulation 13(3A) to which he is a party;][2]

[(*k*) where he is a customer, party to a self-billing agreement within regulation 13(3A), the name, address and VAT registration number of each supplier with whom he has entered into a self-billing agreement.][2]

(2) The Commissioners may—

(*a*) in relation to a trade or business of a description specified by them, or

(*b*) for the purposes of any scheme established by, or under, Regulations made under the Act,

supplement the list of records required in paragraph (1) above by a notice published by them for that purpose.

(3) Every person who, at a time when he is not a taxable person, acquires in the United Kingdom from another member State any goods which are subject to a duty of excise or consist of a new means of transport shall, for the purposes of accounting for VAT, keep such records with respect to the acquisition as may be specified in any notice published by the Commissioners in pursuance of this regulation.

Former regulations—Paras (1), (2): VAT (Accounting and Records) Regulations, SI 1989/2248 reg 2(1), (2); VAT (Accounting and Records) (Amendment) Regulations, SI 1992/3097 reg 3.
Para (3): VAT (Accounting and Records) Regulations, SI 1989/2248 reg 2A; VAT (Accounting and Records) (Amendment) Regulations, SI 1992/3097 reg 4.

Amendments—[1] Para (1)(*da*) inserted by the VAT (Amendment) (No 3) Regulations, SI 1996/1250 reg 8 with effect from 1 June 1996.
[2] Para (1)(*j*), (*k*) inserted by the VAT (Amendment) (No 6) Regulations, SI 2003/3220 regs 1(1)(*b*), 2, 11 with effect from 1 January 2004.

[31A— (1) This regulation applies where a person—

(*a*) makes a supply of investment gold of a description falling within item 1 of Group 15 of Schedule 9 to the Act, or

(*b*) makes a supply of a description falling within item 2 of Group 15 of Schedule 9 to the Act, which subsequently results in the transfer of the possession of the investment gold.

(2) Subject to paragraph (6) below (and save as the Commissioners may otherwise allow in relation to supplies where the value is less than an amount equivalent to 15,000 euro at a rate specified in any notice published by the Commissioners for the purposes of this regulation) in addition to the requirements upon every taxable person under this Part, a person making a supply of a description falling within paragraph (1) above shall—

(*a*) without prejudice to regulations 13 and 14, issue an invoice in respect of the supply containing such details as may be specified in a notice published by the Commissioners for the purposes of this regulation;

(*b*) keep and maintain a record of the supply containing such details as may be specified in a notice published by the Commissioners for the purposes of this regulation;

(*c*) retain such documents in relation to the supply as may be specified in a notice published by the Commissioners for the purposes of this regulation;

(*d*) keep and maintain a record of the recipient of the supply containing such particulars pertaining to the recipient as may be specified in a notice published by the Commissioners for the purposes of this regulation;

(*e*) keep and maintain such other records and documents as may be specified in a notice published by the Commissioners for the purposes of this regulation to allow the proper identification of each recipient of the supply;

(*f*) notify the Commissioners in writing that he is making such supplies within 28 days of the first supply;

(*g*) furnish to the Commissioners such information in relation to his making of the supply as may be specified in a notice published by them.

(3) A taxable person shall keep and maintain, together with the account he is required to keep and maintain under regulation 32 below, a record of exempt supplies of a description falling within item 1 or 2 of Group 15 of Schedule 9 to the Act, that he makes to another taxable person.

(4) Where there is a sale of investment gold, which would if that person were supplying investment gold in the course or furtherance of any business, fall within item 1 or 2 of Group 15 of Schedule 9 to the Act, by a person who is not trading in investment gold, to a person who is so trading, the purchaser shall issue on behalf of the seller an invoice containing such particulars as may be set out in a notice published by the Commissioners for the purposes of this regulation and the seller shall sign such form of declaration as may be set out in a notice published by the Commissioners for the purposes of this regulation.

(5) The records required to be kept and the documents required to be retained under paragraphs (1) to (4) above shall be preserved for a minimum period of 6 years.

(6) Paragraphs (2) to (5) above shall not apply to any person in respect of a supply by him of a description falling within item 1 or 2 of Group 15 of Schedule 9 to the Act the value of which does not exceed £5,000, unless the total value of those supplies to any person over the last 12 months exceeds £10,000.][1]

Amendments—[1] This Regulation inserted by the VAT (Amendment) (No 4) Regulations, SI 1999/3114, regs 2, 4, with effect from 1 January 2000.

[31B Where a person receives a supply of a description falling within article 31A(1) above that person shall retain the purchase invoice in relation to that supply for a minimum period of 6 years.][1]

Amendments—[1] This Regulation inserted by the VAT (Amendment) (No 4) Regulations, SI 1999/3114, regs 2, 4, with effect from 1 January 2000.

[31C Paragraph 10(2) of Schedule 11 to the Act shall apply in relation to supplies of a description falling within items 1 and 2 of Group 15 of Schedule 9 to the Act as it applies in relation to the supply of goods under taxable supplies.][1]

Amendments—[1] This Regulation inserted by the VAT (Amendment) (No 4) Regulations, SI 1999/3114, regs 2, 4, with effect from 1 January 2000.

The VAT account

32— (1) Every taxable person shall keep and maintain, in accordance with this regulation, an account to be known as the VAT account.

(2) The VAT account shall be divided into separate parts relating to the prescribed accounting periods of the taxable person and each such part shall be further divided into 2 portions to be known as "the VAT payable portion" and "the VAT allowable portion".

(3) The VAT payable portion for each prescribed accounting period shall comprise—

(*a*) a total of the output tax due from the taxable person for that period,

(*b*) a total of the output tax due on acquisitions from other member States by the taxable person for that period,

[(*ba*) a total of the tax which the taxable person is required to account for and pay on behalf of the supplier,][1]

(*c*) every correction or adjustment to the VAT payable portion which is required or allowed by regulation 34, 35[, 38, or 38A][1], and

(*d*) every adjustment to the amount of VAT payable by the taxable person for that period which is required, or allowed, by or under any Regulations made under the Act.

(4) The VAT allowable portion for each prescribed period shall comprise—

(*a*) a total of the input tax allowable to the taxable person for that period by virtue of section 26 of the Act,

(*b*) a total of the input tax allowable in respect of acquisitions from other member States by the taxable person for that period by virtue of section 26 of the Act,

(*c*) every correction or adjustment to the VAT allowable portion which is required or allowed by regulation 34, 35 or 38, and

(*d*) every adjustment to the amount of input tax allowable to the taxable person for that period which is required, or allowed, by or under any Regulations made under the Act.

Former regulations—VAT (Accounting and Records) Regulations, SI 1989/2248 reg 4; VAT (Accounting and Records) (Amendment) Regulations, SI 1992/3097 reg 6.

Amendments—[1] Words in para (3)(*b*) inserted, and words in para (3)(*c*) substituted, by the VAT (Amendment) (No 3) Regulations, SI 2007/1418 regs 2, 4 with effect from 1 June 2007.

The register of temporary movement of goods to and from other member States

33— (1) Every taxable person shall keep and maintain, in accordance with this regulation, a register to be known as the register of temporary movement of goods to and from other member States.

(2) Where goods have been moved to or received from another member State and they are to be returned within a period of 2 years of the date of their first removal or receipt, as the case may be, the register shall contain the following information—

(*a*) the date of removal of goods to another member State,

(*b*) the date of receipt of the goods mentioned in sub-paragraph (*a*) above when they are returned from the member State mentioned in that sub-paragraph or another member State,

(*c*) the date of receipt of goods from another member State,

(*d*) the date of removal of the goods mentioned in sub-paragraph (*c*) above when they are returned to the member State mentioned in that sub-paragraph or another member State,

(*e*) a description of the goods sufficient to identify them

(*f*) a description of any process, work or other operation carried out on the goods either in the United Kingdom or in another member State,

(*g*) the consideration for the supply of the goods, and

(*h*) the consideration for the supply of any processing, work or other operation carried out on the goods either in the United Kingdom or another member State.

(3) The Commissioners may in relation to a trade or business of a description specified by them supplement the list of information required in paragraph (2) above by a notice published by them for that purpose.

Former regulations—VAT (Accounting and Records) Regulations, SI 1989/2248 reg 4A; VAT (Accounting and Records) (Amendment) Regulations, SI 1992/3097 reg 7.

[**33A** A person making supplies of a description falling within article 4 of the Value Added Tax (Terminal Markets) Order 1973 shall not be required to keep in relation to those supplies the records specified in regulations 31 (save for paragraph (1)(*a*) of that regulation), 31A, 32 and 33 of these Regulations.][1]

Amendments—[1] This Regulation inserted by the VAT (Amendment) (No 4) Regulations, SI 1999/3114, regs 2, 5, with effect from 1 January 2000.

[**33B** Where a person of a description in article 6 of the Value Added Tax (Terminal Markets) Order 1973 who makes or receives supplies of a description falling within that article, the following Parts of these Regulations shall not apply in relation to those supplies, that is to say—]

(*a*) Part IV;
(*b*) Part V.][1]

Amendments—[1] This Regulation inserted by the VAT (Amendment) (No 4) Regulations, SI 1999/3114, regs 2, 5, with effect from 1 January 2000.

Correction of errors

34— (1) [Subject to paragraph (1A) below][1] this regulation applies where a taxable person has made a return, or returns, to the Controller which overstated or understated his liability to VAT or his entitlement to a payment under section 25(3) of the Act.

[(1A) Subject to paragraph (1B) [and (1C)][3] below, any overstatement or understatement in a return where—

(*a*) a period of [4 years][3] has elapsed since the end of the prescribed accounting period for which the return was made; and
(*b*) the taxable person has not (in relation to that overstatement or understatement) corrected his VAT account in accordance with this regulation before the end of the prescribed accounting period during which that period of [4 years][3] has elapsed,

shall be disregarded for the purposes of this regulation; and in paragraphs (2) to (6) of this regulation "overstatement", "understatement" and related expressions shall be construed accordingly.][1]

[(1B) Paragraph (1A) above does not apply where—

(*a*) the overstatement or understatement is discovered in a prescribed accounting period which begins before 1st May 1997; and
(*b*) the return for that prescribed accounting period has not been made, and was not required to have been made, before that date.][1]

[(1C) Where paragraph (1B) above does not apply, any overstatement or understatement in a return shall be disregarded for the purposes of this regulation where the prescribed accounting period for which the return was made or required to be made ended on or before 31st March 2006.][3]

(2) In this regulation—

(*a*) "under-declarations of liability" means the aggregate of—
 (i) the amount (if any) by which credit for input tax was overstated in any return, and
 (ii) the amount (if any) by which output tax was understated in any return;
(*b*) "over-declarations of liability" means the aggregate of—
 (i) the amount (if any) by which credit for input tax was understated in any return, and
 (ii) the amount (if any) by which output tax was overstated in any return.

(3) Where, in relation to all such overstatements or understatements discovered by the taxable person during a prescribed accounting period, the difference between—

(*a*) under-declarations of liability, and
(*b*) over-declarations of liability,

does not exceed [£50,000][2], the taxable person may correct his VAT account in accordance with this regulation.

[But if Box 6 of the taxable person's return for the prescribed accounting period must contain a total less than £5,000,000, the difference must not for these purposes exceed 1% of that total [unless the difference is £10,000 or less][3].

(Box 6 must contain the total value of sales and all other outputs excluding any VAT – see regulation 25 and Schedule 1 Forms 4 and 5.)][2]

(4) In the VAT payable portion—

(*a*) where the amount of any overstatements of output tax is greater than the amount of any understatements of output tax a negative entry shall be made for the amount of the excess; or
(*b*) where the amount of any understatements of output tax is greater than the amount of any overstatements of output tax a positive entry shall be made for the amount of the excess.

VAT

(5) In the VAT allowable portion—

(*a*) where the amount of any overstatements of credit for input tax is greater than the amount of any understatements of credit for input tax a negative entry shall be made for the amount of the excess; or

(*b*) where the amount of any understatements of credit for input tax is greater than the amount of any overstatements of credit for input tax a positive entry shall be made for the amount of the excess.

(6) Every entry required by this regulation shall—

(*a*) be made in that part of the VAT account which relates to the prescribed accounting period in which the overstatements or understatements in any earlier returns were discovered,

(*b*) make reference to the returns to which it applies, and

(*c*) make reference to any documentation relating to the overstatements or understatements.

(7) Where the conditions referred to in paragraph (3) above do not apply, the VAT account may not be corrected by virtue of this regulation.

Former regulations—VAT (Accounting and Records) Regulations, SI 1989/2248 reg 5; VAT (Accounting and Records) (Amendment) Regulations, SI 1993/761, SI 1994/803.

Cross reference—See VAT Regulations, SI 1995/2518 reg 39(4) (returns correcting earlier returns to which this regulation applies).

Press releases etc—Business Brief 2/98 27-1-98 (VAT: three year time limit for refunds).

Business Brief 13/06 24-8-06 (Court of Appeal Judgment in Michael Fleming t/a Bodycraft).

Amendments—[1] Words in para (1), and paras (1A) and (1B), inserted by the VAT (Amendment) Regulations, SI 1997/1086 reg 5 with effect from 1 May 1997.

[2] In para (3) figure substituted for figure "£2,000", and final two sentences inserted, by the Value Added Tax, etc (Correction of Errors, etc) Regulations, SI 2008/1482 reg 2(1) with effect from 1 July 2008. These amendments only have effect in relation to the overstatements or understatements of liability to VAT in reg 34(3) which taxable persons first discover during their prescribed accounting periods that begin on 1 July 2008 or later: SI 2008/1482 reg 2(2).

[3] In para (1A), words inserted and words substituted for words "3 years", para (1C) inserted, and words in para (3) substituted for words "unless the difference is less than £10,000", by the VAT (Amendment) Regulations, SI 2009/586 regs 2, 4 with effect from 1 April 2009.

35 Where a taxable person has made an error—

(*a*) in accounting for VAT, or

(*b*) in any return made by him,

then, unless he corrects that error in accordance with regulation 34, he shall correct it in such manner and within such time as the Commissioners may require.

Former regulation—VAT (General) Regulations, SI 1985/886 reg 64.

Simon's Tax Cases—*Victoria and Albert Museum Trustees v C&E Comrs* [1996] STC 1016*; *R (on the application of Cardiff County Council) v C&E Comrs* [2002] STC 1318.

Cross reference—See VAT Regulations, SI 1995/2518 reg 39(4) (returns correcting earlier returns to which this regulation applies).

Press releases etc—Business Brief 2/98 27-1-98 (VAT: three year time limit for refunds).

Business Brief 13/06 24-8-06 (Court of Appeal Judgment in Michael Fleming t/a Bodycraft).

Notification of acquisition of goods subject to excise duty by non-taxable persons and payment of VAT

36— (1) Where—

(*a*) a taxable acquisition of goods subject to excise duty takes place in the United Kingdom,

(*b*) the acquisition is not in pursuance of a taxable supply, and

(*c*) the person acquiring the goods is not a taxable person at the time of the acquisition,

the person acquiring the goods shall notify the Commissioners of the acquisition at the time of the acquisition or the arrival of the goods in the United Kingdom, whichever is the later.

(2) The notification shall be in writing in the English language and shall contain the following particulars—

(*a*) the name and current address of the person acquiring the goods,

(*b*) the time of the acquisition,

(*c*) the date when the goods arrived in the United Kingdom,

(*d*) the value of the goods including any excise duty payable, and

(*e*) the VAT due upon the acquisition.

(3) The notification shall include a declaration, signed by the person who is required to make the notification, that all the information entered in it is true and complete.

(4) Any person required to notify the Commissioners of an acquisition of goods subject to excise duty shall pay the VAT due upon the acquisition at the time of notification and, in any event, no later than the last day on which he is required by this regulation to make such notification.

(5) Where a person required to make notification dies or becomes incapacitated and control of his assets passes to another person, being a personal representative, trustee in bankruptcy, receiver, liquidator or person otherwise acting in a representative capacity, that other person shall, so long as he has such control, be required to make the notification referred to in this regulation, provided that the requirement to pay the VAT due upon the acquisition shall apply to that other person only to the extent of the assets of the deceased or incapacitated person over

which he has control and, save to the extent aforesaid, this regulation shall apply to such person so acting in the same way as it would have applied to the deceased or incapacitated person had that person not been deceased or incapacitated.

Former regulations—VAT (General) Regulations, SI 1985/886 reg 64C; VAT (General) (Amendment) Regulations, SI 1992/3102 reg 44.

[Claims for credit for, or repayment of, overstated or overpaid VAT][1]

37 Any claim under section 80 of the Act shall be made in writing to the Commissioners and shall, by reference to such documentary evidence as is in the possession of the claimant, state the amount of the claim and the method by which that amount was calculated.

Former regulation—VAT (Accounting and Records) Regulations, SI 1989/2248 reg 6.
Amendments—[1] Heading substituted by the VAT (Amendment) (No 2) Regulations, SI 2005/2231 reg 2 with effect from 1 September 2005 in relation to claims made under VATA 1994 s 80 on or after that date.

Adjustments in the course of business

38— (1) ...[3] This regulation applies where—

(*a*) there is an increase in consideration for a supply, or
(*b*) there is a decrease in consideration for a supply,

which includes an amount of VAT and the increase or decrease occurs after the end of the prescribed accounting period in which the original supply took place.

[(1A) Subject to paragraph (1B) below, this regulation does not apply to any increase or decrease in consideration which occurs more than 3 years after the end of the prescribed accounting period in which the original supply took place.][1, 3]

[(1B) Paragraph (1A) above does not apply where—

(a) the increase or decrease takes place during a prescribed accounting period beginning before 1st May 1997; and
(b) the return for the prescribed accounting period in which effect is given to the increase or decrease in the business records of the taxable person has not been made, and was not required to have been made, before that date.][1, 3]

[(1C) Where an increase or decrease in consideration relates to a supply in respect of which it is for the recipient, on the supplier's behalf, to account for and pay the tax, the prescribed accounting period referred to in paragraph (1) is that of the recipient, and not the maker, of the supply.

But this paragraph does not apply to the circumstances referred to in regulation 38A.][2]

[Where this regulation applies, both the taxable person who makes the supply and a taxable person who receives the supply shall adjust their respective VAT accounts in accordance with the provisions of this regulation.][3]

(3) [Subject to paragraph (3A) below,][2] the maker of the supply shall—

(*a*) in the case of an increase in consideration, make a positive entry; or
(*b*) in the case of a decrease in consideration, make a negative entry,

for the relevant amount of VAT in the VAT payable portion of his VAT account.

[(3A) Where an increase or decrease in consideration relates to a supply on which the VAT has been accounted for and paid by the recipient of the supply, any entry required to be made under paragraph (3) shall be made in the recipient's VAT account and not that of the supplier.][2]

(4) The recipient of the supply, if he is a taxable person, shall—

(*a*) in the case of an increase in consideration, make a positive entry; or
(*b*) in the case of a decrease in consideration, make a negative entry,

for the relevant amount of VAT in the VAT allowable portion of his VAT account.

(5) Every entry required by this regulation shall, except where paragraph (6) below applies, be made in that part of the VAT account which relates to the prescribed accounting period in which the increase or decrease is given effect in the business accounts of the [relevant][3] taxable person.

(6) Any entry required by this regulation to be made in the VAT account of an insolvent person shall be made in that part of the VAT account which relates to the prescribed accounting period in which the supply was made or received.

(7) None of the circumstances to which this regulation applies is to be regarded as giving rise to any application of regulations 34 and 35.

Former regulation—VAT (Accounting and Records) Regulations, SI 1989/2248 reg 7.
Simon's Tax Cases—*C&E Comrs v McMaster Stores (Scotland) Ltd (in receivership)* [1995] STC 846*.
C&E Comrs v General Motors Acceptance Corp (UK) plc [2004] STC 577.
Amendments—[1] Words in paras (1A) and (1B), inserted by the VAT (Amendment) Regulations, SI 1997/1086 reg 6 with effect from 1 May 1997.
[2] Paras (1C), (3A), and words in para (3) inserted, by the VAT (Amendment) (No 3) Regulations, SI 2007/1418 regs 2, 4(*b*) with effect from 1 June 2007.
[3] In para (1), words "Subject to paragraph (1A) below," repealed, paras (1A), (1B) repealed, para (2) substituted, and in para (5) word inserted, by the VAT (Amendment) Regulations, SI 2009/586 regs 2, 5 with effect from 1 April 2009. Para (2) previously read as follows—

"(2) Where this regulation applies, the taxable person shall adjust his VAT account in accordance with the provisions of this regulation.".

Adjustments where a supply becomes, or ceases to be, a supply to which section 55A(6) of the Act applies (customers to account for tax on supplies of goods of a kind used in missing trader intra-community fraud)

[38A— (1) Where regulation 38 applies and—

(*a*) as a result of an increase in consideration for a supply it becomes one to which section 55A(6) of the Act applies; or

(*b*) as a result of a decrease in consideration for a supply it ceases to be one to which that section applies,

both the maker, and the recipient, of the supply shall make such entries in the VAT payable portion of their VAT accounts as are necessary to account for that fact.

(2) Paragraphs (5) and (6) of regulation 38 shall apply to any entry required by this regulation as they apply to any entry required by that regulation.

(3) None of the circumstances to which this regulation applies is to be regarded as giving rise to any application of regulations 34 and 35.][1]

Amendments—[1] Reg inserted by the VAT (Amendment) (No 3) Regulations, SI 2007/1418 regs 2, 4(*c*) with effect from 1 June 2007.

Calculation of returns

39— (1) Where a person is required by regulations made under the Act to make a return to the Controller, the amounts to be entered on that return shall be determined in accordance with this regulation.

(2) In the box opposite the legend "VAT due in this period on sales and other outputs" shall be entered the aggregate of all the entries in the VAT payable portion of that part of the VAT account which relates to the prescribed accounting period for which the return is made, except that the total of the output tax due in that period on acquisitions from other member States shall be entered instead in the box opposite the legend "VAT due in this period on acquisitions from other EC member States".

(3) In the box opposite the legend "VAT reclaimed in this period on purchases and other inputs" (including acquisitions from other member States) shall be entered the aggregate of all the entries in the VAT allowable portion of that part of the VAT account which relates to the prescribed accounting period for which the return is made.

(4) Where any correction has been made and a return calculated in accordance with these Regulations then any such return shall be regarded as correcting any earlier returns to which regulations 34 and 35 apply.

Former regulations—VAT (Accounting and Records) Regulations, SI 1989/2248 reg 8; VAT (Accounting and Records) (Amendment) Regulations, SI 1992/3097 reg 8.

VAT to be accounted for on returns and payment of VAT

40— [(1) Any person making a return shall in respect of the period to which the return relates account in that return for—

(*a*) all his output tax,

[(*aa*) all VAT which he is required to pay on behalf of the supplier.][4]

(*b*) all VAT for which he is accountable by virtue of Part XVI of these Regulations,

(*c*) all VAT which he is required to pay as a result of the removal of goods from a fiscal warehousing regime, and

(*d*) all VAT which he is required to pay as a result of a supply of specified services (performed on or in relation to goods at a time when they are subject to a warehousing regime) being zero-rated under section 18C(1) of the Act where—

(i) that warehousing regime is one where goods are stored without payment of any duty of excise,

(ii) those goods are subject to a duty of excise,

(iii) those goods have been the subject of an acquisition from another member State and the material time for that acquisition was while those goods were subject to that warehousing regime, and,

(iv) there was no supply of those goods while they were subject to that warehousing regime.

The amounts to be entered on that return shall be determined in accordance with these Regulations.

(2) Any person required to make a return shall pay to the Controller such amount of VAT as is payable by him in respect of the period to which the return relates not later than the last day on which he is required to make that return.

[(2A) Where a return is made in accordance with regulation 25 above using an electronic return system, the relevant payment to the Controller required by paragraph (2) above shall be made solely by means of electronic communications that are acceptable to the Commissioners for this purpose.][2]

(3) The requirements of paragraphs (1) or (2) above shall not apply where the Commissioners allow or direct otherwise.][1]

[(4) A direction under paragraph (3) may in particular allow additional time for a payment mentioned in paragraph (2) that is made by means of electronic communications. The direction may allow different times for different means of payment.][3]

[(5) Later payment so allowed does not of itself constitute a default for the purposes of section 59 of the Act (default surcharge).][3]

Former regulation—VAT (General) Regulations, SI 1985/886 reg 60.
Simon's Tax Cases—*Hindle and another (trading as DJ Baker Bar) v C&E Comrs* [2004] STC 412.
Amendments—[1] This Regulation substituted by the VAT (Amendment) (No 3) Regulations, SI 1996/1250 reg 9 with effect from 1 June 1996.
[2] Para (2A) inserted by the VAT (Amendment) Regulations, SI 2000/258 regs 2, 4 with effect from 1 March 2000.
[3] Paras (4), (5) inserted by the VAT (Amendment) (No 3) Regulations, SI 2004/1675 regs 1(1), (3), 5 with effect from 22 July 2004.
[4] Para (1)(*aa*) inserted by the VAT (Amendment) (No 3) Regulations, SI 2007/1418 regs 2, 4(*d*) with effect from 1 June 2007.

[40A— Where the Commissioners in exercise of their power under section 28(2A) of the Act have directed the manner in which payments on account under section 28 of the Act are to be made, a person who is liable to make such payments shall also pay any amount of VAT payable in respect of a return for any prescribed accounting period in the like manner.][1]

Amendments—[1] This Regulation inserted by the VAT (Amendment) (No 2) Regulations, SI 1996/1198 reg 3 with effect from 1 June 1996.

Accounting etc by reference to the duty point, and prescribed accounting period in which VAT on certain supplies is to be treated as being chargeable

41— (1) Where in respect of—

(*a*) any supply by a taxable person of dutiable goods, or
(*b*) an acquisition by any person from another member State of dutiable goods,

the time of supply or acquisition, as the case may be, precedes the duty point in relation to those goods, the VAT in respect of that supply or acquisition shall be accounted for and paid, and any question as to the inclusion of any duty in the value of the supply or acquisition shall be determined, by reference to the duty point or by reference to such later time as the Commissioners may allow.

(2) …[1]

Former regulations—Para (1): VAT (General) Regulations, SI 1985/886 reg 60A; VAT (General) (Amendment) Regulations, SI 1992/3102 reg 46.
Paras (2), (3): VAT (General) Regulations, SI 1985/886 reg 58ZA; VAT (General) (Amendment) Regulations, SI 1995/1069 reg 4.
Cross reference—See VAT Regulations, SI 1995/2518 reg 6(3) (transfer of a going concern: transferee assuming liabilities of transferor).
Amendments—[1] Paras (2) and (3) deleted by the VAT (Amendment) (No 3) Regulations, SI 1996/1250 reg 10 with effect from 1 June 1996 except that where 28 April 1996 fell within a taxable person's prescribed accounting period which ended on or after 1 June 1996, the amendment had effect in relation to that taxable person from the day after the end of that prescribed accounting period.

Accounting for VAT on the removal of goods

42— (1) This regulation applies where goods have been removed from a member State to a place in any other member State, and that removal falls within any of paragraphs (*d*), (*f*) or (*g*) of article 4 of the Removal Order.

(2) Except where paragraph (3) below applies in respect of the same prescribed accounting period, the owner shall not make any entry in the VAT payable portion of that part of his VAT account which relates to the prescribed accounting period in which he would be liable to account for any VAT chargeable in respect of the removal.

(3) Where—

(*a*) the condition described in article 5 of the Removal Order has not been complied with, and
(*b*) an amount of VAT has become payable,

the owner shall make a positive entry for the relevant amount of VAT in the VAT payable portion of that part of his VAT account which relates to the prescribed accounting period in which the condition was not complied with.

Former regulation—VAT (Removal of Goods) (Accounting) Regulations, SI 1992/3101 reg 3.

Goods removed from warehousing regime

43— (1) This regulation applies to a registered person who is an approved person within the meaning of the Excise Duties (Deferred Payment) Regulations 1992 in respect of goods which are at a specified warehouse.

(2) [Where a person to whom this regulation applies is—

(*a*) the person who is liable under section 18(4)(*b*) of the Act to pay VAT on a supply of goods while the goods are subject to a warehousing regime, or
(*b*) liable under section 18D(2) of the Act to pay VAT on a supply of services to which section 18C(3) of the Act applies (specified services performed on or in relation to goods which are subject to a warehousing regime),

he may pay that VAT at or before the relevant time determined in accordance with paragraph (3) below instead of at the time provided for by sections 18(4)(*b*) or 18D(2)(*a*) of the Act.][1]

(3) For the purposes of paragraph (2) above the relevant time means—

(*a*) in relation to hydrocarbon oils, the 15th day of the month immediately following the month in which the hydrocarbon oils were removed from the warehousing regime;

(*b*) in relation to any other goods subject to a duty of excise, the day (payment day) on which the registered person is required to pay the excise duty on the goods in accordance with regulation 5 of the Excise Duties (Deferred Payment) Regulations 1992.

(4) Where any goods of a kind chargeable to a duty of excise qualify for any relief of that duty, that relief shall be disregarded for the purposes of determining the relevant time under paragraph (3) above.

Amendments—[1] Para (2) substituted by the VAT (Amendment) (No 3) Regulations, SI 1996/1250 reg 11 with effect from 1 June 1996.

[PART VA
REIMBURSEMENT ARRANGEMENTS][1]

Commentary—*De Voil Indirect Tax Service* **V5.159**.

Note—Part VA inserted after Part V by the VAT (Amendment) (No 5) Regulations, SI 1998/59 with effect from 11 February 1998. Regulations 37A to 37H within Part VA were incorrectly numbered. An amending statutory instrument, SI 1999/438, has now been issued. Regulations 37A to 37H have been renumbered in sequence, from 43A to 43H, with effect from 1 April 1999.

Interpretation of Part VA

[43A In this Part—

"claim" means a claim made …[2] under section 80 of the Act for [credit of an amount accounted for to the Commissioners or assessed by them as output tax which was not output tax due to them][2]; and "claimed" and "claimant" shall be construed accordingly;

"reimbursement arrangements" means any arrangements (whether made before, on or after 30th January 1998) for the purposes of a claim which—

(*a*) are made by a claimant for the purpose of securing that he is not unjustly enriched by the [crediting][2] of any amount in pursuance of the claim; and

(*b*) provide for the reimbursement of persons (consumers) who have, for practical purposes, borne the whole or any part of the [original amount brought into account as output tax that was not output tax due][2];

"relevant amount" means that part (which may be the whole) of the amount of a claim which the claimant has reimbursed or intends to reimburse to consumers.][1]

Amendments—[1] This regulation inserted by the VAT (Amendment) (No 5) Regulations, SI 1998/59 with effect from 11 February 1998.

[2] In the definition of "claim", words revoked and words substituted, and in the definition of "reimbursement arrangements", words substituted, by the VAT (Amendment) (No 2) Regulations, SI 2005/2231 reg 3 with effect from 1 September 2005 in relation to claims made under VATA 1994 s 80 on or after that date.

Reimbursement arrangements—general

[43B Without prejudice to regulation 43H below, for the purposes of section 80(3) of the Act (defence by the Commissioners that [crediting][2] by them of an amount claimed would unjustly enrich the claimant) reimbursement arrangements made by a claimant shall be disregarded except where they—

(*a*) include the provisions described in regulation 43C below; and

(*b*) are supported by the undertakings described in regulation 43G below.][1]

Amendments—[1] This regulation inserted by the VAT (Amendment) (No 5) Regulations, SI 1998/59 with effect from 11 February 1998.

[2] Word substituted by the VAT (Amendment) (No 2) Regulations, SI 2005/2231 reg 4 with effect from 1 September 2005 in relation to claims made under VATA 1994 s 80 on or after that date.

Reimbursement arrangements—provisions to be included

[43C The provisions referred to in regulation 43B(*a*) above are that—

(*a*) reimbursement for which the arrangements provide will be completed by no later than 90 days after the [crediting of the amount][2] to which it relates;

(*b*) no deduction will be made from the relevant amount by way of fee or charge (howsoever expressed or effected);

(*c*) reimbursement will be made only in cash or by cheque;

[(*d*) any part of the relevant amount credited to the claimant that is not reimbursed by the time mentioned in paragraph (*a*) above will be notified by the claimant to the Commissioners;][2]

[(*da*) any part of the relevant amount paid (or repaid) to the claimant that is not reimbursed by the time mentioned in paragraph (*a*) above will be repaid by the claimant to the Commissioners;][2]

(*e*) any interest paid by the Commissioners on any relevant amount [paid (or repaid)][2] by them will also be treated by the claimant in the same way as the relevant amount falls to be treated under paragraphs (*a*) and (*b*) above; and

(*f*) the records described in regulation 43E below will be kept by the claimant and produced by him to the Commissioners, or to an officer of theirs in accordance with regulation 43F below.][1]

Amendments—[1] This regulation inserted by the VAT (Amendment) (No 5) Regulations, SI 1998/59 with effect from 11 February 1998.

[2] Words substituted, and paras (*d*), (*da*) substituted for para (*d*) by the VAT (Amendment) (No 2) Regulations, SI 2005/2231 reg 5 with effect from 1 September 2005 in relation to claims made under VATA 1994 s 80 on or after that date.

[Notifications and repayments to the Commissioners

43D The claimant shall give any notification to the Commissioners that he is required to give by virtue of regulation 43C(*d*) above and, without any prior demand, make any repayment to the Commissioners that he is required to make by virtue of regulation 43C(*da*) and (*e*) above within 14 days of the expiration of the 90 days referred to in regulation 43C(*a*) above.][1]

Amendments—[1] This regulation substituted by the VAT (Amendment) (No 2) Regulations, SI 2005/2231 reg 6 with effect from 1 September 2005 in relation to claims made under VATA 1994 s 80 on or after that date.

Records

[43E The claimant shall keep records of the following matters—

(*a*) the names and addresses of those consumers whom he has reimbursed or whom he intends to reimburse;

(*b*) the total amount reimbursed to each such consumer;

(*c*) the amount of interest included in each total amount reimbursed to each consumer;

(*d*) the date that each reimbursement is made.][1]

Amendments—[1] This regulation inserted by the VAT (Amendment) (No 5) Regulations, SI 1998/59 with effect from 11 February 1998.

Production of records

[43F— (1) Where a claimant is given notice in accordance with paragraph (2) below, he shall, in accordance with such notice produce to the Commissioners, or to an officer of theirs, the records that he is required to keep pursuant to regulation 43E above.

(2) A notice given for the purposes of paragraph (1) above shall—

(*a*) be in writing;

(*b*) state the place and time at which, and the date on which the records are to be produced; and

(*c*) be signed and dated by the Commissioners, or by an officer of theirs,

and may be given before or after, or both before and after the Commissioners have [credited][2] the relevant amount to the claimant.][1]

Amendments—[1] This regulation inserted by the VAT (Amendment) (No 5) Regulations, SI 1998/59 with effect from 11 February 1998.

[2] Word in para (2) substituted by the VAT (Amendment) (No 2) Regulations, SI 2005/2231 reg 7 with effect from 1 September 2005 in relation to claims made under VATA 1994 s 80 on or after that date.

Undertakings

[43G— (1) Without prejudice to regulation 43H(*b*) below, the undertakings referred to in regulation 43B(*b*) above shall be given to the Commissioners by the claimant no later than the time at which he makes the claim for which the reimbursement arrangements have been made.

(2) The undertakings shall be in writing, shall be signed and dated by the claimant, and shall be to the effect that—

(*a*) at the date of the undertakings he is able to identify the names and addresses of those consumers whom he has reimbursed or whom he intends to reimburse;

(*b*) he will apply the whole of the relevant amount [credited][2] to him, without any deduction by way of fee or charge or otherwise, to the reimbursement in cash or by cheque, of such consumers by no later than 90 days after his receipt of that amount (except insofar as he has already so reimbursed them);

(*c*) he will apply any interest paid to him on the relevant amount [paid (or repaid)][2] to him wholly to the reimbursement of such consumers by no later than 90 days after his receipt of that interest;

[(*d*) he will notify the Commissioners of the whole or such part of the relevant amount credited to him as he fails to apply in accordance with the undertakings mentioned in sub-paragraphs (*b*) and (*c*) above;][2]

[(*da*) he will repay to the Commissioners without demand the whole or such part of the relevant amount paid (or repaid) to him or of any interest paid to him as he fails to apply in accordance with the undertakings mentioned in sub-paragraphs (*b*) and (*c*) above;][2]

(*e*) he will keep the records described in regulation 43E above; and

(*f*) he will comply with any notice given to him in accordance with regulation 43F above concerning the production of such records.][1]

Amendments—[1] This regulation inserted by the VAT (Amendment) (No 5) Regulations, SI 1998/59 with effect from 11 February 1998.

[2] In para (2), words substituted, and sub-paras (*d*), (*da*) substituted for sub-para (*d*), by the VAT (Amendment) (No 2) Regulations, SI 2005/2231 reg 8 with effect from 1 September 2005 in relation to claims made under VATA 1994 s 80 on or after that date.

Reimbursement arrangements made before 11th February 1998

43H

Amendment—This regulation revoked by the VAT (Amendment) (No 2) Regulations, SI 2005/2231 reg 9 with effect from 1 September 2005 in relation to claims made under VATA 1994 s 80 on or after that date.

PART VI
PAYMENTS ON ACCOUNT

Interpretation of Part VI

44 In this Part—

"body corporate" means a body corporate which is under a duty to make payments on account by virtue of the Value Added Tax (Payments on Account) Order 1993 and "relevant division" means a division of a body corporate by reference to the business of which that body corporate is under such a duty;

"payments on account" has the same meaning as in the Value Added Tax (Payments on Account) Order 1993.

Former regulation—VAT (Payments on Account) (No 2) Regulations, SI 1992/1844 regs 2, 7(1).

Payments on Account

45 Save in a case to which regulation 48 applies, the Commissioners shall give to a taxable person who is under a duty to make payments on account notification in writing of—

(*a*) the amounts that he is under a duty to pay,

(*b*) how those amounts have been calculated, and

(*c*) the times for payment of those amounts.

Former regulation—VAT (Payments on Account) (No 2) Regulations, SI 1992/1844 reg 4.

46 Save in a case to which regulation 48 applies, if in respect of a prescribed accounting period the total amount of the payment on account made by the taxable person exceeds the amount of VAT due from him in respect of that period, the amount of excess shall be paid to him by the Commissioners if and to the extent that it is not required by section 81 of the Act to be set against any sum which he is liable to pay to them.

Former regulation—VAT (Payments on Account) (No 2) Regulations, SI 1992/1844 reg 5.

[46A— (1) A payment on account and a payment in respect of a return to which regulation 40A above applies shall not be treated as having been made by the last day on which it is required to be made unless it is made in such a manner as secures that all the transactions can be completed that need to be completed before the whole of the amount becomes available to the Commissioners.

(2) For the purposes of this regulation and regulation 47 below, references to a payment being made by any day include references to its being made on that day.][1]

Amendments—[1] This regulation inserted by the VAT (Amendment) (No 2) Regulations, SI 1996/1198 reg 4 with effect from 1 June 1996.

47 Where a taxable person fails to make a payment on account by the last day by which he is required to make it, that payment on account shall be recoverable as if it were VAT due from him.

Former regulation—VAT (Payments on Account) (No 2) Regulations, SI 1992/1844 reg 6.

48— (1) The Commissioners shall notify a relevant division in writing of—

(*a*) the amounts of the payments on account that the body corporate is under a duty to make by reference to the business of that division,

(*b*) how those amounts have been calculated, and

(*c*) the times for payment of those amounts.

(2) If in respect of a prescribed accounting period the total amount of the payments on account made by a body corporate by reference to the business of a particular relevant division exceeds the amount of VAT due from the body corporate in respect of that period by reference to that business, the amount of the excess shall be paid to the body corporate through that division by the Commissioners if and to the extent that it is not required by section 81 of the Act to be set against any sum which the body corporate is liable to pay to them.

(3) Section 81 of the Act shall not require any amount which is due to be paid by the Commissioners to a body corporate under paragraph (2) above by reference to the business of a particular relevant division to be set against any sum due from the body corporate otherwise than by reference to that business or to the liabilities of the body corporate arising in connection with that division.

Former regulation—VAT (Payments on Account) (No 2) Regulations, SI 1992/1844 reg 7(2)–(4).

[PART VII
ANNUAL ACCOUNTING][1]

Amendments—[1] This Part (regs 49–55) substituted by the VAT (Annual Accounting) Regulations, SI 1996/542 with effect, in the case of a taxable person who was on 31 March 1996 authorised to use the annual accounting scheme under the VAT Regulations, SI 1995/2518 reg 50, from the first day of his next current accounting year, and in respect of any other taxable person, from 1 April 1996.

Interpretation of Part VII

[49 In this Part—

"authorised person" means a person who has been authorised by the Commissioners in accordance with regulation 50(1), and "authorised" and "authorisation" shall be construed accordingly;

"transitional accounting period" means the period commencing on the first day of a person's prescribed accounting period in which the Commissioners authorise him to use the scheme, and ending on the day immediately preceding the first day of that person's first current accounting year, and is a prescribed accounting period within the meaning of section 25(1) of the Act;

"current accounting year" means the period of 12 months commencing on a date indicated by the Commissioners in their notification of authorisation of a person, or while a person remains authorised the most recent anniversary thereof, and is a prescribed accounting period within the meaning of section 25(1) of the Act;

"the scheme" means the annual accounting scheme established by regulations 50 and 51;

"credit transfer" means the transfer of funds from one bank account to another under a mandate given by the payer to the bank making the transfer;

["the quarterly sum" means—

(*a*) in the case of a taxable person who has been registered for at least 12 months—

(i) immediately preceding the first day of his current accounting year, or

(ii) for the purposes of regulation 51, immediately preceding the first day of his transitional accounting period,

a sum equal to 25 per cent. of the total amount of VAT that he was liable to pay to the Commissioners in respect of those 12 months; or

(*b*) in any other case, a sum equal to 25 per cent of the total amount of VAT that the Commissioners are satisfied he will be liable to pay to the Commissioners in respect of the next 12 months;][2]

"the agreed quarterly sum" means a sum agreed with the Commissioners, not being less than [25 per cent][2] of a taxable person's estimated liability for VAT in his current accounting year;

["the monthly sum" means—

(*a*) in the case of a taxable person who has been registered for at least 12 months—

(i) immediately preceding the first day of his current accounting year, or

(ii) for the purposes of regulation 51, immediately preceding the first day of his transitional accounting period,

a sum equal to 10 per cent of the total amount of VAT that he was liable to pay to the Commissioners in respect of those 12 months; or

(*b*) in any other case, a sum equal to 10 per cent. of the total amount of VAT that the Commissioners are satisfied he will be liable to pay to the Commissioners in respect of the next 12 months;][2]

"the agreed monthly sum" means a sum agreed with the Commissioners, not being less than 10 per cent of a taxable person's estimated liability for VAT, in his current accounting year;

"working day" means any day of the week other than Saturday, Sunday, a bank holiday or a public holiday;

"relevant quarterly date" means the last working day of the fourth and, where a period has such months, the seventh and the tenth months of a transitional accounting period;

"relevant monthly date" means the last working day of the fourth and each successive month of a transitional accounting period.][1]

Amendments—[1] This regulation substituted by the VAT (Annual Accounting) Regulations, SI 1996/542 with effect, in the case of a taxable person who was on 31 March 1996 authorised to use the annual accounting scheme under the VAT Regulations, SI 1995/2518 reg 50, from the first day of his next current accounting year, and in respect of any other taxable person, from 1 April 1996.

[2] Definitions of "the quarterly sum" and "the monthly sum" substituted, and definition of "the agreed monthly sum" amended, by the VAT (Amendment) (No 2) Regulations, SI 2002/1142 regs 1–3 with effect—

(*a*) in the case of a taxable person who is on 24 April 2002 authorised under the Value Added Tax Regulations, SI 1995/2518 reg 50, from the first day of his next prescribed accounting period beginning after that date; and

(*b*) in the case of any other taxable person, from 25 April 2002.

Annual accounting scheme

[50— (1) The Commissioners may, subject to the requirements of this Part, authorise a taxable person to pay and account for VAT by reference to any transitional accounting period, and any subsequent current accounting year at such times, and for such amounts, as may be determined in accordance with the scheme.

(2) A taxable person authorised to pay and account for VAT in accordance with the scheme shall—

(*a*) pay to the Commissioners by credit transfer—

[(i) where the taxable person and Commissioners agree to such payment pattern, the quarterly sum, or as the case may be the agreed quarterly sum, no later than the last working day of each of the fourth, seventh and tenth months of his current accounting year;][2]

(ii) in all other cases, the monthly sum, or as the case may be, the agreed monthly sum, in nine equal monthly instalments, commencing on the last working day of the fourth month of his current accounting year; and

(*b*) make by the last working day of the second month following the end of that current accounting year a return in respect of that year, together with any outstanding payment due to the Commissioners in respect of his liability for VAT for the current accounting year declared on that return.

(3) …[2]][1]

Amendments—[1] This regulation substituted by the VAT (Annual Accounting) Regulations, SI 1996/542 with effect, in the case of a taxable person who was on 31 March 1996 authorised to use the annual accounting scheme under the VAT Regulations, SI 1995/2518 reg 50, from the first day of his next current accounting year, and in respect of any other taxable person, from 1 April 1996.

[2] Para (2)(*a*)(i) substituted, and para (3) revoked, by the VAT (Amendment) (No 2) Regulations, SI 2002/1142 regs 1, 2, 4 with effect—

(*a*) in the case of a taxable person who is on 24 April 2002 authorised under the Value Added Tax Regulations, SI 1995/2518 reg 50, from the first day of his next prescribed accounting period beginning after that date; and

(*b*) in the case of any other taxable person, from 25 April 2002.

[51 An authorised person shall, where in any given case the transitional accounting period is—

(*a*) 4 months or more—

[(i) where the taxable person and Commissioners agree to such payment pattern, pay to the Commissioners by credit transfer on each relevant quarterly date the quarterly sum;][2] or

(ii) in all other cases, pay to the Commissioners by credit transfer on each relevant monthly date the monthly sum; and

(iii) make by the last working day of the second month following the end of his transitional accounting period a return in respect of that period, together with any outstanding payment due to the Commissioners in respect of his liability for VAT declared on that return; or

(*b*) less than 4 months, make by the last working day of the first month following the end of his transitional accounting period a return in respect of that period, together with any outstanding payment due to the Commissioners in respect of his liability for VAT declared on that return.][1]

Amendments—[1] This regulation substituted by the VAT (Annual Accounting) Regulations, SI 1996/542 with effect, in the case of a taxable person who was on 31 March 1996 authorised to use the annual accounting scheme under the VAT Regulations, SI 1995/2518 reg 50, from the first day of his next current accounting year, and in respect of any other taxable person, from 1 April 1996.

[2] Para (*a*)(i) substituted by the VAT (Amendment) (No 2) Regulations, SI 2002/1142 regs 1, 2, 5 with effect—

(*a*) in the case of a taxable person who is on 24 April 2002 authorised under the Value Added Tax Regulations, SI 1995/2518 reg 50, from the first day of his next prescribed accounting period beginning after that date; and

(*b*) in the case of any other taxable person, from 25 April 2002.

Admission to the scheme

[52— (1) A taxable person shall be eligible to apply for authorisation under regulation 50(1) if—

(*a*) …[2]

(*b*) he has reasonable grounds for believing that the value of taxable supplies made or to be made by him in the period of 12 months beginning on the date of his application for authorisation will not exceed [£1,350,000][2];

(*c*) his registration is not in the name of a group under section 43(1) of the Act;

(*d*) his registration is not in the name of a division under section 46(1) of the Act; and

(*e*) he has not in the 12 months preceding the date of his application for authorisation ceased to operate the scheme.

(1A) …[2]

(2) The Commissioners may refuse to authorise a person under regulation 50(1) where they consider it necessary to do so for the protection of the revenue.][1]

Amendments—[1] This regulation substituted by the VAT (Annual Accounting) Regulations, SI 1996/542 with effect, in the case of a taxable person who was on 31 March 1996 authorised to use the annual accounting scheme under the VAT Regulations, SI 1995/2518 reg 50, from the first day of his next current accounting year, and in respect of any other taxable person, from 1 April 1996.

[2] Paras (1)(*a*), (1A) revoked, and figure in para (1)(*b*) substituted, by the VAT (Amendment) Regulations, SI 2006/587 regs 1(2), (5), 2 with effect from 1 April 2006.

[53— (1) An authorised person shall continue to account for VAT in accordance with the scheme until he ceases to be authorised.

(2) An authorised person ceases to be authorised when—

(*a*) at the end of any [transitional accounting period][3] or current accounting year the value of taxable supplies made by him in that period or, as the case may be, year has exceeded [£1,600,000][2]; or

(*b*) his authorisation is terminated in accordance with regulation 54 below;

(*c*) he—

(i) becomes insolvent and ceases to trade, other than for the purpose of disposing of stocks and assets; or

(ii) ceases business or ceases to be registered; or

(iii) dies, becomes bankrupt or incapacitated;

(*d*) he ceases to operate the scheme of his own volition.][1]

Amendments—[1] This regulation substituted by the VAT (Annual Accounting) Regulations, SI 1996/542 with effect, in the case of a taxable person who was on 31 March 1996 authorised to use the annual accounting scheme under the VAT Regulations, SI 1995/2518 reg 50, from the first day of his next current accounting year, and in respect of any other taxable person, from 1 April 1996.

[2] Figure in sub-para (2)(*a*) substituted by the VAT (Amendment) Regulations, SI 2006/587 regs 1(2), (5), 3 with effect from 1 April 2006.

[3] In sub-para (2)(*a*), words substituted by the VAT (Amendment) (No 2) Regulations, SI 2003/1069 regs 1(1), 2, 4 with effect from 10 April 2003.

[54— (1) The Commissioners may terminate an authorisation in any case where—

(*a*) a false statement has been made by or on behalf of an authorised person in relation to his application for authorisation; or

(*b*) an authorised person fails to make by the due date a return in accordance with regulation 50(2)(*b*) or regulation 51(*a*)(iii) or (*b*); or

(*c*) an authorised person fails to make any payment prescribed in regulation 50 or 51; or

(*d*) where they receive a notification in accordance with paragraph (2) below; or

(*e*) at any time during an authorised person's transitional accounting period or current accounting year they have reason to believe, that the value of taxable supplies he will make during the period or as the case may be year, will exceed [£1,600,000][2]; or

(*f*) it is necessary to do so for the protection of the revenue; or

(*g*) an authorised person has not, in relation to a return made by him prior to authorisation, paid to the Commissioners all such sums shown as due thereon; or

(*h*) an authorised person has not, in relation to any assessment made under either section 73 or section 76 of the Act, paid to the Commissioners all such sums shown as due thereon.

(2) Where an authorised person has reason to believe that the value of taxable supplies made by him during a transitional accounting period or current accounting year will exceed [£1,600,000][2], he shall within 30 days notify the Commissioners in writing.][1]

Amendments—[1] This regulation substituted by the VAT (Annual Accounting) Regulations, SI 1996/542 with effect, in the case of a taxable person who was on 31 March 1996 authorised to use the annual accounting scheme under the VAT Regulations, SI 1995/2518 reg 50, from the first day of his next current accounting year, and in respect of any other taxable person, from 1 April 1996.

[2] Figures in paras (1)(*e*), (2) substituted by the VAT (Amendment) Regulations, SI 2006/587 regs 1(2), (5), 3 with effect from 1 April 2006.

[55— (1) The date from which an authorised person ceases to be authorised in accordance with Regulation 53(2) shall be—

(*a*) where regulation 53(2)(*a*) applies, the day following the last day of the relevant transitional accounting period or current accounting year;

(*b*) where regulation 53(2)(*b*) applies, the day on which the Commissioners terminate his authorisation;

(*c*) where regulation 53(2)(*c*) applies, the day on which any one of the events mentioned in that paragraph occurs; and

(*d*) where regulation 53(2)(*d*) applies, the date on which the Commissioners are notified in writing of the authorised persons decision to cease using the scheme.

(2) Where an authorised person ceases to be authorised, he or as the case may be, his representative, shall—

(*a*) if his authorisation ceases before the end of his transitional accounting period or current accounting year, make a return within 2 months of the date specified in paragraph (1)(*b*), (1)(*c*) or (1)(*d*) above, together with any outstanding payment due to the Commissioners in respect of his liability for VAT for that part of the period or year arising before the date he ceased to be authorised; or

(*b*) if his authorisation ceases at the end of his transitional accounting period or current accounting year, make a return together with any outstanding payment due to the Commissioners in respect of his liability for VAT in accordance with regulation 51 or 50 above; and in either case, from the day following the day on which he ceases to be authorised, account for and pay VAT as provided for otherwise than under this Part.][1]

Amendments—[1] This regulation substituted by the VAT (Annual Accounting) Regulations, SI 1996/542 with effect, in the case of a taxable person who was on 31 March 1996 authorised to use the annual accounting scheme under the VAT Regulations, SI 1995/2518 reg 50, from the first day of his next current accounting year, and in respect of any other taxable person, from 1 April 1996.

[PART VIIA
FLAT-RATE SCHEME FOR SMALL BUSINESSES

Interpretation of Part VIIA

55A— (1) In this Part—

…[2]

"capital expenditure goods" means any goods of a capital nature but does not include any goods acquired by a flat-rate trader (whether before he is a flat-rate trader or not)—

(*a*) for the purpose of resale or incorporation into goods supplied by him,

(*b*) for consumption by him within one year, or

(*c*) to generate income by being leased, let or hired;

…[2]

["EDR" means the day with effect from which a person is registered under the Act;][3]

"end date" has the meaning given in regulation 55Q(2);

"flat-rate trader" means a person who is, for the time being, authorised by the Commissioners in accordance with regulation 55B(1);

"relevant purchase" has the meaning given in regulation 55C;

"start date" has the meaning given in regulation 55B(2);

"the scheme" means the flat-rate scheme for small businesses established by this Part;

"the Table" means the table set out in regulation 55K.

(2) For the purposes of this Part, a person is associated with another person at any time if that other person makes supplies in the course or furtherance of a business carried on by him, and—

(*a*) the business of one is under the dominant influence of the other, or

(*b*) the persons are closely bound to one another by financial, economic and organisational links.][1]

[(3) For the purposes of this Part, "relevant date", in relation to a flat-rate trader, means any of the following—

(*a*) his start date;

(*b*) the first day of the prescribed accounting period current at any anniversary of his start date;

(*c*) any day on which he first carries on a new business activity;

(*d*) any day on which he no longer carries on an existing business activity;

(*e*) any day with effect from which the Table is amended in relation to him;

(*f*) where regulation 55JB (reduced rate for newly registered period) applies—

(i) the day that his newly registered period begins, and

(ii) the first anniversary of his EDR.][2]

Amendments—[1] This Part inserted by the VAT (Amendment) (No 2) Regulations, SI 2002/1142 regs 1, 7 with effect from 25 April 2002.

[2] Definition of "amendment date" and "change date" revoked, definition of "EDR" inserted, and para (3) inserted, by the VAT (Amendment) (No 6) Regulations, SI 2003/3220 regs 1(1)(*b*), 2, 18(1) with effect from 1 January 2004.

[Flat-rate scheme for small businesses

55B— (1) The Commissioners may, subject to the requirements of this Part, authorise a taxable person to account for and pay VAT in respect of his relevant supplies in accordance with the scheme with effect from—

(*a*) the beginning of his next prescribed accounting period after the date on which the Commissioners are notified …[2] of his desire to be so authorised, or

(*b*) such earlier or later date as may be agreed between him and the Commissioners.

(2) The date with effect from which a person is so authorised shall be known as his start date.

(3) The Commissioners may refuse to so authorise a person if they consider it is necessary for the protection of the revenue that he is not so authorised.

(4) A flat-rate trader shall continue to account for VAT in accordance with the scheme until his end date.][1]

Amendments—[1] This Part inserted by the VAT (Amendment) (No 2) Regulations, SI 2002/1142 regs 1, 7 with effect from 25 April 2002.

[2] Words revoked by the VAT (Amendment) (No 6) Regulations, SI 2003/3220 regs 1(1)(*b*), 2, 17 with effect from 1 January 2004.

[Relevant supplies and purchases

55C— (1) Subject to paragraphs (3)[, (5) and (6)][2], any—

(*a*) supply of any goods or services to,

(*b*) acquisition of any goods from another member State by, or

(*c*) importation of any goods from a place outside the member States by,

a flat-rate trader is a relevant purchase of his.

(2) Subject to the following provisions of this regulation, any supply made by a person when he is not a flat-rate trader is not a relevant supply of his.

(3) Subject to [paragraphs (4) and (6)][2] below, where—

(*a*) a supply is made to, or made by, a person at a time when he is not a flat-rate trader, and

(*b*) the operative date for VAT accounting purposes is, by virtue of regulation 57 (cash accounting scheme), a date when he is a flat-rate trader,

that supply is a relevant supply or a relevant purchase of his, as the case may be, if otherwise it would not be by virtue of paragraph (2) above.

(4) Where a person—

(*a*) is entitled to any credit for input tax in respect of the supply to, or acquisition or importation by, him of capital expenditure goods,

(*b*) claims any such credit, and

(*c*) makes a supply of those capital expenditure goods,

the supply made by him is not a relevant supply of his, if otherwise it would be.

(5) Where by virtue of any provision of, or made under, the Act a supply is treated as made by a flat-rate trader, whether to himself or otherwise, that supply is neither a relevant supply nor a relevant purchase of his.][1]

[(6) Where a supply of goods to which section 55A(6) of the Act applies (customers to account for tax on supplies of goods of a kind used in missing trader intra-community fraud) is made to, or made by, a flat rate trader, that supply is neither a relevant purchase nor a relevant supply of his.][2]

Amendments—[1] This Part inserted by the VAT (Amendment) (No 2) Regulations, SI 2002/1142 regs 1, 7 with effect from 25 April 2002.

[2] Words in paras (1), (3) substituted, and para (6) inserted, by the VAT (Amendment) (No 3) Regulations, SI 2007/1418 regs 2, 5 with effect from 1 June 2007.

[Method of accounting

55D Subject to [regulations 55H and 55JB][2] below, for any prescribed accounting period of a flat-rate trader, the output tax due from him in respect of his relevant supplies shall be deemed to be the appropriate percentage of his relevant turnover for that period][1]

Amendments—[1] This regulation inserted by the VAT (Amendment) (No 2) Regulations, SI 2002/1142 regs 1, 7 with effect from 25 April 2002.

[2] Words substituted by the VAT (Amendment) (No 6) Regulations, SI 2003/3220 regs 1(1)(*b*), 2, 18(2) with effect from 1 January 2004.

[Input tax

55E— (1) For any prescribed accounting period of a flat-rate trader, he is entitled to credit for input tax in respect of any relevant purchase of his of capital expenditure goods with a value, together with the VAT chargeable, of more than £2,000.

(2) Where paragraph (1) above applies, the whole of the input tax on the goods concerned shall be regarded as used or to be used by the flat-rate trader exclusively in making taxable supplies.

(3) Section 26B(5) of the Act shall not apply to prevent a taxable person from being entitled to credit for input tax in respect of any supply, acquisition or importation by him that is not a relevant purchase of his.

(4) Nothing in this regulation gives an entitlement to credit for input tax where such entitlement is excluded by virtue of any order made under section 25(7) of the Act.][1]

Amendments—[1] This Part inserted by the VAT (Amendment) (No 2) Regulations, SI 2002/1142 regs 1, 7 with effect from 25 April 2002.

[Exceptional claims for VAT relief

55F— (1) This regulation applies where—

(*a*) the first prescribed accounting period for which a taxable person is authorised to account for and pay VAT in accordance with the scheme is the first prescribed accounting period for which he is, or is required to be, registered under the Act, and

(*b*) the taxable person makes a claim in accordance with regulation 111 (exceptional claims for VAT relief).

(2) Where this regulation applies, section 26B(5) of the Act shall not apply to prevent the taxable person from being entitled to credit for input tax in relation to the matters for which he makes the claim described in paragraph (1)(b) above.

(3) Where—

(*a*) this regulation applies, and

(*b*) the Commissioners authorise the claim described in paragraph (1)(b) above,

the whole of the input tax on the goods or services concerned shall be regarded as used or to be used by the taxable person exclusively in making taxable supplies.][1]

Amendments—[1] This Part inserted by the VAT (Amendment) (No 2) Regulations, SI 2002/1142 regs 1, 7 with effect from 25 April 2002.

[Determining relevant turnover

55G— (1) The Commissioners shall prescribe, in a notice published by them, three methods to determine when supplies are to be treated as taking place for the purpose of ascertaining the relevant turnover of a flat-rate trader for a particular period, as follows—

(*a*) "the basic turnover method", which shall be a method based on consideration for supplies taking place in a period;

(*b*) "the cash turnover method", which shall be a method based on the actual consideration received in a period;

(*c*) "the retailer's turnover method", which shall be a method based on the daily gross takings of a retailer.

(2) When exercising their power to prescribe these methods, the Commissioners shall prescribe what rules are to apply when a flat-rate trader ceases to use one of the methods and begins to use a different method.

(3) In any prescribed accounting period, a flat-rate trader must use one of the methods to determine the value of his relevant turnover.][1]

Amendments—[1] This Part inserted by the VAT (Amendment) (No 2) Regulations, SI 2002/1142 regs 1, 7 with effect from 25 April 2002.

[55H— (1) The appropriate percentage to be applied by a flat-rate trader for any prescribed accounting period, or part of a prescribed accounting period (as the case may be), shall be determined in accordance with this regulation and regulations 55JB and 55K.

(2) For any prescribed accounting period—

(*a*) beginning with a relevant date, the appropriate percentage shall be that specified in the Table for the category of business that he is expected, at the relevant date, on reasonable grounds, to carry on in that period;

(*b*) current at his start date but not beginning with his start date, the appropriate percentage shall be that specified in the Table for the category of business that he is expected, at his start date, on reasonable grounds, to carry on in the remainder of the period;

(*c*) not falling within (*a*) or (*b*), the appropriate percentage shall be that applicable to his relevant turnover at the end of the previous prescribed accounting period.

(3) Except that, where a relevant date other than his start date occurs on a day other than the first day of a prescribed accounting period, the following rules shall apply for the remainder of that prescribed accounting period—

(*a*) for the remaining portion, the appropriate percentage shall be that specified in the Table for the category of business that he is expected, at the relevant date, on reasonable grounds, to carry on in that period;

(*b*) "remaining portion" means that part of the prescribed accounting period in which the relevant date occurs—

(i) starting with the relevant date, and

(ii) ending on the last day of that prescribed accounting period;

(*c*) the appropriate percentage specified in sub-paragraph (*a*) shall be applied to his relevant turnover in the remaining portion described;

(*d*) if the rules set out in paragraphs (*a*) to (*c*) apply and then another relevant date occurs in the same prescribed accounting period, then—

(i) the existing remaining portion ends on the day before the latest relevant date,

(ii) another remaining portion begins on the latest relevant date, and

(iii) the rules in paragraph (*a*) to (*c*) shall be applied again in respect of the latest remaining portion.][1]

Amendments—[1] Substituted for regulations 55H–55JA by the VAT (Amendment) (No 6) Regulations, SI 2003/3220 regs 1(1)(*b*), 2, 19(1) with effect from 1 January 2004.

[Reduced appropriate percentage for newly registered period

55JB— (1) This regulation applies where a flat-rate trader's start date falls within one year of his EDR.

(2) Except that this regulation does not apply where—

(*a*) the Commissioners received notification of, or otherwise became fully aware of, his liability to be registered more than one year after his EDR, or

(*b*) his end date or the first anniversary of his EDR falls before 1st January 2004.

(3) At any relevant date on or after 1st January 2004 falling within his newly registered period, the Table shall be read as if each percentage specified in the right-hand column were reduced by one.

(4) A flat-rate trader's "newly registered period" is the period—

(*a*) beginning with the later of—

(i) his start date; and

(ii) the day the Commissioners received notification of, or otherwise became fully aware of, his liability to be registered under the Act, and

(*b*) ending on the day before the first anniversary of his EDR.][1]

Amendments—[1] Inserted by the VAT (Amendment) (No 6) Regulations, SI 2003/3220 regs 1(1)(*b*), 2, 19(2) with effect from 1 January 2004.

[Category of business

55K— (1) Where, at a relevant date, a flat-rate trader is expected, on reasonable grounds, to carry on business in more than one category in the period concerned, paragraph (3) below shall apply.

(2) …[2]

(3) He shall be regarded as being expected, on reasonable grounds, to carry on that category of business which is expected, on reasonable grounds, to be his main business activity in that period.

(4) In paragraph (3) above, his main business activity in a period is to be determined by reference to the respective proportions of his relevant turnover expected, on reasonable grounds, to be generated by each business activity expected, on reasonable grounds, to be carried on in the period.][1]

TABLE

[Category of business	*Appropriate percentage*
Accountancy or book-keeping	11.5
Advertising	8.5
Agricultural services	7
Any other activity not listed elsewhere	9
Architect, civil and structural engineer or surveyor	11
Boarding or care of animals	9.5
Business services that are not listed elsewhere	9.5
Catering services including restaurants and takeaways	10.5
Computer and IT consultancy or data processing	11.5
Computer repair services	10
Dealing in waste or scrap	8.5
Entertainment or journalism	9.5
Estate agency or property management services	9.5
Farming or agriculture that is not listed elsewhere	5.5
Film, radio, television or video production	9.5
Financial services	10.5
Forestry or fishing	8
General building or construction services[(1)]	7.5
Hairdressing or other beauty treatment services	10.5
Hiring or renting goods	7.5
Hotel or accommodation	8.5
Investigation or security	9
Labour-only building or construction services[(1)]	11.5
Laundry or dry-cleaning services	9.5
Lawyer or legal services	12
Library, archive, museum or other cultural activity	7.5
Management consultancy	11

VAT

[Category of business	*Appropriate percentage*
Manufacturing that is not listed elsewhere	7.5
Manufacturing fabricated metal products	8.5
Manufacturing food	7
Manufacturing yarn, textiles or clothing	7.5
Membership organisation	5.5
Mining or quarrying	8
Packaging	7.5
Photography	8.5
Post offices	2
Printing	6.5
Publishing	8.5
Pubs	5.5
Real estate activity not listed elsewhere	11
Repairing personal or household goods	7.5
Repairing vehicles	6.5
Retailing food, confectionary, tobacco, newspapers or children's clothing	2
Retailing pharmaceuticals, medical goods, cosmetics or toiletries	6
Retailing that is not listed elsewhere	5.5
Retailing vehicles or fuel	5.5
Secretarial services	9.5
Social work	8
Sport or recreation	6
Transport or storage, including couriers, freight, removals and taxis	8
Travel agency	8
Veterinary medicine	8
Wholesaling agricultural products	5.5
Wholesaling food	5
Wholesaling that is not listed elsewhere	6

(1) "Labour-only building or construction services" means building or construction services where the value of materials supplied is less than 10 per cent of relevant turnover from such services; any other building or construction services are "general building or construction services".][3]

Cross reference—VAT (Amendment) Regulations, SI 2004/767 reg 2(3) ("his main business activity" in a period (as mentioned in Note 4 below) is to be determined by reference to reg 55K(4) above).

Amendments—[1] This Part inserted by the VAT (Amendment) (No 2) Regulations, SI 2002/1142 regs 1, 7 with effect from 25 April 2002.

[2] Para (2) revoked by the VAT (Amendment) (No 6) Regulations, SI 2003/3220 regs 1(1)(*b*), 2, 18(3) with effect from 1 January 2004.

[3] In para (4), Table substituted by the VAT (Amendment) (No 2) Regulations, SI 2008/3021 regs 2, 4 with effect from 1 December 2008.

[Admission to Scheme

55L— (1) A taxable person shall be eligible to be authorised to account for VAT in accordance with the scheme at any time if—

(*a*) there are reasonable grounds for believing that—

(i) the value of taxable supplies to be made by him in the period of one year then beginning will not exceed [£150,000][2], and

(ii) …[3]

(*b*) he—

(i) is not a tour operator,

(ii) is not required to carry out adjustments in relation to a capital item under Part XV, or

(iii) does not intend to opt to account for the VAT chargeable on a supply made by him by reference to the profit margin on the supply, in accordance with the provisions of any Order made under section 50A of the Act,

(*c*) he has not, in the period of one year preceding that time—

(i) been convicted of any offence in connection with VAT,

(ii) made any payment to compound proceedings in respect of VAT under section 152 of the Customs and Excise Management Act 1979,

(iii) been assessed to a penalty under section 60 of the Act, or

(iv) ceased to operate the scheme, and

(*d*) he is not, and has not been within the past 24 months—

(i) eligible to be registered for VAT in the name of a group under section 43A of the Act,

(ii) registered for VAT in the name of a division under section 46(1) of the Act, or

(iii) associated with another person.

(2) In determining the value of a person's taxable supplies …[3] for the purposes of paragraph (1)(*a*)—

(*a*) any supply of goods or services that are capital assets of the business in the course or furtherance of which they are supplied, and

(*b*) any supply of services treated as made by the recipient by virtue of section 8 of the Act (reverse charge on supplies from abroad),

shall be disregarded.

(3) Notwithstanding the above, where a person has been—

(*a*) eligible to be registered for VAT in the name of a group under section 43A of the Act,

(*b*) registered for VAT in the name of a division under section 46(1) of the Act, or

(*c*) associated with another person,

in the period of 24 months before the date of his application, he shall not be authorised, unless the Commissioners are satisfied that such authorisation poses no risk to the revenue.][1]

Amendments—[1] This Part inserted by the VAT (Amendment) (No 2) Regulations, SI 2002/1142 regs 1, 7 with effect from 25 April 2002.

[2] In sub-para (1)(*a*)(i), "£150,000" substituted for "£100,000", by the VAT (Amendment) (No 2) Regulations, SI 2003/1069 regs 1(1), 2, 7(1) with effect from 10 April 2003.

[3] Para (1)(*a*)(ii) revoked, and in para (2) words "or income" revoked, by the VAT (Amendment) Regulations, SI 2009/586 regs 2, 6 with effect from 1 April 2009. Para (1)(*a*)(ii) previously read as follows—

"(ii) the total value of his income in the period of one year then beginning will not exceed [£187,500][2],".

[Withdrawal from the scheme

55M— (1) Subject to paragraph (2) below, a flat-rate trader ceases to be eligible to be authorised to account for VAT in accordance with the scheme where—

(*a*) at any anniversary of his start date, the total value of his income in the period of one year then ending is more than [£225,000][2],

(*b*) there are reasonable grounds to believe that the total value of his income in the period of 30 days then beginning will exceed [£225,000][2],

(*c*) he becomes a tour operator,

(*d*) he intends to acquire, construct or otherwise obtain a capital item within the meaning of regulation 112(2),

(*e*) he opts to account for the VAT chargeable on a supply made by him by reference to the profit margin on the supply, in accordance with the provisions of any Order made under section 50A of the Act,

(*f*) he becomes—

(i) eligible to be registered for VAT in the name of a group under section 43A of the Act,

(ii) registered for VAT in the name of a division under section 46(1) of the Act, or

(iii) associated with another person,

(*g*) he opts to withdraw from the scheme, or

(*h*) his authorisation is terminated in accordance with regulation 55P below.

(2) A flat-rate trader does not cease to be eligible to be authorised by virtue of paragraph (1)(*a*) above if the Commissioners are satisfied that the total value of his income in the period of one year then beginning will not exceed [£187,500][2].

(3) In determining the value of a flat-rate trader's income for the purposes of paragraphs (1)(*a*) and (*b*) and (2) above, any supply of goods or services that are capital assets of the business in the course or furtherance of which they are supplied, shall be disregarded.

[(4) For the purposes of this regulation, "income" shall be calculated in accordance with the method specified in regulation 55G(1) (determining relevant turnover) used by the business to determine the value of its turnover whilst accounting for VAT under the scheme.

(5) Where a business has used more than one method to determine the value of its turnover whilst accounting for VAT under the scheme, the method referred to in paragraph (4) above shall be the most recent method used.][3]][1]

Amendments—[1] This Part inserted by the VAT (Amendment) (No 2) Regulations, SI 2002/1142 regs 1, 7 with effect from 25 April 2002.

[2] In para (1)(*a*), (*b*), "£225,000" substituted for "£150,000"; and in para (2), "£187,500" substituted for "£125,000"; by the VAT (Amendment) (No 2) Regulations, SI 2003/1069 regs 1(1), 2, 7(2) with effect from 10 April 2003.

[3] Paras (4), (5) inserted by the VAT (Amendment) Regulations, SI 2009/586 regs 2, 7 with effect from 1 April 2009.

[Notification

55N— [(1) Where—

(*a*) at the first day of the prescribed accounting period current at any anniversary of his start date,

(*b*) the appropriate percentage to be applied by a flat-rate trader in accordance with regulation 55H(2)(*a*) for the prescribed accounting period just beginning differs from that applicable to his relevant turnover at the end of the previous prescribed accounting period,

he must notify the Commissioners of that fact within 30 days of the first day of the prescribed accounting period current at the anniversary of his start date.][2]

[(2) Where a flat-rate trader begins to carry on a new business activity or ceases to carry on an existing business activity, he must notify the Commissioners of—

(*a*) that fact,

(*b*) the date that is the relevant date described by regulation 55A(3)(*c*) or (*d*) (as the case may be), and

(*c*) the appropriate percentage to be applied to the period immediately before that relevant date and immediately after it,

within 30 days of that relevant date.][2]

(3) Where any of sub-paragraphs (*a*) to (*g*) of regulation 55M(1) apply, the flat-rate trader shall notify the Commissioners of that fact within 30 days.

(4) Any notification required by this regulation shall be given in writing.][1]

Amendments—[1] This Part inserted by the VAT (Amendment) (No 2) Regulations, SI 2002/1142 regs 1, 7 with effect from 25 April 2002.

[2] Paras (1), (2) substituted by the VAT (Amendment) (No 6) Regulations, SI 2003/3220 regs 1(1)(*b*), 2, 18(4) with effect from 1 January 2004.

[Termination by the Commissioners

55P The Commissioners may terminate the authorisation of a flat-rate trader at any time if—

(*a*) they consider it necessary to do so for the protection of the revenue, or

(*b*) a false statement was made by, or on behalf of, him in relation to his application for authorisation.][1]

Amendments—[1] This Part inserted by the VAT (Amendment) (No 2) Regulations, SI 2002/1142 regs 1, 7 with effect from 25 April 2002.

[Date of withdrawal from the scheme

55Q— (1) The date on which a flat-rate trader ceases to be authorised to account for VAT in accordance with the scheme shall be—

(*a*) where regulation 55M(1)(*a*) applies—

(i) in the case of a person who is authorised in accordance with regulation 50(1) (annual accounting scheme), the end of the prescribed accounting period in which the relevant anniversary occurred, or the end of the month next following, whichever is the earlier, or

(ii) in all other cases, the end of the prescribed accounting period in which the relevant anniversary occurred,

(*b*) where regulation 55M(1)(*b*) applies, the beginning of the period of 30 days in question,

(*c*) where regulation 55M(1)(*c*), (*d*), or (*f*) applies, the date the event occurred,

(*d*) where regulation 55M(1)(*e*) applies, the beginning of the prescribed accounting period for which he makes the election described by that provision,

(*e*) where regulation 55M(1)(*g*) applies, the date on which the Commissioners are notified in writing of his decision to cease using the scheme, or such earlier or later date as may be agreed between them and him, and

(*f*) where regulation 55M(1)(*h*) applies, the date of issue of a notice of termination by the Commissioners or such earlier or later date as may be directed in the notification.

(2) The date with effect from which a person ceases to be so authorised shall be known as his end date.][1]

Amendments—[1] This Part inserted by the VAT (Amendment) (No 2) Regulations, SI 2002/1142 regs 1, 7 with effect from 25 April 2002.

[Self-supply on withdrawal from scheme

55R— (1) This regulation applies where—

(*a*) a person continues to be a taxable person after his end date,

(*b*) for any prescribed accounting period for which he was a flat-rate trader, he was entitled to, and claimed, credit for input tax in respect of any capital expenditure goods, and

(*c*) he did not, whilst he was a flat-rate trader, make a supply of those goods.

(2) Where this regulation applies, those goods shall be treated for the purposes of the Act as being, on the day after his end date, both supplied to him for the purpose of his business and supplied by him in the course or furtherance of his business.

(3) The value of a supply of goods treated under paragraph (2) above as made to or by a person shall be determined as though it were a supply falling within paragraph 6(1) of Schedule 6 to the Act.][1]

Amendments—[1] This Part inserted by the VAT (Amendment) (No 2) Regulations, SI 2002/1142 regs 1, 7 with effect from 25 April 2002.

[Adjustments in respect of stock on hand at withdrawal from scheme

55S— (1) This regulation applies where—

(*a*) a person continues to be a taxable person after his end date,

(*b*) at his end date, he has stock on hand in respect of which he is not entitled to credit for input tax, and

(*c*) the value of the stock on hand referred to in sub-paragraph (*b*) above exceeds the value of his stock on hand in respect of which he was entitled to credit for input tax, at his start date.

(2) Where this regulation applies, the taxable person, for the prescribed accounting period following that in which his end date falls, is entitled to credit for input tax in respect of his stock on hand in such amount as may be determined in accordance with a notice published by the Commissioners.][1]

Amendments—[1] This Part inserted by the VAT (Amendment) (No 2) Regulations, SI 2002/1142 regs 1, 7 with effect from 25 April 2002.

[Amendment by Notice

55T The Commissioners may vary the terms of any method prescribed by them for the purposes of regulations 55G or 55S by publishing a fresh notice or publishing a notice that amends an existing notice.][1]

Amendments—[1] This Part inserted by the VAT (Amendment) (No 2) Regulations, SI 2002/1142 regs 1, 7 with effect from 25 April 2002.

[Reverse charges

55U Section 8 of the Act (reverse charge on supplies from abroad) shall not apply to any relevant supply or relevant purchase of a flat-rate trader.][1]

Amendments—[1] This Part inserted by the VAT (Amendment) (No 2) Regulations, SI 2002/1142 regs 1, 7 with effect from 25 April 2002.

[Bad Debt Relief

55V— (1) This regulation applies where—

(*a*) a person has made a relevant supply,

(*b*) he has used the cash turnover method to determine the value of his relevant turnover for the prescribed accounting period in which the relevant supply was made,

(*c*) he has not accounted for and paid VAT on the supply,

(*d*) the whole or any part of the consideration for the supply has been written off in his accounts as a bad debt, and

(*e*) a period of 6 months (beginning with the date of the supply) has elapsed.

(2) Where this regulation applies—

(*a*) section 36 of the Act (bad debts) and any regulations made thereunder shall apply as if the conditions set out in subsection (1) of that section are satisfied, and

(*b*) the amount of refund of VAT to which the person is entitled under that section shall be the VAT chargeable on the relevant supply described in paragraph (1) above less the flat-rate amount.

(3) In paragraph (2)(*b*) above, the flat-rate amount is—

$A \times B$

where—

A is the appropriate percentage applicable for the prescribed accounting period, or part thereof, in which the relevant supply was made, and

B is the value of the relevant supply together with the VAT chargeable thereon.][1]

Amendments—[1] This Part inserted by the VAT (Amendment) (No 2) Regulations, SI 2002/1142 regs 1, 7 with effect from 25 April 2002.

PART VIII
CASH ACCOUNTING

Interpretation of Part VIII

56 In this Part—

"money" means banknotes or coins;

"notice" means any notice published pursuant to this Part.

Former regulations—VAT (Cash Accounting) Regulations, SI 1987/1427 reg 2; VAT (Cash Accounting) (Amendment) Regulations, SI 1993/762 reg 3.

Cash accounting scheme

57 A taxable person may, subject to this Part and to such conditions as are described in a notice published by the Commissioners, account for VAT in accordance with a scheme (hereinafter referred to in this Part as "the scheme") by which the operative dates for VAT accounting purposes shall be—

(*a*) for output tax, the day on which payment or other consideration is received or the date of any cheque, if later; and

(*b*) for input tax, the date on which payment is made or other consideration is given, or the date of any cheque, if later.

Former regulations—VAT (Cash Accounting) Regulations, SI 1987/1427 reg 3; VAT (Cash Accounting) (Amendment) Regulations, SI 1993/762 reg 4.

[57A— (1) A person shall not account for VAT in accordance with the scheme in respect of any relevant supplies or relevant purchases of his.

(2) In this regulation, "relevant supplies" and "relevant purchases" have the same meanings as in Part VIIA (flat-rate scheme for small businesses).][1]

Amendments—[1] Regulation inserted by the VAT (Amendment) (No 2) Regulations, SI 2002/1142 regs 1, 8 with effect from 25 April 2002.

Admission to the scheme

[58— (1) Without prejudice to paragraph (4) below, a taxable person shall be eligible to begin to operate the scheme from the beginning of any prescribed accounting period if—

(*a*) he has reasonable grounds for believing that the value of taxable supplies to be made by him in the period of one year then beginning will not exceed [£1,350,000][2],

(*b*) he has made all returns which he is required to make, and has—

(i) paid to the Commissioners all such sums shown as due on those returns and on any assessments made either under section 76 of, or Schedule 11 to, the Act, or

(ii) agreed an arrangement with the Commissioners for any outstanding amount of such sums as are referred to in sub-paragraph (i) above to be paid in instalments over a specific period, and

(*c*) he has not in the period of one year preceding that time—

(i) been convicted of any offence in connection with VAT,

(ii) made any payment to compound proceedings in respect of VAT under section 152 of the Customs and Excise Management Act 1979(*c*),

(iii) been assessed to a penalty under section 60 of the Act, or

(iv) by virtue of regulation 64(1), ceased to be entitled to continue to operate the scheme.

(2) The scheme shall not apply to—

(*a*) lease purchase agreements;

(*b*) hire purchase agreements;

(*c*) conditional sale agreements;

(*d*) credit sale agreements;

(*e*) supplies where a VAT invoice is issued and full payment of the amount shown on the invoice is not due for a period in excess of 6 months from the date of the issue of the invoice; …[3]

(*f*) supplies of goods or services in respect of which a VAT invoice is issued in advance of the delivery or making available of the goods or the performance of the services as the case may be[; or

(*g*) supplies of goods in respect of which it is for the recipient, on the supplier's behalf, to account for and pay the VAT.][3].

(3) Sub-paragraph (2)(*f*) above shall not apply where goods have been delivered or made available in part or where services have been performed in part and the VAT invoice in question relates solely to that part of the goods which have been delivered or made available or that part of the services which have been performed.

(4) A person shall not be entitled to begin to operate the scheme if the Commissioners consider it is necessary for the protection of the revenue that he shall not be so entitled.][1]

Amendments—[1] This regulation substituted by the VAT (Amendment) (No 3) Regulations, SI 1997/1614 reg 3 with effect from 3 July 1997.

[2] Figure in sub-para (1)(*a*) substituted by the VAT (Amendment) (No 2) Regulations, SI 2007/768 regs 2, 3 with effect from 1 April 2007.

[3] Words in sub-para (2)(*f*) revoked, and sub-para (2)(*g*) and preceding word "or" inserted, by the VAT (Amendment) (No 3) Regulations, SI 2007/1418 regs 2, 6 with effect from 1 June 2007.

59 Without prejudice to the right of a person to withdraw from the scheme, the Commissioners may vary the terms of the scheme by publishing a fresh notice [or publishing a notice which amends an existing notice][1].

Former regulation—VAT (Cash Accounting) Regulations, SI 1987/1427 reg 5.

Amendments—[1] Words inserted by the VAT (Amendment) (No 3) Regulations, SI 1997/1614 reg 3 with effect from 3 July 1997.

[60— (1) Without prejudice to regulation 64 below, a person shall withdraw from the scheme immediately at the end of a prescribed accounting period of his if the value of taxable supplies made by him in the period of one year ending at the end of the prescribed accounting period in question has exceeded [£1,600,000][2].

(2) Subject to regulations 61 to 63 below a person may withdraw from the scheme at the end of any prescribed accounting period.

(3) The requirements in paragraph (1) above shall not apply where the Commissioners allow or direct otherwise.][1]

Amendments—[1] This regulation substituted by the VAT (Amendment) (No 3) Regulations, SI 1997/1614 reg 5 with effect from 3 July 1997.

[2] Figure in sub-s (1) substituted by the VAT (Amendment) (No 2) Regulations, SI 2007/768 regs 2, 4 with effect from 1 April 2007.

[61— (1) Subject to paragraph (2), a person who ceases to operate the scheme, either of his own volition or because the value of taxable supplies made by him exceeds the level provided for in regulation 60(1), must—

(*a*) settle up, or

(*b*) apply transitional arrangements.

(2) Where the value of taxable supplies made by a person in the period of three months ending at the end of the prescribed accounting period in which he ceased to operate the scheme has exceeded [£1,350,000][2], he may not apply transitional arrangements.

(3) In paragraph (1)(*a*), "settle up" means account for and pay on a return made for the prescribed accounting period in which he ceased to operate the scheme—

(*a*) all VAT that he would have been required to pay to the Commissioners during the time when he operated the scheme, if he had not then been operating the scheme, minus

(*b*) all VAT accounted for and paid to the Commissioners in accordance with the scheme, subject to any adjustment for credit for input tax.

(4) In paragraph (1)(*b*), "apply transitional arrangements" means continue to operate the scheme in respect of his scheme supplies for 6 months after the end of the prescribed accounting period in which he ceased to operate the scheme.

(5) In paragraph (4), "scheme supplies" means supplies made and received while he operated the scheme that are not excluded from the scheme by virtue of regulation 57A or 58 or conditions described in a notice.

(6) Where a person chooses to apply transitional arrangements, he shall account for and pay on a return made for the first prescribed accounting period that ends 6 months or more after the end of the prescribed accounting period in which he ceased to operate the scheme—

(*a*) all VAT that he would have been required to pay to the Commissioners during the time when he operated the scheme, if he had not then been operating the scheme, minus

(*b*) all VAT accounted for and paid to the Commissioners in accordance with the scheme (including any VAT accounted for and paid because he applied transitional arrangements), subject to any adjustment for credit for input tax.][1]

Amendments—[1] This regulation substituted by the VAT (Amendment) Regulations, SI 2004/767 regs 3, 9 with effect from 1 April 2004.

[2] Figure in sub-s (2) substituted by the VAT (Amendment) (No 2) Regulations, SI 2007/768 regs 2, 5 with effect from 1 April 2007.

[62 Where a person operating the scheme becomes insolvent he shall within 2 months of the date of insolvency account for VAT due on all supplies made and received up to the date of insolvency which has not otherwise been accounted for, subject to any credit for input tax.][1]

Amendments—[1] This regulation substituted by the VAT (Amendment) (No 3) Regulations, SI 1997/1614 reg 7 with effect from 3 July 1997.

63— [(1) Where a person operating the scheme ceases business or ceases to be registered he shall within 2 months or such longer period as the Commissioners may allow, make a return accounting for, and pay, VAT due on all supplies made and received up to the date of cessation which has not otherwise been accounted for, subject to any adjustment for credit for input tax.

(2) Where a business or part of a business carried on by a person operating the scheme is transferred as a going concern and regulation 6(1) does not apply, the transferor shall within 2

months or such longer period as the Commissioners may allow, make a return accounting for, and pay, VAT due on all supplies made and received which has not otherwise been accounted for, subject to credit for input tax.][1]

(3) Where a business carried on by a person operating the scheme is transferred in circumstances where regulation [6(1)][2] applies, the transferee shall continue to account for and pay VAT as if he were a person operating the scheme on supplies made and received by the transferor prior to the date of transfer.

Amendments—[1] Paras (1) and (2) substituted by the VAT (Amendment) (No 3) Regulations, SI 1997/1614 reg 8 with effect from 3 July 1997.

[2] Number substituted for "6(2)" by the VAT (Amendment) (No 3) Regulations, SI 1997/1614 reg 8 with effect from 3 July 1997.

Withdrawal from the scheme

[64— (1) A person shall not be entitled to continue to operate the scheme where—

(*a*) he has, while operating the scheme, been convicted of an offence in connection with VAT or has made a payment to compound such proceedings under section 152 of the Customs and Excise Management Act 1979,

(*b*) he has while operating the scheme been assessed to a penalty under section 60 of the Act,

(*c*) he has failed to leave the scheme as required by regulation 60(1) above, or

(*d*) the Commissioners consider it necessary for the protection of the revenue that he shall not be so entitled.

(2) A person who, by virtue of paragraph (1) above, ceases to be entitled to continue to operate the scheme shall account for and pay on a return made for the prescribed accounting period in which he ceased to be so entitled—

(*a*) all VAT which he would have been required to pay to the Commissioners during the time when he operated the scheme, if he had not then been operating the scheme, less

(*b*) all VAT accounted for and paid to the Commissioners in accordance with the scheme, subject to any adjustment for credit for input tax.][1]

Amendments—[1] This regulation substituted by the VAT (Amendment) (No 3) Regulations, SI 1997/1614 reg 9 with effect from 3 July 1997.

[Bad debt relief

64A Where a person accounts for and pays VAT in relation to a supply in accordance with regulation 61(3) or (6) or 64(2), he shall be treated for the purposes of section 36(1)(*a*) of the Act as having accounted for and paid VAT on the supply in the prescribed accounting period in which he ceased to operate the scheme.][1]

Amendments—[1] This regulation inserted by the VAT (Amendment) Regulations, SI 2004/767 regs 3, 10 with effect from 1 April 2004.

Accounting

65— (1) Except in the circumstances set out in regulations 61 to 63, VAT shall be accounted for and paid to the Commissioners by the due date prescribed for the accounting period in which payment or other consideration for the supply is received.

(2) Input tax may be credited either in the prescribed accounting period in which payment or consideration for a supply is given, or in such later period as may be agreed with the Commissioners.

(3) A person operating the scheme shall obtain and keep for a period of 6 years, or such lesser period as the Commissioners may allow, a receipted and dated VAT invoice from any taxable person to whom he has made a payment in money in respect of a taxable supply, and in such circumstances a taxable person must on request provide such a receipted and dated VAT invoice.

(4) A person operating the scheme shall keep for a period of 6 years, or such lesser period as the Commissioners may allow, a copy of any receipt which he gives under paragraph (3) above.

Former regulations—VAT (Cash Accounting) Regulations, SI 1987/1427 reg 12; VAT (Cash Accounting) (Amendment) Regulations, SI 1993/762 reg 8.

PART IX
SUPPLIES BY RETAILERS

Interpretation of Part IX

66 In this Part—

["flat-rate trader" has the meaning given in regulation 55A;][1]

"notice" means any notice or leaflet published by the Commissioners pursuant to this Part;

"scheme" means a method as referred to in regulation 67.

Former regulations—VAT (Supplies by Retailers) Regulations, SI 1972/1148 reg 1(2); VAT (Supplies by Retailers) (Amendment) Regulations, SI 1979/224.

Amendments—[1] Definition of "flat-rate trader" inserted by the VAT (Amendment) (No 2) Regulations, SI 2002/1142 regs 1, 9(*a*) with effect from 25 April 2002.

Retail schemes

67— (1) The Commissioners may permit the value which is to be taken as the value, in any prescribed accounting period or part thereof, of supplies by a retailer which are taxable at other than the zero rate to be determined by a method agreed with that retailer or by any method described in a notice published by the Commissioners for that purpose; and they may publish any notice accordingly.

(2) The Commissioners may vary the terms of any method by—

(*a*) publishing a fresh notice,

(*b*) publishing a notice which amends an existing notice, or

(*c*) adapting any method by agreement with any retailer.

Former regulations—VAT (Supplies by Retailers) Regulations, SI 1972/1148 reg 2; VAT (Supplies by Retailers) (Amendment) Regulations, SI 1979/224.

Simon's Tax Cases—*C&E Comrs v Kingfisher plc* [1994] STC 63*; *C&E Comrs v Co-operative Wholesale Society Ltd* [1995] STC 983*.

68 The Commissioners may refuse to permit the value of taxable supplies to be determined in accordance with a scheme if it appears to them—

(*a*) that the use of any particular scheme does not produce a fair and reasonable valuation during any period,

(*b*) that it is necessary to do so for the protection of the revenue, or

(*c*) that the retailer could reasonably be expected to account for VAT in accordance with regulations made under paragraph 2(1) of Schedule 11 to the Act.

Former regulations—VAT (Supplies by Retailers) Regulations, SI 1972/1148 reg 3; VAT (Supplies by Retailers) (Amendment) Regulations, SI 1987/1712 reg 2.

69 No retailer may at any time use more than one scheme except as provided for in any notice or as the Commissioners may otherwise allow.

Former regulation—VAT (Supplies by Retailers) Regulations, SI 1972/1148 reg 4.

[69A No retailer may use a scheme at any time for which he is a flat-rate trader.][1]

Amendments—[1] Regulation inserted by the VAT (Amendment) (No 2) Regulations, SI 2002/1142 regs 1, 9(*b*) with effect from 25 April 2002.

Notification of use of a scheme

70 ...

Amendments—This regulation revoked by the VAT (Amendment) (No 4) Regulations, SI 1997/2437 with effect from 1 November 1997.

Changing schemes

71[— (1)][1] Save as the Commissioners may otherwise allow, a retailer who accounts for VAT on the basis of taxable supplies valued in accordance with any scheme shall, so long as he remains a taxable person, continue to do so for a period of not less than one year from the adoption of that scheme by him, and any change by a retailer from one scheme to another shall be made at the end of any complete year reckoned from the beginning of the prescribed accounting period in which he first adopted the scheme.

[(2) Paragraph (1) shall not apply where a retailer ceases to operate a scheme solely because he becomes a flat-rate trader.][1]

Former regulation—VAT (Supplies by Retailers) Regulations, SI 1972/1148 reg 6.

Amendments—[1] Para (1) numbered as such, and para (2) added, by the VAT (Amendment) (No 2) Regulations, SI 2002/1142 regs 1, 9(*c*) with effect from 25 April 2002.

Ceasing to use a scheme

72— (1) A retailer shall notify the Commissioners before ceasing to account for VAT on the basis of taxable supplies valued in accordance with these regulations.

(2) A retailer may be required to pay VAT on such proportion as the Commissioners may consider fair and reasonable of any sums due to him at the end of the prescribed accounting period in which he last used a scheme.

Former regulation—VAT (Supplies by Retailers) Regulations, SI 1972/1148 reg 7.

Supplies under Schedule 8, Group 1

73 ...

Amendments—This regulation revoked by the VAT (Amendment) (No 4) Regulations, SI 1997/2437 with effect from 1 November 1997.

Supplies under Schedule 8, Group 12

74 ...

Amendments—This regulation revoked by the VAT (Amendment) (No 4) Regulations, SI 1997/2437 with effect from 1 November 1997.

Change in VAT

75 Where pursuant to any enactment there is a change in the VAT charged on any supply, including a change to or from no VAT being charged on such supply, a retailer using any scheme shall take such steps relating to that scheme as are directed in any notice applicable to him or as may be agreed between him and the Commissioners.

Former regulations—VAT (Supplies by Retailers) Regulations, SI 1972/1148 reg 9; VAT (Supplies by Retailers) (Amendment) Regulations, SI 1975/274.

PART X
TRADING STAMPS

Interpretation of Part X

76 …

Amendments—This Part (regs 76–80) revoked by the VAT (Trading Stamps) Regulations, SI 1995/3043 reg 2, with effect from 1 June 1996.

Trading stamp scheme

77–80 …

Amendments—This Part (regs 76–80) revoked by the VAT (Trading Stamps) Regulations, SI 1995/3043 reg 2, with effect from 1 June 1996.

PART XI
TIME OF SUPPLY AND TIME OF ACQUISITION

Goods for private use and free supplies of services

81— (1) Where the services referred to in paragraph 5(4) of Schedule 4 to the Act are supplied for any period, they shall be treated as being supplied on the last day of the supplier's prescribed accounting period, or of each such accounting period, in which the goods are made available or used.

(2) Where services specified in an order made by the Treasury under section 5(4) of the Act are supplied for any period, they shall be treated as being supplied on the last day of the supplier's prescribed accounting period, or of each such accounting period, in which the services are performed.

Former regulation—VAT (General) Regulations, SI 1985/886 reg 17.

Services from outside the United Kingdom

82 Services which are treated as made by a taxable person under section 8(1) of the Act shall be treated as being supplied when the supplies are paid for or, if the consideration is not in money, on the last day of the prescribed accounting period in which the services are performed.

Former regulation—VAT (General) Regulations, SI 1985/886 reg 18.

Cross references—VAT (Reverse Charge) (Anti-avoidance) Order, SI 1997/1523 art 4 (modification of Reg 82 in relation to telecommunication services).

[Goods supplied by persons outside the United Kingdom

82A Goods which are treated as supplied by a person under section 9A of the Act shall be treated as being supplied when the goods are paid for or, if the consideration is not in money, on the last day of the prescribed accounting period in which the goods are removed or made available.][1]

Amendments—[1] Regulation 82A inserted by the VAT (Amendment) (No 4) Regulations, SI 2004/3140 reg 4 with effect from 1 January 2005 in relation to supplies made on or after that date: SI 2004/3140 reg 2(1).

Time of acquisition

83 Where the time that goods are acquired from another member State falls to be determined in accordance with section 12(1)(*b*) of the Act by reference to the day of the issue, in respect of the transaction in pursuance of which the goods are acquired, of an invoice of such description as the Commissioners may by regulations prescribe, the invoice shall be one which is issued by the supplier [or the customer and which, in either case, is issued under the provisions of the law of the member State where the goods were supplied, corresponding in relation to that member State to the provisions of regulations 13, 13A and 14.][1]

Former regulations—VAT (General) Regulations, SI 1985/886 reg 18A; VAT (General) (Amendment) Regulations, SI 1992/3102 reg 12.

Cross references—See VAT Regulations, SI 1995/2518 reg 18(4) (invoices for certain supplies by intermediate suppliers: treatment as invoices for the purposes of this regulation);

VAT Regulations, SI 1995/2518 reg 19(4) (invoices for certain supplies by persons belonging in other member states: treatment as invoices for the purposes of this regulation).

Amendments—[1] Words substituted by the VAT (Amendment) (No 6) Regulations, SI 2003/3220 regs 1(1)(*b*), 2, 12 with effect from 1 January 2004.

Supplies of land—special cases

84— (1) Where by or under any enactment an interest in, or right over, land is compulsorily purchased and, at the time determined in accordance with section 6(2) or (3) of the Act, the person (the grantor) from whom it is purchased does not know the amount of payment that he is to receive in respect of the purchase then goods or, as the case may require, services shall be treated as supplied each time the grantor receives any payment for the purchase.

(2) [[Subject to paragraphs (3) to (5)][2] below,][1] where a person (the grantor) grants or assigns the fee simple in any land, and at the time of the grant or assignment, the total consideration for it is not determinable, then goods shall be treated as separately and successively supplied at the following times—

(*a*) the time determined in accordance with section 6(2), (4), (5), (6) …[4] or (10) of the Act, as the case may require, and

(*b*) the earlier of the following times—

(i) each time that any part of the consideration which was not determinable at the time mentioned in sub-paragraph (*a*) above is received by the grantor, or

(ii) each time that the grantor issues a VAT invoice in respect of such a part.

[(3) Paragraph (2) above shall not apply in relation to a grant or assignment falling within item 1(*a*) of Group 1 of Schedule 9 to the Act where any of the persons specified in paragraph (4) below intend or expect to occupy the land on a date before a date ten years after completion of the building or civil engineering work on the land, without being in occupation of it [wholly, or substantially wholly,][5] for eligible purposes.][3]

[(4) The persons referred to in paragraph (3) above are—

(*a*) the grantor;

(*b*) any person who, with the intention or in the expectation that occupation of the land on a date before a date ten years after completion of the building or civil engineering work would not be [wholly, or substantially wholly,][5] for eligible purposes—

(i) provides finance for the grantor's development of the land, or

(ii) has entered into any agreement arrangement or understanding (whether or not legally enforceable) to provide finance for the grantor's development of the land;

(*c*) any person who is connected with any person of a description within sub-paragraph (*a*) or (*b*) above.][3]

[(5) For the purposes of this regulation—

(*a*) Note (2) to Group 1 of Schedule 9 to the Act shall apply in determining when a building or civil engineering work is completed;

[(*b*) paragraph 16 of Schedule 10 to the Act shall have effect for determining the meaning of "eligible purposes" and "occupation";

(*ba*) whether a person's occupation is "wholly, or substantially wholly," for eligible purposes shall be determined in the same way as it is for the purposes of paragraph 15 of that Schedule;][5]

(*c*) "the grantor's development of the land" means any acquisition by the grantor of an interest in the land, building or civil engineering work and includes the construction of the building or civil engineering work;

(*d*) "providing finance" has the same meaning as in [paragraph 14(3) of Schedule 10][5] to the Act, subject to any appropriate modifications, but does not include paying the consideration for the grantor's grant or assignment within paragraph (3) above;

(*e*) any question whether one person is connected with another shall be determined in accordance with section 839 [of the Taxes Act; but this is subject to sub-paragraph (*f*);

(*f*) a company is not connected with another company only because both are under the control of—

(i) the Crown,

(ii) a Minister of the Crown,

(iii) a government department, or

(iv) a Northern Ireland department;

(*g*) "company" and "control" have the same meaning as in section 839 of the Taxes Act.][6]][3]

Former regulations—VAT (General) Regulations, SI 1985/886 reg 18B; VAT (General) (Amendment) Regulations, SI 1992/3102 reg 12.

Amendments—[1] Words in para (2) inserted, and paras (3)–(9) inserted, by the VAT (Amendment) (No 3) Regulations, SI 2002/2918 with effect from 28 November 2002 in relation to grants or assignments made after 27 November 2002.

[2] Words in para (2) substituted by the VAT (Amendment) (No 2) Regulations, SI 2003/1069 regs 1(3), 2, 8 in relation to grants or assignments made after 9 April 2003.

[3] Paras (3)–(5) substituted for paras (3)–(9) by the VAT (Amendment) (No 2) Regulations, SI 2003/1069 regs 1(3), 2, 9 in relation to grants or assignments made after 9 April 2003.

[4] Reference revoked by the VAT (Amendment) (No 6) Regulations, SI 2003/3220 regs 1(1)(*b*), 2, 13 with effect from 1 January 2004.

[5] Words in paras (3), (4)(*b*) substituted, in para (5) sub-paras (*b*), (*ba*) substituted for previous sub-para (*b*), and words in para (5)(*d*) substituted, by the Value Added Tax (Buildings and Land) Order, SI 2008/1146, art 6, Sch 1 paras 16, 17 with effect in relation to supplies made on or after 1 June 2008, subject to savings in Sch 2 of the Order.

[6] Words in para (5)(*e*) substituted for words "of the Income and Corporation Taxes Act 1988." by the Value Added Tax (Amendment) (No 3) Regulations, SI 2009/1967 regs 2, 3 with effect from 15 August 2009.

Leases treated as supplies of goods

85— (1) Subject to paragraph (2) below, where the grant of a tenancy or lease is a supply of goods by virtue of paragraph 4 of Schedule 4 to the Act, and the whole or part of the consideration for that grant is payable periodically or from time to time, goods shall be treated as separately and successively supplied at the earlier of the following times—

(*a*) each time that a part of the consideration is received by the supplier, or

(*b*) each time that the supplier issues a VAT invoice relating to the grant.

(2) Where in respect of the grant of a tenancy or lease such as is mentioned in paragraph (1) above the supplier, at or about the beginning of any period not exceeding one year, issues a VAT invoice containing, in addition to the particulars specified in regulation 14, the following particulars—

(*a*) the dates on which any parts of the consideration are to become due for payment in the period,

(*b*) the amount payable (excluding VAT) on each such date, and

(*c*) the rate of VAT in force at the time of the issue of the VAT invoice and the amount of VAT chargeable in accordance with that rate on each of such payments,

goods shall be treated as separately and successively supplied each time that a payment in respect of the tenancy or lease becomes due or is received by the supplier, whichever is the earlier.

(3) Where, on or before any of the dates that a payment is due as stated on an invoice issued as described in paragraph (2) above, there is a change in the VAT chargeable on supplies of the description to which the invoice relates, that invoice shall cease to be treated as a VAT invoice in respect of any such supplies for which payments are due after the change (and not received before the change).

Former regulations—VAT (General) Regulations, SI 1985/886 reg 19; VAT (General) (Amendment) Regulations, SI 1989/1132 reg 3.

Simon's Tax Cases—reg 85(1), *Royal & Sun Alliance Insurance Group plc v C&E Comrs* [2000] STC 933, [2003] STC 832.

Supplies of water, gas or any form of power, heat, refrigeration or ventilation

86— (1) Except in relation to a supply to which subsections (7) and (8) of section 6 of the Act apply, and subject to paragraphs (2) and (3) below, a supply of—

(*a*) water other than—

(i) distilled water, deionised water and water of similar purity, and

(ii) water comprised in any of the excepted items set out in Group 1 of Schedule 8 to the Act, or

(*b*) coal gas, water gas, producer gases or similar gases, or

(*c*) petroleum gases, or other gaseous hydrocarbons, in a gaseous state, or

(*d*) any form of power, heat, refrigeration or ventilation,

shall be treated as taking place each time that a payment in respect of the supply is received by the supplier, or a VAT invoice relating to the supply is issued by the supplier, whichever is the earlier.

(2) Subject to paragraph (3) below, where the whole or part of the consideration for a supply such as is described in paragraph (1)(*a*), (*b*) or (*c*) above or of power in the form of electricity is determined or payable periodically or from time to time, goods shall be treated as separately and successively supplied at the earlier of the following times—

(*a*) each time that a part of the consideration is received by the supplier, or

(*b*) each time that the supplier issues a VAT invoice relating to the supply.

(3) Where separate and successive supplies as described in paragraph (2) above are made under an agreement which provides for successive payments, and the supplier at or about the beginning of any period not exceeding one year, issues a VAT invoice containing, in addition to the particulars specified in regulation 14, the following particulars—

(*a*) the dates on which payments under the agreement are to become due in the period,

(*b*) the amount payable (excluding VAT) on each such date, and

(*c*) the rate of VAT in force at the time of issue of the VAT invoice and the amount of VAT chargeable in accordance with that rate on each of such payments,

goods shall be treated as separately and successively supplied each time that payment in respect of the supply becomes due or is received by the supplier, whichever is the earlier.

(4) Where, on or before any of the dates that a payment is due as stated on an invoice issued as described in paragraph (3) above, there is a change in the VAT chargeable on supplies of the description to which the invoice relates, that invoice shall cease to be treated as a VAT invoice in respect of any such supplies for which payments are due after the change (and not received before the change).

(5) A supply mentioned in paragraph (1)(*a*), (*b*), (*c*) or (*d*) above to which subsections (7) and (8) of section 6 of the Act apply shall be treated as taking place on the day of the issue of a VAT invoice in respect of the supply.

Former regulations—VAT (General) Regulations, SI 1985/886 reg 20; VAT (General) (Amendment) Regulations, SI 1989/1132 reg 4, SI 1992/3102 reg 13.

Acquisitions of water, gas or any form of power, heat, refrigeration or ventilation

87 Where goods described in regulation 86(1)(*a*), (*b*), (*c*) or (*d*) are acquired from another member State and the whole or part of any consideration comprised in the transaction in pursuance of which the goods are acquired is payable periodically, or from time to time, goods shall be treated as separately and successively acquired on each occasion that [an invoice such as is described in regulation 83 is issued.][1]

Former regulations—VAT (General) Regulations, SI 1985/886 reg 20A; VAT (General) (Amendment) Regulations, SI 1992/3102 reg 14.

Amendments—[1] Words substituted by the VAT (Amendment) (No 6) Regulations, SI 2003/3220 regs 1(1)(*b*), 2, 14 with effect from 1 January 2004.

Supplier's goods in possession of buyer

88— (1) Except in relation to a supply mentioned in section 6(2)(*c*) of the Act, or to a supply to which subsections (7) and (8) of section 6 of the Act apply, where goods are supplied under an agreement whereby the supplier retains the property therein until the goods or part of them are appropriated under the agreement by the buyer and in circumstances where the whole or part of the consideration is determined at that time, a supply of any of the goods shall be treated as taking place at the earliest of the following dates—

(*a*) the date of appropriation by the buyer,

(*b*) the date when a VAT invoice is issued by the supplier, or

(*c*) the date when a payment is received by the supplier.

(2) If, within 14 days after appropriation of the goods or part of them by the buyer as mentioned in paragraph (1) above, the supplier issues a VAT invoice in respect of goods appropriated [or a self-billed invoice fulfilling the conditions in regulation 13(3A) is issued by the customer][1], the provisions of section 6(5) of the Act shall apply to that supply.

Former regulations—VAT (General) Regulations, SI 1985/886 reg 21(1), (2); VAT (General) (Amendment) Regulations, SI 1992/3102 reg 15.

Amendments—[1] Words inserted by the VAT (Amendment) (No 6) Regulations, SI 2003/3220 regs 1(1)(*b*), 2, 15 with effect from 1 January 2004.

Retention payments

89 Where any contract [other than one of a description falling within regulation 93 below][1] for the supply of goods (other than for a supply to which subsections (7) and (8) of section 6 of the Act apply) or for the supply of services provides for the retention of any part of the consideration by a person pending full and satisfactory performance of the contract, or any part of it, by the supplier, goods or services (as the case may require) shall be treated as separately and successively supplied at the following times—

(*a*) the time determined in accordance with section 6(2), (3), (4), (5), (6), …[2] (10) or (13) of the Act, as the case may require, and

(*b*) the earlier of the following times—

(i) the time that a payment in respect of any part of the consideration which has been retained, pursuant to the terms of the contract, is received by the supplier, or

(ii) the time that the supplier issues a VAT invoice relating to any such part.

Former regulations—VAT (General) Regulations, SI 1985/886 reg 22; VAT (General) (Amendment) Regulations, SI 1992/3102 reg 16.

Amendments—[1] Words inserted by the VAT (Amendment) (No 5) Regulations, SI 1997/2887 with effect from 1 January 1998.

[2] Reference revoked by the VAT (Amendment) (No 6) Regulations, SI 2003/3220 regs 1(1)(*b*), 2, 16 with effect from 1 January 2004.

Continuous supplies of services

90— (1) Subject to paragraph (2) below, where services[, except those to which regulation 93 applies,][2] are supplied for a period for a consideration the whole or part of which is determined or payable periodically or from time to time, they shall be treated as separately and successively supplied at the earlier of the following times—

(*a*) each time that a payment in respect of the supplies is received by the supplier, or

(*b*) each time that the supplier issues a VAT invoice relating to the supplies.

(2) Where separate and successive supplies of services as described in paragraph (1) above are made under an agreement which provides for successive payments, and the supplier at or about the beginning of any period not exceeding one year, issues a VAT invoice containing, in addition to the particulars specified in regulation 14, the following particulars—

(*a*) the dates on which payments under the agreement are to become due in the period,

(*b*) the amount payable (excluding VAT) on each such date, and

(*c*) the rate of VAT in force at the time of issue of the VAT invoice and the amount of VAT chargeable in accordance with that rate on each of such payments,

services shall be treated as separately and successively supplied each time that a payment in respect of them becomes due or is received by the supplier, whichever is the earlier.

(3) Where, on or before any of the dates that a payment is due as stated on an invoice issued as described in paragraph (2) above, there is a change in the VAT chargeable on supplies of the

description to which the invoice relates, that invoice shall cease to be treated as a VAT invoice in respect of any such supplies for which payments are due after the change (and not received before the change).

[(4) This regulation shall not apply to any relevant services—

(*a*) where the period to which a payment falling within paragraph (1), (2) or (3) above relates, ends before 1st July 1997; or

(*b*) which are treated as supplied on 1st July 1997 by virtue of regulation 90A below.][1]

[(5) In this regulation and in regulations 90A and 90B below, "relevant services" means services within the description contained in paragraph 7A of Schedule 5 to the Act (*c*) which are treated as supplied in the United Kingdom by virtue of [article 18][3] of the Value Added Tax (Place of Supply of Services) Order 1992.][1]

Former regulations—VAT (General) Regulations, SI 1985/886 reg 23; VAT (General) (Amendment) Regulations, SI 1989/1132 reg 5.
Simon's Tax Cases—*C&E Comrs v British Telecom plc* [1996] STC 818*.
Reg 90(1), *B J Rice & Associates v C&E Comrs* [1996] STC 581*; *Royal & Sun Alliance Insurance Group plc v C&E Comrs* [2000] STC 933, [2003] STC 832.
Reg 90(1)(*a*), *C&E Comrs v British Telecom plc* [1995] STC 239*.
Amendments—[1] Paras (4) and (5) inserted by the VAT (Amendment) (No 2) Regulations, SI 1997/1525 with effect from 1 July 1997.
[2] Words inserted by the VAT (Amendment) (No 5) Regulations, SI 1997/2887 with effect from 1 January 1998.
[3] Words amended by the VAT (Amendment) (No 2) Regulations, SI 1998/765 with effect from 18 March 1998.

[**90A** Where—

(*a*) relevant services are supplied for a period for a consideration the whole or part of which is determined or payable periodically or from time to time;

(*b*) the period covered by the payment referred to in sub-paragraph (*c*) below ends on or after 1st July 1997; and

(*c*) a payment in respect of the services was made before 1st July 1997,

the services shall be treated as supplied on 1st July 1997.][1]

Amendments—[1] This regulation inserted by the VAT (Amendment) (No 2) Regulations, SI 1997/1525 with effect from 1 July 1997.

[**90B** Where relevant services are treated as supplied on or after 1st July 1997 by virtue of regulation 90 or 90A above, the supply shall be treated as taking place only to the extent covered by the lower of—

(*a*) the payment; and

(*b*) so much of the payment as is properly attributable to such part of the period covered by the payment as falls after 30th June 1997.][1]

Amendments—[1] This regulation inserted by the VAT (Amendment) (No 2) Regulations, SI 1997/1525 with effect from 1 July 1997.

Royalties and similar payments

91 Where the whole amount of the consideration for a supply of services was not ascertainable at the time when the services were performed and subsequently the use of the benefit of those services by a person other than the supplier gives rise to any payment of consideration for that supply which is—

(*a*) in whole or in part determined or payable periodically or from time to time or at the end of any period,

(*b*) additional to the amount, if any, already payable for the supply, and

(*c*) not a payment to which regulation 90 applies,

a further supply shall be treated as taking place each time that a payment in respect of the use of the benefit of those services is received by the supplier or a VAT invoice is issued by the supplier, whichever is the earlier.

Former regulation—VAT (General) Regulations, SI 1985/886 reg 24.

Supplies of services by barristers and advocates

92 Services supplied by a barrister, or in Scotland, by an advocate, acting in that capacity, shall be treated as taking place at whichever is the earliest of the following times—

(*a*) when the fee in respect of those services is received by the barrister or advocate,

(*b*) when the barrister or advocate issues a VAT invoice in respect of them, or

(*c*) the day when the barrister or advocate ceases to practise as such.

Former regulation—VAT (General) Regulations, SI 1985/886 reg 25.

Supplies in the construction industry

[**93**— (1)Where services, or services together with goods, are supplied in the course of the construction, alteration, demolition, repair or maintenance of a building or any civil engineering work under a contract which provides for payment for such supplies to be made periodically or from time to time, those services or goods and services shall be treated as separately and successively supplied at the earliest of the following times—

(*a*) each time that a payment is received by the supplier,
(*b*) each time that the supplier issues a VAT invoice, or
(*c*) where the services are services to which paragraph (2) below applies, to the extent that they have not already been treated as supplied by virtue of sub-paragraphs (*a*) and (*b*) above—

(i) if the services were performed on or after 9th December 1997 and before 9th June 1999, the day which falls eighteen months after the date on which those services were performed, or
(ii) if the services are performed on or after 9th June 1999, the day on which the services are performed.

(2) This paragraph applies if, at the time the services were, or as the case may require, are performed—

(*a*) it was, or as the case may require, is the intention or expectation of—

(i) the supplier, or
(ii) a person responsible for financing the supplier's cost of supplying the services or services together with goods,

that relevant land would, or as the case may require, will become (whether immediately or eventually) exempt land or, as the case may be, continue (for a period at least) to be such land, or

(*b*) the supplier had, or as the case may require, has received (and used in making his supply) any supply of services or of services together with goods the time of supply of which—

(i) was, or
(ii) but for the issue by the supplier of those services or services together with goods of a VAT invoice (other than one which has been paid in full), would have been,

determined by virtue of paragraph (1)(*c*) above.

(3) For the purposes of this regulation "relevant land" is land on which the building or civil engineering work to which the construction services relate is, or as the case may be, was situated.

(4) In this regulation references to a person's being responsible for financing the supplier's cost of supplying the services or goods and services are references to his being a person who, with the intention or in the expectation that relevant land will become, or continue (for a period at least) to be, exempt land—

(*a*) has provided finance for the supplier's cost of supplying the services or services together with goods, or
(*b*) has entered into any agreement, arrangement or understanding (whether or not legally enforceable) to provide finance for the supplier's cost of supplying the services or services together with goods.

(5) In this regulation references to providing finance for the supplier's cost of supplying services or services together with goods are references to doing any one or more of the following, that is to say—

(*a*) directly or indirectly providing funds for meeting the whole or any part of the supplier's cost of supplying the services or services together with goods,
(*b*) directly or indirectly procuring the provision of such funds by another,
(*c*) directly or indirectly providing funds for discharging, in whole or in part any liability that has been or may be incurred by any person for or in connection with the raising of funds to meet the supplier's cost of supplying the services or services together with goods,
(*d*) directly or indirectly procuring that any such liability is or will be discharged, in whole or in part, by another.

(6) The references in paragraph (5) above to the provision of funds for a purpose referred to in that paragraph include references to—

(*a*) the making of a loan of funds that are or are to be used for that purpose,
(*b*) the provision of any guarantee or other security in relation to such a loan,
(*c*) the provision of any of the consideration for the issue of any shares or other securities issued wholly or partly for raising those funds, or
(*d*) any other transfer of assets or value as a consequence of which any of those funds are made available for that purpose,

but do not include references to funds made available to the supplier by paying to him the whole or any part of the consideration payable for the supply of the services or services together with goods.

(7) In this regulation references to the supplier's cost of supplying the services or services together with goods are to—

(*a*) amounts payable by the supplier for supplies to him of services or of goods used or to be used by him in making the supply of services or of services together with goods, and
(*b*) the supplier's staff and other internal costs of making the supply of services or of services together with goods.

(8) For the purposes of this regulation relevant land is exempt land if—

(*a*) the supplier,

VAT

(*b*) a person responsible for financing the supplier's cost of supplying the services or goods and services, or

(*c*) a person connected with the supplier or with a person responsible for financing the supplier's cost of supplying the services or goods and services,

is in occupation of the land without being in occupation of it wholly or mainly for eligible purposes.

(9) For the purposes of this regulation, but subject to paragraphs (11) and (13) below, a person's occupation at any time of any land is not capable of being occupation for eligible purposes unless he is a taxable person at that time.

(10) Subject to paragraphs (11) and (13) below, a taxable person in occupation of any land shall be taken for the purposes of this regulation to be in occupation of that land for eligible purposes to the extent only that his occupation of that land is for the purpose of making supplies which—

(*a*) are or are to be made in the course or furtherance of a business carried on by him, and

(*b*) are supplies of such a description that any input tax of his which was wholly attributable to those supplies would be input tax for which he would be entitled to credit.

(11) For the purposes of this regulation—

(*a*) occupation of land by a body to which section 33 of the Act applies is occupation of the land for eligible purposes to the extent that the body occupies the land for purposes other than those of a business carried on by that body, and

(*b*) any occupation of land by a government department (within the meaning of section 41 of the Act) is occupation of the land for eligible purposes.

(12) For the purposes of this regulation, where land of which a person is in occupation—

(*a*) is being held by that person in order to be put to use by him for particular purposes, and

(*b*) is not land of which he is in occupation for any other purpose,

that person shall be deemed, for so long as the conditions in sub-paragraphs (*a*) and (*b*) above are satisfied, to be in occupation of the land for the purposes for which he proposes to use it.

(13) Paragraphs (9) to (12) above shall have effect where land is in the occupation of a person who—

(*a*) is not a taxable person, but

(*b*) is a person whose supplies are treated for the purposes of the Act as supplies made by another person who is a taxable person,

as if the person in occupation of the land and that other person were a single taxable person.

(14) For the purposes of this regulation a person shall be taken to be in occupation of any land whether he occupies it alone or together with one or more other persons and whether he occupies all of that land or only part of it.

(15) For the purposes of this regulation, any question as to whether one person is connected with another shall be determined in accordance with section 839 of the Taxes Act[; but this is subject to paragraph (16)][2].

[(16) For the purposes of this regulation—

(*a*) a company is not connected with another company only because both are under the control of—

(i) the Crown,

(ii) a Minister of the Crown,

(iii) a government department, or

(iv) a Northern Ireland department; and

(*b*) "company" and "control" have the same meaning as in section 839 of the Taxes Act][2].][1]

Commentary—*De Voil Indirect Tax Service* **V3.140**.
Former regulation—VAT (General) Regulations, SI 1985/886 reg 26.
Press releases etc—VAT information Sheet 7/99 22-6-99 (new anti-avoidance rules).
Simon's Tax Cases—*Metropolitan Borough of Wirral v C&E Comrs* [1995] STC 597*.
Cross reference—See VAT Regulations, SI 1995/2518 reg 13(4) (authenticated receipts for supplies within this regulation: treatment as VAT invoices).
Amendments—[1] Para substituted by the VAT (Amendment) (No 3) Regulations, SI 1999/1374 with effect from 9 June 1999.
[2] Words in para (15), and whole of para (16), inserted, by the Value Added Tax (Amendment) (No 3) Regulations, SI 2009/1967 regs 2, 4, 5 with effect from 15 August 2009.

General

94 [Subject to regulation 90B above, where under this Part][1] of these Regulations a supply is treated as taking place each time that a payment (however expressed) is received or an invoice is issued, the supply is to be treated as taking place only to the extent covered by the payment or invoice.

Former regulations—VAT (General) Regulations, SI 1985/886 reg 27; VAT (General) (Amendment) Regulations, SI 1992/3102 reg 17.
Amendments—[1] Words substituted for the words "Where under this Part" by the VAT (Amendment) (No 2) Regulations, SI 1997/1525 with effect from 1 July 1997.

[94A In this Part a reference to receipt of payment (however expressed) includes a reference to receipt by a person to whom a right to receive it has been assigned.][1]

Amendments—[1] This regulation inserted by the VAT (Amendment) (No 2) Regulations, SI 1999/599 reg 3, and shall have effect in respect of payments received on or after 10 March 1999.

[94B— (1) This regulation applies in relation to the following supplies where they are provided in the circumstances referred to in paragraph (2) below—

(*a*) supplies falling within regulation 85 above (leases treated as supplies of goods) other than any supply which is exempt by virtue of Group 1 of Schedule 9 to the Act or would be exempt but for the operation of [Part 1 of Schedule 10][2] to the Act;

(*b*) supplies falling within regulation 86(1) to (4) above (supplies of water, gas or any form of power, heat, refrigeration or ventilation);

(*c*) supplies falling within regulation 90 above (continuous supplies of services) other than any supply which is exempt by virtue of Group 1 of Schedule 9 to the Act or would be exempt but for the operation of [Part 1 of Schedule 10][2] to the Act.

(2) The circumstances referred to in paragraph (1) above are—

(*a*) that the person making the supply and the person to whom it is made are connected with each other, or

(*b*) one of those persons is an undertaking in relation to which the other is a group undertaking (except where both undertakings are treated under sections 43A to 43C of the Act as members of the same group), and

(*c*) the supply is subject to the rates of VAT prescribed in section 2 or section 29A of the Act.

(3) But this regulation does not apply where a person can show that a person to whom he has made a supply of a description falling within paragraph (1) above is entitled under sections 25 and 26 of the Act to credit for all of the VAT on that supply.

[(4) For the purposes of paragraph (2)—

(*a*) any question whether one person is connected with another shall be determined in accordance with section 839 of the Taxes Act;

(*b*) a company is not connected with another company only because both are under the control of—

(i) the Crown,
(ii) a Minister of the Crown,
(iii) a government department, or
(iv) a Northern Ireland department;

(*c*) "company" and "control" have the same meaning as in section 839 of the Taxes Act; and

(*d*) "undertaking" and "group undertaking" have the same meaning as in section 1161 of the Companies Act 2006.][3]

(5) Where this regulation applies, goods or services shall, to the extent that they have not already been treated as supplied by virtue of the regulations specified in paragraph (1) above (or any provision of the Act or other regulations made under the Act), and to the extent that they have been provided, be treated as separately and successively supplied—

(*a*) in the case of supplies the provision of which commenced on or before 1st October 2003, at the end of the period of twelve months after that date;

(*b*) in the case of supplies the provision of which commenced after 1st October 2003, at the end of the period of twelve months after the supplies commenced; or

(*c*) where the Commissioners are satisfied that each category of supply has been adequately identified, on such other period end date nominated for each category and falling within the period specified in sub-paragraph (5)(*a*) or (*b*) above as may be notified by the taxable person to the Commissioners in writing,

and thereafter at the end of each subsequent period of twelve months.

(6) But where the person making the supply, within the period of six months after the time applicable under paragraph (5) above either—

(*a*) issues a VAT invoice in respect of it, or

(*b*) receives a payment in respect of it,

the supply shall, to the extent that it has not been treated as taking place at some other time by virtue of the regulations specified in paragraph (1) above (or any provision of the Act or other regulations made under the Act), be treated as taking place at the time the invoice is issued or the payment is received, unless the person making the supply has notified the Commissioners in writing that he elects not to avail himself of this paragraph.

(7) The Commissioners may, at the request of a taxable person, allow paragraph (6) above to apply in relation to supplies made by him (or such supplies as may be specified) as if for the period of six months there were substituted such other period as may be prescribed by them.

(8) A taxable person may after the start of any period to be established under paragraph (5) above—

(*a*) in relation to some or all of his supplies, and

(*b*) where the Commissioners give their approval,

select an alternative period end date falling before the end of that period (which end date but for this paragraph would be established under paragraph (5) above), from which date subsequent periods of twelve months will end.

(9) A date selected and approved under paragraph (8) above shall be the date which establishes the end of the taxable person's current period.

(10) For the purposes of paragraph (8) above, a reference to a period end established under paragraph (5) above includes a reference to a period end established by an earlier application of paragraph (8) above.

(11) Where the supply is one of the leasing of assets, and that leasing depends on one or more other leases of those assets (the superior lease or leases), then the reference in paragraph (2) above to the person making the supply includes a reference to any lessor of a superior lease.

(12) For the purposes of paragraph (11) above, a reference to the leasing of assets includes a reference to any letting, hiring or rental of assets however described, and "lessor" shall be construed accordingly.

(13) For the purposes of this regulation, goods or services are provided at the time when and to the extent that, the recipient receives the benefit of them.

(14) Where this regulation applies, the regulations specified in paragraph (1) above shall not apply to the extent that supplies have been treated as having taken place under this regulation.][1]

Amendments—[1] Regulation 94B inserted by the VAT (Amendment) (No 5) Regulations, SI 2003/2318 regs 2, 3 with effect from 1 October 2003. This insertion has effect for supplies of goods or services the benefit of which was received after the coming into force of SI 2003/2318.

[2] Words in para (1)(*a*), (*c*) substituted by the Value Added Tax (Buildings and Land) Order, SI 2008/1146, art 6, Sch 1 paras 16, 18 with effect in relation to supplies made on or after 1 June 2008, subject to savings in Sch 2 of the Order.

[3] Para (4) substituted by the Value Added Tax (Amendment) (No 3) Regulations, SI 2009/1967 regs 2, 6 with effect from 15 August 2009. Para (4) previously read as follows—

"(4) For the purposes of paragraph (2) above, any question whether a person is connected with another shall be determined in accordance with section 839 of the Income and Corporation Taxes Act 1988 and "undertaking" and "group undertaking" have the same meaning as in section 1161 of the Companies Act 2006.".

Supplies spanning change of rate etc

95 Section 88 of the Act shall apply as if the references in subsection (2) of that section to section 6(4), (5), (6) and (10) of the Act included references to regulations 81, 82, [82A,][2] 84, 85, 86(1) to (4) ...[,][1] 88 to 93 [and 94B][1] of these Regulations.

Former regulations—VAT (General) Regulations, SI 1985/886 reg 28; VAT (General) (Amendment) Regulations, SI 1992/3102 reg 18.

Amendments—[1] This regulation amended by the VAT (Amendment) (No 5) Regulations, SI 2003/2318 regs 2, 4 with effect from 1 October 2003. The amendments have effect for supplies of goods or services the benefit of which was received after the coming into force of SI 2003/2318.

[2] Reference inserted by the VAT (Amendment) (No 4) Regulations, SI 2004/3140 reg 5 with effect from 1 January 2005 in relation to supplies made on or after that date: SI 2004/3140 reg 2(1).

PART XII
VALUATION OF ACQUISITIONS

Interpretation of Part XII

96 In this Part—

"relevant transaction", in relation to any acquisition of goods from another member State, and "relevant time" in relation to any such acquisition, have the meanings given in paragraph 5 of Schedule 7 to the Act.

Former regulation—VAT (Valuation of Acquisitions) Regulations, SI 1992/3099 reg 2(3).

Valuation of acquisitions

97— (1) Subject to paragraph (2) below, the value of the relevant transaction in relation to any goods acquired in the United Kingdom from another member State where—

(*a*) the goods are charged in connection with their removal to the United Kingdom with a duty of excise; or

(*b*) on that removal are subject, in accordance with any provision for the time being having effect for transitional purposes in connection with the accession of any State to the European Communities, to any Community customs duty or agricultural levy of the Economic Community,

shall be taken, for the purposes of the Act, to be the sum of its value apart from paragraph 2 of Schedule 7 to the Act and the amount, so far as not already included in that value, of the excise duty, Community customs duty or, as the case may be, agricultural levy which has been or is to be paid in respect of those goods.

(2) Paragraph (1) above does not apply to a transaction in pursuance of which there is an acquisition of goods which, under subsection (4) of section 18 of the Act, is treated as taking place before the duty point within the meaning of that section.

Former regulation—VAT (Valuation of Acquisitions) Regulations, SI 1992/3099 reg 2(1), (2).

PART XIII
PLACE OF SUPPLY

Distance sales from the United Kingdom

98— (1) Where a person has exercised an option in the United Kingdom corresponding to an option mentioned in paragraph 1(2) of Schedule 2 to the Act, in respect of supplies involving the removal of goods to another member State, he shall notify the Commissioners in writing of the exercise of that option not less than 30 days before the date on which the first supply to which the option relates is made,

(2) The notification referred to in paragraph (1) above shall contain the name of the member State to which the goods have been, or are to be, removed under the direction or control of the person making the supply.

(3) Any person who has notified the Commissioners in accordance with paragraph (1) above shall within 30 days of the date of the first supply as is mentioned in that paragraph furnish to the Commissioners documentary evidence that he has notified the member State of the exercise of his option,

(4) Where a person has notified the Commissioners in accordance with paragraph (1) above he may withdraw his notification by giving a further written notification but that further notification must specify the date upon which the first notification is to be withdrawn, which date must not be earlier than—

(*a*) the 1st January which is, or next follows, the second anniversary of the date of the making of the first supply mentioned above to which the option relates, and

(*b*) the day 30 days after the receipt by the Commissioners of the further notification, and not later than 30 days before the date of the first supply which he intends to make after the withdrawal.

Former regulations—VAT (General) Regulations, SI 1985/886 reg 9A; VAT (General) (Amendment) Regulations, SI 1993/1224.

PART XIV
INPUT TAX AND PARTIAL EXEMPTION

Interpretation of Part XIV and longer periods

99— (1) In this Part—

[(*a*) "exempt input tax" means input tax incurred by a taxable person on goods imported or acquired by, or goods or services supplied to, him in so far as they are used by him or are to be used by him, or a successor of his, in making exempt supplies, or supplies outside the United Kingdom which would be exempt if made in the United Kingdom, other than any input tax which is allowable under regulation [101][5] [[102,][4] 103, 103A or 103B][3];

and "successor" in this paragraph has the same meaning as in regulation 107D;][2]

(*b*) "prescribed accounting period" means—

(i) a prescribed accounting period such as is referred to in regulation 25, or

(ii) a special accounting period, where the first prescribed accounting period would otherwise be 6 months or longer, save that this paragraph shall not apply where the reference to the prescribed accounting period is used solely in order to identify a particular return;

(*c*) "special accounting period" means each of a succession of periods of the same length as the next prescribed accounting period which does not exceed 3 months, and—

(i) the last such period shall end on the day before the commencement of that next prescribed accounting period, and

(ii) the first such period shall commence on the effective date of registration determined in accordance with Schedule 1[, 2, 3 or 3A][1] to the Act and end on the day before the commencement of the second such period;

(*d*) the "tax year" of a taxable person means—

(i) the first period of 12 calendar months commencing on the first day of April, May or June, according to the prescribed accounting periods allocated to him, next following his effective date of registration determined in accordance with Schedule 1[, 2, 3 or 3A][1] to the Act, or

(ii) any subsequent period of 12 calendar months commencing on the day following the end of his first, or any subsequent, tax year,

save that the Commissioners may approve or direct that a tax year shall be a period of other than 12 calendar months or that it shall commence on a date other than that determined in accordance with paragraph (i) or (ii) above;

(*e*) the "registration period" of a taxable person means the period commencing on his effective date of registration determined in accordance with Schedule 1[, 2, 3 or 3A][1] to the Act and ending on the day before the commencement of his first tax year.

(2) In this Part, any reference to goods or services shall be construed as including a reference to anything which is supplied by way of a supply of goods or a supply of services respectively.

(3) The provisions of paragraphs (4), (5), (6) and (7) below shall be used for determining the longer period applicable to taxable persons under this Part.

(4) A taxable person who incurs exempt input tax during any tax year shall have applied to him a longer period which shall correspond with that tax year unless he did not incur exempt input tax during his immediately preceding tax year or registration period, in which case his longer period shall—

(*a*) begin on the first day of the first prescribed accounting period in which he incurs exempt input tax, and

(*b*) end on the last day of that tax year,

except where he incurs exempt input tax only in the last prescribed accounting period of his tax year, in which case no longer period shall be applied to him in respect of that tax year.

(5) A taxable person who incurs exempt input tax during his registration period shall have applied to him a longer period which shall begin on the first day on which he incurs exempt input tax and end on the day before the commencement of his first tax year.

(6) In the case of a taxable person ceasing to be taxable during a longer period applicable to him, that longer period shall end on the day when he ceases to be taxable.

(7) The Commissioners may approve in the case of a taxable person who incurs exempt input tax, or a class of such persons, that a longer period shall apply which need not correspond with a tax year.

Former regulations—Para (1): VAT (General) Regulations, SI 1985/886 reg 29(1); VAT (General) (Amendment) Regulations, SI 1992/645, regs 1–3, SI 1992/3102 reg 19, SI 1993/1639 reg 3.

Para (2): VAT (General) Regulations, SI 1985/886 reg 29(1A); VAT (General) (Amendment) Regulations, SI 1992/3102 reg 19.

Paras (3)–(7): VAT (General) Regulations, SI 1985/886 reg 29(2)–(6); VAT (General) (Amendment) Regulations, SI 1992/645, regs 1–3.

Amendments—[1] Words in para (1)(*c*), (*d*), (*e*) inserted by the VAT (Amendment) (No 3) Regulations, SI 2000/794 regs 2, 6 with effect from 22 March 2000.

[2] Para (1)(*a*) substituted by the VAT (Amendment) Regulations, SI 2002/1074 regs 2, 3, with effect for input tax incurred by a taxable person on goods imported or acquired by, or goods or services supplied to, him after 17 April 2002.

[3] In sub-para (1)(*a*), references substituted by the VAT (Amendment) (No 4) Regulations, SI 2004/3140 reg 9 with effect from 3 December 2004: SI 2004/3140 reg 2(3).

[4] Reference in para (1)(*a*) inserted by the VAT (Amendment) (No 2) Regulations, SI 2007/768 regs 2, 6 with effect from 1 April 2007.

[5] Reference in para (1)(*a*) inserted by the VAT (Amendment) (No 2) Regulations, SI 2009/820 regs 2, 3 with effect in relation to input tax incurred by a taxable person on goods imported or acquired by, or goods or services supplied to, him on or after 1 April 2009. Where 31 March 2009 falls within the prescribed accounting period of a taxable person, the amendments made by SI 2009/820 shall not, in relation to that taxable person, have effect until the day after the end of that prescribed accounting period (SI 2009/820reg 1(2)).

100 Nothing in this Part shall be construed as allowing a taxable person to deduct the whole or any part of VAT on the importation or acquisition by him of goods or the supply to him of goods or services where those goods or services are not used or to be used by him in making supplies in the course or furtherance of a business carried on by him.

Former regulations—VAT (General) Regulations, SI 1985/886 reg 29A; VAT (General) (Amendment) Regulations, SI 1993/1639 reg 4.

Attribution of input tax to taxable supplies

101— (1) Subject to regulation 102 [and [103A][5]][2], the amount of input tax which a taxable person shall be entitled to deduct provisionally shall be that amount which is attributable to taxable supplies in accordance with this regulation.

(2) [Subject to paragraph (8) below and regulation 107(1)(*g*)(ii),][5] in respect of each prescribed accounting period—

(*a*) goods imported or acquired by and …[1] goods or services supplied to, the taxable person in the period shall be identified,

(*b*) there shall be attributed to taxable supplies the whole of the input tax on such of those goods or services as are used or to be used by him exclusively in making taxable supplies,

(*c*) no part of the input tax on such of those goods or services as are used or to be used by him exclusively in making exempt supplies, or in carrying on any activity other than the making of taxable supplies, shall be attributed to taxable supplies, …[5]

(*d*) [where a taxable person does not have an immediately preceding longer period and subject to subparagraph (*e*) below,][5] there shall be attributed to taxable supplies such proportion of the [residual input tax][5] as bears the same ratio to the total of such input tax as the value of taxable supplies made by him bears to the value of all supplies made by him in the period,

[(*e*) the attribution required by subparagraph (*d*) above may be made on the basis of the extent to which the goods or services are used or to be used by him in making taxable supplies,

(*f*) where a taxable person has an immediately preceding longer period and subject to subparagraph (*g*) below, his residual input tax shall be attributed to taxable supplies by reference to the percentage recovery rate for that immediately preceding longer period, and

(*g*) the attribution required by subparagraph (*f*) above may be made using the calculation specified in subparagraph (*d*) above provided that that calculation is used for all the prescribed accounting periods which fall within any longer period applicable to a taxable person.][5]

(3) In calculating the proportion under paragraph (2)(*d*) [or (g)][5] above, there shall be excluded—

(*a*) any sum receivable by the taxable person in respect of any supply of capital goods used by him for the purposes of his business,

(*b*) any sum receivable by the taxable person in respect of any of the following descriptions of supplies made by him, where such supplies are incidental to one or more of his business activities—

[(i) any supply of a description falling within Group 5 of Schedule 9 to the Act,

(ii) any other financial transaction, and

(iii) any real estate transaction,][4]

(*c*) that part of the value of any supply of goods on which output tax is not chargeable by virtue of any order made by the Treasury under section 25(7) of the Act unless the taxable person has imported, acquired or been supplied with the goods for the purpose of selling them, …[5]

(*d*) the value of any supply which, under or by virtue of any provision of the Act, the taxable person makes to himself, [and][5]

(*e*) supplies of a description falling within paragraph (8) below.][5]

(4) The ratio calculated for the purpose of paragraph (2)(*d*)[, (*e*) or (*g*)][5] above shall be expressed as a percentage and, if that percentage is not a whole number, it shall be rounded up [as specified in paragraph (5) below][3].

[(5) The percentage shall be rounded up—

(*a*) where in any prescribed accounting period or longer period which is applied the amount of input tax which is available for attribution under paragraph 2(*d*)[, (*e*) or (*g*)][5] above prior to any such attribution being made does not amount to more than £400,000 per month on average, to the next whole number, and

(*b*) in any other case, to two decimal places.][3]

[(6) For the purposes of this regulation, a "real estate transaction" includes any grant, assignment (including any transfer, disposition or sale), surrender or reverse surrender of any interest in, right over or licence to occupy land.][4]

[(7) In this regulation "taxable supplies" include supplies of a description falling within regulation 103.

(8) Input tax incurred on goods or services acquired by or supplied to a taxable person which are used or to be used by him in whole or in part in making—

(*a*) supplies falling within either item 1 or item 6 of Group 5 of Schedule 9 to the Act; or

(*b*) supplies made from an establishment situated outside the United Kingdom,

shall, whether the supply in question is made within or outside the United Kingdom, be attributed to taxable supplies on the basis of the extent to which the goods or services are used or to be used by him in making taxable supplies.

(9) For the purposes of this regulation in relation to a taxable person—

(*a*) "immediately preceding longer period" means the longer period applicable to him which ends immediately before the longer period in which the prescribed accounting period in respect of which he is making the attribution required by paragraph (2)(*d*) to (*g*) above falls;

(*b*) "percentage recovery rate" means the amount of relevant residual input tax which he was entitled to attribute to taxable supplies under regulation 107(1)(*a*) to (*d*), expressed as a percentage of the total amount of the residual input tax which fell to be so attributed and rounded up in accordance with paragraphs (4) and (5) above;

(*c*) "relevant residual input tax" means all residual input tax other than that which falls to be attributed under paragraph (8) above.

(10) In this regulation "residual input tax" means input tax incurred by a taxable person on goods or services which are used or to be used by him in making both taxable and exempt supplies.][5]

Commentary—*De Voil Indirect Tax Service* **V3.460–V3.467**.

Former regulations—Paras (1), (2): VAT (General) Regulations, SI 1985/886 reg 30(1), (2); VAT (General) (Amendment) Regulations, SI 1992/645 regs 1–3, SI 1992/3102 reg 20.

Paras (3), (4): VAT (General) Regulations, SI 1985/886 reg 30(3), (4); VAT (General) (Amendment) Regulations, SI 1992/645 regs 1–3, SI 1992/3102 reg 20.

Para (5): VAT (General) Regulations, SI 1985/886 reg 30(2A); VAT (General) (Amendment) Regulations, SI 1995/1069 reg 3.

Simon's Tax Cases—*C&E Comrs v Harpcombe Ltd* [1996] STC 726*; *C&E Comrs v Southern Primary Housing Association Ltd* [2003] STC 525; *Banbury Visionplus Ltd v R&C Comrs and other appeals* [2006] STC 1568; *MBNA Europe Bank Ltd v R&C Comrs* [2006] STC 2089; *Royal Bank of Scotland Group plc v R&C Comrs* [2008] STC 1485.

Reg 101(1), *C&E Comrs v Dennis Rye Ltd* [1996] STC 27*.

Reg 101(2), *Dial-a-Phone Ltd v C&E Comrs* [2003] STC 192; [2004] STC 987.

Reg 101(2)(*c*), (*d*), *RAP Group plc v C&E Comrs* [2000] STC 980; *Mayflower Theatre Trust Ltd v R&C Comrs* [2007] STC 880.

Reg 101(2)(*d*), *C&E Comrs v Liverpool Institute for Performing Arts* [2001] STC 891*.

Reg 101(3), *C&E Comrs v JDL Ltd* [2001] STC 1.

Amendments—[1] Words in para (2)(*a*) deleted by the VAT (Amendment) (No 3) Regulations, SI 1996/1250 reg 14, with effect from 1 June 1996 except that where 28 April 1996 fell within a taxable person's prescribed accounting period which ended on or after 1 June 1996, the Amendment has effect in relation to that taxable person from the day after the end of that prescribed accounting period.

[2] In para (1), reference inserted by the VAT (Amendment) (No 4) Regulations, SI 2004/3140 reg 10 with effect from 3 December 2004: SI 2004/3140 reg 2(3).

[3] Words in para (4) substituted for words "to the whole next number", and para (5) inserted, by the VAT (Amendment) Regulations, SI 2005/762 reg 3 with effect from 1 April 2005. Where 31 March 2005 falls within the prescribed accounting

period of a taxable person, the amendments shall not, in relation to that taxable person, have effect until the day after the end of that prescribed accounting period: SI 2005/762 reg 1.

4 In para (3) sub-paras (i)–(iii) substituted for original sub-paras (i)–(v), and para (6) inserted, by the VAT (Amendment) (No 2) Regulations, SI 2007/768 regs 2, 7 with effect from 1 April 2007.

5 In para (1), reference substituted for reference "103B", in para (2), words inserted at beginning, at end of sub-para (*c*) word "and" repealed, in sub-para (*d*) words inserted at beginning and words substituted for words "input tax on such of those goods or services as are used or to be used by him in making both taxable and exempt supplies", and sub-paras (*e*)–(*g*) inserted, in para (3), words inserted, in sub-para (*c*) word "and" repealed, sub-para (*e*) and preceding word "and" inserted, in paras (4), (5), words inserted, and paras (7)–(10) inserted, by the VAT (Amendment) (No 2) Regulations, SI 2009/820 regs 2, 4 with effect in relation to input tax incurred by a taxable person on goods imported or acquired by, or goods or services supplied to, him on or after 1 April 2009. Where 31 March 2009 falls within the prescribed accounting period of a taxable person, the amendments made by SI 2009/820 shall not, in relation to that taxable person, have effect until the day after the end of that prescribed accounting period (SI 2009/820reg 1(2)).

Use of other methods

102— (1) Subject to [paragraphs (2) and (9)][3] below and [regulations 103, 103A and 103B][1], the Commissioners may approve or direct the use by a taxable person of a method other than that specified in regulation 101 ...

[(1A) A method approved or directed under paragraph (1) above—

(*a*) shall be in writing,

(*b*) may attribute input tax which would otherwise fall to be attributed under regulation 103 provided that, where it attributes any such input tax, it shall attribute it all, and

(*c*) shall identify the supplies in respect of which it attributes input tax by reference to the relevant paragraph or paragraphs of section 26(2) of the Act.][3]

(2) Notwithstanding any provision of any method approved or directed to be used under this regulation which purports to have the contrary effect, in calculating the proportion of any input tax on goods or services used or to be used by the taxable person in making both taxable and exempt supplies which is to be treated as attributable to taxable supplies, the value of any supply [of a description falling within regulation [101(3)(*a*) to (*d*)][4] whether made within or outside the United Kingdom][3] shall be excluded.

(3) A taxable person using a method as approved or directed to be used by the Commissioners under paragraph (1) above shall continue to use that method unless the Commissioners approve or direct the termination of its use.

(4) Any direction under paragraph (1) or (3) above shall take effect from the date upon which the Commissioners give such direction or from such later date as they may specify.

[(5) Any approval given or direction made under this regulation shall only have effect if it is in writing in the form of a document which identifies itself as being such an approval or direction.][2]

[(6) Where a taxable person who is using a method which has been approved or directed under this regulation incurs input tax of the description in paragraph (7) below, that input tax shall be attributed to taxable supplies to the extent that the goods or services are used or to be used in making taxable supplies expressed as a proportion of the whole use or intended use.][2]

[(7) The input tax referred to in paragraph (6) above is input tax—

(*a*) the attribution of which to taxable supplies is not prescribed in whole or in part by the method referred to in paragraph (6) above, and

(*b*) which does not fall to be attributed to taxable or other supplies as specified under regulations 103, 103A or 103B.][2]

[(8) Where the input tax specified in paragraph (7)(*a*) above is input tax the attribution of which to taxable supplies is only in part not prescribed by the method, only that part the attribution of which is not so prescribed shall fall within that paragraph.][2]

[(9) With effect from 1st April 2007 the Commissioners shall not approve the use of a method under this regulation unless the taxable person has made a declaration to the effect that to the best of his knowledge and belief the method fairly and reasonably represents the extent to which goods or services are used by or are to be used by him in making taxable supplies.

(10) The declaration referred to in paragraph (9) above shall—

(*a*) be in writing,

(*b*) be signed by the taxable person or by a person authorised to sign it on his behalf, and

(*c*) include a statement that the person signing it has taken reasonable steps to ensure that he is in possession of all relevant information.

(11) Where it appears to the Commissioners that a declaration made under this regulation is incorrect in that—

(*a*) the method does not fairly and reasonably represent the extent to which goods or services are used by or are to be used by the taxable person in making taxable supplies, and

(*b*) the person who signed the declaration knew or ought reasonably to have known this at the time when the declaration was made by the taxable person,

they may subject to paragraph (12) below serve on the taxable person a notice to that effect setting out their reasons in support of that notification and stating the effect of the notice.

(12) The Commissioners shall not serve a notice under this regulation unless they are satisfied that the overall result of the application of the method is an over-deduction of input tax by the taxable person.

(13) Subject to paragraph (14) below, the effect of a notice served under this regulation is that regulation 102B(1) shall apply to the person served with the notice in relation to—

(*a*) prescribed accounting periods commencing on or after the effective date of the method, and

(*b*) longer periods to the extent of that part of the longer period falling on or after the effective date of the method, save that no adjustment shall be required in relation to any part of any prescribed accounting period,

unless or until the method is terminated under regulation 102(3).

(14) In relation to any past prescribed accounting periods, the Commissioners may assess the amount of VAT due to the best of their judgement and notify it to the taxable person unless they allow him to account for the difference in such manner and within such time as they may require.

(15) The service of a notice on a taxable person under this regulation shall be without prejudice to the Commissioners' powers to serve a notice on him under regulation 102A and any notice served under regulation 102A shall take priority in relation to the periods which it covers.

(16) In this regulation "the effective date of the method" is the date when the method to which the declaration relates first takes effect and may predate the date when the declaration was made.

(17) In this regulation and in regulations 102A, 102B, 102C and 107, where paragraph (1A)(*b*) above applies, "taxable supplies" includes supplies of a description falling within regulation 103.][3]

Commentary—*De Voil Indirect Tax Service* **V3.460–V3.467**.

Former regulations—Para (1): VAT (General) Regulations, SI 1985/886 reg 31(1); VAT (General) (Amendment) Regulations, SI 1992/645 regs 1–3, SI 1994/3015 reg 3.

Para (2): VAT (General) Regulations, SI 1985/886 reg 31(1A); VAT (General) (Amendment) Regulations, SI 1994/3015 reg 3.

Paras (3), (4): VAT (General) Regulations, SI 1985/886 reg 31(2), (3); VAT (General) (Amendment) Regulations, SI 1992/645 regs 1–3.

Simon's Tax Cases—*Kwik-Fit (GB) Ltd v C&E Comrs* [1998] STC 159; *Banbury Visionplus Ltd v R&C Comrs and other appeals* [2006] STC 1568; *MBNA Europe Bank Ltd v R&C Comrs* [2006] STC 2089; *DCM (Optical Holdings) Ltd v R&C Comrs* [2008] STC 1294.

Press releases etc—HMRC Brief 23/07, 14-3-07 (guidance on preparing and submitting the new Declaration required for all partial exemption special method applications approved on or after 1 April 2007, including a template for the Declaration).

Amendments—[1] In para (1), references substituted by the VAT (Amendment) (No 4) Regulations, SI 2004/3140 reg 11 with effect from 3 December 2004: SI 2004/3140 reg 2(3).

[2] Paras (5)–(8) inserted by the VAT (Amendment) Regulations, SI 2005/762 reg 4 with effect from 1 April 2005.

[3] Words in para (1) substituted and omitted, paras (1A) and (9)–(17) inserted, and words in para (2) substituted, by the VAT (Amendment) (No 2) Regulations, SI 2007/768 regs 2, 8 with effect from 1 April 2007.

[4] In para (2), words substituted for words "101(3)" by the VAT (Amendment) (No 2) Regulations, SI 2009/820 regs 2, 5 with effect in relation to input tax incurred by a taxable person on goods imported or acquired by, or goods or services supplied to, him on or after 1 April 2009. Where 31 March 2009 falls within the prescribed accounting period of a taxable person, the amendments made by SI 2009/820 shall not, in relation to that taxable person, have effect until the day after the end of that prescribed accounting period (SI 2009/820 reg 1(2)).

[102A— (1) [Notwithstanding the Commissioners' powers to serve a notice under regulation 102,][2] where a taxable person—

(*a*) is for the time being using a method approved or directed under regulation 102, and

(*b*) that method does not fairly and reasonably represent the extent to which goods or services are used by him or are to be used by him in making taxable supplies,

the Commissioners may serve on him a notice to that effect, setting out their reasons in support of that notification and stating the effect of the notice.

(2) The effect of a notice served under this regulation is that regulation 102B shall apply to the person served with the notice in relation to—

(*a*) prescribed accounting periods commencing on or after the date of the notice or such later date as may be specified in the notice, and

(*b*) longer periods to the extent of that part of the longer period falling on or after the date of the notice or such later date as may be specified in the notice.][1]

Amendments—[1] Regulations 102A–102C inserted by the VAT (Amendment) (No 6) Regulations, SI 2003/3220 regs 1(1)(*b*), (2), 2, 21 with effect for input tax incurred by a taxable person on goods imported or acquired by, or goods or services supplied to, him after 31 December 2003.

[2] Words in para (1) inserted by the VAT (Amendment) (No 2) Regulations, SI 2007/768 regs 2, 9 with effect from 1 April 2007.

[102B— (1) Where this regulation applies, a taxable person shall calculate the difference between—

(*a*) the attribution made by him in any prescribed accounting period or longer period, and

(*b*) an attribution which represents the extent to which the goods or services are used by him or are to be used by him in making taxable supplies,

and account for the difference on the return for that prescribed accounting period or on the return on which that longer period adjustment is required to be made, except where the Commissioners allow another return to be used for this purpose.

(2) This regulation shall apply from the date prescribed under regulation 102A(2) or 102C(2), unless or until the method referred to in regulation 102A(1)(*a*) or 102C(1)(*a*) is terminated under regulation 102(3).][1]

Amendments—[1] Regulations 102A–102C inserted by the VAT (Amendment) (No 6) Regulations, SI 2003/3220 regs 1(1)(*b*), (2), 2, 21 with effect for input tax incurred by a taxable person on goods imported or acquired by, or goods or services supplied to, him after 31 December 2003.

[102C— (1) Subject to regulation 102A, where a taxable person—

(*a*) is for the time being using a method approved or directed under regulation 102, and

(*b*) that method does not fairly and reasonably represent the extent to which goods or services are used by him or are to be used by him in making taxable supplies,

the taxable person may serve on the Commissioners a notice to that effect, setting out his reasons in support of that notification.

(2) Where the Commissioners approve a notice served under this regulation, the effect is that regulation 102B shall apply to the person serving the notice in relation to—

(*a*) prescribed accounting periods commencing on or after the date of the notice or such later date as may be specified in the notice, and

(*b*) longer periods to the extent of that part of the longer period falling on or after the date of the notice or such later date as may be specified in the notice.][1]

Amendments—[1] Regulations 102A–102C inserted by the VAT (Amendment) (No 6) Regulations, SI 2003/3220 regs 1(1)(*b*), (2), 2, 21 with effect for input tax incurred by a taxable person on goods imported or acquired by, or goods or services supplied to, him after 31 December 2003.

Attribution of input tax to foreign and specified supplies

103— Other than where it falls to be attributed under [regulation 101 or][4] a method approved or directed by the Commissioners under regulation 102,][3] …[2] Input tax incurred by a taxable person in any prescribed accounting period on goods imported or acquired by, or goods or services supplied to, him which are used or to be used by him in whole or in part in making—

(*a*) supplies outside the United Kingdom which would be taxable supplies if made in the United Kingdom, or

(*b*) supplies specified in an Order under section 26(2)(*c*) of the Act, [other than supplies of a description falling within regulation 103A below,][1]

shall be attributed to taxable supplies to the extent that the goods or services are so used or to be used expressed as a proportion of the whole use or intended use.

(2), (3) …[2]

Former regulations—VAT (General) Regulations, SI 1985/886 reg 32; VAT (General) (Amendment) Regulations, SI 1994/3015 reg 4.

Simon's Tax Cases—*C&E Comrs v Liverpool Institute for Performing Arts* [2001] STC 891*; *MBNA Europe Bank Ltd v R&C Comrs* [2006] STC 2089.

Amendments—[1] Words inserted by the VAT (Amendment) (No 4) Regulations, SI 1999/3114, regs 2, 7, with effect from 1 January 2000.

[2] Paragraph numbering and paras (2), (3) revoked by the VAT (Amendment) (No 4) Regulations, SI 2004/3140 reg 7 with effect from 3 December 2004: SI 2004/3140 reg 2(3).

[3] Words inserted by the VAT (Amendment) (No 2) Regulations, SI 2007/768 regs 2, 10 with effect from 1 April 2007.

[4] Words inserted by the VAT (Amendment) (No 2) Regulations, SI 2009/820 regs 2, 6 with effect in relation to input tax incurred by a taxable person on goods imported or acquired by, or goods or services supplied to, him on or after 1 April 2009. Where 31 March 2009 falls within the prescribed accounting period of a taxable person, the amendments made by SI 2009/820 shall not, in relation to that taxable person, have effect until the day after the end of that prescribed accounting period (SI 2009/820reg 1(2)).

[Attribution of input tax to investment gold][2]

[103A— (1) This regulation applies to a taxable person who makes supplies of a description falling within item 1 or 2 of Group 15 of Schedule 9 to the Act.]

(2) Input tax incurred by him in any prescribed accounting period in respect of supplies by him of a description falling within paragraph (1) above shall be allowable as being attributable to those supplies only to the following extent, that is to say where it is incurred—

(*a*) on investment gold supplied to him which but for an election made under the Value Added Tax (Investment Gold) Order 1999, or but for Note 4(*b*) to Group 15 of Schedule 9 to the Act would have fallen within item 1 or 2 of that Group, or on investment gold acquired by him;

(*b*) on a supply to him, an acquisition by him, or on an importation by him of gold other than investment gold which is to be transformed by him or on his behalf into investment gold;

(*c*) on services supplied to him comprising a change of form, weight or purity of gold.

(3) Where a taxable person produces investment gold or transforms any gold into investment gold he shall also be entitled to credit for input tax incurred by him on any goods or services supplied to him, any acquisitions of goods by him or any importations of goods by him, but only to the extent that they are linked to the production or transformation of that gold into investment gold.

(4) Where input tax has been incurred on goods or services which are used or to be used in making supplies of a description falling within item 1 or 2 of Group 15 of Schedule 9 to the Act and any other supply, that input tax shall be attributed to the supplies falling within item 1 or 2 to the extent that the goods or services are so used or to be used, expressed as a proportion of the whole use or intended use.

(5) Where input tax is attributed to supplies of a description falling within item 1 or 2 of Group 15 to Schedule 9 to the Act under paragraph (4) above, the taxable person shall be entitled to credit for only so much input tax as is reasonably allowable under paragraph (2) or (3) above.

(6) For the purpose of attributing input tax to supplies of a description falling within item 1 or 2 of Group 15 of Schedule 9 to the Act under paragraph (4) above, any input tax of the description in that paragraph shall be deemed to be the only input tax incurred by the taxable person in the prescribed accounting period concerned.][1]

Amendments—[1] This Regulation inserted by the VAT (Amendment) (No 4) Regulations, SI 1999/3114, regs 2, 8, with effect from 1 January 2000.

[2] Heading inserted by the VAT (Amendment) (No 2) Regulations, SI 2007/768 regs 2, 11 with effect from 1 April 2007.

[Attribution of input tax incurred on services and related goods used to make financial supplies

103B— (1) This regulation applies to a taxable person who incurs input tax in the circumstances specified in paragraph (2) below.

(2) [Other than where it falls to be attributed under regulation 101,][2] where—

(*a*) input tax has been incurred by a taxable person in any prescribed accounting period on supplies to him of any of the services specified in paragraph (4) below and of any related goods, and

(*b*) those services and related goods are used or to be used by the taxable person in making both a relevant supply and any other supply, and

(*c*) the relevant supply is incidental to one or more of the taxable person's business activities,

that input tax shall be attributed to taxable supplies to the extent that the services or related goods are so used or to be used expressed as a proportion of the whole use or intended use, notwithstanding any provision of any input tax attribution method that the taxable person is required or allowed to use which purports to have the contrary effect.

(3) In this regulation—

(*a*) "relevant supply" means a supply of a description falling within item 1 or 6 of Group 5 of Schedule 9 to the Act and any supply of the same description which is made in another member State; and

(*b*) "taxable supplies" includes supplies of a description falling within regulation 103.

(4) The services referred to in paragraph (2)(*a*) above are services supplied by—

(*a*) accountants;

(*b*) advertising agencies;

(*c*) bodies which provide listing and registration services;

(*d*) financial advisers;

(*e*) lawyers;

(*f*) marketing consultants;

(*g*) persons who prepare and design documentation; and

(*h*) any person or body which provides similar services to those specified in sub-paragraphs (*a*) to (*g*) above.][1]

Amendments—[1] Regulation 103B inserted by the VAT (Amendment) (No 4) Regulations, SI 2004/3140 reg 8 with effect from 3 December 2004 in relation to input tax incurred by a taxable person on goods imported or acquired by, or goods and services supplied to, him on or after that date: SI 2004/3140 reg 2(2).

[2] Words inserted in para (2) by the VAT (Amendment) (No 2) Regulations, SI 2009/820 regs 2, 7 with effect in relation to input tax incurred by a taxable person on goods imported or acquired by, or goods or services supplied to, him on or after 1 April 2009. Where 31 March 2009 falls within the prescribed accounting period of a taxable person, the amendments made by SI 2009/820 shall not, in relation to that taxable person, have effect until the day after the end of that prescribed accounting period (SI 2009/820reg 1(2)).

Attribution of input tax on self-supplies

104 Where under or by virtue of any provision of the Act a person makes a supply to himself, the input tax on that supply shall not be allowable as attributable to that supply.

Former regulation—VAT (General) Regulations, SI 1985/886 reg 32A; VAT (General) (Amendment) Regulations, SI 1992/645 regs 1–3.

Treatment of input tax attributable to exempt supplies as being attributable to taxable supplies

105 …

Amendments—This regulation revoked by the VAT (Amendment) (No 2) Regulations, SI 1999/599 reg 4, with effect from 10 March 1999, unless the taxable person was registered prior to that date when it shall have effect from the commencement of the first tax year commencing on or after 10 March 1999.

[106— (1) Subject to regulation 106A, where relevant input tax—

(*a*) in any prescribed accounting period, or

(*b*) in the case of a longer period, taken together with the amount of any adjustment in respect of that period under regulation 107B—

(i) does not amount to more than £625 per month on average, and

(ii) does not exceed one half of all his input tax for the period concerned,

all such input tax in that period shall be treated as attributable to taxable supplies.

(2) In the application of paragraph (1) above to a longer period—

(*a*) any treatment of relevant input tax as attributable to taxable supplies in any prescribed accounting period shall be disregarded, and

(*b*) no account shall be taken of any amount or amounts which may be deductible or payable under regulation 115.

(3) For the purposes of this regulation, relevant input tax is input tax attributed under regulations 101, 102, 103, 103A[, 103B][2] and, where the case arises, regulation 107, to exempt supplies or to supplies outside the United Kingdom which would be exempt if made in the United Kingdom (not being supplies specified in an Order made under section 26(2)(*c*) of the Act).][1]

Former regulations—VAT (General) Regulations, SI 1985/886 reg 33A; VAT (General) (Amendment) Regulations, SI 1992/645 regs 1–3, SI 1994/3015 reg 5.

Amendments—[1] Regulation substituted by the VAT (Amendment) Regulations, SI 2002/1074 regs 2, 4 with effect for input tax incurred by a taxable person on goods imported or acquired by, or goods or services supplied to, him after 17 April 2002.

[2] In para (3), reference inserted by the VAT (Amendment) (No 4) Regulations, SI 2004/3140 reg 12 with effect from 3 December 2004: SI 2004/3140 reg 2(3).

[106A— (1) This regulation applies where regulation 107A applies.

(2) Where, taken together with the amount of any adjustment under regulation 107A, input tax attributed under regulations 101, 103[, 103A and 103B][2] to exempt supplies, or to supplies outside the United Kingdom which would be exempt if made in the United Kingdom (in each case not being supplies specified in an Order made under section 26(2)(*c*) of the Act)—

(*a*) does not amount to more than £625 per month on average, and

(*b*) does not exceed one half of all his input tax for the period concerned,

all such input tax in that period shall be treated as attributable to taxable supplies.

(3) Where, in accordance with regulations 101, 103[, 103A and 103B][2], a taxable person has attributed an amount of input tax to exempt supplies, or to supplies outside the United Kingdom which would be exempt if made in the United Kingdom (in each case not being supplies specified in an Order made under section 26(2)(c) of the Act) and, after applying regulation 107A, he is entitled to treat all his input tax as attributable to taxable supplies under paragraph (2) above, he shall—

(*a*) calculate the difference between—

(i) the total amount of input tax for that prescribed accounting period, and

(ii) the amount of input tax deducted in that prescribed accounting period, taken together with the amount of any adjustment under regulation 107A, and

(*b*) include this difference as an under-deduction in a return for the first prescribed accounting period next following the prescribed accounting period referred to in regulation 107A(1), except where the Commissioners allow another return to be used for this purpose.

(4) Where in a prescribed accounting period a taxable person has treated input tax as attributable to taxable supplies under regulation 106(1) but is not entitled to do so because of the operation of paragraph (2) above, he shall include the amount so treated as an over-deduction in a return for the first prescribed accounting period next following the prescribed accounting period referred to in regulation 107A(1), except where the Commissioners allow another return to be used for this purpose.

(5) But where a registered person has his registration cancelled at or before the end of the prescribed accounting period referred to in regulation 107A(1), he shall account for any adjustment under this regulation on his final return.][1]

Amendments—[1] Regulation inserted by the VAT (Amendment) Regulations, SI 2002/1074 regs 2, 5 with effect for input tax incurred by a taxable person on goods imported or acquired by, or goods or services supplied to, him after 17 April 2002.

[2] In paras (2), (3), reference substituted by the VAT (Amendment) (No 4) Regulations, SI 2004/3140 reg 13 with effect from 3 December 2004: SI 2004/3140 reg 2(3).

Adjustment of attribution

107— (1) Where a taxable person to whom a longer period is applicable has provisionally attributed an amount of input tax to taxable supplies in accordance with a method …[2] and save as the Commissioners may dispense with the following requirement to adjust, he …[2]—

[(*a*) shall, subject to subparagraphs (*b*), (*c*) and (*d*) below, determine for the longer period the amount of input tax which is attributable to taxable supplies according to the method used in the prescribed accounting periods,

(*b*) shall, where he has provisionally attributed input tax in accordance with regulation 101(2)(*e*) in any prescribed accounting period, determine for the longer period the amount of residual input tax which is attributable to taxable supplies on the basis of the extent to which the goods or services are used or to be used by him in making taxable supplies,

(*c*) may, where he has not provisionally attributed input tax in accordance with regulation 101(2)(*e*) but was nevertheless entitled to do so, determine for the longer period the amount of residual input tax which is attributable to taxable supplies on the basis of the extent to which the goods or services are used or to be used by him in making taxable supplies, (*d*) shall, where he has provisionally attributed residual input tax under regulation 101(2)(*f*), determine for the longer period the amount of residual input tax which is attributable to taxable supplies using the calculation specified in regulation 101(2)(*d*) subject to the provisions of regulation 101(3) to (5),

(*e*) shall apply the tests set out in regulation 106 to determine whether all input tax in the longer period in question shall be treated as attributable to taxable supplies,

(*f*) shall calculate the difference between the amount of input tax determined to be attributable to taxable supplies under subparagraphs (*a*) to (*e*) above and the amounts of input tax, if any, which were deducted in the returns for the prescribed accounting periods, and

(*g*) shall include any such amount of over-deduction or under-deduction in a return for—

(i) the first prescribed accounting period next following the longer period, or

(ii) the last prescribed accounting period in the longer period,

except where the Commissioners allow another return to be used.][2]

[(2) Where a taxable person makes no adjustment as required by paragraph (1) above, the requirement shall be that the adjustment is made in the return for the first prescribed accounting period next following the longer period.][2]

[(3) But where a registered person has his registration cancelled at or before the end of a longer period, he shall account for any adjustment under this regulation on his final return.][1]

[(4) In this regulation "residual input tax" has the same meaning as in regulation 101(10).][2]

Former regulation—VAT (General) Regulations, SI 1985/886 reg 34; VAT (General) (Amendment) Regulations, SI 1992/645 regs 1–3.

Amendments—[1] Para (3) added by the VAT (Amendment) Regulations, SI 2002/1074 regs 2, 6 with effect for input tax incurred by a taxable person on goods imported or acquired by, or goods or services supplied to, him after 17 April 2002.

[2] In para (1), words ", and where all his exempt input tax in that longer period cannot be treated as attributable to taxable supplies under regulation 106," and "shall" revoked, and sub-paras (*a*)–(*g*) substituted for previous sub-paras (*a*)–(*c*), para (2) substituted, and para (4) inserted, by the VAT (Amendment) (No 2) Regulations, SI 2009/820 regs 2, 8 with effect in relation to input tax incurred by a taxable person on goods imported or acquired by, or goods or services supplied to, him on or after 1 April 2009. Where 31 March 2009 falls within the prescribed accounting period of a taxable person, the amendments made by SI 2009/820 shall not, in relation to that taxable person, have effect until the day after the end of that prescribed accounting period (SI 2009/820reg 1(2)). Paras (1)(*a*)–(*c*), (2) previously read as follows—

"(*a*) determine for the longer period the amount of input tax which is attributable to taxable supplies according to the method used in the prescribed accounting periods,

(*b*) ascertain whether there has been, overall, an over-deduction or an under-deduction of input tax, having regard to the above-mentioned determination and to the sum of the amounts of input tax, if any, which were deducted in the returns for the prescribed accounting periods, and

(*c*) include any such amount of over-deduction or under-deduction in a return for the first prescribed accounting period next following the longer period, except where the Commissioners allow another return to be used for this purpose.".

"(2) Where a taxable person to whom a longer period is applicable has provisionally attributed an amount of input tax to taxable supplies in accordance with a method, and where all his exempt input tax in that longer period can be treated as attributable to taxable supplies under regulation 106, he shall—

(*a*) calculate the difference between the total amount of his input tax for that longer period and the sum of the amounts of input tax deducted in the returns for the prescribed accounting periods, and

(*b*) include any such amount of under-deduction in a return for the first prescribed accounting period next following the longer period, except where the Commissioners allow another return to be used for this purpose.".

[107A— (1) This regulation applies where a taxable person has made an attribution under regulation 101(2)(*b*) and (*d*) and the prescribed accounting period does not form part of a longer period, and the attribution differs substantially from one which represents the extent to which the goods or services are used by him or are to be used by him, or a successor of his, in making taxable supplies.

(2) Where this regulation applies, the taxable person shall calculate the difference and account for it on the return for the first prescribed accounting period next following the prescribed accounting period referred to in paragraph (1) above, except where the Commissioners allow another return to be used for this purpose.

(3) But where a registered person has his registration cancelled at or before the end of the prescribed accounting period referred to in paragraph (1) above, he shall account for any adjustment under this regulation on his final return.][1]

Amendments—[1] Regulations 107A–107E inserted by the VAT (Amendment) Regulations, SI 2002/1074 regs 2, 7 with effect for input tax incurred by a taxable person on goods imported or acquired by, or goods or services supplied to, him after 17 April 2002.

[107B— (1) [Other than where input tax falls to be attributed under regulation 101(8) or regulation 107(1)(*b*) or (*c*),][2] this regulation applies where a taxable person has made an attribution under [regulation 107(1)(*a*) or (*d*)][2] according to the method specified in regulation 101 and that attribution differs substantially from one which represents the extent to which the goods or services are used by him or are to be used by him, or a successor of his, in making taxable supplies.

(2) Where this regulation applies the taxable person shall—

(*a*) calculate the difference, and

(*b*) in addition to any amount required to be included under [regulation 107(1)(g)][2], account for the amount so calculated on the return for the first prescribed accounting period next following the longer period [or the return for the last prescribed accounting period in the longer period if applicable][2], except where the Commissioners allow another return to be used for this purpose.

(3) But where a registered person has his registration cancelled at or before the end of a longer period, he shall account for any adjustment under this regulation on his final return.][1]

Amendments—[1] Regulations 107A–107E inserted by the VAT (Amendment) Regulations, SI 2002/1074 regs 2, 7 with effect for input tax incurred by a taxable person on goods imported or acquired by, or goods or services supplied to, him after 17 April 2002.

[2] In para (1), words inserted and words substituted for words "regulation 107(1)(*a*)", in para (2)(*b*), words substituted for words "regulation 107(1)(*c*)" and words inserted, by the VAT (Amendment) (No 2) Regulations, SI 2009/820 regs 2, 9 with effect in relation to input tax incurred by a taxable person on goods imported or acquired by, or goods or services supplied to, him on or after 1 April 2009. Where 31 March 2009 falls within the prescribed accounting period of a taxable person, the amendments made by SI 2009/820 shall not, in relation to that taxable person, have effect until the day after the end of that prescribed accounting period (SI 2009/820reg 1(2)).

[107C For the purposes of regulations 107A and 107B, a difference is substantial if it exceeds—

(*a*) £50,000; or

(*b*) 50% of the amount of input tax falling to be apportioned under regulation 101(2)(*d*) within the prescribed accounting period referred to in regulation 107A(1), or longer period, as the case may be, but is not less than £25,000.][1]

Amendments—[1] Regulations 107A–107E inserted by the VAT (Amendment) Regulations, SI 2002/1074 regs 2, 7 with effect for input tax incurred by a taxable person on goods imported or acquired by, or goods or services supplied to, him after 17 April 2002.

[107D For the purposes of regulations 107A and 107B a person is the successor of another if he is a person to whom that other person has—

(*a*) transferred assets of his business by a transfer of that business, or part of it, as a going concern; and

(*b*) the transfer of the assets is one falling by virtue of an Order under section 5(3) of the Act to be treated as neither a supply of goods nor a supply of services;

and the reference in this regulation to a person's successor includes references to the successors of his successors through any number of transfers.][1]

Amendments—[1] Regulations 107A–107E inserted by the VAT (Amendment) Regulations, SI 2002/1074 regs 2, 7 with effect for input tax incurred by a taxable person on goods imported or acquired by, or goods or services supplied to, him after 17 April 2002.

[107E— (1) Regulations 107A and 107B shall not apply where the amount of input tax falling to be apportioned under regulation 101(2)(*d*) within the prescribed accounting period referred to in regulation 107A(1), or longer period, as the case may be, does not exceed—

(*a*) in the case of a person who is a group undertaking in relation to one or more other undertakings (other than undertakings which are treated under sections 43A to 43C of the Act as members of the same group as the person), £25,000 per annum, adjusted in proportion for a period that is not 12 months; or

(*b*) in the case of any other person, £50,000 per annum, adjusted in proportion for a period that is not 12 months.

(2) For the purposes of paragraph (1) above, "undertaking" and "group undertaking" have the same meaning as in [section 1161 of the Companies Act 2006][2].][1]

Amendments—[1] Regulations 107A–107E inserted by the VAT (Amendment) Regulations, SI 2002/1074 regs 2, 7 with effect for input tax incurred by a taxable person on goods imported or acquired by, or goods or services supplied to, him after 17 April 2002.

[2] Words in sub-para (2) substituted by the Companies Act 2006 (Consequential Amendments) (Taxes and National Insurance) Order, SI 2008/954 arts 43, 45 with effect from 6 April 2008.

[107F The references in regulations 107C and 107E to an apportionment under regulation 101(2)(*d*) in relation to a longer period include cases where the apportionment is made under regulation 107(1)(*a*) or (*d*) using the calculation specified in regulation 101(2)(*d*).][1]

Amendments—[1] This para inserted by the VAT (Amendment) (No 2) Regulations, SI 2009/820 regs 2, 10 with effect in relation to input tax incurred by a taxable person on goods imported or acquired by, or goods or services supplied to, him on or after 1 April 2009. Where 31 March 2009 falls within the prescribed accounting period of a taxable person, the amendments made by SI 2009/820 shall not, in relation to that taxable person, have effect until the day after the end of that prescribed accounting period (SI 2009/820reg 1(2)).

108— (1) This regulation applies where a taxable person has deducted an amount of input tax which has been attributed to taxable supplies because he intended to use the goods or services in making either—

(*a*) taxable supplies, or

(*b*) both taxable and exempt supplies,

and during a period of 6 years commencing on the first day of the prescribed accounting period in which the attribution was determined and before that intention is fulfilled, he uses or forms an intention to use the goods or services concerned in making exempt supplies or, in the case of an attribution within sub-paragraph (*a*) above, in making both taxable and exempt supplies.

(2) Subject to regulation 110 and save as the Commissioners otherwise allow, where this regulation applies the taxable person shall on the return for the prescribed accounting period in which the use occurs or the intention is formed, as the case may be, account for an amount equal to the input tax which has ceased to be attributable to taxable supplies in accordance with the method which he was required to use when the input tax was first attributed and he shall repay the said amount to the Commissioners.

(3) For the purposes of this regulation any question as to the nature of any supply shall be determined in accordance with the provisions of the Act and any Regulations or Orders made thereunder in force at the time when the input tax was first attributed.

Former regulations—VAT (General) Regulations, SI 1985/886 reg 35; VAT (General) (Amendment) Regulations, SI 1992/645 regs 1–3, SI 1993/1639 reg 6.

Simon's Tax Cases—*C&E Comrs v Svenska International plc* [1999] STC 406*, *C&E Comrs v Wiggett Construction Ltd* [2001] STC 933.

reg 108(1), *Tremerton Ltd v C&E Comrs* [1999] STC 1039.

109— (1) This regulation applies where a taxable person has incurred an amount of input tax which has not been attributed to taxable supplies because he intended to use the goods or services in making either—

(*a*) exempt supplies, or

(*b*) both taxable and exempt supplies,

and during a period of 6 years commencing on the first day of the prescribed accounting period in which the attribution was determined and before that intention is fulfilled, he uses or forms an intention to use the goods or services concerned in making taxable supplies or, in the case of an attribution within sub-paragraph (*a*) above, in making both taxable and exempt supplies.

(2) Subject to regulation 110 and where this regulation applies, the Commissioners shall, on receipt of an application made by the taxable person in such form and manner and containing such particulars as they may direct, pay to him an amount equal to the input tax which has become attributable to taxable supplies in accordance with the method which he was required to use when the input tax was first attributed.

(3) For the purposes of this regulation any question as to the nature of any supply shall be determined in accordance with the provisions of the Act and any Regulations or Orders made thereunder in force at the time when the input tax was first attributed.

Former regulations—VAT (General) Regulations, SI 1985/886 reg 36; VAT (General) (Amendment) Regulations, SI 1992/645 regs 1–3, SI 1993/1639 reg 7.

Simon's Tax Cases—*Royal & Sun Alliance Insurance Group plc v C&E Comrs* [2000] STC 933, [2003] STC 832; *Community Housing Association Ltd v R&C Comrs* [2009] STC 1324.

[110— (1) Subject to paragraph (2) below, in this regulation, in regulations [103B,][2] 108 and 109 above and in Part XV of these Regulations—

(*a*) "exempt supplies" includes supplies outside the United Kingdom which would be exempt if made in the United Kingdom, other than supplies of a description falling within subparagraph (*b*) below; and

(*b*) "taxable supplies" includes supplies of a description falling within regulation [103][2] above.

(2) Subject to paragraph (3) below, for the purposes of identifying the use, or intended use, of goods and services in regulations 108 and 109 above and in Part XV of these Regulations—

(*a*) "exempt supplies" shall be construed as including supplies of a description falling within regulation 103A(1) above, but only to the extent that there is, or would be, no credit for input tax on goods and services under that regulation; and

(*b*) "taxable supplies" shall be construed as including supplies of a description falling within regulation 103A(1) above, but only to the extent that there is, or would be, credit for input tax on goods and services under that regulation.

(3) Any adjustment under regulations 108 and 109 above shall not cause any more or any less input tax to be credited, as the case may be, in respect of supplies of a description falling within regulation 103A(1) above than would be allowed or required under that regulation.

(4) Subject to [regulations 103 and 103B][2], where—

(*a*) regulation 108 or 109 applies,

(*b*) the use to which the goods or services concerned are put, or to which they are intended to be put, includes the making of any supplies outside the United Kingdom, and

(*c*) at the time when the taxable person was first required to attribute the input tax he was not required to use a method approved or directed under regulation 102 or that method did not provide expressly for the attribution of input tax attributable to supplies outside the United Kingdom,

the amount for which the taxable person shall be liable to account under regulation 108 or the amount which he is entitled to be paid under regulation 109, as the case may be, shall be calculated by reference to the extent to which the goods or services concerned are used or intended to be used in making taxable supplies, expressed as a proportion of the whole use or intended use.][1]

Former regulations—VAT (General) Regulations, SI 1985/886 reg 36A; VAT (General) (Amendment) Regulations, SI 1993/1639 reg 8, SI 1994/3015 reg 6.

Amendments—[1] This Regulation substituted by the VAT (Amendment) (No 4) Regulations, SI 1999/3114, regs 2, 9, with effect from 1 January 2000.

[2] Reference inserted in para (1), and references substituted in paras (1)(*b*), (4), by the VAT (Amendment) (No 4) Regulations, SI 2004/3140 reg 14 with effect from 3 December 2004: SI 2004/3140 reg 2(3).

Exceptional claims for VAT relief

111— (1) Subject to paragraphs (2) and (4) below, on a claim made in accordance with paragraph (3) below, the Commissioners may authorise a taxable person to treat as if it were input tax—

(*a*) VAT on the supply of goods or services to the taxable person before the date with effect from which he was, or was required to be, registered, or paid by him on the importation or acquisition of goods before that date, for the purpose of a business which either was carried on or was to be carried on by him at the time of such supply or payment, and

(*b*) in the case of a body corporate, VAT on goods obtained for it before its incorporation, or on the supply of services before that time for its benefit or in connection with its incorporation, provided that the person to whom the supply was made or who paid VAT on the importation or acquisition—

(i) became a member, officer or employee of the body and was reimbursed, or has received an undertaking to be reimbursed, by the body for the whole amount of the price paid for the goods or services,

(ii) was not at the time of the importation, acquisition or supply a taxable person, and

(iii) imported, acquired or was supplied with the goods, or received the services, for the purpose of a business to be carried on by the body and has not used them for any purpose other than such a business.

[(2) No VAT may be treated as if it were input tax under paragraph (1) above—

(*a*) in respect of—

(i) goods or services which had been supplied, or

(ii) save as the Commissioners may otherwise allow, goods which had been consumed,

by the relevant person before the date with effect from which the taxable person was, or was required to be, registered;

(*b*) subject to paragraph (2A)[, (2C) and (2D)][3] below, in respect of goods which had been supplied to, or imported or acquired by, the relevant person more than [4 years][3] before the date with effect from which the taxable person was, or was required to be, registered;

(*c*) in respect of services performed upon goods to which sub-paragraph (*a*) or (*b*) above applies; or

(*d*) in respect of services which had been supplied to the relevant person more than 6 months before the date with effect from which the taxable person was, or was required to be, registered.][1]

[(2A) Paragraph (2)(*b*) above does not apply where—

(*a*) the taxable person was registered before 1st May 1997; and

(*b*) he did not make any returns before that date.

(2B) In paragraph (2) above references to the relevant person are references to—

(*a*) the taxable person; or

(*b*) in the case of paragraph (1)(*b*) above, the person to whom the supply had been made, or who had imported or acquired the goods, as the case may be.][1]

[(2C) Where the relevant person was, or was required to be, registered on or before 1st April 2009, no VAT may be treated as if it were input tax under paragraph (1) above in respect of goods which were supplied to, or imported or acquired by the relevant person more than 3 years before the date with effect from which that person was, or was required to be, registered.

(2D) Where the relevant person was or was required to be registered on or before 31st March 2010 and paragraph (2C) above does not apply, no VAT may be treated as if it were input tax under paragraph (1) above in respect of goods which were supplied to, or imported or acquired by, the relevant person on or before 31st March 2006.][3]

(3) [Subject to paragraph (3A) and (3B) below, a][1] claim under paragraph (1) above shall, save as the Commissioners may otherwise allow, be made on [the first return the taxable person is required to make][2] and, as the Commissioners may require, be supported by invoices and other evidence.

[(3A) Where the taxable person was registered before 1st May 1997 and has not made any returns before that date paragraph (3) above shall have effect as if for the words "the first return the taxable person is required to make" there were substituted the words "the first return the taxable person makes".

(3B) [Subject to paragraph (3C)][3] the Commissioners shall not allow a person to make any claim under paragraph (3) above in terms such that the VAT concerned would fall to be claimed as if it were input tax more than [4 years][3] after the date by which the first return he is required to make is required to be made.][1]

[(3C) The Commissioners shall not allow a person to make any claim under paragraph (3) above in the circumstances where the first return the taxable person was required to make was required to be made on or before 31st March 2006.][3]

(4) A taxable person making a claim under paragraph (1) above shall compile and preserve for such period as the Commissioners may require—

(*a*) in respect of goods, a stock account showing separately quantities purchased, quantities used in the making of other goods, date of purchase and date and manner of subsequent disposals of both such quantities, and

(*b*) in respect of services, a list showing their description, date of purchase and date of disposal, if any.

(5) [Subject to paragraph (6) below][1] if a person who has been, but is no longer, a taxable person makes a claim in such manner and supported by such evidence as the Commissioners may require, they may pay to him the amount of any VAT on the supply of services to him after the date with effect from which he ceased to be, or to be required to be, registered and which was attributable to any taxable supply made by him in the course or furtherance of any business carried on by him when he was, or was required to be, registered.

[(6) Subject to paragraph (7) [and (8)][3] below, no claim under paragraph (5) above may be made more than [4 years][3] after the date on which the supply of services was made.

(7) Paragraph (6) above does not apply where—

(*a*) the person ceased to be, or ceased to be required to be, registered before 1st May 1997; and

(*b*) the supply was made before that date.][1]

[(8) No claim may be made under paragraph (5) above in relation to a supply of services which was made on or before 31st March 2006.][3]

Former regulations—VAT (General) Regulations, SI 1985/886 reg 37; VAT (General) (Amendment) Regulations, SI 1992/645 regs 1–3, SI 1992/3102 reg 22.

Amendments—[1] Para (2) substituted and paras (2A), (2B), (3A), (3B), (6), (7) and words in paras (3), (5) inserted by the VAT (Amendment) Regulations, SI 1997/1086 reg 7 with effect from 1 May 1997.

[2] Words in para (3) substituted by SI 1997/1086 reg 7 with effect from 1 May 1997.

[3] In paras (2)(*b*), (3B), (6), words inserted and words substituted for words "3 years", paras (2C), (2D), (3C), (8) inserted, by the VAT (Amendment) Regulations, SI 2009/586 regs 2, 8 with effect from 1 April 2009.

PART XV
ADJUSTMENTS TO THE DEDUCTION OF INPUT TAX ON CAPITAL ITEMS

Interpretation of Part XV

112— (1) Any expression used in this Part to which a meaning is given in Part XIV of these Regulations shall, unless the contrary intention appears, have the same meaning in this Part as it has in that Part [and in particular, exempt supplies and taxable supplies shall be accorded the same meanings as defined in regulation 110 above][1].

(2) Any reference in this Part to a capital item shall be construed as a reference to a capital item to which this Part applies by virtue of regulation 113, being an item which a person (hereinafter referred to as "the owner") uses in the course or furtherance of a business carried on by him, and for the purpose of that business, otherwise than solely for the purpose of selling the item.

Former regulations—VAT (General) Regulations, SI 1985/886 reg 37A; VAT (General) (Amendment) Regulations, SI 1989/2355 reg 4, SI 1992/645 regs 2, 4.

Press releases etc—Business Brief 30/97 19-12-97 (Statement of practice on a budget change to the capital goods scheme).

Amendments—[1] Words in para (1) inserted by the VAT (Amendment) (No 4) Regulations, SI 1999/3114, regs 2, 10, with effect from 1 January 2000.

Capital items to which this Part applies

113 The capital items to which this Part applies are items of any of the following descriptions—

(*a*) a computer or an item of computer equipment of a value of not less than £50,000 supplied to, or imported or acquired by, the owner,

(*b*) [land, a building or part of a building or a civil engineering work or part of a civil engineering work][1] where the value of the interest therein supplied to the owner, by way of a taxable supply which is not a zero-rated supply, is not less than £250,000 excluding so much of that value as may consist of rent, [(including charges reserved as rent) which is neither payable nor paid more than 12 months in advance nor invoiced for a period in excess of 12 months,][2]

(*c*) a building or part of a building where—

(i) the owner's interest in, right over, or licence to occupy, the building or part of the building is treated as supplied to him under [paragraph 37(3) of Schedule 10][4] to the Act, and

(ii) the value of that supply, determined in accordance with [paragraph 37(5) of that Schedule][4], is not less than £250,000,

(*d*) a building or part of a building where—

(i) the owner's interest in, right over, or licence to occupy, the building or part of the building [was, on or before 1st March 1997, treated][3] as supplied to him under paragraph 6(1) of Schedule 10 to the Act[(as that Schedule stood before being rewritten by article 2 of the Value Added Tax (Buildings and Land) Order 2008)][4], and

(ii) the value of that supply, determined in accordance with paragraph 6(2) of that Schedule[(as that Schedule so stood)][4], [was][3] not less than £250,000, (*e*) a building other than one falling or capable of falling within paragraphs (*c*) or (*d*) above constructed by the owner and first brought into use by him on or after 1st April 1990 where the aggregate of—

(i) the value of taxable grants relating to the land on which the building is constructed made to the owner on or after 1st April 1990, and

(ii) the value of all the taxable supplies of goods and services, other than any that are zero-rated, made or to be made to him for or in connection with the construction of the building on or after 1st April 1990,

is not less than £250,000, …[3]

(*f*) a building which the owner alters, or an extension or an annex which he constructs, where—

(i) additional floor area is created in the altered building, extension or annex, of not less than 10 per cent of the floor area of the building before the alteration in question is carried out, or the extension or annex in question is constructed, and

(ii) the value of all the taxable supplies of goods and services, other than any that are zero-rated, made or to be made to the owner for or in connection with the alteration, extension or annex in question on or after 1st April 1990, is not less than £250,000,

[(*g*) a civil engineering work constructed by the owner and first brought into use by him on or after 3rd July 1997 where the aggregate of—

(i) the value of the taxable grants relating to the land on which the civil engineering work is constructed made to the owner on or after 3rd July 1997, and

(ii) the value of all the taxable supplies of goods and services, other than any that are zero-rated, made or to be made to him for or in connection with the construction of the civil engineering work on or after 3rd July 1997,

is not less than £250,000, and

(*h*) a building which the owner refurbishes or fits out where the value of capital expenditure on the taxable supplies of services and of goods affixed to the building, other than any that are zero-rated, made or to be made to the owner for or in connection with the refurbishment or fitting out in question on or after 3rd July 1997 is not less than £250,000][2]

Former regulations—VAT (General) Regulations, SI 1985/886 reg 37B; VAT (General) (Amendment) Regulations, SI 1989/2355 reg 4, SI 1992/3102 reg 23.

Press releases etc—Business Brief 30/97 19-12-97 (Statement of practice on a budget change to the capital goods scheme).

Amendments—[1] Words in para (*b*) substituted by the VAT (Amendment) (No 3) Regulations, SI 1997/1614 reg 10 with effect from 3 July 1997.

[2] Words in (*b*), and (*g*) and (*h*), inserted by SI 1997/1614 reg 10.

[3] Words in paras (*d*)(i)(*ii*) substituted and words in para (*e*) revoked by SI 1997/1614 reg 10.

[4] Words in para (*c*)(i), (ii) substituted, and words in para (*d*)(i), (ii) inserted, by the Value Added Tax (Buildings and Land) Order, SI 2008/1146, art 6, Sch 1 paras 16, 19 with effect in relation to supplies made on or after 1 June 2008, subject to savings in Sch 2 of the Order.

Period of adjustment

114—(1) The proportion (if any) of the total input tax on a capital item which may be deducted under Part XIV shall be subject to adjustments in accordance with the provisions of this Part.

(2) Adjustments shall be made over a period determined in accordance with the following paragraphs of this regulation.

(3) The period of adjustment relating to a capital item of a description falling within—

(*a*) regulation 113(*a*) shall consist of 5 successive intervals,

(*b*) regulation 113(*b*), where the interest in the land, building or part of the building [or civil engineering work or part of a civil engineering work][1] in question has less than 10 years to run at the time it is supplied to the owner, shall consist of 5 successive intervals, and

(*c*) any other description shall consist of 10 successive intervals,

determined in accordance with [paragraphs (4) to (5B) and (7)][2] below.

(4) Subject to [paragraphs (5A), (5B) and (7)][2] below, the first interval applicable to a capital item shall be determined as follows—

(*a*) where the owner is a registered person when he imports, acquires or is supplied with the item as a capital item, the first interval shall commence on the day of the importation, acquisition or supply and shall end on the day before the commencement of his tax year following that day;

(*b*) where the owner is a registered person when he appropriates to use an item as a capital item, the first interval shall commence on the day he first so uses it and shall end on the day before the commencement of his tax year following that day;

(*c*) where the capital item is of a description falling within regulation 113(*c*), the first interval shall commence on the day the owner's interest in, right over, or licence to occupy, the building or part of the building is treated as supplied to him under [paragraph 37(3) of Schedule 10][3] to the Act and shall end on the day before the commencement of his tax year following that day;

(*d*) where the capital item is of a description falling within regulation 113(*d*), the first interval shall commence on the later of the following days—

(i) 1st April 1990,

(ii) the day the owner first uses the building (or part of the building), and shall end on the day before the commencement of his tax year following the day of commencement of the first interval;

(*e*) where the capital item is of a description falling within regulation 113 [(*e*), (*f*), (*g*) or (*h*)][2], the first interval shall commence on the day the owner first uses the building or the altered building or the extension or annex [or the civil engineering work or the building which has been refurbished or fitted out][1] in question, and shall end on the day before the commencement of his tax year following that day;

(*f*) where the owner is not a registered person when he first uses an item as a capital item, and subsequently—

(i) becomes a registered person, the first interval shall correspond with his registration period, or

(ii) is included among bodies treated as members of a group under section 43 of the Act, the first interval shall correspond with, or be that part still remaining of, the then current tax year of that group.

(5) Subject to [paragraphs (5A), (5B) and (7)][2] below, each subsequent interval applicable to a capital item shall correspond with a longer period applicable to the owner, or if no longer period applies to him, a tax year of his.

[(5A) On the first occasion during the period of adjustment applicable to a capital item that the owner of the item—

(*a*) being a registered person subsequently becomes a member of a group under section 43 of the Act;

(*b*) being a member of a group under section 43 ceases to be a member of that group (whether or not he becomes a member of another such group immediately thereafter); or

(*c*) transfers the item in the course of the transfer of his business or part of his business as a going concern (the item therefore not being treated as supplied) in circumstances where the new owner is not, under regulation 6(1) above, registered with the registration number of and in substitution for the transferor,

the interval then applying shall end on the day before he becomes a member of a group or the day that he ceases to be a member of the group or transfers the business or part of the business (as the case may require) and thereafter each subsequent interval (if any) applicable to the capital item shall end on the successive anniversaries of that day. .][1]

[(5B) Where the extent to which a capital item is used in making taxable supplies does not change between what would, but for this paragraph, have been the first interval and the first subsequent interval applicable to it and the length of the two intervals taken together does not exceed 12 months the first interval applicable to the capital item shall end on what would have been the day that the first subsequent interval expired.][1]

(6) …[2]

[(7) Where the owner of a capital item transfers it during the period of adjustment applicable to it in the course of the transfer of his business or a part of his business as a going concern (the item therefore not being treated as supplied) and the new owner is, under regulation 6(1) above, registered with the registration number of, and in substitution for the transferor, the interval applying to the capital item at the time of the transfer shall end on the last day of the longer period applying to the new owner immediately after the transfer or, if no longer period then applies to him, shall end on the last day of his tax year following the day of transfer.][2]

Former regulations—VAT (General) Regulations, SI 1985/886 reg 37C; VAT (General) (Amendment) Regulations, SI 1989/2355 reg 4, SI 1992/3102 reg 24.

Press releases etc—Business Brief 30/97 19-12-97 (Statement of practice on a budget change to the capital goods scheme).

Amendments—[1] Words in paras (3)(*b*) and (4)(*e*), and paras (5A) and (5B), inserted by the VAT (Amendment) (No 3) Regulations, SI 1997/1614 reg 11 with effect from 3 July 1997.

[2] Words in paras (3), (4) and (5) substituted, para (6) deleted and para (7) substituted by SI 1997/1614 reg 11 with effect from 3 July 1997.

[3] Words in para (4)(*c*) substituted by the Value Added Tax (Buildings and Land) Order, SI 2008/1146, art 6, Sch 1 paras 16, 20 with effect in relation to supplies made on or after 1 June 2008, subject to savings in Sch 2 of the Order.

Method of adjustment

115— (1) Where in a subsequent interval applicable to a capital item, the extent to which it is used in making taxable supplies increases from the extent to which it was so used [or to be used at the time that the original entitlement to deduction of the input tax was determined][4], the owner may deduct for that subsequent interval an amount calculated as follows—

(*a*) where the capital item falls within regulation 114(3)(*a*) or (*b*)—

$$\frac{\text{the total input tax on the capital sum}}{5} \times \text{the adjustment percentage;}$$

(*b*) where the capital item falls within regulation 114(3)(*c*)—

$$\frac{\text{the total input tax on the capital sum}}{10} \times \text{the adjustment percentage;}$$

(2) Where in a subsequent interval applicable to a capital item, the extent to which it is used in making taxable supplies decreases from the extent to which it was so used [or to be used at the

time that the original entitlement to deduction of the input tax was determined][4], the owner shall pay to the Commissioners for that subsequent interval an amount calculated in the manner described in paragraph (1) above.

(3) Where the whole of the owner's interest in a capital item is supplied by him, or the owner is deemed or, but for the fact that the VAT on the deemed supply (whether by virtue of its value or because it is zero-rated or exempt) would have been not more than [the sum specified in paragraph 8(1) of Schedule 4 to the Act][5], would have been deemed to supply a capital item [pursuant to that paragraph][5] during an interval other than the last interval applicable to the capital item, then if the supply (or deemed supply) of the capital item is—

(*a*) a taxable supply, the owner shall be treated as using the capital item for each of the remaining complete intervals applicable to it wholly in making taxable supplies or

(*b*) an exempt supply, the owner shall be treated as not using the capital item for any of the remaining complete intervals applicable to it in making any taxable supplies,

and the owner shall[, except where paragraph (3A) below applies,][2] calculate for each of the remaining complete intervals applicable to it, in accordance with paragraph (1) or (2) above, as the case may require, such amount as he may deduct or such amount as he shall be liable to pay to the Commissioners,

provided that the aggregate of the amounts that he may deduct in relation to a capital item pursuant to this paragraph shall not exceed the output tax chargeable by him on the supply of that capital item.

[(3A) This paragraph applies if the total amount of input tax deducted or deductible by the owner of a capital item as a result of the initial deduction, any adjustments made under paragraph (1) or (2) above and the adjustment which would apart from this paragraph fall to be made under paragraph (3) above would exceed the output tax chargeable by him on the supply of that capital item.][2]

[(3B) Save as the Commissioners may otherwise allow, where paragraph (3A) above applies the owner may deduct, or as the case may require, shall pay to the Commissioners such amount as results in the total amount of input tax deducted or deductible being equal to the output tax chargeable by him on the supply of the capital item.][2]

(4) If a capital item is—

(*a*) irretrievably lost or stolen or is totally destroyed, or

(*b*) is of a kind falling within regulation 114(3)(*b*) and the interest in question expires,

during the period of adjustment applicable to it, no further adjustment shall be made in respect of any remaining complete intervals applicable to it.

(5) For the purposes of this regulation—

["the original entitlement to deduction" means the entitlement to deduction determined in accordance with Part XIV of these Regulations;][4]

"the total input tax on the capital item" means, in relation to a capital item falling within—

(*a*) regulation 113(*a*) or (*b*), the VAT charged on the supply to, or on the importation or acquisition by, the owner of the capital item, other than VAT charged on rent [(including charges reserved as rent) which is neither payable nor paid more than 12 months in advance nor invoiced for a period in excess of 12 months][2] (if any),

(*b*) regulation 113(*c*) or (*d*), the VAT charged on the supply which the owner is treated as making to himself under [paragraph 37(3) of Schedule 10 to the Act, or paragraph 6(1) of that Schedule as it stood before being rewritten by article 2 of the Value Added Tax (Buildings and Land) Order 2008,][6] as the case may require,

(*c*) regulation 113 [(*e*), (*f*), (*g*) or (*h*)][3] the aggregate of the VAT charged on the supplies described in regulation 113 [(*e*), (*f*), (*g*) or (*h*)][3] as the case may require, other than VAT charged on rent (if any),

and shall include, in relation to any capital item, any VAT treated as input tax under regulation 111 which relates to the capital item, other than such VAT charged on rent (if any); and for the purposes of this paragraph reference to the owner shall be construed as references to the person who incurred the total input tax on the capital item;

"the adjustment percentage" means the difference (if any) between the extent, expressed as a percentage, to which the capital item [was used or to be used for the making of taxable supplies at the time the original entitlement to deduction of the input tax was determined][4], and the extent to which it is so used or is treated under paragraph (3) above as being so used in the subsequent interval in question.

(6) [Subject to paragraph (8) below][1] a taxable person claiming any amount pursuant to paragraph (1) above, or liable to pay any amount pursuant to paragraph (2) above, shall include such amount in a return for the second prescribed accounting period next following the interval to which that amount relates, except where the Commissioners allow another return to be used for this purpose, provided that where an interval has come to an end under [regulation 114(5A)][2]—

(*a*) ...[3] because the owner of the capital item has ceased to be a member of a group under section 43 of the Act, any amount claimable from the Commissioners or payable to them (as the case may be) in respect of that interval shall be included in a return for that group for the second prescribed accounting period after the end of the tax year of the group in which the interval in question fell, or

(*b*) …[3] because the owner has transferred part of his business as a going concern, and he remains a registered person after the transfer, any amount claimable from the Commissioners or payable to them (as the case may be) in respect of that interval shall be included in a return by him for the second prescribed accounting period after the end of his tax year in which the interval in question fell,

except where the Commissioners allow another return to be used for this purpose.

(7) [Subject to paragraph (8) below][1] a taxable person claiming any amount or amounts, or liable to pay any amount or amounts, pursuant to paragraph (3) above, shall include such amount or amounts in a return for the second prescribed accounting period next following the interval in which the supply (or deemed supply) in question takes place except where the Commissioners allow another return to be used for this purpose.

[(8) For the purposes of paragraphs (9) and (10) below, a "specified return" means a return specified—

(*a*) in paragraph (6) above,
(*b*) in subparagraph (a) or (b) of that paragraph, or
(*c*) in paragraph (7) above.

(9) Subject to paragraph (10) below, the Commissioners shall not allow the taxable person to use a return other than a specified return unless it is the return for a prescribed accounting period commencing within 4 years of the end of the prescribed accounting period to which the specified return relates.

(10) The Commissioners shall not allow the taxable person to use a return other than a specified return where the specified return is the return for a prescribed accounting period finishing on or before 31st March 2006.][7]

Commentary—*De Voil Indirect Tax Service* **V3.470**.
Former regulations—VAT (General) Regulations, SI 1985/886 reg 37D; VAT (General) (Amendment) Regulations, SI 1989/2355 reg 4.
Press releases etc—Business Brief 30/97 19-12-97 (Statement of practice on a budget change to the capital goods scheme).
Simon's Tax Cases—*Centralan Property Ltd v C&E Comrs* [2006] STC 1542.
Amendments—[1] Words in paras (6) and (7) inserted by the VAT (Amendment) Regulations, SI 1997/1086 reg 8 with effect from 1 May 1997.
[2] Words in para (3), para (3A) and (3B), and words in paras (5)(*a*) and (*b*) inserted by the VAT (Amendment) (No 3) Regulations, SI 1997/1614 reg 12 with effect from 3 July 1997.
[3] Words in para (5)(*c*) substituted and words in paras (6)(*a*) and (*b*) revoked by SI 1997/1614 reg 12 with effect from 3 July 1997.
[4] Words in paras (1), (2) and (5) substituted and new definition of "the original entitlement to deduct" in para (5) inserted by the VAT (Amendment) (No 2) Regulations, SI 1999/599 reg 6 with effect from subsequent adjustment intervals commencing on or after 10 March 1999.
[5] Words in para (3) substituted by the VAT (Amendment) Regulations, SI 2000/258 regs 2, 5 with effect from 1 March 2000.
[6] Words in para (5)(*b*) substituted by the Value Added Tax (Buildings and Land) Order, SI 2008/1146, art 6, Sch 1 paras 16, 21 with effect in relation to supplies made on or after 1 June 2008, subject to savings in Sch 2 of the Order.
[7] Paras (8)–(10) substituted for previous para (8), by the VAT (Amendment) Regulations, SI 2009/586 regs 2, 9 with effect from 1 April 2009. Para (8) previously read as follows—

"(8) The Commissioners shall not allow the taxable person to use a return other than that specified in paragraph (6) above, paragraph (*a*) or (*b*) of that paragraph or paragraph (7) above (in each case, "the specified return"), as the case may be, unless it is the return for a prescribed accounting period commencing within 3 years of the end of the prescribed accounting period to which the specified return relates.".

Ascertainment of taxable use of a capital item

116— (1) Subject to regulation 115(3) [and (3B)][2] and paragraphs (2)[, (A2)][2] and (3) below, for the purposes of this Part, an attribution of the total input tax on the capital item shall be determined for each subsequent interval applicable to it in accordance with the method used under Part XIV for that interval and the proportion of the input tax thereby determined to be attributable to taxable supplies shall be treated as being the extent to which the capital item is used in making taxable supplies in that subsequent interval.

[(A2) Subject to paragraph (2) below, the attribution of the total input tax on a capital item for subsequent intervals determined in accordance with regulation 114(5A) above shall be determined by such method as is agreed with the Commissioners.][2]

(2) In any particular case the Commissioners may allow another method by which, or may direct the manner in which, the extent to which a capital item is used in making taxable supplies in any subsequent interval applicable to it is to be ascertained.

(3) Where the owner of a building which is a capital item of his grants or assigns a tenancy or lease in the whole or any part of that building and that grant or assignment is a zero-rated supply to the extent only as provided by—

(*a*) note [(14)][1] to Group 5 of Schedule 8 to the Act, or
(*b*) that note as applied to Group 6 of that Schedule by note [(3)][1] to Group 6, or
(*c*) paragraph 8 of Schedule 13 to the Act,

any subsequent exempt supply of his arising directly from that grant or assignment shall be disregarded in determining the extent to which the capital item is used in making taxable supplies in any interval applicable to it.

Former regulations—VAT (General) Regulations, SI 1985/886 reg 37E; VAT (General) (Amendment) Regulations, SI 1989/2355 reg 4, SI 1992/645 regs 2, 5.
Press releases etc—Business Brief 30/97 19-12-97 (Statement of practice on a budget change to the capital goods scheme).
Simon's Tax Cases—*C&E Comrs v R & R Pension Fund Trustees* [1996] STC 889*.
Amendments—[1] Figures in para (3) substituted by the VAT (Amendment) Regulations, SI 1995/3147 reg 5, with effect from 1 January 1996.
[2] Words in para (1) above, and para (A2) above, inserted by the VAT (Amendment) (No 3) Regulations, SI 1997/1614 reg 13 with effect from 3 July 1997.

[PART 15A
GOODS USED FOR NON-BUSINESS PURPOSES DURING THEIR ECONOMIC LIFE][1]

Note—The VAT (Amendment) (No 7) Regulations, SI 2007/3099 revoke and replace the VAT (Amendment) (No 6) Regulations, SI 2007/2922. This revocation was necessary owing to a typographical error in the recital powers pursuant to which the No 6 Regulations were made. The No 7 Regulations make the amendments to the VAT Regulations, SI 2003/2518, which were intended to be made by the No 6 Regulations.
Amendments—[1] Part 15A (regs 116A–116N) inserted by the VAT (Amendment) (No 7) Regulations, SI 2007/3099 regs 3, 4 with effect from 1 November 2007: SI 2007/3099 reg 1(2)(*b*).

[Application

116A This Part makes provision for calculating the full cost to a person of providing the supply of services ("relevant supply") that is treated as made pursuant to paragraph 5(4) of Schedule 4 to the Act where goods that are held or used for the purposes of a business are used for private or non-business purposes. Where goods that are held or used for the purposes of a business have an economic life (see regulations 116C, 116D, 116G and 116L) at the time when they are used for private or non-business purposes, the value or part of the value of the relevant supply which is referable to that use on or after 1st November 2007 shall be calculated in accordance with the regulations in this Part.][1]

Amendments—[1] Part 15A (regs 116A–116N) inserted by the VAT (Amendment) (No 7) Regulations, SI 2007/3099 regs 3, 4 with effect from 1 November 2007: SI 2007/3099 reg 1(2)(*b*).

Interpretation of this Part

116B— (1) In this Part—

"full cost of the goods" means the full cost of the goods to the person (being the person making the relevant supply or any of his predecessors) who, in relation to the VAT on the goods mentioned in paragraph 5(5) of Schedule 4 to the Act, is described in that paragraph as being entitled to-

(*a*) credit under sections 25 and 26 of the Act; or

(*b*) a repayment under the scheme made under section 39 of the Act;

"goods" includes land forming part of the assets of, or held or used for the purposes of, a business which is treated as goods for the purposes of paragraph 5 of Schedule 4 to the Act by virtue of paragraph 9 of that Schedule and references to goods being held or used for the purposes of a business shall be construed accordingly;

"predecessor" has the same meaning as it does in paragraph 5 of Schedule 4 to the Act.

(2) In this Part, references to a period of time comprising a number of months shall be computed to two decimal places where that period does not comprise a whole number of months.][1]

Amendments—[1] Part 15A (regs 116A–116N) inserted by the VAT (Amendment) (No 7) Regulations, SI 2007/3099 regs 3, 4 with effect from 1 November 2007: SI 2007/3099 reg 1(2)(*b*).

[Economic life of goods

116C Goods held or used for the purposes of a business have an economic life being (subject to regulations 116G and 116L) the period of time commencing on the day when they are first used for any purpose after they have been supplied to, or acquired or imported by, a person or any of his predecessors and lasting for a period of—

(*a*) 120 months in the case of land, a building or part of a building (but this is subject to regulation 116D);

(*b*) 60 months for all other goods.][1]

Amendments—[1] Part 15A (regs 116A–116N) inserted by the VAT (Amendment) (No 7) Regulations, SI 2007/3099 regs 3, 4 with effect from 1 November 2007: SI 2007/3099 reg 1(2)(*b*).

[116D Where the economic life of the interest of a person, or any of his predecessors, in land, a building or part of a building commences at a time when that interest has less than 120 months to run at that time, it shall be limited to the number of months remaining before expiry of that interest and element B of the formula in regulation 116E and element D of the formula in regulation 116L shall be construed accordingly.][1]

Amendments—[1] Part 15A (regs 116A–116N) inserted by the VAT (Amendment) (No 7) Regulations, SI 2007/3099 regs 3, 4 with effect from 1 November 2007: SI 2007/3099 reg 1(2)(*b*).

[Value of a relevant supply

116E Subject to regulations 116F, 116H and 116I, the value of a relevant supply is the amount determined using the formula—

$$\frac{A}{B} \times (C \times U\%)$$

where—

A is the number of months in the prescribed accounting period during which the relevant supply occurs which fall within the economic life of the goods concerned;

B is the number of months of the economic life of the goods concerned or, in the case of an economic life commencing on 1st November 2007 by virtue of regulation 116L, what would have been its duration if it had been determined according to regulation 116C or 116G as appropriate;

C is the full cost of the goods excluding any increase resulting from a supply of goods or services giving rise to a new economic life; and

U% is the extent, expressed as a percentage, to which the goods are put to any private use or used, or made available for use, for non-business purposes as compared with the total use made of the goods during the part of the prescribed accounting period occurring within the economic life of the goods.][1]

Amendments—[1] Part 15A (regs 116A–116N) inserted by the VAT (Amendment) (No 7) Regulations, SI 2007/3099 regs 3, 4 with effect from 1 November 2007: SI 2007/3099 reg 1(2)(*b*).

[116F Where a prescribed accounting period in which a relevant supply occurs immediately follows a prescribed accounting period during which the goods whose use gives rise to that supply were not used or made available for use for any purpose, element "A" of the formula in regulation 116E shall (without prejudice to any other element of the formula) comprise the total number of months falling within the economic life concerned covered by—

(*a*) the prescribed accounting period in which the relevant supply occurs; and

(*b*) all preceding prescribed accounting periods which commence after the end of the prescribed accounting period during which the goods were last used or made available for use for any purpose before the prescribed accounting period in which the relevant supply occurs.][1]

Amendments—[1] Part 15A (regs 116A–116N) inserted by the VAT (Amendment) (No 7) Regulations, SI 2007/3099 regs 3, 4 with effect from 1 November 2007: SI 2007/3099 reg 1(2)(*b*).

[Later increase in the full cost of goods

116G Where—

(*a*) a supply of goods or services is made to a person or any of his predecessors in respect of any goods held or used for the purposes of a business (whether or not the goods have an economic life in relation to that person at that time);

(*b*) VAT is chargeable on that supply which is eligible (in whole or part) for credit under sections 25 and 26 of the Act or repayment under section 39 of the Act; and

(c) by virtue of that supply, the full cost of the goods is greater than their full cost immediately before that supply,

a new economic life shall, without prejudice to any other economic life having effect in relation to those goods, be treated as commencing in respect of them in accordance with regulation 116C as if they had been supplied, acquired or imported at the time when the supply of goods or services is made.][1]

Amendments—[1] Part 15A (regs 116A–116N) inserted by the VAT (Amendment) (No 7) Regulations, SI 2007/3099 regs 3, 4 with effect from 1 November 2007: SI 2007/3099 reg 1(2)(*b*).

[Value of relevant supplies made during a new economic life

116H Subject to regulation 116I, the calculation of the value of a relevant supply made during a new economic life in accordance with the formula in regulation 116E is varied so that—

C is the increase in the full cost of the goods resulting from the supply of the goods or services giving rise to the new economic life; and

U% is the extent, expressed as a percentage, to which the goods are put to any private use or used, or made available for use, for non-business purposes as compared with the total use made of the goods during the part of the prescribed accounting period occurring during the new economic life of the goods.][1]

Amendments—[1] Part 15A (regs 116A–116N) inserted by the VAT (Amendment) (No 7) Regulations, SI 2007/3099 regs 3, 4 with effect from 1 November 2007: SI 2007/3099 reg 1(2)(*b*).

[Value of relevant supplies of goods which have two or more economic lives

116I Where a relevant supply occurs in relation to goods that have two or more economic lives at the time when they are put to private use or used, or made available for use, for non-business purposes, the value of that supply shall be such amount as represents the total of the amounts calculated in accordance with regulation 116E (as varied by regulation 116H as appropriate) in respect of those economic lives.][1]

Amendments—[1] Part 15A (regs 116A–116N) inserted by the VAT (Amendment) (No 7) Regulations, SI 2007/3099 regs 3, 4 with effect from 1 November 2007: SI 2007/3099 reg 1(2)(*b*).

[Transitional provisions

116J Regulation 116L applies to an economic life that—

(*a*) would be treated as commencing before 1st November 2007 if that regulation did not apply; and

(*b*) relates to goods that, before that day, have been put to any private use or used, or made available for use, for non-business purposes by the person described in regulation 116K or any of his predecessors (whether or not a relevant supply arising from that use has been treated as made before that day).][1]

Amendments—[1] Part 15A (regs 116A–116N) inserted by the VAT (Amendment) (No 7) Regulations, SI 2007/3099 regs 3, 4 with effect from 1 November 2007: SI 2007/3099 reg 1(2)(*b*).

[**116K** The person referred to in regulation 116J(b) is the person who holds or uses the goods concerned for the purposes of his business on 1st November 2007.][1]

Amendments—[1] Part 15A (regs 116A–116N) inserted by the VAT (Amendment) (No 7) Regulations, SI 2007/3099 regs 3, 4 with effect from 1 November 2007: SI 2007/3099 reg 1(2)(*b*).

[**116L** An economic life of goods to which this regulation applies shall be treated as commencing on 1st November 2007 and lasting for the period of time determined using the formula—

$$D \times \frac{(E - F)}{E}$$

where—

D is the number of months which would have been the duration of the economic life concerned if it had commenced in accordance with regulation 116C or had been treated as having commenced in accordance with that regulation by virtue of regulation 116G;

E is the value of element "C" of the formula contained in regulation 116E (as varied where appropriate in relation to that economic life by regulation 116H) for the purpose of determining the whole or, where the use occurs at a time when the goods have two or more economic lives at that time, part of the value of a relevant supply arising from the use of the goods during the economic life concerned;

F is the value determined using the formula—

$$\frac{(G \times 100)}{(X\% \times 100)}$$

where—

G is the total value of relevant supplies of the goods on which VAT has been or will be accounted for in respect of such relevant supplies arising from the goods being put to any private use or used, or made available for use, for non-business purposes before 1st November 2007 (whether or not such supplies are treated as made before or after that day) to the extent that the value of the relevant supplies comprised in the total value was determined by reference to the value of element "E" of the formula used in this regulation in respect of the economic life concerned; and

X% is the extent, expressed as a percentage, to which the goods have been put to any private use or used, or made available for use, for non-business purposes during the period described in regulation 116M as compared with the total use made of the goods in that period.][1]

Amendments—[1] Part 15A (regs 116A–116N) inserted by the VAT (Amendment) (No 7) Regulations, SI 2007/3099 regs 3, 4 with effect from 1 November 2007: SI 2007/3099 reg 1(2)(*b*).

[**116M** The period referred to in regulation 116L is the period of time commencing at the time when the economic life concerned would have commenced if it had commenced in accordance with regulation 116C or had been treated as having commenced in accordance with that regulation by virtue of regulation 116G and ending immediately before 1st November 2007.][1]

Amendments—[1] Part 15A (regs 116A–116N) inserted by the VAT (Amendment) (No 7) Regulations, SI 2007/3099 regs 3, 4 with effect from 1 November 2007: SI 2007/3099 reg 1(2)(*b*).

[**116N** Where a person has claimed deduction of input tax on goods which was incurred within the period of two years ending on 21st March 2007, he may withdraw that claim in whole or part as if it were made in error (but not so as to render him liable to any penalty or payment of interest in respect of that claim) provided that

(*a*) the goods have not been used for any purpose before the claim is withdrawn;

(*b*) he intends or expects that the goods will be put to private or non-business purposes during their economic life;

(*c*) the withdrawal is in respect of-

(i) all of the input tax claimed on the goods; or

(ii) the part of the input tax claimed on the goods which is referable to his intended use of those goods for purposes other than those of his business; and (*d*) the withdrawal is made in accordance with regulation 35 (whatever the amount of the claim that is withdrawn) before 1st February 2008.][1]

Amendments—[1] Part 15A (regs 116A–116N) inserted by the VAT (Amendment) (No 7) Regulations, SI 2007/3099 regs 3, 4 with effect from 1 November 2007: SI 2007/3099 reg 1(2)(*b*).

PART XVI
IMPORTATIONS, EXPORTATIONS AND REMOVALS

Interpretation of Part XVI

117— (1) In regulation 127 "approved inland clearance depot" means any inland premises approved by the Commissioners for the clearance of goods for customs and excise purposes.

(2) For the purposes of regulation 128 "container" means an article of transport equipment (lift-van, moveable tank or other similar structure)—

(*a*) fully or partially enclosed to constitute a compartment intended for containing goods,
(*b*) of a permanent character and accordingly strong enough to be suitable for repeated use,
(*c*) specially designed to facilitate the carriage of goods, by one or more modes of transport, without intermediate reloading,
(*d*) designed for ready handling, particularly when being transferred from one mode of transport to another,
(*e*) designed to be easy to fill and to empty, and
(*f*) having an internal volume of one cubic metre or more,

and the term "container" shall include the accessories and equipment of the container, appropriate for the type concerned, provided that such accessories and equipment are carried with the container, but shall not include vehicles, accessories or spare parts of vehicles, or packaging.

(3) […][2]

[(4) In [regulation][3] 131 "goods" does not include—

(*a*) a motor-vehicle, or
(*b*) a boat intended to be exported under its own power.][1]

(5), (6) …[1]

(7) For the purposes of regulation 129 "overseas authority" means any country other than the United Kingdom or any part of or place in such a country or the government of any such country, part or place.

[(7A) In [regulation][3] 131 the words "overseas visitor" refer to a traveller who is not established within the member States.

(7B) For the purposes of paragraph (7A) above, a traveller is not established within the member States only if that traveller's domicile or habitual residence is situated outside the member States.

(7C) Solely for the purposes of paragraph (7B) above, the traveller's domicile or habitual residence is the place entered as such in a valid—

(*a*) identity document,
(*b*) identity card, or
(*c*) passport.

(7D) A document referred to in subparagraph (*a*), (*b*) or (*c*) of paragraph (7C) above is valid for the purposes of that paragraph only if—

(*a*) it is so recognised by the Commissioners; and
(*b*) it is not misleading as to the traveller's true place of domicile or habitual residence.][2]

(8) In [regulation 132][2] "overseas visitor" means a person who, during the 2 years immediately preceding …[2] the date of the application mentioned in regulation 132, has not been in the member States for more than 365 days, or who, …[2] during the 6 years immediately preceding the date of the application has not been in the member States for more than 1,095 days.

(9) …[3]

(10) In regulations 140 and 144 "customs territory of the Community" has the same meaning as it has for the purposes of Council Regulation (EEC) No 2913 No 92.

[(11) In this Part references to Council Regulation (EEC) No 2913/92 (the Community Customs Code) and Commission Regulation (EEC) No 2454/93 (which contains provisions implementing the Community Customs Code) shall be read as references to those instruments as—

(*a*) amended by the Act concerning the accession of the Czech Republic, the Republic of Estonia, the Republic of Cyprus, the Republic of Latvia, the Republic of Lithuania, the Republic of Hungary, the Republic of Malta, the Republic of Poland, the Republic of Slovenia and the Slovak Republic, signed at Athens on 16th April 2003,
(*b*) amended, modified or otherwise affected by the Act concerning the conditions of Accession of the Republic of Bulgaria and Romania and the adjustments to the Treaties on which the European Union is founded, signed at Luxembourg on 25th April 2005 and Council Regulation (EC) No 1791/2006 (which contains consequential amendments to the Customs Code).][4]

Former regulations—Para (1): VAT (General) Regulations, SI 1985/886 reg 38(1).
Para (2): VAT (General) Regulations, SI 1985/886 reg 38(3).
Paras (3), (4) (as originally enacted): VAT (General) Regulations, SI 1985/886 reg 38(5), (6); VAT (General) (Amendment) Regulations, SI 1992/3102 reg 25.
Paras (5)–(9) (as originally enacted): VAT (General) Regulations, SI 1985/886 reg 38(8)–(12); VAT (General) (Amendment) Regulations, SI 1992/3102 reg 25, SI 1995/913 reg 3.
Para (10): VAT (General) Regulations, SI 1985/886 reg 38(14); VAT (General) (Amendment) Regulations, SI 1995/152 reg 4.
Amendments—[1] Para (4) substituted and paras (5), (6) revoked by the VAT (Amendment) Regulations, SI 1996/210 regs 8, 9, with effect from 1 March 1996.
[2] Para (3) revoked, paras (7A) to (7D) inserted and words in para (8) substituted and revoked by the VAT (Amendment) Regulations, SI 1999/438 reg 10, with effect from 1 April 1999.
[3] Word in paras (4), (7A) substituted for the words "regulations 130 and" and "regulations 130(*a*)(i) and" respectively, and para (9) revoked, by the VAT (Amendment) (No 4) Regulations, SI 2003/1485 regs 2, 5 with effect for supplies made after 30 June 2003.
[4] Para (11) substituted by the VAT (Amendment) (No 3) Regulations, SI 2006/3292 regs 2, 4 with effect from 1 January 2007.

Enactments excepted

118 There shall be excepted from the enactments which are to apply as mentioned in section 16(1) of the Act—

(*a*) the Alcoholic Liquor Duties Act 1979—
(i) section 7 (exemption from duty on spirits in articles used for medical purposes),
(ii) section 8 (repayment of duty on spirits for medical or scientific purposes),
(iii) section 9 (remission of duty on spirits for methylation),
(iv) section 10 (remission of duty on spirits for use in art or manufacture),
(v) section 22(4) (drawback on exportation of tinctures or spirits of wine), and
(vi) sections 42 and 43 (drawback on exportation and warehousing of beer),

(*b*) the Hydrocarbon Oil Duties Act 1979—
(i) section 9 (relief for certain industrial uses),
(ii) section 15 (drawback of duty on exportation etc of certain goods),
(iii) section 16 (drawback of duty on exportation etc of power methylated spirits),
(iv) section 17 (repayment of duty on heavy oil used by horticultural producers),
(v) section 18 (repayment of duty on fuel for ships in home waters),
(vi) section 19 (repayment of duty on fuel used in fishing boats etc),
(vii) section 20 (relief from duty on oil contaminated or accidentally mixed in warehouse), and
(viii) section 20AA (power to allow reliefs),

(*c*) the Customs and Excise Management Act 1979—
(i) section 43(5) (provisions as to duty on re-imported goods),
(ii) section 125(1) and (2) (valuation of goods for the purpose of ad valorem duties),
(iii) section 126 (charge of excise duty on manufactured or composite imported articles), and
(iv) section 127(1)(*b*) (determination of disputes as to duties on imported goods),

(*d*) the Customs and Excise Duties (General Reliefs) Act 1979 other than sections 8 and 9(*b*),
(*e*) the Isle of Man Act 1979, sections 8 and 9 (removal of goods from Isle of Man to United Kingdom), …[1]
(*f*) the Tobacco Products Duty Act 1979, section 2(2) (remission or repayment of duty on tobacco products)[, and
(*g*) the Finance Act 1999, sections 126 and 127 (interest on unpaid customs debts and on certain repayments relating to customs duty)][1].

Former regulations—VAT (General) Regulations, SI 1985/886 reg 39; VAT (General) (Amendment) Regulations, SI 1992/3102 reg 26.
Amendments—[1] Word "and" at end of para (*e*) revoked, and para (*g*) and the word "and" immediately preceding it added by the VAT (Amendment) (No 2) Regulations, SI 2000/634 regs 2, 3 with effect from 1 April 2000.

Regulations excepted

[**119** The provision made by or under the following subordinate legislation shall be excepted from applying as mentioned in section 16(1) of the Act—

(*a*) regulations 16(4) and (5) and 19(1)(*b*) of the Excise Warehousing (Etc) Regulations 1988 (certain removals from warehouse);
(*b*) any regulations made under section 197(2)(*f*) of the Finance Act 1996 (rate of interest on overdue customs duty and on repayments of amounts paid by way of customs duty).][1]

Former regulations—VAT (General) Regulations, SI 1985/886 reg 39B; VAT (General) (Amendment) Regulations, SI 1992/3102 reg 27.
Amendments—[1] This regulation substituted by the VAT (Amendment) (No 2) Regulations, SI 2000/634 regs 2, 4 with effect from 1 April 2000.

Community legislation excepted

120— (1) Council Regulation (EEC) No 918/83 on conditional reliefs from duty on the final importation of goods, and any implementing Regulations made thereunder shall be excepted from the Community legislation which is to apply as mentioned in section 16(1) of the Act.

(2) The following Articles shall be excepted from the Community legislation which is to apply as mentioned in section 16(1) of the Act—

(*a*) in Council Regulation (EEC) No 2913/92 establishing the Community Customs Code—

(i) Articles 126 to 128 (drawback system of inward processing relief),

(ii) …[2]

(iii) Article 137 so far as it relates to partial relief on temporary importation, and Article 142,

(iv) Articles 145 to 160 (outward processing),

(v) …[4] …[1]

(vi) Article 229(*b*) (interest payable on a customs debt),

[(vii) Articles 232(1)(*b*), (2) and (3) (interest on arrears of duty), and

(viii) Article 241, second and third sentences only (interest on certain repayments by the authorities),][1]

[(*b*) in Commission Regulation (EEC) No 2454/93 which contains provisions implementing the Community Customs Code—

(i) Articles 496 to 523, Articles 536 to 544 and Article 550 (but only to the extent that these Articles apply to the drawback system of inward processing relief),

(ii) Article 519 (compensatory interest),

(iii) Articles 585 to 592 (outward processing) (and Articles 496 to 523 to the extent that they are relevant to outward processing),

(iv) …[4]][3]

(3) Council Regulation (EEC) No 2658/87 on the tariff and statistical nomenclature and on the Common Customs Tariff and implementing Regulations made thereunder (end use relief), save and in so far as the said Regulations apply to goods admitted into territorial waters—

(*a*) in order to be incorporated into drilling or production platforms, for purposes of the construction, repair, maintenance, alteration or fitting-out of such platforms, or to link such drilling or production platforms to the mainland of the United Kingdom, or

(*b*) for the fuelling and provisioning of drilling or production platforms,

shall be excepted from the Community legislation which is to apply as mentioned in section 16(1) of the Act.

Former regulations—VAT (General) Regulations, SI 1985/886 reg 40(1)–(3); VAT (General) (Amendment) Regulations, SI 1992/3102 reg 28, SI 1993/3027 regs 2, 3.

Amendments—[1] Words in para (2)(*a*)(v) revoked and para (2)(*a*)(vii), (viii) added by the VAT (Amendment) (No 2) Regulations, SI 2000/634 regs 2, 5 with effect from 1 April 2000.

[2] In para (2), sub-paras (*a*)(ii), (*b*)(ii) revoked by the VAT (Amendment) Regulations, SI 2001/630 reg 3 with effect for goods imported after 31 March 2001.

[3] Sub-para (2)(*b*) substituted by the VAT (Amendment)(No 5) Regulations, SI 2003/2318 regs 2, 5 with effect from 1 October 2003. This substitution has effect for supplies of goods or services the benefit of which was received after the coming into force of SI 2003/2318.

[4] Paras (2)(*a*)(v), (2)(*b*)(iv) revoked by the VAT (Amendment) Regulations, SI 2006/587 regs 1(3), (5), 5 with effect from 6 April 2006.

Adaptations

[121— (1) The provision made by the following enactments shall apply, as mentioned in section 16(1) of the Act, subject to the adaptations prescribed by this regulation.

(2) Section 125(3) of the Customs and Excise Management Act 1979 (valuation of goods) shall have effect as if the reference to the preceding subsections of that section included a reference to section 21 of the Act.

(3) Section 129 of the Finance Act 1999 (recovery of certain amounts by the Commissioners) shall be regarded as providing for the recovery of a repayment of any relevant VAT (import VAT).][1]

Former regulations—VAT (General) Regulations, SI 1985/886 reg 39A; VAT (General) (Amendment) Regulations, SI 1992/3102 reg 27.

Amendments—[1] This regulation substituted by the VAT (Amendment) (No 2) Regulations, SI 2000/634 regs 2, 6 with effect from 1 April 2000.

[121A— (1) The application of the Customs Duties (Deferred Payment) Regulations 1976 in relation to any VAT chargeable on the importation of goods from places outside the member States is subject to the following prescribed adaptations.

(2) In regulation 4(1) (application for approval), regard "security" as being "appropriate security (which may be nil if there is no risk to the payment)".

(3) In regulation 4(2) (security and payment arrangements), regard there being a second sub-paragraph as follows—

"Provided that the amount in question may exceed that of the security in the case of nil security.".

(4) For regulation 4(3) (variations and revocations of approval), regard any Commissioners' variation consequent on the adaptations prescribed by this regulation as only being able to have effect after 30th November 2003.

(5) Before "and" at the end of regulation 8(*a*) (deemed payment for certain purposes at time deferment granted), regard there being—

"(*aa*) Article 74(1) of Council Regulation (EEC) No 2913/92 (Community Customs Code) (no release of goods unless customs debt paid or secured);".][1]

Amendments—[1] This regulation inserted by the VAT (Amendment) (No 5) Regulations, SI 2003/2318 regs 2, 6 with effect from 1 October 2003. This insertion has effect for supplies of goods or services the benefit of which was received after the coming into force of SI 2003/2318.

[121B— (1) The application of Council Regulation (EEC) No 2913/92 (Community Customs Code) in relation to any VAT chargeable on the importation of goods from places outside the member States is subject to the following prescribed adaptations.

(2) But the adaptation in paragraph (5) only applies to the extent that the Commissioners grant deferment of payment of the relevant VAT with nil security.

(3) In Article 218(1) second sub-paragraph (single entry in the accounts), after "secured" regard there being "if required".

(4) In Article 225 first sub-paragraph (deferment of payment conditional on security), after "applicant" regard there being "(but the customs authorities may waive this condition if there is no risk to the payment)".

(5) Regard Article 225 as not being subject to Article 192 (fixing amount of security).][1]

Amendments—[1] This regulation inserted by the VAT (Amendment) (No 5) Regulations, SI 2003/2318 regs 2, 6 with effect from 1 October 2003. This insertion has effect for supplies of goods or services the benefit of which was received after the coming into force of SI 2003/2318.

[121C— (1) The application of Commission Regulation (EEC) No 2454/93 (implementation of Community Customs Code) in relation to any VAT chargeable on the importation of goods from places outside the member States is subject to the following prescribed adaptations.

(2) But the adaptations in paragraphs (3) and (4) only apply to the extent that the Commissioners grant deferment of payment of the relevant VAT with nil security.

(3) Regard Articles 244, 248(1), 257(3), 257(4), 258, 262(1) and 876a(1) (circumstances in which duties have to be or are taken as having to be secured) as providing that the provision of security is at the discretion of the customs authorities.

(4) Regard Articles 244, 248(1), 257(3), 257(4) and 876a(1) (circumstances in which duties have to be secured) as not being subject to Article 192 of Council Regulation (EEC) No 2913/92 (Community Customs Code) (fixing amount of security).][1]

Amendments—[1] This regulation substituted by the VAT (Amendment) (No 5) Regulations, SI 2003/2318 regs 2, 6 with effect from 1 October 2003.

[Adaptations and exceptions for the application of returned goods relief

121D— (1) The application of Council Regulation (EEC) No 2913/92 (Community Customs Code) and Commission Regulation (EEC) No 2454/93 (implementation Regulation) in relation to any VAT chargeable on the importation of goods from places outside the member States is subject to the following prescribed adaptations.

(2) Regard—

(*a*) Articles 185 to 187 of the Community Customs Code (returned Community goods and returned compensating products), and

(*b*) Articles 844 to 856 and Article 882 of the implementation Regulation (returned Community goods and returned compensating products),

as only applying in the case and to the extent of a reimportation to the United Kingdom by the person who originally exported or re-exported the relevant Community goods or compensating products from the VAT territory of the Community.

That VAT territory is the territorial application of Council Directive 77/388/EEC in accordance with Title III of that Directive (territorial application).

(3) Regard the amount of the relief mentioned in Article 186 of the Community Customs Code (returned Community goods) as reduced by the amount of any unpaid VAT.

(4) Regard the amount legally owed in Article 187 of the Community Customs Code (returned compensating products) as reduced by the amount of any paid VAT.

(5) For the purposes of paragraphs (3) and (4)—

(*a*) "VAT" includes value added tax charged in accordance with the law of another member State (see sections 92(1), 92(2) and 96(1) of the Act);

(*b*) "unpaid" refers to any part of the VAT charged and due on—

(i) a supply or acquisition of the goods in a member State before the reimportation, or

(ii) an importation of the goods from outside the member States before the reimportation,

but repaid, remitted or otherwise not paid;

(*c*) "paid" refers to any part of the VAT charged, due and paid on—

(i) a supply or acquisition of the goods in a member State before the reimportation, or

(ii) an importation of the goods from outside the member States before the reimportation, and without any actual, or prospect of, repayment or remission;

(*d*) a sum for which there is or was under the law of a member State an entitlement or right to a deduction or refund within Article 17 of Council Directive 77/388/EEC (origin and scope of the right to deduct) is neither "unpaid" nor "paid".

(6) In the circumstances described by paragraph (7) or (8)—

(*a*) Articles 185 to 187 of the Community Customs Code (returned goods), and

(*b*) Articles 844 to 856 and Article 882 of the implementation Regulation (returned goods),

are excepted from the Community legislation which is to apply as mentioned in section 16(1) of the Act (application of customs legislation in relation to import VAT).

(7) These circumstances are that—

(*a*) the reimporter contemplated by those Articles makes a supply of, or concerning, the goods whilst under the inward processing procedure or in the course of, or after, the relevant exportation, re-exportation or reimportation,

(*b*) the place of that supply for the purposes of VAT is determined by or under section 7 of the Act (place of supply) as being outside the United Kingdom, and

(*c*) the goods nevertheless are or may be stored or physically used in the United Kingdom by or under the direction of that reimporter or the person to whom that supply is made ("recipient").

For these purposes, "reimporter" and "recipient" include someone connected with either person or both persons as determined in accordance with section 839 of the Taxes Act.

(8) These circumstances are that the goods in question were supplied at any time to any person pursuant to regulations 131 to 133 (supplies to persons departing from the member States) or pursuant to any corresponding provision of the Isle of Man.

(9) For the purposes of the Articles of the Community Customs Code and implementation Regulation mentioned in paragraph (2)—

(*a*) regard the description of the customs territory of the Community in Article 3 of the Community Customs Code as being substituted with a description of the VAT territory (see paragraph (2));

(*b*) regard the following references as including a reference to the completion of the formalities referred to in Article 33a(1)(*a*) of Council Directive 77/388/EEC (formalities relating to entry of goods into VAT territory from territory considered a third territory)—

(i) "released for free circulation" in the definition of "Community goods" in Article 4(7), second indent and Article 185(1) of the Community Customs Code;

(ii) "entered" and "declared" for "release for free circulation" in, or for the purposes of, Articles 844(4), 848(1), 848(2), 849(1) and 849(5) of the implementation Regulation;

(*c*) regard the following references as including a reference to the completion of the formalities referred to in Article 33a(2)(*a*) of Council Directive 77/388/EEC (or to a declaration under those formalities) (formalities relating to dispatch or transport of goods from Member State to territory considered a third territory)—

(i) "customs export formalities" in Articles 844(1), 849(1), 849(2) and 849(3) of the implementation Regulation;

(ii) "export declaration" in Article 848(1) of that Regulation;

(iii) "customs formalities relating to their exportation" in Articles 844(4) and 849(1) of that Regulation;

(*d*) regard—

(i) the definition of "import duties" in Article 4(10) of the Community Customs Code as defining instead VAT charged on the importation of goods from places outside the member States in accordance with the Act; and

(ii) the references to "import duty" and "duty" in Article 185(1), second sub-paragraph, second indent and Article 187 of the Community Customs Code as references to such VAT.

(10) The references to Council Directive 77/388/EEC in paragraphs (2), (5)(*d*), (9)(*b*) and (9)(*c*) embrace relevant amendments up to and including 6th April 2006 only.][1]

Amendments—[1] Regulation 121D inserted by the VAT (Amendment) Regulations, SI 2006/587 regs 1(3)–(5), 4 with effect from 6 April 2006. This amendment applies to any reimportation of goods occurring once it is in force.

Postal importations by registered persons in the course of business

122 Goods imported by post from places outside the member States, other than by datapost packet, not exceeding £2,000 in value, or such greater sum as is determined for the time being by the Commissioners, by a registered person in the course of a business carried on by him may, with the authority of the proper officer, be delivered without payment of VAT if—

(*a*) the registered person has given such security as the Commissioners may require, and

(*b*) his registration number is shown on the customs declaration attached to or accompanying the package,

and save as the Commissioners may otherwise allow he shall account for VAT chargeable on the goods on their importation together with any VAT chargeable on the supply of goods or services by him or on the acquisition of goods by him from another member State in a return furnished by him in accordance with these Regulations for the prescribed accounting period during which the goods were imported.

Former regulations—VAT (General) Regulations, SI 1985/886 reg 41; VAT (General) (Amendment) Regulations, SI 1992/3102 reg 29.

Temporary importations

123— (1) Subject to such conditions as the Commissioners may impose, the VAT chargeable on the importation of goods from a place outside the member States shall not be payable where—

(*a*) a taxable person makes a supply of goods which is to be zero-rated in accordance with sub-paragraphs (*a*)(i) and (ii), and (*b*) of section 30(8) of the Act,

(*b*) the goods so imported are the subject of that supply, and

(*c*) the Commissioners are satisfied that—

(i) the importer intends to remove the goods to another member State, and

(ii) the importer is importing the goods in the course of a supply by him of those goods in accordance with the provisions of sub-paragraphs (*a*)(i) and (ii), and (*b*) of section 30(8) of the Act and any Regulations made thereunder.

(2) As a condition of granting the relief afforded by paragraph (1) above the Commissioners may require the deposit of security, the amount of which shall not exceed the amount of VAT chargeable on the importation.

(3) The relief afforded by paragraph (1) above shall continue to apply provided that the importer—

(*a*) removes the goods to another member State within one month of the date of importation or within such longer period as the Commissioners may allow, and

(*b*) supplies the goods in accordance with sub-paragraphs (*a*)(i) and (ii), and (*b*) of section 30(8) of the Act and any Regulations made thereunder.

Former regulations—VAT (General) Regulations, SI 1985/886 reg 42; VAT (General) (Amendment) Regulations, SI 1992/3102 reg 30.

Reimportation of certain goods by non-taxable persons

124

Amendment—Regulation 124 revoked by the VAT (Amendment) Regulations, SI 2006/587 regs 1(3), (5), 5 with effect from 6 April 2006.

Reimportation of certain goods by taxable persons

125

Amendment—Regulation 125 revoked by the VAT (Amendment) Regulations, SI 2006/587 regs 1(3), (5), 5 with effect from 6 April 2006.

Reimportation of goods exported for treatment or process

126 Subject to such conditions as the Commissioners may impose, VAT chargeable on the importation of goods from a place outside the member States which have been temporarily exported from the member States and are reimported after having undergone repair, process or adaptation outside the member States, or after having been made up or reworked outside the member States, shall be payable as if such treatment or process had been carried out in the United Kingdom, if the Commissioners are satisfied that—

(*a*) at the time of exportation the goods were intended to be reimported after completion of the treatment or process outside the member States, and

(*b*) the ownership in the goods was not transferred to any other person at exportation or during the time they were abroad.

Former regulations—VAT (General) Regulations, SI 1985/886 reg 48; VAT (General) (Amendment) Regulations, SI 1992/3102 reg 35.

Supplies to export houses

127 …

Former regulations—VAT (General) Regulations, SI 1985/886 reg 49; VAT (General) (Amendment) Regulations, SI 1992/3102 reg 36.

Amendments—This regulation revoked by the VAT (Amendment) Regulations, SI 1999/438 reg 11, with effect from 1 April 1999.

Export of freight containers

128 Where the Commissioners are satisfied that a container is to be exported to a place outside the member States, its supply, subject to such conditions as they may impose, shall be zero-rated.

Former regulations—VAT (General) Regulations, SI 1985/886 reg 50; VAT (General) (Amendment) Regulations, SI 1992/3102 reg 37.

Supplies to overseas persons

129— (1) Where the Commissioners are satisfied that—

(*a*) goods intended for export to a place outside the member States have been supplied, otherwise than to a taxable person, to—

(i) a person not resident in the United Kingdom,

(ii) a trader who has no business establishment in the United Kingdom from which taxable supplies are made, or

(iii) an overseas authority, and

(*b*) the goods were exported to a place outside the member States,

the supply, subject to such conditions as they may impose, shall be zero-rated.

(2) …[1]

Former regulations—VAT (General) Regulations, SI 1985/886 reg 51; VAT (General) (Amendment) Regulations, SI 1992/3102 reg 38.

Amendments—[1] Para (2) revoked by the VAT (Amendment) (No 4) Regulations, SI 2003/1485 regs 2, 6 with effect for supplies made after 30 June 2003.

Supplies to persons departing from the member States

130 …

Amendment—This regulation revoked by the VAT (Amendment) (No 4) Regulations, SI 2003/1485 regs 2, 6 with effect for supplies made after 30 June 2003.

131— (1) Where the Commissioners are satisfied that—

(*a*) goods have been supplied to a person who is an overseas visitor and who, at the time of the supply, intended to depart from the member States [before the end of the third month following that in which the supply is effected][1] and that the goods should accompany him,

(*b*) save as they may allow, the goods were produced to the competent authorities for the purposes of the common system of VAT in the member State from which the goods were finally exported to a place outside the member States, and

(*c*) the goods were exported to a place outside the member States,

the supply, subject to such conditions as they may impose, shall be zero-rated.

(2) …[2]

Former regulations—VAT (General) Regulations, SI 1985/886 reg 54; VAT (General) (Amendment) Regulations, SI 1992/3102 reg 41.

Amendments—[1] Words in para (1)(*a*) substituted by the VAT (Amendment) Regulations, SI 1995/3147 reg 6, with effect from 1 January 1996.

[2] Para (2) revoked by the VAT (Amendment) (No 4) Regulations, SI 2003/1485 regs 2, 6 with effect for supplies made after 30 June 2003.

132 The Commissioners may, on application by an overseas visitor who intends to depart from the member States within 15 months and remain outside the member States for a period of at least 6 months, permit him within 12 months of his intended departure to purchase, from a registered person, a …[1] motor vehicle without payment of VAT, for subsequent export, and its supply, subject to such conditions as they may impose, shall be zero-rated.

Former regulations—VAT (General) Regulations, SI 1985/886 reg 56; VAT (General) (Amendment) Regulations, SI 1992/3102 reg 43.

Amendments—[1] Word revoked by the VAT (Amendment) Regulations, SI 2000/258 regs 2, 6 with effect from 1 April 2000.

133 The Commissioners may, on application by any person who intends to depart from the member States within 9 months and remain outside the member States for a period of at least 6 months, permit him within 6 months of his intended departure to purchase, from a registered person, a …[1] motor vehicle without payment of VAT, for subsequent export, and its supply, subject to such conditions as they may impose, shall be zero-rated.

Former regulations—VAT (General) Regulations, SI 1985/886 reg 57; VAT (General) (Amendment) Regulations, SI 1992/3102 reg 43.

Amendments—[1] Word revoked by the VAT (Amendment) Regulations, SI 2000/258 regs 2, 6 with effect from 1 April 2000.

Supplies to persons taxable in another member State

134 Where the Commissioners are satisfied that—

(*a*) a supply of goods by a taxable person involves their removal from the United Kingdom,

(*b*) the supply is to a person taxable in another member State,

(*c*) the goods have been removed to another member State, and

(*d*) the goods are not goods in relation to whose supply the taxable person has opted, pursuant to section 50A of the Act, for VAT to be charged by reference to the profit margin on the supply,

the supply, subject to such conditions as they may impose, shall be zero-rated.

Former regulations—VAT (General) Regulations, SI 1985/886 reg 57A; VAT (General) (Amendment) Regulations, SI 1992/3102 reg 44, SI 1995/1280 reg 3.

Supplies of goods subject to excise duty to persons who are not taxable in another member State

135 Where the Commissioners are satisfied that—

(*a*) a supply by a taxable person of goods subject to excise duty involves their removal from the United Kingdom to another member State,

VAT

(*b*) that supply is other than to a person taxable in another member State and the place of supply is not, by virtue of section 7(5) of the Act, treated as outside the United Kingdom,

(*c*) the goods have been removed to another member State in accordance with the provisions of the Excise Goods (Holding, Movement, Warehousing and REDS) Regulations 1992, and

(*d*) the goods are not goods in relation to whose supply the taxable person has opted, pursuant to section 50A of the Act, for VAT to be charged by reference to the profit margin on the supply,

the supply, subject to such conditions as they may impose, shall be zero-rated.

Former regulations—VAT (General) Regulations, SI 1985/886 reg 57B; VAT (General) (Amendment) Regulations, SI 1992/3102 reg 44, SI 1995/1280 reg 4.

Territories to be treated as excluded from or included in the territory of the Community and of the member States

136 For the purposes of the Act the following territories shall be treated as excluded from the territory of the Community—

(*a*) the Channel Islands,

(*b*) Andorra,

(*c*) San Marino, and

(*d*) the Aland Islands.

Former regulations—VAT (General) Regulations, SI 1985/886 reg 57D(1); VAT (General) (Amendment) Regulations, SI 1992/3102 reg 44, SI 1995/152 reg 5.

137 For the purposes of the Act the following territories shall be treated as excluded from the territory of the member States and the territory of the Community—

(*a*) the Canary Islands (Kingdom of Spain),

(*b*) the overseas departments of the French Republic (Guadeloupe, Martinique, Réunion, St. Pierre and Miquelon and French Guiana), and

(*c*) Mount Athos (Hellenic Republic).

Former regulations—VAT (General) Regulations, SI 1985/886 reg 57D(2); VAT (General) (Amendment) Regulations, SI 1992/3102 reg 44.

138— [(1) For the purposes of the Act the territory of the Community shall be treated as excluding—

(*a*) Austria, Finland and Sweden ("the 1995 acceding States"),

(*b*) the Czech Republic, Estonia, Cyprus, Latvia, Lithuania, Hungary, Malta, Poland, Slovakia and Slovenia ("the 2004 acceding States"), and

(*c*) Bulgaria and Romania ("the 2007 acceding states")

in relation to goods to which this regulation applies.][1]

(2) Subject to [paragraph 4][1] below, the goods to which this regulation applies are—

(*a*) goods which are the subject of a supply made in an acceding State before [the date specified in paragraph (5)][1] and which in pursuance of that supply are removed to the United Kingdom on or after [the date specified in paragraph (6)][1] being goods in the case of which provisions of the law of the acceding State in question having effect for purposes corresponding to those of subsection (6)(*a*) or (so far as it applies to exportations) subsection (8) of section 30 of the Act have prevented VAT from being charged on that supply, and

(*b*) goods which were subject to a suspension regime before 1st January 1995, which by virtue of any Community legislation were to remain, for VAT purposes only, subject to that regime for a period beginning with that date and which cease to be subject to that regime on or after 20th October 1995.

(3) For the purposes of paragraph (2)(*b*) above, goods shall be treated as having become subject to a suspension regime if—

(*a*) on their entry into the territory of the Community—

(i) they were placed under a temporary admission procedure with full exemption from import duties, in temporary storage, in a free zone, or under customs warehousing arrangements or inward processing arrangements, or

(ii) they were admitted into the territorial waters of the United Kingdom for the purpose of being incorporated into drilling or production platforms, for the purposes of the construction, repair, maintenance, alteration or fitting-out of such platforms, for the purpose of linking such platforms to the mainland of the United Kingdom, or for the purpose of fuelling or provisioning such platforms, or

(*b*) they were placed under any customs transit procedure in pursuance of a supply made in the course of a business,

and (in the case in question) the time that any Community customs debt in relation to the goods would be incurred in the United Kingdom if the accession to the European Union of the acceding States were disregarded would fall to be determined by reference to the matters mentioned in sub-paragraph (*a*) or (*b*) above.

(4) This regulation does not apply to the following goods—

(*a*) goods which are exported on or after [the date specified in paragraph (6)][1] to a place outside the member States, (*b*) goods which are not means of transport and are removed on or after [the date specified in paragraph (6)][1] from a temporary admission procedure such as is referred to in paragraph (3)(*a*)(i) above, in order to be returned to the person in an acceding State who had exported them from that State,

(*c*) means of transport which are removed on or after [the date specified in paragraph (6)][1] from a temporary admission procedure such as is referred to in paragraph (3)(*a*)(i) above and which—

(i) were first brought into service before [the date specified in paragraph (7)][1], or

(ii) have a value not exceeding £4,000, or

(iii) have been charged in an acceding State with VAT which has not been remitted or refunded by reason of their exportation and to such other tax (if any) to which means of transport of that class or description are normally chargeable.

[(5) For the purposes of paragraphs (2) and (4) the specified date—

(*a*) in relation to the 1995 acceding states is 1st January 1995;

(*b*) in relation to the 2004 acceding states is 1st May 2004; and

(*c*) in relation to the 2007 acceding states is 1st January 2007.

(6) For the purposes of paragraphs (2) and (4) the specified date—

(*a*) in relation to the 1995 acceding states is 20th October 1995;

(*b*) in relation to the 2004 acceding states 1st May 2004; and

(*c*) in relation to the 2007 acceding states 1st January 2007.

(7) For the purposes of paragraph (4)(*c*)(i) the specified date—

(*a*) in relation to the 1995 acceding states is 1st January 1987;

(*b*) in relation to the 2004 acceding states is 1st May 2006; and

(*c*) in relation to the 2007 acceding states is 1st January 1999.][1]

Former regulations—VAT (General) Regulations, SI 1985/886 reg 57DA; VAT (General) (Amendment) Regulations, SI 1995/152 reg 6.

Amendments—[1] Paras (1), (5) and words in paras (2), (4) substituted, by the VAT (Amendment) (No 3) regulations, SI 2006/3292 regs 2, 5 with effect from 1 January 2007.

139 For the purposes of the Act the following territories shall be treated as included in the territory of the member States and the territory of the Community—

(i) the Principality of Monaco (French Republic), …[1]

(ii) the Isle of Man (United Kingdom)[, and

(iii) the United Kingdom Sovereign Base Areas of Akrotiri and Dhekelia (Cyprus).][1]

Former regulations—VAT (General) Regulations, SI 1985/886 reg 57E; VAT (General) (Amendment) Regulations, SI 1992/3102 reg 44.

Amendments—[1] Word in para (i) revoked, and para (iii) and word preceding it inserted, by the VAT (Amendment) (No 2) Regulations, SI 2004/1082 regs 2, 6 with effect from 1 May 2004.

Entry and exit formalities

140— (1) Where goods enter the United Kingdom from the territories prescribed in regulation 136 or 137 the formalities relating to the entry of goods into the customs territory of the Community contained in Council Regulation (EEC) No 2913/92, Commission Regulation (EEC) No 2454/93 and the Customs Controls on Importation of Goods Regulations 1991, shall be completed.

(2) Where goods are exported from the United Kingdom to the territories prescribed in regulation 136 or 137 the formalities relating to the export of goods to a place outside the customs territory of the Community contained in Council Regulation (EEC) No 2913/92 and Commission Regulation (EEC) No 2454/93 shall be completed.

Former regulations—VAT (General) Regulations, SI 1985/886 reg 57F; VAT (General) (Amendment) Regulations, SI 1992/3102 reg 44, SI 1993/3027 regs 2, 4.

Use of the internal Community transit procedure

141 Where goods enter the United Kingdom from the territories prescribed in regulation 136 or 137 and the said goods are intended for another member State, or other destination outside the United Kingdom transport of the goods to which destination involves their passage through another member State, the internal Community transit procedure described in Council Regulation (EEC) No 2913/92 and Commission Regulation (EEC) No 2454/93 shall apply.

Former regulations—VAT (General) Regulations, SI 1985/886 reg 57G; VAT (General) (Amendment) Regulations, SI 1992/3102 reg 44.

Customs and excise legislation to be applied

142 Subject to regulation 143, where goods are imported into the United Kingdom from the territories prescribed in regulation 136 or 137 customs and excise legislation shall apply (so far as relevant) in relation to any VAT chargeable upon such importation with the same exception and adaptations as are prescribed in regulations 118, 119, 120 and 121 in relation to the application of section 16(1) of the Act.

Former regulations—VAT (General) Regulations, SI 1985/886 reg 57H; VAT (General) (Amendment) Regulations, SI 1992/3102 reg 44.

143 Where goods are imported into the United Kingdom from the territories prescribed in regulation 137, section 4 of the Finance (No 2) Act 1992 (enforcement powers) shall apply in relation to any VAT chargeable upon such importation as if references in that section to "member States" excluded the territories prescribed in regulation 137.

Former regulations—VAT (General) Regulations, SI 1985/886 reg 57I; VAT (General) (Amendment) Regulations, SI 1992/3102 reg 44.

144 Where goods are exported from the United Kingdom to the territories prescribed in regulation 136 or 137 the provisions relating to the export of goods to a place outside the customs territory of the Community contained in Council Regulation (EEC) No 2913/92 and Commission Regulation (EEC) No 2454/93 shall apply for the purpose of ensuring the correct application of the zero rate of VAT to such goods.

Former regulations—VAT (General) Regulations, SI 1985 No 886 reg 57J; VAT (General) (Amendment) Regulations, SI 1992/3102 reg 44.

145— (1) Subject to paragraph (2) below, where goods are exported from the United Kingdom to the territories prescribed in regulation 136 or 137 the provisions made by or under the Customs and Excise Management Act 1979 in relation to the exportation of goods to places outside the member States shall apply (so far as relevant) for the purpose of ensuring the correct application of the zero rate of VAT to such goods.

(2) Where goods are being exported from the United Kingdom to the territories prescribed in regulation 137, section 4 of the Finance (No 2) Act 1992 (enforcement powers) shall apply to such goods as if references in that section to "member States" excluded the territories prescribed in regulation 137.

Former regulations—Para (1): VAT (General) Regulations, SI 1985/886 reg 57K; VAT (General) (Amendment) Regulations, SI 1992/3102 reg 44.
Para (2): VAT (General) Regulations, SI 1985/886 reg 57L; VAT (General) (Amendment) Regulations, SI 1992/3102 reg 44.

[PART XVI(A)][1]

FISCAL AND OTHER WAREHOUSING REGIMES

Amendments—[1] This Part inserted by the VAT (Amendment) (No 3) Regulations, SI 1996/1250 reg 13 with effect from 1 June 1996.

Interpretation of Part XVI(A)

145A— (1) In this Part unless the context otherwise requires—

"eligible goods" has the meaning given by section 18B(6);

"fiscal warehouse" includes all fiscal warehouses kept by the same fiscal warehousekeeper;

"material time" has the meaning given by section 18F(1) in the case of a fiscal warehousing regime and section 18(6) in the case of a warehousing regime;

"regulation" or "regulations" refers to the relevant regulation or regulations of these Regulations; and

"section" or "sections" refers to the relevant section or sections of the Act.

(2) For the purposes of this Part, where a fiscal warehousekeeper keeps one or more fiscal warehouses there shall be associated with him a single fiscal warehousing regime; and "relevant fiscal warehousekeeper", "relevant fiscal warehouse", "relevant fiscal warehousing regime", "his fiscal warehouse", "his fiscal warehousing regime" and similar expressions shall be construed in this light.

Fiscal warehousing certificates

145B— (1) The certificate referred to in section 18B(1)(*d*) (certificate relating to acquisitions in or intended for fiscal warehousing) and the certificate referred to in section 18B(2)(*d*) (supplies of goods intended for fiscal warehousing) shall contain the information indicated in the form numbered 17 in Schedule 1 to these Regulations.

(2) A certificate prepared under section 18B(1)(*d*) by an acquirer who is not a taxable person shall be kept by him for a period of six years commencing on the day the certificate is prepared; and he shall produce it to a proper officer when that officer requests him to do so.

Certificates connected with services in fiscal or other warehousing regimes

145C The certificate referred to in section 18C(1)(*c*) (certificate required for the zero-rating of certain services performed on or in relation to goods while those goods are subject to a fiscal or other warehousing regime) shall contain the information indicated in the form numbered 18 in Schedule 1 to these Regulations.

VAT invoices relating to services performed in fiscal or other warehousing regimes

145D— (1) This regulation applies to the invoice referred to in section 18C(1)(*e*) (invoice required for the zero-rating of the supply of certain services performed on or in relation to goods while those goods are subject to a fiscal or other warehousing regime).

(2) The invoice shall be known as a VAT invoice and shall state the following particulars (unless the Commissioners allow any requirement of this paragraph to be relaxed or dispensed with)—

(*a*) an identifying number,
(*b*) the material time of the supply of the services in question,
(*c*) the date of the issue of the invoice,
(*d*) the name, an address and the registration number of the supplier,
(*e*) the name and an address of the person to whom the services are supplied,
(*f*) a description sufficient to identify the nature of the services supplied,
(*g*) the extent of the services and the amount payable, excluding VAT, expressed in sterling,
(*h*) the rate of any cash discount offered,
(*i*) the rate of VAT as zero per cent, and
(*j*) a declaration that in respect of the supply of services in question, the requirements of section 18C(1) will be or have been satisfied.

(3) The supplier of the services in question shall issue the invoice to the person to whom the supply is made within thirty days of the material time of that supply of services (or within such longer period as the Commissioners may allow in general or special directions).

Fiscal warehousing regimes

145E— (1) Upon any eligible goods entering a fiscal warehouse the relevant fiscal warehouse-keeper shall record their entry in his relevant fiscal warehousing record.

(2) Eligible goods shall only be subject to or in a fiscal warehousing regime at any time—

(*a*) while they are allocated to that regime in the relevant fiscal warehousing record;
(*b*) while they are not identified in that record as having been transferred; or,
(*c*) prior to their removal from that regime.

The fiscal warehousing record and stock control

145F— (1) In addition to the records referred to in regulation 31, a fiscal warehousekeeper shall maintain a fiscal warehousing record for any fiscal warehouse in respect of which he is the relevant fiscal warehousekeeper.

(2) The fiscal warehousing record may be maintained in any manner acceptable to the Commissioners. In particular, it shall be capable of—

(*a*) ready use by any proper officer in the course of his duties; and
(*b*) reproduction into a form suitable for any proper officer to readily use at a place other than the relevant fiscal warehouse.

(3) Subject to paragraph (4) below, the fiscal warehousing record shall have the features and shall comply with the requirements set out in Schedule 1A to these Regulations.

(4) In respect of any goods the relevant fiscal warehousing record shall not be required to record events more than six years following—

(*a*) the transfer or removal of those goods from the relevant fiscal warehousing regime; or,
(*b*) the exit of those goods from the relevant fiscal warehouse (in the case of goods which were not allocated to the relevant fiscal warehousing regime).

(5) A fiscal warehousekeeper, upon receiving a request to do so from any proper officer, shall—

(*a*) produce his fiscal warehousing record to that officer and permit him to inspect or take copies of it or of any part of it (as that officer shall require); or,
(*b*) facilitate and permit that officer to inspect any goods which are stored or deposited in his fiscal warehouse (whether or not those goods are allocated to the relevant fiscal warehousing regime).

Fiscal warehousing transfers in the United Kingdom

145G— (1) Subject to paragraphs (2) and (3) below, a fiscal warehousekeeper ("the original fiscal warehousekeeper") may permit eligible goods which are subject to his fiscal warehousing regime ("the original regime") to be transferred to another fiscal warehousing regime ("the other regime") without those goods being treated as removed from the original regime.

(2) The original fiscal warehousekeeper shall not allow eligible goods to exit from his fiscal warehouse in pursuance of this regulation before he receives a written undertaking from the fiscal warehousekeeper in relation to that other fiscal warehousing regime ("the other fiscal warehousekeeper") that, in respect of those eligible goods, the other fiscal warehousekeeper will comply with the requirements of paragraph (3) below.

(3) The other fiscal warehousekeeper, upon the entry of the goods to his fiscal warehouse, shall—

(*a*) record that entry in his fiscal warehousing record; and,
(*b*) allocate those goods to his fiscal warehousing regime.

Furthermore, within 30 days commencing with the day on which those goods left the original fiscal warehouse, he shall—

(*c*) deliver or cause to be delivered to the original fiscal warehousekeeper a certificate in a form acceptable to the Commissioners confirming that he has recorded the entry of those goods to his fiscal warehouse and allocated them to his fiscal warehousing regime; and,
(*d*) retain a copy of that certificate as part of his fiscal warehousing record.

Removal of goods from a fiscal warehousing regime and transfers overseas

145H— (1) Without prejudice to sections 18F(5), 18F(6) and the following paragraphs of this regulation, eligible goods which are allocated to a fiscal warehousing regime shall only be removed from that regime at the time and in any of the following circumstances—

(*a*) when an entry in respect of those eligible goods is made in the relevant fiscal warehousing record which indicates the time and date of their removal from that regime;
(*b*) when the eligible goods are moved outside the fiscal warehouse in respect of which they are allocated to a fiscal warehousing regime (except in the case of movements between fiscal warehouses kept by the same fiscal warehousekeeper); or,
(*c*) at the time immediately preceding a retail sale of those eligible goods.

The person who shall be treated as the person who removes or causes the removal of the relevant goods from the relevant fiscal warehousing regime in any of the circumstances described above shall be, as the case requires, either the person who causes any of those circumstances to occur or, in the case of sub-paragraph (*c*), the person who makes the retail sale referred to there.

(2) Subject to paragraph (3) below, eligible goods which are subject to a fiscal warehousing regime shall not be treated as removed from that regime but shall be treated as transferred or as being in the process of transfer, as the case requires, in any of the following circumstances—

(*a*) where the goods in question are transferred or are in the process of transfer to another fiscal warehousing regime in pursuance of regulation 145G(1) above;
(*b*) where the goods in question are transferred or are in the process of transfer to arrangements which correspond in effect, under the law of another member State, to section 18B(3) (fiscal warehousing) whether or not those arrangements also correspond in effect to section 18C(1) (zero-rating of certain specified services performed in a fiscal or other warehousing regime);
(*c*) where the goods in question are exported or are in the process of being exported to a place outside the member States; or,
(*d*) where the goods in question are moved temporarily to a place other than the relevant fiscal warehouse for repair, processing, treatment or other operations (subject to the prior agreement of and to conditions to be imposed by the Commissioners).

(3) Where any relevant document referred to in paragraph (4) below is not received by the relevant fiscal warehousekeeper within the time period indicated there (commencing on the day on which the relevant eligible goods leave his fiscal warehouse), he shall—

(*a*) make an entry by way of adjustment to his fiscal warehousing record to show the relevant goods as having been removed from his fiscal warehousing regime at the time and on the day when they left;
(*b*) identify in his fiscal warehousing record the person on whose instructions he allowed the goods to leave his fiscal warehouse as the person removing those goods and that person's address and registration number (if any); and,
(*c*) notify the person on whose instructions he allowed the goods to leave his fiscal warehouse that the relevant document has not been received by him in time.

(4) The document and time period referred to in paragraph (3) above is, as the case requires, either—

(*a*) the certificate referred to in regulation 145G(3)(*c*) confirming the completion of a transfer of eligible goods from the relevant fiscal warehousing regime to another fiscal warehousing regime (30 days);
(*b*) a document evidencing the completion of the transfer of the eligible goods from the relevant fiscal warehousing regime directly to arrangements which correspond, in another member State, to fiscal warehousing (60 days); or,
(*c*) a document evidencing the export of the eligible goods from the relevant fiscal warehousing regime to a place outside the member States (60 days).

145I— (1) A fiscal warehousekeeper shall not remove or allow the removal of any eligible goods from his fiscal warehousing regime at any time before—

(*a*) he has inspected and placed on his fiscal warehousing record a copy of the relevant document issued by the Commissioners under regulation 145J(1) (removal document); or,
(*b*) he is provided with the registration number of a person registered under the Act and a written undertaking from that person that any VAT payable by that person as the result of any removal of eligible goods from that fiscal warehousing regime will be accounted for on that person's return in accordance with regulation 40(1)(*c*).

(2) Without prejudice to section 18E, where a fiscal warehousekeeper allows the removal of any eligible goods to take place from his fiscal warehousing regime otherwise than in accordance with this regulation, he shall be jointly and severally liable with the person who removes the goods for the payment of the VAT payable under section 18D(2) to the Commissioners.

(3) Paragraphs (1) and (2) above shall not apply to a removal which is the result of an entry in the relevant fiscal warehousing record made by the relevant fiscal warehousekeeper in compliance with regulation 145H(3)(*a*) (non-receipt of a document following transfer or export).

Payment on removal of goods from a fiscal warehousing regime

145J— (1) The Commissioners may, in respect of a person who is seeking to remove or cause the removal of eligible goods from a fiscal warehousing regime,—

(*a*) accept from or on behalf of that person payment of the VAT payable (if any) as a result of that removal, and

(*b*) issue to that person a document bearing a reference or identification number.

(2) The Commissioners need not act in accordance with paragraph (1) above unless, as the case requires, they are satisfied as to—

(*a*) the value and material time of any supply of the relevant goods in the fiscal warehousing regime which is treated as taking place in the United Kingdom under section 18B(4) and the status of the person who made that supply;

(*b*) the nature and quantity of the relevant eligible goods;

(*c*) the value of any relevant self-supplies of specified services treated as made under section 18C(3) in the course or furtherance of his business by the person who is to remove the relevant goods, or by the person on whose behalf the goods are to be removed, at the time they are removed from the fiscal warehousing regime; and

(*d*) the nature and material time of any relevant supplies of specified services in respect of which the self-supplies referred to in sub-paragraph (*c*) above are treated as being identical (certain supplies of services on or in relation to goods while those goods are subject to the fiscal warehousing regime).

(3) In paragraph (2)(*a*) above 'status' is a reference to whether the person in question—

(*a*) is or is required to be registered under the Act, or

(*b*) would be required to be registered under the Act were it not for paragraph 1(9) of Schedule 1 to the Act, paragraph 1(7) of Schedule 2 to the Act, paragraph 1(6) of Schedule 3 to the Act, or any of those provisions.

[Place of supply of goods subject to warehousing regime

145K— (1) Section 18(1) (supply of goods subject to warehousing regime and before duty point treated as taking place outside the United Kingdom) shall not apply in the following prescribed circumstances.

(2) The circumstances are—

(*a*) that there is a supply of goods that would but for this regulation be treated for the purposes of the Act as taking place outside the United Kingdom by virtue of section 18(1);

(*b*) the whole or part of the business carried on by the supplier of those goods consists in supplying to a number of persons goods to be sold, by them or others, by retail;

(*c*) that supplier is a taxable person (or would be a taxable person but for section 18(1)); and

(*d*) that supply is to a person who is not a taxable person, and

(i) consists in a supply of goods to that person to be sold, by that person, by retail, or

(ii) consists in a supply of goods to that person by retail.][1]

Amendments—[1] This regulation inserted by the VAT (Amendment) (No 2) Regulations, SI 2005/2231 reg 10 with effect from 1 September 2005.

PART XVII
NEW MEANS OF TRANSPORT

Interpretation of Part XVII

146 In this Part—

"claim" means a claim for a refund of VAT made pursuant to section 40 of the Act and "claimant" shall be construed accordingly;

"competent authority" means an authority having powers under the laws in force in any member State to register a vehicle for road use in that member State;

"first entry into service" in relation to a new means of transport means the time determined in relation to that means of transport under regulation 147;

"registration" means registration for road use in a member State corresponding in relation to that member State to registration in accordance with the Vehicles Excise and Registration Act 1994.

Former regulations—VAT (General) Regulations, SI 1985/886 reg 64B(3); VAT (General) (Amendment) Regulations, SI 1992/3102 reg 44; VAT (Refunds in relation to New Means of Transport) Regulations, SI 1992/3100 reg 1(2).

First entry into service of a means of transport

147— (1) For the purposes of section 95 of the Act a means of transport is to be treated as having first entered into service—

(*a*) in the case of a ship or aircraft—

(i) when it is delivered from its manufacturer to its first purchaser or owner, or on its first being made available to its first purchaser or owner, whichever is the earlier, or

(ii) if its manufacturer takes it into use for demonstration purposes, on its being first taken into such use, and

(*b*) in the case of a motorised land vehicle—

(i) on its first registration for road use by the competent authority in the member State of its manufacture or when a liability to register for road use is first incurred in the member State of its manufacture, whichever is the earlier,

(ii) if it is not liable to be registered for road use in the member State of its manufacture, on its removal by its first purchaser or owner, or on its first delivery or on its being made available to its first purchaser, whichever is the earliest, or

(iii) if its manufacturer takes it into use for demonstration purposes, on its first being taken into such use.

(2) Where the times specified in paragraph (1) above cannot be established to the Commissioners' satisfaction, a means of transport is to be treated as having first entered into service on the issue of an invoice relating to the first supply of the means of transport.

Former regulations—VAT (General) Regulations, SI 1985/886 reg 64B(1), (2); VAT (General) (Amendment) Regulations, SI 1992/3102 reg 44.

Notification of acquisition of new means of transport by non-taxable persons and payment of VAT

148— (1) Where—

(*a*) a taxable acquisition of a new means of transport takes place in the United Kingdom,

(*b*) the acquisition is not in pursuance of a taxable supply, and

(*c*) the person acquiring the goods is not a taxable person at the time of the acquisition,

the person acquiring the goods shall notify the Commissioners of the acquisition within 7 days of the time of the acquisition or the arrival of the goods in the United Kingdom, whichever is the later.

(2) The notification shall be in writing in the English language and shall contain the following particulars—

(*a*) the name and current address of the person acquiring the new means of transport,

(*b*) the time of the acquisition,

(*c*) the date when the new means of transport arrived in the United Kingdom,

(*d*) a full description of the new means of transport which shall include any registration mark allocated to it by any competent authority in another member State prior to its arrival in the United Kingdom and any chassis, hull or airframe identification number and engine number,

(*e*) the consideration for the transaction in pursuance of which the new means of transport was acquired,

(*f*) the name and address of the supplier in the member State from which the new means of transport was acquired,

(*g*) the place where the new means of transport can be inspected, and

(*h*) the date of notification.

(3) The notification shall include a declaration, signed by the person who is required to make the notification or a person authorised in that behalf in writing, that all the information entered in it is true and complete.

(4) The notification shall be made at, or sent to, any office designated by the Commissioners for the receipt of such notifications.

(5) Any person required to notify the Commissioners of an acquisition of a new means of transport shall pay the VAT due upon the acquisition at the time of notification or within 30 days of the Commissioners issuing a written demand to him detailing the VAT due and requesting payment.

Former regulations—VAT (General) Regulations, SI 1985/886 reg 64A; VAT (General) (Amendment) Regulations, SI 1992/3102 reg 44.

Refunds in relation to new means of transport

149 A claimant shall make his claim in writing no earlier than one month and no later than 14 days prior to making the supply of the new means of transport by virtue of which the claim arises.

Former regulation—VAT (Refunds in relation to New Means of Transport) Regulations, SI 1992/3100 reg 2.

150 The claim shall be made at, or sent to, any office designated by the Commissioners for the receipt of such claims.

Former regulation—VAT (Refunds in relation to New Means of Transport) Regulations, SI 1992/3100 reg 3.

151 The claim shall contain the following information—

(*a*) the name, current address and telephone number of the claimant,

(*b*) the place where the new means of transport is kept and the times when it may be inspected, (*c*) the name and address of the person who supplied the new means of transport to the claimant,

(*d*) the price paid by the claimant for the supply to him of the new means of transport excluding any VAT,

(*e*) the amount of any VAT paid by the claimant on the supply to him of the new means of transport,

(*f*) the amount of any VAT paid by the claimant on the acquisition of the new means of transport from another member State or on its importation from a place outside the member States,

(*g*) the name and address of the proposed purchaser, the member State to which the new means of transport is to be removed, and the date of the proposed purchase,

(*h*) the price to be paid by the proposed purchaser,

(*i*) a full description of the new means of transport including, in the case of motorised land vehicles, its mileage since its first entry into service and, in the case of ships and aircraft, its hours of use since its first entry into service,

(*j*) in the case of a ship, its length in metres,

(*k*) in the case of an aircraft, its take-off weight in kilograms,

(*l*) in the case of a motorised land vehicle powered by a combustion engine, its displacement or cylinder capacity in cubic centimetres, and in the case of an electrically propelled motorised land vehicle, its maximum power output in kilowatts, described to the nearest tenth of a kilowatt, and

(*m*) the amount of the refund being claimed.

Former regulation—VAT (Refunds in relation to New Means of Transport) Regulations, SI 1992/3100 reg 4.

152 The claim shall be accompanied by the following documents—

(*a*) the invoice issued by the person who supplied the new means of transport to the claimant or such other documentary evidence of purchase as is satisfactory to the Commissioners,

(*b*) in respect of a new means of transport imported from a place outside the member States by the claimant, documentary evidence of its importation and of the VAT paid thereon, and

(*c*) in respect of a new means of transport acquired by the claimant from another member State, documentary evidence of the VAT paid thereon.

Former regulation—VAT (Refunds in relation to New Means of Transport) Regulations, SI 1992/3100 reg 5.

153 The claim shall include a declaration, signed by the claimant or a person authorised by him in that behalf in writing, that all the information entered in or accompanying it is true and complete.

Former regulation—VAT (Refunds in relation to New Means of Transport) Regulations, SI 1992/3100 reg 6.

154 The claim shall be completed by the submission to the Commissioners of—

(*a*) the sales invoice or similar document identifying the new means of transport and showing the price paid by the claimant's customer, and

(*b*) documentary evidence that the new means of transport has been removed to another member State.

Former regulation—VAT (Refunds in relation to New Means of Transport) Regulations, SI 1992/3100 reg 7.

Supplies of new means of transport to persons departing to another member State

155 The Commissioners may, on application by a person who is not taxable in another member State and who intends—

(*a*) to purchase a new means of transport in the United Kingdom, and

(*b*) to remove that new means of transport to another member State,

permit that person to purchase a new means of transport without payment of VAT, for subsequent removal to another member State within 2 months of the date of supply and its supply, subject to such conditions as they may impose, shall be zero-rated.

Former regulations—VAT (General) Regulations, SI 1985/886 reg 57C; VAT (General) (Amendment) Regulations, SI 1992/3102 reg 44.

PART XVIII
BAD DEBT RELIEF (THE OLD SCHEME)

Interpretation of Part XVIII

156–164 …

Amendments—This part revoked by the VAT (Amendment) Regulations, SI 1997/1086 reg 9 with effect from 1 May 1997.

PART XIX
BAD DEBT RELIEF (THE NEW SCHEME)

Interpretation of Part XIX

Note—With effect for the purposes of the making of any refund or repayment after 9 March 1999, but not anything received on or before that day, Part XIX, other than reg 171, of these regulations shall, subject to provisions made under VATA

1994 s 36, be read as if a reference to a payment being received by the claimant includes a payment received by a person to whom a right to receive it has been assigned by virtue of FA 1999 s 12(4).

165 In this Part—

"claim" means a claim in accordance with regulations 166 and 167 for a refund of VAT to which a person is entitled by virtue of section 36 of the Act and "claimant" shall be construed accordingly;

"payment" means any payment or part-payment which is made by any person …[1] by way of consideration for a supply regardless of whether such payment extinguishes the purchaser's debt to the claimant or not;

"purchaser" means a person to whom the claimant made a relevant supply;

"refunds for bad debts account" has the meaning given in regulation 168;

"relevant supply" means any taxable supply upon which a claim is based;

"return" means the return which the claimant is required to make in accordance with regulation 25;

"security" means—

(*a*) in relation to England, Wales and Northern Ireland, any mortgage, charge, lien or other security, and

(*b*) in relation to Scotland, any security (whether heritable or moveable), any floating charge and any right of lien or preference and right of retention (other than a right of compensation or set-off).

Former regulation—VAT (Refunds for Bad Debts) Regulations, SI 1991/371 reg 2.

Amendments—[1] In definition of "payment" words revoked by the VAT Regulations, SI 1999/3029, regs 2, 3 with effect from 1 December 1999.

[Time within which a claim must be made

165A— (1) Subject to paragraph (3) [and (4)][2] below, a claim shall be made within the period of [4 years and 6 months][2] following the later of—

(*a*) the date on which the consideration (or part) which has been written off as a bad debt becomes due and payable to or to the order of the person who made the relevant supply; and

(*b*) the date of the supply.

(2) A person who is entitled to a refund by virtue of section 36 of the Act, but has not made a claim within the period specified in paragraph (1) shall be regarded for the purposes of this Part as having ceased to be entitled to a refund accordingly.

(3) This regulation does not apply insofar as the date mentioned at sub-paragraph (*a*) or (*b*) of paragraph (1) above, whichever is the later, falls before 1st May 1997.

[(4) A person shall be regarded for the purposes of this Part as having ceased to be entitled to a refund where the date mentioned at subparagraph (*a*) or (*b*) of paragraph (1) above, whichever is the later, is on or before 30th September 2005.][2]][1]

Amendments—[1] This regulation inserted by the VAT (Amendment) Regulations, SI 1997/1086 reg 10 with effect from 1 May 1997.

[2] In para (1), words inserted and words substituted for words "3 years and 6 months", and para (4) inserted, by the VAT (Amendment) Regulations, SI 2009/586 regs 2, 10 with effect from 1 April 2009.

The making of a claim to the Commissioners

166— (1) Save as the Commissioners may otherwise allow or direct, the claimant shall make a claim to the Commissioners by including the correct amount of the refund in the box opposite the legend "VAT reclaimed in this period on purchases and other inputs" on his return [for the prescribed accounting period in which he becomes entitled to make the claim or, subject to regulation 165A, any later return][1].

(2) If at a time the claimant becomes entitled to a refund he is no longer required to make returns to the Commissioners he shall make a claim to the Commissioners in such form and manner as they may direct.

Former regulation—VAT (Refunds for Bad Debts) Regulations, SI 1991/371 reg 3.

Amendments—[1] Words in para (1) inserted by the VAT (Amendment) Regulations, SI 1997/1086 reg 11 with effect from 1 May 1997.

[Notice to purchaser of claim

166A Where the purchaser is a taxable person[, and the relevant supply was made before 1st January 2003][2] the claimant shall not before, but within 7 days from, the day he makes a claim give to the purchaser a notice in writing containing the following information—

(*a*) the date of issue of the notice;

(*b*) the date of the claim;

(*c*) the date and number of any VAT invoice issued in relation to each relevant supply;

(*d*) the amount of the consideration for each relevant supply which the claimant has written off as a bad debt;

(*e*) the amount of the claim.][1]

Press releases etc—Business Brief 5/98 10-2-98 (VAT bad debt relief—insolvency practitioners).

Amendments—[1] This regulation inserted by the VAT (Amendment) Regulations, SI 1997/1086 reg 12 with effect from 1 May 1997.

[2] Words inserted by the VAT (Amendment) (No 4) Regulations, SI 2002/3027 regs 2, 3 with effect from 1 January 2003.

Evidence required of the claimant in support of the claim

167 Save as the Commissioners may otherwise allow, the claimant, before he makes a claim, shall hold in respect of each relevant supply—

(*a*) either—

(i) a copy of any VAT invoice which was provided in accordance with Part III of these Regulations, or

(ii) where there was no obligation to provide a VAT invoice, a document which shows the time, nature and purchaser of the relevant goods and services, and the consideration therefore,

(*b*) records or any other documents showing that he has accounted for and paid the VAT thereon, and

(*c*) records or any other documents showing that the consideration has been written off in his accounts as a bad debt.

Former regulation—VAT (Refunds for Bad Debts) Regulations, SI 1991/371 reg 4.

Records required to be kept by the claimant

168— (1) Any person who makes a claim to the Commissioners shall keep a record of that claim.

(2) Save as the Commissioners may otherwise allow, the record referred to in paragraph (1) above shall consist of the following information in respect of each claim made—

(*a*) in respect of each relevant supply for that claim—

(i) the amount of VAT chargeable,

(ii) the prescribed accounting period in which the VAT chargeable was accounted for and paid to the Commissioners,

(iii) the date and number of any invoice issued in relation thereto or, where there is no such invoice, such information as is necessary to identify the time, nature and purchaser thereof, and

(iv) any payment received therefor,

(*b*) the outstanding amount to which the claim relates,

(*c*) the amount of the claim,...[1]

(*d*) the prescribed accounting period in which the claim was made[, and

(*e*) a copy of the notice required to be given in accordance with regulations 166A.][1]

(3) Any records created in pursuance of this regulation shall be kept in a single account to be known as the "refunds for bad debts account".

Former regulation—VAT (Refunds for Bad Debts) Regulations, SI 1991/371 reg 5.

Amendments—[1] Word "and" in para 2(*c*) deleted and para (2)(*e*) and word "and" at end of para (2)(*d*) inserted by the VAT (Amendment) Regulations, SI 1997/1086 reg 13 with effect from 1 May 1997.

Preservation of documents and records and duty to produce

169— (1) Save as the Commissioners may otherwise allow, the claimant shall preserve the documents, invoices and records which he holds in accordance with regulations 167 and 168 for a period of 4 years from the date of the making of the claim.

(2) Upon demand made by an authorised person the claimant shall produce or cause to be produced any such documents, invoices and records for inspection by the authorised person and permit him to remove them at a reasonable time and for a reasonable period.

Former regulation—VAT (Refunds for Bad Debts) Regulations, SI 1991/371 reg 6.

Attribution of payments

170— (1) [Subject to regulation 170A below, where][1]—

(*a*) the claimant made more than one supply (whether taxable or otherwise) to the purchaser, and

(*b*) a payment is received in relation to those supplies,

the payment shall be attributed to each such supply in accordance with the rules set out in paragraphs (2) and (3) below.

(2) The payment shall be attributed to the supply which is the earliest in time and, if not wholly attributed to that supply, thereafter to supplies in the order of the dates on which they were made, except that attribution under this paragraph shall not be made to any supply if the payment was allocated to that supply by the purchaser at the time of payment and the consideration for that supply was paid in full.

(3) Where—

(*a*) the earliest supply and other supplies to which the whole of the payment could be attributed under this regulation occur on one day, or (*b*) the supplies to which the balance of the payment could be attributed under this regulation occur on one day,

the payment shall be attributed to those supplies by multiplying, for each such supply, the payment received by a fraction of which the numerator is the outstanding consideration for that supply and the denominator is the total outstanding consideration for those supplies.

Former regulation—VAT (Refunds for Bad Debts) Regulations, SI 1991/371 reg 7.
Simon's Tax Cases—*Abbey National plc v C&E Comrs* [2006] STC 1.
Amendments—[1] Words substituted by the VAT (Amendment) (No 4) Regulations, SI 2002/3027 regs 2, 4 with effect from 1 January 2003.

[Attribution of payments received under certain credit agreements

[170A— (1) This regulation applies where—

(*a*) the claimant made a supply of goods and, in connection with that supply, a supply of credit;

(*b*) those supplies were made under a hire purchase, conditional sale or credit sale agreement; and

(*c*) a payment is received in relation to those supplies (other than a payment of an amount upon which interest is not charged).

(2) Where the supply of goods was made before 1st September 2006 the payment shall be attributed in accordance with the rule set out in paragraph (5).

(3) Where the supply of goods was made on or after 1st September 2006 and before 1st September 2007 the payment may be attributed in accordance with the rule set out in paragraph (5) or (6).

(4) Where the supply of goods was made on or after 1st September 2007 the payment shall be attributed in accordance with the rule set out in paragraph (6).

(5) Where this paragraph applies, the payment shall be attributed—

(*a*) as to the amount obtained by multiplying it by the fraction A/B, to the supply of credit; and

(*b*) as to the balance, to the supply of goods,

where—

A is the total of the interest on the credit provided under the agreement under which the supplies are made (determined as at the date of the making of the agreement); and
B is the total amount payable under the agreement, less any amount upon which interest is not charged.

(6) Where this paragraph applies, the payment shall be attributed—

(*a*) in respect of payments made on or before termination of the agreement,

(i) as to the amount obtained by multiplying it by the fraction A/B, to the supply of credit; and

(ii) as to the balance, to the supply of goods,

where—

A is the total of the interest on the credit provided under the agreement, less any rebate of interest granted, less any interest attributable to any unpaid instalments prior to the termination; and
B is the total amount payable under the agreement being the total of *A* plus the total for the goods.

"Total for the goods" means the amount due for the goods under the agreement, less any reduction as a consequence of termination, less any amount upon which interest is not charged, less any part of the total due for the goods which is unpaid at the time of termination.

(*b*) in respect of payments made after termination of the agreement, between the supply of goods and the supply of credit according to the proportion of the balances due at the time the payment is made.

(7) Where an agreement provides for a variation of the rate of interest after the date of the making of the agreement then, for the purposes of the calculation in paragraph (5), it shall be assumed that the rate is not varied.][1]

Press releases etc—HMRC Brief 14/07 (Changes to the rules on bad debt relief for goods supplied on credit terms).
Amendments—[1] This regulation substituted by the VAT (Amendment) Regulations, SI 2007/313 regs 2, 3 with effect from 1 March 2007.

Repayment of a refund

[171— (1) Where a claimant—

(*a*) has received a refund upon a claim, and

(*b*) either—

(i) a payment for the relevant supply is subsequently received, or

(ii) a payment is, by virtue of regulation 170 or 170A, treated as attributed to the relevant supply, or

(iii) the consideration for any relevant supply upon which the claim to refund is based is reduced after the claim is made,

he shall repay to the Commissioners such an amount as equals the amount of the refund, or the balance thereof, multiplied by a fraction of which the numerator is the amount so received or attributed, and the denominator is the amount of the outstanding consideration, or such an amount as is equal to the negative entry made in the VAT allowable portion of his VAT account as provided for in regulation 38.][4]

(2) The claimant shall repay to the Commissioners the amount referred to in paragraph (1) above by including that amount in the box opposite the legend "VAT due in this period on sales and other outputs" on his return for the prescribed accounting period in which the payment is received.

(3) Save as the Commissioners may otherwise allow, where the claimant fails to comply with the requirements of regulation 167, 168, 169[, 170 or 170A][2] he shall repay to the Commissioners the amount of the refund obtained by the claim to which the failure to comply relates; and he shall repay the amount by including that amount in the box opposite the legend "VAT due in this period on sales and other outputs" on his return for the prescribed accounting period which the Commissioners shall designate for that purpose.

(4) If at the time the claimant is required to repay any amount, he is no longer required to make returns to the Commissioners, he shall repay such amount to the Commissioners at such time and in such form and manner as they may direct.

[(5) For the purposes of this regulation[, but subject to paragraph (6) below,][3] a reference to payment shall not include a reference to a payment received by a person to whom a right to receive it has been assigned.][1]

[(6) Paragraph (5) above does not apply where any person to whom the right to receive a payment has been assigned (whether by the claimant or any other person) is connected to the claimant.][3]

[(7) Any question for the purposes of paragraph (6) above whether any person is connected to the claimant shall be determined in accordance with section 839 of the Taxes Act.][3]

[(8) Paragraphs (6) and (7) above apply where the right to receive a payment is assigned on or after 11th December 2003.][3]

Former regulation—VAT (Refunds for Bad Debts) Regulations, SI 1991/371 reg 8.

Amendments—[1] Para (5) added by the VAT Regulations, SI 1999/3029, regs 2, 4 with effect from 1 December 1999.
[2] Words substituted by the VAT (Amendment) (No 4) Regulations, SI 2002/3027 regs 2, 6 with effect from 1 January 2003.
[3] Words in para (5) inserted, and paras (6)–(8), inserted by the VAT (Amendment) (No 6) Regulations, SI 2003/3220 regs 1(1)(*a*), 2, 22, 23 with effect from 11 December 2003.
[4] Para (1) substituted by the VAT (Amendment) Regulations, SI 2007/313 regs 2, 4 with effect from 1 March 2007.

Writing off debts

172— (1) This regulation shall apply for the purpose of ascertaining whether, and to what extent, the consideration is to be taken to have been written off as a bad debt.

[(1A) Neither the whole nor any part of the consideration for a supply shall be taken to have been written off in accounts as a bad debt until a period of not less than six months has elapsed from the time when such whole or part first became due and payable to or to the order of the person who made the [relevant supply][2].][1]

[(2) Subject to paragraph (1A) the whole or any part of the consideration for a [relevant supply][2] shall be taken to have been written off as a bad debt when an entry is made in relation to that supply in the refunds for bad debt account in accordance with regulation 168.][1]

(3) Where the claimant owes an amount of money to the purchaser which can be set off, the consideration written off in the accounts shall be reduced by the amount so owed.

(4) Where the claimant holds in relation to the purchaser an enforceable security, the consideration written off in the accounts of the claimant shall be reduced by the value of that security.

Former regulation—VAT (Refunds for Bad Debts) Regulations, SI 1991/371 reg 9.

Amendments—[1] Para (1A) inserted by, and para (2) substituted by, VAT (Amendment) (No 5) Regulations, SI 1996/2960 with effect from 17 December 1996.
[2] Words in paras (1A) and (2) substituted by the VAT (Amendment) Regulations, SI 1997/1086 reg 14 with effect from 1 May 1997.

[Writing off debts—margin schemes

172A— (1) This regulation applies where, by virtue of the claimant's having exercised an option under an order made under section 50A of the Act, the VAT chargeable on the relevant supply is charged by reference to the profit margin.

(2) Where this regulation applies the consideration for the relevant supply which is to be taken to have been written off as a bad debt shall not exceed the relevant amount.

(3) For the purposes of paragraph (2) above the relevant amount is—

(*a*) where either—

(i) no payment has been received in relation to the relevant supply, or

(ii) the total of such payments as have been received does not exceed the non-profit element, the profit margin; or

(*b*) where the total of such payments as have been received exceeds the non-profit element, the amount (if any) by which the consideration for the relevant supply exceeds that total.

(4) In paragraph (3) above—

"non-profit element" means the consideration for the relevant supply less the profit margin.][1]

Amendments—[1] This regulation inserted by the VAT (Amendment) Regulations, SI 1997/1086 reg 15 with effect from 1 May 1997.

[Writing off debts—tour operators margin scheme

172B— (1) This regulation applies where, by virtue of an order under section 53 of the Act, the value of the relevant supply falls to be determined otherwise than in accordance with section 19 of the Act.

(2) Where this regulation applies the consideration for the relevant supply which is to be taken to have been written off as a bad debt shall not exceed the relevant amount.

(3) For the purposes of paragraph (2) above the relevant amount is—

(*a*) where either—

(i) no payment has been received in relation to the relevant supply, or

(ii) the total of any such payments as have been received does not exceed the non-profit element,

the profit element; or

(*b*) where the total of such payments as have been received exceeds the non-profit element, the amount (if any) by which the consideration for the relevant supply exceeds that total.

(4) In this regulation—

"non-profit element" means the consideration for the relevant supply less the profit element;

"profit element" means the sum of—

(*a*) the value of the relevant supply; and

(*b*) the VAT chargeable on the relevant supply.][1]

Amendments—[1] This regulation inserted by the VAT (Amendment) Regulations, SI 1997/1086 reg 15 with effect from 1 May 1997.

[PART XIXA
REPAYMENT OF INPUT TAX WHERE CLAIM MADE UNDER PART XIX][1]

Cross References—See Reg 6(3) above (liability under this Part on transfer of going concern).

Amendments—[1] This part inserted by the VAT (Amendment) Regulations, SI 1997/1086 reg 16 with effect from 1 May 1997.

[Application

172ZC This Part applies where the relevant supply was made before 1st January 2003.][1]

Amendments—[1] This regulation inserted by the VAT (Amendment) (No 4) Regulations, SI 2002/3027 regs 2, 7 with effect from 1 January 2003.

[Interpretation of Part XIXA

172C Any expression used in this Part to which a meaning is given in Part XIX of these Regulations shall, unless the contrary intention appears, have the same meaning in this Part as it has in that Part.][1]

Amendments—[1] This regulation inserted by the VAT (Amendment) Regulations, SI 1997/1086 reg 16 with effect from 1 May 1997.

[Repayment of input tax

172D— (1) Where—

(*a*) a claim has been made; and

(*b*) the purchaser has claimed deduction of the whole or part of the VAT on the relevant supply as input tax ('the deduction'),

the purchaser shall make an entry in his VAT account in accordance with paragraphs (2) and (3) below.

(2) The purchaser shall make a negative entry in the VAT allowable portion of that part of his VAT account which relates to the prescribed accounting period of his in which the claim has been made.

(3) The amount of the negative entry referred to in paragraph (2) above shall be such amount as is found by multiplying the amount of the deduction by a fraction of which the numerator is the amount of the claim and the denominator is the total VAT chargeable on the relevant supply.

(4) None of the circumstances to which this regulation applies is to be regarded as giving rise to any application of regulations 34 and 35.] [1]

Amendments—[1] This regulation inserted by the VAT (Amendment) Regulations, SI 1997/1086 reg 15 with effect from 1 May 1997.

[Restoration of an entitlement to credit for input tax

172E— (1) Where—

(*a*) the purchaser has made an entry in his VAT account in accordance with regulation 172D ("the input tax repayment");

(*b*) he has made the return for the prescribed accounting period concerned, and has paid any VAT payable by him in respect of that period; and

(*c*) the claimant has made a repayment in accordance with regulation 171 in relation to the claim concerned,

the purchaser shall make an entry in his VAT account in accordance with paragraphs (2) and (3) below.

(2) The purchaser shall make a positive entry in the VAT allowable portion of that part of his VAT account which relates to the prescribed accounting period of his in which the repayment has been made.

(3) The amount of the positive entry referred to in paragraph (2) above shall be such amount as is found by multiplying the amount of the input tax repayment by a fraction of which the numerator is the amount repaid by the claimant and the denominator is the total amount of the claim.

(4) None of the circumstances to which this regulation applies is to be regarded as giving rise to any application of regulations 34 and 35.][1]

Amendments—[1] This regulation inserted by the VAT (Amendment) Regulations, SI 1997/1086 reg 16 with effect from 1 May 1997.

[PART XIXB
REPAYMENT OF INPUT TAX WHERE CONSIDERATION NOT PAID][1]

Amendments—[1] This Part inserted by the VAT (Amendment) (No 4) Regulations, SI 2002/3027 regs 2, 8 with effect from 1 January 2003.

[Application

172F This Part applies where the supply in relation to which a person has claimed credit for input tax was made on or after 1st January 2003.][1]

Amendments—[1] This regulation inserted by the VAT (Amendment) (No 4) Regulations, SI 2002/3027 regs 2, 8 with effect from 1 January 2003.

[Interpretation

172G In this Part—

"relevant period" means 6 months following—

(i) the date of the supply, or

(ii) if later, the date on which the consideration for the supply, or (as the case may be) the unpaid part of it, became payable.][1]

Amendments—[1] This regulation inserted by the VAT (Amendment) (No 4) Regulations, SI 2002/3027 regs 2, 8 with effect from 1 January 2003.

[Repayment of input tax

172H— (1) Subject to paragraph (5) below, where a person—

(*a*) has not paid the whole or any part of the consideration for a supply by the end of the relevant period; and

(*b*) has claimed deduction of the whole or part of the VAT on the supply as input tax ("the deduction"),

he shall make an entry in his VAT account in accordance with paragraphs (2) and (3) below.

(2) The person shall make a negative entry in the VAT allowable portion of that part of his VAT account which relates to the prescribed accounting period of his in which the end of the relevant period falls.

(3) The amount of the negative entry referred to in paragraph (2) above shall be such amount as is found by multiplying the amount of the deduction by a fraction of which the numerator is the amount of the consideration for the supply which has not been paid before the end of the relevant period and the denominator is the total consideration for the supply.

(4) None of the circumstances to which this regulation applies is to be regarded as giving rise to any application of regulations 34 and 35.

(5) This regulation does not apply where, for input tax, the operative date for VAT accounting purposes is the date mentioned in regulation 57(*b*) above.][1]

Amendments—[1] This regulation inserted by the VAT (Amendment) (No 4) Regulations, SI 2002/3027 regs 2, 8 with effect from 1 January 2003.

[Restoration of an entitlement to credit for input tax

172I— (1) Where a person—

(*a*) has made an entry in his VAT account in accordance with regulation 172H ("the input tax repayment");

(*b*) has made the return for the prescribed accounting period concerned, and has paid any VAT payable by him in respect of that period; and

(*c*) after the end of the relevant period, has paid the whole or part of the consideration for the supply in relation to which the input tax repayment was made,

he shall make an entry in his VAT account in accordance with paragraphs (2) and (3) below in respect of each such payment made.

(2) The person shall make a positive entry in the VAT allowable portion of that part of his VAT account which relates to the prescribed accounting period of his in which payment of the whole or part of the consideration was made.

(3) The amount of the positive entry referred to in paragraph (2) above shall be such amount as is found by multiplying the amount of the input tax repayment by a fraction of which the numerator is the amount of the payment referred to in paragraph (1) (*c*) above and the denominator is [that consideration for the supply which was not paid before the end of the relevant period][2].

(4) None of the circumstances to which this regulation applies is to be regarded as giving rise to any application of regulations 34 and 35.

(5) …[2]][1]

Amendments—[1] This regulation inserted by the VAT (Amendment) (No 4) Regulations, SI 2002/3027 regs 2, 8 with effect from 1 January 2003.

[2] Words in para (3) substituted, and para (5) revoked, by the VAT (Amendment) Regulations, SI 2003/532 with effect from 1 April 2003.

[Attribution of payments

172J The rules on the attribution of payments in regulation 170 and, as the case may be, [170A(5)][2] above shall apply for determining whether anything paid is to be taken as paid by way of consideration for a particular supply.][1]

Amendments—[1] This regulation inserted by the VAT (Amendment) (No 4) Regulations, SI 2002/3027 regs 2, 8 with effect from 1 January 2003.

[2] Figure substituted by the VAT (Amendment) Regulations, SI 2007/313 regs 2, 5 with effect from 1 March 2007.

[PART 19C
ADJUSTMENT OF OUTPUT TAX IN RESPECT OF SUPPLIES TO WHICH SECTION 55A (6) OF THE ACT APPLIES

172K This Part applies where a person is entitled, by virtue of section 26AB(2) of the Act, to make an adjustment to the amount of VAT which he is required to account for and pay under section 55A(6) of the Act ("the adjustment").][1]

Amendments—[1] Regs 172K–172N inserted by the VAT (Amendment) (No 3) Regulations, SI 2007/1418 regs 2, 7 with effect from 1 June 2007.

Adjustment of output tax

[172L— (1) The person must make the adjustment by making a negative entry in the VAT payable portion of that part of his VAT account which relates to the same prescribed accounting period of his as that in which he is required to make an entry in accordance with regulation 172H(2).

(2) The amount of the negative entry referred to in paragraph (1) above must be equal to the amount of the entry that is required to be made in accordance with regulation 172H(2).][1]

Amendments—[1] Regs 172K–172N inserted by the VAT (Amendment) (No 3) Regulations, SI 2007/1418 regs 2, 7 with effect from 1 June 2007.

Readjustment of output tax

[172M— (1) Where a person—

(*a*) has made an entry in his VAT account in accordance with regulation 172L; and

(*b*) in relation to the same supply, he subsequently makes an entry in his VAT account in accordance with regulation 172I,

he must make an entry in his VAT account in accordance with paragraphs (2) and (3) below.

(2) The person must make a positive entry in the VAT payable portion of that part of his VAT account which relates to the same prescribed accounting period of his as that in which he makes an entry in accordance with regulation 172I.

(3) The amount of the positive entry referred to in paragraph (2) above must be equal to the amount of the entry he makes in accordance with regulation 172I.][1]

Amendments—[1] Regs 172K–172N inserted by the VAT (Amendment) (No 3) Regulations, SI 2007/1418 regs 2, 7 with effect from 1 June 2007.

[172N None of the circumstances to which this Part applies is to be regarded as giving rise to any application of regulations 34 and 35.][1]

Amendments—[1] Regs 172K–172N inserted by the VAT (Amendment) (No 3) Regulations, SI 2007/1418 regs 2, 7 with effect from 1 June 2007.

PART XX
REPAYMENTS TO COMMUNITY TRADERS

Interpretation of Part XX

173— (1) In this Part—

"calendar year" means the period of 12 months beginning with the first day of January in any year;

"claimant" means a person making a claim under this Part or a person on whose behalf such a claim is made;

"official authority" means the authority in a member State designated to issue the certificate referred to in regulation 178(1)(*b*)(i).

(2) For the purposes of this Part, a person is treated as being established in a country if—

(*a*) he has there an establishment from which business transactions are effected, or

(*b*) he has no such establishment (there or elsewhere) but his usual place of residence is there.

(3) For the purposes of this Part—

(*a*) a person carrying on business through a branch or agency in any country is treated as having there an establishment from which business transactions are effected, and

(*b*) "usual place of residence", in relation to a body corporate, means the place where it is legally constituted.

Former regulation—VAT (Repayment to Community Traders) Regulations, SI 1980/1537 reg 2.

Repayment of VAT

174 Subject to the other provisions of this Part a person to whom this Part applies shall be entitled to be repaid VAT charged on goods imported by him from a place outside the member States in respect of which no other relief is available or on supplies made to him in the United Kingdom if that VAT would be input tax of his were he a taxable person in the United Kingdom.

Former regulations—VAT (Repayment to Community Traders) Regulations, SI 1980/1537 reg 3; VAT (Repayment to Community Traders) (Amendment) Regulations, SI 1988/2217 reg 3, SI 1992/3098 reg 3.

Persons to whom this Part applies

175 This Part applies to a person carrying on business in a member State other than the United Kingdom but does not apply to such a person in any period referred to in regulation 179 if during that period—

(*a*) he was established in the United Kingdom, or

(*b*) he made supplies in the United Kingdom of goods or services other than—

(i) transport of freight outside the United Kingdom or to or from a place outside the United Kingdom or services ancillary thereto,

(ii) services where the VAT on the supply is payable solely by the person to whom the services are supplied in accordance with the provisions of section 8 of the Act, and

(iii) goods where the VAT on the supply is payable solely by the person to whom they are supplied as provided for in section [9A or][1] 14 of the Act.

Former regulations—VAT (Repayment to Community Traders) Regulations, SI 1980/1537 reg 4; VAT (Repayment to Community Traders) (Amendment) Regulations, SI 1993/1223 reg 2.

Amendments—[1] Words in sub-para (*b*)(iii) inserted by the VAT (Amendment) (No 4) Regulations, SI 2004/3140 reg 6 with effect from 1 January 2005 in relation to supplies made on or after that date: SI 2004/3140 reg 2(1).

Supplies and importations to which this Part applies

176 This Part applies to any supply of goods or services made in the United Kingdom or to any importation of goods from a place outside the member States but does not apply to—

(*a*) a supply or importation of goods or a supply of services which the claimant has used or intends to use for the purpose of any supply by him in the United Kingdom, or

(*b*) a supply or importation of goods which the claimant has removed or intends to remove to another member State, or which he has exported or intends to export to a place outside the member States.

Former regulations—VAT (Repayment to Community Traders) Regulations, SI 1980/1537 reg 5; VAT (Repayment to Community Traders) (Amendment) Regulations, SI 1988/2217 reg 4, SI 1992/3098 reg 5.

VAT which will not be repaid

177— (1) The following VAT shall not be repaid—

(*a*) VAT charged on a supply which if made to a taxable person would be excluded from any credit under section 25 of the Act,

(*b*) VAT charged on a supply to a travel agent which is for the direct benefit of a traveller other than the travel agent or his employee.

(2) In this regulation a travel agent includes a tour operator and any person who purchases and resupplies services of a kind enjoyed by travellers.

Former regulation—VAT (Repayment to Community Traders) Regulations, SI 1980/1537 reg 6.

Method of claiming

178— (1) A person claiming a repayment of VAT under this Part shall—

(*a*) complete in the English language and send to the Commissioners either the form numbered 15 in Schedule 1 to these Regulations, or a form designed for the purpose by any official authority, containing full information in respect of all the matters specified in the said form and a declaration as therein set out, and

(*b*) at the same time furnish—

(i) a certificate of status issued by the official authority of the member State in which the claimant is established either on the form numbered 16 in Schedule 1 to these Regulations or on the form designed by the official authority for the purpose, and

(ii) such documentary evidence of an entitlement to deduct VAT as may be required of a taxable person claiming a deduction of input tax in accordance with the provisions of regulation 29.

(2) Where the Commissioners are in possession of a certificate of status issued not more than 12 months before the date of the claim, the claimant shall not be required to furnish a further certificate.

(3) The Commissioners shall refuse to accept any document referred to in paragraph (1)(*b*)(ii) above if it bears an official stamp indicating that it had been furnished in support of an earlier claim.

Former regulations—VAT (Repayment to Community Traders) Regulations, SI 1980/1537 reg 7; VAT (Repayment to Community Traders) (Amendment) Regulations, SI 1988/2217 reg 5.

Time within which a claim must be made

179— (1) A claim shall be made not later than 6 months after the end of the calendar year in which the VAT claimed was charged and shall be in respect of VAT charged on supplies or on importations from a place outside the member States made during a period of not less than 3 months and not more than one calendar year, provided that a claim may be in respect of VAT charged on supplies or on importations from a place outside the member States made during a period of less than 3 months where that period represents the final part of a calendar year.

(2) No claim shall be made for less than £16.

(3) No claim shall be made for less than £130 in respect of VAT charged on supplies or on importations from a place outside the member States made during a period of less than one calendar year except where that period represents the final part of a calendar year.

Former regulations—VAT (Repayment to Community Traders) Regulations, SI 1980/1537 reg 8; VAT (Repayment to Community Traders) (Amendment) Regulations, SI 1988/2217 reg 6, SI 1992/3098.

Deduction of bank charges

180 Where any repayment is to be made to a claimant in the country in which he is established, the Commissioners may reduce the amount of the repayment by the amount of any bank charges or costs incurred as a result thereof.

Former regulation—VAT (Repayment to Community Traders) Regulations, SI 1980/1537 reg 9.

Treatment of claim and repayment claimed

181 For the purposes of section 73 of the Act any claim made under this Part shall be treated as a return required under paragraph 2 of Schedule 11 to the Act.

Former regulation—VAT (Repayment to Community Traders) Regulations, SI 1980/1537 reg 10.

182 For the purpose of section 83(*c*) of the Act repayments claimed under this Part shall be treated as the amount of any input tax which may be credited to a person.

Former regulation—VAT (Repayment to Community Traders) Regulations, SI 1980/1537 reg 11.

False, altered or incorrect claims

183 If any claimant furnishes or sends to the Commissioners for the purposes of this Part any document which is false or which has been altered after issue to that person, the Commissioners may refuse to repay any VAT claimed by that claimant for the period of 2 years from the date when the claim, in respect of which the false or altered document was furnished or sent, was made.

Former regulation—VAT (Repayment to Community Traders) Regulations, SI 1980/1537 reg 12.

184 Where any sum has been repaid to a claimant as a result of an incorrect claim, the amount of any subsequent repayment to that claimant may be reduced by the said sum.

Former regulation—VAT (Repayment to Community Traders) Regulations, SI 1980/1537 reg 13.

PART XXI
REPAYMENTS TO THIRD COUNTRY TRADERS

Interpretation of Part XXI

185— (1) In this Part—

"claimant" means a person making a claim under this Part or a person on whose behalf a claim is made and any agent acting on his behalf as his VAT representative;

"official authority" means any-government body or agency in any country which is recognised by the Commissioners as having authority to act for the purposes of this Part;

"prescribed year" means the period of 12 months beginning on the first day of July in any year;

"VAT representative" means any person established in the United Kingdom and registered for VAT purposes in accordance with the provisions of Schedule 1 to the Act who acts as agent on behalf of a claimant;

"third country" means a country other than those comprising the member States of the European Community;

"trader" means a person carrying on a business who is established in a third country and who is not a taxable person in the United Kingdom.

(2) For the purposes of this Part, a person is treated as being established in a country if—

(*a*) he has there a business establishment, or

(*b*) he has no such establishment (there or elsewhere) but his permanent address or usual place of residence is there.

(3) For the purposes of this Part—

(*a*) a person carrying on business through a branch or agency in any country is treated as being established there, and

(*b*) where the person is a body corporate its usual place of residence shall be the place where it is legally constituted.

Former regulation—VAT (Repayments to Third Country Traders) Regulations, SI 1987/2015 reg 2.

Repayments of VAT

186 Subject to the other provisions of this Part a trader shall be entitled to be repaid VAT charged on goods imported by him into the United Kingdom in respect of which no other relief is available or on supplies made to him in the United Kingdom if that VAT would be input tax of his were he a taxable person in the United Kingdom.

Former regulation—VAT (Repayments to Third Country Traders) Regulations, SI 1987/2015 reg 3.

VAT representatives

187 The Commissioners may, as a condition of allowing a repayment under this Part, require a trader to appoint a VAT representative to act on his behalf.

Former regulation—VAT (Repayments to Third Country Traders) Regulations, SI 1987/2015 reg 4.

Persons to whom this Part applies

188— (1) Save as the Commissioners may otherwise allow, a trader to whom this Part applies who is established in a third country having a comparable system of turnover taxes will not be entitled to any refunds under this Part unless that country provides reciprocal arrangements for refunds to be made to taxable persons who are established in the United Kingdom.

(2) This Part shall apply to any trader but not if during any period determined under regulation 192—

(*a*) he was established in any of the member States of the European Community, or

(*b*) he made supplies in the United Kingdom of goods or services other than—

(i) transport of freight outside the United Kingdom to or from a place outside the United Kingdom or services ancillary thereto,

(ii) services where the VAT on the supply is payable solely by the person to whom they are supplied in accordance with the provisions of section 8 of the Act, and

(iii) goods where the VAT on the supply is payable solely by the person to whom they are supplied.

Former regulations—VAT (Repayments to Third Country Traders) Regulations, SI 1987/2015 reg 5; VAT (Repayments to Third Country Traders) (Amendment) Regulations, SI 1993/1222 reg 3.

Supplies and importations to which this Part applies

189 This Part applies to any supply of goods or services made in the United Kingdom or to any importation of goods into the United Kingdom on or after 1st July 1994 but does not apply to any supply or importation which—

(*a*) the trader has used or intends to use for the purpose of any supply by him in the United Kingdom, or

(*b*) has been exported or is intended for exportation from the United Kingdom by or on behalf of the trader.

Former regulation—VAT (Repayments to Third Country Traders) Regulations, SI 1987/2015 reg 6.

VAT which will not be repaid

190— (1) The following VAT shall not be repaid—

(*a*) VAT charged on a supply which if made to a taxable person would be excluded from any credit under section 25 of the Act,

(*b*) VAT charged on a supply to a travel agent which is for the direct benefit of a traveller other than the travel agent or his employee,

[(*c*) VAT charged on a supply used or to be used in making supplies of a description falling within article 3 of the Value Added Tax (Input Tax) (Specified Supplies) Order 1999.][1]

(2) In this regulation a travel agent includes a tour operator or any person who purchases and resupplies services of a kind enjoyed by travellers.

Former regulation—VAT (Repayments to Third Country Traders) Regulations, SI 1987/2015 reg 7.

Amendments—[1] Sub-para (1)(*c*) inserted by the VAT (Amendment) (No 4) Regulations, SI 2004/3140 reg 15 with effect from 3 December 2004 in relation to VAT charged on or after that date: SI 2004/3140 reg 2(4).

Method of claiming

191— (1) A person claiming a repayment of VAT under this Part shall—

(*a*) complete in the English language and send to the Commissioners either the form numbered 9 in Schedule 1 to these Regulations, or a like form produced by any official authority, containing full information in respect of all the matters specified in the said form and a declaration as therein set out, and

(*b*) at the same time furnish—

(i) a certificate of status issued by the official authority of the third country in which the trader is established either on the form numbered 10 in Schedule 1 to these Regulations or on a like form produced by the official authority, and

(ii) such documentary evidence of an entitlement to deduct input tax as may be required of a taxable person claiming a deduction of input tax in accordance with the provisions of regulation 29.

(2) Where the Commissioners are in possession of a certificate of status issued not more than 12 months before the date of the claim, the claimant shall not be required to furnish a further such certificate.

(3) The Commissioners shall refuse to accept any document referred to in paragraph (1)(*b*)(ii) above if it bears an official stamp indicating that it had been furnished in support of an earlier claim.

Former regulation—VAT (Repayments to Third Country Traders) Regulations, SI 1987/2015 reg 8.

Time within which a claim must be made

192— (1) A claim shall be made not later than 6 months after the end of the prescribed year in which the VAT claimed was charged and shall be in respect of VAT charged on supplies or on importations made during a period of not less than 3 months and not more than 12 months, provided that a claim may be made in respect of VAT charged on supplies or on importations made during a period of less than 3 months where that period represents the final part of the prescribed year.

(2) No claim shall be made for less than £16.

(3) No claim shall be made for less than £130 in respect of VAT charged on supplies or on importations made during a period of less than the prescribed year except where that period represents the final part of the prescribed year.

Former regulation—VAT (Repayments to Third Country Traders) Regulations, SI 1987/2015 reg 9.

Deduction of bank charges

193 Where any repayment is to be made to a claimant in the country in which he is established, the Commissioners may reduce the amount of the repayment by the amount of any bank charges or costs incurred as a result thereof.

Treatment of claim and repayment claimed

194 For the purposes of section 73 of the Act any claim made under this Part shall be treated as a return required under paragraph 2 of Schedule 11 to the Act.

Former regulation—VAT (Repayments to Third Country Traders) Regulations, SI 1987/2015 reg 10.

195 For the purpose of section 83(*c*) of the Act repayments claimed under this Part shall be treated as the amount of any input tax which may be credited to a person.

Former regulation—VAT (Repayments to Third Country Traders) Regulations, SI 1987/2015 reg 11.

False, altered or incorrect claims

196 If any claimant furnishes or sends to the Commissioners for the purposes of this Part any document which is false or which has been altered after issue to that person the Commissioners may refuse to repay any VAT claimed by that claimant for the period of 2 years from the date when the claim in respect of which the false or altered documents were furnished or sent, was made.

197 Where any sum has been repaid to a claimant as a result of an incorrect claim, the amount of any subsequent repayment to that claimant may be reduced by the said sum.

PART XXII
REPAYMENT SUPPLEMENT

Computation of period

198 In computing the period of 30 days referred to in section 79(2)(*b*) of the Act, periods referable to the following matters shall be left out of account—

(*a*) the raising and answering of any reasonable inquiry relating to the requisite return or claim,

(*b*) the correction by the Commissioners of any errors or omissions in that requisite return or claim, and

(*c*) in any case to which section 79(1)(*a*) of the Act applies, the following matters, namely—

(i) any such continuing failure to submit returns as is referred to in section 25(5) of the Act, and

(ii) compliance with any such condition as is referred to in paragraph 4(1) of Schedule 11 to the Act.

Former regulation—VAT (Repayment Supplement) Regulation, SI 1988/1343 reg 4.
Simon's Tax Cases—*C&E Comrs v L Rowland & Co (Retail) Ltd* [1992] STC 647*.

Duration of period

199 For the purpose of determining the duration of the periods referred to in regulation 198, the following rules shall apply—

(*a*) in the case of the period mentioned in regulation 198(*a*), it shall be taken to have begun on the date when the Commissioners first raised the inquiry and it shall be taken to have ended on the date when they received a complete answer to their inquiry;

(*b*) in the case of the period mentioned in regulation 198(*b*), it shall be taken to have begun on the date when the error or omission first came to the notice of the Commissioners and it shall be taken to have ended on the date when the error or omission was corrected by them;

(*c*) in the case of the period mentioned in regulation 198(*c*)(i), it shall be determined in accordance with a certificate of the Commissioners under paragraph 14(1)(*b*) of Schedule 11 to the Act;

(*d*) in the case of the period mentioned in regulation 198(*c*)(ii), it shall be taken to have begun on the date of the service of the written notice of the Commissioners which required the production of documents or the giving of security, and it shall be taken to have ended on the date when they received the required documents or the required security.

Former regulation—VAT (Repayment Supplement) Regulations, SI 1988/1343 reg 5.
Simon's Tax Cases—*C&E Comrs v L Rowland & Co (Retail) Ltd* [1992] STC 647*.

PART XXIII
REFUNDS TO "DO-IT-YOURSELF" BUILDERS

Interpretation of Part XXIII

200 In this Part—

"claim" means a claim for refund of VAT made pursuant to section 35 of the Act, and "claimant" shall be construed accordingly;

"relevant building" means a building in respect of which a claimant makes a claim.

Former regulation—VAT ("Do-It-Yourself" Builders) (Refund of Tax) Regulations, SI 1989/2259 reg 2.

Method and time for making claim

201 A claimant shall make his claim in respect of a relevant building by—

(*a*) furnishing to the Commissioners no later than 3 months after the completion of the building [the relevant form for the purposes of the claim][1] containing the full particulars required therein, and

(*b*) at the same time furnishing to them—

(i) a certificate of completion obtained from a local authority or such other documentary evidence of completion of the building as is satisfactory to the Commissioners,

(ii) an invoice showing the registration number of the person supplying the goods, whether or not such an invoice is a VAT invoice, in respect of each supply of goods on which VAT has been paid which have been incorporated into the building or its site,

(iii) in respect of imported goods which have been incorporated into the building or its site, documentary evidence of their importation and of the VAT paid thereon,

(iv) documentary evidence that planning permission for the building had been granted, and

(v) a certificate signed by a quantity surveyor or architect that the goods shown in the claim were or, in his judgement, were likely to have been, incorporated into the building or its site.

Former regulation—VAT ("Do-It-Yourself" Builders) (Refund of Tax) Regulations, SI 1989/2259 reg 3.
Amendments—[1] In para (*a*), words substituted for words "the form numbered 11 in Schedule 1 to these Regulations", by the Value Added Tax (Amendment) (No 3) Regulations, SI 2009/1967 regs 2, 7 with effect from 15 August 2009.

[201A— The relevant form for the purposes of a claim is—

(*a*) Form 11A in Schedule 1 to these Regulations where the claim relates to works described in section 35(1A)(*a*) or (*b*) of the Act;

(*b*) Form 11B in Schedule 1 to these Regulations where the claim relates to works described in section 35(1A)(*c*) of the Act.][1]

Amendments—[1] Reg 201A inserted by the Value Added Tax (Amendment) (No 3) Regulations, SI 2009/1967 regs 2, 8 with effect from 15 August 2009.

PART XXIV
FLAT-RATE SCHEME FOR FARMERS

Interpretation of Part XXIV

202 In this Part—

"certified person" means a person certified as a flat-rate farmer for the purposes of the flat-rate scheme under regulation 203 and "certified" and "certification" shall be construed accordingly.

Former regulation—VAT (Flat-rate Scheme for Farmers) Regulations, SI 1992/3103 reg 1(2).

Flat-rate scheme

203— (1) The Commissioners shall, if the conditions mentioned in regulation 204 are satisfied, certify that a person is a flat-rate farmer for the purposes of the flat-rate scheme (hereinafter in this Part referred to as "the scheme").

(2) Where a person is for the time being certified in accordance with this regulation, then (whether or not that person is a taxable person) any supply of goods or services made by him in the course or furtherance of the relevant part of his business shall be disregarded for the purpose of determining whether he is, has become or has ceased to be liable or entitled to be registered under Schedule 1 to the Act.

Former regulation—VAT (Flat-rate Scheme for Farmers) Regulations, SI 1992/3103 reg 2.

Admission to the scheme

204 The conditions mentioned in regulation 203 are that—

(*a*) the person satisfies the Commissioners that he is carrying on a business involving one or more designated activities,

(*b*) he has not in the 3 years preceding the date of his application for certification—

(i) been convicted of any offence in connection with VAT,

(ii) made any payment to compound proceedings in respect of VAT under section 152 of the Customs and Excise Management Act 1979 as applied by section 72(12) of the Act,

(iii) been assessed to a penalty under section 60 of the Act,

(*c*) he makes an application for certification on the form numbered 14 in Schedule 1 to these Regulations, and

(*d*) he satisfies the Commissioners that he is a person in respect of whom the total of the amounts as are mentioned in regulation 209 relating to supplies made in the year following the date of his certification will not exceed by £3,000 or more the amount of input tax to which he would otherwise be entitled to credit in that year.

Former regulation—VAT (Flat-rate Scheme for Farmers) Regulations, SI 1992/3103 reg 3.

Certification

205 Where the Commissioners certify that a person is a flat-rate farmer for the purposes of the scheme, the certificate issued by the Commissioners shall be effective from—

(*a*) the date on which the application for certification is received by the Commissioners,

(*b*) with the agreement of the Commissioners, an earlier date to that mentioned in sub-paragraph (*a*) above, or

(*c*) if the person so requests, a later date which is no more than 30 days after the date mentioned in sub-paragraph (*a*) above,

provided that any certificate shall not be effective from a date before the date when the person's registration under Schedule 1 or 3 to the Act is cancelled and a certificate shall not be effective from a date earlier than 1st January 1993.

Former regulation—VAT (Flat-rate Scheme for Farmers) Regulations, SI 1992/3103 reg 4.

Cancellation of certificates

206— (1) The Commissioners may cancel a person's certificate in any case where—

(*a*) a statement false in a material particular was made by him or on his behalf in relation to his application for certification,

(*b*) he has been convicted of an offence in connection with VAT or has made a payment to compound such proceedings under section 152 of the Customs and Excise Management Act 1979 as applied by section 72(12) of the Act,

(*c*) he has been assessed to a penalty under section 60 of the Act,

(*d*) he ceases to be involved in designated activities,

(*e*) he dies, becomes bankrupt or incapacitated,

(*f*) he is liable to be registered under Schedule 1 or 3 to the Act,

(*g*) he makes an application in writing for cancellation,

(*h*) he makes an application in writing for registration under Schedule 1 or 3 to the Act, and such application shall be deemed to be an application for cancellation of his certificate,

(*i*) they consider it is necessary to do so for the protection of the revenue, or

(*j*) they are not satisfied that any of the grounds for cancellation of a certificate mentioned in sub-paragraphs (*a*) to (*h*) above do not apply.

(2) Where the Commissioners cancel a person's certificate in accordance with paragraph (1) above, the effective date of the cancellation shall be for each of the cases mentioned respectively in that paragraph as follows—

(*a*) the date when the Commissioners discover that such a statement has been made,

(*b*) the date of his conviction or the date on which a sum is paid to compound proceedings,

(*c*) 30 days after the date when the assessment is notified,

(*d*) the date of the cessation of designated activities,

(*e*) the date on which he died, became bankrupt or incapacitated,

(*f*) the effective date of registration,

(*g*) not less than one year after the effective date of his certificate or such earlier date as the Commissioners may agree,

(*h*) not less than one year after the effective date of his certificate or such earlier date as the Commissioners may agree,

(*i*) the date on which the Commissioners consider a risk to the revenue arises, or

(*j*) the date mentioned in sub-paragraphs (*a*) to (*h*) above as appropriate.

Former regulation—VAT (Flat-rate Scheme for Farmers) Regulations, SI 1992/3103 reg 5.

Death, bankruptcy or incapacity of certified person

207— (1) If a certified person dies or becomes bankrupt or incapacitated, the Commissioners may, from the date on which he died or became bankrupt or incapacitated treat as a certified person any person carrying on those designated activities until some other person is certified in respect of the designated activities or the incapacity ceases, as the case may be; and the provisions of the Act and of any Regulations made thereunder shall apply to any person so treated as though he were a certified person.

(2) Any person carrying on such designated activities shall, within 30 days of commencing to do so, inform the Commissioners in writing of that fact and of the date of the death, or of the nature of the incapacity and the date on which it began.

(3) In relation to a company which is a certified person, the references in regulation 206(1)(*e*) and (2)(*e*) and in paragraph (1) above to the certified person becoming bankrupt or incapacitated shall be construed as references to its going into liquidation or receivership or [entering administration][1].

Former regulation—VAT (Flat-rate Scheme for Farmers) Regulations, SI 1992/3103 reg 6.

Amendments—[1] Words in para (3) substituted by the Enterprise Act 2002 (Insolvency) Order, SI 2003/2096 art 5, Schedule paras 55, 59 with effect from 15 September 2003. However, this amendment does not apply in any case where a petition for an administration order was presented before that date: SI 2003/2096 arts 1, 6.

Further certification

208 Where a person who has been certified and is no longer so certified makes a further application under regulation 204, that person shall not be certified for a period of 3 years from the date of the cancellation of his previous certificate except—

(*a*) the Commissioners may certify from the date of his further application a person who has not been registered under Schedule 1 or 3 to the Act at any time since the cancellation of his previous certificate; and

(*b*) where the circumstances as are mentioned in paragraph 8(1)(*c*) of Schedule 4 to the Act apply, the Commissioners may certify the person mentioned in that paragraph on a date after the expiry of one year from the date of the cancellation of his previous certificate.

Former regulation—VAT (Flat-rate Scheme for Farmers) Regulations, SI 1992/3103 reg 7.

Claims by taxable persons for amounts to be treated as credits for input tax

209— (1)The amount referred to in section 54(4) of the Act and included in the consideration for any taxable supply which is made—

(*a*) in the course or furtherance of the relevant part of his business by a person who is for the time being certified under this part,

(*b*) at a time when that person is not a taxable person, and

(*c*) to a taxable person,

shall be treated, for the purpose of determining the entitlement of the person supplied to credit under sections 25 and 26 of the Act, as VAT on a supply to that person.

(2) Subject to paragraph (3) below and save as the Commissioners may otherwise allow or direct generally or specially, a taxable person claiming entitlement to a credit of an amount as is mentioned in paragraph (1) above shall do so on the return made by him for the prescribed accounting period in which the invoice specified in paragraph (3) below is issued by a certified person.

(3) A taxable person shall not be entitled to credit as is mentioned in paragraph (1) above unless there has been issued an invoice containing the following particulars—

(*a*) an identifying number,

(*b*) the name, address and certificate number of the certified person by whom the invoice is issued,

(*c*) the name and address of the person to whom the goods or services are supplied,

(*d*) the time of the supply,

(*e*) a description of the goods or services supplied,

(*f*) the consideration for the supply or, in the case of any increase or decrease in the consideration, the amount of that increase or decrease excluding the amount as is mentioned in paragraph (1) above, and

(*g*) the amount as is mentioned in paragraph (1) above which amount shall be entitled "Flat-rate Addition" or "FRA".

Former regulation—VAT (Flat-rate Scheme for Farmers) Regulations, SI 1992/3103 reg 8.

Duty to keep records

210— (1) Every certified person shall, for the purposes of the scheme, keep and preserve the following records—

(*a*) his business and accounting records, and

(*b*) copies of all invoices specified in regulation 209(3) issued by him or on his behalf.

(2) Every certified person shall comply with such requirements with respect to the keeping, preservation and production of records as the Commissioners may notify to him.

(3) Every certified person shall keep and preserve such records as are required by paragraph (1) above or by notification for a period of 6 years or such lesser period as the Commissioners may allow.

Former regulation—VAT (Flat-rate Scheme for Farmers) Regulations, SI 1992/3103 reg 9.

Production of records

211— (1) Every certified person shall—

(*a*) upon demand made by an authorised person, produce or cause to be produced for inspection by that person—

(i) at the principal place of business of the person upon whom the demand is made or at such other place as the authorised person may reasonably require, and

(ii) at such time as the authorised person may reasonably require,

any documents specified in regulation 210(1), and

(*b*) permit an authorised person to take copies of, or make extracts from, or remove at a reasonable time and for a reasonable period, any document produced under paragraph (1)(*a*) above.(2) Where a document removed by an authorised person under paragraph (1)(*b*) above is reasonably required for the proper conduct of a business, he shall, as soon as practicable, provide a copy of that document, free of charge, to the person by whom it was produced or caused to be produced.

(3) Where any documents removed under paragraph (1)(*b*) above are lost or damaged, the Commissioners shall be liable to compensate their owner for any expenses reasonably incurred by him in replacing or repairing the documents.

Former regulation—VAT (Flat-rate Scheme for Farmers) Regulations, SI 1992/3103 reg 10.

PART XXV
DISTRESS AND DILIGENCE

[A212 In this Part—

"Job Band" followed by a number between "1" and "12" means the band for the purposes of pay and grading in which the job an officer performs is ranked in the system applicable to Customs and Excise.][1]

Amendments—[1] This Regulation inserted by the VAT (Amendment) (No 4) Regulations, SI 1996/2098 with effect from 2 September 1996.

Distress

212 …

Amendments—This regulation revoked by the Customs and Excise Duties and Other Indirect Taxes Regulations, SI 1997/1431 with effect from 1 July 1997. See SI 1997/1431 for the replacement provisions.

Diligence

213 In Scotland, the following provisions shall have effect—

(*a*) where the Commissioners are empowered to apply to the Sheriff for a warrant to authorise a Sheriff Officer to recover any amount of VAT or any sum recoverable as if it were VAT remaining due and unpaid, any application, and any certificate required to accompany that application, may be made on their behalf by a Collector of Customs and Excise or an officer of rank not below that of [Job Band 7][1];

(*b*) where, during the course of a poinding and sale in accordance with Schedule 5 to the Debtors (Scotland) Act 1987 the Commissioners are entitled as a creditor to do any acts, then any such acts, with the exception of the exercise of the power contained in paragraph 18(3) of that Schedule, may be done on their behalf by a Collector of Customs and Excise or an officer of rank not below that of [Job Band 7][1].

Former regulations—VAT (General) Regulations, SI 1985/886 reg 66; VAT (General) (Amendment) Regulations, SI 1988/2083 reg 2, SI 1993/3027 regs 2, 8.

Amendments—[1] Words in (*a*) and (*b*) above substituted by the VAT (Amendment) (No 4) Regulations, SI 1996/2098 with effect from 2 September 1996.

SCHEDULE 1

Regulation 5(1)

FORM NO 1: APPLICATION FOR VAT REGISTRATION

VAT

Value Added Tax

Application for registration

SPECIMEN

Please read VAT Notice 700/1: **Should I be registered for VAT?** before you begin to complete the application form as the explanatory notes will help you.
If you have any problems completing the form please contact the National Advice Service on 0845 010 9000 or visit our website at www.hmce.gov.uk

You must answer all questions as directed.
Write clearly in black ink and use CAPITAL LETTERS

VAT 1

VAT

Part 1 About the business

Name

1 **Sole proprietors** - please give your full name.

Partnerships - please give your trading name, or if you do not have one please give the names of all partners. You must also complete and return form VAT 2 (available from the National Advice Service or our website).

Corporate or unincorporated bodies - please give the name of the company, club, association, etc.

2 **Do you have a trading name?** (Please tick) ☐ **Yes** ☐ **No**

Please give the trading name of the business.

Status

3 **What is the structure/legal status of the business?** (Please tick)

☐ **Sole proprietor** ☐ **Partnership** (Please complete form VAT 2)

☐ **Corporate body** (e.g. limited company)

Please give incorporation details: Certificate no.

Date of incorporation

Country of incorporation

☐ **Unincorporated body** (e.g. club or association)

Please specify

Business address

4 **Please give the address of your principal place of business. This is where you carry out most of the day-to-day running of the business.** e.g. where you receive and deal with orders.

Postcode

Business phone

Fax number

Mobile phone

E-mail address

Internet address

Business activities

5	**Please tell us about all your current and/or intended business activities.** (Continue on a separate sheet if necessary)	
6	**Are you or any of the partners or directors in the business you are seeking to register through this application, involved in running any other businesses either as a sole proprietor, partner or director?** (Please tick)	☐ Yes ☐ No If **yes**, please give the names of these businesses and VAT registration numbers where appropriate. (Continue on a separate sheet if necessary)
7	**Have you, or any of the partners or directors in the business you are seeking to register through this application, been involved in running any other businesses either as a sole proprietor, partner or director in the past two years?** (Please tick)	☐ Yes ☐ No If **yes**, please give the names of these businesses and VAT registration numbers where appropriate. (Continue on a separate sheet if necessary)
8	**Is your business involved in any other activities registered with or authorised by Customs and Excise?** (Please tick boxes as appropriate)	☐ Excise duties ☐ Imports/exports ☐ Landfill tax ☐ Air passenger duty ☐ Insurance premium tax ☐ Climate change levy ☐ Aggregates levy (From 1/4/2002)
9	**Are you registering as the representative member of a VAT group?** (Please tick)	☐ Yes ☐ No If **yes**, you must provide the additional information set out on forms VAT 50 and VAT 51 (available from the National Advice Service tel: 0845 010 9000 or our website).

Part 2 About the business accounts

VAT returns

10	**Do you expect to receive regular repayments of VAT?** (Please tick)	☐ Yes ☐ No Do not answer **yes** if you believe that the majority of your VAT returns will show an overall payment of tax due to Customs and Excise.

Computer accounts

11 **Is your accounting system computerised?** (Please tick) ☐ **Yes** ☐ **No**

If yes, please give details of the software used in compiling your accounts.

Software

Version

Bank details

12 **Please give details of the bank or building society account that you use for the business.**

Sort code

Account number

or Girobank account number

Part 3 The taxable turnover and date of registration

Start of business

For the purposes of VAT, all the goods or services you supply which are VAT-rated - even zero-rated goods or services - are called 'taxable supplies' whether you are registered for VAT or not. The purchases you make for your business are not your taxable supplies.

13 **Have you made any taxable supplies yet?** (Please tick) ☐ **Yes** ☐ **No**

If yes, give the date of your first taxable supply.
If no, give the date you expect it to be.

Date of first taxable supply

Business transfers

14 **Have you taken over a VAT registered business from someone else as a going concern, or changed the legal entity that owns the business (for example from a sole proprietor to a limited company)?** (Please tick) ☐ **Yes** ☐ **No** (If no proceed to question 18)

If yes, what date did the transfer of the business or change in legal entity take place?

15 **Who was the previous owner?**

16 **What was their VAT number?**

17 **Do you want to keep this number?** (Please tick) ☐ **Yes** ☐ **No**

If yes, you and the previous owner must also complete and return form VAT 68 (available from the National Advice Service tel: 0845 010 9000 or our website). If you do keep the VAT number, remember that you will become liable for the previous owner's VAT debts.

Your taxable turnover and date of registration

We need the following information to determine whether you need to be registered, or whether you are entitled to be registered. The total value of your taxable supplies (see 'Start of business' above) is called your taxable turnover. The question of whether you need to be registered for VAT will depend upon the level of your taxable turnover in any past period of 12 months or less, or on the anticipated level of your taxable turnover in any period then beginning of 30 days alone.

18 **Have your taxable supplies, in the past 12 months or less, gone over the registration limit and/or has there been a point in the past when taxable supplies in the previous 12 months or less exceeded the registration limit?** (Please tick)

☐ **Yes** ☐ **No**

If **yes**, please give the date they exceeded. (The current limits are in Notice 700/1: **Should I be registered for VAT?**)

My taxable supplies exceeded the threshold on

☐☐ ☐☐ ☐☐☐☐

You will be registered from the first day of the second month following, e.g. If your taxable supplies exceeded the threshold in June you will be registered from 1st August.

19 **Do you expect the taxable supplies you will make in the next 30 days alone will exceed the registration limit and/or has there been a date in the past when there were grounds for believing that your taxable supplies would exceed the registration limit in the next 30 days alone?** (Please tick)

☐ **Yes** ☐ **No**

My expectation arose on

☐☐ ☐☐ ☐☐☐☐

You will be registered from the date the expectation arose.

20 **Do you wish to be registered from a date earlier than the date on which you are obliged to be registered?** (Please tick)

☐ **Yes** ☐ **No** (If no proceed to question 23)

21 **From what date would you like to be registered?**

☐☐ ☐☐ ☐☐☐☐ (Proceed to question 23)

Voluntary registration

22 **I am applying for voluntary registration because:** (Please tick)

☐ My taxable turnover is below the current registration threshold.

☐ I am not currently making taxable supplies but intend to in the future.

☐ I am established or have a fixed establishment in the UK and make or intend to make supplies only outside the UK.

I would like to be registered from

☐☐ ☐☐ ☐☐☐☐

Value of your supplies

23 **Please estimate the value of taxable supplies you expect to make in the next 12 months.**

£

24 **Do you expect to make any exempt supplies?**

(For more information about exempt supplies see Notice 700/1: **Should I be registered for VAT?**)
(Please tick)

☐ Yes ☐ No

If **yes**, estimate the value of exempt supplies you expect to make in the next 12 months.

£

25 **EC Trade** (A list of EC Member States is in Notice 700/1: **Should I be registered for VAT?**)

Please tell us the value of goods you are likely to buy from other EC Member States or sell to other EC Member States in the next 12 months

Buy £

Sell £

Exemption from registration

26 **Do you want exemption from registration because your taxable supplies are wholly or mainly zero-rated?**

☐ Yes ☐ No

If **yes**, give the expected value of your zero-rated supplies in the next 12 months.

Zero-rated supplies £

Part 4 Your details and declaration

Home address and National Insurance number

27 **Please give your full home address and your National Insurance number**

- Sole proprietors - give your home address and National Insurance number below.
- Partnerships - give home address and National Insurance numbers of all partners on form VAT 2.
- Corporate bodies - give home address and National Insurance number of the director, company secretary or authorised signatory signing the application form. If you are signing as an authorised signatory include a letter of authorisation signed by a director or company secretary. This must include their home address and National Insurance number.
- Unincorporated bodies - give home address and National Insurance number of the person signing the application form.

Home address
(If you have lived at this address for less than three years please provide details of your previous home address on a separate sheet)

Postcode

National Insurance number
If you do not have a National Insurance number please give your Tax Identification number issued by your country of origin.

National Insurance number

Tax identification number

Declaration

28 **Please sign and date the declaration below**
(Corporate bodies - a director, company secretary or authorised signatory must sign the form)

(Insert full name in BLOCK CAPITALS)

I declare that the information given on this form and accompanying document is true and complete.

Signature

Date

Your position in the business (Please tick one box)

☐ **Proprietor** ☐ **Partner**
☐ **Director** ☐ **Company Secretary**
☐ **Trustee**
Other (Please give details)

Checklist

- Have you signed the form?
- Partnership? **Remember to complete and enclose form VAT 2**
- VAT group? **Remember to complete and enclose forms VAT 50 and VAT 51**
- Corporate body? **Have you completed the incorporation details in question 3?**
- Applying on a voluntary basis because you are not trading yet? **Remember to enclose evidence of your intention to trade such as copies of contracts, details of purchases for your business etc.**
- Taking over a VAT registration number from a previous owner? **Remember to complete and enclose form VAT 68 if you wish to retain the VAT number**
- Involved in land or property-related supplies where you are electing to waive exemption from VAT (opting to tax)? **Have you enclosed details as per Notice 700/1: Should I be registered for VAT?**
- Have you notified the Inland Revenue of your business start up?

What to do next?

When you have completed and signed this form please send it to the address given in Notice 700/1 **Should I be registered for VAT?** Provided you have given all the necessary information we will usually register and give you a VAT registration number within 15 working days of receiving your application form.

Data Protection Act 1998

HM Customs and Excise collects information in order to administer the taxes for which it is responsible (such as VAT, insurance premium tax, excise duties, air passenger duty, landfill tax), and for detecting and preventing crime. Where the law permits we may also obtain information about you from third parties, or give information to them. This would be to check its accuracy, prevent or detect crime or protect public funds in other ways. These third parties may include the police, other government departments and agencies.

Regulation 5(1)

FORM NO: 2: PARTNERSHIP DETAILS

VALUE ADDED TAX

Partnership Details

HM Customs and Excise

For official use only

Date of receipt

Each partner should complete one of the sections below.

Please start at the beginning of each line and leave a space between words.

Please use BLOCK CAPITALS and write clearly in ink.

Registration No. (where known)

1

Full name

Home address

Postcode

Home telephone Mobile telephone

National Insurance Number or Tax Identifier in country of origin

Signature Date

Partner details

2

Full name

Home address

Postcode

Home telephone Mobile telephone

National Insurance Number or Tax Identifier in country of origin

Signature Date

Partner details

3

Full name

Home address

Postcode

Home telephone Mobile telephone

National Insurance Number or Tax Identifier in country of origin

Signature Date

Partner details

4

Full name

Home address

Postcode

Home telephone Mobile telephone

National Insurance Number or Tax Identifier in country of origin

Signature Date

VAT 2 PT (December 2001) *Please continue overleaf*

Partner details

5

Full name

Home address

Postcode

Home telephone Mobile telephone

National Insurance Number or Tax Identifier in country of origin

Signature Date

Partner details

6

Full name

Home address

Postcode

Home telephone Mobile telephone

National Insurance Number or Tax Identifier in country of origin

Signature Date

Partner details

7

Full name

Home address

Postcode

Home telephone Mobile telephone

National Insurance Number or Tax Identifier in country of origin

Signature Date

Partner details

8

Full name

Home address

Postcode

Home telephone Mobile telephone

National Insurance Number or Tax Identifier in country of origin

Signature Date

Partner details

9

Full name

Home address

Postcode

Home telephone Mobile telephone

National Insurance Number or Tax Identifier in country of origin

Signature Date

VAT 2 reverse (1201)

Regulation 6(1)

FORM NO 3: APPLICATION TO USE PREVIOUS OWNER'S VAT REGISTRATION NUMBER FOLLOWING THE TRANSFER OF A BUSINESS AS A GOING CONCERN[4]

Both parts of this Application Form must be filled in

Part 1 To be completed by the new owner
If you are the new legal entity or owner of the business, please read this form carefully and answer all the questions in Part 1.

1. Please give your full name, or your trading name if you have one;

2. Please give your legal status, eg sole proprietor, partnership, limited company

3. I took over the business as a going concern on

4. Please give the name of the previous owner;

5. I apply to use the previous owner's VAT registration number from the above date. The number is;

6. If this application is allowed, I agree to the following conditions:

- I will send in my first VAT return to Customs and Excise, with all the VAT due for the whole of the period shown on the form;
- I will send in any outstanding returns which are due from the previous owner;
- I will pay Customs and Excise any VAT due on supplies made by the previous owner before the business was transferred - including any VAT on stocks and assets kept by the previous owner.
- I agree that any VAT return made by the previous owner for a period after the transfer date will be treated as made by me; and
- I will have no right to claim any money paid by Customs and Excise to the previous owner, before the VAT registration number was transferred.

Signature(s)

(Proprietor, partners, director, company secretary, executor)

Date

Part 2 To be completed by the previous owner
If you are the former legal entity or the previous owner of the business, please read this form carefully and answer all the questions in Part 2.

1. Please give your full name, or your trading name if you have one;

2. Please give your legal status, eg sole proprietor, partnership, limited company

3. I transferred my business / changed my legal status on

4. Please give the name of the new owner;

5. I wish to cancel my VAT registration number from the above date because I am no longer liable or eligible to be registered. I agree to transfer my number to the new owner. The number is

6. If this application is allowed, I agree to the following conditions:

- I will have no right to claim any money paid by Customs and Excise to the new owner.
- I agree that the new owner will be entitled to reclaim any input tax which Customs and Excise would normally have paid to me if the number had not been transferred; and

7. I have retained stocks and assets valued at

£

8. Please give an address where we can contact you after the business has been taken over by the new owner.

Signature(s)

(Proprietor, partners, director, company secretary, executor)

Date

Regulation 6

FORM NO 4: VAT RETURN[4]

Value Added Tax Return
For the period
to

HM Customs and Excise

For Official Use

Registration number | Period

You could be liable to a financial penalty it your completed return and all the VAT payable are not received by the due date.

Due date:

For official use D O R only	

SPECIMEN

Fold Here

Before you fill in this form please read the notes on the back and the VAT leaflet *"Filling in your VAT return"*. Fill in all boxes clearly in ink, and write 'none' where necessary. Don't put a dash or leave any box blank. If there are no pence write **"00"** in the pence column. **Do not** enter more than one amount in any box.

For official use

		£	p
VAT due in this period on **sales** and other outputs	1		
VAT due in this period on **acquisitions** from other **EC Member States**	2		
Total VAT due **(the sum of boxes 1 and 2)**	3		
VAT reclaimed in this period on **purchases** and other inputs (including acquisitions from the EC)	4		
Net VAT to be paid to Customs or reclaimed by you **(Difference between boxes 3 and 4)**	5		
Total value of **sales** and all other outputs excluding any VAT. **Include your box 8 figure**	6		00
Total value of **purchases** and all other inputs excluding any VAT. **Include your box 9 figure**	7		00
Total value of all **supplies** of goods and related services, excluding any VAT, to other **EC Member States**	8		00
Total value of all **acquisitions** of goods and related services, excluding any VAT, from other **EC Member States**	9		00

Retail schemes. If you have used any of the schemes in the period covered by this return, enter the relevant letter(s) in this box.

If you are enclosing a payment please tick this box.

DECLARATION: You, or someone on your behalf, must sign below.

I, ... declare that the
(Full name of signatory in BLOCK LETTERS)

information given above is true and complete.

Signature .... Date .... 19................

A false declaration can result in prosecution.

IB(October 2000)

VAT 100 (Full)

Regulations 23, 25(4)

FORM NO 5: FINAL VAT RETURN[4]

HM Customs and Excise

Final Value Added Tax Return
For the period
to

For Official Use

Registration Number

Period
9999

You could be liable to a financial penalty if your completed return and all the VAT payable are not received by the due date.

Due date:

For official use DOR only	

SPECIMEN

Fold Here

Before you fill in this form please read the notes on the back and the VAT leaflet *"Filling in your VAT return".* Fill in all boxes clearly in ink, and write 'none' where necessary. Don't put a dash or leave any box blank. If there are no pence write **"00"** in the pence column. **Do not** enter more than one amount in any box.

For official use			£	p
	VAT due in this period on **sales** and other outputs	1		
	VAT due in this period on **acquisitions** from other **EC Member States**	2		
	Total VAT due **(the sum of boxes 1 and 2)**	3		
	VAT reclaimed in this period on **purchases** and other inputs (including acquisitions from the EC)	4		
	Net VAT to be paid to Customs or reclaimed by you **(Difference between boxes 3 and 4)**	5		
	Total value of **sales** and all other outputs excluding any VAT. **Include your box 8 figure**	6		00
	Total value of **purchases** and all other inputs excluding any VAT. **Include your box 9 figure**	7		00
	Total value of all **supplies** of goods and related services, excluding any VAT, to other **EC Member States**	8		00
	Total value of all **acquisitions** of goods and related services, excluding any VAT, from other **EC Member States**	9		00

If you are enclosing a payment please tick this box. ☐

DECLARATION: You, or someone on your behalf, must sign below.

I, ...declare that the
(Full name of signatory in BLOCK LETTERS)
information given above is true and complete.

Signature .... Date...

A false declaration can result in prosecution.

VAT 193 (Full) IB(October 2000)

Regulation 5(1)

FORM NO 6: APPLICATION FOR VAT REGISTRATION—DISTANCE SELLING

1. Enter the NAME of the PERSON MAKING DISTANCE SALES to the UK. Write in BLOCK LETTERS and leave a space between words

2. Enter the NAME of the UK TAX REPRESENTATIVE (see note 2)

3. Please give the ADDRESS of the TAX REPRESENTATIVE or the ADDRESS of the PERSON NAMED at box 1 if a tax representative has not been appointed

Phone No.

Postcode

4. Describe your main BUSINESS ACTIVITY IN FULL please (See note 4)

5. Who is the BUSINESS OWNED by? (See Note 5 and tick ONE BOX only)

Sole Proprietor

or Partnership — Please ensure you ALSO complete form VAT 2.

or Limited Company

or Other — Please give details

6. Enter your UK BANK DETAILS or YOUR TAX REPRESENTATIVE'S BANK DETAILS: (See Note 6)

Bank Sort Code — Account Number — or — Giro Bank Account Number

7. Do you use a COMPUTER FOR ACCOUNTING? (See Note 7 and tick one box only) YES NO

8. Has the value of your DISTANCE SALES to customers in the UK exceeded the UK distance selling threshold at any time in the calendar year commencing 1st January 1993 or any subsequent calendar year?

YES — and I exceeded the threshold on — Go to 11

NO — Go to 9

VAT 1A CD 3429/1/N3 (11/92)

9. Have you exercised the OPTION TO MAKE THE PLACE OF SUPPLY THE UK, although you have NOT exceeded the UK threshold? (see note 9)

Tick one box

NO ☐ Go to 10

YES ☐ and the option was exercised in [EC Country] on [| |]

Please enter the date of your first taxable supply in the UK [| |]

---

10. Do you intend to make distance sales of GOODS LIABLE TO EXCISE DUTY to the UK?

NO ☐ Go to 12

YES ☐ Please enter the estimated date of your first taxable supply in the UK. [| |]

---

11. (See note 11 - this is VERY IMPORTANT)

I am REQUIRED TO BE REGISTERED from [| |]

But I would LIKE TO BE REGISTERED from this earlier date [| |] Go to 13

---

12. Do you intend to exercise the OPTION TO MAKE THE PLACE OF SUPPLY of your distance sales the UK?

NO ☐

YES ☐ Please enter the estimated date of your first taxable supply in the UK [| |]

The date from which I wish to be registered is [| |]

---

13. Please enter the ESTIMATED VALUE OF DISTANCE SALES you expect to make to the UK in the next 12 months

£ [ ]

---

14. **Declaration**

I ....

(Full name in BLOCK LETTERS)

declare that all the entered details and information in any accompanying documents are correct and complete

Signature ....

Tick one box

Proprietor	☐	Partner	☐	Director	☐
Company Secretary	☐	Authorised Official (including tax representative)	☐	Trustee	☐

CD 3429/2/N3(11/92)

Regulation 5(1)

FORM NO 7: APPLICATION FOR VAT REGISTRATION—ACQUISITIONS

Value Added Tax

Application for Registration: Acquisitions

*Before you start, please read the Notice "Should I be registered for VAT? - Acquisitions". The notes in part 2 will help you to answer the questions on this form. If you do not answer the questions correctly it may take longer to register you and give you a registration number. Write clearly in **black** ink and use CAPITAL LETTERS.*

1 Please give your full name

- *if you are a limited company give your company name*
- *if you are a partnership give your trading name. If you do not have a trading name give the names of all the partners*

Name:

2 Please give your trading name (if different from the name given at 1)

Trading name:

3 Please give the address of your principal place of business

- *this should be where the day-to-day running of your business takes place*

Business address:

Post code:

Phone no:

Fax no:

SPECIMEN

4 Describe your main business activity (see note 4)

5 Who owns the business?

- *If you are a partnership please remember to fill in form VAT 2 as well as this form*

Please tick ✓

Limited company ☐ Give details from your certificate of incorporation:

Certificate number Date of certificate

Sole proprietor ☐ Partnership ☐

Other ☐ If other, give details below:

6 Please give your bank details

- *this question must be completed in all cases*

Bank sort code Account number

or Girobank account number

Please tick box if you do not have a bank account: ☐

7 Do you use a computer for accounting?

- *if you use a computer let us know the type of computer and software you use, in a separate letter*

Please tick ✓
Yes ☐ No ☐

8 Have you made any acquisitions yet?

- *if you are not sure what **'acquisitions'** means paragraph 1 of the Notice will help you*
- *if you have not yet made any acquisitions **you must enclose evidence** to show that you are going to in the future*

Please tick ✓
Yes ☐ I made my first acquisition on
No ☐ but I intend to start on

9 Have the value of your acquisitions from persons in other EC countries exceeded the registration limit at any time in the calendar year commencing 1 January 1993 or any subsequent calendar year?

Please tick ✓
Yes ☐ I went over the limit on
because the value of my acquisitions from 1 January amounted to £
No ☐ The value of my acquisitions from 1 January amounted to £

10 Do you expect the value of the acquisitions you will make in the next 30 days alone will go over the registration limit?

Please tick ✓
Yes ☐ Go to 11
No ☐ Go to 12

11 From what date must you be registered for VAT?

- *if you have answered Yes to either question 9 or 10 then give the date from which you **have** to be registered (note 11 in part 2 of the Notice will help you)*
- *if you want to be registered from an earlier date fill in the date in the box provided*

I have to be registered from
I would like to be registered from this earlier date

12 I do not need to be registered but I want to be registered

- *only answer this question if you have not yet reached the registration limit but want to be registered on a voluntary basis*

I want to be registered from

13 Do you make taxable supplies in the UK?

Please tick ✓
Yes ☐ Please give the estimated value of taxable supplies you have made in the last 12 months £
No ☐

VAT 1B Page 2(02/97)

14 Do you want exemption from registration because all your acquisitions are zero-rated?

- *if you are asking for exemption from registration enter the expected value of your zero-rated acquisitions in the next 12 months, in the box provided*

Please tick ✓

Yes ☐ Value of zero-rated acquisitions £

No ☐

15 Please complete and sign the declaration

Declaration

I,

(enter your full name in CAPITAL LETTERS) declare that the information given on this form and contained in any accompanying document is true and complete.

Signature

Mr, Mrs, Miss, Ms

Date

Please tick ✓

Proprietor ☐ Director ☐
Trustee ☐ Partner ☐
Company Secretary ☐ Authorised official ☐

For office use

Local office code and registration number

EDR D M Y Stagger Status

Name

Trade name

Trade classification Taxable Turnover

Rept. Vol. 3 Oversize name address Comp. user Group Div Intg Overseas Intg. EC Value of Sales to EC Value of Purchases from EC

Registration	Obligatory/Voluntary	Exemption	Intending	Transfer of Regn No.
Approved - Initial/date				
Refused - Initial/date				
Letter issued - Initial/date	Letter	Letter	Letter	Approval letter

Regulation 5(1)

FORM NO 7A: VAT REGISTRATION NOTIFICATION[2]

Value Added Tax

VAT Registration Notification

This notification form must only be filled in if you have to register because you are making relevant supplies in the UK and you have no place of business here. Section 7 of VAT Notice 700/4 *Registration for VAT: Non-established taxable persons* gives more information about this and will help you to answer the questions on the form.

Please answer all questions. Write clearly in black ink and use CAPITAL LETTERS

Name

1. Sole proprietors - please give your full name.
Partnerships - please give your trading name. If you do not have one, give the names of all partners (*partnerships must also complete form VAT 2*).
Corporate or unincorporated bodies - please give the name of the company, club, association etc.

2. Do you have a trading name? Yes ☐ No ☐

Please give the trading name of the business.

Business address

3. Please give the address of your principal place of business.

Postcode

Phone number

Fax number

Tax representative

4. If you have appointed a tax representative to deal with your VAT matters in the UK please give details below.

Name

Address

Phone number

Postcode

Fax number

VAT1C IB(March 2000)

Status

5. What is the structure/legal status of the business? (*Please tick*)

Sole proprietor ☐ Partnership ☐

Corporate body ☐ (*Please give your company incorporation details*)

Certificate number ☐ Date ☐

Unincorporated body ☐ Please give details ☐

Business activities

6. What does your business do or intend to do? Tell us about your current or intended business activities.

Bank details

7. Please give your UK bank details or your tax representative's bank details.

Sort code ☐ Account number ☐

or

Girobank account number ☐

No bank account (*please tick*) ☐

Computer accounts

8. Is your accounting system computerised?

Yes (*Give details below*) ☐ No ☐

Computer type ☐

Software ☐ Version ☐

Relevant supplies

9. Have you made any relevant supplies yet? (*Please tick one box*)

☐ Yes, I made my first relevant supply on ☐

☐ No, but I expect to make my first relevant supply on ☐

VAT1C IB(March 2000)

10. When did you first have reasonable grounds to believe that you were going to make relevant supplies?

Date [ ]

11. What value of relevant supplies do you expect to make in the next 12 months?

£ [ ]

12. Do you make any other taxable supplies in the UK?

Yes [ ] No [ ]

If, **"*Yes*"**, enter the estimated value of all taxable supplies, other than your relevant supplies, that you expect to make in the UK in the next 12 months.

£ [ ]

Transfer of assets

13. Are you registering because VAT has been recovered by a predecessor in connection with the relevant supplies you have made, or intend to make?

Yes [ ] No [ ]

If **"*Yes*"**, give the name(s) and address(es) of the person(s) who recovered VAT under either the Eighth or Thirteeneth Directive refund schemes.

Exemption

14. Do you want exemption from registration because your relevant supplies are wholly zero-rated?

Yes [ ] No [ ]

If **"*Yes*"**, give the expected value of your zero-rated supplies in the next 12 months.

Zero-rated relevant supplies [ ]

Other VAT registrations

15. Are you involved in, or have you (or any other partners or directors in your business) been involved in any other businesses in the past 5 years?

Yes [ ] No [ ]

If **"*Yes*"**, give the names and VAT registration numbers of these businesses.

(Continue on a separate sheet, if necessary)

Declaration

16. I declare that the information given on this form and contained in any accompanying document is true and complete.

Signature Date

Full name

What is your position in the business? *(Please tick)*

Proprietor Partner Director

Company Secretary Trustee Other

If "Other", give details

Checklist

- Have you answered every question?
- Have you signed the form?
- Partnership? Remember to complete Form VAT2
- Appointing a tax representative? Remember to complete Form VAT1TR

What to do next

When you have completed and signed the form, please send it to the VAT Registration Unit specified in VAT Notice 700/4 *Registration for VAT: Non-established taxable persons.* If you have any problems completing the form please contact the Registration Unit.

Usually we will register you and give you a VAT registration number within 15 working days of receiving your form, provided you have given all the necessary information.

For office use

Local office code and registration number | D M Y | Stagger | Status

Name

Trade name | Trade classification | Taxable turnover

Rept. | Vol. | Oversize name address | Comp. user | Group Div | Intg. | Overseas | Intg. EC | Value of Sales to EC | Value of Purchases from EC

Registration	Obligatory/Voluntary	Exemption	Intending	Transfer of Regn No
Approved - Initial/date				
Refused - Initial/date				
Form issued - Initial/date	VAT9/ other	VAT8	Letter	Approval letter

VAT1C IB(March 2000)

Regulation 10

Form No 8: Appointment of Tax Representative

Appointment of Tax Representative

You should read the notes in the registration booklet *"Should I be registered for VAT? - Distance Selling "* which will help you to answer these questions.
Please write clearly in black ink.

1. Who is the business owned by? Please give the persons full **name** and **address** of the principal place of business.

Phone No. Postcode

Please give the VAT Registration number in EC country of origin

Please give the UK VAT Registration number (if any)

2. Enter the full name and address of the UK Tax Representative

Phone No. Postcode

3. Please give the date of appointment of Tax Representative and VAT registration number (if any)

Date of appointment

VAT Registration number

4. Declaration

We,. .... and
(Full name of PRINCIPAL in BLOCK LETTERS)

....
(Full name of TAX PEPRESENTATIVE in BLOCK LETTERS)

declare that all the entered details and information in any accompanying documents are correct and complete

Signature of Principal .... Date ....

Tick one box

Proprietor ☐ Partner ☐ Director ☐

Company Secretary ☐ Authorised Official ☐ Trustee ☐

Signature of Tax Representative .... Date ....

Tick one box

Proprietor ☐ Partner ☐ Director ☐

Company Secretary ☐ Authorised Official ☐ Trustee ☐

CD 3428/N3(11/92)

Regulation 191(1)

Form No 9: Application by a business person not established in the Community for Refund of VAT

VAT 65A

HM Customs and Excise

Is this your first application? If not, please give Reference No.

Competent authority to which the application is addressed

HM Customs and Excise
VAT Overseas Repayments
8th/13th Directive
Custom House
PO Box 34
LONDONDERRY BT48 7AE
Northern Ireland

APPLICATION
by a business person NOT established in the community for
REFUND OF
VALUE ADDED TAX
Please read the explanatory notes

SPECIMEN

1	Forenames and surname or name of firm of applicant House number and street name Place, country and post code
2	Nature of applicant's business
3	Particulars of the Official Authority and tax/business Registration No. in the country in which the applicant is established or has his/her domicile or normal place of residence
4	Period to which the application refers — From: Month, Year; To: Month, Year
5	Total amount of refund requested (in figures) (see overleaf for itemised list) £
6	The applicant requests the refund of the amount shown in heading 5 in the manner described in heading 7
7	Method of settlement requested (*) Non UK Bank account ☐ UK Bank account ☐ Postal account ☐ Account number Currency of Account — Bank Identifier Code Account in the name of Name and address of the financial body
8	No. of documents enclosed .... Invoices .... Import documents ....
9	The applicant hereby declares (a) that the goods or services specified overleaf were used for the following business activities in the United Kingdom .... (b) that in the United Kingdom during the period covered by this application, he/she engaged in ☐ (*) no supply of goods or services ☐ (*) only the provision of services in respect of which tax is payable solely by the person to whom they are supplied ☐ (*) only in the provision of certain exempted transport services ancillary thereto

(*) Insert x in the appropriate box

(c) that the particulars given in this application are true

The applicant undertakes to pay back any monies wrongfully obtained

At .... on ....
(Place) (Date) (Signature)

Applicant's telephone number .... Applicant's fax number ....

NOTE: Box 10 overleaf **MUST** be completed Applicant's e-mail address ....

10 Statement itemising VAT amounts relating to the period covered by this application

1) Each document submitted should be consecutively numbered starting with 1. The number should be inserted in the top right-hand corner of the face of the document. Enter details across the columns in respect of each invoice etc. submitted. If sufficient space is not available you must use a continuation sheet, headed with your tax registration number, endorsed Box 10 and attached firmly to the application form.

2) You are reminded that when tax is incurred by taxable persons who receive VAT group treatment, the group representative member must apply on behalf of all the members. As the supporting invoices produced will not necessarily be addressed to the representative member, the status certificate must also contain the names of those group members who incurred the tax.

Number	Nature of goods or services	Name, VAT Registration No. (if known) and address of supplier of goods or services	Date and number of invoice or import document	Amount of tax refund applied for	**FOR OFFICIAL USE ONLY**
			C/F		

SPECIMEN

3) Refunds of tax incurred may only be claimed subject to the rules of each state. Brief details of supplies in each member state on which tax cannot be reclaimed are given in HM Customs and Excise Notice 723. Tax incurred on the following supplies will not be refunded by any member state:

(a) supplies of goods which have been or are about to be exported; and

(b) supplies to travel agents which are for the direct benefit of travellers. Under this scheme the term "travel agent" includes tour operators or any person who purchases or re-supplies services to travellers.

Number	Nature of goods or services	Name, VAT Registration No. (if known) and address of supplier of goods or services	Date and number of invoice or import document	Amount of tax refund applied for	**FOR OFFICIAL USE ONLY**
			TOTAL B/F		
			TOTAL		

SPECIMEN

Regulation 191(1)(*b*)

FORM NO 10: CERTIFICATE OF STATUS OF BUSINESS PERSON

Certificate of Status of Business Person

The undersigned ....
(Name and address of official authority)

certifies that ....
(Name of business person)

....
(Nature of activity)

....

....
(Address of the Establishment)

is a registered business person in ....
(Name of county)

*his registration number being [| | | | | | | |]

Date ....

Signature ....

Office date stamp

....
(Name and grade)

*If the applicant does not have a registration number, the official authority should state the reason for this.

VAT 66A CD 3298/N6(07/92) F 8609( )

SPECIMEN

Regulation 201(*a*)

FORM NO 11: VAT REFUNDS FOR DIY BUILDERS

Amendments—Forms 11A (VAT refunds for DIY housebuilders—Claim form for new houses) and 11B (VAT refunds for DIY housebuilders—Claim form for conversions) substituted for previous Form 11, by the Value Added Tax (Amendment) (No 3) Regulations, SI 2009/1967 regs 2, 9 with effect from 15 August 2009. At the time of publication the revised forms were available on the OPSI website at http://www.opsi.gov.uk/si/si2009/pdf/uksi_20091967_en.pdf.

Regulations 21, 22, 23

FORM NO 12: VAT EC SALES LIST

HM Customs and Excise

Value Added Tax

EC Sales list

(Continuation sheet)

VAT Registration Number	Branch/subsidiary Identifier	Calendar Quarter
GB		

For official use D O R only	

	Country Code	Customer's VAT Registration Number	Total value of supplies in pounds sterling (£)	p	Indicator
1				0 0	
2				0 0	
3				0 0	
4				0 0	
5				0 0	
6				0 0	
7				0 0	
8				0 0	
9				0 0	
10				0 0	
11				0 0	
12				0 0	
13				0 0	
14				0 0	
15				0 0	

SPECIMEN

Lines completed (this page only)

VAT 101 A **Page 1** PT1 (April 2004)

Regulation 22(6), 23

FORM NO 13: NEW MEANS OF TRANSPORT FOR REMOVAL FROM THE UK TO ANOTHER MEMBER STATE OF THE EUROPEAN COMMUNITY[6]

New means of transport

Removal from the UK to another member state of the European Community

See notes overleaf before completing.

For the supplier to complete

Title and full name

Full UK address

Phone

VAT Registration number

GB

Details of the new means of transport *(tick one box)*

Motorised land vehicle ☐ Ship ☐ Aircraft ☐

Make	
Model	
Colour	
Registration number	
Date of issue of the plates	
Engine number	
Chassis/Hull/Airframe number	
Name of vessel	
Number of kilometers/hours of navigation/hours of flight (if different from nil)	
Invoice number and date	
Date of supply	
Purchase price	
VAT not paid at time of supply	

I declare that:
- the information given above is correct
- the New Means of Transport described above complies with the definition given in Notice 728 about VAT and the Single Market.

Signature

Date

D D M M Y Y Y Y

For the purchaser to complete

Title and full name

Full UK address *(if applicable)*

Phone

Full address in Member State of destination

Phone

Member State of destination of the new means of transport in which VAT will be paid

Are you a UK Resident? *(Tick one box)*

No ☐ Yes ☐

Are you a serving member of HM Forces or a dependant of a Serving Member of HM Forces? *(Tick one box)*

No ☐ Yes ☐

I declare that:
- the information I have given is correct
- I have read Notice 728 and the notes overleaf
- I intend to remove the New Means of Transport described on this form from the UK to the Member State of Destination within two months of the date of supply
- I intend to notify the fiscal authority in that Member State and pay any tax due
- I understand that if I fail to remove the New Means of Transport described on this form within two months of the date of supply it will become liable to forfeiture and UK taxes will become due.

Signature

Date

D D M M Y Y Y Y

Notes

This form should only be used for removals of new means of transport to other member states of the European Community, by persons not registered for VAT.

Notice 728 (for unregistered purchasers) define what a new means of transport is. They explain the circumstances in which a new means of transport may be obtained free of taxes.

Before completing this form please read the relevant notice and the following information carefully.

You can download the VAT Notices from our website at **www.hmrc.gov.uk** or you can phone our National Advice Service on **0845 01 09 000** for advice.

The following are member states of the EC:

Austria
Belgium
Bulgaria
*Cyprus
Czech Republic
Denmark
Estonia
Finland
France (including Monaco)
Germany
Greece
Hungary
Ireland
Italy
Latvia
Lithuania
Luxembourg
Malta
Netherlands
Poland
Portugal (including the Azores and Maderia)
Romania
Slovakia
Slovenia
Spain (including the Balearic Islands)
Sweden and the UK (including the Isle of Man).

**The European Commission has advised that, as the situation stands at present, the application of the 6th Directive shall be suspended in those area of Cyprus in which the Government of the Republic of Cyprus does not exercise effective control. Transactions with those areas will continue from 1 May 2004 to be treated as non-EU transactions.*

To the supplier

- When this form has been completed send the original to:
  HM Revenue & Customs
  Personal Transport Unit
  Freight Clearance Centre
  Lord Warden Square
  Western Docks
  Dover
  Kent
  CT17 9DN.
- Give the first copy to the purchaser.
- Retain the second copy for your records.
- Attach the third copy to the application for a registration number (this only applies when the new means of transport is a motor vehicle).

To the purchaser

You must remove the new means of transport from the UK to the member state of destination within two months of the date of the supply. The date of supply is the earlier of either:

- the date of the invoice for the purchase of the new means of transport, **or**
- the 15th day of the month after that in which you received the new means of transport or it was despatched to you.

You must notify HM Revenue & Customs immediately if for any reason you change your intention to remove the new means of transport to the member of state of destination within two months of the date of supply.

The supplier will provide you with a copy of this form. You should retain this for production to the tax authority in the member state of destination.

The law relating to this scheme is in section 30(8) of the Value Added Tax Act 1994.

New means of transport

Removal from the UK to another member state of the European Community

See notes overleaf before completing.

For the supplier to complete

Title and full name

Full UK address

Phone

VAT Registration number

GB

Details of the new means of transport *(tick one box)*

Motorised land vehicle ☐ Ship ☐ Aircraft ☐

Make	
Model	
Colour	
Registration number	
Date of issue of the plates	
Engine number	
Chassis/Hull/Airframe number	
Name of vessel	
Number of kilometers/hours of navigation/hours of flight (if different from nil)	
Invoice number and date	
Date of supply	
Purchase price	
VAT not paid at time of supply	

I declare that:

- the information given above is correct
- the New Means of Transport described above complies with the definition given in Notice 728 about VAT and the Single Market.

Signature

Date

D D M M Y Y Y Y

For the purchaser to complete

Title and full name

Full UK address *(if applicable)*

Phone

Full address in Member State of destination

Phone

Member State of destination of the new means of transport in which VAT will be paid

Are you a UK Resident? *(Tick one box)*

No ☐ Yes ☐

Are you a serving member of HM Forces or a dependant of a Serving Member of HM Forces? *(Tick one box)*

No ☐ Yes ☐

I declare that:

- the information I have given is correct
- I have read Notice 728 and the notes overleaf
- I intend to remove the New Means of Transport described on this form from the UK to the Member State of Destination within two months of the date of supply
- I intend to notify the fiscal authority in that Member State and pay any tax due
- I understand that if I fail to remove the New Means of Transport described on this form within two months of the date of supply it will become liable to forfeiture and UK taxes will become due.

Signature

Date

D D M M Y Y Y Y

Notes

This form should only be used for removals of new means of transport to other member states of the European Community, by persons not registered for VAT.

Notice 728 (for unregistered purchasers) define what a new means of transport is. They explain the circumstances in which a new means of transport may be obtained free of taxes.

Before completing this form please read the relevant notice and the following information carefully.

You can download the VAT Notices from our website at **www.hmrc.gov.uk** or you can phone our National Advice Service on **0845 01 09 000** for advice.

The following are member states of the EC:

Austria
Belgium
Bulgaria
*Cyprus
Czech Republic
Denmark
Estonia
Finland
France (including Monaco)
Germany
Greece
Hungary
Ireland
Italy
Latvia
Lithuania
Luxembourg
Malta
Netherlands
Poland
Portugal (including the Azores and Maderia)
Romania
Slovakia
Slovenia
Spain (including the Balearic Islands)
Sweden and the UK (including the Isle of Man).

**The European Commission has advised that, as the situation stands at present, the application of the 6th Directive shall be suspended in those area of Cyprus in which the Government of the Republic of Cyprus does not exercise effective control. Transactions with those areas will continue from 1 May 2004 to be treated as non-EU transactions.*

To the supplier

- When this form has been completed send the original to:
  HM Revenue & Customs
  Personal Transport Unit
  Freight Clearance Centre
  Lord Warden Square
  Western Docks
  Dover
  Kent
  CT17 9DN.
- Give the first copy to the purchaser.
- Retain the second copy for your records.
- Attach the third copy to the application for a registration number (this only applies when the new means of transport is a motor vehicle).

To the purchaser

You must remove the new means of transport from the UK to the member state of destination within two months of the date of the supply. The date of supply is the earlier of either:

- the date of the invoice for the purchase of the new means of transport, **or**
- the 15th day of the month after that in which you received the new means of transport or it was despatched to you.

You must notify HM Revenue & Customs immediately if for any reason you change your intention to remove the new means of transport to the member of state of destination within two months of the date of supply.

The supplier will provide you with a copy of this form. You should retain this for production to the tax authority in the member state of destination.

The law relating to this scheme is in section 30(8) of the Value Added Tax Act 1994.

New means of transport

Removal from the UK to another member state of the European Community

See notes overleaf before completing.

For the supplier to complete

Title and full name

Full UK address

Phone

VAT Registration number

GB

Details of the new means of transport *(tick one box)*

Motorised land vehicle ☐ Ship ☐ Aircraft ☐

Make	
Model	
Colour	
Registration number	
Date of issue of the plates	
Engine number	
Chassis/Hull/Airframe number	
Name of vessel	
Number of kilometers/hours of navigation/hours of flight (if different from nil)	
Invoice number and date	
Date of supply	
Purchase price	
VAT not paid at time of supply	

I declare that:

- the information given above is correct
- the New Means of Transport described above complies with the definition given in Notice 728 about VAT and the Single Market.

Signature

Date D D M M Y Y Y Y

For the purchaser to complete

Title and full name

Full UK address *(if applicable)*

Phone

Full address in Member State of destination

Phone

Member State of destination of the new means of transport in which VAT will be paid

Are you a UK Resident? *(Tick one box)*

No ☐ Yes ☐

Are you a serving member of HM Forces or a dependant of a Serving Member of HM Forces? *(Tick one box)*

No ☐ Yes ☐

I declare that:

- the information I have given is correct
- I have read Notice 728 and the notes overleaf
- I intend to remove the New Means of Transport described on this form from the UK to the Member State of Destination within two months of the date of supply
- I intend to notify the fiscal authority in that Member State and pay any tax due
- I understand that if I fail to remove the New Means of Transport described on this form within two months of the date of supply it will become liable to forfeiture and UK taxes will become due.

Signature

Date D D M M Y Y Y Y

Notes

This form should only be used for removals of new means of transport to other member states of the European Community, by persons not registered for VAT.

Notice 728 (for unregistered purchasers) define what a new means of transport is. They explain the circumstances in which a new means of transport may be obtained free of taxes.

Before completing this form please read the relevant notice and the following information carefully.

You can download the VAT Notices from our website at **www.hmrc.gov.uk** or you can phone our National Advice Service on **0845 01 09 000** for advice.

The following are member states of the EC:

Austria
Belgium
Bulgaria
*Cyprus
Czech Republic
Denmark
Estonia
Finland
France (including Monaco)
Germany
Greece
Hungary
Ireland
Italy
Latvia
Lithuania
Luxembourg
Malta
Netherlands
Poland
Portugal (including the Azores and Maderia)
Romania
Slovakia
Slovenia
Spain (including the Balearic Islands)
Sweden and the UK (including the Isle of Man).

**The European Commission has advised that, as the situation stands at present, the application of the 6th Directive shall be suspended in those area of Cyprus in which the Government of the Republic of Cyprus does not exercise effective control. Transactions with those areas will continue from 1 May 2004 to be treated as non-EU transactions.*

To the supplier

- When this form has been completed send the original to:
  HM Revenue & Customs
  Personal Transport Unit
  Freight Clearance Centre
  Lord Warden Square
  Western Docks
  Dover
  Kent
  CT17 9DN.
- Give the first copy to the purchaser.
- Retain the second copy for your records.
- Attach the third copy to the application for a registration number (this only applies when the new means of transport is a motor vehicle).

To the purchaser

You must remove the new means of transport from the UK to the member state of destination within two months of the date of the supply. The date of supply is the earlier of either:

- the date of the invoice for the purchase of the new means of transport, **or**
- the 15th day of the month after that in which you received the new means of transport or it was despatched to you.

You must notify HM Revenue & Customs immediately if for any reason you change your intention to remove the new means of transport to the member of state of destination within two months of the date of supply.

The supplier will provide you with a copy of this form. You should retain this for production to the tax authority in the member state of destination.

The law relating to this scheme is in section 30(8) of the Value Added Tax Act 1994.

New means of transport

Removal from the UK to another member state of the European Community

See notes overleaf before completing.

For the supplier to complete

Title and full name

Full UK address

Phone

VAT Registration number

GB

Details of the new means of transport *(tick one box)*

Motorised land vehicle ☐ Ship ☐ Aircraft ☐

Make	
Model	
Colour	
Registration number	
Date of issue of the plates	
Engine number	
Chassis/Hull/Airframe number	
Name of vessel	
Number of kilometers/hours of navigation/hours of flight (if different from nil)	
Invoice number and date	
Date of supply	
Purchase price	
VAT not paid at time of supply	

I declare that:

- the information given above is correct
- the New Means of Transport described above complies with the definition given in Notice 728 about VAT and the Single Market.

Signature

Date D D M M Y Y Y Y

For the purchaser to complete

Title and full name

Full UK address *(if applicable)*

Phone

Full address in Member State of destination

Phone

Member State of destination of the new means of transport in which VAT will be paid

Are you a UK Resident? *(Tick one box)*

No ☐ Yes ☐

Are you a serving member of HM Forces or a dependant of a Serving Member of HM Forces? *(Tick one box)*

No ☐ Yes ☐

I declare that:

- the information I have given is correct
- I have read Notice 728 and the notes overleaf
- I intend to remove the New Means of Transport described on this form from the UK to the Member State of Destination within two months of the date of supply
- I intend to notify the fiscal authority in that Member State and pay any tax due
- I understand that if I fail to remove the New Means of Transport described on this form within two months of the date of supply it will become liable to forfeiture and UK taxes will become due.

Signature

Date D D M M Y Y Y Y

Notes

This form should only be used for removals of new means of transport to other member states of the European Community, by persons not registered for VAT.

Notice 728 (for unregistered purchasers) define what a new means of transport is. They explain the circumstances in which a new means of transport may be obtained free of taxes.

Before completing this form please read the relevant notice and the following information carefully.

You can download the VAT Notices from our website at **www.hmrc.gov.uk** or you can phone our National Advice Service on **0845 01 09 000** for advice.

The following are member states of the EC:

Austria
Belgium
Bulgaria
*Cyprus
Czech Republic
Denmark
Estonia
Finland
France (including Monaco)
Germany
Greece
Hungary
Ireland
Italy
Latvia
Lithuania
Luxembourg
Malta
Netherlands
Poland
Portugal (including the Azores and Maderia)
Romania
Slovakia
Slovenia
Spain (including the Balearic Islands)
Sweden and the UK (including the Isle of Man).

**The European Commission has advised that, as the situation stands at present, the application of the 6th Directive shall be suspended in those area of Cyprus in which the Government of the Republic of Cyprus does not exercise effective control. Transactions with those areas will continue from 1 May 2004 to be treated as non-EU transactions.*

To the supplier

- When this form has been completed send the original to:
  HM Revenue & Customs
  Personal Transport Unit
  Freight Clearance Centre
  Lord Warden Square
  Western Docks
  Dover
  Kent
  CT17 9DN.
- Give the first copy to the purchaser.
- Retain the second copy for your records.
- Attach the third copy to the application for a registration number (this only applies when the new means of transport is a motor vehicle).

To the purchaser

You must remove the new means of transport from the UK to the member state of destination within two months of the date of the supply. The date of supply is the earlier of either:

- the date of the invoice for the purchase of the new means of transport, **or**
- the 15th day of the month after that in which you received the new means of transport or it was despatched to you.

You must notify HM Revenue & Customs immediately if for any reason you change your intention to remove the new means of transport to the member of state of destination within two months of the date of supply.

The supplier will provide you with a copy of this form. You should retain this for production to the tax authority in the member state of destination.

The law relating to this scheme is in section 30(8) of the Value Added Tax Act 1994.

Regulation 204(*c*)

Form No 14: Flat Rate Scheme for Agriculture—Application for Certification

HM Customs and Excise

Value Added Tax

Flat Rate Scheme for Agriculture
Application for Certification

Notes to help you complete this form are on the reverse. Please read them carefully

1. Please enter your FULL NAME in BLOCK LETTERS. (See note 1)

2. Please enter the ADDRESS of your BUSINESS. (See note 2)

   Postcode Tel No.

3. Please describe your BUSINESS INCLUDING NON-FARMING ACTIVITIES. (See note 3)

4. Please enter the ESTIMATED VALUE of AGRICULTURAL SUPPLIES you expect to make in the next 12 months. (see note 4)

5. Please enter the ESTIMATED VALUE of SUPPLIES OF OTHER GOODS and SERVICES which you expect to make in the next 12 months. (See note 5)

6. Please enter the DATE from which you wish your CERTIFICATE TO BE EFFECTIVE. (See note 6)

7. Please enter your VAT REGISTRATION NUMBER. Write "NONE" if you are not registered for VAT. (See note 7)

8. **You must complete the following declaration** :

   I..
   (enter your full name in BLOCK LETTERS)
   declare that the information entered on this form is true and complete.
   I apply for cancellation of the VAT registration shown at box 7 above.

   Signature.. Date ....

   Tick one box Proprietor ☐ Director ☐ Trustee ☐
   Partner ☐ Company Secretary ☐ Authorised Official ☐

For Official Use

Initials and Date

All'd LVO TC Abbreviated name

Ref'd EDC

VAT 98 PT (March 2001)

SPECIMEN

Regulation 178(1)(*a*)

FORM NO 15: APPLICATION BY A BUSINESS PERSON ESTABLISHED IN THE COMMUNITY FOR REFUND OF VAT

VAT 65

HM Customs and Excise

Is this your first application? If not, please give Reference No.

Competent authority to which the application is addressed

APPLICATION
by a business person established in the Community for REFUND OF
VALUE ADDED TAX
(Please read the explanatory notes before filling in)

1	Forenames and surname or name of firm of applicant
	House number and street name
	Place, country and post code
2	Nature of applicant's business
3	Particulars of the Official Authority and tax/business Registration No. in the country in which the applicant is established or has his/her domicile or normal place of residence
4	Period to which the application refers — From: Month, Year — To: Month, Year
5	Total amount of refund requested (in figures) (see overleaf for itemised list) £
6	The applicant requests the refund of the amount shown in heading 5 in the manner described in heading 7
7	Method of settlement requested (*) — Non UK Bank account — UK Bank account — Postal account
	Account number
	Currency of Account — Bank Identifier Code
	Account in the name of
	Name and address of the financial body
8	No. of documents enclosed .... Invoices .... Import documents ....

(*) Insert x in the appropriate box

SPECIMEN

9 The applicant hereby declares

(a) that the goods or services specified overleaf were used for the following business activities in the United Kingdom

....

....

....

(b) that in the United Kingdom during the period covered by this application, he/she engaged in

☐ (*) no supply of goods or services

☐ (*) only the provision of services in respect of which tax is payable solely by the person to whom they are supplied

☐ (*) only in the provision of certain exempted transport services ancillary thereto

(*) Insert x in the appropriate box

(c) that the particulars given in this application are true

The applicant undertakes to pay back any monies wrongfully obtained

At .... on ....
(Place) (Date) (Signature)

Applicant's telephone number .... Applicant's fax number ....

NOTE: Box 10 overleaf **MUST** be completed Applicant's e-mail address ....

VAT 65 **Page 1** PT1(April 2002)

10 **Statement itemising VAT amounts relating to the period covered by this application**

1) Each document submitted should be consecutively numbered starting with 1. The number should be inserted in the top right-hand corner of the face of the document. Enter details across the columns in respect of each invoice etc. submitted. If sufficient space is not available you must use a continuation sheet, headed with your tax registration number, endorsed Box 10 and attached firmly to the application form.

2) You are reminded that when tax is incurred by taxable persons who receive VAT group treatment, the group representative member must apply on behalf of all the members. As the supporting invoices produced will not necessarily be addressed to the representative member, the status certificate must also contain the names of those group members who incurred the tax.

Number	Nature of goods or services	Name, VAT Registration No. (if known) and address of supplier of goods or services	Date and number of invoice or import document	Amount of tax refund applied for	FOR OFFICIAL USE ONLY
			C/F		

SPECIMEN

3) Refunds of tax incurred may only be claimed subject to the rules of each state. Brief details of supplies in each member state on which tax cannot be reclaimed are given in HM Customs and Excise Notice 723. Tax incurred on the following supplies will not be refunded by any member state:

(a) supplies of goods which have been or are about to be exported; and

(b) supplies to travel agents which are for the direct benefit of travellers. Under this scheme the term "travel agent" includes tour operators or any person who purchases or re-supplies services to travellers.

Number	Nature of goods or services	Name, VAT Registration No. (if known) and address of supplier of goods or services	Date and number of invoice or import document	Amount of tax refund applied for	**FOR OFFICIAL USE ONLY**
			TOTAL B/F		
			TOTAL		

Regulation 178(1)(*b*)(i)

FORM NO 16: CERTIFICATE OF STATUS OF TAXABLE PERSON

HM Customs and Excise

Certificate of Status of Taxable Person

The undersigned

....

(Name of local VAT office)

certifies that

Name of taxable person

Address

....

....

Nature of activity

is a taxable person for the purposes of Value Added Tax, whose Registration number is

SPECIMEN

Date ....

Office stamp

Signature ....

....

(Name and grade)

VAT 66 CD 1017/N6(07/91) F 5037 (NOV 90) NKBH 9646 50M (11/92)

Regulation 145B

Form No 17[1]

CERTIFICATE REQUIRED TO SECURE RELIEF FROM VAT ON PURCHASED OR ACQUIRED GOODS INTENDED TO BE PLACED IN A FISCAL WAREHOUSING REGIME

Information to be indicated:

I (full name)
(status in company)
of (name and address of company)

declare that (name of company) intends to enter to the fiscal warehousing regime at the fiscal warehouse shown below on (date), or within … days commencing today, the goods indicated below:

– name and address of fiscal warehouse
– authorisation number of the fiscal warehousekeeper
– description of goods
– quantity of goods

I certify that the supply of goods/acquisition is eligible to be relieved from VAT under the following provisions of the Value Added Tax Act 1994 [*delete as appropriate*]:

sections 18B(2)(*d*)/18B(3) (purchases) *or* sections 18B(1)(*d*)/18B(3) (acquisitions).

(signature)
(date)

NOTE: You should be aware that there are severe penalties for making a false declaration. If there is any doubt about the eligibility of the goods or about the fiscal warehouse to which they are being sent you should consult the local Customs and Excise office before preparing the certificate. *A copy of the certificate should be filed with the supplier's invoice and a copy of the delivery note.*

Regulation 145C

Form No 18[1]

CERTIFICATE REQUIRED TO SECURE ZERO-RATING OF SERVICES (OTHER THAN THE SUPPLY OF WAREHOUSING) PERFORMED IN A FISCAL OR OTHER WAREHOUSE

Information to be indicated:

I (full name)
(status in company)
of (name and address of company)

declare that the goods shown below are subject to a fiscal or other warehousing regime at the place indicated below:

– description of goods
– quantity of goods
– warehouse stock number
– name and address of fiscal or other warehouse
– authorisation number of the relevant warehousekeeper/warehouse

and that the following services are to be performed on the goods in the fiscal or other warehouse:

I certify that the supply of services is eligible to be zero-rated for VAT purposes under section 18C(1) of the Value Added Tax Act 1994.

(signature)
(date)

NOTE: You should be aware that there are severe penalties for making a false declaration. If there is any doubt about a supply being entitled to zero-rating you should consult the local Customs and Excise office before signing and giving the certificate. *A copy of the certificate should be filed with the supplier's invoice which should refer to section 18C(1) of the Value Added Tax Act 1994 to be eligible for zero-rating.*

Amendments—[1] Forms 17, 18 added by the VAT (Amendment) (No 3) Regulations, SI 1996/1250 reg 15, Sch 1, with effect from 1 June 1996.

[2] Form 7A inserted by the VAT (Amendment) (No 3) Regulations, SI 2000/794 regs 2, 7 with effect from 22 March 2000.

[3] Forms … 3 substituted by the Value Added Tax (Amendment)(No 3) Regulations, SI 2001/3828 with effect from 1 January 2002.

[4] Forms 4 and 5 substituted by the VAT (Amendment) (No 3) Regulations, SI 2004/1675 reg 1(1), (3), 6, Schedule with effect from 22 July 2004.

[5] Form 1 substituted by the Value Added Tax (Amendment) (No 2) Regulations, SI 2006/2902, reg 3, Sch 1, with effect from 1 December 2006.

[6] Form 13 substituted by the VAT (Amendment) (No 2) Regulations, SI 2007/768 with effect from 1 April 2007

SCHEDULE 1A[1]

Regulation 145F

Amendments—[1] This Schedule inserted by the VAT (Amendment) (No 3) Regulations, SI 1996/1250 reg 16, with effect from 1 June 1996.

The fiscal warehousing record which is referred to in paragraph (3) of regulation 145F shall have the features and comply with the requirements set out below.

1 ***Goods in and out of a fiscal warehouse and its regime***

(*a*) It shall accurately identify any eligible goods which enter or exit the fiscal warehouse, their nature and quantity, and the time and date when they so enter or exit.

(*b*) It shall accurately identify any goods which are not eligible goods and which enter or exit the fiscal warehouse for storage (other than goods which enter for purposes wholly incidental to such storage), their nature and quantity, and time and date when they so enter or exit.

(*c*) It shall accurately identify all eligible goods which are allocated to or removed from the fiscal warehousing regime associated with the relevant fiscal warehousekeeper, the time and date when the allocation or removal takes place, and the location of the eligible goods while they are allocated to the relevant regime.

(*d*) It shall accurately identify as "transferred goods" all eligible goods which are transferred directly from the fiscal warehousing regime to another fiscal warehousing regime, the time and date when the transfer starts, and the address of the fiscal warehouse to which the goods in question are transferred.

(*e*) It shall accurately identify as "transferred goods" all eligible goods which are transferred directly from the fiscal warehousing regime to corresponding arrangements in another member State under regulation 145H(2)(*b*), the date and time when the transfer starts, and the address of the place in the other member State to which the goods in question are transferred.

(*f*) It shall accurately identify as "transferred goods (by reason of export)" all eligible goods which are directly exported from the fiscal warehousing regime to a place outside the member States under regulation 145H(2)(*c*), the date and time when the movement of the goods which is directly associated with the export starts, and the address of the place outside the member States to which the goods in question are consigned.

2 ***Specified services performed in a fiscal warehouse***

It shall accurately identify the nature of any services which are performed on or in relation to eligible goods while those goods are allocated to the relevant fiscal warehousing regime, the date when the services are performed, the particular eligible goods on or in relation to which they are performed, and the name, address and registration number (if any) of the supplier of those services.

3 ***Documents relating to transfers and specified services***

(*a*) It shall include the written undertaking from the other fiscal warehousekeeper relating to a transfer made within the United Kingdom referred to in regulation 145G(2), the certificate from the other fiscal warehousekeeper confirming a transfer made within the United Kingdom referred to in regulation 145G(3)(*c*), and it shall relate them to the relevant transfer.

(*b*) It shall include the copy of the certificate relating to a transfer received by the relevant fiscal warehousekeeper from another fiscal warehousing regime within the United Kingdom referred to in regulation 145G(3)(*d*) and it shall relate that copy to the relevant allocation to his relevant fiscal warehousing regime.

(*c*) It shall include the document relating to the completion of a transfer to corresponding arrangements in another member State referred to in regulation 145H(4)(*b*) and it shall relate that document to the relevant transfer.

(*d*) It shall include the document relating to the completion of an export to a place outside the member States referred to in regulation 145H(4)(*c*) and it shall relate that document to the export in question.

4 ***Procedures where transfers are not completed***

(*a*) It shall be adjusted to show a removal (and not a transfer) where the certificate of transfer within the United Kingdom referred to in regulation 145G(3)(*c*) is not received in time from the other fiscal warehousekeeper.

(*b*) It shall be adjusted to show a removal (and not a transfer) where the document referred to in articles 145H(4)(*b*) or 145H(4)(*c*) concerning goods which have been transferred to corresponding arrangements in another member State, or which have been exported to a place outside the member States, is not received in time.

(*c*) It shall evidence any notification made under regulation 145H(3)(*c*) to the person on whose instructions the goods were allowed to leave the fiscal warehouse.

5 ***Removals from a fiscal warehousing regime***

(*a*) It shall identify the name and address of any person who at any time removes or causes the removal of any goods from the fiscal warehousing regime and that person's registration number if he is registered under the Act.

(*b*) It shall include a copy of the removal document issued by the Commissioners under regulation 145J(1) and shall relate it to the relevant removal.

6 *Miscellaneous*

(*a*) It shall incorporate any modifications to the features or requirements set out in paragraphs 1 to 5 above which the Commissioners may require in respect of the relevant fiscal warehousekeeper.

(*b*) A fiscal warehousekeeper may, with the prior agreement of the Commissioners, maintain a fiscal warehousing record in which any of the features or requirements set out in paragraphs 1 to 5 above are relaxed or dispensed with.

SCHEDULE 2

REVOCATIONS

Regulation 3(1)

Note—The revocations listed in this Schedule have been taken into effect.

1995/2999

Value Added Tax (Refund of Tax) (No 2) Order 1995

Made by the Treasury under VATA 1994 s 33(3)

Made . . . . *22 November 1995*
Laid before the House of Commons . . . . *22 November 1995*
Coming into force . . . . *15 December 1995*

1 This Order may be cited as the Value Added Tax (Refund of Tax) (No 2) Order 1995 and shall come into force on 15th December 1995.

2 The following bodies are hereby specified for the purposes of section 33 of the Value Added Tax Act 1994:

A National Park authority (within the meaning of section 63 of the Environmental Act 1995)
A fire authority constituted by a combination scheme made under section 6 of the Fire Services Act 1947.

1996/1255

Value Added Tax (Fiscal Warehousing) (Treatment of Transactions) Order 1996

Made by the Treasury under VATA 1994 s 5(3)

Made . . . . *8 May 1996*
Laid before the House of Commons . . . . *9 May 1996*
Coming into force . . . . *1 June 1996*

1 This Order may be cited as the Value Added Tax (Fiscal Warehousing) (Treatment of Transactions) Order 1996 and shall come into force on 1st June 1996.

2— (1) In this Order—

"eligible goods" has the meaning given by section 18B(6) of the Act;
"material time" has the meaning given by section 18F(1) of the Act;
"supply" means a supply for the purposes of section 5(2)(*a*) of the Act; and,
"the Act" means the Value Added Tax Act 1994.

(2) In construing article 3(2) below any supply referred to in that article must be treated as taking place at the material time for that supply.

3— (1) A transaction fulfilling the description set out in paragraph (2) below shall be treated as a supply of goods and not as a supply of services.

(2) The description referred to in paragraph (1) above is that there is a supply (which is not a retail transaction) involving the transfer of any undivided share of property in eligible goods and either—

(*a*) that supply takes place while the goods in question are subject to a fiscal warehousing regime, or

(*b*) the transferee causes the goods in question to be placed in a fiscal warehousing regime after receiving that supply but before the supply, if any, which next occurs involving the transfer of any property in those goods.

1997/994

Free Zone (Port of Sheerness) (Substitution of Responsible Authority) Order 1997

Made by the Treasury under CEMA 1979 s 100A(4)(*b*)

Made . . . . *19 March 1997*
Coming into force . . . . *1 April 1997*

1 This Order may be cited as the Free Zone (Port of Sheerness) (Substitution of Responsible Authority) Order 1997 and shall come into force on 1st April 1997.

2 The responsible authority for the area designated a free zone by article 2(1) of the Free Zone (Port of Sheerness) Designation Order 1994 shall, in substitution for the Medway Ports Limited who were appointed by article 3 of that Order, be Port of Sheerness Limited, whose Registered Office is at Maritime Centre, Port of Liverpool, Liverpool L21 1LA.

1997/1431
Distress for Customs and Excise Duties and Other Indirect Taxes Regulations 1997

Made by the Commissioners of Customs and Excise under FA 1997 ss 51(1)–(3)

Made . . . . *9 June 1997*
Laid before House of Commons . . . . *9 June 1997*
Coming into force . . . . *1 July 1997*

Citation and Commencement

1 These Regulations may be cited as The Distress for Customs and Excise Duties and Other Indirect Taxes Regulations 1997 and shall come into force on 1st July 1997.

Interpretation

2— (1) In these Regulations—

"authorised person" means a person acting under the authority of the Commissioners;
"costs" means any costs, charges, expenses and fees;
"officer" means, subject to section 8(2) of the Customs and Excise Management Act 1979, a person commissioned by the Commissioners pursuant to section 6(3) of that Act;
"person in default" means a person who has refused or neglected to pay any relevant tax due from him;
"relevant tax" means any of the following—

...
(*b*) value added tax;
...

"VAT Act" means the Value Added Tax Act 1994;
"walking possession agreement" means an agreement under which, in consideration of any goods and chattels distrained upon being allowed to remain in the custody of the person in default and of the delaying of their sale, that person—

(*a*) acknowledges that the goods and chattels specified in the agreement are under distraint and held in walking possession; and
(*b*) undertakes that, except with the consent of the Commissioners and subject to such conditions as they may impose, he will not remove or allow the removal of any of the specified goods and chattels from the place named in the agreement;

"1994 Act" means Part III of the Finance Act 1994;
"1996 Act" means Part III of the Finance Act 1996;

(2) Any reference in these Regulations to an amount of relevant tax includes a reference to any amount recoverable as if it were an amount of that relevant tax.

Note—Words omitted are not relevant for the purposes of VAT.

Revocations and transitional provisions

3— (1) The Regulations specified in Schedule 3 are hereby revoked to the extent set out there.

(2) Where a warrant is signed before the coming into force of these Regulations, these Regulations shall apply to anything done, after these Regulations come into force, in relation to that warrant or as a consequence of distress being levied.

Levying distress

4— (1) Subject to regulation 5 below, if upon written demand a person neglects or refuses to pay any relevant tax due from him an officer may levy distress on the goods and chattels of that person and by warrant signed by him direct any authorised person to levy such distress.

(2) Where a warrant has been signed, distress shall be levied by or under the direction of, and in the presence of, the authorised person.

(3) Subject to regulation 6 below, distress may be levied on any goods and chattels located at any place whatever including on a public highway.

Restrictions on levying distress

5— (1) ...

(2) Where an amount of VAT is due under section 73(9) of the VAT Act no distress shall be levied before expiry of the last day on which the person who is liable to pay the amount concerned is required, by rules made under paragraph 9 of Schedule 12 to the VAT Act, to serve a notice of appeal with respect to that amount.

Note—Words omitted are not relevant for the purposes of VAT.

Goods and chattels not subject to levy

6 No distress shall be levied on any goods and chattels mentioned in Schedule 1 which at the time of levy are located in a place and used for a purpose mentioned in that Schedule.

Times for levying distress

7— (1) Subject to paragraph (2) below, a levy of distress shall commence only during the period between eight o'clock in the morning and eight o'clock at night on any day of the week but it may be continued thereafter outside that period until the levy is completed.

(2) Where a person holds himself out as conducting any profession, trade or business during hours which are partly within and partly outside, or wholly outside the period mentioned in paragraph (1) above, a levy of distress may be commenced at any time during that period or during the hours of any day in which he holds himself out as conducting that profession, trade or business and it may be continued thereafter outside that period or those hours until the levy is completed.

Costs

8— (1) A person in respect of whose goods and chattels a warrant has been signed shall be liable to pay to an officer or authorised person all costs, in connection with anything done under these Regulations described in column 1 of Schedule 2, as determined in accordance with column 2 of that Schedule.

(2) An authorised person may, after deducting and accounting for the amount of relevant tax to the Commissioners, retain costs from any amount received.

Sale

9 If any person upon whose goods and chattels distress has been levied does not pay the amount of relevant tax due together with costs within 5 days of a levy, an officer or authorised person may sell the distress for payment of the amount of relevant tax and costs; and the officer or authorised person, after deducting and retaining the amount of relevant tax and costs shall restore any surplus to the owner of the goods upon which distress was levied.

Disputes as to costs

10— (1) In the case of any dispute as to costs, the amount of those costs shall be taxed by a district judge of the county court of the district where the distress was levied, and he may make such order as he thinks fit as to the costs of the taxation.

(2) In the application of this regulation to Northern Ireland, in the case of any dispute as to costs, the amount of those costs shall be taxed in the same manner as costs in equity suits or proceedings in the county court in Northern Ireland.

SCHEDULE 1

GOODS AND CHATTELS NOT SUBJECT TO LEVY

Regulation 6

1 Any of the following goods and chattels which are located in a dwelling house at which distress is being levied and are reasonably required for the domestic needs of any person residing in that dwelling house—

(*a*) beds and bedding;
(*b*) household linen;
(*c*) chairs and settees;
(*d*) tables;
(*e*) food;
(*f*) lights and light fittings;
(*g*) heating appliances;
(*h*) curtains;
(*i*) floor coverings;
(*j*) furniture, equipment and utensils used for cooking, storing or eating food;
(*k*) refrigerators;
(*l*) articles used for cleaning, mending, or pressing clothes;
(*m*) articles used for cleaning the home;
(*n*) furniture used for storing—
  (i) clothing, bedding or household linen;
  (ii) articles used for cleaning the home;
  (iii) utensils used for cooking or eating food;
(*o*) articles used for safety in the home;
(*p*) toys for the use of any child within the household;
(*q*) medical aids and medical equipment.

2 Any of the following items which are located in premises used for the purposes of any profession, trade or business—

(*a*) fire fighting equipment for use on the premises;
(*b*) medical aids and medical equipment for use on the premises.

SCHEDULE 2
SCALE OF COSTS

Regulation 8(1)

Matter (*1*)	*Costs* (*2*)
1 For attending to levy distress where payment is made of an amount of relevant tax due and distress is not levied:	£12·50.
2 For levying distress—	
(*a*) where an amount of relevant tax demanded and due does not exceed £100:	£12·50.
(*b*) where an amount of relevant tax demanded and due exceeds £100:	12½% on the first £100, 4% on the next £400, 2½% on the next £1,500, 1% on the next £8,000, ¼% on any additional sum.
3 For taking possession of distrained goods—	
(*a*) where a person remains in physical possession of goods at the place where distress was levied (the person to provide his own food and lodgings):	£4·50 per day.
(*b*) where possession is taken under a walking possession agreement:	£7·00.
4 For appraising goods upon which distress has been levied:	Reasonable costs of appraisement.
5 For arranging removal and storage of goods upon which distress has been levied:	Reasonable costs of arrangement.
6 For removing and storing goods upon which distress has been levied:	Reasonable costs of removal and storage.
7 For advertising the sale of goods upon which distress has been levied:	Reasonable costs of advertising.
8 For selling the distress—	
(*a*) where a sale by auction is held at the auctioneer's premises:	15% of the sum realised.
(*b*) where a sale by auction is held elsewhere:	7½% of the sum realised and auctioneer's reasonable costs.
(*c*) where a sale by other means is undertaken:	7½% of the sum realised and reasonable costs.

9 In addition to any amount specified in this scale in respect of the supply of goods or services on which value added tax is chargeable there may be added a sum equivalent to value added tax at the appropriate rate on that amount.

1997/1523
Value Added Tax (Reverse Charge) (Anti-avoidance) Order 1997

Made by the Treasury under VATA 1994 s 8(5), (7)–(8)

Made . . . . *30 June 1997*
Laid before the House of Commons . . . . *30 June 1997*
Coming into force in accordance with article 1

Citation and commencement

1 This Order may be cited as the Value Added Tax (Reverse Charge) (Anti-avoidance) Order 1997 and shall apply in relation to any services performed on or after 1st July 1997.

Interpretation

2 In this Order—

"the Act" means the Value Added Tax Act 1994;
"the Regulations" means the Value Added Tax Regulations 1995;
"relevant telecommunications services" means services within the description which by virtue of this Order is inserted as paragraph 7A of Schedule 5 to the Act;

"relevant period" means such part of a period over which relevant telecommunications services are performed as falls after 30th June 1997;

"a supply of relevant telecommunications services by virtue of a right" means a supply of relevant telecommunications services performed on or after 1st July 1997 which is made by virtue of the exercise of a right which had been granted before 1st July 1997.

Insertion of telecommunications services into Schedule 5 to the Act

3 [*Amends VATA 1994 Sch 5*]

Modification of the effect of regulation 82 of the Regulations

4— (1) Where a supply of relevant telecommunications services is treated as if it were a taxable supply by virtue of section 8(1) or 43(2B) of the Act, the effect of regulation 82 of the Regulations shall be modified as follows—

(*a*) it shall have no effect in relation to relevant telecommunications services which are performed or which, by virtue of article 10 below, are treated as performed before 1st July 1997;

(*b*) it shall have no effect in relation to relevant telecommunications services which are wholly chargeable to VAT in another member State;

(*c*) where—

(i) relevant telecommunications services are performed on or after 1st July 1997; and

(ii) a payment in respect of those services has been made before that date,

it shall have effect in relation to those services as if the payment was made on 1st July 1997.

(2) Where the circumstances mentioned in paragraph (3) below apply—

(*a*) relevant telecommunications services which are paid for on or after 1st July 1997 shall be treated as being supplied only to the extent covered by the lower of—

(i) so much of the payment as exceeds the part of the payment for the supply by reference to which VAT is chargeable in another member State; and

(ii) so much of the payment as is properly attributable to the relevant period; and

(*b*) relevant telecommunications services which are supplied for a consideration which is not in money shall be treated as being supplied only to the extent covered by the lower of—

(i) so much of the consideration as exceeds the part of the consideration for the supply by reference to which VAT is chargeable in another member State; and

(ii) so much of the consideration as is properly attributable to the relevant period.

(3) The circumstances referred to in paragraph (2) above and article 7 below are that—

(*a*) relevant telecommunications services are performed on or after 1st July 1997; and

(*b*) either—

(i) the services are chargeable to VAT in part in another member State; or

(ii) the period over which the services are performed commenced before 1st July 1997.

Treatment of a right to relevant telecommunications services

5— (1) Subject to article 6 below, where the circumstances mentioned in article 8(3) below apply the time at which and extent to which a supply of relevant telecommunications services by virtue of a right is to be treated as made shall be determined as if the supply of relevant telecommunications services and the right were a single supply of which the supply of the right and each of those supplies constituted different parts.

(2) Without prejudice to the generality of paragraph (1) above, the payment for a right to relevant telecommunications services or the consideration for that right, as the case may be, shall, for the purposes of article 4 above, be treated as if it were the payment or the consideration for the relevant telecommunications services supplied by virtue of the right.

Rights not exercised before 1st July 1997

6 Where—

(*a*) the circumstances mentioned in article 8(3) below apply;

(*b*) a right to relevant telecommunications services is exercised on or after 1st July 1997,

(*c*) the consideration for the right was in money; and

(*d*) a payment in respect of the right was made before 1st July 1997,

the payment shall be deemed to have been made at the time of the exercise of the right.

Value of supply of relevant telecommunications services

7 Where the circumstances mentioned in article 4(3) above apply, the effect of paragraph 8 of Schedule 6 to the Act shall be modified so that the value of the supply treated as made shall be taken—

(*a*) in a case where the consideration for which the relevant telecommunications services were in fact supplied was a consideration in money, to be such amount as is equal to the lower of—

(i) so much of the consideration as exceeds the part of the consideration for the supply by reference to which VAT is chargeable in another member State; and

(ii) so much of the consideration as is properly attributable to the relevant period; and

(*b*) in a case where that consideration did not consist or not wholly consist of money, to be such amount in money as is equivalent to the lower of—

(i) so much of the consideration as exceeds the part of the consideration for the supply by reference to which VAT is chargeable in another member State; and

(ii) so much of the consideration as is properly attributable to the relevant period.

Value of relevant telecommunications services supplied by virtue of a right

8— (1) For the purposes of paragraph 8 of Schedule 6 to the Act and article 7 above, where the circumstances mentioned in paragraph (3) below apply, the consideration for which the relevant telecommunications services were in fact supplied shall be deemed to be the higher of—

(*a*) the consideration for which the services were in fact received; and

(*b*) the lower of—

(i) the open market value of the relevant telecommunications services which were in fact supplied which shall be valued as if they had not been supplied by virtue of the right; and

(ii) the amount determined in accordance with paragraph (2) below.

(2) The amount referred to in paragraph (1)(*b*)(ii) above is the sum of—

(*a*) the consideration for which the relevant telecommunications services were in fact supplied; and

(*b*) the consideration for the right to those services,

reduced by the open market value of the right to the relevant telecommunications services which shall be valued as if the right was a right to those services to be supplied at the open market value for those services determined in accordance with paragraph (1)(*b*)(i) above.

(3) The circumstances referred to in paragraph (1) above are that—

(*a*) there is a supply of relevant telecommunications services by virtue of a right; and

(*b*) the consideration for the relevant telecommunications services which were in fact supplied is less than the open market value of those services which shall be valued as if they had not been supplied by virtue of the right.

Meaning of a right to relevant telecommunications services

9 References in this Order to a right to relevant telecommunications services include references to any right, option or priority with respect to a supply of relevant telecommunications services, and to any interest deriving from any right to relevant telecommunications services.

Time when relevant telecommunications services are treated as performed

10— (1) For the purposes of this Order relevant telecommunications services which are supplied for a consideration the whole or part of which is determined or payable periodically or from time to time or in respect of which statements or invoices are issued periodically or from time to time, shall be treated as performed on the expiration of the period to which a payment, statement or invoice (as the case may be) relates.

(2) Where paragraph (1) above applies the services shall be treated as performed to the extent covered by the payment, statement or invoice.

1997/2558

Value Added Tax (Refund of Tax) Order 1997

Made by the Treasury under VATA 1994 s 33(3)

Made . . . . 27 October 1997
Laid before the House of Commons . . . . . . 28 October 1997
Coming into force . . . . 1 December 1997

1 This Order may be cited as the Value Added Tax (Refund of Tax) Order 1997 and shall come into force on 1 December 1997.

2 The following bodies are hereby specified for the purposes of section 33 of the Value Added Tax Act 1994—

charter trustees established by an Order made under section 17 of the Local Government Act 1992 or by any other statutory instrument made under Part II of that Act.

1998/1461

Air Passenger Duty and Other Indirect Taxes (Interest Rate) Regulations 1998

Made by the Treasury under FA 1996 s 197

Made . . . . 15 June 1998
Laid before the House of Commons . . . . 15 June 1998
Coming into force . . . . 6 July 1998

Citation and commencement

1 These Regulations may be cited as the Air Passenger Duty and Other Indirect Taxes (Interest Rate) Regulations 1998 and shall come into force on 6th July 1998.

Interpretation

2— (1) In these Regulations unless the context otherwise requires—

"established rate" means—

(*a*) on the coming into force of these Regulations, [6 per cent][1] per annum; and

(*b*) in relation to any day after the first reference day after the coming into force of these Regulations, the reference rate found on the immediately preceding reference day;

"operative day" means the [[twelfth][3] working day after the reference day][2];

"reference day" means the […[3] working day following the day on which the most recent meeting of the Monetary Policy Committee of the Bank of England took place][2] ;

"section 197" means section 197 of the Finance Act 1996;

the "relevant enactments" are those referred to in regulations 4(1) and 5(1) below;

"working day" means any day other than a non-business day within the meaning of section 92 of the Bills of Exchange Act 1882.

[(2) In these Regulations the reference rate found on a reference date is the official bank rate determined by the most recent meeting of the Monetary Policy Committee of the Bank of England.][3]

Amendments—[1] Words substituted by the Air Passenger Duty and Other Indirect Taxes (Interest Rate) (Amendment) Regulations, SI 2000/631 regs 2, 3 with effect from 1 April 2000.

[2] In para (1), in definition of "operative day" words substituted for words "sixth day of each month", and in definition of "reference day" words substituted for words "twelfth working day before the next operative day" by the Taxes and Duties (Interest Rate) (Amendment) Regulations, SI 2008/3234 reg 3(1), (2) with effect from 7 January 2009.

[3] In para (1), in definition of "operative day" word substituted for word "eleventh" and in definition of "reference day", word "second" revoked, and para (2) substituted, by the Taxes and Duties (Interest Rate) (Amendment) Regulations, SI 2009/2032 regs 15, 16 with effect from 12 August 2009. Para (2) previously read as follows—

"(2) In these Regulations the reference rate found on a reference day is the percentage per annum found by averaging the base lending rates at close of business on that day of—

(*a*) Bank of Scotland,
(*b*) Barclays Bank plc,
(*c*) Lloyds Bank plc,
(*d*) [HSBC Bank plc],
(*e*) National Westminster Bank plc, and
(*f*) The Royal Bank of Scotland plc,

and, if the result is not a whole number, rounding the result to the nearest such number, with any result midway between two whole numbers rounded down.".

[Applicable rate of interest equal to zero

2A In determining the rate of interest applicable under section 197 for the purposes of any enactments referred to in these Regulations, if the result is less than zero the rate shall be treated as zero for those purposes.][1]

Amendments—[1] Regulation 2A inserted by the Taxes and Duties (Interest Rate) (Amendment) Regulations, SI 2008/3234 reg 3(1), (3) with effect from 7 January 2009.

[2] This regulation revoked by the Taxes and Duties (Interest Rate) (Amendment) Regulations, SI 2009/2032 regs 15, 17 with effect from 12 August 2009.

3 The Air Passenger Duty and Other Indirect Taxes (Interest Rate) Regulations 1997 are hereby revoked.

[Applicable rate of interest payable to the Commissioners of Customs and Excise in connection with excise duties, insurance premium tax, VAT, landfill tax, and customs duty

4— (1) For the purposes of—

(*a*) [section 60(8) of, and paragraphs 7 and 8(1) of Schedule 6 to,][3] the Finance Act 1994,
(*b*) paragraph 21 of Schedule 7 to that Act,
(*c*) [sections 74 and 85A(3)][3] of the Value Added Tax Act 1994,
(*d*) [section 56(5) of and][3] paragraph 26 of Schedule 5 to the Finance Act 1996,
(*e*) paragraph 17 of Schedule 5 to the Finance Act 1997, …[2]
(*f*) section 126 of the Finance Act 1999, […[3]
(*g*) paragraphs 41(2)(*f*), 70(1)(*b*)[, 81(3) and 123(6)][3] of Schedule 6 to the Finance Act 2000 (climate change levy),][2] [and
(*h*) sections 25(2)(*f*)[, 30(3)(f) and 42(6)][3] of, and paragraphs 6 and 8(3)(*a*) of Schedule 5 to, the Finance Act 2001 (aggregates levy),][3]

the rate applicable under section 197 shall, subject to paragraph (2) below, be 8.5 per cent per annum.

(2) Where, on any reference day after the coming into force of these Regulations, the reference rate found on that day differs from the established rate, the rate applicable under section 197 of the Finance Act 1996 for the purposes of the enactments referred to in paragraph (1) above shall, from the next operative day, be the percentage per annum determined in accordance with the formula specified in paragraph (3) below.

(3) The formula specified in this paragraph is—

RR + 2.5,

where RR is the reference rate referred to in paragraph (2) above.][1]

[(4) With effect from 1st November 2001 the rate of interest prescribed in paragraph (1) above for the purposes of paragraph 17 of Schedule 5 to the Finance Act 1997 also applies in the application of that paragraph to assessments under paragraph 14 or 15 of that Schedule as amended by paragraph 19 of Schedule 3 to the Finance Act 2001.][2]

Amendments—[1] This regulation substituted by the Air Passenger Duty and Other Indirect Taxes (Interest Rate) (Amendment) Regulations, SI 2000/631 regs 2, 4 with effect from 1 April 2000.

[2] Word "and" in para (1)(*e*) revoked, and paras (1)(*g*) and (4) added by the Air Passenger Duty and Other Indirect Taxes (Interest Rate) (Amendment) Regulations, SI 2001/3337 regs 1, 2 with effect from 1 November 2001.

[3] The word "and" in para (1)(*f*) revoked, and para (1)(*h*) inserted, by the Air Passenger Duty and Other Indirect Taxes (Interest Rate) (Amendment) Regulations, SI 2003/230 regs 2, 3 with effect from 1 April 2003.

[4] In para (1), in sub-para (*a*) words substituted for words "paragraph 7 of Schedule 6 to", in sub-para (*c*) words substituted for words "section 74", in sub-para (*d*) words inserted, in sub-para (*g*) words substituted for words "and 81(3)", and in sub-para (*h*) words substituted for words "and 30(3)(*f*)", by the Transfer of Tribunal Functions and Revenue and Customs Appeals Order, SI 2009/56 art 3, Sch 2 paras 38, 39 with effect from 1 April 2009.

[Applicable rate of interest payable by the Commissioners of Customs and Excise in connection with air passenger duty, insurance premium tax, VAT, landfill tax, and customs duty

5— (1) For the purposes of—

(*a*) [Parts 2 and 3 of Schedule 3 to the Finance Act 2001 (interest payable on repayments etc)][2],

(*b*) paragraph 22 of Schedule 7 to that Act,

[(*ba*) section 60(6) of the Finance Act 1994,][4]

(*c*) [sections 78 and 85A(2)][4] of the Value Added Tax Act 1994,

(*d*) [section 56(3) and (4) of and][4] paragraph 29 of Schedule 5 to the Finance Act 1996, …[2]

(*e*) section 127 of the Finance Act 1999, […[3]

(*f*) paragraphs 62(3)(*f*)[, 66, 123(4) and 123(5)][4] of Schedule 6 to the Finance Act 2000 (climate change levy)][2][, and

(*g*) [section 42(4) and (5) of and][4] paragraphs 2 and 6(1)(*b*) of Schedule 8 to the Finance Act 2001 (aggregates levy),][3]

the rate applicable under section 197 of the Finance Act 1996 shall be 5 per cent per annum.

(2) Where, on a reference day after the coming into force of these Regulations, the reference rate found on that date differs from the established rate, the rate applicable under section 197 for the purposes of the enactments referred to in paragraph (1) above shall, from the next operative day, be the [higher of—

(*a*) 0.5% per annum, and

(*b*) the percentage per annum found by applying the formula specified in paragraph (3).][5]

[(3) The formula specified in this paragraph is—

RR – 1,

where RR is the reference rate referred to in paragraph (2).][5]

Amendments—[1] This regulation substituted by the Air Passenger Duty and Other Indirect Taxes (Interest Rate) (Amendment) Regulations, SI 2000/631 regs 2, 5 with effect from 1 April 2000.

[2] In para (1), words in sub-para (*a*) substituted, word "and" in sub-para (*d*) revoked, and sub-para (*f*) added by the Air Passenger Duty and Other Indirect Taxes (Interest Rate) (Amendment) Regulations, SI 2001/3337 regs 1, 3 with effect from 1 November 2001.

[3] Word "and" in para (1)(*e*) revoked, and para (1)(*g*) inserted, by the Air Passenger Duty and Other Indirect Taxes (Interest Rate) (Amendment) Regulations, SI 2003/230 regs 2, 4 with effect from 1 April 2003.

[4] In para (1), sub-para (*ba*) inserted, in sub-para (*c*) words substituted for words "section 78", in sub-paras (*d*), (*g*) words inserted, and in sub-para (*f*) words substituted for words "and 66", by the Transfer of Tribunal Functions and Revenue and Customs Appeals Order, SI 2009/56 art 3, Sch 2 paras 38, 40 with effect from 1 April 2009.

[5] In para (2), words substituted, and para (3) substituted, by the Taxes and Duties (Interest Rate) (Amendment) Regulations, SI 2009/2032 regs 15, 17 with effect from 12 August 2009. Words in para (2) previously read as follows—

"percentage per annum determined in accordance with the formula specified in paragraph (3) below.".

Para (3) previously read as follows—

"(3) The formula specified in this paragraph is—

RR – 1,

where RR is the reference rate referred to in paragraph (2) above.".

Effect of change in applicable rate

6 Where the rate applicable under section 197 for the purposes of any of the relevant enactments changes on an operative day by virtue of these Regulations, that change shall have effect for periods beginning on or after the operative day in relation to interest running from before that day as well as in relation to interest running from, or from after that day.

7 Where the rate applicable under section 197 for the purposes of any of the relevant enactments changes on an operative day by virtue of these Regulations, the rate in force immediately prior to any change shall continue to have effect for periods immediately prior to the change and so on in the case of any number of successive changes.

Applicable rate of interest prior to the coming into force of these Regulations

8 The rate applicable under section 197 for interest running from before the date these Regulations come into force in relation to periods prior to that date shall be specified for the relevant enactments in the following Tables—

Table 1
Paragraph 7 of Schedule 6 to the Finance Act 1994

Interest for any period	*Rate*
From 1st November 1994 and before 6th February 1996	5·5 per cent
After 5th February 1996 and before 6th July 1998	6·25 per cent

Table 2
Paragraph 21 of Schedule 7 to the Finance Act 1994

Interest for any period	*Rate*
From 1st October 1994 and before 6th February 1996	5·5 per cent
After 5th February 1996 and before 6th July 1998	6·25 per cent

Table 3
Section 74 of the Value Added Tax Act 1994

Interest for any period	*Rate*
from 1st April 1990 and before 6th November 1990	13 per cent
after 5th November 1990 and before 6th March 1991	12·25 per cent
after 5th March 1991 and before 6th May 1991	11·5 per cent
after 5th May 1991 and before 6th July 1991	10·75 per cent
after 5th July 1991 and before 6th October 1991	10 per cent
after 5th October 1991 and before 6th November 1992	9·25 per cent
after 5th November 1992 and before 6th December 1992	7·75 per cent
after 5th December 1992 and before 6th March 1993	7 per cent
after 5th March 1993 and before 6th January 1994	6·25 per cent
after 5th January 1994 and before 6th October 1994	5·5 per cent
after 5th October 1994 and before 6th March 1995	6·25 per cent
after 5th March 1995 and before 6th February 1996	7 per cent
after 5th February 1996 and before 6th July 1998	6·25 per cent

Table 4
Paragraph 26 of Schedule 5 to the Finance Act 1996

Interest for any period	*Rate*
from 1st April 1997 and before 6th July 1998	6·25 per cent

Table 5
Paragraph 9 of Schedule 6 to the Finance Act 1994

Interest for any period	*Rate*
from 1st November 1994 and before 1st April 1997	8 per cent
after 31st March 1997 and before 6th July 1998	6 per cent

Table 6
Paragraph 22 of Schedule 7 to the Finance Act 1994

Interest for any period	*Rate*
after 1st October 1994 and before 1st April 1997	8 per cent
after 31st March 1997 and before 6th July 1998	6 per cent

Table 7
Section 78 of the Value Added Tax Act 1994

Interest for any period	*Rate*
from 1st April 1973 and before 1st March 1974	8 per cent
after 28th February 1974 and before 1st February 1977	9 per cent
after 31st January 1977 and before 1st March 1979	10 per cent
after 28th February 1979 and before 1st January 1980	12·5 per cent
after 31st December 1979 and before 1st January 1981	15 per cent
after 31st December 1980 and before 1st December 1981	12·5 per cent
after 30th November 1981 and before 1st March 1982	15 per cent
after 28th February 1982 and before 1st July 1982	14 per cent
after 30th June 1982 and before 1st April 1983	13 per cent
after 31st March 1983 and before 1st April 1984	12·5 per cent
after 31st March 1984 and before 1st August 1986	12 per cent
after 31st July 1986 and before 1st January 1987	11·5 per cent
after 31st December 1986 and before 1st April 1987	12·25 per cent
after 31st March 1987 and before 1st November 1987	11·75 per cent
after 31st October 1987 and before 1st December 1987	11·25 per cent
after 30th November 1987 and before 1st May 1988	11 per cent
after 30th April 1988 and before 1st August 1988	9·5 per cent
after 31st July 1988 and before 1st November 1988	11 per cent
after 31st October 1988 and before 1st January 1989	12·25 per cent
after 31st December 1988 and before 1st November 1989	13 per cent
after 31st October 1989 and before 1st April 1991	14·25 per cent
after 31st March 1991 and before [16th October 1991][1]	12 per cent
after 15th October 1991 and before 6th February 1993	10·25 per cent
after 5th February 1993 and before 1st April 1997	8 per cent
after 31st March 1997 and before 6th July 1998	6 per cent

Table 8
Paragraph 29 of Schedule 5 to the Finance Act 1996

Interest for any period	*Rate*
from 1st April 1997 and before 6th July 1998	6 per cent

Amendments—[1] Words in square brackets in Table 7 substituted by the Air Passenger Duty and Other Indirect Taxes (Interest Rate) (Amendment) Regulations, SI 2000/631 regs 2, 6 with effect from 1 April 2000.

1999/2076
Value Added Tax (Refund of Tax) Order 1999

Made by the Treasury under VATA 1994 s 33(3)

Made . . . . 21 July 1999
Laid before the House of Commons . . . . 22 July 1999
Coming into force . . . . 1 September 1999

Commentary—*De Voil Indirect Tax Service* **V6.154, V6.155**.

1 This Order may be cited as the Value Added Tax (Refund of Tax) Order 1999 and shall come into force on 1st September 1999.

2 The Broads Authority (a body corporate established by section 1 of the Norfolk and Suffolk Broads Act 1988) is hereby specified for the purposes of section 33 of the Value Added Tax Act 1994.

1999/3115
Value Added Tax (Importation of Investment Gold) Relief Order 1999

Made by the Treasury under VATA 1994 s 37(1) and FA 1999 s 13(3) and (4)

Made . . . . 19 November 1999
Laid before the House of Commons . . . . 22 November 1999
Coming into force . . . . 1 January 2000

1 This Order may be cited as the Value Added Tax (Importation of Investment Gold) Relief Order 1999 and shall come into force on 1st January 2000.

2 In this Order—

"Investment gold" has the same meaning as in Group 15 of Schedule 9 to the Value Added Tax Act 1994.

3 VAT shall not be chargeable on the importation of investment gold from places outside the member States.

1999/3116
Value Added Tax (Investment Gold) Order 1999

Made by the Treasury under VATA 1994 ss 31(2), 55(6) and 96(9) and FA 1999 s 13(2) and (4)

Made . . . . *19 November 1999*
Laid before the House of Commons . . . . . . *22 November 1999*
Coming into force . . . . *1 January 2000*

Customs and Excise Notices—Notice 701/21: Gold.

Citation, commencement and interpretation

1— (1) This Order may be cited as the Value Added Tax (Investment Gold) Order 1999 and shall come into force on 1st January 2000 and shall have effect in relation to supplies made on or after that date.

(2) In this Order—

"the Commissioners" means the Commissioners of Customs and Excise;

"the Act" means the Value Added Tax Act 1994.

"relevant supply" means a supply of investment gold within the meaning of item 1 or 2 of Group 15 of Schedule 9 to the Act made by a taxable person, to another taxable person and "relevant supplies" shall be construed accordingly.

Exemption for investment gold

2 (*Amends the Value Added Tax Act 1994, Sch 9.*)

Election to waive exemption

3— (1) Subject to paragraphs (2), (6), (7) and (8) below, where an election under this paragraph has effect in relation to a relevant supply by a taxable person who produces or transforms investment gold, which supply would (apart from this paragraph) fall within item 1 or 2 of Group 15 of Schedule 9 to the Act, the supply shall not fall within that Group.

(2) An election under paragraph (1) above (or an election having the like effect) or an election under paragraph (5) below shall apply in respect of an individual relevant supply made and shall have effect on or after the day from which the election is made.

(3) Subject to complying with such conditions as the Commissioners may direct in notices published by them for the purposes of this Order, the Commissioners may permit a taxable person to make elections in respect of relevant supplies by him of a description falling within paragraph (4) below having the like effect to an election under paragraph (1) above.

(4) The supplies referred to in paragraph (3) above are those relevant supplies where the investment gold supplied falls within the description in Note (1)(*a*) contained in Group 15 of Schedule 9 to the Act, made by a taxable person who in the normal course of his business makes supplies of gold for industrial purposes.

(5) Subject to paragraphs (6) to (8) below, where a taxable person has made a relevant supply in respect of which an election under paragraph (1) above (or an election having the like effect) has been made, the supply of services by his agent directly linked to the relevant supply and which supply of services would (apart from this paragraph) fall within item 3 of Group 15 of Schedule 9 to the Act shall, if the agent so elects, not fall within that Group.

(6) A person making a relevant supply in respect of which an election to waive exemption under this article has been made shall comply with such conditions as the Commissioners may specify in notices published by them for the purposes of this Order including conditions relating to the notification of an election.

(7) An election made under paragraph (1) above (or an election having the like effect) and an election made under paragraph (5) above shall be irrevocable.

(8) Where the Commissioners have permitted a person to make elections under paragraph (3) above, they may withdraw that permission where it appears to them to be necessary to do so for the protection of the revenue and accordingly the permission shall cease to have effect from such date as may be specified in a notification from the Commissioners.

Customers to account for tax on supplies of investment gold

4 Section 55(1) to (4) of the Act shall apply to all supplies of a description which but for an election made under article 3 above would fall within item 1 or 2 of Group 15 of Schedule 9 to the Act.

1999/3121
Value Added Tax (Input Tax) (Specified Supplies) Order 1999

Made by the Treasury under VATA 1994 s 26(2)(*c*)

Made . . . . *19 November 1999*
Laid before the House of Commons . . . . . . *22 November 1999*
Coming into force . . . . *1 January 2000*

1 This Order may be cited as the Value Added Tax (Input Tax) (Specified Supplies) Order 1999 and shall come into force on 1st January 2000 and shall have effect in relation to supplies made on or after that date.

2 The supplies described in articles 3 and 4 below are hereby specified for the purposes of section 26(2)(*c*) of the Value Added Tax Act 1994.

3 Services—

(*a*) which are supplied to a person who belongs outside the member States;

(*b*) which are directly linked to the export of goods to a place outside the member States; or

(*c*) which consist of the provision of intermediary services within the meaning of item 4 of Group 2, or item 5 of Group 5, of Schedule 9 to the Value Added Tax Act 1994 in relation to any transaction specified in paragraph (*a*) or (*b*) above,

provided the supply is exempt, or would have been exempt if made in the United Kingdom, by virtue of any item of Group 2, or any of items 1 to 6 and item 8 of Group 5, of Schedule 9 to the Value Added Tax Act 1994.

4 Supplies made either in or outside the United Kingdom which fall, or would fall, within item 1 or 2 of Group 15 of Schedule 9 to the Value Added Tax Act 1994 (investment gold).

5 (Revokes the Value Added Tax (Input Tax) (Specified Supplies) Order 1992, SI 1992/3123.)

2000/1046
Value Added Tax (Refund of Tax) Order 2000

Made by the Treasury under VATA 1994 s 33(3)

Made . . . . *12 April 2000*
Laid before the House of Commons . . . . . . *13 April 2000*
Coming into force . . . . *8 May 2000*

Commentary—*De Voil Indirect Tax Service* **V6.154, V6.155**.

1 This Order may be cited as the Value Added Tax (Refund of Tax) Order 2000 and shall come into force on 8th May 2000.

2 The Greater London Authority (a body corporate established by section 1 of the Greater London Authority Act 1999) is specified for the purposes of section 33 of the Value Added Tax Act 1994.

2000/1515
Value Added Tax (Refund of Tax) (No 2) Order 2000

Made by the Treasury under VATA 1994 s 33(3)

Made . . . . *7 June 2000*
Laid before the House of Commons . . . . . . *8 June 2000*
Coming into force . . . . *3 July 2000*

Commentary—*De Voil Indirect Tax Service* **V6.162**.

1 This Order may be cited as the Value Added Tax (Refund of Tax) (No 2) Order 2000 and shall come into force on 3rd July 2000.

2 The London Fire and Emergency Planning Authority (the body corporate reconstituted by section 328 of, and Schedule 28 to, the Greater London Authority Act 1999) is specified for the purposes of section 33 of the Value Added Tax Act 1994.

2000/1672
Value Added Tax (Refund of Tax) (No 3) Order 2000

Made by the Treasury under VATA 1994 s 33(3)

Made . . . . *26 June 2000*
Laid before the House of Commons . . . . . . *26 June 2000*
Coming into force . . . . *17 July 2000*

Commentary—*De Voil Indirect Tax Service* **V6.162**.

1 This Order may be cited as the Value Added Tax (Refund of Tax) (No 3) Order 2000 and shall come into force on 17th July 2000.

2 Transport for London (the body corporate established by section 154 of the Greater London Authority Act 1999) is specified for the purposes of section 33 of the Value Added Tax Act 1994.

2001/759
Value Added Tax (Electronic Communications) (Incentives) Regulations 2001

Made by the Commissioners of Customs and Excise under FA 2000 Sch 38

Made . . . . *7 March 2001*
Laid before the House of Commons . . . . *8 March 2001*
Coming into force . . . . *1 April 2001*

Amendment—These regulations revoked by the VAT (Amendment) (No 3) Regulations, SI 2004/1675 reg 1(1), (2) with effect from 22 July 2004.

Citation and commencement

1 *These Regulations may be cited as the Value Added Tax (Electronic Communications) (Incentives) Regulations 2001 and come into force on 1st April 2001.*

Interpretation

2 *In these Regulations—*

"the Commissioners" means the Commissioners of Customs and Excise;
"electronic return system" has the meaning given in regulation 25(4B) of the VAT Regulations;
"incentive payment" has the meaning given in regulation 3 below;
"prescribed accounting period" has the meaning given in regulation 2(1) of the VAT Regulations;
"relevant return" means the return referred to in regulation 3(1)(a) below;
"taxable person" has the meaning given in section 3(1) of the Value Added Tax Act 1994;
"VAT Regulations" means the Value Added Tax Regulations 1995.

Incentive for making a VAT return by way of an electronic return system

3— *(1) The Commissioners shall give an incentive in the form of a payment of £50 to any taxable person who—*

(a) makes a return by way of an electronic return system on or after 1st April 2001;
(b) has not previously made such a return on or after that date; and
(c) satisfies the conditions specified in any direction given by the Commissioners under paragraph (2) below.

Such a payment shall be called an "incentive payment".

(2) The Commissioners may give a direction specifying any or all of the following conditions—

(a) that the relevant return is made in compliance with any time limits specified by or under the VAT Regulations;
(b) that the relevant return is made for a prescribed accounting period that is specified in the direction;
(c) that the amount of value added tax that is payable in respect of the period to which the relevant return relates is paid—

(i) by a means of electronic payment that is specified in the direction; and
(ii) in compliance with any time limits specified by or under the VAT Regulations;

(d) that the value of supplies made by the taxable person in the period of 12 months ending on the last day of the prescribed accounting period to which the relevant return relates does not exceed such sum as may be specified.

Withdrawal of an incentive payment and recovery

4— *(1) Where it appears to the Commissioners that a person has failed to satisfy one or more of the conditions specified in a direction given under regulation 3(2) above, they may give notice in writing to that person withdrawing the incentive payment and, where a payment has already been made, may assess the amount so paid and notify it to him.*

(2) The Commissioners may notify an assessment under paragraph (1) above at the same time as they give notice withdrawing the incentive payment.

(3) Subsections (2) to (4) and (8) of section 78A of the Value Added Tax Act 1994 (assessment for interest overpayments) apply in the case of an assessment under paragraph (1) above as they apply in the case of an assessment under section 78A(1) of that Act.

Appeals

5 *An appeal shall lie to a VAT and duties tribunal with respect to—*

(a) an assessment under regulation 4(1) above, or the amount of such an assessment; and
(b) a decision that the conditions of entitlement to an incentive payment are not met.

Directions

6 *Any direction given by the Commissioners under regulation 3(2) above shall be contained in a notice published by them.*

2001/2879
Value Added Tax (Refund of Tax to Museums and Galleries) Order 2001

Made by the Treasury under VATA 1994 s 33A(9)

Made . . . . *9 August 2001*
Laid before the House of Commons . . . . *9 August 2001*
Coming into force . . . . *1 September 2001*

Commentary—*De Voil Indirect Tax Service* **V5.162.**

1 This Order may be cited as the Value Added Tax (Refund of Tax to Museums and Galleries) Order 2001 and comes into force on 1st September 2001.

2 Section 33A of the Value Added Tax Act 1994 applies to the bodies listed in column 1 of the Schedule to this Order.

3 The museums and galleries listed in column 2 of the Schedule are, for the purposes of section 33A of the Value Added Tax Act 1994, relevant museums and galleries in relation to the bodies listed opposite them in the Schedule.

4 Where column 3 of the Schedule indicates a particular date, in the case of the museum or gallery to be found opposite that date, section 33A of the Value Added Tax Act 1994 shall apply as if, in subsection (1)(*c*) of that section, that date were substituted for 1st April 2001.

SCHEDULE

Articles 2, 3 and 4

Column 1	*Column 2*	*Column 3*
Body	*Relevant museums and galleries*	*Later date to be substituted for 1st April 2001*
British Museum	British Museum Great Russell Street London WC1B 3DG	
Imperial War Museum	Imperial War Museum Lambeth Road London SE1 6HZ	1st December 2001
	IWM North Trafford Wharf Road Trafford Park Manchester M17 1TZ	1st April 2002
The National Gallery	The National Gallery Trafalgar Square London WC2N 5ND	
National Maritime Museum	National Maritime Museum Romney Road London SE10 9NF	1st December 2001
National Museums and Galleries on Merseyside	Walker Art Gallery William Brown Street Liverpool L3 8EL	1st December 2001
	[World Museum Liverpool][3] William Brown Street Liverpool L3 8EN	1st December 2001
	Merseyside Maritime Museum Albert Dock Liverpool L3 4AQ	1st December 2001
	[Museum of Liverpool][3] Pier Head Liverpool L3 1PZ	1st December 2001
	The Lady Lever Art Gallery Port Sunlight Village Bebington Wirral Merseyside [CH62 5EQ][3]	1st December 2001
	Sudley House Mossley Hill Road	1st December 2001

Column 1 *Body*	*Column 2* *Relevant museums and galleries*	*Column 3* *Later date to be substituted for 1st April 2001*
	Liverpool L18 8BX	
	[National Conservation Centre][3] Whitechapel Liverpool L1 6HZ	1st December 2001
	[HM Revenue and Customs][3] National Museum Merseyside Maritime Museum Albert Dock Liverpool L3 4AQ	1st December 2001
	[International Slavery Museum Dock Traffic Office Albert Dock Liverpool L3 4AX][3]	[1st April 2006][3]
National Portrait Gallery	National Portrait Gallery St Martin's Place London WC2H 0HE	
Natural History Museum	Natural History Museum Cromwell Road London SW7 5BD	1st December 2001
	Natural History Museum Zoological Museum Akeman Street Tring Herts HP23 6AD	1st December 2001
Royal Armouries	The Royal Armouries Armouries Drive Leeds West Yorkshire LS10 1LT	1st December 2001
	Royal Armouries at Fort Nelson Fort Nelson Down End Road Fareham Hants PO17 6AD	1st December 2001
Science Museum	Science Museum South Kensington London SW7 2DD	1st December 2001
	National Museum of Photography Film and Television Bradford West Yorkshire BD1 1LQ	
	National Railway Museum Leeman Road York YO26 4XJ	1st December 2001
	Science Museum Wroughton Airfield Swindon Wilts SN4 9NS	1st April 2002
	National Coal Mining Museum for England Caphouse Colliery New Road Overton Wakefield West Yorkshire WF4 4RH	

Column 1 *Body*	*Column 2* *Relevant museums and galleries*	*Column 3* *Later date to be substituted for 1st April 2001*
	[Locomotion, The National Railway Museum at Shildon Shildon County Durham DL4 1PQ.][1]	[10th February 2003][1]
Tate Gallery	Tate Britain Millbank London SW1P 4RG	
	Tate Modern Bankside London SE1 9TG	
	Tate Liverpool Albert Dock Liverpool L3 4BB	
Victoria and Albert Museum	Victoria and Albert Museum Cromwell Road London SW7 2RL	22nd November 2001
	Bethnal Green Museum of Childhood Cambridge Heath Road London E2 9PA	22nd November 2001
	Theatre Museum: National Museum of Performing Arts Russell Street Covent Garden London WC2 7PR	22nd November 2001
	Wellington Museum Apsley House 149 Piccadilly Hyde Park Corner London W1J 7NT	
The Wallace Collection	The Wallace Collection Hertford House Manchester Square London W1U 3BN	
The Greater Manchester Museum of Science and Industry	Museum of Science and Industry in Manchester Liverpool Road Castlefield Manchester M3 4FP	1st December 2001
Sir John Soane's Museum	Sir John Soane's Museum 13 Lincoln's Inn Fields London WC2A 3BP	
Museum of London	Museum of London London Wall London EC2Y 5NH	1st December 2001
	Museum of London Archaeological Service Mortimer Wheeler House 46 Eagle Wharf Road London N1	1st March 2002
Geffrye Museum	Geffrye Museum Kingsland Road London E2 8EA	
Horniman Museum	Horniman Museum 100 London Road	

Column 1 *Body*	*Column 2* *Relevant museums and galleries*	*Column 3* *Later date to be substituted for 1st April 2001*
	Forest Hill London SE23 3PQ	
British Library	British Library 96 Euston Road London NW1 2DB (in respect of the historical collections in its galleries, temporary exhibitions and other related public programmes and events)	
The National Army Museum	The National Army Museum Royal Hospital Road Chelsea London SW3 4HT	
The Royal Air Force Museum	The Royal Air Force Museum Hendon London NW9 5LL	1st December 2001
	[The Royal Air Force Museum Cosford Shifnal Shropshire TF11 8UP][3]	[24th August 2005][3]
National Museums & Galleries of Wales	National Museum & Gallery Cathays Park Cardiff CF10 3NP National Museums of Welsh History: Roman Legionary Museum High Street Caerleon NP6 1AE Segontium Roman Fort Museum Beddgelert Road Caernarfon Gwynedd LL55 2LN Museum of Welsh Life St Fagans Cardiff CF5 6XB National Museums of Welsh Industry: Welsh Slate Museum Llanberis Gwynedd LL55 4TY Big Pit, National Mining Museum of Wales Blaenafon Torfaen NP4 9XP Museum of the Welsh Woollen Industry Drefach Felindre Llandysul SA44 5UP Collections Centre Nantgarw Trefforest Industrial Estate Pontypridd CF15 7QT	
	[National Waterfront Museum Swansea Maritime Quarter	[18th October 2001][1]

Column 1 *Body*	*Column 2* *Relevant museums and galleries*	*Column 3* *Later date to be substituted for 1st April 2001*
	Victoria Road Swansea SA1 1SN][1] National Museum of Art: Turner House Plymouth Road Penarth South Glamorgan CF64 3DM	
The National Library of Wales	The National Library of Wales Aberystwyth Ceredigion SY23 3BU (in respect of the historical collections in its galleries, temporary exhibitions and other related public programmes and events)	
National Museums and Galleries of Northern Ireland	Ulster Museum Botanic Gardens Belfast BT9 5AB Armagh County Museum The Mall East Armagh	
National Museums of Scotland	Royal Scottish Museum Chambers Street Edinburgh EH1 1JF Museum of Scotland Chambers Street Edinburgh EH1 1JF National War Museum of Scotland Edinburgh Castle Edinburgh	
National Galleries of Scotland	National Gallery of Scotland The Mound Edinburgh EH2 2EL Scottish National Portrait Gallery Queen Street Edinburgh EH2 1JD Scottish National Gallery of Modern Art Belford Road Edinburgh EH4 3DR Dean Gallery Belford Road Edinburgh EH4 3DR	
National Library of Scotland	National Library of Scotland George IV Bridge Edinburgh EH1 1EW National Library of Scotland 33 Salisbury Place Edinburgh	

Column 1 *Body*	*Column 2* *Relevant museums and galleries*	*Column 3* *Later date to be substituted for 1st April 2001*
	(in respect of the historical collections in its galleries, temporary exhibitions and other related public programmes and events)	
[Keele University	Keele University Art Gallery Keele Arts Keele University, Staffordshire ST5 5BG	1 August 2004
Lancaster University	Peter Scott Gallery Lancaster University Lancaster LA1 4YW	1 August 2004
	Ruskin Library Lancaster University Lancaster LA1 4YH	1 August 2004
London Metropolitan University	The Women's Library London Metropolitan University Old Castle Street London E1 7NT	1 August 2004
Manchester Metropolitan University	Manchester Metropolitan University Special Collections Sir Kenneth Green Library All Saints Manchester M15 6BH	1 August 2004
Middlesex University	Museum of Domestic Design and Architecture Middlesex University Cat Hill Barnet Hertfordshire EN4 8HT	1 August 2004
Queen's University, Belfast	The Naughton Gallery at Queen's and Queen's University Art Collection Lanyon Building Queen's University Belfast BT7 1NN	1 August 2004
School of Oriental and African Studies	Percival David Foundation of Chinese Art 53 Gordon Square London WC1H 0PD	1 August 2004
The Royal Academy of Music	York Gate Collections Royal Academy of Music Marylebone Road London NW1 5HT	1 August 2004
The Royal College of Surgeons of England	Hunterian Museum at the Royal College of Surgeons 35–43 Lincoln's Inn Fields London WC2A 3PE	1 August 2004
University of Aberdeen	Marischal Museum University of Aberdeen Marischal College Broad Street Aberdeen Scotland AB10 1YS	1 August 2004

Column 1 *Body*	*Column 2* *Relevant museums and galleries*	*Column 3* *Later date to be substituted for 1st April 2001*
	Natural Philosophy Collection University of Aberdeen Department of Physics Fraser Noble Building King's College Aberdeen Scotland AB24 3UE	1 August 2004
	Zoology Museum University of Aberdeen Zoology Building Tillydrone Avenue Aberdeen Scotland AB24 2TZ	1 August 2004
University of Birmingham	Barber Institute of Fine Arts University of Birmingham Edgbaston Birmingham B15 2TS	1 August 2004
	Lapworth Museum of Geology University of Birmingham Edgbaston Birmingham B15 2TT	1 August 2004
University of Bristol	University of Bristol Theatre Collection Cantocks Close Bristol BS8 1UP	1 August 2004
University of Cambridge	Sedgwick Museum of Earth Sciences 3 Downing Street Cambridge CB2 3EQ	1 August 2004
	University Museum of Zoology Cambridge Downing Street Cambridge CB2 3EJ	1 August 2004
	The Fitzwilliam Museum Cambridge Trumpington Street Cambridge CB2 1RB	1 August 2004
University College Chichester	Otter Gallery University College Chichester Bishop Otter Campus College Lane Chichester W Sussex PO19 6PE	1 August 2004
University of East Anglia	The Sainsbury Centre for Visual Arts University of East Anglia Norwich NR4 7TJ	28 October 2004
University of Edinburgh	Talbot Rice Gallery The University of Edinburgh Old College South Bridge Edinburgh EH8 9YL	1 August 2004
University of Exeter	The Bill Douglas Centre for the History of Cinema and Popular Culture The Old Library Prince of Wales Road	1 August 2004

Column 1 *Body*	*Column 2* *Relevant museums and galleries*	*Column 3* *Later date to be substituted for 1st April 2001*
	Exeter EX4 4SB	
University of Glamorgan	University of Glamorgan Artworks Collection Oriel y Bont The University of Glamorgan Treforest Pontypridd CF37 1DL	1 August 2004
University of Glasgow	Hunterian Museum Gilbert Scott Building University of Glasgow University Avenue Glasgow G12 8QQ	1 August 2004
	Hunterian Art Gallery 82 Hillhead Street University of Glasgow Glasgow G12 8QQ	1 August 2004
	Zoology Museum Graham Kerr Building University of Glasgow University Avenue Glasgow G12 8QQ	1 August 2004
University of Hull	University of Hull Art Collection University of Hull Hull HU6 7RX	1 August 2004
University of Kent	Centre for the Study of Cartoons and Caricature Templeman Library University of Kent Canterbury CT2 7NU	1 August 2004
University of Manchester	Labour History Archive and Study Centre People's History Museum Head Office 103 Princess Street Manchester M1 6DD	1 August 2004
	The John Rylands Library 150 Deansgate Manchester M3 3EH	1 August 2004
	The Manchester Museum Oxford Road Manchester M13 9PL	1 August 2004
	Whitworth Art Gallery The University of Manchester Oxford Road Manchester M15 6ER	1 August 2004
University of Newcastle upon Tyne	Hancock Museum Barras Bridge Newcastle upon Tyne NE2 4PT	28 February 2005
	Hatton Gallery University of Newcastle upon Tyne Newcastle upon Tyne NE1 7RU	1 August 2004
	Museum of Antiquities University of Newcastle upon Tyne	1 August 2004

Column 1 *Body*	*Column 2* *Relevant museums and galleries*	*Column 3* *Later date to be substituted for 1st April 2001*
	Newcastle upon Tyne NE1 7RU	
	Shefton Museum of Greek Art & Archaeology University of Newcastle upon Tyne Newcastle upon Tyne NE1 7RU	1 August 2004
University of Northumbria at Newcastle	University Gallery and Baring Wing Northumbria University Sandyford Road Newcastle-upon-Tyne NE1 8ST	1 August 2004
University of Oxford	Ashmolean Museum of Art and Archaeology Beaumont Street Oxford OX1 2PH Oxford University Museum of Natural History Parks Road Oxford OX1 3PW	1 August 2004
	Pitt Rivers Museum South Parks Road Oxford OX1 3PP	1 August 2004
	[Museum of the History of Science Broad Street Oxford OX1 3AZ][3]	[1st April 2007][3]
University of Reading	Cole Museum of Zoology School of Animal and Microbial Sciences University of Reading Whiteknights Reading RG6 6AJ	1 August 2004
	Museum of English Rural Life University of Reading Redlands Road Reading RG15EX	1 August 2004
	Ure Museum of Greek Archaeology University of Reading Room 38 HUMUSS Building Whiteknights Reading RG6 6AH	1 August 2004
University of Strathclyde	Collins Gallery University of Strathclyde 22 Richmond Street Glasgow G1 1XQ	1 August 2004
University of Wales Aberystwyth	Ceramics Gallery The University of Wales Buarth Mawr Aberystwyth Ceredigion SY23 1NG	1 August 2004
	School of Art Gallery and Museum The University of Wales	1 August 2004

Column 1	*Column 2*	*Column 3*
Body	*Relevant museums and galleries*	*Later date to be substituted for 1st April 2001*
	Buarth Mawr Aberystwyth Ceredigion SY23 1NG	
University of Wales Swansea	Egypt Centre University of Wales Swansea Singleton Park Swansea SA2 8PP	1 August 2004][2]
[People's History Museum	People's History Museum The Pump House Bridge Street Manchester M3 3ER	9th August 2005
National Football Museum	National Football Museum Sir Tom Finney Way Deepdale Preston PR1 6PA	1st July 2005
University of Liverpool	The Victoria Gallery and Museum The Foundation Building 765 Brownlow Hill Liverpool L69 7ZX	24th October 2005][3]

Amendments—[1] Entries inserted by the VAT (Refund of Tax to Museums and Galleries) Order, SI 2004/1709 with effect from 1 August 2004.
[2] Entries inserted by the VAT (Refund of Tax to Museums and Galleries) (Amendment) Order, SI 2005/1993 with effect from 10 August 2005.
[3] Entries substituted and inserted by the VAT (Refund of Tax to Museums and Galleries) (Amendment) Order, SI 2008/1339 with effect from 1 July 2008.

2001/2880
Free Zone (Southampton) Designation Order 2001

Made by the Treasury under the Customs and Excise Management Act 1979 s 100A

Made . . . . *9 August 2001*
Coming into force . . . . *10 August 2001*

Citation and commencement

1 This Order may be cited as The Free Zone (Southampton) Designation Order 2001 and shall come into force on 10th August 2001.

Designation of area as free zone

2— (1) An area of 3.2436 hectares, in the City of Southampton, Hampshire, shown enclosed by a red line on a map (in this article referred to as "the map"), being of a scale of 1:2500, and signed by a Collector of Customs and Excise, shall be a free zone.

[(2) The map shall be kept by the Commissioners and a copy of the map shall be kept at the offices of the responsible authority.][1]

(3) The map or the copy thereof may, on application, be inspected by members of the public at reasonable hours without charge.

Amendments—[1] Paragraph (2) substituted by the Free Zone Designations (Amendments) Order, SI 2006/1834 art 2 with effect from 1 August 2006.

Appointment of responsible authority

3 The responsible authority for the free zone shall be Southampton Free Trade Zone Limited whose Registered Office is 150 Holborn, London EC1N 2LR.

Period of validity of Order

4 This Order shall have effect for a period of 10 years from the date of coming into force.

Conditions imposed on responsible authority

5 The responsible authority shall—

(*a*) maintain an office in the free zone or at such other place as the Commissioners may allow at which shall be kept any records, for which the responsible authority is responsible, relating to the free zone and the business carried on therein;
(*b*) keep separate accounts in connection with the free zone;
(*c*) provide such information in connection with the free zone and the operation thereof to any person authorised by the Treasury, as that person may reasonably require;
(*d*) provide, free of expense to the Crown, such accommodation and facilities including furniture, fittings and equipment as the Commissioners may reasonably require and such accommodation and facilities shall be properly maintained, heated, lighted, ventilated and kept clean by the responsible authority;
(*e*) provide, free of expense to the Crown, such area of land within the free zone as the Commissioners may reasonably require for the examination of goods and vehicles and shall provide and maintain such appliances and afford such other facilities which are reasonably necessary to enable an account to be taken of any goods or make any examination or search;
(*f*) not permit a person to establish or carry on any trade or business in the free zone unless that person is authorised by the Commissioners to carry on such a trade or business in the free zone.

Health and safety

6 Without prejudice to the responsibilities of persons occupying premises within the free zone, the responsible authority shall ensure that the working conditions within the free zone are safe and without risk to the health and safety of persons employed by the Commissioners and shall comply with any requirements concerning health and safety imposed by any competent authority.

2001/2881
Free Zone (Liverpool) Designation Order 2001

Made by the Treasury under the Customs and Excise Management Act 1979 s 100A

Made . . . . *9 August 2001*
Coming into force . . . . *10 August 2001*

Citation and commencement

1 This Order may be cited as The Free Zone (Liverpool) Designation Order 2001 and shall come into force on 10th August 2001.

Designation of area as free zone

2— (1) An area of 383.28 hectares, in the County of Merseyside, comprising 269.56 hectares in the Metropolitan Borough of Sefton, 77.87 hectares in the Metropolitan Borough of Wirral and 35.85 hectares within the City of Liverpool, shown enclosed by a red line on a map (in this article referred to as "the map"), being of a scale of 1:2500, and signed by a Collector of Customs and Excise, shall be a free zone.

[(2) The map shall be kept by the Commissioners and a copy of the map shall be kept at the offices of the responsible authority.][1]

(3) The map or the copy thereof may, on application, be inspected by members of the public at reasonable hours without charge.

Amendments—[1] Paragraph (2) substituted by the Free Zone Designations (Amendments) Order, SI 2006/1834 art 2 with effect from 1 August 2006.

Appointment of responsible authority

[**3** The responsible authority for the free zone shall be the Mersey Docks and Harbour Company, whose Head Office is at Maritime Centre, Port of Liverpool, Liverpool, L21 1LA.][1]

Amendments—[1] Article substituted by the Free Zone Designations (Amendments) Order, SI 2006/1834 art 3 with effect from 1 August 2006.

Period of validity of Order

4 This Order shall have effect for a period of 10 years from the date of coming into force.

Conditions imposed on responsible authority

5 The responsible authority shall—

(*a*) maintain an office in the free zone or at such other place as the Commissioners may allow at which shall be kept any records, for which the responsible authority is responsible, relating to the free zone and the business carried on therein;
(*b*) keep separate accounts in connection with the free zone;
(*c*) provide such information in connection with the free zone and the operation thereof to any person authorised by the Treasury, as that person may reasonably require;

(*d*) provide, free of expense to the Crown, such accommodation and facilities including furniture, fittings and equipment as the Commissioners may reasonably require and such accommodation and facilities shall be properly maintained, heated, lighted, ventilated and kept clean by the responsible authority;
(*e*) provide, free of expense to the Crown, such area of land within the free zone as the Commissioners may reasonably require for the examination of goods and vehicles and shall provide and maintain such appliances and afford such other facilities which are reasonably necessary to enable an account to be taken of any goods or make any examination or search;
(*f*) not permit a person to establish or carry on any trade or business in the free zone unless that person is authorised by the Commissioners to carry on such a trade or business in the free zone.

Health and safety

6 Without prejudice to the responsibilities of persons occupying premises within the free zone, the responsible authority shall ensure that the working conditions within the free zone are safe and without risk to the health and safety of persons employed by the Commissioners and shall comply with any requirements concerning health and safety imposed by any competent authority.

2001/2882

Free Zone (Prestwick Airport) Designation Order 2001

Made by the Treasury under the Customs and Excise Management Act 1979 s 100A

Made . . . . 9 *August 2001*
Coming into force . . . . 10 *August 2001*

Citation and commencement

1 This Order may be cited as The Free Zone (Prestwick Airport) Designation Order 2001 and shall come into force on 10th August 2001.

Designation of area as free zone

2— (1) An area of 7.0359 acres (2.8475 hectares), in the parish of Ayr in the County of Ayr, shown enclosed by a red line on a map (in this article referred to as "the map"), being of a scale of 1:500, and signed by the Head of Business Services, HM Customs and Excise, Scotland, shall be a free zone.

[(2) The map shall be kept by the Commissioners and a copy of the map shall be kept at the offices of the responsible authority.][1]

(3) The map or the copy thereof may, on application, be inspected by members of the public at reasonable hours without charge.

Amendments—[1] Paragraph (2) substituted by the Free Zone Designations (Amendments) Order, SI 2006/1834 art 2 with effect from 1 August 2006.

Appointment of responsible authority

3 The responsible authority for the free zone shall be Freeport Scotland Ltd whose Registered Office is at County Buildings (Financial Services), Wellington Square, Ayr KA7 2PL.

Period of validity of Order

4 This Order shall have effect for a period of 10 years from the date of coming into force.

Conditions imposed on responsible authority

5 The responsible authority shall—
(*a*) maintain an office in the free zone or at such other place as the Commissioners may allow at which shall be kept any records, for which the responsible authority is responsible, relating to the free zone and the business carried on therein;
(*b*) keep separate accounts in connection with the free zone;
(*c*) provide such information in connection with the free zone and the operation thereof to any person authorised by the Treasury, as that person may reasonably require;
(*d*) provide, free of expense to the Crown, such accommodation and facilities including furniture, fittings and equipment as the Commissioners may reasonably require and such accommodation and facilities shall be properly maintained, heated, lighted, ventilated and kept clean by the responsible authority;
(*e*) provide, free of expense to the Crown, such area of land within the free zone as the Commissioners may reasonably require for the examination of goods and vehicles and shall provide and maintain such appliances and afford such other facilities which are reasonably necessary to enable an account to be taken of any goods or make any examination or search;
(*f*) not permit a person to establish or carry on any trade or business in the free zone unless that person is authorised by the Commissioners to carry on such a trade or business in the free zone.

Health and safety

6 Without prejudice to the responsibility of persons occupying premises within the free zone, the responsible authority shall ensure that the working conditions within the free zone are safe and without risk to the health and safety of persons employed by the Commissioners and shall comply with any requirements concerning health and safety imposed by any competent authority.

2001/3453
Value Added Tax (Refund of Tax) Order 2001

Made by the Treasury under the Value Added Tax Act 1994 s 33(3)

Made . . . . *22 October 2001*
Laid . . . . *23 October 2001*
Coming into force . . . . *1 December 2001*

1 This Order may be cited as the Value Added Tax (Refund of Tax) Order 2001 and shall come into force on 1st December 2001.

2 The Greater London Magistrates' Courts Authority (the body corporate established by section 30A of the Justice of the Peace Act 1997) is specified for the purposes of section 33 of the Value Added Tax Act 1994.

2002/1280
Value Added Tax (Special Provisions) (Amendment) Order 2002

Made by the Treasury under VATA 1994 ss 5(5), 43(2)

Made . . . . *8 May 2002*
Laid before the House of Commons . . . . *9 May 2002*
Coming into force . . . . *1 June 2002*

1— (1) This Order may be cited as the Value Added Tax (Special Provisions) (Amendment) Order 2002 and comes into force on 1st June 2002.

(2) This Order shall not have effect where a person produces printed matter (other than printed matter of a description specified in Group 3 of Schedule 8 to the Value Added Tax Act 1994) from goods—

(*a*) the supply of which to him is treated by virtue of section 6(4) of the Value Added Tax Act 1994 as taking place before 1st June 2002; and

(*b*) which he neither collects nor takes delivery of before that date.

2–4 (*Amend the Value Added Tax* (*Special Provisions*) *Order, SI 1995/1268*)

2002/1418
Free Zone (Port of Tilbury) Designation Order 2002

Made by the Treasury under CEMA 1979 s 100A

Made . . . . *24 May 2002*
Coming into force . . . . *2 June 2002*

Citation and commencement

1 This Order may be cited as The Free Zone (Port of Tilbury) Designation Order 2002 and shall come into force on 2nd June 2002.

Designation of area as free zone

2— (1) An area of 766.9 acres in the Borough of Thurrock in the County of Essex, shown enclosed by a red line on a map (being of a scale of 1:5000), marked "Map referred to in article 2 of the Free Zone (Port of Tilbury) Designation Order 2002" signed by a Deputy Collector of Customs and Excise and dated 19th May 2002, shall be a Free Zone.

[(2) The map shall be kept by the Commissioners and a copy of the map shall be kept at the offices of the responsible authority.][1]

(3) The map or the copy thereof may, on application, be inspected by members of the public at reasonable hours without charge.

Amendments—[1] Paragraph (2) substituted by the Free Zone Designations (Amendments) Order, SI 2006/1834 art 2 with effect from 1 August 2006.

Appointment of responsible authority

3 The responsible authority for the free zone shall be Port of Tilbury London Limited whose Registered Office is at Leslie Ford House, Tilbury Dock, Essex RM18 7EH.

Period of validity of Order

4 This Order shall have effect for a period of 10 years from the date of coming into force.

Conditions imposed on responsible authority

5 The responsible authority shall—

(*a*) maintain an office in the free zone or at such other place as the Commissioners may allow at which shall be kept any records, for which the responsible authority is responsible, relating to the free zone and the business carried on therein;

(*b*) keep separate accounts in connection with the free zone;

(*c*) provide such information in connection with the free zone and the operation thereof to any person authorised by the Treasury, as that person may reasonably require;

(*d*) provide, free of expense to the Crown, such accommodation and facilities including furniture, fittings and equipment as the Commissioners may reasonably require and such accommodation and facilities shall be properly maintained, heated, lighted, ventilated and kept clean by the responsible authority;

(*e*) provide, free of expense to the Crown, such area of land within the free zone as the Commissioners may reasonably require for the examination of goods and vehicles and shall provide and maintain such appliances and afford such other facilities which are reasonably necessary to enable an account to be taken of any goods or make any examination or search;

(*f*) not permit a person to establish or carry on any trade or business in the free zone unless that person is authorised by the Commissioners to carry on such a trade or business in the free zone.

Health and safety

6 Without prejudice to the responsibilities of persons occupying premises within the free zone, the responsible authority shall ensure that the working conditions within the free zone are safe and without risk to the health and safety of persons employed by the Commissioners and shall comply with any requirements concerning health and safety imposed by any competent authority.

2002/1502
Value Added Tax (Cars) (Amendment) Order 2002

Made by the Treasury under VATA 1994 s 50A(1), (5), (8)

Made . . . . 10 June 2002
Laid before the House of Commons . . . . 10 June 2002
Coming into force . . . . 1 July 2002

1— (1) This Order may be cited as the Value Added Tax (Cars) (Amendment) Order 2002 and comes into force on 1st July 2002.

(2) This Order shall not have effect where the taxable person took possession of the motor car pursuant to—

(*a*) an assignment which is an article 5 transaction solely by virtue of article 5(4) of the Value Added Tax (Special Provisions) Order 1995 or a corresponding provision made under the Manx Act; or

(*b*) a transaction forming part of a succession of two or more article 5 transactions, at least one of which was such an assignment,

if the assignment or, where there is a succession of transactions comprising two or more assignments, any of the assignments takes effect before 1st July 2002.

(3) In this article—

"article 5 transaction" means a transaction which is treated as being neither a supply of goods nor a supply of services by virtue of a provision of article 5 of the Value Added Tax (Special Provisions) Order 1995 or a corresponding provision made under the Manx Act;

"the Manx Act" means the Value Added Tax Act 1996.

2 (*amends the Value Added Tax (Cars) Order, SI 1992/3122 art 8*)

2002/1503
Value Added Tax (Special Provisions) (Amendment) (No 2) Order 2002

Made by the Treasury under VATA 1994 s 50A(1), (5), (8)

Made . . . . 10 June 2002
Laid before the House of Commons . . . . 10 June 2002
Coming into force . . . . 1 July 2002

1— (1) This Order may be cited as the Value Added Tax (Special Provisions) (Amendment) (No 2) Order 2002 and comes into force on 1st July 2002.

(2) This Order shall not have effect where the taxable person took possession of the goods pursuant to—

(*a*) an assignment which is an article 5 transaction solely by virtue of article 5(4) of the Value Added Tax (Special Provisions) Order 1995 or a corresponding provision made under the Manx Act; or (*b*) a transaction forming part of a succession of two or more article 5 transactions, at least one of which was such an assignment,

if the assignment or, where there is a succession of transactions comprising two or more assignments, any of the assignments takes effect before 1st July 2002.

(3) In this article—

"article 5 transaction" means a transaction which is treated as being neither a supply of goods nor a supply of services by virtue of a provision of article 5 of the Value Added Tax (Special Provisions) Order 1995 or a corresponding provision made under the Manx Act;

"the Manx Act" means the Value Added Tax Act 1996.

2 (*amends the Value Added Tax (Special Provisions) Order, SI 1995/1268 art 12*)

2002/1935
Value Added Tax (Acquisitions) Relief Order 2002

Made by the Treasury under VATA 1994 s 36A

Made . . . . 25 July 2002
Laid before the House of Commons . . . . 25 July 2002
Coming into force . . . . 15 August 2002

1 This Order may be cited as the Value Added Tax (Acquisitions) Relief Order 2002 and comes into force on 15th August 2002.

2 Subject to article 3 below, no VAT shall be payable on any acquisition from another member State of any goods where, if they were imported from a place outside the member States, relief from payment of VAT would be given by the Value Added Tax (Imported Goods) Relief Order 1984 (as amended from time to time).

3 The relief given by this Order in respect of the acquisition of any goods shall be subject to the same conditions as those to which, by virtue of the Value Added Tax (Imported Goods) Relief Order 1984 (as amended from time to time), relief under that Order would be subject in the case of an importation of those goods.

2003/3113
Customs (Contravention of a Relevant Rule) Regulations 2003

Made by the Treasury under FA 2003 s 26(1), (2), (3), (4), (41)

Made . . . . 2 December 2003
Laid before the House of Commons . . . . 2 December 2003
Coming into force . . . . 23 December 2003

Citation and Commencement

1 These Regulations may be cited as the Customs (Contravention of a Relevant Rule) Regulations 2003 and shall come into force on 23rd December 2003.

Interpretation

2 In these Regulations—

"the Act" means the Customs and Excise Management Act 1979;

"the Accounts and Records Regulations" means the Customs Traders (Accounts and Records) Regulations 1995;

"the Aircraft Report Regulations" means the Aircraft (Customs and Excise) Regulations 1981;

"the 1994 Act" means the Finance Act 1994;

"the Code" means Council Regulation 2913/92/EEC;

"Customs" means the customs authority of the United Kingdom;

"Customs authority of the United Kingdom" has the meaning "the Commissioners" as defined in section 1 of the Act;

for the purpose of the Code and the Implementing Regulation customs authority of the United Kingdom is one of the "customs authorities" defined in Article 4(3) with responsibility for *inter alia* applying customs rules within the territory of the United Kingdom;

"contravene" has the meaning assigned to it by section 24(3) of the Finance Act 2003;

"customs approved treatment or use" has the meaning assigned to it by Article 4(15) of the Code;

"customs procedure" has the meaning assigned to it by Article 4(16) of the Code;

"customs procedure with economic impact" has the meaning assigned to it by Article 84(1)(b) of the Code;

"declaration" has the meaning assigned to it by Article 4(17) of the Code;

"the Implementing Regulation" means Commission Regulation 2454/93/EEC as it implements the Code;

"the Importation Regulations" means the Customs Controls on Importation of Goods Regulations 1991;

"officer" has the meaning assigned to it by section 1 of the Act;

"the Personal Reliefs Order" means the Customs and Excise Duties (Personal Reliefs for Goods Permanently Imported) Order 1992;
"the Postal Packets Regulations" means the Postal Packets (Customs and Excise) Regulations 1986;
"products remaining" has the meaning as defined in Article 104(2) of Council Regulation 918/83/EEC;
"proper officer" means in relation to the person by, with or to whom anything is to be done, the person appointed or authorised in that behalf by the Commissioners;
"relevant rule" has the meaning assigned to it by section 24(3) of the Finance Act 2003;
"relevant tax or duty" has the meaning assigned to it by section 24(2) of the Finance Act 2003;
"the Relief Regulation" means Council Regulation 918/83/EEC;
"the Ship's Report Regulations" means the Ship's Report, Importation and Exportation by Sea Regulations 1981;
"the Transit Regulations" means the Customs and Excise (Transit) Regulations 1993.

Relevant Rule and Amount of Penalty

3— (1) The Schedule to these regulations shall have effect.

(2) An entry in Column 1 of the Schedule specifies the relevant rule or the description of a relevant rule in the case of any relevant tax or duty to which it applies for the purposes of section 26(1) of the Finance Act 2003 (Penalty for contravention of relevant rule).

(3) An entry in Column 2 of the Schedule adjacent to an entry in Column 1 specifies a person, of the description there laid out, who shall be liable to a penalty under section 26 of the Finance Act 2003 (where his conduct contravenes the relevant rule or a relevant rule of the description specified for the purposes of that section).

(4) An entry in Column 3 of the Schedule adjacent to an entry in Columns 1 and 2 specifies for the purposes of section 26(1) of the Finance Act 2003 the maximum amount of the penalty which may be imposed upon a person specified for the purposes of that section as liable for that contravention of that specified relevant rule.

(5) Any description of a relevant rule specified in Column 1 and any description of a person prescribed in Column 2 of the Schedule is without prejudice to the effect of any directly applicable Community provision so described or description of a person responsible contained in that provision so described.

(6) A specified relevant rule or description of a person shall be construed in accordance with the effect and scope of that directly applicable Community provision referred to in Column 1.

SCHEDULE

Regulation 3

Column 1 *Description of relevant Rule/Relevant Rule of a description*	*Column 2* *Person of a description*	*Column 3* *Penalty for contravention*
Report		
Section 35(1) of the Act		
To report in such form and manner containing such particulars as Customs direct.	The master. Person authorised by the master. Commander of the aircraft.	£1,000 £1,000
Ship's Report Regulations: Regulation 3		
Completion of the forms directed by Customs under s 35(1) by the master, or a person authorised by him (as Customs permit).	The master Person authorised by the master.	£1,000 £1,000
Regulation 4		

Column 1 *Description of relevant Rule/Relevant Rule of a description*	*Column 2* *Person of a description*	*Column 3* *Penalty for contravention*
Delivery of a duly completed report: (a) to a boarding officer immediately on request; (b) to the place designated within three hours of the ship having reached its place of loading or unloading; or (c) on the expiration of twenty four hours following arrival within the limits of the port when a ship has not arrived at its place of loading or unloading.	The master. Person authorised by the master.	£1,000 £1,000
Regulation 5		
To retain on board as long as the ship remains within the limits of the port a copy of the form of report for inspection by an officer.	The master.	£1,000
Aircraft Report Regulations:		
Regulation 4(1)		
Delivery to the proper officer of: (a) a General Declaration; (b) particulars of the goods on the aircraft; and (c) a list in duplicate of the stores on board the aircraft.	Commander of the aircraft.	£1,000
Section 35(6) of the Act		
To answer all such question relating to:	The master.	£1,000
(a) the ship or aircraft;	Person authorised by the master.	£1,000
(b) the goods carried therein;		
(c) the crew; and	Commander of the aircraft.	£1,000
(d) the voyage or flight		
as put to him by the proper officer.		
Section 35(7) of the Act		
Where prior to report:	The master.	£1,000
(a) bulk is broken;	Person authorised by the master.	£1,000
(b) stowage of any goods is altered to facilitate unloading of any part thereof before making report;	Commander of the aircraft.	£1,000
(c) any part of the goods are staved, destroyed, thrown overboard; or		
(d) a container opened		
and no proper explanation is given to the satisfaction of Customs.		
Goods brought into the customs territory of the Community (United Kingdom)		

Column 1 *Description of relevant Rule/Relevant Rule of a description*	*Column 2* *Person of a description*	*Column 3* *Penalty for contravention*
Article 38 of the Code		
To convey the goods to the customs office designated or free zone by the route specified, without delay and in accordance with the instructions of Customs.	Person bringing the goods into the Community customs territory.	£1,000
	Any person who assumes responsibility for the carriage of the goods after they have been brought into the Community customs territory.	£1,000
Article 39 of the Code		
Pursuant to Article 39, to inform without delay the Customs of:	In respect of Article 39(1) the person bringing the goods into the Community customs territory; or	£1,000
(a) the inability to comply with Article 38(1) due to unforeseen circumstances or force majeure; and	Any person who assumes responsibility for the carriage of the goods after they have been brought into the customs territory.	£1,000
(b) the precise location of the goods where the unforeseen circumstances or force majeure does not result in the total loss of the goods.	In respect of Article 39(2), the person bringing the vessel or aircraft into the customs territory, or in respect of either provision any other person acting in his place.	£1,000
Presentation of Goods to Customs		
Article 40 of the Code		
To present goods entering the United Kingdom at a customs office or other place designated.	The person who brought the goods into the customs territory of the Community.	£1,000
	The person who assumes responsibility for carriage for the goods following entry into the customs territory.	£1,000
Regulation 3 of the Importation Regulations		
To notify Customs:		
(a) of the arrival of goods in the prescribed form or where approved, by computerised record capable of being printed out; and	The person who brought the goods into the customs territory.	£1,000

Column 1 *Description of relevant Rule/Relevant Rule of a description*	*Column 2* *Person of a description*	*Column 3* *Penalty for contravention*
(b) to make such notification within three hours of the arrival of the ship at the wharf or aircraft at the airport, or if the customs office is closed within one hour following the reopening of the office.	The person who assumes responsibility for carriage of the goods following entry.	£1,000
Article 42 of the Code		
To seek permission of the Customs before examination or sampling of goods in order that they may be assigned a customs approved treatment or use.	The person authorised to assign the goods a customs approved treatment or use.	£1,000
	Any person able to present the goods or to have them presented. A person subject to a specific obligation in relation to goods being assigned to a customs approved treatment or use.	£1,000
	Any person doing so on his behalf.	£1,000
Articles 43 and 44 of the Code and Article 183 of the Implementing Regulation and Regulation 4 of the Importation Regulations		
Upon presentation of the goods or within the period specified a signed summary declaration shall be lodged in the form prescribed. The form shall correspond to the model prescribed by the Customs.	The person who brought the goods into the customs territory.	£1,000
	Any person who assumes responsibility for carriage of the goods following entry into the customs territory.	£1,000
	The person in whose name those above acted.	£1,000
Article 46 of the Code		
Goods shall:		
(a) except in the event of imminent danger, only be unloaded or transhipped from the means of transport with the permission of Customs and in places designated or approved or;	The person who brought the goods into the customs territory.	£1,000
	The person who assumes responsibility for the carriage of the goods following entry into the Customs territory.	£1,000

Column 1 Description of relevant Rule/Relevant Rule of a description	*Column 2 Person of a description*	*Column 3 Penalty for contravention*
(b) be unloaded and unpacked as required by Customs for the purposes of inspecting the goods and means of transport.	The person responsible for the contravention of the Importation Regulations.	£1,000
Where permission is not required, Customs shall be informed forthwith of the unloading or transhipment of the goods.		
Article 47 of the Code		
Goods shall not be removed from their original position without permission of Customs.	The person who brought the goods into the customs territory of the Community.	£1,000
	The person who assumes responsibility for the carriage of goods following entry into the customs territory.	£1,000
Articles 48 and 49 and 59 of the Code and Regulation 5 of the Importation Regulation		
Goods shall be assigned to a customs approved treatment or use within the period prescribed in Article 49.	The person who brought the goods into the customs territory of the Community.	
Entry to a customs approved treatment or use shall be effected by the delivery of an appropriate declaration presented to the proper officer pursuant to regulation 5.	The person who is able to present the goods to customs. The importer within the meaning of the Act	£1,000
	The importer within the meaning of the Act	£1,000
Article 51 of the Code		
Goods in temporary storage shall be stored only at places approved and under the conditions laid down by Customs.	The person bringing the goods into the customs territory of the Community	£1,000
The provision of security where required by Customs.	The person who removed the goods from customs supervision.	£1,000
	The person who participated in such removal.	£1,000
	The person required to fulfil the obligations arising from temporary storage.	£1,000

Column 1 *Description of relevant Rule/Relevant Rule of a description*	*Column 2* *Person of a description*	*Column 3* *Penalty for contravention*
Customs Declarations		
Article 59 of the Code		
Goods intended to be placed under a customs procedure shall be covered by a declaration.	Any person who is able to present the goods in question together with the documents required for the application of the rules governing the procedure.	£2,500
	A specific person (where acceptance of a declaration imposes particular obligations on that specific person).	£2,500
	An agent acting on his behalf.	£2,500
	By a direct agent in the case of a specific person.	£2,500
Articles 62 and 77 of the Code and Article 199 of the Implementing Regulation **Section 167(3) of the Act**		
Declarations shall be:		
(a) made on a form corresponding to the official specimen prescribed for the purpose; (b) signed and contain all the particulars necessary for implementation of the provisions of the customs procedure; and (c) accompanied by all the documents required for implementation of the provisions of the customs procedure.	Any person who is able to present the goods in question together with the documents required for the application of the rules governing the customs procedure. A specific person (where acceptance of a declaration imposes particular obligations on that specific person).	£2,500 £2,500
	By an agent on his behalf.	£2,500
	By a direct agent in the case of a specific person.	£2,500
Simplified Procedures		
Articles 6 and 7 of the Code and Articles 260 to 262 of the Implementing Regulation		
To comply with a condition of an immediately enforceable binding decision of Customs, in respect of an authorisation referred to in Article 260.	The person granted permission to operate simplified procedures.	£2,500

Column 1 *Description of relevant Rule/Relevant Rule of a description*	*Column 2* *Person of a description*	*Column 3* *Penalty for contravention*
	The declarant authorised in accordance with the conditions and in a manner laid down in Article 260 of the Implementing Regulation.	£2,500
Article 76 of the Code and Article 199 of the Implementing Regulation		
Simplified declaration, commercial or administrative document, or entry in the records shall contain particulars necessary for the identification of the goods.	The person granted permission to operate simplified procedures.	£2,500
Where the goods are entered for the procedure in question by means of an entry in the records, the date of such entry must be included.	The declarant authorised in accordance with the conditions and in the manner laid down in Article 260 of the Implementing Regulation.	£2,500
Furnish a supplementary declaration.		
Articles 199 and 260 of the Implementing Regulation		
To make a simplified declaration containing at least the particulars necessary for identification of the goods.	The person granted permission to operate simplified procedures.	£2,500
Where authorised by a general request for release a reference to that authorisation shall be entered on the commercial or administrative document.	The declarant authorised in accordance with the conditions and in a manner laid down in Article 260 of the Implementing Regulation.	£2,500
A simplified declaration shall be accompanied by all documents, production of which may be required to secure the release of goods for free circulation.		
Article 261 of the Implementing Regulation		
That it is possible to guarantee an effective check on compliance with provisions governing release of goods for free circulation.	The person granted permission to operate simplified procedures.	£2,500
	The declarant authorised in accordance with the conditions and in a manner laid down in Article 260 of the Implementing Regulation.	£2,500

Column 1 *Description of relevant Rule/Relevant Rule of a description*	*Column 2* *Person of a description*	*Column 3* *Penalty for contravention*
Local Clearance Procedure		
Articles 6 and 7 of the Code and Articles 263 to 267 , of the Implementing Regulation		
To comply with a condition of an immediately enforceable binding decision of Customs, in respect of an authorisation referred to in Article 263.	The person granted permission to operate simplified procedures	£2,500
	The declarant authorised in accordance with the conditions and in a manner laid down in Article 260 of the Implementing Regulation.	£2,500
Customs Procedure with Economic Impact		
Articles 6, 7, 85 to 87 and 90 of the Code and Articles 505 to 508 of the Implementing Regulation	The person to whom the authorisation for use of any customs procedure with economic impact is issued.	£2,500
To comply with a condition (including special conditions governing the procedure in question) of an immediately enforceable binding decision of Customs, in respect of an authorisation or transferred obligations for use of any customs procedure with economic impact referred to in Articles 85 to 87a	Any person to whom the conditions or obligations of a customs procedure with economic impact are transferred.	£2,500
To notify Customs of all factors arising after the authorisation is granted and which may influence its continuation or content.	Any authorised person.	£2,500
Articles 105 of the Code and Article 528 of the Implementing Regulation		
In respect of customs warehousing, the designated person shall keep stock records of all the goods placed under the customs warehousing procedure in the form approved by Customs.	The designated person.	£1,000
End Use		
Articles 6, 7, 21, 82, 85 to 87 and 90 of the Code and Article 292 and 293 of the Implementing Regulation		
To comply with a condition of an immediately enforceable binding decision of Customs in respect of an authorisation or a transferred obligation under end-use referred to in Article 21 or 82.	The person to whom the authorisation for End Use is issued.	£2,500

Column 1 *Description of relevant Rule/Relevant Rule of a description*	*Column 2* *Person of a description*	*Column 3* *Penalty for contravention*
Free Zones		
Articles 6, 7, 167 and 172 of the Code and Articles 800 and 801 of the Implementing Regulation		
To comply with a condition of an immediately enforceable binding decision of Customs in respect of an approval for a free zone.	The person to whom the approval for a free zone has been granted.	£2,500
Article 105 of the Code and Articles 803 and 804 of the Implementing Regulation		
The person designated shall keep stock records of all the goods placed under the customs warehousing procedure in the form approved by Customs.	The designated person.	£1,000
Transit		
Article 96 of the Code and The Schedule to the Transit Regulations		
Obligation to:		
(a) produce the goods intact at the customs office of destination within the time limit prescribed;	The principal to the transit operation.	£2,500
(b) duly observe the measures adopted by Customs to ensure identification of the goods;		
(c) duly observe the provisions relating to the Community/common transit procedures and comply with any relevant Community provision.	A carrier or recipient of goods who accepts the goods knowing they are moving under Community transit.	£2,500
Article 94(1) of the Code		
To furnish a guarantee.	The principal or authorisation holder.	£2,500
Articles 6 and 7 of the Code and Articles 372 to 376 of the Implementing Regulation		
To comply with a condition of authorisation (including the conditions for use of simplifications and operating and control methods) of an immediately enforceable binding decision of Customs to authorise simplifications of Community transit.	The principal. The consignee.	£2,500 £2,500
Information and Records		
Article 14 of the Code and section 23 of the 1994 Act		

Column 1 *Description of relevant Rule/Relevant Rule of a description*	*Column 2* *Person of a description*	*Column 3* *Penalty for contravention*
Any obligation to provide, furnish, or produce information or documents to Customs (whether subject to time limit or reasonable demand) in such form as may reasonably be required for examination, copying or making extracts or removal for such purposes and whether for a reasonable or specified period.	The person directly or indirectly involved in the customs operation concerned for the purposes of trade in goods.	£1,000
	Any person carrying on a trade or business within the meaning of section 20 of the 1994 Act.	£1,000
Article 16 of the Code and Regulations 3 to 5 and 9 of the Accounts and Records Regulations		
Any obligation for purposes of control by Customs to: (a) keep a record received or issued;	The person directly or indirectly involved in the customs operation concerned for the purposes of trade in goods.	£1,000
(b) preserve a received record and keep and preserve a copy of an issued record;		
(c) preserve a prepared or maintained record which has not been received or issued; (d) keep and preserve a copy of every supplementary declaration made (or made on behalf of the person concerned) or a record of all the information set out in that declaration; (e) keep and preserve a copy of every simplified declaration made (or made on behalf of the person concerned) or a record of all the information set out in that declaration; (f) keep and preserve such other records as Customs may specify in any case or cases in a notice published by them; (g) ensure that any record, kept or preserved which relates to a customs declaration, is so kept or preserved that it is readily apparent that it relates to that declaration; (h) preserve any record or copy of a record for a period of four years (or such lesser period as Customs may require).	A customs trader (any person carrying on a trade or business which consists of or includes any of the activities mentioned in section 20(1) of the 1994 Act).	£1,000
Assistance in Examination of goods		
Articles 241 and 243 of the Implementing Regulation		
To render Customs:	The declarant.	£1,000

Column 1 *Description of relevant Rule/Relevant Rule of a description*	*Column 2* *Person of a description*	*Column 3* *Penalty for contravention*
(a) satisfactory assistance to facilitate examination or sampling of goods; and	The person designated by the declarant to be present at the examination of the goods.	£1,000
(b) where necessary, by a deadline set by that authority.		
Postal Packets		
Articles 49 and 59 of the Code and Article 237(4) of the Implementing Regulation and Regulation 5a and 14 of the Postal Packets Regulations and Regulation 5 of the Importation Regulations		
Where notified by Customs of a requirement to make a declaration, it shall be made in the form determined by them and shall be presented to the proper officer within 28 days.	The addressee of the packet.	£1,000
	Any other person who is, or for the time being, is the importer of the goods within the meaning of the Act.	£1,000
Regulation 9 of the Postal Packets Regulations		
Requirement to have affixed to the bag label a green label in the prescribed form.	The postal operator.	£1,000
	The universal service provider within the meaning of the Postal Services Act 2000.	£1,000
Regulation 11 of the Postal Packets Regulations		
Requirement to perform, in relation to any postal packet or the goods it contains, such duties required by virtue of the customs and excise Acts to be performed by the importer, as Customs may require.	The proper officer of the postal operator.	£1,000
Regulation 12 of the Postal Packets Regulations		
Requirement to:		
(a) produce to the proper officer postal packets arriving in the United Kingdom,	The proper officer of the postal operator.	£1,000
(b) pen for customs examination any packets so produced.		
Regulation 17 of the Postal Packets Regulations		

Column 1 *Description of relevant Rule/Relevant Rule of a description*	*Column 2* *Person of a description*	*Column 3* *Penalty for contravention*
Requirement to deliver to the proper officer any postal packet upon the ground that any goods contained in it are liable to forfeiture.	The proper officer of the postal operator.	£1,000
Preference		
Section 80 of the Act		
(a) To furnish information in such form and within such time as may be specified; (b) To produce for inspection, copying or the taking of extracts, invoices, bills of lading, books or documents specified; as Customs or an officer may require for the purpose of verifying or investigating any certificate or other evidence under any Community requirement;	Any person appearing to the Customs or an officer to have been concerned in any way with the goods, or with any goods from which directly or indirectly they have been produced or manufactured, or to have been concerned with the obtaining or furnishing of the certificate or evidence.	£1,000
	The exporter	£1,000
(i) as to the origin of goods; or (ii) as to payments made or relief from duty allowed in any country or territory.		
Article 199 of the Implementing Regulation **Section 167(3) of the Act** **Community international agreements according to preferential rates of duty**		
Accurate completion of an EUR 1 or equivalent certifying Community origin for goods under any obligation of a particular international agreement entered into by the Community applying as part of the law of the United Kingdom in relation to a relevant tax or duty by virtue of directly applicable Community legislation.	The exporter.	£2,500
Community System of Duty Reliefs		
Articles 7(1), 7(2) and Articles 15(1), 15(2) and Articles 37 and 38 of the Relief Regulation		
To pre-notify the competent authorities and/or pay any unpaid duty where any of the following goods are lent, given as security, hired out, or transferred (whether for consideration or free of charge) within 12 months of acceptance of entry for free circulation, or in respect of Article 37, 36 months where that period is so extended:	In respect of Article 7, the person accorded relief from duties on the importation of the goods on the transfer of their normal place of residence.	£1,000

Column 1 *Description of relevant Rule/Relevant Rule of a description*	*Column 2* *Person of a description*	*Column 3* *Penalty for contravention*
(a) personal property imported upon transfer of normal residence; (b) goods imported on the occasion of a marriage;	In respect of Article 15, the person accorded relief from duties on the importation of the goods on the occasion of a marriage.	£1,000
(c) capital goods and other equipment including that belonging to persons engaged in a liberal profession and to legal persons engaged in a non-profit making activity.	In respect of Articles 37 and 38, the person accorded relief from duties on the importation of capital goods and other equipment.	£1,000
As applied in relation to import VAT under the Personal Reliefs Order: (a) Parts I to IV in relation to Article 7 of the Relief Regulation; (b) Parts I to III and V in relation to Article 15 of the Relief Regulation		
Article 24(1) of the Relief Regulation		
Except where the relief continues to apply in respect of a new secondary residence and in accordance with Article 22(b) and (c), where within a two year period from the date of acceptance of the entry for free circulation of the household effects or within 10 years after of such entry, where the period is so extended in respect of valuable household effects, a secondary residence is hired or transferred to a third person, the import duties on those household effects shall be paid at the rate applicable at the time of the relevant hire or transfer.	The person accorded relief from duties on the importation of household effects to furnish a secondary residence.	£1,000
Article 24(2) of the Relief Regulation		
To pay any relevant duty where the household effects are lent, given as security, hired out, or transferred (whether for consideration or free of charge) within 2 years of acceptance of entry for free circulation or within 10 years after such entry, where the period is so extended in respect of valuable household effects and under the same conditions referred to in Article 24(1).	The person accorded relief from duties on the importation of household effects to furnish a secondary residence.	£1,000
Article 57 **Article 63b** **Article 68** **Articles 76 and 77 of the Relief Regulation**		
To pre-notify the competent authorities where any:	The person accorded relief under Articles 51 and 52(2).	£1,000

Column 1 *Description of relevant Rule/Relevant Rule of a description*	*Column 2* *Person of a description*	*Column 3* *Penalty for contravention*
(a) educational, scientific and cultural materials, scientific instruments and apparatus identified in Articles 51, 53, 54, 56 (for the purposes of Article 57); or		
(b) instruments or apparatus intended for medical research, establishing medical diagnosis or carrying out medical treatment referred to in Article 63a (for the purposes of Article 63b)); or	The recipient bodies accorded relief under Articles 63a(1)	£1,000
(c) goods for charitable or philanthropic organisations (for the purposes of Article 68); or	The organisation benefiting from the relief under Article 68.	£1,000
(d) articles specially designed for the educational, scientific or cultural advancement of blind or education, employment or social advancement of handicapped persons (other than blind persons) (for the purposes of Articles 76 and 77) are lent, hired out, or transferred (whether for consideration or free of charge).	The person, institute or organisation benefiting from the relief under Articles 71 and 72.	£1,000
To pre-pay import duties due, except where the goods are lent, hired out or transferred (whether for consideration or free of charge) to an establishment or organisation which is entitled to benefit from the relief pursuant to:		
(a) Articles 51 or 52(2) (for the purposes of Articles 57 and 63(b));or	The person accorded relief under Articles 51 and 52(2) who lends, hires out or transfers the goods.	£1,000
(b) Articles 65 and 67 (for the purposes of Article 68); or	The organisation benefiting from the relief under Article 68.	£1,000
(c) Article 76(2) (for the purposes of Article 76); or	The person, institute or organisation benefiting from the relief under Articles 71 and 72.	£1,000
(d) Article 77(2) (for the purposes of Article 77)	The person, institute or organisation benefiting from the relief under Articles 71 and 72.	£1,000
and uses the article, instrument or apparatus for purposes which confer such relief.		
Article 59 of the Relief Regulation		
To pre-notify the competent authorities where:		

Column 1 *Description of relevant Rule/Relevant Rule of a description*	*Column 2* *Person of a description*	*Column 3* *Penalty for contravention*
(a) any of the equipment referred to in Article 59a is lent, hired out, or transferred (whether for consideration or free of charge);	The scientific research establishment or organisation benefiting from the relief under Article 59a.	£1,000
(b) an establishment or organisation referred to in Article 59a(1) which no longer fulfils the conditions to qualify for relief or proposes to use the equipment other than for the purposes provided for under that Article.	The scientific research establishment or organisation benefiting from the relief under Article 59a.	£1,000
Without prejudice to the application of Articles 52 and 53:		
(a) in respect of Article 59b(2), to pre-pay import duties due, except where the goods are lent, hired out, or transferred (whether for consideration or free of charge) to an establishment or organisation which is entitled to benefit from the relief pursuant to Article 59a and uses the article, instrument or apparatus for purposes which confer such relief;	The scientific research establishment or organisation benefiting from the relief under Article 59a.	£1,000
(b) in respect of Article 59b(4), for establishments or organisations which cease to fulfil the conditions, to pay import duties due;	The scientific research establishment or organisation benefiting from the relief under Article 59a.	£1,000
(c) in respect of Article 59b(4), equipment used by establishments or organisations benefiting from the relief for purposes other than those provided for under Article 59a, to pay import duties due.	The scientific research establishment or organisation benefiting from the relief under Article 59a.	£1,000
Article 78 of the Relief Regulation		
To inform the competent authorities where the organisation ceases to fulfil the conditions giving entitlement to duty free admission or proposes to use articles admitted duty free for purposes other than those provided for by Articles 71 and 72.	The institute or organisation benefiting from the relief under Articles 71 and 72.	£1,000
In respect of articles:		
(a) remaining in the possession of the institutions or organisations which cease to fulfil the conditions giving entitlement to relief; or	The institute or organisation benefiting from the relief under Articles 71 and 72.	£1,000
(b) used by the institutions or organisations for purposes other than those provided for in Articles 71 and 72,	The institute or organisation benefiting from the relief under Articles 71 and 72.	£1,000
to pay any relevant import duties due.		
Article 83 of the Relief Regulation		

Column 1 *Description of relevant Rule/Relevant Rule of a description*	*Column 2* *Person of a description*	*Column 3* *Penalty for contravention*
To pre-notify the competent authority and pre-pay import duty due where:		
(a) any of the goods referred to in Article 79(1) is lent, hired out or transferred (whether for consideration or free of charge);	The state organisation or other charitable or philanthropic organisation benefiting from the relief under Article 71(1).	£1,000
(b) an organisation referred to in Article 79(1) which no longer fulfils the conditions to qualify for relief or proposes to use the goods other than for the purposes provided for under that Article.		
Articles 100, 104 and 105 of the Relief Regulation		
1 Relieved "products remaining", with the agreement and under the supervision of the competent authority upon completion of examination, analysis or testing to be:	The person accorded relief under Article 100.	£1,000
(a) completely destroyed or rendered commercially valueless; or (b) surrendered to the state without causing it expense; or (c) in justified circumstances, exported outside the customs territory of the Community.		
2 Where Article 104(1) (as set out in 1(a), (b) and (c) above) is not applied, to pay the duty due on the "products remaining".	The person accorded relief under Article 100.	£1,000

2004/674
Recovery of Duties and Taxes etc Due in Other Member States (Corresponding UK Claims, Procedure and Supplementary) Regulations 2004

Made by the Treasury under FA 2002 Sch 39 para 3(1),(2),(3) and the Commissioners of Customs and Excise and the Commissioners of Inland Revenue, under FA 2002 Sch 39 paras 2(2) and 3(4)

Made . . . . *9 March 2004*
Laid before the House of Commons . . . . *10 March 2004*
Coming into force . . . . *1 April 2004*

ARRANGEMENT OF REGULATIONS

PART 1

GENERAL

PART 2

CORRESPONDING UK CLAIMS

PART 3
REQUESTS FOR ASSISTANCE

PART 4
INTEREST

PART 5
ENFORCEMENT OF CORRESPONDING CLAIMS

SCHEDULES:

PART 1
GENERAL

Citation and commencement

1 These Regulations may be cited as the Recovery of Duties and Taxes etc. Due in Other Member States (Corresponding UK Claims, Procedure and Supplementary) Regulations 2004 and shall come into force on 1st April 2004.

Interpretation

2 In these Regulations—

(*a*) "the Act" means the Finance Act 2002;

(*b*) "applicant authority" means an authority in a member State which makes a request for assistance under the Mutual Assistance Recovery Directive;

(*c*) "authorised official" means an official of an applicant authority authorised by that authority to make requests for assistance in accordance with the Mutual Assistance Recovery Directive;

(*d*) "the Board" means the Commissioners of Inland Revenue;

(*e*) "Commission" means the Commission of the European Communities;

(*f*) "Commissioners" mean the Commissioners of Customs and Excise;

(*g*) "consolidated claim" means several foreign claims recoverable from the same person;

(*h*) "contested" means an action contesting a foreign claim or the instrument permitting enforcement brought by an interested party before the competent body of the member State in which the applicant authority is situated in accordance with the laws in force there;

(*i*) "a corresponding UK claim" means a claim in the United Kingdom corresponding to the foreign claim;

(*j*) "costs" includes fees, charges, disbursements, expenses and remuneration;

[(*k*) "Council Directive 2006/112/EC" means that Directive as amended from time to time;

(*l*) "the Directive" means Commission Directive 2002/94/EC, as amended from time to time, being the Directive laying down detailed rules for implementing certain provisions of the Mutual Assistance Recovery Directive;][1]

(*m*) "electronic means" has the same meaning as in Article 2(1) of the Directive;

(*n*) "enforcement action" means action to enforce a foreign claim by way of legal proceedings, distress, diligence or otherwise as might be taken to enforce a corresponding UK claim;

(*o*) "export duties" has the same meaning as in Article 3 of the Mutual Assistance Recovery Directive;

(*p*) "instrument permitting enforcement" means—

(i) any instrument issued by an applicant authority in any member State in relation to a sum claimed by that authority within the jurisdiction of that State; or

(ii) a decision on that claim given in favour of that authority by a court or tribunal or other competent body in that State which permits recovery of that claim in that State or part thereof;

(*q*) "import duties" has the same meaning as in Article 3 of the Mutual Assistance Recovery Directive;

(*r*) "precautionary measures" means measures taken, or to be taken, in order to secure recovery of a foreign claim;

(*s*) "request for assistance" means a request for information, notification, recovery or precautionary measures within the meaning of the Mutual Assistance Recovery Directive.

Amendments—[1] Paras (*k*), (*l*) substituted by the Recovery of Duties and Taxes etc Due in Other Member States (Corresponding UK Claims, Procedure and Supplementary) (Amendment) Regulations, SI 2007/3508 regs 2, 3 with effect from 3 January 2008.

PART 2
CORRESPONDING UK CLAIMS

Corresponding UK claims—duties and taxes

3 For the purposes of Schedule 39 to the Act, column 2 of the table in Schedule 1 prescribes the corresponding UK claim in relation to each foreign claim described in column 1.

PART 3
REQUESTS FOR ASSISTANCE

Requests for information

4—(1) A request for information shall be made in writing in the form specified in Annex I to the Directive. If the request cannot be transmitted by electronic means it shall bear the official stamp of the applicant authority and be signed by an authorised official.

(2) A request for information shall relate to—

(*a*) a debtor;

(*b*) a person liable for settlement of the debt under the law in force in the member State in which the applicant authority is situated; or

(*c*) any third party holding assets belonging to one of the persons mentioned in sub-paragraph (*a*) or (*b*).

(3) The relevant UK authority shall acknowledge receipt of a request for information in writing not later than seven days from the date of such receipt and as appropriate request the applicant authority to provide any additional information necessary to execute the request.

(4) The relevant UK authority shall, not later than six months from the date of acknowledgement of the request, report to the applicant authority the outcome of the investigations which it has conducted in order to obtain the information requested.

(5) The relevant UK authority shall, within a reasonable period following the date upon which that information was obtained, transmit to the applicant authority the information obtained in accordance with the request.

(6) The relevant UK authority shall not be obliged to supply information where—

(*a*) the request was not made in accordance with this regulation;

(*b*) the relevant UK authority would not be able to obtain that information for the purpose of recovery of a corresponding UK claim;

(*c*) the supply of the requested information would disclose any commercial, industrial or professional secret; or

(*d*) disclosure of the information would prejudice the security of the United Kingdom or otherwise be contrary to the law or public policy of the United Kingdom.

(7) An applicant authority may in writing at any time withdraw a request made under this regulation.

Requests for notification of instruments

5—(1) A request for notification of an instrument shall –

(*a*) be made in writing in duplicate in the form specified in Annex II to the Directive;

(*b*) bear the official stamp of the applicant authority;
(*c*) be signed by an authorised official of that authority;
(*d*) be accompanied by two copies of the instrument to be notified.

(2) A request for notification shall relate to a person specified in regulation 4(2).

(3) The relevant UK authority shall—

(*a*) acknowledge receipt of a request for notification in writing not later than seven days after the date of such receipt;
(*b*) take the necessary measures to effect notification immediately upon receipt of the request for notification in accordance with the law applicable to notification of similar instruments in that part of the UK in which notification is given;
(*c*) confirm to the applicant authority, as soon as reasonably practicable, the date the instrument was notified to the person concerned by returning a copy of the request form with the certificate on the reverse completed;
(*d*) not question the validity of the instrument.

(4) The relevant UK authority may request additional information from the applicant authority for the purpose of effecting notification.

(5) For the purposes of this regulation "instrument" means any document or decision including those of a judicial nature which emanate from the member State in which the applicant authority is situated and which relate to a foreign claim.

Requests for recovery or precautionary measures

6— (1) A request for recovery or precautionary measures shall—

(*a*) be made in writing in the form specified in Annex III to the Directive including a declaration that the conditions of the Mutual Assistance Recovery Directive for initiating a request have been fulfilled;
(*b*) bear the official stamp of the applicant authority;
(*c*) be signed by an authorised official of that authority;
(*d*) relate to a person specified in regulation 4(2); and
(*e*) be accompanied by an instrument permitting enforcement.

(2) The amount of the foreign claim stated in the request shall be stated in UK sterling and the currency of the member State in which the applicant authority is situated using the exchange rate specified in regulation 15(2).

(3) The relevant UK authority shall—

(*a*) within seven days of receipt of a request for recovery or precautionary measures—

(i) acknowledge receipt of the request in writing to the applicant authority;
(ii) make a request in writing to the applicant authority to complete the request if it does not contain the full or complete information required by Article 7 of the Mutual Assistance Recovery Directive;

(*b*) where it does not take any enforcement action on a request within three months of receipt, not later than seven days from the end of that period inform the applicant authority in writing of the grounds for its failure to comply with the time limit;
(*c*) within a reasonable time having regard to the particular case, where all or part of the foreign claim cannot be recovered or precautionary measures cannot be taken, so inform the applicant authority, indicating the reasons therefor;
(*d*) no later than at the end of each six month period following the date of acknowledgement of receipt of the request, inform the applicant authority in writing of the status or outcome of any enforcement action;
(*e*) continue, save where prevented by paragraph 4 of Schedule 39 to the Act, any enforcement action or precautionary measures where a request to do so is made by the applicant authority not later than two months from the date of receipt of the notification of the outcome of that action and such request shall be subject to the provisions in these Regulations which applied to the initial request;
(*f*) inform the applicant authority immediately any enforcement action has been taken on a request.

(4) For the purpose of this regulation and regulations 8 to 17 and regulations 20 to 26 a single instrument permitting enforcement which covers more than one foreign claim against a person shall be deemed to constitute a single claim.

(5) A relevant UK authority shall consult the applicant authority where in recovering a foreign claim it intends to allow the debtor time to pay by arrangement or to make payment by instalments (whether or not interest is charged or to be charged on those arrangements).

(6) Except where an enactment or rule of law applicable to a corresponding UK claim requires otherwise, a relevant UK authority shall not be obliged to recover a foreign claim where to do so would, because of the situation of the debtor, create serious economic or social difficulties in the United Kingdom.

Transfer of sums recovered

7— (1) Subject to paragraph (3) the relevant UK authority shall transfer in UK sterling to the applicant authority any sum recovered in respect of a foreign claim not later than one month from the date upon which recovery was effected.

(2) For the purposes of this regulation "sum" shall include any interest including interest charged in the UK.

(3) The relevant UK authority and the applicant authority may agree different arrangements for the transfer of an amount where that amount is less than 1500 Euro.

(4) For the purpose of satisfying a request for recovery any sum recovered shall be deemed to have been recovered in proportion to the foreign claim as expressed in UK sterling.

Contested recovery

8— (1) Any enactment permitting proceedings for the recovery of or precautionary measures in relation to a corresponding UK claim shall apply to a foreign claim which is contested.

(2) …[1].

Amendments—[1] Para (2) revoked by the Recovery of Agricultural Levies Due in Other Member States Regulations, SI 2004/800 regs 2, 3 with effect from 13 April 2004.

Notice of inability to take action or proceedings upon a request for recovery of a contested claim

9 Where, in accordance with paragraph 4 of Schedule 39 to the Act, the relevant UK authority is not permitted to take action for recovery or for a precautionary measure it shall, in writing, advise the competent authority of the reasons within one month of the receipt of the notification by the applicant authority that the foreign claim or instrument permitting enforcement is contested.

Notice of action contesting recovery

10 The relevant UK authority shall notify the applicant authority in writing of any notice of commencement of action in the UK by a person specified in regulation 4(2) for reimbursement of sums recovered or for compensation in relation to recovery of a contested claim.

Reimbursement of sums recovered and compensation

11 Where the result of contesting a foreign claim or instrument permitting enforcement is favourable to the debtor, the applicant authority shall be liable for the reimbursement of any sums recovered, together with any compensation due, in accordance with any law in force in the relevant part of the UK applicable to the corresponding UK claim.

Reimbursement arrangements

12 Where recovery of a foreign claim poses a specific problem, entails a very large amount in costs or relates to the fight against organised crime the relevant UK authority and the applicant authority may agree reimbursement arrangements specific to the case in question.

Notice of cancellation or payment of a claim

13 Where the relevant UK authority undertakes enforcement action or precautionary measures in relation to that foreign claim it shall, upon receipt of notice in writing from the applicant authority as to—

(*a*) payment in satisfaction of that claim; or

(*b*) cancellation or other reason for termination of that claim;

cease any enforcement action or precautionary measures in relation to that claim.

Adjustment of a foreign claim

14— (1) This regulation applies where the amount of a foreign claim is amended for any reason.

(2) Where the amendment leads to a reduction in the amount of the foreign claim—

(*a*) the relevant UK authority shall continue the action which it has undertaken with a view to recovery or to the taking of precautionary measures, but that action shall be limited to the amount still outstanding;

(*b*) if at the time the relevant UK authority is informed of the reduction in the amount of the foreign claim, an amount exceeding the amount still outstanding has already been recovered by it but the transfer procedure referred to in regulation 7 has not yet been initiated, the relevant UK authority shall repay the amount overpaid to the person entitled thereto.

(3) Where the amendment leads to an increase in the amount of the foreign claim—

(*a*) the additional request shall as far as possible be dealt with by the relevant UK authority at the same time as the original request;

(*b*) where, in view of the state of progress of the existing recovery procedure, consolidation of the additional request with the original request is not possible, the relevant UK authority shall be required to comply with the additional request only if it concerns an amount not less than the threshold amount referred to in regulation 15(1).

Minimum amount on requests for assistance

15— (1) A request for assistance shall not be entertained if the foreign claim (whether a single claim or a consolidated claim) is less than 1500 Euro or the sterling equivalent at the time of request.

(2) The rate of exchange to be used for the purposes of these regulations shall be the latest selling rate recorded on the most representative exchange market or markets of the member State in which the applicant authority is situated on the date when the request for assistance is signed.

Limitation on requests for assistance

16— (1) The relevant UK authority shall not be obliged to entertain a request for assistance if the foreign claim is more than five years old.

(2) The point for commencement and calculation of a period of five years shall be—

(*a*) where a foreign claim is not contested, the date the instrument permitting enforcement was established by the applicant authority in accordance with the law in force in the member State in which that authority is situated; or

(*b*) where a foreign claim is contested, the date upon which the applicant authority establishes that the claim or instrument permitting recovery is no longer contested.

Acceptance and transmission of communications

17— (1) The relevant UK authority shall, as far as possible, accept and transmit all information required to be communicated in writing for the purposes of the Mutual Assistance Recovery Directive by electronic means.

(2) Paragraph (1) does not apply to requests for assistance made in accordance with regulations 5 and 6 and the instrument accompanying those requests unless the relevant UK authority and the applicant authority agree to waive paper communication.

Communication of documents and information

18 Documents and information sent to the relevant UK authority pursuant to the Mutual Assistance Recovery Directive may only be communicated by that authority to—

(*a*) the person mentioned in the request for assistance;

(*b*) those persons and authorities responsible for the recovery of the claims, and solely for that purpose; or

(*c*) the judicial authorities dealing with matters concerning the recovery of claims.

Language requirements

19— (1) Save as otherwise agreed by the relevant UK authority, requests for assistance, the instrument permitting enforcement, and any other relevant document addressed to that authority shall be accompanied by a translation of that document in the English language.

(2) All information and particulars communicated to an applicant authority by the relevant UK authority in relation to a request for assistance shall be conveyed in the English language or such other language as is agreed by that authority with the applicant authority.

Limitation

20— (1) The period of limitation or prescription in relation to any issue arising on the recovery of any foreign claim shall be that applicable under the laws in force in the member State in which the applicant authority is situated.

(2) For the purposes of paragraph (1) any step or act taken by the relevant UK authority in recovery of a foreign claim in pursuance of a request for assistance shall be deemed to have been taken in the member State in which the applicant authority is situated where that step or act would, if it had been taken by that applicant authority, have had the effect of suspending or interrupting the period of limitation or prescription in accordance with the laws in force in that member State.

Notice of refusal of requests for assistance

21— (1) Where in accordance with the Mutual Assistance Recovery Directive and the Directive or these Regulations the relevant UK authority decides not to act upon a request for assistance it shall, as soon as practicable after making its decision to refuse a request and any event within three months of the date of acknowledgement of receipt of the request, notify the applicant authority in writing of the reasons for refusal.

(2) In the cases mentioned in regulations 6(6) and 16 a copy of the reasons for refusal shall also be communicated to the Commission within the period specified in paragraph (1).

PART 4
INTEREST

Adaptations

22 Schedule 2 to these Regulations shall have effect.

Interest enforced by the Board

23— (1) A foreign claim corresponding to a UK claim for income tax, capital gains tax or corporation tax carries interest in respect of the principal and any penalty claimed at the rate applicable to the corresponding UK claim under section 178 of the Finance Act 1989 from the date of recognition until payment.

(2) In this regulation "the date of recognition" means the earlier of—

(*a*) the day following the expiry of three months from the date of receipt by the Board of the request for recovery of the foreign claim; and

(*b*) the date the instrument permitting enforcement of the foreign claim is recognised by the Board as an instrument authorising enforcement of the claim in the United Kingdom.

(3) Paragraph (1) above applies even if the date of recognition is a non-business day within the meaning of section 92 of the Bills of Exchange Act 1882.

(4) Interest is payable under this regulation without any deduction of income tax.

(5) For the purposes of this regulation, where—

(*a*) any payment is made by cheque to—

(i) an officer of the Board, or

(ii) the Board, or

(iii) the applicant authority, and

(*b*) the cheque is paid on its first presentation to the banker on whom it is drawn;

the payment shall be treated as made on the day on which the cheque was received by the officer or the Board or the applicant authority.

(6) Interest payable under this regulation shall be recoverable as if it were interest charged under a provision of the Taxes Management Act 1970.

Interest enforced by the Commissioners

24— (1) A foreign claim corresponding to any UK claim—

(*a*) mentioned in column 2 of Part I of Schedule 1, or

(*b*) for insurance premium tax,

shall carry interest in respect of the principal and any penalty claimed at the rate applicable to the corresponding UK claim under section 197 of the Finance Act 1996 from the date of recognition until payment.

(2) In this regulation "the date of recognition" means the earlier of—

(*a*) the day following the expiry of three months from the date of receipt by the Commissioners of the request for recovery of the foreign claim; and

(*b*) the date the instrument permitting enforcement of the foreign claim is recognised by the Commissioners as an instrument authorising enforcement of the claim in the United Kingdom.

(3) Paragraph (1) above applies even if the date of recognition is a non-business day within the meaning of section 92 of the Bills of Exchange Act 1882

(4) Interest is payable under this regulation without any deduction of income tax.

(5) For the purposes of this regulation, where—

(*a*) any payment is made by cheque to—

(i) an officer of Customs and Excise, or

(ii) the Commissioners, or

(iii) the applicant authority, and

(*b*) the cheque is paid on its first presentation to the banker on whom it is drawn,

the payment shall be treated as made on the day on which the cheque was received by the officer or the Commissioners or the applicant authority.

(6) Interest payable under this regulation shall be notified in writing to the person subject to enforcement action in respect of the foreign claim and may be recovered from that person as a debt due to the Crown.

PART 5
ENFORCEMENT OF CORRESPONDING CLAIMS

Evidence

25— (1) An instrument permitting enforcement of a foreign claim recognised by the Board as an instrument authorising enforcement of the claim in the United Kingdom, together with a certificate of a collector that payment of the claim has not been made to him, or, to the best of his knowledge and belief, to any other collector, or to any person acting on his behalf or on behalf of another collector, or to the applicant authority, is sufficient evidence that the sum mentioned in the instrument is unpaid and is due to that authority.

(2) A certificate of a collector that interest is payable under regulation 23(1) and that payment of the interest has not been made to him, or, to the best of his knowledge and belief, to any other collector, or to any person acting on his behalf or on behalf of another collector, or to the applicant authority, is sufficient evidence that the sum mentioned in the instrument is unpaid and is due to that authority.

(3) For the purposes of this regulation, any document purporting to be such a certificate as is mentioned in paragraph (1) and (2) is deemed to be such a certificate unless the contrary is proved.

Enforcement in Scotland

26— (1) For the purposes of enforcement in Scotland, an original, official or certified copy of a decision on a foreign claim by a court, tribunal or other competent body in the member State in which the applicant authority is situated shall be of the same force and effect as an extract of a decree of the Court of Session for the payment of money bearing a warrant for execution.

(2) For the purposes of paragraph (1), a "decision on a foreign claim" means a decision on a foreign claim which permits recovery of that claim in the member State in which the applicant authority is situated or in part thereof.

SCHEDULE 1

CORRESPONDING CLAIMS

Regulation 3

PART 1

Column 1	*Column 2*
1. Foreign Claim	*2. Corresponding UK Claim*
Import duties and export duties charged, in any member State other than the United Kingdom	Import and export duties charged in the United Kingdom
Value added tax (howsoever described) charged in any member State other than the United Kingdom in accordance with the provisions of Council Directive [2006/112/EC][1]	Value added tax charged, in the United Kingdom in accordance with the Value Added Tax Act 1994
Excise duties (howsoever described) charged in any member State other than the United Kingdom upon, – manufactured tobacco, – alcohol and alcoholic beverages, – mineral oils	Excise duty charged, collected or enforced in the United Kingdom in accordance with the Tobacco Products Duty Act 1979, or the Alcoholic Liquor Duties Act 1979, or the Hydrocarbon Oil Duties Act 1979 upon the items described in column 1

Amendments—[1] In column 1, in entry relating to VAT, reference substituted by the Recovery of Duties and Taxes etc Due in Other Member States (Corresponding UK Claims, Procedure and Supplementary) (Amendment) Regulations, SI 2007/3508 regs 2, 4 with effect from 3 January 2008.

PART 2

(Part 2 is not reproduced. See *Tolley's Yellow Tax Handbook*.)

PART 3

Column 1	*Column 2*
1. Foreign claims	*2. Corresponding UK claim*
Refunds, interventions and other measures forming part of the system of total or partial financing of the European Agricultural Guidance and Guarantee Fund (EAGGF), including sums to be collected in connection with these actions charged, levied, collected or paid in any member State other than the United Kingdom.	Those items described in Column 1 charged, levied, collected or paid in the United Kingdom.

Column 1	*Column 2*
1. Foreign claims	*2. Corresponding UK claim*
Levies and other duties provided for under the common organisation of the market for the sugar sector charged in any member State other than the United Kingdom.	Those items described in Column 1 charged in the United Kingdom.
Interest, administrative penalties or fines incurred in any member State other than the United Kingdom relating to a foreign claim described in Column 1 of Parts 1 to 3 of this Schedule	Such interest, administrative penalties or fines as is chargeable in the United Kingdom relating to a corresponding UK claim described in Column 2 of Parts 1 to 3 of this Schedule

SCHEDULE 2
ADAPTATIONS

Regulation 22

Interpretation

1 In this Schedule—

"duties interest" means a foreign claim corresponding to a UK claim for interest on import or export duties …[1];

"IPT interest" means a foreign claim corresponding to a UK claim for interest on insurance premium tax;

"request" means a request for recovery made to the relevant UK authority in accordance with regulation 6 of these Regulations;

"VAT interest" means a foreign claim corresponding to a UK claim for interest on value added tax.

Amendments—[1] Words in definition of "duties interest" revoked by the Recovery of Agricultural Levies Due in Other Member States Regulations, SI 2004/800 regs 2, 4 with effect from 13 April 2004.

Recovery of import duties interest

2— (1) Subsections (2) to (4) and (6) to (8) of section 126 of the Finance Act 1999 shall not apply to duties interest.

(2) In its application to duties interest subsection (1) of section 126 shall apply as if the reference to determination and recovery of the amount of any interest charged in accordance with Article 232 of the Community Customs Code on arrears of customs duty payable to the Commissioners were a reference to the recovery by the Commissioners of an amount of duties interest for which a request has been made.

(3) For the purposes of its application to duties interest subsection (5) of section 126 shall apply as if;

(*a*) the reference to interest the amount of which falls to be determined in accordance with this section were a reference to duties interest to be recovered; and

(*b*) the reference to interest on an amount so determined were a reference to duties interest to be recovered.

Recovery of VAT interest

3— (1) Subsections (1) to (8) and (10) and the expression "unless, or except to the extent that, the assessment is withdrawn or reduced" in subsection (9) of section 76 of the Value Added Tax Act 1994 shall not apply to VAT interest.

(2) In its application to VAT interest subsection (9) of section 76 shall apply as if the reference to an amount being assessed and notified to a person under this section were a reference to an amount of VAT interest specified in a request concerning a person specified in regulation 4(2) of these Regulations in relation to whom a request is made.

Recovery of IPT interest

4— (1) Sub-paragraphs (1) to (7) and (9) and the expression "unless or except to the extent that, the assessment is withdrawn or reduced" in sub-paragraph (8) of paragraph 25 of Schedule 7 to the Finance Act 1994 shall not apply to IPT interest.

(2) In its application to IPT interest sub-paragraph (8) of paragraph 25 shall apply as if the reference to an amount being assessed and notified to any person under this paragraph were a reference to an amount of IPT interest specified in a request concerning a person specified in regulation 4(2) of these Regulations in relation to whom a request is made.

2004/1929
Value Added Tax (Disclosure of Avoidance Schemes) Regulations 2004

Made by the Treasury under VATA 1994 Sch 11A paras 6(2), (3), 9(1) and 13

Made . . . . 22 July 2004
Laid before the House of Commons . . . . 22 July 2004
Coming into force . . . . 1 August 2004

Citation, commencement and interpretation

1— (1) These Regulations may be cited as the Value Added Tax (Disclosure of Avoidance Schemes) Regulations 2004 and come into force on 1st August 2004.

(2) In these Regulations "Schedule 11A" means Schedule 11A to the Value Added Tax Act 1994.

Time of notification

2— (1) Where paragraph 6(1)(*a*) of Schedule 11A applies (VAT return affected by a notifiable scheme), the time prescribed for the purposes of paragraph 6(2) and (3) of that Schedule (duty to notify Commissioners) is the 30th day from the end of the last day specified by or under regulation 25 of the Value Added Tax Regulations 1995 for making the return.

(2) Where paragraph 6(1)(*b*) of Schedule 11A applies (claim for repayment of output tax or an increase in credit for input tax based on a scheme), the time prescribed for the purposes of paragraph 6(2) and (3) of that Schedule is the 30th day from the end of the date the claim is made.

[(3) Where paragraph 6(1)(*c*) of Schedule 11A applies (non-deductible tax less than it would be but for a scheme), the time prescribed for the purposes of paragraph 6(2) and (3) of that Schedule is the 30th day from the end of the last day specified by or under regulation 25 of the Value Added Tax Regulations 1995 for making a return in respect of the relevant prescribed accounting period.

(4) For the purposes of paragraph (3) relevant prescribed accounting period means the period in which the taxable person's non-deductible tax is less than it would be but for any notifiable scheme to which he is party.

(5) Paragraph (1) shall not have effect in relation to any scheme listed in Column 1 of the Schedule where the beginning of the prescribed accounting period for which the VAT return is made is earlier than the date shown opposite that scheme in Column 2 of the Schedule.

(6) Paragraph (2) shall not have effect in relation to any scheme listed in Column 1 of the Schedule where the beginning of the prescribed accounting period in relation to which the claim is made is earlier than the date shown opposite that scheme in Column 2 of the Schedule.][1]

Amendments—[1] Paras (3)–(6) substituted for former paras (3), (4) by the Value Added Tax (Disclosure of Avoidance Schemes) (Amendment) Regulations, SI 2005/2009 arts 2, 3 with effect from 1 August 2005.

Form and manner of notification

3 Notification of a scheme pursuant to paragraph 6(2) or 6(3) of Schedule 11A shall be made in such form and manner as may be specified in a notice published by the Commissioners and not withdrawn by a further notice.

Information to be notified

4— (1) For the purposes of paragraph 6(3) of Schedule 11A (duty to notify the Commissioners of a scheme other than a designated scheme) and paragraph 9(1) of that Schedule (voluntary notification of scheme) the following information is prescribed—

(*a*) any provision designated in accordance with paragraph 4 of Schedule 11A (designation of provisions included in or associated with avoidance schemes) which is included in or associated with the scheme;

(*b*) how the scheme gives rise to a tax advantage, including, insofar as material to the tax advantage—

(i) a description of each arrangement, transaction or series of transactions;
(ii) their sequence;
(iii) their timing, or the intervals between them; and
(iv) the goods or services involved;

(*c*) how the involvement of any party to the scheme contributes to the obtaining of the tax advantage; and

(*d*) any provision having the force of law in the United Kingdom or elsewhere relied upon as giving rise to the tax advantage.

(2) A tax advantage is considered to have been obtained or to be obtained and any arrangement, transaction or series of transactions is considered to have taken place or to take place provided a taxable person has treated or intends to treat it as having been obtained or taken place for the purposes of—

(*a*) a return required under the Value Added Tax Act 1994; …[1]
(*b*) a claim for repayment of output tax or an increase in credit for input tax[; or

(*c*) reducing the amount of his non-deductible tax.][1]

Amendments—[1] In para (2), word "or" at end of sub-para (*a*) revoked, and sub-para (*c*) and preceding word "or" inserted by the Value Added Tax (Disclosure of Avoidance Schemes) (Amendment) Regulations, SI 2005/2009 arts 2, 4 with effect from 1 August 2005.

SCHEDULE

Regulations 2(5) and 2(6)

Row	*Column 1*	*Column 2*
	Scheme	*Date*
(a)	Any scheme allocated a reference number from 1 to 8 by the Value Added Tax (Disclosure of Avoidance Schemes) (Designations) Order 2004.	1st August 2004
(b)	Any scheme that includes, or is associated with, a provision of a description falling within paragraphs 1 to 7 of Schedule 2 to the Value Added Tax (Disclosure of Avoidance Schemes) (Designations) Order 2004.	1st August 2004
(c)	Any scheme allocated the reference number 9 or 10 by the Value Added Tax (Disclosure of Avoidance Schemes) (Designations) Order 2004 and which does not fall within row (b) above.	1st August 2005
(d)	Any scheme that includes, or is associated with, a provision of a description falling within paragraph 8 of Schedule 2 to the Value Added Tax (Disclosure of Avoidance Schemes) (Designations) Order 2004 and which does not fall within rows (a) or (b) above.	1st August 2005][1]

Amendments—[1] Schedule inserted by the Value Added Tax (Disclosure of Avoidance Schemes) (Amendment) Regulations, SI 2005/2009 arts 2, 5 with effect from 1 August 2005.

2004/1931
Value Added Tax (Groups: eligibility) Order 2004

Made by the Treasury under VATA 1994 s 43AA(1)–(4)

Made . . . . *22 July 2004*
Laid before the House of Commons . . . . *22 July 2004*
Coming into force . . . . *1 August 2004*

Citation and commencement

1 This Order may be cited as the Value Added Tax (Groups: eligibility) Order 2004 and comes into force on 1st August 2004.

Modification regarding section 43A of the Value Added Tax Act 1994

2 A body corporate that is a specified body is eligible to be treated as a member of a group if, in addition to satisfying the conditions set out in section 43A(1) of the Value Added Tax Act 1994 ("the Act"), it satisfies both the benefits condition and the consolidated accounts condition.

Specified bodies

3—(1) A body corporate to which this article applies is a specified body for the purposes of this Order if it carries on a relevant business activity and—

(*a*) the value of the group's supplies in the year then ending has exceeded £10 million; or

(*b*) there are reasonable grounds for believing that the value of the group's supplies in the year then beginning will exceed that amount.

(2) For the purposes of determining the value mentioned in sub-paragraph (*b*) of paragraph (1), a body that is not a member of the group shall be deemed to be a member.

(3) Subject to paragraph (4), this article applies to a body corporate which, at any time when the relevant business activity is being carried on—

(*a*) is not a wholly-owned subsidiary of a person who controls all of the other members of the group (or, where the person is or will be a member of the group, all of the other members apart from himself);
(*b*) is managed, directly or indirectly, in respect of the business activity concerned, by a third party in the course or furtherance of a business carried on by him; or
(*c*) is the sole general partner of a limited partnership.

(4) This article does not apply to—

(*a*) a body corporate that controls all of the members of the group (or, where it is a member of the group, all of the members apart from itself);
(*b*) a body corporate whose activities another body corporate is empowered by statute to control;
(*c*) a body corporate whose only activity is acting as the trustee of a pension scheme; or
(*d*) a charity.

(5) In this article—

(*a*) a body corporate is a wholly-owned subsidiary of a person if it is a wholly-owned subsidiary of his within the meaning given by section [1159 of and Schedule 6 to][1] the Companies Act [2006][1], or would be if the person were a company;
(*b*) in determining whether a body corporate is a wholly-owned subsidiary of a person, the membership of any excepted individual who is not acting on behalf of another person shall be disregarded;
(*c*) "pension scheme" means an occupational pension scheme established under a trust and "occupational pension scheme" has the meaning given by section 1 of the Pension Schemes Act 1993.

Amendments—[1] In para (5)(*a*), words substituted for words "736 of" and "1985", by the Companies Act 2006 (Consequential Amendments) (Taxes and National Insurance) Order, SI 2009/1890 art 4(1)(*k*) with effect from 1 October 2009.

Relevant business activities

4— (1) A business activity is a relevant business activity if it involves making one or more supplies of goods or services to one or more members of the group and—

(*a*) those supplies are not incidental to that business activity;
(*b*) at least one of those supplies is or would be chargeable to VAT at a rate other than zero; and
(*c*) the representative member is not or would not be entitled to credit for the whole of the VAT on such supplies as fall within sub-paragraph (*b*) as input tax.

(2) In determining for the purposes of paragraph (1) whether—

(*a*) a body corporate makes any supplies to any members of the group;
(*b*) a supply would be chargeable to VAT at a rate other than zero;
(*c*) the representative member would not be entitled to credit for the whole of the VAT on the supply as input tax, a body corporate that is a member of the group shall be deemed not to be a member.

The benefits condition

5— (1) The benefits condition is satisfied unless more than 50% of the benefits of the relevant business activity accrue, directly or indirectly, to one or more third parties.

(2) For the purposes of paragraph (1), benefits that accrue to a person in his capacity as a member of a body corporate which controls all of the other members of the group (or, where the body is or will be a member of the group, all of the other members apart from itself) shall not be regarded as accruing to a third party.

(3) The following are benefits of a business activity for the purposes of paragraph (1)—

(*a*) profits (whether or not distributed);
(*b*) charges for managing the business activity (including charges for providing staff to manage it);
(*c*) the amounts, if any, by which any other charges made to the body exceed the open market value of the goods or services concerned.

(4) For the purposes of paragraph (1), if there are no such benefits, the business activity shall be deemed to generate profits of £100.

The consolidated accounts condition

6— (1) The consolidated accounts condition is satisfied if—

(*a*) consolidated accounts prepared for a person who controls all of the other members of the group (or, where the person is or will be a member of the group, all of the other members apart from himself) would be required by generally accepted accounting practice to include accounts for the specified body as his subsidiary; and
(*b*) consolidated accounts prepared for a third party would not be required by generally accepted accounting practice to include accounts for the specified body as his subsidiary.

(2) For the purpose of the application of paragraph (1) at a particular time—

(*a*) the reference to consolidated accounts is a reference to consolidated accounts—

(i) for a period including that time, and
(ii) insofar as they relate to that time,

(*b*) any principle of generally accepted accounting practice that permits accounts of a subsidiary undertaking to be excluded from a consolidation as being immaterial shall be disregarded;

(*c*) the reference to consolidated accounts prepared for a person is a reference to consolidated accounts of a kind that could be prepared for him in accordance with generally accepted accounting practice, for which purpose it does not matter—

(i) whether accounts are actually prepared for him (whether for a particular period or at all), or
(ii) in particular, whether he is required to prepare accounts.

(3) In this article "generally accepted accounting practice"—

(*a*) has the meaning given by section 50(1) of the Finance Act 2004;

(*b*) in relation to any time when that section does not have effect, has the meaning given by section 836A of the Income and Corporation Taxes Act 1988.

Interpretation etc

7— (1) In determining—

(*a*) the value of the supplies made by a body corporate that is the sole general partner of a limited partnership (a "general partner");

(*b*) whether a general partner is carrying on a relevant business activity;

(*c*) whether the benefits condition is satisfied in relation to a general partner;

(*d*) whether the consolidated accounts condition is satisfied in relation to a general partner, articles 3(1) and (2), 4(1), 5 and 6 shall apply as if references to the body or specified body, as the case requires, are references to the limited partnership.

(2) A person is a third party for the purposes of this Order if—

(*a*) he does not control the body corporate and all of the other members of the group;

(*b*) a person who controls the body corporate and all of the other members of the group does not control him; and

(*c*) he is not an excepted individual.

(3) An individual is an excepted individual if he is—

(*a*) an employee or director of the body; or

(*b*) where the body is a limited liability partnership, a member of the body.

(4) Any reference in this Order to "the group" is to the group of which the body corporate is a member or to which an application under section 43B(1) or (2)(*a*) of the Act relates, as the case may require.

(5) Any reference in this Order to a person controlling a body corporate includes a reference to his controlling the body together with one or more other individuals with whom he is carrying on a business in partnership.

2004/1933

Value Added Tax (Disclosure of Avoidance Schemes) (Designations) Order 2004

Made by the Treasury under VATA 1994 s 97(3)

Made	*22 July 2004*
Laid before the House of Commons	*22 July 2004*
Coming into force	*1 August 2004*

Citation and commencement

1 This Order may be cited as the Value Added Tax (Disclosure of Avoidance Schemes) (Designations) Order 2004 and comes into force on 1st August 2004.

Interpretation

2— (1) In this Order "the Act" means the Value Added Tax Act 1994.

(2) Any reference in this Order to "Schedule 8" or "Schedule 9" is a reference to that Schedule to the Act.

(3) For the purposes of this Order a person is connected with another where—

(*a*) one of them is an undertaking in relation to which the other is a group undertaking; or

(*b*) both of them are connected to the same trust.

(4) For the purposes of this Order a person is connected to a trust where—

(*a*) he is the settlor of the trust, a trustee or beneficiary of it; or

(*b*) he holds any shares in a company in accordance with the terms of the trust, or is a person on whose behalf such shares are held.

(5) For the purposes of this Order "undertaking" and "group undertaking" have the meaning given by [section 1161 of the Companies Act 2006][1].

(6) A scheme is treated as fitting a description contained in the first column of Schedule 1 to this Order even if any feature of that scheme is not actually present (whether as a matter of law or for any other reason), provided a taxable person has treated that feature as being present for the purpose of making—

(*a*) a return required under the Act; or

(*b*) a claim for the repayment of output tax or an increase in credit for input tax.

(7) A provision is treated as fitting a description contained in Schedule 2 to this Order even if it, or any feature of it, is not actually present (whether as a matter of law or for any other reason), provided a taxable person has treated that feature as being present for the purpose of making—

(*a*) a return required under the Act; or

(*b*) a claim for the repayment of output tax or an increase in credit for input tax.

Amendments—[1] Words in para (5) substituted by the Companies Act 2006 (Consequential Amendments) (Taxes and National Insurance) Order, SI 2008/954 arts 53 with effect from 6 April 2008.

Designation of avoidance schemes and provisions included in or associated with avoidance schemes

3— (1) The schemes described in the first column of Schedule 1 to this Order are designated schemes for the purposes of paragraph 3 of Schedule 11A to the Act and are allocated the reference numbers shown in the second column of Schedule 1.

(2) The provisions described in Schedule 2 to this Order are provisions designated for the purposes of paragraph 4 of Schedule 11A to the Act.

SCHEDULES

SCHEDULE 1

Article 3(1)

Description of Scheme	Reference Number
First grant of a major interest in a building Any scheme comprising or including the first grant of a major interest in any building of a description falling within item 1(*a*) of Group 5 of Schedule 8 (construction of buildings etc.) where— (*a*) the grant is made to a person connected with the grantor; and (*b*) the grantor, or any body corporate treated as a member of a VAT group under section 43 of the Act of which the grantor is a member, attributes to that grant input tax incurred by him— (i) in respect of a service charge relating to the building; or (ii) in connection with any extension, enlargement, repair, maintenance or refurbishment of the building, other than for remedying defects in the original construction.	1
Payment handling service Any scheme comprising or including a retail supply of goods or services together with a linked supply to the same customer, where the total consideration for the retail supply and the linked supply is no different, or not significantly different, from what it would be for the retail sale alone. NOTE "Linked supply" means a supply by the retailer or any other person that— (*a*) relates to the means of payment used for the retail supply; and (*b*) is a supply of a description falling within Group 5 of Schedule 9 (finance).	2
Value shifting Any scheme comprising or including a retail supply of goods or services together with a linked supply to the same customer where— (*a*) the linked supply is a separate supply under the terms of any agreement made by the customer; (*b*) part of the total consideration for the retail supply and the linked supply is attributed to the linked supply by the terms of any such agreement; and (*c*) the total consideration for the retail supply and the linked supply is no different, or not significantly different, from what it would be for the retail supply alone. NOTES (1) "Retail supply" means a supply by retail upon which VAT is charged at the rate in force under section 2(1) of the Act (rate of VAT)	3

Description of Scheme	**Reference Number**

(2) "Linked supply" means a supply of goods or services made by the retailer or any other person which is zero-rated or exempt.

Leaseback agreement **4**

Any scheme comprising or including the supply of goods, or the leasing or letting on hire of goods, ("the relevant supply") by a taxable person to a connected relevant person where—

(*a*) the taxable person or another taxable person connected with him, including the relevant person, is entitled to credit for all the input tax arising on the purchase of the goods;

(*b*) the relevant person uses the goods in the course or furtherance of a business carried on by him, and for the purpose of that business, otherwise than for the purpose of selling, or leasing or letting on hire, the goods; and

(*c*) the relevant person or a person connected with him has directly or indirectly provided funds for meeting more than 90% of the cost of the goods.

NOTES

(1) "Relevant person" means any person who, in respect of the relevant supply, is not entitled to credit for all the input tax wholly attributable to the supplies he makes.

(2) The provision of funds includes—

(*a*) the making of a loan of funds; and

(*b*) the provision of any consideration for the issue of any shares or other securities issued wholly or partly for raising the funds.

(3) The grant, assignment or surrender of a major interest in land is not a supply of goods for the purposes of this scheme.

Extended approval period **5**

Any scheme comprising or including a retail supply of goods where—

(*a*) the goods are sent or taken on approval or sale or return or similar terms;

(*b*) payment for the supply is required in full by the retailer before the expiry of any approval, return or similar period; and

(*c*) for the purposes of accounting for VAT, the retailer treats the goods as supplied on a date after the date on which payment is received in full.

Groups: third party suppliers **6**

Any scheme comprising or including supplies made to one or more group members by a specified body in relation to which the benefits condition is not satisfied.

NOTE

The Value Added Tax (Groups: eligibility) Order 2004 shall apply for the purposes of determining whether—

(*a*) a body corporate is a specified body; and

(*b*) the benefits condition is satisfied in relation to it.

Exempt education or vocational training by a non-profit making body **7**

Any scheme comprising or including the conduct of a relevant business by a non-profit making body where—

(*a*) it receives a relevant supply from a connected taxable person who is not an eligible body; and

(*b*) in any one prescribed accounting period the value of all such relevant supplies is equal to or more than 20% of the cost of making the supplies comprising the relevant business.

NOTES

(1) "Relevant business" means a business whose activities consist wholly or mainly of the supply of education or vocational training to persons who are not taxable persons.

(2) "Non-profit making body" means a body within Note (1)(*e*) of Group 6 of Schedule 9 (Education) which is not otherwise within Note 1.

(3) "Relevant supply" means the supply, including the leasing or letting on hire, for use in a relevant business of—

(*a*) a capital item used in the course or furtherance of the relevant business, and for the purpose of that business, otherwise than solely for the purpose of selling, or leasing or letting on hire, the item;

(*b*) staff;

(*c*) management services;

(*d*) administration services; or

(*e*) accountancy services.

Description of Scheme	Reference Number
(4) "Eligible body" has the meaning given by Note (1) of Group 6 of Schedule 9.	
(5) "Vocational training" has the meaning given by Note (3) of Group 6 of Schedule 9, but does not include vocational training of a description falling within item 5 or 5A of that Group.	
Taxable education or vocational training by a non-eligible body	8
Any scheme comprising or including the conduct of a relevant business by a non-eligible body connected to an eligible body where—	
(*a*) the non-eligible body benefits or intends to benefit the eligible body by way of gift, dividend or otherwise; or	
(*b*) the eligible body makes any supply to the non-eligible body which is a relevant supply and, in any one prescribed accounting period, the value of all such relevant supplies is equal to or more than 20% of the cost of making the supplies comprising the relevant business.	
NOTES	
(1) "Eligible body" has the meaning given by Note (1) of Group 6 of Schedule 9.	
(2) "Relevant business" means a business whose activities consist wholly or mainly of the taxable supply of education or vocational training.	
(3) "Vocational training" has the meaning given by Note (3) of Group 6 of Schedule 9.	
(4) "Relevant supply" means the supply, or leasing or letting on hire, for use in a relevant business of—	
(*a*) a capital item used in the course or furtherance of the relevant business, and for the purpose of that business, otherwise than solely for the purpose of selling, or leasing or letting on hire, the item;	
(*b*) staff;	
(*c*) management services;	
(*d*) administration services; or	
(*e*) accounting services.	
[*Cross-border face-value vouchers*	
Any scheme comprising or including the supply of a relevant service by a person belonging in the United Kingdom (the UK supplier) to a person belonging in a member State other than the United Kingdom (the non-UK recipient) where—	9
(a) the service is used, or intended to be used, in whole or in part, by the non-UK recipient or any other person belonging in another member State for the purposes of supplying a relevant service to a person belonging in the United Kingdom (the retail supply);	
(b) the recipient of the retail supply uses a face-value voucher issued by a person belonging in a country other than the United Kingdom to obtain that supply;	
(c) the person making the retail supply does not account for VAT on that supply in the United Kingdom or any other member State; and	
(d) the UK supplier and the person making the retail supply are connected persons.	
NOTES	
(1) "Face-value voucher" means tokens, stamps or vouchers of a description falling within paragraph 1(1) of Schedule 10A to the Act (face-value vouchers).	
(2) "Relevant service" means a supply of a description specified in any of paragraphs 7A to 7C of Schedule 5 to the Act (services supplied where received).	
(3) References in this scheme to the retail supply shall not include any supply of a relevant service made to a taxable person.	
Surrender of relevant lease	
Any scheme comprising or including the surrender by an occupier of a building of a relevant lease, tenancy or licence to occupy where—	10
(a) the occupier or any person connected to him is a relevant person;	
(b) the building is a capital item for the purposes of regulation 113 of the Value Added Tax Regulations 1995;	

Description of Scheme **Reference Number**

(c) before the surrender the occupier paid relevant VAT and was not entitled to full credit for, or refund of, that VAT under any provision of the Act or regulations;
(d) following the surrender the occupier continues to occupy at least 80% of the area previously occupied; and
(e) following the surrender the occupier pays no relevant VAT or pays less than 50% of the relevant VAT paid before the surrender.
NOTES
(1) Relevant lease, tenancy or licence to occupy means any lease of, tenancy of or licence to occupy the building granted or assigned to the occupier where—
(a) an election under paragraph 2 of Schedule 10 (election to waive exemption) has been made in relation to the building; and
(b) that election has not been revoked in accordance with paragraph 3(5) of Schedule 10.
(2) Relevant person means any person who—
(a) is a lessor of the building;
(b) is an owner of the building for the purposes of regulation 113 of the VAT Regulations 1995; and
(c) has made an election under paragraph 2 of Schedule 10 in relation to the building.
(3) Relevant VAT means VAT on rent paid or payable by the occupier in relation to the building.
(4) Surrender includes any termination by the occupier of the relevant lease, tenancy or licence to occupy where he has entered into any agreement, arrangement or understanding (whether legally binding or not) with the lessor regarding that termination.
(5) Building includes any part of that building.][1]

Amendments—[1] Entry inserted by the VAT (Disclosure of Avoidance Schemes) (Designations) (Amendment) Order, SI 2005/1724 arts 2, 3 with effect from 1 August 2005.

SCHEDULE 2

Article 3(2)

PART 1
Provisions associated with schemes

Confidentiality condition

1 An agreement preventing or limiting the disclosure of how a scheme gives rise to a tax advantage.

The sharing of the tax advantage with another party to the scheme or with the promoter

2— (1) An agreement that the tax advantage to a person accruing from the operation of the scheme be shared to any extent with another party to it or another person promoting it.

(2) A person is a promoter of a scheme if, in the course of a trade, profession or business which involves the provision to other persons of services relating to taxation—

(*a*) he is to any extent responsible for the design of the proposed arrangements; or
(*b*) he invites persons to enter into contracts for the implementation of the proposed arrangements.

Fee payable to a promoter which is in whole or in part contingent on tax savings from the scheme

3— (1) An agreement that payment to a promoter of the scheme be contingent in whole or in part on the tax advantage accruing from the operation of the scheme.

(2) A person is a promoter of a scheme if, in the course of a trade, profession or business which involves the provision to other persons of services relating to taxation—

(*a*) he is to any extent responsible for the design of the proposed arrangements; or
(*b*) he invites persons to enter into contracts for the implementation of the proposed arrangements.

PART 2
Provisions included in schemes

Prepayment between connected parties

4— (1) A payment for a supply of goods or services between connected persons—

(*a*) before the time applicable under section 6(2) or (3) of the Act; or

(*b*) where the supply is a continuous supply and the payment is before the goods or services are provided.

(2) A supply is a continuous supply if it is a supply to which regulation 85 (leases treated as supplies of goods), 86 (supplies of water, gas or any form of power, heat, refrigeration or ventilation), 90 (continuous supply of services), 91 (royalties and similar payments) or 93 (supplies in the construction industry) of the Value Added Tax Regulations 1995 applies.

(3) For the purposes of paragraph (1)(*b*) goods or services are provided at the time when, and to the extent that, the recipient receives the benefit of them.

Funding by loan, share subscription or subscription in securities

5 The funding in whole or in part of a supply of goods or services between connected persons by means of a loan between connected persons or the subscription for shares in, or securities issued by, a connected person.

Off-shore loops

6— (1) A supply of a relevant service which is used or intended to be used, in whole or in part, directly or indirectly, in making to a person belonging in the United Kingdom, a supply which is zero-rated, exempt or treated as made in another country (and not in the United Kingdom) by virtue of section 7(10) of the Act (place of supply of services).

(2) A "relevant service" is a service of a description falling within—

(*a*) article 3(*a*) of the Value Added Tax (Input Tax) (Specified Supplies) Order 1999 (services supplied to a person who belongs outside the member States);

(*b*) article 3(*b*) of that Order (services directly linked to the export of goods to a place outside the member States), insofar as they are supplies of a description falling within item 2 of Group 5 of Schedule 9 (the making of any advance or any credit); or

(*c*) article 3(*c*) of that Order (the provision of intermediary insurance or financial services);

or is a supply of a description specified in any of paragraphs 1 to 8 of Schedule 5 to the Act (services supplied where received), and the recipient of that supply belongs in a country, other than the Isle of Man, which is not a member State.

Property transactions between connected persons

7— (1) A relevant grant where—

(*a*) the grantor or grantee of the interest or right is a person who is not entitled to credit for all the input tax wholly attributable to the supplies he makes;

(*b*) any work of construction, alteration, demolition, repair, maintenance or civil engineering has been or is to be carried out on the land; and

(*c*) the grant is made to a person connected with the grantor.

(2) "Relevant grant" means the grant of any interest in or right over land or of any licence to occupy land or, in relation to land in Scotland, any personal right to call for or be granted any such interest or right, other than a grant of a description falling within item 1 of Group 5 (first grant of a major interest by a person constructing a building designed for dwelling, or intended for use solely for residential or charitable purposes; or by a person converting a non-residential building to residential use) or item 1 of Group 6 (first grant of a major interest in a protected building by a person reconstructing it) of Schedule 8.

(3) "Grant" includes an assignment or surrender and the supply made by the person to whom an interest is surrendered when there is a reverse surrender.

[Issue of face-value vouchers

8— (1) The issue of face-value vouchers for consideration.

(2) Paragraph 1 does not apply where—

(*a*) the issuer expects, on reasonable grounds, that at least 75% of the face-value of the vouchers will be redeemed within three years of the date on which the vouchers were issued; and

(*b*) the vouchers were issued to relevant persons.

(3) A relevant person is

(*a*) any person who is not connected with the issuer; or

(*b*) any body corporate—

(i) which is a member of the same VAT group as the issuer for the purposes of section 43 of the Act; and

(ii) which does not intend to supply the vouchers, directly or indirectly, to any person connected with the issuer outside that VAT group.

(4) "Face-value vouchers" means tokens, stamps or vouchers of a description falling within paragraph 1(1) of Schedule 10A to the Act (face-value vouchers) and "face-value" has the meaning given by paragraph 1(2) of that Schedule.][1]

Amendments—[1] This paragraph inserted by the VAT (Disclosure of Avoidance Schemes) (Designations) (Amendment) Order, SI 2005/1724 arts 2, 4 with effect from 1 August 2005.

2004/3147
VAT (Imported Gas and Electricity) Relief Order 2004

Made . . . . *30 November 2004*
Laid before the House of Commons . . . . . . *2 December 2004*
Coming into force . . . . *1 January 2005*

Whereas it appears necessary to the Treasury that the relief from value added tax provided by this Order should be allowed with a view to conforming with Article 14.1(k) of Council Directive No. 77/388 EEC and Article 249 of the Treaty establishing the European Community:

Now, therefore, the Treasury, in exercise of the powers conferred on them by section 37(1) of the Value Added Tax Act 1994, hereby make the following Order:

1 This Order may be cited as the Value Added Tax (Imported Gas and Electricity) Relief Order 2004 and shall come into force on 1 January 2005 in relation to goods imported on or after that date.

2 The VAT chargeable on the importation from a place outside the member States of-

(*a*) gas through the natural gas distribution network or
(*b*) electricity

shall not be payable.

2004/3148
Value Added Tax (Place of Supply of Goods) Order 2004

Made . . . . *30 November 2004*
Laid before the House of Commons . . . . . . *2 December 2004*
Coming into force . . . . *1 January 2005*

The Treasury, in exercise of the powers conferred on them by sections 7(11) and 9A of the Value Added Tax Act 1994 , hereby make the following Order:

PART 1
PRELIMINARY

Citation and commencement

1— (1) This Order may be cited as the Value Added Tax (place of supply of goods) Order 2004 and shall come into force on 1 January 2005.

(2) Part 3 (supplies of gas and electricity) has effect in relation to supplies made on or after 1 January 2005.

Rules for determining place of supply

2 The rules for determining where a supply of goods is made shall be varied in accordance with the following provisions of this Order.

Revocation

3 The Value Added Tax (Place of Supply of Goods) Order 1992 is hereby revoked.

PART 2
GOODS SUPPLIED ON BOARD SHIPS, AIRCRAFT AND TRAINS

Interpretation of Part 2

4 In this Part—

"Community transport" means the transportation of passengers between the point of departure and the point of arrival in the course of which-

(*a*) there is a stop in a Member State other than that in which lies the point of departure and

(*b*) there is no stop in a country which is not a Member State

"homeward stage" means that part of the return trip which ends at the first stop in the country in which the return trip commenced and which involves only such other stops, if any, as are in Member States where there have previously been stops (in the course of that return trip)

"pleasure cruise" includes a cruise wholly or partly for the purposes of education or training
"point of arrival" means the last place in the Member States where it is expected that passengers who have commenced their journey at a place in a Member State will terminate their journey or, where there is to follow a leg which will involve a stop in a place outside the Member States, the last such place before such leg is undertaken
"point of departure" means the first place in the Member States where it is expected that passengers will commence their journey or, where there has been a leg which involved a stop in a place outside the Member States, the first such place after such leg has been completed
"return trip" means any journey involving two or more countries where it is expected that the means of transport will stop in the country from which it originally departed.

5 Subject to articles 6 to 8, where goods are supplied on board a ship, aircraft or train in the course of a Community transport, those goods shall be treated as supplied at the point of departure.

6 Subject to articles 7 and 8, any goods supplied on board a [ship, aircraft or train][1] in the course of a Community transport for consumption on board shall be treated as supplied outside the Member States.

Amendments—[1] Words substituted for words "ship or aircraft" by the VAT (Place of Supply of Goods) Order, SI 2009/215 arts 2, 3 with effect from 6 April 2009.

7 For the purposes of this Part—

(*a*) part of transportation where it is expected that a different means of transport will be used shall be treated as separate transportation and
(*b*) the homeward stage of a return trip shall be treated as separate transportation.

8 This Part shall not apply to any goods supplied as part of a pleasure cruise.

PART 3
SUPPLIES OF GAS AND ELECTRICITY

Interpretation of Part 3

9 In this Part—

(*a*) "the Act" means the Value Added Tax Act 1994
(*b*) "dealer" means a person whose principal activity in respect of receiving supplies of relevant goods is the re-selling of those goods and whose own consumption of those goods is negligible
(*c*) "relevant goods" means gas supplied through the natural gas distribution network, and electricity
(*d*) "re-selling" for the purposes of article 9(*b*) does not include—

(i) re-sale as part of a single composite supply of other goods or services or
(ii) re-sale as a supply that falls to be disregarded under section 43(1)(*a*) of the Act where relevant goods are to be effectively used and consumed by a member of a VAT group

(*e*) "VAT group" means any bodies corporate treated under sections 43A to 43C of the Act as members of a group.

10 Relevant goods supplied to a dealer shall be treated as supplied at the place where that dealer has established his business or has a fixed establishment to which the relevant goods are supplied or, in the absence of such a place of business or fixed establishment, the place where he has his permanent address or usually resides.

11 Subject to articles 12 and 13, supplies of relevant goods not falling within article 10 above shall be treated as supplied at-

(*a*) the place where the recipient of the supply has effective use and consumption of the goods or
(*b*) in relation to any part of the goods not consumed, the place where the recipient of the supply has established his business or has a fixed establishment to which the goods are supplied, or in the absence of such place of business or fixed establishment, the place where he has his permanent address or usually resides.

12 Where the recipient of supplies of relevant goods supplies those goods as part of a single composite supply of other goods or services, that constitutes effective use and consumption by him of the goods for the purposes of article 11(*a*).

13 The supply of relevant goods to a member of a VAT group, where the goods are effectively used and consumed by a member of that group, shall constitute effective use and consumption of the goods for the purposes of article 11(*a*).

14 For the purposes of section 9A of the Act (reverse charge on gas and electricity supplied by persons outside the United Kingdom) a person is outside the United Kingdom if he has established his business or has a fixed establishment outside the United Kingdom or, in the absence of such a place of business or fixed establishment, the place where he has his permanent address or usually resides is outside the United Kingdom.

2005/1133

Revenue and Customs (Inspections) Regulations 2005

Made by the Treasury under the Commissioners for Revenue and Customs Act 2005 ss 27(1) and (2)

Made . . . . *7 April 2005*
Laid before Parliament . . . . *8 April 2005*
Coming into force . . . . *29 April 2005*

Citation and commencement

1 These Regulations may be cited as the Revenue and Customs (Inspections) Regulations 2005 and shall come into force on 29th April 2005.

Interpretation

2— (1) In these Regulations—

"the Act" means the Commissioners for Revenue and Customs Act 2005;

"appropriate inspectors" means in relation to—

(*a*) an inspection in England and Wales, the inspectors of constabulary,

(*b*) an inspection in Scotland, the inspectors of constabulary and the Scottish inspectors acting jointly,

(*c*) an inspection in Northern Ireland, the Northern Ireland inspectors;

"Chairman" means the Commissioner for the time being designated as chairman of Her Majesty's Revenue and Customs in Letters Patent under section 1(1) of the Act;

"civil penalty" means any penalty for which the Commissioners have power under any enactment to make an assessment or a demand;

"Commissioners" means the Commissioners for Revenue and Customs;

"criminal investigation" means any investigation for the purpose of considering whether an offence has been committed or discovering by whom an offence has been committed;

"Director" means the Director of Revenue and Customs Prosecutions;

"inspectors of constabulary" means Her Majesty's Inspectors of Constabulary;

"officer" means an officer of Revenue and Customs;

"revenue" has the meaning given by section 5(4) of the Act;

"risk" means the likelihood of an officer or the Commissioners doing or omitting to do something which affects—

(*a*) the prevention, detection or investigation of an offence by an officer or the Commissioners,

(*b*) any criminal proceedings in England and Wales conducted by the Director,

(*c*) any criminal proceedings conducted in Scotland under the direction of the Lord Advocate or a procurator fiscal, or

(*d*) any criminal proceedings conducted in Northern Ireland by the Commissioners or the Director of Public Prosecutions for Northern Ireland,

and the possible effect of such an act or omission on the prevention, detection or investigation of that offence or those proceedings.

(2) A reference to the Scottish inspectors or to the Northern Ireland inspectors has the same meaning as in section 27(6) of the Act.

Inspection Functions: England and Wales

3— (1) The inspectors of constabulary may carry out inspections in England and Wales for the purpose of assessing the effectiveness of the following conduct—

(*a*) any acts or omissions of an officer or the Commissioners in connection with the prevention, detection or investigation of an offence by him or them, or

(*b*) any acts or omissions of an officer or the Commissioners in connection with criminal proceedings conducted by the Director.

(2) The inspectors of constabulary may carry out inspections in England and Wales to assess the effectiveness of any matter described in regulation 6.

(3) The inspectors of constabulary may exercise the powers under this regulation on their own initiative or at the request of the Chancellor of the Exchequer or the Commissioners but the Chancellor of the Exchequer may not make a request to carry out an inspection in relation to a particular person.

(4) The chief inspector of constabulary may include in his report under section 54(4) of the Police Act 1996 (annual reports) a report on the Commissioners and officers.

Inspection Functions: Scotland

4— (1) The inspectors of constabulary and the Scottish inspectors may jointly carry out inspections in Scotland for the purpose of assessing the effectiveness of the following conduct—

(*a*) any acts or omissions of an officer or the Commissioners in connection with the prevention, detection or investigation of an offence by him or them, or

(b) any acts or omissions of an officer or the Commissioners in connection with criminal proceedings conducted under the direction of the Lord Advocate or a procurator fiscal.

(2) The inspectors of constabulary and the Scottish inspectors may jointly carry out inspections in Scotland to assess the effectiveness of any matter described in regulation 6.

(3) The inspectors of constabulary and the Scottish inspectors may jointly exercise the powers under this regulation on their own initiative or at the request of the Chancellor of the Exchequer or the Commissioners but the Chancellor of the Exchequer may not make a request to carry out an inspection in relation to a particular person.

Inspection Functions: Northern Ireland

5— (1) The Northern Ireland inspectors may carry out inspections in Northern Ireland for the purpose of assessing the effectiveness of the following conduct—

(a) any acts or omissions of an officer or the Commissioners in connection with the prevention, detection or investigation of an offence by him or them, or

(b) any acts or omissions of an officer or the Commissioners in connection with criminal proceedings conducted in Northern Ireland by the Commissioners or the Director of Public Prosecutions for Northern Ireland.

(2) The Northern Ireland inspectors may carry out inspections in Northern Ireland to assess the effectiveness of any of the matters described in regulation 6.

(3) The Northern Ireland inspectors may exercise the powers under this regulation on their own initiative or at the request of the Chancellor of the Exchequer or the Commissioners but the Chancellor of the Exchequer may not make a request to carry out an inspection in relation to a particular person.

Inspection of means of dealing with risks

6 The matters to which regulations 3(2), 4(2) and 5(2) apply are—

(a) any method devised by or for Her Majesty's Revenue and Customs for identifying and dealing with a risk;

(b) any measures devised by or for Her Majesty's Revenue and Customs for assuring that an officer or the Commissioners are properly applying that method, and

(c) the operation of any such method or measures by an officer or the Commissioners.

Access

7— (1) This regulation applies to an inspection carried out under regulation 3, 4 or 5.

(2) For the purposes of an inspection the Commissioners shall provide to the appropriate inspectors such of the following as are reasonably required by the appropriate inspectors—

(a) access to any premises belonging to the Commissioners;

(b) access to any system operated by or on behalf of the Commissioners for storing and retrieving information electronically;

(c) any information or documents held by the Commissioners.

(3) For the purposes of an inspection an officer shall provide to the appropriate inspectors such information or documents held by him as are reasonably required by the inspectors.

Inspections of guidance

8 The appropriate inspectors may, if the Chancellor of the Exchequer or the Commissioners request them to do so, carry out an inspection of—

(a) the operation of any guidance issued by the Commissioners to officers for assessing or demanding a civil penalty instead of carrying out a criminal investigation into any matter or vice versa, or

(b) the operation of any guidance issued by the Commissioners for using other powers to secure any revenue, for the collection and management of which the Commissioners are responsible, instead of assessing or demanding a civil penalty or carrying out a criminal investigation.

Reports

9— (1) Where—

(a) the inspectors of constabulary carry out an inspection under regulation 3 or 8,

(b) the inspectors of constabulary and the Scottish inspectors jointly carry out an inspection under regulation 4 or 8, or

(c) the Northern Ireland inspectors carry out an inspection under regulation 5 or 8,

they shall provide a report of the inspection to the Chancellor of the Exchequer.

(2) Subject to paragraph (3), the Chancellor of the Exchequer shall arrange for any report received by him to be published.

(3) The Chancellor of the Exchequer may exclude from publication under paragraph (2) any part of a report if, in his opinion, the publication of that part—

(a) would be against the interests of national security;

(*b*) might jeopardise the safety of any person;

(*c*) would contravene section 29(2) of the Act, or

(*d*) might prejudice the prevention or detection of crime or the apprehension or prosecution of offenders.

(4) The Chancellor of the Exchequer shall send a copy of the published report to the Chairman.

(5) The Commissioners shall—

(*a*) prepare comments on the published report;

(*b*) send a copy of the comments to the Chancellor of the Exchequer before such date as may be specified by him;

(*c*) publish the comments in such manner as appears to the Commissioners to be appropriate.

(6) Where the inspectors of constabulary and the Scottish inspectors provide a report of an inspection to the Chancellor of the Exchequer he shall send a copy of the published report to the Scottish Ministers.

Appointment of assistant inspectors and staff officers

10— (1) Section 56 of the Police Act 1996 (appointment of assistant inspectors and staff officers) shall have effect subject to the following modifications—

(*a*) in section 56(1) after "constabulary" insert "for the purpose of carrying out functions under the Revenue and Customs (Inspections) Regulations 2005", and

(*b*) in section 56(2) for "Members of a police force" substitute "Officers of Revenue and Customs".

(2) Section 34 of the Police (Scotland) Act 1967 (appointment of assistant inspectors and staff officers)shall have effect subject to the following modifications—

(*a*) in section 34(1) after "constabulary" insert "for the purpose of carrying out functions under the Revenue and Customs (Inspections) Regulations 2005", and

(*b*) in section 34(1A) for "Constables" substitute "Officers of Revenue and Customs".

Payment

11— (1) The Commissioners shall pay to the inspectors of constabulary, for functions carried out by those inspectors under these Regulations, such amount as may be agreed between the Commissioners and those inspectors or, in the absence of an agreement, such amount as the Treasury, after consultation with the Secretary of State, may determine.

(2) The Commissioners shall pay to the inspectors of constabulary and the Scottish inspectors, for functions carried out jointly by those inspectors under these Regulations, such amount as may be agreed between the Commissioners and those inspectors or, in the absence of an agreement, such amount as the Treasury, after consultation with the Secretary of State and Scottish Ministers, may determine.

(3) The Commissioners shall pay to the Northern Ireland inspectors for functions carried out by those inspectors under these Regulations such amount as may be agreed between the Commissioners and those inspectors or, in the absence of an agreement, such amount as the Treasury, after consultation with the Secretary of State, may determine.

2005/3290

Value Added Tax (Input Tax) (Reimbursement by Employers of Employees' Business Use of Road Fuel) Regulations 2005

Made by HMRC Commissioners under VATA 1994 s 24(6)(*a*)

Made . . . . *30 November 2005*

Laid before the House of Commons . . . . *30 November 2005*

Coming into force . . . . *1 January 2006*

Commentary—*De Voil Indirect Tax Service* **V3.436.**

1 These Regulations may be cited as the Value Added Tax (Input Tax) (Reimbursement by Employers of Employees' Business Use of Road Fuel) Regulations 2005 and come into force on 1st January 2006.

2 Regulation 5 shall apply where—

(*a*) road fuel is supplied to a taxable person (employer) in circumstances where it is delivered to and paid for by his employee acting in his name and on his behalf for use by him (the employee) either in whole or in part for the purposes of the taxable person's business; and

(*b*) the taxable person has agreed to reimburse and does so reimburse his employee for the cost of the road fuel so used in one of the ways specified in regulations 3 and 4.

3 Where all the road fuel is used for the purposes of the taxable person's business, by payment of the actual cost of the road fuel.

4 Where only part of the road fuel is used for the purposes of the taxable person's business, by payment of either—

(*a*) an amount which represents the actual cost of the road fuel so used determined by—

(i) the total distances travelled by the vehicle in which the road fuel is used for the purposes of the taxable person's business; and

(ii) the cylinder capacity of that vehicle; or

(*b*) the actual cost of the road fuel in circumstances where the taxable person will account for output tax on any private use under section 57 of the Value Added Tax Act 1994.

5 Where this regulation applies, subject to regulation 6, the amount of input tax to be deducted by the taxable person under section 24(1) of the Value Added Tax Act 1994 in relation to the supply of road fuel referred to in regulation 2 shall be quantified by reference to the amount paid by him to his employee as reimbursement under regulation 3 or 4, as the case may be.

6 These regulations only apply where the taxable person holds a VAT invoice which contains the details prescribed by regulation 14(1), regulation 14(2) or regulation 16(1) of the Value Added Tax Regulations 1995 as may be applicable and, where so required, is made out to him as the recipient of the supply.

7 In these regulations, "use for the purposes of the taxable person's business" means use for those purposes by the taxable person (employer) in making onward taxable supplies.

2005/3311
Revenue and Customs (Complaints and Misconduct) Regulations 2005

Made by the Treasury under CRCA 2005 ss 28(1) and (2), and 29(3)

Made . . . . 1 December 2005
Laid before Parliament . . . . 2 December 2005
Coming into force . . . . 28 December 2005

Citation, commencement and extent

1— (1) These Regulations may be cited as the Revenue and Customs (Complaints and Misconduct) Regulations 2005 and shall come into force on 28th December 2005.

(2) These Regulations extend to England and Wales.

Interpretation

2 In these Regulations—

"2002 Act" means the Police Reform Act 2002;

"Commission" means the Independent Police Complaints Commission;

"Commissioners" means the Commissioners for Her Majesty's Revenue and Customs;

"Complaints Regulations" means the Police (Complaints and Misconduct) Regulations 2004;

"conduct matter" has the meaning given by section 12 of the 2002 Act;

"functions" has the meaning given by section 51(2)(*a*) of the Commissioners for Revenue and Customs Act 2005;

"Investigatory Powers Order" means the Independent Police Complaints Commission (Investigatory Powers) Order 2004;

"officers" means officers of Revenue and Customs;

"Staff Conduct Regulations" means the Independent Police Complaints Commission (Staff Conduct) Regulations 2004.

Application of provisions of Part 2 of the 2002 Act with modifications

3— (1) The provisions specified in paragraphs (2), (3) and (4) shall apply for the purpose of conferring functions on the Commission in relation to the Commissioners and officers.

(2) Sections 9 to 29 of the 2002 Act shall have effect with the modifications made by Schedule 1 to these Regulations.

(3) Schedule 2 to the 2002 Act shall have effect with the modifications made by Schedule 2 to these Regulations.

(4) Paragraphs 10 to 24, 27 and 29 of Schedule 3 to the 2002 Act shall have effect with the modifications made by Schedule 3 to these Regulations.

(5) Paragraphs 1 to 9, 25, 26 and 28 of Schedule 3 to the 2002 Act shall have effect with the modifications made by Schedule 3 to these Regulations.

(6) The provisions specified in—

(*a*) paragraphs (2), (3) and (4) shall have effect from the date these Regulations come into force;

(*b*) paragraph (5) shall have effect from 1st April 2006.

(7) The references in regulations 5, 8 and 9(1) to Part 2 of the 2002 Act are references to Part 2 of the 2002 Act as modified by Schedules 1, 2 and 3 to these Regulations.

Application of the Investigatory Powers Order, the Complaints Regulations and the Staff Conduct Regulations with modifications

4— (1) The provisions specified in paragraph (2) shall apply for the purpose of conferring functions on the Commission in relation to the Commissioners and officers.

(2) From the date these Regulations come into force—

(*a*) the Investigatory Powers Order shall have effect,

(*b*) the Complaints Regulations shall have effect with the modifications made by Part 1 of Schedule 4 to these Regulations, and

(*c*) the Staff Conduct Regulations shall have effect with the modifications made by Part 2 of Schedule 4 to these Regulations.

(3) The references in regulations 5, 8 and 9(1) to—

(*a*) the Complaints Regulations,

(*b*) the Staff Conduct Regulations,

are references to those Regulations as modified by Parts 1 and 2 of Schedule 4 to these Regulations.

[4A— (1) For the purpose of the application of the Complaints Regulations under regulation 4, the amendments made to those Regulations by the provisions specified in paragraph (2) shall apply.

(2) The provisions specified are—

(*a*) regulation 26 of the Serious Organised Crime and Police Act 2005 (Powers of Arrest) (Consequential Amendments) Order 2005, and

(*b*) regulation 2 of the Police (Complaints and Misconduct) (Amendment) Regulations 2006.

(3) This regulation has effect from 27th July 2006.][1]

Amendments—[1] Regulation inserted by the Revenue and Customs (Complaints and Misconduct) (Amendment) Regulations, SI 2006/1748 reg 3 with effect from 27 July 2006.

Disclosure of information

5 Where the Commission, or any person acting on its behalf, obtains information in the course of performing a function under these Regulations it or he may not disclose it except as permitted by Part 2 of the 2002 Act or the Complaints Regulations.

Use of information

6 Where the Commission, or any person acting on its behalf, obtains information in the course of performing a function under these Regulations it or he may not use it for any purpose other than the performance of a function under these Regulations.

Payments

7— (1) The Commissioners shall pay such amount to the Secretary of State in respect of functions performed by the Commission under these Regulations as may be agreed between the Commissioners and the Commission.

(2) In the absence of an agreement, the Commissioners shall pay such amount in respect of those functions as the Treasury, after consultation with the Secretary of State, shall determine.

Complaints about conduct occurring before 1st April 2006

8 Nothing in Part 2 of the 2002 Act, the Investigatory Powers Order, the Complaints Regulations or the Staff Conduct Regulations shall have effect in relation to a complaint made about the conduct of a Commissioner or an officer occurring before 1st April 2006.

Conduct matter occurring before 1st April 2006

9— (1) Subject to paragraph (2), nothing in Part 2 of the 2002 Act, the Investigatory Powers Order, the Complaints Regulations or the Staff Conduct Regulations shall have effect in relation to a conduct matter relating to the conduct of a Commissioner or an officer occurring before 1st April 2006.

(2) Paragraph (1) does not apply to any conduct matter which the appropriate authority may refer to the Commission under paragraph 13(2) of Schedule 3 to the 2002 Act.

SCHEDULE 1
MODIFICATION OF SECTIONS 9 TO 29 OF THE 2002 ACT

Regulation 3(2)

1 At the end of section 9(3) insert—

"(*g*) any person who holds or has held office or employment as a Commissioner or officer.".

2— (1) Section 10 shall be modified as follows.

(2) In subsection (1) after "the Commission" insert ", in relation to the Commissioners and officers,".

(3) In subsection (1)(*a*) for "police authorities and chief officers" substitute "the Commissioners".

(4) In subsection (1)(*e*) omit "and also of police practice in relation to other matters,".

(5) Omit subsection (1)(*f*).

(6) In subsection (2)(*a*) for "persons serving with the police" substitute—

"Commissioners or officers which the appropriate authority—

(i) has a duty to refer to the Commission under paragraph 4(1) of Schedule 3 or,

(ii) may refer to the Commission under paragraph 4(2) or (3) of Schedule 3;".

(7) In subsection (2)(*b*) for the words from "appears that" to the end substitute—

"appears that—

(i) there may have been conduct by such persons which constitutes or involves the commission of a criminal offence or behaviour justifying disciplinary proceedings, and

(ii) that conduct or behaviour is conduct or behaviour which the appropriate authority has a duty to refer to the Commission under paragraph 13(1) of Schedule 3 or may refer to the Commission under paragraph 13(2) or (3) of that Schedule.".

(8) In subsection (2)(*ba*) for "a person serving with the police" insert "an officer".

(9) Omit subsection (3).

(10) In subsection (4)(*a*) for "subsections (1) and (3)" insert "subsection (1)".

(11) In subsection (5)(*a*) after "functions" insert "in relation to the Commissioners and officers".

(12) Omit subsections (7)(*b*) and (*c*).

(13) In subsection (8) for the words from "control of a police force" to the end substitute "control of Her Majesty's Revenue and Customs by the Commissioners".

3— (1) Section 11 shall be modified as follows.

(2) In subsections (1), (2), (3), and (5) for "Secretary of State" insert "Chancellor of the Exchequer".

(3) Omit subsection (4)(*b*).

(4) In subsection (6) for the words from "under subsection (1)" to the end substitute "under subsection (1) to the Commissioners".

(5) In subsection (7) for the words from "under subsection (3)" to the end substitute "under subsection (3) to the Commissioners".

(6) Omit subsections (8) and (9).

(7) In subsection (10) for paragraphs (*a*) to (*g*) substitute—

"(*a*) the Chancellor of the Exchequer, and

(*b*) the Commissioners."

(8) In the heading for "Reports to the Secretary of State" substitute "Reports to the Chancellor of the Exchequer".

4— (1) Section 12 shall be modified as follows.

(2) In subsections (1) and (2) for "a person serving with the police" substitute "a Commissioner or an officer".

(3) In subsections (2B)(*a*), [(2B)(*b*)][1], (2C)(*a*) and (2D) for "a person serving with the police" (on each occasion the words occur) substitute "an officer".

Amendments—[1] Words inserted by the Revenue and Customs (Complaints and Misconduct) (Amendment) Regulations, SI 2006/1748 reg 4 with effect from 27 July 2006.

5— (1) Section 14 shall be modified as follows.

(2) In subsection (1) for the words from "control of a police force" to the end substitute "control of Her Majesty's Revenue and Customs by the Commissioners".

(3) Omit subsections (2) and (3).

6— (1) Section 15 shall be modified as follows.

(2) In subsection (1)—

(*a*) for the words in paragraph (*a*) substitute "the Commissioners and ";

(*b*) omit paragraph (*b*);

(*c*) for "it or he is" substitute "they are or he is" and for "that force" substitute "Her Majesty's Revenue and Customs".

(3) In subsection (3)—

(*a*) for paragraph (*a*) substitute—

"(*a*) the Commission requires the chief officer of a police force to provide a member of his force for appointment under paragraph 17A or 18A of Schedule 3,";

(*b*) omit paragraphs (*b*) and (*c*);

(*c*) omit "or Director General".

(4) In subsection (4)—

(*a*) omit paragraphs (*c*) and (*d*), and

(*b*) after paragraph (*d*) insert—

"(*e*) the Commissioners,".

(5) In subsection (5)—

(*a*) omit paragraphs (*c*) and (*d*);

(*b*) for "16, 17 or 18" substitute "17A or 18A".

(6) After subsection (5) insert—

"(5A) It shall be the duty of the Head of the Home Civil Service, the Chairman and Commissioners to ensure that a person appointed under paragraph 16,17, 17A, 18 or 18A of Schedule 3 to carry out an investigation is given all such assistance and co-operation in the carrying out of that investigation as that person may reasonably require.".

(7) Omit subsections (6) and (7).

7— (1) Section 16 shall be modified as follows.

(2) In subsection (1)—

(*a*) in paragraph (*a*)—

(i) for "one" substitute "a";

(ii) omit "to another";

(iii) delete "or";

(*b*) at the end of paragraph (*b*) insert "; or";

(*c*) after paragraph (*b*) insert—

"(*c*) a police force provides assistance by agreement under paragraph 17A(2) or 18A(2) of Schedule 3.".

(3) In subsection (2)—

(*a*) in paragraph (*a*) for—

(i) "one police force to another" substitute "a police force",

(ii) "the first force ("the assisting force")" substitute "that force";

(iii) in sub-paragraph (i) for "a member of the other force" substitute "a Commissioner or an officer";

(iv) in sub-paragraph (ii) for "a member of the other force" substitute "an officer";

(*b*) in paragraph (*b*)—

(i) omit "(the assisting force)";

(ii) in sub-paragraph (i) for "not a member of that force" substitute "a Commissioner or an officer";

(iii) in sub-paragraph (ii) for "not a member of that force" substitute "an officer".

(4) In subsection (3)—

(*a*) for "one police force to another" substitute "a police force";

(*b*) for "police authority maintaining that other police force" substitute "appropriate authority";

(*c*) for "the assisting force" substitute "that force";

(*d*) omit "(if any)";

(*e*) in paragraph (*b*)(i) after "generally" insert "and the Commissioners", and

(*f*) in paragraph (*b*)(ii) omit "by one police force to another".

(5) After subsection (3) there shall be inserted—

"(3A) Subsection (3) shall have effect in relation to assistance which a police force provides by agreement under paragraph 17A (2) or 18A (2) of Schedule 3 as if the reference in that subsection to required to be provided were a reference to provided by agreement under paragraph 17A(2) or 18A(2) of Schedule 3.".

(6) Omit subsections (5), (6) and (7).

8— (1) Section 17 shall be modified as follows.

(2) From the beginning of subsection (1) to the end of paragraph (*b*) of that subsection substitute "It shall be the duty of the Commissioners".

(3) In subsection (2)—

(*a*) for the words "every police authority and of every chief officer" substitute "the Commissioners", and

(*b*) in paragraph (*a*) for the words "that authority and or chief officer" substitute "the Commissioners".

(4) In subsection (4)—

(*a*) for the words "a police authority or chief officer" substitute "the Commissioners", and

(*b*) in paragraph (*a*) for the words "that authority and or chief officer" substitute "the Commissioners".

9— (1) Section 18 shall be modified as follows.

(2) In subsection (1)(*a*)—

(*a*) for paragraphs (i) and (ii) substitute "the Commissioners"; and

(*b*) for "that force" substitute "Her Majesty's Revenue and Customs".

(3) In subsection (1) for "the authority or, as the case may be, of the chief officer" substitute "the Commissioners".

(4) In subsection (2)(*a*) for "the force in question" substitute "the Commissioners".

(5) In subsection (3) for "the authority or chief officer" substitute "the Commissioners".

(6) In subsection (5)(*b*) for "police authorities and chief officers" substitute "the Commissioners".

(7) In the heading to the section for "police premises" substitute "Her Majesty's Revenue and Customs premises".

10— (1) Section 22 shall be modified as follows.

(2) In subsection (1) for the words from "guidance" to the end of paragraph (*c*) substitute "guidance to the Commissioners and officers".

(3) In subsection (3)—

(*a*) for paragraph (*a*) substitute—
"(*a*) the Commissioners and";

(*b*) omit paragraph (*b*).

(4) In subsection (4) for "the Secretary of State" substitute "the Chancellor of the Exchequer".

(5) Omit subsection (5)(*c*).

11 Omit sections 25 and 26.

12— (1) Section 29 shall be modified as follows.

(2) In subsection (1)—

(*a*) for the definition of "the appropriate authority" substitute the following definition—
""the appropriate authority"—

(*a*) in relation to the Chairman, the Deputy Chairman, a Commissioner or an officer or in relation to any complaint, matter or

investigation relating to the conduct of such a person, means—

(i) if that person is the Chairman or Deputy Chairman, the Head of the Home Civil Service,

(ii) if that person is a Commissioner, the Chairman, or

(iii) if that person is an officer, the Commissioners" and

(*b*) in relation to a death or serious injury matter and the relevant officer, means the Commissioners.";

(*b*) after the definition of "the appropriate authority" insert—
""the Chairman" means the chairman of the Commissioners";

(*c*) after the definition of "the Commission" insert—
""the Commissioners" means the Commissioners for Her Majesty's Revenue and Customs;";

(*d*) after the definition of "conduct matter" insert—
""the Deputy Chairman" means the Deputy Chairman of the Commissioners";

(*e*) for the definition of "disciplinary proceedings" substitute
""disciplinary proceedings" means any proceedings or management process during which the conduct of the Chairman, Deputy Chairman, a Commissioner or an officer is considered in order to determine whether a sanction or punitive measure should be imposed against him in relation to that conduct;";

(*f*) after the definition of "local resolution" insert the following definition—
""officers" means officers of Revenue and Customs;", and

(*g*) omit the definitions of "local resolution", "relevant force", and "senior officer".

(3) In subsection (1A) for "person serving with the police (within the meaning of section 12(7))" substitute "officer" and for "such person" substitute "such officer".

(4) In subsection (1B) for "persons serving with the police" substitute "officers".

(5) Omit subsection (7).

(6) In subsection (3) for the words from "falling within" to the end of that subsection substitute "who is a Commissioner or an officer (whether at the time of the conduct or any subsequent time)".

(7) In subsection (4)—

(*a*) for paragraph (*a*) substitute—
"(*a*) a person who, at the time when the conduct was supposed to have taken place in relation to him, was a Commissioner or an officer (whether or not he was on duty in his capacity as a Commissioner or officer at that time).";

(*b*) omit paragraph (*b*)(i);

(*c*) for "person falling within subsection (3)(*a*) to (*d*)" substitute "Commissioner or officer".

SCHEDULE 2

MODIFICATION OF SCHEDULE 2 TO THE 2002 ACT

Regulation 3(3)

1 After paragraph 6(2) insert—

"(2A) The Commission may make arrangements with the Commissioners under which officers of Revenue and Customs are engaged on temporary service with the Commission.".

2 In paragraph 17(1)(*c*) after "Secretary of State" insert ", the Treasury".

SCHEDULE 3

MODIFICATION OF SCHEDULE 3 TO THE 2002 ACT

Regulations 3(4) and (5)

1— (1) Paragraph 1 shall be modified as follows.

(2) For sub-paragraph (1) substitute—

"(1) Where—

(*a*) complaint is made to the Head of the Home Civil Service about the conduct of the Chairman or Deputy Chairman, or

(*b*) the Head of the Home Civil Service becomes aware that a complaint about the conduct of the Chairman or Deputy Chairman has been made to the Commission,

the Head of the Home Civil Service shall take all such steps as appear to him to be appropriate for the purposes of Part 2 of this Act for obtaining and preserving evidence relating to the conduct complained of.".

(3) After sub-paragraph (1) insert—

"(1A) Where—

(*a*) a complaint is made to the Chairman about the conduct of a Commissioner, or

(*b*) the Chairman becomes aware that a complaint about the conduct of a Commissioner has been made to the Commission,

the Chairman shall take all such steps as appear to him to be appropriate for the purposes of Part 2 of this Act for obtaining and preserving evidence relating to the conduct complained of.".

(4) For sub-paragraph (2) substitute—

"(2) Where—

(*a*) a complaint is made to the Commissioners about the conduct of an officer, or

(*b*) the Commissioners become aware that a complaint about the conduct of an officer has been made to the Commission,

the Commissioners shall take all such steps as appear to them to be appropriate for the purposes of Part 2 of this Act for obtaining and preserving evidence relating to the conduct complained of.".

(5) For sub-paragraph (3) substitute—

"(3) The duty of the—

(*a*) Head of the Home Civil Service under sub-paragraph (1);

(*b*) Chairman under sub-paragraph (1A);

(*c*) Commissioners under sub-paragraph (2),

must be performed as soon as practicable after the complaint is made or, as the case may be, he or they become aware of it.".

(6) In sub-paragraph (4) for—

(*a*) "he shall" substitute "he or they shall";

(*b*) "he is satisfied" substitute "he is or they are satisfied"; and

(*c*) "appearing to him" substitute "appearing to him or them".

(7) Omit sub-paragraph (5).

(8) In sub-paragraph (6)—

(*a*) for "a chief officer" substitute—

"the—

(*a*) Head of the Home Civil Service;

(*b*) Chairman;

(*c*) Commissioners,";

(*b*) the words after "a chief officer" become full out words;

(*c*) for "he may" substitute "he or they may", and

(*d*) omit "by the police authority maintaining his force or".

2— (1) Paragraph 2 shall be modified as follows.

(2) In sub-paragraph (1)(*a*) for "police authority or chief officer who is" substitute "Head of the Home Civil Service, Chairman or Commissioners who is or are".

(3) In sub-paragraph (2)—

(*a*) for "a police authority, it" substitute "the Head of the Home Civil Service or Chairman, he";

(*b*) in paragraph (*a*) for "it is itself" substitute "he is himself"; and

(*c*) in paragraph (*b*) for "it determines that it" substitute "he determines that he".

(4) In sub-paragraph (3) for—

(*a*) "a chief officer, he shall" substitute "the Commissioners, they shall";

(*b*) "he is himself" substitute "they are themselves"; and

(*c*) "he determines that he is not" substitute "they determine that they are not".

(5) In sub-paragraph (5) for "a police authority or a chief officer gives" substitute "Head of the Home Civil Service, Chairman or Commissioners gives or give".

(6) For sub-paragraph (6) substitute—

"(6) Where—

(*a*) the Head of the Home Civil Service or Chairman determines, in the case of any complaint made to him, that he is himself the appropriate authority,

(*b*) the Commissioners determine, in the case of any complaint made to them, that they are themselves the appropriate authority, or

(*c*) a complaint is notified to the Head of the Home Civil Service, Chairman or Commissioners under this paragraph,

the Head of the Home Civil Service, Chairman or Commissioners shall record the complaint.".

3— (1) Paragraph 3 shall be modified as follows.

(2) In sub-paragraph (1) for "a police authority or chief officer" substitute "the Head of the Home Civil Service, Chairman or Commissioners".

(3) In sub-paragraph (2)—

(*a*) for "police authority or chief officer" and "authority or chief officer" substitute (on each occasion) "Head of the Home Civil Service, Chairman or Commissioners"

(*b*) for "decides" substitute "decides or decide" and

(*c*) in paragraph (*c*) for "that complainant's right to appeal" substitute "whether the complainant has a right to appeal".

(4) In sub-paragraph (3)—

(*a*) for "police authority or chief officer" substitute "Head of the Home Civil Service, Chairman or Commissioners"; and

(*b*) after "paragraph" insert "if, but only if, the failure is in respect of conduct which the Head of the Home Civil Service, Chairman or Commissioners is or are required to refer to the Commission under paragraph 4(1)(*a*) or (*b*).".

(5) In sub-paragraph (4)—

(*a*) in paragraph (*b*) for "police authority or chief officer" substitute "Head of the Home Civil Service, Chairman or Commissioners"; and

(*b*) for "a police authority or chief officer" substitute "the Head of the Home Civil Service, Chairman or Commissioners".

(6) In sub-paragraph (6) for—

(*a*) "police authority or, as the case may be, the chief officer" substitute "Head of the Home Civil Service, Chairman or, as the case may be, the Commissioners"; and

(*b*) "police authority or chief officer" substitute "Head of the Home Civil Service, Chairman or Commissioners".

4— (1) Paragraph 4 shall be modified as follows.

[(1A) After sub-paragraph (1) insert—

"(1A) The obligation on the Head of the Home Civil Service under sub-paragraph (1)(*a*) or (*b*) to refer a complaint about the conduct of a person in respect of whom he is the appropriate authority arises only if the Head of the Home Civil Service is satisfied that the complaint contains an indication that a criminal offence may have been committed by that person.

(1B) The obligation on the Chairman or the Commissioners under sub-paragraph (1)(*a*) or (1)(*b*) to refer a complaint about the conduct of a person in respect of whom he is or they are the appropriate authority arises only if he is or they are satisfied that the complaint contains an indication that the person may have—

(*a*) committed a criminal offence; or

(*b*) behaved in a manner which would justify the bringing of disciplinary proceedings and that such behaviour (if it had taken place) would be likely to lead to the termination of that person's office or employment.'.][1]

(2) In sub-paragraph (3)—

(*a*) for "a police authority" substitute "the Head of the Home Civil Service";

(*b*) in paragraph (*a*) for "chief officer of police of the police force maintained by that authority" substitute "Chairman"; and

(*c*) in paragraph (*b*) for "the police authority" substitute "the Head of the Home Civil Service".

(3) In sub-paragraph (5)(*b*) for "a police authority or chief officer" substitute "the Head of the Home Civil Service, Chairman or Commissioners".

(4) In sub-paragraph (6)—

(*a*) for "A police authority or chief officer which refers" substitute "Where the Head of the Home Civil Service, Chairman or Commissioners refers or refer";

(*b*) after "paragraph" insert "he or they"; and

(*c*) in paragraph (*b*) for "that authority or chief officer" substitute "the Head of the Home Civil Service, Chairman or Commissioners".

Amendments—[1] Sub-para (1A) inserted by the Revenue and Customs (Complaints and Misconduct) (Amendment) Regulations, SI 2006/1748 reg 5 with effect from 27 July 2006.

5— (1) Paragraph 5 shall be modified as follows.

(2) In sub-paragraph (1) for "a police authority or chief officer" substitute "the Head of the Home Civil Service, Chairman or Commissioners".

(3) In sub-paragraph (2) for "paragraph 6" substitute "sub-paragraph (2A)".

(4) After sub-paragraph (2) insert—

"(2A) In a case to which sub-paragraph (2) applies the appropriate authority shall not be required by virtue of any of the provisions of this Schedule to take any action in relation to the complaint but may handle the complaint in whatever manner it thinks fit, or take no action in relation to the complaint.".

(5) For sub-paragraph 3(*b*) substitute—

"(*b*) to the person complained against.".

6— (1) Paragraph 6 shall be modified as follows.

(2) For sub-paragraph (2) substitute—

"(2) The appropriate authority shall not be required by virtue of any provisions of this Schedule to take any action in relation to the complaint but may handle the complaint in whatever manner it thinks fit or take no action in relation to the complaint.".

(3) Omit sub-paragraphs (3) to (7).

7 Omit paragraphs 7, 8 and 9.

8— (1) Paragraph 10 shall be modified as follows.

(2) In sub-paragraph (1)—

(*a*) in paragraph (*a*) for—

(i) "a police authority or chief officer" (on both occasions where it occurs) substitute "the Head of the Home Civil Service, Chairman or Commissioners";

(ii) for "has received" substitute "has or have received"; and

(iii) for "that authority or chief officer" substitute "the Head of the Home Civil Service, Chairman or Commissioners";

(*b*) in paragraph (*b*) for "that authority or chief officer" substitute "the Head of the Home Civil Service, Chairman or Commissioners".

(3) In sub-paragraph (2)—

(*a*) for "The authority or chief officer" substitute "The Head of the Home Civil Service, Chairman or Commissioners";

(*b*) in paragraph (*a*) for "it or, as the case may be, he is" substitute "he is or, as the case may be, they are"; and

(*c*) in paragraph (*b*) for "if it or he is not" substitute "if he is or they are not".

(4) In sub-paragraph (3)—

(*a*) …[1]

(*b*) for "a police authority or chief officer determines" substitute "the Head of the Home Civil Service, Chairman or Commissioners determines or determine";

(*c*) for "it or, as the case may be, he is" substitute "he is, or as the case may be, they are", and

(*d*) for "it or he" substitute "he or they".

(5) …[1]

Amendments—[1] Words omitted are revoked by the Revenue and Customs (Complaints and Misconduct) (Amendment) Regulations, SI 2006/1748 reg 5 with effect from 27 July 2006.

9— (1) Paragraph 11 shall be modified as follows.

(2) In sub-paragraph (1)—

(*a*) …[1];

(*b*) in paragraph (*a*) for "police authority or chief officer who is" substitute "Head of the Home Civil Service, Chairman or Commissioners who is or are".

(3) …[1]

Amendments—[1] Words omitted are revoked by the Revenue and Customs (Complaints and Misconduct) (Amendment) Regulations, SI 2006/1748 reg 5 with effect from 27 July 2006.

10— (1) Paragraph 12 shall be modified as follows.

(2) Omit sub-paragraph (1).

(3) For sub-paragraph (2) substitute—

"(2) Where—

(*a*) the Head of the Home Civil Service becomes aware of any recordable matter relating to the conduct of the Chairman or Deputy Chairman;

(*b*) the Chairman becomes aware of any recordable matter relating to the conduct of a Commissioner; or

(*c*) the Commissioners become aware of any recordable matter relating to the conduct of an officer,

it shall be his or their duty to take all such steps as appear to him or them to be appropriate for the purposes of Part 2 of this Act for obtaining and preserving the evidence relating to that matter.".

(4) For sub-paragraph (3) substitute—

"(3) The duty under sub-paragraph (2) of—

(*a*) the Head of the Home Civil Service;

(*b*) the Chairman;

(*c*) the Commissioners,

must be performed as soon as practicable after he becomes or they become aware of the matter in question.".

(5) In sub-paragraph (4) for—

(*a*) "he shall be under a duty, until he is" substitute "he or they shall be under a duty until he is or they are"; and

(*b*) "appearing to him" substitute "appearing to him or them".

(6) Omit sub-paragraph (5).

(7) In sub-paragraph (6)—

(*a*) for "the chief officer" substitute "the Chairman or Commissioners";

(*b*) for "he may be directed" substitute "he or they may be directed"; and

(*c*) omit "by the police authority maintaining his force or".

11— (1) Paragraph 13 shall be modified as follows.

(2) In sub-paragraph (1) for—

(*a*) "a police authority or a chief officer" substitute "the Head of the Home Civil Service, Chairman or Commissioners", and

(*b*) "the authority or chief officer is" substitute "any of those persons is or are".

[(2A) After sub-paragraph (1) insert—

"(1A) Sub-paragraph (1) is subject to sub-paragraphs (1B) and (1C).

(1B) The obligation on the Head of the Home Civil Service under sub-paragraph (1)(*a*) or (1)(*b*) to refer a recordable conduct matter in respect of a person for whom he is the appropriate authority arises only if the Head of the Home Civil Service is satisfied that the matter is one in respect of which there is an indication that a criminal offence may have been committed by that person.

(1C) The obligation on the Chairman or the Commissioners under sub-paragraph (1)(*a*) or (1)(*b*) to refer a recordable conduct matter in respect of a person for whom he is or they are the appropriate authority arises only if he is or they are satisfied that the matter is one in respect of which there is an indication that the person may have—

(*a*) committed a criminal offence; or

(*b*) behaved in a manner which would justify the bringing of disciplinary proceedings and that such behaviour (if it had taken place) would be likely to lead to the termination of that person's office or employment.".][1]

(3) In sub-paragraph (3)—

(*a*) for "a police authority maintaining any police force" substitute "the Head of the Home Civil Service";

(*b*) in paragraph (*a*) for "chief officer of police of that force" substitute "Chairman"; and

(*c*) in paragraph (*b*) for "police authority" substitute "Head of the Home Civil Service".

(4) In sub-paragraph (5)(*b*) for "a police authority or chief officer" substitute "the Head of the Home Civil Service, Chairman or Commissioners".

(5) In sub-paragraph (6)—

(*a*) in paragraph (*a*) for "a police authority or chief officer refers" substitute "the Head of the Home Civil Service, Chairman or Commissioners refers or refer";

(*b*) in paragraph (*b*) for "that authority or chief officer does not" substitute "the Head of the Home Civil Service, Chairman or Commissioners does or do not"; and

(*c*) for "that authority or chief officer" substitute "the Head of the Home Civil Service, Chairman or Commissioners".

Amendments—[1] Sub-para (2A) inserted by the Revenue and Customs (Complaints and Misconduct) (Amendment) Regulations, SI 2006/1748 reg 5 with effect from 27 July 2006.

12— (1) Paragraph 14 shall be modified as follows.

(2) In sub-paragraph (1) for "a police authority or chief officer" substitute "the Head of the Home Civil Service, Chairman or Commissioners".

(3) In sub-paragraph (2)—

(*a*) after "recordable conduct matter" insert "referred by the Head of the Home Civil Service, Chairman or Commissioners";
(*b*) for "appropriate authority" substitute "Head of the Home Civil Service, Chairman or Commissioners";
(*c*) for "that authority" (on the first occasion those words appear) substitute "by him or them"; and
(*d*) for "that authority" (on the second occasion those words appear) substitute "he or they".

13— (1) Paragraph 14A shall be modified as follows.

(2) For sub-paragraph (1) substitute—

"(1) Where a DSI matter comes to the attention of the Commissioners, being the appropriate authority, it shall be their duty to record that matter.".

14— (1) Paragraph 14B shall be modified as follows.

(2) Omit sub-paragraph (1).

(3) In sub-paragraph (2)—

(*a*) for the words from "Where" to the end of paragraph (*b*) substitute "Where a DSI matter comes to the attention of the Commissioners";
(*b*) for "his duty" substitute "their duty"; and
(*c*) for "to him" substitute "to them".

(4) In sub-paragraph (3) for "chief officer's" substitute "Commissioners'" and for "he becomes" substitute "they become".

(5) In sub-paragraph (4) for "he shall" substitute "they shall", "he is" substitute "they are" and "to him" substitute "to them".

(6) Omit sub-paragraph (5).

(7) In sub-paragraph (6) for "chief officer" substitute "Commissioners", for "he" substitute "they" and omit "by the police authority maintaining his force or".

15— (1) Paragraph 14D shall be modified as follows.

(2) In sub-paragraph (1) for "a police authority or a chief officer" substitute "the Commissioners".

16— (1) Paragraph 15 shall be modified as follows.

(2) After sub-paragraph (4)(*b*) insert—

"(*bb*) an investigation by a police force under the supervision of the Commission;".

(3) In sub-paragraph (4)(*c*) substitute "the appropriate authority" for "that authority".

(4) After sub-paragraph (4)(*c*) insert—

"(*cc*) an investigation by a police force under the management of the Commission;".

(5) After sub-paragraph (4) insert—

"(4A) An investigation relating to any conduct of the Chairman, Deputy Chairman or other Commissioners under this paragraph may only be carried out in the form specified in sub-paragraph (4)(*bb*), (4)(*cc*) or (4)(*d*).".

17— (1) Paragraph 16 shall be modified as follows.

(2) In sub-paragraph (1) omit paragraph (*a*).

(3) Omit sub-paragraph (2).

[(4) For sub-paragraph (3) substitute—

"(3) It shall be the duty of the appropriate authority to appoint an officer to investigate the complaint or matter.".][1]

(5) Omit [sub-paragraphs (4) and (5)][1].

Amendments—[1] Sub-para (4) substituted, and words in sub-para (5) substituted by the Revenue and Customs (Complaints and Misconduct) (Amendment) Regulations, SI 2006/1748 reg 5 with effect from 27 July 2006.

18— (1) Paragraph 17 shall be modified as follows.

(2) In sub-paragraph (2) for the words from "appoint" to the end of the sub-paragraph substitute "appoint an officer to investigate the complaint or matter.".

(3) In sub-paragraph (4)(*a*) for "sub-paragraph 2(*a*) or (*b*)" substitute "sub-paragraph (2)".

(4) Omit sub-paragraphs (6) and (6A).

19 After paragraph 17 insert—

"17A— (1) This paragraph applies where the Commission determines that there should be an investigation by a police force under the supervision of the Commission.

(2) The Commission shall—

(*a*) identify the police force whose force area includes the geographical area to which the subject matter of the complaint, recordable conduct matter or DSI matter most closely relates, and
(*b*) take steps to obtain the agreement of—
(i) the chief officer of police of that force, and
(ii) the appropriate authority,

to the appointment by the Commission of that force to carry out the investigation.

(3) In the event that no agreement is reached under sub-paragraph (2) the Commission may require the chief officer of police of any police force it considers appropriate to carry out the investigation.

(4) A chief officer of police of a police force who agrees to or is required to carry out an investigation shall, if he has not already done so, appoint a person serving with the police who is a member of that force to investigate that complaint.

(5) Sub-paragraphs (3) to (5) and (7) of paragraph 17 shall apply as they apply to an investigation by the appropriate authority which the Commission has determined is one that it should supervise and the references to the appropriate authority in those sub-paragraphs shall be treated as references to the chief officer of police concerned.

(6) An appointment of a person under sub-paragraph (4) or (5) shall be notified by the chief officer of police concerned to the appropriate authority.".

20 After paragraph 18 insert—

"18A— (1) This paragraph applies where the Commission determines that there should be an investigation by a police force under the management of the Commission.

(2) The Commission shall—

(*a*) identify the police force whose force area includes the geographical area to which the subject matter of the complaint, recordable conduct matter or DSI matter most closely relates, and

(*b*) take steps to obtain the agreement of—

(i) the chief officer of police of that force, and

(ii) the appropriate authority,

to the appointment by the Commission of that force to carry out the investigation.

(3) In the event that no agreement is reached under sub-paragraph (2) the Commission may require the chief officer of police of any police force it considers appropriate to carry out the investigation.

(4) A chief officer of police of a police force who agrees to or is required to carry out an investigation shall, if he has not already done so, appoint a person serving with the police who is a member of that force to investigate that complaint or matter.

(5) Sub-paragraphs (3) to (5) of paragraph 17 shall apply as they apply to an investigation by the appropriate authority which the Commission has determined is one that it should supervise and the references to the appropriate authority in those sub-paragraphs shall be treated as references to the chief officer of police concerned.

(6) An appointment of a person under sub-paragraph (4) or (5) shall be notified by the chief officer of police concerned to the appropriate authority.

(7) The person appointed to investigate the complaint or matter shall, in relation to that investigation, be under the direction and control of the Commission.".

21 Omit paragraphs 19(3) and (3A).

22— (1) Paragraph 20 shall be modified as follows.

(2) Omit sub-paragraph (1)(*a*).

(3) In paragraph 20(3) after "Director of Public Prosecutions" insert "or, as the case may be, the Director of Revenue and Customs Prosecutions".

23 Omit paragraphs 20A to 20I.

24— (1) Paragraph 21A shall be modified as follows.

(2) In sub-paragraphs (1) and (3) for "a person serving with the police" substitute "an officer".

(3) In sub-paragraph (1) after "18" insert "or 18A".

(4) In sub-paragraph (3) for "16 or 17" substitute "16, 17 or 17A".

25 In paragraph 22(2) for "17 or 18" substitute "17, 17A, 18 or 18A".

26— (1) In paragraph 23(2)(*c*) after "Director of Public Prosecutions" insert "or the Director of Revenue and Customs Prosecutions".

(2) In paragraphs 23(3), (4) and (6)(*b*) after "Director of Public Prosecutions" insert "or, as the case may be, the Director of Revenue and Customs Prosecutions".

27 In paragraphs 24(2)(*b*), (3), (4) and (6)(*b*) after "Director of Public Prosecutions" insert "or, as the case may be, the Director of Revenue and Customs Prosecutions".

28 In paragraphs 24A(4), 24B(1) and 24C(1) for "a person serving with the police" substitute (on each occasion where the words occur) "an officer".

29 Omit paragraph 25(2A).

30 In paragraph 27(3) for "any person serving with the police" substitute "any officer".

SCHEDULE 4

Regulation 4(2)

PART 1
MODIFICATION OF THE COMPLAINTS REGULATIONS

1 Omit regulation 4.

2— (1) In regulation 6(2) for the words from "consent" to the end of the paragraph substitute—

"consent—

(i) in the case of an investigation carried out by an appointed person who is an officer, of the Director of Revenue and Customs Prosecutions, or

(ii) in any other case, of the Director of Public Prosecutions,

to the imposition thereof."

(2) In regulation 6(3) for—

(*a*) "a chief officer" substitute "the Head of the Home Civil Service, Chairman or Commissioners";

(*b*) "consulting him" substitute "consulting him or them";

(*c*) "he may make" substitute "he or they may make".

3 Omit regulations 7(2)(*b*) and 7(7)(*c*).

4— (1) In regulation 8(1) for "a police authority or chief officer" substitute "the Head of the Home Civil Service, Chairman or Commissioners".

(2) In regulation 8(2)(*c*) for "the police force or police authority which" substitute "the Head of the Home Civil Service, Chairman or Commissioners who".

(3) In regulations 8(3)(*a*) and (7) for "police authority or chief officer" substitute "Head of the Home Civil Service, Chairman or Commissioners".

(4) In regulation 8(5) for "A police authority or chief officer" substitute "The Head of the Home Civil Service, Chairman or Commissioners".

5 Omit regulation 9.

6— (1) Regulation 12 shall be modified as follows.

(2) After paragraph (1)(*b*) insert—

"(*c*) preventing the disclosure of any information held by the Revenue and Customs in connection with a function of the Revenue and Customs which—

(i) is obtained from the Head of the Home Civil Service, Chairman, Commissioners or an officer, and

(ii) relates to a person whose identity is specified in the disclosure or can be deduced from it.".

(3) After paragraph (1) insert—

"(1A) Paragraph (1)(*c*) does not apply to any information about internal administrative arrangements of Her Majesty's Revenue and Customs (whether relating to Commissioners, officers or others).".

(4) After paragraph (2) insert—

"(2A) The Commission shall consult the appropriate authority in any case under paragraph (1)(*c*) before deciding whether or not it is satisfied under paragraph (2).".

(5) After paragraph (3) insert—

"(4) In this regulation "the Revenue and Customs" means—

(*a*) the Commissioners;

(*b*) an officer;

(*c*) a person acting on behalf of the Commissioners or an officer;

(*d*) a committee established by the Commissioners;

(*e*) a member of a committee established by the Commissioners;

(*f*) the Commissioners of Inland Revenue (or any committee or staff of theirs or anyone acting on their behalf);

(*g*) the Commissioners of Customs and Excise (or any committee or staff of theirs or anyone acting on their behalf), and

(*h*) a person specified in section 6(2) or 7(3) of the Commissioners for Revenue and Customs Act 2005.".

7— (1) In regulation 18(1) for "17 or 18" substitute "17, 17A, 18 or 18A".

(2) Omit regulations 18(1)(*d*), (2) and (3).

8 In regulation 21 for "person serving with the police" substitute "Commissioner or an officer".

9 In regulation 24—

(*a*) for "Every police authority and chief officer" substitute "The Head of the Home Civil Service, Chairman and Commissioners", and

(*b*) in paragraphs (*a*) and (*b*) for "it or him" substitute "him or them".

10— (1) In regulation 25(1) for "a police authority or chief officer" substitute "the Head of the Home Civil Service, Chairman or Commissioners".

(2) In regulation 25(3) for "(*a*) and (*b*)" substitute "(*a*), (*b*) and (*c*)".

11— (1) Regulation 26 shall be modified as follows.

(2) In paragraph (1) for—

(*a*) "chief officer" substitute "the Head of the Home Civil Service, Chairman or Commissioners";
(*b*) "on him" substitute "on him or them"; and
(*c*) "an officer" substitute "a person".

(3) In paragraph (2) for sub-paragraphs (*a*) to (*c*) substitute—

"(*a*) in the case of the Head of the Home Civil Service, to a member of the Senior Civil Service;
(*b*) in the case of the Chairman, to a member of the Senior Civil Service employed in the service of the Commissioners;
(*c*) in the case of the Commissioners, to an officer.".

(4) Omit paragraph (3).

(5) For paragraph (4) substitute—

"(4) The Head of the Home Civil Service, Chairman or Commissioners shall not, in any particular case, delegate any power or duty under paragraph (1) to a person who has acted as investigating officer in that case.".

(6) In paragraph (5) for "a chief constable" substitute "the Head of the Home Civil Service, Chairman or Commissioners".

12 Omit regulations 28, 29 and 30.

PART 2
MODIFICATION OF THE STAFF CONDUCT REGULATIONS

1 In regulation 2(3)(*a*)(i) for "person serving with the police" substitute "Commissioner or officer".

2007/1417
Value Added Tax (Section 55A) (Specified Goods and Excepted Supplies) Order 2007

Made by the Treasury under VATA 1994 s 55A(9), (10), (11) and (14)

Made . . . . *10 May 2007*
Laid before the House of Commons . . . . *10 May 2007*
Coming into force . . . . *1 June 2007*

Citation and commencement

1 This Order may be cited as the Value Added Tax (Section 55A) (Specified Goods and Excepted Supplies) Order 2007 and comes into force on 1st June 2007.

Interpretation

2 In this Order—

"public electronic communications service" has the same meaning as in section 151 of the Communications Act 2003;
"specified goods" means goods of a description specified in article 3;
"the Act" means the Value Added Tax Act 1994.

Specified Goods

3 For the purposes of section 55A of the Act (customers to account for tax on supplies of goods of a kind used in missing trader intra-community fraud) the goods of a description specified below are goods to which that section applies—

(*a*) mobile telephones, whether or not they have any function in addition to the transmitting and receiving of spoken messages;
(*b*) integrated circuit devices, such as central processing units and microprocessor units, in a state prior to integration into end user products.

Excepted supplies

4 For the purposes of section 55A of the Act, a supply of a description specified below is an excepted supply—

(*a*) a supply of specified goods where the value of the supply is less than £5000;
(*b*) a supply of specified goods where the supply is of a description specified in an order made under section 50A of the Act (margin schemes) and, in accordance with such an order, the supplier opts to account for the VAT chargeable on the supply on the profit margin on the supply instead of by reference to its value;

(*c*) a supply of a mobile telephone where, at the time a person enters into the agreement to purchase the telephone—

(i) he enters into an agreement (including the renewal or extension of an existing agreement) with a provider of a public electronic communications service for the supply, in relation to that telephone, of such a service, and

(ii) that agreement is not one that requires periodical pre-payments in order to use the service ("Pay as You Go");

(*d*) a transfer or disposal of specified goods for no consideration that is treated as a supply of goods by virtue of paragraph 5(1) of Schedule 4 to the Act.

5 Article 4(*a*) does not apply to a supply of specified goods where—

(*a*) the supply is particularised on the same VAT invoice as a supply, or supplies, of other specified goods, and

(*b*) the total value of the supplies equals or exceeds £5000.

2007/1509
Control of Cash (Penalties) Regulations 2007

Made by the Treasury under ECA 1972 s 2(2), being designated for the purposes of that subsection in relation to measures relating to preventing the use of the financial system for the purpose of money laundering and measures relating to the movement of capital and to payments between Member States and between Member States and countries which are not Member States:

Made . . . . *22 May 2007*
Laid before Parliament . . . . *23 May 2007*
Coming into force . . . . *15 June 2007*

Citation and commencement

1 These Regulations may be cited as the Control of Cash (Penalties) Regulations 2007 and come into force on 15th June 2007.

Interpretation

2 In these Regulations—

"Community Regulation" means European Parliament and Council Regulation (EC) No 1889/2005 on controls of cash entering or leaving the Community

"The Commissioners" means the Commissioners for Her Majesty's Revenue and Customs.

Power to impose penalties

3— (1) The Commissioners may impose a penalty of such amount as they consider appropriate, not exceeding £5000, on a person failing to comply with article 3 of the Community Regulation (obligation to declare cash of a value of 10,000 euros or more).

(2) Where the Commissioners decide to impose a penalty under this regulation, they must forthwith inform the person, in writing, of—

(*a*) their decision to impose the penalty and its amount;

(*b*) their reasons for imposing the penalty;

(*c*) the review procedure; and

(*d*) the right to appeal to a tribunal.

(3) Where a person is liable to a penalty under this regulation, the Commissioners may reduce the penalty to such amount (including nil) as they think proper.

Review procedure

4— (1) Any person who is the subject of a decision to impose a penalty under regulation 3 may by notice in writing to the Commissioners require them to review that decision.

(2) The Commissioners need not review any decision unless the notice requiring the review is given before the end of the period of 45 days beginning with the date on which written notification of the decision was first given to the person requiring the review.

(3) A person may give a notice under this regulation to require a decision to be reviewed for a second or subsequent time only if—

(*a*) the grounds on which he requires the further review are that the Commissioners did not, on any previous review, have the opportunity to consider certain facts or other matters; and

(*b*) he does not, on the further review, require the Commissioners to consider any facts or matters which were considered on a previous review except insofar as they are relevant to any issue to which the facts or matters not previously considered relate.

(4) Where the Commissioners are required under this regulation to review any decision they must either

(*a*) confirm the decision; or

(*b*) withdraw or vary the decision and take such further steps (if any) in consequence of the withdrawal or variation as they consider appropriate.

(5) Where the Commissioners do not, within 45 days beginning with the date on which the review was required by a person, give notice to that person of their determination of the review, they are to be assumed for the purposes of these Regulations to have confirmed the decision.

Appeals to a VAT and duties tribunal

5 An appeal lies to a VAT and duties tribunal with respect to a decision of the Commissioners on a review under regulation 4.

6 On an appeal under regulation 5, the tribunal has the power to—

(*a*) quash or vary any decision of the Commissioners, including the power to reduce any penalty to such amount (including nil) as it thinks proper; and

(*b*) substitute its own decision for any decision quashed on appeal.

7 An appeal shall not be entertained unless—

(*a*) the amount which the Commissioners have imposed by way of a penalty under regulation 2 has been paid to them; or

(*b*) on being satisfied that the appellant would otherwise suffer hardship the Commissioners agree or the tribunal decides that the appeal should be entertained notwithstanding that the amount has not been paid.

Retention of cash detained

8 Where the Commissioners have imposed a penalty under regulation 3 they may deduct from any cash detained pursuant to article 4(2) of the Community Regulation the amount of the penalty, and upon expiry of the period for appealing, or where an appeal has been made upon determination of the appeal, the amount payable shall be forfeit to them.

2007/2126

International Mutual Administrative Assistance in Tax Matters Order 2007

A draft of this Order was laid before the House of Commons in accordance with FA 2006 s 173(7) and approved by a resolution of that House. Accordingly, Her Majesty, in exercise of the powers conferred upon Her by FA 2006 s 173(1)–(3), by and with the advice of Her Privy Council, orders as follows—

Made . . . . 25 July 2007

Commentary—*Simon's Taxes* **A2.304, E6.455**.

Citation

1 This Order may be cited as the International Mutual Administrative Assistance in Tax Matters Order 2007.

Mutual administrative assistance arrangements to have effect

2 It is declared that—

(*a*) arrangements relating to international tax enforcement that fall within the joint Council of Europe/Organisation for Economic Co-operation and Development Convention on Mutual Administrative Assistance in Tax Matters, signed on behalf of the United Kingdom on 24 May 2007, have been made in relation to the other signatory territories, and

(*b*) it is expedient that those arrangements have effect.

2007/2709

Tribunals, Courts and Enforcement Act 2007 (Commencement No 1) Order 2007

Made by the Lord Chancellor under TCEA 2007 s 148(5)

Made . . . . 13 September 2007

1 Citation and interpretation

(1) This Order may be cited as the Tribunals, Courts and Enforcement Act 2007 (Commencement No 1) Order 2007.

(2) In this Order, "the Act" means the Tribunals, Courts and Enforcement Act 2007.

2 Provisions coming into force on 19th September 2007

The following provisions of the Act come into force on 19th September 2007—

(*a*) sections 1, 2, 7(1) and (9), 9(3), 10(3), 11(5)(*f*) and (6) to (8), 13(6), (8)(*f*), (9), (10), (14) and (15), 18(10) and (11), 20(3), (6) and (7), 21(6), 22, 27(5) and (6), 30 to 42, 45(3), 49, 54, 58, 59, 61 and 144(1), (5) and (7);

(*b*) section 46 to the extent that it relates to Schedule 5;

(*c*) section 48(1) to the extent that it relates to the following paragraphs of Schedule 8—

(i) paragraphs 31(1) to (3), 62, 63 and 65(1) and (2); and
(ii) paragraph 65(3) to the extent that it relates to the Senior President of Tribunals;

(*d*) section 48(2) to the extent that it relates to paragraphs 1, 2 and 12(2) of Schedule 9;
(*e*) sections 50(1) to (5) and (7), 51 and 52 for the purposes of paragraph 3 of Schedule 1;
(*f*) section 144(11) to the extent that it relates to Part 1 and section 51;
(*g*) in Schedule 1, paragraphs 1 to 11;
(*h*) in Schedule 4, paragraph 15;
(*i*) Schedule 5;
(*j*) Schedule 6; and
(*k*) in Schedule 7, paragraphs 25(2) to (7) and 26 to 28.

3 Provisions coming into force on 1st November 2007
The following provisions of the Act come into force on 1st November 2007—

(*a*) sections 44, 45(1) and (2) and 146;
(*b*) section 48(1) to the extent that it relates to the following paragraphs of Schedule 8—

(i) paragraphs 2, 3, 8 to 12, 14, 15, 17, 19 to 23, 30(*a*) to (*c*), 32, 33(1) and (2), 49 to 52 and 56 to 61;
(ii) paragraphs 4, 5, 7 and 53 to the extent that they relate to the Administrative Justice and Tribunals Council and to the Scottish Committee of the Administrative Justice and Tribunals Council; and
(iii) paragraph 18 to the extent that it relates to the Administrative Justice and Tribunals Council;

(*c*) in Schedule 7—

(i) paragraphs 1 to 6, 10(1)(*a*) and (*b*), (2)(*a*) and (*b*), (3)(*a*) and (*b*) and (4), 12, 13, 14(1), (2), (3)(*a*) and (4), 15 to 18, 20, 21(1), (2), (4) and (5), 22(1)(*a*) and (*b*) and (2), 23 and 25(1);
(ii) paragraphs 11 and 22(3) to the extent that they relate to the Administrative Justice and Tribunals Council and to the Scottish Committee of the Administrative Justice and Tribunals Council; and
(iii) paragraph 21(6) to the extent that it relates to reports made by the Administrative Justice and Tribunals Council; and

(*d*) in Part 1 of Schedule 23, the entries relating to—

(i) the House of Commons Disqualification Act 1975;
(ii) the Northern Ireland Assembly Disqualification Act 1975;
(iii) the Race Relations Act 1976;
(iv) the Estate Agents Act 1979;
(v) sections 1, 2, 3, 4 and 13(5)(*c*) of the Tribunals and Inquiries Act 1992;
(vi) the Scotland Act 1998 (Cross-Border Public Authorities) (Adaptation of Functions etc) Order 1999 to the extent that Schedule 9 applies to sections 2 and 4 of the Tribunals and Inquiries Act 1992;
(vii) the Freedom of Information Act 2000; and
(viii) the Scottish Public Services Ombudsman Act 2002 (Consequential Provisions and Modifications) Order 2004.

4 Provisions coming into force on 1st December 2007
Section 48(1) of the Act comes into force on 1st December 2007 to the extent that it relates to paragraphs 35 to 39 of Schedule 8.

5 Provisions coming into force on 1st April 2008
The following provisions of the Act come into force on 1st April 2008—

(*a*) sections 139 and 140; and
(*b*) Schedule 22.

6 Provisions coming into force on 1st June 2008
The following provisions of the Act come into force on 1st June 2008—

(*a*) all paragraphs of Schedule 7, except paragraph 24, to the extent that they are not already in force; and
(*b*) section 48(1) to the extent that it relates to the following paragraphs of Schedule 8—

(i) paragraphs 4 and 5 to the extent that they relate to the Welsh Committee of the Administrative Justice and Tribunals Council;
(ii) paragraphs 7, 18 and 53, to the extent that they are not already in force; and
(iii) paragraph 30(*d*).

2007/3298

Transfer of Funds (Information on the Payer) Regulations 2007

Made . . . . *22 November 2007*
Laid before Parliament . . . . *23 November 2007*
Coming into force . . . . *15 December 2007*

The Treasury are a government department designated for the purposes of section 2(2) of the European Communities Act 1972 in relation to the prevention of money laundering and terrorist financing;

The Treasury, in exercise of the powers conferred on them by section 2(2) of the European Communities Act 1972 and by sections 168(4)(*b*), 402(1)(*b*), 417(1) and 428(3) of the Financial Services and Markets Act 2000, make the following Regulations:

PART 1
GENERAL

1 Citation, commencement etc

(1) These Regulations may be cited as the Transfer of Funds (Information on the Payer) Regulations 2007 and come into force on 15th December 2007.

(2) These Regulations are prescribed for the purposes of sections 168(4)(*b*) (appointment of persons to carry out investigations in particular cases) and 402(1)(*b*) (power of the Authority to institute proceedings for certain other offences) of the 2000 Act.

2 Interpretation

(1) In these Regulations—

"the 2000 Act" means the Financial Services and Markets Act 2000;

"authorised person" means a person who is authorised for the purposes of the 2000 Act;

"the Authority" means the Financial Services Authority;

"the Commissioners" means the Commissioners for Her Majesty's Revenue and Customs;

"money laundering" means an act which falls within section 340(11) of the Proceeds of Crime Act 2002;

"notice" means a notice in writing;

"the payments regulation" means Regulation 1781/2006/EC of the European Parliament and of the Council of 15th November 2006 on information on the payer accompanying transfers of funds;

"supervisory authority" in relation to any payment service provider means the supervisory authority specified for such a payment service provider by regulation 3;

"terrorist financing" means an offence under—

(*a*) section 15 (fund-raising), 16 (use and possession), 17 (funding arrangements), 18 (money laundering) or 63 (terrorist finance: jurisdiction) of the Terrorism Act 2000;

(*b*) paragraph 7(2) or (3) of Schedule 3 to the Anti-Terrorism, Crime and Security Act 2001 (freezing orders);

(*c*) article 7, 8 or 10 of the Terrorism (United Nations Measures) Order 2006; or

(*d*) article 7, 8 or 10 of the Al-Qaida and Taliban (United Nations Measures) Order 2006;

(2) Unless otherwise defined, expressions used in these Regulations and the payments regulation have the same meaning as in the payments regulation.

(3) References in these Regulations to numbered Articles are references to Articles of the payments regulation.

PART 2
SUPERVISION

3 Supervisory authorities

(1) The Authority is the supervisory authority for payment service providers who are authorised persons.

(2) The Commissioners are the supervisory authority for payment service providers who are not authorised persons.

4 Duties of supervisory authorities

(1) A supervisory authority must effectively monitor the payment service providers for whom it is the supervisory authority and take necessary measures for the purpose of securing compliance by such payment service providers with the requirements of the payments regulation.

(2) A supervisory authority which, in the course of carrying out any of its functions under these Regulations, knows or suspects that a payment service provider is or has engaged in money laundering or terrorist financing must promptly inform the Serious Organised Crime Agency.

(3) A disclosure made under paragraph (2) is not to be taken to breach any restriction, however imposed, on the disclosure of information.

(4) The functions of the Authority under these Regulations shall be treated for the purposes of Parts 1, 2 and 4 of Schedule 1 to the 2000 Act (the Financial Services Authority) as functions conferred on the Authority under that Act.

5 Costs of supervision

(1) The Authority and the Commissioners may impose charges on payment service providers supervised by them.

(2) Charges levied under paragraph (1) must not exceed such amount as the Authority or the Commissioners (as the case may be) consider will enable them to meet any expenses reasonably incurred by them in carrying out their functions under these Regulations or for any incidental purpose.

(3) Without prejudice to the generality of paragraph (2), a charge may be levied in respect of each of the premises at which a payment service provider carries on (or proposes to carry on) business.

(4) The Authority must apply amounts paid to it by way of penalties imposed under regulation 11 towards expenses incurred in carrying out its functions under these Regulations or for any incidental purpose.

PART 3
ENFORCEMENT

Powers of Supervisory Authorities

6 Interpretation

In this Part—

"officer", except in regulations 10(3) and 16, means—

(*a*) an officer of the Authority, including a member of the Authority's staff or an agent of the Authority; or

(*b*) an officer of Revenue and Customs;

"recorded information" includes information recorded in any form and any document of any nature.

7 Power to require information from, and attendance of, relevant and connected persons

(1) An officer may, by notice to a payment service provider or to a person connected with a payment service provider, require the payment service provider or the connected person, as the case may be—

(*a*) to provide such information as may be specified in the notice;

(*b*) to produce such recorded information as may be so specified; or

(*c*) to attend before an officer at a time and place specified in the notice and answer questions.

(2) For the purposes of paragraph (1), a person is connected with a payment service provider if he is, or has at any time been, in relation to the payment service provider, a person listed in Schedule 1 to these Regulations.

(3) An officer may exercise powers under this regulation only if the information sought to be obtained as a result is reasonably required in connection with the exercise by the supervisory authority for which he acts of its functions under these Regulations.

(4) Where an officer requires information to be provided or produced pursuant to paragraph (1)(*a*) or (*b*)—

(*a*) the notice must set out the reasons why the officer requires the information to be provided or produced; and

(*b*) such information must be provided or produced—

(i) before the end of such reasonable period as may be specified in the notice; and

(ii) at such place as may be so specified.

(5) In relation to information recorded otherwise than in legible form, the power to require production of it includes a power to require the production of a copy of it in legible form or in a form from which it can readily be produced in visible and legible form.

(6) The production of a document does not affect any lien which a person has on the document.

(7) A person may not be required under this regulation to provide or produce information or to answer questions which that person would be entitled to refuse to provide, produce or answer on grounds of legal professional privilege in proceedings in the High Court, except that a lawyer may be required to provide the name and address of his client.

(8) Subject to paragraphs (9) and (10), a statement made by a person in compliance with a requirement imposed on that person under paragraph (1)(*c*) is admissible in evidence in any proceedings, so long as it also complies with any requirements governing the admissibility of evidence in the circumstances in question.

(9) In criminal proceedings in which a person is charged with an offence to which this paragraph applies—

(*a*) no evidence relating to the statement may be adduced; and
(*b*) no question relating to it may be asked,

by or on behalf of the prosecution unless evidence relating to it is adduced, or a question relating to it is asked, in the proceedings by or on behalf of that person.

(10) Paragraph (9) applies to any offence other than one under—

(*a*) section 5 of the Perjury Act 1911 (false statements without oath);
(*b*) section 44(2) of the Criminal Law (Consolidation) (Scotland) Act 1995 (false statements and declarations); or
(*c*) Article 10 of the Perjury (Northern Ireland) Order 1979 (false unsworn statements).

(11) In the application of this regulation to Scotland, the reference in paragraph (7) to—

(*a*) proceedings in the High Court is to be read as a reference to proceedings in the Court of Session; and
(*b*) an entitlement on grounds of legal professional privilege is to be read as a reference to an entitlement on the grounds of confidentiality of communications—

(i) between a professional legal adviser and his client; or
(ii) made in connection with or in contemplation of legal proceedings and for the purposes of those proceedings.

8 Entry, inspection without a warrant etc

(1) Where an officer has reasonable cause to believe that any premises are being used by a payment service provider in connection with the payment service provider's business or professional activities, he may on producing evidence of his authority at any reasonable time—

(*a*) enter the premises;
(*b*) inspect the premises;
(*c*) observe the carrying on of business or professional activities by the payment service provider;
(*d*) inspect any recorded information found on the premises;
(*e*) require any person on the premises to provide an explanation of any recorded information or to state where it may be found;
(*f*) inspect any cash found on the premises.

(2) An officer may take copies of, or make extracts from, any recorded information found under paragraph (1).

(3) Paragraphs (1)(*d*) and (*e*) and (2) do not apply to recorded information which the payment service provider would be entitled to refuse to disclose on grounds of legal professional privilege in proceedings in the High Court, except that a lawyer may be required to provide the name and address of his client and, for this purpose, regulation 7(11) applies to this paragraph as it applies to regulation 7(7).

(4) An officer may exercise powers under this regulation only if the information sought to be obtained as a result is reasonably required in connection with the exercise by the supervisory authority for which he acts of its functions under these Regulations.

(5) In this regulation, "premises" means any premises other than premises used only as a dwelling.

9 Entry to premises under warrant

(1) A justice may issue a warrant under this paragraph if satisfied on information on oath given by an officer that there are reasonable grounds for believing that the first, second or third set of conditions is satisfied.

(2) The first set of conditions is—

(*a*) that there is on the premises specified in the warrant recorded information in relation to which a requirement could be imposed under regulation 7(1)(*b*); and
(*b*) that if such a requirement were to be imposed—

(i) it would not be complied with; or
(ii) the recorded information to which it relates would be removed, tampered with or destroyed.

(3) The second set of conditions is—

(*a*) that a person on whom a requirement has been imposed under regulation 7(1)(*b*) has failed (wholly or in part) to comply with it; and
(*b*) that there is on the premises specified in the warrant recorded information which has been required to be produced.

(4) The third set of conditions is—

(*a*) that an officer has been obstructed in the exercise of a power under regulation 8; and
(*b*) that there is on the premises specified in the warrant recorded information or cash which could be inspected under regulation 8(1)(*d*) or (*f*).

(5) A justice may issue a warrant under this paragraph if satisfied on information on oath given by an officer that there are reasonable grounds for suspecting that—

(*a*) an offence under these Regulations has been, is being or is about to be committed by a payment service provider; and
(*b*) there is on the premises specified in the warrant recorded information relevant to whether that offence has been, or is being or is about to be committed.

(6) A warrant issued under this regulation shall authorise an officer—

(*a*) to enter the premises specified in the warrant;
(*b*) to search the premises and take possession of any recorded information or anything appearing to be recorded information specified in the warrant or to take, in relation to any such recorded information, any other steps which may appear to be necessary for preserving it or preventing interference with it;
(*c*) to take copies of, or extracts from, any recorded information specified in the warrant;
(*d*) to require any person on the premises to provide an explanation of any recorded information appearing to be of the kind specified in the warrant or to state where it may be found;
(*e*) to use such force as may reasonably be necessary.

(7) Where a warrant is issued by a justice under paragraph (1) or (5) on the basis of information on oath given by an officer of the Authority, for "an officer" in paragraph (6) substitute "a constable".

(8) In paragraphs (1), (5) and (7), "justice" means—

(*a*) in relation to England and Wales, a justice of the peace;
(*b*) in relation to Scotland, a justice within the meaning of section 307 of the Criminal Procedure (Scotland) Act 1995 (interpretation);
(*c*) in relation to Northern Ireland, a lay magistrate.

(9) In the application of this regulation to Scotland, the references in paragraphs (1), (5) and (7) to information on oath are to be read as references to evidence on oath.

10 Failure to comply with information requirement

(1) If, on an application made by a supervisory authority it appears to the court that a person (the "information defaulter") has failed to do something that he was required to do under regulation 7(1), the court may make an order under this regulation.

(2) An order under this regulation may require the information defaulter—

(*a*) to do the thing that he failed to do within such period as may be specified in the order;
(*b*) otherwise to take such steps to remedy the consequences of the failure as may be so specified.

(3) If the information defaulter is a body corporate, a partnership or an unincorporated body of persons which is not a partnership, the order may require any officer of the body corporate, partnership or body, who is (wholly or partly) responsible for the failure to meet such costs of the application as are specified in the order.

(4) In this regulation, "court" means—

(*a*) in England and Wales and Northern Ireland, the High Court or the county court;
(*b*) in Scotland, the Court of Session or the sheriff court.

Civil Penalties, Review and Appeals

11 Power to impose civil penalties

(1) A supervisory authority may impose a penalty of such amount as it considers appropriate on a payment service provider in respect of any transfer of funds to which the payments regulation applies—

(*a*) in the case of the payment service provider of the payer, if he fails to comply with any requirement in—

(i) Article 5(1) read with Article 6(1) (information accompanying transfers of funds within the EEA);
(ii) Article 5(2) read with Article 5(3) or (4) (whichever is relevant) (verification of information);
(iii) Article 5(5) (record keeping);
(iv) Article 6(2) (information to be provided following request);
(v) Article 7(1) read with Article 7(2) (information accompanying transfers of funds from the EEA to outside the EEA);

(*b*) in the case of the payment service provider of the payee, if he fails to comply with any requirement in Article 8 (detection of missing information), 9(1) (transfers of funds with missing or incomplete information), 9(2) sub-paragraph 2 (reporting) or 11 (record keeping);
(*c*) in the case of the intermediary payment service provider, if he fails to comply with any requirement in Article 12 (keeping information on the payer with the transfer) or 13(3), (4) or (5) (use of a payment system with technical limitations);

and, for this purpose, "appropriate" means effective, proportionate and dissuasive.

(2) The supervisory authority must not impose a penalty on a person under paragraph (1) where there are reasonable grounds for it to be satisfied that the person took all reasonable steps and exercised all due diligence to ensure that the requirement would be complied with.

(3) In deciding whether a person has failed to comply with any requirement of the payments regulation, the supervisory authority must consider whether the person followed any relevant guidance which was at the time—

(*a*) issued by a supervisory authority or any other appropriate body;
(*b*) approved by the Treasury; and
(*c*) published in a manner approved by the Treasury as suitable in their opinion to bring the guidance to the attention of persons likely to be affected by it.

(4) In paragraph (3), an "appropriate body" means any body which regulates or is representative of any trade, profession, business or employment carried on by the payment service provider.

(5) Where the Commissioners decide to impose a penalty under this regulation, they must give the payment service provider notice of—

(*a*) their decision to impose the penalty and its amount;
(*b*) the reasons for imposing the penalty;
(*c*) the right to a review under regulation 12; and
(*d*) the right to appeal under regulation 13(1)(*b*).

(6) Where the Authority proposes to impose a penalty under this regulation, it must give the payment service provider notice of—

(*a*) its proposal to impose the penalty and the proposed amount;
(*b*) the reasons for imposing the penalty; and
(*c*) the right to make representations to it within a specified period (which may not be less than 28 days).

(7) The Authority must then decide, within a reasonable period, whether to impose a penalty under this regulation and it must give the payment service provider notice of—

(*a*) its decision not to impose a penalty; or
(*b*) the following matters—
 (i) its decision to impose a penalty and the amount;
 (ii) the reasons for its decision; and
 (iii) the right to appeal under regulation 13(1)(*a*).

(8) A penalty imposed under this regulation is payable to the supervisory authority which imposes it.

12 Review procedure

(1) Any payment service provider who is the subject of a decision by the Commissioners to impose a penalty under regulation 11 may by notice to the Commissioners require them to review that decision.

(2) The Commissioners need not review any decision unless the notice requiring the review is given within 45 days beginning with the date on which they first gave notice of the decision to the payment service provider requiring the review.

(3) Where the Commissioners are required under this regulation to review any decision they must either—

(*a*) confirm the decision; or
(*b*) withdraw or vary the decision and take such further steps (if any) in consequence of the withdrawal or variation as they consider appropriate.

(4) Where the Commissioners do not, within 45 days beginning with the date on which the review was required by a payment service provider, give notice to that person of their determination of the review, they are to be taken for the purposes of these Regulations to have confirmed the decision.

13 Appeals

(1) A payment service provider may appeal from a decision by—

(*a*) the Authority under regulation 11(7); and
(*b*) the Commissioners on a review under regulation 12.

(2) An appeal from a decision by—

(*a*) the Authority is to the Financial Services and Markets Tribunal; and
(*b*) the Commissioners is to a VAT and duties tribunal.

(3) The provisions of Part 9 of the 2000 Act (hearings and appeals), subject to the modifications set out in paragraph 1 of Schedule 2, apply in respect of appeals to the Financial Services and Markets Tribunal made under this regulation as they apply in respect of references made to that Tribunal under that Act.

(4) The provisions of Part 5 of the Value Added Tax Act 1994 (appeals), subject to the modifications set out in paragraph 2 of Schedule 2, apply in respect of appeals to a VAT and duties tribunal made under this regulation as they apply in respect of appeals made to such a tribunal under section 83 (appeals) of that Act.

(5) A VAT and duties tribunal hearing an appeal under paragraph (2) has the power to—

(*a*) quash or vary any decision of the supervisory authority, including the power to reduce any penalty to such amount (including nil) as they think proper; and

(*b*) substitute their own decision for any decision quashed on appeal.

Criminal Offences

14 Offences

(1) A payment service provider is guilty of an offence in respect of any transfer of funds to which the payments regulation applies—

(*a*) in the case of the payment service provider of the payer, if he fails to comply with any requirement in—

(i) Article 5(1) read with Article 6(1) (information accompanying transfers of funds within the EEA);

(ii) Article 5(2) read with Article 5(3) or (4) (whichever is relevant) (verification of information);

(iii) Article 5(5) (record keeping);

(iv) Article 6(2) (information to be provided following request);

(v) Article 7(1) read with Article 7(2) (information accompanying transfers of funds from the EEA to outside the EEA);

(*b*) in the case of the payment service provider of the payee, if he fails to comply with any requirement in Article 8 (detection of missing information), 9(1) or the third paragraph of Article 9 (transfers of funds with missing or incomplete information) or Article 11 (record keeping);

(*c*) in the case of the intermediary payment service provider, if he fails to comply with any requirement in Article 12 (keeping information on the payer with the transfer) or 13(3), (4) or (5) (use of a payment system with technical limitations).

(2) A payment service provider who is guilty of an offence under paragraph (1) is liable—

(*a*) on summary conviction, to a fine not exceeding the statutory maximum;

(*b*) on conviction on indictment, to imprisonment for a term not exceeding two years, to a fine or to both.

(3) In deciding whether a person has committed an offence under paragraph (1), the court must consider whether the person followed any relevant guidance which was at the time—

(*a*) issued by a supervisory authority or any other appropriate body;

(*b*) approved by the Treasury; and

(*c*) published in a manner approved by the Treasury as suitable in their opinion to bring the guidance to the attention of persons likely to be affected by it.

(4) In paragraph (3), an "appropriate body" means any body which regulates or is representative of any trade, profession, business or employment carried on by the alleged offender.

(5) A person is not guilty of an offence under this regulation if he took all reasonable steps and exercised all due diligence to avoid committing the offence.

(6) Where a person is convicted of an offence under this regulation, he shall not also be liable to a penalty under regulation 11.

15 Prosecution of offences

(1) Proceedings for an offence under regulation 14 may be instituted by—

(*a*) the Director of Revenue and Customs Prosecutions or by order of the Commissioners;

(*b*) the Director of Public Prosecutions; or

(*c*) the Director of Public Prosecutions for Northern Ireland.

(2) Proceedings for an offence under regulation 14 may be instituted only against a payment service provider or, where the payment service provider is a body corporate, a partnership or an unincorporated association, against any person who is liable to be proceeded against under regulation 16.

(3) Where proceedings under paragraph (1) are instituted by order of the Commissioners, the proceedings must be brought in the name of an officer of Revenue and Customs.

(4) Where the Commissioners investigate, or propose to investigate, any matter with a view to determining—

(*a*) whether there are grounds for believing that an offence under regulation 14 has been committed by any person; or

(*b*) whether a person should be prosecuted for such an offence,

that matter is to be treated as an assigned matter within the meaning of section 1(1) of the Customs and Excise Management Act 1979.

(5) Paragraphs (1) and (3) do not extend to Scotland and, in its application to the Commissioners acting in Scotland, paragraph (4)(*b*) shall be read as referring to the Commissioners determining whether to refer the matter to the Crown Office and Procurator Fiscal Service with a view to the Procurator Fiscal determining whether a person should be prosecuted for such an offence.

16 Offences by bodies corporate etc

(1) If an offence under regulation 14 committed by a body corporate is shown—

(*a*) to have been committed with the consent or the connivance of an officer of the body corporate; or

(*b*) to be attributable to any neglect on his part,

the officer as well as the body corporate is guilty of an offence and liable to be proceeded against and punished accordingly.

(2) If an offence under regulation 14 committed by a partnership is shown—

(*a*) to have been committed with the consent or the connivance of a partner; or

(*b*) to be attributable to any neglect on his part,

the partner as well as the partnership is guilty of an offence and liable to be proceeded against and punished accordingly.

(3) If an offence under regulation 14 committed by an unincorporated association (other than a partnership) is shown—

(*a*) to have been committed with the consent or the connivance of an officer of the association; or

(*b*) to be attributable to any neglect on his part,

the officer as well as the association is guilty of an offence and liable to be proceeded against and punished accordingly.

(4) If the affairs of a body corporate are managed by its members, paragraph (1) applies in relation to the acts and defaults of a member in connection with his functions of management as if he were a director of the body.

(5) Proceedings for an offence alleged to have been committed by a partnership or an unincorporated association must be brought in the name of the partnership or association (and not in that of its members).

(6) A fine imposed on the partnership or association on its conviction of an offence is to be paid out of the funds of the partnership or association.

(7) Rules of court relating to the service of documents are to have effect as if the partnership or association were a body corporate.

(8) In proceedings for an offence brought against the partnership or association—

(*a*) section 33 of the Criminal Justice Act 1925 (procedure on charge of offence against corporation) and Schedule 3 to the Magistrates' Courts Act 1980 (corporations) apply as they do in relation to a body corporate;

(*b*) section 70 of the Criminal Procedure (Scotland) Act 1995 (proceedings against bodies corporate) applies as it does in relation to a body corporate;

(*c*) section 18 of the Criminal Justice (Northern Ireland) Act 1945 (procedure on charge) and Schedule 4 to the Magistrates' Courts (Northern Ireland) Order 1981 (corporations) apply as they do in relation to a body corporate.

(9) In this regulation—

"officer"—

(*a*) in relation to a body corporate, means a director, manager, secretary, chief executive, member of the committee of management, or a person purporting to act in such a capacity; and

(*b*) in relation to an unincorporated association, means any officer of the association or any member of its governing body, or a person purporting to act in such capacity; and

"partner" includes a person purporting to act as a partner.

PART 4
MISCELLANEOUS

17 Recovery of charges and penalties through the court

Any charge or penalty imposed on a payment service provider by a supervisory authority under regulation 5(1) or 11(1) is a debt due from that person to the authority, and is recoverable accordingly.

18 Transfers between the United Kingdom and the Channel Islands and the Isle of Man

In determining whether a person has failed to comply with any requirement in the payments regulation, any transfer of funds between the United Kingdom and—

(*a*) the Channel Islands; or

(*b*) the Isle of Man,

shall be treated as a transfer of funds within the United Kingdom.

SCHEDULE 1

CONNECTED PERSONS

Regulation 7(2)

Corporate Bodies

1 If the payment service provider is a body corporate ("BC"), a person who is or has been—

(*a*) an officer or manager of BC or of a parent undertaking of BC;
(*b*) an employee of BC;
(*c*) an agent of BC or of a parent undertaking of BC

Partnerships

2 If the payment service provider is a partnership, a person who is or has been a member, manager, employee or agent of the partnership.

Unincorporated Associations

3 If the payment service provider is an unincorporated association of persons which is not a partnership, a person who is or has been an officer, manager, employee or agent of the association.

Individuals

4 If the payment service provider is an individual, a person who is or has been an employee or agent of that individual.

SCHEDULE 2

MODIFICATIONS IN RELATION TO APPEALS

Regulation 13(3) and (4)

THE VALUE ADDED TAX ACT 1994

2 Part 5 of the Value Added Tax Act 1994 (appeals) is modified as follows—

(*a*) omit section 84; and
(*b*) in section 87, in paragraph (*a*) of each of subsections (1), (2) and (3), omit ", or is recoverable as, VAT".

Note—Provisions beyond the scope of this publication have not been reproduced.

2008/568
Finance Act 2007, Schedule 24 (Commencement and Transitional Provisions) Order 2008

Made by the Treasury under FA 2007 s 97

Made . . . . *3 March 2008*

1 Citation and interpretation

(1) This Order may be cited as the Finance Act 2007, Schedule 24 (Commencement and Transitional Provisions) Order 2008.

(2) In this Order "Schedule 24" means Schedule 24 to the Finance Act 2007 and a reference to a paragraph (without more) is a reference to that paragraph of Schedule 24.

(3) In this Order—

"HMRC" means Her Majesty's Revenue and Customs;
"relevant documents" means documents given to HMRC of a kind listed in the Table in paragraph 1;
"relevant tax" means any tax mentioned in the Table in paragraph 1; and
"tax period" has the meaning given in paragraph 28(g).

2 Appointed days

The days appointed for the coming into force of Schedule 24 are—

(*a*) 1st April 2008 in relation to relevant documents relating to tax periods commencing on or after that date;
(*b*) 1st April 2008 in relation to assessments falling within paragraph 2 for tax periods commencing on or after that date;
(*c*) 1st July 2008 in relation to relevant documents relating to claims under the Thirteenth Council Directive (arrangements for the refund of value added tax to persons not established in Community territory) for years commencing on or after that date;

(*d*) 1st January 2009 in relation to relevant documents relating to claims under the Eighth Council Directive (arrangements for the refund of value added tax to taxable persons not established in the territory of the country) for years commencing on or after that date;
(*e*) 1st April 2009 in relation to documents relating to all other claims for repayments of relevant tax made on or after 1st April 2009 which are not related to a tax period; and
(*f*) in any other case, 1st April 2009 in relation to documents given where a person's liability to pay relevant tax arises on or after that date.

3 Transitional provision

Notwithstanding article 2, no person shall be liable to a penalty under Schedule 24 in respect of any tax period for which a return is required to be made before 1st April 2009.

4 Saving

Notwithstanding paragraph 29(*d*) (consequential amendments), sections 60 and 61 of the Value Added Tax Act 1994 (VAT evasion) shall continue to have effect with respect to conduct involving dishonesty which does not relate to an inaccuracy in a document or a failure to notify HMRC of an under-assessment by HMRC.

2008/1146
Value Added Tax (Buildings and Land) Order 2008

Made by the Treasury under FA 2006 s 17(1)–(5)

Made . . . . *21 April 2008*
Laid before the House of Commons . . . . *22 April 2008*
Coming into force . . . . *1 June 2008*

1 Citation, commencement and effect

(1) This Order may be cited as the Value Added Tax (Buildings and Land) Order 2008 and comes into force on 1st June 2008.

(2) This Order, apart from article 4, has effect in relation to supplies made on or after 1st June 2008.

(3) Article 4 has effect in relation to supplies made on or after 1st June 2020.

(4) Paragraphs (2) and (3) are subject to Schedule 2 (transitional provisions and savings).

2 Rewrite of Schedule 10 to VATA 1994

(*inserts* new VATA 1994 Sch 10).

3–5

(*These amendments are already in force and are therefore not reproduced*)

6 Consequential amendments, repeals and revocations

Schedule 1 contains consequential amendments, repeals and revocations.

7 Transitional provisions and savings

Schedule 2 contains transitional provisions and savings.

SCHEDULE 1
CONSEQUENTIAL AMENDMENTS, REPEALS AND REVOCATIONS

Article 6

Note—The amendments effected by Sch 1 are already in force and are therefore not reproduced here.

SCHEDULE 2
TRANSITIONAL PROVISIONS AND SAVINGS

Article 7

PART 1
GENERAL PROVISIONS

1 The re-enactment by article 2 of this Order of any provision of Schedule 10 to VATA 1994 in a rewritten form does not affect the continuity of the law.

2 Paragraph 1 does not apply to any change in the law relating to that provision effected by that article.

3 Any thing which—

(*a*) has been done, or has effect as if done, under or for the purposes of a provision (a "superseded provision") of Schedule 10 to VATA 1994 as it stood before being rewritten, and
(*b*) is in force or effective immediately before the commencement of the corresponding rewritten provision,

has effect after that commencement as if done under or for the purposes of the rewritten provision.

4 Any reference (express or implied) in any enactment, instrument or document to—

(*a*) a rewritten provision, or
(*b*) things done or falling to be done under or for the purposes of a rewritten provision,

is to be read as including, in relation to times, circumstances or purposes in relation to which any corresponding superseded provision had effect, a reference to the superseded provision or (as the case may be) things done or falling to be done under or for the purposes of the superseded provision.

5 Any reference (express or implied) in any enactment, instrument or document to—

(*a*) a superseded provision, or
(*b*) things done or falling to be done under or for the purposes of a superseded provision,

is to be read as including, in relation to times, circumstances or purposes in relation to which any corresponding rewritten provision has effect, a reference to the rewritten provision or (as the case may be) things done or falling to be done under or for the purposes of the rewritten provision.

6 Paragraphs 1 to 5 have effect instead of section 17(2) of the Interpretation Act 1978 (but do not affect the operation of any other provision of that Act).

7 Paragraphs 4 and 5 have effect only in so far as the context permits.

PART 2
OTHER PROVISION

Elections made before 1st November 1989

8—(1) An election under paragraph 2 of Schedule 10 to VATA 1994 which was made before 1st November 1989 continues to have effect in accordance with paragraph 3(1)(b) of that Schedule.

(2) In this paragraph any reference to Schedule 10 to VATA 1994 is to that Schedule as it stood before being rewritten by article 2 of this Order.

Elections made before 1st March 1995

9— (1) An election under paragraph 2 of Schedule 10 to VATA 1994 which was made before 1st March 1995 continues to have effect in accordance with paragraph 3(6)(a) of that Schedule.

(2) In this paragraph any reference to Schedule 10 to VATA 1994 is to that Schedule as it stood before being rewritten by article 2 of this Order.

Developers of certain non-residential buildings etc

10 The fact that paragraphs 5 to 7 of Schedule 10 to VATA 1994 (as it stood before being rewritten by article 2 of this Order) are not rewritten by that article is not to affect—

(*a*) the continued operation of Part 15 of the Value Added Tax Regulations 1995 (adjustments to the deduction of input tax on capital items) in relation to supplies treated as made on or before 1st March 1997, or
(*b*) the continued operation of paragraph (*b*) of item 1 in Group 1 of Schedule 9 to VATA 1994, as read with Note (7), in relation to supplies made before 1st June 2020.

Option made before 1st June 2008 specifying a description of land

11 The fact that the words ", or of a description specified," in paragraph 3(2) of Schedule 10 to VATA 1994 (as it stood before being rewritten by article 2 of this Order) are not rewritten by that article is not to affect the continued operation of an option to tax any land—

(*a*) which was made before 1st June 2008, and
(*b*) which specified a description of land.

2008/1948
Taxes (Fees for Payment by Telephone) Regulations 2008

Made by the Commissioners for Her Majesty's Revenue and Customs under FA 2008 s 136(1) and (3)

Made . . . . 22 *July* 2008
Laid before the House of Commons . . . . . . 22 *July* 2008
Coming into force . . . . 13 *August* 2008

1 Citation and commencement

These Regulations may be cited as the Taxes (Fees for Payment by Telephone) Regulations 2008 and shall come into force on 13th August 2008.

2 Fee payable for telephone payments by credit card

(1) Since the Commissioners expect that they will be required to pay a fee in connection with amounts paid by using a credit card, a person who—

(*a*) makes a payment to the Commissioners or a person authorised by the Commissioners, and

(*b*) gives telephone authorisation to make the payment by credit card,

must also pay a fee of 0.91% of the payment.

(2) The fee must be paid by being added to the payment (so that, accordingly, the person must make a single overall payment, consisting of the payment and the fee).

(3) In these Regulations "credit card" means a card which—

(*a*) is a credit-token falling within section 14(1)(*b*) of the Consumer Credit Act 1974, or

(*b*) would be a credit-token falling within that enactment were the card to be given to an individual.

2009/56

Transfer of Tribunal Functions and Revenue and Customs Appeals Order 2009

Made . . . . *18th January 2009*

Coming into force . . . . *1st April 2009*

The Lord Chancellor and the Treasury make the following Order in exercise of the powers conferred by sections 30(1) and (4), 31(1), (2) and (9) and 38 of, and paragraph 30 of Schedule 5 to, the Tribunals, Courts and Enforcement Act 2007 and section 124(1) to (7) of the Finance Act 2008.

A draft of this Order was laid before Parliament and approved by resolution of each House of Parliament in accordance with section 49(5) of the Tribunals, Courts and Enforcement Act 2007 and section 124(9) of the Finance Act 2008.

1 Citation and commencement

(1) This Order may be cited as the Transfer of Tribunal Functions and Revenue and Customs Appeals Order 2009.

(2) This Order comes into force on 1st April 2009.

2 The existing tribunals

In this Order "existing tribunals" means—

(*a*) the Commissioners for the general purposes of the income tax established under section 2 of the Taxes Management Act 1970;

(*b*) the Commissioners for the special purposes of the Income Tax Acts established under section 4 of the Taxes Management Act 1970;

(*c*) the VAT and duties tribunals established under Schedule 12 to the Value Added Tax Act 1994;

(*d*) the tribunal established under section 706 of the Income and Corporation Taxes Act 1988; and

(*e*) the tribunal established under section 704 of the Income Tax Act 2007.

3 Transfer of functions, consequential and other amendments

(1) Schedule 1 contains amendments to primary legislation which—

(*a*) transfer functions of existing tribunals, and

(*b*) make consequential and other provision (including provision about reviews of decisions by Her Majesty's Revenue and Customs).

(2) Schedule 2 contains amendments to secondary legislation which—

(*a*) transfer functions of existing tribunals, and

(*b*) make consequential and other provision (including provision about reviews of decisions by Her Majesty's Revenue and Customs).

4 Abolition of existing tribunals

The existing tribunals (apart from the Commissioners for the general purposes of the income tax) are abolished.

5 Transfer of members of existing tribunals

A person who, immediately before this Order comes into force, holds an office listed in column 1 of any of the following tables is to hold the office or offices listed in the corresponding entry in column 2 of that table—

The Special Commissioners	
1 Office held	2 Office or offices to be held

Commissioner for the special purposes of the Income Tax Acts appointed under section 4 of the Taxes Management Act 1970	Transferred-in judge of the Upper Tribunal
Deputy Commissioner for the special purposes of the Income Tax Acts appointed under section 4A of the Taxes Management Act 1970	Transferred-in judge of the First-tier Tribunal and deputy judge of the Upper Tribunal

VAT and duties tribunals	
1 Office held	*2 Office or offices to be held*
President of VAT and duties tribunals appointed under paragraph 2 of Schedule 12 to the Value Added Tax Act 1994	Transferred-in judge of the Upper Tribunal
Person appointed to a panel of chairmen of a VAT and duties tribunal under paragraph 7 of Schedule 12 to the Value Added Tax Act 1994	Transferred-in judge of the First-tier Tribunal and deputy judge of the Upper Tribunal
Person appointed to a panel of other members of a VAT and duties tribunal under paragraph 7 of Schedule 12 to the Value Added Tax Act 1994	Transferred-in other member of the First-tier Tribunal

Tribunal established under section 706 ICTA 1988	
1 Office held	*2 Office or offices to be held*
Chairman of the tribunal appointed under section 706(1)(*a*) of the Income and Corporation Taxes Act 1988	Transferred-in judge of the Upper Tribunal
Other member of the tribunal appointed under section 706(1)(*b*) of the Income and Corporation Taxes Act 1988	Transferred-in other member of the First-tier Tribunal

Tribunal established under section 704 ITA 2007	
1 Office held	*2 Office or offices to be held*
Chairman of the tribunal appointed under section 704(1)(*a*) of the Income Taxes Act 2007	Transferred-in judge of the Upper Tribunal
Other member of the tribunal appointed under section 704(1)(*b*) of the Income Taxes Act 2007	Transferred-in other member of the First-tier Tribunal

6 Transitionals and savings

Schedule 3 contains—

(*a*) transitional provision, and
(*b*) saving provision.

SCHEDULE 1

CONSEQUENTIAL AMENDMENTS AND SUPPLEMENTAL PROVISIONS—PRIMARY LEGISLATION

Article 3

Note—The amendments made by this Schedule are already in force and are therefore not reproduced.

SCHEDULE 2

CONSEQUENTIAL AMENDMENTS AND SUPPLEMENTAL PROVISIONS—SECONDARY LEGISLATION

Article 3

Note—The amendments made by this Schedule are already in force and are therefore not reproduced.

SCHEDULE 3

TRANSITIONAL AND SAVING PROVISIONS

Article 6

General

1— (1) In this Schedule—

"commencement date" means the date on which this Order comes into force;

"enactment" includes subordinate legislation (within the meaning of the Interpretation Act 1978);

"HMRC" means Her Majesty's Revenue and Customs;

"tribunal" means the First-tier Tribunal or, where determined by or under Tribunal Procedure Rules, the Upper Tribunal.

(2) For the purposes of this Schedule there are "current proceedings" if, before the commencement date—

(*a*) any party has served notice on an existing tribunal for the purpose of beginning proceedings before the existing tribunal, and

(*b*) the existing tribunal has not concluded proceedings arising by virtue of that notice.

Former VAT and duties tribunals matters (except VAT)

2— (1) This paragraph applies in relation to the following decisions—

(*a*) any relevant decision which HMRC notify before the commencement date, unless—

(i) the period to require a review of the decision has expired before that date, or

(ii) a review of the decision has been required before that date;

(*b*) any relevant review decision which HMRC notify before the commencement date unless—

(i) the period to serve notice of appeal against the decision on an existing tribunal has expired before that date, or

(ii) notice of appeal against the decision has been served on an existing tribunal before that date.

(2) On and after the commencement date, the following enactments continue to apply (subject to sub-paragraphs (3) and (4)) as they applied immediately before that date—

(*a*) the review and appeal provisions,

(*b*) rule 4(2) of the Value Added Tax Tribunals Rules 1986, and

(*c*) any other enactments that apply in relation to relevant decisions or relevant review decisions.

(3) Those enactments apply subject to Tribunal Procedure Rules.

(4) Any reference to an existing tribunal is to be substituted with a reference to the tribunal.

(5) Any time period which has started to run before the commencement date and has not expired will continue to apply.

(6) In this paragraph—

"relevant decision" means a decision to which a review and appeal provision applies (apart from a relevant review decision);

"relevant review decision" means a decision—

(*a*) that is made on a review of a relevant decision, and

(*b*) to which a review and appeal provision applies,

and includes a relevant decision that is treated as having been confirmed under a review and appeal provision.

"review and appeal provisions" means—

(*a*) sections 14 to 16 of the Finance Act 1994,

(*b*) sections 59 and 60 of the Finance Act 1994,

(*c*) sections 54 to 56 of the Finance Act 1996,

(*d*) paragraphs 121 to 123 of Schedule 6 to the Finance Act 2000,

(*e*) sections 40 to 42 of the Finance Act 2001,

(*f*) sections 33 to 37 of the Finance Act 2003,

(*g*) regulations 9 to 13 of the Export (Penalty) Regulations 2003,

(*h*) regulations 4 to 7 of the Control of Cash (Penalties) Regulations 2007,

(*i*) regulations 43 and 44 of the Money Laundering Regulations 2007, and (*j*) regulations 12 and 13 of the Transfer of Funds (Information on the Payer) Regulations 2007.

3— (1) This paragraph applies in relation to a relevant decision if, before the commencement date—

(*a*) HMRC have notified the relevant decision, and

(*b*) a review of the decision has begun under a review and appeal provision (whether or not a relevant review decision has been notified).

(2) On and after the commencement date the following enactments continue to apply (subject to sub-paragraphs (3) and (4)), as they applied immediately before that date—

(*a*) the review and appeal provisions,

(*b*) rule 4(2) of the VAT Tribunals Rules 1986, and

(*c*) any other enactments that apply in relation to relevant decisions or relevant review decisions.

(3) Those enactments apply subject to Tribunal Procedure Rules.

(4) Any reference to an existing tribunal is to be substituted with a reference to the tribunal.

(5) Any time period which has started to run before the commencement date and has not expired will continue to apply.

(6) On and after the commencement date, no notification offering or requiring a review may be given under any review and appeal provision or any other enactments that are applicable to the decision as they apply after that date.

(7) In this paragraph "review and appeal provision", "relevant decision" and "relevant review decision" have the same meaning as in paragraph 2.

Former VAT and duties tribunals matters: VAT

4— (1) This paragraph applies if, before the commencement date—

(*a*) HMRC have notified a decision relating to a matter to which section 83 of the Value Added Tax Act 1994 applies, and

(*b*) no party has served notice on a VAT and duties tribunal for the purpose of beginning proceedings before such a tribunal in relation to that decision.

(2) On and after the commencement date, the following enactments continue to apply (subject to sub-paragraphs (3) and (4)) as they applied immediately before that date—

(*a*) the Value Added Tax Act 1994,

(*b*) rule 4(2) of the VAT Tribunals Rules 1986, and

(*c*) any other enactments that are applicable to the decision.

(3) Those enactments apply subject to Tribunal Procedure Rules.

(4) Any reference to an existing tribunal is to be substituted with a reference to the tribunal.

(5) Any time period which has started to run before the commencement date and has not expired will continue to apply.

Matters formerly heard by existing tribunals (*except VAT and duties tribunals*)

5— (1) This paragraph applies if, before the commencement date—

(*a*) a notice of appeal has been given to HMRC; but

(*b*) no party has served notice on an existing tribunal for the purpose of beginning proceedings before the existing tribunal in relation to that appeal.

(2) Where the date on which a review is required or offered falls on or before 31 March 2010, the period for HMRC to give notice of their conclusions for the purposes of the relevant provision is to be 90 days (but without prejudice to any power to agree to a different period).

(3) In this paragraph—

"review" means a review under—

(*a*) section 49B or 49C of the Taxes Management Act 1970, or

(*b*) any other enactment which, as amended by this Order, contains provisions corresponding to section 49B or 49C for review to be required or offered;

"relevant provision" means—

(*a*) in the case of a review under section 49B or 49C of the Taxes Management Act 1970, section 49E(6) of that Act, or

(*b*) in the case of a review under any other enactment amended by this Order, the provision that corresponds to section 49E(6) of the Taxes Management Act 1970 in relation to that review.

Current proceedings

6 Any current proceedings are to continue on and after the commencement date as proceedings before the tribunal.

7— (1) This paragraph applies to current proceedings that are continued before the tribunal by virtue of paragraph 6.

(2) Where a hearing before an existing tribunal (except for the Commissioners for the general purposes of the income tax) began before the commencement date but was not completed by that date, the tribunal must be comprised for the continuation of that hearing of the person or persons who began it.

(3) The tribunal may give any direction to ensure that proceedings are dealt with fairly and justly and, in particular, may—

(*a*) apply any provision in procedural rules which applied to the proceedings before the commencement date; or

(*b*) disapply any provision of Tribunal Procedure Rules.

(4) In sub-paragraph (3) "procedural rules" means any provision (whether called rules or not) regulating practice or procedure before an existing tribunal.

(5) Any direction or order made or given in proceedings which is in force immediately before the commencement date remains in force on and after that date as if it were a direction or order of the tribunal relating to proceedings before that tribunal.

(6) A time period which has started to run before the commencement date and which has not expired will continue to apply.

(7) An order for costs may only be made if, and to the extent that, an order could have been made before the commencement date (on the assumption, in the case of costs actually incurred after that date, that they had been incurred before that date).

Cases to be remitted by courts

8 Any case to be remitted by a court on or after the commencement date in relation to an existing tribunal shall be remitted to the tribunal.

Decisions of VAT and duties tribunals and courts: interest and payment

9— (1) This paragraph applies in relation to any decision of a VAT and duties tribunal made before the commencement date.

(2) On and after that date, the following provisions continue to apply as they applied immediately before that date—

(*a*) section 84(8) of the Value Added Tax Act 1994 (VAT),

(*b*) section 60(6) to (8) of the Finance Act 1994 (insurance premium tax),

(*c*) paragraphs 8 and 10 of Schedule 6 to the Finance Act 1994 (air passenger duty),

(*d*) section 56(3) to (5) of the Finance Act 1996 (landfill tax),

(*e*) paragraph 123(4) to (6) of Schedule 6 to the Finance Act 2000 (climate change levy),

(*f*) section 42(4) to (6) of the Finance Act 2001 (aggregates levy),

(*g*) paragraph 14(4) of Schedule 3 to the Finance Act 2001 (excise and customs).

10— (1) This paragraph applies if an appeal from a decision of a VAT and duties tribunal, or from a court, is made before the commencement date.

(2) Section 85B of the Value Added Tax Act 1994 does not apply in relation to that decision.

Decisions of existing tribunals: rights of appeal, reviews and irregularities

11— (1) This paragraph applies to a decision of an existing tribunal if, immediately before the commencement date—

(*a*) an appeal lies to a court from that decision,

(*b*) an application may be or has been made to an existing tribunal seeking a review of that decision, or

(*c*) the existing tribunal wishes to correct an irregularity.

(2) Except as provided for in sub-paragraph (3), on and after the commencement date such rights of appeal shall lie from the decision as would lie from a decision of the First-tier Tribunal made on or after that date.

(3) Subject to the modifications specified in sub-paragraphs (4) and (5) the following enactments continue to apply for the purposes of a case to be stated, a review, or for correcting an irregularity in respect of any decision of the Commissioners for the general purposes of the income tax made before the commencement date, as if the amendments in this Order had not been made—

(*a*) sections 56 and 58 of the Taxes Management Act 1970,

(*b*) regulations 17 and 20 to 24 of the General Commissioners (Jurisdiction and Procedure) Regulations 1994, and

(*c*) the General Commissioners of Income Tax (Costs) Regulations 2001.

(4) Section 56(6) of the Taxes Management Act 1970 is modified so that for "the Commissioners" there is substituted "the tribunal".

(5) Section 58 of the Taxes Management Act 1970 is modified as follows—

(*a*) omit subsection (2B); and

(*b*) in subsection (2C) omit "or on an appeal under section 56A of this Act".

(6) In article 4 of the Tribunals, Courts and Enforcement Act 2007 (Commencement No 6 and Transitional Provisions) Order 2008—

(*a*) for "section 56 of the 1970 Act (statement of case for opinion of the High Court)" substitute "sections 56(3) and (11) and 58 of the 1970 Act (statement of case for opinion of the High Court) and regulations 17 and 20 to 24 of the General Commissioners (Jurisdiction and Procedure) Regulations 1994 (review of tribunal's final determination, stated case procedures and correction of irregularities)"; and

(*b*) after "commenced" insert ", and the amendments to the 1970 Act and the revocation of the General Commissioners (Jurisdiction and Procedure) Regulations 1994, the General Commissioners (Jurisdiction and Procedure) (Amendment) Regulations 1999, the General Commissioners (Jurisdiction and Procedure) (Amendment) Regulations 2005 and the General Commissioners and Special Commissioners (Jurisdiction and Procedure) (Amendment) Regulations 2007 (as they relate to the General Commissioners) in the Transfer of Tribunal Functions and Revenue and Customs Appeals Order 2009 had not been made".

Existing tribunals—staff

12 Staff appointed to the existing tribunals (except to the Commissioners for the general purposes of the income tax) before the commencement date are, on and after that date, to be treated, for the purpose of any enactment, as if they had been appointed by the Lord Chancellor under section 40(1) of the Tribunals, Courts and Enforcement Act 2007 (tribunal staff and services).

Transitional: general

13— (1) In so far as appropriate in consequence of this Order, a reference in an enactment, instrument or other document to an existing tribunal, or a member or official of an existing tribunal (however expressed) is to be taken to be a reference to the tribunal.

(2) Sub-paragraph (1) does not apply to any reference that is amended by Schedule 1 or 2.

2009/403
Finance Act 2008, Schedule 39 (Appointed Day, Transitional Provision and Savings) Order 2009

Made by the Treasury under FA 2008 s 118(2) and (3)

Made . . . . *26 February 2009*

Citation and interpretation

1— (1) This Order may be cited as the Finance Act 2008, Schedule 39 (Appointed Day, Transitional Provision and Savings) Order 2009.

(2) In this Order a reference to a paragraph (without more) is a reference to that paragraph of Schedule 39 to the Finance Act 2008.

(3) In this Order—

"the Taxes Acts" has the meaning given in section 118(1) of the Taxes Management Act 1970;
"TMA 1970" means the Taxes Management Act 1970;
"VATA 1994" means the Value Added Tax Act 1994.

Appointed days

2— (1) The day appointed for the coming into force of paragraphs 32 to 36 is 1st April 2009.

(2) Subject to article 10(2), the day appointed for the coming into force of paragraphs 1 to 31 and 37 to 66 is 1st April 2010.

Transitional provisions and savings

3 Paragraph 33 is disregarded where, for the purposes of section 33A of VATA 1994 (refunds of VAT to museums and galleries), the day on which the supply was made or the acquisition or importation took place was on or before 31st March 2006.

4 Paragraph 34 is disregarded—

(*a*) where, for the purposes of section 77 of VATA 1994 (assessments: time limits and supplementary assessments), the end of the prescribed accounting period or the importation, acquisition or event giving rise to the penalty, as appropriate, occurred on or before 31st March 2006, and

(*b*) where, after a person's death, a sum is assessed as due by reason of some conduct (however described) of the deceased, including a sum due by way of penalty, interest or surcharge, and the date of the death is on or before 31st March 2006.

5 Paragraph 35 is disregarded where, for the purposes of a claim under section 78 of VATA 1994 (interest in certain cases of official error), the end of the applicable period to which the claim relates was on or before 31st March 2006.

6 Paragraph 36 is disregarded where, for the purposes of section 80 of VATA 1994 (credit for, or repayment of, overstated or overpaid VAT), the relevant date is on or before 31st March 2006.

7 Section 36(1A)(*b*) and (*c*) of TMA 1970 (fraudulent and negligent conduct) shall not apply where the year of assessment is 2008–09 or earlier, except where the assessment on the person

("P") is for the purposes of making good to the Crown a loss of tax attributable to P's negligent conduct or the negligent conduct of a person acting on P's behalf.

8 Paragraph 46(2A)(*b*) and (*c*) of Schedule 18 to the Finance Act 1998 (general time limits for assessments) shall not apply where the end of the accounting period to which the assessment relates is on or before 31st March 2010, except in a case involving negligence on the part of—

(*a*) the company, or

(*b*) a person acting on behalf of the company, or

(*c*) a person who was a partner of the company at the relevant time.

9 Section 77(4A)(*c*) and (*d*) of VATA 1994 (value added tax: assessments: time limits and supplementary assessments) shall not apply where the end of the prescribed accounting period or the importation, acquisition or event giving rise to the penalty, as appropriate, occurred on or before 31 March 2010, except where VAT has been lost in circumstances giving rise to a penalty under section 67 of VATA 1994 (failure to notify and unauthorised issue of invoices).

10— (1) This article applies where an event specified in paragraph 4 below relates to a year of assessment in respect of which a person ("P") has not been given notice under—

(*a*) section 8 of TMA 1970 (personal return),

(*b*) section 8A of TMA 1970 (trustee's return), or

(*c*) section 12AA of TMA 1970 (partnership return),

within one year of the end of the year of assessment.

(2) Where this article applies, the day appointed for the coming into force of paragraphs 1 to 31 and 37 to 65 is 1st April 2012.

(3) But this article does not apply if, as regards P and a year of assessment, any income which ought to have been assessed to income tax or chargeable gains which ought to have been assessed to capital gains tax, have not been assessed, or an assessment to tax has become insufficient, or any relief which has been given has become excessive.

(4) The events referred to in paragraph (1) above are—

(*a*) an assessment on P to income tax or capital gains tax,

(*b*) a claim by or on behalf of P, provided for by any provision of the Taxes Acts, and

(*c*) a notice given by P under section 711 of the Income Tax (Earnings and Pensions Act) 2003 (right to make a return).

(5) Nothing in this article has any application where P is a company.

2009/571
Finance Act 2008, Schedule 40 (Appointed Day, Transitional Provisions and Consequential Amendments) Order 2009

Made by the Treasury under FA 2008 s 122

Made . . . . *9 March 2009*
Laid before the House of Commons . . . . *10 March 2009*
Coming into force . . . . *1 April 2009*

Citation and interpretation

1— (1) This Order may be cited as the Finance Act 2008, Schedule 40 (Appointed Day, Transitional Provisions and Consequential Amendments) Order 2009 and comes into force on 1st April 2009.

(2) In this Order a reference to a paragraph (without more) is a reference to that paragraph of Schedule 40 to the Finance Act 2008.

(3) In this Order—

"filing date", in relation to a relevant document, means—

(i) where the document is required to be given to HMRC, the date by which it is required to be given, and

(ii) where the document is not required to be given to HMRC, the date on which it is given;

"HMRC" means Her Majesty's Revenue and Customs;

"relevant documents" means documents given to HMRC of a kind inserted in the Table in paragraph 1 of Schedule 24 by paragraph 2(4) or (5);

"relevant tax" means any tax inserted in the Table in paragraph 1 of Schedule 24 by paragraph 2(4) or (5);

"Schedule 24" means Schedule 24 to the Finance Act 2007; and

"tax period" has the meaning given in paragraph 28(*g*) of Schedule 24.

Appointed day

2 The day appointed for the coming into force of Schedule 40 to the Finance Act 2008 is 1st April 2009.

3 In their application in relation to penalties payable under paragraph 1 of Schedule 24 (error in taxpayer's document), the entries inserted by paragraph 2(4) and (5) shall have effect in relation to—

(*a*) relevant documents—

(i) which relate to tax periods commencing on or after 1st April 2009, and

(ii) for which the filing date is on or after 1st April 2010;

(*b*) relevant documents relating to all claims for repayments of relevant tax made on or after 1st April 2010 which are not related to a tax period;

(*c*) relevant documents produced under regulations under section 256 of the Inheritance Tax Act 1984 ("IHTA 1984") (regulations about accounts, etc), where the date of death is on or after 1st April 2009; and

(*d*) in any other case, relevant documents given where a person's liability to pay relevant tax arises on or after 1st April 2010.

4 In their application in relation to penalties payable under paragraph 1A of Schedule 24 (error in taxpayer's document attributable to another person), the entries inserted by paragraph 2(4) and (5) shall have effect in relation to—

(*a*) relevant documents—

(i) which relate to tax periods commencing on or after 1st April 2009, and

(ii) for which the filing date is on or after 1st April 2010;

(*b*) relevant documents relating to all claims for repayments of relevant tax made on or after 1st April 2010 which are not related to a tax period;

(*c*) relevant documents produced under regulations under section 256 of IHTA 1984 (regulations about accounts, etc) where the date of death is on or after 1st April 2009; and

(*d*) in any other case, relevant documents given where a person's liability to pay relevant tax arises on or after 1st April 2010.

5 In their application in relation to assessments falling within paragraph 2 of Schedule 24 (under-assessment by HMRC), the entries inserted by paragraph 2(4) and (5) shall have effect in relation to tax periods commencing on or after 1st April 2009, where the filing date for the relevant document is on or after 1st April 2010.

Transitional provisions

6— (1) Paragraph 21 (consequential repeals) repeals the provisions listed in paragraph (2) only in so far as those provisions relate to conduct involving dishonesty which relates to—

(*a*) an inaccuracy in a document, or

(*b*) a failure to notify HMRC of an under-assessment by HMRC.

(2) The provisions referred to in paragraph (1) are—

(*a*) in the Finance Act 1994—

(i) section 8 (penalty for evasion of excise duty), and

(ii) paragraphs 12 and 13 of Schedule 7 (insurance premium tax: civil penalties),

(*b*) paragraphs 18 and 19 of Schedule 5 to the Finance Act 1996 (landfill tax: civil penalties: evasion and misdeclaration or neglect),

(*c*) paragraphs 98 and 99 of Schedule 6 to the Finance Act 2000 (climate change levy: civil penalties: evasion, liability of directors and misdeclaration or neglect),

(*d*) in Schedule 6 to the Finance Act 2001—

(i) paragraphs 7 and 8 (aggregates levy: civil penalties: evasion, liability of directors and misdeclaration or neglect), and

(ii) paragraph 9A(5)(*b*) (penalty under paragraph 7 above),

(*e*) section 133(2) to (4) of the Finance Act 2002 (aggregates levy: amendments to provisions about civil penalties).

7 Notwithstanding paragraph 29(*d*) of Schedule 24 (consequential amendments), sections 60 and 61 of the Value Added Tax Act 1994 (VAT evasion) shall continue to have effect with respect to conduct involving dishonesty which does not relate to an inaccuracy in a document or a failure to notify HMRC of an under-assessment by HMRC.

Consequential amendments to enactments

8 Schedule 1 contains amendments of enactments in consequence of the provisions omitted by paragraph 21 and by paragraph 29 of Schedule 24.

9 Schedule 2 contains consequential amendments to secondary legislation.

SCHEDULE 1

CONSEQUENTIAL AMENDMENTS—PRIMARY LEGISLATION

Article 8

Value Added Tax Act 1994

22 The Value Added Tax Act 1994 is amended as follows.

23 In section 66(7) (failure to submit EC sales statement or statement relating to section 55A)—

(*a*) after "76" insert "and Schedule 24 to the Finance Act 2007", and (*b*) after "any penalty under this section" insert "or that Schedule".

24 In section 69(9)(*c*) (breaches of regulatory provisions) after "section 60 or 63" insert " or a penalty under Schedule 24 to the Finance Act 2007".

25 In section 69A(7)(*a*) (breach of record-keeping requirements etc in relation to transactions in gold) after "section 60" insert "or a penalty for a deliberate inaccuracy under Schedule 24 to the Finance Act 2007".

26 In section 69B(7)(*a*) (breach of record keeping requirements imposed by directions) after "section 60" insert "or a penalty for a deliberate inaccuracy under Schedule 24 to the Finance Act 2007".

27 In paragraph 10(3)(*b*) of Schedule 11A(*a*) (disclosure of avoidance schemes) after "section 60" insert "or a penalty for a deliberate inaccuracy under Schedule 24 to the Finance Act 2007".

SCHEDULE 2

CONSEQUENTIAL AMENDMENTS—SECONDARY LEGISLATION

Article 9

Duty Stamps Regulations 2006

42 The Duty Stamps Regulations 2006 are amended as follows.

43 For regulation 10(8) substitute—

"(8) A relevant penalty is a penalty that has been assessed and notified under Schedule 24 to the Finance Act 2007 (penalties for errors) and that has not been withdrawn or quashed."

2009/1177

Value Added Tax (Refund of Tax to Charter Trustees and Conservators) Order 2009

Made by the Treasury under VATA 1994 s 33(3)(*k*)

Made	*7 May 2009*
Laid before the House of Commons	*8 May 2009*
Coming into force	
Articles 1 and 2	*1 June 2009*
Remainder	*1 April 2010*

1 Citation and commencement

This Order may be cited as the Value Added Tax (Refund of Tax to Charter Trustees and Conservators) Order 2009 and shall come into force—

(*a*) for the purposes of articles 1 and 2 on 1st June 2009, and
(*b*) for all other purposes on 1st April 2010.

2 Charter Trustees

The following bodies are specified for the purposes of section 33 of the Value Added Tax Act 1994—

(*a*) the Charter Trustees for the City of Chester,
(*b*) the Charter Trustees for Crewe,
(*c*) the Charter Trustees for the City of Durham,
(*d*) the Charter Trustees for Ellesmere Port, and
(*e*) the Charter Trustees for Macclesfield.

3 Wimbledon and Putney Commons Conservators

The Wimbledon and Putney Commons Conservators are specified for the purposes of section 33 of the Value Added Tax Act 1994.

VALUE ADDED TAX
EC LEGISLATION

CONTENTS

Note—The following list comprises EC legislation currently in force and reproduced on the following pages.
See below for the full list in chronological order showing legislation which is currently in force, repealed or amending.

EC TREATIES

Treaty Establishing The European Community.

EC COUNCIL DIRECTIVES

67/227: *First Council Directive of 11 April 1967* (repealed by Council Directive 2006/112/EC).

67/228: *Second Council Directive of 11 April 1967 on the harmonisation of legislation of Member States concerning turnover taxes Structure and procedures for application of the common system of value added tax* (repealed by Council Directive 77/388)

69/169: Council Directive of 28 May 1969 on the harmonisation of provisions laid down by law, regulation or administrative action relating to exemption from turnover tax on imports in international travel.

76/308: Council Directive of 15 March 1976 on mutual assistance for the recovery of claims resulting from operations forming part of the system of financing the European Agricultural Guidance and Guarantee Fund, and of agricultural levies and customs duties [and in respect of value added tax].

77/388: *Sixth Council Directive of 17 May 1977* (repealed by Council Directive 2006/112/EC).

77/799: Council Directive of 19 December 1977 concerning mutual assistance by the competent authorities of the Member States in the [fields of direct taxation and value added tax].

78/1035: Council Directive of 19 December 1978 on the exemption from taxes of imports of small consignments of goods of a non-commercial character from third countries. (repealed and replaced by 2006/79/EC)

79/1072: Eighth Council Directive of 6 December 1979.

83/181: Council Directive of 28 March 1983 determining the scope of Article 14(1)(*d*) of Directive 77/388/EEC as regards exemption from value added tax on the final importation of certain goods.

86/560: Thirteenth Council Directive of 17 November 1986.

89/465: *Eighteenth Council Directive of 18 July 1989*. (repealed)

91/680: Council Directive of 16 December 1991 supplementing the common system of VAT and amending Directive 77/388/EEC with a view to the abolition of fiscal frontiers.

92/111: *Council Directive of 14 December 1992 amending Directive 77/388/EEC and introducing simplification measures with regard to value added tax.* (repealed)

94/4: Council Directive of 14 February 1994 amending Directives 69/169/EEC and 77/388/EEC—allowances for travellers from third countries and limits on tax-free purchases in intra-Community travel.

94/5: *Council Directive of 14 February 1994 supplementing the common system of VAT and amending Directive 77/388/EEC with regard to special arrangements applicable to second-hand goods, works of art, collectors' items and antiques.* (repealed)

98/80: *Council Directive of 12 October 1998 supplementing the common system of value added tax and amending Directive 77/388/EEC—special scheme for investment gold.* (repealed)

2002/38: *Council Directive of 7 May 2002 amending and temporarily amending Council Directive 77/388 EEC as regards the value added tax arrangements applicable to radio and television broadcasting services and certain electronically supplied services.* (repealed)

2002/94: *Commission Directive of 9 December 2002 laying down detailed rules for implementing certain provisions of Council Directive 76/308/EEC on mutual assistance for the recovery of claims relating to certain levies, duties, taxes and other measures.* (repealed)

2006/79 Council Directive of 5 October 2006 on the exemption from taxes of imports of small consignments of goods of a non-commercial character from third countries (codified version).

2006/112 Council Directive of 28 November 2006 on the common system of value added tax.

2007/74 Council Directive of 20 December 2007 on the exemption from value added tax and excise duty of goods imported by persons travelling from third countries.

2008/9:	Council Directive of 12 February 2008 laying down detailed rules for the refund of value added tax, provided for in Directive 2006/112/EC, to taxable persons not established in the Member State of refund but established in another Member State.
2008/55:	Council Directive of 26 May 2008 on mutual assistance for the recovery of claims relating to certain levies, duties, taxes and other measures.

EC REGULATIONS

2913/92:	Council Regulation of 12 October 1992 establishing the Community Customs Code (to be repealed by Regulation 450/2008/EC)
3590/92:	*Commission Regulation of 11 December 1992 concerning the statistical information media for statistics on trade between Member States.* (repealed by Commission Regulation 1982/2004/EC art 27)
2454/93:	Commission Regulation of 2 July 1993 laying down provisions for the implementation of Council Regulation No 2913/92/EEC establishing the Community Customs Code.
1798/03:	Council Regulation of 7 October 2003 on administrative cooperation in the field of value added tax and repealing Regulation (EEC) No 218/92
638/04:	Regulation of the European Parliament and of the Council of 31 March 2004 on Community statistics relating to the trading of goods between Member States and repealing Council Regulation (EEC) No 3330/91
1925/04:	Commission Regulation of 29 October 2004 laying down detailed rules for implementing certain provisions of Council Regulation No 1798/2003 concerning administrative cooperation in the field of value-added tax.
1777/05:	Council Regulation of 17 October 2005 laying down implementing measures for Directive 77/388/EEC on the common system of value added tax.
450/2008:	Regulation of the European Parliament and of the Council of 23 April 2008 laying down the Community Customs Code (Modernised Customs Code)

EC DECISIONS

86/356:	Council Decision of 21 July 1986 authorising the UK to apply flat-rate measures in respect of the non-deductible VAT charged on fuel expenditure in company cars.
89/466:	Council Decision of 18 July 1989 authorising derogation from Council Directive 77/388/EEC art 11(A)(1)(*b*).
89/534:	Council Decision authorising derogation from Council Directive 77/388/EEC art 11A(1)(*a*).
92/546:	Council Decision of 23 November 1992 authorising derogation from Council Directive 77/388/EEC art 28e(1).
92/621:	Council Decision of 21 December 1992 authorising application of a particular measure in accordance with Council Directive 77/388/EEC art 22(12)(*b*).
93/111:	Council Decision of 15 February 1993 authorising derogation from Council Directive 77/388/EEC art 17.
93/204:	Council Decision of 5 April 1993 authorising derogation from Council Directive 77/388/EEC arts 5(8) and 21(1)(*a*).
93/609:	Council Decision of 22 November 1993 authorising derogation from Council Directive 77/388/EEC art 22(12)(*a*).
95/252:	Council Decision of 29 June 1995 authorising derogation from Council Directive 77/388/EEC arts 6 and 17.
97/214:	Council Decision of 17 March 1997 authorising derogation from Council Directive 77/388/EEC art 9.
97/375:	*Council Decision of 9 June 1997 authorising derogation from Council Directive 77/388/EEC art 17* (repealed by Council Decision 2007/133/EC art 2).
98/23:	Council Decision of 19 December 1997 authorising the United Kingdom to extend application of a measure derogating from Article 28e(1) of the Sixth Council Directive 77/388/EEC on the harmonisation of the laws of the Member States relating to turnover taxes.
98/198:	Council Decision of 9 March 1998 authorising the United Kingdom to extend application of a measure derogating from Articles 6 and 17 of the Sixth Council Directive (77/388/EEC) on the harmonisation of the laws of the Member States relating to turnover taxes.
2000/185:	Council Decision of 28 February 2000 authorising Member States to apply a reduced rate of VAT to certain labour-intensive services in accordance with the procedure provided for in Article 28(6) of Directive 77/388/EEC.

2006/774:	Council Decision of 7 November 2006 authorising certain Member States to apply a reduced rate of VAT to certain labour-intensive services in accordance with the procedure provided for in Article 28(6) of Directive 77/388/EEC.
2007/133:	Council Decision of 30 January 2007 authorising Estonia, Slovenia, Sweden and the United Kingdom to apply a special measure derogating from Article 167 of Directive 2006/112/EC on the common system of value added tax.
2007/250	Council Decision of 16 April 2007 authorising the United Kingdom to introduce a special measure derogating from Article 193 of Directive 2006/112/EC on the common system of value added tax.

CHRONOLOGICAL LIST OF EC LEGISLATION

Note—This list comprises amending or repealed legislation and legislation currently in force. Amending and repealed titles are printed in italics.

See above for the shorter list comprising legislation currently in force and reproduced on the following pages.

1957

Treaty Establishing The European Community.

1967

67/227: *First Council Directive of 11 April 1967* (repealed by Council Directive 2006/112/EC).

EC 1967/ 67/228: *Second Council Directive of 11 April 1967 on the harmonisation of legislation of Member States concerning turnover taxes Structure and procedures for application of the common system of value added tax* (repealed by Council Directive 77/388)

1969

69/169: Council Directive of 28 May 1969 on the harmonisation of provisions laid down by law, regulation or administrative action relating to exemption from turnover tax on imports in international travel.

69/463: *Third Council Directive of 9 December 1969* (amends Directive 67/227)

1976

76/308: Council Directive of 15 March 1976 on mutual assistance for the recovery of claims resulting from operations forming part of the system of financing the European Agricultural Guidance and Guarantee Fund, and of agricultural levies and customs duties [and in respect of value added tax].

1977

77/388: *Sixth Council Directive of 17 May 1977* (repealed by Council Directive 2006/112/EC).

77/799: Council Directive of 19 December 1977 concerning mutual assistance by the competent authorities of the Member States in the [fields of direct taxation and value added tax].

1978

78/1035: Council Directive of 19 December 1978 on the exemption from taxes of imports of small consignments of goods of a non-commercial character from third countries.

1979

79/1070: *Council Directive of 6 December 1979* (amends Directive 77/799).

79/1072: Eighth Council Directive of 6 December 1979

1980

1224/80: *Council Regulation of 28 May 1980 on the valuation of goods for customs purposes* (repealed by Council Regulation 2913/92 art 251).

1494/80: *Commission Regulation of 11 June 1980 on interpretative notes and generally accepted accounting principles for the purposes of customs value* (repealed by Commission Regulation 2454/93 art 913).

1495/80: *Commission Regulation of 11 June 1980 implementing certain provisions of Articles 1, 3 and 8 of Council Regulations (EEC) No 1224/80 on the valuation of goods for customs purposes* (repealed by Commission Regulation 2454/93 art 913).

1496/80: *Commission Regulation of 11 June 1980 on the declaration of particulars relating to customs value and on documents to be furnished* (repealed by Commission Regulation 2454/93 art 913).

3177/80: *Commission Regulation of 5 December 1980 on the place of introduction to be taken into consideration in applying article 14(2) of Council Regulation (EEC) No 1224/80 on the valuation of goods for customs purposes* (repealed by Commission Regulation 2454/93 art 913).

3179/80: *Commission Regulation of 5 December 1980 on postal charges to be taken into consideration when determining the customs value of goods sent by post* (repealed by Commission Regulation 2454/93 art 913).

1981

1577/81: *Commission Regulation of 12 June 1981 establishing a system of simplified procedures for the determination of the customs value of certain perishable goods* (repealed by Commission Regulation 2454/93 art 913).

1983

83/181: Council Directive of 28 March 1983 determining the scope of Article 14 (1) (*d*) of Directive 77/388/EEC as regards exemption from value added tax on the final importation of certain goods.

3158/83: *Commission Regulation of 9 November 1983 on the incidence of royalties and licence fees in customs value* (repealed by Commission Regulation 2454/93 art 913).

1984

84/386: *Tenth Council Directive of 31 July 1984* (amends Directive 77/388)

2151/84: *Council Regulation of 23 July 1984 on the customs territory of the Community* (repealed by Council Regulation 2913/92 art 251).

1985

1766/85: *Commission Regulation of 27 June 1985 on the rates of exchange to be used in the determination of customs value* (repealed by Commission Regulation 2454/93 art 913).

1986

86/356: *Council Decision of 21 July 1986 authorising the UK to apply flat-rate measures in respect of the non-deductible VAT charged on fuel expenditure in company cars* (Repealed by Council Decision 2006/659/EC art 4, with effect from 30 April 2007)

86/560: Thirteenth Council Directive of 17 November 1986.

1989

89/465: Eighteenth Council Directive of 18 July 1989.

89/466: Council Decision of 18 July 1989 authorising derogation from Council Directive 77/388/EEC art 11(A)(1)(*b*).

89/534: Council Decision authorising derogation from Council Directive 77/388/EEC art 11A(1)(*a*).

1991

91/680: Council Directive of 16 December 1991 supplementing the common system of VAT and amending Directive 77/388/EEC with a view to the abolition of fiscal frontiers.

3330/91: *Council Regulation of 7 November 1991 on the statistics relating to the trading of goods between member States* (repealed by European Parliament and Council Regulation 638/2004 art 15).

1992

92/77: *Council Directive of 19 October 1992* (amends Directive 77/388).

92/111: Council Directive of 14 December 1992 amending Directive 77/388/EEC and introducing simplification measures with regard to value added tax.

92/546: Council Decision of 23 November 1992 authorising derogation from Council Directive 77/388/EEC art 28e(1).

92/621: Council Decision of 21 December 1992 authorising application of a particular measure in accordance with Council Directive 77/388/EEC art 22(12)(*b*).

2256/92: *Commission Regulation of 31 July 1992 on statistical thresholds for the statistics on trade between member States* (repealed by Commission Regulation (EC) 1901/2000 art 49).

2913/92: Council Regulation of 12 October 1992 establishing the Community Customs Code.

3590/92: Commission Regulation of 11 December 1992 concerning the statistical information media for statistics on trade between Member States.

3903/92: *Commission Regulation of 21 December 1992 on air transport costs to be included in customs value* (repealed by Commission Regulation 2454/93 art 913).

1993

93/111: Council Decision of 15 February 1993 authorising derogation from Council Directive 77/388/EEC art 17.

93/204: Council Decision of 5 April 1993 authorising derogation from Council Directive 77/388/EEC arts 5(8) and 21(1)(*a*).

93/563: Council Decision of 25 October 1993 authorising derogation from Council Directive 77/388/EEC arts 2(1) and 17.

93/609: Council Decision of 22 November 1993 authorising derogation from Council Directive 77/388/EEC art 22(12)(*a*).

2454/93: Commission Regulation of 2 July 1993 laying down provisions for the implementation of Council Regulation No 2913/92/EEC establishing the Community Customs Code.

1994

94/4: Council Directive of 14 February 1994 amending Directives 69/169/EEC and 77/388/EEC—allowances for travellers from third countries and limits on tax-free purchases in intra-Community travel.

94/5: Council Directive of 14 February 1994 supplementing the common system of VAT and amending Directive 77/388/EEC with regard to special arrangements applicable to second-hand goods, works of art, collectors' items and antiques.

1995

95/7: *Council Directive of 10 April 1995 amending Directive 77/388/EEC and introducing new simplification measures with regard to VAT—scope of certain exemptions and practical arrangements for implementing them* (amends Directive 77/388/EEC).

95/242: Council Decision of 29 June 1995 authorising derogation from Council Directive 77/388/EEC arts 6 and 17.

1997

97/214: Council Decision of 17 March 1997 authorising derogation from Council Directive 77/388/EEC art 9.

97/375: Council Decision of 9 June 1997 authorising derogation from Council Directive 77/388/EEC art 17.

97/860: Commission Regulation of 14 May 1997 amending Regulation (EEC) No 3046/92 with regard to the reporting of the value of goods.

97/1427: Commission Regulation of 23 July 1997 amending Regulation (EEC) No 2454/93 laying down provisions for the implementation of Council Regulation (EEC) No 2913/92 establishing the Community Customs Code.

1998

75/98: Commission Regulation of 12 January 1998 amending Regulation (EEC) No 2454/93 laying down provisions for the implementation of Council Regulation (EEC) No 2913/92 establishing the Community Customs Code.

98/23: Council Decision of 19 December 1997 authorising the United Kingdom to extend application of a measure derogating from Article 28e(1) of the Sixth Council Directive 77/388/EEC on the harmonisation of the laws of the Member States relating to turnover taxes.

98/198: Council Decision of 9 March 1998 authorising the United Kingdom to extend application of a measure derogating from Articles 6 and 17 of the Sixth Council Directive (77/388/EEC) on the harmonisation of the laws of the Member States relating to turnover taxes.

1677/98: Commission Regulation of 29 July 1998 amending Regulation (EEC) No 2454/93 laying down provisions for the implementation of Council Regulation (EEC) No 2913/92 establishing the Community Customs Code.

98/80: Council Directive of 12 October 1998 supplementing the common system of value added tax and amending Directive 77/388/EEC—special scheme for investment gold.

98/2535: Commission Regulation of 26 November 1998 amending Regulation (EEC) No 3046/92 with regard to information provided by the tax authorities.

98/94/EC: Council Directive of 14 December 1998 amending Directive 94/4/EC and extending the temporary derogation applicable to Germany and Austria.

1999

99/79: Council Decision of 18 January 1999 amending Article 3 of Decision 98/198/EC.

99/49/EC: Council Directive of 25 May 1999 amending, with regard to the level of standard rate, Directive 77/388/EEC on the common system of VAT.

99/59/EC Council Directive of 17 June 1999 amending with regard to the VAT arrangements applicable to telecommunication services, Directive 77/388/EEC.

2000

17/EC: Council Directive of 30 March 2000 amending Directive 77/388/EEC on the common system of VAT: transitional provisions granted to the Republic of Austria and the Portuguese Republic.

65/EC: Council Directive of 17 October 2000 amending Directive 77/388/EEC as regards the determination of the person liable for payment of VAT.

1602/EC: Commission Regulation amending Regulation 2454/93/EEC laying down provisions for the implementation of Council Regulation 2913/92/EEC establishing the Community Customs Code.

2700/EC: Parliament and Council Regulation amending Council Regulation 2913/92/EEC establishing the Community Customs Code.

2787: Commission Regulation amending Regulation (EEC) No 2454/93 laying down provisions for the implementation of Council Regulation 2913/92/EEC establishing the Community Customs Code.

2001

4/EC: amending the sixth Directive (77/388/EEC) on the common system of value added tax, with regard to the length of time during which the minimum standard rate is to be applied

44/EC: amending Directive 76/308/EEC on mutual assistance for the recovery of claims resulting from operations forming part of the system of financing the European Agricultural Guidance and Guarantee Fund, and of agricultural levies and customs duties and in respect of value added tax and certain excise duties

115/EC: amending Directive 77/388/EEC with a view to simplifying, modernising and harmonising the conditions laid down for invoicing in respect of value added tax

2002

38/EC: amending and temporarily amending Council Directive 77/388 EEC as regards the value added tax arrangements applicable to radio and television broadcasting services and certain electronically supplied services.

92/EC: amending Directive 77/388/EEC to extend the facility allowing Member States to apply reduced rates of VAT to certain labour-intensive services

94/EC: laying down detailed rules for implementing certain provisions of Council Directive 76/308/EEC on mutual assistance for the recovery of claims relating to certain levies, duties, taxes and other measures.

954/EC: Council Decision of 3 December 2002 extending the period of application of Decision 2000/185/EC authorising Member States to apply a reduced rate of VAT to certain labour-intensive services in accordance with the procedure provided for in Article 28(6) of Directive 77/388/EEC

2003

881/EC: amending Regulation (EEC) No 2454/93 laying down provisions for the implementation of Council Regulation (EEC) No 2913/92 establishing the Community Customs Code

2005

1777/05: Council Regulation of 17 October 2005 laying down implementing measures for Directive 77/388/EEC on the common system of value added tax

2006

2006/112:	Council Directive of 28 November 2006 on the common system of value added tax.
2006/774:	Council Decision of 7 November 2006 authorising certain Member States to apply a reduced rate of VAT to certain labour-intensive services in accordance with the procedure provided for in Article 28(6) of Directive 77/388/EEC.

2007

2007/133:	Council Decision of 30 January 2007 authorising Estonia, Slovenia, Sweden and the United Kingdom to apply a special measure derogating from Article 167 of Directive 2006/112/EC on the common system of value added tax.
2007/250	Council Decision of 16 April 2007 authorising the United Kingdom to introduce a special measure derogating from Article 193 of Directive 2006/112/EC on the common system of value added tax.

2008

2008/8:	Council Directive of 12 February 2008 amending Directive 2006/112/EC as regards the place of supply of services.
2008/9:	Council Directive of 12 February 2008 laying down detailed rules for the refund of value added tax, provided for in Directive 2006/112/EC, to taxable persons not established in the Member State of refund but established in another Member State.
2008/55:	Council Directive of 26 May 2008 on mutual assistance for the recovery of claims relating to certain levies, duties, taxes and other measures.
67/2008:	Commission Regulation of 25 January 2008 amending Regulation (EC) No 3199/93 on the mutual recognition of procedures for the complete denaturing of alcohol for the purposes of exemption from excise duty.
117/2008:	Council Directive of 16 December 2008 amending Directive 2006/112/EC on the common system of value added tax to combat tax evasion connected with intra-Community transactions.
143/2008:	Council Regulation of 12 February 2008 amending Regulation (EC) No 1798/2003 as regards the introduction of administrative cooperation and the exchange of information concerning the rules relating to the place of supply of services, the special schemes and the refund procedure for value added tax
450/2008:	Regulation of the European Parliament and of the Council of 23 April 2008 laying down the Community Customs Code (Modernised Customs Code)
1179/2008:	Commission Regulation of 28 November 2008 laying down detailed rules for implementing certain provisions of Council Directive 2008/55/EC on mutual assistance for the recovery of claims relating to certain levies, duties, taxes and other measures.
37/2009:	Council Regulation of 16 December 2008 amending Regulation (EC) No 1798/2003 on administrative cooperation in the field of value added tax, in order to combat tax evasion connected with intra-Community transactions.
47/2009:	Council Directive of 5 May 2009 amending Directive 2006/112/EC as regards reduced rates of value added tax.
69/2009:	Council Directive of 25 June 2009 amending Directive 2006/112/EC on the common system of value added tax as regards tax evasion linked to imports.
222/2009:	Regulation of the European Parliament and of the Council of 11 March 2009 amending Regulation (EC) No 638/2004 on Community statistics relating to the trading of goods between Member States.

EC TREATIES

Treaty establishing the European Community

Note—The text of this treaty reflects amendments made by the Treaty of Amsterdam, including the renumbering of articles. The Treaty of Amsterdam (OJ C340 10.11.97 p1) was ratified on 1 May 1999.

PART THREE
COMMUNITY POLICIES

[TITLE VI (EX TITLE V): COMMON RULES ON COMPETITION, TAXATION AND APPROXIMATION OF LAWS][1]

CHAPTER 2—TAX PROVISIONS

Article 90 (ex Article 95)

No Member State shall impose, directly or indirectly, on the products of other Member States any internal taxation of any kind in excess of that imposed directly or indirectly on similar domestic products.

Furthermore, no Member State shall impose on the products of other Member States any internal taxation of such a nature as to afford indirect protection to other products.

Simon's Tax Cases—*EC Commission v Kingdom of Spain* [1993] STC 150*; *EC Commission v Hellenic Republic* [1993] STC 160*; *EC Commission v French Republic* (Case C-276/91) [1997] STC 584*; [1997] *Fazenda Pública v Fricarnes* SA [1997] STC 1348*.

Article 91 (ex Article 96)

Where products are exported to the territory of any Member State, any repayment of internal taxation shall not exceed the internal taxation imposed on them whether directly or indirectly.

Article 92 (ex Article 98)

In the case of charges other than turnover taxes, excise duties and other forms of indirect taxation, remissions and repayments in respect of exports to other Member States may not be granted and countervailing charges in respect of imports from Member States may not be imposed unless the measures contemplated have been previously approved for a limited period by the Council acting by a qualified majority on a proposal from the Commission.

[Article 93 (ex Article 99)

The Council shall, acting unanimously on a proposal from the Commission and after consulting the European Parliament and the Economic and Social Committee, adopt provisions for the harmonisation of legislation concerning turnover taxes, excise duties and other forms of indirect taxation to the extent that such harmonisation is necessary to ensure the establishment and the functioning of the internal market within the time-limit laid down in Article 14.][2]

Simon's Tax Cases—*R v C&E Comrs, ex p Lunn Poly Ltd* [1998] STC 649*; *EC Commission v EU Council (supported by Ireland, Portuguese Republic and United Kingdom)* [2007] STC 1121.

Amendments—[1] Title introduced by article G(17) of the Treaty on European Union signed at Maastricht on 7 February 1992.

[2] This article substituted by the Treaty on European Union signed at Maastricht on 7 February 1992.

CHAPTER 3—APPROXIMATION OF LAWS

[Article 94 (ex Article 100)

The Council shall, acting unanimously on a proposal from the Commission and after consulting the European Parliament and the Economic and Social Committee, issue directives for the approximation of such laws, regulations or administrative provisions of the Member States as directly affect the establishment or functioning of the common market.][1]

Simon's Tax Cases—*EC Commission v EU Council (supported by Ireland, Portuguese Republic and United Kingdom)* [2007] STC 1121.

Amendments—[1] This article substituted by the Treaty on European Union made at Maastricht on 7 February 1992.

[Article 95 (ex Article 100a)][1]

[1 By way of derogation from Article 94 and save where otherwise provided in this Treaty, the following provisions shall apply for the achievement of the objectives set out in Article 14. The Council shall, acting in accordance with the procedure referred to in Article 251 and after consulting the Economic and Social Committee, adopt the measures for the approximation of the provisions laid down by law, regulation or administrative action in Member States which have as their object the establishment and functioning of the internal market.][2]

2. Paragraph 1 shall not apply to fiscal provisions, to those relating to the free movement of persons nor to those relating to the rights and interests of employed persons.

3. The Commission, in its proposals envisaged in paragraph 1 concerning health, safety, environmental protection and consumer protection, will take as a base a high level of protection, taking account in particular of any new development based on scientific facts. Within their respective powers, the European Parliament and the Council will also seek to achieve this objective.

4. If, after the adoption by the Council or by the Commission of a harmonisation measure, a Member State deems it necessary to maintain national provisions on grounds of major needs

referred to in Article 30, or relating to the protection of the environment or the working environment, it shall notify the Commission of these provisions as well as the grounds for maintaining them.

5. Moreover, without prejudice to paragraph 4, if, after the adoption by the Council or by the Commission of a harmonisation measure, a member State deems it necessary to introduce national provisions based on new scientific evidence relating to the protection of the environment or working environment on grounds of a problem specific to that Member State arising after the adoption of the harmonisation measure, it shall notify the Commission of the envisaged provisions as well as the grounds for introducing them.

6. The Commission shall, within six months of the notifications as referred to in paragraphs 4 and 5, approve or reject the national provisions involved after having verified whether or not they are a means of arbitrary discrimination or a disguised restriction on trade between Member States and whether or not they shall constitute an obstacle to the functioning of the internal market.

In the absence of a decision by the Commission within this period the national provisions referred to in paragraphs 4 and 5 shall be deemed to have been approved.

When justified by the complexity of the matter and in the absence of danger for human health, the Commission may notify the Member State concerned that the period referred to in this paragraph may be extended for a further period of six months.

7. When pursuant to paragraph 6, a Member State is authorised to maintain or introduce national provisions derogating from a harmonisation measure, the Commission shall immediately examine whether to propose an adaptation to that measure.

8. When a Member State raises a specific problem on public health in a field which has been the subject of prior harmonisation measures, it shall bring it to the attention of the Commission which shall immediately examine whether to propose appropriate measures to the Council.

9. By way of derogation from the procedure laid down in Articles 226 and 227, the Commission or any Member State may bring the matter directly before the Court of Justice if it considers that another Member State is making improper use of the powers provided for in this Article.

10. The harmonisation measures referred to above shall, in appropriate cases, include a safeguard clause authorising the Member States to take, for one or more of the non-economic reasons referred to in Article 30, provisional measures subject to a Community control procedure.][1]

Simon's Tax Cases—*EC Commission v EU Council (supported by Ireland, Portuguese Republic and United Kingdom)* [2007] STC 1121.

Amendments—[1] This article added by the Single European Act 1987 art 18.

[2] Para 1 substituted by the Treaty on European Union made at Maastricht on 7 February 1992.

Article 96 (ex Article 101)

Where the Commission finds that a difference between the provisions laid down by law, regulation or administrative action in Member States is distorting the conditions of competition in the common market and that the resultant distortion needs to be eliminated, it shall consult the Member States concerned.

If such consultation does not result in an agreement eliminating the distortion in question, the Council shall, on a proposal from the Commission, acting unanimously during the first stage and by a qualified majority thereafter, issue the necessary directives. The Commission and the Council may take any other appropriate measures provided for in this Treaty.

Article 97 (ex Article 102)

1. Where there is reason to fear that the adoption or amendment of a provision laid down by law, regulation or administrative action may cause distortion within the meaning of Article 96, a Member State desiring to proceed therewith shall consult the Commission. After consulting the Member States, the Commission shall recommend to the States concerned such measures as may be appropriate to avoid the distortion in question.

2. If a State desiring to introduce or amend its own provisions does not comply with the recommendation addressed to it by the Commission, other Member States shall not be required, in pursuance of Article 96, to amend their own provisions in order to eliminate such distortion. If the Member State which has ignored the recommendation of the Commission causes distortion detrimental only to itself, the provisions of Article 96 shall not apply.

[TITLE VII (EX TITLE VI): ECONOMIC AND MONETARY POLICY

CHAPTER 1—ECONOMIC POLICY

Article 98 (ex Article 102a)

Member States shall conduct their economic policies with a view to contributing to the achievement of the objectives of the Community, as defined in Article 2, and in the context of the broad guidelines referred to in Article 99(2). The Member States and the Community shall act in accordance with the principle of an open market economy with free competition, favouring an efficient allocation of resources, and in compliance with the principles set out in Article 4.][1]][2]

Amendments—[1] This chapter added by the Single European Act 1987 art 20.
[2] This title amended by virtue of the Treaty on European Union signed at Maastricht in 7 February 1992.

TITLE IX (EX TITLE VII)—COMMON COMMERCIAL POLICY

[Article 133 (ex Article 113)

1. The common commercial policy shall be based on uniform principles, particularly in regard to changes in tariff rates, the conclusion of tariff and trade agreements, the achievement of uniformity in measures of liberalisation, export policy and measures to protect trade such as those to be taken in the event of dumping or subsidies.

2. The Commission shall submit proposals to the Council for implementing the common commercial policy.

3. Where agreements with one or more States or international organisations need to be negotiated, the Commission shall make recommendations to the Council, which shall authorise the Commission to open the necessary negotiations. The Council and the Commission shall be responsible for ensuring that the agreements negotiated are compatible with internal Community policies and rules.

The Commission shall conduct these negotiations in consultation with a special committee appointed by the Council to assist the Commission in this task and within the framework of such directives as the Council may issue to it. The Commission shall report regularly to the special committee on the progress of negotiations.

The relevant provisions of Article 300 shall apply.

4. In exercising the powers conferred upon it by this Article, the Council shall act by a qualified majority.

5. Paragraphs 1 to 4 shall also apply to the negotiation and conclusion of agreements in the fields of trade in services and the commercial aspects of intellectual property, insofar as those agreements are not covered by the said paragraphs and without prejudice to paragraph 6.

By way of derogation from paragraph 4, the Council shall act unanimously when negotiating and concluding an agreement in one of the fields referred to in the first subparagraph, where that agreement includes provisions for which unanimity is required for the adoption of internal rules or where it relates to a field in which the Community has not yet exercised the powers conferred upon it by this Treaty by adopting internal rules.

The Council shall act unanimously with respect to the negotiation and conclusion of a horizontal agreement insofar as it also concerns the preceding subparagraph or the second subparagraph of paragraph 6.

This paragraph shall not affect the right of the Member States to maintain and conclude agreements with third countries or international organisations insofar as such agreements comply with Community law and other relevant international agreements.

6. An agreement may not be concluded by the Council if it includes provisions which would go beyond the Community's internal powers, in particular by leading to harmonisation of the laws or regulations of the Member States in an area for which this Treaty rules out such harmonisation.

In this regard, by way of derogation from the first subparagraph of paragraph 5, agreements relating to trade in cultural and audiovisual services, educational services, and social and human health services, shall fall within the shared competence of the Community and its Member States. Consequently, in addition to a Community decision taken in accordance with the relevant provisions of Article 300, the negotiation of such agreements shall require the common accord of the Member States. Agreements thus negotiated shall be concluded jointly by the Community and the Member States.

The negotiation and conclusion of international agreements in the field of transport shall continue to be governed by the provisions of Title V and Article 300.

7. Without prejudice to the first subparagraph of paragraph 6, the Council, acting unanimously on a proposal from the Commission and after consulting the European Parliament, may extend the application of paragraphs 1 to 4 to international negotiations and agreements on intellectual property insofar as they are not covered by paragraph 5.][1]

Amendments—[1] This article (which was substituted by the Treaty on European Union made at Maastricht on 7 February 1992) is further substituted by the Treaty of Nice, Article 2(8) (OJ C 80; 10.3.2001).

PART FIVE
INSTITUTIONS OF THE COMMUNITY

TITLE I: PROVISIONS GOVERNING THE INSTITUTIONS

CHAPTER 1—THE INSTITUTIONS

Section 4—The Court of Justice

[Article 220 (ex Article 164)

The Court of Justice and the Court of First Instance, each within its jurisdiction, shall ensure that in the interpretation and application of this Treaty the law is observed.

In addition, judicial panels may be attached to the Court of First Instance under the conditions laid down in Article 225a in order to exercise, in certain specific areas, the judicial competence laid down in this Treaty.][1]

Amendments—[1] This article substituted by the Treaty of Nice, Article 2(26) (OJ C 80; 10.3.2001).

[Article 221 (ex Article 165)

The Court of Justice shall consist of one judge per Member State.

The Court of Justice shall sit in chambers or in a Grand Chamber, in accordance with the rules laid down for that purpose in the Statute of the Court of Justice.

When provided for in the Statute, the Court of Justice may also sit as a full Court.][1]

Amendments—[1] This article (which was substituted by the Treaty on European Union made at Maastricht on 7 February 1992) is further substituted by the Treaty of Nice, Article 2(27) (OJ C 80; 10.3.2001).

[Article 222 (ex Article 166)

The Court of Justice shall be assisted by eight Advocates-General. Should the Court of Justice so request, the Council, acting unanimously, may increase the number of Advocates-General.

It shall be the duty of the Advocate-General, acting with complete impartiality and independence, to make, in open court, reasoned submissions on cases which, in accordance with the Statute of the Court of Justice, require his involvement.][1]

Amendments—[1] This article substituted by the Treaty of Nice, Article 2(28) (OJ C 80; 10.3.2001).

[Article 223 (ex Article 167)

The Judges and Advocates General of the Court of Justice shall be chosen from persons whose independence is beyond doubt and who possess the qualifications required for appointment to the highest judicial offices in their respective countries or who are jurisconsults of recognised competence; they shall be appointed by common accord of the governments of the Member States for a term of six years.

Every three years there shall be a partial replacement of the Judges and Advocates-General, in accordance with the conditions laid down in the Statute of the Court of Justice.

The Judges shall elect the President of the Court of Justice from among their number for a term of three years. He may be re-elected.

Retiring Judges and Advocates-General may be reappointed.

The Court of Justice shall appoint its Registrar and lay down the rules governing his service.

The Court of Justice shall establish its Rules of Procedure. Those Rules shall require the approval of the Council, acting by a qualified majority.][1]

Amendments—[1] This article substituted by the Treaty of Nice, Article 2(29) (OJ C 80; 10.3.2001).

[Article 224 (ex Article 168)

The Court of First Instance shall comprise at least one judge per Member State. The number of Judges shall be determined by the Statute of the Court of Justice. The Statute may provide for the Court of First Instance to be assisted by Advocates-General.

The members of the Court of First Instance shall be chosen from persons whose independence is beyond doubt and who possess the ability required for appointment to high judicial office. They shall be appointed by common accord of the governments of the Member States for a term of six years. The membership shall be partially renewed every three years. Retiring members shall be eligible for reappointment.

The Judges shall elect the President of the Court of First Instance from among their number for a term of three years. He may be re-elected.

The Court of First Instance shall appoint its Registrar and lay down the rules governing his service.

The Court of First Instance shall establish its Rules of Procedure in agreement with the Court of Justice. Those Rules shall require the approval of the Council, acting by a qualified majority.

Unless the Statute of the Court of Justice provides otherwise, the provisions of this Treaty relating to the Court of Justice shall apply to the Court of First Instance.][1]

Amendments—[1] This article substituted by the Treaty of Nice, Article 2(30) (OJ C 80; 10.3.2001).

[Article 225 (ex Article 168a)][1]

1. The Court of First Instance shall have jurisdiction to hear and determine at first instance actions or proceedings referred to in Articles 230, 232, 235, 236 and 238, with the exception of those assigned to a judicial panel and those reserved in the Statute for the Court of Justice. The Statute may provide for the Court of First Instance to have jurisdiction for other classes of action or proceeding.

Decisions given by the Court of First Instance under this paragraph may be subject to a right of appeal to the Court of Justice on points of law only, under the conditions and within the limits laid down by the Statute.

2. The Court of First Instance shall have jurisdiction to hear and determine actions or proceedings brought against decisions of the judicial panels set up under Article 225a.

Decisions given by the Court of First Instance under this paragraph may exceptionally be subject to review by the Court of Justice, under the conditions and within the limits laid down by the Statute, where there is a serious risk of the unity or consistency of Community law being affected.

3. The Court of First Instance shall have jurisdiction to hear and determine questions referred for a preliminary ruling under Article 234, in specific areas laid down by the Statute.

Where the Court of First Instance considers that the case requires a decision of principle likely to affect the unity or consistency of Community law, it may refer the case to the Court of Justice for a ruling.

Decisions given by the Court of First Instance on questions referred for a preliminary ruling may exceptionally be subject to review by the Court of Justice, under the conditions and within the limits laid down by the Statute, where there is a serious risk of the unity or consistency of Community law being affected.][1]

Amendments—[1] This article (which was substituted by the Treaty on European Union made at Maastricht on 7 February 1992) is further substituted by the Treaty of Nice, Article 2(31) (OJ C 80; 10.3.2001).

[Article 225a

The Council, acting unanimously on a proposal from the Commission and after consulting the European Parliament and the Court of Justice or at the request of the Court of Justice and after consulting the European Parliament and the Commission, may create judicial panels to hear and determine at first instance certain classes of action or proceeding brought in specific areas.

The decision establishing a judicial panel shall lay down the rules on the organisation of the panel and the extent of the jurisdiction conferred upon it.

Decisions given by judicial panels may be subject to a right of appeal on points of law only or, when provided for in the decision establishing the panel, a right of appeal also on matters of fact, before the Court of First Instance.

The members of the judicial panels shall be chosen from persons whose independence is beyond doubt and who possess the ability required for appointment to judicial office. They shall be appointed by the Council, acting unanimously.

The judicial panels shall establish their Rules of Procedure in agreement with the Court of Justice. Those Rules shall require the approval of the Council, acting by a qualified majority.

Unless the decision establishing the judicial panel provides otherwise, the provisions of this Treaty relating to the Court of Justice and the provisions of the Statute of the Court of Justice shall apply to the judicial panels.][1]

Amendments—[1] This article inserted by the Treaty of Nice, Article 2(32) (OJ C 80; 10.3.2001).

Article 226 (ex Article 169)

If the Commission considers that a Member State has failed to fulfil an obligation under this Treaty, it shall deliver a reasoned opinion on the matter after giving the State concerned the opportunity to submit its observations.

If the State concerned does not comply with the opinion within the period laid down by the Commission, the latter may bring the matter before the Court of Justice.

Simon's Tax Cases—*EC Commission v Federal Republic of Germany* (Case C-74/91) [1996] STC 843*.

Article 227 (ex Article 170)

A Member State which considers that another Member State has failed to fulfil an obligation under this Treaty may bring the matter before the Court of Justice.

Before a Member State brings an action against another Member State for an alleged infringement of an obligation under this Treaty, it shall bring the matter before the Commission.

The Commission shall deliver a reasoned opinion after each of the States concerned has been given the opportunity to submit its own case and its observations on the other party's case both orally and in writing.

If the Commission has not delivered an opinion within three months of the date on which the matter was brought before it, the absence of such opinion shall not prevent the matter from being brought before the Court of Justice.

[Article 228 (ex Article 171)

1. If the Court of Justice finds that a Member State has failed to fulfil an obligation under this Treaty, the State shall be required to take the necessary measures to comply with the judgement of the Court of Justice.

2. If the Commission considers that the Member State concerned has not taken such measures it shall, after giving that State the opportunity to submit its observations, issue a reasoned opinion specifying the points on which the Member State concerned has not complied with the judgement of the Court of Justice.

If the Member State concerned fails to take the necessary measures to comply with the Court's judgement within the time-limit laid down by the Commission, the latter may bring the case before the Court of Justice. In so doing it shall specify the amount of the lump sum or penalty payment to be paid by the Member State concerned which it considers appropriate in the circumstances.

If the Court of Justice finds that the Member State concerned has not complied with its judgement it may impose a lump sum or penalty payment on it.

This procedure shall be without prejudice to Article 227.][1]

Amendments—[1] This article substituted by the Treaty on European Union made at Maastricht on 7 February 1992.

Article 229 (ex Article 172)

[Regulations adopted jointly by the European Parliament and the Council, and by the Council, pursuant to the provisions of this Treaty, may give the Court of Justice unlimited jurisdiction with regard to the penalties provided for in such regulations.][1]

Amendments—[1] This article substituted by the Treaty on European Union made at Maastricht on 7 February 1992.

[Article 229a

Without prejudice to the other provisions of this Treaty, the Council, acting unanimously on a proposal from the Commission and after consulting the European Parliament, may adopt provisions to confer jurisdiction, to the extent that it shall determine, on the Court of Justice in disputes relating to the application of acts adopted on the basis of this Treaty which create Community industrial property rights. The Council shall recommend those provisions to the Member States for adoption in accordance with their respective constitutional requirements.][1]

Amendments—[1] This article inserted by the Treaty of Nice, Article 2(33) (OJ C 80; 10.3.2001).

Article 230 (ex Article 173)

[The Court of Justice shall review the legality of acts adopted jointly by the European Parliament and the Council, of acts of the Council, of the Commission and of the ECB, other than recommendations and opinions, and of acts of the European Parliament intended to produce legal effects *vis-à-vis* third parties.

[It shall for this purpose have jurisdiction in actions brought by a Member State, the European Parliament, the Council or the Commission on grounds of lack of competence, infringement of an essential procedural requirement, infringement of this Treaty or of any rule of law relating to its application, or misuse of powers.][2]

[The Court of Justice shall have jurisdiction under the same conditions in actions brought by the Court of Auditors and by the ECB for the purpose of protecting their prerogatives.][2]

Any natural or legal person may, under the same conditions, institute proceedings against a decision addressed to that person or against a decision which, although in the form of a regulation or a decision addressed to another person, is of direct and individual concern to the former.

The proceedings provided for in this Article shall be instituted within two months of the publication of the measure, or of its notification to the plaintiff, or, in the absence thereof, of the day on which it came to the knowledge of the latter, as the case may be.][1]

Amendments—[1] This article substituted by the Treaty on European Union made at Maastricht on 7 February 1992.
[2] The second and third paragraphs substituted by the Treaty of Nice, Article 2(34) (OJ C 80; 10.3.2001).

Article 231 (ex Article 174)

If the action is well founded, the Court of Justice shall declare the act concerned to be void.

In the case of a regulation, however, the Court of Justice shall, if it considers this necessary, state which of the effects of the regulation which it has declared void shall be considered as definitive.

Article 232 (ex Article 175)

[Should the European Parliament, the Council or the Commission, in infringement of this Treaty, fail to act, the Member States and the other institutions of the Community may bring an action before the Court of Justice to have the infringement established.

The action shall be admissible only if the institution concerned has first been called upon to act. If, within two months of being so called upon, the institution concerned has not defined its position, the action may be brought within a further period of two months.

Any natural or legal person may, under the conditions laid down in the preceding paragraphs, complain to the Court of Justice that an institution of the Community has failed to address to that person any act other than a recommendation or an opinion.

The Court of Justice shall have jurisdiction, under the same conditions, in actions or proceedings brought by the ECB in the areas falling within the latter's field of competence and in actions or proceedings brought against the latter.][1]

Amendments—[1] This article substituted by the Treaty on European Union made at Maastricht on 7 February 1992.

Article 233 (ex Article 176)

[The institution or institutions whose act has been declared void or whose failure to act has been declared contrary to this Treaty shall be required to take the necessary measures to comply with the judgement of the Court of Justice.

This obligation shall not affect any obligation which may result from the application of the second paragraph of Article 288.

This Article shall also apply to the ECB.][1]

Amendments—[1] This article substituted by the Treaty on European Union made at Maastricht on 7 February 1992.

Article 234 (ex Article 177)

[The Court of Justice shall have jurisdiction to give preliminary rulings concerning:

(*a*) the interpretation of this Treaty;

(*b*) the validity and interpretation of acts of the institutions of the Community and of the ECB;

(*c*) the interpretation of the statutes of bodies established by an act of the Council, where those statutes so provide.

Where such a question is raised before any court or tribunal of a Member State, that court or tribunal may, if it considers that a decision on the question is necessary to enable it to give judgement, request the Court of Justice to give a ruling thereon.

Where any such question is raised in a case pending before a court or tribunal of a Member State against whose decision there is no judicial remedy under national law, that court or tribunal shall bring the matter before the Court of Justice.][1]

Simon's Tax Cases—*Church of Scientology of California v C&E Comrs* [1981] STC 65*.

Amendments—[1] This article substituted by the Treaty on European Union made at Maastricht on 7 February 1992.

Article 239 (ex Article 182)

The Court of Justice shall have jurisdiction in any dispute between Member States which relates to the subject matter of this Treaty if the dispute is submitted to it under a special agreement between the parties.

Article 240 (ex Article 183)

Save where jurisdiction is conferred on the Court of Justice by this Treaty, disputes to which the Community is a party shall not on that ground be excluded from the jurisdiction of the courts or tribunals of the Member States.

Article 241 (ex Article 184)

[Notwithstanding the expiry of the period laid down in the fifth paragraph of Article 230, any party may, in proceedings in which a regulation adopted jointly by the European Parliament and the Council, or a regulation of the Council, of the Commission, or of the ECB is in issue, plead the grounds specified in the second paragraph of Article 230 in order to invoke before the Court of Justice the inapplicability of that regulation.][1]

Amendments—[1] This article substituted by the Treaty on European Union made at Maastricht on 7 February 1992.

Article 242 (ex Article 185)

Actions brought before the Court of Justice shall not have suspensory effect. The Court of Justice may, however, if it considers that circumstances so require, order that application of the contested act be suspended.

Article 243 (ex Article 186)

The Court of Justice may in cases before it prescribe any necessary interim measures.

Article 244 (ex Article 187)

The judgements of the Court of Justice shall be enforceable under the conditions laid down in Article 256.

[Article 245 (ex Article 188)

The Statute of the Court of Justice shall be laid down in a separate Protocol.

The Council, acting unanimously at the request of the Court of Justice and after consulting the European Parliament and the Commission, or at the request of the Commission and after consulting the European Parliament and the Court of Justice, may amend the provisions of the Statute, with the exception of Title I.][1]

Amendments—[1] This article substituted by the Treaty of Nice, Article 2(35) (OJ C 80; 10.3.2001).

CHAPTER 2—PROVISIONS COMMON TO SEVERAL INSTITUTIONS

Article 249 (ex Article 189)

[In order to carry out their task and in accordance with the provisions of this Treaty, the European Parliament acting jointly with the Council, the Council and the Commission shall make regulations and issue directives, take decisions, make recommendations or deliver opinions.

A regulation shall have general application. It shall be binding in its entirety and directly applicable in all Member States.

A directive shall be binding, as to the result to be achieved, upon each Member State to which it is addressed, but shall leave to the national authorities the choice of form and methods.

A decision shall be binding in its entirety upon those to whom it is addressed.

Recommendations and opinions shall have no binding force.][1]

Amendments—[1] This article substituted by the Treaty on European Union made at Maastricht on 7 February 1992.

EC COUNCIL DIRECTIVES

First Council Directive
of 11 April 1967
on the harmonisation of legislation of Member States concerning turnover taxes

(67/227/EEC)

Note—See OJ 71, 14.4.67, p 1301.

Repeal—This Directive repealed by Council Directive of 28 November 2006 on the common system of value added tax (2006/112/EC). For correlation table, see Annex XII of that Directive.

THE COUNCIL OF THE EUROPEAN ECONOMIC COMMUNITY,

Having regard to the Treaty establishing the European Economic Community, and in particular Articles 99 and 100 thereof;

Having regard to the proposal from the Commission;

Having regard to the Opinion of the European Parliament;

Having regard to the Opinion of the Economic and Social Committee;

Whereas the main objective of the Treaty is to establish, within the framework of an economic union, a common market within which there is healthy competition and whose characteristics are similar to those of a domestic market;

Whereas the attainment of this objective presupposes the prior application in Member States of legislation concerning turnover taxes such as will not distort conditions of competition or hinder the free movement of goods and services within the common market;

Whereas the legislation at present in force does not meet these requirements; whereas it is therefore in the interest of the common market to achieve such harmonisation of legislation concerning turnover taxes as will eliminate, as far as possible, factors which may distort conditions of competition, whether at national or Community level, and make it possible subsequently to achieve the aim of abolishing the imposition of tax on importation and the remission of tax on exportation in trade between Member States;

Whereas, in the light of the studies made, it has become clear that such harmonisation must result in the abolition of cumulative multi-stage taxes and in the adoption by all Member States of a common system of value added tax;

Whereas a system of value added tax achieves the highest degree of simplicity and of neutrality when the tax is levied in as general a manner as possible and when its scope covers all stages of production and distribution and the provision of services; whereas it is therefore in the interest of the common market and of Member States to adopt a common system which shall also apply to the retail trade;

Whereas, however, the application of that tax to retail trade might in some Member States meet with practical and political difficulties; whereas, therefore, Member States should be permitted, subject to prior consultation, to apply the common system only up to and including the wholesale trade stage, and to apply, as appropriate, a separate complementary tax at the retail stage, or at the preceding stage;

Whereas it is necessary to proceed by stages, since the harmonisation of turnover taxes will lead in Member States to substantial alterations in tax structure and will have appreciable consequences in the budgetary, economic and social fields;

Whereas the replacement of the cumulative multi-stage tax systems in force in the majority of Member States by the common system of value added tax is bound, even if the rates and exemptions are not harmonised at the same time, to result in neutrality in competition, in that within each country similar goods bear the same tax burden, whatever the length of the production and distribution chain, and that in international trade the amount of the tax burden borne by goods is known so that an exact equalisation of that amount may be ensured; whereas, therefore, provision should be made, in the first stage, for adoption by all Member States of the common system of value added tax, without an accompanying harmonisation of rates and exemptions;

Whereas it is not possible to foresee at present how and within what period the harmonisation of turnover taxes can achieve the aim of abolishing the imposition of tax on importation and the remission of tax on exportation in trade between Member States; whereas it is therefore preferable that the second stage and the measures to be taken in respect of that stage should be determined later on the basis of proposals made by the Commission to the Council;

HAS ADOPTED THIS DIRECTIVE:

Article 1

Member States shall replace their present system of turnover taxes by the common system of value added tax defined in Article 2.

In each Member State the legislation to effect this replacement shall be enacted as rapidly as possible, so that it can enter into force on a date to be fixed by the Member State in the light of the conjunctural situation; this date shall not be later than [1 January 1972.][1]

From the entry into force of such legislation, the Member State shall not maintain or introduce any measure providing for flat-rate equalisation of turnover taxes on importation or exportation in trade between Member States.

Application to the United Kingdom—The United Kingdom had until 1 July 1973 to comply with this directive: see Act of Accession (1972), art 152 and Annex XI Part VI point 1.

Cross references—For flat rate equalisation of turnover taxes, see EEC Treaty, art 97 (member states may establish average rates for products or groups of products); Council Directive 68/221/EEC; see OJ L115, 18.5.1968, p 14 (average rates calculated in accordance with this directive; art 1 of the First Council Directive 67/227/EEC; see OJ L171, 14.4.1967, p 1301 (average rates may not be maintained or introduced); and art 3 of the Third Council Directive 69/463/EEC; see OJ L320, 20.12.1969, p 34 (average rates may not be increased).

Amendments—[1] Words substituted by art 1 of the Third Council Directive of 9 December 1969: 69/463/EEC; see OJ L320, 20.12.1969, p 34.

Article 2

The principle of the common system of value added tax involves the application to goods and services of a general tax on consumption exactly proportional to the price of the goods and services, whatever the number of transactions which take place in the production and distribution process before the stage at which tax is charged.

On each transaction, value added tax, calculated on the price of the goods or services at the rate applicable to such goods or services, shall be chargeable after deduction of the amount of value added tax borne directly by the various cost components.

The common system of value added tax shall be applied up to and including the retail trade stage.

. . .[1]

Simon's Tax Cases—*Société Financière d'Investissements SPRL v Belgium* [2000] STC 164; *Belgocodex SA v Belgium* [2000] STC 351; *Midland Bank Plc v C&E Comrs* [2000] STC 501; *C&E Comrs v Southern Primary Housing Association Ltd* [2003] STC 525; *C&E Comrs v Southern Primary Housing Association Ltd* [2004] STC 209.

Amendments—[1] Paragraph repealed by art 36 of the Sixth Council Directive of 17 May 1977: 77/388/EEC; see OJ L145, 13.6.1977, p 1.

Article 3

The Council shall issue, on a proposal from the Commission, a second Directive concerning the structure of, and the procedure for applying, the common system of value added tax.

Cross references—For the directive made, see the Second Council Directive 67/228/EEC; see OJ L71, 14.4.1967, p 1303. This directive ceases to apply in member states in accordance with art 37 of the Sixth Council Directive 77/388/EEC; see OJ L145, 13.6.1977, p 1.

Article 4

In order to enable the Council to discuss this, and if possible to take decisions before the end of the transitional period, the Commission shall submit to the Council, before the end of 1968, proposals as to how and within what period the harmonisation of turnover taxes can achieve the aim of abolishing the imposition of tax on importation and the remission of tax on exportation in trade between Member States, while ensuring the neutrality of those taxes as regards the origin of the goods or services.

In this connection, particular account shall be taken of the relationship between direct and indirect taxes, which differs in the various Member States; of the effects of an alteration in tax systems on the tax and budget policy of Member States; and of the influence which tax systems have on conditions of competition and on social conditions in the Community.

[Article 5] [1]

Amendments—[1] Article 5 repealed by art 36 of the Sixth Council Directive of 17 May 1977: 77/388/EEC; see OJ L145, 13.6.1977, p 1.

Article 6

This Directive is addressed to the Member States.

Second Council Directive of 11 April 1967 on the harmonisation of legislation of Member States concerning turnover taxes Structure and procedures for application of the common system of value added tax

(67/228/EEC)

Commentary—*De Voil Indirect Tax Service* **V1.204**.
Note—See OJ 71, 14.4.1967, p 1303–1312 (DE, FR, IT, NL) English special edition: Series I Chapter 1967 p 0016.
Simon's Tax Cases—*Fleming (trading as Bodycraft) v R&C Comrs; Condé Nast Publications Ltd v R&C Comrs* [2008] STC 324.
Repeal—This Directive repealed by Sixth Council Directive of 17 May 1977 on the harmonisation of the laws of the Member States relating to turnover taxes – common system of value added tax: uniform basis of assessment (Directive 77/388/EEC), subsequently Council Directive of 28 November 2006 on the common system of value added tax (Directive 2006/112/EC).

THE COUNCIL OF THE EUROPEAN ECONOMIC COMMUNITY,

Having regard to the Treaty establishing the European Economic Community, and in particular Articles 99 and 100 thereof;

Having regard to the First Council Directive of 11 April 1967[1] on the harmonisation of legislation of Member States concerning turnover taxes;

Having regard to the proposal from the Commission;.

Having regard to the Opinion of the European Parliament;

Having regard to the Opinion of the Economic and Social Committee;

Whereas the replacement of the turnover taxes in force in Member States by a common system of value added tax is intended as a means of attaining the objectives set out in the First Directive;

Whereas, until the abolition of the imposition of tax on importation and the remission of tax on exportation, it is possible to grant Member States substantial autonomy in determining the rate or differential rates of tax;

Whereas it is also possible to accept on a transitional basis certain differences in the procedure for applying the tax in Member States; whereas it is, however, necessary to make provision for appropriate procedures to ensure neutrality in competition between Member States and to restrict progressively or to abolish the differences in question, so that national systems of value added tax may be brought into alignment, thereby preparing the way for the attainment of the objective set out in Article 4 of the First Directive;

Whereas, in order to enable the system to be applied in a simple and neutral manner, and to keep the standard rate of tax within reasonable limits, it is necessary to limit special systems and exceptional measures;

Whereas the system of value added tax makes it possible, where appropriate, for social and economic reasons, to effect reductions or increases in the tax burden on certain goods and services by means of a differentiation in the rates, but the introduction of zero rates gives rise to difficulties, so that it is highly desirable to limit strictly the number of exemptions and to make the reductions considered necessary by applying reduced rates which are high enough to permit in normal circumstances the deduction of the tax paid at the preceding stage, which moreover achieves in general the same result as that at present obtained by the application of exemptions in cumulative multistage systems;

Whereas it has proved possible to leave Member States themselves to make rules concerning the numerous services whose cost has no influence on the prices of goods, and the systems to be applied in the case of small undertakings, subject, as regards the latter, to prior consultation;

Whereas it has proved necessary to provide for special systems for the application of the value added tax to the agricultural sector and to request the Commission to submit to the Council, as soon as possible proposals to this effect;

Whereas it is necessary to provide for a rather large number of special provisions covering interpretation, derogations and certain detailed application procedures, and to establish a list of the services compulsorily subject to the common system; and whereas these provisions and this list should appear in the Annexes forming an integral part of this Directive;

HAS ADOPTED THIS DIRECTIVE:

Note—[1] OJ No 71, 14.4.1967, p 1301.

Article 1

Member States shall introduce, in accordance with a common system, a tax on turnover (hereinafter called "value added tax").

The structure of, and procedures for applying this tax shall be established by Member States in accordance with the provisions of the following Articles and of Annexes A and B.

Article 2

The following shall be subject to the value added tax:

(*a*) *The supply of goods and the provision of services within the territory of the country by a taxable person against payment;*
(*b*) *the importation of goods.*

Article 3

"Territory of the country" means the territory In which the State concerned applies the value added tax; this territory shall, as a general rule, include the whole of the national territory, including territorial waters.

Article 4

"Taxable person" means any person who independently and habitually engages in transactions pertaining to the activities of producers, traders or persons providing services, whether or not for gain.

Article 5

1. "Supply of goods" means the transfer of the right to dispose of tangible property as owner.

2. The following shall also be considered as supply within the meaning of paragraph 1:

(*a*) *the actual handing over of goods, under a contract which provides for the hiring of goods for a certain period, or the sale on deferred terms of goods, in both cases subject to a clause to the effect that ownership shall pass at the latest upon payment of the final instalment due;*
(*b*) *the transfer, by order of a public authority, of ownership in goods against payment of compensation;*
(*c*) *the transfer of goods pursuant to a contract under which commission is payable on purchase or sale;*
(*d*) *the delivery of moveable property produced under a contract for work, that is to say the handing over by a contractor to his customer of moveable property which he has made from materials and objects entrusted to him by the customer for this purpose, whether or not the contractor has provided a part of the products used;*
(*e*) *the delivery up of works of construction, including those in which moveable property is incorporated in immoveable property.*

3. The following shall be treated as supply against payment:

(*a*) *the appropriation by a taxable person, from his undertaking, of goods which he applies to his own private use or transfers free of charge;*
(*b*) *the use for the needs of his undertaking, by a taxable person, of goods produced or extracted by him or by another person on his behalf.*

4. The place of supply shall be deemed as being:

(*a*) *in cases where the goods are dispatched or transported either by the supplier or by the consignee, or by a third person: the place where the goods were at the time when the dispatch or transport to the consignee began;*
(*b*) *in cases where the goods are not dispatched or transported: the place where the goods were at the time of supply.*

5. The chargeable event shall occur at the moment when delivery is effected. In the case, however, of supply involving payments on account before delivery, it may be provided that the chargeable event shall already have occurred at the moment of issue of the invoice or, at the latest, at the moment of receipt of the payment, in respect of the whole of the amount invoiced or received.

Article 6

1. "Provision of services" means any transaction which does not constitute a supply of goods within the meaning of Article 5.

2. The rules laid down in this Directive as regards the taxation of the provision of services shall be compulsorily applicable only to services listed in Annex B.

3. The place of the provision of service shall, as a general rule, be regarded as being the place where the services provided, the right transferred or granted, or the object hired, is used or enjoyed.

4. The chargeable event shall occur at the moment when the service is provided. In the case, however, of the provision of services of indeterminate length or exceeding a certain period or involving payments on account, it may be provided that the chargeable event shall already have occurred at the moment of issue of the invoice or, at the latest, at the moment of the receipt of the payment on account, in respect of the whole of the amount invoiced or received.

Article 7

1. "Importation of goods" means the entry of such goods into the "territory of the country" within the meaning of Article 3.

2. At importation, the chargeable event shall occur at the time of such entry. Member States may, however, link the chargeable event and the date when payment of value added tax falls due with the chargeable event and the date when payment of customs duties or other import taxes, charges and levies falls due.

The same link may be established, as regards the chargeable event and the date when payment of value added tax falls due, in respect of the supply of imported goods placed under a system of suspension of customs duties or other taxes, charges or levies.

Article 8

The basis of assessment shall be:

(a) in the case of supply of goods and of the provision of services, everything which makes up the consideration for the supply of the goods or the provision of services, including all expenses and taxes except the value added tax itself;

(b) in the case of the transactions referred to in Article 5(3)(a) and (b), the purchase price of the goods or of like goods or, if there is no purchase price, the cost price;

(c) in the case of importation of goods, the customs value, plus all duties, taxes, charges and levies due by reason of importation, except the value added tax itself. The same basis of assessment shall apply when the goods are exempt from customs duties or are not subject to ad valorem customs duties.

In the case of importation of goods, each Member State may add to the basis of assessment the incidental expenses (packing, transport, insurance, etc) arising up to the place of destination which have not been included in that basis.

Article 9

1. The standard rate of value added tax shall be fixed by each Member State at a percentage of the basis of assessment which shall be the same for the supply of goods and for the provision of services.

2. In certain cases, the supply of goods and the provision of services may, however, be subject to increased rates or to reduced rates. Each reduced rate shall be determined in such a manner that the amount of value added tax resulting from the application of this rate shall normally permit the deduction of the whole of the value added tax which is deductible under Article 11.

3. The rate applicable to importation of goods shall be that which is applied in the territory of the country to the supply of like goods.

Article 10

1. The following shall be exempted from value added tax on conditions laid down by each Member State:

(a) the supply of goods consigned or transported to places outside the territory in which the State concerned applies value added tax;

(b) the provision of services relating to goods covered by (a) or in transit.

2. The "provision of services relating to importations of goods may, subject to the consultations mentioned in Article 16, be exempted from value added tax.

3. Each Member State may, subject to the consultations mentioned in Article 16, determine the other exemptions which it considers necessary.

Article 11

1. Where goods and services are used for the purposes of his undertaking, the taxable person shall be authorised to deduct from the tax for which he is liable:

(a) the value added tax invoiced to him in respect of goods supplied to him or in respect of services rendered to him;

(b) the value added tax paid in respect of imported goods;

(c) the value added tax which he has paid in respect of the use of goods referred to in Article 5(3)(b).

2. Value added tax on goods and services used in non-taxable or exempt transactions shall not be deductible.

The taxable person shall however be authorised to make the deduction if the supply of goods or the provision of services takes place abroad or is exempt under Article 10(1) or (2).

As regards goods and services which are used both in transactions giving entitlement to deduction and in transactions which do not give entitlement to deduction, deduction shall only be allowed for that part of the value added tax which is proportional to the amount relating to the transactions giving entitlement to deduction (pro rata rule).

3. The deduction shall be made from the value added tax due for the period during which deductible tax is invoiced in the case of paragraph 1(a) or paid in the case of paragraph 1(b) and (c) (immediate deductions).

In the case of a partial deduction under paragraph 2 the amount of the deduction shall be provisionally, determined in accordance with criteria established by each Member State and finally adjusted after the end of the year when the pro rata figure for the year of acquisition has been calculated.

As regards capital goods, the adjustment shall be effected on the basis of the variations of the pro rata figure which have occurred during a period of five years including the year during which the goods were acquired; the adjustment shall, apply each year to only one-fifth of the tax borne by capital goods.

4. Certain goods and services may be excluded from the deduction system, in particular those capable of being exclusively or partially used for the private needs of the taxable person or of his staff.

Article 12

1. Every taxable person shall keep sufficiently detailed accounts to permit application of the value added tax and inspection by the tax authorities.

2. Every taxable person shall issue an invoice in respect of goods supplied and services provided by him to another taxable person.

3. Every taxable person shall each month lodge a declaration showing, in respect of transactions carried out during the preceding month, all the information required to calculate the tax and the deductions to be made. Every taxable person shall pay the amount of the value added tax when lodging the declaration.

Article 13

Should a Member State consider that, in exceptional cases, special measures should be adopted in order to simplify the charging procedure in respect of the tax or to prevent certain frauds, it shall so inform the Commission and the other Member States.

Should there, within one month, be objections from one or more States or from the Commission, the request for derogation shall be brought before the Council, which shall act on a proposal from the Commission within three months.

Should it appear from the conclusion of the Commission that only a simplification of the charging procedure or a measure designed to prevent fraud is involved, the Council shall act by a qualified majority on the derogation requested.

Should it appear, on the contrary, from those conclusions that the proposed measure might be prejudicial to the very principles of the system introduced by this Directive, and in particular to neutrality in competition between Member States, the Council shall act unanimously.

In either case, the Council shall act in accordance with the same procedure as regards the period of application of such measures.

The State concerned may not apply the proposed measures until the period for entering objections has expired or, where there have been objections, until after the Council's decision, if such decision is favourable.

These provisions shall cease to be applicable when the imposition of tax on importation and the remission of tax on exportation are abolished in trade between Member States.

Article 14

Each Member State may, subject to the consultations mentioned in Article 16, apply to small undertakings whose subjection to the normal system of value added tax would meet with difficulties the special system best suited to national requirements and possibilities.

Cross reference—See Directive 2006/112/EC arts 284, 285.

Article 15

1. The Commission shall submit to the Council, as soon as possible, proposals for Directives on common procedures for applying value added tax to transactions relating to agricultural products.

2. Until the date fixed in the Directive referred to in paragraph 1 for the application of such common procedures, each Member State may, subject to the consultations mentioned in Article 16, apply to undertakings in the agricultural sector whose subjection to the normal system ,of value added tax would meet with difficulties the special system best suited to national requirements and possibilities.

Article 16

Where a Member State must, in accordance with the provisions of this Directive, enter into consultations, it shall refer the matter to the Commission in good time, having regard to the application of Article 102 of the Treaty.

Article 17

With a view to the transition from the present systems of turnover taxes to the common system of value added tax, Member States may:

—adopt transitional measures to levy the tax in advance;

—apply, during a certain transitional period, in respect of capital goods, the method of deduction by annual instalments (deductions pro rata temporis);

—exclude, in whole or in part, during a certain transitional period, capital goods from the deduction system provided for in Article 11;

and, subject to the consultations mentioned in Article 16:

—authorise (in order to grant relief, total or partial, but general in scope, from the turnover tax charged up to the time of introducing value added tax) standard deductions in respect of capital goods not yet written off and of stocks in hand at that time. Member States may, however, restrict such deductions to goods exported during a period of one year from the introduction of value added tax. In that event, such deductions shall only be allowed in respect of stocks in hand at the time referred to above and exported in an unaltered state;

—provide for reduced rates or even exemptions with refund, if appropriate, of the tax paid at the preceding stage, where the total incidence of such measures does not exceed that of the reliefs applied under the present system. Such measures may only be taken for clearly defined social reasons and for the benefit of the final consumer, and may not remain in force after the abolition of the imposition of tax on importation and the remission of tax on exportation in trade between Member States.

Cross reference—See Directive 77/388/EEC arts 24(2)(*a*), 28(1), (2)(*a*).

Article 18

The Commission shall, after consulting the Member States, submit to the Council, for the first time on 1 January 1972 and every two years thereafter, a report on the operation of the common system of value added tax in Member States.

Article 19

The Council shall, in the interest of the common market, adopt at the proper time, on a proposal from the Commission, the appropriate Directives to complete the common system of value added tax, and in particular to restrict progressively or to abolish measures adopted by Member States in derogation from this system, so that national systems of value added tax may be brought into alignment, thereby preparing the way for the attainment of the objective set out in Article 4 of the First Directive.

Article 20

The Annexes shall form an integral part of this Directive.

Article 21

This Directive is addressed to the Member States.

ANNEX A

1. Regarding Article 3

If a Member State intends to apply value added tax in a territory smaller than its national territory, it shall enter into the consultations mentioned in Article 16.

2. Regarding Article 4

The expression "activities of producers, traders, or persons providing services" is to be understood in a wide sense and to cover all economic activities, including, therefore, activities of the extractive industries, agriculture and the professions.

If a Member State intends not to tax certain activities, it should achieve its purpose by means of exemptions rather than by excluding from the scope of the tax persons pursuing such activities.

Member States may also consider as a "taxable person" anyone who engages occasionally in the transactions referred to in Article 4.

The expression "independently" is intended in particular to exclude from taxation wage-earners who are bound to their employer by a contract of service. This expression also makes it possible for each Member State not to consider as separate taxable persons, but as one single taxable person, persons who, although independent from the legal point of view, are, however, organically linked to one another by economic, financial or organisational relationships. Any Member State intending to adopt such a system shall enter into the consultations mentioned in Article 16.

States, regional and local government bodies and other public corporate bodies shall not as a general rule be considered as taxable persons in respect of activities which they pursue in their official capacity as official authorities.

If, however, they pursue activities as producers, traders, or providers of services, they may be considered as liable to tax in respect of such activities.

3. Regarding Article 5(1)

"Tangible property" means both moveable and immoveable tangible property.

The supply of electric current, gas, heat, refrigeration and the like shall be considered as supply of goods.

In case of contribution to a company of the whole or part of the contributor's assets, Member States may regard the benefiting company as the successor in title of the contributor.

4. Regarding Article 5(2)(a)

For the purposes of this Directive, the contract referred to in Article 5(2)(a) must not be subdivided into part hire and part sale, but shall be regarded, as soon as concluded, as a contract involving a taxable supply.

5. Regarding Article 5(2)(d) and (e)

Member States which, for specifically national reasons, cannot consider the transactions referred to in Article 5(2)(d) and (e) as supply shall classify them in the category of provision of services, subjecting them to the rate which would be applicable to them if they were considered as supply.

The following, inter alia, shall be considered as "works of construction":

—the construction of buildings, bridges, roads, ports, etc, in performance of a building contract;
—earth-moving and planting of gardens;
—installation work (of central heating, for example);
—repairs to buildings, other than current maintenance.

6. Regarding Article 5(3)(a)

As regards the appropriation of goods in an unaltered state bought by a taxable person, Member States may, instead of taxing, forbid deduction or adjust it if deduction has already been effected. However, appropriation for giving gifts of small value and samples, which from the tax point of view may be classified as overhead expenses, shall not be considered as taxable supply. Moreover, the provisions of Article 11(2) shall not be applicable to such appropriations.

7. Regarding Article 5(3)(b)

This provision shall only be applied to ensure equality of taxation between, on the one hand, goods purchased and intended for the needs of the undertaking, and in respect of which there is no entitlement to immediate or complete deduction, and, on the other hand, goods produced or extracted by the taxable person or on his behalf by a third person which are also used for the same needs.

8. Regarding Article 5(5)

The "chargeable event" means the event giving rise to the tax.

9. Regarding Article 6(1)

The definition of provision of services given in this paragraph involves classification of, inter alia, the following as provision of services:

—the assignment of intangible property;
—the carrying out of an obligation to refrain from doing something;
—the carrying out of a service rendered by order of a public authority;
—the carrying out of work on goods, if such work is not considered as supply within the meaning of Article 5(2)(d) and (e) as, for example, current maintenance work, the laundering of linen, etc.

This definition shall not prevent taxation by Member States of certain transactions engaged in by a taxable person as services "rendered to oneself" when such a measure proves necessary in order to avoid distortion of competition.

10. Regarding Article. 6(2)

Member States shall refrain, as far as possible, from granting exemption from tax in respect of the provision of the services listed in Annex B.

11. Regarding Article 6(3)

The Council shall, acting unanimously on a proposal from the Commission, lay down, before 1 January 1970, special rules concerning certain services for which such rules may prove necessary, derogating where appropriate from the provisions of Article 6(3). Until those rules have been laid down, each Member State may, in order to simplify the procedure for charging the tax, derogate from the provisions of Article 6(3); it shall, however, take the necessary steps to avoid double taxation or non-taxation.

12. Regarding Article 8

Any Member State which applies value added tax only up to and including the wholesale stage may, in the case of goods sold by retail by a taxable person, reduce the basis of assessment by a certain percentage; the basis thus reduced shall not, however, be lower than the purchase or cost price plus, where appropriate, the amount of the customs duties (including levies), taxes and charges on the goods (except value added tax), even if payment thereof has been suspended.

In the case of importation of goods sold by retail, the same reduction shall be applied to the basis of assessment.

It shall be left to Member States to define, in accordance with their national concepts, the concept of "sale of goods by retail".

Each Member State may, subject to the consultations mentioned in Article 16, law down, as a measure to prevent fraud and in respect of specified goods and services, that, in derogation from Article 8, the basis of assessment shall not be lower than a minimum basis determined by its national law.

13. Regarding Article 8(a)

The expression "consideration" means everything received in return for the supply of goods or the provision of services, including incidental expenses (packing, transport, insurance, etc) that is to say not only the cash amounts charged, but also, for example, the value of the goods received in exchange or, in the case of goods or services supplied by order of a public authority, the amount of the compensation received.

This provision ,shall not, however, prevent each Member State which considers it necessary for the achievement of greater neutrality in competition from being able to exclude from the basis of assessment in respect of supply the incidental expenses arising as from the place of supply as defined in Article 5(4) and to tax such expenses as consideration for the provision of services.

Further, the expenses paid in the name and for the account of the customer which are shown in the accounts of the supplier as transitory items shall not be included in the basis of assessment.

The customs duties and other charges, taxes, etc, paid at importation by agents and other intermediaries in customs clearance including forwarding agents, under their own name, may also be excluded from the basis of assessment corresponding to the services they have provided.

14. Regarding Article 8(c)

In intra-Community trade, Member States shall endeavour to apply to importations of goods a basis of assessment which corresponds, as far as possible, to that used for supply made within the territory of the country; this basis shall include the same components as those taken into account pursuant to Article 8(c).

Until the abolition of the imposition of tax on importation and the remission of tax on exportation in trade between Member States at the latest, and subject to the consultations mentioned in Article 16, each Member State may apply to importations of goods from third countries a basis of assessment which corresponds, as far as possible, to that used for supply within the territory of the country; this basis shall include the same components as those taken into account pursuant to Article 8(c).

15. Regarding Article 9(2)

Where this paragraph is applied to the transport services referred to in Annex B, item 5, it must be so applied as to ensure equality of treatment as between the different modes of transport.

16. Regarding Article 10(1)(a)

Relief from tax as provided for in this provision refers to the supply of goods directly exported, that is to say supply made by the exporter. Member States may, however, extend exemption to supply made at the preceding stage.

17. Regarding Article 10(1)(b)

Member States may, however, refrain from granting this exemption if relief from the value added tax charged on. the provision of these services is effected in favour of the beneficiary of the services by means of deductions. Moreover, Member States may, except in the case of the provision of services relating to goods in transit, restrict such exemption to the provision of services relating to goods the supply of which inside the country is taxable.

18. Regarding Article 10(2)

This provision relates in particular to the provision of international transport services at importation and to port services.

19. Regarding Article 10(2) and (3)

Where these paragraphs are applied to the transport services referred to in Annex B, item 5, they must be so applied as to ensure equality of treatment as between the different modes of transport.

20. Regarding Article 11(1)(a)

In the cases provided for in Article 5(5), second sentence, and Article 6(4), second sentence, the deductions may be made as soon as the invoice is received, even though the goods have not yet been supplied or the services rendered.

21. Regarding Article 11(2), second subparagraph

Member States may, however, restrict the right to deduction to transactions relating to goods the supply of which inside the country is taxable.

22. Regarding Article 11(2), third subparagraph

The pro rata figure shall, in general, be determined in respect of all the transactions carried out by the taxable person (general pro rata figure). However, a taxable person may, exceptionally, obtain administrative permission to determine special pro rata figures for certain sectors of his activities.

23. Regarding Article 11(3), first subparagraph

Subject to the consultations mentioned in Article 16, each Member State may, on conjunctural grounds, partially or wholly exclude capital goods from the deduction system, or apply in respect of such goods, instead of the method of immediate deductions, that of annual instalments (deductions pro rata temporis).

24. Regarding Article 11(3), third subparagraph

Member States may specify certain tolerances in order to limit the number of adjustments in the event of variations in the annual pro rata figure as compared with the initial pro rata figure which served as a basis for deductions in the case of capital goods.

25. Regarding Article 12(2)

The invoice must show separately the price exclusive of tax and the corresponding tax for each different rate, together with any exemption.

Each Member State may, in special cases, provide for derogations from this rule and also from the obligation laid down in Article 12(2). Such derogations, however, must be strictly limited.

Notwithstanding the other measures to be taken by Member States to ensure payment of the tax and to prevent fraud, all persons, whether taxable or not, who show the value added tax on an invoice, must pay the amount thereof.

26. Regarding Article 12(3)

Each Member State may, for practical reasons, shorten the period laid down in Article 12(3) or authorise certain taxable persons to lodge the declaration quarterly, half yearly or annually.

During the first six months of each year, the taxable person shall, where appropriate, lodge a declaration concerning all the previous years' transactions, and including all the particulars necessary for any adjustments.

Each Member State shall, as regards importation of goods, adopt measures governing the procedure in respect of the declaration and of the payment which must ensue.

27. Regarding Article 14

Where this Article is applied to the transport services referred to in Annex B, item 5, it must be so applied as to ensure equality of treatment as between the different modes of transport.

28. Regarding Article 17, fourth indent

Stocks may be valued inter alia by reference to the transactions carried out during preceding years by the taxable persons.

ANNEX B

List of the services referred to in Article 6(2):

1. assignments of patents, trade marks and other similar rights, and the granting of licences in respect of such rights;

2. work, other than that referred to in Article 5(2)(d), on tangible moveable property, carried out for a taxable person;

3. provision of services to prepare or co-ordinate the carrying out of works of construction, as, for example, services provided by architects and by firms providing on-site supervision of works;

4. commercial advertising services;

5. transport and storage of goods, and ancillary services;

6. hiring of tangible moveable property to a taxable person;

7. provision of staff to a taxable person;

8. services provided by consultants, engineers, planning offices and similar services, in scientific, economic or technical fields;

9. the carrying out of an obligation to refrain from exercising, in whole or in part, a business activity or a right included in this list;

10. the services of forwarding agents, brokers, business agents and other independent intermediaries, in so far as they relate to supply or importation of goods or the provision of services included in this list.

Cross reference—See Directive 77/388/EEC Annex F para 2.

Council Directive
of 28 May 1969
on the harmonisation of provisions laid down by law, regulation or administrative action relating to exemption from turnover tax ... on imports in international travel

(69/169/EEC)

Notes—See OJ L133, 4.6.1969, p 6.

The provisions on excise duty laid down in this Directive ceased to apply on 31 December 1992 in respect of relations between member States by virtue of Directive 92/12/EEC art 23(4), OJ L76, 23.3.92, p 1. The words omitted from the text below relate to excise duties and are not relevant to this work.

The provisions of this Directive relating to VAT cease to have effect on 31 December 1992 as regards relations between member States; see Directive 91/680/EEC art 2(3); OJ L376, 31.12.91, p 1.

This Directive repealed by Council Directive 2007/74/EC art 18 with effect from 1 December 2008 (Directive 2007/74/EC art 20). See below for the text of Directive 2007/74/EC.

THE COUNCIL OF THE EUROPEAN COMMUNITIES

Having regard to the Treaty establishing the European Economic Community, and in particular Article 99 thereof,

Having regard to the proposal from the Commission,

Whereas, notwithstanding the achievement of the customs union, which involves the abolition of customs duties and the majority of the charges having equivalent effect in trade between Member States, it is necessary, until harmonisation of indirect taxes has reached an advanced stage, to retain the imposition of tax on importation and the remission of tax on exportation in such trade;

Whereas it is desirable that, even before such harmonisation, the populations of the Member States should become more strongly conscious of the reality of the common market and that to this end measures should be adopted for the greater liberalisation of the system of taxes on imports in travel between Member States; whereas the need for such measures has been emphasised repeatedly by members of the Assembly;

Whereas reductions of this kind in respect of travel constitute a further step in the direction of the reciprocal opening of the markets of the Member States and the creation of conditions similar to those of a domestic market;

Whereas such reductions must be limited to non-commercial importations of goods by travellers; whereas, as a general rule, such goods can only be obtained in the country from which they come (country of exit) already taxed, so that if the country of entry forgoes, within the prescribed limits, charging turnover tax ... on imports, this avoids double taxation without leading to an absence of taxation;

Whereas a Community system of tax reductions on imports has proved necessary also in respect of travel between third countries and the Community;

HAS ADOPTED THIS DIRECTIVE:

Article 1

[1. Goods contained in the personal luggage of travellers coming from third countries shall be exempt from the turnover tax and ... levied on imports if the imported goods have no commercial character and the total value of the goods does not exceed [175][1] European units of account per person.]

2. Member States may reduce this exemption to [90][2] ECU for travellers under fifteen years old.

3. Where the total value per person of several items exceeds the amounts set out in paragraph 1 or the amount fixed pursuant to paragraph 2, as the case may be, exemption up to these amounts shall be granted for such of the items as would, if imported separately, have been granted exemption, it being understood that the value of an individual item cannot be split up.

Amendments—[1] Limit in para (1) substituted for "45" by Council Directive 94/4/EC of 14 February 1994, arts 1, 4 with effect from 3 March 1994 (date on which the Directive was published in the *Official Journal*); see OJ L60, 3.3.94, p 14 and see also p 678, *ante*.

[2] Limit in para (2) substituted for "23" by Council Directive 94/4/EC of 14 February 1994, arts 1, 4.

Article 2

[1. Exemption from turnover tax and excise duty on imports shall apply to goods contained in the personal luggage of travellers coming from Member States of the Community provided that they fulfil the conditions laid down in Articles 9 and 10 of the Treaty, have been acquired subject to the general rules governing taxation on the domestic market of one of the Member States and have no commercial character and that the total value of the goods does not exceed [600][1] ECU per person.]

2. Member States may reduce this exemption up to [150 ECU][2] for travellers under fifteen years old.

3. Where the total value per person of several items exceeds [the amount set out in paragraph 1] or the amount fixed pursuant to paragraph 2, as the case may be, exemption up to these amounts shall be granted for such of the items as would, if imported separately, have been granted exemption, it being understood that the value of an individual item cannot be split up.

[4. Where the travel referred to in paragraph 1:

—involves transit through the territory of a third country; overflying without landing shall not, however, be regarded as transit within the meaning of this Directive,

—begins in a part of the territory of another Member State in which turnover tax and/or excise duty is not chargeable on goods consumed within that territory,

the traveller must be able to establish that the goods transported in his luggage have been acquired subject to the general conditions governing taxation on the domestic market of a Member State and do not qualify for any refunding of turnover tax and/or excise duty, failing which Article 1 shall apply.]

[5. Under no circumstances may the total value of the goods exempted exceed the amount provided for in paragraph 1 or 2.]

[6. Every two years, and for the first time on 31 October 1987 at the latest, the Council, acting in accordance with the procedures provided for by the Treaty on this point, shall adjust the amounts of the exemptions referred to in paragraphs 1 and 2 in order to maintain the genuine value.]

Amendments—[1] Limit in para 1 substituted for "390" by Council Directive 91/191/EEC of 27 March 1991, art 1 with effect from 1 July 1991; see OJ L94, 16.4.1991, p 24.

[2] Limit in para 2 substituted for "100" by Council Directive 91/191/EEC of 27 March 1991, art 1 with effect from 1 July 1991; see OJ L94, 16.4.1991, p 24.

Article 3

For the purposes of this Directive:

1. The value of personal effects which are imported temporarily or are re-imported following their temporary export shall not be taken into consideration for determining the exemption referred to in Articles 1 and 2.

2. Importations shall be regarded as having no commercial character if they:

(a) take place occasionally, and

(b) consist exclusively of goods for the personal or family use of the travellers, or of goods intended as presents; the nature or quantity of such goods must not be such as might indicate that they are being imported for commercial reasons.

[3. "Personal luggage" shall mean the whole of the luggage which a traveller is in a position to submit to the customs authorities upon his arrival, as well as luggage which he submits later to the same authorities, subject to proof that such luggage was registered as accompanied luggage, at the time of his departure, with the company which has been responsible for conveying him.

The definition of "personal luggage" shall not cover portable containers containing fuel. However, for each means of motor transport a quantity of fuel not exceeding 10 litres shall be admitted duty-free in such a container, without prejudice to national provisions governing the possession and transport of fuel.]

Article 4

[1. Without prejudice to national provisions applicable to travellers whose residence is outside Europe, each Member State shall set the following quantitative limits for exemptions from turnover tax and excise duty of the goods listed below:

	I Travel between third countries and the Community	*II Travel between Member States*
(a) Tobacco products—		
cigarettes or	*200*	*300*
cigarillos (cigars of a maximum weight of 3 grammes each) or	*100*	*150*

VAT

	I Travel between third countries and the Community	*II Travel between Member States*
cigars or	*50*	*75*
smoking tobacco	*250 g*	*400 g*
(b) Alcohol and alcoholic beverages— *distilled beverages and spirits of an alcoholic strength exceeding 22% vol; undenatured ethyl alcohol of 80% vol and over*	*a total of 1 litre*	*a total of 1,5 litres*
or distilled beverages and spirits, and aperitifs with a wine or alcohol base, tafia, saké or similar beverages of an alcoholic strength not exceeding 22% vol; sparkling wines, fortified wines and	*a total of 2 litres*	*a total of 3 litres*
—still wines	*a total of 2 litres*	*a total of 5 litres*
(c) Perfumes	*50 g*	*75 g*
and		
toilet waters	*¼ litre*	*⅜ litre*
(d) Coffee	*500 g*	*1,000 g*
or		
coffee extracts and essences	*200 g*	*400 g*
(e) Tea	*100 g*	*200 g*
or		
tea extracts and essences	*40 g*	*80 g*

2. Exemption of the goods mentioned in paragraph 1(a) and (b) shall not be granted to travellers under 17 years of age.

Exemption for the goods mentioned in paragraph 1(d) shall not be granted to travellers under 15 years of age.]

3. Within the quantitative limits set in paragraph 1 and taking account of the restrictions in paragraph 2, the value of the goods listed in paragraph 1 shall not be taken into consideration in determining the exemption referred to in Articles 1 and 2.

[4. Where the travel referred to in Article 2(1).

—involves transit through the territory of a third country; overflying without landing shall not, however, be regarded as transit within the meaning of this Directive,

—begins in a part of the territory of another Member State in which turnover tax and/or excise duty is not chargeable on goods consumed within that territory,

the traveller must be able to establish that the goods transported in his luggage have been acquired subject to the general conditions governing taxation on the domestic market of a Member State and do not qualify for any refunding of turnover tax and/or duty, failing which the quantities set out in paragraph I, column I, shall apply.]

[5. Under no circumstances may the total quantity of goods exempted exceed the quantities provided for in paragraph 1, column II.]

Article 5

[1. Member States may reduce the value and/or quantity of the goods which may be admitted duty free, down to one-tenth of the values and/or quantities provided for in Articles 2 and 4(1), column II, where such goods are imported from another Member State by persons resident in the frontier zone of the importing Member State or in that of the neighbouring Member State, by frontier zone workers, or by the crew of the means of transport used in international travel.

However, duty free entitlement in respect of the goods listed below may be as follows:

(a) Tobacco products	
Cigarettes	*40*
or	
cigarillos (cigars of a maximum weight of 3 grammes each)	*20*
or	
cigars	*10*
or	
smoking tobacco	*50 g*
(b) alcoholic beverages:	
—distilled beverages and spirits, of an alcoholic strength exceeding 22% vol	*0·25 litre*
or	

—distilled beverages and spirits, and aperitifs with a wine or alcohol base of an alcoholic strength not exceeding 22% vol;
sparkling wines, fortified wines *0·50 litre*
and
—still wines *0·50 litre]*

[2. Member States may set lower limits as to value and/or quantity for the exemption of goods when they are imported from a third country by persons resident in the frontier zone, by frontier zone workers or by the crew of the means of transport used in travel between third countries and the Community.]

[3. Member States may set lower limits as to value and/or quantity for the exemption of goods when they are imported from another Member State by members of the armed forces of a Member State, including civilian personnel and spouses and dependent children, stationed in another Member State.]

[4. The restrictions in paragraphs 1 and 2 shall not apply where the persons referred to therein produce evidence to show that they are going beyond the frontier zone or that they are not returning from the frontier zone of the neighbouring Member State or third country.]

These restrictions shall, however, still apply to frontier zone workers and to the crew of the means of transport used in international travel where they import goods when travelling in the course of their work.

[5. In the case of Ireland and the Kingdom of Denmark, in no case shall the restrictions in paragraph 1 be such that those to whom the restrictions apply are able to enjoy a more favourable treatment than that accorded by the limits set out in Articles 7c and 7d. The restrictions set out in paragraph 1 shall be calculated by reference to Articles 2 and 4 (1) column II of the table.][1]

[6. For the purposes of paragraphs 1, 2 and 4:

— "frontier zone" means a zone which, as the crow flies, does not extend more than 15 kilometres from the frontier of a Member State. Each Member State must however include within its frontier zone the local administrative districts part of the territory of which lies within the zone;

— "frontier zone worker" means any person whose normal activities require that he should go to the other side of the frontier on working days.]

[7. Member States may exclude from exemption goods falling within CN codes 7108 and 7109 of the Common Customs Tariff.]

[8. Member States may reduce the quantities of goods referred to in Article 4(1)(a) and (d) for travellers coming from a third country who enter a Member State.]

[9. By way of derogation from Article 4(1), Finland shall be authorised, until [30 November 2008][2] *to apply a maximum quantitative limit of not less than 16 litres for the importation of beer from third countries.]*

Amendments—[1] Para 5 inserted and following paras renumbered by Council Directive 91/191/EEC of 27 March 1991, art 1 with effect from 1 July 1991; see OJ L94, 16.4.1991, p 25.
[2] Date in para 9 substituted by Council Directive 2007/74/EC of 20 December 2007, art 17 with effect from 1 January 2008, see OJ L 346, 29.12.2007 p 6.

Article 6

Amendments—This art repealed by EEC Council Directive 92/111, art 1.25 with effect from 1 January 1993; OJ L384, 30.12.92.

Article 7

[1. For the purposes of this Directive, "European unit of account" (EUA) shall be as defined in the Financial Regulation of 21 December 1977.]

[2. The EUA equivalent in national currency which shall apply for the implementation of this Directive shall be fixed once a year. The rates applicable shall be those obtaining on the first working day of October with effect from 1 January of the following year.]

[3. Member States may round off the amounts in national currency resulting from the conversion of the amounts in EUA provided for in Articles 1 and 2, provided such rounding-off does not exceed 2 EUA.]

[4. Member States may maintain the amounts of the exemptions in force at the time of the annual adjustment provided for in paragraph 2 if, prior to the rounding-off provided for in paragraph 3, conversion of the amounts of the exemptions expressed in EUA would result in a change of less than 5% in the exemption expressed in national currency or to a lowering of this exemption.]

[5. Member States may maintain the existing amount of the exemption if the conversion of the amounts of the exemptions, expressed in ecus, adopted during the adjustment referred to in Articles 2(6) and 7b(4) would result in a change of less than 5% in the exemption expressed in national currency or in a reduction in that exemption.]

[Article 7a

Member States shall, within the framework of intra-Community travel, take the necessary steps to enable travellers to confirm tacitly or by a simple oral declaration that they are complying with the authorised limits and conditions for the duty-free elements.

It shall be open to Member States not to levy turnover tax or excise duty on the import of goods by a traveller when the amount of the tax which should be levied is equal to, or less than, 5 ECU.]

[Article 7b

1. By way of derogation from Article 1(1), Spain is hereby authorised to apply, until 31 December 2000, an allowance of ECU 600 for imports of the goods in question by travellers coming from the Canary Islands, Ceuta and Melilla who enter the territory of Spain as defined in Article 3(2) and (3) of Directive 77/388/EEC.

2. By way of derogation from Article 1(2), Spain shall have the option of reducing that allowance to ECU 150 for travellers under 15 years of age.][1]

Amendments—[1] This article substituted by Council Directive 94/4/EC of 14 February 1994, arts 1(3), 4 with effect from 3 March 1994 (date on which the Directive was published in the Official Journal); see OJ L60, 3.3.94, p 14.

[Article 7c

Notwithstanding Articles 2(1) and 4(1), the Kingdom of Denmark shall be authorised to apply the following quantitative limits until [31 December 1992][2] *for the importation of the goods in question by travellers resident in Denmark after a stay of less than 36 hours outside Denmark:*

Products	
—Cigarettes	*100*
—Distilled beverages and spirits of an alcoholic strength by volume more than 22% vol.	*nil*
—Beer	*12 litres]*[1]

Amendment—[1] This Article substituted by Council Directive 91/191/EEC of 27 March 1991, art 1 with effect from 8 April 1991; see OJ L94, 16.4.1991, p 25.

[2] Date substituted for "31 December 1991" by Council Directive 91/673/EEC of 19 December 1991, art 1 (2); see OJ L373, 31.12.1991, p 33.

[Article 7d

Notwithstanding Article 2(1) and within the limit set out therein, Ireland shall be authorised to apply a quantitative limit of 30 litres of beer for all travellers to Ireland until 31 December 1992.

Notwithstanding Articles 2(1), 4(1) and 7b(1)(b), Ireland shall be authorised to apply the following limits until 31 December 1992 for the import of the goods in question by travellers from Ireland after a stay of less than 24 hours outside Ireland:

(a) for travellers from the Community: ECU 175, but the unit value may not exceed ECU 110;

(b) for beer, 15 litres.][1]

Amendments—[1] This Article added by Council Directive 91/673/EEC of 19 December 1991, art 3; see OJ L373, 31.12.1991, p 33.

Article 8

1. Member States shall bring into force not later than 1 January 1970 the measures necessary to comply with this Directive.

2. Each Member State shall inform the Commission of the measures which it adopts to implement this Directive.

The Commission shall communicate such information to the other Member States.

Article 9

This Directive is addressed to the Member States.

Done at Brussels, 28 May 1969.

Amendments—This Directive has been substantially amended by Directives 72/230/EEC; see OJ L139, 16.6. 1972, p 28; 78/1032/EEC; see OJ L366, 28.12.78, p 28; 78/1033/EEC; see OJ L366, 28.12.1978, p 31; 81/933/EEC; see OJ L338, 25.11.1981, p 24; 82/443/EEC; see OJ L206, 14.7.1982, p 35; 84/231/EEC; see OJ L117, 3.5.1984, p 42; 85/348/EEC; see OJ L183, 16.7.1985, p 24; 87/198/EEC; see OJ L78, 20.3.1987, p 53; 88/664/EEC; see OJ L382, 21.12.1988, p 41; 89/194/EEC; see OJ L73, 17.3.1989, p 47 and 89/220/EEC; see OJ L92, 5.4.1989, p 15.

[Council Directive of 15 March 1976 on mutual assistance for the recovery of claims relating to certain levies, duties, taxes and other measures.][1]

(76/308/EEC)

Note—See OJ L73, 18.3.1976, p 18.

This Directive repealed by Council Directive 2008/55/EC of 26 May 2008, art 25, Annex 1 with effect from 30 June 2008. See below for the text of Directive 2008/55/EC.

Amendments—[1] Title substituted by Council Directive 2001/44/EC art 1, para 1; see OJ L175, 28.6.2001, p 17.

THE COUNCIL OF THE EUROPEAN COMMUNITIES,

Having regard to the Treaty establishing the European Economic Community, and in particular Article 100 thereof,

Having regard to Council Regulation (EEC) No 729/70 of 21 April 1970 on the financing of the common agricultural policy (OJ No L94, 28.4.1970, p 13), as last amended by Regulation (EEC) No 2788/72 (OJ No L295, 30.12.1972, p 1), and in particular Article 8 (3) thereof,

Having regard to the proposal from the Commission,

Having regard to the opinion of the European Parliament (OJ No C19, 12.4.1973, p 38),

Having regard to the opinion of the Economic and Social Committee (OJ No C69, 28.8.1973, p 3),

Whereas it is not at present possible to enforce in one Member State a claim for recovery substantiated by a document drawn up by the authorities of another Member State;

Whereas the fact that national provisions relating to recovery are applicable only within national territories is in itself an obstacle to the establishment and functioning of the common market; whereas this situation prevents Community rules from being fully and fairly applied, particularly in the area of the common agricultural policy, and facilitates fraudulent operations;

Whereas it is therefore necessary to adopt common rules on mutual assistance for recovery;

Whereas these rules must apply both to the recovery of claims resulting from the various measures which form part of the system of total or partial financing of the European Agricultural Guidance and Guarantee Fund and to the recovery of agricultural levies and customs duties within the meaning of Article 2 of Decision 70/243/ECSC, EEC, Euratom of 21 April 1970 on the replacement of financial contributions from Member States by the Communities' own resources (OJ No L94, 28.4.1970, p 19), and of Article 128 of the Act of Accession; whereas they must also apply to the recovery of interest and costs incidental to such claims;

Whereas mutual assistance must consist of the following: the requested authority must on the one hand supply the applicant authority with the information which the latter needs in order to recover claims arising in the Member State in which it is situated and notify the debtor of all instruments relating to such claims emanating from that Member State, and on the other hand it must recover, at the request of the applicant authority, the claims arising in the Member State in which the latter is situated;

Whereas these different forms of assistance must be afforded by the requested authority in compliance with the laws, regulations and administrative provisions governing such matters in the Member State in which it is situated;

Whereas it is necessary to lay down the conditions in accordance with which requests for assistance must be drawn up by the applicant authority and to give a limitative definition of the particular circumstances in which the requested authority may refuse assistance in any given case;

Whereas when the requested authority is required to act on behalf of the applicant authority to recover a claim, it must be able, if the provisions in force in the Member State in which it is situated so permit and with the agreement of the applicant authority, to allow the debtor time to pay or authorise payment by instalment; whereas any interest charged on such payment facilities must also be remitted to the Member State in which the applicant authority is situated;

Whereas, upon a reasoned request from the applicant authority, the requested authority must also be able, in so far as the provisions in force in the Member State in which it is situated so permit, to take precautionary measures to guarantee the recovery of claims arising in the applicant Member State; whereas such claims must not however be given any preferential treatment in the Member State in which the requested authority is situated;

Whereas it is possible that during the recovery procedure in the Member State in which the requested authority is situated the claim or the instrument authorising its enforcement issued in the Member State in which the applicant authority is situated may be contested by the person concerned; whereas it should be laid down in such cases that the person concerned must bring the action contesting the claim before the competent body of the Member State in which the applicant authority is situated and that the requested authority must suspend any enforcement proceedings which it has begun until a decision is taken by the aforementioned body;

Whereas it should be laid down that documents and information communicated in the course of mutual assistance for recovery may not be used for other purposes;

Whereas this Directive should not curtail mutual assistance between particular Member States under bilateral or multilateral agreements or arrangements;

Whereas it is necessary to ensure that mutual assistance functions smoothly and to this end to lay down a Community procedure for determining the detailed rules for the application of such assistance within an appropriate period; whereas it is necessary to set up a committee to organise close and effective collaboration between the Member States and the Commission in this area.

HAS ADOPTED THIS DIRECTIVE:

Article 1

This Directive lays down the rules to be incorporated into the laws, regulations and administrative provisions of the Member States to ensure the recovery in each Member State of the claims referred to in Article 2 which arise in another Member State.

[Article 2

This Directive shall apply to all claims relating to:

(*a*) *refunds, interventions and other measures forming part of the system of total or partial financing of the European Agricultural Guidance and Guarantee Fund* (*EAGGF*), *including sums to be collected in connection with these actions;*

(*b*) *levies and other duties provided for under the common organisation of the market for the sugar sector;*

(*c*) *import duties;*

(*d*) *export duties;*

(*e*) *value added tax;*

(*f*) *excise duties on:*

- *manufactured tobacco,*
- *alcohol and alcoholic beverages,*
- *mineral oils;*

(*g*) *taxes on income and capital;*

(*h*) *taxes on insurance premiums;*

(*i*) *interest, administrative penalties and fines, and costs incidental to the claims referred to in points* (*a*) *to* (*h*), *with the exclusion of any sanction of a criminal nature as determined by the laws in force in the Member State in which the requested authority is situated.*]1

Amendments—1 Substituted by Council Directive 2001/44/EC art 1, para 2; see OJ L175, 28.6.2001, p 17.

Article 3

In this Directive:

— *"applicant authority" means the competent authority of a Member State which makes a request for assistance concerning a claim referred to in Article 2,*

— *"requested authority" means the competent authority of a Member State to which a request for assistance is made,*

[— *"import duties" means customs duties and charges having equivalent effect on imports, and import charges laid down within the framework of the common agricultural policy or in that of specific arrangements applicable to certain goods resulting from the processing of agricultural products,*

— *"export duties" means customs duties and charges having equivalent effect on exports, and export charges laid down within the framework of the common agricultural policy or in that of specific arrangements applicable to certain goods resulting from the processing of agricultural products,*

— *"taxes on income and capital" means those enumerated in Article 1*(*3*) *of Directive 77/799/EEC*(***), *read in conjunction with Article 1*(*4*) *of that Directive,*

— *"taxes on insurance premiums" means:*

in Austria:	(*i*) *Versicherungssteuer* (*ii*) *Feuerschutzsteuer*
in Belgium:	(*i*) *Taxe annuelle sur les contrats d'assurance* (*ii*) *Jaarlijkse taks op de verzekeringscontracten*
in Germany:	(*i*) *Versicherungssteuer* (*ii*) *Feuerschutzsteuer*
in Denmark:	(*i*) *Afgift af lystfartøjsfor-sikringer* (*ii*) *Afgift af ansvarsforsik-ringer for motorkøretøjer m.v.* (*iii*) *Stempelafgift af forsikringspræmier*
in Spain:	*Impuesto sobre la prima de seguros*
in Greece:	(*i*) Φ *ὸ* ρος κυκλου ερνασιϖν (ΦΚΕ) (*ii*) Τέλη *Χ*αρτοση *μ*ου
in France:	*Taxe sur les conventions d'assurances*
in Finland:	(*i*) *Eräistä vakuutusmak-suista suoritettava vero/skatt på vissa försäkring-spremier* (*ii*) *Palosuojelumaksu/brand-skyddsavgift*
in Italy:	*Imposte sulle assicurazioni private ed i contratti vitalizi di cui alla legge 29.10.1967 No 1216*
in Ireland:	*levy on insurance premiums*

in Luxembourg:	*(i) Impôt sur les assurances*
	(ii) Impôt dans l'interêt du service d'incendie
in the Netherlands:	*Assurantiebelasting*
in Portugal:	*Imposto de selo sobre os prémios de seguros*
in Sweden:	*none*
in the United Kingdom:	*insurance premium tax (IPT).*
[in Malta:	*Taxxa fuq Dokumenti u Trasferementi]*[2]
[in Slovenia:	*(i) davek od prometa zavarovalnih poslov*
	(ii) pozarna taska.][2]

This Directive shall also apply to claims relating to identical or analogous taxes which supplement or replace the taxes on insurance premiums referred to in the sixth indent. The competent authorities of the Member States shall communicate to each other and to the Commission the dates of entry into force of such taxes.][1]

(*) Council Directive 77/799/EEC of 19 December 1977 concerning mutual assistance by the competent authorities of the Member States in the field of direct taxation (OJ L336, 27.12.1977, p.15). Directive as last amended by the 1994 Act of Accession.

Amendments—[1] Words inserted by Council Directive 2001/44/EC art 1, para 3; see OJ L175, 28.6.2001, p 17.
[2] Words inserted by the 2003 Act of Accession Annex II Chapter 9 para 2.

Article 4

1. At the request of the applicant authority, the requested authority shall provide any information which would be useful to the applicant authority in the recovery of its claim.

In order to obtain this information, the requested authority shall make use of the powers provided under the laws, regulations or administrative provisions applying to the recovery of similar claims arising in the Member State where that authority is situated.

2. The request for information shall indicate [the name, address and any other relevant information relating to the identification to which the applicant authority normally has access][1] *of the person to whom the information to be provided relates and the nature and amount of the claim in respect of which the request is made.*

3. The requested authority shall not be obliged to supply information:

(a) which it would not be able to obtain for the purpose of recovering similar claims arising in the Member State in which it is situated:

(b) which would disclose any commercial, industrial or professional secrets; or

(c) the disclosure of which would be liable to prejudice the security of or be contrary to the public policy of the State.

4. The requested authority shall inform the applicant authority of the grounds for refusing a request for information.

Note—For detailed rules on implementing paras 2 and 4 see arts 2–7 of the Commission Directive of 4 November 1977: 77/794/EEC; see OJ L333, 24.12.1977, p 11.

Amendments—[1] Words in para (2) substituted by Council Directive 2001/44/EC art 1, para 4; see OJ L175, 28.6.2001, p 17.

Article 5

1. The requested authority shall, at the request of the applicant authority, and in accordance with the rules of law in force for the notification of similar instruments or decisions in the Member State in which the requested authority is situated, notify to the addressee all instruments and decisions, including those of a judicial nature, which emanate from the Member State in which the applicant authority is situated and which relate to a claim and/or to its recovery.

2. The request for notification shall indicate [the name, address and any other relevant information relating to the identification to which the applicant authority normally has access][1] *of the addressee concerned, the nature and the subject of the instrument or decision to be notified, if necessary the name and address of the debtor and the claim to which the instrument or decision relates, and any other useful information.*

3. The requested authority shall promptly inform the applicant authority of the action taken on its request for notification and, more especially, of the date on which the instrument or decision was forwarded to the addressee.

Note—For detailed rules on implementing paras 2 and 3 see arts 8–10 of the Commission Directive of 4 November 1977: 77/794/EEC; see OJ L333, 24.12.1977, p 11.

Amendments—[1] Words in para (2) substituted by Council Directive 2001/44/EC art 1, para 5; see OJ L175, 28.6.2001, p 17.

Article 6

1. At the request of the applicant authority, the requested authority shall, in accordance with the laws, regulations or administrative provisions applying to the recovery of similar claims arising in the Member State in which the requested authority is situated, recover claims which are the subject of an instrument permitting their enforcement.

2. For this purpose any claim in respect of which a request for recovery has been made shall be treated as a claim of the Member State in which the requested authority is situated, except where Article 12 applies.

[Article 7

1. The request for recovery of a claim which the applicant authority addresses to the requested authority must be accompanied by an official or certified copy of the instrument permitting its enforcement, issued in the Member State in which the applicant authority is situated and, if appropriate, by the original or a certified copy of other documents necessary for recovery.

2. The applicant authority may not make a request for recovery unless—

(a) the claim and/or the instrument permitting its enforcement are not contested in the Member State in which it is situated, except in cases where the second subparagraph of Article 12(2) is applied,

(b) it has, in the Member State in which it is situated, applied appropriate recovery procedures available to it on the basis of the instrument referred to in paragraph 1, and the measures taken will not result in the payment in full of the claim.

3. The request for recovery shall indicate—

(a) the name, address and any other relevant information relating to the identification of the person concerned and/or to the third party holding his or her assets;

(b) the name, address and any other relevant information relating to the identification of the applicant authority;

(c) a reference to the instrument permitting its enforcement issued in the Member State in which the applicant authority is situated;

(d) the nature and the amount of the claim, including the principal, the interest, and any other penalties, fines and costs due indicated in the currencies of the Member States in which both authorities are situated;

(e) the date of notification of the instrument to the addressee by the applicant authority and/or by the requested authority;

(f) the date from which and the period during which enforcement is possible under the laws in force in the Member State in which the applicant authority is situated;

(g) any other relevant information.

4. The request for recovery shall also contain a declaration by the applicant authority confirming that the conditions set out in paragraph 2 have been fulfilled.

5. As soon as any relevant information relating to the matter which gave rise to the request for recovery comes to the knowledge of the applicant authority it shall forward it to the requested authority.][1]

Amendments—[1] Arts 7–10 substituted by Council Directive 2001/44/EC art 1, para 6; see OJ L175, 28.6.2001, p 17.

[Article 8

1. The instrument permitting enforcement of the claim shall be directly recognised and automatically treated as an instrument permitting enforcement of a claim of the Member State in which the requested authority is situated.

2. Notwithstanding the first paragraph, the instrument permitting enforcement of the claim may, where appropriate and in accordance with the provisions in force in the Member State in which the requested authority is situated, be accepted as, recognised as, supplemented with, or replaced by an instrument authorising enforcement in the territory of that Member State.

Within three months of the date of receipt of the request for recovery, Member States shall endeavour to complete such acceptance, recognition, supplementing or replacement, except in cases where the third subparagraph is applied. They may not be refused if the instrument permitting enforcement is properly drawn up. The requested authority shall inform the applicant authority of the grounds for exceeding the period of three months.

If any of these formalities should give rise to contestation in connection with the claim and/or the instrument permitting enforcement issued by the applicant authority, Article 12 shall apply.][1]

Amendments—[1] Arts 7–10 substituted by Council Directive 2001/44/EC art 1, para 6; see OJ L175, 28.6.2001, p 17.

[Article 9

1. Claims shall be recovered in the currency of the Member State in which the requested authority is situated. The entire amount of the claim that is recovered by the requested authority shall be remitted by the requested authority to the applicant authority.

2. The requested authority may, where the laws, regulations or administrative provisions in force in the Member State in which it is situated so permit, and after consultations with the applicant authority, allow the debtor time to pay or authorise payment by instalment. Any interest charged by the requested authority in respect of such extra time to pay shall also be remitted to the Member State in which the applicant authority is situated.

From the date on which the instrument permitting enforcement of recovery of the claim has been directly recognised or accepted, recognised, supplemented or replaced in accordance with Article 8, interest will be charged for late payment under the laws, regulations and administrative provisions in force in the Member State in which the requested authority is situated and shall also be remitted to the Member State in which the applicant authority is situated.][1]

Amendments—[1] Arts 7–10 substituted by Council Directive 2001/44/EC art 1, para 6; see OJ L175, 28.6.2001, p 17.

[Article 10

Notwithstanding Article 6(2), the claims to be recovered shall not necessarily benefit from the privileges accorded to similar claims arising in the Member State in which the requested authority is situated.][1]

Amendments—[1] Arts 7–10 substituted by Council Directive 2001/44/EC art 1, para 6; see OJ L175, 28.6.2001, p 17.

Article 11

The requested authority shall inform the applicant authority immediately of the action it has taken on the request for recovery.

Article 12

1. If, in the course of the recovery procedure, the claim and/or the instrument permitting its enforcement issued in the Member State in which the applicant authority is situated are contested by an interested party, the action shall be brought by the latter before the competent body of the Member State in which the applicant authority is situated, in accordance with the laws in force there. This action must be notified by the applicant authority to the requested authority. The party concerned may also notify the requested authority of the action.

2. As soon as the requested authority has received the notification referred to in paragraph 1 either from the applicant authority or from the interested party, it shall suspend the enforcement procedure pending the decision of the body competent in the matter [unless the applicant authority requests otherwise in accordance with the second subparagraph][1]*. Should the requested authority deem it necessary, and without prejudice to Article 13, that authority may take precautionary measures to guarantee recovery in so far as the laws or regulations in force in the Member State in which it is situated allow such action for similar claims.*

[Not withstanding the first subparagraph of paragraph 2, the applicant authority may in accordance with the law, regulations and administrative practices in force in the Member State in which it is situated, request the requested authority to recover a contested claim, in so far as the relevant laws, regulations and administrative practices in force in the Member State in which the requested authority is situated allow such action. If the result of contestation is subsequently favourable to the debtor, the applicant authority shall be liable for the reimbursement of any sums recovered, together with any compensation due, in accordance with the laws in force in the Member State in which the requested authority is situated.][1]

3. Where it is the enforcement measures taken in the Member State in which the requested authority is situated that are being contested the action shall be brought before the competent body of that Member State in accordance with its laws and regulations.

4. Where the competent body before which the action has been brought in accordance with paragraph 1 is a judicial or administrative tribunal, the decision of that tribunal, in so far as it is favourable to the applicant authority and permits recovery of the claim in the Member State in which the applicant authority is situated shall constitute the "instrument permitting enforcement" within the meaning of Articles 6, 7 and 8 and the recovery of the claim shall proceed on the basis of that decision.

Note—For detailed rules on implementing para 1 see arts 16, 17 of the Commission Directive of 4 November 1977: 77/794/EEC; see OJ L333, 24.12.1977, p 11.

Amendments—[1] Words in para (2) added by Council Directive 2001/44/EC art 1, para 7; see OJ L175, 28.6.2001, p 17.

Article 13

On a reasoned request by the applicant authority, the requested authority shall take precautionary measures to ensure recovery of a claim in so far as the laws or regulations in force in the Member State in which it is situated so permit.

In order to give effect to the provisions of the first paragraph, Articles 6, 7(1), (3) and (5), 8, 11, 12 and 14 shall apply mutatis mutandis.

Article 14

[The requested authority shall not be obliged:

(a) to grant the assistance provided for in Articles 6 to 13 if recovery of the claim would, because of the situation of the debtor, create serious economic or social difficulties in the Member State in which that authority is situated, in so far as the laws, regulations and administrative practices in force in the Member State in which the requested authority is situated allow such action for similar national claims;

(b) to grant the assistance provided for in Articles 4 to 13, if the initial request under Article 4, 5 or 6 applies to claims more than five years old, dating from the moment the instrument permitting the recovery is established in accordance with the laws, regulations or administrative practices in force in the Member State in which the applicant authority is situated, to the date of the request. However, in cases where the claim or the instrument is contested, the time limit begins from the

moment at which the applicant State establishes that the claim or the enforcement order permitting recovery may no longer be contested.][1]

The requested authority shall inform the applicant authority of the grounds for refusing a request for assistance. Such reasoned refusal shall also be communicated to the Commission.

Amendments—[1] First paragraph substituted by Council Directive 2001/44/EC art 1, para 8; see OJ L175, 28.6.2001, p 17.

Article 15

1. Questions concerning periods of limitation shall be governed solely by the laws in force in the Member State in which the applicant authority is situated.

2. Steps taken in the recovery of claims by the requested authority in pursuance of a request for assistance, which, if they had been carried out by the applicant authority, would have had the effect of suspending or interrupting the period of limitation according to the laws in force in the Member State in which the applicant authority is situated, shall be deemed to have been taken in the latter State, in so far as that effect is concerned.

Article 16

Documents and information sent to the requested authority pursuant to this Directive may only be communicated by the latter to:

(*a*) *the person mentioned in the request for assistance;*

(*b*) *those persons and authorities responsible for the recovery of the claims, and solely for that purpose;*

(*c*) *the judicial authorities dealing with matters concerning the recovery of the claims.*

Article 17

Requests for assistance [the instrument permitting the enforcement and other relevant documents][1] *shall be accompanied by a translation in the official language, or one of the official languages of the Member State in which the requested authority is situated, without prejudice to the latter authority's right to waive the translation.*

Amendments—[1] Words substituted by Council Directive 2001/44/EC art 1, para 9; see OJ L175, 28.6.2001, p 17.

[Article 18

1. The requested authority shall recover from the person concerned and retain any costs linked to recovery which it incurs, in accordance with the laws and regulations of the Member State in which it is situated that apply to similar claims.

2. Member States shall renounce all claims on each other for the refund of costs resulting from mutual assistance which they grant each other pursuant to this Directive.

3. Where recovery poses a specific problem, concerns a very large amount in costs or relates to the fight against organised crime, the applicant and requested authorities may agree reimbursement arrangements specific to the cases in question.

4. The Member State in which the applicant authority is situated shall remain liable to the Member State in which the requested authority is situated for any costs and any losses incurred as a result of actions held to be unfounded, as far as either the substance of the claim or the validity of the instrument issued by the applicant authority are concerned.][1]

Amendments—[1] Substituted by Council Directive 2001/44/EC art 1, para 10; see OJ L175, 28.6.2001, p 17.

Article 19

Member States shall provide each other with a list of authorities authorised to make or receive requests for assistance.

[Article 20

1. The Commission shall be assisted by a recovery committee (hereinafter referred to as "the Committee"), composed of representatives of the Member States and chaired by the representative of the Commission.

2. Where reference is made to this paragraph, Articles 5 and 7 of Decision 1999/468/EC shall apply.

The period referred to in Article 5(6) of Decision 1999/468/EC shall be set at three months.

3. The Committee shall adopt its own rules of procedure.][1]

Amendments—[1] Substituted by Council Directive 2001/44/EC art 1, para 11; see OJ L175, 28.6.2001, p 17.

Article 21

The committee may examine any matter concerning the application of this Directive raised by its chairman either on his own initiative or at the request of the representative of a Member State.

[Article 22

The detailed rules for implementing Articles 4(2) and (4), 5(2) and (3) and Articles 7, 8, 9, 11, 12(1) and (2), 14, 18(3) and 25 and for determining the means by which communications between the authorities may be transmitted, the rules on conversion, transfer of sums recovered, and the fixing of a minimum amount for claims which may give rise to a request for assistance, shall be adopted in accordance with the procedure laid down in Article 20(2).][1]

Amendments—[1] Substituted by Council Directive 2001/44/EC art 1, para 12; see OJ L175, 28.6.2001, p 17.

Article 23

The provisions of this Directive shall not prevent a greater measure of mutual assistance being afforded either now or in the future by particular Member States under any agreements or arrangements, including those for the notification of legal or extra-legal acts.

Article 24

Member States shall bring into force the measures necessary to comply with this Directive not later than 1 January 1978.

Article 25

Each Member State shall inform the Commission of the measures which it has adopted to implement this Directive. The Commission shall forward this information to the other Member States.

[Each Member State shall inform the Commission annually of the number of requests for information, notification and recovery sent and received each year, the amount of the claims involved and the amounts recovered. The Commission shall report biennially to the European Parliament and the Council on the use made of these arrangements and on the results achieved.][1]

Amendments—[1] Words added by Council Directive 2001/44/EC art 1, para 13; see OJ L175, 28.6.2001, p 17.

Article 26

This Directive is addressed to the Member States.

Sixth Council Directive of 17 May 1977 on the harmonisation of the laws of the Member States relating to turnover taxes—common system of value added tax: uniform basis of assessment

(*77/388/EEC*)

Note—See OJ L145, 13.6.1977, p 1.
Repeal—This Directive repealed by Council Directive of 28 November 2006 on the common system of value added tax (2006/112/EC). For correlation table, see Annex XII of that Directive.
Cross references—See F(No 2)A 1992 s 14(2) (provisions to give effect to the requirements of this Directive as amended by Directive 91/680/EEC in connection with abolition of fiscal frontiers between member States).

THE COUNCIL OF THE EUROPEAN COMMUNITIES

Having regard to the Treaty establishing the European Economic Community, and in particular Articles 99 and 100 thereof,

Having regard to the proposal from the Commission,

Having regard to the opinion of the European Parliament (OJ C40, 8.4.74, p 25),

Having regard to the opinion of the Economic and Social Committee (OJ C139, 12.11.74, p 15),

Whereas all Member States have adopted a system of value added tax in accordance with the first and second Council Directives of 11 April 1967 on the harmonisation of the laws of the Member States relating to turnover taxes (OJ 71, 14.4.67, pp 1301–1367);

Whereas the Decision of 21 April 1970 on the replacement of financial contributions from Member States by the Communities' own resources (OJ L94, 28.4.70, p 19) provides that the budget of the Communities shall, irrespective of other revenue, be financed entirely from the Communities' own resources; whereas these resources are to include those accruing from value added tax and obtained by applying a common rate of tax on a basis of assessment determined in a uniform manner according to Community rules;

Whereas further progress should be made in the effective removal of restrictions on the movement of persons, goods, services and capital and the integration of national economies;

Whereas account should be taken of the objective of abolishing the imposition of tax on the importation and the remission of tax on exportation in trade between Member States; whereas it should be ensured that the common system of turnover taxes is non-discriminatory as regards the origin of goods and services, so that a common market permitting fair competition and resembling a real internal market may ultimately be achieved;

Whereas, to enhance the non-discriminatory nature of the tax, the term "taxable person" must be clarified to enable the Member States to extend it to cover persons who occasionally carry out certain transactions;

Whereas the term "taxable transaction" has led to difficulties, in particular as regards transactions treated as taxable transactions; whereas these concepts must be clarified;

Whereas the determination of the place where taxable transactions are effected has been the subject of conflicts concerning jurisdiction as between Member States, in particular as regards supplies of goods for assembly and the supply of services; whereas although the place where a supply of services is effected should in principle be defined as the place where the person supplying the services has his principal place of business, that place should be defined as being in the country of the person to whom the services are supplied, in particular in the case of certain services supplied between taxable persons where the cost of the services is included in the price of the goods;

Whereas the concepts of chargeable event and of the charge to tax must be harmonised if the introduction and any subsequent alterations of the Community rate are to become operative at the same time in all Member States;

Whereas the taxable base must be harmonised so that the application of the Community rate to taxable transactions leads to comparable results in all the Member States;

Whereas the rates applied by Member States must be such as to allow the normal deduction of the tax applied at the preceding stage;

Whereas a common list of exemptions should be drawn up so that the Communities' own resources may be collected in a uniform manner in all the Member States;

Whereas the rules governing deductions should be harmonised to the extent that they affect the actual amounts collected; whereas the deductible proportion should be calculated in a similar manner in all the Member States;

Whereas it should be specified which persons are liable to pay tax, in particular as regards services supplied by a person established in another country;

Whereas the obligations of taxpayers must be harmonised as far as possible so as to ensure the necessary safeguards for the collection of taxes in a uniform manner in all the Member States; whereas taxpayers should, in particular, make a periodic aggregate return of their transactions, relating to both inputs and outputs where this appears necessary for establishing and monitoring the basis of assessment of own resources;

Whereas Member States should nevertheless be able to retain their special schemes for small undertakings, in accordance with common provisions, and with a view to closer harmonisation; whereas Member States should remain free to apply a special scheme involving flat rate rebates of input value added tax to farmers not covered by normal schemes; whereas the basic principles of this scheme should be established and a common method adopted for calculating the value added of these farmers for the purposes of collecting own resources;

Whereas the uniform application of the provisions of this Directive should be ensured; whereas to this end a Community procedure for consultation should be laid down; whereas the setting up of a Value Added Tax Committee would enable the Member States and the Commission to co-operate closely;

Whereas Member States should be able, within certain limits and subject to certain conditions, to take or retain special measures derogating from this Directive in order to simplify the levying of tax or to avoid fraud or tax avoidance;

Whereas it might appear appropriate to authorise Member States to conclude with non-member countries or international organisations agreements containing derogations from this Directive;

Whereas it is vital to provide for a transitional period to allow national laws in specified fields to be gradually adapted,

HAS ADOPTED THIS DIRECTIVE:

TITLE I: INTRODUCTORY PROVISIONS

Article 1

Member States shall modify their present value added tax systems in accordance with the following Articles.

They shall adopt the necessary laws, regulations and administrative provisions so that the systems as modified enter into force at the earliest opportunity and by 1 January 1978 at the latest.

TITLE II: SCOPE

Article 2

The following shall be subject to value added tax:

1 the supply of goods or services effected for consideration within the territory of the country by a taxable person acting as such;

2 the importation of goods.

Commentary—*De Voil Indirect Tax Service* **V2.101**.

Note—Council Decision 93/563/EEC, art 1 allows derogation from para 1 above.

Simon's Tax Cases—*C&E Comrs v Church Schools Foundation Ltd;* [2001] STC 1661; *C&E Comrs v Polok* [2002] STC 361; *Kretztechnik AG v Finanzamt Linz* [2005] STC 1118; *Hotel Scandic Gåsabäck AB v Riksskatteverket* [2005] STC 1311.

Art 2(1), *Halifax plc and others v C&E Comrs* [2006] STC 919; *University of Huddersfield Higher Education Corporation v C&E Comrs* [2006] STC 980; *Elliniko Dimosio v Karageorgou and others* [2006] STC 1654; *Ministero dell'Economia e delle Finanze and another v FCE Bank plc* [2007] STC 165.

Cross references—See VAT Regulations, SI 1995/2518 reg 10 (implementation of para 1 above).

TITLE III: TERRITORIAL APPLICATION

[Article 3

1. For the purposes of this Directive—

— "territory of a Member State" shall mean the territory of the country as defined in respect of each Member State in paragraphs 2 and 3,

— "Community" and "territory of the Community" shall mean the territory of the Member States as defined in respect of each Member State in paragraphs 2 and 3,

— "third territory" and "third country" shall mean any territory other than those defined in paragraphs 2 and 3 as the territory of a Member State.

2. For the purposes of this Directive, the "territory of the country" shall be the area of application of the Treaty establishing the European Economic Community as defined in respect of each Member State in Article 227.

3. The following territories of individual Member States shall be excluded from the territory of the country:

—Federal Republic of Germany:

the Island of Heligoland,
the territory of Büsingen,

—Kingdom of Spain:

Ceuta,
Melilla,

—Republic of Italy:

Livigno,
Campione d'Italia,
the Italian waters of Lake Lugano.

The following territories of individual Member States shall also be excluded from the territory of the country:

—Kingdom of Spain:

the Canary Islands,

—French Republic:

the overseas departments,

—Hellenic Republic:

Άγιο Όροζ.

[[4. By way of derogation from paragraph 1, in view of:

—the conventions and treaties which the Principality of Monaco and the Isle of Man have concluded respectively with the French Republic and the United Kingdom of Great Britain and Northern Ireland,

—the Treaty concerning the Establishment of the Republic of Cyprus, the Principality of Monaco, the Isle of Man and the United Kingdom Sovereign Base Areas of Akrotiri and Dhekelia shall not be treated for the purpose of the application of this Directive as third territories.][3]

Member States shall take the measures necessary to ensure that transactions originating in or intended for—

— the Principality of Monaco are treated as transactions originating in or intended for the French Republic,

— the Isle of Man are treated as transactions originating in or intended for the United Kingdom of Great Britain and Northern Ireland.][2]

[— the United Kingdom Sovereign Base Areas of Akrotiri and Dhekelia are treated as transactions originating in or intended for the Republic of Cyprus.][3]

5. If the Commission considers that the provisions laid down in paragraphs 3 and 4 are no longer justified, particularly in terms of fair competition or own resources, it shall submit appropriate proposals to the Council.][1]

Amendments—[1] Article 3 replaced by EEC Council Directive 91/680; OJ L376, 31.12.1991, p 1 art 1(1).
[2] Para 4 replaced by EEC Council Directive 92/111, art 1.1; OJ L384, 30.12.92.
[3] In para 4, words replaced and words inserted by the 2003 Act of Accession Protocol No 3 Annex Part Two (OJ L236; 23.9.2003 p 940).

TITLE IV: TAXABLE PERSONS

Article 4

1. "Taxable person" shall mean any person who independently carries out in any place any economic activity specified in paragraph 2, whatever the purpose or results of that activity.

2. The economic activities referred to in paragraph 1 shall comprise all activities of producers, traders and persons supplying services including mining and agricultural activities and activities of the professions. The exploitation of tangible or intangible property for the purpose of obtaining income therefrom on a continuing basis shall also be considered an economic activity.

3. Member States may also treat as a taxable person anyone who carries out, on an occasional basis, a transaction relating to the activities referred to in paragraph 2 and in particular one of the following:

(a) the supply before first occupation of buildings or parts of buildings and the land on which they stand; Member States may determine the conditions of application of this criterion to transformations of buildings and the land on which they stand.

Member States may apply criteria other than that of first occupation, such as the period elapsing between the date of completion of the building and the date of first supply or the period elapsing between the date of first occupation and the date of subsequent supply, provided that these periods do not exceed five years and two years respectively.

"A building" shall be taken to mean any structure fixed to or in the ground;

(b) the supply of building land.

"Building land" shall mean any unimproved or improved land defined as such by the Member States.

4. The use of the word "independently" in paragraph 1 shall exclude employed and other persons from the tax in so far as they are bound to an employer by a contract of employment or by any other legal ties creating the relationship of employer and employee as regards working conditions, remuneration and the employer's liability.

Subject to the consultations provided for in Article 29, each Member State may treat as a single taxable person persons established in the territory of the country who, while legally independent, are closely bound to one another by financial, economic and organisational links.

[A Member State exercising the option provided for in the second subparagraph, may adopt any measures needed to prevent tax evasion or avoidance through the use of this provision.][1]

5. States, regional and local government authorities and other bodies governed by public law shall not be considered taxable persons in respect of the activities or transactions in which they engage as public authorities, even where they collect dues, fees, contributions or payments in connection with these activities or transactions.

However, when they engage in such activities or transactions, they shall be considered taxable persons in respect of these activities or transactions where treatment as non-taxable persons would lead to significant distortions of competition.

In any case, these bodies shall be considered taxable persons in relation to the activities listed in Annex D, provided they are not carried out on such a small scale as to be negligible.

Member States may consider activities of these bodies which are exempt under Article 13 or 28 as activities which they engage in as public authorities.

Commentary—*De Voil Indirect Tax Service* **V2.101, V2.108**.

Simon's Tax Cases—Art 4, *Gabalfrisa SL v Agencia Estatale Administracion Tributaria* [2002] STC 535; *I/S Fini H v Skatteministeriet* [2005] STC 903; *Finanzamt Offenbach am Main-Land v Faxworld Vorgründungsgesellschaft Peter Hünninghausen und Wolfgang Klein GbR* [2005] STC 1192; *Waterschap Zeeuws Vlaanderen v Staatssecretaris van Financiën* [2005] STC 1298; *Elliniko Dimosio v Karageorgou and others* [2006] STC 1654.

Art 4(1), *Intercommunale voor Zeewaterontzilting (in liquidation) v Belgian State* [1996] STC 569; *ICAEW v C&E Comrs* [1999] STC 398; *Halifax plc and others v C&E Comrs* [2006] STC 919; *University of Huddersfield Higher Education Corporation v C&E Comrs* [2006] STC 980.

Art 4(2), *ICAEW v C&E Comrs* [1999] STC 398; *C&E Comrs v Yarburgh Children's Trust* [2002] STC 207; *Cibo Participations SA v Directeur regional des impots du Nord-Pas-de-Calais* [2002] STC 460; *Empresa de Desenvolvimento Mineiro SGPS SA (EDM) v Fazenda Pública (Ministério Público, intervening)* [2005] STC 65.

Art 4(3)(*b*), *Gemeente Emmen v Belastingdienst Grote Ondernemingen* [1996] STC 496.

Art 4(4), *Osman v C&E Comrs* [1989] STC 596; *Ayuntamiento de Sevilla v Recaudadores de las Zonas Primera y Segunda* [1993] STC 659; *C&E Comrs v Thorn Materials Supply Ltd and Thorn Resources Ltd* [1998] STC 725; *C&E Comrs v Barclays Bank plc, CA* [2001] STC 1558.

Art 4(5), *R v C&E Comrs, ex p Greater Manchester Police Authority* [2001] STC 406, *CA; EC Commission v UK* [2000] STC 777; *Fazenda Pública v Câmera Municipal do Porto (Ministério Público, third party)* [2001] STC 560; *Customs and Excise Commissioners v Isle of Wight Council* [2005] STC 257; *Edinburgh Telford College v R&C Comrs* [2006] STC 1291; *Finanzamt Eisleben v Feuerbestattungsverein Halle eV (Lutherstadt Eisleben, joined party)* [2006] STC 2043.

Amendments—[1] Words in sub-para (4) inserted by Council Directive 2006/69/EC art 1(1), with effect from 13 August 2006, (OJ L 221, 12.8.2006, p 9).

TITLE V: TAXABLE TRANSACTIONS

Article 5

Supply of goods

1. "Supply of goods" shall mean the transfer of the right to dispose of tangible property as owner.

2. Electric current, gas, heat, refrigeration and the like shall be considered tangible property.

3. Member States may consider the following to be tangible property:

(a) certain interest in immovable property;

(b) rights in rem giving the holder thereof a right of user over immovable property;

(*c*) *shares or interests equivalent to shares giving the holder thereof de jure or de facto rights of ownership or possession over immovable property or part thereof.*

4. The following shall also be considered supplies within the meaning of paragraph 1:

(*a*) *the transfer, by order made by or in the name of a public authority or in pursuance of the law, of the ownership of property against payment of compensation;*

(*b*) *the actual handing over of goods, pursuant to a contract for the hire of goods for a certain period or for the sale of goods on deferred terms, which provides that in the normal course of events ownership shall pass at the latest upon payment of the final instalment;*

(*c*) *the transfer of goods pursuant to a contract under which commission is payable on purchase or sale.*

[5. Member States may consider the handing over of certain works of construction to be supplies within the meaning of paragraph 1.][1]

6. The application by a taxable person of goods forming part of his business assets for his private use or that of his staff, or the disposal thereof free of charge or more generally their application for purposes other than those of his business, where the value added tax on the goods in question or the component parts thereof was wholly or partly deductible, shall be treated as supplies made for consideration. However, applications for the giving of samples or the making of gifts of small value for the purposes of the taxable person's business shall not be so treated.

7. Member States may treat as supplies made for consideration:

(*a*) *the application by a taxable person for the purposes of his business of goods produced, constructed, extracted, processed, purchased or imported in the course of such business, where the value added tax on such goods, had they been acquired from another taxable person, would not be wholly deductible;*

(*b*) *the application of goods by a taxable person for the purposes of a non-taxable transaction, where the value added tax on such goods became wholly or partly deductible upon their acquisition or upon their application in accordance with sub-paragraph* (*a*);

(*c*) *except in those cases mentioned in paragraph 8, the retention of goods by a taxable person or his successors when he ceases to carry out a taxable economic activity where the value added tax on such goods became wholly or partly deductible upon their acquisition or upon their application in accordance with sub-paragraph* (*a*).

8. In the event of a transfer, whether for consideration or not or as a contribution to a company, of a totality of assets or part thereof, Member States may consider that no supply of goods has taken place and in that event the recipient shall be treated as the successor to the transferor. [Where appropriate, Member States may, in cases where the recipient is not wholly liable to tax, take the measures necessary to prevent distortion of competition. They may also adopt any measures needed to prevent tax evasion or avoidance through the use of this provision.][2]

Cross references—See Council Decision EEC 93/204, art 1; OJ L88, 8.4.93 (derogation from para 8 above granted to the UK).

Simon's Tax Cases—art 5, *Finanzamt Uelzen v Armbrecht* [1995] STC 997.

Art 5(1), *van Tiem v Staatssecretaris van Financiën* [1993] STC 91; *British Airways plc v C&E Comrs* [1996] STC 1127; *, *Stewart (t/a GT Shooting) v C&E Comrs* [2002] STC 255; *Halifax plc and others v C&E Comrs* [2006] STC 919; *University of Huddersfield Higher Education Corporation v C&E Comrs* [2006] STC 980.

Art 5(3)(*b*), *van Tiem v Staatssecretaris van Financiën* [1993] STC 91; *Stichting 'Goed Wonen' v Staatssecretaris van Financiën* [2003] STC 1137.

Art 5(6), *Kuwait Petroleum (GB) Ltd v C&E Comrs* [2001] STC 62; *Finanzamt Burgdorf v Fischer, Finanzamt Düsseldorf-Mettman v Brandenstein* [2001] STC 1356; *Hotel Scandic Gåsabäck AB v Riksskatteverket* [2005] STC 1311; *Church of England Children's Society v Revenue and Customs Commissioners* [2005] STC 1644.

Art 5(7)(*a*), *C&E Comrs v Robert Gordon's College* [1995] STC 1093.

Art 5(8), *Abbey National plc v C&E Comrs* [2001] STC 297; *Zita Modes Sàrl v Administration de l'Enregistrment et des Domaines* [2005] STC 1059; *Finanzamt Offenbach am Main-Land v Faxworld Vorgründungsgesellschaft Peter Hünninghausen und Wolfgang Klein GbR* [2005] STC 1192.

Amendments—[1] Para 5 replaced by EC Council Directive 95/7, art 1(1): OJ L102, 5.5.95, p 18 with effect from 25 May 1995.

[2] Words in para (8) inserted by Council Directive 2006/69/EC art 1(2), with effect from 13 August 2006, (OJ L 221, 12.8.2006, p 9).

Article 6

Supply of services

1. "Supply of services" shall mean any transaction which does not constitute a supply of goods within the meaning of Article 5.

Such transactions may include inter alia:

— *assignments of intangible property whether or not it is the subject of a document establishing title,*

— *obligations to refrain from an act or to tolerate an act or situation,*

— *the performances of services in pursuance of an order made by or in the name of a public authority or in pursuance of the law.*

2. The following shall be treated as supplies of services for consideration:

(*a*) *the use of goods forming part of the assets of a business for the private use of the taxable person or of his staff or more generally for purposes other than those of his business where the value added tax on such goods is wholly or partly deductible;*

(*b*) *supplies of services carried out free of charge by the taxable person for his own private use or that of his staff or more generally for purposes other than those of his business.*

Member States may derogate from the provisions of this paragraph provided that such derogation does not lead to distortion of competition.

3. In order to prevent distortion of competition and subject to the consultations provided for in Article 29, Member States may treat as a supply of services for consideration the supply by a taxable person of a service for the purposes of his undertaking where the value added tax on such a service, had it been supplied by another taxable person, would not be wholly deductible.

4. Where a taxable person acting in his own name but on behalf of another takes part in a supply of services, he shall be considered to have received and supplied those services himself.

5. Article 5(8) shall apply in like manner to the supply of services.

Commentary—*De Voil Indirect Tax Service* **V3.470**.

Simon's Tax Cases—*Mirror Group Newspapers Ltd v Customs and Excise Commissioners* [2000] STC 156; *Swedish State v Stockholm Lindopark AB, Stockholm Lindopark AB v Swedish State* [2001] STC 103; *Trinity Mirror plc (formerly Mirror Group Newspapers Ltd) v C&E Comrs* [2001] STC 192.

art 6(1), *Faaborg-Gelting Linien A/S v Finanzamt Flensburg* (Case C-231/94) [1996] STC 774; *Landboden-Agrardienste GmbH & Co KG v Finanzamt Calau* (Case C-384/95) [1998] STC 171; *Halifax plc and others v C&E Comrs* [2006] STC 919; *University of Huddersfield Higher Education Corporation v C&E Comrs* [2006] STC 980.

art 6(2), *Enkler v Finanzamt Homburg* (Case C-230/94) [1996] STC 1316; *Julius Fillibeck Söhne Gmbh & Co KG v Finanzamt Neustadt* (Case C-258/95) [1998] STC 513; *Hotel Scandic Gåsabäck AB v Riksskatteverket* [2005] STC 1311; *Charles and another v Staatssecretaris van Financiën* [2006] STC 1429.

art 6(2)(*a*), *Victoria and Albert Museum Trustees v C&E Comrs* [1996] STC 1016; *Finanzamt München III v Mohsche* (Case C-193/91) [1997] STC 195; *Seeling v Finanzamt Starnberg* [2003] STC 805.

art 6(3), *C&E Comrs v Robert Gordon's College* [1995] STC 1093.

art 6(5), *Finanzamt Offenbach am Main-Land v Faxworld Vorgründungsgesellschaft Peter Hünninghausen und Wolfgang Klein GbR* [2005] STC 1192.

Article 7

Imports

[1. "Importation of goods" shall mean:

(*a*) *the entry into the Community of goods which do not fulfil the conditions laid down in Articles 9 and 10 of the Treaty establishing the European Economic Community or, where the goods are covered by the Treaty establishing the European Coal and Steel Community, are not in free circulation;*

[(b) the entry into the Community of goods from a third territory, other than the goods covered by (a).][2]

2. The place of import of goods shall be the Member State within the territory of which the goods are when they enter the Community.

3. Notwithstanding paragraph 2, where goods referred to in paragraph 1(a) are, on entry into the Community, placed under one of the arrangements referred to in Article 16(1)(B)[(a), (b), (c) and (d)],[3] *under arrangements for temporary importation with total exemption from import duty or under external transit arrangements, the place of import of such goods shall be the Member State within the territory of which they cease to be covered by those arrangements.*

[Similarly, when goods referred to in paragraph 1(b) are placed, on entry into the Community, under one of the procedures referred to in Article 33a(1)(b) or (c), the place of import shall be the Member State within whose territory this procedure ceases to apply.][4]*]*[1]

Amendments—[1] Article 7 replaced by EEC Council Directive 91/680; OJ L376, 31.12.1991, p 1 art 1(2).

[2] Para 1(*b*) replaced by EEC Council Directive 92/111, art 1.2; OJ L384, 30.12.92.

[3] Words in para 3 added by EEC Council Directive 92/111, art 1.3, OJ L384, 30.12.92.

[4] Words in para 3 replaced by EEC Council Directive 92/111, art 1.3, OJ L384, 30.12.92.

TITLE VI: PLACE OF TAXABLE TRANSACTIONS

Article 8

Supply of goods

1. The place of supply of goods shall be deemed to be:

(*a*) *in the case of goods dispatched or transported either by the supplier or by the person to whom they are supplied or by a third person: the place where the goods are at the time when dispatch or transport to the person to whom they are supplied begins. Where the goods are installed or assembled, with or without a trial run, by or on behalf of the supplier, the place of supply shall be deemed to be the place where the goods are installed or assembled. In cases where the installation or assembly is carried out [in a Member State other than]*[1] *that of the supplier, [the Member State within the territory of which the installation or assembly is carried out]*[1] *shall take any necessary steps to avoid double taxation in that State;*

(*b*) *in the case of goods not dispatched or transported: the place where the goods are when the supply takes place;*

[(c) in the case of goods supplied on board ships, aircraft or trains during the part of a transport of passengers effected in the Community: at the point of the departure of the transport of passengers

[(d) in the case of the supply of gas through the natural gas distribution system, or of electricity, to a taxable dealer: the place where that taxable dealer has established his business or has a fixed

establishment for which the goods are supplied, or, in the absence of such a place of business or fixed establishment, the place where he has his permanent address or usually resides.

"Taxable dealer" for the purposes of this provision means a taxable person whose principal activity in respect of purchases of gas and electricity is reselling such products and whose own consumption of these products is negligible.][5]

[(e) in the case of the supply of gas through the natural gas distribution system, or of electricity, where such a supply is not covered by point (d): the place where the customer has effective use and consumption of the goods. Where all or part of the goods are not in fact consumed by this customer, these non consumed goods are deemed to have been used and consumed at the place where he has established his business or has a fixed establishment for which the goods are supplied. In the absence of such a place of business or fixed establishment, he is deemed to have used and consumed the goods at the place where he has his permanent address or usually resides.][5]

For the purposes of applying this provision—

- *"part of a transport of passengers effected in the Community" shall mean the part of the transport effected, without a stop in a third territory, between the point of departure and the point of arrival of the transport of passengers,*
- *"the point of departure of the transport of passengers" shall mean the first point of passenger embarkation foreseen within the Community, where relevant after a leg outside the Community,*
- *"the point of arrival of the transport of passengers" shall mean the last point of disembarkation of passengers foreseen within the Community of passengers who embarked in the Community, where relevant before a leg outside the Community.*

In the case of a return trip, the return leg shall be considered to be a separate transport.

The Commission shall, by 30 June 1993 at the latest, submit to the Council a report accompanied, if necessary, by appropriate proposals on the place of taxation of goods supplied for consumption and services, including restaurant services, provided for passengers on board ships, aircraft or trains.

By 31 December 1993, after consulting the European Parliament, the Council shall take a unanimous decision on the Commission proposal.

Until 31 December 1993, Member States may exempt or continue to exempt goods supplied for consumption on board whose place of taxation is determined in accordance with the above provisions, with the right to deduct the value added tax paid at an earlier stage.][3]

[2. By way of derogation from paragraph 1(a), where the place of departure of the consignment or transport of goods is in a third territory, the place of supply by the importer as defined in [Article 21(4)][4] *and the place of any subsequent supplies shall be deemed to be within the Member State of import of the goods.]*[2]

Cross references—See VAT (Place of Supply of Goods) Order, SI 1992/3283 (implementation of para 1(*c*) above).

Simon's Tax Cases—art 8(1)(*c*), *Peninsular and Oriental Steam Navigation Co v C&E Comrs* [2000] STC 488; *Köhler v Finanzamt Düsseldorf-Nord* [2006] STC 469.

Amendments—[1] Words in para 1(*a*) substituted by EEC Council Directive 91/680; OJ L376, 31.12.1991, p 1 art 1(3), (4), (5).

[2] Para 2 replaced by EEC Council Directive 91/680; OJ L376, 31.12.1991, p 1 art 1(3), (4), (5).

[3] Para 1(*c*) replaced by EEC Council Directive 92/111, art 1.4; OJ L384, 30.12.92.

[4] Words "Article 21(4)" substituted for "Article 21(2)" by Council Directive 2000/65/EC art 1(6) with effect from 21 October 2000; OJ L269 p 44, 21.10.00. Member states must bring into force the measures necessary to comply with these provisions not later than 31 December 2001.

[5] Para 1(*d*), (*e*) inserted by Council Directive 2003/92/EC art 1(1); OJ L260, 11.10.2003 p 8.

Article 9

Supply of services

1. The place where a service is supplied shall be deemed to be the place where the supplier has established his business or has a fixed establishment from which the service is supplied or, in the absence of such a place of business or fixed establishment, the place where he has his permanent address or usually resides.

2. However:

(a) the place of the supply of services connected with immovable property, including the services of estate agents and experts, and of services for preparing and co-ordinating construction works, such as the services of architects and of firms providing on-site supervision, shall be the place where the property is situated;

(b) the place where transport services are supplied shall be the place where transport takes place, having regard to the distances covered;

(c) the place of the supply of services relating to:

- *cultural, artistic, sporting, scientific, educational, entertainment or similar activities, including the activities of the organisers of such activities, and where appropriate, supply of ancillary services,*
- *ancillary transport activities such as loading, handling and similar activities,*
- *valuations of movable tangible property,*
- *work on movable tangible property.*

shall be the place where those services are physically carried out;

[(d)...][1]

(*e*) *the place where the following services are supplied when performed for customers established outside the Community or for taxable persons established in the Community but not in the same country as the supplier, shall be the place where the customer has established his business or has a fixed establishment to which the service is supplied or, in the absence of such a place, the place where he has his permanent address or usually resides:*

—transfers and assignments of copyrights, patents, licences, trade marks and similar rights,

—advertising services,

—services of consultants, engineers, consultancy bureaux, lawyers, accountants and other similar services, as well as data processing and the supplying of information,

—obligations to refrain from pursuing or exercising, in whole or in part, a business activity or a right referred to in this point (*e*),

—banking, financial and insurance transactions including reinsurance, with the exception of the hire of safes,

—the supply of staff,

—the services of agents who act in the name and for the account of another, when they procure for their principal the services referred to in this point (*e*).

[—the hiring out of movable tangible property with the exception of all forms of transport;][2]

[—the provision of access to, and of transport or transmission through, natural gas and electricity distribution systems and the provision of other directly linked services.][5]

[—Telecommunications. Telecommunications services shall be deemed to be services relating to the transmission, emission or reception of signals, writing, images and sounds or information of any nature by wire, radio, optical or other electromagnetic systems, including the related transfer or assignment of the right to use capacity for such transmission, emission or reception. Telecommunications services within the meaning of this provision shall also include provision of access to global information networks;][3]

[—radio and television broadcasting services,][4]

[—electronically supplied services, inter alia, those described in Annex L.][4]

[(*f*) *the place where services referred to in the last indent of sub-paragraph* (*e*) *are supplied when performed for non-taxable persons who are established, have their permanent address or usually reside in a Member State, by a taxable person who has established his business or has a fixed establishment from which the service is supplied outside the Community or, in the absence of such a place of business or fixed establishment, has his permanent address or usually resides outside the Community, shall be the place where the non-taxable person is established, has his permanent address or usually resides.]*[4]

[3. In order to avoid double taxation, non-taxation or the distortion of competition, the Member States may, with regard to the supply of services referred to in paragraph 2(*e*)*, except for the services referred to in the last indent when supplied to non-taxable persons, and also with regard to the hiring out of forms of transport consider:]*[4]

(*a*) *the place of supply of services, which under this Article would be situated within the territory of the country, as being situated outside the Community where the effective use and enjoyment of the services take place outside the Community;*

(*b*) *the place of supply of services, which under this Article would be situated outside the Community, as being within the territory of the country where the effective use and enjoyment of the services take place within the territory of the country.*

[4. In the case of telecommunications services and radio and television broadcasting services referred to in paragraph 2(*e*) *when performed for non-taxable persons who are established, have their permanent address or usually reside in a Member State, by a taxable person who has established his business or has a fixed establishment from which the service is supplied outside the Community, or in the absence of such a place of business or fixed establishment, has his permanent address or usually resides outside the Community, Member States shall make use of paragraph 3*(*b*)*.]*[4]

Commentary—*De Voil Indirect Tax Service* **V2.101, V3.166, V3.192**.

Note—Council decision 97/214 allows derogation from this Article.

Press releases etc—Written Answer. OJ C140, 21.5.94 (treatment of compensation payments for destroyed or stolen property subject to leasing contracts governed by para 2(*e*) above).

Business Brief 12/98 21.5.98 (Overseas businesses established in the UK through agencies).

Simon's Tax Cases—art 9, *Diversified Agency Services Ltd v C&E Comrs* [1996] STC 398; (*Case C-167/95*) [1997] STC 1287; *C&E Comrs v Chinese Channel (Hong Kong) Ltd* [1998] STC 347, *R (on the application of IDT Card Services Ireland Ltd) v Customs and Excise Commissioners* [2005] STC 314; *R&C Comrs v IDT Card Services Ireland Ltd* [2006] STC 1252.

Art 9(1), *ARO Lease BV v Inspecteur der Belastingdienst Grote Ondernemingen, Amsterdam* (Case C-190/95) [1997] STC 1272; *Lease Plan Luxembourg SA v Belgium* (Case C-390/96) [1998] STC 628; *EC Commission v French Republic* [2001] STC 156; *RAL (Channel Islands) and others v C&E Comrs* [2005] STC 1025; *Ministero dell'Economia e delle Finanze and another v FCE Bank plc* [2007] STC 165.

Art 9(2)(*b*), *EC Commission v Hellenic Republic* (Case C-331\94) [1996] STC 1168; *Reisebüro Binder GmbH v Finanzamt Stuttgart-Körperschaften* (Case C-116/96) [1998] STC 604.

Art 9(2)(*c*), *Dudda v Finanzamt Bergisch Gladbach* (Case C-327/94) [1996] STC 1290; *RAL (Channel Islands) and others v C&E Comrs* [2005] STC 1025; *Ministre de l'Économie, des Finances et de l'Industrie v Gillian Beach Ltd* [2006] STC 1080.

Art 9(2)(*d*), *Hamann v Finanzamt Hamburg-Eimsbüttel* [1991] STC 193.

Art 9(2)(*e*), *EC Commission v Grand Duchy of Luxembourg* (Case C-69/92) [1997] STC 712; *von Hoffmann v Finanzamt Trier* [1997] STC 1321; *Synidcat des Producteurs Independants (SPI) v Ministere de l'Economie, des Finances et de l'Industry* [2001] STC 523; *Design Concept SA v Flanders Expo SA* [2003] STC 912; *R&C Comrs v Zurich Insurance Co* [2006] STC 1694.

Cross references—See VAT (Place of Supply of Services) Order, SI 1992/3121 (implementation of paras 2, 3 above).

Amendments—[1] Para 2(*d*) deleted by art 1 of the Tenth Council Directive of 31 July 1984: 84/386/EEC; see OJ L208, 3.8.1984, p 58.
[2] Words in para 2(*e*) added by art 1 of the Tenth Council Directive of 31 July 1984: 84/386/EEC; see OJ L208. 3.8.1984, p 58.
[3] Indent added to s 9(2)(*e*) and para 4 inserted by Council Directive of 17 June 1999: 99/59/EC; see OJ L162/64, 26.6.1999.
[4] This article is temporarily amended by Council Directive 2002/38 art 1 para 1 (OJ L 128; 15.05.02). Two more indents added to para 2(*e*), and point (*f*) added; the introductory phrase to para 3 substituted, and para 4 substituted, with effect for a period of three years from 1 July 2003: see Council Directive 2002/38/EC art 4.
[5] Indent added to para 2(*e*) by Council Directive 2003/92/EC, art 1(2); OJ L260, 11.10.2003 p 8.

TITLE VII: CHARGEABLE EVENT AND CHARGEABILITY OF TAX

Article 10

1

(*a*) *"Chargeable event" shall mean the occurrence by virtue of which the legal conditions necessary for tax to become chargeable are fulfilled.*

(*b*) *The tax becomes "chargeable" when the tax authority becomes entitled under the law at a given moment to claim the tax from the person liable to pay, notwithstanding that the time of payment may be deferred.*

2. The chargeable event shall occur and the tax shall become chargeable when the goods are delivered or the services are performed. Deliveries of goods other than those referred to in Article 5(4)(b) and supplies of services which give rise to successive statements of account or payments shall be regarded as being completed at the time when the periods to which such statements of account or payments pertain expire. [Member States may in certain cases provide that continuous supplies of goods and services which take place over a period of time shall be regarded as being completed at least at intervals of one year.][2]

However, where a payment is to be made on account before the goods are delivered or the services are performed, the tax shall become chargeable on receipt of the payment and on the amount received.

By way of derogation from the above provisions, Member States may provide that the tax shall become chargeable, for certain transactions or for certain categories of taxable person, either:

—no later than the issue of the invoice …[3]*, or*

—no later than receipt of the price, or

—where an invoice …[3] *is not issued, or is issued late, within a specified period from the date of the chargeable event.*

[3. The chargeable event shall occur and the tax shall become chargeable when the goods are imported. Where goods are placed under one of the arrangements referred to in Article 7(3) on entry into the Community, the chargeable event shall occur and the tax shall become chargeable only when the goods cease to be covered by those arrangements.

However, where imported goods are subject to customs duties, to agricultural levies or to charges having equivalent effect established under a common policy, the chargeable event shall occur and the tax shall become chargeable when the chargeable event for those Community duties occurs and those duties become chargeable.

Where imported goods are not subject to any of those Community duties, Member States shall apply the provisions in force governing customs duties as regards the occurrence of the chargeable event and the moment when the tax becomes chargeable.][1]

Simon's Tax Cases—art 10, *Ufficio IVA di Trapani v Italittica SpA* (Case C-144/94) [1995] STC 1059; *Balocchi v Ministero delle Finanze* [1997] STC 640; *Société Financière d'Investissements SPRL v Belgium* [2000] STC 164.
Art 10(2), *C&E Comrs v British Telecom plc* [1996] STC 818; *BUPA Hospitals Ltd and another v C&E Comrs* [2006] STC 967.
Art 10(3), *Pezzullo Molini Pastifici Mangimifici SpA v Ministero delle Finanze* (Case C-166/94) [1996] STC 1236.

Amendments—[1] Article 10(3) replaced by EEC Council Directive 91/680; OJ L376, 31.12.1991, p 1 art 1(6).
[2] Words in art 10(2) inserted by Council Directive 2000/65/EC art 1(1) with effect from 21 October 2000; OJ L269 p 44, 21.10.00. Member states must bring into force the measures necessary to comply with these provisions not later than 31 December 2001.
[3] Words in art 10(2) revoked by Council Directive 2001/115/EC art 4(1) (see OJ L 015; 17.01.02).

TITLE VIII: TAXABLE AMOUNT

Article 11

A. Within the territory of the country

1. The taxable amount shall be:

(*a*) *in respect of supplies of goods and services other than those referred to in* (*b*), (*c*) *and* (*d*) *below, everything which constitutes the consideration which has been or is to be obtained by the supplier from the purchaser, the customer or a third party for such supplies including subsidies directly linked to the price of such supplies;*

(*b*) *in respect of supplies referred to in Article 5(6) and* (*7*), *the purchase price of the goods or of similar goods or, in the absence of a purchase price, the cost price, determined at the time of supply;*

(c) in respect of supplies referred to in Article 6(2), the full cost to the taxable person of providing the services;

(d) in respect of supplies referred to in Article 6(3), the open market value of the services supplied.

...[6]

2. The taxable amount shall include:

(a) taxes, duties, levies and charges, excluding the value added tax itself;

(b) incidental expenses such as commission, packing, transport and insurance costs charged by the supplier to the purchaser or customer. Expenses covered by a separate agreement may be considered to be incidental expenses by the Member States.

3. The taxable amount shall not include:

(a) price reductions by way of discount for early payment;

(b) price discounts and rebates allowed to the customer and accounted for at the time of the supply;

(c) the amounts received by a taxable person from his purchaser or customer as repayment for expenses paid out in the name and for the account of the latter and which are entered in his books in a suspense account. The taxable person must furnish proof of the actual amount of this expenditure and may not deduct any tax which may have been charged on these transactions.

[4. By way of derogation from paragraphs 1, 2 and 3, Member States which, on 1 January 1993, did not avail themselves of the option provided for in the third sub-paragraph of Article 12(3)(a) may, where they avail themselves of the option provided for in Title B(6), provide that, for the transactions referred to in the second sub-paragraph of Article 12(3)(c), the taxable amount shall be equal to a fraction of the amount determined in accordance with paragraphs 1, 2 and 3.

That fraction shall be determined in such a way that the value added tax thus due is, in any event, equal to at least 5% of the amount determined in accordance with paragraphs 1, 2 and 3.][3]

[5. Member States shall have the option of including in the taxable amount in respect of the supply of goods and services, the value of exempt investment gold within the meaning of Article 26b, which has been provided by the customer to be used as a basis for working and which as a result, loses its VAT exempt investment gold status when such goods and services are supplied. The value to be used is the open market value of the investment gold at the time that those goods and services are supplied.

6. In order to prevent tax evasion or avoidance, Member States may take measures to ensure that the taxable amount in respect of a supply of goods or services shall be the open market value. The option shall be applied only in respect of supplies of goods and services involving family or other close personal ties, management, ownership, membership, financial or legal ties as defined by the Member State. For these purposes legal ties may include the relationship between an employer and employee or the employee's family, or any other closely connected persons.

The option in the first subparagraph may apply only in any of the following circumstances:

(a) where the consideration is lower than the open market value and the recipient of the supply does not have a full right of deduction under Article 17;

(b) where the consideration is lower than the open market value and the supplier does not have a full right of deduction under Article 17 and the supply is subject to an exemption under Article 13 or Article 28(3)(b);

(c) where the consideration is higher than the open market value and the supplier does not have a full right of deduction under Article 17.

Member States may restrict the categories of suppliers or recipients to whom the measures in the first and the second subparagraph shall apply.

Member States shall inform the Committee established in accordance with Article 29 of any new national measure adopted pursuant to the provisions of this paragraph.

7. For the purposes of this Directive, "open market value" shall mean the full amount that, in order to obtain the goods or services in question at that time, a customer at the same marketing stage at which the supply of goods or services takes place, would have to pay, under conditions of fair competition, to a supplier at arm's length within the territory of the Member State in which the supply is subject to tax.

Where no comparable supply of goods or services can be ascertained, "open market value" shall mean, in respect of goods, an amount that is not less than the purchase price of the goods or of similar goods or, in the absence of a purchase price, the cost price, determined at the time of supply; in respect of services it shall mean not less than the full cost to the taxable person of providing the service.][6]

B. Importation of goods

[1. The taxable amount shall be the value for customs purposes, determined in accordance with the Community provisions in force; this shall also apply for the import of goods referred to in Article 7(1)(b).][2]

2. ... (repealed by Directive 91/680)

[3. The taxable amount shall include, in so far as they are not already included:

(a) taxes, duties, levies and other charges due outside the importing Member State and those due by reason of importation, excluding the value added tax to be levied;

(b) incidental expenses, such as commission, packing, transport and insurance costs, incurred up to the first place of destination within the territory of the importing Member State.

"First place of destination" shall mean the place mentioned on the consignment note or any other document by means of which the goods are imported into the importing Member State. In the absence of such an indication, the first place of destination shall be taken to be the place of the first transfer of cargo in the importing Member State.

[The incidental expenses referred to above shall also be included in the taxable amount where they result from transport to another place of destination within the territory of the Community if that place is known when the chargeable event occurs.][5]

4. The taxable amount shall not include those factors referred to in A(3)(a) and (b).

5. When goods have been temporarily exported [from the Community][1] *and are re-imported after having undergone abroad repair, processing or adaptation, or after having been made up or reworked [outside the Community]*[1]*, Member States shall take steps to ensure that the treatment of the goods for value added tax purposes is the same as that which would have applied to the goods in question had the above operations been carried out within the territory of the country.*

[6. By way of derogation from paragraphs 1 to 4, Member States which, on 1 January 1993, did not avail themselves of the option provided for in the third sub-paragraph of Article 12(3)(a) may provide that for imports of the works of art, collectors' items and antiques defined in Article 26a(A)(a), (b) and (c), the taxable amount shall be equal to a fraction of the amount determined in accordance with paragraphs 1 to 4.

That fraction shall be determined in such a way that the value added tax thus due on the import is, in any event, equal to at least 5% of the amount determined in accordance with paragraphs 1 to 4.][4]

C. Miscellaneous provisions

1. In the case of cancellation, refusal or total or partial non-payment, or where the price is reduced after the supply takes place, the taxable amount shall be reduced accordingly under conditions which shall be determined by the Member States.

However, in the case of total or partial non-payment, Member States may derogate from this rule.

[2. Where information for determining the taxable amount on importation is expressed in a currency other than that of the Member State where assessment takes place, the exchange rate shall be determined in accordance with the Community provisions governing the calculation of the value for customs purposes.

Where information for the determination of the taxable amount of a transaction other than an import transaction is expressed in a currency other than that of the Member State where assessment takes place, the exchange rate applicable shall be the latest selling rate recorded, at the time the tax becomes chargeable, on the most representative exchange market or markets of the Member State concerned, or a rate determined by reference to that or those markets, in accordance with the …down by that Member State. However, for some of those transactions or for certain categories of taxable person, Member States may continue to apply the exchange rate determined in accordance with the Community provisions in force governing the calculation of the value for customs purposes.][1]

3. As regards returnable packing costs, Member States may:

—either exclude them from the taxable amount and take the necessary measures to see that this amount is adjusted if the packing is not returned,

—or include them in the taxable amount and take the necessary measures to see that this amount is adjusted where the packing is in fact returned.

Note—Some words are missing in the second paragraph of art 11(C)(2) which is reproduced above as it appears in the EEC Official Journal.

Press releases etc—Business Brief 21/97, 3.10.97 (bad debt relief scheme changes for barter transactions).

Simon's Tax Cases—*Direct Cosmetics Ltd and Laughtons Photographs Ltd v C&E Comrs* [1988] STC 540; *BP Supergas Anonimos Etairia Geniki Emporiki-Viomichaniki kai Antiprossopeion v Greece* (Case C-62/93) [1995] STC 805; *C&E Comrs v Bugeja* [2000] STC 1; *C&E Comrs v Plantiflor Ltd* [2000] STC 137.

Art 11A, *Trafalgar Tours Ltd v C&E Comrs* [1990] STC 127.

Art 11A(1), *Muy's en De Winter's Bouw-en Aannemingsbedrijf BV v Staatssecretaris van Financiën* [1997] STC 665; *Rosgill Group Ltd v C&E Comrs* [1997] STC 811; *Nell Gwynn House Maintenance Fund Trustees v C&E Comrs* [1999] STC 79; *Marks and Spencer plc v C&E Comrs (Case C-62/00)* [2002] STC 1036.

Art 11A(1)*(a)*, *Town and County Factors Ltd v C&E Comrs* (Case C-498/99) [2002] STC 1263; *EC Commission v Federal Republic of Germany (United Kingdom intervening)*, [2003] STC 301; *Yorkshire Co-operatives Ltd v C&E Comrs* [2003] STC 234; *Office des Produits Wallons ASBL v Belgium* [2003] STC 1100; *Lex Services plc v C&E Comrs* [2004] STC 73.

Art 11A(1)*(c)*, *Köhne v Finanzamt München III* [1990] STC 749; *Enkler v Finanzamt Homburg* (Case C-230/94) [1996] STC 1316.

Art 11A(2)*(b)*, *C&E Comrs v British Telecom plc* [1999] STC 758.

Art 11A(3), *Nell Gwynn House Maintenance Fund Trustees v C&E Comrs* [1999] STC 79.

Art 11A(3)*(b)*, *Boots Co plc v C&E Comrs* [1990] STC 387; *Kuwait Petroleum (GB) Ltd v C&E Comrs* [1999] STC 488, [2001] STC 62, *Freemans v C&E Comrs* [2001] STC 960.

Art 11A(3)*(c)*, *C&E Comrs v Plantiflor* [2002] STC 1132.

Art 11C(1), *Elida Gibbs Ltd v C&E Comrs* (Case C-317/94) [1996] STC 1387; *Goldsmiths (Jewellers) Ltd v C&E Comrs* (Case C-330/95) [1997] STC 1073; *Yorkshire Co-operatives Ltd v C&E Comrs* [2003] STC 234.

Amendments—[1] Article 11(B), (C) amended by EEC Council Directive 91/680; OJ L376, 31.12.1991, p 1, art 1(8), (9), (10).

[2] Para (B)(1) replaced by EEC Council Directive 92/111, art 1.5; OJ L384, 30.12.92.

[3] Para (A)(4) added by EEC Council Directive 94/5, arts 1(1), 4; OJ L60, 3.3.94. For commencement, see art 4 of the Directive printed *post*; see p 678.
[4] Para (B)(6) added by EEC Council Directive 94/5, arts 1(1), 4; OJ L60, 3.3.94.
[5] Words in para (B)(3)(*b*) replaced by EC Council Directive 95/7, art 1(2): OJ L102, 5.5.95, p 18 with effect from 25 May 1995.
[6] Words in para (A)(1)(*d*) repealed, and para (A)(5)–(7) inserted, by Council Directive 2006/69/EC art 1(3), with effect from 13 August 2006, (OJ L 221, 12.8.2006, p 9).

TITLE IX: RATES

Article 12

1. The rate applicable to taxable transactions shall be that in force at the time of the chargeable event. However:

(a) in the cases provided for in the second and third sub-paragraphs of Article 10(2), the rate to be used shall be that in force when the tax becomes chargeable;

[(b) in the cases provided for in the second and third sub-paragraphs of Article 10(3), the rate applicable shall be that in force at the time when the tax becomes chargeable.]

2. In the event of changes in the rates, Member States may:

—effect adjustments in the cases provided for in paragraph 1(a) in order to take account of the rate applicable at the time when the goods or services were supplied,

—adopt all appropriate transitional measures.

[3.

[(a) [The standard rate of value added tax shall be fixed by each Member State as a percentage of the taxable amount and shall be the same for the supply of goods and for the supply of services. From 1 January 2006 until 31 December 2010, the standard rate may not be less than 15%.][9]

[The Council shall decide, in accordance with Article 93 of the Treaty, on the level of the standard rate to be applied after 31 December 2010.][9]

[Member states may also apply either one or two reduced rates. These rates shall be fixed as a percentage of the taxable amount which may not be less than 5% and shall apply only to supplies of the categories of goods and services specified in Annex H.][7]

[The third subparagraph shall not apply to the services referred to in the last indent of Article 9(2)(e).][8]

[(b) Member States may apply a reduced rate to supplies of natural gas, electricity and district heating provided that no risk of distortion of competition exists. A Member State intending to apply such a rate must inform the Commission before doing so. The Commission shall give a decision on the existence of a risk of distortion of competition. If the Commission has not taken that decision within three months of the receipt of the information a risk of distortion of competition is deemed not to exist.][10]

[(c) Member States may provide that the reduced rate, or one of the reduced rates, which they apply in accordance with the third paragraph of (a) shall also apply to imports of works of art, collectors' items and antiques as referred to in Article 26a(A)(a), (b) and (c).

Where they avail themselves of this option, Member States may also apply the reduced rate to supplies of works of art, within the meaning of Article 26a(A)(a):

—effected by their creator or his successors in title,

—effected on an occasional basis by a taxable person other than a taxable dealer, where these works of art have been imported by the taxable person himself or where they have been supplied to him by their creator or his successors in title or where they have entitled him to full deduction of value added tax.][4]

(d) … [5]

(e) …][6]

Member States will take all necessary measures to combat fraud in this area from 1 January 1993. These measures may include the introduction of a system of accounting for VAT on supplies of gold between taxable persons in the same Member State which provides for the payment of tax by the buyer on behalf of the seller and a simultaneous right for the buyer to a deduction of the same amount of tax as input tax.][2]

4. …[2] *Each reduced rate shall be so fixed that the amount of value added tax resulting from the application thereof shall be such as in the normal way to permit the deduction therefrom of the whole of the value added tax deductible under the provisions of Article 17.*

[On the basis of a report from the Commission, the Council shall, starting in 1994, review the scope of the reduced rates every two years. The Council, acting unanimously on a proposal from the Commission, may decide to alter the list of goods and services in Annex H.][2]

[By 30 June 2007 at the latest the Commission shall present to the European Parliament and the Council an overall assessment report on the impact of reduced rates applying to locally supplied services, including restaurant services, notably in terms of job creation, economic growth and the proper functioning of the internal market, based on a study carried out by an independent economic think-tank.][10]

[5. Subject to paragraph 3(c), the rate applicable on the importation of goods shall be that applied to the supply of like goods within the territory of the country.][7]

[6. The Portuguese Republic may apply to transactions carried out in the autonomous regions of the Azores and Madeira and to direct imports to those regions, reduced rates in comparison to those applying on the mainland.][1]

Commentary—*De Voil Indirect Tax Service* **V4.401**.
Simon's Tax Cases—*Marks and Spencer plc v C&E Comrs* [2000] STC 16.
Art 12(3)(*a*), *EC Commission v French Republic (Republic of Finland intervening)* [2001] STC 919; *EC Commission v Federal Republic of Germany* [2006] STC 1587.

Amendments—[1] Para 6 added by the Act of Accession 1985, art 26 Annex I Part V point 2; see OJ L302, 15.11.85, p 167.
[2] Para 3 substituted and words in para 4 repealed and added by EEC Council Directive 92/77; see OJ L316, 31.10.92.
[4] Para 3(*c*) replaced by EEC Council Directive 94/5, arts 1(2), 4; OJ L60, 3.3.94. For commencement, see art 4 of the Directive printed *post*.
[5] Para 3(*d*) deleted by EC Council Directive 96/42, art 1, with effect from 1 January 1995; see OJ L170, 9.7.96, p 34.
[6] Para 3(*e*) deleted by EC Council Directive 98/80, art 2; with effect from 17 October 1998; see OJ L281, 17.10.98.
[7] Para 3(*a*) replaced by EC Council Directive 96/95, art 1; OJ L338, 28.12.96.
[8] This article is temporarily amended by Council Directive 2002/38 art 1 para 2 (OJ L 128; 15.05.02). A further sub-paragraph is added to para 3(*a*) with effect for a period of three years from 1 July 2003: see Council Directive 2002/38/EC art 4.
[9] Words in para (3)(*a*) substituted by Council Directive 2005/92 art 1; (see OJ L 345; 28.12.2005, p 19).
[10] Para (3)(*b*) substituted, and words in para (4) substituted, by Council Directive 2006/18 art 1(1); see OJ L 051; 22.2.2006, p 12.

TITLE X: EXEMPTIONS

Article 13

Exemptions within the territory of the country

A. Exemptions for certain activities in the public interest

1. Without prejudice to other Community provisions, Member States shall exempt the following under conditions which they shall lay down for the purpose of ensuring the correct and straightforward application of such exemptions and of preventing any possible evasion, avoidance or abuse:

(*a*) *the supply by the public postal services of services other than passenger transport and telecommunications services, and the supply of goods incidental thereto;*

(*b*) *hospital and medical care and closely related activities undertaken by bodies governed by public law or, under social conditions comparable to those applicable to bodies governed by public law, by hospitals, centres for medical treatment or diagnosis and other duly recognised establishments of a similar nature;*

(*c*) *the provision of medical care in the exercise of the medical and paramedical professions as defined by the Member State concerned;*

(*d*) *supplies of human organs, blood and milk;*

(*e*) *services supplied by dental technicians in their professional capacity and dental prostheses supplied by dentists and dental technicians;*

(*f*) *services supplied by independent groups of persons whose activities are exempt from or are not subject to value added tax, for the purpose of rendering their members the services directly necessary for the exercise of their activity, where these groups merely claim from their members exact reimbursement of their share of the joint expenses, provided that such exemption is not likely to produce distortion of competition;*

(*g*) *the supply of services and of goods closely linked to welfare and social security work, including those supplied by old people's homes, by bodies governed by public law or by other organisations recognised as charitable by the Member State concerned;*

(*h*) *the supply of services and of goods closely linked to the protection of children and young persons by bodies governed by public law or by other organisations recognised as charitable by the Member State concerned;*

(*i*) *children's or young people's education, school or university education, vocational training or retraining, including the supply of services and of goods closely related thereto, provided by bodies governed by public law having such as their aim or by other organisations defined by the Member State concerned as having similar objects;*

(*j*) *tuition given privately by teachers and covering school or university education;*

(*k*) *certain supplies of staff by religious or philosophical institutions for the purpose of sub-paragraphs* (*b*), (*g*), (*h*) *and* (*i*) *of this Article and with a view to spiritual welfare;*

(*l*) *supply of services and goods closely linked thereto for the benefit of their members in return for a subscription fixed in accordance with their rules by non-profit-making organisations with aims of a political, trade-union, religious, patriotic, philosophical, philanthropic or civic nature, provided that this exemption is not likely to cause distortion of competition;*

(*m*) *certain services closely linked to sport or physical education supplied by non-profit-making organisations to persons taking part in sport or physical education;*

(*n*) *certain cultural services and goods closely linked thereto supplied by bodies governed by public law or by other cultural bodies recognised by the Member State concerned;*

(*o*) *the supply of services and goods by organisations whose activities are exempt under the provisions of sub-paragraphs* (*b*), (*g*), (*h*), (*i*), (*l*), (*m*) *and* (*n*) *above in connection with fund-raising events organised exclusively for their own benefit provided that exemption is not likely to cause distortion of competition. Member States may introduce any necessary restrictions in particular as regards the number of events or the amount of receipts which give entitlement to exemption;*

(p) the supply of transport services for sick or injured persons in vehicles specially designed for the purpose by duly authorised bodies;

(q) activities of public radio and television bodies other than those of a commercial nature.

Commentary—*De Voil Indirect Tax Service* **V4.146, V4.161.**
Note—Art 13A(1)(*c*) implemented by the Value Added Tax (Chiropractors) Order, SI 1999/1575 which inserts VATA 1994 Sch 9 Item 1(*cb*), with effect from 29 June 1999.
Simon's Tax Cases—Art 13A(1), *EC Commission v United Kingdom* [1988] STC 251; *Christoph-Dornier-Stiftung für Klinische Psychologie v Finanzamt Gießen* [2005] STC 228.
Art 13A(1)(b), *Gregg v Comrs of Customs and Excise* (Case C-216/97) [1999] STC 934; *C&E Comrs v Kingscrest Associates Ltd (t/a Kingscrest Residential Care Homes)* [2002] STC 490; *Diagnostiko & Therapeftiko Kentro Athinon-Ygeia AE v Ipourgos Ikonomikon* [2006] STC 1349.
Art 13A(1)(*c*), *Barkworth v C&E Comrs* [1988] STC 771; *C&E Comrs v Leightons Ltd* [1995] STC 458; *D v W (Osterreicher Bundesschatz intervening)* [2002] STC 1200; *d'Ambrumenil and another v C&E Comrs Unterpertinger v Pensionsversicherungsanstalt der Arbeiter* [2005] STC 650; *Solleveld and another v Staatssecretaris van Financiën* [2007] STC 71.
Art 13A(1)(*f*), *Assurandør-Societetet, acting on behalf of Taksatorringen v Skatteministeriet* [2006] STC 1842.
Art 13A(1)(*g*), *Yoga for Health Foundation v C&E Comrs* [1984] STC 630; *International Bible Students Association v C&E Comrs* [1988] STC 412; *Bulthuis-Griffioen v Inspector der Omzetbelasting* (Case C-453/93) [1995] STC 954; *Gregg v Comrs of C&E* (Case C-216/97) [1999] STC 934; *Kingscrest Associates Ltd and another v C&E Comrs* [2005] STC 1547.
Art 13A(1)(*i*), [1998] STC 784, *Pilgrims Language Courses Ltd v C&E Comrs* [1999] STC 874; *North of England Zoological Society v C&E Comrs* [1999] STC 1027; *C&E Comrs v University of Leicester Student's Union, CA* [2002] STC 147; *EC Commission v Federal Republic of Germany (Case C-287/00)* [2002] STC 982.
Art 13A(1)(*l*), *Institute of Leisure and Amenity Management v C&E Comrs* [1988] STC 602; *Committee of Directors of Polytechnics v C&E Comrs* [1992] STC 873; *Institute of Motor Industry v C&E Comrs* (Case C-149/97) [1998] STC 1219; *Expert Witness Institute v C&E Comrs, CA* [2002] STC 42.
Art 13A(1)(*m*), *EC Commission v Spain (supported by United Kingdom, intervener)* (Case C-124/96) [1998] STC 1237; *Swedish State v Stockholm Lindopark AB, Stockholm Lindopark AB v Swedish State* [2001] STC 103; *Messenger Leisure Developments Ltd v Revenue and Customs Commissioners* [2005] STC 1078.

2

(a) Member States may make the granting to bodies other than those governed by public law of each exemption provided for in 1(b), (g), (h), (i), (l), (m) and (n) of this Article subject in each individual case to one or more of the following conditions:

—they shall not systematically aim to make a profit, but any profits nevertheless arising shall not be distributed, but shall be assigned to the continuance or improvement of the services supplied,

—they shall be managed and administered on an essentially voluntary basis by persons who have no direct or indirect interest, either themselves or through intermediaries, in the results of the activities concerned,

—they shall charge prices approved by the public authorities or which do not exceed such approved prices or, in respect of those services not subject to approval, prices lower than those charged for similar services by commercial enterprises subject to value added tax,

—exemption of the services concerned shall not be likely to create distortions of competition such as to place at a disadvantage commercial enterprises liable to value added tax.

(b) The supply of services or goods shall not be granted exemption as provided for in (1)(b), (g), (h), (i), (l), (m) and (n) above if:

—it is not essential to the transactions exempted,

—its basic purpose is to obtain additional income for the organisation by carrying out transactions which are in direct competition with those of commercial enterprises liable for value added tax.

Commentary—*De Voil Indirect Tax Service* **V4.146.**
Press releases etc—Business Brief 13/98, 9.6.98 (VAT exemption for osteopaths' service).
Simon's Tax Cases—Art 13A(1)(*b*), *Diagnostiko & Therapeftiko Kentro Athinon-Ygeia AE v Ipourgos Ikonomikon* [2006] STC 1349.
Art 13A(2)(*a*), *C&E Comrs v Bell Concord Educational Trust Ltd* [1989] STC 264; *EC Commission v Spain* (Case C-124/96) [1998] STC 1237.
Art 13A(2)(*b*), *C&E Comrs v Pilgrims Language Courses Ltd* [1998] STC 784.

B. Other exemptions

Without prejudice to other Community provisions, Member States shall exempt the following under conditions which they shall lay down for the purpose of ensuring the correct and straightforward application of the exemptions and of preventing any possible evasion, avoidance or abuse;

(a) insurance and reinsurance transactions, including related services performed by insurance brokers and insurance agents;

(b) the leasing or letting of immovable property excluding:

1 the provisions of accommodation, as defined in the laws of the Member States, in the hotel sector or in sectors with a similar function, including the provision of accommodation in holiday camps or on sites developed for use as camping sites;

2 the letting of premises and sites for parking vehicles;

3 lettings of permanently installed equipment and machinery;

4 hire of safes.

Member States may apply further exclusions to the scope of this exemption;

(*c*) *supplies of goods used wholly for an activity exempted under this Article or under Article 28(3)(b) when these goods have not given rise to the right to deduction, or of goods on the acquisition or production of which, by virtue of Article 17(6), value added tax did not become deductible;*

(*d*) *the following transactions:*

1 the granting and the negotiation of credit and the management of credit by the person granting it;

2 the negotiation of or any dealings in credit guarantees or any other security for money and the management of credit guarantees by the person who is granting the credit;

3 transaction, including negotiation, concerning deposit and current accounts, payments, transfers, debts, cheques and other negotiable instruments, but excluding debt collection and factoring;

4 transactions, including negotiation, concerning currency, bank notes and coins used as legal tender, with the exception of collectors' items; "collectors' items" shall be taken to mean gold, silver or other metal coins or bank notes which are not normally used as legal tender or coins of numismatic interest;

5 transactions, including negotiation, excluding management and safe-keeping, in shares, interests in companies or associations, debentures and other securities, excluding:

—documents establishing title to goods,

—the rights or securities referred to in Article 5(3);

6 management of special investment funds as defined by Member States;

(*e*) *the supply at fact value of postage stamps valid for use for postal services within the territory of the country, fiscal stamps, and other similar stamps;*

(*f*) *betting, lotteries and other forms of gambling, subject to conditions and limitations laid down by each Member State;*

(*g*) *the supply of buildings or parts thereof, and of the land on which they stand, other than as described in Article 4(3)(a);*

(*h*) *the supply of land which has not been built on other than building land as described in Article 4(3)(b).*

Commentary—*De Voil Indirect Tax Service* **V4.111, V4.131, V4.136.**

Simon's Tax Cases—Art 13B(*a*), Item 4, *Century Life plc v C&E Comrs* [2001] STC 38, CA, *Re Forsakringsaktiebolaget Skandia (publ)* [2001] STC 754; *CR Smith Glaziers (Dunfermline) Ltd v C&E Comrs* [2003] STC 419; *Staatssecretaris van Financiën v Arthur Andersen & Co Accountants cs* [2005] STC 508; *Assurandør-Societetet, acting on behalf of Taksatorringen v Skatteministeriet* [2006] STC 1842.

Art 13B(*b*), *Sinclair Collis Ltd v C&E Comrs* [2003] STC 898; *Stichting 'Goed Wonen' v Staatssecretaris van Financiën* [2003] STC 1137; *Belgian State v Temco Europe SA* [2005] STC 1451; *Fonden Marselisborg Lystbådehavn v Skatteministeriet* [2006] STC 1467; *Abbey National plc v C&E Comrs* [2006] STC 1961.

Art 13B(*b*)(1), *Lubbock Fine & Co v C&E Comrs* (Case C-63/92) [1994] STC 101; *Blasi v Finanzamt München I* (Case C-346/95) [1998] STC 336.

Art 13B(*b*)(2), *Skatteministeriet v Henriksen* [1990] STC 768; *Fonden Marselisborg Lystbådehavn v Skatteministeriet* [2006] STC 1467.

Art 13B(*c*), *EC Commission v Italian Republic* (Case C-43/95) [1997] STC 1062; *Jyske Finans A/S v Skatteministeriet (Nordania Finans A/S and BG Factoring A/S intervening)* [2006] STC 1744.

Art 13B(*d*)(1), *Primback Ltd v C&E Comrs* [1996] STC 757; *Muy's en De Winter's Bouw-en Aannemingsbedrijf BV v Staatssecretaris van Financiën* [1997] STC 665; *C&E Comrs v Civil Service Motoring Association Ltd* [1998] STC 111; *C&E Comrs v Lloyds TSB Group Ltd* [1998] STC 528.

Art 13B(*d*)(3), *C&E Comrs v FDR Ltd* [2000] STC 672; *C&E Comrs v BAA plc; Institute of Directors v C&E Comrs* [2003] STC 35, CA; *Finanzamt Groß-Gerau v MKG-Kraftfahrzeuge-Factory GmbH* [2003] STC 951; *Bookit Ltd v R&C Comrs* [2006] STC 1367.

Art 13B(*d*)(3), (5) *Sparekassernes Datacenter (SDC) v Skatteministeriet* (Case C-2/95) [1997] STC 932; *F&I Services Ltd v C&E Comrs* [2000] STC 364; *C&E Comrs v Electronic Data Systems Ltd* [2003] STC 688; *Bookit Ltd v R&C Comrs* [2006] STC 1367.

Art 13B(*d*)(5), *Ivory & Sime Trustlink Ltd v C&E Comrs* [1998] STC 597; *CSC Financial Services Ltd v C&E Comrs (Case C-235/00)* [2002] STC 57.

Art 13B(*d*)(6), *Abbey National plc and another v C&E Comrs* [2006] STC 1136.

Art 13B(*f*), *R v Ryan* [1994] STC 446; *C&E Comrs v Feehan* [1995] STC 75; *Ivory & Sime Trustlink Ltd v C&E Comrs* [1995] STC 708; *United Utilities plc v C&E Comrs* [2006] STC 1423.

Art 13B(*h*), *C&E Comrs v Parkinson* [1989] STC 51; *Gemeente Emmen v Belastingdienst Grote Ondernemingen* (Case C-468/93) [1996] STC 496.

C. Options

Member States may allow taxpayers a right of option for taxation in cases of:

(*a*) *letting and leasing of immovable property;*

(*b*) *the transactions covered in B(d), (g) and (h) above.*

Member States may restrict the scope of this right of option and shall fix the details of its use.

Commentary—*De Voil Indirect Tax Service* **V4.115**.

Simon's Tax Cases—*Belgocodex SA v Belgium* [2000] STC 351; *Stichting 'Goed Wonen' v Staatssecretaris van Financiën* [2003] STC 1137; *Administration de l'enregistrement et des domains, État du grand-duché de Luxembourg v Vermietungsgesellschaft Objekt Kirchberg SARL* [2005] STC 1345; *Marlow Gardner & Cooke Ltd Directors' Pension Scheme v R&C Comrs* [2006] STC 2014.

Article 14

Exemptions on importation

1. Without prejudice to other Community provisions, Member States shall exempt the following under conditions which they shall lay down for the purpose of ensuring the correct and straightforward application of such exemption and of preventing any possible evasion, avoidance or abuse:

(*a*) *final importation of goods of which the supply by a taxable person would in all circumstances be exempted within the country;*
(*b*) *...(repealed by Directive 91/680)*
...[3]
(*d*) *final importation of goods qualifying for exemption from customs duties other than as provided for in the Common Customs Tariff ...*[1] *However, Member States shall have the option of not granting exemption where this would be liable to have a serious effect on conditions of competition ...*[1]*; [This exemption shall also apply to the import of goods, within the meaning of Article 7(1)(b), which would be capable of benefiting from the exemption set out above if they had been imported within the meaning of Article 7(1)(a).]*[2]
(*e*) *reimportation by the person who exported them of goods in the state in which they were exported, where they qualify for exemption from customs duties or would qualify therefor if they were imported from a third country;*
(*f*) *...*[1]
(*g*) *importations of goods:*

—under diplomatic and consular arrangements, which qualify for exemption from customs duties ...[1]*,*
—by international organisations recognised as such by the public authorities of the host country, and by members of such organisations, within the limits and under the conditions laid down by the international conventions establishing the organisations or by headquarters agreements,
—into the territory of Member States which are parties to the North Atlantic Treaty by the armed forces of other States which are parties to that Treaty for the use of such forces or the civilian staff accompanying them or for supplying their messes or canteens where such forces take part in the common defence effort;
[—the exemptions set out in the third indent shall extend to imports by and supplies of goods and services to the forces of the United Kingdom stationed in the island of Cyprus pursuant to the Treaty of Establishment concerning the Republic of Cyprus, dated 16 August 1960, which are for the use of the forces or the civilian staff accompanying them or for supplying their messes or canteens.][5]

(*h*) *importation into ports by sea fishing undertakings of their catches, unprocessed or after undergoing preservation for marketing but before being supplied;*
(*i*) *the supply of services, in connection with the importation of goods where the value of such services is included in the taxable amount in accordance with Article 11B(3)(b);*
(*j*) *importation of gold by Central Banks;*
[(k) import of gas through the natural gas distribution system, or of electricity.][4]

2. The Commission shall submit to the Council at the earliest opportunity proposals designed to lay down Community tax rules clarifying the scope of the exemptions referred to in paragraph 1 and detailed rules for their implementation.

Until the entry into force of these rules, Member States may:
—maintain their national provisions in force on matters related to the above provisions,
—adapt their national provisions to minimise distortion of competition and in particular the non-imposition or double imposition of value added tax within the Community,
—use whatever administrative procedures they consider most appropriate to achieve exemption.

Member States shall inform the Commission, which shall inform the other Member States, of the measures they have adopted and are adopting pursuant to the preceding provisions.

Simon's Tax Cases—art 14(1), *Ministère Public and Ministre des Finances du Royaume de Belgique v Ledoux* [1991] STC 553.
Cross references—See VAT (Imported Goods) Relief Order, SI 1984/746 (provisions implementing para 1(*a*) above).
VAT (Imported Gold) Relief Order, SI 1992/3124 (provisions to conform with para 1(*j*) above).
Customs and Excise (Personal Reliefs for Special Visitors) Order, SI 1992/3156 (provisions implementing para 1(*g*) above);
Council Directive 83/181/EEC (clarifying the scope of art 1(*d*));
Council Directive 85/362/EEC (clarifying the scope of art 14(1)(*c*)).

Amendments—[1] Article 14(1) amended by EEC Council Directive 91/680; OJ L376, 31.12.91, p 1.
[2] Words in para (1)(*d*) added by EEC Council Directive 92/111, art 1.8; OJ L384, 30.12.92.
[3] Para (1)(*c*) deleted by EEC Council Directive 92/111, art 1.8; OJ L384, 30.12.92.
[4] Para 1(*k*) inserted by Council Directive 2003/92/EC, art 1(3); OJ L260, 11.10.2003 p 8.
[5] Words in para 1(*g*) inserted by the 2003 Act of Accession Protocol No 3 Annex Part Three para 2(*a*); OJ L 236; 23.9.2003 p 940.

Article 15

[Exemption of exports from the Community and like transactions and international transport][1]

Without prejudice to other Community provisions Member States shall exempt the following under conditions which they shall lay down for the purpose of ensuring the correct and straightforward application of such exemptions and of preventing any evasion, avoidance or abuse:

1. the supply of goods dispatched or transported to a destination [outside the Community][1]*; by or on behalf of the vendor;*

2. the supply of goods dispatched or transported to a destination [outside the Community][1]*; by or on behalf of a purchaser not established within the territory of the country, with the exception of goods transported by the purchaser himself for the equipping, fuelling and provisioning of pleasure boats and private aircraft or any other means of transport for private use;*

[In the case of the supply of goods to be carried in the personal luggage of travellers, this exemption shall apply on condition that:

—the traveller is not established within the Community,

—the goods are transported to a destination outside the Community before the end of the third month following that in which the supply is effected,

—the total value of the supply, including value added tax, is more than the equivalent in national currency of ECU 175, fixed in accordance with Article 7(2) of Directive 69/169/EEC; however, Member States may exempt a supply with a total value of less than that amount.

For the purposes of applying the second subparagraph:

—a traveller not established within the Community shall be taken to mean a traveller whose domicile or habitual residence is not situated within the Community. For the purposes of this provision, "domicile or habitual residence" shall mean the place entered as such in a passport, identity card or other identity documents which the Member State within whose territory the supply takes place recognises as valid,

—proof of exportation shall be furnished by means of the invoice or other document in lieu thereof, endorsed by the customs office where the goods left the Community.

Each Member State shall transmit to the Commission specimens of the stamps it uses for the endorsement referred to in the second indent of the third subparagraph. The Commission shall transit this information to the tax authorities in the other Member States.][5]

[3. the supply of services consisting of work on movable property acquired or imported for the purpose of undergoing such work within the territory of the Community, and dispatched or transported out of the Community by the person providing the services or by the customer if [not established within the territory of the country][4] *or on behalf of either of them;]*[1]

4. the supply of goods for the fuelling and provisioning of vessels:

(a) used for navigation on the high seas and carrying passengers for reward or used for the purpose of commercial, industrial or fishing activities;

(b) used for rescue or assistance at sea, or for inshore fishing, with the exception, for the latter, of ships' provisions;

(c) of war, as defined in subheading 89.01 A of the Common Customs Tariff, leaving the country and bound for foreign ports or anchorages.

[The Commission shall submit to the Council as soon as possible proposals to establish Community fiscal rules specifying the scope of and practical arrangements for implementing this exemption and the exemptions provided for in (5) to (9). Until these rules come into force, Member States may limit the extent of the exemption provided for in this paragraph.][3]

5. the supply, modification, repair, maintenance, chartering and hiring of the sea-going vessels referred to in paragraph 4(a) and (b) and the supply, hiring, repair and maintenance of equipment—including fishing equipment—incorporated or used therein;

6. the supply, modification, repair, maintenance, chartering and hiring of aircraft used by airlines operating for reward chiefly on international routes, and the supply, hiring, repair and maintenance of equipment incorporated or used therein;

7. the supply of goods for the fuelling and provisioning of aircraft referred to in paragraph 6;

8. the supply of services other than those referred to in paragraph 5, to meet the direct needs of the sea-going vessels referred to in that paragraph or of their cargoes;

9. the supply of services other than those referred to in paragraph 6, to meet the direct needs of aircraft referred to in that paragraph or of their cargoes;

10. supplies of goods and services:

—under diplomatic and consular arrangements,

—to another Member State and intended for the forces of any Member State which is a party to the North Atlantic Treaty, other than the Member State of destination itself, for the use of those forces or of the civilian staff accompanying them, or for supplying their messes or canteens when such forces take part in the common defence effort,][1]

—to international organisations recognised as such by the public authorities of the host country, and to members of such organisations, within the limits and under the conditions laid down by the international conventions establishing the organisations or by headquarters agreements,

—effected within a Member State which is a party to the North Atlantic Treaty and intended either for the use of the forces of other States which are parties to that Treaty or of the civilian staff accompanying them, or for supplying their messes or canteens when such forces take part in the common defence effort.

This exemption shall be [subject to [limitations][3] *laid down by the host Member State]*[1] *until Community tax rules are adopted.*

[In cases where the goods are not dispatched or transported out of the country, and in the case of services, the benefit of the exemption may be given by means of a refund of the tax.][3]

11. supplies of gold to Central Banks;

12. goods supplied to approved bodies which export them [from the Community][1] *as part of their humanitarian, charitable or teaching activities [outside the Community]*[1]*. This exemption may be implemented by means of a refund of the tax;*

[13. The supply of services, including transport and ancillary operations, but excluding the supply of services exempted in accordance with Article 13, where these are directly connected with the export of goods or imports of goods covered by the provisions of Article 7(3) or Article 16(1), Title A.][4]

14. services supplied by brokers and other intermediaries, acting in the name and for account of another person, where they form part of transactions specified in this Article, or of transactions carried out [outside the Community][1].

This exemption does not apply to travel agents who supply in the name and for account of the traveller services which are supplied in other Member States.

[15. The Portuguese Republic may treat sea and air transport between the islands making up the autonomous regions of the Azores and Madeira and between those regions and the mainland in the same way as international transport.][2]

Simon's Tax Cases—art 15, *Staatssecretaris van Financiën v Velker International Oil Co Ltd NV* [1991] STC 640; *Lange v Finanzamt Fürstenfeldbruck* (Case C-111/92) [1997] STC 564.

Cross references—See VATA 1994 Sch 8, Groups 7 and 8 (implementation of paras 3 and 4 above).
Customs and Excise (Personal Reliefs for Special Visitors) Order, SI 1992/3156 (implementation of para 10 above).
VAT (Amendment) Regulations, SI 2000/258 (implementation of para 2 above).

Amendments—[1] Paras 3, 14 amended by EEC Council Directive 91/680; OJ L376, 31.12.1991, p 1.
[2] Para 15 added by the Act of Accession 1985, art 26 Annex I Part V point 2; see OJ L302, 15.11.1985, p 167.
[3] Words in paras 3, 4, 10 replaced by EEC Council Directive 92/111, art 1.9; OJ L384, 30.12.92.
[4] Para 13 replaced by EEC Council Directive 92/111, art 1.9; OJ L384, 30.12.92.
[5] Words in para 2 replaced by Council Directive 95/7, art 1.3: OJ L102, 5.5.95, p 18 with effect from 25 May 1995.

Article 16

Special exemptions linked to international goods traffic

1. Without prejudice to other Community tax provisions, Member States may, subject to the consultations provided for in Article 29, take special measures designed to exempt all or some of the following transactions, provided that they are not aimed at final use and/or consumption and that the amount of value added tax due on cessation of the arrangements on situations referred to at A to E corresponds to the amount of tax which would have been due had each of these transactions been taxed within the territory of the country:

A imports of goods which are intended to be placed under warehousing arrangements other than customs;

B supplies of goods which are intended to be:

(a) produced to customs and, where applicable, placed in temporary storage;
(b) placed in a free zone or in a free warehouse;
(c) placed under customs warehousing arrangements or inward processing arrangements;
(d) admitted into territorial waters:

—in order to be incorporated into drilling or production platforms, for purposes of the construction, repair, maintenance, alteration or fitting-out of such platforms, or to link such drilling or production platforms to the mainland,
—for the fuelling and provisioning of drilling or production platforms;

(e) placed, within the territory of the country, under warehousing arrangements other than customs warehousing.

For the purposes of this Article, warehouses other than customs warehouses shall be taken to be:

—for products subject to excise duty, the places defined as tax warehouses for the purposes of Article 4(b) of Directive 92/12/EEC,
—for goods other than those subject to excise duty, the places defined as such by the Member States. However, Member States may not provide for warehousing arrangements other than customs warehousing where the goods in question are intended to be supplied at the retail stage.

Nevertheless, Member States may provide for such arrangements for goods intended for:

—taxable persons for the purposes of supplies effected under the conditions laid down in Article 28k,
—tax-free shops within the meaning of Article 28k, for the purposes of supplies to travellers taking flights or sea crossings to third countries, where those supplies are exempt pursuant to Article 15,
—taxable persons for the purposes of supplies to travellers on board aircraft or vessels during a flight or sea crossing where the place of arrival is situated outside the Community,
—taxable persons for the purposes of supplies effected free of tax pursuant to Article 15, point 10.

The places referred to in (a), (b), (c) and (d) shall be as defined by the Community customs provisions in force;

C supplies of services relating to the supplies of goods referred to in B;

D supplies of goods and of services carried out:

(a) in the places listed in B(a), (b), (c) and (d) and still subject to one of the situations specified therein;
(b) in the places listed in B(e) and still subject, within the territory of the country, to the situation specified therein.

Where they exercise the option provided for in (a) for transactions effected in customs warehouses, Member States shall take the measures necessary to ensure that they have defined warehousing arrangements other than customs warehousing which permit the provisions in (b) to be applied to the same transactions concerning goods listed in Annex J which are effected in such warehouses other than customs warehouses;

E supplies:

—of goods referred to in Article 7(1)(a) still subject to arrangements for temporary importation with total exemption from import duty or to external transit arrangements,

—of goods referred to in Article 7(1)(b) still subject to the internal Community transit procedure provided for in Article 33a,

as well as supplies of services relating to such supplies.

By way of derogation from the first subparagraph of Article 21(1)(a), the person liable to pay the tax due in accordance with the first subparagraph shall be the person who causes the goods to cease to be covered by the arrangements or situations listed in this paragraph.

When the removal of goods from the arrangements or situations referred to in this paragraph gives rise to importation within the meaning of Article 7(3), the Member State of import shall take the measures necessary to avoid double taxation within the country.][1]

[1a. Where they exercise the option provided for in paragraph 1, Member States shall take the measures necessary to ensure that intra-Community acquisitions of goods intended to be placed under one of the arrangements or in one of the situations referred to in paragraph 1(B) benefit from the same provisions as supplies of goods effected within the country under the same conditions.][1]

2. Subject to the consultation provided for in Article 29, Member States may opt to exempt [intra-Community acquisitions of goods made by a taxable person and][1] *imports for and supplies of goods to a taxable person intending to export them [outside the Community]*[1] *as they are or after processing, as well as supplies of services linked with his export business, up to a maximum equal to the value of his exports during the preceding 12 months.*

[When they take up this option the Member States shall, subject to the consultation provided for in Article 29, extend the benefit of this exemption to intra-Community acquisitions of goods by a taxable person, imports for and supplies of goods to a taxable person intending to supply them, as they are or after processing, under the conditions laid down in Article 28c(A), as well as supplies of services relating to such supplies, up to a maximum equal to the value of his supplies of goods effected under the conditions laid down in Article 28c(A) during the preceding twelve months.

Member States may set a common maximum amount for transactions which they exempt under the first and second subparagraphs.][1]

3. The Commission shall submit to the Council at the earliest opportunity proposals concerning common arrangements for applying value added tax to the transactions referred to in paragraphs 1 and 2.

Cross references—See Council Directive 85/362/EEC (common arrangements for goods subject to temporary importation arrangements).

Amendments—[1] Art 16(1) substituted, para (1A) added and para (2) amended by EC Council Directive 95/7, art 1(9): OJ L102, 5.5.95, p 18 with effect from 25 May 1995.

TITLE XI: DEDUCTIONS

Article 17

Origin and scope of the right to deduct

1. The right to deduct shall arise at the time when the deductible tax becomes chargeable.

[2. In so far as the goods and services are used for the purposes of his taxable transactions, the taxable person shall be entitled to deduct from the tax which he is liable to pay:

[(a) value added tax due or paid within the territory of the country in respect of goods or services supplied or to be supplied to him by another taxable person;][3]

(b) value added tax due or paid in respect of imported goods within the territory of the country;

(c) value added tax due pursuant to Articles 5(7)(a), 6(3) and 28a(6);

(d) value added tax due pursuant to Article 28a(1)(a).][1]

[3. Member States shall also grant every taxable person the right to the deduction or refund of the value added tax referred to in paragraph 2 in so far as the goods and services are used for the purposes of:

(a) transactions relating to the economic activities referred to in Article 4(2), carried out in another country, which would be deductible if they had been performed within the territory of the country;

[(b) transactions which are exempt pursuant to Article 14(1)(g) and (i), 15, 16(1)(B),(C), (D) or (E) or (2) or 28c(A) and (C),][4]*;*

(c) any of the transactions exempt pursuant to Article 13(B)(a) and (d)(1) to (5), when the customer is established outside the Community or when those transactions are directly linked with goods to be exported to a country outside the Community.][1]

[4. The refund of value added tax referred to in paragraph 3 shall be effected:

—to taxable persons who are not established within the territory of the country but who are established in another Member State in accordance with the detailed implementing rules laid down in Directive 79/1072/EEC.
—to taxable persons who are not established within the territory of the Community, in accordance with the detailed implementing rules laid down in Directive 86/560/EEC.]

[For the purposes of applying the above:

(a) the taxable persons referred to in Article 1 of Directive 79/1072/EEC shall also be considered for the purposes of applying the said Directive as taxable persons who are not established in the country when, inside the territory of the country, they have only carried out supplies of goods and services to a person who has been designated as the person liable to pay the tax in accordance with [Article 21(1)(a), (1)(c) or (1)(f) or Article 21(2)(c)][5]*;*
(b) the taxable persons referred to in Article 1 of Directive 86/560/EEC shall also be considered for the purposes of applying the said Directive as taxable persons who are not established in the Community when, inside the territory of the country, they have only carried out supplies of goods and services to a person who has been designated as the person liable to pay the tax in accordance with [Article 21(1)(a), or (1)(f) or Article 21(2)(c)][5]*;*
(c) Directives 79/1072/EEC and 86/560/EEC shall not apply to supplies of goods which are, or may be, exempted under Article 28c(A) when the goods supplied are dispatched or transported by the acquirer or for his account.][2] *]*[1]

5. As regards goods and services to be used by a taxable person both for transactions covered by paragraphs 2 and 3, in respect of which value added tax is deductible, and for transactions in respect of which value added tax is not deductible, only such proportion of the value added tax shall be deductible as is attributable to the former transactions.

This proportion shall be determined, in accordance with Article 19, for all the transactions carried out by the taxable person.

However, Member States may:

(a) authorise the taxable person to determine a proportion for each sector of his business, provided that separate accounts are kept for each sector;
(b) compel the taxable person to determine a proportion for each sector of his business and to keep separate accounts for each sector;
(c) authorise or compel the taxable person to make the deduction on the basis of the use of all or part of the goods and services;
(d) authorise or compel the taxable person to make the deduction in accordance with the rule laid down in the first sub-paragraph, in respect of all goods and services used for all transactions referred to therein;
(e) provide that where the value added tax which is not deductible by the taxable person is insignificant it shall be treated as nil.

6. Before a period of four years at the latest has elapsed from the date of entry into force of this Directive, the Council, acting unanimously on a proposal from the Commission, shall decide what expenditure shall not be eligible for a deduction of value added tax. Value added tax shall in no circumstances be deductible on expenditure which is not strictly business expenditure, such as that on luxuries, amusements or entertainment.

Until the above rules come into force, Member States may retain all the exclusions provided for under their national laws when this Directive comes into force.

7. Subject to the consultation provided for in Article 29, each Member State may, for cyclical economic reasons, totally or partly exclude all or some capital goods or other goods from the system of deductions. To maintain identical conditions of competition, Member States may, instead of refusing deduction, tax the goods manufactured by the taxable person himself or which he has purchased in the country or imported, in such a way that the tax does not exceed the value added tax which would have been charged on the acquisition of similar goods.

Commentary—*De Voil Indirect Tax Service* **V2.101**, **V.3.401**, **V3.460**.
Note—Council Decision 93/563/EEC, art 3 allows derogation from this Article.
Simon's Tax Cases—*Kretztechnik AG v Finanzamt Linz* [2005] STC 1118; *Stichting 'Goed Wonen' v Staatssecretaris van Financiën* [2006] STC 833; *Halifax plc and others v C&E Comrs* [2006] STC 919; *University of Huddersfield Higher Education Corporation v C&E Comrs* [2006] STC 980.
Art 17(2), *EC Commission v French Republic (United Kingdom intervening)* [2003] STC 372, 390; *BUPA Purchasing Ltd and others v C&E Comrs* [2003] STC 1203; *Finanzamt Offenbach am Main-Land v Faxworld Vorgründungsgesellschaft Peter Hünninghausen und Wolfgang Klein GbR* [2005] STC 1192; *Finanzamt Bergisch Gladbach v HE* [2007] STC 128.
Art 17(2)(*a*), *Finanzamt Uelzen v Armbrecht* [1995] STC 997; *C&E Comrs v Southern Primary Housing Association Ltd* [2003] STC 525; *EC Commission v Kingdom of the Netherlands (United Kingdom intervening)* [2003] STC 1506; *C&E Comrs v Southern Primary Housing Association Ltd* [2004] STC 209.
Art 17(5), *Cibo Participations SA v Directeur regional des impots du Nord-Pas-de-Calais* [2002] STC 460; *Dial-a-Phone Ltd v C&E Comrs*, [2003] STC 192; *EC Commission v Kingdom of Spain* [2006] STC 1087; *EC Commission v French Republic (Kingdom of Spain, intervening)* [2006] STC 1098.
Art 17(6), *Group Ltd v C&E Comrs* [1996] STC 898; *Royscot Leasing Ltd v C&E Comrs* [1999] STC 998; *EC Commission v French Republic (United Kingdom intervening)* [2003] STC 372, 390; *Charles and another v Staatssecretaris van Financiën* [2006] STC 1429.
Cross reference—For directives adopted under art 17(4), see the Eighth Council Directive 79/1072/EEC; see OJ L331, 27.12.1979, p 11 and the Thirteenth Council Directive 86/560/EEC; see OJ L326, 21.11.1986, p 40.
VAT (Input Tax) (Specified Supplies) Order, SI 1992/3123 (partial implementation of para 3 above).
VAT Regulations, SI 1995/2518 reg 175 (implementation of para 4 above); reg 188(2)(*b*)(ii) (implementation of para 4 above).

Amendments—[1] Paras 2–4 substituted by Council Directive 91/680/EEC of 16 December 1991 which inserted art 28f(1)with effect from 1 January 1993 for the transitional period specified in art 28l.
[2] Words in para 4 added by Council Directive 92/111/EEC art 1(18); OJ L 384, 30.12.92.
[3] Para 2(*a*) substituted by Council Directive 95/7/EEC art 1(10) with effect from 25 May 1995; OJ L 102, 15.5.95.
[4] Para 3(*b*) (which was substituted by the 2003 Act of Accession Protocol No 3 Annex Part Three para 2(*b*); OJ L 236; 23.9.2003 p 940) substituted by Council Directive 2004/66 art 1, Annex V para 1(*c*); OJ L 168; 1.5.2004 p 35).
[5] Words in para 4 substituted by Council Directive 2006/69/EC art 1(4), with effect from 13 August 2006, (OJ L 221, 12.8.2006, p 9).

Article 18

Rules governing the exercise of the right to deduct

[1. To exercise his right of deduction, a taxable person must:

(a) in respect of deductions pursuant to Article 17(2)(a), hold an invoice drawn up in accordance with Article 22(3);
(b) in respect of deductions pursuant to Article 17(2)(b), hold an import document specifying him as consignee or importer and stating or permitting the calculation of the amount of tax due;
(c) in respect of deductions pursuant to Article 17(2)(c), comply with the formalities established by each Member State;
(d) when he is required to pay the tax as a customer or purchaser where [Article 21(1) or Article 21(2)(c)][2] applies, comply with the formalities laid down by each Member State;
(e) in respect of deductions pursuant to Article 17(2)(d), set out in the declaration provided for in Article 22(4) all the information needed for the amount of the tax due on his intra-Community acquisitions of goods to be calculated and hold an invoice in accordance with Article 22(3).][1]

2. The taxable person shall effect the deduction by subtracting from the total amount of value added tax due for a given tax period the total amount of the tax in respect of which, during the same period, the right to deduct has arisen and can be exercised under the provisions of paragraph 1.

However, Member States may require that as regards taxable persons who carry out occasional transactions as defined in Article 4(3), the right to deduct shall be exercised only at the time of the supply.

3. Member States shall determine the conditions and procedures whereby a taxable person may be authorised to make a deduction which he has not made in accordance with the provisions of paragraphs 1 and 2.

[3a. Member States may authorise a taxable person who does not hold an invoice in accordance with Article 22(3) to make the deduction referred to in Article 17(2)(d); they shall determine the conditions and arrangements for applying this provision.][1]

4. Where for a given tax period the amount of authorised deductions exceeds the amount of tax due, the Member States may either make a refund or carry the excess forward to the following period according to conditions which they shall determine.

However, Member States may refuse to refund or carry forward if the amount of the excess is insignificant.

Commentary—*De Voil Indirect Tax Service* **V3.401**.
Simon's Tax Cases—*Local Authorities Mutual Investment Trust v C&E Comrs* [2004] STC 246 *R (on the application of UK Tradecorp Ltd) v Customs and Excise Commissioners* [2005] STC 138.
art 18(1)(*a*), *Reisdorf v Finanzamt Köln-West* [1997] STC 180; *EC Commission v Kingdom of the Netherlands (United Kingdom intervening)* [2003] STC 1506; *Finanzamt Gummersbach v Bockemühl* [2005] STC 934; *Finanzamt Bergisch Gladbach v HE* [2007] STC 128.
Art 18(4), *Garage Molenheide BVBA, Schepens, Bureau Rik Decan-Business Research & Development NV (BRD) and Sanders BVBA v Belgium* (Joined cases C-286/94, C-340/95, C-401/95 and C-47/96) [1998] STC 126.
Cross references—See Title XVI*a*, arts 28*f* para 2, 28l, *post* (transitional arrangements for the taxation of trade between member States);
VAT Regulations, SI 1995/2518 reg 29(2) (implementation of this article).
Amendments—[1] Para 1 substituted and para 3a inserted by Council Directive 91/680/EEC of 16 December 1991 which inserted art 28f with effect from 1 January 1993 for the transitional period specified in art 28l.
[2] Words in para 1(*d*) substituted by Council Directive 2006/69/EC art 1(5), with effect from 13 August 2006, (OJ L 221, 12.8.2006, p 9).

Article 19

Calculation of the deductible proportion

1. The proportion deductible under the first sub-paragraph of Article 17(5) shall be made up of a fraction having:

—as numerator, the total amount, exclusive of value added tax, of turnover per year attributable to transactions in respect of which value added tax is deductible under Article 17(2) and (3),
—as denominator, the total amount, exclusive of value added tax, of turnover per year attributable to transactions included in the numerator and to transactions in respect of which value added tax is not deductible. The Member States may also include in the denominator the amount of subsidies, other than those specified in Article 11A(1)(a).

The proportion shall be determined on an annual basis, fixed as a percentage and rounded up to a figure not exceeding the next unit.

2. By way of derogation from the provisions of paragraph 1, there shall be excluded from the calculation of the deductible proportion, amounts of turnover attributable to the supplies of capital goods used by the taxable person for the purposes of his business. Amounts of turnover attributable to transactions specified in Article 13B(d), in so far as these are incidental transactions, and to incidental real estate and financial transactions shall also be excluded. Where Member States exercise the option provided under Article 20(5) not to require adjustment in respect of capital goods, they may include disposals of capital goods in the calculation of the deductible proportion.

3. The provisional proportion for a year shall be that calculated on the basis of the preceding year's transactions. In the absence of any such transactions to refer to, or where they were insignificant in amounts, the deductible proportion shall be estimated provisionally, under supervision of the tax authorities, by the taxable person from his own forecasts. However, Member States may retain their current rules.

Deductions made on the basis of such provisional proportion shall be adjusted when the final proportion is fixed during the next year.

Commentary—*De Voil Indirect Tax Service* **V3.460**.
Simon's Tax Cases—art 19, *Dwyer Property Ltd v C&E Comrs* [1995] STC 1035; *C&E Comrs v Liverpool Institute for Performing Arts* [2001] STC 891.
Art 19(1), *Sofitam SA (formerly Satam SA) v Ministre chargé du Budget* (Case C-333/91), ECJ [1997] STC 226; *Floridienne SA and anor v Belgian State* [2000] STC 1044; *EC Commission v Kingdom of Spain* [2006] STC 1087; *EC Commission v French Republic (Kingdom of Spain, intervening)* [2006] STC 1098.
Art 19(2), *Régie Dauphinoise—Cabinet A Forest SARL v Ministre du Budget* (Case C-306/94) [1996] STC 1176; *C&E Comrs v JDL Ltd* [2001] STC 1; *Empresa de Desenvolvimento Mineiro SGPS SA (EDM) v Fazenda Pública (Ministério Público, intervening)* [2005] STC 65.

Article 20

Adjustments of deductions

1. The initial deduction shall be adjusted according to the procedures laid down by the Member States, in particular:

(a) where that deduction was higher or lower than that to which the taxable person was entitled;
(b) where after the return is made some change occurs in the factors used to determine the amount to be deducted, in particular where purchases are cancelled or price reductions are obtained; however, adjustment shall not be made in case of transactions remaining totally or partially unpaid and of destruction, loss or theft of property duly proved or confirmed, nor in the case of applications for the purpose of making gifts of small value and giving samples specified in Article 5(6). However, Member States may require adjustment in cases of transactions remaining totally or partially unpaid and of theft.

2. In the case of capital goods, adjustments shall be spread over five years including that in which the goods were acquired or manufactured. The annual adjustment shall be made only in respect of one-fifth of the tax imposed on the goods. The adjustment shall be made on the basis of the variations in the deduction entitlement in subsequent years in relation to that for the year in which the goods were acquired or manufactured.

By way of derogation from the preceding sub-paragraph, Member States may base the adjustment on a period of five full years starting from the time at which the goods are first used.

[In the case of immovable property acquired as capital goods, the adjustment period may be extended up to 20 years.][1]

3. In the case of supply during the period of adjustment capital goods shall be regarded as if they had still been applied for business use by the taxable person until expiry of the period of adjustment. Such business activities are presumed to be fully taxed in cases where the delivery of the said goods is taxed; they are presumed to be fully exempt where the delivery is exempt. The adjustment shall be made only once for the whole period of adjustment still to be covered.

However, in the latter case, Member States may waive the requirement for adjustment in so far as the purchaser is a taxable person using the capital goods in question solely for transactions in respect of which value added tax is deductible.

4. For the purposes of applying the provisions of paragraphs 2 and 3, Member States may:

—define the concept of capital goods,
—indicate the amount of the tax which is to be taken into consideration for adjustment,
—adopt any suitable measures with a view to ensuring that adjustment does not involve any unjustified advantage,
—permit administrative simplifications.

[Member States may also apply paragraphs 2 and 3 to services which have characteristics similar to those normally attributed to capital goods.][2]

5. If in any Member State the practical effect of applying paragraphs 2 and 3 would be insignificant, that Member State may subject to the consultation provided for in Article 29 forego application of these paragraphs having regard to the need to avoid distortion of competition, the overall tax effect in the Member State concerned and the need for due economy of administration.

6. Where the taxable person transfers from being taxed in the normal way to a special scheme or vice versa, Member States may take all necessary measures to ensure that the taxable person neither benefits nor is prejudiced unjustifiably.

Commentary—*De Voil Indirect Tax Service* **V3.470**.
Simon's Tax Cases—Art 20, *Lennartz v Finanzamt München III* (Case C-97/90) [1995] STC 514; *C&E Comrs v University of Wales College, Cardiff* [1995] STC 611; *Waterschap Zeeuws Vlaanderen v Staatssecretaris van Financiën* [2005] STC 1298; *Stichting 'Goed Wonen' v Staatssecretaris van Financiën* [2006] STC 833.

Art 20(1)(*b*), *Tremerton Ltd v C&E Comrs* [1999] STC 1039; *Finanzamt Burgdorf v Fischer*, *Finanzamt Düsseldorf-Mettman v Brandenstein* [2001] STC 1356.
Art 20(2), *Finanzamt Uelzen v Armbrecht* (Case C-291/92) [1995] STC 997.
Art 20(3), *Centralan Property Ltd v C&E Comrs* [2006] STC 1542.

Amendments—[1] Words in para (2) replaced by EC Council Directive 95/7, art 1(4): OJ L102, 5.5.95, p 18 with effect from 25 May 1995.
[2] Words in para 4 inserted by Council Directive 2006/69/EC art 1(6), with effect from 13 August 2006, (OJ L 221, 12.8.2006, p 9).

TITLE XII: PERSONS LIABLE FOR PAYMENT FOR TAX

[Article 21

Persons liable for payment for tax

1. Under the internal system, the following shall be liable to pay value added tax—

[(a) the taxable person carrying out the taxable supply of goods or of services, except for the cases referred to in (b), (c) and (f). Where the taxable supply of goods or of services is effected by a taxable person who is not established within the territory of the country, Member States may, under the conditions determined by them, lay down that the person liable to pay tax is the person for whom the taxable supply of goods or of services is carried out;][3]

(b) taxable persons to whom services covered by Article 9(2)(e) are supplied or persons who are identified for value added tax purposes within the territory of the country to whom services covered by Article 28b(C), (D), (E) and (F) are supplied, if the services are carried out by a taxable person not established within the territory of the country;

(c) the person to whom the supply of goods is made when the following conditions are met—

—the taxable operation is a supply of goods made under the conditions laid down in Article 28c(E)(3),

—the person to whom the supply of goods is made is another taxable person or a non-taxable legal person identified for the purposes of value added tax within the territory of the country,

—the invoice issued by the taxable person not established within the territory of the country conforms to Article 22(3).

However, Member States may provide a derogation from this obligation, where the taxable person who is not established within the territory of the country has appointed a tax representative in that country;

(d) any person who mentions the value added tax on an invoice …[2]*;*

(e) any person effecting a taxable intra-Community acquisition of goods.

[(f) persons who are identified for value added tax purposes within the territory of the country and to whom goods are supplied under the conditions set out in Article 8(1)(d) or (e), if the supplies are carried out by a taxable person not established within the territory of the country.][3]

2. By way of derogation from the provisions of paragraph 1—

(a) where the person liable to pay tax in accordance with the provisions of paragraph 1 is a taxable person who is not established within the territory of the country, Member States may allow him to appoint a tax representative as the person liable to pay tax. This option shall be subject to conditions and procedures laid down by each Member State;

(b) where the taxable transaction is effected by a taxable person who is not established within the territory of the country and no legal instrument exists, with the country in which that taxable person is established or has his seat, relating to mutual assistance similar in scope to that laid down by Directives 76/308/EEC and 77/799/EEC and by Council Regulation (EEC) No 218/ 92 of 27 January 1992 on administrative co-operation in the field of indirect taxation (VAT), Member States may take steps to provide that the person liable for payment of the tax shall be a tax representative appointed by the non-established taxable person.

[(c) where the following supplies are carried out, Member States may lay down that the person liable to pay tax is the taxable person to whom those supplies are made:

(i) the supply of construction work, including repair, cleaning, maintenance, alteration and demolition services in relation to immovable property, as well as the handing over of construction works considered to be a supply of goods by virtue of Article 5(5);

(ii) the supply of staff engaged in activities covered by (i);

(iii) the supply of immovable property, as referred to in Article 13(B)(g) and (h), where the supplier has opted for taxation of the supply pursuant to point (C)(b) of that Article;

(iv) the supply of used material, used material which cannot be re-used in the same state, scrap, industrial and non industrial waste, recyclable waste, part processed waste and certain goods and services, as identified in Annex M;

(v) the supply of goods provided as security by one taxable person to another in execution of that security;

(vi) the supply of goods following the cession of the reservation of ownership to an assignee and the exercising of this right by the assignee;

(vii) the supply of immovable property sold by the judgment debtor in a compulsory sale procedure.

For the purposes of this point, Member States may provide that a taxable person who also carries out activities or transactions that are not considered to be taxable supplies of goods or services in accordance with Article 2 shall be deemed to be a taxable person in respect of supplies received as referred to in the first subparagraph. A non-taxable body governed by public law, may be deemed to be a taxable person in respect of supplies received as referred to in (v), (vi) and (vii).

For the purposes of this point, Member States may specify the supplies of goods and services covered, and the categories of suppliers or recipients to whom these measures may apply. They may also limit the application of this measure to some of the supplies of goods and services listed in Annex M.

Member States shall inform the Committee established in accordance with Article 29 of any new national measure adopted pursuant to the provisions of this point.][4]

3. In the situations referred to in paragraphs 1 and 2, Member States may provide that someone other than the person liable for payment of the tax shall be held jointly and severally liable for payment of the tax.

4. On importation, value added tax shall be payable by the person or persons designated or accepted as being liable by the Member State into which the goods are imported.][1]

Commentary—*De Voil Indirect Tax Service* **V1.285, V5.186**.

Note—The amendments made by note 3 below were expressed in Council Directive 2003/92 to be made to the version of this article "set out in article 28gh". On a strict reading, this would imply that the amendment be made to the version set out in note 1 below. However, this does not work, and the amendment has been made to the current text of art 21.

Simon's Tax Cases—art 21(1)(*c*), *Finanzamt Osnabrück-Land v Langhorst* (Case C-141/96) [1997] STC 1357; *EMI Group Electronics Ltd v Coldicott* [1997] STC 1372; *Schmeink & Cofreth AG & Co KG v Finanzamt Borken*; *Strobel v Fananzamt Esslingen* (Case C-454/98) [2000] STC 810; *Elliniko Dimosio v Karageorgou and others* [2006] STC 1654.

21(3), *C&E Comrs and another v Federation of Technological Industries and others* [2006] STC 1483.

Cross references—See Council Decision EEC 93/204, art 1; OJ L88, 8.4.93 (derogation from para 1(*a*) above granted to the UK);

VATA 1994 Sch 5 para 9.

Amendments—[1] Article 21 substituted by Council Directive 2000/65/EC art 1(4) with effect from 21 October 2000; OJ L269 p 44, 21.10.00. Member states must bring into force the measures necessary to comply with these provisions not later than 31 December 2001.

[2] Words repealed by Council Directive 2001/115/EC art 4(5); see OJ L 015; 17.01.02.

[3] In para (1), point (*a*) substituted, and point (*f*) inserted, by Council Directive 2003/92 art 1(4), (5) (OJ L 260; 11.10.2003 p 8).

[4] Para 2(*c*) inserted by Council Directive 2006/69/EC art 1(7), with effect from 13 August 2006, (OJ L 221, 12.8.2006, p 9).

TITLE XIII: OBLIGATIONS OF PERSONS LIABLE FOR PAYMENT

[Article 22

Obligations under the internal system:

1

[(a) Every taxable person shall state when his activity as a taxable person commences, changes or ceases. Member States shall, subject to conditions which they lay down, allow the taxable person to make such statements by electronic means, and may also require that electronic means are used.][10]

(b) Without prejudice to (a), every taxable person referred to in Article 28a(1)(a), second subparagraph, shall state that he is effecting intra-Community acquisitions of goods when the conditions for application of the derogation provided for in that Article are not fulfilled.

(c) Member States shall take the measures necessary to identify by means of an individual number:

[—Every taxable person, with the exception of those referred to in Article 28a(4), who, within the territory of the country, effects supplies of goods or of services giving him the right of deduction, other than supplies of goods or of services for which tax is payable solely by the customer or the recipient in accordance with Article 21(1)(a),(b),(c) or (f). However, Member States need not identify certain taxable persons referred to in article 4(3),][12]

—every taxable person referred to in paragraph 1(b) and every taxable person who exercises the option provided for in the third subparagraph of Article 28a(1)(a),

[—every taxable person who, within the territory of the country, effects intra-Community acquisitions of goods for the purposes of his operations relating to the economic activities referred to in Article 4(2) carried out abroad.][2]

(d) Each individual identification number shall have a prefix in accordance with ISO International Standard No 3166—alpha 2—by which the Member State of issue may be identified. [Nevertheless, the Hellenic Republic shall be authorised to use the prefix "EL".][11]

(e) Member States shall take the measures necessary to ensure that their identification systems distinguish the taxable persons referred to in (c) and to ensure the correct application of the transitional arrangements for the taxation of intra-Community transactions as laid down in this Title.

2

(a) Every taxable person shall keep accounts in sufficient detail for value added tax to be applied and inspected by the tax authority.

[(b) Every taxable person shall keep a register of the goods he has dispatched or transported or which have been dispatched or transported on his behalf out of the territory defined in Article 3 but within the Community for the purposes of the transactions referred to in the fifth, sixth and seventh indents of Article 28a(5)(b).

Every taxable person shall keep sufficiently detailed accounts to permit the identification of goods dispatched to him from another Member State by or on behalf of a taxable person identified for purposes of value added tax in that other Member State, in connection with which a service has been provided pursuant to the third or fourth indent of Article 9(2)(c);][9]

[3.

(*a*) *Every taxable person shall ensure that an invoice is issued, either by himself or by his customer or, in his name and on his behalf, by a third party, in respect of goods or services which he has supplied or rendered to another taxable person or to a non-taxable legal person. Every taxable person shall also ensure that an invoice is issued, either by himself or by his customer or, in his name and on his behalf, by a third party, in respect of the supplies of goods referred to in Article 28b(B)(1) and in respect of goods supplied under the conditions laid down in Article 28c(A).*

Every taxable person shall likewise ensure that an invoice is issued, either by himself or by his customer or, in his name and on his behalf, by a third party, in respect of any payment on account made to him before any supplies of goods referred to in the first subparagraph and in respect of any payment on account made to him by another taxable person or non-taxable legal person before the provision of services is completed.

Member States may impose on taxable persons an obligation to issue an invoice in respect of goods or services other than those referred to in the preceding subparagraphs which they have supplied or rendered on their territory. When they do so, Member States may impose fewer obligations in respect of these invoices than those listed under points (b), (c) and (d).

The Member States may release taxable persons from the obligation to issue an invoice in respect of goods or services which they have supplied or rendered in their territory and which are exempt, with or without refund of the tax paid at the preceding stage, pursuant to Article 13, Article 28(2)(a) and Article 28(3)(b).

Any document or message that amends and refers specifically and unambiguously to the initial invoice is to be treated as an invoice. Member States in whose territory goods or services are supplied or rendered may allow some of the obligatory details to be left out of such documents or messages.

Member States may impose time limits for the issue of invoices on taxable persons supplying goods and services in their territory.

Under conditions to be laid down by the Member States in whose territory goods or services are supplied or rendered, a summary invoice may be drawn up for several separate supplies of goods or services.

Invoices may be drawn up by the customer of a taxable person in respect of goods or services supplied or rendered to him by that taxable person, on condition that there is at the outset an agreement between the two parties, and on condition that a procedure exists for the acceptance of each invoice by the taxable person supplying the goods or services. The Member States in whose territory the goods or services are supplied or rendered shall determine the terms and conditions of the agreement and of the acceptance procedures between the taxable person and his customer.

Member States may impose further conditions on the issue of invoices by the customers of taxable persons supplying goods or services on their territory. For example, they may require that such invoices be issued in the name and on behalf of the taxable person. Such conditions must always be the same wherever the customer is established.

Member States may also lay down specific conditions for taxable persons supplying goods or services in their territory in cases where the third party, or the customer, who issues invoices is established in a country with which no legal instrument exists relating to mutual assistance similar in scope to that laid down by Council Directive 76/308/EEC of 15 March 1976 on mutual assistance for the recovery of claims relating to certain levies, duties, taxes and other measures(6), Council Directive 77/799/EEC of 19 December 1977 concerning mutual assistance by the competent authorities of the Member States in the field of direct and indirect taxation(7) and by Council Regulation (EEC) No 218/92 of 27 January 1992 on administrative cooperation in the field of indirect taxation (VAT)(8).

(*b*) *Without prejudice to the specific arrangements laid down by this Directive, only the following details are required for VAT purposes on invoices issued under the first, second and third subparagraphs of point (a):*

—the date of issue;
—a sequential number, based on one or more series, which uniquely identifies the invoice,
—the VAT identification number referred to in paragraph 1(c) under which the taxable person supplied the goods or services;
—where the customer is liable to pay tax on goods supplied or services rendered or has been supplied with goods as referred to in Article 28c(A), the VAT identification number as referred to in paragraph 1(c) under which the goods were supplied or the services rendered to him;
—the full name and address of the taxable person and of his customer;
—the quantity and nature of the goods supplied or the extent and nature of the services rendered;

—the date on which the supply of goods or of services was made or completed or the date on which the payment on account referred to in the second subparagraph of point (a) was made, insofar as that a date can be determined and differs from the date of issue of the invoice;
—the taxable amount per rate or exemption, the unit price exclusive of tax and any discounts or rebates if they are not included in the unit price;
—the VAT rate applied;
—the VAT amount payable, except where a specific arrangement is applied for which this Directive excludes such a detail;
—where an exemption is involved or where the customer is liable to pay the tax, reference to the appropriate provision of this directive, to the corresponding national provision, or to any indication that the supply is exempt or subject to the reverse charge procedure;
—where the intra-Community supply of a new means of transport is involved, the particulars specified in Article 28a(2);
—where the margin scheme is applied, reference to Article 26 or 26a, to the corresponding national provisions, or to any other indication that the margin scheme has been applied;
—where the person liable to pay the tax is a tax representative within the meaning of Article 21(2), the VAT identification number referred to in paragraph 1(c) of that tax representative, together with his full name and address.

Member States may require taxable persons established on their territory and supplying goods or services on their territory to indicate the VAT identification number referred to in paragraph 1(c) of their customer in cases other than those referred to in the fourth indent of the first subparagraph.

Member States shall not require invoices to be signed.

The amounts which appear on the invoice may be expressed in any currency, provided that the amount of tax to be paid is expressed in the national currency of the Member State where the supply of goods or services takes place, using the conversion mechanism laid down in Article 11 C(2).

Where necessary for control purposes, Member States may require invoices in respect of goods supplied or services rendered in their territory and invoices received by taxable persons in their territory to be translated into their national languages.

(c) Invoices issued pursuant to point (a) may be sent either on paper or, subject to an acceptance by the customer, by electronic means.

Invoices sent by electronic means shall be accepted by Member States provided that the authenticity of the origin and integrity of the contents are guaranteed:
—by means of an advanced electronic signature within the meaning of Article 2(2) of Directive 1999/93/EC of the European Parliament and of the Council of 13 December 1999 on a Community framework for electronic signatures(9); Member States may however ask for the advanced electronic signature to be based on a qualified certificate and created by a secure-signature-creation device, within the meaning of Article 2(6) and (10) of the aforementioned Directive;
—or by means of electronic data interchange (EDI) as defined in Article 2 of Commission Recommendation 1994/820/EC of 19 October 1994 relating to the legal aspects of electronic data interchange(10) when the agreement relating to the exchange provides for the use of procedures guaranteeing the authenticity of the origin and integrity of the data; however Member States may, subject to conditions which they lay down, require that an additional summary document on paper is necessary.

Invoices may, however, be sent by other electronic means subject to acceptance by the Member State(s) concerned. The Commission will present, at the latest on 31 December 2008, a report, together with a proposal, if appropriate, amending the conditions on electronic invoicing in order to take account of possible future technological developments in this field.

Member States may not impose on taxable persons supplying goods or services in their territory any other obligations or formalities relating to the transmission of invoices by electronic means. However, they may provide, until 31 December 2005, that the use of such a system is to be subject to prior notification.

Member States may lay down specific conditions for invoices issued by electronic means for goods or services supplied in their territory from a country with which no legal instrument exists relating to mutual assistance similar in scope to that laid down by Directives 76/308/EEC and 77/799/EEC and by Regulation (EEC) No 218/92.

When batches containing several invoices are sent to the same recipient by electronic means, the details that are common to the individual invoices may be mentioned only once if, for each invoice, all the information is accessible.

(d) Every taxable person shall ensure that copies of invoices issued by himself, by his customer or, in his name and on his behalf, by a third party, and all the invoices which he has received are stored.

For the purposes of this Directive, the taxable person may decide the place of storage provided that he makes the invoices or information stored there available without undue delay to the competent authorities whenever they so request. Member States may, however, require taxable persons established in their territory to notify them of the place of storage, if it is outside their territory. Member States may, in addition, require taxable persons established in their territory to store within the country invoices issued by themselves or by their customers or, in their name and on their behalf, by a third party, as well as all the invoices which they have received, when the storage is not by electronic means guaranteeing full on-line access to the data concerned.

The authenticity of the origin and integrity of the content of the invoices, as well as their readability, must be guaranteed throughout the storage period. As regards the invoices referred to in the third subparagraph of point (c), the information they contain may not be altered; it must remain legible throughout the aforementioned period.

The Member States shall determine the period for which taxable persons must store invoices relating to goods or services supplied in their territory and invoices received by taxable persons established in their territory.

In order to ensure that the conditions laid down in the third subparagraph are met, Member States referred to in the fourth subparagraph may require that invoices be stored in the original form in which they were sent, whether paper or electronic. They may also require that when invoices are stored by electronic means, the data guaranteeing the authenticity of the origin and integrity of the content also be stored.

Member States referred to in the fourth subparagraph may impose specific conditions prohibiting or restricting the storage of invoices in a country with which no legal instrument exists relating to mutual assistance similar in scope to that laid down by Directives 76/308/EEC, 77/799/EEC and by Regulation (EEC) No 218/92 and to the right of access by electronic means, download and use referred to in Article 22a.

Member States may, subject to conditions which they lay down, require the storage of invoices received by non-taxable persons.

(e) For the purposes of points (c) and (d), transmission and storage of invoices 'by electronic means' shall mean transmission or making available to the recipient and storage using electronic equipment for processing (including digital compression) and storage of data, and employing wires, radio transmission, optical technologies or other electromagnetic means.

For the purposes of this Directive, Member States shall accept documents or messages in paper or electronic form as invoices if they meet the conditions laid down in this paragraph.][11]

4

[(a) Every taxable person shall submit a return by a deadline to be determined by Member States. That deadline may not be more than two months later than the end of each tax period. The tax period shall be fixed by each Member State at one month, two months or a quarter. Member States may, however, set different periods provided that they do not exceed one year. Member States shall, subject to conditions which they lay down, allow the taxable person to make such returns by electronic means, and may also require that electronic means are used.][10]

(b) The return shall set out all the information needed to calculate the tax that has become chargeable and the deductions to be made including, where appropriate, and in so far as it seems necessary for the establishment of the basis of assessment, the total value of the transactions relative to such tax and deductions and the value of any exempt transactions.

(c) The return shall also set out:

—on the one hand, the total value, less value added tax, of the supplies of goods referred to in Article 28c(A) on which tax has become chargeable during the period.

The following shall also be added: the total value, less value added tax, of the supplies of goods referred to in the second sentence of Article 8(1)(a) and in Article 28b(B)(1) effected within the territory of another Member State for which tax has become chargeable during the return period where the place of departure of the dispatch or transport of the goods is situated in the territory of the country,

[—on the other hand, the total amount, less value-added tax of the intra-Community acquisitions of goods referred to in Article 28a(1) and (6) effected within the territory of the country on which tax has become chargeable.

The following shall also be added: the total value, less value-added tax, of the supplies of goods referred to in the second sentence of Article 8(1)(a) and in Article 28(b)(B)(1) effected in the territory of the country on which tax has become chargeable during the return period, where the place of departure of the dispatch or transport of the goods is situated within the territory of another Member State, and the total amount, less value-added tax, of the supplies of goods made within the territory of the country for which the taxable person has been designated as the person liable for the tax in accordance with Article 28c(E)(3) and under which the tax has become payable in the course of the period covered by the declaration.][3]

5. Every taxable person shall pay the net amount of the value added tax when submitting the regular return. Member States may, however, set a different date for the payment of that amount or may demand an interim payment.

6

[(a) Member States may require a taxable person to submit a statement, including all the particulars specified in paragraph 4, concerning all transactions carried out in the preceding year. That statement shall provide all the information necessary for any adjustments. Member States

shall, subject to conditions which they lay down, allow the taxable person to make such statements by electronic means, and may also require that electronic means are used.][10]

[(b) [Every taxable person identified for value added tax purposes shall also submit a recapitulative statement of the acquirers identified for value added tax purposes to whom he has supplied goods under the conditions provided for in Article 28c(A)(a) and (d), and of consignees identified for value added tax purposes in the transactions referred to in the fifth subparagraph.][9] *]*[4]

[The recapitulative statement shall be drawn up for each calendar quarter within a period and in accordance with procedures to be determined by the Member States, which shall take the measures necessary to ensure that the provisions concerning administrative cooperation in the field of indirect taxation are in any event complied with. Member States shall, subject to conditions which they lay down, allow the taxable person to make such statements by electronic means, and may also require that electronic means are used.][10]

The recapitulative statement shall set out:

—the number by which the taxable person is identified for purposes of value added tax in the territory of the country and under which he effected supplies of goods in the conditions laid down in [Article 28c(A)(a)][5]*,*

[—the number by which each person acquiring goods is identified for purposes of value added tax in another Member State and under which the goods were supplied to him,][9]

—for each person acquiring goods, the total value of the supplies of goods effected by the taxable person. Those amounts shall be declared for the calendar quarter during which the tax became chargeable.

The recapitulative statement shall also set out:

—for the supplies of goods covered by [Article 28c(A)(d)][6]*, the number by means of which the taxable person is identified for purposes of value added tax in the territory of the country, the number by which he is identified in the Member State of arrival of the dispatch or transport [and the total amount of the supplies, determined in accordance with Article 28e(2)]*[7]*,*

—the amounts of adjustments made pursuant to Article 11(C)(1). Those amounts shall be declared for the calendar quarter during which the person acquiring the goods is notified of the adjustment.

...[9]

[In the cases set out in the third subparagraph of Article 28b (A) (2), the taxable person identified for value added tax purposes within the territory of the country shall mention in a clear way on the recapitulative statement:

—the number by which he is identified for value added tax purposes within the territory of the country and under which he carried out the intra-Community acquisition and the subsequent supply of goods,

—the number by which, within the territory of the Member State of arrival of the dispatch or transport of the goods, the consignee of the subsequent supply by the taxable person is identified,

—and, for each consignee, the total amount, less value added tax, of the supplies made by the taxable person within the territory of the Member State of arrival of the dispatch or transport of the goods. These amounts shall be declared for the calendar quarter during which the tax became chargeable][7]

(c) By way of derogation from (b), Member States may:

—require recapitulative statements to be filed on a monthly basis,

—require that recapitulative statements give additional particulars.

(d) In the case of supplies of new means of transport effected under the conditions laid down in Article 28c(A)(b) by a taxable person identified for purposes of value added tax to a purchaser not identified for purposes of value added tax or by a taxable person as defined in Article 28a(4), Member States shall take the measures necessary to ensure that the vendor communicates all the information necessary for value added tax to be applied and inspected by the tax authority.

(e) Member States may require taxable persons who in the territory of the country effect intra-Community acquisitions of goods as defined in Article 28a(1)(a) and (6) to submit statements giving details of such acquisitions provided, however, that such statements may not be required for a period of less than one month.

Member States may also require persons who effect intra-Community acquisitions of new means of transport as defined in Article 28a(1)(b) to provide, when submitting the return referred to in paragraph 4, all the information necessary for value added tax to be applied and inspected by the tax authority.

7. Member States shall take the measures necessary to ensure that those persons who, in accordance with Article 21(1) and (2), are considered to be liable to pay the tax instead of a taxable person not established within the territory of the country comply with the obligations relating to declaration and payment set out in this Article; they shall also take the measures necessary to ensure that those persons who, in accordance with Article 21(3), are held to be jointly and severally liable for payment of the tax comply with the obligations relating to payment set out in this Article.][10]

8. Member States may impose other obligations which they deem necessary for the correct collection of the tax and for the prevention of evasion, subject to the requirement of equal treatment for domestic transactions and transactions carried out between Member States by taxable persons and provided that such obligations do not, in trade between Member States, give rise to formalities connected with the crossing of frontiers.

[The option provided for in the first subparagraph cannot be used to impose additional obligations over and above those laid down in paragraph 3.][11]

9

(*a*) *Member States may release from certain or all obligations:*

—taxable persons carrying out only supplies of goods or of services which are exempt pursuant to Articles 13 and 15,
—taxable persons eligible for the exemption from tax provided for in Article 24 and for the derogation provided for in Article 28a(1)(a), second subparagraph,
—taxable persons carrying out none of the transactions referred to in paragraph 4(c).

[Without prejudice to the provisions laid down in point (d), Member States may not, however, release the taxable persons referred to in the third indent from the obligations referred to in Article 22(3).][11]

(*b*) *Member States may release taxable persons other than those referred to in (a) from certain of the obligations referred to in 2(a).*

(*c*) *Member States may release taxable persons from payment of the tax due where the amount involved is insignificant.*

[(d) Subject to consultation of the Committee provided for in Article 29 and under the conditions which they may lay down, Member States may provide that invoices in respect of goods supplied or services rendered in their territory do not have to fulfil some of the conditions laid down in paragraph 3(b) in the following cases:

—when the amount of the invoice is minor, or
—when commercial or administrative practice in the business sector concerned or the technical conditions under which the invoices are issued make it difficult to comply with all the requirements referred to in paragraph 3(b).

In any case, these invoices must contain the following:

—the date of issue,
—identification of the taxable person,
—identification of the type of goods supplied or services rendered,
—the tax due or the information needed to calculate it.

The simplified arrangements provided for in this point may not be applied to transactions referred to in paragraph 4(c).][11]

[(e) In cases where Member States make use of the option provided for in the third indent of point (a) to refrain from allocating a number as referred to in paragraph 1(c) to taxable persons who do not carry out any of the transactions referred to in paragraph 4(c), and where the supplier or the customer have not been allocated an identification number of this type, the invoice should feature instead another number called the tax reference number, as defined by the Member States concerned.

When the taxable person has been allocated an identification number as referred to in paragraph 1(c), the Member States referred to in the first subparagraph may also require the invoice to show:

—for services rendered referred to in Article 28b(C), (D), (E) and (F) and for supplies of goods referred to in Article 28c(A) and (E) point 3, the number referred to in paragraph 1(c) and the tax reference number of the supplier;
—for other supplies of goods and services, only the tax reference number of the supplier or only the number referred to in paragraph 1(c).][11]

10. Member States shall take measures to ensure that non-taxable legal persons who are liable for the tax payable in respect of intra-Community acquisitions of goods covered by the first subparagraph of Article 28a(1)(a) comply with the above obligations relating to declaration and payment and that they are identified by an individual number as defined in paragraph 1(c), (d) and (e).

11. [In the case of intra-Community acquisitions of products subject to excise duty referred to in Article 28a(1)(c) as well as][8] *in the case of intra-Community acquisitions of new means of transport covered by Article 28a(1)(b), Member States shall adopt arrangements for declaration and subsequent payment.*

12. Acting unanimously on a proposal from the Commission, the Council may authorise any Member State to introduce particular measures to simplify the statement obligations laid down in paragraph 6(b). Such simplification measures, which shall not jeopardise the proper monitoring of intra-Community transactions, may take the following forms:

(*a*) *Member States may authorise taxable persons who meet the following three conditions to file one-year recapitulative statements indicating the numbers by which the persons to whom those taxable persons have supplied goods under the conditions laid down in Article 28c(A) are identified for purposes of value added tax in other Member States:*

—the total annual value, less value added tax, of their supplies of goods or provisions of services, as defined in Articles 5, 6 and 28a(5), does not exceed by more than ECU 35,000 the amount of the annual turnover which is used as a reference for application of the exemption from tax provided for in Article 24,

—the total annual value, less value added tax, of supplies of goods effected by them under the conditions laid down in Article 28c(A) does not exceed the equivalent in national currency of ECU 15,000,

—supplies of goods effected by them under the conditions laid down in Article 28c(A) are other than supplies of new means of transport;

(b) Member States which set at over three months the tax period for which taxable persons must submit the returns provided for in paragraph 4 may authorise such persons to submit recapitulative statements for the same period where those taxable persons meet the following three conditions—

—the overall annual value, less value added tax, of the goods and the services they supply, as defined in Articles 5, 6 and 28a(5), does not exceed the equivalent in national currency of ECU 200,000,

—the total annual value, less value added tax, of supplies of goods effected by them under the conditions laid down in Article 28c(A) does not exceed the equivalent in national currency of ECU 15,000,

—supplies of goods effected by them under the conditions laid down in Article 28c(A) are other than supplies of new means of transport.][1]

Commentary—*De Voil Indirect Tax Service* **V1.285, V2.101, V3.401, V3.415, V5.186.**

Note—The amendment made by note 14 below was expressed in Council Directive 2003/92 to be made to the version of this article "set out in article 28h". On a strict reading, this would imply that the amendment be made to the version set out in note 1 below. However, this does not work, and the amendment has been made to the current text of art 21.

Simon's Tax Cases—art 22, *Bjellica (T/A Eddy's Domestic Appliances) v C&E Comrs* [1995] STC 329; *C&E Comrs and another v Federation of Technological Industries and others* [2006] STC 1483.

Art 22(3), *Reisdorf v Finanzamt Köln-West* (Case C-85/95) [1997] STC 180; *Finanzamt Bergisch Gladbach v HE* [2007] STC 128.

Art 22(3)(*c*), *Finanzamt Osnabrück-Land v Langhorst* (Case C-141/96) [1997] STC 1357; *EMI Group Electronics Ltd v Coldicott* [1997] STC 1372.

Art 22(4), (5), *Balocchi v Ministero delle Finanze* [1997] STC 640.

Art 22(8), *EC Commission v Kingdom of Spain* (Case C-96/91) [1996] STC 672; *Eismann Alto Adige Srl v Ufficio IVA di Bolzano* (Case C-217/94) [1996] STC 1374.

Cross references—See Council Directive 92/111, art 4, para 1; OJ L384, 30.12.92 (member States may provide that information relating to certain transactions referred to in para 6(*b*) of art 22 for which tax becomes payable during January–March 1993 must appear on summary statement for the quarter April–June 1993),

Council Directive 92/111 art 4 para 2 (extension of time limit to 31 December 1993 for adoption of laws, etc under certain provisions of this article);

EEC Council Decision 92/621; OJ L408, 31.12.92 (as provided by para 12 above, the UK is authorised to introduce a particular measure in accordance with para 12(*b*) above to simplify the obligations laid down in para 6(*b*) above regarding recapitulative statements).

Council Decision EC 93/609, *post* (derogation from para 6(*b*) above granted to the UK);

VAT Regulations, SI 1995/2518 regs 5, 6, 13, 14, 16, 20, 36, 148 (implementation of this article);

VAT Regulations, SI 1995/2518 regs 24, 31–34, 37–39 (regulations requiring compliance with para 2 above);

SI 1995/2518 regs 21–23 (regulations requiring compliance with para 6 above).

Amendments—[1] Article 22 substituted by Council Directive 91/680/EEC of 16 December 1991 which inserted art 28h below with effect from 1 January 1993 for the transitional period specified in art 28l.

[2] Words in para 1(*c*) inserted by EEC Council Directive 92/111, art 1(20); OJ L384, 30.12.92.

[3] Words in para 4(*c*) replaced by EEC Council Directive 92/111, art 1(20); OJ L384, 30.12.92.

[4] Para 6(*b*) replaced by EEC Council Directive 92/111, art 1(20); OJ L384, 30.12.92.

[5] Words in para 6(*b*) replaced by EEC Council Directive 92/111, art 1(20); OJ L384, 30.12.92.

[6] Words in para 6(*b*) replaced by EEC Council Directive 92/111, art 1(20); OJ L384, 30.12.92.

[7] Words in para 6(*b*) replaced and words inserted by EEC Council Directive 92/111, art 1(20); OJ L384, 30.12.92.

[8] Words in para 11 inserted by EEC Council Directive 92/111, art 1(20); OJ L384, 30.12.92.

[9] Para (2)(*b*), first indent of second sub-para in para 3(*b*), first sub-para of para 6(*b*) and second indent in third sub-para of para 6(*b*) replaced and the fifth sub-para of para 6(*b*) repealed by EC Council Directive 95/7, art 1(12): OJ L102, 15.5.95, p 18 with effect from 25 May 1995.

[10] Paras 1(*a*), 4(*a*), 6(*a*) and words in para 6(*b*) substituted by Council Directive 2002/38/EC art 2 with effect from 15 May 2002: see OJ L 128; 15.5.02.

[11] Words inserted in para 1(*d*), para 3 substituted, words inserted in paras 8, 9(*a*), and paras 9(*d*), (*e*) inserted, by Council Directive 2001/115/EEC art 2; see OJ L 015, 17.01.02.

[12] In para (1), the first indent in point (*c*) substituted by Council Directive 2003/92 art 1(6); see OJ L 260; 11.10.2003 p 8.

[Article 22a

Right of access to invoices stored by electronic means in another Member State

When a taxable person stores invoices which he issues or receives by an electronic means guaranteeing on-line access to the data and when the place of storage is in a Member State other than that in which he is established, the competent authorities in the Member State in which he is established shall have a right, for the purpose of this directive, to access by electronic means, download and use these invoices within the limits set by the regulations of the Member State where the taxable person is established and as far as that State requires for control purposes.][1]

Amendments—[1] This article inserted by Council Directive 2001/115/EEC art 3; see OJ L 015, 17.01.02.

Article 23

Obligations in respect of imports

As regards imported goods, Member States shall lay down the detailed rules for the making of the declarations and payments.

In particular, Member States may provide that the value added tax payable on importation of goods by taxable persons or persons liable to tax or certain categories of these two need not be paid at the time of importation, on condition that the tax is mentioned as such in a return to be submitted under Article 22(4).

TITLE XIV: SPECIAL SCHEMES

Article 24

Special scheme for small undertakings

1. Member States which might encounter difficulties in applying the normal tax scheme to small undertakings by reason of their activities or structure shall have the option, under such conditions and within such limits as they may set but subject to the consultation provided for in Article 29, of applying simplified procedures such as flat-rate schemes for charging and collecting the tax provided they do not lead to a reduction thereof.

2. Until a date to be fixed by the Council acting unanimously on a proposal from the Commission, but which shall not be later than that on which the charging of tax on imports and the remission of tax on exports in trade between the Member States are abolished:

(a) Member States which have made use of the option under Article 14 of the second Council Directive of 11 April 1967 to introduce exemptions or graduated tax relief may retain them and the arrangements for applying them if they conform with the value added tax system.

Those Member States which apply an exemption from tax to taxable persons whose annual turnover is less than the equivalent in national currency of 5,000 European units of account at the conversion rate of the day on which this Directive is adopted, may increase this exemption up to 5,000 European units of account.

Member States which apply graduated tax relief may neither increase the ceiling of the graduated tax reliefs nor render the conditions for the granting of it more favourable;

(b) Member States which have not made use of this option may grant an exemption from the tax to taxable persons whose annual turnover is at the maximum equal to the equivalent in national currency of 5,000 European units of account at the conversion rate of the day on which this Directive is adopted; where appropriate, they may grant graduated tax relief to taxable persons whose annual turnover exceeds the ceiling fixed by the Member States for the application of exemption;

(c) Member States which apply an exemption from tax to taxable persons whose annual turnover is equal to or higher than the equivalent in national currency of 5,000 European units of account at the conversion rate of the day on which this Directive is adopted, may increase it in order to maintain its value in real terms.

3. The concepts of exemption and graduated tax relief shall apply to the supply of goods and services by small undertakings.

Member States may exclude certain transactions from the arrangements provided for in paragraph 2. The provisions of paragraph 2 shall not, in any case, apply to the transactions referred to in Article 4(3).

[In all circumstances supplies of new means of transport effected under the conditions laid down in Article 28c(A) as well as supplies of goods and services effected by a taxable person who is not established in the territory of the country shall be excluded from the exemption from tax under paragraph 2.][1]

4. The turnover which shall serve as a reference for the purposes of applying the provisions of paragraph 2 shall consist of the amount, exclusive of value added tax, of goods and services supplied as defined in Articles 5 and 6, to the extent that they are taxed, including transactions exempted with refund of tax previously paid in accordance with Article 28(2), and the amount of the transactions exempted pursuant to Article 15, the amount of real property transactions, the financial transactions referred to in Article 13B(d), and insurance services, unless these transactions are ancillary transactions.

However, disposals of tangible or intangible capital assets of an undertaking shall not be taken into account for the purposes of calculating turnover.

5. Taxable persons exempt from tax shall not be entitled to deduct tax in accordance with the provisions of Article 17, nor to show the tax on their invoices …[2]*.*

6. Taxable persons eligible for exemption from tax may opt either for the normal value added tax scheme or for the simplified procedures referred to in paragraph 1. In this case they shall be entitled to any graduated tax relief which may be laid down by national legislation.

7. Subject to the application of paragraph 1, taxable persons enjoying graduated relief shall be treated as taxable persons subject to the normal value added tax scheme.

8. At four-yearly intervals, and for the first time on 1 January 1982, and after consultation of the Member States, the Commission shall report to the Council on the application of the provisions of this Article. It shall as far as may be necessary, and taking into account the needs to ensure the long-term convergence of national regulations, attach to this report proposals for:

(a) improvements to be made to the special scheme for small undertakings;

(b) the adaptation of national systems as regards exemptions and graduated value added tax relief;

(c) the adaptation of the limit of 5,000 European units of account mentioned in paragraph 2.

9. The Council will decide at the appropriate time whether the realisation of the objective referred to in Article 4 of the First Council Directive of 11 April 1967 requires the introduction of a special scheme for small undertakings and will, if appropriate, decide on the limits and common implementing conditions of this scheme. Until the introduction of such a scheme, Member States may retain their own special schemes which they will apply in accordance with the provisions of this Article and of subsequent acts of the Council.

Simon's Tax Cases—*Direct Cosmetics Ltd and Laughtons Photographs Ltd v C&E Comrs* [1988] STC 540; *C&E Comrs v Eastwood Care Homes (Ilkeston) Ltd and others* [2001] STC 1629.

Amendments—[1] Words in para 3 (which were inserted by Council Directive 91/680/EEC of 16 December 1991 which inserted art 28i below from 1 January 1993 for the transitional period specified in art 28l) replaced by Council Directive 92/111/EEC art 1(20); OJ L384, 30.12.92.

[2] Words in para 5 revoked by Council Directive 2001/115/EC art 4(2); see OJ L 015; 17.01.02.

[Article 24a

In implementing Article 24(2) to (6), the following Member States may grant an exemption from value added tax to taxable persons whose annual turnover is less than the equivalent in national currency at the conversion rate on the date of their accession:

—in the Czech Republic: EUR 35 000;
—in Estonia: EUR 16 000;
—in Cyprus: EUR 15 600;
—in Latvia: EUR 17 200;
—in Lithuania: EUR 29 000;
—in Hungary: EUR 35 000;
—in Malta: EUR 37 000 when the economic activity consists principally in the supply of goods, EUR 24 300 when the economic activity consists principally in the supply of services with a low value added (high inputs), and EUR 14 600 in other cases, namely service providers with a high value added (low inputs);
—in Poland: EUR 10 000;
—in Slovenia: EUR 25 000;
—in Slovakia: EUR 35 000.][1]

Amendments—[1] Article 24 bis, which was inserted by the 2003 Act of Accession Annex II Chapter 9 para 3(*a*), is replaced by Article 24a, by virtue of Council Directive 2004/66 art 1, Annex Part V para 1(*a*) (OJ L 168; 1.5.2004 p 35).

Article 25

Common flat-rate scheme for farmers

1. Where the application to farmers of the normal value added tax scheme, or the simplified scheme provided for in Article 24, would give rise to difficulties, Member States may apply to farmers a flat-rate scheme tending to offset the value added tax charged on purchases of goods and services made by the flat-rate farmers pursuant to this Article.

2. For the purposes of this Article, the following definitions shall apply:

"farmer": taxable person who carries on his activity in one of the undertakings defined below,

"agricultural, forestry or fisheries undertakings": an undertaking considered to be such by each Member State within the framework of the production activities listed in Annex A,

"flat-rate farmer": a farmer subject to the flat-rate scheme provided for in paragraphs 3 et seq,

"agricultural products": goods produced by an agricultural, forestry or fisheries undertaking in each Member State as a result of the activities listed in Annex A,

"agricultural service": any service as set out in Annex B supplied by a farmer using his labour force and/or by means of the equipment normally available on the agricultural, forestry or fisheries undertaking operated by him,

"value added tax charge on inputs": the amount of the total value added tax attaching to the goods and services purchased by all agricultural, forestry and fisheries undertakings of each Member State subject to the flat-rate scheme where such tax would be deductible under Article 17 by a farmer subject to the normal value added tax scheme,

"flat-rate compensation percentages": the percentages fixed by Member States in accordance with paragraph 3 and applied by them in the cases specified in paragraph 5 to enable flat-rate farmers to offset at a fixed rate the value added tax charge on inputs,

"flat-rate compensation": the amount arrived at by applying the flat-rate compensation percentage provided for in paragraph 3 to the turnover of the flat-rate farmer in the cases referred to in paragraph 5.

3. Member States shall fix the flat-rate compensation percentages, where necessary, and shall notify the Commission before applying them. Such percentages shall be based on macro-economic statistics for flat-rate farmers alone for the preceding three years. They may not be used to obtain for flat-rate farmers refunds greater than the value added tax charges on imports. Member States shall have the option of reducing such percentages to a nil rate. The percentage may be rounded up or down to the nearest half point.

Member States may fix varying flat-rate compensation percentages for forestry, for the different sub-divisions of agriculture and for fisheries.

4. Member States may release flat-rate farmers from the obligations imposed upon taxable persons by Article 22.

[When they exercise this option, Member States shall take the measures necessary to ensure the correct application of the transitional arrangements for the taxation of intra-Community transactions as laid down in Title XVIa.][1]

[5. The flat-rate percentages provided for in paragraph 3 shall be applied to the prices, exclusive of tax, of:

(a) agricultural products supplied by flat-rate farmers to taxable persons other than those eligible within the territory of the country for the flat-rate scheme provided for in this Article;
(b) agricultural products supplied by flat-rate farmers, under the conditions laid down in Article 28c(A), to non-taxable legal persons not eligible, in the Member State of arrival of the dispatch or transport of the agricultural products thus supplied, for the derogation provided for in Article 28a(1)(a), second sub-paragraph;
(c) agricultural services supplied by flat-rate farmers to taxable persons other than those eligible within the territory of the country for the flat-rate scheme provided for in this Article.

This compensation shall exclude any other form of deduction.][1]

[6. In the case of the supplies of agricultural products and of agricultural services referred to in paragraph 5, Member States shall provide for the flat-rate compensation to be paid either:

(a) by the purchaser or customer. In that event, the taxable purchaser or customer shall be authorised, as provided for in Article 17 and in accordance with the procedures laid down by the Member States, to deduct from the tax for which he is liable within the territory of the country the amount of the flat-rate compensation he has paid to flat-rate farmers.

Member States shall refund to the purchaser or customer the amount of the flat-rate compensation he has paid to flat-rate farmers in respect of any of the following transactions:

—supplies of agricultural products effected under the conditions laid down in Article 28c(A) to taxable persons, or to non-taxable legal persons acting as such in another Member State within which they are not eligible for the derogation provided for in the second subparagraph of Article 28a(1)(a),
—supplies of agricultural products effected under the conditions laid down in Article 15 and in Article 16(1)(B), (D) and (E) to taxable purchasers established outside the Community, provided that the products are used by those purchasers for the purposes of the transactions referred to in Article 17(3)(a) and (b) or for the purposes of services which are deemed to be supplied within the territory of the country and on which tax is payable solely by the customers under Article 21(1)(b),
—supplies of agricultural services to taxable customers established within the Community but in other Member States or to taxable customers established outside the Community, provided that the services are used by those customers for the purposes of the transactions referred to in Article 17(3)(a) and (b) and for the purposes of services which are deemed to be supplied within the territory of the country and on which tax is payable solely by the customers under Article 21(1)(b).

Member States shall determine the method by which the refunds are to be made; in particular, they may apply Article 17(4); or

(b) by the public authorities.][1]

7. Member States shall make all necessary provisions to check properly the payment of the flat-rate compensation to the flat-rate farmers.

8. As regards all supplies of agricultural products and agricultural services other than those covered by paragraph 5, the flat-rate compensation is deemed to be paid by the purchaser or customer.

9. Each Member State may exclude from the flat-rate scheme certain categories of farmers and farmers for whom the application of the normal value added tax scheme, or the simplified scheme provided for in Article 24(1), would not give rise to administrative difficulties.

[Whenever they exercise the option provided for in this Article, Member States shall take all measures necessary to ensure that the same method of taxation is applied to supplies of agricultural products effected under the conditions laid down in Article 28b(B)(1), whether the supply is effected by a flat-rate farmer or by a taxable person other than a flat-rate farmer.][1]

10. Every flat-rate farmer may opt, subject to the rule and conditions to be laid down by each Member State, for application of the normal value added tax scheme or, as the case may be, the simplified scheme provided for in Article 24(1).

11. The Commission shall, before the end of the fifth year following the entry into force of this Directive, present to the Council new proposals concerning the application of the value added tax to transactions in respect of agricultural products and services.

12. …

Note—Para 12 is not relevant to this work.
Simon's Tax Cases—*Finanzamt Rendsburg v Harbs* [2006] STC 340.
Cross references—See VATA 1994 s 54(8) (special treatment for certified farmers as regards registration for VAT purposes).

Amendments—[1] Words in paras 4, 9 added and paras 5 and 6 substituted by Council Directive 91/680/EEC of 16 December 1991 which inserts art 28j; below with effect from 1 January 1993 for the transitional period specified in art 28l.

Article 26

Special scheme for travel agents

1. Member States shall apply value added tax to the operations of travel agents in accordance with the provisions of this Article, where the travel agents deal with customers in their own name and use the supplies and services of other taxable persons in the provision of travel facilities. This Article shall not apply to travel agents who are acting only as intermediaries and accounting for tax in accordance with Article 11 A(3)(c). In this Article travel agents include tour operators.

2. All transactions performed by the travel agent in respect of a journey shall be treated as a single service supplied by the travel agent to the traveller. It shall be taxable in the Member State in which the travel agent has established his business or has a fixed establishment from which the travel agent has provided the services. The taxable amount and the price exclusive of tax, within the meaning of Article 22(3)(b), in respect of this service shall be the travel agent's margin, that is to say, the difference between the total amount to be paid by the traveller, exclusive of value added tax, and the actual cost to the travel agent of supplies and services provided by other taxable persons where these transactions are for the direct benefit of the traveller.

3. If transactions entrusted by the travel agent to other taxable persons are performed by such persons outside the Community, the travel agent's service shall be treated as an exempted intermediary activity under Article 15(14). Where these transactions are performed both inside and outside the Community, only that part of the travel agent's service relating to transactions outside the Community may be exempted.

4. Tax charged to the travel agent by other taxable persons on the transactions described in paragraph 2 which are for the direct benefit of the traveller, shall not be eligible for deduction or refund in any Member State.

Simon's Tax Cases—*C&E Comrs v DFDS A/S* [1997] STC 384; *C&E Comrs v Madgett and Baldwin (T/A Howden Court Hotel) v C&E Comrs* (Joined cases C-308/96 and C-94/97) [1998] STC 1189; *C&E Comrs v First Choice Holidays* [2000] STC 609, [2003] STC 934; *MyTravel plc v C&E Comrs* [2005] STC 1617; *Finanzamt Heidelberg v 1st internationale Sprach- und Studienreisen GmbH* [2006] STC 52.
Cross references—See the VAT (Tour Operators) Order 1987, SI 1987/1806.
Press releases etc—Business Brief 12/98 21.5.98 (Overseas businesses established in the UK through agencies).

[Article 26a

Special arrangements applicable to second-hand goods, works of art, collectors' items and antiques

A Definitions

For the purposes of this Article, and without prejudice to other Community provisions:

(a) works of art shall mean the objects referred to in (a) of Annex I.

However, Member States shall have the option of not considering as 'works of art' the items mentioned in the final three indents in (a) in Annex I;

(b) collectors items shall mean the objects referred to in (b) of Annex I;

(c) antiques shall mean the objects referred to in (c) of Annex I;

(d) second-hand goods shall mean tangible movable property that is suitable for further use as it is or after repair, other than works of art, collectors' items or antiques and other than precious metals or precious stones as defined by the Member States;

(e) taxable dealer shall mean a taxable person who, in the course of his economic activity, purchases or acquires for the purposes of his undertaking, or imports with a view to resale, second-hand goods and/or works of art, collectors' items or antiques, whether that taxable person is acting for himself or on behalf of another person pursuant to a contract under which commission is payable on purchase or sale;

(f) organiser of a sale by public auction shall mean any taxable person who, in the course of his economic activity, offers goods for sale by public auction with a view to handing them over to the highest bidder;

(g) principal of an organiser of a sale by public auction shall mean any person who transmits goods to an organiser of a sale by public auction under a contract under which commission is payable on a sale subject to the following provisions:

—the organiser of the sale by public auction offers the goods for sale in his own name but on behalf of his principal,

—the organiser of the sale by public auction hands over the goods, in his own name but on behalf of his principal, to the highest bidder at the public auction.

B Special arrangements for taxable dealers

1. In respect of supplies of second-hand goods, works of act, collectors' items and antiques effected by taxable dealers, Member States shall apply special arrangements for taxing the profit margin made by the taxable dealer, in accordance with the following provisions.

2. The supplies of goods referred to in paragraph 1 shall be supplies, by a taxable dealer, of second-hand goods, works of art, collectors' items or antiques supplied to him within the Community:

—by a non-taxable person, or
—by another taxable person, in so far as the supply of goods by that other taxable person is exempt in accordance with Article 13(B)(c), or
—by another taxable person in so far as the supply of goods by that other taxable person qualifies for the exemption provided for in Article 24 and involves capital assets, or
—by another taxable dealer, in so far as the supply of goods by that other taxable dealer was subject to value added tax in accordance with these special arrangements.

3. The taxable amount of the supplies of goods referred to in paragraph 2 shall be the profit margin made by the taxable dealer, less the amount of value added tax relating to the profit margin. That profit margin shall be equal to the difference between the selling price charged by the taxable dealer for the goods and the purchase price.

For the purposes of this paragraph, the following definitions shall apply:
—selling price shall mean everything which constitutes the consideration, which has been, or is to be, obtained by the taxable dealer from the purchaser or a third party, including subsidies directly linked to that transaction, taxes, duties, levies and charges and incidental expenses such as commission, packaging, transport and insurance costs charged by the taxable dealer to the purchaser but excluding the amounts referred to in Article 11(A)(3),
—purchase price shall mean everything which constitutes the consideration defined in the first indent, obtained, or to be obtained, from the taxable dealer by his supplier.

4. Member States shall entitle taxable dealers to opt for application of the special arrangements to supplies of:
(a) works of art, collectors' items or antiques which they have imported themselves;
(b) works of art supplied to them by their creators or their successors in title;
(c) works of art supplied to them by a taxable person other than a taxable dealer where the supply by that other taxable person was subject to the reduced rate pursuant to Article 12(3)(c).

Member States shall determine the detailed rules for exercising this option which shall in any event cover a period at least equal to two calendar years.

If the option is taken up, the taxable amount shall be determined in accordance with paragraph 3. For supplies of works of art, collectors' items or antiques which the taxable dealer has imported himself, the purchase price to be taken into account in calculating the margin shall be equal to the taxable amount on importation, determined in accordance with Article 11(B), plus the value added tax due or paid on importation.

5. Where they are effected in the conditions laid down in Article 15, the supplies of second-hand goods, works of art, collectors' items or antiques subject to the special arrangements for taxing the margin shall be exempt.

6. Taxable persons shall not be entitled to deduct from the tax for which they are liable the value added tax due or paid in respect of goods which have been, or are to be, supplied to them by a taxable dealer, in so far as the supply of those goods by the taxable dealer is subject to the special arrangements for taxing the margin.

7. In so far as goods are used for the purpose of supplies by him subject to the special arrangements for taxing the margin, the taxable dealer shall not be entitled to deduct from the tax for which he is liable:
(a) the value added tax due or paid in respect of works of art, collectors' items or antiques which he has imported himself;
(b) the value added tax due or paid in respect of works of which have been, or are to be, supplied to him by their creators or their successors in title;
(c) the value added tax due or paid in respect of works of art which have been, or are to be, supplied to him by a taxable person other than a taxable dealer.

8. Where he is led to apply both the normal arrangements for value added tax and the special arrangements for taxing the margin, the taxable dealer must follow separately in his accounts the transactions falling under each of these arrangements, according to rules laid down by the Member States,

9. The taxable dealer may not indicate separately on the invoices which he issues, ...[2] tax relating to supplies of goods which he makes subject to the special arrangements for taxing the margin.

10. In order to simplify the procedure for charging the tax and subject to the consultation provided for in Article 29, Member States may provide that, for certain transactions or for certain categories of taxable dealers, the taxable amount of supplies of goods subject to the special arrangements for taxing the margin shall be determined for each tax period during which the taxable dealer must submit the return referred to in Article 22(4).

In that event, the taxable amount for supplies of goods to which the same rate of value added tax is applied shall be the total margin made by the taxable dealer less the amount of value added tax relating to that margin.

The total margin shall be equal to the difference between:
—the total amount of supplies of goods subject to the special arrangements for taxing the margin effected by the taxable dealer during the period; that amount shall be equal to the total selling prices determined in accordance with paragraph 3, and

—*the total amount of purchases of goods as referred to in paragraph 2 effected, during that period, by the taxable dealer; that amount shall be equal to the total purchase prices determined in accordance with paragraph 3.*

Member States shall take the necessary measures to ensure that the taxable persons concerned do not enjoy unjustified advantages or sustain unjustified loss.

11. The taxable dealer may apply the normal value added tax arrangements to any supply covered by the special arrangements pursuant to paragraph 2 or 4.

Where the taxable dealer applies the normal value added tax arrangements to:

(a) the supply of a work of art, collectors' item or antique which he has imported himself, he shall be entitled to deduct from his tax liability the value added tax due or paid on the import of those goods;

(b) the supply of a work of art supplied to him by its creator or his successors in title, he shall be entitled to deduct from his tax liability the value added tax due or paid for the work of art supplied to him;

(c) the supply of a work of art supplied to him by a taxable person other than a taxable dealer, he shall be entitled to deduct from his tax liability the value added tax due or paid for the work of art supplied to him.

This right to deduct shall arise at the time when the tax due for the supply in respect of which the taxable dealer opts for application of the normal value added tax arrangements become chargeable.

C Special arrangements for sales by public auction

1. By way of derogation from B, Member States may determine, in accordance with the following provisions, the taxable amount of supplies of second-hand goods, works of art, collectors' items or antiques effected by an organiser of sales by public auction, acting in his own name, pursuant to a contract under which commission is payable on the sale of those goods by public auction, on behalf of:

—*a non-taxable person, or*

—*another taxable person, in so far as the supply of goods, within the meaning of Article 5(4)(c), by that other taxable person is exempt in accordance with Article 13(B)(c), or*

—*another taxable person, in so far as the supply of goods, within the meaning of Article 5(4)(c), by that other taxable person qualifies for the exemption provided for in Article 24 and involves capital assets, or*

—*a taxable dealer, in so far as the supply of goods, within the meaning of Article 5(4)(c), by that other taxable dealer, is subject to tax in accordance with the special arrangements for taxing the margin provided for in B.*

2. The taxable amount of each supply of goods referred to in paragraph 1 shall be the total amount invoiced in accordance with paragraph 4 to the purchaser by the organiser of the sale by public auction, less:

—*the net amount paid or to be paid by the organiser of the sale by public auction to his principal, determined in accordance with paragraph 3, and*

—*the amount of the tax due by the organiser of the sale by public auction in respect of his supply.*

3. The net amount paid or to be paid by the organiser of the sale by public auction to his principal shall be equal to the difference between:

—*the price of the goods at public auction, and*

—*the amount of the commission obtained or to be obtained by the organiser of the sale by public auction from his principal, under the contract whereby commission is payable on the sale.*

4. The organiser of the sale by public auction must issue to the purchaser an invoice …[2] *itemising:*

—*the auction price of the goods,*

—*taxes, dues, levies and charges,*

—*incidental expenses such as commission, packing, transport and insurance costs charged by the organiser to the purchaser of the goods.*

That invoice must not indicate any value added tax separately.

5. The organiser of the sale by public auction to whom the goods were transmitted under a contract whereby commission is payable on a public auction sale must issue a statement to his principal.

That statement must itemise the amount of the transaction, i e the auction price of the goods less the amount of the commission obtained or to be obtained from the principal.

A statement so drawn up shall serve as the invoice which the principal, where he is a taxable person, must issue to the organiser of the sale by public auction in accordance with Article 22(3).

6. Organisers of sales by public auction who supply goods under the conditions laid down in paragraph 1 must indicate in their accounts, in suspense accounts:

—*the amounts obtained or to be obtained from the purchaser of the goods,*

—*the amount reimbursed or to be reimbursed to the vendor of the goods.*

These amounts must be duly substantiated.

7. The supply of goods to a taxable person who is an organiser of sales by public auction shall be regarded as being effected when the sale of those goods by public auction is itself effected.

D Transitional arrangements for the taxation of trade between Member States

During the period referred to in Article 281, Member States shall apply the following provisions:

(a) supplies of new means of transport, within the meaning of Article 28a(2), effected within the conditions laid down in Article 28c(A) shall be excluded from the special arrangements provided for in B and C;

(b) by way of derogation from Article 28a(1)(a), intra-Community acquisitions of second-hand goods, works of art, collectors' items or antiques shall not be subject to value added tax where the vendor is a taxable dealer acting as such and the goods acquired have been subject to tax in the Member State of departure of the dispatch or transport, in accordance with the special arrangements for taxing the margin provided for in B, or where the vendor is an organiser of sales by public auction acting as such and the goods acquired have been subject to tax in the Member State of departure of the dispatch or transport, in accordance with the special arrangements provided for in C;

(c) Articles 28b(B) and 28c(A)(a), (c) and (d) shall not apply to supplies of goods subject to value added tax in accordance with either of the special arrangements laid down in B and C.][1]

Commentary—*De Voil Indirect Tax Service* **V3.532.**

Simon's Tax Cases—Art 26aA(*e*), *Jyske Finans A/S v Skatteministeriet (Nordania Finans A/S and BG Factoring A/S intervening)* [2006] STC 1744.

Amendments—[1] This Article inserted by Council Directive 94/5/EEC, arts 1(3), 4; OJ L60, 3.3.94. For commencement, see art 4 of the Directive.

[2] Words repealed by Council Directive 2001/115/EC art 4(2), (3); see OJ L 015; 17.01.02.

[Article 26b

Special scheme for investment gold

A Definition

For the purposes of this Directive, and without prejudice to other Community provisions: 'investment gold' shall mean:

(i) gold, in the form of a bar or a wafer of weights accepted by the bullion markets, of a purity equal to or greater than 995 thousandths, whether or not represented by securities. Member States may exclude from the scheme small bars or wafers of a weight of 1g or less;

(ii) gold coins which:

—are of a purity equal to or greater than 900 thousandths,

—are minted after 1800,

—are or have been legal tender in the country of origin, and

—are normally sold at a price which does not exceed the open market value of the gold contained in the coins by more than 80%.

Such coins are not, for the purpose of this Directive, considered to be sold for numismatic interest.

Each Member State shall inform the Commission before 1 July each year, starting in 1999, of the coins meeting these criteria which are traded in that Member State. The Commission shall publish a comprehensive list of these coins in the 'C' series of the Official Journal of the European Communities before 1 December each year. Coins included in the published list shall be deemed to fulfil these criteria for the whole year for which the list is published.

Note—See VAT Notice 701/21A, para 3 for the list of investment gold coins.

B Special arrangements applicable to investment gold transactions

Member States shall exempt from value added tax the supply, intra-Community acquisition and importation of investment gold, including investment gold represented by certificates for allocated or unallocated gold or traded on gold accounts and including, in particular, gold loans and swaps, involving a right of ownership or claim in respect of investment gold, as well as transactions concerning investment gold involving futures and forward contracts leading to a transfer of right of ownership or claim in respect of investment gold.

Member States shall also exempt services of agents who act in the name and for the account of another when they intervene in the supply of investment gold for their principal.

C Option to tax

Member States shall allow taxable persons who produce investment gold or transform any gold into investment gold as defined in A a right of option for taxation of supplies of investment gold to another taxable person which would otherwise be exempt under B.

Member States may allow taxable persons, who in their trade normally supply gold for industrial purposes, a right of option for taxation of supplies of investment gold as defined in A(i) to another taxable person, which would otherwise be exempt under B. Member States may restrict the scope of this option.

Where the supplier has exercised a right of option for taxation pursuant to the first or second paragraph, Member States shall allow a right of option for taxation for the agent in respect of the services mentioned in the second paragraph of B.

Member States shall specify the details of the use of these options, and shall inform the Commission of the rules of application for the exercise of these options in that Member State.

D Right of deduction

1. Taxable persons shall be entitled to deduct—

(a) tax due or paid in respect of investment gold supplied to them by a person who has exercised the right of option under C or supplied to them pursuant to the procedure laid down in G;

(b) tax due or paid in respect of supply to them, or intra-Community acquisition or importation by them, of gold other than investment gold which is subsequently transformed by them or on their behalf into investment gold;

(c) tax due or paid in respect of services supplied to them consisting of change of form, weight or purity of gold including investment gold,

if their subsequent supply of this gold is exempt under this Article.

2. Taxable persons who produce investment gold or transform any gold into investment gold, shall be entitled to deduct tax due or paid by them in respect of supplies, or intra-Community acquisition or importation of goods or services linked to the production or transformation of that gold as if their subsequent supply of the gold exempted under this Article were taxable.

E Special obligations for traders in investment gold

Member States shall, as a minimum, ensure that traders in investment gold keep account of all substantial transactions in investment gold and keep the documentation to allow identification of the customer in such transactions.

Traders shall keep this information for a period of at least five years.

Member States may accept equivalent obligations under measures adopted pursuant to other Community legislation, such as Council Directive 91/308/EEC of 10 June 1991 on prevention of the use of the financial system for the purpose of money laundering, to meet the requirements of the first paragraph.

Member States may lay down stricter obligations, in particular on special record keeping or special accounting requirements.

F Reverse charge procedure

By way of derogation from Article 21(1)(a), as amended by Article 28g, in the case of supplies of gold material or semi-manufactured products of a purity of 325 thousandths or greater, or supplies of investment gold where an option referred to in C of this Article has been exercised, Member States may designate the purchaser as the person liable to pay the tax, according to the procedures and conditions, which they shall lay down. When they exercise this option, Member States shall take the measures necessary to ensure that the person designated as liable for the tax due fulfils the obligations to submit a statement and to pay the tax in accordance with Article 22.

G Procedure for transactions on a regulated gold bullion market

1. A Member State may, subject to consultation provided for under Article 29, disapply the exemption for investment gold provided for by this special scheme in respect of specific transactions, other than intra-Community supplies or exports, concerning investment gold taking place in that Member State:

(a) between taxable persons who are members of a bullion market regulated by the Member State concerned, and

(b) where the transaction is between a member of a bullion market regulated by the Member State concerned and another taxable person who is not a member of that market.

Under these circumstances, these transactions shall be taxable and the following shall apply.

2

(a) For transactions under 1(a), for the purpose of simplification, the Member State shall authorise suspension of the tax to be collected as well as dispense with the recording requirements of value added tax.

(b) For transactions under 1(b), the reverse charge procedure under F shall be applicable. Where a non-member of the bullion market would not, other than for these transactions, be liable for registration for VAT in the relevant Member State, the member shall fulfil the fiscal obligations on behalf of the non-member, according to the provisions of that Member State.][1]

Amendments—[1] This Article inserted by Council Directive 98/80/EC, art 1; OJ L281, 17.10.98. For commencement, see art 4 of the Directive printed *post*.

[Article 26c

Special scheme for non-established taxable persons supplying electronic services to non-taxable persons

A Definitions

For the purposes of this Article, the following definitions shall apply without prejudice to other Community provisions:

(a) 'non-established taxable person' means a taxable person who has neither established his business nor has a fixed establishment within the territory of the Community and who is not otherwise required to be identified for tax purposes under Article 22;

(b) 'electronic services' and 'electronically supplied services' means those services referred to in the last indent of Article 9(2)(e);
(c) 'Member State of identification' means the Member State which the non-established taxable person chooses to contact to state when his activity as a taxable person within the territory of the Community commences in accordance with the provisions of this Article;
(d) 'Member State of consumption' means the Member State in which the supply of the electronic services is deemed to take place according to Article 9(2)(f);
(e) 'value added tax return' means the statement containing the information necessary to establish the amount of tax that has become chargeable in each Member State.

B Special scheme for electronically supplied services

1. Member States shall permit a non-established taxable person supplying electronic services to a non-taxable person who is established or has his permanent address or usually resides in a Member State to use a special scheme in accordance with the following provisions. The special scheme shall apply to all those supplies within the Community.

2. The non-established taxable person shall state to the Member State of identification when his activity as a taxable person commences, ceases or changes to the extent that he no longer qualifies for the special scheme. Such a statement shall be made electronically.

The information from the non-established taxable person to the Member State of identification when his taxable activities commence shall contain the following details for the identification: name, postal address, electronic addresses, including websites, national tax number, if any, and a statement that the person is not identified for value added tax purposes within the Community. The non-established taxable person shall notify the Member State of identification of any changes in the submitted information.

3. The Member State of identification shall identify the non-established taxable person by means of an individual number. Based on the information used for this identification, Member States of consumption may keep their own identification systems.

The Member State of identification shall notify the non-established taxable person by electronic means of the identification number allocated to him.

4. The Member State of identification shall exclude the non-established taxable person from the identification register if:

(a) he notifies that he no longer supplies electronic services, or
(b) it otherwise can be assumed that his taxable activities have ended, or
(c) he no longer fulfils the requirements necessary to be allowed to use the special scheme, or
(d) he persistently fails to comply with the rules concerning the special scheme.

5. The non-established taxable person shall submit by electronic means to the Member State of identification a value added tax return for each calendar quarter whether or not electronic services have been supplied. The return shall be submitted within 20 days following the end of the reporting period to which the return refers.

The value added tax return shall set out the identification number and, for each Member State of consumption where tax has become due, the total value, less value added tax, of supplies of electronic services for the reporting period and total amount of the corresponding tax. The applicable tax rates and the total tax due shall also be indicated.

6. The value added tax return shall be made in euro. Member States which have not adopted the euro may require the tax return to be made in their national currencies. If the supplies have been made in other currencies, the exchange rate valid for the last date of the reporting period shall be used when completing the value added tax return. The exchange shall be done following the exchange rates published by the European Central Bank for that day, or, if there is no publication on that day, on the next day of publication.

7. The non-established taxable person shall pay the value added tax when submitting the return. Payment shall be made to a bank account denominated in euro, designated by the Member State of identification. Member States which have not adopted the euro may require the payment to be made to a bank account denominated in their own currency.

8. Notwithstanding Article 1(1) of Directive 86/560/EEC, the non-established taxable person making use of this special scheme shall, instead of making deductions under Article 17(2) of this Directive, be granted a refund according to Directive 86/560/EEC. Articles 2(2),2(3) and 4(2)of Directive 86/560/EEC shall not apply to the refund related to electronic supplies covered by this special scheme.

9. The non-established taxable person shall keep records of the transactions covered by this special scheme in sufficient detail to enable the tax administration of the Member State of consumption to determine that the value added tax return referred to in paragraph 5 is correct. These records should be made available electronically on request to the Member State of identification and to the Member State of consumption. These records shall be maintained for a period of 10 years from the end of the year when the transaction was carried out.

10. Article 21(2)(b) shall not apply to a non-established taxable person who has opted for this special scheme.][1]

Amendments—[1] Article 26c is temporarily inserted by Council Directive 2002/38 art 1 para 3 (OJ L 128; 15.05.02) with effect for a period of three years from 1 July 2003: see Council Directive 2002/38/EC art 4.

TITLE XV: SIMPLIFICATION PROCEDURES

Article 27

[1. The Council, acting unanimously on a proposal from the Commission, may authorise any Member State to introduce special measures for derogation from the provisions of this Directive, in order to simplify the procedure for charging the tax or to prevent certain types of tax evasion or avoidance. Measures intended to simplify the procedure for charging the tax, except to a negligible extent, may not affect the overall amount of the tax revenue of the Member State collected at the stage of final consumption.][1]

[2. A Member State wishing to introduce the measure referred to in paragraph 1 shall send an application to the Commission and provide it with all the necessary information. If the Commission considers that it does not have all the necessary information, it shall contact the Member State concerned within two months of receipt of the application and specify what additional information is required. Once the Commission has all the information it considers necessary for appraisal of the request it shall within one month notify the requesting Member State accordingly and it shall transmit the request, in its original language, to the other Member States.][1]

[3. Within three months of giving the notification referred to in the last sentence of paragraph 2, the Commission shall present to the Council either an appropriate proposal or, should it object to the derogation requested, a communication setting out its objections.][1]

[4. In any event, the procedure set out in paragraphs 2 and 3 shall be completed within eight months of receipt of the application by the Commission.][1]

5. Those Member States which apply on 1 January 1977 special measures of the type referred to in paragraph 1 above may retain them providing they notify the Commission of them before 1 January 1978 and providing that where such derogations are designed to simplify the procedure for charging tax they conform with the requirement laid down in paragraph 1 above.

Simon's Tax Cases—art 27, *C&E Comrs v Next plc* [1995] STC 651; *Primback Ltd v C&E Comrs* [1996] STC 757; *Finanzamt Bergisch Gladbach v Skripalle* (Case C-63/96) [1997] STC 1035; *Finanzamt Sulingen v Sudholz* [2005] STC 747.
Art 27(1), *Genius Holding BV v Staatssecretaris van Financiën* [1991] STC 239; *'K' Line Air Service Europe BV v Eulaerts NV and Belgian State* (Case C-131/91) [1996] STC 597.

Amendments—[1] Paras 1, 2, 3 replaced by Council Directive 2004/7 art 1 (OJ L 027; 30.1.2004 p 44).

TITLE XVI: TRANSITIONAL PROVISIONS

Article 28

1. Any provisions brought into force by the Member States under the provisions of the first four indents of Article 17 of the second Council Directive of 11 April 1967 shall cease to apply, in each Member State, as from the respective dates on which the provisions referred to in the second paragraph of Article 1 of this Directive come into force.

[1a. Until a date which may not be later than 30 June 1999, the United Kingdom of Great Britain and Northern Ireland may, for imports of works of art, collectors' items or antiques which qualified for an exemption on 1 January 1993, apply Article 11(B)(6) in such a way that the value added tax due on importation is, in any event, equal to 2·5% of the amount determined in accordance with Article 11(B)(1) to (4).][3]

[2. Notwithstanding Article 12(3), the following provisions shall apply during the transitional period referred to in Article 281.

(a) Exemptions with refund of the tax paid at the preceding stage and reduced rates lower than the minimum rate laid down in Article 12(3) in respect of the reduced rates, which were in force on 1 January 1991 and which are in accordance with Community law, and satisfy the conditions stated in the last indent of Article 17 of the second Council Directive of 11 April 1967, may be maintained.

Member States shall adopt the measures necessary to ensure the determination of own resources relating to these operations.

In the event that the provisions of this paragraph create for Ireland distortions of competition in the supply of energy products for heating and lighting, Ireland may, on specific request, be authorised by the Commission to apply a reduced rate to such supplies, in accordance with Article 12(3). In that case, Ireland shall submit its request to the Commission together with all necessary information. If the Commission has not taken a decision within three months of receiving the request, Ireland shall be deemed to be authorised to apply the proposed reduced rates.

(b) Member States which, at 1 January 1991 in accordance with Community law, applied exemptions with refund of tax paid at the preceding stage, or reduced rates lower than the minimum laid down in Article 12(3) in respect of the reduced rates, to goods and services other than those specified in Annex H, may apply the reduced rate or one of the two reduced rates provided for in Article 12(3) to any such supplies.

(c) Member States which under the terms of Article 12(3) will be obliged to increase their standard rate as applied at 1 January 1991 by more than 2%, may apply a reduced rate lower than the minimum laid down in Article 12(3) in respect of the reduced rate to supplies of categories of goods and services specified in Annex H. Furthermore, those Member States may

apply such a rate to restaurant services, children's clothing, children's footwear and housing. Member States may not introduce exemptions with refund of the tax at the preceding stage on the basis of this paragraph.

(d) Member States which at 1 January 1991 applied a reduced rate to restaurant services, children's clothing, children's footwear and housing, may continue to apply such a rate to such supplies.

(e) Member States which at 1 January 1991 applied a reduced rate to supplies of goods and services other than those specified in Annex H may apply the reduced rate or one of the two reduced rates provided for in Article 12(3) to such supplies, provided that the rate is not lower than 12%.

[This provision may not apply to supplies of second-hand goods, works of art, collectors' items or antiques subject to value added tax in accordance with one of the special arrangements provided for in Article 26a(B) and (C).][4]

(f) The Hellenic Republic may apply VAT rates up to 30% lower than the corresponding rates applied in mainland Greece in the departments of Lesbos, Chios, Samos, the Dodecanese and the Cyclades, and on the following islands in the Aegean: Thasos, Northern Sporades, Samothrace and Skiros.

(g) On the basis of a report from the Commission, the Council shall, before 31 December 1994, re-examine the provisions of subparagraphs (a) to (f) above in relation to the proper functioning of the internal market in particular. In the event of significant distortions of competition arising, the Council, acting unanimously on a proposal from the Commission, shall adopt appropriate measures.][2]

[(h) Member States which, on 1 January 1993, were availing themselves of the option provided for in Article 5(5)(a) as in force on that date, may apply to supplies under a contract to make up work the rate applicable to the goods after making up.

For the purposes of applying this provision, supplies under a contract to make up work shall be deemed to be delivery by a contractor to his customer of movable property made or assembled by the contractor from materials or objects entrusted to him by the customer for this purpose, whether or not the contractor has provided any part of the materials used.][6]

[(i) Member States may apply a reduced rate to supplies of live plants (including bulbs, roots and the like, cut flowers and ornamental foliage) and wood for use as firewood][7]

[(j) the Republic of Austria may apply one of the two reduced rates provided for in the third subparagraph of Article 12(3)(a) to the letting of immovable property for residential use, provided that the rate is not lower than 10%.

(k) the Portuguese Republic may apply one of the two reduced rates provided for in the third subparagraph of Article 12(3)(a) to restaurant services, provided that the rate is not lower than 12%.][9]

3. During the transitional period referred to in paragraph 4, Member States may:

(a) continue to subject to tax the transactions exempt under Article 13 or 15 set out in Annex E to this Directive;

(b) continue to exempt the activities set out in Annex F under conditions existing in the Member State concerned;

(c) grant to taxable persons the option for taxation of exempt transactions under the conditions set out in Annex G;

(d) continue to apply provisions derogating from the principle of immediate deduction laid down in the first paragraph of Article 18(2);

(e) continue to apply measures derogating from the provisions of Articles 5(4)(c)[5], 6(4) and 11A(3)(c);

(f) provide that for supplies of buildings and building land purchased for the purpose of resale by a taxable person for whom tax on the purchase was not deductible, the taxable amount shall be the difference between the selling price and the purchase price;

(g) by way of derogation from Articles 17(3) and 26(3), continue to exempt without repayment of input tax the services of travel agents referred to in Article 26(3). This derogation shall also apply to travel agents acting in the name and on account of the traveller.

[3a. Pending a decision by the Council, which, under Article 3 of Directive 89/465/EEC, is to act on the abolition of the transitional derogations provided for in paragraph 3, Spain shall be authorised to exempt the transactions referred to in point 2 of Annex F in respect of services rendered by authors and the transactions referred to in points 23 and 25 of Annex F.][1]

4. The transitional period shall last initially for five years as from 1 January 1978. At the latest six months before the end of this period, and subsequently as necessary, the Council shall review the situation with regard to the derogations set out in paragraph 3 on the basis of a report from the Commission and shall unanimously determine on a proposal from the Commission, whether any or all of these derogations shall be abolished.

5. At the end of the transitional period passenger transport shall be taxed in the country of departure for that part of the journey taking place within the Community according to the detailed rules of procedure to be laid down by the Council acting unanimously on a proposal from the Commission.

[6. The Council, acting unanimously on a proposal from the Commission, may authorise any Member State to apply until 31 December 2010 at the latest the reduced rates provided for in the

third subparagraph of Article 12(3)(a) to services listed in a maximum of two of the categories set out in Annex K. In exceptional cases, a Member State may be authorised to apply the reduced rates to services belonging to three of the aforementioned categories.][10]

The services concerned must satisfy the following requirements—

(a) they must be labour-intensive;

(b) they must be largely provided direct to final consumers;

(c) they must be mainly local and not likely to create distortions of competition;

(d) there must be a close link between the lower prices resulting from the rate reduction and the foreseeable increase in demand and employment.

The application of a reduced rate must not prejudice the smooth functioning of the internal market.

[Any Member State wishing to apply for the first time after 31 December 2005 a reduced rate to one or more of the services mentioned in the first subparagraph pursuant to this provision shall inform the Commission before 31 March 2006. It shall communicate to it before that date all relevant particulars concerning the new measures it wishes to introduce, and in particular the following:

(a) scope of the measure and detailed description of the services concerned;

(b) particulars showing that the conditions laid down in the second and third subparagraphs have been met;

(c) particulars showing the budgetary cost of the measure envisaged.][10]

Those Member States authorised to apply the reduced rate referred to in the first sub-paragraph shall, before 1 October 2002, draw up a detailed report containing an overall assessment of the measure's effectiveness in terms notably of job creation and efficiency.

Before 31 December 2002 the Commission shall forward a global evaluation report to the Council and Parliament accompanied, if necessary, by a proposal for appropriate measures for a final decision on the VAT rate applicable to labour-intensive services.][8]

Commentary—*De Voil Indirect Tax Service* **V4.275**.

Simon's Tax Cases—*EC Commission v Federal Republic of Germany* [1996] STC 843; *Marks and Spencer plc v C&E Comrs* [2000] STC 16.

Art 28(2), *EC Commission v United Kingdom* [1988] STC 456; *Jubilee Hall Recreation Centre Ltd v C&E Comrs* [1997] STC 414; *Talacre Beach Caravan Sales Ltd v C&E Comrs* [2006] STC 1671.

Art 28(2)(*a*), *Marks and Spencer plc v C&E Comrs* [1999] STC 205; *Marks and Spencer plc v C&E Comrs, University of Sussex v C&E Comrs* [2004] STC 1.

Art 28(3)(*b*), *Norbury Developments Ltd v C&E Comrs* [1999] STC 511; *Idéal Tourisme SA v Belgian State* [2001] STC 1386.

Art 28(3)(*b*), (*c*), *Finanzamt Goslar v Breitsohl* [2001] STC 355.

Note—Art 17 of the Second Council Directive reads as follows—

Article 17

With a view to the transition from the present systems of turnover taxes to the common system of value added tax, Member States may:

—adopt transitional measures to levy the tax in advance;

—apply, during a certain transitional period, in respect of capital goods, the method of deduction by annual instalments (deductions *pro rata temporis*);

—exclude, in whole or in part, during a certain transitional period, capital goods from the deduction system provided for in Article 11;

and, subject to the consultations mentioned in Article 16:

—authorise (in order to grant relief, total or partial, but general in scope, from the turnover tax charged up to the time of introducing value added tax) standard deductions in respect of capital goods not yet written off and of stocks in hand at that time. Member States may, however, restrict such deductions to goods exported during a period of one year from the introduction of value added tax. In that event, such deductions shall only be allowed in respect of stocks in hand at the time referred to above and exported in an unaltered state;

—provide for reduced rates or even exemptions with refund, if appropriate, of the tax paid at the preceding stage, where the total incidence of such measures does not exceed that of the reliefs applied under the present system. Such measures may only be taken for clearly defined social reasons and for the benefit of the final consumer, and may not remain in force after the abolition of the imposition of tax on importation and the remission of tax on exportation in trade between Member States.

Amendment—[1] Para 3a added by EEC Council Regulation 91/680; OJ L376, 31.12.1991, p 1.

[2] Para 2 replaced by EEC Council Directive 92/77; OJ L316, 31.10.92.

[3] Para 1a inserted by EEC Council Directive 94/5, arts 1(4), 4; OJ L60, 3.3.94. For commencement, see art 4 of the Directive printed *post*.

[4] Words in para 2(*e*) added by EEC Council Directive 94/5, arts 1(5), 4; OJ L60, 3.3.94.

[5] Derogation in para 3(*e*) relating to art 5(4)(*c*) deleted by EEC Council Directive 94/5, arts 1(8), 4; OJ L60, 3.3.94.

[6] Para (2)(*h*) added by EC Council Directive 95/7, art 1(5): OJ L102, 5.5.95, p 18 with effect from 25 May 1995.

[7] Para 2(*i*) added by EC Council Directive 96/42, art 1, with effect from 1 January 1995; see OJ L 170, 9.7.96, p 34.

[8] Para 6 added by EC Council Directive 99/85, art 1(1), with effect from 28 October 1999; see OJ L 277, 28.10.99, p 34.

[9] Para 2(*j*), (*k*) added by EC Council Directive 2000/17, art 1, with effect from 1 January 1999 until the end of the transitional period referred to in Article 281; see OJ L84, 5.4.00, p 24.

[10] Words in para 6 substituted by Council Directive 2006/18 art 1(2); see OJ L 051; 22.2.2006, p 12.

[TITLE XVIA: TRANSITIONAL ARRANGEMENTS FOR THE TAXATION OF TRADE BETWEEN MEMBER STATES]

Note—For the period of application of this Title, see art 28*l* *post*.

Amendments—This Title (arts. 28*a*–28*m*) added by EEC Council Directive 91/680; OJ L376, 31.12.1991, p 1.

Article 28a

Scope

1. The following shall also be subject to value added tax:

(*a*) *intra-Community acquisitions of goods for consideration within the territory of the country by a taxable person acting as such or by a non-taxable legal person where the vendor is a taxable person acting as such who is not eligible for the tax exemption provided for in Article 24 and who is not covered by the arrangements laid down in the second sentence of Article 8*(*1*)(*a*) *or in Article 28b*(*B*)(*1*).

[By way of derogation from the first subparagraph, intra-Community acquisitions of goods made under the conditions set out in paragraph 1a by a taxable person or non-taxable legal person shall not be subject to value added tax.][1]

Member States shall grant taxable persons and non-taxable legal persons eligible under the second subparagraph the right to opt for the general scheme laid down in the first subparagraph. Member States shall determine the detailed rules for the exercise of that option, which shall in any case apply for two calendar years;

(*b*) *intra-Community acquisitions of new means of transport effected for consideration within the country by taxable persons or non-taxable legal persons who qualify for the derogation provided for in the second subparagraph of* (*a*) *or by any other non-taxable person.*

[(*c*) *the intra-Community acquisition of goods which are subject to excise duties effected for consideration within the territory of the country by a taxable person or a non-taxable legal person who qualifies for the derogation referred to in the second subparagraph of point* (*a*), *and for which the excise duties become chargeable within the territory of the country pursuant to Directive 92/12/EEC.]*[2]

[1a. The following shall benefit from the derogation set out in the second subparagraph of paragraph 1(*a*):

(*a*) *intra-Community acquisitions of goods whose supply within the territory of the country would be exempt pursuant to Article 15*(*4*) *to* (*10*);

(*b*) *intra-Community acquisitions of goods other than those at* (*a*), *made—*

—by a taxable person for the purpose of his agricultural, forestry or fisheries undertaking, subject to the flat-rate scheme set out in Article 25, by a taxable person who carries out only supplies of goods or services in respect of which value added tax is not deductible, or by a non-taxable legal person,

—for a total amount not exceeding, during the current calendar year, a threshold which the Member States shall determine but which may not be less than the equivalent in national currency of ECU 10 000, and

—provided that the total amount of intra-Community acquisitions of goods did not, during the previous calendar year, exceed the threshold referred to in the second indent.

The threshold which serves as the reference for the application of the above shall consist of the total amount, exclusive of value added tax due or paid in the Member State from which the goods are dispatched or transported, of intra-Community acquisitions of goods other than new means of transport and other than goods subject to excise duty.][3]

2. For the purposes of this Title:

(*a*) *the following shall be considered as "means of transport": vessels exceeding 7·5 metres in length, aircraft the take-off weight of which exceeds 1,550 kilograms and motorised land vehicles the capacity of which exceeds 48 cubic centimetres or the power of which exceeds 7·2 kilowatts, intended for the transport of persons or goods, except for the vessels and aircraft referred to in Article 15*(*5*) *and* (*6*);

[(*b*) *the means of transport referred to in* (*a*) *shall not be considered to be 'new' where both of the following conditions are simultaneously fulfilled:*

—they were supplied more than three months after the date of first entry into service. However, this period shall be increased to six months for the motorised land vehicles defined in (*a*),

—they have travelled more than 6,000 kilometres in the case of land vehicles, sailed for more than 100 hours in the case of vessels, or flown for more than 40 hours in the case of aircraft.

Member States shall lay down the conditions under which the above facts can be regarded as established.][6]

3. "Intra-Community acquisition of goods" shall mean acquisition of the right to dispose as owner of movable tangible property dispatched or transported to the person acquiring the goods by or on behalf of the vendor or the person acquiring the goods to a Member State other than that from which the goods are dispatched or transported.

Where goods acquired by a non-taxable legal person are dispatched or transported from a third territory and imported by that non-taxable legal person into a Member State other than the Member State of arrival of the goods dispatched or transported, the goods shall be deemed to have been dispatched or transported from the Member State of import. That Member State shall grant the importer as defined in [Article 21(*4*)*]*[8] *a refund of the value added tax paid in connection with the importation of the goods in so far as the importer establishes that his acquisition was subject to value added tax in the Member State of arrival of the goods dispatched or transported.*

4. Any person who from time to time supplies a new means of transport under the conditions laid down in Article 28c(*A*) *shall also be regarded as a taxable person.*

The Member State within the territory of which the supply is effected shall grant the taxable person the right of deduction on the basis of the following provisions:

—the right of deduction shall arise and may be exercised only at the time of the supply,
—the taxable person shall be authorised to deduct the value added tax included in the purchase price or paid on the importation or intra-Community acquisition of the means of transport, up to an amount not exceeding the tax for which he would be liable if the supply were not exempt.

Member States shall lay down detailed rules for the implementation of these provisions.

5. [The following shall be treated as supplies of goods effected for consideration:][7]

(a) …[7]
(b) the transfer by a taxable person of goods from his undertaking to another Member State.

The following shall be regarded as having been transferred to another Member State: any tangible property dispatched or transported by or on behalf of the taxable person out of the territory defined in Article 3 but within the Community for the purposes of his undertaking, other than for the purposes of one of the following transactions:

—the supply of the goods in question by the taxable person within the territory of the Member State of arrival of the dispatch or transport under the conditions laid down in the second sentence of Article 8(1)(a) and in Article 28b(B)(1),
—the supply of the goods in question by the taxable person under the conditions laid down in Article 8(1)(c),
—the supply of the goods in question by the taxable person within the territory of the country under the conditions laid down in Article 15 or in Article 28c(A),
…[7]
[—the supply of a service performed for the taxable person and involving work on the goods in question physically carried out in the Member State in which the dispatch or transport of the goods ends, provided that the goods, after being worked upon, are re-dispatched to that taxable person in the Member State from which they had initially been dispatched or transported.][7]
—temporary use of the goods in question within the territory of the Member State of arrival of the dispatch or transport of the goods for the purposes of the supply of services by the taxable person established within the territory of the Member State of departure of the dispatch or transport of the goods,
—temporary use of the goods in question, for a period not exceeding 24 months, within the territory of another Member State in which the import of the same goods from a third country with a view to temporary use would be eligible for the arrangements for temporary importation with full exemption from import duties.
[—the supply of gas through the natural gas distribution system, or of electricity, under the conditions set out in Article 8(1)(d) or (e).][9]

[However, when one of the conditions to which the benefit of the above is subordinated is no longer met, the goods shall be considered as having been transferred to a destination in another Member State. In this case, the transfer is carried out at the moment that the condition is no longer met.][4]

6. The intra-Community acquisition of goods for consideration shall include the use by a taxable person for the purposes of his undertaking of goods dispatched or transported by or on behalf of that taxable person from another Member State within the territory of which the goods were produced, extracted, processed, purchased, acquired as defined in paragraph 1 or imported by the taxable person within the framework of his undertaking into that other Member State.

[The following shall also be deemed to be an intra-Community acquisition of goods effected for consideration: the appropriation of goods by the forces of a State party to the North Atlantic Treaty, for their use or for the use of the civilian staff accompanying them, which they have not acquired subject to the general rules governing taxation on the domestic market of one of the Member States, when the importation of these goods could not benefit from the exemption set out in Article 14(1)(g).][5]

7. Member States shall take measures to ensure that transactions which would have been classed as "supplies of goods" as defined in paragraph 5 or Article 5 if they had been carried out within the territory of the country by a taxable person acting as such are classed as "intra-Community acquisitions of goods".

Cross references—See VATA 1994 s 95(2) (implementation of para 2(*a*) above);
VAT Regulations, SI 1995/2518 regs 146, 147 (implementation of this article).
VAT Regulations, SI 1995/2518 regs 149–154 (regulations in implementing para 4 above).

Amendments—[1] Words in para 1(*a*) replaced by EEC Council Directive 92/111, art 1.10; OJ L384, 30.12.92.
[2] Para 1(*c*) added by EEC Council Directive 92/111, art 1.10; OJ L384, 30.12.92.
[3] Para 1a inserted by EEC Council Directive 92/111, art 1.10; OJ L384, 30.12.92.
[4] Sub-para added to para 5(*b*) by EEC Council Directive 92/111, art 1.10; OJ L384, 30.12.92.
[5] Sub-para added to para 6 by EEC Council Directive 92/111, art 1.10; OJ L384, 30.12.92.
[6] Para 2(b) replaced by EEC Council Directive 94/5, arts 1(6), 4; OJ L60, 3.3.94. For commencement, see art 4 of the Directive printed post.
[7] The words in the first pair of square brackets in para 5 and words in sub-para (*b*) replaced, and para 5(*a*) and the words omitted from sub-para (*b*) repealed by EC Council Directive 95/7, art 1(6): OJ L102, 5.5.95, p 18 with effect from 25 May 1995.
[8] Words "Article 21(4)" substituted for "Article 21(2)" by Council Directive 2000/65/EC art 1(6) with effect from 21 October 2000; OJ L269 p 44, 21.10.00. Member states must bring into force the measures necessary to comply with these provisions not later than 31 December 2001.
[9] Words in para 5 inserted by Council Directive 2003/92/EC art 1(7); OJ L260, 11.10.2003 p 8.

Article 28b

Place of transactions

A Place of the intra-Community acquisition of goods

1. The place of the intra-Community acquisition of goods shall be deemed to be the place where the goods are at the time when dispatch or transport to the person acquiring them ends.

2. Without prejudice to paragraph 1, the place of the intra-Community acquisition of goods referred to in Article 28a(1)(a) shall, however, be deemed to be within the territory of the Member State which issued the value added tax identification number under which the person acquiring the goods made the acquisition, unless the person acquiring the goods establishes that that acquisition has been subject to tax in accordance with paragraph 1.

If, however, the acquisition is subject to tax in accordance with paragraph 1 in the Member State of arrival of the dispatch or transport of the goods after having been subject to tax in accordance with the first subparagraph, the taxable amount shall be reduced accordingly in the Member State which issued the value added tax identification number under which the person acquiring the goods made the acquisition.

[For the purposes of applying the first subparagraph, the intra-Community acquisition of goods shall be deemed to have been subject to tax in accordance with paragraph 1 when the following conditions have been met—

—the acquirer establishes that he has effected this intra-Community acquisition for the needs of a subsequent supply effected in the Member State referred to in paragraph 1 and for which the consignee has been designated as the person liable for the tax due in accordance with Article 28c(E)(3),

—the obligations for declaration set out in the last subparagraph of Article 22(6)(b) have been satisfied by the acquirer.][1]

B Place of the supply of goods

1. By way of derogation from Article 8(1)(a) and (2), the place of the supply of goods dispatched or transported by or on behalf of the supplier from a Member State other than that of arrival of the dispatch or transport shall be deemed to be the place where the goods are when dispatch or transport to the purchaser ends, where the following conditions are fulfilled:

—the supply of goods is effected for a taxable person eligible for the derogation provided for in the second subparagraph of Article 28a(1)(a), for a non-taxable legal person who is eligible for the same derogation or for any other non-taxable person,

—the supply is of goods other than new means of transport and other than goods supplied after assembly or installation, with or without a trial run, by or on behalf of the supplier.

Where the goods thus supplied are dispatched or transported from a third territory and imported by the supplier into a Member State other than the Member State of arrival of the goods dispatched or transported to the purchaser, they shall be regarded as having been dispatched or transported from the Member State of import.

2. However, where the supply is of goods other than products subject to excise duty, paragraph 1 shall not apply to supplies of goods dispatched or transported to the same Member State of arrival of the dispatch or transport where:

—the total value of such supplies, less value added tax, does not in one calendar year exceed the equivalent in national currency of ECU 100,000, and

—the total value, less value added tax, of the supplies of goods other than products subject to excise duty effected under the conditions laid down in paragraph 1 in the previous calendar year did not exceed the equivalent in national currency of ECU 100,000.

The Member State within the territory of which the goods are when dispatch or transport to the purchaser ends may limit the thresholds referred to above to the equivalent in national currency of ECU 35,000 where that Member State fears that the threshold of ECU 100,000 referred to above would lead to serious distortions of the conditions of competition. Member States which exercise this option shall take the measures necessary to inform the relevant public authorities in the Member State of dispatch or transport of the goods.

Before 31 December 1994, the Commission shall report to the Council on the operation of the special ECU 35,000 thresholds provided for in the preceding subparagraph. In that report the Commission may inform the Council that the abolition of the special thresholds will not lead to serious distortions of the conditions of competition. Until the Council takes a unanimous decision on a Commission proposal, the preceding subparagraph shall remain in force.

3. The Member State within the territory of which the goods are at the time of departure of the dispatch or transport shall grant those taxable persons who effect supplies of goods eligible under paragraph 2 the right to choose that the place of such supplies shall be determined in accordance with paragraph 1.

The Member States concerned shall determine the detailed rules for the exercise of that option, which shall in any case apply for two calendar years.

C Place of the supply of services in the intra-Community transport of goods

1. By way of derogation from Article 9(2)(b), the place of the supply of services in the intra-Community transport of goods shall be determined in accordance with paragraphs 2, 3 and 4. For the purposes of this Title the following definitions shall apply:

— "the intra-Community transport of goods" shall mean transport where the place of departure and the place of arrival are situated within the territories of two different Member States[.][2]

[The transport of goods where the place of departure and the place of arrival are situated within the territory of the country shall be treated as intra-Community transport of goods where such transport is directly linked to transport of goods where the place of departure and the place of arrival are situated within the territories of two different Member States;][2]

— "the place of departure" shall mean the place where the transport of goods actually starts, leaving aside distance actually travelled to the place where the goods are,

— "the place of arrival" shall mean the place where the transport of goods actually ends.

2. The place of the supply of services in the intra-Community transport of goods shall be the place of departure.

3. However, by way of derogation from paragraph 2, the place of the supply of services in the intra-Community transport of goods rendered to customers identified for purposes of value added tax in a Member State other than that of the departure of the transport shall be deemed to be within the territory of the Member State which issued the customer with the value added tax identification number under which the service was rendered to him.

4. Member States need not apply the tax to that part of the transport corresponding to journeys made over waters which do not form part of the territory of the Community as defined in Article 3.

D Place of the supply of services ancillary to the intra-Community transport of goods

By way of derogation from Article 9(2)(c), the place of the supply of services involving activities ancillary to the intra-Community transport of goods, rendered to customers identified for purposes of value added tax in a Member State other than that within the territory of which the services are physically performed, shall be deemed to be within the territory of the Member State which issued the customer with the value added tax identification number under which the service was rendered to him.

E Place of the supply of services rendered by intermediaries

1. By way of derogation from Article 9(1), the place of the supply of services rendered by intermediaries, acting in the name and for the account of other persons, where they form part of the supply of services in the intra-Community transport of goods, shall be the place of departure.

However, where the customer for whom the services rendered by the intermediary are performed is identified for purposes of value added tax in a Member State other than that of the departure of the transport, the place of the supply of services rendered by an intermediary shall be deemed to be within the territory of the Member State which issued the customer with the value added tax identification number under which the service was rendered to him.

2. By way of derogation from Article 9(1), the place of the supply of services rendered by intermediaries acting in the name and for the account of other persons, where they form part of the supply of services the purpose of which is activities ancillary to the intra-Community transport of goods, shall be the place where the ancillary services are physically performed.

However, where the customer of the services rendered by the intermediary is identified for purposes of value added tax in a Member State other than that within the territory of which the ancillary service is physically performed, the place of supply of the services rendered by the intermediary shall be deemed to be within the territory of the Member State which issued the customer with the value added tax identification number under which the service was rendered to him by the intermediary.

3. By way of derogation from Article 9(1), the place of the supply of services rendered by intermediaries acting in the name and for the account of other persons, when such services form part of transactions other than those referred to in paragraph 1 or 2 or in Article 9(2)(e), shall be the place where those transactions are carried out.

However, where the customer is identified for purposes of value added tax in a Member State other than that within the territory of which those transactions are carried out, the place of supply of the services rendered by the intermediary shall be deemed to be within the territory of the Member State which issued the customer with the value added tax identification number under which the service was rendered to him by the intermediary.

[F Place of the supply of services in the case of valuations of or work on movable tangible property

By way of derogation from Article 9(2)(c), the place of the supply of services involving valuations or work on movable tangible property, provided to customers identified for value added tax purposes in a Member State other than the one where those services are physically carried out, shall be deemed to be in the territory of the Member State which issued the customer with the value added tax identification number under which the service was carried out for him.

This derogation shall not apply where the goods are not dispatched or transported out of the Member State where the services were physically carried out.][2]

Cross references—See VAT (Place of Supply of Services) Order, SI 1992/3121 (implementation of paras C, D, E above); VAT Regulations, SI 1995/2518 reg 98 (implementation of para B.3 above);
EEC Council Directive 92/111, art 4, para 2; OJ L384, 30.12.92 (extension of time limit to 31 December 1993 for adoption of laws, etc under certain provisions of this article).

Amendments—[1] Words in para A.2 added by EEC Council Directive 92/111, art 1.11; OJ L384, 30.12.92.
[2] Words in para C(1) and para F inserted and full point in para C(1) replaced by EC Council Directive 95/7, art 1(7): OJ L102, 5.5.95, p 18 with effect from 25 May 1995.

Article 28c

Exemptions

A Exempt supplies of goods

Without prejudice to other Community provisions and subject to conditions which they shall lay down for the purpose of ensuring the correct and straightforward application of the exemptions provided for below and preventing any evasion, avoidance or abuse, Member States shall exempt:

(a) supplies of goods, [as defined in Article 5][4]*, dispatched or transported by or on behalf of the vendor or the person acquiring the goods out of the territory referred to in Article 3 but within the Community, effected for another taxable person or a non-taxable legal person acting as such in a Member State other than that of the departure of the dispatch or transport of the goods.*

This exemption shall not apply to supplies of goods by taxable persons exempt from tax pursuant to Article 24 or to supplies of goods effected for taxable persons or non-taxable legal persons who qualify for the derogation in the second subparagraph of Article 28a(1)(a);

(b) supplies of new means of transport, dispatched or transported to the purchaser by or on behalf of the vendor or the purchaser out of the territory referred to in Article 3 but within the Community, effected for taxable persons or non-taxable legal persons who qualify for the derogation provided for in the second subparagraph of Article 28a(1)(a) or for any other non-taxable person;

[(c) the supply of goods subject to excise duty dispatched or transported to the purchaser, by the vendor, by the purchaser or on his behalf, outside the territory referred to in Article 3 but inside the Community, effected for taxable persons or non-taxable legal persons who qualify for the derogation set out in the second subparagraph of Article 28a(1)(a), when the dispatch or transport of the goods is carried out in accordance with Article 7(4) and (5), or Article 16 of Directive 92/12/EEC.

This exemption shall not apply to supplies of goods subject to excise duty effected by taxable persons who benefit from the exemption from tax set out in Article 24;][1]

[(d) the supply of goods, within the meaning of Article 28a(5)(b), which benefit from the exemptions set out above if they have been made on behalf of another taxable person.][2]

B Exempt intra-Community acquisitions of goods

Without prejudice to other Community provisions and subject to conditions which they shall lay down for the purpose of ensuring the correct and straightforward application of the exemptions provided for below and preventing any evasion, avoidance or abuse, Member States shall exempt:

(a) the intra-Community acquisition of goods the supply of which by taxable persons would in all circumstances be exempt within the territory of the country;

(b) the intra-Community acquisition of goods the importation of which would in all circumstances be exempt under Article 14(1);

(c) the intra-Community acquisition of goods where, pursuant to Article 17(3) and (4), the person acquiring the goods would in all circumstances be entitled to full reimbursement of the value added tax due under Article 28a(1).

C Exempt transport services

Member States shall exempt the supply of intra-Community transport services involved in the dispatch or transport of goods to and from the islands making up the autonomous regions of the Azores and Madeira as well as the dispatch or transport of goods between those islands.

D Exempt importation of goods

Where goods dispatched or transported from a third territory are imported into a Member State other than that of arrival of the dispatch or transport, Member States shall exempt such imports where the supply of such goods by the importer as defined in [Article 21(4)][6] *is exempt in accordance with paragraph A.*

Member States shall lay down the conditions governing this exemption with a view to ensuring its correct and straightforward application and preventing any evasion, avoidance or abuse.

[E Other exemptions

1. (substitutes art 16(1) and adds art 16(1A)).

2. (amends Art 16(2)).

3. Member States shall take specific measures to ensure that value added tax is not charged on the intra-Community acquisition of goods effected, within the meaning of Article 28b(A)(1), within its territory when the following conditions are met—

—the intra-Community acquisition of goods is effected by a taxable person who is not established in the territory of the country but who is identified for value added tax purposes in another Member State,

—the intra-Community acquisition of goods is effected for the purpose of a subsequent supply of goods made by a taxable person in the territory of the country,

—the goods so acquired by this taxable person are directly dispatched or transported from another Member State than that in which he is identified for value added tax purposes and destined for the person for whom he effects the subsequent supply,

—the person to whom the subsequent supply is made is a taxable person or a non-taxable legal person who is identified for value added tax purposes within the territory of the country,

—the person to whom the subsequent supply is made has been designated in accordance with [Article 21(1)(c)][5] as the person liable for the tax due on the supplies effected by the taxable person not established within the territory of the country.][3]

Cross references—See VATA 1994 Sch 8, Group 8, item 14 (implementation of para C above);
Customs and Excise (Personal Reliefs for Special Visitors) Order, SI 1992/3156 (implementation of para B above);
VAT Regulations, SI 1995/2518 regs 134, 135, 155 (implementation of para A above);
VAT Regulations, SI 1995/2518 reg 123 (implementation of para D above);
EEC Council Directive 92/111, art 4, para 2; OJ L384, 30.12.92 (extension of time limit to 31 December 1993 for adoption of laws, etc under certain provisions of this article).

Amendments—[1] Para A(*c*) replaced by EEC Council Directive 92/111, art 1.12; OJ L384, 30.12.92.
[2] Para A(*d*) added by EEC Council Directive 92/111, art 1.12; OJ L384, 30.12.92.
[3] Para E replaced by EEC Council Directive 92/111, art 1.13; OJ L384, 30.12.92.
[4] Words in para (A)(*a*) replaced by EC Council Direction 95/7, art 7(8): OJ L102, 5.5.95, p 18 with effect from 25 May 1995.
[5] Words in fifth indent of art 28c(E)(3) substituted by Council Directive 2000/65/EC art 1(3) with effect from 21 October 2000; OJ L269 p 44, 21.10.00. Member states must bring into force the measures necessary to comply with these provisions not later than 31 December 2001.
[6] Words "Article 21(4)" substituted for "Article 21(2)" by Council Directive 2000/65/EC art 1(6) with effect from 21 October 2000; OJ L269 p 44, 21.10.00. Member states must bring into force the measures necessary to comply with these provisions not later than 31 December 2001.

Article 28d

Chargeable event and chargeability of tax

1. The chargeable event shall occur when the intra-Community acquisition of goods is effected. The intra-Community acquisition of goods shall be regarded as being effected when the supply of similar goods is regarded as being effected within the territory of the country.

2. For the intra-Community acquisition of goods, tax shall become chargeable on the 15th day of the month following that during which the chargeable event occurs.

3. [By way of derogation from paragraph 2, tax shall become chargeable on the issue of the invoice …[3]. provided for in the first subparagraph of Article 22(3)(a) where that invoice …[3] is issued to the person acquiring the goods before the fifteenth day of the month following that during which the taxable event occurs.][1]

4. By way of derogation from Article 10(2) and (3), tax shall become chargeable for supplies of goods effected under the conditions laid down in Article 28c(A) on the 15th day of the month following that during which the chargeable event occurs.

[However, tax shall become chargeable on the issue of the invoice provided for in the first subparagraph of Article 22(3)(a) … where that invoice …[3] is issued before the fifteenth day of the month following that during which the taxable event occurs.][2]

Amendments—[1] Para 3 replaced by EEC Council Directive 92/111, art 1.14; OJ L384, 30.12.92.
[2] Words in para 4 replaced by EEC Council Directive 92/111, art 1.15; OJ L384, 30.12.92.
[3] Words in paras 3, 4 repealed by Council Directive 2001/115/EC art 4(4); see OJ L 015; 17.01.02.

Article 28e

Taxable amount and rate applicable

1. In the case of the intra-Community acquisition of goods, the taxable amount shall be established on the basis of the same elements as those used in accordance with Article 11(A) to determine the taxable amount for supply of the same goods within the territory of the country. [In particular, in the case of the intra-Community acquisition of goods referred to in Article 28a(6), the taxable amount shall be determined in accordance with Article 11(A)(1)(b) and paragraphs 2 and 3.][1]

Member States shall take the measures necessary to ensure that the excise duty due or paid by the person effecting the intra-Community acquisition of a product subject to excise duty is included in the taxable amount in accordance with Article 11(A)(2)(a). [When, after the moment the intra-Community acquisition of goods was effected, the acquirer obtains the refund of excise duties paid in the Member State from which the goods were dispatched or transported, the taxable amount shall be reduced accordingly in the Member State where the intra-Community acquisition took place.][2]

[2. For the supply of goods referred to in Article 28c(A)(d), the taxable amount shall be determined in accordance with Article 11(A)(1)(b) and paragraphs 2 and 3.][3]

[3.][3] *The tax rate applicable to the intra-Community acquisition of goods shall be that in force when the tax becomes chargeable.*

[4.][3] *The tax rate applicable to the intra-Community acquisition of goods shall be that applied to the supply of like goods within the territory of the country.*

Cross references—See VAT Regulations, SI 1995/2518 reg 41(1) (implementation of this article);
EEC Council Directive 92/546, art 1; OJ L351, 2.12.92 (derogation from para 1 above granted to the UK).

Amendments—[1] Words in para 1 replaced by EEC Council Directive 92/111, art 1.16; OJ L384, 30.12.92.
[2] Words in para 1 added by EEC Council Directive 92/111, art 1.16; OJ L384, 30.12.92.
[3] Para 2 inserted by EEC Council Directive 92/111, art 1.17; OJ L384, 30.12.92.

Article 28f

Right of deduction

Notes—Para 1 replaces art 17(2), (3), (4).
Para 2 replaces art 18(1).
Para 3 inserts art 18(3a).

Article 28g

Persons liable for payment of the tax

Note—This article replaces art 21.
Cross references—See EEC Council Directive 92/111, art 4 para 2; OJ L384, 30.12.92 (extension of time limit to 31 December 1993 for adoption of laws, etc under certain provisions of this article).

Article 28h

Obligations of persons liable for payment

Note—This article replaces art 22.

Article 28i

Special scheme for small undertakings

Note—This article amends art 24(3).

Article 28j

Common flat-rate scheme for farmers

Note—Para 1 amends art 25(4).
Para 2 replaces art 25(5), (6).
Para 3 amends art 25(9).

Article 28k

Miscellaneous provisions

The following provisions shall apply until 30 June 1999:

1. Member States may exempt supplies by tax-free shops of goods to be carried away in the personal luggage of travellers taking intra-Community flights or sea crossings to other Member States. For the purposes of this Article:

(a) "tax-free shop" shall mean any establishment situated within an airport or port which fulfils the conditions laid down by the competent public authorities pursuant, in particular, to paragraph 5;

(b) "traveller to another Member State" shall mean any passenger holding a transport document for air or sea travel stating that the immediate destination is an airport or port situated in another Member State;

(c) "intra-Community flight or sea crossing" shall mean any transport, by air or sea, starting within the territory of the country as defined in Article 3, where the actual place of arrival is situated within another Member State.

Supplies of goods effected by tax-free shops shall include supplies of goods effected on board aircraft or vessels during intra-Community passenger transport.

This exemption shall also apply to supplies of goods effected by tax-free shops in either of two Channel Tunnel terminals, for passengers holding valid tickets for the journey between those two terminals.

2. Eligibility for the exemption provided for in paragraph 1 shall apply only to supplies of goods:

[(a) the total value of which per person per journey does not exceed ECU 90.

By way of derogation from Article 28m, Member States shall determine the equivalent in national currency of the above amount in accordance with Article 7(2) of Directive 69/169/EEC.][1]

Where the total value of several items or of several supplies of goods per person per journey exceeds those limits, the exemption shall be granted up to those amounts, on the understanding that the value of an item may not be split;

(*b*) *involving quantities per person per journey not exceeding the limits laid down by the Community provisions in force for the movement of travellers between third countries and the Community.*

The value of supplies of goods effected within the quantitative limits laid down in the previous sub-paragraph shall not be taken into account for the application of (*a*).

3. Member States shall grant every taxable person the right to a deduction or refund of the value added tax referred to in Article 17(2) in so far as the goods and services are used for the purposes of his supplies of goods exempt under this Article.

4. Member States which exercise the option provided for in Article 16(2) shall also grant eligibility under that provision to imports, intra-Community acquisitions and supplies of goods to a taxable person for the purposes of his supplies of goods exempt pursuant to this Article.

5. Member States shall take the measures necessary to ensure the correct and straightforward application of the exemptions provided for in this Article and to prevent any evasion, avoidance or abuse.

Cross references—See VATA 1994 Sch 8, Group 14 (implementation of this article).

Amendments—[1] Words in para 2 substituted by Council Directive 94/4/EC of 14 February 1994, arts 2, 4 with effect from 3 March 1994 (date on which the Directive was published in the Official Journal); see OJ L60, 3.3.94, p 14.

Article 28l

Period of application

The transitional arrangements provided for in this Title shall enter into force on 1 January 1993. Before 31 December 1994 the Commission shall report to the Council on the operation of the transitional arrangements and submit proposals for a definitive system.

The transitional arrangements shall be replaced by a definitive system for the taxation of trade between Member States based in principle on the taxation in the Member State of origin of the goods or services supplied. To that end, after having made a detailed examination of that report and considering that the conditions for transition to the definitive system have been fulfilled satisfactorily, the Council, acting unanimously on a proposal from the Commission and after consulting the European Parliament, shall decide before 31 December 1995 on the arrangements necessary for the entry into force and the operation of the definitive system.

The transitional arrangements shall enter into force for four years and shall accordingly apply until 31 December 1996. The period of application of the transitional arrangements shall be extended automatically until the date of entry into force of the definitive system and in any event until the Council has decided on the definitive system.

[Article 28m

Rate of conversion

To determine the equivalents in their national currencies of amounts expressed in ecus in this Title Member States shall use the rate of exchange applicable on 16 December 1991. However, Bulgaria, the Czech Republic, Estonia, Cyprus, Latvia, Lithuania, Hungary, Malta, Poland, Romania, Slovenia and Slovakia shall use the rate of exchange applicable on the date of their accession.][1]

Amendments—[1] This article substituted by Council Directive 2006/98/EC art 1, Annex Part 2(a) (OJ L 363, 20.12.2006, p 129).

[Article 28n

Transitional measures

1. When goods:

—entered the territory of the country within the meaning of Article 3 before 1 January 1993,

and

—were placed, on entry into the territory of that country, under one of the regimes referred to in Article 14(1)(b) or (c), or Article 16(1)(A),

and

—have not left that regime before 1 January 1993, the provisions in force at the moment the goods were placed under that regime shall continue to apply for the period, as determined by those provisions, the goods remain under that regime.

2. The following shall be deemed to be an import of goods within the meaning of Article 7(1):

(*a*) *the removal, including irregular removal, of goods from the regime referred to in Article 14(1)(c) under which the goods were placed before 1 January 1993 under the conditions set out in paragraph 1;*

(*b*) *the removal, including irregular removal, of goods from the regime referred to in Article 16(1)(A) under which the goods were placed before 1 January 1993 under the conditions set out in paragraph 1;*

(*c*) *the termination of a Community internal transit operation started before 1 January 1993 in the Community for the purpose of supply of goods for consideration made before 1 January 1993 in the Community by a taxable person acting as such;*

(d) the termination of an external transit operation started before 1 January 1993;
(e) any irregularity or offence committed during an external transit operation started under the conditions set out in (c) or any Community external transit operation referred to in (d);
(f) the use within the country, by a taxable or non-taxable person, of goods which have been supplied to him, before 1 January 1993, within another Member State, where the following conditions are met—
—the supply of these goods has been exempted, or was likely to be exempted, pursuant to Article 15(1) and (2),
—the goods were not imported within the country before 1 January 1993.

For the purpose of the application of (c), the expression "Community internal transit operation" shall mean the dispatch or transport of goods under the cover of the internal Community transit arrangement or under the cover of a T2 L document or the intra-Community movement carnet, or the sending of goods by post.

3. In the cases referred to in paragraph 2(a) to (e), the place of import, within the meaning of Article 7(2), shall be the Member State within whose territory the goods cease to be covered by the regime under which they were placed before 1 January 1993.

4. By way of derogation from Article 10(3), the import of the goods within the meaning of paragraph 2 of this Article shall terminate without the occurrence of a chargeable event when:
(a) the imported goods are dispatched or transported outside the Community within the meaning of Article 3;

or

(b) the imported goods, within the meaning of paragraph 2(a), are other than a means of transport and are dispatched or transported to the Member State from which they were exported and to the person who exported them;

or

(c) the imported goods, within the meaning of paragraph 2(a), are means of transport which were acquired or imported before 1 January 1993, in accordance with the general conditions of taxation in force on the domestic market of a Member State, within the meaning of Article 3, and/or have not been subject by reason of their exportation to any exemption from or refund of value added tax.

This condition shall be deemed to be fulfilled when the date of the first use of the means of transport was before 1 January 1985 or when the amount of tax due because of the importation is insignificant.][1]

Amendments—[1] This article added by EEC Council Directive 92/111, art 1.22; OJ L384, 30.12.92.

[TITLE XVIB: TRANSITIONAL PROVISIONS APPLICABLE IN THE FIELD OF SECOND-HAND GOODS, WORKS OF ART, COLLECTORS' ITEMS AND ANTIQUES][1]

Note—For commencement of this Title, see EEC Council Directive 94/5, art 4 printed *post*.
Amendments—[1] This Title (art 28*o*) inserted by EEC Council Directive 94/5, arts 1 (7), 4; OJ L60, 3.3.94. For commencement, see art 4 of the Directive printed *post*.

Article 28o

1. Member States which at 31 December 1992 were applying special tax arrangements other than those provided for in Article 26a(B) to supplies of second-hand means of transport effected by taxable dealers may continue to apply those arrangements during the period referred to in Article 281 in so far as they comply with, or are adjusted to comply with, the following conditions:
(a) the special arrangements shall apply only to supplies of the means of transport referred to in Article 28a(2)(a) and regarded as second-hand goods within the meaning of Article 26a(A)(d), effected by taxable dealers within the meaning of Article 26a(A)(e), and subject to the special tax arrangements for taxing the margin pursuant to Article 26a(B)(1) and (2). Supplies of new means of transport within the meaning of Article 28a(2)(b) that are carried out under the conditions specified in Article 28c(A) shall be excluded from these special arrangements;
(b) the tax due in respect of each supply referred to in (a) is equal to the amount of tax that would be due if that supply had been subject to the normal arrangements for value added tax, less the amount of value added tax regarded as being incorporated in the purchase price of the means of transport by the taxable dealer;
(c) the tax regarded as being incorporated in the purchase price of the means of transport by the taxable dealer shall be calculated according to the following method:
—the purchase price to be taken into account shall be the purchase price within the meaning of Article 26a(B)(3),
—that purchase price paid by the taxable dealer shall be deemed to include the tax that would have been due if the taxable dealer's supplier had subjected the supply to the normal value added tax arrangements,

—the rate to be taken into account shall be the rate applicable within the meaning of Article 12(1), in the Member State within which the place of the supply to the taxable dealer, determined in accordance with Article 8, is deemed to be situated;

(d) the tax due in respect of each supply as referred to in (a), determined in accordance with the provisions of (b), may not be less than the amount of tax that would be due if that supply had been subject to the special arrangements for taxing the margin in accordance with Article 26a(B)(3).

For the application of the above provisions, the Member States have the option of providing that if the supply had been subject to the special arrangements for taxation of the margin, that margin would not have been less than 10% of the selling price, within the meaning of B(3);

(e) the taxable dealer shall not be entitled to indicate separately on the invoices he issues, …[2] tax relating to supplies which he is subjecting to the special arrangements;

(f) taxable persons shall not be entitled to deduct from the tax for which they are liable tax due or paid in respect of second-hand means of transport supplied to them by a taxable dealer, in so far as the supply of those goods by the taxable dealer is subject to the tax arrangements in accordance with (a);

(g) by way of derogation from Article 28a(1)(a), intra-Community acquisitions of means of transport are not subject to value added tax where the vendor is a taxable dealer acting as such and the second-hand means of transport acquired has been subject to the tax, in the Member State of departure of the dispatch or transport, in accordance with (a);

(h) Articles 28b(B) and 28c(A)(a) and (d) shall not apply to supplies of second-hand means of transport subject to tax in accordance with (a).

2. By way of derogation from the first sentence of paragraph 1, the Kingdom of Denmark shall be entitled to apply the special tax arrangements laid down in paragraph 1(a) to (h) during the period referred to in Article 28l.

3. Where they apply the special arrangements for sales by public auction provided for in Article 26a(C), Member States shall also apply these special arrangements to supplies of second-hand means of transport effected by an organiser of sales by public auction acting in his own name, pursuant to a contract under which commission is payable on the sale of those goods by public auction, on behalf of a taxable dealer, in so far as the supply of the second-hand means of transport, within the meaning of Article 5(4)(c), by that other taxable dealer, is subject to tax in accordance with paragraphs 1 and 2.

4. For supplies by a taxable dealer of works of art, collectors' items or antiques that have been supplied to him under the conditions provided for in Article 26a(B)(2), the Federal Republic of Germany shall be entitled, until 30 June 1999, to provide for the possibility for taxable dealers to apply either the special arrangements for taxable dealers, or the normal VAT arrangements according to the following rules:

(a) for the application of the special arrangements for taxable dealers to these supplies of goods, the taxable amount shall be determined in accordance with Article 11(A)(1), (2) and (3);

(b) in so far as the goods are used for the needs of his operations which are taxed in accordance with (a), the taxable dealer shall be authorised to deduct from the tax for which he is liable:

—the value added tax due or paid for works of art, collectors' items or antiques which are or will be supplied to him by another taxable dealer, where the supply by that other taxable dealer has been taxed in accordance with (a),

—the value added tax deemed to be included in the purchase price of the works of art, collectors' items or antiques which are or will be supplied to him by another taxable dealer, where the supply by that other taxable dealer has been subject to value added tax in accordance with the special arrangements for the taxation of the margin provided for in Article 26a(B), in the Member State within whose territory the place of that supply, determined in accordance with Article 8, is deemed to be situated.

This right to deduct shall arise at the time when the tax due for the supply taxed in accordance with (a) becomes chargeable;

(c) for the application of the provisions laid down in the second indent of (b), the purchase price of the works of art, collectors' items or antiques the supply of which by a taxable dealer is taxed in accordance with (a) shall be determined in accordance with Article 26a(B)(3) and the tax deemed to be included in this purchase price shall be calculated according to the following method:

—the purchase price shall be deemed to include the value added tax that would have been due if the taxable margin made by the supplier had been equal to 20% of the purchase price,

—the rate to be taken into account shall be the rate applicable, within the meaning of Article 12(1), in the Member State within whose territory the place of the supply that is subject to the special arrangements for taxation of the profit margin, determined in accordance with Article 8, is deemed to be situated;

(d) where he applies the normal arrangements for value added tax to the supply of a work of art, collectors' item or antique which has been supplied to him by another taxable dealer and where the goods have been taxed in accordance with (a), the taxable dealer shall be authorised to deduct from his tax liability the value added tax referred to in (b);

VAT

(*e*) *the category of rates applicable to these supplies of goods shall be that which was applicable on 1 January 1993;*
(*f*) *for the application of the fourth indent of Article 26a*(*B*)(*2*), *the fourth indent of Article 26a*(*C*)(*1*) *and Article 26a*(*D*)(*b*) *and* (*c*), *the supplies of works of art, collectors' items or antiques, taxed in accordance with* (*a*), *shall be deemed by Member States to be supplies subject to value added tax in accordance with the special arrangements for taxation of the profit margin provided for in Article 26a*(*B*);
(*g*) *where the supplies of works of art, collectors' items or antiques taxed in accordance with* (*a*) *are effected under the conditions provided for in Article 28c*(*A*), *the invoice issued in accordance with Article 22*(*3*) *shall contain an endorsement indicating that the special taxation arrangements for taxing the margin provided for in Article 28o*(*4*) *have been applied.*]1

Amendments—[1] This Title (art 28*o*) inserted by EEC Council Directive 94/5, arts 1(7), 4; OJ L60, 3.3.94. For commencement, see art 4 of the Directive printed *post*.
[2] Words in para 1(*e*) repealed by Council Directive 2001/115/EC art 4(6); see OJ L 015; 17.01.02.

[TITLE XVIC: TRANSITIONAL MEASURES APPLICABLE IN THE CONTEXT OF THE ACCESSION TO THE EUROPEAN UNION OF AUSTRIA, FINLAND AND SWEDEN ON 1 JANUARY 1995, OF THE CZECH REPUBLIC, ESTONIA, CYPRUS, LATVIA, LITHUANIA, HUNGARY, MALTA, POLAND, SLOVENIA AND SLOVAKIA ON 1 MAY 2004, AND OF BULGARIA AND ROMANIA ON 1 JANUARY 2007][1]

Amendments—[1] This Heading replaced by Council Directive 2006/98/EC art 1, Annex Part 2(b) (OJ L 363, 20.12.2006, p 129).

Article 28p

1. For the purpose of applying this Article:

— "Community" shall mean the territory of the Community as defined in Article 3 before accession,
[— "new Member States" shall mean the territory of the Member States acceding to the European Union on 1 January 1995, on 1 May 2004 and on 1 January 2007, as defined for each of those Member States in Article 3 of this Directive,][2]
— "enlarged Community" shall mean the territory of the community as defined in Article 3, after accession.

2. When goods:

—entered the territory of the Community or of one of the new Member States before the date of accession, and
—were placed, on entry into the territory of the Community or of one of the new Member States, under a temporary admission procedure with full exemption from import duties, under one of the regimes referred to in Article 16(*1*)(*B*)(*a*) *to* (*d*) *or under a similar regime in one of the new Member States, and*
—have not left that regime before the date of accession,

the provisions in force at the moment the goods were placed under that regime shall continue to apply until the goods leave this regime, after the date of accession.

3. When goods:

—were placed, before the date of accession, under the common transit procedure or under another customs transit procedure, and
—have not left that procedure before the date of accession,

the provisions in force at the moment the goods were placed under that procedure shall continue to apply until the goods leave this procedure, after the date of accession.

For the purposes of the first indent, "common transit procedure" shall mean the measures for the transport of goods in transit between the Community and the countries of the European Free Trade Association (*EFTA*) *and between the EFTA countries themselves, as provided for in the Convention of 20 May 1987 on a common transit procedure.*

4. The following shall be deemed to be an importation of goods within the meaning of Article 7(*1*) *where it is shown that the goods were in free circulation in one of the new Member States or in the Community;*

(*a*) *the removal, including irregular removal, of goods from a temporary admission procedure under which they were placed before the date of accession under the conditions set out in paragraph 2;*
(*b*) *the removal, including irregular removal, of goods either from one of the regimes referred to in Article 16*(*1*)(*B*)(*a*) *to* (*d*) *or from a similar regime under which they were placed before the date of accession under the conditions set out in paragraph 2;*
(*c*) *the termination of one of the procedures referred to in paragraph 3 which was started before the date of accession in one of new Member States for the purposes of a supply of goods for consideration effected before that date in that Member State by a taxable person acting as such;*

(*d*) *any irregularity or offence committed during one of the procedures referred to in paragraph 3 under the conditions set out at* (*c*).

5. The use after the date of accession within a Member State, by a taxable or non-taxable person, of goods supplied to him before the date of accession within the Community or one of the new Member States shall also be deemed to be an importation of goods within the meaning of Article 7(1) where the following conditions are met:

—*the supply of those goods has been exempted, or was likely to be exempted, either under Article 15(1) and (2) or under a similar provision in the new Member States,*

—*the goods were not imported into one of the new Member States or into the Community before the date of accession.*

6. In the cases referred to in paragraph 4, the place of import within the meaning of Article 7(3) shall be the Member State within whose territory the goods cease to be covered by the regime under which they were placed before the date of accession.

7. By way of derogation from Article 10(3), the importation of goods within the meaning of paragraphs 4 and 5 of this Article shall terminate without the occurrence of a chargeable event when:

(*a*) *the imported goods are dispatched or transported outside the enlarged Community; or*

(*b*) *the imported goods within the meaning of paragraph 4(a) are other than means of transport and are redispatched or transported to the Member State from which they were exported and to the person who exported them; or*

(*c*) *the imported goods within the meaning of paragraph 4(a) are means of transport which were acquired or imported before the date of accession in accordance with the general conditions of taxation in force on the domestic market of one of the new Member States or of one of the Member States of the Community and/or have not been subject, by reason of their exportation, to any exemption from, or refund of, value added tax.*

[This condition shall be deemed to be fulfilled in the following cases:

—*when, in respect of Austria, Finland and Sweden, the date of the first use of the means of transport was before 1 January 1987;*

—*when, in respect of the Czech Republic, Estonia, Cyprus, Latvia, Lithuania, Hungary, Malta, Poland, Slovenia and Slovakia, the date of the first use of the means of transport was before 1 May 1996;*

—*when in respect of Bulgaria and Romania, the date of the first use of the means of transport was before 1 January 1999;*

—*when the amount of tax due by reason of the importation is insignificant.][3]][1]*

Amendments—[1] This title added by EC Council Directive 94/76, art 1; OJ L365, 31.12.94 p 53.
[2] Words in paras (1), (7) replaced by Council Directive 2006/98/EC art 1, Annex Part 2(c), (d) (OJ L 363, 20.12.2006, p 129).
[3] Words in para (7) replaced by the 2003 Act of Accession Annex II Chapter 9 para 3(*d*) (OJ L 236; 23.9.2003 p 555).

TITLE XVII: VALUE ADDED TAX COMMITTEE

Article 29

1. An Advisory Committee on value added tax, hereinafter called "the Committee", is hereby set up.

2. The Committee shall consist of representatives of the Member States and of the Commission.

The chairman of the Committee shall be a representative of the Commission.

Secretarial services for the Committee shall be provided by the Commission.

3. The Committee shall adopt its own rules of procedure.

4. In addition to points subject to the consultation provided for under this Directive, the Committee shall examine questions raised by its chairman, on his own initiative or at the request of the representative of a Member State, which concern the application of the Community provisions on value added tax.

[Article 29a

Implementing measures

The Council, acting unanimously on a proposal from the Commission, shall adopt the measures necessary to implement this Directive.][1]

Amendments—[1] This Article inserted by Council Directive 2004/7 art 2 (OJ L 027; 30.1.2004 p 44).

TITLE XVIII: MISCELLANEOUS

[Article 30

International agreements

1. The Council, acting unanimously on a proposal from the Commission, may authorise any Member State to conclude with a third country or an international organisation an agreement which may contain derogations from this Directive.

2. A Member State wishing to conclude such an agreement shall send an application to the Commission and provide it with all the necessary information. If the Commission considers that it does not have all the necessary information, it shall contact the Member State concerned within two months of receipt of the application and specify what additional information is required. Once the Commission has all the information it considers necessary for appraisal of the request it shall within one month notify the requesting Member State accordingly and it shall transmit the request, in its original language, to the other Member States.

3. Within three months of giving the notification referred to in the last sentence of paragraph 2, the Commission shall present to the Council either an appropriate proposal or, should it object to the derogation requested, a communication setting out its objections.

4. In any event, the procedure set out in paragraphs 2 and 3 shall be completed within eight months of receipt of the application by the Commission.][1]

Amendments—[1] This Article replaced by Council Directive 2004/7 art 3 (OJ L 027; 30.1.2004 p 44).

Article 31

Unit of account

1. The unit of account used in this Directive shall be the European unit of account (EUA) defined by Decision 75/250/EEC (OJ L104, 24.4.75, p 35).

2. When converting this unit of account into national currencies, Member States shall have the option of rounding the amounts resulting from this conversion either upwards or downwards by up to 10 per cent.

Article 32

Second-hand goods

Amendment—This article deleted by EEC Council Directive 94/5, arts 1(9), 4; OJ L60, 3.3.94; with effect as mentioned in art 4 of the Directive printed *post*.

[Article 33] [1]

1. Without prejudice to other Community provisions, in particular those laid down in the Community provisions in force relating to the general arrangements for the holding, movement and monitoring of products subject to excise duty, this Directive shall not prevent a Member State from maintaining or introducing taxes on insurance contracts, taxes on betting and gambling, excise duties, stamp duties and, more generally, any taxes, duties or charges which cannot be characterised as turnover taxes, provided however that those taxes, duties or charges do not, in trade between Member States, give rise to formalities connected with the crossing of frontiers.

2. Any reference in this Directive to products subject to excise duty shall apply to the following products as defined by current Community provisions:

—mineral oils,
—alcohol and alcoholic beverages,
—manufactured tobacco.

Simon's Tax Cases—*Fazenda Pública v Solisnor-Estaleiros Navais SA* (Case C-130/96) [1998] STC 191; *R v C&E Comrs, ex p Lunn Poly Ltd* [1998] STC 649; *SPAR österreichische Warenhandels AG v Finanzlandesdirektion für Salzburg* [1998] STC 960.

Amendments—[1] Article 33 replaced by EEC Council Directive 91/680; OJ L376, 31.12.1991, p 1.

[Article 33a] [1]

[1. Goods referred to in Article 7(1)(b) entering the Community from a territory which forms part of the customs territory of the Community but which is considered as a third territory for the purposes of applying this Directive shall be subject to the following provisions:

(a) the formalities relating to the entry of such goods into the Community shall be the same as those laid down by the Community customs provisions in force for the import of goods into the customs territory of the Community;

(b) when the place of arrival of the dispatch or transport of these goods is situated outside the Member State where they enter the Community, they shall circulate in the Community under the internal Community transit procedure laid down by the Community customs provisions in force, insofar as they have been the subject of a declaration placing them under this regime when the goods entered the Community;

(c) when at the moment of their entry into the Community the goods are found to be in one of the situations which would qualify them, if they were imported within the meaning of Article 7(1)(a), to benefit from one of the arrangements referred to in Article 16(1)(B)(a), (b), (c) and (d), or under a temporary arrangement in full exemption from import duties, the Member States shall take measures ensuring that the goods may remain in the Community under the same conditions as those laid down for the application of such arrangements.

2. Goods not referred to in Article 7(1)(a) dispatched or transported from a Member State to a destination in a territory that forms parts of the customs territory of the Community but which is considered as a third territory for the purposes of applying this Directive shall be subject to the following provisions:

(*a*) *the formalities relating to the export of those goods outside the territory of the Community shall be the same as the Community customs provisions in force in relation to export of goods outside the customs territory of the Community;*

(*b*) *for goods which are temporarily exported outside the Community, in order to be reimported, the Member States shall take the measures necessary to ensure that, on reimportation into the Community, such goods may benefit from the same provisions as if they had been temporarily exported outside the customs territory of the Community.*][1]

Cross references—See VAT Regulations, SI 1995/2518 regs 140, 141 (implementation of this article).

Amendments—[1] This art replaced by EEC Council Directive 92/111, art 1.23; OJ L384, 30.12.92 p 47.

TITLE XIX: FINAL PROVISIONS

Article 34

For the first time on 1 January 1982 and thereafter every two years, the Commission shall, after consulting the Member States, send the Council a report on the application of the common system of value added tax in the Member States. This report shall be transmitted by the Council to the European Parliament.

Article 35

At the appropriate time the Council acting unanimously on a proposal from the Commission, after receiving the opinion of the European Parliament and of the Economic and Social Committee, and in accordance with the interests of the common market, shall adopt further Directives on the common system of value added tax, in particular to restrict progressively or to repeal measures taken by the Member States by way of derogation from the system, in order to achieve complete parallelism of the national value added tax systems and thus permit the attainment of the objective stated in Article 4 of the first Council Directive of 11 April 1967.

Article 36

The fourth paragraph of Article 2 and Article 5 of the first Council Directive of 11 April 1967 are repealed.

Article 37

Second Council Directive 67/228/EEC of 11 April 1967 on value added tax shall cease to have effect in each Member State as from the respective dates on which the provisions of this Directive are brought into application.

Article 38

This Directive is addressed to the Member States.

Done at Brussels, 17 May 1977.

ANNEX A

LIST OF AGRICULTURAL PRODUCTION ACTIVITIES

I CROP PRODUCTION

1. General agriculture, including viticulture

2. Growing of fruit (including olives) and of vegetables, flowers and ornamental plants, both in the open and under glass

3. Production of mushrooms, spices, seeds and propagating materials; nurseries.

II STOCK FARMING TOGETHER WITH CULTIVATION

1. General stock farming

2. Poultry farming

3. Rabbit farming

4. Beekeeping

5. Silkworm farming

6. Snail farming.

III FORESTRY

IV FISHERIES

1. Fresh-water fishing

2. Fish farming

3. Breeding of mussels, oysters and other molluscs and crustaceans

4. Frog farming.

V WHERE A FARMER PROCESSES, USING MEANS NORMALLY EMPLOYED IN AN AGRICULTURAL, FORESTRY OR FISHERIES UNDERTAKING, PRODUCTS DERIVING ESSENTIALLY FROM HIS AGRICULTURAL PRODUCTION, SUCH PROCESSING SHALL ALSO BE REGARDED AS AGRICULTURAL PRODUCTION.

ANNEX B

LIST OF AGRICULTURAL SERVICES

Supplies of agricultural services which normally play a part in agricultural production shall be considered the supply of agricultural services, and include the following in particular:

—field work, reaping and mowing, threshing, baling, collecting, harvesting, sowing and planting

—packing and preparation for market, for example drying, cleaning, grinding, disinfecting and ensilage of agricultural products

—storage of agricultural products

—stock minding, rearing and fattening

—hiring out, for agricultural purposes, of equipment normally used in agricultural, forestry or fisheries undertakings

—technical assistance

—destruction of weeds and pests, dusting and spraying of crops and land

—operation of irrigation and drainage equipment

—lopping, tree felling and other forestry services.

Simon's Tax Cases—*Finanzamt Rendsburg v Harbs* [2006] STC 340.

ANNEX C

COMMON METHOD OF CALCULATION

(*The classification used in this Annex is that used in the Economic Accounts for Agriculture of the Statistical Office of the European Communities* (*SOEC*))

Note—This Annex is not relevant to this work.

ANNEX D

LIST OF THE ACTIVITIES REFERRED TO IN THE THIRD PARAGRAPH OF ARTICLE 4(5)

1. Telecommunications

2. The supply of water, gas, electricity and steam

3. The transport of goods

4. Port and airport services

5. Passenger transport

6. Supply of new goods manufactured for sale

7. The transactions of agricultural intervention agencies in respect of agricultural products carried out pursuant to Regulations on the common organisation of the market in these products

8. The running of trade fairs and exhibitions

9. Warehousing

10. The activities of commercial publicity bodies

11. The activities of travel agencies

12. The running of staff shops, co-operatives and industrial canteens and similar institutions

13. Transactions other than those specified in Article 13 A(*1*)(*q*)*, of radio and television bodies*

ANNEX E

TRANSACTIONS REFERRED TO IN ARTICLE 28(3)(A)

1. …[1]

2. Transactions referred to in Article 13A(*1*)(*e*)

3–6 …[1]

7. Transactions referred to in Article 13A(*1*)(*q*)

8.–10. …[1]

11. Supplies covered by Article 13B(*g*) *in so far as they are made by taxable persons who were entitled to deduction of input tax on the building concerned*

12.–14. …[1]

15. The services of travel agents referred to in Article 26, and those of travel agents acting in the name and on account of the traveller, for journeys outside the Community

Amendments—[1] The transactions referred to in points 1, 3–6, 8–10, and 12–14 abolished with effect from 1 January 1990 by art 1(1) of the Eighteenth Council Directive 89/465/EEC of 18 July 1989; see OJ L 226, 3.8.1989, p 21.

ANNEX F

TRANSACTIONS REFERRED TO IN ARTICLE 28(3)(B)

1. Admission to sporting events

2. Services supplied by authors, artists, performers, lawyers and other members of the liberal professions, other than the medical and paramedical professions, in so far as they are not services specified in Annex B to the second Council Directive of 11 April 1967

3. …[1]

4. …[2]

5. Telecommunications services supplied by public postal services and supplies of goods incidental thereto

6. Services supplied by undertakers and cremation services, together with goods related thereto

7. Transactions carried out by blind persons or workshops for the blind provided these exemptions do not give rise to significant distortion of competition

8. The supply of goods and services to official bodies responsible for the construction, setting out and maintenance of cemeteries, graves and monuments commemorating war dead

9. …[3]

10. Transactions of hospitals not covered by Article 13A(1)(b)

11. …[4]

12. The supply of water by public authorities

13. …[2]

14. …[1]

15. …[2]

16. Supplies of those buildings and land described in Article 4(3)

17. Passenger transport

The transport of goods such as luggage or motor vehicles accompanying passengers and the supply of services related to the transport of passengers, shall only be exempted in so far as the transport of the passengers themselves is exempt

18.–22. …[1]

23. The supply, modification, repair, maintenance, chartering and hiring of aircraft, including equipment incorporated or used therein, used by State institutions

24. …[2]

25. The supply, modification, repair, maintenance, chartering and hiring of warships

26. …[5]

27 The services of travel agents referred to in Article 26, and those of travel agents acting in the name and on account of the traveller, for journeys within the Community

Simon's Tax Cases—Item 6, *Network Insurance Brokers Ltd v C&E Comrs* [1998] STC 742.
Item 16, *Norbury Developments Ltd v C&E Comrs* (Case C-136/97) [1999] STC 511.

Amendments—[1] The transactions referred to in points 3, 14 and 18–22 abolished with effect from 1 January 1990 by art 1(2) of the Eighteenth Council Directive 89/465/EEC of 18 July 1989; see OJ L226, 3.8.1989, p 21.

[2] The transactions referred to in points 4, 13, 15 and 24 abolished with effect from 1 January 1991 by, art 2 of the Eighteenth Council Directive 89/465/EEC of 18 July 1989; see OJ L226, 3.8.1989.

[3] The transaction referred to in point 9 abolished with effect from 1 January 1992 by the Eighteenth Council Directive 89/465/EEC of 18 July 1989, art 2; see OJ L226, 3.8.1989.

[4] The transactions referred to in point 11 abolished with effect from 1 January 1993 by the Eighteenth Council Directive 89/465/EEC of 18 July 1989, art 2; see OJ L226, 3.8.1989.

[5] The transaction referred to in point 26 abolished with effect from 17 October 1998 by EC Council Directive 98/80, art 2; with effect from 17 October 1998; see OJ L281, 17.10.98 printed *post*.

ANNEX G

RIGHT OF OPTION

1. The right of option referred to in Article 28(3)(c) may be granted in the following circumstances:

(a) in the case of transactions specified in Annex E:

Member States which already exempt these supplies but also give the right of option for taxation, may maintain this right of option

(b) in the case of transactions specified in Annex F:

Member States which provisionally maintain the right to exempt such supplies may grant taxable persons the right to opt for taxation

2. Member States already granting a right of option for taxation not covered by the provisions of paragraph 1 above may allow taxpayers exercising it to maintain it until at the latest the end of three years from the date the Directive comes into force.

VAT

[ANNEX H][1]

LIST OF SUPPLIES OF GOODS AND SERVICES WHICH MAY BE SUBJECT TO REDUCED RATES OF VAT

In transposing the categories below which refer to goods into national legislation, Member States may use the combined nomenclature to establish the precise coverage of the category concerned.

Category	*Description*
1	*Foodstuffs (including beverages but excluding alcoholic beverages) for human and animal consumption; live animals, seeds, plants and ingredients normally intended for use in preparation of foodstuffs; products normally intended to be used to supplement or substitute foodstuffs*
2	*Water supplies*
3	*Pharmaceutical products of a kind normally used for health care, prevention of diseases and treatment for medical and veterinary purposes, including products used for contraception and sanitary protection*
4	*Medical equipment, aids and other appliances normally intended to alleviate or treat disability, for the exclusive personal use of the disabled, including the repair of such goods, and children's car seats*
5	*Transport of passengers and their accompanying luggage*
6	*Supply, including on loan by libraries, of books (including brochures, leaflets and similar printed matter, children's picture, drawing or colouring books, music printed or in manuscript, maps and hydrographic or similar charts), newspapers and periodicals, other than material wholly or substantially devoted to advertising matter*
7	*Admissions to shows, theatres, circuses, fairs, amusement parks, concerts, museums, zoos, cinemas, exhibitions and similar cultural events and facilities* *Reception of broadcasting services*
8	*Services supplied by or royalties due to writers, composers and performing artists*
9	*Supply, construction, renovation and alteration of housing provided as part of a social policy*
10	*Supplies of goods and services of a kind normally intended for use in agricultural production but excluding capital goods such as machinery or buildings*
11	*Accommodation provided by hotels and similar establishments including the provision of holiday accommodation and the letting of camping sites and caravan parks*
12	*Admission to sporting events*
13	*Use of sporting facilities*
14	*Supply of goods and services by organisations recognised as charities by Member States and engaged in welfare or social security work, insofar as these supplies are not exempt under Article 13*
15	*Services supplied by undertakers and cremation services, together with the supply of goods related thereto*
16	*Provision of medical and dental care as well as thermal treatment in so far as these services are not exempt under Article 13*
17	*Services supplied in connection with street cleaning, refuse collection and waste treatment, other than the supply of such services by bodies referred to in Article 4(5)*

Amendments—[1] Annex H added by EEC Council Directive 92/77, art 1; OJ L316, 31.10.92 p 1.

[ANNEX I][1]

WORKS OF ART, COLLECTORS' ITEMS AND ANTIQUES

For the purposes of this Directive:

(*a*) *"works of art" shall mean:*

—pictures, collages and similar decorative plaques, paintings and drawings, executed entirely by hand by the artist, other than plans and drawings for architectural, engineering, industrial, commercial, topographical or similar purposes, hand-decorated manufactured articles, theatrical scenery, studio back cloths or the like of painted canvas (CN code 9701),

—original engravings, prints and lithographs, being impressions produced in limited numbers directly in black and white or in colour of one or of several plates executed entirely by hand by the artist, irrespective of the process or of the material employed by him, but not including any mechanical or photomechanical process (CN code 9702 00 00),

—original sculptures and statuary, in any material, provided that they are executed entirely by the artist; sculpture casts the production of which is limited to eight copies and supervised by the artist or his successors in title (CN code 9703 00 00); on an exceptional basis, in cases determined by the Member States, the limit of eight copies may be exceeded for statuary casts produced before 1 January 1989,

—tapestries (CN code 5805 00 00) and wall textiles (CN code 6304 00 00) made by hand from original designs provided by artists, provided that there are not more than eight copies of each,

—individual pieces of ceramics executed entirely by the artist and signed by him,

—enamels on copper, executed entirely by hand, limited to eight numbered copies bearing the signature of the artist or the studio, excluding articles of jewellery and goldsmiths' and silversmiths' wares,

—photographs taken by the artist, printed by him or under his supervision, signed and numbered and limited to 30 copies, all sizes and mounts included;

(b) "collectors' items" shall mean:

—postage or revenue stamps, postmarks, first-day covers, pre-stamped stationery and the like, franked, or if unfranked not being of legal tender and not being intended for use as legal tender (CN code 9704 00 00),

—collections and collectors' pieces of zoological, botanical, mineralogical, anatomical, historical, archaeological, palaeontological, ethnographic or numismatic interest (CN code 9705 00 00);

(c) "antiques" shall mean objects other than works of art or collectors' items, which are more than 100 years old (CN code 9706 00 00).][1]

Amendments—[1] Annex I added by EEC Council Directive 94/5, arts 1(10), 4; OJ L60, 3.3.94. For commencement, see art 4 of the Directive printed *post*.

[ANNEX J][1]

Description of goods	*CN code*
Tin	*8001*
Copper	*7402* *7403* *7405* *7408*
Zinc	*7901*
Nickel	*7502*
Aluminium	*7601*
Lead	*7801*
Indium	*ex 8112 91* *ex 8112 99*
Cereals	*1001 to 1005* *1006: unprocessed rice only* *1007 to 1008*
Oil seeds and oleaginous fruit *Coconuts, Brazil nuts and cashew nuts* *Other nuts* *Olives*	*1201 to 1207* *0801* *0802* *0711 20*
Grains and seeds (including soya beans)	*1201 to 1207*
Coffee, not roasted	*0901 11 00* *0901 12 00*
Tea	*0902*

Description of goods	*CN code*
Cocoa beans, whole or broken, raw or roasted	*1801*
Raw sugar	*1701 11* *1701 12*
Rubber, in primary forms or in plates, sheets or strip	*4001* *4002*
Wool	*5101*
Chemicals in bulk	*Chapters 28 and 29*
Mineral oils (including propane and butane; also including crude petroleum oils)	*2709* *2710* *2711 12* *2711 13*
Silver	*7106*
Platinum (palladium, rhodium)	*7110 11 00* *7110 21 00* *7110 31 00*
Potatoes	*0701*
Vegetable oils and fats and their fractions, whether or not refined, but not chemically modified	*1507 to 1515*

Amendments—[1] Annex J added by EC Council Directive 95/7, art 1(13), Annex, with effect from 25 May 1995; OJ L 102, 5.5.95, p 18.

[ANNEX K][1]

LIST OF SUPPLIES OF SERVICES REFERRED TO IN ARTICLE 28(6)

1. Small services of repairing—
—bicycles,
—shoes and leather goods,
—clothing and household linen (including mending and alteration).

2. Renovation and repairing of private dwellings, excluding materials which form a significant part of the value of the supply.

3. Window cleaning and cleaning in private households.

4. Domestic care services (e g home help and care of the young, elderly, sick or disabled).

5. Hairdressing.][1]

Amendments—[1] Annex K added by EC Council Directive 99/85, art 1(1), Annex, with effect from 28 October 1999; see OJ L 277, 28.10.99, p 34.

[ANNEX L

ILLUSTRATIVE LIST OF ELECTRONICALLY SUPPLIED SERVICES REFERRED TO IN ARTICLE 9(2)(E)

1. Website supply, web-hosting, distance maintenance of programmes and equipment.

2. Supply of software and updating thereof.

3. Supply of images, text and information, and making databases available.

4. Supply of music, films and games, including games of chance and gambling games, and of political, cultural, artistic, sporting, scientific and entertainment broadcasts and events.

5. Supply of distance teaching.

Where the supplier of a service and his customer communicates via electronic mail, this shall not of itself mean that the service performed is an electronic service within the meaning of the last indent of Article 9(2)(e).][1]

Amendments—[1] Annex L added by Council Directive 2002/38 Annex (OJ L 128; 15.05.02).

[ANNEX M

LIST OF SUPPLIES OF GOODS AND SERVICES AS REFERRED TO IN ARTICLE 21(2)(C)(IV)

(a) the supply of ferrous and non ferrous waste, scrap, and used materials including that of semi-finished products resulting from the processing, manufacturing or melting down of ferrous and non-ferrous metals and their alloys;

(b) the supply of ferrous and non-ferrous semi-processed products and certain associated processing services;

(c) the supply of residues and other recyclable materials consisting of ferrous and non-ferrous metals, their alloys, slag, ash, scale and industrial residues containing metals or their alloys and the supply of selection, cutting, fragmenting and pressing services for these products;

(d) the supply of, and certain processing services relating to, ferrous and non-ferrous waste as well as parings, scrap, waste and used and recyclable material consisting of cullet, glass, paper, paperboard and board, rags, bone, leather, imitation leather, parchment, raw hides and skins, tendons and sinews, twine, cordage, rope, cables, rubber and plastic;

(e) the supply of the materials referred to in this annex after processing in the form of cleaning, polishing, selection, cutting, fragmenting, pressing or casting into ingots;

(f) the supply of scrap and waste from the working of base materials.][1]

Amendments—[1] Annex M added by Council Directive 2006/69/EC art 1(8), with effect from 13 August 2006, (OJ L 221, 12.8.2006, p 9).

[Council Directive 77/799/EEC of 19 December 1977 concerning mutual assistance by the competent authorities of the Member States in the field of direct taxation and taxation of insurance premiums][1]

(77/799/EEC)

Note—See OJ L336, 27.12.1977, p 15

Cross references—See Council Directive 2003/93 art 2 (OJ L 264; 15.10.2003 p 23): references made to Directive 77/799/EEC in relation to value added tax shall be construed as references to Council Regulation (EC) 1798/03 (OJ L 264; 15.10.2003 p 1).

Simon's Tax Cases—*EC Commission (supported by Kingdom of Spain, intervener) v United Kingdom* [2006] STC 1944.

Amendments—[1] Title substituted by Council Directive 2004/106 art 1 (1) (OJ L 359; 4.12.2004 p 30).

THE COUNCIL OF THE EUROPEAN COMMUNITIES

Having regard to the Treaty establishing the European Economic Community, and in particular Article 100 thereof,

Having regard to the proposal from the Commission,

Having regard to the opinion of the European Parliament (OJ No C293, 13.12.1976, p 34),

Having regard to the opinion of the Economic and Social Committee (OJ No C56, 7.3.1977, p 66),

Whereas practices of tax evasion and tax avoidance extending across the frontiers of Member States lead to budget losses and violations of the principle of fair taxation and are liable to bring about distortions of capital movements and of conditions of competition; whereas they therefore affect the operation of the common market;

Whereas, for these reasons the Council adopted on 10 February 1975 a resolution on the measures to be taken by the Community in order to combat international tax evasion and avoidance (OJ No C35, 14.2.1975, p 1);

Whereas the international nature of the problem means that national measures, whose effect does not extend beyond national frontiers, are insufficient; whereas collaboration between administrations on the basis of bilateral agreements is also unable to counter new forms of tax evasion and avoidance, which are increasingly assuming a multinational character;

Whereas collaboration between tax administrations within the Community should therefore be strengthened in accordance with common principles and rules;

Whereas the Member States should, on request, exchange information concerning particular cases; whereas the State so requested should make the necessary enquiries to obtain such information;

Whereas the Member States should exchange, even without any request, any information which appears relevant for the correct assessment of taxes on income and on capital, in particular where there appears to be an artificial transfer of profits between enterprises in different Member States or where such transactions are carried out between enterprises in two Member States through a third country in order to obtain tax advantages, or where tax has been or may be evaded or avoided for any reason whatever;

Whereas it is important that officials of the tax administration of one Member State be allowed to be present in the territory of another Member State if both the States concerned consider it desirable;

Whereas care must be taken to ensure that information provided in the course of such collaboration is not disclosed to unauthorised persons, so that the basic rights of citizens and enterprises are safeguarded; whereas it is therefore necessary that the Member States receiving such information should not use it, without the authorisation of the Member State supplying it, other than for the purposes of taxation or to facilitate legal proceedings for failure to observe the tax laws of the receiving State; whereas it is also necessary that the receiving States afford the information the same degree of confidentiality which it enjoyed in the State which provided it, if the latter so requires;

Whereas a Member State which is called upon to carry out enquiries or to provide information shall have the right to refuse to do so where its laws or administrative practices prevent its tax administration from carrying out these enquiries or from collecting or using this information for its own purposes, or where the provision of such information would be contrary to public policy or would lead to the disclosure of a commercial, industrial or professional secret or of a commercial process, or where the Member State for which the information is intended is unable for practical or legal reasons to provide similar information.

Whereas collaboration between the Member States and the Commission is necessary for the permanent study of co-operation procedures and the pooling of experience in the fields considered, and in particular in the field of the artificial transfer of profits within groups of enterprises, with the aim of improving those procedures and of preparing appropriate Community rules,

HAS ADOPTED THIS DIRECTIVE:

Article 1

General provisions

[1. In accordance with the provisions of this Directive the competent authorities of the Member States shall exchange any information that may enable them to effect a correct assessment of taxes on income and on capital, and any information relating to the establishment of taxes on insurance premiums referred to in the sixth indent of Article 3 of Council Directive 76/308/EEC of 15 March 1976 on mutual assistance for the recovery of claims relating to certain levies, duties, taxes and other measures.][1]

2.–4....

[5. The expression "competent authority" means:

in Belgium:

De minister van financiën or an authorised representative
Le ministre des finances or an authorised representative

in Denmark:

Skatteministeren or an authorised representative

in Germany:

Der Bundesminister der Finanzen or an authorised representative

in Greece:

Υπουργειο Οικονομικῶν or an authorised representative

in Spain:

El Ministro de Economia y Hacienda or an authorised representative

in France:

Le ministre de l'économie or an authorised representative

in Ireland:

The Revenue Commissioners or their authorised representative

in Italy:

[il Capo del Dipartimento per le Politiche Fiscali or his authorised representatives][5]

in Luxembourg:

Le ministre de finances or an authorised representative

in the Netherlands:

De minister van financiën or an authorised representative

in Austria:

Der Bundesminister für Finanzen or an authorised representative

in Portugal:

O Ministro das Finanças or an authorised representative

in Finland:

Valtiovarainministeriö or an authorised representative
Finansministeriet or an authorised representative

in Sweden:

[Chefen för Finansdepartementet or his authorised representative][5] *in the United Kingdom:*

[The Commissioners of Customs and Excise or an authorised representative for information required concerning taxes on insurance premiums and excise duty.

The Commissioners of Inland Revenue or an authorised representative for all other information.][3]][2]

[in the Czech Republic:

Ministr financí or an authorised representative][4]

[in Estonia:

Rahandusminister or an authorised representative][4]

[in Cyprus:

Υπουργος Οικονομικϖν or an authorised representative]4

[in Latvia:

Finanšu ministrs or an authorised representative][4]

[in Lithuania:

Finansu ministras or an authorised representative][4]

[in Hungary:

A pénzügyminiszter or an authorised representative][4]

[in Malta:

Il-Ministru responsabbli ghall-Finanzi or an authorised representative][4]

[in Poland:

Minister Finansów or an authorised representative][4]

[in Slovenia:

Minister za finance or an authorised representative][4]

[in Slovakia:

Minister financii or an authorised representative.][4]

[in Bulgaria:

Изпълнителният директор на Националната агенция за приходите

in Romania:

Ministerul Finanţelor Publice or an authorised representative.][6]

Amendments—[1] Para 1 substituted by Council Directive 2004/106 art 1(1) (OJ L 359; 4.12.2004 p 30).

[2] Para 5 substituted by Act of Accession 1994, art 29. Annex I; see OJ L1, 1.1.95, p 212.

[3] Words in paras 1, 5 substituted by Council Directive 2003/93 art 1(2) (OJ L 264; 15.10.2003 p 23).

[4] Words in para 5 inserted by the 2003 Act of Accession Annex II Chapter 9 para 4(*b*) (OJ L 236; 23.9.2003 p 555).

[5] Words in para 5 substituted by Council Directive 2004/56 art 1(1) (OJ L 127, 29.04.2004 p 70).

[6] Words in para 5 inserted by Council Directive 2006/98/EC art 1, Annex Part 3(b) (OJ L 363, 20.12.2006, p 129).

Article 2

Exchange on request

1. The competent authority of a Member State may request the competent authority of another Member State to forward the information referred to in Article 1(1) in a particular case. The competent authority of the requested State need not comply with the request if it appears that the competent authority of the State making the request has not exhausted its own usual sources of information, which it could have utilised, according to the circumstances, to obtain the information requested without running the risk of endangering the attainment of the sought after result.

2. For the purpose of forwarding the information referred to in paragraph 1, the competent authority of the requested Member State shall arrange for the conduct of any enquiries necessary to obtain such information.

[In order to obtain the information sought, the requested authority or the administrative authority to which it has recourse shall proceed as though acting on its own account or at the request of another authority in its own Member State][1]

Amendments—[1] Words in para 2 inserted by Council Directive 2004/56 art 1(2) (OJ L 127, 29.04.2004 p 70).

Article 3

Automatic exchange of information

For categories of cases which they shall determine under the consultation procedure laid down in Article 9, the competent authorities of the Member States shall regularly exchange the information referred to in Article 1(1) without prior request.

Article 4

Spontaneous exchange of information

1. The competent authority of a Member State shall without prior request forward the information referred to in Article 1(1), of which it has knowledge, to the competent authority of any other Member State concerned, in the following circumstances:

(*a*) the competent authority of the one Member State has grounds for supposing that there may be a loss of tax in the other Member State;
(*b*) a person liable to tax obtains a reduction in or an exemption from tax in the one Member State which would give rise to an increase in tax or to liability to tax in the other Member State;
(*c*) business dealings between a person liable to tax in a Member State and a person liable to tax in another Member State are conducted through one or more countries in such a way that a saving in tax may result in one or the other Member State or in both;
(*d*) the competent authority of a Member State has grounds for supposing that a saving of tax may result from artificial transfers of profits within groups of enterprises;
(*e*) information forwarded to the one Member State by the competent authority of the other Member State has enabled information to be obtained which may be relevant in assessing liability to tax in the latter Member State.

2. The competent authorities of the Member States may, under the consultation procedure laid down in Article 9, extend the exchange of information provided for in paragraph 1 to cases other than those specified therein.

3. The competent authorities of the Member States may forward to each other in any other case, without prior request, the information referred to in Article 1(1) of which they have knowledge.

Article 5

Time limit for forwarding information

The competent authority of a Member State which, under the preceding Articles, is called upon to furnish information, shall forward it as swiftly as possible. If it encounters obstacles in furnishing the information or if it refuses to furnish the information, it shall forthwith inform the requesting authority to this effect, indicating the nature of the obstacles or the reasons for its refusal.

Article 6

Collaboration by officials of the State concerned

For the purpose of applying the preceding provisions, the competent authority of the Member State providing the information and the competent authority of the Member State for which the information is intended may agree, under the consultation procedure laid down in Article 9, to authorise the presence in the first Member State of officials of the tax administration of the other Member State. The details for applying this provision shall be determined under the same procedure.

Article 7

Provisions relating to secrecy

[1. All information made known to a Member State under this Directive shall be kept secret in that State in the same manner as information received under its national legislation. In any case, such information:

– may be made available only to the persons directly involved in the assessment of the tax or in the administrative control of this assessment,
– may be made known only in connection with judicial proceedings or administrative proceedings involving sanctions undertaken with a view to, or relating to, the making or reviewing the tax assessment and only to persons who are directly involved in such proceedings; such information may, however, be disclosed during public hearings or in judgements if the competent authority of the Member State supplying the information raises no objection at the time when it first supplies the information,
– shall in no circumstances be used other than for taxation purposes or in connection with judicial proceedings or administrative proceedings involving sanctions undertaken with a view to, or in relation to, the making or reviewing of the tax assessment.

In addition, Member States may provide for the information referred to in the first subparagraph to be used for assessment of other levies, duties and taxes covered by Article 2 of Directive 76/308/EEC.][1]

2. Paragraph 1 shall not oblige a Member State whose legislation or administrative practice lays down, for domestic purposes, narrower limits than those contained in the provisions of that paragraph, to provide information if the State concerned does not undertake to respect those narrower limits.

3. Notwithstanding paragraph 1, the competent authorities of the Member State providing the information may permit it to be used for other purposes in the requesting State, if, under the legislation of the informing State, the information could, in similar circumstances, be used in the informing State for similar purposes.

4. Where a competent authority of a Member State considers that information which it has received from the competent authority of another Member State is likely to be useful to the competent authority of a third Member State, it may transmit it to the latter competent authority with the agreement of the competent authority which supplied the information.

Amendment—[1] Para 1 substituted by Council Directive 2004/56 art 1(3) (OJ L 127, 29.04.2004 p 70).

Article 8

Limits to exchange of information

[1. This Directive does not impose any obligation upon a Member State from which information is requested to carry out inquiries or to communicate information, if it would be contrary to its legislation or administrative practices for the competent authority of that State to conduct such inquiries or to collect the information sought.][1]

2. The provision of information may be refused where it would lead to the disclosure of a commercial, industrial or professional secret or of a commercial process, or of information whose disclosure would be contrary to public policy.

[3. The competent authority of a Member State may decline transmission of information when the Member State requesting it is unable, for reasons of fact or law, to provide the same type of information.][1]

Amendment—[1] Paras 1 and 3 substituted by Council Directive 2004/56 art 1(4) (OJ L 127, 29.04.2004 p 70).

[Article 8a

Notification

1. At the request of the competent authority of a Member State, the competent authority of another Member State shall, in accordance with the rules governing the notification of similar instruments in the requested Member State, notify the addressee of all instruments and decisions which emanate from the administrative authorities of the requesting Member State and concern the application in its territory of legislation on taxes covered by this Directive.

2. Requests for notification shall indicate the subject of the instrument or decision to be notified and shall specify the name and address of the addressee, together with any other information which may facilitate identification of the addressee.

3. The requested authority shall inform the requesting authority immediately of its response to the request for notification and shall notify it, in particular, of the date of notification of the decision or instrument to the addressee.][1]

Amendment—[1] Articles 8a and 8b inserted by Council Directive 2004/56 art 1(5) (OJ L 127, 29.04.2004 p 70).

[Article 8b

Simultaneous controls

1. Where the tax situation of one or more persons liable to tax is of common or complementary interest to two or more Member States, those States may agree to conduct simultaneous controls, in their own territory, with a view to exchanging the information thus obtained, whenever they would appear to be more effective than controls conducted by one Member State alone.

2. The competent authority in each Member State shall identify independently the persons liable to tax whom it intends to propose for simultaneous control. It shall notify the respective competent authorities in the other Member States concerned of the cases which, in its view, should be subject to simultaneous control. It shall give reasons for its choice, as far as possible, by providing the information which led to its decision. It shall specify the period of time during which such controls should be conducted.

3. The competent authority of each Member State concerned shall decide whether it wishes to take part in the simultaneous control. On receipt of a proposal for a simultaneous control, the competent authority shall confirm its agreement or communicate its reasoned refusal to its counterpart authority.

4. Each competent authority of the Member States concerned shall appoint a representative with responsibility for supervising and coordinating the control operation.][1]

Amendment—[1] Articles 8a and 8b inserted by Council Directive 2004/56 art 1(5) (OJ L 127, 29.04.2004 p 70).

Article 9

Consultations

1. For the purposes of the implementation of this Directive, consultations shall be held, if necessary in a Committee, between:

—the competent authorities of the Member States concerned at the request of either, in respect of bilateral questions,

—the competent authorities of all the Member States and the Commission, at the request of one of those authorities or the Commission, in so far as the matters involved are not solely of bilateral interest.

2. The competent authorities of the Member States may communicate directly with each other. The competent authorities of the Member States may by mutual agreement permit authorities designated by them to communicate directly with each other in specified cases or in certain categories of cases.

3. Where the competent authorities make arrangements on bilateral matters covered by this Directive other than as regards individual cases, they shall as soon as possible inform the Commission thereof. The Commission shall in turn notify the competent authorities of the other Member States.

Article 10

Pooling of experience

The Member States shall, together with the Commission, constantly monitor the co-operation procedure provided for in this Directive and shall pool their experience, especially in the field of transfer pricing within groups of enterprises, with a view to improving such co-operation and, where appropriate, drawing up a body of rules in the fields concerned.

Article 11

Applicability of wider-ranging provisions of assistance

The foregoing provisions shall not impede the fulfilment of any wider obligations to exchange information which might flow from other legal acts.

Article 12

Final provisions

1. Member States shall bring into force, the necessary laws, regulations and administrative provisions in order to comply with this Directive not later than 1 January 1979 and shall forthwith communicate them to the Commission.
2. Member States shall communicate to the Commission the texts of any important provisions of national law which they subsequently adopt in the field covered by this Directive.

Article 13

This Directive is addressed to the Member States.

Council Directive of 19 December 1978 on the exemption from taxes of imports of small consignments of goods of a non-commercial character from third countries

(78/1035/EEC)

Note—This Directive repealed by Council Directive 2006/79/EC art 6, Annex 1, Part A (OJ L 286, 17.10.2006, p 15).

Eighth Council Directive of 6 December 1979 on the harmonisation of the laws of the Member States relating to turnover taxes—arrangements for the refund of value added tax to taxable persons not established in the territory of the country

(79/1072/EEC)

Note—See OJ L331, 27.12.1979, p 11.

Prospective amendment—This Directive to be repealed by Council Directive 2008/9/EC of 12 February 2008, art 28(2) with effect from 1 January 2010. However, provisions of this Directive shall continue to apply to refund applications submitted before 1 January 2010. References to this Directive shall be construed as references to Directive 2008/9/EC except for refund applications submitted before 1 January 2010. See below for the text of Directive 2008/9/EC.

THE COUNCIL OF THE EUROPEAN COMMUNITIES

Having regard to the Treaty establishing the European Economic Community,

Having regard to Sixth Council Directive 77/388/EEC of 17 May 1977 on the harmonisation of the laws of the Member States relating to turnover taxes—Common system of value added tax (uniform basis of assessment) (OJ No L145, 13.6.1977, p 1), and particular Article 17(4) thereof,

Having regard to the proposal from the Commission (OJ No C26, 1.2.1978, p 5),

Having regard to the opinion of the European Parliament (OJ No C39, 12.2.1979, p 14),

Having regard to the opinion of the Economic and Social Committee (OJ No C269, 13.11.1978, p 51),

Whereas, pursuant to Article 17(4) of Directive 77/288/EEC, the Council is to adopt Community rules laying down the arrangements governing refunds of value added tax, referred to in paragraph 3 of the said Article, to taxable persons not established in the territory of the country;

Whereas rules are required to ensure that a taxable person established in the territory of one member country can claim for tax which has been invoiced to him in respect of supplies of goods or services in another Member State or which has been paid in respect of imports into that other Member State, thereby avoiding double taxation;

Whereas discrepancies between the arrangements currently in force in Member States, which give rise in some cases to deflection of trade and distortion of competition, should be eliminated;

Whereas the introduction of Community rules in this field will mark progress towards the effective liberalisation of the movement of persons, goods and services, thereby helping to complete the process of economic integration;

Whereas such rules must not lead to the treatment of taxable persons differing according to the Member State in the territory of which they are established;

Whereas certain forms of tax evasion or avoidance should be prevented;

Whereas, under Article 17(4) of Directive 77/388/EEC, Member States may refuse the refund or impose supplementary conditions in the case of taxable persons not established in the territory of the Community; whereas steps should, however, also be taken to ensure that such taxable persons are not eligible for refunds on more favourable terms than those provided for in respect of Community taxable persons;

Whereas, initially, only the Community arrangements contained in this Directive should be adopted; whereas these arrangements provide, in particular, that decisions in respect of applications for refund should be notified within six months of the date on which such applications were lodged; whereas refunds should be made within the same period; whereas, for a period of one year from the final date laid down for the implementation of these arrangements, the Italian Republic should be authorised to notify the decisions taken by its competent services with regard to applications lodged by taxable persons not established within its territory and to make the relevant refunds within nine months, in order to enable the Italian Republic to reorganise the system at present in operation, with a view to applying the Community system;

Whereas further arrangements will have to be adopted by the Council to supplement the Community system; whereas, until the latter arrangements enter into force, Member States will refund the tax on the services and the purchases of goods which are not covered by this Directive, in accordance with the arrangements which they adopt pursuant to Article 17(4) of Directive 77/388/EEC,

HAS ADOPTED THIS DIRECTIVE:

Article 1

For the purposes of this Directive, 'a taxable person not established in the territory of the country' shall mean a person as referred to in Article 4(1) of Directive 77/388/EEC who, during the period referred to in the first and second sentences of the first sub-paragraph of Article 7(1), has had in that country neither the seat of his economic activity, nor a fixed establishment from which business transactions are effected, nor, if no such seat or fixed establishment exists, his domicile or normal place of residence, and who, during the same period, has supplied no goods or services deemed to have been supplied in that country, with the exception of:

(*a*) transport services and services ancillary thereto, exempted pursuant to Article 14(1)(i), Article 15 or Article 16(1), B, C and D of Directive 77/388/EEC;

(*b*) services provided in cases where tax is payable solely by the person to whom they are supplied, pursuant to Article 21(1)(*b*) of Directive 77/388/EEC.

Article 2

Each Member State shall refund to any taxable person who is not established in the territory of the country but who is established in another Member State, subject to the conditions laid down below, any value added tax charged in respect of services or movable property supplied to him by other taxable persons in the territory of the country or charged in respect of the importation of goods into the country, in so far as such goods and services are used for the purposes of the transactions referred to in Article 17(3)(*a*) and (*b*) of Directive 77/388/EEC and of the provision of services referred to in Article 1(*b*).

Simon's Tax Cases—*Ministre du Budget and Ministre de l'Economie et des Finances v Societe Monte Dei Paschi Di Siena* [2001] STC 1029.

Article 3

To qualify for refund, any taxable person as referred to in Article 2 who supplies no goods or services deemed to be supplied in the territory of the country shall :

(*a*) submit to the competent authority referred to in the first paragraph of Article 9 an application modelled on the specimen contained in Annex A, attaching originals of invoices or import documents. Member States shall make available to applicants an explanatory notice which shall in any event contain the minimum information set out in Annex C;

(*b*) produce evidence, in the form of a certificate issued by the official authority of the State in which he is established, that he is a taxable person for the purposes of value added tax in that State. However, where the competent authority referred to in the first paragraph of Article 9 already has such evidence in its possession, the taxable person shall not be bound to produce new evidence for a period of one year from the date of issue of the first certificate by the official authority of the State in which he is established. Member States shall not issue certificates to any taxable persons who benefit from tax exemption pursuant to Article 24(2) of Directive 77/388/EEC;

(*c*) certify by means of a written declaration that he has supplied no goods or services deemed to have been supplied in the territory of the country during the period referred to in the first and second sentences of the first subparagraph of Article 7(1);

(*d*) undertake to repay any sum collected in error.

Press releases etc—Business Brief 6/94 3-3-94 (refunds from Italy: delay: advice on completion of application form: translation of relevant regulations).

Simon's Tax Cases—art 3(*a*), *Société Général des Grandes Sources d'Eaux Minérales Françaises v Bundesamt für Finanzen* [1998] STC 981.

Art 3(*b*), *Debouche v Inspecteur der Invoerrechten en Accijnzen* (Case C-302/93) [1996] STC 1406; *Planzer Luxembourg Sàrl v Bundeszentralamt für Steuern* [2008] STC 1113.

Article 4

To be eligible for the refund, any taxable person as referred to in Article 2 who has supplied in the territory of the country no goods or services deemed to have been supplied in the country other than the services referred to in Article 1(*a*) and (*b*) shall:

(*a*) satisfy the requirements laid down in Article 3(*a*), (*b*) and (*d*);

(*b*) certify by means of a written declaration that, during the period referred to in the first and second sentences of the first subparagraph of Article 7(1), he has supplied no goods or services deemed to have been supplied in the territory of the country other than services referred to in Article 1(*a*) and (*b*).

Article 5

For the purposes of this Directive, goods and services in respect of which tax may be refundable shall satisfy the conditions laid down in Article 17 of Directive 77/388/EEC as applicable in the Member State of refund.

This Directive shall not apply to supplies of goods which are, or may be, exempted under item 2 of Article 15 of Directive 77/388/EEC.

Simon's Tax Cases—*Debouche v Inspecteur der Invoerrechten en Accijnzen* (Case C-302/93) [1996] STC 1406, *Ministre du Budget and Ministre de l'Economie et des Finances v Societe Monte Dei Paschi Di Siena* [2001] STC 1029.

Article 6

Member States may not impose on the taxable persons referred to in Article 2 any obligation, in addition to those referred to in Articles 3 and 4, other than the obligation to provide, in specific cases, the information necessary to determine whether the application for refund is justified.

Article 7

1. The application for refund provided for in Articles 3 and 4 shall relate to invoiced purchases of goods or services or to imports made during a period of not less than three months or not more than one calendar year. Applications may, however, relate to a period of less than three months where the period represents the remainder of a calendar year. Such applications may also relate to invoices or import documents not covered by previous applications and concerning transactions completed during the calendar year in question. Applications shall be submitted to the competent authority referred to in the first paragraph of Article 9 within six months of the end of the calendar year in which the tax became chargeable.

If the application relates to a period of less than one calendar year but not less than three months, the amount for which application is made may not be less than the equivalent in national currency of 200 European units of account; if the application relates to a period of a calendar year or the remainder of a calendar year, the amount may not be less than the equivalent in national currency of 25 European units of account.

2. The European unit of account used shall be that defined in the Finance Regulation of 21 December 1977 (OJ No L 356, 31.12.1977, p 1), as determined on 1 January of the year of the period referred to in the first and second sentences of the first subparagraph of paragraph 1. Member States may round up or down, by up to 10%, the figures resulting from this conversion into national currency.

3. The competent authority referred to in the first paragraph of Article 9 shall stamp each invoice and/or import document to prevent their use for further application and shall return them within one month.

4. Decisions concerning applications for refund shall be announced within six months of the date when the applications, accompanied by all the necessary documents required under this Directive for examination of the application, are submitted to the competent authority referred to in paragraph 3. Refunds shall be made before the end of the above mentioned period, at the applicant's request, in either the Member State of refund or the State in which he is established. In the latter case, the bank charges for the transfer shall be payable by the applicant.

The grounds for refusal of an application shall be stated. Appeals against such refusals may be made to the competent authorities in the Member State concerned, subject to the same conditions as to form and time limits as those governing claims for refunds made by taxable persons established in the same State.

5. Where a refund has been obtained in a fraudulent or in any other irregular manner, the competent authority referred to in paragraph 3 shall proceed directly to recover the amounts wrongly paid and any penalties imposed, in accordance with the procedure applicable in the Member State concerned, without prejudice to the provisions relating to mutual assistance in the recovery of value added tax.

In the case of fraudulent applications which cannot be made the subject of an administrative penalty, in accordance with national legislation, the Member State concerned may refuse for a maximum period of two years from the date on which the fraudulent application was submitted any further refund to the taxable person concerned. Where an administrative penalty has been imposed but has not been paid, the Member State concerned may suspend any further refund to the taxable person concerned until it has been paid.

[Article 8] [1]

Amendments—Article 8 deleted by art 7 of the Thirteenth Council Directive of 17 November 1986: 86/560/EEC; see OJ L326, 21.11.1986, p 40.

Article 9

Member States shall make known, in an appropriate manner, the competent authority to which the application referred to in Article 3(*a*) and in Article 4(*a*) are to be submitted.

The certificates referred to in Article 3(*b*) and in Article 4(*a*), establishing that the person concerned is a taxable person, shall be modelled on the specimens contained in Annex B.

Simon's Tax Cases—*Planzer Luxembourg Sàrl v Bundeszentralamt für Steuern* [2008] STC 1113.

Article 10

Member States shall bring into force the provisions necessary to comply with this Directive no later than 1 January 1981. This Directive shall apply only to applications for refunds concerning value added tax charged on invoiced purchases of goods or services or in imports made as from that date.

Member States shall communicate to the Commission the texts of the main provisions of national law which they adopt in the field covered by this Directive. The Commission shall inform the other Member States thereof.

Article 11

By a way of derogation from Article 7(4), the Italian Republic may, until 1 January 1982, extend the period referred to in this paragraph from six to nine months.

Article 12

Three years after the date referred to in Article 10, the Commission shall, after consulting the Member States, submit a report to the Council on the application of this Directive, and in particular Articles 3, 4 and 7 thereof.

Article 13

This Directive is addressed to the Member States.

ANNEX A

ANNEX A

SPECIMEN

Is this your first application?
If not, please give tax reference number

Receipt stamp

Competent authority to which the application is addressed ▶

Application for refund of value added tax

by a taxable person not established in the country

(Read the explanatory notes before filling in)

1 Surname and forenames or name of firm of applicant

Street and house number

Postal code, place and country

2 Nature of applicant's business

3 Particulars of the tax office and VAT registration number in the country in which the applicant is established or has his domicile or normal place of residence

4 Period to which the application refers — from month year — to month year

5 Total amount of refund requested (in figures) (see overleaf for itemized list)

6 The applicant requests the refund of the amount shown in 5 in the manner described in 7.

(*) insert X in the appropriate box ▶

7 Method of settlement requested (*) Bank account ☐ Postal account ☐

Account number — Code number of financial body

Account in the name of

Name and address of the financial body

8 Number of documents enclosed: .... Invoices: .... Import documents: ....

9 The applicant hereby declares:

(a) that the goods or services specified overleaf were used for his activities as a taxable person during:

....

....

(b) that in the country in which the refund is being requested, and during the period covered by this application, he engaged in:

(*) insert X in the appropriate box ▶

☐ (*) no supply of goods or services,

☐ (*) only the provision of services in respect of which tax is payable solely by the person to whom they are supplied,

☐ (*) only in the provision of certain exempted transport services and services ancillary thereto;

(c) that the particulars given in this application are true.

The applicant undertakes to pay back any monies wrongfully obtained.

.... on ....
(Place) (Date) (Signature)

SPECIMEN

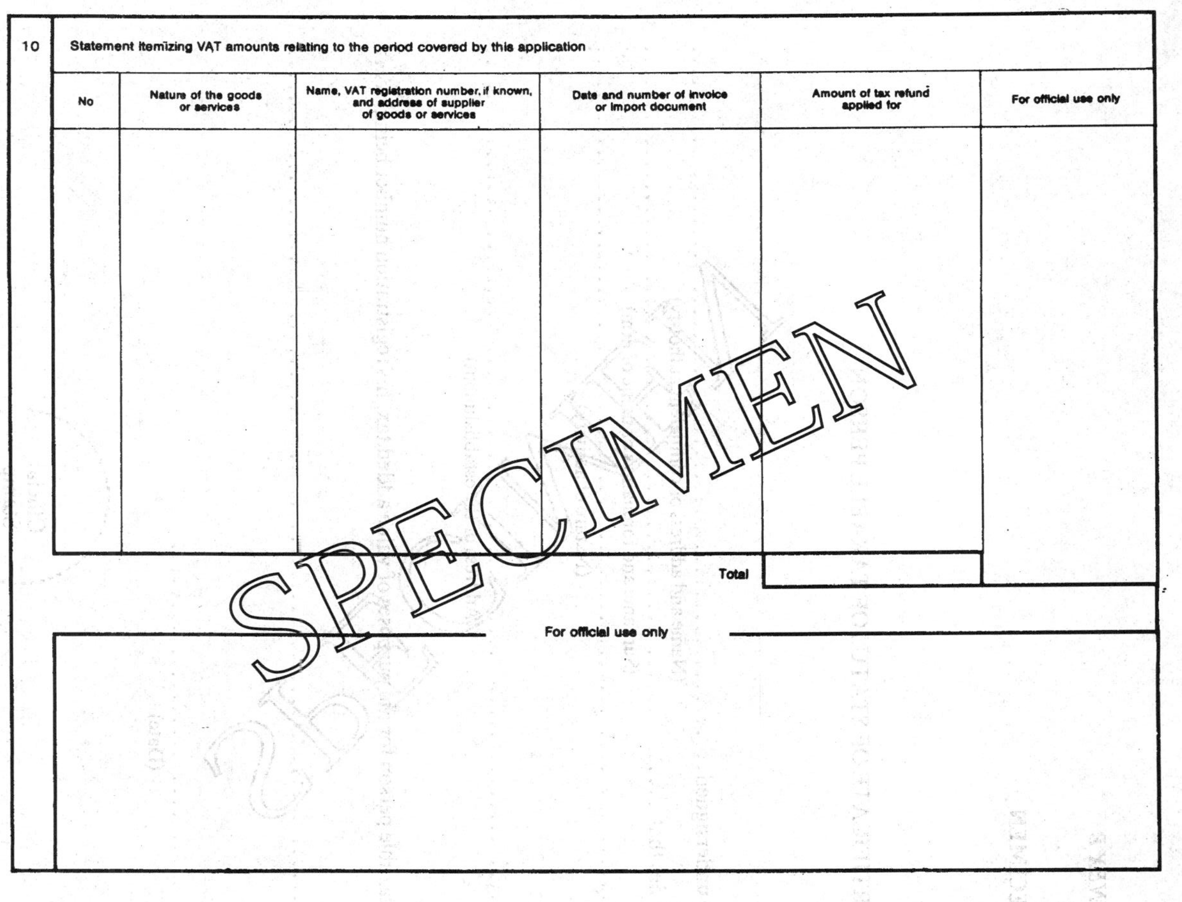

10 Statement itemizing VAT amounts relating to the period covered by this application

No	Nature of the goods or services	Name, VAT registration number, if known, and address of supplier of goods or services	Date and number of invoice or import document	Amount of tax refund applied for	For official use only
			Total		

For official use only

ANNEX B

ANNEX B

SPECIMEN

CERTIFICATE OF STATUS OF TAXABLE PERSON

The undersigned ....
(Name and address of competent authority)

certifies that ....
(Surname and forenames or name of firm)

....
(Nature of activity)

....
(Address of the establishment)

is a taxable person for the purposes of value added tax, his registration number being[1] ....

....

....
(Date)

Official Stamp

....
(Signature, name and grade)

Note.—[1] If the applicant does not have a VAT registration number, the competent authority shall state the reason for this.

ANNEX C

Minimum information to be given in explanatory notes

A. The application shall be drawn up on a form printed in one of the official languages of the European Communities. This form shall, however, be completed in the language of the country of refund.

B. The application shall be completed in block capitals and be submitted, by 30 June of the year following that to which the application relates, to the competent authority of the State to which the application is made (see D below).

C. The VAT registration number in the country of refund shall be given, if it is known to the applicant.

[D. The application shall be submitted to the relevant competent authorities, i e for:

—Belgium:
—Denmark:
—Germany:
—Greece:
—Spain:
—France:
—Ireland:
—Italy:
—Luxembourg:
—the Netherlands:
—Austria:
—Portugal:
—Finland:
—Sweden:
—the United Kingdom:][1]
[—the Czech Republic: Financní úrad pro Prahu 1][2]
[—Estonia: Maksuamet][2]
[—Cyprus: Υπουργειο Οικονομικϖν, Τμημα Τελωνειων, Υπηρεσια ΦΠΑ][2]
[—Latvia: Valsts ienemumu dienesta Lielo nodoklu maksataju parvalde][2]
[—Lithuania: Vilniaus apskrities valstybine mokesčiu inspekcija][2]
[—Hungary: Adó-és Pénzügyi Ellenorzési Hivatal][2]
[—Malta: Id-Dipartiment tat-Taxxa fuq il-Valur Mizÿjud fil-Ministeru tal-Finanzi][2]
[—Poland: Drugi Urzad Skarbowy Warszawa Sródmiescie][2]
[—Slovenia: Davčni urad Ljubljana][2]
[—Slovakia: Danovy úrad Bratislava I][2]
[—Bulgaria: ....;
—Romania: ....][4]

E. The application shall refer to purchases of goods or services invoiced or to imports made during a period of not less than three months or more than one calendar year. However, it may relate to a period of less than three months where this period represents the remainder of a calendar year. Such an application may also relate to invoices or import documents not covered by previous applications and concerning transactions made during the calendar year in question.

F. In 9 (*a*), the applicant shall describe the nature of the activities for which he has acquired the goods or received the services referred to in the application for refund of the tax (e g participation in the International .... Fair, held in .... from .... stand No .... , or international carriage of goods as from .... to .... on ....).

G. The application shall be accompanied by a certificate issued by the official authority of the State in which the applicant is established and which provides evidence that he is a taxable person for the purposes of value added tax in that State. However, where the competent authority referred to in D above already has such evidence in its possession, the applicant shall not be bound to produce new evidence for a period of one year from the date of issue of the first certificate.

H. The application shall be accompanied by the originals of the invoices or import documents showing the amount of value added tax borne by the applicant.

[I. The application may be used for more than one invoice or import document but the total amount of VAT claimed for 19 .... may not be less than:

BEF/LUF ...
DKK ...
DEM ...
GRD ...
PTE ...
FRF ...
IEP ...
ITL ...
NLG ...
ATS ...
ESP ...
FIM ...
SEK ...
GBP ...
[CZK ...][3]
[EEK ...][3]
[CYP ...][3]

[LVL ...][3]
[LTL ...][3]
[HUF ...][3]
[MTL ...][3]
[PLN ...][3]
[SIT ...][3]
[SKK ...][3]
[BGN ...
RON ...[4]]

if the period to which it relates is less than one calendar year but not less than three months or less than:

BEF/LUF ...
DKK ...
DEM ...
GRD ...
PTE ...
FRF ...
IEP ...
ITL ...
NLG ...
ATS ...
ESP ...
FIM ...
SEK ...
GBP ...
[CZK ...][3]
[EEK ...][3]
[CYP ...][3]
[LVL ...][3]
[LTL ...][3]
[HUF ...][3]
[MTL ...][3]
[PLN ...][3]
[SIT ...][3]
[SKK ...][3]
[BGN ...
RON ...][4]

if the period to which it relates is one calendar year or less than three months,][1]

J. Exempted transport services are those carried out in connection with the international carriage of goods, including—subject to certain conditions—transport associated with the transit, export or import of goods.

K. Any refund obtained improperly may render the offender liable to the fines or penalties laid down by the law of the State which has made the refund.

L. The authority in the country of refund reserves the right to make refunds by cheque or money order addressed to the applicant.

Amendments—[1] Points D and I substituted by the Act of Accession of 1994, art 29, Annex I; see OJ L1, 1.1.95, p 213.
[2] Words added to Point D by the 2003 Act of Accession Annex II Chapter 9 para 5(*a*) (OJ L 236; 23.9.2003 p 555).
[3] Words added to Point I by the 2003 Act of Accession Annex II Chapter 9 para 5(*b*), (*c*) (OJ L 236; 23.9.2003 p 555)
[4] Entries added to points D, I by Council Directive 2006/98/EC art 1, Annex Part 4(a)–(c) (OJ L 363, 20.12.2006, p 129).

Council Directive
of 28 March 1983
determining the scope of Article 14(1)(d) of Directive 77/388/EEC as regards exemption from value added tax on the final importation of certain goods

(83/181/EEC)

Note—See OJ L105, 23.4.1983, p.38.
This Directive ceases to have effect on 31 December 1992 as regards relations between member States; see Council Directive 91/680/EEC, art 2(1), *post*.

THE COUNCIL OF THE EUROPEAN COMMUNITIES,

Having regard to the Treaty establishing the European Economic Community, and in particular Articles 99 and 100 thereof,

Having regard to the proposal from the Commission (OJ No C171, 11.7.1980, p 8),

Having regard to the opinion of the European Parliament (OJ No C50, 9.3.1981, p 106),

Having regard to the opinion of the Economic and Social Committee (OJ No C300, 18.11.1980, p 11),

Whereas, pursuant to Article 14(1)(*d*) of Council Directive 77/388/EEC of 17 May 1977 on the harmonisation of the laws of the Member States relating to turnover taxes—Common system of value added tax: uniform basis of assessment (OJ No L145, 13.6.1977, p 1), Member States shall, without prejudice to other Community provisions and under conditions which they shall lay down for the purpose, *inter alia*, of preventing any possible evasion, avoidance or abuse, exempt final importation of goods qualifying for exemption from customs duties other than as provided for in the Common Customs Tariff or which would qualify therefor if they were imported from a third country;

Whereas, in accordance with Article 14(2) of the above mentioned Directive, the Commission is required to submit to the Council proposals designed to lay down Community tax rules clarifying the scope of the exemptions referred to in paragraph 1 of the said Article and detailed rules for their implementation;

Whereas, while it is deemed desirable to achieve the greatest possible degree of uniformity between the system for customs duties and that for value added tax, account should be taken, nevertheless in applying the latter system, of the differences as regards objective and structure between customs duties and value added tax;

Whereas arrangements for value added tax should be introduced that differ according to whether goods are imported from third countries or from other Member States and to the extent necessary to comply with the objectives of tax harmonisation; whereas the exemptions on importation can be granted only on condition that they are not liable to affect the conditions of competition on the home market;

Whereas certain reliefs at present applied in the Member States stem from conventions with third countries or with other Member States which, given their purpose, concern only the signatory Member States; whereas it is not expedient to define at Community level conditions for granting such reliefs; whereas the Member States concerned need merely be authorised to retain them,

HAS ADOPTED THIS DIRECTIVE:

Article 1

1. The scope of the exemptions from value added tax referred to in Article 14(1)(*d*) of Directive 77/388/EEC and the rules for their implementation referred to in Article 14(2) of that Directive shall be defined by this Directive. In accordance with the aforesaid Article, the Member States shall apply the exemptions laid down in this Directive under the conditions fixed by them in order to ensure that such exemptions are correctly and simply applied and to prevent any evasion, avoidance or abuses.

2. For the purposes of this Directive:

(*a*) "imports" means imports as defined in Article 7 of 77/388/EEC and the entry for home use after being subject to one of the systems provided for in Article 16(1)(A) of the said Directive or a system of temporary admission or transit;
(*b*) "personal property" means any property intended for the personal use of the persons concerned or for meeting their households needs.

The following, in particular, shall constitute "personal property":

—household effects,
—cycles and motor-cycles, private motor vehicles and their trailers, camping caravans, pleasure craft and private aeroplanes.

Household provisions appropriate to normal family requirements, household pets and saddle animals shall also constitute "personal property".

The nature or quantity of personal property shall not reflect any commercial interest, nor shall they be intended for an economic activity within the meaning of Article 4 of Directive 77/388/EEC. However, portable instruments of the applied or liberal arts, required by the person concerned for the pursuit of his trade or profession, shall also constitute personal property;

(*c*) "household effects" means personal effects, household linen and furnishings and items of equipment intended for the personal use of the persons concerned or for meeting their household needs;
(*d*) "alcoholic products" means products (beer, wine, aperitifs with a wine or alcohol base, brandies, liqueurs and spirituous beverages, etc) falling within heading Nos [2203][1] to [2208][1] of the Common Customs Tariff;
(*e*) "Community" means the territory of the Member States where Directive 77/388/EEC applies.

Amendment—[1] Figures in art 1(2)(*d*) substituted by art 1 of Commission Directive of 7 March 1989: 89/219/EEC; see OJ L92, 5.4.1989, p 13.

TITLE I
IMPORTATION OF PERSONAL PROPERTY BELONGING TO INDIVIDUALS COMING FROM COUNTRIES SITUATED OUTSIDE THE COMMUNITY

CHAPTER I

Personal property of natural persons transferring their normal place of residence from a third country to the Community

Article 2

Subject to Articles 3 to 10, exemption from VAT on importation shall be granted on personal property imported by natural persons transferring from their normal place of residence from outside the Community to a Member State of the Community.

Article 3

Exemption shall be limited to personal property which:

(*a*) except in special cases justified by the circumstances, has been in the possession of and, in the case of non-consumable goods, used by the person concerned at his former normal place of residence for a minimum of six months before the date on which he ceases to have his normal place of residence outside the Community;

(*b*) is intended to be used for the same purpose at his new normal place of residence.

The Member States may in addition make exemption conditional upon such property having borne either in the country of origin or in the country of departure, the customs and/or fiscal charges to which it is normally liable.

Article 4

Exemption may be granted only to persons whose normal place of residence has been outside the Community for a continuous period of at least 12 months.

However, the competent authorities may grant exceptions to this rule provided that the intention of the person concerned was clearly to reside outside the Community for a continuous period of at least 12 months.

Article 5

Exemption shall not be granted in respect of:

(*a*) alcoholic products;

(*b*) tobacco or tobacco products;

(*c*) commercial means of transport;

(*d*) articles for use in the exercise of a trade or profession, other than portable instruments of the applied or liberal arts.

Vehicles intended for mixed use for commercial or professional purposes may also be excluded from exemption.

Article 6

Except in special cases, exemption shall be granted only in respect of personal property entered for permanent importation within 12 months of the date of establishment, by the person concerned, of his normal place of residence in the Member State of importation.

The personal property may be imported in several separate consignments within the period referred to in the preceding paragraph.

Article 7

1. Until 12 months have elapsed from the date of the declaration for its final importation, personal property which has been imported exempt from tax may not be lent, given as security, hired out or transferred, whether for a consideration or free of charge, without prior notification to the competent authorities.

2. Any loan, giving as security, hiring out or transfer before the expiry of the period referred to in paragraph 1 shall entail payment of the relevant value added tax on the goods concerned, at the rate applying on the date of such loan, giving as security, hiring out or transfer, on the basis of the type of goods and the customs value ascertained or accepted on that date by the competent authorities.

Article 8

1. By way of derogation from the first paragraph of Article 6, exemption may be granted in respect of personal property permanently imported before the person concerned establishes his normal place of residence in the Member State of importation, provided that he undertakes

actually to establish his normal place of residence there within a period of six months. Such undertaking shall be accompanied by a security, the form and amount of which shall be determined by the competent authorities.

2. Where use is made of the provisions of paragraph 1, the period laid down in Article 3 shall be calculated from the date of importation into the Member State concerned.

Article 9

1. Where, owing to occupational commitments, the person concerned leaves the country situated outside the Community where he had his normal place of residence without simultaneously establishing his normal place of residence in the territory of a Member State, although having the intention of ultimately doing so, the competent authorities may authorise exemption in respect of the personal property which he transfers into the said territory for this purpose.

2. Exemption in respect of the personal property referred to in paragraph 1 shall be granted in accordance with the conditions laid down in Articles 2 to 7, on the understanding that:

(*a*) the periods laid down in Article 3(*a*) and the first paragraph of Article 6 shall be calculated from the date of importation;

(*b*) the period referred to in Article 7(1) shall be calculated from the day when the person concerned actually establishes his normal place of residence in the territory of a Member State.

3. Exemption shall also be subject to an undertaking from the person concerned that he will actually establish his normal place of residence in the territory of a Member State within a period laid down by the competent authorities in keeping with the circumstances. The latter may require this undertaking to be accompanied by a security, the form and amount of which they shall determine.

Article 10

The competent authorities may derogate from Article 3(*a*) and (*b*), 5(*c*) and (*d*) and 7 when a person has to transfer his normal place of residence from a country situated outside the Community to the territory of a Member State as a result of exceptional political circumstances.

CHAPTER II

Goods imported on the occasion of a marriage

Article 11

1. Subject to Articles 12 to 15, exemption shall be granted in respect of trousseaux and household effects, whether or not new, belonging to a person transferring his or her normal place of residence from a country outside the Community to the territory of a Member State on the occasion of his or her marriage.

[2. Exemption shall also be granted in respect of presents customarily given on the occasion of a marriage which are received by a person fulfilling the conditions laid down in paragraph 1 from persons having their normal place of residence in a country situated outside the Community. The exemption shall apply to presents of a unit value of not more than 200 ECU. Member States may, however, grant exemption for more than 200 ECU provided that the value of each exempt present does not exceed 1 000 ECU.][1]

3. The Member State may make exemption of the goods referred to in paragraph 1 conditional on their having borne, either in the country of origin or in the country of departure, the customs and/or fiscal charges to which they are normally liable.

Amendments—[1] Para (2) substituted by art 1(1) of the Council Directive of 13 June 1988: 88/331/EEC; see OJ L151, 17.6.88, p 79.

Article 12

1. The exemption referred to in Article 11 may be granted only to persons:

(*a*) whose normal place of residence has been outside the Community for a continuous period of at least 12 months. However, derogations from this rule may be granted provided that the intention of the person concerned was clearly to reside outside the Community for a continuous period of at least 12 months;

(*b*) who produce evidence of their marriage.

Article 13

No exemption shall be granted for alcoholic products, tobacco or tobacco products.

Article 14

1. Save in exceptional circumstances, exemption shall be granted only in respect of goods permanently imported:

—not earlier than two months before the date fixed for the wedding (in this case exemption may be made subject to the lodging of appropriate security, the form and amount of which shall be determined by the competent authorities), and

—not later than four months after the date of the wedding.

2. Goods referred to in Article 11 may be imported in several separate consignments within the period referred to in paragraph 1.

Article 15

1. Until 12 months have elapsed from the date of the declaration for their final importation, goods which have been imported exempt from tax may not be lent, given as security, hired out or transferred, whether for a consideration or free of charge, without prior notification to the competent authorities.

2. Any loan, giving as security, hiring out or transfer before the expiry of the period referred to in paragraph 1 shall entail payment of the relevant value added tax on the goods concerned, at the rate applying on the date of such loan, giving as security, hiring out or transfer, on the basis of the type of goods and the value ascertained or accepted on that date by the competent authorities.

CHAPTER III

Personal property acquired by inheritance

Article 16

Subject to Articles 17 to 19, exemption shall be granted in respect of personal property acquired by inheritance by a natural person having his normal place of residence in a Member State.

Article 17

Exemption shall not be granted in respect of:

(*a*) alcoholic products;
(*b*) tobacco or tobacco products;
(*c*) commercial means of transport;
(*d*) articles for use in the exercise of a trade or profession, other than portable instruments of the applied or liberal arts, which were required for the exercise of the trade or profession of the deceased;
(*e*) stocks of raw materials and finished or semi-finished products;
(*f*) livestock and stocks of agricultural products exceeding the quantities appropriate to normal family requirements.

Article 18

1. Exemption shall be granted only in respect of personal property permanently imported not later than two years from the date on which the person becomes entitled to the goods (final settlement of the inheritance).

However, this period may be extended by the competent authorities on special grounds.

2. The goods may be imported in several separate consignments within the period referred to in paragraph 1.

Article 19

Articles 16 to 18 shall apply *mutatis mutandis* to personal property acquired by inheritance by legal persons engaged in a non-profitmaking activity who are established in the territory of a Member State.

TITLE II

SCHOOL OUTFITS, SCHOLASTIC MATERIALS AND OTHER SCHOLASTIC HOUSEHOLD EFFECTS

Article 20

1. Exemption shall be granted in respect of outfits, scholastic materials and household effects representing the usual furnishings for a student's room and belonging to pupils or students coming to stay in a Member State for the purposes of studying there and intended for their personal use during the period of their studies.

2. For the purposes of this Article:

(*a*) pupil or student means any person enrolled in an educational establishment in order to attend full-time the courses offered therein;
(*b*) outfit means underwear and household linen as well as clothing, whether or not new;
(*c*) scholastic materials means articles and instruments (including calculators and typewriters) normally used by pupils or students for the purposes of their studies.

Article 21

Exemption shall be granted at least once per school year.

TITLE III
IMPORTS OF NEGLIGIBLE VALUE

[Article 22

Goods of a total value not exceeding 10 ECU shall be exempt on admission. Member States may grant exemption for imported goods of a total value of more than 10 ECU but not exceeding 22 ECU. However, Member States may exclude goods which have been imported on mail order from the exemption provided for in the first sentence of the first subparagraph.][1]

Amendments—[1] This art substituted by art 1 of the Council Directive of 13 June 1988: 88/331/EEC; see OJ L151, 17.6.88, p.79.

Article 23

Exemption shall not apply to the following:

(*a*) alcoholic products;
(*b*) perfumes and toilet water;
(*c*) tobacco or tobacco products.

TITLE IV
CAPITAL GOODS AND OTHER EQUIPMENT IMPORTED ON THE TRANSFER OF ACTIVITIES

Article 24

1. Without prejudice to the measures in force in the Member State with regard to industrial and commercial policy, and subject to Articles 25 to 28, Member States may allow exemption, on admission, for imports of capital goods and other equipment belonging to undertakings which definitively cease their activity in the country of departure in order to carry on a similar activity in the Member State into which the goods are imported and which, in accordance with Article 22(1) of Directive 77/388/EEC, have given advance notice to the competent authorities of the Member State of importation of the commencement of such activity.

Where the undertaking transferred is an agricultural holding, its livestock shall also be exempt on admission.

2. For the purposes of paragraph 1:

— "activity" means an economic activity as referred to in Article 4 of Directive 77/388/EEC,
— "undertaking" means an independent economic unit of production or of the service industry.

Article 25

1. The exemption referred to in Article 24 shall be limited to capital goods and equipment which:

(*a*) except in special cases justified by the circumstances, have actually been used in the undertaking for a minimum of 12 months prior to the date on which the undertaking ceased to operate in the country of departure;
(*b*) are intended to be used for the same purposes after the transfer;
(*c*) are to be used for the purposes of an activity not exempted under Article 13 of Directive 77/388/EEC;
(*d*) are appropriate to the nature and size of the undertaking in question.

2. However, Member States may exempt capital goods and equipment imported from another Member State by charitable or philanthropic organisations at the time of the transfer of their principal place of business to the Member State of importation.

Such exemption, shall, however, be granted only on condition that at the time when they were acquired the capital goods and equipment in question were not exempt under Article 15(12) of Directive 77/388/EEC.

3. Pending entry into force of the common rules referred to in the first subparagraph of Article 17(6) of Directive 77/388/EEC, Member States may exclude from the exemption, in whole or in part, capital goods in respect of which they have availed themselves of the second subparagraph of that paragraph.

Article 26

No exemption shall be granted to undertakings established outside the Community and the transfer of which into the territory of a Member State is consequent upon or is for the purpose of merging with, or being absorbed by, an undertaking established in the Community, without a new activity being set up.

Article 27

No exemption shall be granted for:

(*a*) means of transport which are not of the nature of instruments of production or of the service industry;
(*b*) supplies of all kinds intended for human consumption or for animal feed;
(*c*) fuel and stocks of raw materials or finished or semi-finished products;
(*d*) livestock in the possession of dealers.

Article 28
Except in special cases justified by the circumstances, the exemption referred to in Article 24 shall be granted only in respect of capital goods and other equipment imported before the expiry of a period of 12 months from the date when the undertaking ceased its activities in the country of departure.

TITLE V
IMPORTATION OF CERTAIN AGRICULTURAL PRODUCTS AND PRODUCTS INTENDED FOR AGRICULTURAL USE

CHAPTER I

Products obtained by Community farmers on properties located in a State other than the State of importation

Article 29
1. Subject to Articles 30 and 31, agricultural, stock-farming, bee-keeping, horticultural and forestry products from properties located in a country adjoining the territory of the Member State of importation which are operated by agricultural producers having their principal undertaking in that Member State and adjacent to the country concerned shall be exempt on admission.
2. To be eligible under paragraph 1, stock-farming products must be obtained from animals reared, acquired or imported in accordance with the general tax arrangements applicable in the Member State of importation.
3. Pure-bred horses, not more than six months old and born outside the Member State of importation of an animal covered in that State and then exported temporarily to give birth, shall be exempt on admission.

Article 30
Exemption shall be limited to products which have not undergone any treatment other than that which normally follows their harvest or production.

Article 31
Exemption shall be granted only in respect of products imported by the agricultural producer or on his behalf.

Article 32
This Chapter shall apply *mutatis mutandis* to the products of fishing or fish-farming activities carried out in the lakes or waterways bordering the territory of the Member State of importation by fishermen established in that Member State and to the products of hunting activities carried out on such lakes or waterways by sportsmen established in that Member State.

CHAPTER II

Seeds, fertilisers and products for the treatment of soil and crops

Article 33
Subject to Article 34, seeds, fertilisers and products for the treatment of soil and crops, intended for use on property located in a Member State adjoining a country situated outside the Community or another Member State and operated by agricultural producers having their principal undertaking in the said country situated outside the Community or Member State adjacent to the territory of the Member State of importation shall be exempt on admission.

Article 34
1. Exemption shall be limited to the quantities of seeds, fertilisers or other products required for the purpose of operating the property.
2. It shall be granted only for seeds, fertilisers or other products introduced directly into the importing Member State by the agricultural producer or on his behalf.
3. Member States may make exemption conditional upon the granting of reciprocal treatment.

TITLE VI
IMPORTATION OF THERAPEUTIC SUBSTANCES, MEDICINES, LABORATORY ANIMALS AND BIOLOGICAL OR CHEMICAL SUBSTANCES

CHAPTER I

Laboratory animals and biological or chemical substances intended for research

Article 35

1. The following shall be exempt on admission:

(*a*) animals specially prepared and sent free of charge for laboratory use;

(*b*) biological or chemical substances;

—which are imported free of charge from the territory of another Member State, or

—which are imported from countries outside the Community subject to the limits and conditions laid down in [Article 60][1] of Council Regulation (EEC) No 918/83 of 28 March 1983 setting up a community system of reliefs from customs duty.

2. The exemption referred to in paragraph 1 shall be limited to animals and biological or chemical substances which are intended for:

—either public establishments principally engaged in education or scientific research, including those departments of public establishments which are principally engaged in education or scientific research,

—or private establishments principally engaged in education or scientific research and authorised by the competent authorities of the Member States to receive such articles exempt from tax.

Amendments—[1] Words in para (1)(*b*) substituted by art 1 of the Council Directive of 13 June 1988: 88/331/EEC; see OJ L151, 17.6.88, p.79.

CHAPTER II

Therapeutic substances of human origin and blood-grouping and tissue-typing reagents

Article 36

1. Without prejudice to the exemption provided for in Article 14(1)(*a*) of Directive 77/2388/EEC and subject to Article 37, the following shall be exempted:

(*a*) therapeutic substances of human origin;

(*b*) blood-grouping reagents;

(*c*) tissue-typing reagents.

2. For the purposes of paragraph 1:

— "therapeutic substances of human origin" means human blood and its derivatives (whole human blood, dried human plasma, human albumin and fixed solutions of human plasma protein, human immunoglobulin and human fibrinogen),

— "Blood-grouping reagents" means all reagents, whether of human, animal, plant or other origin used for blood-type grouping and for the detection of blood incompatibilities,

— "tissue-typing reagents" means all reagents whether of human, animal, plant or other origin used for the determination of human tissue-types.

Article 37

Exemption shall be limited to products which:

(*a*) are intended for institutions or laboratories approved by the competent authorities, for use exclusively for non-commercial medical or scientific purposes;

(*b*) are accompanied by a certificate of conformity issued by a duly authorised body in the country of departure;

(*c*) are in containers bearing a special label identifying them.

Article 38

Exemption shall include the special packaging essential for the transport of therapeutic substances of human origin or blood-grouping or tissue-typing reagents and also any solvents and accessories needed for their use which may be included in the consignments.

[CHAPTER IIA

Reference substances for the quality control of medical products

Article 38a

Consignments which contain samples of reference substances approved by the World Health Organisation for the quality control of materials used in the manufacture of medicinal products and which are addressed to consignees authorised by the competent authorities of the Member States to receive such consignments free of tax shall be exempt on admission.][1]

Amendments—[1] This chapter inserted by art 1(4) of the Council Directive of 13 June 1988: 88/331/EEC; see OJ L151, 17.6.88, p 79.

CHAPTER III

Pharmaceutical products used at international sports events

Article 39

Pharmaceutical products for human or veterinary medical use by persons or animals participating in international sports events shall, within the limits necessary to meet their requirements during their stay in the Member State of importation, be exempt on admission.

TITLE VII
GOODS FOR CHARITABLE OR PHILANTHROPIC ORGANISATIONS

Article 40

Member States may impose a limit on the quantity or value of the goods referred to in Articles 41 to 55, in order to remedy any abuse and to combat major distortions of competition.

CHAPTER I

Goods imported for general purposes

Article 41

1. Subject to Articles 42 to 44, the following shall be exempt on admission:

(*a*) basic necessities obtained free of charge and imported by State organisations or other charitable or philanthropic organisations, approved by the competent authorities for distribution free of charge to needy persons;

(*b*) goods of every description sent free of charge, by a person or organisation established in a country other than the Member State of importation, and without any commercial intent on the part of the sender, to State organisations or other charitable or philanthropic organisations approved by the competent authorities, to be used for fund-raising at occasional charity events for the benefit of needy persons;

(*c*) equipment and office materials sent free of charge, by a person or organisation established in a country other than the Member State of importation, and without any commercial intent on the part of the sender, to charitable or philanthropic organisations approved by the competent authorities, to be used solely for the purposes of meeting their operating needs or carrying out their stated charitable or philanthropic aims.

2. For the purposes of paragraph 1(*a*) "basic necessities" means those goods required to meet the immediate needs of human beings, e g food, medicine, clothing and bed-clothes.

Article 42

Exemption shall not be granted in respect of:

(*a*) alcoholic products;
(*b*) tobacco or tobacco products;
(*c*) coffee and tea;
(*d*) motor vehicles other than ambulances.

Article 43

Exemption shall be granted only to organisations accounting procedures of which enable the competent authorities to supervise their operations and which offer all the guarantees considered necessary.

Article 44

1. Exempt goods may not be put out by the organisation entitled to exemption for loan, hiring out or transfer, whether for a consideration or free of charge, for purposes other than those laid down in Article 41(*a*) and (*b*), unless the competent authorities have been informed thereof in advance.

2. Should goods and equipment be lent, hired out or transferred to an organisation entitled to benefit from exemption pursuant to Articles 41 and 43, the exemption shall continue to be granted provided that the latter uses the goods and equipment for purposes which confer the right to such exemption.

In other cases, loan, hiring out or transfer shall be subject to prior payment of value added tax at the rate applying on the date of the loan, hiring out or transfer, on the basis of the type of goods and equipment and the value ascertained or accepted on that date by the competent authorities.

Article 45

1. Organisations referred to in Article 41 which cease to fulfil the conditions giving entitlement to exemption, or which are proposing to use goods and equipment exempt on admission for purposes other than those provided for by that Article, shall so inform the competent authorities.

2. Goods remaining in the possession of organisations which cease to fulfil the conditions giving entitlement to exemption shall be liable to the relevant import value added tax at the rate applying on the date on which those conditions cease to be fulfilled, on the basis of the type of goods and equipment and the value as ascertained or accepted on that date by the competent authorities.

3. Goods used by the organisation benefiting from the exemption for purposes other than those provided for in Article 41 shall be liable to the relevant import value added tax at the rate applying on the date on which they are put to another use on the basis of the type of goods and equipment and the value as ascertained on that date by the competent authorities.

CHAPTER II

Articles imported for the benefit of handicapped persons

Article 46

1. Articles specially designed for the education, employment or social advancement of blind or other physically or mentally handicapped persons shall be exempt on admission where:

(*a*) they are imported by institutions or organisations that are principally engaged in the education of or the provision of assistance to handicapped persons and are authorised by the competent authorities of the Member States to receive such articles exempt from tax; and

(*b*) they are donated to such institutions or organisations free of charge and with no commercial intent on the part of the donor.

2. Exemption shall apply to specific spare parts, components or accessories specifically for the articles in question and to the tools to be used for the maintenance, checking, calibration and repair of the said articles, provided that such spare parts, components, accessories or tools are imported at the same time as the said articles or, if imported subsequently, that they can be identified as being intended for articles previously exempt on admission or which would be eligible to be so exempt at the time when such entry is requested for the specific spare parts, components or accessories and tools in question.

3. Articles exempt on admission may not be used for purposes other than the education, employment or social advancement of blind or other handicapped persons.

Article 47

1. Goods exempt on admission may be lent, hired out or transferred, whether for a consideration or free of charge, by the beneficiary institutions or organisations on a non-profitmaking basis to the persons referred to in Article 46 with whom they are concerned, without payment of value added tax on importation.

2. No loan, hiring out or transfer may be effected under conditions other than those provided for in paragraph 1 unless the competent authorities have first been informed.

Should an article be lent, hired out or transferred to an institution or organisation itself entitled to benefit from this exemption, the exemption shall continue to be granted, provided the latter uses the article for purposes which confer the right to such exemption.

In other cases, loan, hiring out or transfer shall be subject to prior payment of value added tax, at the rate applying on the date of the loan, hiring out or transfer, on the basis of the type of goods and the value ascertained or accepted on that date by the competent authorities.

Article 48

1. Institutions or organisations referred to in Article 46 which cease to fulfil the conditions giving entitlement to exemption, or which are proposing to use articles exempt on admission for purposes other than those provided for by that Article shall so inform the competent authorities.

2. Articles remaining in the possession of institutions or organisations which cease to fulfil the conditions giving entitlement to exemption shall be liable to the relevant import value added tax at the rate applying on the date on which those conditions cease to be fulfilled, on the basis of the type of goods and the value ascertained or accepted on that date by the competent authorities.

3. Articles used by the institution or organisation benefiting from the exemption for purposes other than those provided for in Article 46 shall be liable to the relevant import value added tax at the rate applying on the date on which they are put to another use on the basis of the type of goods and the value ascertained or accepted on that date by the competent authorities.

CHAPTER III

Goods imported for the benefit of disaster victims

Article 49

1. Subject to Articles 50 to 55, goods imported by State organisations or other charitable or philanthropic organisations approved by the competent authorities shall be exempt on admission where they are intended:

(*a*) for distribution free of charge to victims of disasters affecting the territory of one or more Member States; or

(*b*) to be made available free of charge to the victims of such disasters, while remaining the property of the organisations in questions.

2. Goods imported by disaster-relief agencies in order to meet their needs during the period of their activity shall also benefit upon admission from the exemption referred to in paragraph 1 under the same conditions.

Article 50

No exemption shall be granted for materials and equipment intended for rebuilding disaster areas.

Article 51

Granting of the exemption shall be subject to a decision by the Commission, acting at the request of the Member State or States concerned in accordance with an emergency procedure entailing the consultation of the other Member States. This decision shall, where necessary, lay down the scope and the conditions of the exemption.

Pending notification of the Commission's decision, Member States affected by a disaster may authorise the suspension of any import value added tax chargeable on goods imported for the purposes described in Article 49, subject to an undertaking by the importing organisation to pay such tax if exemption is not granted.

Article 52

Exemption shall be granted only to organisations the accounting procedures of which enable the competent authorities to supervise their operations and which offer all the guarantees considered necessary.

Article 53

1. The organisations benefiting from the exemption may not lend, hire out or transfer, whether for a consideration or free of charge, the goods referred to in Article 49(1) under conditions other than those laid down in that Article without prior notification thereof to the competent authorities.

2. Should goods be lent, hired out or transferred to an organisation itself entitled to benefit from exemption pursuant to Article 49, the exemption shall continue to be granted, provided the latter uses the goods for purposes which confer the right to such exemption.

In other cases, loan, hiring out or transfer shall be subject to prior payment of value added tax, at the rate applying on the date of the loan, hiring out or transfer, on the basis of the type of goods and the value ascertained or accepted on that date by the competent authorities.

Article 54

1. The goods referred to in Article 49(1)(*b*), after they cease to be used by disaster victims, may not be lent, hired out or transferred, whether for a consideration or free of charge, unless the competent authorities are notified in advance.

2. Should goods be lent, hired out or transferred to an organisation itself entitled to benefit from exemption pursuant to Article 49 or, if appropriate, to an organisation entitled to benefit from exemption pursuant to Article 41(1)(*a*), the exemption shall continue to be granted, provided such organisations use them for purposes which confer the right to such exemption.

In other cases, loan, hiring out or transfer shall be subject to prior payment of value added tax, at the rate applying on the date of the loan, hiring out or transfer, on the basis of the type of goods and the value ascertained or accepted on that date by the competent authorities.

Article 55

1. Organisations referred to in Article 49 which cease to fulfil the conditions giving entitlement to exemption, or which are proposing to use the goods exempt on admission for purposes other than those provided for by that Article shall so inform the competent authorities.

2. In the case of goods remaining in the possession of organisations which cease to fulfil the conditions giving entitlement to exemption, when these are transferred to an organisation itself entitled to benefit from exemption pursuant to this chapter or, if appropriate, to an organisation entitled to benefit from exemption pursuant to Article 41, the exemption shall continue to be granted, provided the organisation uses the goods in question for purposes which confer the

right to such exemptions. In other cases, the goods shall be liable to the relevant import value added tax at the rate applying on the date on which those conditions cease to be fulfilled, on the basis of the type of goods and the value ascertained or accepted on that date by the competent authorities.

3. Goods used by the organisation benefiting from the exemption for purposes other than those provided for in this chapter shall be liable to the relevant import value added tax at the rate applying on the date on which they are put to another use, on the basis of the type of goods and the value ascertained or accepted on that date by the competent authorities.

TITLE VIII
IMPORTATION IN THE CONTEXT OF CERTAIN ASPECTS OF INTERNATIONAL RELATIONS

CHAPTER I

Honorary decorations or awards

Article 56

On production of satisfactory evidence to the competent authorities by the persons concerned, and provided the operations involved are not in any way of a commercial character, exemption shall be granted in respect of:

(*a*) decorations conferred by the government of a country other than the Member State of importation on persons whose normal place of residence is in the latter State;

(*b*) cups, medals and similar articles of an essentially symbolic nature which, having been awarded in a country other than the Member State of importation to persons having their normal place of residence in the latter State as a tribute to their activities in fields such as the arts, the sciences, sport or the public service or in recognition of merit at a particular event, are imported by such persons themselves;

(*c*) cups, medals and similar articles of an essentially symbolic nature which are given free of charge by authorities or persons established in a country other than the Member State of importation, to be presented in the territory of the latter State for the same purposes as those referred to in (*b*).

[(*d*) Awards, trophies and souvenirs of a symbolic nature and of limited value intended for distribution free of charge to persons normally resident in a country other than that of import, at business conferences or similar international events; their nature, unitary value or other features, must not be such as might indicate that they are intended for commercial purposes.][1]

Amendments—[1] Para (*d*) inserted by art 1(5) of the Council Directive of 13 June 1988: 88/331/EEC; see OJ L151, 17.6.88, p 79.

CHAPTER II

Presents received in the context of international relations

Article 57

Without prejudice, where relevant, to the provisions applicable to the international movement of travellers, and subject to Articles 58 and 59, exemption shall be granted in respect of goods:

(*a*) imported by persons who have paid an official visit in a country other than that of their normal residence and who have received such goods on that occasion as gifts from the host authorities;

(*b*) imported by persons coming to pay an official visit in the Member State of importation and who intend to offer them on that occasion as gifts to the host authorities;

(*c*) sent as gifts, in token of friendship or goodwill, by an official body, public authority or group carrying on an activity in the public interest which is located in a country other than the Member State of importation, to an official body, public authority or group carrying on an activity in the public interest which is located in the Member State of importation and approved by the competent authorities to receive such goods exempt from tax.

Article 58

No exemption shall be granted for alcoholic products, tobacco or tobacco products.

Article 59

Exemption shall be granted only:

—where the articles intended as gifts are offered on an occasional basis,

—where they do not, by their nature, value or quantity, reflect any commercial interest,

—if they are not used for commercial purposes.

CHAPTER III

Goods to be used by monarchs or heads of State

Article 60

Exemption from tax, within the limits and under the conditions laid down by the competent authorities, shall be granted in respect of:

(*a*) gifts to reigning monarchs and heads of State;

(*b*) goods to be used or consumed by reigning monarchs and heads of State of another State, or by persons officially representing them, during their official stay in the Member State of importation. However, exemption may be made subject, by the Member State of importation, to reciprocal treatment.

The provisions of the preceding subparagraph are also applicable to persons enjoying prerogatives at international level analogous to those enjoyed by reigning monarchs or heads of State.

TITLE IX
IMPORTATION OF GOODS FOR THE PROMOTION OF TRADE

CHAPTER I

Samples of negligible value

Article 61

1. Without prejudice to Article 65(1)(*a*), samples of goods which are of negligible value and which can be used only to solicit orders for goods of the type they represent shall be exempt on admission.

2. The competent authorities may require that certain articles, to qualify for exemption on admission, be rendered permanently unusable by being torn, perforated, or clearly and indelibly marked, or by any other process, provided such operation does not destroy their character as samples.

For the purposes of paragraph 1, "samples of goods" means any article representing a type of goods whose manner of presentation and quantity, for goods of the same type or quality, rule out its use for any purpose other than that of seeking orders.

CHAPTER II

Printed matter and advertising material

[Article 62] [1]

[Subject to Article 63, printed advertising matter such as catalogues, price lists, directions for use or brochures shall be exempt on admission provided that they relate to:

(*a*) goods for sale or hire by a person established outside the Member State of import, or

(*b*) services offered by a person established in another Member State, or

(*c*) transport, commercial insurance or banking services offered by a person established in a third country.][1]

Amendments—[1] This art substituted by art 1 of the Council Directive of 13 June 1988: 88/331/EEC; see OJ L151, 17.6.88, p 79.

[Article 63] [1]

[The exemption referred to in Article 62 shall be limited to printed advertisements which fulfil the following conditions:

(*a*) printed matter must clearly display the name of the undertaking which produces, sells or hires out the goods, or which offers the services to which it refers;

(*b*) each consignment must contain no more than one document or a single copy of each document if it is made up of several documents. Consignments comprising several copies of the same document may nevertheless be granted exemption provided their total gross weight does not exceed one kilogram;

(*c*) printed matter must not be the subject of grouped consignments from the same consignor to the same consignee.

However, the conditions under (*b*) and (*c*) shall not apply to printed matter relating to either goods for sale or hire or services offered by a person established in another Member State provided that the printed matter has been imported, and will be distributed, free of charge.][1]

Amendments—[1] This art substituted by art 1(6) of the Council Directive of 13 June 1988: 88/331/EEC; see OJ L151, 17.6.88, p 79.

Article 64

Articles for advertising purposes, of no intrinsic commercial value, sent free of charge by suppliers to their customers which, apart from their advertising function, are not capable of being used shall also be exempt on admission.

CHAPTER III

Goods used or consumed at a trade fair or similar event

Article 65

1. Subject to Articles 66 to 69, the following shall be exempt on admission:

(*a*) small representative samples of goods intended for a trade fair or similar event;

(*b*) goods imported solely in order to be demonstrated or in order to demonstrate machines and apparatus displayed at a trade fair or similar event;

(*c*) various materials of little value, such as paints, varnishes and wallpaper, which are to be used in the building, fitting-out and decoration of temporary stands at a trade fair or similar event, which are destroyed by being used;

(*d*) printed matter, catalogues, prospectuses, price lists, advertising posters, calendars, whether or not illustrated, unframed photographs and other articles supplied free of charge in order to advertise goods displayed at a trade fair or similar event.

2. For the purposes of paragraph 1, "trade fair or similar event" means:

(*a*) exhibitions, fairs, shows and similar events connected with trade, industry, agriculture or handicrafts;

(*b*) exhibitions and events held mainly for charitable reasons;

(*c*) exhibitions and events held mainly for scientific, technical, handicraft, artistic, educational or cultural or sporting reasons, for religious reasons or for reasons of worship, trade union activity or tourism, or in order to promote international understanding;

(*d*) meetings of representatives of international organisations or collective bodies;

(*e*) official or commemorative ceremonies and gatherings;

but not exhibitions staged for private purposes in commercial stores or premises to sell goods.

Article 66

The exemption referred to in Article 65(1)(*a*) shall be limited to samples which:

(*a*) are imported free of charge as such or are obtained at the exhibition from goods imported in bulk;

(*b*) are exclusively distributed free of charge to the public at the exhibition for use or consumption by the persons to whom they have been offered;

(*c*) are identifiable as advertising samples of low unitary value;

(*d*) are not easily marketable and, where appropriate, are packaged in such a way that the quantity of the item involved is lower than the smallest quantity of the same item actually sold on the market;

(*e*) in the case of foodstuffs and beverages not packaged as mentioned in (*d*), are consumed on the spot at the exhibition;

(*f*) in their total value and quantity, are appropriate to the nature of the exhibition, the number of visitors and the extent of the exhibitor's participation.

Article 67

The exemption referred to in Article 65(1)(*b*) shall be limited to goods which are:

(*a*) consumed or destroyed at the exhibition, and

(*b*) are appropriate, in their total value and quantity, to the nature of the exhibition, the number of visitors and the extent of the exhibitor's participation.

Article 68

The exemption referred to in Article 65(1)(*d*) shall be limited to printed matter and articles for advertising purposes which:

(*a*) are intended exclusively to be distributed free of charge to the public at the place where the exhibition is held;

(*b*) in their total value and quantity, are appropriate to the nature of the exhibition, the number of visitors and the extent of the exhibitor's participation.

Article 69

The exemption referred to in Article 65(1)(*a*) and (*b*) shall not be granted for:

(*a*) alcoholic products;

(*b*) tobacco or tobacco products

(*c*) fuels, whether solid, liquid or gaseous.

TITLE X

GOODS IMPORTED FOR EXAMINATION, ANALYSIS OR TEST PURPOSES

Article 70

Subject to Articles 71 to 76, goods which are to undergo examination, analysis or tests to determine their composition, quality or other technical characteristics for purposes of information or industrial or commercial research shall be exempt on admission.

Article 71

Without prejudice to Article 74, the exemption referred to in Article 70 shall be granted only on condition that the goods to be examined, analysed or tested are completely used up or destroyed in the course of the examination, analysis or testing.

Article 72

No exemption shall be granted in respect of goods used in examination, analysis or tests which in themselves constitute sales promotion operations.

Article 73

Exemption shall be granted only in respect of the quantities of goods which are strictly necessary for the purpose for which they are imported. These quantities shall in each case be determined by the competent authorities, taking into account the said purpose.

Article 74

1. The exemption referred to in Article 70 shall cover goods which are not completely used up or destroyed during examinations, analysis or testing, provided that the products remaining are, with the agreement and under the supervision of the competent authorities:

—completely destroyed or rendered commercially valueless on completion of examination, analysis or testing, or

—surrendered to the State without causing it any expense, where this is possible under national law, or

—in duly justified circumstances, exported outside the territory of the Member State of importation.

2. For the purposes of paragraph 1, "products remaining" means products resulting from the examinations, analyses or tests or goods not actually used.

Article 75

Save where Article 74(1) is applied, products remaining at the end of the examinations, analyses or tests referred to in Article 70 shall be subject to the relevant import value added tax, at the rate applying on the date of completion of the examinations, analysis or tests, on the basis of the type of goods and the value ascertained or accepted on that date by the competent authorities. However, the interested party may, with the agreement and under the supervision of the competent authorities, convert products remaining to waste or scrap. In this case, the import duties shall be those applying to such waste or scrap at the time of conversion.

Article 76

The period within which the examinations, analysis or tests must be carried out and the administrative formalities to be completed in order to ensure the use of the goods for the purposes intended shall be determined by the competent authorities.

TITLE XI

MISCELLANEOUS EXEMPTIONS

CHAPTER I

Consignments sent to organisations protecting copyright or industrial and commercial patent rights

Article 77

Trademarks, patterns or designs and their supporting documents, as well as applications for patents for invention or the like, to be submitted to the bodies competent to deal with the protection of copyrights or the protection of industrial or commercial patent rights shall be exempt on admission.

CHAPTER II

Tourist information literature

Article 78

The following shall be exempt on admission:

(*a*) documentation (leaflets, brochures, books, magazines, guidebooks, posters, whether or not framed, unframed photographs and photographic enlargements, maps, whether or not illustrated, window transparencies, and illustrated calendars) intended to be distributed free of charge and the principal purpose of which is to encourage the public to visit foreign countries, in particular in order to attend cultural, tourist, sporting, religious or trade or professional meetings or events, provided that such literature contains not more than 25 per cent of private commercial advertising and that the general nature of its promotional aims is evident;

(*b*) foreign hotel lists and yearbooks published by official tourist agencies, or under their auspices, and timetables for foreign transport services, provided that such literature is intended for distribution free of charge and contains not more than 25 per cent of private commercial advertising;

(*c*) reference material supplied to accredited representatives or correspondents appointed by official national tourist agencies and not intended for distribution, ie yearbooks, lists of telephone or telex numbers, hotel lists, fairs catalogues, specimens of craft goods of negligible value, and literature on museums, universities, spas or other similar establishments.

CHAPTER III

Miscellaneous documents and articles

Article 79

The following shall be exempt on admission:

(*a*) documents sent free of charge to the public services of Member States;

(*b*) publications of foreign governments and publications of official international bodies intended for distribution without charge;

(*c*) ballot papers for elections organised by bodies set up in countries other than the Member State of importation;

(*d*) objects to be submitted as evidence or for like purposes to the courts or other official agencies of the Member State;

(*e*) specimen signatures and printed circulars concerning signatures sent as part of customary exchanges of information between public services or banking establishments;

(*f*) official printed matter sent to the central banks of the Member States;

(*g*) reports, statements, notes, prospectuses, application forms and other documents drawn up by companies with headquarters outside the Member State of importation and sent to the bearers or subscribers of securities issued by such companies;

(*h*) recorded media (punched cards, sound recordings, microfilms, etc) used for the transmission of information sent free of charge to the addressee, in so far as exemption does not give rise to abuses or to major distortions of competition;

(*i*) files, archives, printed forms and other documents to be used in international meetings, conferences or congresses, and reports on such gatherings;

(*j*) plans, technical drawings, traced designs, descriptions and other similar documents imported with a view to obtaining or fulfilling orders in a country other than the Member State of importation or to participating in a competition held in that State;

(*k*) documents to be used in examinations held in the Member State of importation by institutions set up in another country;

(*l*) printed forms to be used as official documents in the international movement of vehicles or goods, within the framework of international conventions;

(*m*) printed forms, labels, tickets and similar documents sent by transport undertakings or by undertakings of the hotel industry located in a country other than the Member State of importation to travel agencies set up in that State;

(*n*) printed forms and tickets, bills of lading, way-bills and other commercial or office documents which have been used;

(*o*) official printed forms from national or international authorities, and printed matter conforming to international standards sent for distribution by associations of countries other than the Member State of importation to corresponding associations located in the State;

(*p*) photographs, slides and stereotype mats for photographs, whether or not captioned, sent to press agencies to newspaper or magazine publishers;

(*q*) articles listed in the Annex to this Directive which are produced by the United Nations or one of its specialised agencies whatever the use for which they are intended;

(*r*) collectors' pieces and works of art of an educational, scientific or cultural character which are not intended for sale and which are imported by museums, galleries and other institutions approved by the competent authorities of the Member States for the purpose of duty-free admission of these goods. The exemption is granted only on condition that the articles in question are imported free of charge or, if they are imported against payment, that they are not supplied by a taxable person.

[(*s*) importations of official publications issued under the authority of the country of export, international institutions, regional or local authorities and bodies under public law established in the country of export, and printed matter distributed on the occasion of elections to the European Parliament or on the occasion of national elections in the country in which the printed matter originates by foreign political organisations officially recognised as such in the Member States, insofar as such publications and printed matter have been subject to tax in the country of export and have not benefited from remission of tax on export.][1]

Amendments—[1] Para (*s*) added by art 1(7) of the Council Directive of 13 June 1988: 88/331/EEC; see OJ L151, 17.6.88, p 79.

CHAPTER IV

Ancillary materials for the stowage and protection of goods during their transport

Article 80

The various materials such as rope, straw, cloth, paper and cardboard, wood and plastics which are used for the stowage and protection—including heat protection—of goods during their transport to the territory of a Member State, shall be exempt on admission, provided that:

(*a*) they are not normally re-usable; and

(*b*) the consideration paid for them forms part of the taxable amount as defined in Article 11 of Directive 77/388/EEC.

CHAPTER V

Litter, fodder and feedingstuffs for animals during their transport

Article 81

Litter, fodder and feedingstuffs of any description put on board the means of transport used to convey animals to the territory of a Member State for the purpose of distribution to the said animals during the journey shall be exempt on admission.

CHAPTER VI

[Fuel and lubricants present in land motor vehicles and special containers][1]

[Article 82] [1]

[1. Subject to Articles 83, 84 and 85, the following shall be exempt on admission:

(*a*) fuel contained in the standard tanks of:

—private and commercial motor vehicles and motor cycles;

—special containers;

(*b*) fuel contained in portable tanks carried by private motor vehicles and motor cycles, up to a maximum of 10 litres per vehicle and without prejudice to national provisions on the holding and transport of fuel.

2. For the purpose of paragraph 1:

(*a*) "commercial motor vehicle" means any motorised road vehicle (including tractors with trailers) which, by its type of construction and equipment, is designed for, and capable of transporting, whether for payment or not:

—more than nine persons including the driver,

—goods,

and any road vehicle for a special purpose other than transport as such;

(*b*) "private motor vehicle" means any motor vehicle not covered by the definition set out in (*a*);

(*c*) "standard tanks" means:

—the tanks permanently fixed by the manufacturer to all motor vehicles of the same type as the vehicle in question and whose permanent fitting enables fuel to be used directly, both for the purpose of propulsion and, where appropriate, for the operation, during transport, of refrigeration systems and other systems.

Gas tanks fitted to motor vehicles designed for the direct use of gas as a fuel and tanks fitted to ancillary systems with which the vehicle may be equipped shall also be considered to be standard tanks.

—tanks permanently fixed by the manufacturer to all containers of the same type as the container in question and whose permanent fitting enables fuel to be used directly for the operation, during transport, of refrigeration systems and other systems with which special containers are equipped;

(*d*) "special container" means any container fitted with specially designed apparatus for refrigeration systems, oxygenation systems, thermal insulation systems, or other systems.][1]

Amendments—[1] This art and the preceding heading substituted by the Council Directive of 13 June 1988: 88/331/EEC art 1(9); see OJ L151, 17.6.88, p.79.

[Article 83

Member States may limit the application of the exemption for fuel contained in the standard fuel tanks of commercial motor vehicles [and special containers][2]

(*a*) when the vehicle comes from a third country, to 200 litres per vehicle and per journey;

(*b*) when the vehicle comes from another Member State—

—to 200 litres per vehicle and per journey in the case of vehicles designed for, and capable of, the transport, with or without remuneration, of goods,

—to 600 litres per vehicle and per journey in the case of vehicles designed for, and capable of, the transport, with or without remuneration, of more than nine persons, including the driver.

[(*c*) to 200 litres per special container and per journey.][3]

Acting in accordance with the procedures provided for by the Treaty on this point, the Council shall decide, on a proposal from the Commission, before 1 July 1986, on the increase of the quantity of fuel admitted duty-free and contained in the standard fuel tanks of the vehicles referred to in the first indent of (*b*) of the first sub-paragraph.][1]

Amendments—[1] This art substituted by art 1 of the Council Directive of 8 July 1985: 85/346/EEC; see OJ L183, 16.7.1985, p 21.

[2] Words inserted by art 1 of the Council Directive of 13 June 1988: 88/331/EEC; see OJ L151, 17.6.88, p.79.

[3] Para (*c*) added by art 1 of the Council Directive of 13 June 1988: 88/331/EEC; see OJ L151, 17.6.88, p 79.

Article 84

Member States may limit the amount of fuel exempt on admission in the case of:

[(*a*) commercial motor vehicles engaged in international transport coming from third countries to their frontier zone, to a maximum depth of 25 kilometres as the crow flies, where such transport consists of journeys made by persons residing in that zone;][1]

(*b*) private motor vehicles belonging to persons residing in the frontier zone, to a maximum depth of 15 kilometres as the crow flies, contiguous with a third country.

Amendments—[1] Para (*a*) substituted by art 2 of the Council Directive of 8 July 1985: 85/346/EEC; see OJ L183, 16.7.1985, p 21.

Article 85

Fuel exempt on admission may not be used in a vehicle other than that in which it was imported nor be removed from that vehicle and stored, except during necessary repairs to that vehicle, or transferred for a consideration or free of charge by the person granted the exemption.

Non-compliance with the preceding paragraph shall give rise to application of the import value added tax relating to the products in question at the rate in force on the date of such non-compliance, on the basis of the type of goods and the value ascertained or accepted on that date by the competent authorities.

Article 86

The exemption referred to in Article 82 shall also apply to lubricants carried in motor vehicles and required for their normal operation during the journey in question.

CHAPTER VII

Goods for the construction, upkeep or ornamentation of memorials to, or cemeteries for, war victims

Article 87

Exemption from tax shall be granted in respect of goods imported by organisations authorised for that purpose by the competent authorities, for use in the construction, upkeep or ornamentation of cemeteries and tombs of, and memorials to, war victims of a country other than the Member State of importation who are buried in the latter State.

CHAPTER VIII

Coffins, funerary urns and ornamental funerary articles

Article 88

The following shall be exempt on admission:

(*a*) coffins containing bodies and urns containing the ashes of deceased persons, as well as the flowers, funeral wreaths and other ornamental objects normally accompanying them;

(*b*) flowers, wreaths and other ornamental objects brought by persons resident in a Member State other than that of importation, attending a funeral or coming to decorate graves in the territory of a Member State of importation provided these importations do not reflect, by either their nature of their quantity, any commercial intent.

TITLE XII
GENERAL AND FINAL PROVISIONS

Article 89

Where this Directive provides that the granting of an exemption shall be subject to the fulfilment of certain conditions, the person concerned shall, to the satisfaction of the competent authorities, furnish proof that these conditions have been met.

Article 90

1. The exchange value in national currency of the ECU to be taken into consideration for the purposes of this Directive shall be fixed once a year. The rates to be applied shall be those obtaining on the first working day in October and shall take effect on 1 January the following year.

2. Member States may round off the amounts in national currency arrived at by converting the amounts in ECU.

3. Member States may continue to apply the amounts of the exemptions in force at the time of the annual adjustment provided for in paragraph 1, if conversion of the amounts of the exemptions expressed in ECU leads, before the rounding-off provided for in paragraph 2, to an alteration of less than 5 per cent in the exemption expressed in national currency [or to a reduction in that exemption.][1]

Amendments—[1] Words in para 3. added by the Council Directive of 13 June 1988: 88/331/EEC art 1(11); see OJ L151, 17.6.88, p 79.

Article 91

No provision of this Directive shall prevent Member States from continuing to grant:

(*a*) the privileges and immunities granted by them under cultural, scientific or technical co-operation agreements concluded between them or with third countries;

(*b*) the special exemptions justified by the nature of frontier traffic which are granted by them under frontier agreements concluded between them or with countries outside the Community.

[(*c*) exemptions in the context of agreements entered into on the basis of reciprocity with third countries that are Contracting Parties to the Convention on International Civil Aviation (Chicago 1944) for the purpose of implementing Recommended Practices 4.42 and 4.44 in Annex 9 to the Convention (eighth edition, July 1980).][1]

Amendments—[1] Para (*c*) added by the Council Directive of 13 June 1988: 88/331/EEC; see OJ L151, 17.6.88, p 79.

Article 92

Until the establishment of Community exemptions upon importation, Member States may retain the exemptions granted to:

(*a*) merchant-navy seamen;

(*b*) workers returning to their country after having resided for at least six months outside the importing Member State on account of their occupation.

Article 93

1. Member States shall bring into force the measures necessary to comply with this Directive with effect from 1 July 1984.

2. Member States shall inform the Commission of the measures which they adopt to give effect to this Directive, indicating, where the case arises, those measures which they adopt by simple reference to identical provisions of Regulation (EEC) No 918/83.

Article 94

This Directive is addressed to the Member States.

Done at Brussels, 28 March 1983.

[ANNEX][1]

Visual and auditory materials of an educational, scientific or cultural character

CN code	*Description*
3704 00	Photographic plates, film, paper, paperboard and textiles, exposed but not developed:
ex 3704 00 10	—Plates and film:
	—Cinematograph film, positives, of an educational, scientific or cultural character

CN code	*Description*
ex 3705	Photographic plates and film, exposed and developed, other than cinematograph film:
	—Of an educational, scientific or cultural character
3706	Cinematograph film, exposed and developed, whether or not incorporating sound track or consisting only of sound track:
3706 10	—Of a width of 35 mm or more:
	—Other:
ex 3706 10 99	—Other positives:
	—Newsreels (with or without sound track) depicting events of current news value at the time of importation, and imported up to a limit of two copies of each subject for copying purposes
	—Archival film material (with or without sound track) intended for use in connection with newsreel films
	—Recreational films particularly suited for children and young people
	—Other films of educational, scientific or cultural character
3706 90	—Other:
	—Other:
	—Other positives:
ex 3706 90 51 ex 3706 90 91 ex 3706 90 99	—Newsreels (with or without sound track) depicting events of current news value at the time of importation, and imported up to a limit of two copies of each subject for copying purposes
	—Archival film material (with or without sound track) intended for use in connection with newsreel films
	—Recreational films particularly suited for children and young people
	—Other films of educational, scientific or cultural character:
4911	Other printed matter, including printed pictures and photographs:
	—Other:
4911 99	—Other:
ex 4911 99 90	—Other:
	—Microcards or other information storage media required in computerised information and documentation services of an educational, scientific or cultural character
	—Wall charts designed solely for demonstration and education
ex 8524	Records, tapes and other recorded media for sound or other similarly recorded phenomena including matrices and masters for the production of records, but excluding products of Chapter 37:
	—Of an educational, scientific or cultural character
ex 9023 00	Instruments, apparatus and models, designed for demonstrational purposes (for example, in education or exhibitions), unsuitable for other uses:
	—Patterns, models and wall charts of an educational, scientific or cultural character, designed solely for demonstration and education
	—Mock-ups or visualisations of abstract concepts such as molecular structures or mathematical formulae
Various	Holograms for laser projection
	Multi-media kits
	Materials for programmed instructions, including materials in kit form with the corresponding printed materials

Amendments—[1] Annex substituted by art 1 of Commission Directive of 7 March 1989: 89/219/EEC; see OJ L92, 5.4.1989, p 13.

Thirteenth Council Directive of 17 November 1986 on the harmonisation of the laws of the Member States relating to turnover taxes—arrangements for the refund of value added tax to taxable persons not established in Community territory

(86/560/EEC)

Note—See OJ L326, 21.11.86, p 40.

THE COUNCIL OF THE EUROPEAN COMMUNITIES,

Having regard to the Treaty establishing the European Economic Community, and in particular Articles 99 and 100 thereof,

Having regard to the Sixth Council Directive 77/388/EEC of 17 May 1977 on the harmonisation of the laws of the Member States relating to turnover taxes—Common system of value added tax: uniform basis of assessment (OJ L145, 13.6.77, p 1), and in particular Article 17 (4) thereof,

Having regard to the proposal from the Commission (OJ C223, 27.8.82, p 5, OJ C196, 23.7.83, p 6),

Having regard to the opinion of the European Parliament (OJ C161, 20.6.83, p 111),

Having regard to the opinion of the Economic and Social Committee (OJ C176, 4.7.83, p 22),

Whereas Article 8 of Directive 79/1072/EEC (OJ L331, 27.12.79, p 11) on the arrangements for the refund of value added tax to taxable persons not established in the territory of the country provides that in the case of taxable persons not established in the territory of the Community, Member States may refuse refunds or impose special conditions;

Whereas there is a need to ensure the harmonious development of trade relations between the Community and third countries based on the provisions of Directive 79/1072/EEC, while taking account of the varying situations encountered in third countries;

Whereas certain forms of tax evasion or avoidance should be prevented,

HAS ADOPTED THIS DIRECTIVE—

Article 1

For the purposes of this Directive—

1. "A taxable person not established in the territory of the Community" shall mean a taxable person as referred to in Article 4(1) of Directive 77/388/EEC who, during the period referred to in Article 3(1) of this Directive, has had in that territory neither his business nor a fixed establishment from which business transactions are effected, nor, if no such business or fixed establishment exists, his permanent address or usual place of residence, and who, during the same period, has supplied no goods or services deemed to have been supplied in the Member State referred to in Article 2, with the exception of—

(*a*) transport services and services ancillary thereto, exempted pursuant to Article 14(1)(*i*), Article 15 or Article 16(1), B, C and D of Directive 77/388/EEC;

(*b*) services provided in cases where tax is payable solely by the person to whom they are supplied, pursuant to Article 21(1)(*b*) of Directive 77/388/EEC;

2. "Territory of the Community" shall mean the territories of the Member States in which Directive 77/388/EEC is applicable.

Simon's Tax Cases—*Planzer Luxembourg Sàrl v Bundeszentralamt für Steuern* [2008] STC 1113.

Article 2

1. Without prejudice to Articles 3 and 4, each Member State shall refund to any taxable person not established in the territory of the Community, subject to the conditions set out below, any value added tax charged in respect of services rendered or moveable property supplied to him in the territory or the country by other taxable persons or charged in respect of the importation of goods into the country, in so far as such goods and services are used for the purposes of the transactions referred to in Article 17(3)(*a*) and (*b*) of Directive 77/388/EEC or of the provision of services referred to in point 1(*b*) of Article 1 of this Directive.

2. Member States may make the refunds referred to in paragraph 1 conditional upon the granting by third States of comparable advantages regarding turnover taxes.

3. Member States may require the appointment of a tax representative.

Simon's Tax Cases—*Rizení Letového Provozu CR sp v Bundesamt für Finanzen* [2007] STC 1509.

Article 3

1. The refunds referred to in Article 2(1) shall be granted upon application by the taxable person. Member States shall determine the arrangements for submitting applications, including the time limits for doing so, the period which applications should cover, the authority competent to receive them and the minimum amounts in respect of which applications may be submitted. They shall also determine the arrangements for making refunds, including the time limits for doing so. They shall impose on the applicant such obligations as are necessary to determine whether the application is justified and to prevent fraud, in particular the obligation to provide proof that he is engaged in an economic activity in accordance with Article 4(1) of Directive 77/388/EEC. The applicant must certify, in a written declaration, that, during the period prescribed, he has not carried out any transaction which does not fulfil the conditions laid down in point 1 of Article 1 of this Directive.

2. Refunds may not be granted under conditions more favourable than those applied to Community taxable persons.

Article 4

1. For the purposes of this Directive, eligibility for refunds shall be determined in accordance with Article 17 of Directive 77/388/EEC as applied in the Member State where the refund is paid.

2. Member States may, however, provide for the exclusion of certain expenditure or make refunds subject to additional conditions.

3. This Directive shall not apply to supplies of goods which are or may be exempted under point 2 of Article 15 of Directive 77/388/EEC.

Article 5

1. Member States shall bring into force the laws, regulations and administrative provisions necessary to comply with this Directive by 1 January 1988 at the latest. This Directive shall apply only to applications for refunds concerning value added tax charged on purchases of goods or services invoiced or on imports effected on or after that date.

2. Member States shall communicate to the Commission the main provisions of national law which they adopt in the field covered by this Directive and shall inform the Commission of the use they make of the option afforded by Article 2(2). The Commission shall inform the other Member States thereof.

Article 6

Within three years of the date referred to in Article 5, the Commission shall, after consulting the Member States, submit a report to the Council and to the European Parliament on the application of this Directive, particularly as regards the application of Article 2(2).

Article 7

As from the date on which this Directive is implemented, and at all events by the date mentioned in Article 5, the last sentence of Article 17(4) of Directive 77/388/EEC and Article 8 of Directive 79/1072/EEC shall cease to have effect in each Member State.

Article 8

This Directive is addressed to the Member States.

Done at Brussels, 17 November 1986.

Eighteenth Council Directive of 18 July 1989 on the harmonisation of the laws of the Member States relating to turnover taxes—abolition of certain derogations provided for in article 28(3) of the Sixth Directive, 77/388/EEC

(89/465/EEC)

Note—See OJ L226, 3.8.1989, p 21.

Repeal—This Directive repealed by Council Directive 2006/112/EC Art 411, Annex XII Part A with effect from 1 January 2007 (OJ L 347, 11.12.2006 p 1).

THE COUNCIL OF THE EUROPEAN COMMUNITIES

Having regard to the Treaty establishing the European Economic Community, and in particular Article 99 thereof,

Having regard to the proposal from the Commission.

Having regard to the opinion of the European Parliament (OJ No C125, 11.5.1987, p 27),

Having regard to the opinion of the Economic and Social Committee (OJ No C218, 29.8.1985, p 11),

Whereas Article 28(3) of the Sixth Council Directive, 77/388/EEC, of 17 May 1977 on the harmonisation of the laws of the Member States relating to turnover taxes—Common system of value added tax: uniform basis of assessment (OJ No L145, 13.6.1977, p 1), as last amended by the Act of Accession of Spain and Portugal, allows Member States to apply measures derogating from the normal rules of the common system of value added tax during a transitional period; whereas that period was originally fixed at five years; whereas the Council undertook to act, on a proposal from the Commission, before the expiry of that period, on the abolition, where appropriate, of some or all of those derogations;

Whereas many of those derogations give rise, under the Communities' own resources system, to difficulties in calculating the compensation provided for in Council Regulations (EEC, Euratom) No 1553/89 of 29 May 1989 on the definitive uniform arrangements for the collection of own resources accruing from value added tax (OJ No L155, 7.7.1989, p 9); whereas, in order to ensure that that system operates more efficiently, there are grounds for abolishing those derogations;

Whereas the abolition of those derogations will also contribute to greater neutrality of the value added tax system at Community level;

Whereas some of the said derogations should be abolished respectively from 1 January 1990, 1 January 1991, 1 January 1992 and 1 January 1993;

Whereas, having regard to the provisions of the Act of Accession, the Portuguese Republic may, until 1 January 1994 at the latest, postpone the abolition of the exemption of the transactions referred to in points 3 and 9 in Annex F to Directive 77/338/EEC;

Whereas it is appropriate that, before 1 January 1991, the Council should, on the basis of a Commission report, review the situation with regard to the other derogations provided for in Article 28(3) of Directive 77/388/EEC, including the one referred to in the second subparagraph of point 1 of Article 1 of this Directive, and that it should take a decision, on a proposal from the Commission, on the abolition of these derogations, bearing in mind any distortion of competition which has resulted from their application or which may arise in connection with the future completion of the internal market,

HAS ADOPTED THIS DIRECTIVE

Article 1

Directive 77/388/EEC is hereby amended as follows:

1. With effect from 1 January 1990 the transactions referred to in points 1, 3 to 6, 8, 9, 10, 12, 13 and 14 of Annex E shall be abolished.

Those Member States which, on 1 January 1989, subjected to value added tax the transactions listed in Annex E, points 4 and 5, are authorised to apply the conditions of Article 13A(2)(a), final indent, also to services rendered and goods delivered, as referred to in Article 13A(1)(m) and (n), where such activities are carried out by bodies governed by public law.

2. In Annex F:

(a) The transactions referred to in points 3, 14 and 18 to 22 shall be abolished with effect from 1 January 1990;

(b) The transactions referred to in points 4, 13, 15 and 24 shall be abolished with effect from 1 January 1991;

(c) The transaction referred to in point 9 shall be abolished with effect from 1 January 1992;

(d) The transaction referred to in point 11 shall be abolished with effect from 1 January 1993.

Article 2

The Portuguese Republic may defer until 1 January 1994 at the latest the dates referred to in Article 1, point 2(a), for the deletion of point 3 from Annex F and in Article 1, point 2(c), for the deletion of point 9 from Annex F.

Simon's Tax Cases—*Finanzamt Groß-Gerau v MKG-Kraftfahrzeuge-Factory GmbH* [2003] STC 951.

Article 3

By 1 January 1991 the Council, on the basis of a report from the Commission, shall review the situation with regard to the other derogations laid down in Article 28(3) of Directive 77/388/EEC, including that referred to in the second subparagraph of point 1 of Article 1 of this Directive and, acting on a Commission proposal, shall decide whether these derogations should be abolished, having regard to any distortions of competition which have resulted from their having been applied or which might arise from measures to complete the Internal Market.

Article 4

In respect of the transactions referred to in Article 1, 2 and 3, Member States may take measures concerning deduction of value added tax in order totally or partially to prevent the taxable persons concerned from deriving unwarranted advantages or sustaining unwarranted disadvantages.

Simon's Tax Cases—*Finanzamt Groß-Gerau v MKG-Kraftfahrzeuge-Factory GmbH* [2003] STC 951.

Article 5

1. Member States shall take the necessary measures to comply with this Directive not later than the dates laid down in Article 1 and 2.

2. Member States shall inform the Commission of the main provisions of national law which they adopt in the field governed by this Directive.

Article 6

This Directive is addressed to the Member States.

Council Directive of 16 December 1991 supplementing the common system of value added tax and amending Directive 77/388/EEC with a view to the abolition of fiscal frontiers

(91/680/EEC)

Note—See OJ L376 31.12.1991, p 1.

THE COUNCIL OF THE EUROPEAN COMMUNITIES,

Having regard to the Treaty establishing the European Economic Community, and in particular Article 99 thereof,

Having regard to the proposal from the Commission,

Having regard to the opinion of the European Parliament,

Having regard to the opinion of the Economic and Social Committee,

Whereas Article 8a of the Treaty defines the internal market as an area without internal frontiers in which the free movement of goods, persons, services and capital is ensured in accordance with the provisions of the Treaty;

Whereas the completion of the internal market requires the elimination of fiscal frontiers between Member States and that to that end the imposition of tax on imports and the remission of tax on exports in trade between Member States be definitively abolished;

Whereas fiscal controls at internal frontiers will be definitively abolished as from 1 January 1993 for all transactions between Member States;

Whereas the imposition of tax on imports and the remission of tax on exports must therefore apply only to transactions with territories excluded from the scope of the common system of value added tax;

Whereas, however, in view of the conventions and treaties applicable to them, transactions originating in or intended for the Principality of Monaco and the Isle of Man must be treated as transactions originating in or intended for the French Republic and the United Kingdom of Great Britain and Northern Ireland respectively;

Whereas the abolition of the principle of the imposition of tax on imports in relations between Member States will make provisions on tax exemptions and duty-free allowances superfluous in relations between Member States; whereas, therefore, those provisions should be repealed and the relevant Directives adapted accordingly;

Whereas the achievement of the objective referred to in Article 4 of the First Council Directive of 11 April 1967, as last amended by the Sixth Directive 77/388/EEC, requires that the taxation of trade between Member States be based on the principle of the taxation in the Member State of origin of goods and services supplied without prejudice, as regards Community trade between taxable persons, to the principle that tax revenue from the imposition of tax at the final consumption stage should accrue to the benefit of the Member State in which that final consumption takes place;

Whereas, however, the determination of the definitive system that will bring about the objectives of the common system of value added tax on goods and services supplied between Member States requires conditions that cannot be completely brought about by 31 December 1992;

Whereas, therefore, provision should be made for a transitional phase, beginning on 1 January 1993 and lasting for a limited period, during which provisions intended to facilitate transition to the definitive system for the taxation of trade between Member States, which continues to be the medium-term objective, will be implemented;

Whereas during the transitional period intra-Community transactions carried out by taxable persons other than exempt taxable persons should be taxed in the Member States of destination, at those Member States' rates and under their conditions;

Whereas intra-Community acquisitions of a certain value by exempt persons or by non-taxable legal persons and certain intra-Community distance selling and supplies of new means of transport to individuals or exempt or non-taxable bodies should also be taxed, during the transitional period, in the Member States of destination, at those Member States' rates and under their conditions, in so far as such transactions would, in the absence of special provisions, be likely to cause significant distortions of competition between Member States;

Whereas the necessary pursuit of a reduction of administrative and statistical formalities for undertakings, particularly small and medium-sized undertakings, must be reconciled with the implementation of effective control measures and the need, on both economic and tax grounds, to maintain the quality of Community statistical instruments;

Whereas advantage must be taken of the transitional period of taxation of intra-Community trade to take measures necessary to deal with both the social repercussions in the sectors affected and the regional difficulties, in frontier regions in particular, that might follow the abolition of the imposition of tax on imports and of the remission of tax on exports in trade between Member States; whereas Member States should therefore be authorised, for a period ending on

30 June 1999, to exempt supplies of goods carried out within specified limits by duty-free shops in the context of air and sea travel between Member States;

Whereas the transitional arrangements will enter into force for four years and will accordingly apply until 31 December 1996; whereas they will be replaced by a definitive system for the taxation of trade between Member States based on the principle of the taxation of goods and services supplied in the Member State of origin, so that the objective referred to in Article 4 of the First Council Directive of 11 April 1967 is achieved;

Whereas to that end the Commission will report to the Council before 31 December 1994 on the operation of the transitional arrangements and make proposals for the details of the definitive system for the taxation of trade between Member States; whereas the Council, considering that the conditions for transition to the definitive system have been fulfilled satisfactorily, will decide before 31 December 1995 on the arrangements necessary for the entry into force and the operation of the definitive system, the transitional arrangements being automatically continued until the entry into force of the definitive system and in any event until the Council has decided on the definitive system;

Whereas, accordingly, Directive 77/388/EEC, as last amended by Directive 89/465/EEC should be amended,

HAS ADOPTED THIS DIRECTIVE:

Simon's Tax Cases—*Eismann Alto Adige Srl v Ufficio IVA di Bolzano* [1996] STC 1374.

Article 1

Directive 77/388/EEC is hereby amended as follows:

Note—Amendments made by this article have been incorporated in Directive 77/388/EEC.

Article 2

1. The following Directives shall cease to have effect on 31 December 1992 as regards relations between Member States:

—Directive 83/181/EEC, as last amended by Directive 89/219/EEC,
—Directive 85/362/EEC.

2. The provisions on value added tax laid down in the following Directive shall cease to have effect on 31 December 1992:

—Directive 74/651/EEC, as last amended by Directive 88/663/EEC,
—Directive 83/182/EEC,
—Directive 83/183/EEC, as amended by Directive 89/604/EEC.

3. The provisions of Directive 69/169/EEC as last amended by Directive 91/191/EEC relating to value added tax shall cease to have effect on 31 December 1992 as regards relations between Member States.

Article 3

1. Member States shall adapt their present value added tax systems to this Directive.

They shall bring into force such laws, regulations and administrative provisions as are necessary for their arrangements thus adapted to Article 1(1) to (20) and (22) to (24) and 2 of this Directive to enter into force on 1 January 1993.

2. Member States shall inform the Commission of the provisions which they adopt to apply this Directive.

3. Member States shall communicate to the Commission the texts of the provisions of national law which they adopt in the field governed by this Directive.

4. When Member States adopt such measures they shall include a reference to this Directive or shall accompany them by such a reference on the occasion of their official publication.

The manner in which such references shall be made shall be laid down by the Member States.

Article 4

This Directive is addressed to the Member States.

Council Directive
of 14 December 1992
amending Directive 77/388/EEC and introducing simplification measures with regard to value added tax

(92/111/EEC)

Note—See OJ L384 36.12.1992, p 47.
Repeal—This Directive repealed by Council Directive 2006/112/EC Annex XI with effect from 1 January 2007.

THE COUNCIL OF THE EUROPEAN COMMUNITIES

Having regard to the Treaty establishing the European Economic Community, and in particular Article 99 thereof,

Having regard to the proposal from the Commission,

Having regard to the opinion of the European Parliament,

Having regard to the opinion of the Economic and Social Committee,

Whereas Article 3 of Council Directive 91/680/EEC of 16 December 1991 supplementing the common system of value added tax and amending Directive 77/388/EEC with a view to the abolition of fiscal frontiers sets 1 January 1993 as the date for the entry into force of these provisions in all the Member States;

Whereas in order to facilitate the application of these provisions and to introduce the simplifications needed, it is necessary to supplement the common system of value added tax, as applicable on 1 January 1993, so as to clarify how the tax shall apply to certain operations carried out with third territories and certain operations carried out inside the Community, as well [as] to define the transitional measures between the provisions in force on 31 December 1992 and those which will enter into force as from 1 January 1993;

Whereas in order to guarantee the neutrality of the common system of turnover tax in respect of the origin of goods, the concept of a third territory and the definition of an import must be supplemented;

Whereas certain territories forming part of the Community customs territory are regarded as third territories for the purposes of applying the common system of value added tax; whereas value added tax is therefore applied to trade between the Member States and those territories according to the same principles as apply to any operation between the Community and third countries; whereas it is necessary to ensure that such trade is subject to fiscal provisions equivalent to those which would be applied to operations carried out under the same conditions with territories which are not part of the Community customs territory; whereas as a result of these provisions the Seventeenth Council Directive 85/362/EEC of 16 July 1985 on the harmonisation of the laws of the Member States relating to turnover taxes—Exemption from value added tax on the temporary importation of goods other than means of transport, becomes null and void;

Whereas it is necessary to state exactly how the exemptions relating to certain export operations or equivalent operations will be implemented; whereas it is necessary to adapt the other Directives concerned accordingly;

Whereas it is necessary to clarify the definition of the place of taxation of certain operations carried out on board ships, aircraft or trains transporting passengers inside the Community;

Whereas the transitional arrangements for taxation of trade between the Member States must be supplemented to take account both of the Community provisions relating to excise duties and the need to clarify and simplify the detailed rules for the application of the tax of certain operations which will be carried out between the Member States as from 1 January 1993;

Whereas Council Directive 92/12/EEC of 25 February 1992 on the general arrangements for products subject to excise duty and on the holding, movement and monitoring of such products lays down particular procedures and obligations in relation to declarations in the case of shipments of such products to another Member State; whereas as a result the methods of applying tax to certain supplies and intra-Community acquisitions of products liable to excise duties can be simplified to the benefit both of the persons liable to pay tax and the competent administrations;

Whereas it is necessary to define the scope of the exemptions referred to in Article 28c of Directive 77/388/EEC; whereas it is also necessary to supplement the provisions concerning the chargeability of the tax and the methods of determining the taxable amount of certain intra-Community operations;

Whereas, for taxable operations in the domestic market linked to intra-Community trade in goods which are carried out during the period laid down in Article 281 of Directive 77/388/EEC by taxable persons not established in the Member State referred to in Article 28b(A)(1) of the said Directive, it is necessary to take simplification measures guaranteeing equivalent treatment in all the Member States; whereas to achieve this, the provisions concerning the taxation system and the person liable to tax in respect of such operations must be harmonised;

Whereas in order to take account of the provisions relating to the person liable to pay tax in the domestic market and to avoid certain forms of tax evasion or avoidance, it is necessary to clarify the Community provisions concerning the repayment to taxable persons not established in the country of the value added tax referred to in Article 17(3) of Directive 77/388/EEC as amended by Article 28f of the said Directive;

Whereas the abolition as from 1 January 1993 of tax on imports and tax relief on exports for trade between the Member States makes it necessary to have transitional measures in order to ensure the neutrality of the common system of value added tax and to avoid situations of double-taxation or non-taxation;

Whereas it is therefore necessary to lay down special provisions for cases where a Community procedure, started before 1 January 1993 for the purposes of a supply effected before that date by a taxable person acting as such in respect of goods dispatched or transported to another Member State, is not completed until after 31 December 1992;

Whereas such provisions should also apply to taxable operations carried out before 1 January 1993 to which particular exemptions were applied which as a result delayed the taxable event;

Whereas it is also necessary to lay down special measures for means of transport which, not having been acquired or imported subject to the general domestic tax conditions of a Member State, have benefited, by the application of national measures, from an exemption from tax because of their temporary import from another Member State;

Whereas the application of these transitional measures, both in relation trade between the Member States and to operations with third territories, presupposes supplementing the definition of the operations to be made subject to taxation as from 1 January 1993 and the clarification for such cases of the concepts of the place of taxation, the taxable event and the chargeability of the tax;

Whereas, on account of the current economic situation, the Kingdom of Spain and the Italian Republic have requested that, as a transitional measure, provisions derogating from the principle of immediate deduction laid down in the first subparagraph of Article 18(2) of Directive 77/388/EEC be applied; whereas this request should be granted for a period of two years which may not be extended;

Whereas this Directive lays down common provisions for simplifying the treatment of certain intra-Community operations; whereas, in a number of cases, it is for the Member States to determine the conditions for implementing these provisions; whereas certain Member States will not be able to complete the legislative procedure necessary to adapt their legislation on value added tax within the period laid down; whereas an additional period should therefore be allowed for the implementation of this Directive; whereas a maximum period of twelve months is sufficient for this purpose;

Whereas it is accordingly necessary to amend Directive 77/388/EEC,

HAS ADOPTED THIS DIRECTIVE:

Article 1

Directive 77/388/EEC is hereby amended as follows:

Note—The amendments made by this article have been incorporated in the appropriate provisions of Directive 77/388/EEC.

Article 2

1. As from 1 January 1993 and for a period of two years, which may not be extended, the Kingdom of Spain and the Italian Republic shall be authorised to apply provisions derogating from the principle of immediate deduction provided for in the first subparagraph of Article 18(2). These provisions may not have the effect of delaying by more than one month the time when the right to deduction, having arisen, may be exercised under Article 18(1).

However, for taxable persons who file the returns provided for in Article 22(4) for quarterly tax periods, the Kingdom of Spain and the Italian Republic shall be authorised to provide that the right to deduction which has come into being which could, under Article 18(1), be exercised in a given quarter, may not be exercised until the following quarter. This provision shall only apply where the Kingdom of Spain or the Italian Republic authorises such taxable persons to opt for the filing of monthly returns.

2. By way of derogation from the third subparagraph of Article 15(10), the Portuguese Republic, the French Republic, the Kingdom of the Netherlands and the Federal Republic of Germany shall be authorised, in regard to contracts concluded after 31 December 1992, to abolish the repayment, procedure, where it is prohibited by this Directive by 1 October 1993 at the latest.

Article 3

The Council, acting unanimously on a Commission proposal, shall adopt before 30 June 1993, detailed rules for the taxation of chain transactions between taxable persons, so that such rules may enter into force on 1 January 1994.

Article 4

1. The Member States shall adapt their present value added tax system to the provisions of this Directive.

They shall adopt the necessary laws, regulations and administrative provisions for their adapted systems to enter into force on 1 January 1993.

Member States may, however, provide that information relating to transactions referred to in the last subparagraph of Article 22(6)(b) for which the tax becomes payable during the first three calendar months of 1993 must appear at the latest on the summary statement signed for the second calendar quarter of 1993.

2. By way of derogation from the second subparagraph of paragraph 1, Member States shall be authorised to adopt the necessary laws, regulations and administrative provisions in order to implement by 1 January 1984 at the latest the provisions laid down in the following paragraphs of Article 1—

—paragraph 11,

—paragraph 13, insofar as it relates to Article 28c(E)(3);

—paragraph 19, insofar as it relates to the third subparagraph of Article 21(1)(a),

—paragraph 20, insofar as it relates to obligations in respect of the transactions referred to in the preceding indents.

Member States which, on 1 January 1993, apply measures equivalent to those mentioned above shall adopt the necessary measures to ensure that the principles laid down in Article 22(6) and in current Community provisions on administrative co-operation in the area of indirect taxation are complied with as from 1 January 1993 without fail.

3. By way of derogation from the second subparagraph of paragraph 1, the Federal Republic of Germany shall be authorised to adopt the necessary laws, regulations and administrative provisions in order to implement by 1 October 1993 at the latest the provisions laid down in Article 1(10) with regard to Article 28a(1a)(a).

4. Member States shall inform the Commission of the provisions which they adopt to apply this Directive.

5. Member States shall communicate the provisions of domestic law which they adopt in the field covered by this Directive to the Commission.

6. When Member States adopt these provisions, they shall contain a reference to this Directive or shall be accompanied by such reference on the occasion of their official publication. The methods of making such a reference shall be laid down by the Member States.

Article 5

This Directive is addressed to the Member States.

Council Directive of 14 February 1994 amending Directives 69/169/EEC and 77/388/EEC and increasing the level of allowances for travellers from third countries and the limits on tax-free purchases in intra-Community travel

(94/4/EC)

Note—See OJ L60 03.03.1994, p 14.

THE COUNCIL OF THE EUROPEAN UNION,

Having regard to the Treaty establishing the European Community, and in particular Article 99 thereof,

Having regard to the proposal from the Commission,

Having regard to the opinion of the European Parliament,

Having regard to the opinion of the Economic and Social Committee,

Whereas Article 1(1) of Council Directive 69/169/EEC of 28 May 1969 on the harmonisation of provisions laid down by law, regulation or administrative action relating to exemption from turnover tax and excise duty on imports in international travel provides for allowances in respect of goods contained in the personal luggage of travellers coming from third countries on condition that such imports have no commercial character;

Whereas the total value of the goods eligible for this exemption may not exceed ECU 45 per person; whereas, in accordance with Article 1(2) of Directive 69/169/EEC, Member States may reduce the allowance to ECU 23 for travellers under 15 years of age;

Whereas account must be taken of measures in favour of travellers recommended by specialised international organisations, in particular the measures contained in Annex F.3 to the International Convention on the Simplification and Harmonisation of Customs Procedures;

Whereas these objectives could be attained by increasing the allowances;

Whereas it is necessary to provide, for a limited period, a derogation for Germany, taking into account the economic difficulties likely to be caused by the amount of the allowances, particularly as regards travellers entering the territory of that Member State by land frontiers linking Germany to countries other than Member States and the EFTA members or by means of coastal navigation coming from the said countries;

Whereas there are special links between continental Spain and the Canary Islands, Ceuta and Melilla;

Whereas it is necessary to ensure, during the period when these sales are authorised pursuant to the provisions of Article 28k of Council Directive 77/388/EEC of 17 May 1977 on the harmonisation of the laws of the Member States relating to turnover taxes—Common system of value added tax: uniform basis of assessment, that the real value of goods likely to be sold in tax-free shops to travellers on intra-Community flights or sea crossings is maintained,

HAS ADOPTED THIS DIRECTIVE:

Article 1

Note—Article 1 amends Directive 69/169/EEC, arts 1, 7*b*.

Article 2

Note—Article 2 amends Directive 77/388/EEC, art 28*k*.
Repeal—Article 2 repealed by Council Directive 2006/112/EC Annex XI with effect from 1 January 2007.

Article 3

1. Member States shall bring into force the provisions necessary to comply with this Directive by 1 April 1994 at the latest. They shall forthwith inform the Commission thereof.

When Member States adopt these provisions, they shall contain a reference to this Directive or shall be accompanied by such reference on the occasion of their official publication. The methods of making such a reference shall be laid down by the Member States.

[2. By way of derogation from paragraph 1, the Federal Republic of Germany and the Republic of Austria shall be authorised to bring into force the measures necessary to comply with this Directive by 1 January [2003][2] at the latest for goods imported by travellers entering German or Austrian territory by a land frontier linking Germany or Austria to countries other than Member States and the EFTA members or, where applicable, by means of coastal navigation coming from the said countries.][1]

[However, those Member States shall apply an allowance of not less than ECU 100 from 1 January 1999 to imports by the travellers referred to in the preceding subparagraph. They shall jointly increase that amount gradually, with a view to applying the limit in force in the Community to the said imports by 1 January 2003 at the latest.][3]

3. Member States shall communicate to the Commission the text of the provisions of domestic law which they adopt in the field covered by this Directive.

Amendments—[1] Paragraph 2 replaced by Directive 94/75/EC, art 1; OJ L365, 31.12.1994, p 52.
[2] Words in brackets replaced by Directive 98/94/EC, art 1; OJ L 358, 31.12.1998, p 105, 106 with effect from 31 December 1998.
[3] Replaced by Directive 98/94/EC, art 1; OJ L 358, 31.12.1998, p 105, 106 with effect from 31 December 1998.

Article 4

This Directive shall enter into force on the day of its publication in the *Official Journal of the European Communities*.

Article 5

This Directive is addressed to the Member States.

Council Directive
of 14 February 1994
supplementing the common system of value added tax and amending Directive 77/388/EEC—special arrangements applicable to second-hand goods, works of art, collectors' items and antiques

(94/5/EC)

Note—See OJ L60 03.03.1994, p 16.
Repeal—This Directive repealed by Council Directive 2006/112/EC Annex XI with effect from 1 January 2007.

THE COUNCIL OF THE EUROPEAN UNION,

Having regard to the Treaty establishing the European Community, and in particular Article 99 thereof,

Having regard to the proposal from the Commission,

Having regard to the opinion of the European Parliament,

Having regard to the opinion of the Economic and Social Committee,

Whereas, in accordance with Article 32 of the Sixth Council Directive 77/388/EEC of 17 May 1977 on the harmonisation of the laws of the Member States relating to turnover taxes—Common system of value added tax: uniform basis of assessment, the Council is to adopt a Community taxation system to be applied to used goods, works of art, antiques and collectors' items;

Whereas the present situation, in the absence of Community legislation, continues to be marked by the application of very different systems which cause distortion of competition and deflection of trade both internally and between Member States; whereas these differences also include a lack of harmonisation in the levying of the own resources of the Community; whereas consequently it is necessary to bring this situation to an end as soon as possible;

Whereas the Court of Justice has, in a number of judgements, noted the need to attain a degree of harmonisation which allows double taxation in intra-Community trade to be avoided;

Whereas it is essential to provide, in specific areas, for transitional measures enabling legislation to be gradually adapted;

Whereas, within the internal market, the satisfactory operation of the value added tax mechanisms means that Community rules with the purpose of avoiding double taxation and distortion of competition between taxable persons must be adopted;

Whereas it is accordingly necessary to amend Directive 77/388/EEC,

HAS ADOPTED THIS DIRECTIVE:

Article 1

Note—Article 1 amends Directive 77/388/EEC, arts 11, 12, 28, 28*a*, 32 and inserts in Directive 77/388/EEC arts 26*a*, 28*o* and Annex I.

Article 2

Member States may take measures concerning the right to deduct value added tax in order to avoid the taxable dealers concerned enjoying unjustified advantages or sustaining unjustified loss.

Article 3

Acting unanimously on a proposal from the Commission, the Council may authorise any Member State to introduce particular measures for the purpose of combating fraud, by providing that the tax due in application of the arrangements for taxing the profit margin provided for in Article 26a(B) cannot be less than the amount of tax which would be due if the profit margin were equal to a certain percentage of the selling price. This percentage shall be fixed taking into account the normal profit margins realised by economic operators in the sector concerned.

Article 4

1. Member States shall adapt their present value added tax system to this Directive.

They shall bring into force such laws, regulations and administrative provisions as are necessary for their system thus adapted to enter into force on 1 January 1995 at the latest.

2. Member States shall inform the Commission of the provisions which they adopt to apply this Directive.

3. Member States shall communicate to the Commission the provisions of national law which they adopt in the field covered by this Directive.

4. When Member States adopt such provisions, they shall contain a reference to this Directive or be accompanied by such reference on the occasion of their official publication. The methods of making such a reference shall be laid down by the Member States.

Article 5

This Directive is addressed to the Member States.

Council Directive of 12 October 1998 supplementing the common system of value added tax and amending Directive 77/388/EEC—special scheme for investment gold

(98/80/EC)

Note—See OJ L281 17.10.1998, p 31.
Repeal—This Directive repealed by Council Directive 2006/112/EC Annex XI with effect from 1 January 2007.

THE COUNCIL OF THE EUROPEAN UNION

Having regard to the Treaty establishing the European Community and in particular Article 99 thereof,

Having regard to the proposal from the Commission,

Having regard to the opinion of the European Parliament,

Having regard to the opinion of the Economic and Social Committee,

Whereas, under the sixth Council Directive 77/388/EEC of 17 May 1977 on the harmonisation of the laws of the Member States relating to turnover taxes—common system of value added tax: uniform basis of assessment transactions concerning gold are in principle taxable although, on the basis of the transitional derogation provided for in Article 28(3) in conjunction with point 26 of Annex F to the said Directive, Member States may continue to exempt transactions concerning gold other than gold for industrial use; whereas the application by some Member States of that transitional derogation is the cause of a certain distortion of competition;

Whereas gold does not only serve as an input for production but is also acquired for investment purposes; whereas the application of the normal tax rules constitutes a major obstacle to its use for financial investment purposes and therefore justifies the application of a specific tax scheme for investment gold; whereas such a scheme should also enhance the international competitiveness of the Community gold market;

Whereas supplies of gold for investments purposes are similar in nature to other financial investments often exempted from tax under the current rules of the sixth Directive, and therefore exemption from tax appears to be the most appropriate tax treatment for supplies of investment gold;

Whereas the definition of investment gold should only comprise forms and weights of gold of very high purity as traded in the bullion markets and gold coins the value of which primarily reflects its gold price; whereas, in the case of gold coins, for reasons of transparency, a yearly list of qualifying coins should be drawn up providing security for the operators trading in such coins; whereas the legal security of traders demands that coins included in this list be deemed to fulfil the criteria for exemption of this Directive for the whole year for which the list is valid; whereas such list will be without prejudice to the exemption, on a case-by-case basis, of coins, including newly minted coins which are not included in the list but which meet the criteria laid down in this Directive;

Whereas since a tax exemption does, in principle, not allow for the deduction of input tax while tax on the value of the gold may be charged on previous operations, the deduction of such input tax should be allowed in order to guarantee the advantages of the special scheme and to avoid distortions of competition with regard to imported investment gold;

Whereas the possibility of using gold for both industrial and investment purposes requires the possibility for operators to opt for normal taxation where their activity consists either in the producing of investment gold or transformation of any gold into investment gold, or in the wholesale of such gold when they supply in their normal trade gold for industrial purposes;

Whereas the dual use of gold may offer new opportunities for tax fraud and tax evasion that will require effective control measures to be taken by Member States; whereas a common standard of minimum obligations in accounting and documentation to be held by the operators is therefore desirable although, where this information does already exist pursuant to other Community legislation, a Member State may consider these requirements to be met;

Whereas experience has shown that, with regard to most supplies of gold of more than a certain purity the application of a reverse charge mechanism can help to prevent tax fraud while at the same time alleviating the financing charge for the operation; whereas it is justified to allow Member States to use such mechanism; whereas for importation of gold Article 23 of the Sixth Directive allows, in a similar way, that tax is not paid at the moment of importation provided it is mentioned in the declaration pursuant to Article 22(4) of that Directive;

Whereas transactions carried out on a bullion market regulated by a Member State require further simplifications in their tax treatment because of the huge number and the speed of such operations; whereas Member States are allowed to disapply the special scheme, to suspend tax collection and to dispense with recording requirements;

Whereas since the new tax scheme will replace existing provisions under Article 12(3)(e) and point 26 of Annex F of the Sixth Directive, these provisions should be deleted,

HAS ADOPTED THIS DIRECTIVE

Article 1

Note—Article 1 inserts in Directive 77/388/EEC art 26*b*.

Article 2

Article 12(3)(e) and point 26 of Annex F to Directive 77/388/EEC shall be deleted.

Article 3

1. Member States shall bring into force the laws, regulations and administrative provisions necessary to comply with this Directive on 1 January 2000. They shall forthwith inform the Commission thereof.

When Member States adopt these measures, they shall contain a reference to this Directive or shall be accompanied by such reference on the occasion of their official publication. The methods of making such reference shall be laid down by the Member States.

2. Member States shall communicate to the Commission the text of the provisions of domestic law, which they adopt in the field, governed by this Directive.

Article 4

This Directive shall enter into force on the day of its publication in the Official Journal of the European Communities.

Article 5

This Directive is addressed to the Member States.

Done at Luxembourg, 12 October 1998.

Commentary—*De Voil Indirect Tax Service* **V5.143**.

Council Directive of 7 May 2002 amending and amending temporarily Directive 77/388/EEC as regards the value added tax arrangements applicable to radio and television broadcasting services and certain electronically supplied services

(2002/38/EC)

Repeal—This Directive repealed by Council Directive 2006/112/EC Annex XI with effect from 1 January 2007.

THE COUNCIL OF THE EUROPEAN UNION,

Having regard to the Treaty establishing the European Community, and in particular Article 93 thereof,

Having regard to the proposal from the Commission,

Having regard to the opinion of the European Parliament,

Having regard to the opinion of the Economic and Social Committee,

Whereas:

(1) The rules currently applicable to VAT on radio and television broadcasting services and on electronically supplied services, under Article 9 of the sixth Council Directive 77/388/EEC of 17 May 1977 on the harmonisation of the laws of the Member States relating to turnover taxes—Common system of value added tax: uniform basis of assessment, are inadequate for taxing such services consumed within the Community and for preventing distortions of competition in this area.

(2) In the interests of the proper functioning of the internal market, such distortions should be eliminated and new harmonised rules introduced for this type of activity. Action should be taken to ensure, in particular, that such services where effected for consideration and consumed by customers established in the Community are taxed in the Community and are not taxed if consumed outside the Community.

(3) To this end, radio and television broadcasting services and electronically supplied services provided from third countries to persons established in the Community or from the Community to recipients established in third countries should be taxed at the place of the recipient of the services.

(4) To define electronically supplied services, examples of such services should be included in an annex to the Directive.

(5) To facilitate compliance with fiscal obligations by operators providing electronically supplied services, who are neither established nor required to be identified for tax purposes within the Community, a special scheme should be established. In applying this scheme any operator supplying such services by electronic means to non-taxable persons within the Community, may, if he is not otherwise identified for tax purposes within the Community, opt for identification in a single Member State.

(6) The non-established operator wishing to benefit from the special scheme should comply with the requirements laid down therein, and with any relevant existing provision in the Member State where the services are consumed.

(7) The Member State of identification must under certain conditions be able to exclude a non-established operator from the special scheme.

(8) Where the non-established operator opts for the special scheme, any input value added tax that he has paid with respect to goods and services used by him for the purpose of his taxed activities falling under the special scheme, should be refunded by the Member State where the input value added tax was paid, in accordance with the arrangements of the thirteenth Council Directive 86/560/EEC of 17 November 1986 on the harmonisation of the laws of the Member States relating to turnover taxes—arrangements for the refund of value added tax to taxable persons not established in Community territory. The optional restrictions for refund in Article 2(2) and (3) and Article 4(2) of the same Directive should not be applied.

(9) Subject to conditions which they lay down, Member States should allow certain statements and returns to be made by electronic means, and may also require that electronic means are used.

(10) Those provisions pertaining to the introduction of electronic tax returns and statements should be adopted on a permanent basis. It is desirable to adopt all other provisions for a temporary period of three years which may be extended for practical reasons but should, in any event, based on experience, be reviewed within three years from 1 July 2003.

(11) Directive 77/388/EEC should therefore be amended accordingly,

HAS ADOPTED THIS DIRECTIVE:

Article 1

(*Temporarily amends Directive 77/388/EEC arts 9, 12, temporarily inserts art 26c*).

Article 2

(*Amends Directive 77/388/EEC art 22*).

Article 3

1. Member States shall bring into force the laws, regulations and administrative provisions necessary to comply with this Directive on 1 July 2003. They shall forthwith inform the Commission thereof.

When Member States adopt these measures, they shall contain a reference to this Directive or shall be accompanied by such reference on the occasion of their official publication. Member States shall determine how such reference is to be made.

2. Member States shall communicate to the Commission the text of the provisions of domestic law which they adopt in the field covered by this Directive.

[Article 4

Article 1 shall apply until 31 December 2006][1]

Amendments—[1] This article substituted by Council Directive 2006/58/EC art 1 (OJ L 174, 28.6.2006 p 5).

Article 5

The Council, on the basis of a report from the Commission, shall review the provisions of Article 1 of this Directive before 30 June 2006 and shall either, acting in accordance with Article 93 of the Treaty, adopt measures on an appropriate electronic mechanism on a non-discriminatory basis for charging, declaring, collecting and allocating tax revenue on electronically supplied services with taxation in the place of consumption or, if considered necessary for practical reasons, acting unanimously on the basis of a proposal from the Commission, extend the period mentioned in Article 4.

Article 6

This Directive shall enter into force on the day of its publication in the Official Journal of the European Communities.

Article 7

This Directive is addressed to the Member States.

Done at Brussels, 7 May 2002.

ANNEX

(Inserts Directive 77/388/EEC Annex L).

Commission Directive

of 9 December 2002

laying down detailed rules for implementing certain provisions of Council Directive 76/308/EEC on mutual assistance for the recovery of claims relating to certain levies, duties, taxes and other measures

(2002/94/EC)

Note—See OJ L337, 13.12.2002, p 41.

Repeal—This Directive repealed by Commission Regulation (EC) 1179/2008 art 31 with effect from 1 January 2009 (OJ L 319, 29.11.2008 p 21).

THE COMMISSION OF THE EUROPEAN COMMUNITIES,

Having regard to the Treaty establishing the European Community,

Having regard to Council Directive 76/308/EEC of 15 March 1976 on mutual assistance for the recovery of claims relating to certain levies, duties, taxes and other measures (*OJ L 73, 19.3.1976, p 18*), *as last amended by Directive 2001/44/EC* (*OJ L 175, 28.6.2001, p 17*), *and in particular Article 22 thereof,*

Whereas:

(*1*) *The system of mutual assistance between the competent authorities of Member States, as set out in Directive 76/308/EEC, has been amended as regards the information to be supplied to the applicant authority, the notification of the addressee concerning the applicable instruments and decisions, the adoption of precautionary measures, and the recovery by the requested authority of claims on behalf of the applicant authority.*

(*2*) *As regards each of those aspects, therefore, Commission Directive 77/794/EEC of 4 November 1977 laying down detailed rules for implementing certain provisions of Directive 76/308/EEC on mutual assistance for the recovery of claims resulting from operations forming part of the system of financing the European Agricultural Guidance and Guarantee Fund, and of agricultural levies and customs duties, and in respect of value added tax (OJ L 333, 24.12.1977, p 11), as last amended by Directive 86/489/EEC (OJ L 283, 4.10.1986, p 23), should be amended accordingly.*

(3) Furthermore, detailed rules should be laid down concerning the means by which communications between authorities may be transmitted.

(4) In the interests of clarity, Directive 77/794/EEC should be replaced.

(5) The measures provided for in this Directive are in accordance with the opinion of the Committee on Recovery,

HAS ADOPTED THIS DIRECTIVE:

CHAPTER I

General provisions

Article 1

This Directive lays down the detailed rules for implementing Article 4(2) and (4), Article 5(2) and (3), Article 7, Article 8, Article 9, Article 11, Article 12(1) and (2), Article 14, Article 18(3) and Article 25 of Directive 76/308/EEC.

It also lays down the detailed rules on conversion, transfer of sums recovered, the fixing of a minimum amount for claims which may give rise to a request for assistance, as well as the means by which communications between authorities may be transmitted.

Article 2

For the purposes of this Directive:

1. transmission "by electronic means" shall mean transmission using electronic equipment for processing (including digital compression) of data and employing wires, radio transmission, optical technologies or other electromagnetic means;

2. "CCN/CSI" network shall mean the common platform based on the Common Communication Network (CCN) and Common System Interface (CSI), developed by the Community to ensure all transmissions by electronic means between competent authorities in the area of Customs and Taxation.

CHAPTER II

Requests for information

Article 3

The request for information referred to in Article 4 of Directive 76/308/EEC shall be made out in writing in accordance with the model in Annex I to this Directive. If the request cannot be transmitted by electronic means, it shall bear the official stamp of the applicant authority and shall be signed by an official thereof duly authorised to make such a request.

Where a similar request has been addressed to any other authority, the applicant authority shall indicate in its request for information the name of that authority.

Article 4

The request for information may relate to—

1. the debtor;

2. any person liable for settlement of the claim under the law in force in the Member State in which the applicant authority is situated (hereinafter "the Member State of the applicant authority");

3. any third party holding assets belonging to one of the persons mentioned under point 1 or 2.

Article 5

1. The requested authority shall acknowledge receipt of the request for information in writing as soon as possible and in any event within seven days of such receipt.

2. Immediately upon receipt of the request the requested authority shall, where appropriate, ask the applicant authority to provide any additional information necessary. The applicant authority shall provide all additional necessary information to which it normally has access.

Article 6

1. The requested authority shall transmit each item of requested information to the applicant authority as and when it is obtained.

2. Where all or some of the requested information cannot be obtained within a reasonable time, having regard to the particular case, the requested authority shall so inform the applicant authority, indicating the reasons therefor.

In any event, at the end of six months from the date of acknowledgement of receipt of the request, the requested authority shall inform the applicant authority of the outcome of the investigations which it has conducted in order to obtain the information requested.

In the light of the information received from the requested authority, the applicant authority may request the latter to continue its investigations. That request shall be made in writing within two months of the receipt of the notification of the outcome of the investigations carried out by the requested authority, and shall be treated by the requested authority in accordance with the provisions applying to the initial request.

Article 7

If the requested authority decides not to comply with the request for information, it shall notify the applicant authority in writing of the reasons for the refusal to comply with the request, specifying the provisions of Article 4 of Directive 76/308/EEC on which it relies. Such notification shall be given by the requested authority as soon as it has taken its decision and in any event within three months of the date of the acknowledgement of the receipt of the request.

Article 8

The applicant authority may at any time withdraw the request for information which it has sent to the requested authority. The decision to withdraw shall be transmitted to the requested authority in writing.

CHAPTER III

Requests for notification

Article 9

The request for notification referred to in Article 5 of Directive 76/308/EEC shall be made out in writing in duplicate in accordance with the model in Annex II to this Directive. The said request shall bear the official stamp of the applicant authority and shall be signed by an official thereof duly authorised to make such a request.

Two copies of the instrument or decision, notification of which is requested, shall be attached to the request.

Article 10

The request for notification may relate to any natural or legal person who, in accordance with the law in force in the Member State of the applicant authority, is required to be informed of any instrument or decision which concerns that person.

In so far as such is not indicated in the instrument or decision of which notification is requested, the request for notification shall refer to the rules in force in the Member State of the applicant authority governing the procedure for contestation of the claim or for its recovery.

Article 11

1. The requested authority shall acknowledge receipt of the request for notification in writing as soon as possible and in any event within seven days of such receipt.

Immediately upon receipt of the request for notification, the requested authority shall take the necessary measures to effect notification in accordance with the law in force in the Member State in which it is situated.

If necessary, but without jeopardising the final date for notification indicated in the request for notification, the requested authority shall ask the applicant authority to provide additional information.

The applicant authority shall provide all additional information to which it normally has access.

The requested authority shall in any event not question the validity of the instrument or decision of which notification is requested.

2. The requested authority shall inform the applicant authority of the date of notification as soon as this has been effected, by returning to it one of the copies of the request with the certificate on the reverse side duly completed.

CHAPTER IV

Requests for recovery or for precautionary measures

Article 12

1. Requests for recovery or for precautionary measures referred to in Articles 6 and 13 respectively of Directive 76/308/EEC shall be made out in writing in accordance with the model in Annex III to this Directive.

Such requests, which shall include a declaration that the conditions laid down in Directive 76/308/EEC for initiating the mutual assistance procedure have been fulfilled, shall bear the official stamp of the applicant authority and shall be signed by an official thereof duly authorised to make such a request.

2. The instrument permitting enforcement shall accompany the request for recovery or for precautionary measures. A single instrument may be issued in respect of several claims where they concern one and the same person.

For the purposes of Articles 13 to 20 of this Directive, all claims covered by the same instrument permitting enforcement shall be deemed to constitute a single claim.

Article 13

Requests for recovery or for precautionary measures may relate to any person referred to in Article 4.

Article 14

1. If the currency of the Member State of the requested authority is different from the currency of the Member State of the applicant authority, the applicant authority shall express the amount of the claim to be recovered in both currencies.

2. The rate of exchange to be used for the purposes of paragraph 1 shall be the latest selling rate recorded on the most representative exchange market or markets of the Member State of the applicant authority on the date when the request for recovery is signed.

Article 15

1. The requested authority shall, in writing, as soon as possible and in any event within seven days of receipt of the request for recovery or for precautionary measures—

(a) acknowledge receipt of the request;

(b) ask the applicant authority to complete the request if it does not contain the information or other particulars mentioned in Article 7 of Directive 76/308/EEC.

The applicant authority shall provide all information to which it has access.

2. If the requested authority does not take the requisite action within the three-month period laid down in Article 8 of Directive 76/308/EEC, it shall, as soon as possible and in any event within seven days of the expiry of that period, inform the applicant authority in writing of the grounds for its failure to comply with the time limit.

Article 16

Where, within a reasonable time having regard to the particular case, all or part of the claim cannot be recovered or precautionary measures cannot be taken, the requested authority shall so inform the applicant authority, indicating the reasons therefor.

No later than at the end of each six-month period following the date of acknowledgement of the receipt of the request, the requested authority shall inform the applicant authority of the state of progress or the outcome of the procedure for recovery or for precautionary measures.

In the light of the information received from the requested authority, the applicant authority may request the latter to re-open the procedure for recovery or for precautionary measures. That request shall be made in writing within two months of the receipt of the notification of the outcome of that procedure, and shall be treated by the requested authority in accordance with the provisions applying to the initial request.

Article 17

1. Any action contesting the claim or the instrument permitting its enforcement which is taken in the Member State of the applicant authority shall be notified to the requested authority in writing by the applicant authority immediately after the latter has been informed of such action.

2. If the laws, regulations and administrative practices in force in the Member State of the requested authority do not permit precautionary measures or the recovery requested under the second subparagraph of Article 12(2) of Directive 76/308/EEC, the requested authority shall notify the applicant authority to that effect as soon as possible and in any event within one month of the receipt of the notification referred to in paragraph 1.

3. Any action which is taken in the Member State of the requested authority for reimbursement of sums recovered or for compensation in relation to recovery of contested claims under the second subparagraph of Article 12(2) of Directive 76/308/EEC shall be notified to the applicant authority in writing by the requested authority immediately after the latter has been informed of such action.

The requested authority shall as far as possible involve the applicant authority in the procedures for settling the amount to be reimbursed and the compensation due. Upon a reasoned request from the requested authority, the applicant authority shall transfer the sums reimbursed and the compensation paid within two months of the receipt of that request.

Article 18

1. If the request for recovery or for precautionary measures becomes devoid of purpose as a result of payment of the claim or of its cancellation or for any other reason, the applicant authority shall immediately inform the requested authority in writing so that the latter may stop any action which it has undertaken.

2. Where the amount of the claim which is the subject of the request for recovery or for precautionary measures is adjusted for any reason, the applicant authority shall immediately inform the requested authority in writing, and if necessary issue a new instrument permitting enforcement.

3. If the adjustment entails a reduction in the amount of the claim, the requested authority shall continue the action which it has undertaken with a view to recovery or to the taking of precautionary measures, but that action shall be limited to the amount still outstanding.

If, at the time when the requested authority is informed of the reduction in the amount of the claim, an amount exceeding the amount still outstanding has already been recovered by it but the transfer procedure referred to in Article 19 has not yet been initiated, the requested authority shall repay the amount overpaid to the person entitled thereto.

4. If the adjustment entails an increase in the amount of the claim, the applicant authority shall as soon as possible address to the requested authority an additional request for recovery or for precautionary measures.

That additional request shall, as far as possible, be dealt with by the requested authority at the same time as the original request from the applicant authority. Where, in view of the state of progress of the existing procedure, consolidation of the additional request with the original request is not possible, the requested authority shall be required to comply with the additional request only if it concerns an amount not less than that referred to in Article 25(2).

5. In order to convert the adjusted amount of the claim into the currency of the Member State of the requested authority, the applicant authority shall use the exchange rate used in its original request.

Article 19

Any sum recovered by the requested authority, including, where applicable, the interest referred to in Article 9(2) of Directive 76/308/EEC, shall be transferred to the applicant authority in the currency of the Member State of the requested authority. The transfer shall take place within one month of the date on which recovery was effected.

The competent authorities of the Member States may agree different arrangements for the transfer of amounts below the threshold referred to in Article 25(2) of this Directive.

Article 20

Irrespective of any amounts collected by the requested authority by way of the interest referred to in Article 9(2) of Directive 76/308/EEC, the claim shall be deemed to have been recovered in proportion to the recovery of the amount expressed in the national currency of the Member State of the requested authority, on the basis of the exchange rate referred to in Article 14(2) of this Directive.

CHAPTER V

Transmission of communications

Article 21

1. All information communicated in writing pursuant to this Directive shall, as far as possible, be transmitted only by electronic means, except for—

(a) the request for notification referred to in Article 5 of Directive 76/308/EEC and the instrument or decision of which notification is requested;

(b) requests for recovery or for precautionary measures referred to in Articles 6 and 13 respectively of Directive 76/308/EEC, and the instrument permitting enforcement.

2. The competent authorities of the Member States may agree to waive the communication on paper of the requests and instruments specified in paragraph 1.

Article 22

Each Member State shall designate a central office with principal responsibility for communication by electronic means with other Member States. That office shall be connected to the CCN/CSI network.

Where several authorities are appointed in a Member State for the purpose of applying this Directive, the central office shall be responsible for the forwarding of all communication by electronic means between those authorities and the central offices of other Member States.

Article 23

1. Where the competent authorities of the Member States store information in electronic data bases and exchange such information by electronic means, they shall take all measures necessary to ensure that any information communicated in whatever form pursuant to this Directive is treated as confidential.

It shall be covered by the obligation of professional secrecy and shall enjoy the protection extended to similar information under the national law of the Member State which received it.

2. The information referred to in paragraph 1 may be made available only to the persons and authorities referred to in Article 16 of Directive 76/308/EEC.

Such information may be used in connection with judicial or administrative proceedings initiated for the recovery of levies, duties, taxes and other measures referred to in Article 2 of Directive 76/308/EEC.

Persons duly accredited by the Security Accreditation Authority of the European Commission may have access to this information only in so far as is necessary for the care, maintenance and development of the CCN/CSI network.

3. Where the competent authorities of the Member States communicate by electronic means, they shall take all measures necessary to ensure that all communications are duly authorised.

Article 24

Information and other particulars communicated by the requested authority to the applicant authority shall be conveyed in the official language or one of the official languages of the Member State of the requested authority or in another language agreed between the applicant and requested authorities.

CHAPTER VI

Eligibility and refusal of requests for assistance

Article 25

1. A request for assistance may be made by the applicant authority in respect of either a single claim or several claims where those are recoverable from one and the same person.

2. No request for assistance may be made if the total amount of the relevant claim or claims listed in Article 2 of Directive 76/308/EEC is less than EUR 1500.

Article 26

If the requested authority decides, pursuant to the first paragraph of Article 14 of Directive 76/308/EEC, to refuse a request for assistance, it shall notify the applicant authority in writing of the reasons for the refusal. Such notification shall be given by the requested authority as soon as it has taken its decision and in any event within three months of the date of receipt of the request for assistance.

CHAPTER VII

Reimbursement arrangements

Article 27

Each Member State shall appoint at least one official duly authorised to agree reimbursement arrangements under Article 18(3) of Directive 76/308/EEC.

Article 28

1. If the requested authority decides to request reimbursement arrangements it shall notify the applicant authority in writing of the reasons for its view that recovery of the claim poses a specific problem, entails very high costs or relates to the fight against organised crime.

The requested authority shall append a detailed estimate of the costs for which it requests reimbursement by the applicant authority.

2. The applicant authority shall acknowledge receipt of the request for reimbursement arrangements in writing as soon as possible and in any event within seven days of receipt.

Within two months of the date of acknowledgement of receipt of the said request, the applicant authority shall inform the requested authority whether and to what extent it agrees with the proposed reimbursement arrangements.

3. If no agreement is reached between the applicant and requested authority with respect to reimbursement arrangements, the requested authority shall continue recovery procedures in the normal way.

CHAPTER VIII

Final provisions

Article 29

Each Member State shall inform the Commission before 15 March each year, as far as possible by electronic means, of the use made of the procedures laid down in Directive 76/308/EEC and of the results achieved in the previous calendar year, in accordance with the model in Annex IV to this Directive.

Article 30

The Member States shall bring into force the laws, regulations and administrative provisions necessary to comply with this Directive by 30 April 2003 at the latest. They shall forthwith inform the Commission thereof.

When Member States adopt those provisions, they shall contain a reference to this Directive or be accompanied by such a reference on the occasion of their official publication. Member States shall determine how such reference is to be made.

Article 31

The Commission shall communicate to the other Member States the measures which each Member State takes for implementing this Directive.

Each Member State shall notify the other Member States and the Commission of the name and address of the competent authorities for the purpose of applying this Directive, as well as of the officials authorised to agree arrangements under Article 18(3) of Directive 76/308/EEC.

Article 32

Directive 77/794/EEC is hereby repealed.

References to the repealed Directive shall be construed as references to this Directive.

Article 33

This Directive shall enter into force on the 20th day following that of its publication in the Official Journal of the European Communities.

Article 34

This Directive is addressed to the Member States.

(*Annexes I–IV have not been reproduced*).

Council Directive of 5 October 2006 on the exemption from taxes of imports of small consignments of goods of a non-commercial character from third countries (codified version)

(2006/79/EC)

Note—See OJ L 286, 17.10.2006 p 15.

THE COUNCIL OF THE EUROPEAN UNION,

Having regard to the Treaty establishing the European Community, and in particular Article 93 thereof,

Having regard to the proposal from the Commission,

Having regard to the opinion of the European Parliament[1],

Having regard to the opinion of the European Economic and Social Committee[2],

Whereas:

(1) Council Directive 78/1035/EEC of 19 December 1978 on the exemption from taxes of imports of small consignments of goods of a non-commercial character from third countries[3] has been substantially amended several times[4]. In the interests of clarity and rationality, the said Directive should be codified.

(2) Provision should be made for the exemption from turnover taxes and excise duties of imports of small consignments of goods of a non-commercial character from third countries.

(3) To that end the limits within which such exemption is to be applied should, for practical reasons, be as far as possible the same as those laid down for the Community arrangements for exemption from customs duties in Council Regulation (EEC) No 918/83 of 28 March 1983 setting up a Community system of reliefs from customs duty[5].

(4) It is necessary to set special limits for certain products because of the high level of taxation to which they are at present subject in the Member States.

(5) This Directive should be without prejudice to the obligations of the Member States relating to the time-limits for transposition into national law of the Directives set out in Annex I, Part B,

HAS ADOPTED THIS DIRECTIVE:

Notes—[1] Not yet published in the Official Journal.
[2] Not yet published in the Official Journal.
[3] OJ L 366, 28.12.1978, p. 34. Directive as last amended by the 1994 Act of Accession.
[4] See Annex I, Part A.
[5] OJ L 105, 23.4.1983, p. 1. Regulation as last amended by the 2003 Act of Accession.

Article 1

1. Goods in small consignments of a non-commercial character sent from a third country by private persons to other private persons in a Member State shall be exempt on importation from turnover tax and excise duty.

2. For the purposes of paragraph 1, 'small consignments of a non-commercial character' shall mean consignments which:

(*a*) are of an occasional nature;

(*b*) contain only goods intended for the personal or family use of the consignees, the nature and quantity of which do not indicate that they are being imported for any commercial purpose;

(*c*) contain goods with a total value not exceeding EUR 45;

(*d*) are sent by the sender to the consignee without payment of any kind.

Article 2

1. Article I shall apply to the goods listed below subject to the following quantitative limits:

(*a*) tobacco products

(i) 50 cigarettes,

or

(ii) 25 cigarillos (cigars of a maximum weight of three grams each),

or

(iii) 10 cigars,

or

(iv) 50 grams of smoking tobacco;

(*b*) alcohol and alcoholic beverages:

(i) distilled beverages and spirits of an alcoholic strength exceeding 22% vol.; undenatured ethyl alcohol of 80% vol. and over: one standard bottle (up to 1 litre),

or

(ii) distilled beverages and spirits, and aperitifs with a wine or alcohol base, tafia, saké or similar beverages of an alcoholic strength of 22% vol. or less; sparkling wines, fortified wines: one standard bottle (up to 1 litre),

or

(iii) still wines: two litres;

(*c*) perfumes: 50 grams,

or

toilet waters: 0,25 litre or eight ounces;

(*d*) coffee: 500 grams,

or

coffee extracts and essences: 200 grams;

(*e*) tea: 100 grams,

or

tea extracts and essences: 40 grams.

2. Member States shall have the right to reduce the quantities of the products referred to in paragraph 1 eligible for exemption from turnover tax and excise duties, or to abolish exemption for such products altogether.

Article 3

Any goods listed in Article 2 which are contained in a small consignment of a non-commercial character in quantities exceeding those laid down in the said Article shall be excluded in their entirety from exemption.

Article 4

1. The euro equivalent in national currency which shall apply for the implementation of this Directive shall be fixed once a year. The rates applicable shall be those obtaining on the first working day of October with effect from 1 January of the following year.

2. Member States may round off the amounts in national currency resulting from the conversion of the amounts in euros provided for in Article 1(2), provided such rounding-off does not exceed EUR 2.

3. Member States may maintain the amount of the exemption in force at the time of the annual adjustment provided for in paragraph 1 if, prior to the rounding-off provided for in paragraph 2, conversion of the amount of the exemption expressed in euros would result in a change of less than 5% in the exemption expressed in national currency.

Article 5

Member States shall communicate to the Commission the text of the main provisions of national law which they adopt in the field covered by this Directive. The Commission shall inform the other Member States thereof.

Article 6

Directive 78/1035/EEC shall be repealed, without prejudice to the obligations of the Member States relating to the time-limits for transposition into national law of the Directives set out in Annex I, Part B.

References to the repealed Directive shall be construed as references to this Directive and shall be read in accordance with the correlation table in Annex II.

Article 7

This Directive shall enter into force on the 20th day following its publication in the Official Journal of the European Union.

Article 8

This Directive is addressed to the Member States.

Done at Luxembourg, 5 October 2006.

For the Council

The President

K. Rajamäki

ANNEX I

PART A

REPEALED DIRECTIVE WITH ITS SUCCESSIVE AMENDMENTS

Council Directive 78/1035/EEC[1] (OJ L 366, 28.12.1978, p. 34)	
Council Directive 81/933/EEC (OJ L 338, 25.11.1981, p. 24)	only Article 2
Council Directive 85/576/EEC (OJ L 372, 31.12.1985, p. 30)	

Notes—[1] Directive 78/1035/EEC was also amended by the 1994 Act of Accession.

PART B

TIME-LIMITS FOR TRANSPOSITION INTO NATIONAL LAW

(referred to in Article 6)

Directive	Time-limit for transposition
78/1035/EEC	1 January 1979
81/933/EEC	31 December 1981
85/576/EEC	30 June 1986

ANNEX II

CORRELATION TABLE

Directive 78/1035/EEC	This Directive
Article 1(1)	Article 1(1)
Article 1(2), first indent	Article 1(2)(*a*)
Article 1(2), second indent	Article 1(2)(*b*)
Article 1(2), third indent	Article 1(2)(*c*)
Article 1(2), fourth indent	Article 1(2)(*d*)
Article 2(1)(*a*), from "50 cigarettes" to "50 grams of smoking tobacco"	Article 2(1)(*a*)(i) to (iv)
Article 2(1)(*b*)	Article 2(1)(*b*)
Article 2(1)(*b*), first indent	Article 2(1)(*b*)(i)
Article 2(1)(*b*), second indent	Article 2(1)(*b*)(ii)
Article 2(1)(*b*), third indent	Article 2(1)(*b*)(iii)
Article 2(1)(*c*), (*d*) and (*e*)	Article 2(1)(*c*), (*d*) and (*e*)
Article 2(2)	Article 2(2)
Article 2(3)	—
Article 3	Article 3
Article 4(1)	—
Article 4(2)	Article 4(1)
Article 4(3)	Article 4(2)
Article 4(4)	Article 4(3)
Article 5(1)	—
Article 5(2)	Article 5

	Article 6
—	Article 7
Article 6	Article 8
—	Annex I
—	Annex II

Council Directive
of 28 November 2006
on the common system of value added tax

(2006/112/EC)

Note—This Directive repeals Council Directives 67/227/EEC (First Council Directive of 11 April 1967) and 77/388 (Sixth Council Directive of 17 May 1977). For correlation table, see Annex XII.

THE COUNCIL OF THE EUROPEAN UNION,

Having regard to the Treaty establishing the European Community, and in particular Article 93 thereof,

Having regard to the proposal from the Commission,

Having regard to the Opinion of the European Parliament,

Having regard to the Opinion of the European Economic and Social Committee,

Whereas:

(1) Council Directive 77/388/EEC of 17 May 1977 on the harmonisation of the laws of the Member States relating to turnover taxes — Common system of value added tax: uniform basis of assessment[1] has been significantly amended on several occasions. Now that new amendments are being made to the said Directive, it is desirable, for reasons of clarity and rationalisation that the Directive should be recast.

(2) The recast text should incorporate all those provisions of Council Directive 67/227/EEC of 11 April 1967 on the harmonisation of legislation of Member States concerning turnover taxes[2] which are still applicable. That Directive should therefore be repealed.

(3) To ensure that the provisions are presented in a clear and rational manner, consistent with the principle of better regulation, it is appropriate to recast the structure and the wording of the Directive although this will not, in principle, bring about material changes in the existing legislation. A small number of substantive amendments are however inherent to the recasting exercise and should nevertheless be made. Where such changes are made, these are listed exhaustively in the provisions governing transposition and entry into force.

(4) The attainment of the objective of establishing an internal market presupposes the application in Member States of legislation on turnover taxes that does not distort conditions of competition or hinder the free movement of goods and services. It is therefore necessary to achieve such harmonisation of legislation on turnover taxes by means of a system of value added tax (VAT), such as will eliminate, as far as possible, factors which may distort conditions of competition, whether at national or Community level.

(5) A VAT system achieves the highest degree of simplicity and of neutrality when the tax is levied in as general a manner as possible and when its scope covers all stages of production and distribution, as well as the supply of services. It is therefore in the interests of the internal market and of Member States to adopt a common system which also applies to the retail trade.

(6) It is necessary to proceed by stages, since the harmonisation of turnover taxes leads in Member States to alterations in tax structure and appreciable consequences in the budgetary, economic and social fields.

(7) The common system of VAT should, even if rates and exemptions are not fully harmonised, result in neutrality in competition, such that within the territory of each Member State similar goods and services bear the same tax burden, whatever the length of the production and distribution chain.

(8) Pursuant to Council Decision 2000/597/EC, Euratom, of 29 September 2000 on the system of the European Communities' own resources[3], the budget of the European Communities is to be financed, without prejudice to other revenue, wholly from the Communities' own resources. Those resources are to include those accruing from VAT and obtained through the application of a uniform rate of tax to bases of assessment determined in a uniform manner and in accordance with Community rules.

(9) It is vital to provide for a transitional period to allow national laws in specified fields to be gradually adapted.

(10) During this transitional period, intra-Community transactions carried out by taxable persons other than exempt taxable persons should be taxed in the Member State of destination, in accordance with the rates and conditions set by that Member State.

(11) It is also appropriate that, during that transitional period, intra-Community acquisitions of a certain value, made by exempt persons or by non-taxable legal persons, certain intra-Community distance selling and the supply of new means of transport to individuals or

to exempt or non-taxable bodies should also be taxed in the Member State of destination, in accordance with the rates and conditions set by that Member State, in so far as such transactions would, in the absence of special provisions, be likely to cause significant distortion of competition between Member States.

(12) For reasons connected with their geographic, economic and social situation, certain territories should be excluded from the scope of this Directive.

(13) In order to enhance the non-discriminatory nature of the tax, the term 'taxable person' should be defined in such a way that the Member States may use it to cover persons who occasionally carry out certain transactions.

(14) The term 'taxable transaction' may lead to difficulties, in particular as regards transactions treated as taxable transactions. Those concepts should therefore be clarified.

(15) With a view to facilitating intra-Community trade in work on movable tangible property, it is appropriate to establish the tax arrangements applicable to such transactions when they are carried out for a customer who is identified for VAT purposes in a Member State other than that in which the transaction is physically carried out.

(16) A transport operation within the territory of a Member State should be treated as the intra-Community transport of goods where it is directly linked to a transport operation carried out between Member States, in order to simplify not only the principles and arrangements for taxing those domestic transport services but also the rules applicable to ancillary services and to services supplied by intermediaries who take part in the supply of the various services.

(17) Determination of the place where taxable transactions are carried out may engender conflicts concerning jurisdiction as between Member States, in particular as regards the supply of goods for assembly or the supply of services. Although the place where a supply of services is carried out should in principle be fixed as the place where the supplier has established his place of business, it should be defined as being in the Member State of the customer, in particular in the case of certain services supplied between taxable persons where the cost of the services is included in the price of the goods.

(18) It is necessary to clarify the definition of the place of taxation of certain transactions carried out on board ships, aircraft or trains in the course of passenger transport within the Community.

(19) Electricity and gas are treated as goods for VAT purposes. It is, however, particularly difficult to determine the place of supply. In order to avoid double taxation or non taxation and to attain a genuine internal market free of barriers linked to the VAT regime, the place of supply of gas through the natural gas distribution system, or of electricity, before the goods reach the final stage of consumption, should therefore be the place where the customer has established his business. The supply of electricity and gas at the final stage, that is to say, from traders and distributors to the final consumer, should be taxed at the place where the customer actually uses and consumes the goods.

(20) In the case of the hiring out of movable tangible property, application of the general rule that supplies of services are taxed in the Member State in which the supplier is established may lead to substantial distortion of competition if the lessor and the lessee are established in different Member States and the rates of taxation in those States differ. It is therefore necessary to establish that the place of supply of a service is the place where the customer has established his business or has a fixed establishment for which the service has been supplied or, in the absence thereof, the place where he has his permanent address or usually resides.

(21) However, as regards the hiring out of means of transport, it is appropriate, for reasons of control, to apply strictly the general rule, and thus to regard the place where the supplier has established his business as the place of supply.

(22) All telecommunications services consumed within the Community should be taxed to prevent distortion of competition in that field. To that end, telecommunications services supplied to taxable persons established in the Community or to customers established in third countries should, in principle, be taxed at the place where the customer for the services is established. In order to ensure uniform taxation of telecommunications services which are supplied by taxable persons established in third territories or third countries to non-taxable persons established in the Community and which are effectively used and enjoyed in the Community, Member States should, however, provide for the place of supply to be within the Community.

(23) Also to prevent distortions of competition, radio and television broadcasting services and electronically supplied services provided from third territories or third countries to persons established in the Community, or from the Community to customers established in third territories or third countries, should be taxed at the place of establishment of the customer.

(24) The concepts of chargeable event and of the chargeability of VAT should be harmonised if the introduction of the common system of VAT and of any subsequent amendments thereto are to take effect at the same time in all Member States.

(25) The taxable amount should be harmonised so that the application of VAT to taxable transactions leads to comparable results in all the Member States.

(26) To prevent loss of tax revenues through the use of connected parties to derive tax benefits, it should, in specific limited circumstances, be possible for Member States to intervene as regards the taxable amount of supplies of goods or services and intra-Community acquisitions of goods.

(27) In order to combat tax evasion or avoidance, it should be possible for Member States to include within the taxable amount of a transaction which involves the working of investment gold provided by a customer, the value of that investment gold where, by virtue of being worked, the gold loses its status of investment gold. When they apply these measures, Member States should be allowed a certain degree of discretion.

(28) If distortions are to be avoided, the abolition of fiscal controls at frontiers entails, not only a uniform basis of assessment, but also sufficient alignment as between Member States of a number of rates and rate levels.

(29) The standard rate of VAT in force in the various Member States, combined with the mechanism of the transitional system, ensures that this system functions to an acceptable degree. To prevent divergences in the standard rates of VAT applied by the Member States from leading to structural imbalances in the Community and distortions of competition in some sectors of activity, a minimum standard rate of 15 % should be fixed, subject to review.

(30) In order to preserve neutrality of VAT, the rates applied by Member States should be such as to enable, as a general rule, deduction of the VAT applied at the preceding stage.

(31) During the transitional period, certain derogations concerning the number and the level of rates should be possible.

(32) To achieve a better understanding of the impact of reduced rates, it is necessary for the Commission to prepare an assessment report on the impact of reduced rates applied to locally supplied services, notably in terms of job creation, economic growth and the proper functioning of the internal market.

(33) In order to tackle the problem of unemployment, those Member States wishing to do so should be allowed to experiment with the operation and impact, in terms of job creation, of a reduction in the VAT rate applied to labour-intensive services. That reduction is also likely to reduce the incentive for the businesses concerned to join or remain in the black economy.

(34) However, such a reduction in the VAT rate is not without risk for the smooth functioning of the internal market and for tax neutrality. Provision should therefore be made for an authorisation procedure to be introduced for a period that is fixed but sufficiently long, so that it is possible to assess the impact of the reduced rates applied to locally supplied services. In order to make sure that such a measure remains verifiable and limited, its scope should be closely defined.

(35) A common list of exemptions should be drawn up so that the Communities' own resources may be collected in a uniform manner in all the Member States.

(36) For the benefit both of the persons liable for payment of VAT and the competent administrative authorities, the methods of applying VAT to certain supplies and intra-Community acquisitions of products subject to excise duty should be aligned with the procedures and obligations concerning the duty to declare in the case of shipment of such products to another Member State laid down in Council Directive 92/12/EEC of 25 February 1992 on the general arrangements for products subject to excise duty and on the holding, movement and monitoring of such products[4].

(37) The supply of gas through the natural gas distribution system, and of electricity is taxed at the place of the customer. In order to avoid double taxation, the importation of such products should therefore be exempted from VAT.

(38) In respect of taxable operations in the domestic market linked to intra-Community trade in goods carried out during the transitional period by taxable persons not established within the territory of the Member State in which the intra-Community acquisition of goods takes place, including chain transactions, it is necessary to provide for simplification measures ensuring equal treatment in all the Member States. To that end, the provisions concerning the taxation system and the person liable for payment of the VAT due in respect of such operations should be harmonised. It is however, necessary to exclude in principle from such arrangements goods that are intended to be supplied at the retail stage.

(39) The rules governing deductions should be harmonised to the extent that they affect the actual amounts collected. The deductible proportion should be calculated in a similar manner in all the Member States.

(40) The scheme which allows the adjustment of deductions for capital goods over the lifetime of the asset, according to its actual use, should also be applicable to certain services with the nature of capital goods.

(41) It is appropriate to specify the persons liable for payment of VAT, particularly in the case of services supplied by a person who is not established in the Member State in which the VAT is due.

(42) Member States should be able, in specific cases, to designate the recipient of supplies of goods or services as the person liable for payment of VAT. This should assist Member States in simplifying the rules and countering tax evasion and avoidance in identified sectors and on certain types of transactions.

(43) Member States should be entirely free to designate the person liable for payment of the VAT on importation.

(44) Member States should be able to provide that someone other than the person liable for payment of VAT is to be held jointly and severally liable for its payment.

(45) The obligations of taxable persons should be harmonised as far as possible so as to ensure the necessary safeguards for the collection of VAT in a uniform manner in all the Member States.

(46) The use of electronic invoicing should allow tax authorities to carry out their monitoring activities. It is therefore appropriate, in order to ensure the internal market functions properly, to draw up a list, harmonised at Community level, of the particulars that must appear on invoices and to establish a number of common arrangements governing the use of electronic invoicing and the electronic storage of invoices, as well as for self-billing and the outsourcing of invoicing operations.

(47) Subject to conditions which they lay down, Member States should allow certain statements and returns to be made by electronic means, and may require that electronic means be used.

(48) The necessary pursuit of a reduction in the administrative and statistical formalities to be completed by businesses, particularly small and medium-sized enterprises, should be reconciled with the implementation of effective control measures and the need, on both economic and tax grounds, to maintain the quality of Community statistical instruments.

(49) Member States should be allowed to continue to apply their special schemes for small enterprises, in accordance with common provisions, and with a view to closer harmonisation.

(50) Member States should remain free to apply a special scheme involving flat rate rebates of input VAT to farmers not covered by the normal scheme. The basic principles of that special scheme should be established and a common method adopted, for the purposes of collecting own resources, for calculating the value added by such farmers.

(51) It is appropriate to adopt a Community taxation system to be applied to second-hand goods, works of art, antiques and collectors' items, with a view to preventing double taxation and the distortion of competition as between taxable persons.

(52) The application of the normal VAT rules to gold constitutes a major obstacle to its use for financial investment purposes and therefore justifies the application of a special tax scheme, with a view also to enhancing the international competitiveness of the Community gold market.

(53) The supply of gold for investment purposes is inherently similar to other financial investments which are exempt from VAT. Consequently, exemption appears to be the most appropriate tax treatment for supplies of investment gold.

(54) The definition of investment gold should cover gold coins the value of which primarily reflects the price of the gold contained. For reasons of transparency and legal certainty, a yearly list of coins covered by the investment gold scheme should be drawn up, providing security for the operators trading in such coins. That list should be without prejudice to the exemption of coins which are not included in the list but which meet the criteria laid down in this Directive.

(55) In order to prevent tax evasion while at the same time alleviating the financing burden for the supply of gold of a degree of purity above a certain level, it is justifiable to allow Member States to designate the customer as the person liable for payment of VAT.

(56) In order to facilitate compliance with fiscal obligations by operators providing electronically supplied services, who are neither established nor required to be identified for VAT purposes within the Community, a special scheme should be established. Under that scheme it should be possible for any operator supplying such services by electronic means to non-taxable persons within the Community, if he is not otherwise identified for VAT purposes within the Community, to opt for identification in a single Member State.

(57) It is desirable for the provisions concerning radio and television broadcasting and certain electronically supplied services to be put into place on a temporary basis only and to be reviewed in the light of experience within a short period of time.

(58) It is necessary to promote the uniform application of the provisions of this Directive and to that end an advisory committee on value added tax should be set up to enable the Member States and the Commission to cooperate closely.

(59) Member States should be able, within certain limits and subject to certain conditions, to introduce, or to continue to apply, special measures derogating from this Directive in order to simplify the levying of tax or to prevent certain forms of tax evasion or avoidance.

(60) In order to ensure that a Member State which has submitted a request for derogation is not left in doubt as to what action the Commission plans to take in response, time-limits should be laid down within which the Commission must present to the Council either a proposal for authorisation or a communication setting out its objections.

(61) It is essential to ensure uniform application of the VAT system. Implementing measures are appropriate to realise that aim.

(62) Those measures should, in particular, address the problem of double taxation of cross-border transactions which can occur as the result of divergences between Member States in the application of the rules governing the place where taxable transactions are carried out.

(63) Although the scope of the implementing measures would be limited, those measures would have a budgetary impact which for one or more Member States could be significant. Accordingly, the Council is justified in reserving to itself the right to exercise implementing powers.

VAT

(64) In view of their limited scope, the implementing measures should be adopted by the Council acting unanimously on a proposal from the Commission.

(65) Since, for those reasons, the objectives of this Directive cannot be sufficiently achieved by the Member States and can therefore be better achieved by at Community level, the Community may adopt measures, in accordance with the principle of subsidiarity as set out in Article 5 of the Treaty. In accordance with the principle of proportionality, as set out in that Article, this Directive does not go beyond what is necessary in order to achieve those objectives.

(66) The obligation to transpose this Directive into national law should be confined to those provisions which represent a substantive change as compared with the earlier Directives. The obligation to transpose into national law the provisions which are unchanged arises under the earlier Directives.

(67) This Directive should be without prejudice to the obligations of the Member States in relation to the time-limits for transposition into national law of the Directives listed in Annex XI, Part B,

HAS ADOPTED THIS DIRECTIVE:

[1] OJ L 145, 13.6.1977, p. 1. Directive as last amended by Directive 2006/98/EC (OJ L 221, 12.8.2006, p. 9).
[2] OJ 71, 14.4.1967, p. 1301. Directive as last amended by Directive 69/ 463/EEC (OJ L 320 of 20.12.1969, p. 34).
[3] OJ L 253, 7.10.2000, p. 42.
[4] OJ L 76, 23.3.1992, p. 1. Directive as last amended by Directive 2004/106/EC (OJ L 359, 4.12.2004, p. 30).

ARRANGEMENT OF CONTENTS

TITLE I
SUBJECT MATTER AND SCOPE

Article 1

1. This Directive establishes the common system of value added tax (VAT).

2. The principle of the common system of VAT entails the application to goods and services of a general tax on consumption exactly proportional to the price of the goods and services, however many transactions take place in the production and distribution process before the stage at which the tax is charged.

On each transaction, VAT, calculated on the price of the goods or services at the rate applicable to such goods or services, shall be chargeable after deduction of the amount of VAT borne directly by the various cost components.

The common system of VAT shall be applied up to and including the retail trade stage.

Simon's Tax Cases—Art 1(2), *Société Financière d'Investissements SPRL v Belgium* [2000] STC 164*; *Belgocodex SA v Belgium* [2000] STC 351*; *Midland Bank Plc v C&E Comrs* [2000] STC 501*; *C&E Comrs v Southern Primary Housing Association Ltd* [2003] STC 525*; *C&E Comrs v Southern Primary Housing Association Ltd* [2004] STC 209*; *JD Wetherspoon plc v R&C Comrs* [2009] STC 1022*.

Article 2

1. The following transactions shall be subject to VAT:

(*a*) the supply of goods for consideration within the territory of a Member State by a taxable person acting as such;

(*b*) the intra-Community acquisition of goods for consideration within the territory of a Member State by:

(i) a taxable person acting as such, or a non-taxable legal person, where the vendor is a taxable person acting as such who is not eligible for the exemption for small enterprises provided for in Articles 282 to 292 and who is not covered by Articles 33 or 36;

(ii) in the case of new means of transport, a taxable person, or a non-taxable legal person, whose other acquisitions are not subject to VAT pursuant to Article 3(1), or any other non-taxable person;

(iii) in the case of products subject to excise duty, where the excise duty on the intra-Community acquisition is chargeable, pursuant to Directive 92/12/EEC, within the territory of the Member State, a taxable person, or a non-taxable legal person, whose other acquisitions are not subject to VAT pursuant to Article 3(1);

(*c*) the supply of services for consideration within the territory of a Member State by a taxable person acting as such;

(*d*) the importation of goods.

2. (*a*) For the purposes of point (ii) of paragraph 1(*b*), the following shall be regarded as 'means of transport', where they are intended for the transport of persons or goods:

(i) motorised land vehicles the capacity of which exceeds 48 cubic centimetres or the power of which exceeds 7,2 kilowatts;

(ii) vessels exceeding 7,5 metres in length, with the exception of vessels used for navigation on the high seas and carrying passengers for reward, and of vessels used for the purposes of commercial, industrial or fishing activities, or for rescue or assistance at sea, or for inshore fishing;

(iii) aircraft the take-off weight of which exceeds 1 550 kilograms, with the exception of aircraft used by airlines operating for reward chiefly on international routes.

(*b*) These means of transport shall be regarded as 'new' in the cases:

(i) of motorised land vehicles, where the supply takes place within six months of the date of first entry into service or where the vehicle has travelled for no more than 6 000 kilometres;

(ii) of vessels, where the supply takes place within three months of the date of first entry into service or where the vessel has sailed for no more than 100 hours;

(iii) of aircraft, where the supply takes place within three months of the date of first entry into service or where the aircraft has flown for no more than 40 hours.

(*c*) Member States shall lay down the conditions under which the facts referred to in point (*b*) may be regarded as established.

3. 'Products subject to excise duty' shall mean energy products, alcohol and alcoholic beverages and manufactured tobacco, as defined by current Community legislation, but not gas supplied through the natural gas distribution system or electricity.

Commentary—*De Voil Indirect Tax Service* **V2.101**.

Simon's Tax Cases—*C&E Comrs v Church Schools Foundation Ltd**; [2001] STC 1661*; *C&E Comrs v Polok* [2002] STC 361*; *Kretztechnik AG v Finanzamt Linz* [2005] STC 1118*; *Hotel Scandic Gåsabäck AB v Riksskatteverket* [2005] STC 1311*; *Société thermale d'Eugénie-les-Bains v Ministère de l'Economie, des Finances et de l'Industrie* [2008] STC 2470*.

Art 2(1), *University of Huddersfield Higher Education Corporation v C&E Comrs* [2006] STC 980*; *Elliniko Dimosio v Karageorgou and others* [2006] STC 1654*; *Ministero dell'Economia e delle Finanze and another v FCE Bank plc* [2007] STC 165*; *EC Commission v United Kingdom* [2007] STC 1211*; *Aktiebolaget NN v Skatteverket* [2008] STC 3203*.

Article 3

1. By way of derogation from Article 2(1)(*b*)(i), the following transactions shall not be subject to VAT:

(*a*) the intra-Community acquisition of goods by a taxable person or a non-taxable legal person, where the supply of such goods within the territory of the Member State of acquisition would be exempt pursuant to Articles 148 and 151;

(*b*) the intra-Community acquisition of goods, other than those referred to in point (*a*) and Article 4, and other than new means of transport or products subject to excise duty, by a taxable person for the purposes of his agricultural, forestry or fisheries business subject to the common flat-rate scheme for farmers, or by a taxable person who carries out only supplies of goods or services in respect of which VAT is not deductible, or by a non-taxable legal person.

2. Point (*b*) of paragraph 1 shall apply only if the following conditions are met:

(*a*) during the current calendar year, the total value of intra-Community acquisitions of goods does not exceed a threshold which the Member States shall determine but which may not be less than EUR 10 000 or the equivalent in national currency;

(*b*) during the previous calendar year, the total value of intra-Community acquisitions of goods did not exceed the threshold provided for in point (*a*).

The threshold which serves as the reference shall consist of the total value, exclusive of VAT due or paid in the Member State in which dispatch or transport of the goods began, of the intra-Community acquisitions of goods as referred to under point (*b*) of paragraph 1.

3. Member States shall grant taxable persons and non-taxable legal persons eligible under point (*b*) of paragraph 1 the right to opt for the general scheme provided for in Article 2(1)(*b*)(i).

Member States shall lay down the detailed rules for the exercise of the option referred to in the first subparagraph, which shall in any event cover a period of two calendar years.

Article 4

In addition to the transactions referred to in Article 3, the following transactions shall not be subject to VAT:

(*a*) the intra-Community acquisition of second-hand goods, works of art, collectors' items or antiques, as defined in points (1) to (4) of Article 311(1), where the vendor is a taxable dealer acting as such and VAT has been applied to the goods in the Member State in which their dispatch or transport began, in accordance with the margin scheme provided for in Articles 312 to 325;

(*b*) the intra-Community acquisition of second-hand means of transport, as defined in Article 327(3), where the vendor is a taxable dealer acting as such and VAT has been applied to the means of transport in the Member State in which their dispatch or transport began, in accordance with the transitional arrangements for second-hand means of transport;

(*c*) the intra-Community acquisition of second-hand goods, works of art, collectors' items or antiques, as defined in points (1) to (4) of Article 311(1), where the vendor is an organiser of sales by public auction, acting as such, and VAT has been applied to the goods in the Member State in which their dispatch or transport began, in accordance with the special arrangements for sales by public auction.

TITLE II
TERRITORIAL SCOPE

Article 5

For the purposes of applying this Directive, the following definitions shall apply:

(1) 'Community' and 'territory of the Community' mean the territories of the Member States as defined in point (2);

(2) 'Member State' and 'territory of a Member State' mean the territory of each Member State of the Community to which the Treaty establishing the European Community is applicable, in accordance with Article 299 of that Treaty, with the exception of any territory referred to in Article 6 of this Directive;

(3) 'third territories' means those territories referred to in Article 6;

(4) 'third country' means any State or territory to which the Treaty is not applicable.

Article 6

1. This Directive shall not apply to the following territories forming part of the customs territory of the Community:

(*a*) Mount Athos;
(*b*) the Canary Islands;
(*c*) the French overseas departments;
(*d*) the Åland Islands;
(*e*) the Channel Islands.

2. This Directive shall not apply to the following territories not forming part of the customs territory of the Community:

(*a*) the Island of Heligoland;
(*b*) the territory of Büsingen;
(*c*) Ceuta;
(*d*) Melilla;
(*e*) Livigno;
(*f*) Campione d'Italia;
(*g*) the Italian waters of Lake Lugano.

Article 7

1. In view of the conventions and treaties concluded with France, the United Kingdom and Cyprus respectively, the Principality of Monaco, the Isle of Man and the United Kingdom Sovereign Base Areas of Akrotiri and Dhekelia shall not be regarded, for the purposes of the application of this Directive, as third countries.

2. Member States shall take the measures necessary to ensure that transactions originating in or intended for the Principality of Monaco are treated as transactions originating in or intended for

France, that transactions originating in or intended for the Isle of Man are treated as transactions originating in or intended for the United Kingdom, and that transactions originating in or intended for the United Kingdom Sovereign Base Areas of Akrotiri and Dhekelia are treated as transactions originating in or intended for Cyprus.

Article 8

If the Commission considers that the provisions laid down in Articles 6 and 7 are no longer justified, particularly in terms of fair competition or own resources, it shall present appropriate proposals to the Council.

TITLE III
TAXABLE PERSONS

Article 9

1. 'Taxable person' shall mean any person who, independently, carries out in any place any economic activity, whatever the purpose or results of that activity.

Any activity of producers, traders or persons supplying services, including mining and agricultural activities and activities of the professions, shall be regarded as 'economic activity'. The exploitation of tangible or intangible property for the purposes of obtaining income therefrom on a continuing basis shall in particular be regarded as an economic activity.

2. In addition to the persons referred to in paragraph 1, any person who, on an occasional basis, supplies a new means of transport, which is dispatched or transported to the customer by the vendor or the customer, or on behalf of the vendor or the customer, to a destination outside the territory of a Member State but within the territory of the Community, shall be regarded as a taxable person.

Commentary—*De Voil Indirect Tax Service* **V2.101, V2.108.**
Simon's Tax Cases—Art 9(1), *ICAEW v C&E Comrs* [1999] STC 398*; *C&E Comrs v Yarburgh Children's Trust* [2002] STC 207*; *Cibo Participations SA v Directeur regional des impots du Nord-Pas-de-Calais* [2002] STC 460*; *Empresa de Desenvolvimento Mineiro SGPS SA (EDM) v Fazenda Pública (Ministério Público, intervening)* [2005] STC 65*; *University of Huddersfield Higher Education Corporation v C&E Comrs* [2006] STC 980*; *T-Mobile Austria GmbH and others v Republic of Austria* [2008] STC 184*; *Hutchison 3G UK Ltd and others v C&E Comrs* [2008] STC 218*; *R v Hashash* [2008] STC 1158*; *van der Steen v Inspecteur van de Belastingdienst* [2008] STC 2379*.

Article 10

The condition in Article 9(1) that the economic activity be conducted 'independently' shall exclude employed and other persons from VAT in so far as they are bound to an employer by a contract of employment or by any other legal ties creating the relationship of employer and employee as regards working conditions, remuneration and the employer's liability.

Simon's Tax Cases—*Osman v C&E Comrs* [1989] STC 596*; *Ayuntamiento de Sevilla v Recaudadores de las Zonas Primera y Segunda* [1993] STC 659*; *C&E Comrs v Thorn Materials Supply Ltd and Thorn Resources Ltd* [1998] STC 725*; *C&E Comrs v Barclays Bank plc, CA* [2001] STC 1558*; *van der Steen v Inspecteur van de Belastingdienst* [2008] STC 2379*.

Article 11

After consulting the advisory committee on value added tax (hereafter, the 'VAT Committee'), each Member State may regard as a single taxable person any persons established in the territory of that Member State who, while legally independent, are closely bound to one another by financial, economic and organisational links.

A Member State exercising the option provided for in the first paragraph, may adopt any measures needed to prevent tax evasion or avoidance through the use of this provision.

Simon's Tax Cases—*Osman v C&E Comrs* [1989] STC 596*; *Ayuntamiento de Sevilla v Recaudadores de las Zonas Primera y Segunda* [1993] STC 659*; *C&E Comrs v Thorn Materials Supply Ltd and Thorn Resources Ltd* [1998] STC 725*; *C&E Comrs v Barclays Bank plc, CA* [2001] STC 1558*; *van der Steen v Inspecteur van de Belastingdienst* [2008] STC 2379*.

Article 12

1. Member States may regard as a taxable person anyone who carries out, on an occasional basis, a transaction relating to the activities referred to in the second subparagraph of Article 9(1) and in particular one of the following transactions:

(*a*) the supply, before first occupation, of a building or parts of a building and of the land on which the building stands;

(*b*) the supply of building land.

2. For the purposes of paragraph 1(*a*), 'building' shall mean any structure fixed to or in the ground.

Member States may lay down the detailed rules for applying the criterion referred to in paragraph 1(*a*) to conversions of buildings and may determine what is meant by 'the land on which a building stands'.

Member States may apply criteria other than that of first occupation, such as the period elapsing between the date of completion of the building and the date of first supply, or the period elapsing between the date of first occupation and the date of subsequent supply, provided that those periods do not exceed five years and two years respectively.

3. For the purposes of paragraph 1(*b*), 'building land' shall mean any unimproved or improved land defined as such by the Member States.

Simon's Tax Cases—*Gemeente Emmen v Belastingdienst Grote Ondernemingen* [1996] STC 496*.

Article 13

1. States, regional and local government authorities and other bodies governed by public law shall not be regarded as taxable persons in respect of the activities or transactions in which they engage as public authorities, even where they collect dues, fees, contributions or payments in connection with those activities or transactions.

However, when they engage in such activities or transactions, they shall be regarded as taxable persons in respect of those activities or transactions where their treatment as non-taxable persons would lead to significant distortions of competition.

In any event, bodies governed by public law shall be regarded as taxable persons in respect of the activities listed in Annex I, provided that those activities are not carried out on such a small scale as to be negligible.

2. Member States may regard activities, exempt under Articles 132, 135, 136, 371, 374 to 377, and Article 378(2), Article 379(2), or Articles 380 to 390, engaged in by bodies governed by public law as activities in which those bodies engage as public authorities.

Commentary—*De Voil Indirect Tax Service* **V2.108**.
Simon's Tax Cases—*Fazenda Pública v Câmera Municipal do Porto (Ministério Público, third party)* [2001] STC 560*; *Edinburgh Telford College v R&C Comrs* [2006] STC 1291*; *Finanzamt Eisleben v Feuerbestattungsverein Halle eV (Lutherstadt Eisleben, joined party)* [2006] STC 2043*; *T-Mobile Austria GmbH and others v Republic of Austria* [2008] STC 184*; *Hutchison 3G UK Ltd and others v C&E Comrs* [2008] STC 218*; *R&C Comrs v Isle of Wight Council and others* [2008] STC 614; *Finanzamt Oschatz v Zweckverband zur Trinkwasserversorgung und Abwasserbeseitigung Torgau-Westelbien* [2009] STC 1*; *R&C Comrs v Isle of Wight Council and others* [2009] STC 1098*; *Cambridge University v R&C Comrs* [2009] STC 1288.
Press releases etc—HMRC Brief 28/08, 20-5-08 (interpretation of "bodies governed by public law" and "special legal regime", reconsidered by HMRC).

TITLE IV
TAXABLE TRANSACTIONS

CHAPTER 1
SUPPLY OF GOODS

Article 14

1. 'Supply of goods' shall mean the transfer of the right to dispose of tangible property as owner.

2. In addition to the transaction referred to in paragraph 1, each of the following shall be regarded as a supply of goods:

(*a*) the transfer, by order made by or in the name of a public authority or in pursuance of the law, of the ownership of property against payment of compensation;
(*b*) the actual handing over of goods pursuant to a contract for the hire of goods for a certain period, or for the sale of goods on deferred terms, which provides that in the normal course of events ownership is to pass at the latest upon payment of the final instalment;
(*c*) the transfer of goods pursuant to a contract under which commission is payable on purchase or sale.

3. Member States may regard the handing over of certain works of construction as a supply of goods.

Commentary—*De Voil Indirect Tax Service* **V3.119**.
Simon's Tax Cases—Art 14(1), *van Tiem v Staatssecretaris van Financiën* [1993] STC 91*; *British Airways plc v C&E Comrs* [1996] STC 1127*; *, *Stewart (t/a GT Shooting) v C&E Comrs* [2002] STC 255*; *Halifax plc and others v C&E Comrs* [2006] STC 919*; *University of Huddersfield Higher Education Corporation v C&E Comrs* [2006] STC 980*; *R&C Comrs v Loyalty Management UK Ltd* [2007] STC 536*; *Aktiebolaget NN v Skatteverket* [2008] STC 3203*.
Art 14(2)(*c*), *EC Commission v United Kingdom* [2007] STC 1211*.

Article 15

1. Electricity, gas, heat, refrigeration and the like shall be treated as tangible property.

2. Member States may regard the following as tangible property:

(*a*) certain interests in immovable property;
(*b*) rights in rem giving the holder thereof a right of use over immovable property;
(*c*) shares or interests equivalent to shares giving the holder thereof de jure or de facto rights of ownership or possession over immovable property or part thereof.

Simon's Tax Cases—Art 15(2), *van Tiem v Staatssecretaris van Financiën* [1993] STC 91*; *Stichting 'Goed Wonen' v Staatssecretaris van Financiën* [2003] STC 1137*.

Article 16

The application by a taxable person of goods forming part of his business assets for his private use or for that of his staff, or their disposal free of charge or, more generally, their application for purposes other than those of his business, shall be treated as a supply of goods for consideration, where the VAT on those goods or the component parts thereof was wholly or partly deductible.

However, the application of goods for business use as samples or as gifts of small value shall not be treated as a supply of goods for consideration.

Simon's Tax Cases—*Kuwait Petroleum (GB) Ltd v C&E Comrs* [2001] STC 62*; *Finanzamt Burgdorf v Fischer, Finanzamt Düsseldorf-Mettman v Brandenstein* [2001] STC 1356*; *Hotel Scandic Gåsabäck AB v Riksskatteverket* [2005] STC 1311*; *Church of England Children's Society v Revenue and Customs Commissioners* [2005] STC 1644*.

Article 17

1. The transfer by a taxable person of goods forming part of his business assets to another Member State shall be treated as a supply of goods for consideration.

'Transfer to another Member State' shall mean the dispatch or transport of movable tangible property by or on behalf of the taxable person, for the purposes of his business, to a destination outside the territory of the Member State in which the property is located, but within the Community.

2. The dispatch or transport of goods for the purposes of any of the following transactions shall not be regarded as a transfer to another Member State:

(*a*) the supply of the goods by the taxable person within the territory of the Member State in which the dispatch or transport ends, in accordance with the conditions laid down in Article 33;
(*b*) the supply of the goods, for installation or assembly by or on behalf of the supplier, by the taxable person within the territory of the Member State in which dispatch or transport of the goods ends, in accordance with the conditions laid down in Article 36;
(*c*) the supply of the goods by the taxable person on board a ship, an aircraft or a train in the course of a passenger transport operation, in accordance with the conditions laid down in Article 37;
(*d*) the supply of gas through the natural gas distribution system, or of electricity, in accordance with the conditions laid down in Articles 38 and 39;
(*e*) the supply of the goods by the taxable person within the territory of the Member State, in accordance with the conditions laid down in Articles 138, 146, 147, 148, 151 or 152;
(*f*) the supply of a service performed for the taxable person and consisting of work on the goods in question physically carried out within the territory of the Member State in which dispatch or transport of the goods ends, provided that the goods, after being worked upon, are returned to that taxable person in the Member State from which they were initially dispatched or transported;
(*g*) the temporary use of the goods within the territory of the Member State in which dispatch or transport of the goods ends, for the purposes of the supply of services by the taxable person established within the Member State in which dispatch or transport of the goods began;
(*h*) the temporary use of the goods, for a period not exceeding twenty-four months, within the territory of another Member State, in which the importation of the same goods from a third country with a view to their temporary use would be covered by the arrangements for temporary importation with full exemption from import duties.

3. If one of the conditions governing eligibility under paragraph 2 is no longer met, the goods shall be regarded as having been transferred to another Member State. In such cases, the transfer shall be deemed to take place at the time when that condition ceases to be met.

Article 18

Member States may treat each of the following transactions as a supply of goods for consideration:

(*a*) the application by a taxable person for the purposes of his business of goods produced, constructed, extracted, processed, purchased or imported in the course of such business, where the VAT on such goods, had they been acquired from another taxable person, would not be wholly deductible;
(*b*) the application of goods by a taxable person for the purposes of a non-taxable area of activity, where the VAT on such goods became wholly or partly deductible upon their acquisition or upon their application in accordance with point (*a*);
(*c*) with the exception of the cases referred to in Article 19, the retention of goods by a taxable person, or by his successors, when he ceases to carry out a taxable economic activity, where the VAT on such goods became wholly or partly deductible upon their acquisition or upon their application in accordance with point (*a*).

Simon's Tax Cases—*C&E Comrs v Robert Gordon's College* [1995] STC 1093*; *Gemeente Leusden and another v Staatssecretaris van Financiën* [2007] STC 776*.

Article 19

In the event of a transfer, whether for consideration or not or as a contribution to a company, of a totality of assets or part thereof, Member States may consider that no supply of goods has taken place and that the person to whom the goods are transferred is to be treated as the successor to the transferor.

Member States may, in cases where the recipient is not wholly liable to tax, take the measures necessary to prevent distortion of competition. They may also adopt any measures needed to prevent tax evasion or avoidance through the use of this Article.

Simon's Tax Cases—*Abbey National plc v C&E Comrs* [2001] STC 297*; *Zita Modes Sàrl v Administration de l'Enregistrment et des Domaines* [2005] STC 1059*; *Finanzamt Offenbach am Main-Land v Faxworld Vorgründungsgesellschaft Peter Hünninghausen und Wolfgang Klein GbR* [2005] STC 1192*.

CHAPTER 2
INTRA-COMMUNITY ACQUISITION OF GOODS

Article 20

'Intra-Community acquisition of goods' shall mean the acquisition of the right to dispose as owner of movable tangible property dispatched or transported to the person acquiring the goods, by or on behalf of the vendor or the person acquiring the goods, in a Member State other than that in which dispatch or transport of the goods began.

Where goods acquired by a non-taxable legal person are dispatched or transported from a third territory or a third country and imported by that non-taxable legal person into a Member State other than the Member State in which dispatch or transport of the goods ends, the goods shall be regarded as having been dispatched or transported from the Member State of importation. That Member State shall grant the importer designated or recognised under Article 201 as liable for payment of VAT a refund of the VAT paid in respect of the importation of the goods, provided that the importer establishes that VAT has been applied to his acquisition in the Member State in which dispatch or transport of the goods ends.

Article 21

The application by a taxable person, for the purposes of his business, of goods dispatched or transported by or on behalf of that taxable person from another Member State, within which the goods were produced, extracted, processed, purchased or acquired within the meaning of Article 2(1)(*b*), or into which they were imported by that taxable person for the purposes of his business, shall be treated as an intra-Community acquisition of goods for consideration.

Article 22

The application by the armed forces of a State party to the North Atlantic Treaty, for their use or for the use of the civilian staff accompanying them, of goods which they have not purchased subject to the general rules governing taxation on the domestic market of a Member State shall be treated as an intra-Community acquisition of goods for consideration, where the importation of those goods would not be eligible for the exemption provided for in point (*h*) of Article 143.

Prospective amendments—Article 22 to be substituted by Council Directive 2009/69/EC art 1 with effect from 24 July 2009. The deadline for implementation of this Directive is 1 January 2011 (OJ L 175, 4.7.2009 p 12). Text to read as follows—

> **"Article 22**
>
> The application by the armed forces of a State party to the North Atlantic Treaty, for their use or for the use of the civilian staff accompanying them, of goods which they have not purchased subject to the general rules governing taxation on the domestic market of a Member State shall be treated as an intra-Community acquisition of goods for consideration, where the importation of those goods would not be eligible for the exemption provided for in Article 143(1)(*h*).".

Article 23

Member States shall take the measures necessary to ensure that a transaction which would have been classed as a supply of goods if it had been carried out within their territory by a taxable person acting as such is classed as an intra-Community acquisition of goods.

CHAPTER 3
SUPPLY OF SERVICES

Article 24

1. 'Supply of services' shall mean any transaction which does not constitute a supply of goods.

2. 'Telecommunications services' shall mean services relating to the transmission, emission or reception of signals, words, images and sounds or information of any nature by wire, radio, optical or other electromagnetic systems, including the related transfer or assignment of the right to use capacity for such transmission, emission or reception, with the inclusion of the provision of access to global information networks.

Commentary—*De Voil Indirect Tax Service* **V3.470**.

Simon's Tax Cases—art 24(1), *Faaborg-Gelting Linien A/S v Finanzamt Flensburg* [1996] STC 774*; *Landboden-Agrardienste GmbH & Co KG v Finanzamt Calau* [1998] STC 171*; *Halifax plc and others v C&E Comrs* [2006] STC 919*; *University of Huddersfield Higher Education Corporation v C&E Comrs* [2006] STC 980*; *R&C Comrs v Loyalty Management UK Ltd* [2007] STC 536*.

Article 25

A supply of services may consist, inter alia, in one of the following transactions:

(*a*) the assignment of intangible property, whether or not the subject of a document establishing title;

(*b*) the obligation to refrain from an act, or to tolerate an act or situation;

(*c*) the performance of services in pursuance of an order made by or in the name of a public authority or in pursuance of the law.

Commentary—*De Voil Indirect Tax Service* **V3.470**.

Simon's Tax Cases—*Faaborg-Gelting Linien A/S v Finanzamt Flensburg* (Case C-231/94) [1996] STC 774*; *Landboden-Agrardienste GmbH & Co KG v Finanzamt Calau* (Case C-384/95) [1998] STC 171*; *Halifax plc and others v C&E Comrs* [2006] STC 919*; *University of Huddersfield Higher Education Corporation v C&E Comrs* [2006] STC 980*; *R&C Comrs v Loyalty Management UK Ltd* [2007] STC 536*.

Article 26

1. Each of the following transactions shall be treated as a supply of services for consideration:

(*a*) the use of goods forming part of the assets of a business for the private use of a taxable person or of his staff or, more generally, for purposes other than those of his business, where the VAT on such goods was wholly or partly deductible;

(*b*) the supply of services carried out free of charge by a taxable person for his private use or for that of his staff or, more generally, for purposes other than those of his business.

2. Member States may derogate from paragraph 1, provided that such derogation does not lead to distortion of competition.

Commentary—*De Voil Indirect Tax Service* **V3.470**.

Simon's Tax Cases—*Seeling v Finanzamt Starnberg* [2003] STC 805*; *Finanzamt Offenbach am Main-Land v Faxworld Vorgründungsgesellschaft Peter Hünninghausen und Wolfgang Klein GbR* [2005] STC 1192*; *Hotel Scandic Gåsabäck AB v Riksskatteverket* [2005] STC 1311*; *Charles and another v Staatssecretaris van Financiën* [2006] STC 1429*; *Danfoss A/S and anor v Skatteministeriet* [2009] STC 701*; *Vereniging Noordelijke Land en Tuinbouw Organisatie v Staatssecretaris van Financiën* [2009] STC 935*.

Article 27

In order to prevent distortion of competition and after consulting the VAT Committee, Member States may treat as a supply of services for consideration the supply by a taxable person of a service for the purposes of his business, where the VAT on such a service, were it supplied by another taxable person, would not be wholly deductible.

Article 28

Where a taxable person acting in his own name but on behalf of another person takes part in a supply of services, he shall be deemed to have received and supplied those services himself.

Article 29

Article 19 shall apply in like manner to the supply of services.

CHAPTER 4
IMPORTATION OF GOODS

Article 30

'Importation of goods' shall mean the entry into the Community of goods which are not in free circulation within the meaning of Article 24 of the Treaty.

In addition to the transaction referred to in the first paragraph, the entry into the Community of goods which are in free circulation, coming from a third territory forming part of the customs territory of the Community, shall be regarded as importation of goods.

TITLE V
PLACE OF TAXABLE TRANSACTIONS

CHAPTER 1
PLACE OF SUPPLY OF GOODS

Section 1 Supply of goods without transport

Article 31

Where goods are not dispatched or transported, the place of supply shall be deemed to be the place where the goods are located at the time when the supply takes place.

Simon's Tax Cases—*EMAG Handel Eder OHG v Finanzlandesdirektion für Kärnten* [2007] STC 1461*.

Section 2 Supply of goods with transport

Article 32

Where goods are dispatched or transported by the supplier, or by the customer, or by a third person, the place of supply shall be deemed to be the place where the goods are located at the time when dispatch or transport of the goods to the customer begins.

However, if dispatch or transport of the goods begins in a third territory or third country, both the place of supply by the importer designated or recognised under Article 201 as liable for payment of VAT and the place of any subsequent supply shall be deemed to be within the Member State of importation of the goods.

Simon's Tax Cases—*Aktiebolaget NN v Skatteverket* [2008] STC 3203*.

Article 33

1. By way of derogation from Article 32, the place of supply of goods dispatched or transported by or on behalf of the supplier from a Member State other than that in which dispatch or transport of the goods ends shall be deemed to be the place where the goods are located at the time when dispatch or transport of the goods to the customer ends, where the following conditions are met:

(*a*) the supply of goods is carried out for a taxable person, or a non-taxable legal person, whose intra-Community acquisitions of goods are not subject to VAT pursuant to Article 3 (1) or for any other non-taxable person;

(*b*) the goods supplied are neither new means of transport nor goods supplied after assembly or installation, with or without a trial run, by or on behalf of the supplier.

2. Where the goods supplied are dispatched or transported from a third territory or a third country and imported by the supplier into a Member State other than that in which dispatch or transport of the goods to the customer ends, they shall be regarded as having been dispatched or transported from the Member State of importation.

Article 34

1. Provided the following conditions are met, Article 33 shall not apply to supplies of goods all of which are dispatched or transported to the same Member State, where that Member State is the Member State in which dispatch or transport of the goods ends:

(*a*) the goods supplied are not products subject to excise duty;

(*b*) the total value, exclusive of VAT, of such supplies effected under the conditions laid down in Article 33 within that Member State does not in any one calendar year exceed EUR 100 000 or the equivalent in national currency;

(*c*) the total value, exclusive of VAT, of the supplies of goods, other than products subject to excise duty, effected under the conditions laid down in Article 33 within that Member State did not in the previous calendar year exceed EUR 100 000 or the equivalent in national currency.

2. The Member State within the territory of which the goods are located at the time when their dispatch or transport to the customer ends may limit the threshold referred to in paragraph 1 to EUR 35 000 or the equivalent in national currency, where that Member State fears that the threshold of EUR 100 000 might cause serious distortion of competition.

Member States which exercise the option under the first subparagraph shall take the measures necessary to inform accordingly the competent public authorities in the Member State in which dispatch or transport of the goods begins.

3. The Commission shall present to the Council at the earliest opportunity a report on the operation of the special EUR 35 000 threshold referred to in paragraph 2, accompanied, if necessary, by appropriate proposals.

4. The Member State within the territory of which the goods are located at the time when their dispatch or transport begins shall grant those taxable persons who carry out supplies of goods eligible under paragraph 1 the right to opt for the place of supply to be determined in accordance with Article 33.

The Member States concerned shall lay down the detailed rules governing the exercise of the option referred to in the first subparagraph, which shall in any event cover two calendar years.

Article 35

Articles 33 and 34 shall not apply to supplies of second-hand goods, works of art, collectors' items or antiques, as defined in points (1) to (4) of Article 311(1), nor to supplies of second-hand means of transport, as defined in Article 327(3), subject to VAT in accordance with the relevant special arrangements.

Article 36

Where goods dispatched or transported by the supplier, by the customer or by a third person are installed or assembled, with or without a trial run, by or on behalf of the supplier, the place of supply shall be deemed to be the place where the goods are installed or assembled.

Where the installation or assembly is carried out in a Member State other than that of the supplier, the Member State within the territory of which the installation or assembly is carried out shall take the measures necessary to ensure that there is no double taxation in that Member State.

Simon's Tax Cases—*EMAG Handel Eder OHG v Finanzlandesdirektion für Kärnten* [2007] STC 1461*; *Aktiebolaget NN v Skatteverket* [2008] STC 3203*.

Section 3 Supply of goods on board ships, aircraft or trains

Article 37

1. Where goods are supplied on board ships, aircraft or trains during the section of a passenger transport operation effected within the Community, the place of supply shall be deemed to be at the point of departure of the passenger transport operation.

2. For the purposes of paragraph 1, 'section of a passenger transport operation effected within the Community' shall mean the section of the operation effected, without a stopover outside the Community, between the point of departure and the point of arrival of the passenger transport operation. 'Point of departure of a passenger transport operation' shall mean the first scheduled point of passenger embarkation within the Community, where applicable after a stopover outside the Community.

'Point of arrival of a passenger transport operation' shall mean the last scheduled point of disembarkation within the Community of passengers who embarked in the Community, where applicable before a stopover outside the Community.

In the case of a return trip, the return leg shall be regarded as a separate transport operation.

3. The Commission shall, at the earliest opportunity, present to the Council a report, accompanied if necessary by appropriate proposals, on the place of taxation of the supply of goods for consumption on board and the supply of services, including restaurant services, for passengers on board ships, aircraft or trains.

Pending adoption of the proposals referred to in the first subparagraph, Member States may exempt or continue to exempt, with deductibility of the VAT paid at the preceding stage, the supply of goods for consumption on board in respect of which the place of taxation is determined in accordance with paragraph 1.

Simon's Tax Cases—*Peninsular and Oriental Steam Navigation Co v C&E Comrs* [2000] STC 488*; *Köhler v Finanzamt Düsseldorf-Nord* [2006] STC 469*.

Section 4 Supply of goods through distribution systems

Article 38

1. In the case of the supply of gas through the natural gas distribution system, or of electricity, to a taxable dealer, the place of supply shall be deemed to be the place where that taxable dealer has established his business or has a fixed establishment for which the goods are supplied, or, in the absence of such a place of business or fixed establishment, the place where he has his permanent address or usually resides.

2. For the purposes of paragraph 1, 'taxable dealer' shall mean a taxable person whose principal activity in respect of purchases of gas or electricity is reselling those products and whose own consumption of those products is negligible.

Article 39

In the case of the supply of gas through the natural gas distribution system, or of electricity, where such a supply is not covered by Article 38, the place of supply shall be deemed to be the place where the customer effectively uses and consumes the goods.

Where all or part of the gas or electricity is not effectively consumed by the customer, those non-consumed goods shall be deemed to have been used and consumed at the place where the customer has established his business or has a fixed establishment for which the goods are supplied. In the absence of such a place of business or fixed establishment, the customer shall be deemed to have used and consumed the goods at the place where he has his permanent address or usually resides.

CHAPTER 2

PLACE OF AN INTRA-COMMUNITY ACQUISITION OF GOODS

Article 40

The place of an intra-Community acquisition of goods shall be deemed to be the place where dispatch or transport of the goods to the person acquiring them ends.

Article 41

Without prejudice to Article 40, the place of an intra-Community acquisition of goods as referred to in Article 2(1)(*b*)(i) shall be deemed to be within the territory of the Member State which issued the VAT identification number under which the person acquiring the goods made the acquisition, unless the person acquiring the goods establishes that VAT has been applied to that acquisition in accordance with Article 40.

If VAT is applied to the acquisition in accordance with the first paragraph and subsequently applied, pursuant to Article 40, to the acquisition in the Member State in which dispatch or transport of the goods ends, the taxable amount shall be reduced accordingly in the Member State which issued the VAT identification number under which the person acquiring the goods made the acquisition.

Article 42

The first paragraph of Article 41 shall not apply and VAT shall be deemed to have been applied to the intra-Community acquisition of goods in accordance with Article 40 where the following conditions are met:

(*a*) the person acquiring the goods establishes that he has made the intra-Community acquisition for the purposes of a subsequent supply, within the territory of the Member State identified in accordance with Article 40, for which the person to whom the supply is made has been designated in accordance with Article 197 as liable for payment of VAT;

(*b*) the person acquiring the goods has satisfied the obligations laid down in Article 265 relating to submission of the recapitulative statement.

[CHAPTER 3
PLACE OF SUPPLY OF SERVICES

Section 1 Definitions

Article 43

For the purpose of applying the rules concerning the place of supply of services:

1. a taxable person who also carries out activities or transactions that are not considered to be taxable supplies of goods or services in accordance with Article 2(1) shall be regarded as a taxable person in respect of all services rendered to him;

2. a non-taxable legal person who is identified for VAT purposes shall be regarded as a taxable person.]

Commentary—*De Voil Indirect Tax Service* **V2.101, V3.166, V3.192.**
Simon's Tax Cases—*Lease Plan Luxembourg SA v Belgium* (Case C-390/96) [1998] STC 628*; *EC Commission v French Republic* [2001] STC 156*; *RAL (Channel Islands) and others v C&E Comrs* [2005] STC 1025*; *Ministero dell'Economia e delle Finanze and another v FCE Bank plc* [2007] STC 165*.
Amendments—Chapter 3 substituted by Council Directive 2008/8/EC art 2 with effect from 1 January 2010 (OJ L 44, 20.2.2008 p 11).

[Section 2 General rules

Article 44

The place of supply of services to a taxable person acting as such shall be the place where that person has established his business. However, if those services are provided to a fixed establishment of the taxable person located in a place other than the place where he has established his business, the place of supply of those services shall be the place where that fixed establishment is located. In the absence of such place of establishment or fixed establishment, the place of supply of services shall be the place where the taxable person who receives such services has his permanent address or usually resides.]

Amendments—Chapter 3 substituted by Council Directive 2008/8/EC art 2 with effect from 1 January 2010 (OJ L 44, 20.2.2008 p 11).

[Article 45

The place of supply of services to a non-taxable person shall be the place where the supplier has established his business. However, if those services are provided from a fixed establishment of the supplier located in a place other than the place where he has established his business, the place of supply of those services shall be the place where that fixed establishment is located. In the absence of such place of establishment or fixed establishment, the place of supply of services shall be the place where the supplier has his permanent address or usually resides.]

Simon's Tax Cases—*Heger Rudi GmbH v Finanzamt Graz-Stadt* [2008] STC 2679*.
Amendments—Chapter 3 substituted by Council Directive 2008/8/EC art 2 with effect from 1 January 2010 (OJ L 44, 20.2.2008 p 11).

[Section 3 Particular provisions

Subsection 1 Supply of services by intermediaries

Article 46

The place of supply of services rendered to a non-taxable person by an intermediary acting in the name and on behalf of another person shall be the place where the underlying transaction is supplied in accordance with this Directive.]

Commentary—*De Voil Indirect Tax Service* **V2.101, V3.166, V3.192.**
Simon's Tax Cases—*EC Commission v Hellenic Republic* (Case C-331\94) [1996] STC 1168*; *Reisebüro Binder GmbH v Finanzamt Stuttgart-Körperschaften* (Case C-116/96) [1998] STC 604*.
Amendments—Chapter 3 substituted by Council Directive 2008/8/EC art 2 with effect from 1 January 2010 (OJ L 44, 20.2.2008 p 11).

[Subsection 2 Supply of services connected with immovable property

Article 47

The place of supply of services connected with immovable property, including the services of experts and estate agents, the provision of accommodation in the hotel sector or in sectors with a similar function, such as holiday camps or sites developed for use as camping sites, the granting of rights to use immovable property and services for the preparation and coordination of construction work, such as the services of architects and of firms providing on-site supervision, shall be the place where the immovable property is located.]

Amendments—Chapter 3 substituted by Council Directive 2008/8/EC art 2 with effect from 1 January 2010 (OJ L 44, 20.2.2008 p 11).

[Subsection 3 Supply of transport

Article 48

The place of supply of passenger transport shall be the place where the transport takes place, proportionate to the distances covered.]

Amendments—Chapter 3 substituted by Council Directive 2008/8/EC art 2 with effect from 1 January 2010 (OJ L 44, 20.2.2008 p 11).

[Article 49

The place of supply of the transport of goods, other than the intra-Community transport of goods, to non-taxable persons shall be the place where the transport takes place, proportionate to the distances covered.]

Amendments—Chapter 3 substituted by Council Directive 2008/8/EC art 2 with effect from 1 January 2010 (OJ L 44, 20.2.2008 p 11).

[Article 50

The place of supply of the intra-Community transport of goods to non-taxable persons shall be the place of departure.]

Amendments—Chapter 3 substituted by Council Directive 2008/8/EC art 2 with effect from 1 January 2010 (OJ L 44, 20.2.2008 p 11).

[Article 51

"Intra-Community transport of goods" shall mean any transport of goods in respect of which the place of departure and the place of arrival are situated within the territories of two different Member States.

"Place of departure" shall mean the place where transport of the goods actually begins, irrespective of distances covered in order to reach the place where the goods are located and "place of arrival" shall mean the place where transport of the goods actually ends.]

Amendments—Chapter 3 substituted by Council Directive 2008/8/EC art 2 with effect from 1 January 2010 (OJ L 44, 20.2.2008 p 11).

[Article 52

Member States need not apply VAT to that part of the intra-Community transport of goods to non-taxable persons taking place over waters which do not form part of the territory of the Community.]

Amendments—Chapter 3 substituted by Council Directive 2008/8/EC art 2 with effect from 1 January 2010 (OJ L 44, 20.2.2008 p 11).

[Subsection 4

Supply of cultural, artistic, sporting, scientific, educational, entertainment and similar services, ancillary transport services and valuations of and work on movable property.]

Amendments—Chapter 3 substituted by Council Directive 2008/8/EC art 2 with effect from 1 January 2010 (OJ L 44, 20.2.2008 p 11).

[Article 53

The place of supply of services and ancillary services relating to cultural, artistic, sporting, scientific, educational, entertainment or similar activities, such as fairs and exhibitions, including the supply of services of the organisers of such activities, shall be the place where those activities are physically carried out.]

Amendments—Chapter 3 substituted by Council Directive 2008/8/EC art 2 with effect from 1 January 2010 (OJ L 44, 20.2.2008 p 11).
Articles 53, 54 to be substituted, by Council Directive 2008/8/EC art 3 with effect from 1 January 2011,(OJ L 44, 20.2.2008 p 11).

[Article 54

The place of supply of the following services to non-taxable persons shall be the place where the services are physically carried out:

(*a*) ancillary transport activities such as loading, unloading, handling and similar activities;
(*b*) valuations of and work on movable tangible property.]

Amendments—Chapter 3 substituted by Council Directive 2008/8/EC art 2 with effect from 1 January 2010 (OJ L 44, 20.2.2008 p 11).
Articles 53, 54 to be substituted, by Council Directive 2008/8/EC art 3 with effect from 1 January 2011,(OJ L 44, 20.2.2008 p 11).

[Subsection 5 Supply of restaurant and catering services

Article 55

The place of supply of restaurant and catering services other than those physically carried out on board ships, aircraft or trains during the section of a passenger transport operation effected within the Community, shall be the place where the services are physically carried out.]

Amendments—Chapter 3 substituted by Council Directive 2008/8/EC art 2 with effect from 1 January 2010 (OJ L 44, 20.2.2008 p 11).

[Subsection 6 Hiring of means of transport

Article 56

1. The place of short-term hiring of a means of transport shall be the place where the means of transport is actually put at the disposal of the customer.

2. For the purposes of paragraph 1, "short-term" shall mean the continuous possession or use of the means of transport throughout a period of not more than thirty days and, in the case of vessels, not more than ninety days.]

Amendments—Chapter 3 substituted by Council Directive 2008/8/EC art 2 with effect from 1 January 2010 (OJ L 44, 20.2.2008 p 11).

[Subsection 7 Supply of restaurant and catering services for consumption on board ships, aircraft or trains

Article 57

1. The place of supply of restaurant and catering services which are physically carried out on board ships, aircraft or trains during the section of a passenger transport operation effected within the Community, shall be at the point of departure of the passenger transport operation.

2. For the purposes of paragraph 1, "section of a passenger transport operation effected within the Community" shall mean the section of the operation effected, without a stopover outside the Community, between the point of departure and the point of arrival of the passenger transport operation.

"Point of departure of a passenger transport operation" shall mean the first scheduled point of passenger embarkation within the Community, where applicable after a stopover outside the Community.

"Point of arrival of a passenger transport operation" shall mean the last scheduled point of disembarkation within the Community of passengers who embarked in the Community, where applicable before a stop-over outside the Community.

In the case of a return trip, the return leg shall be regarded as a separate transport operation.]

Amendments—Chapter 3 substituted by Council Directive 2008/8/EC art 2 with effect from 1 January 2010 (OJ L 44, 20.2.2008 p 11).

[Subsection 8 Supply of electronic services to non-taxable persons

Article 58

The place of supply of electronically supplied services, in particular those referred to in Annex II, when supplied to non-taxable persons who are established in a Member State, or who have their permanent address or usually reside in a Member State, by a taxable person who has established his business outside the Community or has a fixed establishment there from which the service is supplied, or who, in the absence of such a place of business or fixed establishment, has his permanent address or usually resides outside the Community, shall be the place where the non-taxable person is established, or where he has his permanent address or usually resides. Where the supplier of a service and the customer communicate via electronic mail, that shall not of itself mean that the service supplied is an electronically supplied service.]

Amendments—Chapter 3 substituted by Council Directive 2008/8/EC art 2 with effect from 1 January 2010 (OJ L 44, 20.2.2008 p 11).
Sub-s 8 to be substituted by Council Directive 2008/8/EC art 5(1) with effect from 1 January 2015 (OJ L 44, 20.2.2008 p 11).

[Subsection 9 Supply of services to non-taxable persons outside the Community

Article 59

The place of supply of the following services to a non-taxable person who is established or has his permanent address or usually resides outside the Community, shall be the place where that person is established, has his permanent address or usually resides:

(*a*) transfers and assignments of copyrights, patents, licences, trade marks and similar rights;
(*b*) advertising services;
(*c*) the services of consultants, engineers, consultancy firms, lawyers, accountants and other similar services, as well as data processing and the provision of information;
(*d*) obligations to refrain from pursuing or exercising, in whole or in part, a business activity or a right referred to in this Article;
(*e*) banking, financial and insurance transactions including reinsurance, with the exception of the hire of safes;
(*f*) the supply of staff;
(*g*) the hiring out of movable tangible property, with the exception of all means of transport;
(*h*) the provision of access to, and of transport or transmission through, natural gas and electricity distribution systems and the provision of other services directly linked thereto;
(*i*) telecommunications services;
(*j*) radio and television broadcasting services;
(*k*) electronically supplied services, in particular those referred to in Annex II.

Where the supplier of a service and the customer communicate via electronic mail, that shall not of itself mean that the service supplied is an electronically supplied service.]

Commentary—*De Voil Indirect Tax Service* **V2.101, V3.166, V3.192.**
Simon's Tax Cases—*EC Commission v Grand Duchy of Luxembourg* (Case C-69/92) [1997] STC 712*; *von Hoffmann v Finanzamt Trier* [1997] STC 1321*; *Synidcat des Producteurs Independants (SPI) v Ministere de l'Economie, des Finances et de l'Industry* [2001] STC 523*; *Design Concept SA v Flanders Expo SA* [2003] STC 912*; *R&C Comrs v Zurich Insurance Co* [2006] STC 1694*; *R&C Comrs v Zurich Insurance Co* [2007] STC 1756*; *EC Commission v Germany* [2008] STC 2906*; *Kollektivavtalsstiftelsen TRR Trygghetsrådet v Skatteverket* [2009] STC 526.
Amendments—Chapter 3 substituted by Council Directive 2008/8/EC art 2 with effect from 1 January 2010 (OJ L 44, 20.2.2008 p 11).
Prospective amendment—In the first and second paras, points (*i*), (*j*), (*k*) to be substituted by Council Directive 2008/8/EC art 5(2) with effect from 1 January 2015 (OJ L 44, 20.2.2008 p 11).

[Subsection 10 Prevention of double taxation or non-taxation

Article 59a

In order to prevent double taxation, non-taxation or distortion of competition, Member States may, with regard to services the place of supply of which is governed by Articles 44, 45, 56 and 59:

(*a*) consider the place of supply of any or all of those services, if situated within their territory, as being situated outside the Community if the effective use and enjoyment of the services takes place outside the Community;
(*b*) consider the place of supply of any or all of those services, if situated outside the Community, as being situated within their territory if the effective use and enjoyment of the services takes place within their territory.

However, this provision shall not apply to the electronically supplied services where those services are rendered to non-taxable persons not established within the Community.]

Amendments—Chapter 3 substituted by Council Directive 2008/8/EC art 2 with effect from 1 January 2010 (OJ L 44, 20.2.2008 p 11).
Prospective amendment—Article 59a to be substituted by Council Directive 2008/8/EC art 5(3) with effect from 1 January 2015 (OJ L 44, 20.2.2008 p 11).

[Article 59b

Member States shall apply Article 59a(*b*) to telecommunications services and radio and television broadcasting services, as referred to in point (*j*) of the first paragraph of Article 59, supplied to non-taxable persons who are established in a Member State, or who have their permanent address or usually reside in a Member State, by a taxable person who has established his business outside the Community or has a fixed establishment there from which the services are supplied, or who, in the absence of such a place of business or fixed establishment, has his permanent address or usually resides outside the Community.]

Prospective amendment—Article 59b to be repealed by Council Directive 2008/8/EC art 5(3) with effect from 1 January 2015 (OJ L 44, 20.2.2008 p 11).

Amendments—Chapter 3 substituted by Council Directive 2008/8/EC art 2 with effect from 1 January 2010 (OJ L 44, 20.2.2008 p 11). Chapter 3 previously read as follows—

"CHAPTER 3
PLACE OF SUPPLY OF SERVICES

Section 1 General rule

Article 43

The place of supply of services shall be deemed to be the place where the supplier has established his business or has a fixed establishment from which the service is supplied, or, in the absence of such a place of business or fixed establishment, the place where he has his permanent address or usually resides.

Section 2 Particular provisions

Subsection 1 Supply of services by intermediaries

Article 44

The place of supply of services by an intermediary acting in the name and on behalf of another person, other than those referred to in Articles 50 and 54 and in Article 56(1), shall be the place where the underlying transaction is supplied in accordance with this Directive.

However, where the customer of the services supplied by the intermediary is identified for VAT purposes in a Member State other than that within the territory of which that transaction is carried out, the place of the supply of services by the intermediary shall be deemed to be within the territory of the Member State which issued the customer with the VAT identification number under which the service was rendered to him.

Subsection 2 Supply of services connected with immovable property

Article 45

The place of supply of services connected with immovable property, including the services of estate agents and experts, and services for the preparation and coordination of construction work, such as the services of architects and of firms providing on-site supervision, shall be the place where the property is located.

Subsection 3 Supply of transport

Article 46

The place of supply of transport other than the intra-Community transport of goods shall be the place where the transport takes place, proportionately in terms of distances covered.

Article 47

The place of supply of intra-Community transport of goods shall be the place of departure of the transport.

However, where intra-Community transport of goods is supplied to customers identified for VAT purposes in a Member State other than that of the departure of the transport, the place of supply shall be deemed to be within the territory of the Member State which issued the customer with the VAT identification number under which the service was rendered to him.

Article 48

'Intra-Community transport of goods' shall mean any transport of goods in respect of which the place of departure and the place of arrival are situated within the territories of two different Member States.

'Place of departure' shall mean the place where transport of the goods actually begins, irrespective of distances covered in order to reach the place where the goods are located.

'Place of arrival' shall mean the place where transport of the goods actually ends.

Article 49

The transport of goods in respect of which the place of departure and the place of arrival are situated within the territory of the same Member State shall be treated as intra-Community transport of goods where such transport is directly linked to transport of goods in respect of which the place of departure and the place of arrival are situated within the territory of two different Member States.

Article 50

The place of the supply of services by an intermediary, acting in the name and on behalf of another person, where the intermediary takes part in the intra-Community transport of goods, shall be the place of departure of the transport.

However, where the customer of the services supplied by the intermediary is identified for VAT purposes in a Member State other than that of the departure of the transport, the place of the supply of services by the intermediary shall be deemed to be within the territory of the Member State which issued the customer with the VAT identification number under which the service was rendered to him.

Article 51

Member States need not apply VAT to that part of the intra-Community transport of goods taking place over waters which do not form part of the territory of the Community.

Subsection 4 Supply of cultural and similar services, ancillary transport services or services relating to movable tangible property

Article 52

The place of supply of the following services shall be the place where the services are physically carried out:

(*a*) cultural, artistic, sporting, scientific, educational, entertainment or similar activities, including the activities of the organisers of such activities and, where appropriate, ancillary services;
(*b*) ancillary transport activities, such as loading, unloading, handling and similar activities;
(*c*) valuations of movable tangible property or work on such property.

Article 53

By way of derogation from Article 52(*b*), the place of supply of services involving activities ancillary to the intra-Community transport of goods, supplied to customers identified for VAT purposes in a Member State other than that in the territory of which the activities are physically carried out, shall be deemed to be within the territory of the Member State which issued the customer with the VAT identification number under which the service was rendered to him.

Article 54

The place of the supply of services by an intermediary, acting in the name and on behalf of another person, where the intermediary takes part in the supply of services consisting in activities ancillary to the intra-Community transport of goods, shall be the place where the ancillary activities are physically carried out.

However, where the customer of the services supplied by the intermediary is identified for VAT purposes in a Member State other than that within the territory of which the ancillary activities are physically carried out, the place of supply of services by the intermediary shall be deemed to be within the territory of the Member State which issued the customer with the VAT identification number under which the service was rendered to him.

Article 55

By way of derogation from Article 52(*c*), the place of supply of services involving the valuation of movable tangible property or work on such property, supplied to customers identified for VAT purposes in a Member State other than that in the territory of which the services are physically carried out, shall be deemed to be within the territory of the Member State which issued the customer with the VAT identification number under which the service was rendered to him.

The derogation referred to in the first paragraph shall apply only where the goods are dispatched or transported out of the Member State in which the services were physically carried out.

Subsection 5 Supply of miscellaneous services

Article 56

1. The place of supply of the following services to customers established outside the Community, or to taxable persons established in the Community but not in the same country as the supplier, shall be the place where the customer has established his business or has a fixed establishment for which the service is supplied, or, in the absence of such a place, the place where he has his permanent address or usually resides:

(*a*) transfers and assignments of copyrights, patents, licences, trade marks and similar rights;
(*b*) advertising services;
(*c*) the services of consultants, engineers, consultancy bureaux, lawyers, accountants and other similar services, as well as data processing and the provision of information;
(*d*) obligations to refrain from pursuing or exercising, in whole or in part, a business activity or a right referred to in this paragraph;
(*e*) banking, financial and insurance transactions, including reinsurance, with the exception of the hire of safes;
(*f*) the supply of staff;
(*g*) the hiring out of movable tangible property, with the exception of all means of transport;
(*h*) the provision of access to, and of transport or transmission through, natural gas and electricity distribution systems and the provision of other services directly linked thereto;
(*i*) telecommunications services;
(*j*) radio and television broadcasting services;
(*k*) electronically supplied services, such as those referred to in Annex II;
(*l*) the supply of services by intermediaries, acting in the name and on behalf of other persons, where those intermediaries take part in the supply of the services referred to in this paragraph.

2. Where the supplier of a service and the customer communicate via electronic mail, that shall not of itself mean that the service supplied is an electronically supplied service for the purposes of point (*k*) of paragraph 1.

3. Points (*j*) and (*k*) of paragraph 1 and paragraph 2 shall apply until 31 December 2009.

Article 57

1. Where the services referred to in point (*k*) of Article 56(1) are supplied to non-taxable persons who are established in a Member State, or who have their permanent address or usually reside in a Member State, by a taxable person who has established his business outside the Community or has a fixed establishment there from which the service is supplied, or who, in the absence of such a place of business or fixed establishment, has his permanent address or usually resides outside the Community, the place of supply shall be the place where the non-taxable person is established, or where he has his permanent address or usually resides.

2. Paragraph 1 shall apply until 31 December 2009.

Subsection 6 Criterion of effective use and enjoyment

Article 58

In order to avoid double taxation, non-taxation or distortion of competition, Member States may, with regard to the supply of the services referred to in Article 56(1) and with regard to the hiring out of means of transport:

(*a*) consider the place of supply of any or all of those services, if situated within their territory, as being situated outside the Community, if the effective use and enjoyment of the services takes place outside the Community;
(*b*) consider the place of supply of any or all of those services, if situated outside the Community, as being situated within their territory, if the effective use and enjoyment of the services takes place within their territory.

However, this provision shall not apply to the services referred to in point (k) of Article 56(1), where those services are rendered to non-taxable persons.

Article 59

1. Member States shall apply Article 58(*b*) to telecommunications services supplied to non-taxable persons who are established in a Member State, or who have their permanent address or usually reside in a Member State, by a taxable person who has established his business outside the Community or has a fixed establishment there from which the services are supplied, or who, in the absence of such a place of business or fixed establishment, has his permanent address or usually resides outside the Community.

2. Until 31 December 2009, Member States shall apply Article 58(*b*) to radio and television broadcasting services, as referred to in Article 56(1)(*j*), supplied to non-taxable persons who are established in a Member State, or who have their permanent address or usually reside in a Member State, by a taxable person who has established his business outside the Community or who has a fixed establishment there from which the services are supplied, or who, in the absence of such a place of business or fixed establishment, has his permanent address or usually resides outside the Community.".

CHAPTER 4

PLACE OF IMPORTATION OF GOODS

Article 60

The place of importation of goods shall be the Member State within whose territory the goods are located when they enter the Community.

Article 61

By way of derogation from Article 60, where, on entry into the Community, goods which are not in free circulation are placed under one of the arrangements or situations referred to in Article 156, or under temporary importation arrangements with total exemption from import duty, or under external transit arrangements, the place of importation of such goods shall be the Member State within whose territory the goods cease to be covered by those arrangements or situations.

Similarly, where, on entry into the Community, goods which are in free circulation are placed under one of the arrangements or situations referred to in Articles 276 and 277, the place of importation shall be the Member State within whose territory the goods cease to be covered by those arrangements or situations.

TITLE VI
CHARGEABLE EVENT AND CHARGEABILITY OF VAT

CHAPTER 1
GENERAL PROVISIONS

Article 62

For the purposes of this Directive:

(1) 'chargeable event' shall mean the occurrence by virtue of which the legal conditions necessary for VAT to become chargeable are fulfilled;

(2) VAT shall become 'chargeable' when the tax authority becomes entitled under the law, at a given moment, to claim the tax from the person liable to pay, even though the time of payment may be deferred.

CHAPTER 2
SUPPLY OF GOODS OR SERVICES

Article 63

The chargeable event shall occur and VAT shall become chargeable when the goods or the services are supplied.

Article 64

1. Where it gives rise to successive statements of account or successive payments, the supply of goods, other than that consisting in the hire of goods for a certain period or the sale of goods on deferred terms, as referred to in point (*b*) of Article 14 (2), or the supply of services shall be regarded as being completed on expiry of the periods to which such statements of account or payments relate.

[2. Supplies of services for which VAT is payable by the customer pursuant to Article 196, which are supplied continuously over a period of more than one year and which do not give rise to statements of account or payments during that period shall be regarded as being completed on expiry of each calendar year until such time as the supply of services comes to an end.

Member States may provide that, in certain cases other than those referred to in the previous paragraph, the continuous supply of goods or services over a period of time is to be regarded as being completed at least at intervals of one year.][1]

Amendments—[1] Para 2 substituted by Council Directive 2008/117/EC art 1 with effect from 21 January 2009. The deadline for implementation of this Directive is 1 January 2010 (OJ L 14, 20.1.2009 p 7). Text previously read as follows—

"2. Member States may provide that, in certain cases, the continuous supply of goods or services over a period of time is to be regarded as being completed at least at intervals of one year.".

Article 65

Where a payment is to be made on account before the goods or services are supplied, VAT shall become chargeable on receipt of the payment and on the amount received.

Article 66

By way of derogation from Articles 63, 64 and 65, Member States may provide that VAT is to become chargeable, in respect of certain transactions or certain categories of taxable person at one of the following times:

(*a*) no later than the time the invoice is issued;

(*b*) no later than the time the payment is received;

(*c*) where an invoice is not issued, or is issued late, within a specified period from the date of the chargeable event.

[The derogation provided for in the first paragraph shall not, however, apply to supplies of services in respect of which VAT is payable by the customer pursuant to Article 196.][1]

Amendments—[1] Para inserted by Council Directive 2008/117/EC art 1 with effect from 21 January 2009. The deadline for implementation of this Directive is 1 January 2010 (OJ L 14, 20.1.2009 p 7).

Article 67

1. Where, in accordance with the conditions laid down in Article 138, goods dispatched or transported to a Member State other than that in which dispatch or transport of the goods begins are supplied VAT-exempt or where goods are transferred VAT-exempt to another Member State by a taxable person for the purposes of his business, VAT shall become chargeable on the 15th day of the month following that in which the chargeable event occurs.

2. By way of derogation from paragraph 1, VAT shall become chargeable on issue of the invoice provided for in Article 220, if that invoice is issued before the 15th day of the month following that in which the chargeable event occurs.

CHAPTER 3

INTRA-COMMUNITY ACQUISITION OF GOODS

Article 68

The chargeable event shall occur when the intra-Community acquisition of goods is made.

The intra-Community acquisition of goods shall be regarded as being made when the supply of similar goods is regarded as being effected within the territory of the relevant Member State.

Article 69

1. In the case of the intra-Community acquisition of goods, VAT shall become chargeable on the 15th day of the month following that in which the chargeable event occurs.

2. By way of derogation from paragraph 1, VAT shall become chargeable on issue of the invoice provided for in Article 220, if that invoice is issued before the 15th day of the month following that in which the chargeable event occurs.

CHAPTER 4

IMPORTATION OF GOODS

Article 70

The chargeable event shall occur and VAT shall become chargeable when the goods are imported.

Article 71

1. Where, on entry into the Community, goods are placed under one of the arrangements or situations referred to in Articles 156, 276 and 277, or under temporary importation arrangements with total exemption from import duty, or under external transit arrangements, the chargeable event shall occur and VAT shall become chargeable only when the goods cease to be covered by those arrangements or situations.

However, where imported goods are subject to customs duties, to agricultural levies or to charges having equivalent effect established under a common policy, the chargeable event shall occur and VAT shall become chargeable when the chargeable event in respect of those duties occurs and those duties become chargeable.

2. Where imported goods are not subject to any of the duties referred to in the second subparagraph of paragraph 1, Member States shall, as regards the chargeable event and the moment when VAT becomes chargeable, apply the provisions in force governing customs duties.

Simon's Tax Cases—*Pezzullo Molini Pastifici Mangimifici SpA v Ministero delle Finanze* (Case C-166/94) [1996] STC 1236*.

TITLE VII

TAXABLE AMOUNT

CHAPTER 4

IMPORTATION OF GOODS

Note—This Chapter number and heading appear to be erroneous. In accordance with the Arrangement of Contents the Chapter number and heading should instead read "Chapter 1 Definition".

Article 72

For the purposes of this Directive, 'open market value' shall mean the full amount that, in order to obtain the goods or services in question at that time, a customer at the same marketing stage at which the supply of goods or services takes place, would have to pay, under conditions of fair competition, to a supplier at arm's length within the territory of the Member State in which the supply is subject to tax.

Where no comparable supply of goods or services can be ascertained, 'open market value' shall mean the following:

(1) in respect of goods, an amount that is not less than the purchase price of the goods or of similar goods or, in the absence of a purchase price, the cost price, determined at the time of supply;

(2) in respect of services, an amount that is not less than the full cost to the taxable person of providing the service.

CHAPTER 2
SUPPLY OF GOODS OR SERVICES

Article 73

In respect of the supply of goods or services, other than as referred to in Articles 74 to 77, the taxable amount shall include everything which constitutes consideration obtained or to be obtained by the supplier, in return for the supply, from the customer or a third party, including subsidies directly linked to the price of the supply.

Simon's Tax Cases—*Town and County Factors Ltd v C&E Comrs* (Case C-498/99) [2002] STC 1263*; *EC Commission v Federal Republic of Germany (United Kingdom intervening)*, [2003] STC 301*; *Yorkshire Co-operatives Ltd v C&E Comrs* [2003] STC 234*; *Office des Produits Wallons ASBL v Belgium* [2003] STC 1100*; *Lex Services plc v C&E Comrs* [2004] STC 73*; *Total UK Ltd v R&C Comrs* [2008] STC 19*; *Ministero dell'Economia e delle Finanze v Part Service Srl* [2008] STC 3132*; *Fiscale eenheid Koninklijke Ahold NV v Staatssecretaris van Financiën* [2009] STC 45*; *JD Wetherspoon plc v R&C Comrs* [2009] STC 1022*.

Article 74

Where a taxable person applies or disposes of goods forming part of his business assets, or where goods are retained by a taxable person, or by his successors, when his taxable economic activity ceases, as referred to in Articles 16 and 18, the taxable amount shall be the purchase price of the goods or of similar goods or, in the absence of a purchase price, the cost price, determined at the time when the application, disposal or retention takes place.

Article 75

In respect of the supply of services, as referred to in Article 26, where goods forming part of the assets of a business are used for private purposes or services are carried out free of charge, the taxable amount shall be the full cost to the taxable person of providing the services.

Simon's Tax Cases—*Köhne v Finanzamt München III* [1990] STC 749*; *Enkler v Finanzamt Homburg* (Case C-230/94) [1996] STC 1316*; *Hausgemeinschaft Jörg und Stefanie Wollny v Finanzamt Landshut* [2008] STC 1618*.

Article 76

In respect of the supply of goods consisting in transfer to another Member State, the taxable amount shall be the purchase price of the goods or of similar goods or, in the absence of a purchase price, the cost price, determined at the time the transfer takes place.

Article 77

In respect of the supply by a taxable person of a service for the purposes of his business, as referred to in Article 27, the taxable amount shall be the open market value of the service supplied.

Article 78

The taxable amount shall include the following factors:

(*a*) taxes, duties, levies and charges, excluding the VAT itself;

(*b*) incidental expenses, such as commission, packing, transport and insurance costs, charged by the supplier to the customer.

For the purposes of point (*b*) of the first paragraph, Member States may regard expenses covered by a separate agreement as incidental expenses.

Simon's Tax Cases—*C&E Comrs v British Telecom plc* [1999] STC 758*.

Article 79

The taxable amount shall not include the following factors:

(*a*) price reductions by way of discount for early payment;

(*b*) price discounts and rebates granted to the customer and obtained by him at the time of the supply;

(*c*) amounts received by a taxable person from the customer, as repayment of expenditure incurred in the name and on

behalf of the customer, and entered in his books in a suspense account.

The taxable person must furnish proof of the actual amount of the expenditure referred to in point (*c*) of the first paragraph and may not deduct any VAT which may have been charged.

Simon's Tax Cases—*Boots Co plc v C&E Comrs* [1990] STC 387*; *Nell Gwynn House Maintenance Fund Trustees v C&E Comrs* [1999] STC 79*; *Kuwait Petroleum (GB) Ltd v C&E Comrs* [2001] STC 62*; *Freemans v C&E Comrs* [2001] STC 960*; *C&E Comrs v Plantiflor* [2002] STC 1132*.

Article 80

1. In order to prevent tax evasion or avoidance, Member States may in any of the following cases take measures to ensure that, in respect of the supply of goods or services involving family or other close personal ties, management, ownership, membership, financial or legal ties as defined by the Member State, the taxable amount is to be the open market value:

(*a*) where the consideration is lower than the open market value and the recipient of the supply does not have a full right of deduction under Articles 167 to 171 and Articles 173 to 177;

(*b*) where the consideration is lower than the open market value and the supplier does not have a full right of deduction under Articles 167 to 171 and Articles 173 to 177 and the supply is subject to an exemption under Articles 132, 135, 136, 371, 375, 376, 377, 378(2), 379(2) or Articles 380 to 390;

(*c*) where the consideration is higher than the open market value and the supplier does not have a full right of deduction under Articles 167 to 171 and Articles 173 to 177.

For the purposes of the first subparagraph, legal ties may include the relationship between an employer and employee or the employee's family, or any other closely connected persons.

2. Where Member States exercise the option provided for in paragraph 1, they may restrict the categories of suppliers or recipients to whom the measures shall apply.

3. Member States shall inform the VAT Committee of national legislative measures adopted pursuant to paragraph 1 in so far as these are not measures authorised by the Council prior to 13 August 2006 in accordance with Article 27 (1) to (4) of Directive 77/388/EEC, and which are continued under paragraph 1 of this Article.

Article 81

Member States which, at 1 January 1993, were not availing themselves of the option under Article 98 of applying a reduced rate may, if they avail themselves of the option under Article 89, provide that in respect of the supply of works of art, as referred to in Article 103(2), the taxable amount is to be equal to a fraction of the amount determined in accordance with Articles 73, 74, 76, 78 and 79.

The fraction referred to in the first paragraph shall be determined in such a way that the VAT thus due is equal to at least 5% of the amount determined in accordance with Articles 73, 74, 76, 78 and 79.

Article 82

Member States may provide that, in respect of the supply of goods and services, the taxable amount is to include the value of exempt investment gold within the meaning of Article 346, which has been provided by the customer to be used as basis for working and which as a result, loses its VAT exempt investment gold status when such goods and services are supplied. The value to be used is the open market value of the investment gold at the time that those goods and services are supplied.

CHAPTER 3

INTRA-COMMUNITY ACQUISITION OF GOODS

Article 83

In respect of the intra-Community acquisition of goods, the taxable amount shall be established on the basis of the same factors as are used in accordance with Chapter 1 to determine the taxable amount for the supply of the same goods within the territory of the Member State concerned. In the case of the transactions, to be treated as intra-Community acquisitions of goods, referred to in Articles 21 and 22, the taxable amount shall be the purchase price of the goods or of similar goods or, in the absence of a purchase price, the cost price, determined at the time of the supply.

Article 84

1. Member States shall take the measures necessary to ensure that the excise duty due from or paid by the person making the intra-Community acquisition of a product subject to excise duty is included in the taxable amount in accordance with point (*a*) of the first paragraph of Article 78.

2. Where, after the intra-Community acquisition of goods has been made, the person acquiring the goods obtains a refund of the excise duty paid in the Member State in which dispatch or transport of the goods began, the taxable amount shall be reduced accordingly in the Member State in the territory of which the acquisition was made.

CHAPTER 4

IMPORTATION OF GOODS

Article 85

In respect of the importation of goods, the taxable amount shall be the value for customs purposes, determined in accordance with the Community provisions in force.

Article 86

1. The taxable amount shall include the following factors, in so far as they are not already included:

(*a*) taxes, duties, levies and other charges due outside the Member State of importation, and those due by reason of importation, excluding the VAT to be levied;

(*b*) incidental expenses, such as commission, packing, transport and insurance costs, incurred up to the first place of destination within the territory of the Member State of importation as well as those resulting from transport to another place of destination within the Community, if that other place is known when the chargeable event occurs.

2. For the purposes of point (*b*) of paragraph 1, 'first place of destination' shall mean the place mentioned on the consignment note or on any other document under which the goods are imported into the Member State of importation. If no such mention is made, the first place of destination shall be deemed to be the place of the first transfer of cargo in the Member State of importation.

Article 87

The taxable amount shall not include the following factors:

(*a*) price reductions by way of discount for early payment;

(*b*) price discounts and rebates granted to the customer and obtained by him at the time of importation.

Article 88

Where goods temporarily exported from the Community are reimported after having undergone, outside the Community, repair, processing, adaptation, making up or re-working, Member States shall take steps to ensure that the tax treatment of the goods for VAT purposes is the same as that which would have been applied had the repair, processing, adaptation, making up or re-working been carried out within their territory.

Article 89

Member States which, at 1 January 1993, were not availing themselves of the option under Article 98 of applying a reduced rate may provide that in respect of the importation of works of art, collectors' items and antiques, as defined in points (2), (3) and (4) of Article 311(1), the taxable amount is to be equal to a fraction of the amount determined in accordance with Articles 85, 86 and 87.

The fraction referred to in the first paragraph shall be determined in such a way that the VAT thus due on the importation is equal to at least 5% of the amount determined in accordance with Articles 85, 86 and 87.

Simon's Tax Cases—*EC Commission v United Kingdom* [2007] STC 1211*.

CHAPTER 5

MISCELLANEOUS PROVISIONS

Article 90

1. In the case of cancellation, refusal or total or partial nonpayment, or where the price is reduced after the supply takes place, the taxable amount shall be reduced accordingly under conditions which shall be determined by the Member States.

2. In the case of total or partial non-payment, Member States may derogate from paragraph 1.

Simon's Tax Cases—*Elida Gibbs Ltd v C&E Comrs* (Case C-317/94) [1996] STC 1387*; *Goldsmiths (Jewellers) Ltd v C&E Comrs* (Case C-330/95) [1997] STC 1073*; *Yorkshire Co-operatives Ltd v C&E Comrs* [2003] STC 234*.

Article 91

1. Where the factors used to determine the taxable amount on importation are expressed in a currency other than that of the Member State in which assessment takes place, the exchange rate shall be determined in accordance with the Community provisions governing the calculation of the value for customs purposes.

2. Where the factors used to determine the taxable amount of a transaction other than the importation of goods are expressed in a currency other than that of the Member State in which assessment takes place, the exchange rate applicable shall be the latest selling rate recorded, at the time VAT becomes chargeable, on the most representative exchange market or markets of the Member State concerned, or a rate determined by reference to that or those markets, in accordance with the rules laid down by that Member State.

However, for some of the transactions referred to in the first subparagraph or for certain categories of taxable persons, Member States may use the exchange rate determined in accordance with the Community provisions in force governing the calculation of the value for customs purposes.

Article 92

As regards the costs of returnable packing material, Member States may take one of the following measures:

(*a*) exclude them from the taxable amount and take the measures necessary to ensure that this amount is adjusted if the packing material is not returned;

(*b*) include them in the taxable amount and take the measures necessary to ensure that this amount is adjusted if the packing material is in fact returned.

TITLE VIII
RATES

CHAPTER 1
APPLICATION OF RATES

Article 93

The rate applicable to taxable transactions shall be that in force at the time of the chargeable event.

However, in the following situations, the rate applicable shall be that in force when VAT becomes chargeable:

(*a*) in the cases referred to in Articles 65 and 66;

(*b*) in the case of an intra-Community acquisition of goods;

(*c*) in the cases, concerning the importation of goods, referred to in the second subparagraph of Article 71(1) and in Article 71(2).

Article 94

1. The rate applicable to the intra-Community acquisition of goods shall be that applied to the supply of like goods within the territory of the Member State.

2. Subject to the option under Article 103(1) of applying a reduced rate to the importation of works of art, collectors' items or antiques, the rate applicable to the importation of goods shall be that applied to the supply of like goods within the territory of the Member State.

Article 95

Where rates are changed, Member States may, in the cases referred to in Articles 65 and 66, effect adjustments in order to take account of the rate applying at the time when the goods or services were supplied.

Member States may also adopt all appropriate transitional measures.

CHAPTER 2
STRUCTURE AND LEVEL OF RATES

Section 1 Standard rate

Article 96

Member States shall apply a standard rate of VAT, which shall be fixed by each Member State as a percentage of the taxable amount and which shall be the same for the supply of goods and for the supply of services.

Article 97

1. From 1 January 2006 until 31 December 2010, the standard rate may not be less than 15%.

2. The Council shall decide, in accordance with Article 93 of the Treaty, on the level of the standard rate to be applied after 31 December 2010.

Commentary—*De Voil Indirect Tax Service* **V4.401**.

Simon's Tax Cases—*EC Commission v French Republic (Republic of Finland intervening)* [2001] STC 919*; *EC Commission v Federal Republic of Germany* [2006] STC 1587*; *Finanzamt Oschatz v Zweckverband zur Trinkwasserversorgung und Abwasserbeseitigung Torgau-Westelbien* [2009] STC 1*

Section 2 Reduced rates

Article 98

1. Member States may apply either one or two reduced rates.

2. The reduced rates shall apply only to supplies of goods or services in the categories set out in Annex III.

[The reduced rates shall not apply to electronically supplied services.][1]

3. When applying the reduced rates provided for in paragraph 1 to categories of goods, Member States may use the Combined Nomenclature to establish the precise coverage of the category concerned.

Commentary—*De Voil Indirect Tax Service* **V4.401**.
Simon's Tax Cases—*EC Commission v French Republic (Republic of Finland intervening)* [2001] STC 919*; *EC Commission v Federal Republic of Germany* [2006] STC 1587*; *Finanzamt Oschatz v Zweckverband zur Trinkwasserversorgung und Abwasserbeseitigung Torgau-Westelbien* [2009] STC 1*.
Amendments—Second sub-para substituted by Council Directive 2008/8/EC art 2(2) with effect from 1 January 2010 (OJ L 44, 20.2.2008 p 11). Text previously read as follows—

"The reduced rates shall not apply to the services referred to in point (k) of Article 56(1).".

Article 99

1. The reduced rates shall be fixed as a percentage of the taxable amount, which may not be less than 5%.

2. Each reduced rate shall be so fixed that the amount of VAT resulting from its application is such that the VAT deductible under Articles 167 to 171 and Articles 173 to 177 can normally be deducted in full.

Article 100

On the basis of a report from the Commission, the Council shall, starting in 1994, review the scope of the reduced rates every two years.

The Council may, in accordance with Article 93 of the Treaty, decide to alter the list of goods and services set out in Annex III.

Article 101

By 30 June 2007 at the latest the Commission shall present to the European Parliament and the Council an overall assessment report on the impact of reduced rates applying to locally supplied services, including restaurant services, notably in terms of job creation, economic growth and the proper functioning of the internal market, based on a study carried out by an independent economic think-tank.

Section 3 Particular provisions

Article 102

Member States may apply a reduced rate to the supply of natural gas, of electricity or of district heating, provided that no risk of distortion of competition thereby arises.

Any Member State intending to apply a reduced rate under the first paragraph must, before doing so, inform the Commission accordingly. The Commission shall decide whether or not there is a risk of distortion of competition. If the Commission has not taken that decision within three months of receipt of the information, no risk of distortion of competition shall be deemed to exist.

Article 103

1. Member States may provide that the reduced rate, or one of the reduced rates, which they apply in accordance with Articles 98 and 99 is also to apply to the importation of works of art, collectors' items and antiques, as defined in points (2), (3) and (4) of Article 311(1).

2. If Member States avail themselves of the option under paragraph 1, they may also apply the reduced rate to the following transactions:

(*a*) the supply of works of art, by their creator or his successors in title;

(*b*) the supply of works of art, on an occasional basis, by a taxable person other than a taxable dealer, where the works of art have been imported by the taxable person himself, or where they have been supplied to him by their creator or his successors in title, or where they have entitled him to full deduction of VAT.

Article 104

Austria may, in the communes of Jungholz and Mittelberg (Kleines Walsertal), apply a second standard rate which is lower than the corresponding rate applied in the rest of Austria but not less than 15%.

[Article 104a

Cyprus may apply one of the two reduced rates provided for in Article 98 to the supply of liquid petroleum gas (LPG) in cylinders.][1]

Amendments—[1] Article 104a inserted by Council Directive 2009/47/EC art 1 with effect from 1 June 2009 (OJ L 116, 9.5.2009 p 18).

[Article 105

1. Portugal may apply one of the two reduced rates provided for in Article 98 to the tolls on bridges in the Lisbon area.

2. Portugal may, in the case of transactions carried out in the autonomous regions of the Azores and Madeira and of direct importation into those regions, apply rates lower than those applying on the mainland.][1]

Amendments—[1] Article 105 substituted by Council Directive 2009/47/EC art 1 with effect from 1 June 2009 (OJ L 116, 9.5.2009 p 18). Text previously read as follows:

"Portugal may, in the case of transactions carried out in the autonomous regions of the Azores and Madeira and of direct importation into those regions, apply rates lower than those applying on the mainland.".

CHAPTER 3

TEMPORARY PROVISIONS FOR PARTICULAR LABOUR-INTENSIVE SERVICES[1]

Amendments—[1] Chapter 3 repealed by Council Directive 2009/47/EC art 1 with effect from 1 June 2009 (OJ L 116, 9.5.2009 p 18).

Article 106

The Council may, acting unanimously on a proposal from the Commission, allow Member States to apply until 31 December 2010 at the latest the reduced rates provided for in Article 98 to services listed in Annex IV.

The reduced rates may be applied to services from no more than two of the categories set out in Annex IV.

In exceptional cases a Member State may be allowed to apply the reduced rates to services from three of those categories.[1]

Amendments—[1] Chapter 3 repealed by Council Directive 2009/47/EC art 1 with effect from 1 June 2009 (OJ L 116, 9.5.2009 p 18).

Article 107

The services referred to in Article 106 must meet the following conditions:

(*a*) *they must be labour-intensive;*
(*b*) *they must largely be provided direct to final consumers;*
(*c*) *they must be mainly local and not likely to cause distortion of competition.*

There must also be a close link between the decrease in prices resulting from the rate reduction and the foreseeable increase in demand and employment. Application of a reduced rate must not prejudice the smooth functioning of the internal market.[1]

Amendments—[1] Chapter 3 repealed by Council Directive 2009/47/EC art 1 with effect from 1 June 2009 (OJ L 116, 9.5.2009 p 18).

Article 108

Any Member State wishing to apply for the first time after 31 December 2005 a reduced rate to one or more of the services referred to in Article 106 pursuant to this Article shall inform the Commission accordingly no later than 31 March 2006. It shall communicate to it before that date all relevant information concerning the new measures it wishes to introduce, in particular the following:

(*a*) *scope of the measure and detailed description of the services concerned;*
(*b*) *particulars showing that the conditions laid down in Article 107 have been met;*
(*c*) *particulars showing the budgetary cost of the measure envisaged.*[1]

Amendments—[1] Chapter 3 repealed by Council Directive 2009/47/EC art 1 with effect from 1 June 2009 (OJ L 116, 9.5.2009 p 18).

CHAPTER 4

SPECIAL PROVISIONS APPLYING UNTIL THE ADOPTION OF DEFINITIVE ARRANGEMENTS

Article 109

Pending introduction of the definitive arrangements referred to in Article 402, the provisions laid down in this Chapter shall apply.

Simon's Tax Cases—*Marks & Spencer plc v R&C Comrs* [2008] STC 1408*.

Article 110

Member States which, at 1 January 1991, were granting exemptions with deductibility of the VAT paid at the preceding stage or applying reduced rates lower than the minimum laid down in Article 99 may continue to grant those exemptions or apply those reduced rates.

The exemptions and reduced rates referred to in the first paragraph must be in accordance with Community law and must have been adopted for clearly defined social reasons and for the benefit of the final consumer.

Article 111

Subject to the conditions laid down in the second paragraph of Article 110, exemptions with deductibility of the VAT paid at the preceding stage may continue to be granted in the following cases:

(*a*) by Finland in respect of the supply of newspapers and periodicals sold by subscription and the printing of publications distributed to the members of corporations for the public good;

(*b*) by Sweden in respect of the supply of newspapers, including radio and cassette newspapers for the visually impaired, pharmaceutical products supplied to hospitals or on prescription, and the production of, or other related services concerning, periodicals of non-profit-making organisations;

[(*c*) by Malta in respect of the supply of foodstuffs for human consumption and pharmaceuticals.][1]

Amendments—[1] Para (*c*) inserted by Council Directive 2009/47/EC art 1 with effect from 1 June 2009 (OJ L 116, 9.5.2009 p 18).

Article 112

If the provisions of Article 110 cause for Ireland distortion of competition in the supply of energy products for heating and lighting, Ireland may, on specific request, be authorised by the Commission to apply a reduced rate to such supplies, in accordance with Articles 98 and 99.

In the case referred to in the first paragraph, Ireland shall submit a request to the Commission, together with all necessary information. If the Commission has not taken a decision within three months of receiving the request, Ireland shall be deemed to be authorised to apply the reduced rates proposed.

Article 113

Member States which, at 1 January 1991, in accordance with Community law, were granting exemptions with deductibility of the VAT paid at the preceding stage or applying reduced rates lower than the minimum laid down in Article 99, in respect of goods and services other than those specified in Annex III, may apply the reduced rate, or one of the two reduced rates, provided for in Article 98 to the supply of such goods or services.

Article 114

1. Member States which, on 1 January 1993, were obliged to increase their standard rate in force at 1 January 1991 by more than 2% may apply a reduced rate lower than the minimum laid down in Article 99 to the supply of goods and services in the categories set out in Annex III.

[The Member States referred to in the first subparagraph may also apply such a rate to children's clothing and children's footwear and housing.][1]

2. Member States may not rely on paragraph 1 to introduce exemptions with deductibility of the VAT paid at the preceding stage.

Amendments—[1] In para 1, second sub-para substituted by Council Directive 2009/47/EC art 1 with effect from 1 June 2009 (OJ L 116, 9.5.2009 p 18). Text previously read as follows—

"The Member States referred to in the first subparagraph may also apply such a rate to restaurant services, children's clothing, children's footwear and housing.".

[Article 115

Member States which, at 1 January 1991, were applying a reduced rate to children's clothing, children's footwear or housing may continue to apply such a rate to the supply of those goods or services.][1]

Amendments—[1] Article 115 substituted by Council Directive 2009/47/EC art 1 with effect from 1 June 2009 (OJ L 116, 9.5.2009 p 18). Text previously read as follows—

"Article 115

Member States which, at 1 January 1991, were applying a reduced rate to restaurant services, children's clothing, children's footwear or housing may continue to apply such a rate to the supply of those goods or services.".

Article 116

Portugal may apply one of the two reduced rates provided for in Article 98 to restaurant services, provided that the rate is not lower than 12%.[1]

Amendments—[1] Article 116 repealed by Council Directive 2009/47/EC art 1 with effect from 1 June 2009 (OJ L 116, 9.5.2009 p 18).

Article 117

1. For the purposes of applying Article 115, Austria may continue to apply a reduced rate to restaurant services.[1]

2. Austria may apply one of the two reduced rates provided for in Article 98 to the letting of immovable property for residential use, provided that the rate is not lower than 10%.

Amendments—[1] Para 1 repealed by Council Directive 2009/47/EC art 1 with effect from 1 June 2009 (OJ L 116, 9.5.2009 p 18).

Article 118

Member States which, at 1 January 1991, were applying a reduced rate to the supply of goods or services other than those specified in Annex III may apply the reduced rate, or one of the two reduced rates, provided for in Article 98 to the supply of those goods or services, provided that the rate is not lower than 12%.

The first paragraph shall not apply to the supply of second-hand goods, works of art, collectors' items or antiques, as defined in points (1) to (4) of Article 311(1), subject to VAT in accordance with the margin scheme provided for in Articles 312 to 325 or the arrangements for sales by public auction.

Article 119

For the purposes of applying Article 118, Austria may apply a reduced rate to wines produced on an agricultural holding by the producer-farmer, provided that the rate is not lower than 12%.

Article 120

Greece may apply rates up to 30% lower than the corresponding rates applied in mainland Greece in the departments of Lesbos, Chios, Samos, the Dodecanese and the Cyclades, and on the islands of Thassos, the Northern Sporades, Samothrace and Skiros.

Article 121

Member States which, at 1 January 1993, regarded work under contract as the supply of goods may apply to the delivery of work under contract the rate applicable to the goods obtained after execution of the work under contract.

For the purposes of applying the first paragraph, 'delivery of work under contract' shall mean the handing over by a contractor to his customer of movable property made or assembled by the contractor from materials or objects entrusted to him by the customer for that purpose, whether or not the contractor has provided any part of the materials used.

Article 122

Member States may apply a reduced rate to the supply of live plants and other floricultural products, including bulbs, roots and the like, cut flowers and ornamental foliage, and of wood for use as firewood.

CHAPTER 5

TEMPORARY PROVISIONS

[Article 123

The Czech Republic may, until 31 December 2010, continue to apply a reduced rate of not less than 5% to the supply of construction work for residential housing not provided as part of a social policy, excluding building materials.][1]

Amendments—[1] Article 123 substituted by Council Directive 2007/75/EC of 20 December 2007, art 1(1) with effect from 1 January 2008.

Article 124

...[1]

Amendments—[1] Article 124 repealed by Council Directive 2007/75/EC of 20 December 2007, art 1(2) with effect from 1 January 2008.

Article 125

1. Cyprus may, [until 31 December 2010][1], continue to grant an exemption with deductibility of VAT paid at the preceding stage in respect of the supply of pharmaceuticals and foodstuffs for human consumption, with the exception of ice cream, ice lollies, frozen yoghurt, water ice and similar products and savoury food products (potato crisps/sticks, puffs and similar products packaged for human consumption without further preparation).

2. Cyprus may continue to apply a reduced rate of not less than 5% to the supply of restaurant services, [until 31 December 2010][1] or until the introduction of definitive arrangements, as referred to in Article 402, whichever is the earlier.[2]

Amendments—[1] Words substituted by Council Directive 2007/75/EC of 20 December 2007, art 1(3) with effect from 1 January 2008.

[2] Para 2 repealed by Council Directive 2009/47/EC art 1 with effect from 1 June 2009 (OJ L 116, 9.5.2009 p 18).

Article 126

...[1]

Amendments—[1] Article 126 repealed by Council Directive 2007/75/EC of 20 December 2007, art 1(4) with effect from 1 January 2008.

Article 127

Malta may, until [31 December 2010][1], continue to grant an exemption with deductibility of VAT paid at the preceding stage in respect of the supply of foodstuffs for human consumption and pharmaceuticals.

Amendments—[1] Words substituted by Council Directive 2007/75/EC of 20 December 2007, art 1(5) with effect from 1 January 2008.

Prospective amendments—Article 127 to be repealed by Council Directive 2009/47/EC art 1 with effect from 1 January 2011 (OJ L 116, 9.5.2009 p 18).

[Article 128

1. Poland may, until 31 December 2010, grant an exemption with deductibility of VAT paid at the preceding stage in respect of the supply of certain books and specialist periodicals.

2. Poland may, until 31 December 2010 or until the introduction of definitive arrangements, as referred to in Article 402, whichever is the earlier, continue to apply a reduced rate of not less than 7% to the supply of restaurant services.[2]

3. Poland may, until 31 December 2010, continue to apply a reduced rate of not less than 3% to the supply of foodstuffs as referred to in point (1) of Annex III.

4. Poland may, until 31 December 2010, continue to apply a reduced rate of not less than 7% to the supply of services, not provided as part of a social policy, for construction, renovation and alteration of housing, excluding building materials, and to the supply before first occupation of residential buildings or parts of residential buildings, as referred to in Article 12(1)(*a*).][1]

Amendments—[1] Article 128 substituted by Council Directive 2007/75/EC of 20 December 2007, art 1(6) with effect from 1 January 2008.

[2] Para 2 repealed by Council Directive 2009/47/EC art 1 with effect from 1 June 2009 (OJ L 116, 9.5.2009 p 18).

Article 129

1. Slovenia may, [until 31 December 2010][1] *or until the introduction of definitive arrangements as referred to in Article 402, whichever is the earlier, continue to apply a reduced rate of not less than 8.5% to the preparation of meals.*[2]

2. Slovenia may, [until 31 December 2010][1], continue to apply a reduced rate of not less than 5% to the supply of construction, renovation and maintenance work for residential housing not provided as part of a social policy, excluding building materials.

Amendments—[1] Words substituted by Council Directive 2007/75/EC of 20 December 2007, art 1(7) with effect from 1 January 2008.

[2] Para 1 repealed by Council Directive 2009/47/EC art 1 with effect from 1 June 2009 (OJ L 116, 9.5.2009 p 18).

Article 130

...[1]

Amendments—[1] Article 130 repealed by Council Directive 2007/75/EC of 20 December 2007, art 1(8) with effect from 1 January 2008.

TITLE IX
EXEMPTIONS

CHAPTER 1
GENERAL PROVISIONS

Article 131

The exemptions provided for in Chapters 2 to 9 shall apply without prejudice to other Community provisions and in accordance with conditions which the Member States shall lay down for the purposes of ensuring the correct and straightforward application of those exemptions and of preventing any possible evasion, avoidance or abuse.

CHAPTER 2
EXEMPTIONS FOR CERTAIN ACTIVITIES IN THE PUBLIC INTEREST

Article 132

1. Member States shall exempt the following transactions:

(*a*) the supply by the public postal services of services other than passenger transport and telecommunications services, and the supply of goods incidental thereto;

(*b*) hospital and medical care and closely related activities undertaken by bodies governed by public law or, under social conditions comparable with those applicable to bodies governed by public law, by hospitals, centres for medical treatment or diagnosis and other duly recognised establishments of a similar nature;

(*c*) the provision of medical care in the exercise of the medical and paramedical professions as defined by the Member State concerned;

(*d*) the supply of human organs, blood and milk;

(*e*) the supply of services by dental technicians in their professional capacity and the supply of dental prostheses by dentists and dental technicians;

(*f*) the supply of services by independent groups of persons, who are carrying on an activity which is exempt from VAT or in relation to which they are not taxable persons, for the purpose of rendering their members the services directly necessary for the exercise of that activity, where those groups merely claim from their members exact reimbursement of their share of the joint expenses, provided that such exemption is not likely to cause distortion of competition;

(*g*) the supply of services and of goods closely linked to welfare and social security work, including those supplied by old people's homes, by bodies governed by public law or by other bodies recognised by the Member State concerned as being devoted to social wellbeing;

(*h*) the supply of services and of goods closely linked to the protection of children and young persons by bodies governed by public law or by other organisations recognised by the Member State concerned as being devoted to social wellbeing;

(*i*) the provision of children's or young people's education, school or university education, vocational training or retraining, including the supply of services and of goods closely related thereto, by bodies governed by public law having such as their aim or by other organisations recognised by the Member State concerned as having similar objects;

(*j*) tuition given privately by teachers and covering school or university education;

(*k*) the supply of staff by religious or philosophical institutions for the purpose of the activities referred to in points (*b*), (*g*), (*h*) and (*i*) and with a view to spiritual welfare;

(*l*) the supply of services, and the supply of goods closely linked thereto, to their members in their common interest in return for a subscription fixed in accordance with their rules by non-profit-making organisations with aims of a political, trade-union, religious, patriotic, philosophical, philanthropic or civic nature, provided that this exemption is not likely to cause distortion of competition;

(*m*) the supply of certain services closely linked to sport or physical education by non-profit-making organisations to persons taking part in sport or physical education;

(*n*) the supply of certain cultural services, and the supply of goods closely linked thereto, by bodies governed by public law or by other cultural bodies recognised by the Member State concerned;

(*o*) the supply of services and goods, by organisations whose activities are exempt pursuant to points (*b*), (*g*), (*h*), (*i*), (*l*), (*m*) and (*n*), in connection with fund-raising events organised exclusively for their own benefit, provided that exemption is not likely to cause distortion of competition;

(*p*) the supply of transport services for sick or injured persons in vehicles specially designed for the purpose, by duly authorised bodies;

(*q*) the activities, other than those of a commercial nature, carried out by public radio and television bodies.

2. For the purposes of point (*o*) of paragraph 1, Member States may introduce any restrictions necessary, in particular as regards the number of events or the amount of receipts which give entitlement to exemption.

Commentary—*De Voil Indirect Tax Service* **V4.146**, **V4.161**.

Simon's Tax Cases—*EC Commission v United Kingdom* [1988] STC 251*; *Christoph-Dornier-Stiftung für Klinische Psychologie v Finanzamt Gießen* [2005] STC 228*.

Art 132(1), *Gregg v Comrs of Customs and Excise* (Case C-216/97) [1999] STC 934*; *C&E Comrs v Kingscrest Associates Ltd (t/a Kingscrest Residential Care Homes)* [2002] STC 490*; *Diagnostiko & Therapeftiko Kentro Athinon-Ygeia AE v Ipourgos Ikonomikon* [2006] STC 1349*.

Art 132(1)(a), *R (on the application of TNT Post UK Ltd) v R&C Comrs* [2009] STC 1438*.

Art 132(1)(*b*), *LuP GmbH v Finanzamt Bochum-Mitte* [2008] STC 1742*.

Art 132(1)(*c*), *C&E Comrs v Leightons Ltd* [1995] STC 458*; *D v W (Osterreicher Bundesschatz intervening)* [2002] STC 1200*; *d'Ambrumenil and another v C&E Comrs Unterpertinger v Pensionsversicherungsanstalt der Arbeiter* [2005] STC 650*; *Solleveld and another v Staatssecretaris van Financiën* [2007] STC 71*; *LuP GmbH v Finanzamt Bochum-Mitte* [2008] STC 1742*.

Art 132(1)(e), *Administration de l'enregistrement et des domaines v Eurodental Sàrl* (Case C-240/05) [2007] STC 275*; *VDP Dental Laboratory NV v Staatssecretaris van Financiën* [2007] STC 474*.

Art 132(1)(*f*), *Assurandør-Societetet, acting on behalf of Taksatorringen v Skatteministeriet* [2006] STC 1842*; *Stichting Centraal Begeleidingsorgaan voor de Intercollegiale Toetsing v Staatssecretaris van Financiën* [2009] STC 869*.

Art 132(1)(*g*), *Bulthuis-Griffioen v Inspector der Omzetbelasting* (Case C-453/93) [1995] STC 954*; *Gregg v Comrs of C&E* (Case C-216/97) [1999] STC 934*; *Kingscrest Associates Ltd and another v C&E Comrs* [2005] STC 1547*; *Staatssecretaris van Financiën v Stichting Kinderopvang Enschede* [2007] STC 294*.

Art 132(1)(*h*), *Staatssecretaris van Financiën v Stichting Kinderopvang Enschede* [2007] STC 294*.

Art 132(1)(*i*), *North of England Zoological Society v C&E Comrs* [1999] STC 1027*; *C&E Comrs v University of Leicester Student's Union, CA* [2002] STC 147*; *EC Commission v Federal Republic of Germany* (*Case C-287/00*) [2002] STC 982*; *Staatssecretaris van Financiën v Stichting Kinderopvang Enschede* [2007] STC 294*; *Stichting Regionaal Opleidingen Centrum Noord-Kennermerland/West-Friesland (Horizon College) v Staatssecretaris van Financiën* [2008] STC 2145*.

Art 132(1)(*j*), *R&C Comrs v Empowerment Enterprises Ltd* [2008] STC 1835; *Haderer v Finanzamt Wilmersdorf* [2008] STC 2171*.

Art 132(1)(*l*), *Institute of Leisure and Amenity Management v C&E Comrs* [1988] STC 602*; *Committee of Directors of Polytechnics v C&E Comrs* [1992] STC 873*; *Institute of Motor Industry v C&E Comrs* (Case C-149/97) [1998] STC 1219*; *Expert Witness Institute v C&E Comrs, CA* [2002] STC 42*; *British Association for Shooting and Conservation Ltd v R&C Comrs* [2009] STC 1421*.

Art 132(1)(*m*), *EC Commission v Spain (supported by United Kingdom, intervener)* (Case C-124/96) [1998] STC 1237*; *Swedish State v Stockholm Lindopark AB, Stockholm Lindopark AB v Swedish State* [2001] STC 103*; *Messenger Leisure Developments Ltd v Revenue and Customs Commissioners* [2005] STC 1078*; *Canterbury Hockey Club and another v R&C Comrs* [2008] STC 3351*.

Art 132(1)(*n*), *Bournemouth Symphony Orchestra v C&E Comrs, Loughborough Festival Opera v R&C Comrs* [2007] STC 198*.

Article 133

Member States may make the granting to bodies other than those governed by public law of each exemption provided for in points (*b*), (*g*), (*h*), (*i*), (*l*), (*m*) and (*n*) of Article 132(1) subject in each individual case to one or more of the following conditions:

(*a*) the bodies in question must not systematically aim to make a profit, and any surpluses nevertheless arising must not be distributed, but must be assigned to the continuance or improvement of the services supplied;

(*b*) those bodies must be managed and administered on an essentially voluntary basis by persons who have no direct or indirect interest, either themselves or through intermediaries, in the results of the activities concerned;

(*c*) those bodies must charge prices which are approved by the public authorities or which do not exceed such approved prices or, in respect of those services not subject to approval, prices lower than those charged for similar services by commercial enterprises subject to VAT;

(*d*) the exemptions must not be likely to cause distortion of competition to the disadvantage of commercial enterprises subject to VAT.

Member States which, pursuant to Annex E of Directive 77/388/ EEC, on 1 January 1989 applied VAT to the transactions referred to in Article 132(1)(*m*) and (*n*) may also apply the conditions provided for in point (*d*) of the first paragraph when the said supply of goods or services by bodies governed by public law is granted exemption.

Commentary—*De Voil Indirect Tax Service* **V4.146.**
Simon's Tax Cases—*C&E Comrs v Bell Concord Educational Trust Ltd* [1989] STC 264*; *EC Commission v Spain* (Case C-124/96) [1998] STC 1237*; *LuP GmbH v Finanzamt Bochum-Mitte* [2008] STC 1742*.

Article 134

The supply of goods or services shall not be granted exemption, as provided for in points (*b*), (*g*), (*h*), (*i*), (*l*), (*m*) and (*n*) of Article 132(1), in the following cases:

(*a*) where the supply is not essential to the transactions exempted;

(*b*) where the basic purpose of the supply is to obtain additional income for the body in question through transactions which are in direct competition with those of commercial enterprises subject to VAT.

Commentary—*De Voil Indirect Tax Service* **V4.146.**
Simon's Tax Cases—*C&E Comrs v Pilgrims Language Courses Ltd* [1998] STC 784*; *Canterbury Hockey Club and another v R&C Comrs* [2008] STC 3351*.

CHAPTER 3

EXEMPTIONS FOR OTHER ACTIVITIES

Article 135

1. Member States shall exempt the following transactions:

(*a*) insurance and reinsurance transactions, including related services performed by insurance brokers and insurance agents;

(*b*) the granting and the negotiation of credit and the management of credit by the person granting it;

(*c*) the negotiation of or any dealings in credit guarantees or any other security for money and the management of credit guarantees by the person who is granting the credit;

(*d*) transactions, including negotiation, concerning deposit and current accounts, payments, transfers, debts, cheques and other negotiable instruments, but excluding debt collection;

(*e*) transactions, including negotiation, concerning currency, bank notes and coins used as legal tender, with the exception of collectors' items, that is to say, gold, silver or other metal coins or bank notes which are not normally used as legal tender or coins of numismatic interest;

(*f*) transactions, including negotiation but not management or safekeeping, in shares, interests in companies or associations, debentures and other securities, but excluding documents establishing title to goods, and the rights or securities referred to in Article 15(2);

(*g*) the management of special investment funds as defined by Member States;

(*h*) the supply at face value of postage stamps valid for use for postal services within their respective territory, fiscal stamps and other similar stamps;

(*i*) betting, lotteries and other forms of gambling, subject to the conditions and limitations laid down by each Member State;

(*j*) the supply of a building or parts thereof, and of the land on which it stands, other than the supply referred to in point (*a*) of Article 12(1);

(*k*) the supply of land which has not been built on other than the supply of building land as referred to in point (*b*) of Article 12(1);

(*l*) the leasing or letting of immovable property.

2. The following shall be excluded from the exemption provided for in point (*l*) of paragraph 1:

(*a*) the provision of accommodation, as defined in the laws of the Member States, in the hotel sector or in sectors with a similar function, including the provision of accommodation in holiday camps or on sites developed for use as camping sites;

(*b*) the letting of premises and sites for the parking of vehicles;

(*c*) the letting of permanently installed equipment and machinery;
(*d*) the hire of safes.

Member States may apply further exclusions to the scope of the exemption referred to in point (l) of paragraph 1.

Commentary—*De Voil Indirect Tax Service* **V4.111**, **V4.131**, **V4.136**.
Simon's Tax Cases—Art 135, *Ford Motor Company Ltd v R&C Comrs* [2008] STC 1016*.
Art 135(1)(*a*), *CR Smith Glaziers (Dunfermline) Ltd v C&E Comrs* [2003] STC 419*; *Staatssecretaris van Financiën v Arthur Andersen & Co Accountants cs* [2005] STC 508*; *Assurandør-Societetet, acting on behalf of Taksatorringen v Skatteministeriet* [2006] STC 1842*; *EC Commission v Hellenic Republic* [2007] STC 194*; *JCM Beheer BV v Staatssecretaris van Financiën* [2008] STC 3360*.
Art 135(1)(*b*), *Primback Ltd v C&E Comrs* [1996] STC 757*; *Muy's en De Winter's Bouw-en Aannemingsbedrijf BV v Staatssecretaris van Financiën* [1997] STC 665*; *C&E Comrs v Civil Service Motoring Association Ltd* [1998] STC 111*; *C&E Comrs v Lloyds TSB Group Ltd* [1998] STC 528*; *Ludwig v Finanzamt Luckenwalde* [2008] STC 1640*.
Art 135(1)(*c*), *Velvet & Steel Immobilien und Handels GmbH v Finanzamt Hamburg-Eimsbüttel* [2008] STC 922*.
Art 135(1)(*d*), *Sinclair Collis Ltd v C&E Comrs* [2003] STC 898*; *Stichting 'Goed Wonen' v Staatssecretaris van Financiën* [2003] STC 1137*; *Belgian State v Temco Europe SA* [2005] STC 1451*; *Fonden Marselisborg Lystbådehavn v Skatteministeriet* [2006] STC 1467*; *Abbey National plc v C&E Comrs* [2006] STC 1961*; *Scottish Exhibition Centre Ltd v R&C Comrs* [2008] STC 967*.
Art 135(1)(*f*) *F&I Services Ltd v C&E Comrs* [2000] STC 364*; *CSC Financial Services Ltd v C&E Comrs* (*Case C-235/00*) [2002] STC 57*; *C&E Comrs v Electronic Data Systems Ltd* [2003] STC 688*; *Bookit Ltd v R&C Comrs* [2006] STC 1367*.
Art 135(1)(*g*), *Abbey National plc and another v C&E Comrs* [2006] STC 1136*; *JP Morgan Fleming Claverhouse Investment Trust plc and another v R&C Comrs* [2008] STC 1180*.
Art 135(1)(*i*), *R v Ryan* [1994] STC 446*; *C&E Comrs v Feehan* [1995] STC 75*; *Ivory & Sime Trustlink Ltd v C&E Comrs* [1995] STC 708*; *United Utilities plc v C&E Comrs* [2006] STC 1423*; *Finanzamt Gladbeck v Linneweber, Finanzamt Herne-West v Akritidis* [2008] STC 1069*.
Art 135(1)(*k*), *C&E Comrs v Parkinson* [1989] STC 51*; *Gemeente Emmen v Belastingdienst Grote Ondernemingen* (Case C-468/93) [1996] STC 496*.
Art 135(1)(*l*), *Ministero della Finanze—Ufficio IVA di Milano v Co.GE.P. Srl* [2008] STC 2744*; *Walderdorff v Finanzamt Waldviertel* [2008] STC 3079*; *Holland (t/a The Studio Hair Company) v R&C Comrs, Vigdor Ltd v R&C Comrs* [2009] STC 150*.
Art 135(2)(*a*), *Lubbock Fine & Co v C&E Comrs* (Case C-63/92) [1994] STC 101*; *Blasi v Finanzamt München I* (Case C-346/95) [1998] STC 336*.
Art 135(2)(*b*), *Skatteministeriet v Henriksen* [1990] STC 768*; *Fonden Marselisborg Lystbådehavn v Skatteministeriet* [2006] STC 1467*.

Article 136

Member States shall exempt the following transactions:

(*a*) the supply of goods used solely for an activity exempted under Articles 132, 135, 371, 375, 376 and 377, Article 378 (2), Article 379(2) and Articles 380 to 390, if those goods have not given rise to deductibility;
(*b*) the supply of goods on the acquisition or application of which VAT was not deductible, pursuant to Article 176.

Article 137

1. Member States may allow taxable persons a right of option for taxation in respect of the following transactions:

(*a*) the financial transactions referred to in points (*b*) to (*g*) of Article 135(1);
(*b*) the supply of a building or of parts thereof, and of the land on which the building stands, other than the supply referred to in point (*a*) of Article 12(1);
(*c*) the supply of land which has not been built on other than the supply of building land referred to in point (*b*) of Article 12(1);
(*d*) the leasing or letting of immovable property.

2. Member States shall lay down the detailed rules governing exercise of the option under paragraph 1.

Member States may restrict the scope of that right of option.

Commentary—*De Voil Indirect Tax Service* **V4.115**.
Simon's Tax Cases—*Belgocodex SA v Belgium* [2000] STC 351*; *Stichting 'Goed Wonen' v Staatssecretaris van Financiën* [2003] STC 1137*; *Administration de l'enregistrement et des domains, État du grand-duché de Luxembourg v Vermietungsgesellschaft Objekt Kirchberg SARL* [2005] STC 1345*; *Marlow Gardner & Cooke Ltd Directors' Pension Scheme v R&C Comrs* [2006] STC 2014; *Proceedings brought by Uudenkaupungin kaupunki* [2008] STC 2329*.

CHAPTER 4
EXEMPTIONS FOR INTRA-COMMUNITY TRANSACTIONS

Section 1 Exemptions related to the supply of goods

Article 138

1. Member States shall exempt the supply of goods dispatched or transported to a destination outside their respective territory but within the Community, by or on behalf of the vendor or the person acquiring the goods, for another taxable person, or for a non-taxable legal person acting as such in a Member State other than that in which dispatch or transport of the goods began.

2. In addition to the supply of goods referred to in paragraph 1, Member States shall exempt the following transactions:

(*a*) the supply of new means of transport, dispatched or transported to the customer at a destination outside their respective territory but within the Community, by or on behalf of the vendor or the customer, for taxable persons, or non-taxable legal persons, whose intra-Community acquisitions of goods are not subject to VAT pursuant to Article 3(1), or for any other non-taxable person;

(*b*) the supply of products subject to excise duty, dispatched or transported to a destination outside their respective territory but within the Community, to the customer, by or on behalf of the vendor or the customer, for taxable persons, or non-taxable legal persons, whose intra-Community acquisitions of goods other than products subject to excise duty are not subject to VAT pursuant to Article 3(1), where those products have been dispatched or transported in accordance with Article 7(4) and (5) or Article 16 of Directive 92/12/EEC;

(*c*) the supply of goods, consisting in a transfer to another Member State, which would have been entitled to exemption under paragraph 1 and points (*a*) and (*b*) if it had been made on behalf of another taxable person.

Simon's Tax Cases—*EMAG Handel Eder OHG v Finanzlandesdirektion für Kärnten* [2007] STC 1461*.

Article 139

1. The exemption provided for in Article 138(1) shall not apply to the supply of goods carried out by taxable persons who are covered by the exemption for small enterprises provided for in Articles 282 to 292.

Nor shall that exemption apply to the supply of goods to taxable persons, or non-taxable legal persons, whose intra-Community acquisitions of goods are not subject to VAT pursuant to Article 3(1).

2. The exemption provided for in Article 138(2)(*b*) shall not apply to the supply of products subject to excise duty by taxable persons who are covered by the exemption for small enterprises provided for in Articles 282 to 292.

3. The exemption provided for in Article 138(1) and (2)(*b*) and (*c*) shall not apply to the supply of goods subject to VAT in accordance with the margin scheme provided for in Articles 312 to 325 or the special arrangements for sales by public auction.

The exemption provided for in Article 138(1) and (2)(*c*) shall not apply to the supply of second-hand means of transport, as defined in Article 327(3), subject to VAT in accordance with the transitional arrangements for second-hand means of transport.

Simon's Tax Cases—*EMAG Handel Eder OHG v Finanzlandesdirektion für Kärnten* [2007] STC 1461*.

Section 2 Exemptions for intra-community acquisitions of goods

Article 140

Member States shall exempt the following transactions:

(*a*) the intra-Community acquisition of goods the supply of which by taxable persons would in all circumstances be exempt within their respective territory;

(*b*) the intra-Community acquisition of goods the importation of which would in all circumstances be exempt under points (*a*), (*b*) and (*c*) and (*e*) to (*l*) of Article 143;

(*c*) the intra-Community acquisition of goods where, pursuant to Articles 170 and 171, the person acquiring the goods would in all circumstances be entitled to full reimbursement of the VAT due under Article 2(1)(*b*).

Prospective amendments—Point (*b*) to be substituted by Council Directive 2009/69/EC art 1 with effect from 24 July 2009. The deadline for implementation of this Directive is 1 January 2011 (OJ L 175, 4.7.2009 p 12). Text to read as follows—

"(*b*) the intra-Community acquisition of goods the importation of which would in all circumstances be exempt under points (*a*), (*b*) and (*c*) and (*e*) to (*l*) of Article 143(1);".

Article 141

Each Member State shall take specific measures to ensure that VAT is not charged on the intra-Community acquisition of goods within its territory, made in accordance with Article 40, where the following conditions are met:

(*a*) the acquisition of goods is made by a taxable person who is not established in the Member State concerned but is identified for VAT purposes in another Member State;

(*b*) the acquisition of goods is made for the purposes of the subsequent supply of those goods, in the Member State concerned, by the taxable person referred to in point (*a*);

(*c*) the goods thus acquired by the taxable person referred to in point (*a*) are directly dispatched or transported, from a Member State other than that in which he is identified for VAT purposes, to the person for whom he is to carry out the subsequent supply;

(*d*) the person to whom the subsequent supply is to be made is another taxable person, or a non-taxable legal person, who is identified for VAT purposes in the Member State concerned;

(*e*) the person referred to in point (*d*) has been designated in accordance with Article 197 as liable for payment of the VAT due on the supply carried out by the taxable person who is not established in the Member State in which the tax is due.

Section 3 Exemptions for certain transport services

Article 142

Member States shall exempt the supply of intra-Community transport of goods to and from the islands making up the autonomous regions of the Azores and Madeira, as well as the supply of transport of goods between those islands.

CHAPTER 5
EXEMPTIONS ON IMPORTATION

Article 143

Member States shall exempt the following transactions:

(*a*) the final importation of goods of which the supply by a taxable person would in all circumstances be exempt within their respective territory;

(*b*) the final importation of goods governed by Council Directives 69/169/EEC ([1]), 83/181/EEC ([2]) and 2006/79/ EC ([3]);

(*c*) the final importation of goods, in free circulation from a third territory forming part of the Community customs territory, which would be entitled to exemption under point (*b*) if they had been imported within the meaning of the first paragraph of Article 30;

(*d*) the importation of goods dispatched or transported from a third territory or a third country into a Member State other than that in which the dispatch or transport of the goods ends, where the supply of such goods by the importer designated or recognised under Article 201 as liable for payment of VAT is exempt under Article 138;

(*e*) the reimportation, by the person who exported them, of goods in the state in which they were exported, where those goods are exempt from customs duties;

(*f*) the importation, under diplomatic and consular arrangements, of goods which are exempt from customs duties;

(*g*) the importation of goods by international bodies recognised as such by the public authorities of the host Member State, or by members of such bodies, within the limits and under the conditions laid down by the international conventions establishing the bodies or by headquarters agreements;

(*h*) the importation of goods, into Member States party to the North Atlantic Treaty, by the armed forces of other States party to that Treaty for the use of those forces or the civilian staff accompanying them or for supplying their messes or canteens where such forces take part in the common defence effort;

(*i*) the importation of goods by the armed forces of the United Kingdom stationed in the island of Cyprus pursuant to the Treaty of Establishment concerning the Republic of Cyprus, dated 16 August 1960, which are for the use of those forces or the civilian staff accompanying them or for supplying their messes or canteens;

(*j*) the importation into ports, by sea fishing undertakings, of their catches, unprocessed or after undergoing preservation for marketing but before being supplied;

(*k*) the importation of gold by central banks;

(*l*) the importation of gas through the natural gas distribution system, or of electricity.

Simon's Tax Cases—*Ministère Public and Ministre des Finances du Royaume de Belgique v Ledoux* [1991] STC 553*.

Notes—[1] Council Directive 69/169/EEC of 28 May 1969 on the harmonisation of provisions laid down by Law, Regulation or Administrative Action relating to exemption from turnover tax and excise duty on imports in international travel (OJ L 133, 4.6.1969, p. 6). Directive as last amended by Directive 2005/93/EC (OJ L 346, 29.12.2005, p. 16).

[2] Council Directive 83/181/EEC of 28 March 1983 determining the scope of Article 14(1)(*d*) of Directive 77/388/EEC as regards exemption from value added tax on the final importation of certain goods (OJ L 105, 23.4.1983, p. 38). Directive as last amended by the 1994 Act of Accession.

[3] Council Directive 2006/79/EC of 5 October 2006 on the exemption from taxes of imports of small consignments of goods of a non-commercial character from third countries (codified version) (OJ L 286, 17.10.2006, p. 15).

Prospective amendments—Introductory words to be substituted, and para 2 to be inserted, by Council Directive 2009/69/EC art 1 with effect from 24 July 2009. The deadline for implementation of this Directive is 1 January 2011 (OJ L 175, 4.7.2009 p 12). Text to read as follows—

"1. Member States shall exempt the following transactions:".

"2. The exemption provided for in paragraph 1(*d*) shall apply in cases when the importation of goods is followed by the supply of goods exempted under Article 138(1) and (2)(c) only if at the time of importation the importer has provided to the competent authorities of the Member State of importation at least the following information:

(*a*) his VAT identification number issued in the Member State of importation or the VAT identification number of his tax representative, liable for payment of the VAT, issued in the Member State of importation;

(*b*) the VAT identification number of the customer, to whom the goods are supplied in accordance with Article 138(1), issued in another Member State, or his own VAT identification number issued in the Member State in which the dispatch or transport of the goods ends when the goods are subject to a transfer in accordance with Article 138(2)(c);

(*c*) the evidence that the imported goods are intended to be transported or dispatched from the Member State of importation to another Member State.

However, Member States may provide that the evidence referred to in point (*c*) be indicated to the competent authorities only upon request.".

Article 144

Member States shall exempt the supply of services relating to the importation of goods where the value of such services is included in the taxable amount in accordance with Article 86(1)(*b*).

Article 145

1. The Commission shall, where appropriate, as soon as possible, present to the Council proposals designed to delimit the scope of the exemptions provided for in Articles 143 and 144 and to lay down the detailed rules for their implementation.

2. Pending the entry into force of the rules referred to in paragraph 1, Member States may maintain their national provisions in force.

Member States may adapt their national provisions so as to minimise distortion of competition and, in particular, to prevent non-taxation or double taxation within the Community.

Member States may use whatever administrative procedures they consider most appropriate to achieve exemption.

3. Member States shall notify to the Commission, which shall inform the other Member States accordingly, the provisions of national law which are in force, in so far as these have not already been notified, and those which they adopt pursuant to paragraph 2.

CHAPTER 6

EXEMPTIONS ON EXPORTATION

Article 146

1. Member States shall exempt the following transactions:

(*a*) the supply of goods dispatched or transported to a destination outside the Community by or on behalf of the vendor;

(*b*) the supply of goods dispatched or transported to a destination outside the Community by or on behalf of a customer not established within their respective territory, with the exception of goods transported by the customer himself for the equipping, fuelling and provisioning of pleasure boats and private aircraft or any other means of transport for private use;

(*c*) the supply of goods to approved bodies which export them out of the Community as part of their humanitarian, charitable or teaching activities outside the Community;

(*d*) the supply of services consisting in work on movable property acquired or imported for the purpose of undergoing such work within the Community, and dispatched or transported out of the Community by the supplier, by the customer if not established within their respective territory or on behalf of either of them;

(*e*) the supply of services, including transport and ancillary transactions, but excluding the supply of services exempted in accordance with Articles 132 and 135, where these are directly connected with the exportation or importation of goods covered by Article 61 and Article 157(1)(*a*).

2. The exemption provided for in point (*c*) of paragraph 1 may be granted by means of a refund of the VAT.

Simon's Tax Cases—Art 146(1)(*e*), *R&C Comrs v EB Central Services Ltd and another* [2008] STC 2209*; *Navicon SA v Administración del Estrado* [2008] STC 2693*; *Netto Supermarket GmbH & Co OHG v Finanzamt Machin* [2008] STC 3280*.

Article 147

1. Where the supply of goods referred to in point (*b*) of Article 146(1) relates to goods to be carried in the personal luggage of travellers, the exemption shall apply only if the following conditions are met:

(*a*) the traveller is not established within the Community;

(*b*) the goods are transported out of the Community before the end of the third month following that in which the supply takes place;

(*c*) the total value of the supply, including VAT, is more than EUR 175 or the equivalent in national currency, fixed annually by applying the conversion rate obtaining on the first working day of October with effect from 1 January of the following year.

However, Member States may exempt a supply with a total value of less than the amount specified in point (*c*) of the first subparagraph.

2. For the purposes of paragraph 1, 'a traveller who is not established within the Community' shall mean a traveller whose permanent address or habitual residence is not located within the Community. In that case 'permanent address or habitual residence' means the place entered as such in a passport, identity card or other document recognised as an identity document by the Member State within whose territory the supply takes place.

Proof of exportation shall be furnished by means of the invoice or other document in lieu thereof, endorsed by the customs office of exit from the Community.

Each Member State shall send to the Commission specimens of the stamps it uses for the endorsement referred to in the second subparagraph. The Commission shall forward that information to the tax authorities of the other Member States.

Simon's Tax Cases—*Netto Supermarket GmbH & Co OHG v Finanzamt Machin* [2008] STC 3280*.

CHAPTER 7

EXEMPTIONS RELATED TO INTERNATIONAL TRANSPORT

Article 148

Member States shall exempt the following transactions:

(*a*) the supply of goods for the fuelling and provisioning of vessels used for navigation on the high seas and carrying passengers for reward or used for the purpose of commercial, industrial or fishing activities, or for rescue or assistance at sea, or for inshore fishing, with the exception, in the case of vessels used for inshore fishing, of ships' provisions;

(*b*) the supply of goods for the fuelling and provisioning of fighting ships, falling within the combined nomenclature (CN) code 8906 10 00, leaving their territory and bound for ports or anchorages outside the Member State concerned;

(*c*) the supply, modification, repair, maintenance, chartering and hiring of the vessels referred to in point (*a*), and the supply, hiring, repair and maintenance of equipment, including fishing equipment, incorporated or used therein;

(*d*) the supply of services other than those referred to in point (*c*), to meet the direct needs of the vessels referred to in point (*a*) or of their cargoes;

(*e*) the supply of goods for the fuelling and provisioning of aircraft used by airlines operating for reward chiefly on international routes;

(*f*) the supply, modification, repair, maintenance, chartering and hiring of the aircraft referred to in point (*e*), and the supply, hiring, repair and maintenance of equipment incorporated or used therein;

(*g*) the supply of services, other than those referred to in point (*f*), to meet the direct needs of the aircraft referred to in point (*e*) or of their cargoes.

Simon's Tax Cases—Art 148(*c*), *R&C Comrs v Stone, The Kei* [2008] STC 2501*; *Navicon SA v Administración del Estrado* [2008] STC 2693*.
Art 148(*g*), *R&C Comrs v EB Central Services Ltd and another* [2008] STC 2209*.

Article 149

Portugal may treat sea and air transport between the islands making up the autonomous regions of the Azores and Madeira and between those regions and the mainland as international transport.

Article 150

1. The Commission shall, where appropriate, as soon as possible, present to the Council proposals designed to delimit the scope of the exemptions provided for in Article 148 and to lay down the detailed rules for their implementation.

2. Pending the entry into force of the provisions referred to in paragraph 1, Member States may limit the scope of the exemptions provided for in points (*a*) and (*b*) of Article 148.

CHAPTER 8

EXEMPTIONS RELATING TO CERTAIN TRANSACTIONS TREATED AS EXPORTS

Article 151

1. Member States shall exempt the following transactions:

(*a*) the supply of goods or services under diplomatic and consular arrangements;

(*b*) the supply of goods or services to international bodies recognised as such by the public authorities of the host Member State, and to members of such bodies, within the limits and under the conditions laid down by the international conventions establishing the bodies or by headquarters agreements;

(*c*) the supply of goods or services within a Member State which is a party to the North Atlantic Treaty, intended either for the armed forces of other States party to that Treaty for the use of those forces, or of the civilian staff accompanying them, or for supplying their messes or canteens when such forces take part in the common defence effort;

(*d*) the supply of goods or services to another Member State, intended for the armed forces of any State which is a party to the North Atlantic Treaty, other than the Member State of destination itself, for the use of those forces, or of the civilian staff accompanying them, or for supplying their messes or canteens when such forces take part in the common defence effort;

(*e*) the supply of goods or services to the armed forces of the United Kingdom stationed in the island of Cyprus pursuant to the Treaty of Establishment concerning the Republic of Cyprus, dated 16 August 1960, which are for the use of those forces, or of the civilian staff accompanying them, or for supplying their messes or canteens.

Pending the adoption of common tax rules, the exemptions provided for in the first subparagraph shall be subject to the limitations laid down by the host Member State.

2. In cases where the goods are not dispatched or transported out of the Member State in which the supply takes place, and in the case of services, the exemption may be granted by means of a refund of the VAT.

Article 152

Member States shall exempt the supply of gold to central banks.

CHAPTER 9

EXEMPTIONS FOR THE SUPPLY OF SERVICES BY INTERMEDIARIES

Article 153

Member States shall exempt the supply of services by intermediaries, acting in the name and on behalf of another person, where they take part in the transactions referred to in Chapters 6, 7 and 8, or of transactions carried out outside the Community.

The exemption referred to in the first paragraph shall not apply to travel agents who, in the name and on behalf of travellers, supply services which are carried out in other Member States.

CHAPTER 10

EXEMPTIONS FOR TRANSACTIONS RELATING TO INTERNATIONAL TRADE

Section 1 Customs warehouses, warehouses other than customs warehouses and similar arrangements

Article 154

For the purposes of this Section, 'warehouses other than customs warehouses' shall, in the case of products subject to excise duty, mean the places defined as tax warehouses by Article 4(*b*) of Directive 92/12/EEC and, in the case of products not subject to excise duty, the places defined as such by the Member States.

Article 155

Without prejudice to other Community tax provisions, Member States may, after consulting the VAT Committee, take special measures designed to exempt all or some of the transactions referred to in this Section, provided that those measures are not aimed at final use or consumption and that the amount of VAT due on cessation of the arrangements or situations referred to in this Section corresponds to the amount of tax which would have been due had each of those transactions been taxed within their territory.

Article 156

1. Member States may exempt the following transactions:

(*a*) the supply of goods which are intended to be presented to customs and, where applicable, placed in temporary storage;

(*b*) the supply of goods which are intended to be placed in a free zone or in a free warehouse;

(*c*) the supply of goods which are intended to be placed under customs warehousing arrangements or inward processing arrangements;

(*d*) the supply of goods which are intended to be admitted into territorial waters in order to be incorporated into drilling or production platforms, for purposes of the construction, repair, maintenance, alteration or fitting-out of such platforms, or to link such drilling or production platforms to the mainland;

(*e*) the supply of goods which are intended to be admitted into territorial waters for the fuelling and provisioning of drilling or production platforms.

2. The places referred to in paragraph 1 shall be those defined as such by the Community customs provisions in force.

Article 157

1. Member States may exempt the following transactions:

(*a*) the importation of goods which are intended to be placed under warehousing arrangements other than customs warehousing;

(*b*) the supply of goods which are intended to be placed, within their territory, under warehousing arrangements other than customs warehousing.

2. Member States may not provide for warehousing arrangements other than customs warehousing for goods which are not subject to excise duty where those goods are intended to be supplied at the retail stage.

Article 158

1. By way of derogation from Article 157(2), Member States may provide for warehousing arrangements other than customs warehousing in the following cases:

(*a*) where the goods are intended for tax-free shops, for the purposes of the supply of goods to be carried in the personal luggage of travellers taking flights or sea crossings to third territories or third countries, where that supply is exempt pursuant to point (*b*) of Article 146(1);

(*b*) where the goods are intended for taxable persons, for the purposes of carrying out supplies to travellers on board an aircraft or a ship in the course of a flight or sea crossing where the place of arrival is situated outside the Community;

(*c*) where the goods are intended for taxable persons, for the purposes of carrying out supplies which are exempt from VAT pursuant to Article 151.

2. Where Member States exercise the option of exemption provided for in point (*a*) of paragraph 1, they shall take the measures necessary to ensure the correct and straightforward application of this exemption and to prevent any evasion, avoidance or abuse.

3. For the purposes of point (*a*) of paragraph 1, 'tax-free shop' shall mean any establishment which is situated within an airport or port and which fulfils the conditions laid down by the competent public authorities.

Article 159

Member States may exempt the supply of services relating to the supply of goods referred to in Article 156, Article 157(1)(*b*) or Article 158.

Article 160

1. Member States may exempt the following transactions:

(*a*) the supply of goods or services carried out in the locations referred to in Article 156(1), where one of the situations specified therein still applies within their territory;

(*b*) the supply of goods or services carried out in the locations referred to in Article 157(1)(*b*) or Article 158, where one of the situations specified in Article 157(1)(*b*) or in Article 158 (1) still applies within their territory.

2. Where Member States exercise the option under point (*a*) of paragraph 1 in respect of transactions effected in customs warehouses, they shall take the measures necessary to provide for warehousing arrangements other than customs warehousing under which point (*b*) of paragraph 1 may be applied to the same transactions when they concern goods listed in Annex V and are carried out in warehouses other than customs warehouses.

Article 161

Member States may exempt supply of the following goods and of services relating thereto:

(*a*) the supply of goods referred to in the first paragraph of Article 30 while they remain covered by arrangements for temporary importation with total exemption from import duty or by external transit arrangements;

(*b*) the supply of goods referred to in the second paragraph of Article 30 while they remain covered by the internal Community transit procedure referred to in Article 276.

Article 162

Where Member States exercise the option provided for in this Section, they shall take the measures necessary to ensure that the intra-Community acquisition of goods intended to be placed under one of the arrangements or in one of the situations referred to in Article 156, Article 157(1)(*b*) or Article 158 is covered by the same provisions as the supply of goods carried out within their territory under the same conditions.

Article 163

If the goods cease to be covered by the arrangements or situations referred to in this Section, thus giving rise to importation for the purposes of Article 61, the Member State of importation shall take the measures necessary to prevent double taxation.

Section 2 Transactions exempted with a view to export and in the framework of trade between the Member States

Article 164

1. Member States may, after consulting the VAT Committee, exempt the following transactions carried out by, or intended for, a taxable person up to an amount equal to the value of the exports carried out by that person during the preceding 12 months:

(*a*) intra-Community acquisitions of goods made by the taxable person, and imports for and supplies of goods to the taxable person, with a view to their exportation from the Community as they are or after processing;

(*b*) supplies of services linked with the export business of the taxable person.

2. Where Member States exercise the option of exemption under paragraph 1, they shall, after consulting the VAT Committee, apply that exemption also to transactions relating to supplies carried out by the taxable person, in accordance with the conditions specified in Article 138, up to an amount equal to the value of the supplies carried out by that person, in accordance with the same conditions, during the preceding 12 months.

Article 165

Member States may set a common maximum amount for transactions which they exempt pursuant to Article 164.

Section 3 Provisions common to Sections 1 and 2

Article 166

The Commission shall, where appropriate, as soon as possible, present to the Council proposals concerning common arrangements for applying VAT to the transactions referred to in Sections 1 and 2.

VAT

TITLE X
DEDUCTIONS

CHAPTER 1

ORIGIN AND SCOPE OF RIGHT OF DEDUCTION

Article 167

A right of deduction shall arise at the time the deductible tax becomes chargeable.

Simon's Tax Cases—*Proceedings brought by Uudenkaupungin kaupunki* [2008] STC 2329*.

Article 168

In so far as the goods and services are used for the purposes of the taxed transactions of a taxable person, the taxable person shall be entitled, in the Member State in which he carries out these transactions, to deduct the following from the VAT which he is liable to pay:

(*a*) the VAT due or paid in that Member State in respect of supplies to him of goods or services, carried out or to be carried out by another taxable person;

(*b*) the VAT due in respect of transactions treated as supplies of goods or services pursuant to Article 18(*a*) and Article 27;

(*c*) the VAT due in respect of intra-Community acquisitions of goods pursuant to Article 2(1)(*b*)(i);

(*d*) the VAT due on transactions treated as intra-Community acquisitions in accordance with Articles 21 and 22;

(*e*) the VAT due or paid in respect of the importation of goods into that Member State.

Article 169

In addition to the deduction referred to in Article 168, the taxable person shall be entitled to deduct the VAT referred to therein in so far as the goods and services are used for the purposes of the following:

(*a*) transactions relating to the activities referred to in the second subparagraph of Article 9(1), carried out outside the Member State in which that tax is due or paid, in respect of which VAT would be deductible if they had been carried out within that Member State;

(*b*) transactions which are exempt pursuant to Articles 138, 142 or 144, Articles 146 to 149, Articles 151, 152, 153 or 156, Article 157(1)(*b*), Articles 158 to 161 or Article 164;

(*c*) transactions which are exempt pursuant to points (*a*) to (*f*) of Article 135(1), where the customer is established outside the Community or where those transactions relate directly to goods to be exported out of the Community.

Article 170

[All taxable persons who, within the meaning of Article 1 of Directive 86/560/EEC [*****], Article 2(1) and Article 3 of Directive 2008/9/EC [******] and Article 171 of this Directive, are not established in the Member State in which they purchase goods and services or import goods subject to VAT shall be entitled to obtain a refund of that VAT insofar as the goods and services are used for the purposes of the following:][1]

(*a*) transactions referred to in Article 169;

(*b*) transactions for which the tax is solely payable by the customer in accordance with Articles 194 to 197 or Article 199.

Amendments—[1] Introductory sentence substituted by Council Directive 2008/8/EC art 2(3) with effect from 1 January 2010 (OJ L 44, 20.2.2008 p 11). Text previously read as follows—

"All taxable persons who, within the meaning of Article 1 of Directive 79/1072/EEC , Article 1 of Directive 86/560/EEC and Article 171 of this Directive, are not established in the Member State in which they purchase goods and services or import goods subject to VAT shall be entitled to obtain a refund of that VAT in so far as the goods and services are used for the purposes of the following:".

Article 171

[1. VAT shall be refunded to taxable persons who are not established in the Member State in which they purchase goods and services or import goods subject to VAT but who are established in another Member State, in accordance with the detailed rules laid down in Directive 2008/9/EC.[1]

The taxable persons referred to in Article 1 of Directive 79/1072/ EEC shall also, for the purposes of applying that Directive, be regarded as taxable persons who are not established in the Member State concerned where, in the Member State in which they purchase goods and services or import goods subject to VAT, they have only carried out the supply of goods or services to a person designated in accordance with Articles 194 to 197 or Article 199 as liable for payment of VAT.

2. VAT shall be refunded to taxable persons who are not established within the territory of the Community in accordance with the detailed implementing rules laid down in Directive 86/560/EEC.

The taxable persons referred to in Article 1 of Directive 86/560/ EEC shall also, for the purposes of applying that Directive, be regarded as taxable persons who are not established in the Community where, in the Member State in which they purchase goods and services or import goods subject to VAT, they have only carried out the supply of goods or services to a person designated in accordance with Articles 194 to 197 or Article 199 as liable for payment of VAT.

[3. Directive 86/560/EEC shall not apply to:

(*a*) amounts of VAT which according to the legislation of the Member State of refund have been incorrectly invoiced;

(*b*) invoiced amounts of VAT in respect of supplies of goods the supply of which is, or may be, exempt pursuant to Article 138 or Article 146(1)(*b*).][1]

Amendments—[1] Paras 1, 3 substituted by Council Directive 2008/8/EC art 2(4) with effect from 1 January 2010 (OJ L 44, 20.2.2008 p 11). Text previously read as follows—

"1. VAT shall be refunded to taxable persons who are not established in the Member State in which they purchase goods and services or import goods subject to VAT but who are established in another Member State, in accordance with the detailed implementing rules laid down in Directive 79/1072/EEC."

"3. Directives 79/1072/EEC[(1)] and 86/560/EEC[(2)] shall not apply to the supply of goods which is, or may be, exempted pursuant to Article 138 where the goods thus supplied are dispatched or transported by or on behalf of the person acquiring the goods."

Notes to former para 3 previously read as follows—

"(1) Eighth Council Directive 79/1072/EEC of 6 December 1979 on the harmonization of the laws of the Member States relating to turnover taxes — Arrangements for the refund of value added tax to taxable persons not established in the territory of the country (OJ L 331, 27.12.1979, p. 11). Directive as last amended by the 2003 Act of Accession.
(2) Thirteenth Council Directive 86/560/EEC of 17 November 1986 on the harmonization of the laws of the Member States relating to turnover taxes – Arrangements for the refund of value added tax to taxable persons not established in Community territory (OJ L 326, 21.11.1986, p. 40).

[Article 171a

Member States may, instead of granting a refund of VAT pursuant to Directives 86/560/EEC or 2008/9/EC on those supplies of goods or services to a taxable person in respect of which the taxable person is liable to pay the tax in accordance with Articles 194 to 197 or Article 199, allow deduction of this tax pursuant to the procedure laid down in Article 168. The existing restrictions pursuant to Article 2(2) and Article 4(2) of Directive 86/560/EEC may be retained.

To that end, Member States may exclude the taxable person who is liable to pay the tax from the refund procedure pursuant to Directives 86/560/EEC or 2008/9/EC.][1]

Amendments—[1] Article 171A inserted by Council Directive 2008/8/EC art 2(4) with effect from 1 January 2010 (OJ L 44, 20.2.2008 p 11).

Article 172

1. Any person who is regarded as a taxable person by reason of the fact that he supplies, on an occasional basis, a new means of transport in accordance with the conditions specified in Article 138(1) and (2)(*a*) shall, in the Member State in which the supply takes place, be entitled to deduct the VAT included in the purchase price or paid in respect of the importation or the intra-Community acquisition of this means of transport, up to an amount not exceeding the amount of VAT for which he would be liable if the supply were not exempt.

A right of deduction shall arise and may be exercised only at the time of supply of the new means of transport.

2. Member States shall lay down detailed rules for the implementation of paragraph 1.

CHAPTER 2

PROPORTIONAL DEDUCTION

Article 173

1. In the case of goods or services used by a taxable person both for transactions in respect of which VAT is deductible pursuant to Articles 168, 169 and 170, and for transactions in respect of which VAT is not deductible, only such proportion of the VAT as is attributable to the former transactions shall be deductible.

The deductible proportion shall be determined, in accordance with Articles 174 and 175, for all the transactions carried out by the taxable person.

2. Member States may take the following measures:

(*a*) authorise the taxable person to determine a proportion for each sector of his business, provided that separate accounts are kept for each sector;

(*b*) require the taxable person to determine a proportion for each sector of his business and to keep separate accounts for each sector;

(*c*) authorise or require the taxable person to make the deduction on the basis of the use made of all or part of the goods and services;

(*d*) authorise or require the taxable person to make the deduction in accordance with the rule laid down in the first subparagraph of paragraph 1, in respect of all goods and services used for all transactions referred to therein;

(*e*) provide that, where the VAT which is not deductible by the taxable person is insignificant, it is to be treated as nil.

Commentary—*De Voil Indirect Tax Service* **V2.101**, **V.3.401**, **V3.460**.
Simon's Tax Cases—*Cibo Participations SA v Directeur regional des impots du Nord-Pas-de-Calais* [2002] STC 460*; *Dial-a-Phone Ltd v C&E Comrs*, [2003] STC 192*; *EC Commission v Kingdom of Spain* [2006] STC 1087*; *EC Commission v French Republic (Kingdom of Spain, intervening)* [2006] STC 1098*; *Proceedings brought by Uudenkaupungin kaupunki* [2008] STC 2329*; *Royal Bank of Scotland Group plc v R&C Comrs* [2009] STC 461*.

Article 174

1. The deductible proportion shall be made up of a fraction comprising the following amounts:

(*a*) as numerator, the total amount, exclusive of VAT, of turnover per year attributable to transactions in respect of which VAT is deductible pursuant to Articles 168 and 169;

(*b*) as denominator, the total amount, exclusive of VAT, of turnover per year attributable to transactions included in the numerator and to transactions in respect of which VAT is not deductible.

Member States may include in the denominator the amount of subsidies, other than those directly linked to the price of supplies of goods or services referred to in Article 73.

2. By way of derogation from paragraph 1, the following amounts shall be excluded from the calculation of the deductible proportion:

(*a*) the amount of turnover attributable to supplies of capital goods used by the taxable person for the purposes of his business;

(*b*) the amount of turnover attributable to incidental real estate and financial transactions;

(*c*) the amount of turnover attributable to the transactions specified in points (*b*) to (*g*) of Article 135(1) in so far as those transactions are incidental.

3. Where Member States exercise the option under Article 191 not to require adjustment in respect of capital goods, they may include disposals of capital goods in the calculation of the deductible proportion.

Commentary—*De Voil Indirect Tax Service* **V3.460**.
Simon's Tax Cases—*Dwyer Property Ltd v C&E Comrs* [1995] STC 1035*; *C&E Comrs v Liverpool Institute for Performing Arts* [2001] STC 891*; *António Jorge Lda v Fazenda Pública* [2008] STC 2533*.
Art 174(1), *Sofitam SA (formerly Satam SA) v Ministre chargé du Budget* (Case C-333/91), ECJ [1997] STC 226*; *Floridienne SA and anor v Belgian State* [2000] STC 1044*; *EC Commission v Kingdom of Spain* [2006] STC 1087*; *EC Commission v French Republic (Kingdom of Spain, intervening)* [2006] STC 1098*; *Royal Bank of Scotland Group plc v R&C Comrs* [2009] STC 461*.
Art 174(2), *Régie Dauphinoise—Cabinet A Forest SARL v Ministre du Budget* (Case C-306/94) [1996] STC 1176*; *C&E Comrs v JDL Ltd* [2001] STC 1*; *Empresa de Desenvolvimento Mineiro SGPS SA (EDM) v Fazenda Pública (Ministério Público, intervening)* [2005] STC 65*; *Nordania Finans A/S and another v Skatteministeriet* [2008] STC 3314*.

Article 175

1. The deductible proportion shall be determined on an annual basis, fixed as a percentage and rounded up to a figure not exceeding the next whole number.

2. The provisional proportion for a year shall be that calculated on the basis of the preceding year's transactions. In the absence of any such transactions to refer to, or where they were insignificant in amount, the deductible proportion shall be estimated provisionally, under the supervision of the tax authorities, by the taxable person on the basis of his own forecasts.

However, Member States may retain the rules in force at 1 January 1979 or, in the case of the Member States which acceded to the Community after that date, on the date of their accession.

3. Deductions made on the basis of such provisional proportions shall be adjusted when the final proportion is fixed during the following year.

Commentary—*De Voil Indirect Tax Service* **V3.460**.
Simon's Tax Cases—*Dwyer Property Ltd v C&E Comrs* [1995] STC 1035*; *C&E Comrs v Liverpool Institute for Performing Arts* [2001] STC 891*; *António Jorge Lda v Fazenda Pública* [2008] STC 2533*.

CHAPTER 3

RESTRICTIONS ON THE RIGHT OF DEDUCTION

Article 176

The Council, acting unanimously on a proposal from the Commission, shall determine the expenditure in respect of which VAT shall not be deductible. VAT shall in no circumstances be deductible in respect of expenditure which is not strictly business expenditure, such as that on luxuries, amusements or entertainment.

Pending the entry into force of the provisions referred to in the first paragraph, Member States may retain all the exclusions provided for under their national laws at 1 January 1979 or, in the case of the Member States which acceded to the Community after that date, on the date of their accession.

Commentary—*De Voil Indirect Tax Service* **V2.101**, **V.3.401**, **V3.460**.
Simon's Tax Cases—*Group Ltd v C&E Comrs* [1996] STC 898*; *Royscot Leasing Ltd v C&E Comrs* [1999] STC 998*; *EC Commission v French Republic (United Kingdom intervening)* [2003] STC 372, 390*; *Charles and another v Staatssecretaris van Financiën* [2006] STC 1429*; *Proceedings brought by Uudenkaupungin kaupunki* [2008] STC 2329*; *Danfoss A/S and anor v Skatteministeriet* [2009] STC 701*.

Article 177

After consulting the VAT Committee, each Member State may, for cyclical economic reasons, totally or partly exclude all or some capital goods or other goods from the system of deductions.

In order to maintain identical conditions of competition, Member States may, instead of refusing deduction, tax goods manufactured by the taxable person himself or goods which he has purchased within the Community, or imported, in such a way that the tax does not exceed the amount of VAT which would be charged on the acquisition of similar goods.

CHAPTER 4
RULES GOVERNING EXERCISE OF THE RIGHT OF DEDUCTION

Article 178

In order to exercise the right of deduction, a taxable person must meet the following conditions:

(*a*) for the purposes of deductions pursuant to Article 168(*a*), in respect of the supply of goods or services, he must hold an invoice drawn up in accordance with Articles 220 to 236 and Articles 238, 239 and 240;

(*b*) for the purposes of deductions pursuant to Article 168(*b*), in respect of transactions treated as the supply of goods or services, he must comply with the formalities as laid down by each Member State;

(*c*) for the purposes of deductions pursuant to Article 168(*c*), in respect of the intra-Community acquisition of goods, he must set out in the VAT return provided for in Article 250 all the information needed for the amount of the VAT due on his intra-Community acquisitions of goods to be calculated and he must hold an invoice drawn up in accordance with Articles 220 to 236;

(*d*) for the purposes of deductions pursuant to Article 168(*d*), in respect of transactions treated as intra-Community acquisitions of goods, he must complete the formalities as laid down by each Member State;

(*e*) for the purposes of deductions pursuant to Article 168(*e*), in respect of the importation of goods, he must hold an import document specifying him as consignee or importer, and stating the amount of VAT due or enabling that amount to be calculated;

(*f*) when required to pay VAT as a customer where Articles 194 to 197 or Article 199 apply, he must comply with the formalities as laid down by each Member State.

Article 179

The taxable person shall make the deduction by subtracting from the total amount of VAT due for a given tax period the total amount of VAT in respect of which, during the same period, the right of deduction has arisen and is exercised in accordance with Article 178.

However, Member States may require that taxable persons who carry out occasional transactions, as defined in Article 12, exercise their right of deduction only at the time of supply.

Article 180

Member States may authorise a taxable person to make a deduction which he has not made in accordance with Articles 178 and 179.

Article 181

Member States may authorise a taxable person who does not hold an invoice drawn up in accordance with Articles 220 to 236 to make the deduction referred to in Article 168(*c*) in respect of his intra-Community acquisitions of goods.

Article 182

Member States shall determine the conditions and detailed rules for applying Articles 180 and 181.

Article 183

Where, for a given tax period, the amount of deductions exceeds the amount of VAT due, the Member States may, in accordance with conditions which they shall determine, either make a refund or carry the excess forward to the following period.

However, Member States may refuse to refund or carry forward if the amount of the excess is insignificant.

Commentary—*De Voil Indirect Tax Service* **V3.401**.
Simon's Tax Cases—*Garage Molenheide BVBA, Schepens, Bureau Rik Decan-Business Research & Development NV (BRD) and Sanders BVBA v Belgium* (Joined cases C-286/94, C-340/95, C-401/95 and C-47/96) [1998] STC 126*.

CHAPTER 5

ADJUSTMENT OF DEDUCTIONS

Article 184

The initial deduction shall be adjusted where it is higher or lower than that to which the taxable person was entitled.

Article 185

1. Adjustment shall, in particular, be made where, after the VAT return is made, some change occurs in the factors used to determine the amount to be deducted, for example where purchases are cancelled or price reductions are obtained.

2. By way of derogation from paragraph 1, no adjustment shall be made in the case of transactions remaining totally or partially unpaid or in the case of destruction, loss or theft of property duly proved or confirmed, or in the case of goods reserved for the purpose of making gifts of small value or of giving samples, as referred to in Article 16.

However, in the case of transactions remaining totally or partially unpaid or in the case of theft, Member States may require adjustment to be made.

Commentary—*De Voil Indirect Tax Service* **V3.470**.
Simon's Tax Cases—*Tremerton Ltd v C&E Comrs* [1999] STC 1039*; *Finanzamt Burgdorf v Fischer, Finanzamt Düsseldorf-Mettman v Brandenstein* [2001] STC 1356*.

Article 186

Member States shall lay down the detailed rules for applying Articles 184 and 185.

Article 187

1. In the case of capital goods, adjustment shall be spread over five years including that in which the goods were acquired or manufactured.

Member States may, however, base the adjustment on a period of five full years starting from the time at which the goods are first used.

In the case of immovable property acquired as capital goods, the adjustment period may be extended up to 20 years.

2. The annual adjustment shall be made only in respect of one-fifth of the VAT charged on the capital goods, or, if the adjustment period has been extended, in respect of the corresponding fraction thereof.

The adjustment referred to in the first subparagraph shall be made on the basis of the variations in the deduction entitlement in subsequent years in relation to that for the year in which the goods were acquired, manufactured or, where applicable, used for the first time.

Commentary—*De Voil Indirect Tax Service* **V3.470**.
Simon's Tax Cases—*Finanzamt Uelzen v Armbrecht* (Case C-291/92) [1995] STC 997*; *Gemeente Leusden and another v Staatssecretaris van Financiën* [2007] STC 776*.

Article 188

1. If supplied during the adjustment period, capital goods shall be treated as if they had been applied to an economic activity of the taxable person up until expiry of the adjustment period.

The economic activity shall be presumed to be fully taxed in cases where the supply of the capital goods is taxed.

The economic activity shall be presumed to be fully exempt in cases where the supply of the capital goods is exempt.

2. The adjustment provided for in paragraph 1 shall be made only once in respect of all the time covered by the adjustment period that remains to run. However, where the supply of capital goods is exempt, Member States may waive the requirement for adjustment in so far as the purchaser is a taxable person using the capital goods in question solely for transactions in respect of which VAT is deductible.

Commentary—*De Voil Indirect Tax Service* **V3.470**.
Simon's Tax Cases—*Centralan Property Ltd v C&E Comrs* [2006] STC 1542*.

Article 189

For the purposes of applying Articles 187 and 188, Member States may take the following measures:

(*a*) define the concept of capital goods;
(*b*) specify the amount of the VAT which is to be taken into consideration for adjustment;
(*c*) adopt any measures needed to ensure that adjustment does not give rise to any unjustified advantage;
(*d*) permit administrative simplifications.

Article 190

For the purposes of Articles 187, 188, 189 and 191, Member States may regard as capital goods those services which have characteristics similar to those normally attributed to capital goods.

Article 191

If, in any Member State, the practical effect of applying Articles 187 and 188 is negligible, that Member State may, after consulting the VAT Committee, refrain from applying those provisions, having regard to the overall impact of VAT in the Member State concerned and the need for administrative simplification, and provided that no distortion of competition thereby arises.

Article 192

Where a taxable person transfers from being taxed in the normal way to a special scheme or vice versa, Member States may take all measures necessary to ensure that the taxable person does not enjoy unjustified advantage or sustain unjustified harm.

[Article 192a

For the purposes of this Section, a taxable person who has a fixed establishment within the territory of the Member State where the tax is due shall be regarded as a taxable person who is not established within that Member State when the following conditions are met:

(*a*) he makes a taxable supply of goods or of services within the territory of that Member State;

(*b*) an establishment which the supplier has within the territory of that Member State does not intervene in that supply.][1]

Amendments—[1] Article 192a inserted by Council Directive 2008/8/EC art 2(5) with effect from 1 January 2010 (OJ L 44, 20.2.2008 p 11).

TITLE XI
OBLIGATIONS OF TAXABLE PERSONS AND CERTAIN NON-TAXABLE PERSONS

CHAPTER 1
OBLIGATION TO PAY

Section 1 Persons liable for payment of VAT to the tax authorities

Article 193

VAT shall be payable by any taxable person carrying out a taxable supply of goods or services, except where it is payable by another person in the cases referred to in Articles 194 to 199 and Article 202.

Article 194

1. Where the taxable supply of goods or services is carried out by a taxable person who is not established in the Member State in which the VAT is due, Member States may provide that the person liable for payment of VAT is the person to whom the goods or services are supplied.

2. Member States shall lay down the conditions for implementation of paragraph 1.

Article 195

VAT shall be payable by any person who is identified for VAT purposes in the Member State in which the tax is due and to whom goods are supplied in the circumstances specified in Articles 38 or 39, if the supplies are carried out by a taxable person not established within that Member State.

[Article 196

VAT shall be payable by any taxable person, or non-taxable legal person identified for VAT purposes, to whom the services referred to in Article 44 are supplied, if the services are supplied by a taxable person not established within the territory of the Member State.][1]

Amendments—[1] Article 196 substituted, by Council Directive 2008/8/EC art 2(7) with effect from 1 January 2010 (OJ L 44, 20.2.2008 p 11). Text previously read as follows—

> **"Article 196**
>
> VAT shall be payable by any taxable person to whom the services referred to in Article 56 are supplied or by any person identified for VAT purposes in the Member State in which the tax is due to whom the services referred to in Articles 44, 47, 50, 53, 54 and 55 are supplied, if the services are supplied by a taxable person not established in that Member State.".

Article 197

1. VAT shall be payable by the person to whom the goods are supplied when the following conditions are met:

(*a*) the taxable transaction is a supply of goods carried out in accordance with the conditions laid down in Article 141;

(*b*) the person to whom the goods are supplied is another taxable person, or a non-taxable legal person, identified for VAT purposes in the Member State in which the supply is carried out;

(*c*) the invoice issued by the taxable person not established in the Member State of the person to whom the goods are supplied is drawn up in accordance with Articles 220 to 236.

2. Where a tax representative is appointed as the person liable for payment of VAT pursuant to Article 204, Member States may provide for a derogation from paragraph 1 of this Article.

Article 198

1. Where specific transactions relating to investment gold between a taxable person who is a member of a regulated gold bullion market and another taxable person who is not a member of that market are taxed pursuant to Article 352, Member States shall designate the customer as the person liable for payment of VAT.

If the customer who is not a member of the regulated gold bullion market is a taxable person required to be identified for VAT purposes in the Member State in which the tax is due solely in respect of the transactions referred to in Article 352, the vendor shall fulfil the tax obligations on behalf of the customer, in accordance with the law of that Member State.

2. Where gold material or semi-manufactured products of a purity of 325 thousandths or greater, or investment gold as defined in Article 344(1) is supplied by a taxable person exercising one of the options under Articles 348, 349 and 350, Member States may designate the customer as the person liable for payment of VAT.

3. Member States shall lay down the procedures and conditions for implementation of paragraphs 1 and 2.

Article 199

1. Member States may provide that the person liable for payment of VAT is the taxable person to whom any of the following supplies are made:

(*a*) the supply of construction work, including repair, cleaning, maintenance, alteration and demolition services in relation to immovable property, as well as the handing over of construction works regarded as a supply of goods pursuant to Article 14(3);

(*b*) the supply of staff engaged in activities covered by point (*a*);

(*c*) the supply of immovable property, as referred to in Article 135(1)(*j*) and (*k*), where the supplier has opted for taxation of the supply pursuant to Article 137;

(*d*) the supply of used material, used material which cannot be re-used in the same state, scrap, industrial and non industrial waste, recyclable waste, part processed waste and certain goods and services, as listed in Annex VI;

(*e*) the supply of goods provided as security by one taxable person to another in execution of that security;

(*f*) the supply of goods following the cession of a reservation of ownership to an assignee and the exercising of this right by the assignee;

(*g*) the supply of immovable property sold by a judgment debtor in a compulsory sale procedure.

2. When applying the option provided for in paragraph 1, Member States may specify the supplies of goods and services covered, and the categories of suppliers or recipients to whom these measures may apply.

3. For the purposes of paragraph 1, Member States may take the following measures:

(*a*) provide that a taxable person who also carries out activities or transactions that are not considered to be taxable supplies of goods or services in accordance with Article 2 shall be regarded as a taxable person in respect of supplies received as referred to in paragraph 1 of this Article;

(*b*) provide that a non-taxable body governed by public law, shall be regarded as a taxable person in respect of supplies received as referred to in points (*e*), (*f*) and (*g*) of paragraph 1.

4. Member States shall inform the VAT Committee of national legislative measures adopted pursuant to paragraph 1 in so far as these are not measures authorised by the Council prior to 13 August 2006 in accordance with Article 27(1) to (4) of Directive 77/388/EEC, and which are continued under paragraph 1 of this Article.

Article 200

VAT shall be payable by any person making a taxable intra-Community acquisition of goods.

Article 201

On importation, VAT shall be payable by any person or persons designated or recognised as liable by the Member State of importation.

Article 202

VAT shall be payable by any person who causes goods to cease to be covered by the arrangements or situations listed in Articles 156, 157, 158, 160 and 161.

Article 203

VAT shall be payable by any person who enters the VAT on an invoice.

Article 204

1. Where, pursuant to Articles 193 to 197 and Articles 199 and 200, the person liable for payment of VAT is a taxable person who is not established in the Member State in which the VAT is due, Member States may allow that person to appoint a tax representative as the person liable for payment of the VAT.

Furthermore, where the taxable transaction is carried out by a taxable person who is not established in the Member State in which the VAT is due and no legal instrument exists, with the country in which that taxable person is established or has his seat, relating to mutual assistance similar in scope to that provided for in Directive 76/308/EEC ([1]) and Regulation (EC) No 1798/2003 ([1]), Member States may take measures to provide that the person liable for payment of VAT is to be a tax representative appointed by the non-established taxable person.

However, Member States may not apply the option referred to in the second subparagraph to a non-established taxable person, within the meaning of point (1) of Article 358, who has opted for the special scheme for electronically supplied services.

2. The option under the first subparagraph of paragraph 1 shall be subject to the conditions and procedures laid down by each Member State.

([1]) Council Directive 76/308/EEC of 15 March 1976 on mutual assistance for the recovery of claims relating to certain levies, duties, taxes and other measures (OJ L 73, 19.3.1976, p. 18.). Directive as last amended by the Act of Accession of 2003.

Prospective amendments—In para 1, third sub-para to be substituted by Council Directive 2008/8/EC art 5(4) with effect from 1 January 2015 (OJ L 44, 20.2.2008 p 11).

Article 205

In the situations referred to in Articles 193 to 200 and Articles 202, 203 and 204, Member States may provide that a person other than the person liable for payment of VAT is to be held jointly and severally liable for payment of VAT.

Section 2 Payment arrangements

Article 206

Any taxable person liable for payment of VAT must pay the net amount of the VAT when submitting the VAT return provided for in Article 250. Member States may, however, set a different date for payment of that amount or may require interim payments to be made.

Article 207

Member States shall take the measures necessary to ensure that persons who are regarded as liable for payment of VAT in the stead of a taxable person not established in their respective territory, in accordance with Articles 194 to 197 and Articles 199 and 204, comply with the payment obligations set out in this Section.

Member States shall also take the measures necessary to ensure that those persons who, in accordance with Article 205, are held to be jointly and severally liable for payment of the VAT comply with these payment obligations.

Article 208

Where Member States designate the customer for investment gold as the person liable for payment of VAT pursuant to Article 198(1) or if, in the case of gold material, semi-manufactured products, or investment gold as defined in Article 344(1), they exercise the option provided for in Article 198(2) of designating the customer as the person liable for payment of VAT, they shall take the measures necessary to ensure that he complies with the payment obligations set out in this Section.

Article 209

Member States shall take the measures necessary to ensure that non-taxable legal persons who are liable for payment of VAT due in respect of intra-Community acquisitions of goods, as referred to in Article 2(1)(*b*)(i), comply with the payment obligations set out in this Section.

Article 210

Member States shall adopt arrangements for payment of VAT on intra-Community acquisitions of new means of transport, as referred to in Article 2(1)(*b*)(ii), and on intra-Community acquisitions of products subject to excise duty, as referred to in Article 2(1)(*b*)(iii).

Article 211

Member States shall lay down the detailed rules for payment in respect of the importation of goods.

In particular, Member States may provide that, in the case of the importation of goods by taxable persons or certain categories thereof, or by persons liable for payment of VAT or certain categories thereof, the VAT due by reason of the importation need not be paid at the time of importation, on condition that it is entered as such in the VAT return to be submitted in accordance with Article 250.

Article 212

Member States may release taxable persons from payment of the VAT due where the amount is insignificant.

CHAPTER 2

IDENTIFICATION

Article 213

1. Every taxable person shall state when his activity as a taxable person commences, changes or ceases.

Member States shall allow, and may require, the statement to be made by electronic means, in accordance with conditions which they lay down.

2. Without prejudice to the first subparagraph of paragraph 1, every taxable person or non-taxable legal person who makes intra-Community acquisitions of goods which are not subject to VAT pursuant to Article 3(1) must state that he makes such acquisitions if the conditions, laid down in that provision, for not making such transactions subject to VAT cease to be fulfilled.

Article 214

1. Member States shall take the measures necessary to ensure that the following persons are identified by means of an individual number:

(*a*) every taxable person, with the exception of those referred to in Article 9(2), who within their respective territory carries out supplies of goods or services in respect of which VAT is deductible, other than supplies of goods or services in respect of which VAT is payable solely by the customer or the person for whom the goods or services are intended, in accordance with Articles 194 to 197 and Article 199;

(*b*) every taxable person, or non-taxable legal person, who makes intra-Community acquisitions of goods subject to VAT pursuant to Article 2(1)(*b*) and every taxable person, or non-taxable legal person, who exercises the option under Article 3(3) of making their intra-Community acquisitions subject to VAT;

(*c*) every taxable person who, within their respective territory, makes intra-Community acquisitions of goods for the purposes of transactions which relate to the activities referred to in the second subparagraph of Article 9(1) and which are carried out outside that territory.

[(*d*) every taxable person who within their respective territory receives services for which he is liable to pay VAT pursuant to Article 196;

(*e*) every taxable person, established within their respective territory, who supplies services within the territory of another Member State for which VAT is payable solely by the recipient pursuant to Article 196.][1]

2. Member States need not identify certain taxable persons who carry out transactions on an occasional basis, as referred to in Article 12.

Amendments—[1] Para 1(*d*), (*e*) inserted, by Council Directive 2008/8/EC art 2(8) with effect from 1 January 2010 (OJ L 44, 20.2.2008 p 11).

Article 215

Each individual VAT identification number shall have a prefix in accordance with ISO code 3166 — alpha 2 — by which the Member State of issue may be identified.

Nevertheless, Greece may use the prefix 'EL'.

Article 216

Member States shall take the measures necessary to ensure that their identification systems enable the taxable persons referred to in Article 214 to be identified and to ensure the correct application of the transitional arrangements for the taxation of intra-Community transactions, as referred to in Article 402.

CHAPTER 3
INVOICING

Section 1 Definition

Article 217

For the purposes of this Chapter, 'transmission or provision by electronic means' shall mean transmission or provision to the addressee of data using electronic equipment for processing (including digital compression) and storage, and employing wire, radio, optical or other electromagnetic means.

Section 2 Concept of invoice

Article 218

For the purposes of this Directive, Member States shall accept documents or messages on paper or in electronic form as invoices if they meet the conditions laid down in this Chapter.

Article 219

Any document or message that amends and refers specifically and unambiguously to the initial invoice shall be treated as an invoice.

Section 3 Issue of invoices

Article 220

Every taxable person shall ensure that, in respect of the following, an invoice is issued, either by himself or by his customer or, in his name and on his behalf, by a third party:

(1) supplies of goods or services which he has made to another taxable person or to a non-taxable legal person;

(2) supplies of goods as referred to in Article 33;

(3) supplies of goods carried out in accordance with the conditions specified in Article 138;

(4) any payment on account made to him before one of the supplies of goods referred to in points (1), (2) and (3) was carried out;

(5) any payment on account made to him by another taxable person or non-taxable legal person before the provision of services was completed.

Article 221

1. Member States may impose on taxable persons an obligation to issue an invoice in respect of supplies of goods or services made in their territory, other than those referred to in Article 220. Member States may, in respect of the invoices referred to in the first subparagraph, impose fewer obligations than those laid down in Articles 226, 230, 233, 244 and 246.

2. Member States may release taxable persons from the obligation laid down in Article 220 to issue an invoice in respect of supplies of goods or services which they have made in their territory and which are exempt, with or without deductibility of the VAT paid at the preceding stage, pursuant to Articles 110 and 111, Article 125(1), Article 127, Article 128 (1), Articles 132, 135, 136, 371, 375, 376 and 377, Article 378 (2), Article 379(2) and Articles 380 to 390.

Article 222

Member States may impose time limits on taxable persons for the issue of invoices when supplying goods or services in their territory.

Article 223

In accordance with conditions to be laid down by the Member States in whose territory goods or services are supplied, a summary invoice may be drawn up for several separate supplies of goods or services.

Article 224

1. Invoices may be drawn up by the customer in respect of the supply to him, by a taxable person, of goods or services, if there is a prior agreement between the two parties and provided that a procedure exists for the acceptance of each invoice by the taxable person supplying the goods or services.

2. The Member States in whose territory the goods or services are supplied shall determine the terms and conditions of such prior agreements and of the acceptance procedures between the taxable person and the customer.

3. Member States may impose further conditions on taxable persons supplying goods or services in their territory concerning the issue of invoices by the customer. They may, in particular, require that such invoices be issued in the name and on behalf of the taxable person.

The conditions referred to in the first subparagraph must always be the same wherever the customer is established.

Article 225

Member States may impose specific conditions on taxable persons supplying goods or services in their territory in cases where the third party, or the customer, who issues invoices is established in a country with which no legal instrument exists relating to mutual assistance similar in scope to that provided for in Directive 76/308/EEC and Regulation (EC) No 1798/2003.

Section 4 Content of invoices

Article 226

Without prejudice to the particular provisions laid down in this Directive, only the following details are required for VAT purposes on invoices issued pursuant to Articles 220 and 221:

(1) the date of issue;
(2) a sequential number, based on one or more series, which uniquely identifies the invoice;
(3) the VAT identification number referred to in Article 214 under which the taxable person supplied the goods or services;
(4) the customer's VAT identification number, as referred to in Article 214, under which the customer received a supply of goods or services in respect of which he is liable for payment of VAT, or received a supply of goods as referred to in Article 138;
(5) the full name and address of the taxable person and of the customer;
(6) the quantity and nature of the goods supplied or the extent and nature of the services rendered;
(7) the date on which the supply of goods or services was made or completed or the date on which the payment on account referred to in points (4) and (5) of Article 220 was made, in so far as that date can be determined and differs from the date of issue of the invoice;
(8) the taxable amount per rate or exemption, the unit price exclusive of VAT and any discounts or rebates if they are not included in the unit price;
(9) the VAT rate applied;
(10) the VAT amount payable, except where a special arrangement is applied under which, in accordance with this Directive, such a detail is excluded;
(11) in the case of an exemption or where the customer is liable for payment of VAT, reference to the applicable provision of this Directive, or to the corresponding national provision, or any other reference indicating that the supply of goods or services is exempt or subject to the reverse charge procedure;
(12) in the case of the supply of a new means of transport made in accordance with the conditions specified in Article 138 (1) and (2)(*a*), the characteristics as identified in point (*b*) of Article 2(2);
(13) where the margin scheme for travel agents is applied, reference to Article 306, or to the corresponding national provisions, or any other reference indicating that the margin scheme has been applied;
(14) where one of the special arrangements applicable to second-hand goods, works of art, collectors' items and antiques is applied, reference to Articles 313, 326 or 333, or to the corresponding national provisions, or any other reference indicating that one of those arrangements has been applied;
(15) where the person liable for payment of VAT is a tax representative for the purposes of Article 204, the VAT identification number, referred to in Article 214, of that tax representative, together with his full name and address.

Article 227

Member States may require taxable persons established in their territory and supplying goods or services there to indicate the VAT identification number, referred to in Article 214, of the customer in cases other than those referred to in point (4) of Article 226.

Article 228

Member States in whose territory goods or services are supplied may allow some of the compulsory details to be omitted from documents or messages treated as invoices pursuant to Article 219.

Article 229

Member States shall not require invoices to be signed.

Article 230

The amounts which appear on the invoice may be expressed in any currency, provided that the amount of VAT payable is expressed in the national currency of the Member State in which the supply of goods or services takes place, using the conversion mechanism laid down in Article 91.

Article 231

For control purposes, Member States may require invoices in respect of supplies of goods or services in their territory and invoices received by taxable persons established in their territory to be translated into their national languages.

Section 5 Sending invoices by electronic means

Article 232

Invoices issued pursuant to Section 2 may be sent on paper or, subject to acceptance by the recipient, they may be sent or made available by electronic means.

Article 233

1. Invoices sent or made available by electronic means shall be accepted by Member States provided that the authenticity of the origin and the integrity of their content are guaranteed by one of the following methods:

(*a*) by means of an advanced electronic signature within the meaning of point (2) of Article 2 of Directive 1999/93/EC of the European Parliament and of the Council of 13 December 1999 on a Community framework for electronic signatures ([1]);

(*b*) by means of electronic data interchange (EDI), as defined in Article 2 of Commission Recommendation 1994/820/EC

of 19 October 1994 relating to the legal aspects of electronic data interchange ([2]), if the agreement relating to the exchange provides for the use of procedures guaranteeing the authenticity of the origin and integrity of the data.

Invoices may, however, be sent or made available by other electronic means, subject to acceptance by the Member States concerned.

2. For the purposes of point (*a*) of the first subparagraph of paragraph 1, Member States may also ask for the advanced electronic signature to be based on a qualified certificate and created by a secure-signature-creation device, within the meaning of points (6) and (10) of Article 2 of Directive 1999/93/EC.

3. For the purposes of point (*b*) of the first subparagraph of paragraph 1, Member States may also, subject to conditions which they lay down, require that an additional summary document on paper be sent.

(1) OJ L 13, 19.1.2000, p. 12.
(2) OJ L 338, 28.12.1994, p. 98.

Article 234

Member States may not impose on taxable persons supplying goods or services in their territory any other obligations or formalities relating to the sending or making available of invoices by electronic means.

Article 235

Member States may lay down specific conditions for invoices issued by electronic means in respect of goods or services supplied in their territory from a country with which no legal instrument exists relating to mutual assistance similar in scope to that provided for in Directive 76/308/EEC and Regulation (EC) No 1798/2003.

Article 236

Where batches containing several invoices are sent or made available to the same recipient by electronic means, the details common to the individual invoices may be mentioned only once if, for each invoice, all the information is accessible.

Article 237

The Commission shall present, at the latest on 31 December 2008, a report and, if appropriate, a proposal amending the conditions applicable to electronic invoicing in order to take account of future technological developments in that field.

Section 6 Simplification measures

Article 238

1. After consulting the VAT Committee, Member States may, in accordance with conditions which they may lay down, provide that in the following cases some of the information required under Article 226 and 230, subject to options taken up by Member States under Articles 227, 228 and 231, need not be entered on invoices in respect of supplies of goods or services in their territory:

(*a*) where the amount of the invoice is minor;

(*b*) where commercial or administrative practice in the business sector concerned or the technical conditions under which the invoices are issued make it difficult to comply with all the obligations referred to in Articles 226 and 230.

2. Invoices must, in any event, contain the following information:

(*a*) the date of issue;

(*b*) identification of the taxable person;

(*c*) identification of the type of goods or services supplied;

(*d*) the VAT amount payable or the information needed to calculate it.

3. The simplified arrangements provided for in paragraph 1 may not be applied to the transactions referred to in Articles 20, 21, 22, 33, 36, 138 and 141.

Article 239

In cases where Member States make use of the option under point (*b*) of the first subparagraph of Article 272(1) of not allocating a VAT identification number to taxable persons who do not carry out any of the transactions referred to in Articles 20, 21, 22, 33, 36, 138 and 141, and where the supplier or the customer has not been allocated an identification number of that type, another number called the tax reference number, as defined by the Member States concerned, shall be entered on the invoice instead.

Article 240

Where the taxable person has been allocated a VAT identification number, the Member States exercising the option under point (*b*) of the first subparagraph of Article 272(1) may also require the invoice to show the following:

(1) in respect of the supply of services, as referred to in Articles 44, 47, 50, 53, 54 and 55, and the supply of goods, as referred to in Articles 138 and 141, the VAT identification number and the tax reference number of the supplier;

(2) in respect of other supplies of goods or services, only the tax reference number of the supplier or only the VAT identification number.

CHAPTER 4
ACCOUNTING

Section 1 Definition

Article 241

For the purposes of this Chapter, 'storage of an invoice by electronic means' shall mean storage of data using electronic equipment for processing (including digital compression) and storage, and employing wire, radio, optical or other electromagnetic means.

Section 2 General obligations

Article 242

Every taxable person shall keep accounts in sufficient detail for VAT to be applied and its application checked by the tax authorities.

Article 243

1. Every taxable person shall keep a register of the goods dispatched or transported, by that person or on his behalf, to a destination outside the territory of the Member State of departure but within the Community for the purposes of transactions consisting in work on those goods or their temporary use as referred to in points (*f*), (*g*) and (*h*) of Article 17 (2).

2. Every taxable person shall keep accounts in sufficient detail to enable the identification of goods dispatched to him from another Member State, by or on behalf of a taxable person identified for VAT purposes in that other Member State, and used for services consisting in valuations of those goods or work on those goods as referred to in point (*c*) of Article 52.

Section 3 Specific obligations relating to the storage of all invoices

Article 244

Every taxable person shall ensure that copies of the invoices issued by himself, or by his customer or, in his name and on his behalf, by a third party, and all the invoices which he has received, are stored.

Article 245

1. For the purposes of this Directive, the taxable person may decide the place of storage of all invoices provided that he makes the invoices or information stored in accordance with Article 244 available to the competent authorities without undue delay whenever they so request.

2. Member States may require taxable persons established in their territory to notify them of the place of storage, if it is outside their territory.

Member States may also require taxable persons established in their territory to store within that territory invoices issued by themselves or by their customers or, in their name and on their behalf, by a third party, as well as all the invoices that they have received, when the storage is not by electronic means guaranteeing full on-line access to the data concerned.

Article 246

The authenticity of the origin and the integrity of the content of the invoices stored, as well as their legibility, must be guaranteed throughout the storage period.

In respect of the invoices referred to in the second subparagraph of Article 233(1), the details they contain may not be altered and must remain legible throughout the storage period.

Article 247

1. Each Member State shall determine the period throughout which taxable persons must ensure the storage of invoices relating to the supply of goods or services in its territory and invoices received by taxable persons established in its territory.

2. In order to ensure that the conditions laid down in Article 246 are met, the Member State referred to in paragraph 1 may require that invoices be stored in the original form in which they were sent or made available, whether paper or electronic. Additionally, in the case of invoices stored by electronic means, the Member State may require that the data guaranteeing the authenticity of the origin of the invoices and the integrity of their content, as provided for in the first paragraph of Article 246, also be stored.

3. The Member State referred to in paragraph 1 may lay down specific conditions prohibiting or restricting the storage of invoices in a country with which no legal instrument exists relating to mutual assistance similar in scope to that provided for in Directive 76/308/EEC and Regulation (EC) No 1798/2003 or to the right referred to in Article 249 to access by electronic means, to download and to use.

Article 248

Member States may, subject to conditions which they lay down, require the storage of invoices received by non-taxable persons.

Section 4 Right of access to invoices stored by electronic means in another Member State

Article 249

Where a taxable person stores invoices which he issues or receives by electronic means guaranteeing on-line access to the data and where the place of storage is in a Member State other than that in which he is established, the competent authorities in the Member State in which he is established shall, for the purposes of this Directive, have the right to access those invoices by electronic means, to download and to use them, within the limits set by the rules of the Member State in which the taxable person is established and in so far as those authorities require for control purposes.

CHAPTER 5

RETURNS

Article 250

1. Every taxable person shall submit a VAT return setting out all the information needed to calculate the tax that has become chargeable and the deductions to be made including, in so far as is necessary for the establishment of the basis of assessment, the total value of the transactions relating to such tax and deductions and the value of any exempt transactions.

2. Member States shall allow, and may require, the VAT return referred to in paragraph 1 to be submitted by electronic means, in accordance with conditions which they lay down.

Article 251

In addition to the information referred to in Article 250, the VAT return covering a given tax period shall show the following:

(*a*) the total value, exclusive of VAT, of the supplies of goods referred to in Article 138 in respect of which VAT has become chargeable during this tax period;

(*b*) the total value, exclusive of VAT, of the supplies of goods referred to in Articles 33 and 36 carried out within the territory of another Member State, in respect of which VAT has become chargeable during this tax period, where the place where dispatch or transport of the goods began is situated in the Member State in which the return must be submitted;

(*c*) the total value, exclusive of VAT, of the intra-Community acquisitions of goods, or transactions treated as such, pursuant to Articles 21 or 22, made in the Member State in which the return must be submitted and in respect of which VAT has become chargeable during this tax period;

(*d*) the total value, exclusive of VAT, of the supplies of goods referred to in Articles 33 and 36 carried out in the Member State in which the return must be submitted and in respect of which VAT has become chargeable during this tax period, where the place where dispatch or transport of the goods began is situated within the territory of another Member State;

(*e*) the total value, exclusive of VAT, of the supplies of goods carried out in the Member State in which the return must be submitted and in respect of which the taxable person has been designated, in accordance with Article 197, as liable for payment of VAT and in respect of which VAT has become chargeable during this tax period.

Article 252

1. The VAT return shall be submitted by a deadline to be determined by Member States. That deadline may not be more than two months after the end of each tax period.

2. The tax period shall be set by each Member State at one month, two months or three months. Member States may, however, set different tax periods provided that those periods do not exceed one year.

Article 253

Sweden may apply a simplified procedure for small and medium-sized enterprises, whereby taxable persons carrying out only transactions taxable at national level may submit VAT returns three months after the end of the annual direct tax period.

Article 254

In the case of supplies of new means of transport carried out in accordance with the conditions specified in Article 138(2)(*a*) by a taxable person identified for VAT purposes for a customer not identified for VAT purposes, or by a taxable person as defined in Article 9(2), Member States shall take the measures necessary to ensure that the vendor communicates all the information needed for VAT to be applied and its application checked by the tax authorities.

Article 255

Where Member States designate the customer of investment gold as the person liable for payment of VAT pursuant to Article 198 (1) or if, in the case of gold material, semi-manufactured products or investment gold as defined in Article 344(1), they exercise the option provided for in Article 198(2) of designating the customer as the person liable for payment of VAT, they shall take the measures necessary to ensure that he complies with the obligations relating to submission of a VAT return set out in this Chapter.

Article 256

Member States shall take the measures necessary to ensure that persons who are regarded as liable for payment of VAT in the stead of a taxable person not established within their territory, in accordance with Articles 194 to 197 and Article 204, comply with the obligations relating to submission of a VAT return, as laid down in this Chapter.

Article 257

Member States shall take the measures necessary to ensure that non-taxable legal persons who are liable for payment of VAT due in respect of intra-Community acquisitions of goods, as referred to in Article 2(1)(*b*)(i), comply with the obligations relating to submission of a VAT return, as laid down in this Chapter.

Article 258

Member States shall lay down detailed rules for the submission of VAT returns in respect of intra-Community acquisitions of new means of transport, as referred to in Article 2(1)(*b*)(ii), and intra-Community acquisitions of products subject to excise duty, as referred to in Article 2(1)(*b*)(iii).

Article 259

Member States may require persons who make intra-Community acquisitions of new means of transport as referred to in Article 2 (1)(*b*)(ii), to provide, when submitting the VAT return, all the information needed for VAT to be applied and its application checked by the tax authorities.

Article 260

Member States shall lay down detailed rules for the submission of VAT returns in respect of the importation of goods.

Article 261

1. Member States may require the taxable person to submit a return showing all the particulars specified in Articles 250 and 251 in respect of all transactions carried out in the preceding year. That return shall provide all the information necessary for any adjustments.

2. Member States shall allow, and may require, the return referred to in paragraph 1 to be submitted by electronic means, in accordance with conditions which they lay down.

CHAPTER 6
RECAPITULATIVE STATEMENTS

[Article 262

Every taxable person identified for VAT purposes shall submit a recapitulative statement of the following:

(*a*) the acquirers identified for VAT purposes to whom he has supplied goods in accordance with the conditions specified in Article 138(1) and (2)(*c*);
(*b*) the persons identified for VAT purposes to whom he has supplied goods which were supplied to him by way of intra-Community acquisitions referred to in Article 42;
(*c*) the taxable persons, and the non-taxable legal persons identified for VAT purposes, to whom he has supplied services, other than services that are exempted from VAT in the Member State where the transaction is taxable, and for which the recipient is liable to pay the tax pursuant to Article 196.][1]

Amendments—[1] Article 262 substituted by Council Directive 2008/8/EC art 2(9) with effect from 1 January 2010 (OJ L 44, 20.2.2008 p 11). Text previously read as follows—

"Article 262

Every taxable person identified for VAT purposes shall submit a recapitulative statement of the acquirers identified for VAT purposes to whom he has supplied goods in accordance with the conditions specified in Article 138(1) and (2)(*c*), and of the persons identified for VAT purposes to whom he has supplied goods which were supplied to him by way of intra-Community acquisitions referred to in Article 42.".

[Article 263

1. The recapitulative statement shall be drawn up for each calendar month within a period not exceeding one month and in accordance with procedures to be determined by the Member States.

1a. However, Member States, in accordance with the conditions and limits which they may lay down, may allow taxable persons to submit the recapitulative statement for each calendar quarter within a time limit not exceeding one month from the end of the quarter, where the total quarterly amount, excluding VAT, of the supplies of goods as referred to in Articles 264(1)(*d*) and 265(1)(*c*) does not exceed either in respect of the quarter concerned or in respect of any of the previous four quarters the sum of EUR 50000 or its equivalent in national currency.

The option provided for in the first subparagraph shall cease to be applicable after the end of the month during which the total value, excluding VAT, of the supplies of goods as referred to in Article 264(1)(*d*) and 265(1)(*c*) exceeds, in respect of the current quarter, the sum of EUR 50000 or its equivalent in national currency. In this case, a recapitulative statement shall be drawn up for the month(s) which has (have) elapsed since the beginning of the quarter, within a time limit not exceeding one month.

1b. Until 31 December 2011, Member States are allowed to set the sum mentioned in paragraph 1a at EUR 100000 or its equivalent in national currency.

1c. In the case of supplies of services as referred to in Article 264(1)(*d*), Member States, in accordance with the conditions and limits which they may lay down, may allow taxable persons to submit the recapitulative statement for each calendar quarter within a time limit not exceeding one month from the end of the quarter.

Member States may, in particular, require the taxable persons who carry out supplies of both goods and services as referred to in Article 264(1)(*d*) to submit the recapitulative statement in accordance with the deadline resulting from paragraphs 1 to 1b.

2. Member States shall allow, and may require, the recapitulative statement referred to in paragraph 1 to be submitted by electronic file transfer, in accordance with conditions which they lay down.][1]

Amendments—[1] Article 263 substituted by Council Directive 2008/117/EC art 1 with effect from 21 January 2009. The deadline for implementation of this Directive is 1 January 2010 (OJ L 14, 20.1.2009 p 7). Text previously read as follows—

"Article 263

1. The recapitulative statement shall be drawn up for each calendar quarter within a period and in accordance with procedures to be determined by the Member States. Member States may, however, provide that recapitulative statements are to be submitted on a monthly basis.

2. Member States shall allow, and may require, the recapitulative statements referred to in paragraph 1 to be submitted by electronic means, in accordance with conditions which they lay down.".

Article 264

1. The recapitulative statement shall set out the following information:

[(*a*) the VAT identification number of the taxable person in the Member State in which the recapitulative statement must be submitted and under which he has carried out the supply of goods in accordance with the conditions specified in Article 138(1) and under which he effected taxable supplies of services in accordance with the conditions laid down in Article 44;
(*b*) the VAT identification number of the person acquiring the goods or receiving the services in a Member State other than that in which the recapitulative statement must be submitted and under which the goods or services were supplied to him;][1]
(*c*) the VAT identification number of the taxable person in the Member State in which the recapitulative statement must be submitted and under which he has carried out a transfer to another Member State, as referred to in Article 138(2)(*c*), and the number by means of which he is identified in the Member State in which the dispatch or transport ended;
[(*d*) for each person who acquired goods or received services, the total value of the supplies of goods and the total value of the supplies of services carried out by the taxable person;][1]

(*e*) in respect of supplies of goods consisting in transfers to another Member State, as referred to in Article 138(2)(*c*), the total value of the supplies, determined in accordance with Article 76;

(*f*) the amounts of adjustments made pursuant to Article 90.

[2. The value referred to in paragraph 1(*d*) shall be declared for the period of submission established in accordance with Article 263(1) to (1*c*) during which VAT became chargeable.

The amounts referred to in paragraph 1(f) shall be declared for the period of submission established in accordance with Article 263(1) to (1*c*) during which the person acquiring the goods was notified of the adjustment.][2]

Amendments—[1] Para 1(*a*), (*b*), (*d*) substituted, by Council Directive 2008/8/EC art 2(10) with effect from 1 January 2010 (OJ L 44, 20.2.2008 p 11). Text previously read as follows—

"(*a*) the VAT identification number of the taxable person in the Member State in which the recapitulative statement must be submitted and under which he has carried out the supply of goods in accordance with the conditions specified in Article 138(1);

(*b*) the VAT identification number of the person acquiring the goods in a Member State other than that in which the recapitulative statement must be submitted and under which the goods were supplied to him;".

"(*d*) for each person who acquired goods, the total value of the supplies of goods carried out by the taxable person;".

[2] Para 2 substituted by Council Directive 2008/117/EC art 1 with effect from 21 January 2009. The deadline for implementation of this Directive is 1 January 2010 (OJ L 14, 20.1.2009 p 7). Text previously read as follows—

"2. The value referred to in point (*d*) of paragraph 1 shall be declared for the calendar quarter during which VAT became chargeable.

The amounts referred to in point (*f*) of paragraph 1 shall be declared for the calendar quarter during which the person acquiring the goods was notified of the adjustment.".

Article 265

1. In the case of intra-Community acquisitions of goods, as referred to in Article 42, the taxable person identified for VAT purposes in the Member State which issued him with the VAT identification number under which he made such acquisitions shall set the following information out clearly on the recapitulative statement:

(*a*) his VAT identification number in that Member State and under which he made the acquisition and subsequent supply of goods;

(*b*) the VAT identification number, in the Member State in which dispatch or transport of the goods ended, of the person to whom the subsequent supply was made by the taxable person;

(*c*) for each person to whom the subsequent supply was made, the total value, exclusive of VAT, of the supplies made by the taxable person in the Member State in which dispatch or transport of the goods ended.

[2. The value referred to in paragraph 1(*c*) shall be declared for the period of submission established in accordance with Article 263(1) to (1*b*) during which VAT became chargeable.][1]

Amendments—[1] Para 2 substituted by Council Directive 2008/117/EC art 1 with effect from 21 January 2009. The deadline for implementation of this Directive is 1 January 2010 (OJ L 14, 20.1.2009 p 7). Text previously read as follows—

"2. The value referred to in point (*c*) of paragraph 1 shall be declared for the calendar quarter during which VAT became chargeable.".

Article 266

By way of derogation from Articles 264 and 265, Member States may provide that additional information is to be given in recapitulative statements.

Article 267

Member States shall take the measures necessary to ensure that those persons who, in accordance with Articles 194 and 204, are regarded as liable for payment of VAT, in the stead of a taxable person who is not established in their territory, comply with the obligation to submit a recapitulative statement as provided for in this Chapter.

Article 268

Member States may require that taxable persons who, in their territory, make intra-Community acquisitions of goods, or transactions treated as such, pursuant to Articles 21 or 22, submit statements giving details of such acquisitions, provided, however, that such statements are not required in respect of a period of less than one month.

Article 269

Acting unanimously on a proposal from the Commission, the Council may authorise any Member State to introduce the special measures provided for in Articles 270 and 271 to simplify the obligation, laid down in this Chapter, to submit a recapitulative statement. Such measures may not jeopardise the proper monitoring of intra-Community transactions.

Article 270

By virtue of the authorisation referred to in Article 269, Member States may permit taxable persons to submit annual recapitulative statements indicating the VAT identification numbers, in another Member State, of the persons to whom those taxable persons have supplied goods in accordance with the conditions specified in Article 138(1) and (2)(*c*), where the taxable persons meet the following three conditions:

(*a*) the total annual value, exclusive of VAT, of their supplies of goods and services does not exceed by more than EUR 35 000, or the equivalent in national currency, the amount of the annual turnover which is used as a reference for application of the exemption for small enterprises provided for in Articles 282 to 292;

(*b*) the total annual value, exclusive of VAT, of supplies of goods carried out by them in accordance with the conditions specified in Article 138 does not exceed EUR 15 000 or the equivalent in national currency;

(*c*) none of the supplies of goods carried out by them in accordance with the conditions specified in Article 138 is a supply of new means of transport.

Article 271

By virtue of the authorisation referred to in Article 269, Member States which set at over three months the tax period in respect of which taxable persons must submit the VAT return provided for in Article 250 may permit such persons to submit recapitulative statements in respect of the same period where those taxable persons meet the following three conditions:

(*a*) the total annual value, exclusive of VAT, of their supplies of goods and services does not exceed EUR 200 000 or the equivalent in national currency;

(*b*) the total annual value, exclusive of VAT, of supplies of goods carried out by them in accordance with the conditions specified in Article 138 does not exceed EUR 15 000 or the equivalent in national currency;

(*c*) none of the supplies of goods carried out by them in accordance with the conditions specified in Article 138 is a supply of new means of transport.

CHAPTER 7

MISCELLANEOUS PROVISIONS

Article 272

1. Member States may release the following taxable persons from certain or all obligations referred to in Chapters 2 to 6:

(*a*) taxable persons whose intra-Community acquisitions of goods are not subject to VAT pursuant to Article 3(1);

(*b*) taxable persons carrying out none of the transactions referred to in Articles 20, 21, 22, 33, 36, 138 and 141;

(*c*) taxable persons carrying out only supplies of goods or of services which are exempt pursuant to Articles 132, 135 and 136, Articles 146 to 149 and Articles 151, 152 or 153;

(*d*) taxable persons covered by the exemption for small enterprises provided for in Articles 282 to 292;

(*e*) taxable persons covered by the common flat-rate scheme for farmers.

Member States may not release the taxable persons referred to in point (*b*) of the first subparagraph from the invoicing obligations laid down in Articles 220 to 236 and Articles 238, 239 and 240.

2. If Member States exercise the option under point (*e*) of the first subparagraph of paragraph 1, they shall take the measures necessary to ensure the correct application of the transitional arrangements for the taxation of intra-Community transactions.

3. Member States may release taxable persons other than those referred to in paragraph 1 from certain of the accounting obligations referred to in Article 242.

Article 273

Member States may impose other obligations which they deem necessary to ensure the correct collection of VAT and to prevent evasion, subject to the requirement of equal treatment as between domestic transactions and transactions carried out between Member States by taxable persons and provided that such obligations do not, in trade between Member States, give rise to formalities connected with the crossing of frontiers.

The option under the first paragraph may not be relied upon in order to impose additional invoicing obligations over and above those laid down in Chapter 3.

CHAPTER 8

OBLIGATIONS RELATING TO CERTAIN IMPORTATIONS AND EXPORTATIONS

Section 1 Imp or t at i on

Article 274

Articles 275, 276 and 277 shall apply to the importation of goods in free circulation which enter the Community from a third territory forming part of the customs territory of the Community.

Article 275

The formalities relating to the importation of the goods referred to in Article 274 shall be the same as those laid down by the Community customs provisions in force for the importation of goods into the customs territory of the Community.

Article 276

Where dispatch or transport of the goods referred to in Article 274 ends at a place situated outside the Member State of their entry into the Community, they shall circulate in the Community under the internal Community transit procedure laid down by the Community customs provisions in force, in so far as they have been the subject of a declaration placing them under that procedure on their entry into the Community.

Article 277

Where, on their entry into the Community, the goods referred to in Article 274 are in one of the situations which would entitle them, if they were imported within the meaning of the first paragraph of Article 30, to be covered by one of the arrangements or situations referred to in Article 156, or by a temporary importation arrangement with full exemption from import duties, Member States shall take the measures necessary to ensure that the goods may remain in the Community under the same conditions as those laid down for the application of those arrangements or situations.

Section 2 Exportation

Article 278

Articles 279 and 280 shall apply to the exportation of goods in free circulation which are dispatched or transported from a Member State to a third territory forming part of the customs territory of the Community.

Article 279

The formalities relating to the exportation of the goods referred to in Article 278 from the territory of the Community shall be the same as those laid down by the Community customs provisions in force for the exportation of goods from the customs territory of the Community.

Article 280

In the case of goods which are temporarily exported from the Community, in order to be reimported, Member States shall take the measures necessary to ensure that, on reimportation into the Community, such goods may be covered by the same provisions as would have applied if they had been temporarily exported from the customs territory of the Community.

TITLE XII
SPECIAL SCHEMES

CHAPTER 1
SPECIAL SCHEME FOR SMALL ENTERPRISES

Section 1 Simplified procedures for charging and collection

Article 281

Member States which might encounter difficulties in applying the normal VAT arrangements to small enterprises, by reason of the activities or structure of such enterprises, may, subject to such conditions and limits as they may set, and after consulting the VAT Committee, apply simplified procedures, such as flat-rate schemes, for charging and collecting VAT provided that they do not lead to a reduction thereof.

Section 2 Exemptions or graduated relief

Article 282

The exemptions and graduated tax relief provided for in this Section shall apply to the supply of goods and services by small enterprises.

Article 283

1. The arrangements provided for in this Section shall not apply to the following transactions:
(*a*) transactions carried out on an occasional basis, as referred to in Article 12;
(*b*) supplies of new means of transport carried out in accordance with the conditions specified in Article 138(1) and (2)(*a*);
(*c*) supplies of goods or services carried out by a taxable person who is not established in the Member State in which the VAT is due.

2. Member States may exclude transactions other than those referred to in paragraph 1 from the arrangements provided for in this Section.

Article 284

1. Member States which have exercised the option under Article 14 of Council Directive 67/228/EEC of 11 April 1967 on the harmonisation of legislation of Member States concerning turnover taxes — Structure and procedures for application of the common system of value added tax [1] of introducing exemptions or graduated tax relief may retain them, and the arrangements for applying them, if they comply with the VAT rules.

2. Member States which, at 17 May 1977, exempted taxable persons whose annual turnover was less than the equivalent in national currency of 5 000 European units of account at the conversion rate on that date, may raise that ceiling up to EUR 5 000.

Member States which applied graduated tax relief may neither raise the ceiling for graduated tax relief nor render the conditions for the granting of it more favourable.

[1] OJ 71, 14.4.1967, p. 1303/67. Directive repealed by Directive 77/ 388/EEC.

Article 285

Member States which have not exercised the option under Article 14 of Directive 67/228/EEC may exempt taxable persons whose annual turnover is no higher than EUR 5 000 or the equivalent in national currency.

The Member States referred to in the first paragraph may grant graduated tax relief to taxable persons whose annual turnover exceeds the ceiling fixed by them for its application.

Article 286

Member States which, at 17 May 1977, exempted taxable persons whose annual turnover was equal to or higher than the equivalent in national currency of 5 000 European units of account at the conversion rate on that date, may raise that ceiling in order to maintain the value of the exemption in real terms.

Article 287

Member States which acceded after 1 January 1978 may exempt taxable persons whose annual turnover is no higher than the equivalent in national currency of the following amounts at the conversion rate on the day of their accession:

(1) Greece: 10 000 European units of account;
(2) Spain: ECU 10 000;
(3) Portugal: ECU 10 000;
(4) Austria: ECU 35 000;
(5) Finland: ECU 10 000;
(6) Sweden: ECU 10 000;
(7) Czech Republic: EUR 35 000;
(8) Estonia: EUR 16 000;
(9) Cyprus: EUR 15 600;
(10) Latvia: EUR 17 200;
(11) Lithuania: EUR 29 000;
(12) Hungary: EUR 35 000;
(13) Malta: EUR 37 000 if the economic activity consists principally in the supply of goods, EUR 24 300 if the economic activity consists principally in the supply of services with a low value added (high inputs), and EUR 14 600 in other cases, namely supplies of services with a high value added (low inputs);
(14) Poland: EUR 10 000;
(15) Slovenia: EUR 25 000;
(16) Slovakia: EUR 35 000.

Article 288

The turnover serving as a reference for the purposes of applying the arrangements provided for in this Section shall consist of the following amounts, exclusive of VAT:

(1) the value of supplies of goods and services, in so far as they are taxed;
(2) the value of transactions which are exempt, with deductibility of the VAT paid at the preceding stage, pursuant to Articles 110 or 111, Article 125(1), Article 127 or Article 128(1);
(3) the value of transactions which are exempt pursuant to Articles 146 to 149 and Articles 151, 152 or 153;
(4) the value of real estate transactions, financial transactions as referred to in points (*b*) to (*g*) of Article 135(1), and insurance services, unless those transactions are ancillary transactions.

However, disposals of the tangible or intangible capital assets of an enterprise shall not be taken into account for the purposes of calculating turnover.

Article 289

Taxable persons exempt from VAT shall not be entitled to deduct VAT in accordance with Articles 167 to 171 and Articles 173 to 177, and may not show the VAT on their invoices.

Article 290

Taxable persons who are entitled to exemption from VAT may opt either for the normal VAT arrangements or for the simplified procedures provided for in Article 281. In this case, they shall be entitled to any graduated tax relief provided for under national legislation.

Article 291

Subject to the application of Article 281, taxable persons enjoying graduated relief shall be regarded as taxable persons subject to the normal VAT arrangements.

Article 292

The arrangements provided for in this Section shall apply until a date to be fixed by the Council in accordance with Article 93 of the Treaty, which may not be later than that on which the definitive arrangements referred to in Article 402 enter into force.

Section 3 Reporting and review

Article 293

Every four years starting from the adoption of this Directive, the Commission shall present to the Council, on the basis of information obtained from the Member States, a report on the application of this Chapter, together, where appropriate and taking into account the need to ensure the long-term convergence of national regulations, with proposals on the following subjects:

(1) improvements to the special scheme for small enterprises;

(2) the adaptation of national systems as regards exemptions and graduated tax relief;

(3) the adaptation of the ceilings provided for in Section 2.

Article 294

The Council shall decide, in accordance with Article 93 of the Treaty, whether a special scheme for small enterprises is necessary under the definitive arrangements and, if appropriate, shall lay down the common limits and conditions for the implementation of that scheme.

CHAPTER 2
COMMON FLAT-RATE SCHEME FOR FARMERS

Article 295

1. For the purposes of this Chapter, the following definitions shall apply:

(1) 'farmer' means any taxable person whose activity is carried out in an agricultural, forestry or fisheries undertaking;

(2) 'agricultural, forestry or fisheries undertaking' means an undertaking regarded as such by each Member State within the framework of the production activities listed in Annex VII;

(3) 'flat-rate farmer' means any farmer covered by the flat-rate scheme provided for in this Chapter;

(4) 'agricultural products' means goods produced by an agricultural, forestry or fisheries undertaking in each Member State as a result of the activities listed in Annex VII;

(5) 'agricultural services' means services, and in particular those listed in Annex VIII, supplied by a farmer using his labour force or the equipment normally employed in the agricultural, forestry or fisheries undertaking operated by him and normally playing a part in agricultural production;

(6) 'input VAT charged' means the amount of the total VAT attaching to the goods and services purchased by all agricultural, forestry and fisheries undertakings of each Member State subject to the flat-rate scheme where such tax would be deductible in accordance with Articles 167, 168 and 169 and Articles 173 to 177 by a farmer subject to the normal VAT arrangements;

(7) 'flat-rate compensation percentages' means the percentages fixed by Member States in accordance with Articles 297, 298 and 299 and applied by them in the cases specified in Article 300 in order to enable flat-rate farmers to offset at a fixed rate the input VAT charged;

(8) 'flat-rate compensation' means the amount arrived at by applying the flat-rate compensation percentage to the turnover of the flat-rate farmer in the cases specified in Article 300.

2. Where a farmer processes, using means normally employed in an agricultural, forestry or fisheries undertaking, products deriving essentially from his agricultural production, such processing activities shall be treated as agricultural production activities, as listed in Annex VII.

Simon's Tax Cases—*Finanzamt Rendsburg v Harbs* [2006] STC 340*.

Article 296

1. Where the application to farmers of the normal VAT arrangements, or the special scheme provided for in Chapter 1, is likely to give rise to difficulties, Member States may apply to farmers, in accordance with this Chapter, a flat-rate scheme designed to offset the VAT charged on purchases of goods and services made by the flat-rate farmers.

2. Each Member State may exclude from the flat-rate scheme certain categories of farmers, as well as farmers for whom application of the normal VAT arrangements, or of the simplified procedures provided for in Article 281, is not likely to give rise to administrative difficulties.

3. Every flat-rate farmer may opt, subject to the rules and conditions to be laid down by each Member State, for application of the normal VAT arrangements or, as the case may be, the simplified procedures provided for in Article 281.

Article 297

Member States shall, where necessary, fix the flat-rate compensation percentages. They may fix varying percentages for forestry, for the different sub-divisions of agriculture and for fisheries.

Member States shall notify the Commission of the flat-rate compensation percentages fixed in accordance with the first paragraph before applying them.

Article 298

The flat-rate compensation percentages shall be calculated on the basis of macro-economic statistics for flat-rate farmers alone for the preceding three years.

The percentages may be rounded up or down to the nearest half-point. Member States may also reduce such percentages to a nil rate.

Article 299

The flat-rate compensation percentages may not have the effect of obtaining for flat-rate farmers refunds greater than the input VAT charged.

Article 300

The flat-rate compensation percentages shall be applied to the prices, exclusive of VAT, of the following goods and services:

(1) agricultural products supplied by flat-rate farmers to taxable persons other than those covered, in the Member State in which these products were supplied, by this flat-rate scheme;

(2) agricultural products supplied by flat-rate farmers, in accordance with the conditions specified in Article 138, to non-taxable legal persons whose intra-Community acquisitions of goods are subject to VAT, pursuant to Article 2(1)(*b*), in the Member State in which dispatch or transport of those agricultural products ends;

(3) agricultural services supplied by flat-rate farmers to taxable persons other than those covered, in the Member State in which these services were supplied, by this flat-rate scheme.

Article 301

1. In the case of the supply of agricultural products or agricultural services specified in Article 300, Member States shall provide that the flat-rate compensation is to be paid either by the customer or by the public authorities.

2. In respect of any supply of agricultural products or agricultural services other than those specified in Article 300, the flat-rate compensation shall be deemed to be paid by the customer.

Article 302

If a flat-rate farmer is entitled to flat-rate compensation, he shall not be entitled to deduction of VAT in respect of activities covered by this flat-rate scheme.

Article 303

1. Where the taxable customer pays flat-rate compensation pursuant to Article 301(1), he shall be entitled, in accordance with the conditions laid down in Articles 167, 168 and 169 and Articles 173 to 177 and the procedures laid down by the Member States, to deduct the compensation amount from the VAT for which he is liable in the Member State in which his taxed transactions are carried out.

2. Member States shall refund to the customer the amount of the flat-rate compensation he has paid in respect of any of the following transactions:

(*a*) the supply of agricultural products, carried out in accordance with the conditions specified in Article 138, to taxable persons, or to non-taxable legal persons, acting as such in another Member State within the territory of which their intra-Community acquisitions of goods are subject to VAT pursuant to Article 2(1)(*b*);

(*b*) the supply of agricultural products, carried out in accordance with the conditions specified in Articles 146, 147, 148 and 156, Article 157(1)(*b*) and Articles 158, 160 and 161, to a taxable customer established outside the Community, in so far as the products are used by that customer for the purposes of the transactions referred to in Article 169(*a*) and (*b*) or for the purposes of supplies of services which are deemed to take place within the territory of the Member State in which the customer is established and in respect of which VAT is payable solely by the customer pursuant to Article 196;

(*c*) the supply of agricultural services to a taxable customer established within the Community but in another Member State or to a taxable customer established outside the Community, in so far as the services are used by the customer for the purposes of the transactions referred to in Article 169(*a*) and (*b*) or for the purposes of supplies of services which are deemed to take place within the territory of the Member State in which the customer is established and in respect of which VAT is payable solely by the customer pursuant to Article 196.

3. Member States shall determine the method by which the refunds provided for in paragraph 2 are to be made. In particular, they may apply the provisions of Directives 79/1072/EEC and 86/560/EEC.

Article 304

Member States shall take all measures necessary to verify payments of flat-rate compensation to flat-rate farmers.

Article 305

Whenever Member States apply this flat-rate scheme, they shall take all measures necessary to ensure that the supply of agricultural products between Member States, carried out in accordance with the conditions specified in Article 33, is always taxed in the same way, whether the supply is effected by a flat-rate farmer or by another taxable person.

CHAPTER 3

SPECIAL SCHEME FOR TRAVEL AGENTS

Article 306

1. Member States shall apply a special VAT scheme, in accordance with this Chapter, to transactions carried out by travel agents who deal with customers in their own name and use supplies of goods or services provided by other taxable persons, in the provision of travel facilities. This special scheme shall not apply to travel agents where they act solely as intermediaries and to whom point (*c*) of the first paragraph of Article 79 applies for the purposes of calculating the taxable amount.

2. For the purposes of this Chapter, tour operators shall be regarded as travel agents.

Article 307

Transactions made, in accordance with the conditions laid down in Article 306, by the travel agent in respect of a journey shall be regarded as a single service supplied by the travel agent to the traveller.

The single service shall be taxable in the Member State in which the travel agent has established his business or has a fixed establishment from which the travel agent has carried out the supply of services.

Article 308

The taxable amount and the price exclusive of VAT, within the meaning of point (8) of Article 226, in respect of the single service provided by the travel agent shall be the travel agent's margin, that is to say, the difference between the total amount, exclusive of VAT, to be paid by the traveller and the actual cost to the travel agent of supplies of goods or services provided by other taxable persons, where those transactions are for the direct benefit of the traveller.

Article 309

If transactions entrusted by the travel agent to other taxable persons are performed by such persons outside the Community, the supply of services carried out by the travel agent shall be treated as an intermediary activity exempted pursuant to Article 153.

If the transactions are performed both inside and outside the Community, only that part of the travel agent's service relating to transactions outside the Community may be exempted.

Article 310

VAT charged to the travel agent by other taxable persons in respect of transactions which are referred to in Article 307 and which are for the direct benefit of the traveller shall not be deductible or refundable in any Member State.

CHAPTER 4
SPECIAL ARRANGEMENTS FOR SECOND-HAND GOODS, WORKS OF ART, COLLECTORS' ITEMS AND ANTIQUES

Section 1 Definitions

Article 311

1. For the purposes of this Chapter, and without prejudice to other Community provisions, the following definitions shall apply:

(1) 'second-hand goods' means movable tangible property that is suitable for further use as it is or after repair, other than works of art, collectors' items or antiques and other than precious metals or precious stones as defined by the Member States;
(2) 'works of art' means the objects listed in Annex IX, Part A;
(3) 'collectors' items' means the objects listed in Annex IX, Part B;
(4) 'antiques' means the objects listed in Annex IX, Part C;
(5) 'taxable dealer' means any taxable person who, in the course of his economic activity and with a view to resale, purchases, or applies for the purposes of his business, or imports, second-hand goods, works of art, collectors' items or antiques, whether that taxable person is acting for himself or on behalf of another person pursuant to a contract under which commission is payable on purchase or sale;
(6) 'organiser of a sale by public auction' means any taxable person who, in the course of his economic activity, offers goods for sale by public auction with a view to handing them over to the highest bidder;
(7) 'principal of an organiser of a sale by public auction' means any person who transmits goods to an organiser of a sale by public auction pursuant to a contract under which commission is payable on a sale.

2. Member States need not regard as works of art the objects listed in points (5), (6) or (7) of Annex IX, Part A.

3. The contract under which commission is payable on a sale, referred to in point (7) of paragraph 1, must provide that the organiser of the sale is to put up the goods for public auction in his own name but on behalf of his principal and that he is to hand over the goods, in his own name but on behalf of his principal, to the highest bidder at the public auction.

Commentary—*De Voil Indirect Tax Service* **V3.532**.
Simon's Tax Cases—Art 311(1)(5), *Jyske Finans A/S v Skatteministeriet (Nordania Finans A/S and BG Factoring A/S intervening)* [2006] STC 1744*.

Section 2 Special arrangements for taxable dealers

Subsection 1 Margin scheme

Article 312

For the purposes of this Subsection, the following definitions shall apply:

(1) 'selling price' means everything which constitutes the consideration obtained or to be obtained by the taxable dealer from the customer or from a third party, including subsidies directly linked to the transaction, taxes, duties, levies and charges and incidental expenses such as commission, packaging, transport and insurance costs charged by the taxable dealer to the customer, but excluding the amounts referred to in Article 79;
(2) 'purchase price' means everything which constitutes the consideration, for the purposes of point (1), obtained or to be obtained from the taxable dealer by his supplier.

Article 313

1. In respect of the supply of second-hand goods, works of art, collectors' items or antiques carried out by taxable dealers, Member States shall apply a special scheme for taxing the profit margin made by the taxable dealer, in accordance with the provisions of this Subsection.

2. Pending introduction of the definitive arrangements referred to in Article 402, the scheme referred to in paragraph 1 of this Article shall not apply to the supply of new means of transport, carried out in accordance with the conditions specified in Article 138(1) and (2)(*a*).

Article 314

The margin scheme shall apply to the supply by a taxable dealer of second-hand goods, works of art, collectors' items or antiques where those goods have been supplied to him within the Community by one of the following persons:

(*a*) a non-taxable person;
(*b*) another taxable person, in so far as the supply of goods by that other taxable person is exempt pursuant to Article 136;
(*c*) another taxable person, in so far as the supply of goods by that other taxable person is covered by the exemption for small enterprises provided for in Articles 282 to 292 and involves capital goods;

(*d*) another taxable dealer, in so far as VAT has been applied to the supply of goods by that other taxable dealer in accordance with this margin scheme.

Article 315

The taxable amount in respect of the supply of goods as referred to in Article 314 shall be the profit margin made by the taxable dealer, less the amount of VAT relating to the profit margin. The profit margin of the taxable dealer shall be equal to the difference between the selling price charged by the taxable dealer for the goods and the purchase price.

Article 316

1. Member States shall grant taxable dealers the right to opt for application of the margin scheme to the following transactions:

(*a*) the supply of works of art, collectors' items or antiques, which the taxable dealer has imported himself;

(*b*) the supply of works of art supplied to the taxable dealer by their creators or their successors in title;

(*c*) the supply of works of art supplied to the taxable dealer by a taxable person other than a taxable dealer where the reduced rate has been applied to that supply pursuant to Article 103.

2. Member States shall lay down the detailed rules for exercise of the option provided for in paragraph 1, which shall in any event cover a period of at least two calendar years.

Article 317

If a taxable dealer exercises the option under Article 316, the taxable amount shall be determined in accordance with Article 315.

In respect of the supply of works of art, collectors' items or antiques which the taxable dealer has imported himself, the purchase price to be taken into account in calculating the profit margin shall be equal to the taxable amount on importation, determined in accordance with Articles 85 to 89, plus the VAT due or paid on importation.

Article 318

1. In order to simplify the procedure for collecting the tax and after consulting the VAT Committee, Member States may provide that, for certain transactions or for certain categories of taxable dealers, the taxable amount in respect of supplies of goods subject to the margin scheme is to be determined for each tax period during which the taxable dealer must submit the VAT return referred to in Article 250.

In the event that such provision is made in accordance with the first subparagraph, the taxable amount in respect of supplies of goods to which the same rate of VAT is applied shall be the total profit margin made by the taxable dealer less the amount of VAT relating to that margin.

2. The total profit margin shall be equal to the difference between the following two amounts:

(*a*) the total value of supplies of goods subject to the margin scheme and carried out by the taxable dealer during the tax period covered by the return, that is to say, the total of the selling prices;

(*b*) the total value of purchases of goods, as referred to in Article 314, effected by the taxable dealer during the tax period covered by the return, that is to say, the total of the purchase prices.

3. Member States shall take the measures necessary to ensure that the taxable dealers referred to in paragraph 1 do not enjoy unjustified advantage or sustain unjustified harm.

Article 319

The taxable dealer may apply the normal VAT arrangements to any supply covered by the margin scheme.

Article 320

1. Where the taxable dealer applies the normal VAT arrangements to the supply of a work of art, a collectors' item or an antique which he has imported himself, he shall be entitled to deduct from the VAT for which he is liable the VAT due or paid on the import.

Where the taxable dealer applies the normal VAT arrangements to the supply of a work of art supplied to him by its creator, or the creator's successors in title, or by a taxable person other than a taxable dealer, he shall be entitled to deduct from the VAT for which he is liable the VAT due or paid in respect of the work of art supplied to him.

2. A right of deduction shall arise at the time when the VAT due on the supply in respect of which the taxable dealer opts for application of the normal VAT arrangements becomes chargeable.

Article 321

If carried out in accordance with the conditions specified in Articles 146, 147, 148 or 151, the supply of second-hand goods, works of art, collectors' items or antiques subject to the margin scheme shall be exempt.

Article 322

In so far as goods are used for the purpose of supplies carried out by him and subject to the margin scheme, the taxable dealer may not deduct the following from the VAT for which he is liable:

(*a*) the VAT due or paid in respect of works of art, collectors' items or antiques which he has imported himself;

(*b*) the VAT due or paid in respect of works of art which have been, or are to be, supplied to him by their creator or by the creator's successors in title;

(*c*) the VAT due or paid in respect of works of art which have been, or are to be, supplied to him by a taxable person other than a taxable dealer.

Article 323

Taxable persons may not deduct from the VAT for which they are liable the VAT due or paid in respect of goods which have been, or are to be, supplied to them by a taxable dealer, in so far as the supply of those goods by the taxable dealer is subject to the margin scheme.

Article 324

Where the taxable dealer applies both the normal VAT arrangements and the margin scheme, he must show separately in his accounts the transactions falling under each of those arrangements, in accordance with the rules laid down by the Member States.

Article 325

The taxable dealer may not enter separately on the invoices which he issues the VAT relating to supplies of goods to which he applies the margin scheme.

Subsection 2 Transitional arrangements for second-hand means of transport

Article 326

Member States which, at 31 December 1992, were applying special tax arrangements other than the margin scheme to the supply by taxable dealers of second-hand means of transport may, pending introduction of the definitive arrangements referred to in Article 402, continue to apply those arrangements in so far as they comply with, or are adjusted to comply with, the conditions laid down in this Subsection.

Denmark is authorised to introduce tax arrangements as referred to in the first paragraph.

Article 327

1. These transitional arrangements shall apply to supplies of second-hand means of transport carried out by taxable dealers, and subject to the margin scheme.

2. These transitional arrangements shall not apply to the supply of new means of transport carried out in accordance with the conditions specified in Article 138(1) and (2)(*a*).

3. For the purposes of paragraph 1, the land vehicles, vessels and aircraft referred to in point (*a*) of Article 2(2) shall be regarded as 'second-hand means of transport' where they are second-hand goods which do not meet the conditions necessary to be regarded as new means of transport.

Article 328

The VAT due in respect of each supply referred to in Article 327 shall be equal to the amount of VAT that would have been due if that supply had been subject to the normal VAT arrangements, less the amount of VAT regarded as being incorporated by the taxable dealer in the purchase price of the means of transport.

Article 329

The VAT regarded as being incorporated by the taxable dealer in the purchase price of the means of transport shall be calculated in accordance with the following method:

(*a*) the purchase price to be taken into account shall be the purchase price within the meaning of point (2) of Article 312;

(*b*) that purchase price paid by the taxable dealer shall be deemed to include the VAT that would have been due if the taxable dealer's supplier had applied the normal VAT arrangements to the supply;

(*c*) the rate to be taken into account shall be the rate applicable, pursuant to Article 93, in the Member State in the territory of which the place of the supply to the taxable dealer, as determined in accordance with Articles 31 and 32, is deemed to be situated.

Article 330

The VAT due in respect of each supply of means of transport as referred to in Article 327(1), determined in accordance with Article 328, may not be less than the amount of VAT that would be due if that supply were subject to the margin scheme.

Member States may provide that, if the supply is subject to the margin scheme, the margin may not be less than 10% of the selling price within the meaning of point (1) of Article 312.

Article 331

Taxable persons may not deduct from the VAT for which they are liable the VAT due or paid in respect of second-hand means of transport supplied to them by a taxable dealer, in so far as the supply of those goods by the taxable dealer is subject to VAT in accordance with these transitional arrangements.

Article 332

The taxable dealer may not enter separately on the invoices he issues the VAT relating to supplies to which he applies these transitional arrangements.

Section 3 Special arrangements for sales by public auction

Article 333

1. Member States may, in accordance with the provisions of this Section, apply special arrangements for taxation of the profit margin made by an organiser of a sale by public auction in respect of the supply of second-hand goods, works of art, collectors' items or antiques by that organiser, acting in his own name and on behalf of the persons referred to in Article 334, pursuant to a contract under which commission is payable on the sale of those goods by public auction.

2. The arrangements referred to in paragraph 1 shall not apply to the supply of new means of transport, carried out in accordance with the conditions specified in Article 138(1) and (2)(*a*).

Article 334

These special arrangements shall apply to supplies carried out by an organiser of a sale by public auction, acting in his own name, on behalf of one of the following persons:

(*a*) a non-taxable person;

(*b*) another taxable person, in so far as the supply of goods, carried out by that taxable person in accordance with a contract under which commission is payable on a sale, is exempt pursuant to Article 136;

(*c*) another taxable person, in so far as the supply of goods, carried out by that taxable person in accordance with a contract under which commission is payable on a sale, is covered by the exemption for small enterprises provided for in Articles 282 to 292 and involves capital goods;

(*d*) a taxable dealer, in so far as the supply of goods, carried out by that taxable dealer in accordance with a contract under which commission is payable on a sale, is subject to VAT in accordance with the margin scheme.

Article 335

The supply of goods to a taxable person who is an organiser of sales by public auction shall be regarded as taking place when the sale of those goods by public auction takes place.

Article 336

The taxable amount in respect of each supply of goods referred to in this Section shall be the total amount invoiced in accordance with Article 339 to the purchaser by the organiser of the sale by public auction, less the following:

(*a*) the net amount paid or to be paid by the organiser of the sale by public auction to his principal, as determined in accordance with Article 337;

(*b*) the amount of the VAT payable by the organiser of the sale by public auction in respect of his supply.

Article 337

The net amount paid or to be paid by the organiser of the sale by public auction to his principal shall be equal to the difference between the auction price of the goods and the amount of the commission obtained or to be obtained by the organiser of the sale by public auction from his principal pursuant to the contract under which commission is payable on the sale.

Article 338

Organisers of sales by public auction who supply goods in accordance with the conditions laid down in Articles 333 and 334 must indicate the following in their accounts, in suspense accounts:

(*a*) the amounts obtained or to be obtained from the purchaser of the goods;

(*b*) the amounts reimbursed or to be reimbursed to the vendor of the goods.

The amounts referred to in the first paragraph must be duly substantiated.

Article 339

The organiser of the sale by public auction must issue to the purchaser an invoice itemising the following:

(*a*) the auction price of the goods;
(*b*) taxes, duties, levies and charges;
(*c*) incidental expenses, such as commission, packing, transport and insurance costs, charged by the organiser to the purchaser of the goods.

The invoice issued by the organiser of the sale by public auction must not indicate any VAT separately.

Article 340

1. The organiser of the sale by public auction to whom the goods have been transmitted pursuant to a contract under which commission is payable on a public auction sale must issue a statement to his principal. The statement issued by the organiser of the sale by public auction must specify separately the amount of the transaction, that is to say, the auction price of the goods less the amount of the commission obtained or to be obtained from the principal.

2. The statement drawn up in accordance with paragraph 1 shall serve as the invoice which the principal, where he is a taxable person, must issue to the organiser of the sale by public auction in accordance with Article 220.

Article 341

Member States which apply the arrangements provided for in this Section shall also apply these arrangements to supplies of second-hand means of transport, as defined in Article 327(3), carried out by an organiser of sales by public auction, acting in his own name, pursuant to a contract under which commission is payable on the sale of those goods by public auction, on behalf of a taxable dealer, in so far as those supplies by that taxable dealer would be subject to VAT in accordance with the transitional arrangements for second-hand means of transport.

Section 4 Measures to prevent distortion of competition and tax evasion

Article 342

Member States may take measures concerning the right of deduction in order to ensure that the taxable dealers covered by special arrangements as provided for in Section 2 do not enjoy unjustified advantage or sustain unjustified harm.

Article 343

Acting unanimously on a proposal from the Commission, the Council may authorise any Member State to introduce special measures to combat tax evasion, pursuant to which the VAT due under the margin scheme may not be less than the amount of VAT which would be due if the profit margin were equal to a certain percentage of the selling price.

The percentage of the selling price shall be fixed in the light of the normal profit margins made by economic operators in the sector concerned.

CHAPTER 5
SPECIAL SCHEME FOR INVESTMENT GOLD

Section 1 General provisions

Article 344

1. For the purposes of this Directive, and without prejudice to other Community provisions, 'investment gold' shall mean:

(1) gold, in the form of a bar or a wafer of weights accepted by the bullion markets, of a purity equal to or greater than 995 thousandths, whether or not represented by securities;
(2) gold coins of a purity equal to or greater than 900 thousandths and minted after 1800, which are or have been legal tender in the country of origin, and are normally sold at a price which does not exceed the open market value of the gold contained in the coins by more than 80%.

2. Member States may exclude from this special scheme small bars or wafers of a weight of 1 g or less.

3. For the purposes of this Directive, the coins referred to in point (2) of paragraph 1 shall not be regarded as sold for numismatic interest.

Article 345

Starting in 1999, each Member State shall inform the Commission by 1 July each year of the coins meeting the criteria laid down in point (2) of Article 344(1) which are traded in that Member State. The Commission shall, before 1 December each year, publish a comprehensive list of those coins in the 'C' series of the *Official Journal of the European Union*. Coins included in the published list shall be deemed to fulfil those criteria throughout the year for which the list is published.

Section 2 Exemption from VAT

Article 346

Member States shall exempt from VAT the supply, the intra-Community acquisition and the importation of investment gold, including investment gold represented by certificates for allocated or unallocated gold or traded on gold accounts and including, in particular, gold loans and swaps, involving a right of ownership or claim in respect of investment gold, as well as transactions concerning investment gold involving futures and forward contracts leading to a transfer of right of ownership or claim in respect of investment gold.

Article 347

Member States shall exempt the services of agents who act in the name and on behalf of another person, when they take part in the supply of investment gold for their principal.

Section 3 Taxation option

Article 348

Member States shall allow taxable persons who produce investment gold or transform gold into investment gold the right to opt for the taxation of supplies of investment gold to another taxable person which would otherwise be exempt pursuant to Article 346.

Article 349

1. Member States may allow taxable persons who, in the course of their economic activity, normally supply gold for industrial purposes, the right to opt for the taxation of supplies of gold bars or wafers, as referred to in point (1) of Article 344(1), to another taxable person, which would otherwise be exempt pursuant to Article 346.
2. Member States may restrict the scope of the option provided for in paragraph 1.

Article 350

Where the supplier has exercised the right under Articles 348 and 349 to opt for taxation, Member States shall allow the agent to opt for taxation of the services referred to in Article 347.

Article 351

Member States shall lay down detailed rules for the exercise of the options provided for in this Section, and shall inform the Commission accordingly.

Section 4 Transactions on a regulated gold bullion market

Article 352

Each Member State may, after consulting the VAT Committee, apply VAT to specific transactions relating to investment gold which take place in that Member State between taxable persons who are members of a gold bullion market regulated by the Member State concerned or between such a taxable person and another taxable person who is not a member of that market. However, the Member State may not apply VAT to supplies carried out in accordance with the conditions specified in Article 138 or to exports of investment gold.

Article 353

Member States which, pursuant to Article 352, tax transactions between taxable persons who are members of a regulated gold bullion market shall, for the purposes of simplification, authorise suspension of the tax to be collected and relieve taxable persons of the accounting requirements in respect of VAT.

Section 5 Special rights and obligations for traders in investment gold

Article 354

Where his subsequent supply of investment gold is exempt pursuant to this Chapter, the taxable person shall be entitled to deduct the following:

(*a*) the VAT due or paid in respect of investment gold supplied to him by a person who has exercised the right of option under Articles 348 and 349 or supplied to him in accordance with Section 4;
(*b*) the VAT due or paid in respect of a supply to him, or in respect of an intra-Community acquisition or importation carried out by him, of gold other than investment gold which is subsequently transformed by him or on his behalf into investment gold;
(*c*) the VAT due or paid in respect of services supplied to him consisting in a change of form, weight or purity of gold including investment gold.

Article 355

Taxable persons who produce investment gold or transform gold into investment gold shall be entitled to deduct the VAT due or paid by them in respect of the supply, intra-Community acquisition or importation of goods or services linked to the production or transformation of that gold, as if the subsequent supply of the gold exempted pursuant to Article 346 were taxed.

Article 356

1. Member States shall ensure that traders in investment gold keep, as a minimum, accounts of all substantial transactions in investment gold and keep the documents which enable the customers in such transactions to be identified.

Traders shall keep the information referred to in the first subparagraph for a period of at least five years.

2. Member States may accept equivalent obligations under measures adopted pursuant to other Community legislation, such as Directive 2005/60/EC of the European Parliament and of the Council of 26 October 2005 on the prevention of the use of the financial system for the purpose of money laundering and terrorist financing ([1]), to comply with the requirements under paragraph 1.

3. Member States may lay down obligations which are more stringent, in particular as regards the keeping of special records or special accounting requirements.

(1) OJ L 309, 25.11.2005, p. 15.

CHAPTER 6

SPECIAL SCHEME FOR NON-ESTABLISHED TAXABLE PERSONS SUPPLYING ELECTRONIC SERVICES TO NON-TAXABLE PERSONS

Prospective amendments—Heading to Chapter 6 to be substituted by Council Directive 2008/8/EC art 5(6) with effect from 1 January 2015 (OJ L 44, 20.2.2008 p 11).

Section 1 General provisions

[Article 357

This Chapter shall apply until 31 December 2014.][1][Article 357

Amendments—[1] This article substituted by Council Directive 2008/8/EC art 1(4) with effect from 1 January 2009 (OJ L 44, 20.2.2008 p 11). This article (as substituted by Council Directive 2006/138/EC) previously read as follows—

"This Chapter shall apply until 31 December 2008."

Prospective amendments—Article 357 to be repealed by Council Directive 2008/8/EC art 5(7) with effect from 1 January 2015 (OJ L 44, 20.2.2008 p 11).

Article 358

For the purposes of this Chapter, and without prejudice to other provisions, the following definitions shall apply:

(1) "non-established taxable person" means a taxable person who has not established his business in the territory of the Community and who has no fixed establishment there and who is not otherwise required to be identified pursuant to Article 214;

[(2) "electronic services" and "electronically supplied services" mean the services referred to in point (k) of the first paragraph of Article 59;][1]

(3) "Member State of identification" means the Member State which the non-established taxable person chooses to contact to state when his activity as a taxable person within the territory of the Community commences in accordance with the provisions of this Chapter;

[(4) "Member State of consumption" means the Member State in which, pursuant to Article 58, the supply of the electronic services is deemed to take place;][1]

(5) "VAT return" means the statement containing the information necessary to establish the amount of VAT due in each Member State.

Amendments—[1] Points (2), (4) substituted, by Council Directive 2008/8/EC art 2(11) with effect from 1 January 2010 (OJ L 44, 20.2.2008 p 11). Text previously read as follows—

"(2) 'electronic services' and 'electronically supplied services' mean the services referred to in point (*k*) of Article 56(1);".

"(4) 'Member State of consumption' means the Member State in which, pursuant to Article 57, the supply of the electronic services is deemed to take place;".

Prospective amendments—Article 358 to be substituted by Council Directive 2008/8/EC art 5(8) with effect from 1 January 2015 (OJ L 44, 20.2.2008 p 11).

Section 2 Special scheme for electronically supplied services

Prospective amendments—Heading to Section 2 to be substituted by Council Directive 2008/8/EC art 5(9) with effect from 1 January 2015 (OJ L 44, 20.2.2008 p 11).

Article 358a to be inserted by Council Directive 2008/8/EC art 5(10) with effect from 1 January 2015 (OJ L 44, 20.2.2008 p 11).

Article 359

Member States shall permit any non-established taxable person supplying electronic services to a non-taxable person who is established in a Member State or who has his permanent address or usually resides in a Member State, to use this special scheme. This scheme applies to all electronic services supplied in the Community.

Prospective amendments—Articles 359–365 to be substituted by Council Directive 2008/8/EC art 5(11) with effect from 1 January 2015 (OJ L 44, 20.2.2008 p 11).

Article 360

The non-established taxable person shall state to the Member State of identification when he commences or ceases his activity as a taxable person, or changes that activity in such a way that he no longer meets the conditions necessary for use of this special scheme. He shall communicate that information electronically.

Prospective amendments—Articles 359–365 to be substituted by Council Directive 2008/8/EC art 5(11) with effect from 1 January 2015 (OJ L 44, 20.2.2008 p 11).

Article 361

1. The information which the non-established taxable person must provide to the Member State of identification when he commences a taxable activity shall contain the following details:

(*a*) name;
(*b*) postal address;
(*c*) electronic addresses, including websites;
(*d*) national tax number, if any;
(*e*) a statement that the person is not identified for VAT purposes within the Community.

2. The non-established taxable person shall notify the Member State of identification of any changes in the information provided.

Prospective amendments—Articles 359–365 to be substituted by Council Directive 2008/8/EC art 5(11) with effect from 1 January 2015 (OJ L 44, 20.2.2008 p 11).

Article 362

The Member State of identification shall allocate to the non-established taxable person an individual VAT identification number and shall notify him of that number by electronic means. On the basis of the information used for that identification, Member States of consumption may have recourse to their own identification systems.

Prospective amendments—Articles 359–365 to be substituted by Council Directive 2008/8/EC art 5(11) with effect from 1 January 2015 (OJ L 44, 20.2.2008 p 11).

Article 363

The Member State of identification shall strike the non-established taxable person from the identification register in the following cases:

(*a*) if he notifies that Member State that he no longer supplies electronic services;
(*b*) if it may otherwise be assumed that his taxable activities have ceased;
(*c*) if he no longer meets the conditions necessary for use of this special scheme;
(*d*) if he persistently fails to comply with the rules relating to this special scheme.

Prospective amendments—Articles 359–365 to be substituted by Council Directive 2008/8/EC art 5(11) with effect from 1 January 2015 (OJ L 44, 20.2.2008 p 11).

Article 364

The non-established taxable person shall submit by electronic means to the Member State of identification a VAT return for each calendar quarter, whether or not electronic services have been supplied. The VAT return shall be submitted within 20 days following the end of the tax period covered by the return.

Prospective amendments—Articles 359–365 to be substituted by Council Directive 2008/8/EC art 5(11) with effect from 1 January 2015 (OJ L 44, 20.2.2008 p 11).

Article 365

The VAT return shall show the identification number and, for each Member State of consumption in which VAT is due, the total value, exclusive of VAT, of supplies of electronic services carried out during the tax period and the total amount of the corresponding VAT. The applicable rates of VAT and the total VAT due must also be indicated on the return.

Prospective amendments—Articles 359–365 to be substituted by Council Directive 2008/8/EC art 5(11) with effect from 1 January 2015 (OJ L 44, 20.2.2008 p 11).

Article 366

1. The VAT return shall be made out in euro.

Member States which have not adopted the euro may require the VAT return to be made out in their national currency. If the supplies have been made in other currencies, the non-established taxable person shall, for the purposes of completing the VAT return, use the exchange rate applying on the last day of the tax period.

2. The conversion shall be made by applying the exchange rates published by the European Central Bank for that day, or, if there is no publication on that day, on the next day of publication.

Prospective amendments—Para 1 to be substituted by Council Directive 2008/8/EC art 5(12) with effect from 1 January 2015 (OJ L 44, 20.2.2008 p 11).

Article 367

The non-established taxable person shall pay the VAT when submitting the VAT return.

Payment shall be made to a bank account denominated in euro, designated by the Member State of identification. Member States which have not adopted the euro may require payment to be made to a bank account denominated in their own currency.

Prospective amendments—Articles 367, 368 to be substituted by Council Directive 2008/8/EC art 5(13) with effect from 1 January 2015 (OJ L 44, 20.2.2008 p 11).

Article 368

The non-established taxable person making use of this special scheme may not deduct VAT pursuant to Article 168 of this Directive. Notwithstanding Article 1(1) of Directive 86/560/EEC, the taxable person in question shall be refunded in accordance with the said Directive. Articles 2(2) and (3) and Article 4(2) of Directive 86/560/EEC shall not apply to refunds relating to electronic services covered by this special scheme.

Prospective amendments—Articles 367, 368 to be substituted by Council Directive 2008/8/EC art 5(13) with effect from 1 January 2015 (OJ L 44, 20.2.2008 p 11).

Article 369

1. The non-established taxable person shall keep records of the transactions covered by this special scheme. Those records must be sufficiently detailed to enable the tax authorities of the Member State of consumption to verify that the VAT return is correct.

2. The records referred to in paragraph 1 must be made available electronically on request to the Member State of identification and to the Member State of consumption.

Those records must be kept for a period of ten years from the end of the year during which the transaction was carried out.

Prospective amendments—Para 1 to be substituted by Council Directive 2008/8/EC art 5(14) with effect from 1 January 2015 (OJ L 44, 20.2.2008 p 11).

New Section 3 (articles 369a–369k) to be inserted by Council Directive 2008/8/EC art 5(15) with effect from 1 January 2015 (OJ L 44, 20.2.2008 p 11).

TITLE XIII
DEROGATIONS

CHAPTER 1
DEROGATIONS APPLYING UNTIL THE ADOPTION OF DEFINITIVE ARRANGEMENTS

Section 1 Derogations for States which were members of the Community on 1 January 1978

Article 370

Member States which, at 1 January 1978, taxed the transactions listed in Annex X, Part A, may continue to tax those transactions.

Article 371

Member States which, at 1 January 1978, exempted the transactions listed in Annex X, Part B, may continue to exempt those transactions, in accordance with the conditions applying in the Member State concerned on that date.

Commentary—*De Voil Indirect Tax Service* **V4.275**.

Simon's Tax Cases—*Norbury Developments Ltd v C&E Comrs* [1999] STC 511*; *Finanzamt Goslar v Breitsohl* [2001] STC 355*; *Idéal Tourisme SA v Belgian State* [2001] STC 1386*.

Article 372

Member States which, at 1 January 1978, applied provisions derogating from the principle of immediate deduction laid down in the first paragraph of Article 179 may continue to apply those provisions.

Article 373

Member States which, at 1 January 1978, applied provisions derogating from Article 28 or from point (*c*) of the first paragraph of Article 79 may continue to apply those provisions.

Article 374

By way of derogation from Articles 169 and 309, Member States which, at 1 January 1978, exempted, without deductibility of the VAT paid at the preceding stage, the services of travel agents, as referred to in Article 309, may continue to exempt those services. That derogation shall apply also in respect of travel agents acting in the name and on behalf of the traveller.

Section 2 Derogations for States which acceded to the Community after 1 January 1978

Article 375

Greece may continue to exempt the transactions listed in points (2), (8), (9), (11) and (12) of Annex X, Part B, in accordance with the conditions applying in that Member State on 1 January 1987.

Article 376

Spain may continue to exempt the supply of services performed by authors, listed in point (2) of Annex X, Part B, and the transactions listed in points (11) and (12) of Annex X, Part B, in accordance with the conditions applying in that Member State on 1 January 1993.

Article 377

Portugal may continue to exempt the transactions listed in points (2), (4), (7), (9), (10) and (13) of Annex X, Part B, in accordance with the conditions applying in that Member State on 1 January 1989.

Article 378

1. Austria may continue to tax the transactions listed in point (2) of Annex X, Part A.

2. For as long as the same exemptions are applied in any of the Member States which were members of the Community on 31 December 1994, Austria may, in accordance with the conditions applying in that Member State on the date of its accession, continue to exempt the following transactions:

(*a*) the transactions listed in points (5) and (9) of Annex X, Part B;

(*b*) with deductibility of the VAT paid at the preceding stage, all parts of international passenger transport operations, carried out by air, sea or inland waterway, other than passenger transport operations on Lake Constance.

Article 379

1. Finland may continue to tax the transactions listed in point (2) of Annex X, Part A, for as long as the same transactions are taxed in any of the Member States which were members of the Community on 31 December 1994.

2. Finland may, in accordance with the conditions applying in that Member State on the date of its accession, continue to exempt the supply of services by authors, artists and performers, listed in point (2) of Annex X, Part B, and the transactions listed in points (5), (9) and (10) of Annex X, Part B, for as long as the same exemptions are applied in any of the Member States which were members of the Community on 31 December 1994.

Article 380

Sweden may, in accordance with the conditions applying in that Member State on the date of its accession, continue to exempt the supply of services by authors, artists and performers, listed in point (2) of Annex X, Part B, and the transactions listed in points (1), (9) and (10) of Annex X, Part B, for as long as the same exemptions are applied in any of the Member States which were members of the Community on 31 December 1994.

Article 381

The Czech Republic may, in accordance with the conditions applying in that Member State on the date of its accession, continue to exempt the international transport of passengers, as referred to in point (10) of Annex X, Part B, for as long as the same exemption is applied in any of the Member States which were members of the Community on 30 April 2004.

Article 382

Estonia may, in accordance with the conditions applying in that Member State on the date of its accession, continue to exempt the international transport of passengers, as referred to in point (10) of Annex X, Part B, for as long as the same exemption is applied in any of the Member States which were members of the Community on 30 April 2004.

Article 383

Cyprus may, in accordance with the conditions applying in that Member State on the date of its accession, continue to exempt the following transactions:

(*a*) the supply of building land referred to in point (9) of Annex X, Part B, until 31 December 2007;

(*b*) the international transport of passengers, as referred to in point (10) of Annex X, Part B, for as long as the same exemption is applied in any of the Member States which were members of the Community on 30 April 2004.

Article 384

For as long as the same exemptions are applied in any of the Member States which were members of the Community on 30 April 2004, Latvia may, in accordance with the conditions applying in that Member State on the date of its accession, continue to exempt the following transactions:

(*a*) the supply of services by authors, artists and performers, as referred to in point (2) of Annex X, Part B;

(*b*) the international transport of passengers, as referred to in point (10) of Annex X, Part B.

Article 385

Lithuania may, in accordance with the conditions applying in that Member State on the date of its accession, continue to exempt the international transport of passengers, as referred to in point (10) of Annex X, Part B, for as long as the same exemption is applied in any of the Member States which were members of the Community on 30 April 2004.

Article 386

Hungary may, in accordance with the conditions applying in that Member State on the date of its accession, continue to exempt the international transport of passengers, as referred to in point (10) of Annex X, Part B, for as long as the same exemption is applied in any of the Member States which were members of the Community on 30 April 2004.

Article 387

For as long as the same exemptions are applied in any of the Member States which were members of the Community on 30 April 2004, Malta may, in accordance with the conditions applying in that Member State on the date of its accession, continue to exempt the following transactions:

(*a*) without deductibility of the VAT paid at the preceding stage, the supply of water by a body governed by public law, as referred to in point (8) of Annex X, Part B;

(*b*) without deductibility of the VAT paid at the preceding stage, the supply of buildings and building land, as referred to in point (9) of Annex X, Part B;

(*c*) with deductibility of the VAT paid at the preceding stage, inland passenger transport, international passenger transport and domestic inter-island sea passenger transport, as referred to in point (10) of Annex X, Part B.

Article 388

Poland may, in accordance with the conditions applying in that Member State on the date of its accession, continue to exempt the international transport of passengers, as referred to in point (10) of Annex X, Part B, for as long as the same exemption is applied in any of the Member States which were members of the Community on 30 April 2004.

Article 389

Slovenia may, in accordance with the conditions applying in that Member State on the date of its accession, continue to exempt the international transport of passengers, as referred to in point (10) of Annex X, Part B, for as long as the same exemption is applied in any of the Member States which were members of the Community on 30 April 2004.

Article 390

Slovakia may, in accordance with the conditions applying in that Member State on the date of its accession, continue to exempt the international transport of passengers, as referred to in point (10) of Annex X, Part B, for as long as the same exemption is applied in any of the Member States which were members of the Community on 30 April 2004.

Section 3 Provisions common to Sections 1 and 2

Article 391

Member States which exempt the transactions referred to in Articles 371, 375, 376 or 377, Article 378(2), Article 379(2) or Articles 380 to 390 may grant taxable persons the right to opt for taxation of those transactions.

Commentary—*De Voil Indirect Tax Service* **V4.275**.

Simon's Tax Cases—*Finanzamt Goslar v Breitsohl* [2001] STC 355*.

Article 392

Member States may provide that, in respect of the supply of buildings and building land purchased for the purpose of resale by a taxable person for whom the VAT on the purchase was not deductible, the taxable amount shall be the difference between the selling price and the purchase price.

Article 393

1. With a view to facilitating the transition to the definitive arrangements referred to in Article 402, the Council shall, on the basis of a report from the Commission, review the situation with regard to the derogations provided for in Sections 1 and 2 and shall, acting in accordance with Article 93 of the Treaty decide whether any or all of those derogations is to be abolished.

2. By way of definitive arrangements, passenger transport shall be taxed in the Member State of departure for that part of the journey taking place within the Community, in accordance with the detailed rules to be laid down by the Council, acting in accordance with Article 93 of the Treaty.

CHAPTER 2

DEROGATIONS SUBJECT TO AUTHORISATION

Section 1 Simplification measures and measures to prevent tax evasion or avoidance

Article 394

Member States which, at 1 January 1977, applied special measures to simplify the procedure for collecting VAT or to prevent certain forms of tax evasion or avoidance may retain them provided that they have notified the Commission accordingly before 1 January 1978 and that such simplification measures comply with the criterion laid down in the second subparagraph of Article 395(1).

Article 395

1. The Council, acting unanimously on a proposal from the Commission, may authorise any Member State to introduce special measures for derogation from the provisions of this Directive, in order to simplify the procedure for collecting VAT or to prevent certain forms of tax evasion or avoidance.

Measures intended to simplify the procedure for collecting VAT may not, except to a negligible extent, affect the overall amount of the tax revenue of the Member State collected at the stage of final consumption.

2. A Member State wishing to introduce the measure referred to in paragraph 1 shall send an application to the Commission and provide it with all the necessary information. If the Commission considers that it does not have all the necessary information, it shall contact the Member State concerned within two months of receipt of the application and specify what additional information is required.

Once the Commission has all the information it considers necessary for appraisal of the request it shall within one month notify the requesting Member State accordingly and it shall transmit the request, in its original language, to the other Member States.

3. Within three months of giving the notification referred to in the second subparagraph of paragraph 2, the Commission shall present to the Council either an appropriate proposal or, should it object to the derogation requested, a communication setting out its objections.

4. The procedure laid down in paragraphs 2 and 3 shall, in any event, be completed within eight months of receipt of the application by the Commission.

Simon's Tax Cases—*C&E Comrs v Next plc* [1995] STC 651*; *Primback Ltd v C&E Comrs* [1996] STC 757*; *Finanzamt Bergisch Gladbach v Skripalle* (Case C-63/96) [1997] STC 1035*; *Finanzamt Sulingen v Sudholz* [2005] STC 747*.
Art 395(1), *Genius Holding BV v Staatssecretaris van Financiën* [1991] STC 239*; *'K' Line Air Service Europe BV v Eulaerts NV and Belgian State* (Case C-131/91) [1996] STC 597*.

Section 2 International agreements

Article 396

1. The Council, acting unanimously on a proposal from the Commission, may authorise any Member State to conclude with a third country or an international body an agreement which may contain derogations from this Directive.

2. A Member State wishing to conclude an agreement as referred to in paragraph 1 shall send an application to the Commission and provide it with all the necessary information. If the Commission considers that it does not have all the necessary information, it shall contact the Member State concerned within two months of receipt of the application and specify what additional information is required.

VAT

Once the Commission has all the information it considers necessary for appraisal of the request it shall within one month notify the requesting Member State accordingly and it shall transmit the request, in its original language, to the other Member States.

3. Within three months of giving the notification referred to in the second subparagraph of paragraph 2, the Commission shall present to the Council either an appropriate proposal or, should it object to the derogation requested, a communication setting out its objections.

4. The procedure laid down in paragraphs 2 and 3 shall, in any event, be completed within eight months of receipt of the application by the Commission.

TITLE XIV
MISCELLANEOUS

CHAPTER 1
IMPLEMENTING MEASURES

Article 397

The Council, acting unanimously on a proposal from the Commission, shall adopt the measures necessary to implement this Directive.

CHAPTER 2
VAT COMMITTEE

Article 398

1. An advisory committee on value added tax, called 'the VAT Committee', is set up.

2. The VAT Committee shall consist of representatives of the Member States and of the Commission.

The chairman of the Committee shall be a representative of the Commission.

Secretarial services for the Committee shall be provided by the Commission.

3. The VAT Committee shall adopt its own rules of procedure.

4. In addition to the points forming the subject of consultation pursuant to this Directive, the VAT Committee shall examine questions raised by its chairman, on his own initiative or at the request of the representative of a Member State, which concern the application of Community provisions on VAT.

Simon's Tax Cases—*Stradasfalti Srl v Agenzia delle Entrate – Ufficio di Trento* [2007] STC 508*.

CHAPTER 3
CONVERSION RATES

Article 399

Without prejudice to any other particular provisions, the equivalents in national currency of the amounts in euro specified in this Directive shall be determined on the basis of the euro conversion rate applicable on 1 January 1999. Member States having acceded to the European Union after that date, which have not adopted the euro as single currency, shall use the euro conversion rate applicable on the date of their accession.

Article 400

When converting the amounts referred to in Article 399 into national currencies, Member States may adjust the amounts resulting from that conversion either upwards or downwards by up to 10%.

CHAPTER 4
OTHER TAXES, DUTIES AND CHARGES

Article 401

Without prejudice to other provisions of Community law, this Directive shall not prevent a Member State from maintaining or introducing taxes on insurance contracts, taxes on betting and gambling, excise duties, stamp duties or, more generally, any taxes, duties or charges which cannot be characterised as turnover taxes, provided that the collecting of those taxes, duties or charges does not give rise, in trade between Member States, to formalities connected with the crossing of frontiers.

Simon's Tax Cases—*KÖGÁZ rt and others v Zala Megyei Közigazgatàsi Hivatal Vezetoje, OTP Garancia Biztositó rt v Vas Megvei Közigazgatàsi Hivatal* [2008] STC 2367*.

TITLE XV
FINAL PROVISIONS

CHAPTER 1
TRANSITIONAL ARRANGEMENTS FOR THE TAXATION OF TRADE BETWEEN MEMBER STATES

Article 402

1. The arrangements provided for in this Directive for the taxation of trade between Member States are transitional and shall be replaced by definitive arrangements based in principle on the taxation in the Member State of origin of the supply of goods or services.

2. Having concluded, upon examination of the report referred to in Article 404, that the conditions for transition to the definitive arrangements are met, the Council shall, acting in accordance with Article 93 of the Treaty, adopt the provisions necessary for the entry into force and for the operation of the definitive arrangements.

Article 403

The Council shall, acting in accordance with Article 93 of the Treaty, adopt Directives appropriate for the purpose of supplementing the common system of VAT and, in particular, for the progressive restriction or the abolition of derogations from that system.

Article 404

Every four years starting from the adoption of this Directive, the Commission shall, on the basis of information obtained from the Member States, present a report to the European Parliament and to the Council on the operation of the common system of VAT in the Member States and, in particular, on the operation of the transitional arrangements for taxing trade between Member States. That report shall be accompanied, where appropriate, by proposals concerning the definitive arrangements.

CHAPTER 2
TRANSITIONAL MEASURES APPLICABLE IN THE CONTEXT OF ACCESSION TO THE EUROPEAN UNION

Article 405

For the purposes of this Chapter, the following definitions shall apply:

(1) 'Community' means the territory of the Community as defined in point (1) of Article 5 before the accession of new Member States;

(2) 'new Member States' means the territory of the Member States which acceded to the European Union after 1 January 1995, as defined for each of those Member States in point (2) of Article 5;

(3) 'enlarged Community' means the territory of the Community as defined in point (1) of Article 5 after the accession of new Member States.

Article 406

The provisions in force at the time the goods were placed under temporary importation arrangements with total exemption from import duty or under one of the arrangements or situations referred to in Article 156, or under similar arrangements or situations in one of the new Member States, shall continue to apply until the goods cease to be covered by these arrangements or situations after the date of accession, where the following conditions are met:

(*a*) the goods entered the Community or one of the new Member States before the date of accession;

(*b*) the goods were placed, on entry into the Community or one of the new Member States, under these arrangements or situations;

(*c*) the goods have not ceased to be covered by these arrangements or situations before the date of accession.

Article 407

The provisions in force at the time the goods were placed under customs transit arrangements shall continue to apply until the goods cease to be covered by these arrangements after the date of accession, where the following conditions are met:

(*a*) the goods were placed, before the date of accession, under customs transit arrangements;

(*b*) the goods have not ceased to be covered by these arrangements before the date of accession.

Article 408

1. The following shall be treated as an importation of goods where it is shown that the goods were in free circulation in one of the new Member States or in the Community:

(*a*) the removal, including irregular removal, of goods from temporary importation arrangements under which they were placed before the date of accession under the conditions provided for in Article 406;
(*b*) the removal, including irregular removal, of goods either from one of the arrangements or situations referred to in Article 156 or from similar arrangements or situations under which they were placed before the date of accession under the conditions provided for in Article 406;
(*c*) the cessation of one of the arrangements referred to in Article 407, started before the date of accession in the territory of one of the new Member States, for the purposes of a supply of goods for consideration effected before that date in the territory of that Member State by a taxable person acting as such;
(*d*) any irregularity or offence committed during customs transit arrangements started under the conditions referred to in point (*c*).

2. In addition to the case referred to in paragraph 1, the use after the date of accession within the territory of a Member State, by a taxable or non-taxable person, of goods supplied to him before the date of accession within the territory of the Community or one of the new Member States shall be treated as an importation of goods where the following conditions are met:

(*a*) the supply of those goods has been exempted, or was likely to be exempted, either under points (*a*) and (*b*) of Article 146(1) or under a similar provision in the new Member States;
(*b*) the goods were not imported into one of the new Member States or into the Community before the date of accession.

Article 409

In the cases referred to in Article 408(1), the place of import within the meaning of Article 61 shall be the Member State within whose territory the goods cease to be covered by the arrangements or situations under which they were placed before the date of accession.

Article 410

1. By way of derogation from Article 71, the importation of goods within the meaning of Article 408 shall terminate without the occurrence of a chargeable event if one of the following conditions is met:

(*a*) the imported goods are dispatched or transported outside the enlarged Community;
(*b*) the imported goods within the meaning of Article 408(1)(*a*) are other than means of transport and are redispatched or transported to the Member State from which they were exported and to the person who exported them;
(*c*) the imported goods within the meaning of Article 408(1)(*a*) are means of transport which were acquired or imported before the date of accession in accordance with the general conditions of taxation in force on the domestic market of

one of the new Member States or of one of the Member States of the Community or which have not been subject, by reason of their exportation, to any exemption from, or refund of, VAT.

2. The condition referred to in paragraph 1(*c*) shall be deemed to be fulfilled in the following cases:

(*a*) when the date of first entry into service of the means of transport was more than eight years before the accession to the European Union.
(*b*) when the amount of tax due by reason of the importation is insignificant.

CHAPTER 3

TRANSPOSITION AND ENTRY INTO FORCE

Article 411

1. Directive 67/227/EEC and Directive 77/388/EEC are repealed, without prejudice to the obligations of the Member States concerning the time-limits, listed in Annex XI, Part B, for the transposition into national law and the implementation of those Directives.

2. References to the repealed Directives shall be construed as references to this Directive and shall be read in accordance with the correlation table in Annex XII.

Article 412

1. Member States shall bring into force the laws, regulations and administrative provisions necessary to comply with Article 2 (3), Article 44, Article 59(1), Article 399 and Annex III, point (18) with effect from 1 January 2008. They shall forthwith communicate to the Commission the text of those provisions and a correlation table between those provisions and this Directive.

When Member States adopt those provisions, they shall contain a reference to this Directive or be accompanied by such a reference on the occasion of their official publication. Member States shall determine how such reference is to be made.

2. Member States shall communicate to the Commission the text of the main provisions of national law which they adopt in the field covered by this Directive.

Article 413

This Directive shall enter into force on 1 January 2007.

Article 414

This Directive is addressed to the Member States.

Done at Brussels, 28 November 2006.

For the Council

The President

E. HEINÄLUOMA

ANNEX I

LIST OF THE ACTIVITIES REFERRED TO IN THE THIRD SUBPARAGRAPH OF ARTICLE 13(1)

(1) Telecommunications services;

(2) supply of water, gas, electricity and thermal energy;

(3) transport of goods;

(4) port and airport services;

(5) passenger transport;

(6) supply of new goods manufactured for sale;

(7) transactions in respect of agricultural products, carried out by agricultural intervention agencies pursuant to Regulations on the common organisation of the market in those products;

(8) organisation of trade fairs and exhibitions;

(9) warehousing;

(10) activities of commercial publicity bodies;

(11) activities of travel agents;

(12) running of staff shops, cooperatives and industrial canteens and similar institutions;

(13) activities carried out by radio and television bodies in so far as these are not exempt pursuant to Article 132(1)(q).

ANNEX II

[INDICATIVE LIST OF THE ELECTRONICALLY SUPPLIED SERVICES REFERRED TO IN ARTICLE 58 AND POINT (K) OF THE FIRST PARAGRAPH OF ARTICLE 59]

Amendments—Heading to Annex II substituted, by Council Directive 2008/8/EC art 2(12) with effect from 1 January 2010 (OJ L 44, 20.2.2008 p 11). Heading previously read as follows—
"Indicative List of the Electronically Supplied Services Referred to in Point (K) of Article 56(1)".

Prospective amendments—Heading to Annex II to be further substituted by Council Directive 2008/8/EC art 5(16) with effect from 1 January 2015 (OJ L 44, 20.2.2008 p 11).

(1) Website supply, web-hosting, distance maintenance of programmes and equipment;

(2) supply of software and updating thereof;

(3) supply of images, text and information and making available of databases;

(4) supply of music, films and games, including games of chance and gambling games, and of political, cultural, artistic, sporting, scientific and entertainment broadcasts and events;

(5) supply of distance teaching.

ANNEX III

LIST OF SUPPLIES OF GOODS AND SERVICES TO WHICH THE REDUCED RATES REFERRED TO IN ARTICLE 98 MAY BE APPLIED

(1) Foodstuffs (including beverages but excluding alcoholic beverages) for human and animal consumption; live animals, seeds, plants and ingredients normally intended for use in the preparation of foodstuffs; products normally used to supplement foodstuffs or as a substitute for foodstuffs;

(2) supply of water;

(3) pharmaceutical products of a kind normally used for health care, prevention of illnesses and as treatment for medical and veterinary purposes, including products used for contraception and sanitary protection;

(4) medical equipment, aids and other appliances normally intended to alleviate or treat disability, for the exclusive personal use of the disabled, including the repair of such goods, and supply of children's car seats;

(5) transport of passengers and their accompanying luggage;

[(6) supply, including on loan by libraries, of books on all physical means of support (including brochures, leaflets and similar printed matter, children's picture, drawing or colouring books, music printed or in manuscript form, maps and hydrographic or similar charts), newspapers and periodicals, other than material wholly or predominantly devoted to advertising;][1]

(7) admission to shows, theatres, circuses, fairs, amusement parks, concerts, museums, zoos, cinemas, exhibitions and similar cultural events and facilities;

(8) reception of radio and television broadcasting services;

(9) supply of services by writers, composers and performing artists, or of the royalties due to them;

(10) provision, construction, renovation and alteration of housing, as part of a social policy;

[(10a) renovation and repairing of private dwellings, excluding materials which account for a significant part of the value of the service supplied;

(10b) window-cleaning and cleaning in private households;][1]

(11) supply of goods and services of a kind normally intended for use in agricultural production but excluding capital goods such as machinery or buildings;

(12) accommodation provided in hotels and similar establishments, including the provision of holiday accommodation and the letting of places on camping or caravan sites;

[(12a) restaurant and catering services, it being possible to exclude the supply of (alcoholic and/or non-alcoholic) beverages;][1]

(13) admission to sporting events;

(14) use of sporting facilities;

(15) supply of goods and services by organisations recognised as being devoted to social wellbeing by Member States and engaged in welfare or social security work, in so far as those transactions are not exempt pursuant to Articles 132, 135 and 136;

(16) supply of services by undertakers and cremation services, and the supply of goods related thereto;

(17) provision of medical and dental care and thermal treatment in so far as those services are not exempt pursuant to points (*b*) to (*e*) of Article 132(1);

(18) supply of services provided in connection with street cleaning, refuse collection and waste treatment, other than the supply of such services by bodies referred to in Article 13.

[(19) minor repairing of bicycles, shoes and leather goods, clothing and household linen (including mending and alteration);

(20) domestic care services such as home help and care of young, elderly, sick or disabled;

(21) hairdressing.][1]

Amendments—[1] Point 6 substituted, and points (10a), (10b), (12a), (19)–(21) inserted, by Council Directive 2009/47/EC art 1, Annex, with effect from 1 June 2009 (OJ L 116, 9.5.2009 p 18). Text previously read as follows—

"(6) supply, including on loan by libraries, of books (including brochures, leaflets and similar printed matter, children's picture, drawing or colouring books, music printed or in manuscript form, maps and hydrographic or similar charts), newspapers and periodicals, other than material wholly or predominantly devoted to advertising;".

Simon's Tax Cases—*Finanzamt Rendsburg v Harbs* [2006] STC 340*.

ANNEX IV

LIST OF THE SERVICES REFERRED TO IN ARTICLE 106

(*1*) *Minor repairing of:*

(*a*) *bicycles;*

(*b*) *shoes and leather goods;*

(*c*) *clothing and household linen* (*including mending and alteration*)*;*

(*2*) *renovation and repairing of private dwellings, excluding materials which account for a significant part of the value of the service supplied;*

(*3*) *window-cleaning and cleaning in private households;*

(*4*) *domestic care services such as home help and care of the young, elderly, sick or disabled;*

(*5*) *hairdressing.*[1]

Amendments—[1] Annex IV repealed by Council Directive 2009/47/EC art 1, Annex, with effect from 1 June 2009 (OJ L 116, 9.5.2009 p 18).

ANNEX V

CATEGORIES OF GOODS COVERED BY WAREHOUSING ARRANGEMENTS OTHER THAN CUSTOMS WAREHOUSING AS PROVIDED FOR UNDER ARTICLE 160(2)

	CN-code	*Description of goods*
(1)	0701	Potatoes
(2)	0711 20	Olives
(3)	0801	Coconuts, Brazil nuts and cashew nuts
(4)	0802	Other nuts

	CN-code	Description of goods
(5)	0901 11 00 0901 12 00	Coffee, not roasted
(6)	0902	Tea
(7)	1001 to 1005 1007 to 1008	Cereals
(8)	1006	Husked rice
(9)	1201 to 1207	Grains and oil seeds (including soya beans) and oleaginous fruits
(10)	1507 to 1515	Vegetable oils and fats and their fractions, whether or not refined, but not chemically modified
(11)	1701 11 1701 12	Raw sugar
(12)	1801	Cocoa beans, whole or broken, raw or roasted
(13)	2709 2710 2711 12 2711 13	Mineral oils (including propane and butane; also including crude petroleum oils)
(14)	Chapters 28 and 29	Chemicals in bulk
(15)	4001 4002	Rubber, in primary forms or in plates, sheets or strip
(16)	5101	Wool
(17)	7106	Silver
(18)	7110 11 00 7110 21 00 7110 31 00	Platinum (palladium, rhodium)
(19)	7402 7403 7405 7408	Copper
(20)	7502	Nickel
(21)	7601	Aluminium
(22)	7801	Lead
(23)	7901	Zinc
(24)	8001	Tin
(25)	ex 8112 92 ex 8112 99	Indium

ANNEX VI

LIST OF SUPPLIES OF GOODS AND SERVICES AS REFERRED TO IN POINT (D) OF ARTICLE 199(1)

(1) Supply of ferrous and non ferrous waste, scrap, and used materials including that of semi-finished products resulting from the processing, manufacturing or melting down of ferrous and non-ferrous metals and their alloys;

(2) supply of ferrous and non-ferrous semi-processed products and certain associated processing services;

(3) supply of residues and other recyclable materials consisting of ferrous and non-ferrous metals, their alloys, slag, ash, scale and industrial residues containing metals or their alloys and supply of selection, cutting, fragmenting and pressing services of these products;

(4) supply of, and certain processing services relating to, ferrous and non-ferrous waste as well as parings, scrap, waste and used and recyclable material consisting of cullet, glass, paper, paperboard and board, rags, bone, leather, imitation leather, parchment, raw hides and skins, tendons and sinews, twine, cordage, rope, cables, rubber and plastic;

(5) supply of the materials referred to in this annex after processing in the form of cleaning, polishing, selection, cutting, fragmenting, pressing or casting into ingots;

(6) supply of scrap and waste from the working of base materials.

ANNEX VII

LIST OF THE AGRICULTURAL PRODUCTION ACTIVITIES REFERRED TO IN POINT (4) OF ARTICLE 295(1)

(1) Crop production:

(*a*) general agriculture, including viticulture;

(*b*) growing of fruit (including olives) and of vegetables, flowers and ornamental plants, both in the open and under glass;
(*c*) production of mushrooms, spices, seeds and propagating materials;
(*d*) running of nurseries;

(2) stock farming together with cultivation:

(*a*) general stock farming;
(*b*) poultry farming;
(*c*) rabbit farming;
(*d*) beekeeping;
(*e*) silkworm farming;
(*f*) snail farming;

(3) forestry;

(4) fisheries:

(*a*) freshwater fishing;
(*b*) fish farming;
(*c*) breeding of mussels, oysters and other molluscs and crustaceans;
(*d*) frog farming.

ANNEX VIII

INDICATIVE LIST OF THE AGRICULTURAL SERVICES REFERRED TO IN POINT (5) OF ARTICLE 295(1)

(1) Field work, reaping and mowing, threshing, baling, collecting, harvesting, sowing and planting;

(2) packing and preparation for market, such as drying, cleaning, grinding, disinfecting and ensilage of agricultural products;

(3) storage of agricultural products;

(4) stock minding, rearing and fattening;

(5) hiring out, for agricultural purposes, of equipment normally used in agricultural, forestry or fisheries undertakings;

(6) technical assistance;

(7) destruction of weeds and pests, dusting and spraying of crops and land;

(8) operation of irrigation and drainage equipment;

(9) lopping, tree felling and other forestry services.

ANNEX IX

WORKS OF ART, COLLECTORS' ITEMS AND ANTIQUES, AS REFERRED TO IN POINTS (2), (3) AND (4) OF ARTICLE 311(1)

PART A

WORKS OF ART

(1) Pictures, collages and similar decorative plaques, paintings and drawings, executed entirely by hand by the artist, other than plans and drawings for architectural, engineering, industrial, commercial, topographical or similar purposes, hand-decorated manufactured articles, theatrical scenery, studio back cloths or the like of painted canvas (CN code 9701);

(2) original engravings, prints and lithographs, being impressions produced in limited numbers directly in black and white or in colour of one or of several plates executed entirely by hand by the artist, irrespective of the process or of the material employed, but not including any mechanical or photomechanical process (CN code 9702 00 00);

(3) original sculptures and statuary, in any material, provided that they are executed entirely by the artist; sculpture casts the production of which is limited to eight copies and supervised by the artist or his successors in title (CN code 9703 00 00); on an exceptional basis, in cases determined by the Member States, the limit of eight copies may be exceeded for statuary casts produced before 1 January 1989;

(4) tapestries (CN code 5805 00 00) and wall textiles (CN code 6304 00 00) made by hand from original designs provided by artists, provided that there are not more than eight copies of each;

(5) individual pieces of ceramics executed entirely by the artist and signed by him;

(6) enamels on copper, executed entirely by hand, limited to eight numbered copies bearing the signature of the artist or the studio, excluding articles of jewellery and goldsmiths' and silversmiths' wares;

(7) photographs taken by the artist, printed by him or under his supervision, signed and numbered and limited to 30 copies, all sizes and mounts included.

PART B
COLLECTORS' ITEMS

(1) Postage or revenue stamps, postmarks, first-day covers, pre-stamped stationery and the like, used, or if unused not current and not intended to be current (CN code 9704 00 00);

(2) collections and collectors' pieces of zoological, botanical, mineralogical, anatomical, historical, archaeological, palaeontological, ethnographic or numismatic interest (CN code 9705 00 00).

PART C
ANTIQUES

Goods, other than works of art or collectors' items, which are more than 100 years old (CN code 9706 00 00).

ANNEX X

LIST OF TRANSACTIONS COVERED BY THE DEROGATIONS REFERRED TO IN ARTICLES 370 AND 371 AND ARTICLES 375 TO 390

PART A
TRANSACTIONS WHICH MEMBER STATES MAY CONTINUE TO TAX

(1) The supply of services by dental technicians in their professional capacity and the supply of dental prostheses by dentists and dental technicians;

(2) the activities of public radio and television bodies other than those of a commercial nature;

(3) the supply of a building, or parts thereof, or of the land on which it stands, other than as referred to in point (*a*) of Article 12(1), where carried out by taxable persons who were entitled to deduction of the VAT paid at the preceding stage in respect of the building concerned;

(4) the supply of the services of travel agents, as referred to in Article 306, and those of travel agents acting in the name and on behalf of the traveller, in relation to journeys outside the Community.

PART B
TRANSACTIONS WHICH MEMBER STATES MAY CONTINUE TO EXEMPT

(1) Admission to sporting events;

(2) the supply of services by authors, artists, performers, lawyers and other members of the liberal professions, other than the medical and paramedical professions, with the exception of the following:

(*a*) assignments of patents, trade marks and other similar rights, and the granting of licences in respect of such rights;
(*b*) work, other than the supply of contract work, on movable tangible property, carried out for a taxable person;
(*c*) services to prepare or coordinate the carrying out of construction work, such as services provided by architects and by firms providing on-site supervision of works;
(*d*) commercial advertising services;
(*e*) transport and storage of goods, and ancillary services;
(*f*) hiring out of movable tangible property to a taxable person;
(*g*) provision of staff to a taxable person;
(*h*) provision of services by consultants, engineers, planning offices and similar services in scientific, economic or technical fields;
(*i*) compliance with an obligation to refrain from exercising, in whole or in part, a business activity or a right covered by points (*a*) to (*h*) or point (*j*);
(*j*) the services of forwarding agents, brokers, business agents and other independent intermediaries, in so far as they relate to the supply or importation of goods or the supply of services covered by points (*a*) to (*i*);

(3) the supply of telecommunications services, and of goods related thereto, by public postal services;

(4) the supply of services by undertakers and cremation services and the supply of goods related thereto;

(5) transactions carried out by blind persons or by workshops for the blind, provided that those exemptions do not cause significant distortion of competition;

(6) the supply of goods and services to official bodies responsible for the construction, setting out and maintenance of cemeteries, graves and monuments commemorating the war dead;

(7) transactions carried out by hospitals not covered by point (*b*) of Article 132(1);

(8) the supply of water by a body governed by public law;

(9) the supply before first occupation of a building, or parts thereof, or of the land on which it stands and the supply of building land, as referred to in Article 12;

(10) the transport of passengers and, in so far as the transport of the passengers is exempt, the transport of goods accompanying them, such as luggage or motor vehicles, or the supply of services relating to the transport of passengers;

(11) the supply, modification, repair, maintenance, chartering and hiring of aircraft used by State institutions, including equipment incorporated or used in such aircraft;

(12) the supply, modification, repair, maintenance, chartering and hiring of fighting ships;

(13) the supply of the services of travel agents, as referred to in Article 306, and those of travel agents acting in the name and on behalf of the traveller, in relation to journeys within the Community.

ANNEX XI

Simon's Tax Cases—Part B, (4), *Network Insurance Brokers Ltd v C&E Comrs* [1998] STC 742*.
Part B, (9), *Norbury Developments Ltd v C&E Comrs* (Case C-136/97) [1999] STC 511*.

PART A
REPEALED DIRECTIVES WITH THEIR SUCCESSIVE AMENDMENTS

(1) Directive 67/227/EEC (OJ 71, 14.4.1967, p. 1301)
Directive 77/388/EEC
(2) Directive 77/388/EEC (OJ L 145, 13.6.1977, p. 1)
Directive 78/583/EEC (OJ L 194, 19.7.1978, p. 16)
Directive 80/368/EEC (OJ L 90, 3.4.1980, p. 41)
Directive 84/386/EEC (OJ L 208, 3.8.1984, p. 58)
Directive 89/465/EEC (OJ L 226, 3.8.1989, p. 21)
Directive 91/680/EEC (OJ L 376, 31.12.1991, p. 1) — (except for Article 2)
Directive 92/77/EEC (OJ L 316, 31.10.1992, p. 1)
Directive 92/111/EEC (OJ L 384, 30.12.1992, p. 47)
Directive 94/4/EC (OJ L 60, 3.3.1994, p. 14) — (only Article 2)
Directive 94/5/EC (OJ L 60, 3.3.1994, p. 16)
Directive 94/76/EC (OJ L 365, 31.12.1994, p. 53)
Directive 95/7/EC (OJ L 102, 5.5.1995, p. 18)
Directive 96/42/EC (OJ L 170, 9.7.1996, p. 34)
Directive 96/95/EC (OJ L 338, 28.12.1996, p. 89)
Directive 98/80/EC (OJ L 281, 17.10.1998, p. 31)
Directive 1999/49/EC (OJ L 139, 2.6.1999, p. 27)
Directive 1999/59/EC (OJ L 162, 26.6.1999, p. 63)
Directive 1999/85/EC (OJ L 277, 28.10.1999, p. 34)
Directive 2000/17/EC (OJ L 84, 5.4.2000, p. 24)
Directive 2000/65/EC (OJ L 269, 21.10.2000, p. 44)
Directive 2001/4/EC (OJ L 22, 24.1.2001, p. 17)
Directive 2001/115/EC (OJ L 15, 17.1.2002, p. 24)
Directive 2002/38/EC (OJ L 128, 15.5.2002, p. 41)
Directive 2002/93/EC (OJ L 331, 7.12.2002, p. 27)
Directive 2003/92/EC (OJ L 260, 11.10.2003, p. 8)
Directive 2004/7/EC (OJ L 27, 30.1.2004, p. 44)
Directive 2004/15/EC (OJ L 52, 21.2.2004, p. 61)
Directive 2004/66/EC (OJ L 168, 1.5.2004, p. 35) — (only Point V of the Annex)
Directive 2005/92/EC (OJ L 345, 28.12.2005, p. 19)
Directive 2006/18/EC (OJ L 51, 22.2.2006, p. 12)
Directive 2006/58/EC (OJ L 174, 28.6.2006, p. 5)
Directive 2006/69/EC (OJ L 221, 12.8.2006, p. 9 — (only Article 1)
Directive 2006/98/EC (OJ L ..., ..., p ... (*) — (only point 2 of the Annex)

PART B
TIME LIMITS FOR TRANSPOSITION INTO NATIONAL LAW (REFERRED TO IN ARTICLE 411)

Directive	*Deadline for transposition*
Directive 67/227/EEC	1 January 1970
Directive 77/388/EEC	1 January 1978
Directive 78/583/EEC	1 January 1979
Directive 80/368/EEC	1 January 1979
Directive 84/386/EEC	1 July 1985
Directive 89/465/EEC	1 January 1990 1 January 1991 1 January 1992 1 January 1993 1 January 1994 for Portugal
Directive 91/680/EEC	1 January 1993
Directive 92/77/EEC	31 December 1992
Directive 92/111/EEC	1 January 1993 1 January 1994 1 October 1993 for Germany
Directive 94/4/EC	1 April 1994
Directive 94/5/EC	1 January 1995
Directive 94/76/EC	1 January 1995
Directive 95/7/EC	1 January 1996 1 January 1997 for Germany and Luxembourg
Directive 96/42/EC	1 January 1995
Directive 96/95/EC	1 January 1997
Directive 98/80/EC	1 January 2000
Directive 1999/49/EC	1 January 1999
Directive 1999/59/EC	1 January 2000
Directive 1999/85/CE	—
Directive 2000/17/EC	—
Directive 2000/65/EC	31 December 2001
Directive 2001/4/EC	1 January 2001
Directive 2001/115/EC	1 January 2004
Directive 2002/38/EC	1 July 2003
Directive 2002/93/EC	—
Directive 2003/92/EC	1 January 2005
Directive 2004/7/EC	30 January 2004
Directive 2004/15/EC	—
Directive 2004/66/EC	1 May 2004
Directive 2005/92/EC	1 January 2006
Directive 2006/18/EC	—
Directive 2006/58/EC	1 July 2006
Directive 2006/69/EC	1 January 2008

ANNEX XII
CORRELATION TABLE

Directive 67/227/EEC	*Directive 77/388/EEC*	*Amending Directives*	*Other acts*	*This Directive*
Article 1, first paragraph				Article 1(1)
Article 1, second and third paragraphs				—
Article 2, first, second and third paragraphs				Article 1(2), first, second and third subparagraphs
Articles 3, 4 and 6				—
	Article 1			—
	Article 2, point (1)			Article 2(1)(a) and (c)
	Article 2, point (2)			Article 2(1)(d)
	Article 3(1), first indent			Article 5, point (2)
	Article 3(1), second indent			Article 5, point (1)
	Article 3(1), third indent			Article 5, points (3) and (4)
	Article 3(2)			—
	Article 3(3), first subparagraph, first indent			Article 6(2)(a) and (b)
	Article 3(3), first subparagraph, second indent			Article 6(2)(c) and (d)
	Article 3(3), first subparagraph, third indent			Article 6(2)(e), (f) and (g)
	Article 3(3) second subparagraph, first indent			Article 6(1)(b)

Directive 67/227/EEC	*Directive 77/388/EEC*	*Amending Directives*	*Other acts*	*This Directive*
	Article 3(3) second subparagraph, second indent			Article 6(1)(c)
	Article 3(3), second subparagraph, third indent			Article 6(1)(a)
	Article 3(4), first subparagraph, first and second indents			Article 7(1)
	Article 3(4), second subparagraph, first second and third indents			Article 7(2)
	Article 3(5)			Article 8
	Article 4(1) and (2)			Article 9(1), first and second subparagraphs
	Article 4(3)(a), first subparagraph, first sentence			Article 12(1)(a)
	Article 4(3)(a), first subparagraph, second sentence			Article 12(2), second subparagraph
	Article 4(3)(a), second subparagraph			Article 12(2), third subparagraph
	Article 4(3)(a), third subparagraph			Article 12(2), first subparagraph
	Article 4(3)(b), first subparagraph			Article 12(1)(b)
	Article 4(3)(b), second subparagraph			Article 12(3)
	Article 4(4), first subparagraph			Article 10

Directive 67/227/EEC	*Directive 77/388/EEC*	*Amending Directives*	*Other acts*	*This Directive*
	Article 4(4), second and third subparagraphs			Article 11, first and second paragraphs
	Article 4(5), first, second and third subparagraphs			Article 13(1), first, second and third subparagraphs
	Article 4(5), fourth subparagraph			Article 13(2)
	Article 5(1)			Article 14(1)
	Article 5(2)			Article 15(1)
	Article 5(3)(a), (b) and (c)			Article 15(2)(a), (b) and (c)
	Article 5(4)(a), (b) and (c)			Article 14(2)(a), (b) and (c)
	Article 5(5)			Article 14(3)
	Article 5(6), first and second sentences			Article 16, first and second paragraphs
	Article 5(7)(a), (b) and (c)			Article 18(a), (b) and (c)
	Article 5(8), first sentence			Article 19, first paragraph
	Article 5(8), second and third sentences			Article 19, second paragraph
	Article 6(1), first subparagraph			Article 24(1)
	Article 6(1), second subparagraph, first, second and third indents			Article 25(a), (b) and (c)
	Article 6(2), first subparagraph, points (a) and (b)			Article 26(1)(a) and (b)

Directive 67/227/EEC	*Directive 77/388/EEC*	*Amending Directives*	*Other acts*	*This Directive*
	Article 6(2), second subparagraph			Article 26(2)
	Article 6(3)			Article 27
	Article 6(4)			Article 28
	Article 6(5)			Article 29
	Article 7(1)(a) and (b)			Article 30, first and second paragraphs
	Article 7(2)			Article 60
	Article 7(3), first and second subparagraphs			Article 61, first and second paragraphs
	Article 8(1)(a), first sentence			Article 32, first paragraph
	Article 8(1)(a), second and third sentences			Article 36, first and second paragraphs
	Article 8(1)(b)			Article 31
	Article 8(1)(c), first subparagraph			Article 37(1)
	Article 8(1)(c), second subparagraph, first indent			Article 37(2), first subparagraph
	Article 8(1)(c), second subparagraph, second and third indents			Article 37(2), second and third subparagraphs
	Article 8(1)(c), third subparagraph			Article 37(2), fourth subparagraph
	Article 8(1)(c), fourth subparagraph			Article 37(3), first subparagraph

Directive 67/227/EEC	*Directive 77/388/EEC*	*Amending Directives*	*Other acts*	*This Directive*
	Article 8(1)(c), fifth subparagraph			—
	Article 8(1)(c), sixth subparagraph			Article 37(3), second subparagraph
	Article 8(1)(d), first and second subparagraphs			Article 38(1) and (2)
	Article 8(1)(e), first sentence			Article 39, first paragraph
	Article 8(1)(e), second and third sentences			Article 39, second paragraph
	Article 8(2)			Article 32, second paragraph
	Article 9(1)			Article 43
	Article 9(2) introductory sentence			—
	Article 9(2)(a)			Article 45
	Article 9(2)(b)			Article 46
	Article 9(2)(c), first and second indents			Article 52(a) and (b)
	Article 9(2)(c), third and fourth indents			Article 52(c)
	Article 9(2)(e), first to sixth indents			Article 56(1)(a) to (f)
	Article 9(2)(e), seventh indent			Article 56(1)(l)
	Article 9(2)(e), eighth indent			Article 56(1)(g)
	Article 9(2)(e), ninth indent			Article 56(1)(h)

Directive 67/227/EEC	*Directive 77/388/EEC*	*Amending Directives*	*Other acts*	*This Directive*
	Article 9(2)(e), tenth indent, first sentence			Article 56(1)(i)
	Article 9(2)(e), tenth indent, second sentence			Article 24(2)
	Article 9(2)(e), tenth indent, third sentence			Article 56(1)(i)
	Article 9(2)(e), eleventh and twelfth indents			Article 56(1)(j) and (k)
	Article 9(2)(f)			Article 57(1)
	Article 9(3)			Article 58, first and second paragraphs
	Article 9(3)(a) and (b)			Article 58, first paragraph, points (a) and (b)
	Article 9(4)			Article 59(1) and (2)
	Article 10(1)(a) and (b)			Article 62, points (1) and (2)
	Article 10(2), first subparagraph, first sentence			Article 63
	Article 10(2), first subparagraph, second and third sentences			Article 64(1) and (2)
	Article 10(2), second subparagraph			Article 65
	Article 10(2), third subparagraph, first, second and third indents			Article 66(a), (b) and (c)
	Article 10(3), first subparagraph, first sentence			Article 70

Directive 67/227/EEC	*Directive 77/388/EEC*	*Amending Directives*	*Other acts*	*This Directive*
	Article 10(3), first subparagraph, second sentence			Article 71(1), first subparagraph
	Article 10(3), second subparagraph			Article 71(1), second subparagraph
	Article 10(3), third subparagraph			Article 71(2)
	Article 11(A)(1)(a)			Article 73
	Article 11(A)(1)(b)			Article 74
	Article 11(A)(1)(c)			Article 75
	Article 11(A)(1)(d)			Article 77
	Article 11(A)(2)(a)			Article 78, first paragraph, point (a)
	Article 11(A)(2)(b), first sentence			Article 78, first paragraph, point (b)
	Article 11(A)(2)(b), second sentence			Article 78, second paragraph
	Article 11(A)(3)(a) and (b)			Article 79, first paragraph, points (a) and (b) Article 87(a) and (b)
	Article 11(A)(3)(c), first sentence			Article 79, first paragraph, point (c)
	Article 11(A)(3)(c), second sentence			Article 79, second paragraph
	Article 11(A)(4),first and second subparagraphs			Article 81, first and second paragraphs

Directive 67/227/EEC	*Directive 77/388/EEC*	*Amending Directives*	*Other acts*	*This Directive*
	Article 11(A)(5)			Article 82
	Article 11(A)(6), first subparagraph, first and second sentences			Article 80(1), first subparagraph
	Article 11(A)(6), first subparagraph, third sentence			Article 80(1), second subparagraph
	Article 11(A)(6), second subparagraph			Article 80(1), first subparagraph
	Article 11(A)(6), third subparagraph			Article 80(2)
	Article 11(A)(6), fourth subparagraph			Article 80(3)
	Article 11(A)(7), first and second subparagraphs			Article 72, first and second paragraphs
	Article 11(B)(1)			Article 85
	Article 11(B)(3)(a)			Article 86(1)(a)
	Article 11(B)(3)(b), first subparagraph			Article 86(1)(b)
	Article 11(B)(3)(b), second subparagraph			Article 86(2)
	Article 11(B)(3)(b), third subparagraph			Article 86(1)(b)
	Article 11(B)(4)			Article 87
	Article 11(B)(5)			Article 88
	Article 11(B)(6), first and second subparagraphs			Article 89, first and second paragraphs

Directive 67/227/EEC	*Directive 77/388/EEC*	*Amending Directives*	*Other acts*	*This Directive*
	Article 11(C)(1), first and second subparagraphs			Article 90(1) and (2)
	Article 11(C)(2), first subparagraph			Article 91(1)
	Article 11(C)(2), second subparagraph, first and second sentences			Article 91(2), first and second subparagraphs
	Article 11(C)(3), first and second indents			Article 92(a) and (b)
	Article 12(1)			Article 93, first paragraph
	Article 12(1)(a)			Article 93, second paragraph, point (a)
	Article 12(1)(b)			Article 93, second paragraph, point (c)
	Article 12(2), first and second indents			Article 95, first and second paragraphs
	Article 12(3)(a), first subparagraph, first sentence			Article 96
	Article 12(3)(a), first subparagraph, second sentence			Article 97(1)
	Article 12(3)(a), second subparagraph			Article 97(2)
	Article 12(3)(a), third subparagraph, first sentence			Article 98(1)
	Article 12(3)(a), third subparagraph, second sentence			Article 98(2), first subparagraph Article 99(1)

Directive 67/227/EEC	*Directive 77/388/EEC*	*Amending Directives*	*Other acts*	*This Directive*
	Article 12(3)(a), fourth subparagraph			Article 98(2), second subparagraph
	Article 12(3)(b), first sentence			Article 102, first paragraph
	Article 12(3)(b), second, third and fourth sentences			Article 102, second paragraph
	Article 12(3)(c), first subparagraph			Article 103(1)
	Article 12(3)(c), second subparagraph, first and second indents			Article 103(2)(a) and (b)
	Article 12(4), first subparagraph			Article 99(2)
	Article 12(4), second subparagraph, first and second sentences			Article 100, first and second paragraphs
	Article 12(4), third subparagraph			Article 101
	Article 12(5)			Article 94(2)
	Article 12(6)			Article 105
	Article 13(A)(1), introductory sentence			Article 131
	Article 13(A)(1)(a) to (n)			Article 132(1)(a) to (n)
	Article 13(A)(1)(o), first sentence			Article 132(1)(o)
	Article 13(A)(1)(o), second sentence			Article 132(2)

Directive 67/227/EEC	*Directive 77/388/EEC*	*Amending Directives*	*Other acts*	*This Directive*
	Article 13(A)(1)(p) and (q)			Article 132(1)(p) and (q)
	Article 13(A)(2)(a), first to fourth indents			Article 133(a) to (d)
	Article 13(A)(2)(b), first and second indents			Article 134(a) and (b)
	Article 13(B), introductory sentence			Article 131
	Article 13(B)(a)			Article 135(1)(a)
	Article 13(B)(b), first subparagraph			Article 135(1)(l)
	Article 13(B)(b), first subparagraph, points (1) to (4)			Article 135(2), first subparagraph, points (a) to (d)
	Article 13(B)(b), second subparagraph			Article 135(2), second subparagraph
	Article 13(B)(c)			Article 136(a) and (b)
	Article 13(B)(d)			—
	Article 13(B)(d), points (1) to (5)			Article 135(1)(b) to (f)
	Article 13(B)(d), point (5), first and second indents			Article 135(1)(f)
	Article 13(B)(d), point (6)			Article 135(1)(g)
	Article 13(B)(e) to (h)			Article 135(1)(h) to (k)
	Article 13(C), first subparagraph, point (a)			Article 137(1)(d)

Directive 67/227/EEC	*Directive 77/388/EEC*	*Amending Directives*	*Other acts*	*This Directive*
	Article 13(C), first subparagraph, point (b)			Article 137(1)(a), (b) and (c)
	Article 13(C), second subparagraph			Article 137(2), first and second subparagraphs
	Article 14(1), introductory sentence			Article 131
	Article 14(1)(a)			Article 140(a)
	Article 14(1)(d), first and second subparagraphs			Article 143(b) and (c)
	Article 14(1)(e)			Article 143(e)
	Article 14(1)(g), first to fourth indents			Article 143(f) to (i)
	Article 14(1)(h)			Article 143(j)
	Article 14(1)(i)			Article 144
	Article 14(1)(j)			Article 143(k)
	Article 14(1)(k)			Article 143(l)
	Article 14(2), first subparagraph			Article 145(1)
	Article 14(2), second subparagraph, first, second and third indents			Article 145(2), first, second and third subparagraphs
	Article 14(2), third subparagraph			Article 145(3)
	Article 15, introductory sentence			Article 131
	Article 15, point (1)			Article 146(1)(a)

Directive 67/227/EEC	*Directive 77/388/EEC*	*Amending Directives*	*Other acts*	*This Directive*
	Article 15, point (2), first subparagraph			Article 146(1)(b)
	Article 15, point (2), second subparagraph, first and second indents			Article 147(1), first subparagraph, points (a) and (b)
	Article 15, point (2), second subparagraph, third indent, first part of the sentence			Article 147(1), first subparagraph, point (c)
	Article 15, point (2), second subparagraph, third indent, second part of the sentence			Article 147(1), second subparagraph
	Article 15, point (2), third subparagraph, first and second indents			Article 147(2), first and second subparagraphs
	Article 15, point (2), fourth subparagraph			Article 147(2), third subparagraph
	Article 15, point (3)			Article 146(1)(d)
	Article 15, point (4), first subparagraph, points (a) and (b)			Article 148(a)
	Article 15, point (4), first subparagraph, point (c)			Article 148(b)
	Article 15, point (4), second subparagraph, first and second sentences			Article 150(1) and (2)
	Article 15, point (5)			Article 148(c)
	Article 15, point (6)			Article 148(f)
	Article 15, point (7)			Article 148(e)

Directive 67/227/EEC	*Directive 77/388/EEC*	*Amending Directives*	*Other acts*	*This Directive*
	Article 15, point (8)			Article 148(d)
	Article 15, point (9)			Article 148(g)
	Article 15, point (10), first subparagraph, first to fourth indents			Article 151(1), first subparagraph, points (a) to (d)
	Article 15, point (10), second subparagraph			Article 151(1), second subparagraph
	Article 15, point (10), third subparagraph			Article 151(2)
	Article 15, point (11)			Article 152
	Article 15, point (12), first sentence			Article 146(1)(c)
	Article 15, point (12), second sentence			Article 146(2)
	Article 15, point (13)			Article 146(1)(e)
	Article 15, point (14), first and second subparagraphs			Article 153, first and second paragraphs
	Article 15, point (15)			Article 149
	Article 16(1)			—
	Article 16(2)			Article 164(1)
	Article 16(3)			Article 166
	Article 17(1)			Article 167
	Article 17(2), (3) and (4)			—
	Article 17(5), first and second subparagraphs			Article 173(1), first and second subparagraphs

Directive 67/227/EEC	*Directive 77/388/EEC*	*Amending Directives*	*Other acts*	*This Directive*
	Article 17(5), third subparagraph, points (a) to (e)			Article 173(2)(a) to (e)
	Article 17(6)			Article 176
	Article 17(7), first and second sentences			Article 177, first and second paragraphs
	Article 18(1)			—
	Article 18(2), first and second subparagraphs			Article 179, first and second paragraphs
	Article 18(3)			Article 180
	Article 18(4), first and second subparagraphs			Article 183, first and second paragraphs
	Article 19(1), first subparagraph, first indent			Article 174(1), first subparagraph, point (a)
	Article 19(1), first subparagraph, second indent, first sentence			Article 174(1), first subparagraph, point (b)
	Article 19(1), first subparagraph, second indent, second sentence			Article 174(1), second subparagraph
	Article 19(1), second subparagraph			Article 175(1)
	Article 19(2), first sentence			Article 174(2)(a)
	Article 19(2), second sentence			Article 174(2)(a) and (b)
	Article 19(2), third sentence			Article 174(3)

Directive 67/227/EEC	*Directive 77/388/EEC*	*Amending Directives*	*Other acts*	*This Directive*
	Article 19(3), first subparagraph, first and second sentences			Article 175(2), first subparagraph
	Article 19(3), first subparagraph, third sentence			Article 175(2), second subparagraph
	Article 19(3), second subparagraph			Article 175(3)
	Article 20(1), introductory sentence			Article 186
	Article 20(1)(a)			Article 184
	Article 20(1)(b), first part of the first sentence			Article 185(1)
	Article 20(1)(b), second part of the first sentence			Article 185(2), first subparagraph
	Article 20(1)(b), second sentence			Article 185(2), second subparagraph
	Article 20(2), first subparagraph, first sentence			Article 187(1), first subparagraph
	Article 20(2), first subparagraph, second and third sentences			Article 187(2), first and second subparagraphs
	Article 20(2), second and third subparagraphs			Article 187(1), second and third subparagraphs
	Article 20(3), first subparagraph, first sentence			Article 188(1), first subparagraph
	Article 20(3), first subparagraph, second sentence			Article 188(1), second and third subparagraphs

Directive 67/227/EEC	*Directive 77/388/EEC*	*Amending Directives*	*Other acts*	*This Directive*
	Article 20(3), first subparagraph, third sentence			Article 188(2)
	Article 20(3), second subparagraph			Article 188(2)
	Article 20(4), first subparagraph, first to fourth indents			Article 189(a) to (d)
	Article 20(4), second subparagraph			Article 190
	Article 20(5)			Article 191
	Article 20(6)			Article 192
	Article 21			—
	Article 22			—
	Article 22a			Article 249
	Article 23, first paragraph			Article 211, first paragraph Article 260
	Article 23, second paragraph			Article 211, second paragraph
	Article 24(1)			Article 281
	Article 24(2)			Article 292
	Article 24(2)(a), first subparagraph			Article 284(1)
	Article 24(2)(a), second and third subparagraphs			Article 284(2), first and second subparagraphs
	Article 24(2)(b), first and second sentences			Article 285, first and second paragraphs

Directive 67/227/EEC	*Directive 77/388/EEC*	*Amending Directives*	*Other acts*	*This Directive*
	Article 24(2)(c)			Article 286
	Article 24(3), first subparagraph			Article 282
	Article 24(3), second subparagraph, first sentence			Article 283(2)
	Article 24(3), second subparagraph, second sentence			Article 283(1)(a)
	Article 24(4), first subparagraph			Article 288, first paragraph, points (1) to (4)
	Article 24(4), second subparagraph			Article 288, second paragraph
	Article 24(5)			Article 289
	Article 24(6)			Article 290
	Article 24(7)			Article 291
	Article 24(8)(a), (b) and (c)			Article 293, points (1), (2) and (3)
	Article 24(9)			Article 294
	Article 24a, first paragraph, first to twelfth indents			Article 287, points (7) to (16)
	Article 25(1)			Article 296(1)
	Article 25(2), first to eighth indents			Article 295(1), points (1) to (8)
	Article 25(3), first subparagraph, first sentence			Article 297, first paragraph, first sentence and second paragraph

Directive 67/227/EEC	*Directive 77/388/EEC*	*Amending Directives*	*Other acts*	*This Directive*
	Article 25(3), first subparagraph, second sentence			Article 298, first paragraph
	Article 25(3), first subparagraph, third sentence			Article 299
	Article 25(3), first subparagraph, fourth and fifth sentences			Article 298, second paragraph
	Article 25(3), second subparagraph			Article 297, first paragraph, second sentence
	Article 25(4), first subparagraph			Article 272(1), first subparagraph, point (e)
	Article 25(5) and (6)			—
	Article 25(7)			Article 304
	Article 25(8)			Article 301(2)
	Article 25(9)			Article 296(2)
	Article 25(10)			Article 296(3)
	Article 25(11) and (12)			—
	Article 26(1) first and second sentences			Article 306(1), first and second subparagraphs
	Article 26(1) third sentence			Article 306(2)
	Article 26(2), first and second sentences			Article 307, first and second paragraphs
	Article 26(2), third sentence			Article 308
	Article 26(3), first and second sentences			Article 309, first and second paragraphs

Directive 67/227/EEC	*Directive 77/388/EEC*	*Amending Directives*	*Other acts*	*This Directive*
	Article 26(4)			Article 310
	Article 26a(A)(a), first subparagraph			Article 311(1), point (2)
	Article 26a(A)(a), second subparagraph			Article 311(2)
	Article 26a(A)(b) and (c)			Article 311(1), points (3) and (4)
	Article 26a(A)(d)			Article 311(1), point (1)
	Article 26a(A)(e) and (f)			Article 311(1), points (5) and (6)
	Article 26a(A)(g), introductory sentence			Article 311(1), point (7)
	Article 26a(A)(g), first and second indents			Article 311(3)
	Article 26a(B)(1)			Article 313(1)
	Article 26a(B)(2)			Article 314
	Article 26a(B)(2), first and second indents			Article 314(a) to (d)
	Article 26a(B)(3), first subparagraph, first and second sentences			Article 315, first and second paragraphs
	Article 26a(B)(3), second subparagraph			Article 312
	Article 26a(B)(3), second subparagraph, first and second indents			Article 312, points (1) and (2)

Directive 67/227/EEC	*Directive 77/388/EEC*	*Amending Directives*	*Other acts*	*This Directive*
	Article 26a(B)(4), first subparagraph			Article 316(1)
	Article 26a(B)(4), first subparagraph, points (a), (b) and (c)			Article 316(1)(a), (b) and (c)
	Article 26a(B)(4), second subparagraph			Article 316(2)
	Article 26a(B)(4), third subparagraph, first and second sentences			Article 317, first and second paragraphs
	Article 26a(B)(5)			Article 321
	Article 26a(B)(6)			Article 323
	Article 26a(B)(7)			Article 322
	Article 26a(B)(7)(a), (b) and (c)			Article 322(a), (b) and (c)
	Article 26a(B)(8)			Article 324
	Article 26a(B)(9)			Article 325
	Article 26a(B)(10) first and second subparagraphs			Article 318(1), first and second subparagraphs
	Article 26a(B)(10), third subparagraph, first and second indents			Article 318(2)(a) and (b)
	Article 26a(B)(10), fourth subparagraph			Article 318(3)
	Article 26a(B)(11), first subparagraph			Article 319

Directive 67/227/EEC	*Directive 77/388/EEC*	*Amending Directives*	*Other acts*	*This Directive*
	Article 26a(B)(11), second subparagraph, point (a)			Article 320(1), first subparagraph
	Article 26a(B)(11), second subparagraph, points (b) and (c)			Article 320(1), second subparagraph
	Article 26a(B)(11), third subparagraph			Article 320(2)
	Article 26a(C)(1), introductory sentence			Article 333(1) Article 334
	Article 26a(C)(1), first to fourth indents			Article 334(a) to (d)
	Article 26a(C)(2), first and second indents			Article 336(a) and (b)
	Article 26a(C)(3)			Article 337
	Article 26a(C)(4), first subparagraph, first, second and third indents			Article 339, first paragraph, points (a), (b) and (c)
	Article 26a(C)(4), second subparagraph			Article 339, second paragraph
	Article 26a(C)(5), first and second subparagraphs			Article 340(1), first and second subparagraphs
	Article 26a(C)(5), third subparagraph			Article 340(2)
	Article 26a(C)(6), first subparagraph, first and second indents			Article 338, first paragraph, points (a) and (b)
	Article 26a(C)(6), second subparagraph			Article 338, second paragraph

Directive 67/227/EEC	*Directive 77/388/EEC*	*Amending Directives*	*Other acts*	*This Directive*
	Article 26a(C)(7)			Article 335
	Article 26a(D), introductory sentence			—
	Article 26a(D)(a)			Article 313(2) Article 333(2)
	Article 26a(D)(b)			Article 4(a) and (c)
	Article 26a(D)(c)			Article 35 Article 139(3), first subparagraph
	Article 26b(A), first subparagraph, point (i), first sentence			Article 344(1), point (1)
	Article 26b(A), first subparagraph, point (i), second sentence			Article 344(2)
	Article 26b(A), first subparagraph, point (ii), first to fourth indents			Article 344(1), point (2)
	Article 26b(A), second subparagraph			Article 344(3)
	Article 26b(A), third subparagraph			Article 345
	Article 26b(B), first subparagraph			Article 346
	Article 26b(B), second subparagraph			Article 347
	Article 26b(C), first subparagraph			Article 348

Directive 67/227/EEC	*Directive 77/388/EEC*	*Amending Directives*	*Other acts*	*This Directive*
	Article 26b(C), second subparagraph, first and second sentences			Article 349(1) and (2)
	Article 26b(C), third subparagraph			Article 350
	Article 26b(C), fourth subparagraph			Article 351
	Article 26b(D)(1)(a), (b) and (c)			Article 354(a), (b) and (c)
	Article 26b(D)(2)			Article 355
	Article 26b(E), first and second subparagraphs			Article 356(1), first and second subparagraphs
	Article 26b(E), third and fourth subparagraphs			Article 356(2) and (3)
	Article 26b(F), first sentence			Article 198(2) and (3)
	Article 26b(F), second sentence			Articles 208 and 255
	Article 26b(G)(1), first subparagraph			Article 352
	Article 26b(G)(1), second subparagraph			—
	Article 26b(G)(2)(a)			Article 353
	Article 26b(G)(2)(b), first and second sentences			Article 198(1) and (3)
	Article 26c(A)(a) to (e)			Article 358, points (1) to (5)
	Article 26c(B)(1)			Article 359

Directive 67/227/EEC	*Directive 77/388/EEC*	*Amending Directives*	*Other acts*	*This Directive*
	Article 26c(B)(2), first subparagraph			Article 360
	Article 26c(B)(2), second subparagraph, first part of the first sentence			Article 361(1)
	Article 26c(B)(2), second subparagraph, second part of the first sentence			Article 361(1)(a) to (e)
	Article 26c(B)(2), second subparagraph, second sentence			Article 361(2)
	Article 26c(B)(3), first and second subparagraphs			Article 362
	Article 26c(B)(4)(a) to (d)			Article 363(a) to (d)
	Article 26c(B)(5), first subparagraph			Article 364
	Article 26c(B)(5), second subparagraph			Article 365
	Article 26c(B)(6), first sentence			Article 366(1), first subparagraph
	Article 26c(B)(6), second and third sentences			Article 366(1), second subparagraph
	Article 26c(B)(6), fourth sentence			Article 366(2)
	Article 26c(B)(7), first sentence			Article 367, first paragraph
	Article 26c(B)(7), second and third sentences			Article 367, second paragraph

Directive 67/227/EEC	*Directive 77/388/EEC*	*Amending Directives*	*Other acts*	*This Directive*
	Article 26c(B)(8)			Article 368
	Article 26c(B)(9), first sentence			Article 369(1)
	Article 26c(B)(9), second and third sentences			Article 369(2), first and second subparagraphs
	Article 26c(B)(10)			Article 204(1), third subparagraph
	Article 27(1) first and second sentences			Article 395(1) first and second subparagraphs
	Article 27(2), first and second sentences			Article 395(2), first subparagraphs
	Article 27(2), third sentence			Article 395(2), second subparagraph
	Article 27(3) and (4)			Article 395(3) and (4)
	Article 27(5)			Article 394
	Article 28(1) and (1a)			—
	Article 28(2), introductory sentence			Article 109
	Article 28(2)(a), first subparagraph			Article 110, first and second paragraphs
	Article 28(2)(a), second subparagraph			—
	Article 28(2)(a), third subparagraph, first sentence			Article 112, first paragraph

VAT

Directive 67/227/EEC	*Directive 77/388/EEC*	*Amending Directives*	*Other acts*	*This Directive*
	Article 28(2)(a), third subparagraph, second and third sentences			Article 112, second paragraph
	Article 28(2)(b)			Article 113
	Article 28(2)(c), first and second sentences			Article 114(1), first and second subparagraphs
	Article 28(2)(c), third sentence			Article 114(2)
	Article 28(2)(d)			Article 115
	Article 28(2)(e), first and second subparagraphs			Article 118, first and second paragraphs
	Article 28(2)(f)			Article 120
	Article 28(2)(g)			—
	Article 28(2)(h), first and second subparagraphs			Article 121, first and second paragraphs
	Article 28(2)(i)			Article 122
	Article 28(2)(j)			Article 117(2)
	Article 28(2)(k)			Article 116
	Article 28(3)(a)			Article 370
	Article 28(3)(b)			Article 371
	Article 28(3)(c)			Article 391
	Article 28(3)(d)			Article 372
	Article 28(3)(e)			Article 373
	Article 28(3)(f)			Article 392

Directive 67/227/EEC	*Directive 77/388/EEC*	*Amending Directives*	*Other acts*	*This Directive*
	Article 28(3)(g)			Article 374
	Article 28(3a)			Article 376
	Article 28(4) and (5)			Article 393(1) and (2)
	Article 28(6), first subparagraph, first sentence			Article 106, first and second paragraphs
	Article 28(6), first subparagraph, second sentence			Article 106, third paragraph
	Article 28(6), second subparagraph, points (a), (b) and (c),			Article 107, first paragraph, points (a), (b) and (c)
	Article 28(6), second subparagraph, point (d)			Article 107, second paragraph
	Article 28(6), third subparagraph			Article 107, second paragraph
	Article 28(6), fourth subparagraph, points (a), (b) and (c)			Article 108(a), (b) and (c)
	Article 28(6), fifth and sixth subparagraphs			—
	Article 28a(1), introductory sentence			Article 2(1)
	Article 28a(1)(a), first subparagraph			Article 2(1)(b)(i)
	Article 28a(1)(a), second subparagraph			Article 3(1)

Directive 67/227/EEC	*Directive 77/388/EEC*	*Amending Directives*	*Other acts*	*This Directive*
	Article 28a(1)(a), third subparagraph			Article 3(3)
	Article 28a(1)(b)			Article 2(1)(b)(ii)
	Article 28a(1)(c)			Article 2(1)(b)(iii)
	Article 28a(1a)(a)			Article 3(1)(a)
	Article 28a(1a)(b), first subparagraph, first indent			Article 3(1)(b)
	Article 28a(1a)(b), first subparagraph, second and third indents			Article 3(2), first subparagraph, points (a) and (b)
	Article 28a(1a)(b), second subparagraph			Article 3(2), second subparagraph
	Article 28a(2), introductory sentence			—
	Article 28a(2)(a)			Article 2(2), point (a) (i), (ii), and (iii)
	Article 28a(2)(b), first subparagraph			Article 2(2), point (b)
	Article 28a(2)(b), first subparagraph, first and second indents			Article 2(2), point (b) (i), (ii), and (iii)
	Article 28a(2)(b), second subparagraph			Article 2(2), point (c)
	Article 28a(3), first and second subparagraphs			Article 20, first and second paragraphs
	Article 28a(4), first subparagraph			Article 9(2)

Directive 67/227/EEC	*Directive 77/388/EEC*	*Amending Directives*	*Other acts*	*This Directive*
	Article 28a(4), second subparagraph, first indent			Article 172(1), second subparagraph
	Article 28a(4), second subparagraph, second indent			Article 172(1), first subparagraph
	Article 28a(4), third subparagraph			Article 172(2)
	Article 28a(5)(b), first subparagraph			Article 17(1), first subparagraph
	Article 28a(5)(b), second subparagraph,			Article 17(1), second subparagraph and (2), introductory sentence
	Article 28a(5)(b), second subparagraph, first indent			Article 17(2)(a) and (b)
	Article 28a(5)(b), second subparagraph, second indent			Article 17(2)(c)
	Article 28a(5)(b), second subparagraph, third indent			Article 17(2)(e)
	Article 28a(5)(b), second subparagraph, fifth, sixth and seventh indents			Article 17(2)(f), (g) and (h)
	Article 28a(5)(b), second subparagraph, eighth indent			Article 17(2)(d)
	Article 28a(5)(b), third subparagraph			Article 17(3)
	Article 28a(6), first subparagraph			Article 21
	Article 28a(6), second subparagraph			Article 22

VAT

Directive 67/227/EEC	*Directive 77/388/EEC*	*Amending Directives*	*Other acts*	*This Directive*
	Article 28a(7)			Article 23
	Article 28b(A)(1)			Article 40
	Article 28b(A)(2), first and second subparagraphs			Article 41, first and second paragraphs
	Article 28b(A)(2), third subparagraph, first and second indents			Article 42(a) and (b)
	Article 28b(B)(1), first subparagraph, first and second indents			Article 33(1)(a) and (b)
	Article 28b(B)(1), second subparagraph			Article 33(2)
	Article 28b(B)(2), first subparagraph			Article 34(1)(a)
	Article 28b(B)(2), first subparagraph, first and second indents			Article 34(1)(b) and (c)
	Article 28b(B)(2), second subparagraph, first and second sentences			Article 34(2), first and second subparagraphs
	Article 28b(B)(2), third subparagraph, first sentence			Article 34(3)
	Article 28b(B)(2), third subparagraph, second and third sentences			—
	Article 28b(B)(3), first and second subparagraphs			Article 34(4), first and second subparagraphs

Directive 67/227/EEC	*Directive 77/388/EEC*	*Amending Directives*	*Other acts*	*This Directive*
	Article 28b(C)(1), first indent, first subparagraph			Article 48, first paragraph
	Article 28b(C)(1), first indent, second subparagraph			Article 49
	Article 28b(C)(1), second and third indents			Article 48, second and third paragraphs
	Article 28b(C)(2) and (3)			Article 47, first and second paragraphs
	Article 28b(C)(4)			Article 51
	Article 28b(D)			Article 53
	Article 28b(E)(1), first and second subparagraphs			Article 50, first and second paragraphs
	Article 28b(E)(2), first and second subparagraphs			Article 54, first and second paragraphs
	Article 28b(E)(3), first and second subparagraphs			Article 44, first and second paragraphs
	Article 28b(F), first and second paragraphs			Article 55, first and second paragraphs
	Article 28c(A), introductory sentence			Article 131
	Article 28c(A)(a), first subparagraph			Article 138(1)
	Article 28c(A)(a), second subparagraph			Article 139(1), first and second subparagraphs
	Article 28c(A)(b)			Article 138(2)(a)

Directive 67/227/EEC	*Directive 77/388/EEC*	*Amending Directives*	*Other acts*	*This Directive*
	Article 28c(A)(c), first subparagraph			Article 138(2)(b)
	Article 28c(A)(c), second subparagraph			Article 139(2)
	Article 28c(A)(d)			Article 138(2)(c)
	Article 28c(B), introductory sentence			Articles 131
	Article 28c(B)(a), (b) and (c)			Article 140(a), (b) and (c)
	Article 28c(C)			Article 142
	Article 28c(D), first subparagraph			Article 143(d)
	Article 28c(D), second subparagraph			Article 131
	Article 28c(E), point (1), first indent, replacing Article 16(1)			
	— paragraph 1, first subparagraph			Article 155
	— paragraph 1, first subparagraph, point (A)			Article 157(1)(a)
	— paragraph 1, first subparagraph, point (B), first subparagraph, points (a), (b) and (c)			Article 156(1)(a), (b) and (c)

Directive 67/227/EEC	*Directive 77/388/EEC*	*Amending Directives*	*Other acts*	*This Directive*
	— paragraph 1, first subparagraph, point (B), first subparagraph, point (d), first and second indents			Article 156(1)(d) and (e)
	— paragraph 1, first subparagraph, point (B), first subparagraph, point (e), first subparagraph			Article 157(1)(b)
	— paragraph 1, first subparagraph, point (B), first subparagraph, point (e), second subparagraph, first indent			Article 154
	— paragraph 1, first subparagraph, point (B), first subparagraph, point (e), second subparagraph, second indent, first sentence			Article 154
	— paragraph 1, first subparagraph, point (B), first subparagraph, point (e), second subparagraph, second indent, second sentence			Article 157(2)

VAT

Directive 67/227/EEC	*Directive 77/388/EEC*	*Amending Directives*	*Other acts*	*This Directive*
	— paragraph 1, first subparagraph, point (B), first subparagraph, point (e), third subparagraph, first indent			—
	— paragraph 1, first subparagraph, point (B), first subparagraph, point (e), third subparagraph, second, third and fourth indents			Article 158(1)(a), (b) and (c)
	— paragraph 1, first subparagraph, point (B), second subparagraph			Article 156(2)
	— paragraph 1, first subparagraph, point (C)			Article 159
	— paragraph 1, first subparagraph, point (D), first subparagraph, points (a) and (b)			Article 160(1)(a) and (b)
	— paragraph 1, first subparagraph, point (D), second subparagraph			Articles 160(2)
	— paragraph 1, first subparagraph, point (E), first and second indents			Article 161(a) and (b)

Directive 67/227/EEC	*Directive 77/388/EEC*	*Amending Directives*	*Other acts*	*This Directive*
	— paragraph 1, second subparagraph			Article 202
	— paragraph 1, third subparagraph			Article 163
	Article 28c(E), point (1), second indent, inserting paragraph 1a into Article 16			
	— paragraph 1a			Article 162
	Article 28c(E), point (2), first indent, amending Article 16(2)			
	— paragraph 2, first subparagraph			Article 164(1)
	Article 28c(E), point (2), second indent, inserting the second and third subparagraphs into Article 16(2)			
	— paragraph 2, second subparagraph			Article 164(2)
	— paragraph 2, third subparagraph			Article 165
	Article 28c(E), point (3), first to fifth indents			Article 141(a) to (e)
	Article 28d(1), first and second sentences			Article 68, first and second paragraphs
	Article 28d(2) and (3)			Article 69(1) and (2)

Directive 67/227/EEC	*Directive 77/388/EEC*	*Amending Directives*	*Other acts*	*This Directive*
	Article 28d(4), first and second subparagraphs			Article 67(1) and (2)
	Article 28e(1), first subparagraph			Article 83
	Article 28e(1), second subparagraph, first and second sentences			Article 84(1) and (2)
	Article 28e(2)			Article 76
	Article 28e(3)			Article 93, second paragraph, point (b)
	Article 28e(4)			Article 94(1)
	Article 28f, point (1) replacing Article 17(2), (3) and (4)			
	— paragraph 2(a)			Article 168(a)
	— paragraph 2(b)			Article 168(e)
	— paragraph 2(c)			Article 168(b) and (d)
	— paragraph 2(d)			Article 168(c)
	— paragraph 3(a), (b) and (c)			Article 169(a), (b) and (c) Article 170(a) and (b)
	— paragraph 4, first subparagraph, first indent			Article 171(1), first subparagraph
	— paragraph 4, first subparagraph, second indent			Article 171(2), first subparagraph

Directive 67/227/EEC	*Directive 77/388/EEC*	*Amending Directives*	*Other acts*	*This Directive*
	— paragraph 4, second subparagraph, point (a)			Article 171(1), second subparagraph
	— paragraph 4, second subparagraph, point (b)			Article 171(2), second subparagraph
	— paragraph 4, second subparagraph, point (c)			Article 171(3)
	Article 28f, point (2) replacing Article 18(1)			
	— paragraph 1(a)			Article 178(a)
	— paragraph 1(b)			Article 178(e)
	— paragraph 1(c)			Article 178(b) and (d)
	— paragraph 1(d)			Article 178(f)
	— paragraph 1(e)			Article 178(c)
	Article 28f, point (3) inserting paragraph 3a into Article 18			
	— paragraph 3a, first part of the sentence			Article 181
	— paragraph 3a, second part of the sentence			Article 182
	Article 28g replacing Article 21			
	— paragraph 1(a), first subparagraph			Article 193
	— paragraph 1(a), second subparagraph			Article 194(1) and (2)
	— paragraph 1(b)			Article 196

Directive 67/227/EEC	*Directive 77/388/EEC*	*Amending Directives*	*Other acts*	*This Directive*
	— paragraph 1(c), first subparagraph, first, second and third indents			Article 197(1)(a), (b) and (c)
	— paragraph 1(c), second subparagraph			Article 197(2)
	— paragraph 1(d)			Article 203
	— paragraph 1(e)			Article 200
	— paragraph 1(f)			Article 195
	— paragraph 2			—
	— paragraph 2(a), first sentence			Article 204(1), first subparagraph
	— paragraph 2(a), second sentence			Article 204(2)
	— paragraph 2(b)			Article 204(1), second subparagraph
	— paragraph 2(c), first subparagraph			Article 199(1)(a) to (g)
	— paragraph 2(c), second, third and fourth subparagraphs			Article 199(2), (3) and (4)
	— paragraph 3			Article 205
	— paragraph 4			Article 201
	Article 28h replacing Article 22			

Directive 67/227/EEC	Directive 77/388/EEC	Amending Directives	Other acts	This Directive
	— paragraph 1(a), first and second sentences			Article 213(1), first and second subparagraphs
	— paragraph 1(b)			Article 213(2)
	— paragraph 1(c), first indent, first sentence			Article 214(1)(a)
	— paragraph 1(c), first indent, second sentence			Article 214(2)
	— paragraph 1(c), second and third indents			Article 214(1)(b) and (c)
	— paragraph 1(d), first and second sentences			Article 215, first and second paragraphs
	— paragraph 1(e)			Article 216
	— paragraph 2(a)			Article 242
	— paragraph 2(b), first and second indents			Article 243(1) and (2)
	— paragraph 3(a), first subparagraph, first sentence			Article 220, point (1)
	— paragraph 3(a), first subparagraph, second sentence			Article 220, points (2) and (3)
	— paragraph 3(a), second subparagraph			Article 220, points (4) and (5)
	— paragraph 3(a), third subparagraph, first and second sentences			Article 221(1), first and second subparagraphs

Directive 67/227/EEC	*Directive 77/388/EEC*	*Amending Directives*	*Other acts*	*This Directive*
	— paragraph 3(a), fourth subparagraph			Article 221(2)
	— paragraph 3(a), fifth subparagraph, first sentence			Article 219
	— paragraph 3(a), fifth subparagraph, second sentence			Article 228
	— paragraph 3(a), sixth subparagraph			Article 222
	— paragraph 3(a), seventh subparagraph			Article 223
	— paragraph 3(a), eighth subparagraph, first and second sentences			Article 224(1) and (2)
	— paragraph 3(a), ninth subparagraph, first and second sentences			Article 224(3), first subparagraph
	— paragraph 3(a), ninth subparagraph, third sentence			Article 224(3), second subparagraph
	— paragraph 3(a), tenth subparagraph			Article 225
	— paragraph 3(b), first subparagraph, first to twelfth indents			Article 226, points (1) to (12)
	— paragraph 3(b), first subparagraph, thirteenth indent			Article 226, points (13) and (14)

Directive 67/227/EEC	*Directive 77/388/EEC*	*Amending Directives*	*Other acts*	*This Directive*
	— paragraph 3(b), first subparagraph, fourteenth indent			Article 226, point (15)
	— paragraph 3(b), second subparagraph			Article 227
	— paragraph 3(b), third subparagraph			Article 229
	— paragraph 3(b), fourth subparagraph			Article 230
	— paragraph 3(b), fifth subparagraph			Article 231
	— paragraph 3(c), first subparagraph			Article 232
	— paragraph 3(c), second subparagraph, introductory sentence			Article 233(1), first subparagraph
	— paragraph 3(c), second subparagraph, first indent, first sentence			Article 233(1), first subparagraph, point (a)
	— paragraph 3(c), second subparagraph, first indent, second sentence			Article 233(2)
	— paragraph 3(c), second subparagraph, second indent, first sentence			Article 233(1), first subparagraph, point (b)
	— paragraph 3(c), second subparagraph, second indent, second sentence			Article 233(3)

Directive 67/227/EEC	*Directive 77/388/EEC*	*Amending Directives*	*Other acts*	*This Directive*
	— paragraph 3(c), third subparagraph, first sentence			Article 233(1), second subparagraph
	— paragraph 3(c), third subparagraph, second sentence			Article 237
	— paragraph 3(c), fourth subparagraph, first and second sentences			Article 234
	— paragraph 3(c), fifth subparagraph			Article 235
	— paragraph 3(c), sixth subparagraph			Article 236
	— paragraph 3(d), first subparagraph			Article 244
	— paragraph 3(d), second subparagraph, first sentence			Article 245(1)
	— paragraph 3(d), second subparagraph, second and third sentences			Article 245(2), first and second subparagraphs
	— paragraph 3(d), third subparagraph, first and second sentences			Article 246, first and second paragraphs
	— paragraph 3(d), fourth, fifth and sixth subparagraphs			Article 247(1), (2) and (3)
	— paragraph 3(d), seventh subparagraph			Article 248

Directive 67/227/EEC	*Directive 77/388/EEC*	*Amending Directives*	*Other acts*	*This Directive*
	— paragraph 3(e), first subparagraph			Articles 217 and 241
	— paragraph 3(e), second subparagraph			Article 218
	— paragraph 4(a), first and second sentences			Article 252(1)
	— paragraph 4(a), third and fourth sentences			Article 252(2), first and second subparagraphs
	— paragraph 4(a), fifth sentence			Article 250(2)
	— paragraph 4(b)			Article 250(1)
	— paragraph 4(c), first indent, first and second subparagraphs			Article 251(a) and (b)
	— paragraph 4(c), second indent, first subparagraph			Article 251(c)
	— paragraph 4(c), second indent, second subparagraph			Article 251(d) and (e)
	— paragraph 5			Article 206
	— paragraph 6(a), first and second sentences			Article 261(1)
	— paragraph 6(a), third sentence			Article 261(2)
	— paragraph 6(b), first subparagraph			Article 262

Directive 67/227/EEC	*Directive 77/388/EEC*	*Amending Directives*	*Other acts*	*This Directive*
	— paragraph 6(b), second subparagraph, first sentence			Article 263(1), first subparagraph
	— paragraph 6(b), second subparagraph, second sentence			Article 263(2)
	— paragraph 6(b), third subparagraph, first and second indents			Article 264(1)(a) and (b)
	— paragraph 6(b), third subparagraph, third indent, first sentence			Article 264(1)(d)
	— paragraph 6(b), third subparagraph, third indent, second sentence			Article 264(2), first subparagraph
	— paragraph 6(b), fourth subparagraph, first indent			Article 264(1)(c) and (e)
	— paragraph 6(b), fourth subparagraph, second indent, first sentence			Article 264(1)(f)
	— paragraph 6(b), fourth subparagraph, second indent, second sentence			Article 264(2), second subparagraph
	— paragraph 6(b), fifth subparagraph, first and second indents			Article 265(1)(a) and (b)
	— paragraph 6(b), fifth subparagraph, third indent, first sentence			Article 265(1)(c)

Directive 67/227/EEC	*Directive 77/388/EEC*	*Amending Directives*	*Other acts*	*This Directive*
	— paragraph 6(b), fifth subparagraph, third indent, second sentence			Article 265(2)
	— paragraph 6(c), first indent			Article 263(1), second subparagraph
	— paragraph 6(c), second indent			Article 266
	— paragraph 6(d)			Article 254
	— paragraph 6(e), first subparagraph			Article 268
	— paragraph 6(e), second subparagraph			Article 259
	— paragraph 7, first part of the sentence			Article 207, first paragraph Article 256 Article 267
	— paragraph 7, second part of the sentence			Article 207, second paragraph
	— paragraph 8, first and second subparagraphs			Article 273, first and second paragraphs
	— paragraph 9(a), first subparagraph, first indent			Article 272(1), first subparagraph, point (c)
	— paragraph 9(a), first subparagraph, second indent			Article 272(1), first subparagraph, points (a) and (d)
	— paragraph 9(a), first subparagraph, third indent			Article 272(1), first subparagraph, point (b)

Directive 67/227/EEC	*Directive 77/388/EEC*	*Amending Directives*	*Other acts*	*This Directive*
	— paragraph 9(a), second subparagraph			Article 272(1), second subparagraph
	— paragraph 9(b)			Article 272(3)
	— paragraph 9(c)			Article 212
	— paragraph 9(d), first subparagraph, first and second indents			Article 238(1)(a) and (b)
	— paragraph 9(d), second subparagraph, first to fourth indents			Article 238(2)(a) to (d)
	— paragraph 9(d), third subparagraph			Article 238(3)
	— paragraph 9(e), first subparagraph			Article 239
	— paragraph 9(e), second subparagraph, first and second indents			Article 240, points (1) and (2)
	— paragraph 10			Articles 209 and 257
	— paragraph 11			Articles 210 and 258
	— paragraph 12, introductory sentence			Article 269
	— paragraph 12(a), first, second and third indents			Article 270(a), (b) and (c)
	— paragraph 12(b), first second and third indents			Article 271(a), (b) and (c)

Directive 67/227/EEC	*Directive 77/388/EEC*	*Amending Directives*	*Other acts*	*This Directive*
	Article 28i inserting a third subparagraph into Article 24(3)			
	— paragraph 3, third subparagraph			Article 283(1)(b) and (c)
	Article 28j, point (1) inserting a second subparagraph into Article 25(4)			
	— paragraph 4, second subparagraph			Article 272(2)
	Article 28j, point (2) replacing Article 25(5) and (6)			
	— paragraph 5, first subparagraph, points (a), (b) and (c)			Article 300, points (1), (2) and (3)
	— paragraph 5, second subparagraph			Article 302
	— paragraph 6(a), first subparagraph, first sentence			Article 301(1)
	— paragraph 6(a), first subparagraph, second sentence			Article 303(1)
	— paragraph 6(a), second subparagraph, first, second and third indents			Article 303(2)(a), (b) and (c)
	— paragraph 6(a), third subparagraph			Article 303(3)

Directive 67/227/EEC	*Directive 77/388/EEC*	*Amending Directives*	*Other acts*	*This Directive*
	— paragraph 6(b)			Article 301(1)
	Article 28j, point (3) inserting a second subparagraph into Article 25(9)			
	— paragraph 9, second subparagraph			Article 305
	Article 28k, point (1), first subparagraph			—
	Article 28k, point (1), second subparagraph, point (a)			Article 158(3)
	Article 28k, point (1), second subparagraph, points (b) and (c)			—
	Article 28k, points (2), (3) and (4)			—
	Article 28k, point (5)			Article 158(2)
	Article 28l, first paragraph			—
	Article 28l, second and third paragraphs			Article 402(1) and (2)
	Article 28l, fourth paragraph			—
	Article 28m			Article 399, first paragraph
	Article 28n			—
	Article 28o(1), introductory sentence			Article 326, first paragraph
	Article 28o(1)(a), first sentence			Article 327(1) and (3)

Directive 67/227/EEC	*Directive 77/388/EEC*	*Amending Directives*	*Other acts*	*This Directive*
	Article 28o(1)(a), second sentence			Article 327(2)
	Article 28o(1)(b)			Article 328
	Article 28o(1)(c), first second and third indents			Article 329(a), (b) and (c)
	Article 28o(1)(d), first and second subparagraphs			Article 330, first and second paragraphs
	Article 28o(1)(e)			Article 332
	Article 28o(1)(f)			Article 331
	Article 28o(1)(g)			Article 4(b)
	Article 28o(1)(h)			Article 35 Article 139(3), second subparagraph
	Article 28o(2)			Article 326, second paragraph
	Article 28o(3)			Article 341
	Article 28o(4)			—
	Article 28p(1), first, second and third indents			Article 405, points (1), (2) and (3)
	Article 28p(2)			Article 406
	Article 28p(3), first subparagraph, first and second indents			Article 407(a) and (b)
	Article 28p(3), second subparagraph			—
	Article 28p(4)(a) to (d)			Article 408(1)(a) to (d)

Directive 67/227/EEC	*Directive 77/388/EEC*	*Amending Directives*	*Other acts*	*This Directive*
	Article 28p(5), first and second indents			Article 408(2)(a) and (b)
	Article 28p(6)			Article 409
	Article 28p(7), first subparagraph, points (a), (b) and (c)			Article 410(1)(a), (b) and (c)
	Article 28p(7), second subparagraph, first indent			—
	Article 28p(7), second subparagraph, second, third and fourth indents			Article 410(2)(a), (b) and (c)
	Article 29(1) to (4)			Article 398(1) to (4)
	Article 29a			Article 397
	Article 30(1)			Article 396(1)
	Article 30(2), first and second sentences			Article 396(2), first subparagraph
	Article 30(2), third sentence			Article 396(2), second subparagraph
	Article 30(3) and (4)			Article 396(3) and (4)
	Article 31(1)			—
	Article 31(2)			Article 400
	Article 33(1)			Article 401
	Article 33(2)			Article 2(3)
	Article 33a(1), introductory sentence			Article 274

Directive 67/227/EEC	*Directive 77/388/EEC*	*Amending Directives*	*Other acts*	*This Directive*
	Article 33a(1)(a)			Article 275
	Article 33a(1)(b)			Article 276
	Article 33a(1)(c)			Article 277
	Article 33a(2), introductory sentence			Article 278
	Article 33a(2)(a)			Article 279
	Article 33a(2)(b)			Article 280
	Article 34			Article 404
	Article 35			Article 403
	Articles 36 and 37			—
	Article 38			Article 414
	Annex A(I)(1) and (2)			Annex VII, point (1)(a) and (b)
	Annex A(I)(3)			Annex VII, points (1)(c) and (d)
	Annex A(II)(1) to (6)			Annex VII, points (2)(a) to (f)
	Annex A(III) and (IV)			Annex VII, points (3) and (4)
	Annex A(IV)(1) to (4)			Annex VII, points (4)(a) to (d)
	Annex A(V)			Article 295(2)
	Annex B, introductory sentence			Article 295(1), point (5)
	Annex B, first to ninth indents			Annex VIII, points (1) to (9)
	Annex C			—

VAT

Directive 67/227/EEC	*Directive 77/388/EEC*	*Amending Directives*	*Other acts*	*This Directive*
	Annex D(1) to (13)			Annex I, points (1) to (13)
	Annex E(2)			Annex X, Part A, point (1)
	Annex E(7)			Annex X, Part A, point (2)
	Annex E(11)			Annex X, Part A, point (3)
	Annex E(15)			Annex X, Part A, point (4)
	Annex F(1)			Annex X, Part B, point (1)
	Annex F(2)			Annex X, Part B, points (2)(a) to (j)
	Annex F(5) to (8)			Annex X, Part B, points (3) to (6)
	Annex F(10)			Annex X, Part B, point (7)
	Annex F(12)			Annex X, Part B, point (8)
	Annex F(16)			Annex X, Part B, point (9)
	Annex F(17), first and second subparagraphs			Annex X, Part B, point (10)
	Annex F(23)			Annex X, Part B, point (11)
	Annex F(25)			Annex X, Part B, point (12)
	Annex F(27)			Annex X, Part B, point (13)
	Annex G(1) and (2)			Article 391
	Annex H, first paragraph			Article 98(3)
	Annex H, second paragraph, introductory sentence			—

Directive 67/227/EEC	*Directive 77/388/EEC*	*Amending Directives*	*Other acts*	*This Directive*
	Annex H, second paragraph, points (1) to (6)			Annex III, points (1) to (6)
	Annex H, second paragraph, point (7), first and second subparagraphs			Annex III, points (7) and (8)
	Annex H, second paragraph, points (8) to (17)			Annex III, points (9) to (18)
	Annex I, introductory sentence			—
	Annex I(a), first to seventh indents			Annex IX, Part A, points (1) to (7)
	Annex I(b), first and second indents			Annex IX, Part B, points (1) and (2)
	Annex I(c)			Annex IX, Part C
	Annex J, introductory sentence			Annex V, introductory sentence
	Annex J			Annex V, points (1) to (25)
	Annex K(1), first, second and third indents			Annex IV, points (1)(a), (b) and (c)
	Annex K(2) to (5)			Annex IV, points (2) to (5)
	Annex L, first paragraph, points (1) to (5)			Annex II, points (1) to (5)
	Annex L, second paragraph			Article 56(2)
	Annex M, points (a) to (f)			Annex VI, points (1) to (6)

Directive 67/227/EEC	*Directive 77/388/EEC*	*Amending Directives*	*Other acts*	*This Directive*
		Article 1, point (1), second subparagraph, of Directive 89/465/EEC		Article 133, second paragraph
		Article 2 of Directive 94/5/EC		Article 342
		Article 3, first and second sentences, of Directive 94/5/EC		Article 343, first and second paragraphs
		Article 4 of Directive 2002/38/EC		Article 56(3) Article 57(2) Article 357
		Article 5 of Directive 2002/38/EC		—
			Annex VIII(II), point (2)(a) of the Act of Accession of Greece	Article 287, point (1)
			Annex VIII(II), point (2)(b) of the Act of Accession of Greece	Article 375
			Annex XXXII(IV), point (3)(a), first indent and second indent, first sentence, of the Act of Accession of Spain and Portugal	Article 287, points (2) and (3)
			Annex XXXII(IV), point (3)(b), first subparagraph, of the Act of Accession of Spain and Portugal	Article 377

Directive 67/227/EEC	*Directive 77/388/EEC*	*Amending Directives*	*Other acts*	*This Directive*
			Annex XV(IX), point (2)(b), first subparagraph, of the Act of Accession of Austria, Finland and Sweden	Article 104
			Annex XV(IX), point (2)(c), first subparagraph, of the Act of Accession of Austria, Finland and Sweden	Article 287, point (4)
			Annex XV(IX), point (2)(f), first subparagraph, of the Act of Accession of Austria, Finland and Sweden	Article 117(1)
			Annex XV(IX), point (2)(g), first subparagraph, of the Act of Accession of Austria, Finland and Sweden	Article 119
			Annex XV(IX), point (2)(h), first subparagraph, first and second indents, of the Act of Accession of Austria, Finland and Sweden	Article 378(1)
			Annex XV(IX), point (2)(i), first subparagraph, first indent, of the Act of Accession of Austria, Finland and Sweden	—
			Annex XV(IX), point (2)(i), first subparagraph, second and third indents, of the Act of Accession of Austria, Finland and Sweden	Article 378(2)(a) and (b)

Directive 67/227/EEC	*Directive 77/388/EEC*	*Amending Directives*	*Other acts*	*This Directive*
			Annex XV(IX), point (2)(j) of the Act of Accession of Austria, Finland and Sweden	Article 287, point (5)
			Annex XV(IX), point (2)(l), first subparagraph, of the Act of Accession of Austria, Finland and Sweden	Article 111(a)
			Annex XV(IX), point (2)(m), first subparagraph, of the Act of Accession of Austria, Finland and Sweden	Article 379(1)
			Annex XV(IX), point (2)(n), first subparagraph, first and second indents, of the Act of Accession of Austria, Finland and Sweden	Article 379(2)
			Annex XV(IX), point (2)(x), first indent, of the Act of Accession of Austria, Finland and Sweden	Article 253
			Annex XV(IX), point (2)(x), second indent, of the Act of Accession of Austria, Finland and Sweden	Article 287, point (6)
			Annex XV(IX), point (2)(z), first subparagraph, of the Act of Accession of Austria, Finland and Sweden	Article 111(b)

Directive 67/227/EEC	*Directive 77/388/EEC*	*Amending Directives*	*Other acts*	*This Directive*
			Annex XV(IX), point (2)(aa), first subparagraph, first and second indents, of the Act of Accession of Austria, Finland and Sweden	Article 380
			Protocol No 2 of the Act of Accession of Austria, Finland and Sweden concerning the Åland Islands	Article 6(1)(d)
			Annex V(5), point (1)(a) of the 2003 Act of Accession of the Czech Republic, Estonia, Cyprus, Latvia, Lithuania, Hungary, Malta, Poland Slovenia and Slovakia	Article 123
			Annex V(5), point (1)(b) of the 2003 Act of Accession	Article 381
			Annex VI(7), point (1)(a) of the 2003 Act of Accession	Article 124
			Annex VI(7), point (1)(b) of the 2003 Act of Accession	Article 382
			Annex VII(7), point (1), first and second subparagraphs, of the 2003 Act of Accession	Article 125(1) and (2)
			Annex VII(7), point (1), third subparagraph, of the 2003 Act of Accession	—
			Annex VII(7), point (1), fourth subparagraph, of the 2003 Act of Accession	Article 383(a)

Directive 67/227/EEC	*Directive 77/388/EEC*	*Amending Directives*	*Other acts*	*This Directive*
			Annex VII(7), point (1), fifth subparagraph, of the 2003 Act of Accession	—
			Annex VII(7), point (1), sixth subparagraph, of the 2003 Act of Accession	Article 383(b)
			Annex VIII(7), point (1)(a) of the 2003 Act of Accession	—
			Annex VIII(7), point (1)(b), second subparagraph, of the 2003 Act of Accession	Article 384(a)
			Annex VIII(7), point (1), third subparagraph, of the 2003 Act of Accession	Article 384(b)
			Annex IX(8), point (1) of the 2003 Act of Accession	Article 385
			Annex X(7), point (1)(a)(i) and (ii) of the 2003 Act of Accession	Article 126(a) and (b)
			Annex X(7), point (1)(c) of the 2003 Act of Accession	Article 386
			Annex XI(7), point (1) of the 2003 Act of Accession	Article 127
			Annex XI(7), point (2)(a) of the 2003 Act of Accession	Article 387(c)
			Annex XI(7), point (2)(b) of the 2003 Act of Accession	Article 387(a)
			Annex XI(7), point (2)(c) of the 2003 Act of Accession	Article 387(b)

Directive 67/227/EEC	*Directive 77/388/EEC*	*Amending Directives*	*Other acts*	*This Directive*
			Annex XII(9), point (1)(a) of the 2003 Act of Accession	Article 128(1) and (2)
			Annex XII(9), point (1)(b) of the 2003 Act of Accession	Article 128(3), (4) and (5)
			Annex XII(9), point (2) of the 2003 Act of Accession	Article 388
			Annex XIII(9), point (1)(a) of the 2003 Act of Accession	Article 129(1) and (2)
			Annex XIII(9), point (1)(b) of the 2003 Act of Accession	Article 389
			Annex XIV(7), first subparagraph, of the 2003 Act of Accession	Article 130(a) and (b)
			Annex XIV(7), second subparagraph, of the 2003 Act of Accession	—
			Annex XIV(7), third subparagraph, of the 2003 Act of Accession	Article 390

Council Directive
of 20 December 2007
on the exemption from value added tax and excise duty of goods imported by persons travelling from third countries

(2007/74/EC)

Note—See OJ L 346, 29.12.2007 p 6.

THE COUNCIL OF THE EUROPEAN UNION,

Having regard to the Treaty establishing the European Community, and in particular Article 93 thereof,

Having regard to the proposal from the Commission,

Having regard to the Opinion of the European Parliament,

Having regard to the Opinion of the European Economic and Social Committee,

Whereas:

(1) Council Directive 69/169/EEC of 28 May 1969 on the harmonisation of provisions laid down by law, regulation or administrative action relating to exemption from turnover tax and excise duty on imports in international travel[1] established a Community system of tax exemptions. While it remains necessary to maintain that system in order to prevent double taxation, as well as in cases where, in view of the conditions under which goods are imported, the usual need to protect the economy is absent, it should still apply only to non-commercial imports of goods in the personal luggage of travellers from third countries.

(2) However, given the number of amendments required, as well as the need to adapt Directive 69/169/EEC to enlargement and to the new external borders of the Community, and to re-structure and simplify certain provisions for the sake of clarity, the complete revision and repeal and replacement of Directive 69/169/EEC is justified.

(3) The quantitative limits and monetary thresholds to which the exemptions are subject should meet the current needs of Member States.

(4) The monetary threshold should take account of changes in the real value of money since the last increase in 1994 and should also reflect the abolition of quantitative limits on goods subject to excise duties in some Member States which will now fall into the general threshold on VAT.

(5) The ease of shopping abroad could cause problems to Member States which share land-borders with third countries with significantly lower prices. It is justifiable, therefore, to set a lower monetary threshold for forms of travel other than air and sea travel.

(6) In the experience of the Commission, the quantities for tobacco products and alcoholic beverages have, in general, been shown to be appropriate and should therefore be maintained.

(7) The quantitative limits for the exemption of excise goods should reflect the current scheme of taxation of such goods in the Member States. Accordingly, it is appropriate to provide for a limit for beer whereas the limits for perfume, coffee and tea should be discontinued.

(8) It is appropriate to allow Member States to set lower limits with regard to the monetary threshold for children and to exclude under-aged persons from the exemptions for tobacco products and alcoholic beverages, in order to ensure a high level of health protection.

(9) Given the need to promote a high level of human health protection for Community citizens, it is appropriate to allow Member States to apply reduced quantitative limits for the exemption of tobacco products.

(10) In order to take account of the special situation of certain people with regard to their location or working environment, it should also be possible for Member States to apply narrower exemptions in the case of frontier workers, persons residing near Community frontiers and the crew of the means of transport used in international travel.

(11) It is to be recalled that Austria shares a land border with Samnauntal, a Swiss enclave where a specific tax system is applied which results in significantly lower taxation than that applicable under the rules applying in the rest of Switzerland and, indeed, in the Kanton of Graubünden of which Samnauntal forms part. In view of that special situation, which has led Austria to apply lower quantitative limits for tobacco products with respect to that enclave in accordance with Article 5(8) of Directive 69/169/EEC, it is appropriate to allow that Member State to apply the lower limit provided for tobacco products by this Directive only to Samnauntal.

(12) For Member States which have not introduced the euro, a mechanism should be set up to enable amounts expressed in national currencies to be converted into euro and thus ensure equal treatment in the Member States.

(13) The amount on which Member States are free not to levy taxes on the import of goods should be increased in order to reflect current monetary values,

HAS ADOPTED THIS DIRECTIVE:

Note—[1] OJ L 133, 4.6.1969 p 6. Directive as last amended by Directive 2005/93/EC (OJ L 346, 29.12.2005 p 16).

CHAPTER 1

SUBJECT-MATTER AND DEFINITIONS

Article 1

This Directive lays down rules relating to the exemption from value added tax (VAT) and excise duty of goods imported in the personal luggage of persons travelling from a third country or from a territory where the Community provisions on VAT or excise duty, or both, as defined in Article 3, do not apply.

Article 2

Where a journey involves transit through the territory of a third country, or begins in a territory as referred to in Article 1, this Directive shall apply if the traveller is unable to establish that the goods transported in his luggage have been acquired subject to the general conditions governing taxation on the domestic market of a Member State and do not qualify for any refunding of VAT or excise duty.

Overflying without landing shall not be regarded as transit.

Article 3

For the purposes of this Directive, the following definitions shall apply:

1. "third country" means any country which is not a Member State of the European Union;

In view of the Fiscal Agreement between France and the Principality of Monaco dated 18 May 1963 and the Agreement of friendship and neighbourly relations between Italy and the Republic of San Marino dated 31 March 1939, Monaco shall not be regarded as a third country and San Marino shall not be regarded as a third country in respect of excise duty;

2. "territory where the Community provisions on VAT or excise duty, or both do not apply" means any territory, other than a territory of a third country, where Directives 2006/112/EC[1] or 92/12/EEC, or both do not apply;

In view of the Agreement between the Governments of the United Kingdom and the Isle of Man on Customs and Excise and associated matters dated 15 October 1979, the Isle of Man shall not be regarded as a territory where the Community provisions on VAT or excise duty, or both do not apply;

3. "air travellers" and "sea travellers" means any passengers travelling by air or sea other than private pleasure-flying or private pleasure-sea-navigation;

4. "private pleasure-flying" and "private pleasure-sea-navigation" means the use of an aircraft or a sea-going vessel by its owner or the natural or legal person who enjoys its use either through hire or through any other means, for purposes other than commercial and in particular other than for the carriage of passengers or goods or for the supply of services for consideration or for the purposes of public authorities;

5. "frontier zone" means a zone which, as the crow flies, does not extend more than 15 kilometres from the frontier of a Member State and which includes the local administrative districts part of the territory of which lies within the zone; Member States may grant exemptions therefrom;

6. "frontier-zone worker" means any person whose normal activities require that he should go to the other side of the frontier on his work days.

Note—[1] OJ L 347, 11.12.2006 p 1. Directive as amended by Directive 2006/138/EC (OJ L 384, 29.12. 2006 p 92).

CHAPTER 2

EXEMPTIONS

SECTION 1

COMMON PROVISIONS

Article 4

Member States shall, on the basis of either monetary thresholds or quantitative limits, exempt from VAT and excise duty goods imported in the personal luggage of travellers, provided that the imports are of a non-commercial character.

Article 5

For the purposes of the application of the exemptions, personal luggage shall be regarded as the whole of the luggage which a traveller is able to present to the customs authorities upon arrival, as well as luggage which he presents later to the same authorities, subject to proof that such luggage was registered as ac-companied luggage, at the time of his departure, with the company which has been responsible for conveying him. Fuel other than that referred to in Article 11 shall not be regarded as personal luggage.

Article 6

For the purposes of the application of the exemptions, imports shall be regarded as being of a non-commercial character if they meet the following conditions:

(a) they take place occasionally;

(b) they consist exclusively of goods for the personal or family use of the travellers, or of goods intended as presents.

The nature or quantity of the goods must not be such as to indicate that they are being imported for commercial reasons.

Article 7

1. Member States shall exempt from VAT and excise duty imports of goods, other than those referred to in Section 3, the total value of which does not exceed EUR 300 per person.

In the case of air and sea travellers, the monetary threshold specified in the first subparagraph shall be EUR 430.

2. Member States may lower the monetary threshold for travellers under 15 years old, whatever their means of transport. However, the monetary threshold may not be lower than EUR 150.

3. For the purposes of applying the monetary thresholds, the value of an individual item may not be split up.

4. The value of the personal luggage of a traveller, which is imported temporarily or is re-imported following its temporary export, and the value of medicinal products required to meet the personal needs of a traveller shall not be taken into consideration for the purposes of applying the exemptions referred to in paragraphs 1 and 2.

SECTION 3
QUANTITATIVE LIMITS

Article 8

1. Member States shall exempt from VAT and excise duty imports of the following types of tobacco product, subject either to the following higher or lower quantitative limits:

(*a*) 200 cigarettes or 40 cigarettes;

(*b*) 100 cigarillos or 20 cigarillos;

(*c*) 50 cigars or 10 cigars;

(*d*) 250g smoking tobacco or 50g smoking tobacco.

Each amount specified in points (*a*) to (*d*) shall represent, for the purposes of paragraph 4, 100% of the total allowance for tobacco products.

Cigarillos are cigars of a maximum weight of 3 grams each.

2. Member States may choose to distinguish between air travellers and other travellers by applying the lower quantitative limits specified in paragraph 1 only to travellers other than air travellers.

3. By derogation from paragraphs 1 and 2, Austria may, as long as the tax system in the Swiss enclave of Samnauntal differs from that applicable in the rest of the Kanton of Graubünden, limit the application of the lower quantitative limit to tobacco products brought into the territory of that Member State by travellers who enter its territory directly from the Swiss enclave of Samnauntal.

4. In the case of any one traveller, the exemption may be applied to any combination of tobacco products, provided that the aggregate of the percentages used up from the individual allowances does not exceed 100%.

Article 9

1. Member States shall exempt from VAT and excise duty alcohol and alcoholic beverages other than still wine and beer, subject to the following quantitative limits:

(*a*) a total of 1 litre of alcohol and alcoholic beverages of an alcoholic strength exceeding 22% vol, or un-denatured ethyl alcohol of 80% vol and over;

(*b*) a total of 2 litres of alcohol and alcoholic beverages of an alcoholic strength not exceeding 22% vol.

Each of the amounts specified in points (*a*) and (*b*) represent, for the purposes of paragraph 2, 100% of the total allowance for alcohol and alcoholic beverages.

2. In the case of any one traveller, the exemption may be applied to any combination of the types of alcohol and alcoholic beverage referred to in paragraph 1, provided that the aggregate of the percentages used up from the individual allowances does not exceed 100%.

3. Member States shall exempt from VAT and excise duty a total of 4 litres of still wine and 16 litres of beer.

Article 10

Exemptions under Articles 8 or 9 shall not apply in the case of travellers under 17 years of age.

Article 11

Member States shall exempt from VAT and excise duty, in the case of any one means of motor transport, the fuel contained in the standard tank and a quantity of fuel not exceeding 10 litres contained in a port-able container.

Article 12

The value of goods referred to in Articles 8, 9 or 11 shall not be taken into consideration for the purposes of applying the exemption provided for in Article 7(1).

CHAPTER 3

SPECIAL CASES

Article 13

1. Member States may lower the monetary thresholds or the quantitative limits, or both, in the case of travellers in the following categories:

(*a*) persons resident in a frontier zone;

(*b*) frontier-zone workers;

(*c*) the crew of a means of transport used to travel from a third country or from a territory where the Community provisions on VAT or excise duty, or both do not apply.

2. Paragraph 1 shall not apply where a traveller in one of the categories listed therein produces evidence to show that he is going beyond the frontier zone of the Member State or that he is not returning from the frontier zone of the neighbouring third country.

However, it shall apply where frontier-zone workers or the crew of the means of transport used in international travel import goods when travelling in the course of their work.

CHAPTER IV

GENERAL AND FINAL PROVISIONS

Article 14

Member States may choose not to levy VAT or excise duty on the import of goods by a traveller when the amount of the tax which should be levied is equal to, or less than, EUR 10.

Article 15

1. The euro equivalent in national currency which shall apply for the implementation of this Directive shall be fixed once a year. The rates applicable shall be those obtaining on the first working day of October. They shall be published in the Official Journal of the European Union and shall apply from 1 January of the following year.

2. Member States may round off the amounts in national currency resulting from the conversion of the amounts in euro provided for in Article 7, provided such rounding-off does not exceed EUR 5.

3. Member States may maintain the monetary thresholds in force at the time of the annual adjustment provided for in paragraph 1 if, prior to the rounding-off provided for in paragraph 2, conversion of the corresponding amounts expressed in euro would result in a change of less than 5% in the exemption expressed in national currency or in a lowering of this exemption.

Article 16

Every four years and for the first time in 2012 the Commission shall forward a report on the implementation of this Directive to the Council, where appropriate accompanied by a proposal for amendment.

Article 17

In Article 5(9) of Directive 69/169/EEC the date of 31 December 2007 shall be replaced by 30 November 2008.

Article 18

Directive 69/169/EEC shall be repealed and replaced by this Directive with effect from 1 December 2008.

References to the repealed Directive shall be construed as references to this Directive and shall be read in accordance with the correlation table in the Annex.

Article 19

1. Member States shall bring into force the laws, regulations and administrative provisions necessary to comply with Articles 1 to 15 of this Directive with effect from 1 December 2008. They shall forthwith communicate to the Commission the text of those measures.

When Member States adopt those measures, they shall contain a reference to this Directive or be accompanied by such reference on the occasion of their official publication. Member States shall determine how such reference is to be made.

2. Member States shall communicate to the Commission the text of the main provisions of national law which they adopt in the field covered by this Directive.

Article 20

This Directive shall enter into force on the day of its publication in the Official Journal of the European Union.

It shall apply with effect from 1 December 2008.

However, Article 17 shall apply with effect from 1 January 2008.

Article 21

This Directive is addressed to the Member States.

Done at Brussels, 20 December 2007.

For the Council
The President
F. Nunes Correia

ANNEX

CORRELATION TABLE

Directive 69/169/EEC	*This Directive*
Article 1(1)	Article 7(1)
Article 1(2)	Article 7(2)
Article 1(3)	Article 7(3)
Article 2	–
Article 3, point one	Article 7(4)
Article 3, point two	Article 6
Article 3, point three, first subparagraph	Article 5
Article 3, point three, second subparagraph	Article 5 and 11
Article 4(1), introductory phrase	Article 8(1) introductory phrase, Article 9(1) introductory phrase
Article 4(1), second column	–
Article 4(1)(*a*), first column	Article 8(1)
Article 4(1)(*b*), first column	Article 9(1)
Article 4(1)(*c*), (*d*) and (*e*), first column	–
Article 4(2) first subparagraph	Article 10
Article 4(2) second subparagraph	–
Article 4(3)	Article 12
Article 4(4)	Article 2
Article 4(5)	–
Article 5(1)	–
Article 5(2)	Article 13(1)
Article 5(3)	–
Article 5(4)	Article 13(2)
Article 5(5)	–
Article 5(6), introductory phrase, first indent	Article 3(5)
Article 5(6), introductory phrase, second indent	Article 3(6)
Article 5(7)	–
Article 5(8)	–
Article 5(9)	–
Article 7(1)	–
Article 7(2)	Article 15(1)
Article 7(3)	Article 15(2)
Article 7(4)	Article 15(3)
Article 7(5)	–
Article 7a(1)	–
Article 7a(2)	Article 14
Article 7b	–
Article 7c	–
Article 7d	–
Article 8(1)	Article 19(1), first subparagraph
Article 8(2), first subparagraph	Article 19(1), first subparagraph
Article 8(2), second subparagraph	–

Article 9 Article 21

Council Directive 2008/9/EC
of 12 February 2008
laying down detailed rules for the refund of value added tax, provided for in Directive 2006/112/EC, to taxable persons not established in the Member State of refund but established in another Member State

(2008/9/EC)

Note—See OJ L 44, 20.02.2008 p 23.

THE COUNCIL OF THE EUROPEAN UNION,

Having regard to the Treaty establishing the European Community, and in particular Article 93 thereof,

Having regard to the proposal from the Commission,

Having regard to the opinion of the European Parliament,[1]

Having regard to the opinion of the European Economic and Social Committee,[2]

Whereas:

(1) Considerable problems are posed, both for the administrative authorities of Member States and for businesses, by the implementing rules laid down by Council Directive 79/1072/EEC of 6 December 1979 on the harmonisation of the laws of the Member States relating to turn-over taxes – Arrangements for the refund of value added tax to taxable persons not established in the territory of the country.[3]

(2) The arrangements laid down in that Directive should be amended in respect of the period within which decisions concerning applications for refund are notified to businesses. At the same time, it should be laid down that businesses too must provide responses within specified periods. In addition, the procedure should be simplified and modernised by allowing for the use of modern technologies.

(3) The new procedure should enhance the position of businesses since the Member States shall be liable to pay interest if the refund is made late and the right of appeal by businesses will be strengthened.

(4) For clarity and better reading purposes, the provision concerning the application of Directive 79/1072/EEC, previously contained in Council Directive 2006/112/EC of 28 November 2006 on the common system of value added tax[4], should now be integrated in this Directive.

(5) Since the objectives of this Directive cannot be sufficiently achieved by the Member States and can therefore, by reason of the scale of the action, be better achieved at Community level, the Community may adopt measures, in accordance with the principle of subsidiarity as set out in Article 5 of the Treaty. In accordance with the principle of proportionality, as set out in that Article, this Directive does not go beyond what is necessary in order to achieve those objectives.

(6) In accordance with point 34 of the Interinstitutional Agreement on better law-making[5], Member States are encouraged to draw up, for themselves and in the interests of the Community, their own tables illustrating, as far as possible, the correlation between this Directive and the transposition measures, and to make them public.

(7) In the interest of clarity, Directive 79/1072/EEC should therefore be repealed, subject to the necessary transitional measures with respect to refund applications introduced before 1 January 2010,

HAS ADOPTED THIS DIRECTIVE:

Notes—[1] OJ C 285 E, 22.11.2006 p 122.

[2] OJ C 28, 3.2.2006 p 86.

[3] OJ L 331, 27.12.1979 p 11. Directive as last amended by Directive 2006/98/EC (OJ L 363, 20.12.2006 p 129).

[4] OJ L 347, 11.12.2006 p 1. Directive as last amended by Directive 2007/75/EC (OJ L 346, 29.12.2007 p 13).

[5] OJ C 321, 31.12.2003 p 1.

Article 1

This Directive lays down the detailed rules for the refund of value added tax (VAT), provided for in Article 170 of Directive 2006/112/EC, to taxable persons not established in the Member State of refund, who meet the conditions laid down in Article 3.

Article 2

For the purposes of this Directive, the following definitions shall apply:

1 "taxable person not established in the Member State of refund" means a taxable person within the meaning of Article 9(1) of Directive 2006/112/EC who is not established in the Member State of refund but established in the territory of another Member State;

2 "Member State of refund" means the Member State in which the VAT was charged to the taxable person not established in the Member State of refund in respect of goods or services supplied to him by other taxable persons in that Member State or in respect of the importation of goods into that Member State;

3 "refund period" means the period mentioned in Article 16 covered by the refund application;

4 "refund application" means the application for refund of VAT charged in the Member State of refund to the taxable person not established in the Member State of refund in respect of goods or services supplied to him by other taxable persons in that Member State or in respect of the importation of goods into that Member State;

5 "applicant" means the taxable person not established in the Member State of refund making the refund application.

Article 3

This Directive shall apply to any taxable person not established in the Member State of refund who meets the following conditions:

(*a*) during the refund period, he has not had in the Member State of refund, the seat of his economic activity, or a fixed establishment from which business transactions were effected, or, if no such seat or fixed establishment existed, his domicile or normal place of residence;

(*b*) during the refund period, he has not supplied any goods or services deemed to have been supplied in the Member State of refund, with the exception of the following transactions:

(i) the supply of transport services and services ancillary thereto, exempted pursuant to Articles 144, 146, 148, 149, 151, 153, 159 or 160 of Directive 2006/112/EC;

(ii) the supply of goods and services to a person who is liable for payment of VAT in accordance with Articles 194 to 197 and Article 199 of Directive 2006/112/EC.

Article 4

This Directive shall not apply to:

(*a*) amounts of VAT which, according to the legislation of the Member State of refund, have been incorrectly invoiced;

(*b*) amounts of VAT which have been invoiced in respect of supplies of goods the supply of which is, or may be, exempt under Article 138 or Article 146(1)(*b*) of Directive 2006/112/EC.

Article 5

Each Member State shall refund to any taxable person not established in the Member State of refund any VAT charged in respect of goods or services supplied to him by other taxable persons in that Member State or in respect of the importation of goods into that Member State, insofar as such goods and services are used for the purposes of the following transactions:

(*a*) transactions referred to in Article 169(*a*) and (*b*) of Directive 2006/112/EC;

(*b*) transactions to a person who is liable for payment of VAT in accordance with Articles 194 to 197 and Article 199 of Directive 2006/112/EC as applied in the Member State of refund.

Without prejudice to Article 6, for the purposes of this Directive, entitlement to an input tax refund shall be determined pursuant to Directive 2006/112/EC as applied in the Member State of refund.

Article 6

To be eligible for a refund in the Member State of refund, a taxable person not established in the Member State of refund has to carry out transactions giving rise to a right of deduction in the Member State of establishment.

When a taxable person not established in the Member State of refund carries out in the Member State in which he is established both transactions giving rise to a right of deduction and transactions not giving rise to a right of deduction in that Member State, only such proportion of the VAT which is refundable in accordance with Article 5 may be refunded by the Member State of refund as is attributable to the former trans-actions in accordance with Article 173 of Directive 2006/112/EC as applied by the Member State of establishment.

Article 7

To obtain a refund of VAT in the Member State of refund, the taxable person not established in the Member State of refund shall address an electronic refund application to that Member State and submit it to the Member State in which he is established via the electronic portal set up by that Member State.

Article 8

1. The refund application shall contain the following information:

(*a*) the applicant's name and full address;

(*b*) an address for contact by electronic means;

(*c*) a description of the applicant's business activity for which the goods and services are acquired;

(*d*) the refund period covered by the application;
(*e*) a declaration by the applicant that he has supplied no goods and services deemed to have been sup-plied in the Member State of refund during the refund period, with the exception of transactions referred to in points (i) and (ii) of Article 3(*b*);
(*f*) the applicant's VAT identification number or tax reference number;
(*g*) bank account details including IBAN and BIC codes.

2. In addition to the information specified in paragraph 1, the refund application shall set out, for each Member State of refund and for each invoice or importation document, the following details:

(*a*) name and full address of the supplier;
(*b*) except in the case of importation, the VAT identification number or tax reference number of the supplier, as allocated by the Member State of refund in accordance with the provisions of Articles 239 and 240 of Directive 2006/112/EC;
(*c*) except in the case of importation, the prefix of the Member State of refund in accordance with Article 215 of Directive 2006/112/EC;
(*d*) date and number of the invoice or importation document;
(*e*) taxable amount and amount of VAT expressed in the currency of the Member State of refund;
(*f*) the amount of deductible VAT calculated in accordance with Article 5 and the second paragraph of Article 6 expressed in the currency of the Member State of refund;
(*g*) where applicable, the deductible proportion calculated in accordance with Article 6, expressed as a percentage;
(*h*) nature of the goods and services acquired, described according to the codes in Article 9.

Article 9

1. In the refund application, the nature of the goods and services acquired shall be described by the following codes:

1 = fuel;

2 = hiring of means of transport;

3 = expenditure relating to means of transport (other than the goods and services referred to under codes 1 and 2);

4 = road tolls and road user charge;

5 = travel expenses, such as taxi fares, public transport fares;

6 = accommodation;

7 = food, drink and restaurant services;

8 = admissions to fairs and exhibitions;

9 = expenditure on luxuries, amusements and entertainment;

10 = other.

If code 10 is used, the nature of the goods and services supplied shall be indicated.

2. The Member State of refund may require the applicant to provide additional electronic coded information as regards each code set out in paragraph 1 to the extent that such information is necessary because of any restrictions on the right of deduction under Directive 2006/112/EC, as applicable in the Member State of refund or for the implementation of a relevant derogation received by the Member State of refund under Articles 395 or 396 of that Directive.

Article 10

Without prejudice to requests for information under Article 20, the Member State of refund may require the applicant to submit by electronic means a copy of the invoice or importation document with the refund application where the taxable amount on an invoice or importation document is EUR 1000 or more or the equivalent in national currency. Where the invoice concerns fuel, the threshold is EUR 250 or the equivalent in national currency.

Article 11

The Member State of refund may require the applicant to provide a description of his business activity by using the harmonised codes determined in accordance with the second subparagraph of Article 34a(3) of Council Regulation (EC) No 1798/2003[1].

Note—[1] OJ L 264, 15.10.2003 p 1.

Article 12

The Member State of refund may specify which language or languages shall be used by the applicant for the provision of information in the refund application or of possible additional information.

Article 13

If subsequent to the submission of the refund application the deductible proportion is adjusted pursuant to Article 175 of Directive 2006/112/EC, the applicant shall make a correction to the amount applied for or already refunded.

The correction shall be made in a refund application during the calendar year following the refund period in question or, if the applicant makes no refund applications during that calendar year, by submitting a separate declaration via the electronic portal established by the Member State of establishment.

Article 14

1. The refund application shall relate to the following:

(*a*) the purchase of goods or services which was invoiced during the refund period, provided that the VAT became chargeable before or at the time of the invoicing, or in respect of which the VAT became chargeable during the refund period, provided that the purchase was invoiced before the tax became chargeable;

(*b*) the importation of goods during the refund period.

2. In addition to the transactions referred to in paragraph 1, the refund application may relate to invoices or import documents not covered by previous refund applications and concerning transactions completed during the calendar year in question.

Article 15

1. The refund application shall be submitted to the Member State of establishment at the latest on 30 September of the calendar year following the refund period. The application shall be considered submitted only if the applicant has filled in all the information required under Articles 8, 9 and 11.

2. The Member State of establishment shall send the applicant an electronic confirmation of receipt with-out delay.

Article 16

The refund period shall not be more than one calendar year or less than three calendar months. Refund applications may, however, relate to a period of less than three months where the period represents the remainder of a calendar year.

Article 17

If the refund application relates to a refund period of less than one calendar year but not less than three months, the amount of VAT for which a refund is applied for may not be less than EUR 400 or the equivalent in national currency.

If the refund application relates to a refund period of a calendar year or the remainder of a calendar year, the amount of VAT may not be less than EUR 50 or the equivalent in national currency.

Article 18

1. The Member State of establishment shall not forward the application to the Member State of refund where, during the refund period, any of the following circumstances apply to the applicant in the Member State of establishment:

(*a*) he is not a taxable person for VAT purposes;

(*b*) he carries out only supplies of goods or of services which are exempt without deductibility of the VAT paid at the preceding stage pursuant to Articles 132, 135, 136, 371, Articles 374 to 377, Article 378(2)(*a*), Article 379(2) or Articles 380 to 390 of Directive 2006/112/EC or provisions providing for identical exemptions contained in the 2005 Act of Accession;

(*c*) he is covered by the exemption for small enterprises provided for in Articles 284, 285, 286 and 287 of Directive 2006/112/EC;

(*d*) he is covered by the common flat-rate scheme for farmers provided for in Articles 296 to 305 of Directive 2006/112/EC.

2. The Member State of establishment shall notify the applicant by electronic means of the decision it has taken pursuant to paragraph 1.

Article 19

1. The Member State of refund shall notify the applicant without delay, by electronic means, of the date on which it received the application.

2. The Member State of refund shall notify the applicant of its decision to approve or refuse the refund application within four months of its receipt by that Member State.

Article 20

1. Where the Member State of refund considers that it does not have all the relevant information on which to make a decision in respect of the whole or part of the refund application, it may request, by electronic means, additional information, in particular from the applicant or from

the competent authorities of the Member State of establishment, within the four-month period referred to in Article 19(2). Where the additional information is requested from someone other than the applicant or a competent authority of a Member State, the request shall be made by electronic means only if such means are available to the recipient of the request.

If necessary, the Member State of refund may request further additional information.

The information requested in accordance with this paragraph may include the submission of the original or a copy of the relevant invoice or import document where the Member State of refund has reasonable doubts regarding the validity or accuracy of a particular claim. In that case, the thresholds mentioned in Article 10 shall not apply.

2. The Member State of refund shall be provided with the information requested under paragraph 1 within one month of the date on which the request reaches the person to whom it is addressed.

Article 21

Where the Member State of refund requests additional information, it shall notify the applicant of its decision to approve or refuse the refund application within two months of receiving the requested information or, if it has not received a reply to its request, within two months of expiry of the time limit laid down in Article 20(2). However, the period available for the decision in respect of the whole or part of the refund application shall always be at least six months from the date of receipt of the application by the Member State of refund.

Where the Member State of refund requests further additional information, it shall notify the applicant of its decision in respect of the whole or part of the refund application within eight months of receipt of the application by that Member State.

Article 22

1. Where the refund application is approved, refunds of the approved amount shall be paid by the Member State of refund at the latest within 10 working days of the expiry of the deadline referred to in Article 19(2) or, where additional or further additional information has been requested, the deadlines referred to in Article 21.

2. The refund shall be paid in the Member State of refund or, at the applicant's request, in any other Member State. In the latter case, any bank charges for the transfer shall be deducted by the Member State of refund from the amount to be paid to the applicant.

Article 23

1. Where the refund application is refused in whole or in part, the grounds for refusal shall be notified by the Member State of refund to the applicant together with the decision.

2. Appeals against decisions to refuse a refund application may be made by the applicant to the competent authorities of the Member State of refund in the forms and within the time limits laid down for appeals in the case of refund applications from persons who are established in that Member State.

If, under the law of the Member State of refund, failure to take a decision on a refund application within the time limits specified in this Directive is not regarded either as approval or as refusal, any administrative or judicial procedures which are available in that situation to taxable persons established in that Member State shall be equally available to the applicant. If no such procedures are available, failure to take a decision on a refund application within these time limits shall mean that the application is deemed to be rejected.

Article 24

1. Where a refund has been obtained in a fraudulent way or otherwise incorrectly, the competent authority in the Member State of refund shall proceed directly to recover the amounts wrongly paid and any penal-ties and interest imposed in accordance with the procedure applicable in the Member State of refund, without prejudice to the provisions on mutual assistance for the recovery of VAT.

2. Where an administrative penalty or interest has been imposed but has not been paid, the Member State of refund may suspend any further refund to the taxable person concerned up to the unpaid amount.

Article 25

The Member State of refund shall take into account as a decrease or increase of the amount of the refund any correction made concerning a previous refund application in accordance with Article 13 or, where a separate declaration is submitted, in the form of separate payment or recovery.

Article 26

Interest shall be due to the applicant by the Member State of refund on the amount of the refund to be paid if the refund is paid after the last date of payment pursuant to Article 22(1).

If the applicant does not submit the additional or further additional information requested to the Member State of refund within the specified time limit, the first paragraph shall not apply. It shall also not apply until the documents to be submitted electronically pursuant to Article 10 have been received by the Member State of refund.

Article 27

1. Interest shall be calculated from the day following the last day for payment of the refund pursuant to Article 22(1) until the day the refund is actually paid.

2. Interest rates shall be equal to the interest rate applicable with respect to refunds of VAT to taxable persons established in the Member State of refund under the national law of that Member State.

If no interest is payable under national law in respect of refunds to established taxable persons, the interest payable shall be equal to the interest or equivalent charge which is applied by the Member State of refund in respect of late payments of VAT by taxable persons.

Article 28

1. This Directive shall apply to refund applications submitted after 31 December 2009.

2. Directive 79/1072/EEC shall be repealed with effect from 1 January 2010. However, its provisions shall continue to apply to refund applications submitted before 1 January 2010.

References to the repealed Directive shall be construed as references to this Directive except for refund applications submitted before 1 January 2010.

Article 29

1. Member States shall bring into force the laws, regulations and administrative provisions necessary to comply with this Directive with effect from 1 January 2010. They shall forthwith inform the Commission thereof.

When such provisions are adopted by Member States, they shall contain a reference to this Directive or be accompanied by such reference on the occasion of their official publication. The methods of making such reference shall be laid down by Member States.

2. Member States shall communicate to the Commission the text of the main provisions of national law which they adopt in the field covered by this Directive.

Article 30

This Directive shall enter into force on the day of its publication in the Official Journal of the European Union.

Article 31

This Directive is addressed to the Member States.

Done at Brussels, 12 February 2008.

For the Council

The President

A. Bajuk

Council Directive
of 26 May 2008
on mutual assistance for the recovery of claims relating to certain levies, duties, taxes and other measures
(Codified version)

(2008/55/EC)

Note—See OJ L 150, 10.06.2008 p 28.

THE COUNCIL OF THE EUROPEAN UNION,

Having regard to the Treaty establishing the European Community, and in particular Articles 93 and 94 thereof,

Having regard to the proposal from the Commission,

Having regard to the opinion of the European Parliament,[1]

Having regard to the opinion of the European Economic and Social Committee,[2]

Whereas:

(1) Council Directive 76/308/EEC of 15 March 1976 on mutual assistance for the recovery of claims relating to certain levies, duties, taxes and other measures[3] has been substantially amended several times[4]. In the interests of clarity and rationality the said Directive should be codified.

(2) The fact that national provisions relating to recovery are applicable only within national territories is in itself an obstacle to the functioning of the internal market. This situation prevents Community rules from being fully and fairly applied, particularly in the area of the common agricultural policy, and facilitates fraudulent operations.
(3) It is necessary to meet the threat to the financial interests of the Community and the Member States and to the internal market posed by the development of fraud so as to safeguard better the competitiveness and fiscal neutrality of the internal market.
(4) It is therefore necessary to adopt common rules on mutual assistance for recovery.
(5) These rules should apply to the recovery of claims resulting from the various measures which form part of the system of total or partial financing of the European Agricultural Guarantee Fund and the European Agricultural Fund for Rural Development, to the recovery of levies and other duties and import and export duties, valued added tax and harmonised excise duties (manufactured tobacco, alcohol and alcoholic beverages and mineral oils), as well as of taxes on income, on capital and on insurance premiums. They should also apply to the recovery of interest, administrative penalties and fines, with the exclusion of any sanction of a criminal nature, and costs incidental to such claims.
(6) Mutual assistance should consist of the following: the requested authority should on the one hand supply the applicant authority with the information which the latter needs in order to recover claims arising in the Member State in which it is situated and notify the debtor of all instruments relating to such claims emanating from that Member State, and on the other hand it should recover, at the request of the applicant authority, the claims arising in the Member State in which the latter is situated.
(7) These different forms of assistance should be afforded by the requested authority in compliance with the laws, regulations and administrative provisions governing such matters in the Member State in which it is situated.
(8) It is necessary to lay down the conditions in accordance with which requests for assistance must be drawn up by the applicant authority and to give a limitative definition of the particular circumstances in which the requested authority may refuse assistance in any given case.
(9) In order to permit more efficient and effective recovery of claims in respect of which a request for recovery has been made, the instrument permitting enforcement of the claim should, in principle, be treated as an instrument of the Member State in which the requested authority is situated.
(10) When the requested authority is required to act on behalf of the applicant authority to recover a claim, it should be able, if the provisions in force in the Member State in which it is situated so permit and with the agreement of the applicant authority, to allow the debtor time to pay or authorise payment by instalment. Any interest charged on such payment facilities should also be remitted to the Member State in which the applicant authority is situated.
(11) Upon a reasoned request from the applicant authority, the requested authority should also be able, in so far as the provisions in force in the Member State in which it is situated so permit, to take precautionary measures to guarantee the recovery of claims arising in the applicant Member State. Such claims should not necessarily benefit from the privileges ac-corded to similar claims arising in the Member State in which the requested authority is situated.
(12) During the recovery procedure in the Member State in which the requested authority is situated the claim or the instrument authorising its enforcement issued in the Member State in which the applicant authority is situated may be contested by the person concerned. It should be laid down in such cases that the person concerned must bring the action contesting the claim before the competent body of the Member State in which the applicant authority is situated and that the requested authority must suspend, unless the applicant authority requests otherwise, any enforcement proceedings which it has begun until a decision is taken by the aforementioned body.
(13) It should be laid down that documents and information communicated in the course of mutual assistance for recovery may not be used for other purposes.
(14) The use of mutual assistance for recovery cannot, save in exceptional circumstances, be based on financial benefits or an interest in the results obtained, but Member States should be able to agree the reimbursement arrangements when recovery poses a specific problem.
(15) This Directive should not curtail mutual assistance between particular Member States under bilateral or multilateral agreements or arrangements.
(16) The measures necessary for the implementation of this Directive should be adopted in accordance with Council Decision 1999/468/EC of 28 June 1999 laying down the procedures for the exercise of implementing powers conferred on the Commission[5].
(17) This Directive should be without prejudice to the obligations of the Member States relating to the time-limits for transposition into national law of the Directives set out in Annex I, Part C,

HAS ADOPTED THIS DIRECTIVE:

Notes—[1] Opinion of 19 June 2007 (not yet published in the Official Journal).
[2] OJ C 93, 27.4.2007 p 15.
[3] OJ L 73, 19.3.1976 p 18. Directive as last amended by the 2003 Act of Accession. The original title of the Directive is "Council Directive 76/308/EEC of 15 March 1976 on mutual assistance for the recovery of claims resulting from operations forming part of the system of financing the European Agricultural Guidance and Guarantee Fund, and of

the agricultural levies and customs duties". It was amended by Directive 79/1071/EEC (OJ L 331, 27.12.1979 p 10), by Directive 92/12/EEC (OJ L 76, 23.3.1992 p 1) and Directive 2001/44/EC (OJ L 175, 28.6.2001 p 17).

[4] See Annex I, Parts A and B.

[5] OJ L 184, 17.7.1999 p 23. Decision as last amended by Decision 2006/512/EC (OJ L 200, 22.7.2006 p 11).

Article 1

This Directive lays down the rules to be incorporated into the laws, regulations and administrative provisions of the Member States to ensure the recovery in each Member State of the claims referred to in Article 2 which arise in another Member State.

Article 2

This Directive shall apply to all claims relating to:

(*a*) refunds, interventions and other measures forming part of the system of total or partial financing of the European Agricultural Guarantee Fund (EAGF) and the European Agricultural Fund for Rural Development (EAFRD), including sums to be collected in connection with these actions;

(*b*) levies and other duties provided for under the common organisation of the market for the sugar sector;

(*c*) import duties;

(*d*) export duties;

(*e*) value added tax;

(*f*) excise duties on:

(i) manufactured tobacco,

(ii) alcohol and alcoholic beverages,

(iii) mineral oils;

(*g*) taxes on income and capital;

(*h*) taxes on insurance premiums;

(*i*) interest, administrative penalties and fines, and costs incidental to the claims referred to in points (*a*) to (*h*), with the exclusion of any sanction of a criminal nature as determined by the laws in force in the Member State in which the requested authority is situated.

It shall also apply to claims relating to taxes which are identical or analogous to the taxes on insurance premiums referred to in Article 3(6) which supplement or replace them. The competent authorities of the Member States shall communicate to each other and to the Commission the dates of entry into force of such taxes.

Article 3

For the purposes of this Directive:

1. "applicant authority" means the competent authority of a Member State which makes a request for assistance concerning a claim referred to in Article 2;

2. "requested authority" means the competent authority of a Member State to which a request for assistance is made;

3. "import duties" means customs duties and charges having equivalent effect on imports, and import charges laid down within the framework of the common agricultural policy or in that of specific arrangements applicable to certain goods resulting from the processing of agricultural products;

4. "export duties" means customs duties and charges having equivalent effect on exports, and export charges laid down within the framework of the common agricultural policy or in that of specific arrangements applicable to certain goods resulting from the processing of agricultural products;

5. "taxes on income and capital" means those enumerated in Article 1(3) of Council Directive (77/799/EEC) of 19 December 1977 concerning mutual assistance by the competent authorities of the Member States in the field of direct taxation and taxation of insurance premiums[1], read in conjunction with Article 1(4) of that Directive;

6. "taxes on insurance premiums" means:

(*a*) in Belgium:

(i) taxe annuelle sur les contrats d'assurance,

(ii) jaarlijkse taks op de verzekeringscontracten;

(*b*) in Denmark:

(i) afgift af lystfartøjsforsikringer,

(ii) afgift af ansvarsforsikringer for motorkøretøjer m.v.,

(iii) stempelafgift af forsikringspræmier;

(*c*) in Germany:

(i) Versicherungssteuer,

(ii) Feuerschutzsteuer;

(*d*) in Greece:

(i) Fòros kklou ergasin (F.K.E),

(ii) Tlh Cartosmou;

(*e*) in Spain: Impuesto sobre las primas de seguros;
(*f*) in France: taxe sur les conventions d'assurances;
(*g*) in Ireland: levy on insurance premiums;
(*h*) in Italy: imposte sulle assicurazioni private ed i contratti vitalizi di cui alla legge 29.10.1967 No 1216;
(*i*) in Luxembourg:
(i) impôt sur les assurances,
(ii) impôt dans l'interêt du service d'incendie;
(*j*) in Malta: taxxa fuq dokumenti u trasferimenti;
(*k*) in the Netherlands: assurantiebelasting;
(*l*) in Austria:
(i) Versicherungssteuer,
(ii) Feuerschutzsteuer;
(*m*) in Portugal: imposto de selo sobre os prémios de seguros;
(*n*) in Slovenia:
(i) davek od promenta zavarovalnih poslov,
(ii) poarna taksa;
(*o*) in Finland:
(i) eräistä vakuutusmaksuista suoritettava vero/skatt på vissa försäkringspremier,
(ii) palosuojelumaksu/brandskyddsavgift;
(*p*) in the United Kingdom: insurance premium tax (IPT).

Note—[1] OJ L 336, 27.12.1977 p 15. Directive as last amended by Directive 2006/98/EC (OJ L 363, 20.12.2006 p 129).

Article 4

1. At the request of the applicant authority, the requested authority shall provide any information which would be useful to the applicant authority in the recovery of its claim.

In order to obtain this information, the requested authority shall make use of the powers provided under the laws, regulations or administrative provisions applying to the recovery of similar claims arising in the Member State where that authority is situated.

2. The request for information shall indicate the name and address of the person to whom the information to be provided relates and any other relevant information relating to the identification to which the applicant authority normally has access and the nature and amount of the claim in respect of which the request is made.

3. The requested authority shall not be obliged to supply information:

(*a*) which it would not be able to obtain for the purpose of recovering similar claims arising in the Member State in which it is situated;
(*b*) which would disclose any commercial, industrial or professional secrets; or
(*c*) the disclosure of which would be liable to prejudice the security of or be contrary to the public policy of the State.

4. The requested authority shall inform the applicant authority of the grounds for refusing a request for in-formation.

Article 5

1. The requested authority shall, at the request of the applicant authority, and in accordance with the rules of law in force for the notification of similar instruments or decisions in the Member State in which the requested authority is situated, notify to the addressee all instruments and decisions, including those of a judicial nature, which emanate from the Member State in which the applicant authority is situated and which relate to a claim and/or to its recovery.

2. The request for notification shall indicate the name and address of the addressee concerned and any other relevant information relating to the identification to which the applicant authority normally has access, the nature and the subject of the instrument or decision to be notified, if necessary the name, and address of the debtor and any other relevant information relating to the identification to which the applicant authority normally has access and the claim to which the instrument or decision relates, and any other useful information.

3. The requested authority shall promptly inform the applicant authority of the action taken on its request for notification and, more especially, of the date on which the instrument or decision was forwarded to the addressee.

Article 6

At the request of the applicant authority, the requested authority shall, in accordance with the laws, regulations or administrative provisions applying to the recovery of similar claims arising in the Member State in which the requested authority is situated, recover claims which are the subject of an instrument permitting their enforcement.

For this purpose any claim in respect of which a request for recovery has been made shall be treated as a claim of the Member State in which the requested authority is situated, except where Article 12 applies.

Article 7

1. The request for recovery of a claim which the applicant authority addresses to the requested authority shall be accompanied by an official or certified copy of the instrument permitting its enforcement, issued in the Member State in which the applicant authority is situated and, if appropriate, by the original or a certified copy of other documents necessary for recovery.

2. The applicant authority may not make a request for recovery unless:

(*a*) the claim and/or the instrument permitting its enforcement are not contested in the Member State in which it is situated, except in cases where the second subparagraph of Article 12(2) applies;

(*b*) it has, in the Member State in which it is situated, applied appropriate recovery procedures available to it on the basis of the instrument referred to in paragraph 1, and the measures taken will not result in the payment in full of the claim.

3. The request for recovery shall indicate:

(*a*) the name, address and any other relevant information relating to the identification of the person concerned and/or to the third party holding his or her assets;

(*b*) the name, address and any other relevant information relating to the identification of the applicant authority;

(*c*) a reference to the instrument permitting its enforcement issued in the Member State in which the applicant authority is situated;

(*d*) the nature and the amount of the claim, including the principal, the interest, and any other penalties, fines and costs due indicated in the currencies of the Member States in which both authorities are situated;

(*e*) the date of notification of the instrument to the addressee by the applicant authority and/or by the requested authority;

(*f*) the date from which and the period during which enforcement is possible under the laws in force in the Member State in which the applicant authority is situated;

(*g*) any other relevant information.

The request for recovery shall also contain a declaration by the applicant authority confirming that the conditions set out in paragraph 2 have been fulfilled.

4. As soon as any relevant information relating to the matter which gave rise to the request for recovery comes to the knowledge of the applicant authority it shall forward it to the requested authority.

Article 8

The instrument permitting enforcement of the claim shall be directly recognised and automatically treated as an instrument permitting enforcement of a claim of the Member State in which the requested authority is situated.

Notwithstanding the first paragraph, the instrument permitting enforcement of the claim may, where appropriate and in accordance with the provisions in force in the Member State in which the requested authority is situated, be accepted as, recognised as, supplemented with, or replaced by an instrument authorising enforcement in the territory of that Member State.

Within three months of the date of receipt of the request for recovery, Member States shall endeavour to complete such acceptance, recognition, supplementing or replacement, except in cases referred to in the fourth paragraph. These formalities may not be refused if the instrument permitting enforcement is properly drawn up. The requested authority shall inform the applicant authority of the grounds for exceeding the period of three months.

If any of these formalities should give rise to contestation in connection with the claim or the instrument permitting enforcement issued by the applicant authority, Article 12 shall apply.

Article 9

1. Claims shall be recovered in the currency of the Member State in which the requested authority is situated. The entire amount of the claim that is recovered by the requested authority shall be remitted by the requested authority to the applicant authority.

2. The requested authority may, where the laws, regulations or administrative provisions in force in the Member State in which it is situated so permit, and after consultations with the applicant authority, allow the debtor time to pay or authorise payment by instalment. Any interest charged by the requested authority in respect of such extra time to pay shall also be remitted to the Member State in which the applicant authority is situated.

From the date on which the instrument permitting enforcement of recovery of the claim has been directly recognised in accordance with the first paragraph of Article 8 or accepted, recognised, supplemented or replaced in accordance with the second paragraph of Article 8, interest will be charged for late payment under the laws, regulations and administrative provisions in force in the Member State in which the re-quested authority is situated and shall also be remitted to the Member State in which the applicant authority is situated.

Article 10

Notwithstanding the second paragraph of Article 6, the claims to be recovered shall not necessarily benefit from the privileges accorded to similar claims arising in the Member State in which the requested authority is situated.

Article 11

The requested authority shall inform the applicant authority immediately of the action it has taken on the request for recovery.

Article 12

1. If, in the course of the recovery procedure, the claim and/or the instrument permitting its enforcement issued in the Member State in which the applicant authority is situated are contested by an interested party, the action shall be brought by the latter before the competent body of the Member State in which the applicant authority is situated, in accordance with the laws in force there. This action shall be notified by the applicant authority to the requested authority. The party concerned may also notify the requested authority of the action.

2. As soon as the requested authority has received the notification referred to in paragraph 1 either from the applicant authority or from the interested party, it shall suspend the enforcement procedure pending the decision of the body competent in the matter, unless the applicant authority requests otherwise in accordance with the second subparagraph of this paragraph. Should the requested authority deem it necessary, and without prejudice to Article 13, that authority may take precautionary measures to guarantee recovery in so far as the laws or regulations in force in the Member State in which it is situated allow such action for similar claims.

The applicant authority may, in accordance with the law, regulations and administrative practices in force in the Member State in which it is situated, request the requested authority to recover a contested claim, in so far as the relevant laws, regulations and administrative practices in force in the Member State in which the requested authority is situated allow such action. If the result of contestation is subsequently favour-able to the debtor, the applicant authority shall be liable for the reimbursement of any sums recovered, together with any compensation due, in accordance with the laws in force in the Member State in which the requested authority is situated.

3. Where it is the enforcement measures taken in the Member State in which the requested authority is situated that are being contested the action shall be brought before the competent body of that Member State in accordance with its laws and regulations.

4. Where the competent body before which the action has been brought in accordance with paragraph 1 is a judicial or administrative tribunal, the decision of that tribunal, in so far as it is favourable to the applicant authority and permits recovery of the claim in the Member State in which the applicant authority is situated, shall constitute the "instrument permitting enforcement" referred to in Articles 6, 7 and 8 and the recovery of the claim shall proceed on the basis of that decision.

Article 13

On a reasoned request by the applicant authority, the requested authority shall take precautionary measures to ensure recovery of a claim in so far as the laws or regulations in force in the Member State in which it is situated so permit.

In order to give effect to the provisions of the first paragraph, Articles 6, 7(1), (3) and (4), 8, 11, 12 and 14 shall apply *mutatis mutandis*.

Article 14

The requested authority shall not be obliged:

(*a*) to grant the assistance provided for in Articles 6 to 13 if recovery of the claim would, because of the situation of the debtor, create serious economic or social difficulties in the Member State in which that authority is situated, in so far as the laws, regulations and administrative practices in force in the Member State in which the requested authority is situated allow such action for similar national claims;

(*b*) to grant the assistance provided for in Articles 4 to 13, if the initial request under Articles 4, 5 or 6 applies to claims more than five years old, dating from the moment the instrument permitting the recovery is established in accordance with the laws, regulations or administrative practices in force in the Member State in which the applicant authority is situated, to the date of the request. However, in cases where the claim or the instrument is contested, the time-limit begins from the moment at which the applicant State establishes that the claim or the instrument permitting recovery may no longer be contested.

The requested authority shall inform the applicant authority of the grounds for refusing a request for assistance. Such reasoned refusal shall also be communicated to the Commission.

Article 15

1. Questions concerning periods of limitation shall be governed solely by the laws in force in the Member State in which the applicant authority is situated.

2. Steps taken in the recovery of claims by the requested authority in pursuance of a request for assistance, which, if they had been carried out by the applicant authority, would have had the effect of suspending or interrupting the period of limitation according to the laws in force in the Member State in which the applicant authority is situated, shall be deemed to have been taken in the latter State, in so far as that effect is concerned.

Article 16

Documents and information sent to the requested authority pursuant to this Directive may only be communicated by the latter to:

(*a*) the person mentioned in the request for assistance;

(*b*) those persons and authorities responsible for the recovery of the claims, and solely for that purpose;

(*c*) the judicial authorities dealing with matters concerning the recovery of the claims.

Article 17

Requests for assistance, the instrument permitting the enforcement and other relevant documents shall be accompanied by a translation in the official language, or one of the official languages of the Member State in which the requested authority is situated, without prejudice to the latter authority's right to waive the translation.

Article 18

1. The requested authority shall recover from the person concerned and retain any costs linked to recovery which it incurs, in accordance with the laws and regulations of the Member State in which it is situated that apply to similar claims.

2. Member States shall renounce all claims on each other for the refund of costs resulting from mutual assistance which they grant each other pursuant to this Directive.

3. Where recovery poses a specific problem, concerns a very large amount in costs or relates to the fight against organised crime, the applicant and requested authorities may agree reimbursement arrangements specific to the cases in question.

4. The Member State in which the applicant authority is situated shall remain liable to the Member State in which the requested authority is situated for any costs and any losses incurred as a result of actions held to be unfounded, as far as either the substance of the claim or the validity of the instrument issued by the applicant authority are concerned.

Article 19

Member States shall provide each other with a list of authorities authorised to make or receive requests for assistance.

Article 20

1. The Commission shall be assisted by the recovery committee (hereinafter referred to as the Committee).

2. Where reference is made to this paragraph, Articles 5 and 7 of Decision 1999/468/EC shall apply.

The period referred to in Article 5(6) of Decision 1999/468/EC shall be set at three months.

Article 21

The Committee may examine any matter concerning the application of this Directive raised by its chairman either on his own initiative or at the request of the representative of a Member State.

Article 22

The detailed rules for implementing Articles 4(2) and (4), 5(2) and (3) and Articles 7, 8, 9, 11, 12(1) and (2), 14, 18(3) and 24 and for determining the means by which communications between the authorities may be transmitted, the rules on conversion, transfer of sums recovered, and the fixing of a minimum amount for claims which may give rise to a request for assistance, shall be adopted in accordance with the procedure referred to in Article 20(2).

Article 23

This Directive shall not prevent a greater measure of mutual assistance being afforded either now or in the future by particular Member States under any agreements or arrangements, including those for the notification of legal or extra-legal acts.

Article 24

Each Member State shall inform the Commission of the measures which it has adopted to implement this Directive.

The Commission shall forward this information to the other Member States.

Each Member State shall inform the Commission annually of the number of requests for information, notification and recovery sent and received each year, the amount of the claims involved and the amounts recovered.

The Commission shall report biennially to the European Parliament and the Council on the application of these arrangements and on the results achieved.

Article 25

Directive 76/308/EEC, as amended by the acts listed in Annex I, Parts A and B, is repealed, without prejudice to the obligations of the Member States relating to the time-limits for transposition into national law of the Directives set out in Annex I, Part C.

References to the repealed Directive shall be construed as references to this Directive and shall be read in accordance with the correlation table in Annex II.

Article 26

This Directive shall enter into force on the 20th day following its publication in the Official Journal of the European Union.

Article 27

This Directive is addressed to the Member States.

Done at Brussels, 26 May 2008.

For the Council

The President

D. Rupel

ANNEX 1

PART A

REPEALED DIRECTIVE WITH ITS SUCCESSIVE AMENDMENTS
(REFERRED TO IN ARTICLE 25)

Directive 76/308/EEC (OJ L 73, 19.3.1976, p. 18).	–
Directive 79/1071/EEC (OJ L 331, 27.12.1979, p. 10).	–
Directive 92/12/EEC (OJ L 76, 23.3.1992, p. 1).	Only Article 30a
Directive 92/108/EEC (OJ L 390, 31.12.1992, p. 124).	Only Article 1, point 9
Directive 2001/44/EC (OJ L 175, 28.6.2001, p. 17).	–

PART B

AMENDED ACTS WHICH ARE NOT REPEALED

1979 Act of Accession

1985 Act of Accession

1994 Act of Accession

2003 Act of Accession

PART C

LIST OF TIME-LIMITS FOR TRANSPOSITION INTO NATIONAL LAW
(REFERRED TO IN ARTICLE 25)

Directive	*Time-limit for transposition*
76/308/EEC	1 January 1978
79/1071/EEC	1 January 1981

92/12/EEC	1 January 1993[1]
92/108/EEC	31 December 1992
2001/44/EC	30 June 2002

Note—[1] With regard to Article 9(3) the Kingdom of Denmark is authorised to introduce the laws, regulations and administrative provisions required for complying with this provisions by 1 January 1993 at the latest.

ANNEX 2

CORRELATION TABLE

Directive 76/308/EEC	*This Directive*
Article 1	Article 1
Article 2, introductory wording, points (*a*) to (*e*)	Article 2, first paragraph, points (*a*) to (*e*)
Article 2, introductory wording, point (*f*) first, second and third indents	Article 2, first paragraph, point (*f*)(i), (ii) and (iii)
Article 2, introductory wording, points (*g*) to (*i*)	Article 2, first paragraph, points (*g*) to (*i*)
Article 3, first paragraph, first to fifth indents	Article 3, first paragraph, points (1) to (5)
Article 3, sixth indent, first paragraph, point (*a*)	Article 3(6)(*l*)
Article 3, sixth indent, first paragraph, point (*b*)	Article 3(6)(*a*)
Article 3, sixth indent, first paragraph, point (*c*)	Article 3(6)(*c*)
Article 3, sixth indent, first paragraph, point (*d*)	Article 3(6)(*b*)
Article 3, sixth indent, first paragraph, point (*e*)	Article 3(6)(*e*)
Article 3, sixth indent, first paragraph, point (*f*)	Article 3(6)(*d*)
Article 3, sixth indent, first paragraph, point (*g*)	Article 3(6)(*f*)
Article 3, sixth indent, first paragraph, point (*h*)	Article 3(6)(*o*)
Article 3, sixth indent, first paragraph, point (*i*)	Article 3(6)(*h*)
Article 3, sixth indent, first paragraph, point (*j*)	Article 3(6)(*g*)
Article 3, sixth indent, first paragraph, point (*k*)	Article 3(6)(*i*)
Article 3, sixth indent, first paragraph, point (*l*)	Article 3(6)(*k*)
Article 3, sixth indent, first paragraph, point (*m*)	Article 3(6)(*m*)
Article 3, sixth indent, first paragraph, point (*n*)	–
Article 3, sixth indent, first paragraph, point (*o*)	Article 3(6)(*p*)
Article 3, sixth indent, first paragraph, point (*p*)	Article 3(6)(*j*)
Article 3, sixth indent, first paragraph, point (*q*)	Article 3(6)(*n*)
Article 3, sixth indent, second paragraph	Article 2, second paragraph
Articles 4 and 5	Articles 4 and 5
Article 6(1)	Article 6 first paragraph
Article 6(2)	Article 6 second paragraph
Article 7(1) and (2)	Article 7(1) and (2)
Article 7(3)	Article 7(3), first subparagraph
Article 7(4)	Article 7(3), second subparagraph
Article 7(5)	Article 7(4)
Article 8(1)	Article 8, first paragraph
Article 8(2), first, second and third paragraphs	Article 8, second, third and fourth paragraphs

Articles 9 to 19	Articles 9 to 19
Article 20(1) and (2)	Article 20(1) and (2)
Article 20(3)	–
Articles 21, 22 and 23	Articles 21, 22 and 23
Article 24	–
Article 25, first paragraph, first and second sentences	Article 24, first and second paragraphs
Article 25, second paragraph, first and second sentences	Article 24, second and third paragraphs
Article 26	Article 27
–	Annex I
–	Annex II

EC REGULATIONS

Council Regulation of 7 November 1991 on the statistics relating to the trading of goods between Member States

(3330/91/EEC)

Note—This Regulation repealed by European Parliament and Council Regulation 638/2004 art 15 (OJ L 102; 7.4.2004 p 1) with effect from 1 January 2005. References to the repealed legislation should be construed as references to European Parliament and Council Regulation 638/2004.

Council Regulation of 27 January 1992 on administrative co-operation in the field of indirect taxation (VAT)

(218/92/EEC)

Note—See OJ L24 01.02.1992, p 1.
Amendment—This regulation repealed by Council Regulation 1798/2003 art 47 (OJ L 264; 15.10.2003 p 1).

Commission Regulation of 31 July 1992 on statistical thresholds for the statistics on trade between Member States

(2256/92/EEC)

Amendments—This regulation repealed by Commission Regulation (EC) 1901/2000 art 49 with effect from 1 January 2001. See OJ L 228 p 28; 08.09.2000.

Council Regulation of 12 October 1992 establishing the Community Customs Code

(2913/92/EEC)

Note—See OJ L302 19.10.1992, p 1.
Prospective repeal—This Regulation to be repealed by Regulation 450/2008/EC of the European Parliament and of the Council of 23 April 2008 laying down the Community Customs Code (Modernised Customs Code) art 186. This repeal to have effect from 24 June 2009 at the earliest (art 188(2)). For the implementation of Regulation 450/2008/EC see art 188 thereof.

CONTENTS

THE COUNCIL OF THE EUROPEAN COMMUNITIES

Having regard to the Treaty establishing the European Economic Community, and in particular Articles 28, 100a and 113 thereof,

Having regard to the proposal from the Commission,

In co-operation with the European Parliament,

Having regard to the opinion of the Economic and Social Committee,

Whereas the Community is based upon a customs union; whereas it is advisable, in the interests both of Community traders and the customs authorities, to assemble in a code the provisions of customs legislation that are at present contained in a large number of Community regulations and directives; whereas this task is of fundamental importance from the standpoint of this internal market;

Whereas such a Community Customs Code (hereinafter called "the Code") must incorporate current customs legislation; whereas it is, nevertheless, advisable to amend that legislation in order to make it more consistent, to simplify it and to remedy certain omissions that still exist with a view to adopting complete Community legislation in this area;

Whereas, based on the concept of an internal market, the code must contain the general rules and procedures which ensure the implementation of the tariff and other measures introduced at Community level in connection with trade in goods between the Community and third countries; whereas it must cover, among other things, the implementation of common agricultural and commercial policy measures taking into account the requirements of these common policies;

Whereas it would appear advisable to specify that this Code is applicable without prejudice to specific provisions laid down in other fields; whereas such specific rules may exist or be introduced in the context, *inter alia*, of legislation relating to agriculture, statistics, commercial policy or own resources;

Whereas, in order to secure a balance between the needs of the customs authorities in regard to ensuring the correct application of customs legislation, on the one hand, and the right of traders to be treated fairly, on the other, the said authorities must be granted, *inter alia*, extensive powers of control and the said traders a right of appeal; whereas the implementation of a customs appeals system will require the United Kingdom to introduce new administrative procedures which cannot be effected before 1 January 1995;

Whereas in view of the paramount importance of external trade for the Community, customs formalities and controls should be abolished or at least kept to a minimum;

Whereas it is important to guarantee the uniform application of this Code and to provide, to that end, for a Community procedure which enables the procedures for its implementation to be adopted within a suitable time; whereas a Customs Code Committee should be set up in order to ensure close and effective co-operation between the Member States and the Commission in this field;

Whereas in adopting the measures required to implement this Code, the utmost care must be taken to prevent any fraud or irregularity liable to affect adversely the General Budget of the European Communities,

HAS ADOPTED THIS REGULATION:

TITLE I: GENERAL PROVISIONS

CHAPTER 1—SCOPE AND BASIC DEFINITIONS

Article 1

Customs rules shall consist of this Code and the provisions adopted at Community level or nationally to implement them. The Code shall apply, without prejudice to special rules laid down in other fields

—to trade between the Community and third countries,

—to goods covered by the Treaty establishing the European Coal and Steel Community, the Treaty establishing the European Economic Community or the Treaty establishing the European Atomic Energy Community.

Article 2

1. Save as otherwise provided, either under international conventions or customary practices of a limited geographic and economic scope or under autonomous Community measures, Community customs rules shall apply uniformly throughout the customs territory of the Community.

2. Certain provisions of customs rules may also apply outside the customs territory of the Community within the framework of either rules governing specific fields or international conventions.

Article 3

[1 The customs territory of the Community shall comprise:

—the territory of the Kingdom of Belgium,

—the territory of the Kingdom of Denmark, except the Faroe Islands and Greenland,

—the territory of the Federal Republic of Germany, except the Island of Heligoland and the territory of Büsingen (Treaty of 23 November 1964 between the Federal Republic of Germany and the Swiss Confederation),

—the territory of the Kingdom of Spain, except Ceuta and Melilla,

—[the territory of the French Republic, except the overseas territories and Saint-Pierre and Miquelon and Mayette,][2]

—the territory of the Hellenic Republic,

—the territory of Ireland,

—the territory of the Italian Republic, except the municipalities of Livigno and Campione d'Italia and the national waters of Lake Lugano which are between the bank and the political frontier of the area between Ponte Tresa and Porto Ceresio,

—the territory of the Grand Duchy of Luxembourg,

—the territory of the Republic of Austria,

—the territory of the Kingdom of the Netherlands in Europe,

—the territory of the Portuguese Republic,

—[the territory of the Republic of Finland,][2]

—the territory of the Kingdom of Sweden,

—the territory of the United Kingdom of Great Britain and Northern Ireland and of the Channel Islands and the Isle of Man.][1]

[—the territory of the Republic of Bulgaria,

—the territory of Romania][4]

[2. The following territories situated outside the territory of the Member States shall, taking the conventions and treaties applicable to them into account, be considered to be part of the customs territory of the Community:

(*a*) FRANCE

The territory of the principality of Monaco as defined in the Customs Convention signed in Paris on 18 May 1963 (Official Journal of the French Republic of 27 September 1963, p. 8679)

(*b*) CYPRUS

The territory of the United Kingdom Sovereign Base Areas of Akrotiri and Dhekelia as defined in the Treaty concerning the Establishment of the Republic of Cyprus, signed in Nicosia on 16 August 1960 (United Kingdom Treaty Series No 4 (1961) Cmnd. 1252).][3]

3. The customs territory of the Community shall include the territorial waters, the inland maritime waters and the airspace of the Member States, and the territories referred to in paragraph 2, except for the territorial waters, the inland maritime waters and the airspace of those territories which are not part of the customs territory of the Community pursuant to paragraph 1.

Amendments—[1] Article 3(1) is substituted by the Act of Accession 1994, art 29, Annex I; see OJ L1, 1.1.95, p 181.
[2] Indents 5 and 13 are substituted by EC Regulation 82/97/EC with effect from 1 January 1997; see OJ L 17, 21.1.97, p 1.
[3] Article 3(2) is substituted by the 2003 Act of Accession Protocol No 3 Annex Part One para 1.
[4] Entries in article 3(1) inserted by Council Regulation 1791/2006/EC art 1, Annex Part 12.

Article 4

For the purposes of this Case, the following definitions shall apply:

(1) "Person" means:

—a natural person,

—a legal person,

—where the possibility is provided for under the rules in force, an association of persons recognised as having the capacity to perform legal acts but lacking the legal status of a legal person.

(2) "Persons established in the Community" means:

—in the case of a natural person, any person who is normally resident there,

—in the case of a legal person or an association of persons, any person that has in the Community its registered office, central headquarters or a permanent business establishment.

(3) "Customs authorities" means the authorities responsible *inter alia* for applying customs rules.

(4) "Customs office" means any office at which all or some of the formalities laid down by customs rules may be completed.

[(4a) "Customs office of entry" means the customs office designated by the customs authorities in accordance with the customs rules to which goods brought into the customs territory of the Community must be conveyed without delay and at which they will be subject to appropriate risk-based entry controls;][3]

[(4b) "Customs office of import" means the customs office designated by the customs authorities in accordance with the customs rules where the formalities for assigning goods brought into the customs territory of the Community to a customs-approved treatment or use, including appropriate risk-based controls, are to be carried out;][3]

[(4c) "Customs office of export" means the customs office designated by the customs authorities in accordance with the customs rules where the formalities for assigning goods leaving the customs territory of the Community to a customs-approved treatment or use, including appropriate risk-based controls, are to be completed;][3]

[(4d) "Customs office of exit" means the customs office designated by the customs authorities in accordance with the customs rules to which goods must be presented before they leave the customs territory of the Community and at which they will be subject to customs controls relating to the completion of exit formalities, and appropriate risk-based controls.][3]

(5) "Decision" means any official act by the customs authorities pertaining to customs rules giving a ruling on a particular case, such act having legal effects on one or more specific or identifiable persons; [this term covers *inter alia*, binding information within the meaning of Article 12.] [1]

(6) "Customs status" means the status of goods as Community or non-Community goods.

(7) "Community goods" means goods:

—[wholly obtained in the customs territory of the Community under the conditions referred to in Article 23 and not incorporating goods imported from countries or territories not forming part of the customs territory of the Community. Goods obtained from goods placed under a suspensive arrangement shall not be deemed to have Community status in cases of special economic importance determined in accordance with the committee procedure,][1]

—imported from countries or territories not forming part of the customs territory of the Community which have been released for free circulation,

—obtained or produced in the customs territory of the Community, either from goods referred to in the second indent alone or from goods referred to in first and second indents.

(8) "Non-Community goods" means goods other than those referred to in sub-paragraph 7.

Without prejudice to Articles 163 and 164, Community goods shall lose their status as such when they are actually removed from the customs territory of the Community.

(9) "Customs debt" means the obligation on a person to pay the amount of the import duties (customs debt on importation) or export duties (customs debt on exportation) which apply to specific goods under the Community provisions in force.

(10) "Import duties" means:

—customs duties and charges having an effect equivalent to customs duties payable on the importation of goods,

—... [1] import charges introduced under the common agricultural policy or under the specific arrangements applicable to certain goods resulting from the processing of agricultural products.

(11) "Export duties" means:

—customs duties and charges having an effect equivalent to customs duties payable on the exportation of goods,

—... [1] export charges introduced under the common agricultural policy or under the specific arrangements applicable to certain goods resulting from the processing of agricultural products.

(12) "Debtor" means any person liable for payment of a customs debt.

(13) "Supervision by the customs authorities" means action taken in general by those authorities with a view to ensuring that customs rules and, where appropriate, other provisions applicable to goods subject to customs supervision are observed.

[(14) "Customs controls" means specific acts performed by the customs authorities in order to ensure the correct application of customs rules and other legislation governing the entry, exit, transit, transfer and end-use of goods moved between the customs territory of the Community and third countries and the presence of goods that do not have Community status; such acts may include examining goods, verifying declaration data and the existence and authenticity of electronic or written documents, examining the accounts of undertakings and other records, inspecting means of transport, inspecting luggage and other goods carried by or on persons and carrying out official inquiries and other similar acts.][3]

(15) "Customs-approved treatment or use of goods" means:

(*a*) the placing of goods under a customs procedure;
(*b*) their entry into a free zone or free warehouse;
(*c*) their re-exportation from the customs territory of the Community;
(*d*) their destruction;
(*e*) their abandonment to the Exchequer.

(16) "Customs procedure" means:

(*a*) release for free circulation;
(*b*) transit;
(*c*) customs warehousing;
(*d*) inward processing;
(*e*) processing under customs control;
(*f*) temporary admission;
(*g*) outward processing;
(*h*) exportation.

(17) "Customs declaration" means the act whereby a person indicates in the prescribed form and manner a wish to place goods under a given customs procedure.

(18) "Declarant" means the person making the customs declaration in his own name or the person in whose name a customs declaration is made.

(19) "Presentation of goods to customs" means the notification to the customs authorities, in the manner laid down, of the arrival of goods at the customs office or at any other place designated or approved by the customs authorities.

(20) "Release of goods" means the act whereby the customs authorities make goods available for the purposes stipulated by the customs procedure under which they are placed.

(21) "Holder of the procedure" means the person on whose behalf the customs declaration was made or the person to whom the rights and obligations of the above mentioned person in respect of a customs procedure have been transferred.

(22) "Holder of the authorisation" means the person to whom an authorisation has been granted.

(23) "Provisions in force" means Community or national provisions.

[(24) "Committee procedure" means either the procedure referred to in Articles 247 and 247a, or in Articles 248 and 248a.][2]

[(25) "Risk" means the likelihood of an event occurring, in connection with the entry, exit, transit, transfer and end-use of goods moved between the customs territory of the Community and third countries and the presence of goods that do not have Community status, which—

—prevents the correct application of Community or national measures, or
—compromises the financial interests of the Community and its Member States, or
—poses a threat to the Community's security and safety, to public health, to the environment or to consumers.][3]

[(26) "Risk management" means the systematic identification of risk and implementation of all measures necessary for limiting exposure to risk. This includes activities such as collecting data and information, analysing and assessing risk, prescribing and taking action and regular monitoring and review of the process and its outcomes, based on international, Community and national sources and strategies.][3]

Amendments—[1] Article 4(5), (7),(10),(11) are amended by EC Regulation 82/97/EC with effect from 1 January 1997; see at L 17, 21.10.97, p 10.
[2] Article 4(24) replaced by EC Regulation 2700/2000/EC with effect from 19 December 2000; see OJ L 311, 12.12.2000, p 17.
[3] Article 4(4a)–(4d), (25), (26) inserted, and article 4(14) substituted, by Parliament and Council Regulation (EC) 648/2005 art 1(1); see OJ L 117; 04.05.2005, p 13.

CHAPTER 2—SUNDRY GENERAL PROVISIONS RELATING IN PARTICULAR TO THE RIGHTS AND OBLIGATIONS OF PERSONS WITH REGARD TO CUSTOMS RULES

SECTION 1
RIGHT OF REPRESENTATION

Article 5

1. Under the conditions set out in Article 64(2) and subject to the provisions adopted within the framework of Article 243(2)(*b*), any person may appoint a representative in his dealings with the customs authorities to perform the acts and formalities laid down by customs rules.

2. Such representation may be:

—direct, in which case the representative shall act in the name of and on behalf of another person, or
—indirect, in which case the representative shall act in his own name but on behalf of another person.

A Member State may restrict the right to make customs declarations:

—by direct representation, or
—by indirect representation,

so that the representative must be a customs agent carrying on his business in that country's territory.

3. Save in the cases referred to in Article 64(2)(*b*) and (3), a representative must be established within the Community.

4. A representative must state that he is acting on behalf of the person represented, specify whether the representation is direct or indirect and be empowered to act as a representative.

A person who fails to state that he is acting in the name of or on behalf of another person or who states that he is acting in the name of or on behalf of another person without being empowered to do so shall be deemed to be acting in his own name and on his own behalf.

5. The customs authorities may require any person stating that he is acting in the name of or on behalf of another person to produce evidence of his powers to act as a representative.

[SECTION 1A
AUTHORISED ECONOMIC OPERATORS][1]

Amendments—[1] Section 1a and Article 5a inserted by Parliament and Council Regulation (EC) 648/2005 art 1(2); see OJ L 117; 04.05.2005, p 13.

Article 5a

1. Customs authorities, if necessary following consultation with other competent authorities, shall grant, subject to the criteria provided for in paragraph 2, the status of "authorised economic operator" to any economic operator established in the customs territory of the Community.

An authorised economic operator shall benefit from facilitations with regard to customs controls relating to security and safety and/or from simplifications provided for under the customs rules.

The status of authorised economic operator shall, subject to the rules and conditions laid down in paragraph 2, be recognised by the customs authorities in all Member States, without prejudice to customs controls. Customs authorities shall, on the basis of the recognition of the status of authorised economic operator and provided that the requirements relating to a specific type of simplification provided for in Community customs legislation are fulfilled, authorise the operator to benefit from that simplification.

2. The criteria for granting the status of authorised economic operator shall include:

—an appropriate record of compliance with customs requirements,

—a satisfactory system of managing commercial and, where appropriate, transport records, which allows appropriate customs controls,

—where appropriate, proven financial solvency, and

—where applicable, appropriate security and safety standards.

The committee procedure shall be used to determine the rules:

—for granting the status of authorised economic operator,

—for granting authorisations for the use of simplifications,

—for establishing which customs authority is competent to grant such status and authorisations,

—for the type and extent of facilitations that may be granted in respect of customs controls relating to security and safety, taking into account the rules for common risk management,

—for consultation with, and provision of information to, other customs authorities;

and the conditions under which:

—an authorisation may be limited to one or more Member States,

—the status of authorised economic operator may be suspended or withdrawn, and

—the requirement of being established in the Community may be waived for specific categories of authorised economic operator, taking into account, in particular, international agreements.][1]

Amendments—[1] Section 1a and Article 5a inserted by Parliament and Council Regulation (EC) 648/2005 art 1(2); see OJ L 117; 04.05.2005, p 13.

SECTION 2
DECISIONS RELATING TO THE APPLICATION OF CUSTOMS RULES

Article 6

1. Where a person requests that the customs authorities take a decision relating to the application of customs rules that person shall supply all the information and documents required by those authorities in order to take a decision.

2. Such decision shall be taken and notified to the applicant at the earliest opportunity.

Where a request for a decision is made in writing, the decision shall be made within a period laid down in accordance with the existing provisions, starting on the date on which the said request is received by the customs authorities. Such a decision must be notified in writing to the applicant.

However, that period may be exceeded where the customs authorities are unable to comply with it. In that case, those authorities shall so inform the applicant before the expiry of the above mentioned period, stating the grounds which justify exceeding it and indicating the further period of time which they consider necessary in order to give a ruling on the request.

3. Decisions adopted by the customs authorities in writing which either reject requests or are detrimental to the persons to whom they are addressed shall set out the grounds on which they are based. They shall refer to the right of appeal provided for in Article 243.

4. Provision may be made for the first sentence of paragraph 3 to apply likewise to other decisions.

Article 7

Save in the cases provided for in the second sub-paragraph of Article 244, decisions adopted shall be immediately enforceable by customs authorities.

Article 8

1. A decision favourable to the person concerned shall be annulled if it was issued on the basis of incorrect or incomplete information and:

—the applicant knew or should reasonably have known that the information was incorrect or incomplete, and

—such decision could not have been taken on the basis of correct or complete information.

2. The persons to whom the decision was addressed shall be notified of its annulment.

3. Annulment shall take effect from the date on which the annulled decision was taken.

Article 9

1. A decision favourable to the person concerned, shall be revoked or amended where, in cases other than those referred to in Article 8, one or more of the conditions laid down for its issue were not or are no longer fulfilled.

2. A decision favourable to the person concerned may be revoked where the person to whom it is addressed fails to fulfil an obligation imposed on him under that decision.

3. The person to whom the decision is addressed shall be notified of its revocation or amendment.

4. The revocation or amendment of the decision shall take effect from the date of notification. However, in exceptional cases where the legitimate interests of the person to whom the decision is addressed so require, the customs authorities may defer the date when revocation or amendment takes effect.

Article 10

Articles 8 and 9 shall be without prejudice to national rules which stipulate that decisions are invalid or become null and void for reasons unconnected with customs legislation.

SECTION 3
INFORMATION

Article 11

1. Any person may request information concerning the application of customs legislation from the customs authorities.

Such a request may be refused where it does not relate to an import or export operation actually envisaged.

2. The information shall be supplied to the applicant free of charge. However, where special costs are incurred by the customs authorities, in particular as a result of analyses or expert reports on goods, or the return of the goods to the applicant, he may be charged the relevant amount.

Article 12

Note—Article 12 is outside the scope of this work.

SECTION 4
OTHER PROVISIONS

[Article 13

1. Customs authorities may, in accordance with the conditions laid down by the provisions in force, carry out all the controls they deem necessary to ensure that customs rules and other legislation governing the entry, exit, transit, transfer and end-use of goods moved between the customs territory of the Community and third countries and the presence of goods that do not have Community status are correctly applied. Customs controls for the purpose of the correct application of Community legislation may be carried out in a third country where an international agreement provides for this.

2. Customs controls, other than spot-checks, shall be based on risk analysis using automated data processing techniques, with the purpose of identifying and quantifying the risks and developing the necessary measures to assess the risks, on the basis of criteria developed at national, Community and, where available, international level.

The committee procedure shall be used for determining a common risk management framework, and for establishing common criteria and priority control areas.

Member States, in cooperation with the Commission, shall establish a computer system for the implementation of risk management.

3. Where controls are performed by authorities other than the customs authorities, such controls shall be performed in close coordination with the customs authorities, wherever possible at the same time and place.

4. In the context of the controls provided for in this Article, customs and other competent authorities, such as veterinary and police authorities, may communicate data received, in connection with the entry, exit, transit, transfer and end-use of goods moved between the customs territory of the Community and third countries and the presence of goods that do not have Community status, between each other and to the customs authorities of the Member States and to the Commission where this is required for the purposes of minimising risk.

Communication of confidential data to the customs authorities and other bodies (e g security agencies) of third countries shall be allowed only in the framework of an international agreement and provided that the data protection provisions in force, in particular Directive 95/46/EC of the European Parliament and of the Council of 24 October 1995 on the protection of individuals with regard to the processing of personal data and on the free movement of such data and Regulation (EC) No 45/2001 of the European Parliament and of the Council of 18 December 2000 on the protection of individuals with regard to the processing of personal data by the Community institutions and bodies and on the free movement of such data are respected.][1]

Amendments—[1] Article 13 substituted by Parliament and Council Regulation (EC) 648/2005 art 1(3); see OJ L 117; 04.05.2005, p 13.

Article 14

For the purposes of applying customs legislation, any person directly or indirectly involved in the operations concerned for the purposes of trade in goods shall provide the customs authorities with all the requisite documents and information, irrespective of the medium used, and all the requisite assistance at their request and by any time limit prescribed.

[Article 15

All information which is by nature confidential or which is provided on a confidential basis shall be covered by the duty of professional secrecy. It shall not be disclosed by the competent authorities without the express permission of the person or authority providing it. The communication of information shall, however, be permitted where the competent authorities are obliged to do so pursuant to the provisions in force, particularly in connection with legal proceedings. Any disclosure or communication of information shall fully comply with prevailing data protection provisions, in particular Directive 95/46/EC and Regulation (EC) No 45/2001.][1]

Amendments—[1] Article 15 substituted by Parliament and Council Regulation (EC) 648/2005 art 1(4); see OJ L 117; 04.05.2005, p 13.

Article 16

The persons concerned shall keep the documents referred to in Article 14 for the purposes of [customs controls][1], for the period laid down in the provisions in force and for at least three calendar years, irrespective of the medium used. That period shall run from the end of the year in which:

(*a*) in the case of goods released for free circulation in circumstances other than those referred to in (*b*) or goods declared for export, from the end of the year in which the declarations for release for free circulation or export are accepted;

(*b*) in the case of goods released for free circulation at a reduced or zero rate of import duty on account of their end-use, from the end of the year in which they cease to be subject to customs supervision;

(*c*) in the case of goods placed under another customs procedure, from the end of the year in which the customs procedure concerned is completed;

(*d*) in the case of goods placed in a free zone or free warehouse, from the end of the year on which they leave the undertaking concerned.

Without prejudice to the provisions of Article 221(3), second sentence, where a check carried out by the customs authorities in respect of a customs debt shows that the relevant entry in the accounts has to be corrected, the documents shall be kept beyond the time limit provided for in the first paragraph for a period sufficient to permit the correction to be made and checked.

Amendments—[1] Words substituted by Parliament and Council Regulation (EC) 648/2005 art 1(5); see OJ L 117; 04.05.2005, p 13.

Article 17

Where a period, date or time limit is laid down pursuant to customs legislation for the purpose of applying legislation, such period shall not be extended and such date or time limit shall not be deferred unless specific provision is made in the legislation concerned.

[Article 18

1. The value of the ecu in national currencies to be applied for the purposes of determining the tariff classification of goods and import duties shall be fixed once a month. The rates to be used for this conversion shall be those published in the *Official Journal of the European Communities* on the penultimate working day of the month. Those rates shall apply throughout the following month.

However, where the rate applicable at the start of the month differs by more than 5% from that published on the penultimate working day before the 15th of that same month, the latter rate shall apply from the 15th until the end of the month in question.

2. The value of the ecu in national currencies to be applied within the framework of customs legislation in cases other than those referred to in paragraph 1 shall be fixed once a year. The rates to be used for this conversion shall be those published in the *Official Journal of the European Communities* on the first working day of October, with effect from 1 January of the following year. If no rate is available for a particular national currency, the rate applicable to that currency shall be that obtaining on the last day for which a rate was published in the *Official Journal of the European Communities*.

3. The customs authorities may round up or down the sum resulting from the conversion into their national currency of an amount expressed in ecus for purposes other than determining the tariff classification of goods or import or export duties.

The rounded-off amount may not differ from the original amount by more than 5%.

The customs authorities may retain unchanged the national-currency value of an amount expressed in ecus if, at the time of the annual adjustment provided for in paragraph 2, the conversion of that amount, prior to the above mentioned rounding-off, results in a variation of less than 5% in the national-currency value or a reduction in that value.][1]

Amendment—[1] Article 18 is substituted by EC regulation 82/97/EC with effect from 1 January 1997; see OJ L 17, 21.1.97.

Article 19
The procedure of the Committee shall be used to determine in which cases and under which conditions the application of customs legislation may be simplified.

TITLE II: FACTORS ON THE BASIS OF WHICH IMPORT DUTIES OR EXPORT DUTIES AND THE OTHER MEASURES PRESCRIBED IN RESPECT OF TRADE IN GOODS ARE APPLIED

Articles 20–26

Note—Articles 20–26 are outside the scope of this work.

CHAPTER 2—ORIGIN OF GOODS

SECTION 2

Article 27
Preferential origin of goods
The rules on preferential origin shall lay down the conditions governing acquisition of origin which goods must fulfil in order to benefit from the measures referred to in Article 20(3)(*d*) or (*e*).
Those rules shall:
(*a*) in the case of goods covered by the agreements referred to in Article 20(3)(*d*), be determined in those agreements;
(*b*) in the case of goods benefiting from the preferential tariff measures referred to in Article 20(3)(*e*), be determined in accordance with the Committee procedure.

CHAPTER 3—VALUE OF GOODS FOR CUSTOMS PURPOSES

Article 28
The provisions of this Chapter shall determine the customs value for the purposes of applying the Customs Tariff of the European Communities and non-tariff measures laid down by Community provisions governing specific fields relating to trade in goods.

Article 29
1. The customs value of imported goods shall be the transaction value, that is, the price actually paid or payable for the goods when sold for export to the customs territory of the Community, adjusted, where necessary, in accordance with Articles 32 and 33, provided:
(*a*) that there are no restrictions as to the disposal or use of the goods by the buyer, other than restrictions which:
—are imposed or required by a law or by the public authorities in the Community,
—limit the geographical area in which the goods may be resold, or
—do not substantially affect the value of the goods;
(*b*) that the sale or price is not subject to some condition or consideration for which a value cannot be determined with respect to the goods being valued;
(*c*) that no part of the proceeds of any subsequent resale, disposal or use of the goods by the buyer will accrue directly or indirectly to the seller, unless an appropriate adjustment can be made in accordance with Article 32; and
(*d*) that the buyer and seller are not related, or, where the buyer and seller are related, that the transaction value is acceptable for customs purposes under paragraph 2.

2

(*a*) In determining whether the transaction value is acceptable for the purposes of paragraph 1, the fact that the buyer and the seller are related shall not in itself be sufficient grounds for regarding the transaction value as unacceptable. Where necessary, the circumstances surrounding the sale shall be examined and the transaction value shall be accepted provided that the relationship did not influence the price. If, in the light of information provided by the declarant or otherwise, the customs authorities have grounds for considering that the relationship influenced the price, they shall communicate their grounds to the declarant and he shall be given a reasonable opportunity to respond. If the declarant so requests, the communication of the grounds shall be in writing.
(*b*) In a sale between related persons, the transaction value shall be accepted and the goods valued in accordance with paragraph 1 wherever the declarant demonstrates that such value closely approximates to one of the following occurring at or about the same time:
(i) the transaction value in sales, between buyers and sellers who are not related in any particular case, of identical or similar goods for export to the Community;
(ii) the customs value of identical or similar goods, as determined under Article 30(2)(*c*);

(iii) the customs value of identical or similar goods, as determined under Article 30(2)(*d*).

In applying the foregoing tests, due account shall be taken of demonstrated differences in commercial levels, quantity levels, the elements enumerated in Article 32 and costs incurred by the seller in sales in which he and the buyer are not related and where such costs are not incurred by the seller in sales in which he and the buyer are related.

(*c*) The tests set forth in sub-paragraph (*b*) are to be used at the initiative of the declarant and only for comparison purposes. Substitute values may not be established under the said sub-paragraph.

3

(*a*) The price actually paid or payable is the total payment made or to be made by the buyer to or for the benefit of the seller for the imported goods and includes all payments made or to be made as a condition of sale of the imported goods by the buyer to the seller or by the buyer to a third party to satisfy an obligation of the seller. The payment need not necessarily take the form of a transfer of money. Payment may be made by way of letters of credit or negotiable instrument and may be made directly or indirectly.

(*b*) Activities, including marketing activities, undertaken by the buyer on his own account, other than those for which an adjustment is provided in Article 32, are not considered to be an indirect payment to the seller, even though they might be regarded as of benefit to the seller or have been undertaken by agreement with the seller, and their cost shall not be added to the price actually paid or payable in determining the customs value of imported goods.

Article 30

1. Where the customs value cannot be determined under Article 29, it is to be determined by proceeding sequentially through sub-paragraphs (*a*), (*b*), (*c*) and (*d*) of paragraph 2 to the first sub-paragraph under which it can be determined, subject to the proviso that the order of application of sub-paragraphs (*c*) and (*d*) shall be reversed if the declarant so requests; it is only when such value cannot be determined under a particular sub-paragraph that the provisions of the next sub-paragraph in a sequence established by virtue of this paragraph can be applied.

2. The customs value as determined under this Article shall be:

(*a*) the transaction value of identical goods sold for export to the Community and exported at or about the same time as the goods being valued;

(*b*) the transaction value of similar goods sold for export to the Community and exported at or about the same time as the goods being valued;

(*c*) the value based on the unit price at which the imported goods for identical or similar imported goods are sold within the Community in the greatest aggregate quantity to persons not related to the sellers;

(*d*) the computed value, consisting of the sum of:

—the cost or value of materials and fabrication or other processing employed in producing the imported goods,

—an amount for profit and general expenses equal to that usually reflected in sales of goods of the same class or kind as the goods being valued which are made by producers in the country of exportation for export to the Community,

—the cost or value of the items referred to in Article 32(1)(*e*).

3. Any further conditions and rules for the application of paragraph 2 above shall be determined in accordance with the committee procedure.

Article 31

1. Where the customs value of imported goods cannot be determined under Articles 29 or 30, it shall be determined, on the basis of data available in the Community, using reasonable means consistent with the principles and general provisions of:

—the agreement on implementation of Article VII of the General Agreement on Tariffs and Trade, [of 1994] [1]

—Article VII of the General Agreement on Tariffs and Trade, [of 1994] [1]

—the provisions of this chapter.

2. No customs value shall be determined under paragraph 1 on the basis of:

(*a*) the selling price in the Community of goods produced in the Community;

(*b*) a system which provides for the acceptance for customs purposes of the higher of two alternative values;

(*c*) the price of goods on the domestic market of the country of exportation;

(*d*) the cost of production, other than computed values which have been determined for identical or similar goods in accordance with Article 30(2)(*d*);

(*e*) prices for export to a country not forming part of the customs territory of the Community;

(*f*) minimum customs values; or

(*g*) arbitrary or fictitious values.

Amendment—[1] Words added to first and second indents by EC Regulation 82/97/EC with effect from 1 January 1997; see OJ L 17, 21.1.97, p 1.

Article 32

1. In determining the customs value under Article 29, there shall be added to the price actually paid or payable for the imported goods:

(*a*) the following, to the extent that they are incurred by the buyer but are not included in the price actually paid or payable for the goods:

(i) commissions and brokerage, except buying commissions,

(ii) the cost of containers which are treated as being one, for customs purposes, with the goods in question,

(iii) the cost of packing, whether for labour or materials;

(*b*) the value, apportioned as appropriate, of the following goods and services where supplied directly or indirectly by the buyer free of charge or at reduced cost for use in connection with the production and sale for export of the imported goods, to the extent that such value has not been included in the price actually paid or payable:

(i) materials, components, parts and similar items incorporated in the imported goods,

(ii) tools, dies, moulds and similar items used in the production of the imported goods,

(iii) materials consumed in the production of the imported goods,

(iv) engineering, development, artwork, design work, and plans and sketches undertaken elsewhere than in the Community and necessary for the production of the imported goods;

(*c*) royalties and licence fees related to the goods being valued that the buyer must pay, either directly or indirectly, as a condition of sale of the goods being valued, to the extent that such royalties and fees are not included in the price actually paid or payable;

(*d*) the value of any part of the proceeds of any subsequent resale, disposal or use of the imported goods that accrues directly or indirectly to the seller;

(*e*)

(i) the cost of transport and insurance of the imported goods, and

(ii) loading and handling charges associated with the transport of the imported goods

to the place of introduction into the customs territory of the Community.

2. Additions to the price actually paid or payable shall be made under this Article only on the basis of objective and quantifiable data.

3. No additions shall be made to the price actually paid or payable in determining the customs value except as provided in this Article.

4. In this Chapter, the term "buying commissions" means fees paid by an importer to his agent for the service of representing him in the purchase of the goods being valued.

5. Notwithstanding paragraph 1(*c*):

(*a*) charges for the right to reproduce the imported goods in the Community shall not be added to the price actually paid or payable for the imported goods in determining the customs value; and

(*b*) payments made by the buyer for the right to distribute or resell the imported goods shall not be added to the price actually paid or payable for the imported goods if such payments are not a condition of the sale for export to the Community of the goods.

Simon's Tax Cases—Art 32(3), *Umbro International Ltd v R&C Comrs* [2009] STC 1345.

Article 33

1. Provided that they are shown separately from the price actually paid or payable, the following shall not be included in the customs value:

(*a*) charges for the transport of goods after their arrival at the place of introduction into the customs territory of the Community;

(*b*) charges for construction, erection, assembly, maintenance or technical assistance, undertaken after importation of imported goods such as industrial plant, machinery or equipment;

(*c*) charges for interest under a financing arrangement entered into by the buyer and relating to the purchase of imported goods, irrespective of whether the finance is provided by the seller or another person, provided that the financing arrangement has been made in writing and where required, the buyer can demonstrate that:

—such goods are actually sold at the price declared as the price actually paid or payable, and

—the claimed rate of interest does not exceed the level for such transactions prevailing in the country where, and at the time when, the finance was provided;

(*d*) charges for the right to reproduce imported goods in the Community;

(*e*) buying commissions;

(*f*) import duties or other charges payable in the Community by reason of the importation or sale of the goods.

Article 34

Specific rules may be laid down in accordance with the procedure of the committee to determine the customs value of carrier media for use in data processing equipment and bearing data or instructions.

Article 35

[Where factors used to determine the customs value of goods are expressed in a currency other than that of the Member State where the valuation is made, the rate of exchange to be used shall be that duly published by the authorities competent in the matter][1].

Such rate shall reflect as effectively as possible the current value of such currency in commercial transactions in terms of the currency of such Member State and shall apply during such period as may be determined in accordance with the procedure of the committee.

Where such a rate does not exist, the rate of exchange to be used shall be determined in accordance with the procedure of the committee.

Amendment—[1] First paragraph of Article 35 replaced by .EC Regulation 2700/2000/EC with effect from 19 December 2000 with effect from 19 December 2000; see OJ L 311, 12.12.2000, p 17.

Article 36

1. The provisions of this chapter shall be without prejudice to the specific provisions regarding the determination of the value for customs purposes of goods released for free circulation after being assigned a different customs-approved treatment or use.

2. By way of derogation from Articles 29, 30 and 31, the customs value of perishable goods usually delivered on consignment may, at the request of the declarant, be determined under simplified rules drawn up for the whole Community in accordance with the committee procedure.

TITLE III: PROVISIONS APPLICABLE TO GOODS BROUGHT INTO THE CUSTOMS TERRITORY OF THE COMMUNITY UNTIL THEY ARE ASSIGNED A CUSTOMS-APPROVED TREATMENT OR USE

CHAPTER 1—ENTRY OF GOODS INTO THE CUSTOMS TERRITORY OF THE COMMUNITY

[Article 36a

1. Goods brought into the customs territory of the Community shall be covered by a summary declaration, with the exception of goods carried on means of transport only passing through the territorial waters or the airspace of the customs territory without a stop within this territory.

2. The summary declaration shall be lodged at the customs office of entry.

Customs authorities may allow the summary declaration to be lodged at another customs office, provided that this office immediately communicates or makes available electronically the necessary particulars to the customs office of entry.

Customs authorities may accept, instead of the lodging of the summary declaration, the lodging of a notification and access to the summary declaration data in the economic operator's computer system.

3. The summary declaration shall be lodged before the goods are brought into the customs territory of the Community.

4. The committee procedure shall be used to establish:

—the time limit by which the summary declaration is to be lodged before the goods are brought into the customs territory of the Community,

—the rules for exceptions from, and variations to, the time limit referred to in the first indent, and

—the conditions under which the requirement for a summary declaration may be waived or adapted,

in accordance with the specific circumstances and for particular types of goods traffic, modes of transport and economic operators and where international agreements provide for special security arrangements.][1]

Amendments—[1] Articles 36a–36c inserted by Parliament and Council Regulation (EC) 648/2005 art 1(6); see OJ L 117; 04.05.2005, p 13.

[Article 36b

1. The committee procedure shall be used to establish a common data set and format for the summary declaration, containing the particulars necessary for risk analysis and the proper application of customs controls, primarily for security and safety purposes, using, where appropriate, international standards and commercial practices.

2. The summary declaration shall be made using a data processing technique. Commercial, port or transport information may be used, provided that it contains the necessary particulars.

Customs authorities may accept paper-based summary declarations in exceptional circumstances, provided that they apply the same level of risk management as that applied to summary declarations made using a data processing technique.

3. The summary declaration shall be lodged by the person who brings the goods, or who assumes responsibility for the carriage of the goods into the customs territory of the Community.

4. Notwithstanding the obligation of the person referred to in paragraph 3, the summary declaration may be lodged instead by:

(*a*) the person in whose name the person referred to in paragraph 3 acts; or

(*b*) any person who is able to present the goods in question or to have them presented to the competent customs authority; or

(*c*) a representative of one of the persons referred to in paragraph 3 or points (*a*) or (*b*).

5. The person referred to in paragraphs 3 and 4 shall, at his request, be authorised to amend one or more particulars of the summary declaration after it has been lodged. However, no amendment shall be possible after the customs authorities:

(*a*) have informed the person who lodged the summary declaration that they intend to examine the goods; or

(*b*) have established that the particulars in questions are incorrect; or

(*c*) have allowed the removal of the goods.][1]

Amendments—[1] Articles 36a–36c inserted by Parliament and Council Regulation (EC) 648/2005 art 1(6); see OJ L 117; 04.05.2005, p 13.

[Article 36c

1. The customs office of entry may waive the lodging of a summary declaration in respect of goods for which, before expiry of the time limit referred to in Article 36a(3) or (4), a customs declaration is lodged. In such case, the customs declaration shall contain at least the particulars necessary for a summary declaration and, until such time as the former is accepted in accordance with Article 63, it shall have the status of a summary declaration.

Customs authorities may allow the customs declaration to be lodged at a customs office of import different from the customs office of entry, provided that this office immediately communicates or makes available electronically the necessary particulars to the customs office of entry.

2. Where the customs declaration is lodged other than by use of data processing technique, the customs authorities shall apply the same level of risk management to the data as that applied to customs declarations made using a data processing technique.][1]

Amendments—[1] Articles 36a–36c inserted by Parliament and Council Regulation (EC) 648/2005 art 1(6); see OJ L 117; 04.05.2005, p 13.

Article 37

1. Goods brought into the customs territory of the Community shall, from the time of their entry, be subject to customs supervision. They may be subject to [customs controls][1] in accordance with the provisions in force.

2. They shall remain under such supervision for as long as necessary to determine their customs status, if appropriate, and in the case of non-Community goods and without prejudice to Article 82(1), until their customs status is changed, they enter a free zone or free warehouse or they are re-exported or destroyed in accordance with Article 182.

Amendments—[1] Words in para (1) substituted by Parliament and Council Regulation (EC) 648/2005 art 1(7); see OJ L 117; 04.05.2005, p 13.

Article 38

1. Goods brought into the customs territory of the Community shall be conveyed by the person bringing them into the Community without delay, by the route specified by the customs authorities and in accordance with their instructions, if any:

(*a*) to the customs office designated by the customs authorities or to any other place designated or approved by those authorities; or,

(*b*) to a free zone, if the goods are to be brought into that free zone direct:

—by sea or air, or

—by land without passing through another part of the customs territory of the Community, where the free zone adjoins the land frontier between a Member State and a third country.

2. Any person who assumes responsibility for the carriage of goods after they have been brought into the customs territory of the Community, *inter alia* as a result of transhipment, shall become responsible for compliance with the obligation laid down in paragraph 1.

3. Goods which, although still outside the customs territory of the Community, may be subject to [customs controls by][1] a Member State under the provisions in force, as a result of *inter alia* an agreement concluded between that Member State and a third country, shall be treated in the same way as goods brought into the customs territory of the Community.

4. Paragraph 1(*a*) shall not preclude implementation of any provisions in force with respect to tourist traffic, frontier traffic, postal traffic or traffic of negligible economic importance, on condition that customs supervision and customs control possibilities are not thereby jeopardised.

[5 Paragraphs 1 to 4 and Articles 36a to 36c and 39 to 53 shall not apply to goods which temporarily leave the customs territory of the Community while moving between two points in that territory by sea or air, provided that the carriage is effected by a direct route and by regular air or shipping services without a stop outside the customs territory of the Community.][2]

6. Paragraph 1 shall not apply to goods on board vessels or aircraft crossing the territorial sea or airspace of the Member States without having as their destination a port or airport situated in those Member States.

Amendments—[1] Words in para (3) substituted by Parliament and Council Regulation (EC) 648/2005 art 1(7); see OJ L 117; 04.05.2005, p 13.

[2] Para (5) substituted by Parliament and Council Regulation (EC) 648/2005 art 1(8); see OJ L 117; 04.05.2005, p 13.

Article 39

1. Where, by reason of unforeseeable circumstances or force majeure, the obligation laid down in Article 38(1) cannot be complied with, the person bound by that obligation or any other person acting in his place shall inform the customs authorities of the situation without delay. Where the unforeseeable circumstances or force majeure do not result in total loss of the goods, the customs authorities shall also be informed of their precise location.

2. Where, by reason of unforeseeable circumstances or force majeure, a vessel or aircraft covered by Article 38(6) is forced to put into port or land temporarily in the customs territory of the Community and the obligation laid down in Article 38(1) cannot be complied with, the person bringing the vessel or aircraft into the customs territory of the Community or any other person acting in his place shall inform the customs authorities of the situation without delay.

3. The customs authorities shall determine the measures to be taken in order to permit customs supervision of the goods referred to in paragraph 1 as well as those on board a vessel or aircraft in the circumstances specified in paragraph 2 and to ensure, where appropriate, that they are subsequently conveyed to a customs office or other place designated or approved by the authorities.

CHAPTER 2—PRESENTATION OF GOODS TO CUSTOMS

[Article 40

Goods entering the customs territory of the Community shall be presented to customs by the person who brings them into that territory or, if appropriate, by the person who assumes responsibility for carriage of the goods following such entry, with the exception of goods carried on means of transport only passing through the territorial waters or the airspace of the customs territory of the Community without a stop within this territory. The person presenting the goods shall make a reference to the summary declaration or customs declaration previously lodged in respect of the goods.][1]

Amendments—[1] Article 40 substituted by Parliament and Council Regulation (EC) 648/2005 art 1(9); see OJ L 117; 04.05.2005, p 13.

Article 41

Article 40 shall not preclude the implementation of rules in force relating to goods:

(*a*) carried by travellers;

(*b*) placed under a customs procedure but not presented to customs.

Article 42

Goods may, once they have been presented to customs, and with the permission of the customs authorities, be examined or samples may be taken, in order that they may be assigned a customs-approved treatment or use. Such permission shall be granted, on request, to the person authorised to assign the goods such treatment or use.

CHAPTER 3—[UNLOADING OF GOODS PRESENTED TO CUSTOMS][1]

Amendments—[1] Title substituted by Parliament and Council Regulation (EC) 648/2005 art 1(10); see OJ L 117; 04.05.2005, p 13.

Articles 43–45

Amendments—Articles 43–45 repealed by Parliament and Council Regulation (EC) 648/2005 art 1(11); see OJ L 117; 04.05.2005, p 13.

Article 46

1. Goods shall be unloaded or transhipped from the means of transport carrying them solely with the permission of the customs authorities in places designated or approved by those customs authorities.

However, such permission shall not be required in the event of the imminent danger necessitating the immediate unloading of all or part of the goods. In that case, the customs authorities shall be informed accordingly forthwith.

2. For the purpose of inspecting goods and the means of transport carrying them, the customs authorities may at any time require goods to be unloaded and unpacked.

Article 47

Goods shall not be removed from their original position without the permission of the customs authorities.

Articles 48–57

Note—Articles 48–57 are outside the scope of this work.

TITLE IV: CUSTOMS—APPROVED TREATMENT OR USE

CHAPTER 1—GENERAL

Article 58

1. Save as otherwise provided, goods may at any time, under the conditions laid down, be assigned any customs-approved treatment or use irrespective of their nature or quantity, or their country of origin, consignment or destination.

2. Paragraph 1 shall not preclude the imposition of prohibitions or restrictions justified on grounds of public morality, public policy or public security, the protection of health and life of humans, animals or plants, the protection of national treasures possessing artistic, historic or archaeological value or the protection of industrial and commercial property.

CHAPTER 2—CUSTOMS PROCEDURES

SECTION 1

PLACING OF GOODS UNDER A CUSTOMS PROCEDURE

Article 59

1. All goods intended to be placed under a customs procedure shall be covered by a declaration for that customs procedure.

2. Community goods declared for an export, outward processing, transit or customs warehousing procedure shall be subject to customs supervision from the time of acceptance of the customs declaration until such time as they leave the customs territory of the Community or are destroyed or the customs declaration is invalidated.

Article 60

Insofar as Community customs legislation lays down no rules on the matter, Member States shall determine the competence of the various customs offices situated in their territory, account being taken, where applicable, of the nature of the goods and the customs procedure under which they are to be placed.

Article 61

The customs declaration shall be made:

(*a*) in writing; or

(*b*) using a data-processing technique where provided for by provisions laid down in accordance with the committee procedure or where authorised by the customs authorities; or

(*c*) by means of a normal declaration or any other act whereby the holder of the goods expresses his wish to place them under a customs procedure, where such a possibility is provided for by the rules adopted in accordance with the committee procedure.

A DECLARATIONS IN WRITING

I Normal procedure

Article 62

1. Declarations in writing shall be made on a form corresponding to the official specimen prescribed for that purpose. They shall be signed and contain all the particulars necessary for implementation of the provisions governing the customs procedure for which the goods are declared.

2. The declaration shall be accompanied by all the documents required for implementation of the provisions governing the customs procedure for which the goods are declared.

Article 63

Declarations which comply with the conditions laid down in Article 62 shall be accepted by the customs authorities immediately, provided that the goods to which they refer are presented to customs.

Article 64

1. Subject to Article 5, a customs declaration may be made by any person who is able to present the goods in question or to have them presented to the competent customs authority, together with all the documents which are required to be produced for the application of the rules governing the customs procedure in respect of which the goods were declared.

2. However,

(*a*) where acceptance of a customs declaration imposes particular obligations on a specific person, the declaration must be made by that person or on his behalf;

(*b*) the declarant must be established in the Community.

However, the condition regarding establishment in the Community shall not apply to persons who:

—make a declaration for transit or temporary importation;

—declare goods on an occasional basis, provided that the customs authorities consider this to be justified.

3. Paragraph 2(*b*) shall not preclude the application by the Member States of bilateral agreements concluded with third countries, or customary practices having similar effect, under which nationals of such countries may make customs declarations in the territory of the Member States in question, subject to reciprocity.

Article 65

The declaration shall, at his request, be authorised to amend one or more of the particulars of the declaration after it has been accepted by customs. The amendment shall not have the effect of rendering the declaration applicable to goods other than those it originally covered.

However, no amendment shall be permitted where authorisation is requested after the customs authorities:

(*a*) have informed the declarant that they intend to examine the goods; or,

(*b*) have established that the particulars in question are incorrect; or,

(*c*) have released the goods.

Article 66

1. The customs authorities shall, at the request of the declarant, invalidate a declaration already accepted where the declarant furnishes proof that goods were declared in error for the customs procedure covered by that declaration or that, as a result of special circumstances, the placing of the goods under the customs procedure for which they were declared is no longer justified.

Nevertheless, where the customs authorities have informed the declarant of their intention to examine the goods, a request for invalidation of the declaration shall not be accepted until after the examination has taken place.

2. The declaration shall not be invalidated after the goods have been released, except in cases defined in accordance with the committee procedure.

3. Invalidation of the declaration shall be without prejudice to the application of the penal provisions in force.

Article 67

Save as otherwise expressly provided, the date to be used for the purposes of all the provisions governing the customs procedure for which the goods are declared shall be the date of acceptance of the declaration by the customs authorities.

Article 68

For the verification of declarations which they have accepted, the customs authorities may:

(*a*) examine the documents covering the declaration and the documents accompanying it. The customs authorities may require the declarant to present other documents for the purpose of verifying the accuracy of the particulars contained in the declaration;

(*b*) examine the goods and take samples for analysis or for detailed examination.

Article 69

1. Transport of the goods to the places where they are to be examined and samples are to be taken, and all the handling necessitated by such examination or taking of samples, shall be carried out by or under the responsibility of the declarant. The costs incurred shall be borne by the declarant.

2. The declarant shall be entitled to be present when the goods are examined and when samples are taken. Where they deem it appropriate, the customs authorities shall require the declarant to

be present or represented when the goods are examined or samples are taken in order to provide them with the assistance necessary to facilitate such examination or taking of samples.

3. Provided that samples are taken in accordance with the provisions in force, the customs authorities shall not be liable for payment of any compensation in respect thereof but shall bear the costs of their analysis or examination.

Article 70

1. Where only part of the goods covered by a declaration are examined, the results of the partial examination shall be taken to apply to all the goods covered by that declaration.

However, the declarant may request a further examination of the goods if he considers that the results of the partial examination are not valid as regards the remainder of the goods declared.

2. For the purposes of paragraph 1, where a declaration form covers two or more items, the particulars relating to each item shall be deemed to constitute a separate declaration.

Article 71

1. The results of verifying the declaration shall be used for the purposes of applying the provisions governing the customs procedure under which the goods are placed.

2. Where the declaration is not verified, the provisions referred to in paragraph 1 shall be applied on the basis of the particulars contained in the declaration.

Article 72

1. The customs authorities shall take the measures necessary to identify the goods where identification is required in order to ensure compliance with the conditions governing the customs procedure for which the said goods have been declared.

2. Means of identification affixed to the goods or means of transport shall be removed or destroyed only by the customs authorities or with their permission unless, as a result of unforeseeable circumstances or force majeure, their removal or destruction is essential to ensure the protection of the goods or means of transport.

Article 73

1. Without prejudice to Article 74, where the conditions for placing the goods under the procedure in question are fulfilled and provided the goods are not subject to any prohibitive or restrictive measures, the customs authorities shall release the goods as soon as the particulars in the declaration have been verified or accepted without verification. The same shall apply where such verification cannot be completed within a reasonable period of time and the goods are no longer required to be present for verification purposes.

2. All the goods covered by the same declaration shall be released at the same time.

For the purposes of this paragraph, where a declaration form covers two or more items, the particulars relating to each item shall be deemed to constitute a separate declaration.

Article 74

1. Where acceptance of a customs declaration gives rise to a customs debt, the goods covered by the declaration shall not be released unless the customs debt has been paid or secured. However, without prejudice to paragraph 2, this provision shall not apply to the temporary importation procedure with partial relief from import duties.

2. Where, pursuant to the provisions governing the customs procedure for which the goods are declared, the customs authorities require the provision of a security, the said goods shall not be released for the customs procedure in question until such security is provided.

Article 75

Any necessary measures, including confiscation and sale, shall be taken to deal with goods which:

(*a*) cannot be released because:

—it has not been possible to undertake or continue examination of the goods within the period prescribed by the customs authorities for reasons attributable to the declarant; or,

—the documents which must be produced before the goods can be placed under the customs procedure requested have not been produced; or,

—payments or security which should have been made or provided in respect of import duties or export duties, as the case may be, have not been made or provided within the period prescribed; or

—they are subject to bans or restrictions;

(*b*) are not removed within a reasonable period after their release.

II. Simplified procedures

Article 76

1. In order to simplify completion of formalities and procedures as far as possible while ensuring that operations are conducted in a proper manner, the customs authorities shall, under conditions laid down in accordance with the committee procedure, grant permission for:

(*a*) the declaration referred to in Article 62 to omit certain of the particulars referred to in paragraph 1 of that Article for some of the documents referred to in paragraph 2 of that Article not to be attached thereto;

(*b*) a commercial or administrative document, accompanied by request for the goods to be placed under the customs procedure in question, to be lodged in place of the declaration referred to in Article 62;

(*c*) the goods to be entered for the procedure in question by means of an entry in the records; in this case, the customs authorities may waive the requirement that the declarant presents the goods to customs.

The simplified declaration, commercial or administrative document or entry in the records must contain at least the particulars necessary for identification of the goods. Where the goods are entered in the records, the date of such entry must be included.

2. Except in cases to be determined in accordance with the committee procedure, the declarant shall furnish a supplementary declaration which may be of a general, periodic or recapitulative nature.

3. Supplementary declarations and the simplified declarations referred to in sub-paragraphs 1(*a*), (*b*) and (*c*), shall be deemed to constitute a single, indivisible instrument taking effect on the date of acceptance of the simplified declarations; in the cases referred to in sub-paragraph 1(*c*), entry in the records shall have the same legal force as acceptance of the declaration referred to in Article 62.

4. Special simplified procedures for the Community transit procedure shall be laid down in accordance with the committee procedure.

B OTHER DECLARATIONS

Article 77

[1][1] Where the customs declaration is made by means of a data-processing technique within the meaning of Article 61(*b*), or by an oral declaration or any other act within the meaning of Article 61(*c*), Articles 62 to 76 shall apply *mutatis mutandis* without prejudice to the principles set out therein.

[2 Where the customs declaration is made by means of a data-processing technique, the customs authorities may allow accompanying documents referred to in Article 62(2) not to be lodged with the declaration. In this case the documents shall be kept at the customs authorities' disposal][1]

Amendments—[1] Paragraph numbered, and Article 77(2) added by EC Regulation 2700/2000/EC with effect from 19 December 2000; see OJ L 311, 12.12.2000, p 17.

C POST-CLEARANCE EXAMINATION OF DECLARATIONS

Article 78

1. The customs authorities may, on their own initiative or at the request of the declarant, amend the declaration after release of the goods.

2. The customs authorities may, after releasing the goods and in order to satisfy themselves as to the accuracy of the particulars contained in the declaration, inspect the commercial documents and data relating to the import or export operations in respect of the goods concerned or to subsequent commercial operations involving those goods. Such inspections may be carried out at the premises of the declarant, of any other person directly or indirectly involved in the said operations in a business capacity or of any other person in possession of the said document and data for business purposes. Those authorities may also examine the goods where it is still possible for them to be produced.

3. Where revision of the declaration or post-clearance examination indicates that the provisions governing the customs procedure concerned have been applied on the basis of incorrect or incomplete information, the customs authorities shall, in accordance with any provisions laid down, take the measures necessary to regularise the situation, taking account of the new information available to them.

SECTION 2
RELEASE FOR FREE CIRCULATION

Article 79

Release for free circulation shall confer on non-Community goods the customs status of Community goods.

It shall entail application of commercial policy measures, completion of the other formalities laid down in respect of the importation of goods and the charging of any duties legally due.

Article 80

1. By way of derogation from Article 67, provided that the import duty chargeable on the goods is one of the duties referred to in the first indent of Article 4(10) and that the rate of duty is reduced after the date of acceptance of the declaration for release for free circulation but before the goods are released, the declarant may request application of the more favourable rate.

2. Paragraph 1 shall not apply where it has not been possible to release the goods for reasons attributable to the declarant alone.

Article 81

Where a consignment is made up of goods falling within different tariff classifications, and dealing with each of those goods in accordance with its tariff classification for the purpose of drawing up the declaration would entail a burden of work and expense disproportionate to the import duties chargeable, the customs authorities may, at the request of the declarant, agree that import duties be charged on the whole consignment on the basis of the tariff classification of the goods which are subject to the highest rate of import duty.

Article 82

1. Where goods are released for free circulation at a reduced or zero rate of duty on account of their end-use, they shall remain under customs supervision. Customs supervision shall end when the conditions laid down for granting such a reduced or zero rate of duty cease to apply, where the goods are exported or destroyed or where the use of the goods for purposes other than those laid down for the application of the reduced or zero rate of duty is permitted subject to payment of the duties due.

2. Articles 88 and 90 shall apply *mutatis mutandis* to the goods referred to in paragraph 1.

Article 83

Goods released for free circulation shall lose their customs status as Community goods where:

(*a*) the declaration for release for free circulation is invalidated after release [...][1] , or

(*b*) the imported duties payable on those goods are repaid or remitted:

—under the inward processing procedure in the form of the drawback system; or

—in respect of defective goods or goods which fail to comply with the terms of the contract, pursuant to Article 238; or

—in situations of the type referred to in Article 239 where repayment or remission is conditional upon the goods being exported or re-exported or being assigned an equivalent customs-approved treatment or use.

Amendment—Words in sub-para(*a*) repealed by EC Regulation 82/97/EC with effect from 1 January 1997; see OJ L17, 21.1.97

SECTION 3

Suspensive arrangements and customs procedures with economic impact

A Provisions common to several procedures

Article 84

1. In Articles 85 to 90:

(*a*) where the term "procedure" is used, it is understood as applying, in the case of non-Community goods, to the following arrangements:

—external transit;
—customs warehousing;
—inward processing in the form of a system of suspension;
—processing under customs control;
—temporary importation;

(*b*) where the term "customs procedure with economic impact" is used, it is understood as applying to the following arrangements:

—customs warehousing;
—inward processing;
—processing under customs control;
—temporary importation;
—outward processing.

2. "Import goods" means goods placed under a suspensive procedure and goods which, under the inward processing procedure in the form of the drawback system, have undergone the formalities for release for free circulation and the formalities provided for in Article 125.

3. "Goods in the unaltered state" means import goods which, under the inward processing procedure or the procedures for processing under customs control, have undergone no form of processing.

Article 85

The use of any customs procedure with economic impact shall be conditional upon authorisation being issued by the customs authorities.

Article 86

Without prejudice to the additional special conditions governing the procedure in question, the authorisation referred to in Article 85 and that referred to in Article 100(1) shall be granted only:

—to persons who offer every guarantee necessary for the proper conduct of the operations;

—where the customs authorities can supervise and monitor the procedure without having to introduce administrative arrangements disproportionate to the economic needs involved.

Article 87

1. The conditions under which the procedure in question is used shall be set out in the authorisation.

2. The holder of the authorisation shall notify the customs authorities of all factors arising after the authorisation was granted which may influence its continuation or content.

[Article 87a

In the cases referred to in the second sentence of the first indent of Article 4 (7), any products or goods obtained from goods placed under a suspensive arrangement shall be considered as being placed under the same arrangement][1]

Amendment—[1] This article was inserted by EC Regulations 82/97/EC with effect from 1 January 1997; see OJ L 21.1.97. p 1.

Article 88

The customs authorities may make the placing of goods under a suspensive arrangement conditional upon the provision of security in order to ensure that any customs debt which may be incurred in respect of those goods will be paid.

Special provisions concerning the provision of security may be laid down in the context of a specific suspensive arrangement.

Article 89

1. A suspensive arrangement with economic impact shall be discharged when a new customs-approved treatment or use is assigned either to the goods placed under that arrangement or to compensating or processed products placed under it.

2. The customs authorities shall take all the measures necessary to regularise the position of goods in respect of which a procedure has not been discharged under the conditions prescribed.

Article 90

The rights and obligations of the holder of a customs procedure with economic impact may, on the conditions laid down by the customs authorities, be transferred successively to other persons who fulfil any conditions laid down in order to benefit from the procedure in question.

Articles 91–200

Note—Articles 91–200 are outside the scope of this work.

CHAPTER 2—INCURRENCE OF A CUSTOMS DEBT

Article 201

1. A customs debt on importation shall be incurred through:

(*a*) the release for free circulation of goods liable to import duties, or

(*b*) the placing of such goods under the temporary importation procedure with partial relief from import duties.

2. A customs debt shall be incurred at the time of acceptance of the customs declaration in question.

3. The debtor shall be the declarant. In the event of indirect representation, the person on whose behalf the customs declaration is made shall also be a debtor.

Where a customs declaration in respect of one of the procedures referred to in paragraph 1 is drawn up on the basis of information which leads to all or part of the duties legally owed not being collected, the persons who provided the information required to draw up the declaration and who knew, or who ought reasonably to have known that such information was false, may also be considered debtors in accordance with the national provisions in force.

Article 202

1. A customs debt on importation shall be incurred through:

(*a*) the unlawful introduction into the customs territory of the Community of goods liable to import duties, or (*b*) the unlawful introduction into another part of that territory of such goods located in a free zone or free warehouse.

For the purpose of this Article, unlawful introduction means any introduction in violation of the provisions of Articles 38 to 41 and the second indent of Article 177.

2. The customs debt shall be incurred at the moment when the goods are unlawfully introduced.

3. The debtors shall be:

—the person who introduced such goods unlawfully,

—any persons who participated in the unlawful introduction of the goods and who were aware or should reasonably have been aware that such introduction was unlawful, and

—any persons who acquired or held the goods in question and who were aware or should reasonably have been aware at the time of acquiring or receiving the goods that they had been introduced unlawfully.

Article 203

1. A customs debt on importation shall be incurred through:

—the unlawful removal from customs supervision of goods liable to import duties.

2. The customs debt shall be incurred at the moment when the goods are removed from customs supervision.

3. The debtors shall be:

—the person who removed the goods from customs supervision,

—any persons who participated in such removal and who were aware or should reasonably have been aware that the goods were being removed from customs supervision,

—any persons who acquired or held the goods in question and who were aware or should reasonably have been aware at the time of acquiring or receiving the goods that they had been removed from customs supervision, and

—where appropriate, the person required to fulfil the obligations arising from temporary storage of the goods or from the use of the customs procedure under which those goods are placed.

Article 204

1. A customs debt on importation shall be incurred through:

(*a*) non-fulfilment of one of the obligations arising, in respect of goods liable to import duties, from their temporary storage or from the use of the customs procedure under which they are placed, or

(*b*) non-compliance with a condition governing the placing of the goods under that procedure or the granting of a reduced or zero rate of import duty by virtue of the end-use of the goods,

in cases other than those referred to in Article 203 unless it is established that those failures have no significant effect on the correct operation of the temporary storage or customs procedure in question.

2. The customs debt shall be incurred either at the moment when the obligation whose non-fulfilment gives rise to the customs debt ceases to be met or at the moment when the goods are placed under the customs procedure concerned where it is established subsequently that a condition governing the placing of the goods under the said procedure or the granting of a reduced or zero rate of import duty by virtue of the end-use of the goods was not in fact fulfilled.

3. The debtor shall be the person who is required, according to the circumstances, either to fulfil the obligations arising, in respect of goods liable to import duties, from their temporary storage or from the use of the customs procedure under which they have been placed, or to comply with the conditions governing the placing of the goods under that procedure.

Article 205

1. A customs debt on importation shall be incurred through:

—the consumption or use, in a free zone or a free warehouse, of goods liable to import duties, under conditions other than those laid down by the legislation in force.

Where goods disappear and where their disappearance cannot be explained to the satisfaction of the customs authorities, those authorities may regard the goods as having been consumed or used in the free zone or the free warehouse.

2. The debt shall be incurred at the moment when the goods are consumed or are first used under conditions other than those laid down by the legislation in force.

3. The debtor shall be the person who consumed or used the goods and any persons who participated in such consumption or use and who were aware or should reasonably have been aware that the goods were being consumed or used under conditions other than those laid down by the legislation in force.

Where customs authorities regard goods which have disappeared as having been consumed or used in the free zone or the free warehouse and it is not possible to apply the preceding paragraph, the person liable for payment of the customs debt shall be the last person known to these authorities to have been in possession of the goods.

Article 206

1. By way of derogation from Articles 202 and 204(1)(*a*), no customs debt on importation shall be deemed to be incurred in respect of specific goods where the person concerned proves that the non-fulfilment of the obligations which arise from:
—the provisions of Articles 38 to 41 and the second indent of Article 177, or
—keeping the goods in question in temporary storage, or
—the use of the customs procedure under which the goods have been placed,

results from the total destruction or irretrievable loss of the said goods as a result of the actual nature of the goods or unforeseeable circumstances or *force majeure*, or as a consequence of authorisation by the customs authorities.

For the purposes of this paragraph, goods shall be irretrievably lost when they are rendered unusable by any person.

2. Nor shall a customs debt on importation be deemed to be incurred in respect of goods released for free circulation at a reduced or zero rate of import duty by virtue of their end-use, where such goods are exported or re-exported with the permission of the customs authorities.

Article 207

Where, in accordance with Article 206(1), no customs debt is deemed to be incurred in respect of goods released for free circulation at a reduced or zero rate of import duty on account of their end-use, any scrap or waste resulting from such destruction shall be deemed to be non-Community goods.

Article 208

Where in accordance with Article 203 or 204 a customs debt is incurred in respect of goods released for free circulation at a reduced rate of import duty on account of their end-use, the amount paid when the goods were released for free circulation shall be deducted from the amount of the customs debt.

This provision shall apply *mutatis mutandis* where a customs debt is incurred in respect of scrap and waste resulting from the destruction of such goods.

Article 209

1. A customs debt on exportation shall be incurred through:
—the exportation from the customs territory of the Community, under cover of a customs declaration, of goods liable to export duties.

2. The customs debt shall be incurred at the time when such customs declaration is accepted.

3. The debtor shall be the declarant. In the event of indirect representation, the person on whose behalf the declaration is made shall also be a debtor.

Article 210

1. A customs debt on exportation shall be incurred through:
—the removal from the customs territory of the Community of goods liable to export duties without a customs declaration.

2. The customs debt shall be incurred at the time when the said goods actually leave that territory.

3. The debtor shall be:
—the person who removed the goods, and
—any persons who participated in such removal and who were aware or should reasonably have been aware that a customs declaration had not been but should have been lodged.

Article 211

1. A customs debt on exportation shall be incurred through:
—failure to comply with the conditions under which the goods were allowed to leave the customs territory of the Community with total or partial relief from export duties.

2. The debt shall be incurred at the time when the goods reach a destination other than that for which they were allowed to leave the customs territory of the Community with total or partial relief from export duties or, should the customs authorities be unable to determine that time, the expiry of the time limit set for the production of evidence that the conditions entitling the goods to such relief have been fulfilled.

3. The debtor shall be the declarant. In the event of indirect representation, the person on whose behalf the declaration is made shall also be a debtor.

Article 212

The customs debt referred to in Articles 201 to 205 and 209 to 211 shall be incurred even if it relates to goods subject to measures of prohibition or restriction on importation or exportation of any kind whatsoever. However, no customs debt shall be incurred on the unlawful introduction into the customs territory of the Community of counterfeit currency or of narcotic drugs and psychotropic substances which do not enter into the economic circuit strictly supervised by the competent authorities with a view to their use for medical and scientific purposes. For the purposes of criminal law as applicable to customs offences, the customs debt shall nevertheless be deemed to have been incurred where, under a Member State's criminal law, customs duties provide the basis for determining penalties, or the existence of a customs debt is grounds for taking criminal proceedings.

[Article 212a

Where customs legislation provides for favourable tariff treatment of goods by reason of their nature or end-use or for relief or total or partial exemption from import or export duties pursuant to Articles 21, 82, 145 or 184 to 187, such favourable tariff treatment, relief or exemption shall also apply in cases where a customs debt is incurred pursuant to Articles 202 to 205, 210 or 211, on condition that the behaviour of the person concerned involves neither fraudulent dealing nor obvious negligence and he produces evidence that the other conditions for the application of favourable treatment, relief or exemption have been satisfied.][1]

Amendments—This Article replaced by EC Regulation 2700/2000/EC with effect from 19 December 2000; see OJ L 311, 12.12.2000, p 17.

Article 213

Where several persons are liable for payment of one customs debt, they shall be jointly and severally liable for such debt.

Article 214

1. Save as otherwise expressly provided by this Code and without prejudice to paragraph 2, the amount of the import duty or export duty applicable to goods shall be determined on the basis of the rules of assessment appropriate to those goods at the time when the customs debt in respect of them is incurred.

2. Where it is not possible to determine precisely when the customs debt is incurred, the time to be taken into account in determining the rules of assessment appropriate to the goods concerned shall be the time when the customs authorities conclude that the goods are in a situation in which a customs debt is incurred.

However, where the information available to the customs authorities enables them to establish that the customs debt was incurred prior to the time when they reached that conclusion, the amount of the import duty or export duty payable on the goods in question shall be determined on the basis of the rules of assessment appropriate to the goods at the earliest time when existence of the customs debt arising from the situation may be established from the information available.

3. Compensatory interest shall be applied, in the circumstances and under the conditions to be defined in the provisions adopted under the committee procedure, in order to prevent the wrongful acquisition of a financial advantage through deferment of the date on which the customs debt was incurred or entered into the accounts.

[Article 215

1. A customs debt shall be incurred—

—at the place where the events from which it arises occur,

—if it is not possible to determine that place, at the place where the customs authorities conclude that the goods are in a situation in which a customs debt is incurred,

—if the goods have been entered for a customs procedure which has not been discharged, and the place cannot be determined pursuant to the first or second indent within a period of time determined, if appropriate, in accordance with the committee procedure, at the place where the goods were either placed under the procedure concerned or were introduced into the Community customs territory under that procedure.

2. Where the information available to the customs authorities enables them to establish that the customs debt was already incurred when the goods were in another place at an earlier date, the customs debt shall be deemed to have been incurred at the place which may be established as the location of the goods at the earliest time when existence of the customs debt may be established.

3. The customs authorities referred to in Article 217(1) are those of the Member State where the customs debt is incurred or is deemed to have been incurred in accordance with this Article.][1]

[4 If a customs authority finds that a customs debt has been incurred under Article 202 in another Member State and the amount of that debt is lower than EUR 5000, the debt shall be deemed to have been incurred in the Member State where the finding was made.][2]

Amendment—[1] This Article was substituted by European Parliament and Council Regulation (EC) 955/1999, Art 1, para 7; see OJ L 119, 7.5.99, p 1.

[2] This paragraph added by EC Regulation 2700/2000/EC with effect from 19 December 2000; see OJ L 311, 12.12.2000, p 17.

Article 216

1. In so far as agreements concluded between the Community and certain third countries provide for the granting on importation into those countries of preferential tariff treatment for goods originating in the Community within the meaning of such agreements, on condition that, where they have been obtained under the inward processing procedure, non-Community goods incorporated in the said originating goods are subject to payment of the import duties payable thereon, the validation of the documents necessary to enable such preferential tariff treatment to be obtained in third countries shall cause a customs debt on importation to be incurred.

2. The moment when such customs debt is incurred shall be deemed to be the moment when the customs authorities accept the export declaration relating to the goods in question.

3. The debtor shall be the declarant. In the event of indirect representation, the person on whose behalf the declaration is made shall also be a debtor.

4. The amount of the import duties corresponding to this customs debt shall be determined under the same conditions as in the case of a customs debt resulting from the acceptance, on the same date, of the declaration for release for free circulation of the goods concerned for the purpose of terminating the inward processing procedure.

Articles 217–232

Note—Articles 217–232 are outside the scope of this work.

CHAPTER 4—EXTINCTION OF CUSTOMS DEBT

Article 233

Without prejudice to the provisions in force relating to the time-barring of a customs debt and non-recovery of such a debt in the event of the legally established insolvency of the debtor, a customs debt shall be extinguished:

(*a*) by payment of the amount of duty;

(*b*) by remission of the amount of duty;

(*c*) where, in respect of goods declared for a customs procedure entailing the obligation to pay duties:

—the customs declaration is invalidated[...][1],

—the goods, before their release, are either seized and simultaneously or subsequently confiscated, destroyed on the instructions of the customs authorities, destroyed or abandoned in accordance with Article 182, or destroyed or irretrievably lost as a result of their actual nature or of unforeseeable circumstances or *force majeure*;

(*d*) where goods in respect of which a customs debt is incurred in accordance with Article 202 are seized upon their unlawful introduction and are simultaneously or subsequently confiscated.

In the event of seizure and confiscation, the customs debt shall, nonetheless for the purposes of the criminal law applicable to customs offences, be deemed not to have been extinguished where, under a Member State's criminal law, customs duties provide the basis for determining penalties or the existence of a customs debt is grounds for taking criminal proceedings.

Amendment—[1] Words in sub-para (*c*) first indent were repealed by EC Regulation 82/97/EC with effect from 1 January 1997; see OJ L17, 21.1.97, p 1.

Article 234

A customs debt, as referred to in Article 216, shall also be extinguished where the formalities carried out in order to enable the preferential tariff treatment referred to in Article 216 to be granted are cancelled.

Articles 235–242

Note—Articles 235–242 are outside the scope of this work.

TITLE VIII: APPEALS

Article 243

1. Any person shall have the right to appeal against decisions taken by the customs authorities which relate to the application of customs legislation, and which concern him directly and individually.

Any person who has applied to the customs authorities for a decision relating to the application of customs legislation and has not obtained a ruling on that request within the period referred to in Article 6(2) shall also be entitled to exercise the right of appeal.

The appeal must be lodged in the Member State where the decision has been taken or applied for.

2. The right of appeal may be exercised:

(*a*) initially, before the customs authorities designated for that purpose by the Member States;

(*b*) subsequently, before an independent body, which may be a judicial authority or an equivalent specialised body, according to the provisions in force in the Member States.

Article 244

The lodging of an appeal shall not cause implementation of the disputed decision to be suspended.

The customs authorities shall, however, suspend implementation of such decision in whole or in part where they have good reason to believe that the disputed decision is inconsistent with customs legislation or that irreparable damage is to be feared for the person concerned.

Where the disputed decision has the effect of causing import duties or export duties to be charged, suspension of implementation of that decision shall be subject to the existence or lodging of a security. However, such security need not be required where such a requirement would be likely, owing to the debtor's circumstances, to cause serious economic or social difficulties.

Article 245

The provisions for the implementation of the appeals procedure shall be determined by the Member States.

Article 246

This title shall not apply to appeals lodged with a view to the annulment or revision of a decision taken by the customs authorities on the basis of criminal law.

TITLE IX: FINAL PROVISIONS

CHAPTER 1—CUSTOMS CODE COMMITTEE

[Article 247

The measures necessary for the implementation of this Regulation, including implementation of the Regulation referred to in Article 184, except for Title VIII and subject to Articles 9 and 10 of Regulation (EEC) No 2658/87(7) and to Article 248 of this Regulation shall be adopted in accordance with the regulatory procedure referred to in Article 247a(2) in compliance with the international commitments entered into by the Community.][1]

Amendments—[1] Articles 247, 247a, 248, 248a, 249 substituted for Articles 247, 248, and 249 by EC Regulation 2700/2000/EC with effect from 19 December 2000; see OJ L 311, 12.12.2000, p 17.

[Article 247a

1. The Commission shall be assisted by a Customs Code Committee (hereinafter referred to as 'the Committee').

2. Where reference is made to this paragraph, Articles 5 and 7 of Decision 1999/468/EC shall apply, having regard to the provisions of Article 8 thereof.

The period laid down in Article 5(6) of Decision 1999/468/EC shall be set at three months.

3. The Committee shall adopt its rules of procedure.][1]

Amendments—[1] Articles 247, 247a, 248, 248a, 249 substituted for Articles 247, 248, and 249 by EC Regulation 2700/2000/EC with effect from 19 December 2000; see OJ L 311, 12.12.2000, p 17.

[Article 248

The measures necessary for implementing Articles 11, 12 and 21 shall be adopted in accordance with the management procedure referred to in Article 248a(2).][1]

Amendments—[1] Articles 247, 247a, 248, 248a, 249 substituted for Articles 247, 248, and 249 by EC Regulation 2700/2000/EC with effect from 19 December 2000; see OJ L 311, 12.12.2000, p 17.

[Article 248a

1. The Commission shall be assisted by a Customs Code Committee, hereinafter referred to as 'the Committee'.

2. Where reference is made to this paragraph, Articles 4 and 7 of Decision 1999/468/EC shall apply.

The period laid down in Article 4(3) of Decision 1999/468/EC shall be set at three months.

3. The Committee shall adopt its rules of procedure.][1]

Amendments—[1] Articles 247, 247a, 248, 248a, 249 substituted for Articles 247, 248, and 249 by EC Regulation 2700/2000/EC with effect from 19 December 2000; see OJ L 311, 12.12.2000, p 17.

[Article 249

The Committee may examine any question concerning customs legislation which is raised by its chairman, either on his own initiative or at the request of a Member State's representative.][1]

Amendments—[1] Articles 247, 247a, 248, 248a, 249 substituted for Articles 247, 248, and 249 by EC Regulation 2700/2000/EC with effect from 19 December 2000; see OJ L 311, 12.12.2000, p 17.

CHAPTER 2—LEGAL EFFECTS IN A MEMBER STATE OF MEASURES TAKEN, DOCUMENTS ISSUED AND FINDINGS MADE IN ANOTHER MEMBER STATE

Article 250

Where a customs procedure is used in several Member States,

—the decisions, identification measures taken or agreed on, and the documents issued by the customs authorities of one Member State shall have the same legal effects in other Member States as such decisions, measures taken and documents issued by the customs authorities of each of those Member States;

—the findings made at the time controls are carried out by the customs authorities of a Member State shall have the same conclusive force in the other Member States as the findings made by the customs authorities of each of those Member States.

CHAPTER 3—OTHER FINAL PROVISIONS

Article 251

1. The following Regulations and Directives are hereby repealed:

—Council Regulation (EEC) No 1224/80 of 28 May 1980 on the valuation of goods for customs purposes, as last amended by the Regulation (EEC) No 4046/89;

—Council Regulation (EEC) No 2151/84 of 23 July 1984 on the customs territory of the Community, as last amended by the Act of Accession of Spain and Portugal.

Note—Repeals within the scope of this work only are mentioned: other repeals have been omitted.

Article 252

Note—Article 252 is outside the scope of this work.

Article 253

This Regulation shall enter into force on the third day following that of its publication in the *Official Journal of the European Communities*.

It shall apply from 1 January 1994.

Title VIII shall not apply to the United Kingdom until 1 January 1995.

However, Article 161 and, in so far as they concern re-exportation, Articles 182 and 183 shall apply from 1 January 1993. In so far as the said Articles make reference to provisions in this Code and until such time as such provisions enter into force, the references shall be deemed to allude to the corresponding provisions in the Regulations and Directives listed in Article 251.

Before 1 October 1993, the Council shall, on the basis of a Commission progress report on discussions regarding the consequences to be drawn from the monetary conversion rate used for the application of common agricultural policy measures, review the problem of trade in goods between the Member States in the context of the internal market. This report shall be accompanied by Commission proposals if any, on which the Council shall take a decision in accordance with the provisions of the Treaty.

Before 1 January 1998, the Council shall, on the basis of a Commission report, review this Code with a view to making such adaptations as may appear necessary taking into account in particular the achievement of the internal market. This report shall be accompanied by proposals, if any, on which the Council shall take a decision in accordance with the provisions of the Treaty.

Note—This Regulation was published in OJ L302, 19.10.92.
This Regulation shall be binding in its entirety and directly applicable in all Member States.

Commission Regulation
of 11 December 1992
concerning the statistical information media for statistics on trade between Member States

(3590/92/EEC)

Note—See OJ L364 12.12.1992, p 32.
Repealed by Commission Regulation 1982/2004/EC art 27 (OJ L 343, 19.11.2004, p 3)

THE COMMISSION OF THE EUROPEAN COMMUNITIES

Having regard to the Treaty establishing the European Economic Community,

Having regard to Council Regulation (EEC) No 3330/91 of 7 November 1991, on the statistics relating to the trading of goods between Member States (OJ L316, 16.11.1991, p 1), as amended by Commission Regulation (EEC) No 3046/92 (OJ L307, 23.10.1992, p 27) and in particular Article 12 thereof,

Whereas, in the context of statistics on trade between Member States, it is necessary to adopt standard statistical forms for regular use by the parties responsible for providing information in order to ensure that the declarations required of them adhere to a consistent format, irrespective of the Member State where they are made; whereas the choice accorded to the parties responsible for providing information by Article 12(2) of the above mentioned Regulation is only available if the Commission sets up the appropriate information media; whereas, moreover, certain Member States would rather use Community media than produce national forms of their own;

Whereas it is important to provide the competent authorities with all the technical details required for the printing of these forms;

Whereas it is advisable in order to ensure uniform treatment of the parties responsible for providing information, to contribute towards the cost of these forms; whereas it is necessary to estimate the amount of Community funds required for this; whereas this amount must be in line with the financial perspective set out in the Interinstitutional Agreement of 29 June 1988 on Budgetary Discipline and Improvement of the Budgetary Procedure (OJ L185, 15.7.1988, p 33); whereas, in compliance with this Agreement, the appropriations actually available must be determined in accordance with budgetary procedure;

Whereas it is necessary to take account of other modes of transmitting information, and, in particular, to promote the use of magnetic or electronic information media;

Whereas the measures provided for in this Regulation reflect the opinion of the Committee on Statistics Relating to the Trading of Goods between Member States,

HAS ADOPTED THIS REGULATION:

Article 1

1. With a view to the drawing-up by the Community and its Member States of statistics on trade between the Member States, the statistical information media provided for in Article 12, paragraph 1, of Council Regulation (EEC) No 3330/91, hereafter referred to as "the basic Regulation", shall be set up in accordance with the provisions of this Regulation.

2. In Member States where no distinction is made between the periodic declaration and the periodic declaration required for tax purposes, the provisions necessary for the setting-up of information media shall, insofar as necessary, be adopted within the framework of Community or national tax regulations, and in conformity with the other implementing provisions of the basic Regulation.

Article 2

Without prejudice to provisions adopted pursuant to Article 34 of the basic Regulation, Intrastat forms N-Dispatch, R-Dispatch and S-Dispatch and N-Arrival, R-Arrival and S-Arrival, specimens of which are annexed to this Regulation, shall be used in conformity with the provisions set out below.

—Forms N shall be used by parties responsible for providing information who are not subject to the dispensations resulting from the assimilation and simplification thresholds fixed by each Member State, nor to the exemption provided for in the following indent.

—Forms R shall be used by parties responsible for providing information whom the competent national authorities have exempted from giving a description of the goods.

—Forms S shall be used by parties responsible for providing information who are subject to the dispensations resulting from the simplification threshold.

Article 3

1. The forms referred to in Article 2 shall consist of a single sheet, which shall be delivered to the competent national authorities.

The Member States may, however, require parties responsible for providing information to retain a copy in accordance with the instructions of the competent national authorities.

2. The forms shall be printed on paper which is suitable for writing and weighs no less than 70 g/m^2.

The colour of the paper used shall be white. The colour of the print shall be red. The paper and the print used must meet the technical requirements of optical character recognition (OCR) equipment.

The fields and subdivisions shall be measured horizontally in units of one-tenth of an inch and vertically in units of one-sixth of an inch.

The forms shall measure 210×297 mm, subject to maximum tolerances as to length of -5 mm and +8 mm.

3. The conditions under which the forms may be produced using reproduction techniques departing from the provisions of paragraph 2, first and second subparagraphs, shall be determined by the Member States, which shall inform the Commission accordingly.

Article 4

The Member States shall, without charge, supply parties responsible for providing information with the forms reproduced in specimen in the Annex hereto.

The Commission shall contribute annually, at the end of the reporting period, to the costs which the Member States have incurred in printing these forms and distributing them via official postal channels. This contribution shall be calculated in proportion to the number of forms which the parties responsible for providing information have actually transmitted to the competent national authorities during the year in question.

Article 5

Parties responsible for providing information who wish to use magnetic or electronic media shall give prior notice of this intention to the national authorities responsible for compiling statistics on trade between Member States. Parties responsible for providing information shall, in this event, comply with any relevant provisions adopted by the Commission and with any national instructions issued by the above mentioned authorities pursuant to the said provisions, bearing in mind the technical equipment available to them. These instructions shall include in their structuring rules the Cusdec message designed and updated by the United Nations Edifact Board—Message Design Group 3, and shall comply with the provisions relating to the Instat subset of that message, which the Commission shall publish in a user manual.

Article 6

1. In derogation from Article 2, parties responsible for providing information who wish to use as an information medium the statistical forms of the Single Administrative Document as provided for in Council 717/91 (OJ L78, 26.3.1991, p 1) shall comply with the instructions issued by the competent national authorities. The latter shall send a copy of these instructions to the Commission.

2. Member States which set up media other than those provided for in Article 2 or Article 5 above, or paragraph 1 of this Article, shall inform the Commission accordingly in advance. They shall send the Commission an example of such media and/or provide details as to their use.

Article 7

This Regulation shall enter into force on the seventh day following that of its publication in the Official Journal of the European Communities.

It shall apply from the date provided for in Article 35, second indent, of the basic Regulation.

This Regulation shall be binding in its entirety and directly applicable in all Member States.

Council Regulation of 5 April 1993 on transit statistics and storage statistics relating to the trading of goods between Member States

(854/93/EEC)

Note—See OJ L90 14.04.1993, p 1.
This regulation is spent.

Commission Regulation of 2 July 1993 laying down provisions for the implementation of Council Regulation No 2913/92/EEC establishing the Community Customs Code

(2454/93/EEC)

Note—See OJ L253 11.11.1993, p 1.

PART I: GENERAL IMPLEMENTING PROVISIONS

TITLE I: GENERAL

TITLE V: CUSTOMS VALUE

THE COMMISSION OF THE EUROPEAN COMMUNITIES,

Having regard to the Treaty establishing the European Economic Community,

Having regard to Council Regulation (EEC) No 2913/92 of 12 October 1992 establishing the Community Customs Code, hereinafter referred to as the "Code", and in particular Article 249 thereof,

Whereas the Code assembled all existing customs legislation in a single legal instrument; whereas at the same time the Code made certain modifications to this legislation to make it more coherent, to simplify it and to plug certain loopholes; whereas it therefore constitutes complete Community legislation in this area;

Whereas the same reasons which led to the adoption of the Code apply equally to the customs implementing legislation; whereas it is therefore desirable to bring together in a single regulation those customs implementing provisions which are currently scattered over a large number of Community regulations and directives;

Whereas the implementing code for the Community Customs Code hereby established should set out existing customs implementing rules; whereas it is nevertheless necessary, in the light of experience:

—to make some amendments in order to adapt the said rules to the provisions of the Code,

—to extend the scope of certain provisions which currently apply only to specific customs procedures in order to take account of the Code's comprehensive application,

—to formulate certain rules more precisely in order to achieve greater legal security in their application;

Whereas the changes made relate mainly to the provisions concerning customs debt;

Whereas it is appropriate to limit the application of Article 791(2) until 1 January 1995 and to review the subject matter in the light of experience gained before that time;

Whereas the measures provided for by this Regulation are in accordance with the opinion of the Customs Code Committee,

HAS ADOPTED THIS REGULATION:

PART ONE
GENERAL IMPLEMENTING PROVISIONS

TITLE I—GENERAL

CHAPTER 1—DEFINITIONS

Article 1

For the purposes of this Regulation:

1. *Code means*:

Council Regulation (EEC) No 2913/92 of 12 October 1992 establishing a Community Customs Code;

[2 *ATA carnet means*:

the international customs document for temporary importation established by virtue of the ATA Convention or the Istanbul Convention;][1]

[3. *Committee means:*

the Customs Code Committee established by Articles 247a and 248a of the Code;][2]

4. *Customs Co-operation Council means:*

the organisation set up by the Convention establishing a Customs Co-operation Council, done at Brussels on 15 December 1950;

5. *Particulars required for identification of the goods means:*

on the one hand, the particulars used to identify the goods commercially allowing the customs authorities to determine the tariff classification and, on the other hand, the quantity of the goods;

6. *Goods of a non-commercial nature means:*

goods whose entry for the customs procedure in question is on an occasional basis and whose nature and quantity indicate that they are intended for the private, personal or family use of the consignees or persons carrying them, or which are clearly intended as gifts;

7. *Commercial policy measures means:*

non-tariff measures established, as part of the common commercial policy, in the form of Community provisions governing the import and export of goods, such as surveillance or safeguard measures, quantitative restrictions or limits and import or export prohibitions;

8. *Customs nomenclature means:*

one of the nomenclatures referred to in Article 20(6) of the Code;

9. *Harmonised System means:*

the Harmonised Commodity Description and Coding System;

[10. *Treaty means:*

the Treaty establishing the European Community;][2]

[11. *Istanbul Convention means:*

the Convention on Temporary Admission agreed at Istanbul on 26 June 1990.][1]

[12. *Economic operator means*:

a person who, in the course of his business, is involved in activities covered by customs legislation.][3]

Amendments—[1] Point 2 replaced and point 11 added by Commission Regulation 1762/95/EC (see OJ L171, 21.7.95, p 8).
[2] Points 3, 10 replaced by Commission Regulation 444/2002 art 1(1) (OJ L 68; 12.3.2002 p 11).
[3] Point 12 added by Commission Regulation 1875/2006/EC (OJ L 360, 19.12.2006, p 64).

[Article 1a

For the purposes of applying Articles 291 to 300, the countries of the Benelux Economic Union shall be considered as a single Member State.][1]

Amendments—[1] Article 1a substituted by Commission Regulation 1602/2000/EC with effect from 1 January 2001; see OJ L 188, 26.08.2000, p 1.

CHAPTER 2—DECISIONS

Article 2

Where a person making a request for a decision is not in a position to provide all the documents and information necessary to give a ruling, the customs authorities shall provide the documents and information at their disposal.

Article 3

A decision concerning security favourable to a person who has signed an undertaking to pay the sums due at the first written request of the customs authorities, shall be revoked where the said undertaking is not fulfilled.

Article 4

A revocation shall not affect goods which, at the moment of its entry into effect, have already been placed under a procedure by virtue of the revoked authorisation.

However, the customs authorities may require that such goods be assigned to a permitted customs-approved treatment or use within the period which they shall set.

[Article 4a

1. Under the conditions and in the manner which they shall determine, and with due regard to the principles laid down by customs rules, the customs authorities may provide that formalities shall be carried out by a data-processing technique.

For this purpose:

— "a data-processing technique" means:

(*a*) the exchange of EDI standard messages with the customs authorities;

(*b*) the introduction of information required for completion of the formalities concerned into customs data-processing systems;

— "EDI" (electronic data interchange) means, the transmission of data structured according to agreed message standards, between one computer system and another, by electronic means,

— "standard message" means a predefined structure recognised for the electronic transmission of data.

2. The conditions laid down for carrying out formalities by a data-processing technique shall include inter alia measures for checking the source of data and for protecting data against the risk of unauthorised access, loss, alteration or destruction.

Article 4b

Where formalities are carried out by a data-processing technique, the customs authorities shall determine the rules for replacement of the handwritten signature by another technique which may be based on the use of codes.][1]

Amendments—[1] Articles 4a and 4b added by Commission Regulation 3665/93/EEC; see OJ L335, 31.12.93, p 1.

[Article 4c

For test programmes using data-processing techniques designed to evaluate possible simplifications, the customs authorities may, for the period strictly necessary to carry out the programme, waive the requirement to provide the following information—

(*a*) the declaration provided for in Article 178(1);

(*b*) by way of derogation from Article 222(1), the particulars relating to certain boxes of the Single Administrative Document which are not necessary for the identification of the goods and which are not the factors on the basis of which import or export duties are applied.

However, the information shall be available on request in the framework of a control operation.

The amount of import duties to be charged in the period covered by a derogation granted pursuant to the first subparagraph shall not be lower than that which would be levied in the absence of a derogation.

Member States wishing to engage in such test programmes shall provide the Commission in advance with full details of the proposed test programme, including its intended duration. They shall also keep the Commission informed of actual implementation and results. The Commission shall inform all the other Member States.][1]

Amendments—[1] Article 4c added by Commission Regulation 2787/2000/EC with effect from 3 January 2001; see OJ L 330 27.12.2000, p 1.

Articles 4d –140

Note—Articles 4d–140 are outside the scope of this work; please refer to Tolley's *Customs Duties Handbook*.

TITLE V—CUSTOMS VALUE

CHAPTER 1—GENERAL PROVISIONS

Article 141

1. In applying the provisions of Articles 28 to 36 of the Code and those of this title, Member States shall comply with the provisions set out in Annex 23.

The provisions as set out in the first column of Annex 23 shall be applied in the light of the interpretative note appearing in the second column.

2. If it is necessary to make reference to generally accepted accounting principles in determining the customs value, the provisions of Annex 24 shall apply.

Article 142

1. For the purposes of this title:

(*a*) "the Agreement" means the Agreement on implementation of Article VII of the General Agreement on Tariffs and Trade concluded in the framework of the multilateral trade negotiations of 1973 to 1979 and referred to in the first indent of Article 31(1) of the Code;

(*b*) "produced goods" includes goods grown, manufactured and mined;

(*c*) "identical goods" means goods produced in the same country which are the same in all respects, including physical characteristics, quality and reputation. Minor differences in appearance shall not preclude goods otherwise conforming to the definition from being regarded as identical;

(*d*) "similar goods" means goods produced in the same country which, although not alike in all respects, have like characteristics and like component materials which enable them to perform the same functions and to be commercially interchangeable; the quality of the goods, their reputation and the existence of a trademark are among the factors to be considered in determining whether goods are similar;

(*e*) "goods of the same class or kind" means goods which fall within a group or range of goods produced by a particular industry or industry sector, and includes identical or similar goods.

2. "Identical goods" and "similar goods", as the case may be, do not include goods which incorporate or reflect engineering, development, artwork, design work, and plans and sketches for which no adjustment has been made under Article 32(1)(*b*)(iv) of the Code because such elements were undertaken in the Community.

Article 143

1. [For the purposes of Title II, Chapter 3 of the Code and of this Title, persons shall be deemed to be related only if—][1]

(*a*) they are officers or directors of one another's businesses;

(*b*) they are legally recognised partners in business;

(*c*) they are employer and employee;

(*d*) any person directly or indirectly owns, controls or holds 5% or more of the outstanding voting stock or shares of both of them;

(*e*) one of them directly or indirectly controls the other;

(*f*) both of them are directly or indirectly controlled by a third person;

(*g*) together they directly or indirectly control a third person; or

(*h*) they are members of the same family. Persons shall be deemed to be members of the same family only if they stand in any of the following relationships to one another;

—husband and wife,
—parent and child,
—brother and sister (whether by whole or half blood),
—grandparent and grandchild,
—uncle or aunt and nephew or niece,
—parent-in-law and son-in-law or daughter-in-law,
—brother-in-law and sister-in-law.

2. For the purposes of this title, persons who are associated in business with one another in that one is the sole agent, sole distributor or sole concessionaire, however described, of the other shall be deemed to be related only if they fall within the criteria of paragraph 1.

Amendments—[1] In para 1 words substituted by Commission Regulation (EC) 46/1999, Art 1, para 8; see OJ L 10, 15.01.99, p 1.

Article 144

1. For the purposes of determining customs value under Article 29 of the Code of goods in regard to which the price has not actually been paid at the material time for valuation for customs purposes, the price payable for settlement at the said time shall as a general rule be taken as the basis for customs value.

2. The Commission and the Member States shall consult within the Committee concerning the application of paragraph 1.

[Article 145

1. Where goods declared for free circulation are part of a larger quantity of the same goods purchased in one transaction, the price actually paid or payable for the purposes of Article 29(1) of the Code shall be that price represented by the proportion of the total price which the quantity so declared bears to the total quantity purchased.

Apportioning the price actually paid or payable shall also apply in the case of the loss of part of a consignment or when the goods being valued have been damaged before entry into free circulation.

2. After release of the goods for free circulation, an adjustment made by the seller, to the benefit of the buyer, of the price actually paid or payable for the goods may be taken into consideration for the determination of the customs value in accordance with Article 29 of the Code, if it is demonstrated to the satisfaction of the customs authorities that:

(*a*) the goods were defective at the moment referred to by Article 67 of the Code;

(*b*) the seller made the adjustment in performance of a warranty obligation provided for in the contract of sale, concluded before release for free circulation of the goods;

(*c*) the defective nature of the goods has not already been taken into account in the relevant sales contract.

3. The price actually paid or payable for the goods, adjusted in accordance with paragraph 2, may be taken into account only if that adjustment was made within a period of 12 months following the date of acceptance of the declaration for entry to free circulation of the goods.][1]

Amendments—[1] Substituted by Commission Regulation (EC) 444/2002, Art 1, para 6; see OJ L68, 12.03.2002, p 11.

Article 146

Where the price actually paid or payable for the purposes of Article 29(1) of the Code includes an amount in respect of any internal tax applicable within the country of origin or export in respect of the goods in question, the said amount shall not be incorporated in the customs value provided that it can be demonstrated to the satisfaction of the customs authorities concerned that the goods in question have been or will be relieved therefrom for the benefit of the buyer.

Article 147

1. For the purposes of Article 29 of the Code, the fact that the goods which are the subject of a sale are declared for free circulation shall be regarded as adequate indication that they were sold for export to the customs territory of the Community. [In the case of successive sales before valuation, only the last sale, which led to the introduction of the goods into the customs territory of the Community, or a sale taking place in the customs territory of the Community before entry for free circulation of the goods shall constitute such indication.

Where a price is declared which relates to a sale taking place before the last sale on the basis of which the goods were introduced into the customs territory of the Community, it must be demonstrated to the satisfaction of the customs authorities that this sale of goods took place for export to the customs territory in question.

The provisions of Articles 178 to 181a shall apply.][1]

2...[1] where goods are used in a third country between the time of sale and the time of entry into free circulation the customs value need not be the transaction value.

3. The buyer need satisfy no condition other than that of being a party to the contract of sale.

Amendments—[1] Words in para 1 replaced and words omitted from para 2 deleted by Commission Regulation 1762/95/EC; see OJ L171, 21.7.95, p 8.

Article 148

Where, in applying Article 29(1)(*b*) of the Code, it is established that the sale or price of imported goods is subject to a condition or consideration the value of which can be determined with respect to the goods being valued, such value shall be regarded as an indirect payment by the buyer to the seller and part of the price actually paid or payable provided that the condition or consideration does not relate to either:

(*a*) an activity to which Article 29(3)(*b*) of the Code applies; or

(*b*) a factor in respect of which an addition is to be made to the price actually paid or payable under the provisions of Article 32 of the Code.

Article 149

1. For the purposes of Article 29(3)(*b*) of the Code, the term "marketing activities" means all activities relating to advertising and promoting the sale of the goods in question and all activities relating to warranties or guarantees in respect of them.

2. Such activities undertaken by the buyer shall be regarded as having been undertaken on his own account even if they are performed in pursuance of an obligation on the buyer following an agreement with the seller.

Article 150

1. In applying Article 30(2)(*a*) of the Code (the transaction value of identical goods), the customs value shall be determined by reference to the transaction value of identical goods in a sale at the same commercial level and in substantially the same quantity as the goods being valued. Where no such sale is found, the transaction value of identical goods sold at a different commercial level and/or in different quantities, adjusted to take account of differences attributable to commercial level and/or to quantity, shall be used, provided that such adjustments can be made on the basis of demonstrated evidence which clearly establishes the reasonableness and accuracy of the adjustment, whether the adjustment leads to an increase or a decrease in the value.

2. Where the costs and charges referred to in Article 32(1)(*e*) of the Code are included in the transaction value, an adjustment shall be made to take account of significant differences in such costs and charges between the imported goods and the identical goods in question arising from differences in distances and modes of transport.

3. If, in applying this Article, more than one transaction value of identical goods is found, the lowest such value shall be used to determine the customs value of the imported goods.

4. In applying this Article, a transaction value for goods produced by a different person shall be taken into account only when no transaction value can be found under paragraph 1 for identical goods produced by the same person as the goods being valued.

5. For the purposes of this Article, the transaction value of identical imported goods means a customs value previously determined under Article 29 of the Code, adjusted as provided for in paragraphs 1 and 2 of this Article.

Article 151

1. In applying Article 30(2)(*b*) of the Code (the transaction value of similar goods), the customs value shall be determined by reference to the transaction value of similar goods in a sale at the same commercial level and in substantially the same quantity as the goods being valued. Where no such sale is found, the transaction value of similar goods sold at a different commercial level and/or in different quantities, adjusted to take account of differences attributable to commercial level and/or to quantity, shall be used, provided that such adjustments can be made on the basis of demonstrated evidence which clearly establishes the reasonableness and accuracy of the adjustment, whether the adjustment leads to an increase or a decrease in the value.

2. Where the costs and charges referred to in Article 32(1)(*e*) of the Code are included in the transaction value, an adjustment shall be made to take account of significant differences in such costs and charges between the imported goods and the similar goods in question arising from differences in distances and modes of transport.

3. If, in applying this Article, more than one transaction value of similar goods is found, the lowest such value shall be used to determine the customs value for the imported goods.

4. In applying this Article, a transaction value for goods produced by a different person shall be taken into account only when no transaction value can be found under paragraph 1 for similar goods produced by the same person as the goods being valued.

5. For the purposes of this Article, the transaction value of similar imported goods means a customs value previously determined under Article 29 of the Code, adjusted as provided for in paragraphs 1 and 2 of this Article.

Article 152

1

(*a*) If the imported goods or identical or similar imported goods are sold in the Community in the condition as imported, the customs value of imported goods, determined in accordance with Article 30(2)(*c*) of the Code, shall be based on the unit price at which the imported goods or identical or similar imported goods are so sold in the greatest aggregate quantity, at or about the time of the importation of the goods being valued, to persons who are not related to the persons from whom they buy such goods, subject to deductions for the following:

(i) either the commissions usually paid or agreed to be paid or the additions usually made for profit and general expenses (including the direct and indirect costs of marketing the goods in question) in connection with sales in the Community of imported goods of the same class or kind;

(ii) the usual costs of transport and insurance and associated costs incurred within the Community;

(iii) the import duties and other charges payable in the Community by reason of the importation or sale of the goods.

[(*aa*) The customs value of certain perishable goods imported on consignment may be directly determined in accordance with Article 30(2)(*c*) of the Code. For this purpose the unit prices shall be notified to the Commission by the Member States and disseminated by the Commission via TARIC in accordance with Article 6 of Council Regulation (EEC) No 2658/87.

The unit prices shall be calculated and notified as follows:

(i) After the deductions provided for in point (*a*), a unit price per 100 kg net for each category of goods shall be notified by the Member States to the Commission. The Member States may fix standard amounts for the costs referred to in point (*a*)(ii) which shall be made known to the Commission.

(ii) The unit price may be used to determine the customs value of the imported goods for periods of 14 days, each period beginning on a Friday.

(iii) The reference period for determining the unit prices shall be the preceding period of 14 days which ends on the Thursday preceding the week during which new unit prices are to be established.

(iv) The unit prices shall be notified by the Member States to the Commission in euro not later than 12 noon on the Monday of the week in which they are disseminated by the

Commission. If that day is a non-working day, notification shall be made on the working day immediately preceding that day. Unit prices shall only apply if this notification is disseminated by the Commission.][1]

(*b*) If neither the imported goods nor identical nor similar imported goods are sold at or about the time of importation of the goods being valued, the customs value of imported goods determined under this Article shall, subject otherwise to the provisions of paragraph 1(*a*), be based on the unit price at which the imported goods or identical or similar imported goods are sold in the Community in the condition as imported at the earliest date after the importation of the goods being valued but before the expiration of 90 days after such importation.

2. If neither the imported goods nor identical nor similar imported goods are sold in the Community in the condition as imported, then, if the importer so requests, the customs value shall be based on the unit price at which the imported goods, after further processing, are sold in the greatest aggregate quantity to persons in the Community who are not related to the persons from whom they buy such goods, due allowance being made for the value added by such processing and the deductions provided for in paragraph 1(*a*).

3. For the purposes of this Article, the unit price at which imported goods are sold in the greatest aggregate quantity is the price at which the greatest number of units is sold in sales to persons who are not related to the persons from whom they buy such goods at the first commercial level after importation at which such sales take place.

4. Any sale in the Community to a person who supplies directly or indirectly free of charge or at reduced cost for use in connection with the production and sale for export of the imported goods any of the elements specified in Article 32(1)(*b*) of the Code should not be taken into account in establishing the unit price for the purposes of this Article.

5. For the purposes of paragraph 1(*b*), the "earliest date" shall be the date by which sales of the imported goods or of identical or similar imported goods are made in sufficient quantity to establish the unit price.

Amendments—[1] Para (*aa*) inserted by Council Regulation (EC) 215/2006 art 1(1); see OJ L 038; 9.2.2006, p 11.

Article 153

1. In applying Article 30(2)(*d*) of the Code (computed value), the customs authorities may not require or compel any person not resident in the Community to produce for examination, or to allow access to, any account or other record for the purposes of determining this value. However, information supplied by the producer of the goods for the purposes of determining the customs value under this Article may be verified in a non-Community country by the customs authorities of a Member State with the agreement of the producer and provided that such authorities give sufficient advance notice to the authorities of the country in question and the latter do not object to the investigation.

2. The cost or value of materials and fabrication referred to in the first indent of Article 30(2)(*d*) of the Code shall include the cost of elements specified in Article 32(1)(*a*)(ii) and (iii) of the Code.

It shall also include the value, duly apportioned, of any product or service specified in Article 32(1)(*b*) of the Code which has been supplied directly or indirectly by the buyer for use in connection with the production of the imported goods. The value of the elements specified in Article 32(1)(*b*)(iv) of the Code which are undertaken in the Community shall be included only to the extent that such elements are charged to the producer.

3. Where information other than that supplied by or on behalf of the producer is used for the purposes of determining a computed value, the customs authorities shall inform the declarant, if the latter so requests, of the source of such information, the data used and the calculations based on such data, subject to Article 15 of the Code.

4. The "general expenses" referred to in the second indent of Article 30(2)(*d*) of the Code, cover the direct and indirect costs of producing and selling the goods for export which are not included under the first indent of Article 30(2)(*d*) of the Code.

Article 154

Where containers referred to in Article 32(1)(*a*)(ii) of the Code are to be the subject of repeated importations, their cost shall, at the request of the declarant, be apportioned, as appropriate, in accordance with generally accepted accounting principles.

Article 155

For the purposes of Article 32(1)(*b*)(iv) of the Code, the cost of research and preliminary design sketches is not to be included in the customs value.

Article 156

Article 33(*c*) of the Code shall apply *mutatis mutandis* where the customs value is determined by applying a method other than the transaction value.

[**Article 156a**

1. The customs authorities may, at the request of the person concerned, authorise:

—by derogation from Article 32(2) of the Code, certain elements which are to be added to the price actually paid or payable, although not quantifiable at the time of incurrence of the customs debt,

—by derogation from Article 33 of the Code, certain charges which are not to be included in the customs value, in cases where the amounts relating to such elements are not shown separately at the time of incurrence of the customs debt,

to be determined on the basis of appropriate and specific criteria.

In such cases, the declared customs value it not to be considered as provisional within the meaning of the second indent of Article 254.

2. The authorisation shall be granted under the following conditions:

(*a*) the carrying out of the procedures provided for by Article 259 would, in the circumstances, represent disproportionate administrative costs;

(*b*) recourse to an application of Articles 30 and 31 of the Code appears to be inappropriate in the particular circumstances;

(*c*) there are valid reasons for considering that the amount of import duties to be charged in the period covered by authorisation will not be lower than that which would be levied in the absence of an authorisation;

(*d*) competitive conditions amongst operators are not distorted.]

Amendment—This article is added by Commission Regulation 1676/96/EC; see OJ L 218 28.8.96, p1.

CHAPTER 2—PROVISIONS CONCERNING ROYALTIES AND LICENCE FEES

Article 157

1. For the purposes of Article 32(1)(*c*) of the Code, royalties and licence fees shall be taken to mean in particular payment for the use of rights relating:

—to the manufacture of imported goods (in particular, patents, designs, models and manufacturing know-how), or

—to the sale for exportation of imported goods (in particular, trade marks, registered designs), or

—to the use or resale of imported goods (in particular, copyright, manufacturing processes inseparably embodied in the imported goods).

2. Without prejudice to Article 32(5) of the Code, when the customs value of imported goods is determined under the provisions of Article 29 of the Code, a royalty or licence fee shall be added to the price actually paid or payable only when this payment:

—is related to the goods being valued, and

—constitutes a condition of sale of those goods.

Article 158

1. When the imported goods are only an ingredient or component of goods manufactured in the Community, an adjustment to the price actually paid or payable for the imported goods shall only be made when the royalty or licence fee relates to those goods.

2. Where goods are imported in an unassembled state or only have to undergo minor processing before resale, such as diluting or packing, this shall not prevent a royalty or licence fee from being considered related to the imported goods.

3. If royalties or licence fees relate partly to the imported goods and partly to other ingredients or component parts added to the goods after their importation, or to post-importation activities or services, an appropriate apportionment shall be made only on the basis of objective and quantifiable data, in accordance with the interpretative note to Article 32(2) of the Code in Annex 23.

Article 159

A royalty or licence fee in respect of the right to use a trade mark is only to be added to the price actually paid or payable for the imported goods where:

—the royalty or licence fee refers to goods which are resold in the same state or which are subject only to minor processing after importation,

—the goods are marketed under the trade mark, affixed before or after importation, for which the royalty or licence fee is paid, and

—the buyer is not free to obtain such goods from other suppliers unrelated to the seller.

Article 160

When the buyer pays royalties or licence fees to a third party, the conditions provided for in Article 157(2) shall not be considered as met unless the seller or a person related to him requires the buyer to make that payment.

Article 161

Where the method of calculation of the amount of a royalty or licence fee derives from the price of the imported goods, it may be assumed in the absence of evidence to the contrary that the payment of that royalty or licence fee is related to the goods to be valued.

However, where the amount of a royalty or licence fee is calculated regardless of the price of the imported goods, the payment of that royalty or licence fee may nevertheless be related to the goods to be valued.

Article 162

In applying Article 32(1)(*c*) of the Code, the country of residence of the recipient of the payment of the royalty or licence fee shall not be a material consideration.

Chapter 3—Provisions concerning the place of introduction into the Community

Article 163

1. For the purposes of Article 32(1)(*e*) and Article 33(*a*) of the Code, the place of introduction into the customs territory of the Community shall be:

(*a*) for goods carried by sea, the port of unloading, or the port of transhipment, subject to transhipment being certified by the customs authorities of that port;

(*b*) for goods carried by sea and then, without transhipment, by inland waterway, the first port where unloading can take place either at the mouth of the river or canal or further inland, subject to proof being furnished to the customs office that the freight to the port of unloading is higher than that to the first port;

(*c*) for goods carried by rail, inland waterway, or road, the place where the first customs office is situated;

(*d*) for goods carried by other means, the place where the land frontier of the customs territory of the Community is crossed.

[2. The customs value of goods introduced into the customs territory of the Community and then carried to a destination in another part of that territory through the territories of Belarus, Russia, Switzerland, Bosnia and Herzegovina, Croatia, the Federal Republic of Yugoslavia or the former Yugoslav Republic of Macedonia shall be determined by reference to the first place of introduction into the customs territory of the Community, provided that goods are carried direct through the territories of those countries by a usual route across such territory to the place of destination.][1]

3. The customs value of goods introduced into the customs territory of the Community and then carried by sea to a destination in another part of that territory shall be determined by reference to the first place of introduction into the customs territory of the Community, provided the goods are carried direct by a usual route to the place of destination.

[4. Paragraphs 2 and 3 of this Article shall also apply where the goods have been unloaded, transhipped or temporarily immobilised in the territories of Belarus, Russia, Switzerland, Bosnia and Herzegovina, Croatia, the Federal Republic of Yugoslavia or the former Yugoslav Republic of Macedonia for reasons related solely to their transport.][1]

5. For goods introduced into the customs territory of the Community and carried directly from one of the French overseas departments to another part of the customs territory of the Community or vice versa, the place of introduction to be taken into consideration shall be the place referred to in paragraphs 1 and 2 situated in that part of the customs territory of the Community from which the goods came, if they were unloaded or transhipped there and this was certified by the customs authorities.

6. When the conditions specified at paragraphs 2, 3 and 5 are not fulfilled, the place of introduction to be taken into consideration shall be the place specified in paragraph 1 situated in that part of the customs territory of the Community to which the goods are consigned.

Amendments—[1] Paras 2, 4 replaced by Commission Regulation 1792/2006/EC art 1, Annex Part 11(4), (5) (OJ L 362, 20.12.2006, p 1).

Chapter 4—Provisions concerning transport costs

Article 164

In applying Article 32(1)(*e*) and 33(*a*) of the Code:

(*a*) where goods are carried by the same mode of transport to a point beyond the place of introduction into the customs territory of the Community, transport costs shall be assessed in proportion to the distance covered outside and inside the customs territory of the Community, unless evidence is produced to the customs authorities to show the costs that would have been incurred under a general compulsory schedule of freight rates for the carriage of the goods to the place of introduction into the customs territory of the Community;

(*b*) where goods are invoiced at a uniform free domicile price which corresponds to the price at the place of introduction, transport costs within the Community shall not be deducted from

that price. However, such deduction shall be allowed if evidence is produced to the customs authorities that the free-frontier price would be lower than the uniform free domicile price;
(*c*) where transport is free or provided by the buyer, transport costs to the place of introduction, calculated in accordance with the schedule of freight rates normally applied for the same modes of transport, shall be included in the customs value.

Article 165
1. All postal charges levied up to the place of destination in respect of goods sent by post shall be included in the customs value of these goods, with the exception of any supplementary postal charge levied in the country of importation.
2. No adjustment to the declared value shall, however, be made in respect of such charges in determining the value of consignments of a non-commercial nature.
3. Paragraphs 1 and 2 are not applicable to goods carried by the express postal services known as EMS-Datapost (in Denmark, EMS-Jetpost, in Germany, EMS-Kurierpostsendungen, in Italy, CAI-Post).

Article 166
The air transport costs to be included in the customs value of goods shall be determined by applying the rules and percentages shown in Annex 25.

CHAPTER 5—VALUATION OF CERTAIN CARRIER MEDIA FOR USE IN ADP EQUIPMENT

Article 167
...[1]

Amendments—[1] Repealed by Commission Regulation (EC) 444/2002, Art 1, para 7; see OJ L68, 12.03.2002, p 11.

CHAPTER 6—PROVISIONS CONCERNING RATES OF EXCHANGE

Article 168
For the purposes of Articles 169 to 171 of this chapter:
(*a*) "rate recorded" shall mean:
—the latest selling rate of exchange recorded for commercial transactions on the most representative exchange market or markets of the Member State concerned, or
—some other description of a rate of exchange so recorded and designated by the Member State as the "rate recorded" provided that it reflects as effectively as possible the current value of the currency in question in commercial transactions;
(*b*) "published" shall mean made generally known in a manner designated by the Member State concerned;
(*c*) "currency" shall mean any monetary unit used as a means of settlement between monetary authorities or on the international market.

Article 169
1. Where factors used to determine the customs value of goods are expressed at the time when that value is determined in a currency other than that of the Member State where the valuation is made, the rate of exchange to be used to determine that value in terms of the currency of the Member State concerned shall be the rate recorded on the second-last Wednesday of a month and published on that or the following day.
2. The rate recorded on the second-last Wednesday of a month shall be used during the following calendar month unless it is superseded by a rate established under Article 171.
3. Where a rate of exchange is not recorded on the second-last Wednesday indicated in paragraph 1, or, if recorded, is not published on that or the following day, the last rate recorded for the currency in question published within the preceding 14 days shall be deemed to be the rate recorded on that Wednesday.

Article 170
Where a rate of exchange cannot be established under the provisions of Article 169, the rate of exchange to be used for the application of Article 35 of the Code shall be designated by the Member State concerned and shall reflect as effectively as possible the current value of the currency in question in commercial transactions in terms of the currency of that Member State.

Article 171
1. Where a rate of exchange recorded on the last Wednesday of a month and published on that or the following day differs by 5% or more from the rate established in accordance with Article 169 for entry into use the following month, it shall replace the latter rate from the first Wednesday of that month as the rate to be applied for the application of Article 35 of the Code.
2. Where in the course of a period of application as referred to in the preceding provisions, a rate of exchange recorded on a Wednesday and published on that or the following day differs by 5%

or more from the rate being used in accordance with this Chapter, it shall replace the latter rate and enter into use on the Wednesday following as the rate to be used for the application of Article 35 of the Code. The replacement rate shall remain in use for the remainder of the current month, provided that this rate is not superseded due to operation of the provisions of the first sentence of this paragraph.

3. Where, in a Member State, a rate of exchange is not recorded on a Wednesday or, if recorded, is not published on that or the following day, the rate recorded shall, for the application in that Member State of paragraphs 1 and 2, be the rate most recently recorded and published prior to that Wednesday.

Article 172

When the customs authorities of a Member State authorise a declarant to furnish or supply at a later date certain details concerning the declaration for free circulation of the goods in the form of a periodic declaration, this authorisation may, at the declarant's request, provide that a single rate be used for conversion into that Member State's currency of elements forming part of the customs value as expressed in a particular currency. In this case, the rate to be used shall be the rate, established in accordance with this Chapter, which is applicable on the first day of the period covered by the declaration in question.

CHAPTER 7—SIMPLIFIED PROCEDURES FOR CERTAIN PERISHABLE GOODS

Articles 173–177

Amendments—Articles 173–177 repealed by Council Regulation (EC) 215/2006 art 1(2); see OJ L 038; 9.2.2006, p 11.

CHAPTER 8—DECLARATIONS OF PARTICULARS AND DOCUMENTS TO BE FURNISHED

Article 178

1. Where it is necessary to establish a customs value for the purposes of Articles 28 to 36 of the Code, a declaration of particulars relating to customs value (value declaration) shall accompany the customs entry made in respect of the imported goods. The value declaration shall be drawn up on a form D.V.1 corresponding to the specimen in Annex 28, supplemented where appropriate by one or more forms D.V.1 *bis* corresponding to the specimen in Annex 29.

[2. The value declaration provided for in paragraph 1 shall be made only by a person established in the Community and in possession of the relevant facts. The second indent of Article 64(2)(b) and Article 64(3) of the Code shall apply *mutatis mutandis*.][1]

3. The customs authorities may waive the requirement of a declaration on the form referred to in paragraph 1 where the customs value of the goods in question cannot be determined under the provisions of Article 29 of the Code. In such cases the person referred to in paragraph 2 shall furnish or cause to be furnished to the customs authorities such other information as may be requested for the purposes of determining the customs value under another Article of the said Code; and such other information shall be supplied in such form and manner as may be prescribed by the customs authorities.

4. The lodging with a customs office of a declaration required by paragraph 1 shall, without prejudice to the possible application of penal provisions, be equivalent to the engagement of responsibility by the person referred to in paragraph 2 in respect of:

—the accuracy and completeness of the particulars given in the declaration,
—the authenticity of the documents produced in support of these particulars, and
—the supply of any additional information or document necessary to establish the customs value of the goods.

5. This Article shall not apply in respect of goods for which the customs value is determined under the simplified procedure system established in accordance with the provisions of Articles 173 to 177.

Amendments—[1] Article 178(2) is replaced by Commission Regulation 1677/98 art 1(1); OJ L 212, 30.07.98, p 18–22 with effect from 6 August 1998.

Article 179

1. Except where it is essential for the correct application of import duties, the customs authorities shall waive the requirement of all or part of the declaration provided for in Article 178(1):

(*a*) where the customs value of the imported goods in a consignment does not exceed [EUR 10000][1], provided that they do not constitute split or multiple consignments from the same consignor to the same consignee; or
(*b*) where the importations involved are of a non-commercial nature; or
(*c*) where the submission of the particulars in question is not necessary for the application of the Customs Tariff of the European Communities or where the customs duties provided for in the Tariff are not chargeable pursuant to specific customs provisions.

2. The amount in ecu referred to in paragraph 1(*a*) shall be converted in accordance with Article 18 of the Code. The customs authorities may round-off upwards or downwards the sum arrived at after conversion.

The customs authorities may maintain unamended the exchange value in national currency of the amount determined in ecu if, at the time of the annual adjustment provided for in Article 18 of the Code, the conversion of this amount, before the rounding-off provided for in this paragraph, leads to an alteration of less than 5% in the exchange value expressed in national currency or to a reduction thereof.

3. In the case of continuing traffic in goods supplied by the same seller to the same buyer under the same commercial conditions, the customs authorities may waive the requirement that all particulars under Article 178(1) be furnished in support of each customs declaration, but shall require them whenever the circumstances change and at least once every three years.

4. A waiver granted under this Article may be withdrawn and the submission of a D.V.1 may be required where it is found that a condition necessary to qualify for that waiver was not or is no longer met.

Amendments—[1] Figure substituted by Commission Regulation (EC) 444/2002, Art 1, para 8; see OJ L68, 12.03.2002, p 11.

Article 180

Where computerised systems are used, or where the goods concerned are the subject of a general, periodic or recapitulative declaration, the customs authorities may authorise variations in the form of presentation of data required for the determination of customs value.

Article 181

1. The person referred to in Article 178(2) shall furnish the customs authorities with a copy of the invoice on the basis of which the value of the imported goods is declared. Where the customs value is declared in writing this copy shall be retained by the customs authorities.

2. In the case of written declarations of the customs value, when the invoice for the imported goods is made out to a person established in a Member State other than that in which the customs value is declared, the declarant shall furnish the customs authorities with two copies of the invoice. One of these copies shall be retained by the customs authorities; the other, bearing the stamp of the office in question and the serial number of the declaration at the said customs office, shall be returned to the declarant for forwarding to the person to whom the invoice is made out.

3. The customs authorities may extend the provisions of paragraph 2 to cases where the person to whom the invoice is made out is established in the Member State in which the customs value is declared.

[Article 181a

1. The customs authorities need not determine the customs valuation of imported goods on the basis of the transaction value method if, in accordance with the procedure set out in paragraph 2, they are not satisfied, on the basis of reasonable doubts, that the declared value represents the total amount paid or payable as referred to in Article 29 of the Code.

2. Where the customs authorities have the doubts described in paragraph 1 they may ask for additional information in accordance with Article 178(4). If those doubts continue, the customs authorities must, before reaching a final decision, notify the person concerned, in writing if requested, of the grounds for those doubts and provide him with a reasonable opportunity to respond. A final decision and the grounds therefor shall be communicated in writing to the person concerned.][1]

Amendments—[1] Article 181a is inserted by Commission Regulation 3254/94/EC; see OJ L346, 31.12.94, p 1.

Articles 181b –197

Note—Articles 181b–197 are outside the scope of this work.

TITLE VII—CUSTOMS DECLARATIONS—NORMAL PROCEDURE

Articles 198–856a

Note—Articles 198–856a are outside the scope of this work.

PART FOUR
CUSTOMS DEBT

Articles 857–912

Note—Articles 857–912g are outside the scope of this work.

PART FIVE
FINAL PROVISIONS

Article 913

The following Regulation and Directives shall be repealed:

—Commission Regulation (EEC) No 1494/80 of 11 June 1980 on interpretative notes and generally accepted accounting principles for the purposes of customs value,

—Commission Regulation (EEC) No 1495/80 of 11 June 1980 implementing certain provisions of Council Regulation (EEC) No 1224/80 on the valuation of goods for customs purposes, as last amended by Regulation (EEC) No 558/91,

—Commission Regulation (EEC) No 1496/80 of 11 June 1980 on the declaration of particulars relating to customs value and on documents to be furnished, as last amended by Regulation (EEC) No 979/93,

—Commission Regulation (EEC) No 3177/80 of 5 December 1980 on the place of introduction to be taken into consideration in applying Article 14(2) of Council Regulation (EEC) No 1224/80 on the valuation of goods for customs purposes, as last amended by Regulation (EEC) No 2779/90,

—Commission Regulation (EEC) No 3179/80 of 5 December 1980 on postal charges to be taken into consideration when determining the customs value of goods sent by post, as last amended by Regulation (EEC) No 1264/90,

—Commission Regulation (EEC) No 1577/81 of 12 June 1981 establishing a system of simplified procedures for the determination of the customs value of certain perishable goods, as last amended by Regulation (EEC) No 3334/90,

—Commission Regulation (EEC) No 3158/83 of 9 November 1983 on the incidence of royalties and licence fees in customs value,

—Commission Regulation (EEC) No 1766/85 of 27 June 1985 on the rates of exchange to be used in the determination of customs value, as last amended by Regulation (EEC) No 593/91,

—Commission Regulation (EEC) No 3903/92 of 21 December 1992 on air transport costs.

Note—Repeals within the scope of this work only are mentioned: other repeals have been omitted.

Article 914

References to the provisions repealed shall be understood as referring to this Regulation.

Article 915

This Regulation shall enter into force on the third day following its publication in the *Official Journal of the European Communities*.

It shall apply from 1 January 1994.

…

This Regulation shall be binding in its entirety and directly applicable in all Member States.

Note—Words omitted are outside the scope of this work.

ANNEX 23
INTERPRETATIVE NOTES ON CUSTOMS VALUE

First column Reference to provisions of the Customs Code	*Second column Notes*
Article 29(1)	The price actually paid or payable refers to the price for the imported goods. Thus the flow of dividends or other payments from the buyer to the seller that do not relate to the imported goods are not part of the customs value.
Article 29(1)(*a*) third indent	An example of such restriction would be the case where a seller requires a buyer of automobiles not to sell or exhibit them prior to a fixed date which represents the beginning of a model year.
Article 29(1)(*b*)	Some examples of this include: (*a*) the seller establishes the price of the imported goods on condition that the buyer will also buy other goods in specified quantities; (*b*) the price of the imported goods is dependent upon the price or prices at which the buyer of the imported goods sells other goods to the seller of the imported goods;

First column Reference to provisions of the Customs Code	*Second column Notes*
	(*c*) the price is established on the basis of a form of payment extraneous to the imported goods, such as where the imported goods are semi-finished goods which have been provided by the seller on condition that he will receive a specified quantity of the finished goods.
	However, conditions or considerations relating to the production or marketing of the imported goods shall not result in rejection of the transaction value. For example, the fact that the buyer furnishes the seller with engineering and plans undertaken in the country of importation shall not result in rejection of the transaction value for the purposes of Article 29(1).
Article 29(2)	**1** Paragraphs 2(*a*) and (*b*) provide different means of establishing the acceptability of a transaction value.
	2 Paragraph 2(*a*) provides that where the buyer and the seller are related, the circumstances surrounding the sale shall be examined and the transaction value shall be accepted as the customs value provided that the relationship did not influence the price. It is not intended that there should be an examination of the circumstances in all cases where the buyer and the seller are related. Such examination will only be required where there are doubts about the acceptability of the price. Where the customs authorities have no doubts about the acceptability of the price, it should be accepted without requesting further information from the declarant. For example, the customs authorities may have previously examined the relationship, or it may already have detailed information concerning the buyer and the seller, and may already be satisfied from such examination or information that the relationship did not influence the price.
	3 Where the customs authorities are unable to accept the transaction value without further inquiry, it should give the declarant an opportunity to supply such further detailed information as may be necessary to enable it to examine the circumstances surrounding the sale. In this context, the customs authorities should be prepared to examine relevant aspects of the transaction, including the way in which the buyer and seller organise their commercial relations and the way in which the price in question was arrived at, in order to determine whether the relationship influenced the price. Where it can be shown that the buyer and seller, although related under the provisions of Article 143 of this Regulation, buy from and sell to each other as if they were not related, this would demonstrate that the price had not been influenced by the relationship. As an example of this, if the price had been settled in a manner consistent with the normal pricing practices of the industry in question or with the way the seller settles prices for sales to buyers who are not related to him, this would demonstrate that the price had not been influenced by the relationship. As a further example, where it is shown that the price is adequate to ensure recovery of all costs plus a profit which is representative of the firm's overall profit realised over a representative period of time (eg on an annual basis) in sales of goods of the same class or kind, this would demonstrate that the price had not been influenced.
	4 Paragraph 2(*b*) provides an opportunity for the declarant to demonstrate that the transaction value closely approximates to a "test" value previously accepted by the customs authorities and is therefore acceptable under the provisions of Article 29. Where a test under paragraph 2(*b*) is met, it is not necessary to examine the question of influence under paragraph 2(*a*). If the customs authorities already have sufficient information to be satisfied, without further detailed inquiries, that one of the tests provided in paragraph (2)(*b*) has been met, there is no reason for them to require the declarant to demonstrate that the test can be met.

First column Reference to provisions of the Customs Code	*Second column Notes*
Article 29(2)(*b*)	A number of factors must be taken into consideration in determining whether one value "closely approximates" to another value. These factors include the nature of the imported goods, the nature of the industry itself, the season in which the goods are imported, and, whether the difference in values is commercially significant. Since these factors may vary from case to case, it would be impossible to apply a uniform standard such as a fixed percentage, in each case. For example, a small difference in value in a case involving one type of goods could be unacceptable while a large difference in a case involving another type of goods might be acceptable in determining whether the transaction value closely approximates to the "test" values set forth in Article 29(2)(*b*).
Article 29(3)(*a*)	An example of an indirect payment would be the settlement by the buyer, whether in whole or in part, of a debt owed by the seller.
Article 30(2)(*a*), (*b*)	**1** In applying these provisions, the customs authorities shall, wherever possible, use a sale of identical or similar goods, as appropriate, at the same commercial level and in substantially the same quantity as the goods being valued. Where no such sale is found, a sale of identical or similar goods, as appropriate, that takes place under any one of the following three conditions may be used: (*a*) a sale at the same commercial level but in a different quantity; (*b*) a sale at a different commercial level but in substantially the same quantity; or (*c*) a sale at a different commercial level and in a different quantity. **2** Having found a sale under any one of these three conditions adjustments will then be made, as the case may be, for: (*a*) quantity factors only; (*b*) commercial level factors only; or (*c*) both commercial level and quantity factors. **3** The expression "and/or" allows the flexibility to use the sales and make the necessary adjustments in any one of the three conditions described above. **4** A condition for adjustment because of different commercial levels or different quantities is that such adjustment, whether it leads to an increase or a decrease in the value, be made only on the basis of demonstrated evidence that clearly establishes the reasonableness and accuracy of the adjustment, e g valid price lists containing prices referring to different levels or different quantities. As an example of this, if the imported goods being valued consist of a shipment of 10 units and the only identical or similar imported goods, as appropriate, for which a transaction value exists involved a sale of 500 units, and it is recognised that the seller grants quantity discounts, the required adjustment may be accomplished by resorting to the seller's price list and using that price applicable to a sale of 10 units. This does not require that a sale had to have been made in quantities of 10 as long as the price list has been established as being bona fide through sales at other quantities. In the absence of such an objective measure, however, the determination of a customs value under the provisions of Article 30(2)(*a*) and (*b*) is not appropriate.
Article 30(2)(*d*)	**1** As a general rule, customs value is determined under these provisions on the basis of information readily available in the Community. In order to determine a computed value, however, it may be necessary to examine the costs of producing the goods being valued and other information which has to be obtained from outside the Community. Furthermore, in most cases the producer of the goods will be outside the jurisdiction of the authorities of the Member States. The use of the computed value method will generally be limited to those cases where the buyer and seller are related, and the producer is prepared to supply to the authorities of the country of importation the necessary costings and to provide facilities for any subsequent verification which may be necessary.

First column Reference to provisions of the Customs Code	*Second column Notes*
	2 The "cost or value" referred to in Article 30(2)(*d*), first indent, is to be determined on the basis of information relating to the production of the goods being valued supplied by or on behalf of the producer. It is to be based upon the commercial accounts of the producer, provided that such accounts are consistent with the generally accepted accounting principles applied in the country where the goods are produced.
	3 The "amount for profit and general expenses" referred to in Article 30(2)(*d*), second indent, is to be determined on the basis of information supplied by or on behalf of the producer unless his figures are inconsistent with those usually reflected in sales of goods of the same class or kind as the goods being valued which are made by producers in the country of exportation for export to the country of importation.
	4 No cost or value of the elements referred to in this Article shall be counted twice in determining the computed value.
	5 It should be noted in this context that the "amount for profit and general expenses" has to be taken as a whole. It follows that if, in any particular case, the producer's profit figure is low and his general expenses are high, his profit and general expenses taken together may nevertheless be consistent with that usually reflected in sales of goods of the same class or kind. Such a situation might occur, for example, if a product were being launched in the Community and the producer accepted a nil or low profit to offset high general expenses associated with the launch. Where the producer can demonstrate that he is taking a low profit on his sales of the imported goods because of particular commercial circumstances, his actual profit figures should be taken into account provided that he has valid commercial reasons to justify them and his pricing policy reflects usual pricing policies in the branch of industry concerned. Such a situation might occur, for example, where producers have been forced to lower prices temporarily because of an unforeseeable drop in demand, or where they sell goods to complement a range of goods being produced in the country of importation and accept a low profit to maintain competitivity. Where the producer's own figures for profit and general expenses are not consistent with those usually reflected in sales of goods of the same class or kind as the goods being valued which are made by producers in the country of exportation for export to the country of importation, the amount for profit and general expenses may be based upon relevant information other than that supplied by or on behalf of the producer of the goods.
	6 Whether certain goods are "of the same class or kind" as other goods must be determined on a case-by-case basis with reference to the circumstances involved. In determining the usual profits and general expenses under the provisions of Article 30(2)(*d*), sales for export to the country of importation of the narrowest group or range of goods, which includes the goods being valued, for which the necessary information can be provided, should be examined. For the purposes of Article 30(2)(*d*), "goods of the same class or kind" must be from the same country as the goods being valued.
Article 31(1)	**1** Customs values determined under the provisions of Article 31(1) should, to the greatest extent possible, be based on previously determined customs values.
	2 The methods of valuation to be employed under Article 31(1) should be those laid down in Articles 29 and 30(2), but a reasonable flexibility in the application of such methods would be in conformity with the aims and provisions of Article 31(1).
	3 Some examples of reasonable flexibility are as follows:
	(*a*) *Identical goods*—the requirement that the identical goods should be exported at or about the same time as the goods being valued could be flexibly interpreted; identical imported goods produced in a country other than the country of exportation of the goods being valued could be the basis for customs valuation; customs values of identical imported goods already determined under the provisions of Article 30(2)(*c*) and (*d*) could be used.

First column Reference to provisions of the Customs Code	*Second column Notes*
	(*b*) *Similar goods*—the requirement that the similar goods should be exported at or about the same time as the goods being valued could be flexibly interpreted; similar imported goods produced in a country other than the country of exportation of the goods being valued could be the basis for customs valuations; customs values of similar imported goods already determined under the provisions of Article 30(2)(*c*) and (*d*) could be used.
	(*c*) *Deductive method*—the requirement that the goods shall have been sold in the "condition as imported" in Article 152(1)(*a*) could be flexibly interpreted; the "90 days" requirement could be administered flexibly.
Article 32(1)(*b*)(ii)	**1** There are two factors involved in the apportionment of the elements specified in Article 32(1)(*b*)(ii) to the imported goods—the value of the element itself and the way in which that value is to be apportioned to the imported goods. The apportionment of these elements should be made in a reasonable manner appropriate to the circumstances and in accordance with generally accepted accounting principles.
	2 Concerning the value of the element, if the buyer acquires the element from a seller not related to him at a given cost, the value of the element is that cost. If the element was produced by the buyer or by a person related to him, its value would be the cost of producing it. If the element had been previously used by the buyer, regardless of whether it had been acquired or produced by him, the original cost of acquisition or production would have to be adjusted downwards to reflect its use in order to arrive at the value of the element.
	3 Once a value has been determined for the element, it is necessary to apportion that value to the imported goods. Various possibilities exist. For example, the value might be apportioned to the first shipment, if the buyer wishes to pay duty on the entire value at one time. As another example, he may request that the value be apportioned over the number of units produced up to the time of the first shipment. As a further example, he may request that the value be apportioned over the entire anticipated production where contracts of firm commitments exist for the production. The method of apportionment used will depend upon the documentation provided by the buyer.
	4 As an illustration of the above, a buyer provides the producer with a mould to be used in the production of the imported goods and contracts with him to buy 10,000 units. By the time of arrival of the first shipment of 1,000 units, the producer has already produced 4,000 units. The buyer may request the customs authorities to apportion the value of the mould over 1,000, 4,000 or 10,000 units.
Article 32(1)(*b*)(iv)	**1** Additions for the elements specified in Article 32(1)(*b*)(iv) should be based on objective and quantifiable data. In order to minimise the burden for both the declarant and customs authorities in determining the values to be added, data readily available in the buyer's commercial record system should be used in so far as possible.
	2 For those elements supplied by the buyer which were purchased or leased by the buyer, the addition would be the cost of the purchase or the lease. No addition shall be made for those elements available in the public domain, other than the cost of obtaining copies of them.
	3 The ease with which it may be possible to calculate the values to be added will depend on a particular firm's structure and management practice, as well as its accounting methods.
	4 For example, it is possible that a firm which imports a variety of products from several countries maintains the records of its design centre outside the country of importation in such a way as to show accurately the costs attributable to a given product. In such cases, a direct adjustment may appropriately be made under the provisions of Article 32.

First column Reference to provisions of the Customs Code	*Second column Notes*
	5 In another case, a firm may carry the cost of the design centre outside the country of importation as a general overhead expense without allocation to specific products. In this instance, an appropriate adjustment could be made under the provisions of Article 32 with respect to the imported goods by apportioning total design centre costs over total production benefiting from the design centre and adding such apportioned cost on a unit basis to imports. **6** Variations in the above circumstances will, of course, require different factors to be considered in determining the proper method of allocation. **7** In cases where the production of the element in question involves a number of countries and over a period of time, the adjustment should be limited to the value actually added to that element outside the country of importation.
Article 32(1)(*c*)	The royalties and licence fees referred to in Article 32(1)(*c*) may include, among other things, payments in respect of patents, trademarks and copyrights.
Article 32(2)	Where objective and quantifiable data do not exist with regard to the additions required to be made under the provisions of Article 32, the transaction value cannot be determined under the provisions of Article 29. As an illustration of this, a royalty is paid on the basis of the price in a sale in the importing country of a litre of a particular product that was imported by the kilogram and made up into a solution after importation. If the royalty is based partially on the imported goods and partially on other factors which have nothing to do with the imported goods (such as when the imported goods are mixed with domestic ingredients and are no longer separately identifiable, or when the royalty cannot be distinguished from special financial arrangements between the buyer and the seller), it would be inappropriate to attempt to make an addition for the royalty. However, if the amount of this royalty is based only on the imported goods and can be readily quantified, an addition to the price actually paid or payable can be made.

Reference to provisions of the Customs Code Implementing Provisions	*Notes*
Article 143(1)(*e*)	One person shall be deemed to control another when the former is legally or operationally in a position to exercise restraint or direction over the latter.
Article 150(1) Article 151(1)	The expression "and/or" allows the flexibility to use the sales and make the necessary adjustments in any one of the three conditions described in paragraph 1 of the interpretative notes to Articles 30(2)(*a*) and (*b*).
Article 152(1)(*a*)(i)	**1** The words "profit and general expenses" should be taken as a whole. The figure for the purposes of this deduction should be determined on the basis of information supplied by the declarant unless his figures are inconsistent with those obtaining in sales in the country of importation of imported goods of the same class or kind. Where the declarant's figures are inconsistent with such figures, the amount for profit and general expenses may be based upon relevant information other than that supplied by the declarant. **2** In determining either the commissions or the usual profits and general expenses under this provision, the question whether certain goods are of the same class or kind as other goods must be determined on a case-by-case basis by reference to the circumstances involved. Sales in the country of importation of the narrowest group or range of imported goods of the same class or kind, which includes the goods being valued, for which the necessary information can be provided, should be examined. For the purposes of this provision, "goods of the same class or kind" includes goods imported from the same country as the goods being valued as well as goods imported from other countries.

First column Reference to provisions of the Customs Code	*Second column Notes*
Article 152(2)	**1** Where this method of valuation is used, deductions made for the value added by further processing shall be based on objective and quantifiable data relating to the cost of such work. Accepted industry formulas, recipes, methods of construction, and other industry practices would form the basis of the calculations. **2** This method of valuation would normally not be applicable when, as a result of the further processing, the imported goods lose their identity. However, there can be instances where, although the identity of the imported goods is lost, the value added by the processing can be determined accurately without unreasonable difficulty. On the other hand, there can also be instances where the imported goods maintain their identity but form such a minor element in the goods sold in the country of importation that the use of this valuation method would be unjustified. In view of the above, each situation of this type must be considered on a case-by-case basis.
Article 152(3)	**1** As an example of this, goods are sold from a price list which grants favourable unit prices for purchases made in larger quantities.

Sale quantity	Unit price	Number of sales	Total quantity sold at each price
One to 10 units	100	10 sales of five units Five sales of three units	65
11 to 25 units	95	Five sales of 11 units	55
Over 25 units	90	One sale of 30 units One sale of 50 units	80
—	—	—	—

The greatest number of units sold at a price is 80; therefore, the unit price in the greatest aggregate quantity is 90.

2 As another example of this, two sales occur. In the first sale 500 units are sold at a price of 95 currency units each. In the second sale 400 units are sold at a price of 90 currency units each. In this example, the greatest number of units sold at a particular price is 500; therefore, the unit price in the greatest aggregate quantity is 95.

3 A third example would be the following situation where various quantities are sold at various prices.

(*a*) Sales

Sale quantity	*Unit price*
40 units	100
30 units	90
15 units	100
50 units	95
25 units	105
35 units	90
5 units	100

(*b*) Total

Total quantity sold	*Unit price*
65	90
50	95
60	100
25	105

In this example, the greatest number of units sold at a particular price is 65; therefore, the unit price in the greatest aggregate quantity is 90.

ANNEX 24

APPLICATION OF GENERALLY ACCEPTED ACCOUNTING PRINCIPLES FOR THE DETERMINATION OF CUSTOMS VALUE

1. "Generally accepted accounting principles" refers to the recognised consensus or substantial authoritative support within a country at a particular time as to which economic resources and obligations should be recorded as assets and liabilities, which changes in assets and liabilities should be recorded, how the assets and liabilities and changes in them should be measured, what information should be disclosed and how it should be disclosed, and which financial statements should be prepared. These standards may be broad guidelines of general application as well as detailed practices and procedures.

2. For the purposes of the application of the customs valuation provisions, the customs administration concerned shall utilise information prepared in a manner consistent with generally accepted accounting principles in the country which is appropriate for the Article in question. For example, the determination of usual profit and general expenses under the provisions of Article 152(1)(*a*)(i) of this Regulation would be carried out utilising information prepared in a manner consistent with generally accepted accounting principles of the country of importation. On the other hand, the determination of usual profit and general expenses under the provisions of Article 30(2)(*d*) of the Code would be carried out utilising information prepared in a manner consistent with generally accepted accounting principles of the country of production. As a further example, the determination of an element provided for in Article 32(1)(*b*)(ii) of the Code undertaken in the country of importation would be carried out utilising information in a manner consistent with the generally accepted accounting principles of that country.

[ANNEX 25

AIR TRANSPORT COSTS TO BE INCLUDED IN THE CUSTOMS VALUE

1. The following table shows—

(*a*) third countries listed by continents and zones[1] (column 1).
(*b*) the percentages which represent the part of the air transport costs from a given third country to the EC to be included in the customs value (column 2).

Notes—[1] The percentages are valid for all airports in a given country unless specific airports of departure are indicated.

2. When goods are shipped from countries or from airports not included in the following table, other than the airports referred to in paragraph 3, the percentage given for the airport nearest to that of departure shall be taken.

3. As regards the French overseas departments of Guadeloupe, Guyana, Martinique and Reunion, of which territories the airports are not included in the table, the following rules shall apply—

(*a*) for goods shipped direct to those departments from third countries, the whole of the air transport cost is to be included in the customs value;
(*b*) for goods shipped to the European part of the Community from third countries and transhipped or unloaded in one of those departments, only the air transport costs which would have been incurred for carrying the goods only as far as the place of transhipment or unloading are to be included in the customs value;
(*c*) for goods shipped to those departments from third countries and transhipped or unloaded in an airport in the European part of the Community, the air transport costs to be included in the customs value are those which result from the application of the percentages given in the following table to the costs which would have been incurred for carrying the goods from the airport of departure to the airport of transhipment or unloading.

The transhipment or unloading shall be certified by an appropriate endorsement by the customs authorities on the air waybill or other air transport document, with the official stamp of the office concerned; failing this certification the provisions of the last subparagraph of Article 163(6) of this Regulation shall apply.

1	*2*
Zone (country) of departure (third country)	*Percentages of the air transport costs to be included in the customs value for zone of arrival EC*
America	

1	*2*
Zone (country) of departure (third country)	*Percentages of the air transport costs to be included in the customs value for zone of arrival EC*
Zone A **Canada:** Gander, Halifax, Moncton, Montreal, Ottawa, Quebec, Toronto, (other airports see zone B) **Greenland**	70
United States of America: Akron, Albany, Atlanta, Baltimore, Boston, Buffalo, Charleston, Chicago, Cincinnati, Columbus, Detroit, Indianapolis, Jacksonville, Kansas City, Lexington, Louisville, Memphis, Milwaukee, Minneapolis, Nashville, New Orleans, New York, Philadelphia, Pittsburgh, St Louis, Washington DC, (other airports see zones B and C)	
Zone B **Canada:** Edmonton, Vancouver, Winnipeg, (other airports see zone A) **United States of America:** Albuquerque, Austin, Billings, Dallas, Denver, Houston, Las Vegas, Los Angeles, Miami, Oklahoma, Phoenix, Portland, Puerto Rico, Salt Lake City, San Francisco, Seattle, (other airports see zones A and C) **Central America** (all countries) **South America** (all countries)	78
Zone C **United States of America:** Anchorage, Fairbanks, Honolulu, Juneau, (other airports see zones A and B)	89
Africa	
Zone D Algeria, Egypt, Libya, Morocco, Tunisia	33
Zone E Benin, Burkina Faso, Cameroon, Cape Verde, Central African Republic, Chad, Côte d'Ivoire, Djibouti, Ethiopia, Gambia, Ghana, Guinea, Guinea-Bissau, Liberia, Mali, Mauritania, Niger, Nigeria, Senegal, Sierra Leone, Sudan, Togo	50
Zone F Burundi, Democratic Republic of Congo, Congo (Brazzaville), Equatorial Guinea, Gabon, Kenya, Rwanda, São Tomé and Principe, Seychelles, Somalia, St. Helena, Tanzania, Uganda	61

1	*2*
Zone (country) of departure (third country)	*Percentages of the air transport costs to be included in the customs value for zone of arrival EC*
Zone G Angola, Botswana, Comoros, Lesotho, Madagascar, Malawi, Mauritius, Mozambique, Namibia, Republic of South Africa, Swaziland, Zambia, Zimbabwe	74
Asia	
Zone H Armenia, Azerbaijan, Georgia, Iran, Iraq, Israel, Jordan, Kuwait, Lebanon, Syria	27
Zone I Bahrain, Muscat and Oman, Qatar, Saudi Arabia, United Arab Emirates, Yemen (Arab Republic)	43
Zone J Afghanistan, Bangladesh, Bhutan, India, Nepal, Pakistan.	46
Zone K Kazakhstan, Kyrgyzstan, Tajikistan, Turkmenistan, Uzbekistan, Russia: Novosibirsk, Omsk, Perm, Sverdlovsk, (other airports see zones L, M, and O)	57
Zone L Brunei, China, Indonesia, Kampuchea, Laos, Macao, Malaysia, Maldives, Mongolia, Myanmar, Philippines, Singapore, Sri Lanka, Taiwan, Thailand, Vietnam Russia: Irkutsk, Kirensk, Krasnoyarsk, (other airports see zones K, M and O)	70
Zone M Japan, Korca (North), Korca (South) Russia: Khabarovsk, Vladivostok, (other airports see zones K, L and O)	83
Australia and Oceania	
Zone N Australia and Oceania	79
Europe	
Zone O Iceland, Russia: Gorky, Kuibishev, Moscow, Orel, Rostov, Volgograd, Voronej, (other airports see zones K, L and M), Ukraine	30

1	*2*
Zone (country) of departure (third country)	*Percentages of the air transport costs to be included in the customs value for zone of arrival EC*
Zone P Albania, Belarus, Bosnia-Herzegovina, …[2], Faroe Islands, Former Yugoslav Republic of Macedonia, Moldova, Norway, …[2], Serbia and Montenegro, Turkey	15
Zone Q Croatia, Switzerland][1]	5

Amendments—[1] Annex 25 replaced by Commission Regulation (EC) 881/2003 Annex III (L 134; 29.05.2003 p 1) with effect from 1 May 2004.

[2] Words repealed by Commission Regulation 1792/2006/EC art 1, Annex Part 11(45) (OJ L 362, 20.12.2006, p 1).

ANNEX 28

Note—Form DV1, European Community—Declaration of Particulars Relating to Customs Value, is not reproduced here.

ANNEX 29

Note—Form DV1 BIS, European Community—Continuation Sheet, is not reproduced here.

Council Regulation of 7 October 2003 on administrative cooperation in the field of value added tax and repealing Regulation (EEC) No 218/92

(1798/2003/EC)

Note—See OJ L 264; 15.10.2003 p 1.

Cross references—See Council Directive 2003/93 art 2 (OJ L 264; 15.10.2003 p 23): references made to Directive 77/799/EEC in relation to value added tax shall be construed as references to Council Regulation (EC) 1798/2003 (OJ L 264; 15.10.2003 p 1).

Simon's Tax Cases—*Silversafe Ltd (in liquidation) and another v Hood and others* [2007] STC 871; *EC Commission v EU Council (supported by Ireland, Portuguese Republic and United Kingdom)* [2007] STC 1121.

THE COUNCIL OF THE EUROPEAN UNION,

Having regard to the Treaty establishing the European Community, and in particular Article 93 thereof,

Having regard to the proposal from the Commission,

Having regard to the opinion of the European Parliament,

Having regard to the opinion of the European Economic and Social Committee,

Whereas:

(1) Tax evasion and tax avoidance extending across the frontiers of Member States lead to budget losses and violations of the principle of fair taxation and are liable to bring about distortions of capital movements and of the conditions of competition. They therefore affect the operation of the internal market.

(2) Combating value added tax (VAT) evasion calls for close cooperation between the administrative authorities in each Member State responsible for the application of the provisions in that field.

(3) The tax harmonisation measures taken to complete the internal market should therefore include the establishment of a common system for the exchange of information between the Member States whereby the Member States' administrative authorities are to assist each other and cooperate with the Commission in order to ensure the proper application of VAT on supplies of goods and services, intra-Community acquisition of goods and importation of goods.

(4) Electronic storage and transmission of certain data for VAT control purposes is indispensable for the proper functioning of the VAT system.

(5) The conditions for the exchange of, and direct access of Member States to, electronically stored data in each Member State should be clearly defined. Operators should have access to certain of such data where required for the fulfilment of their obligations.

(6) The Member State of consumption has primary responsibility for assuring that non-established suppliers comply with their obligations. To this end, the application of the temporary special scheme for electronically supplied services that is provided for in Article 26c of Sixth Council Directive 77/388/EEC of 17 May 1977 on the harmonisation of the laws of Member States relating to turnover taxes, Common system of value added tax: uniform basis of assessment, requires the definition of rules concerning the provision of information and transfer of money between the Member State of identification and the Member State of consumption.

(7) Council Regulation (EEC) No 218/92 of 27 January 1992 on administrative cooperation in the field of indirect taxation (VAT) established in this respect a system of close cooperation amongst the Member States' administrative authorities and between those authorities and the Commission.

(8) Regulation (EEC) No 218/92 supplements Council Directive 77/799/EEC of 19 December 1977 concerning mutual assistance by the competent authorities of the Member States in the field of direct and indirect taxation.

(9) Those two legal instruments have proved to be effective but are no longer able to meet the new requirements of administrative cooperation resulting from the ever closer integration of economies within the internal market.

(10) The existence of two separate instruments for cooperation on VAT has, moreover, hampered effective cooperation between tax administrations.

(11) The rights and obligations of all parties concerned are currently ill-defined. Clearer and binding rules governing cooperation between Member States are therefore necessary.

(12) There is not enough direct contact between local or national anti-fraud offices, with communication between central liaison offices being the rule. This leads to inefficiency, under-use of the arrangements for administrative cooperation and delays in communication. Provision should therefore be made to bring about more direct contacts between services with a view to making cooperation more efficient and faster.

(13) Cooperation is also not intensive enough, in that, apart from the VAT information exchange system (VIES), there are not enough automatic or spontaneous exchanges of information between Member States. Exchanges of information between the respective administrations as well as between administrations and the Commission should be made more intensive and swifter in order to combat fraud more effectively.

(14) The provisions on VAT administrative cooperation of Regulation (EEC) No 218/92 and of Directive 77/799/EEC should therefore be joined and strengthened. For reasons of clarity this should be done in a single new instrument which replaces Regulation (EEC) No 218/92.

(15) This Regulation should not affect other Community measures which contribute to combating VAT fraud.

(16) For the purposes of this Regulation, it is appropriate to consider limitations of certain rights and obligations laid down by Directive 95/46/EC of the European Parliament and of the Council of 24 October 1995 on the protection of individuals with regard to the processing of personal data and on the free movement of such data in order to safeguard the interests referred to in Article 13(1)(*e*) of that Directive.

(17) The measures necessary for the implementation of this Regulation should be adopted in accordance with Council Decision 1999/468/EC of 28 June 1999 laying down the procedures for the exercise of implementing powers conferred on the Commission.

(18) This Regulation respects the fundamental rights and observes the principles which are recognised in particular by the Charter of Fundamental Rights of the European Union,

HAS ADOPTED THIS REGULATION:

CHAPTER I—GENERAL PROVISIONS

Article 1

1. This Regulation lays down the conditions under which the administrative authorities in the Member States responsible for the application of the laws on VAT on supplies of goods and services, intra-Community acquisition of goods and importation of goods are to cooperate with each other and with the Commission to ensure compliance with those laws.

To that end, it lays down rules and procedures to enable the competent authorities of the Member States to cooperate and to exchange with each other any information that may help them to effect a correct assessment of VAT.

This Regulation also lays down rules and procedures for the exchange of certain information by electronic means, in particular as regards VAT on intra-Community transactions.

[For the period provided for in Article 357 of Council Directive 2006/112/EC of 28 November 2006 on the common system of value added tax, it also lays down rules and procedures for the exchange by electronic means of value added tax information on services supplied electronically in accordance with the special scheme provided for in Chapter 6 of Title XII of that Directive and also for any subsequent exchange of information and, as far as services covered by that special scheme are concerned, for the transfer of money between Member States' competent authorities.][1]

2. This Regulation shall not affect the application in the Member States of the rules on mutual assistance in criminal matters.

Amendments—[1] In para 1, fourth sub-para substituted by Council Regulation 143/2008/EC of 12 February 2008, art 1(1) with effect from 1 January 2010. Text previously read as follows—

"For the period provided for in Article 4 of Directive 2002/38/EC(9), it also lays down rules and procedures for the exchange by electronic means of value added tax information on services supplied electronically in accordance with the special scheme provided for in Article 26c of Directive 77/388/EEC, and also for any subsequent exchange of information and, as far as services covered by that special scheme are concerned, for the transfer of money between Member States' competent authorities.".

Prospective amendments—In para 1, fourth sub-para to be further substituted by Council Regulation 143/2008/EC of 12 February 2008, art 2(1) with effect from 1 January 2015.

Article 2

For the purposes of this Regulation:

1. "competent authority of a Member State", means:

—*in Belgium:*

Le ministre des finances

De Minister van financiën,

[— in Bulgaria:

Изпълнителният директор на Националната агенция за приходите,][2]

[—*in the Czech Republic:*

Ministerstvo financí,][1]

—*in Denmark:*

Skatteministeren,

—*in Germany:*

Bundesministerium der Finanzen,

[—*in Estonia:*

Maksuamet,][1]

—*in Greece:*

Υπονργειο Οικονομίαζ και Οικονομικων

—*in Spain:*

El Secretario de Estado de Hacienda,

—*in France:*

le ministre de l'économie, des finances et de l'industrie,

—*in Ireland:*

The Revenue Commissioners,

—*in Italy:*

il Capo del Dipartimento delle Politiche Fiscali,

[—*in Cyprus:*

Υπουργός Οικονομικών ή εξουσιοδοτημένος αντιπρόσωπος του,

—*in Latvia:*

Valsts ienemumu dienests,

—*in Lithuania:*

Valstybine mokesčių inspekcija prie Finansų ministerijos,][1]

—*in Luxembourg:*

L'Administration de l'Enregistrement et des Domaines,

[—in Hungary:

Adó- és Pénzügyi Ellenorzési Hivatal Központi Kapcsolattartó Irodája,

—in Malta:

Dipartiment tat-Taxxa fuq il-Valur Mizjud fil-Ministeru tal-Finanzi u Affarijiet Ekonomici,][1]

—*in the Netherlands:*

De minister van Financiën,

—*in Austria:*

Bundesminister für Finanzen,

[—in Poland:

Minister Finansów,][1]

[— in Romania:

Agenţia Naţionalã de Administrare Fiscalã,][2]

—*in Portugal:*

O Ministro das Finanças,

[—*in Slovenia:*

Ministrstvo za finance,

—*in Slovakia:*

Ministerstvo financií][1]

—*in Finland:*

Valtiovarainministeriö
Finansministeriet,

—*in Sweden:*

Chefen för Finansdepartementet,

—*in the United Kingdom:*

The Commissioners of Customs and Excise;

2. "central liaison office", means the office which has been designated under Article 3(2) with principal responsibility for contacts with other Member States in the field of administrative cooperation;

3. "liaison department", means any office other than the central liaison office with a specific territorial competence or a specialised operational responsibility which has been designated by the competent authority pursuant to Article 3(3) to exchange directly information on the basis of this Regulation;

4. "competent official", means any official who can directly exchange information on the basis of this Regulation for which he has been authorised pursuant to Article 3(4);

5. "requesting authority", means the central liaison office, a liaison department or any competent official of a Member State who makes a request for assistance on behalf of the competent authority;

6. "requested authority", means the central liaison office, a liaison department or any competent official of a Member State who receives a request for assistance on behalf of the competent authority;

7. "intra-Community transactions", means the intra-Community supply of goods or services;

[8. "intra-Community supply of goods" means any supply of goods which must be declared in the recapitulative statement provided for in Article 262 of Directive 2006/112/EC;

9. "intra-Community supply of services" means any supply of services which must be declared in the re-capitulative statement provided for in Article 262 of Directive 2006/112/EC;

10. "intra-Community acquisition of goods" means the acquisition of the right under Article 20 of Directive 2006/112/EC to dispose as owner of moveable tangible property;

11. "VAT identification number" means the number provided for in Articles 214, 215 and 216 of Directive 2006/112/EC;][3]

12. "administrative enquiry", means all the controls, checks and other action taken by Member States in the performance of their duties with a view to ensuring proper application of VAT legislation;

13. "automatic exchange", means the systematic communication of predefined information to another Member State, without prior request, at pre-established regular intervals;

14. "structured automatic exchange", means the systematic communication of predefined information to another Member State, without prior request, as and when that information becomes available;

15. "spontaneous exchange", means the irregular communication without prior request of information to another Member State;

16. "person", means:

(*a*) a natural person;

(*b*) a legal person; or

(*c*) where the legislation in force so provides, an association of persons recognised as having the capacity to perform legal acts but lacking the legal status of a legal person;

17. "to grant access", means to authorise access to the relevant electronic database and to obtain data by electronic means;

18. "by electronic means", means using electronic equipment for the processing (including digital compression) and storage of data, and employing wires, radio transmission, optical technologies or other electromagnetic means;

19. "CCN/CSI network", means the common platform based on the common communication network (CCN) and common system interface (CSI), developed by the Community to ensure all transmissions by electronic means between competent authorities in the area of customs and taxation.

Note—See OJ L 264; 15.10.2003 p 1.

Amendments—[1] Entries inserted by Council Regulation 885/2004 art 1, Annex Part IV para 2 (OJ L 168; 1.5.2004 p 1).

[2] Entries inserted by Council Regulation 1791/2006/EC art 1, Annex Part 7 (OJ L 363, 20.12.2006, p 1).

[3] Points 8–11 substituted by Council Regulation 143/2008/EC of 12 February 2008, art 1(2) with effect from 1 January 2010. Text previously read as follows—

"8. "intra-Community supply of goods", means any supply of goods which must be declared in the recapitulative statement provided for in Article 22(6)(*b*) of Directive 77/388/EEC;

9. "intra-Community supply of services", means any supply of services covered by Article 28b(C), (D), (E) and (F) of Directive 77/388/EEC;

10. "intra-Community acquisition of goods", means acquisition of the right to dispose as owner of movable tangible property under Article 28a(3) of Directive 77/388/EEC;

11. "VAT identification number", means the number provided for in Article 22(1)(*c*), (*d*) and (*e*) of Directive 77/388/EEC;".

Prospective amendments—Existing first para to be renumbered as para 1, and new para 2 to be inserted by Council Regulation 143/2008/EC of 12 February 2008, art 2(2) with effect from 1 January 2015.

Article 3

1. The competent authorities referred to in point 1 of Article 2 are the authorities in whose name this Regulation is to be applied, whether directly or by delegation.

2. Each Member State shall designate a single central liaison office to which principal responsibility shall be delegated for contacts with other Member States in the field of administrative cooperation. It shall inform the Commission and the other Member States thereof.

3. The competent authority of each Member State may designate liaison departments. The central liaison office shall be responsible for keeping the list of those departments up to date and making it available to the central liaison offices of the other Member States concerned.

4. The competent authority of each Member State may in addition designate, under the conditions laid down by it, competent officials who can directly exchange information on the basis of this Regulation. When it does so, it may limit the scope of such designation. The central liaison office shall be responsible for keeping the list of those officials up to date and making it available to the central liaison offices of the other Member States concerned.

5. The officials exchanging information under Articles 11 and 13 shall in any case be deemed to be competent officials for this purpose, in accordance with conditions laid down by the competent authorities.

6. Where a liaison department or a competent official sends or receives a request or a reply to a request for assistance, it shall inform the central liaison office of its Member State under the conditions laid down by the latter.

7. Where a liaison department or a competent official receives a request for assistance requiring action outside its territorial or operational area, it shall forward such request without delay to the central liaison office of its Member State and inform the requesting authority thereof. In such a case, the period laid down in Article 8 shall start the day after the request for assistance has been forwarded to the central liaison office.

Article 4

1. The obligation to give assistance as provided for in this Regulation shall not cover the provision of information or documents obtained by the administrative authorities referred to in Article 1 acting with the authorisation or at the request of the judicial authority.

2. However, where a competent authority has the powers in accordance with national law to communicate the information referred to in paragraph 1, it may be communicated as a part of the administrative cooperation provided for in this Regulation. Any such communication must have the prior authorisation of the judicial authority if the necessity of such authorisation derives from national law.

CHAPTER II—EXCHANGE OF INFORMATION ON REQUEST

SECTION 1—REQUEST FOR INFORMATION AND FOR ADMINISTRATIVE ENQUIRIES

Article 5

1. At the request of the requesting authority, the requested authority shall communicate the information referred to in Article 1, including any information relating to a specific case or cases.

2. For the purpose of forwarding the information referred to in paragraph 1, the requested authority shall arrange for the conduct of any administrative enquiries necessary to obtain such information.

3. The request referred to in paragraph 1 may contain a reasoned request for a specific administrative enquiry. If the Member State takes the view that no administrative enquiry is necessary, it shall immediately inform the requesting authority of the reasons thereof.

4. In order to obtain the information sought or to conduct the administrative enquiry requested, the requested authority or the administrative authority to which it has recourse shall proceed as though acting on its own account or at the request of another authority in its own Member State.

Prospective amendments—Para 3 to be substituted by Council Regulation 143/2008/EC of 12 February 2008, art 2(3) with effect from 1 January 2015.

Article 6

Requests for information and for administrative enquiries pursuant to Article 5 shall, as far as possible, be sent using a standard form adopted in accordance with the procedure referred to in Article 44(2).

Article 7

1. At the request of the requesting authority, the requested authority shall communicate to it any pertinent information it obtains or has in its possession as well as the results of administrative enquiries, in the form of reports, statements and any other documents, or certified true copies or extracts thereof.

2. Original documents shall be provided only where this is not contrary to the provisions in force in the Member State in which the requested authority is established.

SECTION 2—TIME LIMIT FOR PROVIDING INFORMATION

Article 8

The requested authority shall provide the information referred to in Articles 5 and 7 as quickly as possible and no later than three months following the date of receipt of the request.

However, where the requested authority is already in possession of that information, the time limit shall be reduced to a maximum period of one month.

Article 9

In certain special categories of cases, time limits different from the ones provided for in Article 8 may be agreed between the requested and the requesting authorities.

Article 10

Where the requested authority is unable to respond to the request by the deadline, it shall inform the requesting authority in writing forthwith of the reasons for its failure to do so, and when it considers it would be likely to be able to respond.

SECTION 3—PRESENCE IN ADMINISTRATIVE OFFICES AND PARTICIPATION IN ADMINISTRATIVE ENQUIRIES

Article 11

1. By agreement between the requesting authority and the requested authority and in accordance with the arrangements laid down by the latter, officials authorised by the requesting authority may, with a view to exchanging the information referred to in Article 1, be present in the offices where the administrative authorities of the Member State in which the requested authority is established carry out their duties. Where the requested information is contained in documentation to which the officials of the requested authority have access, the officials of the requesting authority shall be given copies of the documentation containing the requested information.

2. By agreement between the requesting authority and the requested authority, and in accordance with the arrangements laid down by the latter, officials designated by the requesting authority may, with a view to exchanging the information referred to in Article 1, be present during the administrative enquiries. Administrative enquiries shall be carried out exclusively by the officials of the requested authority. The requesting authority's officials shall not exercise the powers of inspection conferred on officials of the requested authority. They may, however, have access to the same premises and documents as the latter, through their intermediary and for the sole purpose of the administrative enquiry being carried out.

3. The officials of the requesting authority present in another Member State in accordance with paragraphs 1 and 2 must at all times be able to produce written authority stating their identity and their official capacity.

SECTION 4—SIMULTANEOUS CONTROLS

Article 12

With a view to exchanging the information referred to in Article 1, two or more Member States may agree to conduct simultaneous controls, in their own territory, of the tax situation of one or more taxable persons who are of common or complementary interest, whenever such controls would appear to be more effective than controls carried out by only one Member State.

Article 13

1. A Member State shall identify independently the taxable persons whom it intends to propose for a simultaneous control. The competent authority of that Member State shall notify the competent authority in the other Member States concerned of the cases proposed for simultaneous controls. It shall give reasons for its choice, as far as possible, by providing the information which led to its decision. It shall specify the period of time during which such controls should be conducted.

2. The Member States concerned shall then decide whether they wish to take part in the simultaneous controls. On receipt of a proposal for a simultaneous control, the competent authority of the Member State shall confirm its agreement or communicate its reasoned refusal to its counterpart authority.

3. Each competent authority of the Member States concerned shall appoint a representative to be responsible for supervising and coordinating the control operation.

CHAPTER III—REQUEST FOR ADMINISTRATIVE NOTIFICATION

Article 14

The requested authority shall, at the request of the requesting authority and in accordance with the rules governing the notification of similar instruments in the Member State in which it is established, notify the addressee of all instruments and decisions which emanate from the administrative authorities and concern the application of VAT legislation in the territory of the Member State in which the requesting authority is established.

Article 15

Requests for notification, mentioning the subject of the instrument or decision to be notified, shall indicate the name, address and any other relevant information for identifying the addressee.

Article 16

The requested authority shall inform the requesting authority immediately of its response to the request for notification and notify it, in particular, of the date of notification of the decision or instrument to the addressee.

CHAPTER IV—EXCHANGE OF INFORMATION WITHOUT PRIOR REQUEST

Article 17

Without prejudice to the provisions of Chapters V and VI, the competent authority of each Member State shall, by automatic or structured automatic exchange, forward the information referred to in Article 1 to the competent authority of any other Member State concerned, in the following cases:

1. Where taxation is deemed to take place in the Member State of destination and the effectiveness of the control system necessarily depends on the information provided by the Member State of origin;
2. Where a Member State has grounds to believe that a breach of VAT legislation has been committed or is likely to have been committed in the other Member State;
3. Where there is a risk of tax loss in the other Member State.

Prospective amendments—New para to be inserted at end, by Council Regulation 143/2008/EC of 12 February 2008, art 2(4) with effect from 1 January 2015.

Article 18

The following shall be determined in accordance with the procedure referred to in Article 44(2):

1. The exact categories of information to be exchanged;
2. The frequency of the exchanges;
3. The practical arrangements for the exchange of information.

Each Member State shall determine whether it will take part in the exchange of a particular category of information, as well as whether it will do so in an automatic or structured automatic way.

Prospective amendments—Second para to be substituted by Council Regulation 143/2008/EC of 12 February 2008, art 2(5) with effect from 1 January 2015.

Article 19

The competent authorities of the Member States may, in any case by spontaneous exchange, forward to each other, any information referred to in Article 1 of which they are aware.

Article 20

Member States shall take the necessary administrative and organisational measures to facilitate the exchanges provided for in this Chapter.

Article 21

A Member State cannot be obliged, for the purposes of implementing the provisions of this Chapter, to impose new obligations on persons liable for VAT with a view to collecting information nor to bear disproportionate administrative burdens.

CHAPTER V—STORAGE AND EXCHANGE OF INFORMATION SPECIFIC TO INTRA-COMMUNITY TRANSACTIONS

Article 22

[1. Each Member State shall maintain an electronic database in which it stores and processes the information which it collects pursuant to Chapter 6 of Title XI of Directive 2006/112/EC.][1]

To enable that information to be used in the procedures provided for in this Regulation, the information shall be stored for at least five years from the end of the calendar year in which access to the information is to be granted.

2. Member States shall ensure that their databases are kept up to date, and are complete and accurate.

Criteria shall be defined, in accordance with the procedure referred to in Article 44(2), to determine which changes are not pertinent, essential or useful and therefore need not be made.

Amendments—[1] Para substituted by Council Regulation 143/2008/EC of 12 February 2008, art 1(3) with effect from 1 January 2010. Text previously read as follows—

"1. Each Member State shall maintain an electronic database in which it shall store and process the information that it collects in accordance with Article 22(6)(*b*) in the version given in Article 28h of Directive 77/388/EEC.".

Article 23

On the basis of the data stored in accordance with Article 22, the competent authority of a Member State shall have communicated to it automatically and without delay by any other Member State the following information, to which it may also have direct access:

1. VAT identification numbers issued by the Member State receiving the information;

[2. the total value of all intra-Community supplies of goods and the total value of all intra-Community supplies of services to persons holding a VAT identification number by all operators identified for the purposes of VAT in the Member State providing the information.][1]

[The values referred to in point 2 of the first paragraph shall be expressed in the currency of the Member State providing the information and shall relate to the periods for submission of the recapitulative statements specific to each taxable person which are established in accordance with Article 263 of Directive 2006/112/EC.][2]

Amendments—[1] In point 2, first sub-para substituted by Council Regulation 143/2008/EC of 12 February 2008, art 1(4) with effect from 1 January 2010. Text previously read as follows—

"2. the total value of all intra-Community supplies of goods to persons holding a VAT identification number by all operators identified for the purposes of VAT in the Member State providing the information.".

[2] Second para substituted by Council Regulation (EC) No 37/2009 of 16 December 2008, art 1(1) with effect from 1 January 2010. Text previously read as follows—

"The values referred to in point 2 shall be expressed in the currency of the Member State providing the information and shall relate to calendar quarters.".

Article 24

[On the basis of the data stored in accordance with Article 22 and solely in order to prevent a breach of VAT legislation, the competent authority of a Member State shall, wherever it considers it necessary for the control of intra-Community acquisitions of goods or intra-Community supplies of services taxable in its territory, obtain directly and without delay, or have direct access to by electronic means, any of the following information:

1. the VAT identification numbers of the persons who carried out the supplies of goods and services referred to in point 2 of the first paragraph of Article 23;

2. the total value of supplies of goods and services from each such person to each person holding a VAT identification number referred to in point 1 of the first paragraph of Article 23.][1]

[The values referred to in point 2 of the first paragraph shall be expressed in the currency of the Member State providing the information and shall relate to the periods for submission of the recapitulative statements specific to each taxable person which are established in accordance with Article 263 of Directive 2006/112/EC.][2]

Amendments—[1] First para substituted by Council Regulation 143/2008/EC of 12 February 2008, art 1(5) with effect from 1 January 2010. Text previously read as follows—

"On the basis of the data stored in accordance with Article 22 and solely in order to prevent a breach of VAT legislation, the competent authority of a Member State shall, wherever it considers it necessary for the control of intra-Community acquisitions of goods, obtain directly and without delay, or have direct access to by electronic means, any of the following information:

1. The VAT identification numbers of the persons who effected the supplies referred to in point 2 of Article 23; and

2. The total value of such supplies from each such person to each person holding a VAT identification number referred to in point 1 of Article 23.".

[2] Second para substituted by Council Regulation (EC) No 37/2009 of 16 December 2008, art 1(2) with effect from 1 January 2010. Text previously read as follows—

"The values referred to in point 2 shall be expressed in the currency of the Member State providing the information and shall relate to calendar quarters.".

Article 25

[1. Where the competent authority of a Member State is obliged to grant access to information under Articles 23 and 24, it shall do so as soon as possible and, at the latest, within one month of the end of the period to which the information relates.

2. By way of derogation from paragraph 1, where information is added to a database in the circumstances provided for in Article 22, access to such additional information shall be granted as quickly as possible and no later than one month after the end of the period in which it was collected.][1]

3. The conditions under which access to the corrected information may be granted shall be laid down in accordance with the procedure referred to in Article 44(2).

Amendments—[1] Paras 1, 2 substituted by Council Regulation (EC) No 37/2009 of 16 December 2008, art 1(3) with effect from 1 January 2010. Text previously read as follows—

"1. Where the competent authority of a Member State is obliged to grant access to information under Articles 23 and 24, it shall do so as soon as possible and within three months at the latest of the end of the calendar quarter to which the information relates.

2. By way of derogation from paragraph 1, where information is added to a database in the circumstances provided for in Article 22, access to such additional information shall be granted as quickly as possible and no later than three months from the end of the quarter in which it was collected.".

Article 26

Where, for the purposes of Articles 22 to 25, the competent authorities of the Member States store information in electronic databases and exchange such information by electronic means, they shall take all measures necessary to ensure compliance with Article 41.

Article 27

1. Each Member State shall maintain an electronic database containing a register of persons to whom VAT identification numbers have been issued in that Member State.

2. At any time the competent authority of a Member State may obtain directly or have communicated to it, from the data stored in accordance with Article 22, confirmation of the validity of the VAT identification number under which a person has effected or received an intra-Community supply of goods or services.

On specific request, the requested authority shall also communicate the date of issue and, where appropriate, the expiry date of the VAT identification number.

3. On request, the competent authority shall also provide without delay the name and address of the person to whom the number has been issued, provided that such information is not stored by the requesting authority with a view to possible use at some future time.

[4. The competent authorities of each Member State shall ensure that persons involved in the intra-Community supply of goods or of services and, for the period provided for in Article 357 of Directive 2006/112/EC, non-established taxable persons supplying electronically supplied services, in particular those referred to in Annex II of that Directive, are allowed to obtain confirmation of the validity of the VAT identification number of any specified person.

During the period provided for in Article 357 of Directive 2006/112/EC, the Member States shall provide such confirmation by electronic means in accordance with the procedure referred to in Article 44(2) of this Regulation.][1]

5. Where, for the purposes of paragraphs 1 to 4, the competent authorities of the Member States store information in electronic databases and exchange such information by electronic means, they shall take all measures necessary to ensure compliance with Article 41.

Amendments—[1] Para (4) substituted by Council Regulation 143/2008/EC of 12 February 2008, art 1(6) with effect from 1 January 2010. Text previously read as follows—

"4. The competent authorities of each Member State shall ensure that persons involved in the intra-Community supply of goods or of services and, for the period provided for in Article 4 of Directive 2002/38/EC, persons supplying services referred to in the last indent of Article 9(2)e of Directive 77/388/EEC are allowed to obtain confirmation of the validity of the VAT identification number of any specified person.

For the period provided for in Article 4 of Directive 2002/38/EC Member States shall, in particular, provide such confirmation by electronic means in accordance with the procedure referred to in Article 44(2).".

Prospective amendments—Para 4 to be further substituted by Council Regulation 143/2008/EC of 12 February 2008, art 2(6) with effect from 1 January 2015.

CHAPTER VI—[PROVISIONS CONCERNING THE SPECIAL SCHEME IN CHAPTER 6 OF TITLE XII OF DIRECTIVE 2006/112/EC][1]

Amendments—[1] Heading substituted by Council Regulation 143/2008/EC of 12 February 2008, art 1(7) with effect from 1 January 2010. Text previously read as follows—

"Provisions concerning the special scheme in Article 26c of Directive 77/388/EEC".

Prospective amendments—Heading to be further substituted by Council Regulation 143/2008/EC of 12 February 2008, art 2(7) with effect from 1 January 2015.

[Article 28

The following provisions shall apply concerning the special scheme provided for in Chapter 6 of Title XII of Directive 2006/112/EC. The definitions contained in Article 358 of that Directive shall also apply for the purpose of this Chapter.][1]

Amendments—[1] Article 28 substituted by Council Regulation 143/2008/EC of 12 February 2008, art 1(8) with effect from 1 January 2010. Text previously read as follows—

"Article 28

The following provisions shall apply concerning the special scheme provided for in Article 26c in Directive 77/388/EEC. The definitions contained in point A of that Article shall also apply for the purpose of this Chapter.".

Prospective amendments—Article to be further substituted by Council Regulation 143/2008/EC of 12 February 2008, art 2(8) with effect from 1 January 2015.

Article 29

[1. The information provided by the taxable person not established in the Community to the Member State of identification when his activities commence pursuant to Article 361 of Directive 2006/112/EC shall be submitted in an electronic manner. The technical details, including a common electronic message, shall be determined in accordance with the procedure provided for in Article 44(2) of this Regulation.][1]

2. The Member State of identification shall transmit this information by electronic means to the competent authorities of the other Member States within 10 days from the end of the month during which the information was received from the non-established taxable person. In the same manner the competent authorities of the other Member States shall be informed of the allocated identification number. The technical details, including a common electronic message, by which this information is to be transmitted, shall be determined in accordance with the procedure provided for in Article 44(2).

3. The Member State of identification shall without delay inform by electronic means the competent authorities of the other Members States if a non-established taxable person is excluded from the identification register.

Amendments—[1] Para 1 substituted by Council Regulation 143/2008/EC of 12 February 2008, art 1(9) with effect from 1 January 2010. Text previously read as follows—

"1. The information from the non-established taxable person to the Member State of identification when his activities commence set out in the second subparagraph of Article 26c(B)(2) of Directive 77/388/EEC is to be submitted in an electronic manner. The technical details, including a common electronic message, shall be determined in accordance with the procedure provided for in Article 44(2).".

Prospective amendments—Article to be substituted by Council Regulation 143/2008/EC of 12 February 2008, art 2(9) with effect from 1 January 2015.

Article 30

[The return with the details set out in Article 365 of Directive 2006/112/EC is to be submitted in an electronic manner. The technical details, including a common electronic message, shall be determined in accordance with the procedure provided for in Article 44(2) of this Regulation.][1]

The Member State of identification shall transmit this information by electronic means to the competent authority of the Member State concerned at the latest 10 days after the end of the month that the return was received. Member States which have required the tax return to be made in a national currency other than euro, shall convert the amounts into euro using the exchange rate valid for the last date of the reporting period. The exchange shall be done following the exchange rates published by the European Central Bank for that day, or, if there is no publication on that day, on the next day of publication. The technical details by which this information is to be transmitted shall be determined in accordance with the procedure provided for in Article 44(2).

The Member State of identification shall transmit by electronic means to the Member State of consumption the information needed to link each payment with a relevant quarterly tax return.

Amendments—[1] First para substituted by Council Regulation 143/2008/EC of 12 February 2008, art 1(10) with effect from 1 January 2010. Text previously read as follows—

"The return with the details set out in the second subparagraph of Article 26c(B)(5) of Directive 77/388/EEC is to be submitted in an electronic manner. The technical details, including a common electronic message, shall be determined in accordance with the procedure provided for in Article 44(2).".

Prospective amendments—First para to be further substituted and second para to be substituted, by Council Regulation 143/2008/EC of 12 February 2008, art 2(10) with effect from 1 January 2015.

[Article 31

The provisions in Article 22 of this Regulation shall apply also to information collected by the Member State of identification in accordance with Articles 360, 361, 364 and 365 of Directive 2006/112/EC.][1]

Amendments—[1] Article 31 substituted by Council Regulation 143/2008/EC of 12 February 2008, art 1(11) with effect from 1 January 2010. Text previously read as follows—

"Article 31

The provisions in Article 22 shall apply also to information collected by the Member State of identification in accordance with Article 26c(B)(2) and (5) of Directive 77/388/EEC.".

Prospective amendments—Article to be further substituted by Council Regulation 143/2008/EC of 12 February 2008, art 2(11) with effect from 1 January 2015.

Article 32

The Member State of identification shall ensure that the amount the non-established taxable person has paid is transferred to the bank account denominated in euro, which has been designated by the Member State of consumption to which the payment is due. Member States which required the payments in a national currency other than euro, shall convert the amounts into euro using the exchange rate valid for the last date of the reporting period. The exchange shall be done following the exchange rates published by the European Central Bank for that day, or, if there is no publication on that day, on the next day of publication. The transfer shall take place at the latest 10 days after the end of the month that the payment was received.

If the non-established taxable person does not pay the total tax due, the Member State of identification shall ensure that the payment is transferred to the Member States of consumption in proportion to the tax due in each Member State. The Member State of identification shall inform by electronic means the competent authorities of the Member States of consumption thereof.

Prospective amendments—New para to be inserted at end, by Council Regulation 143/2008/EC of 12 February 2008, art 2(12) with effect from 1 January 2015.

Article 33

Member States shall notify by electronic means the competent authorities of the other Member States of the relevant bank account numbers for receiving payments according to Article 32.

Member States shall without delay notify by electronic means the competent authorities of the other Member States and the Commission of changes in the standard tax rate.

[Article 34

Articles 28 to 33 of this Regulation shall apply for the period provided for in Article 357 of Directive 2006/112/EC.][1]

Amendments—[1] Article 34 substituted by Council Regulation 143/2008/EC of 12 February 2008, art 1(12) with effect from 1 January 2010. Text previously read as follows—

"**Article 34**

Articles 28 to 33 shall apply for a period provided for in Article 4 of Directive 2002/38/EC.".

Prospective amendments—Article to be repealed by Council Regulation 143/2008/EC of 12 February 2008, art 2(13) with effect from 1 January 2015.

CHAPTER VIA—PROVISIONS CONCERNING THE EXCHANGE AND CONSERVATION OF INFORMATION IN THE CONTEXT OF THE PROCEDURE PROVIDED FOR IN DIRECTIVE 2008/9/EC

Article 34a

1. Where the competent authority of the Member State of establishment receives an application for refund of value added tax under Article 5 of Directive 2008/9/EC of 12 February 2008 laying down detailed rules for the refund of value added tax, provided for in Directive 2006/112/EC, to taxable persons not established in the Member State of refund but established in another Member State* and Article 18 of that Directive is not applicable, it shall, within 15 calendar days of its receipt and by electronic means, forward the application to the competent authorities of each Member State of refund concerned with confirmation that the applicant as defined in Article 2(5) of Directive 2008/9/EC is a taxable person for the purposes of value added tax and that the identification or registration number given by this person is valid for the refund period.

2. The competent authorities of each Member State of refund shall notify by electronic means the competent authorities of the other Member States of any information required by them under Article 9(2) of Directive 2008/9/EC. The technical details, including a common electronic message by which this information is to be transmitted, shall be determined in accordance with the procedure provided for in Article 44(2) of this Regulation.

3. The competent authorities of each Member State of refund shall notify by electronic means the competent authorities of the other Member States if they want to make use of the option to require the applicant to provide the description of business activity by harmonised codes as referred to in Article 11 of Directive 2008/9/EC.

The harmonised codes referred to in the first subparagraph shall be determined in accordance with the procedure provided for in Article 44(2) of this Regulation on the basis of the NACE classification established by Regulation (EEC) No 3037/90.][1]

Note—* OJ L 44, 20.2.2008 p 23.

Amendments—[1] Chapter VIa inserted by Council Regulation 143/2008/EC of 12 February 2008, art 1(13) with effect from 1 January 2010.

CHAPTER VII—RELATIONS WITH THE COMMISSION

Article 35

1. The Member States and the Commission shall examine and evaluate how the arrangements for administrative cooperation provided for in this Regulation are working. The Commission shall pool the Member States' experience with the aim of improving the operation of those arrangements.

2. The Member States shall communicate to the Commission any available information relevant to their application of this Regulation.

3. A list of statistical data needed for evaluation of this Regulation shall be determined in accordance with the procedure referred to in Article 44(2). The Member States shall communicate these data to the Commission in so far as they are available and the communication is not likely to involve administrative burdens which would be unjustified.

4. With a view to evaluating the effectiveness of this system of administrative cooperation in combating tax evasion and tax avoidance, Member States may communicate to the Commission any other information referred to in Article 1.

5. The Commission shall forward the information referred to in paragraphs 2, 3 and 4 to the other Member States concerned.

CHAPTER VIII—RELATIONS WITH THIRD COUNTRIES

Article 36

1. When the competent authority of a Member State receives information from a third country, that authority may pass the information on to the competent authorities of Member States which might be interested in it and, in any event, to all those which request it, in so far as permitted by assistance arrangements with that particular third country.

2. Provided the third country concerned has given an undertaking to provide the assistance required to gather evidence of the irregular nature of transactions which appear to contravene VAT legislation, information obtained under this Regulation may be communicated to that third country, with the consent of the competent authorities which supplied the information, in accordance with their domestic provisions applying to the communication of personal data to third countries.

CHAPTER IX—CONDITIONS GOVERNING THE EXCHANGE OF INFORMATION

Article 37

Information communicated pursuant to this Regulation shall, as far as possible, be provided by electronic means under arrangements to be adopted in accordance with the procedure referred to in Article 44(2).

Article 38

Requests for assistance, including requests for notification, and attached documents may be made in any language agreed between the requested and requesting authority. The said requests shall only be accompanied by a translation into the official language or one of the official languages of the Member State in which the requested authority is established, in special cases when the requested authority gives a reason for asking for such a translation.

Article 39

[For the period provided for in Article 357 of Directive 2006/112/EC, the Commission and the Member States shall ensure that such existing or new communication and information exchange systems which are necessary to provide for the exchanges of information described in Articles 29 and 30 of this Regulation are operational. The Commission will be responsible for whatever development of the common communication network/common system interface (CCN/CSI) is necessary to permit the exchange of this information between Member States. Member States will be responsible for whatever development of their systems is necessary to permit this information to be exchanged using the CCN/CSI.][1]

Member States shall waive all claims for the reimbursement of expenses incurred in applying this Regulation except, where appropriate, in respect of fees paid to experts.

Amendments—[1] First para substituted by Council Regulation 143/2008/EC of 12 February 2008, art 1(14) with effect from 1 January 2010. Text previously read as follows—

"For the period provided for in Article 4 of Directive 2002/38/EC, the Commission and the Member States shall ensure that such existing or new communication and information exchange systems which are necessary to provide for the exchanges of information described in Articles 29 and 30 are operational. The Commission will be responsible for whatever development of the common communication network/common system interface (CCN/CSI) is necessary to permit the exchange of this information between Member States. Member States will be responsible for whatever development of their systems is necessary to permit this information to be exchanged using the CCN/CSI.".

Prospective amendments—First para to be further substituted by Council Regulation 143/2008/EC of 12 February 2008, art 2(14) with effect from 1 January 2015.

Article 40

1. The requested authority in one Member State shall provide a requesting authority in another Member State with the information referred to in Article 1 provided that:

(*a*) the number and the nature of the requests for information made by the requesting authority within a specific period do not impose a disproportionate administrative burden on that requested authority;

(*b*) that requesting authority has exhausted the usual sources of information which it could have used in the circumstances to obtain the information requested, without running the risk of jeopardising the achievement of the desired end.

2. This Regulation shall impose no obligation to have enquiries carried out or to provide information if the laws or administrative practices of the Member State which would have to supply the information do not authorise the Member State to carry out those enquiries or collect or use that information for that Member State's own purposes.

3. The competent authority of a Member State may refuse to provide information where the Member State concerned is unable, for legal reasons, to provide similar information. The Commission shall be informed of the grounds of the refusal by the requested Member State.

4. The provision of information may be refused where it would lead to the disclosure of a commercial, industrial or professional secret or of a commercial process, or of information whose disclosure would be contrary to public policy.

5. The requested authority shall inform the requesting authority of the grounds for refusing a request for assistance.

6. A minimum threshold triggering a request for assistance may be adopted in accordance with the procedure referred to in Article 44(2).

Article 41

1. Information communicated in any form pursuant to this Regulation shall be covered by the obligation of official secrecy and enjoy the protection extended to similar information under both the national law of the Member State which received it and the corresponding provisions applicable to Community authorities.

Such information may be used for the purpose of establishing the assessment base or the collection or administrative control of tax for the purpose of establishing the assessment base.

The information may also be used for the assessment of other levies, duties, and taxes covered by Article 2 of Council Directive 76/308/EEC of 15 March 1976 on mutual assistance for the recovery of claims relating to certain levies, duties, taxes and other measures.

In addition, it may be used in connection with judicial proceedings that may involve penalties, initiated as a result of infringements of tax law without prejudice to the general rules and legal provisions governing the rights of defendants and witnesses in such proceedings.

2. Persons duly accredited by the Security Accreditation Authority of the European Commission may have access to this information only in so far as it is necessary for care, maintenance and development of the CCN/CSI network.

3. By way of derogation from paragraph 1, the competent authority of the Member State providing the information shall permit its use for other purposes in the Member State of the requesting authority, if, under the legislation of the Member State of the requested authority, the information can be used for similar purposes.

4. Where the requesting authority considers that information it has received from the requested authority is likely to be useful to the competent authority of a third Member State, it may transmit it to the latter authority. It shall inform the requested authority thereof in advance. The requested authority may require that the transmission of the information to a third party be subject to its prior agreement.

5. Member States shall, for the purpose of the correct application of this Regulation, restrict the scope of the obligations and rights provided for in Article 10, Article 11(1), Articles 12 and 21 of Directive 95/46/EC to the extent required in order to safeguard the interests referred to in Article 13(e) of that Directive.

Article 42

Reports, statements and any other documents, or certified true copies or extracts thereof, obtained by the staff of the requested authority and communicated to the requesting authority under the assistance provided for by this Regulation may be invoked as evidence by the competent bodies of the Member State of the requesting authority on the same basis as similar documents provided by another authority of that country.

Article 43

1. For the purpose of applying this Regulation, Member States shall take all necessary measures to:

(*a*) ensure effective internal coordination between the competent authorities referred to in Article 3;

(*b*) establish direct cooperation between the authorities authorised for the purposes of such coordination;

(*c*) ensure the smooth operation of the information exchange arrangements provided for in this Regulation.

2. The Commission shall communicate to each Member State, as quickly as possible, any information which it receives and which it is able to provide.

CHAPTER X—GENERAL AND FINAL PROVISIONS

Article 44

1. The Commission shall be assisted by the Standing Committee on Administrative Cooperation, (hereinafter referred to as the Committee).

2. Where reference is made to this paragraph, Articles 5 and 7 of Decision 1999/468/EC shall apply, having regard to the provisions of Article 8 thereof.

The period laid down in Article 5(6) of Decision 1999/468/EC shall be set at three months.

3. The Committee shall adopt its rules of procedure.

Article 45

1. Every three years from the date of entry into force of this Regulation, the Commission shall report to the European Parliament and the Council on the application of this Regulation.

2. Member States shall communicate to the Commission the text of any provisions of national law, which they adopt in the field covered by this Regulation.

Article 46

1. The provisions of this Regulation shall be without prejudice to the fulfilment of any wider obligations in relation to mutual assistance ensuing from other legal acts, including bilateral or multilateral agreements.

2. Where the Member States conclude bilateral arrangements on matters covered by this Regulation other than to deal with individual cases, they shall inform the Commission without delay. The Commission shall in turn inform the other Member States.

Article 47

Regulation (EEC) No 218/92 is hereby repealed.

References made to the repealed Regulation shall be construed as references to this Regulation.

Article 48

This Regulation shall enter into force on 1 January 2004.

This Regulation shall be binding in its entirety and directly applicable in all Member States.

Regulation of the European Parliament and of the Council of 31 March 2004 on Community statistics relating to the trading of goods between Member States and repealing Council Regulation (EEC) No 3330/91

(638/2004/EC)

THE EUROPEAN PARLIAMENT AND THE COUNCIL OF THE EUROPEAN UNION,

Having regard to the Treaty establishing the European Community, and in particular Article 285(1) thereof,

Having regard to the proposal from the Commission,

Having regard to the opinion of the European Economic and Social Committee,

Acting in accordance with the procedure laid down in Article 251 of the Treaty,

Whereas:

(1) Council Regulation (EEC) No 3330/91 of 7 November 1991 on the statistics relating to the trading of goods between Member States(3) introduced a completely new system of data collection, which has been simplified on two occasions. In order to improve the transparency of this system and to make it easier to understand, Regulation (EEC) No 3330/91 should be replaced by this Regulation.

(2) This system should be retained, as a sufficiently detailed level of statistical information is still required for the Community policies involved in the development of the internal market and for Community enterprises to analyse their specific markets. Aggregated data also need to be available quickly in order to analyse the development of the Economic and Monetary Union. Member States should have the possibility of collecting information which meets their specific needs.

(3) There is, however, a need to improve the wording of the rules on compiling statistics relating to the trading of goods between Member States so that they can be more easily understood by the companies responsible for providing the data, the national services collecting the data and users.

(4) A system of thresholds should be retained, but in a simplified form, in order to provide a satisfactory response to users' needs whilst reducing the burden of response on the parties responsible for providing statistical information, particularly small and medium-sized enterprises.

(5) A close link should be maintained between the system for collecting statistical information and the fiscal formalities which exist in the context of trade of goods between Member States. This link makes it possible, in particular, to check the quality of the information collected.

(6) The quality of the statistical information produced, its evaluation by means of common indicators and transparency in this field are important objectives, which call for regulation at Community level.

(7) Since the objective of the planned action, namely the creation of a common legal framework for the systematic production of Community statistics relating to the trading of goods between Member States, cannot be sufficiently achieved at national level and can be better achieved at

Community level, the Community may adopt measures, in accordance with the principle of subsidiarity as set out in Article 5 of the Treaty. In accordance with the principle of proportionality, as set out in that Article, this Regulation does not go beyond what is required to achieve this objective.

(8) Council Regulation (EC) No 322/97 of 17 February 1997 on Community statistics provides a reference framework for this Regulation. However, the very detailed level of information in the field of statistics relating to the trading of goods requires specific rules with regard to confidentiality.

(9) It is important to ensure the uniform application of this Regulation and, in order to do so, to make provision for a Community procedure to help determine the implementing arrangements within an appropriate timescale and to make the necessary technical adaptations.

(10) The measures necessary for implementation of this Regulation should be adopted in accordance with Council Decision 1999/468/EC of 28 June 1999 laying down the procedures for the exercise of implementing powers conferred on the Commission,

HAVE ADOPTED THIS REGULATION:

Article 1

Subject matter

This Regulation establishes a common framework for the systematic production of Community statistics relating to the trading of goods between Member States.

Article 2

Definitions

For the purpose of this Regulation, the following definitions shall apply:

(*a*) "goods": all movable property, including electric current;

(*b*) "specific goods or movements": goods or movements which, by their very nature, call for specific provisions, and in particular industrial plants, vessels and aircraft, sea products, goods delivered to vessels and aircraft, staggered consignments, military goods, goods to or from offshore installations, spacecraft, motor vehicle and aircraft parts and waste products;

(*c*) "national authorities": national statistical institutes and other bodies responsible in each Member State for producing Community statistics relating to the trading of goods between Member States;

(*d*) "Community goods":

(i) goods entirely obtained in the customs territory of the Community, without addition of goods from third countries or territories which are not part of the customs territory of the Community;

(ii) goods from third countries or territories which are not part of the customs territory of the Community, which have been released for free circulation in a Member State;

(iii) goods obtained in the customs territory of the Community either from the goods referred to exclusively in point (ii) or from the goods referred to in points (i) and (ii);

(*e*) "Member State of dispatch": the Member State as defined by its statistical territory from which goods are dispatched to a destination in another Member State;

(*f*) "Member State of arrival": the Member State as defined by its statistical territory in which goods arrive from another Member State;

(*g*) "goods in simple circulation between Member States": Community goods dispatched from one Member State to another, which, on the way to the Member State of destination, travel directly through another Member State or stop for reasons related only to the transport of the goods.

Article 3

Scope

1. Statistics relating to the trading of goods between Member States shall cover dispatches and arrivals of goods.

2. Dispatches shall cover the following goods leaving the Member State of dispatch for a destination in another Member State:

(*a*) Community goods, except goods which are in simple circulation between Member States;

(*b*) goods placed in the Member State of dispatch under the inward processing customs procedure or the processing under customs control procedure.

3. Arrivals shall cover the following goods entering the Member State of arrival, which were initially dispatched from another Member State:

(*a*) Community goods, except goods which are in simple circulation between Member States;

(*b*) goods formerly placed in the Member State of dispatch according to the inward processing customs procedure or the processing according to customs control procedure, which are maintained according to the inward processing customs procedure or the processing according to customs control procedure or released for free circulation in the Member State of arrival.

[4. The Commission may adopt different or specific rules applying to specific goods or movements. Those measures, designed to amend non-essential elements of this Regulation, inter alia, by supplementing it, shall be adopted in accordance with the regulatory procedure with scrutiny referred to in Article 14(3).][1]

5. Some goods, a list of which shall be drawn up in accordance with the procedure referred to in Article 14(2), shall be excluded from the statistics for methodological reasons.

Amendments—[1] Para 4 substituted by Parliament and Council Regulation 222/2009 of 11 March 2009 art 1(1) with effect from 1 January 2010. Text previously read as follows—

"4. Different or specific rules, to be determined in accordance with the procedure referred to in Article 14(2), may apply to specific goods or movements.".

Article 4

Statistical territory

1. The statistical territory of the Member States shall correspond to their customs territory as defined in Article 3 of Council Regulation (EEC) No 2913/92 of 12 October 1992 establishing the Community Customs Code.

2. By way of derogation from paragraph 1, the statistical territory of Germany shall include Heligoland.

Article 5

Data sources

1. A specific data collection system, hereinafter referred to as the "Intrastat" system, shall apply for the provision of the statistical information on dispatches and arrivals of Community goods which are not the subject of a single administrative document for customs or fiscal purposes.

2. The statistical information on dispatches and arrivals of other goods shall be provided directly by customs to the national authorities, at least once a month.

3. For specific goods or movements, sources of information other than the Intrastat system or customs declarations may be used.

4. Each Member State shall organise the way Intrastat data is supplied by the parties responsible for providing information. To facilitate the task of these parties, the conditions for increased use of automatic data processing and electronic data transmission shall be promoted by the Commission (Eurostat) and the Member States.

Article 6

Reference period

1. The reference period for the information to be provided in accordance with Article 5 shall be the calendar month of dispatch or arrival of the goods.

[2. The reference period may be adapted by the Commission to take into account the linkage with value added tax (VAT) and customs obligations. Those measures, designed to amend non-essential elements of this Regulation, inter alia, by supplementing it, shall be adopted in accordance with the regulatory procedure with scrutiny referred to in Article 14(3).][1]

Amendments—[1] Para 2 substituted by Parliament and Council Regulation 222/2009 of 11 March 2009 art 1(2) with effect from 1 January 2010. Text previously read as follows—

"2. The reference period may be adapted to take into account the linkage with value added tax (VAT) and customs obligations, pursuant to provisions adopted in accordance with the procedure referred to in Article 14(2).".

Article 7

Parties responsible for providing information

[1. The parties responsible for providing the information for the Intrastat system shall be:

(*a*) the taxable person as defined in Title III of Council Directive 2006/112/EC of 28 November 2006 on the common system of value added tax, in the Member State of dispatch, who:

(i) has concluded the contract, with the exception of transport contracts, giving rise to the dispatch of goods or, failing that;

(ii) dispatches or provides for the dispatch of the goods or, failing that;

(iii) is in possession of the goods which are the subject of the dispatch;

or its tax representative in accordance with Article 204 of Directive 2006/112/EC; and

(*b*) the taxable person as defined in Title III of Directive 2006/112/EC, in the Member State of arrival, who:

(i) has concluded the contract, with the exception of transport contracts, giving rise to the delivery of goods or, failing that;

(ii) takes delivery or provides for delivery of the goods or, failing that;

(iii) is in possession of the goods which are the subject of the delivery;

or its tax representative in accordance with Article 204 of Directive 2006/112/EC.][1]

2. The parties responsible for providing information may transfer the task to a third party, but such transfer shall in no way reduce the responsibility of the said party.

3. Failure by any party responsible for providing information to fulfil his/her obligations under this Regulation shall render him/her liable to the penalties which the Member States shall lay down.

Amendments—[1] Para 1 substituted by Parliament and Council Regulation 222/2009 of 11 March 2009 art 1(3) with effect from 1 January 2010. Text previously read as follows—

"1. The parties responsible for providing the information for the Intrastat system shall be:

(*a*) the natural or legal person registered for VAT in the Member State of dispatch who:

(i) has concluded the contract, with the exception of transport contracts, giving rise to the dispatch of goods or, failing that,

(ii) dispatches or provides for the dispatch of the goods or, failing that,

(iii) is in possession of the goods which are the subject of the dispatch;

(*b*) the natural or legal person registered for VAT in the Member State of arrival who:

(i) has concluded the contract, with the exception of transport contracts, giving rise to the delivery of goods or, failing that,

(ii) takes delivery or provides for delivery of the goods or, failing that,

(iii) is in possession of the goods which are the subject of the delivery.".

Article 8

Registers

1. National authorities shall set up and manage a register of intra-Community operators containing at least the consignors, upon dispatch, and the consignees, upon arrival.

2. In order to identify the parties responsible for providing information referred to in Article 7 and to check the information which is provided, the tax administration responsible in each Member State shall furnish the national authority:

[(*a*) at least once a month, with the lists of taxable persons who have declared that, during the period in question, they have supplied goods to other Member States or acquired goods from other Member States. The lists shall show the total values of the goods declared by each taxable person for fiscal purposes;][1]

(*b*) on its own initiative or at the request of the national authority, with any information provided for fiscal purposes which could improve the quality of statistics.

The arrangements for the communication of the information shall be determined in accordance with the procedure referred to in Article 14(2).

This information shall be treated by the national authority in accordance with the rules applied to it by the tax administration.

3. The tax administration shall bring to the attention of VAT-registered traders the obligations which they may incur as parties responsible for providing the information required by Intrastat.

Amendments—[1] Para 2(*a*) substituted by Parliament and Council Regulation 222/2009 of 11 March 2009 art 1(3) with effect from 1 January 2010. Text previously read as follows—

"(*a*) at least once a month, with the lists of natural or legal persons who have declared that, during the period in question, they have supplied goods to other Member States or acquired goods from other Member States. The lists shall show the total values of the goods declared by each natural or legal person for fiscal purposes;".

Article 9

Intrastat information to be collected

1. The following information shall be collected by the national authorities:

[(*a*) the individual identification number allocated to the party responsible for providing information in accordance with Article 214 of Directive 2006/112/EC;][1]

(*b*) the reference period;

(*c*) the flow (arrival, dispatch);

(*d*) the commodity, identified by the eight-digit code of the Combined Nomenclature as defined in Council Regulation (EEC) No 2658/87 of 23 July 1987 on the tariff and statistical nomenclature and on the Common Customs Tariff;

(*e*) the partner Member State;

(*f*) the value of the goods;

(*g*) the quantity of the goods;

(*h*) the nature of the transaction.

Definitions of the statistical data referred to in points (*e*) to (*h*) are given in the Annex. Where necessary, the arrangements for the collection of this information, particularly the codes to be employed, shall be determined in accordance with the procedure referred to in Article 14(2).

2. Member States may also collect additional information, for example:

(*a*) the identification of the goods, at a more detailed level than the Combined Nomenclature;

(*b*) the country of origin, on arrival;

(*c*) the region of origin, on dispatch, and the region of destination, on arrival;

(*d*) the delivery terms;

(*e*) the mode of transport;

(*f*) the statistical procedure.

[Definitions of the statistical data referred to in points (*e*) to (*h*) are given in the Annex. Where necessary, the Commission shall determine the arrangements for the collection of that information, particularly the codes to be employed. Those measures, designed to amend non-essential elements of this Regulation, inter alia, by supplementing it, shall be adopted in accordance with the regulatory procedure with scrutiny referred to in Article 14(3).][1]

Amendments—[1] Para 1(*a*), and final para, substituted by Parliament and Council Regulation 222/2009 of 11 March 2009 art 1(3) with effect from 1 January 2010. Text previously read as follows—

"(*a*) the identification number allocated to the party responsible for providing information in accordance with Article 22(1)(*c*) of the Sixth Council Directive 77/388/EEC of 17 May 1977 on the harmonisation of the laws of the Member States relating to turnover taxes-common system of value added tax: uniform basis of assessment, in the version given in Article 28h thereof;".

"Definitions of the statistical data referred to in points (*b*) to (*f*) are given in the Annex. Where necessary, the arrangements for the collection of this information, particularly the codes to be employed, shall be determined in accordance with the procedure referred to in Article 14(2).".

Article 10

Simplification within the Intrastat system

1. In order to satisfy users' needs for statistical information without imposing excessive burdens on economic operators, Member States shall define each year thresholds expressed in annual values of intra-Community trade, below which parties are exempted from providing any Intrastat information or may provide simplified information.

2. The thresholds shall be defined by each Member State, separately for arrivals and dispatches.

[3. The thresholds below which parties are exempted from providing any Intrastat information shall be set at a level that ensures that the value of at least 97 % of the total dispatches and at least 95 % of the total arrivals of the relevant Member State's taxable persons is covered.

The Commission shall adapt those Intrastat coverage rates to technical and economic developments, whenever it is possible to reduce them while maintaining statistics which meet the quality indicators and standards in force. Those measures, designed to amend non-essential elements of this Regulation, shall be adopted in accordance with the regulatory procedure with scrutiny referred to in Article 14(3).][1]

4. Member States may define other thresholds below which parties may benefit from the following simplification:

(*a*) exemption from providing information about the quantity of the goods;

(*b*) exemption from providing information about the nature of the transaction;

(*c*) possibility of reporting a maximum of 10 of the detailed relevant subheadings of the Combined Nomenclature, that are the most used in terms of value, and regrouping the other products in accordance with rules determined in accordance with the procedure referred to in Article 14(2).

[The Commission shall specify the conditions for defining those thresholds. Those measures, designed to amend non-essential elements of this Regulation, inter alia, by supplementing it, shall be adopted in accordance with the regulatory procedure with scrutiny referred to in Article 14(3).][1]

[5. Member States may under certain conditions, which meet quality requirements, simplify the information to be provided for small individual transactions. The conditions shall be defined by the Commission. Those measures, designed to amend non-essential elements of this Regulation, inter alia, by supplementing it, shall be adopted in accordance with the regulatory procedure with scrutiny referred to in Article 14(3).][1]

6. The information on the thresholds applied by the Member States shall be sent to the Commission (Eurostat) no later than 31 October of the year preceding the year to which they apply.

Amendments—[1] Para 3 substituted, in para 4, second sub-para substituted, and para 5 substituted, by Parliament and Council Regulation 222/2009 of 11 March 2009 art 1(6) with effect from 1 January 2010. Text previously read as follows—

"3. For defining thresholds below which parties are exempted from providing any Intrastat information, Member States shall ensure that information referred to in Article 9(1), first subparagraph, points (*a*) to (*f*), made available by the parties responsible for providing information, is such that at least 97 % of the relevant Member State's total trade expressed in value is covered.".

"Every Member State applying these thresholds shall ensure that the trade of these parties shall amount to a maximum of 6% of its total trade.".

"5. Member States may, under certain conditions, which meet quality requirements and which shall be defined in accordance with the procedure referred to in Article 14(2), simplify the information to be provided for small individual transactions.".

[Article 11

Statistical confidentiality

Only where the party or parties that have provided information so request shall the national authorities decide whether statistical results which may make it possible to identify the said provider(s) are to be disseminated or are to be amended in such a way that their dissemination does not prejudice statistical confidentiality.][1]

Amendments—[1] Article 11 substituted by Parliament and Council Regulation 222/2009 of 11 March 2009 art 1(7) with effect from 1 January 2010. Text previously read as follows—

"Article 11

Statistical confidentiality

Where the parties who have provided information so request, the national authorities shall decide whether statistical results which make it possible indirectly to identify the said provider(s) are to be disseminated or are to be amended in such a way that their dissemination does not prejudice statistical confidentiality.".

Article 12

Transmission of data to the Commission

1. Member States shall transmit to the Commission (Eurostat) the monthly results of their statistics relating to the trading of goods between Member States no later than:

[(*a*) 40 calendar days after the end of the reference month for the aggregated data to be defined by the Commission. Those measures, designed to amend non-essential elements of this Regulation, inter alia, by supplementing it, shall be adopted in accordance with the regulatory procedure with scrutiny referred to in Article 14(3).][1]

(*b*) 70 calendar days after the end of the reference month in the case of detailed results including the information referred to in Article 9(1), first subparagraph, points (*b*) to (*h*).

As regards the value of the goods, the results shall include the statistical value only, as defined in the Annex.

Member States shall transmit to the Commission (Eurostat) the data which are confidential.

2. Member States shall provide the Commission (Eurostat) with monthly results which cover their total trade in goods by using estimates, where necessary.

[The results of the estimates shall comply with criteria defined by the Commission. Those measures, designed to amend non-essential elements of this Regulation, inter alia, by supplementing it, shall be adopted in accordance with the regulatory procedure with scrutiny referred to in Article 14(3).][1]

3. Member States shall transmit the data to the Commission (Eurostat) in electronic form, in accordance with an interchange standard. The practical arrangements for the transmission of data shall be determined in accordance with the procedure referred to in Article 14(2).

[4. Member States shall transmit to the Commission (Eurostat) annual statistics on trade by business characteristics, namely economic activity carried out by the enterprise according to the section or two-digit level of the common statistical classification of economic activities in the European Community (NACE), as established by Regulation (EC) No 1893/2006 of the European Parliament and of the Council, and size-class measured in terms of number of employees.

Those statistics shall be compiled by linking data on business characteristics recorded according to Regulation (EC) No 177/2008 of the European Parliament and of the Council of 20 February 2008 establishing a common framework for business registers for statistical purposes with the statistics referred to in Article 3 of this Regulation.

Implementing provisions for compiling those statistics shall be determined by the Commission. Those measures, designed to amend non-essential elements of this Regulation, inter alia, by supplementing it, shall be adopted in accordance with the regulatory procedure with scrutiny referred to in Article 14(3).][1]

Amendments—[1] Para 1(*a*) substituted, in para 2 words inserted, and para 4 inserted, by Parliament and Council Regulation 222/2009 of 11 March 2009 art 1(8) with effect from 1 January 2010. Text previously read as follows—

"(*a*) 40 calendar days after the end of the reference month for the aggregated data to be defined in accordance with the procedure referred to in Article 14(2);".

[Article 13

Quality

1. For the purposes of this Regulation, the following quality criteria shall apply to the statistics to be transmitted:

(*a*) "relevance", which refers to the degree to which statistics meet current and potential needs of the users;

(*b*) "accuracy", which refers to the closeness of estimates to the unknown true values;

(*c*) "timeliness", which refers to the period between the availability of the information and the event or phenomenon it describes;

(*d*) "punctuality", which refers to the delay between the date of release of the data and the target date (the date by which the data should have been delivered);

(*e*) "accessibility" and "clarity", which refer to the conditions and modalities by which users can obtain, use and interpret data;

(*f*) "comparability", which refers to the measurement of the impact of differences in applied statistical concepts, measurement tools and procedures where statistics are compared between geographical areas, sectoral domains or over time;

(*g*) "coherence", which refers to the adequacy of the data to be reliably combined in different ways and for various uses.

2. Member States shall provide the Commission (Eurostat) with an annual report on the quality of the statistics transmitted.

3. In applying the quality criteria laid down in paragraph 1 to the statistics covered by this Regulation, the modalities and structure of the quality reports shall be defined in accordance with the regulatory procedure referred to in Article 14(2).

The Commission (Eurostat) shall assess the quality of the statistics transmitted.

4. The Commission shall determine any measures necessary to ensure the quality of the statistics transmitted according to the quality criteria. Those measures, designed to amend non-essential elements of this Regulation, inter alia, by supplementing it, shall be adopted in accordance with the regulatory procedure with scrutiny referred to in Article 14(3).][1]

Amendments—[1] Article 13 substituted by Parliament and Council Regulation 222/2009 of 11 March 2009 art 1(9) with effect from 1 January 2010. Text previously read as follows—

"**Article 13**

Quality

1. Member States shall take all measures necessary to ensure the quality of the data transmitted according to the quality indicators and standards in force.

2. Member States shall present to the Commission (Eurostat) a yearly report on the quality of the data transmitted.

3. The indicators and standards enabling the quality of the data to be assessed, the structure of the quality reports to be presented by the Member States and any measures necessary for assessing or improving the quality of the data shall be determined in accordance with the procedure referred to in Article 14(2).".

Article 14

Committee procedure

1. The Commission shall be assisted by a Committee for the statistics on the trading of goods between Member States.

2. Where reference is made to this paragraph, Articles 5 and 7 of Decision 1999/468/EC shall apply, having regard to the provisions of Article 8 thereof.

The period laid down in Article 5(6) of Decision 1999/468/EC shall be set at three months.

[3. Where reference is made to this paragraph, Article 5a(1) to (4), and Article 7 of Decision 1999/468/EC shall apply, having regard to the provisions of Article 8 thereof.][1]

Amendments—[1] Para 3 substituted by Parliament and Council Regulation 222/2009 of 11 March 2009 art 1(10) with effect from 1 January 2010. Text previously read as follows—

"3. The Committee shall adopt its Rules of Procedure.".

Article 15

Repeal

1. Regulation (EEC) No 3330/91 is hereby repealed.

2. References to the repealed regulation shall be construed as being made to this Regulation.

Article 16

Entry into force

This Regulation shall enter into force on the 20th day following that of its publication in the Official Journal of the European Union.

It shall apply from 1 January 2005.

This Regulation shall be binding in its entirety and directly applicable in all Member States.

ANNEX

DEFINITIONS OF STATISTICAL DATA

1. PARTNER MEMBER STATE

(*a*) The partner Member State is the Member State of consignment, on arrival. This means the presumed Member State of dispatch in cases where goods enter directly from another Member State. Where, before reaching the Member State of arrival, goods have entered one or more Member States in transit and have been subject in those States to halts or legal operations not inherent in their transport (eg change of ownership), the Member State of consignment shall be taken as the last Member State where such halts or operations occurred.

(*b*) The partner Member State is the Member State of destination, on dispatch. This means the last Member State to which it is known, at the time of dispatch, that the goods are to be dispatched.

2. QUANTITY OF THE GOODS

The quantity of the goods can be expressed in two ways:

(*a*) the net mass, which means the actual mass of the goods excluding all packaging;

(*b*) the supplementary units, which mean the possible units measuring quantity other than net mass, as detailed in the annual Commission regulation updating the Combined Nomenclature.

3. VALUE OF THE GOODS

The value of the goods can be expressed in two ways:

[(*a*) the taxable amount, which is the value to be determined for taxation purposes in accordance with Directive 2006/112/EC;][1]

(*b*) the statistical value, which is the value calculated at the national borders of the Member States. It includes only incidental expenses (freight, insurance) incurred, in the case of dispatches, in the part of the journey located on the territory of the Member State of dispatch and, in the case of arrivals, in the part of the journey located outside the territory of the Member State of arrival. It is said to be a fob value (free on board) for dispatches, and a cif value (cost, insurance, freight) for arrivals.

Amendments—[1] Para (*a*) substituted by Parliament and Council Regulation 222/2009 of 11 March 2009 art 1(11) with effect from 1 January 2010. Text previously read as follows—

"(*a*) the taxable amount, which is the value to be determined for taxation purposes in accordance with Directive 77/388/EEC;".

4. NATURE OF THE TRANSACTION

The nature of transaction means the different characteristics (purchase/sale, work under contract, etc.) which are deemed to be useful in distinguishing one transaction from another.

5. COUNTRY OF ORIGIN

(*a*) The country of origin, on arrivals only, means the country where the goods originate.

(*b*) Goods which are wholly obtained or produced in a country originate in that country.

(*c*) Goods whose production involved more than one country shall be deemed to originate in the country where they underwent their last, substantial, economically justified processing or working in a company equipped for that purpose, resulting in the manufacture of a new product or representing an important stage of manufacture.

6. REGION OF ORIGIN OR DESTINATION

(*a*) The region of origin, on dispatch, means the region of the Member State of dispatch where the goods were produced or were erected, assembled, processed, repaired or maintained; failing that, the region of origin is the region where the goods were dispatched, or, failing that, the region where the commercial process took place.

(*b*) The region of destination, on arrival, means the region of the Member State of arrival where the goods are to be consumed or erected, assembled, processed, repaired or maintained; failing that, the region of destination is the region to which the goods are to be dispatched, or, failing that, the region where the commercial process is to take place.

7. DELIVERY TERMS

The delivery terms mean those provisions of the sales contract which lay down the obligations of the seller and the buyer respectively, in accordance with the Incoterms of the International Chamber of Commerce (cif, fob, etc.).

8. MODE OF TRANSPORT

The mode of transport is determined by the active means of transport by which the goods are presumed to be going to leave the statistical territory of the Member State of dispatch, on dispatch, and by the active means of transport by which the goods are presumed to have entered the statistical territory of the Member State of arrival, on arrival.

9. STATISTICAL PROCEDURE

The statistical procedure means the different characteristics which are deemed to be useful in distinguishing different types of arrivals/dispatches for statistical purposes.

Commission Regulation
of 29 October 2004
laying down detailed rules for implementing certain provisions of Council Regulation No 1798/2003 concerning administrative cooperation in the field of value-added tax

(1925/04/EC)

Note—See OJ L331 05.11.2004, p 13

THE COMMISSION OF THE EUROPEAN COMMUNITIES,

Having regard to the Treaty establishing the European Community,

Having regard to Council Regulation (EC) No 1798/2003 of 7 October 2003 on administrative cooperation in the field of value-added tax and repealing Regulation (EEC) No 218/92[1] and, in particular Articles 18, 35 and 37 thereof,

Whereas:

(1) The provisions on VAT administrative cooperation laid down in Regulation (EEC) No 218/92 and Council Directive 77/799/EEC of 19 December 1977 concerning mutual assistance by the competent authorities of the Member States in the field of direct taxation, certain excise duties and taxation of insurance premiums[2] have been merged and strengthened in Regulation (EC) No 1798/2003.

(2) It is necessary to specify the exact categories of information to be exchanged without prior request, as well as the frequency with which those exchanges are to be made, and the relevant practical arrangements.

(3) Arrangements should be laid down for the provision of information communicated pursuant to Regulation (EC) No 1798/2003 by electronic means.

(4) Finally, it is necessary to establish a list of the statistical data needed for the evaluation of Regulation (EC) No 1798/2003.

(5) The measures provided for in this Regulation are in accordance with the opinion of the Standing Committee on Administrative Cooperation,

HAS ADOPTED THIS REGULATION:

Notes—[1] OJ L 264, 15.10.2003, p. 1. Regulation as amended by Regulation (EC) No 885/2004 (OJ L 168, 1.5.2004, p 1).
[2] OJ L 336, 27.12.1977, p. 15. Directive as last amended by Directive 2004/56/EC (OJ L 127, 29.4.2004, p 70).

Article 1

Subject matter

This Regulation lays down detailed rules for implementing Articles 18, 35 and 37 of Regulation (EC) No 1798/2003.

Article 2

Definitions

For the purposes of this Regulation:

1. "missing trader" shall mean a trader registered as a taxable person for VAT purposes who, potentially with a fraudulent intent, acquires or purports to acquire goods or services without payment of VAT and supplies these goods or services with VAT, but does not remit the VAT due to the appropriate national authority.
2. "to hijack a VAT registration" shall mean to use another trader's VAT registration number illicitly.

Article 3

Categories of information to be exchanged without prior request

The categories of information to be the subject of automatic or structured automatic exchange, in accordance with Article 17 of Regulation (EC) No 1798/2003, shall be the following:

1. information on non-established traders;
2. information on new means of transport;
3. information concerning distance selling not subject to VAT in the Member State of origin;
4. information concerning intra-Community transactions presumed to be irregular;
5. information on (potential) "missing traders".

Article 4

Subcategories of information to be exchanged without prior request

1. In respect of non-established traders the information shall relate to the following:
   (*a*) the allocation of VAT identification numbers to taxable persons established in another Member State;
   (*b*) VAT refunds to taxable persons not established in the territory of the country, pursuant to Council Directive 79/1072/EEC[1].
2. In respect of new means of transport, the information shall relate to the following:
   (*a*) supplies exempted in accordance with Article 28c(A)(*b*) of Council Directive 77/388/EEC[2], of new means of transport as defined in Article 28a(2), by persons regarded as taxable persons pursuant to Article 28a(4) who are registered for VAT;
   (*b*) supplies exempted in accordance with Article 28c(A)(*b*) of Directive 77/388/EEC, of new vessels and aircraft as defined in Article 28a(2), by taxable persons registered for VAT, other than those mentioned under point (*a*), to persons not registered for VAT;
   (*c*) supplies exempted in accordance with Article 28c(A)(*b*) of Directive 77/388/EEC, of new motorised land vehicles as defined in Article 28a(2), by taxable persons registered for VAT, other than those mentioned under point (*a*), to persons not registered for VAT.
3. In respect of distance selling not subject to VAT in the Member State of origin, the information shall relate to the following:
   (*a*) supplies above the threshold provided for in Article 28b(B)(2) of Directive 77/388/EEC;
   (*b*) supplies below the threshold provided for in Article 28b(B)(2) of Directive 77/388/EEC, where the taxable person opts for taxation in the Member State of destination in accordance with Article 28b(B)(3) of that Directive.
4. In respect of intra-Community transactions presumed to be irregular, the information shall relate to the following:

(*a*) supplies in cases where it is certain that the value of intra-Community supplies notified under the VAT Information exchange system (VIES) varies significantly from the value of the corresponding intra-Community acquisitions reported;

(*b*) intra-Community supplies of goods not exempted from VAT in accordance with Article 28c(A) of Directive 77/388/EEC to a taxable person established in another Member State.

5. In respect of (potential) "missing traders", the information shall relate to the following:

(*a*) taxable persons for whom a VAT identification number has been cancelled or is no longer valid due to an absence or simulation of economic activity, and who have made intra-Community transactions;

(*b*) taxable persons who are (potential) "missing traders" but whose VAT identification number has not been cancelled;

(*c*) taxable persons who carry out intra-Community supplies and their customers in other Member States in cases where the customer is a (potential) "missing trader" or uses a "hijacked VAT registration".

Notes—[1] OJ L 331, 27.12.1979, p. 11.
[2] OJ L 145, 13.6.1977, p. 1.

Article 5

Notification of participation in the exchange of information

Each Member State shall notify the Commission in writing, within three months from the entry into force of this Regulation, of its decision, taken in accordance with the second paragraph of Article 18 of Regulation (EC) No 1798/2003, as to whether it is going to take part in the exchange of a particular category or subcategory of information referred to in Articles 3 and 4 and, if so, whether it is going to do so in an automatic or structured automatic way. The Commission shall inform the other Member States accordingly.

A Member State which subsequently modifies the categories or subcategories of information which it exchanges or the way in which it takes part in the exchange of information shall notify the Commission accordingly in writing. The Commission shall inform the other Member States accordingly.

Article 6

Frequency of the transmission of the information

In cases where the automatic exchange system is being used, the information shall be provided in accordance with the following timetable:

(*a*) at the latest within three months of the end of the calendar year in which that information has become available, with regard to the categories referred to in Article 3(1) and (3);

(*b*) at the latest within three months of the end of the calendar quarter during which that information has become available, with regard to the categories referred to in Article 3(2).

Information concerning the categories referred to in Article 3(4) and (5) shall be provided as soon as it becomes available.

Article 7

Transmission of communications

1. All information communicated in writing pursuant to Article 37 of Regulation (EC) No 1798/2003 shall, as far as possible, be transmitted only by electronic means via the CCN/CSI network, with the exception of the following:

(*a*) the request for notification referred to in Article 14 of Regulation (EC) No 1798/2003 and the instrument or decision of which notification is requested;

(*b*) original documents provided pursuant to Article 7 of Regulation (EC) No 1798/2003.

2. The competent authorities of the Member States may agree to waive the communication on paper of the information specified in points (*a*) and (*b*) of paragraph 1.

Article 8

Evaluation

The arrangements for administrative cooperation shall be evaluated in accordance with Article 35(1) of Regulation (EC) No 1798/2003, at three-yearly intervals with effect from the entry into force of this Regulation.

Article 9

Statistical data

The list of statistical data referred to in Article 35(3) of Regulation (EC) No 1798/2003 is set out in the Annex.

Each Member State shall, before 30 April each year and as far as possible by electronic means, communicate to the Commission those statistical data, using the model set out in this Annex.

Article 10

Communication of national measures

Member States shall communicate to the Commission the text of any laws, regulations or administrative provisions which they apply in the field covered by this Regulation.

The Commission shall communicate those measures to the other Member States.

Article 11

Entry into force

This Regulation shall enter into force on the twentieth day following that of its publication in the Official Journal of the European Union.

This Regulation shall be binding in its entirety and directly applicable in all Member States.

COUNCIL REGULATION (EC) No 1777/2005
of 17 October 2005
laying down implementing measures for Directive 77/388/EEC on the common system of value added tax

(1777/05/EC)

THE COUNCIL OF THE EUROPEAN UNION,

Having regard to the Treaty establishing the European Community,

Having regard to the Sixth Council Directive 77/388/EEC of 17 May 1977 on the harmonisation of the laws of the Member States relating to turnover taxes — Common system of value added tax: uniform basis of assessment[(1)], hereinafter referred to as 'Directive 77/388/EEC', and in particular Article 29a thereof,

Having regard to the proposal from the Commission,

Whereas:

(1) Directive 77/388/EEC contains rules on value added tax which, in some cases, are subject to interpretation by the Member States. The adoption of common provisions implementing Directive 77/388/EEC should ensure that application of the value added tax system complies more fully with the objective of the internal market, in cases where divergences in application have arisen or may arise which are incompatible with the proper functioning of the said market. These implementing measures are legally binding only from the date of the entry into force of this Regulation and are without prejudice to the validity of the legislation and interpretation previously adopted by the Member States.

(2) It is necessary for the achievement of the basic objective of ensuring a more uniform application of the current value added tax system to lay down rules implementing Directive 77/388/EEC, in particular in respect of taxable persons, the supply of goods and services, and the place of their supply. In accordance with the principle of proportionality as set out in the third subparagraph of Article 5 of the Treaty, this Regulation does not go beyond what is necessary in order to achieve the objective pursued. Since it is binding and directly applicable in all Member States, uniformity of application will be best ensured by a Regulation.

(3) These implementing provisions contain specific rules in response to selective questions of application and are designed to bring uniform treatment throughout the Community to those specific circumstances only. They are therefore not conclusive for other cases and, in view of their formulation, are to be applied restrictively.

(4) The further integration of the internal market has led to an increased need for cooperation by economic operators established in different Member States across internal borders and the development of European economic interest groupings (EEIGs), constituted in accordance with Regulation (EEC) No 2137/85[(2)], it should therefore be provided that such EEIGs are also taxable persons where they supply goods or services for consideration.

(5) The sale of an option as a financial instrument should be treated as a supply of services separate from the underlying transactions to which the option relates.

(6) It is necessary, on the one hand, to establish that a transaction which consists solely of assembling the various parts of a machine provided by a customer must be considered as a supply of services, and, on the other hand, to establish the place of such supply.

(7) Where various services supplied in the framework of organising a funeral form a part of a single service, the rule on the place of supply should also be determined.

(8) Certain specific services such as the assignment of television broadcasting rights in respect of football matches, the translation of texts, services for claiming value added tax refunds, certain services as an agent, the hiring of means of transport and certain electronic services involve cross-border scenarios or even the participation of economic operators established in third countries. The place of supply of these services needs to be clearly determined in order to create greater legal certainty. It should be noted that the services identified as electronic services or otherwise do not constitute a definitive, exhaustive list.

(9) In certain specific circumstances a credit or debit card handling fee which is paid in connection with a transaction should not reduce the taxable amount for the latter.

(10) Vocational training or retraining should include instruction relating directly to a trade or profession as well as any instruction aimed at acquiring or updating knowledge for vocational purposes, regardless of the duration of a course.

(11) 'Platinum nobles' should be treated as being excluded from the exemptions for currency, bank notes and coins.

(12) Goods transported outside the Community by the purchaser thereof and used for the equipping, fuelling or provisioning of means of transport used for non-business purposes by persons other than natural persons, such as bodies governed by public law and associations, should be excluded from the exemption for export transactions.

(13) To guarantee uniform administrative practices for the calculation of the minimum value for exemption on exportation of goods carried in the personal luggage of travellers, the provisions on such calculations should be harmonised.

(14) Electronic import documents should also be admitted to exercise the right to deduct, where they fulfil the same requirements as paper-based documents.

(15) Weights for investment gold which are definitely accepted by the bullion market should be named and a common date for establishing the value of gold coins be determined to ensure equal treatment of economic operators.

(16) The special scheme for taxable persons not established in the Community, supplying electronic services to non-taxable persons established or resident within the Community is subject to certain conditions. Where those conditions are no longer fulfilled, the consequences thereof should, in particular, be made clear.

(17) In the case of intra-Community acquisition of goods, the right of the Member State of acquisition to tax the acquisition should remain unaffected by the value added tax treatment of the transaction in other Member States.

(18) Rules should be established to ensure the uniform treatment of supplies of goods once a supplier has exceeded the distance selling threshold for supplies to another Member State,

HAS ADOPTED THIS REGULATION:

Notes—[1] OJ L 145, 13.6.1977, p. 1. Directive as last amended by Directive 2004/66/EC (OJ L 168, 1.5.2004, p. 35).
[2] OJ L 199, 31.7.1985, p. 1.

CHAPTER I
SUBJECT MATTER

Article 1

This Regulation lays down measures for the implementation of Articles 4, 6, 9, 11, 13, 15, 18, 26b, 26c, 28a and 28b of Directive 77/388/EEC, and of Annex L thereto.

CHAPTER II
TAXABLE PERSONS AND TAXABLE TRANSACTIONS

SECTION 1
(ARTICLE 4 OF DIRECTIVE 77/388/EEC)

Article 2

A European Economic Interest Grouping (EEIG) constituted in accordance with Regulation (EEC) No 2137/85 which supplies goods or services for consideration to its members or to third parties shall be a taxable person within the meaning of Article 4(1) of Directive 77/388/EEC.

SECTION 2
(ARTICLE 6 OF DIRECTIVE 77/388/EEC)

Article 3

1. The sale of an option, where such a sale is a transaction within the scope of point (5) of Article 13(*b*)(*d*) of Directive 77/388/EEC, shall be a supply of services within the meaning of Article 6(1) of that Directive. That supply of services shall be distinct from the underlying operations to which the services relate.

2. Where a taxable person only assembles the different parts of a machine all of which were provided to him by his customer, that transaction shall be a supply of services within the meaning of Article 6(1) of Directive 77/388/EEC.

CHAPTER III

PLACE OF TAXABLE TRANSACTIONS

SECTION 1

(ARTICLE 9(1) OF DIRECTIVE 77/388/EEC)

Article 4

Insofar as they constitute a single service, services supplied in the framework of organising a funeral shall fall within the scope of Article 9(1) of Directive 77/388/EEC.

SECTION 2

(ARTICLE 9(2) OF DIRECTIVE 77/388/EEC)

Article 5

Except where the goods being assembled become part of immovable property, the place of the supply of services specified in Article 3(2) of this Regulation shall be established in accordance with Article 9(2)(*c*) or Article 28b(*f*) of Directive 77/388/EEC.

Article 6

The service of translation of texts shall be covered by Article 9(2)(*e*) of Directive 77/388/EEC.

Article 7

Where a body established in a third country assigns television broadcasting rights in respect of football matches to taxable persons established in the Community, that transaction shall be covered by the first indent of Article 9(2)(*e*) of Directive 77/388/EEC.

Article 8

The supply of services which consist in applying for or receiving refunds under Directive 79/1072/EEC[1] shall be covered by the third indent of Article 9(2)(*e*) of Directive 77/388/EEC.

Note—[1] Eighth Council Directive 79/1072/EEC of 6 December 1979 on the harmonisation of the laws of the Member States relating to turnover taxes — Arrangements for the refund of value added tax to taxable persons not established in the territory of the country (OJ L 331, 27.12.1979, p. 11). Directive as last amended by the 2003 Act of Accession.

Article 9

The supply of services of agents as referred to in the seventh indent of Article 9(2)(*e*) of Directive 77/388/EEC shall cover the services of agents acting in the name and for the account of the recipient of the service procured and services performed by the agents acting in the name and for the account of the provider of the service procured.

Article 10

Trailers and semi-trailers, as well as railway wagons, shall be forms of transport for the purposes of the eighth indent of Article 9(2)(*e*) of Directive 77/388/EEC.

Article 11

1. 'Electronically supplied services' as referred to in the 12th indent of Article 9(2)(*e*) of Directive 77/388/EEC and in Annex L to Directive 77/388/EEC shall include services which are delivered over the Internet or an electronic network and the nature of which renders their supply essentially automated and involving minimal human intervention, and in the absence of information technology is impossible to ensure.

2. The following services, in particular, shall, where delivered over the Internet or an electronic network, be covered by paragraph 1:

(*a*) the supply of digitised products generally, including software and changes to or upgrades of software;
(*b*) services providing or supporting a business or personal presence on an electronic network such as a website or a webpage;
(*c*) services automatically generated from a computer via the Internet or an electronic network, in response to specific data input by the recipient;
(*d*) the transfer for consideration of the right to put goods or services up for sale on an Internet site operating as an online market on which potential buyers make their bids by an automated procedure and on which the parties are notified of a sale by electronic mail automatically generated from a computer;
(*e*) Internet Service Packages (ISP) of information in which the telecommunications component forms an ancillary and subordinate part (ie packages going beyond mere Internet access and including other elements such as content pages giving access to news, weather or travel reports; playgrounds; website hosting; access to online debates etc.);
(*f*) the services listed in Annex I.

Article 12

The following, in particular, shall not be covered by the 12th indent of Article 9(2)(*e*) of Directive 77/388/EEC—

1. Radio and television broadcasting services as referred to in the 11th indent of Article 9(2)(*e*) of Directive 77/388/EEC;

2. Telecommunications services, within the meaning of the 10th indent of Article 9(2)(*e*) of Directive 77/388/EEC;

3. Supplies of the following goods and services—

(*a*) goods, where the order and processing is done electronically;
(*b*) CD-ROMs, floppy disks and similar tangible media;
(*c*) printed matter, such as books, newsletters, newspapers or journals;
(*d*) CDs, audio cassettes;
(*e*) video cassettes, DVDs;
(*f*) games on a CD-ROM;
(*g*) services of professionals such as lawyers and financial consultants, who advise clients by e-mail;
(*h*) teaching services, where the course content is delivered by a teacher over the Internet or an electronic network, (namely via a remote link);
(*i*) offline physical repair services of computer equipment;
(*j*) offline data warehousing services;
(*k*) advertising services, in particular as in newspapers, on posters and on television;
(*l*) telephone helpdesk services;
(*m*) teaching services purely involving correspondence courses, such as postal courses;
(*n*) conventional auctioneers' services reliant on direct human intervention, irrespective of how bids are made;
(*o*) telephone services with a video component, otherwise known as videophone services;
(*p*) access to the Internet and World Wide Web;
(*q*) telephone services provided through the Internet.

CHAPTER IV
TAXABLE AMOUNT

(ARTICLE 11 OF DIRECTIVE 77/388/EEC)

Article 13

Where a supplier of goods or services, as a condition of accepting payment by credit or debit card, requires the customer to pay an amount to himself or another undertaking, and where the total price payable by that customer is unaffected irrespective of how payment is accepted, that amount shall constitute an integral part of the taxable amount for the supply of the goods or services, under Article 11 of Directive 77/388/EEC.

CHAPTER V
EXEMPTIONS

SECTION 1

(ARTICLE 13 OF DIRECTIVE 77/388/EEC)

Article 14

Vocational training or retraining services provided under the conditions set out in Article 13(*a*)(1)(i) of Directive 77/388/EEC shall include instruction relating directly to a trade or profession as well as any instruction aimed at acquiring or updating knowledge for vocational purposes. The duration of a vocational training or retraining course shall be irrelevant for this purpose.

Article 15

The exemption referred to in Article 13(*b*)(*d*)(4) of Directive 77/388/EEC shall not apply to platinum nobles.

SECTION 2

(ARTICLE 15 OF DIRECTIVE 77/388/EEC)

Article 16

'Means of transport for private use' as referred to in the first subparagraph of Article 15(2) of Directive 77/388/EEC shall include means of transport used for non-business purposes by persons other than natural persons, such as bodies governed by public law within the meaning of Article 4(5) of that Directive and associations.

Article 17

In order to determine whether the threshold set by a Member State in accordance with the third indent of the second subparagraph of Article 15(2) of Directive 77/388/EEC has been exceeded, the calculation shall be based on the invoice value. The aggregate value of several goods may be used only if all those goods are included on the same invoice issued by the same taxable person supplying goods to the same customer.

CHAPTER VI
DEDUCTIONS

(ARTICLE 18 OF DIRECTIVE 77/388/EEC)

Article 18

Where the importing Member State has introduced an electronic system for completing customs formalities, the expression 'import document' as referred to in Article 18(1)(*b*) of Directive 77/388/EEC shall cover electronic versions of such documents, provided that they allow for the exercise of the right of deduction to be checked.

CHAPTER VII
SPECIAL SCHEMES

(ARTICLES 26B AND 26C OF DIRECTIVE 77/388/EEC)

Article 19

1. 'Weights accepted by the bullion markets' as referred to in Article 26b(*a*)(i), first paragraph, of Directive 77/388/EEC shall at least cover the units and the weights traded as set out in Annex II to this Regulation.

2. For the purposes of establishing the list referred to in the third subparagraph of Article 26b(*a*) of Directive 77/388/EEC, 'price' and 'open market value' as referred to in the fourth indent of point (ii) of the first subparagraph shall be the price and open market value on 1 April of each year. If 1 April does not fall on a day on which those values are fixed, the values of the next day on which they are fixed shall be used.

Article 20

1. Where, in the course of a calendar quarter, a non-established taxable person using the special scheme provided for in Article 26c(*b*) of Directive 77/388/EEC meets at least one of the criteria for exclusion laid down in Article 26c(*b*)(4), the Member State of identification shall exclude that non-established taxable person from the special scheme. In such cases the non-established taxable person may subsequently be excluded from the special scheme at any time during that quarter. In respect of electronic services supplied prior to exclusion but during the calendar quarter in which exclusion occurs, the non-established taxable person shall submit a return for the entire quarter in accordance with Article 26c(*b*)(5) of Directive 77/388/EEC. The requirement to submit this return shall have no effect on the requirement, if any, to register under the normal rules in a Member State.

2. A Member State of identification which receives a payment in excess of that resulting from the return submitted under Article 26c(*b*)(5) of Directive 77/388/EEC shall reimburse the overpaid amount directly to the taxable person concerned. Where the Member State of identification has received an amount pursuant to a return subsequently found to be incorrect, and that Member State has already distributed that amount among the Member States of consumption, those Member States shall directly reimburse the overpayment to the non-established taxable person and inform the Member State of identification of the adjustment to be made.

3. Any return period (quarter) within the meaning of Article 26c(*b*)(5) of Directive 77/388/EEC shall be a separate return period. Once a return under Article 26c(*b*)(5) of Directive 77/388/EEC has been rendered, any subsequent changes to the figures contained therein may be made only by means of an amendment to that return and not by an adjustment to a subsequent return. Amounts of value added tax paid under Article 26c(*b*)(7) of Directive 77/388/EEC shall be specific to that return. Any subsequent amendments to the amounts paid may be effected only by reference to that return and may not be allocated to another return, or adjusted on a subsequent return.

4. Amounts on value added tax returns made under the special scheme provided for in Article 26c(*b*) of Directive 77/388/EEC shall not be rounded up or down to the nearest whole monetary unit. The exact amount of value added tax shall be reported and remitted.

CHAPTER VIII

TRANSITIONAL MEASURES

(ARTICLES 28A AND 28B OF DIRECTIVE 77/388/EEC)

Article 21

Where an intra-Community acquisition of goods within the meaning of Article 28a of Directive 77/388/EEC has taken place, the Member State in which the dispatch or transport ends shall exercise its power of taxation irrespective of the VAT treatment applied to the transaction in the Member State in which the dispatch or transport began. 29.10.2005 EN Official Journal of the European Union L 288/5 Any request by a supplier of goods for a correction in the tax invoiced by him and reported by him to the Member State where the dispatch or transport of the goods began shall be treated by that State in accordance with its own domestic rules.

Article 22

Where in the course of a calendar year the threshold applied by a Member State in accordance with Article 28b(*b*)(2) of Directive 77/388/EEC is exceeded, Article 28b(*b*) of that Directive shall not modify the place of supplies of goods other than products subject to excise duty carried out in the course of the same calendar year which are made before the threshold applied by the Member State for the calendar year then current is exceeded provided that the supplier:

(*a*) has not exercised the option under Article 28b(*b*)(3) of that Directive and

(*b*) did not exceed the threshold in the course of the preceding calendar year. However, Article 28b(*b*) of Directive 77/388/EEC shall modify the place of the following supplies to the Member State in which the dispatch or transport ends:

(*a*) the supply by which the threshold applied by the Member State for the calendar year then current was exceeded in the course of the same calendar year;

(*b*) any subsequent supplies within that Member State in that calendar year;

(*c*) supplies within that Member State in the calendar year following the calendar year in which the event referred to in point (*a*) occurred.

CHAPTER IX

FINAL PROVISIONS

Article 23

This Regulation shall enter into force on 1 July 2006. Article 13 shall be applicable from 1 January 2006. This Regulation shall be binding in its entirety and directly applicable in all Member States.

Done at Luxembourg, 17 October 2005.

ANNEX I

Article 11

1. Item 1 of Annex L to Directive 77/388/EEC—

(*a*) Website hosting and webpage hosting

(*b*) Automated, online and distance maintenance of programmes

(*c*) Remote systems administration

(*d*) Online data warehousing where specific data is stored and retrieved electronically

(*e*) Online supply of on-demand disc space.

2. Item 2 of Annex L to Directive 77/388/EEC—

(*a*) Accessing or downloading software (including procurement/accountancy programmes and anti-virus software) plus updates

(*b*) Software to block banner adverts showing, otherwise known as Bannerblockers

(*c*) Download drivers, such as software that interfaces computers with peripheral equipment (such as printers)

(*d*) Online automated installation of filters on websites

(*e*) Online automated installation of firewalls.

3. Item 3 of Annex L to Directive 77/388/EEC—

(*a*) Accessing or downloading desktop themes

(*b*) Accessing or downloading photographic or pictorial images or screensavers

(*c*) The digitised content of books and other electronic publications

(*d*) Subscription to online newspapers and journals

(*e*) Weblogs and website statistics

(*f*) Online news, traffic information and weather reports

(*g*) Online information generated automatically by software from specific data input by the customer, such as legal and financial data, (in particular such data as continually updated stock market data, in real time)

(*h*) The provision of advertising space including banner ads on a website/web page (*i*) Use of search engines and Internet directories.

4. Item 4 of Annex L to Directive 77/388/EEC

(*a*) Accessing or downloading of music on to computers and mobile phones
(*b*) Accessing or downloading of jingles, excerpts, ringtones, or other sounds
(*c*) Accessing or downloading of films
(*d*) Downloading of music on to computers and mobile phones
(*e*) Accessing automated online games which are dependent on the Internet, or other similar electronic networks, where players are geographically remote from one another.

5. Item 5 of Annex L to Directive 77/388/EEC

(*a*) Automated distance teaching dependent on the Internet or similar electronic network to function and the supply of which requires limited or no human intervention, including virtual classrooms, except where the Internet or similar electronic network is used as a tool simply for communication between the teacher and student
(*b*) Workbooks completed by pupils online and marked automatically, without human intervention.

ANNEX II

Article 19

Unit	*Weights traded*
Kg	12,5/1
Gram	500/250/100/50/20/10/5/2,5/2
Ounce (1 oz = 31,1035 g)	100/10/5/1/½/¼
Tael (1 tael = 1,193 oz.)[1]	10/5/1
Tola (10 tolas = 3,75 oz.([2]	10

Notes—[1] Tael = a traditional Chinese unit of weight. The nominal fineness of a Hong Kong tael bar is 990 but in Taiwan 5 and 10 tael bars can be 999,9 fineness.
[2] Tola = a traditional Indian unit of weight for gold. The most popular sized bar is 10 tola, 999 fineness.

Regulation of the European Parliament and of the Council of 23 April 2008 laying down the Community Customs Code (Modernised Customs Code)

(450/2008/EC)

Note—See OJ L 145, 04.06.2008 p 1.

CONTENTS

THE EUROPEAN PARLIAMENT AND THE COUNCIL OF THE EUROPEAN UNION,

Having regard to the Treaty establishing the European Community, and in particular Articles 26, 95, 133 and 135 thereof,

Having regard to the proposal from the Commission,

Having regard to the opinion of the European Economic and Social Committee[1],

Acting in accordance with the procedure laid down in Article 251 of the Treaty[2],

Whereas:

(1) The Community is based upon a customs union. It is advisable, in the interests both of economic operators and of the customs authorities in the Community, to assemble current customs legislation in a Community Customs Code (hereinafter referred to as the Code). Based on the concept of an internal market, the Code should contain the general rules and procedures which ensure the implementation of the tariff and other common policy measures introduced at Community level in connection with trade in goods between the Community and countries or territories outside the customs territory of the Community, taking into account the requirements of those common policies. Customs legislation should be better aligned on the provisions relating to the collection of import charges without change to the scope of the tax provisions in force.

(2) In accordance with the Communication from the Commission concerning the protection of the Community's financial interests and the Action Plan for 2004–2005, it is appropriate to adapt the legal framework for the protection of the financial interests of the Community.

(3) Council Regulation (EEC) No 2913/92 of 12 October 1992 establishing the Community Customs Code[3] was based upon integration of the customs procedures applied separately in the respective Member States during the 1980s. That Regulation has been repeatedly and substantially amended since its introduction, in order to address specific problems such as the protection of good faith or the taking into account of security requirements. Further amendments to the Code are necessary as a consequence of the important legal changes which have occurred in recent years, at both Community and international level, such as the expiry of the Treaty establishing the European Coal and Steel Community and the entry into force of the 2003 and 2005 Acts of Accession, as well as the Amendment to the International Convention on the simplification and harmonisation of customs procedures (hereinafter referred to as the revised Kyoto Convention), the accession of the Community to which was approved by Council Decision 2003/231/EC[4]. The time has now come to streamline customs procedures and to take into account the fact that electronic declarations and processing are the rule and paper-based declarations and processing the exception. For all of these reasons, further amendment of the present Code is not sufficient and a complete overhaul is necessary.

(4) It is appropriate to introduce in the Code a legal framework for the application of certain provisions of the customs legislation to trade in goods between parts of the customs territory to which the provisions of Council Directive 2006/112/EC of 28 November 2006 on the common system of value added tax[5] apply and parts of that territory where those provisions do not apply, or to trade between parts where those provisions do not apply. Considering the fact that the goods concerned are Community goods and the fiscal nature of the measures at stake in this intra-Community trade, it is justifiable to introduce, through implementing measures, appropriate simplifications to the customs formalities to be applied to those goods.

(5) The facilitation of legitimate trade and the fight against fraud require simple, rapid and standard customs procedures and processes. It is therefore appropriate, in line with the Communication from the Commission on a simple and paperless environment for customs and trade, to simplify customs legislation, to allow the use of modern tools and technology and to promote further the uniform application of customs legislation and modernised approaches to customs control, thus helping to ensure the basis for efficient and simple clearance procedures. Customs procedures should be merged or aligned and the number of procedures reduced to those that are economically justified, with a view to increasing the competitiveness of business.

(6) The completion of the internal market, the reduction of barriers to international trade and investment and the reinforced need to ensure security and safety at the external borders of the Community have transformed the role of customs authorities giving them a leading role within the supply chain and, in their monitoring and management of international trade, making them a catalyst to the competitiveness of countries and companies. Customs legislation should therefore reflect the new economic reality and the new role and mission of customs authorities.

(7) The use of information and communication technologies, as laid down in the future Decision of the European Parliament and of the Council on a paperless environment for customs and trade, is a key element in ensuring trade facilitation and, at the same time, the

effectiveness of customs controls, thus reducing costs for business and risk for society. It is therefore necessary to establish in the Code the legal framework within which that Decision can be implemented, in particular the legal principle that all customs and trade transactions are to be handled electronically and that information and communication systems for customs operations are to offer, in each Member State, the same facilities to economic operators.

(8) Such use of information and communication technologies should be accompanied by harmonised and standardised application of customs controls by the Member States, to ensure an equivalent level of customs control throughout the Community so as not to give rise to anti-competitive behaviour at the various Community entry and exit points.

(9) In the interests of facilitating business, while at the same time providing for the proper levels of control of goods brought into or out of the customs territory of the Community, it is desirable that the information provided by economic operators be shared, taking account of the relevant data-protection provisions, between customs authorities and with other agencies involved in that control, such as police, border guards, veterinary and environmental authorities, and that controls by the various authorities be harmonised, so that the economic operator need give the information only once and that goods are controlled by those authorities at the same time and at the same place.

(10) In the interests of facilitating certain types of business, all persons should continue to have the right to appoint a representative in their dealings with the customs authorities. However, it should no longer be possible for that right of representation to be reserved under a law laid down by one of the Member States. Furthermore, a customs representative who complies with the criteria for the granting of the status of authorised economic operator, should be entitled to provide his services in a Member State other than the one where he is established.

(11) Compliant and trustworthy economic operators should, as "authorised economic operators", be able to take maximum advantage of widespread use of simplification and, taking account of security and safety aspects, benefit from reduced levels of customs control. They may thus enjoy the status of "customs simplification" authorised economic operator or the status of "security and safety" authorised economic operator. They may be granted one or other status, or both together.

(12) All decisions, that is to say, official acts by the customs authorities pertaining to customs legislation and having legal effect on one or more persons, including binding information issued by those authorities, should be covered by the same rules. Any such decisions should be valid throughout the Community and should be capable of being annulled, amended except where otherwise stipulated, or revoked where they do not conform to the customs legislation or its interpretation.

(13) In accordance with the Charter of Fundamental Rights of the European Union, it is necessary, in addition to the right of appeal against any decision taken by the customs authorities, to provide for the right of every person to be heard before any decision is taken which would adversely affect him.

(14) The streamlining of customs procedures within an electronic environment requires the sharing of responsibilities between the customs authorities of different Member States. It is necessary to ensure an appropriate level of effective, dissuasive and proportionate sanctions throughout the internal market.

(15) In order to secure a balance between, on the one hand, the need for customs authorities to ensure the correct application of customs legislation and, on the other, the right of economic operators to be treated fairly, the customs authorities should be granted extensive powers of control and economic operators a right of appeal.

(16) In order to minimise the risk to the Community, its citizens and its trading partners, the harmonised application of customs controls by the Member States should be based upon a common risk management framework and an electronic system for its implementation. The establishment of a risk management framework common to all Member States should not prevent them from controlling goods by random checks.

(17) It is necessary to establish the factors on the basis of which import or export duties and other measures in respect of trade in goods are applied. It is also appropriate to lay down clear provisions for issuing proofs of origin in the Community, where the exigencies of trade so require.

(18) It is desirable to group together all cases of incurrence of a customs debt on importation, other than following the submission of a customs declaration for release for free circulation or temporary admission with partial relief, in order to avoid difficulties in determining the legal basis on which the customs debt was incurred. The same should apply in cases of incurrence of a customs debt on exportation.

(19) Since the new role of customs authorities implies the sharing of responsibilities and cooperation between inland and border customs offices, the customs debt should, in most cases, be incurred at the place where the debtor is established, as the customs office competent for that place can best supervise the activities of the person concerned.

(20) Furthermore, in line with the revised Kyoto Convention, it is appropriate to provide for a reduced number of cases where administrative cooperation between Member States is required in order to establish the place where the customs debt was incurred and to recover the duties.

(21) The rules for special procedures should allow for the use of a single guarantee for all categories of special procedures and for that guarantee to be comprehensive, covering a number of transactions.

(22) In order to ensure better protection of the financial interests of the Community and of the Member States, a guarantee should cover non-declared or incorrectly declared goods included in a consignment or in a declaration for which it is provided. For the same reason, the undertaking of the guarantor should also cover amounts of import or export duty which fall to be paid following post-release controls.

(23) In order to safeguard the financial interests of the Community and of the Member States and to curb fraudulent practices, arrangements involving graduated measures for the application of a comprehensive guarantee are advisable. Where there is an increased risk of fraud it should be possible to prohibit temporarily the application of the comprehensive guarantee, taking account of the particular situation of the economic operators concerned.

(24) It is appropriate to take account of the good faith of the person concerned in cases where a customs debt is incurred through non-compliance with customs legislation and to minimise the impact of negligence on the part of the debtor.

(25) It is necessary to lay down the principle of how to determine the status of Community goods and the circumstances pertaining to the loss of such status, and to provide a basis for determining when that status remains unaltered in cases where goods temporarily leave the customs territory of the Community.

(26) It is appropriate, where an economic operator has provided, in advance, the information necessary for risk-based controls on the admissibility of the goods, to ensure that quick release of goods is then the rule. Fiscal and trade policy controls should primarily be performed by the customs office competent in respect of the premises of the economic operator.

(27) The rules for customs declarations and for the placing of goods under a customs procedure should be modernised and streamlined, in particular by requiring that customs declarations be, as a rule, made electronically and providing for only one type of simplified declaration.

(28) Since the revised Kyoto Convention favours the lodging, registering and checking of the customs declaration prior to the arrival of the goods and, furthermore, the dissociation of the place where the declaration is lodged from the place where the goods are physically located, it is appropriate to provide for centralised clearance at the place where the economic operator is established. Centralised clearance should include the facility for the use of simplified declarations, deferment of the date of the submission of a complete declaration and required documents, periodic declaration and deferred payment.

(29) In order to help to ensure neutral conditions for competition throughout the Community, it is appropriate to lay down at Community level the rules governing the destruction or disposal otherwise of goods by the customs authorities, these being matters which have previously required national legislation.

(30) It is appropriate to lay down common and simple rules for the special procedures (transit, storage, specific use and processing), supplemented by a small set of rules for each category of special procedure, in order to make it simple for the operator to choose the right procedure, to avoid errors and to reduce the number of post-release recoveries and repayments.

(31) The granting of authorisations for several special procedures with a single guarantee and a single supervising customs office should be facilitated and there should be simple rules on the incurrence of a customs debt in these cases. The basic principle should be that goods placed under a special procedure, or the products made from them, are to be assessed at the time when the customs debt is incurred. However, it should also be possible, where economically justified, to assess the goods at the time when they were placed under a special procedure. The same principles should apply to usual forms of handling.

(32) In view of the increased security-related measures introduced into the Code under Regulation (EC) No 648/2005 of the European Parliament and of the Council of 13 April 2005 amending Council Regulation (EEC) No 2913/92 establishing the Community Customs Code[6], the placing of goods into free zones should become a customs procedure and the goods should be subject to customs controls at entry and with regard to records.

(33) Given that the intention of re-exportation is no longer necessary, the inward processing suspension procedure should be merged with processing under customs control and the inward processing drawback procedure abandoned. This single inward-processing procedure should also cover destruction, except where destruction is carried out by, or under the supervision of, customs.

(34) Security-related measures relating to Community goods brought out of the customs territory of the Community should apply equally to the re-export of non-Community goods. The same basic rules should apply to all types of goods, with the possibility of exceptions where necessary, such as for goods only transiting through the customs territory of the Community.

(35) The measures necessary for the implementation of this Regulation should be adopted in accordance with Council Decision 1999/468/EC of 28 June 1999 laying down the procedure for the exercise of implementing powers conferred on the Commission[7].

(36) It is appropriate to provide for the adoption of measures implementing this Code. These measures should be adopted in accordance with the management and regulatory procedures provided for in Articles 4 and 5 of Decision 1999/468/EC.

(37) In particular, the Commission should be empowered to define the conditions and criteria necessary for the effective application of this Code. Since those measures are of general scope and are designed to amend non-essential elements of this Regulation or to supplement this Regulation by the addition of new non-essential elements, they must be adopted in accordance with the regulatory procedure with scrutiny provided for in Article 5a of Decision 1999/468/EC.

(38) It is appropriate, in order to ensure an effective decision-making process, to examine questions relating to the preparation of a position to be taken by the Community in committees, working groups and panels established by or under international agreements dealing with customs legislation.

(39) In order to simplify and rationalise customs legislation, a number of provisions presently contained in autonomous Community acts have, for the sake of transparency, been incorporated into the Code.

The following Regulations, together with Regulation (EEC) No 2913/92, should therefore be repealed:

Council Regulation (EEC) No 3925/91 of 19 December 1991 concerning the elimination of controls and formalities applicable to the cabin and hold baggage of persons taking an intra-Community flight and the baggage of persons making an intra-Community sea crossing[8] and Council Regulation (EC) No 1207/2001 of 11 June 2001 on procedures to facilitate the issue or the making out in the Community of proofs of origin and the issue of certain approved exporter authorisations under the provisions governing preferential trade between the European Community and certain countries[9].

(40) Since the objectives of this Regulation, namely, to lay down rules and procedures applicable to goods brought into or out of the customs territory of the Community in order to enable the Customs Union to function effectively as a central pillar of the internal market, cannot be sufficiently achieved by the Member States and can therefore be better achieved at Community level, the Community may adopt measures, in accordance with the principle of subsidiarity as set out in Article 5 of the Treaty. In accordance with the principle of proportionality, as set out in that Article, this Regulation does not go beyond what is necessary in order to achieve those objectives,

HAVE ADOPTED THIS REGULATION:

Amendments—[1] OJ C 309, 16.12.2006, p. 22.

[2] Opinion of the European Parliament of 12 December 2006, Council Common Position of 15 October 2007 (OJ C 298 E, 11.12.2007, p. 1) and Position of the European Parliament of 19 February 2008.

[3] OJ L 302, 19.10.1992, p. 1. Regulation as last amended by Regulation (EC) No 1791/2006 (OJ L 363, 20.12.2006, p. 1).

[4] OJ L 86, 3.4.2003, p. 21. Decision as amended by Decision 2004/485/EC (OJ L 162, 30.4.2004, p. 113).

[5] OJ L 347, 11.12.2006, p. 1. Directive as last amended by Directive 2008/8/EC (OJ L 44, 20.2.2008, p. 11).

[6] OJ L 117, 4.5.2005, p. 13.

[7] OJ L 184, 17.7.1999, p. 23. Decision as amended by Decision 2006/512/EC (OJ L 200, 22.7.2006, p. 11).

[8] OJ L 374, 31.12.1991, p. 4. Regulation as amended by Regulation (EC) No 1882/2003 of the European Parliament and of the Council (OJ L 284, 31.10.2003, p. 1).

[9] OJ L 165, 21.6.2001, p. 1. Regulation as last amended by Regulation (EC) No 75/2008 (OJ L 24, 29.1.2008, p. 1).

TITLE I
GENERAL PROVISIONS

CHAPTER 1
SCOPE OF CUSTOMS LEGISLATION, MISSION OF CUSTOMS AND DEFINITIONS

Subject matter and scope

Article 1

1. This Regulation establishes the Community Customs Code, hereinafter referred to as "the Code", laying down the general rules and procedures applicable to goods brought into or out of the customs territory of the Community.

Without prejudice to international law and conventions and Community legislation in other fields, the Code shall apply uniformly throughout the customs territory of the Community.

2. Certain provisions of the customs legislation may apply outside the customs territory of the Community within the framework of legislation governing specific fields or of international conventions.

3. Certain provisions of the customs legislation, including the simplifications for which it provides, shall apply to the trade in goods between parts of the customs territory of the Community to which the provisions of Directive 2006/112/EC apply and parts of that territory where those provisions do not apply, or to trade between parts of that territory where those provisions do not apply.

The measures designed to amend non-essential elements of this Regulation, by supplementing it, laying down the provisions referred to in the first subparagraph and simplified formalities for their implementation, shall be adopted in accordance with the regulatory procedure with scrutiny referred to in Article 184(4). Those measures shall also take account of particular circumstances pertaining to the trade in goods involving only one Member State.

Mission of customs authorities

Article 2

Customs authorities shall be primarily responsible for the supervision of the Community's international trade, thereby contributing to fair and open trade, to the implementation of the external aspects of the internal market, of the common trade policy and of the other common Community policies having a bearing on trade, and to overall supply chain security. Customs authorities shall put in place measures aimed, in particular, at the following:

(*a*) protecting the financial interests of the Community and its Member States;

(*b*) protecting the Community from unfair and illegal trade while supporting legitimate business activity;

(*c*) ensuring the security and safety of the Community and its residents, and the protection of the environment, where appropriate in close cooperation with other authorities;

(*d*) maintaining a proper balance between customs controls and facilitation of legitimate trade.

Customs territory

Article 3

1. The customs territory of the Community shall comprise the following territories, including their territorial waters, internal waters and airspace:

- the territory of the Kingdom of Belgium,
- the territory of the Republic of Bulgaria,
- the territory of the Czech Republic,
- the territory of the Kingdom of Denmark, except the Faeroe Islands and Greenland,
- the territory of the Federal Republic of Germany, except the Island of Heligoland and the territory of Buesingen (Treaty of 23 November 1964 between the Federal Republic of Germany and the Swiss Confederation),
- the territory of the Republic of Estonia,
- the territory of Ireland,
- the territory of the Hellenic Republic,
- the territory of the Kingdom of Spain, except Ceuta and Melilla,
- the territory of the French Republic, except New Caledonia, Mayotte, Saint-Pierre and Miquelon, Wallis and Futuna Islands, French Polynesia and the French Southern and Antarctic Territories,
- the territory of the Italian Republic, except the municipalities of Livigno and Campione d'Italia and the national waters of Lake Lugano which are between the bank and the political frontier of the area between Ponte Tresa and Porto Ceresio,
- the territory of the Republic of Cyprus, in accordance with the provisions of the 2003 Act of Accession,
- the territory of the Republic of Latvia,
- the territory of the Republic of Lithuania,
- the territory of the Grand Duchy of Luxembourg,
- the territory of the Republic of Hungary,
- the territory of Malta,
- the territory of the Kingdom of the Netherlands in Europe,
- the territory of the Republic of Austria,
- the territory of the Republic of Poland,
- the territory of the Portuguese Republic,
- the territory of Romania,
- the territory of the Republic of Slovenia,
- the territory of the Slovak Republic,
- the territory of the Republic of Finland,
- the territory of the Kingdom of Sweden,
- the territory of the United Kingdom of Great Britain and Northern Ireland and of the Channel Islands and the Isle of Man.

2. The following territories, including their territorial waters, internal waters and airspace, situated outside the territory of the Member States shall, taking into account the conventions and treaties applicable to them, be considered to be part of the customs territory of the Community:

(*a*) FRANCE

The territory of Monaco as defined in the Customs Convention signed in Paris on 18 May 1963 (Journal officiel de la République française (Official Journal of the French Republic) of 27 September 1963, p. 8679);

(*b*) CYPRUS

The territory of the United Kingdom Sovereign Base Areas of Akrotiri and Dhekelia as defined in the Treaty concerning the Establishment of the Republic of Cyprus, signed in Nicosia on 16 August 1960 (United Kingdom Treaty Series No 4 (1961) Cmnd. 1252).

Definitions

Article 4

For the purposes of the Code, the following definitions shall apply:

1. "customs authorities" means the customs administrations of the Member States responsible for applying the customs legislation and any other authorities empowered under national law to apply certain customs legislation;

2. "customs legislation" means the body of legislation made up of the following:
   (*a*) the Code and the provisions adopted at Community level and, where appropriate, at national level, to implement it;
   (*b*) the Common Customs Tariff;
   (*c*) the legislation setting up a Community system of reliefs from customs duties;
   (*d*) international agreements containing customs provisions, insofar as they are applicable in the Community;

3. "customs controls" means specific acts performed by the customs authorities in order to ensure the correct application of customs legislation and other legislation governing the entry, exit, transit, transfer, storage and end-use of goods moved between the customs territory of the Community and other territories, and the presence and movement within the customs territory of non-Community goods and goods placed under the end-use procedure;

4. "person" means a natural person, a legal person, and any association of persons which is not a legal person but which is recognised under Community or national law as having the capacity to perform legal acts;

5. "economic operator" means a person who, in the course of his business, is involved in activities covered by customs legislation;

6. "customs representative" means any person appointed by another person to carry out the acts and formalities required under the customs legislation in his dealings with customs authorities;

7. "risk" means the likelihood of an event that may occur, with regard to the entry, exit, transit, transfer or end-use of goods moved between the customs territory of the Community and countries or territories outside that territory and to the presence of goods which do not have Community status, which would have any of the following results:
   (*a*) it would prevent the correct application of Community or national measures;
   (*b*) it would compromise the financial interests of the Community and its Member States;
   (*c*) it would pose a threat to the security and safety of the Community and its residents, to human, animal or plant health, to the environment or to consumers;

8. "customs formalities" means all the operations which must be carried out by the persons concerned and by the customs authorities in order to comply with the customs legislation;

9. "summary declaration" (entry summary declaration and exit summary declaration) means the act whereby, before or at the time of the event, a person informs the customs authorities, in the prescribed form and manner, that goods are to be brought into or out of the customs territory of the Community;

10. "customs declaration" means the act whereby a person indicates in the prescribed form and manner a wish to place goods under a given customs procedure, with an indication, where appropriate, of any specific arrangements to be applied;

11. "declarant" means the person lodging a summary declaration or a re-export notification or making a customs declaration in his own name or the person in whose name such a declaration is made;

12. "customs procedure" means any of the following procedures under which goods may be placed in accordance with this Code:
   (*a*) release for free circulation;
   (*b*) special procedures;
   (*c*) export;

13. "customs debt" means the obligation on a person to pay the amount of import or export duty which applies to specific goods under the customs legislation in force;

14. "debtor" means any person liable for a customs debt;

15. "import duties" means customs duties payable on the importation of goods;

16. "export duties" means customs duties payable on the exportation of goods;

17. "customs status" means the status of goods as Community or non-Community goods;

18. "Community goods" means goods which fall into any of the following categories:
   (*a*) goods wholly obtained in the customs territory of the Community and not incorporating goods imported from countries or territories outside the customs territory of the Community. Goods wholly obtained in the customs territory of the Community shall not have the customs

status of Community goods if they are obtained from goods placed under the external transit procedure, a storage procedure, the temporary admission procedure or the inward-processing procedure in cases determined in accordance with Article 101(2)(*c*);
(*b*) goods brought into the customs territory of the Community from countries or territories outside that territory and released for free circulation;
(*c*) goods obtained or produced in the customs territory of the Community, either solely from goods referred to in point (*b*) or from goods referred to in points (*a*) and (*b*);

19. "non-Community goods" means goods other than those referred to in point (18) or which have lost their customs status as Community goods;

20. "risk management" means the systematic identification of risk and the implementation of all measures necessary for limiting exposure to risk. This includes activities such as collecting data and information, analysing and assessing risk, prescribing and taking action and regular monitoring and review of that process and its outcomes, based on international, Community and national sources and strategies;

21. "release of goods" means the act whereby the customs authorities make goods available for the purposes specified for the customs procedure under which they are placed;

22. "customs supervision" means action taken in general by the customs authorities with a view to ensuring that customs legislation and, where appropriate, other provisions applicable to goods subject to such action are observed;

23. "repayment" means the refunding of any import or export duty that has been paid;

24. "remission" means the waiving of the obligation to pay import or export duties which have not been paid;

25. "processed products" means goods placed under a processing procedure which have undergone processing operations;

26. "person established in the customs territory of the Community" means:
(*a*) in the case of a natural person, any person who has his habitual residence in the customs territory of the Community;
(*b*) in the case of a legal person or an association of persons, any person who has his registered office, central headquarters or a permanent business establishment in the customs territory of the Community;

27. "presentation of goods to customs" means the notification to the customs authorities of the arrival of goods at the customs office or at any other place designated or approved by the customs authorities and the availability of those goods for customs controls;

28. "holder of the goods" means the person who is the owner of the goods or who has a similar right of disposal over them or who has physical control of them;

29. "holder of the procedure" means the person who makes the customs declaration, or on whose behalf the customs declaration is made, or the person to whom the rights and obligations of that person in respect of a customs procedure have been transferred;

30. "commercial policy measures" means non-tariff measures established, as part of the common commercial policy, in the form of Community provisions governing international trade in goods;

31. "processing operations" means any of the following:
(*a*) the working of goods, including erecting or assembling them or fitting them to other goods;
(*b*) the processing of goods;
(*c*) the destruction of goods;
(*d*) the repair of goods, including restoring them and putting them in order;
(*e*) the use of goods which are not to be found in the processed products, but which allow or facilitate the production of those products, even if they are entirely or partially used up in the process (production accessories);

32. "rate of yield" means the quantity or percentage of processed products obtained from the processing of a given quantity of goods placed under a processing procedure;

33. "message" means a communication in a prescribed format containing data transmitted from one person, office or authority to another using information technology and computer networks.

CHAPTER 2

RIGHTS AND OBLIGATIONS OF PERSONS WITH REGARD TO CUSTOMS LEGISLATION

SECTION 1—PROVISION OF INFORMATION

Exchange and storage of data

Article 5

1. All exchanges of data, accompanying documents, decisions and notifications between customs authorities and between economic operators and customs authorities required under

the customs legislation, and the storage of such data as required under the customs legislation, shall be made using electronic data-processing techniques.

The measures designed to amend non-essential elements of this Regulation, by supplementing it, laying down exceptions to the first subparagraph, shall be adopted in accordance with the regulatory procedure with scrutiny referred to in Article 184(4).

Those measures shall define the cases in which and the conditions under which paper or other transactions may be used in place of electronic exchanges of data, taking the following, in particular, into account:

(*a*) the possibility of temporary failure of the customs authorities' computerised systems;
(*b*) the possibility of temporary failure of the economic operator's computerised systems;
(*c*) international conventions and agreements which provide for the use of paper documents;
(*d*) travellers without direct access to the computerised systems and with no means of providing electronic information;
(*e*) practical requirements for declarations to be made orally or by any other act.

2. Except where these are otherwise specifically provided for in the customs legislation, the Commission shall, in accordance with the regulatory procedure referred to in Article 184(2), adopt measures laying down the following:

(*a*) the messages to be exchanged between customs offices, as required for the application of the customs legislation;
(*b*) a common data set and format of the messages to be exchanged under the customs legislation.

The data referred to in point (*b*) of the first subparagraph shall contain the particulars necessary for risk analysis and the proper application of customs controls, using, where appropriate, international standards and commercial practices.

Data protection

Article 6

1. All information acquired by the customs authorities in the course of performing their duties which is by its nature confidential or which is provided on a confidential basis shall be covered by the obligation of professional secrecy. Except as provided for under Article 26(2), such information shall not be disclosed by the competent authorities without the express permission of the person or authority that provided it.

Such information may, however, be disclosed without permission where the customs authorities are obliged or authorised to do so pursuant to the provisions in force, particularly in respect of data protection, or in connection with legal proceedings.

2. Communication of confidential data to the customs authorities and other competent authorities of countries or territories outside the customs territory of the Community shall be permitted only in the framework of an international agreement ensuring an adequate level of data protection.

3. The disclosure or communication of information shall take place in full compliance with data-protection provisions in force.

Exchange of additional information between customs authorities and economic operators

Article 7

1. Customs authorities and economic operators may exchange any information not specifically required under the customs legislation, in particular for the purpose of mutual cooperation in the identification and counteraction of risk. That exchange may take place under a written agreement and may include access to the computer systems of economic operators by the customs authorities.

2. Any information provided by one party to the other in the course of the cooperation referred to in paragraph 1 shall be confidential unless both parties agree otherwise.

Provision of information by the customs authorities

Article 8

1. Any person may request information concerning the application of customs legislation from the customs authorities. Such a request may be refused where it does not relate to an activity pertaining to international trade in goods that is actually envisaged.

2. Customs authorities shall maintain a regular dialogue with economic operators and other authorities involved in international trade in goods. They shall promote transparency by making the customs legislation, general administrative rulings and application forms freely available, wherever practical without charge, and through the Internet.

Provision of information to the customs authorities

Article 9

1. Any person directly or indirectly involved in the accomplishment of customs formalities or in customs controls shall, at the request of the customs authorities and within any time limit

specified, provide those authorities with all the requisite documents and information, in an appropriate form, and all the assistance necessary for the completion of those formalities or controls.

2. The lodging of a summary declaration or customs declaration, or notification, or the submission of an application for an authorisation or any other decision, shall render the person concerned responsible for the following:

(*a*) the accuracy and completeness of the information given in the declaration, notification or application;

(*b*) the authenticity of any documents lodged or made available;

(*c*) where applicable, compliance with all of the obligations relating to the placing of the goods in question under the customs procedure concerned, or to the conduct of the authorised operations.

The first subparagraph shall apply also to the provision of any information in any other form required by or given to the customs authorities.

Where the declaration or notification is lodged, the application is submitted or information is provided by a customs representative of the person concerned, the customs representative shall also be bound by the obligations set out in the first subparagraph.

Electronic systems

Article 10

1. Member States shall cooperate with the Commission with a view to developing, maintaining and employing electronic systems for the exchange of information between customs offices and for the common registration and maintenance of records relating, in particular, to the following:

(*a*) economic operators directly or indirectly involved in the accomplishment of customs formalities;

(*b*) applications and authorisations concerning a customs procedure or the status of authorised economic operator;

(*c*) applications and special decisions granted in accordance with Article 20;

(*d*) common risk management, as referred to in Article 25.

2. The measures designed to amend non-essential elements of this Regulation, by supplementing it, laying down the following:

(*a*) the standard form and content of the data to be registered;

(*b*) maintenance of those data, by the customs authorities of Members States;

(*c*) the rules for access to those data by:

(i) economic operators,

(ii) other competent authorities,

shall be adopted in accordance with the regulatory procedure with scrutiny referred to in Article 184(4).

SECTION 2—CUSTOMS REPRESENTATION

Customs representative

Article 11

1. Any person may appoint a customs representative.

Such representation may be either direct, in which case the customs representative shall act in the name of and on behalf of another person, or indirect, in which case the customs representative shall act in his own name but on behalf of another person.

A customs representative shall be established within the customs territory of the Community.

2. Member States may define, in accordance with Community law, the conditions under which a customs representative may provide services in the Member State where he is established. However, without prejudice to the application of less stringent criteria by the Member State concerned, a customs representative who complies with the criteria laid down in Article 14(*a*) to (*d*) shall be entitled to provide such services in a Member State other than the one where he is established.

3. The measures designed to amend non-essential elements of this Regulation, by supplementing it, laying down in particular, the following:

(*a*) the conditions under which the requirement referred to in the third subparagraph of paragraph 1 may be waived;

(*b*) the conditions under which the entitlement referred to in paragraph 2 may be conferred and proved;

(*c*) any further measures for the implementation of this Article,

shall be adopted in accordance with the regulatory procedure with scrutiny referred to in Article 184(4).

Empowerment

Article 12

1. When dealing with the customs authorities, a customs representative shall state that he is acting on behalf of the person represented and specify whether the representation is direct or indirect.

A person who fails to state that he is acting as a customs representative or who states that he is acting as a customs representative without being empowered to do so shall be deemed to be acting in his own name and on his own behalf.

2. The customs authorities may require any person stating that he is acting as a customs representative to produce evidence of his empowerment by the person represented.

The measures designed to amend non-essential elements of this Regulation, by supplementing it, laying down derogations from the first subparagraph, shall be adopted in accordance with the regulatory procedure with scrutiny referred to in Article 184(4).

SECTION 3—AUTHORISED ECONOMIC OPERATOR

Application and authorisation

Article 13

1. An economic operator who is established in the customs territory of the Community and who meets the conditions set out in Articles 14 and 15 may request the status of authorised economic operator.

The customs authorities shall, if necessary following consultation with other competent authorities, grant that status, which shall be subject to monitoring.

2. The status of authorised economic operator shall consist in two types of authorisations: that of a "customs simplification" authorised economic operator and that of a "security and safety" authorised economic operator.

The first type of authorisation shall enable economic operators to benefit from certain simplifications in accordance with the customs legislation. Under the second type of authorisation the holder thereof shall be entitled to facilitations relating to security and safety.

Both types of authorisations may be held at the same time.

3. The status of authorised economic operator shall, subject to Articles 14 and 15, be recognised by the customs authorities in all Member States, without prejudice to customs controls.

4. Customs authorities shall, on the basis of the recognition of the status of authorised economic operator and provided that the requirements related to a specific type of simplification provided for in the customs legislation are fulfilled, authorise the operator to benefit from that simplification.

5. The status of authorised economic operator may be suspended or revoked in accordance with the conditions laid down pursuant to Article 15(1)(*g*).

6. The authorised economic operator shall notify the customs authorities of all factors arising after that status was granted which may influence its continuation or content.

Granting of status

Article 14

The criteria for the granting of the status of authorised economic operator shall be the following:

(*a*) a record of compliance with customs and tax requirements;
(*b*) a satisfactory system of managing commercial and, where appropriate, transport records, which allows appropriate customs controls;
(*c*) proven solvency;
(*d*) pursuant to Article 13(2), in cases where an authorised economic operator wishes to take advantage of the simplifications provided for in accordance with the customs legislation, practical standards of competence or professional qualifications directly related to the activity carried out;
(*e*) pursuant to Article 13(2), in cases where an authorised economic operator wishes to take advantage of facilitations with regard to customs controls relating to security and safety, appropriate security and safety standards.

Implementing measures

Article 15

1. The measures designed to amend non-essential elements of this Regulation, by supplementing it, laying down rules in respect of the following:

(*a*) the granting of the status of authorised economic operator;
(*b*) the cases in which review of the status of authorised economic operator is to be carried out;

(*c*) the granting of authorisations for the use of simplifications by authorised economic operators;

(*d*) identification of the customs authority competent for the granting of such status and authorisations;

(*e*) the type and extent of facilitations that may be granted to authorised economic operators in respect of customs controls relating to security and safety;

(*f*) consultation with and provision of information to other customs authorities;

(*g*) the conditions under which the status of authorised economic operator may be suspended or revoked;

(*h*) the conditions under which the requirement of being established in the customs territory of the Community may be waived for specific categories of authorised economic operators, taking into account, in particular, international agreements,

shall be adopted in accordance with the regulatory procedure with scrutiny referred to in Article 184(4).

2. Those measures shall take account of the following:

(*a*) the rules adopted pursuant to Article 25(3);

(*b*) professional involvement in activities covered by customs legislation;

(*c*) practical standards of competence or professional qualifications directly related to the activity carried out;

(*d*) the economic operator as the holder of any internationally recognised certificate issued on the basis of relevant international conventions.

SECTION 4—DECISIONS RELATING TO THE APPLICATION OF CUSTOMS LEGISLATION

General provisions

Article 16

1. Where a person requests that the customs authorities take a decision relating to the application of customs legislation, that person shall supply all the information required by those authorities in order for them to be able to take that decision.

A decision may also be requested by, and taken with regard to, several persons, in accordance with the conditions laid down in the customs legislation.

2. Except where otherwise provided for in the customs legislation, a decision as referred to in paragraph 1 shall be taken, and the applicant notified, without delay, and at the latest within four months of the date on which all the information required by the customs authorities in order for them to be able to take that decision is received by those authorities.

However, where the customs authorities are unable to comply with those time limits, they shall inform the applicant of that fact before the expiry of those time limits, stating the reasons and indicating the further period of time which they consider necessary in order to give a decision on the request.

3. Except where otherwise specified in the decision or in the customs legislation, the decision shall take effect from the date on which the applicant receives the decision, or is deemed to have received it. Except in the cases provided for in Article 24(2), decisions adopted shall be enforceable by the customs authorities from that date.

4. Before taking a decision which would adversely affect the person or persons to whom it is addressed, the customs authorities shall communicate the grounds on which they intend to base their decision to the person or persons concerned, who shall be given the opportunity to express their point of view within a period prescribed from the date on which the communication was made.

Following the expiry of that period, the person concerned shall be notified, in the appropriate form, of the decision, which shall set out the grounds on which it is based. The decision shall refer to the right of appeal provided for in Article 23.

5. The measures designed to amend non-essential elements of this Regulation, by supplementing it, laying down the following:

(*a*) the cases in which and conditions under which the first subparagraph of paragraph 4 shall not apply;

(*b*) the period referred to in the first subparagraph of paragraph 4,

shall be adopted in accordance with the regulatory procedure with scrutiny referred to in Article 184(4).

6. Without prejudice to provisions laid down in other fields which specify the cases in which, and the conditions under which, decisions are invalid or become null and void, the customs authorities who issued a decision may at any time annul, amend or revoke it where it does not conform with the customs legislation.

7. Except when a customs authority acts as a judicial authority, the provisions of paragraphs 3, 4 and 6 of this Article and of Articles 17, 18 and 19 shall also apply to decisions taken by the customs authorities without prior request from the person concerned and, in particular, to the notification of a customs debt as provided for in Article 67(3).

Community-wide validity of decisions

Article 17

Except where otherwise requested or specified, decisions taken by the customs authorities which are based upon or related to the application of customs legislation shall be valid throughout the customs territory of the Community.

Annulment of favourable decisions

Article 18

1. The customs authorities shall annul a decision favourable to the person to whom it is addressed if all the following conditions are satisfied:

(*a*) the decision was issued on the basis of incorrect or incomplete information;

(*b*) the applicant knew or ought reasonably to have known that the information was incorrect or incomplete;

(*c*) if the information had been correct and complete, the decision would have been different.

2. The person to whom the decision was addressed shall be notified of its annulment.

3. Annulment shall take effect from the date on which the initial decision took effect, unless otherwise specified in the decision in accordance with the customs legislation.

4. The Commission may, in accordance with the management procedure referred to in Article 184(3), adopt measures for the implementation of this Article, in particular in respect of decisions addressed to several persons.

Revocation and amendment of favourable decisions

Article 19

1. A favourable decision shall be revoked or amended where, in cases other than those referred to in Article 18, one or more of the conditions laid down for its issue were not or are no longer fulfilled.

2. Except where otherwise specified in the customs legislation, a favourable decision addressed to several persons may be revoked only in respect of a person who fails to fulfil an obligation imposed under that decision.

3. The person to whom the decision was addressed shall be notified of its revocation or amendment.

4. Article 16(3) shall apply to the revocation or amendment of the decision.

However, in exceptional cases where the legitimate interests of the person to whom the decision was addressed so require, the customs authorities may defer the date on which revocation or amendment takes effect.

5. The Commission may, in accordance with the management procedure referred to in Article 184(3), adopt measures for the implementation of this Article, in particular in respect of decisions addressed to several persons.

Decisions relating to binding information

Article 20

1. The customs authorities shall, on formal request, issue decisions relating to binding tariff information, hereinafter referred to as "BTI decisions", or decisions relating to binding origin information, hereinafter referred to as "BOI decisions".

Such a request shall be refused in any of the following circumstances:

(*a*) where the application is made, or has already been made, at the same or another customs office, by or on behalf of the holder of a decision in respect of the same goods and, for BOI decisions, under the same circumstances determining the acquisition of origin;

(*b*) where the application does not relate to any intended use of the BTI or BOI decision or any intended use of a customs procedure.

2. BTI or BOI decisions shall be binding only in respect of the tariff classification or determination of the origin of goods.

Those decisions shall be binding on the customs authorities, as against the holder of the decision, only in respect of goods for which customs formalities are completed after the date on which the decision takes effect.

The decisions shall be binding on the holder of the decision, as against the customs authorities, only with effect from the date on which he receives, or is deemed to have received, notification of the decision.

3. BTI or BOI decisions shall be valid for a period of three years from the date on which the decision takes effect.

4. For the application of a BTI or BOI decision in the context of a particular customs procedure, the holder of the decision must be able to prove that:

(*a*) in the case of a BTI decision, the goods declared correspond in every respect to those described in the decision;

(*b*) in the case of a BOI decision, the goods in question and the circumstances determining the acquisition of origin correspond in every respect to the goods and the circumstances described in the decision.

5. By way of derogation from Article 16(6) and Article 18, BTI or BOI decisions shall be annulled where they are based on inaccurate or incomplete information from the applicants.

6. BTI or BOI decisions shall be revoked in accordance with Article 16(6) and Article 19.

They may not be amended.

7. The Commission shall, in accordance with the regulatory procedure referred to in Article 184(2), adopt measures for the implementation of paragraphs 1 to 5 of this Article.

8. Without prejudice to Article 19, the measures designed to amend non-essential elements of this Regulation, by supplementing it, laying down

(*a*) the conditions under which, and the moment when, the BTI or BOI decision ceases to be valid;

(*b*) the conditions under which, and the period of time for which, a decision as referred to in point (*a*) may still be used in respect of binding contracts based upon the decision and concluded before the expiry of its validity;

(*c*) the conditions under which the Commission may issue decisions requesting Member States to revoke or amend a decision relating to binding information and giving different binding information compared with other decisions on the same subject,

shall be adopted in accordance with the regulatory procedure with scrutiny referred to in Article 184(4).

9. The measures designed to amend non-essential elements of this Regulation, by supplementing it, laying down the conditions under which other decisions relating to binding information are to be issued shall be adopted in accordance with the regulatory procedure with scrutiny referred to in Article 184(4).

Section 5—Penalties

Application of penalties

Article 21

1. Each Member State shall provide for penalties for failure to comply with Community customs legislation. Such penalties shall be effective, proportionate and dissuasive.

2. Where administrative penalties are applied, they may take, inter alia, one of the following forms, or both:

(*a*) a pecuniary charge by the customs authorities, including, where appropriate, a settlement applied in place of and in lieu of a criminal penalty;

(*b*) the revocation, suspension or amendment of any authorisation held by the person concerned.

3. Member States shall notify the Commission, within six months from the date of application of this Article, as determined in accordance with Article 188(2), of the national provisions in force as envisaged in paragraph 1 and shall notify it without delay of any subsequent amendment affecting them.

Section 6—Appeals

Decisions taken by a judicial authority

Article 22

Articles 23 and 24 shall not apply to appeals lodged with a view to the annulment, revocation or amendment of a decision relating to the application of customs legislation taken by a judicial authority, or by customs authorities acting as judicial authorities.

Right of appeal

Article 23

1. Any person shall have the right to appeal against any decision taken by the customs authorities relating to the application of customs legislation which concerns him directly and individually.

Any person who has applied to the customs authorities for a decision and has not obtained a decision on that request within the time limits referred to in Article 16(2) shall also be entitled to exercise the right of appeal.

2. The right of appeal may be exercised in at least two steps:

(*a*) initially, before the customs authorities or a judicial authority or other body designated for that purpose by the Member States;

(*b*) subsequently, before a higher independent body, which may be a judicial authority or an equivalent specialised body, according to the provisions in force in the Member States.

3. The appeal must be lodged in the Member State where the decision has been taken or applied for.

4. Member States shall ensure that the appeals procedure enables the prompt confirmation or correction of decisions taken by the customs authorities.

Suspension of implementation

Article 24

1. The submission of an appeal shall not cause implementation of the disputed decision to be suspended.

2. The customs authorities shall, however, suspend implementation of such a decision in whole or in part where they have good reason to believe that the disputed decision is inconsistent with customs legislation or that irreparable damage is to be feared for the person concerned.

3. In the cases referred to in paragraph 2, where the disputed decision has the effect of causing import duties or export duties to be payable, suspension of that decision shall be conditional upon the provision of a guarantee, unless it is established, on the basis of a documented assessment, that such a guarantee would be likely to cause the debtor serious economic or social difficulties.

The Commission may, in accordance with the regulatory procedure referred to in Article 184(2), adopt measures for the implementation of the first subparagraph of this paragraph.

SECTION 7—CONTROL OF GOODS

Customs controls

Article 25

1. The customs authorities may carry out all the customs controls they deem necessary.

Customs controls may in particular consist of examining goods, taking samples, verifying declaration data and the existence and authenticity of documents, examining the accounts of economic operators and other records, inspecting means of transport, inspecting luggage and other goods carried by or on persons and carrying out official enquiries and other similar acts.

2. Customs controls, other than random checks, shall primarily be based on risk analysis using electronic data-processing techniques, with the purpose of identifying and evaluating the risks and developing the necessary counter-measures, on the basis of criteria developed at national, Community and, where available, international level.

Member States, in cooperation with the Commission, shall develop, maintain and employ a common risk management framework, based upon the exchange of risk information and analysis between customs administrations and establishing, inter alia, common risk evaluation criteria, control measures and priority control areas.

Controls based upon such information and criteria shall be carried out without prejudice to other controls carried out in accordance with paragraphs 1 and 2 or with other provisions in force.

3. The Commission, without prejudice to paragraph 2 of this Article, shall, in accordance with the regulatory procedure referred to in Article 184(2), adopt implementing measures laying down the following:

(*a*) common risk management framework;
(*b*) common criteria and priority control areas;
(*c*) the risk information and analysis to be exchanged between customs administrations.

Cooperation between authorities

Article 26

1. Where, in respect of the same goods, controls other than customs controls are to be performed by competent authorities other than the customs authorities, customs authorities shall, in close cooperation with those other authorities, endeavour to have those controls performed, wherever possible, at the same time and place as customs controls (one-stop-shop), with customs authorities having the coordinating role in achieving this.

2. In the framework of the controls referred to in this Section, customs and other competent authorities may, where necessary for the purposes of minimising risk and combating fraud, exchange with each other and with the Commission data received in the context of the entry, exit, transit, transfer, storage and end-use of goods, including postal traffic, moved between the customs territory of the Community and other territories, the presence and movement within the customs territory of non-Community goods and goods placed under the end-use procedure, and the results of any control. Customs authorities and the Commission may also exchange such data with each other for the purpose of ensuring a uniform application of Community customs legislation.

Post-release control

Article 27

The customs authorities may, after releasing the goods and in order to ascertain the accuracy of the particulars contained in the summary or customs declaration, inspect any documents and data relating to the operations in respect of the goods in question or to prior or subsequent commercial operations involving those goods. Those authorities may also examine such goods and/or take samples where it is still possible for them to do so.

Such inspections may be carried out at the premises of the holder of the goods or his representative, of any other person directly or indirectly involved in those operations in a business capacity or of any other person in possession of those documents and data for business purposes.

Intra-Community flights and sea crossings

Article 28

1. Customs controls or formalities shall be carried out in respect of the cabin and hold baggage of persons either taking an intra-Community flight, or making an intra-Community sea crossing, only where the customs legislation provides for such controls or formalities.

2. Paragraph 1 shall apply without prejudice to either of the following:

(*a*) security and safety checks;

(*b*) checks linked to prohibitions or restrictions.

3. The Commission shall, in accordance with the regulatory procedure referred to in Article 184(2), adopt measures for the implementation of this Article, laying down the cases in which and the conditions under which customs controls and formalities may be applied to the following:

(*a*) the cabin and hold baggage of the following:

(i) persons taking a flight in an aircraft which comes from a non-Community airport and which, after a stopover at a Community airport, continues to another Community airport;

(ii) persons taking a flight in an aircraft which stops over at a Community airport before continuing to a non-Community airport;

(iii) persons using a maritime service provided by the same vessel and comprising successive legs departing from, calling at or terminating in a non-Community port;

(iv) persons on board pleasure craft and tourist or business aircraft;

(*b*) cabin and hold baggage:

(i) arriving at a Community airport on board an aircraft coming from a non-Community airport and transferred at that Community airport to another aircraft proceeding on an intra-Community flight;

(ii) loaded at a Community airport onto an aircraft proceeding on an intra-Community flight for transfer at another Community airport to an aircraft whose destination is a non-Community airport.

SECTION 8—KEEPING OF DOCUMENTS AND OTHER INFORMATION; CHARGES AND COSTS

Keeping of documents and other information

Article 29

1. The person concerned shall, for the purposes of customs controls, keep the documents and information referred to in Article 9(1) for at least three calendar years, by any means accessible by and acceptable to the customs authorities.

In the case of goods released for free circulation in circumstances other than those referred to in the third subparagraph, or goods declared for export, that period shall run from the end of the year in which the customs declarations for release for free circulation or export are accepted.

In the case of goods released for free circulation duty-free or at a reduced rate of import duty on account of their end-use, that period shall run from the end of the year in which they cease to be subject to customs supervision.

In the case of goods placed under another customs procedure, that period shall run from the end of the year in which the customs procedure concerned has ended.

2. Without prejudice to Article 68(4), where a customs control in respect of a customs debt shows that the relevant entry in the accounts has to be corrected and the person concerned has been notified of this, the documents and information shall be kept for three years beyond the time limit provided for in paragraph 1 of this Article.

Where an appeal has been lodged or where court proceedings have begun, the documents and information must be kept for the period provided for in paragraph 1 of this Article or until the appeals procedure or court proceedings are terminated, whichever is the later.

Charges and costs

Article 30

1. Customs authorities shall not impose charges for the performance of customs controls or any other application of the customs legislation during the official opening hours of their competent customs offices.

However, the customs authorities may impose charges or recover costs where specific services are rendered, in particular the following:

(*a*) attendance, where requested, by customs staff outside official office hours or at premises other than customs premises;

(*b*) analyses or expert reports on goods and postal fees for the return of goods to an applicant, particularly in respect of decisions taken pursuant to Article 20 or the provision of information in accordance with Article 8(1);

(*c*) the examination or sampling of goods for verification purposes, or the destruction of goods, where costs other than the cost of using customs staff are involved;

(*d*) exceptional control measures, where these are necessary due to the nature of the goods or to potential risk.

2. The measures designed to amend non-essential elements of this Regulation, by supplementing it, laying down measures for the implementation of the second subparagraph of paragraph 1, shall be adopted in accordance with the regulatory procedure with scrutiny referred to in Article 184(4).

CHAPTER 3

CURRENCY CONVERSION AND TIME LIMITS

Currency conversion

Article 31

1. The competent authorities shall publish, and/or make available on the Internet, the rate of exchange applicable where the conversion of currency is necessary for one of the following reasons:

(*a*) because factors used to determine the customs value of goods are expressed in a currency other than that of the Member State where the customs value is determined;

(*b*) because the value of the euro is required in national currencies for the purposes of determining the tariff classification of goods and the amount of import and export duty, including value thresholds in the Community Customs Tariff.

2. Where the conversion of currency is necessary for reasons other than those referred to in paragraph 1, the value of the euro in national currencies to be applied within the framework of the customs legislation shall be fixed at least once a year.

3. The Commission shall, in accordance with the regulatory procedure referred to in Article 184(2), adopt measures for the implementation of this Article.

Time limits

Article 32

1. Where a period, date or time limit is laid down in the customs legislation, such period shall not be extended or reduced and such date or time limit shall not be deferred or brought forward unless specific provision is made in the provisions concerned.

2. The rules applicable to periods, dates and time limits set out in Regulation (EEC, Euratom) No 1182/71 of the Council of 3 June 1971 determining the rules applicable to periods, dates and time limits[1] shall apply, except where otherwise specifically provided for in Community customs legislation.

Amendments—[1] OJ L 124, 8.6.1971, p. 1.

TITLE II

FACTORS ON THE BASIS OF WHICH IMPORT OR EXPORT DUTIES AND OTHER MEASURES IN RESPECT OF TRADE IN GOODS ARE APPLIED

CHAPTER 1

COMMON CUSTOMS TARIFF AND TARIFF CLASSIFICATION OF GOODS

Common Customs Tariff

Article 33

1. Import and export duties due shall be based on the Common Customs Tariff.

Other measures prescribed by Community provisions governing specific fields relating to trade in goods shall, where appropriate, be applied in accordance with the tariff classification of those goods.

2. The Common Customs Tariff shall comprise the following:

(*a*) the Combined Nomenclature of goods as laid down in Council Regulation (EEC) No 2658/87 of 23 July 1987 on the tariff and statistical nomenclature and on the Common Customs Tariff[1];

(*b*) any other nomenclature which is wholly or partly based on the Combined Nomenclature or which provides for further subdivisions to it, and which is established by Community provisions governing specific fields with a view to the application of tariff measures relating to trade in goods;

(*c*) the conventional or normal autonomous customs duties applicable to goods covered by the Combined Nomenclature;

(*d*) the preferential tariff measures contained in agreements which the Community has concluded with certain countries or territories outside the customs territory of the Community or groups of such countries or territories;

(*e*) preferential tariff measures adopted unilaterally by the Community in respect of certain countries or territories outside the customs territory of the Community or groups of such countries or territories;

(*f*) autonomous measures providing for a reduction in or exemption from customs duties on certain goods;

(*g*) favourable tariff treatment specified for certain goods, by reason of their nature or end-use, in the framework of measures referred to under points (*c*) to (*f*) or (*h*);

(*h*) other tariff measures provided for by agricultural or commercial or other Community legislation.

3. Where the goods concerned fulfil the conditions included in the measures laid down in points (*d*) to (*g*) of paragraph 2, the measures referred to in those provisions shall apply, at the request of the declarant, instead of those provided for in point (*c*) of that paragraph. Such application may be made retrospectively, provided that the time limits and conditions laid down in the relevant measure or in the Code are complied with.

4. Where application of the measures referred to in points (*d*) to (*g*) of paragraph 2, or the exemption from measures referred to in point (*h*) thereof, is restricted to a certain volume of imports or exports, such application or exemption shall, in the case of tariff quotas, cease as soon as the specified volume of imports or exports is reached.

In the case of tariff ceilings such application shall cease by virtue of a legal act of the Community.

5. The Commission shall, in accordance with the management procedure referred to in Article 184(3), adopt measures for the implementation of paragraphs 1 and 4 of this Article.

Amendments—[1] OJ L 256, 7.9.1987, p. 1. Regulation as last amended by Regulation (EC) No 275/2008 (OJ L 85, 27.3.2008, p. 3).

Tariff classification of goods

Article 34

1. For the application of the Common Customs Tariff, "tariff classification" of goods shall consist in the determination of one of the subheadings or further subdivisions of the Combined Nomenclature under which those goods are to be classified.

2. For the application of non-tariff measures, "tariff classification" of goods shall consist in the determination of one of the subheadings or further subdivisions of the Combined Nomenclature, or of any other nomenclature which is established by Community provisions and which is wholly or partly based on the Combined Nomenclature or which provides for further subdivisions to it, under which those goods are to be classified.

3. The subheading or further subdivision determined in accordance with paragraphs 1 and 2 shall be used for the purpose of applying the measures linked to that subheading.

CHAPTER 2
ORIGIN OF GOODS

SECTION 1—NON-PREFERENTIAL ORIGIN

Scope

Article 35

Articles 36, 37 and 38 lay down rules for the determination of the non-preferential origin of goods for the purposes of applying the following:

(*a*) the Common Customs Tariff with the exception of the measures referred to in Article 33(2)(*d*) and (*e*);

(*b*) measures, other than tariff measures, established by Community provisions governing specific fields relating to trade in goods;

(*c*) other Community measures relating to the origin of goods.

Acquisition of origin

Article 36

1. Goods wholly obtained in a single country or territory shall be regarded as having their origin in that country or territory.

2. Goods the production of which involved more than one country or territory shall be deemed to originate in the country or territory where they underwent their last substantial transformation.

Proof of origin

Article 37

1. Where an origin has been indicated in the customs declaration pursuant to customs legislation, the customs authorities may require the declarant to prove the origin of the goods.

2. Where proof of origin of goods is provided pursuant to customs legislation or other Community legislation governing specific fields, the customs authorities may, in the event of reasonable doubt, require any additional evidence needed in order to ensure that the indication of origin does comply with the rules laid down by the relevant Community legislation.

3. A document proving origin may be issued in the Community where the exigencies of trade so require.

Implementing measures

Article 38

The Commission shall, in accordance with the regulatory procedure referred to in Article 184(2), adopt measures for the implementation of Articles 36 and 37.

SECTION 2—PREFERENTIAL ORIGIN

Preferential origin of goods

Article 39

1. In order to benefit from the measures referred to in points (*d*) or (*e*) of Article 33(2) or from non-tariff preferential measures, goods shall comply with the rules on preferential origin referred to in paragraphs 2 to 5 of this Article.

2. In the case of goods benefiting from preferential measures contained in agreements which the Community has concluded with certain countries or territories outside the customs territory of the Community or with groups of such countries or territories, the rules on preferential origin shall be laid down in those agreements.

3. In the case of goods benefiting from preferential measures adopted unilaterally by the Community in respect of certain countries or territories outside the customs territory of the Community or groups of such countries or territories, other than those referred to in paragraph 5, the Commission shall, in accordance with the regulatory procedure referred to in Article 184(2), adopt measures laying down the rules on preferential origin.

4. In the case of goods benefiting from preferential measures applicable in trade between the customs territory of the Community and Ceuta and Melilla, as contained in Protocol 2 to the 1985 Act of Accession, the rules on preferential origin shall be adopted in accordance with Article 9 of that Protocol.

5. In the case of goods benefiting from preferential measures contained in preferential arrangements in favour of the overseas countries and territories associated with the Community, the rules on preferential origin shall be adopted in accordance with Article 187 of the Treaty.

6. The Commission shall, in accordance with the regulatory procedure referred to in Article 184(2), adopt measures necessary for the implementation of the rules referred to in paragraphs 2 to 5 of this Article.

CHAPTER 3

VALUE OF GOODS FOR CUSTOMS PURPOSES

Scope

Article 40

The customs value of goods, for the purposes of applying the Common Customs Tariff and non-tariff measures laid down by Community provisions governing specific fields relating to trade in goods, shall be determined in accordance with Articles 41 to 43.

Method of customs valuation based on the transaction value

Article 41

1. The primary basis for the customs value of goods shall be the transaction value, that is the price actually paid or payable for the goods when sold for export to the customs territory of the Community, adjusted, where necessary, in accordance with measures adopted pursuant to Article 43.

2. The price actually paid or payable is the total payment made or to be made by the buyer to the seller or by the buyer to a third party for the benefit of the seller for the imported goods and includes all payments made or to be made as a condition of sale of the imported goods.

3. The transaction value shall apply provided that the following conditions are satisfied:

(*a*) there are no restrictions as to the disposal or use of the goods by the buyer, other than any of the following:

(i) restrictions imposed or required by a law or by the public authorities in the Community;
(ii) limitations of the geographical area in which the goods may be resold;
(iii) restrictions which do not substantially affect the customs value of the goods;

(*b*) the sale or price is not subject to some condition or consideration for which a value cannot be determined with respect to the goods being valued;
(*c*) no part of the proceeds of any subsequent resale, disposal or use of the goods by the buyer will accrue directly or indirectly to the seller, unless an appropriate adjustment can be made in accordance with measures adopted pursuant to Article 43;
(*d*) the buyer and seller are not related or the relationship did not influence the price.

Secondary methods of customs valuation

Article 42

1. Where the customs value of goods cannot be determined under Article 41, it shall be determined by proceeding sequentially from point (*a*) to paragraph 2(*d*) of this Article, until the first point under which the customs value of goods can be determined.

The order of application of points (*c*) and (*d*) shall be reversed if the declarant so requests.

2. The customs value, pursuant to paragraph 1, shall be:

(*a*) the transaction value of identical goods sold for export to the customs territory of the Community and exported at or about the same time as the goods being valued;
(*b*) the transaction value of similar goods sold for export to the customs territory of the Community and exported at or about the same time as the goods being valued;
(*c*) the value based on the unit price at which the imported goods, or identical or similar imported goods, are sold within the customs territory of the Community in the greatest aggregate quantity to persons not related to the sellers;
(*d*) the computed value.

3. Where the customs value cannot be determined under paragraph 1, it shall be determined, on the basis of data available in the customs territory on the Community, using reasonable means consistent with the principles and general provisions of the following:

(*a*) the agreement on implementation of Article VII of the General Agreement on Tariffs and Trade;
(*b*) Article VII of General Agreement on Tariffs and Trade;
(*c*) this chapter.

Implementing measures

Article 43

The Commission shall, in accordance with the regulatory procedure referred to in Article 184(2), adopt the measures laying down the following:

(*a*) the elements which, for the purposes of determining the customs value, must be added to the price actually paid or payable, or which may be excluded;
(*b*) elements which are to be used to determine the computed value;
(*c*) the method of determination of the customs value in specific cases, and with regard to goods for which a customs debt is incurred after the use of a special procedure:
(*d*) any further conditions, provisions and rules necessary for the application of Articles 41 and 42.

TITLE III
CUSTOMS DEBT AND GUARANTEES

CHAPTER 1
INCURRENCE OF A CUSTOMS DEBT

SECTION 1—CUSTOMS DEBT ON IMPORTATION

Release for free circulation and temporary admission

Article 44

1. A customs debt on importation shall be incurred through the placing of non-Community goods liable to import duties under either of the following customs procedures:

(*a*) release for free circulation, including under the end-use provisions;

(*b*) temporary admission with partial relief from import duties.

2. A customs debt shall be incurred at the time of acceptance of the customs declaration.

3. The declarant shall be the debtor. In the event of indirect representation, the person on whose behalf the customs declaration is made shall also be a debtor.

Where a customs declaration in respect of one of the procedures referred to in paragraph 1 is drawn up on the basis of information which leads to all or part of the import duties not being collected, the person who provided the information required to draw up the declaration and who knew, or who ought reasonably to have known, that such information was false shall also be a debtor.

Special provisions relating to non-originating goods

Article 45

1. Where a prohibition of drawback of, or exemption from, import duties applies to non-originating goods used in the manufacture of products for which a proof of origin is issued or made out in the framework of a preferential arrangement between the Community and certain countries or territories outside the customs territory of the Community or groups of such countries or territories, a customs debt on importation shall be incurred in respect of those non-originating goods, through the acceptance of the re-export notification relating to the products in question.

2. Where a customs debt is incurred pursuant to paragraph 1, the amount of import duty corresponding to that debt shall be determined under the same conditions as in the case of a customs debt resulting from the acceptance, on the same date, of the customs declaration for release for free circulation of the non-originating goods used in the manufacture of the products in question for the purpose of ending the inward-processing procedure.

3. Article 44(2) and (3) shall apply mutatis mutandis. However, in the case of non-Community goods as referred to in Article 179, the person who lodges the re-export notification shall be the debtor. In the event of indirect representation, the person on whose behalf the notification is lodged shall also be a debtor.

Customs debt incurred through non-compliance

Article 46

1. For goods liable to import duties, a customs debt on importation shall be incurred through non-compliance with any of the following:

(*a*) one of the obligations laid down in customs legislation concerning the introduction of non-Community goods into the customs territory of the Community, their removal from customs supervision, or the movement, processing, storage, temporary admission or disposal of such goods within that territory;

(*b*) one of the obligations laid down in customs legislation concerning the end-use of goods within the customs territory of the Community;

(*c*) a condition governing the placing of non-Community goods under a customs procedure or the granting, by virtue of the end-use of the goods, of duty exemption or a reduced rate of import duty.

2. The time at which the customs debt is incurred shall be either of the following:

(*a*) the moment when the obligation the non-fulfilment of which gives rise to the customs debt is not met or ceases to be met;

(*b*) the moment when a customs declaration is accepted for the placing of goods under a customs procedure where it is established subsequently that a condition governing the placing of the goods under that procedure or the granting of a duty exemption or a reduced rate of import duty by virtue of the end-use of the goods was not in fact fulfilled.

3. In cases referred to under points (*a*) and (*b*) of paragraph 1, the debtor shall be any of the following:

(*a*) any person who was required to fulfil the obligations concerned;

(*b*) any person who was aware or should reasonably have been aware that an obligation under the customs legislation was not fulfilled and who acted on behalf of the person who was obliged to fulfil the obligation, or who participated in the act which led to the non-fulfilment of the obligation;

(*c*) any person who acquired or held the goods in question and who was aware or should reasonably have been aware at the time of acquiring or receiving the goods that an obligation under the customs legislation was not fulfilled.

4. In cases referred to under point (*c*) of paragraph 1, the debtor shall be the person who is required to comply with the conditions governing the placing of the goods under a customs procedure or declaring the goods concerned under that procedure or the granting of a duty exemption or reduced rate of import duty by virtue of the end-use of the goods.

Where a customs declaration in respect of one of the procedures referred to in paragraph 1 is drawn up, or any information required under the customs legislation relating to the conditions governing the placing of the goods under a customs procedure is given to the customs authorities, which leads to all or part of the import duties not being collected, the person who provided the information required to draw up the declaration and who knew, or who ought reasonably to have known, that such information was false shall also be a debtor.

Deduction of an amount of import duty already paid

Article 47

1. Where a customs debt is incurred, pursuant to Article 46(1), in respect of goods released for free circulation at a reduced rate of import duty on account of their end-use, the amount of import duty paid when the goods were released for free circulation shall be deducted from the amount of the import duty corresponding to the customs debt.

The first subparagraph shall apply mutatis mutandis where a customs debt is incurred in respect of scrap and waste resulting from the destruction of such goods.

2. Where a customs debt is incurred, pursuant to Article 46(1), in respect of goods placed under temporary admission with partial relief from import duties, the amount of import duty paid under partial relief shall be deducted from the amount of the import duty corresponding to the customs debt.

SECTION 2—CUSTOMS DEBT ON EXPORTATION

Export and outward processing

Article 48

1. A customs debt on exportation shall be incurred through the placing of goods liable to export duties under the export procedure or the outward-processing procedure.

2. The customs debt shall be incurred at the time of acceptance of the customs declaration.

3. The declarant shall be the debtor. In the event of indirect representation, the person on whose behalf the customs declaration is made shall also be a debtor.

Where a customs declaration is drawn up on the basis of information which leads to all or part of the export duties not being collected, the person who provided the information required for the declaration and who knew, or who should reasonably have known, that such information was false shall also be a debtor.

Customs debt incurred through non-compliance

Article 49

1. For goods liable to export duties, a customs debt on exportation shall be incurred through non-compliance with either of the following:

(*a*) one of the obligations laid down in customs legislation for the exit of the goods;

(*b*) the conditions under which the goods were allowed to leave the customs territory of the Community with total or partial relief from export duties.

2. The time at which the customs debt is incurred shall be one of the following:

(*a*) the moment at which the goods actually leave the customs territory of the Community without a customs declaration;

(*b*) the moment at which the goods reach a destination other than that for which they were allowed to leave the customs territory of the Community with total or partial relief from export duties;

(*c*) should the customs authorities be unable to determine the moment referred in point (*b*), the expiry of the time limit set for the production of evidence that the conditions entitling the goods to such relief have been fulfilled.

3. In cases referred to under point (*a*) of paragraph 1, the debtor shall be any of the following:

(*a*) any person who was required to fulfil the obligation concerned;

(*b*) any person who was aware or should reasonably have been aware that the obligation concerned was not fulfilled and who acted on behalf of the person who was obliged to fulfil the obligation;

(*c*) any person who participated in the act which led to the non-fulfilment of the obligation and who was aware or should reasonably have been aware that a customs declaration had not been lodged but should have been.

4. In cases referred to under point (*b*) of paragraph 1, the debtor shall be any person who is required to comply with the conditions under which the goods were allowed to leave the customs territory of the Community with total or partial relief from export duties.

SECTION 3—PROVISIONS COMMON TO CUSTOMS DEBTS INCURRED ON IMPORTATION AND EXPORTATION

Prohibitions and restrictions

Article 50

1. The customs debt on importation or exportation shall be incurred even if it relates to goods which are subject to measures of prohibition or restriction on importation or exportation of any kind.

2. However, no customs debt shall be incurred on either of the following:

(*a*) the unlawful introduction into the customs territory of the Community of counterfeit currency;

(*b*) the introduction into the customs territory of the Community of narcotic drugs and psychotropic substances other than where strictly supervised by the competent authorities with a view to their use for medical and scientific purposes.

3. For the purposes of penalties as applicable to customs offences, the customs debt shall nevertheless be deemed to have been incurred where, under the law of a Member State, customs duties or the existence of a customs debt provide the basis for determining penalties.

Several debtors

Article 51

Where several persons are liable for payment of the amount of import or export duty corresponding to one customs debt, they shall be jointly and severally liable for the full amount of the debt.

General rules for calculation of the amount of import or export duty

Article 52

1. The amount of the import or export duty shall be determined on the basis of those rules for calculation of duty which were applicable to the goods concerned at the time at which the customs debt in respect of them was incurred.

2. Where it is not possible to determine precisely the time at which the customs debt is incurred, that time shall be deemed to be the time at which the customs authorities conclude that the goods are in a situation in which a customs debt has been incurred.

However, where the information available to the customs authorities enables them to establish that the customs debt had been incurred prior to the time at which they reached that conclusion, the customs debt shall be deemed to have been incurred at the earliest time that such a situation can be established.

Special rules for calculation of the amount of import duty

Article 53

1. Where costs for storage or usual forms of handling have been incurred within the customs territory of the Community in respect of goods placed under a customs procedure, such costs or the increase in value shall not be taken into account for the calculation of the amount of import duty where satisfactory proof of those costs is provided by the declarant.

However, the customs value, quantity, nature and origin of non-Community goods used in the operations shall be taken into account for the calculation of the amount of import duty.

2. Where the tariff classification of goods placed under a customs procedure changes as a result of usual forms of handling within the customs territory of the Community, the original tariff classification for the goods placed under the procedure shall be applied at the request of the declarant.

3. Where a customs debt is incurred for processed products resulting from the inward-processing procedure, the amount of import duty corresponding to such debt shall, at the request of the declarant, be determined on the basis of the tariff classification, customs value, quantity, nature and origin of the goods placed under the inward-processing procedure at the time of acceptance of the customs declaration relating to those goods.

4. Where customs legislation provides for a favourable tariff treatment of goods, or for relief or total or partial exemption from import or export duties, pursuant to Article 33(2)(*d*) to (*g*), Articles 130 to 133 or Articles 171 to 174, or pursuant to Council Regulation (EEC) No 918/83 of 28 March 1983 setting up a Community system of reliefs from customs duty[1], such favourable tariff treatment, relief or exemption shall also apply in cases where a customs debt is incurred

pursuant to Articles 46 or 49 of this Regulation, on condition that the failure which led to the incurrence of a customs debt did not constitute an attempt at deception.

Notes—[1] OJ L 105, 23.4.1983, p. 1. Regulation as last amended by Regulation (EC) No 274/2008 (OJ L 85, 27.3.2008, p. 1).

Implementing measures

Article 54

The measures designed to amend non-essential elements of this Regulation, by supplementing it, laying down the following:

(*a*) the rules for the calculation of the amount of import or export duty applicable to goods;
(*b*) further special rules for specific procedures;
(*c*) derogations from Articles 52 and 53, in particular to avoid the circumvention of the tariff measures referred to in Article 33(2)(*h*),

shall be adopted in accordance with the regulatory procedure with scrutiny referred to in Article 184(4).

Place where the customs debt is incurred

Article 55

1. A customs debt shall be incurred at the place where the customs declaration or the re-export notification referred to in Articles 44, 45 and 48 is lodged or where the supplementary declaration referred to in Article 110(3) is to be lodged.

In all other cases, the place where a customs debt is incurred shall be the place where the events from which it arises occur.

If it is not possible to determine that place, the customs debt shall be incurred at the place where the customs authorities conclude that the goods are in a situation in which a customs debt is incurred.

2. If the goods have been entered for a customs procedure which has not been discharged, and the place cannot be determined, pursuant to the second or third subparagraphs of paragraph 1, within a specified period of time, the customs debt shall be incurred at the place where the goods were either placed under the procedure concerned or were introduced into the customs territory of the Community under that procedure.

The measures designed to amend non-essential elements of this Regulation, by supplementing it, laying down the period of time referred to in the first subparagraph of this paragraph shall be adopted in accordance with the regulatory procedure with scrutiny referred to in Article 184(4).

3. Where the information available to the customs authorities enables them to establish that the customs debt may have been incurred in several places, the customs debt shall be deemed to have been incurred at the place where it was first incurred.

4. If a customs authority establishes that a customs debt has been incurred under Article 46 or Article 49 in another Member State and the amount of import or export duty corresponding to that debt is lower than EUR 10000, the customs debt shall be deemed to have been incurred in the Member State where the finding was made.

…

CHAPTER 3

RECOVERY AND PAYMENT OF DUTY AND REPAYMENT AND REMISSION OF THE AMOUNT OF IMPORT AND EXPORT DUTY

SECTION 1—DETERMINATION OF THE AMOUNT OF IMPORT OR EXPORT DUTY, NOTIFICATION OF THE CUSTOMS DEBT AND ENTRY IN THE ACCOUNTS

Determination of the amount of import or export duty

Article 66

1. The amount of import or export duty payable shall be determined by the customs authorities responsible for the place where the customs debt is incurred, or is deemed to have been incurred in accordance with Article 55, as soon as they have the necessary information.

2. Without prejudice to Article 27, the customs authorities may accept the amount of import or export duty payable determined by the declarant.

…

SECTION 2

Enforcement of payment and arrears

Article 78

1. Where the amount of import or export duty payable has not been paid within the prescribed period, the customs authorities shall secure payment of that amount by all means available to them under the law of the Member State concerned.

The measures designed to amend non-essential elements of this Regulation, by supplementing it, laying down measures in respect of securing payment from guarantors within the framework of a special procedure, shall be adopted in accordance with the regulatory procedure with scrutiny referred to in Article 184(4).

2. Interest on arrears shall be charged on the amount of import or export duty from the date of expiry of the prescribed period until the date of payment.

The rate of interest on arrears shall be the interest rate applied by the European Central Bank to its most recent main refinancing operation carried out before the first calendar day of the half-year in question (the reference rate), plus two percentage points.

For a Member State which is not participating in the third stage of economic and monetary union, the reference rate referred to above shall be the equivalent rate set by its national central bank. In that case, the reference rate in force on the first calendar day of the half-year in question shall apply for the following six months.

3. Where a customs debt has been notified pursuant to Article 67(3), interest on arrears shall be charged over and above the amount of import or export duty, from the date on which the customs debt was incurred until the date of its notification.

The rate of interest on arrears shall be set in accordance with paragraph 2.

4. The customs authorities may refrain from charging interest on arrears where it is established, on the basis of a documented assessment of the situation of the debtor, that to charge it would create serious economic or social difficulties.

5. The measures designed to amend non-essential elements of this Regulation, by supplementing it, laying down the cases, in terms of time and amounts, in which the customs authorities may waive the collection of interest on arrears, shall be adopted in accordance with the regulatory procedure with scrutiny referred to in Article 184(4).

...

CHAPTER 4

EXTINGUISHMENT OF CUSTOMS DEBT

Extinguishment

Article 86

1. Without prejudice to Article 68 and the provisions in force relating to non-recovery of the amount of import or export duty corresponding to a customs debt in the event of the judicially established insolvency of the debtor, a customs debt on importation or exportation shall be extinguished in any of the following ways:

(*a*) by payment of the amount of import or export duty;

(*b*) subject to paragraph 4, by remission of the amount of import or export duty;

(*c*) where, in respect of goods declared for a customs procedure entailing the obligation to pay duties, the customs declaration is invalidated;

(*d*) where goods liable to import or export duties are confiscated;

(*e*) where goods liable to import or export duties are seized and simultaneously or subsequently confiscated;

(*f*) where goods liable to import and export duties are destroyed under customs supervision or abandoned to the State;

(*g*) where the disappearance of the goods or the non-fulfilment of obligations arising from the customs legislation results from the total destruction or irretrievable loss of those goods as a result of the actual nature of the goods or unforeseeable circumstances or force majeure, or as a consequence of instruction by the customs authorities; for the purpose of this point, goods shall be considered as irretrievably lost when they have been rendered unusable by any person;

(*h*) where the customs debt was incurred pursuant to Article 46 or 49 and where the following conditions are fulfilled:

(i) the failure which led to the incurrence of a customs debt had no significant effect on the correct operation of the customs procedure concerned and did not constitute an attempt at deception;

(ii) all of the formalities necessary to regularise the situation of the goods are subsequently carried out;

(*i*) where goods released for free circulation duty-free, or at a reduced rate of import duty by virtue of their end-use, have been exported with the permission of the customs authorities;

(*j*) where it was incurred pursuant to Article 45 and where the formalities carried out in order to enable the preferential tariff treatment referred to in that Article to be granted are cancelled;

(*k*) where, subject to paragraph 5 of this Article, the customs debt was incurred pursuant to Article 46 and evidence is provided to the satisfaction of the customs authorities that the goods have not been used or consumed and have been exported from the customs territory of the Community.

2. In the event of confiscation, as referred to in paragraph 1(*d*), the customs debt shall, nevertheless, for the purposes of penalties applicable to customs offences, be deemed not to have been extinguished where, under the law of a Member State, customs duties or the existence of a customs debt provide the basis for determining penalties.

3. Where, in accordance with paragraph 1(*g*), a customs debt is extinguished in respect of goods released for free circulation duty-free or at a reduced rate of import duty on account of their end-use, any scrap or waste resulting from their destruction shall be deemed to be non-Community goods.

4. Where several persons are liable for payment of the amount of import or export duty corresponding to the customs debt and remission is granted, the customs debt shall be extinguished only in respect of the person or persons to whom the remission is granted.

5. In the case referred to in paragraph 1(*k*), the customs debt shall not be extinguished in respect of any person or persons who attempted deception.

6. Where the customs debt was incurred pursuant to Article 46, it shall be extinguished with regard to the person whose behaviour did not involve any attempt at deception and who contributed to the fight against fraud.

7. The Commission may, in accordance with the regulatory procedure referred to in Article 184(2), adopt measures for the implementation of this Article.

TITLE IV
GOODS BROUGHT INTO THE CUSTOMS TERRITORY OF THE COMMUNITY

CHAPTER 1
ENTRY SUMMARY DECLARATION

Obligation to lodge an entry summary declaration

Article 87

1. Goods brought into the customs territory of the Community shall be covered by an entry summary declaration, with the exception of means of transport temporarily imported and means of transport and the goods carried thereon only passing through the territorial waters or the airspace of the customs territory of the Community without a stop within that territory.

2. Except where otherwise specified in the customs legislation, an entry summary declaration shall be lodged at the competent customs office before the goods are brought into the customs territory of the Community.

Customs authorities may accept, instead of the lodging of the entry summary declaration, the lodging of a notification and access to the entry summary declaration data in the economic operator's computer system.

3. The measures designed to amend non-essential elements of this Regulation, by supplementing it, laying down the following:

(*a*) the cases, other than those referred to in paragraph 1 of this Article, in which the requirement for an entry summary declaration may be waived or adapted and the conditions under which it may be so waived or adapted;

(*b*) the deadline by which the entry summary declaration is to be lodged or made available before the goods are brought into the customs territory of the Community;

(*c*) the rules for exceptions from and variations to the deadline referred to in point (*b*);

(*d*) the rules for determining the competent customs office at which the entry summary declaration is to be lodged or made available and where risk analysis and risk-based entry controls are to be carried out,

shall be adopted in accordance with the regulatory procedure with scrutiny referred to in Article 184(4).

In adopting those measures, account shall be taken of the following:

(*a*) special circumstances;

(*b*) the application of those measures to certain types of goods traffic, modes of transport or economic operators;

(*c*) international agreements which provide for special security arrangements.

Lodgement and responsible person

Article 88

1. The entry summary declaration shall be lodged using an electronic data-processing technique. Commercial, port or transport information may be used provided it contains the necessary particulars for an entry summary declaration.

Customs authorities may, in exceptional circumstances, accept paper-based entry summary declarations, provided that they apply the same level of risk management as that applied to entry summary declarations made using an electronic data-processing technique and that the requirements for the exchange of such data with other customs offices can be met.

2. The entry summary declaration shall be lodged by the person who brings the goods into the customs territory of the Community or who assumes responsibility for the carriage of the goods into that territory.

3. Notwithstanding the obligations of the person referred to in paragraph 2, the entry summary declaration may be lodged instead by one of the following persons:

(*a*) the importer or consignee or other person in whose name or on whose behalf the person referred to in paragraph 2 acts;

(*b*) any person who is able to present the goods in question or to have them presented to the competent customs authority.

4. Where the entry summary declaration is lodged by a person other than the operator of the means of transport by which the goods are brought on to Community customs territory, that operator shall lodge with the appropriate customs office a notification of arrival in the form of a manifest, a dispatch note or a load sheet containing the information required in order to enable all the goods transported which are to be covered by an entry summary declaration to be identified.

The Commission shall, in accordance with the regulatory procedure referred to in Article 184(2), adopt measures stipulating the information which must appear on the notification of arrival.

Paragraph 1 shall apply, mutatis mutandis, to the notification of arrival mentioned in the first subparagraph of this paragraph.

Amendment of entry summary declaration

Article 89

1. The person who lodges the entry summary declaration shall, at his request, be permitted to amend one or more particulars of that declaration after it has been lodged.

However, no such amendment shall be possible after any of the following events:

(*a*) the customs authorities have informed the person who lodged the entry summary declaration that they intend to examine the goods;

(*b*) the customs authorities have established that the particulars in question are incorrect;

(*c*) the customs authorities have allowed the removal of the goods from the place where they were presented.

2. The measures designed to amend non-essential elements of this Regulation, by supplementing it, laying down exceptions to paragraph 1(*c*) of this Article, defining, in particular, the following:

(*a*) criteria for establishing grounds for amendments after removal;

(*b*) the data elements which may be amended;

(*c*) the time limit after removal within which amendment may be permitted,

shall be adopted in accordance with the regulatory procedure with scrutiny referred to in Article 184(4).

Customs declaration replacing entry summary declaration

Article 90

The competent customs office may waive the lodging of an entry summary declaration in respect of goods for which, prior to the expiry of the deadline referred to in point (*b*) of the first subparagraph of Article 87(3), a customs declaration is lodged. In that case, the customs declaration shall contain at least the particulars necessary for the entry summary declaration. Until such time as the customs declaration is accepted in accordance with Article 112, it shall have the status of an entry summary declaration.

CHAPTER 2

ARRIVAL OF GOODS

SECTION 1—ENTRY OF GOODS INTO THE CUSTOMS TERRITORY OF THE COMMUNITY

Customs supervision

Article 91

1. Goods brought into the customs territory of the Community shall, from the time of their entry, be subject to customs supervision and may be subject to customs controls. Where applicable, they shall be subject to such prohibitions and restrictions as are justified on grounds of, inter alia, public morality, public policy or public security, the protection of the health and life of humans, animals or plants, the protection of the environment, the protection of national treasures possessing artistic, historic or archaeological value and the protection of industrial or commercial property, including controls on drug precursors, goods infringing certain intellectual property rights and cash entering the Community, as well as to the implementation of fishery conservation and management measures and of commercial policy measures.

They shall remain under such supervision for as long as is necessary to determine their customs status and shall not be removed therefrom without the permission of the customs authorities.

Without prejudice to Article 166, Community goods shall not be subject to customs supervision once their customs status is established.

Non-Community goods shall remain under customs supervision until their customs status is changed, or they are re-exported or destroyed.

2. The holder of goods under customs supervision may, with the permission of the customs authorities, at any time examine the goods or take samples, in particular in order to determine their tariff classification, customs value or customs status.

Conveyance to the appropriate place

Article 92

1. The person who brings goods into the customs territory of the Community shall convey them without delay, by the route specified by the customs authorities and in accordance with their instructions, if any, to the customs office designated by the customs authorities, or to any other place designated or approved by those authorities, or into a free zone.

Goods brought into a free zone shall be brought into that free zone directly, either by sea or air or, if by land, without passing through another part of the customs territory of the Community, where the free zone adjoins the land frontier between a Member State and a third country.

The goods shall be presented to the customs authorities in accordance with Article 95.

2. Any person who assumes responsibility for the carriage of goods after they have been brought into the customs territory of the Community shall become responsible for compliance with the obligation laid down in paragraph 1.

3. Goods which, although still outside the customs territory of the Community, may be subject to customs controls by the customs authority of a Member State as a result of an agreement concluded with the relevant country or territory outside the customs territory of the Community, shall be treated in the same way as goods brought into the customs territory of the Community.

4. Paragraph 1 shall not preclude application of any special provisions with respect to letters, postcards and printed matter and their electronic equivalents held on other media or to goods carried by travellers, goods transported within frontier zones or in pipelines and wires as well as any other traffic of negligible economic importance, provided that customs supervision and customs control possibilities are not thereby jeopardised.

5. Paragraph 1 shall not apply to means of transport and goods carried thereon only passing through the territorial waters or the airspace of the customs territory of the Community without a stop within that territory.

Intra-Community air and sea services

Article 93

1. Articles 87 to 90, 92(1) and 94 to 97 shall not apply to goods which have temporarily left the customs territory of the Community while moving between two points in that territory by sea or air, provided that carriage has been effected by a direct route and by an air or regular shipping service without a stop outside the customs territory of the Community.

2. The measures designed to amend non-essential elements of this Regulation, by supplementing it, laying down special provisions for air and regular shipping services, shall be adopted in accordance with the regulatory procedure with scrutiny referred to in Article 184(4).

Conveyance under special circumstances

Article 94

1. Where, by reason of unforeseeable circumstances or force majeure, the obligation laid down in Article 92(1) cannot be complied with, the person bound by that obligation or any other person acting on that person's behalf shall inform the customs authorities of the situation without delay. Where the unforeseeable circumstances or force majeure do not result in total loss of the goods, the customs authorities shall also be informed of their precise location.

2. Where, by reason of unforeseeable circumstances or *force majeure*, a vessel or aircraft covered by Article 92(5) is forced to put into port or to land temporarily in the customs territory of the Community and the obligation laid down in Article 92(1) cannot be complied with, the person who brought the vessel or aircraft into the customs territory of the Community, or any other person acting on that person's behalf, shall inform the customs authorities of the situation without delay.

3. The customs authorities shall determine the measures to be taken in order to permit customs supervision of the goods referred to in paragraph 1, or of the vessel or aircraft and any goods thereon in the circumstances specified in paragraph 2, and to ensure, where appropriate, that they are subsequently conveyed to a customs office or other place designated or approved by the authorities.

SECTION 2—PRESENTATION, UNLOADING AND EXAMINATION OF GOODS

Presentation of goods to customs

Article 95

1. Goods brought into the customs territory of the Community shall be presented to customs immediately upon their arrival at the designated customs office or any other place designated or approved by the customs authorities or in the free zone by one of the following persons:

(*a*) the person who brought the goods into the customs territory of the Community;

(*b*) the person in whose name or on whose behalf the person who brought the goods into that territory acts;

(*c*) the person who assumed responsibility for carriage of the goods after they were brought into the customs territory of the Community.

2. Notwithstanding the obligations of the person described in paragraph 1, presentation of the goods may be effected instead by one of the following persons:

(*a*) any person who immediately places the goods under a customs procedure;

(*b*) the holder of an authorisation for the operation of storage facilities or any person who carries out an activity in a free zone.

3. The person presenting the goods shall make a reference to the entry summary declaration or customs declaration which has been lodged in respect of the goods.

4. Paragraph 1 shall not preclude application of any special provisions with respect to letters, postcards and printed matter and their electronic equivalents held on other media or to goods carried by travellers, goods transported within frontier zones or in pipelines and wires as well as any other traffic of negligible economic importance, provided that customs supervision and customs control possibilities are not thereby jeopardised.

Unloading and examination of goods

Article 96

1. Goods shall be unloaded or trans-shipped from the means of transport carrying them solely with the permission of the customs authorities in places designated or approved by those authorities.

However, such permission shall not be required in the event of an imminent danger necessitating the immediate unloading of all or part of the goods. In that case, the customs authorities shall immediately be informed accordingly.

2. The customs authorities may at any time require goods to be unloaded and unpacked for the purpose of examining them, taking samples or examining the means of transport carrying them.

3. Goods presented to customs shall not be removed from the place where they have been presented without the permission of the customs authorities.

SECTION 3—FORMALITIES AFTER PRESENTATION

Obligation to place non-Community goods under a customs procedure

Article 97

1. Without prejudice to Articles 125 to 127, non-Community goods presented to customs shall be placed under a customs procedure.

2. Except as otherwise provided, the declarant shall be free to choose the customs procedure under which he wishes to place the goods, under the conditions for that procedure, irrespective of their nature or quantity, or their country of origin, consignment or destination.

…

TITLE V

GENERAL RULES ON CUSTOMS STATUS, PLACING GOODS UNDER A CUSTOMS PROCEDURE, VERIFICATION, RELEASE AND DISPOSAL OF GOODS

CHAPTER 1

CUSTOMS STATUS OF GOODS

…

Loss of customs status of Community goods

Article 102

Community goods shall become non-Community goods in the following cases:

(*a*) where they are moved out of the customs territory of the Community, insofar as the rules on internal transit or the measures laid down in accordance with Article 103 do not apply;
(*b*) where they have been placed under the external transit procedure, a storage procedure or the inward-processing procedure, insofar as the customs legislation so allows;
(*c*) where they have been placed under the end-use procedure and are either subsequently abandoned to the State, or are destroyed and waste remains;
(*d*) where the declaration for release of goods for free circulation is invalidated after release in accordance with measures adopted pursuant to the second subparagraph of Article 114(2).
…

CHAPTER 2
PLACING GOODS UNDER A CUSTOMS PROCEDURE

SECTION 1—GENERAL PROVISIONS

Customs declaration of goods and customs supervision of Community goods

Article 104

1. All goods intended to be placed under a customs procedure, except for the free-zone procedure, shall be covered by a customs declaration appropriate for the particular procedure.
2. Community goods declared for export, internal Community transit or outward processing shall be subject to customs supervision from the time of acceptance of the declaration referred to in paragraph 1 until such time as they leave the customs territory of the Community or are abandoned to the State or destroyed or the customs declaration is invalidated.

Competent customs offices

Article 105

1. Except where Community legislation provides otherwise, Member States shall determine the location and competence of the various customs offices situated in their territory.

Member States shall ensure that official opening hours are fixed for those offices that are reasonable and appropriate, taking into account the nature of the traffic and of the goods and the customs procedures under which they are to be placed, so that the flow of international traffic is neither hindered nor distorted.

2. The Commission shall, in accordance with the regulatory procedure referred to in Article 184(2), adopt measures defining the various roles and responsibilities of competent customs offices, and notably of the following:
(*a*) the customs offices of entry, import, export or exit;
(*b*) the customs offices carrying out the formalities for the placing of goods under a customs procedure;
(*c*) the customs offices granting authorisations and supervising customs procedures.

Centralised clearance

Article 106

1. Customs authorities may authorise a person to lodge, or make available, at the customs office responsible for the place where he is established a customs declaration for goods which are presented to customs at another customs office. In such cases, the customs debt shall be deemed to be incurred at the customs office at which the customs declaration is lodged or made available.
2. The customs office at which the customs declaration is lodged or made available shall carry out the formalities for the verification of the declaration, the recovery of the amount of import or export duty corresponding to any customs debt and for granting release of the goods.

3. The customs office at which the goods are presented shall, without prejudice to its own controls for security and safety purposes, carry out any examination justifiably requested by the customs office at which the customs declaration is lodged or made available and shall allow release of the goods, taking into account information received from that office.

4. The measures designed to amend non-essential elements of this Regulation, by supplementing it, laying down in particular, rules in respect of the following:
(*a*) the granting of the authorisation referred to in paragraph 1;
(*b*) the cases in which review of the authorisation is to be carried out;
(*c*) the conditions under which the authorisation is granted;
(*d*) identification of the customs authority competent for the granting of the authorisation;
(*e*) consultation with and provision of information to other customs authorities, where appropriate;
(*f*) the conditions under which the authorisation may be suspended or revoked;
(*g*) the specific role and responsibilities of the competent customs offices involved, particularly in respect of the controls to be applied;
(*h*) the form of, and any time limit for, the completion of formalities,

shall be adopted in accordance with the regulatory procedure with scrutiny referred to in Article 184(4).

Those measures shall take account of the following:

– with regard to point (*c*), where more than one Member State is involved, compliance by the applicant with the criteria laid down in Article 14 for the granting of the status of authorised economic operator,

– with regard to point (*d*), the place where the applicant's main accounts for customs purposes are held or accessible, facilitating audit-based controls, and where at least part of the activities to be covered by the authorisation are to be carried out.

Types of customs declaration

Article 107

1. The customs declaration shall be lodged using an electronic data-processing technique. The customs authorities may allow the customs declaration to take the form of an entry in the declarant's records, provided that the customs authorities have access to those data in the declarant's electronic system and that the requirements for any necessary exchange of such data between customs offices are met.

2. Where this is provided for in the customs legislation, the customs authorities may accept a paper-based customs declaration, or a customs declaration made orally or by any other act whereby goods can be placed under a customs procedure.

3. The Commission shall, in accordance with the regulatory procedure referred to in Article 184(2), adopt measures for the implementation of this Article.

SECTION 2—STANDARD CUSTOMS DECLARATIONS

Content of a declaration and supporting documents

Article 108

1. Customs declarations shall contain all the particulars necessary for application of the provisions governing the customs procedure for which the goods are declared. Customs declarations made using an electronic data-processing technique shall contain an electronic signature or other means of authentication. Paper-based declarations shall be signed.

The Commission shall, in accordance with the regulatory procedure referred to in Article 184(2), adopt measures laying down the specifications to which customs declarations must correspond.

2. The supporting documents required for application of the provisions governing the customs procedure for which the goods are declared shall be made available to the customs authorities at the time when the declaration is lodged.

3. When a customs declaration is lodged using an electronic data-processing technique, the customs authorities may also allow supporting documents to be lodged using that technique. Customs authorities may accept, instead of the lodging of those documents, access to the relevant data in the economic operator's computer system.

However, upon request by the declarant, the customs authorities may allow those documents to be made available after release of the goods.

4. The Commission shall, in accordance with the regulatory procedure referred to in Article 184(2), adopt measures for the implementation of paragraphs 2 and 3 of this Article.

SECTION 3—SIMPLIFIED CUSTOMS DECLARATIONS

Simplified declaration

Article 109

1. The customs authorities shall, provided that the conditions of paragraphs 2 and 3 of this Article are fulfilled, authorise any person to have goods placed under a customs procedure on the basis of a simplified declaration which may omit certain of the particulars and supporting documents referred to in Article 108.

2. The measures designed to amend non-essential elements of this Regulation, by supplementing it, relating to the conditions under which the authorisation referred to in paragraph 1 of this Article is to be given, shall be adopted in accordance with the regulatory procedure with scrutiny referred to in Article 184(4).

3. The Commission may, in accordance with the regulatory procedure referred to in Article 184(2), adopt measures concerning the specifications to which the simplified declarations must correspond.

Supplementary declaration

Article 110

1. In the case of a simplified declaration pursuant to Article 109(1), the declarant shall furnish a supplementary declaration containing the further particulars necessary to complete the customs declaration for the customs procedure concerned.

The supplementary declaration may be of a general, periodic or recapitulative nature.

The measures designed to amend non-essential elements of this Regulation, by supplementing it, laying down exceptions to the first subparagraph of this paragraph, shall be adopted in accordance with the regulatory procedure with scrutiny referred to in Article 184(4).

2. The supplementary declaration and the simplified declaration referred to in Article 109(1) shall be deemed to constitute a single, indivisible instrument taking effect on the date on which the simplified declaration is accepted in accordance with Article 112.

Where the simplified declaration takes the form of an entry in the declarant's records and access to those data by the customs authorities, the declaration shall take effect from the date on which the goods are entered in the records.

3. The place where the supplementary declaration is to be lodged in accordance with the authorisation shall be deemed, for the purposes of Article 55, to be the place where the customs declaration has been lodged.

SECTION 4—PROVISIONS APPLYING TO ALL CUSTOMS DECLARATIONS

Person lodging a declaration

Article 111

1. Without prejudice to Article 110(1), a customs declaration may be made by any person who is able to present or make available all of the documents which are required for the application of the provisions governing the customs procedure in respect of which the goods are declared. That person shall also be able to present the goods in question or to have them presented to the competent customs office.

However, where acceptance of a customs declaration imposes particular obligations on a specific person, the declaration must be made by that person or by his representative.

2. The declarant shall be established in the customs territory of the Community. However, the following declarants shall not be required to be established within the Community:

- persons who lodge a declaration for transit or temporary admission,
- persons who declare goods occasionally, provided that the customs authorities deem this to be justified.

3. The measures designed to amend non-essential elements of this Regulation, by supplementing it, laying down the cases in which, and the conditions under which, the requirements referred to in paragraph 2 may be waived, shall be adopted in accordance with the regulatory procedure with scrutiny referred to in Article 184(4).

Acceptance of a declaration

Article 112

1. Declarations which comply with the conditions laid down in this Chapter shall be accepted by the customs authorities immediately, provided that the goods to which they refer have been presented to customs or, to the satisfaction of the customs authorities, are made available for customs controls.

Where the declaration takes the form of an entry in the declarant's records and access to those data by the customs authorities, the declaration shall be deemed to have been accepted at the moment at which the goods are entered in the records. The customs authorities may, without prejudice to the legal obligations of the declarant or to the application of security and safety controls, waive the obligation for the goods to be presented or to be made available for customs control.

2. Without prejudice to Article 110(2) or the second subparagraph of paragraph 1 of this Article, where a customs declaration is lodged at a customs office other than the office at which the goods are presented, the declaration shall be accepted when the office at which the goods are presented confirms the availability of the goods for customs controls.

3. The date of acceptance of the customs declaration by the customs authorities shall, except where otherwise provided, be the date to be used for the application of the provisions governing the customs procedure for which the goods are declared and for all other import or export formalities.

4. The Commission shall, in accordance with the regulatory procedure referred to in Article 184(2), adopt measures laying down detailed rules for the implementation of this Article.

Amendment of a declaration

Article 113

1. The declarant shall, at his request, be permitted to amend one or more of the particulars of the declaration after the declaration has been accepted by customs. The amendment shall not render the declaration applicable to goods other than those which it originally covered.

2. No such amendment shall be permitted where it is requested after any of the following events:

(*a*) the customs authorities have informed the declarant that they intend to examine the goods;

(*b*) the customs authorities have established that the particulars in question are incorrect;

(*c*) the customs authorities have released the goods.

3. The measures designed to amend non-essential elements of this Regulation, by supplementing it, laying down exceptions to paragraph 2(*c*) of this Article, shall be adopted in accordance with the regulatory procedure with scrutiny referred to in Article 184(4).

Invalidation of a declaration

Article 114

1. The customs authorities shall, at the request of the declarant, invalidate a declaration already accepted in the following cases:

(*a*) where they are satisfied that the goods are immediately to be placed under another customs procedure;

(*b*) where they are satisfied that, as a result of special circumstances, the placing of the goods under the customs procedure for which they were declared is no longer justified.

However, where the customs authorities have informed the declarant of their intention to examine the goods, a request for invalidation of the declaration shall not be accepted before the examination has taken place.

2. The declaration shall not be invalidated after the goods have been released.

The measures designed to amend non-essential elements of this Regulation, by supplementing it, laying down exceptions to the first subparagraph of this paragraph, shall be adopted in accordance with the regulatory procedure with scrutiny referred to in Article 184(4).

SECTION 5—OTHER SIMPLIFICATIONS

Facilitation of the drawing-up of customs declarations for goods falling under different tariff subheadings

Article 115

Where a consignment is made up of goods falling within different tariff subheadings, and dealing with each of those goods in accordance with its tariff subheadings for the purpose of drawing-up the customs declaration would entail a burden of work and expense disproportionate to the import duties chargeable, the customs authorities may, at the request of the declarant, agree that import duties be charged on the whole consignment on the basis of the tariff subheadings of the goods which are subject to the highest rate of import or export duty.

The Commission may, in accordance with the regulatory procedure referred to in Article 184(2), adopt measures for the implementation of this Article.

Simplification of customs formalities and controls

Article 116

1. Customs authorities may authorise simplifications, other than as referred to under Section 3 of this Chapter, of the customs formalities and controls.

2. The measures designed to amend non-essential elements of this Regulation, by supplementing it, laying down in particular rules in respect of the following:

(*a*) the granting of the authorisations referred to in paragraph 1;

(*b*) the cases in which review of the authorisations is to be carried out and the conditions under which their use is to be monitored by the customs authorities;

(*c*) the conditions under which the authorisations are granted;

(*d*) the conditions under which an economic operator may be authorised to carry out certain customs formalities which should in principle be carried out by the customs authorities, including the self-assessment of import and export duties, and to perform certain controls under customs supervision;

(*e*) identification of the customs authority competent for the granting of the authorisations;

(*f*) consultation with and provision of information to other customs authorities, where appropriate;

(*g*) the conditions under which the authorisations may be suspended or revoked;

(*h*) the specific role and responsibilities of the competent customs offices involved, particularly in respect of the controls to be applied;

(*i*) the form of, and any time limit for, the completion of formalities,

shall be adopted in accordance with the regulatory procedure with scrutiny referred to in Article 184(4).

Those measures shall take account of the following:

- the customs formalities to be completed and customs controls to be performed for security and safety purposes on goods brought into or leaving the customs territory of the Community,
- the rules adopted pursuant to Article 25(3),
- with regard to point (*d*), where more than one Member State is involved, the applicant shall hold the status of authorised economic operator in accordance with Article 14,
- with regard to point (*e*), the place where the applicant's main accounts for customs purposes are held or accessible, facilitating audit-based controls, and where at least part of the activities to be covered by the authorisation are to be carried out.

CHAPTER 3
VERIFICATION AND RELEASE OF GOODS

SECTION 1—VERIFICATION

Verification of a customs declaration

Article 117

The customs authorities may, for the purpose of verifying the accuracy of the particulars contained in a customs declaration which they have accepted:

(*a*) examine the declaration and all of the supporting documents;
(*b*) require the declarant to present other documents;
(*c*) examine the goods;
(*d*) take samples for analysis or for detailed examination of the goods.

Examination and sampling of goods

Article 118

1. Transport of the goods to the places where they are to be examined and where samples are to be taken, and all the handling necessitated by such examination or taking of samples, shall be carried out by or under the responsibility of the declarant. The costs incurred shall be borne by the declarant.

2. The declarant shall have the right to be present or represented when the goods are examined and when samples are taken. Where the customs authorities have reasonable grounds for so doing, they may require the declarant to be present or represented when the goods are examined or samples are taken or to provide them with the assistance necessary to facilitate such examination or taking of samples.

3. Provided that samples are taken in accordance with the provisions in force, the customs authorities shall not be liable for payment of any compensation in respect thereof but shall bear the costs of their analysis or examination.

Partial examination and sampling of goods

Article 119

1. Where only part of the goods covered by a customs declaration is examined, or samples are taken, the results of the partial examination, or of the analysis or examination of the samples, shall be taken to apply to all the goods covered by the same declaration.

However, the declarant may request a further examination or sampling of the goods if he considers that the results of the partial examination, or of the analysis or examination of the samples taken, are not valid as regards the remainder of the goods declared. The request shall be granted, provided that the goods have not been released or that, if they have been released, the declarant proves that they have not been altered in any way.

2. For the purposes of paragraph 1, where a customs declaration covers two or more items, the particulars relating to each item shall be deemed to constitute a separate declaration.

3. The Commission shall, in accordance with the management procedure referred to in Article 184(3), adopt measures laying down the procedure to be followed in the event of divergent results of examinations pursuant to paragraph 1 of this Article.

Results of the verification

Article 120

1. The results of verifying the customs declaration shall be used for the application of the provisions governing the customs procedure under which the goods are placed.

2. Where the customs declaration is not verified, paragraph 1 shall apply on the basis of the particulars contained in the declaration.

3. The results of the verification made by the customs authorities shall have the same conclusive force throughout the customs territory of the Community.

Identification measures

Article 121

1. The customs authorities or, where appropriate, economic operators authorised to do so by the customs authorities, shall take the measures necessary to identify the goods where identification is required in order to ensure compliance with the provisions governing the customs procedure for which those goods have been declared.

Those identification measures shall have the same legal effect throughout the customs territory of the Community.

2. Means of identification affixed to the goods or means of transport shall be removed or destroyed only by the customs authorities or, where they are authorised to do so by the customs authorities, by economic operators, unless, as a result of unforeseeable circumstances or force majeure, their removal or destruction is essential to ensure the protection of the goods or the means of transport.

Implementing measures

Article 122

The Commission may, in accordance with the regulatory procedure referred to in Article 184(2), adopt measures for the implementation of this Section.

SECTION 2—RELEASE

Release of the goods

Article 123

1. Without prejudice to Article 117, where the conditions for placing the goods under the procedure concerned are fulfilled and provided that any restriction has been applied and the goods are not subject to any prohibition, the customs authorities shall release the goods as soon as the particulars in the customs declaration have been verified or are accepted without verification.

The first subparagraph shall also apply where verification as referred to in Article 117 cannot be completed within a reasonable period of time and the goods are no longer required to be present for verification purposes.

2. All the goods covered by the same declaration shall be released at the same time.

For the purposes of the first subparagraph, where a customs declaration covers two or more items, the particulars relating to each item shall be deemed to constitute a separate customs declaration.

3. Where the goods are presented at a customs office other than the office at which the customs declaration has been accepted, the customs authorities involved shall exchange the information necessary for the release of the goods, without prejudice to appropriate controls.

Release dependent upon payment of the amount of import or export duty corresponding to the customs debt or provision of a guarantee

Article 124

1. Where the placing of goods under a customs procedure gives rise to a customs debt, the release of the goods shall be conditional upon the payment of the amount of import or export duty corresponding to the customs debt or the provision of a guarantee to cover that debt.

However, without prejudice to the third subparagraph, the first subparagraph shall not apply to temporary admission with partial relief from import duties.

Where, pursuant to the provisions governing the customs procedure for which the goods are declared, the customs authorities require the provision of a guarantee, those goods shall not be released for the customs procedure in question until such guarantee is provided.

2. The Commission may, in accordance with the regulatory procedure referred to in Article 184(2), adopt measures laying down exceptions to the first and third subparagraphs of paragraph 1 of this Article.

CHAPTER 4

DISPOSAL OF GOODS

Destruction of goods

Article 125

Where the customs authorities have reasonable grounds for so doing, they may require goods which have been presented to customs to be destroyed and shall inform the holder of the goods accordingly. The costs of destruction shall be borne by the holder of the goods.

Measures to be taken by the customs authorities

Article 126

1. The customs authorities shall take any necessary measures, including confiscation and sale, or destruction, to dispose of goods in the following cases:

(*a*) where one of the obligations laid down in customs legislation concerning the introduction of non-Community goods into the customs territory of the Community has not been fulfilled, or the goods have been withheld from customs supervision;

(*b*) where the goods cannot be released for any of the following reasons:

(i) it has not been possible, for reasons attributable to the declarant, to undertake or continue examination of the goods within the period prescribed by the customs authorities;

(ii) the documents which must be produced before the goods can be placed under, or released for, the customs procedure requested have not been made available;

(iii) payments or a guarantee which should have been made or provided in respect of import or export duties, as the case may be, have not been made or provided within the period prescribed;

(iv) they are subject to prohibitions or restrictions;

(*c*) where the goods have not been removed within a reasonable period after their release;

(*d*) where, after their release, the goods are found not to have fulfilled the conditions for that release;

(*e*) where goods are abandoned to the State in accordance with Article 127.

2. Non-Community goods which have been abandoned to the State, seized or confiscated shall be deemed to be placed under the temporary storage procedure.

…

TITLE VI
RELEASE FOR FREE CIRCULATION AND RELIEF FROM IMPORT DUTIES

CHAPTER 1
RELEASE FOR FREE CIRCULATION

Scope and effect

Article 129

1. Non-Community goods intended to be put on the Community market or intended for private use or consumption within the Community shall be placed under release for free circulation.

2. Release for free circulation shall entail the following:

(*a*) the collection of any import duties due;

(*b*) the collection, as appropriate, of other charges, as provided for under relevant provisions in force relating to the collection of those charges;

(*c*) the application of commercial policy measures and prohibitions and restrictions insofar as they do not have to be applied at an earlier stage;

(*d*) completion of the other formalities laid down in respect of the importation of the goods.

3. Release for free circulation shall confer on non-Community goods the customs status of Community goods.

…

TITLE VII
SPECIAL PROCEDURES

CHAPTER 1
GENERAL PROVISIONS

Scope

Article 135

Goods may be placed under any of the following categories of special procedures:

(*a*) transit, which shall comprise external and internal transit;

(*b*) storage, which shall comprise temporary storage, customs warehousing and free zones;

(*c*) specific use, which shall comprise temporary admission and end-use;

(*d*) processing, which shall comprise inward and outward processing.

Authorisation

Article 136

1. An authorisation from the customs authorities shall be required for the following:

– the use of the inward or outward-processing procedure, the temporary admission procedure or the end-use procedure,
– the operation of storage facilities for the temporary storage or customs warehousing of goods, except where the storage facility operator is the customs authority itself.

The conditions under which the use of one or more of the procedures referred to above or the operation of storage facilities is permitted shall be set out in the authorisation.

2. The measures designed to amend non-essential elements of this Regulation, by supplementing it, laying down in particular rules in respect of the following:

(*a*) the granting of the authorisation referred to in paragraph 1;
(*b*) the cases in which review of the authorisation is to be carried out;
(*c*) the conditions under which the authorisation is granted;
(*d*) identification of the customs authority competent for the granting of the authorisation;
(*e*) consultation with and provision of information to other customs authorities, where appropriate;
(*f*) the conditions under which the authorisation may be suspended or revoked;
(*g*) the specific role and responsibilities of the competent customs offices involved, particularly in respect of the controls to be applied;
(*h*) the form of, and any time limit for, the completion of formalities,

shall be adopted in accordance with the regulatory procedure with scrutiny referred to in Article 184(4).

Those measures shall take account of the following:

(*a*) with regard to point (*c*) of the first subparagraph, where more than one Member State is involved, compliance by the applicant with the criteria laid down in Article 14 for the granting of the status of authorised economic operator,
(*b*) with regard to point (*d*) of the first subparagraph, the place where the applicant's main accounts for customs purposes are held or accessible, facilitating audit-based controls, and where at least part of the activities to be covered by the authorisation are to be carried out.

3. Except where otherwise provided for in the customs legislation, the authorisation referred to in paragraph 1 shall be granted only to the following persons:

(*a*) persons who are established in the customs territory of the Community;
(*b*) persons who provide the necessary assurance of the proper conduct of the operations and, in cases where a customs debt or other charges may be incurred for goods placed under a special procedure, provide a guarantee in accordance with Article 56;
(*c*) in the case of the temporary admission or inward-processing procedure, the person who uses the goods or arranges for their use or who carries out processing operations on the goods or arranges for them to be carried out, respectively.

The measures designed to amend non-essential elements of this Regulation, by supplementing it, providing for derogations from the first subparagraph of this paragraph, shall be adopted in accordance with the regulatory procedure with scrutiny referred to in Article 184(4).

4. Except where otherwise provided for and in addition to paragraph 3, the authorisation referred to in paragraph 1 shall be granted only where the following conditions are fulfilled:

(*a*) where the customs authorities are able to exercise customs supervision without having to introduce administrative arrangements disproportionate to the economic needs involved;
(*b*) where the essential interests of Community producers would not be adversely affected by an authorisation for a processing procedure (economic conditions).

The essential interests of Community producers shall be deemed not to be adversely affected, as referred to in point (*b*) of the first subparagraph, except where evidence to the contrary exists or where the customs legislation provides that the economic conditions are deemed to be fulfilled.

Where evidence exists that the essential interests of Community producers are likely to be adversely affected, an examination of the economic conditions shall take place in accordance with Article 185.

The Commission shall, in accordance with the regulatory procedure referred to in Article 184(2), adopt measures governing the following:

(*a*) examination of the economic conditions;
(*b*) the determination of cases in which the essential interests of Community producers are likely to be adversely affected, taking into account commercial and agricultural policy measures;
(*c*) the determination of cases in which the economic conditions are deemed to be fulfilled.

5. The holder of the authorisation shall notify the customs authorities of all factors arising after the authorisation was granted which may influence its continuation or content.

Records

Article 137

1. Except for the transit procedure, or where otherwise provided for under the customs legislation, the holder of the authorisation, the holder of the procedure, and all persons carrying on an activity involving the storage, working or processing of goods, or the sale or purchase of goods in free zones, shall keep records in a form approved by the customs authorities.
The records must enable the customs authorities to supervise the procedure concerned, in particular with regard to identification of the goods placed under that procedure, their customs status and their movements.

2. The measures designed to amend non-essential elements of this Regulation, by supplementing it, relating to the implementation of this Article, shall be adopted in accordance with the regulatory procedure with scrutiny referred to in Article 184(4).

Discharge of a procedure

Article 138

1. In cases other than the transit procedure and without prejudice to Article 166, a special procedure shall be discharged when the goods placed under the procedure, or the processed products, are placed under a subsequent customs procedure, have left the customs territory of the Community, or have been destroyed with no waste remaining, or are abandoned to the State in accordance with Article 127.

2. The transit procedure shall be discharged by the customs authorities when they are in a position to establish, on the basis of a comparison of the data available to the customs office of departure and those available to the customs office of destination, that the procedure has ended correctly.

3. The customs authorities shall take all the measures necessary to regularise the situation of the goods in respect of which a procedure has not been discharged under the conditions prescribed.

Transfer of rights and obligations

Article 139

The rights and obligations of the holder of a procedure with regard to goods which have been placed under a special procedure other than transit may, under the conditions laid down by the customs authorities, be fully or partially transferred to other persons who fulfil the conditions laid down for the procedure concerned.

...

CHAPTER 4

SPECIFIC USE

...

SECTION 2—END-USE

End-use procedure

Article 166

1. Under the end-use procedure, goods may be released for free circulation under a duty exemption or at a reduced rate of duty on account of their specific use. They shall remain under customs supervision.

2. Customs supervision under the end-use procedure shall end in the following cases:
   (*a*) where the goods have been used for the purposes laid down for the application of the duty exemption or reduced rate of duty;
   (*b*) where the goods are exported, destroyed or abandoned to the State;
   (*c*) where the goods have been used for purposes other than those laid down for the application of the duty exemption or reduced duty rate and the applicable import duties have been paid.

3. Where a rate of yield is required, Article 167 shall apply *mutatis mutandis* to the end-use procedure.

...

TITLE IX
CUSTOMS CODE COMMITTEE AND FINAL PROVISIONS

CHAPTER 1
CUSTOMS CODE COMMITTEE

Further implementing measures

Article 183

1. The Commission shall, in accordance with the regulatory procedure referred to in Article 184(2), adopt rules for the interoperability of Member States' electronic customs systems as

well as for the relevant Community components to bring about improved cooperation based upon electronic data exchange between customs authorities, between customs authorities and the Commission and between customs authorities and economic operators.

2. The measures designed to amend non-essential elements of this Regulation, by supplementing it, laying down the following:

(*a*) the conditions under which the Commission may issue decisions requesting Member States to revoke or amend a decision – other than those referred to in Article 20(8)(*c*) issued within the framework of the customs legislation which deviates from comparable decisions of other competent authorities and thereby compromises the uniform application of customs legislation;

(*b*) any other implementing measures, where necessary, including where the Community has accepted commitments and obligations in relation to international agreements which require the adaptation of provisions of the Code;

(*c*) further cases and conditions under which the application of this Code may be simplified,

shall be adopted in accordance with the regulatory procedure with scrutiny referred to in Article 184(4).

Committee

Article 184

1. The Commission shall be assisted by the Customs Code Committee, hereinafter referred to as "the Committee".

2. Where reference is made to this paragraph, Articles 5 and 7 of Decision 1999/468/EC shall apply, having regard to the provisions of Article 8 thereof.

The period laid down in Article 5(6) of Decision 1999/468/EC shall be set at three months.

3. Where reference is made to this paragraph, Articles 4 and 7 of Decision 1999/468/EC shall apply, having regard to the provisions of Article 8 thereof.

The period laid down in Article 4(3) of Decision 1999/468/EC shall be set at three months.

4. Where reference is made to this paragraph, Article 5a(1) to (4) and Article 7 of Decision 1999/468/EC shall apply, having regard to the provisions of Article 8 thereof.

Further matters

Article 185

The Committee may examine any question concerning the customs legislation which is raised by its chairman, either on the initiative of the Commission or at the request of a representative of a Member State, and which concerns, in particular, the following:

(*a*) any problems arising from the application of customs legislation;

(*b*) any position to be taken by the Community in committees, working groups and panels established by or under international agreements dealing with customs legislation.

CHAPTER 2

FINAL PROVISIONS

Repeal

Article 186

Regulations (EEC) No 3925/91, (EEC) No 2913/92 and (EC) No 1207/2001 are hereby repealed.

References to the repealed Regulations shall be construed as references to this Regulation and shall be read in accordance with the correlation tables set out in the Annex.

Entry into force

Article 187

This Regulation shall enter into force on the 20th day following its publication in the Official Journal of the European Union.

Application

Article 188

1. The second subparagraph of Article 1(3), second subparagraph of Article 5(1), first subparagraph of Article 5(2), Article 10(2), Article 11(3), second subparagraph of Article 12(2), Article 15(1), Article 16(5), Article 18(4), Article 19(5), Article 20(7), Article 20(8), Article 20(9), second subparagraph of Article 24(3), Article 25(3), Article 28(3), Article 30(2), Article 31(3), Article 33(5), Article 38, Article 39(3), Article 39(6), Article 43, Article 54, second subparagraph of Article 55(2), Article 56(9), Article 57(3), second subparagraph of Article 58, second subparagraph of Article 59(1), Article 62(3), Article 63(3), Article 65(3), third subparagraph of Article 67(1), Article 71, first subparagraph of Article 72(3), Article 76, Article 77(3), second subparagraph of Article 78(1), Article 78(5), Article 85, Article 86(7), first subparagraph of

Article 87(3), second subparagraph of Article 88(4), Article 89(2), Article 93(2), Article 101(2), Article 103, Article 105(2), first subparagraph of Article 106(4), Article 107(3), second subparagraph of Article 108(1), Article 108(4), Article 109(2), Article 109(3), third subparagraph of Article 110(1), Article 111(3), Article 112(4), Article 113(3), second subparagraph of Article 114(2), second subparagraph of Article 115, first subparagraph of Article 116(2), Article 119(3), Article 122, Article 124(2), Article 128, Article 134, first subparagraph of Article 136(2), second subparagraph of Article 136(3), fourth subparagraph of Article 136(4), Article 137(2), Article 140(2), fourth subparagraph of Article 142(1), second subparagraph of Article 142(2), second subparagraph of Article 142(3), Article 143, Article 144(2), second subparagraph of Article 145(3), second subparagraph of Article 148(2), Article 150(3), Article 151(5), first subparagraph of Article 164, second subparagraph of Article 171(3), Article 176(1), Article 177(5), Article 178(3), third subparagraph of Article 181, Article 182(2), Article 183(1) and Article 183(2) shall be applicable from 24 June 2008.

2. All other provisions shall be applicable once the implementing provisions adopted on the basis of the Articles referred to in the paragraph 1 are applicable. The implementing provisions shall enter into force on 24 June 2009 at the earliest.

Notwithstanding the entry into force of the implementing provisions, the provisions of this Regulation referred to in this paragraph shall be applicable on 24 June 2013 at the latest.

3. Article 30(1) shall apply from 1 January 2011.

This Regulation shall be binding in its entirety and directly applicable in all Member States.

Done at Strasbourg, 23 April 2008.

For the European Parliament

The President

H.-G. Pöttering

For the Council

The President

J. Lenari

ANNEX

CORRELATION TABLES

1. REGULATION (EEC) NO 2913/92

Regulation (EEC) No 2913/92	*This Regulation*
Article 1	Article 4
Article 2	Article 1
Article 3	Article 3
Article 4	Article 4
Article 4, points (4a) to (4d)	–
Article 5	Articles 11 and 12
Article 5a	Articles 13, 14 and 15
Article 6	Article 16
Article 7	Article 16
Article 8	Articlc 18
Article 9	Article 19
Article 10	Article 16
Article 11	Articles 8 and 30
Article 12	Article 20
Article 13	Articles 25 and 26
Article 14	Article 9
Article 15	Article 6
Article 16	Article 29
Article 17	Article 32
Article 18	Article 31
Article 19	Articles 116 and 183
Article 20	Articles 33 and 34
Article 21	Article 33
Article 22	Article 35
Article 23	Article 36
Article 24	Article 36
Article 25	–
Article 26	Article 37

Regulation (EEC) No 2913/92	*This Regulation*
Article 27	Article 39
Article 28	Article 40
Article 29	Article 41
Article 30	Article 42
Article 31	Article 42
Article 32	Article 43
Article 33	Article 43
Article 34	Article 43
Article 35	Article 31
Article 36	Article 41
Article 36a	Article 87
Article 36b	Articles 5, 88 and 89
Article 36c	Article 90
Article 37	Article 91
Article 38	Articles 92 and 93
Article 39	Article 94
Article 40	Article 95
Article 41	Article 95
Article 42	Article 91
Article 43	–
Article 44	–
Article 45	–
Article 46	Article 96
Article 47	Article 96
Article 48	Article 97
Article 49	–
Article 50	Articles 98 and 151
Article 51	Articles 151 and 152
Article 52	Article 152
Article 53	Article 151
Article 54	Article 99
Article 55	Article 100
Article 56	Article 125
Article 57	Article 126
Article 58	Articles 91 and 97
Article 59	Article 104
Article 60	Article 105
Article 61	Article 107
Article 62	Article 108
Article 63	Article 112
Article 64	Article 111
Article 65	Article 113
Article 66	Article 114
Article 67	Article 112
Article 68	Article 117
Article 69	Article 118
Article 70	Article 119
Article 71	Article 120
Article 72	Article 121
Article 73	Article 123
Article 74	Article 124
Article 75	Article 126
Article 76	Articles 108, 109, 110 and 112
Article 77	Articles 107 and 108
Article 78	Article 27
Article 79	Article 129
Article 80	–
Article 81	Article 115
Article 82	Article 166
Article 83	Article 102

Regulation (EEC) No 2913/92	*This Regulation*
Article 84	Article 135
Article 85	Article 136
Article 86	Article 136
Article 87	Article 136
Article 87a	–
Article 88	Article 136
Article 89	Article 138
Article 90	Article 139
Article 91	Articles 140 and 144
Article 92	Article 146
Article 93	Article 147
Article 94	Articles 62, 63, 136 and 146
Article 95	Articles 136 and 146
Article 96	Article 146
Article 97	Article 143
Article 98	Articles 143, 148 and 153
Article 99	Article 153
Article 100	Article 136
Article 101	Article 149
Article 102	Article 149
Article 103	–
Article 104	Article 136
Article 105	Article 137
Article 106	Articles 137 and 154
Article 107	Article 137
Article 108	Article 150
Article 109	Articles 141 and 143
Article 110	Article 153
Article 111	Article 140
Article 112	Article 53
Article 113	–
Article 114	Articles 142 and 168
Article 115	Articles 142 and 143
Article 116	Article 136
Article 117	Article 136
Article 118	Article 169
Article 119	Article 167
Article 120	Article 143
Article 121	Articles 52 and 53
Article 122	Articles 52 and 53
Article 123	Article 170
Article 124	–
Article 125	–
Article 126	–
Article 127	–
Article 128	–
Article 129	–
Article 130	Article 168
Article 131	Article 143
Article 132	Article 136
Article 133	Article 136
Article 134	–
Article 135	Article 53
Article 136	Article 53
Article 137	Article 162
Article 138	Article 136
Article 139	Article 162
Article 140	Article 163
Article 141	Article 164
Article 142	Articles 143 and 164

Regulation (EEC) No 2913/92	*This Regulation*
Article 143	Articles 47 and 165
Article 144	Articles 47, 52 and 53
Article 145	Articles 48 and 171
Article 146	Articles 143 and 171
Article 147	Article 136
Article 148	Article 136
Article 149	Article 171
Article 150	Article 171
Article 151	Article 171
Article 152	Article 172
Article 153	Article 171
Article 154	Articles 173 and 174
Article 155	Article 173
Article 156	Article 173
Article 157	Article 174
Article 158	–
Article 159	–
Article 160	–
Article 161	Articles 176, 177 and 178
Article 162	Article 177
Article 163	Article 145
Article 164	Articles 103 and 145
Article 165	Article 143
Article 166	Article 148
Article 167	Articles 155 and 156
Article 168	Article 155
Article 168a	–
Article 169	Articles 157 and 158
Article 170	Articles 157 and 158
Article 171	Article 150
Article 172	Article 156
Article 173	Articles 141 and 159
Article 174	–
Article 175	Article 159
Article 176	Article 137
Article 177	Article 160
Article 178	Article 53
Article 179	–
Article 180	Article 161
Article 181	Article 160
Article 182	Articles 127, 168 and 179
Article 182a	Article 175
Article 182b	Article 176
Article 182c	Articles 176, 179 and 180
Article 182d	Articles 5, 180 and 181
Article 183	Article 177
Article 184	–
Article 185	Articles 130 and 131
Article 186	Article 130
Article 187	Article 132
Article 188	Article 133
Article 189	Article 56
Article 190	Article 58
Article 191	Article 56
Article 192	Articles 57 and 58
Article 193	Article 59
Article 194	Article 59
Article 195	Article 61
Article 196	Article 60
Article 197	Article 59

Regulation (EEC) No 2913/92	*This Regulation*
Article 198	Article 64
Article 199	Article 65
Article 200	-
Article 201	Article 44
Article 202	Article 46
Article 203	Article 46
Article 204	Articles 46 and 86
Article 205	Article 46
Article 206	Articles 46 and 86
Article 207	Article 86
Article 208	Article 47
Article 209	Article 48
Article 210	Article 49
Article 211	Article 49
Article 212	Article 50
Article 212a	Article 53
Article 213	Article 51
Article 214	Articles 52 and 78
Article 215	Articles 55 and 66
Article 216	Article 45
Article 217	Articles 66 and 69
Article 218	Article 70
Article 219	Article 70
Article 220	Articles 70 and 82
Article 221	Articles 67 and 68
Article 222	Article 72
Article 223	Article 73
Article 224	Article 74
Article 225	Article 74
Article 226	Article 74
Article 227	Article 75
Article 228	Article 76
Article 229	Article 77
Article 230	Article 73
Article 231	Article 73
Article 232	Article 78
Article 233	Article 86
Article 234	Article 86
Article 235	Article 4
Article 236	Articles 79, 80, and 84
Article 237	Articles 79 and 84
Article 238	Articles 79, 81 and 84
Article 239	Articles 79, 83, 84, and 85
Article 240	Article 79
Article 241	Article 79
Article 242	Article 79
Article 243	Article 23
Article 244	Article 24
Article 245	Article 23
Article 246	Article 22
Article 247	Article 183
Article 247a	Article 184
Article 248	Article 183
Article 248a	Article 184
Article 249	Article 185
Article 250	Articles 17, 120 and 121
Article 251	Article 186
Article 252	Article 186
Article 253	Article 187

VAT

2. REGULATIONS (EEC) NO 3925/91 AND (EC) NO 1207/2001

Repealed Regulation	*This Regulation*
Regulation (EEC) No 3925/91	Article 28
Regulation (EC) No 1207/2001	Article 39

EC DECISIONS

Council Decision
of 5 October 1984
application of article 27 of the Sixth Council Directive of 17 May 1977 on value added tax authorisation of a derogation, requested by the United Kingdom, with a view to avoiding certain types of fraud or tax evasion

(84/469/EEC)

Note—See OJ L264 05.10.1984, p 27.
This Decision is spent.

Council Decision
of 21 July 1986
authorising the United Kingdom to apply flat-rate measures in respect of the non-deductible value added tax charged on fuel expenditure in company cars

(86/356/EEC)

Note—See OJ L212 03.08.1986, p 35.
Repealed by Council Decision 2006/659/EC art 4, with effect from 30 April 2007 (OJ L 272, 3.10.2006, p 15).

THE COUNCIL OF THE EUROPEAN COMMUNITIES

Having regard to the Treaty establishing the European Economic Community,

Having regard to the sixth Council Directive 77/388/EEC of 17 May 1977 on the harmonisation of the laws of the Member States relating to turnover taxes—Common system of value added tax: uniform basis of assessment, as last amended by Directive 84/386/EEC, and in particular Article 27 thereof,

Having regard to the proposal from the Commission,

Whereas, under the terms of Article 27(1) of Directive 77/388/EEC, the Council, acting unanimously on a proposal from the Commission, may authorise any Member State to introduce special measures for derogation from the provisions of that Directive, in order to simplify the procedure for charging the tax or to prevent certain types of tax evasion or avoidance;

Whereas the United Kingdom has requested authorisation to introduce a special measure designed to determine on a flat-rate basis the proportion of value added tax relating to expenditure on fuel used for private purposes in company cars; whereas that measure derogates from Articles 5(6) and 17(6) of Directive 77/388/EEC;

Whereas it is appropriate to accede to this request subject to certain conditions,

HAS ADOPTED THIS DECISION—

Article 1

The United Kingdom is hereby authorised to fix on a flat-rate basis the proportion of value added tax relating to expenditure on fuel used for private purposes in company cars.

Article 2

For a transitional period, the proportion of the tax referred to in Article 1 may be expressed in fixed amounts determined according to engine capacity or type of vehicle. These fixed amounts shall be adjusted annually in line with changes in the average cost of fuel.

Article 3

Where Article 2 is applied, the United Kingdom shall communicate to the Commission annually the following information, broken down by vehicle category—

1. The average cost of fuel per kilometre.

2. The average distance covered per vehicle each year on private journeys.

3. An estimate of the number of vehicles affected by this Decision.

The system which has been set up will be reviewed on the basis of this information and taking account of the harmonisation of expenditure not eligible for a deduction of value added tax envisaged in Article 17(6) of Directive 77/388/EEC.

Article 4

This Decision shall apply from 23 March 1986.

Article 5

This Decision is addressed to the United Kingdom.

Authorisation
application of article 27 of the Sixth Council Directive of 17 May 1977 on value added tax authorisation of a derogation requested by the government of the United Kingdom

In its request dated 27 June 1986 and supplemented on 3 September 1986 following a request from the Commission for further information, the United Kingdom Government informed the Commission, pursuant to the above provisions, of its intention to introduce a measure derogating from the Sixth Directive.

The purpose of the measure, which replaces a previously notified derogation the scope of which was too broad, remains that of simplifying calculation of VAT in respect of long stays in hotels by assessing on a flat-rate basis the part of the service deemed to correspond to a letting of immovable property exempt under Article 13(B)(*b*)(1) of Sixth VAT Directive (77/388/EEC). However, the measure will henceforth apply only to hotel services provided to individuals themselves occupying the accommodation in question. Accordingly, the previous provision is repealed.

The Commission informed the other Member States, by letter dated 9 October 1986, of the request submitted by the United Kingdom Government.

In accordance with Article 27(4) of the Sixth Directive, the Council Decision authorising this derogation will be deemed to have been adopted if, within two months of the other Member States being informed as described above, neither the Commission nor any Member State has requested that the matter be discussed by the Council.

As neither the Commission nor any Member State has raised the matter within the prescribed time, the Council Decision is deemed to have been adopted on 10 December 1986.

Note—See OJ L359, 19.12.1986, p 59.

Authorisation
application of article 27 of the Sixth Council Directive of 17 May 1977 on value added tax authorisation for a derogation measure requested by the United Kingdom government

In its request dated 6 January 1987 the United Kingdom Government informed the Commission, pursuant to the above provisions, of its intention to introduce measures derogating from the sixth Directive with effect from 1 April 1987.

The purpose of the proposed anti-avoidance measures is to prevent taxable persons artificially reducing the price for supplies or imports of goods or for supplies of services to totally or partially exempt persons with whom they have certain family, legal or business ties specified in national legislation. In such circumstances, the free market value may be taken as the consideration for the transaction, irrespective of whether the latter is actually taxed or not, where otherwise there would be loss of tax.

The Commission informed the other Member States, by letter dated 10 February 1987, of the request submitted by the United Kingdom Government.

In accordance with Article 27(4) of the sixth Directive, the Council's decision will be deemed to have been adopted if, within two months of the other Member States being informed, as described above, neither the Commission nor any Member State has requested that the matter be raised by the Council.

As neither the Commission nor any Member State has requested such action within that period, the Council's decision is deemed to have been adopted on 11 April 1987.

Note—See OJ L132, 21.5.1987, p 22.

Council Decision of 18 July 1989 authorising the United Kingdom to apply a measure derogating from article 11(A)(1)(*b*) of the Sixth Directive 77/388/EEC on the harmonisation of the laws of the Member States relating to turnover taxes

(89/466/EEC)

Note—See OJ L226 03.08.1989, p 23.

THE COUNCIL OF THE EUROPEAN COMMUNITIES

Having regard to the Treaty establishing the European Economic Community,

Having regard to the Sixth Council Directive 77/388/EEC of 17 May 1977 on the harmonisation of the laws of the Member States relating to turnover taxes—Common system of value added tax: uniform basis of assessment (OJ No L145, 13.6.1977, p 1), as last amended by the Act of Accession of Spain and Portugal, and in particular Article 27 thereof,

Having regard to the proposal from the Commission,

Whereas, under Article 27(1) of the Sixth Directive, the Council, acting unanimously on a proposal from the Commission, may authorise any Member State to introduce special measures for derogation from that Directive in order to simplify the procedure for charging the tax or to prevent certain types of tax evasion or avoidance;

Whereas the United Kingdom, by letter addressed to the Commission and registered on 9 January 1989, requested authorisation to introduce a special measure derogating from Article 11 of the said Directive;

Whereas the other Member States were informed of the United Kingdom's request on 9 February 1989;

Whereas, by letter dated 10 April 1989, the Commission, having decided that it had fundamental objections to the United Kingdom Government's request, asked, in accordance with Article 27(4) of the Sixth Directive, that the matter be raised by the Council;

Whereas, by a note dated 10 May 1989, the United Kingdom informed the Council that it was modifying and narrowing the scope of the derogation notified to the Commission on 9 January 1989;

Whereas the United Kingdom currently exempts all building land under Article 28(3)(*b*), read in conjunction with point 16 of Annex F to the Sixth Directive;

Whereas, in order to comply with the spirit of the Court of Justice ruling in Case 416/85, the United Kingdom wishes to tax supplies of buildings and the land on which they stand where these are used for commercial or industrial purposes, while retaining zero rating for supplies of residential buildings and exemption for supplies of building land;

Whereas, in order to simplify the procedure for charging the tax and to prevent certain types of tax evasion or avoidance, the United Kingdom wishes to apply the tax to transactions relating to commercial or industrial buildings and to the land on which they stand before first occupation on the basis of the open market value at the time they are taken into use; whereas, in the case of supply or letting with the developer option for taxation under Article 13(C)(*a*) of the Sixth Directive, this objective is achieved because the price of the supply or the rent necessarily reflects the value of the land at the time of such supply or letting;

Whereas, in order to achieve the objective in question where the building is to be occupied by a taxable person who has constructed it and who is not entitled to full deduction of the tax or where the same taxable person lets the building on an exempt basis under Article 13(B)(*b*) of the Sixth Directive, the United Kingdom intends to make use of the option provided for in Article 5(7)(*a*) and (*b*) of the said Directive to tax such occupation or letting of the property on the basis of its open market value;

Whereas, as a result of the taxable amount being determined by reference to the open market value in this way, the amended request derogates from Article 11(A)(1)(*b*) of the Sixth Directive, which stipulates that, in respect of supplies referred to in Article 5(6) and (7), the taxable amount is the purchase price of the goods or of similar goods or, in the absence of a purchase price, the cost price, determined at the time of supply;

Whereas it is appropriate to accede to the request of the United Kingdom pending deletion of point 16 of Annex F to the Sixth Directive, which permits Member States to exempt temporarily supplies of new buildings and building land;

Whereas the said special measure will not have a negative effect on the European Communities' own resources accruing from value added tax,

HAS ADOPTED THIS DIRECTIVE:

Article 1

By way of derogation from Article 11(A)(1)(*b*) of the Sixth Directive, the United Kingdom is hereby authorised to use the open market value as the taxable amount for the supply, within the meaning of Article 5(7)(*a*) and (*b*) of the said Directive, of buildings or parts of buildings before first occupation and of the land on which they stand.

Article 2

This authorisation shall be granted pending the deletion of point 16 of Annex F to the Sixth Directive.

Article 3

This Directive is addressed to the United Kingdom.

Council Decision
of 29 September 1989
application of article 27 of the Sixth Council Directive of 17 May 1977 on value added tax authorising the United Kingdom to apply, in respect of certain supplies to unregistered resellers, a measure derogating from article 11A(1)(a) of the Sixth Directive 77/388/EEC on the harmonisation of the laws of the Member States relating to turnover taxes

(89/534/EEC)

Note—See OJ L280 29.09.1989, p 54.

THE COUNCIL OF THE EUROPEAN COMMUNITIES

Having regard to the Treaty establishing the European Economic Community,

Having regard to the Sixth Council Directive 77/388/EEC of 17 May 1977 on the harmonisation of the laws of the Member States relating to turnover taxes—Common system of value added tax: uniform basis of assessment, as last amended by the Act of Accession of Spain and Portugal, and in particular Article 27 thereof,

Having regard to the proposal from the Commission,

Whereas, under Article 27(1) of the Sixth Directive, the Council, acting unanimously on a proposal from the Commission, may authorise any Member State to introduce special measures for derogation from that Directive, in order to simplify the procedure for charging the tax or to prevent certain types of tax evasion or avoidance;

Whereas the United Kingdom was authorised by Council Decision 85/369/EEC, deemed to have been adopted on 13 June 1985, in accordance with the procedure laid down by Article 27(4) of the Sixth Directive, to introduce for a two-year period a derogation from the Sixth Directive to combat tax avoidance;

Whereas certain marketing structures based on sales of goods effected by taxable persons to non-taxable persons with a view to their resale at the retail stage result in avoidance of tax at the stage of final consumption;

Whereas, in order to prevent such tax avoidance, the United Kingdom applies a measure permitting the tax authorities to adopt administrative decisions the effect of which is to tax supplies made by the taxable persons operating such marketing structures on the basis of the open market value of the goods at the retail stage;

Whereas that measure constitutes a derogation from Article 11A(1)(*a*) of the Sixth Directive, which stipulates that, within the territory of the country, the taxable amount in respect of supplies of goods is everything which constitutes the consideration which has been, or is to be, obtained by the supplier from the purchaser or a third party for such supplies;

Whereas the United Kingdom was authorised by the Council Decision deemed to have been adopted on 25 May 1987 to extend for two years the derogation authorised by Decision 85/369/EEC;

Whereas the United Kingdom's application for that extension was limited to two years because of the proceedings in Joined Cases 138 and 139/86: reference to the Court of Justice by the "London Value Added Tax Tribunal" for a preliminary ruling in the proceedings pending before that Tribunal between "Direct Cosmetics Ltd" and "Laughtons Photographs Ltd" against "Commissioners of Customs and Excise" on the interpretation of Article 27 of the Sixth Directive and on the validity of Decision 85/369/EEC; whereas, in its judgement of 12 July 1988, the Court of Justice confirmed the validity of that Decision;

Whereas the United Kingdom, by letter received by the Commission on 24 February 1989, requested authorisation to extend the said measure for an indefinite period;

Whereas, in its judgement of 12 July 1988, the Court of Justice ruled *inter alia* that Article 27 of the Sixth Directive permitted the adoption of a derogating measure such as that at issue on condition that the resultant difference in treatment was justified by objective circumstances;

Whereas, in order to satisfy itself that this condition is met, the Commission must be informed of any administrative decisions adopted by the tax authorities in connection with the derogation in question;

Whereas the other Member States were notified of the United Kingdom's request on 22 March 1989; whereas the Council Decision is deemed to have been adopted if, within two months of the other Member States being informed, neither the Commission nor any Member State has requested that the matter be raised by the Council; whereas no such request has been made; whereas the Council's Decision is thus deemed to have been adopted on 24 May 1989;

Whereas the said measure will not have a negative effect on the European Communities' own resources accruing from value added tax,

HAS ADOPTED THIS DECISION:

Article 1

By way of derogation from Article 11A(1)(*a*) of the Sixth Directive, the United Kingdom is hereby authorised to prescribe, in cases where a marketing structure based on the supply of goods through non-taxable persons results in non-taxation at the stage of final consumption, that the taxable amount for supplies to such persons is to be the open market value of the goods as determined at that stage.

Article 2

The United Kingdom shall inform the Commission of any administrative decisions subsequently adopted in connection with the derogation.

Article 3

This Decision is addressed to the United Kingdom.

Council Decision
of 23 November 1992
authorising the United Kingdom to apply a measure derogating from Article 28e(1) of the Sixth Directive 77/388/EEC on the harmonisation of the laws of the Member States relating to turnover taxes

(92/546/EEC)

Note—See OJ L351 02.12.1992, p 34.
This Decision applied until 31 December 1996: see Article 1 below.

THE COUNCIL OF THE EUROPEAN COMMUNITIES

Having regard to the Treaty establishing the European Economic Community,

Having regard to the Sixth Council Directive 77/388/EEC of 17 May 1977 on the harmonisation of the laws of the Member States relating to turnover taxes—Common system of value added tax: uniform basis of assessment, and in particular Article 27 thereof,

Having regard to the proposal from the Commission,

Whereas, pursuant to Article 27(1) of Directive 77/388/EEC, the Council, acting unanimously on a proposal from the Commission, may authorise any Member State to introduce special measures for derogation from that Directive in order to simplify the procedure for charging the tax or to prevent certain types of tax evasion and avoidance;

Whereas Council Directive 91/680/EEC of 16 December 1991 supplementing the common system of value added tax and amending Directive 77/388/EEC with a view to the abolition of fiscal frontiers introduces the concept of intra-Community acquisitions of goods; whereas the arrangements for taxing such acquisitions pose certain problems in the United Kingdom concerning the taxable amount;

Whereas the United Kingdom was authorised by a Council Decision, deemed to have been adopted on 11 April 1987 in accordance with the procedure laid down by Article 27(4) of Directive 77/388/EEC, to introduce in certain circumstances special measures to determine the taxable amount of supplies and importations of goods, and of supplies of services; whereas the authorisation of 11 April 1987 does not extend to cover intra-Community acquisitions;

Whereas the United Kingdom, by letter officially received by the Commission on 27 April 1992, requested the authorised derogation to be extended so as to cover intra-Community acquisitions of goods;

Whereas the other Member States were informed on 21 May 1992 of the United Kingdom's request;

Whereas the purpose of this derogation is to prevent persons having certain family, legal or business ties, specified in national legislation, from artificially reducing the price of intra-Community acquisitions so as to benefit from a more advantageous tax position than would otherwise be possible;

Whereas the measure envisaged by the United Kingdom consists of enabling the relevant authorities to direct that the open market value of the relevant transaction shall be used, where the value of the transaction would otherwise be less than the open market value;

Whereas the proposed measure is limited in scope in so far as it would only be applicable to intra-Community acquisitions made by persons who are not fully taxable persons;

Whereas the proposed measure constitutes a derogation from Article 28e(1) of Directive 77/388/EEC;

Whereas the authorisation requested will be temporary;

Whereas the derogation will have a favourable effect on the Community's own resources arising from value added tax,

HAS ADOPTED THIS DECISION:

Article 1

By way of derogation from Article 28e(1) of Directive 77/388/EEC, the United Kingdom is hereby authorised until 31 December 1996 to introduce a special measure allowing the appropriate authorities to direct that the open market value be taken as the taxable amount for intra-Community acquisitions of goods, where the person by whom the goods are acquired is not a fully taxable person, and where there exist certain family, legal or business ties, specified in the national legislation, between the person by whom the goods are acquired and the supplier.

Article 2

This Decision is addressed to the United Kingdom.

Council Decision of 21 December 1992 authorising the United Kingdom to apply a particular measure in accordance with Article 22(12)(b) of Directive 77/388/EEC

(92/621/EEC)

Note—See OJ L408 31.12.1992, p 17.

THE COUNCIL OF THE EUROPEAN COMMUNITIES

Having regard to the Treaty establishing the European Economic Community,

Having regard to the Sixth Council Directive, 77/388/EEC, of 17 May 1977 on the harmonisation of the laws of the Member States relating to turnover taxes—Common system of value added tax: uniform basis of assessment, and in particular Article 22 thereof,

Having regard to the proposal from the Commission,

Whereas, under Article 22(12) of Directive 77/388/EEC, the Council, acting unanimously on a proposal from the Commission, may authorise any Member State to introduce particular measures to simplify the statement obligations laid down in paragraph 6(*b*) of Article 22; whereas Article 22(12) further stipulates that such simplification measures may not jeopardise the proper monitoring of intra-Community transactions, and may take the forms outlined in subparagraphs (*a*) and (*b*) of Article 22(12);

Whereas the United Kingdom, by letter received by the Commission on 22 May 1992, has requested authorisation for a simplification measure which takes the form laid down in subparagraph (*b*) of Article 22(12);

Whereas the authorisation will be temporary;

Whereas the particular measure will not affect the European Communities' own resources arising from value added tax,

HAS ADOPTED THIS DECISION:

Article 1

As provided for by Article 22(12) of Directive 77/388/EEC, the United Kingdom is hereby authorised, with effect from 1 January 1993 until 31 December 1996 or until the end of the transitional arrangements in the unlikely event that this is later, to introduce a particular measure in accordance with subparagraph (*b*) of Article 22(12), to simplify the obligations laid down in paragraph 6(*b*) of Article 22 regarding recapitulative statements.

Article 2

This Decision is addressed to the United Kingdom.

Council Decision
of 15 February 1993
authorising the United Kingdom to apply an optional measure derogating from Article 17 of the Sixth Directive (77/388/EEC) on the harmonisation of the laws of the Member States relating to turnover taxes

(93/111/EEC)

Note—See OJ L43 20.02.1993, p 46.
This Decision applied until 31 December 1996: see Article 1 below.

THE COUNCIL OF THE EUROPEAN COMMUNITIES

Having regard to the Treaty establishing the European Economic Community,

Having regard to the Sixth Council Directive (77/388/EEC) of 17 May 1977 on the harmonisation of the laws of the Member States relating to turnover taxes—Common system of value added tax: uniform basis of assessment OJ No L145, 13.6.1977, p 1. Directive as last amended by Directive 92/111/EEC (OJ No L384, 31.12.1992, p 47), and in particular Article 27 thereof,

Having regard to the proposal from the Commission,

Whereas, under the terms of Article 27(1) of Directive 77/388/EEC, the Council, acting unanimously on a proposal from the Commission, may authorise any Member State to introduce special measures for derogation from the provisions of that Directive in order to simplify the procedure for charging the tax or to prevent certain types of tax evasion or avoidance;

Whereas the United Kingdom was authorised, by Decision 90/497/EEC (OJ No L276, 6.10.1990, p 45), in accordance with the procedure laid down in Article 27(1) to (4) of Directive 77/388/EEC, to apply a measure derogating from Article 17(1) of the said Directive until 31 December 1992;

Whereas the United Kingdom, by means of a letter dated 26 October 1992 and received by the Commission on 28 October 1992, requested authorisation to extend the said derogation until 31 December 1996;

Whereas the other Member States were informed on 27 November 1992 of the United Kingdom's request;

Whereas this special measure derogating from Article 17(1) of Directive 77/388/EEC forms part of an optional system of taxation for firms with an annual turnover of less than £350 000 based on the third subparagraph of Article 10(2) of the said Directive, which permits payment of tax to be deferred until receipt of the price;

Whereas the United Kingdom wishes to increase the turnover ceiling from £300 000 to £350 000 to take account of inflation;

Whereas that request can be accepted in view of the limited number of firms that have opted for this simplified scheme and the limited duration of the extension in question;

Whereas the derogation concerned has no negative effect on the own resources of the European Communities accruing from VAT,

HAS ADOPTED THIS DECISION:

Article 1

By way of derogation from the provisions of Article 17(1) of Directive 77/388/EEC, the United Kingdom is hereby authorised, until 31 December 1996, to provide within an optional scheme that enterprises with an annual turnover of less than £350 000 must postpone the right of deduction of tax until it has been paid to the supplier.

Article 2

This Decision is addressed to the United Kingdom.

Council Decision
of 5 April 1993
authorising the United Kingdom to apply a measure derogating from Articles 5(8) and 21(1)(a) of the Sixth Council Directive 77/388/EEC on the harmonisation of the laws of the Member States relating to turnover taxes

(93/204/EEC)

Note—See OJ L88 08.04.1993, p 43.
This Decision applied until 31 December 1996: see Article 1 below.

THE COUNCIL OF THE EUROPEAN COMMUNITIES

Having regard to the Treaty establishing the European Economic Community,

Having regard to the Sixth Council Directive 77/388/EEC of 17 May 1977 on the harmonisation of the laws of the Member States relating to turnover taxes—Common system of value added tax: uniform basis of assessment, and in particular Article 27 thereof,

Having regard to the proposal from the Commission,

Whereas pursuant to Article 27(1) of Directive 77/388/EEC the Council, acting unanimously on a proposal from the Commission, may authorise any Member State to introduce special measures for derogation from the provisions of that Directive in order to simplify the procedure for charging the tax or to prevent certain types of tax evasion or avoidance;

Whereas the United Kingdom was authorised by Decision 90/127/EEC, in accordance with the procedure laid down in Article 27(1) to (4) of Directive 77/388/EEC to apply a measure derogating from Articles 5(8) and 21(1)(*a*) of the said Directive;

Whereas the United Kingdom, by means of a letter dated 16 November 1992 and received by the Commission on 18 November 1992, requested authorisation to extend the said derogation until 31 December 1996;

Whereas the other Member States were informed on 18 December 1992 of the United Kingdom's request;

Whereas the purpose of the derogation is to prevent groups of enterprises which are treated as a single taxable person within the meaning of Article 4(4) of Directive 77/388/EEC and which are not entitled to deduct tax in full from being able to benefit from full deduction of the tax on certain transfers of assets made in the United Kingdom pursuant to Article 5(8) of that Directive;

Whereas pursuant to Article 5(8) of Directive 77/388/EEC Member States may, in the event of a transfer, whether for consideration or not or as a contribution to a company, of a totality of assets or part thereof, consider that no supply of goods has taken place and that the recipient is to be treated as the successor to the transferor;

Whereas the United Kingdom makes general use of the option provided for in the said Article 5(8);

Whereas, therefore, the measure planned by the United Kingdom derogates from the said Article 5(8) in that a supply is deemed to take place where part of a totality of assets is transferred to a company which, as a member of a group of enterprises which are treated as a single taxable person within the meaning of Article 4(4) of that Directive, is not entitled to deduct tax in full;

Whereas the measure planned by the United Kingdom also constitutes a derogation form Article 21(1)(*a*) of Directive 77/388/EEC according to which, under the internal system, the person liable for the tax is the taxable person who carries out the taxable transaction;

Whereas that derogation will have a favourable effect on the European Communities' own resources from value added tax,

HAS ADOPTED THIS DECISION:

Article 1

By way of derogation from Articles 5(8) and 21(1)(*a*) of Directive 77/388/EEC, the United Kingdom is hereby authorised to apply until 31 December 1996:

—a provision whereby a supply of goods is deemed to occur where assets, other than the capital goods subject to adjustment of the deductions initially made pursuant to legislation adopted by the United Kingdom on the basis of Article 20 of the said Directive, are totally or partially transferred to a company which is a member of a group of enterprises treated as a single taxable person within the meaning of Article 4(4) of that Directive and which, as a member of that group, is not entitled to deduct tax in full,

—a provision whereby the company which is the recipient of the supply of assets referred to in the first indent becomes liable to tax.

Article 2

This Decision is addressed to the United Kingdom.

Council Decision
of 22 November 1993
authorising the United Kingdom to apply a particular measure in accordance with Article 22(12)(a) of the Sixth Directive 77/388/EEC on the harmonisation of the laws of the Member States relating to turnover taxes

(93/609/EC)

Note—See OJ L292 26.11.1993, p 51.

THE COUNCIL OF THE EUROPEAN UNION,

Having regard to the Treaty establishing the European Community,

Having regard to the Sixth Council Directive 77/388/EEC of 17 May 1977 on the harmonisation of the laws of the Member States relating to turnover taxes—Common system of value added tax: uniform basis of assessment, and in particular Article 22 thereof,

Having regard to the proposal from the Commission,

Whereas, pursuant to Article 22(12) of the Sixth Directive 77/388/EEC, the Council, acting unanimously on a proposal from the Commission, may authorise any Member State to introduce particular measures to simplify the statement obligations laid down in paragraph 6(*b*) of Article 22; whereas Article 22(12) further stipulates that such simplification measures may not jeopardise the proper monitoring of intra-Community transactions, and may take the forms outlined in sub-paragraphs (*a*) and (*b*) of Article 22(12);

Whereas the United Kingdom, by letter received by the Commission on 27 April 1993, has requested authorisation of a simplification measure which takes the form laid down in sub-paragraph (*a*) of Article 22(12);

Whereas the authorisation will be temporary;

Whereas the particular measure will not effect the European Communities' own resources arising from value added tax,

HAS ADOPTED THIS DECISION:

Article 1

As provided for by Article 22(12) of the Sixth Directive 77/388/EEC, the United Kingdom is hereby authorised, with effect from 1 January 1993 until 31 December 1996 or until the end of the transitional arrangements, should this be later, to introduce a particular measure in accordance with sub-paragraph (*a*) of Article 22(12), to simplify the obligations laid down in paragraph 6(*b*) of Article 22 regarding recapitulative statements.

Article 2

This Decision is addressed to the United Kingdom.

Council Decision
of 29 June 1995
authorising the United Kingdom to apply a measure derogating from Articles 6 and 17 of the Sixth Council Directive (77/388/EEC) on the harmonisation of the laws of the Member States relating to turnover taxes

(95/252/EC)

Note—See OJ L159 11.07.1995, p 19.

THE COUNCIL OF THE EUROPEAN UNION,

Having regard to the Treaty establishing the European Community,

Having regard to the Sixth Council Directive (77/388/EEC) of 17 May 1977 on the harmonisation of the laws of the Member States relating to turnover taxes—Common system of value added tax: uniform basis of assessment and in particular Article 27 thereof,

Having regard to the proposal from the Commission,

Whereas, pursuant to Article 27(1) of the Directive 77/388/EEC, the Council, acting unanimously on a proposal from the Commission, may authorise any Member State to introduce special measures for derogation from that Directive, in order to simplify the procedure for charging the tax or to prevent certain types of tax evasion or avoidance;

Whereas, by registered letter to the Commission dated 22 March 1995, the United Kingdom requested authorisation to introduce a measure derogating from Articles 6(2) and 17 of the said Directive;

Whereas, in accordance with Article 27(3) of the said Directive, the other Member States were informed on 20 April 1995 of the request made by the United Kingdom;

Whereas the derogation in question, which forms part of a thorough recasting of the legislation governing the deduction of input tax on cars, aims, firstly, to restrict to 50 per cent the right of the hirer or lessee to deduct input tax on passenger car hire or leasing transactions where the car is used for private purposes and, secondly, to waive the value added tax payable on the private use of the car in question;

Whereas the objective of this input tax restriction is to introduce a flat-rate tax for the private use of cars hired or leased by taxable persons;

Whereas the measure, by reducing the administrative burden on traders, who are not required to keep records of private mileage, constitutes a simplification of the procedure for charging the tax within the meaning of Article 27 of Directive 77/388/EEC;

Whereas the authorisation requested by the United Kingdom can be granted only temporarily, either until the entry into force of the Community rules determining what expenditure will not be eligible for a deduction of value added tax pursuant to the first subparagraph of Article 17(6) of the said Directive or by 31 December 1997 at the latest;

Whereas the derogation in question has no adverse impact on the European Communities' own resources accruing from value added tax,

HAS ADOPTED THIS DECISION:

Article 1

By way of derogation from Article 17(2) and (3) of Directive 77/388/EEC, the United Kingdom is hereby authorised to restrict to 50 per cent the right of the hirer or lessee to deduct input tax on charges for the hire or lease of a passenger car where the car is used for private purposes.

Article 2

By way of derogation from Article 6(2)(*a*) of Directive 77/388/EEC, the United Kingdom is hereby authorised not to treat as supplies of services for consideration the private use of a business car hired or leased by a taxable person.

Article 3

This authorisation shall expire on the date of the entry into force of the Community rules determining what expenditure is not to be eligible for a deduction of value added tax, pursuant to the first subparagraph of Article 17(6) of Directive 77/388/EEC, but not later than 31 December 1997.

Article 4

This Decision is addressed to the United Kingdom.

Council Decision of 17 March 1997 authorising the United Kingdom of Great Britain and Northern Ireland to apply a measure derogating from Article 9 of the Sixth Directive (77/388/EEC) on the harmonisation of the laws of the Member States relating to turnover taxes

(97/214/EC)

Note—See OJ L86 28.03.1997, p 33.
This Decision applied until 31 December 1999: see Article 3 below.

THE COUNCIL OF THE EUROPEAN UNION,

Having regard to the Treaty establishing the European Community,

Having regard to the Sixth Council Directive 77/388/EEC of 17 May 1977 on the harmonisation of the laws of the Member States relating to turnover taxes—Common system of value added tax: uniform basis of assessment, and in particular Article 27 thereof,

Having regard to the proposal from the Commission,

Whereas, pursuant to Article 27(1) of Directive 77/388/EEC, the Council, acting unanimously on a proposal from the Commission, may authorise any Member State to introduce special measures for derogation from that Directive in order to simplify the procedure for charging the tax or to prevent certain types of tax evasion or avoidance;

Whereas, by letter to the Commission registered on 6 December 1996, the United Kingdom of Great Britain and Northern Ireland requested authorisation to introduce a measure derogating from Article 9 of Directive 77/388/EEC;

Whereas the other Member States were informed on 20 December 1996 of the request made by the United Kingdom of Great Britain and Northern Ireland;

Whereas the measure is necessary to counter the tax avoidance effects that have led a growing number of Community taxable and non-taxable persons to purchase telecommunications services outside the Community in order to avoid payment of VAT; whereas the measure is furthermore necessary to discourage suppliers of telecommunications services established in a Member State from establishing themselves outside the Community;

Whereas the measure is also necessary to simplify the procedure for charging the tax insofar as it provides the same tax obligations for customers of telecommunications services regardless of whether these services are performed by suppliers established inside or outside the Community;

Whereas the derogations will not affect, except to a negligible extent, the amount of tax due at the final consumption stage and will not therefore have an adverse effect on the European Communities' own resources arising from value-added tax;

Whereas it is necessary to grant this measure from 1 January 1997 in order to remedy as quickly as possible a situation undermining the competitiveness of European telecommunications companies; whereas from 1 January 1997 the customers and the suppliers of telecommunications services had no longer a legitimate confidence in the continuation of the legislation in force at that date;

Whereas it is desirable that the derogation should be granted until 31 December 1999, or, if a Directive altering the place of taxation of telecommunications services enters into force at an earlier date, until that date, in order to allow the Council to adopt a general Community solution based on the Commission proposal,

HAS ADOPTED THIS DECISION:

Article 1

By way of derogation from Article 9(1) of Directive 77/388/EEC, the United Kingdom of Great Britain and Northern Ireland is authorised to include, within Article 9(2)(*e*) of the Directive, telecommunications services. In the case of a Member State making use of this facility, the provisions of Article 9(3)(*b*) of the Directive shall also apply to these services.

Telecommunications services shall be deemed to be services relating to the transmission, emission or reception of signals, writing, images and sounds or information of any nature by wire, radio, optical or other electromagnetic systems, including the transfer or assignment of the right to use capacity for such transmission, emission or reception.

Article 2

This Decision may be applied to telecommunications services in respect of which the chargeable event took place from 1 January 1997. It will also apply to prepayments made in respect of telecommunications services paid for before the date of implementation of this Decision by the Member State insofar as these prepayments cover supplies of telecommunications services which are performed after the date of implementation.

Article 3

The authorisation specified in this Decision shall apply until 31 December 1999, or, if a Directive altering the place of taxation of telecommunications services enters into force at an earlier date, until that date.

Article 4

This Decision is addressed to the United Kingdom of Great Britain and Northern Ireland.

Council Decision of 9 June 1997 authorising the United Kingdom to apply an optional measure derogating from Article 17 of the sixth Directive (77/388/EEC) on the harmonisation of the Laws of the Member States relating to turnover taxes

(97/375/EC)

Note—See OJ L158 17.06.1997, p 43.
Repealed and replaced by Council Decision 2007/133/EC, art 2 (OJ L 57, 24.2.2007, p 12).

THE COUNCIL OF THE EUROPEAN UNION,

Having regard to the Treaty establishing the European Community,

Having regard to the Sixth Council Directive 77/388/EEC of 17 May 1977 on the harmonisation of the laws of the Member States relating to turnover taxes—Common System of value added tax: uniform basis of assessment, and in particular Article 27 thereof,

Having regard to the proposal from the Commission,

Whereas, under the terms of Article 27(1) of Directive 77/388/EEC, the Council, acting unanimously on a proposal from the Commission, may authorise any Member State to introduce special measure for derogation from the provisions of that Directive in order to simplify the procedure for charging the tax or to prevent certain types of tax evasion or avoidance;

Whereas, the United Kingdom was authorised, by Decision 93/111/EEC. in accordance with the procedure laid down in Article 27 (1) to (4) of Directive 77/388/EEC to apply a measure derogating from Article 17 (1) of the said Directive until 31 December 1996;

Whereas the United Kingdom, by means of a letter registered by the Commission on 19 November 1996, requested authorisation to extend the said derogation;

Whereas the other Member States were informed on 18 December 1996 of the United Kingdom's request;

Whereas this special measure derogating from Article 17 (1) of Directive 77/388/EEC forms part of an optional system of taxation for firms with an annual turnover not higher than £400,000 based on the third subparagraph of Article 10 (2) of the said Directive, which permits payment of tax to be deferred until receipt of the price;

Whereas the United Kingdom seeks authority to increase the turnover ceiling from £350,000 to £400,000 to take account of inflation;

Whereas a derogation can be accepted in view of the number of firms that already have opted for this simplified scheme and the limited duration of this extension;

Whereas the derogation in question does not have a negative effect on the own resources of the European Communities accruing from VAT;

Whereas the Commission adopted on 10 July 1996 a work programme based on a step-by-step approach for progressing towards a new common system of VAT;

Whereas the last package of proposals is to be put forward by mid-1999 and, in order to permit an evaluation of the coherence of the derogation with the global approach of the new common VAT system, the authorisation is granted until 31 December 1999,

HAS ADOPTED THIS DECISION:

[Article 1

By way of derogation from the provisions of Article 17(1) of Sixth Directive 77/388/EEC, the United Kingdom is hereby authorised, until 31 December 2006, to provide, within an optional scheme, that enterprises with an annual turnover not higher than GBP 660000 must postpone the right of deduction of tax until it has been paid to the supplier.][1]

Amendments—[1] *This Article replaced by EC Council Decision 2003/909 art 1 (OJ L 342; 30.12.2003 p 49).*

Article 2

This Decision is addressed to the United Kingdom.

Council Decision
of 19 December 1997
authorising the United Kingdom to extend application of a measure derogating from Article 28e(1) of the Sixth Council Directive 77/388/EEC on the harmonisation of the laws of the Member States relating to turnover taxes

(98/23/EC)

Note—See OJ L8 14.01.1998, p 24.
Repealed by Council Directive 2006/69/EC of 24 July 2006, art 2, Annex II with effect from 12 August 2006.

THE COUNCIL OF THE EUROPEAN UNION,

Having regard to the Treaty establishing the European Community,

Having regard to the Sixth Council Directive 77/388/EEC of 17 May 1977 on the harmonisation of the laws of the Member States relating to turnover taxes—Common system of value-added tax: uniform basis of assessment, and in particular Article 27 thereof,

Having regard to the previous Decision 92/546/EEC,

Having regard to the proposal from the Commission,

Whereas, pursuant to Article 27(1) of Directive 77/388/EEC, the Council, acting unanimously on a proposal from the Commission, may authorise any Member State to introduce or extend special measures for derogation from that Directive in order to simplify the procedure for charging the tax or to prevent certain types of tax evasion and avoidance;

Whereas, by letter registered at the Commission on 21 February 1997, the United Kingdom requested authorisation to extend application of the derogation measure previously granted to it by Decision 92/546/EEC until 31 December 1996;

Whereas the other Member States were informed on 6 May 1997 of the United Kingdom's request;

Whereas, pursuant to Decision 92/546/EEC, the United Kingdom is authorised to introduce a special measure allowing the appropriate authorities to direct that the open-market value be taken as the taxable amount for intra-Community acquisitions of goods where the person acquiring the goods is not a fully taxable person and there are family, legal or business ties, specified in national legislation, between the person acquiring the goods and the supplier;

Whereas Decision 92/546/EEC empowered the United Kingdom to supplement a special measure authorised by Council Decision, deemed to have been adopted on 11 April 1987, permitting the United Kingdom to direct that the open-market value be taken as the taxable amount for supplies of goods and services or imports where the recipient is a totally or partially exempt person and there are family, legal or business ties, specified in national legislation, between the person supplying the goods or services and the recipient or between the person importing the goods and the person to whom payment for them has to be made;

Whereas the purpose of the measure in question is to prevent persons with family, legal or business ties, specified in national legislation, from artificially reducing the prices of taxable transactions;

Whereas according to the case law of the Court of Justice of the European Communities, national derogation measures which are intended to prevent fraud or tax avoidance are to be interpreted strictly and can be used to derogate from the rules for determining the taxable amount only within the limits strictly necessary to achieve this objective;

Whereas, the special measure is to apply only in cases where the administration is able, based on the facts, to conclude that the determination of the taxable amount provided for in Article 28e of Directive 77/388/EEC is influenced by family, business or legal ties between the person who acquires the goods and the supplier; whereas the administration may not act on mere presumptions, and the parties concerned must be allowed to adduce evidence to the contrary where they dispute the level of the open value established by the administration;

Whereas the measure is limited in scope insofar as it will apply only to taxable transactions where the recipient is a totally or partially exempt person;

Whereas, given the limited scope of the derogation, the special measure is proportionate to the aim pursued;

Whereas the Commission adopted on 10 July 1996 a work programme, accompanied by a schedule of proposals, providing for gradual, stage-by-stage progress towards a common VAT system for the internal market;

Whereas, as the final package of proposals is scheduled for mid-1999, the authorization is being granted until 31 December 1999 so as to enable an assessment to be made at that time as to whether the derogation measure is consistent with the overall approach adopted under the new common VAT system;

Whereas this derogation will have an adverse impact on the Communities' own resources arising from VAT,

HAS ADOPTED THIS DECISION:

Article 1

By way of derogation from Article 28e (1) of Directive 77/388/EEC, the United Kingdom is hereby authorized, until [31 December 2006][1], to apply a special measure allowing the appropriate authorities to direct that the open-market value be taken as the taxable amount for intra-Community acquisitions of goods when the following two conditions are met:

—the person who acquires the goods is not a fully taxable person and there are family, legal or business ties specified in national legislation, between the person acquiring the goods and the supplier,

—a number of facts make it possible to conclude that these family, business or legal ties have influenced the determination of the taxable amount provided for in the said Article 28e.

Amendments—[1] Date replaced by EC Council Decision 2003/909 art 2 (OJ L 342; 30.12.2003 p 49).

Article 2

This Decision is addressed to the United Kingdom.

Council Decision of 9 March 1998 authorising the United Kingdom to extend application of a measure derogating from Articles 6 and 17 of the Sixth Council Directive (77/388/EEC) on the harmonisation of the laws of the Member States relating to turnover taxes

(98/198/EC)

Note—See OJ L76 13.03.1998, p 31.
This Decision applied until 31 December 2007: see Article 3 below.

THE COUNCIL OF THE EUROPEAN UNION

Having regard to the Treaty establishing the European Community,

Having regard to the Sixth Council Directive 77/388/EEC of 17 May 1977 on the harmonisation of the laws of the Member States relating to turnover taxes—Common system of value added tax: uniform basis of assessment and in particular Article 27 thereof,

Having regard to the previous Decision 95/252/EC,

Having regard to the proposal from the Commission,

Whereas, pursuant to Article 27(1) of Directive 77/388/EEC, the Council, acting unanimously on a proposal from the Commission, may authorise any Member State to introduce or extend special measures for derogation from that Directive in order to simplify the procedure for charging the tax or to prevent certain types of tax evasion or avoidance;

Whereas, by letter registered at the Commission on 6 October 1997, the United Kingdom requested authorisation to extend application of the derogation previously granted to it by Decision 95/252/EC;

Whereas the other Member States were informed on 23 October 1997 of the United Kingdom's request;

Whereas the United Kingdom was authorised by Decision 95/252/EC to apply until 31 December 1997 a measure derogating from Articles 6 and 17 of Directive 77/388/EEC;

Whereas the derogation in question is designed, firstly, to restrict to 50% the right of the hirer or lessee of a car to deduct the VAT on the hire or leasing transaction where the car is used for private purposes and, secondly, to waive the VAT payable on the private use of the car in question;

Whereas the objective of this restriction of the right to deduct is to tax the private use of cars hired or leased by taxable persons at a flat rate;

Whereas the measure, by reducing the administrative burden on traders, who are not required to keep records of private mileage, constitutes a simplification of the procedure for charging tax within the meaning of Article 27 of Directive 77/388/EEC;

Whereas the Commission adopted on 10 July 1996 a work programme, accompanied by a schedule of proposals, provided for gradual, stage-by-stage progress towards a common VAT system for the internal market;

Whereas the authorisation is being granted until 31 December 1998 so as to enable an assessment to be made at that time as to whether the derogation measure is consistent with the Community approach to limitations of the right to deduct VAT on certain expenditure, which will be adopted under that programme;

Whereas the derogation will not have an adverse impact on the Community's own resources accruing from VAT;

HAS ADOPTED THIS DECISION

Article 1

By way of derogation from Article 17(2) and (3) of Directive 77/388/EEC the United Kingdom is hereby authorised to restrict to 50% the right of the hirer or lessee of a car to deduct the VAT on the cost of hiring or leasing that car where it is used for private purposes.

Article 2

By way of derogation from Article 6(2)(*a*) of Directive 77/388/EEC the United Kingdom is hereby authorised not to treat as supplies of services for consideration the private use of a business car hired or leased by a taxable person.

[Article 3

This authorisation shall expire on the date of entry into force of Community rules determining what expenditure relating to motorised road vehicles is not to be eligible for full deduction of value added tax, but on 31 December 2007 at the latest.][1]

Amendments—[1] This Article replaced by EC Council Decision 2004/855/EC of 7 December 2004.

Article 4

This Decision is addressed to the United Kingdom.

Commentary—*De Voil Indirect Tax service* **V3.449**.
Cross references—See the VAT (Input Tax) Order, SI 1992/3222 art 7(2H).

Council Decision
of 28 February 2000
authorising Member States to apply a reduced rate of VAT to certain labour-intensive services in accordance with the procedure provided for in Article 28(6) of Directive 77/388/EEC

(2000/185/EC)

Note—See OJ L59 04.03.2000, p 10.
Words omitted do not relate to the UK.
This Decision applied until 31 December 2005: see Article 3 below.

THE COUNCIL OF THE EUROPEAN UNION,

Having regard to the Treaty establishing the European Community,

Having regard to Sixth Council Directive 77/388/EEC of 17 May 1977 on the harmonisation of the laws of the Member States relating to turnover taxes—common system of value added tax: uniform basis of assessment, and in particular Article 28(6) thereof,

Having regard to the proposal from the Commission,

Whereas—

(1) Under Article 28(6) of Directive 77/388/EEC, the Council, acting unanimously on a proposal from the Commission, may authorise any Member State that has submitted an application in accordance with the procedure and conditions provided for in that Article, to apply a reduced rate of VAT to certain labour-intensive services.

(2) The services concerned must meet the conditions provided for in the Directive and be included in the list in Annex K to the Directive.

(3) This is an experiment limited to a maximum period of three years running from 1 January 2000 to 31 December 2002.

(4) However, the introduction of such a targeted reduction in the VAT rate entails some risk to the proper operation of the internal market and tax neutrality; provision should therefore be made for an authorisation period for a full and clearly defined three-year period, for the measure to be on an optional basis for Member States, and for its scope to be made subject to strict conditions so that it remains verifiable and limited.

(5) In view of the experimental nature of the measure, a detailed assessment of its impact in terms of job creation and efficiency should be carried out by the Member States which implement it and by the Commission.

(6) The Member States that have submitted an application have complied with the procedure and conditions set out in Directive 77/388/EEC.

(7) Three Member States, France, Luxembourg and the Netherlands have applied for authorisation to apply a reduced rated of VAT exceptionally to a third category of the services listed in Annex K; in each case the reduction in rate in the third of the sectors selected can have only an insignificant economic impact.

(8) The United Kingdom has applied for authorisation to apply a reduced rate of VAT to dwelling-related services only in the Isle of Man; in the light of the specific territorial rules governing the status of the Isle of Man, including Article 299(6)(*c*) of the Treaty, the Treaty on the accession of the United Kingdom and Article 3(4) of Directive 77/388/EEC, and in the light of the fact that the rules on the location of such services will ensure that they are taxed where the dwelling is located, applying a reduced rate of VAT carries no risk of distortion of competition; however, restricting the reduced rate to the Isle of Man is something which can be authorised only as an exceptional measure. In relation to other territories of Member States where the Treaty and Directive 77/388/EEC are fully applicable, such a step could not be taken without jeopardising the principle of applying uniform rates in a single Member State.

(9) The other Member States have been informed about the applications for authorisation.

(10) This Decision will have no impact on the Communities' own resources derived from VAT,

HAS ADOPTED THIS DECISION

Article 1

In accordance with Article 28(6) of Directive 77/388/EEC, the following Member States are hereby authorised to apply the reduced rates provided for in the third sub-paragraph of Article 12(3)(*a*) for a maximum of [six years running from 1 January 2000 to 31 December 2005][1] to the services for which they have submitted applications in accordance with the required procedure, and which are listed under their names below—

…

9 The United Kingdom for one sector, referred to in point 2 of Annex K to Directive 77/388/EEC, but for the Isle of Man only—

renovation and repairing of private dwellings, excluding materials which form a significant part of the value of the supply.

Amendments—[1] Words replaced by EC Council Decision 2004/161 art 1(1) (OJ L 052; 21.2.2004 p 62), itself amended by Corrigendum (OJ L 91; 30.3.2004 p 60).

Article 2

Before 1 October 2002 each of the Member States listed in Article 1 shall draw up a detailed report containing an overall assessment of the measure's effectiveness in terms of job creation and efficiency and forward it to the Commission.

Article 3

This Decision shall take effect on the day of its publication in the Official Journal of the European Communities.

It shall apply from 1 January 2000 to [31 December 2005][1].

Amendments—[1] Words replaced by EC Council Decision 2004/161 art 1(2) (OJ L 052; 21.2.2004 p 62), itself amended by Corrigendum (OJ L 91; 30.3.2004 p 60).

Article 4

This Decision is addressed to the Member States referred to in Article 1.

Done at Brussels, 28 February 2000.

Commentary—*De Voil Indirect Tax Service* **V1.111**.

Council Decision of 25 September 2006 authorising the United Kingdom to introduce a special measure derogating from Articles 5(6) and 11(A)(1)(*b*) of Directive 77/388/EEC on the harmonisation of the laws of the Member States relating to turnover taxes

(2006/659/EC)

Note—See OJ L 272, 03.10.2006 p 15.

THE COUNCIL OF THE EUROPEAN UNION,

Having regard to the Treaty establishing the European Community,

Having regard to the sixth Council Directive 77/388/EEC of 17 May 1977 on the harmonisation of the laws of the Member States relating to turnover taxes — Common system of value added tax: uniform basis of assessment[1], and in particular Article 27(1) thereof,

Having regard to the proposal from the Commission,

Whereas:

(1) By letter registered by the Secretariat-General of the Commission on 7 April 2005, the United Kingdom requested authorisation to derogate from Articles 5(6) and 11(A)(1)(*b*) of Directive 77/388/EEC.

(2) In accordance with Article 27(2) of Directive 77/388/EEC, the Commission informed the other Member States by letter dated 26 October 2005 of the request made by the United Kingdom. By letter dated 27 October 2005, the Commission notified the United Kingdom that it had all the information it considered necessary for appraisal of the request.

(3) The United Kingdom wishes to replace the derogation, provided for by Council Decision 86/356/EEC of 21 July 1986 authorising the United Kingdom to apply flat-rate measures in respect of the non-deductible value added tax charged on fuel expenditure in company cars[2], which authorised special simplification measures in order to determine on a flat-rate basis the proportion of value added tax (VAT) relating to expenditure on fuel in business cars partly used for private purposes. This procedure relieves taxable persons of the need to keep detailed mileage records in order to calculate, for each car, the exact amount of VAT related to private and business motoring. Like this system, the proposed new system will be optional for taxable persons.

(4) The current system is based on the type of fuel used and the engine size of the car. The United Kingdom wishes to amend this system and base it on the level of carbon dioxide (CO2) emissions from the car, as there is a proportional correlation between emissions and fuel consumption and therefore with expenditure on fuel. This means that a flat-rate scale system based on CO2 emissions could achieve the same objective of taxing fuel expenditure incurred by a business for private motoring. At the same time, the United Kingdom also expects to achieve greater accuracy in determining the charge for private consumption by increasing, and therefore refining, the number of scale bands in comparison with the existing bands.

(5) This arrangement has effectively enabled the United Kingdom to simplify the procedure for charging tax in relation to expenditure on fuel for business cars and the proposed system, based on CO2 emissions, will have a similar effect. Private consumption should be more accurately reflected under the new system.

(6) The authorisation should be limited in time, so that in the light of the experience gained up to that date an assessment may be made as to whether or not the derogation is still justified.

(7) Decision 86/356/EEC should be repealed after a certain period but in any case at the entry into force of the national provisions introducing the new special measure, in order to avoid a situation in which authorisations for both systems exist at the same time.

(8) The United Kingdom should inform the Commission of the national provisions introducing the new special measure as soon as they have been adopted and should ensure that this measure will not enter into force before 30 April 2007.

(9) The derogation has no negative impact on the Community's own resources accruing from VAT,

HAS ADOPTED THIS DECISION:

Note—[1] OJ L 145, 13.6.1977, p. 1. Directive as last amended by Directive 2006/69/EC (OJ L 221, 12.8.2006, p. 9).
[2] OJ L 212, 2.8.1986, p. 35.

Article 1

By way of derogation from Articles 5(6) and 11(A)(1)(*b*) of Directive 77/388/EEC, the United Kingdom is authorised, from 1 May 2007 until 31 December 2015, to fix on a flat-rate basis the proportion of value added tax relating to expenditure on fuel used for private purposes in business cars.

Article 2

The proportion of the tax referred to in Article 1 shall be expressed in fixed amounts, established on the basis of the CO_2 emissions level of the type of vehicle, that reflect fuel consumption. The United Kingdom shall adjust these fixed amounts annually to reflect changes in the average cost of fuel.

Article 3

The system set up on the basis of this Decision shall be optional for taxable persons.

Article 4

Decision 86/356/EEC is repealed on 30 April 2007.

The United Kingdom shall inform the Commission of the national provisions referred to in Article 1 as soon as they have been adopted.

Article 5

This Decision is addressed to the United Kingdom of Great Britain and Northern Ireland.

Done at Brussels, 25 September 2006.

Council Decision of 7 November 2006 authorising certain Member States to apply a reduced rate of VAT to certain labour-intensive ser-vices in accordance with the procedure provided for in Article 28(6) of Directive 77/388/EEC

(2006/774/EC)

Notes—See OJ L 314, 15.11.2006 p 28.
This Decision ceases to apply from 1 January 2011 (See Article 18).

THE COUNCIL OF THE EUROPEAN UNION,

Having regard to the Treaty establishing the European Community,

Having regard to Sixth Council Directive 77/388/EEC of 17 May 1977 on the harmonisation of the laws of the Member States relating to turnover taxes – Common system of value added tax: uniform basis of assessment[1], (hereinafter referred to as "the Directive"), and in particular Article 28(6) thereof,

Having regard to the proposal from the Commission,

Whereas:

(1) The Council, acting unanimously on a proposal from the Commission, may authorise any Member State that has submitted an application in accordance with the procedure and conditions provided for by Directive 77/388/EEC to apply a reduced rate of VAT to certain labour-intensive services.

(2) The services concerned must meet the conditions provided for in the Directive and be included in Annex K thereto.

(3) Under Council Decision 2000/185/EC of 28 February 2000 authorising Member States to apply a reduced rate of VAT to certain labour intensive services in accordance with the procedure provided for in Article 28(6) of Directive 77/388/EEC[2], Belgium, Spain, France, Italy, Luxembourg, the Netherlands, Portugal and the United Kingdom (for the Isle of Man only) could apply, until 31 December 2005, a reduced rate of VAT to the labour-intensive services for which they had submitted a request to this effect.

(4) Council Directive 2006/18/EC[3] amends the Directive with regard to reduced rates of value added tax, in order, on the one hand, to extend their application until 31 December 2010, and on the other hand, to allow those Member States that so wish, to avail themselves for the first time of the possibility provided for therein, and permit those Member States that wish to amend the list of services to which they have applied the measures provided for by the Directive in the past, to submit an application for a reduction of the rates to the Commission.

(5) In order to allow those Member States authorised by Decision 2000/185/EC to apply a reduced rate to continue to do so until 31 December 2010, and in the interests of legal clarity, the provisions of that Decision should be included in this Decision for those Member States that have not amended their initial application.

(6) In accordance with the Directive, Greece, which was already authorised by Decision 2000/185/EC to apply a reduced rate for two of the categories listed in Annex K, has submitted a new application extending the scope of its previous authorisation. Greece should therefore be awarded a new authorisation permitting the application of a reduced rate, in accordance with its new application.
(7) The Czech Republic, Cyprus, Latvia, Hungary, Malta, Poland, Slovenia and Finland have submitted applications to apply a reduced rate of VAT to certain labour-intensive services in accordance with the procedure and conditions provided for in the Directive.
(8) Furthermore, the Czech Republic, Hungary, Poland and Greece have submitted applications for authorisation to apply, as an exceptional measure, a reduced rate to three categories of the services listed in Annex K. For each of these four Member States, the reduction in rate in the third of the categories selected can have only an insignificant economic impact.
(9) In order that the Member States concerned may continue to apply reduced rates to certain labour-intensive services, as provided for in Decision 2000/185/EC, this Decision should apply from 1 January 2006.
(10) This Decision will have no impact on the Communities' own resources derived from VAT,
HAS ADOPTED THIS DECISION:

Note—[1] OJ L 145, 13.6.1977 p 1. Directive as last amended by Directive 2006/69/EC (OJ L 221, 12.8.2006 p 9).
[2] OJ L 59, 4.3.2000 p 10. Decision as last amended by Decision 2004/161/EC (OJ L 52, 21.2.2004 p 62).
[3] OJ L 51, 22.2.2006 p 12.

Article 1

In accordance with the first subparagraph of Article 28(6) of Directive 77/388/EEC, Belgium is authorised to apply a reduced rate during the period 1 January 2006 to 31 December 2010 to the following two services referred to in points 1 and 2 of Annex K to that Directive:

(*a*) Small services of repairing:
- bicycles,
- shoes and leather goods,
- clothing and household linen (including mending and alteration);

(*b*) renovation and repairing of private dwellings more than five years old, excluding materials which form a significant part of the value of the supply.

Article 2

In accordance with the first and fourth subparagraphs of Article 28(6) of Directive 77/388/EEC, the Czech Republic is authorised to apply a reduced rate during the period 1 January 2006 to 31 December 2010 to the following three services referred to in points 2, 3 and 4 of Annex K to that Directive:

(*a*) renovation and repairing of private dwellings, excluding materials which form a significant part of the value of the supply;
(*b*) window cleaning and cleaning in private households;
(*c*) domestic care services, (.. home help and care of the young, elderly, sick or disabled).

Article 3

In accordance with the first and fourth subparagraphs of Article 28(6) of Directive 77/388/EEC, Greece is authorised to apply a reduced rate during the period 1 January 2006 to 31 December 2010 to the following three services referred to in points 1, 2 and 4 of Annex K to that Directive:

(*a*) small services of repairing:
- bicycles,
- shoes and leather goods,
- clothing and household linen (including mending and alteration);

(*b*) renovation and repairing of old private dwellings (not constructed recently), excluding materials which form a significant part of the value of the supply;
(*c*) domestic care services, (eg home help and care of the young, elderly, sick or disabled).

Article 4

In accordance with the first subparagraph of Article 28(6) of Directive 77/388/EEC, Spain is authorised to apply a reduced rate during the period 1 January 2006 to 31 December 2010 to the following two services referred to in points 2 and 5 of Annex K to that Directive:

(*a*) bricklaying for the repair of private dwellings, excluding materials which form a significant part of the value of the supply;
(*b*) hairdressing.

Article 5

In accordance with the first subparagraph of Article 28(6) of Directive 77/388/EEC, France is authorised to apply a reduced rate during the period 1 January 2006 to 31 December 2010 to the following three ser-vices referred to in points 2, 3 and 4 of Annex K to that Directive:

(*a*) renovation and repairing of private dwellings completed more than two years ago, excluding materials which form a significant part of the value of the supply;
(*b*) domestic care services (e g home help and care of the young, elderly, sick or disabled);
(*c*) window cleaning and cleaning in private households.

Article 6

In accordance with the first subparagraph of Article 28(6) of Directive 77/388/EEC, Italy is authorised to apply a reduced rate during the period 1 January 2006 to 31 December 2010 to the following two services referred to in points 2 and 4 of Annex K to that Directive:

(*a*) renovation and repairing of private dwellings, excluding materials which form a significant part of the value of the supply;
(*b*) domestic care services (e g home help and care of the young, elderly, sick or disabled).

Article 7

In accordance with the first and fourth subparagraphs of Article 28(6) of Directive 77/388/EEC, Cyprus is authorised to apply a reduced rate during the period 1 January 2006 to 31 December 2010 to the following two services referred to in points 2 and 5 of Annex K to that Directive:

(*a*) renovation and repairing of private dwellings, excluding materials which form a significant part of the value of the supply;
(*b*) hairdressing.

Article 8

In accordance with the first and fourth subparagraphs of Article 28(6) of Directive 77/388/EEC, Latvia is authorised to apply a reduced rate during the period 1 January 2006 to 31 December 2010 to the following two services referred to in points 2 and 5 of Annex K to that Directive:

(*a*) renovation and repairing of private dwellings, excluding materials which form a significant part of the value of the supply;
(*b*) hairdressing.

Article 9

In accordance with the first subparagraph of Article 28(6) of Directive 77/388/EEC, Luxembourg is authorised to apply a reduced rate during the period 1 January 2006 to 31 December 2010 to the following three services referred to in points 1, 3 and 5 of Annex K to that Directive:

(*a*) small services of repairing:
- bicycles,
- shoes and leather goods,
- clothing and household linen (including mending and alteration);

(*b*) hairdressing;
(*c*) window cleaning and cleaning in private households.

Article 10

In accordance with the first and fourth subparagraphs of Article 28(6) of Directive 77/388/EEC, Hungary is authorised to apply a reduced rate during the period 1 January 2006 to 31 December 2010 to the following three services referred to in points 1, 2 and 4 of Annex K to that Directive:

(*a*) small services of repairing:
- bicycles,
- shoes and leather goods,
- clothing and household linen (including mending and alteration);

(*b*) renovation and repairing of private dwellings, excluding materials which form a significant part of the value of the supply;
(*c*) domestic care services (e g home help and care of the young, elderly, sick or disabled).

Article 11

In accordance with the first and fourth subparagraphs of Article 28(6) of Directive 77/388/EEC, Malta is authorised to apply a reduced rate during the period 1 January 2006 to 31 December 2010 to the following two services referred to in points 1 and 4 of Annex K to that Directive:

(*a*) small services of repairing:
- bicycles,
- shoes and leather goods,
- clothing and household linen (including mending and alteration);

(*b*) domestic care services (e g home help and care of the young, elderly, sick or disabled).

Article 12

In accordance with the first subparagraph of Article 28(6) of Directive 77/388/EEC, the Netherlands is authorised to apply a reduced rate during the period 1 January 2006 to 31 December 2010 to the following three services referred to in points 1, 2 and 5 of Annex K to that Directive:

(*a*) small services of repairing:
- bicycles,
- shoes and leather goods,
- clothing and household linen (including mending and alteration);

(*b*) hairdressing;
(*c*) painting and plastering services for the renovation and repairing of private dwellings more than 15 years old, excluding materials which form a significant part of the value of the supply.

Article 13

In accordance with the first and fourth subparagraphs of Article 28(6) of Directive 77/388/EEC, Poland is authorised to apply a reduced rate during the period 1 January 2006 to 31 December 2010 to the following three services referred to in points 1, 2 and 5 of Annex K to that Directive:

(*a*) small services of repairing:
- bicycles,
- shoes and leather goods,
- clothing and household linen (including mending and alteration);

(*b*) renovation and repairing of private dwellings, excluding materials which form a significant part of the value of the supply;
(*c*) hairdressing.

Article 14

In accordance with the first subparagraph of Article 28(6) of Directive 77/388/EEC, Portugal is authorised to apply a reduced rate during the period 1 January 2006 to 31 December 2010 to the following two ser-vices referred to in points 2 and 4 of Annex K to that Directive:

(*a*) renovation and repairing of private dwellings, excluding materials which form a significant part of the value of the supply;
(*b*) domestic care services (eg home help and care of the young, elderly, sick or disabled).

Article 15

In accordance with the first and fourth subparagraphs of Article 28(6) of Directive 77/388/EEC, Slovenia is authorised to apply a reduced rate during the period 1 January 2006 to 31 December 2010 for renovation and repairing of private dwellings, excluding materials which form a significant part of the value of the supply, referred to in point 2 of Annex K to that Directive.

Article 16

In accordance with the first and fourth subparagraphs of Article 28(6) of Directive 77/388/EEC, Finland is authorised to apply a reduced rate during the period 1 January 2006 to 31 December 2010 to the following two services referred to in points 1 and 5 of Annex K to that Directive:

(*a*) small services of repairing:
- bicycles,
- shoes and leather goods,
- clothing and household linen (including mending and alteration);

(*b*) hairdressing.

Article 17

In accordance with the first subparagraph of Article 28(6) of Directive 77/388/EEC, the United Kingdom is authorised to apply a reduced rate during the period 1 January 2006 to 31 December 2010 for renovation and repairing of private dwellings, excluding materials which form a significant part of the value of the supply referred to in point 2 of Annex K to that Directive, but for the Isle of Man only.

Article 18

This Decision shall apply from 1 January 2006 until 31 December 2010.

Article 19

This Decision is addressed to the Kingdom of Belgium, the Czech Republic, the Hellenic Republic, the Kingdom of Spain, the French Republic, the Italian Republic, the Republic of Cyprus, the Republic of Lat-via, the Grand Duchy of Luxembourg, the Republic of Hungary, the Republic of Malta, the Kingdom of the Netherlands, the Republic of Poland, the Portuguese Republic, the Republic of Slovenia, the Republic of Finland and the United Kingdom of Great Britain and Northern Ireland.

Done at Brussels, 7 November 2006.

For the Council

The President

E. Heinäluoma

Council Decision of 30 January 2007 authorising Estonia, Slovenia, Sweden and the United Kingdom to apply a special measure derogating from Article 167 of Directive 2006/112/EC on the common system of value added tax

(2007/133/EC)

Note—See OJ L 057, 24.02.2007 p 12.
This Decision ceases to apply from 1 January 2010 (See Article 3).

THE COUNCIL OF THE EUROPEAN UNION,

Having regard to the Treaty establishing the European Community,

Having regard to Council Directive 2006/112/EC of 28 November 2006 on the common system of value added tax[1], and in particular Article 395(1) thereof,

Having regard to the proposal from the Commission,

Whereas:

(1) In accordance with Article 27 of the Sixth Council Directive 77/388/EEC of 17 May 1977 on the harmonisation of the laws of the Member States relating to turnover taxes — Common system of value added tax: uniform basis of assessment[2], the United Kingdom was authorised by Decision 97/375/EC[3], by way of derogation from Article 17(1) of the said Directive and in order to operate an optional scheme in which tax is accounted for on the basis of cash paid and received (cash accounting), to postpone the right of deduction of input VAT of taxable persons who account for the output VAT for their supplies when they have received the payment of the price from their customers, pursuant to the second indent of the third subparagraph of Article 10(2) of the said Directive, until the input VAT has been paid to the supplier.

(2) By letter registered by the Secretariat-General of the Commission on 26 January 2006, the United Kingdom requested an extension of three years of that derogation. The United Kingdom also requested for the turnover limit for the simplified cash accounting scheme to be increased from GBP 660000 to GBP 1350000.

(3) By letter registered by the Secretariat-General of the Commission on 31 August 2006, Estonia requested a derogation from Article 17(1) of Directive 77/388/EEC to allow the VAT to become deductible by the taxable person when the supplier is paid. This postponement of deduction will apply only under a simplified cash accounting scheme under which taxable persons account for the output VAT for their supplies when they have received payment from their customers, pursuant to the second indent of the third subparagraph of Article 10(2) of the said Directive. Estonia requested that the cash accounting scheme be limited to taxable persons classified as sole proprietors under Estonian law.

(4) By letter registered by the Secretariat-General of the Commission on 27 June 2006, Slovenia requested a derogation from Article 17(1) of Directive 77/388/EEC to allow the VAT to become deductible by the taxable person when the supplier is paid. This postponement of deduction will apply only under a simplified cash accounting scheme under which taxable persons account for the output VAT for their supplies when they have received payment from their customers, pursuant to the second indent of the third subparagraph of Article 10(2) of the said Directive. Slovenia requested that the turnover limit for their simplified cash accounting scheme be set at EUR 208646.

(5) By letter registered by the Secretariat-General of the Commission on 6 April 2006, Sweden requested a derogation from Article 17(1) of Directive 77/388/EEC to allow the VAT to become deductible by the taxable person when the supplier is paid. This postponement of deduction will apply only under a simplified cash accounting scheme under which taxable persons account for the output VAT for their supplies when they have received payment from their customers, pursuant to the second indent of the third subparagraph of Article 10(2) of the said Directive. Sweden requested that the turnover limit for their simplified cash accounting scheme be set at SEK 3000000.

(6) In accordance with Article 27(2) of Directive 77/388/EEC, the Commission informed the other Member States by letter dated 6 October 2006 of the request made by Estonia, by letter dated 6 October 2006 of the request made by Slovenia, by letter dated 4 October 2006 of the request made by Sweden and by letter dated 6 October 2006 of the request made by the United Kingdom. By letter dated 6 October 2006 the Commission notified Sweden and by letters dated 9 October 2006 the Commission notified Estonia, Slovenia and the United Kingdom, that it had all the information it considered necessary for the appraisal of their request.

(7) Directive 77/388/EEC has been recast and repealed by Directive 2006/112/EC. References to the provisions of the former are to be construed as references to the latter.

(8) The cash accounting scheme is a simplification measure for small and medium sized businesses. Regarding the United Kingdom, raising the ceiling for the simplified scheme will allow a greater number of firms to opt for the scheme. The increase of the turnover limit would extend the scheme to a potential additional 57000 businesses. The derogation requested by Estonia will allow 5700 businesses to use the cash accounting scheme. In the case of Slovenia, 62000 businesses will be able to opt for the use of the cash accounting scheme. As for Sweden, the scheme will be available to 630000 businesses.

(9) The Estonian, Slovenian, Swedish and United Kingdom derogations can be accepted in view of the percentage of eligible businesses that could opt for this simplified scheme and the limited duration.

(10) Since taxable persons who have applied the optional scheme in the past should be able to continue using it without interruption, the authorisation given to the United Kingdom should apply from the date of expiry of Decision 97/375/EC. Also as this would allow more taxable persons to adopt the scheme from the beginning of their accounting year, Member States concerned should be allowed to make the optional scheme available as from 1 January 2007.

(11) The derogation in question does not affect the overall amount of the tax revenue of the Member States collected at the stage of final consumption and as a consequence does not have a negative effect on the own resources of the European Communities accruing from VAT.

(12) Given the urgency of the matter, in order to avoid a legal gap, it is imperative to grant an exception to the six-week period mentioned in point I(3) of the Protocol on the role of national Parliaments in the European Union, annexed to the Treaty on European Union and to the Treaties establishing the European Communities,

HAS ADOPTED THIS DECISION:

Note—[1] OJ L 347, 11.12.2006, p. 1. Directive as amended by Directive 2006/138/EC (OJ L 384, 29.12.2006, p. 92).
[2] OJ L 145, 13.6.1977, p. 1. Directive as last amended by Directive 2006/98/EC (OJ L 363, 20.12.2006, p. 129).
[3] OJ L 158, 17.6.1997, p. 43. Decision as last amended by Decision 2003/909/EC (OJ L 342, 30.12.2003, p. 49).

Article 1

By way of derogation from Article 167 of Directive 2006/112/EC, Estonia, Slovenia, Sweden and the United Kingdom are authorised to postpone the right of deduction of the input tax of the taxable persons, as defined in the second paragraph, until the input tax has been paid to their suppliers.

The taxable persons concerned must use a scheme whereby they account for the output VAT for their supplies when they have received the payments from their customers. They must have an annual turnover not higher than EUR 208646 for Slovenia, SEK 3000000 for Sweden and GBP 1350000 for the United Kingdom, or, in the case of Estonia, must be registered as a sole proprietor.

Article 2

Decision 97/375/EC is hereby repealed.

Article 3

This Decision shall apply from 1 January 2007 to 31 December 2009.

[Article 3] [1]

This Decision is addressed to the Republic of Estonia, the Republic of Slovenia, the Kingdom of Sweden and the United Kingdom of Great Britain and Northern Ireland.

Amendments—[1] This article appears to have been misnumbered in the original text.

Done at Brussels, 30 January 2007.

Council Decision of 16 April 2007 authorising the United Kingdom to introduce a special measure derogating from Article 193 of Directive 2006/112/EC on the common system of value added tax

(2007/250/EC)

Note—See OJ L109, 26.04.2007 p 42.

THE COUNCIL OF THE EUROPEAN UNION,

Having regard to the Treaty establishing the European Community,

Having regard to Council Directive 2006/112/EC of 28 November 2006 on the common system of value added tax[1], and in particular Article 395(1) thereof,

Having regard to the proposal from the Commission,

Whereas:

(1) In a letter registered by the Secretariat-General of the Commission on 10 February 2006, the United Kingdom requested authorisation to introduce a special measure derogating from Article 21(1)(*a*) of the Sixth Council Directive 77/388/EEC of 17 May 1977 on the harmonisation of the laws of the Member States relating to turnover taxes — Common system of values added tax: uniform basis of assessment[2].

(2) In accordance with Article 27(2) of Directive 77/388/EEC, the Commission informed the other Member States by letter dated 18 July 2006 of the request made by the United Kingdom. By letter dated 19 July 2006, the Commission notified the United Kingdom that it had all the information it considered necessary for appraisal of the request.

(3) Directive 77/388/EEC has been recast and repealed by Directive 2006/112/EC. References to the provisions of the former are to be construed as references to the latter.

(4) The person liable for payment of the value added tax (VAT), under Article 193 of Directive 2006/112/EC, is the taxable person supplying the goods. The purpose of the derogation requested by the United Kingdom is to place that liability on the taxable person to whom the supplies are made, but only under certain conditions and exclusively in the case of mobile telephones and computer chips/microprocessors.

(5) Within that sector, a significant number of traders engage in tax evasion by not paying VAT to the tax authorities after selling the products. Their customers, however, being in receipt of a valid invoice, remain entitled to a tax deduction. In the most aggressive forms of this tax evasion, the same goods are, via a "carousel" scheme, supplied several times without payment of the VAT to the tax authorities. By designating in those cases the person to whom the goods are supplied as the person liable for the VAT, the derogation would remove the opportunity to engage in that form of tax evasion. However, it would not affect the amount of VAT due.

(6) For the purposes of ensuring the effective operation of the derogation and preventing the tax evasion from being shifted to other products or towards the retail level, the United Kingdom should introduce appropriate control and reporting obligations. The Commission should be informed of the specific measures adopted, and the monitoring and overall evaluation of the operation of the derogation.

(7) The measure is proportionate to the objectives pursued since it is not intended to apply generally, but only to a specific high risk sector comprising certain carefully defined products in relation to which the scale and size of the tax evasion has resulted in considerable tax losses. Furthermore, since that sector is a small one, the derogation cannot be considered equivalent to a general measure.

(8) The authorisation should be valid only for a short period, because it cannot be ascertained with certainty that the objectives of the measure will be achieved, nor can the impact of the measure on the functioning of the VAT system in the United Kingdom and in other Member States be gauged in advance; moreover, the impact of the measure and its implementation on the functioning of the internal market will have to be properly assessed.

(9) The derogation has no negative impact on the Community's own resources accruing from VAT,

HAS ADOPTED THIS DECISION:

Note—[1] OJ L 347, 11.12.2006, p. 1. Directive as last amended by Directive 2006/138/EC (OJ L 384, 29.12.2006, p. 92).
[2] OJ L 145, 13.6.1977, p. 1. Directive as last amended by Directive 2006/98/EC (OJ L 363, 20.12.2006, p. 129).

Article 1

By way of derogation from Article 193 of Directive 2006/112/EC, the United Kingdom is authorised to designate the taxable person to whom supplies of the following goods are made as the person liable to pay VAT:

1. mobile telephones, being devices made or adapted for use in connection with a licensed network and operated on specified frequencies, whether or not they have any other use;
2. integrated circuit devices such as microprocessors and central processing units in a state prior to integration into end user products.

The derogation shall apply in respect of supplies of goods for which the taxable amount is equal to or higher than GBP 5000.

Article 2

The derogation provided for in Article 1 is subject to the United Kingdom introducing appropriate and effective control and reporting obligations on taxable persons that supply goods to which the reverse charge applies in accordance with this Decision.

Article 3

The United Kingdom shall inform the Commission where it has adopted the measures referred to in Articles 1 and 2 and shall, by 31 March 2009, submit a report to the Commission on the overall evaluation of the operation of the measures concerned, in particular as regards the effectiveness of the measure and any evidence of the shifting of tax evasion to other products or to the retail level.

Article 4

This Decision shall expire on 30 April 2009.

Article 5

This Decision is addressed to the United Kingdom of Great Britain and Northern Ireland.

Done at Luxembourg, 16 April 2007.

Council Decision of 5 May 2009 amending Decision 2007/250/EC authorising the United Kingdom to introduce a special measure derogating from Article 193 of Directive 2006/112/EC on the common system of value added tax

(2009/439/EC)

Note—See OJ L 148, 11.6.2009 p 14.

THE COUNCIL OF THE EUROPEAN UNION,

Having regard to the Treaty establishing the European Community,

Having regard to Council Directive 2006/112/EC of 28 November 2006 on the common system of value added tax, and in particular Article 395(1) thereof,

Having regard to the proposal from the Commission,

Whereas:

(1) In a letter registered by the Secretariat-General of the Commission on 28 July 2008, the United Kingdom requested authorisation to continue to apply a special measure derogating from Article 193 of Directive 2006/112/EC as regards the person liable for the payment of value added tax (VAT) to the tax authorities and previously provided for by Council Decision 2007/250/EC of 16 April 2007.

(2) In accordance with Article 395(2) of Directive 2006/112/EC, the Commission informed the other Member States by letter of 17 March 2009 of the request made by the United Kingdom. By letter dated 20 March 2009, the Commission notified the United Kingdom that it had all the information it considered necessary for the appraisal of the request.

(3) The person liable for the payment of VAT under Article 193 of Directive 2006/112/EC is the taxable person supplying the goods. However, the derogating measure enabled the United Kingdom to apply, until 30 April 2009 and under certain conditions, a reverse charge mechanism which implied that the liability for the payment of VAT shifted to the taxable person to whom certain supplies of mobile phones and integrated circuit devices were made, provided the taxable amount of the supply was equal to, or higher than, GBP 5000.

(4) The purpose of that derogating measure was to deal with certain aggressive forms of tax evasion, and in particular with "carousel" schemes whereby goods are supplied several times without VAT being paid to the tax authorities while leaving customers with a valid invoice for VAT deduction. The application of the reverse charge, without actual payment of VAT from the customer to the supplier, removes the possibility of that form of tax evasion.

(5) Given the apparent seriousness of VAT fraud in the United Kingdom, as attested by the information submitted by the United Kingdom, and given the measure's expected preventive effect, the measure remains proportionate since the extension of the derogation is limited to a reasonable period and the measure remains targeted in scope. Furthermore, it does not form the basis of an overall measure for a generalised reverse charge system.

(6) The derogation has no negative impact on the Community's own resources accruing from VAT.

(7) Legal continuity of the measure should be ensured,

HAS ADOPTED THIS DECISION:

Article 1

Article 4 of Council Decision 2007/250/EC is replaced by the following:

> **"Article 4**
>
> This Decision shall expire on 30 April 2011."

Article 2

This Decision shall apply from 1 May 2009.

Article 3

This Decision is addressed to the United Kingdom of Great Britain and Northern Ireland.

Done at Brussels, 5 May 2009.

VALUE ADDED TAX
EXTRA-STATUTORY CONCESSIONS

LIST OF CONCESSIONS

INTERNATIONAL FIELD

ESC 2.1 VAT, excise and customs duties—goods and services

ESC 2.2 VAT, excise and customs duties—UK-manufactured alcoholic liquor and tobacco products purchased by diplomats

ESC 2.3 VAT, excise and customs duties—United States Air Force

ESC 2.4 VAT and customs duty—gifts

ESC 2.5 VAT—American war graves

ESC 2.6 VAT—Supplies to diplomatic missions, international organisations, NATO forces etc in other EC countries

ESC 2.7 VAT and customs duty—certain aircraft ground and security equipment

ESC 2.8 Relief from UK excise duty on alcoholic drinks supplied duty-paid in another Member State for consumption on Eurostar trains which are in UK territory.

CONCESSIONS DESIGNED TO REMOVE INEQUITIES OR ANOMALIES IN ADMINISTRATION

ESC 3.1 VAT—VAT on purchase of road fuel

ESC 3.2 VAT—Group supplies using an overseas member: anticipation of legislative changes

ESC 3.3 Zero rating of supplies of certain goods used in connection with collection of monetary donations

ESC 3.4 VAT—Misunderstanding by a VAT trader

ESC 3.5 *VAT—Misdirection* (obsolete)

ESC 3.6 VAT—Coin-operated machines

ESC 3.7 VAT—VAT on minor promotional items supplied in linked supplies schemes

ESC 3.8 VAT—Use of margin scheme for vehicle sales when incomplete records have been kept

ESC 3.9 VAT—Recoveries under the VAT Act 1994 Schedule 11 paragraph 5

ESC 3.10 VAT—VAT on necessary meals and accommodation provided by recognised representative sporting bodies to amateur sports persons chosen to represent that body in a competition

ESC 3.11 VAT—Incorrect customer declaration

ESC 3.12 VAT—Buses with special facilities for carrying disabled persons

ESC 3.13 VAT—Repayment of import VAT to shipping agents and freight forwarders

ESC 3.14 VAT—Zero-rating of certain supplies of free zone goods

ESC 3.15 VAT—Printed matter published in instalments

ESC 3.16 VAT—Connection to the gas or electricity mains supply

ESC 3.17 VAT—Zero-rating of supplies of training for foreign governments

ESC 3.18 VAT—Exemption for all domestic service charges

ESC 3.19 VAT—Supplies of "relevant goods" to charities

ESC 3.20 VAT—Disapplication of repayment of input tax (Value Added Tax Act 1994 s 36(4A) and the VAT Regulations 1995

ESC 3.21 VAT—Sales of poor quality goods

ESC 3.22 VAT—Valuation of the refurbishment or fitting out of a building for the purposes of the capital goods scheme

ESC 3.23 VAT—Supplies by Financial Ombudsman Services Ltd to ombudsman authorities

ESC 3.24 VAT—Charities who provide care in an institution and also supply goods to disabled persons resident in their own and other institutions.

ESC 3.25 VAT—Resuscitation training models supplied to charities and other eligible bodies for use in first aid training

ESC 3.26 VAT—Works of art, antiques and collectors' items

ESC 3.27 VAT—Use of the Auctioneers' Scheme for sales of goods at auction on behalf of non-taxable persons

ESC 3.28 VAT—Supplies by Financial Services Authority to self-regulating organisations

ESC 3.29 VAT—Charitable buildings

ESC 3.30 VAT—Retail pharmacists

ESC 3.31 VAT—Supplies by the Financial Services Compensation Scheme Ltd (FSCS) to compensation scheme authorities

ESC 3.32 VAT—Electronic face value vouchers

ESC 3.33 VAT—Supplies previously made by the Post Office

ESC 3.34 VAT—Tax reclaimed by museums and galleries covered by Section 33A of the Value Added Tax Act 1994

ESC 3.35 VAT—Apportionment of certain membership subscriptions to non-profit making bodies

ESC 3.36 VAT—Imported works of art, antiques etc

ESC 3.37 VAT—Exemption for supplies of welfare services by private welfare agencies pending registration

INSURANCE PREMIUM TAX—CONCESSIONS DESIGNED TO REMOVE INEQUITIES OR ANOMALIES IN ADMINISTRATION

See *Insurance Premium Tax* post for Concessions 4.1 to 4.6.

LANDFILL TAX—CONCESSIONS DESIGNED TO REMOVE INEQUITIES OR ANOMALIES IN ADMINISTRATION

See *Landfill Tax* post for Concession 5.1.

CLIMATE CHANGE LEVY—CONCESSIONS DESIGNED TO REMOVE INEQUITIES OR ANOMALIES IN ADMINISTRATION

See *Climate Change Levy* post for Concessions 7.1 to 7.4.

FACILITATION OF EXPORTS

ESC 8.1 VAT—Sailaway boats

NON-COMMERCIAL TRANSACTIONS

ESC 9.1 VAT—VAT on goods supplied at duty-free and tax-free shops

ESC 9.2 VAT—Marine fuel

ESC 9.3 VAT and excise duties—Personal reliefs for goods permanently imported from third countries

ESC 9.4 VAT and excise duties—Personal reliefs for goods permanently imported from third countries

ESC 9.5 VAT and excise duties—Personal reliefs for goods permanently imported from third countries

ESC 9.6 VAT and excise duties—Personal reliefs for goods permanently imported from third countries

ESC 9.7 VAT and excise duties—Personal reliefs for goods permanently imported from third countries

CUSTOMS & EXCISE NOTICE 48

July 2009.
This notice cancels and replaces Notice 48 (March 2002). Details of any changes to the previous version can be found in paragraph 1.1 of this notice.

Section 1 Introduction

1.1 WHAT IS THIS NOTICE ABOUT?

This notice gives details of all Customs & Excise extra-statutory concessions (ESCs) in force at the time of going to print.
This notice has been re-written to include details of ESCs that have been granted, or become obsolete, since the last edition. New ESCs are shown in paragraphs 2.7, 3.3, 3.31, 3.32, 3.33, 3.34, 3.35, 6.4 and 7.1. Where possible, the numbering of ESCs that have become obsolete has been reused.

You can access details of any changes to this notice since (July 2002) on our Internet website at www.hmce.gov.uk.

1.2 WHAT IS AN EXTRA-STATUTORY CONCESSION?

In certain circumstances where remission or repayment of revenue is not provided for by law, the Department may allow relief on an extra-statutory basis. Extra-statutory concessions (ESCs) are remissions of revenue that allow relief in specific sets of circumstances to all businesses falling within the relevant conditions. They are authorised when strict application of the law would create a disadvantage or the effect would not be the one intended.

1.3 HOW ARE ESCS APPLIED?

HM Revenue & Customs (HMRC) ESCs are of general application. That is, a concession may be exercised by anyone to whom the circumstances set out in the concessions apply without references to HMRC . However, where an attempt is made to use an ESC for tax avoidance, the Commissioners may withdraw or restrict its application.

1.4 AGREEMENTS WITH TRADE BODIES

In certain trades, particular arrangements for applying VAT and other charges have been agreed with the appropriate trade associations. These are not ESCs and are listed in Notice 700/57 *Administrative agreements entered into with trade bodies.*

1.5 INLAND REVENUE ESCS

Inland Revenue ESCs are published in their Notice IR1 *Extra-Statutory Concessions.*

Section 2 International field

2.1 VAT, EXCISE AND CUSTOMS DUTIES GOODS AND SERVICES

Duty (which includes all import and excise duties) and VAT are remitted or refunded in accordance with agreements with the authorities concerned on—

- goods and services imported by or supplied to visiting forces and their instrumentalities, for the official use of the force, or their instrumentalities;
- goods and services imported by or supplied to NATO military headquarters, organisations or agencies, for their official use;
- United States and Canadian Government expenditure on mutual defence or mutual aid contracts; and
- temporary importations of equipment required by contractors for fulfilling NATO infrastructure contracts or in connection with the provision and maintenance of US forces defence facilities in the United Kingdom.

2.2 VAT, EXCISE AND CUSTOMS DUTIES—UK-MANUFACTURED ALCOHOLIC LIQUOR AND TOBACCO PRODUCTS PURCHASED BY DIPLOMATS

Duty and VAT are remitted on alcoholic liquor and tobacco products of UK manufacture imported by, or supplied to, diplomatic representatives of foreign states in the United Kingdom who are entitled to similar privileges in respect of imported products of foreign manufacture under the Diplomatic Privileges Act 1964.

2.3 VAT AND EXCISE DUTIES—UNITED STATES AIR FORCE

Relief from VAT and/or excise duty is allowed, in accordance with conditions agreed with the United States Air Force, on—

- charges for admission to air shows and open days; and
- goods sold by US forces organisations during air shows and open days to persons not entitled to receive/consume them unless customs charges have been paid.

2.4 VAT AND CUSTOMS DUTY—GIFTS

Duty and VAT are remitted on gifts (whether imported or purchased in the United Kingdom) from United States forces to charitable organisations.

2.5 VAT—AMERICAN WAR GRAVES

In order to place inland purchases on the same footing as imported goods, VAT is remitted on the supply of goods and services to the American Battle Monuments Commission for the maintenance of the American Military Cemetery and Memorial at Maddingley, Cambridge and Brookwood, Surrey.

2.6 VAT—SUPPLIES TO DIPLOMATIC MISSIONS, INTERNATIONAL ORGANISATIONS, NATO FORCES ETC IN OTHER EC COUNTRIES

A VAT registered trader can zero-rate supplies of goods, (other than new means of transport), or services made to entitled persons and bodies resident or situated in other EC countries provided—

- the goods or services are for either the official use of the entitled bodies or for the personal use of entitled members etc thereof;
- the supplier obtains from the customer an application for exemption from VAT under Article 15.10 of the Sixth VAT Directive (or, if not available, a written order/certificate confirming eligibility under that Article);
- in the case of goods, they are removed to another EC country; and
- the supplier obtains and keeps proof of removal of the goods to another EC country within three months of the time of supply. This should be the commercial proof of export or removal normally acceptable for VAT zero-rating purposes.

2.7 VAT AND CUSTOMS DUTY—CERTAIN AIRCRAFT GROUND AND SECURITY EQUIPMENT

The Convention on International Civil Aviation (Chicago Convention) allows relief from duty and VAT for certain ground and security equipment imported into the territory of one Contracting State by an airline of another Contracting State operating an international service. The United Kingdom is a signatory to the Chicago Convention.

Additionally, the United Kingdom has concluded a number of Air Service Agreements which allow, on a reciprocal basis, the various reliefs detailed in the Convention, including the one mentioned above.

We have become aware that end-use relief may be being claimed erroneously in these cases. Aircraft ground and security equipment does not qualify for end-use relief. We are in the process of drawing up a new procedure to enable the relief to be correctly claimed.

In the interim period an extra-statutory concession has been agreed to allow relief for ground and security equipment to be claimed. The following list details those goods which qualify for relief and who is eligible to claim it.

2.7.1 Qualifying goods

The following ground and security equipment for aircraft—

(a) Repair, maintenance and servicing equipment—
  - material for airframes, engines and instruments;
  - specialised aircraft repair kits;
  - starter batteries and carts;
  - maintenance platforms and steps;
  - test equipment for aircraft, aircraft engines, and instruments;
  - aircraft engine heaters and coolers; and
  - ground radio equipment.

(b) Passenger-handling equipment—
  - passenger-loading steps;
  - specialised passenger-weighing devices; and
  - specialised catering equipment.

(c) Cargo-loading equipment—
  - vehicles for moving or loading of baggage, cargo, equipment or supplies;
  - specialised cargo-loading devices; and

- specialised cargo-weighing devices.

(d) Component parts for incorporation into ground equipment including the items listed above.
(e) Security equipment—

- weapon-detecting devices;
- explosives-detecting devices; and
- intrusion detecting devices.

(f) Component parts for incorporation into security equipment.

Claims for relief of duty and VAT under this concession should be addressed to the Entry Processing Unit where the goods will be cleared with a copy of this advice.

Commentary—*De Voil Indirect Tax Service* **V3.336.**
Press releases etc—Concession announced in Business Brief 18/97, 22-8-97.

2.8 RELIEF FROM UK EXCISE DUTY ON ALCOHOLIC DRINKS SUPPLIED DUTY-PAID IN ANOTHER MEMBER STATE FOR CONSUMPTION ON EUROSTAR TRAINS WHICH ARE IN UK TERRITORY

The measure provides a scheme to tax alcohol supplied for consumption on Eurostar trains. The basis for the scheme is that alcoholic drinks loaded in France or Belgium duty paid on journeys commencing from those Member States and destined for the UK will not incur a liability to UK duty when entering the UK. Conversely, such goods loaded for journeys commencing from the UK will be UK duty paid, but will not attract reimbursement when consumed outside UK territory. The revenue effect will therefore be broadly neutral.

Section 3 Concessions designed to remove inequities or anomalies in administration

3.1 VAT—VAT ON PURCHASE OF ROAD FUEL

The Value Added Tax Act 1994 section 56 (formerly Finance Act 1986 section 9) requires payment of a scale charge when road fuel purchased by a business is used for private journeys. However, where a registered person claims no input tax on purchases of road fuel, whether for business or private journeys, the VAT scale charge will not apply.

3.2 VAT—GROUP SUPPLIES USING AN OVERSEAS MEMBER—ANTICIPATION OF LEGISLATIVE CHANGES

With effect from 26 November 1996, a resolution under the Provisional Collection of Taxes Act has created a new tax charge for the representative member of a VAT group, where supplies of a type set out in Schedule 5 to the VAT Act 1994 are purchased by an overseas group member and used for making Schedule 5 supplies to a UK group member. This new tax charge was made permanent when the Finance Act 1997 was passed on 19 March 1997. The new tax charge is given effect by section 41 of the Finance Act, which inserts the new rules into section 43 of the VAT Act 1994 at paragraphs (2A) to (2E).

Committee Stage amendments to what became section 41 reduced the impact of the new tax charge in certain specified circumstances with effect from 19 March 1997, the date when the Finance Act 1997 was passed. The impact will be further reduced when Regulations are made under section 41. This concession will allow groups to account for VAT with effect from 26 November 1996 as though the amendments and Regulations had been in force from that date. The concession falls into two parts.

3.2.1 First part of concession

First, a tax charge under section 41 is triggered where an overseas member of a VAT group has been supplied with services falling within any of paragraphs 1 to 8 of Schedule 5 to the VAT Act 1994 (services to be treated as supplied where received). By concession, no tax charge will be triggered by any such services which are exempt from VAT because they fall within one of the descriptions in Schedule 9 of the Act. This concession applies to supplies made between 26 November 1996 and 19 March 1997. After that date the concession is not needed, because it has been given legal effect by the passing of the Finance Act.

3.2.2 Second part of concession

Second, the amount of the tax charge under section 41 is calculated with reference to the value of the supply by the overseas member to the UK member. By concession, the value for calculating the tax charge may be reduced to the value of the Schedule 5 services purchased by the overseas group member, provided that the group is in a position to provide evidence in the UK of the value of those services, and that those services have not been undervalued. This concession will be given legal effect when Regulations are made under section 41.

Commentary—*De Voil Indirect Tax Service* **V3.193.**

VAT

3.3 VAT: ZERO RATING OF SUPPLIES OF CERTAIN GOODS USED IN CONNECTION WITH COLLECTION OF MONETARY DONATIONS

This concession applies to supplies to a charity of the following goods:

(a) lapel stickers or attachments designed to be worn on the lapel, which are of no intrinsic value, low cost to the charity and are given as a token in acknowledgement of a donation;
(b) component parts of items described in (a) above when supplied for self assembly;
(c) any form of receptacle which:
- is manufactured specifically for the purpose of collecting donated money;
- is used solely for collecting money for charity;
- is, or will be, clearly marked as collecting for a named charity; and
- can be secured by lock or tamper evident seal.

(d) bucket lids, designed to fit buckets and provide a secure seal, for use solely in connection with collecting money for charity;
(e) pre-printed letters the primary purpose of which is to appeal for money for charity (not necessarily including the addressees' particulars);
(f) envelopes used in conjunction with letters described (e) above for forwarding donations, provided that they are over-printed with an appeal request related to that contained in the letter;
(g) outer envelopes used in conjunction with letters described in (e) above, provided that they are over-printed with an appeal request related to that contained in the letter;
(h) pre-printed collecting envelopes appealing for money (of the type used by the welfare charities and which are usually hand delivered to domestic premises); and
(i) stewardship envelopes used for planned giving which, as a minimum requirement, are pre-printed with the name of the relevant place of worship or other charity.

Where this concession applies, the supply may be treated as if it were a zero-rated supply.

This concession applies from 1 April 2000.

The Commissioners may withdraw or restrict the application of this concession if they have reasonable cause to believe it is being abused.

3.4 VAT—MISUNDERSTANDING BY A VAT TRADER

VAT undercharged by a registered trader on account of a bona fide misunderstanding may be remitted provided all the following conditions are fulfilled—

(a) there is no reason to believe that the tax has been knowingly evaded;
(b) there is no evidence of negligence;
(c) the misunderstanding does not concern an aspect of the tax clearly covered in the guidance published by HM Revenue & Customs or in specific instructions to the trader concerned; and
(d) the tax due was not charged, could not now reasonably be expected to be charged to customers, and will not be charged.

Where, at the time the misunderstanding comes to light, there are unfulfilled firm orders from customers, for which the price quoted has been based mistakenly on the assumption that no VAT, or less VAT than properly due, would be chargeable, VAT undercharged may be remitted in respect of such orders provided conditions (a)–(d) above are met.

3.5 VAT—MISDIRECTION

If a Customs and Excise officer, with the full facts before him, has given a clear and unequivocal ruling on VAT in writing or, knowing the full facts, has misled a registered person to his detriment, any assessment of VAT due will be based on the correct ruling from the date the error was brought to the registered person's attention.

Note—HMRC ceased to accept claims under this Concession from 1 April 2009: see HMRC Brief 15/09, 27-3-09.

3.6 VAT—COIN-OPERATED MACHINES

The tax point for supplies made from coin-operated machines is the date the machine is used. As an accounting convenience, however, operators may delay accounting for VAT until the takings are removed from a machine.

For all other purposes the normal tax point rules apply. Therefore in the event of a theft of takings from a machine, VAT must still be accounted for in full on any supplies that have been made from the machine.

3.7 VAT—VAT ON MINOR PROMOTIONAL ITEMS SUPPLIED IN LINKED SUPPLIES SCHEMES

These are schemes in which a minor article is linked, although not necessarily physically linked, with a main article (of either goods or services) and sold with it at a single price. The price paid should normally be apportioned to reflect any difference where the items are liable to VAT at different rates.

However, if the minor article—
(a) is not charged to the customer at a separate price;
(b) costs the supplier no more than 20% of the total cost of the combined supply (excluding VAT); and
(c) costs the supplier no more than—
  – £1 (excluding VAT) if included with goods intended for retail sale; or
  – £5 (excluding VAT) otherwise,

the supplier may account for VAT on the minor article at the same rate as the main article—ie no apportionment is necessary.

3.8 VAT—USE OF MARGIN SCHEME FOR VEHICLE SALES WHEN INCOMPLETE RECORDS HAVE BEEN KEPT

If a dealer in second-hand vehicles who supplies a vehicle in circumstances in which, but for his failure to keep the necessary records relating to either the purchase or to the sale of the vehicle (but not to both), he would be entitled to account for the VAT chargeable on the supply on the profit margin on the supply rather than its value may, provided he satisfies the Commissioners that the mark-up achieved on the supply does not exceed 100%, treat the profit margin on the supply as being equal to—
(a) where he has kept the necessary purchase records, the purchase price; and
(b) where he has kept the necessary sales records, half of the selling price,

and accordingly account for the VAT chargeable on the supply on that profit margin.

Commentary—*De Voil Indirect Tax Service* **V3.534.**
Note—This concession will be withdrawn with effect from 1 April 2010. See the HMRC Technical Note, 'Withdrawal of Extra-statutory Concessions', published April 2009.

3.9 VAT—RECOVERIES UNDER THE VAT ACT 1994 SCHEDULE 11 PARAGRAPH 5

Where an amount is shown or represented as VAT on an invoice issued by a person who is neither registered nor required to be registered for VAT at the time when the invoice is issued, the provisions of Schedule 11 paragraph 5 of the VAT Act 1994 (formerly Schedule 7 paragraph 6 of the VAT Act 1983) enable the Commissioners to require that person to pay an equivalent amount to them. The Act does not provide any relief in respect of related VAT incurred by such a person. On the grounds of equity, a person making such a payment may be permitted to deduct from it the amount of VAT incurred on supplies to him of goods and services that were directly attributable to any invoiced supply in respect of which such payment is required.

Where such a person has made a supply to a taxable person and, on the invoice, showed or represented an amount as VAT, the recipient of the supply has no legal entitlement to treat that amount as his input tax. If it is clear that the taxable person who received the supply has treated such an amount as input tax in good faith, action to recover the amount so deducted may be remitted on grounds of equity.

3.10 VAT—VAT ON NECESSARY MEALS AND ACCOMMODATION PROVIDED BY RECOGNISED REPRESENTATIVE SPORTING BODIES TO AMATEUR SPORTS PERSONS CHOSEN TO REPRESENT THAT BODY IN A COMPETITION

The Value Added Tax (Input Tax) Order 1992 (SI 1992/3222) (formerly the Value Added Tax (Special Provisions) Order 1981 (SI 1981/1741) as amended by the VAT (Special Provisions) (Amendment) Order 1988 (SI 1988/1124)) prevents input tax deduction where goods or services have been provided for the purposes of business entertainment except where this entertainment is of an employee. The effect of this provision is to produce different treatment as between, for example, professional football teams and amateur football teams. This is because the professional players are employees of their clubs and input tax is deductible, while the amateur players are, by definition, not employees and input tax is blocked. This distinction between amateur and professional sportsmen has led to inequity in the VAT treatment of certain amateur representative bodies who are registered for VAT and account for output tax on "gate money" in the same way as professional clubs, but cannot recover VAT on some of their genuine business expenses.

With the overwhelming number of clubs this has provided no problem as members' subscriptions are regarded as being payment, in part, for any accommodation or meals that they may receive when playing for that club. However, problems have been encountered with certain bodies that choose, from affiliated clubs, individual amateur sports persons to represent their country or county. These persons so selected are not full subscribing members of the representational body. They pay a very small nominal subscription, or no subscription at all so the provision in Notice 700/65—entertainment of members of clubs, associations, etc—cannot apply. To remove this inequity of treatment as between professional and amateur bodies, it has been agreed that input tax necessarily incurred on the provision of accommodation and meals for team members selected by such representative bodies may be deductible as input tax. This concession not only applies to selected players but also to the committee members of the body who are to be treated as "persons engaged in the management of a company and deemed to be employees of that company". The concession does not cover alcoholic drinks and tobacco (including cigarettes and cigars) provided for consumption by players and committee members.

3.11 VAT—INCORRECT CUSTOMER DECLARATION

Where a customer provides an incorrect declaration claiming eligibility for zero-rating under Groups 2, 4, 5, 6, 8, 12 or 15 of the zero rate Schedule of the VAT Act 1994, or eligibility for a reduced rate under Group 1 of Schedule 7A for the qualifying use of fuel and power, and where a supplier, despite having taken all reasonable steps to check the validity of the declaration, nonetheless fails to identify the inaccuracy and in good faith makes the supplies concerned at the zero rate, or a reduced rate, HM Revenue & Customs will not seek to recover the tax due from the supplier.

3.12 VAT—BUSES WITH SPECIAL FACILITIES FOR CARRYING DISABLED PERSONS

A vehicle constructed or adapted to have a carrying capacity of less than 12 passengers would not normally qualify for input tax deduction. But where a vehicle which would otherwise have 12 or more seats, has a carrying capacity of less than 12 passengers solely because it is equipped with facilities for persons in wheelchairs, it can be treated, for VAT purposes, as if it had at least 12 seats.

3.13 VAT—REPAYMENT OF IMPORT VAT TO SHIPPING AGENTS AND FREIGHT FORWARDERS

Import VAT may be paid directly to shipping agents and freight forwarders where importers go into liquidation, or where an administrator or administrative receiver has been appointed who certifies that, in his or her opinion, ordinary unsecured creditors would receive nothing in a liquidation, leaving the agents unable to recover VAT paid on their behalf. The importers must have gone into a formal state of insolvency or receivership within 6 months of the date of lodgement of the Customs entry, and the goods must have remained under the agents' control throughout their stay in the UK and have been re-exported unused from the European Community.

3.14 VAT—ZERO-RATING OF CERTAIN SUPPLIES OF FREE ZONE GOODS

From 1 August 1991 the supply of goods subject to import VAT which are free zone goods in the UK may be zero-rated on condition that there is an agreement between the supplier and the customer that the customer will clear the goods for removal from the zone and will take responsibility for payment of the import VAT.

3.15 VAT—PRINTED MATTER PUBLISHED IN INSTALMENTS

Books are zero-rated for VAT under item 1 of Group 3 of Schedule 8 to the VAT Act 1994 (formerly item 1 of Group 3 of Schedule 5 to the VAT Act 1983). However, there is a specialist area of the market known as continuity publishing or part-works where the product is supplied in parts over varying periods but builds up into a greater whole, ie a loose-leaf book. Unless such items, when viewed independently, are books etc at the time of supply, they are not entitled to zero-rating under the present law.

From 1 February 1993 by way of concession, if, at the time of supply, an article is or was not by itself regarded as a book, including a loose-leaf book, qualifying for zero-rating under item 1 of Group 3 of Schedule 8 to the VAT Act 1994, but is or was a part of a larger finite work which itself would fall under item 1 of Group 3 of Schedule 8 as a book, then the individual component parts may also be zero-rated where they are or were being supplied either direct by the publisher or through a distribution chain to the final consumer.

From 26 October 1993 by way of further concession in relation to card-based boxed continuity series publications, such publications, even though not bound or held together other than in or by their container, and having all the other characteristics of a book, will for VAT purposes be treated as a book.

3.16 VAT—CONNECTION TO THE GAS OR ELECTRICITY MAINS SUPPLY

Connection to the gas or electricity mains supply, which would have been a zero-rated supply before 1 April 1994 by virtue of Group 7 of Schedule 5 to the Value Added Tax Act 1983, may continue to be treated as a zero-rated supply provided that—

(a) it is the first connection to the gas or electricity mains supply (as the case may be) of—
- a building, or part of a building, which consists of a dwelling or number of dwellings;
- a building, or part of a building, used solely for a relevant residential purpose (within the meaning of Note 4 to Group 7);
- a building, or part of a building, used by a charity otherwise than in the course or furtherance of a business;

- a residential caravan (that is to say a caravan on a site in respect of which there is no covenant, statutory planning consent or similar permission precluding occupation throughout the year); or
- a houseboat (within the meaning of Group 6 to Note 7G); and

(b) the person receiving the supply does not do so for the purpose of any business carried on by him.

3.17 VAT—ZERO-RATING OF SUPPLIES OF TRAINING FOR FOREIGN GOVERNMENTS

From 1 October 1993 the services of training (not being services comprised in any Group of Schedule 9 to the VAT Act 1994, formerly Schedule 6 to the VAT Act 1983), supplied to a foreign government in furtherance of its sovereign activities (and not its business activities), is liable to VAT at the zero rate provided the supplier retains a statement in writing from that government (or its accredited representative), that the trainees are employed in furtherance of its sovereign activities.

3.18 VAT—EXEMPTION FOR ALL DOMESTIC SERVICE CHARGES

The concession exempts from 1 April 1994 all mandatory service charges or similar charges paid by the occupants of residential property towards the upkeep of the dwellings or block of flats in which they reside and towards the provision of a warden, caretakers, and people performing a similar function for those occupants. The concession does not exempt service charges paid in respect of holiday accommodation as defined in paragraph 1(*e*) of and Notes 11–13 to Group 1, Schedule 9, VAT Act 1994 (formerly paragraph 1(*d*) of and Notes (10), (10A) and (10B) to Group 1, Schedule 6, VAT Act 1983).

3.19 VAT—SUPPLIES OF "RELEVANT GOODS" TO CHARITIES

Where "relevant goods" of a kind described in Note (3) to Group 15 of the Value Added Tax Act 1994 are supplied to a charity—

(a) whose sole purpose and function is to provide a range of care services to meet the personal needs of handicapped people (of which transport might form a part); or

(b) which provides transport services predominantly to handicapped people,

then by concession, the supply of those goods will be zero-rated, as will the repair and maintenance of those goods and the supply of any further goods in connection with that repair and maintenance.

"Handicapped" means chronically sick or disabled.

In order to be eligible for this concession, a charity must demonstrate that it meets the requirements of sub-paragraphs (a) or (b) above by way of—

- its charitable aims and objectives;
- its publicity and advertising material;
- any documents which it has issued for the purpose of obtaining funding from a third party such as a local authority;
- its day-to-day operations; and
- any other evidence that may be relevant.

3.20 VAT—DISAPPLICATION OF REPAYMENT OF INPUT TAX (VALUE ADDED TAX ACT 1994 S 36(4A) AND THE VAT REGULATIONS SI 1995/2518 (AS AMENDED BY THE VAT (AMENDMENT) REGULATIONS SI 1997/1086)

1. Subject to paragraphs 3 and 4 below, section 36(4A) of the VAT Act 1994 will not apply to any person where—

(a) an insolvency procedure has commenced in relation to that person under section 81(4B), (4C) and (5) of the VAT Act 1994;

(b) the claimant's notification of his claim for bad debt relief in accordance with regulation 166A of the Value Added Tax Regulations 1995 (SI 1995/2518), is received after the insolvency procedure has commenced; and

(c) each relevant supply upon which the claim for bad debt relief is based, was made prior to the commencement of the insolvency procedure.

2. Paragraph 1 above applies whether or not the business of the person who is the subject of the insolvency procedure continues to be carried on.

3. Paragraph 1 above does not apply unless the Commissioners have received notification on Form VAT 769 "Notification of Insolvency details", or such other notification as the Commissioners may require, in respect of the insolvency procedure referred to in that paragraph.

4. Paragraph 1 above does not apply in circumstances where its application would give rise to tax avoidance.

The insolvency procedures to which the Concession applies

The insolvency procedures included in section 81 of the Value Added Tax Act 1994 for the purposes of this concession are—

- Bankruptcy.
- Compulsory liquidation (winding up).
- Creditors' voluntary liquidation (voluntary winding up).
- Members' voluntary liquidation (voluntary winding up).
- Administrative Receivership.
- Administrative Order.
- Individual Voluntary Arrangement.
- Company Voluntary Arrangement.
- Scottish Trust Deed.
- Deed of Arrangement.

After further consultations with representatives of insolvency practitioners and colleagues within Customs who deal with insolvency policy, it has been agreed that the application of this concession should be extended to a number of other types of insolvencies that are not included in the strict interpretation of section 81 of the Value Added Tax Act 1994. Accordingly this concession will apply to the following types of insolvency that are not included in section 81.

- Partnership Voluntary Arrangement. (Insolvent Partnerships Order 1994; Insolvent Partnerships Order (Northern Ireland) 1995).
- Partnership Liquidation. (Insolvent Partnerships Order 1994; Insolvent Partnerships Order (Northern Ireland) 1995).
- Partnership Administration Order. (Insolvent Partnerships Order 1994; Insolvent Partnerships Order (Northern Ireland) 1995).
- Sequestration. (Bankruptcy (Scotland) Act 1985; Bankruptcy (Scotland) Act 1993).
- County Court Administration Order. (County Court Act 1984). Scheme of Arrangement. (Companies Act 1985).
- Deceased Persons Administration Order. (Administration of Insolvent Estates of Deceased Persons Order 1986; Administration of Insolvent Estates of Deceased Persons Order (Northern Ireland) 1991).

Application of extra-statutory concession

The effective date for the application of the concession will be the date of the Customs claim in the insolvency. This will be the relevant date of the insolvency and the insolvency meeting date (if applicable).

In Administration Order cases the effective date will be the date of the Administration Order.

Where there is a subsequent insolvency the concession will also apply to that subsequent insolvency.

If an insolvency arrangement fails the insolvency is annulled and the requirement to account for clawback will be reinstated.

The concession will only apply to a provisional liquidation if it is followed by a permanent liquidation. In these circumstances the clawback concession will take effect from the date of the provisional liquidation.

3.21 VAT—SALES OF POOR QUALITY GOODS

By concession, the supply by a charity of any goods which have been donated for sale or the supply of such goods by a taxable person who is covenanted by deed to give all the profits of that supply to a charity, shall be treated as zero-rated, provided that—

(a) the supply is a sale of goods donated to that charity or taxable person; but

(b) the goods, although of a kind which the charity or taxable person makes available to the general public for purchase (whether in a shop or elsewhere) are by reason of their poor quality not fit to be so made available.

3.22 VAT—VALUATION OF THE REFURBISHMENT OR FITTING OUT OF A BUILDING FOR THE PURPOSES OF THE CAPITAL GOODS SCHEME

3.22.1 Part I—Introduction

Regulation 113(*h*) of the VAT Regulations 1995 defines as a capital item (ie an item subject to adjustment under the capital goods scheme)—

> "a building which the owner refurbishes or fits out where the value of capital expenditure on the taxable supplies of services and of goods affixed to the building, other than any that are zero-rated, made or to be made to the owner for or in connection with the refurbishment or fitting-out in question on or after 3rd July 1997 is not less than £250,000."

Some businesses have difficulty in identifying "goods affixed" for the purposes of determining the value of the capital item under this regulation and this concession allows them to include in the calculation the value of capital expenditure on goods which may not have been affixed to the building.

3.22.2 Part II—The concession

A taxable person seeking to determine the value of a capital item under regulation 113(*h*) can include any additional amount of capital expenditure, over and above that incurred on supplies of services and of goods affixed to the building, incurred for or in connection with the refurbishment or fitting out in question.

3.22.3 Part III—Conditions

(1) This concession applies with effect from 1 January 2000.

(2) A taxable person taking advantage of this concession must keep a record of the value of the capital item and of the supplies on the basis of which the value was determined.

(3) A taxable person who has determined the value of a capital item in accordance with this concession must apply the capital goods scheme to the VAT incurred on all the expenditure included in the calculation of the item's value.

3.22.4 Part IV—Warnings and definitions

The Commissioners may withdraw or restrict the application of any part of this concession if they consider that it is being used to avoid tax.

Where expenditure on goods which are not affixed to the building is included in the value of a capital item the requirement to apply the capital goods scheme to the VAT incurred on that expenditure means that adjustments will have to continue to be made even if those goods have been disposed of, unless they are disposed of as part of the disposal of the whole interest in the building when a final adjustment (unless the disposal is made in the last adjustment period applicable to the capital item) must be made in the normal way.

3.23 VAT—SUPPLIES BY FINANCIAL OMBUDSMAN SERVICES LTD TO OMBUDSMAN AUTHORITIES

This concession provides that payments from eight ombudsman authorities for the performance by the Financial Ombudsman Services Ltd (FOS) of the complaint handling duties of the authorities shall not be treated as consideration for any supply in the course of furtherance of any business by FOS.

The payment of any amount at any time by the—

- Office of the Building Societies Ombudsman (OBSO)
- Office of the Banking Ombudsman (OBO)
- Insurance Ombudsman Bureau (IOB)
- Personal Assurance Arbitration Service (PASS)
- PIA Ombudsman Bureau (PIAOB)
- Office of the Investment Ombudsman Bureau (OIOB)
- SFA Complaints Bureau and Arbitration Service (SFACBAS)
- FSA Independent Investigator (FSAII)

to Financial Ombudsman Services Ltd (FOS) for the supply of services by FOS in connection with the ombudsman and complaint handing scheme duties by OBSO, OBO, IOB, PAAS, PIAOB, OIOB, SFACBAS and FSAII (as the case may be) between 1 April 2000 and 1 October 2000 shall not be treated as consideration for any supply in the course of any business carried on by FOS.

3.24 VAT—CHARITIES WHO PROVIDE CARE IN AN INSTITUTION AND ALSO SUPPLY GOODS TO DISABLED PERSONS RESIDENT IN THEIR OWN AND OTHER INSTITUTIONS

1. This concession applies in relation to a supply of goods which, apart from Note (5B) to Group 12 of Schedule 8 to the Value Added Tax 1994, would fall within paragraph (*g*) of item 2 of that Group, where—

(a) the goods are goods other than spectacles or contact lenses, and are designed solely for use by a visually handicapped person;

(b) the goods are supplied by a charity at or below cost;

(c) the recipient of the supply is a resident or is attending the premises of a relevant institution as defined in Note (5I) to the said Group 12; and

(d) the charity is not actively engaged in supplying goods within paragraph (a) above solely to handicapped persons who are resident in or attending the premises of a relevant institution as defined by Note (5I) to the said Group 12 operated, managed or controlled by the charity.

2. Where this concession applies, the supply of the goods may be treated as if it were a zero-rated supply.

3. The Commissioners may withdraw or restrict the application of this concession if they have reasonable cause to believe that it is being abused.

3.25 VAT—RESUSCITATION TRAINING MODELS SUPPLIED TO CHARITIES AND OTHER ELIGIBLE BODIES FOR USE IN FIRST AID TRAINING

1. The concession shall operate to include in Note (3) to Group 15 of Schedule 8 to the Value Added Tax Act 1994, the following—

(a) human resuscitation training models acquired for use in first aid training in either or both cardiopulmonary resuscitation and defibrillation techniques; and

(b) parts and accessories for use in or with the goods described in paragraph (a) above, where the parts and accessories are for use in the training of either or both cardiopulmonary resuscitation and defibrillation techniques.

2. In this concession resuscitation training model means a model which includes a head and torso designed for use in the training of cardiopulmonary resuscitation or defibrillation techniques.

3. In this concession cardiopulmonary resuscitation means a combination of expired air ventilation and chest compression.

4. The Commissioners may withdraw or restrict the application of this concession if they have reasonable cause to believe that it is being abused.

3.26 VAT—WORKS OF ART, ANTIQUES AND COLLECTORS' ITEMS

The Value Added Tax (Treatment of Transactions) Order 1995 (SI 1995/958) relieves from VAT certain transactions by treating them as neither a supply of goods nor a supply of services. This Order may also be applied, in the same way that it applies to works of art, to the following goods—

(a) all works of art falling within paragraph (*a*) of Annex I to Council Directive 77/388/EEC (inserted by Council Directive 94/5/EC) which do not already fall within the said order;

(b) collectors' items falling within paragraph (*b*) of the said Annex I; and

(c) antiques falling within paragraph (*c*) of the said Annex I.

3.27 VAT—USE OF THE AUCTIONEERS' SCHEME FOR SALES OF GOODS AT AUCTION ON BEHALF OF NON-TAXABLE PERSONS

From 1 January 1999, an auctioneer selling, on behalf of a third party vendor who is a non-taxable person, goods which have been grown, made or produced (including bloodstock or livestock reared from birth) by that person, may enter the goods into the auctioneers' scheme provided he holds a certificate from the vendor which includes—

(a) vendor's full name and address;

(b) description of goods and date of sale;

(c) declaration that the vendor is not registered nor required to be registered for VAT;

(d) signature of vendor and date; and

(e) signature of auctioneer and date,

and all other conditions of the scheme are met. The completed certificate must be retained with the relevant records for VAT purposes.

An example of an acceptable certificate is set out below:

AUCTIONEERS' SCHEME FOR SECOND-HAND GOODS, WORKS OF ART, ANTIQUES AND COLLECTORS' ITEMS

Extra-statutory concession number xx
Vendor's Certificate for goods grown, made or produced and sold at auction on behalf of non-taxable persons

I (full name)
of (address)

declare that I am not registered or required to be registered for VAT and that the goods detailed below are to be sold at auction on my behalf by (auctioneer's name)
Description of goods

Date of sale (to be completed by auctioneer)
Signature of vendor
Signature of auctioneer
Date

3.28 VAT—SUPPLIES BY FINANCIAL SERVICES AUTHORITY TO SELF-REGULATING ORGANISATIONS

The payment of any amount at any time by the Investment Management Regulatory Organisation (IMRO); the Personal Investment Authority (PIA); or the Securities and Futures Authority (SFA) to the Financial Services Authority (FSA) for the supply by the FSA in the carrying out of the regulatory functions of IMRO, PIA or SFA (as the case may be) between 1 April 1998 and the coming into effect of the Financial Services and Markets Act 2000, and similar payments by the Registrar of Friendly Societies (RFS); and the Insurance Directorate of HM Treasury (ID) for the supply by FSA in the carrying out of regulatory functions of RFS and ID (as the case may be) between 1 January 1999 and the coming into effect of the Financial Services and Markets Act 2000 shall not be treated as consideration for any supply in the course or furtherance of any business carried on by FSA.

3.29 VAT—CHARITABLE BUILDINGS

3.29.1 Part I—Introduction

Whether or not a building is to be used solely for a relevant charitable purpose is relevant to the VAT liability of supplies of or in relation to the building under Groups 5 (Construction of Buildings, etc.) and 6 (Protected Buildings) of Schedule 8 to the Value Added Tax Act 1994 and Group 1 (Land) of Schedule 9 to that Act. It is also relevant to whether or not a self supply of a building arises under paragraph 1 (Residential and charitable buildings—change of use etc.) of Schedule 10 (Buildings and Land) to that Act and to whether an election to waive exemption in respect of a building may be made under that Schedule. This concession mitigates the legal requirement that the building must be used solely for a qualifying purpose.

3.29.2 Part II—The concession

1—(1) For the purposes of Groups 5 and 6 of Schedule 8, Group 1 of Schedule 9 and Schedule 10 to the Value Added Tax Act 1994 (VATA), and subject to the conditions set out in Part III below, the non-qualifying use of a building can be ignored if the entire building will be used solely for a qualifying purpose for more than 90 per cent of the total time the building is available for use.

(2) Alternatively, the non-qualifying use of an identifiable part of a building can be ignored if that part of the building will be used solely for a qualifying purpose for more than 90 per cent of the total time that part of the building is available for use.

(3) Alternatively, the non-qualifying use of a building can be ignored if 90 per cent or more of the floor space of the entire building will be used solely for a qualifying purpose.

(4) Alternatively, the non-qualifying use of a building can be ignored if the entire building will be used solely for a qualifying purpose by 90 per cent or more of the people using the building (on a head count basis).

3.29.3 Part III—Conditions

2—(1) For any one building only one of the four methods may be used.

(2) The time based test for parts of a building, the floor space test and the head count test may only be used with the written agreement of HM Revenue & Customs .

(3) The floor space and head count tests may not be applied to parts of a building.

(4) The concession must be calculated and applied at the time a relevant supply is made. This is usually when the question arises of whether a building, or part of a building is used or will be used for a relevant charitable purpose.

(5) The concession must be applied in a way which ensures a result which is fair and reasonable to both the taxpayer and HM Revenue & Customs .

(6) This extra-statutory concession applies to supplies made on or after 1 June 2000.

(7) It is a condition of the relief for charitable buildings that they continue to be used for the qualifying purpose for ten years after their completion. If during this ten year period the building (or part of it) is put to a non-qualifying use that exceeds the terms of this concession, VAT must be accounted for on the deemed self supply that arises by virtue of paragraph 1 of Schedule 10 to VATA.

3.29.4 Part IV—Warnings and definitions

3—(1) The Commissioners may withdraw or restrict the application of any part of this concession if they consider that it is being used to avoid tax. A person who uses it for the purposes of tax avoidance will be required to account for tax in accordance with the provisions of the law.

(2) "Qualifying use" and "qualifying purpose" mean use solely for a relevant charitable purpose. Use for a relevant charitable purpose is defined in Note (6) to Group 5 of Schedule 8 to the VAT Act 1994. This Note is imported into Group 6 of that Schedule by Note (3), Group 1 of Schedule 9 by Note (3) and Schedule 10 by paragraph 9.

(3) "Building" includes an annex, constructed to an existing building, which meets the conditions in Note (17)(a) and (b) to Group 5 of Schedule 8 to the VAT Act 1994.

Note—This concession is to be withdrawn following a 12-month transitional period starting on 1 July 2009. During this transitional period, charities will be able to continue to apply ESC 3.29, or choose to apply the revised interpretation of the statutory provision described in HMRC Brief 30/09, published 1-7-09 (changes to the application of the zero-rate to new buildings used for a relevant charitable or residential use). See also VAT Information Sheet 8/09 for more details.

3.30 VAT—RETAIL PHARMACISTS

(1) This concession applies in relation to a supply of goods which, apart from Note (5A) to Group 12 of Schedule 8 to the VAT Act 1994, would fall within Item 1 of that Group, when—

(a) the goods supplied are dispensed to an individual for his/her personal use while he/she is an inpatient or resident or while he/she is attending a relevant institution which is a hospital or nursing home;

(b) the goods are ordered in accordance with section 41 of the National Health Service Act 1977, section 27 of the National Health Service (Scotland) Act 1978 or Article 63 of the Health and Personal Social Services (Northern Ireland) Order 1972;

(c) the goods are dispensed in accordance with the National Health Service (Pharmaceutical Services) Regulations 1992, Schedule 1 to the National Health Service (Pharmaceutical Services) (Scotland) Regulations 1995 or the Pharmaceutical Services Regulations (Northern Ireland) 1997; and

(d) the person dispensing the goods is paid for doing so by—

- the Prescription Pricing Authority;
- the Prescription Information and Pricing Services Division of the Welsh Health Common Services Authority;
- the Pharmacy Practice Division of the Common Services Agency; or
- the Central Services Agency.

(2) Where this concession applies, the supply may be treated as if it were a zero-rated supply.

(3) The Commissioners may withdraw or restrict the application of the concession if they have reasonable cause to believe that it is being abused.

3.31 VAT: SUPPLIES BY THE FINANCIAL SERVICES COMPENSATION SCHEME LTD (FSCS) TO COMPENSATION SCHEME AUTHORITIES

The payment of any amount at any time by the Investors Compensation Scheme (ICS), the Deposit Protection Scheme (DPS), the Building Societies Investor Protection Scheme (BSIPS), the Policyholders Protection Scheme (PPS), the Friendly Societies Protection Scheme (FSPS), and the Section 43 Scheme (S43S) for the supply of services by FSCS in carrying out the compensatory scheme functions of ICS, DPS, BSIPS, PPS, FSPS, and S43S (as the case may be) between 1 February 2001 and the coming into effect of the Financial Services & Markets Act 2000 shall not be treated as consideration for any supply in the course of any business carried on by FSCS.

3.32 VAT: ELECTRONIC FACE VALUE VOUCHERS

1. Under paragraph 5 of Schedule 6 to the VAT Act 1994, where a right to receive goods or services for an amount stated on any token, stamp or voucher is granted for a consideration, the consideration shall be disregarded for the purposes of the Act except to the extent (if any) that it exceeds that amount.

2. The paragraph currently only has application in relation to face value vouchers or similar devices which have a physical form, such as paper vouchers.

3. From 8 March 2001 by way of concession the paragraph shall also apply to face value vouchers or similar devices in electronic form provided that they operate in the same way as their physical counterparts.

4. Paragraph 3 above does not apply in circumstances where its application would give rise to tax avoidance.

3.33 VAT: SUPPLIES PREVIOUSLY MADE BY THE POST OFFICE

The Postal Services Act 2000 replaced each reference to "the Post Office" within VAT legislation with a reference to "the Post Office Company". This concession maintains the scope of existing VAT reliefs following a restructuring of the Post Office corporation immediately prior to the transfer of the property, rights and liabilities of the corporation to the Post Office Company.

This concession extends the reference to the "the Post Office Company" to include a reference to any wholly owned subsidiary of the Post Office Company providing the public postal service, for the purposes of:

(a) the VAT exemption provided for postal services in items 1 and 2 of Group 3, Schedule 9, Value Added Tax 1994, and

(b) the zero rating of transport services provided for in item 4(*b*), Group 8, Schedule 8 to the Value Added Tax Act 1994, and

(c) the interpretation of "datapost packet" provided for in regulation 2 (1) of the Value Added Tax Regulations (SI 1995/2518).

Any reference in this concession to a wholly owned subsidiary shall be construed in accordance with section 736 of the Companies Act 1985.

3.34 VAT: TAX RECLAIMED BY MUSEUMS AND GALLERIES COVERED BY SECTION 33A OF THE VALUE ADDED TAX ACT 1994

1. Scope of this extra-statutory concession

1.1 The Government is committed to free public access to the main national museums and galleries. Ordinarily, when a museum or gallery moves from charging taxable entrance charges to free admission, it loses its entitlement to recover the VAT incurred on the related goods and services it purchases. This is because admitting the public free of charge is not a business activity and thus there is no entitlement to recover input tax in relation to it. The purpose of the scheme in Section 33A of the Value Added Tax Act 1994 ("the Act") is to refund this irrecoverable VAT to the bodies listed in an Order made under Section 33A(9). The entitlement to such refunds will commence from the date the Order takes effect in relation to the museum or gallery listed in it.

1.2 When a person recovers input tax on goods or services and subsequently transfers or uses them for a non-business purpose, a supply of the goods or services is deemed to have been made under paragraphs 5(1) or 5(4) of Schedule 4 to the Act (goods), or under Article 3 of the Value Added Tax (Supply of Services) Order 1993 (SI 1993/1507) (services).

1.3 Furthermore, where input tax had been recovered in relation to a capital item as defined in regulation 113 of the Value Added Tax Regulations 1995, a move from taxable admission charges to non-business free access can have an effect on the proportion of taxable as opposed to exempt use of the capital item. This would result in adjustments of the input tax recovered under the normal operation of the capital goods scheme.

1.4 This extra-statutory concession aims to ensure that the museums and galleries specified in an Order made under Section 33A(9) of the Act are not required to repay input tax, properly recovered at the time on goods and services used in connection with taxable supplies of admitting the public for payment, solely on account of the move to free admission.

1.5 The concession will not be extended to any situation where it appears to the Commissioners that its use will assist in avoiding VAT, and where it appears to them that the concession has been so used it will be treated as never having applied.

2. Operation of this extra-statutory concession

2.1 Each of the following descriptions of transactions shall be treated as neither a supply of goods nor a supply of services, namely:

(a) goods which after purchase are subsequently put to a non-business use giving rise otherwise to a supply under paragraphs 5(1) or 5(4) of Schedule 4 to the Act; and

(b) services which after purchase are subsequently put to a non-business use giving rise otherwise to a supply under Article 3 of the Value Added Tax (Supply of Services) Order 1993.

This is providing in each case, that the change in use of the goods and services arose solely as a direct result of a body listed in an Order made under Section 33A(9) of the Act using the goods or services for the purpose of offering free rights of admission to the museum or gallery to which the Order specifies.

2.2 This paragraph applies to adjustments to the deduction of input tax on capital items under Part XV of the Value Added Tax Regulations 1995. Adjustment will not be required in so far as a change in use of a capital item relates to free admission with related refunds of VAT under Section 33A of the Act. Otherwise, adjustments are not affected. Where this paragraph applies, the owner of a capital item shall in each subsequent interval adjust the total input tax on the capital item and the extent of taxable use of the capital item for the purposes of Part XV as follows:

(a) the total input tax on the capital item shall be deemed to be the proportion that would have been input tax if admissions which have subsequently become free had been free at the time the VAT was incurred; and

(b) the extent of taxable use of the capital item at the time the original entitlement to deduction was determined shall be deemed to be the extent of taxable use at that time if admissions which have subsequently become free had been free at that time.

3. Dates when this extra-statutory concession has effect

3.1 This extra-statutory concession takes effect for each museum or gallery specified in an Order made under Section 33A(9) of the Act on the day appointed in the Order for that museum or gallery, whether or not the day appointed was before the date of publication of this concession.

3.35 VAT: APPORTIONMENT OF CERTAIN MEMBERSHIP SUBSCRIPTIONS TO NON-PROFIT MAKING BODIES

Where a membership body supplies, in return for its membership subscription, a principal benefit, together with one or more ancillary benefits, it will normally have to treat the subscription as being in return for that principal benefit. This means that the body will have to ignore the liability to the VAT of the ancillary benefits and account for VAT on the whole subscription based on the liability to VAT of that principal benefit.

However bodies that are non-profit making and supply a mixture of zero-rated, exempt and/or standard rated benefits to their members in return for their subscriptions, may apportion such subscriptions to reflect the value and VAT liability of those individual benefits, without regard to whether there is one principal benefit. This concession may not be used for the purpose of tax avoidance.

3.36 VAT: IMPORTED WORKS OF ART, ANTIQUES ETC

In case of works of art, antiques etc falling within section 21(5) of the VAT Act 1994, with effect from 1 November 2001, paragraph (*b*) of sub-section 6(D) of that section shall cease to have effect except in cases where conditions have been created artificially for obtaining the advantage of the reduced rate of VAT on importation.

Note—This concession subsequently enacted by the Enactment of Extra-Statutory Concessions Order, SI 2009/730 art 17 with effect in relation to importations on or after 6 April 2009.

3.37 VAT—EXEMPTION FOR SUPPLIES OF WELFARE SERVICES BY PRIVATE WELFARE AGENCIES PENDING REGISTRATION

(1) By concession, the exemption provided for by the amendment to paragraph (*b*) of VATA 1994 Sch 9 Group 7 item 9 made by the Value Added Tax (Health and Welfare) Order (SI 2003/24), with effect from 31 January 2003, shall apply to supplies of welfare services made by a private welfare agency in the following circumstances—

(a) in the case of an agency in England, Wales and Scotland, where that agency—

(i) is required to register under one of the Acts specified at (2) below; and

(ii) is not registered owing to the fact that either—

the regulations providing for the mechanics of such registration and the keeping of registers are not yet in force; or they are, but the agency's application for registration is being processed; or

the date by which it must apply for registration has not yet passed;

(b) in the case of an agency in Northern Ireland, where that agency—

(i) has a reasonable expectation of being required to register under the Health and Personal Social Services (Quality, Improvement and Regulation) (Northern Ireland) Order 2003; and

(ii) is not registered owing to the fact that either—

that Order or the regulations providing for the mechanics of such registration and the keeping of registers are not yet in force;

or they are, and the agency's application for registration is being processed;

or the date by which it must apply for registration has not yet passed;

(c) in the case of any agency, only where it applies the exemption to all supplies of welfare services (as defined in Note (6) to Group 7 of Schedule 9 to the Value Added Tax Act 1994) which it makes.

(2) The relevant Acts are—

(a) in the case of agencies in England and Wales, the Care Standards Act 2000; and

(b) in the case of agencies in Scotland, the Regulation of Care (Scotland) Act 2001.

(3) This concession is subject to the requirement that such an agency applies for registration under the appropriate Act or Order in accordance with the provisions of the relevant regulations no later than the date specified as the date by which an agency must so apply.

(4) This concession shall cease to apply—

i. where an agency is registered under the appropriate Act or Order; or

ii. where an agency has its application for registration refused.

(5) The Commissioners may withdraw or restrict the application of this concession if they have reasonable cause to believe that it is being abused.

Section 8 Facilitation of exports

8.1 VAT—SAILAWAY BOATS

Under regulation 129 of the Value Added Tax Regulations 1995, the supply of a sailaway boat to an overseas resident outside the VAT territory of the Member States may be zero-rated provided the boat is exported to a place outside the Member States within 6 months of the date of delivery, and the supplier obtains satisfactory proof of its eventual export.

As a concession and to prevent loss of UK trade, the supply of a boat to a UK resident may also be zero-rated provided—

(a) the supplier has evidence that the UK resident intends to keep the boat outside the VAT territory of the Member States for a continuous period of at least 12 months; and
(b) the boat is exported, within 2 months of the date of delivery, to a place outside the VAT territory of the Member States; and
(c) the boat is not used for any commercial purposes between the time of supply and exportation; and
(d) the supplier obtains and holds satisfactory evidence of export of the boat directly to a place outside the VAT territory of the Member States on copy 3 of the Form C88 (Single Administrative Document).

The above conditions apply to boats supplied both to UK residents who intend to keep them abroad and to UK residents intending to emigrate.

Section 9 Non-commercial transactions

9.1 VAT—VAT ON GOODS SUPPLIED AT DUTY-FREE AND TAX-FREE SHOPS

The supplier of goods which are liable to VAT and which are supplied to intending passengers at duty-free and tax-free shops approved by the Commissioners may, for those goods which are exported directly to a place outside the VAT territory of the Member States, be regarded as the exporter and zero-rate the supply.

9.2 VAT—MARINE FUEL

Commercial vessels engaged on voyages within UK territorial waters (or within the limits of a port), may receive certain types of marine fuel VAT free providing the conditions set out in Notice 703 *VAT—Exports and removals of goods from the United Kingdom* are met.

This relief extends only to those supplies of fuel which were zero-rated prior to 1 July 1990 under the Value Added Tax Act 1983 Schedule 5 Group 7 item 4. It does not apply to petrol, DERV or lubricating oil.

9.3 VAT AND EXCISE DUTIES—PERSONAL RELIEFS FOR GOODS PERMANENTLY IMPORTED FROM THIRD COUNTRIES

Where property (including motor vehicles) which has been purchased in accordance with the terms of Article 15/10 of Directive 77/388/EEC and which otherwise qualifies for relief from payment of customs charges under Article 11 of the Customs and Excise Duties (Personal Reliefs for Goods Permanently Imported) Order 1992, relief is not to be refused solely by reason of Article 11.2 of that Order.

9.4 VAT AND EXCISE DUTIES—PERSONAL RELIEFS FOR GOODS PERMANENTLY IMPORTED FROM THIRD COUNTRIES

Where property (including motor vehicles) which has been purchased by members of UK forces (or by the civilian staff accompanying them) in countries outside the area of the European Community and which otherwise qualifies for relief from payment of customs charges under Article 11 of the Customs and Excise Duties (Personal Reliefs for Goods Permanently Imported) Order 1992, relief is not to be refused solely by reason of Article 11.2 of that Order.

9.5 VAT AND EXCISE DUTIES—PERSONAL RELIEFS FOR GOODS PERMANENTLY IMPORTED FROM THIRD COUNTRIES

Where property (including motor vehicles) which has been purchased under a UK export scheme by members of the UK diplomatic service, by members of UK forces or by the civilian staff accompanying them or by members of international organisations and which otherwise qualifies for relief from payment of customs charges under Article 11 of the Customs and Excise Duties (Personal Reliefs for Goods Permanently Imported) Order 1992, relief is not to be refused solely by reason of Article 11.2 of that Order.

9.6 VAT AND EXCISE DUTIES—PERSONAL RELIEFS FOR GOODS PERMANENTLY IMPORTED FROM THIRD COUNTRIES

Where personal belongings otherwise qualify for relief under Article 11 of the Customs and Excise Duties (Personal Reliefs for Goods Permanently Imported) Order 1992 save only that the property has not been possessed and used for the specified period, then just as relief can be granted from customs duties as "special cases justified by the circumstances" under Article 3 of Council Regulation 918/83, similar consideration shall apply in respect of VAT and excise duties and relief may be granted accordingly.

9.7 VAT AND EXCISE DUTIES—PERSONAL RELIEFS FOR GOODS PERMANENTLY IMPORTED FROM THIRD COUNTRIES

Where personal belongings otherwise qualify for relief under Article 11 of the Customs and Excise Duties (Personal Reliefs for Goods Permanently Imported) Order 1992 save only that the property is declared for relief outside the specific periods, then just as relief can be granted from customs duties as special cases under Article 6, or under Article 9 of Council Regulation 918/83, similar consideration shall apply in respect of VAT and excise duties and relief may be granted accordingly.

Section 10 Concessions obsolete since last edition of update 1 to Notice 48 (published in October 2000)

10.1 VAT—GROUP SUPPLIES USING AN OVERSEAS MEMBER: TRANSITIONAL RELIEF

10.1.1 General

With effect from 26 November 1996, a resolution under the Provisional Collection of Taxes Act has created a new tax charge for the representative member of a VAT group, where supplies of a type set out in Schedule 5 to the VAT Act 1994 are purchased by an overseas group member and used for making Schedule 5 supplies to a UK group member. This new tax charge was made permanent when the Finance Act 1997 was passed on 19 March 1997. The new tax charge is given effect by section 41 of the Finance Act, which inserts the new rules into section 43 of the VAT Act 1994 at paragraphs (2A) to (2E).

The time of the supply which is taxed under section 41 is the time when the supply is paid for or, if the consideration is not in money, on the last day of the prescribed accounting period in which the services are performed. Under this concession, taxpayers may treat the introduction of the new charge under section 41 as though it were a change in the rate of VAT, and covered by section 88 of the VAT Act 1994.

This means that, where the UK group member has on, or after 26 November 1996, paid for services affected by section 41, but performance of those services took place to any extent before that date, the group may account for tax only on that proportion of the services which were performed on or after 26 November 1996. Further details are contained in Notice 700.

10.1.2 Telecommunications services

Telecommunications services are not currently affected by section 41 because they do not fall within Schedule 5 of the VAT Act 1994. However, it is possible that relevant telecommunications services will be so included shortly. When that happens, appropriate rules will be introduced to determine whether and when VAT should be accounted for on these telecommunications services provided by suppliers outside the UK, but received by customers within the UK. Accordingly, this concession does not apply to telecommunications services.

Commentary—*De Voil Indirect Tax Service* **V3.193.**

10.2 VAT—DEVELOPER'S SELF-SUPPLY ON 1 MARCH 1997

1. The developer's self-supply on 1 March 1997 under paragraph 5(1)(*b*) of Schedule 10 to the Value Added Tax Act 1994 need not be treated as made where—

(a) construction of a building or civil engineering work is still in progress on 1 March 1997 and the value of the developer's potential self-supply including those construction costs in paragraph 6(2)(*b*) of Schedule 10 to the Value Added Tax Act 1994 incurred both before and on or after 28 February 1997, would be less than £100,000; or

(b) a building or civil engineering work was completed before 1 March 1995 and either—

  (i) the building is fully occupied or the civil engineering work is used by a "developer" who is a taxable person for non-business purposes, rather than in connection with making any exempt supplies of goods or services, and consequently the "developer" under paragraph 5(5) of Schedule 10 to the Value Added Tax Act 1994 would have been a taxable person under paragraph 5(4)(*b*) of that Schedule; or

  (ii) the building has been fully occupied or the civil engineering work has been fully used before 1 March 1997; or

  (iii) the building or civil engineering work is the subject of an election to waive exemption, and input tax has been provisionally recovered in the anticipation of granting a taxable interest in it.

2. Examples of buildings or civil engineering works which might be within paragraph 1(*b*)(i) above are non-business NHS hospitals, government offices, and buildings and civil engineering works occupied or used by a local authority or similar body pursuant to its statutory non-business activities.

3. If a "developer"—

(a) has completed the construction of a building or civil engineering work before 1 March 1995; and

(b) considers that the building or work would not have been subject to the developer's self-supply had the provisions in paragraph 5(1)(*a*) of Schedule 10 to the Value Added Tax Act 1994 continued after 28 February 1997, but the situation is not described in paragraphs 1(a) to 1(b) above,

then that person may make an individual request in writing to the Commissioners of HM Revenue & Customs not to be treated as making a developer's self-supply on 1 March 1997.

Any reference in this concession to a building or civil engineering work includes a building or work which has been or is being reconstructed, enlarged or extended.

Commentary—*De Voil Indirect Tax Service* **V3.244.**

VALUE ADDED TAX
VAT NOTICES

CONTENTS

VAT NOTICES IN CURRENT ISSUE

Notice No	*Title*
48	Extra-statutory concessions (2002 with Updates 1 to 3) [see *Extra-statutory concessions* ante]
60	The Intrastat general guide (2004)
101	Deferring duty, VAT and other charges (2009)
160	Enquiries into indirect tax matters (2007)
700	The VAT guide (2002 with Updates 1 and 2) [part reproduced]
700/1	Should I be registered for VAT? (2009 with Updates 1 and 2)
700/2	Group and divisional registration (2004)
700/6	VAT rulings (March 2008)
700/7	Business promotion schemes (2002 with Update 1)
700/8	Disclosure of VAT avoidance schemes (2006) [reproduced]
700/9	Transfer of a business as a going concern (2008)
700/11	Cancelling your registration (with Update 1 and Supplement to Notices 700/1 and 700/11)
700/12	Filling in your VAT return (2002 with Updates 1, 2 and 3)
700/14	Video cassette films: rental and part-exchange (2004)
700/15	The ins and outs of VAT (2002)
700/17	Funded pension schemes (2002)
700/18	Relief from VAT on bad debts (2008 with Update 1)
700/21	Keeping records and accounts (2008)
700/24	Postage and delivery charges (2003)
700/25	Taxis and hire-cars (2002)
700/34	Staff (2005)
700/35	Business gifts and samples (1997)
700/41	Late registration penalty (2002)
700/42	Misdeclaration penalty and repeated misdeclaration penalty (2002)
700/43	Default interest (2003 with Update 1)
700/44	Barristers and advocates (2007)
700/45	How to correct VAT errors and make adjustments or claims (2002 with Updates 1 to 4)
700/46	Agricultural flat rate scheme (2002)
700/47	Confidentiality in VAT matters (tax advisers)—statement of practice (1993)
700/50	Default surcharge (2008 with Update 1)
700/52	Notice of requirement to give security to Customs and Excise (Statement of Practice, 2005, with Update 1)
700/56	Insolvency (2006, with Update 1)
700/57	Administrative agreements entered into with trade bodies (2004 with Update 1) [summary table reproduced]
700/58	Treatment of VAT repayment returns and VAT repayment supplement (2002 with Update 1)
700/60	Payments on account (2003)
700/62	Self billing (2003)
700/63	Electronic invoicing (2007)
700/64	Motoring expenses (2007)
700/65	Business entertainment (2002)
700/67	Registration scheme for racehorse owners (2002)
701/1	Charities (2004 with Updates 1 and 2)
701/2	Welfare (2007)
701/5	Clubs and associations (2002 with Update 1)
701/6	Charity-funded equipment for medical, veterinary, etc uses (2003 with Supplement issued in 1997)
701/7	VAT reliefs for disabled people (2002)
701/8	Postage stamps and philatelic supplies (2003)
701/9	Commodities and terminal markets (2002, with Update 1)
701/10	Zero-rating of books etc (2003 with Update 1)
701/12	Disposals of antiques, works of art etc from historic houses (2002)
701/13	Gaming and amusement machines (2004)
701/14	Food (2002)
701/15	Animals and animal food (2002)

Notice No	*Title*
701/16	Water and sewerage services (2002 with Update 1)
701/18	Woman's sanitary protection products (2002)
701/19	Fuel and power (2002 with Update 1)
701/20	Caravans and houseboats (2004)
701/21	Gold (2002) [part reproduced]
701/21A	Investment gold coins (2009) [part reproduced]
701/22	Tools for the manufacture of goods for export (2002)
701/23	Protective equipment (2002)
701/26	Betting and gaming (2004)
701/27	Bingo (2007)
701/28	Lotteries (2003)
701/30	Education and vocational training (2002 with Update 1)
701/31	Health institutions (2007)
701/32	Burial, cremation and the commemoration of the dead (2006 with Update 1)
701/35	Youth clubs (2004)
701/36	Insurance (2002 with Update 1) [part reproduced]
701/38	Seeds and plants (2003)
701/39	VAT liability law (2004)
701/40	Food processing services (2002)
701/41	Sponsorship (2002)
701/45	Sport (2002)
701/47	Culture (2003 with Updates 1 and 2)
701/48	Corporate purchasing cards (2002 with Update 1) [part reproduced]
701/49	Finance (2009)
701/57	Health professionals (2007)
701/58	Charity advertising and goods connected with collecting donations (2002 with Update 1)
701/59	Motor vehicles for disabled people (2002)
702	VAT: imports (2006)
702/7	Import VAT relief for goods supplied onward to another country in the European Community (2008)
702/8	Fiscal warehousing (2006 with Update 1)
702/9	Warehousing and free zones (updated 2005)
703	Exports and removals of goods from the UK (2006 with Update 1) [reproduced]
703/1	Supply of freight containers for export or removal from the UK (2004 with Updates 1, 2 and 3) [part reproduced]
703/2	Sailaway boats supplied for export outside the EC (2002 with Updates 1 and 2) [reproduced]
703/3	Sailaway boat scheme (2002 with Updates 1 and 2)
704	VAT retail exports (2004 with Update 1) [reproduced]
704/1	VAT refunds for travellers departing from the EC (2004) [reproduced]
705	Buyer's guide to personal exports of motor vehicles to destinations outside the EC (2004 with Update 1) [reproduced]
705A	Supplies of vehicles under the personal export scheme for removal from the EC (2004 with Update 1) [reproduced]
706	Partial exemption (2006)
706/2	Capital goods scheme (2002)
708	Buildings and construction (2008) [part reproduced]
708/6	Energy-saving materials (2002)
709/1	Catering and take-away food (2007 with Update 1)
709/3	Hotels and holiday accommodation (2002 with Updates 1 and 2)
709/5	Tour operators' margin scheme (2004) [part reproduced]
709/6	Travel agents and tour operators (2002)
714	Zero rating young children's clothing and footwear (2002)
718	Margin schemes for second-hand goods, works of art, antiques and collectors' items (2003 with Updates 1, 2 and 3) [part reproduced]
719	VAT refunds for "do-it-yourself" builders and converters (2002 with Update 1)
723	Refunds of VAT in the European Community for EC and non-EC businesses (2003, with Updates 1, 2 and 3)

Notice No	Title
725	The single market (2007, with Updates 1 & 2) [part reproduced]
726	Joint and several liability in the supply of specified goods (2008)
727	Retail schemes (2002, with Update 1) [reproduced]
727/2	Bespoke retail schemes (2006, with Update 1)
727/3	Retail schemes: how to work the point of sale scheme (2002 with Updates 1, 2) [reproduced]
727/4	Retail schemes: how to work the apportionment schemes (2002 with Updates 1, 2) [reproduced]
727/5	Retail schemes: how to work the direct calculation schemes (2002 with Updates 1, 2) [reproduced]
728	New means of transport (2008) [reproduced]
730	*Civil evasion penalty investigations: statement of practice* (superseded by Code of Practice 9 from 1/9/05)
731	Cash accounting (2008) [reproduced]
732	Annual accounting (2006 with Update 1)
733	Flat rate scheme for small businesses (2009 with Update 1) [reproduced]
735	VAT reverse charge for mobile phones and computer chips (2008)
741	Place of supply of services (2008)
742	Land and property (2002 with Updates 1, 2 and 3)
742/3	Scottish land law terms (2002 with Update 1)
742A	Opting to tax land and buildings (2008, Updated 2009) [reproduced]
744A	Passenger transport (2002)
744B	Freight transport and associated services (2006)
744C	Ships, aircraft and associated services (1997)
744D	International services: zero-rating (2002)
747	VAT notices having the force of law (2003) [reproduced]
749	Local authorities and similar bodies (2002)
915	Assessments and time limits: statements of practice (2002)
920	The single currency (1999)
930	What if I don't pay? (2002)
989	Visits by C & E officers (2002)
998	VAT refund scheme for National museums and galleries (2003, with Update 2)
999	Catalogue of publications (2005)
1000	Complaints and putting things right (2002)
Explanatory leaflet	Appeals and applications before the Tribunals (1995) [reproduced in the *Press Releases* section of this work]
CWL4	Fund-raising events: exemption for charities and other qualifying bodies (2001)

VAT INFORMATION SHEETS

5/95	VAT: change to the Tour Operators' Margin Scheme from 1 January 1996
6/95	VAT: NHS dispensing doctors
1/96	VAT: filling in your EC Sales List
3/96	Tour operators' margin scheme—practical implementation of the "airline charter option" following the changes which came into effect on 1 January 1996
4/96	Tour operators' margin scheme—practical implementation of the "agency option" following the changes which came into effect on 1 January 1996
1/97	Tour operators' margin scheme—practical implementation of the "trader to trader (wholesale) option" following the changes which came into effect on 1 January 1996
6/97	Drugs, medicines and aids for the handicapped—liability with effect from 1 January 1998
3/98	Local authorities and NHS—joint stores depots
5/98	Local authorities—supplies to new unitary authorities under local government reorganisation (transitional arrangements)
6/98	Local authority pension funds—VAT treatment and administrative concession
8/98	Charities—supply, repair and maintenance of relevant goods (and correction)
2/99	Local Authorities—agreement of s 33 methods
3/99	VAT—New Deal programme

6/99	Charities—liability of routine domestic tasks
8/99	Opticians—apportionment of charges for supplies of spectacles and dispensing
9/99	Imported works of art, antiques and collectors' pieces—changes to the reduced rate of VAT
10/99	Financial exemptions—changes brought about by the 1999 Finance Order
12/99	VAT on business cars—changes to take effect on 1 December 1999
2/00	Exports and removals—conditions for zero-rating
3/00	Supplies through undisclosed agents—revised VAT treatment
2/01	Single or multiple supplies: how to decide
3/01	VAT—Digitised publications
6/01	Changes to the VAT second-hand margin scheme
1/02	VAT civil evasion cases: a new approach to investigations—Statement of practice
4/02	Budget 2002: VAT—partial exemption – standard method override
1/03	Electronically supplied services and broadcasting services: New EU place of supply rules
2/03	Clarification of VAT treatment of services by financial advisers
3/03	Modernisation of Face Value Vouchers
4/03	Electronically supplied services: A guide to interpretation
5/03	Electronically supplied services: evidence of customer location and status
6/03	Tribunal decision on VAT treatment of repossessed and voluntarily returned cars
7/03	Electronically supplied services: special scheme for non-EU businesses
10/03	Electronically supplied services: supplementary information on the Special Scheme for non-EU businesses
11/03	Electronic Point of Sale (EPOS) systems
12/03	Face value vouchers
13/03	Electronically supplied services: special scheme for non-EU businesses—currency exchange rates for reporting period ending 30 September 2003
14/03	New time of supply rules for on-going supplies
15/03	The VAT treatment of share registration services
16/03	VAT Invoicing changes
17/03	Changes to the VAT flat-rate scheme
1/04	Electronically supplied services: special scheme for non-EU businesses—currency exchange rates for reporting period ending 31 December 2003
3/04	Electronically supplied services: EU Enlargement
4/04	Electronically supplied services: special scheme for non-EU businesses—currency exchange rates for reporting period ending 31 March 2004
5/04	Claims made in the light of GMAC High Court decision: VAT treatment of returned cars and other goods
6/04	Electronically supplied services: special scheme for non-EU businesses—currency exchange rates for reporting period ending 30 June 2004
7/04	Eligibility rules for VAT grouping
8/04	Electronically supplied services: special scheme for non-EU businesses—currency exchange rates for reporting period ending 30 September 2004
9/04	Partial exemption—fair recovery of VAT on costs of incidental financial supplies
10/04	Changes to the place of supply of natural gas and electricity
11/04	Electronically supplied services: special scheme for non-EU businesses—currency exchange rates for reporting period ending 31 December 2004
1/05	E-supplied services: special scheme non-EU businesses—exchange rates
2/05	Electronically supplied services: changes to Greece VAT rate
3/05	Electronically supplied services: Special scheme for non-EU businesses
4/05	Electronically supplied services: change to Portugal VAT rate
5/05	Electronically supplied services: Special scheme for non-EU businesses Sep 2005
6/05	Business travel agents
7/05	Clarification of place of supply policy
8/05	Recovery of VAT by businesses on fuel purchased by employees on their behalf
1/06	Electronically supplied services: currency exchange rates—period ending 12–05
2/06	Electronically supplied services: changes to Hungary VAT rate
3/06	Dispensing Doctors and VAT Registration
4/06	Liability of essential and advanced services supplied in England/Wales under NHS
5/06	Supplies of goods under finance agreements
6/06	Changes to the annual accounting scheme
9/06	Electronically supplied services: Special scheme for non-EU businesses
11/06	Guidance on the VAT treatment of certain Islamic products

1/07	Electronically supplied services: Special scheme for non-EU businesses
2/07	Electronically supplied services: Special scheme for non-EU businesses: VAT rates
3/07	Electronically supplied services: Special scheme for non-EU businesses: Germany
4/07	Electronically supplied services: Special scheme for non-EU businesses
5/07	Health professionals affected by changes to exemption for medical services
6/07	Reverse charge for purchases and sales of mobile phones and computer chips
7/07	Electronically supplied services: special scheme for non-EU businesses
8/07	Reverse charge for purchases and sales of mobile phones and computer chips
9/07	Electronically supplied services: special scheme for non-EU businesses
10/07	Changes to VAT invoicing with effect from October 2007
11/07	Accounting for VAT on standard-rated prescription products
12/07	Transfer of a Going Concern (TOGC): Changes to VAT record-keeping requirements
14/07	HMRC guidance: assets used partly for non-business purposes
15/07	Supply of parts and equipment for qualifying ships and aircraft
1/08	Electronically supplied services: Special Scheme for non-EU businesses
2/08	Electronically supplied services: Special Scheme for non-EU businesses
3/08	*Land and buildings: new Schedule 10 to VATA 1994* [see now Notice 742A]
4/08	Supplies of government grant funded research
5/08	Electronically supplied services: currency exchange rates to June 2008
6/08	Electronically supplied services: Special scheme for non-EU businesses—changes
7/08	VAT: Partial Exemption—adjustments when house builders let their dwellings
9/08	Special scheme for non-EU businesses – exchange rates for period ending Sept 08
10/08	Electronically supplied services: Special scheme for non-EU businesses
11/08	Electronically supplied services: changes to VAT rates
12/08	Electronically supplied services: Special scheme for non-EU businesses: Latvia
1/09	Electronically supplied services: Special scheme for non-EU businesses: changes
2/09	Special scheme for non-EU businesses: exchange rates for period ending Dec 2008
3/09	Withdrawal of the VAT Staff Hire Concession on 1 April 2009
4/09	VAT: Partial Exemption – changes to the standard method
5/09	Special scheme for non-EU businesses – exchange rates for period ending March 2009
6/09	VAT: Opting to tax supplies for land and buildings
7/09	Private use charge: manufacturer's company, dealer demonstrators & rental cars
8/09	Changes to the zero rate used for buildings used for a charitable use
9/09	Special Scheme for non-EU businesses – exchange rates for period ending Jun 2009
10/09	Electronically supplied services: Special scheme for non-EU businesses: changes
11/09	Electronically supplied services: Special scheme for non-EU businesses: changes
12/09	Changes to the operation of the option to tax on supplies of land and build

VAT NOTICES WITH THE FORCE OF LAW

Notice 747
VAT Notices having the force of law

June 2003

Under certain provisions of the Value Added Tax Act 1994, HM Customs & Excise have the power to determine the detailed requirements of VAT. These provisions and conditions are set out either in regulations made by statutory instrument (secondary legislation) or in notices which also have, in whole or in part, statutory authority (tertiary legislation). The notices which contain provisions having the force of law, cross-referenced to the relevant enabling powers, are listed [and reproduced] below.

Notice	*Part having the force of law and its purpose*	*Enabling powers*
Notice 700: The VAT Guide	Paragraph 7.7—values expressed in foreign currency.	VATA 1994 Sch 6 para 11

Notice	*Part having the force of law and its purpose*	*Enabling powers*
Notice 701/21: Gold	Section 3—para 3.1: notification. Section 4—paras 4.3–4.5: further notification requirements; para 4.6: invoicing requirements. Section 6—paras 6.2–6.4: further invoicing requirements. Section 7—paras 7.1–7.7: record-keeping requirements.	VATA 1994 ss 26, 31 VAT regs 1995 reg 31A VAT (Investment Gold) Order 1999 (SI 1999/3116)
Notice 701/21A: Investment Gold Coins	Section 3—list of investment gold coins.	VATA 1994 Sch 9, Group 15 VAT regs 1995 reg 31A VAT (Investment Gold) Order 1999 (SI 1999/3116)
Notice 701/36: Insurance	Paragraph 11.3.1: requirement to keep records Paragraph 11.3.2: relevant VAT invoice to be used when supplying goods or services under a VAT margin scheme	VATA 1994 Sch 11 para 6(1) VAT Regs 1995 regs 31(1) and 31(2) VATA 1994 Legal Note (4)(*c*)(iii) to Item 4 of Group 2, Schedule 9
Notice 701/48: Corporate purchasing cards	Para 3.3—Line Item Detail (LID) invoices. Para 3.4—the Summary VAT invoice.	VATA 1994 Sch 11 para 2 VAT Regs 1995 regs 13 and 14
Notice 703: Exports and removals of goods from the United Kingdom	Principally paras 2.2 and 8.4 but specific conditions relating to the zero-rating of particular types of supplies of goods for export outside the EC, or removal to another EC Member State, are contained throughout the Notice.	VATA 1994 ss 30(6), (8) and (10) VAT Regs 1995 regs 127, 129 and 134
Notice 703/1: Supply of freight containers for export or removal from the United Kingdom	Paras [2.3 and 2.4] contain the conditions which must be met in full in order to zero-rate supplies (by way of sale) of freight containers for export outside the EC or for removal to another EC Member State.	VATA 1994 ss 30(6), (8) and (10) VAT Regs 1995 regs 128, 134
Notice 703/2: Sailaway boats supplied for export outside the European Community	Principally section 3 which sets out the conditions to be complied with, but other paras outline additional conditions which must be met.	VATA 1994 s 30(8) VAT Regs 1995 reg 129
Notice 704: Retail exports	[The] notice expands on the conditions for the retailer to supply goods that can be zero-rated to entitled customers. The parts of this notice which have the force of law are indicated by three asterisks (***) at the beginning and end of the paragraph.	VATA 1994 s 30(8) VAT Regs 1995 regs 130 and 131
Notice 704/1: VAT refunds for travellers departing from the European Community	[The] notice expands on the conditions for travellers departing from the European Community and how they may be able to get a refund on some goods bought by using the Retail Export Scheme.	VATA 1994 s 30(8) VAT Regs 1995 regs 130 and 131
Notice 705: [Buyers guide to personal exports of new motor vehicles to destinations outside the European Community	[Provisions included in boxes within the text].	VATA 1994 s 30(8) VAT Regs 1995 regs 132 and 133

Notice	*Part having the force of law and its purpose*	*Enabling powers*
Notice 705A: VAT: Supplies of vehicles under the Personal Export Scheme for removal from the European Community	[Provisions included in boxes within the text].	VATA 1994 s 30(8) VAT Regs 1995 regs 132 and 133
Notice 708: Buildings and construction	Section 18, para 18.1—Certificate for developers and building contractors in respect of relevant residential and relevant charitable buildings	VATA 1994 Sch 7A, Group 6 para 8(2)(b), Group 7, para 4A(1)(b); Sch 8 Group 5 Note (12)(b)
Notice 709/5: Tour operators' margin scheme	The notice provides that certain goods and services which would otherwise be covered by the Margin Scheme are excluded, and specifies the method of calculation for the Margin Scheme	VATA 1994 s 53 VAT (Tour Operators) Order 1987 SI 1987/1806 arts 3 and 7 as amended by the VAT (Tour Operators) Orders of 1990, 1992 and 1995
Notice 718: Margin Schemes for second-hand goods, works of art, antiques and collectors' items	Section 3: Records and Accounts. Section 6: Global Accounting—records and accounts. Para 6.2—all apart from final sentence. Para 6.3. Para 6.4—final sentence. Para 6.5—all apart from final sub-para. Para 6.6—all apart from final sentence. Para 6.7; Para 6.9. Section 7: The Auctioneers' Scheme—basic principles. Para 7.3—final sentence. Section 8: The Auctioneers' Scheme—records and accounts. Para 8.1; Para 8.2 Section 22: Horses and ponies. Para 22.7—final sub-para.	VATA 1994 s 50A. VAT (Cars) Order 1992 (SI 1992/3122) as amended VAT (Special Provisions) Order 1995 (SI 1995/1268) as amended VAT (Input Tax) Order 1992 (SI 1992/3222) as amended
Notice 725: VAT: The Single Market	[Provisions included in boxes within the text].	VATA 1994 s 30(8) VATA 1994 Sch 7 para 4

VAT

Notice	*Part having the force of law and its purpose*	*Enabling powers*
Notice 727: VAT: Retail schemes	Section 2.1: When should I use a retail scheme? Section 2.2: What if my business makes retail and non-retail sales? Section 2.4: Can I use a retail scheme for sales to other VAT registered businesses? Section 3.4: How does the Point of Sale scheme work? Section 3.7: What factors should I consider before choosing Apportionment Scheme (1)? Section 3.9: What factors should I consider before using Apportionment Scheme (2)? Section 3.12: What factors should I consider before using Direct Calculation scheme(1)? Section 4.1: Can I use a mixture of schemes? Section 4.2: Can I change schemes? Section 4.4: Do I need to keep a record of my Daily Gross Takings? Section 5.1: What is a bespoke scheme? Section 6.1: What must I do when I cease using a retail scheme? Section 6.2: Are there any other rules when ceasing to use a scheme? Section 8.3: What are the conditions for using the catering adaptation? schemes or Apportionment Scheme (1)? Section 8.5: How do I start to use the adaptation? Section 8.6: Do I have to maintain any records? Section 8.7: How do I calculate my output tax under the catering adaptation? Section 8.8: How do I calculate the percentage of my standard-rated sales? Section 9.4: How does the adjustment work if I use the Direct Calculation? Section 9.5: How do I estimate the percentage of zero-rated supplies?	VATA 1994 Sch 11 para 2(6) VAT Regs 1995 Part IX (regs 66–75)
Notice 727/3: Retail schemes: How to work the Point of Scale scheme	Section 2: General rules—paras 2.3–2.5. Section 3: The Point of Sale Scheme—paras 3.2–3.4. Section 4: Mechanics of the Point of Sale Scheme—para 4.2. Section 5: Daily Gross Takings (DGT) checklist—paras 5.1–5.5. Section 6: Special transactions. Section 7: Business promotions—paras 7.2–7.6.	VATA 1994 Sch 11 para 2(6) VAT Regs 1995 Part IX (SI 1995/2518) (regs 66–75)
Notice 727/4: Retail schemes. How to work the Apportionment Schemes	Section 2: General rules—paras 2.3–2.5. Section 3: Basic principles of Apportionment Schemes 1 and 2—paras 3.2–3.6. Section 4: Mechanics of Apportionment Scheme 1—paras 4.2–4.3. Section 5: Mechanics of Apportionment Scheme 2—paras 5.2–5.4. Section 6: Daily Gross Takings (DGT) checklist—paras 6.1–6.5. Section 7: Special transactions. Section 8: Business promotions.	VATA 1994 Sch 11 para 2(6) VAT Regs 1995 Part IX (SI 1995/2518) (regs 66–75)

Notice	*Part having the force of law and its purpose*	*Enabling powers*
Notice 727/5: Retail schemes. How to work the Direct Calculation schemes	Section 2: General rules—paras 2.3–2.5. Section 3: Basic Principles of Direct Calculation Schemes 1 and 2—paras 3.1–3.7. Section 4: Mechanics of the Direct Calculation Schemes (1 and 2)—paras 4.2–4.5. Section 5: Daily Gross Takings (DGT) checklist—paras 5.1–5.5. Section 6: Special transactions. Section 7: Business promotions.	VATA 1994 Sch 11 para 2(6) VAT Regs 1995 Part IX (SI 1995/2518) (regs 66–75)
Notice 728: New Means of Transport	Para 6.1—What happens when I buy an NMT in the UK for removal to another member state? and para 3.6—rate of exchange used to calculate the value of an NMT. Other conditions and procedures to be complied with are set out elsewhere in the Notice	VATA 1994 s 30(8); Sch 7 para 4(2) VAT Regs 1995 reg 155
Notice 731: Cash accounting	Section 2: Basics of cash accounting. Para 2.1—final sub-para. Para 2.3—first sub-para. Para 2.5—final sub-para. Section 3: Records and accounting for VAT. Para 3.2.2—first sub-para. Para 3.3—final sub-para. Para 3.4.1—final sub-para. Para 3.4.2—final sub-para. Section 4: Special rules for particular transactions. Para 4.2—first sub-para. Para 4.3—first sub-para. Para 4.5—first sub-para. Para 4.7—second sub-para. Para 4.8—final sub-para. Section 5: Leaving the cash accounting scheme. Para 5.3—first line, second sub-para. Para 5.6—final sub-para. Para 5.7.2—first sub-para. Para 5.9—final sub-para.	VATA 1994 s 25(1) and Sch 11 para. 2(7) VAT Regs 1995 regs 56–65 as amended by VAT (Amendment) (No 3) Regulations 1997
Notice 733: Flat rate scheme for small businesses	Para 6.4: Records to be kept. Para 7.11: Stock adjustment. Para 9.4: Time of payment. Para 9.5: Value of payment. Para 9.6: Value of Supply. Para 9.7: Ceasing to use the cash-based method. Para 10.3: Value of Daily Gross Takings. Para 10.4: Value of Daily Gross Takings. Para 10.6: Adjustment to Daily Gross Takings.	The primary legislation is contained in the VATA 1994 s 26B, as amended by FA 2002 This is supplemented by more detailed rules in Regs 55A to 55V to the VAT Regulations 1995
Notice 742: Opting to tax land and buildings	[Paras 2.6.3, 3.4.2, 3.6.2, 5.5, 6.3.6, 6.3.8; 8.1.3, 8.1.5, 8.3.3, 8.3.5 and 14.8; and Text within boxes A–L in paragraphs 2.6.4, 3.4.3, 3.6.3, 5.2, 6.3.5, 8.1.2, 8.3.2, 13.10.1, 14.6, 14.8 and 14.11.]	[VATA 1994 Sch 10]

Notice 700
The VAT guide

2002 (with Updates 1 and 2)

7. OUTPUT TAX: INTRODUCTION AND TAX VALUE

…

7.7 Values expressed in a foreign currency

> Paragraph 7.7 in this Notice has the force of law under the VAT Act 1994, Schedule 6, paragraph 11.

For VAT purposes, amounts of money must always be expressed in sterling. If you need to convert an amount from a foreign currency into sterling, you must do so on the following basis:

(*a*) Unless you have adopted one of the alternatives set out below, you must use the UK market selling rate at the time of the supply. The rates published in national newspapers will be acceptable as evidence of the rates at the relevant time; or

(*b*) As an alternative, you may use the period rate of exchange published by Customs and Excise for customs purposes. Our National Advice Service can give you details of particular period rates. You may adopt this alternative for **all** your supplies or for all supplies of a particular class or description. If you opt for only a particular class or description, you should make a note of the details in your records at the time of adoption.

You do not need to notify us in advance if you wish to adopt this alternative, but having made such an option, you cannot then change it without first getting the agreement of the VAT Business Centre for your area; or

(*c*) You may apply in writing to the VAT Business Centre for your area to use a rate—or method of determining a rate—which you use for commercial purposes but which is not covered by (*a*) or (*b*) above.

In considering whether to allow such applications, local VAT offices will take into account—

- whether the proposed rate or method is determined by reference to the UK currency market;
- whether it is objectively verifiable; and
- the frequency with which it is proposed to update it. Forward rates or methods deriving from forward rates are not acceptable.

Whatever rate or method you adopt, the appropriate rate for any supply is that current at the time of the supply.

If you make supplies that fall within the tour operators' margin scheme, see Notice 709/5 "Tour operators' margin scheme" for details of how to convert the value of your purchases.

Commentary—*De Voil Indirect Tax Service* **V3.103.**

Notice 700/8
Disclosure of VAT avoidance schemes

February 2006

This notice cancels and replaces Notice 700/8 (August 2004). It also cancels Business Brief 34/04, part 3 (VAT Avoidance Disclosures Unit – change of address).

Paragraphs 5.2, 5.4, 8.2 and 8.7 of this notice, which explain how to make a notification and where to send it, have the force of law under the VAT (Disclosure of Avoidance Schemes) Regulations 2004, regulation 3. These paragraphs are indicated by being placed in a box.

1 INTRODUCTION

1.1 What is this notice about?

This notice is about what to do when you enter into arrangements or transactions that are intended to give you or any other person a VAT advantage when compared to adopting a different course of action.

This notice does not cover the rules for notifying arrangements relating to Income Tax, Corporation Tax, Capital Gains Tax or Stamp Duty Land Tax. The rules for these taxes are explained in guidance available on the Anti Avoidance Group's page on HM Revenue & Customs' Internet website:

www.hmrc.gov.uk/aiu/index.htm.

1.2 What's changed?

This notice has been revised to include legislative changes made since the last version to the meaning of "tax advantage", the "duty to notify" rules, and the range of "listed schemes" and "hallmarks". It also corrects some minor errors and expands on the guidance to help you identify the schemes that must be notified.

Following restructuring within HM Revenue & Customs, the address for disclosing a notifiable arrangement has also been changed – see paragraphs 5.4 and 8.7.

You can access details of any changes since February 2006 on our Internet website at www.hmrc.gov.uk or by telephoning the National Advice Service on 0845 010 9000.

This notice and others mentioned are available both on paper and on our website.

1.3 Who should read this notice?

You should read this notice if you are, or are liable to be, registered for VAT in the UK, and either—

(a) enter into one of 10 specific arrangements (known in this notice as "listed schemes") that the Treasury have designated as having been, or might be, entered into for the purpose of enabling any person to obtain a VAT advantage; or

(b) enter into, or knowingly become a party to, any other arrangements or transactions that are intended to give you or any other person a VAT advantage and which include, or are associated with, one of 8 "hallmarks" of tax avoidance.

More detailed criteria on whether the rules for "listed schemes" or "hallmarked" schemes affect you can be found from paragraphs 4.1 and 7.1 respectively.

In general, you will not need to read this notice if you, or where you are a member of a corporate group, the whole group, make taxable and exempt supplies totalling below £150,000 per quarterly VAT accounting period or £50,000 if you submit monthly returns.

It is suggested you also read this notice if you devise or sell VAT avoidance, planning or mitigation schemes, arrangements or devices.

1.4 WHAT LAW COVERS THIS NOTICE?

The main relevant law is as follows—

- The meaning of "tax advantage" and "notifiable scheme", and the duty to notify and penalty provisions, are prescribed in: Sch 11A to VATA 1994 (as inserted by s 19 and Sch 2 to the Finance Act 2004 with effect from 1 August 2004; and amended by s 6 and Sch 1 to the Finance (No 2) Act 2005 with effect from 1 August 2005);
- Transitional provisions relating to changes in 2005 to the meaning of "tax advantage" and the duty to notify provisions are found in: the Finance (No 2) Act 2005 s 6, (Appointed Day and Savings Provisions) Order 2005 (SI 2005/2010).
- The "listed schemes" and "hallmarks" are described in: the VAT (Disclosure of Avoidance Schemes) (Designations) Order 2004 (SI 2004/1933) (as amended by the VAT (Disclosure of Avoidance Schemes) (Designations) (Amendment) Order 2005 (SI 2005/1724) with effect from 1 August 2005).
- The time of notification, and information to be notified, is prescribed in: the VAT (Disclosure of Avoidance Schemes) Regulations 2004 (SI 2004/1929) (as amended by the VAT (Disclosure of Avoidance Schemes) (Amendment) Regulations 2005 (SI 2005/2009) with effect from 1 August 2005).

Commentary—*De Voil Indirect Tax Service* **V5.213.**

2 OBTAINING A VAT ADVANTAGE

2.1 Can I structure my affairs so as to obtain a VAT advantage?

Yes, provided what you do is not dishonest. However, under the rules explained in this notice, you may need to formally tell us about what you are doing; and we might decide to challenge whether the structure achieves the intended advantage (see also paragraph 3.10).

Note: If you are required to tell us what you are doing, you may be liable to a *penalty* if you do not provide us on time with the information explained in this notice.

2.2 Can I get a ruling on the arrangements and transactions I'm planning to do?

Notice 700/6 "VAT rulings" explains how you can normally obtain our view on how transactions should be treated for VAT. However, we will not "approve" tax planning arrangements and will refuse to give rulings where we suspect that the transactions are part of a tax avoidance scheme.

2.3 What happens if I obtain a VAT advantage dishonestly?

The matter could be investigated as either a criminal investigation or under the civil investigation of fraud procedures. Civil investigations are undertaken in accordance with Code of Practice 9, which can be accessed at: www.hmrc.gov.uk/leaflets/c11.htm

Commentary—*De Voil Indirect Tax Service* **V5.213.**

3 ABOUT NOTIFYING HM REVENUE & CUSTOMS

3.1 What must I tell HM Revenue and Customs about?

You must tell us about—

- certain arrangements that are named and described in the relevant law (referred to in this notice as "listed schemes") – see paragraph 3.4 below and sections 4 to 6; and
- arrangements and transactions that include or are associated with at least one of a range of designated provisions that are often linked with avoidance (referred to in this notice as "hallmarks" and "hallmarked schemes") – see paragraph 3.6 below and sections 7, 8 and 10.

3.2 Does everyone have to notify?

No. Only taxable persons (ie those who are, or are liable to be, registered for VAT in the UK) have to notify.

Even then, various filters, or tests, may mean you do not have to notify. For example, your turnover may be below the relevant threshold. The detailed rules are explained in sections 4 and 7 for listed schemes and hallmarked schemes respectively.

There is also a voluntary facility that allows any person to register a hallmarked scheme with us. Businesses using one of these registered schemes may be exempt from having to separately notify (see paragraph 7.8 and section 9).

3.2.1 VAT groups

The representative member of a VAT group is responsible for notifying schemes involving group members – see also paragraph 3.3.2.

3.3 Does only the beneficiary of the VAT advantage have to notify?

No. Any taxable person (see paragraph 3.2 above) who is a party to a notifiable scheme may have to tell us about the scheme.

3.3.1 "A party to a scheme"

You are a party to a scheme if you knowingly take part in it.

You are not a party to a scheme if you—

(a) are unwittingly involved in any of the steps of the scheme (ie you have no knowledge of either the existence of the scheme or the role you play in it); or

(b) act purely in an advisory capacity.

3.3.2 VAT groups

Where a member of a VAT group is a contractual party in a notifiable scheme, the duty to disclose falls on the representative member of the group.

The notification should provide the name of the group member who is involved in the scheme as well as the name and registration number of the representative member – see paragraphs 5.2 and 8.2.

3.3.3 What if another party to the scheme has already made a notification?

You must still notify us.

3.3.4 Joint notifications

Where more than one party is obliged to notify us, the parties concerned can make a joint notification. The notification should make it clear that it is a joint notification, who all the parties are that are making the notification, and provide the information set out in paragraph 5.3 or 8.3 as appropriate.

3.4 What are the listed schemes?

The schemes are—

- Scheme 1 – The first grant of a major interest in a building (see paragraphs 6.1 and 6.2);
- Scheme 2 – Payment handling services (see paragraphs 6.1 and 6.3);
- Scheme 3 – Value shifting (see paragraphs 6.1 and 6.4);
- Scheme 4 – Leaseback agreements (see paragraphs 6.1 and 6.5);
- Scheme 5 – Extended approval periods (see paragraphs 6.1 and 6.6);
- Scheme 6 – Groups: third party suppliers (see paragraphs 6.1 and 6.7);
- Scheme 7 – Education and training by a non-profit making body (see paragraphs 6.1 and 6.8);
- Scheme 8 – Education and training by a non-eligible body (see paragraphs 6.1 and 6.9); and
- Scheme 9 – Cross-border face-value vouchers (see paragraphs 6.1 and 6.10); and
- Scheme 10 – Surrender of a relevant lease (see paragraphs 6.1 and 6.11).

3.5 New listed schemes

The range of listed schemes may be updated periodically by the making of a new Treasury Statutory Instrument. We will give one month's notice of the intention to list a new scheme, so that interested parties can let us have their views on the proposals. Notice of such proposed changes will be given on our Internet site at www.hmrc.gov.uk.

3.6 What are the hallmarks?

The hallmarks are—

- Confidentiality condition agreements (see paragraphs 10.1 and 10.2);
- Agreements to share a tax advantage (see paragraphs 10.1 and 10.3);
- Contingent fee agreements (see paragraphs 10.1 and 10.4);
- Prepayments between connected parties (see paragraphs 10.1 and 10.5);
- Funding by loans, share subscriptions or subscriptions in securities (see paragraphs 10.1 and 10.6);
- Off-shore loops (see paragraphs 10.1 and 10.7);
- Property transactions between connected persons (see paragraphs 10.1 and 10.8); and
- The issue of face-value vouchers (see paragraphs 10.1 and 10.9).

3.7 What if HM Revenue & Customs already know I am using a notifiable scheme?

You must still notify us under the rules set out in this notice.

3.8 What don't I have to notify?

There is no "white list" of schemes that do not require notification. If you have a liability to notify us about a scheme, you should do so even if you believe we already know about the type of scheme you are using.

Section 11 explains our view on some frequently encountered issues to do with hallmarked schemes.

3.9 Will my notification be made public?

Notifications are subject to the normal rules of taxpayer confidentiality found in the Commissioners for Revenue & Customs Act 2005 and, other than in the exceptional circumstances allowed for, are not made public. However, if we challenge what you are doing and the matter progresses to the Courts the hearing is likely to be held in public.

3.10 Are all notified arrangements regarded as avoidance and challenged?

No. Whilst we have tried to keep the burden to a minimum, you may have to tell us about arrangements that we do not consider to be avoidance.

We will examine all notifications sent to us and might decide to investigate further, challenging the arrangements where appropriate. This may mean that you are issued with an assessment for an amount of tax that we believe has been incorrectly declared. Should the arrangements give rise to a tax liability over and above what would have been due if the arrangements had not been entered into, an assessment may also be issued for this additional amount.

As well as the notified arrangements, an investigation may include an examination of other arrangements that you use in your business.

Commentary—*De Voil Indirect Tax Service* **V5.213.**

4 LISTED SCHEMES – DECIDING WHETHER YOU MUST NOTIFY

4.1 Decision chart

You must notify use of a listed scheme when *all* of the following tests are met—

Test	*Description*	*Further information*
1	You are a *taxable person*	Paragraph 3.2
2	You are a *party* to a *listed scheme*	Paragraph 3.3 and section 6
3	A *relevant event* occurs	Paragraph 4.2
4	Your *turnover* exceeds either of the minimum thresholds	Paragraphs 4.3
5	You have *not already notified* HM Revenue & Customs, as required under the rules set out in this notice, that you are using the scheme	Paragraph 4.4

Section 5 explains by when you must make your notification, the information it should contain and where to send it.

4.2 Relevant events that trigger notification

The requirement for you to notify is triggered when one of the following events occurs to you—

- You show in a VAT return, in respect of any VAT accounting period starting on or after 1 August 2004, a higher or lower net amount of VAT than would be the case but for the listed scheme.
- You make a claim (such as by submitting a voluntary disclosure), in respect of any VAT accounting period starting on or after 1 August 2004 for which a VAT return has been

submitted, for the repayment of output tax over-declared or input tax credit under-claimed that is greater than would be the case but for the listed scheme.
- The amount of non-deductible VAT (see paragraph 4.2.1 below) you incur, in respect of any VAT accounting period starting on or after 1 August 2005, would have been higher but for the listed scheme.

4.2.1 Non-deductible VAT incurred

VAT is, or would have been, incurred by you when it is, or would have been—

- VAT on the supply to you of any goods or services (including VAT on reverse charges);
- VAT on the acquisition by you from another member state of any goods; or
- VAT paid or payable by you on the importation of any goods from a place outside the EU.

It is, or would have been, non-deductible VAT when it is, or would have been—

- VAT that is input tax, but for which you are not entitled to credit; or
- VAT that is not input tax, and for which you are not entitled to a refund under any provision of VATA 1994.

Commentary—*De Voil Indirect Tax Service* **V5.213.**

4.3 The minimum turnover thresholds

The turnover threshold is measured by reference to the *total* amount of *taxable and exempt* supplies made by—

- you; or
- where you are a member of a corporate group, *the whole group*, made up of the ultimate holding company (or entity) and all its subsidiaries, including you. For this purpose UK company law definitions used for preparing group accounts apply (s 259 of the Companies Act 1985). As a result the group will normally be made up of all the companies shown as subsidiaries in the ultimate parent's consolidated group accounts, plus any companies that are excluded from the consolidation but are subsidiaries for UK company law purposes.

For the purpose of calculating turnover, intra-corporate group transactions are included. However, intra-VAT group transactions are ignored.

4.3.1 The threshold

Your turnover exceeds the minimum threshold when the total amount of *taxable and exempt* supplies made by you (or the wider corporate group as explained above) is, or is greater than—

(a) £600,000 in the year immediately prior to the VAT accounting period that triggers notification (see paragraph 4.2); or
(b) the appropriate proportion of £600,000 in the VAT accounting period immediately prior to the VAT accounting period that triggers notification. (For example, the "appropriate proportion" is one twelfth of £600,000 (ie £50,000) where the VAT accounting period is one month; and one quarter of £600,000 (ie £150,000) where the VAT accounting period is three months.)

4.3.2 Disaggregation

Should we find that a taxable person's business has been split in an attempt to avoid the requirement to make a notification, we will use our powers to direct that the separate entities be treated as one. If it is found later that other entities should have been included in that direction, a supplementary direction can be made to include them. The effect a supplementary direction has on the timing of a notification is explained in paragraph 5.1.5.

Commentary—*De Voil Indirect Tax Service* **V2.190C.**

4.4 Exemption for previously notified schemes

4.4.1 General

The use of some schemes will only trigger one relevant event (see paragraph 4.2). Others, such as a payment handling service, are designed to give an ongoing VAT benefit over time. Consequently, more than one relevant event may occur. The use of such a scheme only has to be notified once.

However, a listed scheme may be used more than once. For example, listed scheme 1 (first grant of a major interest) may be used to remove the VAT cost of refurbishing more than one property. Where this happens, each adoption of the scheme must be notified, but you only need tell us once about each case.

Paragraph 5.3 explains what information to provide.

4.4.2 Listed schemes notified under the rules for hallmarked schemes

The range of listed schemes may change (see paragraph 3.5). If you have previously notified your use of a listed scheme under the rules for hallmarked schemes, you are not required to make a new notification when the scheme becomes "listed".

If the scheme is used again, you must notify the new arrangements – see paragraph 4.4.1.

Commentary—*De Voil Indirect Tax Service* **V5.213.**

5 LISTED SCHEMES – HOW TO NOTIFY HM REVENUE & CUSTOMS

5.1 By what date must I notify HM Revenue & Customs?

Your notification must be made to HM Revenue & Customs within 30 days of—

- in the case of the net amount of VAT shown in a VAT return being different to what would otherwise be the case (see the first bullet at paragraph 4.2), the due date for making the return;
- in the case of a claim being made that is greater than would otherwise be the case (see the second bullet at paragraph 4.2), the making of the claim; or
- in the case of the amount of your non-deductible VAT in respect of a VAT accounting period being less than would otherwise be the case (see the third bullet at paragraph 4.2), the due date for making a return in respect of that accounting period.

For examples of when a notification is due see paragraphs 5.1.3 to 5.1.4.

5.1.1 Early notifications

HM Revenue & Customs will accept early notifications, such as before the relevant event has taken place, provided the scheme has been implemented.

5.1.2 Transitional rules for newly listed schemes

Use of listed schemes 1 to 8 need only be notified when a relevant event takes place in relation to an accounting period starting on or after 1 August 2004.

Use of listed schemes 9 and 10 need only be notified when a relevant event takes place in relation to an accounting period starting on or after 1 August 2005.

5.1.3 Examples of due date for notifying when a return is affected (for listed schemes 1 to 8)

Examples of the notification due date, when the net amount of VAT shown on a return is affected by the scheme, include—

Period of affected VAT return	*Due date for submitting return*	*Notification due*
1 June 2004 to 31 August 2004	30 September 2004	No notification required (return starts before 1 August 2004)
1 August 2004 to 31 August 2004	30 September 2004	30 October 2004
1 August 2004 to 31 October 2004	30 November 2004	30 December 2004
1 September 2004 to 30 November 2004	31 December 2004	30 January 2005
1 October 2004 to 31 December 2004	31 January 2005	2 March 2005

If you pay VAT due on a return by an approved electronic method you may be entitled to an extension to the due date for submitting your return. If this is the case, the due date for notifying a scheme is 30 days after the extended due date for submitting the return.

5.1.4 Examples of due date for notifying when a claim is affected (for listed schemes 1 to 8)

Examples of the notification due date, when the amount of VAT being claimed is affected by use of the scheme, include—

VAT return period covered by affected claim	*Date claim is made*	*Notification due*
1 August 2004 to 31 August 2004	27 November 2004	27 December 2004
1 July 2004 to 30 September 2004	14 January 2005	No notification required (return starts before 1 August 2004)
1 October 2004 to 31 December 2004	29 August 2005	28 September 2005

5.1.5 Directions that taxpayers are treated as one

Where HM Revenue & Customs issue a direction that a number of taxpayers should be treated as one (see paragraph 4.3.2), the due date is determined by reference to the first relevant event (see paragraph 4.2) that takes place following the issue of the direction.

5.2 How do I notify HM Revenue & Customs?

The following rule has the force of law

You must notify us either in writing or by email to the relevant address given at paragraph 5.4. The notification should be prominently headed:

- Disclosure of use of listed scheme – Notification under para 6(2) of Sch 11A to VATA 1994.

and give your:

- business name (if you are the representative member of a VAT group, notifying as a result of a group member being involved in a notifiable scheme, also tell us the name of the member);
- address; and
- VAT registration number.

5.3 What information must I provide?

The only information you must provide is the number of the scheme, which can be found in section 6. Your obligation to notify is fulfilled on receipt of the required information at one of the addresses given in paragraph 5.4.

On some occasions you may use more than one scheme at the same time (see paragraph 4.4). Where this happens you must tell us about all of the schemes of each type that are being used and haven't previously been reported.

For joint notifications, see paragraph 3.3.4.

5.4 Where do I send my notification?

The following rule has the force of law

You must send your notification to either of the addresses given below.

Post to:
VAT Avoidance Disclosures Unit
Anti-Avoidance Group (Intelligence)
HM Revenue & Customs
1st Floor, 22 Kingsway
London WC2B 6NR

Or e-mail to:

vat.avoidance.disclosures.bst@hmrc.gsi.gov.uk

5.5 What if I send my notification to another address?

If you send your notification to an address other than those given in paragraph 5.4 (for example your local office or the National Advice Service), you will not have made a proper notification. Failure to make a proper notification will make you liable to a penalty as explained in section 12.

5.6 How will HM Revenue & Customs deal with my notification?

We will acknowledge receipt of all notifications received at the addresses given in paragraph 5.4, and consider whether we wish to investigate – see paragraph 3.10. If we do not contact you, this does not mean the arrangements are acceptable to us.

If we are already investigating your use of the notified scheme, that investigation will continue as appropriate.

Commentary—*De Voil Indirect Tax Service* **V5.213.**

6 THE LISTED SCHEMES

6.1 Descriptions of the listed schemes

The listed schemes are described in paragraphs 6.2 to 6.9 below. (Note: Arrangements that are not covered by a listed scheme may need to be notified as a hallmarked scheme – see section 7.)

The descriptions are intended only as a guide and are not a substitute for the descriptions contained in the relevant law (see paragraph 1.4). For each scheme there is—

- a list of the identifying features of the scheme;
- an example of arrangements that are covered by the listed scheme; and
- in some cases, examples of ones that are not.

6.1.1 Whether the features of a scheme are present

A feature of a scheme is regarded as being present when it is either—

- present as a matter of fact; or
- a taxable person treats it as being present for the purpose of making a VAT return or

voluntary disclosure, even if it is not actually present (whether as a matter of law or for any other reason). For example, a feature of a scheme may rely on a transaction being a supply for VAT purposes. If, for the purpose of making a return, a taxable person treats the transaction as being such a supply, then the feature is regarded as being present (for the purposes of deciding whether disclosure is required), even if it is subsequently found, say by the Courts, that there has been no supply as a matter of law.

6.1.2 Connected persons

For the purposes of the scheme descriptions a person is connected with another where—

- one of them is an undertaking in relation to which the other is a group undertaking as defined by s 259 of the Companies Act 1985 (essentially, one is the parent or subsidiary undertaking of the other, or both are subsidiaries of a common parent undertaking); or
- both of them are connected to the same trust.

A person is connected to a trust where he—

- is the settlor of the trust, or a trustee or beneficiary of it; or
- holds any shares in a company in accordance with the terms of the trust, or is a person on whose behalf such shares are held.

Commentary—*De Voil Indirect Tax Service* **V5.213.**

6.2 Scheme 1 – The first grant of a major interest in a building

This scheme aims to remove the VAT cost of extending, enlarging, repairing, refurbishing or servicing buildings that are zero-rated when sold by developers.

Examples of the buildings concerned are houses, student halls of residence and buildings used by charities for non-business activities.

6.2.1 The scheme's features

The scheme comprises or includes the following features—

(a) a zero-rated major interest grant is made in the building (see Notice 708 "Buildings and construction") to a connected person (see paragraph 6.1.2); and

(b) the following input tax is attributed to the grant:

- input tax in respect of a service charge relating to the building; or
- input tax in connection with any extension, enlargement, repair, maintenance or refurbishment of the building (other than for remedying defects In the original construction).

6.2.2 Examples of arrangements included in the listed scheme

A housing landlord may seek to use this scheme to recover input tax on the renovation of houses that he had constructed several years earlier. Having decided that some of the houses require major refurbishment, the landlord leases or sells them to a subsidiary in such a way that he attributes to that zero-rated disposal the VAT on the refurbishment, which may be undertaken either before or after the grant. The subsidiary may then simply lease the houses back to the landlord so that he can then let them on again to tenants.

By way of another example, the builder of new halls of residence may try to recover future input tax on repairs and maintenance of the buildings, even though his income from the property at that time will be exempt, by building into the initial zero-rated lease or sale a payment for, and agreement to provide, repairs and maintenance in the future.

6.2.3 Examples of arrangements not included in the listed scheme

This listed scheme does not include arrangements where—

(a) the zero-rated grant is made under VATA 1994, Sch 8, Group 5, Item 1(b) (person converting a non-residential building);

(b) the zero-rated grant is made under VATA 1994, Sch 8, Group 6, Item 1 (substantial reconstruction of a protected building); or

(c) there is no zero-rated grant made to a connected person.

Commentary—*De Voil Indirect Tax Service* **V5.213.**

6.3 Scheme 2 – Payment handling services

This scheme aims to reduce the VAT due on the advertised price of retail goods or services by transforming an element of the price into an exempt payment handling service (such as credit/debit card or cash handling).

6.3.1 The scheme's features

The scheme comprises or includes the following features—

- a retail supply of goods or services;
- a linked supply to the same customer, by the retailer or any person, that relates to the means of payment used for the retail supply and is a supply of a description falling within VATA 1994, Sch 9, Group 5 (finance); and

– the total consideration due for the retail supply and linked supply is no different, or not significantly different, from what it would be for the retail supply alone.

6.3.2 Example of arrangements included in the listed scheme

When a customer presents his goods at the till, and decides to pay by credit or debit card rather than cash, he may be informed that part of the ticket price is being paid to a separate company and is in consideration for processing or accepting his credit card as the means of payment. Agreements signed or agreed by the customer at the point of sale may be alleged to support this. The total amount paid by the customer remains the same whether or not the handling service is actually used or needed by the customer but is separated into a reduced value for the taxable goods and an exempt amount paid to the separate company. There is no comparable reduction in the value for the goods if he chooses to pay by cash.

Commentary—*De Voil Indirect Tax Service* **V5.213.**

6.4 Scheme 3 – Value shifting

This scheme aims to transfer value from standard-rated retail supplies into linked zero-rated or exempt supplies.

6.4.1 The schemes features

The scheme comprises or includes the following features—

(a) a standard-rated retail supply of goods or services;
(b) a linked zero-rated or exempt supply by any person to the same customer;
(c) the linked supply is treated as a separate supply under the terms of an agreement made by the customer;
(d) the terms of the agreement attribute part of the consideration for the retail supply and linked supply to the linked supply; and
(e) the total consideration due for the retail supply and linked supply is no different, or not significantly different, from what it would be for the retail supply alone.

6.4.2 Example of arrangements included in the listed scheme

A retail customer making a large purchase may find that, at the point of sale, he is offered an insurance product with the goods. Rather than paying an additional amount for this cover, the customer will be informed that the ticket price has now been apportioned to cover both the goods and the insurance. If the customer then says he does not want the insurance, there is no reduction of the ticket price to reflect this. The overall price paid by the customer remains the same whether he takes the insurance or not.

6.4.3 Examples of arrangements not included in the listed scheme

Notification is not required when the linked goods or services are supplied free, with no part of the price being attributed to that supply.

Additionally notification is not required for normal business promotion arrangements. For example: a retailer offers a "meal deal" where customers can buy a sandwich, a soft drink and packet of crisps for a single price that is lower than the normal combined price of the three items. When apportioning the cost between the zero-rated and standard-rated items the retailer spreads the discount across all the goods supplied. These arrangements are unlikely to be notifiable as each linked supply would not normally be subject to a separate agreement with the customer; and the total amount payable is likely to be significantly different from what it would be for the standard rated element alone.

Commentary—*De Voil Indirect Tax Service* **V5.213.**

6.5 Scheme 4 – Leaseback agreements

This scheme aims to defer or reduce the VAT cost of acquiring goods by a business that cannot recover all of the input tax on those goods were it to directly buy them itself.

6.5.1 The scheme's features

The scheme comprises or includes the following features—

(a) a person (the "relevant person") receives a supply of goods, or the leasing or letting on hire of goods;
(b) he uses the goods in his business, but is not entitled to full input tax credit for the VAT on the supply to him;
(c) the supply to him is made by a person connected with him (see paragraph 6.1.2);
(d) the supplier, or a person connected with him, is entitled to full input tax credit on the purchase of the goods; and
(e) the relevant person (or a person connected with him) funds (directly or indirectly) more than 90 per cent of the cost of the goods.

For the purposes of this scheme, goods do not include land transactions.

6.5.2 Examples of arrangements included in the listed scheme

A partly exempt trader, such as a bank, requires new computer equipment. The decision is taken that the bank's corporate group will purchase the equipment outright. However, in order to reduce or remove the VAT effect of the irrecoverable input tax, the group acquires the computers in a subsidiary, which then leases them to the bank. Depending on the values and length of the lease, the intention is to spread the irrecoverable VAT cost, or to avoid a proportion of it altogether.

6.5.3 Example of arrangements not included in the listed scheme

Notification is not required for leasing arrangements that are between unconnected parties. For example:

Company "A", an insurance business, requires a new computerised telephone system for its call centres. Rather than buy the equipment outright it decides to lease it. It contracts with Company "B", an unconnected commercial leasing business, to lease the equipment for a five-year period. As Company "B" has no expertise in sourcing the equipment required, it is agreed that Company "A" will purchase the equipment from its usual supplier. Company "A" then sells the equipment to Company "B" who leases it back to Company "A".

Commentary—*De Voil Indirect Tax Service* **V5.213.**

6.6 Scheme 5 – Extended approval periods

This scheme aims to defer accounting for output tax on retail (including mail order) supplies of goods.

6.6.1 The scheme's features

The scheme comprises or includes the following features—

(a) a retail supply of goods where the goods are sent or taken on approval, sale or return, or similar terms;

(b) a requirement that the customer pays in full before any approval, return or similar period expires; and

(c) for the purposes of accounting for VAT, the supplier treats the goods as supplied on a date after the date on which payment is received in full.

6.6.2 Example of arrangements included in the listed scheme

A customer orders goods from an Internet retailer. The retailer is paid on-line when the customer places the order and delivery follows shortly thereafter. The retailer, either due to various guarantees, or specific terms and conditions, seeks to account for VAT on the transaction at a later date, claiming the supply was on "approval" or "sale or return". This is despite the fact that payment has been received, delivery has taken place and, in some cases, the goods have been consumed or used by the customer before the retailer regards the customer as having accepted the goods.

Commentary—*De Voil Indirect Tax Service* **V5.213.**

6.7 Scheme 6 – Groups: third party suppliers

These are schemes that aim to reduce or remove the VAT incurred on bought in taxable services (including outsourced services) by a user that cannot recover all of the input tax charged to it for those services.

6.7.1 The scheme's features

The scheme description is linked to legislation that took effect from 1 August 2004 and which only applies to business that are in VAT groups or intend to join a VAT group where the VAT group concerned has a turnover exceeding £10 million a year. Notification of this scheme only applies to bodies affected by that legislation. VAT Information Sheet 07/04 "Eligibility Rules for VAT Grouping" (**Division V16.5**) gives guidance on the linked legislation.

The scheme comprises or includes the following features—

(a) supplies made to one or more VAT group members by a body that is a specified body for the purposes of the VAT (Groups: eligibility) Order 2004 (SI 2004/1931); and

(b) the benefits condition of the VAT (Groups: eligibility) Order 2004 (SI 2004/1931) is not satisfied.

6.7.2 Example of arrangements included in the listed scheme

A partly exempt business, say company A an insurance company, wants to buy in computer services from third party company B, but wants to reduce the irrecoverable VAT cost of doing this. Companies A and B establish company C, in which A owns 51 per cent of C's shares. Company A includes C in its VAT group. Company B owns the remaining shares in C, but these shares confer rights to 99 per cent of the dividends declared by C and 99 per cent of the assets on winding up.

Company C holds the contract to provide the computer services required by company A from company B and employs the staff to provide the service. Besides the dividends, B also receives benefits from C in the form of a management charge for managing C's activity of providing computer services. As a result almost all of the benefits of company C's activity accrue to company B. Thus company B has access to the profits and benefits of the computer service activity, and company A hopes to avoid a large VAT cost as there will be no VAT charged within the VAT group.

Commentary—*De Voil Indirect Tax Service* **V5.213.**

6.8 Scheme 7—education and training by a non-profit making body

This scheme aims to allow a business providing education or training to avoid charging VAT on supplies to customers by arranging for those supplies to be made through a non-profit making body.

6.8.1 The scheme's features

The scheme comprises or includes the following features—

(a) a non-profit making body conducts a business whose activities consist wholly or mainly of the supply of VAT exempt education or vocational training to persons who are not taxable persons;

(b) it receives any of the following "key supplies", for use in that business, from a connected taxable person (see paragraph 6.1.2) who is not eligible for the exemption (see VATA 1994, Sch 9, Group 6, note 1)–

- a capital item (including leasing or letting on hire of a capital item),
- staff,
- management services,
- administration services, or
- accountancy services; and

(c) in any one VAT return accounting period the value of those key supplies comprise 20 per cent or more of the non-profit making body's costs.

"Non-profit making body" means a body within VATA 1994, Sch 9, Group 6, Note (1)(e), which is not otherwise within Note 1.

"Vocational training" has the meaning given by VATA 1994, Sch 9, Group 6, Note (3) but does not include vocational training of a description falling within item 5 or 5A of that Group.

6.8.2 Example of arrangements included in the listed scheme

A training company such as a driving instruction business, which normally trains private individuals and accounts for VAT out of its income, decides to set up a new non-profit making body to provide the training in the future, exempt from VAT. However, being a non-profit making body it is unable to distribute its profits, and the shareholders of the existing business will lose out. Various agreements may therefore be put in place to act as a mechanism to return those profits to the original training company. For example, the business premises may be leased, the rent for which may be set at a rate directly related to the turnover or profit of the non-profit making body.

Commentary—*De Voil Indirect Tax Service* **V5.213.**

6.9 Scheme 8 – Education and training by a non-eligible body

This scheme aims to enable "eligible bodies" that would otherwise make exempt supplies to make taxable supplies and so avoid incurring irrecoverable input tax. The typical customers involved would be bodies such as NHS Trusts and Local Authorities, but can also include normal commercial bodies.

6.9.1 The scheme's features

This scheme comprises or includes the following features—

(a) a body that is not an eligible body for the purposes of the exemption (see VATA 1994, Sch 9, Group 6, note 1) is connected (see paragraph 6.1.2) to a body that is an eligible body; and

(b) the non-eligible body conducts a business whose activities consist wholly or mainly of the taxable supply of education or vocational training.

In addition, either—

(a) the non-eligible body benefits or intends to benefit the eligible body by way of gift, dividend or otherwise;

or both—

(b) the eligible body makes to the non-eligible body, for use in the non-eligible body's business, any supply (including the leasing or letting on hire) of any of the following "key supplies"–

- a capital item (including the leasing or letting on hire of a capital item),
- staff,
- management services,
- administration services, or
- accountancy services; and

(c) in any one VAT return accounting period the value of those key supplies comprise 20 per cent or more of the non-eligible body's costs.

6.9.2 Example of arrangements included in the listed scheme

An institution, such as a university, has a contract to provide training to employees of a NHS Trust. Normally, the training would be exempt from VAT and thus the VAT on costs involved in providing it would not be recoverable. In order to provide this training, the university needs to build a new facility, but would like to reduce the cost of the irrecoverable VAT on the building. The university may establish a subsidiary that is expressly allowed to distribute its profits, claiming exemption for its training supplies. The subsidiary may have few or no resources, so will need to be provided with those resources by the university under various contracts and agreements. It is also likely that the university would want to access any profits from this activity and may choose to do this by having the subsidiary gift those profits to it under the Gift Aid relief. Thus the university may hope to transform the training into a fully taxable activity and recover the input tax on the new facility in the subsidiary, together with other taxable costs.

Commentary—*De Voil Indirect Tax Service* **V5.213.**

6.10 Scheme 9 – Cross-border face-value vouchers

This scheme aims to avoid paying VAT anywhere in the EU on "relevant services" originating from UK suppliers and provided to UK residents who use face-value vouchers (such as phone cards) to pay for them.

"Relevant services" are telecommunication services, radio and television broadcasting services, and electronically supplied services (such as software, images, music and games supplied over the internet).

6.10.1 The scheme's features

This scheme comprises or includes the following features—

(a) the supply of a "relevant service" from a UK supplier (S) to someone (A) in another EU member state;
(b) a person (B) in another member state B, who may be the same person as A or a different person, uses S's service to supply a "relevant service" to a customer in the UK (the "retail supply");
(c) S (the UK supplier) and B (the person making the retail supply) are connected persons (see paragraph 6.1.2);
(d) the customer is not a taxable person and uses a face-value voucher issued by a non-UK person (C), who may be the same person as B or a different person, to obtain the supply;
(e) B (the person making the retail supply) does not account for VAT on that supply in the UK or any other EU member state.

6.10.2 Example of arrangements included in the listed scheme

A company, UK Supplier Ltd, contracts to supply telecommunication services to a related company, Redeemer Ltd, in another EU member state, such as Ireland.

A second related Irish company, Issuer Ltd, issues phone cards and sells them to UK retailers. The retailers sell the cards to UK customers, who use them to obtain telecommunication services from Redeemer Ltd. The cards say that, when they are used, Redeemer Ltd will provide the telecommunication services. Redeemer Ltd does this by buying in the services under its contract with UK Supplier Ltd.

Redeemer Ltd and Issuer Ltd argue that no VAT is due in Ireland or the UK.

NB Only taxable persons in the UK who are party to the scheme, such as UK Supplier Ltd, are required to notify. UK retailers who are not party to the scheme (because they have no knowledge of their involvement in it), and parties who are not taxable persons in the UK, are not required to notify – see paragraphs 3.2 and 3.3.

6.10.3 Examples of arrangements not included in the listed scheme

Not included are any arrangements where the person that makes the retail supplies to the final consumer belongs outside the EU; or where no UK supplier of a relevant service is involved in the scheme.

Commentary—*De Voil Indirect Tax Service* **V5.213.**

6.11 Scheme 10 – Surrender of a relevant lease

This scheme aims to allow a person to escape, or substantially reduce, the VAT incurred on opted lease rentals whilst remaining in occupation of the building.

6.11.1 The scheme's features

This scheme comprises or includes the following features—

(a) an occupier of a building (or part of a building) agrees with the landlord to the surrender or other early termination of his lease, tenancy or licence to occupy a building;

VAT

(b) the building is a capital item within the meaning of the Capital Goods Scheme (whether or not the adjustment period has expired);

(c) the occupier, or any person connected with him, is a person who–
- is a landlord of the building,
- owns it for the purposes of the Capital Goods Scheme, and
- has elected to waive exemption (also known as "opting to tax") in relation to it;

(d) before the surrender–
- the occupier paid VAT on the rent of the building (or part of the building), and
- was unable to recover this VAT in full; and

(e) following the surrender—
- the occupier continues to occupy at least 80 per cent of the area previously occupied, and
- pays no VAT on the rent, or pays less than 50 per cent of the amount of VAT previously paid (comparing similar rental periods).

6.11.2 Examples of arrangements included in the listed scheme

Included are arrangements whereby—
- the occupier surrenders or terminates a taxable lease early and, despite the existence of an option to tax, the connected landlord makes a grant of a new lease that is exempt from VAT by reason of the option to tax disapplication rules;
- the occupier surrenders or terminates a taxable lease early and, despite the existence of an option to tax, the connected landlord sells the building to the occupier as an exempt from VAT by reason of the option to tax disapplication rules;
- the occupier, who is also a landlord further back in a chain of leases, arranges for all of the leases to be surrendered, leaving the occupier with the building (possibly paying a small amount of taxable ground rent to the ultimate freeholder).

Commentary—*De Voil Indirect Tax Service* **V5.213.**

7 HALLMARKED SCHEMES – DECIDING WHETHER YOU MUST NOTIFY

7.1 Decision chart

You are liable to notify use of a hallmarked scheme when *all* of the following tests are met—

Test	*Description*	*Further information*
1	You are a taxable person	Paragraph 3.2
2	You are a party to a scheme	Paragraphs 3.3 and 7.3
3	That scheme is not a listed scheme	Paragraph 3.4 and section 6
4	The main purpose, or one of the main purposes, of the scheme is for any person to obtain a tax advantage	Paragraph 7.4
5	A relevant event occurs	Paragraph 7.5
6	Your turnover exceeds either of the minimum thresholds	Paragraphs 7.6
7	Your scheme contains one or more hallmarks of avoidance	Paragraph 3.6 and section 10
8	You have not already notified HM Revenue & Customs, under the rules set out in this notice, that you are using the scheme	Paragraph 7.7
9	You have not been provided with a scheme number by someone who has registered the scheme with HM Revenue & Customs	Paragraph 7.8

Section 8 explains by when you must make your notification, the information it should contain and where to send it.

7.2 Protective notifications

If you are unsure whether you meet all of the relevant tests for notification, you may make a protective notification. In doing so you should explain which test, or tests, is causing you difficulty and why.

7.3 What is a scheme?

A scheme is any planned action entered into and includes any arrangements, transaction or series of transactions.

Engaging someone to ensure you claim all the input tax to which you are entitled, utilising an extra-statutory concession or trade facilitation measure open to all, using the grouping provisions, "opting to tax" a property, or negotiating a new partial exemption method are not in themselves schemes. This is the case even if they involve a hallmark of avoidance (see paragraph 3.6 and section 10). However, these features may form part of a scheme. You can find more on this and further examples in Section 11.

7.4 Schemes used for the purpose of obtaining a tax advantage

A scheme is potentially notifiable if the main purpose, or one of the main purposes, of it is for *any person*, who might not be you, to obtain a tax advantage. You may be liable to notify before that advantage is obtained (see paragraph 7.5 below for information on the events that trigger notification), or if you are not the person obtaining the advantage.

You are only required to notify if you are a party to the scheme. If the advantage accrues to another person and you are unaware that this will happen or your role in the scheme, then you are not required to notify – see paragraph 3.3.

7.4.1 What is a "tax advantage"?

A tax advantage happens when, as a result of the scheme—

(a) any taxable person accounts, or will account, for a lower net amount of VAT than would otherwise be the case in respect of a VAT return for any VAT accounting period starting on or after 1 August 2004;

(b) any taxable person obtains, or will obtain, in respect of any VAT accounting period starting on or after 1 August 2004, a VAT repayment that—
 - he would not otherwise obtain,
 - is larger than would otherwise be the case, or
 - is earlier than would otherwise be the case;

(c) any taxable person recovers, or will recover, in respect of any VAT accounting period starting on or after 1 August 2004, input tax before the supplier has to account for the corresponding output tax, and the period between the two events is longer than would otherwise be the case;

(d) the amount of any taxable person's non-deductible VAT (see paragraph 7.4.2), in respect of any VAT accounting period starting on or after 1 August 2005, is less than would otherwise be the case; or

(e) in relation to any person who is not a taxable person, the amount of his non-refundable VAT (see paragraph 7.4.3), at any time on or after 1 August 2005, is less than would otherwise be the case.

7.4.2 Non-deductible VAT

VAT is non-deductible VAT when, in relation to a taxable person, it is—

- VAT that is input tax, but for which he is not entitled to credit; or
- VAT incurred by him that is not input tax and for which he is not entitled to a refund under any provision of VATA 1994.

VAT is incurred by a taxable person when it is—

- VAT on the supply to him of any goods or services (including VAT on reverse charges);
- VAT on the acquisition by him from another member state of any goods; or
- VAT paid or payable by him on the importation of any goods from a place outside the member states.

7.4.3 Non-refundable VAT

VAT is non-refundable VAT when, in relation to a person who is not a taxable person—

(a) it is—
 - VAT on the supply to him of any goods or services;
 - VAT on the acquisition by him from another member state of any goods; or
 - VAT paid or payable by him on the importation of any goods from a place outside the member states; and

(b) it is not VAT that he is entitled to be refunded under any provision of VATA 1994.

7.4.4 Is the obtaining of a tax advantage a main purpose of the scheme?

There is no one factor that determines whether the obtaining of a tax advantage is the main, or one of the main, purposes of a scheme. All surrounding circumstances need to be taken into consideration. They include—

- the overall objectives of the arrangements and transactions (including the objectives of any wider corporate or VAT group to which the parties to the scheme belong; and the objectives of any persons or businesses who control the parties); and
- whether the introduction of any unnecessary, complex or costly steps would have taken place were it not for the tax advantage that can be obtained.

In general, it is likely the main purpose test would be met where, more likely than not, were it not for any VAT advantage arising, the arrangements would either have not been implemented or would have been implemented in a different manner.

Similarly, where there are two or more ways of carrying out a genuine commercial objective and the choice is determined on grounds other than the potential VAT saving but a VAT advantage (when compared to adopting one or more of the alternatives) nevertheless arises, it is unlikely the main purpose test would be met.

7.5 Relevant events that trigger notification

The requirement for you to notify is triggered when one of the following events occurs *to you*—

- You show in a VAT return, in respect of any VAT accounting period starting on or after 1 August 2004 (or 1 August 2005 when the scheme involves only hallmark 8 (face-value vouchers) and no other hallmark), a higher or lower net amount of VAT than would be the case but for the scheme.
- You make a claim (such as by submitting a voluntary disclosure), in respect of any VAT accounting period starting on or after 1 August 2004 for which a VAT return has been submitted (or 1 August 2005 when the scheme involves only hallmark 8 (face-value vouchers) and no other hallmark), for the repayment of output tax over declared or input tax credit under claimed that is greater than would be the case but for the scheme.
- The amount of non-deductible VAT (see paragraph 7.5.1 below) you incur, in respect of any VAT accounting period starting on or after 1 August 2005, would have been higher but for the scheme.

7.5.1 Non-deductible VAT incurred

VAT is, or would have been, incurred by you when it is, or would have been—

- VAT on the supply to you of any goods or services (including VAT on reverse charges);
- VAT on the acquisition by you from another member state of any goods; or
- VAT paid or payable by you on the importation of any goods from a place outside the EU.

It is, or would have been, non-deductible VAT when it is, or would have been—

- VAT that is input tax, but for which you are not entitled to credit; or
- VAT that is not input tax, and for which you are not entitled to a refund under any provision of VATA 1994.

7.6 The minimum turnover thresholds

The turnover threshold is measured by reference to the *total* amount of *taxable and exempt* supplies made by—

- you; or
- where you are a member of a corporate group, *the whole group,* made up of the ultimate holding company (or entity) and all its subsidiaries, including you. For this purpose UK company law definitions used for preparing group accounts apply (s 259 of the Companies Act 1985). As a result the group will normally be made up of all the companies shown as subsidiaries in the ultimate parent's consolidated group accounts, plus any companies that are excluded from the consolidation but are subsidiaries for UK company law purposes.

For the purpose of calculating turnover, intra-corporate group transactions are included. However, intra-VAT group transactions are ignored.

7.6.1 The threshold

Your turnover exceeds the minimum threshold when the total amount of *taxable and exempt* supplies made by you (or the wider corporate group as explained above) is, or is greater than—

(a) £10 million in the year immediately prior to the VAT return period that triggers notification (see paragraph 7.5); or
(b) the appropriate proportion of £10 million in the VAT return period immediately prior to the VAT return period that triggers notification. (For example, the "appropriate proportion" is one twelfth of £10 million (ie £833,334) where the VAT return period is one month; and one quarter of £10 million (ie £2.5 million) where the VAT return period is three months.)

7.6.2 Disaggregation

Should we find that a taxable person's business has been split in an attempt to avoid the requirement to make a notification, we will use our powers to direct that the separate entities be treated as one. If it is found later that other entities should have been included in that direction, a supplementary direction can be made to include them. The effect a supplementary direction has on the timing of a notification is explained in paragraph 8.1.2.

7.7 What if I have already notified HM Revenue & Customs?

You need only notify a scheme once.

If you enter into new arrangements that are structured in the same way as a previously notified scheme you need not notify these new arrangements. (By "structured in the same way", we mean that the details of the scheme required to be notified under paragraph 8.4 and 8.6 are the same. The parties to the scheme and the hallmarks may be different.)

However, if you enter into new arrangements that are structured in a materially different way to a previously notified scheme, you will, subject to the necessary conditions being met (such as the turnover threshold, etc), have to notify use of that scheme irrespective of whether the hallmarks are the same.

For hallmarked schemes that become listed schemes, see paragraph 4.4.2.

7.8 Hallmarked schemes already registered with HM Revenue & Customs

You are not required to notify us about your use of a hallmarked scheme if someone has registered it with us under the Voluntary Registration Scheme (see section 9), and they have advised you of the scheme reference number we have allocated to it (prefixed by the letters VRS). In addition, there is no requirement to enter the reference number on a VAT return or to tell us in advance of any enquiries we wish to make that you hold the number. You should, however, keep a record of when you were advised of it.

We do not publish details of the schemes that have been registered with us, or who have registered them.

Commentary—*De Voil Indirect Tax Service* **V5.213.**

8 HALLMARKED SCHEMES – HOW TO NOTIFY HM REVENUE & CUSTOMS

8.1 By what date must I notify HM Revenue & Customs?

Your notification must be made to HM Revenue & Customs within 30 days of—

- in the case of the net amount of VAT shown in a VAT return being different to what would otherwise be the case (see the first bullet at paragraph 7.5), the due date for making the return;
- in the case of a claim being made that is greater than would otherwise be the case (see the second bullet at paragraph 7.5), the making of the claim; or
- in the case of the amount of your non-deductible VAT in respect of a VAT accounting period being less than would otherwise be the case (see the third bullet at paragraph 7.5), the due date for making a return in respect of that accounting period.

For examples of when a notification is due see paragraphs 5.1.3 to 5.1.4.

8.1.1 Early notifications

HM Revenue & Customs will accept early notifications, such as before the relevant event has taken place, provided the scheme has been implemented.

8.1.2 Directions that taxpayers are treated as one

Where HM Revenue & Customs issue a direction that a number of taxpayers should be treated as one (see paragraph 7.6.2), the due date is determined by reference to the first relevant event (see paragraph 7.5) that takes place following the issue of the direction.

Commentary—*De Voil Indirect Tax Service* **V5.213.**

8.2 How do I notify HM Revenue & Customs?

The following rule has the force of law

> You must notify us either in writing or by email to the relevant address given at paragraph 8.7. The notification should be prominently headed:
>
> - Disclosure of use of hallmarked scheme – Notification under paragraph 6(3) of Sch 11A to VATA 1994.
>
> and give your:
>
> - business name (if you are the representative member of a VAT group, notifying as a result of a group member being involved in a notifiable scheme, also tell us the name of the member);
> - address; and
> - VAT registration number.

Commentary—*De Voil Indirect Tax Service* **V5.213.**

8.3 What information must I provide?

When notifying a hallmarked scheme you *must* provide *all* the following information, to the extent that it is known to you, and explain what information you are unable to provide and why—

- information demonstrating how the scheme works – see paragraph 8.4;
- a statement as to which hallmark or hallmarks are included in or associated with the scheme you are notifying to us – see paragraph 8.5; and

- a statement as to which specific legislation you rely upon for the tax advantage – see paragraph 8.6.

For joint notifications, see paragraph 3.3.4.

Commentary—*De Voil Indirect Tax Service* **V5.213.**

8.4 The workings of the scheme

To make a valid notification you *must* provide sufficient information to show—

- how the scheme works; and
- how the involvement of any party to the scheme contributes to the obtaining of the tax advantage, including, to the extent that it is material to the obtaining of the tax advantage:
- a description of each arrangement, transaction or series of transactions – see paragraph 8.4.1;
- their sequence – see paragraph 8.4.2;
- their timing, or the intervals between them – see paragraph 8.4.3; and
- the goods or services involved – see paragraph 8.4.1.

You are *not required* to quantify the amount or expected amount of the tax advantage.

8.4.1 Describing the scheme

You must provide sufficient information so that HM Revenue & Customs can understand how the tax advantage is obtained. The degree of information to be provided will vary from scheme to scheme and the extent to which you have knowledge of other parties' intentions and circumstances.

For most notifications we recommend you include, along with the description of how the beneficiary obtains the tax advantage—

- a summary of the scheme (ie what the beneficiaries' tax position would be without the scheme, and whether the scheme provides them with an absolute saving or a deferral of a tax burden); and
- a diagrammatic representation of its structure (showing the participants, transaction flows, etc.).

The scheme description need only provide generic information; you do not need to provide the detail that is specific to your circumstances. For example, a step of the scheme could be described as, "building is leased to Company A" rather than, "1 High Street is leased to Bank plc." It follows that you do not need to submit copies of contracts and other documents. However, if you find it easier to explain the scheme by referring to the specific detail of your case, you may do so. You may also submit supplementary documentation if you wish.

Remember, to the extent that it is known to you, you will need to explain how the involvement of any party to the scheme contributes to the obtaining of the tax advantage. In the example given, you should go on and say whether the lease is taxed and, if so, whether any of the tax charged is recoverable by Company A/Bank plc.

8.4.2 Sequence

Where the order of the arrangements or transactions is critical to the workings of the scheme, this should be explained. You should make it clear what the precise sequence is. We recommend listing these as "Step 1", "Step 2", etc.

8.4.3 Timing and interval

Where the timing of, or interval between, arrangements or transactions are critical to the workings of the scheme, this should be explained.

For example, you should explain if the interval between transactions are due to take place within a short period of time of each other to take advantage of a VAT rule; over a long period to cause a VAT "drip feed" effect; or timed to miss or bridge accounting periods.

Commentary—*De Voil Indirect Tax Service* **V5.213.**

8.5 Declaration of hallmarks

This need not be a standalone part of your notification; it can be included as part of your general explanation of the working of the scheme. If you are unsure whether a feature is a hallmark, say why you are unsure.

8.6 The statutory provision

You must let us know the law that you believe gives rise to the tax advantage (see paragraph 7.4.1) derived from use of the scheme. This could be—

- UK law;
- the law of another country, such as where you rely on a different tax treatment; or
- EU law, such as where you rely on the principle of "direct effect" (ie that EU law has effect, irrespective of the provisions of UK VAT law).

Commentary—*De Voil Indirect Tax Service* **V5.213.**

8.7 Where do I send my notification?

The following rule has the force of law

Your must send your notification to either of the following addresses:
Post to:
VAT Avoidance Disclosures Unit
Anti-Avoidance Group (Intelligence)
HM Revenue & Customs
1st Floor, 22 Kingsway
London WC2B 6NR
Or e-mail to:
vat.avoidance.disclosures.bst@hmrc.gsi.gov.uk

8.8 What if I send my notification to another address?

If you send your notification to an address other than those given in paragraph 8.7 (for example to your local office or the National Advice Service), you will not have made a proper notification. Failure to make a proper notification will make you liable to a penalty as explained in Section 12.

8.9 How will HM Revenue & Customs deal with my notification?

We will acknowledge receipt of all notifications received at the addresses given in paragraph 8.7. However, the acknowledgement is not a confirmation that you have met your statutory obligation.

If your notification does not contain all the information set out in paragraphs 8.3 to 8.6, you may be contacted and asked to provide the required information or explain why you are unable to provide it. Only when the information (to the extent that you are able) has been provided will your obligation be discharged. If this is not done within the time limit for making a notification, you will be liable to a penalty as explained in Section 12.

Once the required information has been provided, we will consider whether we wish to investigate further at that time – see paragraph 3.10. If we do not contact you, this does not mean the arrangements are acceptable to us.

If we are already investigating your use of the notified scheme, that action will continue as appropriate.

Commentary—*De Voil Indirect Tax Service* **V5.213.**

9 HALLMARKED SCHEMES – VOLUNTARY REGISTRATION SCHEME

9.1 Why use the Voluntary Registration Scheme?

The principal objective of the rules for hallmarked schemes is to enable HM Revenue & Customs to find out about new and innovative schemes. The Voluntary Registration Scheme enables us to learn about these schemes whilst reducing the burdens on business – they are exempted from having to notify us of their use of the scheme (see paragraph 7.8).

The Voluntary Registration Scheme does not exempt a person from notifying a listed scheme.

9.2 Is it an approval system?

No. Acceptance of an application to register the details of a hallmarked scheme does not mean that we agree with the analysis that has been provided.

9.3 How do I know whether a scheme has already been registered?

We do not publish details of schemes that have been registered with us. If you apply to register a scheme that is the same as, or a variant of, a scheme that somebody else has already registered with us, we will issue you with your own unique reference number.

9.4 Who can register a scheme?

Anyone, including advisers, promoters and trade bodies, can apply to register a scheme; you need not have devised or marketed it yourself.

However, in some cases we may decide not to issue you with a reference number (see paragraph 9.9).

9.5 How do I register a scheme?

You should write or send an e-mail to the address shown in paragraph 8.7, giving us the details of the scheme you wish to register. Please make it clear in your notification that you are applying for a reference number under the Voluntary Registration Scheme.

9.6 Information to be provided

When applying to register a hallmarked scheme, you *must* provide the same information that anyone required to make a notification would. The information required is explained in paragraphs 8.3 to 8.6.

You can apply to register variations of a scheme at the same time, although we may decide to issue different reference numbers for each variation.

9.7 Will HM Revenue & Customs acknowledge my application?

Yes, we will acknowledge your application upon receipt.

9.8 How quickly are reference numbers issued?

Subject to paragraph 9.9 below, we aim to examine applications and issue reference numbers (prefixed by the letters VRS) within ten working days of receipt.

9.9 Will a reference number always be issued?

No, the issue of a reference number is discretionary. Whilst we will normally issue reference numbers in relation to schemes, whether we agree that they work or not, we will not normally issue a reference number in relation to applications that are unclear or ambiguous, or appear to cover several different schemes rather than just one. We will also not issue a reference number for a scheme that appears to be an existing listed scheme.

9.10 What happens if a VRS reference number is not issued?

The normal rules for hallmarked schemes apply – see section 7.

Commentary—*De Voil Indirect Tax Service* **V5.213.**

10 THE HALLMARKS

10.1 Descriptions of the "hallmarks"

The hallmarks are described in paragraphs 10.2 to 10.8 below.

These descriptions are intended to help you decide if they appear in the scheme you are using, so that you will know whether you have to notify your use of the scheme to us. The descriptions are not a substitute for the descriptions contained in the law (see paragraph 1.4). It is your responsibility to decide whether or not a particular hallmark occurs in your scheme.

10.1.1 Connected persons

For the purposes of the hallmark descriptions a person is connected with another where—

- one of them is an undertaking in relation to which the other is a group undertaking as defined by s 259 of the Companies Act 1985 (essentially, one is the parent or subsidiary undertaking of the other, or both are subsidiaries of a common parent undertaking); or
- both of them are connected to the same trust.

A person is connected to a trust where he:

- is the settlor of the trust, or a trustee or beneficiary of it; or
- holds any shares in a company in accordance with the terms of the trust, or is a person on whose behalf such shares are held.

10.2 Confidentiality condition agreements

There is a "confidentiality condition" hallmark when there is an agreement that prevents or limits a person from giving others details of how a scheme gives rise to a tax advantage (see paragraph 7.4.1).

The hallmark is aimed at confidentiality conditions that are intended to protect the competitive advantage of a promoter or creator of the scheme over other promoters, say because it is an innovative scheme, and is often made before a potential user has the full details of the scheme explained to them. It, therefore, applies where—

- a specific condition of confidentiality is imposed; or
- a client specifically undertakes (either in writing or verbally) not to reveal details of how a particular scheme gives rise to a tax advantage.

10.2.1 General confidentiality clauses

It is standard practice for advisers to include a "general confidentiality condition" within their terms of engagement, prohibiting the client from passing on advice to third parties.

You need not regard a general confidentiality clause as being a confidentiality condition hallmark if it is simply imposed in relation to all advice, not merely the scheme in question. However, it is regarded as a hallmark where:

- it is introduced specifically in order to prevent or limit a person from revealing details of how a particular scheme gives rise to a tax advantage; or

- it is specifically drawn to a client's attention by an adviser when introducing a scheme to the client in order to prevent or limit him from revealing details of how the particular scheme gives rise to a tax advantage.

10.3 Agreements to share a tax advantage

There is a "sharing a tax advantage" hallmark when there is an agreement that the tax advantage (see paragraph 7.4.1) accruing from the scheme be shared, to any extent, between the person to whom it accrues and the promoter or any other person who is a party to the scheme.

A "promoter" is anyone who, in the course of their trade, profession or business of providing taxation services, designs or sells the arrangements entered into.

10.4 Contingent fee agreements

There is a "contingent fee" hallmark when there is an agreement that payment to a promoter of a scheme is partly or wholly contingent on the tax advantage (see paragraph 7.4.1) accruing from use of the scheme.

A "promoter" is anyone who, in the course of their trade, profession or business of providing taxation services, designs or sells the arrangements entered into.

10.5 Prepayments between connected persons

There is a "prepayment" hallmark when the operation of a scheme involves a prepayment being made for supplies between connected persons (see paragraph 10.1.1). The prepayment may be of any amount and the time between the prepayment and the actual provision of the goods or services may be of any duration.

10.6 Funding by loans, share subscriptions or subscriptions in securities

This hallmark applies when a supply of goods or services made between two connected persons is funded (in whole or in part)—

- by a loan between connected persons;
- by one person subscribing for shares in another with whom he is connected; or
- by one person subscribing in securities issued by another with whom he is connected.

"Connected persons" is explained at paragraph 10.1.1.

10.7 Off-shore loops

This hallmark applies when certain exported services (which allow the exporter to recover related input tax) are used to provide other services to UK persons, and these "imported" services are not subject to VAT.

In detail it applies when—

(a) a person makes a supply of services covered by—
  - art 3(a) of the VAT (Input Tax) (Specified Supplies) Order 1999 (exempt financial and insurance services supplied to a person who belongs outside the member states of the EU),
  - art 3(b) of the VAT (Input Tax) (Specified Supplies) Order 1999 (services directly linked to the export of goods to a place outside the member states), insofar as they are supplies of a description falling within item 2 of Group 5 of Sch 9 to the VATA 1994 (the making of any advance or any credit),
  - art 3(c) of the VAT (Input Tax) (Specified Supplies) Order 1999 (the provision of certain intermediary insurance or financial services), or
  - paras 1 to 8 of Sch 5 to VATA 1994 (services supplied where received), and the recipient belongs in a country, other than the Isle of Man, which is not a member state of the EU; and

(b) the service is used or intended to be used, in whole or in part, directly or indirectly, in making to a person belonging in the UK a supply which is—
  - zero-rated,
  - exempt, or
  - treated as made in another country (and not the UK) by virtue of s 7(10) of VATA 1994.

10.8 Property transactions between connected persons

This hallmark applies when—

(a) a grant, which is not a zero-rated grant, is made of:
  - any interest in, right over or licence to occupy land, or
  - in relation to land in Scotland, any personal right to call for or be granted any such interest or right;

(b) the grantor or grantee of the interest or right is a person who cannot recover input tax in full;

(c) a work of any construction, alteration, demolition, repair, maintenance or civil engineering has been or is to be carried out on the land; and

(d) the grant is made to a person connected with the grantor (see paragraph 10.1.1).

10.9 Issue of face-value vouchers

This hallmark applies when—

(a) face-value vouchers are issued for consideration; and
(b) either—
– the issuer does not expect at least 75 per cent of the vouchers to be redeemed within three years of them being issued, or
– whatever the expected redemption rate, the vouchers are issued to a connected person (see paragraph 10.1.1) outside of any VAT group to which the issuer belongs.

10.9.1 Expected redemption rates

The expected redemption rate is measured by reference to the face value of the vouchers taken together, for example—

– A business issues £1m worth of vouchers and expects £900,000 worth of those vouchers to be redeemed. That is a 90 per cent expected redemption rate, irrespective of whether the expectation is actually met.
– A business issues vouchers that can be partly redeemed, such as may happen with certain electronic vouchers, and expects 100 per cent of them to be redeemed but on average only 30 per cent of the value to be redeemed. That would be a 30 per cent expected redemption rate, again irrespective of whether the expectation is actually met.

Commentary—*De Voil Indirect Tax Service* **V5.213.**

11 HALLMARKED SCHEMES—FREQUENTLY ASKED QUESTIONS

11.1 Use of extra statutory concessions

Q: I am using an extra statutory concession (ESC). When I use the ESC I could be seen as obtaining a tax advantage. Do I have to notify HM Revenue & Customs under the new rules?

A: No. An ESC is not, in itself, a scheme. It is a remission of revenue that allows relief in specific sets of circumstances to all businesses falling within the relevant conditions. It is authorised when strict application of the law would create an undue disadvantage or the effect would not be the one intended. However, you should remember that if an ESC is used as part of a tax avoidance scheme, that use is likely to be challenged by HM Revenue & Customs. HM Revenue & Customs may also consider withdrawing or restricting the ESC's application.

11.2 Use of partial exemption special methods

Q: I have negotiated a new partial exemption special method (PESM). It gives me a higher rate of input tax recovery compared with my previous method. Do I notify HM Revenue & Customs under the new rules?

A: No, a PESM is not a scheme. When a PESM is agreed with HM Revenue & Customs it is a fair and reasonable estimate of input tax recovery.

11.3 Changes to VAT group structures

Q: On occasions we add or remove a company from our VAT group. Changes to our group generally affect the amount of VAT declared by the group on its returns. Do we notify HM Revenue & Customs under these rules?

A: No. Making such a change does not, in itself, constitute a scheme as it can only be done on application to HM Revenue & Customs.

11.4 VAT audits

Q: I do not have the staff or expertise to check all my purchase invoices to ensure I claim all the input tax I am entitled to. I am therefore going to engage someone to do this for me, who charges a fee contingent on the amount of VAT claimed. This is not being done in conjunction with any other arrangements or transactions. Contingent fees are a hallmark of tax avoidance. Do I notify HM Revenue & Customs under the new rules?

A: No. Simply claiming all input tax to which you are entitled is not a "scheme". You are not implementing arrangements or transactions to gain a tax advantage. You are simply seeking to recover the correct amount of tax.

11.5 Identifying use of hallmarks

Q: I am using a scheme, and am not sure whether it contains any hallmarks of avoidance. Should I notify my use of this scheme to protect myself from the possible imposition of a penalty at a later date?

A: You may make a protective notification if you wish. There is further information on this at paragraph 7.2. Remember, however, the presence of a hallmark of avoidance is not the only test for having to notify a scheme. A scheme is notifiable only if *all* the tests in paragraph 7.1 are met.

If your turnover is below £10 million, for example, you do not have to notify us.

11.6 Subsidiaries funded by share capital or loans

Q: My Company is forming a subsidiary company that will supply it with goods and services. The subsidiary will be funded by share capital or a loan. For the purposes of the law we are connected persons. This is the funding by share subscriptions or loans hallmark. I will have to investigate whether this results in a tax advantage. It is difficult for me to do this, so to be safe should I notify HM Revenue & Customs under the new rules?

A: Not unless all the tests listed in paragraph 7.1 are met. In relation to the tax advantage test, the obtaining a tax advantage has to be a main purpose. The presence of a tax advantage does not automatically cause the test to be met.

12 PENALTIES

Commentary—*De Voil Indirect Tax Service* **V5.213.**

12.1 The penalties

The penalties for failing to make a full notification to us at the correct time are—

- 15 per cent of the VAT saved (see paragraph 12.2 below) for listed schemes; and
- £5,000 for hallmarked schemes.

12.2 What is the VAT saved?

The VAT saved by a taxable person is the aggregate of—

- the amount by which the amount of VAT he has shown as payable in relevant VAT returns is less than the amount that he would have shown were it not for the scheme;
- the amount by which the amount of VAT he has shown as repayable in relevant VAT returns exceeds the amount that he would have shown were it not for the scheme;
- the amount by which the amount he has claimed (for example in a voluntary disclosure) exceeds the amount that he would have claimed were it not for the scheme; and,
- the amount by which the amount of non-deductible VAT (see paragraph 7.4.2) that he would have incurred were it not for the scheme exceeds that which has been incurred (to the extent that it is not already represented in the calculation).

12.2.1 Relevant VAT returns

Relevant VAT returns begin with that in which a tax advantage (see paragraph 7.4.1) first arose and end with the VAT return covering—

- the date on which the person complied with the requirement to notify; or, if earlier,
- the VAT return for the period immediately before HM Revenue & Customs notify the penalty assessment to the taxpayer.

If it is unclear which VAT returns are to be used for the calculation, we will use best judgement to determine which apply and advise you accordingly.

12.3 Will a penalty always be issued?

No, there are a number of circumstances where a penalty will not be issued. We will not issue a penalty if you—

- can demonstrate that you had a reasonable excuse for failing to notify us;
- as a result of the actions which triggered your requirement to notify you:
- are convicted of an offence under VATA 1994 or other legislation; or
- are assessed for a penalty for conduct involving dishonesty under the rules relating to VAT evasion.

Civil investigations into VAT evasion are undertaken in accordance with Code of Practice 9, which can be accessed at: www.hmrc.gov.uk/leaflets/c11.htm

Commentary—*De Voil Indirect Tax Service* **V5.335.**

12.4 Reasonable excuse

No penalty will be payable if you are able to satisfy us, or on appeal, the VAT and Duties Tribunal, that there is a reasonable excuse for your failure to notify us that you are using a scheme. Notice 700/42 "Misdeclaration penalty and repeated misdeclaration penalty" gives more guidance on the term "reasonable excuse". If reasonable excuse does not apply, there may still be grounds for mitigation.

Commentary—*De Voil Indirect Tax Service* **V5.335.**

12.5 Mitigation

A penalty can be reduced if there are mitigating circumstances that fall short of a reasonable excuse.

The law does not define the grounds for mitigation but it specifically *excludes*—

- your lack of funds to pay any tax or penalty due;
- the fact that little or no tax has been lost; and
- the fact that you acted in good faith.

When we consider mitigation we will consider all the facts that led to the failure to notify us. The amount of mitigation allowed will depend on the specific circumstances of your case.

Commentary—*De Voil Indirect Tax Service* **V5.334.**

12.6 Issuing a penalty assessment

If you are liable to a penalty we will notify you in writing of your liability to the penalty and explain—

- the amount of the penalty;
- the reasons for the imposition of the penalty;
- how the penalty has been calculated; and
- the amount of any mitigation allowed.

An assessment for a penalty that is due will be issued even if, before that happens, the taxable person concerned ceases to be a party to the scheme that gave rise to the requirement to notify. Any penalty due is treated as recoverable as if it were VAT due from the assessed person. The penalty cannot be claimed as input tax.

Commentary—*De Voil Indirect Tax Service* **V5.333.**

12.7 Time period for issuing a penalty

No assessment to a penalty can be issued more than two years after we had sufficient facts to enable us to issue one.

13 RECONSIDERATIONS AND APPEALS

13.1 What if I disagree with a penalty or direction?

If you disagree with—

- your liability to a penalty;
- the amount of a penalty; or
- a direction issued in the circumstances explained in paragraphs 4.3.2 and 7.6.2,

you may ask for a reconsideration to be undertaken or appeal to the VAT and Duties Tribunal.

13.2 Reconsiderations

You should write to us within 30 days of the date of the letter in which we notified our decision to you, and ask for a reconsideration to be undertaken if you think that—

- you have a reasonable excuse for the failure to notify (see paragraph 0); or
- there are mitigating circumstances which warrant reduction of the penalty (see paragraph 12.5).

The notification letter will give the address to which you should write asking for a reconsideration to be undertaken.

13.3 Appeals

You also have the right to appeal to an independent VAT and duties tribunal.

The Leaflet Appeals and applications to the Tribunal tells you what to do. You can request a copy of the leaflet by telephoning any of the Tribunal Centres in—

- London (0207 631 4242);
- Manchester (0161 868 6600); and
- Edinburgh (0131 226 3551).

The tribunal can consider whether there is a reasonable excuse and can also increase as well as decrease any amount of mitigation that we have allowed.

Commentary—*De Voil Indirect Tax Service* **V5.262, V5.4.**

Notice 701/21
Gold

2002

Commentary—*De Voil Indirect Tax Service* **V4.186.**
Note—Certain paragraphs within the following extracts have the force of law and these are enclosed within boxes.

3 THE NEED TO NOTIFY EXEMPT SUPPLIES OF INVESTMENT GOLD

3.1 When and how do I have to notify?

The first time that you make an exempt supply of investment gold which exceeds £5,000, or when the value of your supplies of exempt investment gold to any one customer is over £10,000 in any 12 month period, you must notify us within 28 days at the following address—The Gold Team, HM Customs and Excise, Thomas Paine House, Angel Square, Torrens Street, London EC1V 1TA.

If you are required to notify that you trade in investment gold and you are not registered for VAT, you must also provide the following information—

1 Name of company, partnership or sole proprietor.
2. Company incorporation number or details of partners.
3. Address(es).
4. Telephone number.
5. Contact name.
6. Accountant's name, address and telephone number.
7. Associated VAT registration numbers.

The Gold Team will send you an acknowledgement. If, however, you do not receive this within 28 days, you must check that they have received your notification.

You do not need to notify us of subsequent supplies.

4 OPTING TO TAX INVESTMENT GOLD

...

4.3 What if I produce or transform gold into investment gold?

As long as you are a taxable person you may opt to tax any supply of investment gold to another taxable person.

You must notify your local Business Advice Centre if you intend to opt to tax. If you do not receive an acknowledgement within 28 days, you must check that they have received the notification.

4.4 What if I supply gold for industrial purposes?

If you are a taxable person, who as a normal part of your business supplies gold for industrial purposes, you may only opt to tax certain supplies of investment gold, *but you need to get our agreement first.*

To get our agreement to you opting to tax your supplies of investment gold, you must write to your local Business Advice Centre, giving your VAT registration number and confirming that you normally trade in gold for industrial purposes. If they agree they will send you a letter of approval within 28 days. They will normally impose conditions and the letter will also explain what these are and tell you when you can start opting.

We will accept that you normally supply investment gold for industrial purposes if you can show that you do so on a regular basis.

Once you have received our agreement, you may opt to tax supplies of investment gold bars or wafers you make to other taxable persons.

We may however withdraw our approval for the protection of the revenue.

4.5 What if I act as an agent?

If you are acting for a named principal and your principal has opted to tax, you may opt to tax your services in so far as they are related to your principal's "opted" supplies of investment gold.

You must inform your local Business Advice Centre that you intend to opt to tax your services. If you do not receive an acknowledgement within 28 days, you must check that they have received the notification.

4.6 Do I need to alter my invoices?

As opting to tax a transaction is simple—once you have fulfilled the conditions in paragraph 4.3, 4.4 and 4.5, all you need to do is to include the following statement on your invoice.

"We have opted to tax this transaction."

But please note that once you have opted to tax a particular supply you cannot change your mind and exempt it.

…

6 INVOICING REQUIREMENTS FOR TRADING IN EXEMPT INVESTMENT GOLD

…

6.2 When do I need to issue an invoice for sales of exempt investment gold?

You *must* issue an invoice for—

– each sale involving exempt investment gold which exceeds £5,000;
– smaller transactions if the total value of sales to that customer has exceeded £10,000 in the last twelve months.

You must also give each invoice a unique identifying number.

But please note that you do not need to produce the invoice or keep the records described in this section or section 7 or notify us that you trade in investment gold (section 3) if every supply of investment gold you make is for less than £5,000, unless the total value of supplies to an individual customer over the previous twelve months was above £10,000.

6.3 Do I need to raise an invoice if I buy investment gold from a person who does not trade in investment gold?

Yes—you *must* issue an invoice on behalf of the seller if—

– the value of the purchase is more than £5,000; or
– you make more than one purchase from the same supplier and the total value of your purchases from that supplier has gone over £10,000 in the last twelve months.

It must contain all of the relevant details specified in paragraph 6.4.

Also, the invoice must include the following declaration which must be signed by the seller—

"I declare that to the best of my knowledge the details shown on this invoice are correct." (Signature and name).

6.4 What must I show on the invoice for sales of exempt investment gold?

Each invoice *must* contain the following details if appropriate—

– name and address of seller; your name and address (if different to the seller); name and address of the purchaser; delivery address (if different); unique customer reference (see paragraph 7.1(b)).
– date of invoice; delivery date; type of supply (for example, sale).
– your VAT registration number if you, or your principal are registered for VAT, or the seller's VAT registration number (if you are not the seller); and
– a description of the gold supplied;
  – *for bars and wafers*—form, weight and purity, any other identifying feature (including any proprietary mark, hallmark and serial number where applicable); *or*
  – *for investment gold coins*—the coin type, country of origin and whether or not the coin is included on the list of gold coins reproduced in Notice 701/21A "Investment gold coins".
– the number of items; and
– the total amount payable.

…

7 RECORDS TO BE KEPT

7.1 Records to be kept for gold delivered or taken away by your customer

If you sell exempt investment gold which is delivered or available to be taken away by your customer, you must keep the following information as part of your business records. These requirements do not apply if you make supplies described within paragraphs 7.2, 7.3(a), 7.6 and 8.2.

This applies whether or not you are registered for VAT.

➡

(a) *Accounting record*

You must keep and maintain a record showing the following details—

- invoice number;
- invoice date;
- customer reference number;
- customer's VAT registration number (if applicable);
- description of the gold (form, quantity and purity);
- name and address of the agent (if applicable);
- name and address of the purchaser; and
- transaction value.

(b) *Customer record*

You must keep and maintain a record identifying customers who purchase exempt investment gold. This record must have a unique reference number and contain the following information—

- name;
- date of birth;
- current address; and
- telephone number (if available).

You must take reasonable steps to ensure that your customer has given you correct information. In order to do this, you must ask for and examine at least one document from each of the following lists.

List 1	*List 2*
Passport	Telephone bill
Full driving licence	Other utility bill
National Insurance card	Deeds
Birth certificate	Tenancy lease
National identity card	Council tax bill
	Hotel key card (for non-UK residents only)

You may agree alternative satisfactory evidence with your local Business Advice Centre.

If possible, you should keep a copy of the documents you see. You should write on each copy "certified as original document". You must sign and date this declaration.

If it is not possible to keep a copy of the document you see, you must record, as part of your customer record, sufficient details to enable us to obtain a copy if we ask. As a minimum you should record—

- the name of the document;
- the reference number; and
- the name and address of the issuing authority.

You must insist that your customer produces the original document. You must keep the record up to date.

(c) *Method of keeping the required particulars*

Where you are required to keep and maintain the records specified in parts (a) and (b) of this paragraph you may, as an alternative, keep and maintain the details required in a manner which is convenient for your business provided—

- all the details specified are accessible for inspection by a VAT officer; and
- you have agreed the format with your local Business Advice Centre.

7.2 Banks and other financial service businesses

If you are a bank or other financial service business which, for the purposes of the Money Laundering Regulations, SI 1993/1933, is a "relevant financial business" you may, as an alternative to the customer record set out in paragraph 7.1(b), keep and maintain the records specified in those regulations.

Relevant financial businesses to whom this applies must conduct the appropriate identification procedures and keep the required records in the case of all transactions in investment gold where the value of a one-off transaction exceeds 15,000 euro or, where one-off transactions appear linked and their value together exceeds 15,000 euro.

For the purposes of this notice the exchange rate between the euro and the UK pound sterling shall be the annual rate published in the Official Journal of the European Communities (OJEC)—www.europa.eu.int/eur-lex.

7.3 Auctioneers and other agents of investment gold

(a) *Were you are acting in your own name*

If, as an agent or auctioneer, you invoice goods in your own name for goods sold on behalf of a third party vendor, the goods are treated for VAT purposes as supplies both to and by you.

Auctioneers are treated as agents for VAT purposes. For more information about the VAT treatment of transactions by agents see Notice 700 "The VAT guide".

You are considered to be making a supply of services to the vendor in return for commission charged, and if a buyer's premium is charged, you are also making a further supply of services to the buyer.

It is important not to confuse the supply of the goods with the supply of services to the seller or the buyer.

As an agent or auctioneer, you are treated as if you were supplying the goods yourself. The special scheme applies to you in the same way as it would apply to a principal. Supplies involving investment gold or investment gold coins will be exempt, unless you are selling gold upon which an option to tax has been exercised. For more information about opting to tax see section 4. The auctioneer will also have the same rights of deduction (see section 5) and is bound by the same notification, record keeping and accounting obligations (see sections 6, 7, and 8).

It is important that you check with the vendor before the sale whether the gold being sold is investment gold. If you are an auctioneer you should also remember that investment gold coins are not eligible for the Auctioneers' Scheme.

If you are an agent or auctioneer acting in your own name, your supply of services to either the buyer or the seller will be taxable.

(*b*) *Where you are acting in the name of your principal*

If, as an agent or auctioneer, you sell and invoice the goods in the name of your principal, your supply will be exempt (see paragraph 2.2). You may opt to tax these services, if you are registered for VAT and your principal also opts to tax his onward supply of the investment gold (see paragraph 4.5).

7.4 Internet and mail order sales

If you sell investment gold over the internet or by mail order and you fulfil the conditions at (a) or (b) below, you may, instead of keeping the customer record set out at paragraph 7.1(b), keep and maintain the following record—

(a) if your supply is paid for by credit card and the delivery address is also the card holder's address, you must record the name of your customer, the credit card issuer and the card number; or

(b) if your supply is paid for by cheque, you must record the name of your customer, the name of the bank and the account number of your customer.

You must also keep proof of despatch of the investment gold to your customer's address.

7.5 Sales by VAT registered businesses

If you are registered for VAT and you are—

- authorised to opt to tax supplies of investment gold; or
- a producer or transformer of investment gold;

you must keep and maintain with your VAT account, in addition to the records set out in paragraphs 3.1, 6.2, 6.3, and 7.3(a) and 7.6, a record of any supply of investment gold made to another taxable person where you have delivered or otherwise made the gold available to them, and on which you have not opted to tax.

7.6 Sales to VAT registered businesses

If you sell investment gold to another VAT registered business you may, instead of keeping the customer record described at paragraph 7.1(b), ask your customer for their VAT registration number. However, you must check with your local Business Advice Centre that the VAT registration number provided is authentic.

7.7 How long must I keep my records?

You must keep all the documents and records specified in this section for at least six years from the date of the transaction. In the case of regular customers, you must keep your customer record for six years following the most recent supply of investment gold.

If you purchase investment gold you must keep the purchase invoice you receive for at least six years from the date of the transaction.

VAT

Notice 701/21A Investment gold coins

January 2009
This notice cancels and replaces Notice 701/21A (February 2008).

1 INTRODUCTION

1.1 What does this notice cover?

This notice:

— explains that an investment gold coin is exempt from Value Added Tax (VAT) and explains which coins can be considered as investment gold coins (see Section 2) and

— provides revised lists of investment gold coins whose supply is exempt from VAT (in Section 3). Readers are advised that, because there are several changes from previous lists, they should refer directly to the lists for qualifying coins.

You should read this notice alongside Notice 701/21 "Gold" which gives further information about dealing in gold coins.

Commentary—*De Voil Indirect Tax Service* **V4.186.**

1.2 Who should read this notice?

Traders dealing in investment gold coins.

2 INVESTMENT GOLD COINS

2.1 What is an investment gold coin?

An investment gold coin is:

(a) gold coin minted after 1800 that:

— is of a purity of not less than 900 thousandths
— is, or has been, legal tender in its country of origin and
— is of a description of coin that is normally sold at a price that does not exceed 180 per cent of the open market value of the gold contained in the coin or

(b) a gold coin on the lists in Section 3.

A coin not on the lists can still be exempt from VAT if it falls within the description at (a) above. But you must be able to show from your business records that any such coin meets the criteria.

You should treat coins that do not fall within (a) or (b) above as subject to VAT at the standard rate.

Commentary—*De Voil Indirect Tax Service* **V4.186.**

2.2 Coin types

All gold coins that have the same denomination (face value), size and gold fineness as those described at paragraph 2.1 and Section 3, are exempt from VAT.

The definition for VAT purposes is wider than the one which coin experts (numismatists) normally use. This is because changes of superficial design do not alter the gold coin type or description.

So, a gold coin type may be a single issue for one year, or have been produced for almost two centuries, as in the case of the British sovereign.

Commentary—*De Voil Indirect Tax Service* **V4.186.**

2.3 Selling price

Of the three criteria in paragraph 2.1(a), only the selling price of the coin is subjective.

Coins are minted in various finishes and will be sold at a variety of prices. If exemption depended on the actual selling price of an individual coin this would lead to inconsistency. Administration of the exemption would become burdensome for traders and HM Revenue & Customs alike. For this reason, exemption depends on the normal selling price.

Commentary—*De Voil Indirect Tax Service* **V4.186.**

2.4 What is the "normal" selling price?

This is the price that can most usually be demanded for a particular type of coin.

It does not matter that an individual coin is of special interest to collectors; if the usual price of the coin type falls within 180 per cent of the value of the gold contained therein, all coins of that type will be exempt.

Similarly, if a coin type is usually valued at more than 180 per cent of the gold value, because of its interest to collectors, but an individual coin is in such poor condition that it is worth less than 180 per cent of its gold value, that coin (like others of its type), will be subject to VAT at the standard rate.

Commentary—*De Voil Indirect Tax Service* **V4.186.**

2.5 Conditions affecting the normal selling price

The finish influences the normal selling price of coins. Investment gold coins fall into two broad classes.

The first consists of relatively older issues made to circulate as currency.

These will normally be worn from circulation.

The second, generally more recent, are primarily produced as a store of wealth. These may have been issued in a number of finishes and if the majority of a type of coin are in for example 'brilliant uncirculated' condition then, other things being equal, the brilliant uncirculated value will reflect the normal selling price.

On the other hand, if the majority of a particular coin are in "proof" condition, then the value of the proof coin is more likely to reflect the normal selling price. The test of normal selling price must take into account these factors and be based on the condition in which the gold coin type is most frequently traded.

Commentary—*De Voil Indirect Tax Service* **V4.186.**

2.6 Can I use the Margin Scheme for investment gold coins?

No. You cannot sell investment gold coins (see paragraph 2.1) under the Margin Scheme.

If you have mistakenly included investment gold coins as purchases in Margin Scheme stock records, delete the entry and note it accordingly.

If you have included the coins in Global Accounting purchases, remove the items from the scheme and adjust the total purchases in the period. You must also deduct the value you have attributed to the items from your Global Accounting purchase record.

Guidance on correcting errors is in Notice 700/45 "How to correct VAT errors and make adjustments or claims".

Further guidance on the Margin Scheme is in Notice 718 "Margin Schemes for second-hand goods, works of art, antiques and collectors' items".

Commentary—*De Voil Indirect Tax Service* **V4.186.**

2.7 Record keeping requirements for dealers in investment gold coins

There are specific record keeping and notification rules for dealers in investment gold and investment gold coins. These are in Notice 701/21 "Gold".

3 LISTS OF INVESTMENT GOLD COINS

The European Commission publish annually a list of gold coins which must be treated as investment gold coins in all EU member states. **The list has legal force and supplements the law.**

HM Revenue & Customs have added an additional list of gold coins alongside the European Commission list [not reproduced here]. These are gold coins that HM Revenue & Customs recognise as falling within the exemption for investment gold coins.

This second list does not have legal force.

These lists are valid for the year 2009. They are set in alphabetical order, by names of countries and denominations of coins. Within the same category of coins, the list follows the increasing value of the currency.

The denomination of each coin reflects the currency shown on the coins.

However, where the currency on the coin is not shown in roman script, where possible its denomination in the list is shown in brackets.

Commentary—*De Voil Indirect Tax Service* **V4.186.**

TABLE 1: THE EUROPEAN COMMISSION LIST

Country of issue	*Denomination of the coins*
AFGHANISTAN	(20 AFGHANI)
	10000 AFGHANI
	(½ AMANI)
	(1 AMANI)
	(2 AMANI)
	(4 GRAMS)
	(8 GRAMS)

Country of issue	*Denomination of the coins*
	1 TILLA
	2 TILLAS
ALBANIA	20 LEKE
	50 LEKE
	100 LEKE
	200 LEKE
	500 LEKE
	5 POUNDS
ALDERNEY	25 POUNDS
	1000 POUNDS
ANDORRA	50 DINERS
	100 DINERS
	250 DINERS
ANGUILLA	1 SOVEREIGN
	5 DOLLARS
	10 DOLLARS
	20 DOLLARS
	100 DOLLARS
ARGENTINA	1 ARGENTINO
ARUBA	10 FLORIN
	25 FLORIN
AUSTRALIA	5 DOLLARS
	15 DOLLARS
	25 DOLLARS
	50 DOLLARS
	100 DOLLARS
	150 DOLLARS
	200 DOLLARS
	250 DOLLARS
	500 DOLLARS
	1000 DOLLARS
	2500 DOLLARS
	3000 DOLLARS
	10000 DOLLARS
	½ SOVEREIGN (= ½ POUND)
	1 SOVEREIGN (= 1 POUND)
AUSTRIA	10 CORONA (= 10 KRONEN)
	20 CORONA (= 20 KRONEN)
	100 CORONA (= 100 KRONEN)
	1 DUCAT
	(4 DUCATS)
	10 EURO
	25 EURO
	50 EURO
	100 EURO
	4 FLORIN = 10 FRANCS (= 4 GULDEN)
	8 FLORIN = 20 FRANCS (= 8 GULDEN)
	25 SCHILLING
	100 SCHILLING
	200 SCHILLING
	500 SCHILLING
	1000 SCHILLING
	2000 SCHILLING
BAHAMAS	10 DOLLARS
	20 DOLLARS
	25 DOLLARS
	50 DOLLARS
	100 DOLLARS
	150 DOLLARS
	200 DOLLARS

Country of issue	*Denomination of the coins*
	250 DOLLARS
	2500 DOLLARS
BELGIUM	10 ECU
	25 ECU
	50 ECU
	100 ECU
	50 EURO GOLD
	100 EURO
BELIZE	5000 FRANCS
	25 DOLLARS
	50 DOLLARS
	100 DOLLARS
	250 DOLLARS
BERMUDA	10 DOLLARS
	25 DOLLARS
	30 DOLLARS
	50 DOLLARS
	60 DOLLARS
	100 DOLLARS
	200 DOLLARS
	250 DOLLARS
BHUTAN	1 SERTUM
	2 SERTUMS
	5 SERTUMS
BOLIVIA	4000 PESOS BOLIVIANOS
BOTSWANA	5 PULA
	150 PULA
	10 THEBE
BRAZIL	300 CRUZEIROS
	(4 000 REIS)
	(5 000 REIS)
	(6 400 REIS)
	(10 000 REIS)
	(20 000 REIS)
BRITISH VIRGIN ISLES	100 DOLLARS
BULGARIA	10 LEVA
	20 LEVA
	100 LEVA
BURUNDI	10 FRANCS
	25 FRANCS
	50 FRANCS
	100 FRANCS
CANADA	1 DOLLAR
	2 DOLLARS
	5 DOLLARS
	10 DOLLARS
	20 DOLLARS
	50 DOLLARS
	100 DOLLARS
	175 DOLLARS
	200 DOLLARS
	350 DOLLARS
	1 SOVEREIGN
CAYMAN ISLANDS	25 DOLLARS
	50 DOLLARS
	100 DOLLARS
CHAD	250 DOLLARS
	3000 FRANCS
	5000 FRANCS
	10000 FRANCS

Country of issue	*Denomination of the coins*
	20000 FRANCS
CHILE	2 PESOS
	5 PESOS
	10 PESOS
	20 PESOS
	50 PESOS
	100 PESOS
	200 PESOS
CHINA	5/20 YUAN (1/20 oz)
	10/50 YUAN (1/10 oz)
	50/200 YUAN (½ oz)
	100/500 YUAN (1 oz)
	5 (YUAN)
	10 (YUAN)
	20 (YUAN)
	25 (YUAN)
	50 (YUAN)
	100 (YUAN)
	150 (YUAN)
	200 (YUAN)
	250 (YUAN)
	300 (YUAN)
	400 (YUAN)
	450 (YUAN)
	500 (YUAN)
	1000 (YUAN)
COLOMBIA	1 PESO
	2 PESOS
	2 ½ PESOS
	5 PESOS
	10 PESOS
	20 PESOS
	100 PESOS
	200 PESOS
	300 PESOS
	500 PESOS
	1000 PESOS
	1500 PESOS
	2000 PESOS
	15000 PESOS
CONGO	10 FRANCS
	20 FRANCS
	25 FRANCS
	50 FRANCS
	100 FRANCS
COOK ISLANDS	100 DOLLARS
	200 DOLLARS
	250 DOLLARS
COSTA RICA	5 COLONES
	10 COLONES
	20 COLONES
	50 COLONES
	100 COLONES
	200 COLONES
	1500 COLONES
	5000 COLONES
	25000 COLONES
CUBA	4 PESOS
	5 PESOS
	10 PESOS

Country of issue	*Denomination of the coins*
	20 PESOS
	50 PESOS
	100 PESOS
CYPRUS	50 POUNDS
CZECH REPUBLIC	1000 KORUN (1000 Kc)
	2000 KORUN (2000 Kc)
	2500 KORUN (2500 Kc)
	5000 KORUN (5000 Kc)
	10000 KORUN (10000 Kc)
CZECHOSLOVAKIA	1 DUKAT
	2 DUKAT
	5 DUKAT
	10 DUKAT
DENMARK	20 KRONER
DOMINICAN REPUBLIC	30 PESOS
	100 PESOS
	200 PESOS
	250 PESOS
ECUADOR	1 CONDOR
	10 SUCRES
EL SALVADOR	25 COLONES
	50 COLONES
	100 COLONES
	200 COLONES
	250 COLONES
EQUATORIAL GUINEA	250 PESETAS
	500 PESETAS
	750 PESETAS
	1000 PESETAS
	5000 PESETAS
ETHIOPIA	400 BIRR
	600 BIRR
	10 (DOLLARS)
	20 (DOLLARS)
	50 (DOLLARS)
	100(DOLLARS)
	200 (DOLLARS)
FIJI	200 DOLLARS
	250 DOLLARS
FINLAND	100 EURO
FRANCE	¼ EURO
	10 EURO
	20 EURO
	50 EURO
	5 FRANCS
	10 FRANCS
	40 FRANCS
	50 FRANCS
	100 FRANCS
	500 FRANCS
	655, 97 FRANCS
GABON	10 FRANCS
	25 FRANCS
	50 FRANCS
	100 FRANCS
	1000 FRANCS
	3000 FRANCS
	5000 FRANCS

Country of issue	*Denomination of the coins*
	10000 FRANCS
	20000 FRANCS
GAMBIA	200 DALASIS
	500 DALASIS
	1000 DALASIS
GIBRALTAR	1/25 CROWN
	1/10 CROWN
	1/5 CROWN
	1/2 CROWN
	1 CROWN
	2 CROWNS
	50 PENCE
	1 POUND
	5 POUNDS
	25 POUNDS
	50 POUNDS
	100 POUNDS
	1/25 ROYAL
	1/10 ROYAL
	1/5 ROYAL
	½ ROYAL
	1 ROYAL
GUATEMALA	5 QUETZALES
	10 QUETZALES
	20 QUETZALES
GUERNSEY	1 POUND
	5 POUNDS
	10 POUNDS
	25 POUNDS
	50 POUNDS
	100 POUNDS
GUINEA	1000 FRANCS
	2000 FRANCS
	5000 FRANCS
	10000 FRANCS
HAITI	20 GOURDES
	50 GOURDES
	100 GOURDES
	200 GOURDES
	500 GOURDES
	1000 GOURDES
HONDURAS	200 LEMPIRAS
	500 LEMPIRAS
HONG KONG	1000 DOLLARS
HUNGARY	1 DUKAT
	4 FORINT = 10 FRANCS
	8 FORINT = 20 FRANCS
	50 FORINT
	100 FORINT
	200 FORINT
	500 FORINT
	1 000 FORINT
	5 000 FORINT
	10 000 FORINT
	20 000 FORINT
	50 000 FORINT
	100 000 FORINT
	20 KORONA
	100 KORONA
ICELAND	500 KRONUR

Country of issue	*Denomination of the coins*
	10000 KRONUR
INDIA	1 MOHUR
	15 RUPEES
	1 SOVEREIGN
INDONESIA	2000 RUPIAH
	5000 RUPIAH
	10000 RUPIAH
	20000 RUPIAH
	25000 RUPIAH
	100000 RUPIAH
	200000 RUPIAH
IRAN	(½ AZADI)
	(1 AZADI)
	(¼ PAHLAVI)
	(½ PAHLAVI)
	(1 PAHLAVI)
	(2½ PAHLAVI)
	(5 PAHLAVI)
	(10 PAHLAVI)
	500 RIALS
	750 RIALS
	1 000 RIALS
	2 000 RIALS
	50 POUND
IRAQ	(5 DINARS)
	(50 DINARS)
	(100 DINARS)
ISLE OF MAN	1/20 ANGEL
	1/10 ANGEL
	¼ ANGEL
	½ ANGEL
	1 ANGEL
	5 ANGEL
	10 ANGEL
	15 ANGEL
	20 ANGEL
	1/25 CROWN
	1/10 CROWN
	1/5 CROWN
	½ CROWN
	1 CROWN
	50 PENCE
	1 POUND
	2 POUNDS
	5 POUNDS
	50 POUNDS
	(½/SOVEREIGN)
	(1 SOVEREIGN)
	(2 SOVEREIGNS)
	(5 SOVEREIGNS)
ISRAEL	20 LIROT
	50 LIROT
	100 LIROT
	200 LIROT
	500 LIROT
	1 000 LIROT
	5 000 LIROT
	5 NEW SHEQALIM
	10 NEW SHEQALIM
	20 NEW SHEQALIM

Country of issue	*Denomination of the coins*
	5 SHEQALIM
	10 SHEQALIM
	500 SHEQEL
IVORY COAST	10 FRANCS
	25 FRANCS
	50 FRANCS
	100 FRANCS
JAMAICA	100 DOLLARS
	250 DOLLARS
JERSEY	1 POUND
	2 POUNDS
	5 POUNDS
	10 POUNDS
	20 POUNDS
	25 POUNDS
	50 POUNDS
	100 POUNDS
	1 SOVEREIGN
JORDAN	2 DINARS
	5 DINARS
	10 DINARS
	25 DINARS
	50 DINARS
	60 DINARS
KATANGA	5 FRANCS
KENYA	100 SHILLINGS
	250 SHILLINGS
	500 SHILLINGS
KIRIBATI	150 DOLLARS
LATVIA	100 LATU
LESOTHO	1 LOTI
	2 MALOTI
	4 MALOTI
	10 MALOTI
	20 MALOTI
	50 MALOTI
	100 MALOTI
	250 MALOTI
	500 MALOTI
LIBERIA	12 DOLLARS
	20 DOLLARS
	25 DOLLARS
	30 DOLLARS
	50 DOLLARS
	100 DOLLARS
	200 DOLLARS
	250 DOLLARS
	500 DOLLARS
	2500 DOLLARS
LUXEMBOURG	5 EURO
	10 EURO
	20 FRANCS
	40 FRANCS
MACAU	250 PATACAS
	500 PATACAS
	1000 PATACAS
	10000 PATACAS
MALAWI	250 KWACHA
MALAYSIA	100 RINGGIT
	200 RINGGIT

Country of issue	*Denomination of the coins*
	250 RINGGIT
	500 RINGGIT
MALI	10 FRANCS
	25 FRANCS
	50 FRANCS
	100 FRANCS
MALTA	5 (LIRI)
	10 (LIRI)
	20 (LIRI)
	25 (LIRI)
	50 (LIRI)
	100 (LIRI)
	25 LM
	50 EURO
MARSHALL ISLANDS	20 DOLLARS
	50 DOLLARS
	200 DOLLARS
MAURITIUS	100 RUPEES
	200 RUPEES
	250 RUPEES
	500 RUPEES
	1000 RUPEES
MEXICO	2 PESOS
	2½ PESOS
	5 PESOS
	10 PESOS
	20 PESOS
	50 PESOS
	250 PESOS
	500 PESOS
	1 000 PESOS
	2 000 PESOS
	1/20 ONZA
	1/10 ONZA
	¼ ONZA
	½ ONZA
	1 ONZA
MONACO	100 FRANCS
	200 FRANCS
	10 EURO
	20 EURO
	100 EURO
MONGOLIA	750 (TUGRIK)
	1000 (TUGRIK)
NEPAL	1 ASARPHI
	1000 RUPEES
NETHERLANDS	(1 DUKAAT)
	(2 DUKAAT)
	1 GULDEN
	5 GULDEN
	10 EURO
	20 EURO
	50 EURO
NETHERLANDS ANTILLES	5 GULDEN
	10 GULDEN
	50 GULDEN
	100 GULDEN
	300 GULDEN
NEW ZEALAND	10 DOLLARS
	150 DOLLARS

Country of issue	*Denomination of the coins*
NICARAGUA	50 CORDOBAS
	10 FRANCS
	25 FRANCS
	50 FRANCS
NIGER	100 FRANCS
NORWAY	1500 KRONER
OMAN	25 BAISA
	50 BAISA
	100 BAISA
	¼ OMANI RIAL
	½ OMANI RIAL
	OMANI RIAL
	5 OMANI RIALS
	10 OMANI RIALS
	15 OMANI RIALS
	20 OMANI RIALS
	25 OMANI RIALS
	75 OMANI RIALS
PAKISTAN	3000 RUPEES
PANAMA	100 BALBOAS
	500 BALBOAS
PAPUA NEW GUINEA	100 KINA
	1/5 LIBRA
	½ LIBRA
	1 LIBRA
	5 SOLES
	10 SOLES
	20 SOLES
	50 SOLES
PERU	100 SOLES
PHILIPPINES	1000 PISO
	1500 PISO
	5000 PISO
POLAND	50 ZLOTY (Golden Eagle)
	100 ZLOTY (Golden Eagle)
	100 ZLOTY
	200 ZLOTY (Golden Eagle)
	200 ZLOTY
	500 ZLOTY (Golden Eagle)
PORTUGAL	1 ESCUDO
	100 ESCUDOS
	200 ESCUDOS
	500 ESCUDOS
	10000 REIS
	5 EURO
	8 EURO
RHODESIA	10 SHILLINGS
	1 POUND
	5 POUNDS
RUSSIA	25 ROUBLES
	50 ROUBLES
	100 ROUBLES
	200 ROUBLES
	1000 ROUBLES
	10000 ROUBLES
RWANDA	10 FRANCS
	25 FRANCS
	50 FRANCS
	100 FRANCS
SAN MARINO	1 SCUDO

Country of issue	*Denomination of the coins*
	2 SCUDI
	5 SCUDI
	10 SCUDI
	20 EURO
	50 EURO
SAUDI ARABIA	1 GUINEA (= 1 SAUDI POUND)
	10 FRANCS
	25 FRANCS
	50 FRANCS
	100 FRANCS
	250 FRANCS
	500 FRANCS
	1000 FRANCS
SENEGAL	2500 FRANCS
SERBIA	10 DINARA
	20 DINARA
SEYCHELLES	1000 RUPEES
	1500 RUPEES
SIERRA LEONE	¼ GOLDE
	½ GOLDE
	1 GOLDE
	5 GOLDE
	10 GOLDE
	1 LEONE
	20 DOLLARS
	50 DOLLARS
	100 DOLLARS
	250 DOLLARS
	500 DOLLARS
	2500 DOLLARS
SINGAPORE	1 DOLLAR
	2 DOLLARS
	5 DOLLARS
	10 DOLLARS
	20 DOLLARS
	25 DOLLARS
	50 DOLLARS
	100 DOLLARS
	150 DOLLARS
	250 DOLLARS
	500 DOLLARS
SLOVENIA	2500 TOLARS
	5000 TOLARS
	20000 TOLARS
	25000 TOLARS
	100 EURO
	180 EURO
SOLOMON ISLANDS	10 DOLLARS
	25 DOLLARS
	50 DOLLARS
	100 DOLLARS
SOMALIA	20 SHILLINGS
	50 SHILLINGS
	100 SHILLINGS
	200 SHILLINGS
	500 SHILLINGS
	1500 SHILLINGS
SOUTH AFRICA	1/10 KRUGERRAND
	¼ KRUGERRAND
	½ KRUGERRAND

Country of issue	*Denomination of the coins*
	1 KRUGERRAND
	1/10 oz NATURA
	¼ oz NATURA
	½ oz NATURA
	1 oz NATURA
	1/10 PROTEA
	1 PROTEA
	½ POND
	1 POND
	1 RAND
	2 RAND
	5 RAND
	25 RAND
	½ SOVEREIGN (= ½ POUND)
	1 SOVEREIGN (= 1 POUND)
SOUTH KOREA	2500 WON
	20000 WON
	25000 WON
	30000 WON
	50000 WON
SPAIN	2 (ESCUDOS)
	10 (ESCUDOS)
	10 PESETAS
	20 PESETAS
	5 000 PESETAS
	10 000 PESETAS
	20 000 PESETAS
	40 000 PESETAS
	80 000 PESETAS
	200 EURO
	400 EURO
SUDAN	25 POUNDS
	50 POUNDS
	100 POUNDS
SURINAM	100 GULDEN
	2 EMALANGENI
	5 EMALANGENI
	10 EMALANGENI
	20 EMALANGENI
	25 EMALANGENI
	50 EMALANGENI
	100 EMALANGENI
	250 EMALANGENI
SWAZILAND	1 LILANGENI
	20 KRONOR
	1000 KRONOR
SWEDEN	2000 KRONOR
SWITZERLAND	50 FRANCS
	100 FRANCS
SYRIA	(½ POUND)
	(1 POUND)
TANZANIA	1500 SHILINGI
	2000 SHILINGI
THAILAND	(150 BAHT)
	(300 BAHT)
	(400 BAHT)
	(600 BAHT)
	(800 BAHT)
	(1500 BAHT)
	(2500 BAHT)

Country of issue	*Denomination of the coins*
	(3000 BAHT)
	(4000 BAHT)
	(5000 BAHT)
	(6000 BAHT)
TONGA	½ HAU
	1 HAU
	5 HAU
	¼ KOULA
	½ KOULA
	1 KOULA
TUNISIA	2 DINARS
	5 DINARS
	10 DINARS
	20 DINARS
	40 DINARS
	75 DINARS
	10 FRANCS
	20 FRANCS
	100 FRANCS
	5 PIASTRES
TURKEY	(25 KURUSH) (= 25 PIASTRES)
	(50 KURUSH) (= 50 PIASTRES)
	(250 KURUSH) (= 250 PIASTRES)
	(500 KURUSH) (= 500 PIASTRES)
	½ LIRA
	1 LIRA
	500 LIRA
	1000 LIRA
	10000 LIRA
	50000 LIRA
	100000 LIRA
	200000 LIRA
	1000000 LIRA
	60000000 LIRA
TURKS & CAICOS ISLANDS	100 CROWNS
TUVALU	50 DOLLARS
UGANDA	50 SHILLINGS
	100 SHILLINGS
	500 SHILLINGS
	1000 SHILLINGS
UNITED ARAB EMIRATES	(500 DIRHAMS)
	(750 DIRHAMS)
	(1000 DIRHAMS)
UNITED KINGDOM	(1/3 GUINEA)
	(½ GUINEA)
	50 PENCE
	2 POUNDS
	5 POUNDS
	10 POUNDS
	25 POUNDS
	50 POUNDS
	100 POUNDS
	(½ /SOVEREIGN) (= ½ /POUND)
	(2 SOVEREIGNS)
	(5 SOVEREIGNS)
URUGUAY	5000 NUEVO PESOS
	20000 NUEVO PESOS
	5 PESOS
USA	10 DOLLARS (AMERICAN EAGLE)
	1 DOLLAR

Country of issue	Denomination of the coins
	2.5 DOLLARS
	5 DOLLARS
	20 DOLLARS
	25 DOLLARS
	50 DOLLARS
VATICAN	10 LIRE GOLD
	20 LIRE
	100 LIRE GOLD
	20 EURO
	50 EURO
VENEZUELA	(10 BOLIVARES)
	(20 BOLIVARES)
	(100 BOLIVARES)
	1000 BOLIVARES
	3000 BOLIVARES
	3000 BOLIVARES
	5000 BOLIVARES
	10000 BOLIVARES
	5 VENEZOLANOS
WESTERN SAMOA	50 TALA
	100 TALA
YUGOSLAVIA	1 DUCAT
	4 DUCATS
	20 DINARA
	100 DINARA
	200 DINARA
	500 DINARA
	1000 DINARA
	1500 DINARA
	2000 DINARA
	2500 DINARA
	5000 DINARA
ZAIRE	100 ZAIRES
ZAMBIA	250 KWACHA

Notice 701/36 Insurance

2002

Note—This notice cancels and replaces Notice 701/36 (October 1997).

Paragraph 11.3.1 in this Notice has the force of law under VATA 1994 Sch 11 para 6(1), VAT Regulations, SI 1995/2518 reg 31(1), (2), VATA 1994 Sch 9 Group 2 Item 4, Note (4)(*c*)(iii).

11.3 DISCLOSURE PROVISIONS

There are special provisions in UK VAT legislation requiring suppliers to disclose to their customers any amount they charge, in addition to the insurance premium, for arranging the insurance. These provisions are as follows.

If you are:

– a supplier of taxable (but not zero rated) goods or services; and
– insurance is supplied to your customers in connection with the supply of those goods or services; and
– a supply of related services is made in connection with that insurance by either; you, the supplier of the goods or services, or by someone connected to you (as defined by section 839 of the Income and Corporation Taxes Act 1988)

then for any additional amount charged for arranging the insurance to be exempt:

– the amounts (in £'s sterling) of the premium and also of any fee charged in addition to the premium must be identified in writing on a document; and

– that document must be issued to the customer at or before the time the insurance transaction is entered into.

If these conditions are not met, there will continue to be no VAT chargeable on the amount collected by you and passed onto the insurer for the supply of insurance. Any fees or commission you receive for your services of arranging the insurance, however, will be liable to tax at the same rate as the goods or services themselves.

11.3.1 Disclosure procedures for insurance sold over the telephone, Internet etc

We realise that the disclosure provisions laid out in paragraph 11.3 may cause problems for businesses that effect transactions over the telephone, or by some other means of electronic communication, whereby the customer and the salesperson are not physically together when the sale takes place.

Obviously in these circumstances it would not be possible for a document containing the required statements to be given to the customer at or before the time the transaction is entered into.

To overcome this problem, we require a person selling insurance with taxable goods and/or services by electronic means to keep additional records as detailed under step 4 in the table below. VAT legislation allows us to specify which records a taxable business is required to keep and also allows us to supplement, by means of a notice (in this case, this notice), the list of those records.

For an additional fee charged by a supplier selling insurance with other goods or services by electronic means to be exempt, therefore, the following procedure must be implemented:

Step	Procedure
1	The supplier must make full disclosure at the time the insurance transaction takes place. For example, if holidays are being sold over the telephone, the salesperson must inform the customer orally of the amounts in sterling due for the premium and any additional fee charged in connection with the insurance.
2	The supplier must have in place a system whereby sales staff annotate a document (even if this only involves ticking a box) at the time they make oral or electronic disclosure to the customer to indicate that they have done so.
3	The supplier must comply with the legal requirement to prepare a document containing the details laid out in paragraph 11.3 and issue it to the customer (albeit after the insurance transaction has been entered into).
4	The supplier must retain a copy of these records as they would their normal VAT records.

11.3.2 Insurance sold with goods or services under a VAT margin scheme

The legislation states that we may set out in a notice the form of the document to be used for making the disclosure detailed in paragraph 11.3.

Using this notice, therefore, we require a person supplying goods or services under one of the VAT margin schemes to make the required disclosure on the relevant VAT invoice issued by that person.

Information on margin schemes can be found in Notices 718 Margin scheme for second-hand goods, works of art, antiques and collectors' items and 709/5 Tour operators' margin scheme.

Commentary—*De Voil Indirect Tax Service* **V4.121**.

Notice 701/48
Corporate purchasing cards

2002

3.3 The line item detail Vat invoice

Commentary—*De Voil Indirect Tax Service* **V3.415, V3.421**.
Note—This paragraph has the force of law under the VAT Regulations 1995, SI 1995/2518 regs 13, 14.

As the invoice report is issued by the card company or bank to the purchaser, the supplier will not know when it is actually issued. But as the date is normally only relevant for tax point purposes (which have been specially provided for, see para 2.3), Customs has agreed to waive the requirement to show the date of issue contained in the VAT Regulations, SI 1995/2518 reg 14(1)(*c*).

The invoice report issued to the purchaser must, however, show the transmission date for each transaction, so the purchaser will know the date from which input tax can be claimed. The invoice report is, therefore, acceptable as evidence for input tax recovery, subject to the normal rules governing entitlement.

In order to fulfil the requirements of the VAT Regulations, SI 1995/2518 reg 31, suppliers must retain the invoice data transmitted and any invoices from their normal systems which they have produced but not issued.

3.4 The summary VAT invoice

Commentary—*De Voil Indirect Tax Service* **V3.415, V3.421**.
Note—This paragraph has the force of law under SI 1995/2518 regs 14 and 15.

Some suppliers do not have accounting systems capable of transmitting LID invoices but are able to provide summary VAT information. As a general rule, Customs will accept summary VAT invoice reports in support of input tax claims.

The summary VAT invoice reports must contain the following information—

- value of the supply;
- VAT amount charged;
- VAT note;
- time of supply;
- description of the goods;
- supplier's name, address and VAT number; and
- customer's name and address.

If you are capable of transmitting only summary VAT data you must, for purchasing card transactions, continue to generate VAT invoices at the same time for output tax accounting purposes. However, you may discharge your obligation to issue an invoice where single transactions have a value of not more than £5,000 by transmitting the summary VAT information to your bank or card company.

Where the value of a single transaction exceeds £5,000, you must issue a VAT invoice. A single transaction is the total value of purchases made using a card at any one time, for example from one "swipe" of the card. You must also issue a copy of your normal VAT invoice, for any transaction where the value does not exceed £5,000, if you are specifically requested to do so by your customer. In such a case the invoice must be clearly endorsed with the words "Paid by purchasing card—Supplementary VAT invoice".

Notice 703
Export of goods from the United Kingdom

August 2006 (with Update 1)
This notice cancels and replaces Notice 703 (April 2005).

Parts of this notice have the force of law under s 30(6) of VATA 1994 and reg 129 of the VAT Regulations 1995. These parts are indicated by being placed in a box as in the example shown below.

> **The following rule has the force of law**
> The evidence you obtain as proof of export, whether official or commercial or supporting must clearly identify: the supplier, the consignor (where different from the supplier) the customer, the goods, an accurate value, the export destination, and mode of transport and route of the export movement.

1 INTRODUCTION

Commentary—*De Voil Indirect Tax Service* **Division V4.3**.

1.1 What is this notice about?

This notice explains the conditions for zero-rating VAT on an export of goods, that is, when the goods leave the European Community (EC). It also provides guidance on what you should do when you export goods in specific circumstances. Goods delivered from the United Kingdom (UK) to a destination elsewhere in the EC are not exports for VAT purposes. Such transactions are called removals. You can find out more about removals in Notice 725 "The Single Market" .

For information on zero-rating of services performed on goods for export see Notice 741 "Place of supply of services" , and Notice 744D "International services: zero-rating" .

1.2 What's changed?

The following changes to the April 2005 version have been made:

Paragraph	*Alteration*
2.3	Amended to clarify definition of exporter for VAT zero-rating purposes

Paragraph	*Alteration*
2.4	Amended to clarify definition of an overseas person
2.5 to 2.6	Amended to include additional advice for exporters and their agents
2.10	Amended to clarify definition of direct export
2.11	Amended to clarify definition of indirect export
2.16	New paragraph covering goods accidentally lost destroyed or stolen before export
3.3 to 3.6	Amended to clarify conditions for zero-rating direct and indirect exports
3.8	New paragraph on right of appeal
4.13	New paragraph on conditions for zero-rating exports of motor vehicles
4.14	New paragraph on tools used in the UK to manufacture goods for export
5.2 to 5.8	Amended to clarify evidence produced by the New Export System
5.10 to 5.12	New paragraphs covering the New Computerised Transit System
5.13	New paragraph covering evidence of export for goods going by road through the EC to Switzerland, Liechtenstein, Norway, San Marino, Andorra and Romania
6.3	Amended to clarify the position regarding photocopy evidence
7.3	Amended to clarify Merchandise in Baggage procedures
7.5	Amended to clarify evidence available for exports by letter post or airmail
9.2	New paragraph covering direct and indirect retail exports shipped as freight or household effects
11.2 to 11.3	Amended to clarify accounting adjustment if evidence of export not received or goods not exported
12.2 to 12.3	Amended to provide certificate of export from the EC not the UK
13	Deleted because the references to notices giving details of goods/procedures that have special requirements are now located elsewhere in this notice

1.3 Who should read this notice?

You should read this notice if you are a VAT registered person and you intend to export goods or if you are involved in the exportation of goods from the UK to a destination outside the EC as a customs clearing agent, freight forwarder, haulier, warehousekeeper, shipping company or airline.

1.4 What EC law is covered by this notice?

Article 15 of the EC Sixth VAT Directive (77/388/EEC) provides the legal basis for exempting goods dispatched or transported out of the EC. Amongst other things it states that member states shall lay down conditions "for the purpose of ensuring the correct and straightforward application of such exemptions and preventing any evasion, avoidance or abuse". The UK uses the term "zero-rating" rather than "exemption" used in EC law to avoid confusion with the use of exemption elsewhere in UK law.

1.5 Why do we refer to the EC and not the European Union (EU) throughout the notice?

The EU is a collective term. It does not, strictly speaking, have a legal personality.

Where we speak of Community law it is correct to speak of the EC. We have, therefore, retained the term EC throughout the notice.

1.6 What is the UK law relating to exports?

The UK VAT law relating to the zero-rating of exports of goods for VAT purposes can be found in—

- VATA 1994 s 30(6) for direct exports
- VATA 1994 s 30(8) and reg 129 of the VAT Regulations (SI 1995/2518) for indirect exports
- VATA 1994 s 30(10) for circumstances where the conditions for zero-rating are not met.

Additional legislation and Extra Statutory Concessions (ESCs) exist to allow relief from taxation in specific circumstances.

1.7 What is the legal status of this notice?

Under UK VAT law, HM Revenue & Customs may specify conditions to prevent evasion, avoidance or abuse. This notice lays down the conditions, which must be met in full, for goods exported outside the EC to be zero-rated. Plain English has been used wherever possible but as these conditions have legal status, some legal wording has been necessary.

Text shown in boxes has the force of law.

2 THE BASICS

2.1 What is meant by VAT zero-rating?

A zero-rated VAT supply is one which is subject to VAT but where the VAT is at 0 per cent.

Commentary—*De Voil Indirect Tax Service* **V4.201–202, 207.**

2.2 Why does zero-rating apply to exports?

VAT is a tax levied on goods and services consumed in the EC. When goods are exported they are "consumed" outside the EC and to impose VAT on such goods would be contrary to the purpose of the tax. Therefore, the supply of exported goods is zero-rated provided certain conditions are met.

2.3 Who is the "exporter" for VAT zero-rating purposes?

The exporter is the person who, for VAT purposes either—

- supplies or owns goods and exports or arranges for them to be exported to a destination outside the EC, or
- supplies goods to an overseas person, who arranges for the goods to be exported to a destination outside the EC.

Commentary—*De Voil Indirect Tax Service* **V4.201–202, 207.**

2.4 What is meant by "an overseas person"?

This means a person or company who is not resident or registered for VAT in the UK, has no business establishment in the UK from which taxable supplies are made, or is an overseas authority.

Commentary—*De Voil Indirect Tax Service* **V4.326.**

2.5 Can I appoint someone to handle my export transactions?

Yes. You can appoint a freight forwarder, shipping company, airline or other person to handle export transactions and produce the necessary customs export declarations on your behalf. In these circumstances, you must provide your representative with—

- A full description of the goods, including value, quantity and weight. Copies of the export invoice, packing list and technical details of the goods will help your representative to fully and accurately complete the export declaration and transport documents.

We also recommend that you provide your representative with:

- Your UK TURN (Trader's Unique Reference Number – that is your VAT registration number plus 3 digits – see Notice 553 TURN, Pseudo TURN, dummy TURN and Private Importations for details).
- A commercial reference number that your agent should incorporate into the Declaration Unique Consignment Reference (DUCR). DUCRs are key to an export consignment, and are used by many organisations in the exporting process for example, exporters, agents, freight forwarders, airlines, shipping lines and Customs. This will help to provide an audit trail showing the goods you have sold have been physically exported – see section 6 Proof of export.
- Once the export declaration has been made, we strongly advise that you ask your agent to supply the actual DUCR used, and the export entry reference number, as this information will ensure that the export transaction can be easily traced to your records for VAT zero-rating – see paragraphs 3.3 and 3.4 – conditions for zero-rating.

If your agent fails to fulfil any obligations it is you the exporter who becomes liable to account for any VAT which may become chargeable as a result of this failure.

2.6 What are an agent's obligations?

The freight forwarder, shipping company, airline or other person appointed by you, the exporter, or your overseas customer must—

- take reasonable steps to ensure that the goods are as described by the exporter
- ensure that the necessary pre- or post-shipment customs formalities are completed
- ensure that the goods are exported within the time limits specified by the exporter
- keep records of each export transaction
- obtain or provide valid evidence of export (see sections 6 and 7) and send it to the exporter once the goods have been exported.

We also recommend that agents—

- Ask the exporter for their UK TURN for use in Box 2 of the export declaration (for commercial exports it is not acceptable to enter "PR" in box 2).
- Wherever possible use the exporter's TURN and commercial reference as part of the DUCR, and routinely advise the exporter of the DUCR and the CHIEF export entry reference (see section 5 for information about CHIEF). This will help the exporter to provide an audit trail showing that the goods sold have been physically exported.

2.7 Which countries are part of the UK for VAT purposes?

The UK consists of England, Scotland, Wales, Northern Ireland and the waters within 12 nautical miles of their coastlines. Although the Isle of Man has its own VAT authority, sales to the Isle of Man are treated as any other sale within the UK.

The Channel Islands are part of the Customs territory of the EC, but are *outside* the EC, including the UK, for fiscal (VAT) purposes. Supplies of goods sent to the Channel Islands are regarded as exports for VAT purposes and may be zero-rated if the conditions set out in paragraph 3.3 or 3.4 are met. See paragraph 7.2 for information about evidence of export of goods to the Channel Islands.

Commentary—*De Voil Indirect Tax Service* **V1.215**.

2.8 Which countries and territories are part of the EC Fiscal (VAT) area?

- Austria
- Belgium
- Cyprus*
- Czech Republic
- Denmark, except the Faroe Islands and Greenland
- Estonia
- Finland
- France, including Monaco
- Germany, except Busingen and the Isle of Heligoland
- Greece
- Hungary
- The Republic of Ireland
- Italy, except the communes of Livigno and Campione d'Italia and the Italian waters of Lake Lugano
- Latvia
- Lithuania
- Luxembourg
- Malta
- The Netherlands
- Poland
- Portugal, including the Azores and Madeira
- Slovakia
- Spain, including the Balearic Islands but excluding Ceuta and Melilla
- Slovenia
- Sweden
- United Kingdom and the Isle of Man.

[Plus, from 1 January 2007—
- Bulgaria;
- Romania.]

*The European Commission has advised that the application of the Sixth VAT Directive (Directive 77/388/EEC of 17 May 1977) shall be suspended in those areas of Cyprus in which the Government of the Republic of Cyprus does not exercise effective control. Goods to these destinations continue to be eligible for zero-rating as exports.

Note—Para 2.8 amended by Update 1, January 2007.
Commentary—*De Voil Indirect Tax Service* **V1.213**.

2.9 Countries and territories outside the EC fiscal (VAT) area

- The Aland Islands
- Andorra
- The Canary Islands
- The Channel Islands
- The overseas departments of France (Guadeloupe, Martinique, Réunion, St. Pierre and Miquelon, and French Guiana)
- Gibraltar
- Mount Athos
- San Marino
- The Vatican City
- All other countries which do not appear in paragraph 2.8.

Commentary—*De Voil Indirect Tax Service* **V1.213**.

2.10 What is meant by direct exports?

For VAT purposes a direct export occurs when you the supplier send goods to a destination outside the EC, and you are responsible either for arranging the transport yourself or appointing a freight agent. The goods may be exported by any of the following means—

- in your baggage
- in your own transport
- by rail, post or courier service, or
- by a shipping line, airline or freight forwarder employed by you and not by your customer.

Commentary—*De Voil Indirect Tax Service* **V4.311**.

2.11 What is meant by indirect exports?

An indirect export occurs when your overseas customer (as defined in paragraph 2.4) or their agent collects or arranges for the collection of the goods from you the supplier within the UK and then takes them outside the EC. This includes goods collected ex-works (see paragraph 6.6 for further information).

Commentary—*De Voil Indirect Tax Service* **V4.326**.

2.12 What happens if I supply goods to a non-EC branch of a UK VAT registered company?

(a) Where you supply goods directly to a customer outside the EC, and that customer is a branch of a UK VAT registered company, you may zero-rate the supply as a direct export provided—
   - you or your representative arranges for the goods to be sent directly to a non-EC country
   - the overseas delivery address for the goods is shown on the invoice even if the invoice is made out or sent to the associated UK company, or a UK Shared Service Centre for administrative reasons, and
   - the conditions, time limits and evidential requirements for direct exports are met—see paragraph 3.3.

(b) But where your customer or their representative arranges for the goods to be exported outside the EC, this is an indirect export. As the non-EC branch is a taxable person in the UK, it is not an "overseas person" for VAT zero-rating purposes – see paragraph 2.4. This means that the conditions in paragraph 3.4 are not met and the supply cannot be zero-rated. VAT is due at the appropriate UK rate.

Commentary—*De Voil Indirect Tax Service* **V4.326**.

2.13 What is the time of supply of exported goods?

The time of supply determines when a supply of goods or services is treated as taking place. This is called the tax point. In most cases the time of supply will be the earlier of either the date you—

- send the goods to your customer or your customer takes them away, or
- receive full payment for the goods.

For the treatment of deposits and progress payments see paragraph 11.5.

Commentary—*De Voil Indirect Tax Service* **V3.131, V4.307**.

2.14 How do I treat exports where there is no taxable supply?

You need not account for VAT if you—

- supply and export goods which you are to install outside the EC for your customer (the supply takes place in the country where the goods are installed)
- export goods outside the EC temporarily for exhibition or processing, or
- export goods outside the EC on sale or return, where the goods remain your property until they are sold.

However, you must still hold valid proof of export (see sections 6 and 7) to demonstrate to us how you disposed of the goods. You must also declare to us any goods returned to the UK.

2.15 How do I treat transfer of my own goods?

When transferring goods from your UK business to your branch outside the EC you need proof of export as evidence that you have transferred your goods.

Transfer of goods from your UK business to a branch outside the EC is not a supply but you must declare to us any goods returned to the UK, and retain the details. You can deduct any related input tax subject to the normal rules but do not include the value of any transferred goods as an output in Box 6 of your VAT return.

2.16 Goods accidentally lost, destroyed or stolen before export

You must account for VAT on goods destined for export outside the EC which have been accidentally lost, destroyed or stolen in the UK as follows—

- before you supplied them – no VAT is due
- you supplied them for direct export – no VAT is due provided that evidence of loss, destruction or theft is held, for example an insurance claim, police investigation etc
- you supplied them for indirect export – VAT is due at the appropriate rate if the goods have been delivered to or collected by the overseas person, or their agent, in the UK.

Commentary—*De Voil Indirect Tax Service* **V4.339.**

3 CONDITIONS AND TIME LIMITS FOR ZERO-RATING

3.1 General

You must meet certain conditions before you can zero-rate supplies of goods for export. These conditions cover the—

- evidence (either official or commercial) you must hold to prove entitlement to zero-rating
- time limits in which the goods must be physically exported from the EC
- time limits in which you must obtain evidence of export to support zero-rating.

Only exports that comply with these conditions are eligible for zero-rating.

Commentary—*De Voil Indirect Tax Service* **V4.307.**

3.2 Why are conditions necessary?

The conditions set out in regulations and this notice are necessary to ensure only genuine exports are zero-rated whilst keeping VAT export procedures as simple as possible.

3.3 Conditions for zero-rating direct exports

The text in this box has the force of law

A supply of goods sent to a destination outside the EC is liable to the zero rate as a direct export where you—

- ensure that the goods are exported from the EC within the specified time limits (see paragraph 3.5)
- obtain official or commercial evidence of export as appropriate (see paragraphs 6.2 and 6.3) within the specified time limits
- keep supplementary evidence of the export transaction (see paragraph 6.4), *and*
- comply with the law and the conditions of this notice.

You must not zero-rate a direct export where you—

- deliver or post the goods to a customer's address in the EC (including the UK), or
- allow the goods to be collected by or on behalf of your customer even if it is claimed they are for subsequent export. See paragraphs 3.6 and 7.4 for details of deliveries made to another UK trader for groupage, consolidation, processing or incorporation prior to export.

3.4 Conditions for zero-rating indirect exports

The text in this box has the force of law

A supply of goods to an overseas customer (see paragraph 2.4) sent to a destination outside the EC is liable to the zero rate as an indirect export where your overseas customer:

- exports the goods from the EC within the specified time limits (see paragraph 3.5), *and*
- obtains and gives you valid official or commercial evidence of export as appropriate (see paragraphs 6.2 and 6.3) within the specified time limits, and you:
- keeps supplementary evidence of export transactions (see paragraph 6.4), *and*
- complies with the law and the conditions of this notice, *and* the goods are not used between the time of leaving your premises and export, except where specifically authorised elsewhere in this notice or any other VAT notice.

You must not zero-rate an indirect export where the goods are—

- supplied to a private individual who is resident in the UK, or
- supplied to a business registered for VAT in the UK (including an overseas business that has a place of business in the UK from which taxable supplies are made), or
- delivered to, or collected by, a UK customer at a UK address.

If your export transactions do not fit specifically into any of these categories or those listed in sections 3 and 4 contact our National Advice Service for advice prior to export, obtaining a written decision, if necessary.

3.5 What are the time limits for exporting the goods and obtaining evidence?

You must export the goods from the EC and obtain valid evidence of export within the time limits shown in the table below. In all cases the time limits are triggered by the time of supply (see paragraph 12.3).

The text in this box has the force of law

Type of export	*Time limit for exporting goods*	*Time limit for obtaining evidence*
Direct (under the control of the supplier) and indirect (ex-works) exports (see paragraphs 3.3 and 3.4)	3 months	3 months
Supplies of goods involved in groupage or consolidation prior to export (see paragraph 7.4)	3 months	3 months
Exports through auctioneers (see paragraph 7.9)	3 months	3 months
Goods delivered to the Foreign & Commonwealth Office (FCO) for export through diplomatic channels (see paragraph 7.11)	3 months	3 months
Goods ordered by a responsible person of an installation situated outside UK territorial waters (see paragraph 4.8)	3 months	3 months
Goods ordered by the Ministry of Defence (MOD) and other Government Departments provided they are directly exported (see paragraphs 4.9 and 4.11)	3 months	3 months
Goods to be delivered to overseas authorities provided they are ordered through their embassies, High Commissions or UK purchasing agents (see paragraph 4.12)	3 months	3 months
Supplies of goods involved in processing or incorporation prior to export (see paragraph 3.6).	6 months	6 months
Thoroughbred racehorses (subject to conditions to be found in Notice 700/57 "Administrative Agreements entered into with trade bodies"). This notice also sets the conditions for extending the time limits to 12 months.	6 months	6 months

If you have not exported the goods within the time limits, or do not hold the necessary evidence to show that the goods have been physically exported, you must not zero-rate the supply and must account for VAT at the appropriate UK rate (see paragraphs 11.2 and 11.3).

3.6 Conditions for zero-rating goods for export after processing or incorporation

The text in this box has the force of law

When you make a supply of goods to an overseas person for export, but deliver them to a third person in the UK who is also making a taxable supply of goods or services to that overseas person, you can zero-rate the supply provided—

- the goods are only being delivered and *not supplied* to the third person in the UK
- no use is made of the goods other than for processing or incorporation into other goods for export
- the goods are exported from the EC and you obtain evidence of export within the specified time limits and your records show:
- the name and address of the overseas person the invoice number and date
- the description, quantity and value of the goods
- the name and address of the third person in the UK to whom the goods were delivered ➡

- the date by which the goods must be exported and proof of export obtained, and
- the date of actual exportation.

Your records must be able to show that the goods you supplied have been processed or incorporated into the goods exported.

Where such supplies are made, an extension to the normal time limits for exporting the goods and obtaining satisfactory evidence of export is allowed – see paragraph 3.5.

In cases where the third person is not in the UK but in another EC member state the same conditions will generally apply to allow you to zero-rate your supply.

However, you should establish the full facts behind the particular supply in question before assuming that zero-rating is appropriate. If you intend to make such a supply and are unsure as to whether it may be zero-rated, you should contact our National Advice Service.

3.7 What if I can't meet all the conditions?

If you do not meet all the above conditions the supply cannot be zero-rated as an export and you must account for VAT at the appropriate UK rate (see paragraph 11.2).

It is therefore essential that you establish at the time of sale what type of export documentation will be sent to you to support the zero-rating of your supply.

3.8 Right of appeal

If you disagree with a decision we have given, you can ask for it to be reconsidered.

You should certainly do this if—

- you can provide further information, or
- there are facts that you think may not have been fully taken into account.

You may also appeal to an independent VAT and Duties Tribunal. You can find out more about appeals procedures in Notice 700 "The VAT Guide".

4 CONDITIONS FOR ZERO-RATING IN SPECIFIC CIRCUMSTANCES

4.1 Multiple transactions leading to a single movement of goods

Where a single movement of goods is supported by two or more underlying transactions only the final transaction may be zero-rated.

This might happen where more than two businesses are involved. For example, in the scenario shown below three companies are involved in a chain of transactions.

- Company **A** (based outside the EC) orders goods from Company **B** (UK based)
- Company **B** purchases the goods from Company **C** (also UK based) but does not take delivery of the goods
- Company C, at the request of Company B, sends the goods direct to Company **A**

In this scenario there are 2 separate transactions which should be treated as follows:

- Supply of goods from Company **C** to Company **B** is a supply in the UK and must be invoiced at the appropriate rate of UK VAT
- Supply of goods from Company **B** to Company **A** is zero-rated as an export subject to the relevant conditions being met.

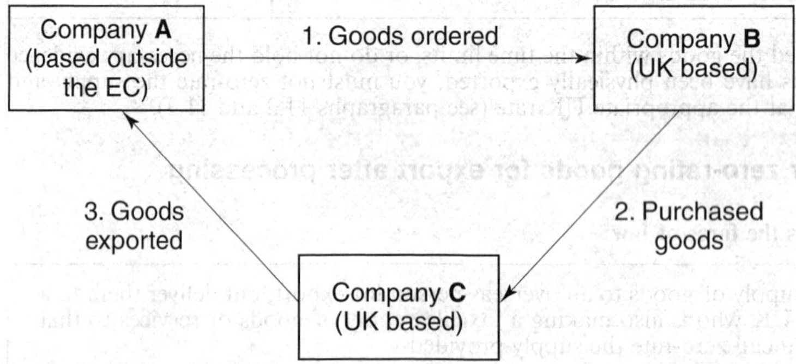

Commentary—*De Voil Indirect Tax Service* **V4.311.**

4.2 How are exports by members of a VAT Group treated?

Formation of a VAT Group is an arrangement that allows two or more corporate bodies to account for VAT as a single taxable person. A VAT group is treated in the same way as a single company registered for VAT on its own. The registration is made in the name of the representative member, who is responsible for completing and rendering the single return on behalf of the group. For further information on VAT groups please refer to VAT Notice 700/2 "Group and divisional registration".

Where an exporter is part of a VAT group registration, purchases between VAT group members are not normally chargeable with VAT. Once a supply is made to an entity outside of the VAT Group the normal rules of export apply.

4.3 Exports from UK free zones

Free zones have no special status for VAT export purposes. You may zero-rate supplies of goods from a free zone for export outside the EC, provided the conditions explained in this notice are met. Supplies made to customers based within a UK free zone should be treated as normal domestic supplies.

4.4 Exports of containers

Supplies of new or second-hand freight containers for export are treated as supplies of goods and can be zero-rated provided that the conditions for export are met. The containers may be used to carry other goods for export during the export movement.

The definition of the term "container" and the conditions to be met before you can zero-rate the supply of a container may be found in Notice 703/1 "Supply of freight containers for export or removal from the United Kingdom".

Commentary—*De Voil Indirect Tax Service* **V4.323.**

4.5 Exports of computer software

Exports of standard ("normalised") computer software packages are regarded as supplies of goods, which may be zero-rated on export from the EC, subject to the conditions in this notice.

Supplies of—

- specific items of software tailored to the individual requirements of a company and
- software transmitted by telephone or other data network are generally regarded as supplies of services and are therefore outside the scope of this notice. You can find further information in Notice 741 "Place of supply of services" .

4.6 Exports of hydrocarbon oils

Hydrocarbon oils are subject to UK excise duty and are normally held in warehouses approved by HM Revenue & Customs until the time of delivery. Sales within these warehouses prior to delivery are disregarded for VAT purposes. See paragraph 7.10 for evidence of export from the EC.

4.7 Exports to oil rigs, etc. and other continental shelf installations

This paragraph applies to the export of goods to structures such as oil rigs, drilling units, accommodation platforms and similar oil or gas exploration / exploitation structures. It also applies to mobile floating structures such as drill ships, tankers, jack-up rigs, semi submersible rigs and Floating Production Storage and Offloading (FPSO) vessels which are often stationed at fixed locations.

Exports to installations outside EC territorial waters

(a) Goods supplied and exported by you to an installation not owned by you

You can zero-rate the supply as a direct export provided that the goods are exported and you obtain valid proof of export within three months of the time of supply.

(b) Goods sent to an installation owned by you

There is no supply as this is a transfer of your own goods (see paragraphs 2.14 and 2.15). However, you must still hold valid proof of export to demonstrate how you disposed of the goods.

(c) Goods sent to replenish your own stocks on an installation not owned by you.

The supply position is the same as at (b) above.

Commentary—*De Voil Indirect Tax Service* **V4.337.**

4.8 Goods supplied for sale on installations which are situated outside UK territorial waters

UK territorial waters consists of the waters within 12 nautical miles of the coastlines of England, Scotland, Wales and Northern Ireland.

The text in this box has the force of law

> You can zero-rate these supplies provided:
>
> - you obtain a written order for the goods from a responsible person on the installation to which the goods are to be sent
>
> ➡

- the goods are supplied either direct to the installation or through an agent for consolidation followed by direct delivery to the installation, and
- you obtain a receipt for the goods, signed by a responsible person on the installation, within three months of the time of supply.

Commentary—*De Voil Indirect Tax Service* **V4.337.**

4.9 Supplies to the Ministry of Defence (MOD) and overseas military establishments

The MOD is registered for VAT in the UK and all supplies to them, or to any military establishment in the UK on their behalf, should include VAT at the appropriate rate.

Direct exports to overseas military and similar installations may be zero-rated provided you comply with the conditions set out in this notice. See paragraphs 4.10 and 10.7 for further information.

4.10 Supplies to regimental shops

Special conditions exist to allow the zero-rating of supplies of goods where the Regiment (or equivalent military unit) is about to be posted to a location outside the EC.

The text in this box has the force of law

You can zero-rate the supply of goods (except new and second-hand motor vehicles) to Regimental shops provided:

- each written order received from the President of the Regimental Institute (PRI) states that the Regiment is about to take up an overseas posting and that the goods ordered will be exported from the EC
- the goods are delivered to the PRI ready packed for shipment no more than 48 hours before the Regiment is due to depart for the overseas posting
- the goods are exported outside the EC, *and*
- you retain a certificate of receipt signed by the PRI which clearly identifies the goods, gives full shipment details and states the date on which they were exported from the EC.

The PRI will keep a full record of such transactions for reference purposes for a period of not less than six years.

Commentary—*De Voil Indirect Tax Service* **V4.336.**

4.11 Supplies to Government Departments other than the Foreign and Commonwealth office (FCO)

You can zero-rate the supply of goods to Government Departments only if you arrange for their direct export to a destination outside the EC and comply with the conditions set out in this notice. For supplies to the FCO see paragraph 7.11.

You must not zero-rate goods for export delivered to Government Departments in the UK even if the goods are ordered for, or by, overseas establishments.

4.12 Supplies to overseas authorities

If you do not meet *all* of the conditions below the supply cannot be zero-rated as an export and you must account for VAT on the supply at the appropriate UK rate.

The text in this box has the force of law

You may zero-rate supplies of goods to overseas authorities which are ordered through their embassies, High Commissions or purchasing agents in the UK, provided:

- you keep a separate record of each transaction (see section 11), including evidence that the supply has been made to an overseas authority, for example the order for the goods, sales invoice made out to the overseas authority, evidence of payment from the overseas authority etc
- the goods are exported and proof of export obtained within three months, as detailed on the form at section 12, and
- the goods are not used between the time of leaving your premises and export, either for their normal purpose or for display, exhibition or copying.

Commentary—*De Voil Indirect Tax Service* **V4.326.**

4.13 Export of motor vehicles

You can zero-rate the supply of any motor vehicle, new or second hand—

- as a direct export under the conditions specified in paragraph 3.3, provided that the vehicle is not used or delivered in the EC before it is exported
- as an indirect export under the conditions specified in paragraph 3.4 provided that the vehicle is not subsequently used except for the trip to the place of departure from the EC, or
- if the vehicle is sold to a private individual under the terms of the Personal Export Scheme – see paragraph 9.1.

Commentary—*De Voil Indirect Tax Service* **V4.334.**

4.14 Tools used in the UK to manufacture goods for export

Notice 701/22 "Tools for manufacture of goods for export" explains the conditions for zero-rating supplies of jigs, patterns, templates, dies, moulds, punches and similar tools used in the UK to manufacture goods for export.

Commentary—*De Voil Indirect Tax Service* **V4.283.**

5 CUSTOMS DECLARATIONS VIA THE NEW EXPORT SYSTEM (NES) AND THE NEW COMPUTERISED TRANSIT SYSTEM (NCTS)

This section covers the evidence generated by NES and NCTS.

Commentary—*De Voil Indirect Tax Service* **V4.308.**

5.1 What is NES?

NES is a system used by freight agents, importers and exporters, to declare import or export entries electronically. If you export goods including those goods that are leaving the EC via other EC member states, you should refer to the procedures and customs requirements described in detail in Notice 275 "Export procedures", and Notice 276 "The new export system".

5.2 How does NES work?

The NES operates via a computer system known as "Customs Handling of Import Export Freight" or CHIEF. When an export declaration is entered to CHIEF it must go through a number of stages before the export procedure is finalised. The stages are—

- Pre-lodgement of data
- Acceptance of data
- Arrival message
- Departure message

At each stage the Status of Entry code and the ICS (Indicate Clearance Status) code will change, and a message showing the current status is generated by NES to the person who submitted the electronic declaration.

5.3 What will NES produce as evidence of export?

Official evidence of export cannot be obtained until the export declaration has been fully discharged. This happens when a departure message is input to CHIEF by either the port inventory system, a nominated loader, or, in some cases, by Customs.

Official evidence will be either—

- a copy of the final goods departed message (see 5.4), or
- a screen print from CHIEF showing the appropriate status codes (see 5.5).

5.4 Goods Departed Message (GDM)

At UK air and seaports a computerised system is used to follow the goods through the port area. Where these systems are linked to NES, an electronic message known as a Goods Departed Message (GDM) will be generated and should be received by the person submitting the export declaration. The GDM is official evidence of export *only* when goods leave the EC from the UK. See paragraph 5.6 below for goods leaving the EC from somewhere other than the UK.

If you, as an exporter or supplier, do not input export declarations yourself, you will not receive the appropriate messages to confirm the goods have been exported from the EC. You should ask your agent or the person who declares the goods on your behalf to supply you with a copy of the final goods departed message appropriate for your exports.

Similarly, if your overseas customer or their agent inputs the export declaration, you should ask for a paper copy of the final goods departed message appropriate to the goods you supplied. If official evidence of export cannot be obtained, you will need to rely on commercial transport evidence as described in paragraphs 6.3 and 6.6.

5.5 Screen print from CHIEF

If you or your agent make your electronic export declarations via CHIEF or the WEB declaration option, an alternative to the Goods Departed Message can be obtained by printing a copy of the screen "DEVD option 2" in CHIEF. This screen print will provide official proof of export *only* when it shows—

- a Status of Entry code 8, *and*
- ICS Code 60.

These codes mean that the goods have actually departed from the EC.

5.6 Exports leaving the EC from somewhere other than the UK

Every export from the UK requires an NES entry irrespective of where the goods leave the EC. However, where the goods are leaving the EC, transiting another EC member state, they must be accompanied by a travelling copy 3 of the Single Administrative Document (SAD). This will be—

- stamped at the point of departure from the EC
- returned to the person presenting it, (who should ensure that it has been stamped), and
- returned to the exporter who will require it as proof of export.

The stamped copy 3 is your official evidence of export.

5.7 Assumed Departure Message

When goods have arrived at the port but for some reason a departure message is not input, CHIEF will issue an Assumed Departure Message within a specified timescale.

This message is not accepted as evidence for VAT zero-rating. Alternative commercial transport evidence as described in paragraph 6.3 must be produced.

5.8 What happens where goods leave from a port or airport where no computerised system is in place?

Where no computerised system is in place at the port or airport, you or your agent or forwarder can arrange with Customs to manually enter a departure message when the goods are exported. In this scenario you or your agent should ask the Customs Officer for a printed copy of the DEVD option 2 screen showing the ICS code 60 (see 5.5) to use as official proof of export. This, together with the supporting supplementary evidence will be accepted as evidence for zero-rating.

5.9 What happens if the goods are not exported?

If for any reason the goods are not exported and an export declaration has been made, the Customs Officer at the declared port of export must be formally advised and the export declaration cancelled. Where goods are supplied in the UK instead, VAT must be accounted for at the appropriate UK rate.

5.10 What is the New Computerised Transit System (NCTS)?

NCTS is a European wide system, based upon electronic declaration and processing, designed to provide better management and control of goods under Community/Common Transit (CT) procedures. In some circumstances you may be required to enter the goods to the CT procedure if the goods you export transit the UK or one or more other member states before leaving the EC. Further details about NCTS and CT requirements can be found on our website at www.hmrc.gov.uk >businesses and corporations > imports and exports > New Computerised Transit System (NCTS) and in the Transit Manual at http://www.europa.eu.int/comm/taxation_customs/customs/procedural_aspect s/transit/common_community/index_en.htm

5.11 How does NCTS work?

The system automatically produces a Transit Accompanying Document (TAD) containing a unique Movement Reference Number (MRN) and bar code. The TAD moves with the goods (rather than a paper copy 3 SAD as described in paragraph 5.6). If the goods are presented intact, together with the TAD, at the office of destination, a message is sent to the office where the NCTS declaration was made.

The CT procedure is then discharged electronically. There is no requirement to return a paper document to the exporter.

5.12 What will NCTS produce as evidence of export?

Where goods have been entered to NCTS, official evidence of export will be confirmation that the CT procedure has been discharged. The exporter or agent can obtain this confirmation from NCTS by entering the unique Movement Reference Number.

(When NCTS is used the Goods Departed Message (GDM) generated by NES is not accepted as evidence for VAT zero-rating. This is because in these circumstances the GDM only confirms that the goods have left the UK, not that the goods have left the EC.)

5.13 Goods travelling by road through the EC to Switzerland, Liechtenstein, Norway, San Marino, Andorra and Romania

Community status goods travelling to the above destinations may be entered to the Community/ Common Transit (CT) procedure either in the UK or at another point in the EC. (Non-community goods must be entered to the CT procedure in the UK.) Full details of the CT requirements can be found in the Transit Manual (see paragraph 5.10). Official evidence for VAT zero-rating will be *either*—

- confirmation that the CT procedure has been discharged (see paragraph 5.12), or
- the stamped copy 3 SAD (see paragraph 5.6) if the goods have not been entered to CT procedure in the UK, or
- the stamped copy 3 SAD, together with confirmation of discharge of the CT procedure if goods have been entered to CT procedure in another member state after leaving the UK.

[Note: Romania joins the EC on 1 January 2007. This paragraph will therefore cease to apply to goods travelling to Romania from that date.]

Note—Para 5.13 amended by Update 1, January 2007.

5.14 What additional documents are required before export of restricted goods?

The export of certain goods is prohibited or restricted. Where the export is one of restricted goods you will need to obtain a licence in addition to the official and commercial transport documentary evidence.

- Under NES the licence must be referenced on the declaration and produced when requested by Customs.
- With a non-NES declaration the licence must accompany the customs declaration.

Further advice on restricted goods may be obtained from—

- Export Control Organisation Helpline Department of Trade & Industry, 4 Abbey Orchard Street, London, SW1P 2HT; email address: eco.help@dti.gsi.gov.uk
- Department of Environment, Tollgate House, Houlton Street, Bristol, BS2 9DJ.
- Department for Culture Media and Sport, Trafalgar Place, 2–4 Cockspur Street, London, SW1Y 5BQ.

6 PROOF OF EXPORT

6.1 What does this section cover?

This section explains the evidence that is required for a supply of goods exported outside the EC to be zero-rated for VAT.

For VAT zero-rating purposes you must produce either official evidence as described in paragraph 6.2 or commercial evidence as described in paragraph 6.3. Equal weight is put on official and commercial transport evidence but both must be supported by supplementary evidence to show that a transaction has taken place, and that the transaction relates to the goods physically exported. If the evidence of export provided is found to be unsatisfactory, VAT zero-rating will not be allowed and the supplier of the goods will be liable to account for the VAT due (see paragraph 11.2).

Commentary—*De Voil Indirect Tax Service* **V4.306.**

6.2 Official evidence

This is produced by Customs, for example Goods Departed Messages (GDM) generated by NES. Alternatively it may be in the form of a Single administrative Document (SAD) endorsed by Customs at the point of exit from the EC, or confirmation of the electronic discharge of an NCTS movement. See section 5 for more detail on how official evidence of export is produced.

6.3 Commercial transport evidence

This describes the physical movement of the goods, for example—

- Authenticated sea-waybills
- Authenticated air-waybills
- PIM/PIEX International consignment notes
- Master air-waybills or bills of lading
- Certificates of shipment containing the full details of the consignment and how it left the EC, or
- International Consignment Note/Lettre de Voiture International (CMR) fully completed by the consignor, the haulier and the receiving consignee, or Freight Transport Association (FTA) own account transport documents fully completed and signed by the receiving customer.

Further details on the purpose of these documents can be found in Notice 275 "Export procedures" and Notice 276 "The new export system".

Photocopy certificates of shipment are not normally acceptable as evidence of export, nor are photocopy bills of lading, sea-waybills or air-waybills (unless authenticated by the shipping or air line).

6.4 What supplementary evidence is available?

You are likely to hold, within your accounting system some or all of the following—

- customer's order
- sales contract
- inter-company correspondence
- copy of export sales invoice
- advice note
- consignment note
- packing list
- insurance and freight charges documentation
- evidence of payment, and/or
- evidence of the receipt of the goods abroad.

You must hold sufficient evidence to prove that a transaction has taken place, though it will probably not be necessary for you to hold all of the items listed.

6.5 What must be shown on export evidence?

The text in this box has the force of law

> The evidence you obtain as proof of export, whether official or commercial, or supporting must clearly identify—
>
> - the supplier
> - the consignor (where different from the supplier)
> - the customer
> - the goods
> - an accurate value
> - the export destination, *and*
> - the mode of transport and route of the export movement.

Vague descriptions of goods, quantities or values are not acceptable. For instance, "various electrical goods" must not be used when the correct description is "2000 mobile phones (Make ABC and Model Number XYZ2000)". An accurate value, for example, £50,000 must be shown and not excluded or replaced by a lower or higher amount.

If the evidence is found to be unsatisfactory you as the supplier will become liable for the VAT due.

6.6 What evidence will I need to obtain to substantiate VAT zero-rating when I do not arrange shipment of the goods?

Typically this occurs when goods are supplied ex-works. If your overseas customer arranges for the goods to be collected from your premises and exported to a place outside the EC member states it can be difficult for you, as the supplier, to obtain adequate proof of export as the carrier is contracted to your overseas customer. For this type of transaction the standard of evidence required to substantiate VAT zero-rating is high.

Before zero-rating the supply and releasing the goods to your customer, you must confirm what evidence of export is to be provided.

If the evidence of export—

- does not show that the goods have left the EC within the appropriate time limits, or
- is found, upon examination, to be unsatisfactory, you, the supplier, *will* become liable for payment of the VAT.

For these reasons you should consider whether to—

- include the requirement for the buyer to provide export evidence as part of the sales contract between you and your customer, and/or
- secure against the possibility that your buyer will fail to provide the proper export evidence by, for example, taking a deposit from your customer equal to the amount of VAT you will be liable to pay if the evidence is not sent to you.

The deposit can be refunded when you obtain evidence that proves the goods were exported.

Evidence must show the goods you supplied have left the EC. Copies of transport documents alone will not be sufficient. Information held must identify the date and route of the movement and the mode of transport involved. It should include the following—

- a written order from your customer which shows their name and address, and the address where the goods are to be delivered
- copy sales invoice showing the invoice number, customer's name and a description of the goods
- delivery address for the goods

6.9 If I am an overseas customer arranging my own export what do I need to do to ensure that I get the benefit of zero-rating?

Once you have collected the goods or arranged for the goods to be taken to the port or airport, for export, you should provide the supplier of the goods with all of the documentary evidence you hold to prove that the goods have been physically exported. You should ensure that the supplier is in possession of this evidence to enable them to meet the time limits for export.

6.10 What if I have lost or mislaid export evidence?

If you have lost or mislaid the official or commercial evidence of export supplied by the ship owner or carrier, duplicate evidence of export may be obtained. The replacement evidence of export must be clearly marked "DUPLICATE EVIDENCE OF EXPORT" and be authenticated and dated by an official of the issuing company.

7 PROOF OF EXPORT FOR ZERO-RATING IN SPECIFIC CIRCUMSTANCES

This section covers the specific evidence of export that you must obtain according to the method of export used. In all cases the official or commercial transport evidence you obtain must be supported by the supplementary information set out in paragraph 6.4 to show that the transaction has taken place.

Commentary—*De Voil Indirect Tax Service* **V4.306, 326.**

7.1 Air and sea freight

If you are using commercial transport documents as proof of export for goods exported outside the EC by—

- Air – you must obtain and keep an authenticated master or house air-waybill endorsed with the flight prefix and number, and the date and place of departure.
- Sea – you must keep one of the copies of the shipped bill of lading or sea-waybill (certifying actual shipment) or, where a shipping company does not issue these, a certificate of shipment given by a responsible official of that company.

7.2 Road freight

The International Consignment Note (CMR) provides evidence of the identity of the contracting parties when goods are transferred by road. It is in three parts and is completed and signed by the sender of the goods, the carrier and the person receiving the goods. Where the overseas customer arranges for the goods to be collected ex-works the CMR alone is not conclusive evidence that the goods in question have left the EC but, where the CMR is used as part of the evidence, it is important that the information is complete and all the details legible.

7.3 Merchandise in Baggage (MIB)

Commercial or business goods exported in accompanied baggage are known as MIB. Commercial evidence of export is normally only available where goods are shipped as manifested freight, as individual consignments or as part of groupage consignments. Currently MIB is outside the scope of the New Export System and you will need to complete a non-electronic paper SAD (Form C88) and follow the procedures below.

Provided the goods and correctly completed SAD copies 2 and 3 are presented to the MIB officer, official certification of copy 3 of the SAD can be obtained for the following—

- Merchandise in Baggage
- Re-export of temporarily imported goods
- Transfers of own goods (see paragraph 2.15)
- Purchases by overseas persons
- Exports where commercial documents are not available (for example where an ATA carnet has been lost).

In all these cases the certified copy 3 of the SAD (Form C88) is your evidence of export.

(a) Where you export the goods

If you export goods in baggage or in a private motor vehicle, you must:

- Include "MIB" in box 44 of the export SAD (C88).
- Arrive well before your scheduled departure time and present copy 2 and copy 3 (marked "for VAT purposes only") of the SAD, with the goods, to the MIB officer at the UK place of export from the EC for the reverse of copy 3 to be certified that goods have been shipped.

Copy 3 will be handed back to you as evidence of export for retention in your records.

(b) Where your customer exports the goods

Where your overseas customer collects the goods from your premises and arranges transportation in baggage or in a private motor vehicle you must:

- Give your customer a completed SAD with your name and VAT number shown in box 2. (This will ensure that your overseas customer does not include your supplies on a single

SAD covering goods purchased from a number of UK suppliers. If they did this, they would be unable to provide you with an original officially certified copy 3 for your records).

Your overseas customer must:

- Arrive well before their scheduled departure time and present copy 2 and copy 3 (marked "for VAT purposes only") of the SAD (Form C88) with the goods, to the MIB officer at the UK place of export from the EC. The MIB officer will certify the reverse of copy 3 to show that goods have been shipped and hand it back to your overseas customer.
- Send you copy 3 as evidence of export for retention in your records.

(c) Leaving the EC via another member state

If you or your customer depart the EC via another member state copy 3 of the SAD (Form C88) will be certified by Customs at the place you leave the EC.

Full details of the MIB procedures are given in Notice 6 Merchandise in Baggage.

7.4 Groupage or consolidation transactions

If you use a freight forwarder, consignments (often coming from several consignors) may be aggregated into one load, known as groupage or consolidation cargo. The freight forwarder must keep copies of the original bill of lading, sea-waybill or air-waybill, and all consignments in the load must be shown on the container or vehicle manifest. You will be issued with a certificate of shipment by the freight forwarder, often supported by an authenticated photocopy of the original bill of lading, a sea-waybill or a house air-waybill. Where such consignments are being exported, the forwarder is usually shown as the consignor in the shipping documents.

(a) Certificate of shipment

Certificates of shipment are usually produced by packers and consolidators involved in road, rail and sea groupage consignments when they themselves receive only a single authenticated transport document from the carrier. The certificate of shipment is an important document, which should be sent to you as soon as the goods have been exported from the EC.

The certificate of shipment must be an original and authenticated by an official of the issuing company unless it is computer produced, on a once-only basis, as a by-product of the issuing company's accounting system.

A properly completed certificate of shipment will help you to meet the evidential requirements described in paragraph 6.1.

(b) What information must be shown?

Although the certificate of shipment can be in any format, it must be an original and will usually contain the following information—

- the name and address of the issuing company
- a unique reference number or issuer's file reference
- the name of the exporter (and VAT number, if known)
- the place, port or airport of loading
- the place, port or airport of shipment
- the name of the export vessel or the aircraft, flight prefix and number
- the date of sailing or flight
- the customer's name
- the destination of the goods
- a full description of the goods exported (including quantity, weight and value)
- the number of packages
- the exporter's invoice number and date if known
- the bill of lading or air-waybill number (if applicable), and
- the identifying number of the vehicle, container or railway wagon.

7.5 Postal exports

Goods exported by post may be zero-rated if they are direct exports and you hold the necessary evidence of posting to an address outside the EC.

(a) Evidence of posting for letter post or airmail (packages up to 2kg)

A fully completed certificate of posting form, presented with the goods for export, and stamped by the Post Office will be your evidence of export. Acceptable forms are—

- Form C&E 132 for single or multiple packages taken to the Post Office. Blank forms may be obtained from our National Advice Service or from our Internet site.
- Form P326 available from the Post Office and used for single packages taken to the Post Office.

Also acceptable is—

- A Certificate of Posting for International Mail, or a Royal Mail Collection Manifest, available from a Royal Mail sales advisor, for use by customers using their Business Collections Service, where the Royal Mail collection driver signs the certificate.

You can find further information on Royal Mail international services on their website at www.royalmail.com.

(*b*) *Evidence of posting for parcels*

Parcelforce Worldwide operates a range of international parcel services. If you use any of these services for a non-EC destination, you will use a bar-coded service label and customs declaration. The customs declaration may either be a paper "despatch pack", or an online version. The information required for both formats is the same.

Whichever version you use, you should be aware of the following points:

- A fully completed customs declaration is required for every parcel (even if you are sending a multiple item consignment) as every parcel may be inspected by Customs on an individual basis.
- A full and clear description of all the items within the parcel is required including quantity, weight, and value of the goods.
- If you arrange for the parcel to be collected from your premises, the collection driver will provide a despatch pack for you to complete (if you have not already completed the declaration) and will then sign the receipt copy. If you have completed and printed your declaration online, the collection driver will sign your online receipt or manifest.
- If the parcel is taken to a Post Office the completed receipt copy from the despatch pack will be handed back to you, together with a printed proof of shipment from the Post Office SmartPost system. This will show the overseas delivery address, date of despatch and unique consignment number (which will match the unique consignment number on your despatch pack customer receipt.) You should keep *both* the proof of shipment and the customer receipt.

In addition to the individual parcel declarations described above, account customers of Parcelforce Worldwide who export on a regular basis also have two additional potential sources of information listing multiple export parcels:

- Worldwide Despatch Manager (WDM) – online users can print a manifest, which lists all despatched parcels.
- Statement of account.

All of the individual parcel declarations, plus either the manifest or the statement of account listing each export will provide proof of export for VAT purposes.

You can find further information on Parcelforce Worldwide International Services, on their website at www.parcelforce.com.

7.6 Exports by courier and fast parcel services

Courier and fast parcel operators specialise in the shipment of small consignments to overseas destinations within guaranteed times.

(*a*) *Operators who do not issue separate certificates of shipment*

Most courier and fast parcel operators do not issue separate certificates of shipment.

The invoice for moving small consignments for export from the EC, which routinely bears details of the unique air-waybill numbers for each shipment, represents normal commercial evidence of export. In addition, many express companies are able to offer a track and trace service via their websites where the movement of consignments can be traced through to the final destination. This information can be printed and can also be used to confirm that the goods have left the EC.

(*b*) *Operators who use the system based upon a Despatch Pack*

A few companies still use a documentary system based upon a Despatch Pack containing accounting data, a Customs export declaration and receipt copies of a house airway bill or consignment note. These packs are issued to customers to complete for each export shipment.

Goods being exported outside the EC must be fully and clearly described with the value shown on the export declaration. A Despatch Pack must be completed for each overseas address and consignee. The driver collecting the parcels will endorse the receipt copy and return it to the consignor. This, plus the statement of account issued by the express operator, listing each export shipment, will provide commercial proof of export.

(*c*) *Use of more than one courier/fast parcel company*

Due to the complexities of the movement of consignments within the courier/fast parcel environment, there is often more than one company involved in the handling and ultimate export of the goods. You as the UK supplier may not be certain as to which courier/fast parcel company has made the export declaration to Customs.

Consequently it may be difficult to obtain official proof of export, leaving you to rely on the commercial evidence of export as described above. If the operator makes a bulk declaration when exporting the goods via another member state, it may not be possible to print a travelling Copy 3 for the individual consignments of the SAD referred to in paragraph 5.6.

In these circumstances, you must use commercial evidence of export, typically fully completed transport documents.

However, where you, as the supplier, are certain that the export declaration has been made by a specific courier/fast parcel company you may rely on either commercial or official evidence as detailed in paragraphs 6.2 and 6.3.

(*d*) *Overseas customer arranging the export by courier*

If your overseas customer arranges for the goods to be exported by courier you should find out what proof of export they will be providing to enable you to zero-rate the supply. More information on what you should do is contained in paragraph 6.6.

7.7 Exports by rail

Rail contractors offer services by rail for parcels and full loads.

(*a*) *Parcels*

If you intend to export parcels by rail, you should establish what evidence of export will be provided to you by the rail contractor. This will normally be a consignment note such as a 5-part PIM/PIEX – International Consignment Note, copy 4 is the exporter's copy and receipt for the goods.

These receipted forms plus the railway statement of account listing each export provide your evidence of export for VAT purposes.

(*b*) *Bulk cargo services*

Rail contractors offer services for the movement of full loads in wagons, containers and swap bodies. Containers and swap bodies are handled by intermediaries who use their own consignment documentation. Full loads in wagons use the 5-part "Convention International des Marchandises par Chemin de Fer" (CIM) consignment note. This contains the "Uniform Rules concerning the contract for International Carriage of goods by rail".

In all cases, the exporter's copy of the consignment note endorsed with a railway stamp is your evidence of export.

7.8 Exports through packers

For goods exported under groupage arrangements, you must obtain a certificate of shipment (see paragraph 7.4) signed by the packer showing a full description of the goods packed for export – including quantity, weight, value, destination, etc.

For single consignments you must obtain commercial evidence of shipment by road, rail, sea or air and a certificate of posting or equivalent evidence of export when exported by other means.

7.9 Exports through auctioneers

Auctioneers act in a number of ways. It is important that you check with the auctioneer before you sell your goods whether they are acting in their own name.

You can find further information on the role of auctioneers in Notice 700 "The VAT Guide" and Notice 718 "Margin schemes for second hand goods, works of art, antiques and collectors' items".

(*a*) *Auctioneer acting in your name*

If you sell goods through an auctioneer who—

- is not acting in their own name, and
- exports the goods,

you may zero-rate your supply provided that you obtain a certificate of export from the auctioneer, in the form set out in paragraph 12.2 or paragraph 12.3 within three months of the date of the auction. The auctioneer must hold valid evidence of export for the goods.

(*b*) *Auctioneer acting in own name*

If you sell goods through an auctioneer who is acting in their own name, the goods are treated as being supplied to the auctioneer and must not be zero-rated by you as an export. The auctioneer will be able to zero-rate the onward supply in the normal way.

7.10 Exports from Customs, Excise and/or fiscal warehouses

A warehousekeeper who holds valid commercial transport evidence that the goods delivered from the warehouse have been exported may provide the registered owner of the goods with a signed and dated document certifying export. It must include the following information—

- name and address of the warehousekeeper
- order number, invoice number and date of transaction
- name and address of the owner of the goods
- details of the stock exported (description, quantity, value, etc)
- name of the export vessel or aircraft flight prefix and number
- port or airport of loading
- date of sailing or departure
- destination of the goods

- bill of lading or air-waybill number (where appropriate)
- identifying number of the container or railway wagon (if used), and
- signature of the warehousekeeper and date.

7.11 Supplies to the Foreign and Commonwealth Office (FCO)

You can zero-rate the supply of goods ordered by British Embassies, High Commissions and diplomats abroad that are delivered to the FCO for export through diplomatic channels within three months of the time of supply. You as the supplier must keep a separate record of each transaction.

To evidence that the supply was made to an overseas person, you must be able to identify the destination of the goods. You should therefore retain documents which contain this information, for example the order. You must also obtain a certificate of receipt from the FCO within three months of the time of the supply of goods. The certificate may be on a copy of the sales invoice or on an itemised list, which you must keep to support your claim to zero-rating.

You must not zero-rate the supply of any other goods ordered by and delivered to the FCO for stock or general distribution.

7.12 Exports to the Channel Islands

Excise goods or goods subject to Customs controls (for example restricted goods) being exported to the Channel Islands will always require a SAD (Form C88) declaration. This may be made using the New Export System (NES).

In the case of goods not subject to Customs or Excise controls one of the following declaration procedures may be used—

- a bulk NES declaration by the shipping line supported by individual Consignment Note and Customs Declarations (CNCD), or
- individual NES declarations by exporters.

Further details may be found in Notice 275 "Export procedures".

At south coast ferry ports a combined CNCD with a supporting itemised schedule of goods exported may be used in place of the SAD and sea waybill for manifested freight.

A CNCD may be on an approved standard commercial document or a partly completed SAD.

Evidence of export for goods sent to the Channel Islands is made up of the following (as appropriate)—

- official proof of export produced by NES – see section 5
- goods shipped by air – an authenticated master air-waybill or house air-waybill (see paragraph 7.1)
- goods carried as Merchandise in Baggage – a Customs certified copy 3 of the SAD (Form C88) (see paragraph 7.3)
- goods shipped through a freight forwarder – a certificate of shipment issued by the freight forwarder (see paragraph 7.4) or an authenticated copy of the CNCD
- goods shipped through a fast parcel or courier service – evidence as per paragraph 7.6, or
- goods shipped directly by the south coast ferry companies – an authenticated copy of the CNCD as described above.

7.13 Exports via EC member states

Where you send goods by road via for example Dover, across the EC before final export, or where you move goods from the UK to an airport in another member state before final export, this is an export via an EC member state.

If you export to non-EC countries via other EC member states, you will require either official proof of export for VAT purposes or commercial transport evidence that the goods have left the EC to substantiate the zero-rating of the supplies.

Official evidence of export will normally be copy 3 of the export SAD (Form C88) or NES equivalent endorsed at the Customs office of exit from the EC – see paragraph 5.6. The office of exit will vary depending on the type of transport used and the nature of the supply. See also paragraph 5.12 for types of official evidence available when goods move under Community/Common Transit (CT) procedures, and paragraph 5.13 for information about goods travelling by road to Switzerland, Liechtenstein, Norway, San Marino, Andorra and Romania.

Where goods subject to excise duty are moving under duty suspension arrangements, the Customs office of exit from the EC will certify the accompanying document (an "attestation" in EC terms) and return it to the consignor as evidence of exportation from the EC. The standard time limit of three months for obtaining the evidence of export applies.

7.14 Channel tunnel

The evidence of export procedures outlined above for exports via other EC member states apply equally to goods transported via the Channel Tunnel.

The arrangements outlined in paragraph 7.7 cover goods carried on through-rail freight services through the Tunnel.

There are Merchandise in Baggage facilities at both the Waterloo International Terminal (for foot passengers) and at Ashford Inland Clearance Depot (for car and coach passengers joining the Tunnel at Cheriton).

8 EXTRA-STATUTORY CONCESSIONS (ESCS)

Two extra-statutory concessions exist which enable zero-rating of VAT on supplies of goods in specific circumstances. Further details may be found in Notice 48 "Extra-Statutory Concessions".

8.1 Duty or tax-free shops (ESC 9.1)

(a) Can I zero-rate the supply of goods made from my "airside" duty or tax-free shop?

ESC 9.1 allows zero-rating of the supply of goods to be carried in the personal luggage of passengers flying directly out of the UK to a non-EC country.

If you operate a duty or tax-free shop at an airport, you can zero-rate the supply of goods for immediate export by travellers departing on flights to destinations outside the EC. Although it is the intending passenger who is exporting the goods, it is the retailer who is treated as the exporter for VAT purposes and therefore needs to evidence that the goods have been exported.

To zero-rate the supply you must provide us with evidence of the sale to an intending passenger for export to a third country.

At the point of sale you should check that—

- the traveller is departing directly to a destination outside the EC, and
- the goods are to be exported.

We must be able to verify the transaction. Acceptable evidence showing that the sale is to an entitled passenger is obtained from the airline boarding card or travel document. This clearly shows the names of passengers, the date of travel and the flight number/destination. Information from the boarding cards or travel documents presented by entitled passengers should be retained by retailers as part of their export evidence.

If you, as a retailer, are unsure about the acceptability of the evidence you propose to use you should contact our National Advice Service. Large businesses controlled by the Large Business Service (LBS) should contact their National Business Manager.

Any agreement reached on acceptability of alternative evidence should be confirmed in writing.

(b) If the customer returns goods as defective can I zero-rate the replacement goods?

If, following the sale, the customer returns the goods as defective and you as the retailer are required to replace them, whether you charge VAT on the value of the replacement goods will depend upon their ultimate destination. If the replacement goods are to be exported they may be zero-rated, subject to the normal export rules.

If they are delivered to an address within the UK or EC member state the original zero-rate sale must be cancelled and the supply is subject to VAT at the appropriate rate.

You can find information on when you may zero-rate supplies to customers registered for VAT in another EC member state in Notice 725 "The Single Market".

Commentary—*De Voil Indirect Tax Service* **V4.338.**

8.2 Relief for marine fuel (ESC 9.2)

Extra Statutory Concession (ESC) 9.2 allows vessels engaged on commercial voyages within UK territorial waters (or within the limits of a port) to receive certain types of marine fuel VAT free.

You can zero-rate such supplies as ships' stores providing—

- you obtain, from the person to whom the marine fuel is to be supplied, a written declaration that the goods are for use as stores on a non-private voyage
- you obtain written confirmation from the master, owner or duly authorised agent of the vessel declaring that the fuel is solely for use on a named ship
- the fuel is sent direct to the ship or addressed and delivered to the master of a named vessel c/o the shipping line or agent, and
- you hold a receipt confirming delivery of the fuel on board the ship, signed by the master or other responsible officer.

The concession described above extends only to those supplies of fuel, which were zero-rated prior to 1 July 1990. It does not apply to petrol, Ultra Low Sulphur Diesel (ULSD) or lubricating oil.

Commentary—*De Voil Indirect Tax Service* **V4.321.**

9 EXPORTS BY RETAILERS

9.1 Export schemes for retailers

- There are a number of exports schemes for retailers selling goods for export by private individuals.

(*a*) *Retail Export Scheme* (*RES*)

The Retail Export Scheme allows participating retailers to refund VAT on goods purchased by entitled customers. You should refer to the conditions laid down in Notice 704 "VAT Retail exports".

(*b*) *Personal Export Scheme for vehicles* (*PES*)

You can zero-rate the supply of a new or second hand motor vehicle for export by your customer in certain circumstances. You should refer to the conditions in Notice 705 "Buyer's guide to personal exports of motor vehicles to destinations outside the EC" and Notice 705A "VAT Supplies of vehicles under the Personal Export Scheme for removal from the EC".

(*c*) *Sailaway Boat Scheme*

The Sailaway Boat Scheme allows boats exported to final destinations outside the EC to be zero-rated for VAT purposes. You can find more details in Notice 703/2 "Sailaway boats supplied for export outside the EC".

9.2 Retail exports shipped as freight or household effects

(*a*) *Direct exports*

If you, as retailer, arrange for goods to be exported outside the EC you may zero-rate the supply provided all the conditions in paragraph 3.3 are met.

(*b*) *Indirect exports*

If your overseas customer arranges for the export of the goods outside the EC you may zero-rate the supply provided all the conditions in paragraph 3.4 are met.

Commentary—*De Voil Indirect Tax Service* **V4.331–335.**

10 STORES FOR USE IN SHIPS, AIRCRAFT OR HOVERCRAFT TO DESTINATIONS OUTSIDE UK

Commentary—*De Voil Indirect Tax Service* **V4.321–322.**

10.1 What is meant by the term "stores"?

Stores are goods for use in a ship, aircraft or hovercraft and include—

- fuel
- goods for running repairs or maintenance, for example lubricants, spare and replacement parts
- goods for general use on board by the crew
- goods for sale by retail to passengers carried on the voyage or flight who intend to use the stores on board only.

10.2 What supplies are eligible for zero-rating?

You can zero-rate supplies of goods classed as "stores" under paragraph 10.1 for the fuelling and provisioning of vessels and aircraft providing—

- They are for use on a voyage or flight with a non-private purpose and with an eventual destination outside the UK. See paragraph 8.2 for details of an Extra Statutory Concession (ESC) covering supplies of marine fuel to vessels for voyages in home waters.
- They are shipped from the UK within three months of supply.
- The conditions outlined in paragraph 10.4 are met.

10.3 Supplies to registered shipping companies etc

If you make supplies to VAT registered shipping lines or airline operators they can choose to have—

- All supplies, including goods for shipment as stores on their ships or aircraft, delivered to their premises.

In these circumstances you must charge VAT at the appropriate rate. The shipping or airline company can deduct input tax subject to the normal rules. (The subsequent transfer of the goods from their premises to the ship or aircraft for use as stores is not then a supply for VAT purposes).

- Supplies of stores made direct to foreign-going craft.

You can zero-rate such supplies provided the goods are eligible for stores relief under paragraph 10.2, and the conditions in paragraph 10.4 are met.

When you receive an order for goods to be shipped as stores you must ensure that you receive clear instructions on how to deal with the supply.

10.4 Conditions for zero-rating supplies to foreign-going vessels and aircraft

Unless *all* these conditions are met there is no eligibility for zero-rating and you must account for VAT at the appropriate UK rate.

The text in this box has the force of law

You can zero-rate eligible supplies of goods to foreign-going vessels and aircraft providing—

- The person to whom the goods are supplied is the end user e g master of the vessel.
- The person to whom the goods are to be supplied declares in writing that the goods are for use as stores on a voyage or flight which is to be made for a non-private purpose.
- You obtain and hold a written order or confirmation given by the master, commander, owner or duly authorised agent of the ship or aircraft. This must include a declaration that the goods are solely for use as stores on a named ship or aircraft that is entitled to receive duty-free stores for the voyage in question, which is to an eventual destination outside the UK. Aircraft making through international flights are eligible to receive VAT-free stores even if the aircraft makes one or more stops in the UK in the course of such a flight.
- You send the goods—
  - direct to the ship or aircraft
  - through freight forwarders for consolidation and delivery direct to the ship or aircraft, or
  - addressed and delivered to the master of a named vessel c/o the shipping line or agent.
- You obtain and hold a receipt confirming delivery of the goods on board the ship or aircraft, signed by the master, commander or other responsible officer of the ship or aircraft. You can accept such a receipt signed by a responsible official of the airline concerned. However airlines using this facility must obtain prior written agreement from Revenue and Customs. They must confirm that the signatory is in a position to provide the receipt based on personal knowledge of flight details and that the airline will maintain documentation enabling Revenue and Customs staff to verify entitlement to relief.
- You have a certificate of export as described in paragraph 7.10 where your supplies are made direct from a warehouse not operated or owned by you to an eligible vessel or aircraft. The advice note issued by the warehousekeeper normally serves this purpose.

Please note the conditions for zero-rating in the following specific circumstances—

- Where there is a supply chain, intermediaries must account for VAT at the appropriate rate.
- If you supply goods to a shore-side storage tank you may not zero-rate the supply *unless* your customer is the exporter of the goods and you hold the necessary evidence.

10.5 Supplies for sale in ships' shops and on board aircraft and for ships' slop chests

The arrangements in paragraphs 10.2, 10.3 and 10.4 apply to goods supplied for sale in ships' shops, etc even though there may be no taxable supply at the time of shipment (for example transfer of own goods, supply on sale or return terms). Where goods have been shipped on a foreign-going ship or aircraft, any later sale of the goods will be a supply outside the UK and there will be no further VAT liability unless they are re-landed in the UK (see paragraph 10.6).

VAT is chargeable on goods sold on board a vessel on a coastwise journey or aircraft on an internal flight.

10.6 Re-landed stores

Where stores are supplied and subsequently re-landed in the UK these are treated as imports and you should follow the procedures in VAT Notice 702 "Imports" .

10.7 Supplies of mess and canteen stores for HM ships

(*a*) *Conditions for zero-rating*

The text in this box has the force of law

You can zero-rate supplies of goods for use as mess and canteen stores on HM ships which are about to leave for a foreign port or a voyage outside UK territorial waters of more than fifteen days duration. The goods must be ordered for the general use on board by members of the ship's company. The Commanding Officer must certify each order: ➡

"HMS ....is deploying from the United Kingdom for service abroad on ....(date) calling at a foreign port or on a voyage outside territorial waters of more than fifteen days' duration and these stores are for use by members of the crew during the deployment".

You must deliver the goods direct to the ship for loading on board, obtain a receipt for them on board and keep it to support your claim for zero-rating.

(b) Sale or return

If you supply duty-free goods on sale or return to messes in HM ships you cannot zero-rate them for VAT purposes when they are sent out to the ship, as there is no taxable supply at that time. The taxable supply occurs only when the goods are adopted, that is when the customer pays for the goods or otherwise indicates his wish to keep them; or at the end of 12 months or any shorter period you have agreed for the goods to be bought or returned (see Notice 700 "The VAT Guide"). You are responsible for ensuring that the messes inform you promptly of when the adoption of the goods took place. If adoption occurs when the vessel is in UK territorial waters the supply is taxable, if outside there is no supply for VAT purposes. Commanders of HM ships will provide suppliers with this information.

(c) Sales of goods in canteens and shops

Where there is no supply at the time of delivery on board, VAT is chargeable at the appropriate rate on sales of goods in canteens and shops on board HM ships in UK ports or on coastwise voyages. If the ship is outside UK territorial waters any sale of goods is outside the scope of VAT and is taxable only if the goods are re-landed in the UK. Notice 700 "The VAT Guide" explains how to deal with this in your records and accounts.

11 RECORDS AND ACCOUNTING FOR VAT

11.1 What records do I need to keep?

Notice 700 "The VAT Guide" contains details of the records and accounts you should keep. In addition you should retain evidence of export as described in sections 6 and 7. It is important that you follow the accounting instructions explained in this section if you do not hold the evidence of export from the EC by the due date.

If you do not follow these rules, you will be liable to be assessed for VAT due on the supplies and may incur default interest and financial penalties as a result.

Commentary—*De Voil Indirect Tax Service* **V4.306, V5.201–211.**

11.2 How do I adjust my accounts if I do not receive evidence of export or if goods are not exported?

If you make an export you can zero-rate the supply in your records when the goods are supplied to your customer. But if you do not—

- obtain and hold the required evidence of export, or
- ensure the goods have been exported within the relevant time limit for the supply, and the supply would normally be standard-rated in the UK, you must account for VAT accordingly.

You must amend your VAT records and account for VAT on the taxable proportion of the invoiced amount or consideration you have received. For a VAT rate of 17.5 per cent the VAT element would be calculated at 7/47.

When you amend your VAT records, you must make an entry equal to the tax on the supplies concerned on the "VAT PAYABLE" side of your VAT account. You must include this amount in Box 1 of your VAT return *for the period in which the relevant time limit expires.*

11.3 What if the goods are exported or I obtain evidence of export after I have accounted for VAT?

If the goods are subsequently exported and/or you later obtain evidence of export you can then zero-rate the supply and adjust your VAT account *for the period in which you obtained the evidence*. This is provided that the goods have not been used in the UK prior to export (unless specifically authorised by Revenue and Customs) and in the case of an *indirect export* – see paragraph 2.11 – the goods have been supplied to an overseas person (as defined in paragraph 2.4).

11.4 How do I account for exported goods, which are subsequently returned damaged?

Where export goods damaged after shipment are relanded in the UK they must be declared to HM Revenue and Customs. If you or a member of a salvage association subsequently sell the goods, the seller must account for VAT, at the appropriate UK rate, on the sale price.

Commentary—*De Voil Indirect Tax Service* **V4.339.**

11.5 How do I account for VAT on deposits and progress payments?

Deposits and progress payments are part payments towards the total cost of a supply received in advance of its completion and have the same VAT liability as the final supply. If the final supply is to be zero-rated as an export, these payments may also be zero-rated.

However, if the goods are not eventually exported or you fail to obtain valid evidence of export you must account for VAT on the total value of the supply, including any deposit, progress or stage payments, on your next VAT return.

12 FORMS

12.1 Example of a certificate of shipment for embassies, High Commissions etc

Certificate of shipment

Date of issue:
Reference:

Supplier
VAT number
Supplier's invoice number and date
Port of loading
Port of shipment
Flight/sailing
Destination
AWB No
HAWB No
Bill of lading No
Sea-waybill No
Number of packages

Description of export goods **Quantity** **Weight** **Value**

(Authorised Signatory)

12.2 Example of a Certificate of export for goods sold at auction and exported direct by the auctioneer as air or sea freight

I, ... (full name of signatory) certify that the article(s) detailed below and sold as Lot No(s) .... at auction by me on .... (date of sale) has/have* been exported from the EC on the undermentioned vessel/aircraft*:

Description of article(s)	*LOT No*	*Value £'s*

Name of export vessel, or aircraft flight prefix and number

Port or airport of loading ....

Date of sailing or departure ....

Destination ....

Bill of lading or air-waybill number (where appropriate) ....

Identifying number of container or railway wagon (if used)..

.... (Signature of auctioneer)

Date..

*Delete as necessary

12.3 Certificate of export for goods sold at auction and exported direct by the auctioneer by parcel post or courier service

I, ... (full name of signatory) certify that the article(s) detailed below and sold as Lot No(s)... at auction by me on .... (date of sale) has/have* been exported from the EC by post/courier service*:

Description of article(s)	*LOT No*	*Value £'s*

Place of posting...

Method of posting (parcel/letter etc)....................................

Date of posting...

Destination..

Certificate(s) of posting numbers held by me..

.... (Signature of auctioneer)

Date...

*Delete as necessary

13 TRADE ASSOCIATION CONTACT DETAILS

You can get further guidance about the commercial aspects of specific exports from freight forwarders, shipping companies or airlines at the appropriate ports or airports.

The Trade Associations listed below may also provide advice—

Automated Customs and International Trade Association (ACITA)
49 Barkham Ride
Wokingham
Berkshire
RG11 4HA

Association of International Courier and Express Services (AICES)
Unit 1B
Gallymead Road
Colnbrook
Berkshire
SL3 0EN

British Exporters Association (BEXA)
Broadway House
Tothill Street
London
SW1H 9NQ

British International Freight Association (BIFA)
Redfern House
Browells Lane
Feltham
Middlesex
W13 7EP

Customs Practitioners Group
100 New Bridge Street
London EC4V 6JA

Electronic Data Interchange Association

148 Buckingham Palace Road
London
SW1W 9TR

Freight Transport Association (FTA)
Hermes House
St John's Road
Tunbridge Wells
Kent TN4 9UZ

The Institute of Export
Export House
64 Clifton Street
London
EC2A 4HB

The Simpler Trade Procedures Board (SITPRO)
(SITPRO offer a free helpline to businesses on all matters relating to International Trade
8th Floor
Oxford House
76 Oxford Street
London
W1D 1BS
E-mail address: info@sitpro.org.uk; or
Tel: 00 44 (0)207 467 7280

Business Information
British Standards Institution
389 Chiswick High Road
London W4 4AL

United Kingdom Oil Industry Taxation Committee (UKOITC)
Total House
4 Lancer Square
London
W8 4EW

Notice 703/1 Supply of freight containers for export or removal from the United Kingdom

2004 (*with Updates 1, 2, 3*)

Commentary—*De Voil Indirect Tax Service* **V4.323.**
Note—Paragraphs 2.3 and 2.4 have the force of law under VATA 1994 s 30(6), 30(8) and SI 1995/2518 regs 128, 134.

2.3 CONDITIONS FOR ZERO-RATING THE SALE OF CONTAINERS TO VAT REGISTERED CUSTOMERS IN OTHER MEMBER STATES

From I January 1993 the removal of a container to another EC Member State is treated as a zero-rated supply provided that all the following conditions are met:

- you obtain your EC customer's VAT registration number (with a 2 digit country code prefix) which you must show on your VAT invoice;
- the containers are sent from the UK to a destination in another EC Member State; and
- within three months of the date of supply, you obtain and hold valid commercial documentary evidence that the containers have been removed from the UK. Examples of acceptable evidence are listed in Notice 703 Exports and removals of goods from the United Kingdom.

If your customer is not registered for VAT in another EC Member State, or all of the above conditions are not met, you cannot zero-rate your supply and you must account for tax on the containers in the UK.

If your EC customer collects or arranges for the collection of the container and its removal from the UK, you should confirm with your customer how the container is to be removed, and what evidence of removal will be available to you.

You may also wish to consider taking a deposit from your customer equal to the amount of VAT you will have to account for if you believe you will not be able to obtain evidence of the type listed in Notice 703.

2.4 CONDITIONS FOR ZERO-RATING THE SALE OF CONTAINERS IN THE UK FOR INDIRECT EXPORT FROM THE EC

To zero-rate the sale of a freight container for export (but not where you export the container direct), you must obtain a written undertaking from your customer that:

- the container will be exported from the EC; and
- will not be used within the EC except for:
  - a single domestic journey before export of the container, on which inland freight may be carried between two points within the UK. This is allowable only if the route brings the container reasonably directly from the point of supply to the place where it is to be loaded with the export cargo, or exported;
  - international movements of goods, which may include a journey within the UK for the purpose of loading or unloading the goods;
- records accounting for the use of the container will be maintained, as specified in paragraph 2.5.

The above conditions, where met, allow a chain of supplies to be zero-rated.

Notice 703/2
Sailaway boats supplied for export outside the European Community

2002 (*with Updates 1and 2*)

Note—Principally section 3 has the force of law under VATA 1994 s 30(8) and SI 1995/2518 reg 129. This sets out the conditions to be complied with for sailaway boats, but other paragraphs outline additional conditions which must be met.

1 SAILAWAY BOATS SUPPLIED FOR EXPORT OUTSIDE THE EUROPEAN COMMUNITY

1.1 What is this notice about?

This notice explains the procedures for zero-rating the supply of a sailaway boat. The notice has been rewritten to improve readability, but the technical content has not changed from the October 1998 edition.

…

1.2 Who should read this notice?

This notice is intended for manufacturers and other suppliers of boats.

1.3 What is the definition of a "sailaway boat"?

A "sailaway boat" is defined as a boat which is to be—

- delivered to the purchaser or their authorised skipper within the EC; and
- exported under its own power to a destination outside the VAT territory of the European Community (EC).

For further information see the destination guide at section 5.4.

1.4 Who can use this scheme?

The scheme can only be used for the private purchase of a boat by—

(a) an *overseas visitor* who intends to export the boat under its own power to a destination outside the EC within six months of the date of delivery. This is normally the date the boat leaves your premises; or

(b) an *EC resident* (or emigrant) who intends to export the boat under its own power to a destination outside the EC within two months of the date of delivery. This is normally the date the boat leaves your premises. The boat must be kept outside the EC for a continuous period of at least 12 months.

The scheme is not to be used for commercial purchases.

1.5 What forms have to be used?

You will need to prove that the boat has been removed from the EC before you can zero-rate the sale in your records. The forms you will need to use are—

- Form VAT 436 —notification of VAT-free purchase of a sailaway boat, and customer's declaration.

  Original copy (1)—copy for certification

Copy (2)—Customs copy
Copy (3)—customer's copy
Copy (4)—supplier's copy

- Form C88 (single administrative document)—copies 1–3
  Copy 1—Community transit copy where applicable (take a copy for your own records)
  Copy 2—for UK Customs
  Copy 3—for certification when the boat finally leaves the EC
- Form C1331—to advise departure from the UK.

The use of the forms vary according to whether a boat departs to a destination outside the EC directly from the UK or via another member state (see section 4).

1.6 Can I include direct exports in this scheme?

If you supply, and arrange delivery of a boat either on a trailer or by using a skipper employed by you to a destination outside the EC, then you must *not* use this scheme. If the boat is not to be used in the EC before it is exported, you can arrange for the boat to be delivered direct to a destination outside the EC free of VAT. For more information about direct exports please see Notice No 703 "Exports and removals of goods from the United Kingdom".

1.7 Does the scheme include boats that are taken to other member states of the EC

No, boats supplied for private use that are removed from the UK to another EC country *cannot be supplied* under the scheme described in this Notice. See Notice No 728 "Motor vehicles, boats, aircraft: intra-EC movements by private persons" for details of how they can be supplied free of VAT.

1.8 Does the scheme cover parts and accessories?

No, but parts or accessories may be supplied under the retail export scheme. Notice No 704 "Retail exports" tells you how to deal with sales you make under the retail export scheme.

2 ACCOUNTING ARRANGEMENTS

2.1 How do I account for VAT?

You must keep a separate record of all boats you sell under the scheme. Your sales invoice must clearly show that the supply of the boat was made under the sailaway boat scheme.

If you do not obtain and hold evidence of export within one month of the date of export you must account for VAT accordingly.

- If you have taken a deposit of the VAT due then it should be brought to account;
- If you have not taken a deposit you must amend your VAT records and account for VAT on the taxable proportion of the invoiced amount or consideration you have received, that is for a VAT rate of 17.5 per cent the VAT element is calculated at 7/47.

When you amend your VAT records you must make an entry equal to the tax on the supplies concerned on the "VAT PAYABLE" side of your account. You must include this amount in Box 1 of your VAT return for the period in which the time limit expires.

2.2 Should I take a deposit of VAT?

The boat is not eligible for zero rated VAT status until Form VAT 436 certified by the Customs office at the place of final departure is received. You are, therefore, strongly advised to treat any sale of a boat under the scheme as liable to VAT until you have received the certified form VAT 436. You may wish to ask your customer for a deposit equal to the amount of VAT, to be refunded when the required evidence of export is received.

If you do not receive the necessary evidence of export you will have to account for the VAT due—even if you did not charge it at the point of sale.

2.3 What should I do if I receive evidence of export after I have accounted for VAT?

If you later obtain evidence that the boat was exported from the EC within the permitted time limits, you can zero-rate the supply and refund any deposit and adjust your VAT account for the period in which you obtained the evidence. You should treat the transaction as a credit in your VAT records. See Notice No 700 "The VAT guide".

3 SELLING CONDITIONS

3.1 What do I have to do prior to the boat being supplied?

Before a boat is supplied you must—

(a) ensure that your customer is entitled to use the scheme (see para 1.4);

(b) ensure that your customer intends to export the boat from the EC within the permitted time limits as outlined in para 1.4;
(c) give your customer a copy of Notice No 703/3 "Sailaway boat scheme" and an application form VAT 436; and
(d) ensure form VAT 436 is fully completed by you and your customer, and Part 2 submitted to the National Unit for Personal Transport (PTU) at least two weeks before due delivery of the boat.

All notifications should be serially numbered in the top right hand corner and submitted to the PTU at the following address: HM Customs & Excise (MSO), National Unit for Personal Transport (PTU), P O Box 242, Dover, Kent, CT17 9GP; Telephone number: 01304 224 556; Fax number: 01304 224 567.

Please ensure that notifications are correct and complete before you accept them. An incorrect or incomplete notification *will be returned* for correction, and this may delay the delivery of the boat.

The PTU will be pleased to give you any help or advice on the purchase of a sailaway boat.

3.2 What should I do at the time of the sale?

At the time of sale you must—

(a) ensure that your customer knows that he/she must not dispose, or attempt to dispose of the boat in the EC by hire, pledge as security*, sale, gift or any other means;
(b) keep a *separate* record of the sale; and
(c) agree how any refund of the deposited VAT will be paid (see para 2.2).

*The boat's documents may only be used as security that is required by the finance house for the purchase of the boat. The boat must not be pledged as security for a separate purchase, for example a car, flat or house.

3.3 What will happen if the order is cancelled?

If, after the notification is processed, the order for the boat is subsequently cancelled by the customer before delivery, you should immediately notify the PTU of—

- the name of the customer;
- details of the boat; and
- the serial number of the notification.

4 EXPORT PROCEDURES

4.1 What must I do if my customer is leaving the UK directly for a destination outside the EC?

You must tell your customer to—

- complete form C1331 "Notice of intended departure";
- make the boat available for inspection by Customs at exportation. (Where possible this should be arranged in advance with the Customs at the port of exportation. Contact numbers can be found in Notice No 8 "Sailing your pleasure craft to and from the United Kingdom");
- take the completed form VAT 436 to the UK Customs office nearest the place of departure. (Customs will retain the C1331 and sign and stamp form VAT 436 to show that the boat has been declared for exportation. The certified form will be returned to your customer); and return the certified form VAT 436 to you. If you give the customer a stamped addressed envelope, Customs may agree to return the form to you on your customer's behalf.

4.2 What must I do if my customer is calling into another member state before finally exporting the boat from the EC?

You must tell your customer to—

- take the completed forms C88 (copies 2 and 3) and VAT 436 to the UK Customs office nearest the place of departure from the UK. Customs will keep copy 2 of the C88 and return copy 3 with form VAT 436 to your customer;
- export the boat from the EC within the time limits laid down in para 1.4;
- take copy 3 of C88 and VAT436 to the Customs office at the place of final departure from the EC for certification; *and*
- return the certified C88 and VAT 436 to you.

You should ensure that your customer understands that you cannot zero-rate the supply of the boat and make the refund of VAT until you have received the Customs certified documents.

4.3 What do I do when I receive the certified evidence of export?

When you receive the Customs certified evidence of export, you should refund any deposit to your customer by the method agreed, and account for the sale in your VAT records as explained in para 2.1.

5 FURTHER INFORMATION

5.1 What will happen if someone wants to re-import a VAT-free boat back into the EC?

If a boat that was supplied tax free at purchase is brought back to the EC it must be declared to Customs in the member state of importation. You should ensure that your customer is fully aware of the need to make an import declaration. VAT will be payable unless some other relief is available.

Commentary—*De Voil Indirect Tax Service* **V3.351.**

5.2 Can I zero rate supplies destined for the Channel Islands

The Channel Islands are outside the EC VAT area and therefore qualify as a final destination for boats supplied VAT-free for export. EC residents who register VAT-free boats in the Channel Islands cannot claim VAT-free temporary importation of such boats into an EC member state. VAT is payable on these importations. However, subject to their meeting the conditions for temporary importation, private persons resident in the Channel Islands may be entitled to import their own boats for their own personal use for up to 18 months without payment of import VAT.

5.3 Notice No 703/3 "Sailaway boat scheme"

Notice No 703/3 explains to boat buyers how the sailaway boat scheme works. You should hold a stock of these for issue to your customers.

5.4 Destination guide

The Sailaway Boat Scheme **must not** *be used for the following destinations*	*The Sailaway Boat Scheme can be used for the following destinations*
The member states of the EC which are—	All countries *not* listed in column 1 and—
Austria	
Belgium	
Denmark	Faroe Islands, Greenland
Finland	Aland Islands
France, including Monaco	French Guiana, Guadeloupe, Martinique, Reunion, St. Pierre and Miquelon
Germany	
Greece	Mount Athos
Republic of Ireland	
Italy	
Luxembourg	
The Netherlands	
Portugal, including the Azores and Madeira	
Spain, and the Balearic Islands	Canary Islands, Ceuta, Melilla
Sweden	
United Kingdom, and the Isle of Man	Channel Islands and Gibraltar
Plus from 1 May 2004	
Cyprus*	
The Czech Republic	
Estonia	
Hungary	
Latvia	
Lithuania	
Malta	
Poland	
The Slovak Republic	
Slovenia	
Plus from 1 January 2007	
Bulgaria	
Romania	

* The European Commission in December 2003 advised that the application of the 6th VAT Directive (Directive 77/388/EEC of 17 May 1977) shall be suspended in those areas of Cyprus in

which the Government of the Republic of Cyprus does not exercise effective control. From 1 May 2004 goods to these destinations continue to be eligible for zero-rating as exports.

Andorra and San Marino are not in the EC for VAT purposes and so the scheme can be used if they are the destination.

GLOSSARY

EC	The European Community consisting of: Austria, Belgium, Denmark, Finland, France, Germany, Greece, Republic of Ireland, Italy, Luxembourg, the Netherlands, Portugal, Spain, Sweden and the United Kingdom. Plus from 1 May 2004 Cyprus*, The Czech Republic, Estonia, Hungary, Latvia, Lithuania, Malta, Poland, the Slovak Republic, and Slovenia. * The European Commission in December 2003 advised that the application of the 6th VAT Directive (Directive 77/388/EEC of 17 May 1977) shall be suspended in those areas of Cyprus in which the Government of the Republic of Cyprus does not exercise effective control. From 1 May 2004 goods to these destinations continue to be eligible for zero-rating as exports **Plus from 1 January 2007** Bulgaria and Romania
UK	The United Kingdom: England, Scotland, Wales, Northern Ireland, (including the Isle of Man but not the Channel Islands or Gibraltar).
Sailaway boat	A vessel supplied VAT free in the UK which is to be exported under its own power to a destination outside the VAT territory of the European Community (EC).
EC resident	A person who has lived in the EC for more than 365 days in the two years before the date they buy the boat; and is leaving the EC for a continuous period of at least 12 months (this includes overseas students and workers who have lived in the EC for more than 365 days in the two years before the date they buy the boat).
Overseas visitor	An overseas visitor is someone who normally lives outside the EC, has not been in the EC for more than 365 days in the two years before the date they buy the boat and intends to leave the EC, within six months of the date of delivery of the boat.

Notice 704
VAT: retail exports

2004 (*with Update 1*)

This notice cancels and replaces Notice 704 (July 2003). Details of any changes to the previous version can be found in paragraph 1.2 of this notice.

Regulation 131 of the VAT Regulations 1995 sets out conditions for using the Retail Export Scheme. This regulation also gives the Commissioners power to impose further conditions which must be met to allow a supply to be zero-rated. Parts of this notice have the force of law under that regulation. These paragraphs are indicated by three asterisks (***) at the beginning and end of the paragraph.

EXAMPLE:

The following text has the force of law

There is no facility to have your refund document stamped in your country of destination

…

CONTENTS

7 Information for travellers
8 Intra EC cruises—special arrangement
9 Fiscal (VAT) territory of the European Community

Commentary—*De Voil Indirect Tax Service* **V4.331.**

1 INTRODUCTION

1.1 What is this notice about?

This notice explains when supplies of goods sold by VAT registered retailers to entitled persons for personal use and exported as accompanied baggage can be zero-rated. In particular, it sets out the conditions that must be complied with by retailers and entitled customers using the VAT Retail Export Scheme.

1.2 What's changed?

The notice has been rewritten to improve readability. In addition, the scheme and conditions have been reviewed and changed and you are strongly recommended to read through this notice to understand where changes have been made. The main changes have been introduced to:

- take account of European Community (EC) enlargement from 1 May 2004 (covered in update 1, issued February 2004);
- limit purchases under the scheme by overseas students and migrant workers to the end of their stay in the EC;
- include the new invoicing requirements arising from implementation of the EC VAT Invoicing Directive; and
- set out conditions for retailers who complete refund forms after the date of sale.

You can access details of any changes to this notice since November 2004 either on our Internet website at www.hmce.gov.uk or by telephoning the National Advice Service on 0845 010 9000.

This notice and others mentioned are available both on paper and on our website.

1.3 Who should read this notice?

This notice is intended for retailers and entitled customers.

1.4 What is the legal status of this notice?

Article 15 of the EC Sixth VAT Directive states that Member States shall lay down conditions "for the purpose of ensuring the correct and straightforward application of such exemptions (zero-rating) and preventing any evasion, avoidance or abuse". Under United Kingdom VAT law, the Commissioners of Customs and Excise may specify conditions in regulations or otherwise impose conditions to meet this requirement.

The VAT Regulations 1995 and this notice lay down the conditions for the VAT Retail Export Scheme which must be met in full for a supply of goods for export outside the EC to be zero-rated. As these conditions have legal status, some legal wording has been necessary but plain English has been used wherever possible.

Text with three asterisks at the beginning and end of the paragraph has the force of law.

1.5 Where can travellers obtain further information?

Retailers and travellers may obtain further information and advice from the National Advice Service on 0845 010 9000; or +44 20 8929 0152 for international callers.

See "Further help and advice" on the inside front cover for full details. This notice and others mentioned are available in hard copy from the National Advice Service and on our website.

A simplified notice aimed specifically at travellers, Notice 704/1 Tax Free Shopping: VAT Refunds for travellers departing from the European Community (EC) highlights the main aspects of the scheme. Notice 704/1 is available in various languages.

Tourist and travel organisations as well as the VAT refund companies distribute information about the VAT Retail Export Scheme.

(Please note that whilst retail export schemes operate throughout the EC they are regulated by the laws of the individual Member States and may differ in significant details from the scheme in the UK. Travellers wishing to purchase goods in another EC Member State should contact the Customs or tax authorities of the Member State for detailed information and advice.)

2 GENERAL PRINCIPLES

2.1 What is the VAT Retail Export Scheme?

The VAT Retail Export Scheme allows:

- certain customers (see paragraph 2.4) to receive a refund of VAT paid on goods exported to destinations outside the European Community (EC) subject to conditions detailed at paragraph 2.3; and

- retailers to zero-rate goods sold to entitled customers when they have the necessary evidence of export and have refunded the VAT to the customer.

This is a voluntary scheme and retailers do not have to operate it. Those who do must ensure that all the conditions set out in this notice are met.

2.2 Is there a minimum sales value?

No. Although retailers may set a minimum sales value below which they will not operate the scheme.

2.3 What conditions apply to the scheme?

The following text has the force of law

***Retailers and refund companies (see paragraph 5.5) may only operate the VAT Retail Export Scheme when they comply with the conditions set out in this notice. Briefly these are:

- the customer must be entitled to use the scheme (see paragraph 2.4);
- the goods must be eligible to be purchased under the scheme (see paragraph 2.6);
- the customer must make the purchase in person and complete the form at the retailer's premises in full (see paragraph 3.1 and 7.4.2);
- the goods must be exported from the EC by the last day of the third month following that in which the goods were purchased;
- the customer must send the retailer or the refund company evidence of export stamped by Customs on an official version of Form VAT 407, an approved version of Form VAT 407 or an officially approved invoice (see Section 4); and
- the retailer or the refund company must not zero-rate the supply until the VAT has been refunded to the customer (see paragraph 5.2).***

2.3.1 Can the time limit for export be extended?

No. The goods must be exported from the EC by the last day of the third month following that in which the goods were purchased.

The following text has the force of law

Retailers and refund companies must not zero-rate goods exported after the last day of the third month following the month in which the goods were purchased-even if the VAT refund document has been stamped in error by a UK or other EC Customs officer.

2.4 Who can buy goods under the scheme?

2.4.1 Overseas visitors

An overseas visitor is a traveller (including a member of the crew of a ship or aircraft) who is not established in the EC. This means a person:

- whose domicile or habitual place of residence is not situated within the EC. A person's "domicile or habitual residence" is the place entered as such on their valid passport, identity card or other acceptable document, such as a driving licence. *The customer must prove their eligibility to use the scheme by providing one or more of these documents;* and
- who intends to leave the UK for a final destination outside the EC, with the goods, by the last day of the third month following that in which the goods were purchased (for example, goods purchased on 1 June must be exported by 30 September); and
- who exports the goods having produced them, their receipts, and the VAT refund document to a Customs officer at the point of departure from the EC.

2.4.2 Overseas visitors studying or working in the UK

Overseas visitors (see paragraph 2.4.1) entering the UK as students or migrant workers are only entitled to purchase goods under the scheme during the last 4 months of their stay in the UK. Such visitors will have been issued with a pre-entry visa from the UK and in the case of work periods of 6 months or more a separate work permit document is issued in the UK. The visa is contained in the overseas person's passport and shows the start and end date for the study or work period authorised. *Retailers should ask to see the visa or work permit before selling goods under the scheme.*

The customer most prove their eligibility to use the scheme by providing evidence that the period of their visit is ending and must:

- intend to leave the EC with the goods by the last day of the third month following that in which the goods were purchased; and
- having left the EC remain outside the EC for a minimum period of 12 months; and
- export the goods having produced them, their receipts, and the VAT refund document to a Customs officer at the point of departure from the EC.

2.4.3 Entitled EC residents

For the purposes of this scheme only, a customer who is established in the EC but intends to permanently leave the EC for a minimum period of 12 months may also be treated as an overseas visitor. To qualify under this provision, the customer must:

- intend to leave the UK with the goods by the last day of the third month following that in which the goods were purchased for an immediate destination outside the EC; and
- remain outside the EC for a period of at least 12 months. The customer must prove their eligibility to use the scheme by providing evidence of their intention to remain outside the EC for at least 12 months. Typically this evidence would be one of the following: overseas work permit, approved visa application, residency permit; and
- export the goods having produced them, their receipts, and the VAT refund document to a Customs officer at the point of departure from the EC.

2.5 Which countries are in the EC?

The VAT territory of the EC is made up of 25 Member States [(27 from 1 January 2007)], including some territories with which certain countries have links. Goods cannot be purchased under this scheme for removal to another Member State. Details of the fiscal (VAT) territory of the EC and of the special territories that are outside the EC for VAT purposes are in Section 9 of this notice.

Note—Para 2.5 amended by Update 1, January 2007.

2.6 What goods can be sold under the scheme?

The following text has the force of law

***Standard-rated goods and lower-rated goods with the exception of those listed below may be sold under the scheme:

- new and second hand motor vehicles for personal export (see Notice 705 Buyer's guide to personal exports of motor vehicles to destinations outside the EC);
- boats sold to visitors who intend to sail them to a destination outside the EC (see Notice 703/2 Sailaway boats supplied for export outside the EC);
- goods over £600 (excluding VAT) in value exported for business purposes (see Notice 703 Export of goods from the United Kingdom);
- goods that will be exported as freight or unaccompanied baggage (see Notice 703 Export of goods from the United Kingdom);
- goods requiring an export licence (but antiques can be sold under the scheme even if they require an export licence);
- unmounted gemstones;
- bullion (over 125g, 2.75 troy ounces or 10 Tolas);
- goods for consumption in the EC-no certification of export will be given for used consumable items, for example, perfume which is wholly or partly consumed in the EC; and
- goods purchased by mail order including those purchased over the Internet (see paragraph 2.8).

Zero-rated goods such as books and children's clothing cannot be sold under the scheme.***

2.7 Can retailers exclude certain goods from the scheme?

Yes, they can if they wish. They do not have to operate the scheme for all lines of goods that they sell.

2.8 Can the scheme be used for sales by mail order or goods sold over the Internet?

No. Goods sold to entitled persons by mail order or over the Internet will fall within the export rules set out in Notice 703 Export of goods from the United Kingdom. However, a mail order company or an Internet retailer with a retail outlet can use the scheme for goods sold from that outlet provided they comply with all the conditions set out in this notice.

2.9 Can the scheme be used for services?

No. **The scheme is for the sale of goods only**. The scheme cannot be used for services supplied to customers such as hotel accommodation, meals and car hire. This applies even where services are sold with the goods, for example labour costs for fitting spare parts to a motor vehicle. Where a vehicle brought into the UK for the use of the overseas visitor requires repairs, the sale of the spare parts only and not the cost of fitting can be included in the scheme.

But see Notice 703 Export of goods from the United Kingdom for guidance on what to do in the case of a vehicle owned by an overseas person and temporarily imported for work. Extended warranty work may not be zero-rated under the VAT Retail Export Scheme.

3 MAKING A SALE UNDER THE VAT RETAIL EXPORT SCHEME

As a retailer, you are strongly advised to keep a stock of VAT Notices 704 and 704/1 to help you explain the scheme to customers who may not have obtained a notice for themselves.

3.1 What to do at the time of sale

Please note that for you to comply with the conditions of the scheme your customer must attend in person at the time of the sale although a third party may pay for the goods. There is no facility under this scheme for a representative to attend in place of the entitled person at the time of the sale.

When customers ask to use the scheme you must:

Step	*Procedure*
1	Check that they are entitled to use the scheme (see paragraph 2.4);
2	Check that the goods are eligible for the scheme (see paragraph 2.6);
3	Check that the customer intends to leave the EC with the goods for a final destination outside the EC by the last day of the third month following that in which the goods were purchased;
4	Fill in a VAT refund document. A responsible member of staff should complete the document. Ensure all sections are fully completed, unused lines are ruled through and the customer and retailer declarations are signed at the time of the sale (see paragraph 4.2 for full details).

In addition give your customer a copy of Notice 704/1 and:

- agree with your customer how the refund will be made. (It would be useful to provide your customer with a reply paid envelope for the refund document to be returned after stamping by Customs);
- explain about any administrative fees;
- mark your customer's sales receipt to indicate that the goods have been included on a VAT refund document. For example: "VAT Export";
- explain that no refunds will be made on items (such as perfume) wholly or partly consumed in the EC;
- advise them to produce their refund document to the Customs officer for stamping at the point of departure from the EC. Explain that failure to do so will mean that a refund will not be paid. The goods and receipts must also be available for inspection if required. (See paragraph 3.4 if the customer is departing the EC on a through (transit) flight);
- advise them to allow plenty of time in which to produce their goods and refund form prior to departure. This is particularly important if they are exporting goods in hold baggage as they may need to allow up to two hours in addition to their advised check in time in case of queues;
- advise them to carry items of high value, for example, jewellery, furs, cameras, watches, silverware, laptop computers and small antiques in their hand baggage; and
- you may also wish to advise your customer to take a photocopy of the VAT refund document once it has been stamped by Customs.

3.2 Refund documents

When you make a sale under the scheme to an entitled person going to a final destination outside the EC you must complete a VAT refund document. The document can be a Form VAT 407 or an officially approved invoice that both you and your customer must sign at the time of the sale.

The document must be the original signed by you or your representative and by your customer-photocopies will not be accepted by Customs at export.

3.3 Issuing VAT 407 Forms

Blank VAT 407 forms must not be issued to members of the public. They must only be issued to VAT registered retailers who operate the VAT Retail Export Scheme.

3.4 Producing goods and refund documents to Customs

You should give customers a copy of Notice 704/1 and advise them that:

- they must produce the VAT refund document to the Customs officer at the point of departure from the EC. The goods and receipts must also be available for inspection if required. The Customs officer will stamp the refund document to show that the goods have been exported and return it to the customer; and
- they should send back to you or to the refund company the refund documents stamped by the UK or EC Customs officer. They should use the reply paid envelope you provide, or hand the documents to the cash refund booth, if appropriate (see paragraph 6.4).

Remember, whilst a single refund document is acceptable, it is recommended that you issue separate VAT refund documents (but make only one administrative charge) if the customer intends to carry some goods in hand baggage and other goods in hold baggage. This is particularly important if the customer is leaving on a through (transit) flight via another EC airport because the goods in hold baggage must be declared before check in, whilst the goods in hand baggage must be declared at the final point of departure from the EC.

3.5 Goods not exported

When customers present the VAT refund documents to the UK or other EC Customs officer, they are making a declaration that all the goods shown on the document are being exported from the EC. Customers sometimes decide not to export goods purchased under the scheme.

You should inform your customer that any goods listed on the VAT refund document not exported from the EC must be clearly *deleted* from the document *before* it is presented to a UK or EC Customs officer for stamping. It is a Customs offence to make a false declaration.

3.6 Charging for administrative or handling expenses

If you intend to deduct an amount from the refund due, to cover administrative or handling expenses, the amount of the administration fee and net refund due must be shown clearly on the VAT refund document. You are strongly advised to explain this charge clearly to your customers when they buy the goods to avoid subsequent confusion or misunderstanding.

3.7 Refunds to customers

When you receive a VAT refund document stamped by UK or other EC Customs, check that all goods have been exported from the EC by the last day of the third month following that in which the goods were purchased.

Where they have, you should make any refund due to your customer by the method agreed at the time of sale.

You cannot zero-rate the sale unless you have a stamped VAT refund document showing that the goods have been exported within the time limit and can show that the refund has been made to your customer.

Refund forms stamped outside the EC are not to be accepted as evidence of export under any circumstances.

4 COMPLETION AND CONTROL OF REFUND FORMS

You may use a Form VAT 407 or adapted invoice for the scheme.

4.1 Form VAT 407

If you use the Form VAT 407 the following versions can be used:

- Form VAT 407 issued by Customs, available free of charge from the National Advice Service;
- your own version of the Form VAT 407, containing the same information as the Customs' version and approved beforehand by Customs; or
- a refund company's version of the Form VAT 407, containing the same information as the Customs' version and approved beforehand by Customs.

4.2 How to complete Form VAT 407

When completing a Form VAT 407 the following instructions must be followed.

PART	Completed by	Procedure
A	Customer	Make sure your customer completes this part legibly in full at the time of sale and signs the declaration.
B	Retailer	(a) Give a full and accurate description of the goods quoting identification numbers, serial numbers or other identifying marks for example hallmarks, together with the quantity (and weight in the case of jewellery) of goods sold. Descriptions such as stock numbers, "see invoice attached", "Jewellery" or "Designer goods" are not acceptable. The description must be clear enough to allow the UK or EC Customs officer to readily identify the goods. (b) Cross through any unused lines on the form. (c) Show – the total amount payable including VAT in both words and figures; – the amount of VAT included in the price; – the amount of any administration fee that will be deducted from the refund; and – the amount of refund that will be paid to the customer.

C	Retailer	(a) Insert the full name of your business, address and VAT number; (b) Insert the date the goods were sold to the customer; and (c) the declaration must be signed either by yourself or another responsible person in your business.
D	Customs Officer	At the point of departure from the EC a Customs officer must stamp the form to validate the export. (Whilst desirable, it is not essential the Customs officer signs the form.)

Customs officers may refuse to stamp refund forms completed incorrectly or not completed in full. For example, forms showing inadequate descriptions of goods may be rejected.

4.3 Officially approved invoice

If you do not use one of the versions of Form VAT 407 described at paragraph 4.1 you may use an officially approved invoice. You should be aware that if you do use an officially approved invoice you must meet the requirements of invoicing legislation. The invoice must include the details set out at paragraph 4.3.1.

4.3.1 What general information is required on an invoice?

Where the total consideration for a supply (including VAT) is less than £250 a simplified invoice may be issued. Simplified invoices must show:

- your name, address and VAT registration number;
- the time of supply;
- a description sufficient to identify the goods supplied;
- the total amount payable including VAT; and
- for each rate of VAT chargeable, the gross amount payable including VAT and the VAT rate applicable.

Where the total consideration for a supply (including VAT) is £250 or more, the invoice must show:

- an identifying number;
- your name, address and VAT registration number;
- date of issue;
- time of supply (tax point-only needs to be shown if different from the date of issue);
- your customer's name (or trading name) and address*;
- a *description* identifying the goods … you are supplying;
- the gross total amount payable excluding VAT;
- the rate of any cash discount offered;
- the unit price (see Notice 700 The VAT guide); and
- the total amount of VAT charged, shown in sterling.

For each *description*, of goods … you must show the:

- quantity of goods …;
- rate of VAT; and
- amount payable excluding VAT.

*Where an approved invoice is used for the scheme the usual address will be your customer's place of residence outside the EC.

Provided your customer agrees, a retailer may issue a modified VAT invoice showing the VAT inclusive amounts of each supply instead of the VAT exclusive values. However, in all other respects the modified invoice should show the details required for a full VAT invoice (see Notice 700 The VAT guide as amended by Update 2 issued February 2004

Remember, you cannot use the VAT Retail Export Scheme for services.

Note—Para 4.3.1 amended by Update 1, January 2007.

4.4 Design and size of own versions of VAT 407s or invoices

The following text has the force of law

- ***The VAT 407 or invoice must closely follow the design of the Customs and Excise version of Form VAT 407…
- It must include the data protection statement shown on the face of the form and the information shown on the reverse side of the Customs and Excise version of Form VAT 407. This includes:
  - the heading "Retail Export Scheme";
  - providing spaces for the retailer's and the customer's declarations as stipulated on the Form VAT 407, including details of the customer's passport/identity number and country of issue, date of arrival in the EC, intended date of departure from the EC;
  - and a separate box not less than 5 cm by 3.5 cm for official stamping by a Customs officer at the customer's point of departure from the EC.

- The total amount payable must be shown in words as well as figures.
- Each VAT 407 or invoice must show the amount of any administrative charge and the net refund due to the customer.***

Note—Para 4.4 amended by Update 1, January 2007.

4.5 Prior approval of own versions of VAT 407s or invoices

You must seek approval beforehand from Customs and Excise if you wish to use your own adapted VAT 407 or invoice for sales made under the scheme.

Remember, if you use an officially approved VAT 407 or invoice you must still make sure that your customer is entitled to use the scheme and that the declarations are completed in full and signed by you (or another responsible person in your business) and your customer at the time of the sale.

4.6 How can I obtain approval from Customs and Excise?

If you do not intend to use the VAT 407 Form issued by Customs and Excise you must send a sample of your own invoice or version of the VAT 407 refund document for approval to Customs & Excise. Addresses can be obtained from the National Advice Service on 0845 010 9000 (see the "Further help and advice" section at the front of this notice for details), or via our Customs and Excise Internet home page by following the links from "contact us" through to Written Enquiries Teams.

4.7 Reply paid envelope

Each year several hundred VAT refund documents are returned to Customs at Heathrow airport for a variety of reasons. This is usually because the postage has not been paid and because the document contains a customs' stamp. Whether using a Form VAT 407, your own or a refund company's version, or an adapted invoice, give your customer the fully completed VAT refund document and a reply paid envelope addressed to either you or the refund company administering the refund. If you do not provide a reply paid envelope, you should make it clear that your customer is responsible for providing the envelope and paying the correct postage.

4.8 Can I complete the VAT refund form before export of the goods for past purchases?

Paragraph 3.2 states that refund forms must be completed at the time of sale. Customers may ask you to complete a refund form to cover past purchases. You may only agree to such requests provided you have adequate security procedures in place to prevent abuse of the scheme. This includes:

- stamping till receipts to show that the goods have been purchased under the Retail Export Scheme, for example "VAT Export".
- your till system allowing you to check that the receipts produced are genuine and can only appear once on a VAT 407 refund document;
- your system allowing you to check whether:
  - a refund for returned goods has already been made for a receipt now produced or
  - a VAT 407 refund document has been issued for goods where a refund for returned goods is now sought.

The following text has the force of law

Where you cannot show that you have adequate security procedures in place, you must continue to complete VAT refund documents at the time of the sale.

4.8.1 Completion of refund documents on production of receipts for past purchases

Where you do have adequate safeguards in place to prevent abuse of the scheme and a customer asks for a refund document to cover a series of purchases over a period of time, you must include only those goods that will be exported by the last day of the third month following that in which the goods were purchased. The purchase date entered on the refund document must be the date of the earliest purchase.

4.9 Control of blank or partly completed VAT refund documents

Whether you use:

- Form VAT 407 issued by Customs;
- a refund company's version of the form; or
- your own officially approved invoice,

you must:

- keep stocks of the blank documents secure;
- not issue blank or partly completed forms to any person outside your business.

4.10 Uncertified export documents

The following text has the force of law

If your customers send you VAT refund documents which have not been stamped by UK or other EC Customs, you cannot zero-rate the supply because export of the goods from the EC has not been certified as required by the scheme.
There are no exceptions to this rule.

4.11 Lost refund documents

4.11.1 Document lost before certification

If your customer has lost the VAT refund document before leaving the EC and asks for another, you can prepare a "DUPLICATE" *clearly marked* as such. The duplicate form and the goods must be produced to the Customs officer at the point of departure from the EC. You should take steps to ensure that should the original document appear it is not processed through your records.

When issuing a duplicate document, you must:

– make sure the original document has not been received and processed by you already;
– be satisfied that a sale took place by the production of till receipts or other information; and
– advise the traveller if they find the original refund document later, it is to be cancelled.

If you later receive the original document ensure it is cancelled.

4.11.2 Document lost after certification

If your customer has lost the VAT refund document after stamping by UK or other EC Customs, you may issue a duplicate only where a photocopy of the stamped original is produced. Duplicates of forms lost after Customs stamping must **not** be issued in any other circumstances.

The duplicate and the photocopy of the original document stamped by Customs must be sent to the Customs officer who stamped the original document. If satisfied, the Customs officer will stamp the duplicate and return it to you so that a refund may be made.

5 ACCOUNTING FOR VAT

5.1 Must I charge VAT at the point of sale?

You must treat any sale of standard-rated and lower-rated goods you make under the scheme as liable to VAT until you have received the VAT refund document appropriately stamped by a UK or other EC Customs officer. It is in your interest to charge VAT at the point of sale, and refund it to your customer only when you get valid evidence of export. Until you receive the necessary evidence of export and make the refund to your customer you will have to account for the VAT due.

5.2 What must I do before zero-rating the sale?

The following text has the force of law

You must obtain the stamped refund document and refund the VAT to your customer by the agreed method. You must retain the stamped refund document and evidence of the refund made to your customer to support the zero-rating of the supply.

If the certified VAT refund document arrives after you have accounted for VAT, you can refund the VAT and zero-rate the sale by reducing your output tax by the relevant amount in box 1 of your VAT return [for the period in which the evidence is received and the refund is made]—see Notice 700 The VAT Guide.

Note—Para 5.2 amended by Update 1, January 2007.

5.3 Retailers using a retail scheme

The individual retail schemes notices (in the 727 series) will explain how you should deal with sales and refunds under the VAT Retail Export Scheme in your retail scheme calculations.

5.4 Retailers not using a retail scheme

You must keep a record of all sales including VAT made under the VAT Retail Export Scheme. When you receive a VAT refund document stamped by a UK or other EC Customs officer and you have refunded the VAT, you can zero-rate the sale in your records.

5.5 Refund companies

You may contract with a refund company to administer the refund on your behalf. Refund companies usually provide an officially approved VAT refund document of their own design for use by retailers. If you use one of these companies, you still have to account for the VAT, as explained in paragraphs 5.1 and 5.2. You must retain the certified VAT refund documents and evidence that the VAT has been refunded in your records to support any zero-rating claimed.

5.6 Concession shops

Many larger stores operate concessions for other retailers within their own stores, where one counter or area sells goods from another retailer's range. Where the sale is rung through the main store tills it is acceptable for the VAT refund document to be issued by the host store (typically at the main customer service desk). In these circumstances the host store is responsible for complying with the conditions of the scheme as set out in this notice and for accounting for the VAT.

However, where the concession operates its own tills and issues receipts in its own right showing its own name and VAT number, any VAT refund documents relating to these purchases must be issued by the concession and not the host store. In these cases the concession is responsible for complying with the conditions of the scheme as set out in this notice and for accounting for the VAT.

5.7 Direct reclaim system

The direct reclaim system involves two distinct transactions. A retailer sells goods to a refund company who immediately sells them on to an eligible traveller. The accounting procedure is as follows:

- The retailer must invoice the sale to the refund company because this is a business-to-business supply, not a retail sale, and account for VAT on the supply. See paragraph 4.3.1 for the information that must be included on a VAT invoice.
- The refund company may use the invoice from the retailer to reclaim input tax on the purchase from the retailer. Notice 700 The VAT Guide provides information on the rules for invoices and claiming input tax.
- The refund company must also account for VAT on the sale to the traveller. It may subsequently zero-rate the supply *but only* where and when all the conditions of the VAT Retail Export Scheme set out in this notice are met.
- The retailer may include the sale to the refund company in their daily gross takings for retail scheme purposes if they wish.

5.8 Sales under the Margin Scheme for second-hand goods, works of art, antiques and collectors' items

If you make sales under the Margin Scheme for second-hand goods, accounting requirements will differ from those that must be fulfilled under the VAT Retail Export Scheme. You can use the two schemes for a single sale if you adapt the VAT refund document as follows:

- head it "Second-hand goods-this document is adapted in accordance with Notice 704, paragraph 5.8";
- leave the line "Amount of VAT included in the price" blank; and
- complete the refund due box.

See also Notice 718 Margin Schemes for second-hand goods, works of art, antiques and collectors' items.

5.9 Sales by auctioneers

If an auctioneer sells goods on your behalf to someone who is entitled to use the Retail Export Scheme and a VAT refund document is completed, you can zero-rate the sale when:

- the VAT refund document stamped by a UK or EC Customs officer is returned to you, and
- you have made the refund to your customer.

However, the VAT Retail Export Scheme can no longer be used for goods exported as freight (see paragraph 6.2). Exports of goods by freight should be made in accordance with the procedures described in Notice 703 Export of goods from the United Kingdom.

If auctioneers are registered for VAT and sell goods in their own name to someone who is entitled to use the scheme then, for VAT purposes, they may be treated as both receiving and making a supply of goods in accordance with Notice 700 The VAT Guide. They can zero-rate the sale provided they hold a VAT refund document stamped by a UK or EC Customs officer and have refunded the VAT to their customer.

5.10 VAT treatment of administration or handling fees

If you deduct an amount from the VAT refund due to cover administrative or handling expenses, the amount you deduct is a consideration for the supply of the service to your customers in connection with the export of goods to a destination outside the EC, and is zero-rated.

6 OTHER INFORMATION

6.1 Goods exported as hold baggage

Customers leaving by air may not always be able to export large or heavy items as hand baggage and customers buying such items should be advised to inform Customs before checking their baggage in. The airline enquiry desk can tell your customer of the Customs arrangements in force, as these vary from airport to airport.

Advise your customer that during busy periods queues are likely. Therefore they may need to allow up to two hours, prior to check in and the security procedures, to produce the goods and refund document. Long queues at the airport will not be accepted as a reason for failing to obtain a Customs stamp on the refund form.

6.2 Goods exported as freight

The concession allowing the Retail Export Scheme to be used for goods exported by travellers as freight (including unaccompanied baggage, courier and post) was withdrawn on 1 July 2003. The procedures for exporting goods by freight are described in Notice 703 Export of goods from the United Kingdom.

6.3 Supplies to diplomats, members of international organisations and NATO forces in other Member States

The scheme cannot be used for such supplies. There are special arrangements under Article 15(10) of the EC Sixth VAT Directive-see Notice 725 The Single Market.

6.4 Cash refund booths

Some refund companies have arrangements with refund booths at ports, airports and border crossing points from which cash refunds can be made to travellers before they leave the EC. In addition some refund companies will pay cash refunds to travellers in local currency at their destinations. The cash booth may charge your customer an additional administrative fee for these facilities. In all cases the customer will need to have their VAT refund document stamped by Customs at the place of departure from the EC.

6.5 Export licensing

Antiques may be exported only on production of a valid export licence to Customs at the point of departure from the UK. Further advice can be obtained from:

The Department for Culture, Media and Sport
2–4 Cockspur Street
LONDON
SW1Y 5DH

If you sell goods that fall into this category you should explain this to your customers. They will probably need your assistance to obtain an export licence.

6.6 Information on other types of exports

Notice 703 Export of goods from the United Kingdom contains further guidance on zero-rating goods sent directly from the UK as freight or by courier or post.

7 INFORMATION FOR TRAVELLERS

7.1 What is the VAT Retail Export Scheme?

While you are in the United Kingdom (UK) you will pay Value Added Tax (VAT) on most goods that you buy. The VAT Retail Export Scheme allows you to claim a VAT refund on some of those goods by following the conditions summarised at paragraph 2.3 of this notice. Many shops in the UK will advertise the scheme as "Tax Free Shopping".

7.2 Do I qualify to use the scheme?

Paragraph 2.4 explains who is entitled to use the scheme.

7.3 Can I use the scheme for everything that I buy?

No. Not all shops operate the scheme; check before you buy. You cannot use the scheme to get a refund of VAT on meals and services such as hotel accommodation, car hire, taxi fares, etc, even though you may have been charged VAT on them.

The scheme may be used for any standard rated and lower-rated goods except those listed in paragraph 2.6 of this notice. There are different rules for these goods. You can get details and copies of the relevant notices from the National Advice Service. See the "Further help and advice" section at the front of this notice for details.

Under certain circumstances business travellers may obtain refunds of VAT paid on services provided and goods consumed in the EC. Notice 723 Refunds of VAT in the European Community for EC and non-EC businesses explains the conditions and how to make a claim. Customs officers at the place the traveller departs the UK are not involved in the refund of VAT on business expenses.

7.4 Making a purchase using the VAT Retail Export Scheme

7.4.1 What must I do before buying the goods?

Check that the retailer operates the scheme. Retailers do not have to operate the scheme, but those who do usually advertise the scheme as "Tax Free Shopping".

7.4.2 How do I buy tax-free goods?

Purchases must always be made by you personally although they may be paid for by a third party. There is no facility under this scheme for a representative to attend in your place at the time of sale.

7.4.3 When you buy the goods:

- tell the retailer that you want to use the scheme;
- ask the retailer to explain how the scheme works. You should make sure you understand what you have to do;
- tell the retailer your country of final destination. The retailer will ask you to provide proof that you are eligible to use the scheme (see paragraph 2.4);
- the retailer will ask you to complete and sign a VAT refund document at the time of sale in his presence. Make sure that you complete part A in full. Incomplete forms will not be stamped by Customs;
- make sure the retailer fully completes part B including an accurate description of the goods and signs the retailer's declaration in part C; and
- discuss with the retailer how the refund will be made, for example, cheque or credit card, how long it will take to receive the refund and any administration charges they will make.

The retailer will then give the completed VAT refund document to you. You may also be given a reply paid envelope. If the retailer does not give you one, you must provide an envelope and pay the postage for the return of the refund form after it has been stamped by Customs.

Remember, you must not allow anyone to sign the refund document on your behalf. If you do so, you will not be entitled to a VAT refund.

7.4.4 What VAT refund document will the retailer give me?

The retailer will give you one of the following documents:

- an official Customs Form VAT 407;
- a shop or refund company's own version of the VAT 407 form; or
- a sales invoice that is headed "Retail Export Scheme" and contains all the details that are shown on a Form VAT 407.

7.4.5 What happens if I return the goods to the shop for a refund or exchange?

If you wish to return goods that have been sold to you under the scheme, either for a full refund or for exchange you must also take your receipt and the VAT refund document back to the retailer. The retailer will delete the entry for the returned goods or cancel the VAT refund document and issue a new one as appropriate.

7.4.6 Can I use the scheme without an approved VAT refund document?

No. You cannot use the scheme without one of the refund documents described in Section 4. These forms are only available from VAT registered retailers who operate the scheme. They are not available to travellers at airports, ports or from Customs and Excise. *Till receipts alone are not acceptable for the scheme as operated in the UK.*

7.5 Exporting the goods

7.5.1 When must I export the goods?

You must export the goods from the EC by the last day of the third month following that in which the goods were purchased. For example, goods purchased on 3 February have to be exported by 31 May.

7.5.2 What must I do when I leave the EC?

(a) Leaving for an immediate destination outside the EC:

- If you **are not** travelling to any other country within the EC, you must present your refund document to Customs at your port or airport of departure when you leave the UK. The goods and receipts must also be available for inspection if required.
- If you are leaving by air and have goods that are too large or heavy to carry on board the aircraft you may pack them in your hold baggage. If you do this, you should contact the Customs officer *before you check in* and produce the goods for examination and the refund document for certification. However, you should always carry high value items in your hand baggage, this includes jewellery, furs, cameras, expensive watches, silverware, laptop computers and small antiques. Contact the airline or airport enquiry desk to check the arrangements in force as these vary from airport to airport.
- During busy periods, queues are likely and you should *allow yourself plenty of time* in which to produce the goods and refund document before departure. This is particularly

important if you are exporting goods in your hold baggage as you may need to allow up to two hours in addition to your advised check in time. *Long queues will not be accepted as a reason for not obtaining a UK or EC Customs' stamp on the refund document.*

- If satisfied that all the conditions of the scheme have been met the Customs officer will stamp your VAT refund documents.

(b) Leaving the EC via another EC country:

If you are departing the EC via another EC country, you must present the goods and the refund document to the Customs authorities of that country.

(c) Leaving the EC on a through (transit) flight **via another EC airport**:

There are special rules for goods being carried on through flights leaving via another EC airport:

- *Hand Baggage*: Goods carried as hand baggage must be produced with the refund document to Customs in the last EC airport before leaving to return home.
- *Hold Baggage*: Goods carried as hold baggage must be produced with the refund document to UK Customs before you check in your baggage.

7.5.3 What should I do if there is no Customs presence?

In most cases you will be able to locate a Customs officer to stamp your refund document. However, some ports and airports do not have a 24-hour Customs presence and at others the Customs export offices are open only when there are departures for immediate destinations outside the EC. At such places there will either be a telephone to speak to Customs or a clearly marked post box to deposit your refund document. *You must ensure that your refund document is fully completed and that the reply paid envelope is not sealed before it is placed in the deposit box.* Customs will collect it and if satisfied that all the conditions of the scheme have been met, they will stamp it and send it to the retailer or refund company to arrange your refund.

Remember, if you are travelling to an EC airport where you will transfer to a flight out of the EC, you must produce the goods carried in your hand baggage and the refund form to Customs at the last point of transfer before departure from the EC.

The following text has the force of law

There is no facility to have your refund document stamped in your country of destination.

7.5.4 Am I making a declaration to Customs when I present the VAT refund document to the Customs officer?

Yes, you are making a declaration that:

- you are eligible to use the scheme; and
- that all the goods shown on the document are being exported from the EC by you.

It is a very serious offence to make a false declaration. This may involve you missing your flight or sailing and the misdeclared goods may be seized and penalties imposed.

7.5.5 What should I do if I decide not to export all of the goods bought under the scheme?

If you decide to leave goods bought under the scheme in the EC, you **must** clearly delete those items from any VAT refund document for certification when you finally leave the EC. This amendment *must be made before* you present the VAT refund document and the remaining goods to Customs for examination and stamping. The VAT refund document must show only the items being exported.

7.5.6 What happens if I cannot produce the goods and /or get the VAT refund document stamped before I leave the EC?

You will not receive any refund of VAT. If, however, you cannot produce the goods because, for example, your baggage has been lost or mislaid, you must tell the Customs officer at the port or airport of departure from the EC. The officer will tell you what action to take.

Your refund document must be stamped by a Customs officer when you leave the EC. Certification by anyone other than an EC Customs officer when you leave the EC is not acceptable. Long queues at the airport will not be accepted as a reason for not getting a UK or EC Customs' stamp on the form. Forms stamped outside the EC are not acceptable.

7.6 Obtaining your refund

Methods for the payment of refunds are set out at paragraphs 7.6.1 and 7.6.2. Whichever method is used, it should have been agreed between you and the retailer when you bought the goods.

Your refund may be reduced by an administration charge. This charge should be clearly shown on your refund document.

If you do not receive your refund within a reasonable time you should write to the retailer – not to Customs and Excise.

7.6.1 How do I obtain my refund?

After your VAT refund document has been stamped and returned to you by Customs you can either:

- post the refund document back to the retailer to arrange payment of your refund; or
- post the refund document back to a VAT refund company to arrange payment of your refund.

7.6.2 Can I obtain a cash refund at the airport?

Not all retailers and airports offer this "Cash Service". The retailer will advise you whether a cash refund is available. In such circumstances you will be advised to hand your refund document to a cash refund booth to arrange immediate payment.

The refund document will be passed to Customs by the cash refund booth. After stamping by Customs the form is sent to the retailer or refund company as evidence that the goods have been exported.

7.7 Lost refund documents

7.7.1 What should I do if I have lost the VAT refund document before stamping?

If the refund document is lost before stamping you should ask the retailer to provide a duplicate document. This must be clearly headed up "DUPLICATE". Produce the duplicate document with the goods to the Customs export officer when you leave the EC. If you find the original refund document later – destroy it.

7.7.2 What should I do if the VAT refund document is lost after stamping?

If the refund document is lost after stamping, unless you can produce a photocopy of the stamped refund document you will not receive a refund of VAT. If, however, you can provide a photocopy of the VAT refund document stamped by Customs at your final departure point from the EC, you can return this to the retailer and ask for a duplicate refund form to be issued and sent for stamping to the original Customs office. The document must be clearly headed up "DUPLICATE".

7.8 What should I do if I bring the goods back into the EC?

If the goods are brought back into the EC at any time they must be declared to Customs in the importing EC Member State-unless they are within the duty or tax-free traveller's allowance limits of that Member State.

However, if you purchased goods as an entitled EC resident (see paragraph 2.4.3) or as a student or migrant worker (see paragraph 2.4.2) and re-import them within 12 months of your departure from the EC, duty and tax free allowances will not apply to the goods as you will have failed to remain outside the EC for at least 12 months. You will have to pay any import duties, including VAT that are due.

8 INTRA EC CRUISES – SPECIAL ARRANGEMENT

8.1 Why is there a need for a special arrangement?

Non-EC passengers on wholly intra EC cruises may not have access to their luggage and purchases made under the VAT Retail Export Scheme from disembarkation until they arrive at their final non-EC destination. They cannot, therefore, produce their goods and VAT refund document to the Customs officer for stamping at their point of final departure from the EC.

Therefore, for wholly intra EC cruises which commence within the UK and where the final port of disembarkation is also within the UK, a special arrangement was introduced on 1 July 2003.

8.2 What is the special arrangement?

8.2.1 Individual purchases below £1000

Cruise operators may produce an omnibus bulk refund document for all eligible goods, below £1000 per item, purchased on board by entitled individual passengers.

The omnibus refund document must accompany the individual passenger's luggage to the airport of departure.

If satisfied the Customs officer will stamp the bulk refund form and return it to the cruise operator. On receipt of the certified bulk refund form, the cruise operator must account for the sales in their VAT records, as explained in Section 5.

The following has the force of law

However, the cruise operator must account for VAT on any goods on the bulk refund form not exported from the EC within the prescribed limits.

8.2.2 Bulk refund documents

The format of the bulk refund document must be approved beforehand by Customs. (See paragraph 4.6 for details).

It must be clearly headed "**Retail Export Scheme**" and must only include those goods that:

- were sold on board the vessel;
- are eligible to be supplied under the VAT Retail Export Scheme (see paragraph 2.6); and
- were supplied to entitled customers (see paragraph 2.4).

It must also give the following details:

- your name, address and VAT registration number;
- your customer's name and usual address;
- your customer's passport number and country of issue;
- a description which clearly identifies the goods and the quantity involved; and
- the amount payable per item. (Where this includes VAT, the amount payable inclusive of VAT and the amount of VAT included in the total price should be shown).

In addition, it must include a retailer declaration as stipulated on the Form VAT 407 signed by a responsible ship's officer, and a separate box not less than 5 cm by 3.5 cm for official certification by Customs and Excise.

8.2.3 Individual purchases £1000 and above

The normal VAT 407 form or equivalent (see paragraph 4.1) must be completed for purchases of £1000 or more per item. The customer must produce the goods and the form for stamping to the Customs officer at the point of final departure from the EC.

9 FISCAL (VAT) TERRITORY OF THE EUROPEAN COMMUNITY

9.1 Countries and territories within the EC fiscal (VAT) area

The following countries and territories are within the EC fiscal (VAT) area:

- Austria
- Belgium
- Cyprus*
- The Czech Republic
- Denmark, except the Faroe Islands and Greenland
- Estonia
- Finland
- France, including Monaco
- Germany, except Busingen and the Isle of Heligoland
- Greece
- Hungary
- The Republic of Ireland
- Italy, except the communes of Livigno and Campione d'Italia and the Italian waters of Lake Lugano
- Latvia
- Lithuania
- Luxembourg
- Malta
- The Netherlands
- Poland
- Portugal, including the Azores and Madeira
- The Slovak Republic
- Slovenia
- Spain, including the Balearic Islands but excluding Ceuta and Melilla
- Sweden
- United Kingdom and the Isle of Man

[Plus, from 1 January 2007—

- Bulgaria,
- Romania.]

* The European Commission has advised that the application of the 6th VAT Directive (Directive 77/388/EEC of 17 May 1977) shall be suspended in those areas of Cyprus in which the Government of the Republic of Cyprus does not exercise effective control. Eligible goods to entitled customers going to these destinations may be sold under this scheme.

Note—Para 9.1 amended by Update 1, January 2007.

9.2 Countries and territories outside the EC fiscal (VAT) area

The following countries and territories are outside the EC fiscal (VAT) area:

- The Channel Islands
- Andorra
- San Marino

- The Aland Islands
- The Canary Islands
- The overseas departments of France (Guadeloupe, Martinique, Réunion, St Pierre and Miquelon and French Guiana)
- Mount Athos
- Gibraltar
- The Vatican City

If you need more information on the VAT territory of the EC, please contact the National Advice Service on 0845 010 9000. (See the inside front cover for details).

Notice 704/1 VAT refunds for travellers departing from the European Community (EC)

2004

1 INTRODUCTION

This Notice tells you how to get a tax refund on goods bought in the UK from shops operating the VAT Retail Export Scheme. Full details on the operation of the Scheme can be found in VAT Notice 704 VAT Retail Exports which is available from shops operating the Scheme, Customs at Ports and Airports or from the National Advice Service on 0845 010 9000. See 'further help and advice' overleaf for more details.

Commentary—*De Voil Indirect Tax Service* **V4.331**.

2 WHAT IS THE VAT RETAIL EXPORT SCHEME?

When you visit the United Kingdom (UK) you will pay Value Added Tax (VAT) on most things that you buy. The VAT Retail Export Scheme allows you to claim a VAT refund on most goods that you buy and export from the European Community (EC). The shopkeeper may deduct an administration fee before making any refund.

3 DO I QUALIFY TO USE THE SCHEME?

Yes if you are an overseas visitor:

(a) an overseas visitor is a traveller who is not established in the European Community (EC) (see (b) below if you are studying or working in the UK). This means that:
  - your domicile or habitual place of residence is not situated within the European Community (EC); and
  - you intend to leave the UK for a final destination outside the EC, with the goods, by the last day of the third month following that in which the goods were purchased; and
  - you export the goods having produced them, their receipts and the VAT refund document to Customs at the point of departure from the EC.

(b) Non-EC residents studying or working in the UK or EC residents may also qualify to use the scheme if they intend to permanently leave the EC for a minimum period of 12 months. To qualify under this provision you must:
  - intend to leave the UK with the goods by the last day of the third month following that in which the goods were purchased for an immediate destination outside the EC; and
  - remain outside the EC for a period of at least 12 months; and
  - export the goods having produced them, their receipts and the VAT refund document to Customs at the point of departure from the EC.

4 WHAT GOODS CAN I BUY UNDER THE SCHEME?

You can buy any goods under the Scheme on which you pay VAT except:

- new or used motor vehicles;
- a boat that you intend to sail to a destination outside the EC;
- goods over £600 in value exported for business purposes (a form C88 must be used for these);
- goods that will be exported as freight;
- goods requiring an export licence (except antiques);
- unmounted gemstones;
- bullion (over 125g, 2.75 troy ounces or 10 Tolas);
- mail order goods including Internet sales.

In addition you cannot obtain a refund of tax on goods which are consumed, or partly consumed, in the EC such as perfume; or service charges such as hotel expenses.

5 WHERE CAN I BUY TAX FREE GOODS?

From any shop operating the VAT Retail Export Scheme. The Scheme is voluntary and shops do not have to operate it. If in doubt you should ask before you buy the goods.

6 WHAT DO I DO WHEN I BUY TAX FREE GOODS?

At the time you buy the goods the retailer will ask you to provide proof that you are eligible to use the Scheme. For example the retailer will ask to see your passport. You will then be asked to complete and sign some simple details on a refund form. The form will be either;

– an official Customs Form VAT 407; or
– a shop or refund company's own version of the VAT 407 form; or
– a VAT Retail Export Scheme sales invoice.

You must have one of these forms, till receipts alone are not acceptable.

The form should be completed at the time you buy the goods in the presence of the retailer. You cannot ask another person to complete and sign these details on your behalf.

You should also agree with the shop how your refund will be repaid to you.

7 WHEN MUST I EXPORT THE GOODS?

You must export the goods from the EC by the last day of the third month following that in which the goods were purchased. For example, goods purchased on 3 February would have to be exported by 31 May.

8 WHAT MUST I DO WHEN I LEAVE THE UK?

(a) Leaving for an immediate destination outside the EC:

If you are not travelling to any other country within the EC, you must present your goods and the refund form to UK Customs at your port or airport of departure. Items that will be checked in as hold baggage must be produced to Customs before you check in your baggage.

During busy periods, queues are likely and you should allow yourself plenty of time in which to produce the goods and refund form prior to departure. This is particularly important if you are exporting goods in your hold baggage as any extra time allowed should be in addition to your advised check in time.

When Customs are satisfied that all the conditions of the Scheme have been met, they will certify and return your refund form to you.

(b) Leaving the EC via another EC country:

If you are departing the EC via another EC country, you must present the goods and the refund form to the Customs authorities of that country.

(c) Leaving the EC on a through (transit) flight via another EC Member State:

There are special rules for goods being carried on through flights leaving via another Member State.

– **Hand Baggage**:

Goods carried as hand baggage must be produced to Customs in the last EC Country with the refund form before leaving to return home.

– **Hold Baggage**:

Goods carried as hold baggage must be produced to Customs in the UK with the refund form before you check in your baggage.

9 WHAT SHOULD I DO IF THERE IS NO CUSTOMS PRESENCE?

In most cases you will be able to locate a Customs Officer to certify your form. However, some of the smaller UK ports and airports do not have a 24 hour Customs presence. At such places there will be either a telephone to ring the officer or a clearly marked Customs post box to deposit your form. Customs will collect the form and if they are satisfied that all the conditions have been met, they will certify it and return it to the retailer to arrange your refund.

There is no facility to have your form certified in your country of destination.

10 HOW DO I OBTAIN MY REFUND?

After your VAT refund form has been certified by Customs you can either:

– post the form back to the retailer to arrange payment of your refund;
– post the form back to a commercial refund company to arrange payment of your refund;
– hand your form to a refund booth to arrange immediate payment.

Whichever method is used should have been agreed between yourself and the retailer when you bought the goods.

Your refund may be reduced by an administration charge. This charge should be clearly shown on your refund form.

If you do not receive your refund within a reasonable time you should write to the retailer – not to Customs and Excise.

11 WHAT SHOULD I DO IF I DECIDE NOT TO EXPORT ALL OF THE GOODS BOUGHT UNDER THE SCHEME?

If you decide to leave goods bought under the Scheme in the EC, you must clearly delete those items from any VAT refund document for certification when you finally leave the EC. This amendment must be made before you present the VAT refund document and the remaining goods to Customs for examination and certification.

The VAT refund document must show only those items which are being exported.

IMPORTANT

YOU WILL NOT RECEIVE A REFUND OF VAT IF THE VAT REFUND DOCUMENT IS NOT FULLY COMPLETED

YOU MUST PRODUCE THE GOODS AND THE VAT REFUND DOCUMENT TO CUSTOMS WHEN YOU LEAVE THE EC

NO GOODS = NO REFUND

FURTHER HELP AND ADVICE

If you need further help or advice or more copies of Customs and Excise Notices, please call the National Advice Service on 0845 010 9000. Lines are open Monday to Friday 8 am to 8 pm.

If you have hearing difficulties please ring the Textphone service on 0845 000 0200.

All calls are charged at the local rate within the UK. Charges may differ from mobile phones.

Alternatively, you can visit our website at www.hmce.gov.uk.

IF YOU HAVE A COMPLAINT

If you have a complaint, contact Customs at your local office or at the port or airport. If they cannot sort out the problem, you should contact the Regional Business Head, the head of Customs for the region. Your local office will tell you how to do this. Ask for a copy of our code of practice on complaints (Notice 1000). If the Regional Business Head does not sort out your complaint, you can then ask the Adjudicator to look into it.

The Adjudicator, whose services are free, is independent.

The address is:

The Adjudicator's Office
Haymarket House
28 Haymarket London SW1Y 4SP
Phone: 020 7930 2292
FAX: 020 7930 2298

Commentary—*De Voil Indirect Tax Service* **V4.331**.

Notice 705
Buyer's guide to personal exports of motor vehicles to destinations outside the EC

2004 (with Update 1)

This notice cancels and replaces Notice 705 (September 1995).

The legal basis for the Personal Export Scheme is in VATA 1994 ss 30(8) and 30(10) and VAT Regulations 1995 (SI 1995/2518), regs 132 and 133. Parts of this notice have the force of law under those regulations. These parts are indicated by being placed in a box as in the example shown below.

EXAMPLE:

The following rule has the force of law

> If you receive a net payment you must include the full value before such deductions (and including VAT) in your scheme turnover. This will usually be the value shown on your sales invoice.

CONTENTS

1 INTRODUCTION

1.1 What is this notice about?

This notice explains the Personal Export Scheme which allows the purchase of motor vehicles free of Value Added Tax (VAT) for temporary use in the United Kingdom (UK) before export to a destination outside the European Community (EC). It sets out the conditions that must be complied with by everyone using this scheme.

De Voil Indirect Tax Service **V4.334.**

1.2 What's changed?

This notice has been re-structured and rewritten to improve readability.

The technical content, apart from amendments to reflect the enlargement of the EC on 1 May 2004, remains unchanged since the September 1995 edition as updated in April 2000.

You can access details of any changes to this notice since March 2004 on our Internet site at www.hmce.gov.uk or by telephoning the National Advice Service on 0845 010 9000.

This notice and others mentioned are available both on paper and on our website.

1.3 Who should read this notice?

This notice is intended for overseas visitors and EC residents who intend to remain outside the EC for at least six months.

1.4 What is the legal status of this notice?

The legal provisions that cover the Personal Export Scheme are contained in the—

- VATA 1994 s 30(8); and 30(10); and
- VAT Regulations 1995 (SI 1995/2518) regs 132 and 133. These regulations allow for specific conditions that have the force of law.

The VAT Regulations 1995 and this notice lay down those conditions which must be met in full for a motor vehicle to be supplied free of VAT for export under the Personal Export Scheme.

2 PURCHASING A VEHICLE UNDER THE PERSONAL EXPORT SCHEME

De Voil Indirect Tax Service **V4.334.**

2.1 What is the Personal Export Scheme?

The Personal Export Scheme (PES) allows entitled customers to purchase a motor vehicle in the UK free of VAT for export outside the European Community. Subject to some restrictions the vehicle may also be used for a limited period in the EC before being finally exported to a destination outside the EC.

Warning: It may be very difficult to import motor vehicles into some countries. You are advised to check with the relevant Embassy or High Commission in the UK before placing an order for a vehicle under the Scheme.

2.2 Can I use the Scheme to purchase a motor vehicle for permanent removal to another EC country?

No. PES can only be used for vehicles that will be exported outside the EC.

For intra EC removals see Notice 728 "New means of transport".

2.3 Can I use the Scheme?

You can use the Scheme if you are—

(a) *an Overseas visitor.* This means that you have *not* been in the EC for more than *either*—

– 365 days in the two years before the date when you apply to use the Scheme; *or*

- 1095 days in the six years before the date when you apply to use the Scheme; *and*
- you intend to leave and remain outside the EC with the motor vehicle for a period of at least six months; *and*
- you comply with all the other conditions of the Scheme.

(b) *an Entitled EC resident*. This means that you have been in the EC for *more than*—
- 365 days in the two years before the date when you apply to use the Scheme; *or*
- 1095 days in the six years before the date when you apply to use the Scheme; and
- you intend to leave and remain outside the EC with the motor vehicle for a period of at least six months; and
- you comply with all the other conditions of the Scheme.

2.4 Which countries are part of the European Community (EC)?

[The VAT territory of the EC is made up of 25 Member States (27 from 1 January 2007)] including some territories with which they have links. Details of the fiscal (VAT) territory of the EC and of the special territories which are outside the EC for VAT purposes are given in section 7.

Note—Para 2.4 amended by Update 1, January 2007.
Commentary—*De Voil Indirect Tax Service* **V1.213.**

2.5 What type of vehicle can I buy under the scheme?

You may use the scheme to buy a new or used motor vehicle, motorcycle or motor caravan but *not* a pedal cycle or trailer caravan.

De Voil Indirect Tax Service **V1.213.**

2.6 Where must I buy the vehicle?

The vehicle must be purchased from a VAT registered business that operates the Personal Export Scheme.

Note: Factory fitted extras can only be supplied VAT-free if they are included on the invoice for the supply of the vehicle at the time of purchase.

De Voil Indirect Tax Service **V4.334.**

2.7 How do I apply to use the Scheme?

The VAT registered business that operates the Scheme will give you an application Form VAT 410.

You must complete the form and sign the declaration. This means that you have read and understand this notice and will comply with *all* the conditions of the Scheme. You must give the completed VAT 410 form back to the supplier who will return the customer copy which you should keep.

Note: You will not be able to obtain a refund of VAT on a motor vehicle where the purchase price paid included VAT even if the vehicle is later exported to a destination outside the EC.

De Voil Indirect Tax Service **V4.334.**

2.8 When may I apply to use the Scheme?

You may apply to use the Scheme if you intend to leave the EC in—
- 15 months or less, if you are an overseas visitor (see paragraph 2.3); or
- 9 months or less, if you are an entitled EC resident (see paragraph 2.3).

De Voil Indirect Tax Service **V4.334.**

2.9 Who may take delivery of the vehicle?

Only you (the applicant) who applied to use the Scheme may take delivery of the vehicle in the UK. No other person may take delivery of the vehicle on your behalf, without the written authority of the Personal Transport Unit (see paragraph 4.4 for contact details).

2.10 Delivery receipts

You will also have to sign a certificate of receipt when you take delivery of the vehicle.

De Voil Indirect Tax Service **V4.334.**

3 USING THE VEHICLE PRIOR TO IT BEING EXPORTED FROM THE EC

3.1 Do I have to insure the vehicle?

Yes. You *must* insure the vehicle before using it.

If you are unable to export the vehicle because it has been stolen or involved in an accident and written-off, the VAT amount not paid at the time of purchase will become due.

It is therefore in your own interest to insure the vehicle for its tax inclusive value at the time of purchase.

3.2 Can anyone else drive the vehicle while it is in the EC?

Yes, but only if *you* are still in the EC. The vehicle can only be driven by another person who—

- has your permission; *and*
- is an entitled person (see paragraph 2.3).

The vehicle may also be driven by your spouse or by a chauffeur.

3.3 How long may I use the vehicle in the UK before finally exporting it?

(a) *Overseas visitors* (see paragraph 2.3)

- If you are an overseas visitor you may take delivery and use the vehicle in the UK during the last 12 months of your stay in the EC.

(b) *Entitled EC resident* (see paragraph 2.3)

- If you are an entitled EC resident you may take delivery and use the vehicle in the UK only during the last six months before you finally leave the EC.

Remember— you must not dispose of, or attempt to dispose of the vehicle in the EC by hire, pledge as security, sale, gift or any other means.

3.4 Can I make a temporary visit abroad with the vehicle?

You may only make a temporary visit to another EC country. If you do take the vehicle to another EC country you can bring the vehicle back to the UK without any Customs formalities *only* if—

- it is returned to the UK before the due date for exportation; *and*
- you still intend to export and depart with the vehicle from the EC by the due date for exportation.

If you intend to make a temporary visit to another EC country with your vehicle, you are advised to check with the relevant fiscal (VAT) authorities of the member state concerned prior to your visit. As your vehicle had been supplied free of VAT you should establish whether you need to comply with any Customs' requirements upon entry into another EC country.

You should *not* make a temporary visit to a *non-EC* country prior to the final date for export shown on the VAT 410 form. If you do, when the vehicle is re-imported into either the UK or another EC country, the VAT amount not paid at the time of purchase will become due, (unless you qualify for relief (see section 6)). You *must* declare the vehicle to Customs at the place of re-importation into the EC and show the customs officer the following document as appropriate—

- for new vehicles – the vehicle registration document (VX302);
- for second hand vehicles – the Form VAT 410.

4 EXPORTING THE VEHICLE

De Voil Indirect Tax Service **V4.334.**

4.1 When must I export the vehicle?

You must export the vehicle when you finally leave the EC. To comply with the conditions of the scheme this must be within—

- 12 months of the date of delivery if you are an overseas visitor (see paragraph 2.3); or
- 6 months of the date of delivery if you are an entitled EC resident (see paragraph 2.3).

4.2 Where can I find the date when the vehicle must be exported?

(a) New Vehicles

The final date for exportation of a new motor vehicle from the EC is shown on the pink registration document (VX302).

(b) Second hand vehicles

The final date for exportation of a second hand motor vehicle is shown on the Form VAT 410.

4.3 What should I do when I finally export the vehicle?

You should notify the Driver Vehicle Licensing Agency Local Office (DVLA LO)—

(a) New vehicles

Complete the tear off section of the pink registration document (VX302) and return it to the DVLA LO as shown on the document.

(b) Second hand vehicles

Complete the relevant section of the V5 registration document and send the entire document to the DVLA LO as shown on the document. The DVLA LO will issue an export certificate to enable the vehicle to be re-registered in the country of destination.

Note: If you intend leaving the UK within 14 days of acquiring the vehicle, tell the motor dealer before you buy so that the dealer can arrange for the DVLA LO to issue you with an export certificate straightaway.

You must make shipping arrangements in good time to ensure that the vehicle is exported by the due date.

If you fail to export the vehicle by the due date, the VAT not paid *at the time you purchased the vehicle* will become payable and the vehicle becomes liable to forfeiture and may be seized.

4.4 What if I cannot export the vehicle by the due date?

You *must* immediately contact—

HM Customs & Excise

Personal Transport Unit
PO Box 242
Dover
Kent
CT17 9GP
Tel: (01304) 664556/7
Fax: (01304) 664567

5 CHANGE OF CIRCUMSTANCES

De Voil Indirect Tax Service **V4.334.**

5.1 What must I do if I change my plans while the vehicle is in the UK?

You *must* immediately contact the PTU (see paragraph 4.4). You can no longer use the vehicle tax-free if, having bought it, you find that—

- you cannot export it by the date shown in the registration document (VX302), or in the case of second-hand vehicles the date on the VAT 410 form; or
- you or the vehicle will not be staying outside the EC for at least six consecutive months from the date of exportation of the vehicle.

You will have to pay the full amount of VAT that you did not pay when you bought the vehicle. The PTU will tell you how to do this.

5.2 What must I do if I change my plans while the vehicle is in another EC country?

If whilst visiting another EC country you decide to remain with the vehicle in that EC country, i.e. the vehicle will not be exported from the EC by the due date for export, you *must* immediately notify the fiscal authorities in the EC country in which you are then staying and pay VAT and any other local taxes due.

6 RE-IMPORTATION OF VEHICLES PREVIOUSLY EXPORTED

De Voil Indirect Tax Service **V4.334.**

6.1 Can I bring the vehicle back to the UK after exportation from the EC?

Yes, but taxes must be paid at importation unless you are eligible for relief from duty and tax as explained in Notice 3 *Bringing your belongings and private motor vehicle to the United Kingdom from outside the European Community*.

6.2 How much tax will I be charged when the vehicle is re-imported into the UK?

If you are eligible for relief under the rules in Notice 3 *Bringing your belongings and private motor vehicle to the United Kingdom from outside the European Community*, no VAT will be charged.

If however—

- the vehicle is re-imported 6 months or more *after* the date for export shown in the registration document (VX302), or in the case of second-hand vehicles the date on the VAT 410 form; or
- you can show that you and the vehicle have remained outside the EC for at least six consecutive months, the VAT payable will be based on the value of the vehicle at the time of re-importation.

> In all other cases, you will be charged the VAT that was not paid when you bought the vehicle.

6.3 Do I need to register and license the vehicle when it is permanently re-imported into the UK?

Yes—unless the vehicle is not to be used or kept on the public roads.

On arrival in the UK you *must* apply immediately to the nearest DVLA Local Office to get your vehicle re-licensed and re-registered. You will need to produce proof of payment of, or exemption from, VAT in order to re-license or re-register the vehicle.

Contact details for the DVLA can be found in the telephone directory.

6.4 What should I do if I re-import the vehicle into another EC country after it was exported from the EC?

You should contact the fiscal (VAT) authority in the EC country in which you are to stay and pay the VAT and any other local taxes due.

7 FISCAL (VAT) TERRITORY OF THE EUROPEAN COMMUNITY

De Voil Indirect Tax Service **V1.213.**

7.1 The following countries and territories are within the EC fiscal (VAT) area—

- Austria;
- Belgium;
- Denmark, except the Faroe Islands and Greenland;
- Finland;
- France, including Monaco;
- Germany, except Busingen and the Isle of Heligoland;
- Greece;
- The Republic of Ireland;
- Italy, except the communes of Livigno and Campione d'Italia and the Italian waters of Lake Lugano;
- Luxembourg;
- The Netherlands;
- Portugal, including the Azores and Madeira;
- Spain, including the Balearic Islands but excluding Ceuta and Melilla;
- Sweden; and
- United Kingdom and the Isle of Man.

Plus from 1 May 2004—

- Cyprus*;
- Czech Republic;
- Estonia;
- Hungary;
- Latvia;
- Lithuania;

- Malta;
- Poland;
- Slovakia; and
- Slovenia.

[Plus, from 1 January 2007—

- Bulgaria;
- Romania.]

*The European Commission in December 2003 advised that the application of the 6th VAT Directive (Directive 77/388/EEC of 17 May 1977) shall be suspended in those areas of Cyprus in which the Government of the Republic of Cyprus does not exercise effective control. From 1 May 2004 goods to these destinations continue to be eligible for zero-rating as exports.

Note—Para 7.1 amended by Update 1, January 2007.

7.2 The following countries and territories are outside the EC fiscal (VAT) area

- The Channel Islands;
- Andorra;
- San Marino;
- The Åland Islands;
- The Canary Islands;
- The overseas departments of France (Guadeloupe, Martinique, Réunion, St. Pierre and Miquelon and French Guiana);
- Mount Athos;
- Cyprus (until 1 May 2004);
- Gibraltar;
- Malta (until 1 May 2004); and
- The Vatican City.

If you need more information on the VAT territory of the EC, please contact our National Advice Service (see paragraph 1.2 for contact details).

Notice 705A
VAT: Supplies of vehicles under the Personal Export Scheme for removal from the EC

March 2004 (with Update 1)

This notice cancels and replaces Notice 705A (October 1995)

The legal basis for the Personal Export Scheme is in VATA 1994 ss 30(8) and 30(10) and VAT Regulations 1995 (SI 1995/2518), regs 132 and 133. Parts of this notice have the force of law under those regulations. These parts are indicated by being placed in a box as in the example shown below.

EXAMPLE:

The following rule has the force of law

> If you receive a net payment you must include the full value before such deductions (and including VAT) in your scheme turnover. This will usually be the value shown on your sales invoice.

CONTENTS

1 INTRODUCTION

1.1 What is this Notice about?

This notice explains the Personal Export Scheme which allows the supply of motor vehicles free of Value Added Tax (VAT) for temporary use in the United Kingdom (UK) before they are exported to a destination outside the European Community (EC). It sets out the conditions that must be complied with by everyone using this Scheme.

De Voil Indirect Tax Service **V4.334.**

1.2 What's changed?

This notice has been re-structured and rewritten to improve readability.

The technical content, apart from amendments to reflect the enlargement of the EC on 1 May 2004, remains unchanged since the October 1995.

You can access details of any changes to this notice since March 2004 on our Internet site at www.hmce.gov.uk or by telephoning the National Advice Service on 0845 010 9000.

This notice and others mentioned are available both on paper and on our website.

1.3 Who should read this notice?

VAT registered traders who wish to supply motor vehicles VAT-free, to overseas visitors and entitled EC residents, for export to a destination *outside* the EC.

1.4 What is the legal status of this notice?

The legal provisions that cover the Personal Export Scheme are contained in the:

- VATA 1994 s 30(8) and 30(10); and
- VAT Regulations 1995 (SI 1995/2518) regs 132 and 133. These regulations allow for specific conditions that have the force of law.

The VAT Regulations 1995 and this notice lay down the conditions which must be met in full for a motor vehicle to be supplied free of VAT for export under the Personal Export Scheme.

2 SUPPLYING A VEHICLE UNDER THE PERSONAL EXPORT SCHEME

De Voil Indirect Tax Service **V4.334.**

2.1 What is the Personal Export Scheme?

The Personal Export Scheme allows you to supply to entitled customers a motor vehicle in the UK free of VAT for export outside the European Community. Subject to some restrictions the vehicle may also be used for a limited period in the EC before being finally exported to a destination outside the EC.

Warning: It may be difficult to import motor vehicles into some countries. To avoid any confusion check with the customer that they have contacted the relevant Embassy or High Commission in the UK before they place an order for a vehicle under the Scheme.

2.2 Can I use the Scheme to supply a motor vehicle for permanent removal to another EC country?

No. The Scheme can only be used for vehicles that will be exported outside the EC.

For intra-EC removals see Notice 728 "New means of transport".

2.3 Which customers can use the Scheme?

The Scheme can be used by customers who are—

(a) *Overseas visitors*: This means that your customer has *not* been in the EC for more than *either*:

- 365 days in the two years before the date when they apply to use the Scheme; *or*
- 1095 days in the six years before the date when they apply to use the Scheme; *and*
- intends to leave and remain outside the EC with the motor vehicle for a period of at least six months; *and*
- complies with all the other conditions of the Scheme.

(b) *Entitled EC residents*: This means your customer *has* been in the EC for *more than*:

- 365 days in the two years before the date when they apply to use the Scheme; *or*
- 1095 days in the six years before the date when they apply to use the Scheme; *and*
- intends to leave and remain outside the EC with the motor vehicle for a period of at least six months; *and*
- complies with all the other conditions of the Scheme.

2.4 Which Countries are part of the European Community (EC)?

[The VAT territory of the EC is made up of 25 Member States (27 from 1 January 2007)] including some territories with which they have links. Details of the fiscal (VAT) territory of the EC and of the special territories which are outside the EC for VAT purposes are given in section 10.

Note—Para 2.4 updated in January 2007.

2.5 What type of vehicle can I sell under the Scheme?

You may use the Scheme to sell motor vehicles, motorcycles or motor caravans but *not* pedal cycles or trailer caravans.

Note: If the price of the vehicle *when purchased* included VAT, your customer will *not* be eligible for a refund even if the vehicle is later exported to a destination outside the EC.

2.6 When can I take an order for a vehicle under the Scheme?

You may take an order under the Scheme if your customer intends to leave the EC in—

- 15 months or less if they are an overseas visitor (see paragraph 2.3); or
- 9 months or less if they are an entitled EC resident (see paragraph 2.3).

2.7 When must the vehicle be exported?

For the purchaser to comply with the conditions of the Scheme the vehicle must be exported within—

- 12 months from the date of delivery if they are an overseas visitor (see paragraph 2.3); or
- 6 months from the date of delivery if they are entitled EC resident (see paragraph 2.3).

3 MAKING A SALE UNDER THE PERSONAL EXPORT SCHEME

De Voil Indirect Tax Service **V4.334.**

3.1 What should I do at the time of sale?

You should verify that your customer is entitled to use the Scheme (see paragraph 2.3). If your customer is entitled to use the Scheme you must give him/her a copy of Notice 705 "VAT: Buyer's guide to personal exports of motor vehicles to destinations outside the EC" and an application form VAT 410. You should explain the conditions of the Scheme to the customer and give him/her time to read Notice 705.

In completing the VAT 410 Form, the applicant declares that they have received, read and understood Notice 705 and will comply with all of the conditions of the scheme listed on the reverse of the form VAT 410.

Warning: It is an offence for applicants to give incorrect information on the VAT 410 form, they should be advised if they do so they may be liable to prosecution.

You can obtain supplies of Notice 705 and VAT 410 Forms from our National Advice Service (NAS) see paragraph 1.2 for contact details.

3.2 The VAT 410 form

The VAT 410 form is carbonated and incorporates 4 copies—

- Part 1 – (*blue*) Customs copy;
- Part 2 – (*green*) Purchaser's copy;
- Part 3 – (*pink*) Supplier's copy; and
- Part 4 – (*yellow*) DVLA LO copy.

All completed application forms *must* be serially numbered in the top right hand corner. Each separate franchise at the same location will require a separate series of numbers. The Customs copy should be forwarded, at least two weeks before the date of delivery of the vehicle, to the Personal Transport Unit at the following address—

HM Customs & Excise

➡

Personal Transport Unit
PO Box 242
Dover
Kent
C17 9PG
Tel: 01304 664556/7
Fax: 01304 664567

Please ensure that application forms are fully completed and correct before you accept them.

An incomplete or incorrect application form *will be returned* to you for correction and this may delay the delivery of the vehicle.

3.3 Invoicing of vehicles and supply of extras

You must supply and invoice VAT-free vehicles direct to the applicant.

Note: Factory fitted extras can only be supplied VAT-free if they are included on the initial invoice for the supply of the vehicle at the time of purchase.

3.4 Insuring the vehicle

You should advise the person purchasing the vehicle to insure the vehicle for its full *tax inclusive* value at the time of purchase.

If the vehicle is not exported, (it may be stolen or involved in an accident and written-off) the VAT amount not paid at the time of purchase will become due.

3.5 What action should I take if an order is cancelled?

If, after the application is approved, the order is subsequently cancelled by the applicant before delivery, you should *immediately* contact the Personal Transport Unit at the address given in paragraph 3.2. The Personal Transport Unit will need the following details—

- the name of the applicant;
- make and model of the vehicle ordered;
- the serial number of the VAT 410 application form; and
- in the case of second-hand vehicles, the vehicle registration number.

3.6 Breach of conditions

If you become aware that a vehicle you supplied under the Scheme has been retained in the United Kingdom beyond the due date for export, or that any other condition of the Scheme has been breached, you should *immediately* notify the PTU.

4 REGISTERING AND LICENSING OF VEHICLES WITH THE DRIVER AND VEHICLE LICENSING AGENCY LOCAL OFFICE (DVLA LO)

De Voil Indirect Tax Service **V4.334.**

4.1 New vehicles

To register the vehicle, you *must* submit an application Form V55 headed prominently in block letters "PERSONAL EXPORT (VAT FREE) VEHICLE" and attach it to the DVLA LO copy (*part 4*) of the Form VAT 410 and send it to one of the DVLA LOs listed in section 11.

4.2 Second hand vehicles

As these vehicles will already have been registered you *must* notify the DVLA LO of the change of keeper and apply for a special tax disc. To do this, you *must* submit to one of the DVLA LOs listed in section 11—

- the completed V5 Registration Document;
- Form V10 (Vehicle Licence Application Form);
- the DVLA LO copy (*part 4*) of the Form VAT 410; also
- Form VX304 if the purchaser of the vehicle is entitled to claim exemption from payment of vehicle excise duty.

➡

The second-hand vehicle must *not* be supplied with any pre-existing tax disc. If a disc is already in force, it should be surrendered separately to the DVLA LO for a refund.

If the customer intends exporting the vehicle within 14 days of purchase, you should complete the V5 Registration Document to notify export *at the same time as notifying the change of keeper to the DVLA LO*. This will ensure that your customer receives an export certificate in good time before leaving the UK.

5 DELIVERY PROCEDURES

De Voil Indirect Tax Service **V4.334.**

5.1 Action before delivery of the vehicle

New vehicles

Before the vehicle is delivered you must complete the details required on pages 5 and 8 of the pink registration book, showing the amount of VAT remitted (not paid), the date of delivery and the final date for export.

Second hand vehicles

If you have followed the procedures in paragraphs 4.2 and 6.2, you do not need to do anything else.

5.2 Who may take delivery of the vehicle?

You must deliver the vehicle to the applicant in the UK.

No one else may take delivery of the vehicle on behalf of the applicant without the written authority from the Personal Transport Unit (see paragraph 3.2 for contact details).

5.3 Delivery receipts

You must retain a dated certificate of receipt for the vehicle signed by the applicant with your records.

5.4 Urgent delivery procedure

This procedure applies only in respect of an overseas visitor who intends to leave the UK *within one month* of their application for a vehicle purchased under the Scheme.

You may also allow delivery within two weeks of completion of the VAT 410 form when the overseas visitor requests an urgent delivery of the motor vehicle due to his/her imminent departure from the UK.

For *all* urgent delivery requests you *must* complete a Certificate for Urgent Delivery (see section 8). You should send copies of Urgent Delivery Certificates by fax to the Personal Transport Unit at least three working days before the date of delivery of the vehicle to the applicant. The certificate *must* be authorised by a sole proprietor, partner, director, company secretary or a duly authorised person at a responsible level.

When you fax the certificate to the Personal Transport Unit you *must* also fax a copy of the VAT 410 form plus, for new vehicles, the V55 Form. You should then post the original papers to the Personal Transport Unit (see paragraph 3.2).

Note: You must *not* use this procedure if the initial application by the customer has been either—

– rejected or returned for amendment; or
– if your customer has made more than one application in any period of 6 months.

5.5 Queries

If you have any doubts or questions before or after delivery of the vehicle which *cannot* be resolved by the NAS (see paragraph 1.2 for contact details), you should consult the PTU at the address shown in paragraph 3.2.

6 WHAT RECORDS MUST I KEEP?

De Voil Indirect Tax Service **V4.334.**

6.1 New vehicles

You must keep available for inspection by our officers—

- the normal VAT records as set out in Notice 700 "The VAT Guide";
- your copy of the VAT 410 form; and
- a separate record of each vehicle supplied under the Scheme showing:
  - the date of delivery;
  - the applicant's name and United Kingdom address;
  - particulars of the vehicle supplied, including type, chassis and registration number;
  - amount of VAT remitted on the delivery price which must include the prices of any accessories, or
  - extras and any delivery charges less any discount allowed; and
- a certificate of receipt for the vehicle, detailing the chassis and registration number which must be signed and dated by the applicant.

6.2 Second-hand vehicles

You should already have a record of second-hand vehicles in your second-hand stock book.

When you sell a second-hand vehicle under the Scheme, you *must* close this stock book entry *and* include a cross-reference to the serial number of the VAT 410 form. Insert "zero-rate" in the VAT rate column of your stock book and "Nil" in the VAT due column.

You must then record the sale separately and include the same details as required for sales of new vehicles.

You can, if you wish, include your second-hand sales with your records of new vehicle sales.

6.3 How long must I keep the records?

Records of all vehicles sold must be retained for a period of six years as specified in Notice 700 "The VAT Guide".

7 ALTERNATIVES TO THE PERSONAL EXPORT SCHEME

De Voil Indirect Tax Service **V4.311.**

7.1 Direct Exports

If your customer does not want to use the vehicle in the UK before it is exported from the EC, you need not supply the vehicle under the scheme. You may be able to supply the vehicle VAT-free as a direct export.

Notice 703 "Exports and removals of goods" from the UK provides more information about direct exports.

8 FORMAT FOR CERTIFICATE FOR URGENT DELIVERY

Certificate for urgent delivery

Applicant's Details:

Name:.. Invoice no:..

Address: ....

....

....

....

....

Post Code: ....

Vehicle Details:

Make: .... Model: ....

Chassis No: .... Registration No: ....

I hereby certify that I have this day personally interviewed

....(*name of applicant*) who assures me that he/she has not applied for or acquired a VAT free motor vehicle under the Personal Export Scheme, as described in Notice 705, within the last 6 months.

I have also inspected his/her passport number .... issued by

....(*name of authority*) and the following documents: (*see * below*)..

....

I have no reason to doubt his/her status as an overseas visitor or his/her declared intention to leave the European Community with the vehicle on (*date*) .... (*see ** below*) and to remain abroad with the vehicle for at least six consecutive months.
Signed: ....
Position in company: ....
Date: ....
* Example: details of car ferry tickets; overseas residence permit; return tickets; confirmatory letters or such evidence as was seen.
** This date must not be later than one month from the date of application.

9 SUPPLIERS CHECKLIST

Have you checked? *You must ensure at the time of application/sale that ...*		*Tick if yes*
1	the customer is eligible to use the Personal Export Scheme (see paragraph 2.3)?	
2	the customer has received and read a copy of the Notice 705 (see paragraph 3.1)?	
3	it is the customer who will personally take delivery of the vehicle in the UK (see paragraph 5.2)?	
4	the customer agrees to comply with all the conditions of the Scheme (see paragraph 3.1)?	
5	you keep a separate record of the vehicle supplied under the Scheme (see paragraph 6)?	
6	the customer is informed they may be liable to prosecution if the information they have given on the VAT 410 application form is incorrect (see paragraph 3.1)	
7	you have completed the VAT 410 (carbonated – 4 part) application form? Copies to be distributed as follows: —copy 1 (*blue*) – Customs copy; —copy 2 (*green*) – Purchasers copy; —copy 3 (*pink*) – Suppliers copy; —copy 4 (yellow) – Vehicle Registration copy – attached to the VRO copy should be either of the following forms— New vehicles: Form V55 authorising the issue of a pink log book (see paragraph 4.1); or Second hand vehicles: —Completed V5 Registration Document; —V10 form (Vehicle licence application), and —VX304 if the purchaser is entitled to claim exemption from payment of vehicle excise duty (see paragraph 4.2)	
8	the customer has been advised to insure the vehicle for the full tax inclusive value at the time of purchase (see paragraph 3.4)	
9	the customer is aware the vehicle must be exported from the EC by the final date for exportation (see paragraph 2.7)	
10	the customer has been informed that— —if their order is cancelled (see paragraph 3.5); or —they change their plans and the vehicle is to remain in the UK/EC, they must immediately contact either the PTU at Dover, (see paragraph 3.2 for contact details) or the VAT fiscal authority in the EC country in which they are to remain	
11	the vehicle is delivered directly to the applicant who completed the VAT 410 Form (see paragraph 5.2)	

12	the applicant signs a dated certificate of receipt for the vehicle, a copy of which should be retained in your records (see paragraph 5.3)	

10 FISCAL (VAT) TERRITORY OF THE EUROPEAN COMMUNITY

De Voil Indirect Tax Service **V1.213.**

10.1 The following countries and territories are within the EC fiscal (VAT) area—

- Austria;
- Belgium;
- Denmark, except the Faroe Islands and Greenland;
- Finland;
- France, including Monaco;
- Germany, except Busingen and the Isle of Heligoland;
- Greece;
- The Republic of Ireland;
- Italy, except the communes of Livigno and Campione d'Italia and the Italian waters of Lake Lugano;
- Luxembourg;
- The Netherlands;
- Portugal, including the Azores and Madeira;
- Spain, including the Balearic Islands but excluding Ceuta and Melilla;
- Sweden; and
- United Kingdom and the Isle of Man.

Plus from 1 May 2004—

- Cyprus*;
- Czech Republic;
- Estonia;
- Hungary;
- Latvia;
- Lithuania;
- Malta;
- Poland;
- Slovakia; and
- Slovenia.

[Plus from 1 January 2007—

- Bulgaria;
- Romania.]

*The European Commission in December 2003 advised that the application of the 6th VAT Directive (Directive 77/388/EEC of 17 May 1977) shall be suspended in those areas of Cyprus in which the Government of the Republic of Cyprus does not exercise effective control. From 1 May 2004 goods to these destinations continue to be eligible for zero-rating as exports.

Note—Text inserted by Update 1, January 2007.

10.2 The following countries and territories are outside the EC fiscal (VAT) area

- The Channel Islands;
- Andorra;
- San Marino;
- The Åland Islands;
- The Canary Islands;
- The overseas departments of France (Guadeloupe, Martinique, Réunion, St. Pierre and Miquelon and French Guiana);
- Mount Athos;
- Cyprus; (until 1 May 2004)
- Gibraltar;
- Malta (until 1 May 2004); and
- The Vatican City.

If you need more information on the VAT territory of the EC, please contact our National Advice Service (see paragraph 1.2 for contact details).

11 DRIVER VEHICLE LICENSING AGENCY—LOCAL OFFICES (DVLA LOS) (FORMERLY VEHICLE REGISTRATION OFFICES VROS)

Beverley
Birmingham
Bristol
Chelmsford
Glasgow
Leeds
Luton
Lincoln
Maidstone
Manchester
Northampton
Norwich
Oxford
Stockton

Details of the DVLA LOs can be found in the telephone directory under: "Environment, Transport & the Regions (Dept of the) – "Road". See their advertisement under Driving and Vehicles.

Commentary—*De Voil Indirect Tax Service* **V4.334.**

Notice 708
Buildings and construction

2008

18. THE CERTIFICATES

18.1 Zero-rated and reduced-rated building work

THIS CERTIFICATE HAS THE FORCE OF LAW
Certificate for zero-rated and reduced-rated building work
1. Address of the building:
2. Name and address of organisation receiving the building work:
VAT Registration number (if registered):
Charity registration (if registered):
3. Date of completion (or estimated date of completion) of the work:
Value (or estimated value) of the supply: £
Name, address and VAT registration number of building contractor:
4. I have read the relevant parts of Notice 708 Buildings and construction and certify that this organisation (in conjunction with any other organisation where applicable) will use the building, or the part of the building, for which zero-rating or reduced-rating is being sought solely for (tick as appropriate ☑):
a relevant charitable purpose, namely by a charity in either or both of the following ways:
otherwise than in the course or furtherance of business, ☑ or
as a village hall or similarly in providing social or recreational facilities for a local community. ☑
a relevant residential purpose, namely as:
(a) a home or other institution providing residential accommodation for children ☑
(b) a home or other institution providing residential accommodation with personal care for persons in need of personal care by reason of old age, disablement, past or present dependence on alcohol or drugs or past or present mental disorder ☑
a hospice ☑
residential accommodation for students or school pupils ☑
residential accommodation for members of any of the armed forces ☑
a monastery, nunnery or similar establishment ☑ or
an institution which is the sole or main residence of at least 90 per cent of its residents ☑
and will not be used as a hospital, prison or similar institution or an hotel, inn or similar establishment.

5. I certify that:
– the information given is complete and accurate; and
– if the building, or a part of the building, for which zero-rated supplies have been obtained, is let or otherwise used for a purpose which is not solely for a relevant residential purpose or relevant charitable purpose within a period of 10 years from the date of its completion, a taxable supply will have been made, and this organisation will account for tax at the standard rate.
Name (print):
Position held:
Signed:
Date:

General warning
1. HMRC reserves the right to alter the format of the certificate through the publication of a new notice. You must ensure that the certificate used is current at the time of issue.
Warnings for the issuer
2. You may be liable to a penalty if you issue a false certificate.
3. You are responsible for the information provided on the completed certificate.
Warnings for the developer
4. You must take all reasonable steps to check the validity of the declaration given to you on this certificate.
5. You must check that you meet all the conditions for zero-rating or reduced-rating your supply – see Notice 708 *Buildings and construction*.

18.2 Zero-rated sales and long leases

THIS CERTIFICATE HAS THE FORCE OF LAW
Certificate for sales and long leases of zero-rated buildings
1. Address of the building:
2. Name and address of organisation buying, or entering into a long lease on, the building (or part of the building):
VAT Registration number (if registered):
Charity registration (if registered):
3. Date (or estimated date) of purchase or commencement of the lease:
Value (or estimated value) of the supply: £
Name, address and VAT registration number of the developer:
4. I have read the relevant parts of Notice 708 *Buildings and construction* and certify that the building, or the part of the building, for which zero-rating is being sought will be used solely for (tick as appropriate ☑):
a relevant charitable purpose, namely by a charity in either or both of the following ways:
(a) otherwise than in the course or furtherance of business ☑ or
(b) as a village hall or similarly in providing social or recreational facilities for a local community. ☑
a relevant residential purpose, namely as:
a home or other institution providing residential accommodation for children ☑
a home or other institution providing residential accommodation with personal care for persons in need of personal care by reason of old age, disablement, past or present dependence on alcohol or drugs or past or present mental disorder ☑
a hospice ☑
residential accommodation for students or school pupils ☑
residential accommodation for members of any of the armed forces ☑
a monastery, nunnery or similar establishment ☑ or
an institution which is the sole or main residence of at least 90 per cent of its residents ☑
and will not be used as a hospital, prison or similar institution or an hotel, inn or similar establishment.
5. I certify that:
– the information given is complete and accurate; and
– if the building, or a part of the building, for which zero-rated supplies have been obtained, is let or otherwise used for a purpose which is not solely for a relevant residential purpose or relevant charitable purpose within a period of 10 years from the date of its completion, a taxable supply will have been made, and this organisation will account for tax at the standard rate.
Name (print):
Position held:
Signed:
Date:

General warning
1. HMRC reserves the right to alter the format of the certificate through the publication of a new notice. You must ensure that the certificate used is current at the time of issue.
Warnings for the issuer
2. You may be liable to a penalty if you issue a false certificate.
3. You are responsible for the information provided on the completed certificate.
Warnings for the developer
4. You must take all reasonable steps to check the validity of the declaration given to you on this certificate.
5. You must also check that you meet all the conditions for zero-rating your supply – see Notice 708 – *Buildings and construction*.

Notice 709/5
Tour operators' margin scheme

2004

Commentary—*De Voil Indirect Tax Service* **V3.591; V6.191, V6.192.**
Note—Sections 8 to 12 have the force of law under VATA 1994 s 53 and SI 1997/1806 arts 3 and 7 as amended.

8 END-OF-YEAR CALCULATION (ANNUAL ADJUSTMENT)

(*referred to in paras 2.6, 5.2, 5.9, 6.1, 6.3, 6.7, 6.8, 7.5, 7.7 and 7.8*)

STEP

1 Working out the total sales of margin scheme packages
Total the VAT-inclusive selling prices of your designated travel services and margin scheme packages supplied during the financial year.
2 Working out the purchase prices of margin scheme supplies
Total the VAT-inclusive purchase prices of the standard-rated designated travel services included in the total at 1.
3 Total the VAT-inclusive purchase prices of the zero-rated designated travel services included in the total at 1.
4 Working out the direct costs of in-house supplies
Total the VAT-exclusive direct costs to you of the standard-rated in-house supplies included in 1. Add a percentage of that amount equivalent to the standard rate of VAT.
5 Total the VAT-exclusive direct costs to you of the zero-rated in-house supplies included in 1.
6 Total the VAT-inclusive direct costs to you of the exempt in-house supplies included in 1. Deduct any input tax that you are entitled to recover on these costs.
7 Total the direct costs to you of the in-house supplies included in 1 that are supplied outside the UK, exclusive of any VAT incurred on these costs that you are entitled to recover. Add to the total an uplift equivalent to the percentage VAT rate applicable to such supplies if you have paid VAT on these supplies to the VAT authorities in another member state.
8 Working out the "costs" of agency supplies
Total the VAT-inclusive amounts paid by you to your principals in respect of the agency supplies included in 1 for which the consideration you receive is standard-rated.
9 Total the VAT-inclusive amounts paid by you to your principals in respect of the agency supplies included in 1 for which the consideration you receive is not standard-rated.
10 Working out the total margin
Add the totals of costs at 2 to 9 inclusive.
11 Calculate the total margin for all the supplies included in 1 by deducting the total at 10 from the total at 1.
12 Apportioning the margin
Calculate the margin for the standard-rated designated travel services by applying the following formula—

$$\frac{\text{total at 2}}{\text{total at 10}} \times \text{total at 11}$$

13 Calculate the margin for the zero-rated designated travel services by applying the following formula—

$$\frac{\text{total at 3}}{\text{total at 10}} \times \text{total at 11}$$

14 Calculate the margin for the standard-rated in-house supplies by applying the following formula—

$$\frac{\text{total at 4}}{\text{total at 10}} \times \text{total at 11}$$

15 Calculate the margin for the zero-rated in-house supplies by applying the following formula—

$$\frac{\text{total at 5}}{\text{total at 10}} \times \text{total at 11}$$

16 Calculate the margin for the exempt in-house supplies by applying the following formula—

$$\frac{\text{total at 6}}{\text{total at 10}} \times \text{total at 11}$$

17 Calculate the margin for the supplies made outside the UK by applying the following formula—

$$\frac{\text{total at 7}}{\text{total at 10}} \times \text{total at 11}$$

18 Calculate the consideration for the standard-rated agency supplies by applying the following formula—

$$\frac{\text{total at 8}}{\text{total at 10}} \times \text{total at 11}$$

19 Calculate the consideration for the non-standard-rated agency supplies by applying the following formula—

$$\frac{\text{total at 9}}{\text{total at 10}} \times \text{total at 11}$$

20 Working out your output tax

Calculate the output VAT due on the designated travel services by applying the following formula—

total at 12 × the VAT fraction

21 Calculate the output VAT due on the standard-rated in-house supplies by applying the following formula—

(total at 4 + total at 14) × the VAT fraction

22 Calculate the output VAT due on the standard-rated agency supplies by applying the following formula—

total at 18 × the VAT fraction

23 Working out sales values

Calculate the VAT-exclusive value of the standard-rated designated travel services by deducting the total at 20 from the total at 12.

24 Calculate the VAT-exclusive value of your standard-rated in-house supplies by applying the following formula—

total at 4 + total at 14 − *total at* 21

25 Calculate the value of your zero-rated in-house supplies by applying the following formula—

total at 5 + *total at* 15

26 Calculate the value of your exempt in-house supplies by applying the following formula

total at 6 + *total at* 16

27 Calculate the value of your in-house supplies which are supplied outside the UK by applying the following formula—

total at 7 + *total at* 15

Working out the annual adjustment

28 Calculate the total output VAT due on your designated travel services and margin scheme packages by adding the totals at 20 to 22 inclusive.

29 Total the provisional output VAT which has been accounted for during the financial year on the supplies included in the total at 1.

30 Deduct the total at 29 from the total at 28. Include the resulting total on your VAT return, either as a payable amount where the amount is positive or as a deductible amount where the amount is negative.

9 ACCOUNTING FOR VAT ON THE PROVISIONAL VALUE OF DESIGNATED TRAVEL SERVICES AND MARGIN SCHEME PACKAGES

(*referred to in paras* 1.2, 2.6, 5.9, 6.3, 6.8, 7.5 and 7.7)

STEP

Working out the provisional percentage

1 Calculate the VAT-inclusive amount of your standard-rated supplies of designated travel services and margin scheme packages for the preceding financial year by adding the totals from steps 4, 12, 14 and 18 of section 8.

2 Calculate the VAT-inclusive standard-rated percentage of the total selling price of all your designated travel services and margin scheme packages for the preceding tax year by applying the following formula—

$$\frac{\text{total at step 1 of Section 9}}{\text{total at step 1 of Section 8}} \times 100$$

Working out the VAT return figures

3 Total the VAT-inclusive selling prices of the designated travel services and margin scheme packages supplied during the prescribed accounting period.

4 Calculate the provisional VAT-inclusive amount of your standard-rated supplies of designated travel services and margin scheme packages made during the prescribed accounting period by applying the following formula—

total at step 3 × *percentage at step* 2

5 Calculate the provisional amount of output VAT due for the prescribed accounting period by applying the following formula—

total at *step* 4 × the VAT fraction

10 SIMPLIFIED END-OF-YEAR CALCULATION (ANNUAL ADJUSTMENT)

(*referred to in paras* 1.2, 2.6, 5.3, 5.9, 6.1, 6.3, 6.7, 6.8, 7.5, 7.7 and 7.8)

STEP

1 Total the VAT-inclusive selling prices of your designated travel services and margin scheme packages supplied during the financial year.

2 Total the VAT-inclusive purchase prices of the designated travel services included in the total at 1.

3 Calculate the VAT-inclusive amount of the supplies included in 1 by deducting the total at 2 from the total at 1.

4 Calculate the total output VAT due on your designated travel services and margin scheme packages by applying the following formula—

total at step 3 × the VAT fraction

5 Calculate the VAT-exclusive value of your designated travel services and margin scheme packages by deducting the total at 4 from the total at 3.

6 Total the provisional output VAT which has been accounted for during the financial year on the supplies included in the total at 1.

7 Deduct the total at 6 from the total at 4. Include the resulting total on your VAT return, either as a payable amount where the amount is positive or as a deductible amount where the amount is negative.

11 ACCOUNTING FOR VAT ON THE PROVISIONAL VALUE OF DESIGNATED TRAVEL SERVICES AND MARGIN SCHEME PACKAGES WHEN THE SIMPLIFIED CALCULATION APPLIES (ALL SUPPLIES STANDARD-RATED)

(*referred to in paras* 1.2, 2.6, 5.9, 6.3, 7.5 and 7.7)

STEP

1 Calculate the VAT-inclusive standard-rated percentage of the total selling price of all your designated travel services and margin scheme packages for the preceding tax year by applying the following formula—

$$\frac{\text{total at step 3 of Section 10}}{\text{total at step 1 of Section 10}} \times 100$$

2 Total the VAT-inclusive selling prices of all of your designated travel services and margin scheme packages supplied during the prescribed accounting period.

3 Calculate the provisional VAT-inclusive amount of your standard-rated supplies of designated travel services and margin scheme packages made during the prescribed accounting period by applying the following formula—

total at step 2 × *percentage at step* 1

4 Calculate the provisional amount of output VAT due for the prescribed accounting period by applying the following formula—

total at *step* 3 × the VAT fraction

5 Calculate the provisional VAT-exclusive value of all of your designated travel services and margin scheme packages made during the prescribed accounting period by deducting the total at 4 from the total at 3.

12 TERTIARY LAW

(*referred to in paras* 1.2, 3.3, 3.4, 5.7, 6.3, 6.5, 7.5, 7.7 and 7.8)

TL1

1 This section shall come into effect on 1 January 1998.

2 The supply of goods or services by a tour operator—

(a) to a person for use by that person for the purpose of that person's business other than by way of re-supply; and

(b) which, but for the VAT (Tour Operators) Order, SI 1987/1806 art 5, would be treated as supplied in another member state;

shall be deemed not to be a designated travel service if, and only if, the tour operator has paid VAT to the relevant VAT authority on his supply in that member state.

3 The supply of goods or services by a tour operator—

(a) to a person for use by that person for the purpose of that person's business other than by way of re-supply; and

(b) which, but for the VAT (Tour Operators) Order, SI 1987/1806 art 5, would be treated as supplied outside the territory of the Community;

may be treated as not being a designated travel service.

4 Where—

(a) goods or services have been acquired by a tour operator prior to the commencement of this section; and

(b) input tax credit has been claimed in respect of those goods or services or part of those goods or services; and

(c) after the commencement of this section the goods or services in respect of which input tax has been claimed are used in the making of a supply to a person for use by that person's business (other than for the purposes of making an onward supply);

that part of the supply referable to goods or services on which input tax has been claimed shall be treated as not being a designated travel service.

TL2

1 This section shall come into effect on 1 January 1998.

2 The supply of goods or services by a tour operator—

(a) who belongs in the United Kingdom; and

(b) which, but for the VAT (Tour Operators) Order, SI 1987/1806 art 5, would be treated as supplied in the United Kingdom; and

(c) made to a body which is entitled to a refund of the tax charged on such supply under either VATA 1994 s 33 or s 39;

may be treated as not being a designated travel service.

TL3

1 This section shall come into effect on 1 January 1998.

2 Where a tour operator, in the same financial year, supplies—

(a) designated travel services or margin scheme packages which are to be enjoyed wholly outside the European Community; and

(b) designated travel services or margin scheme packages which are to be enjoyed wholly or partly within the European Community;

the Commissioners of Customs & Excise may, on being given written notification by the tour operator no later than the due date for rendering his first VAT return for the financial year in which the supplies are to be made, allow the supplies under sub-para (a) to be valued separately from those under sub-para (b).

3 Where a tour operator, under para 2 above, has separately valued supplies of designated travel services or margin scheme packages enjoyed wholly outside the European Community from supplies of designated travel services or margin scheme packages enjoyed wholly or partly within the European Community, the Commissioners of Customs & Excise may, on being given written notification by the tour operator no later than the due date for rendering his first VAT return for any subsequent financial year, allow supplies to be made in such subsequent financial year to be valued using the method specified at Section 8 of this Notice.

TL4

1 This section shall come into effect on 1 January 1998.

2 Where—

(a) a supply of goods or services is acquired by a tour operator for the purpose of supplying a designated travel service; and

(b) the value of the supply to the tour operator is expressed in a currency other than sterling;

the tour operator must convert such value into sterling for the purposes of steps 2 or 3 of section 8 of this Notice or step 2 of section 10 of this Notice.

3 For the purposes of para 2 above, the tour operator must use—

(a) the rate of exchange published in the *Financial Times* using the *Federation of Tour Operators'* base rate current at the time such supplies were costed by the person from whom the tour operator has acquired the goods or services; or

(b) the commercial rate of exchange current at the time that the supplies in his brochure were costed; or

(c) the rate published in the *Financial Times* on the date that the tour operator pays for the supplies; or

(d) the rate of exchange which was applicable to the purchase by the tour operator of the foreign currency which he used to pay for those supplies; or

(e) the period rate of exchange published by Customs & Excise for customs purposes in force at the time the tour operator pays for those supplies.

4 Where the methods at para 3(a) or (b) above are used, the tour operator must publish the rate in any brochure or leaflet in which these supplies are held out for sale.

5 The Commissioners of Customs & Excise may, on being given written notification by a tour operator no later than the due date for rendering his first return of his financial year, allow a different method to be used in that financial year from that used in the previous financial year.

TL5

1 Subject to Section TL3 of section 12 of this Notice, the value of designated travel services, in-house supplies and agency supplies shall be determined by applying the formula set out in Appendix A of this Notice (hereinafter referred to as "the full calculation"), unless during the relevant period all such supplies are liable to VAT at the same rate, in which case the value shall be determined by applying the formula set out in Section 10 of this Notice (hereinafter referred to as "the simplified calculation").

2 The provisional value of designated travel services, in-house supplies and agency supplies shall be determined in accordance with the formula set out in—

(a) Section 9 of this Notice, where the full calculation applies; or

(b) Section 11 of this Notice, where the simplified calculation applies.

3 A tour operator shall be required to account for VAT on the provisional value of his supplies of designated travel services, in-house supplies and agency supplies on the VAT return for the prescribed accounting period in which the supplies are made.

4 The difference between the amount of VAT due on the value of designated travel services, in-house supplies and agency supplies supplied during a tour operator's financial year, and the amount of VAT paid on the provisional value of those supplies, shall be adjusted by the tour operator on the VAT return for the first prescribed accounting period ending after the end of the financial year during which the supplies were made.

TL6

1 For the purpose of Sections 8 to 12 of this Notice—

(a) "in-house supply" means a supply by a tour operator which is neither a designated travel service nor an agency supply;

(b) "agency supply" means a supply arranged by a tour operator between two other persons, in the capacity of an agent or intermediary for either person, for which the tour operator receives a consideration, the value of which is not readily identifiable;

(c) "margin scheme package" means a single transaction which includes one or more designated travel services;

(d) "financial year" means a period corresponding to a tour operator's financial year for accounting purposes;

(e) "direct costs" means costs which are directly and specifically attributable to the provision of in-house supplies, to the extent that they are so attributable;

(f) "VAT fraction" has the same meaning as in Notice No 700 "The VAT guide" Appendix B.

...

Notice 718
Margin schemes for secondhand goods, works of art, antiques and collectors' items

2003 (with Updates 1 and 2)

...

3 RECORDS AND ACCOUNTS

The detailed rules in this section have the force of law.

3.1 What records must I keep?

To use the normal margin scheme you must keep all the records referred to in this section. If you do not, you cannot use the normal margin scheme and will have to pay VAT on the full selling price. The rules in this section are modified if you use one of the other schemes described in this notice (global accounting, auctioneers' scheme, selling horses and ponies) and you must follow the rules in the relevant section.

The normal rules in Notice 700 "The VAT Guide" apply. In addition, to use the normal margin scheme, you must keep—

- a stock book or similar record as described at paragraph 3.3;
- purchase invoices as described at paragraph 3.5;
- copies of sales invoices as described at paragraph 3.7.

Commentary—*De Voil Indirect Tax Service* **V3.536.**

3.2 How long must I keep the records?

The normal rules about business records apply and they must be kept for at least six years. Notice 700 "The VAT Guide" explains a concession to this general rule. But if your stock includes goods which you obtained more than six years ago, you must retain all the evidence which will show your eligibility to margin scheme treatment when you eventually sell them.

3.3 What details do I have to include in my stock book?

Your stock book must be up to date at all times and must include the following information for each item you purchase for resale under the margin scheme (you can include any other information for your own accounting purposes);

Purchase details	*Sales details*
Stock number in numerical sequence	Date of sale
Date of purchase	Sales invoice number
Purchase invoice number	Name of buyer
Purchase price	Selling price or method of disposal
Name of seller	Margin on sale (sales price minus purchase price)
Any unique reference number (for example a car registration number)	VAT due (margin x VAT fraction – 7/47ths with a VAT rate of 17.5%)
Description of the goods (such as make and model)	

You must include your calculations under the appropriate headings in your stock book. If your purchase price exceeds, or is the same as your selling price then no VAT will be due. However, you cannot offset any VAT on goods which are sold at a loss. In these circumstances you should show the VAT due as "Nil" in your stock book.

An example of a margin scheme stock book is included at Section 4.

Commentary—*De Voil Indirect Tax Service* **V3.536.**

3.4 What do I have to do when I buy eligible goods?

When you buy goods which you intend to sell under the margin scheme you must—

Step	*Description*
1	*Check that the goods are eligible for the scheme* (see Section 2). Eligible goods purchased from private individuals or dealers who are not VAT registered can be sold under the scheme. If you buy from another VAT registered dealer it should be clearly indicated on your purchase invoice that the goods are being supplied under the margin scheme (see paragraph 3.5).
2	*Obtain a purchase invoice at the time you buy the goods.* If you buy from another VAT registered dealer, that dealer will make out the invoice. If you buy from an unregistered dealer and he provides you with an invoice, you must ensure that it contains all the details necessary to meet the requirements of paragraph 3.5. If you buy from an unregistered dealer who does not provide an invoice, or from a private individual you must make out the invoice.
3	*Enter the purchase details of the goods in your stock book under the appropriate headings.* The purchase price you enter in your stock book must be the price on the invoice agreed between you and the seller. You must not alter the purchase price and must not add the cost of repair, refurbishment and business overheads.

If you buy a number of items as a single lot but intend to sell them separately, you must allocate a purchase price to each item. If you are using global accounting see Section 5.

If you obtain goods under a transfer of a business as a going concern you should refer to the guidance in paragraphs 24.6 and 24.8.

Banks or financial institutions that obtained goods when the rights in a hire purchase or conditional sale agreement were assigned to them should refer to the guidance in paras 24.7 and 24.8. Anyone that obtains such goods on the transfer of a going concern made by such bodies, should also follow this guidance.

Commentary—*De Voil Indirect Tax Service* **V3.532, 534.**

3.5 What details must be included on purchase invoices?

The following information must always appear on your purchase invoices—

- seller's name and address;
- your name and address;
- stock book number;
- invoice number;
- date of transaction;
- a description of the goods including any unique identification number;
- total price–you must not add any other costs to this price; and
- for goods purchased from another VAT registered dealer, a declaration by the seller that "*Input tax deduction has not been and will not be claimed by me in respect of the goods sold on this invoice*".

Remember, if an amount of VAT is itemised separately on the invoice, the goods are not eligible for onward sale under the margin scheme.

Commentary—*De Voil Indirect Tax Service* **V3.536.**

3.6 What must I do to use the margin scheme for the sale of goods?

If you intend to use the margin scheme when selling eligible goods you must—

Step	*Description*
1	*Ensure that you have followed all the rules relating to the purchase of the goods* (see paragraph 3.4). If you have not, you cannot use the margin scheme for the sale of the goods.
2	*Make out a sales invoice* (see paragraph 3.7 for the details which must be included).
3	*Certify the invoice* "Input tax deduction has not been and will not be claimed by me in respect of the goods sold on this invoice".
4	*Enter the sales details in your stock book* under the appropriate headings.
5	*Issue the invoice to your customer* and keep a copy for your records.

If you include more than one item on your sales invoice you must allocate a selling price to each item.

3.7 What details must I include on sales invoices?

The following information must always appear on your sales invoices—

- your name and address and VAT registration number;
- buyer's name and address;
- stock book number;
- invoice number;
- date of sale;
- a description of the goods including any unique reference number;
- total price–you must not show VAT separately; and
- a declaration "*Input tax deduction has not been and will not be claimed by me in respect of the goods sold on this invoice*".

If you sell an insurance product you should also disclose the full price of this on the invoice, plus any fees you are charging for the product outside the contract of insurance (see Notice "IPT2 A General Guide to IPT").

Commentary—*De Voil Indirect Tax Service* **V3.536.**

3.8 Do I need to keep records for goods on sale or return?

If your stock includes goods supplied to you on a sale or return basis (see Notice 700 "The VAT Guide") you must include, in your stock book or in a separate record of sale or return goods, the following details of the goods—

- the date of transfer of the goods;
- description of goods including any unique identification number–for example car registration;
- name and address of dealer/person transferring the goods; and

– date of sale or return.

Similarly, if any goods are removed from your stock on a sale or return basis to another dealer's premises you should note your stock record with the date and details of the dealer to whom you have transferred the goods.

If you sell goods on behalf of a third party, and you issue an invoice for those goods in your own name, you are acting as an agent for VAT purposes (see paragraph 13.1).

3.9 How do I treat invoices in foreign currencies?

If you are buying and selling eligible goods in a foreign currency (including euros), you must convert any such values to sterling to show the prices for items bought or sold in order to calculate your margin (see table below). If you use global accounting or the auctioneers' scheme see the special rules in paragraphs 6.11 and 8.5 respectively.

Purchase invoices	If your purchase invoice is in a foreign currency, you must convert the values to sterling. If you buy a number of items at an inclusive price and do not intend to sell them as one lot, you must convert the price to sterling and then apportion this amount between the items. You must enter the sterling amounts on an item by item basis in your stock record.
Sales invoices	If you issue a sales invoice in a foreign currency, the invoice must also show the sterling equivalent of the value of the goods. When you sell more than one item on the same invoice, you must show the foreign currency and sterling price for each item on that invoice and enter the sterling amounts in your stock record. If, however, you are selling as one lot goods which you bought as one lot, you need only show a total foreign currency and sterling value for that lot.

To convert amounts in foreign currencies you must use one of the methods outlined in Notice 700 "The VAT Guide". But, whatever method you adopt, the exchange rate to use is that current at the time of supply by, or to, you.

Commentary—*De Voil Indirect Tax Service* **V3.164.**

3.10 How do I fill in my VAT return?

At the end of each tax period you will be sent a VAT return to fill in. To help you complete your VAT return you may find VAT leaflet 700/12 "Filling in your VAT return" useful. You can obtain a copy from our National Advice Service. There are some special rules which you must follow for any goods which you have bought or sold under the margin scheme during the tax period.

– *Box 1.* Include the output tax due on all eligible goods sold in the period covered by the return.
  Box 6. Include the full selling price of all eligible goods sold in the period, less any VAT due on the margin.
– *Box 7.* Include the full purchase price of eligible goods bought in the period.

There is no requirement to include margin scheme purchases or sales in boxes 8 and 9 of your VAT return (see paragraph 15.5).

Commentary—*De Voil Indirect Tax Service* **V3.532.**

. . .

6 GLOBAL ACCOUNTING—RECORDS AND ACCOUNTS

6.1 What records do I need to keep?

You do not need to keep all the detailed records which are required under the normal margin scheme—for instance you do not have to maintain a detailed stock book. Global accounting records do not have to be kept in any set way but they must be complete, up to date and clearly distinguishable from any other records. You must keep records of purchases and sales as described in the following paragraphs together with workings used to calculate the VAT due. You must keep all your records for six years.

If you are unsure about how to maintain your global accounting records you should ask your local VAT Business Advice Centre.

Commentary—*De Voil Indirect Tax Service* **V3.535.**

6.2 What must I do when buying goods under global accounting?

The boxed text below has the force of law

> When you buy goods which you intend to sell under global accounting you must—
> – check that the goods are eligible for global accounting;
> – obtain a purchase invoice. If you buy from another VAT registered dealer the dealer must make out an invoice at the time of sale and certify that it is not a tax invoice. If you buy from an unregistered dealer and he provides you with an invoice, you must ensure that it contains all the details necessary to meet the requirements of para 6.3. If you buy from an unregistered dealer who does not provide an invoice, or from a private individual, you should make out the invoice at the time you buy the goods; and
> – enter the purchase details of the goods in your global accounting purchase records. The purchase price must be the price on the invoice which has been agreed between you and the seller.

You cannot use the scheme if an amount of VAT is shown on the invoice.

Commentary—*De Voil Indirect Tax Service* **V3.535.**

6.3 What details must be included on purchase invoices?

The boxed text below has the force of law

> Purchase invoices must include—
> – your name and address;
> – the seller's name and address;
> – invoice number;
> – date of transaction;
> – description of goods (this must be sufficient to enable us to verify that the goods are eligible for global accounting, for example "four tables, ten chairs" – "assorted goods" is not acceptable);
> – total price, you must not show VAT separately; and
> – an endorsement stating "global accounting invoice".

Commentary—*De Voil Indirect Tax Service* **V3.535.**

6.4 What must I do when selling goods under global accounting?

If you have complied with the purchase conditions above you may use global accounting for the sale of the goods by—

– recording the sale in your usual way, for example, by using a cash register;
– issuing a sales invoice for sales to other VAT registered dealers and keeping a copy of the invoice; and
– transferring your daily takings for eligible goods and/or totals of copy invoices to your global accounting sales record or summary (see paragraph 6.6).

The boxed text below has the force of law

> You must be able to distinguish between sales made under global accounting and other types of transactions at the point of sale.

Commentary—*De Voil Indirect Tax Service* **V3.535.**

6.5 What details must I include on sales invoices?

The boxed text below has the force of law

> You must issue a sales invoice to other VAT registered dealers. These invoices and any other global accounting sales invoice you issue must show the following details—
> – your name, address and VAT registration number;
> – the buyer's name and address;
> – invoice number;
> – date of sale;
> – description of goods (this must be sufficient to enable us to verify that the goods are eligible for global accounting, for example "four tables, ten chairs" – "assorted goods" is not acceptable);
> – total price—you must not show VAT separately; and
> – an endorsement stating "global accounting invoice".

If you are selling an item for more than £500 and do not wish to disclose to the purchaser that you bought the item under global accounting, you may choose to use the following declaration on your sales invoice— "*Input tax deduction has not been and will not be claimed by me in respect of the goods sold on this invoice*". Whichever declaration you use, we must be able to distinguish your global accounting records from any other records.

Commentary—*De Voil Indirect Tax Service* **V3.535.**

6.6 What details should I include in my purchase and sales summaries?

The boxed text below has the force of law

Although you do not have to keep your purchase and sales records or summaries in any particular way, they must include the following details taken from your purchase invoices and any sales invoices you may issue—

- invoice number;
- date of purchase/sale;
- description of goods (this must be sufficient to enable us to verify that the goods are eligible for global accounting, for example "four tables, ten chairs" – "assorted goods" is not acceptable); and
- total price.

Paragraph 5.7 gives an example of how you should work out the VAT due at the end of each period.

Commentary—*De Voil Indirect Tax Service* **V3.535.**

6.7 What if I stop using the scheme or transfer goods as a going concern?

The boxed text below has the force of law

If you cease to use global accounting for any reason—for example you may deregister or transfer your business as a going concern—you must make a closing adjustment to take account of purchases for which you have taken credit, but which have not been sold (your closing stock on hand). The adjustment required in this paragraph does not apply if the total VAT due on your stock on hand is £1,000 or less.

In the final period for which you are using the scheme, you must add the purchase value of your closing stock to your sales figure for that period. In this way you will pay VAT (at cost price) on stock for which you have previously had credit under the scheme. The following is an example of a closing adjustment under global accounting—

At the end of the period calculate—

(a)	Value of purchases during the period	£5,000
(b)	Value of sales during the period	£10,000
(c)	Purchase value of closing stock	£8,000
(d)	Add purchase value of closing stock to sales for period (c + b)	£18,000
(e)	Subtract purchases in this period from sales (d – a)	£13,000
(f)	VAT due on margin (e × 7/47ths)	£1,936.17

You must make a similar adjustment if you transfer goods as part of a transfer of a going concern (TOGC). In that case you should add the purchase value of goods included in the scheme to your sales figure for the period in which the TOGC takes place. This adjustment is separate from the actual TOGC which is not subject to VAT.

Commentary—*De Voil Indirect Tax Service* **V3.535.**

6.8 Do I need to adjust my purchase records for items sold outside the scheme?

If goods, already included in your global accounting purchase records, are sold outside the scheme you must adjust your records accordingly.

When you add up your purchases at the end of the period, you must reduce the total by the purchase value of the goods being sold outside the scheme. Because you may not know the exact purchase value of an item, for example the goods may have been part of a bulk purchase, you must apportion a value. There is no set way of doing this but your method must be fair and reasonable and you must be able to demonstrate to us how the value was determined.

You must retain any such evidence and calculations with your records for six years.

Commentary—*De Voil Indirect Tax Service* **V3.535.**

6.9 How do I treat stolen or destroyed goods?

The boxed text below has the force of law

> Any loss of goods by breakage, theft or destruction must be adjusted by the deduction of their purchase price in your global accounting purchase record.

Commentary—*De Voil Indirect Tax Service* **V3.535.**

6.10 How do I treat repairs and restoration costs?

You may reclaim any VAT you are charged on the cost of business overheads, restoration or repair costs etc as input tax subject to the normal rules. However, you must not add any of these costs to the purchase price of the eligible goods you sell under the scheme.

Commentary—*De Voil Indirect Tax Service* **V3.535.**

6.11 How do I treat global accounting invoices in foreign currencies?

Global accounting invoices will normally only show a total price for the goods you buy and sell under the scheme. But individual items with a purchase value over £500 are not eligible for this scheme and you will need to deduct the value of such items from the purchase invoice total. To do this you should convert any total value in foreign currency (including euros) into sterling and then apportion this figure so as to exclude the item or items with individual purchase values over £500. The net purchase amount in sterling must be entered in your purchase records.

If you issue a global accounting sales invoice you must show the sterling equivalent of the total value of the goods. But, even if you sell more than one item on the same invoice, you need only show the total foreign currency and sterling price on that invoice and enter the sterling amount in your sales record.

To convert amounts in foreign currencies you must use one of the methods outlined in Notice 700 "The VAT Guide". But whatever method you adopt, the exchange rate to use is that current at the time of supply by, or to, you.

Commentary—*De Voil Indirect Tax Service* **V3.535.**

7 THE AUCTIONEERS' SCHEME—BASIC PRINCIPLES

7.1 How does an auctioneer account for VAT on the sale of eligible goods?

If an auctioneer sells eligible goods (see paragraph 25.1) and invoices in his own name he may either—

- account for VAT under the auctioneers' scheme; or
- apply the rules for invoicing as an agent (see paragraph 13.2)

This section and ss 8 to 11 explain the detailed rules which apply to auctioneers operating the auctioneers' scheme.

Section 12 contains information about how a business using the margin scheme or global accounting must treat purchases and sales of eligible goods through an auctioneer.

Commentary—*De Voil Indirect Tax Service* **V3.533.**

7.2 How does the auctioneers' scheme work?

The auctioneers' scheme is a variation of the margin scheme. It allows auctioneers to account for VAT on a margin, the calculation of which involves—

- adding to the hammer price the cost of the auctioneer's services charged to the buyer; and
- deducting from the hammer price the cost of the auctioneer's services charged to the seller.

Paragraph 7.4 provides full guidance on how to calculate the VAT due under the auctioneers' scheme.

If you do not keep all the records referred to, you cannot use the scheme and you may have to pay VAT on the full selling price under the normal VAT rules for agents. Further information on those rules can be found in Notice 700 "The VAT Guide".

It is important that you check with the seller before the sale whether the goods are eligible for inclusion in the auctioneers' scheme.

The auctioneers' scheme and its conditions are for the purposes of calculating your VAT liability and do not affect the legal status of agents or the contractual relationships between auctioneers, vendors and buyers.

Commentary—*De Voil Indirect Tax Service* **V3.533.**

7.3 When can the auctioneers' scheme be used?

To use the scheme the goods must be eligible (see paragraph 25.1) and the seller must be—

- not registered for VAT; or

- a VAT registered person supplying goods under the margin scheme or global accounting; or
- an insurance company selling eligible margin scheme goods which they have acquired as a result of an insurance claim provided that they are sold at auction in the same state; or
- a finance house selling eligible margin scheme goods which they have repossessed provided that they are sold at auction in the same state.

The boxed text below has the force of law.

> You must also comply with the invoicing requirements which are explained at Section 8.

Commentary—*De Voil Indirect Tax Service* **V3.533.**

7.4 How do I calculate VAT on goods I sell under the auctioneers' scheme?

As explained in paragraph 7.2, under the auctioneers' scheme a margin is created by taking into account charges for services the auctioneer makes to the seller and the buyer. To calculate the amount of VAT payable on an individual sale the auctioneer must work from the hammer price—

- *Purchase price*—the hammer price less commission charges (if any) the auctioneer makes to the seller. Specific services other than commission supplied to the seller must be excluded.
- *Selling price*—the hammer price plus any charges for services the auctioneer makes to the buyer (for example, buyer's premium or other commission, incidental expenses such as packing, transport and insurance costs).
- *Margin*—deduct the purchase price from the selling price.
- *Output tax*—multiply the margin by the VAT fraction (7/47ths on a VAT rate of 17.5 per cent).

Paragraph 7.5 explains the charges that can be included in your scheme calculations.

Commentary—*De Voil Indirect Tax Service* **V3.533.**

7.5 Which charges do I include in my auctioneers' scheme calculations?

Vendor's commission and buyer's premium must always be included in your auctioneers' scheme calculations. In addition, you must include any other charges made to the buyer of the goods. These additional charges may include incidental expenses such as packing, transport and insurance costs. The only exception to this rule is if the services are a separate supply in their own right. You must make sure that—

- charges included in your scheme calculations do not show VAT separately; and
- invoices clearly show (for the benefit of both seller and buyer) the respective selling and purchase prices to be used in scheme calculations, (indemnity fees should not be included as part of the purchase price if the insurance policy is provided by an approved insurance company).

Any charges made to the buyer which are not included in your scheme calculations must be invoiced separately and if applicable, VAT charged under the normal rules.

Commentary—*De Voil Indirect Tax Service* **V3.533.**

7.6 How do I treat sales to other EC member states?

Sales made under the auctioneers' scheme to another member state are treated in the same way as sales within the UK. The sales are liable to tax in the UK and no further tax is due in the country of destination. Goods sold under the scheme will not be subject to acquisition VAT when they are taken into another EC member state and should not be included on EC sales lists or boxes 8 and 9 of VAT returns. See Section 15 for further information on buying and selling within the EC.

Commentary—*De Voil Indirect Tax Service* **V3.533.**

7.7 What if I sell zero-rated goods?

Under the auctioneers' scheme a margin is created from the supply of services made to the seller and the buyer. These services are not separately charged with VAT. If you are selling zero-rated goods, for example antique books, the auctioneer's margin is also zero-rated. In the VAT due column of your stock record, insert "nil".

Commentary—*De Voil Indirect Tax Service* **V3.533.**

7.8 How do I treat goods supplied for export?

Goods supplied for export under the auctioneers' scheme can be zero-rated provided you obtain proof of export as detailed in Notice 703 "Exports and removals of goods from the UK". You should calculate your margin in accordance with paragraph 7.4 and once you receive evidence of export you may zero-rate the margin. In the VAT due column of your stock record, insert "nil".

Commentary—*De Voil Indirect Tax Service* **V3.533.**

7.9 How do I work out the time of supply?

Goods sold under the auctioneers' scheme are deemed, for VAT purposes, to be both supplies to the auctioneer and from the auctioneer. There is a common tax point for both supplies and this is determined by reference to the actual sale of the goods at auction. The tax point for both supplies will be the earlier of—

– the handing over of the goods by the auctioneer to the buyer; or
– receipt of payment by the auctioneer.

Commentary—*De Voil Indirect Tax Service* **V3.533.**

7.10 What about selling goods on behalf of a pawnbroker?

You may use the auctioneers' scheme to sell eligible goods on behalf of a pawnbroker provided—

– the pawn value is greater than £75 (£25 before 1/5/98); and
– the pledgor is not VAT registered.

If the pledgor is VAT registered you must account for VAT on the full selling price so it is in your own interest to check the status of the pledgor with the pawnbroker.

Commentary—*De Voil Indirect Tax Service* **V3.533.**

7.11 Can I use the auctioneers' scheme for the sale of new goods on behalf of non-taxable persons?

An Extra Statutory Class Concession (ESCC), introduced with effect from 1 January 1999, allows the auctioneers' scheme to be used for the sale of all goods grown, made or produced (including bloodstock or livestock reared from birth) by non-taxable persons.

As a condition of using the concession, you must obtain a signed certificate from the vendor giving the vendor's name and address, a description of the goods and confirmation that he/she is not registered for VAT nor required to be registered for VAT. You may incorporate the certificate into your existing sales entry in agreement with your local VAT Business Advice Centre. See Section 10 for an example of the certificate.

Commentary—*De Voil Indirect Tax Service* **V3.533.**

8 THE AUCTIONEERS' SCHEME—RECORDS AND ACCOUNTS

8.1 What invoices must I issue for sales made under the auctioneers' scheme?

The whole of this paragraph has the force of law.

For sales made under the scheme, you must issue an invoice to the buyer and the seller.

You must issue to the seller an invoice or statement which includes all the details set out at paragraph 3.5 and you must issue to the buyer an invoice or other document which includes all the details set out at paragraph 3.7. Your purchase invoice/statement and sales invoice must also show—

Purchase Invoice / statement	*Sales invoice*
The hammer price of the goods	*The hammer price* of the goods
Any commission charges made to the seller. You must not show a separate amount of VAT on these charges.	*Any charges for services* (for example buyer's premium) made in connection with the sale of the goods (see paragraph 7.5). You must not show a separate amount of VAT on any of these charges.
The net amount due to the seller (this amount will form your purchase price and the selling price for a VAT registered dealer using the margin scheme).	*The amount due from the buyer* (this amount will form your selling price and will be the purchase price for a VAT registered dealer using the margin scheme).

If the seller and/or buyer are using the margin scheme, their respective selling and purchase prices must be clear from the invoices you issue. This means that the auctioneer should allocate any charges included under the auctioneers' scheme against each lot.

If you are unsure about any of the invoicing and record-keeping requirements you should contact our National Advice Service.

Commentary—*De Voil Indirect Tax Service* **V3.533.**

8.2 Do I have to keep a stock record of goods purchased and sold under the auctioneers' scheme?

The boxed text below has the force of law.

Although you must always keep stock records you do not have to maintain a stock book which is strictly in accordance with the requirements set out at paragraph 3.3. However, if you do not, you must retain sufficient alternative records which provide the same information set out in paragraph 3.3. Examples may include—

- entry forms;
- sales catalogues;
- copies of lots and sales of the day; and
- copies of sales and purchase invoices.

Commentary—*De Voil Indirect Tax Service* **V3.533.**

8.3 Can I include scheme and non-scheme supplies on the same invoice?

If you sell goods to the same buyer under the auctioneers' scheme and under normal accounting, you can include each item on one invoice. If you do choose to include the sales on a single invoice you must ensure that each supply can be clearly distinguished. However, to avoid any confusion for the buyer, you are advised to issue separate invoices.

The buyer must be able to establish the sales price for those items sold under the auctioneers' scheme. This amount will form the purchase price for VAT registered dealers using the margin scheme.

Commentary—*De Voil Indirect Tax Service* **V3.533.**

8.4 Can I re-invoice goods under the normal rules?

If goods have been sold under the auctioneers' scheme and the buyer subsequently decides that they wish to treat the transaction outside the scheme—preferring to pay VAT separately on the hammer price and other charges—you may re-invoice for the transaction under the normal VAT rules provided that—

- you are able to comply with all the relevant VAT regulations for the substitute transaction; and
- at the time of the amendment both you and the buyer hold all the original records relating to the transaction.

If you both agree to this re-invoicing and can meet these conditions you must cancel the first entry in your records and cross-refer to the amended transaction. The replacement invoice which you issue to the buyer must clearly refer to the original transaction and state that it is cancelled and that the buyer should amend their VAT account accordingly.

Re-invoicing cannot be undertaken more than three years after the due date of the VAT return on which the original supply was accounted for. This is because input tax cannot be claimed under the three year cap rules.

Commentary—*De Voil Indirect Tax Service* **V3.533.**

8.5 How do I treat auctioneers' scheme invoices in foreign currencies?

Invoices issued in foreign currencies under the auctioneers' scheme must show the sterling equivalent of each element of the invoice—for example the hammer price of the goods and the amount of commission or other charges due—and not just the total value of the supplies made.

Commentary—*De Voil Indirect Tax Service* **V3.533.**

...

22 HORSES AND PONIES

The scheme can be used only for second-hand horses or ponies. Horses and ponies which you have bred and are selling for the first time are not second-hand. You cannot use the scheme for any horse or pony that you have bought on an invoice which shows VAT separately.

Paragraphs 22.1 to 22.6 of this section explain alternative record keeping requirements based on special three-part forms supplied by The British Equestrian Trade Association (BETA).

Paragraphs 22.7 to 22.11 of this section explain the normal record keeping requirements if you do not use the special three-part forms.

22.1 What is the three-part form?

To sell horses and ponies under the margin scheme you can, as an alternative to the normal margin scheme records, use special three-part forms in numbered sets, with a VAT summary sheet at the back. These are sold by—

The British Equestrian Trade Association (BETA) East Wing, Stockfield Park, Wetherby West Yorkshire LS22 4AW.

You can use this form for each horse or pony you sell or intend to sell under the scheme. If you use the three-part form these are the only stock and sales records you need to keep for the purposes of the margin scheme. You do not need to keep a stock book or invoices as described in Section 3. Part—

- A of the form is your stock record;
- B is your copy sales invoice; and
- C is the customer's purchase invoice.

You must not alter the serial number on the form.

If you do not complete the form correctly, VAT will be due on the full selling price.

As you will need your records to confirm the margin on which you account for VAT you must keep all your records for six years after the date of sale of the goods.

Commentary—*De Voil Indirect Tax Service* **V3.532.**

22.2 Buying a horse or pony

Buying from a private person. If you buy a horse or pony from a private person you must—

- check that it is eligible for the scheme;
- complete the "Description" and "Written Description" sections of Parts A, B and C of the form. You must do this in accordance with the standard laid down by the Royal College of Veterinary Surgeons in their booklet "Colours and Markings of Horses". You can get copies from: The Royal College of Veterinary Surgeons 32 Belgrave Square London SW1.

If the horse or pony is not registered with a recognised Breed Society, Stud Book or Register such as the Welsh Pony and Cob Society or Farm Key Freeze Branding, you and a vet must sign Parts A, B and C of the form to certify that the horse or pony is the one described on the form.

However, if the purchase price of the horse or pony is £500 or less, the vet's signature is not necessary. Similarly, if the horse or pony is registered, the signatures are not necessary;

- give the form a stock number in numerical sequence;
- complete the Purchase Record section on the reverse of Part A; and
- keep all three parts of the form (you will need them when you resell the horse or pony).

Buying from someone who is selling under the Scheme. You should follow the rules above but the seller will give you Part C of the form, which you must keep with your partially completed form. The seller will not have to sign the declaration on the reverse of Part A. If the horse or pony is unregistered and has a purchase price of £500 or more, the Part C you are given should already have been signed by a vet. You need only copy the details of the vet's name, practice etc on to your form—you need not get the vet to sign it.

Commentary—*De Voil Indirect Tax Service* **V3.532.**

22.3 Selling a horse or pony

You must—

- check that you have followed the procedure in paragraph 22.1. If you have not, you cannot use the scheme;
- complete the sales record sections on the reverse of Parts A, B and C;
- complete the VAT Record section on the reverse of Part A. Paragraph 2.11 explains how to work out the VAT due;
- keep Parts A and B;
- give Part C to the buyer; and
- complete the VAT summary sheet.

Commentary—*De Voil Indirect Tax Service* **V3.532.**

22.4 Buying a horse or pony at auction

You should follow the rules in paragraph 22.2. If the horse or pony is being sold under the scheme, the auctioneer will give you Part C of the seller's form (you must keep this part with your own partially completed form).

If the horse or pony is sold by a private person you must get the auctioneer to complete details of his name, address and Lot no. on the reverse of Part A of your form.

Commentary—*De Voil Indirect Tax Service* **V3.532.**

22.5 What if I use the three-part form and sell a horse or pony at auction?

You should tell the auctioneer that your horse or pony is being sold under the scheme and give the auctioneer Parts B and C of your form, which must already be completed as per paragraph 22.1.

After the sale—

- the auctioneer will complete the sales details on the reverse of Parts B and C, adding their name, address and signature;
- Part C will be given to the buyer;
- Part B will be returned to you; and

– you should complete the Sales and VAT Records sections on your Part A.

Commentary—*De Voil Indirect Tax Service* **V3.532.**

22.6 What should the auctioneer do if I use the three-part form?

When you sell a horse or pony on behalf of a person selling it under the Scheme, the vendor will give you Parts B and C of the partially completed form. After the sale you should—

- complete the reverse of Parts B and C;
- give Part C to the buyer;
- return Part B to the seller.

If you have sold a horse or pony on behalf of a person not registered for VAT to a person who is registered, you should complete your name, address and Lot no. on the reverse of Part A of the buyer's form.

Commentary—*De Voil Indirect Tax Service* **V3.532.**

22.7 What records do I have to keep if I don't use the three-part form?

If you prefer not to use the three-part form available from BETA you can maintain the normal records and accounts detailed in Section 3.

The boxed text below has the force of law

> If you do decide to keep normal margin scheme records your stock book must include sufficient details to identify the horse or pony including colour, sex, type (e g chestnut, cob, gelding), age (if known), height, stable name (if known), distinctive markings.

Commentary—*De Voil Indirect Tax Service* **V3.532.**

22.8 Buying a horse or pony and not using the three-part form

If you decide not to use the three-part form you must comply with the conditions set out in paragraphs 3.4 and 3.5. If you do purchase a horse or pony from a VAT registered dealer who uses the three-part form, the dealer will give you part C of that form. You may use this as your purchase invoice and enter the details in your stock book. You must include sufficient details in your stock book to identify the horse or pony—see paragraph 22.7.

Commentary—*De Voil Indirect Tax Service* **V3.532.**

22.9 Selling a horse or pony and not using the three-part form

If you sell a horse or pony and do not use the three-part form you must comply with the conditions set out in paragraphs 3.6 and 3.7.

Commentary—*De Voil Indirect Tax Service* **V3.532.**

22.10 Buying a horse or pony at auction and not using the three-part form

If you buy a horse or pony at auction and you are not using the three-part form you must comply with the conditions set out in paragraph 12.1. If the horse or pony is being sold at auction by a VAT registered dealer who uses the three-part form, the auctioneer will give you part C of that form. You may use this as your purchase invoice and enter the details in your stock book. You must include sufficient details in your stock book to identify the horse or pony—see paragraph 22.7.

Commentary—*De Voil Indirect Tax Service* **V3.532.**

22.11 Selling a horse or pony at auction and not using the three-part form

If you sell a horse or pony at auction and you are not using the three-part form you must comply with the conditions set out in paragraph 12.4.

Commentary—*De Voil Indirect Tax Service* **V3.532.**

…

Notice 725
The single market

January 2007 (*with Update 1*)

This notice cancels and replaces Notice 725 (*October 2002*).

Paragraphs 4.3, 4.4, 4.5, 5.2, and 8.5 of this notice have the force of law under s 30(8) and Schedule 6 paragraph 11 of VATA 1994. These parts are indicated by being placed in a box.

…

4 ZERO-RATING OF SUPPLIES TO VAT REGISTERED CUSTOMERS IN ANOTHER MEMBER STATE – GENERAL REQUIREMENTS

Commentary—*De Voil Indirect Tax Service* **V4.341–V4.356.**

4.1 EC law covered by this section

Article 28C(A) of the EC Sixth Directive (77/388/EEC) states that member states shall exempt certain supplies subject to conditions laid down for the purpose of ensuring the correct and straightforward application of such exemptions (zero-rating) and preventing any evasion, avoidance or abuse. The UK uses the term "zero-rating" rather than "exemption" used in EC law to avoid confusion with the use of exemption elsewhere in UK law.

4.2 UK law on removals

The UK VAT law relating to the zero-rating of removals of goods for VAT purposes can be found in VATA 1994 ss 30(8), 30(10) and the VAT Regulations 1995 reg 134.

4.3 When can a supply of goods be zero-rated?

The text in this box has the force of law

A supply from the UK to a customer in another EC member state is liable to the zero rate where—

- you obtain and show on your VAT sales invoice your customer's EC VAT registration number, including the 2-letter country prefix code; and
- the goods are sent or transported out of the UK to a destination in another EC member state; and
- you obtain and keep valid commercial evidence that the goods have been removed from the UK within the time limits set out at paragraph 4.4.

You must not zero-rate a sale, even if the goods are subsequently removed to another member state, if you—

- supply the goods to a UK VAT registered customer (unless that customer is also registered for VAT in another member state. In such cases they must provide their EC VAT registration number and the goods must be removed to another EC member state);
- deliver to, or allow the goods to be collected by, a UK customer at a UK address; or
- allow the goods to be used in the UK in the period between supply and removal, except where specifically authorised to do so.

Paragraph 4.9 covers the checks that you must undertake to ensure that your customer's EC VAT number is valid.

4.4 Time limits for removal of goods and obtaining evidence of removal

The text in this box has the force of law

In all cases the time limits for removing the goods and obtaining valid evidence of removal will begin from the time of supply. For goods removed to another EC member state the time limits are as follows:

- three months (including supplies of goods involved in groupage or consolidation prior to removal); or
- six months for supplies of goods involved in processing or incorporation prior to removal.

4.5 Goods removed to customers in other member states after processing or incorporation

The text in this box has the force of law

When you make a supply of goods to a VAT registered customer in another member state, but have to deliver them to a third person in the UK who is also making a taxable supply of goods or services to that customer, you can zero-rate the supply provided—

- you obtain and show on your VAT sales invoice your customer's EC VAT registration number, including the 2-letter country prefix code;
- the goods are only being delivered and *not* supplied to the third person in the UK;
- no use is made of the goods other than for processing or incorporation into other goods for removal; and
- you obtain and keep valid commercial evidence that the goods have been removed from the UK within the time limits set out at paragraph 4.4;

and your records show—

- the name, address and VAT number of the customer in the EC;

➡

- the invoice number and date;
- the description, quantity and value of the goods;
- the name and address of the third person in the UK to whom the goods were delivered;
- the date by which the goods must be removed;
- proof of removal obtained from the person responsible for transporting the goods out of the UK; and
- the date the goods were actually removed from the UK.

Your records must be able to show that the goods you supplied have been processed or incorporated into the goods removed from the UK.

In cases where the third person is not in the UK but in another EC member state, the same conditions will generally apply to allow you to zero-rate your supply.

4.6 What should I do if I cannot meet all the conditions in paragraphs 4.3, 4.4 or 4.5?

If you cannot obtain and show a valid EC VAT registration number on your sales invoice you must charge and account for tax in the UK at the appropriate UK rate.

If the goods are not removed or you do not have the evidence of removal within the time limits you must account for VAT as described in paragraph 16.10. No VAT is due on goods which would normally be zero rated when supplied in the UK. You may wish to consider taking a deposit for the VAT (see paragraph 5.5) if you have reason to doubt that the goods will be removed. Extra caution may be advisable if your customer:

- is not previously known to you;
- arranges to collect and transport the goods, or their transport arrives without advance correspondence or notice;
- pays in cash; or
- purchases types or quantities of goods inconsistent with their normal commercial practice.

4.7 How can I obtain my EC customer's VAT registration number?

You will probably have carried out the usual commercial checks such as bank and trade credit worthiness references when you agreed to sell goods to your EC customer. We also strongly recommend that you write to them to ask for their EC VAT registration number, as one of the conditions for zero-rating your supply is that you hold a valid EC VAT number for your customer. After placing the number in your accounting records, you should retain the letter or advice which you have received.

4.8 How can I ensure my EC customers give me their VAT registration numbers?

When writing to your customers ask them to provide you with the number which has been allocated to them for intra-EC trade. This will ensure they do not provide you with an internal tax or fiscal number used only in their own member state.

4.9 Checking the validity of an EC customer's VAT registration number

If you are uncertain whether the number you have been given is valid you should make sure it follows the format at paragraph 16.17. As a preliminary check the validity of a customer's number can be confirmed via the online Europa website at: http://europa.eu.int/comm/taxation_customs/vies/en/vieshome.htm

All member states share these arrangements and businesses in other member states can verify a UK VAT registration number in the same way.

To be certain that your customer's details are correct we strongly recommend that you contact the National Advice Service (see paragraph 1.2). They can validate the VAT number and verify that the name and address you give them is correct.

We further recommend that you consider regularly checking your EC customer's VAT registration number to ensure that the details are still valid and the number has not been deregistered.

4.10 Will I have to account for VAT if my customer's VAT number turns out to be invalid?

No. But only if you—

- have taken all reasonable steps to ensure that your customer is registered for VAT in the EC;
- have obtained and shown your customer's EC VAT number on your VAT sales invoice; and
- hold valid documentary evidence that the goods have left the UK.

4.11 What is meant by "reasonable steps"?

We will not regard you as having taken reasonable steps, as mentioned at paragraph 4.10, to ensure your customer is VAT registered in the EC if, for example—

- the VAT number you quote does not conform to the published format for your customer's member state as shown at paragraphs 16.17; or
- you use a VAT number which we have informed you is invalid; or
- you use a VAT number which you know does not belong to your customer.

4.12 Will VAT be chargeable if reasonable steps are not considered to have been taken?

Yes. You will have to account for VAT at the appropriate rate on the goods in the UK.

4.13 Intra-EC supplies of freight containers

For information about the conditions for zero-rating the sale of a container to a VAT registered customer in another member state, see Notice 703/1 "Supply of freight containers for export or removal from the United Kingdom".

5 ZERO-RATING OF SUPPLIES TO VAT REGISTERED CUSTOMERS IN ANOTHER MEMBER STATE – EVIDENCE OF REMOVAL

Commentary—*De Voil Indirect Tax Service* **V4.351–V4.356.**

5.1 Evidence of removal

A combination of these documents must be used to provide clear evidence that a supply has taken place, and the goods have been removed from the UK—

- the customer's order (including customer's name, VAT number and delivery address for the goods);
- inter-company correspondence;
- copy sales invoice (including a description of the goods, an invoice number and customer's EC VAT number etc.);
- advice note;
- packing list;
- commercial transport document(s) from the carrier responsible for removing the goods from the UK, for example an International Consignment Note (CMR) fully completed by the consignor, the haulier and signed by receiving consignee;
- details of insurance or freight charges;
- bank statements as evidence of payment;
- receipted copy of the consignment note as evidence of receipt of goods abroad; and
- any other documents relevant to the removal of the goods in question which you would normally obtain in the course of your intra-EC business.

Photocopy certificates of shipment or other transport documents are not normally acceptable as evidence of removal unless authenticated with an original stamp and dated by an authorised official of the issuing office.

5.2 What must be shown on documents used as proof of removal?

The text in this box has the force of law

The documents you use as proof of removal must clearly identify the following—

- the supplier;
- the consignor (where different from the supplier);
- the customer;
- the goods;
- an accurate value;
- the mode of transport and route of movement of the goods; and
- the EC destination.

Vague descriptions of goods, quantities or values are not acceptable. For instance, "various electrical goods" must not be used when the correct description is "2000 mobile phones (Make ABC and Model Number XYZ2000)". An accurate value, for example, £50,000 must be shown and not excluded or replaced by a lower or higher amount.

If the evidence is found to be unsatisfactory *you* as the supplier could become *liable* for the VAT due.

5.3 Evidence of removal of goods to the Republic of Ireland across the Irish Land Boundary

The evidence you obtain must clearly show that the goods have left the UK. The types of documentary evidence required are explained in paragraphs 5.1 and 5.2. See also paragraph 5.5 for advice when goods are collected by your customer. Depending on the circumstances of the removal, we recommend that you obtain the following types of evidence to meet the conditions for zero-rating:

If the goods are …	*then commercial evidence should include …*
removed by road by an independent carrier,	a copy of the carrier's invoice or consignment note, supported by evidence that the goods have been delivered to a destination in the Republic of Ireland (eg a receipted copy of the consignment note).
removed by rail,	the consignor's copy of the consignment note signed by the railway official accepting the goods for delivery to your customer.
removed in your own transport,	a copy of the delivery note showing your customer's name, address, EC VAT number and actual delivery address in the Republic of Ireland if different, and a signature of your customer, or their authorised representative, confirming receipt of the goods.
collected by your customer or their authorised representative,	a written order completed by your customer, which shows their name, address, EC VAT number, the name of the authorised representative collecting the goods, the address in the Republic of Ireland where the goods are to be delivered, the vehicle registration number of the transport used, and a signature of your customer, or their authorised representative, confirming receipt of the goods.

Where you sell a motor vehicle, which is collected by your customer or their representative, it may be difficult to obtain satisfactory evidence of removal from the UK. In these circumstances, a copy of the vehicle registration document issued by the authorities in the Republic of Ireland will normally provide satisfactory evidence of removal if supported by other evidence described above and in paragraph 5.1.

5.4 What if I deliver the goods to my customer in another EC member state?

In addition to the examples of acceptable documents relating to the sale listed in paragraph 5.1, travel tickets can also be used to demonstrate that an intra-EC journey took place for the purpose of removing the goods from the UK

5.5 What if my customer collects the goods or arranges for their collection and removal from the UK?

If your VAT registered EC customer is arranging removal of the goods from the UK it can be difficult for you as the supplier to obtain adequate proof of removal as the carrier is contracted to your EC customer. For this type of transaction the standard of evidence required to substantiate VAT zero-rating is high.

Before zero-rating the supply you must ascertain what evidence of removal of the goods from the UK will be provided. You should consider taking a deposit equivalent to the amount of VAT you would have to account for if you do not hold satisfactory evidence of the removal of the goods from the UK. The deposit can be refunded when you obtain evidence that proves the goods were removed within the appropriate time limits.

Evidence must show that the goods you supplied have left the UK. Copies of transport documents alone will not be sufficient. Information held must identify the date and route of the movement of goods and the mode of transport involved. It should include the following:

Item	*Description*
1	Written order from your customer which shows their name, address and EC VAT number and the address where the goods are to be delivered.
2	Copy sales invoice showing customer's name, EC VAT number, a description of the goods and an invoice number.
3	Date of departure of goods from your premises and from the UK.
4	Name and address of the haulier collecting the goods.
5	Registration number of the vehicle collecting the goods and the name and signature of the driver and, where the goods are to be taken out of the UK by a different haulier or vehicle, the name and address of that haulier, that vehicle registration number and a signature for the goods.

Item	Description
6	Route, for example, Channel Tunnel, port of exit.
7	Copy of travel tickets.
8	Name of ferry or shipping company and date of sailing or airway number and airport.
9	Trailer number (if applicable).
10	Full container number (if applicable).
11	Name and address for consolidation, groupage, or processing (if applicable).

5.6 How long must I retain evidence of removal?

You must ensure that the proof of removal is—

- retained for six years; and
- made readily available so that any VAT assurance officer is able to substantiate the zero-rating of your removals.

5.7 Can I use an agent?

You, as the supplier of the goods, or your customer can appoint a freight forwarder, shipping company, airline or other person to handle your intra-EC supplies and produce the necessary evidence of removal.

However, you remain legally responsible for ensuring that the conditions for zero-rating supplies of goods to other EC member states, as set out in paragraphs 4.3, 4.4 and 4.5, are met. This includes obtaining and holding evidence of removal of the goods from the UK.

5.8 Groupage or consolidation transactions

If you use a freight forwarder, consignments (often coming from several consignors) may be aggregated into one load, known as groupage or consolidation cargo. The freight forwarder must keep copies of the original bill of lading, sea-waybill or air-waybill, and all consignments in the load must be shown on the container or vehicle manifest. You will be issued with a certificate of shipment by the freight forwarder, often supported by an authenticated photocopy of the original bill of lading, a sea-waybill or a house air-waybill. Where such consignments are being removed, the forwarder may be shown as the consignor in the shipping documents.

(*a*) *Certificate of shipment*

Certificates of shipment are usually produced by packers and consolidators involved in road, rail and sea groupage consignments when they themselves receive only a single authenticated transport document from the carrier. It is an important document, which should be sent to you as soon as the goods have been removed from the UK.

The certificate of shipment must be an original and authenticated by an official of the issuing company unless it is computer produced, on a once-only basis, as a by-product of the issuing company's accounting system.

A properly completed certificate of shipment will help you to meet the evidential requirements described in paragraph 5.1.

(*b*) *What information must be shown?*

Although the certificate of shipment can be in any format, it must be an original and will usually contain the following information—

- the name and address of the issuing company;
- a unique reference number or issuer's file reference;
- the name of the supplier of the goods (and VAT number if known);
- the place, port or airport of loading;
- the place, port or airport of shipment;
- the name of the ship or the aircraft flight prefix and number;
- the date of sailing or flight;
- the customer's name;
- the destination of the goods;
- a full description of the goods removed to another member state (including quantity, weight and value);
- the number of packages;
- the supplier's invoice number and date if known;
- the bill of lading or air-waybill number (if applicable); and
- the identifying number of the vehicle, container or railway wagon.

5.9 Postal services

Goods sent by post may be zero-rated if they are sent directly to your customer registered for VAT in another EC member state, and you hold the necessary evidence of posting. The receipted forms described in the table below, plus the Parcelforce Worldwide statement of account or parcel manifest listing each parcel or multi-parcel, will provide evidence of removal.

Method of posting	*Evidence required*
Letter post or airmail	A fully completed certificate of posting form presented with the goods, and stamped by the Post Office. Acceptable forms are: –Form C&E 132 for single or multiple packages taken to the Post Office. Blank forms may be obtained from our National Advice Service or from our Internet site; –Form P326 available from the Post Office and used for single packages taken to the Post Office; or –a Certificate of Posting for International Mail Only, or a Royal Mail Collection Manifest, available from a Royal Mail sales advisor, for use by customers using their Business Collections Service, where the Royal Mail collection driver signs the certificate. Further information on Royal Mail international services is available on their website at www.royalmail.com
Parcels	Parcelforce Worldwide operates a range of international parcel services. If you use any of these services you will be provided with: –a service specific barcoded label; –a customs export declaration (for non-EC destinations only); –a copy of the Parcelforce Worldwide conditions of carriage; and –a printed receipt, which is your proof of shipment for all destinations. An individual barcode label must be affixed to every parcel. You do not need to complete the customs export declaration for goods being sent to another EC member state. If you arrange for the parcel to be collected from your premises the collecting driver will sign your printed receipt. This is your proof of shipment for EC destinations. If the parcel is taken to a Post Office, the counter clerk will provide you with a printed proof of shipment from the Post Office SmartPost system. This will show the overseas delivery address, date of dispatch and unique consignment number. You should keep this printed proof of shipment as your evidence of removal. In addition to the individual parcel declarations described above, account customers of Parcelforce Worldwide have two further potential sources of information listing multiple parcel dispatches. These are— –Worldwide Dispatch manager (WDM) – online users can print a manifest which lists all dispatched parcels; and –a Statement of Account. All of the individual parcel declarations, plus either the manifest or the statement of account listing each dispatch will provide proof of removal for VAT purposes. You can find further information on Parcelforce Worldwide International services on their website at www.parcelforce.com

5.10 Couriers and fast parcel services

Courier and fast parcel operators specialise in the shipment of goods to overseas destinations within guaranteed timescales.

(a) Operators who do not issue separate certificates of shipment

Most courier and fast parcel operators do not issue separate certificates of shipment. The invoice for moving goods from the UK, which bears details of the unique airway bill numbers for each shipment, represents normal commercial evidence of removal. In addition, many express companies are able to offer a track and trace service via their websites where the movement of goods can be traced through to the final destination.

This information can be printed and also be used to confirm removal from the UK.

(b) Operators who use the system based upon a Dispatch Pack

A few companies still use a documentary system based upon a Dispatch Pack containing accounting data, a Customs export declaration and receipt copies of the relevant house airway bill or consignment note. These packs are issued to customers to complete for each removal from the UK.

An export declaration does not need to be completed for goods being sent to another EC member state but a Dispatch Pack must be completed for each overseas address and consignee. The driver collecting the parcels will endorse the receipt copy and return it to the consignor. This, plus the statement of account listing each removal, will provide evidence of removal from the UK.

(c) Use of more than one courier/fast parcel company

Due to the complexities of the movement of goods within the courier/fast parcel environment, there is often more than one company involved in the handling and ultimate removal of the goods. Ultimately, you as the UK supplier may not be certain as to which courier/fast parcel company has removed the goods. If you are aware that this may happen you will need to establish what proof of removal you will receive from the company to whom you give your goods. The proof available is described in (a) and (b) above.

(d) Overseas customer arranging the removal by courier

If your EC customer arranges for the goods to be removed by courier you should ascertain what proof of removal they will be providing to enable you to zero-rate the supply. You should consider taking a deposit equivalent to the amount of VAT you would have to account for if you do not hold satisfactory evidence of the removal of the goods from the UK. The deposit can be refunded when you obtain evidence that proves the goods were removed within the appropriate time limits.

…

8 TAX VALUE OF ACQUISITIONS

8.1 Calculating the amount of tax due on an acquisition

The amount of tax due on an acquisition is the tax value multiplied by the appropriate VAT rate.

Commentary—*De Voil Indirect Tax Service* **V3.390.**

8.2 What is the tax value of an acquisition?

This is, usually, what you pay for the goods, it is also called the "consideration".

8.3 What is consideration?

Consideration is any form of payment in money or in kind, including anything which is itself a supply. The consideration includes any payment which you make to cover your supplier's costs in making the supply, such as packing, transport or insurance for which they are responsible under their contract with you.

Commentary—*De Voil Indirect Tax Service* **V3.103.**

8.4 Establishing the tax value of an acquisition

The tax value of your acquisition can be established as follows:

Where …	*then the tax value of your acquisition is …*
the consideration is wholly in money,	the amount paid.
the consideration is non-monetary, for example the supply is made in return for payment in goods or services, or is monetary and nonmonetary,	the monetary equivalent of the consideration calculated by reference to the price, excluding VAT, which you would have to pay if the consideration were monetary.
the consideration involves a discounted amount and you pay the discounted amount,	based on the discounted amount.
the consideration includes the offer of a conditional discount which is dependent upon some future event, for example on condition that you buy more from your supplier, or make payment within a specified period of time,	based on the full amount paid. If you later earn the discount, the tax value is reduced and you can adjust the amount of tax accounted for (but you should only do this where you have not claimed, or have been unable to claim, full input tax credit for that acquisition).
there is no consideration, for example a transfer of own goods (see section 9), or when goods are supplied without charge,	in either case, what it would cost you, or the person transferring the goods to you, to purchase the goods in question at the time of the acquisition.

Commentary—*De Voil Indirect Tax Service* **V3.390.**

8.5 What should I do if the value of an acquisition is in a foreign currency?

Where the value of your acquisition is in a foreign currency, you should convert it to sterling as follows:

The text in this box has the force of law.

For VAT purposes, amounts of money must always be expressed in sterling. If you need to convert an amount from a foreign currency into sterling, you must do so on the following basis:

(a) Unless you have adopted one of the alternatives set out below, you must use the UK market selling rate at the time of the acquisition. The rates published in national newspapers will be acceptable as evidence of the rates at the relevant time.

(b) As an alternative you may use the period rate of exchange published by HMRC for customs purposes. The National Advice Service can give details of particular period rates (see paragraph 1.2).

You may adopt this alternative in respect of all your acquisitions or in respect of all acquisitions of a particular class or description. If you opt in respect only of a particular class or description you should make a note in your records at the time of adoption of the class or description to which your option relates.

You do not need to notify HMRC in advance if you wish to adopt this alternative, but if you make such an option you cannot then change it without first obtaining the agreement of the National Advice Service.

(c) You may apply in writing to the National Advice Service for the use of a rate or of a method of determining a rate which you use for commercial purposes but which is not covered by (a) or (b) above. In considering whether to allow such applications the National Advice Service will take into account whether the proposed rate or method is determined by reference to the UK currency market, whether it is objectively verifiable, and the frequency with which the applicant proposes to update it. Forward rates or methods deriving from forward rates are not acceptable.

Before 1 January 1993 you may have used a rate authorised in writing by Customs and Excise under the concessionary arrangements for supplies which applied up to that date. By concession you may extend this to acquisitions without further notification, unless the rate you use wholly derives from currency markets other than in the UK. Your continued use of these concessionary rates is subject to review by HMRC.

The text in this box has the force of law.

Whatever rate or method you adopt, the appropriate rate for any supply is the one current at the time of supply.

Commentary—*De Voil Indirect Tax Service* **V3.393.**

8.6 Do I include any excise duty in the tax value of an acquisition?

Yes. For goods subject to excise duty or, in the case of EC accessionary states, customs duty or agricultural levy, the value of the acquisition is the value determined according to the principles outlined in this chapter plus the duty and/or levy arising from the removal to the UK.

Commentary—*De Voil Indirect Tax Service* **V3.390.**

…

Notice 727 Retail schemes

2002 (with Update 1)

1 INTRODUCTION

…

1.2 What are retail schemes?

The retail schemes are methods you can use to arrive at the value of your taxable retail sales and to determine what proportion of those sales are taxable at the different rates of VAT. As at 1 September 1997 the VAT rates are—

– standard rate (17.5 per cent);
– lower rate (5 per cent); and
– zero rate (0 per cent).

Most VAT registered businesses take these details from tax invoices issued to customers. These schemes provide an alternative if you are a retailer and you find it difficult to issue invoices for a large number of supplies made direct to the public. Each scheme has a turnover limit.

The boxed text below has the force of law.

> The turnover limits for the schemes apply to the whole of your VAT registration.

Commentary—*De Voil Indirect Tax Service* **V3.551.**

…

1.4 Force of law

Parts of this notice have the force of law under the VAT Regulations 1995, Part IX (regs 66–75). All of Sections 7 and 10 have legal force and supplement the law. Certain paragraphs within other parts of the notice also have legal force and supplement the law. The text of those paragraphs is indicated by a statement and has been placed in a box.

Commentary—*De Voil Indirect Tax Service* **V3.552.**

2 USING RETAIL SCHEMES

2.1 When should I use a retail scheme?

The schemes are intended for businesses who cannot reasonably be expected to account for VAT in the normal way. Under normal accounting there is no requirement for you to issue a tax invoice to customers who are not registered for VAT. But normal accounting does require you to identify, for each supply you make, the tax exclusive value and the VAT, and to be able to produce periodic totals of those amounts.

The boxed text below has the force of law.

> The schemes can be used for retail sales only.

Retail sales are generally low in value and made to a large number of customers in small quantities.

Commentary—*De Voil Indirect Tax Service* **V3.551.**

2.2 What if my business makes retail and non-retail sales?

This paragraph has the force of law.

> If you make a mixture of retail and non retail sales you can use a retail scheme to calculate the tax due on your retail sales only. You must account for non retail sales using the normal method of accounting.

Commentary—*De Voil Indirect Tax Service* **V3.551.**

2.3 How do I choose a retail scheme?

Sections 3 and 5 explain briefly the way in which the different schemes work and how they suit different types of business. You will find further information about individual schemes in the specific retail scheme notice.

If, after reading Sections 3 and 5, you find that you are eligible for more than one scheme you will need to choose the one best suited to your particular business. You should also consider other factors too, such as the complexity of the calculation and the amount of paperwork, record-keeping or stock taking you will need to undertake, relative to the other schemes.

Section 11 shows a comparison in table form. Remember, the valuation of the tax due may vary from scheme to scheme.

Commentary—*De Voil Indirect Tax Service* **V3.561.**

2.4 Can I use a retail scheme for sales to other VAT registered businesses?

This paragraph has the force of law.

> Sales to other VAT registered businesses must not be included in a retail scheme. The exception to this is occasional cash sales, for example a—
>
> – garage supplying petrol to a VAT registered customer; or
> – retail DIY store supplying building materials to a VAT registered builder.

Commentary—*De Voil Indirect Tax Service* **V3.551.**

3 STANDARD SCHEMES

…

3.4 How does the Point of Sale scheme work?

Under the Point of Sale scheme you calculate the tax due on your sales by identifying the correct VAT liability at the time you make the sale.

This usually means using a till system which is capable of distinguishing between goods sold at different rates of VAT. But you can use the scheme if you can separate your sales in another way, for example by using separate tills for different rates.

Once your system has produced the total value of sales at each rate you calculate your output tax by applying the appropriate VAT fraction to the relevant portion of your Daily Gross Takings (see para 4.6).

The boxed text below has the force of law.

> If you make only standard or only lower-rated sales, you must use this scheme.

Commentary—*De Voil Indirect Tax Service* **V3.571.**

. . .

3.7 What factors should I consider before choosing Apportionment scheme (1)?

The scheme is relatively simple. However, if on average, you achieve a higher mark-up for your zero-rated goods than your lower or standard-rated goods, you may find that you pay more VAT if you use Apportionment scheme (1) than you would using another scheme.

The boxed text below has the force of law.

> You can only use the scheme if your total tax exclusive turnover from retail sales does not exceed £1 million;
>
> You cannot use the scheme for supplies of services, or for supplies of goods which you have made or grown yourself, or for supplies of catering.

You can find further information about the Apportionment schemes in Notice 727/4 "How to work the Apportionment Schemes".

Commentary—*De Voil Indirect Tax Service* **V3.572.**

. . .

3.9 What factors should I consider before choosing Apportionment scheme (2)?

The scheme can be complex to operate but if you use it properly, it will provide you with a more accurate valuation of your supplies over a period of time.

The boxed text below has the force of law.

> You can only use the scheme if your total tax exclusive turnover from retail sales does not exceed £130 million;
>
> You must be able to work out the Expected Selling Prices (ESPs) of your stock on hand when you start to use the scheme;
>
> You cannot use the scheme for supplies of services or catering.

You can find further information about the Apportionment schemes in Notice 727/4 "How to work the Apportionment Schemes".

Commentary—*De Voil Indirect Tax Service* **V3.572.**

. . .

3.12 What factors should I consider before choosing Direct Calculation scheme (1)?

Direct Calculation scheme (1) can be relatively simple if you have a small proportion of sales at one rate of VAT. But the scheme can produce inaccuracies if Expected Selling Prices are not calculated accurately. Additionally it can be complex to work out if you sell goods at three rates of VAT, though it may be possible to account for a small number of goods at a third rate outside the scheme.

You should also consider the following—

The boxed text below has the force of law.

> – you cannot use Direct Calculation scheme (1) if your annual tax exclusive retail turnover exceeds £1 million;

➡

- if your minority sales are zero-rated you may not use the scheme for zero-rated services;
- if your minority sales are standard-rated you may not use the scheme for standard-rated services;
- the scheme may not be used for supplies of catering.

You can find further information about the schemes in Notice 727/5 "How to work the Direct Calculation schemes".

Commentary—*De Voil Indirect Tax Service* **V3.573.**

4 SPECIAL RULES ABOUT THE STANDARD SCHEMES

4.1 Can I use a mixture of schemes?

The boxed text below has the force of law.

Normally the retail scheme calculation will be a single calculation for the whole of your VAT registration. You can, if you wish, use the same scheme separately at a number of distinct business locations. But, if you use a scheme other than the Point of Sale scheme (see para 3.4), there may be a need to make adjustments to account for transfers between different parts of the business. You must agree the details of such adjustments with your local VAT Business Advice Centre.

You may find that you need to use different schemes in different parts of your business. Provided you are eligible for the schemes, you can mix the Point of Sale scheme (see para 3.4) with either a Direct Calculation (see paras 3.10 to 3.13) or an Apportionment scheme (see paras 3.6 to 3.9). But, you cannot use different versions of the Direct Calculation or Apportionment schemes and you must not use an Apportionment scheme in some parts of your business and a Direct Calculation scheme in other parts.

Remember, you can always use the normal method of accounting together with any scheme or any allowable mixture for which you are eligible.

Commentary—*De Voil Indirect Tax Service* **V3.562.**

4.2 Can I change schemes?

The boxed text below has the force of law.

You can change schemes at the end of a complete year reckoned from the beginning of the tax period in which you first adopted the scheme. You must use the scheme for twelve months, unless—

- you become ineligible for the scheme you are using; or
- we allow or require an earlier change.

If you become ineligible you must cease to use the scheme from the end of the next complete accounting period.

For example, if you account for VAT by reference to quarters ending March, June, September and December and your turnover makes you ineligible for a scheme during February, you must cease to use that scheme to account for supplies made on or after 1 July.Some schemes require adjustments when you cease to use them, see para 6.1.

Commentary—*De Voil Indirect Tax Service* **V3.563.**

…

4.4 Do I need to keep a record of my Daily Gross Takings (DGT)?

This paragraph has the force of law.

Yes. All the retail schemes require a record of the value of your retail sales called the Daily Gross Takings or DGT. From the day you start to use a scheme you must keep a record of your DGT. You must include in this record—

- all payments for your retail supplies as they are received by you from cash customers;
- the full value, including VAT, of all your credit or other non cash retail sales at the time you make the supply; and
- details of any adjustments made to this record.

Commentary—*De Voil Indirect Tax Service* **V3.556.**

…

5 BESPOKE SCHEMES

5.1 What is a bespoke scheme?

The boxed text below has the force of law.

> If your annual turnover of retail sales, excluding VAT, is above £130 million you cannot use the published standard schemes.
>
> If you think your annual turnover is about to exceed £130 million you should contact HMRC as soon as possible to agree a bespoke scheme.
>
> A bespoke scheme will be tailored to meet the particular requirements of your business and is likely to be an adaptation, to a greater or lesser extent, of one of the published schemes.
>
> You can find further information about bespoke schemes in Notice 727/2 "VAT: Bespoke retail schemes".

Commentary—*De Voil Indirect Tax Service* **V3.552, 574.**

6 CEASING TO USE A RETAIL SCHEME

6.1 What must I do when I cease using a retail scheme?

Depending on the scheme you use, you must follow the rules in the table below. *This paragraph has the force of law.*

Scheme	*Procedure*
Point of Sale	No adjustment on ceasing to use for all or part of a VAT registration.
Apportionment (1)	You must perform a closing adjustment, as for the annual adjustment, even if you leave before the anniversary of starting to use the scheme.
Apportionment (2)	Normally no adjustment is necessary. However, if you are ceasing to use this scheme in part of your business but are continuing to use it in other parts of the registration, make sure that the rolling calculation reflects the Expected Selling Prices of stock now excluded from the Apportionment calculation.
Direct Calculation (1)	Normally no adjustment is necessary.
Direct Calculation (2)	You must make a closing adjustment, as for the annual adjustment, even if you leave before the anniversary of starting to use the scheme. The adjustment must take account of any disposals made during the year which were not by way of retail sale. This is done by excluding from the figures used in the calculation, the value of any goods which were previously part of the scheme calculation but were not a retail sale.

Commentary—*De Voil Indirect Tax Service* **V3.563.**

6.2 Are there any other rules when ceasing to use a scheme?

Apart from these special rules under the retail scheme, you should also remember—

- only goods sold by retail can be included in the retail scheme. If you cease to use a scheme because you transfer part or all of your business as a going concern, the value of stock transferred will have to be excluded from your retail scheme; and
- if you cease to trade, VAT may become due on the value of your stocks and assets (see Notice 700/11 "Cancelling your registration").

We may require additional adjustments where unusual patterns of trade prevent your scheme from producing a fair and reasonable result.

For these reasons you must always tell your local VAT Business Advice Centre if—

The boxed text below has the force of law.

> - you buy or sell part of a business; or
> - the legal entity of your business changes (for example, from sole proprietor to partnership); or
> - you are registered as a group and the composition of the group is to change.

Commentary—*De Voil Indirect Tax Service* **V3.261.**

…

8 CATERING ADAPTATION

This section supplements the rules in the "How to work" notices.

…

8.3 What are the conditions for using the catering adaptation?

This paragraph has the force of law.

> You may use the catering adaptation described in paras 8.7 and 8.8 provided—
> - you can satisfy us that you are unable to operate the Point of Sale scheme;
> - you have reasonable grounds for believing that the tax-exclusive value of your taxable retail catering sales (standard and zero-rated sales) will not exceed £1 million in the next twelve months; and
> - your use of the catering adaptation produces a fair and reasonable result in any period.

Commentary—*De Voil Indirect Tax Service* **V3.565.**

8.4 What happens if I do not comply with the conditions?

If you do not comply with the conditions of the catering adaptation we may—

- assess for the underdeclared VAT arising from unsatisfactory use of the catering adaptation; and/or
- refuse use of the catering adaptation for future periods.

Commentary—*De Voil Indirect Tax Service* **V3.565.**

8.5 How do I start to use the adaptation?

This paragraph has the force of law.

> If you wish to use the adaptation and meet the conditions detailed in para 8.3 you must notify your local VAT Business Advice Centre. Generally we will do no more than acknowledge your letter. You may begin to use the adaptation as soon as you receive our acknowledgement.

Commentary—*De Voil Indirect Tax Service* **V3.565.**

8.6 Do I have to maintain any records?

The boxed text below has the force of law.

> Yes. To use the catering adaptation you must maintain a record of Daily Gross Takings (DGT).

The DGT is not simply a record of cash on hand. Details of the DGT requirements are given in paras 4.4 to 4.6.

Commentary—*De Voil Indirect Tax Service* **V3.565.**

8.7 How do I calculate my output tax under the catering adaptation?

To calculate your output tax on catering sales, follow the procedure in the table below for each tax period. *This paragraph has the force of law.*

Step	*Procedure*	*Result*
1	Establish your Daily Gross Takings (DGT) in accordance with paras 4.4 to 4.6 and the rules contained in the relevant scheme notice.	£ ________
2	Calculate the percentage of your total catering sales made at the standard rate. See the rules covering the making of the calculation in para 8.8.	= %
3	Apply the percentage at Step 2 to the DGT at Step 1.	£ ________

4	Total at Step 3 x VAT fraction. (7/47ths for VAT at 17.5 per cent.)	£ ______ This is your output tax on catering sales for this period.

Commentary—*De Voil Indirect Tax Service* **V3.565.**

8.8 How do I calculate the percentage of my standard-rated sales?

This paragraph has the force of law.

Your method of calculation must be able to satisfy us when we visit that the catering adaptation gives a fair and reasonable result in any period. Whichever way you choose to make your calculation you must always—

- base the calculation on a sample of your actual sales for a representative period. The representative period will depend on the nature of your business but you must be able to satisfy us that it takes account of hourly, daily and seasonal fluctuations;
- retain details of the sample, including the dates and times it took place; and
- carry out a new calculation in each tax period. You must not use a calculation that has been established by a previous owner of the business.

Commentary—*De Voil Indirect Tax Service* **V3.565.**

8.9 What is the legal basis for the catering adaptation?

The catering adaptation is published under VAT Regulations 1995 reg 67.

Commentary—*De Voil Indirect Tax Service* **V3.565.**

9 RETAIL CHEMIST ADJUSTMENT

This section supplements the rules in the "How to work" notices.

9.1 What is the liability of goods supplied on prescription?

The supply of goods dispensed by a registered chemist on the prescription of a medical practitioner is zero-rated under Group 12 of the Zero Rated Schedule of VATA 1994. You can find further information in Notice 701/31 "Health".

Commentary—*De Voil Indirect Tax Service* **V3.566.**

9.2 Why is an adjustment necessary?

Most Group 12 goods dispensed on prescription are standard-rated when purchased by the chemist but zero-rated when supplied to the patient. A number of items supplied on prescription such as gluten free bread, are zero-rated at purchase so a further adjustment is also necessary.

Commentary—*De Voil Indirect Tax Service* **V3.566.**

9.3 Does the adjustment apply to all the retail schemes?

No. If you are using a Point of Sale scheme you will be accounting for VAT at the correct rate. This is because you identify the correct rate of VAT at the time the supply is made and no adjustment is necessary. Also, the Retail Chemist adjustment cannot be used with Apportionment scheme (2).

Other retail schemes require the adjustments explained in para 9.4 in order to reduce the output tax which the scheme would otherwise produce.

If you use a direct calculation scheme, you must normally calculate Expected Selling Prices (ESPs) for your "minority" goods (see paras 3.10 and 3.13). However, if your minority goods are standard-rated sales, you may calculate ESPs on the basis of the zero-rated goods received for resale if this would be simpler for your business.

Commentary—*De Voil Indirect Tax Service* **V3.566.**

9.4 How does the adjustment work if I use the Direct Calculation schemes or Apportionment scheme (1)?

Whether you are using the first or the second Direct Calculation scheme or Apportionment scheme (1) you must make the following adjustment. *This paragraph has the force of law.*

Step	*Procedure*	*Result*

1	Calculate your Daily Gross Takings (DGT) including the total amount from your prescription charges and NHS cheque (less the value of any exempt supplies such as rota payments).	£ ________
2	Work out the output tax as explained in the Direct Calculation schemes notice or Apportionment schemes notice.	£ ________
3	Add up the payments received in the period for all Group 12 goods-even if you did not supply the goods in the period. Remember your NHS cheque may include payments for supplies not zero-rated under Group 12, but exempt or standard-rated. Such amounts must not be included in this total.	£ ________
4	Estimate the value of goods included in step 3 that were zero-rated when you received them (see para 9.5 below).	£ ________
5	Subtract the total at step 4 from the total at step 3.	£ ________
6	To work out the VAT you will have included in step 2 from Group 12 goods, multiply the total at step 5 by the VAT fraction (7/47ths for VAT at 17.5 per cent).	£ ________

Commentary—*De Voil Indirect Tax Service* **V3.566.**

9.5 How do I estimate the percentage of zero-rated supplies?

This paragraph has the force of law.

> The adjustments set out at para 9.4 require you to estimate a value for payments for all Group twelve goods that were zero-rated when you received them (see steps 3 and 4 of para 9.4). You must be able to satisfy us if we visit you that your estimation gives a fair and reasonable valuation in any period. Whichever way you choose to make your estimation you must always—
>
> – base the estimation on a sample of your actual purchases for a representative period. The representative period will depend on the nature of your business but you must take account of seasonal fluctuations, etc;
> – retain details of the sample; and
> – carry out a new estimation in each tax period. You must not use an estimation that has been established by a previous owner of the business.

Commentary—*De Voil Indirect Tax Service* **V3.566.**

10 SPECIAL ARRANGEMENTS FOR FLORISTS

10.1 About this section

This section applies to florists or other retailers who are members of organisations such as Interflora, Teleflorist and Flowergram which facilitate the purchase and delivery of flowers. It—

– supplements the rules in the "How to work" notices;
– replaces Notice 727/1 "Retail florists"; and
– has the force of law under regulation 67 of the VAT Regulations 1995 (SI 1995/2518).

Commentary—*De Voil Indirect Tax Service* **V3.567.**

10.2 Is an adjustment necessary for sales made by florists?

Yes. The adjustments you make will depend on your retail scheme and whether or not you are the member of an organisation such as one of those referred to in para 10.1 who—

– receives payment direct from the customer (the sending member); or
– delivers the flowers and receives payment from the organisation (the executing member).

Commentary—*De Voil Indirect Tax Service* **V3.567.**

10.3 How must I treat invoices issued by the agency?

The documents you receive from the agency may show the output tax which you must pay to us. This is known as "self-billed" output tax because the agency issues the invoice for the sales you make. You should check your agency documentation carefully and bring any tax shown to account outside your retail scheme. You do this by adding the self-billed output tax to any VAT calculated in accordance with your retail scheme.

You should find more about self-billed output tax in your agency documentation. You can find further information in Notice 700 "The VAT Guide" or you can ask your local VAT Business Advice Centre.

Commentary—*De Voil Indirect Tax Service* **V3.567.**

10.4 How does the adjustment work?

Depending on the scheme you use, you should follow the rules in the table below—

	As sending member you must …	*As executing member you must …*
Point of Sale	include the payments received in your Daily Gross Takings when you take the order. (No adjustment is necessary.)	not include payments received from the agency in your Daily Gross Takings; account for any tax due outside your retail scheme.
Apportionment (1) and (2)	identify from agency documentation the value of the sales you make as a sending member and account for any tax due outside your retail scheme; not include the payments for these sales in your Daily Gross Takings under the retail scheme calculation.	account for any tax due outside your retail scheme on the basis of the agency documentation; not include the agency payments in your Daily Gross Takings; exclude the value of flowers from your purchase records if you use the simple scheme-Apportionment scheme (1); adjust your Expected Selling Prices for the value of flowers sent as executing member and accounted for outside the retail scheme if you use Apportionment scheme (2).
Direct Calculation (1) and (2)	identify from agency documentation the value of the sales you make as a sending member and account for any tax due on those amounts outside your retail scheme; not include the payments for these sales in your Daily Gross Takings under the retail scheme calculation.	account for any tax due outside your retail scheme on the basis of the agency documentation; not include agency payments in your Daily Gross Takings; adjust your Expected Selling Prices for the value of flowers sent as executing member and accounted for outside the retail scheme.

Commentary—*De Voil Indirect Tax Service* **V3.567.**

…

Notice 727/3
Retail schemes—how to work the point of sale scheme

2002 with Update 1

1 INTRODUCTION

…

1.4 Force of law

Parts of this notice have the force of law under the VAT Regulations 1995, Part IX (regulations 66–75). All paragraphs in Section 6 and certain paragraphs in other sections have legal force and supplement the law. The text of these paragraphs is placed in a box and indicated by a statement.

Commentary—*De Voil Indirect Tax Service* **V3.552.**

...

2 GENERAL RULES

All boxed text in this section has the force of law (see para 1.4).

2.1 Who can use a retail scheme?

Any retailer who would find it difficult to account for VAT in the normal way can use a retail scheme. Accounting in the normal way does not require you to issue a tax invoice to unregistered customers. But it does require you to identify, for each sale, the tax exclusive value and the VAT and to be able to produce periodic totals of those amounts.

Commentary—*De Voil Indirect Tax Service* **V3.551.**

2.2 Can I use any retail scheme?

No. Some of the schemes have turnover limits (see para 3.2 for guidance on when to use the Point of Sale Scheme).

Otherwise, provided your chosen retail scheme produces a fair and reasonable result you may choose a scheme which suits your business best. Notice 727 "VAT Retail" schemes tells you more about choosing a retail scheme.

Commentary—*De Voil Indirect Tax Service* **V3.571, 574.**

2.3 Can I use the scheme to account for all my retail and non-retail supplies?

> No. Retail schemes can be used for retail supplies only.
>
> If you make a mixture of retail and non-retail sales you must only use a retail scheme to calculate the tax due on your retail sales. You must account for non-retail sales using the normal method of accounting.

2.4 What if my business makes sales to other VAT registered businesses?

> Sales to other VAT registered businesses must not be included in a retail scheme.
>
> The exception to this are occasional cash sales, for example—
>
> - a garage supplying petrol to a VAT registered customer; or
> - a retail DIY store supplying building materials to a VAT registered builder.

Commentary—*De Voil Indirect Tax Service* **V3.551.**

2.5 Can I change schemes?

Yes. You can change schemes at the end of a complete year, reckoned from the beginning of the tax period in which you first adopted the scheme. You must use the scheme for 12 months, unless—

- you become ineligible for the scheme you are using; or
- we allow or require an earlier change.

If you become ineligible you must cease using the scheme from the end of the next complete accounting period.

For example, if you account for VAT by reference to quarters ending March, June, September and December and your turnover makes you ineligible for a scheme during February, you must cease to use that scheme to account for supplies made on or after 1 July.

Commentary—*De Voil Indirect Tax Service* **V3.563.**

2.6 Can I change schemes retrospectively?

No. Retrospective changes to retail schemes are not normally allowed. The VAT and Duty Tribunals have repeatedly confirmed the principle that where you operate a scheme according to the published rules (or an agreed variation), the tax which is due under that scheme is the correct VAT for the period. You cannot change schemes retrospectively simply because another scheme produces a lower or different valuation.

We may allow retrospective change in exceptional cases. If you think you have exceptional grounds for a retrospective change you should write to your local VAT Business Advice Centre giving as much detail as possible.

The maximum period for recalculation following a retrospective change of scheme is three years and you must have been, and remain, eligible to use the new scheme during the full period for which you apply.

Commentary—*De Voil Indirect Tax Service* **V3.563.**

2.7 What should I do if I exceed the turnover limit?

If you think your annual retail turnover (excluding VAT) is about to exceed £130 million you should contact HMRC as soon as possible to agree a bespoke scheme. A bespoke scheme will be tailored to meet the particular requirements of your business and is likely to be a variation of one of the published standard schemes. For further information see Notice 727/2 "Bespoke retail schemes".

3 THE POINT OF SALE SCHEME

All boxed text in this section has the force of law (see para 1.4).

3.1 How does the Point of Sale Scheme work?

The Point of Sale scheme works by identifying the VAT liability of the goods or services you sell at the time you make the sale. This usually means using a till system which can distinguish between goods sold at different rates of VAT. However, we accept any system provided you can separate your sales, for example by using separate tills for different rates.

Commentary—*De Voil Indirect Tax Service* **V3.571.**

3.2 Can I use the Point of Sale Scheme rather than any other Retail Scheme?

> Yes. You can use the Point of Sale scheme if you are a retailer making supplies at two or more rates and you can identify the correct liability of the supplies at the time you make them (see para 2.2 for guidance on how to choose a retail scheme).
>
> However, you must use the Point of Sale scheme rather than any other retail scheme if you make supplies at only one positive rate (that is, all lower-rated or all standard-rated).

Commentary—*De Voil Indirect Tax Service* **V3.562.**

3.3 Can I use other schemes with the Point of Sale Scheme?

> Provided you are eligible to use the schemes, you can mix the Point of Sale scheme with either a Direct Calculation or an Apportionment Scheme.
>
> However, you cannot use different versions of the Apportionment Scheme and you must not mix a Direct Calculation Scheme with an Apportionment Scheme.
>
> NB Normally, the retail scheme uses a single calculation for the whole of your VAT registration. However, it is acceptable if you wish to use the same scheme separately at a number of distinct business locations. Then you may need to make adjustments to account for transfers between different parts of the business and you must agree the details of such adjustments with your local VAT Business Advice Centre.

You can always use the normal method of accounting together with any scheme or any allowable mixture for which you are eligible.

Commentary—*De Voil Indirect Tax Service* **V3.556.**

3.4 Do I need to keep any records?

You must keep—

> – a record of your Daily Gross Takings (DGT) and of how those gross takings are made up, as described in the DGT Checklist in Section 5; and
> – any working papers you use to calculate your output tax.

The normal record keeping requirements also apply. Notice 700 "The VAT Guide" tells you what is needed.

3.5 What if I operate the scheme incorrectly?

Any staff you employ need to be able to operate your system correctly, even at the busiest times. If you operate the scheme incorrectly you could underdeclare your output tax and be subject to an assessment and even a financial penalty.

4 MECHANICS OF THE POINT OF SALE SCHEME

4.1 How do I calculate VAT under the Point of Sale Scheme?

The Point of Sale scheme works by applying the appropriate VAT fraction to your total of positive-rated daily gross takings (DGT) to establish the amount of tax that is due on your eligible retail sales. This gives you your scheme output tax. Section 5 explains the DGT rules in detail.

The VAT fraction is simply a way of calculating the amount of VAT contained in the total gross takings. Notice 700 "The VAT Guide" tells you more about the VAT fraction.

Commentary—*De Voil Indirect Tax Service* **V3.571.**

4.2 Can you explain the scheme calculations step by step?

The boxed text below has the force of law (see para 1.4).

The following table is a step-by-step guide to how you must calculate your VAT using this scheme.

(a) Starting to use the scheme

From the day you start to use the scheme keep a record of your Daily Gross Takings (DGT) at each rate of VAT

(b) At the end of each tax period—

Step 1	Add up your DGT for standard-rated supplies for this tax period	£________
Step 2	Add up your DGT for lower-rated supplies for this tax period, if you have any	£________

(c) To calculate your scheme output tax—

Step 3	Multiply step 1 by 7/47 (VAT at 17.5%)	£________
Step 4	Multiply step 2 by 1/21 (VAT at 5%)	£________
Step 5	Add step 3 to step 4 to get the scheme output tax	£________

Commentary—*De Voil Indirect Tax Service* **V3.571.**

4.3 How do I complete my VAT return?

Your output tax figure is used to complete Box 1 of your VAT return (Form VAT 100). If you are using more than one scheme you must add together the output tax calculated by each scheme as well as any other amounts of output tax due and put the total in Box 1.

To help you fill in your VAT return see Notice 700/12 "Filling in your VAT return". You can get a copy by contacting our National Advice Service.

Commentary—*De Voil Indirect Tax Service* **V3.571.**

5 DAILY GROSS TAKINGS (DGT) CHECKLIST

All boxed text in this section has the force of law (see para 1.4).

The DGT is a record of your retail supplies and is a crucial part of your retail scheme records. It is important that you follow the guidance in this section on how to calculate your DGT.

5.1 What must I include in my Daily Gross Takings (DGT)?

From the day you start using the scheme you must keep a record of your DGT. You must include in your DGT record—

- all payments as they are received by you or on your behalf from cash customers for your retail supplies;
- the full value, including VAT, of all your credit or other non cash retail sales at the time you make the supply; and
- details of any adjustments made to this record.

The DGT record will normally be a till roll or copies of sales vouchers. It is this record and not simply cash on hand which constitutes your DGT.

Commentary—*De Voil Indirect Tax Service* **V3.556, 557.**

5.2 Are all forms of cash payment included in my DGT?

Yes. You must include and record the following in your DGT as they are received from your customers—
- Cash;
- Cheques;
- Debit or credit card vouchers;
- Switch, Delta or similar electronic transactions; and
- Electronic cash.

Commentary—*De Voil Indirect Tax Service* **V3.556, 557.**

5.3 Is my DGT simply a record of cash receipts?

No. You must also include the following in your DGT on the day you make the supply—
- the full value of credit sales (excluding any disclosed exempt charge for credit);
- the value of any goods taken out of the business for your own use;
- the cash value of any payment in kind for retail sales;
- the face value of gift, book and record vouchers redeemed (subject to para 6.17); and
- any other payments for retail sales.

Commentary—*De Voil Indirect Tax Service* **V3.556, 557.**

5.4 What transactions may reduce my DGT?

Your till roll or other record of sales constitutes your DGT and it is this figure which you must use when calculating output tax due under your retail scheme.

However, you may reduce your DGT for the following—

- Counterfeit notes;
- Customer overspends using Shopacheck;
- Illegible credit card transactions (where a customer's account details are not legible on the credit card voucher and therefore cannot be presented and redeemed at the bank);
- Inadvertent acceptance of a cheque guarantee card as a credit card;
- Inadvertent acceptance of foreign currency (where discovered at a later time, for example when cashing up);
- Inadvertent acceptance of out of date coupons which have previously been included in your DGT but which are not honoured by promoters;
- Instalments in respect of credit sales;
- Receipts recorded for exempt supplies;
- Receipts recorded for supplies which are to be accounted for outside the scheme;
- Refunds to customers for overcharges or faulty/unsuitable goods;
- Supervisor's float discrepancies;
- Till breakdowns (where incorrect till readings are recorded due to mechanical faults, for example till programming error, false reading and till reset by engineer);
- Unsigned or dishonoured cheques from cash customers (but not from credit customers);
- Use of training tills (where the till used by staff for training has been returned to the sales floor without the zeroing of figures); and
- Void transactions (where an incorrect transaction has been voided at the time of the error).

Commentary—*De Voil Indirect Tax Service* **V3.556, 557.**

5.5 How may I reduce my DGT for transactions listed in paragraph 5.4?

You must be able to provide evidence to support any adjustments to your DGT figure.

If you make an adjustment but subsequently receive a payment, you must include that payment in your DGT.

You must not reduce your DGT for till shortages which result from theft of cash, fraudulent refunds and voids or poor cash handling by staff. See para 6.31 for further details.

Commentary—*De Voil Indirect Tax Service* **V3.557.**

5.6 What if I am involved in transactions not covered in this section?

If you have a particular type of transaction which is not covered in this section, you may find further help in Section 6. There is also advice on the treatment of business promotions in Section 7.

Commentary—*De Voil Indirect Tax Service* **V3.557.**

6 SPECIAL TRANSACTIONS

All boxed text in this section has the force of law (see para 1.4).

If you have a particular type of transaction which is not covered in this section, obtain advice from your local VAT Business Advice Centre. The address and telephone number are in the phone book under "Customs and Excise".

6.1 Acquisitions from other EC member states

Notice 725 "VAT—The Single Market" explains how you account for VAT on goods purchased (acquisitions) from other EC member states.

Suppliers from elsewhere in the EC will not charge VAT on their sales to you but you will have to account for VAT at the rate applicable to the goods in the UK.

For retail scheme purposes, references in this notice to zero-rated goods apply only to goods which are zero-rated in the UK; goods which you acquire from other EC member states at zero-rate, but which are standard-rated in the UK, must be treated as standard-rated in your retail scheme calculations.

6.2 Amusement and gaming machines

Add the "taxable take" of the machine to your standard-rated Daily Gross Takings on the day you remove the cash and/or tokens from the machine.

For details of how to work out the taxable take, see Notice 701/13 "Gaming and amusement machines".

Commentary—*De Voil Indirect Tax Service* **V3.557.**

6.3 BT phonecards

The sale of BT phonecards is outside the scope of VAT (provided they are not sold for more than their face value). Exclude these sales from your Daily Gross Takings. Account for any commission received from BT outside your retail scheme.

If you deal in other types of phonecards you should consult your local VAT Business Advice Centre. The address and telephone number are in the phone book under "Customs and Excise".

Commentary—*De Voil Indirect Tax Service* **V3.557.**

6.4 Business entertainment/gifts

If you purchase goods specifically to consume in the course of business entertainment or to supply as gifts, or you supply such goods from your normal stock, you must account for any tax due by adding the value of the goods to your Daily Gross Takings at the relevant rate.

Commentary—*De Voil Indirect Tax Service* **V3.557.**

6.5 Business overheads

Exclude from your scheme any purchases of goods or services which are not for resale, for example your business overheads such as gas, electricity and rent.

Commentary—*De Voil Indirect Tax Service* **V3.557.**

6.6 Business promotions

See Section 7 of this notice.

6.7 Cash discounts

If you offer goods on cash discount or early settlement include the discounted value in your Daily Gross Takings at the time of the supply.

Commentary—*De Voil Indirect Tax Service* **V3.557.**

6.8 Catering supplies

See catering supplies in Notice 727 "VAT Retail schemes".

6.9 Credit transactions

Account for output tax on credit retail supplies by including the full value of the goods in your Daily Gross Takings (DGT) at the time you make the supply. Do not wait until you are paid and do not include the instalments in the DGT when they are received.

Additional rules apply depending on the way the credit sales are financed—

Supplies involving a finance company	If you arrange credit for your customer through a finance company you should include the full amount paid by the customer in your DGT at the time you make the supply.
Self-financed credit supplies	If you make a separate charge for credit (additional to the cash price) and you disclose it to the customer this is exempt from VAT and should be excluded from your DGT. NB. If your turnover is less than £1 million and you run a business where your customers do not pay for the goods when they receive them (for example you may be a milkman or newsagent) you may take account of opening and closing debtors in your scheme calculations. Notice 727 "VAT Retail Schemes" provides an example of how to do this.

Commentary—*De Voil Indirect Tax Service* **V3.557.**

6.10 Delivery charges

If, in order to fulfil your contract for the sale of the goods, you also deliver them, then there is a single supply of delivered goods. It does not matter whether the charge you make for delivery is separately itemised or invoiced. Examples of supplies of delivered goods are doorstep deliveries of milk or newspapers. The liability of the delivery charge follows the liability of the goods. In this case include the full amount charged in your Daily Gross Takings.

If you supply goods under a contract that does not require delivery but where, nevertheless, you agree to deliver the goods and make a separate charge, then that charge is for a standard-rated supply of services and any tax due must be accounted for outside your retail scheme.

Commentary—*De Voil Indirect Tax Service* **V3.557.**

6.11 Deposits

Most deposits are an advance payment for a supply and must be included in your Daily Gross Takings (DGT).

➡

However, if you take a deposit for another reason, for example as security to ensure the safe return of goods, you should exclude this amount from your DGT (regardless of whether it is eventually refunded or forfeited).

Commentary—*De Voil Indirect Tax Service* **V3.557.**

6.12 Dishonoured cheques/counterfeit notes

See the entry entitled "Unsigned or dishonoured cheques" in para 5.4.

6.13 Disposal of business assets

If you dispose of a business asset, such as a cash register or a van, you should account for VAT on the sale outside your retail scheme.

Commentary—*De Voil Indirect Tax Service* **V3.557.**

6.14 Exempt supplies

Any payments received for supplies which are exempt from VAT must be excluded from your scheme calculations. If you make exempt supplies, for example the sale of National Lottery tickets or financial services, you will need to consider the rules on partial exemption explained in Notice 706 "Partial exemption" and Notice 706/2 "The capital goods scheme".

Commentary—*De Voil Indirect Tax Service* **V3.557.**

6.15 Exports to countries outside the European Community

Retail Exports	If you make supplies under the terms of the retail export scheme as described in Notice 704 "VAT Retail exports", you should account for tax as follows— (a) Include in your Daily Gross Takings (DGT) all amounts, including VAT, for goods sold for retail export. Do not deduct the refunds which you expect to make to customers. (b) At the end of each tax period add up the amounts for standard-rated goods which have actually been exported. This will be the total of the amounts shown on the officially certified forms returned to you during the period. (c) Calculate notional tax on the total amount at (b), using the VAT fraction that applied at the time when you included the amounts in your DGT. (d) Subtract the notional tax at (c) from your retail scheme output tax.
Direct and Indirect Exports	If you export goods direct, or supply goods in the UK to overseas traders for subsequent indirect export by them, as described in Notice 703 "Exports and removals of goods from the UK", you should exclude these goods (which are supplied as direct or indirect exports) from your retail scheme calculations.

Commentary—*De Voil Indirect Tax Service* **V3.557.**

6.16 Florists

If you are a member of an organisation such as Interflora, Teleflorist and Flowergram, see Notice 727 "VAT Retail schemes".

6.17 Gift, book and record vouchers

If you …	*then …*
sell gift vouchers at a value higher than their face value	the excess is consideration for a supply of services and VAT should be accounted for outside the retail scheme. When you redeem the vouchers you must include their face value in your DGT.

If you …	*then …*
sell gift vouchers at their face value	do not include the amount in your DGT. But, when you redeem the vouchers you must include their face value in your DGT.
sell gift vouchers at a price lower than their face value	do not include the amount in your DGT. When you redeem the voucher, if you have evidence to prove that the voucher was supplied at a discount, then you may include the discounted amount in your DGT. Otherwise you must include the full face value of the voucher in your DGT.
include gift vouchers with other products for a single charge	the supply of the goods and voucher is treated as a multiple supply. This means VAT is only due on that portion of the payment which relates to the goods. You should omit from your DGT that part of the payment which relates to the gift voucher, usually the face value. But you must include in your DGT the face value of the voucher when redeemed by the customer.
issue gift vouchers free of charge	no VAT is due on issue. When the voucher is redeemed for goods no VAT is due unless the cost of the goods exceeds £50. If the cost exceeds £50, VAT is due on the full amount. However, if you also sell such vouchers and are unable to distinguish between the two types at redemption, then you must include the full face value of the voucher in your DGT when it is redeemed.
have purchased a third party's gift vouchers which you intend to issue free of charge (for example in your own promotion)	you normally have not been charged VAT. Equally, you do not have to account for any VAT when you give them away.
redeem gift vouchers and issue tax invoices to VAT registered businesses	you must account for these sales outside your retail scheme.

Commentary—*De Voil Indirect Tax Service* **V3.557.**

6.18 Goods bought at one rate and sold at another

For some goods the rate of tax you charge depends on how they are offered for sale. For example, meat is zero-rated when sold for human consumption but the same meat becomes standard-rated when sold as pet food. If you—

- are a chemist see Notice 727 "VAT Retail schemes".
- sell take-away food see Notice 709/1 "Catering and take-away food and the Catering Adaptation" in Notice 727 "VAT Retail schemes".
- sell young children's clothing see Notice 714 "Young children's clothing and footwear".

As the retailer, you are responsible for ensuring that the correct liability for VAT is applied when you sell goods. If you make a mistake you may underdeclare the amount of tax due, and so may be liable to an assessment and interest to correct the error.

Commentary—*De Voil Indirect Tax Service* **V3.557.**

6.19 Goods sold on "sale or return" or similar terms

You should keep a separate record of goods supplied on a "sale or return" basis. You should only include the amount due for these in your Daily Gross Takings (DGT) when the customer has adopted the goods. If the customer pays a deposit see para 6.11.

De Voil Indirect Tax Service **V3.557.**

6.20 Imports

If you import goods from countries outside the European Community, you should read Notice 702 "Imports".

6.21 Part-exchange

When you accept goods or services in part-exchange, you should include in your Daily Gross Takings the full selling price, including VAT, of the goods you supply.
If you resell goods you have accepted in part-exchange you may be able to use the Second-hand margin scheme see Notice 718 "Margin scheme for second-hand goods, works of art, antiques and collectors' items". If, however, you are unable to use that scheme you should include the part exchange goods in your retail scheme.

De Voil Indirect Tax Service **V3.557.**

6.22 Private or personal use of goods

Tax is due on any positive-rated goods purchased for resale but which you take out of your business for private or personal use. You must add the value of such goods to your Daily Gross Takings.

Commentary—*De Voil Indirect Tax Service* **V3.557.**

6.23 Refunds

You may deduct amounts which are refunded or credited to customers from your Daily Gross Takings, to a maximum of the amount originally charged.

Commentary—*De Voil Indirect Tax Service* **V3.557.**

6.24 Rented payphones

If you rent a payphone from BT or another supplier you are making supplies to users of the telephone and VAT is due on these supplies. Include the money from the payphone in your standard-rated Daily Gross Takings.

Commentary—*De Voil Indirect Tax Service* **V3.557.**

6.25 Retail sales to persons from other EC member states

Supplies made in the UK to persons from other EC member states should be accounted for as normal domestic retail sales.
Special arrangements apply to Distance Selling. This is where goods are sold to unregistered persons in other EC member states and the supplier is responsible for delivery to the customer. You can find out more about it in Notice 725 "VAT—The Single Market".

Commentary—*De Voil Indirect Tax Service* **V3.557.**

6.26 Road fuel

If you use road fuel for private motoring you must account for VAT on this outside the retail scheme, using the rules set out in Notice 700/64 "Motoring expenses".

Commentary—*De Voil Indirect Tax Service* **V3.557.**

6.27 Sale of discount vouchers or cards

If you sell discount vouchers or cards entitling the holder to discounts on purchases from you, you must include the payment received in your Daily Gross Takings (DGT).
For example, if the voucher or card can only be used for purchases of zero-rated goods, you should add the payments received for the voucher or card to your zero-rated DGT. ➡

> If you sell discount vouchers or cards entitling the holder to discounts at several traders, this is a standard-rated supply and you must add the payments received to your standard-rated DGT.

Commentary—*De Voil Indirect Tax Service* **V3.557.**

6.28 Saving stamps, travel cards and pools coupons

> These should be dealt with outside your scheme.

Commentary—*De Voil Indirect Tax Service* **V3.557.**

6.29 Sale or assignment of debts

> If you sell or assign debts due from your customers, no adjustment to your VAT account is necessary since you will already have included the correct amount when you made the supply.

Commentary—*De Voil Indirect Tax Service* **V3.557.**

6.30 Second-hand goods

> You may be able to use the special scheme for second-hand goods see Notice 718 "Margin scheme for second-hand goods, works of art, antiques and collectors' items".
>
> Alternatively, sales of second-hand goods should be accounted for within your retail scheme in the same way as new goods.

Commentary—*De Voil Indirect Tax Service* **V3.557.**

6.31 Theft, shrinkage, leakage and stock losses

> If you find that there are unexplained accounting discrepancies between stock and sales, you must consider the extent to which this is attributable to unrecorded sales, such as to the theft of cash by staff, and add the value back to your Daily Gross Takings.
>
> Where possible these adjustments should be allocated to the specific VAT period in which the theft took place. Otherwise, such shrinkage should be apportioned across relevant tax periods on a fair and reasonable basis.
>
> Unless you have evidence of the liability of the unaccounted supplies, adjustments must be in line with the usual proportion of standard against zero-rated supplies.

Commentary—*De Voil Indirect Tax Service* **V3.557.**

7 BUSINESS PROMOTIONS

All boxed text in this section has the force of law (see para 1.4).

7.1 About business promotion schemes in general

The general guidelines on the business promotion schemes covered in this section are given in Notice 700/7 "Business promotion schemes".

The VAT treatment under your retail scheme depends on whether the promotion is funded solely by you as the retailer or by, or together with, a third party such as the manufacturer.

If you wish to operate a particular promotion scheme which is not covered here you should contact your local VAT Business Advice Centre. The address and telephone number are in the phone book under "Customs and Excise". The timing of this adjustment should follow the rule in para 7.6(c).

Commentary—*De Voil Indirect Tax Service* **V3.557.**

7.2 Discount vouchers

As part payment	When you take a discount voucher as part payment, you should include only the amount of money received from your customer in your DGT. If you subsequently receive payment for the coupon from another source you must include the extra amount in your DGT.
Handling charges	If you make a further charge to a manufacturer for handling the coupons, this is payment for a supply which is exempt from VAT and should be excluded from your DGT.
Sale	If you sell discount vouchers—see para 6.27 of this notice.

Commentary—*De Voil Indirect Tax Service* **V3.557.**

7.3 Vouchers with no values or amounts but redeemable for whole items

Vouchers issued by you to customers making a specific purchase or purchases	No VAT is due upon issue and no further VAT is due when the voucher is used by the customer to obtain the reward goods.
Vouchers issued freely by you	No VAT is due upon issue. When the voucher is redeemed for goods no VAT is due unless the cost of the goods is over £50. VAT is then due on the value of those goods. See also para 6.4 regarding business gifts.
Vouchers issued by another person but redeemable with you	They are likely to be subject to the terms and conditions of that person's promotion. For example, you may be given certain stocks to give away on behalf of that person. Notice 700/7 "Business promotion schemes" contains further information. Alternatively, contact your local VAT Business Advice Centre. The address and telephone number are in the phone book under "Customs and Excise".

Commentary—*De Voil Indirect Tax Service* **V3.557.**

7.4 Vouchers redeemed for cash with you

If you redeem vouchers for cash, the cash payment is outside the scope of VAT. You must not alter your Daily Gross Takings (DGT) by the cash paid out.

Commentary—*De Voil Indirect Tax Service* **V3.557.**

7.5 Gift vouchers

See para 6.17 of this notice.

Commentary—*De Voil Indirect Tax Service* **V3.557.**

7.6 Goods linked in a promotion

These include promotions where—

Two different articles are sold for a single price in a combined offer, for example—

- a washing machine with an iron; or
- a jar of coffee with a packet of chocolate biscuits.

A number of same articles are sold in a multibuy offer, for example—

– "buy two and get a third free".

(a) If both articles are liable at the same rate of tax (as the washing machine/iron combined offer and the multibuy examples above), then there are no additional rules to follow under the Point of Sale scheme.

(b) If the articles are liable at different rates of tax (as the coffee/ biscuits combined offer in the examples above), then there are additional rules to apportion the selling price—

– you may use the method explained in Notice 700 "The VAT Guide"; or
– in the case of goods linked by the manufacturer, you may treat the articles in accordance with the information shown on the supplier's invoice. For example, if the invoice shows separate prices and amounts of tax, you may apportion your selling price on the same basis.

As a concession, where the minor article satisfies the criteria set out in Notice 700/7 "Business promotion schemes", you may account for VAT on the minor item at the same rate as the main article.

If an apportionment of the selling price is necessary, you must separate the amount allocated to the zero-rated article from your standard-rated takings before carrying out your scheme calculation.

(c) If a manufacturer or joint sponsor contributes towards payment for goods, then strictly speaking, when you receive a contribution from a manufacturer or joint sponsor representing partial payment for goods supplied to a customer, you should account for this in the period the goods are supplied.

However, as a concession, you may account for such contributions in the period you receive them from the manufacturer or joint sponsor.

(d) If a manufacturer or joint sponsor contributes, for example towards advertising, then you have made a separate supply of services and this must be dealt with outside your retail scheme.

Commentary—*De Voil Indirect Tax Service* **V3.557.**

…

Notice 727/4
Retail schemes—how to work the apportionment schemes

2002 with Updates 1 and 2

1 INTRODUCTION

…

1.4 Force of law

Parts of this notice have the force of law under the VAT Regulations 1995, Part IX (regulations 66–75). All paragraphs in Section 7 and certain paragraphs in other sections have legal force and supplement the law. The text of these paragraphs is placed in a box and indicated by a statement.

Commentary—*De Voil Indirect Tax Service* **V3.552.**

…

2 GENERAL RULES

All boxed text in this section has the force of law (see para 1.4).

2.1 Who can use a retail scheme?

Any retailer who would find it difficult to account for VAT in the normal way can use a retail scheme. Accounting in the normal way does not require you to issue a tax invoice to unregistered customers. But it does require you to identify, for each sale, the tax exclusive value and the VAT and to be able to produce periodic totals of those amounts.

Commentary—*De Voil Indirect Tax Service* **V3.551.**

2.2 Can I use any retail scheme?

No. Some of the schemes have turnover limits (see para 3.4 for guidance on the Apportionment Schemes).

Otherwise, provided your chosen retail scheme produces a fair and reasonable result you may choose the scheme which suits your business best. Notice 727 "VAT Retail schemes" tells you more about choosing a retail scheme.

Commentary—*De Voil Indirect Tax Service* **V3.571, 574.**

2.3 Can I use the scheme to account for all my retail and non-retail supplies?

> No. Retail schemes can be used for retail supplies only.
>
> If you make a mixture of retail and non-retail sales you must only use a retail scheme to calculate the tax due on your retail sales. You must account for non-retail sales using the normal method of accounting.

2.4 What if my business makes sales to other VAT registered businesses?

> Sales to other VAT registered businesses must not be included in a retail scheme.
>
> The exception to this is occasional cash sales, for example—
>
> – a garage supplying petrol to a VAT registered customer; or
>
> – a retail DIY store supplying building materials to a VAT registered builder.

Commentary—*De Voil Indirect Tax Service* **V3.551.**

2.5 Can I change schemes?

> Yes. You can change schemes at the end of a complete year, reckoned from the beginning of the tax period in which you first adopted the scheme. You must use the scheme for 12 months, unless—
>
> – you become ineligible for the scheme you are using; or
>
> – we allow or require an earlier change.
>
> If you become ineligible you must cease using the scheme from the end of the next complete accounting period.

For example, if you account for VAT by reference to quarters ending March, June, September and December and your turnover makes you ineligible for a particular scheme during February, you must cease to use that scheme to account for supplies made on or after 1 July.

Some schemes require adjustments when you cease using them (see paras 3.5 for guidance on the Apportionment Schemes).

Commentary—*De Voil Indirect Tax Service* **V3.563.**

2.6 Can I change schemes retrospectively?

No. Retrospective changes to retail schemes are not normally allowed. The VAT and Duty Tribunals have repeatedly confirmed the principle that where you operate a scheme according to the published rules (or an agreed variation), the tax due under that scheme is the correct VAT for the period. You cannot change schemes retrospectively simply because another scheme produces a lower or different valuation.

We may allow retrospective change in exceptional cases. If you think you have exceptional grounds for a retrospective change you should write to your local VAT Business Advice Centre giving as much detail as possible.

The maximum period for recalculation following a retrospective change of scheme is three years and you must have been, and remain, eligible to use the new scheme during the full period for which you apply.

Commentary—*De Voil Indirect Tax Service* **V3.563.**

3 BASIC PRINCIPLES OF APPORTIONMENT SCHEMES 1 AND 2

All boxed text in this section has the force of law (see para 1.4).

Unless stated otherwise, this section applies to both Apportionment Schemes 1 and 2.

3.1 How do the Apportionment Schemes work?

3.1.1 Apportionment Scheme 1

Apportionment Scheme 1 is the simpler scheme designed for smaller businesses with a tax exclusive turnover not exceeding £1 million. You work out the value of your purchases for retail sale at different rates of VAT and apply the proportions of those purchase values to your sales.

For example, if—

- 50 per cent of the value of your goods purchased for retail sale are standard rated;
- 30 per cent are lower-rated; and
- 20 per cent zero-rated,

your takings are treated as standard-rated, lower-rated and zero-rated in the same proportions. You then calculate your output tax by applying the relevant VAT fraction (or fractions if more than one positive rate is used) to these positive-rated takings figures.

Once a year you make a similar calculation based on your purchases for the year. This is compared with the tax you have paid to correct any over or under payment.

This scheme is relatively simple. However, if, on average, you achieve a higher mark-up for your zero-rated goods than your lower or standard-rated goods, you may find that you pay more tax if you use the simple Apportionment scheme than you would using another scheme.

3.1.2 Apportionment Scheme 2

Apportionment Scheme 2 is available to businesses with retail turnover, excluding VAT, not exceeding £130 million. You calculate the Expected Selling Prices (ESPs) of standard and lower-rated goods you receive for retail sale (para 5.3). You then work out the ratio of these to the ESPs of all goods received for retail sale and apply this ratio to your takings.

For example, if—

- 60 per cent of the ESPs of all goods you receive for retail sale are standard-rated; and
- 40 per cent are zero-rated,
- then 60 per cent of your takings are treated as standard-rated and 40 per cent as zero-rated. You then calculate your output tax by applying the relevant VAT fraction to these figures for takings.

This scheme can be complex to operate but, if worked properly, will provide a more accurate valuation of your supplies over a period of time.

Commentary—*De Voil Indirect Tax Service* **V3.572.**

3.2 Can I use other schemes with the Apportionment Schemes?

Yes. Provided you are eligible to use the schemes—

- you can mix the Point of Sale scheme with either of the Apportionment Schemes; but
- you cannot mix different versions of the Apportionment Schemes and you must not use an Apportionment Scheme in some parts of your business and a Direct Calculation Scheme in others.

NB Normally, the retail scheme uses a single calculation for the whole of your VAT registration. However, if you wish you can use the same scheme separately at a number of distinct business locations. But you may then need to make adjustments to account for transfers between different parts of the business and you must agree the details of such adjustments with your local VAT Business Advice Centre.

You can always use the normal method of accounting together with any scheme or any allowable mixture for which you are eligible.

Commentary—*De Voil Indirect Tax Service* **V3.572.**

3.3 Do I need to keep any records?

Yes. For both Apportionment Schemes 1 and 2 you must keep—

- a record of your Daily Gross Takings (DGT) and of how those gross takings are made up, as described in the DGT Checklist in Section 6; and
- any working papers you use to calculate your output tax.

Additionally, for Apportionment Scheme 2, you must keep—

- a record of your Expected Selling Prices (ESPs) as explained in para 5.3.

The normal record keeping requirements also apply. Notice 700 "The VAT Guide" tells you what is needed.

Commentary—*De Voil Indirect Tax Service* **V3.556.**

3.4 What should I do if I exceed the turnover limit?

The turnover limit for the scheme applies to the whole of your VAT registration.

3.4.1 Apportionment Scheme 1

If you think your annual tax exclusive turnover is about to exceed £1 million you should consider Apportionment Scheme 2 or any of the other standard retail schemes (para 2.2).

3.4.2 Apportionment Scheme 2

If you think your annual retail turnover, excluding VAT, is about to exceed £130 million you should contact HMRC as soon as possible to agree a bespoke scheme. A bespoke scheme will be tailored to meet the particular requirements of your business and is likely to be a variation of one of the published standard schemes. For further information see Notice 727/2 "Bespoke retail schemes".

3.5 What must I do when I cease to use the Apportionment Schemes?

3.5.1 Apportionment Scheme 1

> When you cease to use Scheme 1, you must perform a closing adjustment, as for the annual adjustment (see para 4.3.2), even if you leave before your scheme's first anniversary.

3.5.2 Apportionment Scheme 2

> When you cease to use Scheme 2, no adjustment is normally required. However, if you cease to use the scheme in one part of your business but continue to use it in other parts, make sure that the rolling calculation reflects the stock/Expected Selling Prices (ESPs) now excluded from the apportionment calculation.

3.6 Are there any other rules when I cease to use the Apportionment Schemes?

Apart from making the adjustments as explained in para 3.5, you should also remember—

- you can only include goods sold by retail in your scheme. If you transfer part or all of your business as a going concern and you cease to use the scheme, you will have to exclude the value of the stock which has been transferred from your retail scheme;
- if you cease to trade, VAT may become due on the value of your stocks and assets (see Notice 700/11 "Cancelling your registration"); and
- we may require additional adjustments where unusual patterns of trade prevent your chosen scheme from producing a fair and reasonable result.

> For these reasons you must always tell your VAT Business Advice Centre if you are—
> - intending to buy or sell part of a business; or
> - changing the legal entity of your business (for example, from sole proprietor to partnership); or
> - registered as a group and the composition of the group is to change.

4 MECHANICS OF APPORTIONMENT SCHEME 1

All boxed text in this section has the force of law (see para 1.4).

4.1 How do I calculate VAT under Apportionment Scheme 1?

The scheme works by applying the appropriate VAT fraction(s) to your total of positive-rated Daily Gross Takings (DGT) to establish the amount of tax that is due on your eligible retail sales. This gives you your scheme output tax. Section 6 explains the DGT rules in detail.

The VAT fraction is simply a way of calculating the amount of VAT contained in the total gross takings. Notice 700 "The VAT Guide" **(Part V8)** tells you more about the VAT fraction.

Commentary—*De Voil Indirect Tax Service* **V3.572.**

4.2 Starting to use Apportionment Scheme 1

> When you start to use the scheme remember—
> - you must not include goods you have in stock as goods received in the period. However, if you have stock items which you intend to sell and not restock, you may include these in your calculation, unless these goods have already been allowed for by you in a previous scheme;
> - the scheme is only for goods bought for retail sale. If you sell goods you have made or grown yourself, you will need to account for them outside the scheme; and
> - if you supply services or catering, you will need to account for them outside the scheme.

Commentary—*De Voil Indirect Tax Service* **V3.572.**

…

5 MECHANICS OF APPORTIONMENT SCHEME 2

All boxed text in this section has the force of law (see para 1.4).

5.1 How do I calculate VAT under Apportionment Scheme 2?

The scheme works by applying the appropriate VAT fraction(s) to your total of positive-rated Daily Gross Takings (DGT) to establish the amount of tax that is due on your eligible retail sales. This gives you your scheme output tax. Section 6 explains the DGT rules in detail.

The VAT fraction is simply a way of calculating the amount of VAT contained in the total gross takings. Notice 700 "The VAT Guide" tells you more about the VAT fraction.

Commentary—*De Voil Indirect Tax Service* **V3.572.**

5.2 Starting to use Apportionment Scheme 2

When you start to use the scheme remember—

- you will need to work out the Expected Selling Prices (ESPs) of goods in stock at each rate of tax and to use a rolling calculation as described in para 5.3; and
- if you supply services or catering, you will need to account for them outside the scheme.

Commentary—*De Voil Indirect Tax Service* **V3.572.**

5.3 Expected Selling Prices (ESPs) calculations for Scheme 2

To use this scheme you need to calculate ESPs and make adjustments to them as detailed here.

5.3.1 How do I calculate ESPs for Scheme 2?

How you calculate your ESPs has a direct effect on the tax you pay under the scheme. You must therefore calculate your ESPs as realistically and accurately as possible to reflect factors which might prevent you from achieving the price.

For example—

- price changes–increases and decreases, for example, sell by date reductions;
- special offers and promotion schemes;
- wastage;
- freezer breakdowns;
- breakages;
- shrinkage-pilferage and loss of stock; and
- bad debts that have been written off in the period.

The list is not exhaustive. If you are aware of other factors which affect your ESPs you must make the appropriate adjustments.

You can calculate your ESPs in any way that produces a fair and reasonable result but you must always be consistent in the method you use (both within one period and from one period to another). You must also record any adjustments and keep the working papers with your retail scheme calculations.

5.3.2 What must I not include in my ESP calculations for Scheme 2?

ESPs are used to calculate the value of your retail sales at different rates. Therefore, you must not include in your calculation—

- wholesale sales;
- goods bought for private use; or
- disposals of stock resulting from a sale of all or part of the business.

5.3.3 What if I have difficulty in making ESP adjustments for Scheme 2?

If you have difficulty in making these adjustments, you may need to use another scheme. However, your local office may—

- agree a method of sampling where reductions cannot be established accurately; or
- agree to the omission of certain adjustments where the effect does not distort your retail scheme.

Commentary—*De Voil Indirect Tax Service* **V3.572.**

5.4 Apportionment Scheme 2 calculations

The following is a step-by-step guide to how you must calculate your VAT using this scheme.

5.4.1 Expected Selling Prices (ESPs) of your opening stock

When you start to use the scheme you must establish the ESPs of your opening stock of goods for retail sale at each rate as follows—

Step 1	Work out the ESPs, including VAT, of standard-rated goods for retail sale in stock.	£______ Standard-rated stock
Step 2	Work out the ESPs, including VAT, of lower-rated goods for retail sale in stock.	£______ Low-rated stock
Step 3	Work out the ESPs, including VAT, of all goods for retail sale in stock.	£______ Total stock

If possible, you should carry out physical stock taking. Otherwise, you may use the ESP values of the goods you received for retail sale in the three months before you started to use the scheme.

5.4.2 Quarterly returns: Output tax for your first three periods

For each of your first three tax periods calculate your output tax for the period as follows—

Step 1 Add up your Daily Gross Takings for this tax period only £______

Step 2 Add up the Expected Selling Prices (ESPs), including VAT, of the standard-rated goods— £______
—received, made or grown for retail sale since you started to use the scheme;
—acquired from other European Community (EC) States since you started to use the scheme; plus
—your standard-rated stock figure at 5.4.1.

Step 3 Add up the ESPs, including VAT, of lower-rated goods— £______
—received, made or grown for retail sale since you started to use the scheme;
—acquired from other EC States since you started to use the scheme; plus
—your lower-rated stock figure at 5.4.1.

Step 4 Add up the ESPs, including VAT, of all goods-standard, lower and zero-rated— £______
—received, made or grown for retail sale since you started the scheme;
—acquired from other EC States since you started to use the scheme; plus
—your total stock figure at 5.4.1.

At the end of each tax period use these figures to work out what proportion of your Daily Gross Takings comes from sales at the positive rates of VAT—

Step 5 Total at step 1 × 7/47 (VAT at 17.5%) × Total at step 2
Total at step 4
£______

Step 6 Total at step 1 × 1/21 (VAT at 5%) × Total at step 3
Total at step 4
£______

Step 7 Total at steps 5 and 6 £______
This is your output tax for Apportionment Scheme 2

5.4.3 Quarterly returns—Output tax for your fourth and subsequent periods

For the fourth quarterly and all later quarterly periods you calculate your output tax for the period as follows—

Ignore the stock that you had in hand when you started to use the scheme

Step 1 Add up the Daily Gross Takings for this tax period only £______

Step 2 Add up the Expected Selling Prices (ESPs), including VAT, of standard-rated goods— £______
—received, made or grown for resale; or
—acquired from other EC States, in this period and the three previous tax periods

Step 3 Add up the ESPs, including VAT, of lower-rated goods— £________
—received, made or grown for resale; or
—acquired from other EC States in this period and the three previous tax periods

Step 4 Add up the ESPs, including VAT, of all goods, standard, lower and zero-rated—
—received, made or grown for resale; or
—acquired from other EC States, in this period and the three previous tax periods

At the end of each tax period, use these figures to work out what proportion of your Daily Gross Takings comes from sales at the positive rates of VAT—

Step 5 Total at step 1 × 7/47 (VAT at 17.5%) × Total at step 2
Total at step 4
£________

Step 6 Total at step 1 × 1/21 (VAT at 5%) × Total at step 3
Total at step 4
£________

Step 7 Total at steps 5 and 6 £________
This is your output tax for Apportionment Scheme 2

5.4.4 Monthly returns: Output tax for your first eleven periods

The method at para 5.4.2 applies for working out your output tax for the first eleven monthly returns.

5.4.5 Monthly returns—Output tax for your twelfth and subsequent periods

The method at para 5.4.3 applies for working out your output tax for the twelfth and later monthly returns. But as you make 12 returns in a year, you must include the previous 11 tax periods.

Commentary—*De Voil Indirect Tax Service* **V3.572.**

…

6 DAILY GROSS TAKINGS (DGT) CHECKLIST

All boxed text in this section has the force of law (see para 1.4).

The DGT is a record of your retail supplies and is a crucial part of your retail scheme records. It is important that you follow the guidance in this section on how to calculate your DGT.

6.1 What must I include in my Daily Gross Takings (DGT)?

From the day you start using the scheme you must keep a record of your DGT. You must include in your DGT record—

- all payments as they are received by you or on your behalf from cash customers for your retail supplies;
- the full value, including VAT, of all your credit or other non cash retail sales at the time you make the supply; and
- details of any adjustments made to this record.

The DGT record will normally be a till roll or copies of sales vouchers. It is this record and not simply cash on hand which constitutes your DGT.

Commentary—*De Voil Indirect Tax Service* **V3.556, 557.**

6.2 Are all forms of cash payment included in my DGT?

Yes. You must include and record the following in your DGT as they are received from your customers—

- Cash;
- Cheques;
- Debit or credit card vouchers;
- Switch, Delta or similar electronic transactions; and
- Electronic cash

Commentary—*De Voil Indirect Tax Service* **V3.557.**

6.3 Is my DGT simply a record of cash receipts?

No. You must also include the following in your DGT on the day you make the supply—

- the full value of credit sales (excluding any disclosed exempt charge for credit);
- the value of any goods taken out of the business for your own use;
- the cash value of any payment in kind for retail sales;
- the face value of gift, book and record vouchers redeemed (subject to para 7.18); and
- any other payments for retail sales.

Commentary—*De Voil Indirect Tax Service* **V3.557.**

6.4 What transactions may reduce my DGT?

Your till roll or other record of sales constitutes your DGT and it is this figure which you must use when calculating output tax due under your retail scheme.

However, you may reduce your DGT for the following—

- Counterfeit notes;
- Customer overspends using Shopacheck;
- Illegible credit card transactions (where a customer's account details are not legible on the credit card voucher and therefore cannot be presented and redeemed at the bank);
- Inadvertent acceptance of a cheque guarantee card as a credit card;
- Inadvertent acceptance of foreign currency (where discovered at a later time, for example when cashing up);
- Inadvertent acceptance of out of date coupons which have previously been included in your DGT but which are not honoured by promoters;
- Instalments in respect of credit sales;
- Receipts recorded for exempt supplies;
- Receipts recorded for goods or services which are to be accounted for outside the scheme;
- Refunds to customers for overcharges or faulty/unsuitable goods;
- Supervisor's float discrepancies;
- Till breakdowns (where incorrect till readings are recorded due to mechanical faults, for example till programming error, false reading and till reset by engineer);
- Unsigned or dishonoured cheques from cash customers (but not from credit customers);
- Use of training tills (where the till used by staff for training has been returned to the sales floor without the zeroing of figures); and
- Void transactions (where an incorrect transaction has been voided at the time of the error).

Commentary—*De Voil Indirect Tax Service* **V3.557.**

6.5 How may I reduce my DGT for transactions listed in para 6.4?

You must be able to provide evidence to support any adjustments to your DGT figure.

If you make an adjustment but subsequently receive a payment, you must include that payment in your DGT.

You must not reduce your DGT for till shortages which result from theft of cash, fraudulent refunds and voids or poor cash handling by staff. See para 7.34 for further details.

Commentary—*De Voil Indirect Tax Service* **V3.557.**

6.6 What if I am involved in transactions not covered in this section?

If you have a particular type of transaction which is not covered in this section, you must check Sections 7 and 8 to see if any of the rules there apply to your business before using the Apportionment Schemes to calculate your tax.

Commentary—*De Voil Indirect Tax Service* **V3.557.**

7 SPECIAL TRANSACTIONS

All boxed text in this section has the force of law (see para 1.4).

If you have a particular type of transaction which is not covered in this section, you should ask for advice from your local VAT Business Advice Centre. The address and telephone number are in the phone book under "Customs and Excise".

7.1 Acquisitions from other EC member states

Notice 725 "VAT—The Single Market" explains how you account for VAT on goods purchased (acquisitions) from other EC member states.

Suppliers from elsewhere in the EC will not charge VAT on their sales to you but you will have to account for VAT at the rate applicable to the goods in the UK.

For retail scheme purposes, references in this notice to zero-rated goods apply only to goods which are zero-rated in the UK; goods which you acquire from other EC member states at zero-rate, but which are standard-rated in the UK, must be treated as standard-rated in your retail scheme calculations.

Commentary—*De Voil Indirect Tax Service* **V3.557.**

7.2 Amusement and gaming machines

If you are using either of the Apportionment Schemes, you should exclude from your Daily Gross Takings the takings from the machines and account for the VAT due as explained in VAT Notice 701/13 "Gaming and amusements machines".

Commentary—*De Voil Indirect Tax Service* **V3.557.**

7.3 BT Phonecards

The sale of BT unused phonecards is outside the scope of VAT (provided they are not sold for more than their face value). Exclude these sales from your Daily Gross Takings. Account for any commission received from BT outside your retail scheme.

If you deal in other types of phonecards you should consult your local VAT Business Advice Centre.

Commentary—*De Voil Indirect Tax Service* **V3.557.**

7.4 Business entertainment / gifts

If you purchase goods specifically to consume in the course of business entertainment or to supply as gifts, you must account for any tax due outside your scheme.

If you supply these goods from your normal stock and operate—

- Apportionment Scheme 1, include the full value of the item in your Daily Gross Takings (DGT).
- Apportionments Scheme 2, include the full value of the item in your DGT and make the necessary adjustment to your ESPs for such goods.

Commentary—*De Voil Indirect Tax Service* **V3.557.**

7.5 Business overheads

Exclude from your scheme any purchases of goods or services which are not for resale, for example your business overheads such as gas, electricity and rent.

Commentary—*De Voil Indirect Tax Service* **V3.557.**

7.6 Business promotions

See Section 8.

7.7 Cash discounts

If you offer goods on cash discount or early settlement include the discounted value in your Daily Gross Takings at the time of the supply.

Commentary—*De Voil Indirect Tax Service* **V3.557.**

7.8 Catering supplies

See catering supplies in Notice 727 "VAT Retail schemes".

7.9 Chemists

See VAT Notice 727 "VAT Retail schemes".

7.10 Credit transactions

Account for output tax on credit retail supplies by including the full value of the goods in your Daily Gross Takings (DGT) at the time you make the supply. Do not wait until you are paid and do not include the instalments in the DGT when they are received.
Additional rules apply depending on the way the credit sales are financed—

Supplies involving a finance company	If you arrange credit for your customer through a finance company, our view is that in most cases you should include the full amount paid by the customer in your DGT at the time you make the supply. However, in some circumstances VAT may only be due on the amount you receive from the finance company. Business Brief 15/96 explains the circumstances in which this treatment may be appropriate.
Self-financed credit supplies	If you make a separate charge for credit (additional to the cash price) and you disclose it to the customer, this is exempt from VAT and should be excluded from your DGT. NB If your turnover is less than £1 million and you run a business where your customers do not pay for the goods when they receive them (for example, you may be a milkman or newsagent), you may take account of opening and closing debtors in your scheme calculations. Notice 727 "VAT Retail Schemes" provides an example of how to do this.

Commentary—*De Voil Indirect Tax Service* **V3.557.**

7.11 Delivery charges

If, in order to fulfil your contract for the sale of the goods, you also deliver them, then there is a single supply of delivered goods. It does not matter whether the charge you make for delivery is separately itemised or invoiced. Examples of supplies of delivered goods are doorstep deliveries of milk or newspapers. The liability of the delivery charge follows the liability of the goods. In this case include the full amount charged in your Daily Gross Takings.

If you supply goods under a contract that does not require delivery but where, nevertheless, you agree to deliver the goods and make a separate charge, then that charge is for a standard-rated supply of services and any tax due must be accounted for outside your retail scheme.

However, under—

- Apportionment Scheme 1, you must not make any adjustment to the record of purchases.
- Apportionment Scheme 2, you must allow for the delivery charge element in the calculation of ESPs.

You will find more about delivery charges and delivered goods in Notice 700 "The VAT Guide" and Notice 700/24 "Postage and delivery charges".

Commentary—*De Voil Indirect Tax Service* **V3.557.**

7.12 Deposits

Most deposits are advance payments for supplies and must be included in your Daily Gross Takings (DGT).

However, if you take a deposit for another reason, for example as security to ensure the safe return of goods you have hired out and you either refund it when the goods are returned safely or you forfeit it to compensate you for loss or damage, you should exclude this amount from your DGT.

Commentary—*De Voil Indirect Tax Service* **V3.557.**

7.13 Dishonoured cheques / counterfeit notes

See the entry entitled "Unsigned or dishonoured cheques" in para 6.4.

7.14 Disposal of business assets

If you dispose of a business asset, such as a cash register or a van, you should account for VAT on the sale outside your retail scheme.

Commentary—*De Voil Indirect Tax Service* **V3.557.**

7.15 Exempt supplies

Any payments received for supplies which are exempt from VAT must be excluded from your scheme calculations.
If you make exempt supplies, for example the sale of National Lottery tickets or financial services, you will need to consider the rules on partial exemption explained in Notice 706 "Partial exemption" and Notice 706/2 "The capital goods scheme".

Commentary—*De Voil Indirect Tax Service* **V3.557.**

7.16 Exports to countries outside the European Community

For—

- Retail Exports, if you make supplies for retail exports (including supplies to UK residents going abroad and to crew of ships and aircraft), under the terms of the retail export scheme as described in Notice 704 "VAT Retail exports"; and
- Direct and Indirect Exports, if you export goods direct, or supply goods in the UK to overseas traders for subsequent indirect export by them, as described in VAT Notice 703 "Exports and removals of goods from the UK",

you must allow for those exports in your scheme calculation as follows—

For either Retail Exports or Direct and Indirect Exports—

(a) Include in your Daily Gross Takings (DGT) all amounts, including VAT, for goods sold for retail export or sent for export.
(b) At the end of each tax period add up the amounts for standard-rated goods which have actually been exported or sent for export.
(c) Calculate notional tax on the total amount at (b), using the VAT fraction that applied at the time when you included the amounts in your DGT.
(d) Subtract the notional tax at (c) from your scheme output tax.

For Direct and Indirect Exports only—

(e) where you do not obtain proof of shipment within three months of the date on which you supplied the goods for export, you must enter the notional tax on those goods already calculated at (b) as an addition to the VAT PAYABLE side of your VAT account for the current tax period.

Commentary—*De Voil Indirect Tax Service* **V3.557.**

7.17 Florists

If you are a member of an organisation such as Interflora, Teleflorist or Flowergram, see Notice 727 "VAT Retail schemes".

Commentary—*De Voil Indirect Tax Service* **V3.567.**

7.18 Gift, book and record vouchers

If you ...	*then ...*
sell gift vouchers at a value higher than their face value	the excess is consideration for a supply of services and VAT should be accounted for on it outside the retail scheme. When you redeem the vouchers you must include their face value in your Daily Gross Takings (DGT).

sell gift vouchers at their face value	do not include the amount in your DGT. But, when you redeem the vouchers you must include their face value in your DGT.
sell gift vouchers at a price lower than their face value	do not include the amount in your DGT. When you redeem the voucher, if you have evidence to prove that that voucher was supplied at a discount, then you may include the discounted amount in your DGT. Otherwise you must include the full face value of the voucher in your DGT.
include gift vouchers with other products for a single charge	the supply of the goods and voucher is treated as a multiple supply. This means VAT is only due on that portion of the payment which relates to the goods. You should omit from your DGT that part of the payment which relates to the gift voucher, usually the face value. But you must include in your DGT the face value of the voucher when redeemed by the customer.
issue gift vouchers free of charge	no VAT is due on the issue. When the voucher is redeemed for goods no VAT is due unless the cost of the goods exceeds £50. If the cost exceeds £50, VAT is due on the full amount. However, if you also sell such vouchers and are unable to distinguish between the two types at redemption, then you must include the full face value of the voucher in your DGT when it is redeemed.
have purchased a third party's gift vouchers which you intend to issue free of charge (for example in your own promotion)	you will not normally have been charged VAT. Equally, you do not have to account for any VAT when you give them away.
redeem gift vouchers and issue tax invoices to VAT registered businesses	you must account for these sales outside your retail scheme.

Commentary—*De Voil Indirect Tax Service* **V3.557.**

7.19 Goods bought at one rate and sold at another

For some goods the rate of tax you charge depends on how they are offered for sale. For example, meat is zero-rated when sold for human consumption but the same meat becomes standard-rated when sold as pet food.

If you are a chemist see Notice 727 "VAT Retail schemes".

If you sell take-away food see VAT Notice 709/2 "Catering and take-away food and the Catering Adaptation" in Notice 727 "VAT Retail schemes".

If you sell young children's clothing see Notice 714 "Young children's clothing and footwear".

All other goods you buy at one rate of tax and sell at another should be treated as follows—

You must keep separate stocks of the goods that you put up or hold out for sale at the different tax rates. When they are received you must enter them in your records of goods received for resale at the tax rate that will apply when they are sold.

If you hold a common stock of those goods that you draw on to sell at different tax rates, depending on the scheme you are using, you must enter in your scheme records their cost to you or their ESP, at the tax rate that applied when you received them. But, when they are put up or held out for sale at the other tax rate, you must—

(a) deduct the appropriate amounts from your scheme records at the tax rate that applied when you received the goods; and

(b) enter the corresponding amounts in your scheme records at the tax rate that applies when you sell them.

As the retailer, you are responsible for ensuring that the correct liability for VAT is applied when you sell goods. If you make a mistake you may underdeclare the amount of tax due, and so may be liable to an assessment and interest to correct the error.

Commentary—*De Voil Indirect Tax Service* **V3.557.**

7.20 Goods bought from unregistered suppliers

If you buy goods for retail sale from suppliers who are not registered for VAT, you must include these goods in your scheme calculation at the appropriate rate.

Commentary—*De Voil Indirect Tax Service* **V3.557.**

7.21 Goods sold on "sale or return" or similar terms

You should keep a separate record of goods supplied on a "sale or return" basis. You should only include the amount due for these in your Daily Gross Takings (DGT) when the customer has adopted the goods.

Commentary—*De Voil Indirect Tax Service* **V3.557.**

7.22 Imports

If you import goods from countries outside the European Community, you should read Notice 702 "Imports".

De Voil Indirect Tax Service **V3.557.**

7.23 Part-exchange

When you accept goods or services in part-exchange, you should include in your Daily Gross Takings the full selling price, including VAT, of the goods you supply.

If you resell goods you have accepted in part-exchange you may be able to use the Second-hand Margin Scheme (see Notice 718 "Margin Scheme for second-hand goods, works of art, antiques and collectors' items"). If, however, you are unable to use that scheme you should include the goods previously taken in part exchange in your retail scheme.

Commentary—*De Voil Indirect Tax Service* **V3.557.**

7.24 Private or personal use of goods

Tax is due on any positive-rated goods purchased for retail sale but which you take out of your business for private or personal use (see Notice 700 "The VAT Guide"). You must add the value of such goods to your Daily Gross Takings.

If you operate—

- Apportionment scheme 1, include the full value of the item in your DGT.
- Apportionment scheme 2, include the full value of the item in your DGT and make any necessary adjustments to your ESPs.

Commentary—*De Voil Indirect Tax Service* **V3.557.**

7.25 Recall of goods by manufacturers

If a manufacturer recalls contaminated or otherwise faulty goods you must adjust your—

- purchase records if you use Apportionment Scheme 1; or
- ESP records if you use Apportionment Scheme 2.

Commentary—*De Voil Indirect Tax Service* **V3.557.**

7.26 Refunds to customers

You may deduct from your Daily Gross Takings amounts which are refunded or credited to customers in respect of taxable supplies of goods to a maximum of the amount originally charged.

Commentary—*De Voil Indirect Tax Service* **V3.557.**

7.27 Rented payphones

If you rent a payphone from BT or another supplier, you are making supplies to users of the payphone and VAT is due on these supplies. As this is a service the supplies must be dealt with outside the Apportionment Schemes.

Commentary—*De Voil Indirect Tax Service* **V3.557.**

7.28 Retail sales to persons from other EC member states

Supplies made in the UK to persons from other EC member states should be accounted for as normal domestic retail sales.
Special arrangements apply to Distance Selling. This is where goods are sold to unregistered persons in other EC member states and the supplier is responsible for delivery to the customer. You can find out more about it in Notice 725 "VAT—The Single Market" and Notice 700/1A "Distance Selling".

Commentary—*De Voil Indirect Tax Service* **V3.557.**

7.29 Road fuel

If you use road fuel for private motoring you must account for VAT on this outside the retail scheme, using the rules set out in Notice 700/64 "Motoring expenses".

Commentary—*De Voil Indirect Tax Service* **V3.557.**

7.30 Sale of discount vouchers or cards

If you sell discount vouchers or cards entitling the holder to discounts on purchases—

- from you, you must include the payment received in your Daily Gross Takings; or
- with several traders, this is a separate standard-rated supply of services and must be dealt with outside your scheme.

Commentary—*De Voil Indirect Tax Service* **V3.557.**

7.31 Sale or assignment of debts

If you sell or assign debts due from your customers, no adjustment to your VAT account is necessary since you will already have included the correct amount when you made the supply.

Commentary—*De Voil Indirect Tax Service* **V3.557.**

7.32 Saving stamps, travel cards and pools coupons

These should be dealt with outside your scheme.

Commentary—*De Voil Indirect Tax Service* **V3.557.**

7.33 Second-hand goods

You may be able to use the special scheme for second-hand goods (see Notice 718 "Margin scheme for second-hand goods, works of art, antiques and collectors' items").
Alternatively, sales of second-hand goods should be accounted for within your retail scheme in the same way as new goods.

Commentary—*De Voil Indirect Tax Service* **V3.557.**

7.34 Theft, shrinkage, leakage and stock losses

If you find that there are unexplained accounting discrepancies between stock and sales, you must consider the extent to which this is attributable to unrecorded sales, such as to the theft of cash by staff, and add the value back to your Daily Gross Takings. ➡

Where possible these adjustments should be allocated to the specific VAT period in which the theft took place. Otherwise, such shrinkage should be apportioned across relevant tax periods on a fair and reasonable basis. Unless you have evidence of the liability of the unaccounted supplies, adjustments must be in line with the usual proportion of standard against zero-rated supplies. When you do this exercise, you will need to consider whether the shrinkage for which you have adjusted your DGT requires you to further adjust your ESPs.

Commentary—*De Voil Indirect Tax Service* **V3.557.**

8 BUSINESS PROMOTIONS

All boxed text in this section has the force of law (see para 1.4).

The general guidelines on the business promotion schemes covered in this section are given in Notice 700/7 "Business promotion schemes".

The VAT treatment under your retail scheme depends on whether the promotion is funded solely by you as the retailer or by, or together with, a third party such as the manufacturer.

If you wish to operate a particular promotion scheme which is not covered here you should contact your local VAT Business Advice Centre. The address and telephone number are in the phone book under "Customs and Excise".

8.1 Discount vouchers

As part payment	When you take a discount voucher as part payment, you should include only the amount of money received from your customer in your Daily Gross Takings (DGT). If you subsequently receive payment for the voucher from another source you must include the extra amount in your DGT. The timing of the adjustment should follow the rule under the heading "When to account for manufacturer's contributions" in para 8.5.
Handling charges	If you make a further charge to a manufacturer for handling the vouchers, this is payment for a supply which is exempt from VAT and should be excluded from your DGT.
Sale	If you sell discount vouchers—see para 7.30.

Commentary—*De Voil Indirect Tax Service* **V3.557.**

8.2 Vouchers with no values or amounts but redeemable for whole items

Vouchers issued by you to customers making a specific purchase or purchases	No VAT is due upon issue and no further VAT is due when the voucher is used by the customer to obtain the reward goods. However, under Apportionment Scheme 2, you must adjust your ESPs for the reward goods.
Vouchers issued freely by you	No VAT is due upon issue. When the voucher is redeemed for goods no VAT is due unless the cost of the goods is over £50. VAT is then due on the value of those goods at the time you give them away and you must add that value to your DGT. You must also adjust the ESPs of the goods concerned under Apportionment scheme 2.

Vouchers issued by another person but redeemable with you	They are likely to be subject to the terms and conditions of that person's promotion. For example, you may be given certain stocks to give away on behalf of that person. These stocks must not be included in your retail scheme calculations. Notice 700/7 "Business promotion schemes" contains further information. Alternatively, contact your local VAT Business Advice Centre. The address and telephone number are in the phone book under 'Customs and Excise'.

Commentary—*De Voil Indirect Tax Service* **V3.557.**

8.3 Vouchers redeemed for cash with you

If you redeem vouchers for cash, the cash payment is outside the scope of VAT. You must not alter your Daily Gross Takings by the cash paid out.

Commentary—*De Voil Indirect Tax Service* **V3.557.**

8.4 Gift vouchers

See para 7.18.

8.5 Goods linked in a promotion

These include promotions where—

Two different articles are sold for a single price in a combined offer, for example—

- a washing machine with an iron; or
- a jar of coffee with a packet of chocolate biscuits.

A number of same articles are sold in a multibuy offer, for example—

"buy two and get a third free".

It is necessary to distinguish between business promotions where the supplier or sponsor contributes in whole or in part to the cost of the promotion, and those which are wholly sponsored by the retailer. This affects both how you treat your Daily Gross Takings (DGT) and how you carry out the rest of the calculation.	
Apportionment Scheme 1 Where such a contribution is received, it must be included in the DGT. No adjustment to purchases will be necessary for these promotions.	
Apportionment Scheme 2 Where such a contribution is received, it must be included in the DGT. You may also have to make appropriate adjustments to your Expected Selling Prices (ESPs). If the supplier/ manufacturer or sponsor makes—	
A full contribution	You should not make any ESP adjustments.
A partial contribution	You should adjust ESPs for the appropriate goods to the extent of the amount not supported by the manufacturer or sponsor.
No contribution	you will have to make an appropriate adjustment to the ESPs of the promotion goods.
If the promotion goods are liable at different rates of tax (as in the example of linked coffee and chocolate biscuits), there are additional rules to reflect the variation in your ESPs. You may— – use the method explained in Notice 700 "The VAT Guide"; or – in the case of goods linked by the manufacturer, treat the articles in accordance with the information shown on the supplier's invoice.	

For example, if the invoice shows separate prices and amounts of tax, you may apportion the ESPs of the linked goods on the same basis. As a concession, where the minor article satisfies the criteria set out in Notice 700/7 "Business promotion schemes", you may account for VAT on the minor article at the same rate as the main article. If you wish to take advantage of this concession, you will need to adjust the record of purchases or the ESPs of the promotion goods as appropriate.
When to account for manufacturer's contributions Strictly speaking, when you receive a contribution from a manufacturer or joint sponsor representing partial payment for goods supplied to a customer, you should account for this in the period the goods are supplied. However, as a concession, you may account for such contributions in the period they are received from the manufacturer or joint sponsor.
If a manufacturer or joint sponsor contributes, for example towards advertising, you have made a separate supply of services and this must be dealt with outside your retail scheme.

Commentary—*De Voil Indirect Tax Service* **V3.557.**

…

Notice 727/5
Retail schemes—how to work the direct calculation schemes

2002 with Updates 1 and 2

This notice cancels and replaces Notice 727/5 (August 1997)

1 INTRODUCTION

1.1 What is this notice about?

This notice tells you about Direct Calculation Schemes 1 and 2, two of the standard Retail Schemes. It explains the general rules applicable to the schemes, how the schemes work (including the calculation of VAT), and what records you should keep-especially your Daily Gross Takings (DGT) and your Expected Selling Prices (ESPs) records.

This notice has been restructured to improve readability, but the technical content has not been changed from the August 1997 edition (as amended/supplemented by updates).

This notice and others mentioned are available both on paper and on our Internet website at www.hmce.gov.uk.

Commentary—*De Voil Indirect Tax Service* **V3.571.**

1.2 Who should read this notice?

You should read this if—

- you are a VAT registered business making retail sales;
- you are unable to account for VAT on those sales in the normal way (see para 2.1); and
- your annual turnover, excluding VAT, does not exceed £130 million.

Commentary—*De Voil Indirect Tax Service* **V3.571.**

1.3 Are there other retail schemes?

Yes. Other standard retail schemes are the Point of Sale Scheme and the Apportionment Schemes. Businesses whose annual retail turnover exceeds £130 million cannot use a standard scheme. Instead they can agree a bespoke retail scheme (see para 3.5).

Commentary—*De Voil Indirect Tax Service* **V3.552.**

1.4 Force of law

Parts of this notice have the force of law under the VAT Regulations 1995, Part IX (regs 66–75). All paragraphs in Section 6 and certain paragraphs in other sections have legal force and supplement the law. The text of these paragraphs is placed in a box and indicated by a statement.

Commentary—*De Voil Indirect Tax Service* **V3.552.**

1.5 Where can I find out about the other schemes?

You will find a general introduction to retail schemes as well as guidance on choosing a retail scheme in Notice 727 "VAT Retail Schemes".

Details of the other schemes can be found in—
Notice 727/2 "Bespoke Retail Schemes";
Notice 727/3 "How to work the Point of Sale Scheme"; and
Notice 727/4 "How to work the Apportionment Schemes".

2 GENERAL RULES

All boxed text in this section has the force of law (see para 1.4).

2.1 Who can use a retail scheme?

Any retailer who would find it difficult to account for VAT in the normal way can use a retail scheme. Accounting in the normal way does not require you to issue a tax invoice to unregistered customers. But it does require you to identify, for each sale, the tax exclusive value and the VAT and to be able to produce periodic totals of those amounts.

Commentary—*De Voil Indirect Tax Service* **V3.551.**

2.2 Can I use any retail scheme?

No. Some of the schemes have turnover limits (see para 3.5 for guidance on the Direct Calculation Schemes).

Otherwise, provided your chosen retail scheme produces a fair and reasonable result you may choose the scheme which suits your business best. Notice 727 "VAT Retail schemes" tells you more about choosing a retail scheme.

De Voil Indirect Tax Service **V3.571, 574.**

2.3 Can I use the scheme to account for all my retail and non-retail supplies?

No. Retail schemes can be used for retail supplies only.

If you make a mixture of retail and non-retail sales you must only use a retail scheme to calculate the tax due on your retail sales. You must account for non-retail sales using the normal method of accounting.

2.4 What if my business makes sales to other VAT registered businesses?

Sales to other VAT registered businesses must not be included in a retail scheme.

The exception to this are occasional cash sales, for example—

- a garage supplying petrol to a VAT registered customer; or
- a retail DIY store supplying building materials to a VAT registered builder.

Commentary—*De Voil Indirect Tax Service* **V3.551.**

2.5 Can I change schemes?

Yes. You can change schemes at the end of a complete year, reckoned from the beginning of the tax period in which you first adopted the scheme. You must use the scheme for 12 months, unless—

- you become ineligible for the scheme you are using; or
- we allow or require an earlier change.

If you become ineligible you must cease using the scheme from the end of the next complete accounting period.

For example, if you account for VAT by reference to quarters ending March, June, September and December and your turnover makes you ineligible for a scheme during February, you must cease to use that scheme to account for supplies made on or after 1 July. Some schemes require adjustments when you cease using them (see para 3.6 for guidance on the Direct Calculation Schemes).

Commentary—*De Voil Indirect Tax Service* **V3.563.**

2.6 Can I change schemes retrospectively?

No. Retrospective changes to retail schemes are not normally allowed. The VAT and Duty Tribunals have repeatedly confirmed the principle that where you operate a scheme according to the published rules (or an agreed variation), the tax due under that scheme is the correct VAT for the period. You cannot change schemes retrospectively simply because another scheme produces a lower or different valuation.

We may allow retrospective change in exceptional cases. If you think you have exceptional grounds for a retrospective change you should write to your local VAT Business Advice Centre giving as much detail as possible.

The maximum period for recalculation following a retrospective change of scheme is three years and you must have been, and remain, eligible to use the new scheme during the full period for which you apply.

Commentary—*De Voil Indirect Tax Service* **V3.563.**

3 BASIC PRINCIPLES OF DIRECT CALCULATION SCHEMES 1 AND 2

All boxed text in this section has the force of law (see para 1.4).

Unless stated otherwise, this section applies to both Direct Calculation Schemes 1 and 2.

3.1 How do the Direct Calculation Schemes work?

The schemes work by calculating the Expected Selling Price (ESPs) of goods for retail sale at one or two rates of VAT in order to establish the proportion of your Daily Gross Takings (DGT) on which VAT is due.

> You must always calculate the Expected Selling Prices of your "minority goods". These are the goods at the rate of tax which forms the smallest proportion of your retail supplies. But see an exception to this rule in 4.2.1.

For example, if you make—

- 60 per cent standard-rated sales; and
- 40 per cent zero-rated sales,

your minority goods are your zero-rated goods. You therefore calculate the Expected Selling Prices (ESPs) for your zero-rated goods received, made or grown for retail sale and then deduct this from your Daily Gross Takings. This gives you your figure for standard-rated sales, to which you apply the VAT fraction to arrive at your output tax liability.

On the other hand, if you make—

- 60 per cent zero-rated sales; and
- 40 per cent standard-rated sales,

your minority goods are your standard-rated goods. You calculate the ESPs for your standard-rated goods received, made or grown for retail sale. You then apply the VAT fraction to this figure to arrive at your output tax liability.

Commentary—*De Voil Indirect Tax Service* **V3.573.**

3.2 What other rules are there when using the Direct Calculation Schemes?

Both schemes work mainly on the premise that you supply goods at two rates of tax (standard and zero). For calculation purposes, if you supply goods at all three rates (standard, lower and zero), the lower-rated supplies are always assumed to be the second minority goods (see Section 4).

Scheme 2 operates in the same way as Scheme 1, but requires an annual stock adjustment to correct any under or overpayment of VAT during the year (see para 4.5).

You should also note—

> - if your minority goods are zero-rated you cannot use the schemes for zero-rated supplies of services;
> - if your minority goods are standard-rated you cannot use the schemes for standard-rated supplies of services; and
> - you may not use the schemes for supplies of catering.

If you set Expected Selling Prices (ESPs) for standard-rated goods and your standard-rated stock has a slow turnover you should be aware that the scheme may not be the best suited to your business, as you will pay VAT in the period in which the goods are received and not necessarily when they are sold.

The Direct Calculation scheme can be relatively simple if you have a small proportion of supplies at one rate. But the scheme can produce significant inaccuracies if Expected Selling Prices are not calculated accurately. Additionally it can be complex to work if you sell goods at three rates of tax, though it may be possible to account for a small number of goods at a third rate outside the scheme.

Commentary—*De Voil Indirect Tax Service* **V3.573.**

3.3 Can I use other schemes with the Direct Calculation Schemes?

> Yes. Provided you are eligible to use the schemes— ➜

> – you can mix the Point of Sale Scheme with either of the Direct Calculation Scheme; but
> – you cannot mix different versions of the Direct Calculation Schemes and you must not use a Direct Calculation Scheme in some parts of your business and an Apportionment Scheme in others.
>
> NB Normally, the retail scheme uses a single calculation for the whole of your VAT registration. However, if you wish you can use the same scheme separately at a number of distinct business locations. But you may then need to make adjustments to account for transfers between different parts of the business and you must agree the details of such adjustments with your local VAT Business Advice Centre.

You can always use the normal method of accounting together with any scheme or any allowable mixture for which you are eligible.

Commentary—*De Voil Indirect Tax Service* **V3.562.**

3.4 Do I need to keep any records?

> Yes. You must keep—
> – a record of your Daily Gross Takings (DGT) and how those gross takings are made up, as described in the DGT Checklist in Section 5;
> – any working papers you use to calculate your output tax; and
> – a record of your Expected Selling Prices (ESPs) as explained in para 4.3.

The normal record keeping requirements also apply. Notice 700 "The VAT Guide" tells you what is needed.

Commentary—*De Voil Indirect Tax Service* **V3.566.**

3.5 What should I do if I exceed the turnover limits?

Direct Calculation Scheme 1 is available to businesses with an annual tax exclusive retail turnover not exceeding £1 million. If you think your annual tax exclusive turnover is about to exceed £1 million you should consider Direct Calculation Scheme 2 or any of the other standard retail schemes (para 2.2).

Direct Calculation Scheme 2 is available to businesses with an annual retail turnover, excluding VAT, between £1 million and £130 million. If you think your annual turnover, excluding VAT, is about to exceed £130 million you should contact HMRC as soon as possible to agree a bespoke scheme. A bespoke scheme will be tailored to meet the particular requirements of your business and is likely to be a variation of one of the published standard schemes. For further information see Notice 727/2 "Bespoke retail schemes".

> For both Schemes 1 and 2, the turnover limits apply to the whole of your VAT registration.
>
> If your turnover is over £1 million and you wish to use a Direct Calculation scheme you must operate Scheme 2.

3.6 What must I do when I cease to use the Direct Calculation Schemes?

> Direct Calculation Scheme 1—No adjustment is normally required.
>
> Direct Calculation Scheme 2—You must do a closing adjustment, as for the annual adjustment (para 4.5), even if you leave before the anniversary of starting to use the scheme. The adjustment must include the tax periods since your last adjustment and must take account of any disposals made during the year which were not by way of retail sale. You do this by excluding from the figures used in your calculation the value of any goods which were previously part of the retail scheme but have not been sold by way of retail. You must also make an adjustment if a part of your business leaves the scheme.

Commentary—*De Voil Indirect Tax Service* **V3.573.**

3.7 Are there any other rules when I cease to use the schemes?

Apart from making the adjustments as explained in para 3.6, you should also remember—

– you can only include retail sale of goods in your scheme. If you transfer part or all of your business as a going concern and you cease to use the scheme, you will have to exclude the value of the stock which has been transferred from your retail scheme;

– if you cease to trade, VAT may become due on the value of your stocks and assets (see Notice 700/11 "Cancelling your registration"); and

– we may require additional adjustments where unusual patterns of trade prevent your chosen scheme from producing a fair and reasonable result.

> For these reasons you must always tell your VAT Business Advice Centre if you are—
> – intending to buy or sell part of a business; or
> – changing the legal entity of your business (for example, from sole proprietor to partnership); or
> – registered as a group and the composition of the group is to change.

Commentary—*De Voil Indirect Tax Service* **V3.261.**

4 MECHANICS OF THE DIRECT CALCULATION SCHEMES (1 AND 2)

All boxed text in this section has the force of law (see para 1.4).

Apart from the requirement under Scheme 2 to carry out a stock-take and to make an annual adjustment (para 4.5), both Direct Calculation Schemes work in very much the same way. Unless stated otherwise, the rules in this section apply to both schemes.

The calculations (for both zero- and standard-rated minority goods detailed here) assume that the second minority goods are liable to tax at the lower rate.

4.1 How do I calculate VAT under the Direct Calculation Schemes?

The Direct Calculation Schemes work by applying the appropriate VAT fraction(s) to your total of positive-rated Daily Gross Takings (DGT) to establish the amount of tax that is due on your eligible retail sales. This gives you your scheme output tax. Section 5 explains the DGT rules in detail.

The VAT fraction is simply a way of calculating the amount of VAT contained in the total gross takings. Notice 700 "The VAT Guide" tells you more about the VAT fraction.

Commentary—*De Voil Indirect Tax Service* **V3.573.**

4.2 Starting to use the Direct Calculation Schemes

4.2.1 Before you start to use the Direct Calculation Schemes

Before you start to use a Direct Calculation scheme you have to decide which goods you are going to set Expected Selling Prices (ESPs) for. You will have to estimate whether the larger portion of your sales is standard-rated or zero-rated. If you also make lower-rated supplies you will have to consider these in making your estimate.

> You must calculate your ESPs for the goods forming the smallest proportion (your minority goods) of your supplies. (See the example in para 3.1).
>
> Once you have started to set ESPs for minority goods, you must continue to set ESPs for that rate of goods for the whole of the retail scheme year.
>
> However, retailers using Direct Calculation Scheme 1 may mark up the "majority" goods if it is more straightforward for them to do so.

For example, newsagents will probably find it easier to set ESPs for their majority sales of magazines and newspapers. There will be fewer purchase records for these than for their minority standard rated sales of tobacco and confectionery which may come from a variety of sources.

4.2.2 When you start to use the Direct Calculation Schemes

> When you start to use the scheme remember—
>
> for Direct Calculation Schemes 1 or 2, you must not include goods you have in stock as goods received in the period. However, if you have stock items which you intend to sell and not restock, you may include these in your calculation for the first period, unless these goods have already been allowed for by you in a previous scheme; and
>
> additionally for Direct Calculation Scheme 2, you must know the ESPs of the minority goods in stock, although you will not need to use this information until the annual adjustment is due.

Commentary—*De Voil Indirect Tax Service* **V3.573.**

4.3 Expected Selling Prices (ESPs)

To use this scheme you need to calculate ESPs and make adjustments to them as detailed here.

4.3.1 How do I calculate ESPs?

> How you calculate your ESPs has a direct effect on the tax you pay under the scheme. You must therefore calculate your ESPs as accurately as possible.

You can calculate your ESPs in any way that produces a fair and reasonable result. However, you must always use the same method and you must also make the adjustments described in para 4.3.3.

The most common methods of calculating ESPs are—

(a) mark up each line of goods—this is the most accurate method; or
(b) mark up classes of goods—for example vegetables or confectionery; or
(c) use recommended retail prices.

> You can only use method (b) if—
>
> – you are unable to mark up each line, as in (a) above;
> – the variation in mark up within the group is no more than 10 per cent;
> – the mark up is reviewed each quarter; and
> – the class of goods has a commercial basis and is not constructed artificially.
>
> You can only use method (c) if—
>
> – you are able to record the recommended retail selling price (RRP) on receipt of the goods; and
> – your invoices or other supplier documentation show the tax inclusive RRP of each separate line of goods, distinguish standard-rated, lower-rated and zero-rated sales and total goods at each rate of tax.

4.3.2 What must I not include in my ESP calculations?

> ESPs are used to calculate the value of your retail sales at different rates. Therefore, you must not include in your calculation—
>
> – wholesale sales;
> – goods bought for private use; or
> – disposals of stock resulting from a sale of all or part of the business.

4.3.3 ESP Adjustment

> As ESPs will rarely be fully achieved in your retail scheme you must make adjustments at the end of each tax period to take account of factors which might affect the selling price.
>
> For example—
>
> – price changes—increases and decreases, for example, sell by date reductions;
> – special offers and promotion schemes;
> – wastage;
> – freezer breakdowns;
> – breakages;
> – shrinkage—pilferage and loss of stock; and
> – bad debts that have been written off in the period.
>
> This list is not exhaustive; if you are aware of other factors which affect your ESPs you must make the appropriate adjustment.
>
> How you make these adjustments is up to you but you must always be consistent in the method you use (both within one period and from one period to another). You must also record any adjustments and keep the working papers with your retail scheme calculations.

4.3.4 What if I have difficulty in making ESP adjustments?

If you have difficulty in making these adjustments, you may need to use another scheme. However, your local office may:

– agree a method of sampling where reductions cannot be established accurately; or
– agree to the omission of certain adjustments where the effect does not distort your retail scheme.

Commentary—*De Voil Indirect Tax Service* **V3.573.**

4.4 Direct Calculation Schemes 1 and 2 calculations

> If you are using Direct Calculation Scheme 2 you must also make the adjustment described in para 4.5 after you have calculated your output tax for the fourth quarter, and you must account for any difference on your return for that quarter.

The following is a step-by-step guide to how you must calculate your VAT using Schemes 1 or 2.

4.4.1 Setting ESPs for zero-rated goods

The calculation assumes that the second minority goods are liable to tax at the lower rate.

If you set ESPs for zero-rated goods then you should make your scheme calculation as follows—

Step 1	Add up your Daily Gross Takings (DGT) for this tax period (see Section 5)	£________
Step 2	Add up the Expected Selling Prices (ESPs) of your zero-rated goods received, made or grown for retail sale in the tax period (adjusted as in para 4.3.3)	£________
Step 3	Deduct the total at step 2 from the total at step 1 to work out the standard-rated element of your takings	
Step 4	Multiply the total at step 3 by 7/47 (VAT at 17.5 per cent) If you make supplies at only two rates of tax, this is your Scheme 1 or 2 output tax	

If you also make supplies at the lower rate you will need to make the following additional calculation—

Step 5	Add up the Expected Selling Prices (ESPs) of your lower-rated goods received, made or grown for retail sale in the tax period (adjusted as in para 4.3.3)	£________
Step 6	Multiply the figure at step 5 by 1/21 (VAT at 5 per cent)	£________
Step 7	Multiply the figure at step 5 by 7/47 (VAT at 17.5 per cent)	£________
Step 8	Deduct the tax figure at step 6 from the tax figure at step 7	£________
Step 9	Reduce the figure for output tax at step 4 by the figure at step 8 to arrive at your scheme output tax	£________

4.4.2 *Setting ESPs for standard-rated goods*

The calculation assumes that the second minority goods are liable to tax at the lower rate.

If you set ESPs for standard-rated goods then you should make your scheme calculation as follows—

Step 1	Add up your Daily Gross Takings (DGT) for this tax period (see para 5). Although this is not used in this calculation, it is still a requirement of operating the scheme and is also used in completing your VAT return	£________
Step 2	Add up the Expected Selling Prices (ESPs) of your standard-rated goods received, made or grown for retail sale in the tax period (adjusted as in para 4.3.3)	£________

Step 3	Multiply the figure at step 2 by 7/47 (VAT at 17.5 per cent) If you make supplies at only two rates of tax, this is your Scheme 1 or 2 output tax	£_______
If you also make supplies at the lower rate you will need to make the following additional calculation—		
Step 4	Add up the ESPs of your lower-rated goods received, made or grown for retail sale in the tax period (adjusted as in para 4.3.3)	£_______
Step 5	Multiply the figure at step 4 by 1/21 (VAT at 5 per cent)	£_______
Step 6	Add the tax figure at step 5 to the tax figure at step 3	£_______

Commentary—*De Voil Indirect Tax Service* **V3.573.**

4.5 Annual adjustment (for Direct Calculation Scheme 2 only)

This sub-section details the annual adjustment required if you use Direct Calculation Scheme 2.

Scheme 2 is based on your retail trade over a full year. This year runs from the beginning of the first tax period in which you use the scheme.

At the end of each year you make an adjustment to reflect the actual sales made by your retail outlets during the year. It compares the movement in stock and levels of goods received, made or grown for retail resale, with what has been accounted for under the scheme calculations for the year.

> Once you have calculated your output tax due under the retail scheme for the fourth quarter, as in para 4.4, you must carry out the annual adjustment as described below.

4.5.1 If you set ESPs for zero-rated goods

The adjustment assumes that the second minority goods are liable to tax at the lower rate.

The adjustment must take account of any disposals since the last adjustment which were not made by way of retail sale. You do this by excluding from the figures used in the calculation the value of any goods which were previously part of the scheme calculation, or included in the opening stock figure, but have not been sold by way of retail. The adjustment is also required if a part of your business leaves the scheme.		
Step 1	When you begin to use the scheme establish the Expected Selling Prices (ESPs) of your opening stock of zero-rated goods for retail sale making any necessary adjustments as in para 4.3.3	£_______
Step 2	Add up your Daily Gross Takings (DGT) for the four quarters	£_______
Step 3	Total the ESPs of your zero-rated goods received, made or grown for retail sale in the four quarters, adjusted as in para 4.3.3, and add the opening zero-rated stock figure at step 1	£_______

Step 4	At the end of the scheme year, or when you cease to use the scheme, establish the ESPs of your closing stock of zero-rated goods for retail sale. (This becomes your opening zero-rated stock figure for the next year)	£________
Step 5	Deduct the figure at step 4 from the figure at step 3. This gives the ESPs for the zero-rated goods you have sold by retail in the year	£________
If you make supplies at only two rates of tax complete steps 6–9. If you make supplies at three rates of tax, omit steps 6–9 and go to step 10.		
Step 6	Deduct the figure at step 5 from the figure at step 2. This gives you your standard-rated takings for the year	£________
Step 7	Multiply the figure at 6 by 7/47 (VAT at 17.5 per cent)	£________
Step 8	Add up the output tax you have paid under the retail scheme in the four quarters	£________
Step 9	If the figure at step 7 is greater than the figure at step 8 you have paid too little tax and you should add the difference to your output tax in the fourth quarter. If the figure at step 7 is smaller than the figure at step 8 you have paid too much tax and you should deduct the difference from your output tax in the fourth quarter.	£________
Steps 10–20 are only necessary if you make supplies at three rates of tax.		
Step 10	When you begin to use the scheme establish the ESPs of your opening stock of lower-rated goods for retail sale, making any necessary adjustments as in para 4.3.3	£________
Step 11	Total the ESPs of your lower-rated goods received, made or grown for retail sale in the four quarters, adjusted as in para 4.3.3, and add the opening lower-rated stock figure at step 10	£________
Step 12	At the end of the scheme year, or when you cease to use the scheme, establish the ESPs of your closing stock of lower-rated goods for retail sale (this becomes your opening lower-rated stock for next year)	£________
Step 13	Deduct the figure at step 12 from the figure at step 11. This gives the ESPs for the lower-rated goods you have sold by retail in the year	£________

Step 14	Multiply the figure at step 13 by 1/21 (VAT at 5 per cent)	£________
Step 15	Add together the figure for total ESPs for zero-rated goods you have sold by retail in the year at step 5 and the figure at step 13	£________
Step 16	Deduct the figure at step 15 from the figure at step 2. This gives you your standard-rated takings for the year	£________
Step 17	Multiply the figure at step 16 by 7/47 (VAT at 17.5 per cent)	£________
Step 18	Add together the figures at step 14 and step 17 to arrive at the output tax due under the retail scheme	£________
Step 19	Add up the output tax you have paid under the retail scheme in the four quarters	£________
Step 20	If the figure at step 18 is greater than the figure at step 19 you have paid too little tax and you should add the difference to your output tax in the fourth quarter. If the figure at step 18 is smaller than the figure at step 19 you have paid too much tax and you should deduct the difference from your output tax in the fourth quarter.	

4.5.2 *If you set ESPs for standard-rated goods*

The adjustment assumes that the second minority goods are liable to tax at the lower rate.

The adjustment must take account of any disposals since the last adjustment which were not made by way of retail sale. You do this by excluding from the figures used in the calculation the value of any goods which were previously part of the scheme calculation, or included in the opening stock figure, but have not been sold by way of retail. The adjustment is also required if a part of your business leaves the scheme.

Step 1	When you begin to use the scheme establish the Expected Selling Prices (ESPs) of your opening stock of standard-rated goods for retail sale, making any necessary adjustments as in para 4.3.3	£________
Step 2	Total the ESPs of your standard-rated goods received, made or grown for retail sale in the four quarters, adjusted as in para 4.3.3	£________
Step 3	Add together the totals at step 1 and step 2	£________
Step 4	At the end of the scheme year, or when you cease to use the scheme, establish the ESPs of your closing stock of standard-rated goods for retail sale. (This becomes your standard-rated opening stock figure for the next year)	£________

VAT

Step 5	Deduct the figure at step 4 from the figure at step 3. This gives the ESPs for the standard-rated goods you have sold by retail sale in the year	£_______
Step 6	Multiply the figure at step 5 by 7/47 (VAT at 17.5 per cent)	£_______
Step 7	Add up the output tax you have paid under the retail scheme in the four quarters	£_______
Step 8	If the figure at step 6 is greater than the figure at step 7 you have paid too little tax for your standard-rated supplies of goods and you should add the difference to your output tax in the fourth quarter. If the figure at step 6 is smaller than the figure at step 7 you have paid too much tax for your standard-rated supplies of goods and you should deduct the difference from your output tax in the fourth quarter.	

If you also make supplies at the lower rate repeat steps 1–8 substituting "lower-rated" for "standard-rated", and at step 6 "1/21" for "7/47".

Commentary—*De Voil Indirect Tax Service* **V3.573.**

4.6 How do I complete my VAT return?

Your output tax figure is used to complete Box 1 of your VAT return (Form VAT 100). If you are using more than one scheme you must add together the output tax calculated from each scheme as well as any other amounts of output tax which are due, and put the total in Box 1.

To help you fill in your VAT return see VAT Notice 700/12 "Filling in your VAT return". You can get a copy by contacting our National Advice Service.

Commentary—*De Voil Indirect Tax Service* **V3.573.**

5 DAILY GROSS TAKINGS (DGT) CHECKLIST

All boxed text in this section has the force of law (see para 1.4).

The DGT is a record of your retail supplies and is a crucial part of your retail scheme records. It is important that you follow the guidance in this section on how to calculate your DGT.

5.1 What must I include in my Daily Gross Takings (DGT)?

From the day you start using the scheme you must keep a record of your DGT. You must include in your DGT record—

- all payments as they are received by you or on your behalf from cash customers for your retail supplies;
- the full value, including VAT, of all your credit or other non cash retail sales at the time you make the supply; and
- details of any adjustments made to this record.

The DGT record will normally be a till roll or copies of sales vouchers. It is this record and not simply cash on hand which constitutes your DGT.

Commentary—*De Voil Indirect Tax Service* **V3.556, 557.**

5.2 Are all forms of cash payment included in my DGT?

Yes. You must include and record the following in your DGT as they are received from your customers—
- Cash;
- Cheques;
- Debit or credit card vouchers;
- Switch, Delta or similar electronic transactions; and
- Electronic cash.

Commentary—*De Voil Indirect Tax Service* **V3.557.**

5.3 Is my DGT simply a record of cash receipts?

No. You must also include the following in your DGT on the day you make the supply—
- the full value of credit sales (excluding any disclosed exempt charge for credit);
- the value of any goods taken out of the business for your own use;
- the cash value of any payment in kind for retail sales;
- the face value of gift, book and record vouchers redeemed (subject to para 6.17); and
- any other payments for retail sales.

5.4 What transactions may reduce my DGT?

Your till roll or other record of sales constitutes your DGT and it is this figure which you must use when calculating output tax due under your retail scheme.

However, you may reduce your DGT for the following—
- Counterfeit notes;
- Customer overspends using Shopacheck;
- Illegible credit card transactions (where a customer's account details are not legible on the credit card voucher and therefore cannot be presented and redeemed at the bank);
- Inadvertent acceptance of a cheque guarantee card as a credit card;
- Inadvertent acceptance of foreign currency (where discovered at a later time, for example when cashing up);
- Inadvertent acceptance of out of date coupons which have previously been included in your DGT but which are not honoured by promoters;
- Instalments in respect of credit sales;
- Receipts recorded for exempt supplies;
- Receipts recorded for goods or services which are to be accounted for outside the scheme;
- Refunds to customers for overcharges or faulty/unsuitable goods;
- Supervisor's float discrepancies;
- Till breakdowns (where incorrect till readings are recorded due to mechanical faults, for example till programming error, false reading and till reset by engineer);
- Unsigned or dishonoured cheques from cash customers (but not from credit customers);
- Use of training tills (where the till used by staff for training has been returned to the sales floor without the zeroing of figures); and
- Void transactions (where an incorrect transaction has been voided at the time of the error).

Commentary—*De Voil Indirect Tax Service* **V3.557.**

5.5 How may I reduce my DGT for transactions listed in para 5.4?

You must be able to provide evidence to support any adjustments to your DGT figure.

If you make an adjustment but subsequently receive a payment, you must include that payment in your DGT.

You must not reduce your DGT for till shortages which result from theft of cash, fraudulent refunds and voids or poor cash handling by staff. See para 6.33 for further details.

Commentary—*De Voil Indirect Tax Service* **V3.557.**

VAT

5.6 What if I am involved in transactions not covered in this section?

If you have a particular type of transaction which is not covered in this section, you must check Sections 6 and 7 to see if any of the rules there apply to your business before using the Direct Calculation Schemes to calculate your tax.

Commentary—*De Voil Indirect Tax Service* **V3.557.**

6 SPECIAL TRANSACTIONS

All boxed text in this section has the force of law (see para 1.4).

If you have a particular type of transaction which is not covered in this section, you should ask for advice from your local VAT Business Advice Centre. The address and telephone number are in the phone book under "Customs and Excise".

6.1 Acquisitions from other EC member states

> Notice 725 "VAT—The Single Market" explains how you account for VAT on goods purchased (acquisitions) from other EC member states.
>
> Suppliers from elsewhere in the EC will not charge VAT on their sales to you but you will have to account for VAT at the rate applicable to the goods in the UK.
>
> For retail scheme purposes, references in this notice to zero-rated goods apply only to goods which are zero-rated in the UK; goods which you acquire from other EC member states at zero-rate, but which are standard-rated in the UK, must be treated as standard-rated in your retail scheme calculations.

Commentary—*De Voil Indirect Tax Service* **V3.557.**

6.2 Amusement and gaming machines

> Where your minority goods are—
>
> – zero-rated (and lower-rated where applicable, as described in para 4.4.1), add the cash and/or tokens from the machine to your Daily Gross Takings on the day that you remove them from the machine; or
> – standard-rated (and lower-rated where applicable, as described in para 4.4.2), exclude the takings from your scheme calculations and account for the tax as explained in VAT Notice 701/13 "Gaming and amusement machines".

Commentary—*De Voil Indirect Tax Service* **V3.557.**

6.3 BT Phonecards

> The sale of unused BT phonecards is outside the scope of VAT (provided they are not sold for more than face value). Exclude these sales from your Daily Gross Takings. Account for any commission received from BT outside your retail scheme.
>
> If you deal in other types of phonecards you should consult your local VAT Business Advice Centre.

Commentary—*De Voil Indirect Tax Service* **V3.557.**

6.4 Business entertainment / gifts

> If you purchase goods specifically to consume in the course of business entertainment or to supply as gifts, you must account for any tax due outside your scheme.
>
> If you use or supply these goods from your normal stock you can account for any tax due under your retail scheme as follows—
>
> – if the goods are lower or standard-rated and your minority goods are zero-rated, you must add the value of the supply to your Daily Gross Takings (DGT); or
> – if your minority goods are lower or standard-rated, no addition to the DGT is necessary but you must adjust the ESP to reflect the value to be accounted for.

Commentary—*De Voil Indirect Tax Service* **V3.557.**

6.5 Business overheads

> Exclude from your scheme any purchases of goods or services which are not for resale, for example your business overheads such as gas, electricity and rent.

6.6 Business promotions

See Section 7.

6.7 Catering supplies

See catering supplies in Notice 727 "VAT Retail schemes".

6.8 Chemists

See VAT Notice 727 "VAT Retail schemes".

6.9 Credit transactions

Account for output tax on credit retail supplies by including the full value of the goods in your Daily Gross Takings (DGT) at the time you make the supply. Do not wait until you are paid and do not include the instalments in the DGT when they are received. Additional rules apply depending on the way the credit sales are financed:	
Supplies involving a finance company	If you arrange credit for your customer through a finance company, our view is that in most cases you should include the full amount paid by the customer in your DGT at the time you make the supply. However, in some circumstances VAT may only be due on the amount you receive from the finance company. Business Brief 15/96 explains the circumstances in which this treatment may be appropriate.
Self-financed credit supplies	If you make a separate charge for credit (additional to the cash price) and you disclose it to the customer, this is exempt from VAT and should be excluded from your DGT. NB If your turnover is less than £1 million and you run a business where your customers do not pay for the goods when they receive them (for example, you may be a milkman or newsagent), you may take account of opening and closing debtors in your scheme calculations. Notice 727 "VAT Retail Schemes" provides an example of how to do this.

Commentary—*De Voil Indirect Tax Service* **V3.557.**

6.10 Delivery charges

If, in order to fulfil your contract for the sale of the goods, you also deliver them, then there is a single supply of delivered goods. It does not matter whether the charge you make for delivery is separately itemised or invoiced. Examples of supplies of delivered goods are doorstep deliveries of milk or newspapers. The liability of the delivery charge follows the liability of the goods. In this case include the full amount charged in your Daily Gross Takings and also allow for the delivery charge element in the ESP calculation.

If you supply goods under a contract that does not require delivery but where, nevertheless, you agree to deliver the goods and make a separate charge, then that charge is for a standard-rated supply of services. You can include the supply of goods in your Daily Gross Takings (DGT) but how you treat the delivery charges depends on which rate of goods you are marking up. For—

- **zero-rated minority goods**, include the delivery charges in your DGT; or
- **standard-rated minority goods,** you can add back as part of your standard rated sales figure the service charge which will not be included in your ESP calculation. If you do not do this, you must account for the tax due on the charges outside your retail scheme.

You will find more about delivery charges and delivered goods in Notice 700 "The VAT Guide" and Notice 700/24 "Postage and delivery charges".

Commentary—*De Voil Indirect Tax Service* **V3.557.**

6.11 Deposits

Most deposits are advance payments for supplies and must be included in your Daily Gross Takings (DGT).

However, if you take a deposit for another reason, for example as security to ensure the safe return of goods you have hired out and you either refund it when the goods are ➡

returned safely or you forfeit it to compensate you for loss or damage, you should exclude this amount from your DGT.

Commentary—*De Voil Indirect Tax Service* **V3.557.**

6.12 Dishonoured cheques/counterfeit notes

See the entry entitled "Unsigned or dishonoured cheques" in para 5.4.

6.13 Disposal of business assets

If you dispose of a business asset, such as a cash register or a van, you should account for VAT on the sale outside your retail scheme.

Commentary—*De Voil Indirect Tax Service* **V3.557.**

6.14 Exempt supplies

Any payments received for supplies which are exempt from VAT must be excluded from your scheme calculations.

If you make exempt supplies, for example the sale of National Lottery tickets or financial services, you will need to consider the rules on partial exemption explained in Notice 706 "Partial exemption" and Notice 706/2 "The capital goods scheme".

Commentary—*De Voil Indirect Tax Service* **V3.557.**

6.15 Exports to countries outside the European Community

You must allow for the following exports in your scheme calculations (as set out in 6.15.1 and 6.15.2)—

- Retail Exports: If you make supplies for retail exports (including supplies to UK residents going abroad and to crew of ships and aircraft), under the terms of the retail export scheme as described in Notice 704 "VAT Retail exports"; and
- Direct and Indirect Exports: If you export goods direct, or supply goods in the UK to overseas traders for subsequent indirect export by them, as described in VAT Notice 703 "Exports and removals of goods from the UK".

NB For Direct Exports, if you are unable to supply the evidence of exportation, you will be held accountable for the tax. Therefore, if you do not arrange the exportation yourself, you should consider asking your customer for a deposit (equal to the amount of tax for which you will be accountable if your customer does not supply the evidence).

If you make retail sales to persons from other EC member states see para 6.27.

6.15.1 Scheme 1 or 2 calculation for zero-rated minority goods

You must follow the normal scheme rules but—

For either Retail Exports or Direct and Indirect Exports

(a) Include in your Daily Gross Takings (DGT) all amounts, including VAT, for goods sold for retail export or sent for export.

(b) At the end of each tax period add up the amounts for standard-rated goods which have actually been exported or sent for export.

(c) Calculate notional tax on the total amount at (b), using the VAT fraction that applied at the time when you included the amounts in your DGT.

(d) Subtract the notional tax at (c) from your scheme output tax.

For Direct and Indirect Exports only—

(e) where you do not obtain proof of shipment within three months of the date on which you supplied the goods for export, you must enter the notional tax on those goods already calculated at (b) as an addition to the VAT PAYABLE side of your VAT account for the current tax period.

6.15.2 Scheme 1 or 2 calculation for standard-rated minority goods

Follow the method set out in para 4.4, but at the end of each tax period—

For either Retail Exports or Direct and Indirect Exports—

(a) Add up the original Expected Selling Prices (ESPs) including VAT, of the standard-rated goods sold for retail export or sent for export.

(b) Calculate notional tax on the total at (a) using the VAT fraction that applied at the time when you included the amounts in your scheme calculations.

(c) Subtract the notional tax at (b) from your scheme output tax.

For Direct Exports only—

(d) Where you do not obtain proof of shipment within three months of the date on which you supplied any goods for export, you must include the notional tax on those goods already calculated at (b) as an addition to the VAT PAYABLE side of your VAT account for the current tax period.

6.16 Florists

If you are a member of an organisation such as Interflora, Teleflorist and Flowergram, see Notice 727 "VAT Retail schemes".

6.17 Gift, book and record vouchers

If you …	*then …*
sell gift vouchers at a value higher than their face value	the excess is consideration for a supply of services and VAT should be accounted for on it outside the retail scheme. When you redeem the vouchers you must include their face value in your Daily Gross Takings (DGT).
sell gift vouchers at their face value	do not include the amount in your DGT. But, when you redeem the vouchers you must include their face value in your DGT.
sell gift vouchers at a price lower than their face value	do not include the amount in your DGT. When you redeem the voucher, if you have evidence to prove that that voucher was supplied at a discount, then you may include the discounted amount in your DGT. Otherwise you must include the full face value of the voucher in your DGT.
include gift vouchers with other products for a single charge	the supply of the goods and voucher is treated as a multiple supply. This means VAT is only due on that portion of the payment which relates to the goods. You should omit from your DGT that part of the payment which relates to the gift voucher, usually the face value. But you must include in your DGT the face value of the voucher when redeemed by the customer.
issue gift vouchers free of charge	No VAT is due on the issue. When the voucher is redeemed for goods no VAT is due unless the cost of the goods exceeds £50. If the cost exceeds £50, VAT is due on the full amount. However, if you also sell such vouchers and are unable to distinguish between the two types at redemption, then you must include the full face value of the voucher in your DGT when it is redeemed.
have purchased a third party's gift vouchers which you intend to issue free of charge (for example in your own promotion)	you will not normally have been charged VAT. Equally, you do not have to account for any VAT when you give them away.
redeem gift vouchers and issue tax invoices to VAT registered businesses	You must account for these sales outside your retail scheme.

Commentary—*De Voil Indirect Tax Service* **V3.557.**

6.18 Goods bought at one rate and sold at another

For some goods the rate of tax you charge depends on how they are offered for sale. For example, meat is zero-rated when sold for human consumption but the same meat becomes standard-rated when sold as pet food.

➡

If you are a chemist see Notice 727 "VAT Retail schemes".

If you sell take-away food see VAT Notice 709/2 "Catering and take-away food" and the Catering Adaptation in Notice 727 "VAT Retail schemes".

If you sell young children's clothing see Notice 714 "Young children's clothing and footwear".

All other goods you buy at one rate of tax and sell at another should be treated as follows—

- You must keep separate stocks of the goods that you put up or hold out for sale at the different tax rates. When they are received you must enter them in your records of goods received for resale at the tax rate that will apply when they are sold.
- If you hold a common stock of those goods that you draw on to sell at different tax rates, depending on the scheme you are using, you must enter in your scheme records their cost to you or their ESP, at the tax rate that applied when you received them. But, when they are put up or held out for sale at the other tax rate, you must–
  (a) deduct the appropriate amounts from your scheme records at the tax rate that applied when you received the goods; and
  (b) enter the corresponding amounts in your scheme records at the tax rate that applies when you sell them.

As the retailer, you are responsible for ensuring that the correct liability for VAT is applied when you sell goods. If you make a mistake you may underdeclare the amount of tax due, and so may be liable to an assessment and interest to correct the error.

Commentary—*De Voil Indirect Tax Service* **V3.557.**

6.19 Goods bought from unregistered suppliers

If you buy goods for retail sale from suppliers who are not registered for VAT, you must include in your ESP calculation only those goods which are taxable at your minority rate.

Commentary—*De Voil Indirect Tax Service* **V3.557.**

6.20 Goods sold on "sale or return" or similar terms

You should keep a separate record of goods supplied on a "sale or return" basis. You should only include the amount due for these in your Daily Gross Takings when the customer has adopted the goods.

If the customer pays a deposit see 6.11.

Commentary—*De Voil Indirect Tax Service* **V3.557.**

6.21 Imports

If you import goods from countries outside the European Community, you should read Notice 702 "Imports".

6.22 Part-exchange

When you accept goods or services in part-exchange, you should include in your Daily Gross Takings the full selling price, including VAT, of the goods you supply.

If you resell goods you have accepted in part-exchange you may be able to use the Second-hand Margin Scheme (see Notice 718 "Margin scheme for second-hand goods, works of art, antiques and collectors' items"). If, however, you are unable to use that scheme you should include the goods previously taken in part exchange in your retail scheme.

Commentary—*De Voil Indirect Tax Service* **V3.557.**

6.23 Private or personal use of goods

Tax is due on any positive-rated goods purchased for retail sale but which you take out of your business for personal or private use (see Notice 700 "The VAT Guide"). You must add the value of such goods—

- to your Daily Gross Takings (DGT), if your minority goods are zero-rated; or
- to your ESPs and DGT to reflect the value due, if your minority goods are lower or standard-rated.

Commentary—*De Voil Indirect Tax Service* **V3.557.**

6.24 Recall of goods by manufacturers

If a manufacturer recalls contaminated or otherwise faulty goods, you must adjust your ESP records.

Commentary—*De Voil Indirect Tax Service* **V3.557.**

6.25 Refunds to customers

You may deduct from your Daily Gross Takings amounts which are refunded or credited to customers in respect of taxable supplies of goods or services to a maximum of the amount originally charged.

Commentary—*De Voil Indirect Tax Service* **V3.557.**

6.26 Rented payphones

If you rent a payphone from BT or another supplier, you make supplies to users of the payphone and VAT is due on these supplies. You must account for the VAT as follows—

- for zero or lower-rated minority goods, include the money removed from the payphone in your Daily Gross Takings; or
- for standard-rated minority goods, deal with the money received from the payphone outside your Direct Calculation scheme.

Commentary—*De Voil Indirect Tax Service* **V3.557.**

6.27 Retail sales to persons from other EC member states

Supplies made in the UK to persons from other EC member states should be accounted for as normal domestic retail sales.

Special arrangements apply to Distance Selling. This is where goods are sold to unregistered persons in other EC Member States and the supplier is responsible for delivery to the customer. You can find out more about it in Notice 725 "VAT—The Single Market" and Notice 700/1A "Distance Selling".

Commentary—*De Voil Indirect Tax Service* **V3.557.**

6.28 Road fuel

If you use road fuel for private motoring you must account for VAT on this outside the retail scheme, using the rules set out in Notice 700/64 "Motoring expenses".

Commentary—*De Voil Indirect Tax Service* **V3.557.**

6.29 Sale of discount vouchers or cards

If you sell discount vouchers or cards entitling the holder to discounts on purchases—

- from you, you must include the payment received in your Daily Gross Takings; or
- with several traders, this is a separate standard-rated supply of services and must be dealt with outside your scheme.

Commentary—*De Voil Indirect Tax Service* **V3.557.**

6.30 Sale or assignment of debts

If you sell or assign debts due from your customers, no adjustment to your VAT account is necessary since you will already have included the correct amount when you made the supply.

Commentary—*De Voil Indirect Tax Service* **V3.557.**

6.31 Saving stamps, travel cards and pools coupons

These should be dealt with outside your scheme.

Commentary—*De Voil Indirect Tax Service* **V3.557.**

6.32 Second-hand goods

You may be able to use the special scheme for second-hand goods (see Notice 718 "Margin scheme for second-hand goods, works of art, antiques and collectors' items").

Alternatively, sales of second-hand goods should be accounted for within your retail scheme in the same way as new goods.

Commentary—*De Voil Indirect Tax Service* **V3.557.**

6.33 Theft, shrinkage, leakage and stock losses

If you find that there are unexplained accounting discrepancies between stock and sales, you must consider the extent to which this is attributable to unrecorded sales, such as to the theft of cash by staff, and add the value back to your Daily Gross Takings.

Where possible these adjustments should be allocated to the specific VAT period in which the theft took place. Otherwise, such shrinkage should be apportioned across relevant tax periods on a fair and reasonable basis;

Unless you have evidence of the liability of the unaccounted supplies, adjustments must be in line with the usual proportion of standard against zero-rated supplies; and

When you do this exercise, you will need to consider whether the shrinkage for which you have adjusted your DGT requires you to further adjust your ESPs.

Commentary—*De Voil Indirect Tax Service* **V3.557.**

7 BUSINESS PROMOTIONS

All boxed text in this section has the force of law (see para 1.4).

The general guidelines on the business promotion schemes covered in this section are given in Notice 700/7 "Business promotion schemes".

The VAT treatment under your retail scheme depends on whether the promotion is funded solely by you as the retailer or by, or together with, a third party such as the manufacturer.

If you wish to operate a particular promotion scheme which is not covered here you should contact your local VAT Business Advice Centre. The address and telephone number are in the phone book under "Customs and Excise".

7.1 Discount vouchers

As part payment	When you take a discount voucher as part payment, you should include only the amount of money received from your customer in your Daily Gross Takings (DGT). If you subsequently receive payment for the voucher from another source you must include the extra amount in your DGT. The timing of the adjustment should follow the rule under the heading "When to account for manufacturer's contributions" in para 7.5.
Handling charges	If you make a further charge to a manufacturer for handling the vouchers, this is payment for a supply which is exempt from VAT and should be excluded from your DGT.
Sale	If you sell discount vouchers—see para 6.29.

Commentary—*De Voil Indirect Tax Service* **V3.557.**

7.2 Vouchers with no values or amounts but redeemable for whole items

Vouchers issued by you to customers making a specific purchase or purchases	No VAT is due upon issue and no further VAT is due when the voucher is used by the customer to obtain the reward goods. However, you must adjust your ESPs for the reward goods.
Vouchers issued freely by you	No VAT is due upon issue. When the voucher is redeemed for goods no VAT is due unless the cost of the goods is over £50. VAT is then due on the value of those goods at the time you give them away and you must add that value to your DGT. See also para 6.4 regarding business gifts.
Vouchers issued by another person but redeemable with you	They are likely to be subject to the terms and conditions of that person's promotion. For example, you may be given certain stocks to give away on behalf of that person. These stocks must not be included in your retail scheme calculations. Notice 700/7 "Business promotion schemes" contains further information. Alternatively, contact your local VAT Business Advice Centre. The address and telephone number are in the phone book under "Customs and Excise".

Commentary—*De Voil Indirect Tax Service* **V3.557.**

7.3 Vouchers redeemed for cash with you

If you redeem vouchers for cash, the cash payment is outside the scope of VAT. You must not alter your Daily Gross Takings by the cash paid out.

Commentary—*De Voil Indirect Tax Service* **V3.557.**

7.4 Gift vouchers

See para 6.17.

7.5 Goods linked in a promotion

These include promotions where—

Two different articles are sold for a single price in a combined offer, for example—

- a washing machine with an iron; or
- a jar of coffee with a packet of chocolate biscuits.

A number of same articles are sold in a multibuy offer, for example—

- "buy two and get a third free".

If both articles are liable at the same rate of tax (as in the examples of linked washing machine/ iron and same article multibuy), there are no additional rules to follow under the Direct Calculation Schemes.
If the articles are liable at different rates of tax (as in the example of linked coffee and chocolate biscuits), there are additional rules to apportion the selling price— –you may use the method explained in Notice 700 "The VAT Guide"; or –in the case of goods linked by the manufacturer, you may treat the articles in accordance with the information shown on the supplier's invoice. For example, if the invoice shows separate prices and amounts of tax, you may apportion your Expected Selling Price (ESPs) on the same basis. As a concession, where the minor article satisfies the criteria set out in Notice 700/7 "Business promotion schemes", you may account for VAT on the minor item at the same rate as the main article.

If an apportionment of the selling price is necessary, you must separate the amount allocated to the lower or zero-rated article from your standard-rated takings before carrying out your scheme calculation.
When to account for manufacturer's contributions Strictly speaking, when you receive a contribution from a manufacturer or joint sponsor representing partial payment for goods supplied to a customer, you should account for this in the period the goods are supplied. However, as a concession, you may account for such contributions in the period they are received from the manufacturer or joint sponsor.
Correcting ESPs You will need to adjust your ESPs if the contribution is for the class of goods which you have marked up in your retail scheme. If you receive from the supplier or sponsor— –a full contribution, do not adjust your ESPs; –a partial contribution, adjust your ESPs for the appropriate goods to the extent of the amount not supported by the sponsor or manufacturer; or –no contribution, make an appropriate adjustment to the ESPs of the promotion goods.
If a manufacturer or joint sponsor contributes, for example towards advertising, you have made a separate supply of services and this must be dealt with outside your scheme.

Commentary—*De Voil Indirect Tax Service* **V3.557.**

…

Notice 728
New means of transport

September 2008

This notice cancels and replaces Notice 728 (February 2003).

Paragraph 3.6 of this notice has the force of law under VATA 1994, Sch 6, Item 11(2). Paragraph 6.1 of this notice has the force of law under the VAT Regulations 1995, Regulation 155. These paragraphs are indicated by being placed in a box.

EXAMPLE:

The following rule has the force of law If you receive a net payment you must include the full value before such deductions (including VAT) in your scheme turnover. This will usually be the value shown on your sales invoice.

1 INTRODUCTION

1.1 What is the notice about?

It explains how VAT applies to new means of transport.

In the EC most goods are charged with VAT in the country in which they are purchased. However for a new vehicle, boat or aircraft, VAT will be due in the member state of destination if:

- it falls within the definition of "New Means of Transport" (NMT), and
- it is sold to a customer who intends to take it to another member state.

The definition of a Means of Transport within this notice and when it is "New" is common to all EC member states and is only for the purpose of determining when VAT is due. Other agencies for example, the DVLA may have different definitions.

1.2 Tertiary legislation

Paragraphs 3.6 and 6.1 have the force of law.

1.3 What's changed?

The technical content is largely unchanged but some clarifications are inserted in paragraphs 2.1, 3.5, 6.2, 6.9. This revision also amends and corrects the address of the Personal Transport Unit (PTU) in paragraphs 3.2 and 8.11 and the DVLA office details in section 10.

1.4 Who should read this notice?

Anyone considering obtaining a vehicle, boat or aircraft in another member state with the intention of bringing it into the UK and vice versa.

2 HOW TO IDENTIFY AND DEAL WITH NEW MEANS OF TRANSPORT

2.1 What is a "means of transport"?

A "means of transport" is any of the following when it is intended for the transport of passengers or goods:

- a boat more than 7.5 metres long (about 24.6 feet)
- an aircraft with a take-off weight of more than 1550 kilograms (about 4417lb), *or*
- a motorised land vehicle which:
  - has an engine with a displacement or cylinder capacity of more than 48 cubic centimetres, or
  - is constructed or adapted to be electrically propelled using more than 7.2 kilowatts (about 9.65 horsepower).

Vehicles, which are not suitable for use on public roads: for example

- off road motorcycles
- combine harvesters
- motorised lawnmower also
- hot air balloons

are *not* means of transport and should not be supplied under the scheme; they are subject to tax in member state of supply.

However, for example, a farm tractor can haul goods on the public roads and is an NMT.

Commentary—*De Voil Indirect Tax Service* **V1.294.**

2.2 When is a means of transport not new?

A vessel or aircraft or a motorised land vehicle is *not* new when *all* the following conditions are met:

A vessel or aircraft is not new	—when more than three months have elapsed since the date of its first entry into service (see paragraph 2.3), and —it has, since its first entry into service, travelled under its own power for more than —100 hours if it is a boat, or —40 hours if it is an aircraft.
A motorised land vehicle is not new	—when more than six months have elapsed since the date of its first entry into service (see paragraph 2.3), and —it has, since its first entry into service, travelled under its own power for more than 6000 kilometres.

Commentary—*De Voil Indirect Tax Service* **V1.294.**

2.3 What does "first entered into service" mean?

For boats or aircraft it is the earlier of

- the date it was delivered from its manufacturer to its first purchaser or owner, or
- the date it was first made available to its first purchaser or owner, or
- the date it was first taken into use for demonstration purposes, by the manufacturer.

For motorised land vehicles it is the earlier of

- the date it was first registered for road use in the member state of manufacture, or
- the date when it was first liable to be registered for road use there.

For motorised vehicles which are removed from member state of supply without being registered for the road, it is the earlier of

- the date it was made available to the first purchaser, or
- the date it was taken into use for demonstration purposes by its manufacturer or sole concessionaire

See also paragraph 2.4.

Commentary—*De Voil Indirect Tax Service* **V1.294.**

2.4 What happens if HM Revenue & Customs is not satisfied with the date of first entry?

If we are not satisfied that a date of first entry into service has been established in accordance with the guidelines at paragraph 2.3, the NMT may be treated as having first entered into service on the date when the invoice relating to its first supply was issued.

Commentary—*De Voil Indirect Tax Service* **V1.294.**

2.5 Is your vehicle, boat or aircraft an NMT?

If your answer is yes then go to paragraph 2.6 or if it is no then go to section 5.

2.6 How should I treat the acquisition or supply of an NMT?

This depends on whether you are VAT-registered or a person/business not registrable for VAT – see table below.

Persons not registrable for VAT	*VAT-registered person/business*
—Purchasing an NMT in another member state and bringing it to the UK (see section 3) —Bringing back an NMT to the UK by members of NATO forces (see section 4) —Bringing means of transport which are not new to the UK (see section 5) —Purchasing an NMT in the UK for removal to another member state (see section 6) —VAT refunds for non-registrable persons of an NMT for removal to other member state (see section 7) —Registration, licensing, type approval and Insurance (see section 9)	—Purchase of an NMT in another member state and bringing it to UK (see section 8) —Supply of an NMT in the UK for removal to other member state (see section 8) —Purchase of an NMT in the UK for removal to another member state by a registered business in another member state (see section 8)

3 PURCHASING AN NMT IN ANOTHER MEMBER STATE AND BRINGING IT TO THE UK

3.1 When do I notify HMRC about the NMT I have brought to the UK?

If you are a private individual (or a business or legal entity which is not registrable for VAT in the UK) and you purchase an NMT in another member state to bring to the UK, you *must* notify us *within 7 days of its arrival in the UK or its acquisition, whichever is the later*. You may be liable to a financial penalty if you do not notify us within 7 days.

Commentary—*De Voil Indirect Tax Service* **V5.127.**

3.2 How do I make the notification?

To make the notification you must use Form VAT 415, which is available from our NAS, and DVLA Local Offices or can be down loaded from our website. The notification must be in English.

The completed form should either be sent by post to	or
HM Revenue & Customs Personal Transport Unit Freight Clearance Centre Lord Warden Square Dover Western Docks Dover Kent CT17 9DN	be completed and handed to the DVLA Local Office (see section 10) when you license and register your vehicle.

Please note: that the Personal Transport Unit only accepts postal notifications, as there are no public enquiry counters and if the notification is made via a DVLA Local Office, they will send the necessary documents to us.

Commentary—*De Voil Indirect Tax Service* **V5.127.**

3.3 Which documents should accompany my notification form?

To process your notification we will need to see a copy of the final purchase invoice, showing:

- the chassis number
- the price paid, *and*
- any invoices for accessories purchased with the vehicle.

We can process your notification more quickly if it is accompanied by these documents.

Commentary—*De Voil Indirect Tax Service* **V5.127.**

3.4 When is the VAT due?

VAT is due at the time of acquisition. This is either:

– the fifteenth day of the month following the one in which the NMT was made available to, or taken away by, the customer (sometimes referred to as the date of removal), *or*
– the date of issue of the tax invoice, whichever is earlier.

Commentary—*De Voil Indirect Tax Service* **V3.388.**

3.5 How is the VAT that is due calculated?

We will *only* calculate how much VAT you owe when the documents stated in paragraph 3.3 are received. The VAT is calculated on the total amount you have paid for the NMT (excluding all trade-ins, part-exchanges or special discounts not freely available to the general public), including any extras you had fitted to it at the time it was supplied, plus any delivery or incidental charges made by your supplier.

Commentary—*De Voil Indirect Tax Service* **V3.390.**

3.6 What rate of exchange is used in the calculation?

This information has the force of law.

> For VAT purposes, amounts of money must always be expressed in sterling. If the invoice for your NMT is in another currency, including the Euro, the Personal Transport Unit (PTU) will convert it into sterling using the rate of exchange current at time of acquisition.
>
> This is normally done using the Revenue & Customs' period rate of exchange, which closely reflects the UK market rate. However, you may make a specific request in writing at the time of notification to use the actual market rate applicable on the date of acquisition. The rates published in national newspapers will be acceptable as evidence of the rate at the relevant time. Rates obtained before the acquisition date are not acceptable.
>
> If you do not request the use of market rate at the time of your notification, the Revenue & Customs' period rate will be used automatically.

Commentary—*De Voil Indirect Tax Service* **V3.393.**

3.7 Can I obtain an estimate of the VAT due on the NMT first?

Yes, you can obtain an estimate if you wish to know in advance how much VAT you would have to pay. You should contact the NAS, but *please note* that the final charges may differ because of exchange rate fluctuations or changes to the value of the NMT.

3.8 When do I actually pay the VAT?

We will calculate the amount of VAT you owe and send you a demand for payment.

Please do not send any payment, before you receive the demand, because the amount you calculate could vary due to the different exchange rates used. You must pay the amount of VAT on the demand *within 30 days* of the date on which it was issued.

Commentary—*De Voil Indirect Tax Service* **V5.127.**

3.9 What if I fail to notify HMRC or fail to pay the VAT due?

If you fail to notify us that you have brought an NMT to the UK or if you fail to pay when we send you the demand, you may be liable to a financial penalty in addition to the VAT, which is due.

Commentary—*De Voil Indirect Tax Service* **V5.349.**

3.10 Under what circumstances may VAT not be payable?

All movements of NMT to the UK are liable to VAT, except where the NMT is a vehicle constructed or adapted for a disabled person. For more information on VAT relief for people with disabilities see Notice 701/7 "VAT reliefs for disabled people". See also paragraph 3.11.

Commentary—*De Voil Indirect Tax Service* **V4.281.**

3.11 Are there any more circumstances when VAT may not be payable?

Yes, you may be entitled to claim relief from VAT that is due when you remove your NMT to the UK if you meet the conditions below.

If you are *and*

—a diplomat, or
—a member of an officially recognised international organisation, or
—a member of NATO or the civilian staff accompanying them

you are returning from service in another member state. Section 4 has more information on whether you qualify for the relief.

3.12 Can I use another person to obtain and bring the NMT to the UK?

Yes, you can use another person, as an intermediary or agent, to assist you in obtaining your NMT and bringing it to the UK. See also paragraph 3.13.

3.13 Who is then responsible for notifying HMRC and for paying the VAT?

If you use an agent or intermediary to obtain and bring the NMT to the UK and the supplier's invoice is raised in your name and given to you by the intermediary, *you* are still the person responsible for notifying HMRC that the NMT has been brought to the UK and for paying the VAT that is due. The declaration on the notification of acquisition (Form VAT 415) should, at all times, be completed by you (the acquirer) and not the intermediary. Any penalties, which result from late notification or payment, will be due from you even if your intermediary caused the delay.

Agents who are VAT registered and acting in their own name in relation to the supply of the NMT should use the procedure in section 8.

3.14 Must I keep a record of my NMT purchase?

You must keep your NMT purchase invoice and proof that you have paid the VAT for six years from the date of purchase. You could be asked to demonstrate that the VAT on your NMT has been paid.

If you decide to sell your NMT within the six-year period you are advised to pass your proof of VAT payment to the new owner.

Commentary—*De Voil Indirect Tax Service* **V5.202.**

3.15 What if I bought the NMT from a non-taxable person and it was already tax paid in that member state?

The supply of the NMT should be zero-rated. The supplier of the NMT should seek a refund of taxes paid from their own member state's fiscal authority and acquisition tax will be due in the UK.

4 NATO FORCES AND DIPLOMATS BRINGING NMTS TO THE UK FROM ANOTHER MEMBER STATE

4.1 As a returning member of the NATO forces/civilian staff, can I claim relief from VAT when I bring my NMT back to the UK?

You can only claim entitlement to VAT relief if you comply with the notification requirements described in section 3. If you meet these requirements you can claim relief at the end of your tour on permanent posting back to the UK. You *must* be in possession of Form BFG 414 if returning from Germany or Form BFC 414 from Cyprus, in order to register your vehicle.

These forms are available from (respectively):

Customs and Immigration
British Forces Liaison
Germany, BFPO40

or

SBA Customs
RAF Akrotiri
BFPO57

If you are returning from any other member state you must provide HMRC with evidence to show that the host authority relieved the tax. If returning with an NMT use VAT Form 415, in all other circumstances a Form 414 must be used.

4.2 I am a diplomat returning to the UK from another member state with my NMT. Can I claim relief from VAT?

You can claim relief if you produce *both* evidence of your tax-free status from your head of mission *and* confirmation that the host member state has granted you relief on your NMT.

5 BRINGING MEANS OF TRANSPORT WHICH ARE NOT NEW TO THE UK

5.1 What if I am bringing a motor vehicle, boat or aircraft, which is not an NMT into the UK?

If you bring the means of transport to the UK from another member state, you will not have to pay UK VAT if:

- it is no longer a "New Means of Transport" as defined in section 2, *and*
- you have paid VAT on its purchase in the member state of supply.

However, the vehicle will be subject to the UK licensing and insurance requirements, which are explained in section 9. You must contact your nearest DVLA Local Office (see section 10) at the earliest opportunity. The DVLA Local Office will ask you to complete the HM Revenue & Customs Form VAT 414 to confirm that UK VAT is not due.

5.2 What if I live in another member state but bring my means of transport on temporary visits to the UK?

If you are normally resident (see paragraph 5.3) in another member state and you bring your means of transport with you on a temporary visit to the UK, you do not have to notify HMRC or pay VAT on it.

5.3 What does "normally resident" mean?

Where you have spent at least 185 days in the last twelve months because of your work and personal connections. But if:

- you have no work connections, *or*
- your work and personal connections are in different countries,

then you will usually be considered to be resident in the country where your personal connections are.

5.4 What should I do if I decide to stay and keep my means of transport in the UK?

If your plans change, and you decide to stay in the UK and keep your means of transport here, you do not need to notify HMRC unless either:

- it was supplied to you tax-free because of your special status in the member state in which you have been living or working, *and*
- the supply took place within the six months prior to your arrival in the UK, if it is a vehicle, or three months if it is a vessel or aircraft, *or*
- it was supplied to you tax-free for removal from the member state of supply, and no EC taxes have been paid on it.

5.5 Do I need to complete Form VAT 414?

Where you are not required to notify HMRC about the arrival of your vehicle in the UK, you may be asked to complete a Form VAT 414 at the time of vehicle registration. This informs us of your vehicle's details for confirmation that there is no UK taxes due.

6 PURCHASING AN NMT IN THE UK FOR REMOVAL TO ANOTHER MEMBER STATE

Commentary—*De Voil Indirect Tax Service* **V4.356.**

6.1 What happens when I buy an NMT in the UK for removal to another member state?

This information is given in the box below.

This information has the force of law.

If you buy an NMT in the UK to take to another member state, you will be liable for the VAT on the value of the NMT when you arrive there. To ensure that the purchase of the NMT is free of UK VAT, you must comply with certain conditions. These are:

- the means of transport must be "new"
- you or your authorised chauffeur, pilot or skipper must personally take delivery of the new means of transport in the UK
- you must remove it from the UK to the member state of destination within two months of the date of supply to you, *and*
- you must complete and sign a declaration on a Form VAT 411, stating your intention to remove the NMT from the UK and pay any VAT due in the member state of destination. Your supplier must complete their part of the form.

6.2 Can an NMT be purchased using a Finance House?

Yes, but normally this will mean the dealer is selling the vehicle to the finance house who in turn sell it to you. If that is the case then you must make sure it is the finance house that is shown as the supplier and the dealer must send the second copy of Form VAT 411 to the finance house for their retention.

6.3 What is Form VAT 411?

Form VAT 411 is your declaration that you will take the NMT to another member state within two months and pay the VAT there. It is also your supplier's declaration that they have supplied an NMT to you for removal from the UK.

6.4 How is the Form VAT 411 used?

The form is made up of an original (the top sheet) and three copies. When it has been properly completed, your supplier will send the original copy to us (see paragraph 8.11) and give the first copy to you. The supplier will keep the second copy of the form as part of their business records, and, if the NMT is a vehicle, they will use the third copy to register it for road use if you are going to drive it out of the UK.

6.5 Can I use the vehicle on UK roads before removal to another member state?

You must not use your vehicle on UK roads unless it has been licensed and registered, and is properly insured. Section 9 contains more information on this.

6.6 What if I am unable to remove the NMT due to circumstances beyond my control?

If you purchase an NMT and then find that because of circumstances beyond your control, you are unable to remove it, you should inform us immediately by writing to the address given in paragraph 3.2. See also paragraph 6.7.

When we receive your letter we will calculate the VAT due and send you a demand, which you must pay immediately.

6.7 What happens if I fail to or am unable to remove the NMT within the period allowed?

If you fail or are unable to remove your NMT from the UK within the two-month period allowed, you should inform HMRC and pay the VAT, which is due. Failure to do so may make your NMT liable to forfeiture.

6.8 Are these NMT exempt from "type approval"?

You can find more information on 'type approval' and how it affects NMTs from paragraphs 9.7 onwards.

6.9 Is there anything else I must do?

When an NMT (that is a vehicle) is finally removed from the UK, the DVLA require the tear-off portion of the VX302 to be completed and collected by the HMRC officer at the final port. HMRC will return the tear-off portion to the DVLA. In the case of a temporary removal to another EC member state, say for a holiday, the VX302 is not required to be completed. If it is then it can cause problems on return to the UK as the licence is cancelled.

7 VAT REFUNDS FOR NON-REGISTRABLE PERSONS OF AN NMT FOR REMOVAL TO OTHER MEMBER STATES

7.1 Who is entitled to a refund?

You may be entitled to a refund of VAT if you satisfy *all* the following conditions:

- you are not registrable for VAT in the UK
- you are selling your NMT to another person, and that person intends to remove the NMT to another member state within two months of the date of supply, and
- you can demonstrate that you have paid UK VAT on your NMT.

7.2 How do I claim my refund?

To claim your refund you should write to the PTU (address at paragraph 3.2) at least 14 days (but no more than one month) before you expect to sell your NMT. You can use the form at section 11 to do this.

When we receive your notification (see also paragraph 7.3) we will advise you if we want to examine the NMT before you sell it, to confirm its eligibility for refund.

7.3 What documents should I submit with the claim form?

Before any refund is made we will need to see *all* the following documents:

- proof of your original purchase (normally the invoice or import entry)
- evidence that you have paid VAT
- proof of your sale, normally this would be your bill of sale and evidence that you have received payment, and
- that the NMT has been removed to another member state.

7.4 What happens if I cannot produce the documents listed at paragraph 7.3?

No refund will be given until you have produced documents showing all these things. (Your documents will be returned to you promptly.)

7.5 How will my VAT refund be calculated?

The amount of VAT refunded to you will depend on the value of the supply you make to your customer, but it cannot exceed that amount of VAT, which you have already paid when you obtained the NMT.

8 ACQUISITION AND SUPPLY OF NMTS BY VAT REGISTERED PERSONS AND BUSINESSES

Commentary—*De Voil Indirect Tax Service* **V3.366–V3.398; V4.341–V4.361; V5.272.**

8.1 How do I obtain an NMT from another member state?

You should provide the supplier or vendor with your UK VAT registration number to enable them to zero-rate the supply of the vehicle to you.

8.2 How do I account for VAT on an NMT purchased in another member state for removal to the UK?

If you are registered for VAT in the UK and you buy a VAT-free NMT from a person registered in another EC member state, you should account for VAT due on your normal VAT return for the period in which you acquired the NMT. See also paragraph 8.3

8.3 Do I have to do anything else?

If the NMT is a vehicle, it must be licensed and registered before it is used on public roads. When you apply to register a vehicle on your own behalf, or on behalf of a customer, the DVLA Local Office (see section 10) will ask you to complete a Form VAT 414 declaring the VAT-free status of the vehicle and the VAT registration number you have used to make the acquisition into the UK. You should also see paragraphs 9.7 to 9.10 for type approval requirements before registration.

8.4 Do I still account for acquisition VAT if I make an onward supply of the NMT in the UK?

Yes, you must account for acquisition tax on the vehicles you acquire. If they form part of your stock in trade, you may recover input tax equal to the amount of acquisition tax you declared. You must charge output tax on the full value of the supply to your customer.

8.5 What if I arrange the supply of an NMT from an EC supplier direct to a customer in the UK?

If you arrange the supply of an NMT from a supplier in another EC member state direct to a customer in the UK, you are acting as an intermediary. If you act in this way for a person who is not registered for VAT in the UK, you may as part of your service (and subject to your customer's authorisation) notify the acquisition of the NMT to the Personnel Transport Unit (PTU) on behalf of your principal using the procedures described in section 3, but see also paragraph 8.6.

8.6 Who will be responsible for the declaration and payment of VAT?

The customer, or acquirer if he is the principal, is responsible for the declaration you make on their behalf and for the payment of the VAT, which is due. You may however make the payment on their behalf. When you trade as an intermediary you must make sure that the customer is provided with the sales invoice from the supplier and the invoice clearly shows the name and address of the acquirer of the NMT and the amount they have paid to the supplier. You should also distinguish clearly between:

- transactions in which you act as an intermediary, and
- the transactions in which you acquire and supply an NMT to the order of a person in the UK, in which case the provisions of paragraph 8.2 may apply.

8.7 What are the conditions for zero-rating the supply of NMT in the UK for removal to another member state?

Assuming you are registered for VAT in the UK, these depend on whether:

- your customer is VAT registered in the member state of destination – see paragraph 8.8, or
- your customer is not VAT registered in the member state of destination – see paragraph 8.9.

8.8 What conditions should I meet if my customer is VAT registered in the member state of destination?

You must meet *all* the conditions below in order to zero-rate the supply to your customer who will be liable for any VAT in their member state:

- you must show on your VAT invoice your customer's VAT registration number (with the two-digit country code prefix, see Notice 725 "The Single Market"), *and*
- the NMT must be despatched or transported to another member state within two months of the date you issue the invoice for the supply, *and*
- you must hold valid commercial documentary evidence, which confirms that the NMT has been removed from the UK
- you should also see paragraph 8.10.

8.9 What conditions should I meet if my customer is not VAT registered in the member state of destination?

You must meet all the conditions in order to zero-rate the supply to your customer who will be liable for any VAT in their member state:

- the means of transport must qualify as "new", see section 2
- the NMT must be removed from the UK to another member state within two months of the date of supply, *and*
- you and your customer must make a joint declaration about the transaction on a Form VAT 411. If this form is not completed properly, you will not be entitled to zero-rate the supply – see paragraphs 6.2 & 6.6

8.10 Should I complete the EC Sales List (ESL) form for this transaction?

You should only complete the ESL form when your customers are registered for VAT in another member state showing the customers EC registration number and value of supplies made in the calendar quarter. For more information please see Notice 725 "The Single Market".

8.11 Where should I send the completed VAT 411?

You must send all originals to:

HM Revenue & Customs
Personal Transport Unit
Freight Clearance Centre
Lord Warden Square
Dover Western Docks
Dover
Kent
CT17 9DN

See also paragraph 8.12.

8.12 Must I submit the Form VAT 411 within a certain deadline?

Yes, you must submit this within six weeks of the end of the calendar quarter in which you have made the supply.

8.13 What if I am VAT registered in another member state but buy an NMT in the UK for removal?

If you are registered for VAT in another EC member state and you buy an NMT from a VAT registered person in the UK for removal to that State your supplier may zero rate the supply under normal rules – see Notice 725 "The Single Market".

To benefit from zero-rating you must remove the NMT from the UK within two months of the time of supply. You must account for any tax due on the acquisition in the member state of destination, under the laws of that State.

For information on licensing, registration and insurance (if the NMT is a motorised land vehicle and you intend to use it on UK roads before removal) see section 9.

8.14 What happens if the NMT is not removed from the UK?

You will be liable to pay UK taxes on your NMT if it is not removed from the UK. You may therefore wish to insure it for its tax-inclusive value for the length of time it remains in the UK. See section 9 for the importance of type approval for vehicles kept in the UK.

8.15 I have purchased an unregistered NMT from a UK VAT registered supplier. Who is responsible for declaring acquisition tax?

The first acquirer of the vehicle into the UK is responsible for declaring acquisition tax on his VAT return. The onward supply of the vehicle to business is a standard-rated supply in the UK for which a normal VAT invoice should be issued.

8.16 If I am not the acquirer of the vehicle into the UK then who should complete the VAT 414 at the time of registration?

The acquirer of the NMT should provide you with a part-completed VAT 414 detailing the vehicle particulars, their name, address and their VAT registration number as acquirer. It must be signed and dated. You should only add the name and address of the registered keeper prior to submission to the DVLA Local Office (see section 10).

9 REGISTRATION, LICENSING, TYPE APPROVAL AND INSURANCE

9.1 Must I license and register the NMT that I brought to the UK from another member state?

Yes, all vehicles used on the UK roads *must* be licensed and registered. If you purchase an NMT in another member state and bring it to the UK, the vehicle must be registered and licensed as soon as possible after arrival. You are not legally entitled to use or keep the vehicle on UK public roads until it has been licensed and registered in the UK.

9.2 Do I need to register an NMT purchased in the UK for removal to another member state?

If you purchase an NMT in the UK for removal to another EC member state and the vehicle is not already registered for road use in the UK, it will be allocated a registration number in a special "VAT-free" series of numbers. This allows it to be identified as tax-free for the length of time it remains in the UK prior to removal. The supplier of the vehicle will obtain the number for you by presenting copy 3 of the Form VAT 411 at one of the DVLA Local Offices (VROs) listed in section 10.

9.3 In what other circumstances do I need to register the NMT?

If you are VAT registered in another EC member state and have purchased an unregistered NMT that will be used on the road before removal from the UK, you should register the vehicle for road use. Form VAT 411A should be completed and be presented to the DVLA Local Office (see section 10) who will allocate a registration mark in the tax-free series.

9.4 What if I decide to keep the vehicle in the UK permanently?

If your plans change and you decide to keep the vehicle in the UK permanently, you cannot retain the 'VAT Free' registration mark. In these circumstances you should contact the Personal Transport Unit (PTU) for advice.

9.5 Should I insure the NMT that I purchased in the UK for removal to another member state?

If you buy an NMT in the UK for removal to another member state you should insure it for its *full value* including UK VAT. If for any reason (for example, an accident) it is not removed from the UK, you will be liable for any UK VAT which was not charged at the time the NMT was supplied to you.

It is a legal requirement that you must be insured against third-party liabilities before you drive a vehicle on UK roads. If your vehicle is registered in the UK, its use must be covered by a policy of insurance issued by an authorised insurer (a member of the Motor Insurers Bureau).

9.6 What if I am a visitor to the UK?

If you are a visitor to the UK you need no further insurance if your vehicle is:

- covered by a valid "Green Card", or
- normally based and currently insured in another member state.

9.7 What is "type approval"?

'Type approval' is the official recognition that the vehicle has satisfied certain international safety standards. You cannot licence and register a vehicle in the UK unless it is type-approved or otherwise exempt. For type approval purposes a motor vehicle is:

- a passenger vehicle with four or more wheels, or three wheels if it has a maximum gross weight of more than 1,000 kilograms, intended to carry no more than eight passengers, excluding the driver, *or*

- a three-wheeled passenger vehicle with a maximum gross weight of under 1,000 kilograms, if it has either a maximum speed of more than 50 kilometres per hour or an engine capacity of more than 50 cubic centimetres, *or*
- a goods vehicle.

9.8 What happens if I supply in the UK for removal to another member state a vehicle which is not "ype approved"?

If you supply in the UK for removal to another member state a vehicle, which is *not* type approved, and your customer changes their mind about removal and keeps the vehicle in the UK, it may not be licensed and registered here.

9.9 Are NMTs exempt from type approval?

NMT vehicles supplied in the UK are exempted from UK type approval requirements for as long as they are relieved from VAT whilst awaiting removal from the UK. If the vehicle is not removed and as a consequence becomes liable to UK VAT, the exemption from type approval is withdrawn. The absence of type approval may affect your ability to register the vehicle in the UK for permanent use on UK roads.

9.10 Where can I find more information on type approval?

You can find out more about type approval from:

The Vehicle Certification Agency
1 The Eastgate Office Centre
Eastgate Road
Bristol
BS5 6XX
Phone: 0117 951 5151

10 LIST OF DVLA LOCAL OFFICES

Office	*Address*	*Phone number*
Scotland		
Aberdeen	Greyfriars House Gallowgate Aberdeen AB10 1WG	0870 850 0007
Dundee	Caledonian House Greenmarket Dundee DD1 4QP	0870 850 0007
Edinburgh	Wallace House Lochside Avenue Edinburgh EH12 9DJ	0870 850 0007
Glasgow	46 West Campbell Street Glasgow G2 6TT	0870 850 0007
Inverness	Longman House 28 Longman Road Inverness IV1 1SF	0870 850 0007
Northern England		
Beverley	Crosskill House Mill Lane Beverley HU17 9JB	0870 850 0007
Carlisle	Ground Floor 3 Merchants Drive Parkhouse CA3 0JW	0870 850 0007
Chester	Norroy House Nuns Road Chester CH1 2ND	0870 850 0007

VAT

Office	*Address*	*Phone number*
Leeds	1st Floor 42 Eastgate Leeds LS2 7DQ	0870 850 0007
Manchester	Trafford House Chester Road Manchester M32 0SL	0870 850 0007
Newcastle-upon- Tyne	Eagle Star House Regent Farm Road Newcastle-upon-Tyne NE3 3QF	0870 850 0007
Preston	Unit A Fulwood Park Caxton Road Fulwood Preston PR2 9NZ	0870 850 0007
Sheffield	Cedar House Hallamshire Court 63 Napier Street Sheffield S11 8HA	0870 850 0007
Stockton-on-Tees	St Marks House St Marks Court Thornaby Stockton-on-Tees TS17 6QR	0870 850 0007
Midlands		
Birmingham	30 Granbury Avenue Garretts Green Birmingham B33 0SD	0870 850 0007
Northampton	Wooton Hall Park Northampton NN4 0GA	0870 850 0007
Nottingham	Nottingham Business Park Unit 6 Orchard Place Off Woodhouse Way Nottingham NG8 6PX	0870 850 0007
Shrewsbury	Stafford Drive Battlefield Ent Park Shrewsbury SY1 3BF	0870 850 0007
Worcester	Clerkenleap Barn Broomhall Kempsey WR5 3HR	0870 850 0007
Eastern England		
Chelmsford	Swift House 18 Hoffmanns Way Chelmsford CM1 1GU	0870 850 0007
Ipswich	Podium Level St Clare House Greyfriars Ipswich IP1 1UT	0870 850 0007
Lincoln	Firth House Firth Court Lincoln LN5 7WD	
Office Closed		

Office	*Address*	*Phone number*
Norwich	11 Prince of Wales Road Norwich NR1 1UP	0870 850 0007
Peterborough	88 Lincoln Road Peterborough PE1 2ST	0870 850 0007
London & Southern England		
Bournemouth	Ground Floor Bourne Gate 25 Bourne Valley Road Poole BH12 1DR	01202 5585531
Brighton	4th Floor Mocatta House Trafalgar Place Brighton BN1 4UE	01273 692271
Maidstone	Coronet House 11 Queen Anne Road Maidstone ME14 1XB	01662 675432
Oxford	Ground Floor 3 Cambridge Terrace Oxford OX1 1RW	01865 724056
Portsmouth	5th Floor The Connect Centre Kingston Crescent North End Portsmouth PO2 8AH	02392 639421
Theale	Building B Theale House Brunel Road Theale RG7 4AQ	0870 241 5161
Sidcup	12–18 Station Road Sidcup DA15 7EQ	020 8302 2134
London	Borehamwood Units 2 & 3 Elstree Gate Elstree Way Borehamwood WD6 1JD	0870 241 1269
Wimbledon	Ground Floor Connect House 133–137 Alexandra Road London SW19 7JY	0870 600 6767
West of England		
Bristol	Northleigh House Lime Kiln Close Stoke Gifford BS34 8SR	0117 969 2211
Exeter	Hanover House Manaton Close Matford Business Park Marsh Barton Trading Estate Exeter EX2 8EF	01392 824330
Truro	Pydar House Pydar Street Truro TR1 2TG	01872 278635
Wales		

Office	*Address*	*Phone number*
Bangor	Penrhos Road Penrhosgarnedd Bangor LL57 2JF	01248 351822
Cardiff	Archway House 77 Ty Glas Avenue Llanishen CF14 5DX	0292 075 3355
Swansea	Unit 1B Sandringham Park Swansea Vale Llansamlet Swansea SA6 7HG	01792 783900
Northern Ireland		
Coleraine	Vehicle Licensing Central Office County Hall Castlerock Road Coleraine Co. Londonderry BT51 3HS	01265 44133

11 APPLICATION FOR A REFUND OF VAT

Information on completing this form is given in section 7.

NEW MEANS OF TRANSPORT: APPLICATION FOR A REFUND OF VAT

Your details

Surname (Mr/Mrs/Miss/Dr) …

Forenames …

Full Address …

Telephone …

Details of the original supply to you

Name and address of supplier …

The price paid by you (exclusive of VAT) …

The amount of VAT paid …

Details of the proposed sale by you

Name and address of proposed purchaser …

Name of the EC Member State to which the New Means of Transport is to be removed: ….

Date of proposed sale by you …

Sale price …

DETAILS OF THE NEW MEANS OF TRANSPORT

	Motorised Land Vehicle	*Boat*	*Aircraft*
Make			
Model			
Colour			
Registration No.			
Engine No			
Length in metres	xxxxxxxxxxx		xxxxxxxxxx
Take off weight (kg)	xxxxxxxxxxx	xxxxxxxxxxx	
Chassis/Hull/ Airframe No			

Mileage since first entry into service		xxxxxxxxxxx	xxxxxxxxxx
Cubic centimetres/ kilowatts		xxxxxxxxxxx	xxxxxxxxxx
Hours of use since first entry into service	xxxxxxxxxxx		

Place in the UK where the New Means of Transport is currently kept

Dates and times when the New Means of Transport may be inspected

Amount of refund being claimed …

I declare that the information I have given and the documents relating to this claim are true and complete.

Signature …

Date …

Please note: no repayment will be considered until Customs have examined your proof of purchase, evidence of payment of VAT, proof of the sale in question and evidence of removal from the UK.

12 GLOSSARY

Throughout this notice the following terms have the meanings shown:

Term	*Meaning*
EC	The European Community: Austria, Belgium, Bulgaria, *Cyprus, Czech Republic, Denmark (except the Faroe Islands and Greenland), Estonia, Finland, France (including Monaco), Germany, Greece, Hungary, Ireland , Italy, Latvia, Lithuania, Luxembourg, Malta, Netherlands, Poland, Portugal (including Azores and Maderia), Romania, Slovakia, Slovinia, Spain (not the Canary Islands), Sweden, and the UK. *The European Commission has advised that, as the situation stands at present, the application of the Principal VAT Directive shall be suspended in those area of Cyprus in which the Government of the Republic of Cyprus does not exercise effective control. Transactions with those areas will continue from 1 May 2004 to be treated as non-EC transactions
UK	The United Kingdom: England, Scotland, Wales, Northern Ireland, (including the Isle of Man but not the Channel Islands).
Another member state	Any member state of the European Community other than the UK.
NMT	New Means of Transport (see the definition in paragraph 2.1).
First entry into service	See paragraph 2.3.

Notice 731
Cash accounting

July 2008

This notice cancels and replaces Notice 731 (April 2004)

The legal basis for the cash accounting scheme is in the VAT Regulations 1995, regulations 56–65. Parts of this notice have the force of law under these regulations. These parts are indicated by being placed in a box.

Example: The following text has the force of law

> You cannot retrospectively apply the cash accounting scheme to your business.

1 INTRODUCTION

1.1 What is this notice about?

This notice explains how the cash accounting scheme works and the conditions you must meet if you want to use it.

Commentary—*De Voil Indirect Tax Service* **V2.199.**

1.2 What's changed?

The notice has been rewritten to make the rules of the scheme clearer. The only changes of substance are new accounting rules for cheques, credit card payments and payments collected by third parties (paragraphs 4.4 to 4.5 and 5.2 to 5.3).

You can access details of any changes to this notice since July 2008 either on our Internet website at www.hmrc.gov.uk or by phoning our advice service on 0845 010 9000.

1.3 What is the cash accounting scheme?

The scheme allows you to account for VAT (output tax) on your sales on the basis of payments you receive, rather than on tax invoices you issue. This is different from the normal rules that require you to account for VAT on your sales when you issue a VAT invoice, even if your customer has not paid you.

However, if you choose to use the scheme, you can only reclaim the VAT incurred on your purchases (*input tax*) once you pay your supplier. Under the normal method of accounting for VAT you can reclaim VAT on purchases you make as soon as you receive a VAT invoice even if you have not paid your supplier.

1.4 Is the scheme suitable for my business?

The scheme could help your cash flow, because in general you do not have to pay VAT to us until your customer has paid you. The scheme will be especially helpful if you give your customers extended credit or suffer a lot of "bad debts".

However, the scheme may not give you any benefit if you:

- are usually paid as soon as you make a sale;
- regularly reclaim more VAT than you pay; or
- make continuous supplies of services.

If you find the scheme is of no benefit, you can stop using it at the end of a VAT accounting period and return to the normal method of accounting for VAT. For more information, see paragraph 6.1.

1.5 Additional rules which have force of law

The rules about cash accounting are set out in the VAT Regulations 1995. Some additional rules made under Regulations 57 and 59 are included in this notice. Their inclusion means that they have the force of law. The text relating to those rules have been placed in a box.

2 BASICS OF CASH ACCOUNTING

2.1 Am I eligible to use the scheme?

You are eligible to start using the scheme if you meet the following conditions:

- you expect the value of your taxable supplies in the next year will be £1,350,000 or less. To work out the value of your taxable supplies, see paragraph 2.2;
- you have no VAT returns outstanding;
- you have not been convicted of a VAT offence in the last year;
- you have not accepted an offer to compound proceedings in connection with a VAT offence in the last year;
- you have not been assessed to a penalty for VAT evasion involving dishonest conduct in the last year;
- you do not owe us any money or if you do, you have made arrangements with us to clear the total amount of your outstanding VAT payments (including surcharges and/or penalties);
- we have not written to you withdrawing use of the scheme during the last year;
- we have not written to you and denied you access to the scheme; and
- you comply with the conditions set out in this notice.

Commentary—*De Voil Indirect Tax Service* **V2.199.**

2.2 How do I work out the value of my taxable supplies for joining the scheme?

Your taxable supplies are the value excluding VAT, of standard, lower and zero-rated supplies you expect to make. Do not include the value of any exempt supplies or the value of any expected sale of capital assets.

2.3 How do I estimate what my future taxable supplies will be?

If you have been registered for less than 12 months, the simplest way is to estimate in the same way you did when you completed Form VAT 1 *Value Added Tax: Application for Registration.* If you have been registered for 12 months or more, you can use the value of your past year's taxable supplies as a guide.

If you believe these methods are not a good indicator of your future taxable supplies, you can make the estimate in any reasonable way.

You might use:

- your business plans;
- information relating to pre-registration business activity; or
- business information from a previous owner.

2.4 What if I estimate that my VAT turnover will not exceed £1,350,000 in the coming year and I am wrong?

We will not penalise you for this provided you can show that there were reasonable grounds for your estimate.

If your estimate of turnover had no reasonable estimate we will immediately remove you from the scheme. So it is sensible to keep a record of how the estimate was made.

2.5 What do I do if the value of my taxable supplies exceeds £1,350,000?

Once you have joined the scheme you may continue to use it until the annual value of your taxable supplies including the disposal of stock and capital assets, but excluding VAT, reaches £1,600,000.

If this figure is exceeded, you will have to leave the scheme at the end of your current tax period and use the normal method of accounting in future. For example:

If your VAT quarter ends on	*and your taxable supplies in the 12 months then ending*	*you must leave the scheme on*
30 November	Exceeded £1,600,000	30 November and begin normal VAT accounting from 1 December.

An exception to this rule for one-off sales is explained in paragraph 2.6.

You should monitor the amount of your taxable supplies regularly so that you have time to modify your books and records if you have to leave the scheme.

If you do leave the scheme, you must bring all outstanding VAT to account in accordance with paragraph 6.4.

2.6 What if my taxable supplies exceed £1,600,000 because of a "one-off" increase in sales?

If you exceed the £1,600,000 limit because of a one-off increase in sales, you may be able to remain on cash accounting on condition that you meet *all* of the following criteria:

- the "one off" increase has not happened before and is not expected to happen again, for example, the sale of a capital asset
- the sale arose from a genuine commercial activity
- there are reasonable grounds for believing that the value of your taxable supplies in the next 12 months will be below £1,350,000.

You must keep a record of how you came to your decision to remain on the scheme. If we find that you do not meet all the conditions then we may exclude you from the scheme immediately, or from the date your ineligible use began.

2.7 Must I use the scheme for all aspects of my business?

The following text has force of law

> Subject to the exceptions listed below you must use the cash accounting scheme for the whole of your VAT registered business.

The transactions below are excluded from cash accounting both to simplify the scheme and assist the cash flow of small businesses:

- goods that you buy or sell under lease purchase, hire purchase, conditional sale or credit sale agreements
- goods imported or acquired from another European Community member state (EC) (or goods removed from a Customs warehouse or free zone). For further information see paragraph 5.5
- certain goods on which the purchaser must account for output tax on his VAT return on the suppliers behalf due to the reverse charge (for further information see VAT Notice 735).

The transactions below are excluded from cash accounting to prevent abuse of the scheme:

- supplies where you issue a VAT invoice and payment of that invoice is not due in full within 6 months of the date it was issued;
- supplies of goods or services where you issue a VAT invoice in advance of making the supply or providing the goods.

Transactions excluded from the scheme must be accounted for under the normal VAT accounting rules as explained in Notice 700 "The VAT Guide".

2.8 Can I use any other schemes when I am on the cash accounting scheme?

If you use the cash accounting scheme you may also be able to use the annual accounting scheme. This scheme allows you to even out your VAT payments as you pay monthly or quarterly instalments based on an estimate of your annual VAT liability. At the end of the year you complete a single VAT return and pay any balance due. For further information see Notice 732 "Annual accounting".

The flat rate scheme cannot be used with cash accounting but it does have its own cash based method. For more information see Notice 733 "Flat rate scheme" (Part V8).

3 STARTING TO USE THE CASH ACCOUNTING SCHEME

3.1 How do I start to use the cash accounting scheme?

The following text has force of law

> You cannot retrospectively apply the cash accounting scheme to your business.

If your business is already registered for VAT and you are eligible to use the scheme (see paragraph 2.1) you may use the scheme from the start of your next VAT period.

There is no need to apply to use the scheme but you must avoid accounting for VAT twice on any supplies made or received before you began to use the scheme.

The following text has force of law and is designed to avoid you paying (or claiming) VAT twice when you change your method of accounting

> In order to do this you must, from the date you start to use the scheme, identify and separate in your records any payments you receive or make for transactions already accounted for under the normal method of VAT accounting. Exclude such payments from your scheme records.

Commentary—*De Voil Indirect Tax Service* **V2.199.**

3.2 I am a new VAT registration, how do I calculate my VAT due?

If you use the scheme from the first date of your VAT registration you may be eligible to reclaim, as though it was input tax, VAT on certain purchases made prior to being registered. For more information see Notice 700 "The VAT Guide".

For example, you may be able to reclaim VAT on:

- initial stocks;
- tools;
- machinery;
- office furniture; or
- other capital equipment.

If you choose to use the scheme from the date of your VAT registration, you must recover the VAT on such purchases as follows:

The following text has force of law

> If you have already paid for the qualifying goods and services, reclaim the VAT as though it was input tax on your first VAT return.
>
> If you pay for the goods or services after you have registered for VAT, claim the VAT, as though it was input tax, in the tax period in which you pay for them.

4 RECORDS AND ACCOUNTING FOR VAT

4.1 Record keeping

Most of the rules about record keeping are the same whether or not you use the scheme. The normal requirements are contained in VAT Notice 700 "The VAT Guide" and Notice 700/21

"Keeping records and accounts". However, there are some extra rules that apply only to the cash accounting scheme and these are explained below.

Note: This section contains only the general rules that apply to all businesses using the scheme. You must check Section 5 for details of special rules that apply to particular transactions.

Commentary—*De Voil Indirect Tax Service* **V2.199, V5.201.**

4.2 Are there any special rules for invoices?

If you receive payment in coins or notes from a customer you must, if asked, endorse the customer's copy of your sales invoice with the amount that they have paid and the date it was paid.

Similarly, *if you pay a supplier in coins or notes,* you must ensure that they endorse your copy of the purchase invoice with the amount you have paid and the date it was paid.

4.3 Do I have to keep any other records?

The following text has force of law

In order to operate the cash accounting scheme, your records must clearly cross refer payments:

- *received* by you, or on your behalf, to your corresponding sales invoice;
- *made* by you to the corresponding purchase invoice;
- *made or received* to the normal commercial evidence (such as bank statements, cheque stubs, paying-in slips.

The easiest way to do this is to keep a cash book summarising all payments made and received, with separate columns for VAT. Whatever form your records take, they should always be complete and up to date.

If you are in any doubt about how to keep your records, contact our advice service (see paragraph 1.2 for contact details) for guidance.

4.4 When must I account for the VAT on my sales?

VAT on your sales (*output tax*) must be accounted for on the VAT return for the accounting period in which you receive a payment from your customer. For the purposes of the scheme, the date you are paid depends on the way in which your customer pays you. The rules are as follows:

If you are paid by	*Then the date you receive payment is*
cash (coins or notes)	the date you receive the money.
giro, standing order or direct debit	the date your bank account is credited with such a payment.

The following text has force of law

If you are paid by credit or debit card: you receive payment on the date you make out a sales voucher for the payment (not when you actually receive payment from the card provider).
If the credit or debit card payment is not honoured, then you do not have to account for the VAT. If you have already accounted for the VAT you can adjust your VAT account, or make a refund claim in line with Notice 700/45 "How to correct VAT errors and make adjustments or claims". If you later receive a payment for the supply, then you must account for the VAT due on that payment.

If you are paid by cheque: you receive payment on the date you receive the cheque, or the date on the cheque, whichever is later.
If the cheque is not honoured, then you do not have to account for the VAT. If you have already accounted for the VAT you can adjust your VAT account, or make a refund claim in line with Notice 700/45 "How to correct VAT errors and make adjustments or claims". If you later receive a payment for the supply, then you must account for the VAT due on that payment.

Commentary—*De Voil Indirect Tax Service* **V5.109.**

4.5 When can I reclaim VAT incurred on my purchases and expenses?

Once you start to use the scheme you claim the VAT you incur on your purchases and expenses (*input tax*) on the VAT return for the tax period in which you make a payment to your supplier. For the purposes of the scheme the date you pay depends on the way in which you make a payment. The rules are as follows:

If you pay by	*Then the date you make payment is*
cash (coins or notes)	the date you pay the money. But remember – you need a receipted invoice to claim back VAT on purchases you have paid for in this way (see paragraph 4.2).

Giro, standing order or direct debit	the date your bank account is debited with such a payment.

The following text has force of law

> **If you pay by credit or debit card:** the date of payment is the date a sales voucher is made out for the payment.
>
> **If you pay by cheque:** the date of payment is the date you send the cheque, or the date on the cheque, whichever is later. If your cheque is not honoured, you cannot reclaim the VAT. If you have already accounted for the VAT you should adjust your VAT account, or make a voluntary disclosure in line with Notice 700/45 "How to correct VAT errors and make adjustments or claims".

Paragraphs 5.7 to 5.10 (inclusive) contain further information relating to payments.

Commentary—*De Voil Indirect Tax Service* **V3.418.**

4.6 Partial exemption

If you incur input tax on goods and services that you use or intend to use in the making of exempt supplies, you may not be able to claim all your input tax. This is known as partial exemption. If you are partly exempt, you should see Notice 706 "Partial exemption".

Under the normal method of accounting for VAT, businesses who are partly exempt will usually make a calculation to establish the correct amount of input tax claimable, based on purchases and sales made during a tax period.

Partly exempt businesses who use the scheme must base such a calculation on payments made and received in a tax period.

4.7 How do I fill in my VAT return?

When you fill in your VAT return remember that the amounts of VAT due and deductible are based on payments received and made, not on invoices issued. For the purposes of the scheme the "Value of Outputs" and the "Value of Inputs" are the amounts of payments you have received or made exclusive of VAT.

Remember, if you make supplies to other EC member states the amount you put in Box 8 of the VAT return should be the total value of all supplies of goods and services made, exclusive of VAT, and not the total of payments received.

5 SPECIAL RULES FOR PARTICULAR TRANSACTIONS

5.1 Deposits

The rules about deposits are in Notice 700 "The VAT Guide". If you receive or pay a deposit which serves as an advance payment, you must account for it in accordance with the rules in paragraphs 4.4 and 4.5.

VAT does not apply to deposits taken as a security to ensure the safe return of goods, whether you refund it upon return of the goods or retain it to compensate you for loss or damage.

Commentary—*De Voil Indirect Tax Service* **V2.199.**

5.2 Payments collected by agents on your behalf

The following text has force of law

> If an agent collects payments on your behalf, you must account for VAT on the supply in the VAT period in which your agent collects payment from your customer.
>
> The value on which VAT is due, is the amount of the taxable debt that the agent collects from your customer, not the amount of credit given to you by the agent (see section 5.8 for more information).

5.3 Factoring

The following text has force of law

> **Recourse agreements (that is where you remain responsible for bearing any loss resulting from an unpaid debt).**
>
> If you have assigned to a factor a debt in respect of a taxable supply you have made while using the cash accounting scheme, you must account for output tax on the supply in the VAT period in which your factor collects payment from your customer.
>
> The value on which VAT is due, is the amount that the factor collects from your customer in relation to taxable supplies, not any lesser amount paid to you by the factor (see ➡

section 5.8). If the factor is unable to collect all (or part) of the debt, then you must account for that amount under the normal rules, in line with paragraph 4.4.

Non-recourse agreements (that is where the factor accepts the risk of any loss resulting from your customer's debt).

If you have assigned to a factor a debt in respect of a taxable supply you have made while using the cash accounting scheme, you must account for output tax on the supply in the VAT period in which your factor collects payment from your customer.

The value on which VAT is due, is the amount that the factor collects from your customer in relation to taxable supplies, not any lesser amount paid to you by the factor (see section 5.8).

If the factor is unable to collect all (or part) of the debt on your behalf, then you must account for output tax on the uncollected element of the debt, in the period in which any advance made against that debt is written off by the factor.

If, however, the factor re-assigns all or part of the debt back to you under a recourse clause, then you may be able to claim bad debt relief, subject to paragraph 6.6.

Commentary—*De Voil Indirect Tax Service* **V5.156.**

5.4 Selling debts

The following text has force of law

If you sell a debt for a taxable supply you made while using the cash accounting scheme, you must account for VAT on the supply in the VAT period in which the debt is sold.

You must account for the output tax on the full value of the supply to which the debt relates, not on any lesser amount which you receive when you sell the debt.

5.5 Imports and EC acquisitions

The following text has force of law

You cannot use the cash accounting scheme for goods you import, acquire from a business registered in another EC member state or remove from a Customs warehouse or free zone.

You must account for VAT on such purchases under the normal VAT rules as explained in Notice 700 "The VAT Guide". You can, however, use the scheme to account for VAT on the onward supply of such goods.

Full details of the VAT import and warehouse requirements are in Notice 702 "VAT: Imports".

5.6 Exports and supplies to other EC member states

If you use the scheme and export goods or despatch them to another EC member state but don't receive the evidence of export/supply within the time limits allowed, you must account for the VAT that becomes due. This means that you account for VAT on any payments already received.

If you receive further payments for such goods you must account for VAT on these payments when you receive them.

If you later obtain evidence of export/supply you can then zero-rate the supply and adjust your VAT account for the tax period in which you obtained the evidence.

Full details of the VAT documentary evidence of export requirements are in Notice 703 "VAT: Exports and removals of goods from the United Kingdom" or, for retail exports, Notice 704 "VAT: Retail exports".

Further information regarding acquisitions from and despatches to other EC member states can be found in Notice 725 "VAT: The Single Market".

5.7 Part payments

This paragraph explains what to do if you receive part payment for an invoice in circumstances where you still expect to receive the rest of the payment. Paragraph 5.8 deals with part payments where your customer has made a deduction before paying your invoice.

The following text has force of law

If you make or receive payments which:

- are a partial payment of an invoice; or
- cover more than one invoice; or
- relate to an invoice for supplies at different rates of tax;

you must allocate the payment to the invoices in the order in which you issue or receive them.

Where you make or receive partial payment of an invoice and VAT is not identified separately you must treat the payment as VAT inclusive. Where you make or receive payments which relate to an invoice for supplies at different rates of tax you must apportion the amount paid or received between the different rates and treat the amounts on which VAT is due at the standard or lower rate as VAT inclusive.

Examples of how this can be done are shown in Section 8.

5.8 Payments received net of deductions

The following text has force of law

If you receive a net payment you must account for VAT on the full value of taxable supplies made by you before such deductions. This will usually be the value shown on your VAT invoice — remember not to include any amounts that are for supplies that do not attract VAT.

Some examples of payments that you may receive that are net of deductions are payments:

- where commission has been deducted by your customer; or
- where commission or payment for expenses has been deducted by a factor or agent collecting money on your behalf (see paragraph 5.2 and 5.3 for more information); or
- where commission or payment for expenses has been deducted by an auctioneer selling goods on your behalf; or
- made by an employer/contractor who has deducted income tax.

5.9 Payments in kind (for example, barter, part exchange)

The general rules about payments in kind are in Notice 700 "The VAT Guide". If you pay or are paid fully or partly in kind, such as by barter or part exchange, you must still account for VAT each time you make or receive a "payment". You receive/make "payment" on the date you receive/supply the goods or services agreed in lieu of money.

You must account for VAT on the full tax value of the supply which is usually the price, excluding VAT, which a customer would have to pay for the supply if they had paid for it with money only.

5.10 Payments received and made in a foreign currency

If you issue VAT invoices in a foreign currency, including euro, you must follow the rules in the relevant paragraphs of Notice 700 "The VAT Guide". If the invoice is paid in full, you will not need to convert the foreign currency payment into sterling for the purposes of the scheme. You must always declare the sterling amount of VAT due on the supply as shown on the invoice.

5.11 What about partial payments?

If you receive a partial payment in a foreign currency against an invoice expressed in:

- *both a foreign currency and sterling* you will need to calculate the amount of VAT included in the payment by determining what proportion of the total amount due on the invoice is being paid and applying that proportion to the total VAT due.

For example, if the payment in the foreign currency represents half of the total foreign currency amount due on an invoice, you must declare half of the sterling VAT figure as shown on the invoice.

- *sterling only* you will need to convert the foreign currency payment into sterling using one of the methods outlined in Notice 700 "The VAT Guide". For the purposes of the scheme, you must be consistent in the method used. But whatever method you adopt, the exchange rate to be used is that current at the time of the supply by you. This may not be the same as the exchange rate which applies at the time you receive payment. Once you have established what the sterling equivalent of the foreign currency payment is and what proportion of the total sterling amount due this represents, you can then determine how much of the payment is VAT.

The above rules also apply if you pay for supplies from other UK businesses in a foreign currency.

Note. This section cannot deal with all the possible situations you may encounter. If you have difficulty in dealing with a transaction, please do not guess the answer. Contact our advice service (see paragraph 1.2 for contact details).

5.12 What do I do if the price agreed for a supply changes?

Any increase or decrease in consideration for a supply must be evidenced by the issue of a credit or debit note.

Where a further payment or refund is then received or made, this should be recorded in your payment record as normal.

For information on credit notes see Notice 700 "The VAT Guide".

6 LEAVING THE SCHEME

6.1 What if I want to leave the scheme?

The following text has force of law

> You can only leave the scheme at the end of a tax period.

You must then use the normal method of accounting for VAT from the beginning of the next tax period. You must bring all outstanding VAT to account in accordance with paragraph 6.4.

Commentary—*De Voil Indirect Tax Service* **V2.199, V5.102.**

6.2 When must I stop using the scheme?

You must stop using the scheme if:

- you cannot comply with the record keeping requirements set out in this notice;
- during a period of one year (ending at the end of a tax period) the value of your taxable supplies, including disposal of stock and capital assets but excluding VAT, exceeds £1,600,000;
- we write to you withdrawing use of the scheme;
- you are convicted of a VAT offence;
- you accept an offer to compound proceedings in connection with a VAT offence;
- you are assessed to a penalty for VAT evasion involving dishonest conduct.

6.3 May I re-join the scheme after leaving it?

If you leave the scheme voluntarily or because the value of your taxable supplies exceeded £1,600,000, you may begin to use the scheme again from the start of a tax period, provided you are eligible to do so as detailed in paragraph 2.1.

6.4 How do I account for VAT if I leave the scheme voluntarily or because my turnover has exceeded the ceiling?

When you leave the scheme there may be supplies that you have made for which you have not been paid and as a result you have not accounted for any VAT. You will need to account for this VAT even if you have not been paid by the customer. There may also be cases where you have not paid your suppliers and you have not yet claimed your input tax. You are entitled to claim this input tax subject to the normal VAT rules. You may choose either to:

- account for all your outstanding VAT due in the period in which you stop using the scheme. This may be simpler but could have a serious effect on your cash flow if the amounts of unpaid VAT on supplies you have made are high. As an alternative you can opt for a further six months in which to account for the outstanding VAT.

Please note that you cannot opt for a further six months in which to account for the outstanding VAT if:

- we have withdrawn use of the scheme from you, or
- the value of your taxable supplies has exceeded £1,600,000 and the value of your supplies made in the previous three months totalled more than £1,350,000.

You do not need to notify us which method you have chosen.

6.5 How do I account for VAT if I use the six-month option?

To avoid double accounting you will need to keep your normal cash accounting records for the supplies you made and received while you used the scheme. In particular you will need to keep a record of payments you make and receive during the six months. In addition, you will need to keep separate records required under normal VAT accounting for new supplies you make and receive after you left the scheme.

Commentary—*De Voil Indirect Tax Service* **V5.103.**

6.6 Do I have to account for outstanding VAT on "bad" debts when I leave the scheme?

One advantage of the cash accounting scheme is that you do not have to account for VAT on bad debts. However, if you stop using cash accounting, you have to account for VAT on supplies you have made and received even if they have not been paid for (see paragraph 6.4).

If you have not received any payment then you may be able to claim relief for your bad debts which meet the conditions of the bad debt relief scheme.

The key conditions are:

- that it is six months from the date on which the debt became due and payable or the supply was made, whichever is later;
- you can provide evidence that the bad debt has been written off in your "refunds for bad debts" account; and

- for supplies made prior to 1 January 2003, where your customer is registered for VAT, you have notified your customer of your claim for bad debt relief.

For more information see Notice 700/18 "VAT relief on bad debts".

Commentary—*De Voil Indirect Tax Service* **V5.156.**

6.7 What do I do if use of the scheme is withdrawn or I am told I cannot use the scheme?

You will be advised in writing if we decide to deny you access or withdraw use of the scheme from you. If you are using the scheme the letter will specify when you must stop using the scheme and when you must account for the outstanding tax due on supplies made and received while using the scheme (further details on how to do this are in section 6.4).

If you disagree with our decision to deny you access to the scheme or withdraw use of the scheme, you may ask us to reconsider.

You should do this within 30 days of the date of our decision and you should let us know if you:

- think that there are facts that may not have been fully considered; or
- can provide further information.

6.8 Is there anything else I can do?

You can also appeal against our decision to a VAT and Duties Tribunal.

The Leaflet "Appeals and applications to the Tribunal" tells you what to do. You can request a copy of the leaflet by phoning the Tribunal Centres in either:

London **020 7631 4242**

Manchester 0161 868 6600

Edinburgh 0131 226 3551

6.9 I've appealed to a VAT Tribunal. May I continue to use the scheme?

If you have appealed to a VAT tribunal about our decision to:

- deny you access to use the scheme;
- withdraw use of the scheme on the grounds of protection of the revenue; or
- not to allow you to continue to use the scheme once you have exceeded the tolerance you must not use the scheme until your appeal is resolved.

If you have appealed against any other matter, then we will normally allow continued use of the scheme, pending the outcome of the appeal. However, if we consider that an appeal facilitates manipulation of the scheme, we may withdraw use of the scheme for the protection of the revenue and you will not be able to use it until the appeal is settled.

Contact our advice service (see paragraph 1.2 for contact details) for further guidance on this matter.

6.10 What do I do if I cease trading?

If you cease trading, you may continue to use the scheme while you dispose of any remaining stocks or assets. Once your VAT registration is cancelled you must follow the rules in paragraph 6.12.

Commentary—*De Voil Indirect Tax Service* **V2.199.**

6.11 What happens if my business becomes insolvent?

If your business becomes insolvent, you will need to account on your pre-insolvency VAT return for all VAT on supplies made and received by you before the date of your insolvency which has not yet been accounted for under the scheme.

Where trading continues after the relevant date, the office holder responsible for the business may continue to use the scheme subject to the rules set out in this notice.

The following text has force of law

> If the office holder does continue to use the cash accounting scheme they must, from the date of insolvency, separate in the business records any payments the business receives or makes for transactions already accounted for on the pre-insolvency VAT return.

Further details relating to insolvency matters are in Notice 700/56 "VAT: Insolvency".

Commentary—*De Voil Indirect Tax Service* **V2.199.**

6.12 What if I deregister?

You will have two months to submit your final return after you deregister. On this return you must account for all outstanding VAT on supplies made and received prior to deregistration.

This applies even if you have not been paid, but you can also reclaim any VAT provided that you have the tax invoices. If some of the outstanding tax relates to bad debts you may claim relief as detailed in paragraph 6.6.

You may also need to account for VAT on the value of any stocks and assets you still have. For further information see Notice 700/11 "Cancelling your registration".

Commentary—*De Voil Indirect Tax Service* **V2.199.**

7 TRANSFER OF A GOING CONCERN

7.1 What if I sell or buy a business as a going concern and the VAT registration number has not been transferred?

Where the whole of a business which uses the scheme is transferred as a going concern and the existing owner cancels the VAT registration of that business, he must follow the rules in paragraph 6.12. The new owner can then choose, subject to eligibility, whether or not to use the scheme.

7.2 What if I sell or buy as a going concern a business which is using the scheme and the VAT registration number has been transferred?

The following text has force of law

> If you sell your business as a going concern and the new owner takes over your VAT registration number, you must advise the new owner that you are using the cash accounting scheme.

The new owner must continue to operate the scheme and account for payments for supplies and purchases made by the previous owner, as if the new owner had made them.

If the new owner does not want to continue to use the scheme, they must leave the scheme as soon as possible and follow the rules in paragraph 6.4.

Remember, outstanding VAT must be accounted for on the return for the tax period in which the new owner stopped using the scheme.

If only part of a business is transferred as a going concern, you should contact our advice service (see paragraph 1.2 for contact details).

Commentary—*De Voil Indirect Tax Service* **V2.199.**

8 ACCOUNTING FOR PART PAYMENTS

(referred to in 5.7)

8.1 Accounting for VAT when a part payment is made against one invoice

Invoice A

Standard-rated goods	£1000.00
VAT	£175.00
Total	**£1175.00**

Step	*Action*
Step 1	If a payment of £750.00 is made against invoice A, determine what percentage of that payment represents VAT as follows— $$\frac{\text{Amount of money received}}{\text{Total invoice amount}} \times 100 = \text{Percentage of VAT due}$$ for example $$\frac{£750.00}{£1175.00} \times 100 = 64\%$$
Step 2	Multiply the amount of VAT charged by the percentage calculated at *Step 1.* for example £175.00 x 64% = £112.00

In this example £112.00 of the £750.00 payment received should be accounted for as VAT.

The remaining £63.00 VAT still due to Customs (£175.00 – £112.00 = £63.00) should be accounted for when further payment is received.

8.2 Accounting for VAT on a single payment made against more than one invoice, or against invoices for supplies at different rates of tax

Invoice B		*Invoice C*	
Date 01/05/98		*Date 26/05/98*	
Standard-rated goods	£1000.00	Standard-rated goods	£2000.00
VAT	£175.00	Zero-rated goods	£1000.00
Total	**£1175.00**	VAT	£350.00
		Total	**£3350.00**

If a payment of £2500.00 is made against invoices B and C which does not relate to any particular supply you should allocate it as follows:

Step	*Action*
Step 1	Allocate £1175.00 of the £2500.00 to the earliest supply ie invoice B and account for VAT of £175.00. The balance of the payment of £1325.00 (£2500.00 – £1175.00 = £1325.00) should then be allocated against the later supply, ie invoice C, as follows:
Step 2	Calculate what percentage of the remaining £1325.00 represents VAT against invoice C. (Remaining amount of money available ÷ Total amount still owed to you (that is invoice C) x 100 = Percentage of invoice paid. for example (£1325.00 ÷ £3350.00) x 100 = 39%
Step 3	Multiply the amount of VAT due on invoice C by the percentage calculated at Step 2 for example £350.00 x 39% = £136.50

In this example £311.50 (£175.00 + £136.50 = £311.50) of the £2500.00 payment should be accounted for as VAT against the £525.00 VAT due. (£175.00 + £350.00 = £525.00).

The remaining £213.50 VAT still due (£350.00 – £136.50) should be accounted for when you receive further payment.

Notice 733
Flat rate scheme for small businesses

March 2007 (with Update 1)

This notice cancels and replaces Notice 733 (February 2004).

The legal basis for the flat rate scheme is in the VAT Regulations 1995, regs 55A–55V, 57A and 69A. Parts of this notice have the force of law under those regulations. These parts are indicated by being placed in a box as in the example shown below.

Example:

The following rule has the force of law

> If you receive a net payment, you must include the full value before such deductions (and including VAT) in your scheme turnover. This will usually be the value shown on your sales invoice.

1 INTRODUCTION

1.1 What is this notice about?

This notice describes the flat rate scheme for small businesses.

Section 2 gives an overview to help you decide whether the scheme can help your business.

If you decide the scheme may help your business the rest of the notice contains the detailed rules on operating the scheme and explains how to apply.

Many of the normal VAT rules apply to the flat rate scheme. So if you can't find the answer to your question in this notice, remember the basics of VAT can be found in Notice 700 "The VAT Guide".

Commentary—*De Voil Indirect Tax Service* **V2.119B.**

1.2 What has changed?

This revised notice replaces the February 2004 edition. Some changes have been made to improve the layout and clarity. The new guidance is—

- a new paragraph on what to do if you leave the scheme because you deregister – paragraph 12.4
- a new paragraph on how florists account for VAT under the scheme – paragraph 10.7
- a description of how barristers chambers can use Method 3 with the scheme – section 13 and
- a new section on how to claim input tax outside the scheme when you buy capital expenditure goods that cost £2,000 or more – section 15.

Those parts of this notice that have the force of law are marked clearly.

2 BASICS OF THE FLAT RATE SCHEME

Commentary—*De Voil Indirect Tax Service* **V2.199B.**

2.1 What is the flat rate scheme?

The flat rate scheme is designed to help small businesses by taking some of the work out of recording VAT sales and purchases. If you use the scheme you apply a single percentage to your turnover in a VAT period. The result is the VAT you pay to HM Revenue & Customs.

2.2 How will it help me?

The main benefit of the scheme is the time saved recording VAT on sales and purchases. This can also take some of the stress out of completing VAT returns at the quarter end. And because you can easily calculate how much VAT you owe on takings, it can help you to manage cash flow.

2.3 Will all businesses benefit?

Not every business will enjoy all the benefits of the scheme. For example, if your customers are VAT registered you will have to calculate the VAT and issue VAT invoices in the normal way. Businesses who buy and sell goods from outside the UK can find the scheme more complex and if you do this make sure you understand the rules in 6.4.

Also, some businesses using the flat rate scheme may pay more VAT than they would on normal accounting. This is because the flat rates are averages. You can estimate the effect on your business by using the ready reckoner on our website at www.hmrc.gov.uk/business/services/vat-flat-rate.htm

2.4 What about input tax?

Input tax is the VAT charged to you by other businesses. Under normal VAT accounting, you claim this back from us on your quarterly VAT return. If you use the flat rate scheme, you do not recover input tax or VAT on imports or acquisitions. This is because the flat rates are calculated to represent the net VAT you need to pay to us. In other words, an allowance for input tax is built into the flat rates.

There are special rules when you buy high value capital goods. Section 15 explains how you can claim back the VAT on these purchases.

2.5 Who can join the scheme?

The scheme is for businesses with a turnover no more than £150,000 a year, *excluding* VAT. There are some additional rules to stop abuse of the scheme. If you want to know more, section 3 explains the joining conditions in more detail. The flat rate scheme is a simpler method of working out the VAT you have to pay to us and so is unsuitable where you regularly receive repayments from us.

2.6 How do I join?

You can apply by post, telephone, or email. Section 5 gives full details.

2.7 Can I combine the flat rate scheme with other schemes?

The table below shows which other schemes you can use with the flat rate scheme.

Scheme	*May be used with flat rate scheme?*	*Further information*

Annual accounting	Yes	Combining the annual accounting scheme with the flat rate scheme can mean you: —spend less time working out how much VAT you owe —avoid a big bill by evening out your VAT over the year —submit only one VAT return a year. If you wish to join both schemes, Notice 732 "Annual accounting" contains a joint application form. If you are already using one of the schemes and wish to use the other, complete the form for the scheme you have not yet joined.
Cash accounting	No	but the flat rate scheme has its own cash based method that is very similar to the cash accounting scheme. See section 9.
Retail schemes	No	but the flat rate scheme has its own retail based method that is very similar to ordinary retail schemes. If you want to leave a retail scheme to join the flat rate scheme, simply follow the rules about ceasing to use the retail scheme in Notice 727 "Retail schemes".
Margin scheme for second-hand goods	No	If you sell a significant proportion of second-hand goods using margin schemes or the auctioneers' scheme, the flat rate scheme will be of limited value to your business. This is because the flat rate scheme calculates VAT on the total received for your sale rather than on the margin.

3 ELIGIBILITY AND CONDITIONS OF THE SCHEME

Commentary—*De Voil Indirect Tax Service* **V2.199B.**

3.1 Who can join?

The flat rate scheme is for small businesses. You can apply to use the scheme if there are reasonable grounds for believing that your taxable turnover (excluding VAT) in the next year will be £150,000 or less.

3.2 How do I work out my taxable turnover?

For this test, leave out any anticipated sales of capital assets but include all of the following-

– the value of your standard rate, zero rate and reduced rate supplies
– your turnover from the sale of second-hand goods sold outside the margin scheme. See Notice 718 "Margin schemes" and
– any sales of investment gold that are covered by VATA s 55. See Notice 701/21 "Gold".

Remember to *leave out* any VAT when doing this test.

3.3 How do I work out my total income for Test 2?

…

3.4 How do I know what my future turnover is going to be?

You may forecast this in any reasonable way. If you have been registered for VAT for 12 months or more, the turnover declared on your returns may be a reasonable guide but take into account any expected changes. If you are not VAT registered when you apply for the scheme, you may forecast your turnover by looking at—

– any period of trading before you apply

- the turnover of the previous business owner or
- information on business plans or loan applications.

3.5 What if my future turnover rises above my forecast?

If your forecast turns out to be too low, we will not penalise you provided there were reasonable grounds for what you forecast. So it is sensible to keep a record of the figures you used to calculate your future turnover.

If your forecast had no reasonable basis, we may exclude you from the scheme immediately, or from the date your ineligible use began.

3.6 What if my turnover rises once I have joined the scheme?

You may stay in the scheme provided your total income (including VAT) for the year just gone has not risen above £225,000. Make this check on each anniversary of your business joining the flat rate scheme. You must leave the scheme if your turnover increases so that there are grounds for believing that the total value of your income will rise above £225,000 in the next 30 days alone. **Important Note.** You become eligible for the scheme based on the level of your taxable turnover, but the test of continuing eligibility for the scheme is based on all income (including exempt income). This could mean that, if you have a very high level of exempt income, in extreme cases you could be eligible to join but have to leave immediately. This is unlikely to happen in practice because the scheme is not suitable for businesses with high levels of exempt turnover. **See paragraph 6.2 for further details.** See section 12 for further details about leaving the scheme.

3.7 Who cannot join the scheme?

You cannot join the scheme if *any* of the following apply—

- you are not registered for VAT
- you use the second-hand margin scheme or the auctioneers' scheme
- you are required to use the tour operator's margin scheme
- you are required to operate the Capital Goods Scheme for certain capital items (see paragraph 15.6)
- you have stopped using the flat rate scheme in the 12 months before the date of your new application
- in the 12 months before your application you have either—
  - accepted a compound penalty offer or been convicted of an offence in connection with VAT or
  - been assessed with a penalty for conduct involving dishonesty
- you are, or within the past 24 months have been, registered for VAT in the name of either a—
  - VAT group (see paragraph 3.8) or
  - division
- you are, or within the past 24 months have been, eligible for VAT group treatment (see paragraph 3.8)
- your business is "associated" with another one in the special way explained in paragraph 3.9.

3.8 Can I use the scheme if I am in a VAT group?

VAT groups are for incorporated businesses which are linked to other incorporated businesses by common control or ownership. If you are eligible to be in a VAT group, even if you are not currently in one, then you cannot use the flat rate scheme. If you become eligible to join a VAT group after you join the scheme, then you must leave the scheme with effect from the date you become eligible.

For details of eligibility to join a group see Notice 700/2 "Group and divisional registration".

If your business has been eligible to join a VAT group in the last two years, but is not eligible at the time you apply, we can let you use the scheme if we agree in writing that your former eligibility is not a risk to the revenue.

3.9 What if my business is closely linked with another business?

There is a rule which stops "associated" businesses joining the flat rate scheme. Paragraph 3.10 explains some exceptions to this rule.

If you are unsure whether the particular relationship between your business and another constitutes "association" then please contact our National Advice Service.

You are associated with another business in this special sense if—

- one business is under the dominant influence of another
- two businesses are closely bound by financial, economic and organisational links or
- another company has the right to give directions to you
- in practice your company habitually complies with the directions of another. The test here is a test of the commercial reality rather than of the legal form.

If your business has been associated in this way with another in the last two years, but is not associated at the time you apply, we can let you use the scheme if we agree in writing that your former association is not a risk to the revenue.

3.10 I have a close connection with another business – does this mean we are "associated"?

Not necessarily. Businesses are not generally "associated" in this special sense where a normal commercial relationship exists.

Example 1

A business is not associated with its customer's company just because it supplies them with the goods they request in the form they request them.

Example 2

A husband and wife are each separately VAT registered in different types of business. Even if they share premises, provided this is charged at a market rate, they will not be "associated".

4 DETERMINING YOUR FLAT RATE PERCENTAGE

Commentary—*De Voil Indirect Tax Service* **V2.199B.**

4.1 Which flat rate applies to my business?

The flat rate you use depends on the business sector that you belong in. All the sectors are in the table in paragraph 4.3. The correct sector is the one that most closely describes what your business will be doing in the coming year. The easiest way to identify your sector is by using the online ready reckoner at www.hmrc.gov.uk/business/services/vat-flat-rate.htm This also shows you which businesses we think belong in each sector.

If you cannot go online, then go through the following steps.

Step	*What you need to do*	*Please remember*
1	See if your business is mentioned in the table in paragraph 4.3	The descriptions of the sectors are not technical and use ordinary English. So if there is a match or a close fit, use that sector.
2	Check the table again to make sure your business is not mentioned in a composite sector	Some of the sectors refer to more than one business type.
3	If there is no sector that mentions your business, look at the sectors for "Businesses not mentioned elsewhere"	There is one for retail, one for business services and one for manufacturing.
4	If you still haven't found a sector you can use "Any other activity not listed elsewhere".	However, if you are still unsure, or unhappy with your choice, you can phone our National Advice Service on 0845 010 9000 Tell the National Advice Service that you have followed Steps 1 to 3 above.

4.2 What if I get the sector wrong?

We will not normally check your choice of sector when we process your application.

So if you have made a mistake you may pay too much tax or too little. Paying too little could mean that you are faced with an unexpected VAT bill at a later date.

However, if we approve you to join the scheme, we will not change your choice of sector retrospectively as long as your choice was reasonable. It will be sensible to keep a record of why you chose your sector in case you need to show us that your choice was reasonable.

4.3 The trade sectors and flat rates

The table below shows the trade sectors and flat rate percentages in alphabetical order.

Trade sector (from 1 April 2004)	*Flat rate percentage*
Accountancy or book-keeping	13
Advertising	9.5
Agricultural services	7.5
Any other activity not listed elsewhere	10

Trade sector (from 1 April 2004)	*Flat rate percentage*
Architect, civil and structural engineer or surveyor	12.5
Boarding or care of animals	10.5
Business services that are not listed elsewhere	11
Catering services, including restaurants and takeaways	12
Computer and IT consultancy or data processing	13
Computer repair services	11
Dealing in waste or scrap	9.5
Entertainment or journalism	11
Estate agency or property management services	11
Farming or agriculture that is not listed elsewhere	6
Film, radio, television or video production	10.5
Financial services	11.5
Forestry or fishing	9
General building or construction services Note: Use "General building" if the value of materials supplied is more than 10% of your turnover. If the value of the materials is less than this, use the "Labour only" flat rate.	8.5
Hairdressing or other beauty treatment services	12
Hiring or renting goods	8.5
Hotel or accommodation	9.5
Investigation or security	10
Labour-only building or construction services Note: Use "Labour-only" if the value of materials supplied is less than 10% of your turnover. If the value of the materials is more than this, use the 'General building' flat rate.	13.5
Laundry or dry-cleaning services	11
Lawyer or legal services	13
Library, archive, museum or other cultural activity	7.5
Management consultancy	12.5
Manufacturing food	7.5
Manufacturing that is not listed elsewhere	8.5
Manufacturing yarn, textiles or clothing	8.5
Manufacturing fabricated metal products	10
Membership organisation	5.5
Mining or quarrying	9
Packaging	8.5
Photography	9.5
Post Offices	2
Printing	7.5
Pubs	5.5
Publishing	9.5
Real estate activity not listed elsewhere	12
Repairing personal or household goods	8.5
Repairing vehicles	7.5
Retailing food, confectionery, tobacco, newspapers or children's clothing	2
Retailing pharmaceuticals, medical goods, cosmetics or toiletries	7
Retailing vehicles or fuel	7
Retailing that is not listed elsewhere	6
Secretarial services	11
Social work	8.5
Sport or recreation	7
Transport or storage, including couriers, freight, removals and taxis	9
Travel agency	9
Veterinary medicine	9.5
Wholesaling agricultural products	6
Wholesaling food	5.5
Wholesaling that is not listed elsewhere	7

Note—Appropriate percentages amended to reflect the temporary reduction in the standard rate of VAT (to 15%) from 1 December 2008 until 1 January 2010. For amended percentages see Annex E of HMRC publication "VAT–Change in the standard rate: a detailed guide for VAT-registered businesses", 24 November 2008.

4.4 Business activities that are the source of common enquiry

The table below gives the trade sector for particular business activities, which have been the subject of common enquiries to our National Advice Service.

Business activity	*Trade sector*	*Flat rate percentage*
Engineering consultants and designers	—Architects, civil and structural engineers	12.5
Agents	—Business services that are not listed elsewhere	11
Barristers	—Lawyers or legal services	13
Florists	—Retailing that is not listed elsewhere	6
Agronomists	—Management consultancy	12.5

4.5 Reduction of 1 per cent for new VAT registrations

If you are in your first year of VAT registration you get a 1 per cent reduction in flat rate. This means you can take 1 per cent off the flat rate you apply to your turnover, until the day before your first anniversary of becoming VAT registered.

Example 1

A business registers for VAT on 1 December 2005 and uses the flat rate scheme from that date with a flat rate of 10%. From 1 December 2005 to 30 November 2006 it can use 9% if there are no changes to the business during this time.

Example 2

A business registers for VAT on 6 January 2006 but does not join the flat rate scheme until 1 July 2006 at a rate of 6%. From 1 July 2006 to 5 January 2007 it may use 5% if there are no changes to the business during this time.

4.6 What if my business fits into more than one sector?

If your business includes supplies in two or more sectors, you must apply the percentage appropriate to your main business activity as measured by turnover.

Choose the sector for which your business gets the greater part of its turnover. Do not split your turnover, or apply more than one percentage.

Example:

If a taxi business does some car repairs, it will have to decide which of the two activities will generate the larger amount of turnover and apply the appropriate flat rate percentage to the whole of its VAT inclusive turnover.

If the taxi part of the business …	*and the car repair part of the business …*	*the business*
expects to generate turnover of £40,000 (including VAT) in the next year	expects to generate turnover (including VAT) of £15,000 in the next year	should apply the flat rate percentage for a taxi business of 9% to the total VAT inclusive turnover for both parts of the business. If this total was £55,000, the business would pay £4,950 in that year.

4.7 What if the balance between parts of my business changes?

If the balance changes but you continue to do all the same activities, carry on using the percentage that was appropriate at the start of the year until the anniversary of you joining the scheme. Review the balance between the parts of the business each year. Make this review for the first day of the VAT period in which the anniversary of you joining the scheme falls. If on that date the balance has changed, or you expect it to change over the year ahead, switch to the trade sector for the larger portion of your expected business.

This may also mean that your flat rate changes. If this occurs use the new flat rate from the start of the VAT period in which your anniversary falls; not just from the anniversary to the end of the period.

4.8 What if I start or stop a business activity during the year?

If you stop a business activity or start a new one during the year, you will need to check if the flat rate scheme is still the better way to calculate your VAT. The change may mean you are no longer eligible to use the scheme – see paragraph 12.2. If you are still eligible to use the scheme, consider which business activity forms the larger part of your expected business. Do this in the way described in paragraph 4.7. Apply the appropriate percentage from the date of the change in your business until your next anniversary of joining the scheme, or the next change to your business – whichever comes first.

If you change flat rate percentages you must write and tell us within 30 days of the change taking place. You should write to the National Advice Service, Written Enquiries Section. Enquiries.estn@hmrc.gsi.gov.uk.

4.9 What if the Table of flat rates changes?

If the flat rate for your trade sector changes, then you must use the new flat rate from the start date for your sector as published in the new Table. In these circumstances you do not have to write and tell us that you have started to use a different rate.

4.10 How do I deal with two flat rates in one VAT period?

Where a change in flat rate occurs in the middle of your VAT accounting period you will have to do two calculations for that period. The first calculation will be from the beginning of the period to the day before the start date for the new flat rate and the other from the start date to the end of the period.

4.11 What if the start date for a new table coincides with changes to my business?

If the start date coincides with the day you would otherwise make a change under the rules in paragraph 4.8 then make the change as normal but use the rate on the new table. If there is more than one change or table amendment in your accounting period (more likely for annual accounters), then you will need more than two VAT calculations for the period. Do each in the way outlined in paragraph 4.8.

5 APPLYING FOR THE SCHEME

Commentary—*De Voil Indirect Tax Service* **V2.199B.**

5.1 When can I apply?

You can apply at the time you register for VAT, or any later time. If you apply near the time of your VAT registration, you can start using the scheme from the date you are registered for VAT. Try not to delay your application if you wish to use the scheme from your date of registration.

5.2 How can I apply?

By post

There is an application form in section 17 of this notice, or if you are reading this notice on the web click here VAT 600 FRS Flat rate scheme application by post.

Postal applications should be sent to our National Registration Service at the following address:

National Registration Service
HM Revenue & Customs
Imperial House
77 Victoria Street
Grimsby
Lincolnshire
DN31 1DB

If you are registering for VAT, you can enclose the form with your Form VAT 1 Application for Registration.

By email

Download the scheme application form VAT 600 FRS Flat rate scheme application by post.

Fill it in on your computer and send it to: frsapplications@hmrc.gov.uk.

Please send questions or correspondence to our National Advice Service, not this address.

By phone

Call our National Advice Service on 0845 010 9000.

5.3 How do I fill in the application form?

The table below will help you to fill in the form. If you are in doubt please telephone our National Advice Service.

Section A

Business name	Use your normal business name. If you are already registered for VAT, this should be the name on your VAT Certificate of Registration.
Business Address	This is your principal place of business. Again, if you are already registered for VAT, this should be the address on your VAT Certificate of Registration.
Telephone number	You do not have to give this, but it may help us to process your application more quickly if we can telephone you to clear up questions about your application
VAT registration number	If you have not been advised of a VAT registration number, leave this blank. Make sure you send the scheme application to the same office as you sent the VAT 1 Notification of VAT registration.
Section B	
Main business activity	Decide which of the sectors in section 4 most accurately describes your business. If your business covers more than one sector, use the sector that is the main part of your business. Decide which is the main part by the amount of turnover each makes.
Flat rate percentage	This is the percentage for your sector as shown in the table in section 4. Insert the full flat rate for your sector even if you are entitled to the 1% discount.
Section B	
Start date	This will normally be from the beginning of the VAT period after we receive your application. We will confirm your actual start date in writing. –If you would prefer to start using the scheme from another date, write the date and reason in the box provided – see paragraph 5.5 for further information.
Section C	
Signature and date	The form should be signed and dated by the owner, a partner, or a director of the business that is applying. A signature is not required on an electronic application. Just type your name in the box.

If your accountant or other representative applies by phone for you to use the scheme, we will send you a copy of the application form completed by us for your records. If there are any errors on it please contact us immediately.

5.4 Do I need to keep a copy of my application?

Yes. This is a good idea and will help if you have to contact us about your application. Please also note the office to which you send it.

5.5 When can I start to use the scheme?

We will notify you in writing if your application is successful. The letter will tell you the date you can start to use the scheme. This will normally be from the start of the VAT period following receipt of your application. Earlier or later start dates can be agreed.

When considering an earlier or later start date, we will consider all the facts including the timing of your application and your compliance record. We will not normally allow you to go back and use the scheme for periods for which you have already calculated your VAT liability.

5.6 What if I don't receive a reply to my application?

We will deal with your application under our Taxpayer's Charter standards. If you do not hear from us within 30 calendar days, please contact the office to which you sent the application to check that it has been received.

6 DETERMINING YOUR FLAT RATE TURNOVER

Commentary—*De Voil Indirect Tax Service* **V2.199B.**

6.1 How do I work out my flat rate turnover?

It is important to get this right. If you include items that are not part of the turnover, you will pay too much VAT. If you leave out items, you will pay too little VAT and could be assessed and have to pay a penalty and interest.

The turnover to which you apply the flat rate is *all* that you receive including the VAT.

There are three ways of calculating your turnover. They are:

Method	*Description*
Basic turnover	This is principally for those who deal mainly with other VAT registered businesses. If you are used to accounting for VAT on an invoice basis, this can be the simplest to operate. For details see section 8.
Cash based turnover	This method is the flat rate scheme equivalent of cash accounting. It is based, not on the time you make the supply, but on the time you are paid for your goods or services. This can be helpful if you give extended credit or your customers pay you late. For details see section 9.
Retailer's turnover	This is essentially the same as a retail scheme and is best if you are a retailer selling goods to the public. For details see section 10. Whichever method you use, you must use that method for at least 12 months.

6.2 What must I include in my flat rate turnover?

Your flat rate turnover is all the supplies your business makes, including VAT. This means *all* of the following—

- the *VAT inclusive* sales and takings for standard rate, zero rate and reduced rate supplies
- the value of exempt supplies, such as any rental income, bank interest on a business account or lottery commission. These examples are not exhaustive and you can find out more about exempt income in Notice 700 The VAT Guide.

You can find out more about exempt income in Notice 700 "The VAT Guide"

- supplies of capital expenditure goods, unless they are supplies on which VAT has to be calculated outside the flat rate scheme in accordance with paragraph 15.9 and
- the value of any despatches to other member states of the EC if you are making intra EC supplies. For details see Notice 725 "The Single Market".

Note: As exempt and zero rate supplies are included in flat rate turnover you apply the flat rate percentage to the exempt and zero rate turnover. You may pay more VAT by being on the scheme if these supplies are a larger proportion of your business turnover than the average for your trade sector.

6.3 What income do I exclude from my flat rate turnover?

You exclude from your flat rate turnover—

- private income, for example income from shares
- the proceeds from the sale of goods you own but which have not been used in your business
- any sales of gold that are covered by VATA s 55 – see Notice 701/21 "Gold"
- non-business income and any supplies outside the scope of UK VAT and
- sales of capital expenditure goods on which you have claimed input tax.

6.4 Special circumstances

Depending on the specific details of your business before you work out your flat rate turnover you may also need to take account of the following—

If your business	*then*
sells goods to other member states of the EU	include this income in your flat rate turnover. If your business has a higher proportion of this type of sale than others in your trade sector you may find that operating the flat rate scheme puts you at a disadvantage compared to your competitors.

If your business	*then*
sells services to other member states of the EU	if your supplies are outside the scope of VAT, leave them out of your flat rate turnover. This will depend on the place of supply of the services – see Notice 741 "Place of supply of services".
buys goods from other member states of the EU	you must account for VAT on these acquisitions in box 2 of your VAT return. Acquisition tax is payable at the standard rate of VAT and not at the flat rate. For full details about intra-Community trade see Notice 725 "The Single Market".
purchases services from outside the UK to which the reverse charge applies	you do not make any adjustment to your flat rate turnover for these supplies. For more information about reverse charges, see Notice 700 "The VAT Guide".
is partly exempt	you are treated on the scheme as fully taxable and do not have to make any partial exemption calculations. You must, however, include your exempt income in your flat rate turnover.
incurs motoring expenses	you do not have to pay any road fuel scale charges since you are not reclaiming any input tax on the road fuel your business uses.
sells second-hand goods	you can include these sales in your flat rate turnover, but you will pay more VAT than if you leave the scheme and use the second hand margin scheme. Including second hand sales is the simplest option and if you only make occasional sales of second-hand goods you may consider this simplicity is worth the extra expense. You cannot, however, use the flat rate scheme and the margin scheme at the same time. You can find more about the second hand margin scheme in Notice 718 "Margin schemes for second-hand goods, works of art, antiques and collectors' items".
is acting as an agent	if you pay amounts to third parties as an agent and debit your client with the precise amounts paid out, you may be able to treat them as disbursements. If you are making such disbursements, then the money received for them is not part of your flat rate turnover. For further information about disbursements see Notice 700 "The VAT Guide".

7 KEEPING RECORDS AND FILLING IN YOUR VAT RETURN

Commentary—*De Voil Indirect Tax Service* **V2.199B, V5.201–211.**

7.1 Must I keep a VAT account?

Yes. If the only VAT to be accounted for is the VAT calculated under the flat rate scheme, just record that in the VAT payable portion of your VAT account. For further details of the VAT account see Notice 700 "The VAT Guide".

In some cases, however, you may have VAT to account for outside the flat rate scheme, for example the single purchase or disposal of capital expenditure goods of more than £2,000 in value. You should enter this in your VAT account in the normal way, in addition to your flat rate VAT.

Commentary—*De Voil Indirect Tax Service* **V5.211.**

7.2 Do I need to keep any special records?

Yes.

This rule has the force of law

> You must keep a record of your flat rate calculation showing— ➡

– your flat rate turnover for the VAT accounting period
– the flat rate percentage you have used
– the tax calculated as due.

This record must be kept with your VAT account.

Commentary—*De Voil Indirect Tax Service* **V2.199B.**

7.3 Do I still need to issue VAT invoices?

Yes. You must still issue VAT invoices to your VAT registered customers. Your customers will treat these as normal VAT invoices. When you come to calculate the scheme turnover, do not forget to include the VAT inclusive total of any invoices you have issued into the method of working out turnover that you are using (see paragraph 6.2). You must keep copies of all sales invoices that you issue to your VAT registered customers.

7.4 How do I calculate the VAT on these invoices?

Record VAT on your sales invoices using the normal rate for the supply (standard, reduced or zero rate or exempt) and not the flat rate percentage assigned to your trade sector. At the end of the VAT period you add up the VAT inclusive total of all your supplies whether you gave a VAT invoice or not and apply the flat rate percentage to this total to give the amount of VAT you must pay to us.

7.5 How do I fill in my VAT return?

Filling in your VAT return is different on the scheme from the normal VAT rules because you are calculating net tax without reference to output tax and input tax.

Follow the rules in the Table below where they differ from those on the VAT return form. If the value for any box is none, write none in the box. Do not leave any box blank.

Filling in your VAT return

Box 1	Use this for the VAT due under the flat rate scheme (see box 6 below). You may have other output tax to include in the box such as the sale of capital expenditure goods on which you have claimed input tax separately while using the flat rate scheme. See paragraph 15.9.
Box 2	In this box you must account for VAT on any goods you buy from other EC member states at the standard rate of VAT and not at your flat rate.
Box 3	Will be the sum of boxes 1 + 2 in the normal way.
Box 4	Will usually be none. If you are filling in a paper VAT return write 'none'. If you are filling in an online return, leave as '£0.00'. However, there may be a claim if you: –make a single purchase of capital expenditure goods of more than £2,000 in value (including VAT), see paragraph 15.2 –can recover VAT on stocks and assets on hand at registration, see paragraph 7.6, or –are making a claim for bad debt relief. As with goods and services you buy from suppliers in the UK, you must not normally claim VAT on any acquisitions of goods and related services from other EC Member States. However, you can normally claim for any single purchase of capital expenditure goods of £2,000 or more value, including VAT. For more details, see paragraph 15.2.
Box 5	Will be the result of box 3 minus box 4 in the normal way.
Box 6	Enter the turnover to which you applied the flat rate scheme percentage, including VAT. You should also include the value, excluding VAT, of any supplies accounted for outside the flat rate scheme, such as the sale of capital expenditure goods. For example: if your VAT inclusive turnover is £10,000 and your flat rate is 8% put the £10,000 in this box and include the £800 in box 1.

Box 7	Will usually be none, except where— –you made a single purchase of capital expenditure goods costing more than £2,000 (including VAT) and you are claiming the input tax in box 4 or –you have acquired goods from other member states of the EU. Put the VAT exclusive value in this box.
Boxes 8 and 9	Use in the normal way.

Commentary—*De Voil Indirect Tax Service* **V5.211.**

7.6 Can I recover VAT on stock and assets I have on hand at registration?

Yes. Record the claim for eligible VAT in your VAT account for your first VAT return.

For details of the rules for claims, see Notice 700/1 "Should I be registered for VAT?"

If you do claim VAT on capital assets on hand at registration and dispose of them later, you must account for VAT at the standard rate of VAT under the normal VAT rules.

Commentary—*De Voil Indirect Tax Service* **V2.199B.**

7.7 Common errors made on VAT returns

- Failure to include any VAT on EC acquisitions in box 2.
- Failure to account for VAT on EC acquisitions in box 2 at the standard rate.
- "None" (or "£0.00" for online returns) missed out of box 4.
- Forgetting to include rental income in the turnover to which the flat rate is applied.
- Exempt income is not included in the turnover to which the flat rate is applied.
- VAT exclusive figure is put in box 6.

7.8 How do I prepare business accounts for income tax purposes while I am using the flat rate scheme?

It is expected that accounts for businesses who are using the scheme will be prepared using gross receipts, less the flat rate VAT percentage, for turnover and that expenses will include the irrecoverable input VAT.

For both VAT and income tax purposes, there is a requirement to keep a record of sales and purchases. But, for businesses using the scheme, that record does not have to analyse gross, VAT and net separately. The records need only be complete, orderly and easy to follow.

See Notice 700/12 "Filling in your return" for further details.

7.9 How do I pay my return?

You can pay by cheque, postal order or electronic means. You may get extra time to pay and submit your return if you pay by electronic means.

If you use the flat rate scheme and annual accounting scheme together, then you must pay by electronic means. For further details on payment see Notice 700 "The VAT Guide".

Commentary—*De Voil Indirect Tax Service* **V5.109.**

7.10 Can I send my VAT return over the Internet?

Yes. To use our online VAT return service you must also pay any VAT due by electronic means.

If you wish to use this facility you must register and enrol through the Government Gateway at www.gateway.gov.uk. You can access the Gateway directly, or through our website www.hmrc.gov.uk.

Commentary—*De Voil Indirect Tax Service* **V5.101A.**

7.11 Can penalties apply to flat rate scheme users?

Yes. Surcharge is applied in the normal way if you send your return in late or pay any VAT due after the due date. For details see Notice 700/50 "Default surcharge". Businesses with a turnover up to £150,000 are issued with a letter offering help and advice on how to avoid late returns and payments the first time they pay late.

If you make errors on your VAT return, then you may be liable to a misdeclaration penalty as well as being assessed for any VAT and default interest due. See Notice 700/42 "Misdeclaration penalty and repeated misdeclaration penalty" and Notice 700/43 "Default Interest".

Commentary—*De Voil Indirect Tax Service* **Division V5.3.**

8 THE BASIC TURNOVER METHOD

Commentary—*De Voil Indirect Tax Service* **V2.199B.**

8.1 How do I use the basic turnover method?

Apply the flat rate percentage for your business to the VAT inclusive total of the supplies that have their tax point in the VAT accounting period.

Tax points are worked out using the normal VAT rules for time of supply. If you issue VAT invoices, this is often the date you issue an invoice. But in some circumstances it will be the date you receive payment, or the date you complete a service or make goods available to your customer.

The detailed rules which you must follow are in Notice 700 "The VAT Guide".

9 THE CASH BASED TURNOVER METHOD

Commentary—*De Voil Indirect Tax Service* **V2.199B.**

9.1 How do I use the cash based turnover method?

Apply the flat rate percentage to the VAT inclusive supplies for which you have been *paid* in the accounting period.

The following rule has the force of law

> *Cash (coins or notes):* you receive payment on the date you receive the money. *Cheques:* you receive payment on the date you receive the cheque, or the date on the cheque, whichever is the later. If the cheque is not honoured you do not need to account for the VAT. If you have already accounted for the VAT you can adjust your records accordingly.
>
> *Giro, standing order or direct debit:* you receive payment on the date your bank account is credited with such a payment.
>
> *Credit or debit card:* you receive payment on the date you make out a sales voucher for a credit/debit card payment (not when you actually get paid by the card provider).

9.2 Change of tax rate or insolvency

In these special circumstances, the *basic* turnover method tax point will determine the treatment of your supplies.

9.3 What if I used Cash accounting before joining the flat rate scheme?

You carry on as before. There is no need to pay the VAT your customers owe you when you change schemes. Include any payments you receive whilst using the flat rate scheme in the total to which you apply your flat rate percentage. Notice 731 "Cash accounting" gives information about the Cash accounting scheme.

9.4 What if I receive a payment "net of deductions"?

The following rule has the force of law.

> If you receive a net payment, you must include the full value before such deductions (and including the relevant VAT) in your scheme turnover. This will usually be the value shown on your sales invoice.

Some examples of payments that you may receive that are net of deductions are:

- where commission has been deducted by your customer
- where commission or payment for expenses has been deducted by a factor or agent collecting money on your behalf
- where commission or payment for expenses has been deducted by an auctioneer selling goods on your behalf
- payments made by an employer/contractor who has deducted income tax.

9.5 What if I receive payments in kind (for example, barter, part exchange)?

The following rule has the force of law.

> If you are paid fully or partly in kind, such as by barter or part exchange, you must include the value including VAT in your flat rate turnover each time you make or receive a "payment". You receive 'payment' on the date you receive the goods or services agreed in lieu of money.
>
> You must account for VAT on the full value of the supply, which is the price, including VAT, which a customer would have to pay for the supply if they had paid for it with money only.

The general rules about payments in kind are in Notice 700 "The VAT Guide".

9.6 What if I want to stop using the cash based method?

The following rule has the force of law.

> If at any time you stop using the cash based accounting method, you must account for VAT on all the supplies made by you while you were using the method for which payment has not been received.
>
> The supplies must be included in your scheme turnover in the return for the period in which you cease to use the cash based method.
>
> The only exception to this is if you cease to use the FRS, but immediately start to use the cash accounting scheme described in Notice 731 "Cash accounting".

You may be able to balance this adjustment with a claim for relief for stocks on hand (paragraph 12.8), or a claim for bad debts (section 14).

10 THE RETAILER'S TURNOVER METHOD

Commentary—*De Voil Indirect Tax Service* **V2.199B.**

10.1 What is the retailer's turnover method?

This method is based on your daily takings. You record payments from your customers as you receive them (for example, through your till) and total the takings daily.

You calculate your daily takings using the guidance at 10.2 to 10.7 below.

To work out your flat rate turnover, you then add to your takings any other items of income your business receives, including those from outside the retail environment.

You may find it helpful to make weekly and monthly totals.

At the end of your VAT accounting period, you apply the flat rate percentage to your flat rate turnover for that period.

Examples of other items of income your business receives might be—

- rent from a flat above the shop
- installation or callout charges if they are invoiced for, rather than going through your till
- disclosed exempt charge for credit.

10.2 What do I include in daily takings?

The following rule has the force of law.

> You must include and record the following in your daily takings as they are received from your customers—
>
> - cash
> - cheques
> - debit or credit card vouchers
> - Switch, Delta or similar electronic transactions
> - electronic cash.

10.3 What non-cash sales do I include in daily takings?

The following rule has the force of law.

> In addition to cash payments you must add the following to, and record in, your daily takings, on the day you make the supply—
>
> - the full value of credit sales
> - the cash value of any payment in kind for retail sales
> - the face value of gift, book and record vouchers redeemed
> - any other payments for retail sales.

10.4 May I make any deductions from my daily takings?

Yes. Your till roll or other record of sales together with the additions explained above constitutes your daily takings and it is this figure which you must start with when calculating your flat rate VAT. You may, however, reduce this daily takings figure with the amount of any of the following—

- void transactions – where an incorrect transaction has been voided at the time of the error
- illegible credit card transactions – where a customer's account details are unclear on the credit card voucher and therefore cannot be presented and redeemed at the bank
- unsigned or dishonoured cheques from cash customers – but not from credit customers
- counterfeit notes
- where a cheque guarantee card is accepted incorrectly as a credit card

- acceptance of out of date coupons which have previously been included in the daily takings but which are not honoured by promoters
- supervisor's float discrepancies
- till breakdowns – where incorrect till readings are recorded due to mechanical faults, for example a till programming error, false reading and till reset by engineer
- use of training tills – where the till used by staff for training has been returned to the sales floor without the zeroing of figures
- customer overspends using Shopacheck
- inadvertent acceptance of foreign currency – where discovered at a later time, for example when cashing up
- receipts for goods or services which are to be accounted for outside the flat rate scheme
- refunds given to customers in respect of taxable supplies to cover accidental overcharges or where goods are unsuitable or faulty
- instalments for credit sales.

10.5 What are the rules for making adjustments to my daily takings?

If you wish to adjust your daily takings, the following rules apply.

The following rule has the force of law.

- you must be able to provide evidence to support any adjustments to your daily takings figure
- if you make an adjustment but receive a payment later, the amount must be included in your daily takings
- you must not make any reductions from daily takings for till shortages that result from theft of cash, fraudulent refunds and voids or poor cash handling by staff.

For further details about cash handling, see Notice 727/3 "Retail schemes: How to work the Point of Sale scheme".

10.6 Are there other rules about daily takings?

Yes. If you are involved in part-exchange, sale or return, credit sales, deposits, vouchers, coupons, or other special transactions, you will have to make other adjustments to your daily takings. Notice 727/3 "Retail schemes: How to work the Point of Sale scheme" will help. The rules for these adjustments apply to businesses using the flat rate scheme in the same way that they apply to businesses using the normal VAT system. If you are in doubt then please contact our National Advice Service.

10.7 Special rules for florists

Special rules apply if you are a member of organisations such as Interflora, Teleflorist or Flowergram.

- When you receive payment direct from your customer, you are the sending member and must include the amount the customer pays you in your daily gross takings.
- When you deliver flowers ordered by customers at another florist, you are the executing member and you must add the order value and the VAT shown, from the monthly Agency self billed invoice, to your flat rate turnover. This will be the gross figure.
- When orders taken by you are delivered by other florists, the invoice from the agency will show the value of these orders as a purchase figure plus VAT. The figures shown may be net or gross depending on which agency is used. *The input tax is always shown but this amount cannot be reclaimed under the flat rate scheme.*

11 CHANGES TO YOUR BUSINESS

Commentary—*De Voil Indirect Tax Service* **V2.199B.**

11.1 What if my business grows?

If your business grows but you remain eligible to use the flat rate scheme you do not need to take any further action. You must check your turnover at least once a year on your anniversary of joining the scheme. If you are expecting sales of £225,000 or more in the next month you should check that you do not exceed the "forward look" test in paragraph 12.2(b).

11.2 What if the increase in my turnover is a one-off?

If, when you do your annual check you find that your turnover has gone above the £225,000 limit but you expect that your turnover in the next year will fall below £187,500 in the next year, you may be able to remain on the scheme with our agreement. If you wish to remain on the scheme in those circumstances, apply in writing to:

HMRC
National Advice Service
Written Enquiries Section

Alexander House
Victoria Avenue
Southend On Sea
Essex
SS99 1BD.

You will need to demonstrate that:

- your VAT inclusive total turnover in the coming year will not exceed £187,500
- the increase was the result of unexpected business activity which has not occurred before and is not expected to recur
- the increase arose from genuine commercial activity.

If, however, the increase occurred in such a way that you must leave the scheme in the circumstances described in paragraph 12.2(b), then you cannot remain on the scheme even if the three conditions above are met.

11.3 What if the nature of my business changes?

If you change the nature of your business but remain eligible to use the flat rate scheme, apply the appropriate flat rate percentage for the trade sector for the new type of business from the date of the change. You must write and tell us about the change within 30 days of the date of the change. This should be recorded with your VAT account as explained in paragraph 7.2.

11.4 What if a business change makes me ineligible to use the flat rate scheme?

If the change in your business results in you becoming ineligible to use the flat rate scheme you must write and tell us and start accounting for VAT in the standard way. See paragraph 12.2 for the rules on what makes you ineligible to continue using the scheme and when you must leave.

12 LEAVING THE SCHEME

Commentary—*De Voil Indirect Tax Service* **V2.199B.**

12.1 When can I leave the scheme?

If you wish to leave the scheme you must write and tell us. We would expect that most businesses will leave at the end of an accounting period. However, you may leave voluntarily at any time. We will confirm the date you left the scheme in writing.

12.2 When must I leave the scheme?

The table below details circumstances that can cause you to become ineligible to continue using the scheme and the date on which you must leave the scheme.

Ref	*If you become ineligible because*	*then you must leave the scheme with effect from*
(a)	At the anniversary of your start date your total income (including VAT) in the year then ending (excluding sales of capital assets) is more than £225,000. If you use the basic turnover method, your total income is determined by the value of invoices you have issued. If you use the cash-based turnover method, your total income is determined by the actual payments you have received.	for businesses on quarterly VAT returns: —the end of the VAT period containing your anniversary; or for annual accounters: —the end of the month after the month containing your FRS anniversary, or the end of your current annual VAT period, whichever comes first.
(b)	there are reasonable grounds to believe the total value of your turnover for the next 30 days alone will be more than £225,000 (excluding sales of capital assets).	the beginning of the period of 30 days.
(c)	you become a tour operator and have to account for VAT using the Tour Operator's Margin Scheme.	the date you became a tour operator.
(d)	you intend, or expect, to buy assets that are covered by the capital goods scheme (see paragraph 15.6).	the date your intention or expectation occurred.

Ref	*If you become ineligible because*	*then you must leave the scheme with effect from*
(e)	you become eligible for VAT group treatment, or register in the name of divisions	the date you become eligible or registered in divisions.
(f)	you become associated with another business in the way described in paragraph 3.9.	the date you become associated.
(g)	you decide to account for VAT using the second hand margin scheme or the auctioneer's scheme.	the beginning of the VAT period in which you decide to use either scheme.

12.3 How often do I have to check my turnover?

You have to make sure that your turnover has not risen above the limit in paragraph 12.2(a) and (b) each year, on your anniversary of joining the scheme.

If your business is growing rapidly, you will need to check at least monthly that you do not become ineligible by virtue of the rule in 12.2(b).

12.4 What must I do if I deregister?

If you deregister you must account for output tax on your final VAT return for—

- sales made on the last day of registration
- the value of any capital expenditure goods or any pre-registration stock, on which you recovered input tax at the time of registration and which are still on hand at the date of deregistration.

12.5 Can you withdraw the scheme from me?

Yes. We may withdraw the scheme at any time for the protection of the revenue. We will specify the date of withdrawal in our notice of withdrawal.

Additionally, if we withdraw the scheme because you were never eligible to use it, we will backdate the withdrawal to the time when you started to use the scheme and you will have to account normally for VAT from then.

12.6 Can I rejoin the scheme?

Yes. If you meet the requirements again, you can rejoin. But you will not be eligible to rejoin for a period of 12 months.

12.7 What must I do after leaving the scheme?

If you are deregistering refer to paragraph 12.4. In general, moving to the normal VAT rules is straightforward but in some circumstances you may need to make extra adjustments to ensure your VAT returns are accurate. The table below gives details.

If	*Then*
you stop using the scheme in the middle of a VAT accounting period,	you must do two calculations when you complete your next VAT return: —the first calculation will be for the portion of the period you used the scheme —the other calculation will be for the rest of the period, using normal VAT rules. This will give you two sets of figures for the period you stop using the scheme. Add these together when you complete your VAT return.
you use the cash based method under the flat rate scheme and you do not move immediately to the cash accounting scheme (see Notice 731 "Cash accounting").	you must make the adjustment described in paragraph 9.5 when you leave the scheme.
the value of your stock has increased while you have been on the scheme	you may be eligible to recover additional VAT on stock which you have on hand when you leave the scheme – see paragraph 12.8.

12.8 What do I do about stock on hand when I leave the scheme?

You may be able to make a stock adjustment and claim input tax when you leave the scheme. Follow the steps in the table at paragraph 12.9 below to find out if and how, you need to make an adjustment. To do this you will need to value your stock. You do not need to do a formal stock-take for the purpose of valuing your stock, but your figures must be reasonable. It makes sense to keep a record of how you valued your stock in case we query the figures.

12.9 How do I make the stock adjustment?

Paragraph 12.8 explains circumstances in which you may be able to recover additional input tax when you leave the scheme if your stock of standard rated items has increased. This is voluntary. The following table explains how you make the adjustment.

This table has the force of law.

Step	*What you need to do*	*Example*
1	Work out the VAT exclusive value of stock on hand on which you had recovered input tax before you joined the flat rate scheme. (Remember, if you were previously on cash accounting, this will be based on stock for you had paid for which you had paid.)	£10,000
2	Work out the VAT exclusive value of stock on hand on which you will be unable to recover input tax after you stop using the flat rate scheme.	£20,000
3	Subtract the figure at Step 1 from the figure at Step 2. (If the figure at Step 1 is larger than the figure at Step 2, you will not be entitled to the adjustment. No further action is necessary.)	£20,000 – £10,000 = £10,000
4	Multiply the result of Step 3 by the standard rate of VAT.	£10,000 × 17.5% = £1,750
5	Claim the VAT calculated at Step 4 in the VAT recoverable portion of your VAT account in the first return you make after leaving the flat rate scheme.	£1,750 recoverable from us as a result of FRS stock adjustment.

13 BARRISTERS

13.1 Can barristers use the flat rate scheme?

Barristers whose chambers use any of the methods of accounting for common expenses may use the scheme. However, those chambers using method 3 (sometimes known as the combination method) must follow the rules below if they have any members using the flat rate scheme. Chambers must ensure that input tax claims are apportioned and only relate to those barristers who are not on the scheme.

Example:

- A chambers has ten barristers, two of whom use the flat rate scheme. The common fund has paid £11,750.00, including VAT, on goods purchased. If none of the barristers were using the scheme, they could have claimed £1,750.00 input tax.
- However, as two of them use the flat rate scheme the chambers must apportion the input tax. If 30% of the input tax is apportioned to the two barristers on the flat rate scheme, the chambers, through the nominated member of the common fund, can only claim 70% (ie £1,225.00) of the VAT paid on the goods. This is the input tax relating to the eight barristers not using the scheme.
- The remaining 30% cannot be claimed as the two barristers using the flat rate scheme have already had their input tax taken into account in their flat rate percentage.

13.2 Do barristers using the scheme have to keep special records?

Chambers choosing to use the adaptation of method 3 explained above, must ensure that barristers do not claim input tax while they use the scheme.

They must put in place a system that monitors the input tax claimed for common expenses. This system must contain records that show—

- The value of the original VAT invoice.
- The amount and percentage of input tax claimed back by the nominated member for each VAT invoice.
- How the input tax is apportioned to the individual barristers.
- How the input tax reclaimed is calculated for each VAT invoice.

The records of all members of chambers using the flat rate scheme must be made available during a visit to the chambers by an officer from HMRC.

Barristers on the flat rate scheme whose chambers use method 3 must ensure that the nominated member does not claim input tax on their behalf.

14 BAD DEBT RELIEF

Commentary—*De Voil Indirect Tax Service* **V2.199B.**

14.1 Can I claim bad debt relief if I use the flat rate scheme?

Bad debt relief arises if you account for and pay output tax on supplies for which you are not paid later. The rules are explained in Notice 700/18 "Relief from VAT on bad debts" and these will apply to you.

If you use the *basic* or *retailer's* turnover methods of flat rate accounting, you can claim relief on eligible supplies at the standard rate of VAT, rather than the flat rate.

This is because the flat rate includes an allowance for input tax which only occurs if you have been paid by your customer. As you will not have been paid, you will not have had full credit for any input tax.

If you are using the cash turnover method, the rule for claiming bad debt relief are different, as explained at paragraph 14.2 below.

14.2 What if I use the cash turnover method of accounting?

If you use the cash turnover method of accounting you may be eligible for bad debt relief if—

- you have not been paid by your customer and it has been six months since you made the supplies
- you have not accounted for and paid tax on the supply
- you have written off the debt in your accounts.

If you meet all these conditions, your claim will be for the difference between the VAT you charged to your customer and the amount you would have declared to us had you been paid. As with businesses that use the basic and retailer's methods, this is because your flat rate takes account of input tax that you would otherwise have been entitled to, if you had been paid by your customer.

You can make the adjustment as follows:

Step	*What you need to do*	*Example*
1	Identify the VAT in the unpaid supply	Total price = £1,175 VAT= £175
2	Calculate the VAT that would have been paid under the flat rate scheme if your customer had paid you. That is the total owed (including VAT) multiplied by your flat rate scheme percentage.	£1,175 x (say) 10% = £117.50
3	Subtract the sum of step 2 from the sum of step 1	£175 – £117.50 = £57.50
4	Step 3 is your special allowance under the flat rate scheme. Include it in your VAT account in your next return.	£57.50 is added to the VAT deductible portion of your VAT account and creates a claim or reduces the VAT payable.

15 CAPITAL EXPENDITURE GOODS

Commentary—*De Voil Indirect Tax Service* **V2.199B.**

15.1 Definition of "capital expenditure goods" on which input tax can be claimed

Normally, capital goods are those goods which are bought to be used in the business but are not used up by it, except through normal wear and tear over a number of years – for example a van, a computer or a bottling machine but not the fuel, printer paper or bottles that go into them.

Capital expenditure goods in the flat rate scheme are capital goods that would fall into the above definition, but also specifically exclude any goods bought to—

- resell
- incorporate into other goods for onward supply
- consume (or completely use) within one year
- generate business income by being leased, let or hired
- goods covered by the capital goods scheme (see paragraph 15.6.).

Nothing in this section allows a business using the flat rate scheme to reclaim VAT on goods which it would not be able to claim under the normal VAT rules.

15.2 Reclaim of VAT on capital expenditure goods

If you use the flat rate scheme, you can reclaim the VAT you have been charged on a single purchase of capital expenditure goods where the amount of the purchase, including VAT, is £2,000 or more.

You deal with these capital expenditure goods outside the flat rate scheme. This means that you claim the input tax in box 4 of your VAT return.

If the supply is—

- more than one purchase
- under £2,000 including VAT or
- of services

then no VAT is claimable, as this input tax is already taken into account in the calculation of your flat rate percentage.

15.3 What counts as a single purchase of capital goods?

The normal VAT rules are used to determine whether any particular supply is one, or more than one, purchase and whether supplies are of goods or services.

Examples of a single purchase are—

- *A computer package* (computer, printer, camera, scanner, speakers etc.) bought as one package is one purchase of capital expenditure goods. If the package costs £2,000 or more (incl. VAT) then input tax can be claimed.
- *Items of kitchen equipment* (a pizza oven, a fridge and a dishwasher) bought for a restaurant. If all the items are from one supplier at one time, then they count as one purchase of capital expenditure goods. If they are from three different suppliers, or at three different times then they will be three purchases and each must be £2,000 or more (inc VAT) to qualify for a reclaim of VAT.

15.4 What counts as goods and services?

- *A van leased/hired to your business*, counts as one continuous supply of services, as ownership will never transfer to your business. For more information on "lease, let, or hire" see paragraph 15.7.
- *A van bought on hire purchase* is a supply of capital expenditure goods because ownership will eventually transfer to your business. If this cost £2,000 or more (incl VAT) then input tax can be claimed.
- *A builder builds an extension* to his business premises supplying all materials himself and including their cost in his final bill. No VAT is claimable, as this construction is a supply of services, not of capital expenditure goods.

15.5 What counts as capital or non-capital goods?

- *A shopkeeper buys bricks, cement and fittings* from his local builder's merchant intending to employ a builder to convert them into an extension of the business premises. No VAT is reclaimable as bricks etc. are not capital expenditure goods.
- *A shop is bought freehold for a retail business* to operate from. If a former owner has opted to tax the property, VAT will be payable on the purchase of these capital expenditure goods and input tax can be claimed.

15.6 What if I intend, or expect, to buy assets that are covered by the capital goods scheme?

If you intend, or expect, to buy such goods you must leave the flat rate scheme and write and tell us immediately. The capital goods scheme applies to—

- computers and items of computer equipment with a VAT exclusive value of £50,000 or more
- land and buildings, civil engineering works and refurbishments of a VAT-exclusive value of £250,000 or more.

For more information, see Notice 706/2 "Capital goods scheme".

15.7 What if goods are bought to 'lease, let or hire'

Where capital goods are bought with the intention of generating income from them either directly (for example boats for hire on a boating lake, hire of bouncy castles or marquees) or indirectly (for example company van used for deliveries during week and hired out at weekends), then they are not capital expenditure goods no matter how much they cost.

15.8 Apportionments for private use

To help simplify the flat rate scheme, where VAT on capital expenditure goods is reclaimable, the intended use of those items is treated as wholly for taxable supplies.

This means that you do not apportion input tax to cover any planned private or exempt use of the goods. This is different to the normal VAT rules.

Example

– if employees are allowed free use of the company van at weekends to move goods or
– a business video camera is used free by a friend of the proprietor to video a family wedding,

then there is no restriction of input tax or payment of output tax under the flat rate scheme.

15.9 Output tax due on disposal of capital expenditure goods

Where you have reclaimed input tax on capital expenditure goods, then you must account for output tax at the standard VAT rate (not at the flat rate) on the disposal price of those goods when they are eventually sold out of the business.

Example

A business on the scheme buys a delivery van for £6,000 inc VAT of £893.61 and it is not used for anything else. As the van is capital expenditure goods, VAT can be reclaimed. When the business later sells or part exchanges the van, say for £2000, it must account for the VAT on this amount at 17.5%, not at the flat rate.

16 APPEALS

Commentary—*De Voil Indirect Tax Service* **V2.199B, Division V5.4.**

16.1 What if I disagree with your decision about my use of the flat rate scheme?

You can ask us to reconsider our decision. Write to the office with whose decision you disagree saying why you disagree. A different officer will review the decision.

You can also appeal to the independent VAT and Duties Tribunal if—

- we refuse to authorise your use of the scheme
- we remove you from the scheme
- you disagree the category and the flat rate percentage that applies to your business.

16.2 Can I carry on using the scheme if I have appealed?

If you have appealed about our decision to withdraw or refuse use of the scheme, you must not use the scheme until your appeal is resolved. If you have appealed against any other matter, such as an assessment, we will normally allow you to continue to use the scheme pending the outcome of the appeal.

17 FORM VAT 600 FRS

[not reproduced]

Notice 742A
Opting to tax land and buildings

June 2008 (*updated July 2009*)

CONTENTS

FOREWORD

This notice cancels and replaces Notice 742A (March 2002). It also cancels Information Sheet 03/08. Details of any changes to the previous version can be found in paragraph 1.2 of this notice.

The following areas of this notice have the force of law under Schedule 10 of the VAT Act 1994—

The text within boxes in paragraphs 2.6.3, 3.4.2, 3.6.2, 5.5, 6.3.6, 6.3.8, 8.1.3, 8.1.5, 8.3.3, 8.3.5 and 14.8, which explains how to make a notification or application and what information it should contain.

The text within boxes A–L in paragraphs 2.6.4, 3.4.3, 3.6.3, 5.2, 6.3.5, 8.1.2, 8.3.2, 13.10.1, 14.6, 14.8 and 14.11.

EXAMPLE:

The following statement has the force of the law.

> Notification of the exclusion of a new building from the effect of an option to tax (*for the purpose of paragraph 27 of Schedule 10 to the VAT Act 1994*) must be made on form **VAT 1614F** and must contain the information requested on that form.

FURTHER HELP AND ADVICE

If you need general advice or more copies of HM Revenue & Customs notices, please ring our advice service on **0845 010 9000. You can call between 8.00 am and 8.00 pm, Monday to Friday.**

If you have **hearing difficulties**, please ring the **Textphone** service on **0845 000 0200**.

If you would like to speak to someone in **Welsh**, please ring **0845 010 0300, between 8.00 am and 6.00 pm, Monday to Friday**.

OTHER NOTICES ON THIS OR RELATED SUBJECTS

706 "Partial exemption"

706/2 "Capital goods scheme"

708 "Buildings and construction"

742 "Land and property"

1. INTRODUCTION

1.1 What is this notice about?

This notice explains the effect of an option to tax and will help you to decide whether to exercise that option. It will tell you whether you need permission from us before you can opt to tax, and how to notify us of your decision. Prior to 1 June 2008, the option to tax was also referred to as the election to waive exemption. From 1 June 2008, it is only referred to as the option to tax.

We recommend that you also read Notice 742 "Land and property" which gives basic information relating to supplies of land.

This notice assumes that you have a working knowledge of basic Value Added Tax (VAT) principles, as outlined in Notice 700 "The VAT Guide".

This notice and others mentioned are available both on paper and on our Internet website at **www.hmrc.gov.uk**.

1.2 What's changed?

This notice replaces Information sheet 03/08 and notice 742A "Opting to tax land and buildings" (March 2002 edition). The notice has been revised to incorporate updates 1, 2 and 3 into the text, and provides additional guidance on changes introduced with effect from 1 June 2008. The main changes are as follows.

- new rules providing that an option to tax affects land and buildings on the same site, with transitional rules, and ability to exclude new buildings from the scope of an option to tax (section 2).
- new certificate for buildings to be converted to dwellings etc and new ability for intermediaries to disapply the option to tax (section 3)
- new certificate for land sold to housing associations (section 3)
- new rules for ceasing to be a relevant associate of an opter (section 6)
- extension to the "cooling off" period for revoking an option to tax (section 8)
- introduction of automatic revocation of the option to tax where no interest has been held for 6 years (section 8)
- introduction of rules governing the revocation of an option to tax after 20 years (section 8)
- revised definition of occupation for the anti-avoidance test including new exclusion for automatic teller machines (section 13)
- introduction of a new way to opt to tax (a real estate election) (section 14).

1.3 What effect does an option to tax have?

Supplies of land and buildings, such as freehold sales, leasing or renting, are normally exempt from VAT. This means that no VAT is payable, but the person making the supply cannot normally recover any of the VAT incurred on their own expenses.

However, you can opt to tax land. For the purposes of VAT, the term "land" includes any buildings or structures permanently affixed to it. You do not need to own the land in order to opt to tax. Once you have opted to tax all the supplies you make of your interest in the land or buildings will normally be standard-rated. And you will normally be able to recover any VAT you incur in making those supplies.

1.4 Who should read this notice?

You should read this notice if you make, or intend to make supplies of any interest in land, buildings or civil engineering works.

1.5 What law covers this notice?

The area of VAT law which specifies the supplies of land and buildings that are exempt from VAT is Group 1 of Schedule 9 to the Value Added Tax Act 1994. The law detailing the option to tax is found in Schedule 10 to the Value Added Tax Act 1994.

The following areas of this notice have the force of the law:

(1) All forms/certificates listed in **Annex 1**

(2) The following boxes

Box A time at which the construction of a new building is taken to begin for the purposes of excluding it from the effect of an option to tax (section 2, paragraph 2.6.4)

Box B timing of certificates to disapply the option to tax for buildings intended for conversion into dwellings etc (section 3, paragraph 3.4.3)

Box C timing of certificates to disapply the option to tax for land supplied to housing associations (section 3, paragraph 3.6.3)

Box D automatic permission conditions (section 5, paragraph 5.2)

Box E conditions for a body corporate to cease to be a relevant associate of an opter (section 6, paragraph 6.3.5)

Box F additional condition for revoking an option within the 6 month "cooling off" period (section 8, paragraph 8.1.2)

Box G conditions for revoking an option to tax after 20 years (section 8, paragraph 8.3.2).

Box H meaning of "wholly" and "substantially wholly" for eligible purposes (section 13, paragraph 13.10.1)

Box J conversion (at time of making a real estate election) of single options into separate options (section 14, paragraph 14.6)

Box K information to be provided with notification of a real estate election (section 14, paragraph 14.8)

Box L information to be provided by maker of real estate election when required to do so (section 14, paragraph 14.11).

Commentary—*De Voil Indirect Tax Service* **V4.114–V4.116.**

2. THE SCOPE OF AN OPTION TO TAX

2.1 What am I opting to tax?

You are opting to tax land. For the purposes of VAT, the term "land" includes buildings. When you opt to tax you can specify an area of land or a "building". Commonly, you will specify a "building" because that is the prominent feature of the land.

From 1 June 2008, if you specify a building, the option to tax will continue to apply to the land on which the building stood if the building is demolished and to any future buildings constructed on the land. If you specify land, the option will apply to any future buildings constructed on the land, but you can specifically exclude new buildings from the effect of an option to tax if you wish to. See paragraph 2.4 for details.

2.2 What constitutes a "building"?

Usually it will be clear what constitutes a "building", for instance an office block or a factory. However in some instances the law treats more than one building as being a single "building" for the purpose of the option to tax. These are:

- buildings that are, or if not yet built are planned to be, linked. Please see paragraph 2.3 for more information on links and
- a complex consisting of a number of units grouped around a fully enclosed concourse, such as a shopping mall.

2.3 What is a "link"?

A link is an internal access or a covered walkway between buildings the purpose of which is to allow movement of goods and people.

It does not include:

- a car park, either above or below ground
- a public thoroughfare or
- a statutory requirement, such as a fire escape.

2.4 What is covered by the option to tax?

We use a number of basic principles to determine how far your option to tax extends over the land and associated buildings.

Option	*Principle*
Land	your option to tax covers all the land, and any buildings or civil engineering works which are part of the land. your option to tax will cover the discrete area of land that you specify, and will not affect any adjoining land. From 1 June 2008, if you construct a new building on land that you have opted, the building will be covered by the option to tax unless you notify us that you wish to exclude the building from the effect of the option (paragraph 2.6 explains how to do this).
Buildings	your option to tax will cover the whole of the building, and the land under and immediately around that building such as forecourts and yards. If your interest in the building is restricted to one floor, your option to tax will still cover the remaining floors of the building. if the building stands in a large area of land, how far the option to tax extends over the land depends on how far the services of the building can be utilised. For example, a racecourse grandstand may provide electricity and shelter for stalls, or other facilities, within its peripheral area. An option to tax on the grandstand would extend over the whole area of land that uses the benefits. From 1 June 2008, if the building is demolished or destroyed, your option to tax will still apply to the land on which the building stood and to any future buildings that are constructed on the land. However, if: —you opted to tax before 1 June 2008, and —it is clear from your notification that the option was made on the building only you can, if you wish, treat the option as revoked once the building is demolished. You do not need to notify us before revoking but you should retain evidence in case it is requested in the future.

2.5 What if I make changes to a building after I have opted to tax?

If you make changes to a building after you have opted to tax you will need to consider whether your option to tax covers those changes. This table below sets out the basic principles for the most common changes made.

Change	*Principle*
Extensions	if you have opted to tax a building and you extend it at a later date, upwards, downwards or sideways, your option to tax will apply to the whole of the extended building.
Linked buildings	if prior to their completion buildings are linked by an internal access or covered walkway (see paragraph 2.3 for more information on what is meant by a "link") they are treated as a single building and an option to tax will apply to both parts. If a link is created after both buildings are completed, the option to tax will not flow through with the link.
Forming a complex	If you have a group of units that have been treated as separate buildings for the option to tax and you later decide to enclose them, the option to tax will not spread to the un-opted units.

2.6 Excluding a new building from the effect of an option to tax

2.6.1 When can I exclude a new building from the effect of an option?

If you construct a new building on opted land (and that building is not within the curtilage of an existing building) you may exclude the new building (and land within its curtilage) from the effect of the option to tax.

If you decide to do this, the new building will be permanently excluded from the effect of your existing option to tax. But you may, if you wish, make a fresh option to tax in the future, subject to obtaining permission from us if appropriate (see section 5).

2.6.2 Requirement to notify the exclusion

You must notify the exclusion **before the earliest of the following times** (which is when the exclusion will take effect):

- when a grant of an interest in the building is first made
- when the new building, or any part of it, is first used
- when the new building is completed.

Under no circumstances can we accept late notification.

2.6.3 How do I notify you?

The following statement has the force of the law.

> Notification of the exclusion of a new building from the effect of an option to tax (*for the purpose of paragraph 27 of Schedule 10 to the VAT Act 1994*) must be made on **form VAT 1614F** and must contain the information requested on that form.

You can download **form VAT 1614F** from **www.hmrc.gov.uk** or obtain it from our advice service on **0845 010 9000**.

2.6.4 When does construction of a building begin?

You cannot exclude a building before construction has begun. The time when construction of a building begins is determined by **Box A** below.

Box A

This boxed text below has the force of the law.

> The time at which the construction of a new building is taken to begin for the purposes of excluding it from the effect of an option to tax (for the purposes of paragraph 27(7) of Schedule 10 to the VAT Act 1994).
>
> Construction of a building begins when it progresses above the level of the building's foundations.

Commentary—*De Voil Indirect Tax Service* **V4.116**.

3. SUPPLIES NOT AFFECTED BY AN OPTION TO TAX

3.1 What supplies are not affected by an option to tax?

There are some supplies where, even if you have opted to tax, the option will not apply. **If you make any of the supplies described in this section your supplies will remain exempt from VAT even if you have opted to tax. This may have an impact on how much input tax you can claim.**

3.2 Buildings designed or adapted and intended for use as dwellings

Your option to tax will not apply if you supply a building, or part of a building, that is designed or adapted as a dwelling (such as a house), or as a number of dwellings (such as a block of flats), and the purchaser or tenant informs you that they intend to use it as a dwelling.

3.3 Buildings designed or adapted and intended to be used for relevant residential purposes

Your option to tax will not apply if you supply a building, or part of a building that is designed or adapted for use for a relevant residential purpose (such as a nursing home) and the purchaser or tenant informs you that they will be using it solely for a relevant residential purpose.

Where a building or part of a building is used for both relevant residential purposes and business purposes, your option to tax will not apply to the part used for relevant residential purposes, provided that the different functions are carried out in clearly defined areas. In these circumstances the value of your supply should be fairly apportioned between the exempt and taxable elements. A building used for a relevant residential purpose is one in which some of the facilities, such as dining rooms and bathrooms, are shared, but this does not include use as a hospital, prison, hotel or similar establishment. Examples include residential homes for children, the elderly or disabled persons and student halls of residence. See Notice 708 "Buildings and Construction" for full definitions and further details.

3.4 Buildings for conversion into dwellings etc.

Your option to tax will not apply if you supply a building or part of a building that is not designed or adapted as a dwelling (or number of dwellings) or for a relevant residential purpose if you receive a certificate from the recipient of your supply (by the time described in paragraphs 3.4.3. and 3.4.4 below) certifying that the building or part of the building is intended for use as a dwelling or number of dwellings or solely for a relevant residential purpose.

3.4.1 When can I issue a certificate?

As a recipient of a supply, you may certify that a building or part of a building is intended for use as a dwelling or solely for a relevant residential purpose only if you

- intend to use the building (or part of the building) as a dwelling or solely for a relevant residential purpose,
- intend to convert the building (or part of a building) with a view to it being used as a dwelling or solely for a relevant residential purpose, or
- are a "relevant intermediary" (see 3.4.2 below).

You may not issue a certificate if the building is to be put to a non-qualifying use for a period before being used as a dwelling or solely for a relevant residential purpose. However, minor or incidental non-qualifying use is disregarded.

3.4.2 What form must the certificate take?

The following statement has the force of the law.

> Certification of intention to use a building (or part of a building) as a dwelling or dwellings or solely for a relevant residential purpose (*for the purpose of paragraph 6 of Schedule 10 to the VAT Act 1994*) must be made on form **VAT 1614D** and must contain the information requested on that form.

You can download form **VAT 1614D** from www.hmrc.gov.uk or obtain it from our advice service on 0845 010 9000.

3.4.3 When should the certificate be provided?

As a supplier, if you receive a certificate by the time set out in **Box B** below, you **must** exempt your supply of the building or part of the building to which the certificate relates.

Box B

This boxed text below has the force of the law.

> **Time by which a certificate of intended use as a dwelling (or dwellings) or solely for a relevant residential purpose must be given to the seller making the supply (for the purpose of paragraph 6(2) of Schedule 10 to the Value Added Tax Act 1994)**

The certificate must be given before the price for the grant to the recipient by the seller is legally fixed, e g by exchange of contracts, letters or missives, or the signing of heads of agreement.

3.4.4 Can I accept a certificate after the time specified in Box B?

If you receive a certificate after the time the price for the grant has been legally fixed, you do not have to accept the certificate, but may do so at your discretion, but only in respect of supplies that arise after the certificate is given. For example, if you have granted a lease for periodic rental payments, you may only exempt the rental supplies that take place after you receive a certificate. If you sell the freehold, you may only exempt the supply if it takes place after you receive a certificate (in the case of freehold sales, the supply would typically take place at completion).

3.4.5 What is a "relevant intermediary"?

You are a "relevant intermediary" if you are purchasing an interest in a building or part of a building and—

- you intend to dispose of the whole of the interest you are purchasing to another, and
- your prospective purchaser has given you a certificate certifying that he:
  - intends to convert the building (or part of it) with a view to it being used as a dwelling or solely for a relevant residential purpose, or
  - is himself a "relevant intermediary".

If you are a "relevant intermediary", the certificate you receive from your prospective purchaser serves two purposes.

(1) it will enable you to issue a certificate to disapply your supplier's option to tax (so that your purchase of the building, or relevant part, is exempt)

(2) it will disapply your own option to tax (if you have made one) when you come to supply the building on to your purchaser (so that your sale of the building, or relevant part, is exempt).

3.4.6 What if only part of building is intended for use as a dwelling or for a relevant residential purpose?

If only part of the building is intended for use as a dwelling or solely for a relevant residential purpose, the certificate should make it clear that this is the case and must contain a description of the qualifying part. The option to tax will apply to the part of the building that is not intended for the qualifying use and the value of the supply should be fairly apportioned between the exempt and taxable elements. You can find out more about apportionment in Notice 700 "The VAT Guide".

3.4.7 What if I make more than one supply of an interest in the building?

If you make more than one supply of a relevant interest in a building to the person who has given you the certificate (for example, because you have granted a lease for periodic rental payments), your option will be disapplied in relation to all subsequent supplies that arise from the same grant in the building or parts of the building covered by the certificate.

3.5 Buildings to be used solely for a relevant charitable purpose

Your option to tax will not apply if you supply a building, or part of a building, and the purchaser or tenant informs you that they will be using it solely for a relevant charitable purpose, other than as an office for general administration e g head office functions of the charity. Where a building or part of a building is used for relevant charitable purposes and business or general administration purposes, your option to tax will not apply to the part used for relevant charitable purposes, provided that the different functions are carried out in clearly defined areas. In these circumstances the value of your supply should be fairly apportioned between the exempt and taxable elements. Relevant charitable purpose means use by a charity for its non-business activities, or as a village hall or similarly to provide social or recreational facilities for a local community. Please see Notice 701/1 "Charities" for more information on non-business activities carried out by such bodies.

3.6 Land sold to a relevant housing association

Your option to tax will not apply if you supply land to a relevant housing association which provides you with a certificate (by the time described in paragraphs 3.6.3 and 3.6.4) certifying that, after any necessary demolition work, dwellings or relevant residential buildings will be constructed on the land.

3.6.1 What is a relevant housing association?

A relevant housing association is a:

- registered social landlord within the meaning of Part 1 of the Housing Act 1996
- registered social landlord within the meaning of the Housing (Scotland) Act 2001 or
- registered housing association within the meaning of Part 2 of the Housing (Northern Ireland) Order 1992.

3.6.2 What form must the certificate take?

The following statement has the force of the law.

> Certification by a relevant housing association that land is to be used (after any necessary demolition work) for the construction of a building or buildings intended for use as a dwelling or number of dwellings or solely for a relevant residential purpose (*for the purpose of paragraph 10 of Schedule 10 to the VAT Act 1994*) must be made on certificate VAT 1614G and must contain the information requested on that form.

You can download certificate **VAT 1614G** from **www.hmrc.gov.uk** or obtain it from our advice service on **0845 010 9000**.

3.6.3 When must the certificate be provided?

As a supplier, if you receive a certificate by the time set out in **Box C** below, you **must** exempt your supply of the land to which the certificate relates.

Box C

This boxed text below has the force of the law.

> **Time by which a certificate of intended use of the land for constructing a dwelling, a number of dwellings, or solely for a relevant residential purpose must be given to the person making the supply (for the purpose of paragraph 10(2) of Schedule 10 to the Value Added Tax Act 1994)**

The certificate must be given before the price for the grant to the recipient by the seller is legally fixed, e g exchange of contracts, by missives or letters, or the signing of heads of agreement.

3.6.4 Can I accept a certificate after the time specified in Box C?

If you receive a certificate after the time the price for the grant has been legally fixed, you do not have to accept the certificate, but may do so at your discretion, but only in respect of supplies that arise after the certificate is given. For example, if you have granted a lease for periodic rental payments, you may only exempt the rental supplies that take place after you receive a certificate. If you sell the freehold, you may only exempt the supply if it takes place after you receive a certificate (in the case of freehold sales, the supply would typically take place at completion).

3.7 Land sold to a "DIY" housebuilder

Your option to tax will not apply if you supply land to someone who will build a dwelling on it for their own use, and not in the course or furtherance of any business carried on by them.

3.8 Pitches for residential caravans

Your option to tax will not apply if you supply a pitch for a permanent residential caravan. A residential caravan is one where residence is permitted throughout the year, and is not restricted by planning consent, covenant or similar provision.

3.9 Moorings for residential houseboats

Your option to tax will not apply if you supply facilities for the mooring or berthing of a residential houseboat. A houseboat is a floating decked structure that is designed or adapted for use solely as a place of permanent habitation. A houseboat does not have the means of, nor is capable of being readily adapted for, self-propulsion. A residential houseboat is one where residence is permitted throughout the year, and is not restricted by planning consent, covenant or similar provision.

3.10 Building to be used for both commercial and residential purposes

You may supply a building, or part of a building, which the purchaser or tenant will be using partly for commercial and partly for residential purposes, such as a flat above a shop. If that is the case you must apportion your supply between the taxable element of the shop and the exempt (or zero-rated) element of the dwelling. You may choose the method of apportionment but it must provide a fair and reasonable result. You can find out more about apportionment in Notice 700 "The VAT Guide".

3.11 Land or building affected by the anti-avoidance measures

The option to tax has no effect in relation to supplies resulting from a grant that falls within the anti-avoidance measures described within section 13.

Commentary—*De Voil Indirect Tax Service* **V4.116**.

4. HOW TO OPT TO TAX

4.1 What do I need to do if I want to opt to tax?

There are two stages in opting to tax. The first stage is making the decision to opt. This may take place at a board meeting or similar, or less formally. However you reach your decision, we recommend that you keep a written record, showing clear details of the land or buildings you are opting to tax, and the date you made your decision.

If you have previously made exempt supplies of the land or building you may need our permission before you can opt to tax. You can find more information about this in section 5.

The second stage is to notify us of your decision in writing. Paragraph 4.2 explains how you should do this.

4.2 Notification of an option to tax

4.2.1 When should I notify my option to tax?

For your option to tax to be valid you must make your notification within 30 days of your decision.

4.2.2 What should I include on my notification?

Your notification must state clearly what land or buildings you are opting to tax, and the date from which the option has effect (see paragraph 4.3). We suggest you use the Notification Form **VAT 1614A** which you can obtain from our National Advice Service. If you are opting to tax discrete areas of land we suggest that you send a map or plan clearly showing the opted land with your notification. If you are opting a building that has a postal address please give it in full including the postcode.

It would speed up our processing of your notification if you include your VAT registration number, or if your registration is pending, your VAT Registration Unit reference number.

It is important that an appropriate person signs the notification and any accompanying list or schedule. Please see section 7 for more information.

4.2.3 Where should I send my notification?

If you are already registered for VAT, your notification should be made to our centralised Option To Tax Unit in writing, either:

- by post to Option To Tax National Unit, HM Revenue & Customs, Portcullis House, 21 India Street, Glasgow, G2 4PZ; or
- by fax to 0141 555 3367.

If you are not registered but need or wish to be registered for VAT as a result of your option to tax, your application to register for VAT and your notification of the option to tax should be submitted together to your regional VAT Registration Unit. Your VAT Registration Unit depends on your business postcode. See also paragraph 6.1.

The correct VAT Registration Unit for your business postcode can be found:

- by accessing www.hmrc.gov.uk or
- by telephoning our advice service on 0845 010 9000; or
- in the notice "Supplement to notices 700/1 and 700/11", also available on the website or from our advice service.

4.2.4 Will I receive an acknowledgement of my notification?

We will normally acknowledge receipt of your notification within 15 working days although this is not necessary for the option to tax to have legal effect. You should not delay charging VAT just because you have not received our acknowledgement.

4.2.5 What if I am notifying an option to tax in relation to land or buildings which are being transferred as a going concern?

You should read paragraph 11.2.

4.3 What is the effective date of my option to tax?

Your option to tax will have effect from the date of your decision, or any later date that you have specified, providing you notify us within 30 days of making your decision. If you realise that you did not notify us within 30 days, you should contact us immediately.

In no circumstances can an option to tax have effect from a date before you made your decision to opt.

4.4 Who is bound by the option to tax?

It is for you alone to decide whether to opt to tax any land or buildings. If you do decide to opt to tax, only the supplies you make of your interest in the land or building will be affected. Your option to tax will not affect supplies made by anyone else. For example, if you are selling an opted building the purchaser has the choice of whether to opt to tax or not. Similarly, if your tenant is sub-letting, they too have this same choice. For this reason, we suggest that you inform your tenant of your decision at the earliest opportunity so that they may safeguard their right to recover input tax by opting to tax, should they wish to.

4.5 What happens if I make an option but at the time of making it intend to revoke it under the "cooling-off" period?

If, at the time of making an option you intend to revoke it during the "cooling-off" period (see paragraph 8.1), the option is treated as invalid.

Commentary—*De Voil Indirect Tax Service* **V4.116.**

5. PERMISSION TO OPT TO TAX

5.1 When do I need permission from Customs?

If you have made, or intend to make, any exempt supplies of the land or buildings within the 10 years prior to the date you wish your option to take effect, you will need our written permission to opt to tax unless you meet one or more of the automatic permission conditions set out below.

5.2 Automatic permission

Since 1 March 1995 you have not needed to obtain our written permission before you opt to tax provided you meet the conditions we have set out in a notice. The conditions have changed from time to time. If you meet any of the 4 conditions set out in **Box D** below you do not need written permission before you opt to tax:

Box D

These conditions have the force of law and came into force on 2 March 2005

Number	Condition
1.	It is a mixed-use development and the only exempt supplies have been in relation to the dwellings.

2. You do not wish to recover any input tax in relation to the land or building incurred before your option to tax has effect; and
—the consideration for your exempt supplies has, up to the date when your option to tax is to take effect, been solely by way of rents or service charges and excludes any premiums or payments in respect of occupation after the date on which the option takes effect. Regular rental and/or service charge payments can be ignored for the purposes of this condition. Payments are considered regular where the intervals between them are no more than a year and where each represents a commercial or genuine arms length value; and
—the only input tax relating to the land or building that you expect to recover after the option to tax takes effect will be on overheads, such as regular rental payments, service charges, repairs and maintenance costs. If you expect to claim input tax in relation to refurbishment or redevelopment of the building you will not meet this condition.
Notes: When deciding whether you meet this condition you should disregard:
—VAT refundable to local authorities and other bodies under section 33(2)(*b*) of the Value Added Tax Act 1994;
—any input tax you can otherwise recover by virtue of the partial exemption de minimis rules (Regulation 106, VAT Regulations 1995); and
—any input tax you are entitled to recover on general business overheads not specifically related to the land or building, such as audit fees.
3. The only input tax you wish to recover in relation to the land or building incurred before your option to tax takes effect relates solely to tax charged by your tenant or tenants upon surrender of a lease; and
—the building or relevant part of the building has been unoccupied between the date of the surrender and the date the option to tax is to take effect; and
—there will be no further exempt supplies of the land or building; and
—you do not intend or expect that you will occupy the land or building other than for taxable purposes.
4. The exempt supplies have been incidental to the main use of the land or building. For example, where you have occupied a building for taxable purposes the following would be seen as incidental to the main use and the condition would be met:
—allowing an advertising hoarding to be displayed;
—granting space for the erection of a radio mast;
—receiving income from an electricity sub-station.
The letting of space to an occupying tenant, however minor, is not incidental.

5.3 What do I need to do if I meet one of the conditions?

If you meet one of the conditions and you decide that you want to opt to tax you still need to write to us to notify your option. You should state in your notification that, although you have made previous exempt supplies of the land or building, you satisfy the conditions for automatic permission. Section 4 gives more information on notifying an option and the records you need to keep.

5.4 What if I don't meet any of the conditions?

If you do not meet any of the conditions for automatic permission you must obtain our written permission before you can opt to tax.

5.5 How do I apply for permission?

The following statement has the force of the law.

> An application for prior permission to opt to tax (*for the purpose of paragraphs 28 and 29 of Schedule 10 to the Value Added Tax Act 1994*) must be made on form **VAT 1614H** and must contain the information requested on that form.

You can download application form **VAT 1614H** from **www.hmrc.gov.uk** or obtain it from our advice service on **0845 010 9000**.

5.6 When will my option take effect?

Once permission is granted, your option will automatically take effect from your application date, or from any later date you request in your application. For applications made on or after 1 June 2008, there is no need for you to notify your option to tax separately once permission is granted.

If you wish your option to take effect from your application date, we recommend you keep evidence of the date you submit the application form (such as a certificate of posting).

5.7 When will you grant permission?

We cannot grant you permission to opt to tax until you provide all the information requested in application form **1614H** and any additional information that we may ask for. Occasionally we will refuse permission, if we are not satisfied that granting permission would result in a fair and reasonable attribution of input tax. Once we have come to an agreement with you in writing as to the attribution of input tax (if necessary) and are satisfied that permission can be granted, we will grant you written permission and your option will automatically take effect from the date of your application or any later date you requested in your application.

5.8 What if I fail to ask for permission?

If you notify us of an option to tax without obtaining permission, and it comes to light at a later stage that you should have obtained prior permission, we have the discretion to treat the option as if it was validly made.

We will generally only exercise this discretion in cases of genuine error, or where tax would otherwise be at risk.

If you think this should apply to you, please write to the Option to Tax National Unit (paragraph 4.2.3 shows how you may contact them) with details of your situation.

Commentary—*De Voil Indirect Tax Service* **V4.116**.

6. OPTION TO TAX AND VAT REGISTRATION

6.1 Liability to register for VAT

If you are not already registered for VAT, you should read VAT Notice 700/1 "Should I be registered for VAT?" If you are required to, or wish to register you should complete an application form and send it to the appropriate Registration office (listed in VAT Notice 700/1). The Registration office will need to be satisfied that you will be making taxable supplies, so you should send your option to tax notification with your application form, see paragraph 4.2.3. If you need our permission before opting to tax, you cannot register before we have given permission so you should also enclose a copy of your written permission with your application.

If your turnover falls below the registration threshold and you deregister, the option to tax does not cease because you have deregistered. Please see section 12 for more details.

Commentary—*De Voil Indirect Tax Service* **V2.144, V4.116**.

6.2 How long must I keep records?

You must keep your correspondence and any record of your decision to opt to tax for a minimum of 6 years. An option to tax cannot normally be revoked until at least 20 years have passed (see section 8). We strongly recommend you keep your option to tax records for longer than 6 years.

Commentary—*De Voil Indirect Tax Service* **V5.202**.

6.3 How does the option to tax affect group registrations?

6.3.1 What is a "relevant associate"?

An option to tax made by a member of a VAT group is generally binding upon other members of the same VAT group. A body corporate that is bound by another body corporate's option to tax under these rules is known as a "relevant associate" of the opter. If you are a relevant associate, you must normally charge VAT on any supplies you make of the opted property, even after you have left the VAT group.

For information about VAT Groups, please see notice 700/2 "Group and Divisional Registration".

You become a "relevant associate" if:

– you are in the same VAT group as the opter when the option first has effect,
– you are in the same VAT group as the opter at any later time when the opter has an interest in the opted property, or
– you are in the same VAT group as another "relevant associate" of the opter when that relevant associate has an interest in the opted property.

6.3.2 When do I cease to be a "relevant associate"?

You cease to be a "relevant associate" in one of three ways.

– by meeting the basic conditions explained below and automatically ceasing to be a relevant associate (see paragraph 6.3.3 below)
– by meeting all of the specified conditions set out in **Box E** below and notifying us on form **VAT 1614B** (see paragraph 6.3.6 below)
– by obtaining our permission (see paragraph 6.3.7 below).

6.3.3 Automatically ceasing to be a relevant associate

You will automatically cease to be a relevant associate in relation to an opted property if you meet **all** of the following conditions

– You are no longer in the VAT group in which you became a relevant associate, **and**

– You do not hold any interest in the opted property, and are not owed any payment for disposal of such an interest, **and**
– You are not "connected" with any person who is the opter or relevant associate and who holds an interest in the land.

If you meet all of these conditions, you automatically cease to be a relevant associate from the time that all three conditions are met. There is no need for you to notify us or to seek permission.

6.3.4 When do you consider a person to be connected with another?

We use the test in section 839 of the Income and Corporation Taxes Act 1968 to determine whether people are connected. Examples of connected persons are:

– Your husband or wife
– Your relatives
– Your husband's or wife's relatives
– Your business partners and their husbands, wives and relatives
– A company that you control, either by yourself or with any of the persons listed above; or
– The trustees of a settlement of which you are a settlor, or of which a person who is still alive and is connected with you is a settlor.

Relative means a brother, sister, ancestor or lineal descendent. It does not include nephews, nieces, uncles and aunts.

Commentary—*De Voil Indirect Tax Service* **V1.296**.

6.3.5 Specified conditions for ceasing to be a relevant associate

If you do not meet the basic conditions set out in paragraph 6.3.3. above, you can cease to be a relevant associate of an opter if:

– you meet all of the conditions specified in **Box E** below, and
– you notify us on form **VAT 1614B** (see paragraph 6.3.6 below).

Box E

The boxed text below has the force of the law

Conditions for a body corporate to cease to be treated as a relevant associate of an opter (for the purpose of paragraph 3(5)(*a*) of Schedule 10 to the Value Added Tax Act 1994 ("the VAT Act 1994")).

A body corporate ceases to be a relevant associate of an opter at the time when it meets all of the following conditions:

1. The grouping condition

The body corporate has ceased to be treated as a member of the VAT group (see section 43 of the VAT Act 1994) by virtue of which it became a relevant associate of the opter.

2. The 20 year condition

The body corporate has:

– held any relevant interest in the building or land acquired whilst a member of that VAT group for a period of at least 20 years; and
– been treated as a relevant associate of the opter for a period of at least 20 years.

3. The capital item condition

Any land or building that is subject to the option is not, in relation to the body corporate, subject to input tax adjustment as a capital item under the capital goods scheme.

4. The valuation condition

The body corporate, or a person connected with it, has not, within a period of ten years ending on the date that the body corporate ceases to be a relevant associate, made a supply of a relevant interest in the building or land that is subject to the option that:

– was for a consideration that was less than the open market value of that supply; or
– arose from a relevant grant.

5. The pre-payment condition

No supply of goods or services has been made for a consideration to the body corporate (or to a person connected with it) which will be wholly or partly attributable to a supply or other use of the land or buildings made by that body (or by a person connected with it) more than 12 months later.

Explanatory Note 1

"Relevant interest in the building or land" means an interest in, right over or licence to occupy the building or land (or any part of it).

Explanatory Note 2

"Relevant grant" means a grant that the grantor intends or expects will give rise to a supply for a consideration significantly greater than any consideration for any earlier ➡

supply arising from the grant (except as a result of a rent review determined according to normal commercial practice).

6.3.6 How do I notify you?

The following statement has the force of the law.

Notification of cessation to be a relevant associate (*for the purpose of paragraph 4 of Schedule 10 to the Value Added Tax Act 1994*) must be made on form **VAT 1614B** and must contain the information requested on that form.

You can download application form **VAT 1614B** from **www.hmrc.gov.uk** or obtain it from our advice service on **0845 010 9000**.

6.3.7 Applying for permission to cease to be a relevant associate

If you do not meet the all of the conditions set out in 6.3.2 or **Box E** above, you may apply for permission to cease to be a relevant associate.

We will not give you permission unless both conditions 1 and 2 of **Box E** are met.

6.3.8 What form should my application take?

The following statement has the force of the law.

Application for permission to cease to be a relevant associate (*for the purpose of paragraph 4 of Schedule 10 to the Value Added Tax Act 1994*) must be made on form **VAT 1614B** and must contain the information requested on that form.

You can download application form **VAT 1614B** from **www.hmrc.gov.uk** or obtain it from our advice service on **0845 010 9000**.

6.3.9 In what circumstances will you grant permission?

We will not grant permission unless you meet conditions 1 and 2 of **Box E** above.

In deciding whether or not to grant permission, we will give particular consideration to whether or not you or a third party has received a VAT benefit as a result of your actions.

For example, a case could arise where, one year before applying for permission to cease to be treated as a relevant associate, you pre pay for the following three years' cleaning services and, in anticipation of ceasing to be a relevant associate, only deduct one third of the input tax charged. Whilst you fail to meet the pre-payment condition (condition 5 of **Box E**), we would nevertheless grant permission, since your recovery of input tax is fair and reasonable. If you had deducted all of the input tax on the cleaning services, permission would be refused, unless the law provided some means by which the original input tax deduction could be adjusted.

6.3.10 If you grant permission, when will I cease to be a relevant associate?

You will cease to be a relevant associate from the date permission is granted. We can only specify an earlier date in cases where you previously gave a notification of ceasing to be a relevant associate believing, in error, that you met the conditions in **Box E** above. In such cases we may allow the date stated in the notification, but only where we are satisfied that the reasons for failing to meet the conditions are insignificant.

In granting permission, we can apply conditions. In cases where these are subsequently broken we may treat the original application for permission as invalid.

7. RESPONSIBILITY FOR OPTING TO TAX

7.1 Who is responsible for making the decision and notifying the option to tax?

The person responsible for making the decision and notifying the option to tax depends on the type of legal entity holding (or intending to hold) the interest in the land or building, and who within that entity has the authority to make decisions concerning VAT. In most cases it will be the sole proprietor, one or more partners (or trustees), a director or an authorised administrator. If you have appointed a third party to notify an option to tax on your behalf, we require written confirmation that the third party is authorised to do so. We would also wish to be notified if you withdraw that authority. The following paragraphs explain who is responsible in other, slightly more unusual situations.

Commentary—*De Voil Indirect Tax Service* **V4.116**.

7.2 Beneficial owners

In some cases there may be both a beneficial owner and a legal owner of land or buildings. An example of this is a bare trust, where a trustee is the legal owner but the benefit of the income from the land or building passes to the beneficial owner. For VAT purposes it is the beneficial owner who is making the supply of the land or building. It is the beneficial owner who should opt to tax, and who must account for any VAT due on the supply and claim any input tax that arises.

This is not the case, however, where the beneficiaries are numerous, such as unit trusts and pension funds. In such situations the person making the supply is the trustee who holds the legal interest and receives the immediate benefit of the consideration.

Commentary—*De Voil Indirect Tax Service* **V2.116**.

7.3 Joint owners

Joint ownership will arise if you and another person buy land or buildings together, or if you sell a part share of your land or building to someone else. If you are a joint owner it is likely that the only supply that can be made of the jointly owned land or building is by you and the other person together.

You and the other person should together notify a single option to tax if you want supplies of the jointly owned land or building to be standard-rated. The taxable supply of the land or building is then made by both of you as one taxable person. To account for output tax and to be able to recover input tax, you and the other person should register for VAT together as if a partnership, even if you are not in partnership for any other purpose.

7.4 Limited partnerships

A limited partnership is made up of one or more "general" partners, who have unlimited liability, and one or more "limited" partners, who are not liable for debts and obligations of the firm. A limited partner is unable to take part in the management and running of the partnership business, and where we find that a limited partner is doing so, we will treat them as a general partner.

If there is only one general partner and one or more limited partners, the general partner is treated as a sole proprietor for VAT registration purposes. Likewise if there are two or more general partners and one or more limited partners, the general partners are treated as a partnership for VAT registration purposes. It is the general partner(s) who should opt to tax and account for any VAT due on the supply and claim any input tax that arises.

Where title to the land or building is held jointly in the names of the general partner(s) **and** the limited partner(s), only the titleholders can make any supplies of that land or building together. That suggests that the limited partner is involved in the management and running of the partnership, and as such we treat them as a general partner and amend the VAT registration to reflect that. If the partnership decides to opt to tax, one or more of the partners should sign the notification.

Commentary—*De Voil Indirect Tax Service* **V2.110**.

7.5 Limited liability partnerships

A limited liability partnership has a separate legal status from its members and is able to enter into contracts in its own right. This means that the individual members of the limited liability partnership are protected from debts or liabilities arising from negligence, wrongful acts or conduct of another member, employee or agent of the partnership.

A limited liability partnership is a corporate body and is liable to register for VAT, subject to the normal registration rules. If the partnership decides to opt to tax, one or more members must sign the notification.

Commentary—*De Voil Indirect Tax Service* **V2.113**.

8. REVOKING AN OPTION TO TAX

8.1 Revoking an option to tax within the 6 month "cooling-off" period

8.1.1 When can I revoke without prior permission?

If you change your mind within 6 months of the effective date of your option to tax, you can revoke your option to tax if you meet all the conditions set out in a) to e) and **Box F** of paragraph 8.1.2 below. You will not need our prior permission but you must notify us before the end of the 6 month period and your notification must be made on form **VAT 1614C** (see paragraph 8.1.3 below).

8.1.2 What are the conditions for revoking?

(a) no more than six months have passed since the day on which the option had effect;
(b) no use, including your own occupation, has been made of the land since the option had effect;
(c) no tax has become chargeable on a supply of the land as a result of the option;
(d) no transfer of a going concern has occurred; and
(e) you have notified the revocation to HMRC on form **1614C**.

An additional condition is set out in **Box F** below. To revoke your option to tax you must either satisfy the additional condition or obtain our permission. Where we grant permission we may impose conditions.

Box F

The contents of this box have the force of the law.

> Revoking an option within 6 months of the option first having effect (under paragraph 23(4) of Schedule 10 to the Value Added Tax Act 1994 ("the VAT Act 1994")).
>
> **Additional condition**
>
> The revocation of an option to tax under paragraph 23 of Schedule 10 to the VAT Act 1994 is effective only if none of the input tax of the person who made the option (or a relevant associate of that person) is allowable for credit as being attributable to supplies that are excluded from Group 1 of Schedule 9 to the VAT Act 1994 by virtue of the option.
>
> **Explanatory Note**
>
> For the purposes of the condition, input tax of the person who made the option shall not be regarded as allowable for credit if:
>
> (a) in the event of the option being revoked, that person would be liable to repay to the Commissioners an amount equal to that input tax by virtue of regulation 108 of the Value Added Tax Regulations 1995 ("the VAT Regulations 1995");
>
> (b) that person is entitled to deduct it provisionally as attributable to taxable supplies by virtue of regulation 101 of the VAT Regulations 1995, or a method approved or directed by the Commissioners pursuant to regulation 102 of those regulations but it is not input tax on goods or services used or to be used by that person exclusively in making supplies that do not fall within Group 1 of Schedule 9 to the VAT Act 1994 by virtue of the option; or
>
> (c) it is input tax on a capital item, subject to adjustments in accordance with part 15 of the VAT Regulations 1995.
>
> **Prior permission granted by the Commissioners.**
>
> The additional condition specified above is not applicable where the taxpayer gets the prior permission of the Commissioners on an application made to them before the end of the 6 month period mentioned in paragraph 23(a) of Schedule 10 to the VAT Act 1994. The Commissioners may specify conditions subject to which their permission is given and, if any of those conditions are broken, may treat the revocation as if it had not been made.

8.1.3 How do I notify you?

The following statement has the force of the law.

> Notification of revocation of an option to tax within the 6 month "cooling off" period (*for the purpose of paragraph 23 of Schedule 10 to the VAT Act 1994*) must be made on form **VAT 1614C** and must contain the information requested on that form.

You can download form **VAT 1614C** from **www.hmrc.gov.uk** or obtain it from our advice service on **0845 010 9000**.

8.1.4 When can I seek permission to revoke?

You can seek permission to revoke if you meet conditions a) to e) of paragraph 8.1.2 above but fail to meet the additional condition specified in **Box F**.

8.1.5 How do I apply for permission?

The following statement has the force of the law.

> Application for permission to revoke an option to tax within the 6 month "cooling off period" (*for the purpose of paragraph 23 of Schedule 10 to the VAT Act 1994*) must be made on form **VAT 1614C** and must contain the information requested on that form.

You can download form **VAT 1614C** from **www.hmrc.gov.uk** or obtain it from our advice service on **0845 010 9000**.

You must submit your application within 6 months of the effective date of your option to tax. Your application for permission will also be treated as notification of your revocation, so there is no requirement to make a separate notification once permission is granted.

When considering whether to grant permission, we will give particular consideration to whether you or a third party have received a VAT benefit as a result of your action.

8.1.6 When does the revocation take effect?

The revocation of an option to tax during its "cooling-off" period has effect from the day on which the option was exercised. However, the revocation of an option to tax may be tax disregarded where any conditions set by HMRC when granting permission to revoke are not met.

8.1.7 How should I adjust my input tax after I have revoked my option?

If you revoke an option to tax under the "cooling off" rules, you should adjust your input tax in accordance with the appropriate rules explained in notice 706 "Partial Exemption" and notice 706/2 "Capital Goods Scheme".

8.1.8 How does the "cooling off" period apply in relation to real estate elections?

If you choose, at the time of making a real estate election, to convert existing "global options" into separate options to tax, you cannot revoke these new separate options under the "cooling-off" period.

See section 14 for information about real estate elections.

8.2 Revoking an option where no interest has been held for more than 6 years

An option to tax exercised by any person in relation to a property where no interest has been held for over 6 years is treated as being automatically revoked from the end of the 6 year period.

However, the 6 year revocation does not apply where the opter has been a member of a VAT group during any time in the relevant 6 year period and any relevant associate of the opter (including those who were relevant associates prior to the start of the relevant 6 year period) has left the VAT group with a relevant interest in the property.

A "relevant 6 year period" means any period of 6 years commencing with when then opter or any relevant associate of the opter, ceases to have any relevant interest in the building.

For the meaning of "relevant associate", see paragraph 6.3.1.

8.3 Revoking an option where more than 20 years have elapsed since it first had effect

8.3.1 When can I revoke without prior permission?

You may revoke an option to tax where more than 20 years have elapsed since the option first had effect if you meet either condition 1 or conditions 2–5 of **Box G** below. You will not need our permission, but you must notify us on form **VAT 1614J** (see paragraph 8.3.3 below).

8.3.2 What are the conditions for revoking?

Box G

The following statement has the force of the law.

Conditions for revoking an option to tax when more than 20 years have elapsed since a relevant interest was first held in an opted building or land and the option first had effect (for the purposes of paragraph 25(1)(a) of Schedule 10 to the Value Added Tax Act 1994 ("the VAT Act 1994")).

A taxpayer may revoke an option to tax made by the taxpayer if either condition 1 below or all of conditions 2 to 5 are met.

1. The relevant interest condition

2. The 20 year condition

The taxpayer or a relevant associate connected to the taxpayer held a relevant interest in the building or land at a time,

- when the option first has effect; and
- more than 20 years before the option is revoked.

3. The capital item condition

4. The valuation condition

The taxpayer or a relevant associate connected to the taxpayer has made no supply of a relevant interest in the building or land subject to the option in the 10 years immediately before revocation of the option that:

- was for a consideration that was less than the open market value of that supply, or
- arose from a relevant grant

5. The pre-payment condition

Explanatory Note 1

"Taxpayer" means—

(a) a person who exercised the option to tax or is treated as making that option by virtue of a real estate election pursuant to paragraph 21 of Schedule 10 to the Act; and ➡

(b) in relation to an option to tax treated as exercised by virtue of a real estate election made pursuant to paragraph 21 of Schedule 10 to the VAT Act 1994 by a body corporate treated as a member of a group under sections 43A to 43D of the Act other than the person described in (a) above, the body corporate whose relevant interest gave rise to the option to tax.

Explanatory Note 2

Explanatory Note 3

Explanatory Note 4

In relation to condition 2 above, it does not matter whether, at the time the option is revoked, the taxpayer continues to hold the relevant interest in the building or land that meets the condition.

Explanatory Note 5

For the purpose of condition 3—

(1) land or buildings that fall for input tax adjustment as a capital item under Part 15 of the VAT Regulations shall not be regarded as so doing if the relevant amount does not exceed £10,000;

(2) the relevant amount is the total of the amounts that the taxpayer or a relevant associate connected to the taxpayer would be required to pay to the Commissioners pursuant to regulation 115(2) of the VAT Regulations in respect of intervals ending after the revocation of the option if—

(a) that person were a taxable person during such intervals; and

(b) the land or building concerned were used, after the revocation of the option, only for making supplies that are not taxable supplies.

Explanatory Note 6

Explanatory Note 7

"Relevant Associate" means – A body corporate as defined in paragraph 3 of Schedule 10 to the Act.

Note—Box G was updated in July 2009, with effect from 1 August 2009: see VAT Information Note 12/09.

8.3.3 How do I notify you?

The following statement has the force of the law.

Notification of revocation of an option to tax after 20 years (*for the purpose of paragraph 25 of Schedule 10 to the VAT Act 1994*) must be made on form **VAT 1614J** and must contain the information requested on that form.

You can download form **VAT 1614J** from **www.hmrc.gov.uk** or obtain it from our advice service on **0845 010 9000**.

8.3.4 When can I seek permission to revoke?

If you do not meet the conditions in **Box G** you may still seek our permission to revoke. However, we cannot give you permission unless condition 2 of **Box G** is met.

8.3.5 How do I apply for permission?

The following statement has the force of the law.

Application for permission to revoke an option to tax after 20 years (*for the purpose of paragraph 25 of Schedule 10 to the VAT Act 1994*) must be made on form **VAT 1614J** and must contain the information requested on that form.

You can download form **VAT 1614J** from **www.hmrc.gov.uk** or obtain it from our advice service on **0845 010 9000**.

8.3.6 In what circumstances will you grant permission?

We will not grant permission unless you meet condition 2 of **Box G** above.

In deciding whether or not to grant permission, we will give particular consideration to whether or not you or a third party has received a VAT benefit as a result of your actions.

For example, a case could arise where, one year before applying for permission to revoke, you pre pay for the following three years' cleaning services and, because of your intention to revoke, you only deduct one third of the input tax charged. Whilst you fail to meet the pre-payment condition (condition 5 of **Box G**), we would nevertheless grant permission, since your recovery of input tax is fair and reasonable. If you had deducted all of the input tax on the cleaning services, permission would be refused, unless the law provided some means by which the original input tax deduction could be adjusted.

8.3.7 If you grant permission, when will my revocation take effect?

Once we have granted permission, the revocation will have effect from the day permission is granted. We can only specify an earlier date in cases where you previously gave a notification of revocation believing, in error, that you met the conditions in **Box G** above. In such cases we may allow the revocation to be effective from the date stated in the original notification, but only where we are satisfied that the reasons for failing to meet the conditions are insignificant.

In granting permission we may specify further conditions subject to which the permission is given. If any of these conditions are subsequently broken we may treat the revocation as if it had not been made.

Commentary—*De Voil Indirect Tax Service* **V4.116**.

9. INPUT TAX

9.1 Rules on reclaiming input tax

Once you have opted to tax your entitlement to recover any input tax you incur will depend on the liability of the supplies you make:

If you make …	**then you will normally be …**
taxable supplies of the land or buildings	able to recover any input tax relating to those supplies
wholly exempt supplies of the land or building (see section 3)	unable to recover any input tax relating to those supplies
supplies that are both taxable and exempt, for example you may have opted to tax a building that is to be used for both commercial and residential purposes	able to recover only the input tax relating to the taxable supply. Notice 706 "Partial exemption" explains how to work out how much input tax relates to taxable supplies.

9.2 What about input tax I incurred before I opted to tax?

9.2.1 May I recover input tax relating to supplies of land or buildings if the supplies are taxable in their own right?

Yes. For example, a freehold sale of a commercial building within 3 years of its completion is always standard-rated.

But many supplies of land and buildings will only become taxable as a result of an option to tax. **If you have not opted to tax, your supplies will be exempt from VAT and input tax relating to the supplies will be exempt input tax and irrecoverable** (there are exceptions to this general rule and you should see paragraph 9.2.6 below for details).

9.2.2 May I recover input tax now that relates to future supplies?

Yes, in certain circumstances. Input tax incurred prior to the making of supplies can be recoverable where you have a clear intention, at the time the costs are incurred, that the supplies of the buildings or land will be taxable. **An option to tax is by far the best evidence of an intention to make taxable supplies for land and property transactions.**

Where, in exceptional circumstances, you wish to delay the making of the option until a future date you may still be able to recover the input tax relating to supplies which will follow the option. This will only be the case, however, where you are able to produce unequivocal documentary evidence, at the time you wish to reclaim your input tax, that you intend your supplies to be taxable.

9.2.3 What types of documents will be accepted as evidence that I intend to make taxable supplies?

A list of examples of the types of documents that may contain evidence of intention is shown below. The list is not intended to be exhaustive and whether a particular document provides the evidence will very much depend upon its content.

It is unlikely that any single document alone will provide sufficient evidence and you are advised to hold a number of separate documents to prove your intention. Customs will normally consider evidence as satisfactory where it involves third parties and shows a firm commitment to the making of taxable supplies. For example:

- A signed agreement/contract that specifies that the vendor will opt to tax prior to the sale.
- An investment appraisal or business plan accepted by a bank, that confirms that supplies will be treated as taxable.
- Marketing literature that has been distributed to the public and where the scale and type of distribution, together with the nature of the advertisement itself, makes it clear that taxable supplies will be made.
- Instructions or advice from professional advisers that specifies the VAT treatment, together with confirmation of your acceptance of the advice.
- Any other similar document that shows that the intention is to make taxable supplies.

We cannot give a list of unacceptable documents. However, any document that merely sets out an option or number of options will not be accepted as unequivocal documentary evidence of an intention to make taxable supplies.

9.2.4 Having recovered input tax relating to future taxable supplies, what action should I take?

- Any documents used as evidence of intention must be retained and made available to HMRC on request.
- Where the intention to make taxable supplies changes, a record must be kept of the date these changes occurred together with appropriate evidence. HMRC must also be informed of the change as soon as possible. Input tax on costs that relate to exempt supplies cannot normally be deducted. Furthermore, VAT previously deducted before the intention changed may need to be adjusted and repaid to HMRC. Please see Notice 706 "Partial exemption" for details.
- **An option to tax must be made and notified to HMRC prior to any supplies of the land or buildings being made.**

9.2.5 Are there any other circumstances in which input tax incurred prior to an option to tax can be recovered?

There are two.

- Where, prior to supplies being made, your intention to make exempt supplies changes to an intention to make taxable supplies you may be able to recover previously exempt input tax under the "payback" rule. You will find more about the payback rule in Notice 706 "Partial exemption". Where, however, your change of intention is not accompanied by an option to tax you will need to retain suitable evidence of your new intention (see paragraph 9.2.3 above); and
- where you made exempt supplies of the land or building before opting to tax and incurred exempt input tax you may be able to recover this under the permission procedure explained in section 5.

9.3 What about speculative and abortive costs?

As a developer you may spend time and effort investigating potential projects such as looking for sites and assessing their suitability. Where you have:

- a clear intention of what supplies you intend to make you must attribute the input tax incurred to the liability of the intended supply; or
- no firm intention of what supplies you will make, the input tax on the costs you incur is "residual" for partial exemption purposes.

Some potential projects are not followed through, and in the end no supplies are actually made. If up to the time of aborting the project you have no firm intention regarding the liability of the supplies you wish to make (and as a result are unable to attribute the input tax to the liability of the intended supply), the related input tax should be left as residual.

When you decide to proceed with a project you will have a clear intention as to what supplies you will make. (It is normally at this point that you decide whether to opt to tax for land and property supplies.) If you had not attributed the input tax previously you should then adjust the input tax accordingly under the "payback" and "clawback" rules. Input tax on the ongoing costs should be attributed to the expected taxable or exempt supplies.

You can find further information in Notice 706 "Partial exemption".

Commentary—*De Voil Indirect Tax Service* **V3.461**.

9.4 What about the VAT I incurred prior to my registration?

You may find that you become registered for VAT as a result of opting to tax. Special rules apply to all newly registered persons under which they may be entitled to claim relief for VAT incurred on supplies they obtained before registration. Relief is restricted on supplies of services to those received not more than 6 months before your registration. This restriction may lead to inequitable treatment compared with a business carrying out similar activities, but who was already VAT registered when the tax was incurred. If you consider you have suffered because of this you should write to the Option To Tax National Unit (paragraph 4.2.3 shows how you may contact them) and explain your circumstances.

In all cases relief for VAT incurred before registration is restricted to tax which can be directly attributed to a taxable activity. If you incurred tax before registration that was attributable both to exempt supplies before registration as well as taxable supplies after registration, the relief will be restricted proportionately.

9.5 Capital goods scheme

If you acquire land or buildings which are considered to be capital items for the purposes of this scheme, you must review their use in your business over a series of intervals, normally lasting 10 years. If there is a change in the extent to which they are used for making taxable supplies you must make an input tax adjustment to take account of this. You will find more information about how the scheme works in the Notice 706/2 "Capital goods scheme".

Commentary—*De Voil Indirect Tax Service* **V3.463, V3.470, V4.116**.

10. TIME OF SUPPLY (TAX POINT)

10.1 Normal tax point rules

The normal tax point rules apply to all supplies of land or buildings. These rules are explained in detail in Notice 700 "The VAT Guide".

If you make leasehold supplies and have opted to tax, a tax point will normally occur when you either issue a tax invoice or receive a payment, whichever is the earlier.

If you are selling the freehold of land or a building a basic tax point will normally occur at the time of legal completion under the terms of the contract, when the freehold is conveyed to the purchaser. The equivalent under Scottish land law is the time of delivery of the disposition. Any payments you receive after the basic tax point do not create a tax point. If you issue a VAT invoice within 14 days after the basic tax point, then the date of issue of that invoice becomes the tax point. If you issue a VAT invoice or receive a payment before the basic tax point, then an actual tax point will be created by whichever happens first, to the extent of the amount invoiced or payment received.

10.2 Does a deposit create a tax point?

Often on the sale of land or buildings, the purchaser pays a deposit at exchange of contracts, followed by payment of the balance on the completion date. An independent stakeholder usually holds the deposit until completion, and the seller receives no payment until that time. In these circumstances, the deposit payment will not create a tax point. It follows that if the deposit is paid directly to the seller or their agent, the payment does create a tax point. In both cases, an earlier tax point arises if a tax invoice is issued before the seller receives any payment.

10.3 What if I receive arrears of rent following my option to tax?

In a tenanted building, a tax point might not occur until you receive payment. In these circumstances, if you opt to tax after the rent becomes due but before it is paid, you must account for output tax on the rental receipt. This is the case even if the payment covers a period before your option to tax took effect.

Commentary—*De Voil Indirect Tax Service* **V3.131–V3.143**.

11. TRANSFER OF A BUSINESS AS A GOING CONCERN

11.1 What does "transferring a business as a going concern" mean?

Notice 700/9 "Transfer of a business as a going concern" explains the VAT position if you are selling your business or part of it. Subject to special VAT rules applying, the sale of the assets of a business, or part of it, will not be treated as a supply for VAT purposes. The sales affected will be those where a business, or part of a business, is capable of separate operation after the sale has taken place, and it is sold as a going concern.

11.2 What if I am transferring land or buildings as part of a transfer of a going concern?

If you have opted to tax the land or buildings being transferred **and**:

- you meet all the conditions specified in Notice 700/9; and
- the purchaser has opted to tax, and
- with effect from 18th March 2004, the purchaser has notified you that their option to tax will not be disapplied in respect of supplies they intend to make of the land or building (see Section 13),

the transfer of the land or buildings as part of a transfer of a going concern is not a taxable supply.

However, the TOGC provisions only apply where the purchaser has notified the option to tax to us before or on the relevant date. The option must also be effective from that date or earlier. By "notified" we mean that the purchaser has properly addressed, pre-paid and posted the letter to us. The declaration that the option will not be disapplied must also be made by the relevant date. The relevant date is the time of the supply; which is normally the date of the transfer, but will also include receipt of a deposit if that is paid in advance of the date of the transfer (unless the deposit is paid to an independent stakeholder). Further information on tax points can be found in section 10 of this Notice.

However, if you are transferring:

- land or buildings which are new (less than 3 years old) or unfinished buildings or civil engineering work which would normally be standard rated, or
- land or buildings on which you have opted to tax

and the purchaser has either:

- not opted to tax the land or building, or
- not notified you that the option to tax will not be disapplied,

then the conditions for a transfer of a going concern will not have been met in respect of the land or buildings. You will have to charge VAT on the sale of the land or building.

The following table will help you to decide whether the conditions for a transfer of a going concern have been met.

Commercial land or building, ordinarily exempt

Has seller opted to tax (Building over 3 years old)?	Has the purchaser opted to tax?	Will the purchaser's option to tax be disapplied?	Transfer of a going concern provisions met?
Yes	Yes	Yes	No
Yes	No	N/A	No
Yes	Yes	No	Yes
No	No	N/A	Yes
No	Yes	Yes	Yes
No	Yes	No	Yes

New building (less than 3 years old), ordinarily standard-rated

Has seller opted to tax?	Has the purchaser opted to tax?	Will the purchaser's option to tax be disapplied?	Transfer of a going concern provisions met?
Yes	Yes	Yes	No
Yes	No	N/A	No
Yes	Yes	No	Yes
No	No	N/A	No
No	Yes	Yes	No
No	Yes	No	Yes

Commentary—*De Voil Indirect Tax Service* **V4.116**.

11.3 What about the input tax I incur on transfer expenses?

The way you treat input tax incurred in relation to a transfer of a going concern depends on whether you are the transferor (the person disposing of the business), or the transferee (the person acquiring the business).

11.3.1 Transferor

As a transferor of a going concern, the transfer of assets of a going concern is neither a supply of goods nor a supply of services for VAT purposes (see Notice 700/9 "Transfer of a business as a going concern").

Following the European Court of Justice decision in the case of *Abbey National plc* (C-408/98), we now accept that, from 1 August 2001, the input tax on expenses that relate wholly to the transfer (for example legal fees) should be treated as an overhead of that part of the business being transferred. Where that part of the business makes:

- only taxable supplies, the input tax is fully recoverable;
- only exempt supplies, the input tax is wholly non-recoverable; and
- both taxable and exempt supplies, the input tax is residual and recoverable in accordance with the partial exemption method in place.

Prior to the Abbey National plc decision, our policy was that input tax incurred on expenses which related to the transfer of assets were considered to be residual tax, and the value of input tax recoverable was calculated in accordance with the partial exemption method in place.

If you are partly exempt and your partial exemption method fails to achieve a fair and reasonable result, we may, exceptionally, be prepared to approve an alternative method, which has retrospective effect.

However, we will seek to ensure that any such method provides for a fair and reasonable recovery of input tax.

11.3.2 Transferee

If you are the transferee of a going concern and acquire assets for your business, the input tax on costs that relate wholly to the acquisition of those assets will be recoverable to the extent to which they will be used in making taxable supplies. Therefore, where they are to be used in making:

- only taxable supplies, the input tax is fully recoverable;
- only exempt supplies, the input tax is wholly non-recoverable; and
- both taxable and exempt supplies, the input tax is residual and recoverable in accordance with the partial exemption method in place.

Please note this applies only to acquisitions of businesses by way of a transfer of a going concern. Any input tax on expenses related to any other form of acquisition, such as the acquisition of shares in a business, should be treated as residual input tax, and recoverable in accordance with the partial exemption method in place.

if you acquire …	And you …	your VAT group may …
a business or its assets as a going concern	are a member of a VAT group registration that is partly exempt; or becomes partly exempt during the tax year in which the transfer takes place	have to account for VAT on certain assets as a supply both to and by the group. Notice 700/9 "Transfer of a business as a going concern" gives full details

Commentary—*De Voil Indirect Tax Service* **V3.461**.

11.4 What if the land or buildings are in the capital goods scheme?

If you are transferring land or buildings which are capital items for purposes of the capital goods scheme, you should make the purchaser aware of any capital goods scheme adjustments you have made and provide sufficient information to enable the purchaser to carry out any future adjustments under the scheme that might be necessary.

If you have acquired land or buildings that are capital items, you are responsible for continuing the capital goods scheme, and making any further adjustments of input tax required under the scheme, until the intervals are complete.

Further detailed information regarding the operation of the scheme can be found in Notice 706/2 "Capital goods scheme".

Commentary—*De Voil Indirect Tax Service* **V2.226**.

12. DEREGISTRATION

12.1 What happens to my option to tax if I deregister?

Your option to tax is not cancelled if you deregister. If you deregister due to a fall in turnover, and then at a later date your income increases above the VAT threshold, the option to tax will still have effect and you must apply to register again.

You may deregister because you are selling your business as a transfer of a going concern. If that is the case, and you are disposing of land or buildings that are capital items for the purposes of the capital goods scheme as part of the transfer, you should inform the purchaser of any adjustments you have made under the scheme.

If the opted land or building is an asset on hand at deregistration you may have to account for output tax in respect of it. For more information please see Notice 700/11 "Cancelling your registration".

13. ANTI-AVOIDANCE MEASURES

13.1 Why do HMRC need the anti-avoidance measures?

Some traders whose supplies are wholly or partly exempt, are not entitled to recover all of the input tax they incur on the purchase of land or buildings, or on major construction projects. As a result, some of these organisations enter into arrangements designed to either increase the amount of input tax they can claim, or to spread the VAT cost of the purchase or construction over a number of years.

To counter this, we introduced an anti-avoidance test. The test is applied each time a grant is made and if caught, the option to tax will not have effect (it will be "disapplied") in respect of the supplies that arise from that particular grant.

From 18 March 2004, new conditions were introduced that extend the disapplication of the option to tax and these may now also impact on the VAT treatment of a transfer as a going concern (TOGC) of a property.

If you are an organisation that normally receives credit for most of the input tax you incur, for example you are fully taxable, then you are unlikely to be affected by the anti-avoidance measures detailed in this section.

13.2 What is the test?

The test is as follows:

If, at the time of the grant of land or buildings:

(1) the development is, or is expected to become, a capital item for the purposes of the capital goods scheme, either for the grantor, a person to whom the development is transferred or a person treated as the grantor (see paragraph 13.4.3 below); **and**

(2) it is the intention or expectation of the grantor or the person treated as the grantor (see

paragraph 13.4.3 below) or the person responsible for financing the grantor's development, that the building will be occupied by them or a person connected to them; **and**

(3) the person occupying the development will be doing so other than wholly or substantially wholly for eligible purposes,

then the option to tax will not have effect in respect of supplies that arise from that particular grant.

The following paragraphs will explain what the test means and how it is to be applied to each grant.

13.3 When was the test introduced?

The test was introduced on 19 March 1997 and only affects supplies made from that date. The anti-avoidance measure does not apply to any grants made before 26 November 1996 and does not apply to grants made between 26 November 1996 and 30 November 1999 if the terms of the grant were agreed in writing before 26 November 1996.

Between 19 March 1997 and 9 March 1999 the anti-avoidance measure only affected grants where the development was a capital item at the time of the grant. From 10 March 1999 we extended the anti-avoidance measure to include situations where, although at the time of the grant the development was not a capital item, it was intended or expected that it would become one at a future date. Part of the extended measure required businesses that had made grants between 19 March 1997 and 9 March 1999 to re-visit those grants, and where appropriate, to treat the date of the grant as 10 March 1999.

The anti avoidance measures were further extended from 18 March 2004. From that date, when a supply is made by a person other than the person who made the grant (eg where a lease has been granted by one person and then assigned to another) that person is treated as making the grant that gave rise to the supply and they are required to apply the option to tax disapplication test (see paragraph 13.2 above). Changes were also made to the rules for determining whether the sale of an interest in land can be treated as a TOGC given that it is now possible for a transferee's option to tax to be disapplied.

13.4 Grants and supplies

13.4.1 What is a grant and who is the grantor?

The word "grant" refers to the act that transfers the land or building, such as a freehold sale of land or a building, the leasing or licensing of land or a building, or the assignment or surrender of that lease, licence or let.

The grantor is the person who sells, leases, licences or lets any of the land or buildings and can be anywhere in the "chain" of people who have an interest in the land or buildings concerned. For example, a freeholder may sell land to another party who constructs a new commercial building on the land to let to another business, who will occupy the building for its own use. In this case there are two grantors: the seller of the land and the business which constructs and leases the new commercial building. It follows that if the occupying business goes on to sub-let part of the building to another business, there would then be three grantors. **The test should be applied to each grant made.**

13.4.2 What do HMRC mean by supplies arising from a grant?

In the case of a freehold sale there is normally a single supply at the time of completion. For leases, however, it is usual for there to be a succession of supplies following the grant. These are treated as made when you either issue an invoice or receive payment (the earlier of the two). Payment would also include any non-monetary consideration.

13.4.3 What if I make supplies under a grant that was originally made by another person?

If, from 18 March 2004, you make a supply under a grant that was originally made by another person then, for the purposes of part 1 of the test in paragraph 13.2, you are treated as if you had made the grant. The grant is treated as made on the date of your first supply of the land.

Where, for the purposes of the test, you are treated as the person who made the grant, you will need to determine whether you satisfy the other elements of the anti-avoidance test and, as a result, your option to tax is disapplied. However, in such circumstances the test is still satisfied (and your option disapplied) where your grant is treated as made after the expiry of your capital goods scheme adjustment period. For example, where there is an intention that the building will be occupied by someone connected to you and will not be used for eligible purposes, then even if your first supply (see paragraph 13.4.2) occurs after the building has ceased to be capital item for the CGS, your option to tax will still be disapplied. This overcomes an avoidance scheme that involved deferring the supplies made under the grant until the land is no longer a capital item.

13.5 How do HMRC establish a person's intention or expectation?

The option to tax has no effect in relation to the supplies arising from the grant if either the grantor, or the person responsible for financing the grantor for that particular development, knows or expects that either one of them, or any party connected to them, will occupy the building for other than eligible purposes (see paragraph 13.10). There does not have to be an intention to avoid VAT for the grant to be caught by the test.

We will consider commercial documents and other evidence such as minutes of meetings, business plans and finance requests to establish the intention and expectation of the businesses that are involved in the particular development.

13.6 What do HMRC mean by finance?

For the purpose of the anti-avoidance measure we regard finance as:

- directly or indirectly providing all or part of the funds for the development;
- directly or indirectly obtaining those funds from another person;
- directly or indirectly providing the funds for discharging all or part of the owner's borrowing for the development; or
- directly or indirectly procuring that such a liability will be discharged by another.

Finance could take many different forms, such as loans, guaranteeing a loan, purchase of shares or securities which finance a development of land, share issues or premium deals.

13.7 When do HMRC consider someone to be responsible for financing a development?

For the purposes of the anti-avoidance measure a person is only deemed to have been responsible for financing a development if two key conditions are met:

(a) at the time the finance is provided, or the agreement to provide the finance is entered into, the person providing the finance must intend or expect that he or the grantor, or somebody connected to either of them, will occupy the particular development for other than eligible purposes; **and**

(b) the funds must be for the purpose of financing the purchase, construction or refurbishment of that development.

If either of these conditions is not met, a person will not be deemed to be responsible for financing the development, even if he has provided the funds to meet part or all of the cost of the development.

13.8 When do HMRC consider a person to be connected with another?

We use the test in section 839 of the Income and Corporation Taxes Act 1988 to determine whether people are connected. Examples of connected persons are:

- your husband or wife;
- your relatives;
- your husband's or wife's relatives;
- your business partners and their husbands, wives and relatives;
- a company that you control, either by yourself or with any of the persons listed above; or
- the trustees of a settlement of which you are a settlor, or of which a person who is still alive and who is connected with you is a settlor.

Relative means a brother, sister, ancestor or lineal descendant. It does not include nephews, nieces, uncles and aunts.

13.9 What do HMRC mean by occupied?

A person is in occupation of a building or land if it has the right to occupy it as if it were the owner and exclude any other person from enjoyment of such a right. Normally they will have been granted a legal interest in or licence to occupy the land, but this might not always be the case. For example, a person is considered to be in occupation where this is by agreement or "de facto". It is not a requirement that the person has an exclusive right of occupation or is utilising all of the land for all of the time in order for them to be considered as occupying it.

13.10 When is occupation "wholly" or "substantially wholly" for eligible purposes?

13.10.1 What is "wholly" or "substantially wholly"?

The anti-avoidance measure examines whether the grantor or the person responsible for financing the development intend that the development will be occupied other than "wholly" or "substantially wholly" for eligible purposes.

The terms "wholly" or "substantially wholly" are defined in **Box H** below

Box H

The boxed text below has the force of the law

Meaning of "wholly" and "substantially wholly" for eligible purposes (for the purpose of paragraph 15(5) of Schedule 10 to the Value Added Tax Act 1994)

Expression	*Meaning*
Occupation "wholly" for eligible purposes	Land occupied 100% for eligible purposes
Occupation "substantially wholly" for eligible purposes,	Land occupied at least 80% for eligible purposes

13.10.2 What are "eligible purposes"?

For someone to be in occupation of the development for eligible purposes they must be occupying it for the purpose of making taxable supplies, or for other supplies which entitle them to credit for their input tax.

Some organisations are always treated as occupying a development for eligible purposes and these include National Health Service Trusts and government departments. Occupation by local authorities or other bodies, such as police and fire authorities, are treated as eligible provided the occupation is for taxable or non-business purposes.

Occupation that arises only because of an automatic teller machine (ATM) fixed to the land is treated as for eligible purposes.

The following are examples of businesses and organisations that may occupy a development for other than eligible purposes:

- businesses, such as insurance companies and banks, making exempt supplies;
- someone who is not, or is not required to be, VAT registered.

Organisations, such as charities, who undertake non-business activities would **not** generally be in occupation for eligible purposes

13.11 What land or buildings are covered by the capital goods scheme?

The anti-avoidance measure only applies to land and buildings that are, or will become, capital items for the purpose of the capital goods scheme. Generally, a capital item comes within the scheme when it is either bought, or first used.

Examples of land and buildings covered by the capital goods scheme are:

- land, a building or part of a building, where the value of the interest supplied to the person buying or leasing it is £250,000 or more;
- a building constructed by the owner where the total value of goods and services received in connection with the construction is £250,000 or more;
- a building which the owner alters, or an extension or annex which he constructs, where additional floor area of at least 10% is created and the value of the goods and services received in connection with the works is £250,000 or more;
- a building which the owner refurbishes or fits out where the value of the capital expenditure on the services received and the goods affixed to the building in connection with the works is £250,000 or more; or
- any of the above acquired from the owner during the capital goods scheme adjustment period by way of a transfer of a going concern (see section 11 for more information).

You will find more information about capital items and how the scheme works in Notice 706/2 "Capital goods scheme".

Commentary—*De Voil Indirect Tax Service* **V3.47O**.

13.12 What do HMRC mean by supplies arising from a grant?

New rules governing transfers of a going concern involving land or buildings came into effect on 18 March 2004. Transferees who are acquiring interests in land or buildings that are either new (less than three years old) or older buildings that have been opted to tax, must not only notify their option to tax by the relevant date but must now, also by the relevant date, notify the transferor whether or not their option to tax will be disapplied. If the option will be disapplied, the sale cannot be de-supplied by a TOGC and VAT must be accounted for.

The new notification requirement has been drafted into VAT law as part of measures to deal with avoidance schemes which make use of the TOGC arrangements. Under the new TOGC rules transferees are required to undertake a new hypothetical test when considering whether land or buildings will be a capital item in their hands. Under the test transferees need to consider whether there are any circumstances in which the building being transferred would become for them a capital item.

If there are, and this would lead to their option to tax being disapplied, they would be unable to provide the notification necessary for the transfer to be treated as a TOGC. This means the transfer of the building would have to be treated as a taxable supply. Section 11 gives further guidance on the effect of the new provisions.

Commentary—*De Voil Indirect Tax Service* **V4.116**.

14. REAL ESTATE ELECTIONS ("REE")

14.1 What is a REE?

If you have made a real estate election ("REE"), you will be treated (with certain exceptions) as having opted to tax every property in which you acquire a "relevant interest" after making the REE. You do not therefore need to notify individual options in relation to properties you acquire after making a REE. Where the person making a REE is in a VAT group, special rules apply to relevant associates (see paragraphs 14.12 to 14.14 below).

Under a REE, each property is treated as individually opted, with all the normal rules for an individual option applying. This means that you can individually revoke the option on each property if the applicable conditions are met. For example, if you have made a REE but you do not wish a property in which you acquire a relevant interest to be opted, you may revoke the option under the "cooling-off" provisions (see paragraph 8.1 above) and the option is treated as though it was never made.

14.2 When does an option to tax under a REE have effect?

An option to tax only has effect under a REE in relation to land in which you subsequently acquire a relevant interest. The option in respect of such a property has effect from the start of the day on which you acquire it.

14.3 Can I opt to tax a property in which I do not hold an interest?

If you wish to make an option to tax on land in respect of which you do not hold a relevant interest, or if you wish an option to have effect earlier than the day on which you acquire a relevant interest, you may do so by making a separately notified option to tax. Such an option will take the form of a single option relating to the land specified. If such a single option covers several properties, it may only be revoked during the cooling-off period or after 20 years have elapsed, if all the properties it covers meet the appropriate conditions.

14.4 Are any properties excluded from the effects of a REE?

A REE will have no effect in relation to property in which you acquire a relevant interest after making it, in the following situations:

- if you have already opted to tax a property (after making the REE) with effect from a time before you acquired a relevant interest in it.
- if you had already opted to tax a property before making the REE and continue to hold that interest.
- if you held a relevant interest in a property at the time you made a REE and still hold that interest when you later acquire a further (different) interest in the property.
- if you already hold a relevant interest in a property which is not otherwise subject to an option to tax and have made exempt supplies within the last 10 years.

14.5 What happens to a property I have previously opted but no longer have an interest in at the time of making a REE?

When you make a REE, any existing option to tax you have made in relation to property in which you do not hold a relevant interest is revoked. If an existing option covers more than one property, it only continues to have effect in relation to any properties in which you hold a relevant interest at the time of making the REE and the remainder of that original option is revoked.

For example, a situation might arise where you have acquired, or are in the process of acquiring, some or all of the land within a given area with a view to re-development. Before making a REE, you might have had an option to tax covering the whole area. If you make a REE, your option is revoked on any property within that area in which you do not hold a relevant interest at that time.

Although you cannot retain an option on property in which you have no relevant interest at the time you make the REE, you may make a new option in respect of that property and notify it so that it has effect immediately after the REE has been made.

14.6 Single options held at the time the REE is made which include more than one parcel of land

Where, before you make a REE, you have an option to tax in relation to land or buildings which comprise separate parcels of land (or which could be divided into separate parcels), you may treat that option as if it were separate options to tax each of those parcels. This choice is only available in relation to land or buildings in which you have a relevant interest at the time you make the REE. Each parcel of land that is to be treated as being separately opted must meet the conditions set out in **Box J** below.

Box J

The boxed text below has the force of the law

Conversion of an option to tax land exercised before a real estate election into separate options to tax land in which a relevant interest is held at the time when the real estate election is made (for the purpose of paragraph 22(6) of Schedule 10 to the Value Added Tax Act 1994.

A person making a real estate election may treat an option to tax made before the real estate election is made as though there were separate options to tax of individual parcels of that land. Each parcel of land that is to be treated as being separately opted must:

1. be identified by at least one of the following—its postal address, land registry title number, map or plan or other description; and
2. meet the conditions relating to the scope of an option contained in paragraph 18 of Schedule 10 to the VAT Act 1994.

14.7 Summary of the effect of a REE on new and existing options

The following treatment will apply to the new and existing options:

(a) Any option to tax taken out on an individual property where a relevant interest in that property is held at the time of making the REE will be unaffected by the making of the REE.

(b) Any option to tax taken out on an individual property where a relevant interest in that property is not held at the time of making the REE is immediately revoked.

(c) Any property on which there is no option to tax and exempt supplies have previously been made, will be unaffected by the making of a REE. An option to tax will be subject to permission (see section 5 above).

(d) Any option to tax made on a larger parcel of land (incl. buildings) will be revoked to the extent that a relevant interest is not held (if the relevant interest is held in all of the land covered by the option, clearly there will be no revocation). If you are in this position, following revocation you have two choices:

(e) you may continue with the remainder of the existing option as in (a) above; or,

(f) you may take the remainder of the land to which the option still applies and convert that into smaller parcels of land, each subject to its own option to tax. The original option now ceases to exist as it has been converted to new options and/or revoked (see conditions in **Box J**).

If a person making a REE decides to adopt (d) (ii) above then the following conditions apply to the newly created options:

(a) For the purposes of the 20 year revocation rule in section 8.3, these new options are treated as having effect from the time at which the original option had effect.

(b) The six month revocation "cooling-off period" in section 8.1 does not apply to the new options.

14.8 How do I notify a real estate election?

If you make a REE, you must notify it to HMRC within 30 days of having made it, or such longer period as they may allow.

The following statement has the force of the law.

Notification of a real estate election (*for the purpose of paragraphs 21 and 22 of Schedule 10 to the Value Added Tax Act 1994*) must be made on form **VAT 1614E** and must contain the information requested on that form.

You can download form **VAT 1614E** from **www.hmrc.gov.uk** or obtain it from our advice service on **0845 010 9000**.

If you hold relevant interests in any properties other than in dwellings or buildings designed or adapted for use as a dwelling, you must, in addition to notifying the REE, provide a list of all properties in which you hold a relevant interest at the time you notify the REE. You must send this list to HMRC within the time specified for notifying the REE; otherwise the REE will not be effective. This list must contain the information specified in **Box K** below and clearly identify any parcels of land subject to separate options to tax from the time of making the REE.

Box K

The boxed text below has the force of the law.

Information to be provided with a notification of a real estate election by a person holding one or more relevant interests in land or buildings (for the purpose of paragraph 21(7) of Schedule 10 to the Value Added Tax Act 1994 ("the VAT Act 1994")).

The notification of a real estate election must contain the required information in relation to any land or buildings (other than buildings designed or adapted for use as a dwelling or a number of dwellings) in which the person making a real estate election holds a relevant interest at the time the REE is made.

➡

The required information must be provided by way of a list specifying the following in respect of each property (other than dwellings or buildings designed or adapted for use as a dwelling) in which the person holds a relevant interest:

1. a description of the land or buildings, identified by reference to postal address, land registry title number, map, plan or other description;
2. in the case of land or buildings in respect of which no option to tax made by the maker of a real estate election has effect, the date of acquisition of a relevant interest in that land or buildings;
3. in the case of land or buildings in respect of which an option to tax made by the maker of a real estate election has effect, the date when the relevant interest in the land or building was first acquired or, if later, the date when the option first had effect;
4. where an option has effect in relation to two or more separately listed parcels of land or buildings, they must be identified as being subject to the same option.

Explanatory Note 1

"Relevant interest" .has the same meaning as in paragraph 21(12) of Schedule 10 to the VAT Act 1994.

Explanatory Note 2

If the person making a real estate election has more than one relevant interest in a parcel of land or a building that were acquired at different times, only the date of acquisition of the most recently acquired relevant interest is to be provided.

Explanatory Note 3

If the person making a real estate election is required to provide the date when an option first had effect in relation to a parcel of land or a buildings and that date is unknown, that person should record that fact and enter an approximate date, using that person's best judgement, and provide a written explanation of why that date is considered reasonable.

14.9 What do I do if I have no record of the date an option to tax first had effect?

If you make a REE and do not have a record of the date when an option first had effect in relation to land or building, explanatory note 3 to **Box K** allows you to provide an approximate date, using your best judgment. You also have to provide an explanation of why you consider that date is reasonable. HMRC will normally accept lists with such dates without further enquiry, but reserve the right to review them either as part of their general assurance and tax maintenance work, or as a result of a specific event (eg notification of the revocation of an option to tax).

14.10 Incomplete or incorrect lists

If you submit an incomplete list or one which contains incorrect information, you should submit a revised and current up-dated list to your Client Relationship Manager or, if you do not have one, to the National Option to Tax Unit in Glasgow, as soon as you identify the error.

14.11 What information must I provide after a real estate election has been made?

If you have made a REE, HMRC may, at any time, require you to provide within 30 days (or such longer period as they may allow) a list of all properties and parcels of land you hold at that time, together with details of all acquisitions, disposals and conversions to dwellings made since you last provided a list. In such a case, you have to provide the information set out in **Box L** below.

Box L

The boxed text below has the force of the law.

Information to be provided by the maker of a real estate election when required to do so by the Commissioners (under paragraph 21(8) of Schedule 10 to the Value Added Tax Act 1994 ("the VAT Act 1994")).

When required to do so, the maker of a real estate election must provide to the Commissioners the following information in relation to any land or buildings (other than buildings designed or adapted for use as a dwelling) in which that person or a relevant group member:

- holds a relevant interest at the time of providing the required information; or
- has ceased to hold a relevant interest since making a real estate election or, if later, since the last occasion on which the maker of the real estate election provided such information to the Commissioners
- information set out in Part A of this box is to be provided in respect of every such property; the information set out in Part B is to be provided in respect of every such ➡

property in which a relevant interest has been acquired or disposed of by the maker of the real estate election or a relevant group member since the date of the last such list, if any.

Part A.

In respect of any land or building in which the maker of a real estate election or a relevant group member holds a relevant interest or has ceased to hold such an interest as described above, the following information must be provided by way of a list specifying:

1. the description of the land or buildings identified by reference to its postal address, land registry title number, map, plan or other description;
2. In the case of land or buildings in respect of which no option to tax made by the maker of a real estate election or relevant group member has effect, the date of acquisition of the relevant interest in the land or buildings;
3. In the case of land or buildings in respect of which an option to tax made by the maker of a real estate election or a relevant group member has effect, the date when the relevant interest in the land or building was acquired or, if later, the date when the option first had effect;
4. where an option has effect in relation to two or more separately listed parcels of land or buildings, they must be identified as being subject to the same option.

Part B.

The following information must be provided in respect of every property in which a relevant interest has been acquired or disposed of by the maker or the real estate election or a relevant group member since the date of the last such list, if any, by way of a list specifying:

1. As appropriate, the date of the maker of the real estate election or a relevant group member:
   - acquiring a relevant interest in land or buildings in which that person has no other relevant interest;
   - ceasing to hold a relevant interest in land or buildings without retaining another relevant interest in that property;
   - opting to tax land or buildings otherwise than by virtue of a real estate election;
   - converting a building or buildings into a dwelling or dwellings;
   - excluding a new building from the effect of an option; and
   - revoking an option to tax in relation to land or buildings;

identifying the land or building to which each occurrence relates.

2. The VAT-exclusive value of the supply of a relevant interest acquired or disposed of by the maker of a real estate election or relevant group member.
3. The VAT (if any) charged on the supply of a relevant interest by the maker of a real estate election or, where the supply occurred before its admission to the group, the relevant group member.

Explanatory Note 1

"***Relevant interest***" and "***relevant group member***" have the same meanings as they do in paragraph 21(12) of Schedule 10 to the VAT Act 1994.

Explanatory Note 2

Where the maker of a real estate election or relevant group member has more than one relevant interest in the same land or building that were acquired at different times, only the date of acquisition of the most recently acquired relevant interest is to be provided.

Explanatory Note 3

In the case of land or a building in which an interest has been held before the date of a real estate election, the date of the occurrence of the making of an option to tax by the person making a real estate election or a relevant group member is the date when that option first has effect.

Explanatory Note 4

The date of the occurrence of the revocation of an option is the date from which the revocation has effect.

Explanatory Note 5

The requirement to provide the information set out in Parts A and B above does not apply to the revocation of an option to tax by virtue of paragraph 23 ("the cooling off" period) or paragraph 24 (lapse of 6 years since having a relevant interest) of Schedule 10 to the VAT Act 1994.

14.12 How are REE's treated in VAT groups?

In a VAT group, any relevant interests held in property can be held by any group member and any option to tax can also be made by any group member (although the declaration of any tax liability will be made by the VAT group representative member). Any member of a VAT group can make a REE although we expect that normally this will be done by the VAT group representative member. When a REE is made, the member making the REE will need to consider all the property holdings and options to tax made by every member of the VAT Group.

14.13 What is the effect of a REE on VAT group members?

At the time of making a REE, the following treatment will apply:

(a) Any option to tax previously taken out on an individual property of any VAT group member where that property is still held will be unaffected by the making of the REE. The original opter remains the opter.

(b) Any option to tax taken out on an individual property by any VAT group member where a relevant interest in that property is not held by any member of the VAT group (including the member making the REE) will immediately be revoked (but see d) below). However, where a member of the VAT group (a "relevant associate") has ceased to be member of the VAT group without also ceasing to be a relevant associate, the option is not revoked.

(c) Any property of any VAT group member on which there is no option to tax and on which exempt supplies have previously been made, will be unaffected by the making of a REE. Any option to tax will be subject to permission (please see section 5).

(d) Any option to tax made on a larger parcel of land (inc buildings) by a VAT group member will be revoked to the extent that a relevant interest is not held by any member of that VAT group (if a relevant interest is held in all of the land covered by the option, clearly there will be no revocation). If you are in this position, you have two choices following any revocation:

(e) you may continue with the remainder of the existing option as in (a) above; or,

(f) you may take the remainder of the land to which the option still applies and convert that into smaller parcels of land, each subject to it own option to tax. These new options become options of the member making the REE, irrespective of which VAT group member made the original option. That original option now ceases to exist as it has been converted to new options and/or revoked. The original opter (if not the member making REE) now becomes a relevant associate in respect of these new options. These new parcels subject to separate options must be clearly shown on the list you send to us with the notification of your REE (see **Box K** above)

14.14 Conditions applying to options on new "parcels" of land

If a member of a VAT group makes a REE and decides to adopt the option in paragraph 14.13 (d)(ii) above, then the following conditions apply to the newly created options:

(a) For the purposes of the 20 year revocation rule, these new options are treated as having effect from the time at which the original option had effect.

(b) For the purposes of the rules governing relevant associates, these new options are treated as having effect from the time the REE is made

(c) The six month revocation "cooling-off period" described in section 8.1 does not apply to the new options.

(d) If a relevant associate subsequently leaves the VAT group with an interest in the property, the 6 year revocation rule see section 8.2 does not apply.

14.15 How can I revoke a REE?

Once you have made a REE, it cannot be revoked but HMRC have the power to withdraw a REE if you repeatedly do not comply with its terms and conditions.

If the REE is withdrawn, a further REE may be made at a subsequent time, but only following our permission. If HMRC agree to a new application for a REE, paragraph 14.6 above will not apply to the new REE.

15. ANNEX 1

All the following Forms and Certificates have the force of law and must be used where appropriate. They can be downloaded from the HMRC website, www.hmrc.gov.uk or obtained from our advice service on 0845 010 9000.

VAT 1614B – Ceasing to be a relevant associate

VAT 1614C – Revoking an option to tax within 6 months (the "cooling off" period)

VAT 1614D – Certificate to disapply the option: Buildings to be converted into dwellings etc.

VAT 1614E – Notification of a real estate election

VAT 1614F – Notification of the exclusion of a new building from the effect of an option to tax

VAT 1614G – Certificate to disapply the option: Land sold to Housing associations

VAT 1614H – Application for permission to opt

VAT 1614J – Revoking an option after 20 years.

Commentary—*De Voil Indirect Tax Service* **V4.116.**

ADMINISTRATIVE AGREEMENTS WITH TRADE BODIES

Notice 700/57
Administrative agreements entered into with trade bodies

2004 with Update 1

Note—HM Customs & Excise have made available details of a number of agreements made with trade bodies. These agreements permit members of the trade bodies to use procedures to meet their obligations under VAT law which take into account their individual circumstances.

The agreements made available, and covered by Notice 700/57, are listed in the table below.

Trade body	*Agreement*	*Remarks*
London Bullion Market Association	Supplies of bullion	
The Brewers' Society	Deduction of input tax incurred in respect of brewers' tenanted estate	
Association of British Factors and Discounters	Partial exemption and factors	
Finance Houses Association Ltd	Finance houses and partial exemption	
Association of British Insurers	Recovery of input tax incurred in UK in connection with supplies by branches outside the European Community	
Association of Investment Trust Companies	Partial exemption	
The British Printing Industries Federation	Apportionment of subsidy publishing supplies	
Marine, aviation and transport insurance underwriters	Claims related to input tax and associated imported services	
Association of British Insurers, Lloyd's of London, the Institute of London Underwriters, the British Insurance and Investment Association	Coding supplies of marine, aviation and transport (MAT) insurance services	
National Caravan Council Limited, British Holiday and Home Park Association Limited	Method of valuing removable contents sold with zero-rated caravans	
Association of Unit Trust and Investment Managers	VAT liability of charges made in connection with Personal Equity Plans (PEPs)	
British Bankers' Association	VAT liability of electronic banking/cash management services	
British Vehicle Rental and Leasing Association	Car leasing and repairs and maintenance services	Effective from 1 August 1995
Society of Motor Manufacturers and Traders	Calculating output tax on the self-supply of a motor vehicle	Effective from 1 August 1992
Gaming Board for Great Britain; British Casino Association	Competitions in card rooms	January 1998
British Phonographic Society	VAT liability of promotional samples given free of charge	March 1998
Thoroughbred Breeders Association	Arrangements under which racehorse owners may register for VAT and the procedures that must be followed	March 1993
British Horseracing Board	Revised arrangements under which racehorse owners may register for VAT and the procedures that must be followed	January 1998

Trade body	*Agreement*	*Remarks*
British Horseracing Board; Thoroughbred Breeders Association	Racehorses applied permanently to personal or other non-business use	
British Horseracing Board; Thoroughbred Breeders Association	Keeping of stallions at stud	
British Horseracing Board; Thoroughbred Breeders Association	Racehorses and time limits for exportation	
Meat and Livestock Commission	VAT treatment of levies collected (invoiced) from 1 October 1990 by the Commission from operators of slaughterhouses and exporters of live animals	
Society of Motor Manufacturers and Traders Ltd	How the one tonne payload test will be applied in practice to double cab pick-ups	
Society of Motor Manufacturers and Traders Ltd	Simplified method by which motor manufacturers, importers and wholesale distributors may calculate the VAT due on the private use of stock in trade cars provided to directors and employees free of charge	
Retail Motor Industry Federation	Simplified method by which retail motor dealers may calculate the VAT due on the private use of demonstrator cars provided to directors and employees free of charge	
British Vehicle Rental and Leasing Association	Simplified method which daily rental companies may use to calculate the VAT due on the incidental private use of their hire fleets	

VALUE ADDED TAX
PRESS RELEASES ETC

CONTENTS

LIST OF PRESS RELEASES, ETC

12 March 1980. Hansard	Costs in High Court and above.
10 December 1982. PN 790	Sales of goodwill.
27 April 1984. PN 909	Part 1 motorcycle test.
24 July 1986. Hansard	Costs in tribunal appeals.
19 November 1987. PN 82/87	Settlement of disputes.
26 April 1989. Hansard	CEMA 1979 s 152.
9 August 1989. PN 58/89	Treatment of certain agricultural grant schemes.
29 July 1992. BB 12/92	VAT on expenses of sale of dwellings bequeathed to charities.
9 September 1992. The Law Society	Settlement of disputes.
14 October 1992. The Law Society	Mesne profits.
28 October 1992. The Law Society	Payment of third party costs.
22 April 1993. BB 12/93	Payments to a retail consortium.
10 September 1993. PN 59/93	VAT recovery by holding companies.
12 September 1994. BB 17/94	VAT on private use of business services.
12 September 1994. BB 17/94	VAT on milk quotas.
8 December 1994. BB 24/94	Sale of property under a power of sale—recovery of VAT on costs incurred by mortgage lenders.
28 March 1995. BB 6/95	VAT on viability studies.
18 May 1995. BB 9/95	Services supplied between local authorities.
31 July 1995. BB 15/95	VAT on business cars.
24 June 1996.	Statement of practice on the new VATA 1994 Sch 9A.
1 July 1996. BB 13/96	VAT exemption for supplies of Government-funded vocational training.
27 August 1996. BB 18/96	Recovery of tax incurred on repairs, maintenance, renovation etc to farmhouses.
17 October 1996. BB 21/96	MOT test charges.
27 March 1997. BB 9/97	Extension of "capping" to claims for refunds other than for amounts overpaid as VAT.
5 June 1997. BB 12/97	Taxable acquisition of yachts in the United Kingdom.
21 July 1997. BB 16/97	VAT changes for bonuses given by car manufactures to dealers or fleet buyers.
24 September 1997. BB 20/97	Vacuum cleaners, air purification and similar anti-allergen products.
10 November 1997. BB 25/97	Herbal product to be standard-rated.
19 December 1997. BB 30/97	Statement of Practice on a budget change to the capital goods scheme.
22 December 1997. BB 31/97	Refusing applications for group treatment to protect the revenue.
7 January 1998. BB 1/98	VAT changes to fleet leasing bonuses.
7 January 1998. BB 1/98	Installation or assembly of imported goods.
21 May 1998. BB 12/98	VAT place of supply rules change for veterinary services.
21 May 1998. BB 12/98	Overseas businesses established in the UK through agencies.
11 September 1998. BB 18/98	Review of the liability of sweetened dried fruit.
15 September 1998. BB 19/98	Local authorities: works in default.
18 December 1998. BB 26/98	VAT groups and transfers of going concerns (TOGCs).
13 January 1999. BB 1/99	The single currency (the euro).
24 February 1999. BB 5/99	Ship design services.
31 March 1999. BB 8/99	The three year cap and partial exemption.
21 April 1999 BB 9/99	Contracting out of vehicle removal/recovery by police authorities: treatment of statutory fees retained by contractors.
17 November 1999. BB 23/99	VAT appeals.
22 December 1999. BB 28/99	Treatment of EC grant aid for the processing of dried fodder.

22 February 2000. BB 3/00	Imported works of art, antiques and collectors' items.
17 March 2000. BB 4/00	VAT and cemeteries.
11 April 2000. BB 6/00	Debt enforcement services provided by Under Sheriffs and Sheriffs' Officers.
18 May 2000. BB 7/00	Approved alterations to protected buildings. Supplies of soft landscaping. VAT treatment of vehicle clamping and tow-away fees.
28 September. 2000 BB 13/00	Bloodstock—sale of additional nominations by stallion syndicates.
20 February 2001. BB 3/01	Court of Appeal decision rules pension review services are VAT exempt.
2 July 2001. BB 8/01	Opting to tax buildings to be converted to dwellings.
11 September 2001. BB 12/01	Partial exemption—supplies to be excluded from the standard method calculation.
29 November 2001. BB 18/01	Reduced rate for supplies of small (de minimis) quantities of fuel oil, gas oil or kerosene.
6 December 2001. BB 19/01	Bad debt relief on goods supplied by hire purchase or conditional sale.
12 February 2002. BB 3/02	Single and multiple supplies—sale of spectacles and contact lenses.
9 May 2002. BB 13/02	Bad debt relief and the treatment of proceeds from the sale of repossessed cars.
5 August 2002. BB 22/02	Three year cap—Marks and Spencer—ECJ judgment, Case C-62/00; [2002] STC 1036.
20 August 2002. BB 23/02	Attribution of input tax incurred on professional services when a company acquires shares in another company in exchange for shares in itself.
8 October 2002. BB 27/02	Extension of transitional period for capping limits—*Marks & Spencer Plc v C&E Comrs*, CJEC Case C-62/00 [2002] STC 1036—Addendum to Business Brief 22/2002—*Grundig Italiana SpA v Ministero delle Finanze*, CJEC Case 255/00.
19 November 2002. BB 30/02	Policy statement on the treatment of applications to leave a VAT group. VAT groups—protection of the revenue.
1 July 2003. BB 7/03	Exemption of call centre services in the insurance sector.
25 July 2003. BB 11/03	Building and construction: grants of a major interest by members of VAT groups. Treatment of communal areas in blocks of flats.
30 September 2003. BB 18/03	VAT on supplies made to operators of vending, amusement and similar machines following the judgment in the case of *Sinclair Collis*. Exemption of intermediary services provided in the finance sector. The VAT position of two new PFI arrangements.
13 November 2003. BB 21/03	Treatment of cage accessories for use in specialised laboratory caging.
10 December 2003. BB 27/03	Partial exemption—special method override Notice.
9 June 2004. BB 16/04	Definition of a motorcar.
1 July 2004. BB 17/04	Excise/VAT – Intra-EC ships, aircraft and trains: retail sale of goods for on board consumption.
2 August 2004. BB 20/04	Gas and electricity suppliers: new extra-statutory concession for bad debts.

10 August 2004. BB 21/04	VAT position of share issues and partnership contributions following the European Court of Justice decision in Kaphag Renditefonds.
14 September 2004. BB 25/04	Customs' policy on assessments following *C&E v Laura Ashley* [2004] STC 635 (High Court) and *DFS Furniture Company v C&E* [2004] STC 559 (Court of Appeal).
26 October 2004. BB 25/04	Place of supply of trading allowances in greenhouse gas emissions.
	Correcting liability errors.
19 November 2004. BB 30/04	VAT and partnership 'shares'.
15 December 2004. BB 34/04	Partial exemption: Floor-area based special methods in the retail sector.
10 February 2005. BB 2/05	Supplies of nursery and crèche facilities by a charity.
4 April 2005. BB 9/05	Hot take-away food.
18 May 2005. BB 11/05	Judgment of the European Court of Justice (ECJ) in the case of Arthur Andersen & co Accountants (C-472/03).
	Zero rating for protected buildings—definition of garage.
15 June 2005. BB 12/05	Aligning VAT accounting periods.
	Clarification of the VAT position of share issues following the European Court of Justice decision in Kretztechnik.
	Landlord inducements to tenants entering leases.
5 July 2005. BB 13/05	Belated notification of an option to tax land and buildings—Clarification of HM Revenue & Customs' policy.
28 July 2005. BB 14/05	Partial exemption—Tribunal decision in *National Provident Institution* (*NPI*).
16 September 2005. BB 18/05	New civil investigation of fraud procedures.
10 October 2005. BB 19/05	High Court decision: Church of England Children's Society.
23 November 2005. BB 21/05	Clarification of the treatment of foreign exchange transactions (forex).
	Further clarification of the VAT position of share issues following the European Court of Justice's decision in *Kretztechnik*.
1 December 2005. BB 22/05	Judgment of the court of appeal in the case of *Ivor Jacobs* ([2005] EWCA Civ 930).
	Further clarification on the VAT position of share issues made to customers outside the EU.
5 December 2005. BB 23/05	VAT exemption for insurance-related services.
18 January 2006. BB 1/06	Company formation services with ancillary printed matter—clarification of treatment post CPP.
	Hotel conference/function facilities: revised interpretation of law on VAT treatment.
9 March 2006. BB 3/06	Beauty procedures performed using class 3B or 4 lasers and/or intense pulse light (IPL) machines—clarification of liability.
24 March 2006. BB 4/06	Off-street car parking provided by local authorities.
12 April 2006. BB 5/06	Interim position following the Court of Session's decision in Edinburgh's Telford College.
27 June 2006. BB 7/06	Exemption for the management of authorised collective investment schemes.
7 July 2006. BB 8/06	Clarification of the treatment of travel agent funded discounts.
17 July 2006. BB 9/06	Clarification of HMRC's policy following the Court of Appeal's decision in *Newnham College*.
7 August 2006. BB 11/06	Partial exemption—higher education sector variable tuition fees

21 August 2006. BB 12/06	Position following the Court of Appeal judgment in *Compass Contract Services Limited*.
24 August 2006. BB 13/06	3-Year Cap on making claims—Court of Appeal Judgment in *Michael Fleming t/a Bodycraft*.
	3-Year Cap on making claims—Court of Appeal Judgment in *Condé Nast Publications Ltd*.
27 September 2006. BB 15/06	Gaming machines—accounting for VAT.
	The reduced value rule for long-stay guests in hotels—revised interpretation of the law on VAT treatment.
13 October 2006. BB 16/06	Changes to VAT law in light of the Gambling Act.
	Publication of tax avoidance scheme disclosure statistics.
	Liability of private tuition.
	Liability of condoms supplied to charities providing care or medical treatment.
19 October 2006. BB 17/06	Partial exemption: bookmakers—recovery of VAT on specialist television services and equipment.
	Disposable barbecues.
27 October 2006. HMRC	Motor trade issues: car derived vans and combi vans.
30 October 2006. BB 18/06	Liability of agents' credit and debit card handling services.
9 November 2006. BB 20/06	Gaming machines—impact of the Linneweber decision.
22 December 2006. BB 23/06	First grant of a major interest in residential property: attribution of input tax and the capital goods scheme.
	Final Business Brief.
26 January 2007. HMRC Brief 05/07	Further clarification of the treatment of foreign exchange transactions (forex) and transactions in other financial instruments.
30 January 2007. HMRC Brief 06/07	Changes to the exemption for medical services from 1 May 2007.
1 February 2007. HMRC Brief 07/07	Cash bingo: accounting for VAT on participation and session fees.
6 February 2007. HMRC Brief 08/07	Manufacturers' "cash back" payments.
6 February 2007. HMRC Brief 10/07	Liability of private tuition.
6 February 2007. HMRC Brief 11/07	VAT schemes for luxury yachts.
9 February 2007. HMRC Brief 12/07	Changes to the cash accounting scheme.
12 February 2007. HMRC Brief 13/07	Fuel scale charge; new CO_2 basis.
13 February 2007. HMRC Brief 14/07	Changes to the rules on bad debt relief for goods supplied on credit terms.
14 March 2007. HMRC Brief 23/07	Partial exemption: special method approvals.
20 March 2007. HMRC Brief 24/07	Proposed reverse charge accounting for businesses trading in mobile telephones and computer chips: announcement of targeted implementation and details of how the rules will operate in practice; and exposure of draft legislation for comment.
22 March 2007. HMRC Brief 27/07	Cultural exemption – clarification of "direct or indirect financial interest" [VATA 1994 Sch 9 Group 13 Note 2(c)].
22 March 2007. HMRC Brief 28/07	VAT treatment of contracted out local authority leisure services.
30 March 2007. HMRC Brief 31/07	Partial exemption: VAT recovery on overhead costs relating to supplies of hire purchase.
10 April 2007. HMRC Brief 36/07	Input tax deduction without a valid VAT invoice: Revised Statement of Practice.
10 April 2007. Statement of Practice	VAT Strategy: Input tax deduction without a valid VAT invoice.

14 June 2007. HMRC Brief 45/07	Partial exemption – VAT deduction by theatres on production costs.
28 June 2007. HMRC Brief 48/07	Introduction of a reduced rate for the supply of smoking cessation products.
24 July 2007. HMRC Brief 51/07	Changes to the VAT Invoicing Regulations with effect from 1 October 2007.
14 August 2007. HMRC Brief 55/07	Revised treatment of VAT incurred on home computers made available by employers to their employees.
22 August 2007. HMRC Brief 58/07	Claims in respect of fund management services.
11 October 2007. HMRC Brief 61/07	Teleos and others (VAT—Intra-Community trade).
11 October 2007. HMRC Brief 62/07	Commission earned by sub-agents in the travel industry.
5 November 2007. HMRC Brief 65/07	JP Morgan Fleming Claverhouse Trust plc – fund management services.
5 November 2007. HMRC Brief 66/07	Treatment of the construction of houses or flats in the grounds of existing care homes, nursing homes or similar buildings.
21 November 2007. HMRC Brief 69/07	The decision of the tribunal in InsuranceWide.com Services Ltd.
19 December 2007. HMRC Brief 75/07	Intrastat – thresholds from 1 January 2008.
3 January 2008. HMRC Brief 1/08	Partial exemption – Cheshire Racing Tribunal Decision.
20 February 2008. HMRC Brief 7/08	Three year time limit for VAT claims.
4 March 2008. HMRC Brief 13/08	Access to Intrastat data.
4 March 2008. HMRC Brief 14/08	Animal rescue charities – VAT liability of the sale of abandoned dogs and cats.
11 March 2008. HMRC Brief 16/08	Valuation of imported goods: Customs valuation declarations and general valuation statements.
1 April 2008. HMRC Brief 19/08	New penalties for errors in returns and documents.
22 April 2008. HMRC Brief 24/08	Land and buildings – new VATA 1994 Sch 10 including changes to the option to tax.
20 May 2008. HMRC Brief 27/08	Interpretation of Article 13 of the Principal VAT Directive: "bodies governed by public law" and "special legal regime".
30 May 2008. HMRC Brief 28/08	Land & buildings – announcing a new revised Notice 742A "Opting to tax land and buildings and associated forms and certificates".
18 June 2008. HMRC Brief 29/08	Learn how your clients can avoid penalties
19 June 2008. HMRC Brief 30/08	Partial exemption: launch of consultation.
27 June 2008. HMRC Brief 31/08	Set off where right to claim overdeclared tax is transferred
18 July 2008. HMRC Guidance Notes	HMRC set-off across taxes following Finance Bill 2008
24 July 2008. HMRC Brief 35/08	VAT exemption for fund management services
25 July 2008. HMRC Brief 34/08	Partial exemption – retrospective claims for input tax by higher education institutions (HEIs)
1 August 2008. HMRC Brief 38/08	Default interest and net errors of less than £2000
6 August 2008. HMRC Brief 36/08	VAT treatment of charity challenge events
15 September 2008. HMRC Brief 44/08	Partial exemption—VAT adjustments when house builders let their dwellings before selling them
17 September 2008. HMRC Brief 46/08	Court of Appeal decision in the case of Loyalty Management (UK) Ltd (LMUK) – HMRC position, pending outcome of appeal to the House of Lords
1 October 2008. HMRC Brief 48/08	Exemption for fund management services
17 October 2008. HMRC Brief 52/08	VAT on fuel used for propelling private pleasure craft and private pleasure flying

22 October 2008. HMRC Brief 53/08	EC sales lists
28 October 2008. HMRC Brief 54/08	New zero-rated dwellings – whether arrangements are abusive
8 December 2008. HMRC Brief 57/08	Excess charges in non-local authority car parks
17 December 2008. HMRC Brief 60/08	Loyalty Management (UK) Ltd
23 December 2008. HMRC Brief 61/08	Intrastat—changes from 1 January 2009
7 January 2009. HMRC Brief 63/08	The decisions of the VAT Tribunal in the cases of the Rank Group plc, in respect of the supply of Mechanised Cash Bingo (MCB) and gaming machine takings
26 January 2009. HMRC Brief 2/09	VAT package and anti-fraud measures implementation update
19 February 2009. HMRC Brief 5/09	Marks & Spencer Plc Judgment: VAT claims and unjust enrichment
23 February 2009. HMRC Brief 6/09	Claims for retrospective application of Extra-Statutory Concession (ESC) 3.35
16 March 2009. HMRC Brief 10/09	Tribunal reform
19 March 2009. HMRC Brief 8/09	VAT staff hire concession
19 March 2009. HMRC Brief 13/09	Leisure Trusts providing all-inclusive membership schemes
20 March 2009. HMRC Brief 14/09	VAT repayment claims and statutory interest: treatment for the purposes of direct tax
27 March 2009. HMRC Brief 15/09	Extra Statutory Concession (ESC) 3.5—Misdirection
31 March 2009. HMRC Brief 18/09	Implications to the Bad Debt Relief conditions as a result of the Tribunal decision in Times Right Marketing Ltd
1 April 2009. HMRC Brief 19/09	Partial exemption – changes to the standard method
8 April 2009. HMRC Brief 27/09	Changes to the Tour Operators' Margin Scheme
20 April 2009. HMRC Brief 28/09	Reverse charge accounting for businesses trading in mobile telephones and computer chips: renewal of EU derogation
14 May 2009. HMRC Brief 31/09	Tax implications of the vehicle scrappage scheme
1 June 2009. HMRC Brief 32/09	Decision of the Court of Appeal in respect of Procter & Gamble UK
9 June 2009. HMRC Brief 33/09	HMRC's policy following the judgment in Newnham College
18 June 2009. HMRC Brief 34/09	Reverse charge accounting for businesses trading in mobile telephones and computer chips: renewal of EU derogation
8 July 2009. HMRC Brief 36/09	VAT treatment of deposits relating to sales of land on which dwellings are to be constructed
9 July 2009. HMRC Brief 38/09	"Dutch barges" and similar vessels designed for and used as permanent residential accommodation by owners
14 July 2009. HMRC Brief 40/09	Decision of the High Court in respect of Rank (mechanised cash bingo and gaming machines)
20 July 2009. HMRC Brief 41/09	Three-year cap for VAT claims – Court of Session decision in Scottish Equitable
23 July 2009. HMRC Brief 43/09	Psychologists' services

PRESS RELEASES, ETC

12 March 1980. Hansard

Costs in High Court and above

Mr Eggar asked the Chancellor of the Exchequer if he will indicate the policy of Her Majesty's Customs & Excise and the Inland Revenue with regard to costs in the High Court and superior courts of appeal.

Mr Peter Rees gave the following answer: The general rule in the appeal courts is that the losing party risks having to pay the other side's costs, and I do not think it would be right to treat tax cases differently as a matter of course. However, both revenue departments exercise their discretion on matters of costs, and are willing in appropriate circumstances, and in particular where it is they who are appealing against an adverse decision, to consider waiving their claims to costs or making other arrangements. Influential factors include the risk of financial hardship to the other party and whether the case is one of significant interest to taxpayers as a whole, turning on a point of law in need of clarification. If the revenue departments are to come to an arrangement of this nature, they would expect to do so in advance of the hearing and following an approach by the taxpayer involved.

HC Written Answer Vol 980 col 572.

Commentary—*De Voil Indirect Tax Service* **V5.476.**

10 December 1982. Press Notice 790

Sales of goodwill

From 1 January 1983 Customs & Excise will treat all sales of the goodwill of a business as taxable supplies except where they are specifically relieved by law.

Unidentifiable goodwill, valued as the residual difference between the business as a whole and the sum of its identifiable assets, is currently treated as outside the scope of VAT.

Normally goodwill is sold as part of the assets of a business transferred as a going concern. Such sales will be relieved from tax if the transfer meets the provisions of the [VAT (Special Provisions) Order 1995 SI 1995/1268 art 5].

NOTE

Sales of goodwill which can be specifically identified as an asset of the business have always been treated as taxable supplies of services (eg, use of a trade mark or trading name, lists of customers etc).

Commentary—*De Voil Indirect Tax Service* **V7.130.**
Cross-references—VATA 1994 s 5.

27 April 1984. Press Notice 909

Part 1 motorcycle test

Customs and Excise announce that with effect from 11 June 1984 fees charged by the Department of Transport (DTp) and training bodies appointed by the DTp for Part 1 of the motorcycle driving test will be liable to VAT at the standard rate.

The driving test for motor cyclists is a two part test administered by the DTp. Part 1 of the test may be conducted by appointed training bodies as well as DTp. Part 2 may only be conducted by the DTp. The appointed training bodies are free to set and retain their fees for the Part 1 test. For VAT purposes these bodies are making a taxable supply to the motor cyclist in the course of their business. It has always been an important principle of VAT that the tax should, as far as possible, apply equally in the public and private sectors and the DTp will therefore be required to account for VAT on the fees it charges for Part 1 tests.

The DTp will continue to supply Part 2 of the motorcycle test and other motor vehicle driving tests as part of its statutory obligation and the fees involved will remain outside the scope of the tax.

Training courses supplied by appointed bodies have always been taxable at the standard rate and this is unchanged by the new arrangements.

Commentary—*De Voil Indirect Tax Service* **V2.242.**

24 July 1986. Hansard

Costs in tribunal appeals

[Note: As a general rule, Customs and Excise do not seek costs against unsuccessful appellants. They do, however, ask for costs in certain narrowly defined cases so as to provide protection for public funds and the general body of taxpayers. They will therefore seek to continue to ask for costs at those exceptional tribunal hearings of substantial and complex cases where large sums are involved and which are comparable with High Court Cases, unless the appeal involves an important general point of law, requiring clarification. They will also continue to consider seeking costs where the appellant has misused the tribunal procedure—for example in frivolous or vexatious cases, or where the appellant has failed to appear or to be represented at a mutually arranged hearing without sufficient explanation, or where the appellant has first produced at a hearing relevant evidence which ought properly to have been disclosed at an earlier stage and which could have saved public funds had it been produced timeously.]

The new penalty provisions and rights of appeal to the Value Added Tax Tribunals has made no change to this policy. Customs & Excise, with the agreement of the Council on Tribunals, consider that appeals against penalties imposed under [VATA 1994 s 60] on the grounds that a person has evaded VAT and his conduct has involved dishonesty, fall to be considered as being comparable with High Court cases. Where such appeals are unsuccessful, Customs & Excise will normally seek an award of costs.

In all cases the question whether or not costs should be awarded will, of course, remain entirely within the discretion of the Tribunal concerned and the amount of any such award will be fixed either by that Tribunal, or by the High Court as provided by Tribunal procedure rules.

Customs & Excise, in consultation with the Council on Tribunals, will continue to keep their policy under careful scrutiny.

HC Written Answer Vol 102 col 459–460.

Commentary—*De Voil Indirect Tax Service* **V5.483**.
Cross-references—VAT Tribunal Rules, SI 1986/590 reg 29.

19 November 1987. Press Notice 82/87

Settlement of disputes

Customs & Excise have reviewed their policy on the VAT treatment of payments made under out-of-court settlements of disputes, after proceedings have been commenced by service of originating process (or appointment of an arbitrator).

They now take the view that, where such payments are in essence compensatory and do not relate directly to supplies of goods or services, they are outside the scope of VAT. This will be so even if the settlement is expressed in terms that the payment is consideration for the plaintiff's agreement to abandon his rights to bring legal proceedings. But payments will remain taxable if, and to the extent, that they are the consideration for specific taxable supplies by the plaintiff, eg where the dispute concerns payment for an earlier supply, or where the plaintiff grants future rights to exploit copyright material under the settlement.

These changes of policy may be applied from 19 November 1987.

NOTE

Customs & Excise had previously taken the view that all payments under out-of-court settlements were generally taxable. The revised VAT liability brings the VAT treatment of out-of-court settlements into line with the VAT treatment of payments under court orders.

Commentary—*De Voil Indirect Tax Service* **V3.102**.
Cross references—VATA 1994 s 5.

26 April 1989. Hansard

CEMA 1979 s 152

Mr Quentin Davies asked the Chancellor of the Exchequer if he will make a statement on the circumstances in which the Commissioners of Customs and Excise will disclose particulars of cases where proceedings for offences are compounded under CEMA 1979 s 152.

Mr Lilley: CEMA 1979 s 152 is the most recent re-enactment of the Commissioners' long-standing power to compound proceedings, that is to offer an alleged offender the option of paying a penalty out of court rather than be prosecuted. This power is used to resolve the majority of customs or excise offences, and enables them to be dealt with efficiently and effectively without burdening the courts or tying up Customs and Excise staff in lengthy court hearings. Hitherto, details of compounded settlements have not usually been made public.

The Commissioners, having reviewed their policy on disclosure of compounded settlements, have decided that in respect of settlements made on or after 1 June 1989, details will be disclosed in the following circumstances—

It will be the Commissioners' invariable practice to disclose details

(a) to other Government Departments whose statutory responsibilities are directly affected; and
(b) to the courts for sentencing purposes after conviction, in cases where there has been an earlier compounded settlement for a similar matter within the time limits specified for offences by the Rehabilitation of Offenders Act.

The Commissioners will also disclose compounded settlements under two other circumstances

(c) to employers when it is apparent that—
  (i) the nature of the employment has facilitated the offence; or
  (ii) where drugs offences or indications of serious alcohol abuse are involved, the nature of the employment or duties requires a high degree of unimpaired judgment or faculties,

(d) in response to enquiries from Parliament or the media about cases which have excited public attention, if disclosure is considered to be in the public interest.

In all cases, persons considering an offer to compound for an alleged offence will be warned when the offer is made that details of the settlement may be disclosed in the circumstances set out at (a) or (d) above.

HC Written Answer Vol 151, cols 562, 563.

Commentary—*De Voil Indirect Tax Service* **V5.304, V5.305**.

9 August 1989. Press Notice 58/89

Treatment of certain agricultural grant schemes

Customs & Excise have been considering whether the voluntary surrender of right by landowners and farmers in return for the payment of certain grants should be liable to VAT at the standard rate, e g the surrender by a farmer of his milk quota in return for the payment of a grant by the Ministry of Agriculture, Fisheries and Food.

Customs have consulted other member states and the EC Commission. These discussions have not yet been finally concluded, and Treasury Ministers have therefore decided that VAT should not be applied in the meantime, and in any case not before 1 April 1991.

Customs' discussions have centred on grant payments to "outgoers" under the milk quota arrangements and the set-aside schemes but the same issues arise on other grant schemes.

The decision to suspend the application of VAT applies to these grant schemes and similar schemes, in particular those listed below:

MINISTRY OF AGRICULTURE, FISHERIES AND FOOD

Farm Woodland Schemes
Set Aside Scheme
Agriculture Act 1986 Section 18 (Environmentally Sensitive Areas)
Outgoers under the Milk (Cessation of Production) Act 1985

DEPARTMENT OF THE ENVIRONMENT

Nature Conservancy Council management agreements
Countryside Premium Scheme for Set Aside Land
Countryside Commission Community Forests Scheme

FORESTRY COMMISSION

Woodland Grant Scheme
Farm Woodland Scheme

Cross references—VATA 1994 s 5.

29 July 1992. Business Brief 12/92

VAT on expenses of sale of dwellings bequeathed to charities

Customs and Excise have recently received a number of queries on the sale of bequeathed dwellings or land, and the circumstances under which charities may be treated as making zero-rates supplies of bequeathed property in cases where the charities have never acquired legal title (VATA 1983 Sch 5 Group 16 item 1 as amended [now VATA 1994 Sch 8 Group 15]).

Following legal advice we have decided that buildings and land are not covered at all by the provisions of Group 16 item 1 [now Group 15], because they are not "goods which have been donated for sale".

Moreover in most cases the dwelling or land concerned would not have been a business asset of either the deceased person or the charity. Any supply of the property flowing from the bequest would normally be outside the scope of VAT, so a charity would not be able to claim input VAT on the expenses of the sale.

Any previous rulings given by the Department on bequeathed buildings and land, and Group 16 item 1 [now Group 15], are now cancelled, except where any charity can show it has relied on such a ruling to zero-rate a supply taking place before 1 August 1992.

Commentary—*De Voil Indirect Tax Service* **V4.266.**

9 September 1992. The Law Society

Settlement of disputes

A meeting with HM Customs & Excise was held on 23 October 1991 ...

The Law Society said that the tribunal decision in Cooper Chasney Ltd (No 4898) had generated comment and correspondence within the VAT sub-committee of the Law Society's revenue law committee on the basis that it might be understood as throwing doubt on the guidance contained in Customs' press notice of 19 November 1987.

An approach was therefore made to Customs, which had replied that it did not consider the decision to be in conflict with the press notice. The Law Society, however, felt there were several aspects of the settlement of disputes where VAT treatment is not straightforward and that further clarification was necessary. It was important that solicitors should be applying the correct principles and assurance from Customs with a view to giving agreed guidance to the profession would be welcome.

Customs & Excise's original approach had been that giving up a right to sue somebody in return for payment was a taxable supply and it satisfied [VATA 1994 s 5(2)(b)], which provides that anything which is not a supply of goods but is done for a consideration (including, if so done, the granting, assignment or surrender of any right) is a supply of services (if done in the course of furtherance of a business).

There had never been any question that if a payment by way of compensation was made pursuant to a court order, this was outside the scope. However, given that basic principle, and the uncertainty surrounding out-of-court settlements prior to the issue of the press notice, it had seemed that Customs was forcing taxpayers to go all the way through the courts and not to enter any settlement by way of compromise, in order to guarantee that any payment would not attract VAT. Customs had reviewed its policy in the light of the decision in the case of Whites Metal Company (No 2400) where the VAT tribunal had held that services were not supplied by a plaintiff to a defendant in reaching a settlement of an action in tort.

9 SEPTEMBER 1992. PRESS NOTICE 82/87

The press notice had been issued with the object of restricting its application to genuine disputes only. If a settlement agreement was worded in terms that the plaintiff was giving up rights to sue the defendant in exchange for a sum of money, this was not a supply. If the agreement not to sue and to settle out of court confirmed a previously agreed price, or confirmed a reduction to a previously agreed price, VAT would be adjusted, using the credit note mechanism, by reference to the price finally agreed. The situation when payment was made subject to a court order remained unchanged.

Since the press notice had been issued, very few cases had been brought to VAT headquarters. Cooper Chasney and Edenroc were notable exceptions. Customs believed that both these decisions were in accordance with the press notice. Local offices had been dealing with queries. However, it was the Law Society's view that the lack of cases which had been brought could indicate unawareness of the potential traps where elements of a settlement could attract a VAT liability.

Customs had considered when drafting the press notice, the particular example of royalties when there had been an inadvertent breach of copyright. If payment was partly to compensate for a past breach, and partly for permission to use in the future the material subject to copyright, there should be a reasonable apportionment. A distinction needed to be drawn. Payment by way of compensation in respect of a past transgression was outside the scope but payment in consideration of allowing the future use of the copyright material was in respect of a taxable supply.

In the Law Society's view, the facts of Cooper Chasney were perhaps more straightforward than difficulties which could be experienced in practice. In that case, the plaintiff had expressly allowed the defendant to use the name "Infolink" in the future (a name which the plaintiff had previously used in his business), but the terms of the settlement were that, in return for payment to the plaintiff by the defendant of an agreed sum, the plaintiff reverted to his own name (Cooper Chasney Ltd) and agreed to discontinue proceeding against the defendant. It was clear that the elements of the agreement went beyond breaches which were alleged to have occurred in the past and giving up a right to sue.

Customs said that in deciding what the payment in the settlement of a dispute was for, it looks carefully at the words used by the parties (as in Cooper Chasney, where an agreement had been entered into which had been set out in the decision) and taxes the parties accordingly.

The Law Society asked if Customs was happy that press notice 82/87 was correct and it confirmed it was satisfied with the general approach and did not think it should be extended, for example, on the basis of the decisions in *Neville Russell v C & E Comrs* [1987] VATTR 194 and *Gleneagles Hotel plc v C & E Comrs* [1986] VATTR 196, to indicate that anything done in exchange for consideration is a supply.

Customs did not consider that a person had an intrinsic right to sue so that by not suing, a person was not necessarily giving up any right. Customs thought the position could be analysed by saying that a person was really exercising an option not to enforce an alleged wrong, rather than giving up any right. The acceptance of an offer not to sue is taken because the reason for wanting to sue in the first place is settled on receipt of payment.

Customs agreed that if VAT was never mentioned in negotiating a settlement, the plaintiff could suddenly find that the amount of cash he or she received in settlement was reduced by VAT. There was a suggestion that this could be avoided by adding to the agreement for settlements the words "VAT will be added [to the agreed sum] if applicable". However, it would obviously be preferable to issue clear guidance to avoid the necessity of requiring such terms automatically to be added to settlement wordings.

The Law Society asked if Customs agreed that liquidated damages paid under contracts were also outside the scope and Customs confirmed this. Such cases would not involve litigation but were within the spirit of the press notice. If a contract contained provisions for damages in respect of a breach, this would generally be within the press notice, but if a plaintiff was giving up a separate right, for example, this right to receive notice, this could be a taxable supply.

Customs has agreed a "joint statement of practice" (JSP) with the principal leasing associations in order to avoid contractual arguments and any ambiguity over the correct VAT treatment of termination payments and rebates/refunds of rentals arising under equipment leases. The object of the JSP is to establish a common treatment which provides that:

1 all lease termination payments may be treated as being in respect of taxable supplies, ie of the right to terminate. Here the termination payment is usually calculated by reference to the amount of rental payments outstanding under the primary lease period; and

2 where, on expiry or termination of an equipment lease, the lessee receives from the lessor a rebate or refund of rentals, no adjustment for VAT previously charged need be made. However, credit notes should be endorsed "this is not a credit note for VAT purposes".

Importantly, the JSP does not override any contractual arrangements in force. If the lessors wish to revert to the terms of their original agreements, they may do so. For example, lease termination payments may arise on default by a lessee which are by way of liquidated damages and therefore outside the scope of VAT.

Taxpayers who were not within the major leasing associations could rely on this agreement but they would not necessarily be aware of it. It was confirmed that local VAT offices had knowledge of it.

The Law Society's letter to the solicitor's office at Customs of 18 June had listed examples of where it had sought Customs' guidance on specific issues. These were raised for discussion and the following answers given:

1 Customs confirmed that press notice 82/87 covered only payments made after proceedings had commenced. If it was clear that payments had been made before proceedings had been commenced, but such payments would not be within s 3(2)(b), Customs would extend outside the scope treatment to such payments.

2 In the area of involuntary supplies (eg a dispute concerning right of light for which damages are awarded) Customs confirmed that only damages in respect of past infringements would be outside the scope. Where a settlement covered past infringements, and also permission to continue in the future the conduct which gave rise to those infringements, Customs would accept a reasonable apportionment.

The Law Society asked about the case where the court required a party to give up a right (eg a right of light or an intellectual property right) in exchange for a payment from the other party. Customs said that this was a difficult point which it would need to consider further. Art 6 (1) of the sixth directive was relevant where it referred to "tolerating an act or situation" as a possible supply for VAT purposes.

Questions concerning rights of light can cause problems. Much depends on whether a payment is made in return for the right to take someone else's light or whether it is compensation for the loss of light subsequent to an adjacent building being constructed. It could be argued in exceptional circumstances that the court is deciding what level of consideration is due in return for the granting of the right. However, it is thought that in the majority of cases the payment will be damages imposed upon the payer by the court and therefore outside the scope of VAT. For example, in cases where the court decides that light may be taken and that compensation is payable this will be seen as outside the scope of VAT—there is no consensual element.

3 Where litigation has involved a supply on which VAT had already been accounted for (but the price was not paid) and the result is a reduction in the price paid for the supply, it may be necessary for a supplier to issue a credit note in order to recover part of the VAT which he or she had previously accounted for and not received. Customs confirmed that, in such a case, the credit note could be accepted as valid and it would prima facie be necessary for the recipient of the supply to repay to Customs the tax which he or she had already claimed back.

4 By way of clarification as to when damages were considered to be compensatory and when such payments would constitute consideration for taxable supplies, Customs offered the example of a local authority digging up a pavement in front of a parade of shops. Compensation for loss of trade suffered as a result of its action paid by the local authority to a shop-keeper would not be regarded as a taxable supply. However, if a shop-keeper was paid by the local authority to allow it to work on his or her land, the payment would be consideration for a taxable supply.

Customs said that it would want to consider in greater detail the question of warranty claims. For example, in a standard rated property transaction, where a warranty had understated the rent and the contract provided for a reduction in the purchase price in such a situation, the procedure set out in **3**, above would apply and the vendor would have to issue a credit note to recover that part of the VAT previously accounted for.

The example of net assets of a business having been overstated in warranties given on sale was not so relevant since if it was a question of shares, it would be in the realm of exempt supplies anyway. Compensation in these circumstances would be regarded as outside the scope unless the agreement provided for a reduction in price.

5 Where the settlement involved cross supplies (other than the mere surrender of the right of action) tax would be payable by each party, without netting off, according to the nature of the supply. The situation may arise that there may be a consideration paid in return for a party agreeing to enter into an agreement. For example, in the property industry, reverse premiums may be paid to a potential tenant in consideration of the tenant agreeing to enter into a property lease or for agreeing to carry out building, refurbishment or demolition works, viz Neville Russell and Battersea Leisure.

If the supply under the agreement was, e g free services, VAT would not be due.

6 Customs confirmed that interest on damages is outside the scope of VAT. It has been confirmed in the European decision in *BAZ Bausystem AG v Finanzant Munchen fur Korperschaften* [1982] ECR 2527 that interest would not increase consideration for a supply.

If an international breach had occurred, the same basic principles should be followed. For example, [VATA 1994 Sch 5] should not apply to a cross border giving up of rights. Apparently, the Dutch and the Germans had had bilateral discussions and had confirmed that they would apply outside the scope treatment on the same basis as in the UK.

The Law Society's Gazette 9 September 1992 p 32.

Cross reference—VATA 1994 Sch 5.

14 October 1992. The Law Society

Mesne profits

Following an enquiry from a member of the profession, the Revenue Law Committee has been in correspondence with Customs as to what extent VAT is relevant to an award of mesne profits.

The Commissioners of Customs & Excise agree that mesne profits are damages for trespass (*Bramwell v Bramwell* [1942] 1 All ER 137). Such damages can only be recovered in respect of a defendant's continued occupation of premises after that right of occupation has expired. As such, an award of mesne profits is not consideration for a supply.

Where a landlord has elected to waive exemption from VAT under the provisions of [VATA 1994 Sch 10 paras 2–4], and arrears of rent accrue, in respect of which the landlord sues the tenant, in addition to a claim for mesne profits, the landlord will clearly have made a taxable supply, and non-payment of the rent by the tenant would not affect the landlord's liability to account for tax on the grant of the lease (the supply) subject to any cash accounting considerations.

If the landlord is not on cash accounting, tax points for the period in respect of which he is claiming arrears of rent will already have been determined under [the VAT Regulations SI 1995/2518 reg 85(1)(*b*) or (2) or 90(1)(*b*) or (2)] as the case may require.

If the landlord is on cash accounting, payments received both pursuant to and by way of settlement of litigation will be viewed by the Commissioners as referable in the first instance to being in satisfaction of rent (ie consideration for the grant). Therefore, if the total amount of the settlement is equal to or less than the arrears of rent, the whole of the settlement will be viewed by the Commissioners as payment received by the landlord in respect of the grant.

The Law Society's Gazette 14 October 1992 p 16.

Cross reference—VATA 1994 s 5.

28 October 1992. The Law Society

Payment of third party costs

[An article was published in the Law Society's Gazette on 24 October 1990 entitled "Payment of another party's costs". The article has been agreed with Customs & Excise and set out the rules which apply when a solicitor's costs are paid by a person other than the person to whom the solicitor's services are supplied. Recent discussions between members of the VAT Sub-Committee of the Law Society's Revenue Law Committee and Customs & Excise have led to the agreement with Customs of new guidance, which is set out below.]

It should be noted that this guidance incorporates a change of practice by Customs and that in certain circumstances, set out below, VAT will be chargeable where this had previously been accepted not to be the case.

"THE INDEMNITY PRINCIPLE"

The October 1990 article stated that when a person other than the solicitor's own client is paying the solicitor's costs, the liability of the paying party is one of indemnity only, and thus in itself outside the scope of VAT. In fact, such payment will only be regarded as outside the scope in certain circumstances, for example, as follows—

(*a*) where following completion of litigation (or arbitration), one party is ordered to pay the other party's costs;

(*b*) where a party to a transaction undertakes to pay the other party's costs, and the matter does not proceed to completion, so the costs are "abortive".

However, there are other circumstances where the payment of costs by a third party is regarded as consideration for the supply for VAT purposes. One specific example of such a situation would be where a transaction obliges one party to be responsible for the costs of the other relating to that transaction, in which case payment will be regarded as part of the consideration for the supply (provided the transaction proceeds to completion).

It is worth restating the following general principles which apply when the payment is on an indemnity basis—

(*a*) the solicitor whose costs are to be paid should deliver a tax invoice to his own client. If his client is not a registered taxable person, it is permissible to deliver a VAT inclusive bill without distinguishing the VAT element, although this would not be common practice;

(*b*) if the solicitor's client is a registered fully taxable person, and the supply of legal services is obtained for the purpose of the client's business, the client will be entitled to an input tax credit in which case the indemnifying party need only pay the costs exclusive of VAT;

(*c*) if the solicitor's client is not a registered fully taxable person and cannot obtain input tax credit, the indemnifying party is liable to pay the costs and VAT as well. However, the indemnifying party cannot recover the VAT;

(*d*) where the solicitor's client is a partly exempt registered taxable person, para (*b*) above applies only to the extent that the client can obtain credit for input tax. Paragraph (*c*) applies to the balance;

(*e*) *in no circumstances may a tax invoice be issued by the client's solicitor to the paying party* who is not in law entitled to receive an input tax credit as the services have not been rendered to him. The paying party should therefore receive a note of the other party's costs in such terms that the note cannot be mistaken for a tax invoice issued to the paying party.

For solicitors' services in insurance cases, please refer to previous guidance on this subject which has been published in the Law Society's Gazette on 16 January 1985 and 15 January 1986.

"WHEN PAYMENT CONSTITUTES PART OF THE CONSIDERATION FOR THE SUPPLY"

It is clearly stated in Customs & Excise Notice 742B (Property ownership) para 15 that payment by a tenant of a landlord's costs incurred in respect of the grant of a lease or licence would be regarded as part of the consideration for the supply by the landlord to the tenant. The practical implications will depend on whether the landlord has elected to waive exemption from VAT in relation to the property. If no election to waive exemption has been made, the landlord would not be entitled to an input tax credit on his costs, so the tenant would be required to pay the gross costs including the VAT element: there will have been no taxable supply, so the tenant will not receive a VAT invoice and will be unable to recover as input tax the VAT he has paid to the landlord.

If the landlord has elected to waive exemption, so VAT is payable in respect of the rent or premium, the landlord can recover the VAT element of the costs, and the tenant will only be required to pay the net amount of the landlord's costs, but to that net amount, the landlord will add a VAT charge.

In effect, the amount paid by the tenant would be the same whether or not the landlord has elected to waive exemption, but only if the landlord has done so will the tenant receive a tax invoice from the landlord, and be able to recover the VAT element if the tenant is a registered taxable person.

CHANGE OF POLICY

It has recently become apparent that Customs will also regard payment of costs which have been incurred by a landlord in respect of the exercise by a tenant of an existing right under the lease or licence as constituting part of the consideration for the supply by the landlord to tenant (and thus potentially subject to VAT as described in the paragraph above headed "When payment constitutes part of the consideration for the supply"). This represents a change from the agreed guidance published on 24 October 1990, and it has been agreed that the effective date for the new regime will be 1 December 1992. It is accepted that if, under the terms of the lease, a landlord cannot unreasonably withhold his consent to the tenant's exercising a right, or where the tenant is permitted to exercise a right without the landlord's consent, but subject to payment by the tenant of the landlord's costs, this will be regarded as an existing right. However, where the landlord has absolute discretion as to whether consent is to be granted for the exercise of a right, payment of costs incurred by the landlord is regarded as consideration for a separate supply, on which the landlord will charge VAT unless the right sought to be exercised would constitute an exempt supply.

The contents of this article supersede the article which was published in the Law Society's Gazette on 11 July 1990, entitled "VAT and notices of assignment" which should now be disregarded.

The Law Society's Gazette 28 October 1992.

Cross reference—VATA 1994 s 5.
Customs & Excise Notices—See C&E Notice 742, para 4.10.

22 April 1993. Business Brief 12/93

Payments to a retail consortium

Retailers may join together to form a purchasing consortium for the purposes of negotiating lower prices for the goods they purchase.

The terms of agreement between different consortia and the suppliers of goods can vary, but a common feature is for the suppliers to make periodic payments to the [purchasing consortium]. The purpose of this brief is to confirm the correct VAT treatment of payments made by suppliers/manufacturers of goods to a purchasing consortium.

Payments made by a manufacturer or supplier to a consortium, are regarded as the consideration for a taxable supply of services, by the consortium, of introducing the manufacturer/supplier to a larger customer base. The purchasing consortium is therefore required to account for output tax at the standard rate on all such receipts.

This view was upheld at a VAT tribunal (Landmark Cash and Carry Ltd [1980] VATTR 1, London, November 1979), although it has since become apparent that some traders may have been treating these payments incorrectly. In particular, traders should note that the payments do not fall to be treated as contingent discounts under Notice 700 para 16 because the consortium does not purchase or take ownership of the goods.

Commentary—*De Voil Indirect Tax Service* **V3.102.**
Cross reference—VATA 1994 s 5.

10 September 1993. Press Notice 59/93

VAT recovery by holding companies

In the light of business responses to a Customs & Excise consultative paper, only minor changes will be made from 1 October to the treatment of VAT on costs incurred by holding companies.

The position of the vast majority of holding companies with active trading subsidiaries will remain unchanged.

GENERAL APPROACH FOR THE FUTURE

Customs will continue to keep the VAT recovery by holding companies under review and will be monitoring developments in Europe, particularly emerging case law from the European Court of Justice.

They accept that any wider changes in the VAT treatment of holding companies would only occur as the result of the adoption of a uniform approach by all member states. If EC proposals on this subject were to be brought forward at any time in the future, Customs would consult with interested parties to allow them the opportunity to comment further.

MINOR CHANGES

Where holding companies are unregistered they cannot by definition recover tax.

But there are VAT registered holding companies who are neither active trading companies in their own right, nor are grouped with active trading subsidiaries making taxable supplies outside the VAT group, nor providing genuine management services to separate trading subsidiaries. Many are in effect investment vehicles with no active involvement in trading subsidiaries and are often grouped with a subsidiary supplying management services to them.

In the case of those types of holding companies, and those companies alone, when they incur costs on the following items they will not be able to recover the tax as it will not be regarded by Customs as relating to any taxable supply. These items are costs incurred in acquiring another company; disposing of a subsidiary; restructuring costs relating to the group or any subsidiary; and investment costs incurred on holdings held.

NOTE

In its simplest sense a holding company describes a company with shareholdings in one or more subsidiaries. But their structures and purpose are much more diverse, ranging from companies with minimal activities where shares are held in subsidiaries and dividends received, but no part is played in the management of the investment, to businesses fully integrated with trading subsidiaries and where the holding company is actively concerned with the supervision and management of the subsidiaries.

The basic functions of a holding company are to acquire and hold shares in subsidiaries, from which it receives dividends; defend itself and its subsidiaries from takeovers; and make disposals. From time to time it may invest, deposit or lend money, and issue or sell shares. Some of these activities are outside the scope of VAT, while others are exempt. A company which had no other activities would not be eligible for VAT registration and would not be able to recover any of the tax it incurred on purchases.

However, holding companies are liable to be registered for VAT, where they have taxable trading activities, supply management services to subsidiaries, or are included in a VAT group with trading subsidiaries.

A consultation paper was issued by Customs on 24 June. Most of the responses to the paper touched upon the importance of a level playing field across Europe so as not to erode the international competitiveness of British business or encourage holding companies to locate elsewhere.

Commentary—*De Voil Indirect Tax Service* **V3.461**.

12 September 1994. Business Brief 17/94

VAT on private use of business services

An order exists to ensure that private or non-business use of services is taxed where initially the tax was recovered because the services were originally purchased wholly for business purposes. There is already a similar provision for goods.

The Value Added Tax (Supply of Services) Order 1983, SI 1983/1507 came into effect on 1 August 1993. The following information replaces and supplements the information in Business Brief 23/93 (26 July 1993) [not reproduced] in the light of comments received from business organisations.

AREAS AFFECTED

Most services by their nature are consumed at the point of delivery. However, some services are akin to goods in that they provide a tangible benefit that is used over time and whose use can therefore change. Examples are building construction and refurbishment, computer software and sporting rights.

A supply under the order occurs if the taxpayer has properly treated all the tax incurred as his input tax and no apportionment has been made under VATA 1994 s 24(5) and there is a subsequent permanent change of use to private or non-business use.

In principle a tax charge also arises if a taxpayer changes the nature of the use of services temporarily from business to non-business use. But a minor or occasional change of use should be ignored. In practice most supplies under the order will occur where the change of use is permanent.

There may also occasionally be circumstances where services are purchased by businesses for purposes similar to a business gift of goods. The taxpayer's purpose is a wholly business one but the services are used for a purpose unconnected with the business. One example is an employee's holiday paid for by the employer as an acknowledgment of exceptional performance.

In such cases a supply under the order occurs, parallel to that under VATA 1994 Sch 4 para 5 for business gifts of goods, where services are supplied to a business which are to be provided free of charge for private non-business use.

The order does not create a tax liability for expenditure that is used for the purposes of the business such as—the maintenance or running costs of a company car fleet, retraining prior to redundancy, subsistence, relocation expenses, information technology supplied for homeworking, domestic accommodation and outplacement.

Some businesses have asked how the order affects the private use of leased business cars. That is taxed by means of the blocking of input tax deduction on the purchase of the cars.

HOW IT WORKS

The point at which tax becomes due is at the end of each accounting period in which a supply under the order takes place.

If a taxpayer changes the use of services permanently from a business to a non-business use he should formally account for the full amount of tax due on the non-business use. There are no set rules about calculating this.

Although services are not subject to depreciation, a taxpayer can use his normal accounting convention for depreciating comparable business assets. Using the asset depreciation method, the value on which tax would be due could be—the cost of services multiplied by the projected period of non-business use, this total being divided by the total period over which comparable assets are normally depreciated.

Alternatively, he may use any other fair and reasonable basis to value the cost to him of the private or other non-business use.

The taxpayer should not account for tax beyond the point at which the asset is fully depreciated to nil value, or the accumulated tax accounted for equals the amount of the input tax on the service as has proved to be not attributable to business use, whichever is the earlier.

Commentary—*De Voil Indirect Tax Service* **V3.216**.
Cross-reference—VATA 1994 s 5.

12 September 1994. Business Brief 17/94

VAT on milk quotas

Recent amendments to the Dairy Products Quotas Regulations allow the transfer of milk quotas without land in certain circumstances. This is a derogation from the general principle of quota attached to land. The supply or transfer of a milk quota without land qualifies as a supply of services, and is therefore standard rated.

However, when the transfer of a milk quota is linked with a supply of land under one agreement, this is regarded as one supply for VAT purposes. It doesn't matter if the land is sold freehold or as a leasehold transfer. The VAT liability of the quota will be the same as the VAT liability for the land, even if separate identifiable sums are paid for the land and the quota, or if the invoice details are split between the land and the quota.

If a milk quota is transferred with a grazing licence there are two separate supplies, one of animal feeding stuffs, through the grazing licence which is zero rated, and the other of the quota which is standard rated.

Commentary—*De Voil Indirect Tax Service* **V3.105; V4.111**.
Cross-reference—VATA 1994 Sch 9, Group 1.

8 December 1994. Business Brief 24/94

Sale of property under a power of sale—recovery of VAT on costs incurred by mortgage lenders

Customs & Excise have reconsidered the VAT treatment of costs incurred by mortgage lenders when selling property to realise their security in circumstances where a borrower has defaulted on a loan.

This Business Brief explains the reasons for this and sets out the arrangements which will apply for the future. It also sets out the position on payment of claims for past periods.

BACKGROUND

Business Brief 20/93 [30 June 1993] indicated that Customs were prepared to see lenders as agents of the borrower in arranging the sale of repossessed property, and hence allow them to claim bad debt relief (BDR), where appropriate, on the VAT incurred on selling costs.

However, Customs subsequently became aware that the order of attribution of the proceeds of sale under the Law of Property Act 1925 s 105 might override the Bad Debt Relief Regulations. This is because under s 105 the proceeds of sale are allocated first to costs such as those incurred in selling the property, which threw some considerable doubt over whether a bad debt was created on which relief could be claimed.

Doubts arose also about the status of lenders as agents and there was concern that some claims had included costs which went beyond the terms of the Business Brief. Customs therefore issued a further Business Brief 5/94 [1 March 1994] suspending the processing of claims, until such time as they could take legal advice and examine more fully the issues involved.

CURRENT POSITION

Having taken Counsel's advice, Customs are of the view that there is a good argument that in arranging the sale of repossessed property, mortgagees act under rights conferred by the mortgage agreement, and not as agents of the borrower. However, Customs believe they can rely on the wider interpretation of "agent" contained in the Sixth VAT Directive [Directive 77/388/EEC] in maintaining their current view on agency, as laid out in Business Brief 20/93. They face more difficulty with the Law of Property Act 1925 s 105, as it may override the order of attribution in the Bad Debt Relief Regulations, but again the matter is not free from doubt.

In the circumstances, Customs believe that the finely balanced nature of the legal advice allows some freedom of choice and they are re-introducing a form of easement.

NEW ARRANGEMENTS

General

The easement is strictly for the purposes of allowing a measure of relief for VAT on bad debts and depends crucially on Customs taking a relaxed view of the supply position. Lenders must not extend this treatment more widely in accounting for VAT within their businesses.

The new arrangements will apply to bad debt relief claims relating to supplies made on or after 1 July 1994. The overall aim is to provide relief to lenders where they suffer sticking tax on the costs of selling property in circumstances where borrowers have defaulted—in effect where the net proceeds of sale are reduced because the VAT element of the costs has not been recovered.

In principle, the easement covers costs incurred by lenders in arranging the sale of repossessed property and also to selling costs incurred when property is sold through a Law of Property Act receiver. It is emphasised that, with the single exception of build-out costs, the arrangements apply only to sale costs, and not to any incurred in relation to letting.

Although the Law of Property Act does not apply in Scotland, there are analogous provisions in the Conveyancing and Feudal Reform (Scotland) Act 1970 s 27. The arrangements therefore apply equally to Scotland.

Basic principle

Under the new arrangements, lenders can be seen as agents of the borrowers in relation to the costs of sale whether or not the mortgage deed specifies such a relationship, As an agent, the lender may treat the selling costs incurred as supplies made to them and by them under VATA 1994 s 47(3). The order of attribution of the sale proceeds in the Bad Debt Relief Regulations can then be applied and bad debt relief claimed as appropriate in accordance with normal rules.

These new arrangements apply only to costs relating directly to the sale of property, which would ordinarily have been incurred by the borrower had he arranged the sale himself. Examples of such costs include charges for professional services connected with the sale e g legal and estate agency fees.

The easement does not include costs incurred on services provided to, and used by, the lender as principal, even though they may be charged on to the borrower under the mortgage deed. Examples of such costs include legal fees associated with taking possession, and locksmiths' fees for securing the property. Costs incurred in pursuing claims against a valuer for negligence are also excluded.

OTHER EXPENSES

The position of certain other expenses incurred by lenders was discussed at recent meeting with trade representatives. Treatment of these under the new arrangements is outlined below.

LAW OF PROPERTY ACT RECEIVERS' CHARGES

Law of Property Act receivers' charges which relate specifically to the sale (not letting) of the property and any costs incurred by them in respect of the sale can be regarded as falling within the scope of the new arrangements, but only where the proceeds of sale received by lenders have been reduced by the VAT element of the charges. Where this happens, lenders may be regarded as acting as agents for the borrower in paying the costs.

This means that Customs are not prepared to apply this arrangement where the Law of Property Act receiver recovers the VAT incurred on behalf of a VAT registered borrower and this is reflected in the proceeds passed to the lender. This may occur, for example, where the Law of Property Act receiver has control of the borrower's VAT returns.

BUILD-OUT COSTS

These are expenses incurred on completion of a partly-completed building or major refurbishment of the property before sale. Customs' legal advice is that lenders incur such costs as principals and do not make any onward supplies to the borrower even though the costs are charged on under the terms of the mortgage deed. It was argued at the recent meetings with trade representatives that strict application of this line would create a hidden VAT charge in respect of buildings whose sale is zero-rated.

Customs are sympathetic to this view and are therefore prepared, very exceptionally, to treat the onward charge of the build-out costs as a supply by the lender as principal to the borrower, where the sale of the building by the borrower is the subject of a taxable supply or the transfer of a going concern for VAT purposes. In the case of build-out costs only, Customs are also prepared to see a supply where the property is the subject of a taxable let and output tax on the rents has been accounted for to Customs.

Customs are not prepared to see an onward supply (creating an entitlement to bad debt relief) when the sale of the building is exempt, where the VAT incurred on building costs would be sticking tax. Customs believe it would be quite wrong to allow recovery of tax by lenders in these circumstances. The arrangements will also not apply if the proceeds of sale or rent received by lenders reflect any input tax on build-out costs recovered by the borrower.

REPAIRS AND MAINTENANCE

Lenders can be seen as agents of the borrower in incurring these expenses and may use the VATA 1994 s 47(3) invoicing procedure to qualify for bad debt relief.

IN-HOUSE SERVICES

If lenders use their own in-house estate agencies or solicitors to deal with the sale, they may, exceptionally, be regarded as making a supply of those services as principal to the borrower under the new arrangements. However lenders may adopt this treatment in order to claim bad debt relief only where output tax has been accounted for on the supply to the borrower in accordance with normal rules.

RECORDS

There is no requirement on lenders to adopt the above arrangements but, if they wish to do so, the normal VAT invoicing and record keeping requirements must be followed for all supplies concerned.

PAST CLAIMS

The new arrangements outlined above are not being applied to claims in respect of supplies made on or before 30 June 1994. For past claims Customs are prepared to accept the wider application sought by lenders following Business Brief 20/93 and will allow relief in respect of all selling costs incurred before the above date, including build-out costs and Law of Property Act receivers' charges.

However, with the exception of build-out costs, those attributable to the letting out of property are excluded, as are those incurred by lenders in pursuing negligence claims against valuers. Customs do not accept that the latter are costs relating to the sale of property. In relation to in-house services, claims for past periods will be allowed only where a VAT charge to the borrower has been raised and output tax has been accounted for to Customs.

Any claims blocked as a result of Business Brief 5/94 will be released. Similarly, any claims held back by lenders because of the Business Brief may now be lodged in the normal way. Claimants are advised to contact their local VAT office to arrange the most suitable way to action their claims.

Commentary—*De Voil Indirect Tax Service* **V5.156**.
Cross-references—VATA 1994 ss 24, 36, 47 and Sch 4 para 7.

28 March 1995. Business Brief 6/95

VAT on viability studies

Both the trade and Customs have experienced difficulties in determining who receives the services of an investigating accountant and who is entitled to recover the VAT on those services.

Customs has therefore reviewed its policy and the following new arrangements have been agreed with the Society of Insolvency Practitioners, and will take effect from 1 May 1995.

CHANGES

From May 1, accountants who are engaged to conduct viability studies will be making supplies of their services to the person who has commissioned the work, instructed them, and who also receives the end product. The direction of the supply does not necessarily follow the direction of the payment for the services. The fact that the company may ultimately pay does not mean that the supply is received by the company. Accountants should issue invoices only to those persons to whom they are providing their services.

Where the company commissions the work and receives the report, the investigating accountant is making a supply to the company. The supply is received by the company for the purpose of its business and the company is entitled to recover the input tax subject to the normal rules. The accountant should therefore issue invoices to the company to allow this recovery. This will apply even if the bank or another third party receives a copy of the report. Acknowledgement of a separate duty of care to the bank by the accountant will not prejudice this supply route, or the ability of the company to recover the VAT on the costs of the viability study.

Where the bank commissions the work and receives the report, the investigating accountant is making a supply to the bank. The supply is received by the bank for the purpose of its business and the bank is entitled to recover the input tax subject to the normal rules. The accountant must issue invoices to the bank. This treatment will apply even if the company ultimately pays for the work, and receives copies of the report.

In some instances the bank receives one report and the company another. An example is where the bank requires a confidential security review as part of the investigation. The accountant might receive instructions only from the company, or separate instructions from both the company and the bank. In either case the accountant makes two separate supplies, one to the bank, and one to the company, and should issue two separate invoices.

Each supply is received for the purpose of the particular business, and both the bank and the company are entitled to recover the input tax invoiced to them subject to the normal rules.

If the company and bank issue joint instructions and both receive the same work product, the accountant's supply is made equally to both. The accountant should issue invoices to both the bank and the company, each for 50 per cent of the cost, and both recipients may recover input tax subject to the normal rules.

There may be circumstances where the company commissions the work, but does not receive any report. In this case the accountant's supply is made to the company, but is not used by the company for the purpose of its business. Therefore neither the bank nor the company is entitled to recover any input tax.

Commentary—*De Voil Indirect Tax Service* **V3.421**.
Cross reference—VATA 1994 s 24.

18 May 1995. Business Brief 9/95

Services supplied between local authorities

Customs & Excise sought the views of interested parties in Business Brief 19/94 (not reproduced) on a possible alteration to the rules governing the VAT status of supplies of services between local authorities. The consultation period has now finished and it has been decided on the basis of the views expressed not to extend the scope of the tax to include services supplied between local authorities for the time being.

Since 1 July 1994 all supplies of goods between local authorities have to be treated as business supplies. This policy was adopted in the light of the *Commune di Carpaneto Piacentimo* ruling from the European Court of Justice, and following a consultation exercise. When the business ruling was introduced it was not extended to cover services as potential problems were foreseen when supplies were made under a statutory obligation; these must remain non-business and outside the scope of the tax.

Representations were initially made to Customs recommending the extension of the business ruling to cover services supplied between local authorities. The aim was to achieve greater simplification and improved consistency in the application of the tax.

However the majority of those who responded expressed the view that the ruling should not be extended. In accepting this opinion Customs, bearing in mind the decision in the *Carpaneto* judgment may, at some future date, need to look again at the VAT status of the supply of services other than those made under statutory obligations or a special legal regime.

PRACTICE STATEMENT

The treatment of services between local authorities should therefore be dealt with as set out in the following practice statement.

The supply of services made under a statutory obligation and not in competition with the private sector should be treated as non-business.

The supply of services not made under a statutory obligation and not in competition with the private sector should be treated as non-business, but may be taxed if both parties agree.

The supply of services made under a statutory obligation but in competition with the private sector should be treated as business and are subject to the appropriate rate of VAT.

The supply of any services which are in competition with the private sector on a significant scale, ie nationally, should be treated as business and are subject to the appropriate rate of VAT.

The supply of services that includes any supply of goods should be treated as business and are subject to the appropriate rate of VAT.

Commentary—*De Voil Indirect Tax Service* **V2.108, V2.242**.
Cross references—VATA 1994 ss 33 and 42.
Definition—"Local authority", s 96(1), (4).

31 July 1995. Business Brief 15/95

VAT on business cars

In this Business Brief we outline further developments to the VAT treatment of business cars which will take effect from 1 August 1995. This follows on from Business Brief 10/95 [not reproduced] where we outlined the major VAT changes that will affect such cars.

LEGISLATION

The European Council adopted a decision on 29 June to allow the UK to derogate from the Sixth VAT Directive arts 6, 17.

Three Treasury Orders were made on 29 June and laid before Parliament on 30 June. Two of the orders required approval by a resolution of the House of Commons which was provided on 17 July. The orders will all come into force on 1 August 1995.

The orders are the VAT (Input Tax) (Amendment) (No 3) Order 1995, SI 1995/1666; the VAT (Cars) (Amendment) (No 2) Order, SI 1995/1667; and the VAT (Supply of Services) (Amendment) Order 1995, SI 1995/1668.

CUT-OVER ARRANGEMENTS

In Business Brief 10/95 we explained that businesses will be able to recover VAT incurred on cars obtained on or after August for "wholly business purposes."

The change is linked to the "N" registration prefix for cars. However some "N" registration cars will be the subject of prior invoicing or prepayment. The proposed legislation therefore contains a cut-over provision that will allow a business to elect to treat as a qualifying car, a car it obtains before 1 August 1995 for wholly business purposes, but which is not first registered until on or after that date. A business cannot do this if it makes a letting or hire of the car before 1 August 1995.

A business may make the election described above on a car by car basis, or it may make a single election for all cars falling within the scope of the election provision. A bulk election will need to identify by registration number each car covered by the election.

If a business elects to adopt a car as a qualifying car as described above, it will become entitled to recover input tax incurred on the supply or importation of that car before 1 August 1995. The right to deduct tax incurred before 1 August will arise in the first VAT return period commencing on or after 1 August and not at the time the tax was incurred. The amount claimed must be clearly identified in the VAT account for that period beginning on or after 1 August.

If a car is adopted as a qualifying car it will be treated as such for all transactions on or after 1 August 1995. If it is let on hire to a business that intends to use it for business and private purposes, the 50 per cent input tax restriction will apply to VAT on the leasing charge as described in Business Brief 10/95. VAT must be charged on the full value of the car on its sale or disposal.

INVOICING ARRANGEMENTS

Customs has agreed with a main leasing trade organisation a recommended form of invoice for leasing companies to adopt for lettings to business customers on or after 1 August. The recommended format will clearly identify whether or not the car is a qualifying car. If the car is a qualifying car the invoice will also clearly identify the amount of tax which is potentially subject to the 50 per cent input tax restriction on leasing charges. Leasing companies should take care not to indicate the actual amount of tax the customer can recover as this will depend upon the customer's specific circumstances.

We intend to introduce VAT Regulations requiring businesses leasing cars to VAT registered businesses to specify whether or not the car is "a qualifying car under art 7(2) of the VAT (Input Tax) Order 1992 (as amended)".

Businesses are reminded that if an invoice for leasing charges is issued before 1 August the car concerned cannot be treated as a qualifying car.

CHANGES IN "WHOLLY BUSINESS PURPOSES"

We wish to make clear that in order to claim input tax relief on a car on the basis that the car is to be used for wholly business purposes, the business must, at the time the tax is incurred, genuinely have no intention to make that car available for private use.

Customs will look closely at all claims where there has been a purported change of intention following input tax recovery. Taxpayers are reminded that incorrect claims to relief will result in assessment with consequential interest and penalties, where appropriate.

EXCESS MILEAGE CHARGES

Where a leasing company makes rental of a car consisting of separate supplies of leasing and maintenance, Customs has agreed that any excess mileage charge may be split between the leasing and maintenance elements. One simple way of doing this would be to split the excess mileage charge on exactly the same basis as the overall rental charge.

Leasing companies may adopt another form of split, but if they do so they will be required to demonstrate from their records that the proportion attributed to maintenance is a fair and reasonable allocation of the costs incurred. Excess mileage charges must not be attributed solely to maintenance.

Commentary—*De Voil Indirect Tax Service* **V3.410, V3.443**.

Cross references—Council Decision 95/252/EC arts 1, 2.
VAT (Cars) Order, SI 1992/3122.
VAT (Input Tax) Order, SI 1992/3222 arts 4, 7.
VAT (Supply of Services) Order, SI 1993/1507.

24 June 1996.

Statement of practice on the new VATA 1994 Sch 9A

1 INTRODUCTION

1.1 The following sets out how Customs & Excise will seek to apply the new anti-avoidance provisions for VAT groups introduced in FA 1996. This statement has been produced jointly by the Chartered Institute of Taxation and Customs & Excise, who have incorporated comments from other professional bodies. Its purpose is solely to clarify Customs & Excise's policy in this area; it does not qualify the relevant legislation, nor does it affect a taxpayer's rights of appeal to an independent VAT tribunal.

2 WHY IS THIS LEGISLATION REQUIRED?

2.1 The new provisions are designed for use only against certain categories of avoidance scheme which rely on the existence of the group registration provision contained in VATA 1994 s 43. Section 43(1)(*a*) provides that any supply of goods or services between members of the same VAT group shall be disregarded, but the schemes in question seek to exploit the "disregard" provision for the sole purpose of reducing the VAT on supplies of goods and services purchased by the group from external sources.

2.2 In addition to providing an administrative convenience to the taxpayer, a tax benefit inevitably results through the normal operation of the disregard provision, which prevents supplies between members of the group registration from being taxed or treated as exempt supplies. The tax benefit which results naturally from group registration is not necessarily VAT avoidance and Customs & Excise accept some loss of tax from the facilitation measure. The following is an example of VAT group arrangements that fall outside the scope of these anti-avoidance provisions.

Example

A company carries on a variety of activities in separate divisions. These divisions "supply" goods and services to each other but, as they are all part of the one body corporate, no supply is made for VAT purposes and no output tax occurs. Input tax recovery is determined according to the taxable status of the company as a whole.

If the same business were to be carried on by a number of separately registered companies, all members of the same group of companies, then these supplies would be supplies for VAT purposes. Should any member of the group be VAT exempt, or otherwise be unable to recover its VAT in full, a VAT cost will have arisen which would not have arisen had the business been run in a single company but in separate divisions.

If all the companies are put into a single VAT group registration then the VAT position of the group is the same as a single company with divisions. No charge to output tax would arise on supplies between members of the group, but equally, no input tax could be claimed in connection with those internal supplies: recovery of such tax would be subject to the tax status and activities of the group as a whole.

2.3 Customs & Excise will, however, seek to use the new provisions where avoidance of VAT over and above such savings arise out of the facilitation measures. Examples of instances where they would seek to take action are given below.

Examples

Entry schemes

A typical entry scheme would involve the supplier acquiring goods and services, and recovering the associated VAT before moving the assets into the user's business (either by transferring the assets to another company in the user's VAT group or by joining the group itself). A common feature of such schemes is that periodic payments due from the user under the contract are staged so as to ensure that the greater part falls due when supplier and user are within the same VAT group.

Exit schemes

Under a typical exit scheme, a company wishing to use goods and services subject to VAT which it cannot recover (the "user") acts in concert with a central purchasing company (the "supplier") within its existing VAT group. The user enters into a contract with the supplier and makes a substantial pre-payment. The supplier then leaves the group, purchases the relevant goods or services and supplies them to the user. The supplier takes full recovery of VAT on the goods and services, but accounts for VAT only on the balance of the purchase price. The user is therefore able to reduce the amount of irrecoverable VAT it would otherwise have suffered on goods and services purchased for its business. NB: Customs & Excise are currently appealing a tribunal decision in connection with one such scheme.

2.4 These examples are illustrative only and Customs & Excise will seek to apply the provisions to any similar scheme or its variation. Features common to such avoidance schemes are that input tax deduction is taken against standard-rated supplies, but output tax does not fall on the full value of those supplies because they are treated to some extent as being made between members of the same VAT group and so are disregarded for VAT. The simplest means of bringing the disregard into play is by moving a company in to or out of a VAT group at a critical moment. But a similar result could be secured by entering into some other transaction, such as the transfer of assets or the assignment of an agreement to or from a group member (see also para 3.5 below covering the definition of transaction in the context of a relevant event).

3 SCOPE OF THE NEW PROVISIONS

3.1 FA 1996 s 31, Sch 4 insert a new VATA 1994 Sch 9A. Essentially, this increases the powers available to Customs & Excise in connection with the registration of VAT groups under VATA 1994 s 43.

3.2 The new powers enable the Commissioners of Customs & Excise to direct that—

- separately registered companies eligible to be treated as members of a VAT group may be compelled to group from a specified date; or
- a company within a group may be compelled to leave a group from a specified date; and
- a supply within a group initially treated as a disregarded supply may subsequently be subjected to tax.

3.3 To neutralise fully the tax advantage gained by an avoidance scheme, a direction may require assumptions to be made in connection with matters arising prior to its issue. Special provisions enable an assessment to be issued to recover tax which would have been due had those assumptions reflected the actual position.

Conditions for the issue of a direction under the new Sch 9A

3.4 A direction may only be issued where all of the following conditions are present—

- A relevant event (defined at para 3.5 below) has occurred which meets conditions which but for the occurrence of that event would not be fulfilled;

The conditions qualifying the relevant event are—

- that there has been, or will or may be, a standard-rated (or partly standard-rated) supply on which the output tax due falls to be charged otherwise than by reference to its full value; and
- the charging of VAT at less than full value gives rise or would give rise to a tax advantage.

3.5 Relevant event. A relevant event is defined as occurring when a company joins or leaves a VAT group registration, or when it enters into any transaction. The word "transaction" is capable of being given a very wide meaning when considered in isolation, but the key to understanding how Customs & Excise will interpret this in the context of the provisions is that a relevant event occurs when a taxpayer enters into a transaction. Generally Customs & Excise will take this to mean when the taxpayer enters into a contract or other disposition, such as a gift.

Example

Take a lease of a building. Each payment of rent could be regarded as a transaction in itself. However, the mere payment of rent would not be regarded as covered by the term "enters into any transaction" as used in the legislation.

Customs & Excise will regard the entering into of the lease by the landlord or tenant as a relevant event which would (if the other conditions are met), potentially bring a company within the scope of the provisions. Other examples falling within the scope of the provisions are an agreement for a lease, an assignment, variation or surrender. The performance of obligations under the lease, (e g the carrying out of repairs or the payment of rent), would not normally be caught unless, exceptionally, such obligation constituted the entering into of a separate contract.

3.6 Full value condition. In the context of these measures, a supply at less than full value (the undercharged supply) means only those supplies which to any extent have been, or will be, disregarded under VATA 1994 s 43 because they arise between VAT group members. Supplies which, although not disregarded under s 43, are less than full value for other reasons are not covered. Customs & Excise could not, for instance, compulsorily group the parties to a lease and lease-back agreement under arrangements that had nothing to do with the operation of an intra-group disregard. This is not to say that other measures would not apply.

3.7 Tax advantage. A tax advantage is defined as arising in circumstances where an input tax credit or payment under VATA 1994 s 39 is taken on goods and services used to make the undercharged supply. It is not essential that the right to a tax credit or payment should be that of the supplier of the undercharged supply. The legislation specifically provides that the condition is also fulfilled where the supplier acquires the goods and/or services tax free under the provisions relating to the transfer of a business as a going concern, and the transferor or some previous owner of the business had been entitled to an input tax credit. The following example based on an entry scheme illustrates why this is necessary.

Example

A partly exempt group of companies (the PX group) wishes to reduce the VAT on computer equipment. It therefore arranges for the equipment to be provided by an associated company, Newco 1, which operates a leasing business.

Newco 1 purchases the necessary equipment and deducts input tax under its own VAT registration against its intended supplies of leasing services to the PX group.

Before entering into a lease agreement Newco 1 transfers its business, including the assets for use by PX group, as a going concern to another associated company, Newco 2. The transfer is not subject to VAT.

Newco 2 enters into a leasing agreement with PX group and after an appropriate period joins the group to ensure that the major part of the lease rentals fall to be disregarded. Overall, the arrangements deliver the tax advantage which Sch 9A is intended to counter even though Newco 2 has not itself had any entitlement to an input tax credit.

In providing that in such cases the transferor and the transferee shall be treated as the same person the legislation ensures that such arrangements are not excluded from the scope of these anti-avoidance measures.

3.8 Other provisions deem that, for the purpose of determining whether the input tax credit is used to make an undercharged supply, separate right to goods or services (including options or priorities in connection with goods or services), and the goods and services themselves shall be treated as a single supply. The intention is to ensure that variations of avoidance schemes such as that in the following example are covered.

Example

PX Group comprising companies A and B wishes to mitigate VAT on purchase of computer equipment.

A pays B 90% of cost for an option to purchase the equipment at a nominal value and the supply falls to be disregarded.

B leaves the group and registers in its own right.

A exercises its option and B supplies the goods to A after purchasing the goods and deducting input tax thereon. The argument could run that the input tax deduction was attributable only to the supply of the goods and not to the option. Without the special provision, therefore, there would not be an undercharged supply enabling a direction to be issued.

By providing that the supply of the option and the supply of the goods are to be treated as a single supply, the legislation ensures that such schemes are brought within the scope of Sch 9A.

3.9 Summary of conditions. Taken together, the conditions require that the relevant event must generate a situation where standard-rated supplies, which have given rise to an input tax credit by any person, are not taxed on their full value, so leading to a tax advantage because input tax deduction is disproportionately greater than the corresponding output tax—essentially the tax advantage of an avoidance scheme such as those described earlier must be present.

Partially completed schemes

3.10 Where Customs & Excise have evidence that a scheme has been implemented (there has been a relevant event) then they can make a direction in anticipation of the conditions for the scheme being met. Clear examples of such evidence would be a lease which, because of an entry scheme, becomes an intra-group lease (even though further rental payments have yet to be made since the relevant event) and an uncompleted purchase contract. A direction cannot be issued in anticipation of the relevant event itself.

Commercial transactions

3.11 Even where a tax advantage arises, Sch 9A will not apply where the relevant event was carried through for a commercial purpose or purposes unconnected with the avoidance of VAT. This recognises the fact that in the vast majority of cases businesses are moved into and out of VAT groups for reasons which have no avoidance motivation whatsoever (eg a relevant event might be motivated solely for administration reasons following a change of ownership of a business). The example given at Annex 1 illustrates arrangements which Customs & Excise would accept as being motivated by a genuine commercial purpose.

3.12 However, it is important to realise that where, in addition to an acceptable commercial purpose, Customs & Excise also identify other main purposes indicating VAT avoidance, they will seek to use their powers to nullify the VAT advantage derived. Examples of mixed motive transactions are given at Annexes 2, 3, along with an indication of how Customs & Excise would view the transactions in question. While the examples are rather complex, they are intended to illustrate the basic point that no direction will be issued where Customs & Excise are satisfied that it is not one of the main purposes of the arrangement to gain a VAT advantage by having a supply disregarded in a VAT group while obtaining input tax recovery in respect of it.

3.13 In deciding issues concerning commercial purpose, Customs & Excise would be prepared to consider the term in its broadest sense where the context of any particular case allowed. The taxable trading arm of a charity, for example, would not be denied a claim to commercial purpose merely because it is part of a non-profit making body.

Time limit on directions

3.14 A direction cannot be given more than six years after the relevant event, or six years after the entitlement to input tax which gave rise to the tax advantage, whichever is the later.

3.15 A direction cannot be given unless the relevant event occurs on or after 29 November 1995.

3.16 However, where a direction is appropriate, it can rely on assumptions about transactions made before that date without any limit (but see para 3.18 below).

Right of appeal

3.17 Taxpayers have full rights of appeal to the VAT tribunal against the issue by Customs & Excise of any direction or assessments issued under these provisions. The tribunal is entitled to consider all relevant facts and decide whether or not the conditions had been fulfilled. In addition the tribunal will be able to decide whether there had been a genuine commercial purpose.

Powers of direction—how far back will Customs & Excise go?

3.18 Customs & Excise will not seek application of any direction from a date earlier than that required to nullify the tax advantage derived from the relevant event. Usually this will be the first day of the prescribed accounting period in which the scheme commences or the relevant event occurs (whichever is the earlier). In calculating an assessment for unpaid tax according to assumptions applying to periods prior to issue of the direction, only those supplies relevant to delivery of the tax advantage will be taken into account. The assessment amount itself will be capped so that it does not exceed what, in the judgment of Customs & Excise is the actual revenue loss arising. This means that input tax that would have been deductible on the basis of the assumptions in the direction can be taken into account in appropriate cases. All other supplies made by the parties involved will be unaffected so there will be no need for any retrospective VAT accounting adjustment in their regard. In short, the intention is that the provisions will be applied so as not to make the actions of Customs & Excise disproportionate to the mischief involved.

3.19 Nevertheless, Customs & Excise will apply these provisions vigorously where an attempt to avoid VAT is made (see also para 6.3 on responsibility for authorising directions).

Is a grouping or degrouping direction irrevocable?

3.20 Once the particular tax advantage of the scheme targeted has been corrected satisfactorily, Customs & Excise will consider any subsequent application to join or leave a group subject to their normal powers of discretion in such matters.

4 RECORDS

4.1 It is not intended that these provisions should increase the record keeping requirements of taxpayers to enable either Customs & Excise to assess under, or taxpayers to comply with, these provisions. If neither the company degrouped nor the remainder of the group have accurate records to determine the value and nature of transactions between them then an assessment will be made on the best judgment of Customs & Excise from all available records, either obtained from or made available to Customs & Excise by the taxpayer.

4.2 Where a direction covers times after its issue the consequences of the direction will materially affect the treatment of any supplies from the date specified in the direction and such supplies will be subject to the normal accounting requirements for VAT. So, for example, a de-grouping direction could result in a separate registration being set up for the company concerned and it will have to make returns and pay tax accordingly.

5 CALCULATION OF CHARGE TO VAT

Disregarded supplies

5.1 Where a direction is made to treat a supply as not being disregarded between group members then tax will become payable according to its value (adjusted as appropriate to take account of any direction issued under VATA 1994 Sch 6 para 1 if the supply is less than market value). A credit will be allowed for that part of the tax which would have been deductible according to the partial exemption method of the VAT group registration.

Degrouping

5.2 Where the direction degroups a company from a group registration then (to the extent that the direction has force for tax periods after it is issued see para 4.2 above) all supplies made by that company to all other members of the group, and all supplies made by other members of the group to that company will, from the date specified in the direction, be treated as taxable supplies. Action in relation to assumptions for events prior to issue of the direction will be covered by the new powers of assessment and only those transactions relevant to the tax advantage will be affected (see para 3.18).

Mandatory grouping

5.3 Normally, the purpose of a direction to group companies together will be for Customs & Excise to recoup any excess claim to input tax. In such cases, the amount of tax to be charged will be the amount of input tax recovered less the amount which would otherwise have been recoverable in accordance with the partial exemption method of the appropriate VAT group registration. A credit will also be allowed in connection with any output tax charged between the parties which would not have been due according to the assumptions specified in the direction.

Transitional provisions

5.4 The new provisions overlap with existing VAT group anti-avoidance provisions contained in VATA 1994 s 43(1A) in that they are available for use in cases where the relevant event occurs on or after 29 November 1995. But s 43(1A) remains in force for cases prior to its repeal on 29 April 1996 (Royal Assent for FA 1996). Customs & Excise will not use the powers under Sch 9A if an assessment under s 43(1A) could be raised to correct the mischief from an avoidance scheme.

Interaction with capital goods scheme

5.5 It is possible that assets to which the capital goods scheme applies will become the subject of a direction. Indeed, the transfer of such goods to or from a VAT group registration could qualify as a relevant event meeting the necessary conditions for triggering the new provisions. In deciding whether there is a tax advantage justifying issue of a direction Customs & Excise will take into account the impact of the capital goods scheme.

Interaction with VATA 1994 s 44

5.6 The fact that the transfer of a business results in a charge to tax under the provisions of VATA 1994 s 44 (these are to remain in force) will not preclude Customs & Excise from exercising the new powers. However, in such cases where a direction is considered necessary, credit will be allowed in calculating an assessment for unpaid tax against a charge under s 44 which would not have been due according to the assumptions specified in the direction.

6 IF CUSTOMS & EXCISE SUSPECT VAT AVOIDANCE

6.1 If Customs & Excise believe a VAT avoidance scheme has been implemented then, save where fraud is also suspected, a Customs & Excise officer will discuss his concerns with the taxpayer and invite an explanation as to whether or not, for example, a particular transaction falls outside the powers under the commercial purpose test.

6.2 If Customs & Excise are subsequently satisfied that a direction and assessment should be made, then their intentions will be set out in a pre-direction letter against which the taxpayer can ask for an internal review. In taking a decision in any one case, Customs & Excise will consider all relevant circumstances including the appropriate form of direction and its future effects. Where more than one remedy is available, Customs & Excise will be prepared to adopt the taxpayer's preferred option providing this does not impose an increased administrative burden (and, obviously, the loss from the avoidance scheme is still neutralised).

Who will be responsible for authorising the issue of directions?

6.3 Implementation of the new provisions is to be closely monitored and for the next two years, at least, it has been agreed that no direction or assessment will be issued under these provisions without the authorisation of Customs & Excise Head Office, at the address given below—HM Customs & Excise, VAT Policy Directorate, VAT Collection Division (Registration Branch), Fourth Floor South West, Queens Dock, Liverpool L74 4AB.

ANNEX 1

The following illustrates the type of case where, should a tax advantage arise from the stated transactions alone, Customs & Excise would accept a genuine commercial reason as prevailing—

There is a movement of a company or a business to a group registration directly following the purchase of the entire issued share capital of a company or the assets of a business as a going concern where—

- the sale is for full consideration;
- the buyer has no interest in the business of the seller and the seller has no interest in the business of the buyer, either before or after the transaction apart from the sale, and

the sale is not associated with any other operation, transaction or arrangement whereby the business (or the part of the business) of the company or any part of the issued share capital of the capital which is sold, or any interest in that business or company, may revert to the seller or to any person who has an interest in the business of the seller.

ANNEX 2
EXAMPLE OF ARRANGEMENT WHERE CUSTOMS & EXCISE WOULD USE THEIR POWERS UNDER SCHEDULE 9A

1 Background

A partly exempt group of companies (the PX group) wishes to buy a large number of new personal computers for £1 million plus any VAT.

2 Commercial considerations

In structuring this purchase the PX group considers four main factors—

- *how to* finance the purchase. The group wishes to fund about half of the purchase price from its own resources, paying the balance over a four year period;
- the accounting treatment of the purchase. The group does not wish to increase the gearing in its group balance sheet;
- the direct tax treatment of the purchase. The group is not expecting to make a profit this year for corporation tax purposes, although it expects to return to profitability in the relatively near future;
- the VAT cost *of the purchase*. The group wishes to minimise the incidence of irrecoverable VAT suffered.

3 Structure chosen

The above factors having been considered, the following steps take place—

- the PX group sets up a new company (Newco) and registers it as part of its VAT group;
- having taken advice on their precise terms, the PX group executes—
  - (*a*) a leasing agreement between Newco and the other PX group companies, this agreement requiring an immediate 50% deposit in respect of each computer to be leased (total £500,000); and
  - (*b*) an agreement to sell Newco to an unrelated Finance House (F Ltd) for a nominal sum;
- the deposit is paid and Newco is sold to F Ltd;
- Newco leaves the PX VAT group;
- Newco buys the computers for £1 million plus VAT, recovering the VAT in full;
- Newco begins to make leasing charges to the PX group. These will eventually amount to £800,000 plus VAT over the four year period.

4 Summary of effects of structure

The PX group has taken legal advice to the effect that—

- its arrangements do not involve it in significantly greater commercial risk than a straightforward leasing agreement;
- because of the precise terms of the agreement, the computers will not be included in the group balance sheet;
- the precise terms of the agreement will allow Newco to claim capital allowances on the purchase of the computers at a time when the consequent direct tax losses can be surrendered to other members of the F Ltd loss relief group, this benefit having been factored into the leasing charge;
- the arrangements have the effect of;
- spreading the irrecoverable VAT suffered on the purchase over a four year period; and
- reducing the absolute amount of irrecoverable VAT by 20%;
- however, the PX group is advised that these VAT efficiencies will be reversed if Customs & Excise issue a direction and assessment under VATA 1994 Sch 9A.

5 Customs & Excise view of structure

Customs & Excise would consider that an arrangement such as that described above has a number of main purposes. Customs & Excise would further consider that one of these main purposes (namely the desire to generate a VAT saving by having Newco obtain full input tax recovery against outputs some of which are disregarded under s 43(1)(*a*)) is not a genuine commercial purpose within the meaning of Sch 9A para 2. Following the procedure outlined in part 5 of this statement of practice, therefore, Customs & Excise would issue a direction in these circumstances (most probably to the effect that the 50% deposit should not have been disregarded under s 43(1)(*a*)). An assessment would follow the direction.

ANNEX 3
EXAMPLE OF ARRANGEMENT WHERE CUSTOMS & EXCISE WOULD NOT USE THEIR POWERS UNDER SCHEDULE 9A

1 Background

A partly exempt group of companies (the PX group) wishes to sell one of its head office buildings, which is surplus to requirements following a downsizing exercise. All of the PX group companies are included in a single VAT group. The property is owned by P Ltd, the group property company, and used by M Ltd, the group management services company. M Ltd pays (and has historically paid) annual rentals in advance on 1 January under a formal 15 year lease. The PX group has elected to waive exemption in respect of all of its properties, although this currently has no effect in respect of the rentals paid by M Ltd, these being disregarded under s 43(1)(*a*).

It is now May 1996, and the PX group wishes to dispose of the property on or around December 1997, when M Ltd's lease (coincidentally) runs out. It will be difficult to relocate M Ltd's staff before that date. However, the directors have already found a willing buyer for the property. The buyer is unrelated to the PX group.

2 Commercial considerations

In structuring this purchase the PX group considers four main factors—

- cash flow. The group would like to make the disposal as soon as possible, using the proceeds to pay off expensive debt.
- accounting. The group would like the profit on disposal of the building to be included in this year's results if possible.
- direct tax. The gain on disposal of the building can be sheltered if the disposal takes place this year.
- VAT. As a matter of policy the group manages the irrecoverable VAT on all of its overheads.

3 Structure chosen

The directors manage to agree with the purchaser the following arrangements—

- P Ltd will sell the freehold of the property to the purchaser on 1 July 1996;
- however, the freehold will be subject to M Ltd's lease, which will have 18 months to run by then;
- the purchaser will opt to tax the property prior to sale so that the transaction can be treated as the transfer of a business as a going concern for VAT purposes;
- in order to avoid the situation where the purchaser charges M Ltd VAT on the final year's rent, M Ltd pays the final year's rent to P Ltd before the sale takes place, an adjustment being made to the sale price to reflect this.

4 Summary of effects of structure

The structure meets all of the group's commercial objectives. However, the group's advisers are concerned that the advance payment of rent by M Ltd might lead to Customs & Excise issuing a direction and assessment under Sch 9A.

5 Customs & Excise approach to the arrangements

Customs & Excise would not issue a direction based on the above facts. Even though the final year's rent is advanced in order to avoid the incidence of irrecoverable VAT, it is not considered that this would have been a main purpose of the sale of the property.

Commentary—*De Voil Indirect Tax Service* **V2.105**.
Cross reference—VATA 1994 Sch 9A para 1.

1 July 1996. Business Brief 13/96

VAT exemption for supplies of Government-funded vocational training

Training providers and further education colleges should note that, with immediate effect, supplies of training, re-training or work experience paid for using Further Education Funding Council (FEFC) funds will qualify for VAT exemption under VATA 1994 Sch 9 Group 6 item 5.

Customs & Excise accept that, in these circumstances, the consideration payable is ultimately a charge to funds provided pursuant to arrangements made under the Employment and Training Act 1973 s 2. This maintains the VAT exempt status of vocational training, previously funded through the Department of Employment.

Similar supplies paid for by further education colleges in Scotland and Wales under parallel funding arrangements will also qualify for exemption under this item.

The exemption applies only to the extent that the consideration payable is ultimately a charge to such funds. This means that where a college pays for a particular training course using both FEFC funds and money available to it from other sources (for example a specific subsidy from industry, or accumulated tuition fees) then apportionment will be necessary to determine the extent to which exemption under item 5 applies. In such cases, where the training is purchased from a body that is not eligible as defined in Group 6 note 1, the single supply will comprise both exempt and standard-rated elements.

To ease this process of apportionment, colleges may opt to apply a global formula rather than perform a separate calculation each time they buy in a supply of vocational training. In other words, it is open for each college to express its annual FEFC allocation as a percentage of its total income for the year. It may then simply apply this percentage to each purchase of vocational training made in the subsequent year in order to arrive at the proportion that qualifies for exemption under item 5.

Commentary—*De Voil Indirect Tax Service* **V4.141**.
Cross reference—VATA 1994 Sch 9 Group 6 Item 5.

27 August 1996. Business Brief 18/96

Recovery of tax incurred on repairs, maintenance, renovation etc to farmhouses

Following a number of VAT tribunal decisions Customs & Excise have reviewed their approach to input tax claims made by sole proprietors and partnerships in relation to farmhouses. The following sets out guidelines which have been agreed with the National Farmers' Union.

However, it must be pointed out that this does not give an automatic entitlement to recover an amount of tax. Businesses should continue to consider their own particular circumstances, and use the guidelines below to assess the proportion of tax that is claimable.

THE GUIDELINES

In the case of a normal working farm where the VAT registered person is actively engaged in running it, 70% of tax incurred on repairs, maintenance and renovations, may be recovered as input tax. This position is in line with that adopted by VAT tribunals who have found that in those given circumstances the dominant purpose was to allow the farming business to be carried on, and allowed 70% of the tax to be claimed.

However, where the building work is more associated with an alteration, e g building an extension, the amount that may be recovered will depend on the purpose for the construction. If the circumstances are such that the dominant purpose is a business one then 70% can be claimed. But if the dominant purpose is a personal one we would expect the claim to be 40% or less, and in some cases, depending on the facts, none of the VAT incurred would be recoverable.

Where farming is not a full-time business and occupation for the VAT registered person, i e income is received from either full-time employment or other sources, the amount of tax that may be claimed will be considerably less. With these kind of cases VAT tribunals have accepted somewhere between 10% and 30% of tax incurred is claimable on the grounds that the dominant purpose is a personal one. Businesses should therefore assess their particular circumstances, and make claims within those parameters.

RETROSPECTIVE CLAIMS

Customs policy reflects the High Court judgment in the case of *The Victoria and Albert Museum Trustees v C & E Comrs* [1996] STC 1016. The museum wished to revisit past input tax claims on the grounds that it could have used a different and more favourable method to calculate its input tax. The court held there had been no error of law or fact, and consequently the museum were not permitted to revisit those earlier tax periods. The three year capping set out in News Release 42/96 [not reproduced] also has to be considered.

(*a*) Where a trader has claimed input tax of less than 70% without reference to Customs & Excise.

In this situation a retrospective claim is not allowable. The trader has assessed the input tax recovery position, and made a claim. There has been no error in law or fact to be corrected.

(*b*) Where a trader has claimed input tax based on an officer's decision, or has been assessed.

In this instance a retrospective claim may be made but any claim will be subject to the three year capping. Where the business self-assessed its input tax at less than 70%, a refund claim will be allowed to the extent of the percentage self-assessed.

LIMITED COMPANIES

Where the occupant of the farmhouse is a director of the company, or a person connected with the director of the company, different legislation applies. This means that only tax on supplies that are used for other than domestic purposes is claimable as input tax. If a room is used partly for business and partly for domestic purposes, VAT will only be recoverable to the extent of the business use and suitable records will need to be kept to justify the proportion of tax being claimed.

Commentary—*De Voil Indirect Tax Service* **V3.408.**
Cross reference—VATA 1994 s 24.

17 October 1996. Business Brief 21/96

MOT test charges

Following a review of their policy on the VAT treatment of Ministry of Transport (MOT) tests, Customs & Excise are introducing changes to operate from 1 November 1996, which will simplify the law in this area.

We are also clarifying the conditions which must be met, if the MOT test fee charged by the test centre to an unapproved garage and recharged to the latter's customer, is to be treated as a disbursement.

THE REVISED POSITION

The charge for an MOT test provided direct by a test centre to its customers is outside the scope of VAT, provided it does not exceed the statutory maximum.

The discount given by a test centre to an unapproved garage will be treated as a normal trade discount and will no longer be seen as consideration for a taxable supply by the unapproved garage either to the test centre or its customer.

Any amount charged by an unapproved garage to its customer over and above the amount charged by the test centre is consideration for its own service of arranging the test as agent of the customer and is taxable at the standard rate. Where the unapproved garage shows the exact amount charged by the test centre separately on the invoice to the customer, and meets the other conditions of para 10.8 of the VAT Guide, it may treat this element as a disbursement and also outside the scope of VAT.

If the unapproved garage chooses not to treat the amount charged by the test centre as a disbursement, or otherwise does not satisfy all the conditions set out in para 10.8 of the VAT Guide, it must account for VAT on the full invoiced amount.

We carried out the review because we recently became aware that our policy is creating difficulties for the trade and our own staff alike. Previous policy was formulated at a time when it was customary for test centres to charge the statutory fee and charge a lower amount only where an unapproved garage delivered a customer's vehicle for testing.

However, many test centres now offer discounts to all customers. Depending on the contractual situation, we have seen the discount as consideration either for a supply by the unapproved garage to the test centre of introducing a customer, or for a supply by the unapproved garage to its customer of arranging for the MOT test to be done. This has been the main difficulty because neither the trade nor local VAT audit staff have any easy way of knowing how much the test centre might normally charge.

We also found there was confusion about the procedures to be adopted where the unapproved garages were treating the charges raised by the test centre as a disbursement on behalf of their customers.

Commentary—*De Voil Indirect Tax Service* **V3.113.**
Cross reference—VATA 1994 s 5.

27 March 1997. Business Brief 9/97

Extension of "capping" to claims for refunds other than for amounts overpaid as VAT

Customs and Excise laid secondary legislation on 26 March 1997 which introduces a three year time limit— "the cap"—for corrections and adjustments including refund claims for input tax not covered by FA 1997 [The VAT(Amendment) Regulations, SI 1997/1086].

On 18 July 1996, the then Paymaster General announced the introduction of a three year time limit on claims, mainly from payment traders, for refunds of amounts overpaid as VAT. However, no similar provisions were introduced for capping claims by way of secondary legislation, and there remained a number of methods of reclaiming VAT which were not subject to a three year cap. The legislation introduced on 26 March 1997 corrects this anomaly.

The changes will take effect on 1 May 1997 and will mainly affect repayment traders.

For ease of reference, any corrections and adjustments including refund claims for input tax are referred to as "claims" in the following text.

THE EFFECT OF THE CHANGES

The amendments extend a three year time limit to—

Late claims for input tax. If a business did not claim input tax on the proper return, it cannot claim input tax on a later return made more than three years after the date when the input tax should have been claimed.

Correction of errors. Errors cannot be corrected more than three years after the period in which the errors arose. This is regardless of whether the correction is made within the VAT account (for errors not exceeding £2,000 in net value) or by informing the local VAT office (net errors over £2,000). A transitional provision allows businesses to correct errors if they have not yet rendered the return in which they discovered the errors, that return is for a prescribed accounting period which begins before 1 May 1997, and it has not been made or required to have been made before 1 May 1997.

Adjustment to take account of an increase or decrease in consideration. Businesses cannot make an adjustment where the increase/decrease in consideration takes place more than three years after the end of the prescribed accounting period in which the original supply took place. A transitional provision allows businesses to adjust for increases/decreases without restriction if they have not yet rendered the return which they should make the adjustment, that return is for a prescribed accounting period which begins before 1 May 1997, and it has not been made or required to have been made before 1 May 1997.

Pre-registration expenses. Newly registered businesses can no longer reclaim VAT incurred on goods (including VAT on services performed on these goods) bought more than three years before the effective date on which they registered for VAT. This does not apply where someone registered before the regulations came into force and has yet to make their first return. Businesses must now also claim tax incurred before registration on the first return they are required to make rather than the first return they do make. Claims for VAT on pre-registration expenses must also be claimed within three years of the due date of the first return the business was required to make.

Post-deregistration expenses. Businesses which have deregistered from VAT can no longer reclaim VAT incurred after deregistration, if it was incurred more than three years before the claim. This does not apply to businesses which had deregistered and received the supply before these amendment regulations were made.

Adjustments under the capital goods scheme. Customs can no longer allow businesses to make belated adjustments to input tax incurred on capital goods items if the adjustment is made on a return for a prescribed accounting period which is more than three years after the end of the accounting period when the adjustment should have been made.

Claims for bad debt relief. Claims must now be made within three years six months of when the consideration for the supply was due or the date of supply, whichever was the later. This does not apply to claims for bad debt relief for any supplies where the consideration became due before the amendment regulations were made.

These changes take effect from 1 May 1997 and only affect claims or adjustments made on or after that date.

. . .

CLAIMS AND ADJUSTMENTS UNAFFECTED BY THE CHANGES

A number of claims dating back more than three years are not affected by the changes to the law. These include—

Returns following compulsory backdated registration for VAT. Where a business is registered for VAT with retrospective effect, it will be able to claim input tax on its first return and should account for output tax due even if the tax was incurred more than three years previously. (Businesses who choose to register for VAT voluntarily can only backdate their registration three years from the date of application).

Claims made under the regulations prior to 1 May 1997. These are not subject to the three year time limit, provided that—

(*a*) they were not claims for refunds of amounts overpaid as VAT — ie section 80 refund claims and;

(*b*) they were valid claims—e g it had been established that either United Kingdom law was ultra vires EC law, or that the Commissioners' interpretation of United Kingdom law was defective in some way, although it does not necessarily mean that Customs has agreed the claims; and

(*c*) that the claims were made in the proper form.

REVIEW

Customs will be reviewing the position of claims and adjustments in more detail to ensure that the three year time limit operates fairly and equitably.

. . .

Commentary—*De Voil Indirect Tax Service* **V3.404**.

5 June 1997. Business Brief 12/97

Taxable acquisition of yachts in the United Kingdom

Customs & Excise have agreed to introduce a temporary arrangement concerning the liability to account for VAT on the taxable acquisition of yachts in the United Kingdom, in certain limited circumstances. This follows representations made on behalf of owners of large yachts and is effective immediately.

Where a VAT-registered business in the United Kingdom buys a yacht from a supplier in another Member State, and the yacht is being removed from that Member State to the place where it will be hired on charter, acquisition VAT may be accounted for in the United Kingdom without the need for the yacht to actually come here. The normal rules will apply for recovery of any input tax that is incurred and for accounting for output tax on any supplies subsequently made.

This arrangement does not affect the VAT treatment of yachts being imported into the EU from third countries, and will be kept under review.

Commentary—*De Voil Indirect Tax Service* **V3.173**.

21 July 1997. Business Brief 16/97

VAT changes for bonuses given by car manufactures to dealers or fleet buyers

Fleet buyer bonuses are given by manufactures or sole concessionaires to customers who make bulk purchases of their vehicles. Dealer demonstrator bonuses are payments made, or credits allowed, by car manufactures or sole concessionaires to dealers, when the dealer agrees to adopt the car as a demonstrator vehicle.

In the past it has been common practice to treat the bonuses as the payment for a supply of services by dealers and customers, so VAT was due from the dealer or customer on this supply.

Following the decision by the European Court of Justice in Elida Gibbs Ltd, which established that discounts can be given by a supplier for his goods to someone other than his direct customer, we now accept that these bonus payments will normally be treated as discounts by manufacturers and sole concessionaires which reduce the value of their supplies. Values should also be adjusted by dealers in their second hand stock books.

In many cases the net effect of this change will not alter the net tax due. However, if businesses believe that they have overpaid VAT in the past three years they should contact their local VAT Business Advice Centre listed under Customs & Excise in the telephone book.

Commentary—*De Voil Indirect Tax Service* **V3.103–3.104**.

24 September 1997. Business Brief 20/97

Vacuum cleaners, air purification and similar anti-allergen products

Customs & Excise have undertaken and have completed a review of the VAT liability of vacuum cleaners, air purification products and similar allergy relief products. The review concluded that such products are standard-rated and not zero-rated under provisions relating to equipment "designed solely" for disabled people (Business Briefs 16/96 and 17/96).

Since 26 August 1996, all supplies of such products have been liable to VAT at the standard rate irrespective of to whom they are supplied.

This confirmation will help to provide certainty for suppliers and customers alike, and will prevent considerable distortion in the trade, particularly for vacuum cleaner suppliers. Previously VAT treatment of these products had been inconsistent. For further information traders and their advisers should contact their local VAT business advice centre listed under Customs & Excise in the telephone book.

10 November 1997. Business Brief 25/97

Herbal product to be standard-rated

From 1 February supplies of Khat (Catha edulis) are standard-rated. Previously this herbal stimulant had been zero-rated as a food product.

In the light of evidence suggesting that Khat is being increasingly used as a stimulant drug, it is now not regarded as a food product and is properly standard-rated.

...

19 December 1997. Business Brief 30/97

Statement of Practice on a budget change to the capital goods scheme

1 INTRODUCTION

1.1 Changes to the capital goods scheme announced at the time of the July 1997 budget included a test to be applied on the disposal of a capital item by the owner during the adjustment period. The test compares the total amount of input tax deducted or deductible on a capital item with the amount of output tax due on the disposal of that item. For the purposes of this Statement of Practice and the examples annexed, this test will be known as "the disposal test".

1.2 The policy objective underlying the disposal test is to ensure that partly exempt businesses such as banks, building societies, insurance companies, educational establishments, sports clubs, providers of private health care and the like, do not obtain an unjustified tax advantage by being able to recover the input tax they incur on land or property which is to be used for exempt purposes.

1.3 The change was announced as part of a package of anti-avoidance measures in the 1997 Budget. It was introduced by the Value Added Tax (Amendment) (No 3) Regulations, SI 1997/1614 and came into force with effect from 3 July 1997.

1.4 It is not intended that the disposal test should be applied to bona fide commercial transactions. The legislation gives Customs & Excise the power to exclude individual transactions and this power will be used either generally or specifically in cases that do not appear to Customs & Excise to involve unjustified tax advantage. So, for example, given the policy objective, the disposal test will not be applied to sales of computer equipment.

1.5 The purpose of this Statement of Practice is to clarify Customs & Excise policy in this area. It does not qualify the relevant legislation, nor does it affect a taxpayer's right of appeal to an independent VAT tribunal.

2 BACKGROUND

2.1 Generally, businesses making taxable supplies can recover VAT on goods and services they buy in for their business (input tax). Businesses making exempt supplies cannot normally recover their input tax. Businesses which make both taxable and exempt supplies can recover input tax to the extent that the goods and services on which it is incurred are used to make taxable supplies.

2.2 The capital goods scheme recognises that certain major capital assets (capital items) are not consumed immediately but are used by businesses over a number of years. It is designed to be fair to both businesses and the Exchequer. The scheme applies to—

- certain land and buildings where the VAT bearing costs of purchase or development (acquisition) amount to £250,000 or more, with an adjustment period of 10 intervals;
- items of computer equipment of a value of £50,000 or more, with an adjustment period of 5 intervals.

2.3 An interval normally equates with the partial exemption tax year. In the first interval the owner deducts input tax incurred on a capital item to the extent that the item is used or to be used in making taxable supplies. He must then review his use of the item over the relevant adjustment period. In each subsequent interval, if the extent of taxable use differs from that which governed the initial recovery of input tax, the owner must make an adjustment. The adjustment is calculated by comparing the percentage of taxable use in the subsequent interval with the initial recovery percentage.

2.4 For example, input tax is deducted in full when a property is acquired, because it is being used exclusively in making taxable supplies. In a subsequent interval the use to which it is put changes from fully taxable to fully exempt. The owner must pay back 1/10th of the input tax originally claimed. If the owner continues to use the property for exempt purposes, similar adjustments will have to be made (and amounts paid back) at the end of each interval for the remainder of the adjustment period.

2.5 The legal basis of the scheme is Part XV of the Value Added Tax Regulations [SI 1995/2518] (regs 112–116). Further information about the scheme can be found in VAT Leaflet 706/2/90 "Capital goods scheme—input tax on computers, land and buildings for use in your business".

3 DISPOSAL OF A CAPITAL ITEM

3.1 The period of adjustment is brought to an end by the outright disposal of the capital item during the adjustment period. In effect, on termination the item is treated as if it were used for the remainder of the adjustment period in making the supply which gives rise to the termination. So, where the capital item is sold and the sale is a taxable supply, the item is treated as being used in all remaining complete intervals for the making of taxable supplies. The owner must make a final adjustment in respect of all remaining intervals to reflect this.

3.2 Prior to 3 July 1997 businesses could acquire a new commercial building as a capital item and recover all of the input tax by putting the item to taxable use in the first interval. At the beginning of interval 2, the owner could make a very substantial exempt supply (say a 999 year lease—which is not an outright disposal because the freehold interest remains) and then immediately sell the freehold of the building—that sale being a compulsory taxable supply. Because there was an exempt lease, the value of the freehold sale was very low and there was output tax only on that very low value. The taxable sale of the capital item ensured the recovery of a high proportion of the input tax incurred while very little output tax was paid. The building then ceased to be a capital item. This results in an unjustified tax advantage and is the sort of arrangement that the new rule is designed to counter.

4 THE INTRODUCTION OF A TEST ON DISPOSAL

4.1 With effect from 3 July 1997 where the owner of a capital item disposes of it and the total input tax deducted is greater than the output tax due on the supply of the item, the owner is required to make an adjustment so that the input tax recoverable does not exceed the output tax chargeable on the supply of the item. The input tax recoverable is the aggregate of—

- the initial deduction of input tax incurred on the purchase or development of the item;
- any adjustments made previously in respect of the item under the scheme; and
- any adjustment that would otherwise be required due to the disposal of the item.

5 APPLICATION OF THE PROVISION

5.1 In principle the disposal test is wide ranging and impacts on many disposals of capital items. In practice it will only be applied where the owner of a capital item would otherwise gain an unjustified tax advantage, and then the tax charge will be limited to an adjustment amount that would ensure no unjustified tax advantage arises. The legislation includes a "save as the Commissioners otherwise allow" provision to enable Customs & Excise to exclude individual transcriptions. This power will be used to exclude the application of the disposal test in cases that do not appear to Customs & Excise to involve unjustified tax advantage. It will not be applied—

- to sales of computer equipment;
- where an owner disposes of an item at a loss due to market conditions (such as a general downturn in property prices);
- where the value of the item has depreciated;
- where the value of the item is reduced for other legitimate reasons (such as accepting a lower price to effect a quick sale);
- where the amount of output tax on disposal is less than the total input tax claimed only due to a reduction in the VAT rate;
- where the item is used only for taxable (including zero-rated) purposes throughout the adjustment period (which includes the final disposal).

5.2 Where there is no unjustified tax advantage a business should not apply the disposal test and in such circumstances it is not necessary to apply to Customs & Excise for a specific ruling. A business need only apply the disposal test where it has entered into arrangements for tax mitigation affecting the particular capital item or its disposal. In cases of doubt or difficulty businesses should contact the local VAT office. Examples of where the disposal test should and should not be applied are set out in the annex.

5.3 Where there is an unjustified tax advantage businesses will need to work out the amount of tax to be adjusted. To do this, they will need to calculate the net tax advantage and then work out how much of the net tax advantage is unjustified. The net tax advantage is the overall benefit derived from the avoidance device. Normally the benefit is that the owner is able to secure the amount of input tax that would still be subject to adjustment under the scheme, were it not for the sale of the capital item. In order to achieve this benefit a taxable supply is made. The net tax advantage would therefore be the amount of input tax secured by the sale less any output tax due on the sale. Some form of apportionment needs to be applied to work out how much of the net tax advantage is unjustified.

Normally this could be achieved by using the ratio that the value of the final taxable sale bears to the value of both the exempt supply and the final taxable sale (see example 4 in the annex).

5.4 If Customs & Excise consider that the disposal of a capital item has resulted in an unjustified tax advantage to the owner the provision will be vigorously enforced. Implementation of the provision is to be closely monitored. For the next two years, where the provision is enforced and a business requests a review of that decision, any review will be carried out by the Partial Exemption Branch, Commercial Division, VAT Policy Directorate.

5.5 This Statement of Practice may be changed or disapplied if used for the purposes of avoidance of tax.

ANNEX 1—EXAMPLES

Example 1

A business acquires the freehold of a newly constructed commercial property for £2 million plus VAT on 1 June 1995. The business immediately occupies the building for its own business purposes. The business is partly exempt with a recovery rate of 50 per cent and is therefore only able to deduct half of the input tax incurred under the normal partial exemption rules.

The business continues to use the building for taxable and exempt purposes for the remainder of the tax year ending on 30 April 1996 (the end of the first interval) and for the following tax year (the second interval) there is a small capital goods scheme adjustment made in respect of the second interval because the overall recovery rate increases.

During the third interval, on 1 August 1997, the business disposes of the property by way of a taxable supply (sold within three years of completion of the construction of the building) for £2 million plus VAT. As a consequence the business is required to carry out a final adjustment and is able to deduct 7/10ths of the input tax previously restricted. The disposal test does not affect the recovery of the 7/10ths because the output tax on disposal is greater than the input tax claimed in the adjustment period.

Example 2

A business completes the construction of a £20 million office block, the whole cost of which had borne VAT, on 1 June 1995 and immediately occupies the building for its own business purposes. The business is partly exempt with a recovery rate of 50 per cent and is therefore only able to deduct half of the input tax incurred.

The business continues to use the building for taxable and exempt purposes for the remainder of the tax year ending on 30 April 1996 (the end of the first interval) and for the following tax year (the second interval). There is a small capital goods scheme adjustment made in respect of the second interval because the overall recovery rate increased.

During the third interval, on 1 August 1997, following a downturn in property prices, the business disposes of the property by way of a taxable supply (sold within three years of completion of construction of the building) for its open market value of £16 million plus VAT. As a consequence the business is required to carry out a final adjustment and is able to deduct 7/10ths of the input tax previously restricted. Since the output tax on disposal is less than the input tax claimed in the adjustment period, the disposal test applies. However, the owner is not required to pay any amount back to Customs & Excise because the building was sold at an open market price and not to obtain an unjustified tax advantage.

Example 3

A business acquires the 20 year leasehold interest in an office block for a premium of £10 million plus VAT (the previous owner having opted to tax) on 1 June 1995. The business immediately occupies the building for its own business purposes. The business is partly exempt with a recovery rate of 65 per cent and is therefore only able to deduct that proportion of the input tax incurred.

The business continues to use the building for taxable and exempt purposes for the remainder of the tax year ending on 31 March 1996 (the end of the first interval) and for the following six tax years (the second to the seventh intervals). There are some small capital goods scheme adjustments made in respect of the later intervals because the overall recovery rate increases or decreases as the case may be.

During the eighth interval, on 1 August 2003, following an expansion in their business, the business relocates to new premises and sells the remaining 12 years leasehold interest in the existing office block to a third party as an exempt supply (not having opted) at an open market price. As a consequence the business is required to carry out a final adjustment in respect of the ninth and tenth intervals and pay back 2/10ths of the input tax previously recovered in the first interval. In addition, since the output tax on disposal is less than the input tax claimed in the adjustment period, the disposal test applies. However, the owner is not required to pay any amount back to Customs & Excise because the building was sold at an open market price and there was no attempt to obtain an unjustified tax advantage. The capital goods scheme adjustments have adequately reflected the exempt use to which the property will be put for the remaining two complete intervals.

Example 4

On 1 June 1997 a developer completes a £25 million commercial development, the whole cost of which had borne VAT (£4,375,000). The developer opts to tax the building and leases it out on a two year lease to a third party tenant at a market rent plus VAT. The developer is therefore able to deduct all the input tax incurred on the development under the normal partial exemption rules.

The business continues to let the building on a taxable lease for the remainder of the tax year ending on 31 March 1998 (the end of the first interval) and for the following tax year (the second interval). A capital goods scheme adjustment is therefore not required for the second interval.

On 1 June 1999 (part way through the third interval) the developer grants a 99 year lease at a premium of £24 million and a peppercorn rent to its wholly owned subsidiary. The subsidiary is wholly exempt. FA 1997 s 37 (VATA 1994 Sch 10 para 2(3AA)) operates so as to disapply the developer's option to tax so that the premium is not subject to VAT. At the end of the third interval there is therefore an adjustment in respect of 1/10th (£437,500) of the initial input tax incurred and a proportion of 1/10th (because there was some taxable use in the first part of the third interval) is paid back to Customs & Excise (assuming a recovery rate of 50%—£218,750).

On 1 May 2000 the developer sells the freehold, subject to the 99 year lease for £250,000 plus VAT, to the wholly owned subsidiary (a compulsory taxable supply). The sale effectively ends the fourth interval. Since the building is used for exempt purposes up to the sale there is an adjustment in respect of 1/10th of the initial input tax incurred. It is a full 1/10th that is restricted because the item is only used for exempt purposes up to the disposal of the item.

As a consequence of the low value taxable disposal, since there is no change in the extent of taxable use the business is not required to carry out a final adjustment. But since the output tax on disposal is less than the input tax claimed in the adjustment period, the disposal test applies. In this instance there is an unjustified tax advantage because the high value exempt grant in the third interval enables a low value taxable sale of the freehold. At the same time the taxable sale enables full recovery of input tax in respect of the remaining six intervals (the fifth to the tenth) while only 1/10th of the input tax is restricted (in the fourth interval) to reflect the exempt grant—

Interval	*Input tax claim*	*Output tax declared*	*Difference*
1–10	(4,375,000)		4,375,000
2–10			4,375,000
3–10	(218,750)		4,156,250
4–10	(437,500)	(43,750)	3,762,500
5–10			3,762,500

In principle £3,762,500 would be due. But the net tax advantage is that the owner is able to secure the amount of input tax that would still be subject to adjustment under the scheme (intervals 5–10), were it not for the sale of the capital item and in order to achieve this benefit a taxable supply is made.

The amount of input tax involved is 6/10ths of £4,375,000–£2,625,000. The amount of output tax involved is £43,750. The net tax advantage is therefore £2,581,250.

Some form of fair and reasonable apportionment needs to be applied to work out how much of the net tax advantage is unjustified. This could be achieved by using the ratio that the value of the final taxable sale bears to the value of both the exempt supply and the final taxable sale—

$$\frac{250,000}{24,250,000} \text{ or } \frac{1}{97} £\,2,581,250 = £\,26,611 \text{ taxable use}$$

$$£2,554,639 \text{ exempt use.}$$

Thus, in practice the disposal test would be applied, but the amount due to Customs & Excise would be the value of the unjustified tax advantage—£2,554,639.

...

22 December 1997. Business Brief 31/97

Refusing applications for group treatment to protect the revenue

Corporate bodies which are under common control and meet certain other conditions (such as residence and established place of business) are eligible to be treated as a group for VAT purposes (under VATA 1994 s 43). However, we can, and do, refuse applications for group treatment where we consider that it is necessary to do so for the protection of the revenue.

A few recent cases where we have refused applications for VAT group treatment have shown that there is some confusion over the circumstances in which these powers may be invoked. This announcement does not represent any change in policy but is intended to clarify our position and remove any grounds for misunderstanding.

POLICY ON REFUSING APPLICATIONS

Applications for VAT group treatment (whether they are to form a new group, to change the composition of an existing group or to change the representative member) may be refused for the protection of the revenue where that treatment would put at risk our ability to collect the revenue or where it would lead to a significant tax advantage, either for the group itself or for its suppliers or customers. We make a judgment on whether there is a significant tax advantage on the facts of each case, taking into consideration the scheme of VAT as a whole.

However, as a general guide, applications for group treatment may be refused where proposed group members have a poor compliance record which might pose a threat to our ability to collect the revenue (for example, where they have consistently failed to pay VAT debts).

They may also be refused if we have reason to believe that the applicants intend to use the grouping facility in order to operate a VAT avoidance scheme.

Applications are also refused where group treatment would create a distortion in the VAT liability of the group's supplies. For example, where grouping would lead to exempt supplies becoming taxable with a consequent increase in entitlement to recovery of input tax; or it would lead to a significant revenue loss. For example where the group's entitlement to recover previously irrecoverable input tax is increased; the irrecoverable input tax that the group incurs is reduced; or revenue loss results from a reduction of the group's liability to output tax.

These are only broad examples of situations where our revenue protection powers can be used and this should not be taken as an exhaustive list.

For further information on VAT group treatment in general traders and their advisers should obtain VAT Notice 700/2 ("Registration for VAT—group treatment") from their local VAT business advice centre listed under Customs & Excise in the telephone book.

7 January 1998. Business Brief 1/98

VAT changes to fleet leasing bonuses

This business brief explains a change in Customs & Excise's approach to the treatment of "fleet leasing bonus" payments—also known as fleet support payments.

BACKGROUND

A "fleet leasing bonus" is a payment made by a car manufacturer or dealer to a business who has leased a number of vehicles previously sold by the manufacturer or dealer to intermediaries. In the past it has been common practice to treat the bonus payment as the consideration for a supply of services by the customer, so VAT was due from the customer on this supply.

REVISED POSITION

Following the European Court of Justice judgment in Elida Gibbs, which established that discounts can be given by a supplier for his goods to someone other than his direct customer, we now accept that fleet leasing bonus payments will normally be treated as discounts. This interpretation follows that applied to bonus payments given by car manufacturers to businesses that buy fleets, detailed in Business Brief 16/97.

This change means that businesses that have received such payments will, in many cases, have overpaid VAT. Treating the payment as a discount rather than as the consideration for a supply of services will mean that no output tax can be due from the customer. However, as a discount the payment will also reduce the input tax recovered by the customer (if any) on the lease payments. For example where 50 per cent of the VAT incurred on the lease payments has been recovered, the bonus payment will reduce the VAT originally claimed by 7/47 × (50% × gross bonus payment).

If businesses believe that they have overpaid VAT in the past three years they should contact their local VAT business advice centre listed under Customs & Excise in the telephone book.

7 January 1998. Business Brief 1/98

Installation or assembly of imported goods

Customs & Excise confirm that the place of supply concession which allows one-off supplies of installed or assembled goods in the UK to be treated as made outside the UK continues to operate.

The concession applies only where the supplier is not registered for VAT in the UK and the supply is a one off with no further UK business anticipated. In addition the goods must be imported into the UK from outside the EC, the customer must act as the importer of the goods and the full value including installation and assembly costs must be shown on the import entry.

VAT due will be collected at import thus avoiding the need for the supplier to register for VAT in respect of a one off supply.

Further information may be obtained from Bob Gilligan, Place of Supply Branch, 4th Floor East, New King's Beam House, 22 Upper Ground, London. Telephone number 0171 865 5397.

Commentary—*De Voil Indirect Tax Service* **V3.381**.

21 May 1998. Business Brief 12/98

VAT place of supply rules change for veterinary services

This business brief explains the place of supply rules for supplies of veterinary services which are to be changed with effect from 1 June 1998.

BACKGROUND

Previously, veterinary services were supplied where they were performed. Therefore, if a UK veterinary surgeon supplied services to a French customer which were physically performed in Germany, the place of supply would have been Germany, and the supply would have been taxable there. However, the European Court of Justice (ECJ) has now ruled that veterinary services are supplied where the supplier belongs.

THE CHANGES

From 1 June 1998 the place of supply for veterinary services will be where the supplier belongs. Supplies of veterinary services by persons belonging in the UK are supplied in the UK and the UK VAT is due, subject to the normal registration rules.

Thus, a UK veterinary surgeon providing veterinary services to a French customer, which are physically performed in Germany, will be making supplies in the UK and UK VAT is due.

...

Commentary—*De Voil Indirect Tax Service* **V3.183**.

21 May 1998. Business Brief 12/98

Overseas businesses established in the UK through agencies

This business brief explains the implications of decisions by the European Court of Justice (ECJ) in the case of *DFDS A/S* (C-260/95) ([1997] STC 384) and the High Court in *Chinese Channel* (*Hong Kong*) *Ltd* (CCHK) ([1998] STC 347) for businesses established overseas which carry on business in the UK through agencies.

BACKGROUND

Business Brief 26/96 outlined the case of *WH Payne & Co* ([1995] V & DR 490). The Tribunal commented that treating a person who carries on a business in a country through a branch or agency as having an establishment in that country (VATA 1994 s 9(5)(*a*)) was inconsistent with the EC Sixth VAT Directive (art 9). The Brief explained that Customs & Excise did not agree that the UK's "branch or agency" provisions were inconsistent with EC law. Customs & Excise would, therefore, continue to regard companies established overseas, which carried on a business through a branch or agency in the UK, as having a fixed establishment in the UK.

The subsequent case of CCHK looked at whether broadcasting services were supplied from its business establishment in Hong Kong or from a fixed establishment created by the agency of an associated company in the UK, Chinese Channel (UK) Ltd (CCUK). In finding that the supplies were made from Hong Kong, the Tribunal again cast doubt on the consistency of UK law (VATA 1994 s 9(5)(*a*)) with EC legislation (art 9) and held that "agency" could not extend to a separate company. Customs & Excise appealed to the High Court.

In the interim, the ECJ delivered its judgment in the case of *DFDS A/S*. The issue was whether a tour operator whose business was established in Denmark was supplying its services from a fixed establishment in the UK created by the agency of its UK subsidiary company (Sixth VAT Directive (art 26)).

COURT DECISIONS

In *DFDS A/S*, the ECJ stated that in determining whether DFDS A/S was established in the UK, it was necessary to ascertain whether or not the UK company, DFDS Ltd, was independent. The fact that DFDS Ltd was a separate legal entity with its own offices was insufficient to demonstrate independence. The ECJ found that there were several factors which showed DFDS Ltd was a mere auxiliary organ of its parent. In particular, DFDS Ltd was wholly owned by its parent and had various contractual obligations imposed upon it. The ECJ held that DFDS Ltd was of the requisite minimum size in terms of its human and technical resources to provide the services, especially in view of the large number of employees and the terms under which it provided services to customers. It concluded that DFDS A/S had a fixed establishment in the UK from which the services were provided.

In *Chinese Channel*, the High Court relied upon the direct effect of the Sixth Directive in interpreting domestic law. It found that the Tribunal's struggle to find consistency between EC law (art 9(1) of the Sixth VAT Directive) and UK law (VATA 1994 s 9(5)(*a*)) was unnecessary and relied upon the ECJ's decision in *DFDS A/S*. The High Court held that because the establishment rules in the Sixth Directive's arts 9 and 26 were similar, DFDS A/S had application to services generally. The High Court said that although the typical agency was a subsidiary acting as a mere auxiliary organ of its overseas parent, it was not restricted to that description. The High Court stressed that what mattered was the reality, function and substance, and not any mere label or legal form. It added that since CCUK was an associate of CCHK, bore no financial risk and could not act for CCHK's competitors, the Tribunal might have concluded that CCUK was not independent had it not misdirected itself that its status as a separate legal entity precluded such a finding.

However, the High Court upheld the Tribunal's decision on the facts of the case. Customs & Excise were unable to impugn successfully the Tribunal's conclusion that, having assessed the contribution made by CCHK and CCUK, the service was supplied from Hong Kong. The High Court found that it was not just a matter of comparing the activities of the two establishments. Rather, it was necessary to consider the significance of those activities and the part they played in contributing to the service supplied. It did not follow that because CCUK had employed a far greater number of staff and spent more man hours than CCHK that CCUK made an equal or greater contribution to the service. It held that because most of the programmes originated in Hong Kong and by far the larger part of their broadcasting activity took place there, the Tribunal had been correct to conclude that the supplies had been made from the Hong Kong establishment.

WHEN AN OVERSEAS BUSINESS HAS A UK FIXED ESTABLISHMENT THROUGH AN AGENCY

Customs & Excise consider that these judgments support their existing policy that an agency creates a fixed establishment of its principal. However, these cases enable Customs & Excise to clarify the circumstances in which such agencies are treated as establishments of their principals.

A UK subsidiary or associate of an overseas business or a UK business unrelated to the overseas business is treated as the latter's UK fixed establishment if it meets the following criteria—

(1) it is of a certain minimum size with the permanent human and technical resources necessary for providing (or receiving) services;
(2) it is not, in function and substance, operating independently of the overseas business; and
(3) it actually supplies (or receives) the service.

If you are an overseas business carrying on business in the UK through such an agency, you are treated as having a fixed establishment here. The VAT implications of this are further explained in Notice 741 "VAT—place of supply of services".

When examining a specific case, our officers will have particular regard for the actual arrangements which exist between the prima facie agency and its principal, rather than any mere wording in contracts.

FURTHER ADVICE AND INFORMATION

If you are unsure whether you are making supplies through (or to) such agencies, you should contact your local VAT business advice centre.

Commentary—*De Voil Indirect Tax Service* **V3.221**.

11 September 1998. Business Brief 18/98

Review of the liability of sweetened dried fruit

Customs have completed a review of the VAT liability of sweetened dried fruit and the following areas have been clarified. Sweetened dried fruit sold as suitable for both snacking and home baking can be zero-rated irrespective of bag size.

Sweetened dried fruit sold as confectionery remains standard-rated. Dried fruit that is naturally sweet and has had no sweetening matter added to it remains zero-rated. An Update to VAT Notice 701/14: "Food", is available from local VAT business advice centres listed under Customs & Excise in the telephone directory.

Customs will not seek to recover VAT where a zero-rated ruling was originally given and this has changed to standard-rated as a result of the review, but in such cases the correct liability must be applied from 1 January 1999. Where a standard-rated ruling has changed to zero-rated, repayments will be subject both to capping and unjust enrichment considerations.

Commentary—*De Voil Indirect Tax Service* **V4.221, V4.226**.

15 September 1998. Business Brief 19/98

Local authorities—works in default

In [*Glasgow City Council v C & E Comrs* (1998) VAT Decision 15491 (unreported),] the Edinburgh VAT and Duties Tribunal ruled on the liability of works in default and the subsequent recovery of costs under the Housing (Scotland) Act 1987 ss 108, 109.

This Act requires local authorities in Scotland to serve a repair notice to the owner of a property that they consider is in disrepair. If the owner does not comply with the notice the council is empowered to arrange for the work to be carried out and recover the cost of the work from the owner. The Tribunal decided that, in these specific circumstances there was no supply for VAT purposes by the Council.

The decision only applies to works in default carried out by Scottish local authorities under ss 108, 109 of the Act. However Customs are taking this opportunity to clarify their guidance on the treatment of all types of default works throughout the UK.

VAT LIABILITY OF WORKS IN DEFAULT

Local authorities are empowered, by specific legislative provisions, to issue notices requiring that works are carried out in a number of situations. The recipient of the notice may or may not comply.

When the recipient of the notice agrees to the work being carried out and arranges the work with either a contractor or with the authority then the supply of the contractor's services is to the recipient of the notice. If the authority arranges the contractor's supplies on the recipient's behalf they may treat these supplies as being to the authority and by the authority under VATA 1994 s 47(3).

If the recipient of the notice refuses to comply the authority may exercise its statutory powers, have the work carried out and recover the cost of the works from the recipient. In these circumstances the authority is not making a supply for VAT purposes.

RECOVERY OF VAT

Only when the supply of the works is to the local authority—as in the *Glasgow City Council* case—may it recover the VAT charged by the contractor. Where the authority makes an onward taxable supply in the course or furtherance of business, the VAT incurred will be recoverable as input tax under VATA 1994 s 25. Where the authority does not make a taxable supply but imposes the works under its statutory powers, as described above, VAT recovery will be under VATA 1994 s 33.

…

Commentary—*De Voil Indirect Tax Service* **V5.162, V2.108, V6.153A, V3.125, V3.221, V3.423**.

18 December 1998. Business Brief 26/98

VAT groups and transfers of going concerns (TOGCs)

This Business Brief clarifies Customs' policy on whether there can be a transfer of a property rental business as a going concern where the landlord and the tenant or the purchaser and the tenant are members of the same VAT group.

BACKGROUND

In *C & E Comrs v Kingfisher plc* [1994] STC 19 the High Court found that members of a VAT group are to be considered a single taxable person for VAT purposes. The status of individual members of VAT groups has also been recently considered by the House of Lords in *C & E Comrs v Thorn Materials Supply Ltd and Thorn Resources Ltd* [1998] STC 725 which came to the same conclusion. A question raised by those decisions is whether there can be a TOGC when the sole business activity constitutes supplies from one group member to another. With property rental between group members, if the rental supply is disregarded under VATA 1994 s 43(1)(*a*), it is simply as though the taxable person (the group) is occupying the property itself. Therefore, where a group member landlord sells a property which is tenanted by another group member, it is doubtful that a business exists which is making relevant supplies capable of transfer as a going concern. Conversely, where a landlord sells a property which is tenanted by a company that is a member of the new landlord's VAT group, the business ceases after the transfer because the tenant and the new landlord effectively become one taxable person.

Customs policy is as follows.

The following situations will not be considered to be TOGCs—

1 Where the purchaser of the property rental business is a member of the same VAT group as the existing tenant.

2 Where a member of a VAT group sells a property, which is being rented to another member of the group, to a third party.

The following situation will be considered to be a TOGC—

3 Where the tenant who is a member of the landlord's VAT group is only one of a number of tenants. The presence of a tenant or tenants outside the group means that the whole transaction can still be treated as a TOGC.

IMPLEMENTATION DATE

This policy will take effect from 1 January 1999. Transactions prior to this date will not be affected. If transfers of the type described at (1) and (2) take place after 1 January 1999 they can still be treated as TOGCs if a deposit or other part-payment of the purchase price is received by the seller before that date. An amendment will be made to Notice No 700/9.

For further information businesses and their advisors should contact their local VAT business advice centre listed under Customs and Excise in the telephone book.

Commentary—*De Voil Indirect Tax Service* **V2.226**.

13 January 1999. Business Brief 1/99

The Single Currency (the euro)

From 1 January 1999 eleven European countries adopted a single currency (the euro).

Although the UK is not one of the countries joining in the first wave, the introduction of the euro is likely to affect a wide range of UK businesses. This Business Brief explains the impact upon HM Customs & excise's requirements. There are two main issues, paying taxes and duties in euro and accounting and invoicing in euro.

1. PAYING TAXES AND DUTIES IN EURO

UK businesses can now pay Customs & excise taxes and duties (including arrears) in most cashless forms of the euro. Notes and coins will not be introduced until 2002. However, all declarations must continue to be made in sterling, including VAT returns and intrastat declarations.

Exchange Rate Fluctuations

When paying in euro, the exchange rate will fluctuate between the time payment is initiated or sent to Customs & excise and the time it is cleared. Businesses will be credited with the sterling value received by Customs and Excise. The repayment of overpayments to businesses and the payment of underpayments to Customs & Excise will be dealt with using existing debt management practices.

The shorter the delay between the time payment is made and the time it is cleared may help to minimise this fluctuation. Payments will be processed most quickly through the use of CHAPS euro (Clearing House Automated Payment System)-an electronic same day funds transfer system.

BACS direct debit

Most methods of payment can be used to pay in euro. One of the main exceptions is BACS direct debit. Although BACS direct credit is available, banks are not making BACS euro direct debit available at this time. The main impact of this is that importers who wish to use the duty deferment facility, of which one of the requirements is that direct debit be used, must continue to pay in sterling.

Conversion Costs

The costs incurred by Customs & Excise in converting euro tax and duty payments into sterling will not be passed on to businesses and will be borne by the Department.

Repayments

All repayments will continue to be made by Customs & Excise in sterling – the currency of the UK.

2. EURO ACCOUNTING AND INVOICING IN THE UK

Invoicing

Customs & Excise have simplified the current requirements for tax invoices issued in currencies other than sterling, in order to facilitate the euro.

If businesses issue tax invoices in euro the invoice must also show the sterling equivalent of the total net value of goods and services at each rate of VAT and the amount of VAT, if any, at each rate.

These rules are set out in HM Customs & Excise's Public Notice 700, paragraphs 6.3 and 3.1(f) but it is not now necessary to make line by line conversions.

The sterling VAT amount on tax invoices is to be used by both the supplier and the customer for VAT accounting purposes ie suppliers must declare the sterling VAT amounts on their sales invoices as output tax and their customers must use the same amounts for input tax purposes. These are necessary requirements in order to preserve the integrity of the tax. VAT and Duty accounts VAT and duty accounts must continue to be maintained in sterling.

Exchange Rates

There are 3 alternative methods that can be used to convert an amount from euro into sterling on invoices (Public notice 700, paragraph 3.1 (f)):

the UK market selling rate at the time of the supply – rates published in national newspapers are acceptable as evidence of the rates at the relevant time;

the period rate of exchange published by Customs & Excise for customs purposes; or—

you may apply in writing to the VAT Business Advice Centre for your area for the use of a rate or method of determining a rate which you use for commercial purposes but which is not covered by the two alternatives above.

Declarations

All declarations must continue to be made in sterling, including VAT returns and intrastat declarations. The one exception is Box 22 on the Single Administrative Document which is used for imports and exports, where euro values can be used.

24 February 1999. Business Brief 5/99

Ship design services

This Business Brief gives Customs' position regarding ship design services. In June 1995, a tribunal (*Cholerton Ltd v C & E Comrs* (1995) VAT Decision 13387 unreported) held that, in certain circumstances, design services were integral to the modification of a ship, despite the fact that Cholerton did not carry out the modification services. The design services were found to be zero-rated.

At the time, Customs accepted the decision and have since allowed businesses supplying design services in identical circumstances to zero-rate their supplies. However, we have now reviewed our policy. We consider that the tribunal failed to take into account that Cholerton was contracted to supply only design services and therefore made no supply of modification services to which the design services could be integral.

Accordingly, with effect from 1 July 1999, Customs will treat design services supplied in the UK as integral to the supply, modification or conversion of a qualifying ship only where a supplier specifically contracts with a customer to design and supply, modify or convert a qualifying ship. In other circumstances, design services will be standard-rated and deductible, subject to the normal rules.

For further information businesses and their advisors should contact their local VAT business advice centre listed under Customs and Excise in the telephone book.

Commentary—*De Voil Indirect Tax Service* **V4.251**.

31 March 1999. Business Brief 8/99

The three year cap and partial exemption

This Business Brief clarifies Customs' policy about how the three year cap affects businesses' partial exemption position, illustrated by a number of examples.

BACKGROUND

The purpose of the three year cap is to provide certainty and stability for both the Exchequer and the tax payer. The provisions are not intended to have any impact on the normal system of deduction and adjustments to deduction as set out in the VAT Regulations.

Any trader or business currently operating the partial exemption rules correctly will not be affected by the three year cap. This also applies to businesses which discover a mistake and make the necessary correction within the three year time limit. In other words, the three year cap only affects businesses who do not claim the input tax to which they were entitled or claim input tax to which they were not entitled, and fail to correct this within three years.

In addition, if a business fails to make an initial deduction of input tax (or gets the initial deduction wrong) and the error falls in a period which is more than three years old, the error cannot be corrected in the partial exemption annual adjustment even if the adjustment itself is not capped. However, even though the unclaimed amount of input tax cannot be reclaimed because it is capped, the annual adjustment itself should be based on the true amounts of input and output tax.

EXAMPLES

The effects of the three year cap are illustrated in the following examples—

(i) A partly exempt business (makes both exempt and taxable supplies) fails to use a partial exemption method and does not claim any input tax for a number of years. After an audit, the business submits a refund claim, in which the first quarter of the third tax year is "capped" (ie more than three years old) but the annual adjustment period itself is not "capped" (it falls within the three year period). Can the input tax in that period be recovered in the annual adjustment?

No—The trader, by failing to recover input tax in the relevant period, has failed to exercise the right to deduct. The trader is not able to claim this "capped" amount in the annual adjustment.

(ii) A partly exempt business calculates deductible input tax in accordance with his partial exemption method. In the first two quarters he fails the *de minimis* limits and so correctly restricts his exempt input tax. In the second two quarters he is able to benefit from the *de minimis* limits and so correctly recovers all his input tax in those quarters. At the end of the year he is able to benefit from the *de minimis* rules for the year as a whole but does not apply them. If he discovers this mistake within three years from the last day of the annual adjustment quarter is he able to correct it?

Yes—The partly exempt trader has correctly applied the *de minimis* rules to each quarter. Since it is at the time of the annual adjustment that the *de minimis* rules are applied to all the input tax incurred in the previous four quarters, it is at that time that any exempt input tax previously restricted may be recovered.

However, where a trader was entitled to apply the *de minimis* rules to a particular period but did not do so, and that period was "capped", any affected input tax falling in that period may not be recovered in the final *de minimis* calculation at the time of the annual adjustment (which itself is not "capped"). This is because the trader failed to exercise the right to deduct within the three year period.

(iii) A business with an agreed partial exemption method mistakenly treats taxable input tax as exempt. Can this input tax be recovered at the time of the annual adjustment if the input tax is proper to a period which is "capped" (but the annual adjustment is not "capped")?

No—We would not allow the trader to recover the exempt input tax at the time of the annual adjustment. The trader has mistakenly treated taxable input tax as exempt, and so he has failed to recover it.

Similarly, if the trader had incorrectly claimed exempt input tax and the input tax was proper to a period which was "capped", we would be unable to recover it under the assessment provisions in that period or the period of the annual adjustment (even if it was not "capped").

Customs are aware that, because of the complexity of the three year cap, we have agreed some claims and settled them as if the annual adjustment can be used to override the cap, effectively giving some claimants a repayment to which they were not entitled. We do not propose to revisit any of these claims, but all future claims will be treated on a proper basis.

…

Commentary—*De Voil Indirect Tax Service* **V3.405, V3.461–V3.466.**
Regulations—See VAT Regulations, SI 1995/2518 regs 99–111 (regulations made under VATA 1994 s 26(3)).
Cross references—See VATA 1994 s 26(3) (for powers to make regulations for securing a fair and reasonable attribution of input tax).
See also the VAT Regulations, SI 1995/2518 regs 29(1A), 34(1A) (time limit for claiming repayments).

21 April 1999. Business Brief 9/99

Contracting out of vehicle removal/recovery by police authorities—treatment of statutory fees retained by contractors

The purpose of this business brief is to clarify the VAT treatment of statutory fees collected and retained by contractors who provide motor vehicle recovery services to police authorities.

Police forces have powers in various circumstances to remove and, where appropriate, store vehicles. Any associated statutory fees are outside the scope of VAT when levied by the police on the motorist or owner of the vehicle. However, the task of removing vehicles is now commonly contracted out by police authorities. These arrangements often include collection of fees by the contractors on behalf of the police. Where this occurs, the fees paid to the contractor are not consideration for any supply by the contractors to the motorist or vehicle owner, and are outside the scope of VAT.

However, under their agreements with the police authority or with an intermediary management company acting on behalf of the police authority, contractors may be entitled to retain some or all of the amounts which they have collected. Where this occurs the retained amount represents consideration for a supply of recovery services by the contractors to the police authority, and is liable to VAT at the standard rate. As well as accounting for VAT, the contractor should issue a VAT invoice to the police authority, who are entitled to recover the VAT charged subject to the normal rules.

ACTION FOR BUSINESSES

Customs have become increasingly aware that the VAT treatment of the retained fees is inconsistent, and that tax is not being accounted for properly in some cases. Therefore, any contractors engaged in vehicle recovery on behalf of a police authority should review their accounting procedures with the authority. Where VAT is not being accounted for in the manner set out above, arrangements should now be put in place for the future. In order to allow contractors time to re-organise their existing procedures, implementation of the correct VAT treatment is to take effect from 1 August 1999.

...

Commentary—*De Voil Indirect Tax Service* **V3.103**.

22 April 1999. Business Brief, 10/99

Tour operators' margin scheme (TOMS)

This business brief explains Customs' position in light of the ECJ decision in *C & E Comrs v Madgett & Baldwin t/a Howden Court Hotel* [[1998] STC 1189]. The hotel, in Torquay, supplies inclusive packages to tourists from the north of England. The packages comprise coach transport between the hotel and customers' home towns, a stay at the hotel for several days and coach excursions. The coach transport is bought-in by the hotel.

DEFINITION OF TOUR OPERATOR

The first issue before the ECJ was to determine whether the hotel's activities were those of a tour operator and therefore subject to VAT under the TOMS. The Court supported Customs' policy that the TOMS applies in principle to anyone who buys in and resells services for the direct benefit of a traveller, but added two new criteria to Customs' definition. The first was that the travel services must be bought in and resold "habitually". The second was that bought-in travel services which take up a small proportion of the package price are "ancillary" in relation to the main supply and would not justify a supplier being regarded as a tour operator. The Court's example of "ancillary" was a taxi ride between a hotel and a local railway station.

APPORTIONMENT OF PACKAGES WHICH INCLUDE IN-HOUSE SUPPLIES

The second issue before the ECJ related to the method of determining the value of the in-house element of the packages. In Madgett & Baldwin's case, the VAT on the margin of the bought-in element was the same whichever method was used. The Court held that, bearing this in mind, the operator was entitled to use a method based on the market value of the in-house supplies when the cost-based calculation required complex sub-apportionment exercises, and when it was possible to identify the in-house element of the package by a market value-based method.

THE WAY FORWARD

Customs see the decision as being primarily about simplification, rather than the amount of VAT paid by tour operators, and consider that the cost-based apportionment set out in Notice No 709/5 "Tour operators' margin scheme" remains a valid method of valuing in-house supplies. Customs intend to use the decision to simplify the TOMS and reduce the number of traders affected by it and will be consulting with the industry and other interested parties. A technical discussion document will be issued in May, exploring practical issues such as the interpretation and application of the terms "habitually", "ancillary" and "market value". Customs envisage this period of consultation running through to the autumn, with appropriate changes to the TOMS being made in due course.

The timing of these changes (and so any revision of Notice No 709/5) is uncertain at this stage, but they are unlikely to be implemented before April 2000. In the meantime, traders should continue to use the TOMS as set out in Notice No 709/5. Subject to capping, any changes which are beneficial to traders may be applied retrospectively. To protect themselves against the effects of capping, traders who consider that they have "overpaid" VAT may lodge a claim with their VAT business advice centre before changes are implemented.

Commentary—*De Voil Indirect Tax Service* **V3.591–593**.

22 April 1999. Business Brief 10/99

Passenger transport services which include catering

This business brief explains Customs' position following the *Sea Containers* case which considered the VAT position of passenger transport supplied with catering on a railway train. There were a number of different types of supply all of which included in-house catering which was promoted as high quality in advertising material. The supplies included—

- charter of the whole train plus crew, with separately negotiated catering;
- charter of the whole train plus crew, with catering included in a single price;
- round trips sold to individual passengers which included high quality catering, such as five course meals and champagne lunches; and

– a stopping trip sold to individual passengers who could alight before the return journey, again including catering.

The issue for the tribunal was whether there were single supplies of zero-rated passenger transport, or separate supplies of transport and standard-rated catering. The tribunal found that in each case there were separate supplies.

Customs consider that this decision, in conjunction with the remarks of the European Court of Justice on single and multiple supplies in another recent case (*Card Protection Plan v C & E Comrs* (Case C–349/96)[1999] STC 270 confirms their current policy. Where an element of catering is included with scheduled passenger transport for no extra charge (such as a meal included in the price of an airline ticket) there is a single supply of passenger transport. Where catering, or other elements such as discos, receptions etc are included as a feature of leisure travel, there are separate supplies, and the catering and other extras are taxable at the standard rate.

…

Commentary—*De Voil Indirect Tax Service* **V3.105, V4.227, 251.**

17 November 1999. Business Brief 23/99

VAT appeals

BACKGROUND

This Business Brief sets out Customs' position on applications for "strike out" and dismissal of appeals following the tribunal's decision in the P W Coleman case [*P W Coleman v C & E Comrs* (1999) VAT Decision 15906, see *Simon's Weekly Tax Intelligence* 1999 p 870]. Customs can apply for an appeal not to proceed to a full hearing (a "strike out" or dismissal) if certain conditions have not been met by the appellants. *P W Coleman* was the lead case in an applications hearing involving four appellants which looked at these conditions.

THE TRIBUNAL'S DECISION

The tribunal found some pre-appeal conditions in VAT law to be acceptable—the requirement for tax in dispute to be paid—allowing an appeal against an assessment to proceed only if the return has been rendered for the period assessed.

The first condition is acceptable because it contains a hardship provision and Customs' decision on that is reviewable by the tribunal. The second condition is proportionate and complementary to the VAT system as it ensures that a return has been rendered for a period subject to a disputed assessment.

However, the tribunal found the condition that all returns and payments have to be up to date before an appeal can be entertained denies access to the tribunal and goes beyond proportionality. The tribunal decided that the appellants had directly enforceable Community Rights to have their appeals heard by a tribunal stemming from Directive 77/388/EEC, which overrode the relevant conditions of VATA 1994.

CUSTOMS' POSITION

Customs have decided not to appeal against the tribunal's decision. Customs are considering whether to suggest an amendment to the pre-conditions which caused the tribunal concern. In the meantime Customs will not apply for appeals to be struck out solely because returns and payments are outstanding for VAT periods not under dispute. However, Customs will continue to make applications for strike out or dismissal in appropriate cases where a return has not been rendered for a VAT period subject to a disputed assessment, or where the tax in dispute has not been paid. A similar line will be taken for appeals concerning insurance premium tax and landfill tax.

Commentary—*De Voil Indirect Tax Service* **V5.421, 422.**

22 December 1999. Business Brief 28/99

Treatment of EC grant aid for the processing of dried fodder

The purpose of this business brief is to notify a change to the VAT treatment of EC grants paid by the Intervention Board to processors of dried animal fodder.

DETAILS OF CHANGE

Until now the UK has not treated such payments as consideration for supplies by processors, but has regarded them as outside the scope of VAT. However, following an approach by the

European Commission, the UK has agreed that these particular payments will be treated as falling within the scope of the tax. This does not involve a change in UK policy in relation to other EC grants.

ACTION FOR DRIED FODDER PROCESSORS

Since supplies of animal fodder are zero-rated no VAT is due on these grants. But processors who supply dried fodder must include the value of grants received in the total value of sales in box 6 of their VAT returns. This also applies to grants received where a business processes the grass of a third party and returns it to them after drying (although Customs understand that this does not happen at present in the UK). However, where the grants relate to fodder for the processors' own use, there is no supply by the processor for VAT purposes, and grants should continue to be treated as outside the scope of VAT. This change will take effect from 1 January 2000.

FURTHER ADVICE

For further advice and information, processors and their advisers should contact their local VAT office, listed under Customs & Excise in the telephone book.

Commentary—*De Voil Indirect Tax Service* **V4.221** (Zero-rating: animal feeding stuffs).

22 February 2000. Business Brief 3/00

Imported works of art, antiques and collectors' items

With the change in the rate of import VAT on works of art, antiques and collectors' items in July 1999 [see Customs & Excise news release dated 2 July 1999, *Simon's Weekly Tax Intelligence* 1999 p 1156], an anti-avoidance measure was introduced to prevent the artificial movement of such items by people seeking to gain a tax advantage from the reduced rate of import VAT. This means that only qualifying imported goods, which have not been exported from the UK in the previous 12 months, are eligible for the 5% effective reduced rate of import VAT.

In practice, however, works of art and similar goods are sent outside the UK for various legitimate commercial reasons, and often return within 12 months. For instance, goods may be sent for exhibition, prior to auction in the UK, or sent on a sale or return basis and returned unsold. The anti-avoidance provision was not intended to disrupt businesses engaged legitimately in such activities and, in many cases, there are specific reliefs which override the "12 month" rule.

GOODS HELD IN TEMPORARY IMPORTATION (TI) ARRANGEMENTS

Goods which are held under a TI regime are not regarded, for VAT purposes, as having been "imported" into the UK. For VAT, goods are not treated as imported until the customs duty debt is incurred (for instance, on removal from TI to home use). Consequently, goods which are removed from TI and sent outside the EU are not considered to have been exported for VAT purposes, and therefore will not be caught by the "12 month" rule. This covers, for example, goods held under TI, intended for sale by auction in the UK, but sent to third countries for exhibition prior to auction.

GOODS NOT HELD IN TI ARRANGEMENTS

For goods sent outside the member states "on approval", or for goods exported for sale by auction, but which fail to sell and have to be returned to the UK within 12 months, "returned goods relief" may apply. Value Added Tax Regulations, SI 1995/2518 reg 125 allows such goods to be relieved from VAT at importation where they remain the property of the taxable person who exported them. Provided all the conditions of the relief are satisfied such goods qualify for full relief from VAT on importation, and will not be affected by the "12 month" rule.

For goods exported from the UK for repair or restoration work and returned to the UK within 12 months, "outward processing relief" may apply. Value Added Tax Regulations, SI 1995/2518 reg 126 allows the original value of the goods (ie the value at export) to be relieved from VAT at importation, where they have been sent outside the EU for process or repair and are subsequently returned without a change of ownership. Provided all the conditions of the relief are satisfied such goods will not be affected by the "12 month" rule. However, VAT at the standard rate is due on the price charged for the repair or restoration.

For goods which are exported from the EU, sold, and imported back into the UK within 12 months, there are no VAT reliefs available. Consequently they will normally attract VAT at 17.5% on importation. However, Customs have agreed that, if goods were exported from the UK prior to the introduction of the new rules on 28 July 1999, businesses should not be disadvantaged. Where businesses would not have known about the "12 month" rule at the time of exportation, then, where appropriate, goods will still qualify for import VAT at the 5% rate, following importation into the UK within the 12 month limit.

17 March 2000. Business Brief 4/00

VAT and cemeteries

This business brief explains Customs' position following the tribunal decision in *Rhondda Cynon Taff County Borough Council* [(1999) VAT Decision 16496 unreported].

BACKGROUND

Since the inception of VAT local authorities have been able to recover the tax incurred in making insignificant exempt supplies under what is now VATA 1994, s 33. In this particular case the appellant argued that the provision and maintenance of cemeteries by local authorities, which Customs has always treated as exempt business activity, was non-business. As a result tax incurred by them in making such supplies did not count for partial exemption purposes and could be recovered as non-business under s 33. The tribunal agreed and concluded that the provision and maintenance of cemeteries by a local authority was not a business activity for VAT purposes, as it had been carried out by them under a special legal regime applicable to public authorities. In reaching this decision the tribunal considered the detailed legal structures which apply to local authorities who operate cemeteries. It also concluded that as there are so few privately owned cemeteries the non-business ruling would not distort competition.

NEW POSITION

Customs has concluded that the decision only applies to the provision and maintenance of local authority operated cemeteries. This includes the grant of a right to an exclusive burial, the right to place and maintain a tombstone, the keeping and storage of the plans and records of burials, general maintenance, and any actions intended to remove dangerous obstructions, e.g collapsed vaults or broken headstones.

Local authority cemeteries may also offer further services, such as the provision of books of remembrance and the erection of headstones for which a charge is made. As the provision of these services is not covered by the special legal regime applicable to cemeteries, they remain business activities of the local authority.

CREMATORIA

Some local authorities also provide crematoria. While crematoria are governed by special legal provisions, similar to those which apply to cemeteries, the higher incidence of privately owned crematoria means that a distortion of competition would result if local authorities were allowed to treat these activities as non-business. Where local authorities operate sites which contain both cemeteries and crematoria and they have exceeded the partial exemption *de minimis* limits, a business/non-business apportionment will have be made between the activities.

For further advice and information, please contact your local business advice centre, listed under Customs and Excise in the telephone directory.

Commentary—*De Voil Indirect Tax Service* **V5.162**.

11 April 2000. Business Brief 6/00

Debt enforcement services provided by Under Sheriffs and Sheriffs' Officers

This business brief explains changes with effect from 1 April 2000 to the VAT treatment of services provided by Under Sheriffs and Sheriffs' Officers in enforcing judgment debts.

BACKGROUND

Customs previously regarded services provided by Under Sheriffs and Sheriffs' Officers in enforcing High Court judgment debts and those of the County Court transferred to the High Court for enforcement as supplies to the High Sheriffs. As the High Sheriffs are not in business for VAT purposes, the tax on these services was not recoverable by them.

NEW VAT TREATMENT

Following an approach by the Under Sheriffs Association, and with the agreement of the Sheriffs' Officers' Association, Customs are now prepared to treat these debt enforcement services as supplies by Under Sheriffs to creditors. This means that, from 1 April 2000, where such creditors are registered for VAT, they will be able to recover tax charged by Under Sheriffs and Sheriffs' Officers, subject to the normal rules.

Therefore, while Under Sheriffs and Sheriffs' Officers may collect fees for their enforcement services from debtors, they should issue VAT invoices only to creditors in all cases. Any documents issued to debtors should make it clear that they are not VAT invoices.

For further information traders should contact their local Customs & Excise business advice centre listed under Customs & Excise in the telephone book.

Commentary—*De Voil Indirect Tax Service* **V5.173** (Enforcement: distress and diligence) and **V3.401** (Relief for tax chargeable, paid or payable.)

18 May 2000. Business Brief 7/00

VAT treatment of vehicle clamping and tow-away fees

This business brief clarifies the VAT treatment of vehicle clamping and tow-away fees, in particular, where they are retained by parking enforcement contractors.

BACKGROUND

Parking enforcement contractors are increasingly used by landowners to enforce parking restrictions on their premises. Vehicles found to be parked without authority are normally clamped or towed away. To secure the release of the vehicle, the owner must pay a fee to the contractor.

In collecting this fee, the contractor is acting as an agent for the landowner. At that point, the fee represents damages or compensation for the trespass suffered by the landowner. The fee is outside the scope of VAT so far as the landowner is concerned, and VAT should not be included in the fee charged to vehicle owners.

VAT TREATMENT OF CONTRACTORS' FEES

However, under the terms of the agreement with the landowner, it is normal practice for the contractor to be paid by retaining all or some of the amounts collected in fees. Where this happens, the amount retained represents consideration for the taxable supply of parking enforcement services by the contractor to the landowner.

The contractor must account for VAT on this amount at the standard rate and, where necessary, issue a VAT invoice to the landowner. VAT will also be due on any additional management charge to the landowner.

For further advice and information traders and their advisers should contact their local VAT office, listed under Customs & Excise in the telephone directory.

Commentary—*De Voil Indirect Tax Service* **V3.102** (Meaning of "supply"); **V3.103** (Meaning of "consideration").

28 September 2000. Business Brief 13/00

Bloodstock—sale of additional nominations by stallion syndicates

This business brief explains changes to the VAT treatment of additional nominations sold by stallion syndicates. The changes will take effect from 1 November 2000.

BACKGROUND

When a colt is to become a stallion standing at stud, it is often syndicated, usually into 40 shares. Each share entitles its owner to one nomination. This lets the owner nominate one mare to be covered by the stallion each breeding season. Each syndicate appoints a secretary, usually a bloodstock agency or a firm of solicitors, to deal with its financial and practical arrangements.

Until recently any additional nominations over and above the initial 40 have been sold through the secretary and the income has been distributed to the members. As the sums involved were low and likely to be below the VAT registration threshold, Customs accepted that these supplies could be treated as not subject to VAT. However, as stallions are now managing up to 100 coverings in a season, this VAT treatment is no longer appropriate.

NEW VAT TREATMENT

From 1 November 2000 the sale of additional stallion nominations will be treated as supplies in the course of business by the syndicates, which will render them liable to VAT registration. However, the bloodstock industry has said that the syndicates do not wish to be registered as partnerships. Customs are therefore prepared to treat syndicate secretaries as agents acting in their own names, but on behalf of the syndicates.

The accounting arrangements which follow have been discussed and agreed with the British Horseracing Board.

Secretaries will raise an invoice in their own name when the supply of an additional nomination is made. Where a secretary's turnover exceeds or is expected to exceed the current VAT registration threshold, the invoice should bear the secretary's own VAT registration number. It should be for the full value of the nomination plus VAT.

When secretaries pass money on to the syndicate members, the members will raise an invoice to the secretary for their share. This will be an invoice bearing the appropriate VAT if the member is registered. Any VAT charged may be treated as input VAT by the secretary.

Any money passed to members will count towards the calculation of their taxable turnover for VAT registration purposes.

The tax point for the supply by the member to the secretary will be the same as that of the supply by the secretary to the purchaser of the nomination.

The stud farm will raise a VAT invoice to the secretary for the keep of the stallion and the secretary will raise a VAT invoice to the stud for the nominations given in return for the keep.

Any input tax incurred by the secretary on behalf of the syndicate may be recovered by the secretary. The secretary will pass these charges on in full to the members of the syndicate and raise a VAT invoice charging output tax on the onward supply.

Where a syndicate does not wish to use these arrangements, it will be required to register for VAT in its own right if its turnover exceeds or is expected to exceed the current VAT registration threshold.

For further information, traders and their advisers should contact their local VAT office, listed under Customs & Excise in the telephone directory.

Commentary—*De Voil Indirect Tax Service* **V6.114** (Bloodstock: syndicates).

20 February 2001. Business Brief 3/01

Court of Appeal decision rules pension review services are VAT exempt

The Court of Appeal has ruled in the case of *Century Life plc* [[2001] STC 38] that the company's pension review services are exempt from VAT, because they are insurance related services provided by insurance agents. The supplies at issue were pension review services, carried out as a result of the Financial Services Authority (FSA)-inspired review of possible pension mis-selling. Customs have decided not to seek leave to appeal to the House of Lords. This business brief explains the implications of the judgment for businesses which think they might be affected.

THE JUDGMENT

Before this judgment, Customs' view was that Century Life merely assisted an insurer, in this case Lincoln Assurance Limited, to comply with the regulatory requirements of the FSA. As a result, Customs believed that these services were not covered by the exemption as Century Life were not introducing or administering insurance contracts.

The Court said that Century Life's services were "intimately related to" insurance policies and that there was "a close nexus" between them and the insurance transaction concerned. And since Customs had accepted that the day to day business of Century Life could properly be characterised as that of "insurance agent", the Court judged the services in question to be exempt.

Since pension review services of the kind performed by Century Life have been ruled to be sufficiently closely "related to insurance", it follows that they are exempt when the "Century Life criteria" are met. However, the judgment does not necessarily apply to other services which are outsourced by insurers to insurance brokers or agents. Each case must be treated on its merits.

THE "CENTURY LIFE CRITERIA"

When someone reviews an insurer's personal pension policies for mis-selling, and during the course of this acts as an insurance broker or agent, having contact with insured persons on behalf of insurers, Customs will accept that the exemption applies to them.

If you think that your business meets these criteria, but you have already accounted for VAT on such services, you can make an adjustment to your VAT accounts as set out in Customs' Notice 700/45 "How to correct errors and make adjustments or claims" para 1.5. Alternatively, you can make a claim for repayment of the VAT taking into account any overclaimed input tax. Such claims will be paid subject to the conditions set out below—

- you must be able to produce suitable evidence that your case exactly fits the "Century Life criteria";
- you must be able to substantiate the amount claimed;
- you will need to look back at earlier attributions of input tax (any input tax incurred on goods and services used exclusively for these pension review services is now attributable to an exempt supply), substituting exempt values for taxable values in your partial exemption calculation and deducting the resulting "exempt input tax" from overpaid output tax in determining the amount of the claim.

Adjustments and refunds are subject to capping after three years.

If Customs can show that you effectively did not bear the burden of the tax, they may reject the claim on the grounds that it would unjustly enrich you. For example, this may have happened because you passed the tax on to someone else without losing profit by doing so, and are unable, or don't intend, to pass on the repayment.

A notification to Customs that you intend making a claim in the future is not a valid claim.

If you have been charged VAT by businesses whose supplies were exempt as a result of this decision, you cannot treat it as your input tax. You will need to make an adjustment to your VAT account to reverse any overclaimed input tax.

FURTHER INFORMATION

Further information can be found in Notice 700/45, entitled "How to correct VAT errors or make adjustments or claims". Businesses and their advisers can also contact their local VAT business advice centre, listed under Customs & Excise in the telephone directory.

Commentary—*De Voil Indirect Tax Service* **V3.221** (Supplies by and through agents).

2 July 2001. Business Brief 8/01

Opting to tax buildings to be converted to dwellings

This business brief is about how Customs & Excise will implement a Tribunal decision on how the option to tax buildings applies to buildings, those which will be converted into dwellings (the VAT Duties Tribunal decision in the case of *SEH Holdings Ltd,* LON/98/1362).

TRIBUNAL DECISION

An option to tax cannot apply to a building or part of a building intended for use as a dwelling. The question for the tribunal was whether it could apply to the sale of a building (in this case a pub) that would eventually be converted into dwellings. However the sale was to someone who was not carrying out the conversion work but had the intention to sell the building to someone else another party on the same day.

The tribunal concluded that the option to tax did apply to the sale of the building. They decided that the person selling the building has only to consider the intended use of the building by the immediate purchaser, and that their intention has to be made known to the person selling the building at the time of the sale. This provides certainty for the person selling the building.

CUSTOMS POLICY

In the light of the tribunal's decision, Customs policy is that where the immediate purchaser of a building (which the vendor had opted to tax) does not intend to use the building himself as a dwelling nor to convert the building into dwellings for sale or rent, the vendor must account for VAT on the sale of the building.

As the previously published guidance by Customs on this type of transaction was not clear, we will not insist on this policy being applied to previous transactions. However, traders should apply this new policy to transactions taking place on or after 1 August 2001.

There is no change to policy in cases where the immediate purchaser of an opted building does intend to use the building as a dwelling or to convert it to dwellings for sale or rent. In these circumstances, the sale of the building remains exempt unless vendor and purchaser have agreed that the sale should be taxable.

AUCTION SALES

Customs are aware that there may be particular problems at auctions because the vendor is not normally aware of the purchaser prior to the auction day. The vendor may have difficulty in finding out what the purchaser intends to do with the building, at the time he has to decide whether to charge VAT or not if he has opted to tax the building. Similarly a purchaser who intends to convert a non-residential property into dwellings, and sell them zero-rated, may also find it difficult to agree with the vendor in writing, prior to the auction date, that the option to tax should still apply to the sale of the building.

Customs are currently reviewing this area of policy and will include the problems of auction sales. In the meantime we suggest that the purchaser should discuss any problem he is facing with the vendor or his representatives prior to the completion date so that they can agree to apply the correct VAT liability.

Customs recognise that in applying the decision strictly, there may be certain circumstances when the VAT charged becomes an additional cost and that this may discourage some developers from converting commercial property into dwellings. Consequently any business, which needs further advice on applying the decision, should contact their local VAT office.

Commentary—*De Voil Indirect Tax Service* **V4.115**.

11 September 2001. Business Brief 12/01

Partial exemption—supplies to be excluded from the standard method calculation

This business brief provides further clarification of Customs & Excise policy previously outlined in Business Brief 8/99 following the House of Lords decision of 23 May 2001 in the *Liverpool Institute of Performing Arts* (LIPA) case (see [2001] STC 891).

WHAT WAS THE LIPA CASE ABOUT?

The LIPA case was about the scope of the partial exemption "standard method" (as described by reg 101 in VAT Regulations, SI 1995/2516) and what supplies should be included in it. Customs argued that the "standard method" calculation determines the deduction of VAT relating to supplies made within the UK and does not determine the deduction of VAT relating to supplies made outside the UK.

WHAT DID THE HOUSE OF LORDS DECIDE?

The House of Lords agreed with Customs. It found that two separate regimes exist, under the VAT Regulations 1995, for determining the amount of VAT that a taxpayer can deduct—

- Regulation 101 (the "standard method") which determines the deduction of VAT relating to supplies made within the UK; and,
- Regulation 103(1) which determines the deduction of VAT relating to supplies made outside the UK.

Regulation 101 cannot therefore be used to determine the amount of VAT to be deducted relating to supplies made outside of the UK.

WHAT ARE THE SUPPLIES THAT FALL WITHIN REG 103(1)?

Regulation 103(1) supplies fall into two categories—

(*a*) Those that would be taxable if they were made within the UK (known as "foreign" supplies but referred to by the House of Lords as "out of country" supplies), e g advertising services; and,

(*b*) Those that would be exempt if they were made within the UK and which are specified in an Order under VATA 1994 s 26(2)(*c*) (known as "specified" exempt supplies) e g certain finance and insurance supplies made by a UK based business to a customer who "belongs" outside of the European Union.

HOW DOES REG 103(1) WORK?

Regulation 103(1) determines the amount of VAT that can be deducted on the basis of use. It is up to the taxpayer to decide how this can be achieved. Any method of calculation is acceptable to Customs provided the result is both fair and reasonable. If the result is not fair and reasonable Customs can raise an assessment to rectify the position.

IF REG 103(1) DEALS WITH "SPECIFIED" EXEMPT SUPPLIES HOW DO I DEAL WITH "NON-SPECIFIED" EXEMPT SUPPLIES?

"Non-specified" exempt supplies are those supplies made outside of the UK that would be exempt if they were made within the UK, but which are not specified in an Order under VATA 1994 s 26(2)(*c*).

The House of Lords confirmed that these supplies are to be given a similar treatment to exempt supplies made in the UK. Whilst the VAT incurred in making these supplies cannot be deducted, the value of these supplies must be included within the "standard method" calculation.

WHAT IF I MAKE SUPPLIES THAT FALL UNDER BOTH REGS 101 AND 103(1)?

If you make taxable and exempt supplies in the UK as well as making supplies outside of the UK, then both regs 101 and 103(1) need to be applied. Regulation 103(1) is always to be applied first. For example—

Step 1—determine the amount of VAT incurred that relates to "out of country" and "specified" exempt supplies. This is done on the basis of use in accordance with reg 103(1). This VAT may be deducted.

Step 2—the remaining VAT incurred that relates to taxable and exempt UK supplies and "non-specified" exempt supplies is dealt with under reg 101. The proportion that can be deducted equals the value of taxable supplies divided by the total value of taxable, and exempt UK supplies and "non-specified" exempt supplies (subject to the requirement to exclude the values of certain distorting supplies). Remember, the values of "out of country" and "specified" exempt supplies dealt with at step 1 are not to be included.

WHAT IF I USE A PARTIAL EXEMPTION "SPECIAL METHOD" INSTEAD OF THE "STANDARD METHOD"?

Customs can approve or direct that a partial exemption "special method" be used instead of the "standard method". Whilst Customs can approve a "special method" to deal with "out of country" and "specified" exempt supplies they cannot direct you to use one. If your approved "special method" already deals with "out of country" and "specified" exempt supplies then you need not take any action following the House of Lords decision. But, if your "special method" does not deal with these supplies then you need to deal with them under reg 103(1) before you apply your "special method".

If you have any further questions please telephone the National Advice Service on 0845 0109 000.

Commentary—*De Voil Indirect Tax Service* **V3.464**.

29 November 2001. Business Brief 18/01

Reduced rate for supplies of small (*de minimis*) quantities of fuel oil, gas oil or kerosene

This business brief article clarifies Customs' policy on supplies of small quantities of oil.

BACKGROUND

Provided it is not for use as road fuel, a supply to an end-user of a small quantity (not more than 2,300 litres) of fuel oil, gas oil or kerosene is treated as if it is for domestic use, and is subject to the reduced rate of VAT. There has been some confusion about how the reduced rate should apply when there is more than one delivery to the same site on the same day.

CUSTOMS' POLICY

In general, Customs regard a supply as comprising all deliveries to the same customer at the same site on the same day. This will be the case even if you raise separate delivery notes or invoices. Deliveries that take place on different days, or to different sites, are regarded as separate supplies, even if you issue a single invoice for more than one delivery.

The following examples help to explain these general principles—

SAME DAY DELIVERIES TO DIFFERENT TANKS

A business customer has two tanks on the same site. You fill both tanks on the same day and raise a separate invoice for each "drop". The amount supplied is the total amount delivered to both tanks. If this amount is above the 2,300 litre (*de minimis*) limit, your supply is standard-rated.

SEPARATE ORDERS ON DIFFERENT DAYS—SAME DAY DELIVERY

A customer places an order for 2,000 litres of gas oil but two days later, before it is delivered, orders a further 1,000 litres for delivery to a different tank on the same site at the same time. The amount supplied is the total amount delivered to both tanks. Your supply is standard-rated.

SEPARATE ORDERS ON THE SAME DAY

A customer places an order for 2,000 litres of gas oil. Later the same day the customer contacts you again and asks for a further delivery of 1,000 litres to a different tank on the same site. If both deliveries are made on the same day, the total amount of 3,000 litres is regarded as a single supply and is standard rated. If the orders are actually delivered on two different days the reduced rate could apply to both deliveries.

SHARED TANKS

You deliver oil to a group of farmers who share a common tank. Each farmer's part of the delivery is regarded as a separate supply and invoiced separately. Any supply to a farmer below the 2,300 litre (*de minimis*) limits will attract the reduced rate.

FURTHER INFORMATION

This clarification of the *de minimis* limit has been agreed with the oil industry. Businesses that have not been applying the *de minimis* limit in this way will be required to follow this policy from 1 June 2002. This will allow them time to make any necessary changes to their accounting systems.

Revised guidance will be included in VAT Notice 701/19 Fuel and power, which is currently being updated. For further advice contact our National Advice Service on 0845 010 9000.

Commentary—*De Voil Indirect Tax Service* **V4.406.**

6 December 2001. Business Brief 19/01

Bad debt relief on goods supplied by hire purchase or conditional sale

This business brief announces changes to bad debt relief entitlement for goods supplied on hire purchase or conditional sale.

ATTRIBUTION OF PAYMENTS TO GOODS OR FINANCE

Bad debt relief can be claimed on supplies of goods made by way of hire purchase or conditional sale where the customer has defaulted.

Supplies made by hire purchase or conditional sale have two components—a supply of goods and a supply of associated finance.

When determining how much bad debt relief can be recovered, the supplier has had to allocate any payments received from their customer to the supply of the goods first and to the supply of finance only after the goods have been "paid in full". Finance companies have pointed out that this is unfair.

NEW TREATMENT

With immediate effect, suppliers can allocate each payment received from defaulting customers to goods and to finance in the same ratio as the total cost of goods and the total cost of finance to the customer. Further guidance is available in Annex 1 to this business brief.

Suppliers can re-calculate previous bad debt relief claims by applying this new policy and submitting a voluntary disclosure. All claims will be capped to three years starting six months from when the payment was due from the customer.

REPOSSESSED GOODS

In determining how much bad debt relief can be claimed, a supplier who has supplied goods by hire purchase or conditional sale has to deduct the proceeds from the disposal of any repossessed goods from the outstanding debt of their customer.

The disposal of these repossessed goods is subject to VAT where the customer has acquired the goods for a business purpose or where the supplier has changed their condition prior to re-selling them. Otherwise, the disposal of repossessed goods is relieved from VAT.

NEW TREATMENT

With immediate effect, where the disposal of the repossessed goods will be subject to VAT, suppliers no longer have to deduct the proceeds of the disposal from the outstanding debt of their customer, when claiming bad debt relief. Only the payments made by the customer have to be deducted.

There are no changes to the current policy where the disposal of repossessed goods will not be subject to VAT. In these cases the proceeds of the disposal, as well as the payments made by the customer must still be deducted from the outstanding debt. Further guidance is available in Annex 1 to this business brief.

Suppliers can re-calculate previous bad debt relief claims by applying this new policy and submitting a voluntary disclosure. All claims will be capped to three years starting six months from when the payment was due from the customer.

If you have any further questions please contact our national advice service on 0845 010 9000.

This release and other information about Customs & Excise can be found at www.hmce.gov.uk.

ANNEX 1—TECHNICAL DETAIL OF CHANGES TO BAD DEBT RELIEF

Attribution of payments in calculating entitlement to BDR

Current policy

A purchase made by a customer of goods by hire purchase ("HP") or conditional sale ("CS") consists of two supplies for VAT purposes. There is a supply of goods (taxable) and a supply of financial services (exempt). The time of supply for goods is typically when they are made available to the customer (VATA 1994 s 6) and the time of supply of the finance (VAT Regulations 1995 reg 90) is when payment is made.

Subject to meeting record keeping and timing conditions of the scheme, BDR arises when a customer defaults and the debt is unpaid. In determining how much BDR is recoverable, the supplier needs to allocate the payments received to the supply which occurred first (VAT Regulations 1995 reg 170(2)). In the case of HP and CS agreements, it will be the supply of goods that occurs first.

The impact of these rules has meant that suppliers have been allocating all the payments received against the goods in the first instance and only to the finance after the goods have been "paid in full".

Change in policy

While still believing the above analysis is correct in law, the Commissioners recognise that the outcome is not fair in relation to the commercial treatment of the transactions. Therefore with immediate effect, suppliers who make supplies under HP and CS agreements can apply the allocation rules set out in VAT Regulations 1995 reg 170(3). Now each payment can be allocated to interest and to goods in the same ratio as the total cost of the goods and total cost of the interest to the customer.

For example, if a car cost £8,000 and the interest over the life of the agreement is £2,000, each payment can be allocated 80% goods and 20% interest.

The Commissioners are currently considering whether a consequential amendment to the law is required to reinforce this new policy.

Treatment of repossessed goods

Current policy

The treatment of the sale of repossessed goods fall broadly into two groups—

- second hand goods (except cars); and
- cars.

While there are similarities, each group is dealt with by separate Orders. To remove the question of doubt, although goods may have originally been supplied new, by the time they are repossessed, they are considered to be second-hand within the meaning of these Orders.

Second-hand goods (except cars)

Subject to meeting the qualifying conditions below, the sale of repossessed second-hand goods (except cars) is treated as neither a supply of goods nor services ("de-supplied") under VAT (Special Provisions) Order, SI 1995/1268 art 4(1)(*a*). The qualifying conditions are that the goods are sold in the same condition as they were when repossessed and that, if the customer had sold them, they would not have been chargeable with VAT on the full price (eg because the customer had not acquired them for a business purpose or they were margin scheme supplies, etc).

If any goods do not qualify under art 4(1)(*a*) to be de-supplied because their condition has been changed or they would have been chargeable with VAT if disposed of by the customer, then their sale is a taxable supply. As the supplier never originally acquired the goods under any circumstances within VAT (Special Provisions) Order, SI 1995/1268 art 12(3), their disposal is not eligible as a margin scheme supply.

Cars

The treatment for cars is very similar to that of other goods. In the VAT (Cars) Order, SI 1992/3122 art 4(1)(*a*), the supply of a car which has been repossessed is de-supplied providing it is sold in the same condition and, under art 4(1A), providing the customer has not been able to deduct some or all of the input tax charged on the car.

If any cars do not qualify under art 4(1)(*a*) to be de-supplied because their condition has been changed or the customer has deducted some or all input tax charged upon it, its sale is a taxable supply. The disposal of these cars after repossession are not margin scheme supplies as the supplier never acquired them under any circumstances within art 8(2).

Recovery of bad debt relief

In determining how much BDR can be claimed, the supplier needs to identify how much consideration (which is attributable to the goods) has been received from the customer and the how much consideration (net of VAT if the sale is not de-supplied) has been received from the sale of the repossessed goods. These two amounts should be deducted from the original supply of the goods to the customer under the HP or CS agreement. Any outstanding balance that is attributable to the goods can, after applying the VAT fraction, be deducted as BDR.

For example, a car is supplied for £8,000 (including VAT of £1,191.49) plus £2,000 interest. It is repossessed and sold for £1,500. The customer has made payments totalling £3,000 (that is all attributable to supply of the goods). Providing six months have passed since the payment was due, a notification letter has been issued and the other record keeping requirements of the BDR scheme have been met, a BDR claim of £521.28 (£3,500 x 7/47) can be made.

If the sale of the repossessed car is a taxable supply, the net value raised from the sale will be £1,276.59 (the balance of £223.41 being VAT). As a result, the BDR claim would be will be £554.55 (£3,723.41 x 7/47).

Same condition

The condition of goods has been changed if any improvements, repairs, replacement parts or the generally making good of any damage has been carried out. The cleaning of goods generally does not affect the condition nor does the inclusion of instruction manuals if they are otherwise missing.

Change in policy

The policy change relates solely to conditions where the disposal of the repossessed goods is not de- supplied. There are no other policy changes in relation to repossessed goods.

With immediate effect, where the disposal of the repossessed goods will be subject to VAT, suppliers no longer have to deduct the proceeds of the disposal from the outstanding debt of their customer when claiming bad debt relief. BDR claims can now be based upon the amount actually paid by their customer providing the record keeping (including the notification letter) and time limit requirements of the scheme are met.

For example, a car is supplied for £8,000 (including VAT of £1,191.49) plus £2,000 interest. The customer has made payments totalling £3,000 that have been split £2,400 to the car and £600 to interest (following the new policy on attribution of payments). Providing six months have passed since the payment was due, a notification letter has been issued and the other record keeping requirements of the BDR scheme have been met, a BDR claim of £834.04 (£5,600 x 7/47) can be made. The sale of the repossessed car will be subject to VAT at 17.5%.

Retrospective application of these new policies

Suppliers can re-calculate previous BDR claims by applying the new policies for the attribution of payments and of the treatment of repossessed goods and submit a voluntary disclosure. Any claim will be capped to three years starting six months from when the consideration was due and payable by the customer.

Any suppliers who have not submitted any BDR claims can do so subject to being capped as above.

Commentary—*De Voil Indirect Tax Service* **V5.156, V3.117, V3.114**.

12 February 2002. Business Brief 3/02

Single and multiple supplies—sale of spectacles and contact lenses

Business Brief 2/01 set out Customs' policy as to whether a transaction consists of a single supply or two or more independent supplies for VAT purposes. The policy, which followed judgments of the European Court and House of Lords in the case of *Card Protection Plan*, has since been confirmed in a number of cases in the courts and VAT tribunal.

This Business Brief provides further clarification of Customs policy in this area, following the decision of the VAT Tribunal in the cases of *Southport Vision Plus* and *Leightons Ltd and Eye-Tech Ltd*. These cases concerned the sale of spectacles and contact lenses by dispensing opticians. The Tribunal found in favour of the appellants that this should be regarded as two separate supplies—one of standard rated goods and the other of exempt dispensing services. The supply of dispensed spectacles and contact lenses therefore continues to be treated in the same way as since 1995. The sight test and supplies of dispensing services independent of the supply of spectacles or contact lenses continue to be exempt.

The treatment of dispensed hearing aids, which is similar to that of dispensed spectacles and contact lenses, also remains unchanged.

Customs & Excise are not appealing this ruling. However, we wish to clarify our views on two aspects of the Tribunal's reasoning.

THE PROPORTION OF COST

The Tribunal took into account the existing agreement between Customs & Excise and opticians that dispensing services are a relatively high percentage of the total price of dispensed spectacles and contact lenses. *Card Protection Plan* established the principle that a single price is not a decisive indicator that there is a single supply. In the light of the Tribunal decision, Customs accept that if a distinct service element represents 50% or more of the price of a bundle of goods and services, it will be a strong indicator that this service is not ancillary to a principal supply of any other goods or services in that bundle and that the consideration may need to be apportioned accordingly.

However Customs also believe that this should not be allowed to open scope for avoidance. It will therefore not accept such an argument where it believes that there has been manipulation of values. It will continue to challenge the apportionment and any attempt to use manipulated values in a way that might distort a decision about whether a transaction is a single supply or multiple supplies.

ANCILLARY ELEMENTS

One of the tests established in *Card Protection Plan* is that a service should be regarded as ancillary to a principal supply if it does not constitute an aim in itself but a means of better enjoying the principal service supplied. In the opticians cases, the Tribunal concluded that the dispensing service cannot be regarded as a means of "better enjoying" the optical appliance, which, in the Tribunal's view, could not be enjoyed at all without the dispensing service.

If taken too widely, that line of reasoning would imply that a service would only be regarded as ancillary where it was, in effect, an optional part of the package. Customs continue to believe that the primary test remains what the customer thinks they are buying. A service can be regarded as an ancillary part of a single supply even where it is a compulsory part of the transaction.

Commentary—*De Voil Indirect Tax Service* **V3.106, V4.186.**

9 May 2002. Business Brief 13/02

Bad debt relief and the treatment of proceeds from the sale of repossessed cars

Business Brief 19/01 set out the Commissioners revised policy with respect to the treatment of proceeds from the sale of repossessed cars. The change in policy was introduced to alleviate the possibility of double taxation when new cars were repossessed and sold, where the sale after repossession was a taxable supply with VAT due on the full value. In such cases the proceeds from the sale of the repossessed car do not need to be deducted from the outstanding debt when calculating entitlement to bad debt relief. In case of any doubt this change only applies where the initial sale was of a new car.

Commentary—*De Voil Indirect Tax Service* **V3.117, V5.156.**

5 August 2002. Business brief 22/02

Three year cap—Marks & Spencer—ECJ judgment, Case C-62/00; [2002] STC 1036

BACKGROUND

Prior to 18 July 1996 if a trader discovered that he had paid more VAT to Customs & Excise than he ought to have, he had six years from the date on which the overpayment was made, or six years from the date on which he discovered his error, in which to make a claim to recover it from Customs. Where claims were made within six years of the date of discovery of an overpayment, they could go back to the inception of the tax in 1973.

On 18 July 1996, in the face of rising claims, the then Paymaster General announced that the time limit for claiming overpayments of VAT was to be reduced to three years. This meant that amounts overpaid more than three years before the date on which a claim was made could not be recovered. This change was applied to all claims made on or after 18 July 1996 and to all claims which had been made before that date but which had not yet been processed and paid. The capping legislation is contained in VATA 1994 s 80.

This change was enacted on 4 December 1996 by a resolution passed by Parliament under the Provisional Collection of Taxes Act 1968, which deemed the change to have had effect from 18 July 1996.

The manner in which this three year time limit was introduced, by FA 1997 s 47(2), was challenged in the courts by Marks and Spencer (M&S) and, during the course of this litigation the Court of Appeal sought the guidance of the ECJ on whether the manner of the introduction of the three year time limit was contrary to the principles of Community law.

Specifically, the Court of Appeal asked the ECJ whether it was permissible in Community law to shorten the time allowed for a person to claim repayment of amounts paid by way of VAT, which they overpaid in breach of directly effective rights conferred on them by the European 6th VAT Directive (the 6th Directive), to which the UK had not given effect in its domestic legislation and to do so with retrospective effect.

THE JUDGMENT OF THE ECJ

The ECJ delivered its judgment on 11 July 2002 and held that the UK had acted contrary to the principles of Community law in that it had failed to implement properly provisions of the 6th Directive, which conferred directly effective rights on taxpayers, and had then retrospectively shortened the time limit within which taxpayers could exercise their rights to repayment.

The ECJ held that when the UK introduced the new time limit they ought to have introduced it with a transitional period, beginning on the date on which the change was enacted, ie 4 December 1996. During this transitional period taxpayers who had directly effective rights under the

6th Directive, which had not been properly implemented in UK law, would have been able to exercise those rights before the new time limits were legitimately imposed.

The ECJ did not hold that it is contrary to Community law to impose time limits on the right to repayment of amounts paid by way of VAT contrary to directly effective provisions of the 6th Directive, but that it is contrary to Community law to impose those time limits with retrospective effect.

It is not the case that the UK capping legislation has been rendered invalid as a result of the fact that we failed to make provision for a transitional period when the three year time limit was introduced. A three year limitation period is, and remains, in force.

PRACTICAL EFFECTS OF THE JUDGMENT

Customs will now give effect, albeit retrospectively, to a transitional regime for when the three year time limit was introduced in 1996 to allow taxpayers to make the claims that they ought to have been able to make at the time. This transitional regime will apply from 4 December 1996 to 31 March 1997.

The judgment of the ECJ only actually requires that Customs give effect to this transitional period for those taxpayers who overpaid amounts by way of VAT in breach of directly effective rights of the 6th Directive as a result of the UK's failure to give proper effect to the Directive and were prevented, by the manner in which the three year time limit was introduced, from recovering those amounts.

However, if Customs had provided for a transitional regime at the time when the three year time limit was introduced, it would not have been applied in such a selective manner. Customs will not, therefore, restrict payment of claims only to those who would benefit from a strict interpretation of the ECJ's judgment in *Marks & Spencer*.

Taxpayers can now make claims under VATA 1994 s 80 for repayment of amounts overpaid, regardless of the cause of the overpayment, subject to the following criteria.

CLAIMS

Customs are now inviting all taxpayers to submit claims to their local VAT offices where—

- they made claims before 31 March 1997, which were capped (either by Customs or by them in expectation that no more than three years would be paid); or
- they made claims before 31 March 1997, which were repaid in full and amounts more than three years old were then clawed back by Customs by means of a recovery assessment; or
- they made no claim but can demonstrate that they discovered the error before 31 March 1997; and
- in all cases, the overpayments of VAT were made before 4 December 1996.

If you consider that you fall within the above parameters, you will have until 31 March 2003 to submit claims.

Claims may be refused in whole or in part if Customs are satisfied that repayment would lead to the unjust enrichment of the claimant.

CLAIMS WHICH DO NOT FALL WITHIN THE SCOPE OF THIS BUSINESS BRIEF

Claims made after 31 March 1997 will be subject to the three year time limit. For example, if between 1 April 1973 and 4 December 1996 you accounted for VAT at the standard rate on supplies, which ought to have been exempted from VAT, and you discovered the error on or after 1 April 1997, it will be limited to the amounts overpaid in the three years before the date on which the claim is made.

Claims relating to overpayments made after 4 December 1996 will be subject to the three year time limit. For example, a claim made after 5 December 1999 in respect of an overpayment made on 5 December 1996 will be out of time.

FORM OF CLAIM

Claims must be made in writing and must include—

- a statement of the amount being claimed and the method of calculation;
- the dates on which the overpayments were made;
- a copy of your original claim (where appropriate);
- copies of documents, schedules, etc. used in support of the application;
- the prescribed accounting periods in respect of which the claim for recovery of the overpayment was made;
- the reason for the claim;
- the reason why you will not be unjustly enriched if a repayment is now made; and
- any claim for interest that you consider you are entitled to make, and the reasons why you consider that your claim arose as the result of an error by Customs.

Claims should only be made for the net amount overpaid for any given prescribed accounting period. If you overpaid output tax during an accounting period on supplies which ought to have been exempted, and in the same accounting period you recovered more input tax than you ought, you should only submit a claim for that period for the amount of output tax over declared, less the amount of input tax over deducted i e the net overpayment.

ASSESSMENTS

When the time limit for making claims for overpaid VAT was reduced from six years to three, with effect from 18 July 1996, Customs' power to make assessments was also reduced by the same amount with effect from the same date. This remains unchanged.

Commentary—*De Voil Indirect Tax Service* **V5.159**.
Cross reference—See Business Brief 27/02 (extension of transitional period for capping limits).

20 August 2002. Business Brief 23/02

Attribution of input tax incurred on professional services when a company acquires shares in another company in exchange for shares in itself

BACKGROUND

This Business Brief article sets out Custom's policy following the decision of 24 June of the VAT and Duties Tribunal in the Southampton Leisure (LON/99/0466) appeal.

The appeal was concerned with the attribution of input tax incurred on certain professional services by the business, when it issued shares to the shareholders of Southampton Football Club Limited in exchange for their shares. Customs' view was that the services were used exclusively for the purposes of an exempt issue of shares, whereas the taxpayer's view was that the services were used in making both taxable and exempt supplies.

TRIBUNAL'S DECISION

The tribunal partly allowed the appeal. Whilst it supported Customs' view that the services relating to the public relations exercise was exclusively related to the issue of shares, the tribunal found that supplies of services, which included certain tasks namely—

- acting as financial advisor;
- the drafting of service contracts for the directors;
- the due diligence review of the target company's affairs—the investigation of title and/ or the valuation of that company's property;
- coordinating the transaction; and
- were not used exclusively in making the exempt supply of the issue of shares. As a result, the tax incurred on those supplies should be treated as residual input tax.

Customs have decided not to appeal the tribunal's decision.

IMPLICATIONS

Customs now accept that any taxed supplies of professional services, which include any of the above tasks in the circumstances of a merger and acquisition or management buy-out, has to some extent a direct and immediate link with the whole of the taxpayer's business. The tax incurred is residual input tax and is attributable to taxable supplies by reference to that person's partial exemption method. However, where a taxed supply of professional services is partly used in making an issue of shares to a person belonging outside the European Union, then the deductible proportion of tax is to be determined on a "use" basis under regulation 103(2) of the VAT Regulations 1995.

WHAT THE DECISION DOES NOT AFFECT

Customs take the view that the decision has no application where shares are issued for subscription. For example, an initial public offer or rights issue. In these instances, the taxed professional services relating to the offer are used exclusively for the purposes of the exempt supply of an issue of shares. But Customs do accept that any services providing general advice on the means of capital raising (provided it is just that) is part of the business' overheads and that the tax incurred on any such services should be treated as residual input tax. In most offers the decision to issue shares is taken at the outset and the question of any general advice simply does not arise.

CLAIMS

Customs will, subject to the normal capping rules, accept claims for overpaid tax. This will largely arise where a business, in the course of a merger or acquisition or management buy-out activity, has wholly attributed to exempt supplies and so treated as irrecoverable an amount of input tax incurred on a supply of professional services, but which following the tribunal's approach in Southampton Leisure ought to have been attributed to both taxable and exempt supplies. The amount of overpaid tax being the deductible proportion of (what is now accepted to be) residual input tax.

8 October 2002. Business Brief 27/02

Extension of transitional period for capping limits—Marks & Spencer Plc v C&E Comrs, CJEC Case C-62/00 [2002] STC 1036—Addendum to Business Brief 22/02—Grundig Italiana SpA v Ministero delle Finanze, CJEC Case 255/00

BACKGROUND

On 5 August 2002 Customs & Excise published Business Brief 22/02, which set out how we intended to give effect to the judgment of the European Court of Justice (ECJ) in *Marks & Spencer*. In that case, the ECJ held that when shortening the time limit for claiming amounts overpaid by way of tax in breach of Community law, member states must make provision for a transitional period during which taxpayers who have rights to make a claim under the "old" law can exercise those rights before they are finally extinguished by the "new" law.

Business Brief 22/02 recognised that there had been no transitional period when the three-year capping legislation was introduced in 1996. It went on to establish, retrospectively, a transitional period to run from 4 December 1996 (the date on which the resolution under the Provisional Collection of Taxes Act 1968 was passed by Parliament) until 31 March 1997 (90 days after 4 December, rounded up to the end of the month).

ECJ JUDGMENT IN GRUNDIG ITALIANA

The length of the transitional period was based on the opinion of the Advocate General in *Grundig Italiana*, a case in which the issue before the ECJ was whether a 90 day transitional period was reasonable where the time limit for submitting claims to recover amounts of overpaid tax is reduced from five years to three.

The Advocate General concluded that it was for the national courts to determine, as a question of fact, whether a transitional period rendered it impossible in practice or excessively difficult for a taxpayer to recover tax he had overpaid. The Advocate General held that the question was not one to which the ECJ could give an answer. However, he said nothing to suggest that the 90 day transitional period applied by the Italians was unreasonable.

On 24 September the ECJ handed down its judgment and, declining to follow the Advocate General, held that where time limits for claiming overpayments of tax are shortened from, for example, five or ten years to three, provision must be made for a transitional period of at least six months.

As a result, the transitional period set out in Business Brief 22/02 is extended by three months and will now be deemed to have run from 4 December 1996 to 30 June 1997 and taxpayers are now invited to submit, or resubmit, claims where:

- they made claims before 30 June 1997, which were capped (either by Customs or by them in expectation that no more than three years would be paid);
- or they made claims before 30 June 1997, which were repaid in full and amounts more than three years old were then clawed back by Customs by means of a recovery assessment;
- or they made no claim but can demonstrate that they discovered the error before 30 June 1997; and in all cases, the overpayments of VAT were made before 4 December 1996.

The deadline for making claims is also extended by three months to 30 June 2003. Requests for an extension will be given sympathetic consideration where taxpayers can demonstrate that they are experiencing real difficulties in meeting the deadline.

Both *Marks & Spencer* and *Grundig Italiana* are landmark cases in this area of Community law. Customs & Excise apologise for any inconvenience caused to taxpayers by the change contained in this Business Brief, but believe that it is right to give taxpayers the benefit of the current thinking of the European Court.

Commentary—*De Voil Indirect Tax Service* **V5.159**.

19 November 2002. Business Brief 30/02

Policy statement on the treatment of applications to leave a VAT group

This Business Brief is issued as a result of recent representations to Customs following the Court of Appeal decision in the case of *Customs and Excise v Barclays Bank PLC* [2001] EWCA Civ 1513, [2001] STC 1558. This article clarifies how Customs and Excise intend to deal with applications for a company to leave a VAT group.

The Court of Appeal ruled in October 2001 that Customs were not obliged to exclude a company from a VAT group as soon as the company ceased to be controlled by the group holding company. As a result of this ruling, Customs were able to prevent the company leaving the VAT group before FA 1995 s 25 came into effect on 1 March 1995. FA 1995 introduced an "exit charge" for companies leaving a VAT group in certain circumstances and would have applied in this case, increasing the amount of VAT due from Barclays.

Businesses and tax advisers are concerned that keeping a company in a VAT group after the company has been sold to a third party may cause commercial difficulties. In practice, it would be rare for Customs to set a later date for cases. Normally Customs policy will be to agree the date requested by the selling group. Customs will set a later date only if VAT avoidance is involved or is likely to arise through obtaining an earlier date.

Applications to leave a VAT group should continue to be made to Customs in the normal way as set out in Public Notice 700/2 Group treatment, indicating the date that the company wishes to leave the VAT group.

Commentary—*De Voil Indirect Tax Service* **V2.113**.

19 November 2002. Business Brief 30/02

VAT groups—protection of the revenue

This article provides businesses with further guidance about VAT grouping structures. Customs will not use their revenue protection powers to challenge acceptable grouping structures.

VAT GROUPING RULES

The VAT grouping rules are a business facilitation measure. They allow members of a VAT group to disregard, for VAT purposes, any supplies between group members, with only one VAT return then being required for the whole VAT group. As a result, a company which decides to set up subsidiaries to carry on parts of its business will be treated for VAT purposes in the same way as if it had decided to carry on the business through branches of a single company.

Two companies can join a VAT group provided both are established (or have a fixed establishment) in the UK and both meet the control criteria, i e one of them controls the other, or they are both controlled by one person, or by two or more individuals carrying on business in a partnership.

Full details of the VAT grouping rules are in Public Notice 700/2.

REVENUE PROTECTION POWERS

The VAT grouping legislation gives Customs the power to prevent a company joining a VAT group and to remove an existing member from a VAT group where this is considered necessary for the protection of the revenue. (Business Briefs 15/99 and 01/01 provide more information about these powers.) One aim of these revenue protection powers is to prevent a company from using contrived structures which seek to extend the benefits of VAT grouping to supplies from what is, in effect, a third party supplier.

One example of a contrived structure which Customs have and will continue to challenge is the so-called A-B share scheme. This involves the setting up of a company where the VAT group holding company (the customer) will have "A" shares and a third party supplier, e g of IT services, will have "B" shares. Typically, while the "A" shares may attract some dividend, the "B" shares will entitle the third party supplier to all or the majority of the profits. The holding company will have the right to appoint the majority of the board of directors of the company, thus meeting the control criteria for eligibility to VAT grouping. The result is contrary to the VAT system and enables partly exempt VAT groups to avoid paying VAT on bought-in services.

ACCEPTABLE GROUPING STRUCTURES

As a general principle, Customs consider that the VAT grouping of two corporate bodies (A and B) is acceptable where A's corporate group either receives or has the ability to control 50% or more of the "economic benefits" of running B's business, provided that the determination of the "economic benefits" is not manipulated to divert benefits to a third party through, for example, high management charges; special dividend payments or other charges, payments or arrangements.

Customs will consider challenging any grouping structure which does not meet this general principle, unless the amount of VAT revenue at stake is nil or too low to justify action.

Examples of normal commercial structures which Customs consider acceptable and therefore would not be challenged are set out below. These are provided for guidance only. In all grouping cases, Customs will apply the principles set out above when determining whether to challenge any particular grouping scheme.

Example 1: VAT grouping does not affect the net VAT revenue to a significant extent

A jointly owned supplier S is VAT grouped with one of its owners C, to whom it provides various taxable services. In the absence of VAT grouping, C would be able to recover all or substantially all the VAT it would pay on S's services. Customs would not take action under Business Brief 01/01 because such action would not be necessary for the protection of the revenue. The position would be similar if all of S's services to C were exempt or zero-rated.

Example 2: 50:50 joint ventures

JV is jointly owned by companies P and Q, and has issued "A" shares to P and "B" shares to Q. It is VAT grouped with P by the "A" shares giving P a slim majority of the voting rights at general meetings. In reality, P and Q share approximately equally in the investment in JV and receive similar shares of its profits. JV is not a subsidiary of either P or Q for UK group accounts purposes. Customs would normally see such grouping as acceptable subject to the caveat under the general rule above that there were no arrangements for Q to obtain significantly more than 50% of the benefits from running JV's business, eg by levying management charges tailored to remove most of JV's profits.

Commentary—*De Voil Indirect Tax Service* **V2.113**.

1 July 2003. Business Brief 7/03

Exemption of call centre services in the insurance sector

Following a recent VAT and Duties Tribunal decision, this article explains Customs' revised policy on the VAT treatment of call centre services where the call centre is attempting to sell insurance by cold calling and is able to put the insurer "on risk" at the point of sale.

THE TRIBUNAL DECISION

The appeal involved TeleTech, a company providing call centre and IT support services to a wide range of clients. The decision related to the services supplied to an insurance company. TeleTech cold called people using contact lists provided by the insurer and attempted to sell them health insurance products. The products were very straightforward and the telephone operatives were selected mainly for their expertise in call handling and selling. Only a small percentage of calls led to sales and TeleTech was paid on a flat fee rather than commission basis.

Customs ruled that TeleTech's services fell outside the exemption for insurance related services, arguing that TeleTech's services were principally of an advertising/promotional nature. The Tribunal allowed TeleTech's appeal on the grounds that TeleTech was selling or trying to sell insurance policies as agents. The decisive factor being that, where calls led to sales, TeleTech was able to put the insurer on risk and the customer on cover. The Tribunal Chairman also observed that the manner of remuneration (ie whether by flat fee or commission) had no bearing on the VAT treatment.

REVISED VAT TREATMENT

As a result of this decision, Customs now accept that call centre services, such as those supplied by TeleTech, are VAT exempt insurance related services where the call centre is able to put the insurer on risk at the point of sale without referral back to the insurer.

Due to the unique nature of the insurance exemption, Customs see this decision as applying only to call centre services supplied in connection with insurance. Customs do not see the decision as having any implications for cases concerning the VAT liability of call centre services supplied to other sectors.

Businesses that think this decision applies to them, but have already accounted for VAT on such services, can make an adjustment to their VAT accounts for overpayments that total less than £2,000 net of any input tax over-claimed or for such overpayments exceeding £2,000. Claims must be submitted to your local Business Advice Centre for repayment, as set out in detail in Section 4 of Customs' Notice 700/45 "How to correct errors and make adjustments or claims".

All adjustments or claims must take into account any over-claimed input tax and are limited to a three-year period as explained in detail in Notice 700/45. Such claims will be paid subject to the conditions set out below—

- Businesses must be able to produce suitable evidence that the services in question qualify for exemption on the basis outlined above, and must be able to substantiate the amount claimed.
- Businesses will need to look back at earlier attributions of input tax (any input tax incurred on goods and services used exclusively for these call centre services is now attributable to an exempt supply), substituting exempt values for taxable values in the partial exemption calculation and deducting the resulting 'exempt input tax' from overpaid output tax in determining the amount of the claim.

If Customs can show that a business effectively did not bear the burden of the tax, it may reject the claim on the grounds that it would unjustly enrich a business. For example, this may have happened because a business passed the tax on to someone else without losing profit by doing so, and are unable, or don't intend, to pass on the repayment. Further details can be found in Notice 700/45 Section 14.

A notification to Customs that a business intends making a claim in the future is not a valid claim.

FURTHER INFORMATION

Further information can be found in Public Notice 700/45 "How to correct VAT errors or make adjustments or claims" or by contacting the National Advice Service on 0845 010 9000.

25 July 2003. Business Brief 11/03

Building and construction: grants of a major interest by members of VAT groups

The first grant of a major interest in a new dwelling, communal residential building or charitable building is zero-rated. "Grant of a major interest" means a freehold sale or a long lease in a building. This Business Brief article clarifies Customs' policy in relation to grants of major interest in zero-rated buildings by VAT groups in the rare situation when a group member makes more than one grant of a major interest in a building, the first of which is to another group member.

Where a major interest in a building is granted by one member of a VAT group to another, the grant should not be considered to be the "first grant of a major interest" in that building by that group member for the purpose of zero-rating.

In effect this means that the first grant of a major interest to a person outside the group can be zero-rated, regardless of the previous activity within the VAT group, so long as the group member making the grant is a person constructing (or converting) the building and it meets all the other criteria.

FURTHER INFORMATION

For further information please contact the National Advice Service on 0845 010 9000.

Commentary—*De Voil Indirect Tax Service* **V2.190; V4.233.**

25 July 2003. Business Brief 11/03

Treatment of communal areas in blocks of flats

This Business Brief article announces Customs' new policy on communal areas in new buildings containing two or more dwellings. Typically these buildings are blocks of flats, which consist of individual dwellings and areas for the use of all residents, such as a lounge, laundry and refuse area. The first sale of each flat is zero-rated and the buyer also acquires a right to use the communal areas.

Where the communal areas are only used by residents and their guests, Customs accept that the construction of the whole building is zero-rated. Where the communal areas are partly used by others, for example if they contain leisure or gym facilities, whether or not for a charge, then the construction of the communal areas is standard-rated.

Where a building contains both a non-residential part and a dwelling, such as a shop with a flat above, zero-rating continues to apply only to the extent that the building is designed as a dwelling.

FURTHER INFORMATION

For further information please contact the National Advice Service on 0845 010 9000.

30 September 2003. Business Brief 18/03

Exemption of intermediary services provided in the finance sector

Following a Court of Appeal decision, this article explains Customs' revised policy on the VAT treatment of services provided by a body that introduces its members, supporters or customers to a credit card provider and undertakes work preparatory to the provision of the credit card.

In a joined Court of Appeal hearing concerning co-branded (affinity) credit card schemes, both British Airports Authority (BAA) and Institute of Directors (IoD) successfully argued that their services of introducing members, supporters or customers to two different banks for the purposes of issuing a credit card were exempt from VAT as the negotiation of credit.

As part of its introductory service, BAA targeted suitable applicants, issued applications, assisted in the completion of the forms, and screened and processed them when they were returned. In the case of IoD, the introductory service supplied included providing a list of suitable members, encouraging members to apply, assisting them with their applications, and validating completed forms.

Customs argued that neither BAA nor IoD were financial intermediaries because they did not provide services that directly affected the underlying credit transactions. Rather they were providing a taxable marketing and promotional service to the banks.

LEGAL DECISIONS

BAA successfully challenged Customs' view in both the Tribunal and High Court. The IoD was defeated in the Tribunal. Both cases were heard jointly in the Court of Appeal.

In rejecting Customs' arguments, the Court of Appeal said that the deciding factor was how the services of BAA and IoD should be characterised and that the High Court had been correct in describing BAA's services as the negotiation of credit. There was an introduction of applicants to a source of credit, and the promotion and marketing element was just an "essential preliminary".

Customs has not appealed.

IMPLICATIONS

As a result of these judgments, a body that introduces its members, supporters or customers to a credit card provider and undertakes work preparatory to the provision of the credit card is providing exempt negotiation or intermediary services.

The decision clarifies UK law and, as a result, Customs accept that it is no longer necessary for the introducer to be capable of affecting the terms of the principal financial service for the exemption to apply.

Exemption, therefore, applies where an intermediary—

- stands between the parties to a contract in the performance of a distinct act of mediation;
- brings the two parties to the contract together; and
- undertakes "work preparatory" such as completing or assisting with the completion of application forms, forwarding forms to the credit card company, and making representations on behalf of either party.

Customs do not view marketing and promotional services supplied in isolation, nor the performing of clerical functions such as providing a list of names or access to a database as exempt intermediary services.

CHARITIES

Under a specific concession outlined in paragraph 11(a) of Public Notice 701/01/95 "Charities", Customs currently allows charities to treat part of their taxable income in respect of affinity credit cards as if it were outside the scope of VAT. However, as a result of the judgment in BAA and the IoD each charity will need to consider whether these supplies are now VAT exempt. Charities that continue to have taxable affinity credit card schemes can continue to treat their income as before.

INFORMATION ON MAKING CLAIMS OR ADJUSTMENTS

Businesses that think this Business Brief article applies to them but have already accounted for VAT on such services, may claim any resulting payment due to them from Customs by using one of the following methods, subject to statutory time limits.

1 If the net value of the adjustments is £2000 or less, businesses may amend their VAT account and include the value of the adjustment on their current VAT return.

2 If the net value of adjustments is more than £2000, a separate claim for payment should be submitted to the local Business Advice Centre. (Businesses cannot make this adjustment on their VAT return).

Both the above methods and how to make a claim are explained in detail in VAT Notice 700/45 "How to correct VAT errors and make adjustments or claims".

All adjustments or claims must take into account any over-claimed input tax and are limited to a three- year period as explained in detail in Notice 700/45. Such claims will be considered subject to the conditions set out below—

- Businesses must be able to produce suitable evidence that the services in question qualify for exemption on the basis outlined above, and must be able to substantiate the amount claimed.
- Businesses will need to look back at earlier attributions of input tax (any input tax incurred on goods and services used exclusively for these services is now attributable to an exempt supply), substituting exempt values for taxable values in the partial exemption calculation and deducting the resulting 'exempt input tax' from overpaid output tax in determining the amount of the claim.
- Businesses that have acquired a capital item (as defined in SI 1995/2518) and have

undertaken an original deduction and/or interval adjustments over the last three years will need to recalculate those figures in order to compensate for the (potential) increased exempt use.

Customs may reject a claim on the grounds that payment would unjustly enrich a business. For example, this may have happened because a business passed the tax on to someone else and are unable, or do not intend, to pass on the repayment. Further details can be found in Notice 700/45 Section 14.

A notification to Customs that a business intends making a claim in the future is not a valid claim. The views expressed in this Business Brief article are those of HM Customs & Excise.

FURTHER INFORMATION

If taxpayers have any queries about the liability of their supplies they should contact Customs' National Advice Service on 0845 010 9000 (Text phone 0845 000 0200).

30 September 2003. Business Brief 18/03

The VAT position of two new PFI arrangements

ISSUE

This Business Brief is intended to clarify the extent to which government departments and NHS bodies can recover the VAT they incur on two new types of PFI (Private Finance Initiative) arrangement, referred to respectively as "Composite Trade" ("Contract Debtor") and "NHS LIFT". What follows are general views, and they do not replace the need to look carefully at the circumstances of each case.

BACKGROUND

Under section 41(3) of the VAT Act 1994, government departments and health service bodies are eligible to recover VAT incurred on a range of services purchased in connection with their non-business activities.

The range of services which are eligible for section 41(3) refunds are listed in a Treasury direction published annually in the London, Edinburgh and Belfast Gazettes—the current Direction was published on 10 January 2003, having taken effect from 2 December 2002. It lists 75 different types of services as "Headings", in respect of which VAT may be recovered.

Headings 45 and 53 are relevant to the "Composite Trade" and "NHS LIFT" PFI arrangements. These state—

HEADING 45

Operation of hospitals, health care establishments and health care facilities and the provision of any related services.

HEADING 53

Provision under a PFI agreement of accommodation for office or other government use, together with management or other services in connection with that accommodation.

Both headings are concerned with PFI and PPP arrangements for buildings, which involve the transfer of risk to bodies outside government.

"COMPOSITE TRADE" ARRANGEMENTS

In most PFI arrangements concerning government real estate the property is acquired by the PFI contractor, with the government department or health service bodies having a lesser interest or a licence. This transfers risk in the property to the PFI contractor.

Under the "Composite Trade" structure, however, the main interest in the property remains vested in the government department or in the health service body, rather than passing to the PFI contractor.

This departure from the normal concept of transferring risk does not stop the PFI contractors' supplies to the government department or the health service body from falling within headings 45 or 53 of the Treasury direction. Provided the supply is of a description falling within either of those headings, then a government department or a health service body will be entitled to recover the VAT levied on the Facilities Management Charge, subject to the other rules laid down by the Treasury.

"NHS LIFT" ARRANGEMENTS

"NHS LIFT" (Local Improvement Finance Trusts) arrangements are intended to consolidate and deliver a wide range of local healthcare services from purpose built facilities. The services will primarily be made by local PCTs (Primary Care Trusts), local authority welfare services and GPs. But the intention is also to involve dentists, chemists etc.

To date, NHS LIFT arrangements have varied, which means that it is not possible to give a single, blanket piece of advice that applies to all such projects. However, Customs believe that in all cases, the question will generally be the extent to which the project qualifies for refunds under heading 45. The answer to this will depend upon the level of health related services that are provided in the building in question, otherwise than in the course of business, and the extent to which the NHS LIFT company is involved in the operation of a health care establishment.

In Customs' view the simple granting of a lease in a building is insufficient to qualify for refund under heading 45, even where it is the equivalent of a landlord repairing and maintaining lease. Customs consider that two requirements must be satisfied before heading 45 can apply. Firstly the building must either be a hospital, or be used to provide health care facilities. Secondly the supply by the PFI contractor to the health service body must be of the operation of that hospital or establishment.

For example, if the building is used for diagnostic work, treating patients and/or patient counselling, Customs accept that it is a health care establishment. Where the NHS LIFT company plays an active role in the operation of that establishment, providing in addition to cleaning and maintenance services, advice in deciding what healthcare services are needed for the local community, how to bring together these services, where to locate the building and, possibly, establishing links with the various health and care agencies, Customs would accept the requirements of heading 45 as being fully satisfied.

An NHS LIFT company would also be involved in the operation of the building if it provided and operated medical equipment.

These examples are nor exhaustive, and cases should be considered on their individual merits, paying regard to the two principles explained above.

13 November 2003. Business Brief 21/03

Treatment of cage accessories for use in specialised laboratory caging

This Business Brief article announces Customs' new policy on certain cage accessories supplied to eligible bodies for use in specialised laboratory caging following a Tribunal decision.

The zero rate applies to supplies of certain types of goods to eligible bodies such as not-for-profit research institutions. These goods include medical, scientific and laboratory equipment for use in medical or veterinary research and any parts or accessories for use in or with such laboratory equipment.

Following a recent VAT Tribunal decision (18247), Customs accept that cage and tray liners and research grade litter, bedding and nesting materials are accessories when designed for use in or with specialised laboratory caging. As a result supplies of these products will qualify for zero-rating when supplied to eligible bodies (see Notice 701/6 "Charity Funded Equipment for medical, veterinary etc uses" for a full list of eligible bodies).

Traders who have previously accounted for VAT on supplies to eligible bodies of these products for use in specialised laboratory caging, can make a claim to their local Business Advice Centre for repayment, as set out in detail in Section 4 of Notice 700/45 "How to correct errors and make adjustments or claims". All claims are limited to a three-year period and will be subject to unjust enrichment considerations as explained in detail in Notice 700/45.

OTHER PRODUCTS

The Tribunal also made some informal comments on the liability of certain other products, namely anaesthetic equipment; surgical instruments; autopsy equipment; surgical scissors; and operating lamps for surgery. These did not amount to a decision. In order to determine whether these goods will qualify for zero-rating when supplied to eligible bodies, a business must ask itself whether the criteria in Notice 701/6 have been met.

Other products, such as environmental enrichment products, were not considered by the Tribunal. Customs maintain that supplies of these products will not qualify for zero-rating when supplied to eligible bodies.

10 December 2003. Business Brief 27/03

Partial exemption—special method override Notice

This Business Brief article describes the effect of the special method override Notice announced in today's pre-Budget Report and which comes into force from 1 January 2004.

SUMMARY

The special method override Notice (Notice) only affects partly exempt businesses that operate a partial exemption special method and where Customs have—

- served a Notice on the business; or,
- approved a Notice served by the business.

A Notice allows Customs or business to correct the results of an unfair special method until a replacement method is implemented.

No other businesses are affected by this measure.

BACKGROUND

A business that makes both taxable and exempt supplies is known as partly exempt and must apply a partial exemption method to calculate how much of the VAT it incurs on its costs and purchases it can deduct. A partial exemption method is supposed to ensure that the business can deduct a fair and reasonable amount of VAT on costs and purchases that are "used or will be used" in making taxable supplies ("the principle of use").

Most partly exempt businesses operate the standard method of partial exemption but some businesses, particularly the most complex ones, operate a special method that has been customised to their needs and approved or directed by Customs. Further details on partial exemption can be found in VAT Notice 706 "Partial Exemption" www.hmce.gov.uk/forms/notices/706.

From time to time, for example when business circumstances change, a special method might no longer meet the principle of use and a new method must be found. Preparing a new special method can take time, especially for a large or complex business, and because a new method cannot normally be backdated Customs or the business can lose out as a result.

NEW MEASURE

A Notice allows either Customs or business to introduce an override with immediate effect, to correct the results of an unfair method until a replacement method is implemented. A business should then correct the results of its special method to ensure that VAT deducted fairly and reasonably reflects the principle of use. Corrections commence from a current or future date specified within the Notice and must continue each time the special method is applied (including any year end adjustment) until a replacement method is implemented. This means that neither Customs nor the business need be disadvantaged whilst a replacement special method is being prepared.

SITUATIONS COVERED BY THE NEW NOTICE

A Notice is intended to be a temporary measure and Customs expect its use to be rare. Customs will only issue or approve a Notice where—

- They have clear evidence that the current special method does not fairly and reasonably reflect the principle of use; and
- They are satisfied that preparing a replacement method will not conclude quickly and that Customs or business would otherwise lose out.

Customs will serve a Notice only when—

- They have attempted, unsuccessfully, to persuade the business to comply, and have the evidence to show this; and,
- They have decided that direction of a special method is not appropriate.

SERVING AND APPROVING A NOTICE

A Notice must specify—

- that it is a special method override notice;
- the current or future date from which it takes effect; and,
- the reasons why the current special method does not meet the principle of use.

When Customs serve a Notice they will also explain its practical effect, for example what a business must do to comply. When Customs approve a Notice served by a business, they will do so in writing as soon as possible and ideally within 30 days of receipt. Decisions on serving a Notice will be taken by a central team.

COMPLYING WITH A NOTICE

To comply with a Notice a business must for each VAT return period (including any year end adjustment)—

- determine the amount of deductible VAT using its current special method;
- determine the amount of deductible VAT in accordance with the principle of use; and,
- account for any difference between these amounts as a Notice correction.

In most cases the reasons given by Customs or business in the Notice will provide a basis for determining the Notice correction. However, a business must still consider its whole method and determine whether there are any other aspects that would otherwise give an unfair result. The Notice correction must therefore ensure that each time a VAT return is prepared, the amount of VAT deducted fairly and reasonably reflects the extent that costs and purchases are used or will be used in making taxable supplies (the principle of use).

If a business does not make corrections to the amount of VAT deducted, and Customs conclude that a Notice correction should have been made, then Customs will make the correction by way of VAT assessment.

RIGHT OF APPEAL

A business can appeal to the VAT and Duties Tribunal against—

- Customs' decision to serve a Notice;
- Customs' decision not to approve a Notice; and,
- any VAT assessments made under a Notice.

Commentary—*De Voil Indirect Tax Service V3.462.*

24 December 2003. Business Brief 30/03

Exemption of "debt negotiation services"

This Business Brief article has been issued to clarify Customs' change in policy on the VAT liability of "debt negotiation services", following the Tribunal decision in the case of *Debt Management Associates*. As a result of this change, the services of "debt negotiation", provided by an intermediary, will be exempt from VAT.

WHAT ARE "DEBT NEGOTIATION SERVICES"?

"Debt negotiation services" typically seek to acquire favourable repayment terms for a debtor who is experiencing difficulty in making repayments under terms already in place.

This type of service may include one or more of the following—

- taking details of income and expenditure, along with details of the creditor(s) and the amounts outstanding, and preparing and presenting a payment plan to the creditor;
- agreeing to act on behalf of such a debtor with the creditor in negotiating the payment plan; or
- agreeing to receive payments from the debtor and passing these payments on to the creditors (with or without first extracting a fee or commission for doing so).

Turning to what is meant by "negotiation", Customs considers that it refers to the activity of an intermediary providing a distinct act of mediation. The purpose of such intermediation is to do all that is necessary in order for two parties to enter into a contract, without the person who is acting as an intermediary having any interest of his own in the terms of the contract. Therefore, provided you bring together the two parties, act between those parties, and attempt to mediate a change to the payment terms you are "negotiating debts".

However, if you are merely providing a service typically undertaken by a company as part of its contract this will not be "negotiation of debts". For example—

- if you issue letters to the debtor on behalf of the creditor demanding payment; or
- if you seek to locate a debtor on behalf of the creditor; or
- if you provide accounting services to the creditor (ie you monitor the debtor's payment account and notify the creditor of any defaulted payments).

This list is not exhaustive.

If you provide a service containing both 'negotiation of debts' and one or more of the services listed above you will need to determine what element predominates. VAT Information Sheet 02/01: "Single or multiple supplies—how to decide" can assist you and is available online at www.hmce.gov.uk/forms/notices/info0201 If you have further questions please contact the National Advice Service on 0845 010 9000.

LIABILITY OF DEBT RE-NEGOTIATION SERVICES

Prior to the *Debt Management Associates* decision Customs' policy had been to tax the services of debt negotiation at the standard rate.

Customs now accept that where a business negotiates payment terms between two parties this is "negotiating debts" and within the scope of the finance exemption which applies to the provision of intermediary services by a person acting in an intermediary capacity and is thus exempt from VAT.

CLAIMS FOR REFUNDS OF VAT

Businesses that think this Business Brief article applies to them, but have already accounted for VAT on such services, may make a claim to their local Business Advice Centre for repayment, as set out in detail in Section 4 of Customs' Notice 700/45 "How to correct errors and make adjustments or claim" available from www.hmce.gov.uk/forms/notices/700–45. All claims are limited to a three-year period and will be subject to unjust enrichment considerations as explained in section 14 of Customs Notice 700/45.

All adjustments or claims must take into account any over-claimed input tax as well as any over declared output tax. Such claims will be considered subject to the conditions set out below—

- Businesses must be able to produce suitable evidence that the services in question qualify for exemption on the basis outlined above, and must be able to substantiate the amount claimed.
- Businesses will need to look back at earlier attributions of input tax to previously considered taxable supplies (including attributions to intended taxable supplies). This VAT will now directly relate to (revised) exempt supplies (or intended exempt supplies) and is therefore exempt input tax and fully restricted. In addition, where the business has apportioned VAT in accordance with the standard method, or a calculation under a special method, there must be a re-calculation of that method by substituting (reducing) the original taxable elements of the fraction by the revised (increased) exempt elements.

A notification to Customs that a business intends making a claim in the future is not a valid claim.

9 June 2004. Business Brief 16/04

VAT – definition of a motorcar

This Business Brief clarifies Customs' interpretation of the definition of a motorcar as contained in the Value Added Tax (Cars) Order 1992.

BACKGROUND

The UK operates a 'block' on the deduction of input tax on the purchase of a vehicle that is defined in VAT legislation as a motorcar. As a result of this block, most businesses that purchase motorcars are unable to recover the VAT they have incurred. In broad terms, the purpose of the block is to prevent recovery of input tax on vehicles whose physical attributes make them suitable for private motoring. It is important, therefore, for business to know the status of their vehicles under the terms of the legislation, as this will affect the deductibility of VAT on their purchase.

The clarification is necessary in the light of recent developments in the car-derived van market, which have resulted in the manufacture of vehicles that have blurred the distinction between cars and vans. This means that these vehicles are difficult to categorise in relation to the definition of motorcars in VAT legislation.

In response, Customs have issued new guidance, produced in consultation with manufacturers, which clarifies our treatment of car-derived vans and highlights the correct interpretation of the legal definition when considering combination vans. This guidance is available on request from the Customs' National Advice Service on 0845 010 9000.

VEHICLES AFFECTED AND THEIR VAT TREATMENT

The vehicles affected are certain car-derived vans and the combination van.

CAR-DERIVED VANS

Many car-derived vans pose no problem with regard to our current definition of a motor car, in that they are clearly vans or non-motor cars for VAT purposes e g they have no rear seats, metal side panels to the rear of the front seats, a load area which is highly unsuitable for carrying passengers etc.

However a number of models, where the vehicle starts off life as a car and is subsequently altered, cannot be so clearly defined. It is these vehicles which are the focus of this brief [and also an HMRC announcement of 27 October 2006].

On the exterior, these vehicles look like a motorcar but their interior has been altered to give the appearance and functionality of a van. The rear seats and seat belts along with their mountings have been completely removed and the rear area of the shell is fitted with a new floor panel to create a load area. In addition, the side 'windows' to the rear of the driver's seat are fitted with immovable opaque panels.

Customs will *not* view such a "car-derived" vehicle as a motorcar for VAT purposes, if:

- the technical criteria specified in Customs guidance are met by the manufacturer. The criteria relate to how any alterations to the vehicle have been effected
- the adaptations give the vehicle the functionality of a commercial vehicle. As such, the removal of a bench seat or similar from what is essentially a two-seater car would not automatically satisfy Customs' requirements and
- the space that remains behind the front row of seats is highly unsuitable for carrying passengers.

It may be difficult for businesses to satisfy themselves fully that all of the technical criteria have been met. At present, Customs, in partnership with the manufacturers, are developing a list of car-derived vans on which VAT can be deducted, subject to the normal rules. This list will be available shortly on the Customs' website. In the meantime, if businesses are in any doubt, they should obtain confirmation in writing from the vendor that the vehicle meets the technical criteria.

Customs consulted the manufacturers on the technical criterion in September 2003. As such, if businesses have bought such a car-derived van prior to 1 October 2003, it is unlikely that it will satisfy all of the technical criteria set out in Customs' guidance. However, where the vehicle has the appearance of a car-derived van as defined above, in such circumstances, Customs will allow that vehicle to be treated as a non-motor car for VAT purposes, and the VAT incurred can be recovered, subject to the normal rules.

COMBINATION VANS

While these vehicles have the appearance of vans, they are designed to be fitted with or include additional seats behind the front row of seats to enable the carriage of passengers.

Such vehicles are motorcars for VAT purposes except in the case of:

— larger vehicles which have a payload of more than one tonne (these vehicles are automatically excluded from becoming motor cars by the one tonne payload test contained in legislation) and

— those vehicles where the dedicated load area (ie that load area which is completely unaffected by the additional seating) is of a sufficient size compared to the passenger area to make the carriage of goods the predominant use of the vehicle.

— If businesses have previously bought a combination van, which does not fall within the exceptions above, it is a motorcar under VAT legislation. If businesses have recovered the VAT incurred on the purchase, they must make an adjustment to correct this overclaim.

Commentary—*De Voil Indirect Tax Service* **V3.443**.

Notes—See HMRC announcement of 27 October 2006 concerning clarification of the definition of car-derived vans. Also see Business Brief 13/06 with regard to retrospective claims for VAT overdeclared by motor retailers following the *Marks and Spencer* European Court decision.

1 July 2004. Business Brief 17/04

Excise/VAT – Intra-EC ships, aircraft and trains: retail sale of goods for on board consumption

This Business Brief article is aimed primarily at businesses involved in the retail sale of goods to travellers on board intra-EC ships, aircraft and trains. It expands on, and clarifies, the definition of goods for on board consumption. These sales remained relieved from VAT when duty free sales to intra-Community travellers were withdrawn in 1999.

The treatment detailed in this Business Brief article has been agreed following consultation with the Passenger Shipping Association.

DEFINITION OF 'ON BOARD CONSUMPTION'

Goods sold for consumption on board ships and aircraft, such as food, drink and tobacco are relieved from excise duty and VAT. However, goods sold for consumption on board trains are relieved from VAT only; sales of tobacco are excise duty paid.

All sales of these commodities from an on board bar or restaurant are treated as being for immediate consumption. However the sale of alcohol and tobacco will carry certain conditions and restrictions. These restrictions are listed in section 37 of Notice 202.

For VAT purposes food, confectionery and soft drink sold anywhere on board a ship or aircraft are treated as goods consumed on board and relieved of VAT; as long as it is self-evident that these products are of a type that are more suitable for on board consumption than gift purchase or home use. Products that by virtue of their nature of packaging are clearly not suitable to be treated as consumed on board (such as boxes of chocolates or tins of biscuits) are subject to VAT in the normal way, even if these products are actually consumed on board the ship or the aircraft.

As smoking is not permitted on board aircraft, no sales of tobacco products will qualify as consumption on board.

2 August 2004. Business Brief 20/04

Gas and electricity suppliers: new extra-statutory concession for bad debts

This Business Brief article outlines a new Extra-Statutory Concession, enabling suppliers of gas and electricity to obtain relief from VAT on debts owed by domestic customers, after the suppliers have accepted the transfer of a domestic customer and their debt from another supply company.

BACKGROUND

The VAT Bad Debt Relief scheme enables VAT registered businesses to recover some or all of the VAT they have declared and paid in respect of their supplies, where their customer has failed to pay. Under the terms of the scheme, the person who makes the supply is the only person entitled to claim VAT Bad Debt Relief.

This concession supports Government policy to allow greater flexibility for domestic fuel and power consumers by enabling them to change suppliers even if they have a debt.

CHANGES

The ESC applies where a domestic customer who is in debt to one supplier changes supplier, and the debt is transferred to the new supplier. The new supplier may claim bad debt relief on any part of the debt that remains outstanding six months after the date of transfer.

TIMING

The ESC takes effect today, Monday 2 August 2004.

THE EXTRA-STATUTORY CONCESSION

1. Where a contract for the supply of gas or electricity is substituted by a new contract ("novation") as a result of a domestic consumer transferring from one supplier to another, then, by concession, the new supplier may claim bad debt relief on a supply of gas or electricity made by the former supplier to that consumer, provided that all of the conditions in paragraph 2 below are satisfied.
2. The conditions referred to in paragraph 1 above are:
   (a) the whole or any part of the consideration for the supply is outstanding at the time of the novation
   (b) the whole of the debt is transferred to the new supplier
   (c) at the time of the novation, the former supplier (if he has not already done so) accounts for VAT on the supply at the appropriate rate or, if he has already received a refund upon a claim for bad debt relief in relation to that supply, repays to the Commissioners the amount of that refund
   (d) the claim is not made until six months after payment for the novation and takes account
   (e) both the former of any payments made by the customer after the date of the novation supplier and the new supplier have evidence of:
      (i) the value of the debt (including the VAT amount) that has been transferred and
      (ii) the date of payment for the novation
   (f) the new supplier has a copy of the document issued by him to the consumer to recover the debt (not required if a pre-payment meter is in use).
3. In this concession:

"domestic consumer" means a person to whom fuel or power is supplied for domestic use

"domestic use" has the same meaning as in Group 1 of Schedule 7A to the Value Added Tax Act 1994

"gas" means gas that is conveyed through pipes to premises by a licensed gas transporter and

"licensed gas transporter" means any person authorised by a licence under section 7 of the Gas Act 1986 (as amended) to supply gas through pipes to any premises.

4. This concession does not apply in circumstances where its application would give rise to tax avoidance.

10 August 2004. Business Brief 21/04

VAT position of share issues and partnership contributions following the European Court of Justice decision in Kaphag Renditefonds

This Business Brief clarifies Customs' position on two issues arising from the decision of the European Court of Justice in the German case of *KapHag Renditefonds v Finanzamt Charlottenburg* (Case C-442/01):

A Whether the issue of shares constitutes a supply for VAT purposes; and

B The VAT position of contributions to partnerships.

The case of KapHag concerned the admission of a new partner into a partnership on payment of a capital contribution. The European Court held that no supply was being made by either the individual partners or the partnership to the incoming partner in return for the capital contribution.

A WHETHER THE ISSUE OF SHARES CONSTITUTES A SUPPLY

The KapHag decision has been cited as authority for the view that an issue of shares by a company is similarly not a supply for VAT purposes. It is claimed that an issue of shares therefore falls outside the terms of Item 6 of Group 5 of Schedule 9 to the Value Added Tax Act 1994. That Item exempts from VAT:

"The issue, transfer or receipt of, or any dealing with, any security or secondary security ..."

It is Customs' view that the formation or variation of a partnership arrangement is wholly distinguishable from the position where a company issues shares in return for consideration. KapHag was concerned solely with the issues surrounding a partnership. The VAT treatment of share issues has been considered by the Court of Appeal in Trinity Mirror plc ([2001] STC 192) where it was held that an issue of shares by a company did constitute a supply of services for VAT purposes and these fall to be exempt under Item 6 of Group 5 of Schedule 9 to the Act. In most circumstances there will then be a restriction of input tax under the partial exemption rules. Further information is available from VAT Notice 706 Partial Exemption.

B CONTRIBUTIONS TO PARTNERSHIPS

Partnerships to which this section applies include "normal" partnerships of individuals or corporate bodies, limited partnerships whose members are individuals or corporate bodies, overseas limited partnerships that are registered as "normal" partnerships or corporate bodies and limited liability partnerships.

Background

In KapHag, the incoming partner was contributing cash in return for admission into the partnership but it will often be the case that the contribution is in the form of other assets. For example, a new partner's contribution may comprise land or interests in land. The European Court's decision tacitly accepted the Advocate-General's Opinion that the same principles would apply whether the contribution consisted of cash or other assets. Whatever the nature of the assets comprising the contribution, there is no reciprocal supply from the partnership. However, where the assets are not cash, the making of the partnership contribution may have other VAT consequences.

The Advocate-General was satisfied that there was "no doubt that the new partner is effecting an act of disposal of his assets, for which the admission to the partnership is not the consideration" (Paragraph 33 of the Opinion). Such a disposal can therefore have VAT consequences when the partner contributing the assets is a VAT registered person. These consequences will vary depending on the nature of the assets being contributed.

KapHag establishes that nothing is provided by the partnership in return for the assets contributed, therefore any such disposal by the incoming partner is made for no consideration. The VAT Act provides that certain things are subject to VAT even when they are provided or done for no consideration. Customs' view is that all those provisions will still apply where there is no consideration when there is a contribution to partnership assets. A VAT registered person may therefore have to account for tax if he contributes assets to the partnership in the circumstances described in the Act. The VAT consequences can be considered under several main heads:

(i) Contribution to partnership comprising services;
(ii) Contribution to partnership comprising goods other than land;
(iii) Contribution to partnership comprising land or interests in land;
(iv) Whether contribution to partnership can constitute the transfer of a going concern;
(v) How the partnership can reclaim the output tax accounted for by an incoming partner on his contribution as its input tax;
(vi) Capital Goods Scheme consequences; and
(vii) Transfer of assets out of a partnership.

(i) Contribution to partnership comprising services

A partnership contribution may comprise services rather than goods – examples of this could be a trademark or trading logo or the use of an asset the ownership of which is retained by the incoming partner. Two legislative provisions set out the circumstances in which such a contribution may be regarded as a taxable supply, paragraph 5(4) of Schedule 4 to the VAT Act and the Value Added Tax (Supply of Services) Order 1993 (SI 1993/1507).

A supply can arise under paragraph 5(4) where a taxable person applies business goods to private use or makes them available for purposes other than those of his business. The taxable person or his predecessor must have been entitled to input tax under sections 25 and 26 of the VAT Act on the supply of those goods (or anything comprised in them) to him.

The Supply of Services Order similarly provides that a supply arises where a taxable person applies bought-in services to private or non-business use for no consideration where he has been entitled to input tax credit under sections 25 and 26. The value of such a supply cannot exceed the taxable person's input tax entitlement.

Where the above criteria are satisfied, a VAT registered incoming partner will have to account for tax on the supply of services that he is regarded as making in the disposal of the services from his existing business. The partnership may be able to recover this as its input tax where the contributed services are to be used for its business. The procedure for doing this is described at (v) below.

(ii) Contribution to partnership comprising goods other than land

If a partnership contribution comprises goods other than land that a taxable person (the transferor) held as assets, then a deemed supply will be generated as a result of Paragraph 5(1) of Schedule 4 to the VAT Act. This deemed supply does not require there to be consideration when the goods are transferred. It does however only apply where the taxable person disposing of the goods, or their predecessor, if for example they obtained the goods by way of a TOGC, was entitled to full or partial credit for the VAT charged when the goods were supplied to him. Where such a deemed supply arises, the incoming partner will have to account for VAT. The partnership may be able to recover this as its input tax where the contributed assets are to be used for its business. The procedure for doing this is described at (v) below.

(iii) Contribution to partnership comprising land or interests in land

The VAT treatment of land or interests in land also depends upon whether the incoming partner or his predecessor was entitled to deduct input tax in relation to the property that he is contributing to the partnership. For example, if he had opted to tax the property, or it was inherently taxable like new freehold commercial property, there may be a deemed supply as described at (ii) above. The incoming partner will then have to account for VAT on this supply. As with other contributed goods, the partnership may be entitled to recover this as input tax where the property is to be used for the partnership's business. The procedure for doing this is described at (v) below.

Please note all submitted notifications of an option to tax need to be signed by "an authorised signatory" as described in paragraph 7.1 of VAT Notice 742A Opting to tax Land & Buildings.

(iv) Whether contribution to partnership can constitute the transfer of a going concern

It is possible that when assets are transferred by way of a partnership contribution that this could qualify to be treated as a transfer of a going concern (Section 49 of the VAT Act and Article 5 of the VAT (Special Provisions) Order 1995 (SI 1995/1268)). If the contribution meets the conditions to be treated as a transfer of a going concern no VAT will be due from the transferor.

(v) How the partnership can reclaim the output tax accounted for by an incoming partner on his contribution as its input tax

When an incoming partner contributes goods and/or services (on which VAT is due as described above) and the partnership uses them for its business purposes, the partnership can recover the VAT as input tax subject to the normal rules. The incoming partner cannot issue a tax invoice, but in order to provide the partnership with acceptable evidence to support a claim for recovery of input tax, he may use his normal invoicing documentation overwritten with the following statement:

> "Certificate for Tax on Partnership Contribution
>
> No payment is necessary for these goods/services. Output tax has been accounted for on the supply."

The incoming partner must show full details of the goods and/or services on the documentation and the amount of VAT shown must be the amount of output tax accounted for to Customs and Excise.

(vi) Capital Goods Scheme consequences

Where the capital contribution is in the form of an interest in land or a computer, it may be an existing capital item of the incoming partner under the Capital Goods Scheme (CGS). If the transfer to the partnership constitutes a supply which is a disposal of an existing CGS item, then this will wind up the existing CGS item and a disposal adjustment may be due. If the transfer constitutes a TOGC then this will end the current interval for the incoming partner and the partnership will then be responsible for making adjustments for any remaining intervals.

As transfers of assets capital contributions will always constitute either a supply or a TOGC, any existing CGS items will always either be subject to a disposal adjustment or continuing CGS adjustments.

Even if the asset transferred as a capital contribution is not a CGS item in the hands of the incoming partner, it may create a new CGS item for the partnership when its transfer constitutes a supply. If this happens the partnership will need to make adjustments in subsequent intervals in the normal way.

The CGS is further explained in VAT Notice 706/2 Capital Goods Scheme.

(vii) Transfer of assets out of a partnership

KapHag was only concerned with assets moving into a partnership in the form of a partnership contribution. It did not cover the reverse situation, where partnership assets are paid out to an outgoing partner or otherwise disposed of by the partnership for no consideration. Where a transfer of assets out of a partnership for no consideration occurs, one of the following sets of circumstances will apply.

(a) If the incoming partner accounted for output tax when he contributed the assets to the partnership and the partnership was entitled to recover all or part of this as its input tax, there will be a subsequent supply by the partnership when the same assets are transferred out unless the transfer out now satisfies the TOGC criteria.

(b) If no output tax was accounted for when the assets were contributed to the partnership because they constituted a TOGC, the transfer out of the same assets will be a deemed supply upon which the partnership will have to account for tax unless the TOGC criteria are again satisfied.

(c) The partnership may be transferring out more assets than those originally contributed to it. Although the original contribution to the partnership may not have been a TOGC, the subsequent transfer out may now satisfy the TOGC criteria. If it does, no VAT will be due from the partnership.

(d) The original contribution to the partnership may have been a TOGC but the partnership may now be transferring out less of the assets than were originally contributed. Unless the assets being transferred out still meet the TOGC criteria in their own right, there may be a deemed supply upon which the partnership will have to account for the appropriate tax. As explained at (ii) and (iii) above, the entitlement of the partnership or its predecessor to deduct input tax in relation to the items that are the subject of the transfer out will determine whether or not there is a supply.

Application of section 45 of the VAT Act 1994

In the past, there was uncertainty as to whether it was section 45(1) of the VAT Act that led to there being no supply from a partnership to an incoming partner. That section provides for the registration of partnerships in the following terms:

"45(1) The registration under this Act of persons—

(a) carrying on a business in partnership, or

(b) carrying on in partnership any other activities in the course or furtherance of which they acquire goods from other member States,

may be in the name of the firm; and no account shall be taken, in determining for any purpose of this Act whether goods or services are supplied to or by such persons or are acquired by such persons from another member State, of any change in the partnership."

Partnerships in England and Wales have no legal identity. A new partner joining a partnership, or old one leaving it, would result in a new partnership rather than change the composition of the existing one. Without s.45(1), deregistration and registration would be necessary every time a partner joined or left. The purpose of s.45(1) is to ensure continuity by providing that a business carried on in a firm's name is treated as a continuing business irrespective of changes in its composition. The situation addressed by s.45(1) is therefore entirely different to that considered in KapHag.

14 September 2004. Business Brief 25/04

Customs' policy on assessments following the judgments of the High Court in C&E v Laura Ashley and the Court of Appeal in DFS Furniture Company v C&E

This Business Brief clarifies Customs' policy on assessments following recent court judgments in Laura Ashley and DFS. Taxpayers are not asked to take any action as a consequence of this Business Brief.

GENERAL

The recent judgments in Laura Ashley, in the High Court, and DFS, in the Court of Appeal, are concerned with the validity of VAT recovery assessments, i e assessments made to recover money paid, repaid or credited to taxpayers in error. The judgments raised several points that Customs regarded as 'unsettled' and so we petitioned the House of Lords to hear a further appeal in the DFS case to clarify the position for the benefit of Customs and taxpayers alike. That petition was unsuccessful and so the DFS litigation is now at an end.

In dealing with the validity of recovery assessments, the court judgments, by implication, raise an issue of a more general nature about the effect of a finding that any assessment raised by Customs is invalid. It is Customs view that the proper course for a taxpayer to take if the taxpayer has been assessed and believes the assessment to be incorrect for any reason is to ask Customs to review the decision and, if still unsatisfied, to make a timely appeal to the VAT & Duties Tribunal.

Where an underdeclaration of tax has been correctly established but the related assessment, which has been paid but not appealed, is subsequently acknowledged to be technically flawed, for example where it was made for the wrong accounting period, Customs will not withdraw the assessment. There will not be any reason to do so. In addition, and subject always to the VAT appeal provisions, no repayment of money paid against a technically flawed but otherwise correct assessment will be made.

This general policy in no way alters Customs' obligation and commitment to make every effort to ensure that assessments for arrears of tax are correct in all respects.

The Laura Ashley and DFS judgments

The effect of these judgments, taken together, is that:

(*a*) assessment time limits cannot begin to run from the date of a court judgment, or its delivery;

but there is continuing uncertainty about:

(*b*) whether an assessment to recover money repaid or credited to a taxpayer as a result of a mistake of law is properly made under VATA 1994 s 80(4A) or s 73(2);

(*c*) whether, for a recovery assessment, time limits can run from the date a repayment is made; and

(*d*) which prescribed accounting period should be assessed when a recovery assessment is made under S73(2).

Customs future practice

1 Assessments time limits running from a court judgment

The law as currently interpreted by the courts in *C&E Comrs v DFS Furniture Company plc* [2004] STC 559 is that a court judgment, or its delivery, is not a fact for the purposes of the 'evidence of facts' time limit rules for making assessments. Customs now accept the DFS judgment on this point and will make no more assessments that rely solely on a court judgment as evidence of facts.

Where past recovery assessments have relied on a court judgment, it is probable that the repayment being recovered was made following a mistake of law. Any tax paid on the recovery assessment was properly due on remedy of the mistake of law.

Some appeals challenging the validity of recovery assessments have been lodged and stood over behind DFS. These appeals will now be reviewed by Customs and the appellants informed of the outcome as soon as possible.

2 Assessments made to recover money repaid or credited following a mistake of law

The judgment in *C&E Comrs v DFS Furniture Company plc* includes obiter dicta remarks which might be taken as suggesting that amounts repaid under VATA 1994 s (80)(1) following a mistake of law were only properly recoverable by assessment made under VATA 1994 s 73(2), subject to the time limits in VATA 1994 s 73(6)(*a*). Customs do not accept this approach.

For the time being, Customs will continue to make assessments under VATA 1994 s 80(4A) for recovery of amounts repaid under s 80(1). However, to protect the Exchequer in the event that the Court of Appeal in DFS is right, we will also assess in the alternative under s 73(2).

Whether past assessments were made under VATA 1994 s 80(4A) or s 73(2) it was appropriate for Customs to recover amounts repaid that ought not to have been repaid.

3 Recovery assessments time limits running from the date the incorrect repayment was made

The Court of Appeal in *C&E Comrs v DFS Furniture Company plc* appears to have taken the view that repayment is not itself a fact for the purposes of the 'evidence of facts' time limit rules for making assessments.

Customs do not think that many, if any, recovery assessments will have been made that rely on the fact of repayment to satisfy the evidence of facts time limit rules. Where at the time of considering a repayment claim Customs are already out of time to make a recovery assessment, we will take account of the obiter dicta remarks in *C&E Comrs v DFS Furniture Company plc* and not repay unless the claimant signs an undertaking to return any payment with interest in the event that the underlying issue is finally determined in Customs' favour.

4. The period to assess under s 73(2)

There are now three apparently conflicting judgments of the courts concerning the period Customs should assess when a recovery assessment is made under VATA 1994 s 73(2).

Customs have taken the period to assess as the period for which a return was made that contained the incorrect claim; or, following the judgment of the Court of Appeal in *C&E v Croydon Hotel and Leisure Co Ltd* [1996] STC 1105, the period in which a voluntary disclosure containing the incorrect claim was made. On this basis, the time limits applying to incorrect returns and to incorrect voluntary disclosures are consistent.

The judgment of the High Court in *C&E v Laura Ashley* [2004] STC 635 was that the period to assess should have been the period to which the relevant tax related, i e the assessment made under VATA 1994 s 73(2) to recover a repayment or credit wrongly given following a voluntary disclosure of an error in an earlier period should have been made for that earlier period.

Finally, the Court of Appeal in *C&E Comrs v DFS Furniture Company plc* [2004] STC 559 took the view that, in similar but not identical circumstances, the period to assess was the period current when the repayment was made.

Until these apparently conflicting judgments are resolved, Customs may in future need to protect tax in certain cases by making assessments in the alternative or by means of enforceable undertakings.

Where, following a court judgment against Customs on, for example, a liability point, Customs are appealing to have that judgment reversed, we would normally meet the claim of another taxpayer in a similar position and raise a recovery assessment to protect the revenue in the expectation that Customs' appeal will succeed. The Laura Ashley judgment may mean that such a protective assessment for an earlier period would be out of time under existing assessment time limit rules. In those circumstances, Customs will not pay a claim unless the claimant signs an undertaking to return any payment with interest in the event that the matter is finally determined in Customs' favour.

For the past, no corrective action is required, as any taxpayer who paid a recovery assessment made under VATA 1994 s 73(2) will have paid an amount that was properly due.

26 October 2004. Business Brief 28/04

Place of supply of trading allowances in greenhouse gas emissions

This Business Brief article announces Customs' policy in determining the place of supply of emissions allowances when traded across borders. This follows extensive discussions in Europe on the EU Emissions Trading Scheme (EU ETS) and ensures consistency with other member States, removing the possibility for double or no taxation.

BACKGROUND

The EU ETS sets out the rules for a scheme in greenhouse gas emission allowance trading within the Community. It is likely to come into force on 1 January 2005. However, in advance of that date all member States have agreed the rules for determining the place of supply of those allowances for VAT purposes. Whilst the UK initially considered that the place of supply of such supplies would come under the 'basic rule' (ie taxed in the country where the supplier is based), we have now agreed, as the result of representations made by businesses and discussions with other Member States, that for cross-border supplies of allowances, the place of supply should be the place where the customer belongs. This approach aligns our place of supply treatment with other Member States and therefore avoids instances of double taxation.

PLACE OF SUPPLY RULES

This only affects supplies of allowances when they are traded across borders; there is no change to the place of supply of supplies within a country (which continue to be taxed where the supplier is based, subject to the normal rules).

For supplies across borders, emissions trading in allowances will be treated as supplied where received (falling within Schedule 5 of the VAT Act 1994 and Article 9(2)(e) of the Sixth VAT Directive).

The place of supply of brokers' services needs to be determined separately. As the place of supply for cross-border transactions in allowances is where they are received, the broker's supply will take place where that broker's customer belongs, regardless of where the actual emissions allowances are sold. According to the normal rules, a broker is regarded as such when sufficient intermediation is performed.

Introduction is not sufficient-where the service is one of mere introduction, the supply will be seen in accordance with the basic rule ie where the introducer belongs.

EFFECTIVE DATE

This policy will be implemented from the date of this Business Brief. However, suppliers may continue to treat their supplies as basic rule for contracts entered into before this date.

26 October 2004. Business Brief 28/04

Correcting liability errors

Business Brief 16/03 explained Customs' practice of announcing changes to policies and our interpretation of the law in Business Briefs. It went on to restate the policy set out in earlier Business Brief 14/94 concerning over- and underpayments arising when announced changes are not implemented by businesses. This Business Brief expands on that policy statement and deals more generally with the tax implications of changes in policy and in the interpretation of the law.

CHANGES IN POLICY

Generally, a change in Customs' policy is not applied retrospectively. Most changes will be announced in a Business Brief and in VAT Notes issued to all registered traders. They will be applied either from a current date or from some future date in order to give businesses time to prepare for the change or perhaps to provide for a transitional period so that businesses have an opportunity, for example, to benefit from an existing policy before a less beneficial policy is introduced.

CHANGES IN INTERPRETATION OF THE LAW

Significant changes in Customs' interpretation of the law will also be announced in a Business Brief and in VAT Notes issued to all registered traders. Unlike a prospective policy change, however, a change in our interpretation of the law, which will usually take place as a result of litigation, means that, in Customs' view, the relevant legislative provision should always have been applied in accordance with the revised interpretation.

For example, the High Court ruled in Kingscrest Associates Ltd [2002] STC 490 that the exemption in UK and EC law for care provided in hospitals and other similar establishments did not apply to non-medical care provided commercially in residential homes for children and young adults with learning difficulties. The effect of this decision was that certain supplies previously regarded as exempt were, and had always been, liable to VAT.

Changes in our interpretation of the law are therefore essentially retrospective. Where past declaration errors were made on returns on the basis of Customs' interpretation of the law, there are three general principles that will apply in correcting matters. These principles also reflect our views, supported by decisions in *Sunningdale Golf Club* [1997] V&DR 79 and *Barclays Bank PLC* LON/02/815 (decision number 18410) that businesses cannot take the benefit of a change in interpretation of the law without the burden.

1. Customs will not expect or require businesses to correct past declaration errors, which were made on the basis of Customs interpretation of the law. Businesses will only be required to apply the new interpretation of the law from a current or future date, which we will announce. Where the new interpretation means that additional tax is due, this date will normally be after every registered trader has been informed of the change via VAT Notes.
2. If, following a Customs announcement of its new interpretation of the law, a business chooses to correct historical errors we will accept the corrections provided the neutrality of the tax is respected and the business is no better off, and the Exchequer no worse off, than they would have been if the mistaken interpretation had not been made.
3. Where Customs exercise a discretion not to collect arrears of tax due, including circumstances covered by the existing misdirection class concession, we shall do so in a manner consistent with the above principles.

Examples to illustrate how these general principles apply in particular circumstances are provided in an annexe to this Business Brief.

THE MISDIRECTION CLASS CONCESSION

The misdirection class concession says that:

> "If a Customs and Excise officer, with the full facts before him, has given a clear and unequivocal ruling on VAT in writing or, knowing the full facts, has misled a registered person to his detriment, any assessment of VAT due will be based on the correct ruling from the date the error was brought to the registered person's attention."

In operating the misdirection class concession Customs' policy is

- to apply the concession to net tax due in a period, i e output tax net of input tax and not to the tax undercharged;
- to apply the concession across periods so that where the output tax and the related input tax fall in different periods like consequences shall ensue as if the input tax and output tax fell in the same period; and
- not to apply the concession where the tax undercharged has or is to be charged on to customers.

This statement of practice applies to all cases where relief under the misdirection class concession is appropriate and is not limited to cases where there has been a mistaken interpretation of the law by Customs.

ANNEX

Example 1 Taxable supplies treated by Customs as exempt: businesses not previously registered for VAT

Where taxable supplies have been treated incorrectly by Customs as exempt, we will normally accept that the misdirection class concession applies and will only require the supplies to be taxable from a future date. This means that businesses will not usually be required to register in respect of previous supplies that were treated as exempt on the basis of Customs interpretation of the law at the time that the supply was made.

A business may choose, however, to register for VAT belatedly in respect of these supplies. In that event the business will normally be asked to complete a long first period return, covering the period from the effective date of registration to the end of the current period, or the date of deregistration if that is appropriate. This is the arrears period. Where taxable turnover is below the registration threshold, the backdating of any voluntary registration will be limited to three years and the long first period adjusted accordingly.

The long first period return must be completed showing any amounts due as output tax for the period covered as well as amounts claimed as input tax. Having chosen to register for VAT, the business must render accurate returns and declare the correct VAT liability. A return completed without fully accounting for output tax, on the basis that none was charged as a result of Customs' mistaken interpretation of the law, will be treated by Customs as a return in error.

Where the net tax position for the arrears period is that a repayment is due, Customs will repay this amount as a VAT credit due under section 25(3) of the VAT Act 1994.

Where the net tax position for the arrears period is that an amount is due to Customs and that amount has not been declared or not paid, we will remit the tax due under the misdirection class concession. The class concession here will be applied to net tax due (and not to output tax) and only across the whole of the arrears period.

A business that has registered belatedly may want to issue belated invoices to customers for VAT. Where, following the change in Customs' view of the law, a business issues additional invoices to recover undercharged VAT from his customers, the concession in the previous paragraph will not apply and he must account for and pay any VAT due. If additional invoices are issued to some customers and not others, relief under the misdirection class concession will only be available on amounts of VAT not charged, net of associated input tax.

Generally, then, there would in this example be no advantage to the taxpayer in being registered for VAT retrospectively unless large amounts of input tax were incurred in the arrears period on capital or overhead expenses.

Example 2 Taxable supplies treated as exempt; businesses registered for VAT

Where supplies have been incorrectly treated by Customs as exempt but are in fact taxable, once again we will normally accept that the misdirection class concession applies and only require that the supplies be treated as taxable from a future date.

However, a VAT registered trader may choose to correct the errors of the past by submitting a voluntary disclosure or repayment claim. Any such voluntary disclosure or repayment claim must be made in accordance with Customs' Notice 700/45 How to correct VAT errors and make adjustments or claims. All corrections must be made within time limits, and claims may be subject to an unjust enrichment defence, as detailed in the Notice.

Subject to the three year limitation period, any voluntary disclosure or repayment claim made should be for all prescribed accounting periods in which Customs' mistaken interpretation of the law has resulted in incorrect tax declarations or payments. Any voluntary disclosure or repayment claim must declare any amounts due as output tax as well as amounts being claimed as input tax and take account of all errors in the periods.

Should a voluntary disclosure for overdeclared tax or repayment claim fail to take into account all errors or all affected accounting periods, then Customs will set-off any amounts owed to us in other periods as a result of the same error.

Where the net tax position for all the periods is that a repayment is due, Customs will repay that amount.

Where, the net tax position is that an amount of VAT is due to us, which has not been paid, we will normally, by discretion, remit this tax, under the misdirection class concession. This means that where the errors are as a result of a taxable supply being treated as exempt, we will not assess for any net tax, i e the excess of output tax not charged over input tax that is deductible.

Where, despite Customs earlier view of the law, a business has treated the supplies all along as taxable and charged VAT to customers no corrective action will be appropriate. Where, following the change in Customs' view of the law, a business issues additional invoices to recover undercharged VAT from his customers, the concession in the previous paragraph will not apply and he must account for and pay any VAT due. If additional invoices are issued to some customers and not others, relief under the misdirection class concession will only be available on amounts of VAT not charged on additional invoices, net of associated input tax. The requirement that any corrections made must be made to all periods, will not apply where underdeclared tax is charged on and the underpayment voluntarily declared and paid to Customs.

Once again, it is likely that there is no material benefit to be gained by correcting the errors of the past unless the business has incurred substantial amounts of input tax on capital or overhead expenses.

Example 3 Exempt or taxable supplies treated as taxable at a higher rate, eg zero or lower rate treated as standard rate; voluntary disclosures from VAT registered traders.

Where supplies have been incorrectly treated by Customs as taxable but are in fact exempt, or are taxable at a lower rate, businesses may choose to correct the errors of the past. Any voluntary disclosure / repayment claim should be made as described in Customs' Notice 700/45 How to correct VAT errors and make adjustments or claims.

Subject to the three year limitation period, any voluntary disclosure / repayment claim should be for all prescribed accounting periods in which the liability error occurred, subject to time limits. When preparing a voluntary disclosure / repayment claim businesses must take account of all errors in the periods, declaring any input tax claimed in error and output tax overdeclared / overpaid.

Should a voluntary disclosure / repayment claim not take into account all errors or all affected accounting periods, then Customs will seek to set-off any amounts owed to us, for these periods against the amount claimed in other periods.

Where the net tax position for all the periods is that a repayment is due to the business, Customs will repay that amount, subject to repayment not unjustly enriching them. Unjust enrichment is dealt with in Notice 700/45 How to correct VAT errors and make adjustments or claims.

19 November 2004. Business Brief 30/04

VAT and partnership 'shares'

BACKGROUND

Business Brief 21/04 clarified Customs' policy on share issues and partnership contributions following the European Court of Justice (ECJ) decision in KapHag Renditefonds (C-442/01). That Business Brief did not deal with the VAT position of transfers of partnership interests ('shares'). This Business Brief explains the VAT treatment of transactions involving the transfer of a partner's 'share'.

IS THE DISPOSAL OF A 'SHARE' IN A PARTNERSHIP A SUPPLY?

KapHag established that a partnership entity or the existing partners are making no supply when a new partner is admitted in return for making a capital contribution. The question arises whether the subsequent disposal by the partner of that 'share' in the partnership is a supply for VAT purposes. It is important to bear in mind that this 'share' is distinct from the assets that were contributed by the partner when they joined the partnership. Therefore, even though the selling price of the 'share' may be determined by the value of those assets, they are not the subject of the later sale, which has its own liability for VAT purposes.

Although the ECJ has not considered this type of transaction with respect to partnership 'shares', there have been a number of cases where it has given a decision in respect of transactions involving shares in companies. The cases of *Polysar* (C-60/90), *Harnas* and *Helm* (C-C-80/95), *Wellcome Trust* (C-155/94) and *Regie Dauphinoise* (C-306/94) have established that the mere acquisition and holding of shares in a company is not to be regarded as an economic activity. However, it has stated that transactions in shares or interests in companies and associations may constitute economic activity in three situations:

(*a*) Where the transactions constitute the direct, permanent and necessary extension of an economic activity.

(*b*) Where the transactions are effected in order to secure a direct or indirect involvement in the management of a company in which the holding is acquired.

(*c*) Where the transactions are effected as part of a commercial share-dealing activity.

Customs considers that the same principles apply to transactions involving partnership 'shares'. This means that in some circumstances the disposal of a partnership 'share' will not constitute a supply and in others it will.

Circumstances in which the disposal of a partnership 'share' will not constitute a supply

This list is not exhaustive. The most common situations in which the disposal of a partnership 'share' by a partner will not be a supply are likely to be:

1 *The 'share' is disposed of for no consideration* – A 'share' in a partnership comprises services rather than goods. When services are transferred, assigned or otherwise disposed of for no consideration, they do not constitute any supply for VAT purposes.

2 *The 'share' being sold was acquired simply as an investment* – Where a partner has acquired his 'share' merely to secure a share in any future profits and has had no involvement in running the partnership, the subsequent sale or assignment of that 'share' for consideration will not be an economic activity. This will not constitute any supply for VAT purposes.

Circumstances in which the disposal of a partnership 'share' will constitute a supply

Again, this list is not exhaustive. The most common situations in which the disposal of a partnership 'share' by a partner will be a supply are likely to be:

1 *Where the partnership 'share' was acquired and disposed of as a direct extension of the*

partner's economic activities – Where a partner is a taxable person in their own right, the partnership 'share' may have been acquired in the course or furtherance of their own economic activities. If that is the case, the subsequent transfer or assignment of that 'share' for a consideration will also be economic activity of that taxable person. For example, the partner may have a business asset to be sold and, rather than selling the asset directly, may have contributed that asset into a partnership and sold the resultant partnership 'share' instead. The sale of that partnership 'share' will constitute a supply for VAT purposes.

2 *Where the partnership 'share' was acquired in order to obtain an active role in the business of the partnership* – Where a partner is a taxable person in their own right and had acquired the partnership 'share' in order to actively participate in, or control, the business of the partnership, then the sale of that 'share' can be economic activity on the partner's part. The sale of the 'share' will constitute a supply for VAT purposes.

3 *Where the partnership 'share' was acquired as part of a commercial partnership 'share-dealing' activity* – A partner who is a taxable person may have a business of dealing in partnership 'shares'. This will be economic activity on the partner's part. Sales or assignments of the partnership 'shares' that were acquired in the course of this activity that are for a consideration will constitute supplies for VAT purposes.

For the avoidance of any doubt, you should note that supplies of partnership 'shares' in the above circumstances cannot be disregarded by virtue of section 45(1) of the VAT Act 1994. As Business Brief 21/04 explained, the purpose of s.45 (1) is to ensure continuity by providing that changes in the composition of a partnership do not create the need for a partnership to deregister and re-register for VAT every time the partners change. It also makes it unnecessary to take account of any changes in the composition of the partnership when determining what supplies have been made or received by the partnership business. The section has no effect upon any supply that one of the partners may be making as a taxable person in their own right.

LIABILITY OF SUPPLIES OF PARTNERSHIP SHARES

In those circumstances where the disposal of a partnership 'share' is a supply, that supply will be an exempt financial service.

TREATMENT OF VAT ON ASSOCIATED PURCHASES

Where the disposal of an existing partnership 'share' is not a supply, the VAT incurred in connection with the disposal will normally not be input tax. Where the disposal is a supply, the related VAT will be input tax, but recovery will normally be fully restricted under the partial exemption rules as the supply is exempt. This is subject to the de minimis provisions (see VAT Notice 706 'Partial Exemption').

APPLICATION TO PAST TRANSACTIONS

This Business Brief clarifies existing policy and the above principles will be applied to all future transactions. Where a past transaction has been treated differently from the above and resulted in an underdeclaration Customs will take no further action. If a past transaction has been treated differently and resulted in an overdeclaration, businesses may use the voluntary disclosure procedure to reclaim the VAT. Any such claims will be subject to the 'three-year capping rules' and rules relating to the payment of statutory interest.

15 December 2004. Business Brief 34/04

Partial exemption: floor-area based special methods in the retail sector

This Business Brief article sets out Customs' view on the use of floor-area based calculations in partial exemption special methods (special methods), particularly in the retail sector. No other businesses are affected.

This brief deals with questions put to Customs following the Tribunal's decision in the case of *Optika Ltd* VTD 18627 (Optika). There is no change of Customs' policy. Further information on partial exemption is available in Notice 706 'Partial Exemption'.

BACKGROUND

Optika, a retail optician, appealed against Customs' rejection of their proposed floor-area based special method. The Tribunal agreed with Customs because, in Optika's case, a floor-area based special method did not give a fair and reasonable result. A method is likely to be fair and reasonable if it:

– Can be operated by the business,
– Can be checked by Customs, and
– Produces a fair result.

In the right circumstances, floor-area based methods will meet all these conditions and Customs will approve them.

FLOOR-AREA BASED SPECIAL METHODS

Floor-area based special methods are likely to be acceptable when:

– Most of the business's VAT bearing costs relate to their premises, and
– Most of the floor-area of those premises is used for either wholly taxable or wholly exempt activities, with only minor areas relating to both.

FLOOR-AREA IN THE RETAIL SECTOR-THE IMPACT OF OPTIKA

Floor-area based special methods are seldom fair and reasonable for retailers. The following features from the Optika case illustrate this:

* NOTIONAL SPLITS OF 'MIXED USE' AREAS: Few areas of Optika's premises were exclusively used for taxable or exempt activities. Optika's proposals therefore required notional splits of mixed-use floor-areas in order to create any workable calculation. Methods that require significant notional splits are unacceptable due to the inherent uncertainties in making and checking them.

* WEIGHTING OF FLOOR AREAS: The method proposed by Optika required a weighting of floor areas with those at the front of the premises having far greater impact on the amount of tax deductible. Optika argued this reflected a system of weightings (known as zoning) commonly used by landlords to calculate rental charges. However, just because zoning is used to calculate an overall rent, this does not mean that more is charged for some areas than for others. Each rental is a single supply covering the entire premises.

* USE OF RETAIL AREAS: Optika's proposals assumed that the use made of the retail area and the shop front related to their taxable products. However the shop front attracted customers to purchase all of their products and much of the selling of exempt products took place in the retail area. Consequently the shop front and retail area are related to both taxable and exempt sales. Because the proposals were based on a mistaken assumption, they were unacceptable.

Many retailers share some or all of these features, either generally or in specific floor-area based special method proposals. Where this occurs floor-area based special methods will not be approved.

FLOOR-AREA IN THE RETAIL SECTOR—GENERAL

The sale of exempt products is often an important and consistent part of the trading activities of retailers, making a significant contribution to profits. For example when finance or insurance is standardly offered and actively marketed on goods being sold. Many retailers advertise and sell both taxable and exempt products in a large proportion of their premises. Where these factors are present, floor-area is unlikely to prove capable of providing a good basis for a special method.

Customs will refuse to approve any method that includes one or more of the features confirmed as unacceptable in the Optika case. Customs will seek to amend or replace any such existing methods that come to light. Businesses who feel that their current special method might not be fair and reasonable, based on the content of this brief, should contact their local VAT office or Customs' National Advice Service.

10 February 2005. Business Brief 2/05

Supplies of nursery and crèche facilities by a charity

This Business Brief article is issued to clarify Customs' position on the business status of supplies of nursery and crèche facilities where those supplies are made by a charity. This issue first arose as a result of the High Court case of *Yarburgh Children's Trust* (see Business Brief 4/03) and has recently been tested again in the High Court case of *St Paul's Community Project Ltd.*

In the earlier case of *Yarburgh*, the Court decided that the charity was not making supplies by way of business. Despite that decision, Customs' position remained that the provision of nursery and crèche facilities in such circumstances was a business activity for VAT purposes. However, in the more recent case of St Paul's, the Court's decision has again gone in favour of the charity. The Court found that the intrinsic nature of the enterprise was not the carrying on of a business, identifying the distinguishing features as the social concern for the welfare of disadvantaged children, lack of commerciality in setting fees and the overall intention simply to cover costs.

Customs do not agree that these features point to the activities being non-business because we consider that the charity is making supplies of services for consideration in much the same way as a commercial nursery. However, taking into account all the circumstances in this case, Customs have decided not to appeal further.

This means Customs will now accept that the provision of nursery and crèche facilities by charities, along the same lines as those in *Yarburgh Children's Trust* and *St Paul's Community Project Ltd*, is not a business activity for VAT purposes.

BACKGROUND

Both *Yarburgh Children's Trust* and *St Paul's Community Project Ltd* are charities which undertake to provide nursery and crèche facilities for pre-school age children as part of their charitable objectives. Both organisations charge fees for their services, which are set at a level designed to ensure that they merely cover their costs. They both undertook construction of new nursery premises. Such supplies would normally be subject to VAT but there are provisions in UK law which allow construction work to be zero-rated where buildings are used by a charity otherwise than in the course of business. Zero-rating can be beneficial to charities, if they undertake exempt activities and the amount of VAT they recover would be heavily restricted. Customs denied zero-rating on the grounds that these charities were making business supplies. The High Court has taken the opposing view that neither charity is in business for VAT purposes.

CUSTOMS' POLICY

It remains Customs' long standing policy that a business activity is possible even in the absence of a profit motive. Customs believe that this approach is consistent with UK and EC legislation and is supported by a number of decisions of the UK and European Courts. Many charities with activities not motivated by profit and whose fees are subsidised by public funds or donations benefit from such activities being business for VAT purposes, because they are able to recover VAT incurred in relation to those activities. It would not be beneficial for the charity sector as a whole if charitable activities were all regarded as non-business, as it would deny them recovery of input tax. In cases that are not broadly in line with *St Paul's* or *Yarburgh*, Customs shall continue to apply the business test, in order to determine whether the supplies concerned are being made by way of business.

WHAT CONSTITUTES A BUSINESS ACTIVITY FOR VAT PURPOSES?

As neither UK nor EC legislation has provided an exhaustive definition or test for determining if an activity is business, the meaning of business and economic activity has emerged from a body of case law. This has given rise to the business test, which consists of six elements or indicators that the Courts have seen as being characteristic of a business. These are not a checklist and a business may have some, but not all, of the features indicated. Instead they are a set of tools designed to help compare activities where there is some uncertainty about their nature with features of activities that are clearly business. In most cases, it will be clear that an activity is business but, where difficulties arise, Customs will apply this business test. The elements of this test were set out in Business Brief 4/03 and are reproduced below.

- Is the activity a serious undertaking earnestly pursued? (This considers whether the activity is carried on for business or daily work rather than pleasure or daily enjoyment.)
- Is the activity an occupation or function that is actively pursued with reasonable or recognisable continuity? (When considering this test one should consider how frequently the supplies will be made.)
- Does the activity have a certain measure of substance in terms of the quarterly or annual value of taxable supplies made?
- Is the activity conducted in a regular manner and on sound and recognised business principles?
- Is the activity predominately concerned with the making of taxable supplies for a consideration? (This has in many instances been seen as the most important and arguably the most problematic indicator. In the appeal of The Institute of Chartered Accountants England & Wales, the House of Lords found that the test must be read as asking 'what is the real nature of the activity' ie is the real nature of the activity the making of taxable supplies for consideration or is it something else?)
- Are the taxable supplies that are being made of a kind which, subject to differences of detail, are commonly made by those who seek to profit from them?

22 February 2005. Business Brief 3/05

Clarification of the liability of the supply of lifts to educational institutions

This Business Brief sets out Customs' policy on the VAT treatment of lifts installed in educational institutions.

BACKGROUND

Educational institutions which have charitable status, such as grant-maintained schools and universities, can receive the supply and installation of lifts to facilitate the movement of disabled staff and pupils between floors in certain buildings at the zero rate of VAT. For such supplies to qualify for zero-rating, the building must be used by the educational institution for the provision of a permanent or temporary residence or a day-centre for disabled people. The relevant legislation is Items 17 and 18 to Group 12 of Schedule 8 of the VAT Act 1994.

As a consequence of comments made by the High Court in 1997 in the Help the Aged appeal (CO2399), Customs formed the view that educational institutions could be regarded as day-centres providing care for disabled people and therefore the installation of lifts in their non-residential buildings could be zero-rated under the above provisions, providing all other conditions were met.

Customs subsequently reconsidered our understanding of the comments made by the High Court, which concerned the interpretation of a different piece of legislation, and decided our original view of them was incorrect. Whilst having a duty of care, especially to disabled people, educational institutions, generally, do not provide care in a day-centre and the High Court's comments did not suggest that they do. Customs' policy therefore reverted to the scope of the zero-rating being limited to the supply of lifts installed in residential accommodation.

However, as a concession, where an educational institution could demonstrate that they had made a decision to proceed with the purchase and installation of a lift in non-residential accommodation before 1 January 2004, on the basis of our former policy, then zero-rating would apply. Additionally, Customs agreed that any lifts zero-rated in this way could also benefit from the zero-rating of their future repair and maintenance under the provisions of Item 5 of Group 12 to Schedule 8 of the VAT Act 1994.

Unfortunately, the changes in policy were not widely publicised at the time and we have recently been made aware that not all those concerned were aware of them. Customs have therefore decided to publicise the change of policy by means of this Business Brief. Customs have also decided to extend the transitional arrangements so that where a contract for the installation of a lift in non-residential accommodation has been entered into before 31 March 2005; we accept that the supply can be zero-rated providing all other conditions have been met. Where the installation of a lift has been zero-rated under these arrangements, subsequent supplies of repair and maintenance of that lift can also be zero-rated.

Where a contract for the installation of a lift in non-residential accommodation is entered into after that date the supply of installation services and any subsequent supplies of repair and maintenance will be standard-rated.

Where a supplier has accounted for VAT on past supplies and is satisfied that all other conditions have been met, subject to the statutory time limits, they may make a claim for the overpaid VAT in one of the following ways:

1 If the net value of the total adjustments is £2,000 or less, suppliers may amend their VAT account and include the value of the adjustment on their current VAT return.
2 If the net value of the total adjustments is more than £2,000, a separate claim for payment should be submitted to the local Business Advice Centre (suppliers cannot make this adjustment on their VAT returns).

Both of the above methods and how to make a claim are explained in VAT Notice 700/45 'How to correct VAT errors & make adjustments or claims'.

NB: Customs may reject a claim on the grounds that payment would unjustly enrich a supplier. For example, this may happen if the supplier is unable or does not intend to pass on the repayment to his customer. Further details can be found in VAT Notice 700/45.

This Business Brief does not apply to lift installations in those buildings where an educational institution provides permanent or temporary residence, which remains zero-rated, provided all other conditions are met.

4 April 2005. Business Brief 9/05

Hot take-away food

This Business Brief clarifies Customs policy on the treatment of hot take-away food in light of recent VAT Tribunal decisions. It includes some minor amendments to policy, and replaces the guidance previously published in Business Brief 26/02.

Most food is zero-rated for VAT purposes. But hot take-away food and drink is standard-rated, whether sold from a traditional take-away, supermarket or any other outlet. Standard rating applies where the supplier's main intention in heating the food is to enable it to be consumed hot or warm (regardless of whether, in practice, the food is always consumed hot or warm). Standard rating applies irrespective of the customer's intention, the place of consumption or whether the food is collected or delivered.

CAN HOT FOOD BE ZERO-RATED?

You can only zero-rate hot food if your main purpose in heating the food is other than to enable it to be consumed hot or warm. For example, newly baked bread is often warm when sold, but is not normally heated for the purpose of enabling it to be consumed hot or warm.

In some cases suppliers have stated that they have other reasons for heating food and supplying it hot or warm. Supplies in such cases may qualify for zero-rating, but only where the circumstances (ie the nature of the product and the way in which it is stored, displayed, advertised, packaged and supplied) support the contention that the supplier's main purpose is other than to enable the food to be consumed hot. For example, items like chips, hot dogs, burgers and baked potatoes are always standard rated when sold hot because they are clearly intended to be eaten hot.

HOW DO I KNOW IF I CAN ZERO-RATE HOT FOOD?

You can only zero-rate hot food if your main reason for heating the food is other than to enable it to be consumed hot or warm. Any such claims must be consistent with the circumstances under which the hot food is supplied (see below). It is important to consider all of your reasons for heating the food before deciding on the VAT liability of your supplies. Often you may have more than one purpose in heating the food, in which case you must decide which is the dominant purpose.

On the basis of Tribunal and court findings, Customs consider the following to be relevant indicators:

Type of outlet—If advertised as a take-away food outlet, supplies of hot food will be standard-rated.

What happens to the food between the time it is cooked or heated and the time it is handed to the customer—If efforts are made to keep it hot, this may be an indicator for standard rating, whereas if it is left to cool naturally for a period of time this may be an indicator for zero-rating.

Type of packaging used—If food is packaged to retain heat, this would be an indicator for standard rating. However, the reverse does not necessarily apply, since food intended for immediate consumption will often be sold in packaging that is not heat retentive.

Availability of condiments, napkins and utensils-This would be an indicator for standard rating.

The way in which the food is advertised and promoted, including in-store signage and any wording shown on packaging.

Food hygiene regulations-Customs accept that in some cases food may be kept hot partly for the purpose of complying with food hygiene regulations. However, the requirement to comply with these regulations will often not be an aim in itself for the supplier, but merely a consequence of supplying food for consumption whilst hot or warm. If this is the case, then the supplies will be standard rated.

Palatability—If an item is generally accepted to be unpalatable when cold, this would be an indicator for standard rating. However, the reverse does not necessarily apply-The fact that an item remains palatable when cold does not preclude the possibility that it has been heated for the purpose of enabling it to be consumed hot.

18 May 2005. Business Brief 11/05

Judgment of the European Court of Justice (ECJ) in the case of Arthur Andersen & co Accountants (C-472/03)

On 3 March 2005, the ECJ released its judgment in the case of Arthur Andersen. This Business Brief article outlines the findings of the Court, details how HM Revenue & Customs (HMRC) interpret these findings in relation to the current UK VAT exemption for insurance-related services and explains the position for businesses that consider they may be affected by the judgment.

The case, which was referred to the ECJ by the Netherlands Supreme Court, concerned the VAT liability of certain 'back office' services provided by Andersen Consulting Management Consultants (ACMC) to a life insurance company. ACMC used qualified personnel to undertake most of the activities related to insurance on behalf of the insurer including the issuing, management and cancellation of policies, the management of claims and, in most cases, taking decisions that bound the insurer to enter into insurance contracts.

The question put to the ECJ was whether such 'back office' activities carried out for an insurance company were exempt from VAT under Article 13B(a) of the Sixth Directive as "related services performed by insurance brokers and insurance agents".

To fall within the VAT exemption, ACMC had to qualify as either insurance brokers or insurance agents. The ECJ held that the essential characteristic of insurance brokers was that they had complete freedom as to choice of insurer for their clients and that, although insurance agents were tied to a particular insurer, their essential characteristic was that they introduced prospective customers to that insurer. As ACMC did not qualify on either count, their services were taxable at the standard rate.

HMRC's view is that the judgment means the UK VAT exemption for insurance-related services in Group 2 of Schedule 9 to the VAT Act 1994 is currently drawn too widely and, to bring it into line with the judgment, it will need to be amended.

UK law currently provides exemption for certain insurance administration and claims handling services including, for example, the provision of claims handling services by loss adjusters under delegated authority and the administration of policies on behalf of the insurer. Following the

ECJ judgment, however, such services should only fall within the VAT exemption for insurance-related services where the provider had also previously introduced the policyholder to the insurer.

HMRC believe that the judgment does not preclude exemption where the provider does not itself have direct contact with the customer, provided that it sub-contracts the introductory service to a sub-agent, and there is a direct contractual link between the principal agent and the agent providing the introductory service. However, the power to bind the insurer to enter into contracts is not in itself enough to gain exemption.

Implementation of the judgment will lead to VAT becoming chargeable on many of the outsourced services currently provided to insurers. Where insurers use these outsourced services to provide exempt insurance services within the EU, this VAT will be irrecoverable.

HMRC are currently meeting insurance industry representative bodies and providers of the affected services to discuss the impact of this judgment. Following these preliminary discussions, there will be a 12 week formal consultation period on how the judgment is to be implemented in the UK, the proposed changes to UK legislation and the impact implementation will have on the affected industries. It is important to note, however, that the ECJ judgment is binding on member states and the consultation will therefore focus on how and when that implementation will take place. It is intended that the consultation document should be published in July 2005.

No action will be taken to change UK law or policy until formal consultation is complete. In the meantime, businesses can rely on UK law and policy on insurance-related services as it is currently explained in HMRC guidance and notices. There will be no change in the scope of the UK VAT exemption for insurance-related services until UK law has been amended.

If, however, you consider that your business is affected by the judgment, you do not have to wait for the UK law to be amended but are able to rely directly on EU law as outlined by the ECJ in its decision. This means that, whilst you do not have to do so, you can, if you wish:

- apply the revised VAT liability to your services from a current date; or
- make an adjustment retrospectively.

Information on how to make any adjustments to VAT previously paid can be found in VAT Notice 700/45 'How to correct VAT errors and make adjustments or claims'. Additional information on correcting VAT liability errors can be found in Customs' Business Brief 28/04

18 May 2005. Business Brief 11/05

Zero rating for protected buildings—definition of garage

This Business Brief article sets out HM Revenue & Customs' (HMRC) revised policy on what constitutes a "garage" for the purpose of the zero ratings relating to listed buildings which are dwellings.

It follows a decision of the VAT & Duties Tribunal in the case of *Grange Builders (Quainton) Ltd* (LON/02/982).

BACKGROUND

The law provides zero rating for approved alterations to a listed building designed to remain as or become a dwelling or number of dwellings and also for the first grant, by the person reconstructing such a building, of a major interest in the building or part of the building, or its site.

For the purpose of the zero rating, such a building can include a garage (occupied together with the dwelling), either constructed at the same time as the building or, where the building has been substantially reconstructed, at the same time as that reconstruction.

HMRC have always considered that in order for the alteration works to a garage to qualify for zero rating, it was necessary for the garage to have been constructed as a garage.

Therefore HMRC would not have seen the zero rate as applying to the alteration of a building (or part of a building) that was in use as a garage if it had not been constructed as a garage at the same time as the dwelling had been constructed (or substantially reconstructed).

THE TRIBUNAL DECISION

The Tribunal found that, for the alteration of a garage to qualify for zero rating, the building does not have to have been constructed as a garage or used as a garage since the time of the construction (or substantial reconstruction) of the dwelling. It held that a small timber-framed barn that was listed as part of the dwelling and in use as a garage was part of the listed dwelling for the purpose of the zero rating because:

- the barn had been constructed at the same time as the listed dwelling; and
- it had been used as a garage for a significant period before being altered.

HM REVENUE & CUSTOMS' REVISED POLICY

HMRC now accept that, provided a garage is in use as a garage before the alteration or reconstruction takes place and continues to be used as one afterwards, it is not necessary for the garage to have been constructed as a garage (ie as an enclosure for the storage of motor vehicles). It can also have been constructed as something different e g a barn.

The other criteria for zero rating must still be met; these are:

- listing (the garage must be listed, either in its own right or through the deeming provisions of planning law);
- occupation (the garage must be occupied together with the dwelling); and
- time of construction (the garage must have been either constructed at the same time as the listed dwelling or, where the dwelling has been substantially reconstructed, at the same time as that reconstruction).

VAT TREATMENT OF PAST SUPPLIES

Where a supplier has accounted for VAT on past supplies, they may make a claim for the overpaid VAT, subject to the three-year statutory time limits, in one of the following ways:

(a) If the net value of the total adjustments is £2,000 or less, suppliers may amend their VAT account and include the value of the adjustment on their current VAT return.

(b) If the net value of the total adjustments is more than £2,000, a separate claim for payment should be submitted to the local Business Advice Centre (suppliers cannot make this adjustment on their VAT returns).

Both of the above methods and how to make a claim are explained in VAT Notice 700/45 'How to correct VAT errors and make adjustments or claims'.

NB: HMRC may reject a claim on the grounds that payment would unjustly enrich a supplier. For example, this may happen if the supplier is unable or does not intend to pass on the repayment to his customer. Further details can be found in VAT Notice 700/45.

15 June 2005. Business Brief 12/05

Aligning VAT accounting periods

This Business Brief article explains and further publicises HM Revenue & Customs' existing policy on the use of the power to align VAT accounting periods.

BACKGROUND

HM Revenue & Customs continue to be concerned about situations in which businesses 'stagger' their VAT accounting periods in order to gain an unjustified and unintended cash flow benefit at the expense of the revenue.

One familiar example is the routing of export sales through a subsidiary which is outside the VAT group, or main VAT registration. In these cases, the export company has zero rated outputs and makes monthly repayment claims. By contrast, output tax on the supply to the subsidiary is standard rated and only brought to account by the parent or other associated company once a quarter. There is, accordingly, a cashflow benefit to the corporate group.

HM REVENUE & CUSTOMS' POLICY ON ALIGNMENT

HM Revenue & Customs have a discretionary power in Regulation 25 (VAT Regulations 1995) to align VAT periods between the associated businesses, thereby removing the cashflow benefit. They may exercise that power by either withdrawing existing permission for monthly periods or by directing a variation to accounting periods. HM Revenue & Customs intend to continue to exercise this power where there is little or no commercial rationale for the VAT period 'stagger' between the associated businesses besides obtaining the cashflow advantage. They may do so, notwithstanding that the usual policy for businesses expecting to make regular claims for repayment of VAT in other factual situations is to allow monthly returns.

There is no intention to use these powers except in cases where a significant cash flow advantage arises and there is a need to protect the revenue.

HM REVENUE & CUSTOMS' USE OF THE REGULATION 25 POWERS

There is no right of appeal to the VAT and Duties Tribunal against the use of the regulation 25 powers. However, the use of the power is subject to judicial review and new guidance shortly to be issued to staff will emphasise the need for exercise of the powers to be proportionate and to take into account all relevant information. That guidance will be available soon through the normal channels.

15 June 2005. Business Brief 12/05

Clarification of the VAT position of share issues following the European Court of Justice decision in Kretztechnik

Note—See also Business Brief 21/05, published 23 November 2005, for further information.

This Business Brief article is an update on HM Revenue & Customs' position on the VAT treatment of share issues and subsequent input tax recovery, following the decision in *Kretztechnik AG v Finanzamt Linz* (Case C-465/03).

THE DECISION

On 26 May 2005, the European Court of Justice (ECJ) gave its judgment in *Kretztechnik*. The ECJ had been asked to rule upon whether or not a first issue of shares by a public limited company is a supply and whether or not the VAT incurred on the costs of such an issue is deductible input tax. The judgment endorsed the earlier Opinion given by the Advocate General on 24 February 2005, ruling that such an issue is not a supply and that the VAT incurred on the costs is recoverable to the extent that the company's outputs are taxable transactions.

REVISED TREATMENT OF SHARE ISSUE TRANSACTIONS

Until now, HM Revenue & Customs' treatment of share issues has been guided by the Court of Appeal decision in *Trinity Mirror plc v C&E Commissioners* [2001] STC 192. This had established that the issue of shares in the UK by a company for the purpose of financing its business was an exempt supply under Item 6 of Group 5 of Schedule 9 to the VAT Act 1994. Any input tax that was attributable to the costs of making the issue was therefore generally not deductible. *Kretztechnik* has now established that this treatment is incorrect.

Companies that make a first issue of shares in circumstances that are the same as those in Kretztechnik's case are now entitled to recover the input tax incurred on the costs of the issue to the extent that they make taxable supplies. Therefore companies with wholly taxable outputs will be entitled to recover all of the relevant input tax, while those with both exempt and taxable outputs will be entitled to recover a proportion in accordance with their partial exemption method. Claims for input tax in respect of past share issues will be accepted subject to the three-year 'capping' rules. Notice 700/45 'How to correct VAT errors and make adjustments or claims' gives detailed guidance on capping and claim procedures.

There are a number of other situations in which a company may issue shares where the circumstances will differ greatly from those which existed in *Kretztechnik*. In particular, a share issue may take place as part of a company merger, demerger or other restructuring. HM Revenue & Customs are taking legal advice on the extent to which *Kretztechnik* applies to these other share issue situations and further guidance will be issued to businesses after this advice has been received. Any claims for repayment received in the interim will be acknowledged but not processed until this advice has been received.

TRANSACTIONS INVOLVING ISSUES OF FINANCIAL INSTRUMENTS AND SECURITIES OTHER THAN SHARES

Businesses may raise capital through the issue of financial instruments or securities other than shares, like bonds, debentures or loan notes. *Kretztechnik* was concerned solely with issues of shares and the ECJ did not comment upon the extent to which the same principles would apply to other types of issues. HM Revenue & Customs are obtaining legal advice on whether or not other issue transactions are affected and will issue further guidance after the position has been reviewed. Any claims for repayment received in the interim will be acknowledged but not processed until this advice has been received.

15 June 2005. Business Brief 12/05

Landlord inducements to tenants entering leases

This Business Brief article provides revised guidance on the VAT status of inducement payments by landlords to tenants. It replaces earlier guidance in Business Brief 04/03, dated 27 May 2003.

BUSINESS BRIEF 04/03

Business Brief 04/03 set out Customs' policy following the European Court of Justice (ECJ) and High Court decisions in the case of Trinity Mirror plc (formerly Mirror Group plc).

In paragraph 26 of the ECJ's judgment, it was held that a "tenant who undertakes, even in return for a payment from the landlord, solely to become a tenant and pay the rent does not, so far as that action is concerned, make a supply of services to the landlord". The High Court subsequently held that paragraph 26 of the ECJ judgment is narrowly drawn, and Business Brief 04/03 sought to give guidance on that.

In line with the High Court ruling, Business Brief 04/03 advised that "a prospective tenant receiving an inducement payment would make a taxable supply by affording the landlord the advantage of being bound by the lease obligations the tenant has to fulfil." In effect, this meant any such obligations other than to pay the rent (e g to redecorate the demised area every five years) would be sufficient to make the inducement payment consideration for a taxable supply.

CHANGE OF POLICY

Following representations from and detailed discussions with various bodies, HM Revenue & Customs now accept that lease obligations, to which tenants are normally bound, do not constitute supplies for which inducement payments on entering leases are consideration.

HM Revenue & Customs believe that the majority of such payments are therefore likely to be outside the scope of VAT as they are no more than inducements to tenants to take leases and to observe the obligations in them. There will be a taxable supply only where a payment is linked to benefits a tenant provides outside normal lease terms. However, merely putting such a benefit as an obligation in a lease will not mean it ceases to be a taxable transaction.

It is considered that this change of policy now effectively puts inducement payments on a similar VAT footing to rent free periods, in being mainly outside the scope of VAT and only a taxable consideration when directly linked to a specific benefit supplied by a tenant to a landlord.

Examples of taxable benefits by tenants that may be supplied in return for such inducements are:

- Carrying out building works to improve the property by undertaking necessary repairs or upgrading the property
- Carrying out fitting-out or refurbishment works for which the landlord has responsibility and is paying the tenant to undertake.
- Acting as anchor tenant

HM Revenue & Customs accept that this is a difficult area where the undertakings of landlords and tenants can change a number of times in the course of negotiating a tenancy. HM Revenue & Customs will therefore seek as much documentation as possible before reaching a decision. HM Revenue & Customs will not assume that there has been a supply and agree that less specific indicators do not determine the issue. For example, publicity indicating that Company X is to take a lease in a development does not, in itself, determine that the company is an anchor tenant.

Equally, undertakings to use improved materials as part of continuous repairs under a tenant repairing lease would not constitute a taxable benefit to the landlord under the first example above.

PAST TRANSACTIONS

The policy change referred to above may mean that there have been certain cases where tax has been charged wrongly in respect of landlord inducements under the guidelines in Business Brief 04/03.

Tenants who have wrongly declared output tax on inducements received are not obliged to adjust their VAT position. However, if they choose to, then, subject to the three-year capping provisions, they should proceed in accordance with VAT Notice 700/45 'How to Correct Errors and make adjustments or claims'.

Option 1

In accordance with paragraph 3.4 of Notice 700/45, where both the tenant and the landlord are registered for VAT, and provided they both agree, tenants may raise credit notes to their landlords and both parties would then adjust their VAT account.

Option 2

Alternatively where the landlord is not registered for VAT, tenants may choose to make a claim under Section 80 of the VAT Act 1994 for overpaid tax. Any such claim would be subject to the three-year capping provisions and the unjust enrichment defence. Sections 5 and 14 of Notice 700/45 refer.

Note that if past transactions are revisited there may be implications as regards deductible input tax-see below.

In all cases where tenants choose to correct past transactions it will be necessary to:

- review the attribution of any input tax incurred on costs, where that attribution was based on those costs being cost components of the taxable supply now being reversed out, and make any resultant adjustments, and
- revisit their partial exemption calculations for the prescribed and longer periods involved as necessary.

Whichever method tenants choose to correct the incorrect treatment of inducements as supplies, landlords must reduce their input tax deductions in respect of the inducements to the extent that they ultimately recovered or were entitled to recover input tax previously. This could also require partial exemption calculations to be revisited if an inputs based method is used or to determine whether de-minimis limits are exceeded.

Commentary—*De Voil Indirect Tax Service* **V4.111.**

5 July 2005. Business Brief 13/05

Belated notification of an option to tax land and buildings—Clarification of HM Revenue & Customs' policy

This Business Brief clarifies HM Revenue & Customs' (HMRC) policy in relation to the exercise of their discretion to accept a belated notification of an option to tax land and buildings. In particular, it explains the distinction between a belated notification and a retrospective or backdated option. This clarification is given following a rise in the number of attempts to notify options to tax that are retrospective or backdated.

WHO IS AFFECTED?

All those who seek acknowledgement of a decision to opt to tax (sometimes known as an election to waive exemption) outside the 30-day time limit.

BACKGROUND

There are two distinct stages in the process of opting to tax. The first is making the decision to opt, the 'election'. The second is notifying HMRC of that decision, in writing, within 30 days of the date that the decision was made.

Of course, HMRC must be satisfied that the trader was legally entitled to opt to tax. If a trader has made previous exempt supplies of the property, they may require our prior written permission to opt to tax. If permission is required, the trader cannot make a valid election until our permission has been received. The circumstances when permission is required are detailed in VAT Notice 742A Opting to tax land and buildings, Section 5.

RETROSPECTIVE OR BACKDATED OPTIONS

The option has effect from the day on which the election is made or any later day specified in the election. This means that no option to tax can take effect from a date prior to the date on which the trader decided to make the election. This would be a backdated or retrospective option and HMRC has no discretion under the law to accept or acknowledge that it is valid.

BELATED NOTIFICATION OF AN OPTION

However, HMRC has discretion to accept a notification of an option to tax later than the prescribed time limit of 30 days after the decision to opt was made. The discretion is designed to cover situations where a trader has genuinely made the decision to opt to tax, but has failed to notify it to HMRC in time. Before considering whether to exercise this discretion, we would need to be satisfied that the decision was made on the date stated in the written notification.

EXERCISING THE DISCRETION

HMRC will usually accept a belated notification if a trader provides evidence, such as the minutes of a Board or management meeting, or correspondence referring to the decision. However, we accept that this is sometimes not available, so in its absence we would normally accept a statement from the responsible person, plus evidence that

- all the relevant facts have been given;
- output tax has been properly charged and accounted for from the date of the supposed election; and
- input tax recovery in respect of the land or building is consistent with the trader having made taxable supplies of it.

There may be other circumstances where we would accept a belated notification, but this would depend on the individual circumstances of the case.

Conversely, HMRC may not accept that a decision to opt was taken, even when the above conditions are met, if for example—

- there has been correspondence concerning or investigation into the liability of supplies of the property in question since the supposed date of the option, and no mention of the option to tax was made;
- the trader or his representative has previously put forward an alternative explanation for the charging of output tax (for example, that the supply was not of land and buildings, or was of a sports facility).

Moreover, HMRC reserves the right to refuse to accept the belated notification if to do so would produce an unfair result, or if the exercise of the discretion was sought in connection with a tax avoidance scheme.

28 July 2005. Business Brief 14/05

Partial exemption—Tribunal decision in National Provident Institution (NPI)

This Business Brief gives the Commissioners' views on the VAT and Duties Tribunal's decision in the *NPI* appeal (Decision No 18944) that was released on 18 February 2005.

The *NPI* case concerned recovery of input tax by an insurance company that made supplies of securities outside the EU. There is no change to the Commissioners' policy, which is explained below.

BACKGROUND

NPI made three sorts of supply for VAT purposes—

(a) taxable supplies of property (which it had opted to tax);
(b) exempt supplies of insurance (pensions, life assurance and annuities), exempt supplies of securities in the UK and in the EU; and
(c) specified supplies of securities outside the EU.

NPI was entitled to recover input tax on overheads that related to its taxable supplies and to its specified supplies. NPI used the standard method of partial exemption (PE), which determines the VAT recovery only in respect of taxable supplies. It is well established that the recovery of VAT on specified supplies has to be determined separately and before the recovery of VAT on taxable supplies.

Apportionment of input tax is therefore carried out in two stages—

(i) between specified supplies and other supplies (both taxable and exempt) on the basis of the relative use of input tax in making each category of supply; and
(ii) between taxable supplies and exempt supplies on the basis of the standard method or an approved special method.

Subject to the Commissioners' approval, these two stages can be combined into a single calculation, always provided that this achieves a fair and reasonable result.

NPI sought recovery of input tax through a single combined calculation on the basis of values. The Commissioners had not approved that calculation and did not consider that it achieved a fair and reasonable result. The Commissioners therefore applied a two-stage calculation using firstly a staff count and secondly values.

THE TRIBUNAL'S DECISION

The Tribunal reviewed the evidence presented and concluded that there was no demonstrable link between input tax on overheads and staff numbers because the main costs were consultant's fees and the like. It also found that the headcount had been estimated and was thus unreliable. The Tribunal therefore concluded that the Commissioners' method was unsafe. In the circumstances, since no other method had been put to the Tribunal, it held that the use of residual input tax in making specified supplies should be determined according to the proportion that the value of specified supplies bore to the value of all supplies.

THE COMMISSIONERS' VIEWS

The Commissioners have decided not to appeal because the decision was made on the facts of the case. They do not consider that it has any wider application for that reason.

Notwithstanding the Tribunal's views in the *NPI* case, the Commissioners consider that sales of securities will normally be distortive when they are included with other sorts of supply in a combined values-based calculation. This will, for example, be the case when the supplies of securities consume proportionately less by way of taxed overheads for each £1 in value than other supplies. This will work unfairly against the taxpayer when the recovery rate for securities transactions is less than that for insurance transactions and against HMRC when it is greater. For any values-based calculation to secure a fair and reasonable apportionment, there must be a proportionate and broadly similar link between the use of taxed overheads and the values of all the supplies in the PE calculation. Such a link would assume that, pound for pound, premium income consumed the same amount of taxed overheads as sales of securities. The Commissioners consider that will rarely be the true position.

USE OF VALUES-BASED PROXIES FOR "USE"

There is no change in the Commissioners' policy. Any proxy for use that secures a fair and reasonable apportionment of input tax to specified supplies is acceptable.

In the right circumstances, the Commissioners will not object to a values-based method for calculating recovery of input tax in respect of specified supplies. It will rarely however, be acceptable to mix securities with other different activities in a single outputs-based calculation. In such cases, a values-based approach will not give a fair and reasonable result because it is likely to significantly under- or over-state the extent to which input tax is used in making recoverable supplies.

FURTHER INFORMATION

Further information on partial exemption is available in VAT Notice 706 "Partial Exemption".

Commentary—*De Voil Indirect Tax Service* **V3.464.**

16 September 2005. Business Brief 18/05

New civil investigation of fraud procedures

Both HM Customs & Excise and the Inland Revenue had procedures for tackling suspected serious tax fraud using civil powers. The former Inland Revenue's Hansard procedures and all former Customs & Excise Civil Evasion procedures are being replaced with a new single Civil Investigations of Fraud procedure for HMRC. (The only exception is the Customs Duties Civil Evasion Penalties applied to travellers at port and airport controls).

1 SEPTEMBER 2005 START AND NEW CODE OF PRACTICE 9 (2005)

The new Civil Investigation of Fraud procedure came into effect on 1 September 2005 for new cases with a new Code of Practice 9 (2005).

Existing cases will be worked to a conclusion under the old Hansard procedures (Code of Practice 9), New Approach or C&E Notice 730.

Initially the new procedure will only be used by officers serving in HMRC Special Civil Investigations. Use by other specialist teams within HMRC is under consideration.

THE CHANGES

- The new procedure is wholly civil, removing the threat of prosecution for the original tax offence—a change from the Inland Revenue's Hansard procedure.
- HMRC will retain the option to consider prosecution for a materially false disclosure or materially false statement with intent to deceive.
- Interviews will no longer be conducted under caution and tape-recorded.
- Investigations under the new Civil Investigation of Fraud procedure will cover both direct and indirect taxes where appropriate.

OUTLINE OF THE CIVIL INVESTIGATION OF FRAUD PROCEDURE

Where HMRC suspect serious tax fraud and decides to proceed via a civil rather than a criminal investigation, the taxpayer will be given one opportunity to secure maximum benefit by making a full disclosure of all irregularities within the direct and indirect tax regimes. If they take that opportunity the investigation will proceed more quickly, efficiently and advantageously for both the taxpayer and HMRC.

If a taxpayer decides not to make a full disclosure and co-operate, HMRC will conduct their own investigation, using statutory information powers if necessary. If irregularities are discovered they will issue formal assessments and pursue collection of unpaid tax with interest. Any penalties due are likely to be significantly higher to reflect the fact that the taxpayer did not take the opportunity given to them to disclose.

Once the decision by HMRC has been made to follow a civil route for investigation and the procedure is offered to the taxpayer, HMRC retain no underlying threat of prosecution for the original tax loss.

PROSECUTION FOR TAX FRAUD

HMRC reserve complete discretion to pursue a criminal investigation with a view to prosecution where they consider it necessary and appropriate. Where HMRC decide to use the Civil Investigation of Fraud procedure it will not prosecute for the original tax offence. However if materially false statements are made or materially false documents are provided with intent to deceive, HMRC may conduct a criminal investigation with a view to a prosecution of that conduct.

SINGLE MEETINGS TO DISCUSS INDIRECT AND DIRECT TAX MATTERS

Once the new procedure is introduced, where suspicions of irregularities cut across direct and indirect taxes, a single meeting will be held to cover all regimes. During this meeting it will be made clear to the taxpayer whether questions are relevant to direct taxes, indirect taxes or both.

DISCLOSURE REPORTS

Any disclosure reports prepared by professional advisers will now be expected to cover direct and indirect tax irregularities in the same document. We anticipate there will be cost savings and other benefits to the taxpayer in submitting a single disclosure report.

CIVIL INVESTIGATION OF FRAUD AND THE HUMAN RIGHTS ACT

We believe the new procedure is compliant with the Human Rights Act. The civil fraud processes previously operated by both departments have received considerable scrutiny in terms of Human Rights and, in particular, Article 6 "Right to a fair trial". The views of the courts in the lead Human Rights Act rulings of *Han & Yau* and *Gill & Gill* together with advice from leading counsel have provided the principles for designing the new procedure. The recent case of *Khan v C & E Comrs* (2005) has endorsed these principles and safeguards have been built into the new procedure.

CONSULTATION

This change is being made after consultation with relevant Representative Bodies.

Commentary—*De Voil Indirect Tax Service* **V5.224A, V5.311.**

10 October 2005. Business Brief 19/05.

High Court decision: Church of England Children's Society

This Business Brief outlines the decision of the High Court in *Church of England Children's Society (CECS)* [2005] EWHC 1692 (Ch) in favour of the charity, and how HM Revenue & Customs intend to apply the decision. HMRC have decided not to appeal.

BACKGROUND

CECS is a charity with a wide range of activities. To raise funds, it engages professional fundraisers to secure regular donations from members of the public. Those donating at least £5 per month receive a copy of the charity's newsletter three times a year.

The VAT Tribunal decided that—

- the fundraisers' fees related to the non-business activity of seeking donations, so the VAT incurred on them was not recoverable
- the newsletters were not zero-rated supplies of printed matter. However, they were deemed zero-rated gifts of business assets and input tax on their production and distribution costs was recoverable following the decision of the High Court in *West Herts College* [2001] STC 1245.

CECS appealed to the High Court against the first part of the Tribunal's decision and HMRC cross-appealed on the second part.

HIGH COURT DECISION

Fundraising fees

The High Court decided that if funds raised by donation by CECS were used to fund its taxable business activities, it was entitled to recover related input tax. It followed the recent judgment of the ECJ in *Kretztechnik AG v Finanzamt Linz* (Case C-465/03). In that case, the ECJ ruled that, where the capital-raising transaction to which costs most closely relate falls outside the scope of VAT because it is not a supply of goods or services, the costs can relate to the organisation as a whole. In other words, if the capital-raising transaction is for the purpose of the business's economic activity in general, the transaction has a direct and immediate link with the whole economic activity of the taxable person. VAT on the transaction is recoverable to the extent that the taxable person is making taxable supplies.

The CECS decision has wider implications than the use of professional fundraisers by charities. Subject to the guidance below, it could impact on the recovery of any VAT incurred in securing donations or legacies to support the work of a charity.

Deemed supplies

The Court also upheld the Tribunal's decision that the newsletter was a deemed zero-rated supply of printed matter and that input tax on the production and distribution costs could be recovered because it related to that taxable deemed supply.

THE WAY FORWARD

Fundraising costs

Where funds are raised solely for a restricted charitable purpose involving wholly non-business activities, the VAT incurred on raising those funds is not input tax and is not recoverable.

Conversely, where the funds raised are used wholly to support the making of business supplies, all of the VAT incurred on fundraising costs can be treated as input tax. The recovery of this input tax will depend upon whether these business supplies are taxable or exempt. Where fundraising input tax is wholly attributable to the making of taxable supplies by the charity, it can be recovered in full, subject to the normal rules. On the other hand, where fundraising input tax is wholly attributable to the making of exempt supplies by the charity, none of it will be recoverable, subject to the partial exemption de minimis limits.

So where a charity which has non-business and business activities incurs VAT on fundraising costs and the funds raised support various activities of the charity, the VAT incurred can only be recoverable input tax to the extent that the funds raised will support taxable business supplies. In practice this means that VAT incurred on fundraising costs must first be subject to an initial business/non-business apportionment to determine how much of the VAT incurred may be treated as input tax. Then, in circumstances where the charity has exempt business activities, this input tax is further subject to the partial exemption rules.

In some cases, a charity's existing business /non-business apportionment method and partial exemption method will produce a fair and reasonable basis by which input tax can be recovered. However, where this is not the case, HMRC will consider proposals for alternative methods. If exceptional circumstances exist, HMRC may allow alternative methods to be applied retrospectively, provided it is fair and reasonable for the charity as a whole.

Deemed supplies

The High Court decision has confirmed that input tax relating to a deemed supply is recoverable where the deemed supply is taxable.

However, in order for there to be a deemed supply, the gifted goods must first be business assets. This means that a charity purchasing or acquiring goods in order to give them away in the furtherance of its non-business charitable purposes would not be able to recover the VAT incurred on the purchase or acquisition of those goods. Following changes to the rules on gifts of business assets with effect from 1 October 2003, there is no longer a deemed supply where the total cost of production of newsletters provided to any donor does not exceed £50 in a twelve month period. Where input tax is incurred on business assets that are given away, but those gifts are not deemed supplies, the attribution of the input tax will be based on the business reasons behind making the gifts. Where input tax is incurred on business assets that are given away, and some of those gifts are deemed supplies whereas others are not, the attribution of the input tax will take both the deemed supplies and the underlying purpose behind making the gifts into account.

Examples

- If a religious charity incurs VAT producing and distributing bibles that it gifts to local hotels for use by guests, the VAT is not input tax and is not recoverable even if the bibles exceed the £50 cost rules that apply to deemed supplies. This is because giving away bibles is not a business activity and VAT incurred cannot therefore be input tax. However, if the charity produced bibles for gifts and for sale, then VAT incurred would be partly input tax.
- If the charity produces religious newsletters that advertise its business activities, VAT incurred will be input tax because of the advertisements. Furthermore, if the newsletters satisfy the deemed supply rules, then the input tax will be fully recoverable even if the charity's business activities are heavily exempt.

MAKING CLAIMS FOR REPAYMENT OF TAX

Charities that wish to make claims for input tax may do so by making a voluntary disclosure to their local VAT office in accordance with guidance in Notice 700/45 "How to correct VAT errors and make adjustments or claims", subject to the time limit in reg 29(1A) of the VAT Regulations 1995. This restricts late claims for input tax to three years from the due date of the return for the prescribed accounting period in which the input tax was chargeable.

Commentary—*De Voil Indirect Tax Service* **V3.211, 212.**

23 November 2005. Business Brief 21/05.

Clarification of the treatment of foreign exchange transactions (forex)

This Business Brief clarifies HM Revenue and Customs' (HMRC) policy regarding forex transactions, following the Tribunal decision in *Willis Pension Fund Trustees Limited* (Willis) (2005) VAT Decision 19183. HMRC have decided not to appeal this decision.

BACKGROUND

Willis was the Trustee of the Willis Pension Fund, which was a pension scheme for the employees of the Willis Group Holding Limited group of companies. The scheme held various investments, including a number of overseas investments and equities. As a result, the sterling value of these assets was subject to exchange rate fluctuations. Willis entered into forex deals with various UK banks, using the services of a third party to conduct the transactions, in order to hedge or minimise the pension scheme's exposure to adverse exchange rate fluctuations. Willis did not offer a spread or charge a separate fee or commission, but relied on the movements in exchange rates in order to minimise their losses and, where possible, make a profit. The question before the Tribunal was whether in entering these transactions, Willis made a supply for VAT purposes.

Currently, HMRC's policy relies upon the European Court of Justice (ECJ) decision in *First National Bank of Chicago* (FNBC) C-172/96. FNBC entered forex transactions as a market maker. Although they did not charge a specific commission, they relied in part on the spread that they offered (that is, they set a buying price and selling price for each currency thereby offering a spread to the customer), in order to make a profit. The ECJ decided that the forex transactions entered into by FNBC were supplies of services and that the consideration for those services was the net result of the transactions over a period of time. HMRC applied this decision to all forex transactions and treated the supplies as exempt under VATA 1994 Sch 9 Group 5 item 1. As a result, businesses that entered into transactions with UK or EU institutions had a restriction placed on the recovery of any associated input tax. Conversely, businesses that entered into transactions with overseas institutions would have been entitled to recover the associated input tax in full under the VAT (Input Tax) (Specified Supplies) Order 1999.

THE DECISION

The Tribunal had to decide whether Willis provided any service to the counterparty when it entered into a foreign exchange transaction. Willis did not charge a fee or commission on the deal and did not factor a spread into its arrangements. Willis simply made the best deals it could from counterparties such as banks. The Tribunal decided that any "profit" retained by Willis from the forex transactions was not the consideration for a supply because it simply resulted from fluctuations in market rates. Willis entered into foreign exchange transactions solely to hedge against currency risks on its investment holdings.

HMRC now accept that there were no supplies made by Willis in respect of the hedging transactions and that this decision will apply to any business entering forex transactions on the same basis as Willis.

HMRC are considering whether this decision has wider application. Further guidance will be issued in due course.

INPUT TAX TREATMENT

HMRC now accept that any VAT paid on associated costs of forex hedging transactions such as those carried out by Willis relates to the business as a whole. It is residual input tax, which can be recovered subject to the partial exemption method used.

CLAIMS FOR OVERPAID INPUT TAX

Claims for input tax in respect of past forex transactions can be made subject to the three-year capping rules. Public Notice 700/45, "How to correct VAT errors and make adjustments or claims" provides further guidance on the capping rules and claim procedures. This will need to take into account any overclaim caused by recovery of the input tax relating to transactions with non-EU counterparties, under the specified supplies order.

Businesses that have recovered the associated input tax because they have entered into forex transactions in a similar way to Willis with non-EU counterparties, may need to consider whether all or part of that input tax should now be restricted following this decision.

Note—See also R&C Brief 5/07, published on 26-1-07.
Commentary—*De Voil Indirect Tax Service* **V3.152, V3.461, V6.126.**

23 November 2005. Business Brief 21/05

Further clarification of the VAT position of share issues following the European Court of Justice's decision in Kretztechnik

Business Brief 12/05 explained HM Revenue and Customs' position on the VAT treatment of share issues and subsequent input tax recovery, following the decision in *Kretztechnik A.G. -v- Finanzamt Linz* (Case C-465/03). This Business Brief article contains additional guidance, with specific implementation dates underlined.

REVISED TREATMENT OF SHARE ISSUE TRANSACTIONS

Business Brief 12/05 advised that companies making a new issue of shares to raise capital for their business, in circumstances identical to those in *Kretztechnik's* case, were not making any supply but were entitled to treat the VAT on the costs of the issue as input tax. Companies that make both taxable and exempt supplies should recover a proportion of the input tax in accordance with their partial exemption method that applied at the time of the issue.

The following guidance explains the VAT position of share transactions where the circumstances differ from those in *Kretztechnik*.

TRANSACTIONS INVOLVING ISSUES OF OTHER TYPES OF SHARES

Businesses may issue shares of different types. For example, there may be an issue of preference shares, a special rights issue, a bonus issue or issue of scrip dividends. *Kretztechnik* principles are applicable to all such share issues and these are now to be regarded as non-supplies for VAT purposes.

TRANSACTIONS INVOLVING ISSUES BY DIFFERENT TYPES OF COMPANIES

Kretztechnik was a public limited company but the body issuing shares could be another type of company, a private company for example. Provided that the issuer's motivation is, like Kretztechnik's, the raising of capital, issues of shares by these other types of company will also be non-supplies for VAT purposes.

TRANSACTIONS INVOLVING THE ISSUE OF FINANCIAL INSTRUMENTS OR SECURITIES OTHER THAN SHARES

The issue of other types of security, such as bonds, debentures or loan notes, should also be treated as non-supplies when the purpose of the issue is to raise capital for the issuer's business. The input tax consequences will be the same as for an issue of shares. Similarly, the issue of shares or units in collective investment funds such as open-ended investment companies or authorised unit trusts will not be supplies for VAT purposes.

SHARES AND OTHER SECURITIES ISSUED IN OTHER SITUATIONS

An issue of shares or other securities may be one of several transactions that take place in the context of wider arrangements. For example, they may be issued in order to effect a company takeover or as part of a company restructuring through merger or demerger. When the issue does take place as part of such wider arrangements, it should still be regarded as a non-supply for VAT purposes.

MAKING CLAIMS

Claims for unrecovered input tax in respect of past issues of shares and other securities can be made subject to the three-year "capping" rules. Such claims need to take into account any input tax that has been over-claimed because it has been attributed to an issue of securities outside the EU. Public Notice 700/45 "How to correct VAT errors and make adjustments or claims" gives detailed guidance on capping and claim procedures.

TRANSFERS OF EXISTING SHARES

Transfers of existing shares for a consideration will continue to be exempt supplies provided that the supplies occur in the course of business activity. In such cases, the input tax that relates to the transfer will be exempt input tax and only recoverable to the extent that the shares have been sold to purchasers outside the EU.

LIABILITY CONSEQUENCES

There are no changes to the exemption for financial services arising from the judgment. Transactions that are no longer supplies, such as issues of shares, will no longer have a corresponding VAT liability such as exemption. However, intermediary and underwriting services in relation to such transactions will continue to be exempt.

CONSEQUENCES FOR THE VAT (INPUT TAX) (SPECIFIED SUPPLIES) ORDER 1999

Input tax on issues of shares made outside the EU

Prior to *Kretztechnik*, issues of shares and other securities to customers belonging outside the EU were treated as specified supplies. This meant that the input tax on related costs could be recovered. From the date of publication of this Business Brief this treatment will no longer apply unless—

(a) You have chosen to apply the *Kretztechnik* treatment to other issues before that date; or
(b) You are making a claim for retrospective recovery of input tax.

The changes announced in paragraph 2 of Business Brief 32/04 will still apply to other incidental financial transactions not affected by *Kretztechnik*.

Input tax incurred by intermediaries in share issues

The changes in this paragraph are effective only from 1 January 2006.

Previously, intermediaries could treat the following transactions as specified supplies—

(a) arranging an issue of shares or other securities on behalf of an issuer belonging outside the EU;
(b) arranging an issue of shares or other securities on behalf of an issuer (wherever they belonged) to recipients outside the EU.

This meant that the input tax on related costs could be recovered whether or not the intermediary's customer belonged outside the EU, provided the issue was made to someone belonging outside the EU. This was because this underlying issue of shares was treated as a supply for VAT purposes.

Following *Kretztechnik*, the situation has changed and, from 1 January 2006, only the services described at (*a*) above will be treated as specified supplies. This is because the underlying issue of shares by the intermediary's customer to the non-EU purchaser is no longer a supply. However, intermediary services to their own customers, as long as they belong outside the EU, is still a specified supply under the Specified Supplies Order.

There is no change to the position of intermediaries who arrange supplies of existing shares or other securities.

Impact of *Kretztechnik* upon the *Water Hall Group* decision

In *Water Hall Group plc*, a VAT Tribunal found that, when shares were issued to a UK company acting as nominee for purchasers belonging outside the EU, the input tax relating to those shares could not be reclaimed by the issuer because the supply was to the UK nominee rather than the non-EU purchasers. In Business Brief 02/05, HMRC announced that businesses should apply the Water Hall decision to issues of shares in the same circumstances. The situation would then be reviewed following release of the *Kretztechnik* decision.

This review has now been completed. HMRC's conclusion is that *Water Hall* no longer has any application. In *Kretztechnik*, an issue of shares was found not to be a supply for VAT purposes, so the question of who is making or receiving the supply no longer arises. We consider that transactions involving sales of existing shares are fundamentally different from share issues because they are capable of constituting supplies. Such transactions were not considered in Water Hall and that decision does not therefore apply to them. Supplies of existing shares are to be regarded as being made to or by the person who actually makes the purchase or sale of the shares. Where the actual purchaser is not known to the seller, the place of belonging of a nominee account for the purchaser, if known, may be used to determine the place of supply. If neither is known, you should treat the supply as made in the UK or refer to the special rules in paragraph 9.2 of Public Notice 701/49 "Finance and securities".

Note—See also Business Brief 22/05, 1 December 2005, below for further clarification on the VAT position of share issues made to customers outside the EU.
Commentary—*De Voil Indirect Tax Service* **V2.236, V3.464, V4.136E.**

1 December 2005. Business Brief 22/05.

Judgment of the court of appeal in the case of *Ivor Jacobs* ([2005] EWCA Civ 930)

This Business Brief article sets out HM Revenue & Customs' (HMRC) revised policy on the recovery of VAT by those using the "VAT refunds for DIY builders and converters" scheme in cases where a mixed use building (used for non-residential and residential use) is converted into dwellings in light of the judgment of the Court of Appeal in the case of *Ivor Jacobs* (C3/2004/2457).

BACKGROUND

Mr Jacobs had converted a former residential school for boys into one large dwelling for his own occupation and three flats. His claim for a VAT refund under the provisions of the "VAT refunds for DIY builders and converters" scheme was rejected because none of the four resulting dwellings had been created exclusively from the conversion of the non-residential part of the school.

Mr Jacobs appealed against the above decision to a VAT Tribunal. The Tribunal found that, when looked at as a whole i e a "primary use" test, the school was entirely non-residential and its conversion qualified for the refund scheme.

HMRC appealed the Tribunal's decision to the High Court. The High Court rejected the Tribunal's "primary use" test and held that the school was in part residential and in part non-residential. However the High Court also rejected HMRC's view that any additional dwelling must be created entirely from the non-residential part. It held that the VAT incurred on converting the non-residential part used in creating the four dwellings was recoverable through the scheme. This is because converting the school had created additional dwellings, the school having contained one dwelling before conversion and four afterwards. The VAT incurred on the conversion of the residential part of the school was not recoverable.

The Court of Appeal unanimously dismissed HMRC's appeal and endorsed the High Court's judgment.

HM REVENUE & CUSTOMS' REVISED POLICY

HMRC now accept that, for the purposes of the DIY Refund Scheme, the conversion of a building that contains both a residential part and a non-residential part comes within the scope of the Scheme so long as the conversion results in an additional dwelling being created. It is no longer necessary for the additional dwelling to be created exclusively from the non-residential part. However, VAT recovery is restricted to the conversion of the non-residential part.

BUILDERS AND DEVELOPERS

HMRC do not consider that the Court of Appeal decision has any impact in similar situations where a building, which is part residential/part non-residential, is being converted into a number of dwellings and the number of dwellings present post-conversion is greater than the number of dwellings present pre-conversion.

Items 1(b) and 3(a) of Group 5 to Schedule 8, VATA 1994 restrict the zero-rating to the dwelling(s) deriving from the conversion of the non-residential part. Our policy remains that the zero rate will not apply to any dwelling(s) deriving (whether in whole or in part) from the conversion of the residential part.

VAT TREATMENT OF PAST SUPPLIES

DIY house builders, who have converted property that was part residential/part non-residential and have increased the number of dwellings in the building overall, are invited to submit claims for VAT incurred on eligible expenditure in converting the non-residential part of the building into a part of the resulting dwellings.

HMRC will only entertain claims in respect of such conversions completed no later than three years prior to the date of this Business Brief.

Commentary—*De Voil Indirect Tax Service* **V4.232.**

1 December 2005. Business Brief 22/05.

Further clarification on the VAT position of share issues made to customers outside the EU

We have had one or two enquiries on Business Brief 21/05 which explained HM Revenue and Customs' position on share issues following the decision in the European case of *Kretztechnik AG* (Case C-465/03). This item clarifies the situation regarding issues of shares and other securities made outside the EU.

CONSEQUENCES FOR THE VAT (INPUT TAX) (SPECIFIED SUPPLIES) ORDER 1999 INPUT TAX ON ISSUES OF SHARES MADE OUTSIDE THE EU

Prior to *Kretztechnik*, issues of shares and other securities to customers belonging outside the EU were treated as specified supplies. This meant that the input tax on related costs could be recovered under the Specified Supplies Order. From 29 November 2005, this treatment will no longer apply to new shares and securities issued outside the EU as they are no longer supplies, although input tax will still be recoverable on the related costs provided the issue is made for the purposes of a fully taxable business. If the issue is made for the purposes of a partly exempt business, then a proportion of the input tax will be recoverable under the business' normal partial exemption method.

The changes announced in paragraph 2 of Business Brief 32/04 will still apply to other incidental financial transactions not affected by *Kretztechnik*.

Commentary—*De Voil Indirect Tax Service* **V2.236, V3.464, V4.136E.**

5 December 2005. Business Brief 23/05.

VAT exemption for insurance-related services

The Government has considered responses to the HMRC consultation concerning VAT and insurance related services following the ECJ judgment in *Arthur Andersen & Co Accountants* (case C-472/03). The Government has noted that the VAT treatment of financial services and insurance will now be subject to review by the European Commission in the near future, and has decided to delay its decision regarding implementation of this ECJ judgment. The Government will monitor the progress of the review in deciding when to make the necessary changes to UK law and will provide industry with sufficient notice in advance of implementation.

Commentary—*De Voil Indirect Tax Service* **V4.123.**

18 January 2006. Business Brief 1/06

Company formation services with ancillary printed matter—clarification of treatment post CPP

The Commissioners are aware that traders providing company formation services may be incorrectly treating some supplies as separate zero-rated supplies of printed matter and standard-rated services.

This Business Brief article clarifies HMRC guidance previously issued. HMRC confirms its view, in the light of the Card Protection Plan case, on the correct treatment of these supplies. It aims to ensure that all traders providing such services treat them correctly for VAT purposes.

Furthermore there may be cases where traders have attempted to secure a competitive advantage over traders that have been treating the supplies correctly by using this incorrect treatment as a basis for value shifting by invoicing a breakdown of the package price.

BACKGROUND

Business Brief 2/01, issued on 16 February 2001, explained the ECJ and House of Lords decisions in the case of *Card Protection Plan (CPP)* (ECJ C-349/96). These decisions clarified how businesses are required to decide whether they are making single or multiple supplies for VAT purposes. The Business Brief required businesses to make necessary changes in treatment by 1 June 2001.

VAT Info Sheet 2/01 further advised businesses how to determine the proper VAT liability of supplies consisting of separately identifiable goods and services. It also advised affected businesses to review the VAT treatment of similar supplies against the tests set out in that sheet and to implement the necessary changes.

Despite this publicity, the company formation industry has in many cases failed to review such supplies post-CPP with the result that, in some cases, suppliers have continued incorrectly to zero-rate supplies of printed matter which are ancillary to supplies of company formation services.

TREATMENT OF COMPANY FORMATION SERVICE PACKAGES INCLUDING ANCILLARY PRINTED MATTER

HMRC's view is that where there is a single advertised price for a company formation package that includes some printed matter (for example a number of copies of the printed and perhaps bound Memorandum & Articles of Association), there is a single standard-rated supply of company formation services. This supply is the principal supply to which the supply of printed matter is ancillary.

The supply of the service by a registration agent of preparing and lodging the original Memorandum and Articles of Association with the Registrar of Companies is wholly standard-rated. In this situation, one or more copies of documents, such as the Certificates of Incorporation and the Memorandum and Articles of Association may be provided. Where these are provided in hard copy form (as opposed to digital format), the question arises as to whether there is a single supply of company registration services to which the supply of printed matter is ancillary, or separate supplies of zero-rated printed matter and standard-rated services.

The judgment in *Card Protection Plan* (ECJ C-349/96) set out a number of relevant criteria, namely:

- Where a transaction comprises a number of features or acts, regard must be had to all the circumstances in which it takes place.
- Where a supply is a single supply from an economic point of view, it should not be artificially split so as to distort the functioning of the VAT system.
- There is a single supply, in particular, in cases where one or more elements of a transaction are to be regarded as constituting the principal service, with other elements being ancillary to that principal service.
- While the charging of a single price is not decisive, the fact that several elements are supplied for a single price may indicate a single supply.

Therefore where a customer acquiring a registered company also receives hard copy documents as part of a fixed-price package, he would normally be seen as receiving a single supply of company formation services rather than separate supplies of company registration services and printed matter.

Where additional copies of documentation are offered as an option for additional payment, there may be either a single supply or multiple supplies.

Action required by businesses making supplies of company formation service packages

Businesses to which this Business Brief applies must review their VAT treatment of these supplies and ensure that any necessary changes are implemented.

Where there has been historic incorrect treatment businesses should account for underpaid output tax by using one of the following methods:

- If the net value of all adjustments is £2000 or less, businesses may amend their VAT account and include the value of the adjustment on their current VAT return.
- If the net value of all adjustments is more than £2000, a separate payment should be submitted to the local Business Advice Centre. (Businesses may not make this adjustment on their VAT return).

Where there has been historic incorrect treatment but businesses can positively evidence misdirection by HMRC, then the correct treatment should be applied from a point not later than the date of this Business Brief.

In cases where misdirection is accepted, HMRC reserves the right to take action where it appears that the incorrect treatment has been used as the basis for value-shifting by invoicing an incorrect breakdown of the package price.

18 January 2006. Business Brief 1/06

Hotel conference/function facilities: revised interpretation of law on VAT treatment

This Business Brief article announces changes in HM Revenue & Customs' interpretation of the law on the VAT treatment of hotel conference/function facilities. This change will be incorporated in an update to VAT Notice 709/3, "Hotels and Holiday Accommodation", to be issued in due course.

The change being made affects the liability of supplies of rooms by hotels that are to be used for meetings, conferences and similar functions. There is no change to the treatment of supplies of rooms where the primary use will be for the purpose of supplies of catering, such as dinner/dances, wedding receptions, etc. Supplies of rooms for such purposes are always taxable supplies.

BACKGROUND

Hotels and other establishments often provide rooms for meetings, conferences and similar functions organised by third parties. It is usual for them to make inclusive charges depending on the requirements of individual delegates. It is the general practice for hotels and similar providers to charge organisers on a delegate or attendee basis (referred to as the "delegate rate"), i e the charge will be determined according to the number of delegates requiring:

- use of conference room only;
- use of conference room plus meal(s) ('8 hour conference delegate rate'); or
- use of conference room plus meals and overnight sleeping accommodation ('24 hour conference delegate rate').

The supply of a conference/function room on its own in these circumstances is exempt from VAT (unless an option to tax has been made). Where, in addition to the use of the conference/function room, a meal is provided to delegates and an inclusive charge made (the 8 hour delegate rate), each element is treated as a separate supply, so whilst the conference room continues to be exempt from VAT (unless an option to tax has been made), the part of the consideration relating to the provision of food is taxable (unless the provision of refreshments is minimal, such as tea and biscuits). However; where the 24-hour conference delegate rate has been applied and an inclusive charge made, HMRC has until now seen the charge as consideration for a single taxable supply of use of the entire hotel's facilities including conference/function facilities, sleeping accommodation and food.

REVISED INTERPRETATION OF THE LAW

Where a room is provided for a meeting, conference or similar function organised by a third party (but not where the primary purpose is for a supply of catering—see above), HMRC now accepts that the provision of conference/function room hire, meals and sleeping accommodation under the 24 hour delegate rate, even where made in return for an inclusive charge, should be treated as separate supplies. These will be taxable supplies, with the exception of the conference/function room hire, which will be an exempt supply, unless the hotel has opted to tax its supplies.

In cases where a single consideration is paid for supplies having different liabilities, for example where a charge for room hire is made under the 24-hour delegate rate by a hotel which has not opted to tax its room hire, a fair and reasonable apportionment of the consideration must be made.

There is no change to the treatment of 8-hour delegate charges.

Where hotels organise and run conferences or similar events themselves and charge for entry to delegates, their supplies are always taxable supplies.

MAKING CLAIMS OR ADJUSTMENTS

Hotels that have made an option to tax will be unaffected by the change and should continue to charge tax on their supplies. For other hotels and businesses, the change described above should be implemented from the date of this Business Brief and there is no requirement to make adjustments in respect of supplies made prior to this date. However, where hotels or other establishments wish to make a claim to HMRC for a repayment of output tax incorrectly paid, they may do so, subject to the conditions set out below, by using one of the following methods (full details are given in VAT Notice 700/45 How to correct VAT errors and make adjustments or claims):

- where the total of previous errors do not exceed £2000 net tax, an adjustment may be made to your current VAT return, or
- where the total previous errors exceed £2000 net tax a separate claim should be submitted to HMRC (in these cases the errors must not be corrected through your VAT returns). Details of where to send your claim can be obtained from the HM Revenue & Customs National Advice Service on 0845 010 9000.

All adjustments or claims are limited to a three-year period and will be subject to the following conditions:

- All claims must take into account input tax that has been claimed, but which under the revised interpretation will not relate to taxable supplies.
- Businesses must be able to produce evidence that they accounted for VAT in the circumstances described above, and must be able to substantiate the amount claimed.

Subject to the three-year limitation period, any claim should be for all prescribed accounting periods in which the liability error occurred.

Should a claim not take into account all errors or all affected accounting periods, then HMRC will seek to set-off amounts owed to us for these periods against amounts claimed in other periods.

HMRC may reject all or part of a claim if repayment would unjustly enrich the claimant. More details on 'unjust enrichment' can be found at part 14 of VAT Notice 700/45 "How to correct VAT errors and make adjustments or claims".

A notification to HMRC that a business intends making a claim in the future is not a valid claim.

FUTURE VAT IMPLICATIONS FOR HOTELS AND SIMILAR PROVIDERS

You should treat supplies in the way described above. Some hotels will now be making exempt supplies as a result of these changes. The input tax that they incur will, as a result, be subject to partial exemption rules and some restriction on the amount they can reclaim may follow. Details can be found in VAT Notice 706, "Partial Exemption". If hotels prefer, they can continue to treat their supplies as taxable (and thereby be entitled to continue claiming their input tax in full) by opting to tax. Details about how to do this are given in VAT Notice 742A, "Opting to tax land and buildings". Hotels that have already made exempt supplies of the meeting room may require permission for an option to tax and they will find further details in Section 5 of Notice 742A.

Where you are in any doubt about the correct treatment please contact the National Advice Service on the telephone number below.

Commentary—*De Voil Indirect Tax Service* **V4.113**.

9 March 2006. Business Brief 3/06

Beauty procedures performed using class 3B or 4 lasers and/or intense pulse light (IPL) machines—clarification of liability

HMRC have become aware that some businesses providing beauty procedures using class 3B or 4 lasers and/or IPL machines may be incorrectly treating their supplies as VAT-exempt health services rather than standard rated supplies of beauty treatment. This Business Brief article is issued to assist those businesses to determine the correct liability of these services.

BACKGROUND

Following the establishment of the Healthcare Commission under the Care Standards Act 2000, certain procedures using prescribed techniques or prescribed technologies became regulated for the first time. Among these were the use of class 3B and 4 lasers and IPL machines.

This has led to establishments such as beauty salons, where class 3B and 4 lasers and/or IPL machines are used (for instance, for removing unwanted hair), being classified as independent hospitals for the purposes of the Care Standards legislation.

TREATMENT OF SUPPLIES MADE USING CLASS 3B AND 4 LASERS AND/OR IPL MACHINES

Where the procedure utilising this equipment is supplied as part of a treatment programme drawn up by a registered health professional following the diagnosis of a medical condition, this treatment is exempt from VAT.

But where it is carried out for a cosmetic reason rather than as an element of medical or surgical treatment, this service is taxable at the standard rate of VAT.

Action required by businesses making non-medical supplies using class 3B and 4 lasers and/or IPL machines

Businesses to which this Business Brief applies must review their VAT treatment of these supplies and ensure that any necessary changes are implemented.

Where businesses have previously been incorrectly treating non-medical supplies as exempt, they should account for any net tax underdeclared by using one of the following methods:

If the net value of all adjustments is £2000 or less, businesses may amend their VAT account and include the value of the adjustment on their current VAT return.

If the net value of all adjustments is more than £2000, a separate payment should be submitted to the local Business Advice Centre. (Businesses may not make this adjustment on their VAT return).

Both of the above methods and how to make a claim are explained in VAT Notice 700/45 'How to correct VAT errors and make adjustments or claims'.

If a voluntary disclosure is not made, and Customs discover the error, the taxpayer may be liable to a misdeclaration penalty.

Where there has been historic incorrect treatment but businesses can positively evidence misdirection by HMRC, then the correct treatment should be applied from a point not later than the date of this Business Brief. Further information can be found in Notice 700/6 "VAT rulings".

Commentary—*De Voil Indirect Tax Service* **V4.146**.

24 March 2006. Business Brief 4/06

Off-street car parking provided by local authorities

The VAT and Duties Tribunal has decided that the Isle of Wight Council and three other local authorities do not have to charge VAT on car parking in their areas. This Business Brief article explains action that HM Revenue and Customs (HMRC) will be taking pending an appeal.

BACKGROUND

Under Article 4(5) of the EC Sixth VAT Directive, activities of public bodies are not regarded as being carried on by way of business for VAT purposes, if they do so under a statutory regime that is unique to the public sector ("special legal regime"), unless this would significantly distort competition with private sector bodies carrying on the same activity.

In an earlier decision (LON/00/653) dated 6 April 2004, the Tribunal found that the Isle of Wight Council provides off-street car parking spaces under such a special legal regime, and consequently this should not be regarded as a business activity for VAT purposes. However, because it considered that the UK has not properly implemented Article 4(5) into national law, the Tribunal did not consider whether such treatment would significantly distort competition (see Business Brief 18/04).

In November 2004 the High Court found that in assessing the applicability of Article 4(5) to a particular case, it is necessary to consider both the legal regime governing an activity and the issue of competition. Consequently the case was referred back to the Tribunal to consider arguments on competition.

THE TRIBUNAL'S DECISION

The Tribunal decided that the non-taxation of local authority off-street car parks does not significantly distort competition in the appellants' geographical areas. It concluded that distortion of the market by public authorities is generally inherent, because Article 4(5) provides that they do not have to charge VAT even though other providers of the same service might have to charge VAT. Consequently, taxation on the grounds of significant distortions of competition should be applied only in the most exceptional of circumstances. Additionally, it found that, in the case of car parking, competition must be looked at in the circumstances prevailing in individual local authorities and not on a nationwide basis.

HMRC'S RESPONSE

HMRC believes that the Tribunal has not taken full account of the EU case law that relates to the application of Article 4(5), including the principle of fiscal neutrality, which was argued at the hearing. Consequently, HMRC does not agree with this decision of the Tribunal and an appeal will accordingly be lodged with the High Court.

FURTHER ACTION

HMRC will consider making repayments to the 4 local authorities involved in the appeal. Any refunds would be subject to the unjust enrichment rules as summarised in the VAT Guide (Notice 700 paragraph 19.13).

As expressed the decision is confined to the circumstances of the four appellant local authorities in question. Theirs were the only circumstances that were considered by the Tribunal. It would be inappropriate for other local authorities to claim refunds of output tax declared on off-street parking simply on the basis of this decision, and any such claim will not be accepted. They should continue to account for VAT based on HMRC's view of the law. Where appropriate, HMRC will continue to make protective assessments or to disallow protective claims received. Should a higher court subsequently rule that HMRC's original decision was correct, we would seek repayment of any amounts previously paid. Interest and penalties will also be sought as appropriate. There is more information about this in para 8 of VAT Notice 700/45 and in Business Brief 28/04.

Commentary—*De Voil Indirect Tax Service* **V3.407.**

12 April 2006. BB 5/06

Interim position following the Court of Session's decision in Edinburgh's Telford College

This Business Brief article explains that HM Revenue & Customs (HMRC) is currently considering the judgment of the Court of Session in the case of *Edinburgh's Telford College* (ETC) [2006] CSIH 13, XA18/05, XA 22/05, released on 22 February 2006, and a further Business Brief will be issued when this process is concluded.

Background

ETC is a further education (FE) college, created by statute. It provides a mixture of further and higher education courses (Scottish Qualifications Framework Levels 4 to 8) which are funded under an agreement with the Scottish Education Funding Council (SEFC).

ETC incurred VAT on the construction of a campus building used for a mixture of non-business activities and activities which give rise to supplies that are either taxable or exempt from VAT. ETC argued that when it provides further and higher education courses, it engages as a public authority and consequently this activity is outside the scope of VAT under Article 4(5) of the Sixth VAT Directive—whether or not fees are charged.

On the basis of this argument, and following the judgments of the European Court of Justice in the cases of *Lennartz v Finanzamt Munchen III* (C-97/90) and *Seeling v Finanzamt Starnberg* (C-269/00) ("Lennartz accounting"), ETC wanted to recover in full the VAT incurred on the campus building. Under Lennartz accounting, when a taxable person incurs VAT on the purchase of an asset for mixed business and non-business use, they can recover the VAT attributable to taxable and non-business use in full and then account for output tax on the ongoing non-business use. In the case of land and buildings, output tax must be accounted for over a maximum period of 20 years.

The Tribunal found that—

- ETC did not act as a public authority when delivering FE and HE courses funded by SEFC. This was because it considered ETC's educational supplies to be made under ordinary commercial contracts with its students.
- It is not necessary to exclude from Lennartz accounting any use of an asset to make supplies that are exempt from VAT. On this basis, the Tribunal upheld ETC's claim to recover all the VAT incurred on the construction of the campus building, even though it is used in part to make exempt supplies; and, as a result,
- HMRC was wrong not to have approved a proposed sectorised PE special method.

The Court of Session's finding

ETC appealed on the first point and HMRC cross-appealed on the second and third points. ETC did not contest HMRC's cross appeal, which was accepted by the Court, and thus the original claim was reduced to take into account the use of the campus building to make exempt supplies. The Court accepted ETC's argument that it engages as a public authority when delivering FE and HE courses. This was on the basis of the legal structure of ETC's managing body and of the legal requirements that relate to its funding stream. As such the Court held that this education was provided in a non-business capacity.

HMRC's position

The judgment of the Court of Session is currently being carefully considered, but HMRC are advised that—should it decide to appeal the case further—we have until 19 May 2006 in which to take the necessary action. A further Business Brief will be issued shortly, which will explain HMRC's response to the judgment and give any further guidance that may be necessary. However, the outcome of this case confirms HMRC's existing guidance that Lennartz accounting does not permit full recovery of VAT when an asset is partially used to make supplies which are exempt from VAT.

Note—See HMRC Brief 27/08, issued 22-5-08 (Interpretation of Article 13 of the Principal VAT Directive: "bodies governed by public law" and "special legal regime").

27 June 2006. Business Brief 7/06

Exemption for the management of authorised collective investment schemes

This Business Brief article announces changes to HMRC's policy concerning the VAT exemption for the management of authorised collective investment schemes, following the judgment of the European Court of Justice (ECJ) in case C-169/04, *Abbey National Plc & Inscape Investment Fund* ("Abbey"), on 4 May 2006.

It updates the section of Business Brief 10/03 headed 'What constitutes "management"?' and the changes apply from 1 October 2006.

BACKGROUND

Article 13B(d)(6) of the Sixth VAT Directive exempts "Management of special investment funds as defined by Member States". The United Kingdom applies this exemption to the management of authorised unit trusts (AUTs), and of the scheme property of open-ended investment companies (OEICs). The exemption is effected in UK law by items 9 and 10 of Group 5, Schedule 9 to the VAT Act 1994.

HMRC's policy has been to apply the exemption to fund management in a strict sense, ie where it involves the assessment of financial risks, the making of investment decisions as to both the selection and disposal of assets under management and a direct involvement in the transactions concerning the assets of the fund, mainly in securities. Services not comprising such investment management functions, such as fund accounting and administration services, were regarded as taxable.

Abbey challenged this interpretation and appealed to the VAT & Duties Tribunal against VAT charged to it on fund accounting and administration services and also against VAT charged to its funds on depository and trustee services. The case was referred to the ECJ, which delivered its judgment on 4 May 2006.

THE ABBEY JUDGMENT

Firstly, the court has ruled that "management" in Article 13B(d)(6) has its own independent meaning in Community law and Member States' discretion to define "management of special investment funds" relates only to the meaning of special investment funds and not to the activities which constitute "management" of such funds.

In considering the services at issue in the appeal, the court made reference to the UCITS Directive, as amended (European Council Directive 85/611/EEC, setting out common EU regulatory requirements for undertakings for collective investment in transferable securities—"UCITS").

It found that the services of trustees or depositories, such as those set out in Articles 7(1) and (3) and 14(1) and (3) of the UCITS Directive, are not covered by the concept of management and are therefore excluded from exemption. This affirms HMRC's policy in respect of such services and they continue to be subject to VAT.

For fund accounting and administration services, the court found that they would qualify as management of special investment funds for the purposes of the VAT exemption if, "viewed broadly, they form a distinct whole and are specific to, and essential for, the management of those funds".

REVISED INTERPRETATION OF THE LAW

Again by reference to the UCITS Directive, the court viewed that tasks, such as those set out in Annex II to the Directive under the heading 'Administration', and which are functions specific to special investment funds, are capable of coming within the scope of the exemption. Under this heading are:

(a) legal and fund management accounting services;
(b) customer inquiries;
(c) valuation and pricing (including tax returns);

(d) regulatory compliance monitoring;
(e) maintenance of unit-holder register;
(f) distribution of income;
(g) unit issues and redemptions;
(h) contract settlements (including certificate dispatch);
(i) record keeping.

The court also found that the exemption does not in principle preclude the management of special investment funds being broken down into a number of separate services which may come within the meaning of "management" for the purpose of the exemption.

HMRC accept that, to benefit from the exemption, it is not necessary that a third party provider of fund administration services performs all of the administration functions required by regulations such as those listed in Annex II to the UCITS Directive (and applicable to UK funds under Financial Services Authority sourcebook rules). It is, however, necessary that the services must, viewed broadly, form a distinct whole fulfilling in effect the specific essential functions of management. In other words, the service must be recognisable in its own right as a service of fund administration.

Just because a particular operation (such as each of those listed in Annex II) is a requirement of regulations it does not necessarily mean that it is exempt if provided in isolation. For example, legal services such as advice or drafting may be required to ensure that certain documents, eg a trust deed or fund prospectus, are valid and comply with the regulations, but this does not mean that the legal service is one of exempt fund administration. Similarly, an external audit of accounts does not of itself assume the characteristics of a fund administration service.

To be exempt, it is necessary for the service to be distinct as a fund administration service. This "distinctiveness" is normally attained by the bundling, into a single supply, of numerous operations that are typical of the administrative management of eg an OEIC. In deciding whether the overall service is distinct as fund administration, both the number of specific operations and their individual characteristics need to be taken into account.

For example, the daily valuation of assets is of particular importance and relevance to OEICs and AUTs in determining the price of shares or units and so this, together with related accounting and reporting functions would be sufficiently distinctive as a fund administration service. However, a service such as "price feeding" of information consisting of the market value of individual stocks, provided to the person carrying out the fund asset valuation, is not in itself a fund administration service.

As a further example, the maintenance of a register of shareholders does not, in isolation, represent a fund administration service. However, if the service is combined with the issue and redemption of the units or shares and collating the number of shares in issue for the purpose of establishing the daily price of the units, such a package takes on the distinct characteristics of fund administration and will be exempt.

HMRC are satisfied that the bundle of services provided by the Bank of New York in the Abbey case is exempt. This consisted of computing the amount of income and the price of units or shares, the valuation of assets, accounting, the preparation of statements for the distribution of income, the provision of information and documentation for periodic accounts, income forecasts and tax returns, as well as data processing, record-keeping and customer inquiries.

There are a number of businesses which provide specialist fund administration services in respect of AUTs and OEICs. In many cases, these services comprise a package of functions which, together, will satisfy the criteria for the exemption. However, as with some of the examples above, certain services or bundles of services cannot be viewed as a distinct service of fund administration. For instance, the legal services referred to above might be described as "specific to, and essential for", the management of the fund but they are not fund administration services.

If the criteria for exemption are satisfied, it should also be noted that a person providing such a package of services will generally be viewed as making a single exempt supply of fund administration services in respect of each fund where the manager has delegated the administrative functions. The fact that each element may be priced separately on a rate card does not affect this.

In summary, HMRC accept that, in accordance with the judgment, services which, viewed broadly, are distinct as fund administration services, and are specific to and essential for the management of AUTs or OEICs are exempt.

MAKING CLAIMS OR ADJUSTMENTS

Businesses that that have taxed fund administration services which satisfy the criteria above should exempt such services made from 1 October 2006. There is no requirement to make adjustments in respect of supplies made prior to this date. However, where businesses wish to make a claim to HMRC for a repayment of output tax incorrectly paid, they may do so, subject to the conditions set out below, by using one of the following methods (full details are given in VAT Notice 700/45 "How to correct VAT errors and make adjustments or claims"):

- Where the total of previous errors does not exceed £2000 net tax, an adjustment may be made to your current VAT return.
- Where the total of previous errors exceeds £2000 net tax, a separate claim should be

submitted to HMRC (in these cases the errors must not be corrected through your VAT returns). Details of where to send your claim can be obtained from update 2 to VAT Notice 700/45 "How to correct VAT errors and make adjustments or claims" or the HM Revenue & Customs National Advice Service on 0845 010 9000.

All adjustments or claims are limited to a three-year period and will be subject to the following conditions:

- All claims must take into account input tax that has been claimed, but which under the revised interpretation will not relate to taxable supplies.
- Businesses must be able to produce evidence that they accounted for VAT in the circumstances described above, and must be able to substantiate the amount claimed.

Subject to the three-year limitation period, any claim should be for all prescribed accounting periods in which the liability error occurred.

Should a claim not take into account all errors or all affected accounting periods, then HMRC will seek to set-off amounts owed to us for these periods against amounts claimed in other periods.

HMRC may reject all or part of a claim if repayment would unjustly enrich the claimant. More details on 'unjust enrichment' can be found at part 14 of VAT Notice 700/45 "How to correct VAT errors and make adjustments or claims".

A notification to HMRC that a business intends making a claim in the future is not a valid claim.

Businesses that have lodged "protective" claims pending the judgments should review them to ensure that they comply with the criteria of the judgment explained in this Business Brief and satisfy the above conditions. In particular, any claims in respect of the services of trustees or depositories should be excluded, as the ECJ confirmed HMRC's view that the supply of these services is taxable at the standard rate.

Commentary—*De Voil Indirect Tax Service* **V4.136H**.

Note—See HMRC Brief 65/07: HMRC withdraw from the appeal in *JP Morgan Fleming Claverhouse Trust plc*.

7 July 2006. Business Brief 8/06

Clarification of the treatment of travel agent funded discounts

This Business Brief article sets out the VAT treatment of supplies by tour operators in cases where agents offer discounts to the travelling customer, following the judgment in the case of First Choice Holidays plc (C-149/01). It also explains what action HM Revenue & Customs (HMRC) will take in relation to voluntary disclosures and assessments resulting from the application of Business Brief 33/02.

BACKGROUND

Within the travel industry it is common practice for tour operators to sell travel services (e g holidays) through travel agents and for travel agents to offer the traveller discounts on these services. The way discounts are operated can differ depending on the contractual obligations between the tour operator and travel agent. In some circumstances, tour operators agree to discounts being given by the travel agent on the understanding that the tour operator will only receive the discounted price the customer pays. In others, the travel agent itself subsidises the discount to the traveller and pays the tour operator the full advertised selling price of any travel services sold. This article affects only the latter circumstances and confirms that the tour operator must account for VAT on the full, advertised price.

In cases where the tour operator has offered the discount and receives only the reduced amount from the travel agent, that is the value to be used when calculating the selling price for VAT purposes. However, where the agent has subsidised the discount to the traveller, there has been some dispute as to the value of the selling price for VAT purposes.

THE COURT OF APPEAL DECISION

The Court of Appeal referred the case of First Choice Holidays to the ECJ which set down its judgment in June 2003, concluding that "the 'total amount to be paid by the traveller' … includes the additional amount that a travel agent … must … pay to the tour operator on top of the price paid by the traveller and which corresponds in amount to the discount given by the travel agent to the traveller on the price of the holiday stated in the tour operator's brochure."

Now that litigation has been completed HMRC are able to set out the final position.

CONSEQUENCES OF THIS JUDGMENT

The judgment means that there is no change to HMRC's policy on discounts within the Tour Operators' Margin Scheme (TOMS), which is that the consideration for travel services is the total received by a tour operator, including any discount offered by a travel agent. As such, this is the amount that should be used to calculate the selling price for VAT purposes and, where applicable, entered into the TOMS calculation. It also confirms that there is no separate supply of a 'right to a discount', as found by the High Court.

BUSINESS BRIEF 32/02

Following the High Court's judgment in this case, Business Brief 33/02 explained how the High Court decision could be applied.

The Business Brief allowed tour operators to use the discounted price in their current TOMS calculations if they wished to, providing they took account of both parts of the High Court judgment. Those who did so were issued with protective preferred and alternative assessments, pending the final outcome of the litigation. The preferred assessments (payable immediately) calculated the additional VAT due if HMRC's view prevailed. The alternative assessments (payment suspended) calculated the additional VAT due on the separate 'top up' supplies if the High Court judgment stood.

The Business Brief also permitted tour operators and travel agents to submit protective voluntary disclosure claims for VAT they considered had been overpaid on previous VAT returns, as a result of tour operators calculating their TOMS on undiscounted holiday values and travel agents not having claimed input tax, on the supply of services to them, by the tour operator.

WAY FORWARD

Now the litigation is concluded, these arrangements need to be revisited. HMRC will be taking corrective action as follows: where tour operators have already declared and paid VAT in line with HMRC's view (either via their VAT returns or by paying the preferred protective assessments issued to them), the VAT paid should already be correct. Protective alternative assessments, issued to tour operators, based on the High Court view of transactions, will now be withdrawn and voluntary disclosure claims utilising the High Court decision will be formally rejected (if this has not already been done). Any protective assessments issued to travel agents who reclaimed input tax on separate 'top up' supplies made to them by tour operators will now be enforced, because it has been determined there were no such supplies and therefore there was no entitlement to input tax.

APPEALS

Businesses who have previously lodged appeals with the VAT and Duties Tribunal that were stayed pending the Court of Appeal decision in this case, are now invited to withdraw them.

FURTHER INFORMATION

Guidance can be found in VAT Notices 709/5 Tour Operators' Margin Scheme and 709/6 Travel Agents and Tour Operators.

Commentary—*De Voil Indirect Tax Service* **V3.591, V3.594**.

17 July 2006. Business Brief 9/06

Clarification of HMRC's policy following the Court of Appeal's decision in Newnham College

This Business Brief article announces that the House of Lords has given HMRC leave to appeal the decision of the Court of Appeal in the case of *The Principal and Fellows of Newnham College Cambridge* (CA [2006] EWCA Civ 285; [2006] All ER (D) 368(Mar)). It also provides interim guidance for those businesses affected by the Court of Appeal decision.

THE ISSUE

The case concerns whether or not Newnham is in occupation of the college library. If so, their option to tax the library would be disapplied—as such occupation would be for the purpose of making exempt supplies of education—in which case, VAT incurred on rebuilding and refurbishment of the library would be irrecoverable. The Court of Appeal ruled in Newnham's favour.

BACKGROUND

HMRC contended that Newnham is in occupation of the library through its students' use of the library and the presence of staff seconded from Newnham to a subsidiary company to run the library. Newnham argued that the term "in occupation" in the anti-avoidance provisions must have the same meaning as the term "licence to occupy" in the exemption provisions. Newnham maintained that it has not been granted a licence to occupy the building and is not therefore in occupation. Accordingly, its option to tax still applies and the VAT incurred on the building works is recoverable.

The Court of Appeal ruled that to be "in occupation" of land requires more than a right to use that land. It requires some degree of control over the use by others (ie some degree of control over what those who are not also "in occupation" of the land can do on the land). The Court of Appeal found that Newnham did not have such a degree of control.

HMRC have been granted leave to appeal the decision to the House of Lords.

HMRC'S VIEW AND PRACTICAL IMPLICATIONS

Until the House of Lords has given its decision, businesses whose circumstances are identical to Newnham's may continue to apply their option to tax. Where businesses do so, HMRC may issue assessments for the tax it believes is due to protect its position. No action will be taken to enforce payment of such assessments until the final outcome of the Newnham case is known. If the final decision is in HMRC's favour, we will require payment of the assessed tax with interest.

Based on the Court of Appeal decision, businesses that were wrongly denied input tax recovery or have accounted for and paid VAT on similar supplies but now find that the relevant option to tax is disapplied, may submit claims for overpaid tax to their local Business Advice Centre. These will be subject to a three-year limitation period. All adjustments or claims must take into account any overclaimed input tax as well as any overdeclared output tax, and overdeclared output tax will be subject to the unjust enrichment provisions.

HMRC will seek claimants' agreement that such claims be held over until the House of Lords' decision is announced. Otherwise, HMRC will make a protective assessment for any amounts repaid. These assessments will have to be paid with interest if the Court of Appeal decision is overturned. A further Business Brief will be issued when the House of Lords decision is known.

Further information about claims can be found in HMRC Notice 700/45 "How to correct VAT errors or make adjustments or claims".

7 August 2006. Business Brief 11/06

Partial exemption—higher education sector variable tuition fees

This Business Brief article concerns the potential detrimental impact of variable tuition fees (VTFs) on the partial exemption (PE) methods of higher education institutions (HEIs). Specialist PE terms are explained in HMRC Notice 706—Partial Exemption.

BACKGROUND

Many HEIs use a PE special method in which input tax on their overhead costs is apportioned by reference to the value of their taxable and exempt supplies. Such a values-based method is easy to operate, responsive to normal business change, and generally works well provided the value of supplies is proportionate to the consumption of VAT-bearing, overhead costs.

The supply of VAT-exempt education by a HEI is heavily subsidised by grant income. This means that the charge to the student, which is the value of the supply for VAT purposes, is often below cost. Unless an adjustment is made to reflect the subsidy, a values-based method will misallocate overhead input tax so will not be fair and reasonable. HMRC believe the easiest way to correct for the subsidy is for the HEI to include its teaching support grant in its method as if it were part of the value of its supplies.

VARIABLE TUITION FEES

The introduction of VTFs from 1 August 2006 increases the value of exempt education. This is because VTFs are charged to students even if a third party subsequently pays them. However, as HMRC understand is often the case, HEIs will return part of the VTFs to students as bursaries rather than use them solely for additional expenditure. If this happens, a values-based method might misallocate overhead input tax to the detriment of the HEI.

CORRECTING AN UNFAIR METHOD

HMRC will approve any PE method that is fair and reasonable for the HEI as a whole. HMRC are firmly of the view that a values-based method works well for a HEI provided sensible adjustments are made to correct for subsidies and receipts that are disbursed rather than expended (thereby reflecting the fact that a grant-subsidised HEI will normally price its supplies so as to cover its costs). But, in order to be acceptable, an adjustment must be clearly justified, transparent and objectively determined—an arbitrary adjustment can never be accepted. Where a HEI returns part of the VTF as a statutory bursary under its Access Agreement with the Office for Fair Access, this may provide a suitable basis for adjustment.

WHAT SHOULD HEIS DO?

If you consider that your PE method is no longer fair and reasonable because of the introduction of VTFs, you are invited to contact your local VAT Office with proposals for a new method (this applies even where HMRC have directed your special method). Alternatively, you may wish to serve a Special Method Override Notice (Notice) on HMRC to correct your method as an interim solution until a new method is approved.

Commentary—*De Voil Indirect Tax Service* **V3.462, V6.225.**

21 August 2006. Business Brief 12/06

Position following the Court of Appeal judgment in Compass Contract Services Limited

This Business Brief article explains the position taken by HMRC following the judgment of the Court of Appeal in the case of *Compass Contract Services UK Limited ("Compass")* ([2006] EWCA Civ 730), released on 9 June 2006. HMRC have decided not to petition the House of Lords for leave to appeal against the judgment of the Court.

BACKGROUND

All supplies of food and drink in the course of catering are standard-rated. Catering is defined (VAT Act 1994 Schedule 8 Group 1) as including supplies of food or drink for consumption on the premises on which they are supplied (as well as hot take-away food), but it is not limited to such supplies.

Compass is a contract catering company that supplies food to staff working at BBC Television Centre. The VAT Tribunal found that the supply of cold food sold from Compass' retail outlets to those staff was zero-rated because there was no supply of catering and that the premises that Compass made their supplies from were the retail units occupied by them and not the whole BBC TV Centre site. The food was therefore not supplied for consumption on the premises on which it was supplied.

HMRC appealed directly to the Court of Appeal and its decision has addressed two main issues:

THE COURT OF APPEAL

"Catering per se"

The Court endorsed the approach set down in the *Safeway Stores plc* case ([1997] STC 163) to be taken in determining what a supply in the course of catering is.

Principally, this is that as no single factor is decisive in determining whether a supply is in the course of catering, all factors need to be considered when looking at the supplies being made.

This finding does not change the position that the sale of cold food by a retailer is standard-rated when sold in the course of catering (see VAT Notice 709/1 section 2). The decision of the Court re-emphasises the approach to take when looking at whether such a supply is being made in the course of catering.

"Premises"

VAT is always chargeable at the standard rate on the supply of food and drink for consumption on the premises on which they are supplied.

The Court of Appeal agreed with the Tribunal that Compass' premises consisted solely of their retail units and not BBC TV Centre as a whole (a restricted access premises). Therefore the sale of cold food to be taken for consumption away from Compass's retail units was zero-rated.

HMRC's previous policy on premises is set out in VAT Notice 709/1 section 3.1, and this advises that:

> Premises fall within two categories, those to which the public has unrestricted access and those to which access is only allowed with permission of some sort.
>
> Restricted access sites, such as secure office buildings, sports stadium, amusement parks and cinemas. Here, the premises are the whole of the building or site. This means that all supplies of food and drink will be standard-rated even if it is taken away from the point of sale.
>
> Unrestricted access sites, such as restaurants, shopping malls, hospitals, bus stations and railway stations (including those with platform ticket barriers). Here, the premises are confined to the outlet itself plus any associated facilities, such as table and chairs outside a café, whether or not you provide these facilities.

However, the judgment in Compass states that:

> "the sandwiches were in fact supplied by Compass to retail customers at six particular outlets located at various points in the larger site, not everywhere or anywhere in the BBC Television Centre site. The geographical situation and the physical extent of the retail units under the control of Compass and to which customers have access are sufficiently identified to be regarded or recognisable as separate premises at which supplies of food are made to Compass customers within the meaning of Note (3)(a). No food is consumed in the

Compass units themselves. That is where the supplies are made. It follows that the sandwiches supplied by Compass are not supplied for the purposes of being consumed on the premises on which they are supplied".

REVISED POLICY ON THE MEANING OF "PREMISES"

Following the Compass case HMRC have reconsidered their policy on "premises". The main change is that at restricted access sites a retailer will now be considered to occupy only that unit from which the sales of food have been made rather than the larger overall premises. However, the "premises" also includes any facilities provided to enable the purchasers to consume the food at the unit, such as areas of seating and tables within, and adjacent to, the retail unit, whether owned by the landlord or the retailer, but clearly for the use of the food retailer's customers.

This means that, unless the retailers supplies of cold food are in the course of catering (see section on Catering per se, above), the supply of cold food for consumption away from the immediate premises, elsewhere in the restricted access premises, will be zero-rated.

VAT NOTICE 709/1

An updated version of VAT Notice 709/1 will be released shortly to reflect this change to policy.

APPORTIONMENT

Where a retailer is unable to distinguish between standard-rated and zero-rated sales of cold food at the point of sale, the liability must be apportioned. However, the apportionment must be fair and reasonable and the retailer must be able to evidence and support the calculations made.

INFORMATION ON MAKING CLAIMS OR ADJUSTMENTS

Businesses making supplies of a similar nature to those made by Compass in this case will need to review the liability of the supplies that they have made. Businesses that have accounted for and paid VAT on supplies that they now consider to be zero-rated may submit claims for overpaid tax to their local Business Advice Centre. This will be subject to a three-year limitation period and unjust enrichment provisions.

Further information about claims can be found in VAT Notice 700/45 "How to correct VAT errors or make adjustments or claims" and Business Briefs 25/04 and 28/04.

24 August 2006. Business Brief 13/06

3-Year Cap on making claims—Court of Appeal Judgment in Michael Fleming t/a Bodycraft

This Business Brief article explains HM Revenue & Customs' (HMRC) position following the judgment of the Court of Appeal in *Michael Fleming (t/a Bodycraft) v CRC (Condé Nast Publications Ltd intervening)* [2006] EWCA Civ 70; [2006] STC 864; [2006] All ER (D) 199 (Feb) (Fleming). The court decided the case against HMRC but has granted permission to appeal to the House of Lords and HMRC are doing so.

Pending the outcome of the appeal to the House of Lords, HMRC will give effect to the Court of Appeal's judgment for those who wish to make a claim, under the terms of this Business Brief, which includes a requirement to repay, with interest, in the event that this judgment is overturned. Many taxpayers may choose to await the final outcome of the litigation. In either event, claims arising out of this litigation will carry an entitlement to make a claim for statutory, simple interest (under VATA 1994 s 78).

BACKGROUND

In 1996 and 1997, the Government introduced a 3-year limitation period on claims for repayment of overpaid VAT, the correction of errors and late claims to input tax. It is now accepted, following the ECJ's judgment in *Marks & Spencer Plc v C&E Comrs* [2002] STC 1036 (M&S), that the statutory 3-year limitation periods (introduced with no express transitional periods during which taxpayers were able to make claims under the pre-existing rules) were, in certain cases, wrongly relied upon by HMRC against taxpayers.

Business Brief 22/02 invited claims under VATA 1994 s 80 for repayment of amounts paid incorrectly as VAT. Taxpayers were not, at that time, invited to submit or re-submit claims which had, or would have, been subject to the capping measures introduced, for example in the Value Added Tax Regulations 1995, SI 1995/2518 reg 29(1A), with effect from 1 May 1997.

The exclusion of claims (particularly those made under SI 1995/2518, reg 29 (input tax)) from the scope of Business Brief 22/02, and the refusal of claims made in accordance with it, led to a number of appeals to the VAT & Duties Tribunal challenging both the manner in which the relevant 3-year limitation periods were enacted and HMRC's response to the M&S judgment. Many of these appeals were decided in favour of HMRC but the Court of Appeal in Fleming found against them and held that persons whose right to deduct input tax arose before the date on which the new time limit was enacted, that is to say before 1 May 1997, should be allowed to claim without imposition of the 3-year cap.

IMPLICATIONS OF THE FLEMING JUDGMENT

The Court of Appeal's judgment has implications beyond late claims for input tax. HMRC accept, for present purposes, that any claim, under SI 1995/2518 regs 29, 34 or 35, or VATA 1994 s 80 arising before the enactment of the respective capping measures, is effectively uncapped. However, this does not mean that the 3-year time limits, as they operate currently since the date of their enactment, are themselves contrary to Community law or in any sense invalid.

MAKING A CLAIM

Taxpayers who believe that they are entitled to benefit from the Court of Appeal's judgment in Fleming, and who wish to claim without waiting until the matter is finally determined in the House of Lords, should proceed as follows—

Where a claim, relating to an event more than three years earlier, has already been made and remains "active", either because no appealable decision has yet been given by HMRC or because the matter is subject to appeal, taxpayers should write to HMRC (see the address below) asking for their claim to be considered in accordance with this Business Brief.

In all other cases, a fresh claim can be made where an amount—

- has been improperly paid as VAT before 4 December 1996;
- has been overdeclared as output tax in an accounting period ending before 4 December 1996; or
- became deductible as input tax on or before 30 April 1997 and has not yet been deducted.

In all cases, the claimant must sign an undertaking to the effect that, if the ultimate determination of litigation removes his entitlement, any credit given, or money paid, to him, will be returned to HMRC with interest. A copy of the undertaking is provided at the Annexe.

Claims falling within the scope of VATA 1994 s 80 will be paid only where HMRC are satisfied that to pay the claim will not result in the unjust enrichment of the claimant.

Form of claim

New claims must be made in writing and must include—

- a statement of the amount being claimed;
- the reason for the claim;
- the method of calculation in as much detail as possible;
- the prescribed accounting periods in respect of which claims are being made, allocating amounts to periods;
- the dates on which any overpayments, overdeclarations or underclaims were made and, if the overpayment was made pursuant to an assessment or voluntary disclosure, the date on which the assessment or disclosure was made;
- copies of all documents, schedules, etc. used in support of the claim;
- the reasons why you will not be unjustly enriched, where appropriate, if a credit is now given or a repayment made; and
- any claim for statutory, simple interest (under VATA 1994 s 78) that you consider you are entitled to make.

Claims (whether made under VATA 1994 s 80 or under SI 1995/2518, reg 29) will only be paid or credited on a net basis. For example, if you overdeclared output tax during a given accounting period on supplies which ought to have been exempt, and in the same accounting period you recovered more input tax than you ought, the input tax wrongly recovered will be set off against the overdeclared output tax and only the balance will be paid or credited. Conversely, if, in a given accounting period you have understated your input tax entitlement but you have also understated your output tax liability, your claim should be for any net credit due.

All claims are to be sent to the Voluntary Disclosure Team at—

HM Revenue & Customs, "Fleming" Claims Team (Leeds), Queens Dock, Liverpool, Merseyside, L74 4AA.

Telephone enquiries in relation to the submission of claims or to claims that have already been submitted to the Claims Team may be made on 0113 389 4432.

Commentary—*De Voil Indirect Tax Service* **V3.405.**
Note—See HMRC Brief 7/08 issued following the House of Lords decisions on *Michael Fleming* and *Condé Nast.*

24 August 2006. Business Brief 13/06

3-YEAR CAP ON MAKING CLAIMS—COURT OF APPEAL JUDGMENT IN CONDÉ NAST PUBLICATIONS LTD

This Business Brief article explains HMRC's position following the Court of Appeal judgment in *Condé Nast Publications Ltd v CRC* [2006] EWCA Civ 976 (Condé Nast).

Taxpayers need take no action as a consequence of this article. Any taxpayer who is likely to benefit from the Court of Appeal's judgment in Condé Nast will benefit from its judgment in Fleming and can lodge, or pursue, a claim as explained in the previous article in this Business Brief.

Like Fleming, Condé Nast concerned claims refused by HMRC on the basis that they were capped by a 3-year limitation period that, it is now accepted, should have been introduced with an express transitional period during which taxpayers ought to have been able to make claims under the pre-existing rules.

The Court of Appeal hearing Condé Nast was bound by, and followed, its majority judgment in Fleming and disposed of the appeal on that basis. However, the Condé Nast litigation raises an important issue not present on the facts of the Fleming case.

HMRC's view is that, in the absence of a transitional period expressly provided for in legislation, the capping provisions should only be disapplied to the extent necessary to give effect to a taxpayer's Community law rights, where, in individual cases, it was made impossible to exercise those rights by the manner in which the cap was introduced.

It should not be disapplied generally in respect of all claims arising before the capping legislation as was decided by the Court of Appeal. Consequently, HMRC argue that, if a taxpayer would not have put in a claim even had a transitional period been provided when the cap was introduced, the absence of a transitional period cannot be said to have infringed his Community law rights by preventing him from making his claim and the 3-year time limit should not be disapplied.

The Court of Appeal decided this point against HMRC. As it has significance in the event that the House of Lords overturns the judgment in Fleming, HMRC have now petitioned their Lordships for leave to appeal against the Court of Appeal's judgment in Condé Nast.

ANNEX

Undertaking to repay VAT and statutory interest

The Commissioners for HM Revenue and Customs ("the Commissioners") agree to credit the account of [ ] ("the Claimant") with the principal sum of VAT of £ [ ] without the need for any further court action by the Claimant. If that results in the Commissioners owing a net sum to the Claimant then the Commissioners agree to pay that net sum to the Claimant [with the appropriate amount of statutory interest].

In return, the Claimant agrees that, if the effect of the decision of the courts, in *Michael Fleming (t/a Bodycraft) v HMRC* [2006] EWCA Civ 70, *Condé Nast Publications Limited v HMRC* [2006] EWCA Civ 976 or any other case, is that the Claimant was not entitled to the credit described above (or any part of the credit), the credit (or part of the credit) will be cancelled and the Claimant will repay all or the appropriate part of any net sum and statutory interest paid to it by the Commissioners.

The Claimant also agrees to pay simple interest, at the rate set under FA 1996 s 197, on any net sum and statutory interest repaid from the date it is paid to the Claimant by the Commissioners to the date it is repaid to the Commissioners.

The Claimant agrees to make the repayments described above, and pay interest thereon, within 28 days of a demand being made by the Commissioners.

Signed—

For the Commissioners for Her Majesty's Revenue & Customs

Name—

Signature—

Date—

For the Claimant

Name—

Signature—

Date—

Commentary—*De Voil Indirect Tax Service* **V3.405**.
Note—See HMRC Brief 7/08 issued following the House of Lords decisions on *Michael Fleming* and *Condé Nast*.

27 September 2006. Business Brief 15/06

Gaming machines—accounting for VAT

In Business Brief 23/05 (issued on 5 December 2005), we advised that the change to the definition of a gaming machine for VAT purposes created certainty by confirming that where the element of chance in the game is provided is not relevant. This followed attempts to avoid VAT by reconfiguring and developing machines so that the random number generator (RNG), which determined the outcome of the game, was sited outside the machine. HMRC consider that the majority of these machines were in fact gaming machines, even before the change in the definition in December 2005, despite having their RNGs fitted outside the main body of the machine. As such, VAT should have been accounted for, and the machines licensed as gaming machines.

It has come to our attention that some businesses failed to license or account for VAT on these machines or have submitted claims to HMRC requesting repayment of VAT that had been paid.

As VAT was correctly payable on these machines, repayments will not be made and, where tax has been underdeclared, assessments will be issued. If you consider you have been misdirected, you should advise your local Business Centre.

27 September 2006. Business Brief 15/06

The reduced value rule for long-stay guests in hotels—revised interpretation of the law on VAT treatment

This Business Brief article announces a change in HM Revenue & Customs' (HMRC) interpretation of the law regarding the application of the reduced value rule for long-stay guests in hotels. This change has been incorporated in an update to VAT Notice 709/3—Hotels and Holiday Accommodation, issued recently.

The change affects the treatment of supplies of overnight accommodation made by hotels (which includes inns, boarding houses and similar establishments), where the accommodation is provided to individuals for periods exceeding 28 days. Stays of up to and including 28 days are unaffected by the change and will continue to be subject to VAT at the standard rate.

BACKGROUND

Many people, for a variety of reasons, "live" in hotels or similar establishments for long periods. As the exemption from VAT for supplies of residential accommodation (for example in houses and flats) does not extend to the accommodation provided by hotels, such people would be disadvantaged. In order to provide greater consistency of treatment, a special valuation rule has the effect of treating supplies of accommodation by hotels as VAT-free from the 29th day of a person's stay. The rule (often referred to as "the reduced value rule") restricts the VAT charge to the part of the payment that is not for accommodation. As a result, where an inclusive charge is made, VAT continues to be due on the part of the charge that relates to meals and drinks, plus other services and facilities provided with the accommodation. Details of how to arrive at the part of the charge subject to tax are given in *Notice 709/03—Hotels and holiday accommodation*. The supply of the accommodation does not become an exempt supply, so there is no restriction to the amount of input tax the hotel can claim as a result of the rule.

It has been the view of HMRC that the rule only applies where the supply of the accommodation is made to the individual who will occupy it and that where the supply of the accommodation is to third parties, such as local authorities, VAT is applicable to the total charge regardless of the length of the individual's stay.

REVISED INTERPRETATION OF THE LAW

Following the recent decision of the Tribunal in the case of *Afro Caribbean Housing Association* [2006] SWTI 1374, HMRC now accepts that the reduced value rule is not limited to situations where the VAT supply is made to the individuals occupying the accommodation. This means, that where, for example, hotels contract with local authorities or other organisations for the provision of accommodation, for example to homeless people or asylum seekers, this can qualify for treatment under the reduced value rule.

However, there are no other changes to HMRC's interpretation of the rule, which means that it still only applies where the same individual is using the accommodation for a continuous period that exceeds 28 days (the first 28 days of each individual's stay is always subject to VAT on the full value). It does not apply, for example, where accommodation is block-booked by companies for periods over 28 days and is used by a number of different individuals for individual periods of less than 28 days. It also does not apply to holiday accommodation. *Notice 709/3—Hotels and holiday accommodation* describes in detail how the rule works.

MAKING CLAIMS OR ADJUSTMENTS

The change described above should be implemented from the date of this Business Brief and there is no requirement to make adjustments in respect of supplies made prior to this date. However, where hotels or other establishments wish to make a claim to HMRC for a repayment of output tax incorrectly paid, they may do so, subject to the conditions set out below, by using one of the following methods (full details are given in *VAT Notice 700/45—How to correct VAT errors and make adjustments or claims*)—

– where the total of previous errors do not exceed £2000 net tax, an adjustment may be made to your current VAT return; or
– where the total previous errors exceed £2000 net tax a separate claim should be submitted to HMRC (in these cases the errors must not be corrected through your VAT returns).

Details of where to send your claim can be obtained from update 2 to *VAT Notice 700/45—How to correct VAT errors and make adjustments or claims* or the HMRC National Advice Service on 0845 010 9000.

All adjustments or claims are limited to a three-year period and businesses must be able to produce evidence that they accounted for VAT in the circumstances described above, and must be able to substantiate the amount claimed. Subject to the three-year limitation period, any claim should also be for all prescribed accounting periods in which the error occurred. Should a claim not take into account all errors or all affected accounting periods, then HMRC will seek to set-off amounts owed to us for these periods against amounts claimed in other periods.

HMRC may reject all or part of a claim if repayment would unjustly enrich the claimant. More details on "unjust enrichment" can be found at part 14 of *VAT Notice 700/45—How to correct VAT errors and make adjustments or claims*.

A notification to HMRC that a business intends making a claim in the future is not a valid claim.

Where you are in any doubt about the correct treatment please contact the National Advice Service on 0845 010 9000.

Commentary—*De Voil Indirect Tax Service* **V4.113.**

13 October 2006. Business Brief 16/06

Changes to VAT law in light of the Gambling Act

In Business Brief 23/05 (issued on 5 December 2005), we advised that the definition of "gaming machine" for VAT liability purposes in VATA 1994 Sch 9 Group 4 was to be amended by Treasury Order. This was intended to ensure that all gaming machines were excluded from the exemption, and so liable to VAT. In the process of doing this, we updated some of the elements of the definition by reference to GA 2005. VATA 1994 s 23, which includes a corresponding definition of a gaming machine in the provision which determines the value on which VAT is accounted for on gaming machine takings, was amended in FA 2006, with retrospective effect from 6 December 2005.

Two new Treasury Orders have been laid before Parliament that will come into effect on 1 November 2006. The new Orders continue to update VAT law in light of GA 2005, and will—

- remove the separate definition of "gaming machine" from Group 4, replacing it by a cross-reference to the identical definition in section 23;
- provide a new definition of "game of chance" in Group 4 and section 23, replacing the cross reference to the Gambling Act definition;
- ensure that the definition of "game of chance" is the same across the UK for both Group 4 and section 23;
- restore the application of VAT to pinball machines; and
- ensure that any game of chance which is not played for a prize does not fall within the exemption.

DEFINITION OF "GAMING MACHINE"

At present, section 23 and Group 4 contain identical definitions of "gaming machine". The new Group 4 Order replaces the definition of "gaming machine" in Group 4 with a cross-reference to the section 23 definition, which is itself amended by the other Order.

NEW DEFINITIONS OF "GAMBLING" AND "GAME OF CHANCE"

The definition of "gambling" was introduced into Group 4 and section 23 by inserting cross-references to the definitions of "betting" and "gaming" in the Gambling Act. The new Order amending section 23 replaces the cross-references to the Gambling Act with stand-alone definitions of "game of chance", based on provisions in GA 2005 s 6 and s 239. "Betting" is no longer to be defined. The new definition of "game of chance" in Group 4 applies for the use of the term in defining the scope of the exemption whether or not the game is played on a machine.

PINBALL MACHINES AND OTHER GAMES OF CHANCE NOT PLAYED FOR A PRIZE

The takings from pinball machines had inadvertently been brought within the scope of the exemption by the PBR Order, when the Gambling Act concept of gaming was imported into VAT legislation dealing with gaming machines. VAT exemption is currently available for the provision of facilities for playing a game of chance, whether or not for a prize. Gaming machines are excluded from the scope of this exemption. Before the PBR order was introduced, pinball machines were taxed as gaming machines as it was not a requirement for a gaming machine to offer a prize. However, the PBR order applied GA 2005 s 6(1), which provides that gaming is playing a game of chance for a prize, to the definition of gaming machines. Although this meant that pinball machines were excluded from the definition of gaming machines, as they do not offer prizes, they still qualified for VAT exemption as the provisions of facilities for playing a game of chance.

In future, only a game of chance played for a prize, whether or not played on a machine, will qualify for exemption in any event. "Prize" will be defined so as to exclude the opportunity to play the game again ("free plays").

Consequently, traders who have been accounting for VAT on pinball machines takings in the period from 6 December 2005 to 31 October 2006 may make a claim to HMRC for a repayment of output tax incorrectly paid, subject to the conditions set out below, by using one of the following (full details can be found in VAT Notice 700/45 *How to correct VAT errors or make adjustments or claims*—

- where the total of previous errors does not exceed £2000 net tax, an adjustment may be made to your current VAT return; and
- where the total of previous errors exceeds £2000 net tax a separate claim should be submitted to HMRC (in these cases the errors must not be corrected through your VAT returns).

Details of where to send your claim can be obtained from the HMRC National Advice Service on 0845 010 9000.

All adjustments or claims will be subject to the following conditions—

- all claims must take into account input tax that has been claimed, but which, while pinball machine takings were exempt, did not relate to taxable supplies; and
- businesses must be able to produce evidence that they accounted for VAT in the circumstances described above, and must be able to substantiate the amount claimed.

Any claim should be for all prescribed accounting periods in which the liability error occurred. Should a claim not take into account all errors or all affected accounting periods, then HMRC will seek to set-off amounts owed to us for these periods against amounts claimed in other periods.

HMRC may reject all or part of a claim if repayment would unjustly enrich the claimant. More details on "unjust enrichment" can be found at part 14 of VAT Notice 700/45 *How to correct VAT errors and make adjustments or claims.*

Commentary—*De Voil Indirect Tax Service* **V4.131.**

13 October 2006. Business Brief 16/06

Publication of tax avoidance scheme disclosure statistics

This Business Brief article announces HMRC's intention to publish the number of disclosures of tax avoidance schemes received.

BACKGROUND

In 2004 disclosure rules were introduced requiring promoters and users to notify details of certain direct tax and VAT arrangements to HMRC. The rules were extended to Stamp Duty Land Tax (SDLT) in 2005, and from 1 August 2006 to the whole of Income Tax, Corporation Tax and Capital Gains Tax.

Since the introduction of the rules, tax professionals, business and others have shown a great deal of interest in the total number of disclosures made, and have made many requests to HMRC for the information. These have included requests under the terms of FoIA 2000. As the disclosure rules were developed in collaboration with tax professionals and business, HMRC see making the information more accessible part of its continuing commitment to this collaboration. Publication of the information is not inconsistent with the strict rules on taxpayer confidentiality and the provisions of the FoIA 2000.

WHAT WILL BE PUBLISHED

Starting on 31 October 2006 HMRC will publish the total number of disclosures that have been made up to 30 September 2006. The information will appear in two tables, one for direct tax and SDLT and the other for VAT. The statistics will be updated in April and October of subsequent years.

Each tax within a table, with the exception of SDLT, is subdivided by category of scheme. For direct tax the categories are financial and employment up to 31 July 2006, and hallmark from 1 August 2006 onwards.

FOR VAT THE CATEGORIES ARE LISTED AND HALLMARK.

Within these categories the totals received will be given as six-monthly totals (for the six months ending 31 March and 30 September each year) and annual totals (for the financial year ending 31 March). An exception to giving a six-monthly total is for the six months ending 30 September 2006, as this covers the 1 August 2006 change of categories for direct tax disclosures. In this case the totals for each category will be for the period that they are applicable. The latest totals published will always be provisional, and will only be finalised when the statistics are next updated.

Information on the history of the disclosure rules and further details on interpreting the statistics will be published alongside the tables. The information note will give details of the total number of voluntary registration scheme (VAT hallmark) disclosures received to date.

WHERE TO FIND THE STATISTICS

The statistics will be published on HMRC's website—http://www.hmrc.gov.uk. Go to the home page and look for the link to the statistics under "What's New" (bottom of screen), otherwise from the home page use the link to the "Practitioner Zone" (top right hand corner) and then use the link under Library to "Anti Avoidance Group". From here follow further links to the statistics.

NEXT PUBLISHING DATE

The updated totals to 31 March 2007 will be published on 30 April 2007.

Commentary—*De Voil Indirect Tax Service* **V5.213.**

13 October 2006. Business Brief 16/06

Liability of private tuition

HMRC's policy on the liability of private tuition is set out in VAT Notice 701/30 *Education and vocational training*, section 6. This advises that the VAT exemption for private tuition only applies to sole proprietors and partnerships who teach a subject that is taught regularly in a number of schools or universities.

It has come to our attention that some businesses that supply private tuition have incorrectly exempted their supplies from VAT. This follows a Tribunal decision in the case of *Empowerment Enterprises Ltd*, which found that the exemption extended to tuition provided by directors of limited companies and those employed by sole proprietors, partnerships or limited companies.

HMRC appealed against the Tribunal's findings and the Court of Session, confirming that exemption is only available to sole proprietors and partnerships.

Therefore, all suppliers of private education should ensure that they are applying the correct liability to their supplies. Additionally, if you have been using the incorrect liability, you will need to account for any unpaid VAT as follows—

- where the total of previous errors does not exceed £2000 net tax, an adjustment may be made to your current VAT return; or
- where the total of previous errors exceeds £2000 net tax, a separate voluntary disclosure should be submitted to HMRC (in these cases the errors must not be corrected through your VAT returns).

Details of where to send your claim can be obtained from update 2 to VAT Notice 700/45—*How to correct VAT errors and make adjustments or claims* or from the HMRC National Advice Service on 0845 010 9000.

Commentary—*De Voil Indirect Tax Service* **V4.141.**
Simon's Tax Cases—*R&C Commissioners v Empowerment Enterprises Ltd* [2006] CSIH 46.

13 October 2006. Business Brief 16/06

Liability of condoms supplied to charities providing care or medical treatment

This business brief article explains HMRC's position as a result of the Tribunal's decision in the case of *Pasante Healthcare Ltd* [LON/06/118 (VTD 19724)].

BACKGROUND

The supply of a "medicinal product" to a charity providing care or medical or surgical treatment is zero-rated (VATA 1994, Sch 8, Group 15). Pasante Healthcare Ltd supplied condoms to a charity that provides free and confidential sexual health advice and contraception to young people. It contended that condoms are medicinal products within the terms of the Act, and therefore should be zero-rated when supplied to such a charity.

In order to qualify as a medicinal product the law requires that they be "administered". HMRC contended that the distribution of condoms by a charity did not meet the legal test.

DECISION

The Tribunal agreed with the appellant that a condom falls within the legal definition of a medicinal product as condoms distributed by a sexual health charity are administered within the terms of the legislation.

THE WAY FORWARD

HMRC have decided not to appeal the tribunal's decision. Businesses supplying condoms in similar circumstances to those of Pasante's should zero rate their supplies

The decision does not affect supplies of condoms to customers other than charities providing care, medical or surgical treatment. They will continue to be liable to the reduced rate of VAT, which applied to contraceptive products, with effect from 1 July 2006.

INFORMATION ON MAKING CLAIMS OR ADJUSTMENTS

Businesses that have accounted for and paid VAT on supplies of condoms that are now consider to be zero-rated may submit claims for overpaid tax to their local Business Advice Centre. These will be subject to a three-year limitation period and unjust enrichment provisions.

More information about claims can be found in VAT Notice 700/45 *How to correct VAT errors or make adjustments or claims* and Business Briefs 25/04 and 28/04.

FURTHER INFORMATION

For further information and advice, please contact HMRC Charity Helpline on 0845 302 0203.

Commentary—*De Voil Indirect Tax Service* **V4.146.**

19 October 2006. Business Brief 17/06

Partial exemption: bookmakers—recovery of VAT on specialist television services and equipment

This Business Brief article clarifies HMRC policy on the recovery of VAT incurred by bookmakers on specialist TV services, following the Tribunal decision in the case of *Town and County Factors (TCF)*, VTD 19616 [but see Note below]. It uses a number of specialist terms, which are fully explained in Public Notice 706, Partial Exemption.

BACKGROUND

Betting shops often incur VAT on specialist TV services and equipment on which they screen racing and sporting events, including those for which exempt bets are accepted. TCF argued that VAT incurred on TV facilities was partly recoverable because they had a direct and immediate link with taxable supplies of gaming machines and refreshments, as well as exempt supplies of betting. HMRC's view was that the costs related wholly to exempt supplies so that no VAT was recoverable.

The Tribunal supported TCF, finding on the facts of the case that VAT incurred on specialist racing TV was residual because TCF added content to the broadcasts advertising their taxable services and because TV attracts customers into shops to play gaming machines. The Tribunal also found that VAT relating to Sky Sports was residual as the costs related to all of the activities of the betting shop even though the broadcasts did not carry adverts for their taxable services.

HMRC'S POLICY FOLLOWING TCF

HMRC are not appealing the decision. HMRC accept that bookmakers who add content to specialist racing TV to advertise their taxable services, may now treat the VAT as residual. HMRC remain of the view that, where no such content is added, the VAT incurred is wholly related to exempt betting and is not recoverable.

HMRC accept that bookmakers may treat VAT incurred on Sky Sports as residual because the broadcasts are not exclusively related to exempt betting. VAT incurred on TV equipment is also residual provided it is used for broadcasts that relate to both taxable and exempt supplies. If the equipment is used wholly for specialist racing TV, then the VAT incurred is irrecoverable.

PARTIAL EXEMPTION METHODS

Even where VAT on specialist racing TV is residual, the amount of taxable use is likely to be very small compared with overhead costs such as lighting and heating. As a result existing Partial Exemption (PE) methods may no longer produce a fair and reasonable result and may need to be amended.

HMRC may seek to replace an unfair method or to prospectively amend its result. If you consider that your PE method is no longer fair and reasonable you should contact your Local Business Advice Centre with proposals for a new method.

CLAIMS FOR UNDER-RECOVERED INPUT TAX

Bookmakers may wish to claim input tax which, in the light of this Business Brief, was incorrectly treated as exempt. Claims should be submitted to the Local Business Advice Centre. They must use the PE method applicable to each accounting period unless there are exceptional circumstances as to why an alternative method is needed. All claims are subject to the relevant time limits.

Further information about making claims can be found in Public Notice 700/45 How to correct VAT errors or make adjustments or claims and Business Briefs 25/04 and 28/04.

Note—See now HMRC Brief 1/08 (following the decision in *Cheshire Racing Ltd*, HMRC now accept that SIS services have a direct and immediate link to gaming machine supplies made by bookmakers).
Commentary—*De Voil Indirect Tax Service* **V6.296.**

19 October 2006. Business Brief 17/06

Disposable barbecues

HM Revenue & Customs (HMRC) have been asked to clarify the VAT treatment of the sale of disposable barbecues. Some retailers have been treating such sales as reduced rate or mixed rate supplies (part standard-rated; part reduced-rated). The correct VAT treatment is that the sale of disposable barbecues is a single standard-rated supply, subject to VAT at 17.5 per cent.

Any errors made on previous VAT returns in respect of such supplies must be corrected in accordance with the conditions set out below, by using one of the following methods (full details are given in VAT Notice 700/45 How to correct VAT errors and make adjustments or claims):

- where the total of previous errors does not exceed £2000 net tax, an adjustment may be made to your current VAT return, or
- where the total of previous errors exceeds £2000 net tax a separate written disclosure should be submitted to HMRC (in these cases the errors must not be corrected through your VAT returns). Details of where to send your disclosure can be obtained from Update 2 to VAT Notice 700/45 How to correct VAT errors and make adjustments or claims or the HMRC National Advice Service on 0845 010 9000.

All adjustments are limited to a three-year period.

If in quantifying errors made, any business considers that the extra-statutory concessions relating to misdirection or misunderstanding apply, they should submit a complete report to HMRC. Details of these ESCs (3.4 and 3.5) and the circumstances under which HMRC will remit, or not assess, VAT undercharged are in Public Notice 48 Extra Statutory Concessions.

Where you are in any doubt about the correct treatment please contact the National Advice Service on 0845 010 9000.

Commentary—*De Voil Indirect Tax Service* **V3.103.**

27 October 2006. HMRC website

Motor trade issues: car derived vans and combi vans

Customs has issued a Business Brief 16/04 which clarifies Customs' interpretation of the definition of a motor car as contained in the Value Added Tax (Cars) Order 1992.

Many car-derived vans pose no problem with regard to our current definition of a motor car, in that they are clearly vans or non-motor cars for VAT purposes e g they have no rear seats, metal side panels to the rear of the front seats, a load area which is highly unsuitable for carrying passengers etc.

The clarification is necessary in the light of recent developments in the car-derived van market, which have resulted in the manufacture of vehicles with a payload of less than one tonne that have blurred the distinction between cars and vans. This means that these vehicles are difficult to categorise in relation to the definition of motorcars in VAT legislation.

The Business Brief refers to a list of car-derived vans on which VAT may be deducted (subject to the normal rules) as they are not seen as cars VAT purposes. The list [on HMRC's website] has been compiled by Customs and is based on information supplied by manufacturers. At any one time it may not be complete or up to date where models change or information has not been provided.

The list is specific to vehicles which are produced or converted by the manufacturers or sole concessionaires and which have been notified to Customs. Vehicles from other sources are not shown and may not meet the criteria to be treated as commercial vehicles.

In these cases it is the responsibility of the purchaser to obtain confirmation in writing from the vendor that the vehicle meets the technical criteria.

Vendors can request the guidance on the technical criteria from the Customs National Advice Service on tel: 0845 101 9000.

Commentary—*De Voil Indirect Tax Service* **V3.443.**

30 October 2006. Business Brief 18/06

Liability of agents' credit and debit card handling services

This Business Brief article announces HMRC's revised policy on the VAT liability of credit and debit card handling services supplied by agents, following the end of litigation in the cases of *Bookit Ltd* (Bookit) and *Scottish Exhibition Centre Ltd* (SEC).It replaces item 2 of Business Brief 21/05 and item 1 of Business Brief 17/98, both of which are now withdrawn. Public Notice 701/49, *Finance*, will be updated in due course.

SUMMARY

The House of Lords has refused HMRC's petition to appeal the Court of Appeal judgment in *Bookit* (EWCA Civ 550) [2006] STC 1367 and HMRC will not be seeking leave to appeal the judgment of the Court of Session in the case of *SEC* ([2006] Scot CS CSIH-42).The effect of the end of litigation in these two cases is that debit and credit card handling services provided by agents are VAT exempt where a key identified component is present in the service. Claims held pending the outcome of these cases will now be reviewed for payment and any assessments raised by HMRC for under-declared tax will be withdrawn where appropriate.

BACKGROUND

The Bookit case concerned the supply of Odeon cinema tickets. Customers wishing to purchase cinema tickets remotely, e g by phone or Internet, were redirected to Odeon's agent, Bookit, who charged the customer an additional fee over and above the price of the ticket for their service. Bookit contended this fee was for credit or debit card handling services and was VAT-exempt as a transaction concerning payments or transfers. The tribunal found that Bookit was providing a taxable card handling service to the customer in return for the additional fee. The High Court, in overturning the tribunal's decision, found that Bookit was carrying out an exempt card handling service. The Court of Appeal, in upholding the High Court judgment, found that the supply by Bookit to the customer included the following components:

- obtaining the card information with the necessary security information from the customer;
- transmitting that information to the card issuers;
- receiving the authorisation codes from the card issuers; and
- transmitting the card information with the necessary security information and the card issuers' authorisation codes to Girobank.

The Court found that the tribunal had been correct in finding components (i) to (iii) to be taxable, but because the fourth component was part of Bookit's service to the customer, and had the effect that funds were transferred to its account with Girobank, exemption was available to Bookit. The *SEC* case concerned the supply of tickets to events held in the Scottish Exhibition and Conference Centre in Glasgow. SEC acted as agent of the promoter in the selling of tickets and charged an additional fee to customers on tickets that were paid for by credit and debit card. SEC contended this fee was for card handling services and was VAT exempt. The tribunal found in HMRC's favour, stating that SEC was providing a single taxable booking service, with the taxable card handling service representing an ancillary aspect enhancing the main service. The Court of Session overturned the tribunal decision, finding that SEC was carrying out an exempt card handling service. The Court based its judgment on the decision of the Court of Appeal in Bookit and on an assumption of similar facts. HMRC do not therefore draw a distinction between the two judgments.

IMPLICATIONS OF THE JUDGMENTS

The judgments have provided further guidance on when a service of credit or debit card handling by an agent is VAT-exempt. If an agent, acting for the supplier of the goods or services, makes a charge to the customer over and above the price of the actual goods or services, for a separately identifiable service of handling payment by credit or debit card, and that service includes the fourth component listed above, then the additional charge will be exempt under item 1, Group 5 of Schedule 9 to the VAT Act 1994. However, where an agent provides some or all of the first three components without providing the fourth, the charge is taxable at the standard rate of VAT. Charges levied on the cardholder for payment by credit and debit card in any other circumstances will not fall within the exemption for financial services and the normal VAT treatment will apply. The judgments do not alter the general principle that the taxable amount for a supply of goods or services includes all payments which the supplier requires the customer to make as a condition of receiving the supply. If, for example, a supplier of goods or services requires a customer to pay an additional charge, above that of the price of the actual goods or services, for payment by credit or debit card, that charge is further consideration for the purchase of those goods or services and VAT is payable on that amount in accordance with the VAT treatment of the goods or services.

INFORMATION ON MAKING CLAIMS OR ADJUSTMENTS

Agents supplying card handling services that meet the criteria set out above, and who have been treating the charge as taxable at the standard rate, should exempt such services from the date of this Business Brief. Conversely, agents supplying card handling services that do not meet the criteria set out above, and have been treating those services as exempt, should now charge tax. There is no requirement to make adjustments in respect of earlier supplies. However, where businesses wish to make a claim to HMRC for a repayment of output tax incorrectly paid, they may do so, subject to the conditions set out below, by using one of the following methods (full details are given in VAT Notice 700/45 *How to correct VAT errors and make adjustments or claims*):

- where the total of previous errors does not exceed £2,000 net tax, an adjustment may be made to your current VAT return.
- where the total of previous errors exceeds £2,000 net tax, a separate claim should be submitted to HMRC (in these cases the errors must not be corrected through your VAT returns). Details of where to send your claim can be obtained from update 2 to VAT Notice 700/45 *How to correct VAT errors and make adjustments or claims* or the HM Revenue & Customs National Advice Service on 0845 010 9000.

All adjustments or claims are limited to a three-year period (subject to Business Brief 13/06) and will be subject to the following conditions:

- all claims must take into account input tax that has been claimed, but which under the revised interpretation will not relate to taxable supplies.
- businesses must be able to produce evidence that they accounted for VAT in the circumstances described above, and must be able to substantiate the amount claimed.

Subject to the three-year limitation period, any claim should be for all prescribed accounting periods in which the liability error occurred. Should a claim not take into account all errors or all affected accounting periods, then HMRC will seek to set-off amounts owed to us for these periods against amounts claimed in other periods. HMRC may reject all or part of a claim if repayment would unjustly enrich the claimant. More details on 'unjust enrichment' can be found at part 14 of VAT Notice 700/45 *How to correct VAT errors and make adjustments or claims*. A notification to HMRC that a business intends making a claim in the future is not a valid claim. HMRC will review claims by businesses for exemption of supplies of debit and credit card handling services, and businesses can expect requests to be challenged vigorously where there is evidence of underlying artificiality or abuse. If there is any doubt about the correct VAT treatment of your services, please contact the National Advice Service on 0845 010 9000.

Commentary—*De Voil Indirect Tax Service* **V4.136I.**

9 November 2006. Business Brief 20/06

Gaming machines—impact of the Linneweber decision

HMRC are aware that following a case in the European Court of Justice (*Edith Linneweber*: C-453/02) [2005] All ER (D) 254 (Feb), many businesses that operate gaming machines claim that they over-declared VAT on the takings from these machines for the period prior to 6 December 2005. This is when the definition of a gaming machine was amended (see Article 5 of Business Brief 23/05 dated 5 December 2005). Business Brief 23/05 stated that: "There have also been suggestions that because certain machines now in use fall outside the definition of a taxable gaming machine, UK law breaches the European Community principle of fiscal neutrality. We do not accept that the avoidance is successful nor that there is any breach of fiscal neutrality."

Despite this, many businesses have submitted voluntary disclosures to recover VAT they consider was not due, with others adjusting their VAT returns, simply stating that the reason for doing so is because of the *Linneweber* decision. The case of Linneweber considered the European principle of fiscal neutrality as it applies to VAT, specifically looking at the different tax treatment that had been applied to identical gaming machines in Germany solely on the basis that the machines were situated in different locations. The UK has not applied different VAT liabilities to identical gaming machines and HMRC do not accept that the UK's tax treatment of gaming machines breached the principle of fiscal neutrality.

If you nevertheless consider that your gaming machine takings have been treated differently from the takings of other identical or substantially similar machines, and that you are entitled to a refund of VAT, HMRC will consider your claim.

However, as HMRC do not accept that the tax treatment of gaming machines was contrary to EC law, claims will only be considered if they are supported by evidence that:

- your machines are identical or substantially the same as those that you are comparing them with;
- these machines are treated differently for VAT purposes; and
- this has caused distortion of competition for your business. Claims received without this evidence will be rejected. Businesses that have adjusted their VAT returns because of the

Linneweber decision should reconsider these adjustments as they will be scrutinised and assessments made where necessary with interest and penalties added as appropriate.

Commentary—*De Voil Indirect Tax Service* **V3.264.**

22 December 2006. Business Brief 23/06

First grant of a major interest in residential property: attribution of input tax and the capital goods scheme

This Business Brief article confirms and explains HMRC policy regarding input tax incurred on the construction of residential property where the developer sells a long leasehold interest separately from the freehold interest.

BACKGROUND

The first grant of a major interest (freehold sale or lease exceeding 21 years) in residential property by its developer is zero-rated, under VAT Act 1994, Schedule 8, Group 5. However, all subsequent grants in the property are VAT exempt. VAT on costs relating to zero-rated supplies is fully recoverable whereas VAT relating to exempt supplies is not normally recoverable. Detailed rules on the liability of supplies of buildings are in Notice 708, on partial exemption in Notice 706 and on the capital goods scheme in Notice 706/2.

ATTRIBUTION OF INPUT TAX

When a residential property is constructed or results from the conversion of a non-residential property and the developer makes a first grant of a major interest in that property, any input tax incurred is recoverable in full. This is because the input tax is wholly attributed to that taxable first grant. This is the case even where the value of the first grant does not represent full equity in the property, such as in shared ownership schemes run by housing associations.

APPLICATION OF THE CAPITAL GOODS SCHEME (CGS)

Regulations 112(2) and 113 of the VAT Regulations 1995 set out when a building will be a capital item for the purposes of the CGS. If a developer constructs a residential property and the first grant of a major interest in the building is a long lease, he is using the building for a business purpose other than solely for the purpose of selling the building. As a result, the developer will have to treat the building as a capital item. The input tax incurred on the construction of the building and wholly attributed to the zero-rated long lease will have to be adjusted through the CGS should a subsequent exempt grant be made of the building. If a developer constructs a residential property and the first grant of a major interest is the sale of the freehold, the developer is using the building solely for the purpose of selling the building and will not have to treat the building as a capital item.

EXAMPLES

There are essentially three ways a developer might grant all the leases and the reversionary interest in the freehold of a residential property (typically a block of flats):

(a) All flats sold followed by the freehold—the sale of each individual flat will be zero-rated as first grant of a major interest. While the developer will hold a capital item, when the freehold is sold, we consider that this will only be exempt to the extent that it relates to those areas of the building that were previously the subject of the zero-rated grants of individual flats. Most of the sale of the freehold will be zero-rated because it relates to the common parts that have not been subject to any previous supply. These circumstances are part of the sale of new dwellings for which the zero-rating was designed. Furthermore any CGS adjustments would be negligible. Accordingly there is no need for CGS adjustments in this example.

(b) Freehold sold before any flats are sold—the sale of the freehold will be a zero-rated grant and since no leases had been granted, would not be a capital item (by virtue of Reg 112(2), VAT Regulations 1995). Since the freehold is zero-rated, all input tax incurred on the construction costs will be fully deductible. As the new freeholder, the purchaser will normally make any exempt grants of leases to buyers of flats. Even where the consideration for such sales accrues to the developer, so that VAT law treats the developer as the person supplying the flat, this will not impact on the initial deduction of input tax by the developer. It may, however, have implications for any input tax incurred on selling costs.

(c) Freehold sold after some flats have been sold—the flats sold before the freehold has been supplied will each be a zero-rated first grant of a major interest. While the developer will hold a capital item, when the freehold is sold, we consider that this will only be exempt to the extent that it relates to those areas of the building that were previously the subject of the zero-rated grants of individual flats. Most of the supply of the freehold will be zero-rated relating to the common parts and unsold flats that haven't been subject to any previous supply. As per example (a) above, no CGS adjustments are needed. If, under the agreement for sale, the developer has retained the right to receive the monies from the sale of the remaining unsold flats, the considerations set out in example (b) above apply.

OTHER RESIDENTIAL PROPERTY

The first grant of a major interest in a relevant residential property (eg a care home) is zero-rated. Under Reg 116(3), VAT Regulations 1995, in determining any CGS adjustments in subsequent years, the developer disregards any exempt supply arising directly from that grant (including all rents due under that lease). Even though the developer holds a capital item, providing he makes no exempt supplies other than those arising from that zero-rated grant, he will retain full deduction of the input tax on the construction of the development. However, if the developer makes a new grant, like selling the freehold, this is the second grant in the building and will be exempt. In this situation CGS adjustments are likely to be required and CGS calculations must be carried out.

Commentary—*De Voil Indirect Tax Service* **V3.470**.

22 December 2006. Business Brief 23/06

Final Business Brief

This is the last Business Brief that HMRC will issue. There has been a substantial decrease in demand for a paper product in recent years. When we consulted subscribers earlier this year their feedback was that a move to an online-only service was appropriate. An online-only service means that HMRC can get information published far more quickly. Business Briefs were originally published by the former HM Customs & Excise and dealt with changes in indirect tax policy. In the former Inland Revenue a similar publication 'Tax Bulletin' covered direct tax matters. HMRC are taking this opportunity to combine the two publications into a single online-only bulletin—'Revenue & Customs Brief'. Revenue & Customs Brief will appear in the Library section of our website at http://www.hmrc.gov.uk/library.htm, and will go live from 1 January 2007.

26 January 2007. HMRC Brief 5/07

Further clarification of the treatment of foreign exchange transactions (forex) and transactions in other financial instruments

Business Brief 21/05 explained HMRC's position following the tribunal decision in *Willis Pension Fund Trustees Limited (Willis)* [VTD 19183] and the implications of the decision for other businesses conducting forex transactions. The Tribunal found that the forex transactions Willis entered into were not supplies for VAT purposes.

This Brief article sets out HMRC's view on when forex transactions are supplies for VAT purposes and the implications this has for VAT recovery. It also outlines HMRC's view on any wider application of the decision to transactions in other financial instruments.

DETERMINING IF YOUR FOREX TRANSACTIONS ARE SUPPLIES FOR VAT PURPOSES

The tribunal decision in Willis applied to a very specific set of circumstances and, whilst some general principles can be drawn from the decision, care needs to be taken when seeking to give it wider application. The European Court of Justice (ECJ) judgment in *First National Bank of Chicago (FNBC)* [C-172/96] is the leading authority on the VAT treatment of forex transactions.

In Willis, forex deals were entered into for the purposes of "hedging". This is a term that is variously defined, but "hedging" is about reducing exposure to risk of loss resulting from fluctuations in some commodity or financial market. What is relevant for VAT purposes is whether any underlying trade is performed to achieve that objective. "Hedging" is not in itself a test for determining whether or not there is a supply for VAT purposes.

In general, forex transactions are supplies for VAT purposes if you adopt a spread position over a period of time when buying and selling currency. This applies whether this is being done for your own account, in support of other areas of your business, or to reduce any exposure position in forex that you hold. A spread position means a difference between a bid price and a sell price from which you would expect to derive a profit. These forex transactions would include both "spot" and "forward" transactions, as envisaged by the FNBC judgment.

Most businesses actively involved in forex trading should readily be able to identify whether their forex transactions fall under the FNBC principle of adopting a spread position. If uncertainties remain, you should consider whether, in selling a currency, you are in a position to set the selling price. If so, you are able to determine the consideration you receive by setting a spread, even if only mimicking market movements, and your forex transactions are likely to be supplies for VAT purposes.

Where your forex transactions are supplies, the consideration will be the net result of all your forex transactions over a period of time and would be exempt under VATA 1994, Sch. 9, Group 5, Item 1. Any forex transactions, for which you charge an attributable fee or commission, would also be exempt supplies under Item 1.

The following are examples of circumstances when it is unlikely that your forex transactions would be seen as supplies for VAT purposes:

– a business simply exchanging one currency for another to realise foreign earnings into sterling, for example, or to acquire currency to settle liabilities incurred outside the UK, is unlikely to be seen as making supplies for VAT purposes provided such transactions are not part of a wider economic activity being carried out for an identifiable consideration
– a business entering into forward forex deals in order to limit its exposure to forex fluctuations in respect of future obligations is unlikely to be seen as making supplies for VAT purposes provided such transactions are not part of a wider economic activity being carried out for an identifiable consideration.

Businesses with a corporate treasury operation active in the financial markets may need to look carefully at their forex transactions. If no spread position is being taken and no profit being actively sought, it is unlikely that any forex transactions would be regarded as supplies. However, a number of larger businesses have corporate treasury operations that are much more pro-active, either externally or internally, within their commercial groups. For example, a business might typically run a "forex desk" in a similar manner to any other financial institution or market maker more traditionally associated with forex dealing. Such businesses are likely to be taking a spread position and would be making supplies. All their forex transactions, whether spot or forward and whether proprietary or in support of other activities or areas of the business, should be treated as forex supplies.

Intermediaries acting in relation to a forex transaction can exempt their intermediary services under item 5, Group 5 of Schedule 9. This applies whether or not the underlying forex transaction is a supply for VAT purposes.

HOW YOUR INPUT TAX RECOVERY WILL BE AFFECTED

The normal input tax recovery rules will apply. Businesses making exempt financial supplies cannot normally recover the VAT attributable to those supplies unless the recipient of those supplies is located outside the EU (in which case recovery is allowed under the VAT (Input Tax)(Specified Supplies) Order 1999). Businesses involved in forex transactions which are not seen as supplies for VAT purposes are able to recover the VAT attributable to those transactions as residual input tax, subject to the partial exemption method used. However, there is no right of recovery under the Specified Supplies Order for such transactions.

Supplies by financial intermediaries can attract recovery under the Specified Supplies Order if the recipient of the intermediaries' supply is based outside the EU, or if the underlying forex transaction is itself a supply which is made outside the EU. There is no right of recovery under the Specified Supplies Order, however, where the recipient of an intermediary's supply is based in the UK or elsewhere in the EU but the underlying transaction is not a supply for VAT purposes. Intermediaries arranging non-EU forex transactions will therefore need to determine whether the underlying transaction is a supply.

Businesses may wish to seek clarification on their present partial exemption methods, and some methods may need to be revised. There are provisions for excluding, in certain circumstances, incidental financial transactions from values-based calculations in partial exemption methods and the provisions of Regulation 106 of the VAT Regulations 1995 allow for de minimis levels of exempt input tax to be treated as attributable to taxable supplies. For further information on this, please refer to VAT Notice 706 *Partial exemption*. Whilst HMRC would wish to avoid disproportionate changes, any proposed changes will need to result in a fair and reasonable method.

WIDER APPLICATION IN RESPECT OF TRANSACTIONS IN OTHER FINANCIAL INSTRUMENTS

The Willis Tribunal made reference in its decision to interest rate swaps. It suggested that, in its view, there would only be a supply when it was possible to identify the consideration being obtained by a party entering into the contract.

There would appear to be nothing arising directly out of Willis that indicates a shortfall in HMRC's current approach to the VAT treatment of other financial instruments and it is, therefore, not intended to revise existing published policy. HMRC do, however, recognise that there may be particular circumstances where Willis principles could apply to transactions in other financial instrument transactions and HMRC would consider such cases on an individual basis.

30 January 2007. HMRC Brief 06/07

Changes to the exemption for medical services from 1 May 2007

This Revenue & Customs Brief announces the implementation of changes to the exemption from VAT for medical services, following the European Court of Justice (ECJ) decision in the case of *Dr Peter d'Ambrumenil and Dispute Resolution Services* (C-307/01). It follows on from earlier Business Briefs 29/03, 18/05 and 04/06.

The changes will take effect from 1 May 2007 subject to House of Commons approval. They affect certain services provided by health professionals registered on a statutory professional register who are registered for VAT. They will not impact on primary health care and core NHS services, which will remain free from VAT.

BACKGROUND

The ECJ decision concerned the VAT exemption for health services provided by health professionals registered on a statutory professional register. The court held that this exemption is restricted to "medical care", which it defined as those services **intended principally to protect (including maintain or restore) the health of an individual**. Medical services which are primarily for the purpose of enabling a third party to take a decision—many of which are currently exempt from VAT under UK law—are taxable. This means that VAT liability is dependent on the purpose for which the supply is made—referred to as the "purpose test".

Business Brief 18/05 issued on 16 September 2005 announced a three month consultation entitled "VAT: A review of the scope of the VAT exemption for medical services". This consultation primarily sought to gather information about the activities of health professionals, and the impact that the ECJ decision may have on the health sector and its clients. This consultation exercise has now been completed and a summary of responses received to this consultation is attached.

In response to the consultation responses and in conjunction with the British Medical Association and British Dental Association, HMRC have drawn up detailed guidance on the application of the purpose test to key services.

UK law will be amended with effect from 1 May 2007 in order to limit the exemption from VAT for health services to those services which constitute the provision of "medical care".

SERVICES AFFECTED

The services most affected by the changes are:

- witness testimony/reports for litigation, compensation or benefit purposes
- reports/medicals for the purpose of providing certain fitness certificates and
- some occupational health services.

These services will become liable to VAT at 17.5 per cent from 1 May 2007. However, this summary is not exhaustive, and health providers should consider the liability of all their services in conjunction with the guidance given in Notice 701/57 *Health professionals* (January 2007). If they remain uncertain as to the liability of any of their services having read the guidance, they should contact the National Advice Service on 0845 010 9000.

ACTION REQUIRED

The changes will affect health service providers registered on a statutory professional register who provide affected services and whose total taxable income is now over the VAT registration threshold, or who are already VAT registered.

Where the health provider is not already VAT registered, they will need to consider their turnover and if the value of all their taxable supplies, including the income from affected services, is over the registration threshold, they will need to register for VAT at the appropriate time in accordance with the guidelines on VAT registration, Notice 700/1 *Should I be registered for VAT?* They will then have to account for VAT on all their taxable supplies, but will be able to reclaim VAT on those purchases and expenses which relate to taxable supplies, in accordance with the normal VAT recovery rules and, in particular, the partial exemption regulations.

Registered health professionals who are already registered for VAT, for example, as a result of dispensing changes which took effect on 1 April 2006, will need to ensure that they account for VAT as appropriate on any affected services.

INSURANCE-RELATED MEDICAL SERVICES

Business Brief 29/03 issued in December 2003 gave details of certain services—such as conducting a medical to assess the level of insurance premiums—which were specifically considered by the ECJ and ruled to be outside the scope of the health exemption, and therefore taxable. The Business Brief explained that doctors and other health professionals were not required to take any action to register for VAT or charge VAT on these services until such time as HMRC formally implemented the changes.

Although such services will no longer qualify under the health exemption, in a recent tribunal case—*Morganash Ltd* (MAN/05/0749)—a ruling was given that medical services which were undertaken for the purpose of enabling a provider of life assurance to decide whether to accept a proposal for a policy fall within the scope of the UK exemption for insurance-related services, pending the implementation of the ECJ decision in the case of *Andersen* (C-472/03). HMRC have decided not to appeal this case and, as a result, accept that insurance-related medical services related to the setting up of contracts, the administration of policies or handling of claims, will remain exempt from VAT, pending any amendment of the UK exemption for insurance services.

Further, the following services will qualify as exempt under the health exemption as being principally for the purposes of protecting, maintaining or restoring the health of the individual concerned:

- health screening under private medical insurance policies—these are regular check-ups to detect early signs of disease;
- income/credit protection insurance—medical services where the policy holder has fallen ill (as opposed to losing their job) which are aimed at assisting the individual in returning to a normal life;
- motor insurance—where medical services are provided under a policy to assist in enabling an injured motorist to return to full health and/or work. (Note—this does not include medicals undertaken for DVLA purposes to ensure initial or continued fitness to drive which are liable to VAT at the standard rate);
- any other medical service provided in connection with an insurance policy where the principal aim is to assist in restoring the health of the individual.

Medical services provided for the purpose of valuing insurance policies for tax purposes, such as inheritance tax, will become liable to VAT at 17.5 per cent.

FURTHER ADVICE

HMRC will shortly be issuing an Information Sheet giving advice on VAT registration and accounting issues for those affected by the changes.

1 February 2007. HMRC Brief 07/07

Cash bingo: accounting for VAT on participation and session fees

This brief is about participation and session fees paid by cash bingo players. It clarifies HM Revenue & Customs' policy on how to calculate those fees for VAT purposes.

BACKGROUND

Participation and session fees charged for taking part in bingo played for cash prizes on premises licensed or registered under Part II of the Gaming Act 1968 (sometimes termed "mainstage" cash bingo) are consideration for standard-rated supplies. Stake money—the amount risked by the player, all of which must be returned as winnings—is not payment for a supply and so is outside the scope of VAT.

Where participation and session fees and stake money are received together in one composite amount charged to players, bingo promoters must work out how much of the payment is stake and how much is the participation and session fee in order to determine how much VAT is due. Section 3.2 of Notice 701/27 *Bingo* explains how to do this.

We have received enquiries from some bingo promoters performing the VAT calculation on a game-by-game basis, asking whether they are acting correctly and these have prompted the issue of this clarification.

CALCULATING THE VAT DUE

When a player pays to participate in all or part of a bingo session, the supply made by the promoter is the right to participate in the number of games during that session for which they have received payment. As a player cannot participate in further sessions unless they make further payment, the supply to the player is completed when the session ends. In these circumstances the amount of VAT due on participation and session charges should properly be calculated on a session-by-session basis by deducting the stake money arising in each individual session from the total amount (less any admission fees) paid by players to participate in that same session. Where money from other sources is added to the stake money received in the session in order to meet guaranteed prizes, that additional money cannot be used to reduce the value for VAT of the participation and session charges paid for taking part in that session.

Where a player pays to take part in an additional game ("flyer") that does not form part of the session charge, this is a separate supply of the right to participate in that further game. The VAT due on fees charged for participating in additional games should be calculated on a game-by-game basis.

Where a promoter provides facilities for participating in linked games or a national game, in which players located at more than one venue all participate in the same game, charges received at all the promoter's participating venues should be aggregated in order to calculate the amount of VAT due on par fees relating to the linked game or national game.

Promoters should not perform a single calculation for the whole of each VAT return period, aggregating stake money and receipts taken for all bingo played during that time.

Notice 701/27 *Bingo* will be updated.

MAKING CLAIMS OR ADJUSTMENTS

Bingo promoters that have calculated the VAT due on participation and session charges on a game-by-game basis, and who now find that they have done so incorrectly, may make a claim to HMRC for a repayment of any resulting overdeclaration, subject to the conditions set out in Notice 700/45 *How to correct VAT errors or make adjustments or claims*. In particular, businesses should note that:

– where the total of previous errors does not exceed £2000 net tax, an adjustment may be made to your current VAT return but
– where the total of previous errors exceeds £2000 net tax a separate claim should be submitted to HMRC (in these cases the errors must not be corrected through your VAT returns).

HMRC may reject all or part of a claim if repayment would unjustly enrich the claimant. More information about unjust enrichment can be found at part 14 of Notice 700/45.

Advice about where to send your claim can be obtained from HMRC's National Advice Service on 0845 010 9000.

6 February 2007. HMRC Brief 08/07

Manufacturers' "cash back" payments

This Revenue and Customs Brief article explains the VAT treatment of "cash backs" and what businesses should do if they pay or receive "cash backs", or have paid or received them in the past.

BACKGROUND

The term "cash back" refers to a payment usually made by a manufacturer directly (or via a recovery agency) to the customer of a wholesaler or retailer—mostly in recognition of the volume of purchases. Similar payments may also be made under manufacturers' discount schemes, or may be referred to as volume bonuses or described in similar terms. Such payments occur outside the direct supply chain and as a result credit notes should not be used.

HMRC have become aware that some businesses have been accounting for "cash back" payments incorrectly. Some manufacturers have reduced their output tax, some have not. Some have made retrospective claims for overpaid output tax, but the recipients of those "cash backs" have not necessarily reduced their input tax.

VAT TREATMENT

The treatment of payments of this nature was laid down by the European Court of Justice (ECJ) in two cases: *Elida Gibbs* (C-317/94) and *Commission v Germany* (C-427/98). HMRC's policy is set out in VAT Notice 700/7 *Business Promotion Schemes* Section 7.5, which states that manufacturers are entitled to reduce the output tax on their sales in respect of the "cash backs", provided that they charged and accounted for VAT on their original supply.

If you are VAT-registered and you receive a "cash back" that relates to a taxable supply, this reduces the taxable value of your purchase, and you must reduce your input tax in the proportion in which you claimed it.

WAY FORWARD

Until 1 March 2007, providing—

– manufacturers have not reduced their output tax, and
– recipients have not reduced their input tax, and
– both parties have agreed to make no adjustments for the past, present and future,

HMRC will not require adjustments to be made in these circumstances, will not assess for over-claimed input tax, and will consider withdrawing any such assessments that have already been raised, subject to the usual three year limitation.

If manufacturers break the agreement, change their minds at a later date, and do adjust their output tax, HMRC will assess recipients in line with assessment time limits.

Where manufacturers have already adjusted their output tax and recipients have failed to adjust their input tax, HMRC will assess for over-claimed input tax, or defend assessments already issued.

In practice, where a manufacturer has not made a claim to reduce their output tax in respect to any "cash back" payments made prior to 1 March 2007, HMRC would assume an agreement between the parties. If however a manufacturer subsequently makes a claim for periods prior to 1 March 2007, HMRC continue to reserve the right to take action in respect to any failure to adjust input tax by the recipient.

A recipient of a "cash back" payment prior to 1 March 2007 remains responsible for identifying if there is a need to reduce their input tax. In cases of doubt they must determine the VAT treatment applied by the manufacturer and apply the guidance given.

From 1 March 2007, businesses should correctly make the necessary adjustments as outlined above. Businesses providing "cash backs" are entitled to reduce their output tax provided that they charged and accounted for VAT on their original supply.

If you are VAT-registered and you receive a "cash back", this reduces the taxable value of your purchase, and you must reduce your input tax accordingly. HMRC will assess for over-claimed input tax where these adjustments are not made.

Any "cash back" payment from manufacturer to customer, that does not affect the wholesaler, does not require the wholesaler to make any VAT adjustment.

CROSS BORDER "CASH BACKS"

Where "cash backs" are paid between businesses in different EU member states (MS), no VAT adjustments should be made. This means in practice:

- where a UK manufacturer pays a "cash back" to a recipient in another MS, the manufacturer cannot reduce his output tax; and
- where a UK recipient receives a "cash back" from a manufacturer in another MS, no input tax deduction is required by the recipient.

CHANGE OF LIABILITY IN THE SUPPLY CHAIN

Where the VAT liability of the goods changes in the supply chain (eg where a charity buys certain goods zero-rated from the wholesaler which were standard-rated for VAT when supplied by the manufacturer), manufacturers cannot reduce their output tax in relation to the "cash back" paid to the charity. Where the 'cash back' relates to goods that were supplied VAT-free to a business receiving the 'cash back', no adjustments should be made.

6 February 2007. HMRC Brief 10/07

Liability of private tuition

HMRC's policy on the liability of private tuition is set out in Notice 701/30 (*Education and vocational training*), section 6. This advises that the VAT exemption for private tuition only applies to sole proprietors and partnerships who teach a subject that is taught regularly in a number of schools or universities.

It has come to our attention that some businesses that supply private tuition have incorrectly exempted their supplies from VAT. This follows a Tribunal decision in the case of *Empowerment Enterprises Ltd*, which found that the exemption extended to tuition provided by directors of limited companies and those employed by sole proprietors, partnerships or limited companies.

HMRC appealed against the Tribunal's findings and the Court of Session allowed the appeal, confirming that exemption is only available to sole proprietors and partnerships.

Therefore, all suppliers of private education should ensure that they are applying the correct liability to their supplies. Additionally, if you have been using the incorrect liability, you will need to account for any unpaid VAT as follows (full details are given in VAT Notice 700/45: *How to correct VAT errors and make adjustments or claims*):

- where the total of previous errors does not exceed £2000 net tax, an adjustment may be made to your current VAT return, or
- where the total of previous errors exceeds £2000 net tax, a separate voluntary disclosure should be submitted to HMRC (in these cases the errors must not be corrected through your VAT returns).

Details of where to send your claim can be obtained from update 2 to VAT Notice 700/45: *How to correct VAT errors and make adjustments or claims*, or from the HMRC National Advice Service.

6 February 2007. HMRC Brief 11/07

VAT schemes for luxury yachts

We are aware that various advisors are promoting VAT schemes through which private individuals incur little or no VAT on the purchase of pleasure craft (both sailing and motor vessels), particularly at the top end of the market. The purpose of this Brief is to describe the key features of the schemes and to announce that we have serious concerns about the validity of the VAT treatment which is claimed for the schemes.

Under the schemes, the user acquires a new vessel which purportedly has 'VAT paid' status while, in reality, paying no VAT (or a minimal amount of VAT).

The schemes fall broadly into two categories – cross-border leasing and artificial chartering to the private funder. Both categories share the following common features:

- They involve a contrived leasing or chartering arrangement of a vessel which is predominantly for the recreational use of an individual.
- The individual provides the funds that are used to pay for the vessel either directly or indirectly (maybe by lending money to an intermediary).
- Registered title to the vessel is held by a special purpose entity (otherwise known as a special purpose vehicle or "SPV") which is controlled (directly or indirectly) either by the individual or by the scheme provider. This SPV may be simply a shell company – also known as a "brass plate" company, bought off the shelf and with nominee directors standing in front of whoever really benefits.
- The SPV purports to use the vessel in a chartering or leasing business. It does not incur VAT (either through a zero-rated export if the SPV is outside the EU, or otherwise by recovering as input tax any VAT charged on the supply).
- The vessel is chartered or leased to the individual. No VAT (or only a minimal amount of VAT) is charged on the lease or charter payments.

Where there is evidence to suggest that a vessel has been supplied through one of these schemes we shall carry out a full investigation of the facts surrounding the supply and take any necessary action.

Commentary—*De Voil Indirect Tax Service* **V3.173**.

9 February 2007. HMRC Brief 12/07

Changes to the cash accounting scheme

This Revenue & Customs Brief explains changes to the Cash Accounting Scheme which will take effect from 1 April 2007.

The changes are:

- The annual turnover limit below which businesses can start to use the scheme, will increase from £660,000 to £1.35 million.
- The annual turnover limit above which businesses must leave the scheme, will increase from £825,000 to £1.6 million.

The scheme allows eligible businesses to account for and pay VAT to HMRC only when they receive payment from their customers. A condition of this treatment is that users of the scheme can only recover VAT on purchases when they pay their suppliers.

For most businesses the scheme offers a cash flow benefit and provides automatic relief from VAT on bad debts without the need to apply for Bad Debt Relief.

Commentary—*De Voil Indirect Tax Service* **V2.199**.

12 February 2007. HMRC Brief 13/07

Fuel scale charge; new CO_2 basis

This Revenue and Customs Brief announces changes to the VAT fuel scale charge. These changes will come into effect on 1 May 2007 and businesses must use the new scales from the start of their first accounting period beginning on or after this date. We are announcing the change early to allow businesses time to familiarise themselves with the new charges and make any necessary IT system changes.

The existing VAT fuel scale charge, which is based on the engine size and fuel type of a car, will be replaced by a fuel scale charge based solely on the CO_2 rating of a car. The new table, which mirrors that used for direct tax purposes, will have 21 bands with 5g/km increments. An outline of the bands is produced at **Annex A**.

The complete new table, which will be available following Budget 2007 as an amendment to Notice 700/64 *Motoring Expenses*, will provide business with the actual scale charge for a car within a particular band. Apart from the change to a CO_2 basis, the system will operate in exactly the same way as the existing VAT fuel scale charge. We have provided an example with illustrative figures in **Annex A**.

In keeping with the existing fuel scale charge, the CO_2 based system will be subject to an annual review to ensure that the charge reflects changes in fuel prices. The figures produced at Budget 2007 will have been reviewed and, as with the current system, will be extant for one year. This change is not intended as a revenue raising measure and the switch to a CO_2 basis will be revenue neutral overall.

Many businesses will already be aware of the underlying concept of the CO_2 based system from using direct tax schemes (company car tax and company car fuel benefit) as well as the new system for Vehicle Excise Duty. For businesses unaware of their CO_2 rating, a number of publicly available websites provide details on vehicles' official CO_2 emission levels and we have included the details of one such site for ease of reference.

Vehicle Certification Agency—CO_2 Database: http://www.vcacarfueldata.org.uk/search/search.asp

ANNEX A

Charge table:
Quarterly Returns

CO_2 emissions, g/km	*VAT Fuel Scale Charge*	*VAT on charge*	*Net amount*
140 or under			
145			
150			
155			
160			
165			
170			
175	£346.00*	£51.53*	£294.47*
180			
185			
190			
195			
200			
205			
210			
215			
220			
225			
230			
235			
240 or over			

* **Notional figures for illustrative purposes only**. The actual levels of new charges will be published at Budget 2007, and will reflect both the new structure and fuel prices at that time. The levels of the new charges will differ from those in the table above.

Example

Current Position

A business pays the current VAT fuel scale charge on a 2006 Vauxhall Vectra petrol 1.8i 4 door saloon; it pays a quarterly output tax charge of £51.53 and enters £294 in to the net outputs box on the return.

The CO_2 rating for this vehicle is 175 g/km.

Following 1 May 2007 changes

The new fuel scale charge, which must be used from the start of your first accounting period beginning on or after 1 May 2007, can be found by looking along the band which covers

171 g/km – 175g/km. In this illustrative example, the new quarterly output tax charge is £51.53 and again the business enters £294 in to the net outputs box on the return.

The new system will determine the fuel scale charge by CO_2 rating alone and there will be no adjustments for fuel type. The exception will be for vehicles too old to have an official CO_2 rating; these businesses will be assigned a set band in the new system based on engine capacity alone.

13 February 2007. HMRC Brief 14/07

Changes to the rules on bad debt relief for goods supplied on credit terms

This article concerns changes to the bad debt relief provisions in respect of claims relating to goods supplied on credit terms, including hire-purchase, conditional sale and credit sale agreements. The new rules reflect existing commercial accounting methods and result in a more accurate bad debt relief figure for the supplier.

BACKGROUND

In VAT Information Sheet 05/04 we set out our policy on claims relating to overpaid VAT following conclusion of the litigation in the case of *General Motors Acceptance Corporation UK Ltd.* We then explained, in VAT Information Sheet 05/06, the changes we were making to close a loophole concerning goods sold, for a second time, by finance companies. We also announced in paragraph 6 of that Information Sheet that we intended to amend the bad debt relief rules to allow businesses to use the same basis for calculating bad debt relief as for the reduction of the original selling price. This article explains the changes we are now making to those rules.

WHY PAYMENTS FOR GOODS AND CREDIT AFFECT COMPUTATION OF BAD DEBT RELIEF

Where a business supplies goods on credit they make two supplies – goods (taxable) and credit (exempt). The supplier must account for VAT on the supply of goods at the outset (the normal time of supply rules apply). However, sometimes agreements are terminated because customers default.

If a customer makes some of the periodic payments before defaulting, these payments will cover both the goods and interest. In order to work out the amount of bad debt relief claimable on the goods, the supplier will need to look back at the payments the customer made before defaulting and allocate them between the goods and interest. They will then be able to calculate how much remains unpaid for the goods and so how much of the output tax they previously paid can be reclaimed as bad debt relief.

NEW LEGISLATION

The new rules will be contained in regulation 170A of the Value Added Tax Regulations 1995 (SI 1995/2518) (as amended) which, in addition to the existing rule, now contains another method of calculation.

INTERACTION WITH EXISTING COMMERCIAL PRACTICE

Previously, the legislation used a "straight-line" methodology. The new legislation will, for the first time, reflect existing commercial practice. Thus, for suppliers, the numbers you feed into the calculation will be based upon whatever commercial method you use, for example an actuarial method or the "Rule of 78". The ultimate purpose of the calculation is to arrive at the amount outstanding in respect of the goods element, which is used for calculating the amount of bad debt relief. The new method will result in a figure which accurately reflects the commercial basis of apportionment adopted by suppliers.

VOLUNTARY TERMINATION OF AGREEMENTS

These provisions apply only to situations where, upon default, customers still owe money. If your customer invokes a right, for example under consumer credit law, to end the agreement early (so-called "voluntary terminations"), they will not normally owe any money and bad debt relief should not apply.

BAD DEBT RELIEF CLAIMS FOR SUPPLIES MADE BEFORE 1 SEPTEMBER 2006

When allocating payments made by defaulting customers between capital and interest, the existing calculation at paragraph 5 of regulation 170A must be used.

BAD DEBT RELIEF CLAIMS FOR SUPPLIES MADE ON OR AFTER 1 SEPTEMBER 2006 AND BEFORE 1 SEPTEMBER 2007

For this transitional period, suppliers may choose between either the existing method (paragraph 5 of regulation 170A), or the new method (article 6 of regulation 170A). You do not have to notify your defaulting customers which method you have used, because they will continue to use the "straight-line" method.

You may if you wish calculate claims using the old method initially and then re-compute the claim using the new method. You can then adjust the difference. This is of course, subject to the normal capping rules.

BAD DEBT RELIEF CLAIMS FOR SUPPLIES MADE ON OR AFTER 1 SEPTEMBER 2007

When allocating payments made by defaulting customers between capital and interest, the new method of calculation at paragraph 6 of regulation 170A must be used.

INPUT TAX TO BE REPAID TO HMRC BY DEFAULTING CUSTOMERS

If you are a defaulting customer who must repay to HMRC VAT you previously reclaimed on the goods, you are unaffected by these changes – you must continue to use the "straight-line" method, whether the supplies were made before, on or after 1 September 2006.

PAYMENTS RECEIVED BY SUPPLIERS AFTER TERMINATION OF A CREDIT AGREEMENT

If you receive payments after the termination of a credit agreement, these should be allocated between the goods and credit according to the proportion of the balances due at the time payment is made. You will then need to re-visit any bad debt relief claim you previously made since the amount outstanding in respect of the goods will have changed.

REDUCTION IN THE PRICE OF A SUPPLY AFTER A BAD DEBT RELIEF REFUND

If you, as supplier, reduce your selling price after you have received a bad debt relief refund in relation to that supply, then you must repay the VAT element of the price reduction to HMRC. This is because, in reducing the selling price, you will be able to reduce the VAT you originally accounted for and therefore should not also receive bad debt relief as well.

14 March 2007. HMRC Brief 23/07

Partial exemption: special method approvals

This article provides further guidance on preparing and submitting the new Declaration that is required for all partial exemption special method applications that are approved on or after 1 April 2007. This article should be read in conjunction with the guidance at: [http://www.hmrc.gov.uk/ria/vat-partial-amendments-qa.pdf].

Further guidance on partial exemption is in Public Notice 706.

BACKGROUND

With effect from 1 April, HMRC will only approve a special method if the business has declared it to be fair and reasonable. The Declaration requires a reasonable person to take reasonable steps to ensure the proposed method is fair. If HMRC approves a method but subsequently discovers the person signing the Declaration did not act reasonably, it could override the method and require the business to recover VAT in accordance with the principle of use. This will improve equity between businesses and lessen the risk of unfair methods enabling HMRC to offer speedier approval increasing business certainty and reducing administrative costs.

HOW SHOULD THE DECLARATION BE MADE?

The Declaration can be made by completing the template in Annex A. It should clearly identify the business, the method to which it relates, and the signatory.

WHEN SHOULD THE DECLARATION BE MADE?

In most cases, the Declaration would accompany the special method proposal inviting HMRC to give approval. HMRC will review the method and unless problems are found, transpose it onto a special method letter adding standard clauses, glossary terms and routine references to ensure clarity, before returning it to the business. Provided the business is content that the method reflects its proposal, it can adopt it as agreed without further correspondence. There is no longer a requirement for the business to sign and return a copy of its finalised method, further saving administrative cost.

In some cases, the business will wish to discuss its draft special method before making a firm proposal to ensure it accords with guidance and partial exemption principles. In these cases, the Declaration should not be made until the special method has been fully developed, otherwise a new Declaration will be required before approval can be given. Similarly, if HMRC consider that a proposed method cannot be approved, despite the accompanying Declaration, it will discuss with the business giving reasons and invite a new proposal and Declaration.

ANNEX A

Partial Exemption—Special Method Declaration

Name of Business:

Address:

VAT Registration Number:

This Declaration is in accordance with paragraphs (9) and (10) of regulation 102 of the VAT Regulations 1995.

As

- [the taxable person (i.e. where the signatory is a sole proprietor)]
- [the person authorised by the taxable person to sign this declaration on its behalf]1

, I hereby declare that to the best of my knowledge and belief, the proposed special method [state precisely where the method is set out] fairly and reasonably represents the extent to which goods or services are used or to be used in making taxable supplies.

I also confirm that I have taken reasonable steps to ensure that I am in possession of all relevant information before making this declaration.

Name (print):

Signed:

Position (print):

Date:

[1] Please delete as appropriate.

Commentary—*De Voil Indirect Tax Service* **V3.462.**

20 March 2007. HMRC Brief 24/07

Proposed reverse charge accounting for businesses trading in mobile telephones and computer chips: announcement of targeted implementation and details of how the rules will operate in practice; and exposure of draft legislation for comment

WHO NEEDS TO READ THIS?

Businesses buying and/or selling any of the following goods:

1. Mobile telephones; and
2. Integrated circuit devices, such as microprocessors and central processing units, in a state prior to integration into end user products.

BACKGROUND

Business Briefs 10/06 and 14/06 gave notice of the Government's intention to implement reverse charge accounting arrangements for certain goods ("the reverse charge"), subject to an EU derogation. Business Brief 19/06 gave a commitment to provide UK business with about 8 weeks notice of the implementation of the reverse charge.

On 19 March 2007 the Government announced the **implementation of the reverse charge for mobile phones and computer chips with effect from 1 June 2007**. The reverse charge will **not apply** to the other goods mentioned in the earlier business Briefs.

The purpose of this Business Brief is to:

A. provide:

(i) confirmation of the timing of the introduction of the reverse charge, and of the goods to which it will apply;
(ii) guidance on the application of reverse charge accounting to mobile phone contracts;
(iii) guidance, to both retailers and wholesalers, on the operation of the de minimis rules;
(iv) clarification of the proposed anti-disaggregation provisions;

(v) guidance to certain customers, such as charities and Local Authorities, purchasing goods for business and non-business purposes;

(vi) guidance on the impact of reverse charge accounting on Payments on Account;

(vii) outline details of Reverse Charge Sales Lists, including notifying HMRC when the first supplies under the reverse charge are made;

(viii) other details of how the new rules will operate in practice (completion of the VAT return; invoicing; the impact on the Cash Accounting Scheme, the Flat Rate Scheme and the second-hand margin scheme; and "light touch" on penalties); and

B. expose the draft secondary legislation for urgent comment before it is laid in May 2007. Comments are invited by no later than 11 April 2007.

A. (I) TIMING AND SCOPE OF IMPLEMENTATION

Following negotiations with our European partners, the Government has decided to target the reverse charge accounting mechanism on mobile phones and computer chips only (detailed in categories 1 and 2 above) with effect from 1 June 2007. Reverse charge accounting will therefore not apply to electronic storage media used in connection with computers, mobile phones or certain other electronic devices, and electronic devices used for the storage, processing or recording of electronic data (categories 3 and 4 in Business Brief 14/06). Communication devices such as Blackberrys fall within the definition of a mobile phone and therefore will come within the scope of the reverse charge.

A. (II) APPLICATION OF REVERSE CHARGE ACCOUNTING TO MOBILE PHONE CONTRACTS

Mobile phones which are supplied with an airtime contract are excluded from the scope of reverse charge accounting. This includes replacement phones and upgrades supplied under the terms of an airtime contract. However, reverse charge accounting **will** apply to "Pay as You Go" ("Prepay") phones.

A. (III) OPERATION OF THE DE MINIMIS LIMIT

Business Brief 10/06 advised that the reverse charge would only apply to supplies of the specified goods with a VAT-exclusive value of £1000 or more, when made within the UK to a VAT-registered business and are to be used for business purposes. The Government has decided to raise this limit to **£5000**, which will apply to the total value of goods subject to the reverse charge supplied together and detailed on a single invoice. Normal VAT accounting continues to apply to supplies of these goods below that value.

Retailers, including internet retailers

The *de minimis* limit is intended to relieve retailers of the need to carry out the necessary checks to establish whether a customer is VAT-registered and is purchasing the goods for a business purpose. Raising the de minimis limit to £5000 should reduce the number of sales made by retailers to other businesses where reverse charge accounting could apply.

Nevertheless, we recognise that there will still be a limited number of cases where the value of a sale at the retail stage exceeds this de minimis threshold, and that in a retail environment it may be difficult to carry out the necessary checks. If, for a transaction over £5000 in value, a retailer is unable to carry out these checks to his satisfaction, then VAT should be charged in the normal way. Such a situation may also arise with internet sales from retail sites, which should be treated in the same way. However, retailers and internet suppliers already have their own checks, usually based on the value (for example, above £10,000) or quantity of the goods, to prevent fraud or money laundering. We would expect them to apply similar checks to prevent manipulation of the £5000 limit.

Wholesalers and other suppliers

Circumstances in other trading environments, such as the wholesale market, are different because suppliers normally have a more established relationship with their customers, which means that they are in a better position to carry out checks on their bona fides, including for the purpose of applying the reverse charge.

HMRC are often asked what additional checks businesses should make in order to demonstrate that they have taken reasonable steps to establish whether the reverse charge applies. It is very difficult to be specific because industries and relationships vary widely.

We are aware that legitimate businesses carry out several commercial checks on their suppliers and customers covering various risks, such as to ensure acceptable use of the goods by the customer. In most instances, these checks will be adequate for reverse charge purposes, provided they are properly evidenced, unless the supplier has doubts about the reliability of the customer.

Businesses selling goods under the reverse charge procedure need to obtain the VAT registration numbers of affected customers, as they will be required for the Reverse Charge Sales Lists. In general, there will be no need to verify VAT registration numbers of customers with an established trading relationship, unless there are specific doubts, but it may be prudent to verify the VAT registration number of new customers.

Where businesses trade with customers without satisfying themselves as to their bona fides, they may be liable to pay to HMRC any tax lost as a result.

A. (IV) ANTI-DISAGGREGATION PROVISIONS

In earlier consultation on the operation of the reverse charge, anti-disaggregation provisions had been suggested to prevent the possibility of manipulation of the de minimis limit, below which the reverse charge will not apply. However, the consultation process identified that businesses would have practical difficulties in implementing such provisions. In the light of these concerns, the Government has decided not to introduce anti-disaggregation provisions in relation to reverse charge accounting. However, any attempt to manipulate the de minimis limit of £5000 will be vigorously challenged.

A. (V) CHARITIES AND LOCAL AUTHORITIES

Some customers, such as charities and Local Authorities, may purchase goods to which the reverse charge applies which will be used partly for business and partly for non-business purposes. In such cases, the reverse charge applies: the customer should account for output tax under the reverse charge procedure and apply the appropriate restriction to the deduction of the resulting input VAT.

A. (VI) PAYMENTS ON ACCOUNT

The Payments on Account (POA) scheme requires businesses with a net VAT liability of £2 million per year or more to make monthly payments on account. Under the current POA rules, the introduction of the reverse charge would have the effect of bringing some businesses within the scope of the POA scheme, or increasing the monthly payments for some businesses already within the scheme. Legislation will be introduced to amend the POA scheme to allow affected businesses to apply to HMRC to exclude the output tax due under the reverse charge from the calculation to establish whether a business is in the POA scheme or the size of monthly payments a business in the scheme has to make.

A. (VII) REVERSE CHARGE SALES LISTS

The following is an outline of how Reverse Charge Sales Lists (RCSLs) will operate:

- the RCSL system will be web-based, accessed through the Government Gateway;
- businesses will have to notify HMRC within 30 days of making their first supply to which the reverse charge applies, and also when they cease to make such supplies;
- if they subsequently re-commence making such supplies, they will have to renotify HMRC;
- businesses making sales to which the reverse charge applied must submit a list for each period, or make a "nil declaration" for any period that the business did not make any relevant supplies but had not notified cessation of such supplies;
- RCSLs may be submitted by keying data on-line or submitting bulk data via a CSV (comma-separated value) file;
- RCSLs, covering the same period as the VAT return, must be submitted within 30 days of the end of the business's VAT return period in which the supplies are made; and
- the information required will be, for each customer, their VAT registration number and the total value of reverse charge supplies made each calendar month to that customer.

The technical specification for the RCSL CSV file for bulk upload is published on the HMRC website (via "VAT Reverse Charge for mobile phones, and computer chips" on the HMRC VAT internet page).

A. (VIII) OTHER PRACTICAL ISSUES

Completion of the VAT return

Suppliers of goods under reverse charge accounting must **not** enter in Box 1 of the VAT return any output tax on sales to which the reverse charge applies, but must enter the value of such sales in Box 6.

Customers must enter in Box 1 of the VAT return the output tax on purchases to which the reverse charge applies, but must **not** enter the value of such purchases in Box 6. They must reclaim the input tax on their reverse charge purchases in Box 4 of the VAT return and include the value of the purchases in Box 7, in the normal way.

Invoicing

When making a sale to which reverse charge accounting applies, suppliers must show all the information normally required to be shown on a VAT invoice and must also annotate the invoice to make it clear that the reverse charge applies and that the customer is required to account for the VAT. The amount of VAT due under the reverse charge rules must be clearly stated on the invoice but should not be included in the amount shown as total VAT charged. The precise wording is not prescribed in law and discussions with business have highlighted the need to keep the annotation short. Either of the following would be acceptable:

– customer to pay output tax of £X to HMRC;
– UK customer to pay O/T of £X to HMRC.

Alternatively, any of the following would also be acceptable, provided that the amount of tax is shown elsewhere on the invoice (but not in box for total output tax charged):

– VAT Act 1994 s 55A applies;
– s 55A VATA 1994 applies;
– customer to account for the VAT to HMRC;
– Reverse charge supply—customer to pay the VAT to HMRC;
– customer to pay VAT to HMRC;
– UK customer to pay VAT to HMRC.

Cash accounting scheme

Businesses using the cash accounting scheme which purchase or sell goods to which the reverse charge applies should exclude these transactions from the scheme and account for them under the reverse charge accounting provisions.

Flat rate scheme

It is unlikely that many businesses using the flat rate scheme will be involved in transactions of goods to which the reverse charge applies but, if they are, they should exclude these from the scheme and account for VAT in accordance with the reverse charge accounting provisions.

Second-hand margin scheme

Where relevant goods are sold under a second-hand margin scheme, the reverse charge will not apply.

Penalties—"light touch"

HMRC understand the difficulties businesses may have in implementing the reverse charge and will, where there is no loss of tax, apply a light touch in dealing with errors that occur in the first six months after introduction of the reverse charge.

B. DRAFT LEGISLATION

Section 19 Finance Act 2006 introduced a new s 55A and s 26AB into the VAT Act 1994, as well as amending other provisions of the Act. These will be brought into effect from 1 June 2007. Under the powers contained in these provisions and existing powers in the VAT Act, the following statutory instruments will be made:

1. the Value Added Tax (Section 55A) (Specified Goods and Excepted Supplies) Order, which details the goods to which the reverse charge applies and supplies which will be excluded from the reverse charge [see http://www.hmrc.gov.uk/briefs/vat/2407-annexa.pdf];
2. the Value Added Tax (Payments on Account) (Amendment) Order, which amends the payment on account rules [see http://www.hmrc.gov.uk/briefs/vat/2407-annexb.pdf];
3. the Value Added Tax (Administration, Collection and Enforcement) Order to amend para 2(3B) of Schedule 11 to the VAT Act to allow regulations to be made to facilitate the introduction of reverse charge sales lists [see http://www.hmrc.gov.uk/briefs/vat/2407-annexc.pdf];
4. the Value Added Tax (Amendment) Regulations, which amend regulations relating to bad debt adjustments, the cash accounting and flat rate schemes and introduce the details of the reverse charge sales lists [see http://www.hmrc.gov.uk/briefs/vat/2407-annexd.pdf]. They also make consequential changes to the VAT accounting regulations.
5. the Value Added Tax (Amendment) (No 2) Regulations implementing regulations relating to the cessation and recommencement of reverse charge sales lists [see http://www.hmrc.gov.uk/briefs/vat/2407-annexe.pdf].

A copy of the draft legislation is attached for information and any comment. Comments should be sent as soon as possible please (and by no later than 11 April 2007) by email to Anti VAT Fraud [see HMRC website for email form and draft legislation].

FURTHER DIALOGUE WITH BUSINESS

HMRC remain committed to working closely with affected businesses and their advisers – as well as the software developers that support those businesses – to facilitate a smooth implementation of the reverse charge.

Further guidance material will be issued before the end of March, and, as necessary, meetings and/or workshops will be organised (depending on need and demand).

In the meantime any specific questions comments or concerns – about the terms of this Business Brief or more generally – can be sent by email to Anti VAT Fraud.

Commentary—*De Voil Indirect Tax Service* **V3.231, V3.233**.

22 March 2007. HMRC Brief 27/07

Cultural exemption – clarification of "direct or indirect financial interest" [VATA 1994 Sch 9 Group 13 Note 2(c)]

This Brief provides guidelines, in the light of recent Court of Appeal Judgments in the cases of *Bournemouth Symphony Orchestra* (C3/2005/1681) and *Longborough Festival Opera* (C3/2006/0369), on how to interpret the term "direct or indirect financial interest". This is for the purpose of the exemption for cultural services contained in Group 13 of Schedule 9 to the VAT Act 1994. The term is relevant because one of the conditions for exemption for services provided by an "eligible body" under Item 2 of that Group is that the body "is managed and administered on a voluntary basis by persons who have no direct or indirect financial interest in its activities" (Note 2(c) refers).

This brief supersedes the advice given on this topic in paragraphs 4.9 to 4.11 of VAT Notice 701/47 Culture and paragraphs 2.2 and 2.3 of section 2 of chapter 28 of V1–7 (HMRC guidance). Update 1 to VAT Notice 701/47 will be available on our website shortly.

The key change from existing guidance is that any direct or indirect financial interest only affects entitlement to exemption if it is actual, not potential. It is now our view that a person who is managing and administering the cultural body can be seen to have a direct or indirect financial interest in its activities only when:

- the person receives any payments for services supplied to the cultural body above the market rate, paid as routine overheads, or receives any payments which are profit-related (whether below, at or above market rates); and
- there is a link between the payments and the person's participation in the direction of the cultural body's activities.

This means that payments to individuals for services of managing and administering the body are not financial interests if:

- they are allowed by the constitution;
- the recipient is excluded from any decision-making regarding the award of any contract to themselves;
- the payments are not above market rates; and
- are not linked to profits.

There is no financial interest where the only potential is for a financial loss – for example, where a risk is underwritten or guaranteed – so that the guarantor only stands to lose money and not gain money as a result.

It is not possible to give exhaustive guidance to cover every eventuality, and the advice given here is intended as a general guideline only.

Commentary—*De Voil Indirect Tax Service* **V4.176**.

22 March 2007. HMRC Brief 28/07

VAT treatment of contracted out local authority leisure services

The **memorandum of understanding** that was jointly agreed by Customs and Excise and the Chartered Institute of Public Finance and Accountancy (CIPFA) in 1991 was reviewed in 2006 and this Business Brief contains the revised version, which supersedes the earlier version (published in Business Brief 11/99). The revisions have been agreed with CIPFA.

1. INTRODUCTION

1.1 This memorandum of understanding sets out how VAT is to be applied to the various supplies that can arise in the provision of local authority leisure services. The contents have been jointly agreed by HM Revenue & Customs and CIPFA. The primary purpose is to identify the types of supply that will normally be encountered and to confirm their correct VAT treatment. It should be noted, however, that the contents will be subject to review from time to time to reflect changing commercial practice and any VAT Tribunal or Court decisions in this area of the tax.

2. BACKGROUND

2.1 Local authorities may be involved in the provision of leisure services in a number of ways:

- by a direct service organisation (DSO) within the local authority's own leisure services department;
- through a non-profit distributing organisation (NPDO), e g a charitable trust or industrial and provident society, in which the authority may have a degree of representation;
- through a wholly commercial independently owned "for profit" leisure management contractor.

2.2 In the case of a DSO, all supplies continue to be made by the local authority and the VAT accounting position is as described at paragraph 5.1 below. However, where the leisure facilities have been developed, owned and operated by the local authority, and the authority then agrees with an NPDO or commercial operator that it will take over the operation of the leisure facilities subject to the authority's conditions, this process is known as "contracting out". The various arrangements that flow from the contracting out process can give rise to a number of potential supplies for VAT purposes.

3. WHO IS MAKING THE SUPPLY OF THE LEISURE FACILITIES?

3.1 Deciding who is actually making the supplies to the users of the leisure facilities is perhaps the single most important aspect to be established, as the appropriate VAT treatment is dependent on this factor. To answer this question, all the relevant documentation e.g. the invitation to tender, the final contract/agreements, back letters and leases or licences and the operational arrangements that are adopted should be considered, to determine the intentions of the parties.

NPDO contractors

3.2 Where operation of the leisure facilities is to be taken over by an NPDO contractor, it is common practice for the relevant premises to be leased to it by the local authority in return for the payment of a peppercorn rent. Thereafter, the NPDO will act as a principal in making supplies to users of the facilities.

Independent contractors

3.3 An independent contractor will, in most cases, be engaged to run the leisure facilities as a principal. However, there can be instances where the contractor will agree to act as an agent of the authority in running certain facilities. In the past, ambiguous written agreements led to uncertainty over the status of some independent contractors. In many cases, the agreements failed to make clear that it was always intended by both parties for the contractor to act as a principal in making supplies to the general public and other users. To avoid such problems, current agreements should make clear the status of the contractor and fully reflect the arrangements under which the parties are to operate.

4. VAT TREATMENT OF PAYMENTS BETWEEN PARTIES

4.1 Local authorities may make payments to operators of leisure facilities. However, the nature of these payments can vary and their VAT treatment depends on the circumstances in which they are paid. In some cases they are simply a grant and are therefore outside the scope of VAT. In other cases, such amounts can represent consideration for a supply or third party consideration. Each case needs to be decided on its own facts.

4.2 Distinguishing between grants and payments can be difficult, especially when interchangeable terms are used, such as "deficit funding". Where funding is freely given, with nothing supplied in return, then the payment is not consideration for any supply. This is normally the case with grants paid by public bodies. Conversely, where funding is given in return for specific goods or services, then that payment is consideration for a supply.

4.3 In recent years it has become increasingly common for grant monies to be awarded on condition that the recipient enters into a service level agreement and agrees to meet targets set out in that document. The funding body may even be entitled to quarterly progress reports. This does not of itself mean that a supply is being made in return for the funding. These agreements are often drawn up purely to ensure that the funds are used for the intended purpose, or "good housekeeping".

4.4 To decide whether funding is a grant or consideration for a supply the following questions must be asked.

- Does the donor receive anything in return for the funding?
- If the donor does not benefit, does a third party benefit instead? And if so, is there a direct link between the money paid by the funder and the supply received by the third party?
- Are there any conditions attached to the funding, which go beyond setting out the terms under which the funds are allocated and the requirement to account for how the funds are used (commonly referred to as "good housekeeping")?

In the case of leisure centres, it is important to consider issues such as the historical provision of the facilities and the relationship between the parties. The answer to these questions will often indicate the nature of the payment.

4.5 For example, where leisure facilities are developed and owned by an operator who merely seeks financial support from the local authority for what has always been the operator's own facilities, then this support is likely to be grant funding which is outside the scope of VAT.

4.6 Where, however, leisure facilities have been developed, owned and operated by the local authority, and the authority then contracts out the operation of those facilities – imposing conditions upon the contractor – any payments made by the authority to the contractor are more likely to be consideration for the contractor's supply of agreeing to take over the provision of leisure services under the conditions imposed by the authority.

4.7 Such arrangements, where payments are found to be consideration, can give rise to various supplies depending upon whether the contractor is acting as an agent of the local authority or as a principal. Some VAT consequences of these are described below.

4.7.1 Principal agreements i.e. where the NPDO or independent contractor supplies the facilities to the user

(a) Contractors' responsibilities

- The payments made by the local authority to the contractor are usually in the form of an annual management fee and/or a variable "contractor's deficit", normally intended to make good any overall shortfall between the takings and operating costs. Under the circumstances described in para 4.6 above, this may represent the consideration for a standard-rated supply by the contractor of agreeing to operate the leisure facilities subject to the authority's conditions.
- In some circumstances a contractor may be obliged to repay some of the gross/net profits to the local authority if, for example, they exceed an agreed level over a period of time (a "contractor's surplus"). These payments normally represent a reduction in the management fee payable by the local authority and VAT credit note procedures will apply.
- Where any monies paid over by the local authority to the contractor are directly linked to prices charged to users, then such payments may represent third party consideration for use of the facilities. The contractor is therefore obliged to account for VAT on the same basis as the normal takings and this cannot be recovered as input tax by the local authority.

(b) Local authorities' responsibilities

- With the exception of where payments represent third party consideration as described above, any VAT charged to the local authority by a contractor acting as principal in respect of the management fee or deficit funding will be recoverable in full by the authority subject to the normal rules. VAT charged by the contractor in these circumstances is not attributable to any lease or licence to occupy granted by the local authority to the contractor.
- There will be a liability on the part of the authority to account for output tax (subject to an option to tax having been exercised), on any amounts received in respect of the grant to the contractor of a tenancy or a license to occupy the leisure facilities. However, where there is no rent or a peppercorn rent payable by the contractor, the grant of the tenancy or licence to occupy will normally represent a supply for no consideration.
- Where there is neither monetary payment nor non-monetary consideration from the contractor to the local authority for a lease or licence to occupy, this is seen as a non-business transaction for the local authority. Any VAT which the authority incurs on costs attributable to the premises will be recoverable under section 33 of the VAT Act 1994 subject to the normal rules.
- Under some arrangements the contractor is obliged, as a condition of taking over the running of the leisure facilities as a principal, to periodically pay an agreed fee to the local authority. Provided this is not rent payable in connection with the granting of a tenancy or licence to occupy the leisure facilities, it will normally represent consideration for a standard-rated supply of the granting of the right to operate the facilities by the local authority to the contractor.

4.7.2 Agency agreements

- The contractor is liable to account for VAT on its supply of agency services to the local authority. Consideration for this supply will comprise any amounts paid to the contractor by the local authority and any amounts retained by the contractor from the takings.
- The VAT charged by the contractor to the local authority will be attributable to the supplies which the authority makes from that facility. It must be apportioned between taxable and exempt supplies in accordance with the authority's section 33 refund method (ie its partial exemption method), and will be recoverable subject to the authority's partial exemption position.
- Any amounts paid over by the contractor to the local authority in respect of the takings collected on behalf of the local authority, will be outside the scope of VAT so far as the contractor is concerned. The liability to account for VAT on the takings remains with the local authority (see paragraph 5.1).
- In some cases the contractor may incur operating expenses as agent for the local authority. Where the supplies are subject to VAT, any entitlement to input tax deduction rests with the local authority. However, if the contractor acts in its own name in relation to the expenses there is a requirement under section 47(2A) VATA 1994 in the case of goods, for the supply to be treated as being made to and by the agent. Where this applies the contractor may recover the VAT involved as input tax (subject to the normal rules) and is required to account for output tax on the onward supply to the authority.

Supplies of services may (if the parties wish) be treated in the same way under section 47(3). There is a requirement to account for the tax on the onward supply in the same tax period as it was recovered.

5. LIABILITY OF SUPPLIES TO USERS OF THE LEISURE FACILITIES

Where supplies are made by a local authority

5.1 The supply of leisure activities will continue to be made by the local authority in circumstances where a DSO is set up or where a contractor is brought in to run the facilities as an agent of the authority. In these circumstances the local authority is liable to account for VAT on the takings at the standard rate for all supplies other than those that may be exempt under the VAT Act 1994, schedule 9, group 1(m) (note 16) (Single lets for over 24 hours and a series of single lets to the same person) – see Notice 742 Land & Property– and group 6 (education) – see Notice 701/30 Education & Vocational Training.

Where supplies are made by a NPDO contractor

5.2 The liability to account for VAT on the takings rests with the NPDO. Some supplies may be taxable and others eligible for exemption under the VAT Act 1994, schedule 9, group 1(m) (note 16) and group 6 (see paragraph 5.1 above), or group 10 (sporting services supplied by non-profit making organisations and competition entry fees – see Notice 701/45 Sport).

Where supplies are made by an independent contractor

5.3 Where the contractor acts as a principal any supplies made to the users of the leisure facilities will be liable to VAT at the standard rate unless exempt under the VAT Act 1994, schedule 9, group 1(m) (note 16) (see paragraph 5.1 above) and group 10 (Item 1) (competition entry fees – see para 5.2 above).

Further supplies made by either contractor to users

5.4 There may be further supplies made in the course of operating leisure facilities such as room hire, crèche facilities and catering franchises. The liability of these will vary and may include additional exempt supplies.

6. FURTHER ADVICE

6.1 This memorandum covers only the basic arrangements that can apply to the operation of contracted-out local authority leisure services. Those involved should consult the HMRC National Advice Service on 0845 010 9000 if they require further guidance on any of these aspects, or if there is anything not covered specifically.

Commentary—*De Voil Indirect Tax Service* **V6.295, V6.305**.

30 March 2007. HMRC Brief 31/07

Partial exemption: VAT recovery on overhead costs relating to supplies of hire purchase

This article explains HMRC's policy on attributing VAT on overhead costs to supplies made under hire-purchase (HP) agreements. It affects businesses that make supplies under HP agreements to consumers, but does not apply to those who arrange such supplies and receive a commission. HMRC are aware that policy is not being applied consistently, so this article confirms the policy to be applied from 1 April 2007. This article also refers to the Tribunal decision *Royal Bank of Scotland* [VTD 19983] regarding VAT recovery and HP agreements.

BACKGROUND TO VAT RECOVERY

An HP transaction involves the supply of goods on credit terms. Provided the charge for credit is clearly identified to the customer, an HP transaction is treated as two supplies for VAT purposes, comprising:

– a supply of goods which is subject to VAT; and,
– a supply of credit which is exempt from VAT.

Businesses making both taxable and exempt supplies must apply a partial exemption method to apportion VAT on overhead costs (such as lighting and heating) to recover that VAT to the extent that the costs are 'used' for making taxable supplies.

The European Court of Justice (ECJ) has established the principles that apply to the recovery of input tax and the Court of Appeal in *Dial-a-phone* [2004] STC 987 confirmed that these principles also applied in UK law.

Costs are therefore "used" to make taxable supplies of goods or services within the meaning of the partial exemption regulations, if they:

– have a direct and immediate link with the taxable transaction (see *BLP* case C-4/94);

- are borne directly by the cost components of a taxable transaction (see *Midland Bank plc* case C-98/98);
- are costs of the various components of the price (see *DA and EA Rompelman* case C-268/83).

These are different aspects of a single test to determine whether VAT is recoverable.

In applying these ECJ principles, HMRC's view is that in order for costs to be a cost component of a taxable transaction, the costs should normally be reflected in the selling price of the taxable transaction. In other words, there is an objective test for determining VAT recovery, in that VAT on costs is not recoverable unless the costs are reflected in the selling price of the taxable supply.

VAT RECOVERY FOR HP TRANSACTIONS

Normally it is clear when VAT on costs is recoverable. This is because goods and services are either sold independently, each priced to reflect the costs incurred, or if they are supplied together, the price of each item reflects both direct costs and overheads.

In most HP transactions, the goods are resold at cost without any margin to cover overhead costs. As there is no margin on the HP goods, the cost of the overheads will normally be built into the price of the supply of credit. In this scenario, HMRC's view is that the overheads are purely cost components of the exempt supply. Otherwise the business would continually enjoy net VAT refunds despite:

- making no zero-rated or reduced rate supplies; and
- charging a total consideration under the HP agreement that fully recovers its costs and an element of profit.

Where overheads are used to make both HP transactions and other supplies on which VAT is charged (such as taxable purchase option fees or sales of repossessed goods), then some VAT on overhead costs is recoverable. In this scenario the partial exemption method should reflect the extent to which the overhead costs are a cost component of the prices of the supplies in question.

EXISTING METHODS

Businesses using special methods will need to review them to ensure that they are fair and reasonable in accordance with the above principles. If an existing method is not fair and reasonable, the business concerned should contact HMRC to discuss a new method going forward. In approving new methods, or reviewing existing methods, HMRC will ensure that methods fairly attribute VAT to taxable supplies taking account of this article.

HP businesses using the standard method will need to consider the standard method override provisions and, if necessary, apply for a special method. In doing this the above principles for HP transactions will need to be taken into account. Further guidance is available in VAT Notice 706 "Partial exemption".

ROYAL BANK OF SCOTLAND

In February, the Scottish Tribunal released its decision in the Royal Bank of Scotland (RBS) case regarding VAT recovery and HP transactions. RBS appealed HMRC's refusal to approve a replacement partial exemption method in which HP transactions would be treated as two transactions, one taxable and one exempt such that 50% of the VAT on related overhead costs would be recoverable. The Tribunal found for RBS. HMRC have lodged an appeal to the Court of Session. The cost component point was not tested because the appeal predated this Revenue and Customs Brief.

10 April 2007. HMRC Brief 36/07

Input tax deduction without a valid VAT invoice: Revised Statement of Practice

This Revenue & Customs Brief announces the publication of "Input tax deduction without a valid VAT invoice – Statement of Practice March 07". It replaces "Input tax deduction without a valid VAT invoice – Statement of Practice July 03".

It should be read by all taxpayers dealing in any of the goods subject to widespread fraud and abuse, namely:

a. Computers and any other equipment, including parts, accessories and software, made or adapted for use in connection with computers or computer systems.
b. Telephones and any other equipment, including parts and accessories, made or adapted for use in connection with telephones or telecommunications.
c. Alcohol—those alcoholic liquors liable to excise duty, which are defined by section 1 of the Alcoholic Liquor Duties Act 1979 or in any regulations made under that Act (e.g. spirits, wines and fortified wines, made-wines, beer, cider and perry).
d. Oils—all oils that are held out for sale as road fuel.

The revised version of the statement of practice continues to apply in cases where an invalid invoice is held. It does not apply where HMRC are not satisfied that a supply has taken place or are questioning the underlying supply. It incorporates a number of changes to reflect developments in this area and includes:

- clarification on your right to deduct input tax in circumstances where HMRC question whether there is an underlying supply;
- information about invoices reflecting amendments to Regulations 14 (Contents of VAT invoice) and 16 (Retailers' invoices) of the Value Added Tax Regulations 1995 brought about by SI 2003/3220;
- details of the requirement to provide evidence of a supply having being made in circumstances where no valid invoice is held; how such a supply must be for its recipient's business; details of checks needing to be made to establish the bona fides of a supplier; evidence of normal commercial arrangements, including payment arrangements and details of how the relationship between the supplier and buyer was established.

This Revenue & Customs Brief takes effect from the date of its publication. HMRC guidance will be updated shortly to reflect these changes.

STATEMENT OF PRACTICE: VAT STRATEGY—INPUT TAX DEDUCTION WITHOUT A VALID VAT INVOICE

1. This Statement of Practice explains and clarifies HMRC's policy in respect of claims for input tax supported by invalid VAT invoices. It also explains why amendments were made to section 24(6)(a) and paragraph 4(1) of Schedule 11 to the Value Added Tax Act 1994 (VATA), and regulation 29(2) of the Value Added Tax Regulations 1995 to introduce new measures. These changes were effective from **16 April 2003** and apply to supplies made on or after this date. The statement of practice was first issued in July 2003 and has now been revised to provide clearer guidance and the updated legal position. This guidance does not apply to situations where HMRC may deny recovery of input tax for other reasons such as "abuse" of the right to deduct.

Why were changes needed?

2. These changes were made to address the increasing threat to VAT receipts by the use of invalid VAT invoices and are part of the Government's strategy to address fraud, avoidance and non-compliance in the VAT system. They are a proportionate and necessary response to a systematic and widespread attack on the VAT system, where the use of invalid VAT invoices is becoming an increasing pressure on revenue receipts, particularly in those business sectors involved in the supply of the goods listed at Appendix 3. In addition to the revenue loss, this has led to distortion of competition.

3. For the vast majority of business there will be no change, and for businesses trading within the targeted sectors the measure will only impact if you have an invalid invoice. If you are a VAT-registered business, and you have been issued with an invoice that is invalid, you should be able to return to your supplier and ask them for a valid VAT invoice that complies with the legislation. If for some reason you cannot, this Statement of Practice sets out whether or not you may be entitled to input tax recovery. In most cases, provided businesses continue to undertake normal commercial checks to ensure their supplier and the supplies they receive are "*bona fide*" prior to doing any trade, it is likely they will be able to satisfy HMRC that the input tax is deductible.

The "right to deduct" principles

4. The basic principle of EU and UK law underlying input tax recovery is that of neutrality. In practice, this means that any business that makes taxable supplies has the right to deduct the VAT incurred on goods or services that form a cost component of those supplies. EU and UK law also provides for rules governing the exercise of the right to deduct VAT. These fundamental VAT principles governing the recovery of VAT are not being changed.

5. A business has incurred input tax if the following conditions are met:

- there has actually been a supply of goods or services;
- that supply takes place in the UK;
- it is taxable at a positive rate of VAT;
- the supplier is a taxable person, ie someone either registered for VAT in the UK, or required to be registered;
- the supply is made to the person claiming the deduction;
- the recipient is a taxable person at the time the tax was incurred; and
- the recipient intends to use the goods or services for his business purposes.

6. If you are a taxable person, in order to exercise your basic right to deduct input tax, you must hold **a valid VAT invoice**. Without a valid VAT invoice, there is no right to deduct input tax. However, in the absence of such an invoice, you may still be able to make claims for input tax, but these claims are subject to HMRC's discretion. This of course assumes that a taxable supply has taken place. Where HMRC question the fact that an underlying supply has taken place, these provisions do not apply.

What legislative changes have been made?

7. The change to section 24(6)(a), VATA permits HMRC to consider evidence other than that contained in documents when exercising their discretion (paragraph 4(1) of schedule 11 is merely a consequential amendment to this change). Before this change, regulation 29(2) permitted HMRC to accept alternative **documentary** evidence to support input tax deduction without a valid VAT invoice. The amendment to regulation 29(2) simply permits HMRC, in applying their discretion, to consider evidence other than just documents.

What constitutes a valid VAT invoice?

8. A valid VAT invoice is one that meets the full legal requirements as set out in regulations 13 and 14 of the Value Added Tax Regulations 1995 (Statutory Instrument 1995/2518). The contents of a valid VAT invoice should show the following information (as set out in regulation 14(1)):

(a) an identifying number;
(b) the time of the supply;
(c) the date of the issue of the document;
(d) the name, address and registration number of the supplier;
(e) the name and address of the person to whom the goods or services are supplied;
(f) [omitted by SI 2003/3220, reg 7(a)];
(g) a description sufficient to identify the goods or services supplied;
(h) for each description, the quantity of the goods or the extent of the services, and the rate of VAT and the amount payable, excluding VAT, expressed in any currency;
(i) the gross total amount payable, excluding VAT, expressed in any currency;
(j) the rate of any cash discount offered;
(k) [omitted by SI 2003/3220, reg 7(a)];
(l) the total amount of VAT chargeable, expressed in sterling;
(m) the unit price.

A self-billed invoice is not a valid invoice unless the recipient meets the conditions for self-billing in Reg 13 (3A) and (3B). The conditions for self-billing are also set out in Notice 700/62 Self-Billing.

9. A taxable person may issue either a less detailed tax invoice where the charge made for an individual supply is £250 or less including VAT, or a modified tax invoice with the agreement of customer. If this is the case, not all of the above information is required. Information about less detailed and modified tax invoices can be found in Section 16.6 of Public Notice 700 (The VAT Guide). Copies can be obtained from the National Advice Service on 0845 010 9000 or downloaded from HMRC's web site at www.hmrc.gov.uk.

What is an invalid VAT invoice?

10. An invoice that falls short of any of the requirements laid down in Reg 14(1) of SI 1995/2518 is an invalid invoice—see Paragraph 8 above. This includes situations where some or all of the details do not relate to the person/business that made the supply or the details shown are those of a company that has gone into liquidation **or is missing at the time the supply is made**.

What do I do if I have an invalid VAT invoice?

11. The simplest thing is to ask your supplier to issue a valid VAT invoice (suppliers are legally obliged to do this). HMRC If a taxable supply has taken place but a revised invoice cannot be obtained HMRC may apply their discretion to allow recovery of input tax.

How do I know I have an invalid VAT invoice?

12. The first step is to ensure that you hold an invoice that contains all the right information. It is difficult to spot an invalid invoice where a false name, address or VAT number has been used. HMRC have established a team who can confirm that supplied VAT registration details are current, valid and match information held by HMRC. This is **not** authorisation of a transaction with that VAT registration, but can help, along with other checks to verify the legitimacy of your supplier. Such information can be obtained by telephoning 01737 734 then 516, 577, 612 or 761.

Invalid invoice and HMRC's discretion

A proper exercise of HMRC's discretion can only be undertaken when there is sufficient evidence to satisfy the Commissioners that a supply has taken place. Where a supply has taken place, but the invoice to support this is invalid, the Commissioners may exercise their discretion and allow a claim for input tax credit. For Supplies/transactions involving goods stated in Appendix 3 HMRC will need to be satisfied that:

- The supply as stated on the invoice did take place.
- There is other evidence to show that the supply/transaction occurred.
- The supply made is in furtherance of the trader's business.
- The trader has undertaken normal commercial checks to establish the bona fide of the supply and supplier.

– Normal commercial arrangements are in place—this can include payment arrangements and how the relationship between the supplier/buyer was established.

What do I do if my checks indicate that a fraud exists?

15. If your checks indicate that there may be a fraud you should consider whether you wish to continue with the transaction. You may also wish to inform HMRC Confidential on 0800 595 000.

I have an invalid VAT invoice; can I still recover input tax?

16. Not automatically. However, HMRC may apply their discretion and still allow recovery.

How will HMRC apply their discretion?

17. For supplies of goods not listed at Appendix 3, claimants will need to be able to answer most of the questions at Appendix 2 satisfactorily. In most cases, this will be little more than providing alternative evidence to show that the supply of goods or services has been made (this has always been HMRC's policy).

18. For supplies of goods listed at Appendix 3, claimants will be expected to be able to answer questions relating to the supply in question including all or nearly all of the questions at Appendix 2. In addition, they are likely to be asked further questions by HMRC in order to test whether they took reasonable care in respect of transactions to ensure that their supplier and the supply were "bona fide".

19. As long as the claimant can provide satisfactory answers to the questions at Appendix 2 and to any additional questions that may be asked, input tax deduction will be permitted.

20. Decisions on when to disallow VAT claims will only be made after an independent central review of the case has been carried out.

Can I appeal against HMRC's decision?

21. If HMRC refuse to allow deduction of input tax under this Statement of Practice, unsuccessful claimants can first ask for a reconsideration of the decision. Should that be unsuccessful, they will then be able to appeal against HMRC's decision to the VAT & Duties Tribunal.

APPENDIX 1

[Flow chart not reproduced]

APPENDIX 2

Questions* to determine whether there is a right to deduct in the absence of a valid VAT invoice

1. Do you have alternative documentary evidence other than an invoice (eg supplier statement)?
2. Do you have evidence of receipt of a taxable supply on which VAT has been charged?
3. Do you have evidence of payment?
4. Do you have evidence of how the goods/services have been consumed within your business or their onward supply?
5. How did you know that the supplier existed?
6. How was your relationship with the supplier established? For example:
   - How was contact made?
   - Do you know where the supplier operates from (have you been there)?
   - How do you contact them?
   - How do you know they can supply the goods or services?
   - If goods, how do you know the goods are not stolen?
   - How do you return faulty supplies?

*This list is not exhaustive and additional questions may be asked in individual circumstances

APPENDIX 3

Supplies of goods subject to widespread fraud and abuse

(a) **Computers and any other equipment**, including parts, accessories and software, made or adapted for use in connection with computers or computer systems.

(b) **Telephones and any other equipment**, including parts and accessories, made or adapted for use in connection with telephones or telecommunications.

(c) **Alcohol**—those alcoholic liquors liable to excise duty, which are defined by section 1 of the Alcoholic Liquor Duties Act 1979 or in any regulations made under that Act (eg spirits, wines and fortified wines, made-wines, beer, cider and perry).

(d) **Oils**—all oils that are held out for sale as road fuel.

14 June 2007. HMRC Brief 45/07

Partial exemption – VAT deduction by theatres on production costs

HMRC has revised its policy on input tax recovery on the costs of staging shows (production costs) for which the theatre's admissions are VAT exempt. It follows the judgment of the Court of Appeal in the case of *Mayflower Theatre Trust Ltd* ([2006] EWCA Civ 116) (MTT). It replaces the first article in Business Brief 12/06, which is now withdrawn. Further information on partial exemption can be found in Public Notice 706.

THE DISPUTE

MTT bought in performances (production services) under contract from touring companies. The supply of production services was a single supply for VAT purposes. HMRC maintained that none of the input tax was deductible because it related solely to supplies of exempt admission. MTT argued that the input tax was partly deductible (residual) because the production costs had a direct and immediate link not only to exempt admissions, but also to taxable supplies such as catering, programme sales and corporate sponsorship.

THE COURT OF APPEAL DECISION

The Tribunal found for HMRC but this was overturned in the High Court. The High Court allowed residual treatment concluding that the production costs were sufficiently linked to what the court described as "taxable tickets" which formed part of a single taxable supply of corporate sponsorship.

The Court of Appeal rejected the "taxable tickets" argument, and a further argument that the costs were overheads of the business as a whole. However, the Court of Appeal found that the production services included the provision of raw material that was essential for the printing of taxable programmes such as logos, photographs and casting information. Accordingly, the input tax was residual. HMRC has decided not to appeal this decision.

THE NEW HMRC POLICY

Theatres which receive single supplies of production services from touring companies, that include material essential for the printing of programmes, may treat the input tax as residual. This applies even where that programme material is a minor part of the contract.

Theatres that stage their own shows may receive supplies such as costumes or scenery. These supplies will not be residual. This is because the costs have a direct and immediate link with admissions and not with the printing of programmes even though costumes and scenery might be visible in subsequent programme photographs.

IMPACT ON THEATRES

The vast majority of theatres use the partial exemption standard method to apportion residual input tax between taxable and exempt supplies. This works well provided VAT bearing costs are used in proportion to the value of supplies made. However, residual production services are used almost entirely for exempt admissions with only a minimal link to taxable programmes. The Court of Appeal recognised that this led to an over-recovery of input tax.

Since 18 April 2002, if the standard method results in an over (or under) recovery of input tax which is classed as "substantial" then the recovery must be re-calculated in accordance with the "actual use" of the costs in question. This is known as the Standard Method Override (SMO). Further information on the SMO, including the definition of "substantial" can be found in the public notice.

Major theatres which buy in large numbers of shows are the ones most likely to trigger the SMO and thus need to undertake a "use-based" calculation for their costs.

A "use-based" calculation is any calculation that fairly reflects how costs are used. As production services only have a direct and immediate link with box office sales and programme sales, a fair calculation could be:

Recoverable input tax on production services

$$= \frac{\text{Value of programme sales}}{\text{Value of programme sales plus value of box office sales}} \times \text{Input tax incurred on production services}$$

Theatres operating the standard method which regularly receive production services that are residual may wish to seek approval for a special method to avoid the risk of triggering the SMO.

CLAIMS FOR UNDER-RECOVERED INPUT TAX

Theatres may wish to claim input tax which, in the light of this HMRC Brief, was incorrectly treated as exempt. They must use the partial exemption method in place when the input tax was

VAT

incurred unless there are exceptional reasons why an alternative method is needed in which case full details should be submitted with the claim. Theatres using the standard method must consider the SMO when making a claim and all claims are subject to the normal three year time limit.

Theatres that have reclaimed input tax on the basis of the High Court's decision, but whose production costs exclude essential material for programmes, will now be subject to assessment with interest due.

Further information about making claims can be found in Public Notice 700/45 How to correct VAT errors and make adjustments or claims and in Business Briefs 25/04 and 28/04.

Commentary—*De Voil Indirect Tax Service* **V4.176**.

28 June 2007. HMRC Brief 48/07

Introduction of a reduced rate for the supply of smoking cessation products

With effect from 1 July 2007, the supply of smoking cessation products will be eligible for the reduced rate of VAT (5%).

This relief will be in force for a period of one year and its introduction will coincide with the ban on smoking in public places in England.

SCOPE OF THE REDUCED RATE

A new group will be added to Schedule 7A of the VAT Act 1994 to introduce the reduced rate to supplies of smoking cessation products, which are pharmaceutical products designed to help people to stop smoking tobacco.

The reduced rate will apply to non-prescribed sales of nicotine patches, nicotine gums, nicotine inhalators, lozenges and other pharmaceutical products held out for sale for the primary purpose of helping people to stop smoking.

The supply of smoking cessation products on a prescription by a medical practitioner will continue to be zero rated.

FURTHER ADVICE

Anyone who remains uncertain as to the liability of the supply of smoking cessation products should contact the National Advice Service.

24 July 2007. HMRC Brief 51/07

Changes to the VAT Invoicing Regulations with effect from 1 October 2007

VAT regulation changes were made on 23 July 2007 and make minor modifications to the format of invoices which are effective from 1 October 2007.

The changes follow infraction proceedings begun by the European Commission. Consultation suggests that the effects on most UK businesses will be minor. Businesses most likely to be affected are **those**:

- using the margin scheme for second-hand goods, antiques, works of art, and collectors' items;
- involved in making travel related supplies that fall within the scope of the Tour Operators' Margin Scheme;
- involved in intra EU supplies of goods and services;
- making supplies where the customer accounts for the VAT.

THE CHANGES

1. The number on the invoice

Regulation 14(1)(*a*) will be amended to include a requirement for an invoice to bear a sequential number based on one or more series which uniquely identify the document.

Consultation supported the view of HMRC that this formal legal change will have little impact on the way invoices are numbered by the majority of businesses.

2. Reference to the second-hand margin schemes

Regulation 14 will be changed to add a requirement that invoices under the special arrangements for second-hand goods, antiques, works of art and collectors' items must include a reference to the nature of the treatment, which accords with the Directive. That means a reference to either the relevant EC or UK legislation, or including any other indication of the treatment.

3. Reference to the Tour Operators' Margin Scheme (TOMS)

Regulation 14 will be changed to add a requirement that invoices under TOMS must include a reference to the nature of the treatment, which accords with the Directive.

Businesses can include a reference to the relevant EC or UK legislation, or include any other indication of the treatment. The choice of legend is a matter for individual businesses to decide.

The new rule only applies to those occasions when an invoice is issued to another taxable person.

4. Reference to the reverse charge or exemption (including zero rate dispatches to other member States)

Regulations will be changed to add a requirement that zero rate dispatches and exempt or reverse charge invoices will require a reference to the grounds for the treatment when the supply is to a business customer based in another member State.

Businesses can include a reference to the relevant EC or UK legislation, or include any other indication of the treatment. The choice of legend is a matter for individual businesses to decide.

Regulation 14 will be amended to make it clear that the requirement also applies to UK supplies where the customer accounts for the VAT, such as the gold scheme (VATA 1994 s 55) or any reverse charge requirement introduced under Missing Trader Intra-Community (MTIC) rules in VATA 1994, s 55A.

The regulations make it clear that a requirement to issue invoices for exempt supplies only arises when the supply is business to business, across an EU border, and an invoice is required by the member State of receipt. Because practice varies widely across member States, HMRC guidance is that businesses should be guided by their customers.

5. References required

The regulations will be changed to make it clear that an invoice issued under the following procedures must contain a reference to the relevant EC or UK legislation, or include any other indication of the treatment. The choice of legend is a matter for individual businesses to decide:

- regulation17(2)(*b*) covering section 14(6) supplies to persons belonging in other member States
- regulation 18(2)(*d*) covering section 14(1) supplies by intermediate suppliers, and
- regulation 19(2)(*d*) covering section 14(2) supplies by persons belonging in other member States.

FURTHER INFORMATION

VAT Information Sheet 10/2007 provides additional details concerning the changes, together with a list of frequently asked questions (FAQs) that you may find helpful. Further information in relation to the consultation and the background to the changes can be found on the Joint VAT Consultative Committee (JVCC) page of the HMRC internet site, which includes two VAT invoicing consultation documents.

If you need further information about VAT invoicing, please ring the National Advice Service.

Commentary—*De Voil Indirect Tax Service* **V3.511**.

14 August 2007. HMRC Brief 55/07

Revised treatment of VAT incurred on home computers made available by employers to their employees

This Revenue and Customs Brief sets out HMRC's revised policy on the VAT treatment of computers made available by employers for use in their employee's homes; this follows withdrawal of the tax exemption which allowed employers to loan computer equipment to their employees tax free.

BACKGROUND

In April 1999 the Government introduced a direct tax exemption which enabled employers to loan a computer to their employees tax-free. The objective was to help increase access to computers and help employees increase their IT literacy skills. In January 2004 the Government launched the Home Computer Initiative which encouraged employers and employees to take advantage of the exemption and sought to make it as straightforward as possible for employers to lend computer equipment to their employees.

At that time the former HM Customs and Excise considered that, while there would undoubtedly be some private use of the computer—usually requiring some restriction on VAT recovery—in the circumstances of the HCI there would be wider benefits to the business and so the VAT treatment should mirror the approach taken for direct tax. Consequently, as long as there was some business use, any VAT incurred, could be deducted in full without any adjustment for private use.

Following a review of the HCI the direct tax exemption was withdrawn with effect from 6 April 2006. Consequently HMRC have now reviewed the VAT position.

HMRC'S REVISED POLICY

HMRC's policy to allow full VAT recovery without any adjustment for private use, in circumstances where there is any business use, is withdrawn from the date of this Revenue and Customs Brief.

With immediate effect businesses must consider why the computer is being provided to the employee to determine the level of VAT that can be claimed. Businesses will only be able to claim full VAT recovery without any requirement to account for VAT on any private use (subject of course to any restriction in respect of exempt supplies) where the provision of a computer is necessary for the employee to carry out the duties of his employment. In these circumstances HMRC's view is that it is unlikely that any private use will be significant when compared with the business need for providing the computer in the first place. This mirrors the approach taken for direct tax concerning exemptions for work related benefits in kind where there is no significant private use.

Where a business cannot demonstrate that it is necessary to provide an employee with a computer in order to carry out the duties of his employment then only a portion of the VAT incurred will be recoverable as input tax. HMRC will accept any method of apportioning the VAT incurred as long as the result fairly and reasonably reflects the extent of business use. In order to minimise your administrative burdens you may be able to agree a set percentage with HMRC based on a representative period.

TRANSITIONAL PROVISIONS

Where a business continues to provide a computer under an existing HCI agreement full VAT recovery can continue until the agreement (normally 3 years) has expired. For further information on these transitional provisions please refer to direct tax guidance EIM2699.

WHAT IF THE BUSINESS IS NOT THE RECIPIENT OF THE SUPPLY?

Please note that it is a basic principle of the VAT system that VAT can only be recovered as input tax where the supply is to the taxable person or business. So, in circumstances where the supply of the computer is to the employee the business cannot recover the VAT incurred on that supply as input tax.

Commentary—*De Voil Indirect Tax Service* **V3.471**.

22 August 2007. HMRC Brief 52/07

Place of supply of trading allowances in greenhouse gas emissions (update)

Commentary—*De Voil Indirect Tax Service* **V3.193**.
Note—This Brief has been cancelled and incorporated into Notice 741 "Place of supply of services".

22 August 2007. HMRC Brief 58/07

Claims in respect of fund management services

BACKGROUND

The EC VAT Directive (formerly the Sixth Directive) exempts 'management of special investment funds as defined by member states'. The UK applies this exemption to the management of authorised unit trusts (AUTs), open-ended investment companies (OEICs) and trust-based schemes. The UK has not applied this exemption to the management of other funds, including investment trust companies (ITCs).

In 2004, JP Morgan Fleming Claverhouse Trust plc, an ITC, appealed to the VAT Tribunal against the VAT charged to it on investment management services. This appeal was joined by the Association of Investment Trust Companies (now the AIC) and the Tribunal referred 3 questions to the European Court of Justice (ECJ). In its judgment of 28 June 2007, the ECJ has given guidance to the Tribunal to determine whether the management of ITCs should be VAT exempt.

CLAIMS CONCERNING THE MANAGEMENT OF ITCS

We have received a number of claims for overpaid VAT on the management of ITCs since the litigation began in 2004. The claims concerning such services have been held over pending the final outcome in the litigation, and will be addressed in due course.

CLAIMS CONCERNING THE MANAGEMENT OF FUNDS OTHER THAN ITCS

Since the ECJ judgment, we have also received a number of claims for overpaid VAT in respect of the management of other funds not at issue in the litigation. Such claims have generally contained a request that they be held pending the final outcome in the *JP Morgan Fleming Claverhouse* case, using the ECJ judgment as support for the claims.

We take the view that this case does not concern the management of funds other than ITCs and that the ECJ judgment is clear in that it does not address the issues that arise concerning such other funds. There is thus no basis for HMRC to accept these claims, nor any current litigation against which to justify holding over the claims. Accordingly, any such claims in respect of the management of funds other than ITCs will be refused. This is in line with our existing published guidance (see paragraph 2.7 of "V1–33: VAT refunds – unjust enrichment – statutory interest – ex-gratia payments").

Commentary—*De Voil Indirect Tax Service* **V4.136H.**
Note—See HMRC Brief 65/07: HMRC withdraw from the appeal in *JP Morgan Fleming Claverhouse Trust plc.*

11 October 2007. HMRC Brief 61/07

Teleos and others (VAT—Intra-Community trade)

The European Court of Justice (ECJ) gave its judgement in this case (reference C-409/04; [2007] All ER (D) 160 (Sep)) on 27 September 2007.

The key points in the decision are:

– goods must physically leave the territory of the Member State of supply to qualify for zero rating;

If a supplier:

– acts in good faith and submits evidence establishing a right to zero-rate an intra Community transaction; and
– has no involvement in tax evasion and takes every reasonable measure in their power to ensure that the transaction did not lead to their participation in tax evasion,
– then the Member State cannot hold the supplier to account for the VAT on those goods if the information relied on subsequently proves to be false.

BACKGROUND

This case involved the purported removal of mobile phones to a VAT registered customer in Spain. No VAT is due in the UK on such transactions provided the supplier meets certain conditions set by HMRC. The principal conditions are that the supplier must obtain their customer's VAT registration number and they must obtain proof that the goods have been removed to another Member State.

Teleos treated all their supplies in this case as intra-EC transactions and did not account for any VAT (referred to as zero-rating for VAT purposes in the UK). To support their claim for VAT zero-rating they relied on commercial road transport documents as proof that the goods had been removed to another Member State. The documents subsequently proved to be false so HMRC disallowed VAT zero-rating and assessed. The ECJ decision is in response to a reference from the High Court following an application by Teleos (and others) to review the Commissioners decision on zero rating.

IMPACT IN THIS CASE

The case will go back to the administrative court to consider the taxpayer's application in the light of the ECJ's ruling. The Commissioners are examining their decision in that case and the case of the other parties to the litigation.

WIDER IMPLICATIONS OF THE DECISION

The Court ruled that EC law on intra-Community supply and intra-Community acquisition are rules governing the physical movement of goods from one Member State to another. Consequently, to obtain the exemption, physical movement of goods from the supplying Member State to another Member State must be established. This accords with the United Kingdom's submissions, and it remains for the supplier of the goods to furnish the proof that the conditions for zero rating are fulfilled. The conditions in UK law and in public notices will continue to govern the entitlement to zero rating.

The Court's decision also limits the Commissioners' ability to recover from the supplier, tax lost through incorrect zero rating in the circumstances of the Teleos case. In restricting the ability to assess in such cases, the court was balancing the benefit of legal certainty for suppliers who act in good faith with the need to have stringent conditions to prevent fraud and abuse. The good faith of the supplier, the steps they took, and whether they are established as not participating in fraud are critical factors in deciding whether they can be obliged to account for VAT after the event.

Indeed, the judgement makes it clear that it is not contrary to Community law to require the supplier to take every step which could be reasonably required of them to satisfy themselves that the transaction which they are effecting does not result in his participation in tax evasion. The judgement is therefore consistent with the line of ECJ cases which underpin HMRC's approach to MTIC fraud and underlines that rights under EC VAT law cannot routinely be enjoyed where the taxpayer in question knew or could have known that they were participating in tax evasion.

CASES ON ALL FOURS

HMRC expect few cases to be on all fours with Teleos. Anyone who considers that an assessment for zero rating falls on the basis of the Teleos decision in the ECJ should make a claim subject to the time limits for such claims. Further information about making claims can be found in Public Notice 700/45 "How to correct VAT errors or make adjustments or claims" and Business Brief 28/04.

Commentary—*De Voil Indirect Tax Service* **V4.343**.

11 October 2007. HMRC Brief 62/07

Commission earned by sub-agents in the travel industry

This Revenue & Customs Brief sets out a change in our interpretation of how VAT law applies to the treatment of commission earned by sub-agents in the travel industry.

Para 2.6 of Public Notice 709/6 "Travel agents and tour operators" states:

> "If you are acting as a sub-agent (that is an intermediary acting for another intermediary), then your services, which are supplied in the UK, are standard- rated."

There is no change if sub-agents provide services which facilitate the making of supplies, such as a simple introduction. In this case, the place of supply for this service is where the sub-agents are established. Where this is in the UK, their commission will be liable to VAT at the standard rate.

However, if sub-agents are involved in the making of arrangements for travel services, then the place of their supply will follow the normal rules for supplies by intermediaries. This will depend on:

- where the underlying arranged supply is made; and
- (where this is in the EU) whether the customer is EU VAT registered.

VAT Notice 741 "Place of supply of services" sets out these rules in more detail.

The liability of the sub-agents' supplies for which they receive the commission will follow that of the underlying supply. Where they are involved in the provision of specific supplies of zero-rated passenger transport, their commission for those transactions will also be zero-rated. Where they are involved in the provision of a package supplied by a UK tour operator under the Tour Operators' Margin Scheme, their commission will continue to be standard-rated.

The "making of arrangements for" travel services does not include supplies of market research, advertising, promotional or similar services. Supplies of these services will continue to be standard-rated, as will payments received from the providers of computerised reservations systems in respect of travel agents' use of these sites.

The vast majority of supplies made by sub-agents are to other VAT registered businesses, which are able to recover tax deducted. This change, therefore, will be broadly revenue neutral.

Businesses are not required to correct past declaration errors which were made on the basis of our earlier interpretation of the law. The second article of Business Brief 28/04 sets out our policy on correcting liability errors and gives more information on how to do this.

Businesses may apply the zero rate, where appropriate, with immediate effect, and otherwise should do so no later than 1 November 2007.

Commentary—*De Voil Indirect Tax Service* **V16.904**.

5 November 2007. HMRC Brief 65/07

JP Morgan Fleming Claverhouse Trust plc – fund management services

This Revenue & Customs Brief announces that HMRC have withdrawn from the appeal in *JP Morgan Fleming Claverhouse Trust plc*.

On 28 June 2007, the European Court of Justice (ECJ) delivered its judgment in this case which gave guidance for the VAT Tribunal to decide, on the facts, whether fund management services provided to investment trust companies (ITCs) should be exempt from VAT.

After careful consideration of the ECJ judgment, we now accept that fund management services supplied to ITCs are exempt and have withdrawn from the appeal. We remain of the view, published in HMRC Brief 58/07, that the judgment does not apply to funds other than ITCs.

SUPPLIES AFFECTED BY THIS DECISION

In an earlier ECJ judgment in Abbey National, it was ruled that the exemption for 'management' of funds covers not only investment management services, but also certain administrative services if, viewed broadly, they form a distinct whole and are specific to, and essential for, the management of the fund.

We published detailed guidance on this in Business Brief 07/06, but it should be noted that the Abbey judgment focused on authorised investment funds such as authorised unit trusts and open-ended investment companies. In this context, the court referred to the UCITS Directive, which sets out certain administrative functions that these funds are required to carry out.

Our revised policy was to exempt services, usually made up of several elements, forming single supplies which are recognisable in their own right as fund administration services. On the other hand, we made it clear that just because a service is a requirement of the regulations does not mean that it is exempt – for example, some legal services may be specific to and essential for the administration of the fund, but they remain legal services, not fund administration services.

Although ITCs are not subject to the same form of regulation, we believe the same principles should apply. For ITCs, services which are specific to, and essential for their administration (or provisions relating solely to ITCs) may be exempt if, viewed broadly, they form a distinct whole recognisable as a fund administration service. More generic management services, such as company secretarial services and accounting, remain taxable if they are not otherwise subsumed into a single composite supply of fund administration services.

IMPLEMENTATION

Businesses may exempt fund management services supplied to ITCs, but we cannot require this until such time as the UK law is amended. We expect to consult informally with key stakeholders in the coming weeks on possible legal changes in this regard.

CLAIMS FOR OVERSTATED OR OVERPAID VAT

Any claims for overstated or overpaid VAT on fund management services supplied to ITCs will now be dealt with in accordance with our Business Brief 28/04 – Correcting liability errors; Notice 700/45 – *How to correct VAT errors and make adjustments or claims*; and published guidance V1–33: VAT refunds – unjust enrichment – statutory interest – ex-gratia payments.

Commentary—*De Voil Indirect Tax Service* **V4.136H**.

5 November 2007. HMRC Brief 66/07

Treatment of the construction of houses or flats in the grounds of existing care homes, nursing homes or similar buildings

This brief sets out HMRC's policy on the VAT treatment of the construction, and first major interest grant of, "independent living" units within the curtilage or grounds of residential care homes. (A "first major interest grant" is defined as the freehold sale or a lease in excess of 21 years, (20 years in Scotland.))

In order for services of the construction, or first major interest grant, of such units to qualify for zero-rating, they must qualify either as buildings "designed as dwellings" or as buildings "intended for use solely for a relevant residential purpose", within the meaning of the these terms as defined in the VAT Act 1994.

Although "independent living" units generally have all of the physical characteristics of a "dwelling", the units only qualify for zero-rating if they meet all the conditions laid down in Note 2 to Group 5 of Schedule 8 to the VAT Act 1994. Where such units have a stipulation in their planning permission that they cannot be used separately from the care homes, of which they form a part, the construction of such units is ineligible for the zero rate, as is the first grant of a major interest in such units.

We have also been asked to consider whether the new units form a building (or buildings) that are "intended for use solely for a relevant residential purpose" thus qualifying the construction of the units for the zero rate.

In our view, the units do not qualify for the zero rate because, if personal care is provided to the occupants of the units, it is either not provided as a zero-rated home or institution would provide personal care or, if it is, it is provided as part of an existing home or institution.

Finally, we consider that such a unit would not qualify for zero-rating as "an institution which is the sole or main residence of at least 90 per cent of its residents", because the units are not institutions.

Commentary—*De Voil Indirect Tax Service* **V4.232, V4.411**.

21 November 2007. HMRC Brief 69/07

The decision of the tribunal in InsuranceWide.com Services Ltd

This concerns the VAT treatment of insurance introductory services following the VAT tribunal decision in *InsuranceWide.com Services Ltd (InsuranceWide)*. The tribunal found that certain internet services provided to insurers and brokers in connection with the arranging of insurance policies do not fall within the exemption for insurance related services provided by insurance brokers and agents and are liable to VAT at the standard rate.

BACKGROUND

InsuranceWide provides an online comparison website service, putting potential customers in touch with insurers via a click-through from its website to that of an insurer or insurance broker. It receives commission from the insurers based on the number of contracts that result from the introductions. Over the years, the services provided by InsuranceWide have changed as technology has developed.

In 2002 InsuranceWide introduced a system known as the InsuranceWide Wizard which automated the selection process by obtaining and recording the essential information required by insurers and applying that information to guide each prospective customer through to the most appropriate insurer or insurers. This information is discussed regularly with insurers to ensure it is kept up to date.

THE DECISION

The Tribunal found that none of the services provided by InsuranceWide fell within the VAT exemption because InsuranceWide was not an insurance agent. InsuranceWide specifically disclaimed being an agent on its website and was found to be playing no part in the negotiation of the contracts. Neither did InsuranceWide have the power to bind the insurance company which the tribunal found to be one of the indicators of an agency relationship (although not it itself determinative for VAT purposes).

Having found against the Appellant on this basis, the tribunal then went on to consider whether any of the services provided by InsuranceWide qualified as the "services of an insurance intermediary" (under UK law) or insurance "related services" (under EU law) which would have made them exempt had InsuranceWide been an insurance agent.

The tribunal found that, in performing the non-Wizard services, InsuranceWide's role was not that of a mediator between the parties to a contract of insurance. It found that InsuranceWide was "nothing more than an introducer and its role ….cannot be properly distinguished from that of an advertiser in that via its website it had no interaction with either party beyond making the one aware of the other and providing a means of one contacting the other."

After the introduction of the Wizard, however, the tribunal found that InsuranceWide's services went beyond that of a mere promoter of, and introducer to, insurance companies and would qualify for exemption under both UK and EU law when provided by an insurance agent or broker. In particular the tribunal highlighted the regular negotiations with insurers about the range and price of products, the saving of time for both the insurers and would be insureds by referring only suitable applicants to appropriate insurers and assisting with the completion of forms.

IMPLICATIONS OF THE DECISION

The decision in InsuranceWide confirms HMRC's current published policy in this area (see in particular paragraph 10.5 of Notice 701/36, *Insurance*) and, as such, does not have implications for any of the insurance-related services that HMRC currently see as falling within the VAT exemption.

Whilst certain services provided via the internet were found to be liable to VAT, HMRC do not see the decision as applying to all internet services and accept that, where the necessary criteria are met, some internet services can fall within the VAT exemption and it is the arrangements between the parties and the nature of the services themselves that determines the VAT liability and not the means by which those services are delivered.

HMRC see the decision as applying, in particular, to advertising/promotional type services such as internet "click through" services and mail-shot and leaflet distribution services where the provider does little more than put one party in touch with the other and plays no part in any interaction between the parties once that introduction has been made. Such services are specifically excluded from the VAT exemption and are taxable regardless of whether (as with InsuranceWide's co-branded websites) the products are promoted in the name of the provider of the service, the provider is an insurance agent or broker by profession, or whether payment is made by fee or commission.

In circumstances (which would include certain "affinity" arrangements) where the provider is clearly acting as an agent of an insurer or insurers and is playing a more active role in arranging the policies than mere introduction – for example, negotiating terms and conditions of the insurance contacts, assisting with forms/queries and actively recommending/endorsing the insurance product/s – VAT exemption continues to apply.

Commentary—*De Voil Indirect Tax Service* **V4.123**.

19 December 2007. HMRC Brief 75/07

Intrastat – thresholds from 1 January 2008

This Revenue & Customs Brief article explains that the Intrastat thresholds will remain unchanged in 2008 from those set on 1 January 2007 and explains how businesses trading with other EU Member States will be affected by this.

INTRASTAT THRESHOLDS

- The exemption threshold remains at £260,000.
- The delivery terms threshold remains at £14,500,000.

BACKGROUND

Community legislation requires the UK to collect information on intra-EU trade for statistical purposes and sets minimum requirements for the quantity of trade covered. These requirements determine the level at which the exemption threshold is set in the UK. The same threshold is applied independently to arrivals (intra-EU imports) and dispatches (intra-EU exports).

Those traders with an annual intra-EU trade in goods above the specified exemption threshold are required to provide monthly statistical returns (Intrastat Supplementary Declarations).

Community legislation requires the UK to collect information to enable the accurate calculation of statistical value. These requirements determine the level at which the delivery terms threshold is set in the UK. The same threshold for delivery terms applies to arrivals and dispatches.

Traders with annual EU trade above the delivery terms threshold are required to supply additional information relating to delivery terms on their statistical returns.

FURTHER INFORMATION

Further information on trade statistics can be found online at http://www.uktradeinfo.com/ or by phoning uktradeinfo Customer Services on 01702 367485.

For further information and advice on submitting Intrastat declarations, please contact the National Advice Service 0845 010 9000.

Commentary—*De Voil Indirect Tax Service* **V5.276**.

3 January 2008. HMRC Brief 1/08

Partial exemption – Cheshire Racing Tribunal Decision

This Revenue & Customs Brief article announces HMRC's revised policy about recovery of input tax on Satellite Information System (SIS) services received by bookmakers following the Tribunal decision in the case of *Cheshire Racing Ltd* (VTD 20283). It updates Article 1 in Business Brief 17/06 that also concerns SIS. It uses a number of specialist terms, which are fully explained in Public Notice 706, Partial Exemption.

BACKGROUND

SIS provides live coverage of horse and dog racing, real time odds, results information and commentary and opinion from pundits. Historically, HMRC's view was that this information related directly to the over the counter betting activity of Bookmakers, which is exempt for VAT purposes.

In the appeal of *Town and County Factors* (VTD 19616) the Tribunal found that there was a sufficient link between SIS costs and taxable supplies made, such that the costs were residual for partial exemption purposes. The Commissioners subsequently issued Business Brief 17/06 which set out how HMRC viewed the logic and wider application of the decision. The Business Brief stated that where the bookmaker contributed additional content to the SIS service so that it partly related to their taxable supplies, then the input tax incurred was residual for that bookmaker.

CHESHIRE RACING (VTD 20283)

Cheshire Racing Ltd disagreed with HMRC's view. They argued that input tax on SIS should be residual even though they did not add additional content. They felt that VAT incurred on the specialist TV services was partly recoverable because it had a direct and immediate link with taxable supplies from gaming machines, as well as betting.

In deciding in favour of Cheshire Racing Ltd, the Tribunal found as a fact there was a direct and immediate link between the content of the SIS broadcast and gaming machine income. This applied even when the bookmaker added no additional information to SIS.

HMRC'S POLICY FOLLOWING CHESHIRE RACING LTD

HMRC are not appealing the decision and now accepts that SIS services have a direct and immediate link to gaming machine supplies made by bookmakers as the SIS provides commentary relevant to those machines.

CLAIMS FOR UNDER-RECOVERED INPUT TAX

Bookmakers may wish to claim input tax which, in the light of this Revenue and Customs Brief, was incorrectly treated as exempt. Claims should be submitted to the Local Business Advice Centre. They must use the partial exemption method applicable to each accounting period unless there are exceptional circumstances as to why an alternative method is needed. In this case they should apply to HMRC to use an alternative special method. All claims are subject to the relevant time limits.

Further information about making claims can be found in Public Notice 700/45 How to correct VAT errors or make adjustments or claims and Business Brief 28/04.

Commentary—*De Voil Indirect Tax Service* **V4.131**.

20 February 2008. HMRC Brief 7/08

Three year time limit for VAT claims

The recent House of Lords decisions in the cases of *Michael Fleming (t/a Bodycraft) v HMRC (Fleming)* and *Condé Nast Publications Ltd v HMRC (Condé Nast)* disapplied the three year time limit for input tax claims in respect of which the entitlement to deduct accrued before 1 May 1997.

HMRC consider that the terms of the judgment also apply to claims to recover VAT overpaid or overdeclared in accounting periods ending before 4 December 1996.

CLAIMS

As a result claims may now be made for:

– output tax overpaid or overdeclared in accounting periods ending before 4 December 1996
– input tax in respect of which the entitlement to deduct arose in accounting periods ending before 1 May 1997

Claims must be submitted to:

HM Revenue & Customs
"Fleming" Claims Team (Leeds)
Queens Dock
Liverpool
Merseyside
L74 4AA

Telephone enquiries in relation to the submission of claims or to claims that have already been submitted to the Claims Team may be made on Tel 0113 389 4432.

Claims relating to accounting periods ending on or after 4 December 1996 (for output tax) or 1 May 1997 (for input tax) are capped at three years.

UNDERTAKINGS

Claims will now be paid, following verification, without the need to provide an undertaking to repay HMRC.

Claimants who have had their claims paid on condition that they provide an undertaking to repay in the event that the House of Lords found in favour of HMRC, are released from those undertakings. No further action is required by claimants.

FURTHER ANNOUNCEMENT

HMRC are still considering the full implications of the judgment and will make a further announcement in due course.

BACKGROUND

In 1996 the government reduced the time limit for claiming overpaid VAT to three years from the date of the overpayment. A similar three year time limit was also introduced for input tax claims in 1997. Both provisions had retrospective, as well as prospective, effect, i e they applied to claims that arose in accounting periods both before and after the enactment of the legislation. Neither contained transitional provisions to allow claims to be made for a limited period under the old rules, before the new time limits came into effect.

The absence of such transitional arrangements was held to breach Community law, in the ECJ judgment in Marks and Spencer plc in July 2002. In August and October 2002, HMRC sought to remedy the position by introducing an administrative transitional regime (Business Briefs 22/02 and 27/02). In January 2008 the House of Lords in Fleming and Condé Nast held that, in the absence of transitional arrangements in 1997, the three year cap had to be disapplied for input tax claims in respect of which the rights to deduct had accrued at 1 May 1997.

HMRC consider that the terms of the judgment are such that they cannot rely on the administrative transitional regime introduced for output tax claims. They accept that the three year cap must therefore be disapplied for such claims where the rights had accrued at 4 December 1996.

Commentary—*De Voil Indirect Tax Service* **V3.405, V5.159C**.

4 March 2008. HMRC Brief 13/08

Access to Intrastat data

This Revenue & Customs Brief announces the introduction of a new VAT regulation. This will make clear that HM Revenue & Customs (HMRC) may use for VAT purposes the data already collected for Intrastat purposes.

The new regulation will not require businesses to provide any additional information. Although it applies to those businesses which supply or acquire EC goods over the (current) annual threshold of £260,000 (net of VAT and Excise duty) and which are therefore required to submit monthly "Intrastat declarations", these businesses need take no action as a result of the change in the law, which comes into effect on 1 April 2008.

BACKGROUND

"Intrastat" is the EU-based system for the collection of statistics on the trade in goods between Member States.

Within the UK, intra-EU trade statistics are compiled from two sources:

– from the aggregate net value of EC supplies (sales) and acquisitions (purchases) which all VAT registered businesses are required to declare on their VAT returns, used to estimate the total value of trade;
– from detailed transaction information provided by those businesses, approximately 32,500 which supply or acquire EC goods over the (current) annual threshold of £260,000 (net of VAT and Excise duty) and which are therefore required to submit monthly "Intrastat declarations".

Data from these sources can support HMRC strategy to counter Missing Trader Intra-Community (MTIC) fraud, a sophisticated and systematic criminal attack on the VAT system, which has reduced VAT revenues by an estimated £2 billion to £3 billion in 2005/06 and £1 billion to £2 billion in 2006/07.

However, under current legislation the full extent to which this data can be used for HMRC VAT enforcement purposes is unclear. The position in law is therefore being regularised, so as to make clear that the data provided for Intrastat purposes is to be provided for VAT purposes as well.

ACTION REQUIRED

No action is required over and above that already required to submit Intrastat declarations. As of 1 April 2008, the data as provided on Intrastat declarations will be provided for both Intrastat and VAT purposes. Affected businesses are therefore still required to provide the information once only, in the same format and at no additional cost. They will not be required to store a second copy of the declaration in their VAT records. New Intrastat forms which make clear the dual purpose of the data in an amended heading to the form will be available shortly.

PENALTIES

Although any breach of the new VAT regulation will in principle become subject to a potential penalty under VAT provisions already in place, the VAT penalty provision does not apply where a person is convicted of an offence in relation to Intrastat. Accordingly, affected taxpayers cannot, once the new VAT regulation is in place, become liable to two penalties, under both VAT and Intrastat regimes for failing to submit the Intrastat declaration (or for completing it inaccurately).

Commentary—*De Voil Indirect Tax Service* **V5.276**, **V5.345**.

4 March 2008. HMRC Brief 14/08

Animal rescue charities – VAT liability of the sale of abandoned dogs and cats

This brief explains the VAT liability of the sale of abandoned animals by a charity following the Tribunal decision in the case of Gables Farm Dogs and Cats Home [*Gablesfarm Dog and Cats Home* VTD 20519].

BACKGROUND

Gables Farm Dogs and Cats Home is a charity that rescues lost, unwanted and homeless cats and dogs many of which are subsequently sold to new owners. It receives unwanted cats and dogs from owners as well as strays and abandoned animals given by local authority dog wardens, the police, and members of the public.

Subject to certain conditions the sale of donated goods by a charity is zero-rated and HMRC's view was that only animals given to the home by their original owners could be regarded as "donated" within the terms of the legislation.

The Tribunal found that the charity took steps to return genuinely lost animals to their owners and those it offered for re-homing had been deliberately abandoned. In these circumstances the animals given to the charity by the local authority, the police and members of the public were donated and therefore zero-rated when sold.

HMRC POLICY FOLLOWING GABLES FARM DOGS AND CATS HOME

HMRC are not appealing the Tribunal's decision and accept that charities selling animals in similar circumstances should zero-rate their supplies.

MAKING CLAIMS FOR PAST SALES

Charities that have accounted for and paid VAT on sales of animals that are now considered to be zero-rated may submit claims for overpaid tax to their Local Business Advice Centre. All claims are subject to the relevant time limits and unjust enrichment provisions.

More information about making claims can be found in VAT Notice 700/45 "How to correct VAT errors or make adjustments or claims" and Business Brief 28/04.

FURTHER INFORMATION

For further information and advice, please contact our Charities Helpline on 0845 302 0203.

Commentary—*De Voil Indirect Tax Service* **V4.261**.

11 March 2008. HMRC Brief 16/08

Valuation of imported goods: Customs valuation declarations and general valuation statements

This Revenue and Customs Brief announces our plans to introduce changes to current procedures that require a valuation declaration form C105 or C109 to be completed by importers or their agents.

BACKGROUND

EC Regulations require that a declaration of particulars, relating to the customs value, shall accompany the customs entry made in respect of imported goods. The C105 is an official form on which the importer, or their agent, records information about the valuation of the imported goods in a single consignment for customs duty and import VAT purposes. Importers are required to provide a completed valuation declaration of particulars with their customs entries when the value of the imported goods exceeds a threshold limit of £6,500.

The C109 is a numbered document, the details of which are quoted on entry documents and used instead of individual valuation declarations for a period not exceeding three years.

REVISED PROCEDURE

So that you do not have to routinely provide information about your importations, we are relaxing the requirement for a valuation declaration to be completed for 99 per cent of all import entry declarations. In future, importers will only be required to complete a valuation declaration on request, for example in respect of import declarations examined by our officers on a post-importation audit.

The new procedure will also mean that there will be no need to complete and register General Valuation Statements, Form C109.

The changes will be introduced on 1 April 2008.

Further information can be found in Customs Information Paper (08)19.

1 April 2008. HMRC Brief 19/08

New penalties for errors in returns and documents

INTRODUCTION

This brief explains how the new penalties will affect our customers and their advisers.

HM Revenue & Customs (HMRC) inherited a confusing variety of penalty charging powers. The new penalties are one of the first pieces of cross cutting legislation designed to make the tax system simpler and more consistent. It follows consultation with our customers and other interested parties during the Review of Powers, Deterrents and Safeguards.

The legislation aims to help those who try to comply, and come down hard on those who don't. The clear messages for customers are that:

- if they take reasonable care when completing their returns they will not be penalised;
- if they do not take reasonable care, errors will be penalised and the penalties will be higher if the error is deliberate;
- disclosing errors to us early will substantially reduce any penalty due.

TAXES AFFECTED

The new penalties are for errors on returns and documents initially for VAT, PAYE, National Insurance, Capital Gains Tax, Income Tax, Corporation Tax and the Construction Industry Scheme.

For these taxes, it applies to returns or other documents for tax periods starting on or after 1 April 2008 that are due to be filed on or after 1 April 2009. The legislation is Schedule 24 of Finance Act 2007.

WHEN CAN A PENALTY FOR INACCURACY BE CHARGED?

Two conditions must be satisfied before we can charge a penalty.

1. The document given to HMRC must contain an inaccuracy that leads to:
   - an understatement of the person's liability to tax;
   - a false or inflated statement of a loss by the person;
   - a false or inflated claim to repayment of tax;
2. The inaccuracy must be careless, deliberate or deliberate and concealed.

A penalty can also be charged where, in the absence of a return, we issue an assessment which is too low and the person does not take reasonable steps to tell us of the under-assessment within 30 days of the date of the assessment.

HOW IS THE PENALTY CALCULATED?

There is no penalty if a person takes reasonable care but submits an incorrect return. However, if the person later discovers the error but does not take reasonable steps to tell us about it, the inaccuracy will be treated as careless.

The penalty percentages are applied to the additional tax due as a result of correcting the error (known as the potential lost revenue). There is a different measure of potential lost revenue where the error results in an overstated loss:

- the penalty is up to 30 per cent of the potential lost revenue if the error is careless;
- the penalty is up to 70 per cent of the potential lost revenue if the error is deliberate;
- the penalty is up to 100 per cent of the potential lost revenue if the error is deliberate and the person conceals it.

The penalty chargeable where tax has been under-assessed because of the customer's failure to send us a return is 30 per cent of the potential lost revenue.

HOW CAN PENALTIES BE REDUCED?

There can be a substantial reduction in the level of penalty charged for unprompted disclosure of errors. A disclosure is unprompted if it is made at a time when the person making it has no reason to believe that HMRC has discovered, or is about to discover, the error.

Further reductions can be given based on the quality of the disclosure. The more a person tells, helps or gives access to HMRC the more the penalty may be reduced.

To calculate the reduction for disclosure we will consider three elements of disclosure. To what extent is the customer?

- telling HMRC about their error;
- helping HMRC work out what extra tax is due;
- giving HMRC access to their records to check their figures.

The reductions are made because we want to encourage people to come forward when they think there is a problem with their tax affairs, or they have not met a requirement.

REASONABLE CARE

Each person has a responsibility to take reasonable care. But what is necessary for each person to meet that responsibility has to be viewed in the light of their abilities and circumstances.

For example, we would not expect the same level of knowledge or expertise from a self-employed and unrepresented individual as from a large multi-national company. We expect a higher degree of care to be taken over large and complex matters than simple straightforward ones.

Every person is expected to make and keep sufficient records for them to provide a complete and accurate return. A person with simple, straightforward tax affairs needs to keep a simple system of records, which are followed and regularly updated. A person with larger and more complex tax affairs will need to put in place more sophisticated systems and maintain them equally carefully.

We believe it is reasonable to expect a person who encounters a transaction or other event with which they are not familiar to take care to check the correct tax treatment or to seek suitable advice. We expect people to take their tax seriously.

SOME PENALTIES MAY BE SUSPENDED

Suspension is intended to support those who try to meet their obligations by helping them to avoid penalties for inaccuracies in the future.

Only a penalty for failing to take reasonable care can be considered for suspension. Suspension conditions will be agreed and set and if they are met the penalty will be cancelled. If they are not met the penalty becomes payable. The period of suspension can be for up to two years.

For example, if a careless inaccuracy is due to poor record-keeping one of the conditions of suspension could be that specified improvements are made to the way records are kept. This will help the customer avoid future errors.

We will consider the taxpayer's general compliance behaviour, the level of disclosure and the nature of the inaccuracy before deciding whether to suspend the penalty.

OTHER TAXES

The 2008 Finance Bill makes provision to extend the new penalties to cover incorrect returns for the other taxes and duties HMRC administer. We expect the new provisions will apply for periods commencing on or after 1 April 2009 where the return is due to be filed on or after 1 April 2010 – see Budget Notice 96.

MORE INFORMATION

Please check the Frequently Asked Questions (FAQs) and the technical guidance in the Compliance Handbook on [www.hmrc.gov.uk/about/new-penalties/index.htmIssued 1 April 2008].

22 April 2008. HMRC Brief 24/08

Land and buildings – new VATA 1994 Sch 10 including changes to the option to tax

This Brief announces the introduction of a new Schedule 10 to the VAT Act 1994 that becomes effective from the 1 June 2008 following the announcement in Budget Note 79 at Budget 2008.

BACKGROUND

Schedule 10 to the VAT Act 1994 deals primarily with the option to tax supplies of land and buildings and was introduced following the European Court's ruling that the UK had to tax the construction of non-domestic buildings. Following a series of amendments needed to block various avoidance schemes; this legislation has become increasingly more complex to follow. The new Schedule 10 has been rewritten in the Tax Law rewrite style, which greatly improves the layout of the legislation as well as simplifying the language.

In addition, in 1995 changes were made to Schedule 10 that allowed revocation of an option to tax 20 years after it had been made. This means the first options eligible for revocation will take place in 2009. This new legislation therefore also includes the rules for revocation and also some changes necessary for its smooth operation. Finally, in line with suggestions received from business, the new legislation includes several changes designed to facilitate business.

During its development, this new legislation has been subject to two public consultations in 2004 and 2005 and legislation was introduced in the Finance Act 2006 to enable the existing Schedule 10 to be replaced by statutory instrument. A further, limited consultation on the initial drafts of the proposed legislation took place in August 2007 with all those who replied to the earlier public consultations.

WHAT IS BEING PUBLISHED?

In addition to a Treasury Order being laid containing the new Schedule 10, we are also publishing an Information Sheet 03/08 which includes guidance for the changes, together with the tertiary legislation (elements of the guidance which have the force of law). This document also includes destination and derivation tables to help business navigate its way around the changes.

An update to Public Notice 742A "Opting to tax land and buildings", to include the material in the Information Sheet, will be issued within two months.

LEGISLATIVE CHANGES

The following areas have changed or are new:

- new rules for relevant associates;
- introduction of certificates to disapply an option to tax for buildings to be converted into dwellings and land supplied to housing associations;
- introduction of disapplication of the option to tax for intermediaries supplying buildings to be converted into dwellings etc;
- revised definition of occupation, including a new exclusion for automatic teller machines;
- introduction of a new way to opt to tax (a real estate election) which does not require individual notifications of each option (see other changes section below);
- extension and changes to the cooling off period;
- automatic revocation of an option to tax after six years if no interest has been held in a property during that time;
- introduction of rules governing the revocation of an option to tax after 20 years;
- provision that in future, an option to tax applies to both the land and buildings on the same site – with a special transitional rule for existing options;
- a new ability to exclude a new building and land within its curtilage from an option to tax;
- new appeal rights;
- repeal of legislation concerning the developer's self supply charge and developmental tenancies (Item 1(*b*) of Group 1 of Schedule 9 to the VAT Act 1994) and also co-owners of land (section 51A of the VAT Act 1994);

EXPLANATION OF THESE CHANGES

All the Schedule 10 changes are fully explained in Information Sheet 03/08 which includes guidance on each change together with tertiary legislation where appropriate. New forms which will have the force of law will be produced before 1June, to support and allow the smooth operation of the new rules.

OTHER CHANGES

At present, a small number of taxpayers, typically large taxpayers, have what has become known as a global option to tax. This option to tax is effectively an option on the whole of the UK, and is typically expressed as follows:

> "I opt to tax the whole of the UK" or more commonly "I opt to tax all the land I currently own and all that I acquire in the future".

While there is no problem with retaining these global options, HM Revenue & Customs (HMRC) has in some cases, by concession, allowed the cooling off period to apply to each property as it is acquired. Under the normal rules, the cooling off period can only apply to the option to tax itself and so should expire three months after the option was made (this will be extended to six months from 1 June 2008). Because of the introduction of the new real estate election, this concession will be withdrawn with effect from 31 July 2009. This should allow sufficient time for those with a global option to decide whether to retain it without a cooling-off period in future, or to convert their global option into a new real estate election.

FURTHER INFORMATION

Further information can be obtained on HMRC's website or through the National Advice Service (NAS) on Tel 0845 010 9000.

Information Sheet 03/08 providing guidance and further detail is available and will supersede or compliment existing guidance as appropriate. A new Notice 742A "Opting to tax land and buildings" and new guidance will be available as soon as possible.

Commentary—*De Voil Indirect Tax Service* **V4.115.**

20 May 2008. HMRC Brief 27/08

Interpretation of Article 13 of the Principal VAT Directive: "bodies governed by public law" and "special legal regime"

HM Revenue and Customs has reconsidered its interpretation of the terms "bodies governed by public law" and "special legal regime" in the context of article 13(1) of the Principal VAT Directive (Directive 2006/112/EC) ("article 13(1)") as well as the application of this provision.

Our current interpretation is based on the decisions in the Court of Session's judgment in *Edinburgh Telford College (ETC)* [2006] CSIH 13 XA 18/05; XA 22/05, [2006] STC 1291, the High Court's judgment in *Riverside Housing Association (Riverside)* [2006] EWHC 2383 (CH), [2006] STC 2072 and the decision of the VAT and Duties Tribunal in *The Chancellors, Masters and Scholars of the University of Cambridge (Cambridge University)* LON/05/0958 (VTD 20610).

This Revenue & Customs Brief explains HMRCs' current thinking on the matter. While the Brief is of immediate interest to further and higher education providers, it may be relevant to other bodies as well.

BACKGROUND

1. Legal position

Under article 13(1), "states, regional and local government authorities and other bodies governed by public law" are not regarded as taxable persons when they engage in activities as "public authorities". Case law has confirmed that such public bodies engage as public authorities when they undertake their duties under a legal regime which applies to them and not to other bodies (a "special legal regime"). This is subject to certain mandatory exclusions and competition criteria.

This provision therefore only applies to the types of body specified, and only in the circumstances when they engage as public authorities. In any other circumstance the normal VAT rules apply.

2. ETC

ETC is a further education college providing further education as defined in the Further and Higher Education (Scotland) Act 1992 (amended by the F&HE (Scotland) Act 2005) and is funded by the Scottish Education Funding Council.

ETC argued that, when it provided further education courses for which it charged fees, it did so as a "public authority" within the meaning of article 13(1) so that it should not be treated as a taxable person in respect of that activity—taking the provision of such education outside the scope of VAT. There was no dispute over courses which are wholly funded through grants paid by the Scottish Further Education Funding Council which are outside the scope of VAT as the grant funding is not consideration for any supply either to the funding provider or to the students.

The Court of Session agreed with ETC, finding that the College's activities were undertaken under the umbrella of a special legal regime deriving from the Further & Higher Education (Scotland) Act 1992, the Scottish Further Education Funding Council (Establishment) (Scotland) Order 1998 and implemented in the funding agreement between the Scottish Further Education Funding Council and the College. The essence of the dispute was whether (as ETC argued) it is necessary to make judgements based on the wider legal regime governing the management and conduct of an activity, or (as HMRC argued) to focus solely upon the legal regime governing the delivery of a particular service. Although cases must be examined in the light of their own facts and on their own merits, HMRC accept that it is necessary to consider the wider legal regime.

The question of whether or not ETC was a body governed by public law was not considered by either the VAT and Duties Tribunal or the Court of Session because HMRC had accepted that the College was such a body. However, the High Court decision in Riverside has led HMRC to reconsider its interpretation of what is meant by a "body governed by public law" for the purposes of article 13(1) and to revise its policy in this area as set out below. This policy change will be reflected in changes to the current guidance on the meaning of a "body governed by public law" which is currently to be found at paragraph 3.7 of V1–14.

3. Riverside

Riverside is a large social housing provider registered with the Housing Corporation as a "Registered Social Landlord" (RSL). So far as is relevant hereto, Riverside argued that its activities were non-business on the basis that it was a body governed by public law for the purposes of article 13(1) and that the Housing Corporation rules, to which RSLs must adhere, amounted to a special legal regime. That contention was rejected by the Tribunal and the High Court.

Even though Riverside was subsidised by Government funds and required by statute to adhere to certain rules applying to RSLs, its supplies of social housing were nevertheless held to be made in the course of business.

In referring to article 13(1), the Tribunal stated that: "The provision clearly contemplates government organisations which are institutions of a democratic state and the European jurisprudence on the topic shows that the concept of a public body is to be narrowly construed ...... It is in my view clear from the legislation itself, interpreted in accordance with the jurisprudence of the Court of Justice, that the 'other bodies' contemplated by the article are those of a kind similar to government bodies, carrying out quasi-governmental functions, of which examples might be the Financial Services Authority and the Housing Corporation itself, with organisations such as the Institute of Chartered Accountants when undertaking its regulatory role. Riverside, by contrast, does not have a regulatory or similar role; it is itself the subject of regulation. It is a private sector organisation which happens to undertake functions on behalf of the state, but that does not make it a public body".

BODY GOVERNED BY PUBLIC LAW

In the light of the decision in Riverside, HMRC have concluded that the term "body governed by public law" in article 13(1) is narrow in application. HMRC consider that a body will only satisfy this criterion if it is a public sector body which forms a part of the UK's public administration, such as a government department, a local authority or a non-departmental public body. Article 13(1) is not intended to enable other bodies to claim special treatment merely because they have delegated powers, are regulated in some way by the State, are funded by public money or are subject to certain specific rules in the pursuit of their activities.

This view has recently been endorsed by the VAT and Duties Tribunal in the Cambridge University case.

Accordingly HMRC no longer accept that the generality of FE and HE providers are bodies governed by public law as defined in article 13(1).

A number of FE and HE bodies have sought to rely on article 13(1) to support an argument for entitlement to zero-rating under Group 5 of Schedule 8 and/or reduced rating under Schedule 7A to the VAT Act. FE and HE bodies should be aware that HMRC do not agree that such bodies can assume that they fall within this provision: rather it is necessary to examine the facts of each case separately.

Further, HMRC are of the view that, even were a body to come within article 13(1) in respect of a particular activity, that would serve only to take supplies in respect of that activity outside the scope of VAT and would not affect the liability of supplies made to that body.

Commentary—*De Voil Indirect Tax Service* **V2.108**.

30 May 2008. HMRC Brief 28/08

Land & buildings – announcing a new revised Notice 742A "Opting to tax land and buildings and associated forms and certificates"

This brief announces a new revised Notice 742A "Opting to tax land and buildings and the publication of a number of new forms and certificates".

BACKGROUND

1. Following consultation, a new Schedule 10 to the VAT Act 1994 (which deals with the option to tax of land and buildings), comes into effect on 1 June 2008. In addition to being re-written in a more simplified style to improve the understanding of the legislation, the new Schedule 10 also introduces the right for businesses to revoke an option to tax. This includes necessary changes to facilitate revocation and a few minor additional changes requested by business.

WHAT IS BEING PUBLISHED?

2. On 1 June 2008, we are publishing on our website a new revised Notice 742A. This revised notice replaces the March 2002 version and its three updates and also consolidates Information Sheet 03/08 which detailed the changes following the introduction of the new Schedule 10. Information Sheet 03/08 is withdrawn from 31 May 2008.

3. In addition, we are publishing a series of new and updated forms and certificates dealing with the option to tax (again available on our website). These forms and certificates, like the clearly marked boxed text in notice 742A, are tertiary legislation and have force of law. The use of these forms and certificates is therefore compulsory although HMRC will, until further notice, continue to accept notification of an option to tax (form 1614A) in a different format (subject to **all** of the same required information being provided).

OTHER CHANGES

4. We are grateful for the comments received from business on Information Sheet 03/08 and the new legislation. We have taken the opportunity in the revised Notice 742A to make some minor changes to clarify the guidance and tertiary legislation. The changes we have made to what was shown in Information Sheet 03/08 are as follows:

- the identifying letter for each piece of tertiary legislation (boxed text) has been changed to fit within the structure of the new notice;
- in Box E – the valuation condition – we have made the time when the 10 year period ends clearer;
- in Box G – all conditions – we have made it clearer that consideration must be given not only to the opter but also to any relevant associate of the opter and includes two additional explanatory notes to explain what 'connected' and 'relevant associate' means;
- in Box G – the 20 year condition – we have removed the confusion surrounding the words 'had effect';
- in Box K – we have made it clear that the time of notification is the time the Real Estate Election is made;
- in paragraph 8.1.4 of the revised Notice 742A, we have made it clearer that permission for revocation within the six month cooling-off period can only be considered if the taxpayer has met conditions a) to e) in paragraph 8.1.2 but fails to meet the condition in Box F.

18 June 2008. HMRC Brief 29/08

Learn how your clients can avoid penalties

We have published a learning package (http://www.hmrc.gov.uk/about/new-penalties/NPA/HTML/NPA_menu.html) to help agents and taxpayers understand the new penalty regime.

This package, published on our website www.hmrc.gov.uk, is also being rolled out to 28,000 of our staff.

The module takes less than half an hour to complete and provides an overview of the new system.

It will help advisers understand the potential impact on their clients. During this financial year they have the opportunity to help their clients identify and correct potential errors and weaknesses in their systems before the new penalty regime starts from 1 April 2009.

THE NEW PENALTIES

The key points are:

- the new penalties are one of the first pieces of cross-cutting legislation designed to make the tax system simpler and more consistent;
- if taxpayers take reasonable care to get their tax right, we will not penalise them, even if they make a mistake;
- if they do not take reasonable care, errors will be penalised and the penalties will be higher if the error is deliberate;
- telling us about errors, especially if this is unprompted, can substantially reduce any penalty due.

Most people take care to fill in their tax returns and documents correctly. We want to encourage that and help them get it right. It uses penalties to stop people who do not take care from gaining an unfair advantage.

TAXES AFFECTED

The new penalties are for errors on returns and documents initially for Income Tax, VAT, PAYE and NICs paid by employers, Capital Gains Tax, Corporation Tax and the Construction Industry Scheme.

For these taxes, it applies to returns or other documents for tax periods starting on or after 1 April 2008 that are due to be filed on or after 1 April 2009. The relevant legislation is Schedule 24 of Finance Act 2007.

This year's Budget proposed to extend the new penalties to almost all the taxes we collect – see Budget Notice 96 – http://www.hmrc.gov.uk/budget2008/bn96.pdfMore information.

In addition to the learning module, our internet page for new penalties, has frequently asked questions, a leaflet, and technical guidance, which are updated. There is an email address for queries.

HMRC Brief 19/08 also explains in more detail how the penalties work.

19 June 2008. HMRC Brief 30/08

Partial exemption: launch of consultation

This Revenue and Customs Brief article announces the launch of a consultation on ideas to simplify the VAT partial exemption rules to reduce compliance costs for businesses. The consultation invites comments and suggestions on the three partial exemption areas identified as simplification priorities by businesses:

- standard method;
- *de minimis* rules;
- Capital Goods Scheme (CGS).

It also invites comments on possibly combining partial exemption and business/non-business calculations.

Partly exempt businesses and their representatives are encouraged to participate to help cut compliance costs. Further information on partial exemption is available in Public Notice 706 "Partial Exemption".

BACKGROUND

VAT on costs relating to taxable supplies is recoverable, whereas VAT relating to exempt supplies is normally irrecoverable. A business that incurs VAT on costs relating to taxable and exempt supplies is partly exempt and must apply the partial exemption rules to calculate how much VAT it can recover.

There are around 140,000 partly exempt businesses including financial service providers, property companies, educational organisations, charities, gaming operators and undertakers. Around 120,000 of these, mainly smaller-sized businesses, operate the standard method, which is a simple turnover-based calculation set out in law.

Around 100,000 small partly exempt businesses benefit from being able to recover VAT relating to exempt supplies that is deemed insignificant under the *de minimis* rules. This is meant to relieve small businesses of the burden of restricting VAT relating to exempt supplies.

Some expenditure on capital items, mainly relating to land and buildings, falls within the CGS. This requires businesses to review the extent to which capital items are used in making taxable supplies for a period of up to ten years, making adjustments to previously recovered VAT where necessary. Most large businesses incur expenditure on capital items.

CONSULTATION

The consultation was launched on 19 June with publication of the consultation document on the HMRC website. Businesses and representative bodies are invited to suggest ways to simplify partial exemption and comment on a number of ideas for simplification. Responses from smaller-sized businesses and their representatives that regularly perform partial exemption calculations are particularly encouraged as they are likely to be affected most and have most to contribute. With this in mind, technical and legal content has been kept to a minimum. The consultation will end on 30 September 2008.

FURTHER INFORMATION

If you have any queries please contact Patrick Wilson on 020 7147 0595 or by email Patrick Wilson [see HMRC website for email form].

Commentary—*De Voil Indirect Tax Service* **V3.461**.

27 June 2008. HMRC Brief 31/08

Set off where right to claim overdeclared tax is transferred

BACKGROUND

A new clause has been introduced into the Finance Bill currently before Parliament. The purpose of the new clause is to close off a potential avoidance opportunity that has arisen as a result of a recent judgment of the Court of Appeal.

In *Revenue & Customs Comrs v Midlands Co-operative Society* [2008] All ER (D) 121 (Apr), the Court held that a right to make a claim for overpaid or overdeclared VAT can be transferred, assigned or sold. Prior to this judgment, HM Revenue & Customs (HMRC) had taken the view that only the person who had overpaid or overdeclared the VAT was entitled to make a claim to recover it. Where a person makes such a claim HMRC are required to set-off against it any outstanding liabilities of the claimant.

The avoidance opportunity arises because there is no provision under current law for HMRC to set-off the liabilities of the person who originally overstated the VAT liability ("the original creditor") if the claim for the VAT overpaid or overdeclared is made by somebody else ("the current creditor"), as a result of the transfer of the right to make a claim. As a consequence, by transferring the right to make a claim, taxpayers can avoid the set-off procedures.

SET-OFF AND UNJUST ENRICHMENT

The new clause operates by putting the current creditor in the shoes of the original creditor for the purposes of setting off liabilities. It provides that, where the original creditor transfers the right to claim overpaid or overdeclared tax to the current creditor, the latter will not receive any more from HMRC than if the original creditor had made the claim.

Whilst the Midlands judgment concerned VAT, it has wider implications; the current procedure for claiming overpaid VAT is replicated for all of the indirect taxes administered by HMRC. The potential for avoidance therefore exists for all indirect taxes. We also consider that the avoidance opportunity may also exist in relation to claims for error or mistake relief for direct taxes.

The avoidance opportunity that arises as a result of this judgment is not restricted to set-off. HMRC has the power to refuse any indirect tax claim where it can show that meeting the claim would unjustly enrich the claimant, because the economic burden of the overcharged tax has been passed on to customers.

However, this defence against payment of a claim does not apply where the claimant was not the person who originally overpaid or overdeclared the tax being claimed. It is therefore possible for the original creditor to sidestep the unjust enrichment provisions by transferring the right to make a claim to another.

The new clause addresses this by again putting the current creditor in the shoes of the original creditor for the purposes of the unjust enrichment provisions. HMRC will be able to refuse to pay a current creditor's claim where they can establish that payment of the claim to the original creditor would have unjustly enriched that original creditor.

PRACTICAL EFFECTS OF THE NEW CLAUSE

The new clause does not make the current creditor liable for the debts of the original creditor. It simply ensures that the current creditor cannot receive a sum greater than the amount the original creditor would have received had they made the claim.

The new clause provides that the amount due from HMRC on a claim on a transferred right will be determined by first setting off the amount of the outstanding liabilities of the original creditor and then any liabilities of the current creditor. The set-off of the original creditor's amounts due to HMRC will discharge the obligations of the original creditor to HMRC and vice versa. Set-off will be of amounts still outstanding at the time when the claim is met.

A current creditor will be able to appeal to a Tribunal or to the Special Commissioners against a decision of HMRC to refuse to pay a claim in whole or in part. Any such appeal would be against the refusal to pay the claim or the decision to reduce it.

The provisions of the new clause will apply to all of the taxes (including excise) administered by HMRC. It will apply to all transfers of rights to make a claim for overpaid tax taking place on or after 25 June 2008.

Commentary—*De Voil Indirect Tax Service* **V5.159B**.

18 July 2008. HMRC Guidance Notes

HMRC set-off across taxes following Finance Bill 2008

THE POLICY

1.1 For many years HMRC has set-off repayments against outstanding debts within tax systems and between Income Tax and National Insurance Contributions (NICs). The judgment of Walker LJ in the case of *Mellham v Burton* [2006] STC 908 confirmed set-off as a normal business principle.

1.2 Set-off reduces costs for taxpayers and HMRC alike and reduces the number of payment transactions and non-productive contacts with HMRC. New legislation in the Finance Bill 2008 (Part 7 Chapter 5) now extends the principle of set-off across a wider range of debts administered by HMRC.

1.3 The new proposals also remove the need to seek authority from taxpayers before the set-off takes place. However, HMRC must still advise the taxpayer in writing what has been done.

CURRENT PROCEDURES

1.4 A great many set-offs already take place every day, within both direct taxes and indirect taxes. The vast majority of these reallocations take place automatically, supported by established procedures for reallocating payments clerically. Guidance is available to staff making set-offs from indirect to direct taxes and vice versa.

FROM NOW ON

1.5 HMRC may make a set-off at any time where an amount is due from and payable to HMRC for the same legal person or entity at the same time.

1.6 Where HMRC is obliged to set-off under specific legislation, these continue to take priority. Examples of such set-offs are for NICs, VAT, Landfill Tax, Aggregates Levy and Excise Drawback, and existing HMRC systems support these mandatory set-offs.

1.7 Going forward, set-off will be at HMRC's discretion or at the taxpayer's request. In particular, set off will mean that:

- Repayments are set only against established debts. "Established debt" is a quantified debt that is correctly payable either based on a return from the taxpayer or which has been assessed and either the appeal has been determined, or the period for appeal has passed.
- Payments are allocated using the framework of existing rules; where the aim is always to allocate to taxpayer's best advantage as outlined in DMBM240010 (www.hmrc.gov.uk/manuals/dmbmanual/DMBM240010.htm).
- Self Assessment (SA) repayments will still be set automatically against SA Payments on Account within the same parameters as they are now.
- Repayments assigned to charity under the SA Donate Scheme will continue to be made to that charity. Other assignments will be secondary to set-off.

1.8 There will be no monetary limit to the amount set-off, but HMRC may choose not to exercise set-off for small amounts if it is clearly uneconomical or unproductive to do so.

1.9 Ministers gave assurances about tax credits and child benefit in the Parliamentary debate on the Bill. HMRC will not use ongoing Tax Credit or Child Benefit awards to pay other tax debts. Where it comes to recovering overpayments arising from a Tax Credit or Child Benefit award, we will not disturb arrangements in place to recover the debt. And finally HMRC will only set other tax repayments against Tax Credit or Child Benefit overpayments when requested to do so by the customer.

1.10 Following Royal Assent, the process will operate largely as it does now with cases for set-off being identified as part of the normal day-to-day work. Set-off across taxes remains a manual process.

1.11 Except in very limited circumstances which are covered by guidance, HMRC will not hold up repayments where they are not already aware of a debt. When pursuing debts, HMRC staff will not in every case check for possible repayments unless they are aware that one is likely. However where staff discover that an overpayment and an outstanding debt exist, every effort should be made to set one against the other.

IMPACT ON THE TAXPAYER

1.12 Greater use of set-off will reduce costs for customers by reducing the number of payment transactions and the number of non-productive contacts. HMRC will no longer seek the authority of the taxpayer to set-off payments due and debts accrued. There is no formal appeal against set-off, but HMRC may consider a taxpayer's specific concerns where a set-off has been made. HMRC will always notify the taxpayer in writing that set-off has taken place.

IMPACT ON HMRC

1.13 The new legislation is expected to have little impact within HMRC generally as Debt Management and Banking will be operating largely within current business rules, and set-off will be managed from within current resources.

1.14 The main impact will be felt in setting-off some indirect tax repayments against direct tax debts.

24 July 2008. HMRC Brief 35/08

VAT exemption for fund management services

At Budget 2008, it was announced that the VAT exemption for fund management services would be amended with effect from 1 October 2008. The amending legislation, explanatory memorandum, and draft guidance have now been published on our website. This Revenue & Customs Brief provides some detail about the amendment and information for businesses wishing to submit claims for overpaid VAT in the light of these changes.

BACKGROUND

EU VAT law exempts "the management of special investment funds as defined by Member States". The UK interpretation of this was challenged and, following the ECJ judgment in *JP Morgan Fleming Claverhouse Investment Trust plc*, we accepted that closed-ended investment undertakings, such as investment trust companies (ITCs), should be defined for the purposes of the exemption.

The amendment gives effect to this judgment in UK law and, in particular, defines "closed-ended collective investment undertaking" by reference to certain criteria which must be satisfied. These are that:

- its sole object is the investment of capital, raised from the public, wholly or mainly in securities;
- it manages its assets on the principle of spreading investment risk;
- all of its ordinary shares (of each class if there is more than one) or equivalent units are included in the official list maintained by the Financial Services Authority pursuant to section 74(1) of the Financial Services and Markets Act 2000; and
- all of its ordinary shares (of each class if there is more than one) or equivalent units are admitted to trading on a regulated market situated or operating in the United Kingdom.

For further details of this, you may wish to refer to the draft guidance.

CLAIMS FOR OVERSTATED OR OVERPAID VAT

Although the amended law comes into effect on 1 October 2008, it represents the situation as it should have been since 1 January 1990 when the exemption was first introduced. There is no requirement to make adjustments in respect of supplies made prior to 1 October 2008. However, businesses which have accounted for VAT on fund management services which qualify for exemption under the amended legislation may wish to submit claims to us for output tax over-accounted for (see VAT Notice 700/45 "How to correct VAT errors and make adjustments or claims").

All adjustments or claims are limited to a three-year period (except those that are subject to the recent House of Lords judgments in *Michael Fleming (t/a Bodycraft)* and *Condé Nast Publications Ltd*—see HMRC Brief 7/08). Businesses must be able to produce evidence that they have accounted for VAT on the relevant services and must be able to substantiate the amount claimed. Subject to the three-year limitation period, any claim should also be for all prescribed accounting periods in which the error occurred. Should a claim not take into account all errors or all affected accounting periods, then we will seek to set-off amounts owed to us for these periods against amounts claimed in other periods.

We may reject all or part of a claim if repayment would unjustly enrich the claimant. More details on "unjust enrichment" can be found at part 14 of VAT Notice 700/45, referred to above. All claims for overstated or overpaid VAT will be dealt with in accordance with our Business Brief 28/04— "Correcting liability errors".

Commentary—*De Voil Indirect Tax Service* **V4.136H**.

25 July 2008. HMRC Brief 34/08

Partial exemption – retrospective claims for input tax by higher education institutions (HEIs)

This Revenue & Customs brief article sets out HM Revenue & Customs (HMRC) policy on retrospective claims by Higher Education Institutions (HEIs) that operated a Partial Exemption (PE) method agreed under the Committee of Vice Chancellors & Principals (CVCP) guidelines. This article takes account of the Tribunal decision in the cases of *Wadham College Oxford & Merton College Oxford* [VTD 20233]. It uses a number of specialist terms that are fully explained in Public Notice 706, "Partial Exemption".

BACKGROUND

Prior to 1997, when the CVCP guidelines were withdrawn, many HEIs chose to determine their recoverable input tax using a simplified partial exemption method described in the guidelines as the CVCP method. Recoverable input tax was calculated as a fixed percentage of the output tax payable on certain taxable supplies (known as tunnelled supplies). For some HEIs, the tunnels did not deal with all taxable supplies and these HEIs had the option to agree additional "tunnels" for any other supplies, or, if they preferred, to agree their own special method instead.

DISPUTE

In 2003, Wadham College Oxford & Merton College Oxford submitted retrospective claims for the period 1973 to 1994 on the basis that the CVCP method had not allowed them to fully recover the residual input tax they were entitled to on general overhead costs. We rejected the claims on the basis of the calculations made.

TRIBUNAL DECISION

In hearing the appeal, the Tribunal considered two issues in detail:

- whether the fixed percentages of the CVCP method gave credit for input tax incurred on general overheads used partly for tunnelled, taxable supplies;

– how to calculate any unclaimed input tax that related to additional taxable supplies not covered by the tunnels.

On the first point, the Tribunal concluded that the CVCP method provided credit for all the input tax they were entitled to in respect of the tunnelled, taxable supplies: both directly attributable and general overhead costs. So, unless the HEI made additional taxable supplies, not covered by the tunnels, then no further claim was due. On the second point, the Tribunal rejected both the appellants' proposed calculation and the method we put forward which included the values of all of the supplies of the HEI (including tunnelled supplies). The Tribunal invited both parties to reach agreement.

HMRC POLICY

We conclude that an HEI operating the CVCP method would only be entitled to claim further input tax if:

– it made taxable supplies not covered by the tunnels in the CVCP method;
– there was no agreement as to how input tax on these taxable supplies would be recovered.

Any entitlement to claim further input tax should be calculated using an appropriate methodology based on the use of the costs incurred.

SUBMITTING CLAIMS

The House of Lords decision in *Condé Nast* and *Fleming* established that the three-year time limit contained in regulation 29(1A) of the VAT Regulations 1995 cannot be applied in relation to input tax incurred, but not yet deducted, in accounting periods ending before 1 May 1997. Claims in respect of those accounting periods may be made at any time until 31 March 2009 (see HMRC Brief 7/08 published on 20 February 2008 and Clause 116 of the Finance Bill 2008 [FA 2008 s 118]).

HEIs that operated a method based on the CVCP guidelines and who made taxable supplies not covered by the partial exemption method may now wish to make claims in line with this article and Budget Notice 78.

If HEIs are uncertain as to whether they have sufficient evidence to demonstrate that additional taxable supplies existed, they may wish to contact their local VAT office for assistance. Once it is established that they made taxable supplies not covered by the PE method, we will only accept claims based on reasonable estimations with supporting evidence.

Commentary—*De Voil Indirect Tax Service* **V6.222**, **V6.230**.

1 August 2008. HMRC Brief 38/08

Default interest and net errors of less than £2000

The current practice, described in paragraph 2.4 of Notice 700/43 (Default Interest) and note 4 on form VAT 652, of not charging default interest on net errors of £2000 or less separately notified to HMRC, will continue until the end of August 2008. However, following the decision in *Wilkinson v Commissioners of Inland Revenue* [2005] UKHL 30, [2006] STC 270, this practice is not considered lawful and will be withdrawn with effect from 1 September 2008. This means therefore that all error notifications (previously known as voluntary disclosures) requiring an assessment may be subject to a default interest charge, irrespective of the amount involved. However as before, *de minimis* net errors can continue to be corrected on a VAT return and will not attract interest.

Commentary—*De Voil Indirect Tax Service* **V5.108**.

6 August 2008. HMRC Brief 36/08

VAT treatment of charity challenge events

This Brief announces HMRC's revised guidance on charity challenge events, including those that qualify for the VAT Charity Fundraising Exemption.

BACKGROUND

Many charities use charity challenge events, for example running, walking and cycling events, to raise funds through sponsorship of the individuals who take part.

Following representations from the charity sector HMRC have been working with the sector to produce revised guidance to assist charities to determine the correct VAT liability of such events.

THE CHANGES

HMRC has now produced revised guidance with examples and a flowchart to be used with the guidance. The revised guidance is included as updates to Notice 701/1 "Charities" and Notice CWL4 "Fund-raising events: Exemption for charities and other qualifying bodies".

Update 1 to CWL4 revises the existing guidance in Section 3.15 of that Notice and cross-refers to the more detailed guidance now included as Update 2 to Notice 701/1 that introduces a revised section 5.9.4, cross-referenced to a new section 10 of that Notice.

TRANSITIONAL PROVISIONS

The guidance will have effect from 31 July 2008. However, HMRC is aware that some charities are likely to have signed contracts sometime before the events are due to take place. HMRC therefore accepts that where a contract for an event has been signed or negotiation with suppliers has started or the event has been publicised prior to the publication of the new guidance, charities can account for VAT using their previous procedures.

CLAIMS

Charities may wish to revisit their previous records and make claims for VAT incorrectly treated in respect of previous contracts.

More information about making claims can be found in VAT Notice 700/45 "How to correct VAT errors or make adjustments or claims" and Business Brief 28/04.

FURTHER INFORMATION

For further information and advice, please contact HMRC Charities Helpline on 0845 302 0203.

Commentary—*De Voil Indirect Tax Service* **V4.171**.

15 September 2008. HMRC Brief 44/08

Partial exemption—VAT adjustments when house builders let their dwellings before selling them

We have published an Information Sheet 7/08 which provides guidance, including worked examples, on the VAT implications when house builders decide to temporarily let their dwellings before selling them.

This Information Sheet is in response to recent enquiries from the house building sector and takes account of the High Court decision in the joined cases of *Curtis Henderson and Briararch* [1992] STC 732 which arose in the early 1990s. The key points to which the Information Sheet refers are:

- if you temporarily let a dwelling before selling it, you may affect the VAT you can recover on your costs;
- many house builders who temporarily let a dwelling will not be affected but you need to check this to avoid making VAT mistakes;
- there is an easy way to check if you are affected by applying what we describe here as a "simple check for *de minimis*".

If you fail this check, you may have to:

- adjust the VAT previously recovered on your submitted VAT returns;
- restrict the VAT to be recovered on your current and future VAT returns;
- both adjust your past VAT recovery and restrict your future VAT recovery.

If you need to adjust VAT previously recovered, exceptionally and if you prefer, you may be able to do this without contacting us.

FURTHER INFORMATION

Further information can be obtained from our website or through the National Advice service on Tel 0845 010 9000. Information Sheet 7/08 provides guidance and further detail is available and supersedes or compliments existing guidance, as appropriate.

Commentary—*De Voil Indirect Tax Service* **V3.461**.

17 September 2008. HMRC Brief 46/08

Court of Appeal decision in the case of Loyalty Management (UK) Ltd (LMUK) – HMRC position, pending outcome of appeal to the House of Lords

This brief confirms that the House of Lords has given us leave to appeal the decision of the Court of Appeal in the case of *Loyalty Management (UK) Ltd* C3/2006/1560 NCN: [2007] EWCA Civ 938 (LMUK). It also provides interim guidance, pending the outcome of our appeal, for those businesses affected by this decision.

BACKGROUND

LMUK runs the Nectar Loyalty Scheme, whereby members of the public can register as "Collectors" and accumulate Nectar points when they buy qualifying goods or services from "Sponsors". Collectors are able to exchange these points for rewards of goods or services with specific suppliers, known as "Redeemers". The Redeemer notifies LMUK of the number of points redeemed on a monthly basis and receives payment from LMUK for these points based on a contractually agreed amount for the points. This payment is described as the "Service Charge".

LMUK considers that the Service Charge payment is consideration for "redemption services" supplied to it by Redeemers. It contends that these supplies of services are wholly standard rated and that the Redeemers should issue LMUK with tax invoices. LMUK regards the amounts charged as VAT on these invoices as its input tax. It accepts that the Redeemer makes a supply of the Reward goods or services to the Collector but only to the extent that the Redeemer receives monetary consideration from the Collector.

We view the payment of the Service Charge by LMUK as third party consideration for the supplies of reward goods and services by the Redeemers to the Collectors, not as consideration for the supply of redemption services to LMUK. As a result, none of the VAT charged by redeemers is recoverable by LMUK as its input tax as the supplies have not been made to LMUK but to the Collector.

The Court of Appeal found that, on the facts of the case, there is a taxable supply of redemption services by redeemers to LMUK in respect of which LMUK is entitled to input tax credit. The payment made to the Redeemer by LMUK was held to be consideration for those services. The Court confirmed that all such payments from LMUK to Redeemers were consideration for fully standard rated supplies (redemption services).

We have appealed the decision to the House of Lords, who gave leave and decided to refer the matter to the European Court of Justice. It will be some while before the final outcome of this litigation is known.

OUR GUIDANCE ON TREATMENT OF SUPPLIES AND CLAIMS PENDING THE OUTCOME OF OUR APPEAL TO THE HOUSE OF LORDS

The Court of Appeal decision represents the law as it currently stands. Therefore, Redeemers, although not party to the litigation, are nonetheless affected by it. Redeemers need to ensure that the treatment of the Service Charge accords with that decision, and that LMUK can benefit from the decision.

As we do not agree with the Court of Appeal's reasoning and have appealed to the House of Lords, we will continue to proceed on the basis of our view of the law in relation to all parties, including LMUK. This is consistent with Notice 700/45 "How to correct VAT errors and make adjustments or claims", section 8 and paragraph 8.6 in particular.

If our appeal fails, corrective action, Notice 700/45 "How to correct VAT errors and make adjustments or claims", as per paragraph 8.7, will apply.

Redeemers are obliged to account for output tax due on the value of the full consideration received from LMUK. Where this is not done, we will seek to assess the amounts of output tax due, subject to the usual time limits. Redeemers thus affected may wish to make protective claims for the additional VAT due, in the event that our appeal is ultimately successful.

LMUK are entitled to reclaim input tax on output tax charged to it by Redeemers to the extent that such claims are supported by the proper evidence, in which case we will ensure assessments are in place to protect our position pending the outcome of our appeal.

Redeemers – supply of rewards for no consideration

Since the consideration paid by LMUK is currently seen to be for redemption services, rewards are being supplied by Redeemers to Collectors without consideration or, where the collector pays cash in addition to points, for partial consideration.

The Court's view was that when payment for the "reward" was partly cash (from the Collector) and partly points, the supply was to the Collector to the extent he paid for it. Therefore, the decision does not affect supplies of rewards by redeemers to Collectors for partial consideration.

However, our view is that, where the supply by a Redeemer of a reward of goods is made wholly for points, and the redeemer is entitled to input tax deduction, the Redeemer is making a supply of those goods (under Schedule 4(5) to the VAT Act 1994). VAT will be due, subject to the normal business gift rules. Notice 700/7 "Business Promotion Schemes covers the treatment of gifts".

Where Redeemers have not and/or do not account for output tax due on these gifts, we will protectively assess for any output tax arising subject to the usual time limits pending the outcome of the litigation. Where Redeemers do, or have, accounted for output tax due on these gifts, they may wish to make protective claims in the event that our litigation is ultimately successful.

Treatment of similar loyalty schemes

The Court of Appeal's decision was based on the specific facts of the case. Therefore, we will continue to look at claims for similarity on a case-by-case basis. It is our view that, until the LMUK litigation is finally concluded, it is not clear on what basis other schemes might be seen as materially similar for VAT purposes.

Consequently, if any other loyalty scheme promoter has claimed or taken an input tax deduction in relation to payments it has made for goods or services provided to members of the scheme by a third party, for example, Redeemer/Supplier, we will disallow such a claim and invite an appeal to the VAT and Duties Tribunal against that decision. Where we see that there might be some similarity with the situation in LMUK, we will make an application to stay the Tribunal proceedings, pending the final outcome of our appeal in LMUK.

As a consequence of a promoter claiming input tax deduction which we have disallowed as third party consideration, we will look at the situation of the third party suppliers of rewards in those schemes and protectively assess against the eventuality that the payments are for services akin to redemption services in the LMUK case. The position of supplies of rewards for no consideration will be considered for protective assessment. In that case, those affected may wish to make protective claims in the event that our litigation is ultimately successful.

For further help or advice, please contact the National Advice Service on Tel 0845 010 9000 or Tel 0845 000 0200 (text phone).

Commentary—*De Voil Indirect Tax Service* **V3.118, V3.409**.
Note—See also HMRC Brief 60/08, issued on 17 December 2008.

1 October 2008. HMRC Brief 48/08

Exemption for fund management services

Changes to the VAT exemption for fund management services from 1 October 2008 were announced at this year's Budget in BN74. The Value Added Tax (Finance) Order 2008 (SI 2008/1892) was laid in July to effect these changes.

Following further representations and consultation with stakeholders, the Order has been replaced to clarify the scope of certain of the changes and to introduce a *de minimis* provision. These amendments concern fund management services in respect of "recognised overseas schemes" which are collective investment schemes established outside the UK, but are "recognised" by the Financial Services Authority in order for them to be marketed within the UK.

The first change concerns funds which are constituted as "umbrellas" containing a number of distinct sub-funds. In such a case, only management services provided in respect of each sub-fund marketed to UK investors are exempt. This follows the policy originally described in the draft guidance, now updated, and this is now made clear in the amended legislation.

The second change introduces a *de minimis* provision, whereby the management of a recognised overseas scheme (or each sub-fund if an umbrella), which is not for the time being marketed in the UK, and has never been marketed in the UK, or has less than 5 per cent of its shares or units held by, or on behalf of, UK investors falls outside the VAT exemption.

The Value Added Tax (Finance) (No 2) Order 2008 makes these changes and the draft guidance has been updated pending its inclusion in the guidance manuals [see HMRC website at http://www.hmrc.gov.uk/budget2008/vat-fund-management-guidance.htm].

Commentary—*De Voil Indirect Tax Service* **V4.139G**.

17 October 2008. HMRC Brief 52/08

VAT on fuel used for propelling private pleasure craft and private pleasure flying

The reduced rate of VAT will continue to apply to supplies of fuel oil, gas oil and kerosene used as fuel for propelling private pleasure craft and kerosene used as fuel for private pleasure flying after 31 October 2008. This rate applies even though the derogations allowing reduced or nil excise duty rates have expired.

BACKGROUND

The reduced rate of VAT applies to supplies of fuel oil, gas oil and kerosene, which are used for domestic or charity non-business purposes, provided that the goods benefit from a rebated rate of excise duty. This includes supplies of not more than 2,300 litres, which are deemed to be supplied for domestic use.

However, from 1 November 2008:

- heavy oil (mainly red diesel, which is a gas oil) used as fuel for propelling private pleasure craft
- kerosene (avtur) used as fuel for private pleasure flying

will effectively attract the full rate of excise duty (see HMRC Briefs 49/08 and 50/08). To enable the reduced VAT rate to continue, the excise duty criterion will be removed from these particular supplies.

LEGISLATION

The VAT (Reduced Rate) (Supplies of Domestic Fuel or Power) Order 2008 (SI 2008/2676) comes into effect on 1 November.

FURTHER INFORMATION

Further information can be obtained from our website or through the National Advice service on Tel 0845 010 9000. VAT Notice 701/19 "Fuel and power" will be updated in due course.

Commentary—*De Voil Indirect Tax Service* **V4.406**.

22 October 2008. HMRC Brief 53/08

EC Sales lists

This article publicises a new requirement that businesses provide us with EC Sales Lists for certain taxable supplies of services from 1 January 2010. This requirement affects all UK businesses that make taxable supplies of services to business customers in other EU countries where the customer is required to account for VAT under the reverse charge procedure.

BACKGROUND

A package of changes to the EC VAT system was agreed by EU Finance Ministers in December 2007 and adopted in February 2008. The changes will modernise and simplify the current rules relating to cross-border supplies of services and to the recovery of VAT on purchases made in other EU countries. The changes will take place between 1 January 2010 and 1 January 2015 and we will consult on the UK implementing legislation later this year. The package includes:

- changes to the rules on the place of supply of services for Business-to-Business (B2B) and Business-to-Consumer (B2C) transactions
- a requirement to complete EC Sales Lists for supplies of taxable services to which the reverse charge applies
- the introduction of an optional One Stop Scheme for B2C supplies of telecoms, broadcasting and electronically supplied services
- the introduction of an electronic VAT refund scheme
- enhanced Administrative Co-operation between Member States to support these changes

ACTION REQUIRED NOW

This brief is only concerned with the second item above. Currently EC Sales Lists are only required for B2B intra-EC supplies of goods. However, from 1 January 2010 EC Sales lists will also be required for intra-EC taxable supplies of services to which the reverse charge applies. They will not be required for:

- supplies which are exempt from VAT according to the rules in the Member State where the supply takes place
- B2B supplies where the recipient is not VAT registered
- B2C supplies

We wish to ensure that UK businesses are fully aware of this requirement so that they can start considering what arrangements or systems they may need to put in place to gather the information needed to complete EC Sales Lists, particularly if these are, or will need to be, electronic systems that will require change. At the present time we anticipate using the same form that is used for reporting goods (VAT 101) and to require the following data:

- country code
- customer's VAT Registration Number
- total value of supplies in sterling
- an indicator will also be required to identify services

Under the VAT Package legislation that was adopted in February, from 1 January 2010 businesses will have to submit EC Sales Lists for taxable supplies of services subject to the reverse charge on a quarterly basis. However, Member States are currently discussing a European Commission anti-fraud proposal which includes a provision that from 1 January 2010 all EC Sales Lists should be submitted on a monthly basis. We have received a number of comments from UK businesses objecting to the introduction of a monthly requirement in respect of supplies of services. We are feeding those responses into the European discussions and we will report the outcome of the negotiations as soon as we are able.

We will be discussing the above changes with software developers and will issue further detailed information on this and other aspects of the VAT package as we are able. In the interim, any queries on this Revenue & Customs Brief or the VAT package in general should be made by email – vat.package@hmrc.gsi.gov.uk.

Commentary—*De Voil Indirect Tax Service* **V3.233, V3.425**.
Note—See also HMRC Brief 2/09, 26-1-09 (VAT package and anti-fraud measures implementation update).

28 October 2008. HMRC Brief 54/08

New zero-rated dwellings – whether arrangements are abusive

1. This brief is for house builders who have built or are building new dwellings with the intention, when they are completed, of selling either the freehold interest or a long lease of over 21 years (at least 20 years in Scotland) in each of the properties.

2. Several such house builders have sought guidance on whether HM Revenue & Customs (HMRC) considers certain transactions involving the supply of new dwellings to be abusive. This brief identifies those situations that HMRC considers not to be abusive.

BACKGROUND

3. The first grant of a major interest (freehold sale or a long lease of over 21 years (at least 20 years in Scotland)) of a new dwelling is zero rated. This allows the house builder to recover all the input tax they have incurred in connection with the development (subject to the normal rules about blocked input tax) and to sell the dwelling without adding VAT.

4. In the current economic climate, many house builders have found that they are unable to sell new dwellings. For most, this leaves them with the choice of leaving them empty until they find a buyer, or renting them out in the short term while they wait for the housing market to recover in order to sell them.

5. Revenue & Customs Brief 44/08 and Information Sheet 07/08 (both published on 15 September 2008) provide guidance for house builders renting out new dwellings on short term lets while retaining the intention to sell a major interest in the dwellings when the markets recover. As those documents explain, short term lets of this kind can sometimes give rise to adjustments of input tax previously recovered.

APPROACH MADE

6. HMRC have been asked about the possibility that house builders might, in advance of any short term lets, make the first grant of a major interest in the completed dwellings to a connected person, who would not be a member of a VAT group with the house builder. This zero-rated sale might remove the need for the kind of adjustments explained in Information Sheet 07/08. The suggestion put to HMRC is that the connected person would then rent out the properties until such a time as they could be sold. The rentals would be exempt and not give rise to input tax deduction on ongoing costs including the costs of the eventual sale (for example estate agency and legal costs). However, deduction of the VAT associated with the original construction would have been secured. We have been asked whether we would see this arrangement as abusive from a VAT point of view. This brief does not attempt to address any other tax consequences that might flow from such transactions or any commercial or legal issues.

IS THIS INTENDED STRUCTURE ABUSIVE?

7. For a scheme to be abusive, it must (as well as having the essential aim of saving VAT) produce a result contrary to the purpose of the VAT legislation. HMRC believe that Parliament intended that the construction of new dwellings should be relieved from VAT. The first grant mechanism introduced by Parliament does achieve this but it relies on the assumption that there will always be a grant of a major interest around the time the dwelling is complete, so ensuring deduction of VAT on all appropriate costs.

8. In HMRC's view, the arrangement set out in paragraph 6 above does not produce a result contrary to the purpose of the legislation, but rather ensures that a transaction of the kind Parliament envisaged will actually take place at the appropriate time. That view rests on the assumption that the purpose of the zero rating provisions associated with new dwellings is to relieve fully from VAT the provision of precisely that – new dwellings. That means that all the costs (save on blocked goods such as washing machines, carpets etc – see Section 13 of Notice 708 Buildings and Construction for more details) associated with producing a new house should either not carry VAT, or carry VAT that is deductible in full.

9. However, whilst we believe it is the policy objective that new dwellings should be zero rated, that does not extend to other goods or services that might be packaged up with the supply of a dwelling. HMRC consider it abusive when a major interest is granted with an essential aim of deducting VAT on costs such as repair, maintenance and refurbishment of dwellings (other than for remedying defects in the original construction) the relief of those kinds of costs not falling within the policy objective as we see it. These types of arrangements are likely to be challenged.

SUMMARY

10. In short, HMRC agree that the arrangement outlined in paragraph 6 above is one that they would not see as abusive and so would not seek to challenge. However, if the VAT deducted goes beyond the VAT that would normally be deducted in relation to the supply of the new dwelling (for example VAT on costs such as repairs, maintenance or refurbishment, which is not normally deductible) such arrangements are likely to be challenged as abusive.

FURTHER INFORMATION

11. For further information and advice contact the HMRC VAT and Excise helpline on Tel 0845 010 9000.

Commentary—*De Voil Indirect Tax Service* **V4.233, V4.238.**

8 December 2008. HMRC Brief 57/08

Excess charges in non-local authority car parks

This Revenue & Customs Brief explains our revised policy on VAT on excess charges and other penalties levied in non-local authority car parks and what you should do if you have incorrectly accounted for VAT on such charges. Certain excess charges which have to date been regarded as further consideration for a taxable supply of parking are now regarded as outside the scope of VAT.

BACKGROUND

Business Brief 19/02 explained our policy on the VAT treatment of excess charges in off-street car parks following the tribunal case of *Bristol City Council* (LON/99/261, [VTD 17665]) ("BCC"). The Tribunal had concluded that excess charges levied by the Council in its off-street car parks were outside the scope of VAT because they were levied pursuant to the Road Traffic Regulation Act 1984 and were not part of the contract entered into between the driver and the council. We accepted that the decision would also apply to other local authorities operating off-street car parks under the same statutory framework.

However, where off-street car parks were not operated by local authorities, we considered that excess charges would normally be subject to VAT because they arose under the terms of the contract between the driver and car park operator. This followed the rationale adopted by the Tribunal in the case of *J G Leigh t/a Moor Lane Video* (LON/89/83X [VTD 5098]), which concerned additional charges for videos held by customers beyond the agreed period of hire.

REVISED POLICY

We have recently reconsidered that policy in the light of new legal advice and have concluded that, in the case of BCC, the Tribunal's decision was founded as much upon the contractual relationship as the statutory regime. Therefore, we now accept that there is a difference between the situation where the contract under which parking is supplied allows for an extension of the original terms, for which additional consideration will be payable, and the situation where the driver is not permitted to extend the original terms and a penalty for breach of contract ensues if this in fact happens. Thus, where a car park operator makes an offer of parking under clear terms and conditions, setting punitive fines for their breach, the fines constitute penalties for breaching the contract, rather than additional consideration for using the facilities. Consequently, they are outside the scope of VAT. Since the same contractual relationships arise between drivers and local authority car park operators as arise between drivers and other car park operators, we have also concluded that the VAT treatment of excess charges will be the same for **all** car park operators.

EXCESS CHARGES NOT SUBJECT TO VAT

The penalty charges that will no longer be subject to VAT are those that are levied where a driver is in breach of the terms of the contract with the car park operator. The commonest situations where a driver may be in breach of the contract are:

- no parking ticket on display;
- underpayment;
- overstaying purchased parking time;
- returning within a specified time;
- parking outside marked bays;
- parking in bays set aside for disabled drivers or parents with children.

EXCESS CHARGES SUBJECT TO VAT

Where the terms and conditions make it clear that the driver can continue to use the facilities after a set period upon payment of a further amount without being in breach of the contract –

for example, no charge for an initial three hours parking but £70 if that period is exceeded – then the payment will be consideration for use of the facilities and subject to VAT.

EXCESS CHARGES RETAINED BY CONTRACTORS

Some parking site owners contract out the management and operation of their parking sites and allow the contractor to retain all or part of the penalties collected. Any such payments retained by the contractor will constitute further consideration for their services supplied to the parking site owner and are subject to VAT.

WHAT NEXT?

If you believe that you have accounted for VAT when you should not have done, you may make a claim for the overpaid tax in line with the provisions of Notice 700/45: "How to correct errors on your VAT Return". Please note that such claims will be subject to "capping" and may also be subject to the unjust enrichment provisions.

Commentary—*De Voil Indirect Tax Service* **V2.201**, **V3.104**.

17 December 2008. HMRC Brief 60/08

Loyalty Management (UK) Ltd

VAT: Court of Appeal decision in the case of Loyalty Management (UK) Ltd—further clarification of HMRC position, pending outcome of appeal to the House of Lords

In October 2007 HM Revenue & Customs (HMRC) lost the *Loyalty Management (UK) Ltd* [2007] All ER (D) 66 (Oct) (LMUK) case C3/2006/1560, concerning the VAT treatment of payments for Nectar scheme rewards, in the Court of Appeal. The Court of Appeal decided that the payments made by LMUK to Nectar scheme 'Redeemers', known as 'service charges', were for taxable supplies of 'redemption services' by the Redeemer to LMUK. LMUK is entitled to claim input tax on the amounts it has paid to Redeemers, so long as that decision remains in effect.

We were granted leave to appeal to the House of Lords, which have referred the matter, as well as the appeal in *Baxi Group Ltd*, to the European Court of Justice without full hearing. Our position, pending the resolution of the litigation, was set out in Revenue & Customs Brief 46/08 issued on 17 September 2008, and included guidance to Redeemers, that they should treat the service charges as consideration for supplies by them to LMUK, and so issue tax invoices to LMUK for VAT on these amounts. They may submit protective claims, if appropriate, in case we succeed in the litigation in the end.

This brief clarifies that Redeemers in the Nectar scheme who are not correctly treating the supplies in accordance with the guidance set out in Revenue & Customs Brief 46/08 must now do so from 17 September 2008, which is the date that the brief took effect. Any guidance given to any Redeemer prior to that date, which was different to the guidance in that brief, is withdrawn from the date of Revenue & Customs Brief 46/08. The treatment advised in that brief will continue in effect until further notice.

For further help or advice, please contact the National Advice Service on Tel 0845 010 9000 or 0845 000 0200 (text phone).

Commentary—*De Voil Indirect Tax Service* **V3.118, V3.409**.

23 December 2008. HMRC Brief 61/08

Intrastat—changes from 1 January 2009

This Revenue and Customs Brief explains how businesses trading with other EU Member States could be affected by changes from 1 January 2009 and also gives advance notification of a further change that is expected to take place from 1 January 2010.

CHANGES IN INTRASTAT THRESHOLDS FROM 1 JANUARY 2009

- The exemption threshold is increased from £260,000 to £270,000;
- The delivery terms threshold is increased from £14,500,000 to £16,000,000.

BACKGROUND

Community legislation requires the UK to collect information on intra-EU trade in goods for statistical purposes and sets minimum requirements for the quantity of trade covered. Currently EU Member States are required to collect data on a minimum of 97 per cent of the value of their EU trade in goods within the Intrastat system. These requirements determine the level at which the exemption threshold is set in the UK. The same threshold is applied independently to arrivals (intra-EU imports) and dispatches (intra-EU exports).

Those traders with an annual intra-EU trade in goods above the specified exemption threshold are required to provide monthly statistical returns (Intrastat Supplementary declarations).

Community legislation also requires the UK to collect information to enable the accurate calculation of statistical value. This requirement determines the level at which the delivery terms threshold is set in the UK.

Traders with an annual EU trade above the delivery terms threshold are required to supply additional information relating to delivery terms on their Intrastat statistical returns.

The revised thresholds are implemented by Statutory Instrument 2008/2847.

CHANGES FOR 2010

HM Revenue & Customs (HMRC) is committed to the simplification of the Intrastat system with the aim of reducing the burden on business while maintaining the quality of the trade statistics provided to users.

We have been working with other Member States over the past year on a revision to the current Community legislation that will allow us to remove some small traders from the Intrastat system.

We expect the revised regulation to be published at the end of this year or early in 2009 and will provide further details in due course.

FURTHER INFORMATION

Further information on trade statistics can be found online at www.uktradeinfo.com or by phoning uktradeinfo Customer Services on 01702 367485.

7 January 2009. HMRC Brief 63/08

The decisions of the VAT Tribunal in the cases of the Rank Group plc, in respect of the supply of Mechanised Cash Bingo (MCB) and gaming machine takings

BACKGROUND

This Brief concerns the VAT liability of MCB and gaming machine takings, following the VAT Tribunal decisions in the cases involving the Rank Group.

In a decision dated 27 May 2008[1] the Tribunal decided that the VAT treatment of MCB provided by Rank was in breach of fiscal neutrality and consequently these supplies should be exempt from VAT.

In a further interim decision dated 19 August 2008[2], the Tribunal found that there had been a prima facie breach of fiscal neutrality in the VAT treatment of Rank's gaming machine takings and that these should have been treated as being exempt from VAT before 6 December 2005, when UK law was changed to make all gaming machine takings taxable. A second Tribunal hearing to hear further aspects of this issue is to be held in October 2009.

HM Revenue & Customs (HMRC) has appealed against both decisions and the High Court hearings are expected to be held in March or April 2009.

Notes—[1] *The Rank Group plc*, LON/06/1243, VTD 20668.
[2] *The Rank Group plc (No 2)*, LON/06/875, VTD 20777.

IMPLICATIONS

VAT: Our view of the law remains unchanged in that VAT is and always has been properly due on supplies of MCB and on the takings of gaming machines. Therefore, businesses should continue to account for VAT on such supplies.

VAT Tribunal decisions are only binding on the specific case heard, as it is only the facts of that specific case that are considered in full. In line with HMRC's normal policy, as we continue to maintain that our view of the law is correct, no other businesses are affected by the decisions and therefore no claims for alleged overpayments of VAT by other operators can be considered until the conclusion of this litigation.

Bingo Duty: In order to protect our position in law, 'protective assessments' of bingo duty will be raised to safeguard revenue. These assessments will be issued to reflect the fact that if there is no VAT to deduct from bingo receipts, then additional bingo duty is due These assessments will not be enforced unless HMRC loses on the substantive VAT liability issue.

Commentary—*De Voil Indirect Tax Service* **V3.264, V4.131.**

26 January 2009. HMRC Brief 2/09

VAT package and anti-fraud measures implementation update

Adoption of EU Council directive and regulation relating to EC Sales Lists and time of supply of services (update to Revenue & Customs Brief 53/08)

On 16 December 2008, the EU Council adopted a Directive 2008/117/EC and a Regulation (37/2009) relating to EC Sales Lists (ESLs) and the time of supply of services subject to the reverse charge.

The implementation date for these new measures is 1 January 2010. This Revenue & Customs Brief gives some information about how these measures will be implemented in the United Kingdom. It should be read in conjunction with Revenue & Customs Brief 53/08.

The main changes relate to the submission of ESLs. In principle, the new Directive provides that these should normally be submitted monthly, but it allows Member States to offer their businesses certain options. The United Kingdom intends to implement these as follows:

- ESLs relating to services may be submitted quarterly, relating to calendar quarters.
- From 1 January 2010, ESLs relating to goods may be submitted quarterly, relating to calendar quarters, provided that the value (excluding VAT) of supplies of goods to other Member States has not exceeded £70,000 in any of the previous 4 quarters.
- A business entitled to submit quarterly ESLs for goods can continue to do so unless the value of supplies of goods to other Member States exceeds £70,000 (excluding VAT) per quarter from 1 January 2010 to 31 December 2011 or £35,000 (excluding VAT) per quarter from 1 January 2012 onwards.
- If a business exceeds the quarterly goods threshold by the end of the first or second month in a quarter, an ESL must be submitted at the end of that month, covering the month or months in that quarter. Lists must be submitted monthly from then.
- Once a business is on a monthly cycle, because it has exceeded the threshold in any quarter, it must continue to submit monthly ESLs for goods until the value of its intra-Community trade in goods has been below the threshold for five consecutive quarters – it may then revert to quarterly submission if its trade remains below the threshold.
- A business required to submit monthly ESLs relating to goods may still submit ESLs relating to services quarterly.
- Any business may submit ESLs for goods and/or services monthly, if it wishes.

The other change to ESLs is that the time, within which both UK businesses and then HM Revenue & Customs (HMRC) must carry out their respective ESL obligations, has been reduced from three months to one. We intend to discuss this issue with business to explore how implementation can balance the needs of business and HMRC. Our current thinking is that businesses that submit paper ESLs would have 14 days from the end of the (last) month to do so. This period would be extended to 21 days for electronic submission of ESLs.

Finally, the Directive makes changes to the time of supply of services rules for services supplied to businesses in another Member State where the customer has to account for VAT under the 'reverse charge'. The changes are:

- the time of supply of such services will be the earlier of when the service is completed or when payment is made.
- for continuous supplies of services, the time of supply will be linked to the end of each billing or payment period, but where no invoice or other accounting document is issued or payment made during the year, the time of supply will be the end of each calendar year.

These changes will determine not only when the customer has to account for VAT under the reverse charge when the service is received from a supplier in another Member State, but also when a supplier is required to include the transaction on an ESL.

We intend to discuss implementation of the new time of supply rules with businesses, to understand their current accounting practices and their concerns about the changes likely to be needed. Our objective in implementing the rules will be to do so in a way which is as easy as possible for businesses to apply, and minimises additional burdens, while remaining consistent with the provisions of the Directive.

A consultation document covering changes to the place of supply rules for services being phased in from 1 January 2010 and the introduction of a requirement to complete ESLs for reverse charge services was issued on 22 December 2008. The deadline for comments on the draft legislation contained in the consultation paper is 13 February 2009. We will be holding consultation seminars in Central London on 2 and 6 February 2009 and intend to cover the issues arising from the changes set out in this Brief at those events. If you are interested in attending please email vat.package@hmrc.gsi.gov.uk.

Commentary—*De Voil Indirect Tax Service* **V3.233**, **V3.425**.

19 February 2009. HMRC Brief 5/09

Marks & Spencer Plc Judgment: VAT claims and unjust enrichment

Marks & Spencer Plc v CRC [2009] UKHL 8 – Judgment of the House of Lords – VAT claims made before 26 May 2005 no longer subject to unjust enrichment

BACKGROUND

Where a business has accounted for too much VAT and makes a claim to recover it, HM Revenue & Customs (HMRC) can refuse to pay that claim if they can show that payment would unjustly enrich the claimant. However, until the law was changed in 2005, this unjust enrichment defence could only be used against a specific category of claimants. This meant that it was possible that a claim by one business could be refused whilst a similar claim from another business could not.

Marks & Spencer fell within the former category and challenged the discriminatory nature of the legislation.

THE HOUSE OF LORDS JUDGMENT

In light of the House of Lords judgment, issued on 4 February 2009 [*Marks and Spencer plc v Revenue and Customs Commissioners* [2009] All ER (D) 39 (Feb), [2009] STC 452], the unjust enrichment defence will no longer be used against any claim made before 26 May 2005 (the date on which the law was amended to remove the discrimination referred to above).

CLAIMS MADE BEFORE 26 MAY 2005

Claims made before 26 May 2005 that were refused by HMRC on the grounds of unjust enrichment and have still not been settled will now be paid, subject to verification. Claims where the unjust enrichment defence was not challenged or was upheld, in the courts, may be resubmitted for consideration, subject to the relevant time limits.

CLAIMS MADE ON OR AFTER 26 MAY 2005

As a result of the change in the law made in the Finance (No 2) Act 2005, which applies the unjust enrichment defence to all categories of claimants, the judgment of the House of Lords does not affect any claim made on or after 26 May 2005.

23 February 2009. HMRC Brief 6/09

Claims for retrospective application of Extra-Statutory Concession (ESC) 3.35

ESC 3.35 permits non-profit making membership bodies that supply a single package of benefits to their members to apportion their subscriptions to reflect the value and VAT liability of the individual benefits, without regard to whether there is one principal benefit.

A practical example is where the principal benefit of a membership subscription is standard-rated, but there are ancillary benefits which, if supplied in their own right, would be zero-rated and/or exempt. In such a case, the body may apportion the subscription to reflect the different elements, rather than treating the whole subscription as standard-rated.

HM Revenue & Customs (HMRC) is aware that some bodies have been using the ESC to rework previously submitted VAT returns, and have submitted claims for "overpaid" VAT. In our view, the ESC may not be used to make retrospective adjustments, as such returns were correct in law. HMRC will therefore reject any such claims.

In some cases the claims have alleged 100 per cent zero rating, due to the principal benefit being zero-rated. Such cases will be given due consideration by HMRC, provided the claim is based on the application of the law, as opposed to retrospective use of the ESC.

Commentary—*De Voil Indirect Tax Service* **V3.105**.

16 March 2009. HMRC Brief 10/09

Tribunals reform

This Revenue & Customs Brief outlines the new tax appeals system and HMRC's new internal review process, due to be implemented from 1 April 2009.

INTRODUCTION

From 1 April 2009 there will be a major change to the current system of tax tribunals. To coincide with this, HMRC is changing the way it handles disagreements about tax. The new review process will help provide a more consistent approach to the way we seek to resolve disputes with those who disagree with appealable tax decisions made by HMRC.

At the moment, there are three main tribunals which deal with appeals against HMRC decisions. From April, these tribunals will be abolished and replaced by a single Tax Chamber in the First-tier Tribunal which will consider all disputes and hear appeals in relation to both direct and indirect tax.

NEW TRIBUNAL

The Tribunals, Courts and Enforcement Act 2007 introduced two new bodies, the First-tier Tribunal and the Upper Tribunal. Over time most existing tribunal jurisdictions including the tax tribunals will be transferring into the new bodies. The new system went live on 3 November 2008. These new statutory bodies are administered by the Tribunals Service which is part of the Ministry of Justice.

Both First-tier and Upper Tribunals are divided into "chambers" where similar types of appeal are heard. On 3 November when appeals formerly heard by the Social Security Appeals Tribunal successfully transferred to the First-tier Social Entitlement Chamber.

Tax appeals will transfer to a new First-tier Chamber, to be known as the Tax Chamber, on 1 April. A right of appeal against decisions of the First-tier Tax Chamber will also be created to a new chamber in the Upper Tribunal to be known as the Finance and Tax Chamber.

The First-tier Tribunal will deal with the vast majority of appeals, apart from a very small number of the most complex appeals that will transfer to the Upper Tribunal at first instance. The Upper Tribunal will mainly deal with appeals against decisions of the First-tier Tribunal. Work within each tier of the tribunal will be organised into specialist chambers, one of which will deal with tax.

The reforms will affect everyone who disagrees with one of our tax decisions and may wish to have it reviewed, or to make an appeal. As part of the reforms, the General Commissioners and Special Commissioners of Income Tax, the Section 706/704 Tribunal and the VAT & Duties Tribunals will be abolished after 31 March 2009 and their existing functions will transfer into the new First-tier Tax Chamber.

Some straightforward appeals will in future usually be dealt with on paper without the need for HMRC or customers to attend a hearing.

Where a hearing is needed the Tribunals Service will arrange this. Most appeals will be heard at one of a national network of tribunal hearing centres.

INTERNAL REVIEW

To coincide with tribunal reform, our customers will be entitled to request an internal review of appealable tax decisions. This new legal right to a review will replace reconsiderations and mandatory reviews in indirect taxes (mandatory reviews will remain for decisions about the restoration of seized goods).

Reviews will be optional and will be done by a trained review officer, who has not previously been involved with that decision, who will be able to offer a balanced and objective view. In the vast majority of cases the review officer will be outside the immediate line management chain of the decision maker.

We must complete reviews within 45 days (unless another period is agreed with the customer). If customers do not want a review, or if they do not agree with the result of the review, they can appeal to the tribunal for a decision.

FURTHER INFORMATION

You can find out more about tribunals reform and internal reviews from the Tribunals Reform Project (http://www.hmrc.gov.uk/about/tribunals-reform.htm) and more about changes to the tax tribunals from the Tribunals Service website (http://www.financeandtaxtribunals.gov.uk/taxAppealsModernisation.htm).

19 March 2009. HMRC Brief 8/09

VAT staff hire concession

As announced at Budget 2008 the VAT Staff Hire Concession, which applies to supplies of staff by employment bureaux, is to be withdrawn from 1 April 2009. This brief is intended to remind affected businesses of its withdrawal and to set out the VAT treatment that should be applied from 1 April. VAT Information Sheet 03/09 issued on 19 March 2009 contains more detailed guidance.

The concession is set out in Part A of the Statement of Practice in Notice 700/34 "Staff" and in Business Brief 2/04. It enables businesses making supplies of their own staff to exclude from the value of their supply the remuneration element and any PAYE (Pay As You Earn), National Insurance Contributions, pension contributions and similar payments relating to the worker provided such payments are made directly to the worker by the hirer, or a payroll company separate from the employment business supplying the staff. Such employment businesses have thus charged VAT solely on their profit margin and not on the full value of their supply.

Parts B and C of the Statement of Practice in Notice 700/34 "Staff" are unaffected and will not be withdrawn on 1 April 2009.

Business Brief 10/04 allowed employment bureaux that did not fall within the conditions of the Staff Hire Concession, because they made supplies of staff using self-employed workers, to choose whether to act as agents or principals for VAT purposes until the review of the Staff Hire Concession was completed. As announced at Budget 2008, this concession will also be withdrawn from 1 April 2009.

From 1 April 2009, in line with normal VAT principles, businesses making supplies of staff must charge and account for VAT on the full value of their supply. The correct VAT treatment following withdrawal is as follows:

If you act as a principal (eg employment business) in making a supply of staff using either:

- your own employees (which includes a director of your company) engaged under a contract of services
- self-employed workers who make their supplies to you under a contract for services

then VAT will be due on the full value of the supply (not just the profit margin).

If you act as an agent in providing introductory services of finding employment for workers or workers for your client and the workers enter into a direct contractual relationship with the client, who pays them, then VAT is due on your intermediary service only (based on your commission received). Such supplies are unaffected by the Staff Hire Concession and so will be unaffected by its withdrawal.

If you are making a supply of services other than staff, for example, supplies of care services, then your supply may qualify for exemption from VAT. See Notice 701/57 "Health professionals" for more information and the qualifying criteria. If your supply is of services other than staff it is unaffected by the Staff Hire Concession and so will be unaffected by its withdrawal.

If you are unsure of the correct VAT treatment of your supplies you should consult Notice 700/34 "Staff" and Notice 701/57 "Health professionals". You may also contact our National Advice Service Helpline on Tel 0845 010 9000, by email: National Advice Service Helpline, or in writing at:

HM Revenue & Customs
National Advice Service
Written Enquiries Section
Alexander House
Victoria Avenue
Southend
Essex
SS99 1BD

Please include your VAT registration number and the name and address of your business in any correspondence. If you are not VAT registered please include your name and address.

Our Clearance procedure is also available in which we will give our view of the correct tax treatment of your transaction. You can use this procedure where you have demonstrated that there is material uncertainty and that the issue is commercially significant. For further guidance on this see "Clearance service for businesses—how to get certainty on significant business tax issues".

ACCOUNTING PROCEDURES AROUND 1 APRIL 2009

The normal time of supply (tax point) rules will apply. However, in respect of supplies spanning 1 April 2009, the Staff Hire Concession will be available to the extent that the service is performed prior to 1 April 2009. For example, if you raise an invoice or receive a payment on Friday 3 April, the concession will by then have been withdrawn. But you may, if you wish, account for VAT on the basis of the value of the services actually performed before and after the withdrawal of the concession, ie you may apportion the consideration for the services between:

- those services performed before 1 April, in respect of which the Staff Hire Concession is available;
- those services performed on or after 1 April, in respect of which the Staff Hire Concession will no longer be available.

Commentary—*De Voil Indirect Tax Service* **V3.221**.

19 March 2009. HMRC Brief 13/09

Leisure Trusts providing all-inclusive membership schemes

THE ISSUE

HMRC is amending its interpretation of the law and therefore its guidance on the VAT treatment of membership schemes allowing unlimited access to leisure facilities in a leisure centre. Businesses that will be most affected are community leisure centres that are run by non-profit making trusts. Supplies made by commercial organisations are not affected and remain taxable at the standard rate.

This brief supersedes the advice given in Revenue & Customs Brief 50/07.

BACKGROUND

Supplies of services closely linked with and essential to sport or physical education, in which an individual takes part, are exempt from VAT when supplied by an "eligible body" (essentially a non-profit making body not subject to commercial influence) as set out in the Value Added Tax Act 1994, Schedule 9, Group 10 (Sport, Sports Competitions and Physical Education). Previously, HMRC's view was that where a scheme offers, over a period, unlimited use of a variety of both taxable and exempt facilities, typically in return for a monthly or annual payment, there is generally a single supply of the standard rated right to use the facilities. However, following representations from the leisure industry and taking into account the comments made in the Court of Appeal in *Revenue and Customs Comrs v Weight Watchers (UK) Ltd* [2008] STC 2313 about the typical consumer, we no longer see the supply as a right to use the services but as being the supply of underlying services.

The Weight Watchers case indicated that it is appropriate to look at the transaction from the viewpoint of the typical consumer, rather than the supplier. The extent of the linkage between the relevant transactions must be considered from an economic point of view. So regarded, the question then is whether it would be artificial to split the transaction into separate supplies. If it would be artificial, then there will be a single supply and the predominant element from the viewpoint of the typical consumer, will determine whether the supply is exempt or standard rated.

REVISED APPROACH

VAT liability depends on the nature of the supply which has to be decided at the time the all-inclusive fee is paid. Where the supply is a single supply that would be artificial to split there can only be one overarching liability. In most cases, the typical consumer who purchases an all-inclusive package will have access to a range of facilities at the leisure centre. Usually most of these facilities would, if supplied individually, be exempt as "services closely linked with and essential to sport or physical education in which the individual is taking part', (for example use of the swimming pool, showers, changing rooms).Therefore, in cases where the predominant reason for purchasing an all-inclusive package is to use the range of available sports facilities, the single supply is exempt.

In some instances packages may include facilities that would be standard-rated if supplied on their own e.g. sauna facilities. However, providing that the predominant reason that the typical consumer purchases the package is to use the (exempt) sports services, the supply of the package is still exempt.

If the predominant reason a typical consumer purchases an all-inclusive package is to make use of standard rated facilities the single supply is standard rated.

EFFECTS OF THE CHANGE

The effect of this change is that non-profit making bodies, including leisure trusts which were previously charging VAT on their all-inclusive packages, will in the majority of cases have to treat them as exempt. If businesses make both exempt and taxable supplies they will be partly exempt and will have to apply the partial exemption rules to determine how much of the input tax incurred on their costs can be deducted. The partial exemption rules are set out and explained in Notice 706 "Partial Exemption".

Notice 701/45 "Sport" will be amended in due course.

CAPITAL GOODS SCHEME (CGS) ITEMS; THE EFFECT OF THE CHANGE

The CGS applies to buildings and some items of computer hardware. It adjusts input tax claimed on building related capital expenditure for any changes in use over a ten year period. It includes both purchases of buildings and subsequent capital expenditure such as refurbishments. If a business is transferred as a going concern (TOGC) and a building subject to the CGS is one of the assets transferred then the new owner must continue the adjustments. The CGS rules are set out and explained in Notice 706/2 "The Capital Goods Scheme".

After affected bodies begin treating their supplies as exempt there will be an apparent change of use from taxable to exempt. However, the policy change represents what the true liability always was, assuming that sports providers have not changed the way they operate. The CGS adjusts the true amount that was initially claimable ignoring any errors that may have occurred whether they can be corrected or not. Therefore, no significant CGS adjustments are likely provided that the way sports facilities are supplied has not changed since any capital expenditure was incurred. If you are concerned that the CGS may significantly affect you then please contact your local VAT office.

If sports providers acquired a CGS building asset as part of a TOGC then the CGS may require adjustments if the previous owner deducted and was properly entitled to deduct input tax on the item. This is likely if the previous owner was a Local Authority. If you are concerned that these circumstances may apply to you then please contact your local VAT office.

MAKING CLAIMS OR ADJUSTMENTS

The change described should be implemented from 1 April 2009 and there is no requirement to make adjustments in respect of supplies made prior to this date. However, where a business wishes to make a claim to HMRC for a repayment of output tax incorrectly accounted for, they may do so, subject to the conditions set out below, by using one of the following methods.

Claims for overpaid output tax must be net of any over-claimed input tax calculated under the partial exemption rules:

Claims can be made either by adjustment to the current VAT return or by submitting a written claim to HMRC.

An adjustment may be made to your current VAT return, but the value of the errors must not exceed the greater of either £10,000 or 1 per cent of the box 6 figure on the claimant's VAT return for the VAT return period of discovery, subject to an upper limit of £50,000.

Where the errors exceed the limits set out above, a written claim should be submitted to HMRC (in these cases the errors must not be corrected through the claimant's returns).

Details of where to send your claim can be obtained from update 2 to VAT Notice 700/45 "How to correct VAT errors and make adjustments or claims" from the HM Revenue & Customs National Advice Service on 0845 010 9000.

All adjustments or claims are limited to a three-year period or after 1 April 2010 a four-year period (except those that are subject to the House of Lords decisions in the cases of *Michael Fleming (t/a Bodycraft) v HMRC (Fleming)* and *Condé Nast Publications Ltd v HMRC (Condé Nast)* see Business Brief 07/08).

Businesses must be able to produce evidence that they accounted for VAT in the circumstances described above, and must be able to substantiate the amount claimed. Any such claims must be submitted by 31 March 2009. Should a claim not take into account all errors or all affected accounting periods, then HMRC will seek to set-off amounts owed for these periods against amounts claimed in other periods.

HMRC may reject all or part of a claim if repayment would unjustly enrich the claimant. More details on "unjust enrichment" can be found at part 14 of VAT Notice 700/45 "How to correct VAT errors and make adjustments or claims".

A notification to HMRC that a business intends making a claim in the future is not a valid claim. All claims for overstated or overpaid VAT will be dealt with in accordance with our Business Brief 28/04 "Correcting liability errors".

Where you are in any doubt about the correct treatment please contact the National Advice Service.

Commentary—*De Voil Indirect Tax Service* **V3.105**, **V4.161**.

20 March 2009. HMRC Brief 14/09

VAT repayment claims and statutory interest: treatment for the purposes of direct tax

BACKGROUND

A number of European Court of Justice Judgments in recent years have resulted in substantial repayments by way of overpaid VAT and Statutory Interest being made to traders for periods covering many years. HM Revenue & Customs (HMRC) has recently legislated to ensure that from 1 April 2009 VAT repayments arising from any "new mistake of law decision" by the courts will be subject to a four year cap (increased from three years with effect from 1 April 2009). However, traders have up until 31 March 2009 to submit claims for periods as far back as the introduction of VAT in 1973 and it is anticipated that significant repayments will be made. These claims for repayment are often referred to as "Fleming" claims.

Section 80 VATA 1994 (as amended by section 3 of the Finance (No 2) Act 2005) is the statutory provision which enables the majority of claims to be made for repayment of output tax overdeclared because of a mistake either of law or fact.

This brief is not intended to provide a definitive technical analysis of the treatment for direct tax purposes of amounts repaid. The circumstances and considerations vary dependent on the particular circumstances of each case. It does however summarise the department's fundamental position and approach for direct tax purposes, as it applies in relation to these repayments.

TRADING INCOME

It has been suggested by some that as a matter of legal principle, receipts of refunds of VAT credited to the profit and loss account are outside the scope of Corporation Tax. HMRC does not agree with this view, firstly because there is no legal authority in support of this assertion and secondly because what is being repaid is not VAT.

The financial accounts prepared at the time are commonly prepared on a VAT exclusive basis and therefore the original turnover and Case 1 profits were reduced by the excessive amount incorrectly paid over as VAT. The repayment of amounts in respect of VAT, originally wrongly declared, are simply returns to the taxpayer of amounts which would have formed part of the taxpayer's trading receipts.

The reality is that a trader has simply calculated a higher sale price to the customer, because of a mistaken view of the law at the date of the transaction. Having subsequently become aware of the incorrect view of the law at the time of the transaction and that the additional amount received from the customer is not VAT, then clearly the amount is a trade receipt in exactly the same way as if it had resulted from any other mistake e g giving the wrong change.

The repayments represent sums that arose from the sale of goods or services in the ordinary course of its trading activities. The fact that amounts were paid to (the former) Customs and Excise in the belief that they were output tax properly due on those supplies, does not alter their trading character for Case 1 purposes.

RECEIPT OF INTEREST

Statutory Interest received in respect of the repayments is interest for tax purposes. While the interest does not arise from any loan relationship as defined by section 81 Finance Act 1996 because it does not arise from the lending of money, section 100 operates to bring interest on money debts within the scope of the loan relationship rules. The period to which a payment relates is the period in which it would properly be recognised under Generally Accepted Accountancy Practice.

CURRENT ENQUIRIES

HMRC's view is that that the repayments and interest are demonstrably part of the taxable income of the business and therefore chargeable to direct tax as trading income and interest respectively. However, there are some businesses who are contending that the repayment and/or the interest are not taxable. HMRC view this as a priority compliance risk and will continue to challenge such cases in accordance with our Litigation and Settlement Strategy.

IDENTIFYING NON-COMPLIANCE

A co-ordinated project is now ongoing to ensure that all current and future non-compliance risk is identified and addressed in a consistent manner, with particular reference to "Fleming" claims. Where potential non-compliance is identified, an intervention will be undertaken to establish the necessary facts.

27 March 2009. HMRC Brief 15/09

Extra Statutory Concession (ESC) 3.5—Misdirection

ESC 3.5 Misdirection gave the view of HM Revenue & Customs (HMRC) of the circumstances in which they would regard themselves as bound by incorrect advice given to customers in respect of Value Added Tax (VAT) and Insurance Premium Tax (IPT).

HMRC are required by law to collect all the taxes, duties and levies under their care, but they have a limited degree of discretion in specific circumstances. In recent years, there have been a number of cases before the courts which have defined the circumstances in which HMRC can regard themselves as bound by incorrect advice. More information is available on the Internet "When you can rely on advice provided by HMRC". ESC 3.5 Misdirection is therefore no longer necessary because it has been overtaken by other published guidance.

HMRC will not accept any further claims under this ESC from 1 April 2009. Customers who think they have received incorrect advice from HMRC in respect of VAT or IPT should see the guidance above for further help, or contact the National Advice Service on Tel 0845 010 9000. There will be no change in service to our customers, as they will still be able to ask us to consider their case if they feel they have been wrongly advised by HMRC.

This does not affect customers who think they have over declared tax, as such cases will continue to be considered under the relevant sections of the Value Added Tax Act 1994, and Finance Acts 1994 and 1997.

Commentary—*De Voil Indirect Tax Service* **V1.274**.

31 March 2009. HMRC Brief 18/09

Implications to the Bad Debt Relief conditions as a result of the Tribunal decision in Times Right Marketing Ltd

This brief announces a change in the treatment of VAT Bad Debt Relief claims made when the net VAT due on a return has not been paid or has been partly paid.

It follows the VAT Tribunal decision in Times Right Marketing Limited (TRML) (In Liquidation) LON/2006/1376.

BACKGROUND

If you make supplies of goods or services to a customer and have not been paid you may be able to claim relief from VAT on your bad debts. In order to claim relief you will have to satisfy all the conditions set out in HM Revenue & Customs (HMRC) Notice 700/18, 'Relief for VAT on bad debts'. One of the conditions is that you must already have accounted for and paid VAT on the supplies you want to claim bad debt relief on.

TRML appealed against a decision by HMRC to reject a claim for Bad Debt Relief (BDR) on the grounds that they had not originally paid the output VAT due. The Tribunal found that the deduction of input tax from output tax due should be seen as in effect payment of that output tax.

IMPLICATIONS OF THE DECISION

We now accept that where a BDR claim is made, payment will be taken to have been made to the extent that output tax is covered by deductible input tax.

The following examples provide further clarification. Please note these examples do not necessarily cover all scenarios that could arise. The amount of BDR to be claimed is included in Box 4 of the supplier's VAT Return, in the VAT period which covers the date they fulfill the conditions to make a claim, or a later period, subject to the usual time limits. For illustrative purposes this figure is shown separately here. It is assumed that all other BDR conditions have been satisfied.

£120,000 is taken to be the amount of VAT on bad debts over six months old at the time of the 2009–08 return.

Example 1 – Supplier has not paid net tax due in any period

	03/08	**06/08**	**09/08**
	£	**£**	**£**
Output tax	200,000	250,000	225,000
Input tax	110,000	112,000	111,000
BDR (in Box 4)			30,000 *
Net tax due	90,000	138,000	104,000
Tax paid	Nil	Nil	Nil

*Allowable BDR in period 09/08 is £30,000 calculated as follows:

VAT related to bad debts on supplies made in period 03/08—£120,000

Less unpaid net tax due in period 03/08 90,000

Maximum 03/08 bad debts available for relief six months later in period 09/08 30,000*

The amount of 03/08 BDR reclaimable in 09/08 has been restricted to the excess of input tax over output tax due on non-bad debt supplies, i e £110,000 input tax – £80,000 output tax.

Example 2 – Supplier has partly paid period 03/08 by the time of submitting their 09/08 return

	03/08	**06/08**	**09/08**
	£	**£**	**£**
Output tax	200,000	250,000	225,000
Input tax	110,000	112,000	111,000
BDR (in Box 4)			50,000 *
Net tax due	90,000	138,000	84,000
Tax paid	Nil	Nil	Nil

*Allowable BDR claim in 09/08 is £50,000 calculated as follows:

VAT related to bad debts on supplies made in period 03/08 £120,000

Less unpaid net tax in period 03/08 70,000

Maximum 03/08 bad debts available for relief six months later in period 09/08 50,000*

The amount of 03/08 BDR reclaimable in 09/08 has been restricted to the excess of input tax over output tax due on non-bad debt supplies. £110,000 input tax – £60,000 (£80,000 – £20,000) output tax.

WHAT HAPPENS IF CHANGES OCCUR AFTER I HAVE MADE MY CLAIM, AS ABOVE?

Where BDR has been claimed on the basis of the interpretation of payment made as set out above, it is possible that the figures for tax paid or input tax due may change after the date of the claim. For example, as a result of additional payment of tax, or alterations to that period's input tax or output tax figures for the period by credit note or the correction of errors by voluntary disclosure or assessment.

In these circumstances the basis of the claim should be recalculated to see if the amount of BDR needs to be changed. If so, correction should be made on your next VAT Return, or if necessary by voluntary disclosure, subject to the normal time limits.

WHAT DOES THIS CHANGE MEAN?

This change in our policy only applies in circumstances relating to what constitutes paid for the purposes of claiming BDR. It does not alter the other conditions you need to satisfy before claiming BDR. It should be understood that BDR can only be reclaimed to the extent that the output tax has actually been paid. This brief clarifies what paid means. We will not be repaying in cash output tax that has not been paid to us in the first place on the original supplies. Revisions to HMRC guidance and Notice 700/18, 'Relief for VAT on bad debts' will be made in due course.

Taxpayers or their advisers who consider making retrospective claims for repayment of under-claimed BDR as a result of this brief are advised that normal BDR time limits apply. Claims must be made within three years and six months of either the date on which the consideration that was written off as BDR was due and payable or the date of the supply.

For further information on the matters covered in this brief or on BDR generally you should contact HMRC on 0845 010 9000.

Commentary—*De Voil Indirect Tax Service* **V5.156**.

1 April 2009. HMRC Brief 19/09

Partial exemption – changes to the standard method

This Revenue and Customs Brief article announces four changes to the partial exemption standard method that take effect from 1 April 2009.

1. in-year provisional recovery rate
2. early annual adjustment
3. use-based option for new partly exempt businesses
4. widening the scope of the standard method.

The changes are being made following responses to the consultation on ideas to simplify the partial exemption rules confirmed strong support for their implementation.

The first three changes are optional and businesses can benefit from them without seeking approval from HM Revenue & Customs (HMRC). Change four is compulsory and affects businesses that make:

- supplies of services to customers outside the UK
- certain financial supplies such as shares and bonds
- supplies made from establishments located outside the UK

FURTHER INFORMATION

Further information can be found in VAT Information Sheet 04/09 which supersedes or compliments existing guidance as appropriate. Legislation will shortly be published on the HMRC website.

Commentary—*De Voil Indirect Tax Service* **V3.461**.

8 April 2009. HMRC Brief 27/09

Changes to the Tour Operators' Margin Scheme

This brief publicises changes to be made to the Tour Operators' Margin Scheme in order to comply fully with EU law. The changes are to take effect from 1 January 2010.

INTRODUCTION

This brief publicises changes to be made to the Tour Operators' Margin Scheme (TOMS) in order to comply fully with EU law. The changes are to take effect from 1 January 2010.

BRIEF OUTLINE OF THE SPECIAL SCHEME FOR TRAVEL AGENTS

The special scheme for travel agents is a VAT accounting scheme and simplification measure for tour operators and other travel service providers based in the EU. Under the normal VAT rules, those businesses buying and selling various elements of their travel packages in different Member States would be liable to register and account for VAT in each of the Member States concerned. The special scheme enables tour operators to register in just the Member State in which they are established, rather than in all Member States where they provide travel services, thus significantly reducing their administrative burdens. Under the scheme, the supply of a travel package is treated as a single supply taxable at the standard rate of VAT, and operators account for VAT on their profit margin in the Member State where they are established, but are prevented from recovering input tax incurred on scheme purchases.

BACKGROUND

The European Commission has written to the UK raising concerns about aspects of the UK's operation of the TOMS and opining that the UK arrangements in respect of these issues were not fully compatible with the VAT Directive (2006/112 EC).

Following legal advice, the UK has accepted that aspects of the scheme were not implemented properly and gave a commitment to amend the TOMS, in order to comply with European law. These aspects concern:

- supplies to business customers for subsequent resale
- supplies to business customers for their own consumption and supplies of educational school trips
- use of market values in respect of in house supplies

Separately, the European Commission commenced formal infraction proceedings against eight Member States for their operation of the TOMS. This did not include the UK.

CONSULTATION

As the UK had no option but to make these changes, HMRC consulted informally with industry representative bodies, the JVCC and other professional bodies in the three month period ended 31 August 2008. The consultation, by necessity, was limited in scope and its purpose was to ensure that the changes are introduced in as business-friendly a manner as possible, with an appropriate transitional period. HMRC considered that 1 April 2009 would be a reasonable implementation date for the changes but, as a result of responses to the consultation, decided that 1 January 2010 would give businesses more time to prepare for the changes. HMRC were unable to announce these changes earlier as we had to seek some further clarification from the European Commission.

CHANGES TO BE MADE

Supplies to business customers for resale (the "opt in")

As a concession (set out in paragraph 3.2 of Notice 709/5), HMRC has allowed tour operators who generally engage in normal holiday sales to the travelling public but occasionally sell to other travel businesses for onward resale the option of accounting for tax on the latter in the special scheme. This was intended to ease the administrative difficulties that operators might otherwise incur in having to use the normal VAT rules to account for occasional supplies of travel services to other businesses.

The UK has had to accept that the VAT Directive refers to supplies made to the "traveller". The "traveller" is the person who consumes the travel, and so the scheme should not be used when the travel service is sold to a person other than the traveller, such as when supplies are made to business customers for resale. Those tour operators affected will have to change their practices from 1 January 2010 to account for the VAT due under the normal VAT rules. In some cases, this may give rise to a requirement to register for VAT in other Member States.

Supplies to businesses for their own consumption and the provision of school trips ("the opt out")

The UK includes travel services which are supplied to other businesses for their own consumption in the special scheme.

However, tour operators have been allowed to opt out of the scheme in respect of such supplies. This has meant that business customers have been able to recover VAT charged on those supplies subject to the normal rules. HMRC has also treated the provision of school trips as a non business activity for VAT purposes and allowed them also to be excluded from the special scheme, enabling local authorities to recover the VAT charged in relation to Local Education Authority schools.

The Commission has clarified that the term "traveller" should not be restricted to the physical person who consumes a travel package, but also covers legal persons that consume the travel package, for example, businesses which pay for employee travel, and the supply of school trips to local authorities. Accordingly, Article 3(3) of the Value Added Tax (Tour Operators) Order 1987 will be revoked with effect from 1 January 2010. This means that from that date businesses receiving supplies of travel services from tour operators will no longer be able to recover VAT on such supplies. Those LEA schools that previously took advantage of the concession set out at paragraph 3.4 of Public Notice 709/5 will no longer be able to recover VAT on UK school trips purchased from tour operators. There will be no change for trips organised directly by a school, such as day trips involving coach transport to a zoo or museum. Non LEA schools (including Grant Maintained and Foundation schools) and youth clubs or colleges were not entitled to claim the concession, and are unaffected by this change.

MARKET VALUES

The current UK TOMS calculation (as detailed in Notice 709/5) requires the margin to be apportioned with reference to the actual costs incurred by the operator in putting together the package. However, the European Court of Justice (ECJ) decision in the case of *MyTravel* (C-291/03) [2005] STC 1617 ruled that, where it is possible to establish an appropriate market value for that part of the selling price which corresponds to the in house supplies, this should be used to apportion the selling price between in house and bought in components. The margin can then be calculated on each of these elements, and the tax computation completed accordingly.

The Court also said, however, that the cost based method could be used where this accurately reflected the actual structure of the package. The ECJ did not elaborate on what it meant by this term but HMRC consider that, as the cost based method assumes a fixed percentage mark up across all elements of the package, the tour operator's package would also have to be on a fixed mark up basis to meet this criterion. If it is not possible to determine a market value, tour operators can continue to use the current cost based method.

The ECJ left it to the national tax authorities and, where appropriate, the Courts, to assess whether it is possible to identify the part of the package corresponding to the in house services on the basis of their market value and, in this context, to determine the most appropriate market. Whilst the concept of market values is complex, and it is not always easy to determine exactly what a market value is in this context, drawing from the various Court findings, it would appear that certain parameters should be taken into account when deciding whether it is possible to establish such a value:

- The market value (selling price) must be within the context of the tour operator's business, e g a tour operator could not use the price of a scheduled airline flight in determining a market value of the flight forming part of a package holiday.
- The market value must be on a like-for-like basis, i e it should be determined on the basis of the price of similar services supplied by the taxable person, and not forming part of a package. If the taxable person does not provide similar services, it may be possible to use the price of services provided by other taxable persons, provided that they can be shown to be comparable.
- Across the board averages may be used if correctly weighted and reviewed regularly.

It is clear from this that market values need to be considered on a case by case basis. Where such values are to be used, they will simply slot into the current calculation method at the appropriate point. The tertiary legislation setting out the market value calculation will be included in the revised Public Notice 709/5 in due course. In the meantime, it is attached in draft as an annex to this brief, together with some examples of calculations (at the 17.5% rate of VAT) using market values. Although the tertiary legislation is not yet in place, in the light of the European Court decision, businesses may of course choose to use market values now where appropriate.

TOMS CALCULATION EXAMPLE 1 ALL IN HOUSE SUPPLIES CALCULATED BY MARKET VALUE

Package price £1000

Being the price paid for the full package by the holidaymaker

In-house MV SR £300

Being the market value of STD rate in-house supplied included in the package.

Bought-in SR cost £75

Bought-in ZR cost £250

Being the cost of the bought-in supplies that form part of the package

Using the matrix

Post the £1000 to box M1 and the £300 to box M2 of the market value matrix.

This works through to £700 in Box M5 which is then posted to Box 1 of the main margin scheme calculation.

The £75 is then posted to Box 2 and the £250 posted to Box 3.

The rest of the boxes can then be calculated based on the information (above) that has now been posted.

MARKET VALUE CALCULATION (ANNUAL ADJUSTMENT)

This section has the force of law and is referred to in paragraphs xx

This section only applies to packages or parts of packages being apportioned by the market value of the in-house element of the package. On completion of all the steps M1-M5 you must then follow the steps in the cost-based calculation in section 9, taking forward the figures from this section as instructed

Step	Boxes requiring "raw data" entry are in white, boxes which "process" that data are in grey.	
	Calculate the value of sales of margin scheme packages	
M1	Total the VAT-inclusive selling prices of all your designated travel services and margin scheme packages supplied during the financial year including any that are not "market value" packages.	1000
	Working out the market value	
M2	Total the VAT inclusive market value of the standard-rated in-house supplies at M1—carry forward this figure to step 21 of section 9	300
M3	Total the VAT inclusive market value of the zero- rated and outside the scope in-house travel services at M1—carry forward this figure to step 26 of section 9	-
M4	Total the VAT inclusive market value of the in-house supplies at step M2 + step M3	300
	Working out selling value of designated travel services and non-market value in-house supplies.	
M5	Deduct the total at step M4 from the total at step M1—carry forward this figure to step 1 of section 9	700

COST-BASED CALCULATION (ANNUAL ADJUSTMENT)

This section has the force of law and is referred to in paragraphs.

This section applies to packages being apportioned by reference to the costs of the in-house element of the package, and imports the figures calculated by the market value method in section 8, where that method is used for all or some of the travel packages. Do not include values already entered in section 8 unless explicitly stated

Step	Boxes requiring "raw data" entry are in white, boxes which "process" that data are in grey.
	Working out the total sales of margin scheme packages

Step		
1	Bring forward the total calculated at step M5 of section 8. If Section 8 is not used then enter the VAT-inclusive selling prices of your designated travel services and margin scheme packages supplied during the financial year.	700
	Working out the purchase prices of margin scheme supplies	
2	Total the VAT-inclusive purchase prices of the standard-rated designated travel services included in the total at step 1.	75
3	Total the VAT-inclusive purchase prices of the non standard-rated designated travel services (supplies enjoyed outside the EU) included in the total at step 1.	250
	Working out the direct costs of in-house supplies. Steps 4 to 7 can be ignored where a market value is applied to all in-house supplies under section 8	
4	Total the VAT-exclusive direct costs to you of the standard-rated in-house supplies included in step 1. Add a percentage of that amount equivalent to the standard rate of VAT.	-
5	Total the VAT-exclusive direct costs to you of the zero-rated in-house supplies included in step 1.	-
6	Total the VAT-inclusive direct costs to you of the exempt in-house supplies included in step 1. Deduct any input tax that you are entitled to recover on these costs.	-
7	Total the direct costs to you of the in-house supplies included in step 1 that are supplied outside the UK, exclusive of any VAT incurred on these costs that you are entitled to recover. Add to the total an uplift equivalent to the percentage VAT rate applicable to such supplies if you have accounted for VAT on these supplies to the VAT authorities in another member state.	-
	Working out the "costs" of agency supplies	
8	Total the VAT-inclusive amounts paid by you to your principals in respect of the agency supplies included in step 1 for which the consideration you receive is standard-rated	-
9	Total the VAT-inclusive amounts paid by you to your principals in respect of the agency supplies included in step 1 for which the consideration you receive is not standard-rated	-
	Working out the total margin	
10	Add the totals of costs at steps 2 to 9 inclusive.	325

Step	Description	Amount
11	Calculate the total margin for all the supplies included in step 1 by deducting the total at step 10 from the total at step 1.	375
	Apportioning the margin	
12	Calculate the margin for the standard-rated designated travel services by applying the following formula— total at step 2 x total at step 11 total at step10	86.54
13	Calculate the margin for the zero-rated designated travel services by applying the following formula— total at step 3 x total at step 11 total at step 10	288.46
	Steps 14 to 17 can be ignored where a market value is applied to all in-house supplies under section 8	
14	Calculate the margin for the standard-rated in-house supplies by applying the following formula— total at step 4 x total at step 11 total at step 10	-
15	Calculate the margin for the zero-rated in-house supplies by applying the following formula— total at step 5 x total at step 11 total at step10	-
16	Calculate the margin for the exempt in-house supplies by applying the following formula— total at step 6 x total at step11 total at step 10	-
17	Calculate the margin for the in-house supplies made outside the UK by applying the following formula— total at step 7 x total at step 11 total at step10	-
18	Calculate the consideration for the standard-rated agency supplies by applying the following formula— total at step 8 x total at step 11 total at step 10	
19	Calculate the consideration for the non-standard-rated agency supplies by applying the following formula— total at step 9 x total at step 11 total at step 10	
	Working out your output tax	
20	Calculate the output VAT due on the designated travel services by applying the following formula— total at step 12 x the VAT fraction	12.89
21	Calculate the output VAT due on the standard-rated in-house supplies by applying the following formula— (total at step 4 + total at step 14 + total calculated at step M2 of section 8) x the VAT fraction.	44.68

22	Calculate the output VAT due on the standard-rated agency supplies by applying the following formula— total at step 18 x the VAT fraction	-
	Working out sales values	
23	Calculate the VAT-exclusive value of the standard-rated designated travel services by deducting the total at step 20 from the total at step 12.	73.65
24	Note the value of the zero-rated designated travel services at step 13	288.46
25	Calculate the VAT-exclusive value of your standard-rated in-house supplies by applying the following formula— (total at step 4 + total at step 14 + total calculated at step M2 of section 8)–total at step 21	255.32
26	Calculate the value of the zero rated supplies made within the scheme by applying the following formula— (total at step 5 + total at step 15 + total calculated at step M3 of section 8)	-
27	Calculate the value of your exempt in-house supplies made by applying the following formula— total at step 6 + total at step 16	-
28	Calculate the value of your in-house supplies which are supplied outside the UK by applying the following formula— total at step 7 + total at step 17	-
29	Calculate the total VAT exclusive value of the supplies— Total of steps 23 to 28. Include this total in box 6 of your VAT return.	617.43
	Working out the annual adjustment	
30	Calculate the total output VAT due on your designated travel services and margin scheme packages by adding the totals at steps 20 to 22 inclusive.	57.57
31	Total the provisional output VAT which has been accounted for during the financial year on the supplies included in the total at step 1.	-
32	Deduct the total at step 31 from the total at step 30. Include the resulting total in box 1 of your VAT return, either as a payable amount where the amount is positive or as a deductible amount where the amount is negative.	57.57

TOMS CALCULATION EXAMPLE 2 MIXTURE OF MARKET VALUE AND COST BASED IN HOUSE SUPPLIES

Package price £10,000

Being the price paid for the full packages by the holidaymaker

In-house MV SR £3,500
In-house MV ZR £1,000
Being the market value of in-house supplies included in the packages.
Bought-in SR cost £1,700
Bought-in ZR cost £0
Being the cost of the bought-in supplies that form part of the packages
In-house (non-MV) SR £100 + VAT =£117.50
In-house (non-MV) ZR £700
In-house (non-MV) Os £220
Agency SR £1000
Agency ZR £100
Using the matrix
Post the £10000 to box M1, the £3500 to box M2 and £1000 to box M3 of the market value matrix.
This works through to £5500 in Box M5 which is then posted to Box 1 of the main margin scheme calculation.
The £1700 is then posted to Box 2,
£117.50 to Box 4,
£700 to Box 5,
£220 to Box 7,
£1000 to Box 8,
£100 to Box 9
The rest of the boxes can then be calculated based on the information (above) that has now been posted.

MARKET VALUE CALCULATION (ANNUAL ADJUSTMENT)

This section has the force of law and is referred to in paragraphs xx

This section only applies to packages or parts of packages being apportioned by the market value of the in-house element of the package. On completion of all the steps M1-M5 you must then follow the steps in the cost-based calculation in section 9, taking forward the figures from this section as instructed

Step	Boxes requiring "raw data" entry are in white, boxes which "process" that data are in grey.	
	Calculate the value of sales of margin scheme packages	
M1	Total the VAT-inclusive selling prices of all your designated travel services and margin scheme packages supplied during the financial year including any that are not "market value" packages.	10000
	Working out the market value	
M2	Total the VAT inclusive market value of the standard-rated in-house supplies at M1—carry forward this figure to step 21 of section 9	3500
M3	Total the VAT inclusive market value of the zero- rated and outside the scope in-house travel services at M1—carry forward this figure to step 26 of section 9	1000
M4	Total the VAT inclusive market value of the in-house supplies at step M2 + step M3	4500
	Working out selling value of designated travel services and non-market value in-house supplies.	

M5	Deduct the total at step M4 from the total at step M1—carry forward this figure to step 1 of section 9	5500

COST-BASED CALCULATION (ANNUAL ADJUSTMENT)

This section has the force of law and is referred to in paragraphs.

This section applies to packages being apportioned by reference to the costs of the in-house element of the package, and imports the figures calculated by the market value method in section 8, where that method is used for all or some of the travel packages. Do not include values already entered in section 8 unless explicitly stated

Step	Boxes requiring "raw data" entry are in white, boxes which "process" that data are in grey.	
	Working out the total sales of margin scheme packages	
1	Bring forward the total calculated at step M5 of section 8. If Section 8 is not used then enter the VAT-inclusive selling prices of your designated travel services and margin scheme packages supplied during the financial year.	5500
	Working out the purchase prices of margin scheme supplies	
2	Total the VAT-inclusive purchase prices of the standard-rated designated travel services included in the total at step 1.	1700
3	Total the VAT-inclusive purchase prices of the non standard-rated designated travel services (supplies enjoyed outside the EU) included in the total at step 1.	-
	Working out the direct costs of in-house supplies. Steps 4 to 7 can be ignored where a market value is applied to all in-house supplies under section 8	
4	Total the VAT-exclusive direct costs to you of the standard-rated in-house supplies included in step 1. Add a percentage of that amount equivalent to the standard rate of VAT.	117.50
5	Total the VAT-exclusive direct costs to you of the zero-rated in-house supplies included in step 1.	700
6	Total the VAT-inclusive direct costs to you of the exempt in-house supplies included in step 1. Deduct any input tax that you are entitled to recover on these costs.	-

Step	Description	Amount
7	Total the direct costs to you of the in-house supplies included in step 1 that are supplied outside the UK, exclusive of any VAT incurred on these costs that you are entitled to recover. Add to the total an uplift equivalent to the percentage VAT rate applicable to such supplies if you have accounted for VAT on these supplies to the VAT authorities in another member state.	220
	Working out the "costs" of agency supplies	
8	Total the VAT-inclusive amounts paid by you to your principals in respect of the agency supplies included in step 1 for which the consideration you receive is standard-rated	1000
9	Total the VAT-inclusive amounts paid by you to your principals in respect of the agency supplies included in step 1 for which the consideration you receive is not standard-rated	100
	Working out the total margin	
10	Add the totals of costs at steps 2 to 9 inclusive.	3837.50
11	Calculate the total margin for all the supplies included in step 1 by deducting the total at step 10 from the total at step 1.	1662.50
	Apportioning the margin	
12	Calculate the margin for the standard-rated designated travel services by applying the following formula— total at step 2 x total at step 11 total at step10	736.48
13	Calculate the margin for the zero-rated designated travel services by applying the following formula— total at step 3 x total at step 11 total at step 10	-
	Steps 14 to 17 can be ignored where a market value is applied to all in-house supplies under section 8	
14	Calculate the margin for the standard-rated in-house supplies by applying the following formula— total at step 4 x total at step 11 total at step 10	50.90
15	Calculate the margin for the zero-rated in-house supplies by applying the following formula— total at step 5 x total at step 11 total at step10	303.26

16	Calculate the margin for the exempt in-house supplies by applying the following formula— total at step 6 x total at step11 total at step 10	-
17	Calculate the margin for the in-house supplies made outside the UK by applying the following formula— total at step 7 x total at step 11 total at step10	95.31
18	Calculate the consideration for the standard-rated agency supplies by applying the following formula— total at step 8 x total at step 11 total at step 10	433.22
19	Calculate the consideration for the non-standard-rated agency supplies by applying the following formula— total at step 9 x total at step 11 total at step 10	43.32
	Working out your output tax	
20	Calculate the output VAT due on the designated travel services by applying the following formula— total at step 12 x the VAT fraction	109.69
21	Calculate the output VAT due on the standard-rated in-house supplies by applying the following formula— (total at step 4 + total at step 14 + total calculated at step M2 of section 8) x the VAT fraction.	546.36
22	Calculate the output VAT due on the standard-rated agency supplies by applying the following formula— total at step 18 x the VAT fraction	64.52
	Working out sales values	
23	Calculate the VAT-exclusive value of the standard-rated designated travel services by deducting the total at step 20 from the total at step 12.	626.79
24	Note the value of the zero-rated designated travel services at step 13	-
25	Calculate the VAT-exclusive value of your standard-rated in-house supplies by applying the following formula— (total at step 4 + total at step 14 + total calculated at step M2 of section 8)–total at step 21	3122.05
26	Calculate the value of the zero rated supplies made within the scheme by applying the following formula— (total at step 5 + total at step 15 + total calculated at step M3 of section 8)	2003.26

27	Calculate the value of your exempt in-house supplies made by applying the following formula— total at step 6 + total at step 16	-
28	Calculate the value of your in-house supplies which are supplied outside the UK by applying the following formula— total at step 7 + total at step 17	316.31
29	Calculate the total VAT exclusive value of the supplies—Total of steps 23 to 28. Include this total in box 6 of your VAT return.	6067.41
	Working out the annual adjustment	
30	Calculate the total output VAT due on your designated travel services and margin scheme packages by adding the totals at steps 20 to 22 inclusive.	720.57
31	Total the provisional output VAT which has been accounted for during the financial year on the supplies included in the total at step 1.	-
32	Deduct the total at step 31 from the total at step 30. Include the resulting total in box 1 of your VAT return, either as a payable amount where the amount is positive or as a deductible amount where the amount is negative.	720.57

TOMS CALCULATION EXAMPLE 3 PROVISIONAL CALCULATION

For the purpose of this exercise assume the year just gone is the summation of example 1 and example 2 Value of box 4 £117.50

Value of box 12 £823.02

Value of box 14 £50.90

Value of box 18 £433.22

Value of box M2 £3800

Total £5224.64

Value of box (M1) £11,000

Value of supplies this ¼ £3000

Using the matrix

Post the £5224.64 to box 1

Calculate the provisional percentage (47.49%) in box 2.

Post £3000 to box 3

Multiply £3000 x 47.5% to calculate provisional Std Rate supplies

Extract the VAT from that figure (7/47 in this example)

ACCOUNTING FOR VAT ON THE PROVISIONAL VALUE OF DESIGNATED TRAVEL SERVICES AND MARGIN SCHEME PACKAGES

THIS SECTION HAS THE FORCE OF LAW and is referred to in paragraphs

Step	Working out the provisional percentage

1	Calculate the VAT-inclusive amount of your standard-rated supplies of designated travel services and margin scheme packages for the preceding financial year by adding the totals from steps 4, 12, 14 and 18 of section 9, together with the total M2 in the market value calculation in section 8.	5224.64
2	Calculate the VAT-inclusive standard-rated percentage of the total selling price of all your designated travel services and margin scheme packages for the preceding tax year by applying them one of following formulae— If you have used a market value to value in-house supplies total at step 1 of this section x 100 total at step M1 of section 8 If you have not used a market value to value in-house supplies total at step 1 of this section x 100 total at step 1 of section 9	47.5%
	Working out the VAT return figures	
3	Total the VAT-inclusive selling prices of the designated travel services and margin scheme packages supplied during the prescribed accounting period.	3000
4	Calculate the provisional VAT-inclusive amount of your standard-rated supplies of designated travel services and margin scheme packages made during the prescribed accounting period by applying the following formula— total at step 3 x percentage at step 2	1424
5	Calculate the provisional amount of output VAT due for the prescribed accounting period by applying the following formula: total at step 4 x the VAT fraction	212.23

TERTIARY LAW

This section has the force of law and is referred to in paragraphs

TL1

1 This section shall come into effect on 1 January 1998.

2 Where a tour operator, in the same financial year, supplies:

- designated travel services or margin scheme packages which are to be enjoyed wholly outside the European Community
- designated travel services or margin scheme packages which are to be enjoyed wholly or partly within the European Community

the Commissioners of Customs and Excise may, on being given written notification by the tour operator no later than the due date for rendering his first VAT return for the financial year in which the supplies are to be made, allow the supplies under sub-paragraph (a) to be valued separately from those under sub-paragraph (b).

3 Where a tour operator, under paragraph 2 above, has separately valued supplies of designated travel services or margin scheme packages enjoyed wholly outside the European Community from supplies of designated travel services or margin scheme packages enjoyed wholly or partly within the European Community, the Commissioners of Customs and Excise may, on being given written notification by the tour operator no later than the due date for rendering his first VAT return for any subsequent financial year, allow supplies to be made in such subsequent financial year to be valued using the method specified at sections 8 and 9 of this Notice.

TL2

1 This section shall come into effect on 1 January 1998.

2 Where:

– a supply of goods or services is acquired by a tour operator for the purpose of supplying a designated travel service
– the value of the supply to the tour operator is expressed in a currency other than sterling

the tour operator must convert such value into sterling for the purposes of steps 2 and 3 of section 9 of this Notice or step 2 of section 11 of this Notice.

3 For the purposes of paragraph 2 above, the tour operator must use one of the following:

– the rate of exchange published in the Financial Times using the Federation of Tour Operators' base rate current at the time such supplies were costed by the person from whom the tour operator has acquired the goods or services
– the commercial rate of exchange current at the time that the supplies in his brochure were costed
– the rate published in the Financial Times on the date that the tour operator pays for the supplies
– the rate of exchange which was applicable to the purchase by the tour operator of the foreign currency which he used to pay for those supplies
– the period rate of exchange published by Customs and Excise for customs purposes in force at the time the tour operator pays for those supplies

4 Where the methods at paragraph 3(a) or (b) above are used, the tour operator must publish the rate in any brochure or leaflet in which these supplies are held out for sale.

5 The Commissioners of Customs and Excise may, on being given written notification by a tour operator no later than the due date for rendering his first return of his financial year, allow a different method to be used in that financial year from that used in the previous financial year.

TL3

1 This section shall come into effect on 1st January 2010.

2 Where possible the value of any in-house supplies shall be valued by reference to their market value and the value of designated travel services and agency supplies shall be determined by applying the formula set out in section 8 of this Notice (hereinafter referred to as the "market value calculation"), unless during the relevant period all such supplies are liable to VAT at the same rate, in which case the value shall be determined by applying the formula set out in section 11 of this Notice (hereinafter referred to as "the simplified calculation").

3 On completing the steps in the market value calculation the figures produced must be entered into the cost-based calculation as detailed in section 9 together with any packages, or parts of packages, for which the market value calculation is not being done.

4 Where the cost-based calculation in TL4 accurately reflects the structure of the package holidays you may opt to use the cost-based calculation for all packages regardless of whether a market value can be established for some or all of the packages and section 8 calculations may be ignored.

5 Where the market value calculation has been used a tour operator may only cease to use that method where it becomes impossible to continue to determine a market value of the supply in question or where the cost-based calculation accurately reflects the structure of the package.

TL4

1 Subject to Section TL1 and TL3 of section 13 of this Notice, the value of designated travel services, in-house supplies and agency supplies shall be determined by applying the formula set out in section 9 of this Notice (hereinafter referred to as the "cost-based calculation"), unless during the relevant period all such supplies are liable to VAT at the same rate, in which case the value shall be determined by applying the formula set out in section 11 of this Notice (hereinafter referred to as "the simplified calculation").

2 The provisional value of designated travel services, in-house supplies and agency supplies shall be determined in accordance with the formula set out in:

– section 10 of this Notice, where the cost-based calculation applies
– section 12 of this Notice, where the simplified calculation applies

3 A tour operator shall be required to account for VAT on the provisional value of his supplies of designated travel services, in-house supplies and agency supplies on the VAT return for the prescribed accounting period in which the supplies are made.

4 The difference between the amount of VAT due on the value of designated travel services, in-house supplies and agency supplies supplied during a tour operator's financial year, and the amount of VAT paid on the provisional value of those supplies, shall be adjusted by the tour operator on the VAT return for the first prescribed accounting period ending after the end of the financial year during which the supplies were made.

TL5

1 For the purpose of sections 8 to 13 of this Notice:

- (a) "in-house supply" means a supply by a tour operator which is neither a designated travel service nor an agency supply;
- (b) "market value" means the selling price of the in-house element of a "margin scheme package" were it to be sold independent of the package in an arms-length transaction to an unconnected person.
- (c) "cost based method" means the calculation in section 9 of this Notice.
- (d) "agency supply" means a supply arranged by a tour operator between two other persons, in the capacity of an agent or intermediary for either person, for which the tour operator receives a consideration, the value of which is not readily identifiable;
- (e) "margin scheme package" means a single transaction which includes one or more designated travel services;
- (f) "financial year" means a period corresponding to a tour operator's financial year for accounting purposes;
- (g) "direct costs" means costs which are directly and specifically attributable to the provision of in-house supplies, to the extent that they are so attributable;
- (h) "VAT fraction" has the same meaning as in Notice 700 The VAT Guide.

Commentary—*De Voil Indirect Tax Service* **V6.369**

20 April 2009. HMRC Brief 28/09

Reverse charge accounting for businesses trading in mobile telephones and computer chips: renewal of EU derogation

WHO NEEDS TO READ THIS?

Businesses buying and/or selling any of the following goods:

1. Mobile telephones
2. Integrated circuit devices, such as microprocessors and central processing units, in a state prior to integration into end user products

BACKGROUND

The reverse charge for mobile phones and computer chips was implemented with effect from 1 June 2007 to remove the opportunity for fraudsters to use these goods to perpetrate missing trader intra-community (MTIC) carousel fraud. As an exception to the normal accounting rules for VAT the UK has a derogation from EU law to apply this anti-fraud measure, which runs until 30 April 2009. The Government announced in its Pre-Budget Report 2008 that it had applied for a renewal of the derogation. The purpose of this Revenue & Customs Brief is to provide:

i. information on renewal of the derogation
ii. guidance on the application of the reverse charge in the event that the renewal is not concluded by 30 April 2009

(I) RENEWAL OF THE DEROGATION

On 10 March 2009 the European Council of Finance Ministers (ECOFIN) agreed, in principle, to the renewal of the UK's derogation until April 2011. The Government is working with the Commission and the Member States to ensure that the legal text is adopted as soon as possible. We anticipate that it will be agreed within the next few weeks. Formal agreement to the renewal text, however, may not be concluded before 30 April, in which case there would be a short gap between the expiry of the derogation and its renewal. If there is a gap, it is expected to be temporary as we expect that the extension of the derogation will apply retrospectively from 1 May 2009 resulting in an unbroken legal vires for the reverse charge. UK law will therefore remain unchanged.

(II) APPLICATION OF THE REVERSE CHARGE

If there is a temporary gap in the derogation, businesses that make or receive business-to-business supplies of mobile phones and/or computer chips with a value of £5,000 or more should continue to apply the reverse charge. Suppliers should also continue to complete and submit Reverse Charge Sales lists for these supplies. Businesses that apply the reverse charge and comply with UK law will not be subject to any penalties as a consequence of any temporary gap in the EU derogation. If a business does not apply the reverse charge during any temporary gap in the derogation, it may be liable to pay to HM Revenue & Customs (HMRC) any tax lost or to have its input tax denied.

FURTHER INFORMATION

For further information on the reverse charge for mobile phones and computer chips please see Public Notice 735: "VAT Reverse charge for mobile phones and computer chips".

Commentary—*De Voil Indirect Tax Service* **V3.233, V3.425.**

14 May 2009. HMRC Brief 31/09

Tax implications of the vehicle scrappage scheme

The government announced at Budget 2009 the introduction of a temporary vehicle scrappage scheme. It is a voluntary scheme which will be administered by participating motor manufacturers and dealers, along with the Department for Business, Enterprise and Regulatory Reform (BERR). Information about it can be found on the BERR website and at Directgov – Motoring. You may also contact BERR's enquiry unit on Tel 020 7215 5000, or email the BERR Automotive Unit with "scrappage" entered in the subject heading.

A. VAT AND DIRECT TAX PROFITS IMPLICATIONS

Vehicles supplied under the scheme will be subject to the normal VAT and direct tax rules. The purpose of this brief is to explain how those rules apply to the £1,000 subsidy payable by BERR on qualifying supplies made under their scheme, plus the £1,000 discount paid by the manufacturer.

Manufacturers

If you are a manufacturer participating in the scheme you will be providing a £1,000 subsidy to the final consumer (over and above any other subsidy or discount you might provide), even though you have no direct contractual relationship with them. You may treat the VAT on your contribution as a discount to the output tax you have paid to HMRC on your sale of the car. You may therefore reduce your output tax by the appropriate VAT amount (which on a gross payment of £1,000 and the current standard rate of VAT of 15 per cent means £130.43). Any such adjustment should be made in the period in which it takes effect in the business records of the manufacturer. This treatment is in accordance with the decision of the European Court of Justice in *Elida Gibbs Ltd v Commissioners of Customs and Excise* [1996] STC 1387 and *Commission v Germany (Taxation)* [2003] STC 301. Guidance on the VAT treatment of such payments by manufacturers was given previously in Revenue and Customs Brief 08/07.

You must not reduce your output tax in respect of BERR's £1,000 contribution. Under the terms of the scheme, BERR will pay you £1,000, but you must pass it on to the dealer within 14 days who, in turn, is obliged to ensure that the final consumer receives the benefit of that sum. You are thus acting as a conduit, receiving and passing on BERR's third party payment to the dealer. The £1,000 subsidy provided by BERR is not a discount on the value of your supply, and so you should make no adjustment in respect of that payment.

For direct tax purposes BERR's £1,000 contribution has no overall effect on the trading profits of the manufacturer. The corresponding £1,000 payable by the manufacturer to the dealer will be an allowable deduction for the purposes of computing the profits of the manufacturing trade.

Dealers

If you are a dealer participating in the Scheme and the manufacturer uses the arrangements above, the cost of the new vehicle received by you is unaffected, and you should make no adjustments to the VAT you pay to the manufacturer, or claim from HMRC as input tax. As explained above, the manufacturer is not providing a £1,000 (or greater) discount to you as part of the Scheme – they are providing it to your customer. Your selling price for the vehicle has not changed and you must not reduce your output tax. Whatever your final VAT-inclusive ("On The Road ") selling price of the new vehicle is, under the Scheme your customer pays £2,000 less, with the balance of the consideration being made up of the two £1,000 subsidies. Under the Scheme, it is important that it is clear to your customer that they are paying £2,000 less than would otherwise be the case – see Directgov – Motoring (http://www.direct.gov.uk/en/Motoring/BuyingAndSellingAVehicle/AdviceOnBuyingAndSellingAVehicle/DG_177693)

The effect of the Scheme on the dealer is neutral for the purposes of computing trading profits. The £2,000 reduction in the sale proceeds received from the customer is matched by the £2,000 trade receipt received in the form of the subsidies paid to the dealer under the scheme.

Customers

Customers buying a new vehicle under the scheme will pay £2,000 less for the vehicle, since BERR will be paying £1,000, and the vehicle manufacturer will be paying £1,000 towards the cost of the purchase. The subsidies will be settled between the manufacturer, dealer and BERR so you will not physically be paid these amounts.

If you are VAT-registered and buy a new car or van under the scheme, you may need to reduce your input tax in respect of the manufacturer's discount. However, you only need to consider this if you are entitled to claim VAT on the purchase of a vehicle – for example, on certain commercial vehicles, or a car that is intended to be used primarily as a taxi; driving instruction car, or self-drive hire (but see paragraph 3.1 of VAT Notice 700/64 "Motoring expenses"). If, under the normal VAT rules, you are entitled to reclaim the VAT you are charged on the purchase of a new vehicle and you buy one under the Scheme, you must reduce the input tax you claim in proportion to the manufacturer's discount. This is because, at the beginning of the chain of transactions culminating in your purchasing the vehicle, the manufacturer will have reduced its output tax. Therefore, since the manufacturer contributes £1,000 and the standard rate of VAT is 15 per cent, you must reduce your input tax by £130.43. You will not receive an amended invoice or credit note. This is the normal VAT treatment for business customers receiving such manufacturer's discounts – see Revenue and Customs Brief 08/07.

B. CAPITAL ALLOWANCES

A business purchaser of a vehicle under the scheme will only be able to claim capital allowances on the net cost to it (after the two subsidies have been deducted). However, the vehicle surrendered by the business consumer will be scrapped and therefore it has no value as a vehicle, in terms of the scrappage scheme. The two subsidies given as deductions from the purchase price will not constitute taxable disposal receipts for capital allowances purposes.

If you need further advice and are a large business with an allocated Customer Relationship Manager, you should consult them. Otherwise you should contact our National Advice Service Helpline on Tel 0845 010 9000, or by Enquiries.estn@hmrc.gsi.gov.uk, or by writing to:

HM Revenue & Customs
National Advice Service
Written Enquiries Section
Alexander House
Victoria Avenue
Southend
Essex
SS99 1BD

Please include your VAT registration number and the name and address of your business in any correspondence. If you are not VAT registered please include your name and address.

1 June 2009. HMRC Brief 32/09

Decision of the Court of Appeal in respect of Procter & Gamble UK

VAT: Liability of regular "Pringles" (a savoury snack product): the decision of the Court of Appeal in respect of Procter & Gamble UK [2009] All ER (D) 177 (May)

The Court of Appeal issued its decision in this case on 20 May 2009. The judgment is in HM Revenue & Customs (HMRC) favour and confirms that the sale of regular "Pringles" is standard-rated for VAT.

BACKGROUND

Proctor & Gamble manufacture "Pringles", a savoury snack product, commonly sold in retail outlets.

Although food is generally zero-rated, some items, including potato crisps and similar products made from the potato or from potato flour or from potato starch are excluded from zero-rating and charged with VAT at the standard rate.

Procter & Gamble appealed to the VAT Tribunal on the grounds that a "Pringle" was not similar to a crisp and that it was not wholly or mainly made from a potato product. The Tribunal did not accept this argument and found in favour of HMRC.

Procter & Gamble subsequently appealed to the High Court which found in their favour and decided that regular "Pringles" were eligible for zero-rating because they were not wholly or mainly made from potato.

HMRC appealed to the Court of Appeal which has upheld the Tribunal's original decision.

IMPLICATIONS OF THIS JUDGMENT

The judgment confirms HMRC's view that "Pringles" are standard-rated for VAT and always have been.

Therefore, any business that chose to stop charging VAT on "Pringles" as a result of the High Court decision must now resume charging VAT on all such sales. Tax must also be accounted for, for the period from when zero-rating was applied to the current date.

An adjustment may be made to your current VAT return, but the value of the errors must not exceed the greater of either £10,000 or 1 per cent of the box 6 figure on the VAT return for the VAT return period of discovery, subject to an upper limit of £50,000.

Where the errors exceed the limits set out above, a written notification detailing the error should be submitted to HMRC (in these cases the errors must not be corrected through the use of VAT returns).

Details of where to send your notification can be obtained from update 2 to VAT Notice 700/45 "How to correct VAT errors and make adjustments or claims" from the HM Revenue & Customs National Advice Service on Tel 0845 010 9000.

Any claims for overpaid VAT lodged as a result of the High Court decision will now be rejected.

If you have any queries about this please contact the National Advice Service.

Commentary—*De Voil Indirect Tax Service* **V4.226**.

9 June 2009. HMRC Brief 33/09

HMRC's policy following the judgment in Newnham College

This Revenue and Customs Brief announces HM Revenue and Customs' (HMRC) revised interpretation of the law following the judgment of the House of Lords in the case of *The Principal and Fellows of Newnham College in the University of Cambridge* [2008] UKHL 23, [2008] 2 All ER 863. It also provides guidance for those businesses affected by the judgment.

THE ISSUE

The case before the House of Lords concerned whether Newnham was "in occupation" of the college library. If they were, their option to tax the library would be disapplied and their occupation would be for the purpose of making supplies of exempt education. Consequently, the VAT incurred on the rebuilding and refurbishment of the library would be irrecoverable. The House of Lords upheld the judgment of the Court of Appeal and found in Newnham's favour. They concluded that Newnham was not in occupation and, as a result, that their option to tax was not disapplied.

HMRC'S REVISED INTERPRETATION OF LAW

HMRC now accept that physical presence alone is not the correct test of occupation for the purposes of what is now VATA 1994 Schedule 10 Paragraphs 12 to 17 (the "anti-avoidance test"). Following the House of Lords judgment, a person is considered to be "in occupation" if, in addition to physical presence which occupation normally entails, they have the right to occupy the property as if they are the owner and to exclude others from enjoyment of such a right. This means a person must have actual possession of the land along with a degree of permanence and control. Such a right will normally result from the grant of a legal interest or licence to occupy. Occupation could also, however, be by agreement or de facto and it is therefore necessary to take account of the day to day arrangements, particularly where these differ from the contractual terms. An exclusive right of occupation is not a requirement; an agreement might, for example, allow for joint occupation. Equally, it is not necessary for a person to be utilising all of the land for all of the time for them to be considered as occupying it.

A person whose interest in land is subject to an inferior interest, such as to prevent him from having rights of occupation for the time being, is not "in occupation" for the purposes of the anti-avoidance test until the inferior interest expires. It should be noted, however, that an important feature of the test is that it is forward looking and takes account of the intended or expected occupation of the building at any time during the Capital Goods Scheme (CGS) adjustment period. As a result, a person who has granted an inferior interest but intends during that adjustment period to occupy the land himself would intend to be "in occupation" for the purposes of the anti-avoidance test and so must consider whether his intended occupation was for eligible purposes.

However, a person can ignore the following types of occupation for the purposes of the test:

1. Occupation which is purely for the purpose of making his rental supplies under the grant, since those are the very supplies whose liability he is trying to determine by applying the test. For example:

(a) occupation by the grantor between the date of the grant and the start of occupation by the tenant which is for the purpose of undertaking refurbishment or repairs,

(b) occupation by maintenance, security or reception staff (or similar), unless it is for the purpose of providing ongoing services separate from the letting itself.

2. Occupation at a future date, but within the CGS adjustment period, which is solely for the purpose of re-letting the property or making a fresh grant.

PRACTICAL IMPLICATIONS

Businesses that were wrongly denied input tax recovery may submit claims to their local Business Advice Centre. These will be subject to a three-year limitation period (four years from

1 April 2009, subject to a transitional period). All such adjustments or claims must take account of any underdeclared output tax as a result of incorrectly treating the option to tax as disapplied.

Further information about claims can be found in Notice 700/45 "How to correct VAT errors or make adjustments or claims".

Commentary—*De Voil Indirect Tax Service* **V4.116**.

18 June 2009. HMRC Brief 34/09

Reverse charge accounting for businesses trading in mobile telephones and computer chips: renewal of EU derogation

WHO NEEDS TO READ THIS?

Businesses buying and/or selling any of the following goods:

(1) Mobile telephones

(2) Integrated circuit devices, such as microprocessors and central processing units, in a state prior to integration into end user products

Further to Revenue & Customs brief 28/09 HMRC can now confirm that the Government's application to renew the derogation was formerly agreed on 5 May 2009 by the European Council of Finance Ministers (ECOFIN). The agreement has retroactive effect from 1 May 2009 meaning that legal vires for the reverse charge is unbroken.

BACKGROUND

The reverse charge for mobile phones and computer chips was implemented with effect from 1 June 2007 to remove the opportunity for fraudsters to use these goods to perpetrate missing trader intra-community (MTIC) carousel fraud. As an exception to the normal accounting rules for VAT the UK has a derogation from EU law to apply this anti-fraud measure, which ran until 30 April 2009. The Government announced in its Pre-Budget Report 2008 that it had applied for a renewal of the derogation.

On 10 March 2009 the ECOFIN agreed, in principle, to the renewal of the UK's derogation until April 2011 and it is this decision that has now been formerly ratified and published under Official Journal reference 2009/439/EC.

FURTHER INFORMATION

For further information on the reverse charge for mobile phones and computer chips please see Public Notice 735: VAT Reverse charge for mobile phones and computer chips.

1 July 2009. HMRC Brief 39/09

Changes to the application of the zero-rate to new buildings used for a relevant charitable or residential use

This Brief announces a change in HM Revenue & Customs (HMRC) interpretation of the legal provisions that apply the zero rate to new buildings used for a relevant charitable purpose, and the withdrawal of Extra Statutory Concession (ESC) 3.29 and two related concessions. VAT Information Sheet 08/09 provides further detail.

BACKGROUND

A building intended to be used solely for a relevant charitable purpose (non-business use) can be zero-rated if the charity provides their developer with an appropriate certificate before the first supply is made.

If, however, the building is put to a business use within ten years of the building's completion, VAT must be paid to HMRC (a change in use charge) to reflect that the building has ceased to be eligible to benefit from the zero-rate.

Under Extra Statutory Concession 3.29, HMRC has permitted zero-rating where a building was used 90 per cent or more for a relevant charitable use. No change of use charge arises in a case where a building ceases to be eligible if it was zero rated only as a result of the application of this concession.

The two related concessions, the "switching areas" concession (where the overall use of the building was unchanged) and the "look through" concession, (where the occupiers' use of the building was for a relevant charitable purpose) enabled some business use of a building to be disregarded.

OUTCOME OF REVIEW

Having fully considered the application of the provision and considered appropriate decisions of the higher courts, HMRC now recognise that the term "solely", as used in the phrase "solely for a relevant residential or relevant charitable purpose", can incorporate an appropriate de minimis margin. And in order to avoid unnecessary disputes in marginal cases, HMRC will accept that this statutory condition is satisfied if the relevant use of the building by the charity is 95 per cent or more.

In the light of this change of view, the ESC is no longer considered to be necessary or appropriate. It will therefore be withdrawn, subject to a 12 month transitional period, as described below.

WAY FORWARD

A person can now rely on this revised interpretation of "solely" that is, 95 per cent or more, to determine whether a building will be eligible for the zero rate or not.

For this purpose, use for a relevant charitable purpose does not have to be calculated using one of the three methods described in ESC 3.29. Any method may be used to calculate the qualifying use of the building, so long as it is fair and reasonable. Prior approval from HMRC for any method of calculation is not required.

If a building is zero rated as a result of applying this new interpretation, there will be a change of use charge if it ceases to be eligible within ten years of the buildings completion.

ESC 3.29 and the two connected concessions will now be withdrawn, subject to a 12 month transitional period starting on 1 July 2009. During this transitional period, charities will be able to continue to apply ESC 3.29, or choose to apply the revised interpretation of the statutory provision described above.

Further details are in VAT Information Sheet 08/09.

The meaning of the term "solely" will depend on the legal context in which it occurs and on the nature of the underlying transactions to which any particular piece of legislation is directed. The revised interpretation described above applies only to the construction of the phrase "solely for a relevant residential or relevant charitable purpose" as used in the context of Groups 5 and 6 of Schedule 8, Group 1 of Schedule 9 and Part 2 of Schedule 10 to the VAT Act 1994.

FURTHER INFORMATION

If you have any enquiries about this Brief, please contact the National Advice Service on Tel. **0845 010 9000** or, if a charity, the Charity Helpline on **0845 302 0203**.

8 July 2009. HMRC Brief 36/2009

VAT treatment of deposits relating to sales of land on which dwellings are to be constructed

This Revenue & Customs Brief clarifies HM Revenue and Customs' (HMRC) view on how deposits paid in relation to sales of land, and in particular sales by developers to registered social landlords (RSLs), should be treated.

BACKGROUND

Where development land is sold to RSLs, it is normal for a deposit to be paid at the time of exchange of contracts when construction has not commenced and the land is bare land. In many cases this deposit will be held by a stakeholder and will not create a tax point for VAT purposes until it is released to the vendor (or vendor's agent), normally at the time of completion. Completion of the sale will in most cases occur at a time when construction of the dwellings has commenced and progressed beyond what is commonly known as the "golden brick", that is, beyond foundation level. This means the supply can normally be zero-rated.

It has, however, become increasingly common for the deposit to be made available to the vendor at the time of exchange when the land is still bare land. This has raised questions about the VAT treatment of the deposit, and in particular, whether it can be treated as part payment for the future zero-rated supply.

HMRC'S INTERPRETATION OF THE CORRECT VAT TREATMENT

HMRC takes the view that where the deposit is released to the vendor and it is clear from the contract or agreement that what will be supplied at completion, or the time of the grant, will be partly completed dwellings (beyond "golden brick"), the deposit is part payment for the grant/supply that will occur at that time. It follows that the VAT liability of the deposit is determined by the anticipated nature of the supply and that zero-rating will be appropriate if it is intended that the conditions for zero-rating will be satisfied at the time of completion. For example, there must be a clear intention that the vendor will have commenced construction of the dwellings at that time and acquired "person constructing" status.

It is possible that the state of the land at completion will differ from that which was anticipated and where this is the case it will be necessary to revisit the VAT treatment of the deposit. It is not possible to give more detailed guidance as the position will depend upon the facts and contractual terms applicable in the particular case. Where taxpayers are uncertain about the correct treatment they should refer to the National Advice Service by phoning 0845 010 9000.

Commentary—*De Voil Indirect Tax Service* **V4.116, V6.270.**

9 July 2009. HMRC Brief 38/09

"Dutch barges" and similar vessels designed for and used as permanent residential accommodation by owners

WHO NEEDS TO READ THIS?

Businesses making supplies of:

- vessels to be used for permanent residential living by the owner;
- certain goods and services to the owners of vessels used for permanent residential living by the owner.

This brief also withdraws Section 4 of Business Brief 35/04 "VAT – clarification of the VAT liability of ships supplied to customers who intend to use them as residential accommodation".

BACKGROUND

"Qualifying ships" – are zero-rated for VAT purposes. A "qualifying ship" is defined as a ship which is not less than 15 gross tons and is neither designed nor adapted for use for recreation or pleasure. The law is set out in the Value Added Tax Act 1994, Schedule 8, Group 8, Item 1 and legal note A1(a).

"Houseboats" – are covered by a separate zero-rate. For VAT purposes, "houseboats" are boats designed as living accommodation that do not have, and cannot be fitted with, a means of propulsion. If a boat can be fitted with a means of propulsion, it is not a "houseboat". The law is set out in the Value Added Tax Act 1994, Schedule 8, Group 9, Item 2.

H M REVENUE & CUSTOMS (HMRC) POLICY

In the light of the High Court decision in the case of Lt Cmdr Colin Stone [2008] STC 2501, [2008] EWHC 1249 (Ch), HMRC are changing their long-standing policy on the liability of vessels used as residential accommodation, excluding houseboats, for VAT purposes. This case concerned the VAT liability of the supply of "Dutch barges" acquired for the purpose of being used as a permanent residence.

The High Court decided that the supply of the vessel was entitled to zero-rating under the terms of UK law, because it was designed to be lived in as a permanent home and, therefore, not designed for use as recreation or pleasure.

HMRC consider that many of these and similar vessels, although designed for use as a permanent residence, can also be designed for use as recreation or pleasure and are perfectly capable of being so used. It was never the intention that UK legislation should provide for the supply of such vessels to benefit from zero-rating but, following Tribunal and Court decisions over time, HMRC have found it increasingly difficult to apply a consistent and coherent policy around the borderlines in this area.

HMRC do not rule out a wider review of policy and legislation in this area. However, in the meantime, we have decided to treat Dutch barges and similar vessels that are designed and supplied for use as the permanent residence of the customer as qualifying ships and eligible for zero-rating. As vessels of less than 15 gross tons can never be zero-rated regardless of their design, the majority of narrow boats designed for permanent residential use will not meet this requirement and their supply will continue to be standard-rated.

As a result of this policy change some supplies of goods and services to the owners of such vessels may also be zero-rated by suppliers.

These include:

- repairs and maintenance of the vessel itself; this does not extend to the domestic equipment and fittings on board;
- modification or conversion of the vessel itself provided that it remains a qualifying ship after modification or conversion; this does not extend to domestic equipment and fittings;
- parts and equipment ordinarily installed or incorporated in the propulsion, navigation, communications or structure of a ship; this does not extend to domestic equipment and fittings.

Further details can be found in Notice 744C.

EVIDENCE OF INTENTION

In keeping with normal rules, suppliers will have to hold evidence to satisfy HMRC that the supply is entitled to zero-rating. This may be in the form of contractual or other documentary evidence. HMRC would also advise suppliers to obtain a declaration from their customers that the vessel is to be designed for use as a permanent residence and intended for such use. We would suggest that suppliers use the format set out for the Undertaking of Use in Notice 744C, adapted as necessary where the supply is one of the vessel itself. Customers should be aware that HMRC have powers to impose penalties where false documentation is used to obtain a tax advantage.

PAST SUPPLIES AND CLAIMS

Customers who have been previously charged VAT on a supply that is now covered by this policy must approach the person who made the supply to them to obtain a refund of VAT. They should not contact HMRC as we have no legal powers to refund tax direct to customers. Suppliers who wish to claim a refund of VAT charged to customers on a supply covered by this policy must submit their claims in accordance with the published rules and subject to the normal repayment, unjust enrichment and capping criteria to HMRC.

FURTHER INFORMATION

For further information on houseboats please see Public Notice 701/20: "VAT Caravans and Houseboats".

For further information on qualifying ships please read Public Notice 744C: "VAT Ships, aircraft and associated services".

For additional information on parts and equipment please read Information Sheet 15/07 "VAT: Supply of parts and equipment for qualifying ships and aircraft".

Or contact our National Advice Service Helpline on Tel 0845 010 9000, or by email, or by writing to: HM Revenue & Customs, National Advice Service, Written Enquiries Section, Alexander House, Victoria Avenue, Southend, Essex, SS99 1BD.

Commentary—*De Voil Indirect Tax Service* **V4.251, V4.275.**

14 July 2009. HMRC Brief 40/09

Decision of the High Court in respect of Rank (mechanised cash bingo and gaming machines)

The High Court issued its decision in this case on 8 June 2009 – the judgment being in Rank's favour [see *Revenue and Customs Commissioners v The Rank Group* [2009] All ER (D) 65 (Jun)]. It confirmed that there had been a breach of fiscal neutrality in the tax treatment of the supply of mechanised cash bingo (MCB). This means that participation fees for playing MCB should have been exempt from VAT and businesses can now submit claims to HM Revenue & Customs (HMRC) for repayment of any output tax wrongly accounted for, subject to the guidelines below.

In relation to gaming machines, the High Court judgment relates to an appeal against an interim ruling of the VAT Tribunal. As the Tribunal has not yet ruled in respect of Rank's full appeal, HMRC will not at this time consider any claims relating to this issue.

BACKGROUND

Rank, which operates Mecca bingo halls, claimed there had been inconsistencies in the way VAT had been applied to the participation fees customers paid to play MCB and to the takings of gaming machines.

Last year the VAT Tribunal ruled there had been a breach of fiscal neutrality in the case of MCB as some participation fees were taxed while others were exempt. (Fiscal neutrality means that similar supplies must be treated the same for tax purposes to avoid any distortion of competition). The High Court has agreed with the Tribunal's decision that all participation fees for MCB should have been exempt from VAT.

The VAT Tribunal also issued an interim decision regarding the way HMRC taxed gaming machines, stating there had been a breach of fiscal neutrality in some cases and over a short period of time before the law was changed in December 2005.

IMPLICATIONS OF THIS JUDGMENT

HMRC will now consider claims for output tax wrongly accounted for by bingo operators on MCB participation fees.

As bingo duty is charged on the VAT-exclusive value of participation fees, this judgment will have an effect on bingo duty declarations although HMRC is still considering the precise implications. However, HMRC will now enforce those bingo duty assessments already made. Further assessments to bingo duty may be made as appropriate.

As the gaming machine case is continuing, with a VAT Tribunal hearing later this year, HMRC will not credit any claims on this issue.

MAKING CLAIMS OR ADJUSTMENTS

Where a business wishes to make a claim to HMRC for output tax wrongly accounted for in respect of MCB participation fees, they may do so, although evidence must be produced that output tax was accounted for, to substantiate the amount claimed.

All claims will be subject to the four-year time limit in section 80(4) of the VAT Act 1994 (as amended) and no claim for periods ending on or prior to 31 March 2006 will be considered.

Correcting the error on your VAT return

Overdeclarations of output tax can also be corrected by adjusting the current VAT return if the net amount of all errors in the accounting periods being corrected is:

- £10,000 or less; or
- less than £50,000 and less than 1 per cent of the box 6 figure on the VAT return in which the adjustment is being effected

These de minimis levels apply to the entire "claim". Thus if your "claim" is for ten accounting periods, it is the net overdeclaration for all ten periods that must be within these levels.

Under regulation 34(1A) of the VAT Regulations 1995 (as amended), all adjustments must be made within four years after the end of the accounting period in which the overdeclaration was made but no accounting period can be adjusted if it ended on or before 31 March 2006.

FURTHER INFORMATION

Details of where to send your claim can be obtained from update 2 to VAT Notice 700/45 – "How to correct VAT errors and make adjustments or claims" from the HM Revenue & Customs National Advice Service on 0845 010 9000.

HMRC may reject all or part of a claim if repayment would unjustly enrich the claimant. More details on "unjust enrichment" can be found at part 14 of VAT Notice 700/45.

There may be direct tax implications where amounts of overdeclared output tax are repaid to businesses and your attention is drawn to R&C Brief 14/09 issued previously.

Where you are in any doubt about the correct treatment please contact the National Advice Service.

20 July 2009. HMRC Brief 41/09

Three-year cap for VAT claims – Court of Session decision in Scottish Equitable

Three-year cap for VAT claims – CRC v Scottish Equitable Plc (unreported) – Order of the Inner House of the Court of Session

THE JUDGMENT OF THE INNER HOUSE

In an Order handed down on 2 July, the court overturned the 2006 decision of the VAT and Duties Tribunal that the introduction of the three-year time limit without a transitional period in 1996 meant that it had never been lawfully enacted.

The Inner House held that the Tribunal was wrong to decide that the absence of transitional provisions, that enabled claims to be made under the old time limits before the new time limit took effect, meant that the provisions were void. The court stressed that it was well recognised that national legislation which breaches Community law is not void and noted that the Tribunal had failed to recognise the difference between rights to claim that accrued before the enactment of the three-year cap and those that accrued afterwards.

The Inner House followed the judgment of the House of Lords in *CRC v Fleming (t/a Bodycraft)* [2008] STC 324 in which the Law Lords held that the three-year time limit should be disapplied in relation to rights to claims that had accrued before its enactment and that that disapplication should continue until the expiry of an adequate, prospective transitional period.

There will be no application for leave to appeal to the House of Lords.

CURRENT CASE LAW ON TIME LIMITS

There are a number of judgments of the European Court of Justice (including *Marks & Spencer Plc v CCE* [2002] STC 1036) confirming that the imposition of reasonable time limits does not breach principles of Community law and that they are necessary to provide legal certainty for both the citizen and the state.

The judgment of the House of Lords in Fleming (referred to above) led to the enactment of section 121, Finance Act 2008. This provided businesses with a prospective transitional period of twelve months, ending on 31 March 2009, in which claims could be made for accounting periods ending before the introduction of the new time limits.

The Inner House in Scottish Equitable has taken the same view as the High Court in *Local Authorities Mutual Investment Trust v CCE* [2004] STC 246, which held that VAT claims for accounting periods ending after the enactment of the new time limit were properly capped.

STATUS OF VAT TIME LIMITS

All VAT claims are now capped at four years, or back to 1 April 2006, whichever is the shorter – see section 80(4) of the VAT Act 1994 as amended by Articles 2 and 6 of the Finance Act 2008, Schedule 39 (Appointed Day, Savings and Transitional Provisions) Order 2009, SI 2009/403 (output tax claims) and regulation 29(1A) of the VAT Regulations 1995 as amended by regulation 3 of the VAT (Amendment) Regulations 2009, SI 2009/586.

APPEALS ON-HOLD BEHIND THIS LITIGATION

A significant number of appeals to the First Tier Tribunal (Tax Chamber) are on-hold, pending the outcome of this litigation. Appellants will need to consider, in the light of the recent order, whether they wish to withdraw their appeal or proceed to a full hearing. HM Revenue & Customs are now taking steps to have these appeals restored to the Tribunal list so that, where necessary, a hearing date can be fixed.

Commentary—*De Voil Indirect Tax Service* **V3.405**, **V5.159C**.

23 July 2009. HMRC Brief 43/09

Psychologists' services

With effect from 1 July 2009 practitioner psychologists are regulated by the Health Professionals Council meaning that any supplies of medical care they make became exempt from VAT from that date. Practitioner psychologists come under seven domains: clinical, counselling, educational, forensic, health, occupational, and sport/exercise. Psychologists who work purely in academic research and experimental psychology and who do not offer services to the general public are excluded from regulation meaning that there will be no change in the VAT treatment of their services.

By "medical care" we mean any service relating to the protection, maintenance or restoration of the health of the person concerned, including mental health. Medical care would include services such as counselling, working with children with emotional problems, dealing with criminals' behavioural problems or running stress management courses.

However, as is the case for all health professionals, the VAT exemption excludes services that are not primarily for the benefit of the patient, for example, assessing a patient's mental condition for legal reasons at the behest of a third party. This is because the primary purpose of such services is to enable a court to take a decision on whether the patient is fit to stand trial rather than any immediate concern about the patient's mental health.

Appeals. 2007

VAT APPEALS

Appeals and applications to the Tribunals—explanatory leaflet

Notes—VAT tribunals were renamed VAT and duties tribunals with effect from 1 July 1994: see FA 1994 ss 7, 19; FA 1994 s 7 (Appointed Day) Order, SI 1994/1690 art 2.

The VAT and Duties Tribunal was replaced from 1 April 2009. Both direct and indirect tax appeals now fall within the remit of the Tax Chamber of the First-tier Tribunal. For further guidance see Tribunals Service guidance following this explanatory leaflet, which is retained for information purposes only.

I INFORMATION YOU NEED TO KNOW

1 What are the VAT and duties tribunals for?

You have the right to appeal to a VAT and duties tribunal against certain decisions of HMRC (or the Treasury in the Isle of Man) about value added tax.

The Chairmen, the members and the tribunal staff are entirely independent of HMRC.

This leaflet explains what sorts of decisions can be appealed against and how you may bring a case before a tribunal. It does not try to list legal references and is not itself part of the law. Should you or your adviser wish to consult the law the main Acts of Parliament and Statutory Instruments are [VATA 1994 and subsequent Finance Acts; the VAT Tribunals Rules 1986 (SI 1986/590)]. This leaflet cannot deal with some unusual types of case which arise only occasionally, but I hope most of those who want to appeal will find it helpful.

VAT and Duties Tribunals are there to give taxpayers a way of getting a hearing in court when HMRC have given a decision with which they disagree.

The tribunals are run by the Tribunals Service, an executive agency of the Department of Constitional Affairs (in Scotland, the Scottish Executive) and they work under the supervision of the Council on Tribunals, 81 Chancery Lane, London WC2A 1BQ and of its Scottish Committee, 120 George Street, Edinburgh EH2 4HH.

2 What should I do first?

You can ask HMRC to reconsider the decision. Many disagreements can be settled by discussion or correspondence with HMRC without your having to go to a tribunal. If you can give further information or you think there are facts which have not been taken into account by HMRC, contact them first.

If you ask HMRC to reconsider a decision you should also ask for a letter giving you extra time in which you may appeal to a tribunal. (See paragraph 9 which deals with time limits).

3 How much will it cost me to appeal?

The tribunals do not charge any fee for dealing with appeals. Your own costs in preparing your appeal will depend on the difficulty of your case and whether you decide to handle your appeal yourself or instruct a representative. You may instruct a solicitor, an accountant, or any other person (qualified or not) to act as your representative.

Public funding (formerly legal aid) is not normally available for appeals to the Tribunals. However if your appeal is against a penalty for tax evasion (dishonest conduct) you maybe eligible. The Tribunal will tell you about this when acknowledging your appeal.

You should also read paragraph 28 which deals with the award of costs and interest, and Appendix D which sets out the practice of HMRC with regard to costs.

4 What can I appeal against?

The tribunals do not have power to consider every kind of review decision of HMRC. The main areas that the tribunals deal with are tax assessments and penalties. Some of the commonest matters appealed against include—

- registration disputes;
- the amount of tax;
- a requirement to give security;
- a default surcharge (for late returns);
- a penalty for misdeclaration or neglect (for an error in a return);
- liability rulings such as a refusal to repay input tax or a decision that supplies are standard-rated.

There are several other less common appealable matters. You can find out what they are from the tribunal centre, and they are listed in Appendix B.

In doubtful cases, the tribunal will rule whether it has power to deal with a matter or not.

5 Is the procedure the same for all appeals?

No. There are three categories of appeal and the procedure differs with each. They are:

A Penalty for Tax Evasion (*Dishonest Conduct*) (*known as "Category 1 appeals"*)

These are appeals against penalties for dishonest evasion of tax, with or without an appeal against an associated assessment. These appeals are **not** dealt with in this leaflet. The tribunal centre can tell you about the procedure. You may also wish to consult a professional adviser.

B General Penalties (*known as "Category 2 appeals"*)

There are four types of penalties against which Category 2 appeals may be made. What happens is set out in paragraph 6.

(i) Default surcharge (late returns or late payments):

Appeals can be made on grounds of reasonable excuse. This means arguing that you should not be required to pay the surcharge because you had a reasonable excuse for whatever went wrong, or because the return was posted, with the tax, in time to get to the VAT Central Unit by the due date.

The tribunal has no power to mitigate (that is, reduce the amount of) the surcharge provided it is correctly calculated, but only to allow or dismiss the appeal outright for each surcharge.

(ii) Penalty for misdeclaration or neglect:

BOTH dismissal of the penalty on grounds of **reasonable excuse** (see (i) above), AND **mitigation** (that is, a reduction in the penalty) **can** be asked for in the same appeal.

(iii) Late registration penalty (that is, civil penalty for failure to notify liability to register):

The position is the same as for penalties for misdeclaration or neglect (see (ii) above).

(iv) Reduction of a penalty for tax evasion (dishonest conduct):

An appeal can be made by a person seeking mitigation (a reduction) of the penalty. Note, however, that appeal against liability to the penalty is a Category 1 appeal (see (A) above).

C Assessments (known as "Category 3 appeals")

This category includes all matters **except** those solely concerning reasonable excuses or penalties. What happens is set out in Paragraph 7. Common examples include appeals against decisions by HMRC regarding—

- assessments to tax
- refusals to allow claims for input tax
- rulings as to liability for tax on supplies of goods or services
- refusals to allow bad debt relief
- requirements to provide security as a condition of continuing to trade
- refusals to allow a Special Scheme to be used.

6 What happens on a Category 2 appeal?

In a reasonable excuse appeal, you **must** set out in the Notice of Appeal details of the reasonable excuse which you want to offer including, for example, the date the return was posted if that is the point you want to make. If this is left out, the tribunal centre may ask you to amend the Notice of Appeal so as to show the nature or your reasonable excuse.

If you are asking for the penalty to be mitigated, it will help if you state your reasons why it should be reduced.

When the tribunal centre has received, registered and acknowledged an appeal, it sends a copy of the Notice of Appeal to HMRC. No statement of case or list of documents is required from you or HMRC.

Accordingly, subject to any preliminary matters which may be raised in the appeal, the tribunal then sends a notice of the hearing date to you and HMRC.

7 What happens on a Category 3 appeal?

In a Category 3 appeal, a copy of the Notice of Appeal is notified by the tribunal centre to HMRC. Within 30 days of the date of notification of the Notice of Appeal (see paragraph 10) HMRC have to serve a Statement of Case setting out the matters and facts upon which they rely to support the disputed decision. At the same time, they have to serve a list of the documents they intend to produce at the hearing; you have the right to see and take copies of those documents. A copy of the statement of case and a list of documents received from HMRC will be sent to you by the tribunal centre.

You must also send to the tribunal a list of any documents you intend to produce (see paragraph 22). However, there may be other matters to settle first or HMRC may be unable to meet the time limit (see paragraph 11).

II APPEALING

8 How do I appeal?

You must first complete a Notice of Appeal and send or fax it to, or hand it in at, the tribunal centre for your area (see Appendix A) with a copy of the disputed decision. You should NOT send it to an office of HMRC. It is better to use the Notice of Appeal form (Trib 1) available from:

(a) any of our Tribunal Centres;
(b) the tribunal's website at www.financeandtaxtribunals.gov.uk or;
(c) telephoning the HMRC's national advice centre on 0845 010 9000.

You, as appellant, or someone authorised to represent you, must sign the Notice of Appeal. All documents will be sent to your representative, if you have one—otherwise they will be sent to you. If your or your representative's address changes during the course of the case, the tribunal centre must be told. Do **not** send payments of tax, etc to the tribunal centre.

9 Is there a time limit for me to appeal?

Yes. An appeal must normally be made within **30 days** of the disputed decision. However, HMRC may extend this period in correspondence with you. If the original 30 days, or an extended period, have expired, you should tick box (iii) in Part B of the Notice of Appeal form to show your wish to apply for an extension of time. Depending on the circumstances there may have to be a hearing to decide whether an extension of time should be allowed.

10 Will the tribunal acknowledge receipt of my Notice of Appeal?

Yes. The tribunal will acknowledge receipt ("service") of any documents you send. The acknowledgment of the Notice of Appeal will normally state the date of service on the tribunal and the date of notification to HMRC of the appeal and will give a tribunal reference number for the appeal. Certain time limits start from these dates (see below).

11 What happens if I cannot meet a time limit, or wish to apply for a direction?

A There are several occasions during the early stages of an appeal when one or other of the parties may be required to do something within a fixed period. For example, you may have to lodge a list of documents and HMRC may have to produce a statement of case; in both cases there is a time limit. You, or HMRC, may wish to apply for an extension of the time limit. The tribunal will consider each application on its merits.

B On other occasions you or HMRC may wish to apply to the tribunal for a direction about something else, for example, to apply for further and better particulars of the other party's case, or for all proceedings in the case to be stood over (suspended) for a set period.

C A party who wants to make such an application must write to the tribunal centre giving his name and address, the tribunal reference number of the appeal, the direction sought, and the grounds (that is, the reasons why the extension of time or other direction is sought).

D A copy of the application will be sent by the tribunal centre to the other party, who has 14 days to consent or object to the application. If the other party does not oppose the application, the tribunal may allow it without a hearing. If it is opposed, the tribunal centre will arrange a preliminary hearing to decide the issue, and will tell you the hearing date. The hearing will be in private unless the tribunal directs otherwise. It is sometimes possible to conduct applications hearings by telephone link. If you think this would be appropriate in your case get in touch with the relevant Tribunal Centre.

12 Are there any conditions I must meet?

Yes.

You cannot appeal against a tax assessment or the amount of a tax assessment in respect of an accounting period unless you have made a VAT return for that period to HMRC. This rule does not apply when the issue in the period is whether you were required to make a return for that period.

13 Will I have to pay the amount of tax in dispute before my appeal can be heard?

If your appeal is about—

- an assessment of tax or the amount of such an assessment or,
- an assessment to recover input tax, or
- the tax chargeable on a supply of goods or services, or
- the tax chargeable on the importation of goods,

a tribunal normally cannot hear your appeal unless the tax in dispute has been paid or deposited with HMRC.

However, the tribunal does have the power to waive this requirement to pay the tax in dispute, and HMRC also may consent to this (see below).

14 How do I apply for my appeal to be heard without payment of the disputed tax?

A As mentioned above, a tribunal cannot hear an appeal which relates to disputed tax unless **either** you have paid or deposited the tax in dispute, **or** the tribunal (or HMRC) have waived that requirement. If paying or depositing the disputed tax would cause you financial **hardship**, you should first write to HMRC asking them to waive the requirement. It is essential for you to demonstrate your financial position to them so that they can consider the matter fully (by means of evidence of assets, liabilities, income and expenditure; you may for example need to send them copies of your bank statements).

B If HMRC do not agree to waive the requirement, you may apply to the tribunal by making a tick in box (a) of Part C of the Notice of Appeal form; this is a "hardship application". If HMRC oppose your hardship application, the tribunal centre will arrange a hearing to decide whether or not to allow it. The hearing will be in private unless the tribunal directs otherwise.

You should have already supplied evidence of your financial position: if you have failed to do so, the last opportunity to present such evidence will be the hearing, and you must provide a list of the documents you wish to rely on in advance of the hearing.

C If the requirement to pay the tax is waived but, subsequently, you lose your appeal, you may have to pay interest on the amount of disputed tax payable to HMRC as a result of the Tribunal's decision. Conversely, if you lose your hardship application but subsequently win your appeal, HMRC are liable to pay you interest on tax which you had to pay or deposit to enable your appeal to proceed and which they have to pay back.

15 Will I have to pay penalties, surcharges or interest before my appeal can be heard?

No. When an appeal is about a penalty, surcharge or an amount of interest you do not have to pay it before your appeal can be heard.

III THE HEARING

16 When and where will my appeal be heard?

The tribunal centre listing office will send you a notice telling you the date, time and place of the hearing. You will always get at least 14 days' notice of a hearing unless both you and HMRC have agreed to shorter notice.

Hearings take place at tribunal centres in London, Manchester and Edinburgh. The tribunal also arranges to hear appeals in many other places (for example, Aberdeen, Belfast, Birmingham, Bristol, Cardiff, Newcastle, Plymouth and York) on request. If you have moved to a new address you can have your appeal hearing at the nearest practicable tribunal centre.

17 What if I wish to postpone a tribunal hearing?

A tribunal is usually reluctant to postpone a hearing, but if it is essential for you to seek a postponement:

(*a*) you or your representative should immediately ask the tribunal listing office by telephone, followed by a letter or fax;
(*b*) you should give your reasons for asking for a postponement;
(*c*) you should be prepared to agree an alternative hearing date when you and your witnesses will be ready;
(*d*) if your reason includes illness you should be ready to supply a medical certificate;
(*e*) an engagement elsewhere is not normally sufficient reason to justify a postponement; you should be ready to explain why the other engagement takes priority over the tribunal hearing.

Where an application to take a hearing out of the list is received within four working days of the hearing date the hearing will only be taken out if there is a compelling reason for doing so, e g serious illness or accident. In other cases late applications to postpone will be heard by the Tribunal at the start of the hearing.

You should not assume a hearing will be cancelled because you have asked; a hearing once appointed remains **on** unless the tribunal states that it has been cancelled.

18 Can I withdraw my appeal?

Yes. You can withdraw your appeal at any time but you should tell the tribunal centre in writing as soon as possible. If you decide to withdraw your appeal, or an application, **after a date for a hearing has been fixed** you should let the tribunal centre know **immediately** by telephone or fax.

HMRC may ask for an order for costs against you if they attend a hearing where you fail to attend or be represented. (See Appendix D).

19 What if I fail to attend a tribunal hearing?

If for any reason you do not attend on the hearing date the tribunal can hear the case in your absence. But if it does, you may, within 14 days of the date of the written decision, apply to have the tribunal decision set aside and your case reinstated. Your application must give the reasons for your failure to attend. The tribunal will consider your application and, if necessary, arrange for a hearing to decide the issue.

You should remember the risk of costs (paragraph 28).

20 Does the burden of proof lie upon me or upon HMRC?

In almost all appeals, at the start the "burden of proof" is upon you. This means it is up to you to show why the disputed assessment, penalty or decision is wrong. When the appeal is against a dishonesty penalty, the burden is on HMRC, who must satisfy the Tribunal that you were dishonest.

You will need to put evidence before the tribunal which will establish the facts, figures, dates, etc. If you need to call witnesses or produce documents, it is up to you to see to it that they are all available at the hearing of the appeal.

21 What documents will I need?

Any documents which you intend to refer to or rely on in support of your case must be available at the hearing. This may include invoices, books of accounts, bank statements, contracts, export documents, etc.

If you are in doubt about whether a document will be needed, your best course is to bring it with you. You should not assume that the hearing will be adjourned to another occasion to enable the documents to be produced.

22 Do the documents have to be disclosed in advance?

Yes. In **Category 3** appeals, each party must disclose to the other party all the documents they intend to rely on at the hearing, and must do so well in advance of the hearing. Each party supplies to the tribunal a list of their documents, along with an offer either to supply copies of them or to allow them to be inspected by a representative of the other side. See also paragraph 7.

If you introduce at the hearing documents of which the other party is unaware, there may have to be a time-wasting adjournment, and you may be ordered to pay the costs of the wasted hearing.

In **Category 2** appeals, it is not compulsory to disclose documents in advance, but you will need to bring with you any documents you are relying on for proof that you have a reasonable excuse or, if this is your case, that the return was posted within reasonable time. Also it is helpful to the tribunal if the parties supply copies of documents prior to the hearing. Appendix C lists evidence you may need to bring in some surcharge cases.

23 I need the evidence of a witness to prove my case; what do I do?

Normally it is up to you to arrange for your witnesses to attend the hearing ready to give their evidence. If a witness is reluctant to attend, the tribunal has power to compel attendance by means of a **witness summons**; the tribunal centre can tell you how this can be obtained.

If you think the evidence of a witness is necessary, but it is not likely to be disputed by HMRC, you can serve (by sending it to the tribunal centre) a Witness Statement, that is the witness's evidence, in writing, signed and dated by him or her. If HMRC do not object to the statement, the tribunal can read the statement and it will not be necessary for the witness to attend the hearing. If HMRC do object, you should bring the witness to the hearing; if you do not, his or her evidence cannot be taken into account. HMRC may serve statements on you; if you do not accept what the witnesses say, you must object promptly, following the instructions the tribunal will send to you. If you do not object to the statements, the tribunal will read them and take account of what the witnesses say. Please note that HMRC do not have to bring a witness to the hearing if you object to his or her statement; they can simply do without the evidence if they wish. If you want to ask that witness questions, you must ensure that HMRC will be bringing him or her and, if not, issue and serve witness summons.

24 What if some of the evidence is agreed, but some is disputed?

If you wish, you may approach HMRC to discuss the case with them and possibly produce an agreed statement of facts, an agreed bundle of documents, agreed accounts, a summary of those matters not agreed, etc. This would simplify preparations for the hearing and save time and money. The tribunal finds agreed statements, etc, helpful.

25 What happens at an appeal hearing?

Appeals are normally heard in public. You or your representative must bring all the documents on which you rely in support of your case and arrange for the attendance of all the witnesses you need (see paragraphs 21, 22 and 23).

The party upon whom the burden of proof rests (normally you but see paragraph 20) will begin. You should introduce the case by explaining what it is about, giving a summary of the facts and indicating how the law applies to the facts.

You will need to explain what is already agreed, what is in dispute, what evidence you are putting forward and the basic points you are making. It is important for each party, in the course of presenting the case, to bring out the essential facts. You should state quite clearly why the decision of HMRC was wrong.

When the first party has introduced its case, and called evidence, the other party will open its case, call evidence (if any) in the same way, and make submissions including its answers to the first party's case. The first party then has a right of reply, but may not raise new issues unless the tribunal allows.

Witnesses usually give evidence on oath or affirmation. After being examined (questioned) by the party calling him, the witness may be cross-examined by the other party, re-examined and perhaps questioned also by the tribunal.

26 Will the tribunal help me put forward my case?

If you are not used to court proceedings, the chairman will help you with your case as far as he can. However, it is likely that the chairman will have little knowledge of the case before the hearing, and will not have seen correspondence between you and HMRC. If it helps, the chairman may ask the HMRC representative to explain initially the basis of their decision. Though the chairman will help you, he cannot argue your case for you.

27 What happens at the end of the hearing?

The tribunal may announce its decision there and then, or may reserve it to be given in writing later. In either case, the reasons for the decision will be given, and a copy of the written decision signed by the chairman will be sent to you.

In Category 2 appeals, provided both parties agree, the tribunal may issue a brief direction recording the outcome instead of a full decision.

28 Can I ask for an award of costs if my appeal succeeds? And what about costs if I lose?

If your appeal is either wholly or partly successful you can ask for costs. If you do ask for costs you will have to give clear details as to how they are made up. You may also ask the tribunal to direct that HMRC repay with interest any tax paid or deposited by you in order to have your appeal heard.

If you lose your appeal HMRC are entitled to ask that you pay their costs. (See Appendix D for a statement of HMRC policy about this.) If you made a successful hardship application and thereby avoided paying or depositing the disputed tax before the hearing of your appeal you may have to pay interest on that tax if you lose your appeal (see paragraph 14C).

APPENDIX A

The address of the London Tribunal Centre is—

15–19 Bedford Avenue, London WC1B 3AS, Telephone No: 020 7612 9700, Fax No: 020 7436 4150; email: vatlon@tribunals.gsi.gov.uk. The public entrance is at 45 Bedford Square, London WC1B 3DN.

The London Tribunal Centre deals with appeals against decisions sent to addresses in Southern England, East Anglia, S Wales, and those sent to addresses outside the UK.

The address of the Manchester Tribunal Centre is—

9th Floor, West Point, 501 Chester Road, Old Trafford, Manchester M16 5HU; Telephone No: 0161 868 6600; Fax No: 0161 876 4479; email: vatman@tribunals.gsi.gov.uk.

The Manchester Tribunal Centre deals with appeals against decisions sent to addresses in the Midlands, Northern England, N Wales, Northern Ireland and the Isle of Man.

The address of the Edinburgh Tribunal Centre is—

George House, 126 George Street, EDINBURGH EH2 4HH; Telephone No: 0131 271 4330; Fax No: 0131 271 4399; Email: email@vatscotland.org.uk.

The Edinburgh Tribunal Centre deals with appeals against decisions sent to addresses in Scotland.

APPENDIX B
LIST OF APPEALABLE MATTERS

The following lists most of the decisions of HMRC concerning VAT (not in strict legal terms) against which you can appeal:

Appeals against decisions with respect to any of the following matters are Category 3 appeals—

- an assessment to tax or the amount of an assessment
- the registration or cancellation of the registration of any taxable person
- a refusal to allow group registration or a change in a group registration
- a refusal to exempt a trader from registration or to allow voluntary registration as a taxable person
- the tax chargeable on a supply of goods or services, or on an importation of goods
- the amount of any input tax allowable
- the proportion of any supplies which may be taken as taxable supplies, for example, by a partially exempt trader
- the amount of a refund to a person constructing a new home
- a refund of tax in respect of a bad debt
- a refund of tax paid on an importation for private purposes of another person's goods
- a direction that the value of supplies shall be their open market value
- a refusal to allow a retailer to use one of the Special Schemes
- a requirement in relation to invoices produced by a computer
- a requirement that a trader should provide security for any tax payable
- a direction that two or more taxable persons should be registered as one
- a refusal to repay tax on grounds of unjust enrichment
- a refusal to allow a taxable person to join the cash accounting scheme or the cancellation of cash accounting scheme facilities.

Category 2 appeals concern a default surcharge (late returns), late registration penalty, penalty for misdeclaration or neglect (wrong returns) or an appeal for mitigation (reduction) of a penalty for tax evasion (dishonest conduct).

Category 1 appeals are solely against the imposition of a penalty for tax evasion (dishonest conduct) and against any related tax assessment.

APPENDIX C
EVIDENCE IN SURCHARGE APPEALS

(*a*) If you are saying that you posted your VAT return and the tax due on it in time to reach the VAT Central Unit at Southend by the due date, it will be for you to satisfy the tribunal of this.

The following are examples of the sorts of evidence (from witnesses and documents) that could help your case. You should bring them with you to the hearing.

(1) your post book, if you have one;
(2) any certificate from the Post Office that the return was posted;
(3) the person who signed the return (if it was not you);
(4) anyone who handled the return after it was signed, including the person who posted it (if it was not you);
(5) your cheque book stubs covering the period when the payment was made;
(6) your bank statements for the period when payment was made;
(7) any other evidence or any other witness that will help the tribunal.

(*b*) If you are saying that the return was not sent in in time because someone was ill, you should bring with you to the hearing records showing exactly when the person concerned was away and, if possible, a medical certificate giving particulars of the illness and details of any time spent in hospital because of it.

(*c*) If you say your bank failed to meet your cheque for VAT by some mistake, you should try to get a letter from the bank admitting the mistake and bring it to the hearing.

(*d*) If you keep a VAT file containing the correspondence between you and HMRC and the documents you receive from them, you should bring that file with you.

You should consider whether you should send copies of any of the documents mentioned above to HMRC (or make them available for inspection) before the hearing; it is possible they might lead them to accept your case.

APPENDIX D
HMRC POLICY ABOUT COSTS

The following is an extract from a written answer by the Minister of State, Treasury, (the Hon Peter Brooke MP [Hansard Vol 102, 24 July 1986 Cols 459–460]) to a parliamentary question:

> "As a general rule, Customs & Excise do not seek costs against unsuccessful appellants. They do, however, ask for costs in certain narrowly defined cases so as to provide protection for public funds and the general body of taxpayers. They will therefore seek to continue to ask for costs at those exceptional tribunal hearings of substantial and complex cases where large sums are involved and which are comparable with High Court cases, unless the appeal involves an important general point of law, requiring clarification. They will also continue to consider seeking costs where the appellant has misused the tribunal procedures—for example in frivolous or vexatious cases, or where the appellant has failed to appear or to be represented at a mutually arranged hearing without sufficient explanation, or where the appellant has first produced at a hearing relevant evidence which ought properly to have been disclosed at an earlier stage and which could have saved public funds had it been produced timeously.
>
> The new penalty provisions and right of appeal to the value added tax tribunals have made no change to this policy."

HMRC consider that appeals involving tax avoidance schemes and any other form of artificial avoidance will generally be substantial and complex in nature and that they may seek costs in such cases.

Issued by the President of VAT and Duties Tribunals, 2007.

The Tribunals Service. March 2009

Making an appeal

1. THE TRIBUNALS SERVICE

The Tribunals Service is part of the Ministry of Justice and provides administrative support for the Tribunals' judiciary who hear cases and decide appeals. The tax appeals system was created on 1 April 2009, and this provides for tax appeals to be heard in a First-tier Tax Chamber, with a right of appeal with permission to the Upper Tribunal. The tax appeals system is totally independent of Her Majesty's Revenue and Customs (HMRC).

2. ABOUT THIS BOOKLET

This booklet is designed to provide you with useful information about how to appeal against a decision of HMRC and how to make your appeal to the Tax Chamber of the First-tier Tribunal.

We explain what decisions can be appealed against and how you may bring a case before the tax tribunal. This booklet aims to give you the essential information you need to make your appeal, though it cannot cover all circumstances.

3. WHAT IS THE TAX TRIBUNAL?

The First-tier Tribunal is divided into several Chambers, one of which is the Tax Chamber. Throughout this booklet this Tax Chamber is referred to as the tax tribunal. The tax tribunal hears the full range of appeals against HMRC decisions in relation to direct and indirect tax cases (explained in paragraph 4 below). It has a single set of procedural rules giving it the flexibility to deal with the whole range of tax matters from the straightforward to the complex. The tax tribunal is completely independent of HMRC, and cases are heard by Judges and other Members who are qualified to hear cases. Annex A provides a list of the types of tax appeal the tribunal can deal with.

4. APPEAL RIGHTS

You can appeal only where the law gives you a right of appeal. Not every HMRC decision on a tax matter carries a right of appeal. When you do have a right of appeal the official letter from HMRC giving the decision will make this clear. The tribunal will determine, in doubtful cases, if it has the jurisdiction (which means the power) to deal with the dispute or not.

The main areas that the tribunal deals with are tax assessments and penalties. A list of the more common tax decisions made by HMRC that can be appealed to the tribunal can be found at Annex A. This is not a complete list and appeals against tax credit decisions are dealt with in the Social Entitlement Chamber and not by the tax tribunal.

Direct tax refers to tax that is usually levied directly off an organisation or an individual person, such as income tax or corporation tax. Indirect tax refers to tax that is usually levied on goods or services rather than on an individual or organisations, such as VAT or Customs Duties.

5. THE TRIBUNAL'S POWERS

In deciding whether to appeal or not, you need to know what the tribunal can and can't do for you. The tribunal does not have unlimited powers. It can only do what the law gives it the power to do. Sometimes, if it accepts that your appeal is valid, it can replace the decision you are appealing against with the decision it thinks should have been made. In other cases it can only direct HMRC to reconsider their decision. If it does not accept that your appeal is valid it will uphold the decision you are appealing against.

6. DECIDING WHETHER TO APPEAL

Before making your appeal, you should know that the tribunal cannot:

Change the law. It has to apply the law as it stands, even if that leads to an outcome that you think is unfair

Deal with administrative complaints about the conduct of HMRC officials. (If you are unhappy with the way HMRC have dealt with your tax affairs, please refer to their guidance on how to complain on the HMRC website http://www.hmrc.gov.uk/dealingwith/complain.htm.)

We cannot advise you whether you have a case or whether you are likely to win or lose your appeal nor can we tell you if you should appeal or not. HMRC, in their decision letter, will have told you whether you have a right of appeal to the tribunal.

Many people who make an appeal choose to get professional advice and support with it.

If you do decide to get advice, please do so at the earliest opportunity – when you are thinking about appealing. Please do not leave it until your appeal is well under way as we may not be able to put your appeal on hold whilst you are seeking representation. If you face a delay in getting advice please keep an eye on the time-limit for appealing.

In indirect tax appeals, the tax tribunal cannot hear an appeal that relates to disputed tax unless either you have paid or deposited the tax in dispute, or the Tribunal (or HMRC) have waived that requirement.

In direct tax, the payment of the tax in dispute is usually postponed pending the outcome of the appeal, and this is not an issue.

7. HARDSHIP CASES – APPLYING FOR YOUR APPEAL TO BE HEARD WITHOUT PAYMENT OF THE DISPUTED TAX

This relates to indirect tax only. The tribunal cannot hear an appeal which relates to disputed tax unless either you have paid or deposited the tax in dispute, or the Tribunal (or HMRC) have waived that requirement. If paying or depositing the disputed tax would cause you financial hardship, you should first write to HMRC asking them to waive the requirement. It is essential that you demonstrate your financial position to them so that they can consider the matter fully. If HMRC do not agree to waive the requirement, you may apply to the tribunal to consider the matter. If HMRC oppose your hardship request, we will arrange a tribunal hearing to decide whether or not to allow it.

To make an application for hardship to the tribunal after receiving HMRC's decision on the matter, you should complete the relevant section on the Notice of Appeal Form and send it to us.

8. WHAT WILL IT COST ME TO APPEAL

You do not need to pay a fee to appeal to the tax tribunal. However, we also do not pay travelling expenses for attending a tribunal hearing. Your own costs in preparing your appeal will depend on the difficulty of your case and whether you decide to handle your appeal yourself or instruct a tax adviser such as a solicitor or accountant.

The tribunal can, in some rare circumstances, make an award of costs against either of the parties. An award of costs is where the tribunal decides that either you or HMRC should pay the costs of the other party in taking their case.

There would be an award of costs against you only where the tribunal considered that you had behaved unreasonably, or in certain circumstances where the tribunal had categorised your case as Complex. You will be given further information if the awarding of costs is a possibility.

9. WHAT SHOULD I DO FIRST?

Before you can make your appeal, you must first have an appeal-able written decision from HMRC with which you disagree. HMRC will have informed you of your options if you disagree with a decision.

You should consider your options seriously before appealing, including asking HMRC to look again at the decision as many disagreements can be settled by discussion or correspondence with HMRC without you actually having to go to a tribunal. HMRC are able to offer a formal internal review of your decision by a reviewer who will have had no previous involvement with your dispute. If you do not wish to engage these processes you can still appeal directly to the tribunal.

10. TIME LIMIT FOR APPEALING

You will normally have 30 days to appeal a disputed HMRC decision. If you make use of HMRC's review process you will have 30 days to appeal from the date they tell you the outcome. The time limit runs from both the original decision and any decision following review. The letter you receive from HMRC, both the original decision and any decision following review, will confirm the time you have for appealing.

If you are making your appeal outside the time limit, you must give reasons to the tribunal in writing.

11. WHERE DO I OBTAIN A NOTICE OF APPEAL?

Appeals to the tax tribunal must be made in writing. When you decide to make your appeal to the tax tribunal, you are strongly advised to complete a Notice of Appeal form and send it to the address at the bottom of the form.

You can download the Notice of Appeal form from our website at http://www.tribunals.gov.uk. If you do not have access to the internet, please phone us on 0845 223 8080 and we will send you a copy.

12. COMPLETING THE NOTICE OF APPEAL

The Notice of Appeal form is an important document as the details contained in this form will be used to process your appeal to a tribunal hearing, and to ensure we convene a panel that is appropriate for determining your case. It helps the tribunal to consider your case fairly and also helps us contact you with information about how your appeal is progressing.

A separate information sheet with guidance notes on completing the Notice of Appeal is available on our website and will be sent to you with the Notice of Appeal if you ask us to send you one. Please phone us on 0845 223 8080 to request this.

The completed Notices of Appeal should be sent to:

Tribunals Service
Tax
2nd Floor
54 Hagley Road
Birmingham
B16 8PE
Telephone: 0845 223 8080

If you prefer to complete the Notice of Appeal electronically, you can send it to us at: taxappeals@tribunals.gsi.gov.uk.

The tribunal will acknowledge receipt of your appeal in writing. You will be given a Tribunal Service Reference Number which you should quote whenever you contact us. At this stage, we will also notify HMRC of your appeal.

13. CASE CATEGORISATION

When you appeal to the tax tribunal, it will put your appeal in one of four categories: Default Paper, Basic, Standard or Complex. Which of the four categories your appeal is allocated to is dependent on the nature and complexity of your appeal.

When we acknowledge your appeal, we will tell you in writing which category your appeal has been allocated, and how your appeal will proceed. We will keep you or your representative informed of progress throughout your appeal. Please note, however, that if you have a representative, we will only send correspondence to them. If you disagree with the way your case has been categorised you should contact the tribunal.

Default Paper cases, by their nature, are generally decided by the tribunal after reading the Notice of Appeal and the other written material provided by you and HMRC. Default Paper cases are dealt with without a hearing, though you may ask for your appeal to be decided at a hearing. If you or HMRC request a hearing or it is decided there should be a hearing by the tribunal, you will be expected to attend. HMRC will also send a representative to the hearing.

Basic category appeals are dealt with at informal hearings (see paragraph 14 below).

The vast majority of appeals within the Standard and Complex categories will be registered at our Tribunals Service Centre in Birmingham but will then be passed to other Tax tribunal offices in London, Manchester and Edinburgh. We will advise you in writing if we transfer your appeal.

Tax appeals are heard at a number of venues across the UK and we will, where possible, arrange for your appeal to be heard at a venue reasonably close to where you live or work. Sometimes, however, due to the size or complexity of an appeal, we may not be able to do this but we will let you know as soon as possible.

There may be occasions during the appeal process when judicial direction on your appeal will be sought. If this is required, we will inform you of the directions and any associated time limits which may apply. In more complex cases, you may be asked to attend a hearing at which a Judge will make directions.

14. STATEMENT OF CASE AND NEXT STEPS

The next step will usually be for the tribunal to request a statement of case from HMRC, except in relation to basic category cases. A statement of case is a written statement of HMRC's position on your case. It will normally contain information such as the legislation under which the appealed decision was made, HMRC's position on the case and any other relevant information associated with the appeal.

Default Paper category (where there is no hearing)

A case categorised as default paper is generally decided when the tribunal has read the Notice of Appeal and other written material provided by you and HMRC. When we have notified HMRC that you have made an appeal against a decision which falls into this category, HMRC have 42 days to provide a statement of case to the tribunal. When the statement of case has been prepared, HMRC will send a copy to you.

You may provide a written response to the statement of case within 30 days of it being sent to you. You should send your response, if you wish to make one, to us and send a copy to HMRC. Please remember to quote your Tribunals Service reference number when writing to us and your HMRC reference number when corresponding with them. Unless you have asked for an oral hearing, the case will be decided by the tribunal when you have provided your response, or if you do not provide one, when the 30 day time limit has expired. The tribunal will send you its response as soon as possible after considering your case.

Basic Category (where there is an informal hearing)

The tribunal does not normally require a statement of case to be produced by HMRC for cases categorised as Basic. If your case is categorised in this way it will be listed for a hearing. You are expected to attend the hearing, when you will be given the opportunity to put forward your case, show the Tribunal any relevant documents you have and, if you wish, call witnesses. HMRC will also attend, and they may put their case, produce documents and call witnesses at the hearing. The hearing will be informal, and the tribunal will usually tell you what it has decided at the end of the hearing.

Standard and Complex categories

When we have notified HMRC that you have made an appeal against a decision in the Standard and Complex categories, HMRC have 60 days to provide a statement of case to the tribunal. The statement of case will contain similar information to that described above for the default paper category, though the facts and issues are likely to be much more complex. As with default paper cases, when HMRC have prepared the statement of case they will send a copy to you.

You will normally have 42 days from receipt of the statement of case from HMRC in which to provide to the tribunal and HMRC a list of the documents which you will rely on at the tribunal hearing. HMRC also have to provide a list of documents and copy their list to you. The tribunal may also make any other direction at this time as to what may be required of you, and may determine that your case requires more intensive case management. You will have the opportunity to express your views on how your case should be managed.

15. WHEN AND WHERE WILL MY APPEAL BE HEARD?

Hearings in the tax tribunal take place at a network of venues across the UK and we will arrange your appeal, where possible, at a venue which is local to you.

If your appeal is categorised as Basic, Standard or Complex, you should attend your hearing. For more information about the process of informing you of your hearing, please see paragraph 16 below.

16. NOTIFICATION OF HEARING

If your appeal is to be decided at a hearing, we will write to you notifying you of the date, time and venue of your hearing. We will give you at least 14 days notice of a hearing, unless both you and HMRC agree to a shorter period. However, we will usually give at least a month's notice.

You should tell us immediately in writing if the date we set for your tribunal hearing is not convenient and give the reasons why you cannot attend. We will then write to you to tell you whether your postponement request has been granted or not. For appeals in the Standard and Complex categories, we will ask you in advance about dates which are inconvenient for you. In these cases, the tribunal will be less willing to agree to a postponement, though it will do so for good reason, such as sudden illness.

Appellants in the Basic category appeals will usually be asked to attend at either 10:00 or 14:00 on the day of the hearing. In the Standard and Complex categories you will be given a set time to attend and the case may last a number of days.

The time to arrive at the venue is given in your notice of hearing letter, and it is the latest time by which you should arrive at the tribunal venue. If you are likely to be late for your hearing, please telephone us and we will relay a message to the tribunal.

For further information of what can happen at your hearing, please refer to the booklet "At your hearing".

17. WITHDRAWALS OF APPEALS

You can withdraw your appeal at any time. Should you wish to withdraw your appeal, you should write to us immediately. If HMRC decide to concede the matter in dispute, they will write to both the tribunal and you.

ANNEX A: WHAT TYPE OF APPEALS DOES THE TAX TRIBUNAL DEAL WITH?

The tax tribunal deals with appeals against decisions about tax made by HMRC. These include:

Direct tax

- income tax
- corporation tax
- capital gains tax
- national insurance contributions
- statutory payments
- inheritance tax
- petroleum revenue tax
- student loans
- stamp duty land tax
- tax collected under Pay as You Earn and the Construction Industry Scheme

Indirect tax

- value added tax (VAT)
- customs duty
- excise duties including:
- alcoholic liquor duties
- hydrocarbon oils duties (ie petrol, diesel, heating fuel etc)
- tobacco products duty
- bingo duty
- gaming duty
- general betting duty
- lottery duty
- pool betting duty
- remote gaming duty
- aggregates levy
- air passenger duty
- climate change levy
- insurance premium tax
- landfill tax

The tax tribunal also deals with appeals against decisions made by HMRC in relation to the Money Laundering Regulations 2007.

The above list contains the most common types of HMRC decisions.

VAT INDEX

Defined words and phrases are listed separately at the end.

VAT

BOATS
acquisition in settlement of insurance claim, SI 1992/3129 art 4
facilities for mooring, anchoring, berthing or storing, VATA 1994 Sch 9 Group 1 item 1(*k*)
handicapped person, designed or adapted for, VATA 1994 Sch 8 Group 12 item 2(i)
lifeboat, VATA 1994 Sch 8 Group 8 item 3
repossession under finance agreement, SI 1992/3129 art 4
sailaway, ESC 8.1
supplied for export outside EC, Notice 703/2
used—
exclusion of input tax credit, SI 1992/3222 art 4
relief for certain supplies, SI 1992/3129 art 8

BODY CORPORATE. *See also* GROUP OF COMPANIES
business carried on in divisions, VATA 1994 s 46(1)
domestic accommodation for directors, VATA 1994 s 24(3)
incorporation of, goods and services acquired before, SI 1995/2518 reg 111
insolvency, priority of tax in, IA 1986 s 175, Sch 6,
liability of director, VATA 1994 s 61
liquidator of, SI 1995/2518 reg 9(1), (3)
officer of, liability to criminal penalties, CEMA 1979 s 171(4)
persons exercising control of, VATA 1994 s 43
receiver of, SI 1995/2518 reg 9(1), (3)
registration of, goods and services acquired before, SI 1995/2518 reg 111, VATA 1994
subsidiary, CA 1985 s 736
voting rights, reference to, CA 1985 s 736A

BONDED WAREHOUSE
generally, VATA 1994 s 18

BONDS
exemption, VATA 1994 Sch 9 Group 5 item 6, 7 note (5)

BOOKLET
zero-rating, VATA 1994 Sch 8 Group 3 item 1

BOOKMAKERS
pitches, treatment of, RI 210
specialist television services and equipment, recovery of VAT on, PR 19/10/06, PR 3/1/08

BOOKS
zero-rating—
children's picture and painting, VATA 1994 Sch 8 Group 3 item 3
generally, VATA 1994 Sch 8 Group 3
minor accessories supplied with, VATA 1994 Sch 8 Group 3 item 6
talking books for handicapped and blind, VATA 1994 Sch 8 Group 4

BOOTS. *See* CLOTHING AND FOOTWEAR

BRITISH BROADCASTING CORPORATION
refund of tax, VATA 1994 s 33

BROADS AUTHORITY
refund of tax, SI 1999/2076

BUILDERS. *See* DO-IT-YOURSELF BUILDER

BUILDING REGULATION FEES
VAT on, in England and Wales, PR 5/3/97

BUILDINGS
adjustment to deduction of input tax, SI 1995/2518 reg 112

BUILDINGS – *contd*
alterations, VATA 1994 Sch 8 note 9
building materials, VATA 1994 Sch 8 Group 5 item 4, Sch 8 Group 6 item 3
change of use, VATA 1994 Sch 10
commercial buildings—
constructed, exempt use or supply, VATA 1994 Sch 10 para 5
refurbished, exempt use or supply, VATA 1994 Sch 10 para 5
transfer of going concern, anti-avoidance, PR 22/4/03
consideration accruing to other than to grantor, VATA 1994 Sch 10 para 8
construction, VATA 1994 Sch 8 Group 5
self-supply of services, SI 1989/472
conversion, VATA 1994 Sch 8 Group 5
changed numbers of dwellings, meaning, VATA 1994 Sch A1 para 10
house in multiple occupation, meaning, VATA 1994 Sch A1 para 11
qualifying—
meaning, VATA 1994 Sch A1 para 9
planning consent and building control approval, obtaining, VATA 1994 Sch A1 para 15
related garage works, VATA 1994 Sch A1 para 14
qualifying residential purpose, VATA 1994 Sch A1 paras 17–21
reduced rate of VAT, VATA 1994 Sch A1 paras 6–8, Sch 7A para 4A
services, qualifying, VATA 1994 Sch A1 paras 16, 21
special residential—
meaning, VATA 1994 Sch A1 para 12
supplies to intended user, reduced rate for, VATA 1994 Sch A1 para 13
co-owners, registration of, VATA 1994 s 51A
developers of non-residential buildings, VATA 1994 Sch 10 paras 5–7
do-it-yourself builder, refund of tax to, VATA 1994 s 35, SI 1989/2259; PR 25/7/03, PR 9/12/03
election to waive exemption, VATA 1994 Sch 10 paras 2–4
flats, treatment of communal areas in, PR 25/7/03
goods installed in, disallowance of input tax credit, SI 1992/3222 art 6
grant of major interest, VATA 1994 Sch 8 Group 5 item 1
lease. *See* LEASE
listed. *See* PROTECTED BUILDINGS
major interest, grant by member of VAT group, PR 25/7/03
meaning, SI 1995/2518 reg 2
new freehold, sale where consideration not determined, PR 29/11/02
new, used for relevant charitable or residential use, PR 1/7/09
new zero-rated dwellings, where arrangements abusive, PR 28/10/08
protected. *See* PROTECTED BUILDINGS
residential and charitable, VATA 1994 Sch 10 para 1
services related to overseas building, VATA 1994 Sch 8 Group 7
soft landscaping, supplies of, PR 18/5/00
stage payments, time of supply, SI 1995/2518 reg 93
transitional provisions, VATA 1994 Sch 13 para 10

BUILDINGS – *contd*
zero-rated and reduced-rated work, certificate, Notice 708 para 18.1, PR 27/6/02
zero-rated sales and long leases, certificate, Notice 708 para 18.2, PR 27/6/02
BURIAL AND CREMATION
American war graves, ESC 2.5
exemption, VATA 1994 Sch 9 Group 8, PR 17/3/00
local authority, PR 17/3/00
import relief on items connected with, 83/181/EEC art 88
BUS
special facilities for carrying disabled persons, ESC 3.12
BUSINESS
admission charges, VATA 1994 s 94(2)(*b*)
assets. *See* BUSINESS ASSETS
artificial separation of business activities, counter-acting, VATA 1994 Sch 1 paras 1A, 2
associations deemed to be carrying on, VATA 1994 s 94(2)
change of name, constitution or ownership of, notification of, SI 1995/2518 reg 5 (2)
disposal of, assets or liabilities of, SI 1992/3129 art 5
meaning, VATA 1994 s 94
office not treated, VATA 1994 s 94(4)
person, certificate of status of, SI 1995/2518 Sch 1 Form 10
transfer to member of group, VATA 1994 s 44
BUSINESS ASSETS
deemed supply, at deregistration, VATA 1994 Sch 4 para 7
disposal, VATA 1994 s 94(6), Sch 4
held at cessation of business, VATA 1994 Sch 4 para 8
private or non-business use, imported goods, VATA 1994 s 27
removal from member states, VATA 1994 Sch 4 para 6
sale by third party, VATA 1994 Sch 4 para 6
time of supply, VATA 1994 s 6(12)
transfer as going concern, VATA 1994 s 49
group of companies, VATA 1994 s 44
BUSINESS ENTERTAINING
exclusion of input tax credit, SI 1992/3222 art 5
BUSINESS GIFT
cost to donor no more than £10.00, VATA 1994 Sch 4 para 5(2)(*a*)
valuation, VATA 1994 Sch 6 para 6(1)(*a*)
BUSINESS PROMOTION SCHEME
reward goods, treatment of, PR 5/8/99
value of goods exchanged for trading stamps, VATA 1994 s 19
BUSINESS SERVICES
private use of, PR 12/9/94

CAMPING
grant of facilities, VATA 1994 Sch 9 Group 1 item 1(*g*)
CAPITAL GAINS TAX
disposals of heritage objects, exemption, VATA 1994 Sch 9 Group 11 item 4
CAPITAL GOODS
credit for input tax on, SI 1995/2518 regs 112–116
importation, exemption on, 83/181/EEC arts 24–38
refurbishment or fitting out work, valuing, ESC 3.22; PR 26/1/00
CAPITAL GOODS – *contd*
tax relief, VATA 1994 s 34
CAPITAL TRANSFER TAX
disposals of heritage objects, exemption, VATA 1994 Sch 9 Group 11 item 1
CAR PARK
non-local authority, excess charges, PR 8/12/08
CARAVAN
acquisition in settlement of insurance claim, SI 1992/3129 art 4
holiday accommodation, VATA 1994 Sch 9 Group 1 item 1
option to tax, excluded, VATA 1994 Sch 10 para 2(2)
pitches and facilities, VATA 1994 Sch 9 Group 1 item 1(*f*)
repossession under finance agreement, SI 1992/3129 art 4
used—
exclusion of input tax credit, SI 1992/3222 art 4
relief for certain supplies, SI 1992/3129 art 8
zero-rating, VATA 1994 Sch 8 Group 9 item 1; PR 13/11/03
CARS. *See* **COMPANY CAR; MOTOR CAR**
CASH
control of, penalties, SI 2007/1509
CASH ACCOUNTING SCHEME
accounting for VAT, SI 1995/2518 reg 65
admission to scheme, SI 1995/2518 reg 58
changes to, PR 9/2/07
eligibility for scheme, SI 1995/2518 reg 58
guide to, Notice 731
insolvency, SI 1995/2518 reg 62
leaving, cancellation of registration, SI 1995/2518 reg 61
sale of business, SI 1995/2518 reg 63
operation of, Notice 731
regulations, VATA 1994 Sch 11 para 2(7)
selling business, SI 1995/2518 reg 63
turnover limit, SI 1995/2518 reg 58
variation of, SI 1995/2518 reg 59
withdrawal from, enforced, SI 1995/2518 regs 60–64
voluntary, SI 1995/2518 regs 60, 61
CASH BACK
payments, VAT treatment of, PR 6/2/07
CASSETTE PLAYERS
blind person, zero-rating, VATA 1994 Sch 8 Group 4 item 2(*a*)
CATERING
employer provided, value of supply, VATA 1994 Sch 6 para 10(1)(*a*)
food supplied in the course of, VATA 1994 Sch 8 Group 1
supplies by groups, VATA 1994 s 44(4)
supplies in course of, PR 21/8/06
take-away food, VATA 1994 Sch 8 Group 1 note (3)
CEMETERIES. *See* **BURIAL AND CREMATION**
CENTRAL BANK
gold supplied to and by, VATA 1994 Sch 8 Group 10
another member state, supply to, SI 1992/3132
importation of, SI 1992/3124
CERTIFICATE OF DEPOSIT
exemption, VATA 1994 Sch 9 Group 5 items 6, 7, note (5)
CESSATION OF BUSINESS
deemed supply of stock held, VATA 1994 Sch 4 para 8
CHANGE OF USE
relevant charitable or residential building, VATA 1994 Sch 10 para 1

COMMISSIONERS OF CUSTOMS AND EXCISE – *contd*
facilities, power to require, CEMA 1979 s 158
interest payable—
given by way of credit, VATA 1994 s 81(1), (2)
official error, VATA 1994 s 78
meaning, VATA 1994 s 96(1)
power to—
free zones, SI 1984/1177 reg 3
require production of evidence, VATA 1994 Sch 11 para 4
require security, VATA 1994 Sch 11 para 4
regulations. *See* REGULATIONS
VAT law changes, interpretation of, PR 6/7/94
COMMUNITY CUSTOMS CODE
Committee, 450/2008/EC arts 183–185
currency conversion, 450/2008/EC art 31
customs procedure, placing goods under, 450/2008/EC arts 104–107
customs status of goods, 450/2008/EC art 102
customs territory, 450/2008/EC art 3
goods brought into—
arrival of goods, 450/2008/EC arts 91–94
entry summary declaration, 450/2008/EC arts 87–90
entry of goods, 450/2008/EC arts 87–90
presentation, unloading and examination, 450/2008/EC arts 95–97
definitions in Code establishing, 450/2008/EC art 4
disposal of goods, 450/2008/EC art 125, 126
duties based on, 450/2008/EC art 33
end-use procedure, 450/2008/EC art 166
formalities and controls, simplification, 450/2008/EC art 116
free circulation, release of goods for, 450/2008/EC art 129
mission of customs authorities, 450/2008/EC art 2
modernised, 450/2008/EC
origin of goods, 450/2008/EC arts 35–39
provisions for the implementation of, 2454/93/EEC
recovery and payment of duty, 450/2008/EC arts 66, 78
release of goods, 450/2008/EC art s123, 24
rights and duties of persons—
appeals, 450/2008/EC arts 22–24
application of customs legislation, decisions relating to, 450/2008/EC arts 16–20
authorised economic operator, 450/2008/EC arts 13–15
control of goods, 450/2008/EC arts 25–28
customs representation, 450/2008/EC arts 11, 12
data protection, 450/2008/EC art 6
documents and other information, keeping, 450/2008/EC arts 29, 30
information, provision of, 450/2008/EC arts 5–10
penalties, 450/2008/EC art 21
special procedures, 450/2008/EC arts 135–139
tariff classification of goods, 450/2008/EC art 34
time limits, 450/2008/EC art 32
COMMUNITY TRADER
repayment of tax to, SI 1995/2518
COMPANY. *See* BODY CORPORATE; GROUP OF COMPANIES
COMPANY CAR
fuel for private use, VATA 1994 ss 56, 57
COMPLAINTS
handling, PR 17/5/02
COMPLIANCE
powers to enforce, VATA 1994 s 73
COMPUTER
admissibility of computer produced documents, VATA 1994 Sch 11 para 6(6)
data processing. *See* DATA PROCESSING
home, made available by employer, PR 14/8/07
input tax, adjustment of, SI 1995/2518 regs 112–116
meaning, VATA 1994 s 96(6)
preparation of tax invoice, VATA 1994 Sch 11 para 3
preservation of information, VATA 1994 Sch 11 para 6
self-supply, VATA 1994 s 44(4)
zero-rating, VATA 1994 Sch 8 Group 15 note (3a)
CONFECTIONERY. *See* FOOD
CONFIRMING HOUSE
exemption, VATA 1994 Sch 9 Group 5
CONNECTED PERSON
acquisition from other member states, VATA 1994 Sch 7 para 1(5)
value of supply, VATA 1994 Sch 6 para 1(4)
CONSIDERATION
acquisition from other member states, VATA 1994 s 20
apportionment, VATA 1994 s 33(4)
discounts for prompt payment, VATA 1994 Sch 6 para 4
fuel for private use, VATA 1994 s 57
gaming machines—
generally, VATA 1994 s 23(1)
tokens, VATA 1994 s 23(2)
value of supply, VATA 1994 s 23(3)
paid by third party, VATA 1994 Sch 6 para 12
received by person other than grantor, VATA 1994 Sch 10 para 8
value—
provision for employees, VATA 1994 Sch 6 para 10(1)
supply of goods and services, VATA 1994 s 29
tokens, stamps and vouchers, VATA 1994 Sch 6 para 5
CONSTRUCTION INDUSTRY
authenticated receipt treated as tax invoice, SI 1995/2518 reg 13(4)
exemption, VATA 1994 Sch 9 Group 1
self-supply of materials, SI 1989/472
time of supply, SI 1995/2518 reg 93
zero-rating, VATA 1994 Sch 8 Groups 5 and 6
CONSTRUCTION SERVICES. *See* BUILDING; CIVIL ENGINEERING WORK; CONSTRUCTION INDUSTRY; LAND
CONSULTANCY SERVICES
reverse charge, VATA 1994 s 8
supplied where received, VATA 1994 Sch 5 para 3
CONTRACT
effect of change of rate of tax, VATA 1994 s 89
VATA 1994
CONTROL POWERS
arrest of persons, CEMA 1979 ss 167, 168
CO-OWNERS
registration, VATA 1994 s 51A

COPYRIGHT
services supplied where received, VATA 1994 Sch 5 para 1
transfer or assignment—
reverse charge, VATA 1994 s 8
zero-rating to overseas, VATA 1994 Sch 8 Group 7
COSTS
award and direction by tribunal, SI 1986/590 reg 29
COUNCIL ON TRIBUNALS
abolition, TCEA 2007 s 45
Scottish Committee, abolition, TCEA 2007 s 45
COURT OF APPEAL
appeal from VAT tribunal, VATA 1994 s 86, SI 1986/2288
Upper Tribunal, appeal from—
proceedings, TCEA 2007 s 14
right of, TCEA 2007 s 13
COURT OF SESSION
Lord President, delegation of functions by, TCEA 2007 s 46
CRASH HELMETS. *See* MOTORCYCLE
CREDIT CARD
exemption, Sch 9 Group 5 note (4)
handling services, liability of, PR 30/10/06
CREDIT NOTES
change in rate of tax on, SI 1995/2518 reg 15
CROWN
liability to VAT, VATA 1994 s 41
CROWN ESTATE COMMISSIONERS
supplies to and by, VATA 1994 s 41
CRUISE
holiday, tax treatment, PR 15/7/96
river, tax treatment, PR 15/7/96
CULTURAL SERVICES
activities, admission to, PR 10/12/03
direct or indirect financial interest, PR 22/3/07
eligible body, supply of services by, VATA 1994 Sch 9 Group 13 item 2
generally, VATA 1994 Sch 9 Group 13
performed outside UK, VATA 1994 Sch 8 Group 7
public body, supply of services by, VATA 1994 Sch 9 Group 13 item 1
CURRENCY
treated as money, VATA 1994 s 96(1)
CURRENT ACCOUNT
exemption, VATA 1994 Sch 9 Group 5
CUSTOMS AND EXCISE ACT 1979
application, VATA 1994 s 16
CUSTOMS AND EXCISE AIRPORT
meaning, CEMA 1979 s 21
CUSTOMS AND EXCISE COMMISSIONERS. *See* COMMISSIONERS OF CUSTOMS AND EXCISE
CUSTOMS DEBT
extinguishment, 450/2008/EC art 86
incurrence, 450/2008/EC arts 44–55
CUSTOMS DECLARATIONS
acceptance, 450/2008/EC art 112
amendment, 450/2008/EC art 113
examination and sampling of goods, 450/2008/EC arts 118, 119
goods under different tariff subheadings, 450/2008/EC art 115
identification procedures, 450/2008/EC art 121
invalidation, 450/2008/EC art 114
person lodging, 450/2008/EC art 111
simplified, 450/2008/EC art 109
standard, 450/2008/EC art 108
supplementation, 450/2008/EC art 110
verification, 450/2008/EC arts 117–120
CUSTOMS DUTY
Community Customs Code, 2454/93/EEC
CUSTOMS DUTY – *contd*
deferred payments, SI 1976/1223
postal packets, SI 1986/260
CUSTOMS ENTRY
zero-rating, VATA 1994 Sch 8 Group 13 item 1
CUSTOMS VALUE
air transport costs, including, 2454/93/EEC art 166, annex 25
carrier media, 2454/93/EEC art 167
declaration of particulars, 2454/93/EEC arts 178–181a
documents to be furnished, 2454/93/EEC arts 178–181a
generally, 450/2008/EC arts 40–43
generally accepted accounting principles, 2454/93/EEC annex 24
goods sent by post, 2454/93/EEC art 165
interpretative notes on, 2454/93/EEC annex 23
perishable goods, simplified procedures for, 2454/93/EEC arts 173–177
place of introduction of goods, 2454/93/EEC art 163
rates of exchange, 2454/93/EEC arts 168–172
royalties and licence fees, incidence of, 2454/93/EEC arts 157–162
transport costs, 2454/93/EEC arts 164–166
CUSTOMS WAREHOUSE
meaning, CEMA 1979 s 1(1)

DATA PROCESSING
zero-rating, VATA 1994 Sch 8 Group 7
DEATH
appellant or applicant to VAT tribunal, SI 1986/590 reg 13
continuation of registration on, SI 1995/2518 reg 9
notification of, to Commissioners, SI 1995/2518 reg 9
payment of tax, SI 1995/2518 regs 25(1), 54, 63
returns, furnishing, SI 1995/2518 regs 25(1), 54, 63
taxable person, of, SI 1995/2518 reg 9
termination of prescribed accounting period on, SI 1995/2518 reg 25(3)
DEBENTURES
exemption, VATA 1994 Sch 9 Group 5 items 6, 7 note (5)
DEBT
bad. *See* BAD DEBT RELIEF
enforcement services, treatment of, PR 11/4/00
goods sold in satisfaction of, VATA 1994 Sch 4 para 7, Sch 11 para 2(1), (2)
DEBIT CARDS
handling services, liability of, PR 30/10/06
DEDUCTIONS
adjustments, 2006/112/EC arts 184–192
origin and scope of right to deduct, 2006/112/EC arts 167–172
proportional, 2006/112/EC arts 173–175
restrictions on right of, 2006/112/EC arts 176, 177
rules governing exercise of right to deduct, 2006/112/EC arts 178–183
DEEMED SUPPLY
agent, VATA 1994 s 16
assets held at deregistration, VATA 1994 Sch 4 para 8(1), (2)
charge to tax, VATA 1994 s 1(1)
fuel for private use, VATA 1994 s 56(6)
gaming machine, VATA 1994 s 23
motor car self supplied, SI 1992/3122 reg 5

VAT

DEEMED SUPPLY – *contd*
removal of goods to another member state, VATA 1994 Sch 4 para 6, SI 1992/3111
services of office holder, VATA 1994 s 95(7)
services received from abroad, VATA 1994 s 8
stationery self supplied, SI 1992/3129 art 7
zero-rated transactions, VATA 1994 s 30(5)
DEFAULT INTEREST
appeal against assessment, VATA 1994 s 82, 83(*q*)
assessment, VATA 1994 s 76, 77
net errors less that £2000, PR 1/8/08
period of, VATA 1994 s 74
prescribed rate, VATA 1994 s 59
DEFAULT SURCHARGE
amount, VATA 1994 s 59(4), (5)
appeal, VATA 1994 s 83(n)
assessment, VATA 1994 s 76, 77
default, meaning, VATA 1994 s 59(1), (1A)
exempted defaults, VATA 1994 s 59(7), (9)
generally, VATA 1994 s 59
payments on account—
aggregate value of defaults, calculating, VATA 1994 s 59A(6), (7)
amount, VATA 1994 s 59A(4), (5)
continuation of surcharge period, VATA 1994 s 59A(3)
default left out of account, VATA 1994 s 59A(10), (11)
exempted defaults, VATA 1994 s 59A(8),(9)
generally, VATA 1994 s 59A
method of payment, VATA 1994 s 59A(12), (13)
person in default, VATA 1994 s 59A(1)
surcharge liability notice, service of, VATA 1994 s 59A(2)
surcharge period, VATA 1994 s 59A(2)
rate, VATA 1994 s 59(1)
surcharge period generally, VATA 1994 s 59(2)
DELIVERY CHARGES
supplies of, PR 20/8/02
DEMOLITION
property situated abroad, VATA 1994 Sch 8 Group 7
DENTAL TECHNICIAN
exemption, VATA 1994 Sch 9 Group 7 item 2
DENTIST
exemption, VATA 1994 Sch 9 Group 7 item 2
DEPOSIT ACCOUNT
exemption, VATA 1994 Sch 9 Group 5 item 8
DEPOSITS
time of supply, VATA 1994 s 6(4)
DEREGISTRATION
acquisitions from other member states, VATA 1994 Sch 3 para 2(1)
appeal against decision, VATA 1994 s 83(*a*)
assessment, VATA 1994 s 73(3)
circumstances—
ceasing to be liable to registration, VATA 1994 Sch 1 para 13
ceasing to make taxable supplies, VATA 1994 Sch 1 paras 3–4 11
void registration, VATA 1994 Sch 1 para 18
refund of tax, VATA 1994 s 24(6)
supplies from other member states, VATA 1994 Sch 2 para 2
DEVELOPMENT CORPORATION
refund of tax to, VATA 1994 s 33(3)
DIETICIAN
exemption, VATA 1994 Sch 9 Group 7
DILIGENCE
enforcement, FA 1997 s 52
recovery of tax by, SI 1995/2518 reg 213
DIPLOMATS
importation of goods, reliefs for
alcohol and tobacco products, ESC 2.2
conditions attaching to, SI 1992/3156 arts 3–4
entitled persons, SI 1992/3156 art 14
motor vehicles, SI 1992/3156 art 16
remission or refund, duty or tax subject to, SI 1992/3156 art 17
tobacco or alcohol products, SI 1992/3156 art 15
DIRECT SELLERS
direction as to value of supply, VATA 1994 Sch 6 para 2
DIRECTIONS
anti-avoidance provisions. *See under* ANTI-AVOIDANCE PROVISIONS
registration, VATA 1994 Sch 1 para 2
value of supplies—
acquisitions, VATA 1994 Sch 7,
open market value, VATA 1994 Sch 6 para 1(1)–(3)
DIRECTORS
holder of office, VATA 1994 s 25(7)
liability for evasion of tax—
appeal, VATA 1994 s 83(*n*), (*o*)
assessment, VATA 1994 s 76, 77
generally, VATA 1994 s 61
meaning, VATA 1994 s 24(7)
provision of domestic accommodation, VATA 1994 s 24(3)
DISABILITY LIVING ALLOWANCE
meaning, VATA 1994 Sch 8 Group 12 note (7)
person in receipt, VATA 1994 Sch 8 Group 12 item 14
DISABLED PERSONS. ***See*** **HANDICAPPED PERSONS**
DISASTERS
victims, goods for benefit of, 83/181/EEC arts 49–55
DISCLOSURE OF INFORMATION. ***See also*** **INFORMATION**
defence, FA 1989 s 182(7)
EEC member states, between, 77/799/EEC, 79/1070
extension of powers, ACSA 2001 s 17
generally, FA 1989 s 182
Isle of Man Customs & Excise service, IMA 1979 s 10
lawful authority, made with, FA 1989 s 182(6)
offence, whether constituting, FA 1989 s 182
overseas purposes, for, ACSA 2001 s 18
penalties, VATA 1994 s 91(3), FA 1989 s 182 (8)
Revenue departments, held by, ACSA 2001 s 19
statistical purposes, VATA 1994 s 91
tax functions, held in exercise of, FA 1989 s 182
DISCOUNT
imported goods, VATA 1994 s 20(3)
prompt payment, VATA 1994 Sch 6 para 4(1)
staff, PR 15/6/92
DISHONEST CONDUCT. ***See*** **EVASION OF TAX; OFFENCES; PENALTIES**
DISPOSAL OF ASSETS
generally, VATA 1994 s 94(6)
DISPUTES
settlement, PR 19/11/87, PR 9/9/92

DISTANCE SALES
option, exercise of, SI 1995/2518 reg 98
DISTRESS
enforcement, FA 1997 s 51
recovery of tax, VATA 1994 Sch 11 para 5(4), SI 1995/2518 reg 212, SI 1997/1431 reg 5
DOCTOR
exemption, VATA 1994 Sch 9 Group 7 item 1(*a*)
DOCTORS DEPUTISING SERVICE
exemption, VATA 1994 Sch 9 Group 7 item 5
DOCUMENTS
admissibility, VATA 1994 Sch 11 para 6(6)
bad debt relief, SI 1995/2518 reg 169
compensation for loss or damage, VATA 1994 Sch 11 para 7(1)
computer produced, VATA 1994 Sch 11 para 6(4)
failure to keep, VATA 1994 s 73(1)
false, VATA 1994 s 72
meaning, VATA 1994 s 96(1), (6)
power to inspect, copy and remove, VATA 1994 Sch 11 para 7
production, VATA 1994 Sch 11 para 7
removal under search warrant, VATA 1994 Sch 11 paras 11–13
DO-IT-YOURSELF BUILDER
appeal to tribunal, VATA 1994 s 83(*g*)
claims by, SI 1995/2518 regs 200, 201 Sch 1
refund of tax, VATA 1994 s 35, SI 1995/2518 Sch 1 Form 11
DOMESTIC ACCOMMODATION. *See* ACCOMMODATION
DOMESTIC APPLIANCES
supply with new buildings, VATA 1994 Sch 8 Group 5 note (12)
DOMESTIC SERVICE CHARGES
exemption for, ESC 3.18
DONATIONS
charities, VATA 1994 Sch 8 Group 5 items 1, 2
goods used in connection with collection of, ESC 3.3
DRAINAGE BOARD
refund of tax, VATA 1994 s 33(3)
DRUGS
personally administered, VAT liability, PR 6/2/03, PR 13/11/03
zero-rating—
generally, SI 1995/2518 reg 74
goods on prescription, VATA 1994 Sch 8 Group 12
supplied to charities, VATA 1994 Sch 8 Group 15
DUTIABLE GOODS
regulations, VATA 1994 Sch 11 para 2(8)
removal to UK, VATA 1994 Sch 9 para 3
warehoused goods. *See* WAREHOUSE
DUTY-FREE SHOPS
goods supplied at, ESC 9.1
DWELLING. *See* BUILDING

EC/EU
acquisition of goods from another member state—
assessment, VATA 1994 s 75
meaning, VATA 1994 s 11
place of supply, VATA 1994 s 13
scope of tax, VATA 1994 s 10
timing, VATA 1994 s 12
valuation, VATA 1994 Sch 7
value, VATA 1994 s 20
administrative co-operation, 1798/2003/EC, 1925/2004/EC
alphabetical codes, SI 1995/2518 reg 2(1)

EC/EU – *contd*
approximation of laws, EC Treaty arts 100–102
common system of VAT—
conversion rates, 2006/112/EC arts 399, 400
derogations, 2006/112/EC arts 370–396, Annex X
implementation of Directive, 1777/2005/EC, 2006/112/EC art 397
principal Directive, PR 11/12/06
subject matter and scope of, 2006/112/EC arts 1–4
territorial scope, 2006/112/EC arts 5–8
transitional provisions, 2006/112/EC arts 402–411
VAT Committee, 2006/112/EC art 398
Court of Justice, EC Treaty arts 164–188
Customs Code. *See* COMMUNITY CUSTOMS CODE
custom controls, VATA 1994 s 16
Customs territory, 450/2008/EC art 3
dried animal fodder, grant aid for, PR 22/12/99
duties and taxes due in other Member States, recovery of, SI 2004/674
excluded territories, SI 1995/2518 regs 136, 137
importation of goods, VATA 1994 s 15
included territories, SI 1995/2518 reg 139
intra-Community acquisitions—
accounting for tax—
duty point, by reference, to, SI 1995/2518 reg 41(1)
value shown on invoice, by reference to, SI 1995/2518 reg 26
gas, of, SI 1995/2518 reg 87
heat, of, SI 1995/2518 reg 87
non-taxable persons, notification and payment of tax by, SI 1995/2518 reg 36
power, of, SI 1995/2518 reg 87
refrigeration of, SI 1995/2518 reg 87
taxable amount for, 92/546
time of, SI 1995/2518 reg 83
valuation of, SI 1992/2099
ventilation, SI 1995/2518 reg 87
water, of, SI 1995/2518 reg 87
legislation, EC Treaty, art 189
member state, removal of goods from—
accounting for, SI 1995/2518
definitions, SI 1992/3111 art 2
establishment in member state, SI 1992/3111 art 3
place of supply, SI 1992/3111 art 4
mutual assistance, SI 2004/674, 77/799/EEC, 2002/94/EC, 2008/55/EC
refund of tax, VATA 1994 s 39
sales list, SI 1995/2518 Sch 1 Form 12, PR 11/10/08
sales statements,
definitions, SI 1995/2518 reg 21
final, SI 1995/2518 reg 23
submission of, SI 1992/3096 reg 5
single currency, implications of UK business, PR 13/1/99
single market, Notice 725
small non-commercial consignment, SI 1986/939
statistics of trade, 638/2004/EC
tax provisions, EC Treaty, arts 95–99
taxation under laws of other member states, VATA 1994 s 92
temporary movement of goods, register of, SI 1995/2518 reg 33
territories included in references to other member states, VATA 1994 s 93

VAT

EC/EU – *contd*
transitional provisions, 2006/112/EC arts 402–411
triangular transactions, VATA 1994 s 14
valuation of acquisitions, VATA 1994 s 20
ECCLESIASTICAL BUILDING
alteration, VATA 1994 Sch 8 Group 6 item 2
E-COMMERCE
Directive, PR 9/5/02
EC SALES STATEMENTS
acquisitions, VATA 1994 Sch 11 para 2(3)
EC sales list (VAT 101), SI 1995/2518 regs 21–23, Sch 1 Form 12, PR 22/10/08
failure to submit, VATA 1994 s 66
inaccuracies, VATA 1994 s 65
meaning, VATA 1994 s 65(6), 66(9)
penalties, VATA 1994 ss 76, 77
EDUCATION
campus building, construction of, PR 12/4/06
eligible body, meaning, VATA 1994 Sch 9 Group 6 note (1)
exemption, VATA 1994 Sch 9 Group 6 items 1–6
higher education institutions, retrospective claims for input tax, PR 25/7/08
library, occupation of, PR 9/6/09
private tuition, PR 13/10/06, PR 6/2/07
variable tuition fees, PR 7/8/06
vocational training, VATA 1994 Sch 9 Group 6 note (3)
youth club, VATA 1994 Sch 9 Group 6 note (6)
ELECTION TO WAIVE EXEMPTION. *See* OPTION TO TAX
ELECTRICAL APPLIANCES
supply to new building, VATA 1994 Sch 8 Group 5 note (12)
ELECTRICITY
connection to mains supply, ESC 3.16
supplied by persons outside UK, reverse charge, VATA 1994 s 9A
ELECTRONIC COMMUNICATIONS
incentives for use of, FA 2000 s 132, Sch 38, SI 2001/759
mandatory e-filing, FA 2002 s 135, FA 2003 s 204
power to provide for use of, FA 1999 s 132
use under other provisions, FA 1999 s 133, FA 2002 s 136, FA 2003 s 205
ELECTRONICALLY SUPPLIED SERVICES
place of supply, 2006/112/EC Annex II
special accounting scheme—
appeals, VATA 1994 Sch 3B para 20
definitions, VATA 1994 Sch 3B para 23
establishment of, VATA 1994 s 3A
general provisions, 2006/112/EC arts 357–369
liability for VAT, VATA 1994 Sch 3B para 10
non-UK tax, payment on account, VATA 1994 Sch 3B para 21
payment of VAT, VATA 1994 Sch 3B para 13
qualifying supplies, VATA 1994 Sch 3B para 3
records, VATA 1994 Sch 3B paras 14, 15
refund of UK tax, VATA 1994 Sch 3B para 22
register, VATA 1994 Sch 3B para 1
registered persons, conditions, VATA 1994 Sch 3B para 2
ELECTRONICALLY SUPPLIED SERVICES – *contd*
special accounting scheme – *contd*
registration—
cancellation, VATA 1994 Sch 3B para 8
changes, obligation to notify, VATA 1994 Sch 3B para 7
conditions, VATA 1994 Sch 3B para 2
date of, VATA 1994 Sch 3B para 5
number, VATA 1994 Sch 3B para 6
obligations following, VATA 1994 Sch 3B paras 10–15
persistent defaulter, of, VATA 1994 Sch 3B para 9
request, VATA 1994 Sch 3B para 4
returns, VATA 1994 Sch 3B paras 11, 12, 18(6)
understatement or overstatement of VAT, VATA 1994 Sch 3B para 16
VAT provisions, application of, VATA 1994 Sch 3B paras 17–22
VAT registration, VATA 1994 Sch 3B paras 17, 18
VAT representatives, VATA 1994 Sch 3B para 19
ELIGIBLE INSTITUTIONS. *See also* EDUCATION
for educated, meaning, VATA 1994 Sch 9 Group 6 note (1)
EMPLOYEE
domestic accommodation supplied—
generally, VATA 1994 Sch 6 para 10(1)
value, VATA 1994 Sch 6 para 10(2)
fuel for private use, VATA 1994 s 56, 57
mobile phone provided to, PR 2/7/99
services—
reverse charge, VATA 1994 s 8
supplied to overseas person, VATA 1994 Sch 8 Group 7
staff hire concession, PR 19/3/09
ENFORCEMENT. *See* ADMINISTRATION AND COLLECTION
ENGINEER
services—
reverse charge, VATA 1994 s 8
supplied where received, VATA 1994 Sch 5 para 3
zero-rating, VATA 1994 Sch 8 Group 7
ENTERTAINMENT
services performed abroad, VATA 1994 Sch 8 para 7
ENFORCEMENT OF JUDGMENTS
commencement of provisions, SI 2007/2709
county court—
transfer of enforcement, TCEA 2007 s 67
warrants of control, TCEA 2007 s 69
goods, taking control of—
amended provisions, TCEA 2007 Sch 13
application of proceeds, TCEA 2007 Sch 12 para 50
assignee or nominee, application to, TCEA 2007 Sch 12 para 61
best price, obtaining, TCEA 2007 Sch 12 para 37
binding property in goods, TCEA 2007 Sch 12 para 4
care of goods, TCEA 2007 Sch 12 para 35
common law rules, replacement of, TCEA 2007 s 65
costs, TCEA 2007 Sch 12 para 62
creditor, remedies available to, TCEA 2007 Sch 12 para 67
Crown preference, abolition, TCEA 2007 s 88

ENFORCEMENT OF JUDGMENTS – *contd*
goods, taking control of – *contd*
Crown, provisions binding, TCEA 2007 s 89
debtor, remedies available to, TCEA 2007 Sch 12 para 66
enactment, writ or warrant, procedure under, TCEA 2007 s 62
enforcement agents—
acting as, TCEA 2007 s 63
certificate to act as, TCEA 2007 s 64
entry on premises, TCEA 2007 Sch 12 paras 14–30
exempt individuals, TCEA 2007 s 63
inventory by, TCEA 2007 Sch 12 para 34
meaning, TCEA 2007 Sch 12 para 2
reasonable force, use of, TCEA 2007 Sch 12 paras 17–22
goods other than securities, abandonment, TCEA 2007 Sch 12 paras 52–54
goods which may be taken, TCEA 2007 Sch 12 para 9
highway, goods on, TCEA 2007 Sch 12 paras 31–33
insolvency provisions, relation to, TCEA 2007 Sch 12 para 69
interpretation, TCEA 2007 Sch 12 Pt 1
limitation of liability, TCEA 2007 Sch 12 paras 63–65
means of, TCEA 2007 Sch 12 para 13
notice of enforcement, TCEA 2007 Sch 12 para 7
offences, TCEA 2007 Sch 12 para 68
power of High Court to stay execution, TCEA 2007 s 70
pre-commencement enforcement, TCEA 2007 s 66
procedure, TCEA 2007 Sch 12 Pt 2
regulations, TCEA 2007 s 90
sale, TCEA 2007 Sch 12 paras 38–46
securities, abandonment, TCEA 2007 Sch 12 paras 55–57
securities, holding and disposal of, TCEA 2007 Sch 12 paras 47–49
third party, goods claimed by, TCEA 2007 Sch 12 para 60
time limit, TCEA 2007 Sch 12 para 8
title, passing, TCEA 2007 Sch 12 para 51
valuation, TCEA 2007 Sch 12 para 36
value of goods, TCEA 2007 Sch 12 para 12
magistrates' courts, warrants of control, TCEA 2007 s 68
ENTRY AND SEARCH
fraud, VATA 1994 s 72, Sch 11 para 10(3), (4)
power to search—
authorised person, VATA 1994 Sch 11 para 10(1), CEMA 1979 s 100F
entry and inspection, VATA 1994 Sch 11 para 10(2)
powers conferred by warrant, VATA 1994 Sch 11 para 10(5)
ERRORS IN RETURN
correction of, SI 1995/2518 reg 34
ESTABLISHMENT
place of belonging, VATA 1994 s 9
EUROPEAN COMMUNITIES/UNION. *See* **EC/EU**
EUROSTAR
trains, alcoholic drinks served on, ESC 2.7
EVASION OF TAX
appeal, VATA 1994 s 83(*n*)
assessment, VATA 1994 s 76, 77
conduct involving dishonesty, VATA 1994 s 60
EVASION OF TAX – *contd*
imported goods, VATA 1994 s 72(10)
investigation of, PR 28/3/02
liability of directors, VATA 1994 s 61
mitigation, VATA 1994 s 70
penalties. *See* PENALTIES
EVIDENCE
bad debt relief, SI 1995/2518 reg 167
certificate of Commissioners, VATA 1994 Sch 11 para 14
computer documents, VATA 1994 Sch 11 para 6(6)
tribunal, at, SI 1986/590 r 21A, 28
EXAMINATION SERVICES
exemption, VATA 1994 Sch 9 Group 6 item 3
meaning, VATA 1994 Sch 9 Group 6 note (4)
EXCISE WAREHOUSE
procedures for goods, SI 1988/890 regs 10–19
returns and records, SI 1988/809 regs 20–25, Schs 2, 3
S 46 goods, SI 1988/809 reg 10A
warehoused goods—
duty chargeable on, SI 1988/809 regs 26–30
operations on, SI 1988/809 Sch 1
EXEMPTION
ambulance services, VATA 1994 Sch 9 Group 7 item 11
banking, VATA 1994 Sch 9 Group 5
betting, gaming and lotteries, VATA 1994 Sch 9 Group 4
burial and cremations, VATA 1994 Sch 9 Group 8
capital goods, VATA 1994 s 34
charities fund-raising, VATA 1994 Sch 9 Group 12 item 1
credit transactions, VATA 1994 Sch 9 Group 5
cultural services, VATA 1994 Sch 9 Group 13
education, research or vocational training—
eligible body, meaning, VATA 1994 Sch 9 Group 6 note (1)
examination services, VATA 1994 Sch 9 Group 6 item 3
generally, VATA 1994 Sch 9 Group 6
teaching English as a foreign language, PR 18/8/99
youth clubs, VATA 1994 Sch 9 Group 9 item 6
election to tax, VATA 1994 Sch 10 paras 2, 4
exportation, 2006/112/EC arts 146, 147
exports, transactions treated as, 2006/112/EC arts 151, 152
fund management services, PR 24/7/08, PR 1/10/08
fund-raising events by charities, VATA 1994 Sch 9 Group 12
generally, VATA 1994 s 31, 2006/112/EC art 131
health and welfare—
ambulance services, VATA 1994 Sch 9 Group 7 item 11
chemists, VATA 1994 Sch 9 Group 7 item 3
chiropractors, PR 18/8/99
dental technician, VATA 1994 Sch 9 Group 7 item 2(*c*)
dentists, VATA 1994 Sch 7 Group 7 item 2
doctors, VATA 1994 Sch 9 Group 7 item 1(*a*)
generally, VATA 1994 Sch 9 Group 7
health visitors, VATA 1994 Sch 7 Group 7 item (*d*)

EXEMPTION – *contd*
health and welfare – *contd*
hearing aid dispensers, VATA 1994 Sch 7 Group 7 item (*e*)
human blood, VATA 1994 Sch 9 Group 7 item 6
human organs, VATA 1994 Sch 9 Group 7 item 8
medical care and surgical treatment, VATA 1994 Sch 9 Group 7 item 4
medical services, PR 30/01/7
midwives, VATA 1994 Sch 7 Group 7 item (*d*)
nurses, VATA 1994 Sch 7 Group 7 item (*d*)
opticians, VATA 1994 Sch 9 Group 7 item 1(*b*)
welfare services, VATA 1994 Sch 9 Group 7 item 9 note (7)
importation of goods, 2006/112/EC arts 143–145
intermediaries, supply of services by, 2006/112/EC art 153
intra-Community transactions, 2006/112/EC arts 138–142
investment gold, VATA 1994 Sch 9 Group 15
insurance, VATA 1994 Sch 9 Group 2
call centre services, PR 1/7/03
international trade, transactions relating to, 2006/112/EC arts 154–166, Annex V
international transport, 2006/112/EC arts 148–150
land—
election to tax, VATA 1994 Sch 10 paras 2–4
grant of interest, right over, VATA 1994 Sch 9 Group 1 item 1
list of, 2006/112/EC arts 135–137
postal services, VATA 1994 Sch 9 Group 3
private tuition, VATA 1994 Sch 9 Group 6 item 12
professional bodies, VATA 1994 Sch 9 Group 9
public interest activities, 2006/112/EC arts 132–134
public interest bodies, VATA 1994 Sch 9 Group 9
reinsurance, VATA 1994 Sch 9 Group 2
schools, VATA 1994 Sch 9 Group 6
securities, VATA 1994 Sch 9 Group 5 item 6
sports, sports competitions and physical education, VATA 1994 Sch 9 Group 10
supplies where input tax cannot be recovered, VATA 1994 Sch 9 Group 14
trade unions, VATA 1994 Sch 9 Group 9
unit trust management, VATA 1994 Sch 9 Group 5 item 9
universities, VATA 1994 Sch 9 Group 6
vocational training, VATA 1994 Sch 9 Group 6
works of art, VATA 1994 Sch 9 Group 11
youth club, VATA 1994 Sch 9 Group 6 item 6

EXEMPT SUPPLY
tax invoice, for, SI 1995/2518 reg 14(4)

EXHIBITION, FAIR
zero-rating, VATA 1994 Sch 8 Group 7

EXPORT
air and sea freight, Notice 703 para 7
arrivals and dispatches, provision of information, SI 1995/2518 regs 23E, 23F
computer software, of, Notice 703 para 4
conditions, VATA 1994 s 30(6)

EXPORT – *contd*
containers, of, Notice 703 para 4
exemptions, 2006/112/EC arts 151, 152
extra-statutory concessions, Notice 703 para 8
forfeiture of goods, VATA 1994 s 30(10)
forms, Notice 703 para 12
government departments, supplies to, Notice 703 para 4
hydrocarbon oils, of, Notice 703 para 4
intra-EC cruises, Notice 704 para 5
military establishments, to, Notice 703 para 4
multiple transactions, Notice 703 para 4
New Export System and New Computerised Transit System, customs declarations via, Notice 703 para 5
oil rigs etc, to, Notice 703 para 4
other EC member states, to, Notice 704 para 8
overseas authorities, supplies to, Notice 703 para 4
postal, Notice 703 para 7
proof of, Notice 703 paras 6, 7
records and accounts, Notice 703 para 11
regimental shops, to, Notice 703 para 4
removal of goods from UK, Notice 703
retail export scheme, SI 1995/2518 regs 52–54; Notice 704
changes to, PR 1/7/03
retailers, by, Notice 703 para 9
ships, aircraft or hovercraft, stores for use in, Notice 703 para 10
time of, CEMA 1979 s 5
tools used for manufacture of goods for, Notice 703 para 4
travellers, information for, Notice 704 para 4
UK free zones, from, Notice 703 para 4
VAT group, by members of, Notice 703 para 4
zero-rating—
application of, Notice 703 para 2
charity, VATA 1994 Sch 8 Group 15 items 2, 3
conditions and time limits, Notice 703 paras 3, 4
financial services, VATA 1994 Sch 8
goods, VATA 1994 s 30(6)
handling goods, VATA 1994 Sch 8 Group 8
insurance, VATA 1994 Sch 8 Group 7
international defence project, VATA 1994 Sch 8 Group 13
overseas authority, VATA 1994 Sch 8 Group 13

EXPORTATION OF GOODS
containers, SI 1995/2518 reg 1282518
exemptions, 2006/112/EC arts 146, 147
formalities, 2454/93, SI 1995/2518 reg 140
overseas persons, supplies to, SI 1995/2518 reg 129
persons departing from the EC, supplies to, SI 1995/2518 regs 130–133

FARMERS
certification, VATA 1994 s 54
flat rate scheme. *See* FLAT RATE SCHEME FOR FARMERS

FARMHOUSE
recovery of tax incurred on repairs, renovation etc, PR 27/8/96

FINANCIAL OMBUDSMAN SERVICES LTD
supplies by, ESC 3.23

FINANCIAL SERVICES
exemption, VATA 1994 Sch 9 Group 4, PR 16/7/02

FINANCIAL SERVICES – *contd*
intermediary, PR 30/9/03
reverse charge, VATA 1994 ss 8, 9
zero-rating, VATA 1994 Sch 8 Group 7
FINANCIAL SERVICES AUTHORITY
self-regulating organisations, supplies to, ESC 3.28
FINANCIAL SERVICES COMPENSATION SCHEME LTD
supplies by, ESC 3.31
FINANCIAL STATEMENTS
inspection by customs officers, VATA 1994 Sch 11 para 7
FIRE AND CIVIL DEFENCE AUTHORITY
refund of tax, SI 1985/1101
FIREARMS
acquisition in settlement of insurance claim, SI 1992/3129 art 4
meaning of, SI 1992/3129 art 2
repossession under finance agreement, SI 1992/3129 art 2
used—
appeal, VATA 1994 s 83(*m*)
qualifying conditions, VATA 1994 s 54
relief for certain supplies, SI 1992/3129 art 8
FISHING RIGHTS
liability, VATA 1994 Sch 9 Group 1
FLAT RATE SCHEME FOR FARMERS
admission, SI 1995/2518 reg 206
appeal, VATA 1994 s 83(*m*)
certificate—
cancellation, SI 1995/2518 reg 206
effective date, SI 1995/2518 reg 205
certification—
application, SI 1995/2518 Sch 1 Form 14
Commissioners, by, SI 1995/2518 reg 203
further, SI 1995/2518 reg 208
certified person—
bankruptcy of, SI 1995/2518 reg 207
death, SI 1995/2518 reg 207
incapacity, SI 1995/2518 reg 207
meaning, SI 1995/2518 reg 202
credit for input tax, claims for amounts to be treated as, SI 1995/2518 reg 209
EC provisions, 2006/112/EC arts 295–305, Annexes VII, VIII
percentage addition, SI 1992/3221
qualifying conditions, VATA 1994 s 54
records—
duty to keep, SI 1995/2518 reg 210
production of, SI 1995/2518 reg 211
FLAT RATE SCHEME FOR SMALL BUSINESSES
accounting, method of, SI 1995/2518 reg 55D
admission to, SI 1995/2518 reg 55L
amendment by notice, SI 1995/2518 reg 55T
appropriate percentage applied, SI 1995/2518 regs 55H, 55J
differing, notification of, SI 1995/2518 reg 55N
associated persons, SI 1995/2518 reg 55A(2)
authorisation, SI 1995/2518 reg 55B
termination, SI 1995/2518 reg 55P
bad debt relief, SI 1995/2518 reg 55V
categories of business, SI 1995/2518 reg 55K
changes to, PR 10/12/03
definitions, SI 1995/2518 reg 55A
determination of liability under, VATA 1994 s 26B
flat rate percentage, determining, Notice 733
FLAT RATE SCHEME FOR SMALL BUSINESSES – *contd*
input tax credit, SI 1995/2518 reg 55E
newly registered period, reduced appropriate percentage for, SI 1995/2518 reg 55JB
operation of scheme, Notice 733
postal and courier services, PR 3/3/04
profits, computation of, RI 246
regulations, power to make, VATA 1994 s 26B
relevant supplies and purchases, SI 1995/2518 reg 55C
relevant turnover, determining, SI 1995/2518 reg 55G
relief, exceptional claims for, SI 1995/2518 reg 55F
reverse charges, SI 1995/2518 reg 55U
withdrawal from, SI 1995/2518 reg 55M
date of, SI 1995/2518 reg 55Q
self-supply on, SI 1995/2518 reg 55R
stock on hand, adjustments for, SI 1995/2518 reg 55S
FLORISTS
retail scheme, use of, Notice 727 para 10
FOOD. *See also* CATERING
animal food. *See* ANIMAL FEEDING STUFFS
hot take-away, VATA 1994 Sch 8 Group 1, PR 2/10/02
prawn crackers, liability of, PR 15/2/99
Pringles, nature of, PR 1/6/09
supplies by retailers, SI 1995/2518 reg 73
supply in the course of catering, VATA 1994 Sch 8 Group 1
sweetened dried fruit, liability of, PR 11/9/98
value of supply to employee, VATA 1994 Sch 6 para 10(1), (2)
zero-rating, VATA 1994 Sch 8 Group 1
FOOTWEAR. *See* CLOTHING AND FOOTWEAR
FOREIGN CURRENCY
acquisition, VATA 1994 Sch 7 para 4
value, VATA 1994 Sch 6 para 11
FOREIGN EXCHANGE
transactions, treatment of, PR 26/0/07
FOREIGN GOVERNMENT
zero-rating of supplies of training for, ESC 3.17
FORMS
application for registration (VAT 1), SI 1995/2518 reg 5(1), Sch 1
acquisitions in respect of (VAT 1B), SI 1995/2518 reg 5(1), Sch 1
distance sales in respect of (VAT 1A), SI 1995/2518 reg 5(1), Sch 1
partnership by (VAT 2), SI 1995/2518 reg 5(1), Sch 1
appointment of tax representative (Form 8), SI 1995/2518 reg 10, Sch 1
diplomats, purchase of EC vehicle (C428), SI 1992/3156 Sch 1
EC sales list (VAT 101), SI 1995/2518 regs 21–23, Sch 1 Form 12
flat rate scheme for farmers, application for certification (VAT 98), SI 1995/2518 Sch 1
generally, SI 1995/2518 reg 2 (3)
refund of tax, third country trader, SI 1995/2518 Sch 1
DIY builders, SI 1995/2518 Sch 1
transfer of business as a going concern (form 3), SI 1995/2518 reg 6 (1), Sch 1
VAT return (VAT 100), SI 1995/2518 reg 25(1), Sch 1
final (VAT 193), SI 1995/2518 reg 25(4), Sch 1

VAT

VAT

VAT

INSOLVENCY – *contd*
preferential debts, categories, IA 1986 s 386—
Customs & Excise, due to, B(S)A 1985 Sch 3, IA 1986 Sch 6, para 3
general provision, IA 1986 s 175
priority of debts, B(S)A 1985 s 51, IA 1986 s 328
relevant date, IA 1986 s 387
repayment of input tax, disapplication of provisions, ESC 3.20
set off credits, VATA 1994 s 81—
transitional provisions, VATA 1994 Sch 13 para 12, FA 1997 s 49

INSTALMENT CREDIT FINANCE
exemption, VATA 1994 Sch 9 Group 5
supply of goods, VATA 1994 Sch 4 para 1
zero-rating, VATA 1994 Sch 8 Group 8

INSURANCE
agents, VATA 1994 Sch 9 Group 2 item 4
back office services, PR 18/5/05
brokers, VATA 1994 Sch 9 Group 2 item 4
call centre services, exemption, PR 1/7/03
claim under policy of, goods acquired in settlement of, SI 1992/3129 art 4
disclosure, Notice 701/36
exemption, VATA 1994 Sch 9 Group 2, PR 5/12/05
Export Credits Guarantee Department, provision by, VATA 1994 Sch 9 Group 2 item 3
intermediary, services of, VATA 1994 Sch 9 Group 2 item 4 notes (1)–(10)
accountants, PR 15/3/90
introductory services, PR 21/11/07
provider—
generally, VATA 1994 Sch 9 item 1
resident outside UK, VATA 1994 Sch 9 item 2
services—
intermediaries other than brokers, of, PR 15/3/90
reverse charge, VATA 1994 s 8
supplied where received, VATA 1994 Sch 5 para 5

INTELLECTUAL PROPERTY. *See* COPYRIGHT; PATENT; TRADEMARK

INTENDING TRADER
deregistration, VATA 1994 Sch 1 paras 11, 12
registration, VATA 1994 Sch 1 paras 9, 10

INTEREST
appeal, VATA 1994 s 83(s)
applicable rate, SI 1998/1461
assessment, VATA 1994 s 76, 77
exemption, VATA 1994 Sch 9 Group 5
given by way of credits and set off of credits, VATA 1994 s 81 FA 1997 s 49
official error, in case of, VATA 1994 s 78, FA 1996 s 183, SI 1997/1015–1016
overpayment—
assessment for overpayment of, VATA 1994 s 78A
claims, PR 24/8/06
period, VATA 1994 s 74
prescribed rate—
generally, SI 1996/165, SI 1997/1015–1016; PR 9/12/03
meaning, VATA 1994 s 74(6)
setting, FA 1996 s 197
recovery of tax, VATA 1994 s 74, FA 1996 s 183
refund. *See under* REFUND OF TAX
repayment supplement, VATA 1994 s 79
zero-rating, VATA 1994 Sch 8 Group 7

INTERNATIONAL COLLABORATION AGREEMENTS,
zero-rating, VATA 1994 Sch 8 Group 13 items 2, 3

INTERNATIONAL SERVICES
zero-rating, VATA 1994 Sch 8 Group 7

INTERNATIONAL TRADE
Blueprint report, PR 24/5/02
customs civil penalties, PR 3/12/03

INTERNATIONAL TRAVEL
Imports by persons travelling from third countries, 2007/74/EC

INTERNET
service packages, treatment of, PR 14/3/02

INVESTMENT TRUSTS
management, VAT treatment, PR 29/11/02

INVOICE
meaning, VATA 1994 s 96(1)
tax. *See* TAX INVOICE

ISLE OF MAN
Act of Tynwald, proof of, IMA 1979 s 12
common duties—
enforcement of Isle of Man judgements for, IMA 1979 s 4
Isle of Man share of, IMA 1979 s 2
offences relating to, IMA 1979 s 5
recovery of, chargeable in the Isle of Man, IMA 1979 s 3
tax as, IMA 1979 s 1
provisions applying to, SI 1982/1067, SI 1982/1068
transfer of functions to, authorities, IMA 1979 s 11
transitional provisions, VATA 1994 Sch 13 para 23
UK as part of, for tax purposes, IMA 1979 s 13

ISSUE OF SECURITIES
exemption, VATA 1994 Sch 9 Group 5 item 1

JOINT PORT LOCAL AUTHORITY
refund of tax, VATA 1994 s 33

JOURNAL
charity advertisement, VATA 1994 Sch 8 Group 15 item 8
zero-rating, VATA 1994 Sch 8 Group 3 item 2

JUDGMENT DEBT
action to recover, application for information—
power to make, TCEA 2007 s 95
unauthorised use or disclosure of information, TCEA 2007 s 102
use of information, TCEA 2007 s 101
court, action by, TCEA 2007 s 96
departmental information request—
information requested, TCEA 2007 s 97
meaning, TCEA 2007 s 97
power to make, TCEA 2007 s 97
responding to, TCEA 2007 s 99
information order—
meaning, TCEA 2007 s 98
power to make, TCEA 2007 s 96
required information not held, failure to disclose in case of, TCEA 2007 s 100
information regulations, TCEA 2007 s 103

JUDICIAL APPOINTMENTS COMMISSION
Senior President of tribunals, selection of, TCEA 2007 Sch 1 Pt 2

JUDICIAL REVIEW
tribunal, in. *See* TRIBUNAL

JUDICIARY
training, guidance or welfare, co-operation, TCEA 2007 s 47
JURY SERVICE
exemption, VATA 1994 Sch 12 para 8
JUSTICE OF THE PEACE
issue of warrant, VATA 1994 Sch 11 paras 11–13

KNITTING PATTERNS
liability of, PR 18/4/91

LABORATORY
cage accessories, treatment of, PR 13/11/03
LAND
assignment or surrender, VATA 1994 Sch 9 Group 1 item 1 note (1)
compulsory purchase of, SI 1995/2518 reg 84
co-owners, registration of, VATA 1994 s 51A
election to tax, VATA 1994 Sch 10 paras 2–4
freehold, grant of. *See* FREEHOLD
grant made without consideration, VATA 1994 Sch 4 paras 5, 9
grant or assignment of fee simple, consideration not determinable for, SI 1995/2518 reg 84
held at date of deregistration, VATA 1994 Sch 4 paras 8, 9
interests in, VATA 1994 Sch 9 Group 1 item 1
lease. *See* LEASE
major interest, VATA 1994 s 96(1)
self-supply, VATA 1994 s 44(4)
services relating to, place of supply, SI 1992/3121 art 5
situated abroad, VATA 1994 Sch 8 Group 1 item 1
supply of, VATA 1994 Sch 9 Group 1
surrender, VATA 1994 Sch 9 Group 1 note (1)
LAVATORY
supply to handicapped person, VATA 1994 Sch 8 Group 12 item 10
LEAFLET
advertising by charities, VATA 1994 Sch 8 Group 15 item 8
zero-rating, VATA 1994 Sch 8 Group 3 item 1
LEARNED SOCIETY
exemption, VATA 1994 Sch 9 Group 9
LEASE
building used for—
charitable purpose, VATA 1994 Sch 8 Group 5 item note 4, Group 6
residential purpose, VATA 1994 Sch 8 Groups 2, 6
dwelling, VATA 1994 Sch 8 Groups 5, 6
grant, VATA 1994 Sch 9 Group 1
holiday accommodation, VATA 1994 Sch 9 Group 1
inducements to enter into, PR 15/6/05
listed building, VATA 1994 Sch 9 Group 6
mesne profits, PR 14/10/92
monument, VATA 1994 Sch 8 Group 6
protected building, VATA 1994 Sch 8 Group 6
rent—
apportionment, PR 17/5/91
rent-free periods, PR 17/12/91
reverse surrender, VATA 1994 Sch 9 Group 1 item 1 notes (1), (1A)
supply of goods as, SI 1995/2518 reg 85
treatment as supply of goods, VATA 1994 Sch 4 para 4
LEGACIES
imported, relief for, CED(GR)A 1979 s 7, SI 1992/3193 art 21
LEGAL AID
VAT treatment of payments, PR 17/3/00
LEGAL SERVICES
insurance claims, VATA 1994 Sch 9 Group 2 note (8)
medico-legal services, PR 19/12/96
reverse charge, VATA 1994 s 8
supplied where received, VATA 1994 Sch 5 para 3
supply to overseas person, VATA 1994 Sch 8 Group 9
third party, payment of costs by, PR 28/10/92
time of supply, SI 1995/2518 reg 92
LEISURE CENTRE
All-inclusive membership schemes, 19/3/09
LEISURE SERVICES
contracted out by local authority, PR 22/3/07
LIABILITY TO TAX
generally, VATA 1994 s 1
LICENCE
services supplied where received, VATA 1994 Sch 5 para 1
transfer or assignment—
reverse charge, VATA 1994 s 8
zero-rating, VATA 1994 Sch 8 Group 9
LIFEBOAT
meaning, VATA 1994 Sch 8 Group 8 note (3)
zero-rating, VATA 1994 Sch 8 Group 8 item 3
LIFT
supply to handicapped person, VATA 1994 Sch 8 Group 12 item 2, 16–18
LIGHTHOUSE AUTHORITY
refund of tax, VATA 1994 s 33(3)
LINKED SUPPLIES SCHEMES
minor promotional items supplied in, ESC 3.7
LIQUIDATION. *See* INSOLVENCY
LISTED BUILDINGS. *See* PROTECTED BUILDINGS
LIVERPOOL FREE ZONE
designation of, SI 1999/3122, SI 2001/2881 art 2
health and safety, SI 2001/2881 art 6
responsible authority for, conditions imposed on, SI 2001/2881 art 5
LLOYD'S INSURANCE MARKET
VAT arrangements for, PR 22/12/99
LOCAL AUTHORITY
leisure services, contracted out, PR 22/3/07
meaning, VATA 1994 s 96(4)
refund of tax, VATA 1994 s 33
registration, VATA 1994 s 42
works in default by, PR 15/9/98
LONDON FIRE AND CIVIL DEFENCE AUTHORITY
refund of tax, SI 1985/1101
LONDON FIRE AND EMERGENCY PLANNING AUTHORITY
refund of tax, SI 2000/1515
LONDON RESIDUARY BODY
refund of tax, SI 1985/1101
LONG STAY ACCOMMODATION. *See* ACCOMMODATION
LORD CHIEF JUSTICE
delegation of functions by, TCEA 2007 s 46

LOYALTY SCHEME
VAT treatment, PR 17/9/08, PR 17/12/08

MACHINERY AND PLANT
capital goods tax relief, VATA 1994 s 34
MACHINE TOOLS SUPPLIED TO OVERSEAS AUTHORITY
zero-rating, VATA 1994 Sch 8 Group 13
MAGAZINE
advertising by charities, VATA 1994 Sch 8, Group 15 item 8
zero-rating, VATA 1994 Sch 8 Group 3
MAGISTRATES COURT COMMITTEE
refund of tax, SI 1986/336
MAP
zero-rating, VATA 1994 Sch 8 Group 3
MARGIN SCHEMES
bad debt relief, SI 1995/2518 reg 172A
calculation of output tax, VATA 1994 s 50A(1)
eligible supplies, VATA 1994 s 50A(2)
global accounting, VATA 1994 s 50A(7)
guide to, Notice 718, PR 10/6/02
MARINE FUEL
tax relief, ESC 9.2
MEAL
provided by employer, VATA 1994 Sch 6 para 10(1), (2)
MEDIA
advertising by charity, VATA 1994 Sch 8 Group 15
MEDIATION
tribunals, in, TCEA 2007 s 24
MEDICAL CARE
exemption, VATA 1994 Sch 9 Group 7 item 4
provided by charities, VATA 1994 Sch 8 Group 15 item 9
MEDICAL EQUIPMENT
zero-rating, VATA 1994 Sch 8 Group 12 items 2–7
MEDICAL LABORATORY TECHNICIAN
exemption, VATA 1994 Sch 9 Group 7
MEDICAL PRACTITIONER
exemption, VATA 1994 Sch 9 Group 7
zero-rating, VATA 1994 Sch 8 Group 12 item 1A
MEDICAL RESEARCH
charities, VATA 1994 Sch 8 Group 15 items 9, 10
MEDICAL SERVICES
exemption, VATA 1994 Sch 9 Group 7
changes in, PR 30/1/07
import relief. SI 1984/746 Sch 2, 83/181/EEC art 38(*a*)
medico-legal services, tax treatment, PR 19/12/96
MEDICO-LEGAL SERVICES
VAT liability, PR 19/12/96
MEMBER STATES. *See* **EC**
METROPOLITAN COUNTY AUTHORITIES
refund of tax, SI 1985/1101
MIDWIFE
exemption, VATA 1994 Sch 9 Group 7 item 1(*d*)
MILK QUOTA
tax treatment, PR 12/9/94
MISDECLARATION
incorrect customer declaration, ESC 3.11
penalty. *See* PENALTIES
repeated, VATA 1994 s 64
resulting in loss of tax, VATA 1994 s 63
MISDIRECTION
revised assessment of VAT, ESC 3.5, PR 27/3/09
MISUNDERSTANDING
undercharge of VAT, ESC 3.4

MONEY
cash, control of, SI 2007/1509
exemption, VATA 1994 Sch 9 Group 5
MOORING
facilities, VATA 1994 Sch 9 Group 1 item 1(*k*)
meaning, VATA 1994 Sch 9 Group 1 note (15)
MORTGAGE
aircraft, supply of, repossessed under, SI 1992/3129 art 4
lender, sale of property under power of sale, PR 8/12/94
marine, supply of ship, repossessed under, SI 1992/3129 art 4
MOT TEST CHARGES
tax treatment, PR 17/10/96
MOTOR ASSESSOR
services, VATA 1994 Sch 9 Group 2 note (1)
MOTOR CAR
Article 5 transaction, SI 2002/1502
demonstrator, PR 1/3/04
diplomat, purchase by, SI 1992/3156 art 16
exclusion of input tax credit, SI 1992/3222 art 7
fuel. *See* FUEL
handicapped person, VATA 1994 Sch 8 Group 12
meaning, 2518, SI 1992/3122 art 2, SI 1992/3222 art 2
overseas visitor, supply to, of, SI 1995/2518 reg 132
parking facilities, VATA 1994 Sch 9 Group 1 item 1(*h*)
person departing from UK, SI 1995/2518 reg 113
Personal Export Scheme—
buyer's guide, Notice 705
supplies for removal from EC, Notice 705A
repossessed, sale of, PR 9/5/02
salary sacrifice, SI 1992/630
second-hand, SI 1992/3122 art 8
self supply of, SI 1992/3122 arts 5–7
stock in trade, use for consideration less than market value, VATA 1994 Sch 6 para 1A
treatment of transactions, SI 1992/3122 art 4
visiting forces, purchase by, SI 1992/3156 reg 19
MOTOR CYCLE
acquisition in settlement of insurance claim, SI 1992/3129 art 4
driving test, PR 27/4/84
meaning, SI 1992/3129 art 2
protective helmet, VATA 1994 Sch 8 Group 16 item 3
second hand—
exclusion of input tax credit, SI 1992/3222 art 4
relief for certain supplies, SI 1992/3129 art 8
repossession under finance agreement, SI 1992/3129 art 4
MOTOR VEHICLE
car derived vans and combi vans, PR 27/10/06
Personal Export Scheme—
buyer's guide, Notice 705
supplies for removal from EC, Notice 705A
MUSEUMS AND GALLERIES
admission to, PR 10/12/03
tax reclaimed by, ESC 3.4

MUSIC
printed, duplicated or manuscript, VATA 1994 Sch 8 Group 3

NATIONAL RIVERS AUTHORITY
refund of VAT, SI 1989/1217
NEGLECT
penalties. *See* PENALTIES
resulting understatement, VATA 1994 s 63(1)
NEW MEANS OF TRANSPORT. *See* TRANSPORT
NEW TOWN COMMISSION
refund of tax, VATA 1994 s 33
NEWSPAPERS
zero-rating, VATA 1994 Sch 8 Group 3—
advertisement by charity, VATA 1994 Sch 8 Group 15 item 8
NEWS PROVIDERS
refund of tax, VATA 1994 s 33
NON-PROFIT MAKING ORGANISATION
exemption—
competition entry fees, VATA 1994 Sch 9 Group 10
education, training and research, VATA 1994 Sch 9 Group 6 items 2, 4, 5
fund raising events for charity, VATA 1994 Sch 9 Group 12 item 2
health and welfare services, VATA 1994 Sch 9 Group 7 item 9
subscriptions to defined bodies, VATA 1994 Sch 9 Group 9
meaning, VATA 1994 Sch 9 Group 10 note (3)
membership subscriptions, apportionment, ESC 3.35, PR 23/2/09
NON-RESIDENTIAL BUILDINGS
developers, VATA 1994 Sch 10 paras 5–7
meaning, VATA 1994 Sch 8 Group 5 note (7)
NORTHERN IRELAND
application of VAT, VATA 1994 ss 1, 7
computer, meaning, VATA 1994 s 96(6)(b)
copy, meaning, VATA 1994 s 96(6)(b)
document, meaning, VATA 1994 s 96(6)(b)
enforcement of tribunal decisions, VATA 1994 s 87(3)
Lord Chief Justice, delegation of functions by, TCEA 2007 s 46
Upper Tribunal, provision for appeals to, TCEA 2007 s 34
recovery of tax, VATA 1994 Sch 11 para 5(4)
refund of tax to Government, VATA 1994 s 99
Upper Tribunal, provision for appeals to, TCEA 2007 s 34
NORTHUMBRIA INTERIM POLICE AUTHORITY
refund of tax, SI 1985/1101
NOTICES
partnerships, by—
generally, SI 1995/2518 reg 7(1)
Scotland, SI 1995/2518 reg 7(2)
NOTIFICATION
bankruptcy, death or incapacity of an individual, SI 1995/2518 reg 9
business establishment opened in Isle of Man, SI 1982/1067 reg 11
ceasing to make taxable supplies, VATA 1994 Sch 1 paras 11, 12
change in—
constitution of partnership, SI 1995/2518 regs 5, 6

NOTIFICATION – *contd*
change in – *contd*
name, constitution or ownership of business, SI 1995/2518 reg 5(2)
registered particulars, SI 1995/2518 regs 5, 6
installation or assembly of goods in UK, SI 1995/2518 reg 12
liability and registration, VATA 1994 Sch 1 paras 5–8
liquidation or receivership or body corporate, SI 1995/2518 reg 9
partnership, by, SI 1995/2518 regs 5(1), 7
penalties for failure to notify, VATA 1994 s 67
registration—
liability to, SI 1995/2518, regs 5, 6
end of liability, SI 1995/2518 reg 5(3)
service, VATA 1994 s 98
tax representative, appointment of, SI 1995/2518 reg 10
triangulation supplies, SI 1995/2518 reg 11
NURSE
exemption, VATA 1994 Sch 9 Group 7 item 1(*d*)
NURSERIES
exemption, VATA 1994 Sch 9 Group 7
NURSING HOME
exemption, VATA 1994 Sch 9 Group 7
existing, construction of houses or flats in grounds of, PR 5/11/07

OCCUPATIONAL THERAPIST
exemption, VATA 1994 Sch 9 Group 7
OFFENCES
breach of walking possession agreements, VATA 1994 s 68
common duties of UK and Isle of Man, IMA 1979 s 5
contravention of relevant rule, penalty for, SI 2003/3113
evasion of tax. *See* EVASION OF TAX
failure to make return, VATA 1994 s 73
failure to notify of acquisition, VATA 1994 s 67
failure to notify of registration, VATA 1994 s 67
failure to submit EC sales statements, VATA 1994 s 66
false information, providing, VATA 1994 s 72
fraudulent evasion of tax, VATA 1994 s 72
goods used in breach of condition, CED(GR)A 1979 s 13C
inaccuracies in EC sales statements, VATA 1994 s 65
incorrect certificates, VATA 1994 s 62
neglect, VATA 1994 s 63
outlying enactments, saving for, CEMA 1979 s 156
power of arrest, VATA 1994 s 72(9)
proceedings for, CEMA 1979 ss 45–48
receiving goods knowing tax to be evaded, VATA 1994 s 72(10)
repeated misdeclarations, VATA 1994 s 63, 64
statistics of trade, in relation to, SI 1992/2790 reg 6
unauthorised disclosure of information, VATA 1994 s 91(4)
unauthorised issue of invoices, VATA 1994 s 67
untrue declarations, etc, CEMA 1979 s 167
OFFICE
meaning, VATA 1994 s 94

OFFICE FOR NATIONAL STATISTICS
disclosure of information to, VATA 1994 s 91
OFFICIAL ERROR
appeal, VATA 1994 s 83(s)
interest, VATA 1994 s 78
OMBUDSMAN AUTHORITIES
supplies to, ESC 3.23
OPEN MARKET VALUE. *See* VALUE
OPTICAL APPLIANCE
exemption, VATA 1994 Sch 9 Group 7
OPTICIAN
exemption, VATA 1994 Sch 9 Group 7 item 1(b)
refund of tax to, RI 129
OPTION TO TAX (ELECTION TO WAIVE EXEMPTION)
amended provisions, guidelines, PR 22/4/08
belated notification of, PR 5/7/05
charities and relevant residential users, disapplication by, PR 19/3/04
effect of, VATA 1994 Sch 10 paras 2–4
contracts, VATA 1994 s 89
guide to, Notice 742A
manner of election, VATA 1994 Sch 10 paras 2, 3
policy on, PR 28/3/02
properties subject to, PR 5/8/99
revised Notice 742A, PR 30/5/08
OUTPUT TAX
accounting for, SI 1995/2518 regs 2(1), 25, 40(a), 108(2)
bad debt relief. *See* BAD DEBT RELIEF
calculation, VATA 1994 Sch 4 para 7, SI 1995/2518 reg 27—
goods sold under a power, SI 1995/2518 reg 27
horses and ponies, SI 1988/1099
motor cars, SI 1992/3122 art 8
second-hand goods, SI 1992/3129 art 8
tour operators' services, SI 1987/1806
estimation, SI 1995/2518 reg 28
foreign currency, amounts expressed in, Notice 700 para 7.3
general provisions, VATA 1994 s 24
margin scheme, VATA 1994 ss 32, 50A
meaning, VATA 1994 s 24(2), Notice 700 para 7.1
missing trader inter-community fraud, adjustment in relation to supplies, VATA 1994 s 26AB
persons liable, VATA 1994 s 1(2)
security, VATA 1994 Sch 11 para 4(2)
tax value, meaning, Notice 700 para 7.2
tour operators. *See* TOUR OPERATORS
OVERDECLARED TAX
transfer of right, set-off, PR 27/6/08
OVERPAID TAX
recovery—
claim for, limitation, PR 24/8/06
generally, SI 1995/2518 reg 37
time limit, PR 5/8/02, PR 8/10/02
OVERSEAS PERSON
EC trader, VATA 1994 Sch 9 Group 7
overseas body, VATA 1994 Sch 8 Group 13
overseas branch, VATA 1994 Sch 8 Group 13
overseas trader, VATA 1994 Sch 8 Group 13
registration of agent, VATA 1994 s 47
OVERSEAS RESIDENT. *See* OVERSEAS PERSON
OVERSEAS SUPPLIER
customers, accounting through, SI 1995/2518 reg 11
OVERSEAS TRADER *See* OVERSEAS PERSON
OVERSTATEMENT OF TAX,
persistent misdeclaration, VATA 1994 s 64
serious misdeclaration, VATA 1994 s 63

PAMPHLET
advertising by charities, VATA 1994 Sch 8 Group 15 item 8
zero-rating, VATA 1994 Sch 8 Group 3
PARKING FACILITIES
exemption, VATA 1994 Sch 9 Group 1 item 1(*h*)
PARTIAL EXEMPTION
attribution of input tax—
adjustment of, SI 1995/2518 regs 107–110
change in intended use, SI 1995/2518 regs 114–116
exempt supplies, SI 1995/2518 reg 105
method of—
foreign supplies, SI 1995/2518 reg 103
self-supplies, SI 1995/2518 reg 104
special, SI 1995/2518 regs 102–102C
special method override notice, PR 10/12/03
specified exempt supplies, SI 1995/2518 regs 103–106
standard, SI 1995/2518 reg 101, PR 11/9/01
bookmakers, services received by, PR 3/1/08
building, adjustment of input tax, SI 1995/2518 regs 112–116
capital items (capital goods scheme), SI 1995/2518 regs 112–116
computers and computer equipment, SI 1995/2518 regs 112–116
consultation, launch of, PR 19/6/08
exempt input tax, SI 1995/2518 reg 99(1)
generally, VATA 1994 s 26
higher education institutions, retrospective claims for input tax, PR 25/7/08
house builders letting dwellings before sale, adjustments, PR 15/9/08
special methods approvals, PR 14/3/07
standard method, changes to, PR 1/4/09
supplies on hire purchase, overhead costs, PR 30/3/07
supplies outside EU, recovery of input tax, PR 28/7/05
tax year, SI 1995/2518 reg 99(1)
three year cap, effect of, PR 31/3/99
PARTNERSHIPS
appeal to VAT tribunal by partners, SI 1986/590 reg 12
business carried on by, VATA 1994 s 46(2)
deemed partnership, VATA 1994 Sch 1 para 2(7)
details, SI 1995/2518 Sch 1 Form 2
fuel for private use—
consideration, VATA 1994 s 57
generally, VATA 1994 s 56
generally, VATA 1994 s 45
notices by—
generally, SI 1995/2518 reg 7(1)
Scotland, SI 1995/2518 reg 7(2)
notification of liability to register by, SI 1995/2518 reg 5(1)
PASSAGE
widening for handicapped persons, VATA 1994 Sch 8 Group 12 item 8
PASSENGER
transportation, VATA 1994 Sch 8 Group 8

VAT

PASSENGER TRANSPORT AUTHORITY
refund of tax, VATA 1994 s 33, SI 1985/1101
PATENT
transfer or assignment—
reverse charge, VATA 1994 s 8
zero-rating, VATA 1994 Sch 8 Group 7
PAWNBROKER
disposal of goods to pawnor, SI 1986/896
PAWNOR
disposal of goods by pawnbroker to, SI 1986/896
PAYMENT OF VAT
amounts less than 1.00, VATA 1994 Sch 11 para 2
appeal, VATA 1994 s 83
breach of provisions—
assessment, VATA 1994 ss 76, 77
generally, VATA 1994 s 69
credit for input tax, VATA 1994 ss 25, 26
errors—
correction of, SI 1995/2518 reg 35
voluntary disclosure, SI 1995/2518 reg 34
goods sold in satisfaction of debt, VATA 1994 Sch 4 para 7, Sch 11 para 2(1)
imported goods—
deposit, CEMA 1979 ss 43(1), 44
postponed accounting scheme, SI 1995/2518 reg 122
security, CEMA 1979 s 37B
input tax, VATA 1994 s 24
output tax, VATA 1994 s 24
payment by reference to accounting periods, VATA 1994 s 25(1)
payment by telephone, fees for, SI 2008/1948
payments on account—
body corporate, SI 1995/2518 reg 48
calculation of amounts, SI 1993/2001 arts 11–15
cessation of duty, SI 1993/2001 art 7
divisions, business carried on in, SI 1993/2001 art 16
duty to pay, SI 1993/2001 art 4
eligible persons, SI 1993/2001 art 5
excess, repayment of, SI 1995/2518 reg 46
failure to make, SI 1995/2518 reg 47
generally, VATA 1994 s 28, SI 1995/2518 regs 40A, 45–48
groups of companies, SI 1993/2001 art 17
missing trader intra-community fraud, supplies used in, SI 1993/2001 art 2A
notification in writing, SI 1992/1844 regs 4, 7, SI 1995/2518 reg 45
overpayment, SI 1995/2518 reg 46
time for payments, SI 1993/2001 arts 8–9
penalties for non-payment, VATA 1994 s 66, 76
procedure—
goods sold in satisfaction of a debt, SI 1995/2518 reg 27
Post Office, to, SI 1986/260 reg 15
postponed accounting system, SI 1995/2518 reg 122
proper officer, to, CEMA 1979 s 43
repayment, VATA 1994 s 25(3)
standing deposit, CEMA 1979 s 44
tax returns, SI 1995/2518 reg 40(2), (3), SI 1995/2518 regs 40A, 46A
security, VATA 1994 s 73
shipping and forwarding agent, by, CEMA 1979 s 43(1)
time limit, SI 1995/2518 regs 25, 40(2), (3), 50, 54, 62, 63

PAYMENT OF VAT – *contd*
unpaid tax—
distress for, SI 1995/2518 reg 212
traders in supply chain, joint and several liability of, VATA 1994 s 77A
warehoused goods, time of, VATA 1994 s 18(4)–(5A)
PENALTIES
avoidance of, PR 18/6/08
breach of regulations, VATA 1994 s 69
breach of walking possession agreements, VATA 1994 s 68
contravention of relevant rule, for, SI 2003/3113
demands, FA 2003 s 30
errors, for, FA 2007 Sch 24, 1/4/08
evasion of tax, VATA 1994 s 72, FA 2003 s 25
directors of body corporate, liability of, FA 2003 s 28
reduction of penalty, FA 2003 s 29
time limit for demands, FA 2003 s 31
failure to make returns, VATA 1994 s 73
failure to notify, VATA 1994 s 67
false information, providing, VATA 1994 s 72
fraudulent evasion of tax, VATA 1994 s 72
imposition of liability, FA 2003 s 24
income tax or corporation tax purposes, not to be deducted for, TA 1988 s 827(1E)
international trade, in area of, PR 3/12/03
misdeclaration, VATA 1994 s 63
repeated, VATA 1994 s 64
mitigation, VATA 1994 s 70
negligence, VATA 1994 ss 70, 76, 77
regulations and orders, FA 2003 s 41
relevant rule, contravention of, FA 2003 s 26
appeal—
bringing, FA 2003 s 33F
right to, FA 2003 s 33
exceptions, FA 2003 s 27
no prosecution after demand notice, FA 2003 s 32
reasonable excuse, FA 2003 s 27
review of decisions—
appeals, FA 2003 ss 36, 37
further, FA 2003 s 34
nature of, FA 2003 s 33E
offer of, FA 2003 s 33A
out of time, FA 2003 s 33D
power of Commissioners on, FA 2003 s 35
requirement, FA 2003 s 33B
right to, FA 2003 s 33
time, extensions of, FA 2003 s 33C
time limit, FA 2003 s 34
time limit for demands, FA 2003 s 31
relevant tax or duty, on, FA 2003 s 24(2)
service of notices, FA 2003 s 39
statements and documents, admissibility of, FA 2003 s 36
unauthorised disclosure of information, VATA 1994 s 91
unauthorised issue of invoices, VATA 1994 s 67
PENSIONS
fund management, VAT treatment, PR 29/11/02, PR 22/8/07, PR 5/11/07
funded, recovery of input tax by employers, PR 10/10/05
review services, PR 20/2/01
PERIODICAL
zero-rating, VATA 1994 Sch 8 Group 3
PERSISTENT MISDECLARATION
penalties, VATA 1994 s 64

PERSON
belonging, VATA 1994 s 9
intending to make taxable supplies, VATA 1994 Sch 1 paras 9, 14, 15
notification, VATA 1994 Sch 11 para 2(4), (5)
PET FOOD. *See* ANIMAL FEEDING STUFFS
PETROL. *See* FUEL
PHARMACISTS
retail, supplies by, ESC 3.30
PHOTOGRAPHS
admissibility in evidence, VATA 1994 Sch 11 paras 12(4)–(7), 14(2)
PHYSIOTHERAPIST
exemption, VATA 1994 Sch 9 Group 7 item 2
PICTURE BOOKS
zero-rating, VATA 1994 Sch 8 Group 3
PILOTAGE SERVICES
zero-rating, VATA 1994 Sch 8 Group 8 item 7
PLACE OF SUPPLY
acquisition of goods, VATA 1994 ss 13, 18, SI 1992/3283, 2006/112/EC arts 31–39
generally, SI 1992/3121
rules for determining, VATA 1994 s 7
services, of, VATA 1994 s 7, 2006/112/EC arts 43–59
country in which supplied, determining, VATA 1994 s 7A
customer's registration number, SI 1992/3121 art 14
hire of transport, SI 1992/3121 arts 17–18
intermediaries, of, SI 1992/3121 arts 11–13
land relating to, SI 1992/3121 art 5
performed, where, SI 1992/3121 art 15
received, where, SI 1992/3121 art 16
rules for determining, SI 1992/3121 arts 4, 18
special rules, VATA 1994 Sch 4A
supplier or recipient, place to which belonging, VATA 1994 s 9
transport, SI 1992/3121 arts 6–10
services supplied where received, VATA 1994 Sch 5
PLANT AND MACHINERY
generally, VATA 1994 s 34
PLANTS
zero-rating, VATA 1994 Sch 8 Group 1
PLAY GROUPS
exemption, VATA 1994 Sch 9 Group 7
POLICE AUTHORITY
refund of tax, VATA 1994 s 33, SI 1985/1101
vehicle removal/recovery, contracting out of, PR 21/4/99
POLITICAL PARTY
subscription income, VATA 1994 s 94
PORTS
authorities, refund of tax, VATA 1994 s 33
zero-rating, VATA 1994 Sch 8 Group 8
POST OFFICE
collection of tax on postal imports, SI 1986/260
supplies previously made by, ESC 3.33
POSTAL PACKETS
conveyance, exemption, VATA 1994 Sch 9 Group 3
customs and excise enactments, application of, PSA 2000 s 105
Customs requirements, SI 1986/260
meaning, VATA 1994 Sch 9 Group 3 note(1)
postponed accounting system, SI 1995/2518 reg 122
POSTAL SERVICES
exemption, VATA 1994 Sch 9 Group 3, PR 18/5/00
POSTPONED ACCOUNTING SYSTEM
payment of tax, SI 1995/2518 reg 122
POWERS
access to recorded information, VATA 1994 Sch 11 para 11
enforcing compliance, VATA 1994 s 73
entry, search and inspection of premises, VATA 1994 Sch 11 para 10
power of arrest, VATA 1994 s 72(9)
power to inspect, copy and remove documents, VATA 1994 Sch 11 para 7
power to obtain information, VATA 1994 Sch 11 para 7
power to open and check gaming machines, VATA 1994 s 66
power to take samples, VATA 1994 Sch 11 para 8
trader required to account for goods, VATA 1994 s 73
visiting uncooperative traders, VATA 1994 s 73(4), (7)
PREMISES
entry to. *See* ENTRY AND SEARCH
PRESCRIBED ACCOUNTING PERIOD
aligning, PR 15/6/05
fuel for private use, VATA 1994 s 56(7)–(9)
generally, VATA 1994 s 25(1)
length, SI 1995/2518 reg 25
meaning, VATA 1994 s 57(1), SI 1995/2518 regs 2(1), 25
tax charged in different period, VATA 1994 Sch 11 para 2(10)(*a*)
PRESCRIPTION
zero-rating, VATA 1994 Sch 8 Group 12 item 1
PRESTWICK AIRPORT FREE ZONE
designation, SI 1994/143, SI 2001/2882 art 2
health and safety, SI 2001/2882 art 6
responsible authority—
appointment, SI 2001/2882 art 3
conditions imposed on, SI 2001/2882 art 5
PRINTED MATTER
import relief, SI 1984/746 Sch 2
instalments, published in, ESC 3.15
self supply, SI 1992/3129 art 7, SI 2002/1280
zero-rating, VATA 1994 Sch 8, group 3
PRIVATE FINANCE INITIATIVE
VAT position, PR 30/9/03
PRIVATE TUITION
exemption, VATA 1994 Sch 9 Group 6 item 3
PROBATION COMMITTEE
refund of tax, SI 1986/336
PROFESSION
business, VATA 1994 s 94
PROFESSIONAL ASSOCIATION
exemption, VATA 1994 Sch 6 Groups 9, 12
PROFESSIONAL BODIES
subscriptions, exemption, VATA 1994 Sch 9 Group 9
PROJECT ORGANISATION FOR SELF BUILD PROJECTS
refund scheme, VATA 1994 s 35
PROTECTED BUILDINGS
approved alteration, VATA 1994 Sch 8 Group 6 note (6), PR 18/5/00
garage, definition, PR 18/5/05
liability of works to, PR 25/7/03
meaning, VATA 1994 Sch 8 Group 6 note (1)

PROTECTED BUILDINGS – *contd*
zero-rating, VATA 1994 Sch 8 Group 6, PR 22/11/96
PROTECTIVE CLOTHING. *See* CLOTHING AND FOOTWEAR
PUBLIC BODIES. *See also* LOCAL AUTHORITY
interpretation, PR 20/5/08
meaning, VATA 1994 Sch 9 Group 7 note (5)
refund of tax, VATA 1994 s 33
PUBLIC DOMAIN
bodies with objects in, VATA 1994 s 94
PUBLIC INTEREST BODIES
subscriptions, exemption, VATA 1994 Sch 9 Group 9
PUBLICATIONS
zero-rating, VATA 1994 Sch 8 Group 3
PURCHASE TAX
vehicle re-imported to UK, VATA 1994 Sch 13 para 3

QUARTER
meaning, VATA 1994 s 96(1)

RADIO
advertising by charities, VATA 1994 Sch 8 Group 15 item 8
supplies to the blind, VATA 1994 Sch 8 Group 4 item 2
RADIOGRAPHER
exemption, VATA 1994 Sch 9 Group 7 item 1(*c*)
RAMP
construction for handicapped person, VATA 1994 Sch 8 Group 12 items 8, 9, 11
RATE OF TAX
application of, 2006/112/EC arts 93–95
change in—
adjustments of contracts, VATA 1994 s 89
effect, SI 1995/2518 reg 15
failure of resolution order, PCTA 1968
flat rate scheme for farmers, percentage addition, SI 1992/3221
supplementary charge, FA 2009 Sch 3 Pt 1
administration, FA 2009 Sch 3 Pt 5
exceptions, FA 2009 Sch 3 Pt 2
interpretation, FA 2009 Sch 3 Pt 5
liability and amount, FA 2009 Sch 3 Pt 3
listed supplies, FA 2009 Sch 3 Pt 4
supplies spanning, VATA 1994 s 88
fuel and power, on, VATA 1994 s 2(1A)–(1C), Sch A1
Provisional Collection of Taxes Act 1968, VATA 1994 s 90
reduced, VATA 1994 s 29A, 2006/112/EC arts 98–101, Annex III
conversion of buildings, for, VATA 1994 Sch A1 paras 6–8, Sch 7A para 4A
definitive arrangements, special provisions applying until adoption of, 2006/112/EC arts 109–122
fuel, for, VATA 1994 s 2(1A), (1B), Sch A1
labour-intensive services, for, 2006/112/EC arts 106–108, Annex IV, 2006/774
smoking cessation products, supply of, PR 28/6/07
special residential building, supplies to intended user, VATA 1994 Sch A1 para 13

RATE OF TAX – *contd*
reduced, VATA 1994 s 29A, 2006/112/EC arts 98–101, Annex III – *contd*
temporary provisions, 2006/112/EC arts 123–130
standard, VATA 1994 s 2, 2006/112/EC arts 96, 97
structure and level of, 2006/112/EC arts 96–105
REASONABLE EXCUSE
failure to notify of acquisitions, VATA 1994 s 67(8)
failure to submit EC sales statements, VATA 1994 s 66(7)(*b*)
insufficient funds, VATA 1994 s 71(1)(*a*)
misdeclaration, VATA 1994 s 63(10)(*a*)
reliance on another to perform task, VATA 1994 s 71(1)(*b*)
unauthorised issue of invoices, VATA 1994 s 67(8)
RECEIVER FOR THE METROPOLITAN POLICE DISTRICT
refund of tax, VATA 1994 s 33
RECIPIENT OF SERVICES
invoice provided, VATA 1994 s 29
place of belonging, VATA 1994 s 9
RECKONABLE DATE
date from which interest runs, VATA 1994 s 74
RECORDED INFORMATION
generally, VATA 1994 Sch 11 para 11
RECORDS. *See also* DOCUMENTS; TAX RETURN
bad debt relief. *See* BAD DEBT RELIEF
breach of requirements, VATA 1994 s 69B
Commissioners powers, VATA 1994 Sch 11 para 6(1)
computer records, VATA 1994 Sch 11 para 6(6)
duty to keep, VATA 1994 Sch 11 para 6, SI 1995/2518 reg 31
failure to keep, VATA 1994 s 69(1)
farmers flat rate scheme, VATA 1994 s 56(4)(*d*)—
duty to keep records, SI 1995/2518 reg 210
production of, SI 1995/2518 reg 211
free zone goods, SI 1984/1177 reg 24
gold, transactions in, VATA 1994 s 69A
horses and ponies, SI 1983/1099 art 3(*c*)
motor cars, SI 1992/3122 art 8(2)(*d*)
orders for access, VATA 1994 Sch 11 para 11
preservation, VATA 1994 Sch 11 para 6(3)—
discharge of duty, VATA 1994 Sch 11 para 6(4), (5)
second hand goods, SI 1992/3129 art 8(3)(*c*)
statistics of trade, SI 1992/2790 reg 5, 638/2004/EC
VAT account, SI 1995/2518 reg 32
RECOVERY OF TAX. *See* ADMINISTRATION AND COLLECTION
REFRIGERATION
supply, VATA 1994 Sch 4 para 3
zero-rating, VATA 1994 Sch 8 Group 15
REFUND OF TAX
appeal, VATA 1994 s 83(*d*)
British Broadcasting Authority, VATA 1994 s 33
Broads Authority, SI 1999/2076
capital goods, VATA 1994 s 34
capping of claims, PR 27/3/97
certain bodies, SI 1973/2121, SI 1976/2028, SI 1985/1101, SI 1986/286, SI 1986/532
change in tax rate, VATA 1994 s 90

REFUND OF TAX – *contd*
charter trustees, SI 1986/336, SI 2009/1177
claims—
disposal of assets, registration in respect of, VATA 1994 Sch 3A
time limit, PR 14/12/99
Commissions for Local Administration, to, SI 1976/2028
Community traders, to, SI 1980/1537
Conservators, SI 2009/1177
construction of certain buildings, VATA 1994 s 35
deregistration. *See* DEREGISTRATION
development corporation, VATA 1994 s 33
discretion, VATA 1994 s 46(1)
do-it-yourself builders, VATA 1994 s 35
drainage boards, VATA 1994 s 33
EC trader, VATA 1994 s 39
eligible persons, VATA 1994 s 25
exemption, following election to waive, PR 16/8/96
extension of 30 day period, SI 1995/2518
farmers in business overseas, VATA 1994 s 54(5)
Fire and Civil Defence Authority, SI 1985/1101
forwarding of claims to other member States, VATA 1994 s 39A
generally, SI 1995/1978, SI 1995/2999
goods imported for private use, VATA 1994 s 27
government departments, VATA 1994 s 41
Greater London Authority, SI 2000/1046
Greater London Magistrates' Courts Authority, SI 2001/3453
Inner London Education Authority, SI 1985/1101
Inner London Interim Education Authority, SI 1985/1101
interest—
awarded by tribunal, VATA 1994 s 73(2)
claim in writing, need for, VATA 1994 s 78(10)
delay caused by claimant's conduct, VATA 1994 s 78(8A)–(9)
paid to claimant, VATA 1994 s 78(1)
statutory, PR 20/3/09
time limit for making claim, VATA 1994 s 78(11)
lighthouse authorities, VATA 1994 s 33
local authorities, VATA 1994 s 33
London Fire and Civil Defence Authority, SI 1985/1101
London Fire and Emergency Planning Authority, SI 2000/1515
London Residuary Body, SI 1985/1101
magistrates courts committee, SI 1986/336
museums and galleries, to, VATA 1994 s 33A
National Rivers Authority, SI 1989/1217
news provider, nominated, VATA 1994 s 33
Northern Ireland Government, VATA 1994 s 99
Northumbria Interim Police Authority, SI 1985/1101
offset against amount due from trader, VATA 1994 s 49
option to tax made, where, PR 16/8/96
opticians, to, RI 129
overpaid tax—
arrangements for reimbursing taxpayer, VATA 1994 s 80A
assessments of amounts due, VATA 1994 s 80B
claims, limitation, PR 24/8/06

REFUND OF TAX – *contd*
overpaid tax – *contd*
generally, VATA 1994 s 80
statutory interest, PR 20/2/09
unjust enrichment, PR 19/2/09
Passenger Transport Authority, SI 1985/1101
police authority, VATA 1994 s 33, SI 1985/1101
port authority, VATA 1994 s 33
power to withhold, VATA 1994 s 25
probation committee, SI 1986/336
Provisional Collection of Taxes Act 1968, VATA 1994 s 90(3)
reimbursement—
arrangements made before 11 February 1998, SI 1995/2518 reg 43H
arrangements, meaning, SI 1995/2518 reg 43A
claim, meaning, SI 1995/2518 reg 43A
interest, SI 1995/2518 reg 43C
means of, SI 1995/2518 reg 43C
records, SI 1995/2518 regs 43E, 43F
relevant amount, SI 1995/2516, reg 43A
repayments, making, SI 1995/2518 reg 43D
undertakings, SI 1995/2518 reg 43G
unjust enrichment, arrangements disregarded as, SI 1995/2518 reg 43B
repayment supplement, VATA 1994 s 79
Residuary Body, SI 1985/1101
Set-off, PR 18/7/08
statutory bodies, VATA 1994 s 33
taxable persons not established in Member State of refund but in another Member State, 2008/9/EC
taxable person not established in territory of country, to, 79/1072, 86/560
third country traders to, SI 1995/2518
transport authority, VATA 1994 s 33
travellers departing from EC, Notice 704/1
UK traders in other EU states, VAT incurred by, PR 24/6/03
water authorities, VATA 1994 s 33, SI 1973/2121

REGISTER OF TAXABLE PERSONS
change in registered particulars, VATA 1994 Sch 1 paras 11, 13, SI 1995/2518 reg 5(2)
register kept by Commissioners, VATA 1994 Sch 1 para 19

REGISTRATION
acquisitions from other member states—
cancellation, VATA 1994 Sch 3 para 6
conditions for, VATA 1994 Sch 3 para 7
entitlement for registration, VATA 1994 Sch 3 para 4
exemption, VATA 1994 Sch 3 para 8
generally, VATA 1994 Sch 3
liability, VATA 1994 Sch 3 paras 1, 2, SI 1996/2950/1628
matters affecting continuance of registration, VATA 1994 Sch 3 para 5
notification, VATA 1994 Sch 3 para 3
relevant acquisition, meaning, VATA 1994 Sch 3 para 11
appeal, VATA 1994 s 83(*a*)
application forms, SI 1995/2518 reg 5(1), Sch 1, Forms 1, 6, 7
artificial separation of business activities, counteracting, VATA 1994 Sch 1 paras 1A, 2
associations, VATA 1994 s 46(3)
cancellation, VATA 1994 Sch 1 para 13, SI 1995/2518 reg 5(3)

REGISTRATION – *contd*
change in particulars, VATA 1994 Sch 1 para 13(3)
co-owners of buildings and land, VATA 1994 s 51A
deregistration. *See* DEREGISTRATION
direction—
conditions, VATA 1994 Sch 1 para 2(2)
service, VATA 1994 Sch 1 para 2(3)
supplementary direction, VATA 1994 Sch 1 para 2(4)
discretion, VATA 1994 Sch 1 para 1(3)
disposal of assets for which VAT repayment claimed, in respect of, VATA 1994 Sch 3A
division of business, VATA 1994 s 46(1)
entitlement, VATA 1994 Sch 1 para 9, 10
exemption, VATA 1994 Sch 1 para 14
failure to notify of liability, VATA 1994 s 67
group of companies, VATA 1994 s 43
intending trader, VATA 1994 Sch 1 paras 9, 10
liability—
cessation of liability, VATA 1994 Sch 1 para 3
end of, notification, VATA 1994 Sch 1 para 11
generally, VATA 1994 Sch 1 paras 1–7
limits—
generally, VATA 1994 Sch 1 para 1(2), (3)
supplies from other member states, VATA 1994 Sch 2 para 1(1), (7)
local authorities, VATA 1994 s 42
notification—
failure to make—
generally, VATA 1994 s 4, 67(1)
penalty, VATA 1994 ss 67(1), 72(11)
form, VATA 1994 Sch 1 para 17, SI 1995/2518 Sch 1
liability, VATA 1994 Sch 1 para 5(1)
partnership, VATA 1994 s 45
persons previously exempt, VATA 1994 Sch 1 para 14
power to vary specified sums, VATA 1994 Sch 1 para 15
quarter, meaning, VATA 1994 s 96(1)
register, VATA 1994 s 3
registrable, meaning, VATA 1994 Sch 1 para 18
representative member of Group of companies, VATA 1994 s 43,
single taxable person, VATA 1994 Sch 1 paras 1A, 2
supplies from other member states, VATA 1994 Sch 2—
cancellation, VATA 1994 Sch 2 para 6
conditions for, VATA 1994 Sch 2 para 7
liability, VATA 1994 Sch 2 paras 1, 2
notification, VATA 1994 Sch 2 para 3—
affecting continuance of registration, VATA 1994 Sch 2 para 5
relevant supply, meaning, VATA 1994 Sch 2 para 10
request for registration, VATA 1994 Sch 2 para 4
taxable person, meaning, VATA 1994 s 3
transfer of business as a going concern, VATA 1994 s 49, Sch 1 para 1(2)
VAT groups, PR 12/7/99
abuses, PR 29/1/04
application to leave, PR 19/11/02
duplication, VATA 1994 s 43D
eligibility, power to alter, VATA 1994 s 43AA
revenue, protection of, PR 19/11/02

REGISTRATION – *contd*
VAT groups, PR 12/7/99 – *contd*
supplier and customer from different organisations in, PR 10/1/01
VAT representatives, of, VATA 1994 s 48(4)
voluntary, VATA 1994 Sch 1 paras 9, 10
REGISTRATION CERTIFICATE
particulars, VATA 1994 Sch 1 paras 11, 12
REGULATIONS
accounting for tax, VATA 1994 Sch 11 para 2
breach of, VATA 1994 s 69
contravention of relevant rule, penalty for, SI 2003/3113
fiscal warehousing, as to, VATA 1994 ss 18D(3), 18F(7), (8)
imported goods, VATA 1994 ss 37(2), (3), 38
meaning, VATA 1994 s 96(1)
parliamentary procedure, VATA 1994 s 97
payment of VAT, deferring, VATA 1994 s 18D(3)
recovery of tax, VATA 1994 Sch 11 para 5(4)
tax representatives, VATA 1994 s 48(6)
transfers of going concerns, VATA 1994 s 49(2), (3)
unincorporated bodies, VATA 1994 s 46
value of supply, SI 1995/2518
REINSURANCE
exemption, VATA 1994 Sch 9 Group 2
services—
reverse charge, VATA 1994 s 8
supplied where received, VATA 1994 Sch 5 para 5
RELEVANT PURPOSE
change of use, VATA 1994 Sch 10 para 1
charitable, VATA 1994 Sch 8 Group 6
residential, VATA 1994 Sch 8 Group 6
RELIEFS. *See* **BAD DEBT RELIEF; EXEMPTION; IMPORT RELIEF; INPUT TAX; TEMPORARY IMPORTATION RELIEF; ZERO-RATING**
RELIGIOUS COMMUNITY
business carried on, VATA 1994 s 95(3)
exemption, VATA 1994 Sch 9 Group 7 item 10
RENT. *See* LEASE
REPAIRS AND MAINTENANCE
farmhouse, to, recovery of tax, PR 27/8/96
handicapped aids, VATA 1994 Sch 8 Group 12 item 5
protected buildings, VATA 1994 Sch 8 Group 6 note (6)
talking books, VATA 1994 Sch 8 Group 4 item 1(1)
REPAYMENT OF TAX. *See* **REFUND OF TAX**
REPAYMENT SUPPLEMENT
qualifying refunds, VATA 1994 s 79
REPOSSESSED GOODS
treated as neither a supply of goods or services, SI 1992/3129 art 4
REPRESENTATIVE MEMBER
registration, VATA 1994 s 43
REPRESENTATIVES
appointment form, SI 1995/2518 Sch 1 Form 8
enforcement by diligence, VATA 1994 s 48, SI 1997/1432
enforcement by distress, VATA 1994 s 48, SI 1997/1432
obligation, VATA 1994 s 48, SI 1995/2518 regs 10, 30
return, SI 1995/2518 reg 25(3)

RESEARCH
exemption, VATA 1994 Sch 9 Group 6 item 1
RESIDENTIAL CARE
liability of, PR 16/7/01, PR 21/3/02
existing home, construction of houses or flats in grounds of, PR 5/11/07
RESIDENTIAL PURPOSE
change of use of building, VATA 1994 Sch 10 para 1
option to tax excluded, VATA 1994 Sch 10 para 2(2)
relevant residential purpose, meaning, VATA 1994 Sch 8 Group 5 note (3)
RESIDUARY BODY
refund of tax, SI 1985/1101
RETAIL SCHEME
appeal, VATA 1994 s 83(*y*)
apportionment, Notice 727/4
direct calculation, Notice 727/5
guide to, Notice 727
point of sale, Notice 727/3
regulations, VATA 1994 Sch 11 para 2(6)
RETAILER
calculation of output tax, VATA 1994 s 30(8)
consortium, payments to, PR 22/4/93
invoice, SI 1995/2518 reg 71
methods for calculating output tax, caterers' scheme, SI 1995/2518 reg 73
requirement to issue tax invoice, SI 1995/2518 reg 16
scheme agreed with Commissioners, SI 1995/2518 reg 67
value of supply by, SI 1995/2518
RETENTION PAYMENT
item of supply, SI 1995/2518 reg 89
RETURN. *See* VAT RETURN
REVERSE CHARGE
cessation and recommencement of relevant supplies, notification of, SI 1995/2518 reg 23D
first relevant supply, notification of, SI 1995/2518 reg 23B
gas and electricity supplied by persons outside UK, on, VATA 1994 s 9A
input tax credit, VATA 1994 ss 8(1), 24(1), (2), SI 1995/2518 reg 29(2)
interpretation, SI 1995/2518 reg 23A
mobile telephones and computer chips, businesses trading in, PR 20/3/07, PR 20/4/09, PR 18.6.09
services received from abroad, VATA 1994 s 8, SI 1997/1523
services supplied where received, VATA 1994 Sch 5
statements, submission of, SI 1995/2518 reg 23C
supplies disregarded for partial exemption, VATA 1994 s 8(3), SI 1997/1523
REVERSE SURRENDER
exemption, VATA 1994 Sch 9 Group 1 item 1 notes (1), (1A)
RIVER CRUISE
tax treatment, PR 15/7/96
ROAD FUEL. *See* FUEL
ROAD VEHICLE. *See* COMPANY CAR; MOTOR CAR; VEHICLE
ROYALTIES
time of supply, SI 1995/2518 reg 91

SALE OR RETURN
time of supply, VATA 1994 s 6
SALES INVOICE. *See* TAX INVOICE
SALVAGE
zero-rating, VATA 1994 Sch 8 Group 8 item 8
SAMPLES
Commissioners power to take, VATA 1994 Sch 11 para 8(1)
compensation, VATA 1994 Sch 11 para 8(3)
gift to actual or potential customers, VATA 1994 Sch 4 para 5(2)(*b*), (3)
SAVINGS ACCOUNT
exemption, VATA 1994 Sch 9, Group 5 item 8
SCHOOL. *See* EDUCATION
SCIENTIFIC COLLECTION
acquisition in settlement of insurance claim, SI 1992/3129 art 4
exemption, VATA 1994 Sch 9 Group 11
import relief, SI 1984/746 art 5, Sch 2
margin scheme, VATA 1994 s 50A
SCIENTIFIC EQUIPMENT
zero-rating, VATA 1994 Sch 8 Group 15
SCIENTIFIC SERVICES
zero-rating, VATA 1994 Sch 8 Group 7
SCOTLAND
assignment, VATA 1994 s 96(1)
copy, meaning, VATA 1994 s 96(7)
distress, VATA 1994 Sch 11 para 5
document, meaning, VATA 1994 s 96(7)
enforcement of tribunal decisions, VATA 1994 s 87(2)
entry and search, VATA 1994 Sch 11 para 10
evidence, VATA 1994 Sch 11 para 6
insolvency, VATA 1994 Sch 11 para 15
order for access to recorded information, VATA 1994 Sch 11 para 11
partnership, notices by, SI 1995/2518 reg 7(2)
recovery of tax, VATA 1994 Sch 11 para 5(5), (6), (9), SI 1995/2518 reg 213
SEARCH. *See* ENTRY AND SEARCH
SECOND HAND GOODS
margin schemes, VATA 1994 ss 32, 50A, SI 1992/3129 art 8, PR 10/6/02, Notice 718
special scheme, 2006/112/EC arts 311–343, Annex IX
SECONDARY SECURITIES
exemption, VATA 1994 Sch 9 Group 5 item 6
SECURITIES
exemption, VATA 1994 Sch 9 Group 5 item 6
SECURITY FOR TAX
appeal, VATA 1994 s 83(1)
failure to provide, VATA 1994 s 72(11)
provision, VATA 1994 Sch 11 para 4
recovery of tax, VATA 1994 Sch 11 para 5(10)
requirement to give, CEMA 1979 s 157
SEEDS
zero-rating, VATA 1994 Sch 8 Group 1
SELF-BILLING INVOICE
procedure, VATA 1994 ss 6(9), 29
SELF-BUILD PROJECTS
refund scheme, VATA 1994 s 35(1)
SELF-SUPPLY
capital items, VATA 1994 s 44(4)
construction services, SI 1989/472
developers of non-residential buildings, VATA 1994 Sch 10 para 6
generally, VATA 1994 s 5
group of companies, VATA 1994 s 43, SI 1992/2122 art 7
input tax, credit—
attribution of, SI 1995/2518 reg 104
generally, VATA 1994 ss 24(1), (2), 80
motor cars, SI 1992/3122 arts 5–7
printed matter, treatment of, SI 1995/1268 art 11
time of supply, VATA 1994 s 6

SELF-SUPPLY – *contd*
Treasury orders, VATA 1994 s 5(5), (6)
SERVICE OF NOTICES
generally, VATA 1994 s 98
partnership's registered name, VATA 1994 s 45(4)
SERIOUS MISDECLARATION. *See also* MISDECLARATION
consequences, VATA 1994 s 63
SERVICES. *See also* PLACE OF SUPPLY, SUPPLY; SUPPLY OF SERVICES
change in rate of tax, VATA 1994 s 89
consideration, supplied without, SI 1995/2518 reg 81
continuous supply, SI 1995/2518 regs 90, 90A, 90B
deregistration, received after, SI 1995/2518 reg 111(5)
imported, relief on, ESC 2.1
incorporation, received before, SI 1995/2518 reg 111
partly used for business purposes, VATA 1994 s 24(5)
registration, received before, SI 1995/2518 reg 111
self-supply, VATA 1994 s 5
SET-OFF CREDITS
Commissioners' power, VATA 1994 s 81(3)
transitional provisions, VATA 1994 Sch 13 para 21
SEWAGE SERVICES
zero-rating, VATA 1994 Sch 8 Group 2
SHARES
charities, dealing by, PR 17/10/96
exchanges, attribution of input tax on professional services, PR 20/8/02
exemption, VATA 1994 Sch 9 Group 5 item 6, 7 note (5)
issues, VAT position, PR 15/6/05
SHEERNESS (PORT OF) FREE ZONE
designation, SI 1994/2898 art 2
duration, SI 1994/2898 art 4
health and safety, SI 1994/2898 art 7
responsible authority, SI 1994/2898 art 3, SI 1997/994
duties of, SI 1994/2898 arts 5, 6
SHEET MUSIC. *See* MUSIC
SHIP
design services, PR 24/2/99
facilities for—
mooring or storage, VATA 1994 Sch 9 Group 1
playing game of chance aboard, VATA 1994 Sch 9 Group 4
handling services, VATA 1994 Sch 8 Group 8 item 6
meaning, VATA 1994 s 96(1)
pilotage services, VATA 1994 Sch 8 Group 8 item 7
shipbuilder's relief, abolition, PR 14/1/04
stores for use in, Notice 703 para 10
supplies, repair or maintenance, VATA 1994 Sch 8 Group 8 items 1, 2A, 2B
zero-rating—
charter or hire, VATA 1994 Sch 8 Group 8
classification, VATA 1994 Sch 8 Group 8
handling in port, VATA 1994 Sch 8 Group 8
repair and maintenance, VATA 1994 Sch 8 Group 8
survey of, VATA 1994 Sch 8 Group 8
transport of passengers, VATA 1994 Sch 8 Group 8
SHOES. *See* CLOTHING AND FOOTWEAR
SHOOTING RIGHTS
liability for VAT, VATA 1994 Sch 9 Group 1
SIMPLIFICATION PROCEDURES
provision, 2006/112/EC arts 238–240
SINGLE CURRENCY
UK business, effect of adoption on, PR 13/1/99
SINGLE TAXABLE PERSON
generally, VATA 1994 Sch 1 paras 1A, 2, 2006/112/EC art 11
SMALL ENTERPRISES
Special schemes, 2006/112/EC arts 281–294
SMOKING CESSATION PRODUCTS
reduced rate for, PR 28/6/07
SOLICITOR
insurance claims, VATA 1994 Sch 9 Group 2
reverse charge, VATA 1994 s 8
supply to overseas person, VATA 1994 Sch 8, Group 7
SOUTHAMPTON FREE ZONE
designation, SI 2001/2880 art 2
health and safety, SI 2001/2880 art 6
responsible authority—
appointment, SI 2001/2880 art 3
conditions imposed on, SI 2001/2880 art 5
SPECIAL ACCOUNTING SCHEME. *See* ELECTRONICALLY SUPPLIED SERVICES
SPIRITS. *See* ALCOHOLIC BEVERAGE
SPIRITUAL WELFARE
exemption, VATA 1994 Sch 9 Group 7 item 10
SPORT
clubs, VAT repayments and interest received by, RI 109
exemption, VATA 1994 Sch 9 Group 10
facilities for playing, VATA 1994 Sch 9 Group 1
letting
fund-raising events, VATA 1994 Sch 9 Group 12 note (3)(*b*)
meals and accommodation provided, VAT on, ESC 3.10
services performed abroad, VATA 1994 Sch 8 Group 7
SPORTING RIGHTS
liability for VAT, VATA 1994 Sch 9 Group 1 item 1(*c*) note (8)
STAMPS, TOKENS AND VOUCHERS
treatment, VATA 1994 s 23, Sch 6 para 5
STANDARD RATE. *See* RATE OF TAX
STATEMENTS
admissibility of computer statements, VATA 1994 Sch 11 para 6(6)
STATIONERY
self supply of, SI 1992/3129 art 7
STATISTICS OF TRADE
ancillary costs sample surveys, SI 1992/2790 reg 4A
assimilation threshold, SI 1992/2790 reg 3
collection system, 91/3330 arts 6–16
Committee, 91/3330 arts 29–30
Community, 638/2004/EC
evidence, SI 1992/2970 regs 7–8
implementing regulation, 92/3046
Intrastat System—
access to data, PR 4/3/08
application, SI 1992/2790 reg 2, 91/3330 art 7, 92/2256 art 1, 92/3046
changes to, PR 23/12/08
revised thresholds, PR 11/12/06, PR 19/12/07
offences, SI 1992/2790 reg 6
recorded information, access to, SI 1992/2790 regs 9–11
records, SI 1992/2790 reg 5
regulations, 91/3330, 92/2256
supplementary declarations, SI 1992/2790 regs 3–4, Sch.

STATISTICS OF TRADE – *contd*
thresholds, 92/2256
STATUTORY BODY
refund of tax, VATA 1994 s 33(3), SI 1973/2121, SI 1976/2028, SI 1985/1101, SI 1986/336, SI 1986/532, SI 1989/1217
STATUTORY INSTRUMENTS
annulment, VATA 1994 s 97(2), (5)
change in rate of tax, VATA 1994 s 2(1)
STATUTORY WATER UNDERTAKER
refund of tax, VATA 1994 s 33(3)
STOCKS
exemption, VATA 1994 Sch 9 Group 5 items 6, 7
STORAGE
ships/aircraft, VATA 1994 Sch 9 Group 1 item 1(k)
STORES
zero-rating of goods supplied, VATA 1994 s 30(6)
STUDENTS
importation reliefs, SI 1992/3193 art 16
SUBSCRIPTION
club, association or organisation, VATA 1994 s 94(2), (3), Sch 6 Group 4
exemption—
trade union, professional and public interest bodies, VATA 1994 Sch 9 Group 9
youth club, VATA 1994 Sch 9 Group 6
gaming club, VATA 1994 Sch 6 Group 4 note (1)(*a*)
SUMMONS
non-compliance, VATA 1994 Sch 12 para 10
witness, SI 1986/590 r 11, 22
SUPPLY
disregarded for VAT purposes, SI 1986/869, SI 1992/630, SI 1992/3129 arts 4–5
exempt, determining whether, after grant of interest etc, VATA 1994 s 96 (10A)
input tax, SI 1995/2518 reg 29
neither goods nor services, SI 1986/896, SI 1992/630, SI 1992/3129 arts 4–5
place of—
goods, SI 1992/3283
services, SI 1992/3121
single or multiple, PR 15/2/01
zero-rated, determining whether, after grant of interest etc, VATA 1994 s 96 (10A)
SUPPLY OF GOODS
agent, VATA 1994 s 47(1)–(2A)
appeal, VATA 1994 s 83(*b*)
apportionment of tax, VATA 1994 s 24(5)
approval on, VATA 1994 s 6(2)
business assets—
ceases to be taxable, VATA 1994 Sch 4 para 8
disposed of, VATA 1994 Sch 4, para 5
gift of, VATA 1994 Sch 4 para 5(2)
removal from member states, VATA 1994 Sch 4 para 6
capital goods, VATA 1994 s 34
change in rate of tax, VATA 1994 s 88—
adjustment of contract, VATA 1994 s 89
charge to tax, VATA 1994 s 1–3, 2006/112/EC arts 63–67
classification, VATA 1994 s 5, Sch 4
deemed. *See* DEEMED SUPPLY
discounts for prompt payment, VATA 1994 Sch 6 para 4(1)
distinguished from supply of services, VATA 1994 Sch 4
do-it-yourself builders, VATA 1994 s 35
exemptions. *See* EXEMPTIONS
SUPPLY OF GOODS – *contd*
generally, VATA 1994 s 5
gift of business assets, VATA 1994 Sch 4 para 5(2)
government departments, VATA 1994 s 41
group of companies, VATA 1994 s 43
heat, VATA 1994 Sch 4 para 3
input tax, VATA 1994 s 24
intermediate, supplies by, SI 1995/2518 regs 11, 18
intra-community acquisition, 2006/112/EC arts 20–23
lease, as, SI 1995/2518 reg 85
major interest in land, VATA 1994 Sch 4 para 4
meaning, 2006/112/EC art 14
output tax, VATA 1994 s 24
partner's liability for tax, VATA 1994 s 45(5)
persons belonging in another member state, to, SI 1995/2518 regs 11, 18
persons belonging in other member states, SI 1995/2518 regs 12, 19
place of supply., VATA 1994 s 7, 2006/112/EC arts 31–39. *See also* PLACE OF SUPPLY
power, VATA 1994 Sch 4 para 3
refrigeration, VATA 1994 Sch 4 para 3
refund of tax. *See* REFUND OF TAX
self supply. *See* SELF SUPPLY
taxable amount, 2006/112/EC arts 73–82
taxable supply, meaning, VATA 1994 s 4
taxable transactions, 2006/112/EC arts 14–19
timing. *See* TIME OF SUPPLY
tour operators, VATA 1994 s 53
transfer of possession of goods, VATA 1994 Sch 4 para 1(2)
treasury orders, VATA 1994 s 5
unincorporated bodies, VATA 1994 s 46(3)
value. *See* VALUE
ventilation, VATA 1994 Sch 4 para 3
water, supply of as, SI 1989/1114
zero-rating, VATA 1994 s 30
SUPPLY OF NEITHER GOODS NOR SERVICES
generally, VATA 1994 s 18, 43(1)
SUPPLY OF SERVICES
acts or omission, VATA 1994 Sch 5 para 4
agent, VATA 1994 s 47(3)
appeal, VATA 1994 s 83(*b*)
apportionment of tax, VATA 1994 s 24(5)
change in rate of tax, VATA 1994 s 88, 89
charge to tax, VATA 1994 s 1 3, 2006/112/EC arts 63–67
continuous, SI 1995/2518 regs 90, 90A, 90B
deemed, non-business use, SI 1993/1507
services received from abroad, VATA 1994 s 8
exemption. *See* EXEMPTIONS
gaming machines. *See* GAMING MACHINES
generally, VATA 1994 s 5
group of companies, VATA 1994 s 43
input tax, VATA 1994 s 24
meaning, 2006/112/EC art 24
output tax, VATA 1994 s 24
place of supply. *See* PLACE OF SUPPLY
place where recipient belongs, VATA 1994 s 9
private use of assets, VATA 1994 Sch 4 para 5(4), (5)
rate of tax, VATA 1994 s 2(1)(*a*)
recipient. *See* RECIPIENT OF SERVICES
refund of tax, VATA 1994 s 33
self supply. *See* SELF SUPPLY

TAX INVOICE – *contd*
time, SI 1995/2518 reg 13(5)
unauthorised issue—
effect on input tax credit, SI 1995/2518 reg 29
mitigation, VATA 1994 s 70
penalty, VATA 1994 s 67
VAT invoice, meaning, VATA 1994 s 6(15)
zero-rated supplies—
distinguished, SI 1995/2518 reg 14(4)
excepted, SI 1995/2518 reg 20
TAX POINT. *See* TIME OF SUPPLY
TAX REPRESENTATIVE
appointment , VATA 1994 s 48
notification of appointment, SI 1995/2518 reg 10
service of notices, VATA 1994 s 98
TELECOMMUNICATIONS
anti-avoidance provisions, SI 1997/1523
continuous supplies of services, SI 1995/2518 regs 90 90A, 90B
services supplied where received , VATA 1994 Sch 5 para 7A, SI 1997/1523 reg 3
TELEGRAPHIC TRANSFER
fees, treatment of, PR 18/11/92
TELEVISION
advertising by charities, VATA 1994 Sch 8 Group 15 item 8
TEMPLATES
zero-rating, VATA 1994 Sch 8 Group 13 item 3
TEMPORARY IMPORTATION EXEMPTION
Community legislation relating to. SI 1992/3111 Sch
meaning, SI 1992/3111 art 4
supply, treatment of, SI 1992/3130
TENANCY. *See* LEASE
TENT
camping facilities, VATA 1994 Sch 9 Group 1 item 1(*g*)
TERMINAL MARKETS
generally, SI 1973/173
Treasury orders, VATA 1994 s 50
TERRITORIAL SEA
extension of tax, VATA 1994 s 96(1)
TERRORISM
disclosure of information—
extension of powers, ACSA 2001 s 17, Sch 4
interpretation, ACSA 2001 s 20
overseas purposes, restriction in case of, ACSA 2001 s 18
revenue departments, held by, ACSA 2001 s 19
THEATRE
accommodation, VATA 1994 Sch 9 Group 1 item 1(l)
admission, VATA 1994 s 94
production costs, VAT deduction, PR 14/6/07
THIRD COUNTRY TRADER
repayment of tax, SI 1995/2518
TILBURY (PORT OF) FREE ZONE
designation, SI 2002/1418 art 2
duration, SI 2002/1418 art 4
health and safety, SI 2002/1418 art 6
responsible authority—
appointment, SI 2002/1418 art 3
duties, SI 2002/1418 art 5
TIMBER
granting right to fell and remove, VATA 1994 Sch 9 Group 1 item 1(l)
TIME LIMITS
assessment, VATA 1994 s 73(6), 77
documents, VATA 1994 Sch 11 para 12
election to tax, VATA 1994 Sch 10 para 3(6)

TIME LIMITS – *contd*
errors, correction of, SI 1995/2518 reg 34(1A)VATA 1994
input tax, three-year limit, SI 1995/2518 reg 29(1A)
invoices, VATA 1994 Sch 11 para 2(2)
notification—
ceasing to make taxable supplies, VATA 1994 Sch 1 para 11
change in registered particulars, VATA 1994 Sch 1 paras 11–13(3)
liability to register, VATA 1994 Sch 1 paras 5, 6
official error, payment of interest in case of, VATA 1994 s 78 (11)
recovery of tax, VATA 1994 s 80(4), (5)
retention of records, VATA 1994 Sch 11 para 6(3)
TIME OF SUPPLY
acquisition of goods—
generally, VATA 1994 s 12
triangular transactions, VATA 1994 s 14(4)
warehousing, VATA 1994 s 18
alteration by Commissioners, VATA 1994 s 6(10)
basic tax point, VATA 1994 s 6(1)–(3)
change of rate of tax, SI 1995/2518 reg 95
election for basic tax point to apply, VATA 1994 s 88(2)
free zone goods, VATA 1994 s 17(5)(*b*)
fuel for private use, VATA 1994 s 56(6)
gas, SI 1995/2518 reg 86
generally, VATA 1994 s 6, SI 1995/2518 reg 94
gift of goods, VATA 1994 s 6(12)
goods—
approval, sale or return, VATA 1994 s 6(2), (4)
buyer's possession, SI 1995/2518 reg 88
private use, for, SI 1995/2518 reg 81(1)
retention payments, SI 1995/2518 reg 89
invoice issued—
after basic tax point, VATA 1994 s 6(5), (6)
before basic tax point, VATA 1994 s 6(4)
land—
compulsory purchase, SI 1995/2518 reg 82(1)
consideration not determinable, SI 1995/2518 reg 82(2)
leases, SI 1995/2518 reg 85
meaning, VATA 1994 s 6(15)
payment received before basic tax point, VATA 1994 s 6(4)
power, heat, refrigeration or ventilation, SI 1995/2518 reg 86
receipt of payment, reference to, SI 1995/2518 reg 94A
regulations, VATA 1994 s 88(3), Sch 11 para 2(9)
removal of goods, VATA 1994 s 6
royalties, SI 1995/2518 reg 91
self-supplied, VATA 1994 s 6(11)
services—
barristers and advocates, SI 1995/2518 reg 92
construction industry, SI 1995/2518 reg 93
continuous supplies of, SI 1995/2518 reg 90
free supplies of, SI 1995/2518 reg 81(2)
outside the UK, from, SI 1995/2518 reg 82
private use of goods, SI 1995/2518 reg 81(1)

TIME OF SUPPLY – *contd*
services – *contd*
retention payments, SI 1995/2518 reg 89
together with goods in construction industry, SI 1995/2518 reg 93
transaction treated as a supply, VATA 1994 ss 6, 56
water, SI 1995/2518 reg 86
TIME SHARING
holiday accommodation, VATA 1994 Sch 8 Group 7 item 7
TOBACCO
products—
diplomats, import by, SI 1992/3156 art 15
small non-commercial consignment, SI 1986/939
travellers' allowance, SI 1994/955
tax-free shops, zero-rating, VATA 1994 Sch 8 Group 14
TOILET WATER
travellers' allowance, SI 1994/955
TOKENS
gaming machines, VATA 1994 s 23(3)
valuation, VATA 1994 Sch 6 para 5
TOPOGRAPHICAL PLAN
zero-rating, VATA 1994 Sch 8 Group 3
TOUR OPERATORS
bad debt relief, SI 1995/2518 reg 172B
discounts funded by, PR 7/7/06
margin scheme—
changes to, PR 8/4/09
designated travel services, incidental supplies, SI 1987/1806 art 14
meaning, SI 1987/1806 art 3
place of supply, SI 1987/1806 art 5
tax chargeable on, SI 1987/1806 art 10
time of supply, SI 1987/1806 art 4
value, SI 1987/1806 arts 7–9
meaning, VATA 1994 s 53(3)
special schemes for, SI 1987/1806, 2006/112/EC arts 306–310
sub-agents, commission earned by, PR 11/10/07
supplies of goods and services, VATA 1994 s 53
TOWAGE
zero-rating, VATA 1994 Sch 8 Group 8 item 8
TRADE ASSOCIATION
exemption, VATA 1994 Sch 9 Group 9
TRADE UNION
exemption, VATA 1994 Sch 9 Group 9
TRADEMARK
transfer or assignment—
reverse charge, VATA 1994 s 8
services supplied where received, VATA 1994 Sch 5 para 1
zero-rating to overseas, VATA 1994 Sch 8 Group 7
TRADING STAMPS
schemes, VATA 1994 s 52
value of goods exchanged for, VATA 1994 Sch 6 para 5
TRAINING
exemption, VATA 1994 Sch 9 Group 6
zero-rating, VATA 1994 Sch 8 Group 7
TRANSFER OF BUSINESS AS GOING CONCERN
capital goods scheme, SI 1995/2518 reg 114
generally, VATA 1994 s 49, SI 1995/1268 reg 5
property, treatment of, PR 20/7/99
review of rules, PR 9/8/08
second-hand cars, SI 1992/3122 reg 8(c)(d)
supply made in course of furtherance of business, VATA 1994 s 94(6)
TRANSFER OF BUSINESS AS GOING CONCERN – *contd*
transfer to members of Group, VATA 1994 s 44, PR 18/12/98
TRANSFER OF FUNDS, INFORMATION ON PAYER
appeals, SI 2007/3298 reg 13, Sch 2
charges and penalties, recovery of, SI 2007/3298 reg 17
civil penalties, SI 2007/3298 reg 11
connected persons, SI 2007/3298 Sch 1
information requirement, failure to comply, SI 2007/3298 reg 10
offences, SI 2007/3298 reg 14
bodies corporate, etc, by, SI 2007/3298 reg 16
prosecution, SI 2007/3298 reg 15
review procedure, SI 2007/3298 reg 12
supervision, costs of, SI 2007/3298 reg 5
supervisory authorities—
duties of, SI 2007/3298 reg 4
entry and inspection of premises, SI 2007/3298 regs 8, 9
Financial Services Authority as, SI 2007/3298 reg 3
powers, SI 2007/3298 regs 6–10
UK and Channel Islands and Isle of Man, transfers between, SI 2007/3298 reg 18
TRANSITIONAL PROVISIONS
assessments, VATA 1994 Sch 13 para 20
bad debt relief, VATA 1994 Sch 13 para 9
generally, VATA 1994 Sch 13 para 1
importation of goods, VATA 1994 Sch 13 para 19
introduction of VATA, VATA 1994 Sch 13 para 3
Isle of Man, VATA 1994 Sch 13 para 23
offences and penalties, VATA 1994 Sch 13 paras 11–18
overseas suppliers account through their customers, VATA 1994 Sch 13 para 6
president, chairman of tribunals, VATA 1994 Sch 13 para 5
set-off of credits, VATA 1994 Sch 13 para 21, FA 1997 s 49
supplies during construction of buildings and works, VATA 1994 Sch 13 para 10
supply in accordance with pre 1975 arrangements, VATA 1994 Sch 13 para 4
validity of subordinate legislation, VATA 1994 Sch 13 para 2
VAT tribunals, VATA 1994 Sch 13 para 22
zero rated supplies of goods and services, VATA 1994 Sch 13 para 8
TRANSPORT. *See also* AIRCRAFT; SHIP
Community—
meaning, SI 1992/3283 art 3
supply of goods, place of, SI 1992/3283 arts 4–5
hire, place of, SI 1992/3121 arts 17–18
international, exemptions, 2006/112/EC arts 148–150
new means of—
application of Vat to, Notice 728
first entry into service, SI 1995/2518 regs 146, 147
form, SI 1995/2518 Sch 1 Form 13
meaning, VATA 1994 s 95
non-taxable persons, notification and payment of tax, SI 1995/2518 reg 148
persons departing to another member state, supply to, SI 1995/2518 reg 155
refund to tax, claim for, SI 1995/2518

TRANSPORT – *contd*
place of supply, SI 1992/3121 arts 6–10
TRANSPORT AUTHORITIES
refund of tax, VATA 1994 s 33
TRAVEL AGENTS. *See* TOUR OPERATORS
TREASURY ORDERS
acquisition from other members states, VATA 1994 s 11(4)
credit for input tax, VATA 1994 s 25(7)
default interest, VATA 1994 s 74(6)
exemption, VATA 1994 s 30
generally, VATA 1994 s 97
import relief, VATA 1994 s 37(1)
payments on account of tax, VATA 1994 s 28, SI 1995/2518 art 40A
place of supply, VATA 1994 s 7(11)
rate of tax, VATA 1994 s 2(2), (3)
repayment supplement, VATA 1994 s 79(7)
tax as common duty of UK and Isle of Man, IMA 1979 s 1(2), (3)
terminal markets, VATA 1994 s 50
tour operators, VATA 1994 s 53
value of certain goods, VATA 1994 s 22(4), (5)
TREATMENT OR PROCESS
goods reimported after, SI 1995/2518 reg 126
tax treatment, VATA 1994 s 22
TRIANGULATION
place of supply, SI 1995/2518 regs 17, 18, VATA 1994 s 14
TRIBUNAL
accommodation, provision of, TCEA 2007 s 41
Administrative Council. *See* ADMINISTRATIVE JUSTICE AND TRIBUNALS COUNCIL
commencement of provisions, SI 2007/2709
efficient and effective system, general duty as to, TCEA 2007 s 39
fees, TCEA 2007 s 42
First-tier Tribunal—
appeal tribunal, as, FA 1994 s 7
assessors, TCEA 2007 s 28
chambers—
Acting President, TCEA 2007 Sch 4 para 6
Deputy President, TCEA 2007 Sch 4 para 5
judges and members of, TCEA 2007 Sch 4 Pt 2
organisation into, TCEA 2007 s 7
president of, TCEA 2007 s 7, Sch 4
costs or expenses in, TCEA 2007 s 29
decision, review of, TCEA 2007 s 9
establishment of, TCEA 2007 s 3
judges of, TCEA 2007 ss 4, 6
appointment of, TCEA 2007 Sch 2 para 1
neither appointed nor transferred in, TCEA 2007 Sch 2 para 6
oaths, TCEA 2007 Sch 2 para 9
removal from office, TCEA 2007 Sch 2 para 3
remuneration, allowances and expenses, TCEA 2007 Sch 2 para 5
terms of appointment, TCEA 2007 Sch 2 para 4
training, TCEA 2007 Sch 2 para 8
members of, TCEA 2007 ss 4, 7
appointment of, TCEA 2007 Sch 2 para 2
neither appointed nor transferred in, TCEA 2007 Sch 2 para 7
oaths, TCEA 2007 Sch 2 para 9
removal from office, TCEA 2007 Sch 2 para 3

TRIBUNAL – *contd*
First-tier Tribunal – *contd*
members of, TCEA 2007 ss 4, 7 – *contd*
remuneration, allowances and expenses, TCEA 2007 Sch 2 para 5
terms of appointment, TCEA 2007 Sch 2 para 4
training, TCEA 2007 Sch 2 para 8
point of law, right of appeal on, TCEA 2007 s 11
practice directions, TCEA 2007 s 23
Senior President presiding over, TCEA 2007 s 3
sittings, location of, TCEA 2007 s 26
sums payable in pursuance of decision, recovery of, TCEA 2007 s 27
judiciary, independence, TCEA 2007 s 1
meditation, provision for, TCEA 2007 s 24
orders and regulations, TCEA 2007 s 49
reform, PR 16/3/09
Senior President—
appointment, TCEA 2007 s 2
delegation of functions, TCEA 2007 s 8
First-tier Tribunal, presiding over, TCEA 2007 s 3
functions of, TCEA 2007 Sch 1 Pt 4
oath, TCEA 2007 Sch 1 Pt 3
recommendations for appointment, TCEA 2007 Sch 1 Pt 1
removal from office, TCEA 2007 Sch 1 Pt 3
remuneration, allowances and expenses, TCEA 2007 Sch 1 Pt 3
report, TCEA 2007 s 43
resignation, TCEA 2007 Sch 1 Pt 3
selection by Judicial Appointments Committee, TCEA 2007 Sch 1 Pt 2
tenure, TCEA 2007 Sch 1 Pt 3
terms of office, TCEA 2007 Sch 1 Pt 3
Upper Tribunal, presiding over, TCEA 2007 s 3
services, TCEA 2007 s 40
staff, TCEA 2007 s 40
transfer of functions—
abolition of tribunals, TCEA 2007 s 31
amendment of lists of tribunals, TCEA 2007 s 37
authorised decision-maker, meaning, TCEA 2007 s 31
consequential amendments, SI 2009/56 Sch s 1, 2
existing tribunals, meaning, SI 2009/56 reg 2
Ministerial responsibility, transfer of, TCEA 2007 s 35
office holders, TCEA 2007 s 31
order for, TCEA 2007 ss 30, 31
orders, form of, TCEA 2007 s 38
procedural rules, power to make, TCEA 2007 s 36
relevant tribunals, TCEA 2007 Sch 6
Scotland, in, TCEA 2007 s 30
transitional and saving provisions, SI 2009/56 Sch 3
Wales, in, TCEA 2007 s 30
transfer of members, SI 2009/56 reg 5
Tribunal Procedure Committee—
expenses, TCEA 2007 Sch 5 para 26
Lord Chancellor's appointees, TCEA 2007 Sch 5 para 21
Lord Chief Justice's appointees, TCEA 2007 Sch 5 para 22
Lord President's appointees, TCEA 2007 Sch 5 para 23
membership, TCEA 2007 Sch 5 para 20

TRIBUNAL – *contd*
Tribunal Procedure Committee – *contd*
rules, making, TCEA 2007 Sch 5 Pt 3
Senior President's appointees, TCEA 2007 Sch 5 para 24
Tribunal Procedure Rules–
amendment of legislation in connection with, TCEA 2007 Sch 5 Pt 4
ancillary powers, TCEA 2007 Sch 5 para 16
arbitration, TCEA 2007 Sch 5 para 14
Committee, making by, TCEA 2007 Sch 5 Pt 3
concurrent functions, TCEA 2007 Sch 5 para 2
content of, TCEA 2007 s 22, Sch 5 para 1
costs and expenses, TCEA 2007 Sch 5 para 12
differential provisions, TCEA 2007 Sch 5 para 19
errors, correction of, TCEA 2007 Sch 5 para 15
evidence, witnesses and attendance, TCEA 2007 Sch 5 para 10
hearings, TCEA 2007 Sch 5 para 7
information, use of, TCEA 2007 Sch 5 para 11
meditation, provision for, TCEA 2007 s 24
own initiative, tribunal acting of, TCEA 2007 Sch 5 para 6
power to make, exercise of, TCEA 2007 s 22
practice directions, reference to, TCEA 2007 Sch 5 para 17
presumptions, TCEA 2007 Sch 5 para 18
procedural grounds, setting-aside of decisions on, TCEA 2007 Sch 5 para 15
proceedings without notice, TCEA 2007 Sch 5 para 8
repeat applications, TCEA 2007 Sch 5 para 5
representation, TCEA 2007 Sch 5 para 9
set-off and interest, TCEA 2007 Sch 5 para 13
staff, delegation of functions to, TCEA 2007 Sch 5 para 3
time limits, TCEA 2007 Sch 5 para 4
Upper Tribunal—
appeal from—
proceedings, TCEA 2007 s 14
right of, TCEA 2007 s 13
appeal to—
point of law, on, TCEA 2007 s 11
proceedings, TCEA 2007 s 12
right of, TCEA 2007 s 11
tribunals in Northern Ireland, from, TCEA 2007 s 34
tribunals in Scotland, from, TCEA 2007 s 33
tribunals in Wales, from, TCEA 2007 s 32
assessors, TCEA 2007 s 28
chambers—
Acting President, TCEA 2007 Sch 4 para 6
Deputy President, TCEA 2007 Sch 4 para 5
judges and members of, TCEA 2007 Sch 4 Pt 2
organisation into, TCEA 2007 s 7
president of, TCEA 2007 s 7, Sch 4
costs or expenses in, TCEA 2007 s 29
decision, review of, TCEA 2007 s 10
establishment of, TCEA 2007 s 3

TRIBUNAL – *contd*
Upper Tribunal – *contd*
judges of, TCEA 2007 s 5
appointment of, TCEA 2007 Sch 3 para 1
deputy, TCEA 2007 Sch 3 para 7
neither appointed nor transferred in, TCEA 2007 Sch 3 para 6
oaths, TCEA 2007 Sch 3 para 10
removal from office, TCEA 2007 Sch 3 para 3
remuneration, allowances and expenses, TCEA 2007 Sch 3 para 5
terms of appointment, TCEA 2007 Sch 3 para 4
training, TCEA 2007 Sch 3 para 9
judicial review—
application for relief, TCEA 2007 s 16
Court of Session, transfer of applications from, TCEA 2007 s 20
High Court, transfer of application from, TCEA 2007 s 19
High Court, transfer of application to, TCEA 2007 s 18
jurisdiction, TCEA 2007 s 15
limits of jurisdiction, TCEA 2007 s 18
quashing orders, TCEA 2007 s 17
Scotland, jurisdiction relating to, TCEA 2007 s 21
members of, TCEA 2007 ss 5, 6
appointment of, TCEA 2007 Sch 3 para 2
neither appointed nor transferred in, TCEA 2007 Sch 3 para 8
oaths, TCEA 2007 Sch 3 para 10
removal from office, TCEA 2007 Sch 3 para 3
remuneration, allowances and expenses, TCEA 2007 Sch 3 para 5
terms of appointment, TCEA 2007 Sch 3 para 4
training, TCEA 2007 Sch 3 para 9
practice directions, TCEA 2007 s 23
Senior President presiding over, TCEA 2007 s 3
sittings, location of, TCEA 2007 s 26
sums payable in pursuance of decision, recovery of, TCEA 2007 s 27
supplementary powers, TCEA 2007 s 25
VAT and duties. *See* VAT AND DUTIES TRIBUNAL

TURNOVER TAXES
harmonisation, 67/228/EEC, 93/609/EEC
international travel, exemption from in, 2007/74/EC

UNDERWRITER
issue of securities and secondary securities, VATA 1994 Sch 9 Group 5

UNINCORPORATED BODIES. *See* CLUBS AND ASSOCIATIONS

UNITED KINGDOM
registration of person making supply outside, VATA 1994 Sch 1 para 14
supplies made, VATA 1994 s 4
territorial extent, VATA 1994 s 96(11)

UNITED STATES AIR FORCE
VAT reliefs, ESC 2.3

UNIT TRUST SCHEMES
exemption, VATA 1994 Sch 9 Group 5 item 6 note (5)

UNIT TRUST SCHEMES – *contd*
investment management services, PR 18/4/01
management, VATA 1994 Sch 9 Group 5 item 9 note (6)

UNIVERSITY. *See* EDUCATION

VALUE
accommodation, provision of—
employees, VATA 1994 Sch 6 para 10
period over 4 weeks, VATA 1994 Sch 6 para 9
acquisitions from member states, VATA 1994 s 20, Sch 7
aircraft, adapted, VATA 1994 s 22(3), (4)
antique, imported, VATA 1994 s 21(4)
appeal, VATA 1994 s 83(*v*), (*w*), (*x*)
assets supplied at deregistration, VATA 1994 Sch 6 para 6
cash discount, VATA 1994 Sch 6 para 4
catering supplied to employees, VATA 1994 Sch 6 para 10
collector's pieces, imported, VATA 1994 s 21(4)
connected person—
importation from, VATA 1994 Sch 6 para 12
supply to, VATA 1994 Sch 6 para 1(4)
consideration, VATA 1994 s 9, Sch 4 para 1
conversion of foreign currency, VATA 1994 Sch 6 para 11
deregistration. *See* DEREGISTRATION
designated travel services, SI 1987/1806 reg 7
direction, VATA 1994 Sch 6 para 1—
to direct seller, VATA 1994 Sch 6 para 2
discount for prompt payment, VATA 1994 Sch 6 para 4
gaming machines, VATA 1994 s 23(2)—
tokens, VATA 1994 s 23(2), (3)
generally, VATA 1994 s 19
goods—
adapted for recreation of pleasure, VATA 1994 s 22
generally, 2454/93/EEC arts 141–181, Annex 23
hovercraft, adapted, VATA 1994 s 22(3), (4)
imported goods, VATA 1994 s 21
incidental expenses, VATA 1994 s 19
monetary consideration, VATA 1994 s 19(2)
motor car, self-supplied, VATA 1994 Sch 6 para 6
non-monetary consideration, VATA 1994 s 19(3), PR 9/10/01
open market value, VATA 1994 s 19(5), Sch 6 para 1(1)
part-money consideration, VATA 1994 s 19(3)
price in money, VATA 1994 s 21(2)
removal of goods to UK, VATA 1994 Sch 9 para 3
residential/charitable buildings, VATA 1994 Sch 10 para 1(6)
retailers, SI 1995/2518
services—
generally, VATA 1994 s 19
received from abroad, VATA 1994 s 8(4)
stamps, VATA 1994 Sch 6 para 5
supply of goods—
by employer, VATA 1994 Sch 6 para 10
expressed in foreign currency, VATA 1994 Sch 6 para 11
Treasury order, VATA 1994 Sch 6 para 6

VALUE – *contd*
supply of services—
by employer, VATA 1994 Sch 6 para 10
expressed in foreign currency, VATA 1994 Sch 6 para 11
Treasury order, VATA 1994 Sch 6 para 6
tokens, VATA 1994 Sch 6 para 5
trading stamps, VATA 1994 Sch 6 para 5
voucher, VATA 1994 Sch 6 para 5, SI 1973/293
work of art, VATA 1994 s 21(4)

VAT AGREEMENTS
trade bodies, made with, Notice 700/57

VAT INVOICE. *See* TAX INVOICE

VAT AND DUTIES TRIBUNALS
affidavits and depositions in other legal proceedings, admissibility, SI 1986/590 r 21A
appeal—
acknowledgement of notice of appeal, SI 1986/590 r 5
amendment, SI 1986/590 r 14
appeal does not lie or cannot be entertained, SI 1986/590 r 6
assessment, VATA 1994 s 83(*p*), (*q*), (*r*)
bad debt relief, VATA 1994 s 83(*h*)
computer produced invoices, VATA 1994 s 83(*z*)
consent, allowed by, SI 1986/590 r 17
correction for under-assessment, VATA 1994 s 84(5)
costs—
award of, SI 1986/590 r 29
direction as to, SI 1986/590 r 29
credit for income tax, VATA 1994 s 83(4), (11)
death or insolvency of appellant or applicant, SI 1986/590 r 13
directions—
method of application, SI 1986/590 r 11
powers to give, SI 1986/590 r 19
directors liability for evasion of tax, VATA 1994 s 83(*n*), (*o*)
dismissal of directions, SI 1986/590 r 18
enforcement of registered or recorded decisions, VATA 1994 s 87
evasion of tax involving dishonesty, VATA 1994 s 83(*n*)
evasion penalty appeal. *See under* APPEALS
explanatory leaflet, PR Appeals
extension of time, SI 1986/590 r 19
further and better particulars, SI 1986/590 r 9
generally, VATA 1994 s 83
group of companies, VATA 1994 s 83(*k*)
imported goods, VATA 1994 s 83(*b*), (*f*)
interest awarded by tribunal, VATA 1994 s 84(8)
interest in cases of official error, VATA 1994 s 83(*s*)
method of, SI 1986/590 r 3
partnership, by, SI 1986/590 r 12
payment made, VATA 1994 s 83(4)
prior decision, dependent on, VATA 1994 s 84(10)
recovery assessment, against, restrictions on, VATA 1994 s 84(3A)
recovery of overpaid tax, VATA 1994 s 83(*t*)
refund of tax, do it yourself builders, VATA 1994 s 83(*g*)
refund of tax, place of acquisition, VATA 1994 s 83(*d*)

VAT

VAT AND DUTIES TRIBUNALS – *contd*
appeal – *contd*
registration, VATA 1994 s 83(*u*), 84(7)
retail schemes, VATA 1994 s 83(*y*)
returns, VATA 1994 s 84(2)
security for tax, VATA 1994 s 83(1)
service at tribunal centre, SI 1986/590 r 31
settlement by agreement, VATA 1994 s 85
statement of case, SI 1986/590 r 7, 8, 8A
striking out, SI 1986/590 r 18
third parties, summonses to, SI 1986/590 r 22
time for, SI 1986/590 r 4
transfer between tribunal centres of, SI 1986/590 r 15
value of acquisition, VATA 1994 s 83(*w*)
value of supply, VATA 1994 s 83(*v*), (*x*)
centre, transfer of appeal or application between, SI 1986/590 r 15
composition, VATA 1994 Sch 12 para 5
Court of Appeal, to, VATA 1994 s 86, SI 1986/2288, SI 1986/590 r 30A
documents—
disclosure, inspection and production, SI 1986/590 r 20
formal service, SI 1986/590 r 10
sending of to parties, SI 1986/590 r 32
establishment, VATA 1994 Sch 12 para 1
hearing—
decision or direction at, SI 1986/590 r 30
directions hearing, notice of, SI 1986/590 r 23(4)
evidence at, SI 1986/590 r 28
failure to appear, SI 1986/590 r 26
notice, SI 1986/590 r 23
procedure, SI 1986/590 r 27
public or private, SI 1986/590 r 24
representation, SI 1986/590 r 25
jurisdiction, VATA 1994 s 82(2)
jury service exemption, VATA 1994 Sch 12 para 8
membership, VATA 1994 Sch 12 paras 6, 7
president, of, VATA 1994 Sch 12 paras 2, 3
procedural rules, VATA 1994 Sch 12 paras 9, 10
reform, PR 16/3/09
Registrar, delegation of powers, SI 1986/590 r 33
sittings, VATA 1994 Sch 12 para 4
transfer of functions, SI 2009/56
witnesses—
statements, SI 1986/590 r 21
summonses, SI 1986/590 r 22

VAT RETURN
accounting for tax, SI 1995/2518 reg 40(1), (3)
assessment, VATA 1994 s 73(1)
calculation, SI 1995/2518 reg 39
correction, SI 1995/2518 reg 34
electronic, SI 1995/2518, reg 25 (4A)–(4K); PR 18/5/00
errors, SI 1995/2518 reg 35
failure to make, VATA 1994 s 73, 84(2)
forms, SI 1995/2518 reg 25(1), Sch 1 Forms 4, 5
generally, 2006/112/EC arts 250–261
goods sold in satisfaction of debt, VATA 1994 Sch 4 para 7
incomplete or incorrect assessment, VATA 1994 Sch 11 para 2(10)(*b*), (*c*)
making, VATA 1994 Sch 11 para 2(1)

VAT RETURN – *contd*
obligation—
to furnish bankruptcy, insolvency, death or incapacity of registered person, SI 1995/2518 reg 25(3)
ceasing to be registered or a taxable person, SI 1995/2518 reg 25(4)
direction of Commissioners, SI 1995/2518 reg 25(2)
generally, SI 1995/2518 reg 25

VEHICLES. *See also* MOTOR CAR
clamping, treatment of, PR 18/5/00
diplomats, SI 1992/3156 art 16
fuel. *See* FUEL
hire, PR 23/8/82
parking facilities, VATA 1994 Sch 9 Group 1
scappage scheme, tax implications of, PR 14/5/09
tow-away fees, PR 18/5/00
visiting forces, SI 1992/3156 art 19
zero-rating—
supply to person leaving UK, SI 1995/2518 regs 132, 133

VENDING MACHINE
supplies to operators of, PR 30/9/03

VENTILATION
supply, VATA 1994 Sch 4 para 3

VESSEL
permanent residential accommodation, used for, PR 9/79/09

VIDEO EQUIPMENT
zero-rating, VATA 1994 Sch 8 Group 16

VILLAGE HALLS
construction, VATA 1994 Sch 8 Group 5

VISITING FORCES
conditions attaching to, SI 1992/3156 arts 5–13
entitled persons, SI 1992/3156 art 18
gift of goods, SI 1992/3156 art 21
motor vehicles, SI 1992/3156 arts 19, 22, Sch
warehouse, removal of goods from, SI 1992/3156 art 20

VOLUNTARY BODIES. *See also* CHARITIES
self build projects, VATA 1994 s 35

VOCATIONAL TRAINING
exemption, VATA 1994 Sch 9 Group 6
meaning, VATA 1994 Sch 9 Group 6 note (3)

VOLUNTARY DISCLOSURE
misdeclarations, VATA 1994 s 63(10)(*b*)

VOUCHERS
electronic face-value, PR 2/7/01, ESC 3.32
face-value, PR 27/5/03
credit, treatment of, VATA 1994 Sch 10A para 3
issue as supply of services, VATA 1994 Sch 10A para 2
meaning, VATA 1994 Sch 10A para 1
other goods and services, supplied with, VATA 1994 Sch 10A para 7
postage stamp as consideration for, VATA 1994 Sch 10A para 5
rate categories of supplies, VATA 1994 Sch 10A para 8(2)
retailer, treatment of, VATA 1994 Sch 10A para 4
supply, charge on, VATA 1994 Sch 10A para 6
valuation, VATA 1994 Sch 6 para 5

WALKING POSSESSION AGREEMENTS
assessment, VATA 1994 ss 76, 77
meaning, VATA 1994 s 68(2)
penalty for breach, VATA 1994 s 68

WAREHOUSE, *See also* BONDED WAREHOUSE; CUSTOMS WAREHOUSE; EXCISE WAREHOUSE; FREE WAREHOUSE
acquisition or supply of goods—
dutiable goods, meaning, VATA 1994 s 18(6)
duty point, meaning, VATA 1994 s 18(6)
material time, meaning, VATA 1994 s 18(6)
regulations, VATA 1994 s 18(5), (5A)
warehouse, meaning, VATA 1994 s 18(6)
certificate connected with services, SI 1995/2518 reg 145C
fiscal warehousing—
application, procedure on, VATA 1994 s 18A(7)
approval, VATA 1994 s 18A(1), (8)
assessment for failure to pay tax, VATA 1994 s 73(7A)
certificates, SI 1995/2518 regs 145B, 145C
cessation, VATA 1994 s 18A(5)
charge in nature of goods, VATA 1994 s 18F(4)
conditions, imposition of, VATA 1994 s 18A(6)
deficient goods, VATA 1994 s 18E
eligible goods, VATA 1994 s 18B(6), Sch 5A
entitlement to keep fiscal warehouse, VATA 1994 s 18A(2)
fiscal warehouse, meaning, VATA 1994 s 18A(3), SI 1995/2518 reg 145A(1)
fiscal warehousekeeper, meaning, VATA 1994 ss 18A(1), 18F(1), SI 1995/2518 reg 145A(2)
generally, VATA 1994 ss 18A, 18F
goods ceasing to be eligible, VATA 1994 s 18F(5)
matters for consideration by Commissioners, VATA 1994 s 18A(4)
missing goods, VATA 1994 s 18E
record and stock control, SI 1995/2518 reg 145F, Sch 1A
regime—
generally, SI 1995/2518 reg 145E
interpretation, SI 1995/2518 reg 145A(2)
stock control and record, SI 1995/2518 reg 145F, Sch 1A
regulations, power to make, VATA 1994 ss 18D(3), 18F(7), (8)
relief—
certificate to secure, SI 1995/2518 Sch 1 Form 17
generally, VATA 1994 s 18B
purchased or acquired goods, certificate to secure relief on, SI 1995/2518 Sch 1 Form 17
removal of goods—
accountability, VATA 1994 s 18D
circumstances in which allowed, SI 1995/2518 reg 145H(1)
deemed removal, VATA 1994 s 18F(6)
failure to pay tax, VATA 1994 s 73(7B)
payment of VAT, SI 1995/2518 reg 43, SI 1995/2518 reg 145J
prohibition on, SI 1995/2518 reg 145I
relevant documents, procedure on non-receipt of, SI 1995/2518 reg 145H(3), (4)

WAREHOUSE – *contd*
fiscal warehousing – *contd*
removal of goods – *contd*
supply of services, VATA 1994 s 18C
transferred, treated as, SI 1995/2518 reg 145H(2)
withdrawal of approval, VATA 1994 s 18A(6), (8)
withdrawal of status, VATA 1994 s 18A(6)
zero-rated supplies, VATA 1994 s 18C
services, certificate connected with, SI 1995/2518 reg 145C
stock control and record, SI 1995/2518 reg 145F Sch 1A
supply of goods, transaction treated as, SI 1966/1255
transfers in the UK, SI 1995/2518 reg 145G
VAT invoices relating to services performed in, SI 1995/2518 reg 145D
zero-rating of services performed in, certificate to secure, SI 1995/2518 Sch 1 Form 18
VAT invoices relating to services performed in, SI 1995/2518 reg 145D

WASHROOM
supply to handicapped person, VATA 1994 Sch 8 Group 12

WATER
refund of tax to authority, VATA 1994 s 33(3), SI 1973/2121
supply of goods, as, SI 1989/1114
time of supply, SI 1995/2518 reg 86
zero-rating, VATA 1994 Sch 8 Group 2

WELFARE SERVICES. *See also* HEALTH AND WELFARE
exemption, VATA 1994 Sch 9 Group 7 item 10

WELFARE SPIRITUAL
exemption, VATA 1994 Sch 9 Group 7 item 10

WINDING UP. *See* INSOLVENCY

WINE
tax free shops, VATA 1994 Sch 8 Group 14
zero-rating, VATA 1994 Sch 8 Group 1

WIRELESS SET
zero-rating of supplies to blind, VATA 1994 Sch 8 Group 4

WOODLAND. *See* LAND; TIMBER

WORKS OF ART
acquisition in settlement of insurance claims, SI 1992/3129 art 4
exclusion of input tax credit, SI 1992/3222 art 4
imported, tax rate, ESC 3.36, PR 15/4/02
import relief, SI 1984/746 Sch 2
margin scheme, PR 10/6/02, Notice 718
meaning, VATA 1994 s 21(6), SI 1992/3129 art 2, SI 1992/3222 art 2
relief for certain supplies, SI 1992/3129 art 4
repossession under finance agreement, SI 1992/3129 art 4
sales from stately homes, VATA 1994 Sch 9 Group 11
special scheme, 2006/112/EC arts 311–343, Annex IX
treatment of supplies, ESC 3.26

YACHT
luxury, VAT schemes, PR 6/2/07
taxable acquisition, PR 5/6/97

YOUTH CLUB
exemption, VATA 1994 Sch 9 Group 6 item 6
meaning, VATA 1994 Sch 9 Group 6 note (6)

ZERO-RATING
aircraft, VATA 1994 Sch 8, Group 8 item 2
air navigation services, VATA 1994 Sch 8 Group 8 item 6A
alcoholic beverages, VATA 1994 Sch 8 Group 1
animal feeding stuffs, VATA 1994 Sch 8 Group 1 general item 2
animals for human consumption, VATA 1994 Sch 8 Group 1 general item 4
bank notes, VATA 1994 Sch 8 Group 11
biscuits, VATA 1994 Sch 8 Group 1
books, VATA 1994 Sch 8 Group 3 item 1
boots, protective, VATA 1994 Sch 8 Group 16
building materials, VATA 1994 Sch 8 Group 5 item 4, Sch 8 Group 6 item 3
caravans, VATA 1994 Sch 8 Group 9 item 1
charities—
advertising, VATA 1994 Sch 8 Group 15 item 8
aids for handicapped persons, VATA 1994 Sch 8 Group 12
building, VATA 1994 Sch 10 Group 1
construction of buildings, VATA 1994 Sch 8 Group 5
donations, VATA 1994 Sch 8 Group 15 items 1, 2
eligible body, meaning, VATA 1994 Sch 8 Group 15 note 4
medical or surgical treatment, VATA 1994 Sch 8 Group 15 item 9
medical or veterinary research, VATA 1994 Sch 8 Group 15 item 10
talking books, VATA 1994 Sch 8 Group 4
wireless sets for the blind, VATA 1994 Sch 8 Group 4
children's picture and painting books, VATA 1994 Sch 8 Group 3 item 3
clothing and footwear, VATA 1994 Sch 8 Group 16
confectionery, VATA 1994 Sch 8 Group 1 excepted item 2
construction of dwellings, VATA 1994 Sch 8 Group 5
conversion of buildings, VATA 1994 Sch 8 Group 5
dairy products, VATA 1994 Sch 8 Group 1
dental supplies, VATA 1994 Sch 8 Group 12
diplomatic missions, organisations etc, ESC 8.2
drugs and medicines, VATA 1994 Sch 8 Group 12
exports. *See* EXPORT
food, VATA 1994 Sch 8 Group 1 general item 1
generally, VATA 1994 s 30
gold, VATA 1994 Sch 8 Group 10
handicapped person—
aids, VATA 1994 Sch 8 Group 12
supply of services for adapting aids, VATA 1994 Sch 8 Group 12
hot food, VATA 1994 Sch 8 Group 1 general item 1
houseboats, VATA 1994 Sch 8 Group 9 item 2
imports, VATA 1994 Sch 8 Group 13

ZERO-RATING – *contd*
incontinence products, PR 30/7/96, PR 5/3/97
international services, VATA 1994 Sch 8 Group 7
intra-Community supply and acquisition, PR 11/10/07
invalid carriages, VATA 1994 Sch 8 Group 12
letting on hire, VATA 1994 s 30
lifeboats, VATA 1994 Sch 8 Group 8 item 3
magazines, VATA 1994 Sch 8 Group 3 item 2
maps, charts and topographical plans, VATA 1994 Sch 8 Group 3 item 5
medical supplies and services, VATA 1994 Sch 8 Group 12
newspapers and journals, VATA 1994 Sch 8 Group 3 item 2
pet foods, VATA 1994 Sch 8 Group 1 excepted item 6
pilotage services, VATA 1994 Sch 8 Group 8 item 7
potato products, VATA 1994 Sch 8 Group 1 excepted item 5
protected buildings, VATA 1994 Sch 8 Group 6
protective helmet, VATA 1994 Sch 8 Group 16
relevant goods, meaning, VATA 1994 Sch 8 Group 15 note (3)
repair and maintenance, VATA 1994 Sch 8 Group 15 items 6, 7
residential and charitable buildings construction, VATA 1994 Sch 8 Group 5
salvage services, VATA 1994 Sch 8 Group 8 item 8
savoury snacks, VATA 1994 Sch 8 Group 1 excepted item 5
seeds, VATA 1994 Sch 8 Group 1 general item 3
services performed in warehouse, certificate to secure, SI 1995/2518 Sch 1 Form 18
sewerage services, VATA 1994 Sch 8 Group 2
sheet music, VATA 1994 Sch 8 Group 3
ships, VATA 1994 Sch 8 Group 8 item 1
surgical appliances, VATA 1994 Sch 8 Group 12
talking books, VATA 1994 Sch 8 Group 4
tax free shops, VATA 1994 Sch 8 Group 14
tax invoices, SI 1995/2518 regs 13(4), 16
towage services, VATA 1994 Sch 8, Group 8 item 8
transport—
designated travel services outside EC, VATA 1994 Sch 8 Group 8 item 12
salvage or towage services, VATA 1994 Sch 8 Group 8 item 8
supply, repair or maintenance of aircraft, VATA 1994 Sch 8 Group 8 item 2
supply, repair or maintenance of lifeboats, VATA 1994 Sch 8 Group 8 item 3
supply, repair or maintenance of ships, VATA 1994 Sch 8 Group 8 item 1
survey of ships and aircraft, VATA 1994 Sch 8 Group 8 item 9
transport of passengers, VATA 1994 Sch 8 Group 8 item 4
transport of goods outside member states, VATA 1994 Sch 8 Group 8 item 5

ZERO-RATING – *contd*
transport – *contd*
transport to and from Azores or Madeira, VATA 1994 Sch 8 Group 8 item 13

ZERO-RATING – *contd*
water, VATA 1994 Sch 8 Group 2
wireless sets for the blind, VATA 1994 Sch 8 Group 4

WORDS AND PHRASES

Words in brackets indicate the context in which the word or phrase is used.

acquisition of goods from other member states, VATA 1994, s 11
adjustment percentage, SI 1995/2518 reg 115(5)
administration order, VATA 1994 s 81(5)(*a*)
administrative receiver, VATA 1994 s 81(5)(*a*)
advanced electronic signature, SI 1995/2518 reg A13
agricultural, forestry or fisheries undertaking, 2006/112/EC art 295
agricultural products, 2006/112/EC art 295
agricultural services, 2006/112/EC art 295
air navigation services, VATA 1994 Sch 8 Group 8 note (6A)
air travellers, 2007/74/EC art 3
aircraft mortgage, SI 1995/1268 art 2
alcoholic products, EC 83/181 art 1
alphabetical code, SI 1995/2518 reg 2
alteration, VATA 1994 Sch 7A para 2, Sch 8 Group 6 note (6)
ancillary transport services, SI 1992/3121 art 2
animal, VATA 1994 Sch 8 Group 1 note (2), Group 15 note (2), Group 16 note (3)
another member state, VATA 1994 s 96(1)
antiques, SI 1995/1268 art 2, SI 1992/3222 art 2, 2006/112/EC art 311
appeal tribunal, FA 2003 s 24(3)
applicable period, VATA 1994 s 78(4)
applicant authority, SI 2004/674 reg 2
approved alteration, VATA 1994 Sch 8 Group 6 note (6)
approved inland clearance depot, SI 1995/2518 reg 117(1)
approved place, SI 1984/1176 reg 3
arrivals and dispatches, SI 1995/2518 reg 23E
Article 5 transaction, SI 1992/3122 art 8(8), SI 1995/1268 art 12(10), SI 2001/1502 art 1(3), SI 2001/1503 art 1(3)
assignment, VATA 1994 s 96(1)
authorised official, SI 2004/674 reg 2
authorised person, VATA 1994 s 96(1)

bad debt relief, VATA 1994 s 36, SI 1995/2518, regs 167–167A
basic period, SI 1993/2001 art 2(1)
belonging in a country, VATA 1994 s 9(2), (3)
booster cushion, VATA 1994 Sch A1 para 7
booster seat, VATA 1994 Sch A1 para 7
building materials, VATA 1994 Sch A1 para 22, Sch 8 Group 5 note (22)
business, VATA 1994 s 94
business gift, VATA 1994 Sch 4 para 5(2ZA)

capital expenditure goods, SI 1995/2518 reg 55A(1)
central heating system, VATA 1994 Sch 7A para 4A
changed number of dwellings conversion, VATA 1994 Sch A1 para 10
Channel Tunnel terminal, VATA 1994 Sch 8 Group 14 note (2)
chargeable event, 2006/112/EC art 62
chargeable operation, SI 1984/1177 reg 2
charity, VATA 1994 Sch 9 Group 12 note (2)
children's car seats, VATA 1994 Sch A1 para 7
claim (reimbursement) SI 1995/2518, reg 43A
clothing, VATA 1994 Sch 8 Group 16 note (1)
CO_2 emissions figure, VATA 1994 s 57(9)
Collector, SI 1995/2518 reg 2(1)
collector's items, 2006/112/EC art 311, SI 1992/3222 art 2, SI 1995/1268 art 2
commercial policy measures, 450/2008/EC art 4
Commissioners, VATA 1994 s 96(1)
Community, SI 1995/2518 reg 2(1),
Community Customs Code, FA 2003 s 24(3)
Community customs rules, FA 2003 s 26(9)
Community export duty, FA 2003 s 24(3)
Community goods, SI 1984/1177 reg 2, 638/2004/EC art 2, 450/2008/EC art 4
Community import duty, FA 2003 s 24(3)
Community relief, CED(GR)A 1979 s 7
Community transport, SI 1992/3283 art 3
conduct, ACSA 2001 s 20(3)
consolidated claim, SI 2004/674 reg 2
container, SI 1995/2518 reg 117(2)
contested, SI 2004/674 reg 2
Continental Shelf, SI 1995/2518 reg 2(1)
contract work, SI 1995/2518, reg 21
control, VATA 1994 s 43(8)
Controller, SI 1995/2518 reg 2(1), SI 1993/2001 art 2
Convention rights, HRA 1998 s 1
copy, VATA 1994 s 96(1)
corresponding UK claim, SI 2004/674 reg 2
cost (of business gift), VATA 1994 Sch 4 para 5(2ZA)
credit voucher, VATA 1994 Sch 10A para 3
criminal conduct, ACSA 2001 s 20(3)
criminal investigation, ACSA 2001 s 20(1)
customs authorities, 450/2008/EC art 4
customs controls, 450/2008/EC art 4
customs debt, 450/2008/EC art 4
customs declaration, 450/2008/EC art 4
customs duty of a preferential tariff country, FA 2003 s 24(3)
customs legislation, 450/2008/EC art 4
customs procedure, 450/2008/EC art 4
customs representative, 450/2008/EC art 4
customs status, 450/2008/EC art 4
customs supervision, 450/2008/EC art 4
customs warehouse, CEMA 1979 s 1(1)

datapost packet, SI 1995/2518 reg 2(1)
date of notification, SI 1985/590 r 2
demand notice, FA 2003 s 24(3)
de-supplied transaction, SI 1992/3122 art 8(8), SI 1995/1268 art 12(10)
designated travel service, VATA 1994 Sch 8 Group 8 note (8), SI 1987/1806 art 3
designed as a dwelling, VATA 1994 Sch 8 Group 5 note (2), Sch 8 Group 6 note (2)
developer, VATA 1994 Sch 10 para 5(5)
director, VATA 1994 s 24(7)
document, VATA 1994 s 96(1)
dutiable alcoholic liquor, SI 2000/426 reg 6

dutiable goods, VATA 1994 s 18(6)
duty point, VATA 1994 ss 18(6), 18F(1)

EC certificate of conformity, VATA 1994 s 57(9)
EC sales statement, VATA 1994 ss 65(6), 66(9)
economic operator, 450/2008/EC art 4
EDI message, SI 1995/2518 reg A13
electronic communications, FA 1999 s 132(10), FA 2000 Sch 38 para 8(1)
electronic data interchange, SI 1995/2518 reg A13
electronic return system, SI 1995/2518 reg 25(4A)
electronic signature, SI 1995/2518 reg A13
electronic storage of invoices, SI 1995/2518 reg A13
electronic transmission, SI 1995/2518 reg A13
eligible body, VATA 1994 Sch 8 Group 15 note (4), Sch 9 Group 6 note (1)
eligible goods, VATA 1994 ss 18B(6), 18F(1)
employment, VATA 1994 s 56(10)
enforcement action, SI 2004/674 reg 2
examination services, VATA 1994 Sch 9 group 6 note (4)
excluded service, VATA 1994 Sch 8 Group 6 note (3)
exempt input tax, SI 1995/2518 reg 99(1)
exiting tribunals, SI 2009/56 reg 2
export duties, 450/2008/EC art 4

face-value voucher, VATA 1994 Sch 10A para 1
farmer, 2006/112/EC art 295
fee simple, VATA 1994 s 96(1)
finance agreement, SI 1992/3132 art 2, SI 1995/1268 art 2
fiscal or other warehousing regime, SI 1995/2518 reg 2(1)
fiscal warehouse, VATA 1994 s 18A(3), SI 1995, No 2518 reg 145A(1)
fiscal warehousekeeper, VATA 1994 s 18F(1), SI 1995, No 2518 reg 145A(2)
fiscal warehousing regime, VATA 1994, s 18F(2)), SI 1995, No 2518 reg 145A(2)
flat-rate trader, SI 1995/2518 reg 55A(1)
food, VATA 1994 Sch 8 Group 1 note (1)
foreign postal packet, PSA 2000 s 105
free zone goods, VATA 1994 s 17(3)
frontier zone, 2007/74/EC art 3
frontier zone worker, 2007/74/EC art 3
fuel for private use, VATA 1994 s 56(3)(*a*)
fuel oil, VATA 1994 Sch A1 para 4(4)
full cost of goods, SI 1995/2518 reg 116B
fund-raising event, VATA 1994 Sch 9 Group 12 note (1)
fur skin, VATA 1994 Sch 8 Group 16 note (3)

gambling, VATA 1994 s 23(B)
game of chance, VATA 1994 s 23(7), Sch 9 Group 4 note (2)
gaming machine, VATA 1994 s 23(4), Sch 9 Group 4 note (3)
garage works, VATA 1994 Sch A1 para 14(2)
gas oil, VATA 1994 Sch A1 para, 4(5)
general representative, FA 1994 s 57(16A0)
goods, SI 1995/2518 reg 117(4), 638/2004/EC art 2
goods of the same class or kind, EC 2454/93 art 142
government department, VATA 1994 s 41(6)

grant, VATA 1994 Sch 8 Group 5 note (1), Sch 9 Group 1 note (1)
gross amount of tax, VATA 1994 s 63(5)

handicapped, VATA 1994 Sch 8 Group 12 note (3), Group 15 note (5)
hardship direction, SI 1986/590 r 2
heavy oil, VATA 1994 Sch A1 para 4(7)
holder of goods, 450/2008/EC art 4
holder of procedure, 450/2008/EC art 4
homeward stage, SI 1992/3283 art 3
hot food, VATA 1994 Sch 8 Group 1 note (3)(*b*)
house in multiple occupation conversion, VATA 1994 Sch A1 para 11
houseboat, VATA 1994 Sch A1 para 3(4), Sch 8 Group 9 item 2, Sch 9 Group 1 note (10), Sch 10 para 3(7A)
household effects, EC 83/181 art 1
hovercraft, VATA 1994 s 96(1)

identical goods, EC 2454/93 art 142
import duties 450/2008/EC art 4
import VAT, FA 2003 s 24(3)
importation of goods, 2006/112/EC art 30
imports, EC 83/181 art 1
individual, VATA 1994 s 57(1)
information, ACSA 2001 s 20(1)
input tax, VATA 1994 s 24(1)(2)
insolvent person, SI 1995/2518, reg 24
instrument permitting enforcement, SI 2004/674 reg 2
insurer, SI 1992/3122 art 2, SI 1995/1268 art 2
interim trustee, VATA 1994 s 96(1)
international collaboration arrangement, VATA 1994 Sch 8 Group 13 note (1)
intra-Community acquisition of goods, 2006/112/EC art 20
intra-Community transport of goods, SI 1992/3121 art 2
investment gold, VATA 1994 Sch 9 Group 15
invoice, VATA 1994 s 96(1)

Job Band, SI 1995/2518 reg A212

kerosene, VATA 1994 Sch A1 para 4(6)

legislation, FA 1999 s 132(10)
lifeboat, VATA 1994 Sch 8 Group 8 note (4)
local authority, VATA 1994 s 96(4)
longer period, SI 1995/2518 reg 99(3)–(6)

major interest, VATA 1994 s 96(1)
managing officer, VATA 1994 s 61(6)
marine mortgage, SI 1995/1268 art 2
material time, VATA 1994 ss 18(6), 18F(1)
means of transport, VATA 1994 s 95
medicinal product, VATA 1994 Sch 8 Group 15 note (11)
Member State of refund, 2008/9/EC Art 2
Message, 450/2008/EC art 4
mitigation appeal, SI 1985/590 r 2
money, VATA 1994 s 96(1), SI 1995/2518 reg 56
monthly sum, SI 1995/2518 reg 49
mooring, VATA 1994 Sch 9 Group 1 note (15)
motor car, SI 1992/3122 art 2, SI 1992/3222 art 2
multiple occupancy dwelling, VATA 1994 Sch A1 para 8(3)

national authorities, 638/2004/EC art 2
new means of transport, VATA 1994 s 95
non-Community goods, 450/2008/EC art 4

non-residential, VATA 1994 Sch 8 Group 5 note (7)
non-refundable tax, VATA 1994 Sch 11A para 2A
notifiable scheme, VATA Sch 11A para 5

open market value, VATA 1994 s 19(5), 2006/112/EC art 72
original entitlement to deduct, SI 1995/2518, reg 115(5)
output tax, VATA 1994 s 24(1), (2), Notice 700 para 7.1
outstanding amount, VATA 1994 s 36(3)
overseas authority, VATA 1994 Sch 8 Group 13 note (2), SI 1995/2518 reg 117(7)
overseas body, VATA 1994 Sch 8 Group 13 note (3)
overseas trader, VATA 1994 Sch 8 Group 13 note (4)
overseas visitor, SI 1995/2518 reg 117(7A)(8)

participant in special scheme, VATA 1994 Sch 3B para 16(5)
permanent trustee, VATA 1994 s 96(1)
person, 450/2008/EC art 4
person established in customs territory of the Community, 450/2008/EC art 4
personal property, EC 83/181 art 1
pleasure cruise, SI 1992/3121 art 2, SI 1992/3283 art 3
point of arrival, SI 1992/3283 art 3
point of departure, SI 1992/3283 art 3
port, VATA 1994 Sch 8 Group 8
postal packet, VATA 1994 Sch 9 Group 3 note (1)
precautionary measures, SI 2004/674 reg 2
preferential tariff country, FA 2003 s 24(3)
prescribed accounting period, VATA 1994 s 25(1), 57(1), SI 1995/2518 regs 2(1), 99(1)
prescribed rate, VATA 1994 s 74(6)
presentation of goods to customs, 450/2008/EC art 4
primary legislation, HRA 1998 s 21
printed matter, SI 1992/3222 art 2
private pleasure-flying, 2007/74/EC art 3
private pleasure-sea-navigation, 2007/74/EC art 3
processed products, 450/2008/EC art 4
processing operations, 450/2008/EC art 4
processing work, SI 1995/2518 reg 21
produced goods, EC 2454/93 art 142
proper officer, SI 1995/2518 reg 2(1), SI 1986/590 r 2
protected building, VATA 1994 Sch 8 Group 6 note (1)
public body, VATA 1994 Sch 9 Group 7 note (5), Group 13 note (1)

qualifying body, VATA 1994 Sch 9 Group 12 note (3)
qualifying conversion, VATA 1994 Sch A1 para 9
qualifying residential purpose, VATA 1994 Sch A1 para 17
qualifying residential premises, VATA 1994 Sch 7A para 2(1)
quarter, VATA 1994 s 96(1)
quarterly sum, SI 1995/2518 reg 49

rate of yield, 450/2008/EC art 4
reasonable excuse appeal, SI 1985/590 r 2
refund application, 2008/9/EC art 2
refund period, 2008/9/EC art 2
registered housing association, VATA 1994 Sch 8 Group 5 note (21), Sch 10 para 3(8)
registered in another member state, SI 1995/2518 reg 21
registered person, SI 1995/2518 reg 2
registration, VATA 1994 Sch 1 para 18
registration number, SI 1995/2518 reg 2(1), SI 1992/3121 art 2
registration period, SI 1995/2518 reg 99(1)
regulations, VATA 1994 s 96(1)
reimbursement arrangements, SI 1995/2518, reg 43A
release of goods, 450/2008/EC art 4
relevant amount, VATA 1994 s 63(4), 66(6); SI 1995/2518, reg 43A
relevant associate, VATA 1994 Sch 10 para 3(7)
relevant charitable purpose, VATA 1994 Sch 8 Group 5 note (6)
relevant establishment, VATA 1994 SCH 8 group 15 note (4B)
relevant goods, VATA 1994 Sch 8 Group 15 note (3)
relevant housing association, VATA 1994 Sch 8 Group 5 note (21)
relevant journey, VATA 1994 Sch 8 Group 14 note (3)
relevant land, SI 1995/2518, reg 93
relevant residential purpose, VATA 1994 Sch 8 Group 5 note (4), Sch A1 para 3(2)
relevant return, VATA 1994 s 78(7)
relevant supply, SI 1995/2518 reg 23A
relevant time, VATA 1994 Sch 3 para 3(3), Sch 7 para 5
relevant transaction, VATA 1994 Sch 7 para 5
renewable source heating system, VATA 1994 Sch 7A para B
repayment, 450/2008/EC art 4
representative, FA 2003 s 24(3)
request for assistance, SI 2004/674 reg 2
retailer voucher, VATA 1994 Sch 10A para 4
return trip, SI 1992/3283 art 3
reverse surrender, VATA 1994 Sch 9 Group 1 note (1A)
risk, 450/2008/EC art 4
risk management, 450/2008/EC art 4

safety seat, VATA 1994 Sch A1 para 7
sea travellers, 2007/74/EC art 3
seasonal pitch, VATA 1994 Sch 9 Group 1 note (14)
second hand goods, 2006/112/EC art 311
security, SI 1995/2518 reg 165
ship, VATA 1994 s 96(1), SI 1995/2518 reg 117(9)
signatory, SI 1995/2518 reg A13
similar establishment, VATA 1994 Sch 9 Group 1 note (9)
similar goods, EC 2454/93, art 142
single household dwelling, VATA 1994 Sch 38 para 8(2)
special accounting period, SI 1995/2518 reg 99(1)
special container, SI 1984/746 Group 10
special residential conversion, VATA 1994 Sch A1 para 12
special scheme return, VATA 1994 Sch 3B para 18(6)
specific goods or movements, 638/2004/EC art 2
specified date, SI 1995/2518 reg 2(1)
standard tanks, SI 1984/746 Group 10
statement, SI 1995/2518 reg 23A
submission date, VATA 1994 s 65(6)
subordinate legislation, HRA 1998 s 21
subsidiary, CA 1985 s 736
summary declaration, 450/2008/EC art 4
supplementary declaration, SI 1992/2790 reg 1

supply, VATA 1994 s 5, Sch 4
supply of goods, 2006/112/EC art 14
supply of qualifying services, VATA 1994 Sch A1 paras 16, 21
supply of services, VATA 1994 s 5(2)(*b*), 2006/112/EC art 24

tax, VATA 1994 s 96(1)
tax authorities, FA 1999 s 132(10), FA 2000 Sch 38 para 8(1)
tax free shop, VATA 1994 Sch 8 Group 14 note (2)
tax invoice, VATA 1994 s 3(1), 2006/112/EC art 217
tax value, Notice 700 para 7.2
tax year, SI 1995/2518 reg 99(1)
taxable acquisition, VATA 1994 s 96(1)
taxable person, VATA 1994 s 96(1), 2006/112/EC art 9
taxable person not established in Member State of refund, 2008/9/EC Art 2
taxable person not established in the territory of the country, EC 79/1072 art 1, EC 86/560 art 1
taxable supply, VATA 1994 s 96(1)
taxation matter, FA 2000 Sch 38 para 8(1)
territory of a member state, 2006/112/EC art 5
territory of the Community, 2006/112/EC art 5
terrorist financing, SI 2007/3298 reg 2(1)
third country, 2006/112/EC art 5, 2007/74/EC art 3
tobacco products, SI 2000/426 reg 6
total entitlement on capital item, SI 1995/2518, reg 115(5)
total value, SI 1995/2518 reg 21
tour operator, VATA 1994 s 53(3)
traveller, VATA 1994 Sch 8 Group 14 note (4)
tribunal, VATA 1994 s 82
trust deed, VATA 1994 s 81(5)(*c*)

UK approval certificate, VATA 1994 s 57(9)
unauthorised person, VATA 1994 s 67(2)

VAT, VATA 1994 s 96(1)
VAT credit, VATA 1994 s 25(3)
VAT invoice, VATA 1994 s 6(15)
VAT representative, VATA 1994 s 48
vehicle, VATA 1994 s 56(10)
vocational training, VATA 1994 Sch 9 Group 6 note (8)

walking possession agreement, VATA 1994 s 68(2)
warehouse, VATA 1994 s 18(6)
welfare services, VATA 1994 Sch 9 Group 7 note (6)
women's sanitary protection products, VATA 1994 Sch A1 para 6
work of art, VATA 1994 s 21(6), SI 1992/3222 art 2, SI 1995/1268 reg 2, 2006/112/EC art 311

STAMP TAXES

CONTENTS

STATUTES

STAMP DUTIES MANAGEMENT ACT 1891

(54 & 55 Vict. Chapter 38)

ARRANGEMENT OF SECTIONS

An Act to consolidate the Law relating to the Management of Stamp Duties.

[21st July 1891]

Application of Act

1 Act to apply to all stamp duties

All duties for the time being chargeable by law as stamp duties shall be under the care and management of the Commissioners, and this Act shall apply to all such duties and to all fees which are for the time being directed to be collected or received by means of stamps.

Mode of recovering Money received for Duty

2 Moneys received for duty and not appropriated to be recoverable in High Court

(1) Every person who, having received any sum of money as or for any duty, or any fee collected by means of a stamp, does not apply the money to the due payment of the duty or fee, and improperly withholds or detains the same, shall be accountable for the amount of the duty or fee, and the same shall be a debt from him to Her Majesty, and recoverable as such accordingly.

(2), (3) …[1]

Amendments—[1] Sub-ss (2), (3) repealed by FA 1999 s 115, Sch 18 para 6, Sch 20 Pt V(4) with effect from 1 October 1999.

Sale of Stamps

3–8

...

Amendments—These sections repealed by FA 1999 s 115, Sch 18 para 6, Sch 20 Pt V(4) with effect from 1 October 1999.

Allowance for Spoiled Stamps

9 Procedure for obtaining allowance

Subject to such regulations as the Commissioners may think proper to make, and to the production of such evidence by statutory declaration or otherwise as the Commissioners may require, allowance is to be made by the Commissioners for stamps spoiled in the cases hereinafter mentioned; (that is to say,):

(1) The stamp on any material inadvertently and undesignedly spoiled, obliterated, or by any means rendered unfit for the purpose intended, before the material bears the signature of any person or any instrument written thereon is executed by any party:

(2), (3) ...[4]

(4) The stamp on any bill of exchange signed by or on behalf of the drawer which has not been accepted or made use of in any manner whatever or delivered out of his hands for any purpose other than by way of tender for acceptance:

(5) The stamp on any promissory note signed by or on behalf of the maker which has not been made use of in any manner whatever or delivered out of his hands:

(6) The stamp on any bill of exchange or promissory note which from any omission or error has been spoiled or rendered useless, although the same, being a bill of exchange, may have been accepted or indorsed, or, being a promissory note, may have been delivered to the payee, provided that another completed and duly stamped bill of exchange or promissory note is produced identical in every particular, except in the correction of the error or omission, with the spoiled bill or note:

(7) The stamp used for any of the following instruments; that is to say,

(*a*) An instrument executed by any party thereto, but afterwards found to be absolutely void from the beginning:

(*b*) An instrument executed by any party thereto, but afterwards found unfit, by reason of any error or mistake therein, for the purpose originally intended:

(*c*) An instrument executed by any party thereto which has not been made use of for any purpose whatever, and which by reason of the inability or refusal of some necessary party to sign the same or to complete the transaction according to the instrument, is incomplete and insufficient for the purpose for which it was intended:

(*d*) An instrument executed by any party thereto, which by reason of the refusal of any person to act under the same, or for want of enrolment or registration within the time required by law, fails of the intended purpose or becomes void:

(*e*) An instrument executed by any party thereto ...[3] which becomes useless in consequence of the transaction intended to be thereby effected being effected by some other instrument duly stamped:

Provided as follows:—

(*a*) That the application for relief is made within [two years][1] after the stamp has been spoiled or become useless or in the case of an executed instrument after the date of the instrument, or, if it is not dated, within [two years][1] after the execution thereof by the person by whom it was first or alone executed or within such further time as the Commissioners may prescribe in the case of any instrument sent abroad for execution or when from unavoidable circumstances any instrument for which another has been substituted cannot be produced within the said period;

(*b*) That in the case of an executed instrument no legal proceeding has been commenced in which the instrument could or would have been given or offered in evidence, and that the instrument is given up to be cancelled;

(*c*) ...[2]

Amendments—[1] Words in sub-s (7), proviso (*a*) in both places, substituted by the Revenue Act 1898 s 13.

[2] Sub-s (7)(*c*) repealed by the Statute Law (Repeals) Act 1993 s 1(1), Sch 1 Pt IX.

[3] Words omitted from sub-s (7) repealed by FA 1996 Sch 39 Pt III para 10(1), (2), (4), (5), Sch 41 Pt VIII(4), with effect from 29 April 1996, except in relation to an instrument which has been accidentally spoiled if an application for allowance under this section was made before that date.

[4] Sub-ss (2) and (3) repealed by FA 1999 s 115, Sch 18 para 6, Sch 20 Pt V(4) with effect from 1 October 1999.

10 Allowance for misused stamps

When any person has inadvertently used for an instrument liable to duty a stamp of greater value than was necessary, or has inadvertently used a stamp for an instrument not liable to any duty, the Commissioners may, on application made within [two years][1] after the date of the instrument, or, if it is not dated, within [two years][1] after the execution thereof by the person by whom it was first or alone executed, and upon the instrument, if liable to duty, being stamped with the proper duty, cancel and allow as spoiled the stamp so misused.

Amendments—[1] Words, in both places, substituted by the Revenue Act 1898 s 13.

11 Allowance how to be made

In any case in which allowance is made for spoiled or misused stamps the Commissioners may give in lieu thereof other stamps of the same denomination and value, or if required, and they think proper, stamps of any other denomination to the same amount in value, or in their discretion, the same value in money, [...][1].

Amendments—[1] Words repealed by FA 1999 s 115, Sch 18 para 6, Sch 20 Pt V(4) with effect from 1 October 1999.

12 Stamps not wanted may be repurchased by the Commissioners

Amendments—This section repealed by FA 1999 s 115, Sch 18 para 6, Sch 20 Pt V(4) with effect from 1 October 1999.

[Allowance for Lost or Spoiled Instruments][1]

[12A Lost or spoiled instruments

(1) This section applies where the Commissioners are satisfied that:

(*a*) an instrument which was executed and duly stamped ("the original instrument") has been accidentally lost or spoiled; and

(*b*) in place of the original instrument, another instrument made between the same persons and for the same purpose ("the replacement instrument") has been executed; and

(*c*) an application for relief under this section is made to the Commissioners; and either

(*d*) where the original instrument has been lost, the applicant undertakes to deliver it up to the Commissioners to be cancelled if it is subsequently found; or

(*e*) where the original instrument has been spoiled:

(i) the application is made within two years after the date of the original instrument, or if it is not dated, within two years after the time when it was executed, or within such further time as the Commissioners may allow; and

(ii) no legal proceeding has been commenced in which the original instrument has been or could or would have been given or offered in evidence; and

(iii) the original instrument is delivered up to the Commissioners to be cancelled.

(2) Where this section applies:

(*a*) the replacement instrument shall not be chargeable with any duty, but shall be stamped with the duty with which it would otherwise have been chargeable in accordance with the law in force at the time when it was executed, and shall be deemed for all purposes to be duly stamped; and

(*b*) if any duty, interest [or penalty][2] was paid in respect of the replacement instrument before the application was made, the Commissioners shall pay to such person as they consider appropriate an amount equal to the duty, interest [or penalty][2] so paid.

(3) For the purposes of this section the Commissioners may require the applicant to produce such evidence by statutory declaration or otherwise as they think fit.][1]

Amendments—[1] This section and preceding cross heading inserted by FA 1996 Sch 39 Pt III para 10(1), (3), (4), (5), with effect from 29 April 1996, except in relation to an instrument which has been accidentally spoiled if an application for allowance under s 9 of this Act was made before that date.

[2] Words in sub-s (2)(*b*) substituted by FA 1999 s 114, Sch 17 para 2 with effect in relation to penalties in respect of things done or omitted after 30 September 1999.

Offences relating to Stamps

13 [Offences in relation to dies and stamps][2]

[(1)][3] [A person commits an offence who][3] does, or causes or procures to be done, or knowingly aids, abets, or assists in doing, any of the acts following; that is to say,

(1), (2) ...[1]

(3) Fraudulently prints or makes an impression upon any material from a genuine die;

(4) Fraudulently cuts, tears, or in any way removes from any material any stamp, with intent that any use should be made of such stamp or of any part thereof;

(5) Fraudulently mutilates any stamp, with intent that any use should be made of any part of such stamp;

(6) Fraudulently fixes or places upon any material or upon any stamp, any stamp or part of a stamp which, whether fraudulently or not, has been cut, torn, or in any way removed from any other material, or out of or from any other stamp;

(7) Fraudulently erases or otherwise either really or apparently removes from any stamped material any name, sum, date, or other matter or thing whatsoever thereon written, with the intent that any use should be made of the stamp upon such material;

(8) Knowingly sells or exposes for sale or utters or uses ...[1] any stamp which has been fraudulently printed or impressed from a genuine die;

(9) Knowingly, and without lawful excuse (the proof whereof shall lie on the person accused) has in his possession ...[1] any stamp which has been fraudulently printed or impressed from a genuine die, or any stamp or part of a stamp which has been fraudulently cut, torn, or otherwise removed from any material, or any stamp which has been fraudulently mutilated, or any stamped material out of which any name, sum, date, or other matter or thing has been fraudulently erased or otherwise either really or apparently removed, ...[4]

[(2) A person guilty of an offence under this section is liable—

(*a*) on summary conviction, to imprisonment for a term not exceeding six months or a fine not exceeding the statutory maximum, or both;

(*b*) on conviction on indictment, to imprisonment for a term not exceeding ten years or a fine, or both.][5]

Cross references—See the Criminal Justice Act 1948 s 1 (references to penal servitude or to imprisonment with hard labour are to be construed as sentence to imprisonment only);
Criminal Law Act 1967 s 1 (abolition of distinction between felony and misdemeanour);
Magistrates' Courts Act 1980 s 17, Sch 1 para 12 (offences under this section triable on indictment or triable summarily).

Amendments—[1] Sub-paras (1), (2) and words in sub-paras (8), (9) repealed by the Forgery Act 1913 s 20 and Schedule.
[2] Words in heading substituted by FA 1999 s 115, Sch 18 para 5(1), (2) with effect in relation to things done or omitted after 30 September 1999.
[3] Sub-s (1) numbered as such and words therein substituted by FA 1999 s 115, Sch 18 para 5(1), (3), with effect in relation to things done or omitted after 30 September 1999.
[4] Words in sub-para (9) repealed by FA 1999 s 115, Sch 18 para 5(1), (4) Sch 20 Pt V(3) with effect in relation to things done or omitted after 30 September 1999.
[5] Sub-s (2) inserted by FA 1999 s 115, Sch 18 para 5 with effect in relation to things done or omitted after 30 September 1999.

16 Proceedings for detection of forged dies, etc

On information given before a justice upon oath that there is just cause to suspect any person of being guilty of any of the offences aforesaid, such justice may, by a warrant under his hand, cause every house, room, shop, building, or place belonging to or occupied by the suspected person, or where he is suspected of being or having been in any way engaged or concerned in the commission of any such offence, or of secreting any machinery, implements, or utensils applicable to the commission of any such offence, to be searched, and if upon such search any of the said several matters and things are found, the same may be seized and carried away, and shall afterwards be delivered over to the Commissioners.

Cross references—See Revenue Act 1898, s 12 (application of this section to the manufacture of paper used for excise licences).

17–20

...

Amendments—Sections 17–20 repealed by FA 1999 s 115, Sch 18 para 6, Sch 20 Pt V(4) with effect from 1 October 1999.

21 Penalty for frauds in relation to duties

Any person who practices or is concerned in any fraudulent act, contrivance, or device, not specially provided for by law, with intent to defraud Her Majesty of any duty shall incur [a penalty not exceeding £3,000][1].

Amendments—[1] Words substituted by FA 1999 s 114, Sch 17 para 2 with effect in relation to penalties in respect of things done or omitted after 30 September 1999.

Miscellaneous

22 As to discontinuance of dies

Whenever the Commissioners determine to discontinue the use of any die, and provide a new die to be used in lieu thereof, and give public notice thereof in the [London, Edinburgh and Belfast Gazettes][1], then from and after any day to be stated in the notice (such day not being within one month after the same is so published) the new die shall be the only lawful die for denoting the duty chargeable in any case in which the discontinued die would have been used; and every instrument first executed by any person, or bearing date after the day so stated, and stamped with the discontinued die, shall be deemed to be not duly stamped:

Provided as follows:

(*a*) If any instrument stamped as last aforesaid, and first executed after the day so stated at any place out of the United Kingdom, is brought to the Commissioners within fourteen days after it has been received in the United Kingdom, then upon proof of the facts to the satisfaction of the Commissioners the stamp thereon shall be cancelled, and the instrument shall be stamped with the same amount of duty by means of the lawful die, without the payment of any penalty:

(*b*) All persons having in their possession any material stamped with the discontinued die, and which by reason of the providing of such new die has been rendered useless, may at any time within six months after the day stated in the notice send the same to the chief office or one of the head offices, and the Commissioners may thereupon cause the stamp on such material to be cancelled, and the same material, or, if the Commissioners think fit, any other material, to be stamped with the new die, in lieu of and to an equal amount with the stamp so cancelled.

Cross references—See Revenue Act 1898 s 10 (application of this section to notices issued under that section).

Amendments—[1] Words substituted by FA 1998 s 150 with effect from 31 July 1998.

23 Application of Act to excise labels

The provisions of this Act in reference to offences relating to stamps shall apply to any label now or hereafter provided by the Commissioners for denoting any [duty of excise other than a duty of excise chargeable on goods imported into the United Kingdom][1], and any label so provided shall be deemed to be included in the term "stamp" as defined by this Act.

Amendments—[1] Words substituted by the Customs and Excise Management Act 1979 Sch 4 para 12, Table, Pt I, with effect from 1 April 1979.

24 Declarations, how to be made

Any statutory declaration to be made in pursuance of or for the purposes of this or any other Act for the time being in force relating to duties may be made before any of the Commissioners, or any officer or person authorised by them in that behalf, or before any commissioner for oaths or any justice or notary public in any part of the United Kingdom, or at any place out of the United Kingdom, before any person duly authorised to administer oaths there.

Cross references—See Revenue Act 1898 s 7 (6) (application of this section to affidavits and oaths).

25 Mode of granting licences

Amendments—This section repealed by FA 1999 s 115, Sch 18 para 6, Sch 20 Pt V(4) with effect from 1 October 1999.

26 Recovery of fines

Amendments—This section repealed by FA 1999 Sch 20 Pt V(3) with effect in relation to things done or omitted from 1 October 1999.

27 Definitions

In this Act, unless the context otherwise requires—

The expression "Commissioners" means Commissioners of Inland Revenue:

The expression "officer" means officer of Inland Revenue:

The expression "chief office" means chief office of Inland Revenue:

The expression "head offices" means the head office of Inland Revenue in Edinburgh and Dublin:

The expression "duty" means any stamp duty for the time being chargeable by law:

The expression "material" includes every sort of material upon which words or figures can be expressed:

The expression "instrument" includes every written document:

The expression "die" includes any plate, type, tool, or implement whatever used under the direction of the Commissioners for expressing or denoting any duty, or rate of duty, or the fact that any duty or rate of duty or penalty has been paid, or that an instrument is duly stamped, or is not chargeable with any duty or for denoting any fee, and also any part of any such plate, type, tool, or implement:

The expressions "forge" and "forged" include counterfeit and counterfeited:

The expression "stamp" means as well a stamp impressed by means of a die as an adhesive stamp for denoting any duty or fee:

The expression "stamped" is applicable as well to instruments and material impressed with stamps by means of a die as to instruments and material having adhesive stamps affixed thereto:

The expressions "executed" and "execution" [have the same meaning as in the Stamp Act 1891][1]:

The expression "justice" means justice of the peace.

Amendments—[1] Words in the definition of "executed" and "execution" substituted by FA 1994 s 239(2), (3).

Short Title

30 Short title

This Act may be cited as the Stamp Duties Management Act, 1891.

STAMP ACT 1891

(54 & 55 Vict. Chapter 39)

ARRANGEMENT OF SECTIONS

PART I
REGULATIONS APPLICABLE TO INSTRUMENTS GENERALLY

Charge of duty upon Instruments

An Act to consolidate the Enactments granting and relating to the Stamp Duties upon Instruments and certain other enactments relating to Stamp Duties.

[21st July 1891]

Construction—FA 1899, Pt II to be construed together with this Act; see FA 1899, s 14;
FA 1907 Pt II to be construed together with this Act; see FA 1907 s 30(2);
RA 1909 Pt II to be construed together with this Act; see RA 1909 s 12(1);
FA 1930 Pt IV to be construed together with this Act; see FA 1930 s 53(4);
FA 1946 Pt VII to be construed together with this Act; see FA 1946 s 67(7);
FA 1947 Pt VI to be construed together with this Act; see FA 1947 s 74(7);
FA 1948 Pt VII to be construed together with this Act; see FA 1948 s 82(6);
FA 1949 Pt IV to be construed together with this Act; see FA 1949 s 52(5);
FA 1952 s 74 to be construed as one with this Act; see FA 1952 s 74(5);
FA 1953 s 31 to be construed as one with this Act; see FA 1953 s 31(3);
FA 1959 Pt IV to be construed as one with this Act; see FA 1959 s 37(2);
FA 1960 s 74 to be construed as one with this Act; see FA 1960 s 74(9);
FA 1963 Pt IV to be construed as one with this Act; see FA 1963 s 73(4);
FA 1964 s 23 to be construed as one with this Act; see FA 1964 s 23(3);
FA 1965 s 90 to be construed as one with this Act; see FA 1965 s 90(6);
FA 1966 Pt VIII, so far as it relates to stamp duties, to be construed as one with this Act; see FA 1966 s 53(2);
FA 1967 Pt V to be construed as one with this Act; see FA 1967 s 45(3);
FA 1970 Pt III, so far as it relates to stamp duties, to be construed as one with this Act; see FA 1970 s 36(5);
FA 1973 Pt V to be construed as one with this Act; see FA 1973 s 59(3);
FA 1974 Sch 11 to be construed as one with this Act; see FA 1974 s 57(3);
FA 1976 s 127 to be construed as one with this Act; see FA 1976 s 127(5);
FA 1985 Pt III to be construed as one with this Act; see FA 1985 s 98(4);
FA 1986 Pt III to be construed as one with this Act; see FA 1986 s 114(4);
FA 1987 Pt III, except s 56 and Sch 7 (stamp duty reserve tax), to be construed as one with this Act; see FA 1987 s 72(4);
FA 1988 ss 140, 141, 143 to be construed as one with this Act; see FA 1988 ss 140(5), 141(5), 143(8);
FA 1990 ss 107–109 to be construed as one with this Act; see FA 1990 s 111(2);
FA 1994 Pt VI to be construed as one with this Act; see FA 1994 s 257(3).
FA 1995 Pt V to be construed as one with this Act; see FA 1995 s 161(3).
FA 1996 s 186 to be construed as one with this Act; see FA 1996 s 186(4).
FA 1999 Pt VI, so far as it relates to stamp duties, to be construed as one with this Act; see FA 1999 s 123(1)(*a*).
FA 2000 ss 118–122, 128, 129, 131, Schs 33 and 34 to be construed as one with this Act; see FA 2000 ss 118(9), 119(10), 120(9), 121(9), 122(7), 128(9), 129(4), 131(7), Sch 33, para 9(2).
FA 2001 s 92 and Sch 30 to be construed as one with this Act; see FA 2001 s 92(7).
FA 2002 ss 111, 113, 115, 116 and Schs 34–37 to be construed as one with this Act; see FA 2002 s 116(3), Sch 34, para 11, Sch 35 para 12, and Sch 36 para 10.
FA 2003 s 125 to be construed as one with this Act; see FA 2003 s 125(3).
FA 2003 s 128 to be construed as one with this Act; see FA 2003 s 128(6).
FA 2003 s 129 to be construed as one with this Act; see FA 2003 s 129(7).
FA 2003 Sch 15 para 33 to be construed as one with this Act; see FA 2003 Sch 15 para 33(9).

PART I

REGULATIONS APPLICABLE TO INSTRUMENTS GENERALLY

Charge of Duty upon Instruments

1 Charge of duties in schedule

Statement of Practice SP 11/91—Interaction of stamp duty and VAT: stamp duty to be calculated on VAT-inclusive consideration.

Amendments—This section repealed by FA 1999 Sch 20 Pt V(2) with effect in relation to instruments executed, or bearer instruments issued, from 1 October 1999, subject to the provisions in FA 1999 Sch 20 Pt V(2) Note 2. Previously the text read—

"From and after the commencement of this Act the stamp duties to be charged for the use of Her Majesty upon the several instruments specified in the First Schedule to this Act shall be the several duties in the said schedule specified, which duties shall be in substitution for the duties theretofore chargeable under the enactments repealed by this Act, and shall be subject to the exemptions contained in this Act and in any other Act for the time being in force."

2 All duties to be paid according to regulations of Act

All stamp duties for the time being chargeable by law upon any instruments are to be paid and denoted according to the regulations in this Act contained, and except where express provision is made to the contrary are to be denoted by impressed stamps only.

3 How instruments are to be written and stamped

(1) Every instrument written upon stamped material is to be written in such manner, and every instrument partly or wholly written before being stamped is to be so stamped, that the stamp may appear on the face of the instrument, and cannot be used for or applied to any other instrument written upon the same piece of material.

(2) If more than one instrument be written upon the same piece of material, every one of the instruments is to be separately and distinctly stamped with the duty with which it is chargeable.

Cross references—See FA 1988 s 143(7) (UK company shares paired with foreign company shares; this section not to apply in relation to a bearer instrument issued after 8 December 1987 representing shares in the UK or foreign companies or a right to an allotment of or to subscribe for such shares).

4 Instruments to be separately charged with duty in certain cases

Except where express provision to the contrary is made by this or any other Act—

(*a*) An instrument containing or relating to several distinct matters is to be separately and distinctly charged, as if it were a separate instrument, with duty in respect of each of the matters;

(*b*) An instrument made for any consideration in respect whereof it is chargeable with *ad valorem* duty, and also for any further or other valuable consideration or considerations, is to be separately and distinctly charged, as if it were a separate instrument, with duty in respect of each of the considerations.

Cross references—See FA 1989 s 173(2) (insurance: abolition of certain duties).

5 Facts and circumstances affecting duty to be set forth in instruments

All the facts and circumstances affecting the liability of any instrument to duty, or the amount of the duty with which any instrument is chargeable, are to be fully and truly set forth in the instrument; and every person who, with intent to defraud Her Majesty,

(*a*) executes any instrument in which all the said facts and circumstances are not fully and truly set forth; or

(*b*) being employed or concerned in or about the preparation of any instrument, neglects or omits fully and truly to set forth therein all the said facts and circumstances;

shall incur [a penalty not exceeding £3,000][1].

Simon's Tax Cases—*Re Brown Root McDermott Fabricators Ltd's and anor's application* [1996] STC 483; *Parinv (Hatfield) Ltd v IRC* [1998] STC 305.

Amendments—[1] Words substituted by FA 1999 s 114, Sch 17 para 3 with effect in relation to penalties in respect of things done or omitted after 30 September 1999.

6 Mode of calculating *ad valorem* duty in certain cases

(1) Where an instrument is chargeable with *ad valorem* duty in respect of—

(*a*) any money in any foreign or colonial currency, or

(*b*) any stock or marketable security,

the duty shall be calculated on the value, on the day of the date of the instrument, of the money in British currency according to the current rate of exchange, or of the stock or security according to the average price thereof.

(2) Where an instrument contains a statement of current rate of exchange, or average price, as the case may require, and is stamped in accordance with that statement, it is, so far as regards the subject matter of the statement, to be deemed duly stamped, unless or until it is shown that the statement is untrue, and that the instrument is in fact insufficiently stamped.

Cross references—See FA 1985 s 88 (this section to apply instead of FA 1899, s 12 to instruments executed after 31 July 1985).

Use of Adhesive Stamps

9 Penalty for frauds in relation to adhesive stamps

(1) If any person—

(*a*) fraudulently removes or causes to be removed from any instrument any adhesive stamp, or affixes to any other instrument or uses for any postal purposes any adhesive stamp which has been so removed, with intent that the stamp may be used again; or

(*b*) sells or offers for sale, or utters, any adhesive stamp which has been so removed or utters any instrument, having thereon any adhesive stamp which has to his knowledge been so removed as aforesaid;

[he is liable to a penalty not exceeding £3,000][2].

(2) …[1]

Cross references—See the Revenue Act 1898, s 7 ("instrument" includes any postal packet within the meaning of the Post Office Protection Act 1884; fines incurred under this section may be recovered summarily).

Amendments—[1] Sub-s (2) repealed by the Revenue Act 1898, s 7(4).

[2] Words in sub-s (1) substituted by FA 1999 s 114, Sch 17 para 3 with effect in relation to penalties in respect of things done or omitted after 30 September 1999.

Appropriated Stamps and Denoting Stamps

11 Denoting stamps

Where the duty with which an instrument is chargeable depends in any manner upon the duty paid upon another instrument, the payment of the last-mentioned duty shall, upon application to the Commissioners and production of both the instruments, be denoted upon the first-mentioned instrument in such manner as the Commissioners think fit.

Cross references—See FA 1984 s 111(2) (application of this section where an agreement for a lease for a term exceeding 35 years is duly stamped and a conveyance, transfer, etc is subject to the agreement).

Adjudication Stamps

[12 Adjudication by Commissioners][1]

[(1) Subject to such regulations as the Commissioners may think fit to make, the Commissioners may be required by any person to adjudicate with reference to any executed instrument upon the questions—

(*a*) whether it is chargeable with duty;

(*b*) with what amount of duty it is chargeable;

(*c*) whether any penalty is payable under section 15B (penalty on late stamping);

(*d*) what penalty is in their opinion correct and appropriate.

(2) The Commissioners may require to be furnished with an abstract of the instrument and with such evidence as they may require as to the facts and circumstances relevant to those questions.

(3) The Commissioners shall give notice of their decision upon those questions to the person by whom the adjudication was required.

(4) If the Commissioners decide that the instrument is not chargeable with any duty, it may be stamped with a particular stamp denoting that it has been the subject of adjudication and is not chargeable with any duty.

(5) If the Commissioners decide that the instrument is chargeable with duty and assess the amount of duty chargeable, the instrument when stamped in accordance with their decision may be stamped with a particular stamp denoting that it has been the subject of adjudication and is duly stamped.

(6) Every instrument stamped in accordance with subsection (4) or (5) shall be admissible in evidence and available for all purposes notwithstanding any objection relating to duty.][1]

Press releases etc—Principal Registry, Family Division 28-2-78 (application for grant of representation: production of deed or instrument to Probate Registry: presentation to Controller of Stamps for preliminary adjudication).

Simon's Tax Cases—s 12(1), *Marx v Estates and General Investments Ltd* [1975] STC 671.

s 12(2), *Parinv (Hatfield) Ltd v IRC* [1998] STC 305.

Cross references—See FA 2000 Sch 32 para 4(2) (instruments ceasing to be stamped even if instrument has been stamped in accordance with sub-s (5) above).

FA 2000 Sch 32 para 4(3) (sub-s (6) above does not apply to an instrument ceasing to be stamped at any time when it is not duly stamped).

FA 2000 Sch 32 para 7 (application of this section in relation to any additional duty chargeable on an instrument to which FA 2000 Sch 32 applies).

Amendments—[1] This section substituted by FA 1999 s 109(3), Sch 12 para 1 with effect for instruments executed after 30 September 1999. This does not apply to transfers or other instruments relating to units under a unit trust scheme by virtue of FA 1999 s 122. Previously the text read—.

"**12 Assessment of duty by Commissioners**

(1) Subject to such regulations as the Commissioners may think fit to make, the Commissioners may be required by any person to express their opinion with reference to any executed instrument upon the following questions:

(*a*) whether it is chargeable with any duty;

(*b*) with what amount of duty it is chargeable.

(2) The Commissioners may require to be furnished with an abstract of the instrument, and also with such evidence as they may deem necessary, in order to show to their satisfaction whether all the facts and circumstances affecting the liability of the instrument to duty, or the amount of the duty chargeable thereon, are fully and truly set forth therein.

(3) If the Commissioners are of opinion that the instrument is not chargeable with any duty, it may be stamped with a particular stamp denoting that it is not chargeable with any duty.

(4) If the Commissioners are of opinion that the instrument is chargeable with duty, they shall assess the duty with which it is in their opinion chargeable, and when the instrument is stamped in accordance with the assessment it may be stamped with a particular stamp denoting that it is duly stamped.

(5) Every instrument stamped with the particular stamp denoting either that it is not chargeable with any duty, or is duly stamped, shall be admissible in evidence, and available for all purposes notwithstanding any objection relating to duty.

(6) Provided as follows:

(*a*) An instrument upon which the duty has been assessed by the Commissioners shall not, if it is unstamped or insufficiently stamped, be stamped otherwise than in accordance with the assessment;

(*b*) Nothing in this section ... shall authorise the stamping after the execution thereof of any instrument which by law cannot be stamped after execution;

(*c*) A statutory declaration made for the purpose of this section shall not be used against any person making the same in any proceeding whatever, except in an inquiry as to the duty with which the instrument to which it relates is chargeable; and every person by whom any such declaration is made shall, on payment of the duty chargeable upon the instrument to which it relates, be relieved from any fine or disability to which he may be liable by reason of the omission to state truly in the instrument any fact or circumstances required by this Act as stated therein."

[12A Adjudication: supplementary provisions][1]

[(1) An instrument which has been the subject of adjudication by the Commissioners under section 12 shall not, if it is unstamped or insufficiently stamped, be stamped otherwise than in accordance with the Commissioners' decision on the adjudication.

(2) If without reasonable excuse any such instrument is not duly stamped within 30 days after the date on which the Commissioners gave notice of their decision, or such longer period as the Commissioners may allow, the person by whom the adjudication was required is liable to a penalty not exceeding £300.

(3) A statutory declaration made for the purposes of section 12 shall not be used against the person making it in any proceedings whatever, except in an inquiry as to the duty with which the instrument to which it relates is chargeable or as to the penalty payable on stamping that instrument.

(4) Every person by whom any such declaration is made shall, on payment of the duty chargeable upon the instrument to which it relates, and any interest or penalty payable on stamping, be relieved from any penalty to which he may be liable by reason of the omission to state truly in the instrument any fact or circumstance required by this Act to be so stated.][1]

Cross references—See FA 2000 Sch 32 para 5 (sub-s (1) above does not prevent an instrument to which FA 2000 Sch 32 applies which is stamped with less than the appropriate amount of duty from being stamped with additional duty).
FA 2000 Sch 32 para 7 (application of this section in relation to any additional duty chargeable on an instrument to which FA 2000 Sch 32 applies).

Amendments—[1] This section inserted by FA 1999 s 109(3), Sch 12 para 1 with effect in relation to instruments executed after 30 September 1999. This does not apply to transfers or other instruments relating to units under a unit trust scheme by virtue of FA 1999 s 122.

[13 Appeal against Commissioners' decision on adjudication][1]

[(1) A person who is dissatisfied with a decision of the Commissioners on an adjudication under section 12 may appeal against it.

(2) The appeal must be brought within 30 days of notice of the decision on the adjudication being given under section 12(3).

(3) An appeal may only be brought on payment of—

(*a*) duty and any penalty in conformity with the Commissioners' decision, and

(*b*) any interest that in conformity with that decision would be payable on stamping the instrument on the day on which the appeal is brought.

(4) An appeal which relates only to the penalty payable on late stamping may be brought to the [First-tier Tribunal][2] in accordance with section 13A below.

(5) Any other appeal may be brought in accordance with section 13B below to the High Court of the part of the United Kingdom in which the case has arisen.][1]

Press releases etc—Law Society 18-7-90 (if no appeal received and no duty paid within 28 days, one reminder is issued; after further 14 days document is returned unstamped).

Cross references—See FA 1965 s 91 (courts may order repayment of sums with such interests as the courts may determine).
FA 2000 Sch 32 para 7 (application of this section in relation to any additional duty chargeable on an instrument to which FA 2000 Sch 32 applies).

Amendments—[1] This section substituted by FA 1999 s 109(3), Sch 12 para 2 with effect in relation to instruments executed after 30 September 1999. This does not apply to transfers or other instruments relating to units under a unit trust scheme by virtue of FA 1999 s 122. Previously the text read:

"13 Persons dissatisfied may appeal

(1) Any person who is dissatisfied with the assessment of the Commissioners may, within twenty-one days after the date of the assessment, and on payment of duty in conformity therewith, appeal against the assessment to the High Court of the part of the United Kingdom in which the case has arisen, and may for that purpose require the Commissioners to state and sign a case, setting forth the question upon which their opinion was required, and the assessment made by them.

(2) The Commissioners shall thereupon state and sign a case and deliver the same to the person by whom it is required, and the case may, within seven days thereafter, be set down by him for hearing.

(3) Upon the hearing of the case the court shall determine the question submitted, and, if the instrument in question is in the opinion of the court chargeable with any duty, shall assess the duty with which it is chargeable.

(4) If it is decided by the court that the assessment of the Commissioners is erroneous, any excess of duty which may have been paid in conformity with the erroneous assessment, together with any fine or penalty which may have been paid in consequence thereof, shall be ordered by the court to be repaid to the appellant …

(5) …"

[2] Words in sub-s (4) substituted for words "Special Commissioners" by the Transfer of Tribunal Functions and Revenue and Customs Appeals Order, SI 2009/56 art 3, Sch 1 paras 1, 2 with effect from 1 April 2009.

[13A Appeal to the [First-tier Tribunal][2]][1]

[(1) The following provisions apply in relation to an appeal under section 13(4).

(2) Notice of appeal must be given in writing to the Commissioners, specifying the grounds of appeal.

(3), (4) …[2]

(5) On the appeal the [First-tier Tribunal][2] may—

(*a*) if it appears …[2] that no penalty should be paid, set the decision aside;

(*b*) if the amount determined appears …[2] to be appropriate, confirm the decision;

(*c*) if the amount determined appears …[2] to be excessive, reduce it to such other amount (including nil) as [the tribunal considers][2] appropriate;

(*d*) if the amount determined appears …[2] to be insufficient, increase it to such amount as [the tribunal considers][2] appropriate.

(6) …[2]

[(7) In addition to any right of appeal on a point of law under section 11(2) of the Tribunals, Courts and Enforcement Act 2007, the person liable to the penalty may appeal to the Upper Tribunal against the amount of the penalty which has been determined under subsection (5), but not against any decision which falls under section 11(5)(*d*) or (*e*) of that Act and was made in connection with the determination of the amount of the penalty.

(7A) Section 11(3) and (4) of the Tribunals, Courts and Enforcement Act 2007 applies to the right of appeal under subsection (7) as it applies to the right of appeal under section 11(2) of that Act.][2]

(8) On an appeal under subsection (7) the [Upper Tribunal][2] has the same powers as are conferred on the [First-tier Tribunal][2] by subsection (5) above.][1]

Cross references—FA 2000 Sch 32 para 7 (application of this section in relation to any additional duty chargeable on an instrument to which FA 2000 Sch 32 applies).

Amendments—[1] This section inserted by FA 1999 s 109(3), Sch 12 para 2 with effect in relation to instruments executed after 30 September 1999. This does not apply to transfers or other instruments relating to units under a unit trust scheme by virtue of FA 1999 s 122.

[2] Words in heading substituted for words "Special Commissioners", sub-ss (3), (4), (6) repealed, in sub-s (5) words substituted and repealed, sub-ss (7), (7A) substituted for previous sub-s (7), and words in sub-s (8) substituted, by the Transfer of Tribunal Functions and Revenue and Customs Appeals Order, SI 2009/56 art 3, Sch 1 paras 1, 3 with effect from 1 April 2009. This section previously read as follows—

"(1) The following provisions apply in relation to an appeal under section 13(4).

(2) Notice of appeal must be given in writing to the Commissioners, specifying the grounds of appeal.

(3) On the hearing of the appeal the Special Commissioners may allow the appellant to put forward a ground not specified in the notice of appeal, and take it into consideration, if satisfied that the omission was not wilful or unreasonable.

(4) The powers conferred by sections 46A(1)(*c*) and (2) to (4) and sections 56B to 56D of the Taxes Management Act 1970 (power of Lord Chancellor to make regulations as to jurisdiction, practice and procedure in relation to appeals) are exercisable in relation to appeals to which this section applies.

(5) On the appeal the Special Commissioners may—

(*a*) if it appears to them that no penalty should be paid, set the decision aside;

(*b*) if the amount determined appears to them to be appropriate, confirm the decision;

(*c*) if the amount determined appears to them to be excessive, reduce it to such other amount (including nil) as they consider appropriate;

(*d*) if the amount determined appears to them to be insufficient, increase it to such amount as they consider appropriate.

(6) Section 56A of the Taxes Management Act 1970 (general right of appeal on point of law) applies in relation to a decision of the Special Commissioners under this section.

(7) Without prejudice to that right of appeal, an appeal lies against the amount of a penalty determined by the Special Commissioners under this section, at the instance of the person liable to the penalty, to the High Court.

(8) On an appeal under subsection (7) the court has the same powers as are conferred on the Special Commissioners by subsection (5) above.".

[13B Appeal to the High Court][1]

[(1) The following provisions apply in relation to an appeal under section 13(5).

(2) The appellant may for the purposes of the appeal require the Commissioners to state and sign a case setting out the questions upon which they were required to adjudicate and their decision upon them.

(3) The Commissioners shall thereupon state and sign a case and deliver the same to the person by whom it is required, and the case may, within 30 days thereafter, be set down by him for hearing.

(4) On the appeal the court shall determine the questions submitted and may give such directions as it thinks fit with respect to the repayment of any duty or penalty paid in conformity with the Commissioners' decision.][1]

Cross references—FA 2000 Sch 32 para 7 (application of this section in relation to any additional duty chargeable on an instrument to which FA 2000 Sch 32 applies).

Amendments—[1] This section inserted by FA 1999 s 109(3), Sch 12 para 2 with effect in relation to instruments executed after 30 September 1999. This does not apply to transfers or other instruments relating to units under a unit trust scheme by virtue of FA 1999 s 122.

Production of Instruments in Evidence

14 Terms upon which instruments not duly stamped may be received in evidence

(1) Upon the production of an instrument chargeable with any duty as evidence in any court of civil judicature in any part of the United Kingdom, or before any arbitrator or referee, notice shall be taken by the judge arbitrator, or referee of any omission or insufficiency of the stamp thereon, and [the instrument may][1], on payment to the officer of the court whose duty it is to read the instrument, or to the arbitrator or referee, of the amount of the unpaid duty, and [any interest or penalty][1] payable on stamping the same, and of a further sum of one pound, be received in evidence, saving all just exceptions on other grounds.

(2) The officer, or arbitrator, or referee receiving [the duty and any interest or penalty][1] shall give a receipt for the same, and make an entry in a book kept for that purpose of the payment and of the amount thereof, and shall communicate to the Commissioners the name or title of the

proceeding in which, and of the party from whom, he received [the duty and any interest or penalty][1], and the date and description of the instrument, and shall pay over to such person as the Commissioners may appoint the money received by him for [the duty and any interest or penalty][1].

(3) On production to the Commissioners of any instrument in respect of which [any duty, interest or penalty][1] has been paid, together with the receipt, the payment of [the duty, interest and penalty][1] shall be denoted on the instrument.

(4) Save as aforesaid, an instrument executed in any part of the United Kingdom, or relating, wheresoever executed, to any property situate, or to any matter or thing done or to be done, in any part of the United Kingdom, shall not, except in criminal proceedings, be given in evidence, or be available for any purpose whatever, unless it is duly stamped in accordance with the law in force at the time when it was [executed][1].

Simon's Tax Cases—s 14(4), *Terrapin International Ltd v IRC* [1976] STC 197; *Re Brown Root McDermott Fabricators Ltd's and anor's application* [1996] STC 483; *Parinv (Hatfield) Ltd v IRC* [1998] STC 305.

HMRC Interpretation RI 174—*(Parinv (Hatfield) Ltd v IRC [1996] STC 933*—off-shore declaration of trust ineffective to avoid ad valorem duty on subsequent transfers).

Cross references—See FA 1984 s 109(3), (4) (reduction of stamp duty on conveyances and transfers with effect from 20 March 1984; how sub-s (4) of this section applies to instruments executed after 12 March 1984 but stamped after 19 March 1984);

FA 1984 s 110(4) (extension of stamp duty relief on sales at discount with effect from 20 March 1984; how sub-s (4) of this section applies to instruments executed after 12 March 1984 but stamped after 19 March 1984);

FA 1985 s 82(7) (abolition of stamp duty in respect of gifts inter vivos from 26 March 1985; instruments executed after 18 March 1985 which are stamped after 25 March 1985; modification of sub-s (4) above);

FA 1985 s 85(4) (abolition of certain fixed duties from 26 March 1985; modification of sub-s (4) above);

FA 1988 s 140(3) (abolition of unit trust instrument duty; modification of sub-s (4) above where a trust instrument executed after 15 March 1988 is not stamped before 22 March 1988 and where a trust instrument in respect of a property becoming trust property after 15 March 1988 is not stamped before 22 March 1988);

FA 1988 s 141(3) (abolition of duty on documents relating to transactions of capital companies; modification of sub-s (4) above where the relevant document in respect of a transaction occurring after 15 March 1988 is not stamped before 22 March 1988);

FA 1988 s 141(3) (abolition of duty on documents relating to transactions of capital companies; modification of sub-s (4) above where an exempt transaction occurs before 16 March 1988 in respect of which a relevant event occurs after 15 March 1988 and the relevant duty is not paid before 22 March 1988);

FA 1993 s 201(3) (increase in stamp duty threshold from 16 March 1993 in respect of conveyance or transfer on sale; applicable law for the purposes of sub-s (4) above);

FA 1993 s 204(3) (method of denoting stamp duty to be prescribed by Treasury regulations; for the purposes of sub-s (4) above the method is to be that in force when an instrument was first executed);

FA 1994 ss 244(5), 245(8) (with effect from an appointed day, instruments on transfer of land in Northern Ireland are required to be produced to the Commissioners and no instrument will be deemed for the purposes of this section to be duly stamped unless it is so produced).

FA 2000 Sch 32 para 4(3) (sub-s (1) above does not apply to an instrument if it cease to be stamped, at any time when it is not duly stamped, unless the unpaid duty and any interest or penalty is paid in accordance with sub-s (1)).

FA 2000 Sch 32 para 6 (application of sub-s (4) in relation to any instrument to which FA 2000 Sch 32 applies).

FA 2002 s 115(5)(*a*) (where an instrument is chargeable with duty under FA 2002 s 115, sub-s (4) above does not apply in relation to it until after the period specified in FA 2002 s 115(2)).

FA 2008 ss 98(6), 99(3), 100(4) (for the purposes of sub-s (4) the law in force at the time of execution of an instrument executed on or after 13 March 2008 but before 19 March 2008, and not stamped before 19 March 2008, is deemed to be the law as varied in accordance with FA 2008 ss 98, 99, 100, Sch 32).

Amendments—[1] Words in sub-ss (1)–(4) substituted by FA 1999 s 109(3), Sch 12 para 3 with effect in relation to instruments executed after 30 September 1999. This does not apply to transfers or other instruments relating to units under a unit trust scheme by virtue of FA 1999 s 122.

Stamping of Instruments after Execution

[15 Stamping after execution][1]

[(1) An unstamped or insufficiently stamped instrument may be stamped after being executed on payment of the unpaid duty and any interest or penalty payable.

(2) Any interest or penalty payable on stamping shall be denoted on the instrument by a particular stamp.][1]

Cross references—See FA 1986 ss 69(5), 72(3) (instruments transferring relevant securities of UK companies to specified persons; extension of sub-s (2) above to such instruments and persons);

FA 1994 s 240 (where an agreement for a lease and the lease giving effect to the agreement are presented together for stamping, the agreement is treated, for penalty, if any, under this section, as executed on the date on which the lease was first executed).

FA 2000 Sch 32 para 7 (application of this section in relation to any additional duty chargeable on an instrument to which FA 2000 Sch 32 applies).

Amendments—[1] This section substituted by FA 1999 s 109(1) with effect in relation to instruments executed after 30 September 1999. This does not apply to transfers or other instruments relating to units under a unit trust scheme by virtue of FA 1999 s 122. Previously the text read:

"**15 Penalty upon stamping instruments after execution**

(1) Save where other express provision is in this Act made, any unstamped or insufficiently stamped instrument may be stamped after the execution thereof, on payment of the unpaid duty and penalty of ten pounds, and also by way of further penalty, where the unpaid duty exceeds ten pounds, of interest on such duty, at the rate of five pounds per centum per annum, from the day upon which the instrument was first executed up to the time when the amount of interest is equal to the unpaid duty.

(2) In the case of such instruments hereinafter mentioned as are chargeable with *ad valorem* duty, the following provisions shall have effect:

(*a*) The instrument, unless it is written upon duly stamped material, shall be duly stamped with the proper *ad valorem* duty before the expiration of thirty days after it is first executed, or after it has been first received in the United Kingdom in case it is first executed at any place out of the United Kingdom, unless the opinion of the Commissioners with respect to the amount of duty with which the instrument is chargeable, has, before such expiration, been required under the provisions of this Act:

(*b*) If the opinion of the Commissioners with respect to any such instrument has been required, the instrument shall be stamped in accordance with the assessment of the Commissioners within fourteen days after notice of the assessment:

(*c*) If any such instrument executed after the sixteenth day of May one thousand eight hundred and eighty-eight has not been or is not duly stamped in conformity with the foregoing provisions of this subsection, the person in that behalf herein-after specified shall incur a fine of ten pounds, and in addition to the penalty payable on stamping the instrument there shall be paid a further penalty equivalent to the stamp duty thereon, unless a reasonable excuse for the delay in stamping, or the omission to stamp, or the insufficiency of stamp, be afforded to the satisfaction of the Commissioners, or of the court, judge, arbitrator, or referee before whom it is produced:

(*d*) The instruments and persons to which the provisions of this subsection are to apply are as follows—

Title of Instrument as described in the First Schedule to this Act	*Person liable to Penalty*
Bond, covenant, or instrument of any kind whatsoever.	The obligee, covenantee, or other person taking the security.
Conveyance on sale.	The vendee or transferee.
Lease or tack.	The lessee.
[Agreement for lease or tack chargeable under section 75.]	[The person contracting for the lease or tack to be granted to him or another.]
…	…
[*Unit Trust Instrument*.][2]	[*The trustees*.]

(3) Provided that save where other express provision is made by this Act in relation to any particular instrument:

(*a*) Any unstamped or insufficiently stamped instrument which has been first executed at any place out of the United Kingdom, may be stamped, at any time within thirty days after it has been first received in the United Kingdom, on payment of the unpaid duty only: and

(*b*) The Commissioners may, if they think fit, … mitigate or remit any penalty payable on stamping.

(4) The payment of any penalty payable on stamping is to be denoted on the instrument by a particular stamp."

[15A Late stamping: interest][1]

[(1) Interest is payable on the stamping of an instrument which—

(*a*) is chargeable with *ad valorem* duty, and

(*b*) is not duly stamped within 30 days after the day on which the instrument was executed (whether in the United Kingdom or elsewhere).

(2) Interest is payable on the amount of the unpaid duty from the end of the period of 30 days mentioned in subsection (1)(*b*) until the duty is paid.

If an amount is lodged with the Commissioners in respect of the duty, the amount on which interest is payable is reduced by that amount.

(3) Interest shall be calculated at the rate applicable under section 178 of the Finance Act 1989 (power of Treasury to prescribe rates of interest).

(4) The amount of interest shall be rounded down (if necessary) to the nearest multiple of £5.

No interest is payable if that amount is less than £25.

(5) Interest under this section shall be paid without any deduction of income tax and shall not be taken into account in computing income or profits for any tax purposes.][1]

Cross references—FA 2000 Sch 32 para 7 (application of this section in relation to any additional duty chargeable on an instrument to which FA 2000 Sch 32 applies).

FA 2002 s 115(5)(*b*) (where an instrument is chargeable with duty under FA 2002 s 115, this section applies in relation to it as if it had been executed at the end of the period specified in FA 2002 s 115(2)).

Amendments—[1] This section inserted by FA 1999 s 109(1) with effect in relation to instruments executed after 30 September 1999. This does not apply to transfers or other instruments relating to units under a unit trust scheme by virtue of FA 1999 s 122.

[15B Late stamping: penalties][1]

[(1) A penalty is payable on the stamping of an instrument which is not presented for stamping within 30 days after—

(*a*) if the instrument is executed in the United Kingdom [or relates to land in the United Kingdom][2], the day on which it is so executed;

(*b*) if the instrument is executed outside the United Kingdom [and does not relate to land in the United Kingdom][2], the day on which it is first received in the United Kingdom.

[(1A) For the purposes of subsection (1) every instrument that (whether or not it also relates to any other transaction) relates to a transaction which to any extent involves land in the United Kingdom is an instrument relating to land in the United Kingdom.][2]

(2) If the instrument is presented for stamping within one year after the end of the 30-day period mentioned in subsection (1), the maximum penalty is £300 or the amount of the unpaid duty, whichever is less.

(3) If the instrument is not presented for stamping until after the end of the one-year period mentioned in subsection (2), the maximum penalty is £300 or the amount of the unpaid duty, whichever is greater.

(4) The Commissioners may, if they think fit, mitigate or remit any penalty payable on stamping.

(5) No penalty is payable if there is a reasonable excuse for the delay in presenting the instrument for stamping.][1]

Cross references—FA 2000 Sch 32 para 7 (application of this section in relation to any additional duty chargeable on an instrument to which FA 2000 Sch 32 applies).

FA 2002 s 115(5)(*b*) (where an instrument is chargeable with duty under FA 2002 s 115, this section applies in relation to it as if it had been executed at the end of the period specified in FA 2002 s 115(2)).

Amendments—[1] This section inserted by FA 1999 s 109(1) with effect in relation to instruments executed after 30 September 1999. This does not apply to transfers or other instruments relating to units under a unit trust scheme by virtue of FA 1999 s 122.

[2] Words in sub-s (1) inserted, and sub-s (1A) inserted, by FA 2002 s 114 with effect for instruments executed after 23 July 2002.

Entries upon Rolls, Books, etc

16 Rolls, books etc, to be open to inspection

Every public officer having in his custody any rolls, books, records, papers, documents, or proceedings, the inspection whereof may tend to secure any duty, or to prove or lead to the discovery of any fraud or omission in relation to any duty, shall at all reasonable times permit any person thereto authorised by the Commissioners to inspect the rolls, books, records, papers, documents, and proceedings, and to take such notes and extracts as he may deem necessary, without fee or reward, and in case of refusal shall for every offence incur [a penalty not exceeding £300][1].

Cross references—See FA 1946 s 56 ("public officers" includes the trustees and managers of a unit trust scheme, and their agents, officers or servants).

Amendments—[1] Words substituted by FA 1999 s 114, Sch 17 para 3 with effect in relation to penalties in respect of things done or omitted after 30 September 1999.

17 Penalty for enrolling, etc, instrument not duly stamped

If any person whose office it is to enrol, register, or enter in or upon any rolls, books, or records any instrument chargeable with duty, enrols, registers, or enters any such instrument not being duly stamped, he shall incur [a penalty not exceeding £300][1].

Amendments—[1] Words in sub-s (1) substituted by FA 1999 s 114, Sch 17 para 3 with effect in relation to penalties in respect of things done or omitted after 30 September 1999.

PART II
REGULATIONS APPLICABLE TO PARTICULAR INSTRUMENTS

Instruments of Apprenticeship

25 Meaning of instrument of apprenticeship

Every writing relating to the service or tuition of any apprentice, clerk, or servant placed with any master to learn any profession, trade, or employment (except articles of clerkship to a solicitor or law agent or writer to the signet) is to be deemed an instrument of apprenticeship.

Amendments—This section repealed by the Statute Law (Repeals) Act 2008 s 1, Sch 1 Part 8 with effect from 21 July 2008.

Bills of Sale

41 Bills of sale

A bill of sale is not to be registered under any Act for the time being in force relating to the registration of bills of sale unless the original, duly stamped, is produced to the proper officer.

Charter-parties

49 Provisions as to duty on charter-party

(1) For the purposes of this Act the expression "charter-party" includes any agreement or contract for the charter of any ship or vessel or any memorandum, letter, or other writing between the captain, master, or owner of any ship or vessel, and any other person for or relating to the freight or conveyance of any money, goods, or effects on board of the ship or vessel.

(2) …[1, 2]

Amendments—[1] Sub-s (2) repealed by FA 1949 s 52(10), Sch 11 Pt V and FA (Northern Ireland) 1949 s 16, Sch 4 Pt II.

[2] This section repealed by the Statute Law (Repeals) Act 2008 s 1, Sch 1 Part 8 with effect from 21 July 2008.

Conveyances on Sale

54 Meaning of "conveyance on sale"

Amendments—This section repealed by FA 1999 Sch 20 Pt V(2) with effect in relation to instruments executed, or bearer instruments issued, from 1 October 1999, subject to the provisions in FA 1999 Sch 20 Pt V(2) Note 2. Previously the text read:

"For the purposes of this Act the expression "conveyance on sale" includes every instrument, and every decree or order of any court or of any commissioners, whereby any property, or any estate or interest in any property, upon the sale thereof is transferred to or vested in a purchaser, or any other person on his behalf or by his direction.".

55 How *ad valorem* duty to be calculated in respect of stock and securities

(1) Where the consideration, or any part of the consideration, for a conveyance on sale consists of any stock or marketable security, the conveyance is to be charged with *ad valorem* duty in respect of the value of the stock or security.

[(1A) For the purposes of subsection (1), it is immaterial—

(*a*) whether, at the time of the execution of the conveyance on sale, the stock or marketable security is or has been issued or is to be issued; and

(*b*) in a case where the stock or marketable security is to be issued, when it is to be, or is, issued and whether the issue is certain or contingent.][1]

(2) Where the consideration, or any part of the consideration, for a conveyance on sale consists of any security not being a marketable security, the conveyance is to be charged with *ad valorem* duty in respect of the amount due on the day of the date thereof for principal and interest upon the security.

Amendments—[1] Sub-s (1A) inserted by FA 2000 s 126(1), (2), with effect for instruments executed after 27 July 2000.

56 How consideration consisting of periodical payments to be charged

(1) Where the consideration, or any part of the consideration, for a conveyance on sale consists of money payable periodically for a definite period not exceeding twenty years, so that the total amount to be paid can be previously ascertained, the conveyance is to be charged in respect of that consideration with *ad valorem* duty on such total amount.

(2) Where the consideration, or any part of the consideration, for a conveyance on sale consists of money payable periodically for a definite period exceeding twenty years or in perpetuity, or for any indefinite period not terminable with life, the conveyance is to be charged in respect of that consideration with *ad valorem* duty on the total amount which will or may, according to the terms of sale, be payable during the period of twenty years next after the day of the date of the instrument.

(3) Where the consideration, or any part of the consideration, for a conveyance on sale consists of money payable periodically during any life or lives, the conveyance is to be charged in respect of that consideration with *ad valorem* duty on the amount which will or may, according to the terms of sale, be payable during the period of twelve years next after the day of the date of the instrument.

(4) …[1]

Statement of Practice SP 11/91—Interaction of stamp duty and VAT; stamp duty to be calculated on the VAT-inclusive consideration.

Simon's Tax Cases—s 56(2), *Quietlece v IRC* [1983] STC 17; *Blendett Ltd v IRC* [1984] STC 95.

Amendments—[1] Sub-s (4) repealed by FA 1971 s 69, Sch 14 Pt VI, and FA (Northern Ireland) 1971 s 9, Sch 3 Pt I.

57 How conveyance in consideration of a debt, etc, to be charged

Where any property is conveyed to any person in consideration, wholly or in part, of any debt due to him, or subject either certainly or contingently to the payment or transfer of any money or stock, whether being or constituting a charge or incumbrance upon the property or not, the debt, money, or stock is to be deemed the whole or part, as the case may be, of the consideration in respect whereof the conveyance is chargeable with *ad valorem* duty.

Regulations—See the Stamp Duty (Exempt Instruments) Regulations, SI 1987/516.

SP 6/90—Conveyances and transfers of property subject to a debt.

Cross references—See FA 1980 s 102 (reduction in consideration where the debt exceeds the value of the property transferred in payment thereof);

FA 1981 s 107(1), (4) (sale of houses at discount by local authorities; notwithstanding this section, the discount not chargeable with stamp duty in respect of instruments executed after 22 March 1981);

F(No 2)A 1983 s 15(1) (this section not to apply in relation to conveyances or transfers by which disposal of land is effected by constituency associations of political parties on reorganisation of constituencies).

58 Direction as to duty in certain cases

(1) Where property contracted to be sold for one consideration for the whole is conveyed to the purchaser in separate parts or parcels by different instruments, the consideration is to be apportioned in such manner as the parties think fit, so that a distinct consideration for each separate part or parcel is set forth in the conveyance relating thereto, and such conveyance is to be charged with *ad valorem* duty in respect of such distinct consideration.

(2) Where property contracted to be purchased for one consideration for the whole by two or more persons jointly, or by any person for himself and others, or wholly for others, is conveyed in parts or parcels by separate instruments to the persons by or for whom the same was purchased for distinct parts of the consideration, the conveyance of each separate part or parcel is to be charged with *ad valorem* duty in respect of the distinct part of the consideration therein specified.

(3) Where there are several instruments of conveyance for completing the purchaser's title to property sold, the principal instrument of conveyance only is to be charged with *ad valorem* duty, and the other instruments are to be respectively charged with such other duty as they may be liable to, but the last-mentioned duty shall not exceed the *ad valorem* duty payable in respect of the principal instrument.

(4) Where a person having contracted for the purchase of any property, but not having obtained a conveyance thereof, contracts to sell the same to any other person, and the property is in consequence conveyed immediately to the sub-purchaser [then, except where—

(*a*) the chargeable consideration moving from the sub-purchaser is less than the value of the property immediately before the contract of sale to him, and

(*b*) the conveyance is not one to which section 107 of the Finance Act 1981 (sales of houses at discount by local authorities etc) applies][1],

the conveyance is to be charged with *ad valorem* duty in respect only of the consideration moving from the sub-purchaser.

(5) Where a person having contracted for the purchase of any property but not having obtained a conveyance contracts to sell the whole, or any part or parts thereof, to any other person or persons, and the property is in consequence conveyed by the original seller to different persons in parts or parcels [then, except where the aggregate of the chargeable consideration for the sale of all such parts or parcels is less than the value of the whole of the property immediately before the contract for their sale or, as the case may be, the first contract for the sale of any of them][1], the conveyance of each part or parcel is to be charged with *ad valorem* duty in respect only of the consideration moving from the sub-purchaser thereof, without regard to the amount or value of the original consideration.

(6) Where a sub-purchaser takes an actual conveyance of the interest of the person immediately selling to him, which is chargeable with *ad valorem* duty in respect of the consideration moving from him, and is duly stamped accordingly, any conveyance to be afterwards made to him of the same property by the original seller shall be chargeable only with such other duty as it may be liable to, but the last-mentioned duty shall not exceed the *ad valorem* duty.

[(7) Any reference in subsection (4) or subsection (5) of this section to chargeable consideration is a reference to consideration which falls to be brought into account in determining the duty (if any) chargeable on the conveyance to the sub-purchaser or, as the case may be, on the conveyance of each of the parts or parcels in question; and in any case where it is necessary for the purposes of either of those subsections to determine [the value at any time of any property, that value shall be taken to be the price which the property might reasonably be expected to fetch on a sale at that time in the open market][3].][2]

Cross references—See FA 1963 s 67(5) (application of this section to "purchaser" and "sale" in that section);

Simon's Tax Cases—s 58(1), *Re Brown Root McDermott Fabricators Ltd's and anor's application* [1996] STC 483.

Modifications—FA 1991 s 112 (modification of this section, with effect from an appointed day, where property mentioned in sub-ss (1), (2) above includes exempt property as defined).

FA 2000 Sch 34 para 3 (modification of this section where part of the property referred to in sub-ss (1), (2) above consists of intellectual property).

FA 2001 Sch 30 para 2(1) (modification of this section where any part or parcel of the property referred to in sub-s (1) above consists of an estate or interest in land situated wholly or partly in a disadvantaged area).

FA 2001 Sch 30 para 2(2) (modification of this section where any part or parcel of the property referred to in sub-s (2) above consists of an estate or interest in land situated wholly or partly in a disadvantaged area, and both or (as the case may be) all the relevant persons are connected with one another).

FA 2003 Sch 20 para 2 (modification of sub-s (1) above where part of the property referred to therein consists of stock and marketable securities).

FA 2003 Sch 20 para 2 (modification of sub-s (2) above where part of the property referred to therein consists of stock and marketable securities and both (or, as the case may be, all) of the relevant persons are connected with one another).

Amendments—[1] Words in sub-ss (4), (5) inserted by FA 1984 s 112(1), (2), (4) where the contract for the sub-sale or the first contract for the sub-sale of a part is entered into after 19 March 1984.

[2] Sub-s (7) inserted by FA 1984 s 112(3), (4).

[3] Words in sub-s (7) substituted by FA 1985 s 82(2), (8) with effect from 26 March 1985.

59 Certain contracts to be chargeable as conveyances on sale

Cross references—See FA 1958 s 34 (instruments chargeable by reference to this heading disregarded for the purposes of that section);

Electricity Act 1989 s 103 (electricity treated as goods for the purposes of this section);

Electricity (Northern Ireland Consequential Amendments) Order, SI 1992/232 (electricity in Northern Ireland treated as goods for the purposes of this section).

Amendments—This section repealed by FA 1999 Sch 20 Pt V(2) with effect in relation to instruments executed, or bearer instruments issued, from 1 October 1999, subject to the provisions in FA 1999 Sch 20 Pt V(2) Note 2. Previously the text read:

"(1) Any contract or agreement … for the sale of any equitable estate or interest in any property whatsoever, or for the sale of any estate or interest in any property except lands, tenements, hereditaments, or heritages, or property locally situate out of the United Kingdom, or goods, wares or merchandise, or stock, or marketable securities, or any ship or vessel, or part interest, share, or property of or in any ship or vessel, shall be charged with the same *ad valorem* duty, to be paid by the purchaser, as if it were an actual conveyance on sale of the estate, interest, or property contracted or agreed to be sold.

(2) Where the purchaser has paid the said *ad valorem* duty and before having obtained a conveyance or transfer of the property, enters into a contract or agreement for the sale of the same, the contract or agreement shall be charged, if the consideration for that sale is in excess of the consideration for the original sale, with the *ad valorem* duty payable in respect of such excess consideration, [but shall not otherwise be chargeable …].

(3) Where duty has been duly paid in conformity with the foregoing provisions, the conveyance or transfer made to the purchaser or sub-purchaser, or any other person on his behalf or by his direction, shall not be chargeable with any duty, and the Commissioners, upon application, either shall denote the payment of the *ad valorem* duty upon the conveyance or transfer, or shall transfer the *ad valorem* duty thereto upon production of the contract or agreement, or contracts or agreements, duly stamped.

(4) …

(5) [Provided that where any such contract or agreement … would, apart from this section, not be chargeable with any duty], and a conveyance or transfer made in conformity with the contract or agreement is presented to the Commissioners for stamping with the *ad valorem* duty chargeable thereon within the period of six months after the first execution of the contract or agreement, or within such longer period as the Commissioners may think reasonable in the

circumstances of the case, the conveyance or transfer shall be stamped accordingly, and the same, and the said contract or agreement, shall be deemed to be duly stamped. Nothing in this proviso shall alter or affect the provisions as to the stamping of a conveyance or transfer after the execution thereof.

(6) Provided also, that the *ad valorem* duty paid upon any such contract or agreement shall be returned by the Commissioners in case the contract or agreement be afterwards rescinded or annulled, or for any other reason be not substantially performed or carried into effect, so as to operate as or be followed by a conveyance or transfer."

60 As to sale of an annuity or right not before in existence

Where upon the sale of any annuity or other right not before in existence such annuity or other right is not created by actual grant or conveyance, but is only secured by bond, warrant of attorney, covenant, contract, or otherwise, the bond or other instrument, or some one of such instruments, if there be more than one, is to be charged with the same duty as an actual grant or conveyance, and is for the purposes of this Act to be deemed an instrument of conveyance on sale.

61 Principal instrument, how to be ascertained

(1) In the cases hereinafter specified the principal instrument is to be ascertained in the following manner:

(*a*), (*b*) …[1]

(*c*) Where in Scotland there is a disposition or assignation executed by the seller, and any other instrument is executed for completing the title, the disposition or assignation is to be deemed the principal instrument.

(2) In any other case the parties may determine for themselves which of several instruments is to be deemed the principal instrument, and may pay the *ad valorem* duty thereon accordingly.

Simon's Tax Cases—s 61(2), *Parinv (Hatfield) Ltd v IRC* [1998] STC 305.

Amendments—[1] Sub-s (1)(*a*), (*b*) repealed by FA 1949 s 52, Sch 11 Pt V, and FA (Northern Ireland) 1949 s 16, Sch 4 Pt II.

Conveyances on any Occasion except Sale or Mortgage

62 What is to be deemed a conveyance on any occasion, not being a sale or mortgage

Concession G5—Transfer of stock from persons to themselves operating as executors' assent.

Statement of Practice SP 11/91—Interaction of stamp duty and VAT: stamp duty to be calculated on the VAT-inclusive consideration.

Cross references—See FA 1902 s 9 (extension of proviso to the retirement of a trustee).

Amendments—This section repealed by FA 1999 Sch 20 Pt V(2) with effect in relation to instruments executed, or bearer instruments issued, from 1 October 1999, subject to the provisions in FA 1999 Sch 20 Pt V(2) Note 2. Previously the text read:

"Every instrument, and every decree or order of any court or of any commissioners, whereby any property on any occasion, except a sale or mortgage, is transferred to or vested in any person, is to be charged with duty as a conveyance or transfer of property.

Provided that a conveyance or transfer made for effectuating the appointment of a new trustee is not to be charged with any higher duty than [50p]."

Duplicates and Counterparts

72 Provision as to duplicates and counterparts

Cross-references—See SDMA 1891 s 12A (Stamping of replicas of documents which have been spoilt or lost).

Amendments—This section repealed by FA 1999 Sch 20 Pt V(2) with effect in relation to instruments executed, or bearer instruments issued, from 1 October 1999, subject to the provisions in FA 1999 Sch 20 Pt V(2) Note 2. Previously the text read:

"The duplicate or counterpart of an instrument chargeable with duty (except the counterpart of an instrument chargeable as a lease, such counterpart not being executed by or on behalf of any lessor or grantor), is not to be deemed duly stamped unless it is stamped as an original instrument, or unless it appears by some stamp impressed thereon that the full and proper duty has been paid upon the original instrument of which it is the duplicate or counterpart."

Exchange and Partition or Division

73 As to exchange, etc

Cross references—See FA 1994 s 241(3), (6) (this section ceases to apply to exchange of property and accordingly in relation to instruments giving effect to the exchange executed after 7 December 1993 in pursuance of contracts made on or after 30 November 1993). See consequential *Amendments* below.

Amendments—This section repealed by FA 1999 Sch 20 Pt V(2) with effect in relation to instruments executed, or bearer instruments issued, from 1 October 1999, subject to the provisions in FA 1999 Sch 20 Pt V(2) Note 2. Previously the text read:

"Where … upon the partition or division of any [estate or interest in land] any consideration exceeding in amount or value one hundred pounds is paid or given, or agreed to be paid or given, for equality, the principal or only instrument whereby the … partition or division is effected is to be charged with the same *ad valorem* duty as a conveyance on sale for the consideration, and with that duty only; and where in any such case there are several instruments for completing the title of either party, the principal instrument is to be ascertained, and the other instruments are to be charged with duty in the manner hereinbefore provided in the case of several instruments of conveyance."

Leases

75 Agreements *for not more than thirty-five years* to be charged as leases

Statement of Practice SP 11/91—Interaction of stamp duty and VAT: stamp duty to be calculated on the VAT-inclusive consideration.

Stamp Taxes

Amendments—This section repealed by FA 1999 Sch 20 Pt V(2) with effect in relation to instruments executed, or bearer instruments issued, from 1 October 1999, subject to the provisions in FA 1999 Sch 20 Pt V(2) Note 2. Previously the text read:

"(1) An agreement for a lease or tack, or with respect to the letting of any lands, tenements, or heritable subjects for any term …, or for any indefinite term, is to be charged with the same duty as if it were an actual lease or tack made for the term and consideration mentioned in the agreement.

[(2) Where duty has been duly paid on an agreement for a lease or tack and, subsequent to that agreement, a lease or tack is granted which either—

(*a*) is in conformity with the agreement, or

(*b*) relates to substantially the same property and term as the agreement,

then the duty which would otherwise be charged on the lease or tack shall be reduced (or, as the case may be, extinguished) by the deduction therefrom of the duty paid on the agreement.]"

77 Directions as to duty in certain cases

(1) A [lease][3], or agreement for a [lease][3], or with respect to any letting, is not to be charged with any duty in respect of any penal rent, or increased rent in the nature of a penal rent, thereby reserved or agreed to be reserved or made payable, or by reason of being made in consideration of the surrender or abandonment of any existing lease, tack, or agreement of or relating to the same subject matter.

(2) A lease made for any consideration in respect whereof it is chargeable with *ad valorem* duty, and in further consideration either of a covenant by the lessee to make, or of his having previously made, any substantial improvement of or addition to the property demised to him, or of any covenant relating to the matter of the lease, is not to be charged with any duty in respect of such further consideration.

(3), (4) …[1]

(5) …[2]

Statement of Practice SP 11/91—Interaction of stamp duty and VAT: stamp duty to be calculated on the VAT-inclusive consideration.

Revenue and other press releases—IR Tax Bulletin August 1995 paras 13–15 (Stamp Office will not seek to refuse exemption under this section merely on the grounds of *de minimis* changes in the property subject to the lease).

Cross references—See the Revenue Act 1909 s 8 (non-application of this section as respects any further consideration in the lease).

Amendments—[1] Sub-ss (3), (4) repealed by FA 1963 ss 56(4), 73(8)(*b*), Sch 14 Pt IV, and FA (Northern Ireland) 1963 ss 5(4), 21, Sch 3 Pt II.

[2] Sub-s (5) repealed by FA 1999 Sch 20 Pt V(2) with effect in relation to instruments executed, or bearer instruments issued, from 1 October 1999, subject to the provisions in FA 1999 Sch 20 Pt V(2) Note 2. Previously the text read:

"(5) An instrument whereby the rent reserved by any other instrument chargeable with duty and duly stamped as a lease or tack is increased is not to be charged with duty otherwise than as a lease or tack in consideration of the additional rent thereby made payable."

[3] "Lease" substituted for the words "lease or tack" by FA 1999 s 112(4), Sch 14 para 2 with effect in relation to instruments executed after 30 September 1999. This does not apply to transfers or other instruments relating to units under a unit trust scheme by virtue of FA 1999 s 122.

Marketable Securities …

83 Penalty on issuing, etc, foreign, etc, security not duly stamped

Every person who in the United Kingdom …[2] assigns, transfers, negotiates, …[2] any foreign security or [Commonwealth][1] government security not being duly stamped, shall incur [a penalty not exceeding £300][3].

Cross references—See FA 1990 ss 109(1), 111(1) (this section not to apply from an appointed day).

Note—This section was to be repealed by FA 1990 Sch 19 Pt VI with effect from an appointed day in accordance with FA 1990 ss 107–111. The Treasury order specifying the appointed day for the purposes of FA 1990 ss 107–110 was to coincide with the start of paperless trading under the Stock Exchange's planned TAURUS system (IR press release, 20-3-90). However, on 11-3-93 the London Stock Exchange News Release 6/93 announced that TAURUS had been abandoned.

Amendments—[1] Word substituted by FA 1963 s 62(4), and FA (Northern Ireland) 1963 s 11(3).

[2] Words repealed by FA 1973 s 59(7), Sch 22 Pt V.

[3] Words substituted by FA 1999 s 114, Sch 17 para 3 with effect in relation to penalties in respect of things done or omitted after 30 September 1999.

Stock Certificates to Bearer

109 Penalty for issuing stock certificate unstamped

(1) Where the holder of a stock certificate to bearer has been entered on the register of the local authority as the owner of the share of stock described in the certificate, the certificate shall be forthwith cancelled so as to be incapable of being re-issued to any person.

(2) …[1]

Cross references—See FA 1899 s 5(2) (application of this section to any instrument chargeable with stamp duty as a stock certificate to bearer, and as if "company or body of persons" were mentioned as well as "local authority");

FA 1990 ss 109(2)(*a*), 111(1) (this section not to apply from an appointed day).

Note—Sub-s (1) was to be repealed by FA 1990 Sch 19 Pt VI with effect from an appointed day in accordance with FA 1990 ss 107–111. The Treasury order specifying the appointed day for the purposes of FA 1990 ss 107–110 was to coincide with the start of paperless trading under the Stock Exchange's planned TAURUS system (IR press release, 20-3-90). However, on 11-3-93 the London Stock Exchange News Release 6/93 announced that TAURUS had been abandoned.

Amendments—[1] Sub-s (2) repealed by FA 1963 s 73(8)(*b*), Sch 14 Pt IV, and FA (Northern Ireland) 1963 s 21, Sch 3 Pt II.

Warrants for Goods

111 Provisions as to warrants for goods

(1) For the purposes of this Act the expression "warrant for goods" means any document or writing, being evidence of the title of any person therein named, or his assigns, or the holder thereof, to the property in any goods, wares, or merchandise lying in any warehouse or dock, or upon any wharf, and signed or certified by or on behalf of the person having the custody of the goods, wares, or merchandise.

(2), (3) …[1, 2]

Amendments—[1] Sub-ss (2), (3) repealed by FA 1949 s 52(10), Sch 11 Pt V, and FA (Northern Ireland) 1949 s 16, Sch 4 Pt II.
[2] This section repealed by the Statute Law (Repeals) Act 2008 s 1, Sch 1 Part 8 with effect from 21 July 2008.

PART III

SUPPLEMENTAL

Miscellaneous

117 Conditions and agreements as to stamp duty void

Every condition of sale framed with the view of precluding objection or requisition upon the ground of absence or insufficiency of stamp upon any instrument executed after the sixteenth day of May one thousand eight hundred and eighty-eight, and every contract, arrangement, or undertaking for assuming the liability on account of absence or insufficiency of stamp upon any such instrument or indemnifying against such liability, absence, or insufficiency, shall be void.

119 Instruments relating to Crown property

Except where express provision to the contrary is made by this or any other Act, an instrument relating to property belonging to the Crown, or being the private property of the sovereign, is to be charged with the same duty as an instrument of the same kind relating to property belonging to a subject.

121 Recovery of penalties

Cross references—See FA 1986 ss 68(6), 71(6) (extension of this section to fines imposed for failure to inform the Commissioners of certain facts in relation to depository receipts and clearance services).
Note—The functions of the Lord Advocate are hereby transferred to the Advocate General for Scotland by virtue of the Transfer of Functions (Lord Advocate and Advocate General for Scotland) Order, SI 1999/679.
Amendments—This section repealed by FA 1999 Sch 20 Pt V(3) with effect in relation to things done or omitted from 1 October 1999.

122 Definitions

(1) In this Act, unless the context otherwise requires,—

The expression "Commissioners" means Commissioners of Inland Revenue:

The expression "material" includes every sort of material upon which words or figures can be expressed:

The expression "instrument" includes every written document:

The expression "stamp" means as well a stamp impressed by means of a die as an adhesive stamp:

The expression "stamped", with reference to instruments and material, applies as well to instruments and material impressed with stamps by means of a die as to instruments and material having adhesive stamps affixed thereto:

The expressions "executed" and "execution", with reference to instruments not under seal, mean signed and signature [(but subject to subsection (1A) of this section)][3]:

The expression "money" includes all sums expressed in British or in any foreign or colonial currency:

The expression "stock" includes any share in any stocks or funds transferable [by the Registrar of Government Stock][6] …[5], [any strip (within the meaning of section 47 of the Finance Act 1942) of any such stocks or funds,][4] …[1], and any share in the stocks or funds of any foreign or colonial state or government, or in the capital stock or funded debt of any county council, corporation, company, or society in the United Kingdom, or of any foreign or colonial corporation, company, or society:

The expression "marketable security" means a security of such a description as to be capable of being sold in any stock market in the United Kingdom:

The expression "steward" of a manor includes deputy steward.[7]

[The expression "tribunal" means the First-tier Tribunal or, where determined by or under Tribunal Procedure Rules, the Upper Tribunal][8]

[(1A) For the purposes of this Act a deed (or, in Scotland, a deed for which delivery is required) shall be treated as executed when it is delivered or, if it is delivered subject to conditions, when the conditions are fulfilled.][2]

(2) In the application of this Act to Scotland expressions referring to the High Court shall be construed as referring to the Court of Session sitting as the Court of Exchequer.

Stamp Taxes

Cross references—See FA 1946 s 54(1) ("stock" includes units under a unit trust scheme);
FA 1986 s 81(2) (transactions transferring stock carried out by a market maker in the ordinary course of his business; modification of the definition of "stamp" in sub-s (1) above in respect of stamp denoting exemption from stamp duty).
Amendments—[1] Words in the definition "stock" repealed by the Statute Law (Repeals) Act 1993 s 1(1), Sch 1 Pt IX.
[2] Sub-s (1A) inserted by FA 1994 s 239(1), (3) in relation to any instrument except one which, on or before 7 December 1993, has been executed for the purposes of this Act as it has effect before this amendment.
[3] Words in the definition of "executed" and "execution" in sub-s (1) added by FA 1994 s 239(1), (3) in relation to any instrument except one which, on or before 7 December 1993, has been executed for the purposes of this Act as it has effect before this amendment.
[4] Words in the definition "stock" inserted by FA 1996 Sch 40 para 1.
[5] Words in the definition of "stock" repealed by the Irish Registers of Government Stock (Closure and Transfer) Order, SI 2002/2521 art 10(2), Sch 2, Pt I with effect from 28 October 2002.
[6] Words in the definition of "stock" substituted by Government Stock (Consequential and Transitional Provision) (No 2) Order, SI 2004/1662, art 1, Schedule para 6 with effect from 1 July 2004.
[7] Words repealed by the Statute Law (Repeals) Act 2008 s 1, Sch 1 Pt 8 with effect from 21 July 2008.
[8] Definition of the expression "tribunal" inserted by the Transfer of Tribunal Functions and Revenue and Customs Appeals Order, SI 2009/56 art 3, Sch 1 paras 1, 4 with effect from 1 April 2009.

Repeal; Commencement; Short title

124 Commencement

This Act shall come into operation on the first day of January one thousand eight hundred and ninety-two.

125 Short title

This Act may be cited as the Stamp Act, 1891.

SCHEDULES

FIRST SCHEDULE

STAMP DUTIES ON INSTRUMENTS

Section 1

Statement of Practice SP 11/91—Interaction of stamp duty and VAT: stamp duty to be calculated on the VAT-inclusive consideration.
Simon's Tax Cases—*Marx v Estates and General Investments Ltd* [1975] STC 671; *Coventry City Council v IRC* [1978] STC 151; *Cummins Engine Co Ltd v IRC* [1981] STC 604; *L M Tenancies 1 plc v IRC* [1998] STC 326.
Notes—This schedule repealed by FA 1999 Sch 20 Pt V(2) with effect in relation to instruments executed, or bearer instruments issued, from 1 October 1999, subject to the provisions in FA 1999 Sch 20 Pt V(2)
For instruments executed, or bearer instruments issued before 1 October 1999, see the text below.
Any reference (express or implied) in any enactment, instrument or other document to any of the headings in Schedule 1 to the Stamp Act 1891 (other than the heading "Bearer Instrument") shall be construed, so far as is required for continuing its effect, as being or, as the case may require, including a reference to the corresponding provision of FA 1999 Sch 13.
Any reference (express or implied) in any enactment, instrument or other document to the heading "Bearer Instrument" in Schedule 1 to the Stamp Act 1891 shall be construed, so far as is required for continuing its effect, as being or, as the case may require, including a reference to FA 1999 Sch 15.

AGREEMENT for a lease or tack, or for any letting.
See LEASE or TACK, and section 75.

AGREEMENT for sale of property.
See CONVEYANCE ON SALE, and section 59.

ANNUITY, conveyance in consideration of:
See CONVEYANCE ON SALE, and section 56.
purchase of:
See CONVEYANCE ON SALE, and section 60.
instruments relating to, upon any other occasion:
See BOND, COVENANT, etc.

ASSIGNMENT or ASSIGNATION.
Upon a sale, or otherwise.
See CONVEYANCE.

[BEARER INSTRUMENT

(1) Inland bearer instrument (other than deposit certificate for overseas stock).	*Duty of an amount equal to three times the transfer duty.*
(2) Overseas bearer instrument (other than deposit certificate for overseas stock or bearer instrument by usage).	*Duty of an amount equal to three times the transfer duty.*
(3) Instrument excepted from paragraph (1) or (2) of this heading.	*Duty of 10p for every £50 or part of £50] of the market value.*

[BEARER INSTRUMENT

(4) Inland or overseas bearer instrument given in substitution for a like instrument duly stamped ad valorem (whether under this heading or not).	*Duty of 10p.*

EXEMPTIONS

1. Instrument constituting, or used for transferring, stock which is exempt from all stamp duties on transfer by virtue of General Exemption (1) in this Schedule or of any other enactment.

2 …

3. Renounceable letter of allotment, letter of rights or other similar instrument where the rights under the letter or instrument are renounceable not later than six months after the issue of the letter or instrument.

BILL OF SALE—

Absolute. See Conveyance on Sale.
And see section 41.

BOND in relation to any annuity upon the original creation and sale thereof.

See CONVEYANCE ON SALE, *and section 60.*

BOND, COVENANT, or INSTRUMENT of any kind whatsoever:

(1) Being the only or principal or primary security for any annuity (except upon the original creation thereof by way of sale or security, and except a superannuation annuity), or for any sum or sums of money at stated periods, not being interest for any principal sum secured by a duly stamped instrument, nor rent reserved by a lease or tack:

For a definite and certain period, so that the total amount to be ultimately payable can be ascertained.	*The same* ad valorem *duty as a bond or covenant for such total amount.*
For the term of life or any other indefinite period: For every £5, and also for any fractional part of £5, of the annuity or sum periodically payable	*10p*

(2) Being a collateral or auxiliary or additional or substituted security for any of the above mentioned purposes where the principal or primary instrument is duly stamped:

Where the total amount to be ultimately payable can be ascertained	*The same* ad valorem *duty as a bond or covenant of the same kind for such total amount.*
In any other case:	
For every £10 and also for any fractional part of £10 of the annuity or sum periodically payable	*5p*

(3) …

BOND given pursuant to the directions of any Act, or of the Commissioners or the Commissioners of Customs, or any of their officers, for or in respect of any of the duties of excise or customs, or for preventing frauds or evasions thereof, or for any other matter or thing relating thereto:

Note—Instruments under this heading are exempt from all stamp duties and the words and figures were repealed by FA 1949 ss 35, 52(10), Sch 8 Pt I, Sch 11 Pt V and FA (Northern Ireland) 1949 ss 8, 16, Sch 2 Pts I, II.

BOND on obtaining letters of administration in … Ireland, or a confirmation of testament in Scotland …

CONVEYANCE or TRANSFER on sale—

Of any property …:
… And see sections 54, 55, 56, 57, 58, 59, 60 and 61.

CONVEYANCE or TRANSFER of any kind not hereinbefore described	*50p*

And see section 62.

COUNTERPART.

See DUPLICATE.

COVENANT in relation to any annuity upon the original creation and sale thereof.

See CONVEYANCE ON SALE, *and section 60.*

COVENANT in relation to any annuity (except upon the original creation and sale thereof) or to other periodical payments.

See BOND, COVENANT, *& c.*

DECLARATION of any use or trust of or concerning any property by any writing, not being a will, or an instrument chargeable with ad valorem duty as a unit trust instrument	*50p*

Stamp Taxes

DISPOSITION of heritable property in Scotland to singular successors or purchasers.

See CONVEYANCE ON SALE.

DISPOSITION of heritable property in Scotland to a purchaser, containing a clause declaring all or any part of the purchase money a real burden upon, or affecting, the heritable property thereby disposed, or any part thereof.

See CONVEYANCE ON SALE...

DISPOSITION in Scotland, containing constitution of feu or ground annual right.

See CONVEYANCE ON SALE, *and section 56.*

DISPOSITION in Scotland of any property or of any right or interest therein not described in this schedule — *50p*

DUPLICATE or COUNTERPART of any instrument chargeable with any duty:

Where such duty does not amount to 50p — { *The same duty as the original instrument.*

In any other case — *50p*

And see section 72.

FEU CONTRACT in Scotland.

See CONVEYANCE ON SALE, *and section 56.*

LEASE or TACK—

(1) …

(2) For any definite term less than a year:

(a) Of any furnished dwelling-house or apartments where the rent for such term exceeds £500 — *£1*

(b) Of any lands, tenements, or heritable subjects except or otherwise than as aforesaid. — *The same duty as a lease for a year at the rent reserved for the definite term.*

(3) For any other definite term or for any indefinite term:

Of any lands, tenements, or heritable subjects—

Where the consideration, or any part of the consideration, moving either to the lessor or to any other person, consists of any money, stock, security or other property:

In respect of such consideration — *The same duty as a conveyance on a sale for the same consideration.*

Where the consideration or any part of the consideration is any rent:

In respect of such consideration:

If the rent, whether reserved as a yearly rent or otherwise, is at a rate or average rate:

	[If the term does not exceed 7 years or is indefinite	*If the term exceeds 7 years but does not exceed 35 years*	*If the term exceeds 35 years but does not exceed 100 years*	*If the term exceeds 100 years*
	£p	*£p*	*£p*	*£p*
Not exceeding £5 per annum.	*Nil*	*0.10*	*0.60*	*1.20*
Exceeding £5 and not exceeding £10.	*Nil*	*0.20*	*1.20*	*2.40*
Exceeding £10 and not exceeding £15.	*Nil*	*0.30*	*1.80*	*3.60*
Exceeding £15 and not exceeding £20.	*Nil*	*0.40*	*2.40*	*4.80*
Exceeding £20 and not exceeding £25.	*Nil*	*0.50*	*3.00*	*6.00*
Exceeding £25 and not exceeding £50.	*Nil*	*1.00*	*6.00*	*12.00*
Exceeding £50 and not exceeding £75.	*Nil*	*1.50*	*9.00*	*18.00*
Exceeding £75 and not exceeding £100.	*Nil*	*2.00*	*12.00*	*24.00*

	[If the term does not exceed 7 years or is indefinite	*If the term exceeds 7 years but does not exceed 35 years*	*If the term exceeds 35 years but does not exceed 100 years*	*If the term exceeds 100 years*
Exceeding £100 and not exceeding £150.	*Nil*	*3.00*	*18.00*	*36.00*
Exceeding £150 and not exceeding £200.	*Nil*	*4.00*	*24.00*	*48.00*
Exceeding £200 and not exceeding £250.	*Nil*	*5.00*	*30.00*	*60.00*
Exceeding £250 and not exceeding £300.	*Nil*	*6.00*	*36.00*	*72.00*
Exceeding £300 and not exceeding £350.	*Nil*	*7.00*	*42.00*	*84.00*
Exceeding £350 and not exceeding £400.	*Nil*	*8.00*	*48.00*	*96.00*
Exceeding £400 and not exceeding £450.	*Nil*	*9.00*	*54.00*	*108.00*
Exceeding £450 and not exceeding £500.	*Nil*	*10.00*	*60.00*	*120.00*
Exceeding £500: for any full sum of £50 and also for any fractional part thereof.	*0.50*	*1.00*	*6.00*	*12.00]*

(4) Of any other kind whatsoever not hereinbefore described *2.00*

And see sections 75, … 77 …

MORTGAGE, BOND, DEBENTURE, COVENANT (except a marketable security otherwise specially charged with duty), and WARRANT OF ATTORNEY to confess and enter up judgment.

(1) Being the only or principal or primary security (other than an equitable mortgage) for the payment or repayment of money—

Not exceeding £300	*5p for every £50 or part of £50 of the amount secured.*
Exceeding £300	*10p for every £100 or part of £100 of the amount secured*

(2) Being a collateral, or auxiliary, or additional, or substituted security (other than an equitable mortgage), or by way of further assurance for the above-mentioned purpose where principal or primary security is duly stamped:

For every £200 and also for any fractional part of £200 of the amount secured *5p*

(3) Being an equitable mortgage:

For every £100, and any fractional part of £100, of the amount secured *5p*

(4) TRANSFER ASSIGNMENT, DISPOSITION or ASSIGNATION of any mortgage, bond, debenture, or covenant (except a marketable security), or of any money or stock secured by any such instrument, or by any warrant of attorney to enter up judgment, or by any judgment within the meaning of the Judgments Enforcement (Northern Ireland) Order 1981:

For every £200 and also for any fractional part of £200, of the amount transferred, assigned, or disposed, exclusive of interest which is not in arrear	*5p*
And also where any further money is added to the money already secured	*The same duty as a principal security for such further money.*

(5) RECONVEYANCE, RELEASE, DISCHARGE, SURRENDER, RESURRENDER, WARRANT TO VACATE, or RENUNCIATION [in whole or in part] of any such security as aforesaid, or of the money thereby secured:

For every £200 and also for any fractional part of £200 of the total amount or value of the money at any time secured *5p*

Note—FA 1971 s 64 abolished stamp duties under this heading.

PARTITION or DIVISION—Instruments effecting:

Stamp Taxes

In the case specified in section 73, see that section.

In any other case *50p*

RELEASE or RENUNCIATION of any property, or of any right or interest in any property—

Upon a sale.

See CONVEYANCE ON SALE.

…

In any other case *50p*

RENUNCIATION.

See …RELEASE.

SUPERANNUATION ANNUITY.

See BOND, COVENANT, &C.

SURRENDER—

…

Of any … kind whatsoever not chargeable with duty as a conveyance on sale … *50p*

TACK of lands, &c, in Scotland.

See LEASE OR TACK.

TRANSFER.

See CONVEYANCE OR TRANSFER.

General exemptions from all stamp duties

(1) Transfer of shares in the Government or Parliamentary stocks or funds or strips (within the meaning of section 47 of the Finance Act 1942) of such stocks or funds.

(2) Instruments for the sale, transfer, or other disposition either absolutely … or otherwise, of any ship or vessel, or any part, interest, share, or property of or in any ship or vessel.

(3) …

(4) Testaments, testamentary instruments, and disposition mortis causa in Scotland.

(5) …

(6) Instruments made by, to, or with the Commissioners of Works for any of the purposes of the Act 15 & 16 Vict., c 28.

Act 15 & 16 Vict c 28—i e Commissioners of Works Act 1852.

Notes—This schedule repealed by FA 1999 Sch 20 Pt V(2) with effect in relation to instruments executed, or bearer instruments issued, from 1 October 1999, subject to the provisions in FA 1999 Sch 20 Pt V(2)

For instruments executed, or bearer instruments issued before 1 October 1999, see the text above.

The word "transfer" substituted for the words "conveyance or transfer" in enactments relating to stamp duty: FA 2003 Sch 20 para 3.

FINANCE ACT 1895

(58 & 59 Vict. Chapter 16)

PART II
STAMPS

12 Collection of stamp duty in cases of property vested by Act or purchased under statutory power

Where after the passing of this Act, by virtue of any Act, whether passed before or after this Act, either—

(*a*) any [stock or marketable securities are][1] vested by way of sale in any person; or

(*b*) any person is authorised to purchase [stock or marketable securities][1];

such person shall within three months after the passing of the Act, or the date of vesting, whichever is later, or after the completion of the purchase, as the case may be, produce to the Commissioners of Inland Revenue a copy of the Act printed by the Queen's printer of Acts of Parliament or some instrument relating to the vesting in the first case, and an instrument of [transfer][1] of the property in the other case, duly stamped with the *ad valorem* duty payable upon a [transfer][1] on sale of the property; and in default of such production, the duty with interest thereon at the rate of five per cent. per annum from the passing of the Act, date of vesting, or completion of the purchase, as the case may be, shall be a debt to Her Majesty from such person.

Cross references—See FA 1991 s 114 (modification of FA 1949 s 36 where the Act mentioned in this section and by virtue of which property is vested or a person is authorised to purchase property is passed on or after an appointed day).

FA 2000 Sch 34 para 5 (where property consists wholly of intellectual property no instrument of conveyance need be produced to the Commissioners under this section).
FA 2003 s 125(2) (this section does not apply to property other than stock or marketable securities).
Amendments—[1] Words substituted by FA 2003 s 125(4), Sch 20 para 4 with effect—
(*a*) in relation to instruments effecting land transactions that—
(i) are SDLT transactions within the meaning of FA 2003 Sch 19 or
(ii) would be such transactions but for an exemption or relief from stamp duty land tax;
(*b*) in relation to other instruments, if they are executed on or after the implementation date for the purposes of stamp duty land tax.
The implementation date is 1 December 2003 (by virtue of SI 2003/2899).
FA 2003 s 125 and Sch 20 have effect subject to FA 2003 Sch 15 para 13(2), (3).

FINANCE ACT 1898

(61 & 62 Vict. Chapter 10)

PART II
STAMPS

6 Removal of doubt as to 54 & 55 Vict c 39, ss 54, 57, so far as regards foreclosure decrees

For the removal of doubts with reference to the effect of sections fifty-four and fifty-seven of the Stamp Act 1891, it is hereby declared that the definition of "conveyance on sale" in the said section fifty-four includes a decree or order for, or having the effect of an order for, foreclosure. Provided that—

(*a*) the *ad valorem* stamp duty upon any such decree or order shall not exceed the duty on a sum equal to the value of the property to which the decree or order relates, and where the decree or order states the value that statement shall be conclusive for the purpose of determining the amount of the duty; and
(*b*) where *ad valorem* stamp duty is paid upon such decree or order, any conveyance following upon such decree or order shall be exempt from the *ad valorem* stamp duty.

REVENUE ACT 1898

(61 & 62 Vict. Chapter 46)

PART II
STAMPS

7 Amendments of 54 & 55 Vict c 39

(1) …[2]

(2) Any document referring to any Act or enactment repealed by the Stamp Act 1891, shall unless the context otherwise requires be construed to refer to that Act or the corresponding enactment in that Act.

(3) …[1]

(4) The expression "instrument" in section nine of the Stamp Act 1891, includes any postal packet within the meaning of the [Postal Services Act 2000][4], and subsection two of the said section is hereby repealed.

(5) …[3]

(6) Section twenty-four of the Stamp Duties Management Act 1891, is hereby declared to apply to affidavits and oaths as well as to statutory declarations.

Amendments—[1] Sub-s (3) repealed by the Statute Law Revision Act 1908.
[2] Sub-s (1) repealed by F(1909–10)A 1910, s 96, Sch 6.
[3] Sub-s (5) repealed by FA 1999 Sch 20 Pt V(3) with effect in relation to things done or omitted from 1 October 1999.
[4] Words in sub-s (4) substituted by the Postal Services Act 2000 (Consequential Modifications No 1) Order, SI 2001/1149 art 3(1), Sch 1 para 6 with effect from 26 March 2001.

10 Amendment of 54 & 55 Vict c 38, s 22

(1) Whenever the Commissioners of Inland Revenue give public notice in the London, Edinburgh, Belfast and Dublin Gazettes that the use of any die, as defined by the Stamp Duties Management Act 1891, has been discontinued, then, whether a new die has been provided or not, from and after any day to be stated in the notice (that day not being within one month after the notice is so published), that die shall not be a lawful die for denoting the payment of duty,

and every instrument first executed by any person, or bearing date, after the day stated in the notice, and stamped with duty denoted by the discontinued die, shall be deemed to be not duly stamped.

(2) The provisos to section twenty-two of the Stamp Duties Management Act 1891, shall apply, subject to the necessary modifications, where a notice is published under this section in the same manner as they apply where a notice is published under that section.

(3) ...[1]

Amendments—[1] Sub-s (3) repealed by the Post Office Act 1969 s 141, Sch 11 Pt II.

12 Extension of certain sections of 54 & 55 Vict c 38, to paper used for excise licences

Sections fourteen, fifteen, and sixteen of the Stamp Duties Management Act 1891 (which relate to frauds in connection with the manufacture of paper), shall extend to paper used for excise licences, in like manner as if it were paper provided by the Commissioners of Inland Revenue for receiving the impression of a die.

FINANCE ACT 1899

(62 & 63 Vict. Chapter 9)

PART II
STAMPS

5 Extension of stamp duty on share warrants and stock certificates to bearer

(1) ...[1]

(2) ...[2] section one hundred and nine of the Stamp Act 1891 (which relates to the penalty for issuing stock certificates unstamped), shall apply to any instrument chargeable with stamp duty ...[2] as a stock certificate to bearer in the same manner as it applies to the stock certificates to bearer named in that section, and as if "company or body of persons" were mentioned in subsection one of that section as well as "local authority".

Cross references—See FA 1990 ss 109(2)(*b*), 111(1) (sub-s (2) not to apply with effect from an appointed day).

Note—Sub-s (2) was to be repealed by FA 1990 Sch 19 Pt VI with effect from an appointed day in accordance with FA 1990 ss 107–111. The Treasury order specifying the appointed day for the purposes of FA 1990 ss 107–110 was to coincide with the start of paperless trading under the Stock Exchange's planned TAURUS system (IR press release, 20-3-90). However, on 11-3-93 the London Stock Exchange News Release 6/93 announced that TAURUS had been abandoned.

Amendments—[1] Sub-s (1) repealed by FA 1963 ss 59(1), (3), 73(8)(*b*), Sch 14 Pt IV, and FA (Northern Ireland) 1963 ss 8(1), 21, Sch 3 Pt II.

[2] Words in sub-s (2), in both places, repealed by FA 1963 ss 59(1), (3), 73(8)(*b*), Sch 14 Pt IV, and FA (Northern Ireland) 1963 s 21, Sch 3 Pt II.

14 Construction of Part of Act

This Part of this Act shall be construed together with the Stamp Act 1891.

FINANCE ACT 1900

(63 & 64 Vict. Chapter 7)

PART II
STAMPS

10 Conveyances on sale

A conveyance on sale made for any consideration in respect whereof it is chargeable with *ad valorem* duty, and in further consideration of a covenant by the purchaser to make, or of his having previously made, any substantial improvement of or addition to the property conveyed to him, or of any covenant relating to the subject matter of the conveyance, is not chargeable, and shall be deemed not to have been chargeable, with any duty in respect of such further consideration.

FINANCE ACT 1902

(2 Edw. 7 Chapter 7)

PART II
STAMPS

9 Amendment of 54 & 55 Vict c 39, s 62

Amendments—This section repealed by FA 1999 Sch 20 Pt V(2) with effect in relation to instruments executed, or bearer instruments issued, from 1 October 1999, subject to the provisions in FA 1999 Sch 20 Pt V(2) Note 2. Previously the text read:

"The provision of section sixty-two of the Stamp Act 1891, limiting to [50p] the duty on conveyances or transfers made for effectuating the appointment of a new trustee, shall apply to any conveyance or transfer for effectuating the retirement of a trustee, although no new trustee is appointed."

This Act repealed in full by the Statute Law (Repeals) Act 2008 s 1, Sch 1 Pt 8 with effect from 21 July 2008.

REVENUE ACT 1903

(3 Edw. 7 Chapter 46)

PART II
STAMPS

7 Reduction of stamp duty in the case of substituted securities

Amendments—This section repealed by FA 1999 Sch 20 Pt V(2) with effect in relation to instruments executed, or bearer instruments issued, from 1 October 1999, subject to the provisions in FA 1999 Sch 20 Pt V(2) Note 2. Previously the text read:

"The whole amount of duty payable under or by reference to paragraph two of the heading "Mortgage, Bond, Debenture, Covenant, and Warrant of Attorney", in the First Schedule to the Stamp Act 1891, on any instrument being a collateral or auxiliary or additional or substituted security, or by way of further assurance, shall not exceed [50p]."

FINANCE ACT 1907

(7 Edw. 7 Chapter 13)

PART II
STAMPS

7 Stamping of hire-purchase agreement

Any agreement for or relating to the supply of goods on hire, whereby the goods in consideration of periodical payments will or may become the property of the person to whom they are supplied [shall not be charged with any stamp duty][1].

Amendments—[1] Words substituted by FA 1985 s 85(2), (3) in respect of instruments executed after 25 March 1985 and instruments executed after 18 March 1985 which are not stamped before 26 March 1985.

PART VII
GENERAL

30 Construction, and short title

(1) …[1]

(2) …[2]

Part II of this Act shall be construed together with the Stamp Act 1891.

…[2]

(3) This Act may be cited as the Finance Act 1907.

Amendments—[1] Sub-s (1) repealed by the Statute Law Revision Act 1927.

[2] Words in sub-s (2) repealed by the Statute Law Revision Act 1927, the Customs and Excise Act 1952 s 320, Sch 12 Pt I and FA 1975 ss 52(2), 59(5), Sch 13 Pt I.

REVENUE ACT 1909

(9 Edw. 7 Chapter 43)

PART II
STAMPS

8 Amendment of section 77 of the Stamp Act 1891

The provisions of subsection (2) of section seventy-seven of the Stamp Act 1891 (which exempt a lease from stamp duty in respect of certain further considerations) shall not apply as respects any further consideration in the lease consisting of a covenant which if it were contained in a separate deed would be chargeable with *ad valorem* stamp duty, and accordingly the lease shall in any such case be charged with duty in respect of any such further consideration under section four of the said Act.

PART III
MISCELLANEOUS

12 Construction, and short title

(1) …[2] Part II of this Act shall be construed together with the Stamp Act 1891, and the Acts amending that Act.

(2) …[1]

(3) This Act may be cited as the Revenue Act 1909.

Amendments—[1] Sub-s (2) repealed by the Statute Law Revision Act 1927.
[2] Words in sub-s (1) repealed by the Customs and Excise Act 1952 s 320, Sch 12 Pt I.

FINANCE ACT 1928

(18 & 19 Geo. 5 Chapter 17)

PART III
MISCELLANEOUS

30 Exemptions from income tax, estate duty and stamp duties in case of trust funds and gifts for reduction of National Debt

(1) …[1]

(2)–(3) …[2]

(4) Any instrument by which any property is transferred to trustees to be held upon trust in accordance with directions which are valid and effective under the said section nine or by which any property is conveyed by way of absolute gift to the National Debt Commissioners to be applied by them in reduction of the National Debt shall be exempt from stamp duty.

Amendments—[1] Sub-s (1) repealed by ICTA 1952 s 527, Sch 25 Pt I.
[2] Sub-ss (2), (3) repealed by FA 1975 ss 52(2), 59(5), Sch 13 Pt I.

35 Construction, short title, application and repeal

(1) …[3]

(2) …[2]

(3) Any reference in this Act to any enactment shall be construed as a reference to that enactment as amended by any subsequent enactment, including this Act.

(4) This Act may be cited as the Finance Act 1928.

(5) Such provisions of this Act as relate to matters with respect to which the Parliament of Northern Ireland has power to make laws shall not extend to Northern Ireland.

(6) …[1]

Amendments—[1] Sub-s (6) repealed by the Statute Law Revision Act 1950.
[2] Sub-s (2) repealed by the Statute Law Revision Act 1953.
[3] Sub-s (1) repealed by the Statute Law (Repeals) Act 1986.

FINANCE ACT 1930

(20 & 21 Geo. 5 Chapter 28)

PART IV
STAMPS

42 Relief from transfer stamp duty in case of transfer of property as between associated companies

(1) Stamp duty under [Part I of Schedule 13 to the Finance Act 1999 ([transfer][9] on sale)][6], shall not be chargeable on an instrument to which this section applies:

Provided that no such instrument shall be deemed to be duly stamped unless either it is stamped with the duty to which it would but for this section be liable, or it has in accordance with the provisions of section twelve of the said Act been stamped with a particular stamp denoting either that it is not chargeable with any duty or that it is duly stamped.

[(2) This section applies to any instrument as respects which it is shown to the satisfaction of the Commissioners [that—

(*a*) the effect of the instrument is to convey or transfer a beneficial interest in property from one body corporate [("the transferor") to another ("the transferee")][8], and

(*b*) the bodies in question are associated at the time the instrument is executed][2]][1]

[unless at the time the instrument is executed arrangements are in existence by virtue of which at that or some later time any person has or could obtain, or any persons together have or could obtain, control of the transferee but not of the transferor.][7]

[(2A) For the purposes of this section bodies corporate are associated at a particular time if at that time one is the parent of the other or another body corporate is the parent of each.][2]

[(2B) For the purposes of this section one body corporate is the parent of another at a particular time if at that time the first body—

[(*a*)][7] is beneficial owner of not less than 75 per cent of the ordinary share capital of the second body][3];

[(*b*) is beneficially entitled to not less than 75 per cent of any profits available for distribution to equity holders of the second body; and

(*c*) would be beneficially entitled to not less than 75 per cent of any assets of the second body available for distribution to its equity holders on a winding-up.][7]

[(3) The ownership referred to in [paragraph (*a*) of][7] subsection [(2B)][4] is ownership either directly or through another body corporate or other bodies corporate, or partly directly and partly through another body corporate or other bodies corporate, and Part I of Schedule 4 to the Finance Act 1938 (determination of amount of capital held through other bodies corporate) shall apply for the purposes of [that paragraph][8] ...[4]][1]

[(4) In this section "ordinary share capital", in relation to a body corporate, means all the issued share capital (by whatever name called) of the body corporate, other than capital the holders of which have a right to a dividend at a fixed rate but have no other right to share in the profits of the body corporate.][5]

[(5) Schedule 18 to the Income and Corporation Taxes Act 1988 shall apply for the purposes of paragraphs (*b*) and (*c*) of subsection (2B) as it applies for the purposes of paragraphs (*a*) and (*b*) of section 413(7) of that Act; but this is subject to subsection (6).

(6) In determining for the purposes of this section whether a body corporate is the parent of the transferor, paragraphs 5(3) and 5B to 5E of Schedule 18 to the Income and Corporation Taxes Act 1988 shall not apply for the purposes of paragraph (*b*) or (*c*) of subsection (2B).

(7) In this section, "control" shall be construed in accordance with section 840 of the Income and Corporation Taxes Act 1988.][7]

Cross references—See FA 1967 s 27(3) (this section shall not apply to any instrument executed on or after 1 August 1967 unless it is shown to the satisfaction of the Commissioners that the instrument was not executed in pursuance of or in connection with an arrangement specified under that section).

See Stamp Duty and Stamp Duty Reserve Tax (Open-ended Investment Companies) Regulations, SI 1997/1156 reg 11 (disapplication of s 42 as regards any beneficial interest in property transferred to or from an open-ended investment company).

Statement of Practice SP 3/98—Stamp duty—group relief.

Amendments—[1] Sub-ss (2), (3) substituted by FA 1967 s 27(2).

[2] Words in sub-s (2) substituted by FA 1995 s 149(2), (7), in relation to instruments executed after 30 April 1995.

[3] Sub-ss (2A), (2B) inserted by FA 1995 s 149(3), (7) in relation to instruments executed after 30 April 1995.

[4] Word in sub-s (3) substituted and words omitted repealed by FA 1995 s 149(4), (7), Sch 29, Pt X, in relation to instruments executed after 30 April 1995.

[5] Sub-s (4) inserted by FA 1995 s 149(5), (7) in relation to instruments executed after 30 April 1995.

[6] Words in sub-s (1) substituted by FA 1999 s 112(4), Sch 14 para 3 with effect in relation to instruments executed after 30 September 1999. This does not apply to transfers or other instruments relating to units under a unit trust scheme by virtue of FA 1999 s 122. Previously the text read "the heading 'Conveyance or Transfer on Sale' in the First Schedule to the Stamp Act 1891".

[7] Words in sub-s (2) after para (*b*), in sub-s (2B) reference to "(*a*)" and whole of paras (*b*), (*c*), and words in sub-s (3) inserted, and sub-ss (5), (6), (7) inserted by FA 2000 s 123(3), (4), (5)(*a*), (6), with effect for instruments executed after 27 July 2000.

[8] Words in sub-s (2) substituted for "to another", words in sub-s (3) substituted for "this section" by FA 2000 s 123(2), (5)(*b*), with effect for instruments executed after 28 July 2000.
[9] The word "transfer" substituted for the words "conveyance or transfer" in enactments relating to stamp duty by FA 2003 Sch 20 para 3.

PART VI
MISCELLANEOUS AND GENERAL

53 Construction, short title, application and repeal

(1) ...[3]

(2) ...[2]

(3) ...[4]

(4) Part IV of this Act shall be construed as one with the Stamp Act 1891.

(5) Any reference in this Act to any enactment shall be construed as a reference to that enactment as amended by any subsequent enactment, including this Act.

(6) This Act may be cited as the Finance Act 1930.

(7) Such of the provisions of this Act as relate to matters with respect to which the Parliament of Northern Ireland has power to make laws shall not extend to Northern Ireland.

(8) ...[1]

Amendments—[1] Sub-s (8) repealed by the Statute Law Revision Act 1950.
[2] Sub-s (2) repealed by the Statute Law Revision Act 1953.
[3] Sub-s (1) repealed by FA 1964 s 26(7), Sch 9.
[4] Sub-s (3) repealed by FA 1975 ss 52(2), 59(5), Sch 13 Pt I.

FINANCE ACT 1931

(21 & 22 Geo. 5 Chapter 28)

PART III
LAND VALUE TAX

28 Production to Commissioners of instruments transferring land

(1) On the occasion of—

(*a*) any transfer on sale of the fee simple of land;
(*b*) the grant of any lease of land for a term of seven or more years;
(*c*) any transfer on sale of any such lease;

it shall be the duty of the transferee, lessee, or proposed lessee to produce to the Commissioners the instrument by means of which the transfer is effected, or the lease granted or agreed to be granted, as the case may be, and to comply with the requirements of the Second Schedule to this Act, and if he fails so to produce any such instrument within thirty days after the execution thereof or, in the case of an instrument first executed at any place out of Great Britain after the instrument is first received in Great Britain, or fails to comply with the requirements of the said Schedule, he shall be liable on summary conviction to a fine not exceeding [level 3 on the standard scale][1].

(2) Where in accordance with the provisions of the last foregoing subsection any agreement for any lease of land for a term of seven or more years has been produced to the Commissioners, and the requirements of the said Second Schedule with respect thereto are complied with, it shall not be necessary under this section to produce to the Commissioners the instrument granting the lease in pursuance of the agreement or to comply with the requirements of the said Schedule with respect thereto, unless that instrument is inconsistent with the agreement, but the Commissioners shall, if any such instrument is produced to them and application is made for that purpose, denote on the instrument that the instrument has been so produced.

(3) This section shall not apply with respect to any instrument which relates[

(*a*)][4] solely to incorporeal hereditaments or to a grave or right of burial ...[2][; or
(*b*) to an SDLT transaction within the meaning of paragraph 1(2) of Schedule 19 to the Finance Act 2003.][4]

(4) Notwithstanding anything in section twelve of the Stamp Act 1891, no instrument required by this section to be produced to the Commissioners shall be deemed, for the purposes of section fourteen of that Act, to be duly stamped unless it is stamped with a stamp denoting that the instrument has been so produced.

(5) This section shall come into operation on the first day of September, nineteen hundred and thirty-one.

[(6) …][3]

Press releases etc—IR Tax Bulletin August 1995 para 28 (an agreement for lease presented with the lease giving effect to it within 30 days of execution of the lease will satisfy the requirements of s 28 above).

Cross references—See FA 1985 s 89(1) (this section not to apply in relation to instruments prescribed by regulations made by statutory instruments).

Amendments—[1] Words substituted by virtue of the Criminal Justice Act 1982 ss 38, 46 (replacing previous increase in fine by Land Commission Act 1967 s 87(1), Sch 14, to £50).

[2] Words in sub-s (3) repealed by the Land Commission Act 1967 s 101, Sch 17.

[3] Sub-s (6) inserted by the Land Commission Act 1967 s 87(1), Sch 14, and repealed by the Statute Law (Repeals) Act 1998 Sch 1 Pt IV Group 2 with effect from 19 November 1998.

[4] Sub-s (3)(*a*) numbered as such, and sub-s (3)(*b*) inserted by the Stamp Duty Land Tax (Consequential Amendment of Enactments) Regulations, SI 2003/2867, reg 2, Schedule para 4 with effect from 1 December 2003.

34 Provisions as to expenses

Any expenses incurred by the Commissioners …[1] for the purposes of this Part of this Act …[1] shall be paid out of moneys provided by Parliament.

Amendments—[1] Words repealed by FA 1934 ss 27, 30, Sch 4.

44 Construction, short title, application and repeal

(1) …[3]

(2) …[2]

(3) Any reference in this Act to any enactment shall be construed as a reference to that enactment as amended by any subsequent enactment, including this Act.

(4) This Act may be cited as the Finance Act 1931.

(5) Such of the provisions of this Act as relate to matters with respect to which the Parliament of Northern Ireland has power to make laws shall not extend to Northern Ireland.

(6) …[1]

Amendments—[1] Sub-s (6) repealed by the Statute Law Revision Act 1950.

[2] Sub-s (2) repealed by the Statute Law Revision Act 1953.

[3] Sub-s (1) repealed by the Statute Law (Repeals) Act 1971.

SCHEDULES

[SCHEDULE 2

REQUIREMENTS IN CONNECTION WITH PRODUCTION OF INSTRUMENTS OF TRANSFER

1 Any person required by section 28 of this Act to produce any instrument to the Commissioners shall furnish to the Commissioners with the instrument a document (signed by the transferee or lessee or by some person on his behalf and showing his address) giving particulars—

(*a*) of the description of the instrument;

(*b*) of the date of the instrument;

(*c*) of the names and addresses of the transferor and transferee or lessor and lessee;

(*d*) of the situation of the land to which the transaction relates, including any dimensions stated in the instrument and, if necessary for the identification of the land, a description of the boundaries of the land, or a plan;

(*e*) of the estate or interest transferred, including, where the transaction is the assignment or grant of a lease or the transfer of a fee simple subject to a lease, the term of the lease, the date of the commencement of the term and the rent reserved;

(*f*) of the consideration, if any, other than the rent shown under sub-paragraph (*e*), showing separately any capital payment, any debt released, any debt covenanted to be paid or to which the transaction is made subject, any periodical payment (including any charge) covenanted to be paid, any terms surrendered, any land exchanged and any other thing representing money or money's worth comprised in the consideration for the transaction;

(*g*) of any minerals, mineral rights, sporting rights, timber or easements reserved, and of any restrictions, covenants or conditions affecting the value of the estate or interest transferred or granted; and

(*h*) of the information given to the transferee or lessee by any relevant authority when requested, in connection with the transaction, to state what entries (if any) relating to the land to which the transaction relates were shown in any relevant register.

2 In paragraph 1(*h*)—

(*a*) in relation to land in England or Wales—

"relevant authority" means a local planning authority within the meaning of the Town and Country Planning Act 1990, and

"relevant register" means a register kept by the authority under section 69(1) of that Act;

(*b*) in relation to land in Scotland—

"relevant authority" means a local authority within the meaning of the Town and Country Planning (Scotland) Act 1997, and "relevant register" means a register kept by the authority under section 36(1) of that Act.][1]

Cross references—See FA 1985 s 89(2) (exemption from s 28 of this Act in relation to prescribed instruments; powers to obtain particulars mentioned in this Schedule in respect of such exempt instruments).

Amendments—[1] Sch 2 substituted by the Statute Law (Repeals) Act 1998 Sch 2 para 10 with effect from 19 November 1998.

FINANCE ACT 1938

(1 & 2 Geo. 6 Chapter 46)

PART V
NATIONAL DEFENCE CONTRIBUTION

42 Further provisions as to subsidiary companies

(1) For the purposes of this section and section twenty-two of the Finance Act 1937 (which provides for the amalgamation for the purposes of the national defence contribution of the profits or losses of bodies corporate with the profits or losses of their subsidiaries), a body corporate shall be deemed to be a subsidiary of another body corporate if and so long as not less than three-quarters of its ordinary share capital is owned by that other body corporate, whether directly or through another body corporate or other bodies corporate, or partly directly and partly through another body corporate or other bodies corporate.

(2) The amount of ordinary share capital of one body corporate owned by a second body corporate through another body corporate or other bodies corporate, or partly directly and partly through another body corporate or other bodies corporate, shall be determined in accordance with the provisions of Part I of the Fourth Schedule to this Act.

(3) In this section and Part I of the said Schedule references to ownership shall be construed as references to beneficial ownership, and the expression "ordinary share capital", in relation to a body corporate, means all the issued share capital (by whatever name called) of the body corporate, other than capital the holders whereof have a right to a dividend at a fixed rate or a rate fluctuating in accordance with the standard rate of income tax, but have no other right to share in the profits of the body corporate.

PART VII
MISCELLANEOUS AND GENERAL

55 Short title, construction, extent and repeals

(1) This Act may be cited as the Finance Act 1938.

(2) …[3]

(3) …[2]

(4) …[4]

(5) Any reference in this Act to any other enactment shall be construed as a reference to that enactment as amended by any subsequent enactment, (unless the context otherwise requires) this Act.

(6) Such of the provisions of this Act as relate to matters with respect to which the Parliament of Northern Ireland has power to make laws shall not extend to Northern Ireland.

(7) …[1]

Amendments—[1] Sub-s (7) repealed by the Statute Law Revision Act 1950.
[2] Sub-s (3) repealed by the Statute Law Revision Act 1953.
[3] Sub-s (2) repealed by F(No 2)A 1964 s 10(4), Sch 4.
[4] Sub-s (4) repealed by FA 1975 ss 52(2), 59(5), Sch 13 Pt I.

SCHEDULES

FOURTH SCHEDULE

PROVISIONS RELATING TO SUBSIDIARY COMPANIES FOR PURPOSE OF NATIONAL DEFENCE CONTRIBUTION

Section 42

PART I

PROVISIONS FOR DETERMINING AMOUNT OF CAPITAL HELD THROUGH OTHER BODIES CORPORATE

(1) Where, in the case of a number of bodies corporate, the first directly owns ordinary share capital of the second and the second directly owns ordinary share capital of the third, then, for

the purposes of this Schedule, the first shall be deemed to own ordinary share capital of the third through the second, and, if the third directly owns ordinary share capital of a fourth, the first shall be deemed to own ordinary share capital of the fourth through the second and third, and the second shall be deemed to own ordinary share capital of the fourth through the third, and so on.

(2) In this Part of this Schedule—

(*a*) any number of bodies corporate of which the first directly owns ordinary share capital of the next and the next directly owns ordinary share capital of the next but one and so on, and, if they are more than three, any three or more of them, are referred to as "a series";
(*b*) in any series—

(i) that body corporate which owns ordinary share capital of another through the remainder is referred to as "the first owner";
(ii) that other body corporate the ordinary share capital of which is so owned is referred to as "the last owned body corporate";
(iii) the remainder, if one only, is referred to as an "intermediary" and, if more than one, referred to as "a chain of intermediaries";

(*c*) a body corporate in a series which directly owns ordinary share capital of another body corporate in the series is referred to as an "owner";
(*d*) any two bodies corporate in a series of which one owns ordinary share capital of the other directly, and not through one or more of the other bodies corporate in the series, are referred to as being directly related to one another.

(3) Where every owner in a series owns the whole of the ordinary share capital of the body corporate to which it is directly related, the first owner shall be deemed to own through the intermediary or chain of intermediaries the whole of the ordinary share capital of the last owned body corporate.

(4) Where one of the owners in a series owns a fraction of the ordinary share capital of the body corporate to which it is directly related, and every other owner in the series owns the whole of the ordinary share capital of the body corporate to which it is directly related, the first owner shall be deemed to own that fraction of the ordinary share capital of the last owned body corporate through the intermediary or chain of intermediaries.

(5) Where—

(*a*) each of two or more of the owners in a series owns a fraction, and every other owner in the series owns the whole, of the ordinary share capital of the body corporate to which it is directly related; or
(*b*) every owner in a series owns a fraction of the ordinary share capital of the body corporate to which it is directly related;

the first owner shall be deemed to own through the intermediary or chain of intermediaries such fraction of the ordinary share capital of the last owned body corporate as results from the multiplication of those fractions.

(6) Where the first owner in any series owns a fraction of the ordinary share capital of the last owned body corporate in that series through the intermediary or chain of intermediaries in that series, and also owns another fraction or other fractions of the ordinary share capital of the last owned body corporate, either—

(*a*) directly; or
(*b*) through an intermediary or intermediaries which is not a member or are not members of that series; or
(*c*) through a chain or chains of intermediaries of which one or some or all are not members of that series; or
(*d*) in a case where the series consists of more than three bodies corporate, through an intermediary or intermediaries which is a member or are members of the series, or through a chain or chains of intermediaries consisting of some but not all of the bodies corporate of which the chain of intermediaries in the series consists;

then, for the purpose of ascertaining the amount of the ordinary share capital of the last owned body corporate owned by the first owner, all those fractions shall be aggregated and the first owner shall be deemed to own the sum of those fractions.

FINANCE ACT 1944

(7 & 8 Geo. 6 Chapter 23)

PART VII

MISCELLANEOUS

45 Exemption of certain assignments by seamen from stamp duty

Stamp duty shall not be charged, and shall be deemed never to have been chargeable, on any assignment rendered valid by Regulation forty-seven D of the Defence (General) Regulations 1939 (which relates to assignments of wages in payment of contributions to certain bodies representing the interests of or providing benefits for seamen).

49 Short title, construction, extent and repeals

(1) This Act may be cited as the Finance Act 1944.

(2) ...[5]

(3) ...[4]

(4) ...[3]

(5) ...[1]

(6) ...[6]

(7) Any reference in this Act to any other enactment shall, except so far as the context otherwise requires, be constructed as a reference to that enactment as amended by or under any other enactment, including this Act.

(8) The provisions of the Fourth Schedule to this Act shall, if provision in that behalf is made by an Act of the Parliament of Northern Ireland, apply with any necessary modifications to death duties payable in Northern Ireland as they apply to death duties payable in England, but save as aforesaid such of the provisions of this Act as relate to matters with respect to which the Parliament of Northern Ireland has power to make laws shall not extend to Northern Ireland.

(9) ...[2]

Amendments—[1] Sub-s (5) is spent (and *repealed* by the Statute Law (Repeals) Act 2008 s 1, Sch 1 Pt 8 with effect from 21 July 2008).

[2] Sub-s (9) repealed by the Statute Law Revision Act 1950.

[3] Sub-s (4) repealed by the Statute Law Revision Act 1953.

[4] Sub-s (3) repealed by the Purchase Tax Act 1963 s 41 (1), Sch 4 Pt I.

[5] Sub-s (2) repealed by the Statute Law (Repeals) Act 1971.

[6] Sub-s (6) repealed by FA 1975 ss 52(2), (3), 59(5), Sch 13 Pt I.

FINANCE ACT 1946

(9 & 10 Geo. 6 Chapter 64)

PART VII

STAMP DUTY

Cross references—See FA 1963 s 65 (references to a unit trust scheme shall be deemed not to include references to (*a*) any common investment scheme or common deposit scheme under the Charities Act 1960 ss 22, 22A, or under Charities Act 1993 ss 24, 25(*b*) any unit trust scheme the units in which are, under the trust instrument, required to be held only by bodies of persons established for charitable purposes only, or trustees of trusts so established);

FA 1981 s 110 (references in this Part to unit trust schemes not to include pooled pension funds of exempt occupational pension schemes);

Stamp Duty and Stamp Duty Reserve Tax (Definition of Unit Trust Scheme) Regulations, SI 1992/197 (exemption from stamp duty in relation to transfer of units of a scheme made under the Administration of Justice Act 1982 s 42(1)).

Stamp Duty and Stamp Duty Reserve Tax (Pension Funds Pooling Schemes) Regulations, SI 1996/1584 (exemption from stamp duty in relation to transfers of units of a pension fund pooling scheme).

52 Exemption from stamp duty of documents connected with nationalisation schemes

Where, by any Act passed after the beginning of the present Session which embodies any scheme for the carrying on of any industry or part of an industry, or of any undertaking, under national ownership or control, provision is made for the transfer of any property, as part of the initial putting into force of the scheme, to the Crown or to a body corporate constituted for the purposes of that scheme or any previous scheme for such national ownership or control as aforesaid—

(*a*) in considering whether any and if so what duty is payable under section twelve of the Finance Act 1895 (which requires Acts to be stamped as conveyances on sale in certain cases) the consideration for the transfer shall be left out of account;

(*b*) ...[1]
(*c*) stamp duty shall not be payable on any conveyance, agreement or assignment made or instrument executed solely for the purpose of giving effect to the transfer.

Amendments—[1] Para (*b*) repealed by FA 1973 s 59(7), Sch 22 Pt V.

54 Units under unit trust schemes to be treated as stock

Amendments—This section repealed by FA 1999 s 139, Sch 20 Pt V(5) with effect in relation to instruments executed from 6 February 2000.

56 Supplemental provisions

Amendments—This section repealed by FA 1999 s 139, Sch 20 Pt V(5) with effect in relation to instruments executed from 6 February 2000

57 Interpretation of Part VII

Regulations—See the Stamp Duty and Stamp Duty Reserve Tax (Definitions of Unit Trust Scheme) Regulations, SI 1988/268;
Stamp Duty and Stamp Duty Reserve Tax (Definition of Unit Trust Scheme) Regulations, SI 1992/197.
Cross references—See Stamp Duty and Stamp Duty Reserve Tax (Open-ended Investment Companies) Regulations, SI 1997/1156 reg 3 (sub-ss (1A) and (1B) above have effect in relation to open-ended investment companies as for unit trust schemes).
Amendments—This section repealed by FA 1999 s 139, Sch 20 Pt V(5) with effect in relation to instruments executed from 6 February 2000. The repeals of sub-ss (1A) and (1B) have effect subject to FA 1999 Sch 19 para 17(4). This section was replaced by FA 1999, Sch 19 para 17(3).

67 Short title, construction, extent and repeals

(1) This Act may be cited as the Finance Act 1946.
(2) ...[5]
(3) ...[4]
(4) ...[3]
(5) ...[1]
(6) ...[6]
(7) Part VII of this Act shall be construed as one with the Stamp Act 1891.
(8) Any reference in this Act to any other enactment shall, except so far as the context otherwise requires, be construed as a reference to that enactment as amended by or under any other enactment, including this Act.
(9) Save as otherwise expressly provided, such of the provisions of this Act as relate to matters with respect to which the Parliament of Northern Ireland has power to make laws shall not extend to Northern Ireland.
(10), (11) ...[2]

Amendments—[1] Sub-s (5) is spent.
[2] Sub-s (10), (11) repealed by the Statute Law Revision Act 1950.
[3] Sub-s (4) repealed by the Statute Law Revision Act 1953.
[4] Sub-s (3) repealed by the Purchase Tax Act 1963 s 41(1), Sch 4 Pt I.
[5] Sub-s (2) repealed by the Statute Law (Repeals) Act 1971.
[6] Sub-s (6) repealed by FA 1975 ss 52(2), 59(5), Sch 13 Pt I.

FINANCE ACT 1947

(10 & 11 Geo. 6 Chapter 35)

PART VI

STAMP DUTIES

57 Exemption of transfers of stock guaranteed by Treasury

(1) Where the payment of principal and interest on any stock to which this section applies is guaranteed by the Treasury, transfers of the stock shall be exempt from all stamp duties.
(2) This section applies to ...[2]
...[1]
...[2]
...[1]
...[2] any ...[2] stock to which it may be applied by direction of the Treasury, being stock issued by a body corporate constituted for the purposes of any scheme for the carrying on of any industry or part of an industry, or of any undertaking, under national ownership or control which may be embodied in any Act passed after the beginning of the present Session.

Notes—Transfers of the following stocks are exempt from stamp duty under this provision by reason of directions given by the Treasury:—
British Electricity 3 per cent Guaranteed Stock 1968–1973.
British Electricity 3 per cent Guaranteed Stock 1974–1977.
British Electricity 3 per cent Guaranteed Stock 1976–1979.
British Electricity 4 per cent Guaranteed Stock 1974–1979.
British Gas 3 per cent Guaranteed Stock 1990–1995.
British Gas 4 per cent Guaranteed Stock 1969–1972.
Various British Transport Stocks were also exempted by direction of the Treasury but these have been renamed by the Transport Act 1962 s 36 and now fall within General Exemption (1) Stamp Act 1891.
This section was to be repealed by FA 1990 Sch 19 Pt VI with effect from an appointed day in accordance with FA 1990 ss 107–111. The Treasury order specifying the appointed day for the purposes of FA 1990 ss 107–110 was to coincide with the start of paperless trading under the Stock Exchange's planned TAURUS system (IR press release, 20-3-90). However, on 11-3-93 the London Stock Exchange News Release 6/93 announced that TAURUS had been abandoned.
Amendments—[1] Words in sub-s (2) repealed by the Air Corporations Act 1949 s 41, Sch 3.
[2] Words in sub-s (2) repealed by the Electricity Act 1989 s 112(4), Sch 18.

PART VII
MISCELLANEOUS

74 Short title, construction, extent and repeals

(1) This Act may be cited as the Finance Act 1947.
(2) …[3]
(3) …[2]
(4), (5) …[1]
(6) …[4]
(7) Part VI of this Act shall be construed as one with the Stamp Act 1891.
(8) …[1]
(9) Any reference in this Act to any other enactment shall, except so far as the context otherwise requires, be construed as a reference to that enactment as amended by or under any other enactment, including this Act.
(10) Such of the provisions of this Act as relate to matters with respect to which the Parliament of Northern Ireland has power to make laws shall not extend to Northern Ireland.
(11) …[1]

Amendments—[1] Sub-ss (4), (5), (8), (11) are spent (and sub-s (8) *repealed* by the Statute Law (Repeals) Act 2008 s 1, Sch 1 Pt 8 with effect from 21 July 2008)).
[2] Sub-s (3) repealed by the Purchase Tax Act 1963 s 41(1), Sch 4 Pt I.
[3] Sub-s (2) repealed by FA 1964 s 26(7), Sch 9.
[4] Sub-s (6) repealed by FA 1975 ss 52(2), 59(5), Sch 13 Pt I.

FINANCE ACT 1949

(12, 13 & 14 Geo. 6 Chapter 47)

PART IV
STAMP DUTIES

35 Abolition of and exemptions from other duties

Amendments—This section repealed by FA 1999 Sch 20 Pt V(2) with effect in relation to instruments executed, or bearer instruments issued, from 1 October 1999, subject to the provisions in FA 1999 Sch 20 Pt V(2) Note 2. Previously the text read:
"(1) In relation to instruments made or executed on or after the date of the passing of this Act, the Stamp Act 1891, shall have effect as if it had been enacted
(*a*) without the headings or parts of headings in the First Schedule thereto which are mentioned in Part I of the Eighth Schedule to this Act (and are not so mentioned only in an exemption); but
(*b*) with the exemptions provided for by the said Part I.
(2) The composition mentioned in Part II of the said Eighth Schedule shall no longer be payable, and the duties so mentioned are abolished.
(3) …".

36 Amendments as to conveyances on sale

(1) …[1]
(2) …[1]
(3) …[1]
(4) Section twelve of the Finance Act 1895 (which relates to duty on property vested by Act or purchased under statutory powers), shall not require any person who is authorised after the coming into force of this section to purchase any property as mentioned in the said section twelve to include in the instrument of conveyance required by that section to be produced to the

Commissioners any goods, wares or merchandise forming part of the property nor, if the property consists wholly of goods, wares or merchandise, to produce any instrument of conveyance thereof to the Commissioners.[2]

Cross references—See FA 1991 s 114 (modification of sub-s (4) above, with effect from an appointed day, where exempt property, as defined, is acquired under FA 1895, s 12).

Amendments—[1] Sub-ss (1), (2), (3) repealed by FA 1956 s 44(9), Sch 5 Pt II.

[2] Sub-s (4) is to be amended and sub-s (5) added by FA 1991, s 110(7) with effect from a day to be appointed, where exempt property, as defined, is acquired under FA 1895, s 12.

PART VII

MISCELLANEOUS

52 Short title, construction, extent and repeals

(1) This Act may be cited as the Finance Act 1949.

(2) …[1]

(3) …[2]

(4) …[3]

(5) Part IV of this Act shall be construed as one with the Stamp Act 1891.

(6) …[4]

(7) …[1]

(8) Any reference in this Act to any other enactment shall, except so far as the context otherwise requires, be construed as a reference to that enactment as amended by or under any other enactment, including this Act.

(9) Save as otherwise expressly provided, such of the provisions of this Act as relate to matters with respect to which the Parliament of Northern Ireland has power to make laws shall not extend to Northern Ireland.

(10) …[1]

(11) …

Note—Sub-s (11) is not relevant to this work.

Amendments—[1] Sub-ss (2), (7), (10) are spent.

[2] Sub-s (3) is repealed by the Statute Law Revision Act 1953.

[3] Sub-s (4) repealed by FA 1975 ss 52(2), 59(5), Sch 13 Pt I.

[4] Sub-s (6) repealed by the Statute Law (Repeals) Act 1989.

FINANCE ACT 1951

(14 & 15 Geo. 6 Chapter 43)

PART V

MISCELLANEOUS

42 Exemption from stamp duties of transfers of International Bank stock

(1) Transfers of any stock of the International Bank for Reconstruction and Development shall be exempt from all stamp duties.

(2) This section shall have effect as from the twenty-sixth day of April, nineteen hundred and fifty-one.

Note—This section was to be repealed by FA 1990 Sch 19 Pt VI with effect from an appointed day in accordance with FA 1990 ss 107–111. The Treasury order specifying the appointed day for the purposes of FA 1990 ss 107–110 was to coincide with the start of paperless trading under the Stock Exchange's planned TAURUS system (IR press release, 20-3-90). However, on 11-3-93 the London Stock Exchange News Release 6/93 announced that TAURUS had been abandoned.

44 Short title, construction, extent and repeals

(1) This Act may be cited as the Finance Act 1951.

(2) …[1]

(3) …[2]

(4) …[1]

(5) …[5]

(6) …[3]

(7) …

(8) Such of the provisions of this Act as relate to matters with respect to which the Parliament of Northern Ireland has power to make laws shall not extend to Northern Ireland.

(9) …[4]

Note—Sub-s (7) is not relevant to this work.

Amendments—[1] Sub-ss (2), (4) are spent.
[2] Sub-s (3) repealed by the Statute Law Revision Act 1953.
[3] Sub-s (6) repealed by the Statute Law (Repeals) Act 1971.
[4] Sub-s (9) repealed by the Statute Law (Repeals) Act 1974.
[5] Sub-s (5) repealed by FA 1975 ss 52(2), 59(5), Sch 13 Pt I.

FINANCE ACT 1952

(15 & 16 Geo. 6 & 1 Eliz. 2 Chapter 33)

PART VI

MISCELLANEOUS AND GENERAL

74 Stamp duties (exemption for certain transfers to joint boards or joint committees of local authorities)

(1) Where provision is made either—

(*a*) …[3]

(*b*) by an order under the Public Health Act 1936 or the Local Government (Scotland) Act 1947 for the transfer of any property to a joint board constituted under section six of the said Act of 1936 or to a joint board or joint committee constituted under section one hundred and nineteen or one hundred and twenty of the said Act of 1947, as the case may be, [from another local authority][1];

then, in considering whether any and if so what duty is payable under section twelve of the Finance Act 1895, (which relates to the stamp duty payable in connection with certain statutory conveyances), the consideration for the transfer shall be left out of account.

(2) … [3]

(3) No stamp duty shall be payable on any conveyance, agreement or assignment made, or instrument executed, solely for the purpose of giving effect to a transfer of property to a joint board or joint committee constituted under section one hundred and nineteen or one hundred and twenty of the Local Government (Scotland) Act 1947 [from another local authority][1].

(4) In this section ["local authority" has the meaning assigned to it by section [842A][4] of the Income and Corporation Taxes Act 1988][2].

(5) This section shall be construed as one with the Stamp Act 1891.

Amendments—[1] Words in sub-ss (1)(*b*), (3) substituted by FA 1974 s 52, Sch 12 para 6.
[2] Words in sub-s (4) substituted by TA 1988 Sch 29 para 32 Table.
[3] Sub-ss (1)(*a*), (2) repealed by the Water Act 1989 Sch 27 Pt I with effect from 1 September 1989 by virtue of SI 1989/1530.
[4] Section number in sub-s (4) substituted by FA 1990 s 127(3), (4), Sch 18 para 1 with effect from 1 April 1990.

76 Short title, construction, extent and repeals

(1) This Act may be cited as the Finance Act 1952.

(2) …[1]

(3) …[2]

(4) …[3]

(5) …[1]

(6) Any reference in this Act to any other enactment shall, except so far as the context otherwise requires, be construed as a reference to that enactment as amended or applied by or under any other enactment, including this Act.

(7) Such of the provisions of Parts I and VI of this Act as relate to matters with respect to which the Parliament of Northern Ireland has power to make laws shall not extend to Northern Ireland.

(8) The enactments specified in the Fourteenth Schedule to this Act are hereby repealed to the extent mentioned in the third column of that Schedule, but this repeal has effect—

(*a*)–(*b*) …[4]

(*c*)–(*d*) …[4]

Note—Sub-s (8)(*c*) is not relevant to this work.

Amendments—[1] Sub-s (2), (5), are spent (and *repealed* by the Statute Law (Repeals) Act 2008 s 1, Sch 1 Pt 8 with effect from 21 July 2008).
[2] Sub-s (3) repealed by the Purchase Tax Act 1963 s 41(1), Sch 4 Pt I.
[3] Sub-s (4) repealed by the Income and Corporation Taxes Act 1970 s 538(1), Sch 16.
[4] Sub-s (8)(*a*), (*b*), (*d*) repealed by the Statute Law (Repeals) Act 1974.

FINANCE ACT 1953

(1 & 2 Eliz. 2 Chapter 34)

PART IV

MISCELLANEOUS AND GENERAL

31 Stamp duties

(1) There shall be exempt from all stamp duties instruments of the following descriptions, being instruments made or executed for the purposes of any savings committee, savings group or other similar body affiliated to the National Savings Committee or the Scottish Savings Committee, that is to say—

(*a*) …[2]

(*b*) …[2] any agreement …[3] whereby a person so acting makes himself responsible for money, stamps or other things supplied for the purposes of the body he acts for.

(2) …[1]

(3) This section shall be construed as one with the Stamp Act 1891.

Amendments—[1] Sub-s (2) repealed by FA 1958 s 40, Sch 9 Pt III, and FA 1963 s 73(8), Sch 14 Pt IV.
[2] Sub-s (1)(*a*) and words in sub-s (1)(*b*) repealed by FA 1970 s 36(8), Sch 8 Pt V.
[3] Words in sub-s (1)(*b*) repealed by FA 1971 s 69, Sch 14 Pt VI.

35 Short title, construction, extent and repeals

(1) This Act may be cited as the Finance Act 1953.

(2) …[4]

(3) …[1]

(4) …[2]

(5) Any reference in this Act to any other enactment shall, except so far as the context otherwise requires, be construed as a reference to that enactment as amended or applied by or under any other enactment, including this Act.

(6) Such of the provisions of this Act as relate to matters in respect of which the Parliament of Northern Ireland has power to make laws shall not extend to Northern Ireland, but nothing in this subsection shall affect the application to Northern Ireland of section thirty-three of this Act.

(7) …[3]

Amendments—[1] Sub-s (3) repealed by the Purchase Tax Act 1963 s 41(1), Sch 4 Pt I.
[2] Sub-s (4)(*a*), (*b*) repealed by the Income and Corporation Taxes Act 1970 s 538(1), Sch 16, and sub-s (4)(*c*) is spent (sub-s (4) *repealed* by the Statute Law (Repeals) Act 2008 s 1, Sch 1 Pt 8 with effect from 21 July 2008).
[3] Sub-s (7) repealed by the Statute Law (Repeals) Act 1974.
[4] Sub-s (2) repealed by the Customs and Excise Management Act 1979 s 177(3), Sch 6 Pt I.

FINANCE ACT 1958

(6 & 7 Eliz. 2 Chapter 56)

PART VI

STAMP DUTIES

34 Conveyances on sale, etc

(1)–(3) …[1]

(4) …[3]

(5)–(7) …[1]

(8) …[2]

(9), (10) …[1]

Cross references—See FA 1963 s 55 (certificate in respect of certain conveyances or transfers on sale to be in the form described in sub-s (4) above).

Amendments—[1] Sub-ss (1)–(3), (5)–(7), (9) and (10) repealed by FA 1963 s 73(8), Sch 14 Pt IV.
[2] Sub-s (8) repealed by FA 1970 s 36(8), Sch 8 Pt V.
[3] Sub-s (4) repealed by FA 1999 Sch 20 Pt V(2) with effect in relation to instruments executed, or bearer instruments issued, from 1 October 1999, subject to the provisions in FA 1999 Sch 20 Pt V(2) Note 2. Previously the text read:

"(4) References in this section to an instrument being certified at a particular amount mean that it contains a statement certifying that the transaction effected by the instrument does not form part of a larger transaction or series of transactions in respect of which the amount or value, or aggregate amount or value, of the consideration exceeds that amount; and for this purpose—

(*a*) any sale or contract or agreement for the sale of goods, wares or merchandise shall be disregarded in the case either—

(i) of an instrument chargeable under the said heading "Conveyance or Transfer on sale", other than an actual conveyance or transfer of the goods, wares or merchandise (with or without other property); or

(ii) of an instrument chargeable by reference to that heading under section fifty-nine of the Stamp Act 1891 (which makes a contract or agreement for sale of certain property chargeable with duty as if it were an actual conveyance on sale); and

(*b*) any such statement as aforesaid shall be construed as leaving out of account any matter which in accordance with paragraph (*a*) of this subsection is to be disregarded.".

FINANCE ACT 1959

(7 & 8 Eliz. 2 Chapter 58)

PART IV

STAMP DUTIES

30 Stamp duty on policies of insurance

(1)–(3) …[1]

(4) …[5]

(*a*)–(*b*) …[3]

(*c*) …[1]

…[3] …[5]

(5) …[4]

(6) Notwithstanding the repeal of section ninety-three of the Stamp Act 1891, a contract for such insurance as is mentioned in section five hundred and six of the Merchant Shipping Act 1894, shall continue to be admissible in evidence although not embodied in a marine policy as required by section twenty-two of the Marine Insurance Act 1906.

(7) This section shall apply in relation to instruments made or executed after the beginning of August, nineteen hundred and fifty-nine.

Amendments—[1] Sub-ss (1)–(3) and (4) (*c*) repealed by FA 1970 s 36(8), Sch 8 Pt IV.
[3] Sub-s (4)(*a*), (*b*), and the words omitted from sub-s (4) repealed by the Statute Law (Repeals) Act 1976 Sch 1, Pt XVIII.
[4] Sub-s (5) repealed by the Statute Law (Repeals) Act 1976 Sch 1, Pt XVIII.
[5] Words in sub-s (4) repealed by FA 1989 Sch 17 Pt IX.

PART V

MISCELLANEOUS

37 Short title, construction, extent and repeal

(1) This Act may be cited as the Finance Act 1959.

(2) Parts I to IV of this Act shall be construed as one with the enactments mentioned in this subsection respectively, that is to say—

(*a*) …[3]

(*b*) …[1]

(*c*) …[2]

(*d*) Part IV with the Stamp Act 1891.

(3) Any reference in this Act to any other enactment shall, except so far as the context otherwise requires, be construed as a reference to that enactment as amended or applied by or under any other enactment including this Act.

(4) Such of the provisions of this Act as relate to matters in respect of which the Parliament of Northern Ireland has power to make laws shall not extend to Northern Ireland.

(5) The enactments specified in the Eighth Schedule to this Act are hereby repealed to the extent mentioned in the third column of that Schedule, and, except as otherwise provided in that column, the said repeals shall have effect—

(*a*) …

(*b*) in the case of the enactments specified in Part II thereof, in relation to instruments made or executed after the beginning of August, nineteen hundred and fifty-nine;

(*c*) in the case of the enactments specified in Part III thereof, in relation to any yearly period beginning after the fifth day of April, nineteen hundred and fifty-nine; and

(*d*) …

Note—Sub-s (5)(*a*), (*d*) are not relevant to this work.

Amendments—[1] Sub-s (2)(*b*) repealed by the Purchase Tax Act 1963 s 41(1), Sch 4 Pt I.
[2] Sub-s (2)(*c*) repealed by TA 1970 s 538(1), Sch 16.
[3] Sub-s (2)(*a*) repealed by CEMA 1979 s 177(3), Sch 6 Pt I.

FINANCE ACT 1960

(8 & 9 Eliz. 2 Chapter 44)

PART V
MISCELLANEOUS

74 Visiting forces and allied headquarters (stamp duty exemptions)

(1) Subsections (2) to (4) of this section shall have effect with a view to conferring exemptions from stamp duty (corresponding to exemptions applicable in the case of Her Majesty's forces) in relation to any visiting force of a designated country, and in those subsections "a force" means any such visiting force as aforesaid.

(2) There shall be exempted from all stamp duties any contract, conveyance or other document made with a view to building or enlarging barracks or camps for a force, or to facilitating the training in the United Kingdom of a force, or to promoting the health or efficiency of a force.

(3), (4) ...[1]

(5) Subsections (2) to (4) of this section shall have effect in relation to any designated allied headquarters as if—

(*a*) the headquarters were a visiting force of a designated country;
(*b*) the members of that force consisted of such of the persons serving at or attached to the headquarters as are members of the armed forces of a designated country;
(*c*) the references to the country to which a force belongs included both any designated allied headquarters and, in relation to any such person as aforesaid, the country of whose armed forces he is a member.

(6) For the purposes of this section—

(*a*) "allied headquarters" means any international military headquarters established or to be established under the North Atlantic Treaty;
(*b*) "designated" means designated for the purpose in question by or under any Order in Council;
(*c*) "visiting force" means any body, contingent or detachment of a country's forces which is for the time being or is to be present in the United Kingdom on the invitation of Her Majesty's Government in the United Kingdom.

(7) Any Order in Council under this section may be varied or revoked by a subsequent Order in Council.

(8) ...[2]

(9) This section shall be construed as one with the Stamp Act 1891.

Cross references—See the Visiting Forces and Allied Headquarters (Stamp Duties) (Designation) Order, SI 1961/581 (visiting forces and headquarters);
The Visiting Forces (Stamp Duties) (Designation) Order, SI 1964/925 (visiting forces).
Amendments—[1] Sub-ss (3), (4) repealed by FA 1970 s 36(8), Sch 8 Pt V.
[2] Sub-s (8) repealed by the Northern Ireland Constitution Act 1973 s 41(1), Sch 6 Pt I.

[74A Visiting forces and allied headquarters (stamp duty land tax exemptions)

(1) This section has effect with a view to conferring exemptions from stamp duty land tax corresponding to exemptions applicable in the case of Her Majesty's forces in relation to any visiting force of a designated country.

In this section "a force" means any such visiting force.

(2) A land transaction entered into with a view to building or enlarging barracks or camps for a force, or to facilitating the training in the United Kingdom of a force, or to promoting the health or efficiency of a force, is exempt from charge for the purposes of stamp duty land tax.

(3) Relief under this section must be claimed in a land transaction return or an amendment of such a return.

(4) Subsection (2) of this section has effect in relation to any designated allied headquarters as if—

(*a*) the headquarters were a visiting force of a designated country;
(*b*) the members of that force consisted of such of the persons serving at or attached to the headquarters as are members of the armed forces of a designated country;
(*c*) the references to the country to which a force belongs included both any designated allied headquarters and, in relation to any such person as is mentioned in paragraph (*b*), the country of whose armed forces he is a member.

(5) For the purposes of this section—

(*a*) "allied headquarters" means any international military headquarters established or to be established under the North Atlantic Treaty;
(*b*) "designated" means designated for the purpose in question by or under any Order in Council;

(*c*) "visiting force" means any body, contingent or detachment of country's forces which is for the time being or is to be present in the United Kingdom on the invitation of Her Majesty's Government in the United Kingdom;

(*d*) "land transaction" has the meaning given by section 43(1) of the Finance Act 2003;

(*e*) "land transaction return" has the meaning given by section 76(1) of that Act.][1]

Amendments—[1] Section 74A inserted by the Stamp Duty Land Tax (Consequential Amendment of Enactments) Regulations, SI 2003/2867, reg 2, Schedule, para 6 with effect from 1 December 2003.

STOCK TRANSFER ACT 1963

(1963 Chapter 18)

1 Simplified transfer of securities

(1) Registered securities to which this section applies may be transferred by means of an instrument under hand in the form set out in Schedule 1 to this Act (in this Act referred to as a stock transfer), executed by the transferor only and specifying (in addition to the particulars of the consideration, of the description and number or amount of the securities, and of the person by whom the transfer is made) the full name and address of the transferee.

(2) The execution of a stock transfer need not be attested; and where such a transfer has been executed for the purpose of a stock exchange transaction, the particulars of the consideration and of the transferee may either be inserted in that transfer or, as the case may require, supplied by means of separate instruments in the form set out in Schedule 2 to this Act (in this Act referred to as brokers transfers), identifying the stock transfer and specifying the securities to which each instrument relates and the consideration paid for those securities.

(3) Nothing in this section shall be construed as affecting the validity of any instrument which would be effective to transfer securities apart from this section; and any instrument purporting to be made in any form which was common or usual before the commencement of this Act, or any other form authorised or required for that purpose apart from this section, shall be sufficient, whether or not it is completed in accordance with the form, if it complies with the requirements as to execution and contents which apply to a stock transfer.

(4) This section applies to fully paid up registered securities of any description, being—

(*a*) securities issued by any company within the meaning of the [Companies Act 1985][3] except a company limited by guarantee or an unlimited company;

(*b*) securities issued by any body (other than a company within the meaning of the said Act) incorporated in Great Britain by or under any enactment or by Royal Charter except a building society within the meaning of the Building Societies Act [1986][4] or a society registered under the Industrial and Provident Societies Act 1893;

(*c*) securities issued by the Government of the United Kingdom, except stock or bonds in [the National Savings Stock Register][2] …[1], and except national savings certificates;

(*d*) securities issued by any local authority;

[(*e*) units of an authorised unit trust scheme or a recognised scheme within the meaning of [Part 17 of the Financial Services and Markets Act 2000][7]][5].

[(*f*) shares issued by an open-ended investment company within the meaning of the open-ended Investment Companies Regulations 2001.][6]

Amendments—[1] Words in sub-s 4 (*c*) repealed by FA 1964 ss 24, 26(7), Sch 8 para 10, Sch 9.

[2] Words in sub-s (4)(*c*) substituted by the Post Office Act 1969 s 108(1) (*f*).

[3] Words in sub-s (4)(*a*) substituted by the Companies Consolidation (Consequential Provisions) Act 1985 s 30, Sch 2.

[4] Figures in sub-s (4) (*b*) substituted by the Building Societies Act 1986 s 120(1), Sch 18 Pt I para 5.

[5] Sub-s (4)(*e*) substituted by the Financial Services Act 1986 s 212(2), Sch 16 para 4(*a*).

[6] Sub-s (4)(*f*) substituted by the open-ended Investment Companies Regulations, SI 2001/1228 reg 84, Sch 7 para 2 with effect from 1 December 2001 (by virtue of SI 2001/3538).

[7] Words in sub-s (4)(*e*) substituted by the Financial Services and Markets Act 2000 (Consequential Amendments and Repeals) Order, SI 2001/3649 art 270 with effect from 1 December 2001.

2 Supplementary provisions as to simplified transfer

(1) Section 1 of this Act shall have effect in relation to the transfer of any securities to which that section applies notwithstanding anything to the contrary in any enactment or instrument relating to the transfer of those securities; but nothing in that section affects—

(*a*) any right to refuse to register a person as the holder of any securities on any ground other than the form in which those securities purport to be transferred to him; or

(*b*) any enactment or rule of law regulating the execution of documents by companies or other bodies corporate, or any articles of association or other instrument regulating the execution of documents by any particular company or body corporate.

(2) Subject to the provisions of this section, any enactment or instrument relating to the transfer of securities to which section 1 of this Act applies shall, with any necessary modifications, apply in relation to an instrument of transfer to which it applies apart from this subsection; and without prejudice to the generality of the foregoing provision, [the references to an instrument of

transfer in section 775 of the Companies Act 2006 (certification of instrument of transfer)][5] shall be construed as including a reference to a broker's transfer.

(3) In relation to the transfer of securities by means of a stock transfer and a brokers transfer—

(*a*) any reference in any enactment or instrument (including in particular [section 770(1)(*a*) of the Companies Act 2006 (registration of transfer)][5] ...[3]) to the delivery or lodging of an instrument (or proper instrument) of transfer shall be construed as a reference to the delivery or lodging of the stock transfer and the brokers transfer;

(*b*) any such reference to the date on which an instrument of transfer is delivered or lodged shall be construed as a reference to the date by which the later of those transfers to be delivered or lodged has been delivered or lodged; and

(*c*) subject to the foregoing provisions of this subsection, the brokers transfer (and not the stock transfer) shall be deemed to be the [transfer][4] for the purposes of the enactments relating to stamp duty[2].

(4) ...[1]

Amendments—[1] Sub-s (4) repealed by the Requirements of Writing (Scotland) Act 1995 s 14(2), Sch 5.
[2] Sub-s (3)(*c*) and preceding word "and" repealed by FA 1990, Sch 19, Part VI with effect from a day to be appointed.
[3] Words in sub-s (3)(*a*) repealed by FA 1999 Sch 20 Pt V(5) with effect in relation to instruments executed from 6 February 2000.
[4] The word "transfer" substituted for the words "conveyance or transfer" in enactments relating to stamp duty by FA 2003 Sch 20 para 3.
[5] Words in sub-ss (2), (3)(*a*) substituted by the Companies Act 2006 (Consequential Amendments etc) Order, SI 2008/948 art 3(1), Sch 1 para 37 with effect from 6 April 2008.

Stamp Taxes

3 Additional provisions as to transfer forms

(1) References in this Act to the forms set out in Schedule 1 and Schedule 2 include reference to forms substantially corresponding to those forms respectively.

(2) The Treasury may by order amend the said Schedules either by altering the forms set out therein or by substituting different forms for those forms or by the addition of forms for use as alternatives to those forms; and references in this Act to the forms set out in those Schedules (including references in this section) shall be construed accordingly.

(3) Any order under subsection (2) of this section which substitutes a different form for a form set out in Schedule 1 to this Act may direct that subsection (3) of section 1 of this Act shall apply, with any necessary modifications, in relation to the form for which that form is substituted as it applies to any form which was common or usual before the commencement of this Act.

(4) Any order of the Treasury under this section shall be made by statutory instrument, and may be varied or revoked by a subsequent order; and any statutory instrument made by virtue of this section shall be subject to annulment in pursuance of a resolution of either House of Parliament.

[(5) An order under subsection (2) of this section may—

(*a*) provide for forms on which some of the particulars mentioned in subsection (1) of section 1 of this Act are not required to be specified;

(*b*) provide for that section to have effect, in relation to such forms as are mentioned in the preceding paragraph or other forms specified in the order, subject to such amendments as are so specified (which may include an amendment of the reference in subsection (1) of that section to an instrument under hand);

(*c*) provide for all or any of the provisions of the order to have effect in such cases only as are specified in the order.][1]

Amendments—[1] Sub-s (5) inserted by the Stock Exchange (Completion of Bargains) Act 1976 ss 6, 7(4), and extends to Northern Ireland in accordance with the provisions of s 5(1), (2) of this Act. It came into effect on 12 February 1979 by virtue of SI 1979/55.

4 Interpretation

(1) In this Act the following expressions have the meanings hereby respectively assigned to them, that is to say—

"local authority" means, in relation to England and Wales,

[[(*a*) a billing authority or a precepting authority, as defined in section 69 of the Local Government Finance Act 1992;

[(*aa*) a fire and rescue authority in Wales constituted by a scheme under section 2 of the Fire and Rescue Services Act 2004 or a scheme to which section 4 of that Act applies;][3]][2]

(*b*) a levying body within the meaning of section 74 of [the Local Government Finance Act 1988][3]; and

(*c*) a body as regards which section 75 of that Act applies,][1]

and, in relation to Scotland, a county council, a town council and any statutory authority, commissioners or trustees to whom section 270 of the Local Government (Scotland) Act 1947 applies;

"registered securities" means transferable securities the holders of which are entered in a register (whether maintained in Great Britain or not);

"securities" means shares, stock, debentures, debenture stock, loan stock, bonds, units of a [collective investment scheme within the meaning of the [Financial Services and Markets Act 2000][3], and other securities of any description;

"stock exchange transaction" means a sale and purchase of securities in which each of the parties is a member of a stock exchange acting in the ordinary course of his business as such or is acting through the agency of such a member;

"stock exchange" means the Stock Exchange, London, and any other stock exchange (whether in Great Britain or not) which is declared by order of the Treasury to be a recognised stock exchange for the purposes of this Act.

(2) Any order of the Treasury under this section shall be made by statutory instrument, and may be varied or revoked by a subsequent order.

Amendments—[1] Paras (*a*)–(*c*) in the definition of "local authority" substituted by the Local Government Finance (Repeals, Savings and Consequential Amendments) Order, SI 1990/776 art 8, Sch 3 para 8.

[2] Para (*a*) in the definition of "local authority" substituted for para (*a*) by the Local Government Finance Act 1992 s 117(1), Sch 13 para 12.

[3] Para (*aa*) in the definition of "local authority" and words in para (*b*) substituted by the Fire and Rescue Services Act 2004 s 53, Sch 1 para 18 with effect from 1 October 2004 (by virtue of SI 2004/2304). In Wales, the Fire and Rescue Services Act, in so far as it was not already in force, came into force on 10 November 2004 (by virtue of SI 2004/2917).

[4] Words in the definition of "securities" substituted by the Financial Services and Markets Act 2000 (Consequential Amendments and Repeals) Order, SI 2001/3649 art 271 with effect from 1 December 2001.

5 Application to Northern Ireland

(1) This Act, so far as it applies to things done outside Great Britain, extends to Northern Ireland.

(2) Without prejudice to subsection (1) of this section, the provisions of this Act affecting securities issued by the Government of the United Kingdom shall apply to any such securities entered in a register maintained in Northern Ireland.

(3) ...[1]

(4) Except as provided by this section, this Act shall not extend to Northern Ireland.

Amendments—[1] Sub-s (3) repealed by the Northern Ireland Constitution Act 1973 s 41(1), Sch 6 Pt I.

FINANCE ACT 1963

(1963 Chapter 25)

An Act to grant certain duties, to alter other duties, and to amend the law relating to the National Debt and the Public Revenue, and to make further provision in connection with Finance

[31st July 1963]

PART IV

STAMP DUTIES

Reduction of duties

55 Reduced duty on conveyance or transfer on sale

Amendments—This section repealed by FA 1999 Sch 20 Pt V(2) with effect in relation to instruments executed, or bearer instruments issued, from 1 October 1999, subject to the provisions in FA 1999 Sch 20 Pt V(2) Note 2. Previously the text read:

"(1) Subject to subsections (1A) to (3) below and to the following provisions of this Part of this Act, the stamp duty chargeable under the heading "Conveyance or Transfer on sale" in Schedule 1 to the Stamp Act 1891 shall be charged by reference to the amount or value of the consideration for the sale at the following rates, that is to say—

(*a*) where the amount or value of the consideration is £60,000 or under and the instrument is certified, as described in section 34(4) of the Finance Act 1958 at £60,000, nil;

(*b*) where paragraph (*a*) above does not apply and—

(i) the amount or value of the consideration does not exceed £500, and

(ii) the instrument is certified as described in section 34(4) of the Finance Act 1958 at £250,000, the rate of 50p for every £50 or part of £50 of the consideration;

(*c*) where paragraph (*a*) above does not apply and—

(i) the amount or value of the consideration exceeds £500 but does not exceed £250,000, and

(ii) the instrument is certified as described in section 34(4) of the Finance Act 1958 at £250,000, the rate of £1 for every £100 or part of £100 of the consideration;

(*d*) where paragraphs (*a*) to (*c*) above do not apply and—

(i) the amount or value of the consideration does not exceed £500,000, and

(ii) the instrument is certified as described in section 34(4) of the Finance Act 1958 at £500,000, the rate of [£2.50p] for every £100 or part of £100 of the consideration; and

(*e*) in any other case the rate of [£3.50p] for every £100 or part of £100 of the consideration;]

and any duty chargeable by reference to that heading shall be charged accordingly.

(1A) In relation to duty chargeable under or by reference to the heading mentioned in subsection (1) above as it applies to a conveyance or transfer of stock or marketable securities, that subsection shall have effect as if for the words from "following rates" to the end of paragraph (*e*) there were substituted the words "rate of 50p for every £100 or part of £100 of the consideration".

(2) In relation to duty chargeable by reference to the heading mentioned in subsection (1) above by virtue of the heading "Lease or Tack" in the said Schedule 1 in a case where part of the consideration consists of rent and that rent exceeds £600 a year, subsection (1) above shall have effect as if

(*a*) paragraph (*a*) and, in paragraphs (*b*) and (*c*), the words "paragraph (*a*) above does not apply and" were omitted and

(*b*) in paragraph (*d*) for the words "paragraphs (*a*) to (*c*)" there were substituted the words "paragraphs (*b*) and (*c*)".

(3) Nothing in this section shall affect any enactment imposing an upper limit on the amount of duty chargeable *ad valorem*.

(4) ..."

56 Reduced duty on leases

Amendments—This section repealed by FA 1999 Sch 20 Pt V(2) with effect in relation to instruments executed, or bearer instruments issued, from 1 October 1999, subject to the provisions in FA 1999 Sch 20 Pt V(2) Note 2. Previously the text read:

"(1), (2) ...

(3) For the purposes of the said heading a lease granted for a fixed term and thereafter until determined shall be treated as a lease for a definite term equal to the fixed term together with such further period as must elapse before the earliest date at which the lease can be determined; and section 75 of the said Act of 1891 (agreements for leases) shall be construed accordingly.

(4) Section 76, subsections (3) and (4) of section 77 and section 78 of the said Act of 1891 shall cease to have effect."

57 Miscellaneous reductions

Amendments—This section repealed by FA 1999 Sch 20 Pt V(2) with effect in relation to instruments executed, or bearer instruments issued from 1 October 1999, subject to the provisions in FA 1999 Sch 20 Pt V(2) Note 2. Previously the text read:

"(1)The rates of stamp duty chargeable under or by reference to the following headings or parts of headings in Schedule 1 to the Stamp Act 1891, that is to say—

Bond, Covenant or Instrument of any kind whatsoever

...

Mortgage, Bond, Debenture, Covenant and Warrant of Attorney,

...

shall be those at which the duty would be chargeable if section 52 of the Finance Act 1947 (which doubled the rates) had not been enacted.

(2)..."

Bearer Instruments

59 Stamp duty on bearer instruments

Amendments—This section repealed by FA 1999 Sch 20 Pt V(2) with effect in relation to instruments executed, or bearer instruments issued, from 1 October 1999, subject to the provisions in FA 1999 Sch 20 Pt V(2) Note 2. Previously the text read:

"(1) ...

(2) For the purposes of the heading set out in subsection (1) above—

(*a*) "inland bearer instrument" means any of the following instruments issued by or on behalf of any company or body of persons corporate or unincorporate formed or established in the United Kingdom, that is to say—

(i) any marketable security transferable by delivery;

(ii) any share warrant or stock certificate to bearer and any instrument to bearer (by whatever name called) having the like effect as such a warrant or certificate;

(iii) any deposit certificate to bearer;

(iv) any other instrument to bearer by means of which any stock can be transferred;

(*b*) "overseas bearer instrument" means an instrument issued otherwise than by or on behalf of any such company or body of persons as is mentioned in paragraph (*a*) above, being an instrument described in sub-paragraphs (i) to (iv) of that paragraph or a bearer instrument by usage;

(*c*) "deposit certificate" means an instrument acknowledging the deposit of stock and entitling the bearer to rights (whether expressed as units or otherwise) in or in relation to the stock deposited or equivalent stock; and "deposit certificate for overseas stock" means a deposit certificate in respect of stock of any one company or body of persons not being such a company or body as is mentioned in paragraphs (*a*) above;

(*d*) "bearer instrument by usage" means an instrument not described in the said sub-paragraphs (i) to (iv) which is used for the purpose of transferring the right to any stock, being an instrument delivery of which is treated by usage as sufficient for the purpose of a sale on the market, whether that delivery constitutes a legal transfer or not;

...

(3) For the purposes of the said heading "the transfer duty" means the duty which would be chargeable under the heading "Conveyance or Transfer on sale" in the said Schedule 1 in respect of an instrument in writing transferring the stock constituted by or transferable by means of the inland or overseas bearer instrument in question for a consideration equal to the market value of that stock; and the instrument so postulated shall be taken to transfer the stock on the day of issue or transfer (depending on whether section 60(1) or (2) of this Act applies) and to be executed in pursuance of a contract made on that day.

(4) For the purposes of this section and the two next following sections, "stock" includes securities, and references to stock include references to any interest in, or in any fraction of, stock or in any dividends or other rights arising out of stock and any right to an allotment of or to subscribe for stock; "transfer" includes negotiation and "transferable", "transferred" and "transferring" shall be construed accordingly; and a bearer instrument by usage used for the purpose of transferring the right to any stock shall be treated as transferring that stock on delivery of the instrument, and as issued by the person by whom or on whose behalf it was first issued, whether or not it was then capable of being used for transferring the right to the stock without execution by the holder.

(5)...".

60 Payment of duty

Amendments—This section repealed by FA 1999 Sch 20 Pt V(2) with effect in relation to instruments executed, or bearer instruments issued, from 1 October 1999, subject to the provisions in FA 1999 Sch 20 Pt V(2) Note 2. Previously the text read:

"(1) Duty under the heading set out in subsection (1) of section 59 of this Act shall be chargeable on issue in the case of the following instruments that is to say—

(*a*) any instrument issued in Great Britain; and

(*b*) any instrument issued by or on behalf of a company or body of persons corporate or unincorporate formed or established in Great Britain, not being a foreign loan security:

and for the purposes of this subsection "foreign loan security" means a security issued outside the United Kingdom in respect of a loan which is expressed in a currency other than sterling and is neither offered for subscription in the United Kingdom nor offered for subscription with a view to an offer for sale in the United Kingdom of securities in respect of the loan.

(2) Duty under the said heading in respect of any instrument not chargeable under subsection (1) above shall be chargeable on transfer in Great Britain of the stock constituted by or transferable by means of the instrument: Provided that the duty chargeable by virtue of this subsection on the transfer of stock shall be chargeable only where duty would be chargeable under or by reference to the heading "Conveyance or Transfer on sale" in Schedule 1 to the Stamp Act 1891 if the transfer were effected by an instrument not being a bearer instrument.

(3) Any instrument which is chargeable under the said heading on issue shall, before being issued, be produced to the Commissioners (together with such particulars in writing of the instrument as the Commissioners may require) and shall be deemed to be duly stamped if, and only if, it is stamped with a particular stamp denoting that it has been produced to the Commissioners: and within six weeks of the date on which any such instrument is issued, or such longer time as the Commissioners may allow, a statement in writing containing the date of issue and such further particulars as the Commissioners may require in respect of that instrument shall be delivered to the Commissioners, and the duty chargeable in respect of that instrument shall be paid to the Commissioners on delivery of that statement or within such longer time as the Commissioners may allow.

(4) If default is made in complying with subsection (3) above in respect of any instrument, the person by whom or on whose behalf the instrument is issued, and any person who acts as the agent of that person for the purposes of the issue, shall be liable to a fine not exceeding the aggregate of £50 and an amount equal to the stamp duty chargeable in respect of that instrument, and shall also be liable to pay to Her Majesty the duty chargeable in respect of that instrument and interest on the duty at the rate of five per cent per annum from the date of the default.

(5) Where any instrument which is chargeable under the said heading on transfer of the stock constituted by or transferable by means of the instrument is presented to the Commissioners for stamping, the person presenting it, and the owner of the instrument, shall furnish to the Commissioners such particulars in writing as they may require for determining the amount of duty chargeable on that instrument.

(6) Any person who in Great Britain transfers, or is concerned as broker or agent in transferring, any stock by or by means of any such instrument as is mentioned in subsection (5) above shall, if the instrument is not duly stamped, be liable to a fine not exceeding the aggregate of £50 and an amount equal to the stamp duty chargeable in respect of that instrument, and shall also be liable to pay to Her Majesty the duty chargeable in respect of that instrument and interest on the duty at the rate of five per cent per annum from the date of the transfer in question.

(7) If any person, in furnishing particulars under this section in respect of any instrument, wilfully or negligently furnishes any particulars which are false in any material respect, he shall be liable to a fine not exceeding the aggregate of £50 and an amount equal to twice the amount by which the stamp duty which ought to be charged in respect of that instrument exceeds the stamp duty paid in respect thereof.

(8) Where any such instrument as is mentioned in subsection (5) above has been stamped *ad valorem* or with a stamp indicating that it is chargeable under paragraph (4) of the said heading and with the duty specified in that paragraph, that instrument shall be deemed for all purposes other than subsection (7) above to have been duly stamped.

(9) Any instrument which is deemed to be duly stamped by virtue of subsection (3) or (8) of this section shall be deemed to be duly stamped in Northern Ireland, and any instrument which is deemed to be duly stamped by virtue of the corresponding provisions in force in Northern Ireland shall be deemed to be duly stamped in Great Britain."

61 Ascertainment of market value

Amendments—This section repealed by FA 1999 Sch 20 Pt V(2) with effect in relation to instruments executed, or bearer instruments issued, from 1 October 1999, subject to the provisions in FA 1999 Sch 20 Pt V(2) Note 2. Previously the text read:

"(1) In relation to an instrument which is chargeable on issue, the market value of the stock constituted by or transferable by means of that instrument shall be taken for the purposes of section 59 of this Act to be—

(*a*) where the stock was offered for public subscription (whether in registered or in bearer form) within twelve months before the issue of the instrument, the amount subscribed for the stock;

(*b*) in any other case, the value of the stock on the first day within one month after the issue of the instrument on which stock of that description is dealt in on a stock exchange in the United Kingdom or, if stock of that description is not so dealt in, the value of the stock immediately after the issue of the instrument.

(2) In relation to an instrument which is chargeable on transfer of the stock constituted by or transferable by means of that instrument, the market value of that stock shall be taken for the purposes of the said section 59 to be the value of that stock—

(*a*) in the case of a transfer pursuant to a contract of sale, on the date when the contract is made;

(*b*) in any other case, on the day preceding that on which the instrument is presented to the Commissioners for stamping, or, if it is not so presented, on the date of the transfer."

Miscellaneous

62 Commonwealth stock

Amendments—This section repealed by FA 1999 Sch 20 Pt V(2) with effect in relation to instruments executed, or bearer instruments issued, from 1 October 1999, subject to the provisions in FA 1999 Sch 20 Pt V(2) Note 2. Previously the text read:

"(1) In Schedule 1 to the Stamp Act 1891, the heading "Conveyance or Transfer whether on sale or otherwise" (which relates to Canadian and colonial stock) shall be omitted, and any transfer of stock to which that heading applied shall be chargeable with stamp duty under the heading appropriate to a like transfer of other stock.

(2)–(6) ..."

63 Securities for annual and other payments

Amendments—This section repealed by FA 1999 Sch 20 Pt V(2) with effect in relation to instruments executed, or bearer instruments issued, from 1 October 1999, subject to the provisions in FA 1999 Sch 20 Pt V(2) Note 2. Previously the text read:

"In determining whether an instrument is—

(*a*) the only principal or primary security for any annuity or for any sum or sums of money within the meaning of paragraph (1) of the heading "Bond, Covenant or Instrument of any kind whatsoever" in Schedule I to the Stamp Act 1891; or

(b) the only, principal or primary security for the payment or repayment of money within the meaning of paragraph (1) of the heading "Mortgage, Bond, Debenture, Covenant and Warrant of Attorney" in that Schedule,

no account shall be taken of any other instrument which is a security for the same annuity, sum or sums, or for the same payment or repayment, as the case may be, or for any part thereof, unless that other instrument is chargeable with stamp duty under either of the said paragraphs and is duly stamped."

65 Miscellaneous exemptions

(1) ...[1]

(2) ...[2]

(3) No stamp duty shall be chargeable in respect of any form of application for legal aid under the Legal Aid and Advice Acts 1949 and 1960 or the Legal Aid (Scotland) Acts, 1949 and 1960, or in respect of any form relating to the offer and acceptance of a certificate pursuant to an application for legal aid under those Acts.[3]

Cross references—See FA 1985 s 81 (renunciation of rights to company shares; sub-s (1) above not to apply to instruments if the rights are renounced under them after 31 July 1985 except where an offer for the rights became unconditional before 28 June 1985).

Amendments—[1] Sub-s (1) repealed by FA 1999 Sch 20 Pt V(2) with effect in relation to instruments executed, or bearer instruments issued, from 1 October 1999, subject to the provisions in FA 1999 Sch 20 Pt V(2) Note 2. Previously the text read:

'(1) Any instrument which is exempt from duty under the heading set out in section 59(1) of this Act by virtue of exemption 3 in that heading or would be so exempt if it were otherwise chargeable under that heading shall be exempt from stamp duty under or by reference to the heading "Conveyance or Transfer on sale" in Schedule 1 to the Stamp Act 1891.'

[2] Sub-s (2) repealed by FA 1999 Sch 20 Pt V(5) with effect in relation to instruments executed from 6 February 2000.

[3] Sub-s (3) repealed by the Statute Law (Repeals) Act 2008 s 1, Sch 1 Pt 8 with effect from 21 July 2008.

67 Prohibition of circulation of blank transfers

(1) Where a transfer in blank relating to registered stock of any description has been delivered, pursuant to a sale of that stock, to or to the order of the purchaser or any person acting on his behalf, any person who in Great Britain parts with possession of that transfer, or who removes it or causes or permits it to be removed from Great Britain, before it has been duly completed shall be liable to a [penalty][3] not exceeding the aggregate of [£300][3] and an amount equal to twice the stamp duty chargeable in respect of that transfer.

(2) For the purposes of this section "transfer in blank" means a transfer in which the name of the transferee has not been inserted, and a transfer shall be treated as duly completed if, and only if, the name of the transferee is inserted therein, being the name of—

(*a*) the purchaser of the stock under the sale;

(*b*) a person entitled to a charge upon the stock for money lent to that purchaser;

(*c*) a nominee holding as a bare trustee for that purchaser or for any such person as is mentioned in paragraph (*b*) above; or

(*d*) a person acting as the agent of that purchaser for the purposes of the sale.

(3) ...[1]

[(4) In this section—

(*a*) "stock" includes securities;

(*b*) references to stock include any interest in, or in any fraction of, stock or in any dividends or other rights arising out of stock and any right to an allotment of or to subscribe for stock; and

(*c*) "transfer" includes any instrument used for transferring stock.

(4A) Nothing in this section applies to—

(*a*) an instrument which is chargeable with duty at the rate specified in paragraph 5 of Schedule 15 to the Finance Act 1999 (certain bearer instruments issued by or on behalf of non-UK companies) and is duly stamped, or

(*b*) renounceable letters of allotment, letters of rights or other similar instruments where the rights under the letter or other instrument are renounceable not later than six months after its issue.][2]

(5) References in this section to the purchaser ...[1] of any stock include references to any person to whom the rights of the purchaser ...[1] are transmitted by operation of law; and in relation to a transfer chargeable with duty in accordance with section 58(4) or (5) of the Stamp Act 1891 (transfers to sub-purchasers) references in this section to the purchaser and a sale shall be construed as references to the sub-purchaser and a sub-sale.

(6) This section shall come into force on such date as the Treasury may by order made by statutory instrument direct.

Note—This section came into force on 26 October 1963 by virtue of the Registered Securities (Completion of Blank Transfers) Order, SI 1963/1743.

This section was to be repealed by FA 1990 Sch 19 Pt VI with effect from an appointed day in accordance with FA 1990 ss 107–111. The Treasury order specifying the appointed day for the purposes of FA 1990 ss 107–110 was to coincide with the start of paperless trading under the Stock Exchange's planned TAURUS system (IR press release, 20-3-90). However, on 11-3-93 the London Stock Exchange News Release 6/93 announced that TAURUS had been abandoned.

Cross references—See FA 1990 ss 109(3), 111(1) (this section not to apply with effect from an appointed day).

Amendments—[1] Sub-s (3) and words in sub-s (5) repealed by FA 1985 s 98(6), Sch 27 Pt IX(1).

[2] Sub-s (4) substituted by sub-ss (4) and (4A) by FA 1999 s 113(3), Sch 16 para 2 with effect in relation to bearer instruments issued after 30 September 1999. For prospective repeal of FA 1999 s 113, Sch 16 para 2 see FA 1999 s 123(3). Previously the text read:

'(4) In this section references to stock shall be construed in accordance with subsection (4) of section 59 of this Act, and "transfer" includes any instrument used for transferring stock; but nothing in this section applies—

(*a*) to any instrument which is chargeable with duty under paragraph (3) of the heading "Bearer Instrument" set out in subsection (1) of that section and is duly stamped or

(*b*) to any instrument which is exempt from duty by virtue of exemption 3 in that heading, or would be so exempt if it were otherwise chargeable under that heading.'

[3] Words and figures in sub-s (1) substituted by FA 1999 s 114, Sch 17 para 6 with effect in relation to penalties in respect of things done or omitted after 30 September 1999. For prospective repeal of FA 1999 Sch 17 para 6 see FA 1999 s 123(3). Previously the text read 'fine' and '£50'.

PART V
MISCELLANEOUS

73 Short title, commencement, construction, extent, amendments and repeals

(1) This Act may be cited as the Finance Act 1963.

(2) Part IV of this Act (except section 67) shall come into force on the 1st August 1963.

(3) …[2]

(4) …[1] Part IV shall be construed as one with the Stamp Act 1891.

(5) Any reference in this Act to any other enactment shall, except so far as the context otherwise requires, be construed as a reference to that enactment as amended or applied by or under any other enactment, including this Act.

(6) Such of the provisions of this Act as relate to matters in respect of which the Parliament of Northern Ireland has power to make laws shall not extend to Northern Ireland.

(7) …

(8) The enactments mentioned in Schedule 14 to this Act—

(*a*) so far as they are mentioned in Part I of that Schedule are hereby repealed to the extent mentioned in the second column of that Part as from the date specified in relation thereto in the third column of that Part;

(*b*) so far as they are mentioned in any other Part of that Schedule are hereby repealed to the extent mentioned in the third column of that Part,

but subject as regards the repeals contained in any Part of that Schedule to any provision in relation thereto made at the end of that Part.

(9) The provisions of Schedules 13 and 14 to this Act as to the operation or effect of repeals contained in those Schedules are without prejudice to the provisions of section 38(2) of the Interpretation Act 1889.

Note—Sub-s (7) is not relevant to this work.

Amendments—[1] Words repealed by TA 1970 ss 538(1), 539(1), Sch 16, FA 1975 ss 50, 52(2), (3), 59, Sch 13 Pt I and CEMA 1979 s 177(3), Sch 6 Pt I.

[2] Sub-s (3) repealed by CEMA 1979 s 177(3), Sch 6 Pt I.

FINANCE ACT 1965

(1965 Chapter 25)

PART V
MISCELLANEOUS AND GENERAL

90 Stamp duty: conveyances and transfers

(1) Subject to the provisions of this section, any instrument whereby property is conveyed or transferred to any person in contemplation of a sale of that property shall be treated for the purposes of the Stamp Act 1891 as a [transfer][3] on sale of that property for a consideration equal to the value of that property.

(2) If on a claim made to the Commissioners not later than two years after the making or execution of an instrument chargeable with duty in accordance with subsection (1) of this section, it is shown to their satisfaction—

(*a*) that the sale in contemplation of which the instrument was made or executed has not taken place and the property has been reconveyed or re-transferred to the person from whom it was conveyed or transferred or to a person to whom his rights have been transmitted on death or bankruptcy; or

(*b*) that the sale has taken place for a consideration which is less than the value in respect of which duty was paid on the instrument by virtue of this section,

the Commissioners shall repay the duty paid by virtue of this section, in a case falling under paragraph (*a*) of this subsection, so far as it exceeds the stamp duty which would have been payable apart from this section and, in a case falling under paragraph (*b*) of this subsection, so far as it exceeds the stamp duty which would have been payable if the instrument had been stamped in accordance with subsection (1) of this section in respect of a value equal to the consideration in question:

…[1]

(3) No instrument chargeable with duty in accordance with subsection (1) of this section shall be deemed to be duly stamped unless the Commissioners have been required to express their opinion thereon under section 12 of the said Act of 1891 and have expressed their opinion thereon in accordance with that section.

(4) The foregoing provisions of this section shall apply whether or not an instrument conveys or transfers other property in addition to the property in contemplation of the sale of which it is made or executed, but those provisions shall not affect the stamp duty chargeable on the instrument in respect of that other property.

(5) For the purposes ...[1] of subsection (1) of this section, the value of property conveyed or transferred by an instrument chargeable with duty in accordance with [that subsection][2] shall be determined without regard to—

(*a*) any power (whether or not contained in the instrument) on the exercise of which the property, or any part of or any interest in, the property, may be re-vested in the person from whom it was conveyed or transferred or in any person on his behalf;

(*b*) any annuity reserved out of the property or any part of it, or any life or other interest so reserved, being an interest which is subject to forfeiture;

but if on a claim made to the Commissioners not later than two years after the making or execution of the instrument it is shown to their satisfaction that any such power as is mentioned in paragraph (*a*) of this subsection has been exercised in relation to the property and the property or any property representing it has been re-conveyed or re-transferred in the whole or in part in consequence of that exercise the Commissioners shall repay the stamp duty paid by virtue of this subsection, in a case where the whole of such property has been so re-conveyed or re-transferred, so far as it exceeds the stamp duty which would have been payable apart from this subsection and, in any other case, so far as it exceeds the stamp duty which would have been payable if the instrument had operated to convey or transfer only such property as is not so re-conveyed or re-transferred.

(6) This section shall be construed as one with the said Act of 1891.

(7) This section shall come into force on 1st August 1965.

Amendments—[1] Words in sub-ss (2), (5) repealed by FA 1985 s 98(6), Sch 27 Pt IX(1).
[2] Words in sub-s (5) substituted by FA 1985 s 82(3).
[3] The word "transfer" substituted for the words "conveyance or transfer" in enactments relating to stamp duty by FA 2003 Sch 20 para 3.

91 Interest where stamp duty repaid under judgment

Amendments—This section repealed by FA 1999 Sch 20 Pt V(1) with effect from 1 October 1999, subject to the provisions in FA 1999 Sch 20 Pt V(1) Note 2. Previously the text read:
'Where under section 13(4) of the Stamp Act 1891 (appeals against assessment of stamp duty) a court orders any sum to be repaid by the Commissioners of Inland Revenue, the court may order it to be repaid with such interest as the court may determine.'

97 Short title, construction, extent and repeal

(1) This Act may be cited as the Finance Act 1965.

(2) ...[1]

(3) Any reference in this Act to any other enactment shall, except so far as the context otherwise requires, be construed as a reference to that enactment as amended or applied by or under any enactment, including this Act.

(4) Save as otherwise expressly provided, such of the provisions of this Act as relate to matters in respect of which the Parliament of Northern Ireland has power to make laws shall not extend to Northern Ireland.

(5) ...

Note—Sub-s (5) is not relevant to this work.
Amendments—[1] Sub-s (2) repealed by TA 1970 s 538(1), Sch 16.

FINANCE ACT 1966

(1966 Chapter 18)

PART VII

MISCELLANEOUS

45 Harbour reorganisation schemes: corporation tax and stamp duty

(1)–(4)...[1]

(5) Where a certified harbour reorganisation scheme contains provision for the transfer of an undertaking, or of any other description of property, to a harbour authority, then, in

Stamp Taxes

considering whether any and if so what duty is payable under section 12 of the Finance Act 1895 (which relates to the stamp duty payable in connection with certain statutory conveyances), the consideration for the transfer shall be left out of account; and no stamp duty shall be payable on any contract or agreement for any such transfer if the contract or agreement is conditional on the making and certification of a harbour reorganisation scheme.

(6) In this section—

"harbour authority" has the same meaning as in the Harbours Act 1964;

"harbour reorganisation scheme" means any statutory provision providing for the management by a harbour authority of any harbour or group of harbours in the United Kingdom, and "certified", in relation to any harbour reorganisation scheme, means certified by a Minister of the Crown or Government department as so providing with a view to securing, in the public interest, the efficient and economical development of the harbour or harbours in question;

...[1]

and in this section and in Schedule 12 to this Act "transferor", in relation to any trade, means the body from whom the trade is transferred, whether or not the transfer is effected by that body.

(7) ...[1]

Amendments—[1] Sub-ss (1)–(4), (7) and words omitted from sub-s (6) repealed by TA 1970 s 538(1), Sch 16.

53 Short title, construction, extent and repeals

(1) This Act may be cited as the Finance Act 1966.

(2) In this Act ...[1] so much of Part VII as relates to stamp duties shall be construed as one with the Stamp Act 1891.

(3) Any reference in this Act to any other enactment shall, except so far as the context otherwise requires, be construed as a reference to that enactment as amended or applied by or under any other enactment, including this Act.

(4) Except as otherwise expressly provided, such of the provisions of this Act as relate to matters in respect of which the Parliament of Northern Ireland has power to make laws shall not extend to Northern Ireland.

(5) ...[3]

(6) ...[2]

(7) ...

Note—Words omitted from sub-s (2) are not relevant to this work.
Sub-s (7) is not relevant to this work.

Amendments—[1] Words in sub-s (2) repealed in part by TA 1970 s 538(1), Sch 16 and FA 1975 ss 52(2), (3), 59(5), Sch 13 Pt I.
[2] Sub-s (6) repealed by the Statute Law (Repeals) Act 1978.
[3] Sub-s (5) repealed by the Statute Law (Repeals) Act 1989.

FINANCE ACT 1967

(1967 Chapter 54)

PART V

STAMP DUTIES

27 Conveyances and transfers on sale: reduction of duty, and amendment of provisions for exemption

(1) ...[1]

(2) ...

(3) The said section 42 shall not apply to any instrument executed on or after the said 1st August unless it is also shown to the satisfaction of the Commissioners that the instrument was not executed in pursuance of or in connection with an arrangement whereunder—

(*a*) the consideration, or any part of the consideration, for the [transfer][3] was to be provided or received, directly or indirectly, by a person other than a body corporate which at the time of the execution of the instrument was associated within the meaning of the said section 42 with either the transferor or the transferee (meaning, respectively, the body from whom and the body to whom the beneficial interest was conveyed or transferred), or

(*b*) the said interest was previously conveyed or transferred, directly or indirectly, by such a person, or

(*c*) the transferor and the transferee were to cease to be associated within the meaning of the said section 42 by reason of [the transferor or a third body corporate ceasing to be the transferee's parent (within the meaning of the said section 42)][2];

and, without prejudice to the generality of paragraph (*a*) above, an arrangement shall be treated as within that paragraph if it is one whereunder the transferor or the transferee or a body corporate associated with either as there mentioned, was to be enabled to provide any of the consideration, or was to part with any of it, by or in consequence of the carrying out of a transaction or transactions involving, or any of them involving, a payment or other disposition by a person other than a body corporate so associated.

This subsection shall, as respects instruments executed on or after the said 1st August, have effect in substitution for section 50 of the Finance Act 1938.

Note:—Sub-s (2) substitutes FA 1930, s 42(2), (3) for s 42(2).
Statement of Practice SP 3/98—Stamp duty—group relief.
Amendments—[1] Sub-s (1) repealed by FA 1972 s 134, Sch 28 Pt XI.
[2] Words in sub-s (3)(*c*) substituted by FA 1995 s 149(6), (7) in relation to instruments executed after 30 April 1995.
[3] The word "transfer" substituted for the words "conveyance or transfer" in enactments relating to stamp duty by FA 2003 Sch 20 para 3.

30 Exemption for bearer instruments relating to stock in foreign currencies

Amendments—This section repealed by FA 1999 Sch 20 Pt V(2) with effect in relation to instruments executed, or bearer instruments issued, from 1 October 1999, subject to the provisions in FA 1999 Sch 20 Pt V(2) Note 2. Previously the text read:

'(1) Subject to subsection (2) below, no duty shall be chargeable under the heading "Bearer Instrument" in Schedule 1 to the Stamp Act 1891 on the issue on or after 1st August 1967 of any instrument which relates to stock expressed in any currency other than sterling or in any units of account defined by reference to more than one currency (whether or not including sterling), or on the transfer on or after that date of the stock constituted by, or transferable by means of, any such instrument.

(2) Where the stock to which any instrument relates consists of a loan for the repayment of which there is an option between sterling and one or more other currencies, that subsection shall apply to the instrument if the option is exercisable only by the holder of the stock, and shall not apply to it in any other case.

(3) Where the capital stock of any company or body of persons is not expressed in terms of any currency, it shall be treated for the purposes of subsection (1) above as expressed in the currency of the territory under the law of which the company or body is formed or established; and a unit under a unit trust scheme, or a share in a foreign mutual fund, shall be treated for the purposes of this section as capital stock of a company or body formed or established in the territory by the law of which the scheme or fund is governed.

(4) ...

(5) In this section—

"foreign mutual fund" means a fund administered under arrangements governed by the law of a territory outside the United Kingdom whereby subscribers to the fund are entitled to participate in, or receive payments by reference to, profits or income arising to the fund from the acquisition, holding, management or disposal of investments, and "share", in relation to a foreign mutual fund, means the right of a subscriber, or of another in his right, to participate in, or receive payments by reference to, profits or income so arising;

...

"stock", except in the expression "capital stock", shall be construed in accordance with section 59(4) of the Finance Act 1963; and

"unit trust scheme", and "unit" in relation to a unit trust scheme have the meanings given to them by section 57 of the Finance Act 1946.'

PART VI
MISCELLANEOUS

45 Citation, interpretation, construction, extent and repeals

(1) This Act may be cited as the Finance Act 1967.

(2) ...

(3) In this Act—

(*a*), (*b*) ...
(*c*) ...
(*d*)–(*f*) ...
(*g*) Part V shall be construed as one with the Stamp Act 1891.
(*h*) ...

(4), (5) ...

(6) Any reference in this Act to any other enactment shall, except so far as the context otherwise requires, be construed as a reference to that enactment as amended or applied by or under any other enactment, including this Act.

(7) Except as otherwise expressly provided, such of the provisions of this Act as relate to matters in respect of which the Parliament of Northern Ireland has power to make laws shall not extend to Northern Ireland.

(8) The enactments mentioned in Schedule 16 to this Act are hereby repealed to the extent mentioned in the third column of that Schedule, but subject to any provision in relation thereto made at the end of any Part of that Schedule.

Note—Sub-s (2), (3)(*a*), (*b*), (*c*), (*d*), (*e*), (*f*), (*h*), (4), (5) are either repealed or not relevant to stamp duty. Sub-s (2) is spent.

Stamp Taxes

PROVISIONAL COLLECTION OF TAXES ACT 1968

(1968 Chapter 2)

1 Temporary statutory effect of House of Commons resolutions affecting ..., stamp duty reserve tax,[2] ...

(1) This section applies only to ..., [stamp duty reserve tax,][3] [stamp duty land tax,][9]...

(1A) ...[4]

(2) Subject to that, and to the provisions of subsections (4) to (8) below, where the House of Commons passes a resolution which—

(*a*) provides for the renewal for a further period of any tax in force or imposed during the previous financial year (whether at the same or a different rate, and whether with or without modifications) or for the variation or abolition of any existing tax, and

(*b*) contains a declaration that it is expedient in the public interest that the resolution should have statutory effect under the provisions of this Act,

the resolution shall, for the period specified in the next following subsection, have statutory effect as if contained in an Act of Parliament and, where the resolution provides for the renewal of a tax, all enactments which were in force with reference to that tax as last imposed by Act of Parliament shall during that period have full force and effect with respect to the tax as renewed by the resolution.

In this section references to the renewal of a tax include references to its reimposition, and references to the abolition of a tax include references to its repeal.

(3) The said period is—

(*a*) in the case of a resolution passed in [November or December][5] in any year, one expiring with [5th May in the next calendar year][6];

[(*aa*) in the case of a resolution passed in February or March in any year, one expiring with 5th August in the same calendar year; and][8]

(*b*) in the case of any other resolution, one expiring at the end of four months after the date on which it is expressed to take effect or, if no such date is expressed, after the date on which it is passed.

(4) A resolution shall cease to have statutory effect under this section unless within the next [thirty][7] days on which the House of Commons sits after the day on which the resolution is passed—

(*a*) a Bill renewing, varying or, as the case may be, abolishing the tax is read a second time by the House, or

(*b*) a Bill is amended by the House [in Committee or on Report, or by any [Public Bill Committee][10] of the House][1] so as to include provision for the renewal, variation or, as the case may be, abolition of the tax.

(5) a resolution shall also cease to have statutory effect under this section if—

(*a*) the provisions giving effect to it are rejected during the passage of the Bill containing them through the House, or

(*b*) an Act comes into operation renewing, varying or, as the case may be, abolishing the tax, or

(*c*) Parliament is dissolved or prorogued.

(6) Where, in the case of a resolution providing for the renewal or variation of a tax, the resolution ceases to have statutory effect by virtue of subsection (4) or (5) above, or the period specified in subsection (3) above terminates, before an Act comes into operation renewing or varying the tax, any money paid in pursuance of the resolution shall be repaid or made good, and any deduction made in pursuance of the resolution shall be deemed to be an unauthorised deduction.

(7) Where any tax as renewed or varied by a resolution is modified by the Act renewing or varying the tax, any money paid in pursuance of the resolution which would not have been payable under the new conditions affecting the tax shall be repaid or made good, and any deduction made in pursuance of the resolution shall, so far as it would not have been authorised under the new conditions affecting the tax, be deemed to be an unauthorised deduction.

(8) When during any session a resolution has had statutory effect under this section, statutory effect shall not be again given under this section in the same session to the same resolution or to a resolution having the same effect.

Note—Words omitted from the heading and sub-s (1) are not relevant for the purposes of stamp duty.
Sub-s (1A) is not relevant for the purposes of stamp duty.

Amendments—[1] Words in sub-s (4)(*b*) added by FA 1968 s 60.

[2] Words in the heading inserted by virtue of FA 1986 s 86(3).

[3] Words in sub-s (1) inserted by FA 1986 s 86(3).

[4] Sub-s (1A) repealed by FA 1993 ss 205(3), 213, Sch 23 Pt VI in relation to resolutions passed after 27 July 1993.

[5] Words in sub-s (3)(*a*) substituted for the words "March or April" by FA 1993 s 205 (4), (7) in relation to resolutions passed after 27 July 1993.

[6] Words in sub-s (3)(*a*) substituted for the words "5th August in the same calendar year" by FA 1993 s 205 (4), (7) in relation to resolutions passed after 27 July 1993.

[7] Word in sub-s (4) substituted for the word "twenty-five" by FA 1993 s 205(5), (7) in relation to resolutions passed after 27 July 1993.
[8] Words in sub-s (3) inserted by F(No2)A 1997 s 50 in relation to resolutions passed after 31 July 1997.
[9] Words inserted by FA 2003 s 123(1), Sch 18 para 1 with effect in accordance with FA 2003 s 124, Sch 19.
[10] Words in sub-s (4)(*b*) substituted by FA 2007 s 112(1) with effect from 19 July 2007.

TAXES MANAGEMENT ACT 1970

(1970 Chapter 9)

Note—For the relevant text of this Act as applicable to stamp duty reserve tax, see the Stamp Duty Reserve Tax Regulations, SI 1986/1711 reg 20 and Schedule.

FINANCE ACT 1970

(1970 Chapter 24)

PART III

MISCELLANEOUS

Stamp Duties

32 Abolition of certain stamp duties, and amendments as to rates and other matters

Amendments—This section repealed by FA 1999 Sch 20 Pt V(2) with effect in relation to instruments executed, or bearer instruments issued, from 1 October 1999, subject to the provisions in FA 1999 Sch 20 Pt V(2) Note 2. Previously the text read:

"The provisions of Schedule 7 to this Act shall have effect, being—

(*a*) in the case of those in Part I of that Schedule, provisions abolishing, or consequential on the abolition of, certain stamp duties,

(*b*) in the case of those in Part II of that Schedule, provisions making general amendments of or in connection with the enactments relating to stamp duties, and

(*c*) in the case of those in Part III of that Schedule, special provisions required for the purposes of those enactments in connection with the introduction of the new currency provided for by the Decimal Currency Act, 1967."

33 Composition by stock exchanges in respect of transfer duty

(1) The Commissioners may enter into an agreement with, or with persons acting on behalf of, [any recognised investment exchange or recognised clearing house][4] for the composition, in accordance with the provisions of this section, of the stamp duty chargeable under or by reference to [Part I or paragraph 16 of Schedule 13 to the Finance Act 1999 ([transfer][5] on sale or otherwise)][1] on such instruments as may be specified in the agreement, …[2]

…[4]

(2) An agreement under this section shall provide—

(*a*) for every instrument to which the agreement relates to bear on its face an indication of the amount of stamp duty chargeable thereon,

(*b*) for the issue in respect of every such instrument by or on behalf of the [recognised investment exchange or recognised clearing house][4], of a certificate (which may relate to more than one such instrument) to the effect that stamp duty to the amount so indicated has been, or will be, accounted for to the Commissioners,

(*c*) for the delivery to the Commissioners, by or on behalf of the [recognised investment exchange or recognised clearing house][4], of periodical accounts in respect of instruments to which the agreement relates, giving such particulars with respect thereto as may be specified in the agreement, and

(*d*) for the payment to the Commissioners, by or on behalf of the [recognised investment exchange or recognised clearing house][4], and on the delivery of any such account, of the aggregate amount of the stamp duty chargeable as mentioned in subsection (1) above on instruments to which the agreement relates during the period to which the account relates;

and any such agreement may contain such other terms and conditions as the Commissioners think proper.

(3) …[3]

(4) An instrument to which an agreement under this section relates and in respect of which a certificate to the effect mentioned in subsection (2) (*b*) above has been issued by or on behalf of the [recognised investment exchange or recognised clearing house][4], in question shall be treated for the purposes of the Stamp Act 1891 as stamped with the amount of duty indicated on the face of the instrument.

Stamp Taxes

(5) A [recognised investment exchange or recognised clearing house][4], or person making default in delivering any account required by an agreement under this section, or in paying any amount in accordance with such an agreement, shall be liable to a fine not exceeding £50 for any day during which the default continues; and, in addition, every amount payable under such an agreement shall bear interest at the rate of 5 per cent. per annum, recoverable by Her Majesty, from the due date for delivery of the account by reference to which it is payable until the actual date of payment.

(6) Except in so far as the context otherwise requires, any reference to a stamp in section 9 or 10 of the Stamp Duties Management Act, 1891 (allowances for spoiled stamps) shall include a reference to any indication of an amount of stamp duty on the face of any instrument to which an agreement under this section relates.

[(7) In this section "recognised investment exchange" and "recognised clearing house" have the meanings given by section 285(1) of the Financial Services and Markets Act 2000.][4]

Cross references—See FA 1976 s 127(7) (extension of this section to Northern Ireland);
FA 1986 s 84(3), (6) (stamp duty exemption with effect from an appointed date on an instrument effecting a transfer of stock if an agreement under this section is in force at the time of the transfer).

Notes—This section was to be repealed by FA 1990 Sch 19 Pt VI with effect from an appointed day in accordance with FA 1990 ss 107–111. The Treasury order specifying the appointed day for the purposes of FA 1990 ss 107–110 was to coincide with the start of paperless trading under the Stock Exchange's planned TAURUS system (IR press release, 20-3-90). However, on 11-3-93 the London Stock Exchange News Release 6/93 announced that TAURUS had been abandoned.

Amendments—[1] Words in sub-s (1) substituted by FA 1999 s 112(4), Sch 14 para 5 with effect in relation to instruments executed after 30 September 1999. This does not apply to transfers or other instruments relating to units under a unit trust scheme by virtue of FA 1999 s 122. For prospective repeal of FA 1999 Sch 14 para 5 see FA 1999 s 123(3). Previously the text read 'the heading "Conveyance or Transfer on Sale" [or "Conveyance or Transfer of any kind not hereinbefore described"] in Schedule 1 to the Stamp Act 1891'.

[2] Words in sub-s (1) repealed by FA 1976 s 132(5), Sch 15 Pt VI.

[3] Sub-s (3) repealed by FA 1976 ss 127(4), 132(5), Sch 15 Pt VI.

[4] Words in sub-ss (1), (2)(*b*)–(*d*), (4), (5) substituted; and sub-s (7) added; by the Financial Services and Markets Act 2000 (Consequential Amendments) (Taxes) Order, SI 2001/3629 art 4 with effect from 1 December 2001 (immediately after the coming into force of the Financial Services and Markets Act 2000 ss 411, 432(1), Sch 20).

[5] The word "transfer" substituted for the words "conveyance or transfer" in enactments relating to stamp duty by FA 2003 Sch 20 para 3.

36 Citation, interpretation, construction, extent and repeals

(1) This Act may be cited as the Finance Act, 1970.

(2) In this Act—

(*a*) except where the context otherwise requires, "the Board" means the Commissioners of Inland Revenue,

(*b*), (*c*) …

(3) …[1]

(4) …

(5) Part III of this Act, so far as it relates to stamp duties, shall be construed as one with the Stamp Act 1891.

(6) Any reference in this Act to any other enactment shall, except so far as the context otherwise requires, be construed as a reference to that enactment as amended or applied by or under any other enactment, including this Act.

(7) Except as otherwise expressly provided such of the provisions of this Act as relate to matters in respect of which the Parliament of Northern Ireland has power to make laws shall not extend to Northern Ireland.

(8) The enactments mentioned in Schedule 8 to this Act (which include enactments which are spent or otherwise unnecessary) are hereby repealed to the extent mentioned in the third column of that Schedule, but subject to any provision in relation thereto made at the end of any Part of that Schedule.

Note—Sub-ss (2)(*b*), (*c*) and (4) are not relevant to this work.

Amendments—[1] Sub-s (3) repealed by CEMA 1979 s 177(3), Sch 6 Pt I.

SCHEDULES

SCHEDULE 7

STAMP DUTIES

Section 32

Note—This Schedule repealed by FA 1999 Sch 20 Pt V(2) with effect in relation to instruments executed, or bearer instruments issued, from 1 October 1999, subject to the provisions in FA 1999 Sch 20 Pt V(2) Note 2. For instruments executed, or bearer instruments issued before 1 October 1999, the text should read:

PART I

ABOLITION OF CERTAIN DUTIES

Duties abolished as from 1st August 1970

1— *(1) This paragraph has effect as from 1st August 1970.*

(2) The following stamp duties are hereby abolished—

(a) the duty of 6d. specified in Schedule 1 to the Stamp Act 1891 under the heading beginning "Agreement or any Memorandum of an Agreement" (the provisions consequential on this abolition being those contained in sub-paragraph (3) below);

(b) the duty of 6d. specified in that Schedule under the heading "Policy of Insurance other than Life Insurance" inserted by section 30(1) of the Finance Act 1959 (and so that a policy of insurance other than life insurance shall be exempt from all stamp duties);

(c) the duty of £10 or £6 imposed on a certificate of registration for an alkali or other works by section 9(6) of the Alkali, &c Works Regulation Act 1906 as amended by section 47 of the Finance Act 1922; and

(d) the duty of 10s. imposed on the memorandum and on the articles of association of a company by virtue of section 3 and section 9 (c) respectively of the Companies Act 1948 (which provide that each of those documents is to be stamped as if it were a deed).

(3) In consequence of sub-paragraph (2) (a) above—

(a) …

(b) …

(c) …

Stamp Taxes

Duties abolished as from 1st February 1971

2— *(1) This paragraph has effect as from 1st February 1971.*

(2) The following stamp duties are hereby abolished—

(a) the duty of 2d. specified in Schedule 1 to the Stamp Act 1891 under the heading beginning "Bill of Exchanges or Promissory Note" inserted by Section 33 (1) of the Finance Act 1961 and

(b) the duty of 2d. specified in that Schedule under the heading beginning "Receipt".

(3) No application for relief in respect of the duty referred to in sub-paragraph (2) (a) above may be made under any of sections 9 to 12 of the Stamp Duties Management Act 1891 (spoiled, misused and unwanted stamps); and no repayment shall be made under any agreement entered into under section 39 of the Finance Act 1956 (composition for the said duty by bankers) in respect of any form supplied by a banker to a customer and returned to the banker unused or spoiled on or after the said 1st February.

PART II

GENERAL AMENDMENTS

3 *This Part of this Schedule, except paragraph 5, has effect as from 1st August 1970.*

Bearer Instruments

6— *(1)–(3) …*

(4) Where an overseas bearer instrument in respect of a loan expressed in sterling has been stamped ad valorem, *or with the denoting stamp referred to in section 60(3) of the Finance Act 1963 or with duty under paragraph (4) of the said heading, duty shall not be charged under that heading by reason only that the instrument is amended on its face pursuant to an agreement for the variation of any of its original terms or conditions.*

Conveyance or transfer on sale

13— *(1) Section 114 of the Stamp Act 1891 (composition for stamp duty on transfers of colonial etc, stock) shall cease to have effect, but transfers of any stock in respect of which payments have been made under that section shall continue to be exempt from stamp duty.*

(2) …

Mortgages, etc

16— *(1)–(3) …*

(4) The duty chargeable under paragraph (4) of the said heading on the transfer, assignment, disposition or assignation to any person of, or of the money or stock secured by, any collateral, auxiliary, additional or substituted security (including any instrument by way of further assurance) shall not exceed 50p. if a transfer, assignment, disposition or assignation to the same person of (or, as the case may be, of the money or stock secured by) the principal or primary security has been duly stamped with the duty chargeable under that paragraph.

(5) …; and the duty chargeable under that paragraph shall not in any case exceed 50p.

PART III

SPECIAL PROVISIONS CONNECTED WITH THE NEW CURRENCY

Late stamping, etc

19— *(1) Where immediately before 15th February 1971 any instrument chargeable with stamp duty is either not stamped or overstamped or insufficiently stamped, the amount of duty then chargeable, or properly chargeable, on the instrument, or, in the case of an insufficiently stamped instrument, the amount of additional duty then chargeable thereon, shall thereafter become, for all the purposes of the enactments relating to stamp duties—*

(a) the equivalent of that amount in the new currency, reduced where that equivalent is not a multiple of 5p to the nearest such multiple, or

(b) 5p if the said equivalent is less than 10p.

(2) In sub-paragraph (1) above, "the new currency" means the new currency of the United Kingdom provided for by the Decimal Currency Act 1967.

Note—This schedule repealed by FA 1999 Sch 20 Pt V(2) with effect in relation to instruments executed, or bearer instruments issued, from 1 October 1999, subject to the provisions in FA 1999 Sch 20 Pt V(2) Note 2. For instruments executed, or bearer instruments issued before 1 October 1999, see the above text.

FINANCE ACT 1971

(1971 Chapter 68)

PART V

MISCELLANEOUS

64 Stamp duty—abolition of duty on bonds, mortgages etc

Amendments—This section repealed by FA 1999 Sch 20 Pt V(2) with effect in relation to instruments executed, or bearer instruments issued, from 1 October 1999, subject to the provisions in FA 1999 Sch 20 Pt V(2) Note 2. Previously the text read:

'(1) The following stamp duties are hereby abolished—

(*a*) except as respects any instrument increasing the rent reserved by another instrument, the duties chargeable by virtue of paragraph (1) and paragraph (2) (securities for annuities other than superannuation annuities and for certain other periodic sums) of the heading in Schedule 1 to the Stamp Act 1891 "Bond, Covenant, or Instrument of any kind whatsoever",

(*b*) the duties chargeable by virtue of the heading in that Schedule "Bond of any kind whatsoever not specifically charged with any duty", and

(*c*) the duties chargeable by virtue of the heading in that Schedule beginning "Mortgage, Bond, Debenture, Covenant".

(2) Subject to section 4 of the said Act of 1891 (separate charges on instruments containing or relating to several distinct matters) …, any instrument which, but for subsection (1) above, would be chargeable with duty under a heading mentioned in that subsection shall not be chargeable with duty under any other heading in the said Schedule 1.

(3) For the avoidance of doubt it is hereby declared that paragraph (*c*) of subsection (1) above does not affect the amount of any duty chargeable under the said Schedule 1 by reference to the heading mentioned in that paragraph.

(4) This section has effect as from 1st August 1971.'

69 Citation, interpretation, construction, extent and repeals

(1) This Act may be cited as the Finance Act 1971.

(2), (3) …

(4) Except so far as the context otherwise requires, any reference in this Act to any enactment shall be construed as a reference to that enactment as amended, and as including a reference to that enactment as applied, by or under any other enactment, including this Act.

(5), (6) …

(7) The enactments mentioned in Schedule 14 to this Act (Part VI of which includes certain obsolete enactments) are hereby repealed to the extent mentioned in the third column of that Schedule, but subject to any provision at the end of any Part of that Schedule.

Note—Sub-ss (2), (3), (5), (6) are not relevant to this work.

FINANCE ACT 1972

(1972 Chapter 41)

PART VII

MISCELLANEOUS

126 Abolition of stamp duty on bank notes and of bankers' licences

Amendments—This section repealed by FA 1999 Sch 20 Pt V(2) with effect in relation to instruments executed, or bearer instruments issued, from 1 October 1999, subject to the provisions in FA 1999 Sch 20 Pt V(2) Note 2. Previously the text read:

'(1) The following are hereby abolished—

(*a*) the stamp duty chargeable by virtue of the heading "BANK NOTE" in Schedule 1 to the Stamp Act 1891;

(*b*) the licences required to be taken out under section 24 of the Stamp Act 1815 (licences for bankers etc issuing certain promissory notes).

(2) This section takes effect on 25th June 1972; and if on or after that date and before the passing of this Act a person pays any duty in respect of a licence of the kind mentioned in subsection (1)(*b*) above which would not have been payable if this Act had then been in force the Commissioners of Inland Revenue shall, on application made to them within two years after the date of payment, repay the duty.'

FINANCE ACT 1973

(1973 Chapter 51)

PART V
STAMP DUTY

47 Stamp duty on documents relating to chargeable transactions of capital companies

(1) If at the time, or as a result, of the occurrence after 31st July 1973 of any of the transactions relating to a capital company which are specified in Part I of Schedule 19 to this Act (in this section referred to as "chargeable transactions")

(a) the place of effective management of the capital company is in Great Britain, or

(b) the registered office of the capital company is in Great Britain but the place of its effective management is outside the member States,

then, subject to subsection (2) below, there shall be delivered to the Commissioners, within one month of the transaction, a statement in such form and containing such particulars with respect to the transaction as the Commissioners may prescribe.

(2) The obligation to deliver a statement to the Commissioners under subsection (1) above shall not apply in relation to a chargeable transaction falling within sub-paragraph (a) or sub-paragraph (b) of paragraph 1 of Schedule 19 to this Act if the transaction consists of or includes—

(a) the formation of a company which is to be incorporated with limited liability under the [Companies Act 1985][1] and is to have a share capital, or

(b) an allotment of shares in respect of which there is a duty under section 52 (1) of that Act to deliver a return to the registrar of companies, or

(c) the registration of a limited partnership (which is effected by sending or delivering a statement under section 8 of the Limited Partnerships Act 1907 to the registrar of companies), or

(d) such a change in the contribution or liability of a member of a limited partnership as gives rise to a duty under section 9 of the Limited Partnerships Act 1907 to send or deliver a statement thereof to the registrar of companies.

(3) In any case where, by virtue of subsection (2) (a) above, there is no obligation to deliver to the Commissioners a statement under subsection (1) above with respect to a chargeable transaction, a statement with respect thereto shall be delivered to the registrar of companies, in addition to the memorandum and articles to be delivered under [section 10 (1) of the Companies Act 1985][1], and

(a) that statement shall be registered by the registrar of companies upon the stamp duty chargeable in accordance with subsection (5) below being paid, and

(b) unless that statement is so registered, the registrar of companies shall not register the memorandum and articles under [section 12 of the Companies Act 1985][1].

(4) If, by virtue of subsection (2) above, there is no obligation to deliver to the Commissioners a statement under subsection (1) above with respect to a chargeable transaction, then

(a) the return or statement required to be delivered or sent to the registrar of companies as mentioned in subsection (2) above, or

(b) the statement required to be delivered to the registrar of companies under subsection (3) above,

shall contain the like particulars with respect to the transaction as would be required to be contained in a statement under subsection (1) above if the obligation under that subsection did apply.

(5) Subject to subsection (6) below, where a chargeable transaction occurs, the relevant document shall be charged with ad valorem *stamp duty of £1 for every £100 or part of £100 of the amount determined in relation to that document under Part II of Schedule 19 to this Act.*

(6) If the relevant document relates to a chargeable transaction which, by virtue of Part III of Schedule 19 to this Act, is an exempt transaction for the purposes of this section then, except as provided in that Part, stamp duty shall not be chargeable on the document under subsection (5) above, but the document shall not be treated as duly stamped unless it is stamped, in accordance with section 12 of the Stamp Act 1891, with a particular stamp denoting either that it is not chargeable with any duty or that it is duly stamped.

(7) *If a chargeable transaction occurs and the stamp duty (if any) chargeable in accordance with this section on the relevant document is not paid within one month from the date of the transaction,—*

(*a*) *the duty, if any, which is so chargeable shall be a debt due to Her Majesty from the capital company to which the transaction relates, or, if that capital company is not a body corporate, shall be a debt due to Her Majesty for which each of the members of the capital company shall be jointly and severally liable; and*

(*b*) *the capital company or, if it is not a body corporate, each of its members jointly and severally shall incur a fine equal to 5 per cent of the duty chargeable and a similar fine for every month from the date of the transaction, other than the first, during which the duty remains unpaid.*

(8) *The supplementary provisions in Part IV of Schedule 19 to this Act shall have effect in relation to chargeable transactions and, in consequence of the provisions of this section, the amendments in Part V of that Schedule shall have effect.*

(9) *In this section and in Schedule 19 to this Act —*

"registered office", in relation to a limited partnership formed in accordance with the Limited Partnerships Act 1907 means the principal place of business of the partnership;

"the relevant document", in relation to a chargeable transaction, means the statement required to be delivered under subsection (1) above or, if subsection (2) above applies,—

(*a*) *the return or statement required to be delivered or sent to the registrar of companies as mentioned in subsection (2) above, or*

(*b*) *the statement required to be delivered to the registrar of companies under subsection (3) above.*[2]

Simon's Tax Cases—*Cambridge Petroleum Royalties Ltd v IRC* [1982] STC 325; *Swithland Investments Ltd and anor v IRC* [1990] STC 448.

Amendments—[1] Words in sub-s (2) (*a*), (3) substituted by the Companies Consolidation (Consequential Provisions) Act 1985 Sch 2 with effect from 1 July 1985.

[2] This section repealed by FA 1988 Sch 14 Pt XI with effect from 22 March 1988, but is reproduced here for the purposes of FA 1988 s 141(4).

50 Temporary statutory effect of House of Commons resolution affecting stamp duties

(1) Where the House of Commons passes a resolution which—

(*a*) provides for the variation or abolition of an existing stamp duty ...[1]; and

(*b*) is expressed to have effect for a period stated in the resolution in accordance with the following provisions of this section; and

(*c*) contains a declaration that it is expedient in the public interest that the resolution should have statutory effect under the provisions of this section;

then, subject to subsection (3) of this section, the resolution shall for the period so stated have statutory effect as if contained in an Act of Parliament.

(2) The period to be stated in a resolution is a period expressed as beginning on a date so stated and ending on, or thirty-one days or such less number of days as may be so stated after, the earliest of the dates mentioned in this subsection; and those dates are—

(*a*) the [thirtieth][2] day on which, after the day the resolution is passed, the House of Commons sits without a Bill containing provisions to the same effect as the resolution being read a second time and without a Bill being amended (whether by the House or a Committee of the House or a [Public Bill Committee][4] so as to include such provisions;

(*b*) the rejection of such provisions during the passage through the House of a Bill containing them;

(*c*) the dissolution or prorogation of Parliament; and

(*d*) the expiration of the period of [six][3] months beginning with the day on which the resolution takes effect.

(3) A resolution shall cease to have statutory effect under this section if an Act comes into operation varying or abolishing the duty.

(4) The ending of the period for which a resolution has statutory effect under the provisions of this section shall not affect the validity of anything done during that period.

Cross references—See F(No 2)A 1975 s 72 (extension of this section to Northern Ireland).

Amendments—[1] Words in sub-s (1)(*a*) repealed by FA 1975 Sch 13 Pt I, with effect from 13 March 1975.

[2] Word in sub-s (2)(*a*) substituted by FA 1993 s 207 in relation to resolutions passed after 27 July 1993.

[3] Word in sub-s (2)(*d*) substituted by FA 1993 s 207 in relation to resolutions passed after 27 July 1993.

[4] Words in sub-s (2)(*a*) substituted by FA 2007 s 112(1) with effect from 19 July 2007.

PART VI

MISCELLANEOUS AND GENERAL

54 Amendments consequential on establishment of The Stock Exchange

(1) In the enactments relating to ... stamp duty—

(*a*) references to the Stock Exchange, London or the London Stock Exchange, a stock exchange in the United Kingdom or a recognised stock exchange in the United Kingdom shall be construed as references to The Stock Exchange;

(*b*) references to quotation on a stock exchange in the United Kingdom or a recognised stock exchange in the United Kingdom shall be construed as references to listing in the Official List of The Stock Exchange; and

(*c*) references to a member of a stock exchange in the United Kingdom shall be construed as references to a member of The Stock Exchange;

and those enactments shall have effect subject to the amendments specified in Schedule 21 to this Act.

(2) This section shall be deemed to have come into operation on 25th March 1973 but shall not affect the operation of any enactment in relation to anything done before that day.

Amendments—Words omitted from sub-s (1) repealed by TA 1988 s 844(4), Sch 31.

59 Citation, interpretation, construction, extent and repeals

(1) This Act may be cited as the Finance Act 1973.

(2) …

(3) In this Act—

(*a*) …[2]

(*b*) …[3]

(*c*) …

(*d*) …[1]

(*e*) Part V shall be construed as one with the Stamp Act 1891.

(4) Except so far as the context otherwise requires, any reference in this Act to any enactment shall be construed as a reference to that enactment as amended, and as including a reference to that enactment as applied, by or under any other enactment, including this Act.

(5) Except as otherwise expressly provided, such of the provisions of this Act as relate to matters in respect of which the Parliament of Northern Ireland has power to make laws do not extend to Northern Ireland.

(6) If the Parliament of Northern Ireland passes provisions amending or replacing any enactment of that Parliament referred to in this Act the reference shall be construed as a reference to the enactment as so amended or, as the case may be, as a reference to those provisions.

(7) The enactments mentioned in Schedule 22 to this Act (which include certain enactments which had ceased to have effect before the commencement of this Act) are hereby repealed to the extent specified in the third column of that Schedule, but subject to any provision at the end of any Part of that Schedule.

Note—Sub-ss (2), (3) (*c*) are not relevant to this work.

Amendments—[1] Sub-s (3) (*d*) repealed by FA 1975 ss 57(2), 59(5), Sch 13 Pt I.

[2] Sub-s (3)(*a*) repealed by CEMA 1979 s 177(3), Sch 6 Pt I.

[3] Sub-s (3)(*b*) repealed by VATA 1983 s 50(2), Sch 11.

SCHEDULES

SCHEDULE 19

STAMP DUTY ON DOCUMENTS RELATING TO CHARGEABLE TRANSACTIONS OF CAPITAL COMPANIES

Section 47

PART III

EXEMPT TRANSACTIONS

10— *(1) A chargeable transaction shall be an exempt transaction for the purposes of section 47 of this Act if it is shown to the satisfaction of the Commissioners—*

(a) that, by virtue of the transaction, a capital company which is in the process of being formed or which is already in existence

(i) has acquired share capital of another capital company to the extent that, after the transaction, not less than 75 per cent of the issued share capital of that other company is beneficially owned by the first company, or

(ii) has acquired the whole or any part of the undertaking of another capital company, and

(b) that the conditions specified in sub-paragraph (2) below are fulfilled in relation to the transaction;

and in this paragraph the first company mentioned in paragraph (a) above is referred to as "the acquiring company" and the other company mentioned in sub-paragraph (i) or (ii) of that paragraph is referred to as "the acquired company".

(2) The conditions referred to in sub-paragraph (1) above are

Stamp Taxes

(a) that the place of effective management or the registered office of the acquired company is in a member State; and

(b) that so much, if any, of the consideration (taking no account of such part thereof as consists of the assumption or discharge by the acquiring company of liabilities of the acquired company) for the acquisition referred to in that sub-paragraph as does not consist

(i) where shares are to be acquired, of the issue of shares in the acquiring company to the holders of shares in the acquired company in exchange for the shares held by them in the acquired company,

(ii) where the whole or any part of the undertaking is to be acquired, of the issue of shares in the acquiring company to the acquired company or to holders of shares in the acquired company,

consists wholly of a payment in cash which does not exceed 10 per cent of the nominal value of the shares which make up the balance of the consideration.

(3) If, at any time within the period of five years beginning with the occurrence of a chargeable transaction which is an exempt transaction falling within paragraph (a) (i) of sub-paragraph (1) above, the acquiring company

(a) ceases to retain at least 75 per cent of the issued share capital of the acquired company, or

(b) disposes of any of the shares in the acquired company which it held immediately after the occurrence of the chargeable transaction,

duty shall then become chargeable, and shall be payable in accordance with sub-paragraph (4) below; but for the purpose of determining whether paragraph (a) or paragraph (b) above applies, any disposal of shares shall be disregarded if it is effected

(i) by a transfer forming part of a chargeable transaction which is itself an exempt transaction by virtue of any provision of sub-paragraph (1) above, or

(ii) in the course of the winding-up of the acquiring company.

(4) If sub-paragraph (3) above applies, then, within one month of the date on which the holding of share capital referred to in paragraph (a) of that sub-paragraph first falls below 75 per cent or, as the case may be, the date of the first disposal of any of the shares referred to in paragraph (b) of that sub-paragraph (in this paragraph referred to as "the date of charge"), there shall be paid to the Commissioners duty corresponding to the stamp duty which would have been charged under subsection (5) of section 47 of this Act on the relevant document if the chargeable transaction had not been an exempt transaction.

(5) If sub-paragraph (4) above applies, subsection (7) of section 47 of this Act shall apply

(a) as if the chargeable transaction had never been an exempt transaction; and

(b) as if for the reference in that subsection to the date of the transaction there were substituted a reference to the date of charge;

and, in addition, interest on the duty payable under that sub-paragraph at the rate of 5 per cent per annum from the date when the chargeable transaction occurred to the date of charge shall be a debt due to Her Majesty from the acquiring company.

[(6) This paragraph applies also where the acquired company is a corporation or body of persons which is not a capital company for the purposes of this Schedule but which is treated as such in another member State; and paragraph 3 (1) above shall apply for the interpretation of this sub-paragraph as it applies for the interpretation of paragraph 1 above.][1]

Amendments—[1] Sub-para (6) added by FA 1976 s 128.
This Schedule repealed by FA 1988 Sch 14 Pt XI with effect from 22 March 1988.
This paragraph is reproduced here for the purposes of FA 1988 s 141(4).

FINANCE ACT 1974

(1974 Chapter 30)

PART IV
MISCELLANEOUS AND GENERAL

49 Increase of certain stamp duties

Amendments—This section repealed by FA 1999 Sch 20 Pt V(2) with effect in relation to instruments executed, or bearer instruments issued, from 1 October 1999, subject to the provisions in FA 1999 Sch 20 Pt V(2) Note 2. Previously the text read:

"(1) The provisions of Schedule 11 to this Act shall have effect, being provisions increasing, or connected with the increase of, certain stamp duties.

(2)–(3) …"

57 Citation, interpretation, construction and repeals

(1) This Act may be cited as the Finance Act 1974.

(2) ...

(3) In this Act—

(*a*)–(*d*)...[1, 2, 3]

(4) Except so far as the context otherwise requires, any reference in this Act to any enactment shall be construed as a reference to that enactment as amended, and as including a reference to that enactment as applied, by or under any other enactment, including this Act.

(5) If the Northern Ireland Assembly passes provisions amending or replacing any enactment of the Parliament of Northern Ireland, or any Order in Council made under section 1(3) of the Northern Ireland (Temporary Provisions) Act 1972 referred to in this Act, the reference shall be construed as a reference to the enactment or order as so amended or, as the case may be, as a reference to those provisions.

(6) The enactments mentioned in Schedule 14 to this Act (which include certain enactments which had ceased to have effect before the commencement of this Act) are hereby repealed to the extent specified in the third column of that Schedule, but subject to any provision at the end of any Part of that Schedule.

Note—Sub-ss (2), (3)(*b*) are not relevant to this work.

Amendments—[1] Sub-s (3)(*a*) repealed in part by CEMA 1979 s 177(3), Sch 6 Pt I and VATA 1983 s 50(2), Sch 11; remainder of that subsection is spent.

[2] Sub-s (3)(*c*) repealed by FA 1985 s 98(6), Sch 27 Pt X.

[3] Sub-s (3)(*d*) repealed by FA 1999 Sch 20 Pt V(2) with effect in relation to instruments executed, or bearer instruments issued, from 1 October 1999, subject to the provisions in FA 1999 Sch 20 Pt V(2) Note 2. Previously the text read:

"(*d*) Schedule 11 shall be construed as one with the Stamp Act 1891.".

Stamp Taxes

SCHEDULE 11

INCREASE OF CERTAIN STAMP DUTIES

Section 49

Note—This schedule repealed by FA 1999 Sch 20 Pt V(2) with effect in relation to instruments executed, or bearer instruments issued, from 1 October 1999, subject to the provisions in FA 1999 Sch 20 Pt V(2) Note 2. For instruments executed, or bearer instruments issued before 1 October 1999, the text should read:

PART I

PROVISIONS HAVING EFFECT IN GREAT BRITAIN

1— *(1) This Part of this Schedule, except paragraphs 6 and 7, shall be deemed to have had effect as from 1st May 1974; and paragraphs 6 (1) and 7 shall have effect as from 1st August, 1974.*

(2) This Part of this Schedule shall not extend to Northern Ireland.

(3) The Commissioners may make such arrangements operating for such period as they may think proper for the charge of duty on any instrument giving effect to a stock exchange transaction (as defined in section 4 of the Stock Transfer Act 1963) in respect of which settlement was due before 1st May 1974 to be the same as if this Act had not been passed, and any instrument stamped in accordance with such arrangements shall be deemed to be duly stamped for all purposes.

PART II

PROVISIONS HAVING EFFECT IN NORTHERN IRELAND

11— *(1) This Part of this Schedule shall have effect as from 1st August 1974.*

(2) This Part of this Schedule shall not extend to Great Britain.

(3) The Commissioners may make such arrangements operating for such period as they may think proper for the charge of duty on any instrument giving effect to a stock exchange transaction (as defined in section 4 of the Stock Transfer Act (Northern Ireland) 1963) in respect of which settlement was due before 1st August 1974 to be the same as if this Act had not been passed, and any instrument stamped in accordance with such arrangements shall be deemed to be duly stamped for all purposes.

Note—This schedule repealed by FA 1999 Sch 20 Pt V(2) with effect in relation to instruments executed, or bearer instruments issued, from 1 October 1999, subject to the provisions in FA 1999 Sch 20 Pt V(2) Note 2. For instruments executed, or bearer instruments issued before 1 October 1999, see the above text.

FINANCE (NO 2) ACT 1975

(1975 Chapter 45)

PART IV

MISCELLANEOUS AND GENERAL

72 Extension of Finance Act 1973 s 50 to stamp duties in Northern Ireland

Section 50 of the Finance Act 1973 (temporary statutory effect of House of Commons resolution affecting stamp duties) shall extend to Northern Ireland and apply to stamp duties having effect there as well as to stamp duties having effect in Great Britain.

FINANCE ACT 1976

(1976 Chapter 40)

PART V

MISCELLANEOUS AND SUPPLEMENTARY

127 Stamp duty: stock exchange transfers

(1) Stamp duty shall not be chargeable on any transfer to a stock exchange nominee …[1]

(2) … [2]

(3) … [3]

(4) …

(5) This section shall be construed as one with the Stamp Act 1891 and in this section—

…[3]

"stock exchange nominee" means any person designated for the purposes of this section as a nominee of The Stock Exchange by an order made by the Secretary of State;

…[3]

(6) The power to make an order under subsection (5) above shall be exercisable by statutory instrument and includes power to vary or revoke a previous order.

(7) Section 33 of the Finance Act 1970 shall extend to Northern Ireland; and in the application of that section …[3] to Northern Ireland for any reference to the Stock Transfer Act 1963 there shall be substituted a reference to the Stock Transfer Act (Northern Ireland) 1963.

Note—Sub-ss (1), (4)–(7) were to be repealed by FA 1990 Sch 19 Pt VI with effect from an appointed day in accordance with FA 1990 ss 107–111. The Treasury order specifying the appointed day for the purposes of FA 1990 ss 107–110 was to coincide with the start of paperless trading under the Stock Exchange's planned TAURUS system (IR press release, 20-3-90). However, on 11-3-93 the London Stock Exchange News Release 6/93 announced that TAURUS had been abandoned.

Sub-s (4) amends FA 1970 s 33(1),

SEPON Limited have been designated as a nominee of The Stock Exchange under sub-s (5), by The Stock Exchange (Designation of Nominees) (Stamp Duty) Order, SI 1979/370 which came into operation on 30 March 1979.

Cross references—See FA 1986 s 88(1)(*a*) (stamp duty reserve tax on instruments relating to agreements to transfer chargeable securities for consideration),

FA 1986 s 97(2)(*a*) (stamp duty reserve tax exemption on instruments relating to arrangements to provide clearance services),

FA 1989 s 175 (stamp duty and stamp duty reserve tax exemptions in certain circumstances involving stock exchange nominees),

FA 1989 s 176 (relief from double stamp duty reserve tax and stamp duty reserve tax exemption in certain circumstances involving stock exchange nominees).

Amendments—[1] Words in sub-s (1) repealed by FA 1986 s 84(1), (4), Sch 23, Pt IX(4) in relation to any transfer giving effect to a transaction carried out on or after 27 October 1986 (ie the day on which The Stock Exchange rule prohibiting a person from carrying on business as both a broker and a jobber is abolished).

[2] Sub-s (2) repealed by FA 1986 s 85(4), Sch 23, Pt IX(4) in relation to any transfer giving effect to a transaction carried out on or after 27 October 1986.

[3] Sub-s (3), the definitions of "jobber" and "stock exchange transaction" in sub-s (5) and the words "and this section" in sub-s (7) repealed by FA 1986 s 114(6), Sch 23 Pt IX(4) with effect from 20 March 1989 by virtue of FA 1986 (Stamp Duty Repeals) Order, SI 1989/291.

131 Inter-American Development Bank

(1) The following provisions of this section shall have effect on the United Kingdom's becoming a member of the Inter-American Development Bank ("the Bank").

(2) …

(3) No stamp duty shall be chargeable [Schedule 15 to the Finance Act 1999 (bearer instruments)][1] on the issue of any instrument by the Bank or on the transfer of the stock constituted by, or transferable by means of, any instrument issued by the Bank.

Notes—Sub-s (2) is not relevant to this work.

Sub-s (3) was to be repealed by FA 1990 Sch 19 Pt VI with effect from an appointed day in accordance with FA 1990 ss 107–111. The Treasury order specifying the appointed day for the purposes of FA 1990 ss 107–110 was to coincide with the start of paperless trading under the Stock Exchange's planned TAURUS system (IR press release, 20-3-90). However, on 11-3-93 the London Stock Exchange News Release 6/93 announced that TAURUS had been abandoned.

Amendments—[1] Words in sub-s (3) substituted by FA 1999 s 113(3), Sch 16 para 3 with effect in relation to bearer instruments issued after 30 September 1999. For prospective repeal of FA 1999 s 113, Sch 16 para 3 see FA 1999 s 123(3). Previously the text read 'under the heading "Bearer Instrument" in Schedule 1 to the Stamp Act 1891'.

INTERPRETATION ACT 1978

(1978 Chapter 30)

Note—See under VAT Statutes, *ante*.

FINANCE ACT 1980

(1980 Chapter 48)

PART V

STAMP DUTY

97 Shared ownership transactions

(1) A lease to which this section applies shall, instead of being chargeable with stamp duty under [Part II of Schedule 13 to the Finance Act 1999 (lease)][9], be chargeable with stamp duty under [Part I of that Schedule ([transfer][10] on sale)][9] as if it were a conveyance for a consideration equal to the value [or sum][1] stated in the lease in accordance with subsection (2)(*d*) below; and where stamp duty has been paid on a lease in accordance with this section stamp duty shall not be chargeable under that Act on any instrument executed in pursuance of the lease whereby the reversion is transferred to the lessee.

(2) This section applies to any lease granted by a body mentioned in subsection (3) below, being a lease which—

(*a*) is of a dwelling for the exclusive use of the lessee or, if there are joint lessees, of those lessees;

[(*b*) is granted partly in consideration of a premium calculated by reference to—

(i) the market value of the dwelling, or

(ii) a sum calculated by reference to that value, and partly in consideration of rent][2];

(*c*) provides for the lessee to acquire the reversion; and

(*d*) contains a statement of the market value referred to in [paragraph (*b*) (i) above or, as the case may be, the sum referred to in paragraph (*b*) (ii) above][2] and a statement to the effect that the parties intend duty to be charged in accordance with this section by reference to that value [or as the case may be, to that sum][3].

(3) The bodies referred to in subsection (2) above are—

[(*a*) a local housing authority within the meaning of the Housing Act 1985;

(*b*) a housing association [within the meaning of][6] the Housing Associations Act 1985 or [Part VII][6] of the Housing (Northern Ireland) Order 1981;][4]

(*c*) a development corporation established by an order made, or having effect as if made, under the New Towns Act 1965;

[(*cc*) a housing action trust established under Part III of the Housing Act 1988;][7]

(*d*) the Commission for the New Towns;

(*e*) …[8]

(*f*) the Northern Ireland Housing Executive;

(*g*) …[5]

(4) For the purposes of subsection (1) above an instrument transferring a reversion shall not be regarded as executed in pursuance of a lease in respect of which duty has been paid in accordance with this section unless it contains a statement to the effect that it has been so executed.

Cross references—See FA 1981 s 108(5), (6), (7) (stamp duty on a lease of a house granted by a body referred to in sub-s (3) above in consideration of rent and premium, lease instrument being executed after 22 March 1981);

FA 1987 s 54(2), (3), (4) (extension of the application of this section to leases granted by and to certain persons after 31 July 1987 under shared ownership schemes of local authorities and housing associations).

Amendments—[1] Words in sub-s (1) inserted by FA 1981 s 108(2), (7), with effect from 23 March 1981.

[2] Sub-s (2)(*b*) and words in sub-s (2)(*d*) substituted by FA 1981 s 108(3), (4), (7), in relation to lease instruments executed after 22 March 1981.

[3] Words in sub-s (2)(*d*) added by FA 1981 s 108(3)(*b*), (7), with effect from 23 March 1981.
[4] Sub-s (3)(*a*), (*b*) substituted by the Housing (Consequential Provisions) Act 1985 s 6(2), Sch 2 para 43, with effect from 1 April 1986.
[5] Sub-s (3)(*g*) repealed by the Housing (Consequential Provisions) Act 1985 s 6(2), Sch 1 Pt I, with effect from 1 April 1986.
[6] Words in sub-s (3)(*b*) substituted by FA 1987 s 54(1).
[7] Sub-s (3)(*cc*) inserted by FA 1988 s 142(1).
[8] Sub-s (3)(*e*) repealed by the Government of Wales Act 1998 Sch 18 Pt IV, with effect from 1 October 1998 by virtue of The Government of Wales Act 1998 (Commencement No 1) Order, SI 1998/2244.
[9] Words in sub-s (1) substituted by FA 1999 s 112(4), Sch 14 para 6 with effect in relation to instruments executed after 30 September 1999. This does not apply to transfers or other instruments relating to units under a unit trust scheme by virtue of FA 1999 s 122. Previously the text read 'the heading "Lease or Tack" in Schedule 1 to the Stamp Act 1891' and 'the heading "Conveyance or Transfer on Sale" in that Schedule' respectively.
[10] The word "transfer" substituted for the words "conveyance or transfer" in enactments relating to stamp duty by FA 2003 Sch 20 para 3.

98 Maintenance funds for historic buildings

(1) No stamp duty shall be chargeable on any instrument whereby property ceases to be comprised in a settlement if as a result of the property or part of it becoming comprised in another settlement (otherwise than by virtue of the instrument itself) there is by virtue of [paragraph 9 (1) or 17 (1) of Schedule 4 to the Capital Transfer Tax Act 1984 there is no charge to capital transfer tax in respect of the property ceasing to be comprised in the settlement or a reduced charge to that tax by virtue of paragraph 9 (4) or 17 (4) of that Schedule][1]; but where only part of the property becomes comprised in the other settlement this subsection shall not affect the stamp duty chargeable on the instrument by reference to the other part.

(2) An instrument in respect of which stamp duty is not chargeable by virtue only of this section or in respect of which the duty chargeable is reduced by virtue of this section shall not be treated as duly stamped unless it is stamped in accordance with section 12 of the Stamp Act 1891 with a stamp denoting that it is not chargeable with any duty or that it is duly stamped.

Cross references—See FA 1986 s 100 (CTT to be known as inheritance tax and CTTA 1984 as Inheritance Tax Act 1984 with effect from 25 July 1986 and references in this section to CTT to be construed accordingly).
Amendments—[1] Words in sub-s (1) substituted by IHTA 1984 Sch 8 para 19 with effect from 1 January 1985.

101 Unit trusts

Amendments—This section repealed by FA 1999 Sch 20 Pt V(5) with effect in relation to instruments executed from 6 February 2000.

102 Conveyance in consideration of debt

(1) Where—

(*a*) any property is conveyed to any person wholly or in part in consideration of a debt due to him; and

(*b*) apart from this section the consideration in respect of which the conveyance would be chargeable with *ad valorem* duty by virtue of section 57 of the Stamp Act 1891 (which deems the debt to be the consideration) would exceed the value of the property conveyed,

that consideration shall be treated as reduced to that value.

(2) Where subsection (1) above applies in relation to any conveyance, it shall not be treated as duly stamped unless it is stamped in accordance with section 12 of the said Act of 1891 with a stamp denoting that it is not chargeable with any duty or that it is duly stamped.

FINANCE ACT 1981

(1981 Chapter 35)

PART VI

STAMP DUTY

107 Sale of houses at discount by local authorities etc

(1) Where a [transfer][18] to which this section applies is subject contingently to the payment of any money (whether by virtue of that [transfer][18] or otherwise), then, notwithstanding section 57 of the Stamp Act 1891 that money shall not be deemed to be part of the consideration in respect of which the [transfer][18] is chargeable with *ad valorem* duty.

(2) …[3]

(3) This section applies to any [transfer][18] on sale of a dwelling-house (including the grant of a lease) at a discount by—

(*a*) any Minister of the Crown or Northern Ireland department;

(*b*) a [local housing authority within the meaning of the Housing Act 1985][4], a county council, a district council within the meaning of the Local Government Act (Northern

Ireland) 1972 or in Scotland a [council constituted under section 2 of the Local Government etc (Scotland) Act 1994][10], the common good of such a council or any trust under its control;

(*c*) the Housing Corporation;

[(*ca*) …;][8]

(*d*) *[Scottish Homes]*[9];

(*e*) the Northern Ireland Housing Executive;

[(*ea*) a registered social landlord within the meaning of Part 1 of the Housing Act 1996;][12]

(*f*) a housing association registered[—;

(i) in Scotland under the Housing Association Act 1985, or

(ii) in Northern Ireland, under Part II of the Housing (Northern Ireland) Order 1992][13]

[(*ff*) a housing action trust established under Part III of the Housing Act 1988;][7]

(*g*) a development corporation established by an order made or having effect as if made under the New Towns Act 1965 or the New Towns (Scotland) Act 1968 or an urban development corporation established by an order made under section 135 of the Local Government, Planning and Land Act 1980;

(*h*) the Commission for the New Towns or a new town commission established under section 7 of the New Towns Act (Northern Ireland) 1965;

(*i*) …[15];

(*j*) the Council of the Isles of Scilly;

(*k*) a police authority within the meaning of [section 101(1) of the Police Act 1996][11] or section 2(1) or 19(9)(*b*) of the Police (Scotland) Act 1967 or [the Northern Ireland Policing Board][16];

(*ka*) …[17]

(*l*) an Education and Libraries Board established under the Education and Libraries (Northern Ireland) Order 1972;

(*m*) any person mentioned in paragraph (*e*), (i), (*j*) or (*l*) of section 1(10) of the Tenants' Rights, Etc. (Scotland) Act 1980;

[(*n*) the United Kingdom Atomic Energy Authority;][1]

[(*o*) such other body as the Treasury may, by order made by statutory instrument, prescribe for the purposes of this section.][2]

[(3A) This section also applies to any [transfer][18] on sale of a dwelling house where the [transfer][18] is made pursuant to a sub-sale made at a discount by a body falling within [subsection (3) (*ea*) or (*f*)][14] above.][1]

[(3B) This section also applies to a [transfer][18] on sale (including the grant of a lease) by a person against whom the right to buy under Part V of the Housing Act 1985 exercisable by virtue of section 171A of that Act (preservation of right to buy on disposal to private sector landlord) to a person who is the qualifying person for the purposes of the preserved right to buy and in relation to whom that dwelling-house is the qualifying dwelling-house.][6]

[(3C) A grant under section 20 or 21 of the Housing Act 1996 (purchase grants in respect of disposals at a discount by registered social landlords) shall not be treated as part of the consideration for a [transfer][18] to which this section applies made by a body falling within subsection (3)(*ea*) above.][12]

(4) This section applies to instruments executed on or after 23rd March 1981 and shall be deemed to have come into force on that date.

Cross references—See Stamp Act 1891, s 58 (4) (conveyances or transfers to which this section applies resulting from sub-sales).

Amendments—[1] Sub-s (3)(*n*) and sub-s (3A) added by FA 1984 s 110(1)–(4) with respect to instruments executed after 19 March 1984 or executed after 12 March 1984 and stamped after 19 March 1984.

[2] Sub-s (3)(*o*) added by FA 1984 s 110(1), (5) with respect to instruments executed after 26 July 1984.

[3] Sub-s (2) repealed by FA 1985 Sch 27, Pt IX(1).

[4] Words in sub-s (3)(*b*) substituted by the Housing (Consequential Provisions) Act 1985 s 6(2), Sch 2 para 48, with effect from 1 April 1986.

[6] Sub-s (3B) inserted by the Housing and Planning Act 1986 Sch 5 para 18 with effect from 17 August 1992.

[7] Sub-s (3) (*ff*) inserted by FA 1988 s 142(2).

[8] Sub-s (3)(*ca*) inserted by the Housing Act 1988 Sch 17 para 105, and repealed by the Government of Wales Act 1998 Sch 18 Pt VI with effect from 1 November 1998 by virtue of the Government of Wales Act 1998 (Commencement No 1) Order, SI 1998/2244.

[9] Words in sub-s (3) (*d*) substituted by the Housing (Scotland) Act 1988 s 3(3), Sch 2 para 1.

[10] Words in sub-s (3)(*b*) substituted for the words "regional, district or islands council" by the Local Government etc (Scotland) Act 1994 s 180(1), Sch 13 para 123, as from a day to be appointed.

[11] Words in sub-s (3)(*k*) substituted by the Police Act 1996 s 103(1), Sch 7 Pt II para 33.

[12] Sub-s (3)(*ea*) and (3C) inserted by the Housing Act 1996 s 55(1), Sch 3 para 1 with effect from 1 October 1996.

[13] Words in sub-s (3)(*f*) substituted for the words "under the Housing Associations Act 1985 or Article 124 of the Housing (Northern Ireland) Order 1981" by the Housing Act 1996 s 55(1), Sch 3 para 1 with effect from 1 October 1996.

[14] Words in sub-s (3A) substituted for the words "subsection (3)(*f*)" by the Housing Act 1996 s 55(1), Sch 3 para 1 with effect from 1 October 1996.

[15] Sub-s (3)(*i*) repealed by the Government of Wales Act 1998 Sch 18 Pt IV with effect from 1 October 1998 by virtue of the Government of Wales Act 1998 (Commencement No 1) Order, SI 1998/2244.

[16] Words in sub-s (3)(*k*) substituted by the Police (Northern Ireland) Act 2000 s 78(1), Sch 6 para 7 with effect from 4 November 2001 (by virtue of SR 2001/396).

[17] Sub-s (3)(*ka*) repealed by the Criminal Justice and Police Act 2001 ss 128(1), 138(2), Sch 6 para 64, Sch 7 para 5 with effect from 1 April 2002 (by virtue of SI 2002/344).

[18] The word "transfer" substituted for the words "conveyance or transfer" in enactments relating to stamp duty by FA 2003 Sch 20 para 3.

Prospective amendments—Sub-s (3)(*d*) to be repealed by the Housing (Scotland) Act 2001 s 112, Sch 10 para 8 with effect from a date to be appointed.

Stamp Taxes

108 Shared ownership transactions

(1) Section 97 of the Finance Act 1980 (shared ownership transactions) shall have effect with the amendments specified in subsections (2) to (4) below.

(2)–(4) …

(5) Where a lease is granted by a body mentioned in subsection (3) of the said section 97 which—

(*a*) is of a dwelling for the exclusive use of the lessee or, if there are joint lessees, of those lessees;

(*b*) provides that the lessee may on payment of a sum require the terms of the lease to be altered so that the rent payable under it is reduced;

(*c*) is granted partly in consideration of rent and partly in consideration of a premium calculated by reference to—

(i) the premium obtainable on the open market for the grant of a lease containing the same terms as the lease but with the substitution for the rent payable under the lease of the minimum rent, or

(ii) a sum calculated by reference to that premium; and

(*d*) contains a statement of the minimum rent and the premium referred to in paragraph (*c*) (i) above or, as the case may be, the sum referred to in paragraph (*c*) (ii) above and a statement to the effect that the parties intend duty to be charged in accordance with this section by reference to that rent and that premium or, as the case may be, that sum,

the lease shall be chargeable to stamp duty as if the premium paid by the lessee were equal to the premium or, as the case may be, the sum, stated in the lease in accordance with paragraph (*d*) above and the rent payable were as so stated.

(6) In subsection (5) above "minimum rent" in relation to any lease means the lowest rent which could become payable under the lease if it were altered as mentioned in paragraph (*b*) of that subsection at the date when the lease is granted.

(7) This section applies to instruments executed on or after 23rd March 1981 and shall be deemed to have come into force on that date.

Cross references—See FA 1987 s 54(2), (3), (4) (extension of the application of sub-ss (5), (6) above to leases granted by and to certain persons after 31 July 1987 under shared ownership schemes of local authorities and housing associations).

110 Pooled pension funds

Amendments—This section repealed by FA 1999 s 139, Sch 20 Pt V(5) with effect for instruments executed from 6 February 2000.

FINANCE ACT 1982

(1982 Chapter 39)

PART V

STAMP DUTY

129 Exemption from duty on grants, transfers to charities, etc

(1) Where any conveyance, transfer or lease is made or agreed to be made to a body of persons established for charitable purposes only or to the trustees of a trust so established or to the Trustees of the National Heritage Memorial Fund [or to the National Endowment for Science, Technology and the Arts][2], no stamp duty shall be chargeable [under Part I or II, *or paragraph 16,*[3] of Schedule 13 to the Finance Act 1999][1] on the instrument by which the conveyance, transfer or lease, or the agreement for it, is effected.

(2) An instrument in respect of which stamp duty is not chargeable by virtue only of subsection (1) above shall not be treated as duly stamped unless it is stamped in accordance with section 12 of the Stamp Act 1891 with a stamp denoting that it is not chargeable with any duty.

(3) This section applies to instruments executed on or after 22nd March 1982 and shall be deemed to have come into force on that date.

Cross references—See FA 1983 s 46(3)(*c*) (stamp duty exemption under this section for Historic Buildings and Monuments Commission for England).

Amendments—[1] Words in sub-s (1) substituted by FA 1999 s 112(4), Sch 14 para 7 with effect in relation to instruments executed after 30 September 1999. This does not apply to transfers or other instruments relating to units under a unit trust scheme by virtue of FA 1999 s 122. Previously the text read 'by virtue of any of the following headings in Schedule 1 to the Stamp Act 1891, namely, "Conveyance or Transfer on Sale", "Conveyance or Transfer of any kind not hereinbefore described" and "Lease or Tack",'.

[2] Words in sub-s (1) inserted by the National Lottery Act 1998 s 24 with effect from 2 July 1998.

[3] Words in sub-s (1) repealed by FA 2008 s 99, Sch 32 para 12 with effect in relation to instruments executed on or after 13 March 2008 and not stamped before 19 March 2008.

This amendment does not have effect in relation to an instrument effecting a land transaction or a duplicate or counterpart of such an instrument. "Land transaction" has the same meaning as in FA 2003 Pt 4, except that it does not include a transfer of an interest in a property-investment partnership (within the meaning of FA 2003 Sch 15) (FA 2008 s 99, Sch 32 para 22).

FINANCE ACT 1983

(1983 Chapter 28)

PART IV
MISCELLANEOUS AND SUPPLEMENTARY

Miscellaneous

46 Historic Buildings and Monuments Commission for England

(1)–(2) …[3]

(3) For the purposes of the enactments set out below, the [Historic Buildings and Monuments Commission][4] shall be treated as a body of persons established for charitable purposes only—

(*a*) …[3]

(*b*) …[3]

(*c*) …[2] section 129 of the Finance Act 1982 (reliefs from stamp duty).

(4) …[2]

(5) …[1]

Amendments—[1] Sub-s (5) repealed by IHTA 1984 s 277, Sch 9.
[2] Words in sub-s (3)(*c*) and sub-s (4) repealed by FA 1985 s 98(6), Sch 27 Pt IX(2).
[3] Sub-s (1), (2), (3)(*a*), (*b*) repealed by TA 1988 s 844(4), Sch 31.
[4] Words in sub-s (3) substituted by TA 1988 Sch 29 para 32 Table.

FINANCE (NO 2) ACT 1983

(1983 Chapter 49)

PART III
MISCELLANEOUS AND SUPPLEMENTARY

15 Relief from stamp duty for local constituency associations of political parties on reorganisation of constituencies

(1) In a case falling within paragraph (*a*) or paragraph (*b*) of subsection (4) of section [7 above, section 57 of the Stamp Act 1891 shall not apply in relation to a [transfer][3] by which the disposal or, in the case of paragraph (*b*), either of the disposals referred to in that paragraph is effected.][1]

(2) …[2]

Notes—Relevant provisions of s 7 referred to in sub-s (1) above are—

"7 Relief for local constituency associations of political parties on reorganisation of constituencies

(1) In this section "relevant date" means the date of coming into operation of an Order in Council under section 3 of the House of Commons (Redistribution of Seats) Act 1949 (orders specifying new parliamentary constituencies) and, in relation to any relevant date,—

(*a*) "former parliamentary constituency" means an area which, for the purposes of parliamentary elections, was a constituency immediately before that date but is no longer such a constituency after that date; and

(*b*) "new parliamentary constituency" means an area which, for the purposes of parliamentary elections, is a constituency immediately after that date but was not such a constituency before that date.

(2) In this section "local constituency association" means an unincorporated association (whether described as an association, a branch or otherwise) whose primary purpose is to further the aims of a political party in an area which at any time is or was the same or substantially the same as the area of a parliamentary constituency or two or more parliamentary constituencies and, in relation to any relevant date,—

(*a*) "existing association" means a local constituency association whose area was the same, or substantially the same, as the area of a former parliamentary constituency or two or more such constituencies; and

(*b*) "new association" means a local constituency association whose area is the same, or substantially the same, as the area of a new parliamentary constituency or two or more such constituencies.

(3) For the purposes of this section, a new association is a successor to an existing association if any part of the existing association's area is comprised in the new association's area.

(4) In any case where, before, on or after a relevant date,—

(*a*) an existing association disposes of land to a new association which is a successor to the existing association, or

(*b*) an existing association disposes of land to a body (whether corporate or unincorporated) which is an organ of the political party concerned and, as soon as practicable thereafter, that body disposes of the land to a new association which is a successor to the existing association,

the parties to the disposal or, where paragraph (*b*) above applies, to each of the disposals, shall be treated for the purposes of corporation tax in respect of chargeable gains or, as the case may require, capital gains tax as if the land

Stamp Taxes

disposed of were acquired from the existing association or the body making the disposal for a consideration of such an amount as would secure that on the disposal neither a gain nor a loss accrued to that association or body."

Amendments—[1] Words in sub-s (1) substituted by FA 1985 s 82(4) in relation to instruments executed after 25 March 1985 and instruments executed after 18 March 1985 which are stamped after 25 March 1985.

[2] Sub-s (2) repealed by FA 1985 s 98(6), Sch 27 Pt IX(1).

[3] The word "transfer" substituted for the words "conveyance or transfer" in enactments relating to stamp duty by FA 2003 Sch 20 para 3.

FINANCE ACT 1984

(1984 Chapter 43)

PART IV

STAMP DUTY

109 Reduction of stamp duty on conveyances and transfers

Amendments—This section repealed by FA 1999 Sch 20 Pt V(2) with effect in relation to instruments executed, or bearer instruments issued, from 1 October 1999, subject to the provisions in FA 1999 Sch 20 Pt V(2) Note 2. Previously the text read:

"(1) (*amends* FA 1963 s 55(1), (2) and FA (Northern Ireland) 1963 s 4(1), (2)).

(2) (*repeals* FA 1974 Sch 11 Pt III).

(3) Subject to subsection (4) below, subsections (1) and (2) above apply—

(*a*) to instruments executed on or after 20th March 1984; and

(*b*) to instruments executed on or after 13th March 1984 which are stamped on or after 20th March 1984;

and, for the purposes of section 14(4) of the Stamp Act 1891 (instruments not to be given in evidence etc unless stamped in accordance with the law in force at the time of first execution), the law in force at the time of execution of an instrument falling within paragraph (*b*) above shall be deemed to be that as varied in accordance with subsections (1) and (2) above.

(4) In the case of an instrument giving effect to a stock exchange transaction, as defined in section 4 of the Stock Transfer Act 1963 subsections (1) to (3) above do not apply unless the transaction takes place on or after 12th March 1984 and is one in respect of which settlement is due on or after 13th March 1984.

(5) This section shall be deemed to have come into force on 20th March 1984."

110 Extension of stamp duty relief on sales at discount

(1)–(3) (*amend* FA 1981 s 107(3) and *insert* s 107(3A)).

(4) Subsections (2) and (3) above have effect with respect to instruments—

(*a*) executed on or after 20th March 1984, or

(*b*) executed on or after 13th March 1984 and stamped on or after 20th March 1984,

and, for the purposes of section 14(4) of the Stamp Act 1891 (instruments not to be given in evidence etc unless stamped in accordance with the law in force at the time of first execution), the law in force at the time of execution of an instrument falling within paragraph (*b*) above shall be deemed to be that as varied in accordance with subsections (2) and (3) above.

(5) (*amends* FA 1981 s 107(3)).

111 Agreements for leases

(1) …[2]

(2) In any case where—

(*a*) an interest in land is conveyed or transferred subject to an agreement for a [lease][3] for a term exceeding 35 years, or

(*b*) a [lease][3] is granted subject to an agreement for a [lease][3] for a term exceeding 35 years,

then, whether or not the conveyance, transfer, [lease][3] is expressed to be so subject, it shall not be taken to be duly stamped unless there is denoted upon the conveyance, transfer, [lease][3] the duty paid on the agreement; and section 11 of the Stamp Act 1891 shall have effect for this purpose as if the duty chargeable on the conveyance, transfer, [lease][3] depended on the duty paid on the agreement.

(3) For the purposes of subsection (2) above, an interest conveyed or transferred or, as the case may be, a [lease][3] granted is not to be regarded as subject to an agreement for a [lease][3] if that agreement is directly enforceable against another interest in the land in relation to which the interest conveyed or transferred or, as the case may be, the [lease][3] granted is a superior interest.

(4) …[1]

(5) This section applies to any agreement for a [lease][3] entered into on or after 20th March 1984 and shall be deemed to have come into force on that date.

Amendments—[1] Sub-s (4) repealed by FA 1999 Sch 20 Pt V(1) with effect from 1 October 1999, subject to the provisions in FA 1999 Sch 20 Pt V(1) Note 2. Previously the text amended the Stamp Act 1891 s 15(2).

[2] Sub-s (1) repealed by FA 1999 Sch 20 Pt V(2) with effect in relation to instruments executed, or bearer instruments issued, from 1 October 1999, subject to the provisions in FA 1999 Sch 20 Pt V(2) Note 2. Previously the text amended the Stamp Act 1891 s 75(1) and substituted s 75(2)).

[3] "Lease" substituted for the words "lease or tack" throughout the section by FA 1999 s 112(4), Sch 14 para 2 with effect in relation to instruments executed after 30 September 1999. This does not apply to transfers or other instruments relating to units under a unit trust scheme by virtue of FA 1999 s 122.

PART VI
MISCELLANEOUS AND SUPPLEMENTARY

Miscellaneous

126 Tax exemptions in relation to designated international organisations

(1) Where—

(*a*) the United Kingdom or any of the Communities is a member of an international organisation; and

(*b*) the agreement under which it became a member provides for exemption from tax, in relation to the organisation, of the kind for which provision is made by this section;

the Treasury may, by order made by statutory instrument, designate that organisation for the purposes of this section.

(2) Where an organisation has been so designated, the provisions mentioned in subsection (3) below shall, with the exception of any which may be excluded by the designation order, apply in relation to that organisation.

(3) The provisions are—

(*a*) …[2]

(*b*) …

(*c*) no stamp duty shall be chargeable under [Schedule 15 to the Finance Act 1999 (bearer instruments)][5] on the issue of any instrument by the organisation or on the transfer of the stock constituted by, or transferable by means of, any instrument issued by the organisation;

[(*d*) no stamp duty reserve tax shall be chargeable under section 93 (depositary receipts) or 96 (clearance services) of the Finance Act 1986 in respect of the issue of securities by the organisation.][3]

[(4) The Treasury may, by order made by statutory instrument, designate any of the Communities or the European Investment Bank for the purposes of this section, and references in subsections (2) and (3) above to an organisation designated for the purposes of this section include references to a body so designated by virtue of this subsection.][1]

[(5) Subsection (3) above, as it applies by virtue of subsection (4) above, shall be read as if the words "under [Schedule 15 to the Finance Act 1999 (bearer instruments)][5]" were omitted.][4]

Note—Words omitted from sub-s (3) are not relevant to stamp duty.

Cross references—See FA 1985 s 96(2) (revocation or variation of the provisions giving stamp duty exemption in respect of issues and transfers of loan stock of European Communities and Investment Bank);

FA 1986 ss 78(4), 79(3) (stamp duty exemption on an instrument transferring loan capital issued or raised by an organisation which is designated under this section at the time of transfer).

Amendments—[1] Sub-s (4) inserted by FA 1985 s 96(1).

[2] Sub-s (3)(*a*) repealed by TA 1988 s 844(4), Sch 31.

[3] Sub-s (3)(*d*) inserted by FA 1990 s 114(1) and applies in relation to the issue of securities by a designated organisation or body according to FA 1990 s 114(2), (3).

[4] Sub-s (5) inserted by FA 1985 s 96(1).

[5] Words in sub-ss (3)(*c*) and (5) substituted by FA 1999 s 113(3), Sch 16 para 4 with effect in relation to bearer instruments issued after 30 September 1999. For prospective repeal of FA 1999 s 113, Sch 16 para 4 see FA 1999 s 123(3). Previously the text read 'the heading "Bearer Instrument" in Schedule 1 to the Stamp Act 1891'.

FINANCE ACT 1985

(1985 Chapter 54)

An Act to grant certain duties, to alter other duties, and to amend the law relating to the National Debt and the Public Revenue, and to make further provision in connection with Finance

[25th July 1985]

PART III
STAMP DUTY

81 Renounceable letters of allotment etc

(1) Subsection (2) below applies where there is an arrangement whereby—

(*a*) rights under an instrument are renounced in favour of a person (A),

(*b*) the rights are rights to shares in a company (company B), and

(*c*) A, or a person connected with A, or A and such a person together, has or have control of company B or will have such control in consequence of the arrangement.

[(2) The instrument shall not be exempt by virtue of paragraph 24(*d*) of Schedule 13 to the Finance Act 1999 (renounceable letters of allotment, etc) from stamp duty under or by reference to Part I of that Schedule ([transfer][3] on sale).][2]

(3) References in this section to shares in company B include references to its loan capital to which [section 79(4) of the Finance Act 1986 does not apply by virtue of section 79(5) or (6)][2] (convertible loan capital and excessive return capital).

(4) In this section "shares" includes stock.

(5) For the purposes of this section a person has control of company B if he has power to control company B's affairs by virtue of holding shares in, or possessing voting power in relation to, company B or any other body corporate.

(6) For the purposes of this section one person is connected with another if he would be so connected for the purposes of the [Taxation of Chargeable Gains Tax Act 1992][1].

(7) This section applies to instruments if rights are renounced under them on or after 1st August 1985, except where the arrangement concerned includes an offer for the rights and on or before 27th June 1985 the offer became unconditional as to acceptances.

Cross references—See FA 1986 s 78(10) (in construing sub-s (3) above, the effect of FA 1986 s 78 (loan capital) to be ignored).

Notes—This section was to be repealed by FA 1990 Sch 19 Pt VI with effect from an appointed day in accordance with FA 1990 ss 107–111. The Treasury order specifying the appointed day for the purposes of FA 1990 ss 107–110 was to coincide with the start of paperless trading under the Stock Exchange's planned TAURUS system (IR press release, 20-3-90). However, on 11-3-93 the London Stock Exchange News Release 6/93 announced that TAURUS had been abandoned.

Amendments—[1] Words in sub-s (6) substituted by TCGA 1992 s 290(1), Sch 10 para 9.

[2] Sub-s (2) and words in sub-s (3) substituted by FA 1999 s 112(4), Sch 14 para 8 with effect in relation to instruments executed after 30 September 1999. This does not apply to transfers or other instruments relating to units under a unit trust scheme by virtue of FA 1999 s 122. For prospective repeal of FA 1999 Sch 14 para 8 see FA 1999 s 123(3). Previously the text read:

"(2) The instrument shall not be exempt by virtue of section 65 (1) of the Finance Act 1963 (renounceable letters of allotment etc) or section 14(1) of the Finance Act (Northern Ireland) 1963 (corresponding provision for Northern Ireland) from stamp duty under or by reference to the heading "Conveyance or Transfer on Sale" in Schedule 1 to the Stamp Act 1891.' and

'section 126(1) of the Finance Act 1976 does not apply by virtue of section 126(2) or (3)' respectively.".

[3] The word "transfer" substituted for the words "conveyance or transfer" in enactments relating to stamp duty by FA 2003 Sch 20 para 3.

82 Gifts inter vivos

(1) The stamp duty chargeable by virtue of section 74 of the Finance (1909–10) Act 1910 (gifts inter vivos) is abolished.

(2) (*amends* Stamp Act 1891, s 58 (7)).

(3) (*amends* FA 1965 s 90(5) and FA (Northern Ireland) 1965, s 4(5)).

(4) (*amends* F(No 2)A 1983 s 15(1)).

(5) *An instrument*—

(*a*) *in respect of which stamp duty would be chargeable by virtue of section 74 of the 1910 Act apart from this section, and*

(*b*) *on which stamp duty is not chargeable under [Part I of Schedule 13 to the Finance Act 1999 ([transfer][2] on sale)][1],*

shall not be deemed to be duly stamped unless it has, in accordance with section 12 of the 1891 Act, been stamped with a particular stamp denoting that it is duly stamped or that it is not chargeable with any duty.[3]

(6) This section applies to—

(*a*) instruments executed on or after 26th March 1985, and

(*b*) instruments executed on or after 19th March 1985 which are stamped on or after 26th March 1985.

(7) For the purposes of section 14 (4) of the Stamp Act 1891 (instruments not to be given in evidence etc unless stamped in accordance with the law in force at the time of first execution), the law in force at the time of execution of an instrument falling within subsection (6) (*b*) above shall be deemed to be that as varied in accordance with this section.

(8) The preceding provisions of this section shall be deemed to have come into operation on 26th March 1985.

(9) *Subsection* (*5*) *above does not apply to an instrument which is required by regulations under section 87* (*1*) *or* (*2*) *below to be certified.*[3]

Cross references—See the Stamp Duty (Exempt Instruments) Regulations, SI 1987/516 for certain instruments executed after 30 April 1987 to which sub-s (5) above does not apply.

Amendments—[1] Words in sub-s (5) substituted by FA 1999 s 112(4), Sch 14 para 9 with effect in relation to instruments executed after 30 September 1999. This does not apply to transfers or other instruments relating to units under a unit trust scheme by virtue of FA 1999 s 122. Previously the text read 'the heading "Conveyance or Transfer on Sale" in Schedule 1 to the Stamp Act 1891'.

[2] The word "transfer" substituted for the words "conveyance or transfer" in enactments relating to stamp duty by FA 2003 Sch 20 para 3.

[3] Sub-ss (5), (9) repealed by FA 2008 s 100(1) with effect in relation to instruments executed on or after 13 March 2008, other than instruments effecting a land transaction (within the meaning of FA 2008 Sch 32 para 22).

83 Transfers in connection with divorce[, dissolution of civil partnership,][4] etc

(1) Stamp duty under [Part I of Schedule 13 to the Finance Act 1999 ([transfer][3] on sale)][2] shall not be chargeable on an instrument by which property is conveyed or transferred from one party to a marriage to the other if the instrument—

(*a*) is executed in pursuance of an order of a court made on granting in respect of the parties a decree of divorce, nullity of marriage or judicial separation, or

(*b*) is executed in pursuance of an order of a court which is made in connection with the dissolution or annulment of the marriage or the parties' judicial separation and which is made at any time after the granting of such a decree, or

[(*bb*) is executed in pursuance of an order of a court which is made at any time under section 22A, 23A or 24A of the Matrimonial Causes Act 1973, or][1]

(*c*) is executed at any time in pursuance of an agreement of the parties made in contemplation of or otherwise in connection with the dissolution or annulment of the marriage[, their judicial separation or the making of a separation order in respect of them][1].

[(1A) Stamp duty under Part 1 of Schedule 13 to the Finance Act 1999 shall not be chargeable on an instrument by which property is conveyed or transferred from one party to a civil partnership to the other if the instrument—

(*a*) is executed in pursuance of an order of a court made on granting in respect of the parties an order or decree for the dissolution or annulment of the civil partnership or their judicial separation;

(*b*) is executed in pursuance of an order of a court which is made in connection with the dissolution or annulment of the civil partnership or the parties' judicial separation and which is made at any time after the granting of such an order or decree for dissolution, annulment or judicial separation as mentioned in paragraph (*a*);

(*c*) is executed in pursuance of an order of a court which is made at any time under any provision of Schedule 5 to the Civil Partnership Act 2004 that corresponds to section 22A, 23A or 24A of the Matrimonial Causes Act 1973; or

(*d*) is executed at any time in pursuance of an agreement of the parties made in contemplation of or otherwise in connection with the dissolution or annulment of the civil partnership, their judicial separation or the making of a separation order in respect of them.][4]

(2) *An instrument in respect of which stamp duty is not chargeable under the heading mentioned in subsection (1) [or (1A)][4] above by virtue only of that subsection shall be chargeable under this subsection with stamp duty of [£5]*[2].[5]

(3) This section applies to instruments executed on or after 26th March 1985 and shall be deemed to have come into operation on that date.

Cross references—See the Stamp Duty (Exempt Instruments) Regulations, SI 1987/516 for stamp duty exemption in respect of certain instruments executed after 30 April 1987 otherwise chargeable under this section.

Amendments—[1] Sub-s (1)(*bb*) inserted and words in sub-s (1)(*c*) substituted (for "or their judicial separation") by the Family Law Act 1996 s 66(1), Sch 8 Pt I para 33, subject to a saving in s 66(2), Sch 9 para 5.

[2] Words in sub-s (1) and figures in sub-s (2) substituted by FA 1999 s 112(4), Sch 14 para 10 with effect in relation to instruments executed after 30 September 1999. This does not apply to transfers or other instruments relating to units under a unit trust scheme by virtue of FA 1999 s 122. Previously the text read 'the heading "Conveyance or Transfer on Sale" in Schedule 1 to the Stamp Act 1891' and '50p'.

[3] The word "transfer" substituted for the words "conveyance or transfer" in enactments relating to stamp duty by FA 2003 Sch 20 para 3.

[4] Sub-s (1A), words in sub-s (2) and words in heading, inserted by Tax and Civil Partnership Regulations, SI 2005/3229 regs 40, 41 with effect from 5 December 2005 (reg 1(1)).

[5] Sub-s (2) repealed by FA 2008 s 99, Sch 32 paras 1, 2 with effect in relation to instruments executed on or after 13 March 2008 and not stamped before 19 March 2008.

This amendment does not have effect in relation to an instrument effecting a land transaction or a duplicate or counterpart of such an instrument. "Land transaction" has the same meaning as in FA 2003 Pt 4, except that it does not include a transfer of an interest in a property-investment partnership (within the meaning of FA 2003 Sch 15) (FA 2008 s 99, Sch 32 para 22).

84 Death: varying dispositions, and appropriations

(1) Where, within the period of two years after a person's death, any of the dispositions (whether effected by will, under the law relating to intestacy or otherwise) of the property of which he was competent to dispose are varied by an instrument executed by the persons or any of the persons who benefit or would benefit under the dispositions, stamp duty under [Part I of Schedule 13 to the Finance Act 1999 ([transfer][2] on sale)][1] shall not be chargeable on the instrument.

(2) Subsection (1) above does not apply where the variation is made for any consideration in money or money's worth other than consideration consisting of the making of a variation in respect of another of the dispositions.

(3) Subsection (1) above applies whether or not the administration of the estate is complete or the property has been distributed in accordance with the original dispositions.

(4) Where property is appropriated by a personal representative in or towards satisfaction of a general legacy of money, stamp duty under the heading mentioned in subsection (1) above shall not be chargeable on an instrument giving effect to the appropriation.

(5) Where on an intestacy property is appropriated by a personal representative in or towards satisfaction of any interest of a surviving [spouse or civil partner][3] in the intestate's estate, stamp duty under the heading mentioned in subsection (1) above shall not be chargeable on an instrument giving effect to the appropriation.

(6) The reference in subsection (5) above to an interest in the intestate's estate—

(*a*) includes a reference to the capital value of a life interest which the surviving [spouse or civil partner][3] has under the Intestates' Estates Act 1952 elected to have redeemed, and

(*b*) in Scotland, includes a reference to prior rights (within the meaning of the Succession (Scotland) Act 1964) but, without prejudice to subsection (7) below, not to such rights as are mentioned in that subsection.

(7) Where in Scotland, on an intestacy or otherwise, property is appropriated by a personal representative in or towards satisfaction of the right of a husband to *jus relicti*, of a wife to *jus* [*relictae*, of issue to *legitim* or rights under section 131 of the Civil Partnership Act 2004, or of a civil partner to rights under section 131 of that Act][3], stamp duty under the heading mentioned in subsection (1) above shall not be chargeable on an instrument giving effect to the appropriation.

(8), (9) …[4]

(10) Subject to subsection (11) below, this section applies to instruments executed on or after 26th March 1985 and shall be deemed to have come into operation on that date.

(11) Subsections (5) to (7) above …[4] apply to instruments executed on or after 1st August 1985.

Cross references—See the Stamp Duty (Exempt Instruments) Regulations, SI 1987/516 for stamp duty exemption in respect of certain instruments executed after 30 April 1987 otherwise chargeable under this section.

Amendments—[1] Words in sub-s (1) and figures in sub-s (8) substituted by FA 1999 s 112(4), Sch 14 para 11 with effect in relation to instruments executed after 30 September 1999. This does not apply to transfers or other instruments relating to units under a unit trust scheme by virtue of FA 1999 s 122. Previously the text read 'the heading "Conveyance or Transfer on Sale" in Schedule 1 to the Stamp Act 1891' and '50p'.

[2] The word "transfer" substituted for the words "conveyance or transfer" in enactments relating to stamp duty by FA 2003 Sch 20 para 3.

[3] Words in sub-ss (5), (6)(*a*) inserted, and words in sub-s (7) substituted by Tax and Civil Partnership Regulations, SI 2005/3229, regs 40, 42, with effect from 5 December 2005 (reg 1(1)).

[4] Sub-ss (8), (9), and words "and, so far as it relates to subsection (5) or (7), subsection (8) above" in sub-s (11), repealed by FA 2008 s 99, Sch 32 paras 1, 3 with effect in relation to instruments executed on or after 13 March 2008 and not stamped before 19 March 2008. Sub-ss (8), (9) previously read as follows—

"(8) An instrument in respect of which stamp duty is not chargeable under the heading mentioned in subsection (1) above by virtue only of subsection (1), (4), (5) or (7) above shall be chargeable under this subsection with stamp duty of [£5].

(9) But an instrument which is chargeable under subsection (8) above shall not be treated as duly stamped unless it has, in accordance with section 12 of the Stamp Act 1891, been stamped with a particular stamp denoting that it is duly stamped.".

This amendment does not have effect in relation to an instrument effecting a land transaction or a duplicate or counterpart of such an instrument. "Land transaction" has the same meaning as in FA 2003 Part 4, except that it does not include a transfer of an interest in a property-investment partnership (within the meaning of FA 2003 Sch 15) (FA 2008 s 99, Sch 32 para 22).

85 Repeal of certain fixed duties

(1) (*repeals certain headings in* Stamp Act 1891 Sch 1).

(2) (*amends* FA 1907 s 7).

(3) This section and that Schedule apply to—

(*a*) instruments executed on or after 26th March 1985, and

(*b*) instruments executed on or after 19th March 1985 which are not stamped before 26th March 1985.

(4) For the purposes of section 14(4) of the Stamp Act 1891 (instruments not to be given in evidence etc unless stamped in accordance with the law in force at the time of first execution), the law in force at the time of execution of an instrument falling within subsection (3)(*b*) above shall be deemed to be that as varied in accordance with this section.

(5) This section and that Schedule shall be deemed to have come into operation on 26th March 1985.

86 Abolition of duty on contract notes

(*repeals* F(1909–10)A 1910, s 77 (1), (2)).

87 Certificates

(1) The Commissioners may make regulations providing that an instrument which is of a kind specified in them—

(*a*) shall be certified to be an instrument of that kind, and

(*b*) shall not be treated as duly stamped if it is not so certified.

(2) The Treasury may make regulations providing that an instrument which is of a kind specified in them, and which would apart from this subsection be chargeable with stamp duty of a fixed amount under any provision so specified, shall not be charged with such duty under that provision if it is certified to be an instrument of that kind.

(3) Certification under this section shall be by such method as the regulations may specify, and in particular they may provide for a certificate to be borne by or attached to or otherwise associated with an instrument in such manner as they may specify.

(4) A certificate under this section shall be in such form and signed by such person as the regulations may specify.

(5) Regulations under this section may contain such incidental or consequential provisions as the Commissioners or Treasury (as the case may be) think fit.

(6) Regulations under this section may make different provision for different cases or descriptions of case.

(7) The power to make regulations under this section shall be exercisable by statutory instrument subject to annulment in pursuance of a resolution of the House of Commons.

88 Exchange rates

Section 12 of the Finance Act 1899 (fixed exchange rate for foreign currency) shall not apply to instruments executed on or after 1st August 1985, and section 6 of the Stamp Act 1891 (exchange rate at date of instrument) shall apply to instruments to which section 12 of the 1899 Act would apply if this Act had not been passed.

89 Exemption from section 28 of Finance Act 1931

(1) Section 28 of the Finance Act 1931 (production to Commissioners of instruments transferring land and furnishing of particulars) shall not apply in relation to any instrument (an "exempt instrument") which falls within any class prescribed for the purposes of this section by regulations made by the Commissioners.

(2) Regulations under this section may—

(*a*) provide that the particulars mentioned in Schedule 2 to the 1931 Act shall be furnished to the Commissioners, in accordance with the requirements of the regulations, in respect of exempt instruments or such descriptions of exempt instruments as may be prescribed by the regulations;

(*b*) make different provision in relation to different cases or kinds of case and in respect of different parts of Great Britain.

(3) Any person who fails to comply with any requirement imposed by regulations made under this section shall be liable on summary conviction to a fine not exceeding level 3 on the standard scale …[1]

(4) The power to make regulations under this section shall be exercisable by statutory instrument; and a statutory instrument containing regulations under this section shall be subject to annulment in pursuance of a resolution of the House of Commons.

(5) Section 35 (*x*) of the 1931 Act (which gives power by regulations to exempt certain instruments in Scotland where particulars are obtained through the General Register of Sasines and which is superseded by the power given by this section) shall cease to have effect.

(6) Regulations made under section 35 (*x*) shall have effect after the commencement of this section as if they were made under this section and as if they imposed on the Keeper of the Registers of Scotland the duty mentioned in section 35 (*x*).

Regulations—See The Stamp Duty (Exempt Instruments) Regulations, SI 1985/1688.
Amendments—[1] Words in sub-s (3) repealed by the Statute Law (Repeals) Act 1993 s 1(1), Sch 1 Pt XIV.

PART V

MISCELLANEOUS AND SUPPLEMENTARY

96 European Communities and Investment Bank: exemptions

(1) (*inserts* FA 1984 s 126(4), (5)).

(2) An order made by virtue of subsection (4) of section 126 of the Finance Act 1984 may revoke or vary the European Communities (Loan Stock) (Stamp Duties) Order 1972 (which provides for exemption from stamp duty in respect of issues and transfers of loan stock of the bodies referred to in that subsection, other than the Economic Community).

98 Short title, interpretation, construction and repeals

(1) This Act may be cited as the Finance Act 1985.

(2)–(3) (*not relevant to stamp duty*).

(4) Part III of this Act shall be construed as one with the Stamp Act 1891.

(5) (*not relevant to stamp duty*).

(6) The enactments specified in Schedule 27 to this Act are hereby repealed to the extent specified in the third column of that Schedule, but subject to any provision at the end of any Part of that Schedule.

FINANCE ACT 1986

(1986 Chapter 41)

ARRANGEMENT OF SECTIONS

PART III
STAMP DUTY

PART IV
STAMP DUTY RESERVE TAX

An Act to grant certain duties, to alter other duties, and to amend the law relating to the National Debt and the Public Revenue, and to make further provision in connection with Finance

[25th July 1986]

PART III

STAMP DUTY

Securities

64 Stock or marketable securities: reduction of rate

Amendments—This section repealed by FA 1999 Sch 20 Pt V(2) with effect in relation to instruments executed, or bearer instruments issued, from 1 October 1999, subject to the provisions in FA 1999 Sch 20 Pt V(2) Note 2. Previously the text amended FA 1963 s 55 *and FA (Northern Ireland) 1963 s 4.*

65 Bearers: consequential provisions etc

Amendments—This section repealed by FA 1999 Sch 20 Pt V(2) with effect in relation to instruments executed, or bearer instruments issued, from 1 October 1999, subject to the provisions in FA 1999 Sch 20 Pt V(2) Note 2. Previously the text amended SA 1891, Sch 1 heading "Bearer Instrument", FA 1963 s 59(3) and FA (Northern Ireland) 1963, s 8.

66 Company's purchase of own shares

(1) This section applies where a company purchases its own shares under section [690][3] of the Companies Act [2006][3] …[3].

(2) [Any return which relates to any of the shares][1] purchased and is delivered to the registrar of companies under section [707][3]][1] of that Act …[3] shall be charged with stamp duty, and treated for all purposes of the Stamp Act 1891, as if it were an instrument transferring the shares [to which it relates][1] on sale to the company in pursuance of the contract (or contracts) of purchase concerned.

(2A) …[2]

(3) Subject to subsection (4) below, this section applies to any [such return][3] which is delivered to the registrar of companies on or after the day of The Stock Exchange reforms.

(4) This section does not apply to any return to the extent that the shares to which it relates were purchased under a contract entered into before the day of The Stock Exchange reforms.

(5) In this section "the day of The Stock Exchange reforms" means the day on which the rule of The Stock Exchange that prohibits a person from carrying on business as both a broker and a jobber is abolished.

Note—This section was to be repealed by FA 1990 Sch 19 Pt VI with effect from an appointed day in accordance with FA 1990 ss 107–111. The Treasury order specifying the appointed day for the purposes of FA 1990 ss 107–110 was to coincide with the start of paperless trading under the Stock Exchange's planned TAURUS system (IR press release, 20-3-90). However, on 11-3-93 the London Stock Exchange News Release 6/93 announced that TAURUS had been abandoned.

Amendments—[1] Words in sub-s (2) substituted and inserted; and reference in sub-ss (2), (3) inserted by FA 2003 s 195, Sch 40 para 2 with effect for any acquisition of shares by a company on or after 1 December 2003 (by virtue of SI 2003/3077).

[2] Sub-s (2A) repealed by FA 2008 s 99, Sch 32 paras 4, 5 with effect in relation to instruments executed on or after 13 March 2008 and not stamped before 19 March 2008. Sub-s (2A) previously read as follows—

"(2A) Any return which relates to the cancellation of any of the shares purchased and is delivered to the registrar of companies under section 169A of the Companies Act 1985 shall be chargeable under this subsection with stamp duty of £5.".

[3] In sub-s (1), figures substituted for figures "162" and "1985", and words "or Article 47 of the Companies (Northern Ireland) Order 1982" repealed, in sub-s (2), reference substituted for reference "169(1) or (1B)", and words " or, as the

case may be, Article 53 of that Order" repealed, and in sub-s (3), words substituted for words "return under section 169[(1) or (1B] of the Companies Act 1985 or Article 53 of the Companies (Northern Ireland) Order 1982,", by the Companies Act 2006 (Consequential Amendments) (Taxes and National Insurance) Order, SI 2009/1890 art 7(*a*)–(*c*) with effect from 1 October 2009.

Depositary receipts

67 Depositary receipts

(1) Subject to subsection (9) below, subsection (2) or (3) below (as the case may be) applies where an instrument [(other than a bearer instrument)][6] transfers relevant securities of a company incorporated in the United Kingdom to a person who at the time of the transfer falls within subsection (6), (7) or (8) below.

[(2) If stamp duty is chargeable on the instrument under Part I of Schedule 13 to the Finance Act 1999 ([transfer][4] on sale), the rate at which that duty is chargeable is 1.5% of the amount or value of the consideration for the sale to which the instrument gives effect.

(3) [In any other case—

(*a*) stamp duty is chargeable on the instrument under this subsection, and

(*b*)][7] subject to subsection (5), the rate at which that duty is chargeable is 1.5% of the value of the securities at the date the instrument is executed.][2]

(4) …[1]

(5) In a case where—

(*a*) securities are issued, or securities sold are transferred, and (in either case) they are to be paid for in instalments,

(*b*) the person to whom they are issued or transferred holds them and transfers them to another person when the last instalment is paid,

(*c*) the transfer to the other person is effected by an instrument in the case of which subsection (3) above applies,

(*d*) before the execution of the instrument mentioned in paragraph (*c*) above an instrument is received by a person falling (at the time of the receipt) within subsection (6), (7) or (8) below,

(*e*) the instrument so received evidences all the rights which (by virtue of the terms under which the securities are issued or sold as mentioned in paragraph (*a*) above) subsist in respect of them at the time of the receipt, and

(*f*) the instrument mentioned in paragraph (*c*) above contains a statement that paragraphs (*a*), (*b*) and (*e*) above are fulfilled,

subsection (3) above shall have effect as if the reference to the value there mentioned were to an amount (if any) equal to the total of the instalments payable, less those paid before the transfer to the other person is effected.

(6) A person falls within this subsection if his business is exclusively that of holding relevant securities—

(*a*) as nominee or agent for a person whose business is or includes issuing depositary receipts for relevant securities, and

(*b*) for the purposes of such part of the business mentioned in paragraph (*a*) above as consists of issuing such depositary receipts (in a case where the business does not consist exclusively of that).

(7) A person falls within this subsection if—

(*a*) he is specified for the purposes of this subsection by the Treasury by order made by statutory instrument, and

(*b*) his business is or includes issuing depositary receipts for relevant securities.

(8) A person falls within this subsection if—

(*a*) he is specified for the purposes of this subsection by the Treasury by order made by statutory instrument,

(*b*) he does not fall within subsection (6) above but his business includes holding relevant securities as nominee or agent for a person who falls within subsection (7)(*b*) above at the time of the transfer, and

(*c*) he holds relevant securities as nominee or agent for such a person, for the purposes of such part of that person's business as consists of issuing depositary receipts for relevant securities (in a case where that business does not consist exclusively of that).

(9) Where an instrument transfers relevant securities of a company incorporated in the United Kingdom—

(*a*) to a company which at the time of the transfer falls within subsection (6) above *and is resident in the United Kingdom*[3], and

(*b*) from a company which at that time falls within that subsection *and is so resident*[3],

subsections (2) to (5) above shall not apply and [stamp duty is not chargeable on the instrument][5].

[(9A) In this section "bearer instrument" has the meaning given in paragraph 3 of Schedule 15 to the Finance Act 1999.][6]

(10) This section applies to any instrument executed on or after the day on which the rule of The Stock Exchange that prohibits a person from carrying on business as both a broker and a jobber is abolished.

Cross references—See FA 1988 s 143(6) (UK company shares paired with foreign company shares; in relation to certain instruments transferring paired shares and executed after 29 July 1988, the foreign company to be treated for the purposes of this section as incorporated in the UK);
FA 1990 ss 108(8), 111(1) (abolition of stamp duty with effect from an appointed day on transfer of securities).

Note—This section was to be repealed by FA 1990 Sch 19 Pt VI with effect from an appointed day in accordance with FA 1990 ss 107–111. The Treasury order specifying the appointed day for the purposes of FA 1990 ss 107–110 was to coincide with the start of paperless trading under the Stock Exchange's planned TAURUS system (IR press release, 20-3-90). However, on 11-3-93 the London Stock Exchange News Release 6/93 announced that TAURUS had been abandoned.

Amendments—[1] Sub-s (4) repealed by FA 1997 s 99(1), Sch 18 Pt VII with effect for any instrument executed on or after 20 October 1997 (the date appointed under FA 1997 s 97 by virtue of SI 1997/2428) except an instrument which transfers relevant securities which were acquired by the transferor before that date. Previously the text read:

"(4) Subsection (3) above shall have effect as if "£1.50" read "£1" in a case where—

(*a*) at the time of the transfer the transferor is a qualified dealer in securities of the kind concerned or a nominee of such a qualified dealer,

(*b*) the transfer is made for the purposes of the dealer's business,

(*c*) at the time of the transfer the dealer is not a market maker in securities of the kind concerned, and

(*d*) the instrument contains a statement that paragraphs (*a*) to (*c*) above are fulfilled."

[2] Sub-ss (2) and (3) substituted by FA 1999 s 112(4), Sch 14 para 12 with effect in relation to instruments executed after 30 September 1999. This does not apply to transfers or other instruments relating to units under a unit trust scheme by virtue of FA 1999 s 122. For prospective repeal of FA 1999 Sch 14 para 12 see FA 1999 s 123(3). Previously the text read:

"(2) If stamp duty is chargeable on the instrument under the heading "Conveyance or Transfer on Sale" in Schedule 1 to the Stamp Act 1891, the rate at which the duty is charged under that heading shall be the rate of £1.50 for every £100 or part of £100 of the amount or value of the consideration for the sale to which the instrument gives effect.

(3) If stamp duty is chargeable on the instrument under the heading "Conveyance or Transfer of any kind not hereinbefore described" in Schedule 1 to the Stamp Act 1891, the rate at which the duty is charged under that heading shall (subject to [subsection] (5) below) be the rate of £1.50 for every £100 or part of £100 of the value of the securities at the date the instrument is executed."

[3] Words in sub-s (9) repealed by FA 2000 s 134(3), (5), Sch 40 Pt III with effect for stamp duty purposes for instruments executed after 28 July 2000 and for stamp duty reserve tax purposes for securities transferred after 28 July 2000.

[4] The word "transfer" substituted for the words "conveyance or transfer" in enactments relating to stamp duty by FA 2003 Sch 20 para 3.

[5] In sub-s (9), words "the stamp duty chargeable on the instrument is £5" substituted by FA 2008 s 99, Sch 32 paras 4, 6 with effect in relation to instruments executed on or after 13 March 2008 and not stamped before 19 March 2008.

[6] Words in sub-s (1) and whole of sub-s (9A) inserted, and words in sub-s (3) substituted by FA 2008 s 99, Sch 32 paras 13, 14 with effect in relation to instruments executed on or after 13 March 2008 and not stamped before 19 March 2008. If a day is appointed under FA 1990 s 111 (abolition day), FA 2008 Sch 32 paras 14, 15 cease to have effect in accordance with FA 1990 s 108 (FA 2008 s 99, Sch 32 para 23).

Sub-s (3) previously read as follows—

"(3) If stamp duty is chargeable on the instrument under paragraph 16 of Schedule 13 to the Finance Act 1999 (transfer otherwise than on sale), then, subject to subsection (5), the rate at which that duty is chargeable is 1.5% of the value of the securities at the date the instrument is executed.".

68 Depositary receipts: notification

(1) A person whose business is or includes issuing depositary receipts for relevant securities of a company incorporated in the United Kingdom shall notify the Commissioners of that fact before the end of the period of one month beginning with the date on which he first issues such depositary receipts.

(2) A person whose business includes (but does not exclusively consist of) holding relevant securities (being securities of a company incorporated in the United Kingdom)—

(*a*) as nominee or agent for a person whose business is or includes issuing depositary receipts for relevant securities, and

(*b*) for the purposes of such part of the business mentioned in paragraph (*a*) above as consists of issuing such depositary receipts (in a case where the business does not consist exclusively of that),

shall notify the Commissioners of that fact before the end of the period of one month beginning with the date on which he first holds such relevant securities as such a nominee or agent and for such purposes.

(3) A company which is incorporated in the United Kingdom and becomes aware that any shares in the company are held by a person such as is mentioned in subsection (1) or (2) above shall notify the Commissioners of that fact before the end of the period of one month beginning with the date on which the company first becomes aware of that fact.

(4) A person who fails to comply with subsection (1) or (2) above shall be liable to a [penalty][1] not exceeding £1,000.

(5) A company which fails to comply with subsection (3) above shall be liable to a [penalty][1] not exceeding £100.

(6) …[2]

Cross references—See FA 1988 s 143(6) (UK company shares paired with foreign company shares; in relation to certain instruments transferring paired shares and executed after 29 July 1988, the foreign company to be treated for the purposes of this section as incorporated in the UK);
FA 1990 ss 109(4), (5), 111(1) (abolition of the requirement of notification under sub-ss (1), (2), (3) with effect from an appointed day).

Note—This section was to be repealed by FA 1990 Sch 19 Pt VI with effect from an appointed day in accordance with FA 1990 ss 107–111. The Treasury order specifying the appointed day for the purposes of FA 1990 ss 107–110 was to coincide with the start of paperless trading under the Stock Exchange's planned TAURUS system (IR press release, 20-3-90). However, on 11-3-93 the London Stock Exchange News Release 6/93 announced that TAURUS had been abandoned.

Amendments—[1] Words in sub-ss (4) and (5) substituted by FA 1999 s 114, Sch 17 para 8 with effect in relation to penalties in respect of things done or omitted after 30 September 1999. For prospective repeal of FA 1999 Sch 17 para 8 see FA 1999 s 123(3). Previously the text read 'fine'.

[2] Sub-s (6) repealed by FA 1999 Sch 20 Pt V(3) with effect in relation to things done or omitted from 1 October 1999.

69 Depositary receipts: supplementary

(1) For the purposes of sections 67 and 68 above a depositary receipt for relevant securities is an instrument acknowledging—

(*a*) that a person holds relevant securities or evidence of the right to receive them, and

(*b*) that another person is entitled to rights, whether expressed as units or otherwise, in or in relation to relevant securities of the same kind, including the right to receive such securities (or evidence of the right to receive them) from the person mentioned in paragraph (*a*) above,

except that for those purposes a depositary receipt for relevant securities does not include an instrument acknowledging rights in or in relation to securities if they are issued or sold under terms providing for payment in instalments and for the issue of the instrument as evidence that an instalment has been paid.

(2) The Treasury may by regulations provide that for subsection (1) above (as it has effect for the time being) there shall be substituted a subsection containing a different definition of a depositary receipt for the purposes of sections 67 and 68 above.

(3) References in this section and sections 67 and 68 above to relevant securities, or to relevant securities of a company, are to shares in or stock or marketable securities of any company (which, unless otherwise stated, need not be incorporated in the United Kingdom).

(4) For the purposes of section 67 (3) above the value of securities at the date the instrument is executed shall be taken to be the price they might reasonably be expected to fetch on a sale at that time in the open market.

(5) …[2]

(6)–(8) …[1]

(9) The power to make regulations or an order under this section shall be exercisable by statutory instrument subject to annulment in pursuance of a resolution of the House of Commons.

Note—This section was to be repealed by FA 1990 Sch 19 Pt VI with effect from an appointed day in accordance with FA 1990 ss 107–111. The Treasury order specifying the appointed day for the purposes of FA 1990 ss 107–110 was to coincide with the start of paperless trading under the Stock Exchange's planned TAURUS system (IR press release, 20-3-90). However, on 11-3-93 the London Stock Exchange News Release 6/93 announced that TAURUS had been abandoned.

Amendments—[1] Sub-ss (6) to (8) repealed by FA 1997 s 99(2), Sch 18 Pt VII with effect for any instrument executed on or after 20 October 1997 (the date appointed under FA 1997 s 97 by virtue of SI 1997/2428) except an instrument which transfers relevant securities which were acquired by the transferor before that date. Previously the text read:

"(6) For the purposes of section 67 (4) above a person is a qualified dealer in securities of a particular kind if he deals in securities of that kind and—

(*a*) is a member of a recognised stock exchange (within the meaning given by section 841 of the Taxes Act 1988, or

(*b*) is designated a qualified dealer by order made by the Treasury.

(7) For the purposes of section 67 (4) above a person is a market maker in securities of a particular kind if he—

(*a*) holds himself out at all normal times in compliance with the rules of The Stock Exchange as willing to buy and sell securities of that kind at a price specified by him, and

(*b*) is recognised as doing so by the Council of The Stock Exchange.

(8) The Treasury may by regulations provide that for subsection (7) above (as it has effect for the time being) there shall be substituted a subsection containing a different definition of a market maker for the purposes of section 67 (4) above."

[2] Sub-s (5) repealed by FA 1999 Sch 20 Pt V(1) with effect from 1 October 1999, subject to the provisions in FA 1999 Sch 20 Pt V(1) Note 2. Previously the text read:

"(5) Where section 67 (3) above applies, section 15 (2) of the Stamp Act 1891 (stamping of instruments after execution) shall have effect as if the instrument were specified in the first column of the table in paragraph (*d*) and the transferee were specified (opposite the instrument) in the second."

Clearance services

70 Clearance services

(1) Subject to subsection (9) [and section 97A][2] below, subsection (2) or (3) below (as the case may be) applies where an instrument [(other than a bearer instrument)][8] transfers relevant securities of a company incorporated in the United Kingdom to a person who at the time of the transfer falls within subsection (6), (7) or (8) below.

[(2) If stamp duty is chargeable on the instrument under Part I of Schedule 13 to the Finance Act 1999 ([transfer][6] on sale), the rate at which that duty is chargeable is 1.5% of the amount or value of the consideration for the sale to which the instrument gives effect.

(3) [In any other case—

(*a*) stamp duty is chargeable on the instrument under this subsection, and

(*b*)][8] subject to subsection (5), the rate at which that duty is chargeable is 1.5% of the value of the securities at the date the instrument is executed.][4]

(4) …[3]

(5) In a case where—

(*a*) securities are issued, or securities sold are transferred, and (in either case) they are to be paid for in instalments,

(*b*) the person to whom they are issued or transferred holds them and transfers them to another person when the last instalment is paid,

(*c*) the transfer to the other person is effected by an instrument in the case of which subsection (3) above applies,
(*d*) before the execution of the instrument mentioned in paragraph (*c*) above an instrument is received by a person falling (at the time of the receipt) within subsection (6), (7) or (8) below,
(*e*) the instrument so received evidences all the rights which (by virtue of the terms under which the securities are issued or sold as mentioned in paragraph (*a*) above) subsist in respect of them at the time of the receipt, and
(*f*) the instrument mentioned in paragraph (*c*) above contains a statement that paragraphs (*a*), (*b*) and (*e*) above are fulfilled,

subsection (3) above shall have effect as if the reference to the value there mentioned were to an amount (if any) equal to the total of the instalments payable, less those paid before the transfer to the other person is effected.

(6) A person falls within this subsection if his business is exclusively that of holding [shares, stock or other marketable][1] securities—

(*a*) as nominee or agent for a person whose business is or includes the provision of clearance services for the purchase and sale of relevant securities, and
(*b*) for the purposes of such part of the business mentioned in paragraph (*a*) above as consists of the provision of such clearance services (in a case where the business does not consist exclusively of that).

(7) A person falls within this subsection if—

(*a*) he is specified for the purposes of this subsection by the Treasury by order made by statutory instrument, and
(*b*) his business is or includes the provision of clearance services for the purchase and sale of relevant securities.

(8) A person falls within this subsection if—

(*a*) he is specified for the purposes of this subsection by the Treasury by order made by statutory instrument,
(*b*) he does not fall within subsection (6) above but his business includes holding relevant securities as nominee or agent for a person who falls within subsection (7) (*b*) above at the time of the transfer, and
(*c*) he holds relevant securities as nominee or agent for such a person, for the purposes of such part of that person's business as consists of the provision of clearance services for the purchase and sale of relevant securities (in a case where that business does not consist exclusively of that).

(9) Where an instrument transfers relevant securities of a company incorporated in the United Kingdom—

(*a*) to a company which at the time of the transfer falls within subsection (6) above …[5], and
(*b*) from a company which at that time falls within that subsection …[5],

subsections (2) to (5) above shall not apply and [stamp duty is not chargeable on the instrument][7].

[(9A) In this section "bearer instrument" has the meaning given in paragraph 3 of Schedule 15 to the Finance Act 1999.][8]

(10) This section applies to any instrument executed on or after the day on which the rule of The Stock Exchange that prohibits a person from carrying on business as both a broker and a jobber is abolished.

Cross references—See FA 1986 s 97A (disapplication of this section in relation to clearance services where an election is made under s 97A(1)).
FA 1988 s 143(6) (UK company shares paired with foreign company shares; in relation to certain instruments transferring paired shares and executed after 29 July 1988, the foreign company to be treated for the purposes of this section as incorporated in the UK);
FA 1990 ss 108(8), 111(1) (abolition of stamp duty with effect from an appointed day on transfer of securities).

Note—This section was to be repealed by FA 1990 Sch 19 Pt VI with effect from an appointed day in accordance with FA 1990 ss 107–111. The Treasury order specifying the appointed day for the purposes of FA 1990 ss 107–110 was to coincide with the start of paperless trading under the Stock Exchange's planned TAURUS system (IR press release, 20-3-90). However, on 11-3-93 the London Stock Exchange News Release 6/93 announced that TAURUS had been abandoned.

Amendments—[1] Words in sub-s (6) substituted by FA 1987 s 52 in relation to instruments executed after 31 July 1987.
[2] Words in sub-s (1) inserted by FA 1996 s 182(1), (6), with effect from 1 July 1996.
[3] Sub-s (4) repealed by FA 1997 s 99 (3), Sch 18 Pt VII with effect for any instrument executed on or after 20 October 1997 (the date appointed under FA 1997 s 97 by virtue of SI 1997/2428) except an instrument which transfers relevant securities which were acquired by the transferor before that date. Previously the text read:
"(4) Subsection (3) above shall have effect as if "£1.50" read "£1" in a case where—
(*a*) at the time of the transfer the transferor is a qualified dealer in securities of the kind concerned or a nominee of such a qualified dealer,
(*b*) the transfer is made for the purposes of the dealer's business,
(*c*) at the time of the transfer the dealer is not a market maker in securities of the kind concerned, and
(*d*) the instrument contains a statement that paragraphs (*a*) to (*c*) above are fulfilled."
[4] Sub-ss (2) and (3) substituted by FA 1999 s 112(4), Sch 14 para 13 with effect in relation to instruments executed after 30 September 1999. This does not apply to transfers or other instruments relating to units under a unit trust scheme by virtue of FA 1999 s 122. For prospective repeal of FA 1999 Sch 14 para 13 see FA 1999 s 123(3). Previously the text read:
"(2) If stamp duty is chargeable on the instrument under the heading "Conveyance or Transfer on Sale" in Schedule 1 to the Stamp Act 1891, the rate at which the duty is charged under that heading shall be the rate of £1.50 for every £100 or part of £100 of the amount or value of the consideration for the sale to which the instrument gives effect.

(3) If stamp duty is chargeable on the instrument under the heading "Conveyance or Transfer of any kind not hereinbefore described" in Schedule 1 to the Stamp Act 1891, the rate at which the duty is charged under that heading shall (subject to [subsection] (5) below) be the rate of £1.50 for every £100 or part of £100 of the value of the securities at the date the instrument is executed."

[5] Words in sub-s (9) repealed by FA 2000 s 134(3), (5), Sch 40 Pt III with effect for stamp duty purposes for instruments executed after 28 July 2000 and for stamp duty reserve tax purposes for securities transferred after 28 July 2000.

[6] The word "transfer" substituted for the words "conveyance or transfer" in enactments relating to stamp duty by FA 2003 Sch 20 para 3.

[7] In sub-s (9), words "the stamp duty chargeable on the instrument is £5" substituted by FA 2008 s 99, Sch 32 paras 4, 7 with effect in relation to instruments executed on or after 13 March 2008 and not stamped before 19 March 2008.

[8] Words in sub-s (1) and whole of sub-s (9A) inserted, and words in sub-s (3) substituted by FA 2008 s 99, Sch 32 paras 13, 15 with effect in relation to instruments executed on or after 13 March 2008 and not stamped before 19 March 2008. If a day is appointed under FA 1990 s 111 (abolition day), FA 2008 Sch 32 paras 14, 15 cease to have effect in accordance with FA 1990 s 108 (FA 2008 s 99, Sch 32 para 23).
Sub-s (3) previously read as follows—
"(3) If stamp duty is chargeable on the instrument under paragraph 16 of Schedule 13 to the Finance Act 1999 (transfer otherwise than on sale), then, subject to subsection (5), the rate at which that duty is chargeable is 1.5% of the value of the securities at the date the instrument is executed."

71 Clearance services: notification

(1) A person whose business is or includes the provision of clearance services for the purchase and sale of relevant securities of a company incorporated in the United Kingdom shall notify the Commissioners of that fact before the end of the period of one month beginning with the date on which he first provides such clearance services.

(2) A person whose business includes (but does not exclusively consist of) holding relevant securities (being securities of a company incorporated in the United Kingdom)—

(*a*) as nominee or agent for a person whose business is or includes the provision of clearance services for the purchase and sale of relevant securities, and

(*b*) for the purposes of such part of the business mentioned in paragraph (*a*) above as consists of the provision of such clearance services (in a case where the business does not consist exclusively of that),

shall notify the Commissioners of that fact before the end of the period of one month beginning with the date on which he first holds such relevant securities as such a nominee or agent and for such purposes.

(3) A company which is incorporated in the United Kingdom and becomes aware that any shares in the company are held by a person such as is mentioned in subsection (1) or (2) above shall notify the Commissioners of that fact before the end of the period of one month beginning with the date on which the company first becomes aware of that fact.

(4) A person who fails to comply with subsection (1) or (2) above shall be liable to a [penalty][1] not exceeding £1,000.

(5) A company which fails to comply with subsection (3) above shall be liable to a [penalty][1] not exceeding £100.

(6) …[2]

Cross references—See FA 1988 s 143(6) (UK company shares paired with foreign company shares; in relation to certain instruments transferring paired shares and executed after 29 July 1988, the foreign company to be treated for the purposes of this section as incorporated in the UK);
FA 1990 ss 109(4), (5), 111(1) (abolition of the requirement of notification under sub-ss (1), (2), (3) with effect from an appointed day).

Note—This section was to be repealed by FA 1990 Sch 19 Pt VI with effect from an appointed day in accordance with FA 1990 ss 107–111. The Treasury order specifying the appointed day for the purposes of FA 1990 ss 107–110 was to coincide with the start of paperless trading under the Stock Exchange's planned TAURUS system (IR press release, 20-3-90). However, on 11-3-93 the London Stock Exchange News Release 6/93 announced that TAURUS had been abandoned.

Amendments—[1] Words in sub-ss (4) and (5) substituted by FA 1999 s 114, Sch 17 para 8 with effect in relation to penalties in respect of things done or omitted after 30 September 1999.

[2] Sub-s (6) repealed by FA 1999 Sch 20 Pt V(3) with effect in relation to things done or omitted from 1 October 1999.

72 Clearance services: supplementary

(1) References in sections 70 and 71 above to relevant securities, or to relevant securities of a company, are to shares in or stock or marketable securities of any company (which, unless otherwise stated, need not be incorporated in the United Kingdom).

(2) For the purposes of section 70(3) above the value of securities at the date the instrument is executed shall be taken to be the price they might reasonably be expected to fetch on a sale at that time in the open market.

(3) …[2]

(4) …[1]

Note—This section was to be repealed by FA 1990 Sch 19 Pt VI with effect from an appointed day in accordance with FA 1990 ss 107–111. The Treasury order specifying the appointed day for the purposes of FA 1990 ss 107–110 was to coincide with the start of paperless trading under the Stock Exchange's planned TAURUS system (IR press release, 20-3-90). However, on 11-3-93 the London Stock Exchange News Release 6/93 announced that TAURUS had been abandoned.

Amendments—[1] Sub-s (4) repealed by FA 1997 s 99 (4), Sch 18 Pt VII with effect for any instrument executed on or after 20 October 1997 (the date appointed under FA 1997 s 97 by virtue of SI 1997/2428) except an instrument which transfers relevant securities which were acquired by the transferor before that date. Previously the text read:
"(4) For the purposes of section 70(4) above 'qualified dealer' and 'market maker' have at any particular time the same meanings as they have at that time for the purposes of section 67 (4) above."

[2] Sub-s (3) repealed by FA 1999 Sch 20 Pt V(1) with effect from 1 October 1999, subject to the provisions in FA 1999 Sch 20 Pt V(1) Note 2. Previously the text read:

"(3) Where section 70(3) above applies, section 15 (2) of the Stamp Act 1891 (stamping of instruments after execution) shall have effect as if the instrument were specified in the first column of the table in paragraph (*d*) and the transferee were specified (opposite the instrument) in the second."

[Transfers between depositary receipt system and clearance system

72A Transfers between depositary receipt system and clearance system

(1) Where an instrument transfers relevant securities of a company incorporated in the United Kingdom between a depositary receipt system and a clearance system—

(*a*) the provisions of section 67(2) to (5) or, as the case may be, section 70(2) to (5) above shall not apply, and

[(*b*) stamp duty is not chargeable on the instrument.][2]

(2) A transfer between a depositary receipt system and a clearance system means a transfer—

(*a*) from (or to) a company that at the time of the transfer falls within section 67(6) above, and

(*b*) to (or from) a company that at that time falls within section 70(6) above.

(3) This section does not apply to a transfer from a clearance system (that is, from such a company as is mentioned in subsection (2)(*b*) above) if at the time of the transfer an election is in force under section 97A below in relation to the clearance services for the purposes of which the securities are held immediately before the transfer.][1]

Amendments—[1] This section inserted by FA 2000 s 134(1), (5) with effect for stamp duty purposes for instruments executed after 28 July 2000.

[2] Sub-s (1)(*b*) substituted by FA 2008 s 99, Sch 32 paras 4, 8 with effect in relation to instruments executed on or after 13 March 2008 and not stamped before 19 March 2008. Sub-s (1)(*b*) previously read as follows—

"(*b*) the stamp duty chargeable on the instrument is £5.".

Reconstructions and acquisitions

73 Reconstructions etc: amendments

Amendments—This section repealed by s 114(6) of, and Sch 23, Pt IX(1) to, this Act (this section amended FA 1927 s 55; FA 1980 Sch 18 para 12; FA 1985 ss 78, 79).

74 Reconstructions etc: repeals

(*repeals* FA 1927 s 55; FA (Northern Ireland) 1928, s 4; FA 1980 Sch 18, para 12(1), (1A); FA 1985 ss 78, 79, 80 *and amends* FA 1980 Sch 18 para 12(3)).

75 Acquisitions: reliefs

(1) This section applies where a company (the acquiring company) acquires the whole or part of an undertaking of another company (the target company) in pursuance of a scheme for the reconstruction of the target company.

(2) If the first and second conditions (as defined below) are fulfilled, stamp duty under [Part I of Schedule 13 to the Finance Act 1999 ([transfer][3] on sale)][1] shall not be chargeable on an instrument executed for the purposes of or in connection with the transfer of the undertaking or part.

(3) An instrument on which stamp duty is not chargeable by virtue only of subsection (2) above shall not be taken to be duly stamped unless it is stamped with the duty to which it would be liable but for that subsection or it has, in accordance with section 12 of the Stamp Act 1891, been stamped with a particular stamp denoting that it is not chargeable with any duty.

(4) The first condition is …[4] that the consideration for the acquisition—

(*a*) consists of or includes the issue of [non-redeemable][2] shares in the acquiring company to all the shareholders of the target company;

(*b*) includes nothing else (if anything) but the assumption or discharge by the acquiring company of liabilities of the target company.

[In paragraph (*a*) above, "non-redeemable shares" means shares which are not redeemable shares.][2]

(5) The second condition is that—

(*a*) the acquisition is effected for bona fide commercial reasons and does not form part of a scheme or arrangement of which the main purpose, or one of the main purposes, is avoidance of liability to stamp duty, income tax, corporation tax or capital gains tax,

(*b*) after the acquisition has been made, each shareholder of each of the companies is a shareholder of the other, and

(*c*) after the acquisition has been made, the proportion of shares of one of the companies held by any shareholder is the same[, or as nearly as may be the same,][4] as the proportion of shares of the other company held by that shareholder.

[(5A) If immediately before the acquisition the target company or the acquiring company holds any of its own shares, the shares are to be treated for the purposes of subsections (4) and (5) as having been cancelled before the acquisition (and, accordingly, the company is to be treated as if it were not a shareholder of itself).][5]

(6) This section applies to any instrument which is executed after 24th March 1986 unless it is executed in pursuance of an unconditional contract made on or before 18th March 1986.

(7) This section shall be deemed to have come into force on 25th March 1986.

Press releases etc—ICAEW TR631 August 1986 (relief not available on company partition).
Cross references—See Stamp Duty and Stamp Duty Reserve Tax (Open-ended Investment Companies) Regulations, SI 1997/1156 , Reg 12 (this section not to apply as regards open-ended investment companies).
Amendments—[1] Words in sub-s (2) substituted by FA 1999 s 112(4), Sch 14 para 14 with effect in relation to instruments executed after 30 September 1999. This does not apply to transfers or other instruments relating to units under a unit trust scheme by virtue of FA 1999 s 122. Previously the text read 'the heading "Conveyance or Transfer on Sale" in Schedule 1 to the Stamp Act 1891'.
[2] Words in sub-s (4) inserted by FA 2000 s 127(1)–(3), with effect for instruments executed after 28 July 2000.
[3] The word "transfer" substituted for the words "conveyance or transfer" in enactments relating to stamp duty by FA 2003 Sch 20 para 3.
[4] Words "that the registered office of the acquiring company is in the United Kingdom and" in sub-s (4) repealed, words in sub-s (5)(*c*) inserted by FA 2006 s 169(2), s 178, Sch 26 Pt 7(5) with effect in relation to instruments executed after 19 July 2006.
[5] Sub-s (5A) inserted by FA 2007 s 74(1), (4) with effect in relation to any instrument executed on or after the day on which FA 2007 is passed (19 July 2007).

76 Acquisitions: further provisions about reliefs

(1) This section applies where a company (the acquiring company) acquires the whole or part of an undertaking of another company (the target company).

(2) If [the first and second conditions (as defined below)][3] is fulfilled, and stamp duty under [Part I of Schedule 13 to the Finance Act 1999 ([transfer][4] on sale)][1] is chargeable on an instrument executed for the purposes of or in connection with—

(*a*) the transfer of the undertaking or part, or

(*b*) the assignment to the acquiring company by a creditor of the target company of any relevant debts (secured or unsecured) owed by the target company,

the rate at which the duty is charged under that heading shall not exceed that mentioned in subsection (4) below.

(3) [The first condition][3] is …[5] that the consideration for the acquisition—

(*a*) consists of or includes the issue of [non-redeemable shares (within the meaning of section 75(4)(*a*) above)][2] in the acquiring company to the target company or to all or any of its shareholders;

(*b*) includes nothing else (if anything) but cash not exceeding 10 per cent of the nominal value of those shares, or the assumption or discharge by the acquiring company of liabilities of the target company, or both.

[(3A) The second condition applies only in relation to an instrument transferring land in the United Kingdom and is that the acquiring company is not associated with another company that is a party to arrangements with the target company relating to shares of the acquiring company issued in connection with the transfer of the undertaking or part.][3]

[(3B) Where an instrument transfers land in the United Kingdom together with other property, the provisions of this section apply as if there were two separate instruments, one relating to land in the United Kingdom and the other relating to other property.][3]

(4) The rate is [0.5%][1] of the amount or value of the consideration for the sale to which the instrument gives effect.

(5) An instrument on which, by virtue only of [this section][3], the rate at which stamp duty is charged is not to exceed that mentioned in subsection (4) above shall not be taken to be duly stamped unless it is stamped with the duty to which it would be liable but for [this section][3] or it has, in accordance with section 12 of the Stamp Act 1891, been stamped with a particular stamp denoting that it is duly stamped.

(6) In subsection (2)(*b*) above "relevant debts" means—

(*a*) any debt in the case of which the assignor is a bank or trade creditor, and

(*b*) any other debt incurred not less than two years before the date on which the instrument is executed.

[(6A) For the purposes of subsection (3A) above—

(*a*) companies are associated if one has control of the other or both are controlled by the same person or persons, and

(*b*) "arrangements" includes any scheme, agreement or understanding, whether or not legally enforceable.

The references in paragraph (*a*) above to control shall be construed in accordance with section 416 of the Taxes Act 1988.][3]

(7) This section applies to any instrument executed on or after the day on which the rule of The Stock Exchange that prohibits a person from carrying on business as both a broker and a jobber is abolished.

Cross references—See FA 2002 s 113, Sch 25 (withdrawal of the relief for company acquisitions where the claim to the relief on an instrument includes a transfer of land to an acquiring company, and control of the acquiring company changes within two years of the execution of that instrument).
Stamp Duty and Stamp Duty Reserve Tax (Open-ended Investment Companies) Regulations, SI 1997/1156 , Reg 12 (this section not to apply as regards open-ended investment companies).

Amendments—[1] Words in sub-ss (2) and (4) substituted by FA 1999 s 112(4), Sch 14 para 15 with effect in relation to instruments executed after 30 September 1999. This does not apply to transfers or other instruments relating to units under a unit trust scheme by virtue of FA 1999 s 122. Previously the text read 'the heading "Conveyance or Transfer on Sale" in Schedule 1 to the Stamp Act 1891' and 'the rate of 50p for every £100 or part of £100' respectively.

[2] Words in sub-s (3)(*a*) substituted for "shares" by FA 2000 s 127(4), with effect for instruments executed after 28 July 2000.

[3] Words in sub-ss (2), (3), (5) substituted, and sub-ss (3A), (3B), (6A) inserted, by FA 2002 s 112 with effect for instruments executed after 23 April 2002. These amendments are deemed to have come into force on 24 April 2002. They do not apply to an instrument giving effect to a contract made before 18 April 2002, unless—

(*a*) the instrument is made in consequence of the exercise after that date of any option, right of pre-emption or similar right, or

(*b*) the instrument transfers the property in question to, or vests it in, a person other than the purchaser under the contract because of an assignment (or, in Scotland, assignation) or further contract made after that date.

[4] The word "transfer" substituted for the words "conveyance or transfer" in enactments relating to stamp duty by FA 2003 Sch 20 para 3.

[5] Words "that the registered office of the acquiring company is in the United Kingdom and" in sub-s (3) repealed by FA 2006 s 169(3), s 178, Sch 26 Pt 7(5) with effect in relation to instruments executed after 19 July 2006.

77 Acquisition of target company's share capital

(1) Stamp duty under [Part I of Schedule 13 to the Finance Act 1999 ([transfer][2] on sale)][1] shall not be chargeable on an instrument transferring shares in one company (the target company) to another company (the acquiring company) if the conditions mentioned in subsection (3) below are fulfilled.

(2) An instrument on which stamp duty is not chargeable by virtue only of subsection (1) above shall not be taken to be duly stamped unless it is stamped with the duty to which it would be liable but for that subsection or it has, in accordance with section 12 of the Stamp Act 1891, been stamped with a particular stamp denoting that it is not chargeable with any duty.

(3) The conditions are that—

(*a*) …[3]

(*b*) the transfer forms part of an arrangement by which the acquiring company acquires the whole of the issued share capital of the target company,

(*c*) the acquisition is effected for bona fide commercial reasons and does not form part of a scheme or arrangement of which the main purpose, or one of the main purposes, is avoidance of liability to stamp duty, stamp duty reserve tax, income tax, corporation tax or capital gains tax,

(*d*) the consideration for the acquisition consists only of the issue of shares in the acquiring company to the shareholders of the target company,

(*e*) after the acquisition has been made, each person who immediately before it was made was a shareholder of the target company is a shareholder of the acquiring company,

(*f*) after the acquisition has been made, the shares in the acquiring company are of the same classes as were the shares in the target company immediately before the acquisition was made,

(*g*) after the acquisition has been made, the number of shares of any particular class in the acquiring company bears to all the shares in that company the same proportion[, or as nearly as may be the same proportion,][3] as the number of shares of that class in the target company bore to all the shares in that company immediately before the acquisition was made, and

(*h*) after the acquisition has been made, the proportion of shares of any particular class in the acquiring company held by any particular shareholder is the same[, or as nearly as may be the same,][3] as the proportion of shares of that class in the target company held by him immediately before the acquisition was made.

[(3A) If immediately before the acquisition the target company or the acquiring company holds any of its own shares, the shares are to be treated for the purposes of subsection (3) as having been cancelled before the acquisition (and, accordingly, the company is to be treated as if it were not a shareholder of itself).][4]

(4) In this section references to shares and to share capital include references to stock.

(5) This section applies to any instrument executed on or after 1st August 1986.[1]

Cross references—See Stamp Duty and Stamp Duty Reserve Tax (Open-ended Investment Companies) Regulations, SI 1997/1156 reg 12 (this section not to apply as regards open-ended investment companies).

Notes—This section was to be repealed by FA 1990 Sch 19 Pt VI with effect from an appointed day in accordance with FA 1990 ss 107–111. The Treasury order specifying the appointed day for the purposes of FA 1990 ss 107–110 was to coincide with the start of paperless trading under the Stock Exchange's planned TAURUS system (IR press release, 20-3-90). However, on 11-3-93 the London Stock Exchange News Release 6/93 announced that TAURUS had been abandoned.

Amendments—[1] Words in sub-s (1) substituted by FA 1999 s 112(4), Sch 14 para 16 with effect in relation to instruments executed after 30 September 1999. This does not apply to transfers or other instruments relating to units under a unit trust scheme by virtue of FA 1999 s 122. For prospective repeal of FA 1999 Sch 14 para 16 see FA 1999 s 123(3). Previously the text read 'the heading "Conveyance or Transfer on Sale" in Schedule 1 to the Stamp Act 1891'.

[2] The word "transfer" substituted for the words "conveyance or transfer" in enactments relating to stamp duty by FA 2003 Sch 20 para 3.

[3] In sub-s (3), para (*a*) repealed, words in paras (*g*), (*h*) inserted by FA 2006 s 169(4), s 178, Sch 26 Pt 7(5) with effect in relation to instruments executed after 19 July 2006. Sub-s (3)(*a*) previously read as follows—

"the registered office of the acquiring company is in the United Kingdom,".

[4] Sub-s (3A) inserted by FA 2007 s 74(2), (4) with effect in relation to any instrument executed on or after the day on which FA 2007 is passed (19 July 2007).

Loan capital, letters of allotment, etc

78 Loan capital

(1)–(6) …[2]

(7) In this section "loan capital" means—

(*a*) any debenture stock, corporation stock or funded debt, by whatever name known, issued by a body corporate or other body of persons (which here includes a local authority and any body whether formed or established in the United Kingdom or elsewhere);
(*b*) any capital raised by such a body if the capital is borrowed or has the character of borrowed money, and whether it is in the form of stock or any other form;
(*c*) stock or marketable securities issued by the government of any country or territory outside the United Kingdom.
[(*d*) any capital raised under arrangements which fall within section 48A of the Finance Act 2005 [or section 507 of the Corporation Tax Act 2009][4] (alternative finance investment bonds).][3]

(8) …[2]

(9) In this section "designated international organisation" means an international organisation designated for the purposes of section [324 of the Taxes Act 1988][1] by an order made under subsection (1) of that section.

(10)–(14) …[2]

Cross references—See FA 1986 s 79 (references to this section in sub-ss (7), (9), (10) and (14) above include a reference to s 79).

Amendments—[1] Words in sub-s (9) substituted by TA 1988 Sch 29 para 32 Table.
[2] Sub-ss (1)–(6), (8) and (10)–(14) repealed by FA 1999 Sch 20 Pt V(2) with effect in relation to instruments executed, or bearer instruments issued, from 1 October 1999, subject to the provisions in FA 1999 Sch 20 Pt V(2) Note 2. Previously the text read:
"(1) This section (which reproduces the effect of a resolution having statutory effect under section 50 of the Finance Act 1973 for the period beginning on 25th March 1986 and ending on 6th July 1986) shall be deemed to have had effect during, and only during, that period.
(2) The following provisions shall not apply.
(*a*) in section 62 of the Finance Act 1963 subsections (2) and (6) (commonwealth stock);
(*b*) in section 11 of the Finance Act (Northern Ireland) 1963, subsections (2) and (5) (commonwealth stock);
(*c*) section 29 of the Finance Act 1967 (local authority capital);
(*d*) section 6 of the Finance Act (Northern Ireland) 1967 (local authority capital);
(*e*) section 126 of the Finance Act 1976 (loan capital).
(3) Stamp duty under the heading "Bearer Instrument" in Schedule 1 to the Stamp Act 1891 shall not be chargeable on the issue of an instrument which relates to loan capital or on the transfer of the loan capital constituted by, or transferable by means of, such an instrument.
(4) Stamp duty shall not be chargeable on an instrument which transfers loan capital issued or raised by—
(*a*) the financial support fund of the Organisation for Economic Co-operation and Development,
(*b*) the Inter-American Development Bank, or
(*c*) an organisation which was a designated international organisation at the time of the transfer (whether or not it was such an organisation at the time the loan capital was issued or raised).
(5) Stamp duty shall not be chargeable on an instrument which transfers short-term loan capital.
(6) Where stamp duty under the heading "Conveyance or Transfer on Sale" in Schedule 1 to the Stamp Act 1891 is chargeable on an instrument which transfers loan capital, the rate at which the duty is charged under that heading shall be the rate of 50p for every £100 or part of £100 of the amount or value of the consideration for the sale to which the instrument gives effect.
(8) In this section "short-term loan capital" means loan capital the date (or latest date) for the repayment of which is not more than 5 years after the date on which it is issued or raised.
(10) In construing sections 80(3) and 81 (3) of the Finance Act 1985 (definitions by reference to section 126 of the Finance Act 1976) the effect of this section shall be ignored.
(11) This section applies to any instrument which falls within section 60(1) of the Finance Act 1963 and is issued after 24th March 1986 and before 7th July 1986.
(12) This section applies to any instrument which falls within section 60(2) of that Act if the loan capital constituted by or transferable by means of it is transferred after 24th March 1986 and before 7th July 1986.
(13) This section applies, in the case of instruments not falling within section 60(1) or (2) of that Act, to any instrument which is executed after 24th March 1986 and before 7th July 1986, unless it is executed in pursuance of a contract made on or before 18th March 1986.
(14) In this section references to section 60(1) of the Finance Act 1963 include references to section 9(1)(*a*) of the Finance Act (Northern Ireland) 1963 and references to section 60(2) of the former Act include references to section 9(1)(*b*) of the latter.".
[3] Sub-s (7)(*d*) inserted by FA 2008 s 154(1), (2) with effect in relation to instruments executed on or after 21 July 2008 (and for this purpose it does not matter when the arrangements falling within FA 2005 s 48A are made).
[4] In sub-s (7)(*d*), words inserted by CTA 2009 s 1322, Sch 1 paras 322, 323. CTA 2009 applies for corporation tax purposes for accounting periods ending on or after 1 April 2009 and for income tax and capital gains tax purposes for the tax year 2009–10 and subsequent tax years.

79 Loan capital: new provisions

(1) …[3]

(2) Stamp duty under [Schedule 15 to the Finance Act 1999 (bearer instruments)][2] shall not be chargeable on the issue of an instrument which relates to loan capital or on the transfer of the loan capital constituted by, or transferable by means of, such an instrument.

(3) Stamp duty shall not be chargeable on an instrument which transfers loan capital issued or raised by—

(*a*) the financial support fund of the Organisation for Economic Co-operation and Development,
(*b*) the Inter-American Development Bank, or
(*c*) an organisation which was a designated international organisation at the time of the transfer (whether or not it was such an organisation at the time the loan capital was issued or raised).

(4) Subject to subsections (5) and (6) below, stamp duty shall not be chargeable on an instrument which transfers any other loan capital.

(5) Subsection (4) above does not apply to an instrument transferring loan capital which, at the time the instrument is executed, carries a right (exercisable then or later) of conversion into shares or other securities, or to the acquisition of shares or other securities, including loan capital of the same description.

(6) Subject to [subsections (7) to (7B)][7] below, subsection (4) above does not apply to an instrument transferring loan capital which, at the time the instrument is executed or any earlier time, carries or has carried—

(*a*) a right to interest the amount of which exceeds a reasonable commercial return on the nominal amount of the capital,

(*b*) a right to interest the amount of which falls or has fallen to be determined to any extent by reference to the results of, or of any part of, a business or to the value of any property, or

(*c*) a right on repayment to an amount which exceeds the nominal amount of the capital and is not reasonably comparable with what is generally repayable (in respect of a similar nominal amount of capital) under the terms of issue of loan capital listed in the Official List of The Stock Exchange.

(7) Subsection (4) above shall not be prevented from applying to an instrument by virtue of subsection (6) (*a*) or (*c*) above by reason only that the loan capital concerned carries a right to interest, or (as the case may be) to an amount payable on repayment, determined to any extent by reference to an index showing changes in the general level of prices payable in the United Kingdom over a period substantially corresponding to the period between the issue or raising of the loan capital and its repayment.

[(7A) Subsection (4) above shall not be prevented from applying to an instrument by virtue of subsection (6)(*b*) above by reason only that the loan capital concerned carries a right to interest which—

(*a*) reduces in the event of the results of a business or part of a business improving, or the value of any property increasing, or

(*b*) increases in the event of the results of a business or part of a business deteriorating, or the value of any property diminishing.][5]

[(7B) Subsection (4) shall not be prevented from applying to a capital market instrument by virtue of subsection (6)(*b*) by reason only that the capital market investment concerned carries or has carried a right to interest which ceases or reduces if, or to the extent that, the issuer, after meeting or providing for other obligations specified in the capital market arrangement concerned, has insufficient funds available from that capital market arrangement to pay all or part of the interest otherwise due.][7]

[(8) Where stamp duty is chargeable under Part I of Schedule 13 of the Finance Act 1999 ([transfer][6] on sale) on an instrument which transfers loan capital, the rate at which duty is charged under that Part shall be 0.5% of the amount or value of the consideration for the sale to which the instrument gives effect.][1]

[(8A) In the application of this section to loan capital that falls within paragraph (*d*) of section 78(7) (alternative finance investment bonds)—

(*a*) subsection (6) has effect as if—

(i) paragraph (*a*) were omitted, and

(ii) for paragraph (*c*) there were substituted—

"(*c*) a right at the end of the bond term (within the meaning of section 48A(1) of the Finance Act 2005 [or section 507(1) of the Corporation Tax Act 2009][9]) to a payment of an amount that exceeds the aggregate of—

(i) the amount paid for the issue of the bond, and

(ii) the notional payment amount;

and for this purpose the "notional payment amount" means the amount of the payments that would represent a reasonable commercial return (within the meaning of section 48A(1) of the Finance Act 2005 [or section 507(1) of the Corporation Tax Act 2009][9]) on the bond over the bond term, less the amount of the payments actually made.",

(*b*) subsections (6)(*b*), (7), (7A), (7B) and (13) have effect as if references to interest were references to additional payments ("additional payments" having the same meaning as in section 48A of the Finance Act 2005 [or section 507 of the Corporation Tax Act 2009][9]), and

(*c*) subsections (7B) and (13) also have effect as if—

(i) references to a capital market investment were references to the loan capital falling within paragraph (*d*) of section 78(7), and

(ii) references to a capital market arrangement were to the arrangements under which that loan capital is raised.][8]

(9)–(11) …[3]

(12) Subsections (7), (9), …[4] of section 78 above shall apply as if references to that section included references to this.

[(13) In this section—

"capital market instrument" means an instrument transferring a capital market investment issued as part of a capital market arrangement, and

Stamp Taxes

"capital market investment" and "capital market arrangement" have the same meaning as in section 72B of the Insolvency Act 1986 (see paragraphs 1 to 3 of Schedule 2A to that Act).][7]

Statement of Practice SP 3/84—FA 1976 s 126(2) (precursor of sub-s (5) above) did not exclude from exemption loan capital carrying an unexpired right to conversion into or acquisition of loan capital which itself is within the exemption.

Cross references—See FA 1987 s 50(3)(*b*), (*c*) (further exemption under other headings in Stamp Act 1891, Sch 1 for instruments falling under this section).

Notes—Sub-ss (2)–(8) and words in sub-s (12) were to be repealed by FA 1990 Sch 19 Pt VI with effect from an appointed day in accordance with FA 1990 ss 107–111. The Treasury order specifying the appointed day for the purposes of FA 1990 ss 107–110 was to coincide with the start of paperless trading under the Stock Exchange's planned TAURUS system (IR press release, 20-3-90). However, on 11-3-93 the London Stock Exchange News Release 6/93 announced that TAURUS had been abandoned.

Amendments—[1] Sub-s (8) substituted by FA 1999 s 112(4), Sch 14 para 17 with effect in relation to instruments executed after 30 September 1999. This does not apply to transfers or other instruments relating to units under a unit trust scheme by virtue of FA 1999 s 122. For prospective repeal of FA 1999 Sch 14 para 17 see FA 1999 s 123(3). Previously the text read:

"(8) Where stamp duty under the heading "Conveyance or Transfer on Sale" in Schedule 1 to the Stamp Act 1891 is chargeable on an instrument which transfers loan capital, the rate at which the duty is charged under that heading shall be the rate of 50p for every £100 or part of £100 of the amount or value of the consideration for the sale to which the instrument gives effect."

[2] Words in sub-s (2) substituted by FA 1999 s 113(3), Sch 16 para 5 with effect in relation to bearer instruments issued after 30 September 1999. For prospective repeal of FA 1999 s 113, Sch 16 para 5 see FA 1999 s 123(3). Previously the text read 'the heading "Bearer Instrument" in Schedule 1 to the Stamp Act 1891'.

[3] Sub-ss (1), (9)–(11) repealed by FA 1999 Sch 20 Pt V(2) with effect in relation to instruments executed, or bearer instruments issued, from 1 October 1999, subject to the provisions in FA 1999 Sch 20 Pt V(2) Note 2. Previously the text read:

"(1) The following provisions shall cease to have effect—

(*a*) in section 62 of the Finance Act 1963 subsections (2) and (6) (commonwealth stock);

(*b*) in section 11 of the Finance Act (Northern Ireland) 1963, subsections (2) and (5) (commonwealth stock);

(*c*) section 29 of the Finance Act 1967 (local authority capital);

(*d*) section 6 of the Finance Act (Northern Ireland) 1967 (local authority capital);

(*e*) section 126 of the Finance Act 1976 (loan capital).

(9) This section applies to any instrument which falls within section 60(1) of the Finance Act 1963 and is issued after 31st July 1986.

(10) This section applies to any instrument which falls within section 60(2) of that Act if the loan capital constituted by or transferable by means of it is transferred after 31st July 1986.

(11) This section applies, in the case of instruments not falling within section 60(1) or (2) of that Act, to any instrument which is executed after 31st July 1986."

[4] Words in sub-s (12) repealed by FA 1999 Sch 20 Pt V(2) with effect in relation to instruments executed, or bearer instruments issued, from 1 October 1999, subject to the provisions in FA 1999 Sch 20 Pt V(2) Note 2. Previously the text read '(10) and (14)'.

[5] Sub-s (7A) inserted by FA 2000 s 133(1). For the purposes of stamp duty, this amendment has effect for instruments executed after 20 March 2000. For the purposes of stamp duty reserve tax, this amendment has effect in accordance with the commencement provisions set out in FA 2000 s 133(3) (broadly with effect after 20 March 2000).

[6] The word "transfer" substituted for the words "conveyance or transfer" in enactments relating to stamp duty by FA 2003 Sch 20 para 3.

[7] Words in sub-s (6) substituted for words "subsection (7)", and sub-ss (7B), (13) inserted, by FA 2008 s 101 with effect in relation to any instrument executed on or after 21 July 2008.

[8] Sub-s (8A) inserted by FA 2008 s 154(1), (4) with effect in relation to any instrument executed on or after 21 July 2008 (and for this purpose it does not matter when the arrangements falling within FA 2005 s 48A are made).

[9] In sub-s (8A)(*a*)(ii), in substituted sub-s (6)(*c*), words inserted in both places, and in sub-s (8A)(*b*), words inserted, by CTA 2009 s 1322, Sch 1 paras 322, 324. CTA 2009 applies for corporation tax purposes for accounting periods ending on or after 1 April 2009 and for income tax and capital gains tax purposes for the tax year 2009–10 and subsequent tax years.

80 Bearer letters of allotment etc

Amendments—This section repealed by FA 1999 Sch 20 Pt V(2) with effect in relation to instruments executed, or bearer instruments issued, from 1 October 1999, subject to the provisions in FA 1999 Sch 20 Pt V(2) Note 2. Previously the text read:

"(1) In Schedule 1 to the Stamp Act 1891, in the heading "Bearer Instrument", paragraph 2 of the exemptions (bearer letter of allotment etc required to be surrendered not later than six months after issue) shall be omitted.

(2) This section applies to any instrument which falls within section 60(1) of the Finance Act 1963 and is issued after 24th March 1986, unless it is issued by a company in pursuance of a general offer for its shares and the offer became unconditional as to acceptances on or before 18th March 1986.

(3) This section applies to any instrument which falls within section 60(2) of that Act if the stock constituted by or transferable by means of it is transferred after 24th March 1986.

(4) In this section the reference to section 60(1) of the Finance Act 1963 includes a reference to section 9(1)(*a*) of the Finance Act (Northern Ireland) 1963 and the reference to section 60(2) of the former Act includes a reference to section 9(1) (*b*) of the latter.

(5) This section shall be deemed to have come into force on 25th March 1986.""

Changes in financial institutions

[80A Sales to intermediaries

[(1) Stamp duty shall not be chargeable on an instrument transferring stock of a particular kind on sale to a person or the person's nominee if—

(*a*) the person is a member of a regulated market on which stock of that kind is regularly traded; and

(*b*) the person is an intermediary and is recognised as such by the market in accordance with arrangements approved by the Commissioners.][2]

[(1A) Stamp duty shall not be chargeable on an instrument transferring stock of a particular kind on sale to a person or the person's nominee if—

(*a*) the person is a member of a multilateral trading facility, or a recognised foreign exchange, on which stock of that kind is regularly traded;

(*b*) the person is an intermediary and is recognised as such by the facility or exchange in accordance with arrangements approved by the Commissioners; and
(*c*) the sale is effected on the facility or exchange.][2]

[(1B) Stamp duty shall not be chargeable on an instrument transferring stock of a particular kind on sale to a person or the person's nominee if—

(*a*) the person is an intermediary who is approved for the purposes of this section by the Commissioners; and
(*b*) stock of that kind is regularly traded on a regulated market.][2]

[(1C) Stamp duty shall not be chargeable on an instrument transferring stock of a particular kind on sale to a person or the person's nominee if—

(*a*) the person is an intermediary who is approved for the purposes of this section by the Commissioners;
(*b*) stock of that kind is regularly traded on a multilateral trading facility or a recognised foreign exchange; and
(*c*) the sale is effected on the facility or exchange.][2]

[(2) Stamp duty shall not be chargeable on an instrument transferring stock of a particular kind on sale to a person or the person's nominee if—

(*a*) the person is a member of a regulated market, a multilateral trading facility or a recognised foreign options exchange;
(*b*) options to buy or sell stock of that kind are regularly traded on, and are listed by or quoted on, that market, facility or exchange;
(*c*) the person is an options intermediary and is recognised as such by that market, facility or exchange in accordance with arrangements approved by the Commissioners; and
(*d*) stock of that kind is regularly traded on a regulated market.][2]

[(2A) Stamp duty shall not be chargeable on an instrument transferring stock of a particular kind on sale to a person or the person's nominee if—

(*a*) the person is a member of a regulated market, a multilateral trading facility or a recognised foreign options exchange;
(*b*) options to buy or sell stock of that kind are regularly traded on, and are listed by or quoted on, that market, facility or exchange;
(*c*) the person is an options intermediary and is recognised as such by that market, facility or exchange in accordance with arrangements approved by the Commissioners; and
(*d*) the sale is effected on a relevant qualifying exchange on which stock of that kind is regularly traded or is effected on a relevant qualifying exchange pursuant to the exercise of a relevant option and options to buy or sell stock of that kind are regularly traded on, and are listed by or quoted on, that exchange;

and in paragraph (*d*) "relevant qualifying exchange" means a multilateral trading facility, a recognised foreign options exchange or a recognised foreign exchange.][2]

[(2B) Stamp duty shall not be chargeable on an instrument transferring stock of a particular kind on sale to a person or the person's nominee if—

(*a*) the person is an options intermediary who is approved for the purposes of this section by the Commissioners;
(*b*) options to buy or sell stock of that kind are regularly traded on, and are listed by or quoted on, a regulated market, a multilateral trading facility or a recognised foreign options exchange; and
(*c*) stock of that kind is regularly traded on a regulated market.][2]

[(2C) Stamp duty shall not be chargeable on an instrument transferring stock of a particular kind on sale to a person or the person's nominee if—

(*a*) the person is an options intermediary who is approved for the purposes of this section by the Commissioners;
(*b*) options to buy or sell stock of that kind are regularly traded on, and are listed by or quoted on, a regulated market, a multilateral trading facility or a recognised foreign options exchange; and
(*c*) the sale is effected on a relevant qualifying exchange on which stock of that kind is regularly traded or is effected on a relevant qualifying exchange pursuant to the exercise of a relevant option and options to buy or sell stock of that kind are regularly traded on, and are listed by or quoted on, that exchange;

and in paragraph (*c*) "relevant qualifying exchange" means a multilateral trading facility, a recognised foreign options exchange or a recognised foreign exchange.][2]

(4) For the purposes of this section—

(*a*) an intermediary is a person who carries on a bona fide business of dealing in stock and does not carry on an excluded business; and
(*b*) an options intermediary is a person who carries on a bona fide business of dealing in quoted or listed options to buy or sell stock and does not carry on an excluded business.

(5) The excluded businesses are the following—

(*a*) any business which consists wholly or mainly in the making or managing of investments;

(*b*) any business which consists wholly or mainly in, or is carried on wholly or mainly for the purpose of, providing services to persons who are connected with the person carrying on the business;

(*c*) any business which consists in insurance business;

(*d*) any business which consists in managing or acting as trustee in relation to a pension scheme or which is carried on by the manager or trustee of such a scheme in connection with or for the purposes of the scheme;

(*e*) any business which consists in operating or acting as trustee in relation to a collective investment scheme or is carried on by the operator or trustee of such a scheme in connection with or for the purposes of the scheme.

(6) A sale is effected on [a facility or][2] an exchange for the purposes of [this section][2] if (and only if)—

(*a*) it is subject to the rules of [the facility or exchange][2]; and

(*b*) it is reported to [the facility or exchange][2] in accordance with the rules of [the facility or exchange][2].

[(6A) The Commissioners may approve a person for the purposes of this section only if the person is authorised under the law of an EEA State to provide any of the investment services or activities listed in Section A 2 or 3 of Annex I to the Directive (execution of orders on behalf of clients and dealing on own account), whether or not the person is authorised under the Directive.][2]

(7) An instrument on which stamp duty is not chargeable by virtue only of this section shall not be deemed to be duly stamped unless it has been stamped with a stamp denoting that it is not chargeable with any duty; and notwithstanding anything in section 122(1) of the Stamp Act 1891, the stamp may be a stamp of such kind as the Commissioners may prescribe.][1]

Cross references—See FA 2002 s 117 (the Treasury may by regulations extend the application of this section to any market that is not a recognised exchange but is prescribed by order under the Financial Services and Markets Act 2000 s 118(3)).

Stamp Duty and Stamp Duty Reserve Tax (Extension of Exceptions relating to Recognised Exchanges) Regulations, SI 2002/1975 (with effect from 26 July 2002, the application of the provision specified in FA 2002 s 117(2) (which includes this section) is extended to the market known as OFEX).

F(No 2)A 2005 s 50 (power of the Treasury to extend the application of this section to any market which is not a recognised exchange, but is a multilateral trading facility or (assuming compliance with the provisions of Title II of the European Parliament and Council Directive 2004/39/EC) would be such a facility).

Modifications—Stamp Duty and Stamp Duty Reserve Tax (Extension of Exceptions relating to Recognised Exchanges) Regulations, SI 2005/1990 regs 3, 4 (modification of this section in its application to prescribed multilateral trading facilities. For definition of "prescribed multilateral trading facility" see SI 2005/1990 reg 2).

Amendments—[1] This section inserted by FA 1997, s 97(1) with effect from 20 October 1997 as appointed by SI 1997/2428, and repealed by FA 1997 Sch 18 Pt VII with effect from the day appointed under FA 1990 s 111.

[2] Sub-ss (1)–(2C) substituted for sub-ss (1)–(3); in sub-s (6), words inserted, and words substituted for the words "subsection (1) or (2) above", and "the exchange" (wherever occurring); and sub-s (6A) inserted, by FA 2007 s 73, Sch 21 para 1 with effect in relation to any instrument executed on or after 1 November 2007: FA 2007 Sch 21 para 1(5).

Sub-ss (1)–(3) previously read as follows—

"(1) Stamp duty shall not be chargeable on an instrument transferring stock of a particular kind on sale to a person or his nominee if—

(*a*) the person is a member of an EEA exchange, or a recognised foreign exchange, on which stock of that kind is regularly traded;

(*b*) the person is an intermediary and is recognised as an intermediary by the exchange in accordance with arrangements approved by the Commissioners; and

(*c*) the sale is effected on the exchange.

(2) Stamp duty shall not be chargeable on an instrument transferring stock of a particular kind on sale to a person or his nominee if—

(*a*) the person is a member of an EEA exchange or a recognised foreign options exchange;

(*b*) options to buy or sell stock of that kind are regularly traded on that exchange and are listed by or quoted on that exchange;

(*c*) the person is an options intermediary and is recognised as an options intermediary by that exchange in accordance with arrangements approved by the Commissioners; and

(*d*) the sale is effected on an EEA exchange, or a recognised foreign exchange, on which stock of that kind is regularly traded or subsection (3) below applies.

(3) This subsection applies if—

(*a*) the sale is effected on an EEA exchange, or a recognised foreign options exchange, pursuant to the exercise of a relevant option; and

(*b*) options to buy or sell stock of the kind concerned are regularly traded on that exchange and are listed by or quoted on that exchange.".

[80B Intermediaries: supplementary

(1) For the purposes of section 80A above the question whether a person is connected with another shall be determined in accordance with the provisions of section 839 of the Income and Corporation Taxes Act 1988.

(2) In section 80A above and this section—

"collective investment scheme" has the meaning given in section [235 of the Financial Services and Markets Act 2000][3];

["the Directive" means Directive 2004/39/EC of the European Parliament and of the Council of 21 April 2004 on markets in financial instruments, as amended from time to time;][4]

…[4]

"EEA State"[, in relation to any time, means a State which at that time is a member State or any other State which at that time][4] is a contracting party to the agreement on the European Economic Area signed at Oporto on the 2nd May 1992 as adjusted by the Protocol signed at Brussels on the 17th March 1993 [(as modified or supplemented from time to time)][4];

["insurance business" means business which consists of the effecting or carrying out of contracts of insurance and, for the purposes of this definition, "contract of insurance" has the meaning given in Article 3(1) of the Financial Services and Markets Act 2000 (Regulated Activities) Order 2001;

"the operator", in relation to a collective investment scheme, shall be construed in accordance with section 237(2) of the Financial Services and Markets Act 2000;][3]

"quoted or listed options" means options which are quoted on or listed by an EEA exchange or a recognised foreign options exchange;

"stock" includes any marketable security;

["trustee", in relation to a collective investment scheme, means a trustee or a depositary within the meaning given in section 237(2) of the Financial Services and Markets Act 2000.][3]

[(2A) Each of the following expressions—

"multilateral trading facility", and

"regulated market",

has the same meaning in section 80A above as it has for the purposes of the Directive.][4]

(3) In section 80A above "recognised foreign exchange" means a market which—

(*a*) is not in an EEA State; and

(*b*) is specified in regulations made by the Treasury under this subsection.

(4) In section 80A above and this section "recognised foreign options exchange" means a market which—

(*a*) is not in an EEA State; and

(*b*) is specified in regulations made by the Treasury under this subsection.

(5) In section 80A above "the exercise of a relevant option" means—

(*a*) the exercise by the options intermediary concerned of an option to buy stock; or

(*b*) the exercise of an option binding the options intermediary concerned to buy stock.

[(5A) The Treasury may by regulations amend section 80A above and this section (as they have effect for the time being) in order to extend the exemption from duty under that section][4]

(6) The Treasury may by regulations provide that section 80A above shall not have effect in relation to instruments executed in pursuance of kinds of agreement specified in the regulations.

(7) The Treasury may by regulations provide that if—

(*a*) an instrument falls within [any of subsections (1) to (2C)][4] of section 80A above, and

(*b*) stamp duty would be chargeable on the instrument apart from that section,

stamp duty shall be chargeable on the instrument at a rate, specified in the regulations, which shall not exceed [0.1%][2] of the consideration for the sale.

(8) The Treasury may by regulations change the meaning of "intermediary" or "options intermediary" for the purposes of section 80A above by amending subsection (4) or (5) of that section (as it has effect for the time being).

(9) The power to make regulations under subsections (3) to (8) above shall be exercisable by statutory instrument subject to annulment in pursuance of a resolution of the House of Commons.][1]

Amendments—[1] This section inserted by FA 1997, s 97(1) with effect from 20 October 1997 as appointed by SI 1997/2428, and repealed by FA 1997 Sch 18 Pt VII with effect from the day appointed under FA 1990 s 111.

[2] Words in sub-s (7) substituted by FA 1999 s 112(4), Sch 14 para 18 with effect in relation to instruments executed after 30 September 1999. This does not apply to transfers or other instruments relating to units under a unit trust scheme by virtue of FA 1999 s 122. For prospective repeal of FA 1999 Sch 14 para 18 see FA 1999 s 123(3). Previously the text read '10p for every £100 or part of £100'.

[3] Words in definition of "collective investment scheme" substituted, and definition of "insurance business", "trustee" and "the operator" substituted by the Financial Services and Markets Act 2000 (Consequential Amendments) (Taxes) Order, SI 2001/3629 arts 6, 7 with effect for any instrument executed after 30 November 2001.

[4] In sub-s (2), definition inserted, definition of "EEA exchange" repealed, and words "means a State which" in definition of "EEA State" substituted, and words inserted; sub-ss (2A), (5A) inserted; and in sub-s (7), words substituted for the words "subsection (1) or (2)" by FA 2007 ss 73, 114, Sch 21 para 2, Sch 27 Pt 4(2) with effect in relation to any instrument executed on or after 1 November 2007: FA 2007 Sch 21 para 1(5).

Definition of "EEA exchange" previously read as follows—

" 'EEA exchange' means a market which appears on the list drawn up by an EEA State pursuant to Article 16 of European Communities Council Directive No 93/22/EEC on investment services in the securities field;".

[80C Repurchases and stock lending

(1) This section applies where a person (A) has entered into an arrangement with another person (B) under which—

(*a*) B is to transfer stock of a particular kind to A or his nominee, and

(*b*) stock of the same kind and amount is to be transferred by A or his nominee to B or his nominee,

and the conditions set out in subsection [(2A) or][3] (3) below are fulfilled.

(2) Stamp duty shall not be chargeable on an instrument transferring stock to B or his nominee or A or his nominee in accordance with the arrangement.

[(2A) The conditions in this subsection are—

(*a*) that A or B is authorised under the law of an EEA State to provide any of the investment services or activities listed in Section A 2 or 3 of Annex I to the Directive (execution of orders on behalf of clients and dealing on own account) in relation to stock of the kind concerned, whether or not A or B is authorised under the Directive; and

(*b*) that stock of the kind concerned is regularly traded on a regulated market.][3]

(3) The conditions [in this subsection][3] are—

(*a*) that the arrangement is effected on [a regulated market, a multilateral trading facility][3] or a recognised foreign exchange; and

(*b*) that stock of the kind concerned is regularly traded on that [market, facility or][3] exchange.

(4) An arrangement does not fall within subsection (1) above if—

(*a*) the arrangement is not such as would be entered into by persons dealing with each other at arm's length; or

(*b*) under the arrangement any of the benefits or risks arising from fluctuations, before the transfer to B or his nominee takes place, in the market value of the stock accrues to, or falls on, A.

(5) An instrument on which stamp duty is not chargeable by virtue only of subsection (2) above shall not be deemed to be duly stamped unless it has been stamped with a stamp denoting that it is not chargeable with any duty; and notwithstanding anything in section 122(1) of the Stamp Act 1891, the stamp may be a stamp of such kind as the Commissioners may prescribe.

(6) An arrangement is effected on [a market, a facility or][3] an exchange for the purposes of subsection (3) above if (and only if)

(*a*) it is subject to the rules of [the market, facility or exchange][3]; and

(*b*) it is reported to [the market, facility or exchange][3] in accordance with the rules of [the market, facility or exchange][3].

(7) In this section—

["the Directive" has the meaning given in section 80B(2) above;

"EEA State" has the meaning given in section 80B(2) above;][3]

...[3]

"recognised foreign exchange" has the meaning given in section 80B(3) above.

[(7A) Each of the following expressions—

"multilateral trading facility", and

"regulated market",

has the same meaning in this section as it has for the purposes of the Directive.][3]

(8) The Treasury may by regulations provide that if stamp duty would be chargeable on an instrument but for subsection (2) above, stamp duty shall be chargeable on the instrument at a rate, specified in the regulations, which shall not exceed [0.1%][2] of the consideration for the transfer.

(9) The Treasury may by regulations amend this section (as it has effect for the time being) in order—

(*a*) to change the conditions for exemption from duty under this section; or

(*b*) to provide that this section does not apply in relation to kinds of arrangement specified in the regulations.

(10) The power to make regulations under subsection (8) or (9) above shall be exercisable by statutory instrument subject to annulment in pursuance of a resolution of the House of Commons.][1]

Cross references—See FA 2002 s 117 (the Treasury may by regulations extend the application of this section to any market that is not a recognised exchange but is prescribed by order under the Financial Services and Markets Act 2000 s 118(3)).

European Single Currency (Taxes) Regulations, SI 1998/3177 regs 25, 27 and 29 for details on replacement of stock in a euroconversion.

Stamp Duty and Stamp Duty Reserve Tax (Extension of Exceptions relating to Recognised Exchanges) Regulations, SI 2002/1975 (with effect from 26 July 2002, the application of the provision specified in FA 2002 s 117(2) (which includes this section) is extended to the market known as OFEX).

F(No 2)A 2005 s 50 (power of the Treasury to extend the application of this section to any market which is not a recognised exchange, but is a multilateral trading facility or (assuming compliance with the provisions of Title II of the European Parliament and Council Directive 2004/39/EC) would be such a facility).

Modifications—Stamp Duty and Stamp Duty Reserve Tax (Extension of Exceptions relating to Recognised Exchanges) Regulations, SI 2005/1990 regs 3, 5 (modification of this section in its application to prescibed multilateral trading facilities. For definition of "prescribed multilateral trading facility" see SI 2005/1990 reg 2).

Amendments—[1] This section inserted by FA 1997, s 98(1) in relation to instruments executed on or after 20 October 1997 as appointed by SI 1997/2428, and repealed by FA 1997 Sch 18 Pt VII with effect from the day appointed under FA 1990 s 111.

[2] Words in sub-s (8) substituted by FA 1999 s 112(4), Sch 14 para 19 with effect in relation to instruments executed after 30 September 1999. This does not apply to transfers or other instruments relating to units under a unit trust scheme by virtue of FA 1999 s 122. For prospective repeal of FA 1999 Sch 14 para 19 see FA 1999 s 123(3). Previously the text read '10p for every £100 or part of £100'.

[3] Words in sub-ss (1), (3), (6), (7) inserted; sub-ss (2A), (7A) inserted; in sub-s (3), words substituted for the words "an EEA exchange"; in sub-s (6), words substituted for the words "the exchange" wherever occurring; in sub-s (7), definition of "EEA exchange" and following word "and" repealed, by FA 2007 ss 73, 114, Sch 21 para 5, Sch 27 Pt 4(2) with effect in relation to any instrument executed on or after 1 November 2007.

Definition of "EEA exchange" previously read as follows—

"'EEA exchange' has the meaning given in section 80B(2) above;".

[80D Repurchases and stock lending: replacement stock on insolvency

(1) This section applies where—

(*a*) A and B have entered into an arrangement falling within section 80C(1),

(*b*) the conditions in subsection (2A) or (3) of that section are met,

(*c*) stock is transferred to A or A's nominee, and

(*d*) the conditions in subsection (2) below are met.

(2) The conditions in this subsection are that—

(*a*) A and B are not connected persons within the meaning of section 839 of the Taxes Act 1988,

(*b*) after B has transferred stock under the arrangement, A or B becomes insolvent,

(*c*) it becomes apparent (whether before or after the insolvency occurs) that, as a result of the insolvency, stock will not be transferred to B or B's nominee in accordance with the arrangement,

(*d*) the party who does not become insolvent ("the solvent party") or the solvent party's nominee acquires replacement stock, and

(*e*) the replacement stock is acquired before the end of the period of 30 days beginning with the day on which the insolvency occurs ("the insolvency date").

(3) Where collateral is provided under the arrangement (or under arrangements of which that arrangement forms part), stamp duty is not chargeable on any instrument transferring to the solvent party or the solvent party's nominee—

(*a*) replacement stock acquired using the collateral (whether directly or indirectly), or

(*b*) where the solvent party uses the whole of the value of the collateral to acquire replacement stock, any further replacement stock.

(4) Where no collateral is provided as mentioned in subsection (3), stamp duty is not chargeable on any instrument transferring replacement stock to the solvent party or the solvent party's nominee.

(5) Subsections (3) and (4) may apply as regards more than one instrument (and where those subsections apply as regards more than one instrument, the instruments may be executed by different persons).

(6) But those subsections apply only as regards replacement stock up to the amount of stock which will not be transferred as a result of the insolvency.

(7) An instrument on which stamp duty is not chargeable by virtue only of subsection (3) or (4) is not to be deemed to be duly stamped unless it has been stamped with a stamp denoting that it is not chargeable with any duty.

(8) Despite section 122(1) of the Stamp Act 1891, the stamp mentioned in subsection (7) may be a stamp of such kind as the Commissioners for Her Majesty's Revenue and Customs may prescribe.

(9) For the purposes of this section, a person becomes insolvent—

(*a*) if a company voluntary arrangement takes effect under Part 1 of the Insolvency Act 1986,

(*b*) if an administration application (within the meaning of Schedule B1 to that Act) is made or a receiver or manager, or an administrative receiver, is appointed,

(*c*) on the commencement of a creditor's voluntary winding up (within the meaning of Part 4 of that Act) or a winding up by the court under Chapter 6 of that Part,

(*d*) if an individual voluntary arrangement takes effect under Part 8 of that Act,

(*e*) on the presentation of a bankruptcy petition (within the meaning of Part 9 of that Act),

(*f*) if a compromise or arrangement takes effect under Part 26 of the Companies Act 2006,

(*g*) if a bank insolvency order takes effect under Part 2 of the Banking Act 2009,

(*h*) if a bank administration order takes effect under Part 3 of that Act, or

(*i*) on the occurrence of any corresponding event which has effect under or as a result of the law of Scotland or Northern Ireland or a country or territory outside the United Kingdom.

(10) In this section—

"collateral" means an amount of money or other property which is payable to, or made available for the benefit of, a party to an arrangement or that party's nominee for the purpose of securing the discharge of the requirement to transfer stock to that party or the nominee;

"replacement stock", in the event of a party to an arrangement becoming insolvent, is stock of the same kind as the stock which will not be transferred to the other party or that party's nominee as a result of the insolvency.][1]

Amendments—[1] Section 80D inserted by FA 2009 s 83, Sch 37 paras 1, 2 with effect where the insolvency in question occurs on or after 1 September 2008. FA 2009 s 83(3). FA 2009 s 83 and FA 2009 Sch 37 cease to have effect—

(a) in relation to the amendments made to Part 3 of FA 1986, when the repeal of sections 80 to 85 of that Act (by Part 6 of Schedule 19 to, and in accordance with sections 107 to 109 of, FA 1990) comes into force, and

(b) in relation to the amendments made to Part 4 of FA 1986, when the repeal of that Part (by Part 7 of Schedule 19 to, and in accordance with section 110 of, FA 1990) comes into force.

81 Sales to market makers

Amendments—This section repealed by FA 1997 s 97(2), Sch 18 Pt VII with effect from 20 October 1997 as appointed by SI 1997/2428. Previously this section was repealed by FA 1990 Sch 19 Pt VI with effect from an appointed day in accordance with FA 1990 ss 107–111. The Treasury order specifying the appointed day for the purposes of FA 1990 ss 107–110 was to coincide with the start of paperless trading under the Stock Exchange's planned TAURUS system (IR press release, 20-3-90). However, on 11-3-93 the London Stock Exchange News Release 6/93 announced that TAURUS had been abandoned.

82 Borrowing of stock by market makers

Amendments—This section repealed by FA 1997 s 98(2), Sch 18 Pt VII with effect from 20 October 1997 as appointed by SI 1997/2428. This section previously repealed by FA 1990 Sch 19 Pt VI with effect from an appointed day in accordance with FA 1990 ss 107–111. The Treasury order specifying the appointed day for the purposes of FA 1990 ss 107–110 was to coincide with the start of paperless trading under the Stock Exchange's planned TAURUS system (IR press release, 20-3-90). However, on 11-3-93 the London Stock Exchange News Release 6/93 announced that TAURUS had been abandoned.

83 Composition agreements

(*amended* FA 1970 s 33 *and is repealed by the* Financial Services and Markets Act 2000 (Consequential Amendments) (Taxes) Order, SI 2001/3629 art 109, Schedule *with effect from 1 December 2001*).

84 Miscellaneous exemptions

(1) (*amends* FA 1976 s 127(1)).

(2) Stamp duty shall not be chargeable on an instrument effecting a transfer of stock if—

(*a*) the transferee is a recognised investment exchange or a nominee of a recognised investment exchange, and

(*b*) an agreement which relates to the stamp duty which would (apart from this subsection) be chargeable on the instrument, and was made between the Commissioners and the investment exchange under section 33 of the Finance Act 1970 is in force at the time of the transfer.

(3) Stamp duty shall not be chargeable on an instrument effecting a transfer of stock if—

(*a*) the transferee is a recognised clearing house or a nominee of a recognised clearing house, and

(*b*) an agreement which relates to the stamp duty which would (apart from this subsection) be chargeable on the instrument, and was made between the Commissioners and the clearing house under section 33 of the Finance Act 1970 is in force at the time of the transfer.

(4) (*amends* FA 1976 s 127(1)).

(5) Subsection (2) above applies to any instrument giving effect to a transaction carried out on or after such day as the Commissioners may appoint by order made by statutory instrument.

(6) Subsection (3) above applies to any instrument giving effect to a transaction carried out on or after such day as the Commissioners may appoint by order made by statutory instrument.

Note—This section was to be repealed by FA 1990 Sch 19 Pt VI with effect from an appointed day in accordance with FA 1990 ss 107–111. The Treasury order specifying the appointed day for the purposes of FA 1990 ss 107–110 was to coincide with the start of paperless trading under the Stock Exchange's planned TAURUS system (IR press release, 20-3-90). However, on 11-3-93 the London Stock Exchange News Release 6/93 announced that TAURUS had been abandoned.

85 Supplementary

(1) (*amend* FA 1920 s 42(1)).

(2)–(4) (*spent*).

(5) In sections 81, 82 and 84 above and this section—

(*a*) "the day of The Stock Exchange reforms" means the day on which the rule of The Stock Exchange that prohibits a person from carrying on business as both a broker and a jobber is abolished,

(*b*) references to a recognised investment exchange are to a recognised investment exchange within the meaning [given by section 285(1)(*a*) of the Financial Services and Markets Act 2000][1], and

(*c*) references to a recognised clearing house are to a recognised clearing house within the meaning [given by section 285(1)(*b*) of the Financial Services and Markets Act 2000][1], and

(*d*) "stock" includes marketable security.

Notes—The day of The Stock Exchange reforms was 27 October 1986.

This section was to be repealed by FA 1990 Sch 19 Pt VI with effect from an appointed day in accordance with FA 1990 ss 107–111. The Treasury order specifying the appointed day for the purposes of FA 1990 ss 107–110 was to coincide with the start of paperless trading under the Stock Exchange's planned TAURUS system (IR press release, 20-3-90). However, on 11-3-93 the London Stock Exchange News Release 6/93 announced that TAURUS had been abandoned.

Amendments—[1] Words in sub-s (5)(*b*), (*c*) substituted by the Financial Services and Markets Act 2000 (Consequential Amendments) (Taxes) Order, SI 2001/3629 arts 6, 8 with effect for any instrument executed after 30 November 2001.

PART IV

STAMP DUTY RESERVE TAX

Construction—FA 1999 Pt VI, so far as it relates to stamp duty reserve tax, to be construed as one with Pt IV of this Act; see FA 1999 s 123(1)(*a*).

Cross references—See FA 1989 ss 175, 176 (stock exchange nominees exempt from stamp duty reserve tax in prescribed circumstances);

FA 1990 ss 110, 111(1) (abolition of stamp duty reserve tax with effect from an appointed day).

Note—This Part was to be repealed by FA 1990 Sch 19 Pt VI with effect from an appointed day in accordance with FA 1990 ss 107–111. The Treasury order specifying the appointed day for the purposes of FA 1990 ss 107–110 was to coincide with the start of paperless trading under the Stock Exchange's planned TAURUS system (IR press release, 20-3-90). However, on 11-3-93 the London Stock Exchange News Release 6/93 announced that TAURUS had been abandoned.

Introduction

86 The tax: introduction

(1) A tax, to be known as stamp duty reserve tax, shall be charged in accordance with this Part of this Act.

(2) The tax shall be under the care and management of the Board.

(3) Section 1 of the Provisional Collection of Taxes Act 1968 shall apply to the tax; and accordingly in subsection (1) of that section after the words "petroleum revenue tax" there shall be inserted the words "stamp duty reserve tax".

[(4) Stamp duty reserve tax shall be chargeable in accordance with the provisions of this Part of this Act—

(*a*) whether the agreement, transfer, issue or appropriation in question is made or effected in the United Kingdom or elsewhere, and

(*b*) whether or not any party is resident or situate in any part of the United Kingdom.][1]

Cross references—See FA 1990 ss 110, 111(1) (abolition of stamp duty reserve tax with effect from an appointed day).

Amendments—[1] Sub-s (4) added by FA 1996 s 187(1), with effect (i) in relation to an agreement, if the agreement is conditional and the condition is satisfied on or after 1 July 1996 or the agreement is not conditional and is made on or after that date, and (ii) in relation to a transfer, issue or appropriation made or effected on or after 1 July 1996.

The principal charge

87 The principal charge

(1) This section applies where a person (A) agrees with another person (B) to transfer chargeable securities (whether or not to B) for consideration in money or money's worth.

(2) There shall be a charge to stamp duty reserve tax under this section on …[1, 2] the relevant day, …[1].

(3) In subsection (2) above "the relevant day" means—

(*a*) in a case where the agreement is conditional, the day on which the condition is satisfied, and

(*b*) in any other case, the day on which the agreement is made.

(4) …[1]

(5)…[1]

(6) Tax under this section shall be charged at the rate of [0.5 per cent][2] of the amount of value of the consideration mentioned in subsection (1) above.

(7) For the purposes of subsection (6) above the value of any consideration not consisting of money shall be taken to be the price it might reasonably be expected to fetch on a sale in the open market at the time the agreement mentioned in subsection (1) above is made.

[(7A) Where—

(*a*) there would be no charge to tax under this section, or

(*b*) there would, under section 92 below, be a repayment or cancellation of tax,

in relation to some of the chargeable securities to which the agreement between A and B relates if separate agreements had been made between them for the transfer of those securities and for the transfer of the remainder, this section and sections 88(5) and 92 below shall have effect as if such separate agreements had been made.][3]

(7B) …[3]

(8) …[3]

(9) This section applies where the agreement to transfer is made on or after the day on which the rule of The Stock Exchange that prohibits a person from carrying on business as both a broker and a jobber is abolished.

(10) This section has effect subject to sections 88 to 90 below.

Simon's Tax Cases—s 87(1) *Save & Prosper Securities Ltd v IRC* [2000] STC (SCD) 408.

Cross references—See FA 1990 ss 110(1), (2), 111(1) (abolition of stamp duty reserve tax with effect from an appointed day);
FA 1997 s 100 (mergers of authorised unit trusts);
FA1997 s 101 (direction to hold trust property on other trusts);
Stamp Duty and Stamp Duty Reserve Tax (Definition of Unit Trust Scheme) Regulations, SI 1992/197 (units of a scheme made under the Administration of Justice Act 1982 s 42(1) are not chargeable securities).
Stamp Duty and Stamp Duty Reserve Tax (Open-ended Investment Companies) Regulations, SI 1997/1156 regs 8 and 10 (exemption from stamp duty on conversion of an authorised unit trust to an open-ended investment company and exemption from stamp duty reserve tax on the amalgamation of an authorised unit trust with an open-ended investment company).
FA 2009 Sch 56 (penalty for failure to make payments on time).

Amendments—[1] In sub-s (2), the words omitted and the whole of sub-ss (4), (5), (8) repealed by FA 1996 ss 188(1), (5), 192(1), (6), Sch 41 Pt VII, with effect in relation to an agreement to transfer securities if the agreement is conditional and the condition is satisfied on or after 1 July 1996 or the agreement is not conditional and is made on or after that date.

[2] Words in sub-s (6) substituted by FA 1996 s 194(1), (7)(*a*), with effect where the agreement to transfer is conditional and the condition is satisfied on or after 1 July 1996 or the agreement is not conditional and is made on or after that date.

Stamp Taxes

[3] Sub-s (7A) substituted and sub-s (7B) repealed by FA 1997 s 106(2), (3), Sch 18 Part VII in relation to an agreement to transfer securities if the agreement is conditional and the condition is satisfied on or after 4 January 1997 or the agreement is not conditional and is made on or after that date.

88 [Special cases][13]

(1) An instrument on which stamp duty is not chargeable by virtue of—

[(*aa*) paragraph 24(*d*) of Schedule 13 to the Finance Act 1999 (renounceable letters of allotment etc.),][1]

(*a*) section 127(1) of the Finance Act 1976 (transfer to stock exchange nominee), or

(*b*) section 84(2) or (3) above [, or

(*c*) Part I of Schedule 19 to the Finance Act 1999 (transfers etc of units in unit trusts),][16]

shall be disregarded in construing [section 92(1A) and (1B) below][6].

[(1A) An instrument on which stamp duty is not chargeable by virtue of section 186 of the Finance Act 1996 (transfers of securities to members of electronic transfer systems etc) shall be disregarded in construing [section 92(1A) and (1B) below][6] unless—

(*a*) the transfer is made by a stock exchange nominee; and

(*b*) the maximum stamp duty chargeable on the instrument, apart from section 186 of the Finance Act 1996, would be [£5][15];

and in this subsection "stock exchange nominee" means a person designated for the purposes of section 127 of the Finance Act 1976 as a nominee of The Stock Exchange by an order made by the Secretary of State under subsection (5) of that section.][2]

[(1B) An instrument on which stamp duty is not chargeable by virtue of section 42 of the Finance Act 1930 or section 11 of the Finance Act (Northern Ireland) 1954 (transfer between associated bodies corporate) shall be disregarded in construing [section 92(1A) and (1B) below][6] in any case where—

(*a*) the property mentioned in section 42(2)(*a*) of the Finance Act 1930 or, as the case may be, section 11(2)(*a*) of the Finance Act (Northern Ireland) 1954 consists of [or includes][10] chargeable securities of any particular kind acquired in the period of two years ending with the day on which the instrument was executed; and

(*b*) the body corporate from which the [transfer][17] there mentioned is effected acquired [any of those chargeable securities][11]—

(i) in a transaction which was given effect by an instrument of transfer on which stamp duty was not chargeable by virtue of section [80A][7] above;

(ii) in pursuance of an agreement to transfer securities as regards which section 87 above did not apply by virtue of section [88A][8] above; ...[11]

[(ii*a*) in pursuance of an agreement to transfer securities which was made for the purpose of performing the obligation to transfer chargeable securities described in [section 89AA(1)(*a*) below and as regards which section 87 above did not apply by virtue of section 89AA(2) below];[14] or][11]

(iii) in circumstances with regard to which the charge to stamp duty or stamp duty reserve tax was treated as not arising by virtue of regulations under section 116 or 117 of the Finance Act 1991.][3]

[(1C) Where—

(*a*) there is an arrangement falling within subsection (1) of section 80C above (stamp duty relief for transfers in accordance with certain arrangements for B to transfer stock to A or his nominee and for A or his nominee to transfer stock of the same kind and amount back to B or his nominee), and

(*b*) under the arrangement stock is transferred to A or his nominee by an instrument on which stamp duty is not chargeable by virtue only of section 80C(2) above, but

(*c*) it becomes apparent that stock of the same kind or amount will not be transferred to B or his nominee by A or his nominee in accordance with the arrangement,

[then, if section 80D does not apply,][18] the instrument shall be disregarded in construing section 92(1A) and (1B) below.][9]

[(1D) Where—

(*a*) an instrument transferring stock in accordance with an arrangement is stamped under section 80C(5) above, but

(*b*) the instrument should not have been so stamped because the arrangement fell within section 80C(4)(*a*) or (*b*) above, and

(*c*) apart from section 80C above stamp duty would have been chargeable on the instrument,

the instrument shall be deemed to be duly stamped under section 80C(5) above, but shall be disregarded in construing section 92(1A) and (1B) below.][9]

(2)–(3)...[4]

[(4) If chargeable securities cannot (apart from this subsection) be identified for the purposes of subsection (1B) above, securities shall be taken as follows, that is to say, securities of the same kind acquired later in the period of two years there mentioned (and not taken for the purposes of that subsection in relation to an earlier instrument) shall be taken before securities acquired earlier in that period.][12]

[(5) If, in the case of an agreement (or of two or more agreements between the same parties) to transfer chargeable securities—

(*a*) the conditions in section 92(1A) and (1B) below are not satisfied by virtue only of the application of subsection (1B) above in relation to the instrument (or any one or more of the two or more instruments) in question, but

(*b*) not all of the chargeable securities falling to be regarded for the purposes of that subsection as transferred by the instrument (or by the two or more instruments between them) were acquired as mentioned in paragraphs (*a*) and (*b*) of that subsection,

stamp duty reserve tax shall be repaid or cancelled under section 92 below in accordance with subsection (5A) below.][12]

[(5A) Any repayment or cancellation of tax falling to be made by virtue of subsection (5) above shall be determined as if (without prejudice to section 87(7A) above) there had instead of the agreement (or the two or more agreements) in question been—

(*a*) a separate agreement (or two or more separate agreements) relating to such of the securities as were acquired as mentioned in paragraphs (*a*) and (*b*) of subsection (1B) above, and

(*b*) a single separate agreement relating to such of the securities as do not fall within those paragraphs,

and as if the instrument in question (or the two or more instruments in question between them) had related only to such of the securities as do not fall within those paragraphs.][12]

[(6) Where a person enters into an agreement for securities to be transferred to him or his nominee, the securities shall be treated for the purposes of subsections (1B)(*a*) and (4) above as acquired by that person at the time when he enters into the agreement, unless the agreement is conditional, in which case they shall be taken to be acquired by him when the condition is satisfied.][5]

Stamp Taxes

Cross references—See FA 1990 ss 110, 111(1) (abolition of stamp duty reserve tax with effect from an appointed day).

Amendments—[1] Sub-s (1)(*aa*), (*ab*) substituted by FA 1999 s 112(4), Sch 14 para 20 with effect in relation to instruments executed after 30 September 1999. This does not apply to transfers or other instruments relating to units under a unit trust scheme by virtue of FA 1999 s 122. For prospective repeal of FA 1999 Sch 14 para 20 see FA 1999 s 123(3). Previously the text read:

"[(*aa*) section 65(1) of the Finance Act 1963 (renounceable letters of allotment etc),]

[(*ab*) section 14(1) of the Finance Act (Northern Ireland) 1963 (renounceable letters of allotment etc),]"

[2] Sub-s (1A) inserted by FA 1996 s 189, with effect in relation to an agreement to transfer securities if an instrument is executed after 30 June 1996 in pursuance of the agreement.

[3] Sub-s (1B) inserted by FA 1996 s 190(1), (3), with effect where the instrument on which stamp duty is not chargeable by virtue of FA 1930 s 42, or FA(NI) 1954 s 11, is executed on or after 4 January 1996 in pursuance of an agreement to transfer securities made on or after that date.

[4] Sub-ss (2), (3) repealed by FA 1996 s 188(3), (5), Sch 41 Pt VII, with effect in relation to an agreement to transfer securities if the agreement is conditional and the condition is satisfied on or after 1 July 1996 or the agreement is not conditional and is made on or after that date.

[5] Sub-ss (4)–(6) added by FA 1996 s 190(2), (3), with effect where the instrument on which stamp duty is not chargeable by virtue of FA 1930 s 42, or FA(NI) 1954 s 11, is executed on or after 4 January 1996 in pursuance of an agreement to transfer securities made on or after that date.

[6] Words in sub-ss (1), (1A), (1B) substituted by FA 1996 s 192(2), (6), with effect in relation to an agreement to transfer securities if the agreement is conditional and the condition is satisfied on or after 1 July 1996 or the agreement is not conditional and is made on or after that date.

[7] Section number in sub-s (1B)(*b*)(i) substituted for "81" by FA 1997 s 97(3) in relation to an agreement to transfer chargeable securities if the securities were acquired in a transaction with effect from 20 October 1997 as appointed by SI 1997/2428.

[8] Section number in sub-s (1B)(*b*)(ii) substituted for "89" by FA 1997 s 102(3) in relation to property consisting of chargeable securities if the securities were acquired in pursuance of an agreement to transfer securities (*a*) in the case of an agreement which is not conditional, if the agreement is made on or after 20 October 1997 as appointed by SI 1997/2428; and (*b*) in the case of a conditional agreement, if the condition is satisfied on or after that day.

[9] Sub-ss (1C) and (1D) inserted by FA 1997 s 103 (4) in relation to instruments executed on or after 20 October 1997 as appointed by SI 1997/2428.

[10] Words in sub-s (1B)(*a*) inserted by FA 1997 s 106(5) where the instrument is executed on or after 4 January 1997 in pursuance of an agreement to transfer securities made on or after that date.

[11] Words in sub-s (1B)(*b*) substituted, in sub-s (1B)(ii) deleted, and sub-s (1B)(iia) inserted by FA 1997 s 106(5) where the instrument is executed on or after 4 January 1997 in pursuance of an agreement to transfer securities made on or after that date.

[12] Sub-ss (4), (5) and (5A) substituted for sub-ss (4) and (5) by FA 1997 s 106(6) where the instrument is executed on or after 4 January 1997 in pursuance of an agreement to transfer securities on or after that date.

[13] Heading substituted by FA 1997 s 106(7).

[14] Words in sub-s (1B)(iia) substituted for the words "paragraph (*a*) of subsection (1) of section 89B below as regards which section 87 above did not apply by virtue of that subsection" by FA 1997 s 103(3) in relation to property consisting of chargeable securities if the securities were acquired in pursuance of (*a*) an agreement to transfer securities which is not conditional if the agreement is made on or after 20 October 1997 as appointed by SI 1997/2428; and (*b*) a conditional agreement if the condition is satisfied on or after that date.

[15] Figures in sub-s (1A) substituted by FA 1999 s 112(4), Sch 14 para 20 with effect in relation to instruments executed after 30 September 1999. This does not apply to transfers or other instruments relating to units under a unit trust scheme by virtue of FA 1999 s 122. For prospective repeal of FA 1999 Sch 14 para 20 see FA 1999 s 123(3). Previously the text read '50p'.

[16] Word in sub-s (1)(*b*) and sub-s (1)(*c*) inserted by FA 1999 Sch 19 para 10 with effect from 6 February 2000.

[17] The word "transfer" substituted for the words "conveyance or transfer" in enactments relating to stamp duty by FA 2003 Sch 20 para 3.

[18] In sub-s (1C), words inserted by FA 2009 s 83, Sch 37 paras 1, 3 with effect where the insolvency in question occurs on or after 1 September 2008. FA 2009 s 83(3). FA 2009 s 83 and Sch 37 cease to have effect—

(a) in relation to the amendments made to Part 3 of FA 1986, when the repeal of sections 80 to 85 of that Act (by Part 6 of Schedule 19 to, and in accordance with sections 107 to 109 of, FA 1990) comes into force, and

(b) in relation to the amendments made to Part 4 of FA 1986, when the repeal of that Part (by Part 7 of Schedule 19 to, and in accordance with section 110 of, FA 1990) comes into force.

[88A Section 87: exceptions for intermediaries

[(1) Section 87 above shall not apply as regards an agreement to transfer securities of a particular kind to B or B's nominee if—

(*a*) B is a member of a regulated market on which securities of that kind are regularly traded; and

(*b*) B is an intermediary and is recognised as such by the market in accordance with arrangements approved by the Commissioners for Her Majesty's Revenue and Customs ("the Commissioners").][2]

[(1A) Section 87 above shall not apply as regards an agreement to transfer securities of a particular kind to B or B's nominee if—

(*a*) B is a member of a multilateral trading facility, or a recognised foreign exchange, on which securities of that kind are regularly traded;

(*b*) B is an intermediary and is recognised as such by the facility or exchange in accordance with arrangements approved by the Commissioners; and

(*c*) the agreement is effected on the facility or exchange.][2]

[(1B) Section 87 above shall not apply as regards an agreement to transfer securities of a particular kind to B or B's nominee if—

(*a*) B is an intermediary who is approved for the purposes of this section by the Commissioners; and

(*b*) securities of that kind are regularly traded on a regulated market.][2]

[(1C) Section 87 above shall not apply as regards an agreement to transfer securities of a particular kind to B or B's nominee if—

(*a*) B is an intermediary who is approved for the purposes of this section by the Commissioners;

(*b*) securities of that kind are regularly traded on a multilateral trading facility or a recognised foreign exchange; and

(*c*) the agreement is effected on the facility or exchange.][2]

[(2) Section 87 above shall not apply as regards an agreement to transfer securities of a particular kind to B or B's nominee if—

(*a*) B is a member of a regulated market, a multilateral trading facility or a recognised foreign options exchange;

(*b*) options to buy or sell securities of that kind are regularly traded on, and are listed by or quoted on, that market, facility or exchange;

(*c*) B is an options intermediary and is recognised as such by that market, facility or exchange in accordance with arrangements approved by the Commissioners; and

(*d*) securities of that kind are regularly traded on a regulated market.][2]

[(2A) Section 87 above shall not apply as regards an agreement to transfer securities of a particular kind to B or B's nominee if—

(*a*) B is a member of a regulated market, a multilateral trading facility or a recognised foreign options exchange;

(*b*) options to buy or sell securities of that kind are regularly traded on, and are listed by or quoted on, that market, facility or exchange;

(*c*) B is an options intermediary and is recognised as such by that market, facility or exchange in accordance with arrangements approved by the Commissioners; and

(*d*) the agreement is effected on a relevant qualifying exchange on which securities of that kind are regularly traded or is effected on a relevant qualifying exchange pursuant to the exercise of a relevant option and options to buy or sell securities of that kind are regularly traded on, and are listed by or quoted on, that exchange;

and in paragraph (*d*) "relevant qualifying exchange" means a multilateral trading facility, a recognised foreign options exchange or a recognised foreign exchange.][2]

[(2B) Section 87 above shall not apply as regards an agreement to transfer securities of a particular kind to B or B's nominee if—

(*a*) B is an options intermediary who is approved for the purposes of this section by the Commissioners;

(*b*) options to buy or sell securities of that kind are regularly traded on, and are listed by or quoted on, a regulated market, a multilateral trading facility or a recognised foreign options exchange; and

(*c*) securities of that kind are regularly traded on a regulated market.][2]

[(2C) Section 87 above shall not apply as regards an agreement to transfer securities of a particular kind to B or B's nominee if—

(*a*) B is an options intermediary who is approved for the purposes of this section by the Commissioners;

(*b*) options to buy or sell securities of that kind are regularly traded on, and are listed by or quoted on, a regulated market, a multilateral trading facility or a recognised foreign options exchange; and

(*c*) the agreement is effected on a relevant qualifying exchange on which securities of that kind are regularly traded or is effected on a relevant qualifying exchange pursuant to the exercise of a relevant option and options to buy or sell securities of that kind are regularly traded on, and are listed by or quoted on, that exchange;

and in paragraph (*c*) "relevant qualifying exchange" means a multilateral trading facility, a recognised foreign options exchange or a recognised foreign exchange.][2]

(4) For the purposes of this section—

(*a*) an intermediary is a person who carries on a bona fide business of dealing in chargeable securities and does not carry on an excluded business; and

(*b*) an options intermediary is a person who carries on a bona fide business of dealing in quoted or listed options to buy or sell chargeable securities and does not carry on an excluded business.

(5) The excluded businesses are the following—

(*a*) any business which consists wholly or mainly in the making or managing of investments;

(*b*) any business which consists wholly or mainly in, or is carried on wholly or mainly for the purpose of, providing services to persons who are connected with the person carrying on the business;

(*c*) any business which consists in insurance business;

(*d*) any business which consists in managing or acting as trustee in relation to a pension scheme or which is carried on by the manager or trustee of such a scheme in connection with or for the purposes of the scheme;

(*e*) any business which consists in operating or acting as trustee in relation to a collective investment scheme or is carried on by the operator or trustee of such a scheme in connection with or for the purposes of the scheme.

(6) An agreement is effected on [a facility or][2] an exchange for the purposes of [this section][2] if (and only if)—

(*a*) it is subject to the rules of [the facility or exchange][2]; and

(*b*) it is reported to [the facility or exchange][2] in accordance with the rules of [the facility or exchange][2].][1]

[(6A) The Commissioners may approve a person for the purposes of this section only if the person is authorised under the law of an EEA State to provide any of the investment services or activities listed in Section A 2 or 3 of Annex I to the Directive (execution of orders on behalf of clients and dealing on own account), whether or not the person is authorised under the Directive.][2]

Cross references—See FA 2002 s 117 (the Treasury may by regulations extend the application of this section to any market that is not a recognised exchange but is prescribed by order under the Financial Services and Markets Act 2000 s 118(3)).

Stamp Duty and Stamp Duty Reserve Tax (Extension of Exceptions relating to Recognised Exchanges) Regulations, SI 2002/1975 (with effect from 26 July 2002, the application of the provision specified in FA 2002 s 117(2) (which includes this section) is extended to the market known as OFEX).

F(No 2)A 2005 s 50 (power of the Treasury to extend the application of this section to any market which is not a recognised exchange, but is a multilateral trading facility or (assuming compliance with the provisions of Title II of the European Parliament and Council Directive 2004/39/EC) would be such a facility).

Modifications—Stamp Duty and Stamp Duty Reserve Tax (Extension of Exceptions relating to Recognised Exchanges) Regulations, SI 2005/1990 regs 3, 6 (modification of this section in its application to prescibed multilateral trading facilities. For definition of "prescribed multilateral trading facility" see SI 2005/1990 reg 2).

Amendments—[1] This section inserted by FA 1997 s 102(1) in relation to an agreement to transfer securities (*a*) in the case of an agreement which is not conditional, if the agreement is made on or after 20 October 1997 as appointed by SI 1997/2428; and (*b*) in the case of a conditional agreement, if the condition is satisfied on or after that date and repealed by FA 1997 Sch 18 Part VII with effect from the day appointed under FA 1990 s 111.

[2] Sub-ss (1)–(2C) substituted for sub-ss (1)–(3); in sub-s (6), words inserted, and words substituted for the words "subsection (1) or (2) above", and "the exchange" (wherever occurring); and sub-s (6A) inserted, by FA 2007 s 73, Sch 21 para 3 with effect in relation to any agreement to transfer securities—

(*a*) in a case where the agreement is conditional, if the condition is satisfied on or after 1 November 2007, and

(*b*) in any other case, if the agreement is made on or after that date.: FA 2007 Sch 21 para 3(5).

Sub-ss (1)–(3) previously read as follows—

"(1) Section 87 above shall not apply as regards an agreement to transfer securities of a particular kind to B or his nominee if—

(*a*) B is a member of an EEA exchange, or a recognised foreign exchange, on which securities of that kind are regularly traded;

(*b*) B is an intermediary and is recognised as an intermediary by the exchange in accordance with arrangements approved by the Board; and

(*c*) the agreement is effected on the exchange.

(2) Section 87 above shall not apply as regards an agreement to transfer securities of a particular kind to B or his nominee if—

(*a*) B is a member of an EEA exchange or a recognised foreign options exchange;

(*b*) options to buy or sell securities of that kind are regularly traded on that exchange and are listed by or quoted on that exchange;

(*c*) B is an options intermediary and is recognised as an options intermediary by that exchange in accordance with arrangements approved by the Board; and

(*d*) the agreement is effected on an EEA exchange, or a recognised foreign exchange, on which securities of that kind are regularly traded or subsection (3) below applies.

(3) This subsection applies if—

(*a*) the agreement is effected on an EEA exchange, or a recognised foreign options exchange, pursuant to the exercise of a relevant option; and

(*b*) options to buy or sell securities of the kind concerned are regularly traded on that exchange and are listed by or quoted on that exchange.".

[88B Intermediaries: supplementary

(1) For the purposes of section 88A above the question whether a person is connected with another shall be determined in accordance with the provisions of section 839 of the Income and Corporation Taxes Act 1988.

(2) In section 88A above and this section—

"collective investment scheme" has the meaning given in section [235 of the Financial Services and Markets Act 2000][2];

["the Directive" means Directive 2004/39/EC of the European Parliament and of the Council of 21 April 2004 on markets in financial instruments, as amended from time to time;][3]

...[3]

"EEA State"[, in relation to any time, means a State which at that time is a member State or any other State which at that time][3] is a contracting party to the agreement on the European Economic Area signed at Oporto on the 2nd May 1992 as adjusted by the Protocol signed at Brussels on the 17th March 1993 [(as modified or supplemented from time to time)][3];

["insurance business" means business which consists of the effecting or carrying out of contracts of insurance and, for the purposes of this definition, "contract of insurance" has the meaning given by Article 3(1) of the Financial Services and Markets Act 2000 (Regulated Activities) Order 2001;

"the operator", in relation to a collective investment scheme, shall be construed in accordance with section 237(2) of the Financial Services and Markets Act 2000;][2]

"quoted or listed options" means options which are quoted on or listed by an EEA exchange or a recognised foreign options exchange;

"recognised foreign exchange" and "recognised foreign options exchange" have the meanings given, respectively, by subsections (3) and (4) of section 80B above;

["trustee", in relation to a collective investment scheme, means a trustee or a depositary within the meaning given in section 237(2) of the Financial Services and Markets Act 2000.][2]

[(2A) Each of the following expressions—

"multilateral trading facility", and

"regulated market",

has the same meaning in section 88A above as it has for the purposes of the Directive.][3]

(3) In section 88A above "the exercise of a relevant option" means—

(*a*) the exercise by B of an option to buy securities; or

(*b*) the exercise of an option binding B to buy securities.

[(3A) The Treasury may by regulations amend section 88A above and this section (as they have effect for the time being) in order to extend the exemption from tax under that section.][3]

(4) The Treasury may by regulations provide that section 88A above shall not have effect in relation to kinds of agreement specified in the regulations.

(5) The Treasury may by regulations provide that if—

(*a*) an agreement falls within [any of subsections (1) to (2C)][3] of section 88A above, and

(*b*) section 87 above would, apart from section 88A, apply to the agreement,

section 87 shall apply to the agreement but with the substitution of a rate of tax not exceeding 0.1 per cent for the rate specified in subsection (6) of that section.

(6) The Treasury may by regulations change the meaning of "intermediary" or "options intermediary" for the purposes of section 88A above by amending subsection (3) or (5) of that section (as it has effect for the time being).

(7) The power to make regulations under subsections [(3A)][3] to (6) above shall be exercisable by statutory instrument subject to annulment in pursuance of a resolution of the House of Commons.][1]

Amendments—[1] This section inserted by FA 1997 s 100(1) in relation to an agreement to transfer securities (*a*) in the case of an agreement which is not conditional, if the agreement is made on or after 20 October 1997 as appointed by SI 1997/2428; and (*b*) in the case of a conditional agreement, if the condition is satisfied on or after that date and repealed by FA 1997 Sch 18 Part VII with effect from the day appointed under FA 1990 s 111.

[2] Words in definition of "collective investment scheme", and definitions of "insurance business", and "the trustee" and "the operator", substituted by the Financial Services and Markets Act 2000 (Consequential Amendments) (Taxes) Order, SI 2001/3629 arts 6, 9. SI 2001/3629 art 9 has effect in relation to—

(*a*) an agreement to transfer chargeable securities which is not conditional, if the agreement is made after 30 November 2001;

(*b*) a conditional agreement to transfer such securities, if the condition is satisfied after that date.

[3] In sub-s (2), definition inserted, definition of "EEA exchange" repealed, and words "means a State which" in definition of "EEA State" substituted, and words inserted; sub-ss (2A), (3A) inserted; and in sub-s (5), words substituted for the words "subsection (1) or (2)"; and in sub-s (7), figure substituted for "(4)", by FA 2007 ss 73, 114, Sch 21 para 4, Sch 27 Pt 4(2) with effect in relation to any agreement to transfer securities—

(*a*) in a case where the agreement is conditional, if the condition is satisfied on or after 1 November 2007, and

(*b*) in any other case, if the agreement is made on or after that date.

Definition of "EEA exchange" previously read as follows—

" 'EEA exchange' means a market which appears on the list drawn up by an EEA State pursuant to Article 16 of European Communities Council Directive No 93/22/EEC on investment services in the securities field;".

89 Section 87: exceptions for market makers etc

Cross references—See FA 1990 ss 110, 111(1) (abolition of stamp duty reserve tax with effect from an appointed day).

Amendments—This section repealed by FA 1997 s 102(2), Sch 18 Part VII in relation to an agreement to transfer securities (*a*) in the case of an agreement which is not conditional, if the agreement is made on or after 20 October 1997 as appointed by SI 1997/2428; and (*b*) in the case of a conditional agreement, if the condition is satisfied on or after that date.

[89A Section 87: exceptions for public issues

(1) Section 87 above shall not apply as regards an agreement to transfer securities other than units under a unit trust scheme to B or B's nominee if—

(*a*) the agreement is part of an arrangement, entered into by B in the ordinary course of B's business as an issuing house, under which B (as principal) is to offer the securities for sale to the public,

(*b*) the agreement is conditional upon the admission of the securities to the Official List of The Stock Exchange,

(*c*) the consideration under the agreement for each security is the same as the price at which B is to offer the security for sale, and

(*d*) B sells the securities in accordance with the arrangement referred to in paragraph (*a*) above.

(2) Section 87 above shall not apply as regards an agreement if the securities to which the agreement relates are newly subscribed securities other than units under a unit trust scheme and—

(*a*) the agreement is made in pursuance of an offer to the public made by A (as principal) under an arrangement entered into in the ordinary course of A's business as an issuing house,

(*b*) a right of allotment in respect of, or to subscribe for, the securities has been acquired by A under an agreement which is part of the arrangement,

(*c*) both those agreements are conditional upon the admission of the securities to the Official List of The Stock Exchange, and

(*d*) the consideration for each security is the same under both agreements;

and for the purposes of this subsection, "newly subscribed securities" are securities which, in pursuance of the arrangement referred to in paragraph (*a*) above, are issued wholly for new consideration.

(3) Section 87 above shall not apply as regards an agreement if the securities to which the agreement relates are registered securities other than units under a unit trust scheme and—

(*a*) the agreement is made in pursuance of an offer to the public made by A,

(*b*) the agreement is conditional upon the admission of the securities to the Official List of The Stock Exchange, and

(*c*) under the agreement A issues to B or his nominee a renounceable letter of acceptance, or similar instrument, in respect of the securities.

(4) The Treasury may by regulations amend paragraph (*b*) of subsection (1) above, paragraph (*c*) of subsection (2) above, and paragraph (*b*) of subsection (3) above (as they have effect for the time being); and the power to make regulations under this section shall be exercisable by statutory instrument subject to annulment in pursuance of a resolution of the House of Commons.][1]

Cross references—See FA 1990 ss 110, 111(1) (abolition of stamp duty reserve tax with effect from an appointed day).

Amendments—[1] This section inserted by F (No 2) A 1987, s 100 (1) in relation to agreements to transfer securities made after 7 May 1987.

[89AA Section 87: exception for repurchases and stock lending

(1) This section applies where a person (P) has entered into an arrangement with another person (Q) under which—

(*a*) Q is to transfer chargeable securities of a particular kind to P or his nominee, and

(*b*) chargeable securities of the same kind and amount are to be transferred by P or his nominee to Q or his nominee,

and the conditions set out in subsection [(2A) or][2] (3) below are fulfilled.

(2) Section 87 above shall not apply as regards an agreement to transfer chargeable securities to P or his nominee or Q or his nominee in accordance with the arrangement.

[(2A) The conditions in this subsection are—

(*a*) that P or Q is authorised under the law of an EEA State to provide any of the investment services or activities listed in Section A 2 or 3 of Annex I to the Directive (execution of orders on behalf of clients and dealing on own account) in relation to securities of the kind concerned, whether or not P or Q is authorised under the Directive; …[3]

(*b*) that securities of the kind concerned are regularly traded on a regulated market[; and

(*c*) that chargeable securities are transferred to P or his nominee and Q or his nominee in pursuance of the arrangement.][3]][2]

(3) The conditions [in this subsection][2] are—

(*a*) that the agreement is effected on [a regulated market, a multilateral trading facility][2] or a recognised foreign exchange;

(*b*) that securities of the kind concerned are regularly traded on that [market, facility or][2] exchange; and

(*c*) that chargeable securities are transferred to P or his nominee and Q or his nominee in pursuance of the arrangement.

(4) An arrangement does not fall within subsection (1) above if—

(*a*) the arrangement is not such as would be entered into by persons dealing with each other at arm's length; or

(*b*) under the arrangement any of the benefits or risks arising from fluctuations, before the transfer to Q or his nominee takes place, in the market value of the chargeable securities accrues to, or falls on, P.

(5) An agreement is effected on [a market, a facility or][2] an exchange for the purposes of subsection (3) above if (and only if)—

(*a*) it is subject to the rules of [the market, facility or exchange][2]; and

(*b*) it is reported to [the market, facility or exchange][2] in accordance with the rules of [the market, facility or exchange][2].

(6) In this section—

["the Directive" has the meaning given in section 88B(2) above;

"EEA State" has the meaning given in section 88B(2) above;][2]

...[2]

"recognised foreign exchange" has the meaning given in section 80B(3) above.

[(6A) Each of the following expressions—

"multilateral trading facility", and

"regulated market",

has the same meaning in this section as it has for the purposes of the Directive.][2]

(7) The Treasury may by regulations provide that if section 87 would apply as regards an agreement but for subsection (2) above, section 87 shall apply as regards the agreement but with the substitution of a rate of tax not exceeding 0.1 per cent. for the rate specified in subsection (6) of that section.

(8) The Treasury may by regulations amend this section (as it has effect for the time being) in order—

(*a*) to change the conditions for exemption from tax under this section; or

(*b*) to provide that this section does not apply in relation to kinds of arrangement specified in the regulations.

(9) The power to make regulations under subsection (7) or (8) above shall be exercisable by statutory instrument subject to annulment in pursuance of a resolution of the House of Commons.][1]

Cross references—See FA 2002 s 117 (the Treasury may by regulations extend the application of this section to any market that is not a recognised exchange but is prescribed by order under the Financial Services and Markets Act 2000 s 118(3)).

European Single Currency (Taxes) Regulations, SI 1998/3177 regs 26 and 28 for details on replacement of chargeable securities in a euroconversion.

Stamp Duty and Stamp Duty Reserve Tax (Extension of Exceptions relating to Recognised Exchanges) Regulations, SI 2002/1975 (with effect from 26 July 2002, the application of the provision specified in FA 2002 s 117(2) (which includes this section) is extended to the market known as OFEX).

F(No 2)A 2005 s 50 (power of the Treasury to extend the application of this section to any market which is not a recognised exchange, but is a multilateral trading facility or (assuming compliance with the provisions of Title II of the European Parliament and Council Directive 2004/39/EC), would be such a facility).

Modifications—Stamp Duty and Stamp Duty Reserve Tax (Extension of Exceptions relating to Recognised Exchanges) Regulations, SI 2005/1990 regs 3, 7 (modification of this section in its application to prescibed multilateral trading facilities. For definition of "prescribed multilateral trading facility" see SI 2005/1990 reg 2).

Amendments—[1] This section inserted by FA 1997 s 103(1), in relation to an agreement to transfer securities (*a*) in the case of an agreement which is not conditional, if the agreement is made on or after 20 October 1997 as appointed by SI 1997/2428; and (*b*) in the case of a conditional agreement, if the condition is satisfied on or after that date and repealed by FA 1997 Sch 18 Part VII with effect from the day appointed under FA 1990 s 111.

[2] Words in sub-ss (1), (3), (5), (6) inserted; sub-ss (2A), (6A) inserted; in sub-s (3), words substituted for the words "an EEA exchange"; in sub-s (5), words substituted for the words "the exchange" wherever occurring; and in sub-s (6), definition of "EEA exchange" repealed, by FA 2007 ss 73, 114, Sch 21 para 6, Sch 27 Pt 4(2) with effect in relation to any agreement to transfer securities—

(*a*) in a case where the agreement is conditional, if the condition is satisfied on or after 1 November 2007, and

(*b*) in any other case, if the agreement is made on or after that date.

Definition of "EEA exchange" previously read as follows—

" 'EEA exchange' has the meaning given in section 88B(2) above;".

[3] In sub-s (2A) word "and" at end of para (*a*) repealed, and para (*c*) and preceding word "and" inserted, by the Stamp Duty Reserve Tax (Amendment of section 89AA of the Finance Act 1986) Regulations, SI 2008/3236 reg 2 with effect in a case where the agreement is conditional, if the condition is satisfied on or after 18 December 2008, and in any other case, if the agreement is made on or after that date.

[89AB Section 87: exception for repurchases and stock lending in case of insolvency

(1) This section applies where—

(*a*) P and Q have entered into an arrangement falling within section 89AA(1),

(*b*) the only reason that the conditions in subsection (2A) or (3) of that section are not met is that chargeable securities of the same kind and amount as those transferred to P or P's nominee are not transferred to Q or Q's nominee, and

(*c*) the conditions in subsection (2) below are met.

(2) The conditions in this subsection are that—

(*a*) P and Q are not connected persons within the meaning of section 839 of the Taxes Act 1988,

(*b*) after Q has transferred securities under the arrangement, either P or Q becomes insolvent, (*c*) it becomes apparent (whether before or after the insolvency occurs) that, as a result of the insolvency, securities will not be transferred to Q or Q's nominee in accordance with the arrangement.

(3) Section 87 does not apply as regards an agreement to transfer chargeable securities to P or P's nominee, or Q or Q's nominee, in accordance with the arrangement.

(4) Subsections (5) and (6) apply if—

(*a*) the party who does not become insolvent ("the solvent party") or the solvent party's nominee acquires replacement securities, and

(*b*) the replacement securities are acquired before the end of the period of 30 days beginning with the day on which the insolvency occurs ("the insolvency date").

(5) Where collateral is provided under the arrangement (or under arrangements of which that arrangement forms part), section 87 does not apply as regards any agreement to transfer to the solvent party or the solvent party's nominee—

(*a*) replacement securities acquired using the collateral (whether directly or indirectly), or

(*b*) where the solvent party uses the whole of the value of the collateral to acquire replacement securities, any further replacement securities.

(6) Where no collateral is provided as mentioned in subsection (5), section 87 does not apply as regards any agreement to transfer replacement securities to the solvent party or the solvent party's nominee.

(7) Subsections (5) and (6) may apply as regards more than one agreement (and where those subsections apply as regards more than one agreement, the agreements may be with different persons).

(8) But those subsections apply only as regards replacement securities up to the amount of securities which will not be transferred as a result of the insolvency.

(9) For the purposes of this section, a person becomes insolvent—

(*a*) if a company voluntary arrangement takes effect under Part 1 of the Insolvency Act 1986,

(*b*) if an administration application (within the meaning of Schedule B1 to that Act) is made or a receiver or manager, or an administrative receiver, is appointed,

(*c*) on the commencement of a creditor's voluntary winding up (within the meaning of Part 4 of that Act) or a winding up by the court under Chapter 6 of that Part,

(*d*) if an individual voluntary arrangement takes effect under Part 8 of that Act,

(*e*) on the presentation of a bankruptcy petition (within the meaning of Part 9 of that Act),

(*f*) if a compromise or arrangement takes effect under Part 26 of the Companies Act 2006,

(*g*) if a bank insolvency order takes effect under Part 2 of the Banking Act 2009,

(*h*) if a bank administration order takes effect under Part 3 of that Act, or

(*i*) on the occurrence of any corresponding event which has effect under or as a result of the law of Scotland or Northern Ireland or a country or territory outside the United Kingdom.

(10) In this section—

"collateral" means an amount of money or other property which is payable to, or made available for the benefit of, a party to an arrangement or that party's nominee for the purpose of securing the discharge of the requirement to transfer securities to that party or the nominee;

"replacement securities", in the event of a party to an arrangement becoming insolvent, are chargeable securities of the same kind as the securities which will not be transferred to the other party or that party's nominee as a result of the insolvency.][1]

Amendments—[1] Section 89AB inserted by FA 2009 s 83, Sch 37 paras 4, 5 with effect where the insolvency in question occurs on or after 1 September 2008. FA 2009 s 83(3). FA 2009 s 83 and FA 2009 Sch 37 cease to have effect—

(a) in relation to the amendments made to Part 3 of FA 1986, when the repeal of sections 80 to 85 of that Act (by Part 6 of Schedule 19 to, and in accordance with sections 107 to 109 of, FA 1990) comes into force, and

(b) in relation to the amendments made to Part 4 of FA 1986, when the repeal of that Part (by Part 7 of Schedule 19 to, and in accordance with section 110 of, FA 1990) comes into force.

[89B Section 87: exceptions for stock lending and collateral security arrangements]

Cross references—See FA 1990 ss 110, 111(1) (abolition of stamp duty reserve tax with effect from an appointed day).

Amendments—This section inserted by FA 1996 s 191, with effect in relation to agreements to transfer chargeable securities in pursuance of an arrangement entered into after 30 June 1996 and repealed by FA 1997 s 103(2), Sch 18 Pt VII in relation to an agreement to transfer securities (*a*) in the case of an agreement which is not conditional, if the agreement is made on or after 20 October 1997 as appointed by SI 1997/2428; and (*b*) in the case of a conditional agreement, if the condition is satisfied on or after that date.

90 Section 87: other exceptions

(1) Section 87 above shall not apply as regards an agreement to transfer a unit under a unit trust scheme [to or from the managers][12] under the scheme.

[(1A) Section 87 above shall not apply as regards an agreement to transfer a unit under a unit trust scheme if an instrument executed at the same time as the agreement and giving effect to the agreement would be exempt from stamp duty (if stamp duty were otherwise chargeable) by virtue of—

(*a*) section 42 of the Finance Act 1930 or section 11 of the Finance Act (Northern Ireland) 1954 (transfers between associated companies), or (*b*) regulations under section 87(2) of the Finance Act 1985 (power to exempt instruments from stamp duty of fixed amount).][12][, or

(*c*) section 96 of the Finance Act 1997 (demutualisation of insurance companies).][16]

[(1B) Section 87 above shall not apply as regards an agreement to transfer trust property to the unit holder on the surrender to the managers of a unit under a unit trust scheme.

The reference here to the surrender of a unit has the same meaning as in Part II of Schedule 19 to the Finance Act 1999.][13]

(2) …[14]

(3) Section 87 above shall not apply as regards an agreement to transfer securities constituted by or transferable by means of—

[(*a*) a non-UK bearer instrument;][6]

(*b*) …[2]

[(3A) Section 87 above shall not apply as regards an agreement to transfer chargeable securities constituted by or transferable by means of [a UK bearer instrument][7] unless subsection (3B), (3C) or (3E) below applies to the instrument.][3]

[(3B) This subsection applies to any instrument which falls within [the exemption conferred by paragraph 16 of Schedule 15 to the Finance Act 1999 (renounceable letters of allotment etc.)][7] (renounceable letter of allotment etc where rights are renounceable not later than six months after issue).][3]

[(3C) This subsection applies to an instrument if—

(*a*) the instrument was issued by a body corporate incorporated in the United Kingdom [(other than an SE which has its registered office outside the United Kingdom following a transfer in accordance with Article 8 of Council Regulation (EC) 2157/2001 on the Statute for a European Company (Societas Europaea))][17];

[(*b*) stamp duty under Schedule 15 to the Finance Act 1999 was not chargeable on the issue of the instrument by virtue only of the exemption conferred by paragraph 17 of that Schedule (non-sterling bearer instruments); and][8]

(*c*) the instrument is not exempt.][3]

[(3D) An instrument is exempt for the purposes of subsection (3C) above if—

(*a*) the chargeable securities in question are, or a depositary receipt for them is, listed on a recognised stock exchange; and

(*b*) the agreement to transfer those securities is not made in contemplation of, or as part of an arrangement for, a takeover of the body corporate which issued such instrument.][3]

[(3E) This subsection applies to an instrument if—

(*a*) the instrument was issued by a body corporate incorporated in the United Kingdom [(other than an SE which has its registered office outside the United Kingdom following a transfer in accordance with Article 8 of Council Regulation (EC) 2157/2001 on the Statute for a European Company (Societas Europaea))][17];

[(*b*) stamp duty under Schedule 15 to the Finance Act 1999 was not chargeable on the issue of the instrument—

(i) by virtue only of the exemption conferred by section 79(2) above (bearer instruments relating to loan capital), or

(ii) by virtue only of that provision and paragraph 17 of that Schedule (non-sterling bearer instruments);][9]

(*c*) by virtue of section 79(5) (convertible loan capital) or 79(6) (loan capital carrying special rights) above, stamp duty would be chargeable on an instrument transferring the loan capital to which the instrument relates; and

(*d*) the instrument is not exempt.][3]

[(3F) An instrument is exempt for the purposes of subsection (3E) above if—

(*a*) the chargeable securities in question are, or a depositary receipt for them is, listed on a recognised stock exchange;

(*b*) the agreement to transfer those securities is not made in contemplation of, or as part of an arrangement for, a takeover of the body corporate which issued the instrument; and

(*c*) those securities do not carry any right of the kind described in section 79(5) above (right of conversion into, or acquisition of, shares or other securities) by the exercise of which [chargeable securities which are not listed][10] on a recognised stock exchange may be obtained.][3]

(4) Section 87 above shall not apply as regards an agreement which forms part of an arrangement falling within section 93 (1) or 96 (1) below.

[(5) Section 87 above shall not apply as regards an agreement to transfer securities which the Board are satisfied are held, when the agreement is made, [for the purposes of a business][11] within subsection (6) below.][1]

[(6) [A business is within this subsection if, or so far as, it consists of][11] that of holding shares, stock or other marketable securities—

(*a*) as nominee or agent for a person whose business is or includes the provision of clearance services for the purchase and sale of shares, stock or other marketable securities, and (*b*) for the purpose of such part of the business mentioned in paragraph (*a*) above as consists of the provision of such clearance services (in a case where the business does not consist exclusively of that);

and in this subsection, "marketable securities" shall be construed in accordance with section 122(1) of the Stamp Act 1891.][1]

[(7) Section 87 above shall not apply as regards an agreement to transfer securities to—

(*a*) a body of persons established for charitable purposes only, or
(*b*) the trustees of a trust so established, or
(*c*) the Trustees of the National Heritage Memorial Fund, or
(*d*) the Historic Buildings and Monuments Commission for England.][1]

[or

(e) the National Endowment for Science, Technology and the Arts.][5]

[(7A) Section 87 above does not apply as regards an agreement to transfer any shares in a company which are held by the company (whether in accordance with section [724][19] of the Companies Act [2006][19] (treasury shares) or otherwise).][15]

[(8) for the purposes of subsections (3D) and (3F) above—

(*a*) references to a depositary receipt for chargeable securities shall be construed in accordance with section 94(1) below;

[(*b*) references to anything listed on a recognised stock exchange shall be construed in accordance with section 1005 of the Income Tax Act 2007;][18]

(*c*) there is a takeover of a body corporate if a person, on his own or together with connected persons, loses or acquires control of it.][4]

[(9) For the purposes of subsection (8) above—

(*a*) any question whether a person is connected with another shall be determined in accordance with section 286 of the Taxation of Chargeable Gains Act 1992;

(*b*) "control" shall be construed in accordance with section 416 of the Income and Corporation Taxes Act 1988.][4]

Stamp Taxes

Cross references—See FA 1986 s 97A(3), (4) (exclusion from charge to stamp duty reserve tax under sub-ss (4), (5) above does not apply to agreements connected with clearance services where an election is made under s 97A(1)).
FA 1990 ss 110, 111(1) (abolition of stamp duty reserve tax with effect from an appointed day).

Amendments—[1] Sub-ss (5), (6), (7) substituted and added by FA 1987 Sch 7 paras 1, 5, 6 and deemed always to have had effect.

[2] Sub-s (3)(*b*) repealed by FA 1997 s 105(1), (4), Sch 18 Pt VII with effect in relation to an agreement if the inland bearer instrument in question was issued on or after 26 November 1996 and (*a*) in the case of an agreement which is not conditional, the agreement is made on or after that date, or (*b*) in the case of a conditional agreement, the condition is satisfied on or after that date.

[3] Sub-ss (3A)–(3F) inserted by FA 1997 s 105(2), (4) with effect as in note 2 above.

[4] Sub-ss (8),(9) added by FA 1997 s 105(3), (4) with effect as in note 2 above.

[5] Sub-s (7)(*e*) inserted by the National Lottery Act 1998 s 24 with effect from 2 July 1998.

[6] Sub-s (3)(*a*) substituted by FA 1999 s 113(3), Sch 16 para 6 with effect in relation to bearer instruments issued after 30 September 1999. For prospective repeal of FA 1999 s 113, Sch 16 para 6 see FA 1999 s 123(3). Previously the text read:
"(*a*) an overseas bearer instrument, within the meaning of the heading "Bearer Instrument" in Schedule 1 to the Stamp Act 1891;"

[7] Words in sub-ss (3A) and (3B) substituted by FA 1999 s 113(3), Sch 16 para 6 with effect in relation to bearer instruments issued after 30 September 1999. For prospective repeal of FA 1999 s 113, Sch 16 para 6 see FA 1999 s 123(3). Previously the text read 'the heading "Bearer Instrument" in Schedule 1 to the Stamp Act 1891' and 'exemption 3 in the heading "Bearer Instrument" in Schedule 1 to the Stamp Act 1891' respectively.

[8] Sub-s (3C)(*b*) substituted by FA 1999 s 113(3), Sch 16 para 6 with effect in relation to bearer instruments issued after 30 September 1999. For prospective repeal of FA 1999 s 113, Sch 16 para 6 see FA 1999 s 123(3). Previously the text read:
"(*b*) stamp duty under the heading "Bearer Instrument" in Schedule 1 to the Stamp Act 1891 was not chargeable on the issue of the instrument by virtue only of—
(i) section 30 of the Finance Act 1967 (exemption for bearer instruments relating to stock in foreign currencies); or
(ii) section 7 of the Finance Act (Northern Ireland) 1967 (which makes similar provision for Northern Ireland); and".

[9] Sub-s (3E)(*b*) substituted by FA 1999 s 113(3), Sch 16 para 6 with effect in relation to bearer instruments issued after 30 September 1999. For prospective repeal of FA 1999 s 113, Sch 16 para 6 see FA 1999 s 123(3). Previously the text read:
"(*b*) stamp duty under the heading "Bearer Instrument" in Schedule 1 to the Stamp Act 1891 was not chargeable on the issue of the instrument—
(i) by virtue only of subsection (2) of section 79 above (exemption for bearer instruments relating to loan capital); or
(ii) by virtue only of that subsection and one or other of the provisions mentioned in subsection (3C)(*b*)(i) and (ii) above;".

[10] Words in sub-s (3F)(*c*) substituted by FA 1999 s 120(2) with effect in relation to instruments issued from 9 March 1999. For prospective repeal of FA 1999 s 120 see FA 1999 s 123(3).

[11] Words in sub-ss (5) and (6) substituted by FA 1999 s 120(3) with effect in relation to agreements to transfer securities made from 9 March 1999. For prospective repeal of FA 1999 s 120 see FA 1999 s 123(3).

[12] Words "to the managers" in sub-s (1) substituted and sub-s (1A) inserted by FA 1999 Sch 19 para 11 with effect from 6 February 2000, where this is the relevant day for the purposes of FA 1986 s 87.

[13] Sub-s (1B) inserted by FA 1999 Sch 19 para 11 with effect from 6 February 2000, where the surrender is within the meaning of FA 1999 Sch 19 Pt II.

[14] Sub-s (2) repealed by FA 1999 Sch 20 Pt V(5) with effect in relation to instruments executed from 6 February 2000.

[15] Sub-s (7A) inserted by FA 2003 s 195, Sch 40 para 3 with effect for any acquisition of shares by a company on or after 1 December 2003 (by virtue of SI 2003/3077).

[16] In sub-s (1A), para (*c*) and preceding word ", or" inserted by FA 2005 s 97(2), (5) with effect where the relevant day for the purposes of FA 1986 s 87 falls on or after 7 April 2005.

[17] Words in sub-ss (3C)(*a*), (3E)(*a*) inserted by F(No 2)A 2005 s 58(1), (2) with effect for the purposes of determining whether or not stamp duty or stamp duty reserve tax is chargeable in respect of anything done on or after 1 April 2005: F(No 2)A 2005 s 58(4).

[18] Sub-s (8)(*b*) substituted by FA 2007 s 109, Sch 26 para 6 with effect from 19 July 2007.

[19] In sub-s (7A), figures substituted for figures "162A" and "1985", by the Companies Act 2006 (Consequential Amendments) (Taxes and National Insurance) Order, SI 2009/1890 art 7(*d*) with effect from 1 October 2009.

91 Liability to tax

(1) Where tax is charged under section 87 above as regards an agreement, B shall be liable for the tax.

(2) …[1]

Cross references—See FA 1990 ss 110, 111(1) (abolition of stamp duty reserve tax with effect from an appointed day).

Amendments—[1] Sub-s (2) repealed by F (No 2) A 1987, s 100 (2), Sch 9, Pt IV, and the repeal is deemed always to have had effect.

92 Repayment or cancellation of tax

(1) If, as regards an agreement to transfer securities to B or his nominee, tax is charged under section 87 above and it is proved to the Board's satisfaction that at a time [on or after the relevant day (as defined in section 87(3))][5] but before the expiry of the period of six years [beginning with that day][5] the conditions mentioned in [subsections (1A) and (1B) below][6] have been fulfilled, [subsections (2) to (4A) of this section shall apply].[6]

[(1A) The first condition is that an instrument is (or instruments are) executed in pursuance of the agreement and the instrument transfers (or the instruments between them transfer) to B or, as the case may be, to his nominee all the chargeable securities to which the agreement relates.][7]

[(1B) The second condition is that the instrument (or each instrument) transferring the chargeable securities to which the agreement relates—

(*a*) so far as those securities are stock or marketable securities within the meaning of section 125 of the Finance Act 2003 (abolition of stamp duty except on instruments relating to stock or marketable securities)—

(i) is duly stamped in accordance with the enactments relating to stamp duty, or

(ii) is not chargeable with stamp duty or otherwise required to be stamped under those enactments; or

(*b*) so far as those securities are not stock or marketable securities within the meaning of that section, is an instrument that, disregarding that section, would not be chargeable with any *ad valorem* stamp duty under those enactments.][9]

[(1C) If, as regards an agreement to transfer shares in a company to that company ("the own-shares agreement")—

(*a*) tax is charged under section 87 above, and

(*b*) it is proved to the Board's satisfaction that at a time in the period of six years beginning on the relevant day (as defined in section 87(3)) the conditions mentioned in subsection (1D) have been fulfilled in respect of those shares,

subsections (2) to (4A) apply.][10]

[(1D) The conditions referred to in subsection (1C) are—

(*a*) that, in relation to the transfer made in pursuance of the own-shares agreement, a return has been made in respect of each of those shares in accordance with section [707][11] of the Companies Act [2006][11] (disclosure by company of purchase of own shares), and

(*b*) that any such return has been duly stamped in accordance with section 66.][10]

(2) If any of the tax charged has been paid, and a claim for repayment is made within the period of six years mentioned in subsection (1) [or, as the case may be, (1C)][10] above, the tax paid shall be repaid; and where the tax paid is not less than £25 it shall be repaid with interest on it at the [rate applicable under section 178 of the Finance Act 1989][2] from [the date on which the payment was made until the order for repayment is issued][3].

(3) To the extent that the tax charged has not been paid, the charge shall be cancelled by virtue of this subsection.

(4) …[4]

[(4A) Interest paid under subsection (2) above shall not constitute income for any tax purposes.][1]

(5) …[4]

[(6) In this section "the enactments relating to stamp duty" means the Stamp Act 1891 and any enactment which amends or is required to be construed together with that Act.][7]

[(7) This section shall have effect in relation to a person to whom the chargeable securities are transferred by way of security for a loan to B as it has effect in relation to a nominee of B.][8]

Note—For the rate applicable under FA 1989 s 178, see SI 1989/1297 *post*.

Cross references—See FA 1986 s 88(1), (1A), (1B) (certain instruments to be disregarded in construing sub-ss (1A), (1B) above).

FA 1990 ss 110, 111(1) (abolition of stamp duty reserve tax with effect from an appointed day).

Amendments—[1] Sub-s (4A) inserted by FA 1987 Sch 7 paras 1, 7 and deemed always to have had effect.

[2] Words in sub-s (2) substituted by FA 1989 s 179(1) (*f*).

[3] Words in sub-s (2) substituted by FA 1989 s 180(5), (7) and deemed always to have had effect.

[4] Sub-ss (4), (5) repealed by FA 1989 Sch 17 Pt X with effect from 18 August 1989 by virtue of FA 1989 s 178(1) (Appointed Day No 1) Order, SI 1989/1298.

[5] Words in sub-s (1) substituted by FA 1996 s 188(4), (5), with effect in relation to an agreement to transfer securities if the agreement is conditional and the condition is satisfied on or after 1 July 1996 or the agreement is not conditional and is made on or after that date.

[6] Words in sub-s (1) substituted by FA 1996 s 192(3), (6), with effect in relation to an agreement to transfer securities if the agreement is conditional and the condition is satisfied on or after 1 July 1996 or the agreement is not conditional and is made on or after that date.
[7] Sub-ss (1A), (1B) inserted (but see fn 9 below) and sub-s (6) added by FA 1996 s 192(4), (5), (6), with effect in relation to an agreement to transfer securities if the agreement is conditional and the condition is satisfied on or after 1 July 1996 or the agreement is not conditional and is made on or after that date.
[8] Sub-s (7) inserted by FA 1997 s 106(8), (9) in relation to an agreement to transfer securities if the agreement is conditional and the conditions satisfied on or after 4 January 1997 or the agreement is not conditional and is made on or after that date.
[9] Sub-s (1B) substituted by the Stamp Duty and Stamp Duty Land Tax (Consequential Amendment of Enactments) Regulations, SI 2003/2868, regs 3, 4 with effect from 1 December 2003. Sub-s (1B) (as inserted by FA 1996) previously read as follows—

"(1B) The second condition is that the instrument (or each instrument) transferring the chargeable securities to which the agreement relates is duly stamped in accordance with the enactments relating to stamp duty if it is an instrument which, under those enactments, is chargeable with stamp duty or otherwise required to be stamped."

[10] Sub-ss (1C), (1D) inserted, and words in sub-s (2) inserted, by FA 2003 s 195, Sch 40 para 4 with effect for any acquisition of shares by a company on or after 1 December 2003 (by virtue of SI 2003/3077).
[11] In sub-s (1D)(*a*), references substituted for references "169(1) or (1B)" and "1985", by the Companies Act 2006 (Consequential Amendments) (Taxes and National Insurance) Order, SI 2009/1890 art 7(*e*) with effect from 1 October 2009.

Other charges

Stamp Taxes

93 Depositary receipts

(1) Subject to subsection (7) below and section 95 below, there shall be a charge to stamp duty reserve tax under this section where in pursuance of an arrangement—

(*a*) a person falling within subsection (2) below has issued or is to issue a depositary receipt for chargeable securities, and

(*b*) chargeable securities of the same kind and amount are transferred or issued to [the person mentioned in paragraph (*a*) above or][1] a person falling within subsection (3) below, or are appropriated by [the person mentioned in paragraph (*a*) above or a person falling within subsection (3) below][2] towards the eventual satisfaction of the entitlement of the receipt's holder to receive chargeable securities.

(2) A person falls within this subsection if his business is or includes issuing depositary receipts for chargeable securities.

(3) A person falls within this subsection if his business is or includes holding chargeable securities as nominee or agent for the person who has issued or is to issue the depositary receipt.

(4) Subject to subsections [(6) and][6](7) below, tax under this section shall be charged at the rate of [1.5 per cent][3] of the following—

(*a*) in a case where the securities are issued, their price when issued;

(*b*) in a case where the securities are transferred for consideration in money or money's worth, the amount or value of the consideration;

(*c*) in any other case, the value of the securities.

(5) ...[5]

(6) In a case where—

(*a*) securities are issued, or securities sold are transferred, and (in either case) they are to be paid for in instalments,

(*b*) the person to whom they are issued or transferred holds them and transfers them to another person when the last instalment is paid,

(*c*) subsection (4) (*c*) above applies in the case of the transfer to the other person,

(*d*) before the making of the transfer to the other person an instrument is received by a person falling within [subsection (2) or (3)][2] above,

(*e*) the instrument so received evidences all the rights which (by virtue of the terms under which the securities are issued or sold as mentioned in paragraph (*a*) above) subsist in respect of them at the time of the receipt, and

(*f*) the transfer to the other person is effected by an instrument containing a statement that paragraphs (*a*), (*b*) and (*e*) above are fulfilled,

subsection (4)(*c*) above shall have effect as if the reference to the value there mentioned were to an amount (if any) equal to the total of the instalments payable, less those paid before the transfer to the other person is effected.

(7) Where tax is (or would apart from this subsection be) charged under this section in respect of a transfer of securities, and *ad valorem* stamp duty is chargeable on any instrument effecting the transfer, then—

(*a*) if the amount of the duty is less than the amount of tax found by virtue of [subsections (4) and][7] (6) above, the tax charged under this section shall be the amount so found less the amount of the duty;

(*b*) in any other case, there shall be no charge to tax under this section in respect of the transfer.

(8) Where tax is charged under the preceding provisions of this section, the person liable for the tax shall (subject to subsection (9) below) be the person who has issued or is to issue the depositary receipt.

(9) Where tax is charged under the preceding provisions of this section in a case where securities are transferred, and at the time of the transfer the person who has issued or is to issue the

depositary receipt is not resident in the United Kingdom and has no branch or agency in the United Kingdom, the person liable for the tax shall be the person to whom the securities are transferred.

(10) Where chargeable securities are issued or transferred on sale under terms providing for payment in instalments and for an issue of other chargeable securities, and (apart from this subsection) tax would be charged under this section in respect of that issue, tax shall not be so charged but—

(*a*) if any of the instalments becomes payable by a person falling within subsection (2) or (3) above, there shall be a charge to stamp duty reserve tax under this section when the instalment becomes payable;

(*b*) the charge shall be at the rate of [1.5 per cent of the amount][4] of the instalment payable;

(*c*) the person liable to pay the instalment shall be liable for the tax.

(11) Subject to subsection (12) below, this section applies where securities are transferred, issued or appropriated after 18th March 1986 (whenever the arrangement was made).

(12) This section does not apply, in the case of securities which are transferred, if the Board are satisfied that they were acquired or appropriated by the transferor on or before 18th March 1986 for or towards the eventual satisfaction of the entitlement of a person to receive securities of the same kind under a depositary receipt (whether issued on or before that date or to be issued after that date).

Cross references—See FA 1984 s 126(3)(*d*) (no stamp duty reserve tax chargeable under this section in respect of issue of securities by designated international organisations);
FA 1990 ss 110(1), (3), (5), 111(1) (abolition of stamp duty reserve tax with effect from an appointed day),
FA 1990 ss 110(7), 111(1) (abolition of stamp duty reserve tax not to have effect where before the appointed day securities are issued or transferred on sale under terms mentioned in sub-s (10) above).
FA 2009 Sch 56 (penalty for failure to make payments on time).

Amendments—[1] Words in sub-s (1)(*b*) inserted by FA 1996 s 193(1), (2)(*a*), (4), with effect (i) in relation to the charge to tax under sub-s (1) of this section, where securities are transferred, issued or appropriated after 30 June 1996 (whenever the arrangement was made), and (ii) in relation to the charge to tax under sub-s (10) of this section, in relation to instalments payable after 30 June 1996.

[2] Words in sub-ss (1)(*b*) and (6) substituted by FA 1996 s 193(1), (2)(*b*), (3), (4), with effect (i) in relation to the charge to tax under sub-s (1) of this section, where securities are transferred, issued or appropriated after 30 June 1996 (whenever the arrangement was made), and (ii) in relation to the charge to tax under sub-s (10) of this section, in relation to instalments payable after 30 June 1996.

[3] Words in sub-ss (4) and (5) substituted by FA 1996 s 194(2)(*a*), (*b*), (7)(*b*), with effect, in relation to the charge to tax under sub-s (1) of this section, where securities are transferred, issued or appropriated after 30 June 1996 (whenever the arrangement was made).

[4] Words in sub-s (10) substituted by FA 1996 s 194(2)(*c*), (7)(*c*), with effect, in relation to the charge to tax under sub-s (10) of this section, in relation to instalments payable after 30 June 1996.

[5] Sub-s (5) repealed by FA 1997 s 104(1), Sch 18 Pt VII where securities are transferred on or after 20 October 1997 (the day appointed for the purposes of FA 1997 s 102 by virtue of SI 1997/2428) unless the securities were acquired by the transferor before that date. Previously the text read:

"(5)In a case where the securities are transferred and—

(*a*) the transfer is effected by an instrument on which stamp duty under the heading 'Conveyance or Transfer of any kind not hereinbefore described' in Schedule 1 to the Stamp Act 1891 is chargeable,

(*b*) at the time of the transfer the transferor is a qualified dealer in securities of the kind concerned or a nominee of such a qualified dealer,

(*c*) the transfer is made for the purposes of the dealer's business,

(*d*) at the time of the transfer the dealer is not a market maker in securities of the kind concerned, and

(*e*) the instrument contains a statement that paragraphs (*b*) to (*d*) above are fulfilled,

subsection (4) above shall have effect [as if '1.5 per cent' read '1 per cent'."

[6] Words in sub-s(4) substituted for "(5) to" by FA 1997 s 104(2) with effect as in note 5 above.

[7] Words in sub-s (7) substituted for "subsections (4) to" by FA 1997 s 104(2) with effect as in note 5 above.

94 Depositary receipts: supplementary

(1) For the purposes of section 93 above a depositary receipt for chargeable securities is an instrument acknowledging—

(*a*) that a person holds chargeable securities or evidence of the right to receive them, and

(*b*) that another person is entitled to rights, whether expressed as units or otherwise, in or in relation to chargeable securities of the same kind, including the right to receive such securities (or evidence of the right to receive them) from the person mentioned in paragraph (*a*) above,

except that for those purposes a depositary receipt for chargeable securities does not include an instrument acknowledging rights in or in relation to securities if they are issued or sold under terms providing for payment in instalments and for the issue of the instrument as evidence that an instalment has been paid.

(2) The Treasury may by regulations provide that for subsection (1) above (as it has effect for the time being) there shall be substituted a subsection containing a different definition of a depositary receipt for the purposes of section 93 above.

(3) For the purposes of section 93(4) (*b*) above the value of any consideration not consisting of money shall be taken to be the price it might reasonably be expected to fetch on a sale in the open market at the time the securities are transferred.

(4) For the purposes of section 93(4) (*c*) above the value of the securities shall be taken to be the price they might reasonably be expected to fetch on a sale in the open market at the time they are transferred or appropriated (as the case may be).

(5)–(7) …[2]

(8) …[1]

(9) The power to make regulations or an order under this section shall be exercisable by statutory instrument subject to annulment in pursuance of a resolution of the House of Commons.

Cross references—See FA 1990 ss 110, 111(1) (abolition of stamp duty reserve tax with effect from an appointed day).

Amendments—[1] Sub-s (8) repealed by FA 1996 s 194(3), (7)(*b*), Sch 41 Pt VII, with effect, in relation to the charge to tax under s 93(1) of this Act, where securities are transferred, issued or appropriated after 30 June 1996 (whenever the arrangement was made).

[2] Sub-ss (5)–(7) repealed by FA 1997 s 104(2), Sch 18 Pt VII where securities are transferred on or after 20 October 1997 (the day appointed for the purposes of FA 1997 s 102 by virtue of SI 1997/2428) unless the securities were acquired by the transferor before that date. Previously the text read:

"(5) For the purposes of section 93(5) above a person is a qualified dealer in securities of a particular kind if he deals in securities of that kind and—

(*a*) is a member of a recognised stock exchange (within the meaning given by section 841 of the Taxes Act 1988), or

(*b*) is designated a qualified dealer by order made by the Treasury.

(6) For the purposes of section 93(5) above a person is a market maker in securities of a particular kind if he—

(*a*) holds himself out at all normal times in compliance with the rules of The Stock Exchange as willing to buy and sell securities of that kind at a price specified by him, and

(*b*) is recognised as doing so by the Council of The Stock Exchange.

(7) The Treasury may by regulations provide that for subsection (6) above (as it has effect for the time being) there shall be substituted a subsection containing a different definition of a market maker for the purposes of section 93 (5) above."

95 Depositary receipts: exceptions

(1) Where securities are transferred—

(*a*) to a company which at the time of the transfer falls within subsection (6) of section 67 above *and is resident in the United Kingdom*[5], and

(*b*) from a company which at that time falls within that subsection *and is so resident*[5],

there shall be no charge to tax under section 93 above in respect of the transfer.

[(2) There shall be no charge to tax under section 93 above in respect of a transfer, issue or appropriation of a UK bearer instrument, except in the case of—

(*a*) an instrument within the exemption conferred by paragraph 16 of Schedule 15 to the Finance Act 1999 (renounceable letters of allotment etc where rights are renounceable not later than six months after issue), or

(*b*) an instrument within the exemption conferred by paragraph 17 of that Schedule (non-sterling instruments) which—

(i) does not raise new capital, and

(ii) is not issued in exchange for an instrument raising new capital.][2]

[(2A) For the purpose of subsection (2)(*b*)—

(*a*) an instrument is regarded as raising new capital only if the condition in subsection (2B) is met, and

(*b*) an instrument is regarded as issued in exchange for an instrument raising new capital only if the conditions in subsection (2C) are met.

(2B) The condition mentioned in subsection (2A)(*a*) is that the instrument—

(*a*) is issued in conjunction with—

(i) the issue of relevant securities for which only cash is subscribed, or

(ii) the granting of rights to subscribe for relevant securities which are granted for a cash consideration only and exercisable only by means of a cash subscription; or

(*b*) is issued to give effect to the exercise of such rights as are mentioned in paragraph (*a*)(ii).

(2C) The conditions mentioned in subsection (2A)(*b*) are that—

(*a*) the instrument is issued in conjunction with the issue of relevant securities by a company in exchange for relevant securities issued by another company, and

(*b*) immediately before the exchange an instrument relating to those other securities—

(i) was regarded for the purposes of subsection (2)(*b*) as raising new capital or as issued in exchange for an instrument raising new capital, or

(ii) would have been so regarded if the amendments made to this section by section 117 of the Finance Act 1999 had been in force at the time of its issue,

and accordingly was or would have been within the exception conferred by subsection (2).

(2D) For the purposes of subsections (2B) and (2C) 'relevant securities' means chargeable securities which are either—

(*a*) shares the holders of which have a right to a dividend at a fixed rate but have no other right to share in the profits of the company, or

(*b*) loan capital within the meaning of section 78 above,

and which, in either case, do not carry any rights (of conversion or otherwise) by the exercise of which chargeable securities other than relevant securities may be obtained.][3]

(3) There shall be no charge to tax under section 93 above in respect of an issue by a company (company X) of securities in exchange for shares in another company (company Y) where company X—

(*a*) has control of company Y, or

(*b*) will have such control in consequence of the exchange or of an offer as a result of which the exchange is made [and the shares in company Y are held under a depositary receipt scheme][1].

(4) For the purposes of subsection (3) above company X has control of company Y if company X has power to control company Y's affairs by virtue of holding shares in, or possessing voting power in relation to, company Y or any other body corporate.

[(5) For the purposes of subsection (3) above, the cases where shares are held under a depositary receipt scheme are those cases where, in pursuance of an arrangement,—

(*a*) a depositary receipt for chargeable securities has been, or is to be, issued by a person falling within section 93(2) above in respect of the shares in question or shares of the same kind and amount; and

(*b*) the shares in question are held by that person, or by a person whose business is or includes holding chargeable securities as nominee or agent for that person, towards the eventual satisfaction of the entitlement of the receipt's holder to receive chargeable securities.

[(6) Where an arrangement is entered into under which—

(*a*) a company issues securities to persons in respect of their holdings of securities issued by another company, and

(*b*) the securities issued by the other company are cancelled,

the issue shall be treated for the purposes of this section as an issue of securities in exchange for securities issued by the other company.][4]

(7) In this section "depositary receipt for chargeable securities" has the same meaning as in section 93 above (see section 94 above).][1]

Cross references—See FA 1990 ss 110, 111(1) (abolition of stamp duty reserve tax with effect from an appointed day).

Amendments—[1] Words in sub-s (3), and sub-ss (5), (6) and (7) inserted by FA 1998 s 151 with effect where the issue by company X referred to in FA 1986 ss 95(3), (6), 97(4) or (7) is an issue on or after 1 May 1998.

[2] Sub-s (2) substituted by FA 1999 s 113(3), Sch 16 para 7 with effect in relation to bearer instruments issued after 30 September 1999. For prospective repeal of FA 1999 s 113, Sch 16 para 7, ss 116 and 117 see FA 1999 s 123(3). FA 1999 s 116 provides transitional arrangements for bearer instruments issued between 30 January 1999 and 8 March 1999; the text of sub-s (2) should read:

"(2)There shall be no charge to tax under section 93 above in respect of a transfer, issue or appropriation of an inland bearer instrument, within the meaning of the heading 'Bearer Instrument' in Schedule 1 to the Stamp Act 1891, except in the case of—

(*a*) an instrument within exemption 3 in that heading (renounceable letters of allotment etc where rights are renounceable not later than six months after issue); or

(*b*) an instrument within the stamp duty exemption for non-sterling instruments which is issued in connection with a company merger or takeover (whether or not involving the company issuing the instrument).

In paragraph (*b*) 'the stamp duty exemption for non-sterling instruments' means the exemption from stamp duty provided for by section 30 of the Finance Act 1967 or section 7 of the Finance Act (Northern Ireland) 1967."

FA 1999 s 117 provides transitional arrangements for bearer instruments issued between 9 March 1999 and 30 September 1999; the text of sub-s (2) should read:

"(2)There shall be no charge to tax under section 93 above in respect of a transfer, issue or appropriation of an inland bearer instrument, within the meaning of the heading 'Bearer Instrument' in Schedule 1 to the Stamp Act 1891, except in the case of—

(*a*) an instrument within exemption 3 in that heading (renounceable letters of allotment etc where rights are renounceable not later than six months after issue); or

(*b*) an instrument within the stamp duty exemption for non-sterling instruments which—

(i) does not raise new capital, and

(ii) is not issued in exchange for an instrument raising new capital.

In paragraph (*b*) 'the stamp duty exemption for non-sterling instruments' means the exemption from stamp duty provided for by section 30 of the Finance Act 1967 or section 7 of the Finance Act (Northern Ireland) 1967."

[3] Sub-ss (2A), (2B), (2C), (2D) inserted by FA 1999 s 117(2) with effect in relation to any bearer instrument issued after 8 March 1999, except one giving effect to an agreement for a company merger or takeover entered into in writing by the companies involved before 30 January 1999.

[4] Sub-s (6) substituted by FA 1999 s 117(3) with effect in relation to any bearer instrument issued after 8 March 1999, except one giving effect to an agreement for a company merger or takeover entered into in writing by the companies involved before 30 January 1999.

[5] Words in sub-s (1) repealed by FA 2000 s 134(3), (5), Sch 40 Pt III with effect for stamp duty purposes for instruments executed after 28 July 2000 and for stamp duty reserve tax purposes for securities transferred after 28 July 2000.

[95A Depositary receipts: exception for replacement securities][1]

[(1) There shall be no charge to tax under section 93 above in respect of the transfer, issue or appropriation of chargeable securities ("the new securities") issued by a company in place of existing securities of the same company ("the old securities") if the following conditions are met.

(2) The first condition is that the old securities are held under a depositary receipt scheme.

(3) The second condition is that—

(*a*) there was a charge to tax under section 93 above in respect of the transfer, issue or appropriation—

(i) of the old securities, or

(ii) of earlier securities in relation to which on a previous application of this section those securities were the new securities,

or there would have been such a charge if that section had been in force; or

(*b*) there would have been such a charge but for section 95(2) or (3) above.

(4) The third condition is that there is an arrangement under which—

(*a*) the new securities are transferred, issued or appropriated as mentioned in section 93(1)(*b*), and

(*b*) the old securities are cancelled.

(5) For the purposes of subsection (2) above the cases in which securities are held under a depositary receipt scheme are those specified (in relation to shares) in section 95(5) above.

(6) The exception provided by this section applies only to the extent that the value of the new securities immediately after their issue does not exceed the value of the old securities immediately before the issue of the new securities.][1]

Amendments—[1] This section inserted by FA 1999 s 118(1) with effect in relation to securities issued from 1 May 1998. For prospective repeal of FA 1999 s 118 see FA 1999 s 123(3).

96 Clearance services

(1) Subject to subsection (5) below and [sections 97 and 97A][1] below, there shall be a charge to stamp duty reserve tax under this section where—

(*a*) a person (A) whose business is or includes the provision of clearance services for the purchase and sale of chargeable securities has entered into an arrangement to provide such clearance services for another person, and

(*b*) in pursuance of the arrangement, chargeable securities are transferred or issued to A or to a person whose business is or includes holding chargeable securities as nominee for A.

(2) Subject to subsections [(4) and][6] (5) below, tax under this section shall be charged at the rate of [1.5 per cent][2] of the following—

(*a*) in a case where the securities are issued, their price when issued;

(*b*) in a case where the securities are transferred for consideration in money or money's worth, the amount or value of the consideration;

(*c*) in any other case, the value of the securities.

(3) …[5]

(4) In a case where—

(*a*) securities are issued, or securities sold are transferred, and (in either case) they are to be paid for in instalments,

(*b*) the person to whom they are issued or transferred holds them and transfers them to another person when the last instalment is paid,

(*c*) subsection (2) (*c*) above applies in the case of the transfer to the other person,

(*d*) before the making of the transfer to the other person an instrument is received by A or a person whose business is or includes holding chargeable securities as nominee for A,

(*e*) the instrument so received evidences all the rights which (by virtue of the terms under which the securities are issued or sold as mentioned in paragraph (*a*) above) subsist in respect of them at the time of the receipt, and

(*f*) the transfer to the other person is effected by an instrument containing a statement that paragraphs (*a*), (*b*) and (*e*) above are fulfilled,

subsection (2) (*c*) above shall have effect as if the reference to the value there mentioned were to an amount (if any) equal to the total of the instalments payable, less those paid before the transfer to the other person is effected.

(5) Where tax is (or would apart from this subsection be) charged under this section in respect of a transfer of securities and *ad valorem* stamp duty is chargeable on any instrument effecting the transfer, then—

(*a*) if the amount of the duty is less than the amount of tax found by virtue of [subsections (2) and][7] (4) above, the tax charged under this section shall be the amount so found less the amount of the duty;

(*b*) in any other case, there shall be no charge to tax under this section in respect of the transfer.

(6) Where tax is charged under the preceding provisions of this section, the person liable for the tax shall (subject to subsection (7) below) be A.

(7) Where tax is charged under the preceding provisions of this section in a case where securities are transferred to a person other than A, and at the time of the transfer A is not resident in the United Kingdom and has no branch or agency in the United Kingdom, the person liable for the tax shall be the person to whom the securities are transferred.

(8) Where chargeable securities are issued or transferred on sale under terms providing for payment in instalments and for an issue of other chargeable securities, and (apart from this subsection) tax would be charged under this section in respect of that issue, tax shall not be so charged but—

(*a*) if any of the instalments becomes payable by A or by a person whose business is or includes holding chargeable securities as nominee for A, there shall be a charge to stamp duty reserve tax under this section when the instalment becomes payable;

(*b*) the charge shall be at the rate of [1.5 per cent of the amount][3] of the instalment payable;

(*c*) the person liable to pay the instalment shall be liable for the tax.

(9) For the purposes of subsection (2) (*b*) above the value of any consideration not consisting of money shall be taken to be the price it might reasonably be expected to fetch on a sale in the open market at the time the securities are transferred.

Stamp Taxes

(10) For the purposes of subsection (2) (*c*) above the value of securities shall be taken to be the price they might reasonably be expected to fetch on a sale in the open market at the time they are transferred.

(11) …[5]

(12)…[4]

(13) Subject to subsection (14) below, this section applies where securities are transferred or issued after 18th March 1986 (whenever the arrangement was made).

(14) This section does not apply, in the case of securities which are transferred, if the Board are satisfied—

(*a*) that on or before 18th March 1986 the transferor (or, where the transferor transfers as agent, the principal) agreed to sell securities of the same kind and amount to the person (other than A) referred to in subsection (1) (*a*) above, and

(*b*) that the transfer is effected in pursuance of that agreement.

Cross references—See FA 1984 s 126(3)(*d*) (no stamp duty reserve tax chargeable under this section in respect of issue of securities by designated international organisations);
FA 1986 s 97A(3), (4) (disapplication of this section where an election is made under s 97A(1)).
FA 1986 s 97A(11) (deemed transfer of securities within sub-s (1) above where an election for an alternative system of charge in respect of clearance services is terminated).
FA 1990 ss 110(1), (4), (6), 111(1) (abolition of stamp duty reserve tax with effect from an appointed day),
FA 1990 ss 110(8), 111(1) (abolition of stamp duty reserve tax not to have effect where before the appointed day securities are issued or transferred on sale under terms mentioned in sub-s (8) above).
FA 2009 Sch 56 (penalty for failure to make payments on time).

Amendments—[1] Words in sub-s (1) substituted by FA 1996 s 196(2), (6), with effect from 1 July 1996.

[2] Words in sub-ss (2), (3) substituted by FA 1996 s 194(4)(*a*), (*b*), (7)(*d*), with effect, in relation to the charge to tax under sub-s (1) of this section, where securities are transferred or issued after 30 June 1996 (whenever the arrangement was made).

[3] Words in sub-s (8) substituted by FA 1996 s 194(4)(*c*), (7)(*e*), with effect, in relation to the charge of tax under sub-s (8) of this section, in relation to instalments payable after 30 June 1996.

[4] Sub-s (12) repealed by FA 1996 ss 194(5), (7)(*d*), Sch 41 Pt VII, with effect, in relation to the charge to tax under sub-s (1) of this section, where securities are transferred or issued after 30 June 1996 (whenever the arrangement was made).

[5] Sub-ss (3) and (11) repealed by FA 1997 s 104(3)(4), Sch 18 Pt VII where securities are transferred on or after 20 October 1997 (the day appointed for the purposes of FA 1997 s 102 by virtue of SI 1997/2428) unless the securities were acquired by the transferor before that date. Previously the text read as follows—

"(3) In a case where the securities are transferred and—

(*a*) the transfer is effected by an instrument on which stamp duty under the heading 'Conveyance or Transfer of any kind not hereinbefore described' in Schedule 1 to the Stamp Act 1891 is chargeable,

(*b*) at the time of the transfer the transferor is a qualified dealer in securities of the kind concerned or a nominee of such a qualified dealer,

(*c*) the transfer is made for the purposes of the dealer's business,

(*d*) at the time of the transfer the dealer is not a market maker in securities of the kind concerned, and

(*e*) the instrument contains a statement that paragraphs (*b*) to (*d*) above are fulfilled,

subsection (2) above shall have effect [as if '1.5 per cent' read '1 per cent'."

"(11) For the purposes of subsection (3) above 'qualified dealer' and 'market maker' have at any particular time the same meanings as they have at that time for the purposes of section 93(5) above."

[6] Words in sub-s (2) substituted for the words "(3) to" by FA 1997, s 104(4) with effect as in note 5 above.

[7] Words in sub-s (5)(*a*) substituted for the words "subsections (2) to" by FA 1997, s 104(4) with effect as in note 5 above.

97 Clearance services: exceptions

(1) Where securities are transferred—

(*a*) to a company which at the time of the transfer falls within subsection (6) of section 70 above *and is resident in the United Kingdom*[6], and

(*b*) from a company which at that time falls within that subsection *and is so resident*[6],

there shall be no charge to tax under section 96 above in respect of the transfer.

(2) …[1]

[(3) There shall be no charge to tax under section 96 above in respect of a transfer or issue of a UK bearer instrument, except in the case of—

(*a*) an instrument within the exemption conferred by paragraph 16 of Schedule 15 to the Finance Act 1999 (renounceable letters of allotment etc. where rights are renounceable not later than six months after issue), or

(*b*) an instrument within the exemption conferred by paragraph 17 of that Schedule (non-sterling instruments) which—

(i) does not raise new capital, and

(ii) is not issued in exchange for an instrument raising new capital.][3]

[(3A) For the purpose of subsection (3)(*b*)—

(*a*) an instrument is regarded as raising new capital only if the condition in subsection (3B) is met, and

(*b*) an instrument is regarded as issued in exchange for an instrument raising new capital only if the conditions in subsection (3C) are met.

(3B) The condition mentioned in subsection (3A)(*a*) is that the instrument—

(*a*) is issued in conjunction with—

(i) the issue of relevant securities for which only cash is subscribed, or

(ii) the granting of rights to subscribe for relevant securities which are granted for a cash consideration only and exercisable only by means of a cash subscription; or (*b*) is issued to give effect to the exercise of such rights as are mentioned in paragraph (*a*)(ii).

(3C) The conditions mentioned in subsection (3A)(*b*) are that—

(*a*) the instrument is issued in conjunction with the issue of relevant securities by a company in exchange for relevant securities issued by another company, and

(*b*) immediately before the exchange an instrument relating to those other securities—

(i) was regarded for the purposes of subsection (3)(*b*) as raising new capital or as issued in exchange for an instrument raising new capital, or

(ii) would have been so regarded if the amendments made to this section by section 117 of the Finance Act 1999 had been in force at the time of its issue,

and accordingly was or would have been within the exception conferred by subsection (3).

(3D) For the purposes of subsections (3B) and (3C) 'relevant securities' means chargeable securities which are either—

(*a*) shares the holders of which have a right to a dividend at a fixed rate but have no other right to share in the profits of the company, or

(*b*) loan capital within the meaning of section 78 above,

and which, in either case, do not carry any rights (of conversion or otherwise) by the exercise of which chargeable securities other than relevant securities may be obtained.][4]

(4) There shall be no charge to tax under section 96 above in respect of an issue by a company (company X) of securities in exchange for shares in another company (company Y) where company X—

(*a*) has control of company Y, or

(*b*) will have such control in consequence of the exchange or of an offer as a result of which the exchange is made

[and the shares in company Y are held under a clearance services scheme.][2]

(5) For the purposes of subsection (4) above company X has control of company Y if company X has power to control company Y's affairs by virtue of holding shares in, or possessing voting power in relation to, company Y or any other body corporate.

[(6) For the purposes of subsection (4) above, the cases where shares are held under a clearance services scheme are those cases where—

(*a*) an arrangement falling within paragraph (*a*) of subsection (1) of section 96 above has been entered into; and

(*b*) in pursuance of that arrangement, the shares are held by the person referred to in that paragraph as A or by a person whose business is or includes holding chargeable securities as nominee for that person.][2]

[(7) Where an arrangement is entered into under which—

(*a*) a company issues securities to persons in respect of their holdings of securities issued by another company, and

(*b*) the securities issued by the other company are cancelled,

the issue shall be treated for the purposes of this section as an issue of securities in exchange for securities issued by the other company.][5]

Cross references—See FA 1990 ss 110, 111(1) (abolition of stamp duty reserve tax with effect from an appointed day).

Amendments—[1] Sub-s (2) repealed by FA 1996 s 196(4), Sch 41 Pt VII, with effect in relation to any transfer effected after 30 June 1996.

[2] Words in sub-s (4), and sub-s (6) inserted by FA 1998 s 151 with effect where the issue by company X referred to in FA 1986 ss 95(3), (6), 97(4) or (7) is an issue on or after 1 May 1998.

[3] Sub-s (3) substituted by FA 1999 s 113(3), Sch 16 para 8 with effect in relation to bearer instruments issued after 30 September 1999. For prospective repeal of FA 1999 s 113, Sch 16 para 8, ss 105 and 106 see FA 1999 s 123(3). FA 1999 s 116 provides transitional arrangements for bearer instruments issued between 30 January 1999 and 8 March 1999; the text of sub-s (3) should read:

"(3)There shall be no charge to tax under section 96 above in respect of a transfer or issue of an inland bearer instrument, within the meaning of the heading "Bearer Instrument" in Schedule 1 to the Stamp Act 1891, except in the case of—

(*a*) an instrument within exemption 3 in that heading (renounceable letters of allotment etc where rights are renounceable not later than six months after issue); or

(*b*) an instrument within the stamp duty exemption for non-sterling instruments which is issued in connection with a company merger or takeover (whether or not involving the company issuing the instrument).

In paragraph (*b*) 'the stamp duty exemption for non-sterling instruments' means the exemption from stamp duty provided for by section 30 of the Finance Act 1967 or section 7 of the Finance Act (Northern Ireland) 1967."

FA 1999 s 117 provides transitional arrangements for bearer instruments issued between 9 March 1999 and 30 September 1999; the text of sub-s (3) should read:

"(3)There shall be no charge to tax under section 96 above in respect of a transfer or issue of an inland bearer instrument, within the meaning of the heading "Bearer Instrument" in Schedule 1 to the Stamp Act 1891, except in the case of—

(*a*) an instrument within exemption 3 in that heading (renounceable letters of allotment etc. where rights are renounceable not later than six months after issue); or

(*b*) an instrument within the stamp duty exemption for non-sterling instruments which —

(i) does not raise new capital, and

(ii) is not issued in exchange for an instrument raising new capital.

In paragraph (*b*) 'the stamp duty exemption for non-sterling instruments' means the exemption from stamp duty provided for by section 30 of the Finance Act 1967 or section 7 of the Finance Act (Northern Ireland) 1967."

[4] Sub-ss (3A), (3B), (3C), (3D) inserted by FA 1999 s 117(5) with effect in relation to any bearer instrument issued after 8 March 1999, except one giving effect to an agreement for a company merger or takeover entered into in writing by the companies involved before 30 January 1999.

Stamp Taxes

[5] Sub-s (7) substituted by FA 1999 s 117(6) with effect in relation to any bearer instrument issued after 8 March 1999, except one giving effect to an agreement for a company merger or takeover entered into in writing by the companies involved before 30 January 1999.

[6] Words in sub-s (1) repealed by FA 2000 s 134(3), (5), Sch 40 Pt III with effect for stamp duty purposes for instruments executed after 28 July 2000 and for stamp duty reserve tax purposes for securities transferred after 28 July 2000.

[97AA Clearance services: further exception][1]

[(1) There shall be no charge to tax under section 96 above in respect of the transfer or issue of chargeable securities ("the new securities") issued by a company in place of existing securities of the same company ("the old securities") if the following conditions are met.

(2) The first condition is that the old securities are held under a clearance services scheme.

(3) The second condition is that—

(*a*) there was a charge to tax under section 96 above in respect of the transfer or issue—

(i) of the old securities, or

(ii) of earlier securities in relation to which on a previous application of this section those securities were the new securities,

or there would have been such a charge if that section had been in force; or

(*b*) there would have been such a charge but for section 97(3) or (4) above.

(4) The third condition is that there is an arrangement under which—

(*a*) the new securities are transferred or issued as mentioned in section 96(1)(*b*), and

(*b*) the old securities are cancelled.

(5) For the purposes of subsection (2) above the cases in which securities are held under a clearance services scheme are those specified (in relation to shares) in section 97(6) above.

(6) The exception provided by this section applies only to the extent that the value of the new securities immediately after their issue does not exceed the value of the old securities immediately before the issue of the new securities.][1]

Amendments—[1] This section inserted by FA 1999 s 118(3) with effect in relation to securities issued from 1 May 1998. For prospective repeal of FA 1999 s 118 see FA 1999 s 123(3).

[97A Clearance services: election for alternative system of charge

(1) A person whose business is or includes the provision of clearance services for the purchase and sale of chargeable securities or relevant securities (an "operator") may, with the approval of the Board, elect that stamp duty and stamp duty reserve tax shall be chargeable in accordance with this section in connection with those clearance services.

(2) An election under subsection (1) above—

(*a*) shall come into force on such date as may be notified to the operator by the Board in giving their approval; and

(*b*) shall continue in force unless and until it is terminated in accordance with the following provisions of this section.

(3) If and so long as an election under subsection (1) above is in force, stamp duty or stamp duty reserve tax (as the case may require) shall, in connection with the clearance services to which the election relates, be chargeable in relation to—

(*a*) a transfer or issue falling within section 70(1) or 96(1) above,

(*b*) an agreement falling within section 90(4) above by virtue of section 96(1) above, or

(*c*) an agreement falling within section 90(5) above,

as it would be chargeable apart from sections 70, 90(4) and (5) and 96 above.

(4) Where stamp duty or stamp duty reserve tax is chargeable by virtue of subsection (3) above in relation to a transfer, issue or agreement, sections 70, 90(4) and (5) and 96 above shall not have effect in relation to that transfer, issue or agreement.

(5) Nothing in subsection (3) or (4) above affects the application of section 70 or 96 above in relation to a transfer falling within section 70(1) or 96(1) above by the operator or his nominee to, or to a nominee of, another operator in relation to whom no election under subsection (1) above is for the time being in force.

(6) The Board may require the operator, as a condition of the approval of his election under subsection (1) above, to make and maintain such arrangements as they may consider satisfactory—

(*a*) for the collection of stamp duty reserve tax chargeable in accordance with this section, and

(*b*) for complying, or securing compliance, with the provisions of this Part and of regulations under section 98 below, so far as relating to such tax.

(7) Where the operator is not resident in the United Kingdom and has no branch or agency in the United Kingdom, the Board may require him, as a condition of the approval of his election under subsection (1) above, to appoint and, so long as the election remains in force, maintain a tax representative.

(8) A person shall not be an operator's tax representative under this section unless that person—

(*a*) has a business establishment in the United Kingdom, and (*b*) is approved by the Board.

(9) A person who is at any time an operator's tax representative under this section—

(*a*) shall be entitled to act on the operator's behalf for the purposes of stamp duty and stamp duty reserve tax in connection with the clearance services to which the operator's election under subsection (1) above relates,

(*b*) shall secure (where appropriate by acting on the operator's behalf) the operator's compliance with and discharge of the obligations and liabilities to which the operator is subject, in connection with the clearance services to which the operator's election under subsection (1) above relates, by virtue of legislation relating to stamp duty or stamp duty reserve tax (including obligations and liabilities arising before he became the operator's tax representative), and

(*c*) shall be personally liable in respect of any failure to secure the operator's compliance with or discharge of any such obligation or liability, and in respect of anything done for purposes connected with acting on the operator's behalf,

as if the obligations and liabilities imposed on the operator were imposed jointly and severally on the tax representative and the operator.

(10) An election under subsection (1) above may be terminated—

(*a*) by not less than thirty days' notice given by the operator to the Board or by the Board to the operator; or

(*b*) if there is or has been a breach of a condition of the approval of the election imposed by virtue of subsection (6) or (7) above, by a notice—

(i) given by the Board to the operator,

(ii) taking effect on the giving of the notice or at such later time as may be specified in the notice, and

(iii) stating that it is given by reason of the breach of condition.

(11) Where an election under subsection (1) above is terminated, section 96 above shall have effect as if chargeable securities of the same amounts and kinds as are, immediately before the termination, held by the operator or his nominee in connection with the provision of the clearance services, had, immediately after the termination, been transferred to the operator or, as the case may be, to the nominee by a transfer falling within subsection (1) of that section.

(12) In this section "relevant securities" has the same meaning as in section 70 above.][1]

[(13) Nothing in section 70(9) or 97(1) above has effect to prevent a charge to stamp duty or stamp duty reserve tax arising—

(*a*) on a transfer to which subsection (5) above applies, or

(*b*) on a deemed transfer under subsection (11) above.][2]

Cross references—See FA 1990 ss 108, 110, 111(1) (abolition of stamp duty and stamp duty reserve tax with effect from an appointed day).

Amendments—[1] This section inserted by FA 1996 s 196(3), (6), with effect from 1 July 1996.

[2] Sub-s (13) inserted by FA 2000 s 134(4), (5) with effect for stamp duty purposes for instruments executed after 28 July 2000 and for stamp duty reserve tax purposes for securities transferred after 28 July 2000.

[97B Transfer between depositary receipt system and clearance system

(1) There shall be no charge to tax under section 93 or 96 above where securities are transferred between a depositary receipt system and a clearance system.

(2) A transfer between a depositary receipt system and a clearance system means a transfer—

(*a*) from (or to) a company which at the time of the transfer falls within section 67(6) above, and

(*b*) to (or from) a company which at that time falls within section 70(6) above.

(3) This section does not apply to a transfer from a clearance system (that is, from such a company as is mentioned in subsection (2)(*b*) above) if at the time of the transfer an election is in force under section 97A above in relation to the clearance services for the purposes of which the securities are held immediately before the transfer.][1]

Amendments—[1] This section inserted by FA 2000 s 134(2), (5) with effect for stamp duty reserve tax purposes for securities transferred after 28 July 2000.

General

98 Administration etc

(1) The Treasury may make regulations—

(*a*) providing that provisions of the Taxes Management Act 1970 specified in the regulations shall apply in relation to stamp duty reserve tax as they apply in relation to a tax within the meaning of that Act, with such modifications (specified in the regulations) as they think fit;

(*b*) making with regard to stamp duty reserve tax such further provision as they think fit in relation to administration, assessment, collection and recovery.

[(1A) The power conferred on the Treasury by subsection (1) above includes power to make provision conferring or imposing on the Board functions which involve the exercise of a discretion.][1]

(2) The power to make regulations under subsection (1) above shall be exercisable by statutory instrument subject to annulment in pursuance of a resolution of the House of Commons.

Regulations—See the Stamp Duty Reserve Tax Regulations, SI 1986/1711; the Stamp Duty and Stamp Duty Reserve Tax (Definition of Unit Trust Scheme and Open-ended Investment Company) Regulations, SI 2001/964.
Cross references—See FA 1989 s 177 (prescribed form for the manner in which notice and information are to be given with regard to stamp duty reserve tax);
FA 1990 ss 110, 111(1) (abolition of stamp duty reserve tax with effect from an appointed day).
FA 2004 s 313(4)(*d*) (disclosure of tax avoidance schemes: no liability to a penalty under this section by reason of any failure to include in any return or account any reference number or information required by virtue of FA 2004 s 313(3)(*a*).
FA 2009 Sch 55 (penalty for failure to make returns etc).
FA 2009 Sch 56 (penalty for failure to make payments on time).
Amendments—[1] Sub-s (1A) inserted by FA 1996 s 195.

99 Interpretation

(1) This section applies for the purposes of this Part of this Act.

[(1A) "Bearer instrument" has the same meaning as in Schedule 15 to the Finance Act 1999. An instrument is a "UK bearer instrument" or "non-UK bearer instrument" according to whether it is issued by or on behalf of a UK company or a non-UK company within the meaning of that Schedule.][10]

(2) "The Board" means the Commissioners of Inland Revenue.

[(3) Subject to the following provisions of this section, "chargeable securities" means—

(*a*) stocks, shares or loan capital,

(*b*) interests in, or in dividends or other rights arising out of, stocks, shares or loan capital,

(*c*) rights to allotments of or to subscribe for, or options to acquire, stocks, shares or loan capital, and

(*d*) units under a unit trust scheme.][1]

[(4) "Chargeable securities" does not include securities falling within paragraph (*a*), (*b*) or (*c*) of subsection (3) above which are issued or raised by a body corporate not incorporated in the United Kingdom unless—

(*a*) they are registered in a register kept in the United Kingdom by or on behalf of the body corporate by which they are issued or raised, or

(*b*) in the case of shares, they are paired with shares issued by a body corporate incorporated in the United Kingdom, or

(*c*) in the case of securities falling within paragraph (*b*) or (*c*) of subsection (3) above, paragraph (*a*) or (*b*) above applies to the stocks, shares or loan capital to which they relate][1][, or

(*d*) they are issued or raised by an SE (whether or not in the course of its formation in accordance with Article 2 of Council Regulation (EC) 2157/2001 on the Statute for a European Company (Societas Europaea)) and, at the time when it falls to be determined whether the securities are chargeable securities, the SE has its registered office in the United Kingdom.][15]

[(4A) "Chargeable securities" does not include securities falling within paragraph (*a*), (*b*) or (*c*) of subsection (3) above if—

(*a*) they are securities issued or raised by an SE (whether or not in the course of its formation in accordance with Article 2 of Council Regulation (EC) 2157/2001 on the Statute for a European Company (Societas Europaea)), and

(*b*) at the time when it falls to be determined whether the securities are chargeable securities, the SE has its registered office outside the United Kingdom;][15]

[(5) "Chargeable securities" does not include securities falling within paragraph (*a*), (*b*) or (*c*) of subsection (3) above if—

(*a*) in the case of stock or marketable securities within the meaning of section 125 of the Finance Act 2003 (abolition of stamp duty except on instruments relating to stock or marketable securities), they are securities the transfer of which is exempt from all stamp duties;

(*b*) in any other case, they are securities the transfer of which, disregarding that section, would be exempt from all stamp duties.][14]

[(5ZA) "Chargeable securities" does not include securities falling within paragraph (*b*) or (*c*) of subsection (3) above if the stocks, shares or loan capital to which the securities relate—

(*a*) are stock or marketable securities within the meaning of section 125 of the Finance Act 2003 (abolition of stamp duty except on instruments relating to stock or marketable securities) the transfer of which is exempt from all stamp duties, or

(*b*) are securities the transfer of which, disregarding that section, would be exempt from all stamp duties.][14]

[(5A) "Chargeable securities" does not include a unit under a unit trust scheme if—

(*a*) all the trustees under the scheme are resident outside the United Kingdom and the unit is not registered in a register kept in the United Kingdom by or on behalf of the trustees under the scheme; or

(*b*) under the terms of the scheme the trust property can only be invested in exempt investments.

(5B) For the purposes of subsection (5A)(*b*)—

(*a*) an investment other than an interest under a collective investment scheme is an exempt investment if, and only if—

(i) it is not an investment on the transfer of which *ad valorem* stamp duty would be chargeable, …[14]

[(ia) it is not an investment on the acquisition of which stamp duty land tax would be chargeable under Part 4 of the Finance Act 2003, and][14]

(ii) it is not a chargeable security;

(*b*) an interest under a collective investment scheme is an exempt investment if, and only if, the scheme is an authorised unit trust scheme or an open-ended investment company and under the terms of the scheme the property subject to the scheme—

(i) cannot be invested in such a way that income can arise to the trustees or the company that will be chargeable to tax in their hands otherwise than under Case III of Schedule D, and

(ii) can only be invested in exempt investments;

(*c*) a derivative is an exempt investment if, and only if, it relates wholly to one or more exempt investments; and

(*d*) funds held for the purposes of the day to day management of the unit trust scheme are not regarded as investments.

[In this subsection "an authorised unit trust scheme", "collective investment scheme" and "an open-ended investment company" have the same meanings as in Part 17 of the Financial Services and Markets Act 2000.][13]][12]

[(6) "Chargeable securities" does not include interests in depositary receipts for stocks or shares.][1]

[(6A) For the purposes of subsection (4) above, shares issued by a body corporate which is not incorporated in the United Kingdom ("the foreign company") are paired with shares issued by a body corporate which is so incorporated ("the UK company") where—

(*a*) the articles of association of the UK company and the equivalent instruments governing the foreign company each provide that no share in the company to which they relate may be transferred otherwise than as part of a unit comprising one share in that company and one share in the other, and

(*b*) such units have been offered for sale to the public in the United Kingdom and, at the same time, [other][7] such units have been offered for sale to the public at a broadly equivalent price in the country in which the foreign company is incorporated.][1]

[(6B) For the purposes of subsection (4) above, shares issued by a body corporate which is not incorporated in the United Kingdom ("the foreign company") are paired with shares issued by a body corporate which is so incorporated ("the UK company") where—

(*a*) the articles of association of the UK company and the equivalent instruments governing the foreign company each provide that no share in the company to which they relate may be transferred otherwise than as part of a unit comprising one share in that company and one share in the other, and

(*b*) the shares issued by the foreign company, and the shares issued by the UK company, are issued to give effect to an allotment of the shares (as part of such units) as fully or partly paid bonus shares.][8]

(7) A depositary receipt for stocks or shares is an instrument acknowledging—

(*a*) that a person holds stocks or shares or evidence of the right to receive them, and

(*b*) that another person is entitled to rights, whether expressed as units or otherwise, in or in relation to stocks or shares of the same kind, including the right to receive such stocks or shares (or evidence of the right to receive them) from the person mentioned in paragraph (*a*) above,

except that a depositary receipt for stocks or shares does not include an instrument acknowledging rights in or in relation to stocks or shares if they are issued or sold under terms providing for payment in instalments and for the issue of the instrument as evidence that an instalment has been paid.

(8) The Treasury may by regulations provide that for subsection (7) above (as it has effect for the time being) there shall be substituted a subsection containing a different definition of a depositary receipt; and the power to make regulations under this subsection shall be exercisable by statutory instrument subject to annulment in pursuance of a resolution of the House of Commons.

[(9) "Unit trust scheme" and related expressions have the meanings given by Part IV of Schedule 19 to the Finance Act 1999.][2]

[(9A) But "unit trust scheme" does not include arrangements falling within section 48A of the Finance Act 2005 [or section 507 of the Corporation Tax Act 2009][17] (alternative finance investment bonds).][16]

(10) In interpreting "chargeable securities" in sections 93, 94, [95,][9] [95A,][11] [96, [97][9][,97AA][11] and 97A][5] above—

[(*a*) paragraph (*a*) of subsection (4) above and the reference to that paragraph in paragraph (*c*) of that subsection shall be ignored, and][3]

(*b*) the effect of [section 133(3) of the Companies Act 2006 (transactions in shares registered in overseas branch register)][18] shall be ignored for the purposes of subsection (5) above.

[(11) In interpreting "chargeable securities" in section 93 or 96 above in a case where—

(*a*) newly subscribed shares, or

(*b*) securities falling within paragraph (*b*) or (*c*) of subsection (3) above which relate to newly subscribed shares,

are issued in pursuance of an arrangement such as is mentioned in that section (or an arrangement which would be such an arrangement if the securities issued were chargeable securities), paragraph (*b*) of subsection (4) above and the reference to that paragraph in paragraph (*c*) of that subsection shall be ignored.][4]

[(12) In subsection (11) above, "newly subscribed shares" means shares issued wholly for new consideration in pursuance of an offer for sale to the public.][4]

[(13) Where the calculation of any tax in accordance with the provisions of this Part results in an amount which is not a multiple of one penny, the amount so calculated shall be rounded to the nearest penny, taking any ½p as nearest to the next whole penny above.][6]

Cross references—See FA 1990 ss 110, 111(1) (abolition of stamp duty reserve tax with effect from an appointed day); FA 1990 s 113 (modifications of sub-ss (6A), (9) and insertion of sub-s (6B) in specified circumstances).
FA 1999 Sch 15 (bearer instruments).

Modification—Sub-ss (5), (5A) modified and sub-s (5C) inserted, in relation to open-ended investment companies, by the Stamp Duty and Stamp Duty Reserve Tax (Open-ended Investment Companies) Regulations, SI 1997/1156, regs 4, 4B, as amended by the Stamp Duty and Stamp Duty Reserve Tax (Open-ended Investment Companies) (Amendment No 2) Regulations, SI 1999/3261, reg 5, and the Stamp Duty and Stamp Duty Reserve Tax (Definition of Unit Trust Scheme and Open-ended Investment Company) Regulations, SI 2001/964 with effect for sub-ss (5), (5A) from 6 February 2000, and for sub-s (5C) from 6 April 2001.

Amendments—[1] Sub-ss (3)–(6A) substituted for sub-ss (3)–(6) by FA 1988 s 144(2), (6) in relation to—

(*a*) agreements to transfer chargeable securities made after 8 December 1987; and

(*b*) transfer, issue or appropriation of chargeable securities after 8 December 1987 in pursuance of an arrangement whenever made.

[2] Sub-s (9) substituted by FA 1999 Sch 19 para 12 with effect from 6 February 2000.

[3] Sub-s (10)(*a*) substituted by FA 1988 s 144(4), (6).

[4] Sub-ss (11), (12) added by FA 1988 s 144(5), (6) with effect as described in [1] above.

[5] Words in sub-s (10) substituted for the words "and 96" by FA 1996 s 196(5), (6), with effect from 1 July 1996.

[6] Sub-s (13) inserted by FA 1996 s 180(6).

[7] Words in sub-ss (6A) inserted and amended by FA 1990 s 113 with effect from 26 July 1990.

[8] Sub-s (6B) inserted by FA 1990 s 113 with effect from 26 July 1990.

[9] Words in sub-s (10) inserted by FA 1998 s 151 with effect where the issue by company X referred to in FA 1986 ss 95(3), (6), 97(4) or (7) is an issue on or after 1 May 1998.

[10] Sub-s (1A) inserted by FA 1999 s 113(3), Sch 16 para 9 with effect in relation to bearer instruments issued after 30 September 1999. For prospective repeal of FA 1999 s 113, Sch 16 para 9 see FA 1999 s 123(3).

[11] Words in sub-s (10) inserted by FA 1999 s 118(2), (4) with effect in relation to securities issued from 1 May 1998. For prospective repeal of FA 1999 s 118 see FA 1999 s 123(3).

[12] Words in sub-s (5), and sub-ss (5A) and (5B) inserted by FA 1999 Sch 19 para 12 with effect from 6 February 2000.

[13] Words in sub-s (5B) substituted by the Financial Services and Markets Act 2000 (Consequential Amendments) (Taxes) Order, SI 2001/3629 arts 6, 10. SI 2001/3629 art 19 has effect in relation to—

(*a*) an agreement to transfer chargeable securities which is not conditional, if the agreement is made after 30 November 2001;

(*b*) a conditional agreement to transfer such securities, if the condition is satisfied after that date.

[14] Sub-ss (5), (5ZA) substituted for sub-s (5), and in sub-s (5B), para (*a*)(ia) inserted, by the Stamp Duty and Stamp Duty Land Tax (Consequential Amendment of Enactments) Regulations, SI 2003/2868 regs 3, 5 with effect from 1 December 2003.

[15] Sub-ss (4)(*d*), (4A) inserted by F(No 2)A 2005 s 57 with effect for the purpose of determining, in relation to anything occurring on or after 1 April 2005, whether securities (whenever issued or raised) are chargeable securities for the purposes of FA 1986 Pt IV.

[16] Sub-s (9A) inserted by FA 2008 s 154(1), (5) with effect in relation to:

(a) agreements to transfer chargeable securities made on or after 21 July 2008, and

(b) the transfer, issue or appropriation of chargeable securities after that day in pursuance of an agreement made after that day;

(and for this purpose it does not matter when the arrangements falling within FA 2005 s 48A are made).

[17] In sub-s (9A), words inserted by CTA 2009 s 1322, Sch 1 paras 322, 325. CTA 2009 applies for corporation tax purposes for accounting periods ending on or after 1 April 2009 and for income tax and capital gains tax purposes for the tax year 2009–10 and subsequent tax years.

[18] In sub-s (10)(*b*), words substituted for words "paragraph 8 of Schedule 14 to the Companies Act 1985 (share registered overseas) and of section 118 of the Companies Act (Northern Ireland) 1960 and paragraph 7 of Schedule 14 to the Companies (Northern Ireland) Order 1986 (equivalent provision for Northern Ireland)", by the Companies Act 2006 (Consequential Amendments) (Taxes and National Insurance) Order, SI 2009/1890 art 7(*f*) with effect from 1 October 2009.

PART VII

MISCELLANEOUS AND SUPPLEMENTARY

114 Short title, interpretation, construction and repeals

(1) This Act may be cited as the Finance Act 1986.

(2), (3) …

(4) Part III of this Act shall be construed as one with the Stamp Act 1891.

(5) …

(6) The enactments and Orders specified in Schedule 23 to this Act are hereby repealed to the extent specified in the third column of that Schedule, but subject to any provision at the end of any Part of that Schedule.

Note—Sub-ss (2), (3), (5) are not relevant to stamp duty.

BUILDING SOCIETIES ACT 1986

(1986 Chapter 53)

An Act to make fresh provision with respect to building societies and further provision with respect to conveyancing services

[25th July 1986]

PART XI
MISCELLANEOUS AND SUPPLEMENTARY AND CONVEYANCING SERVICES

Miscellaneous and supplementary

109 Exemption from stamp duty

[(1)][1] The following instruments shall be exempted from all such stamp duties (if any) as apart from this section would be chargeable on them, that is to say—

(*a*) any copy of the rules of a building society;
(*b*) any transfer of a share in a building society;
(*c*) any bond or other security to be given to, or on account of, a building society or by an officer of a building society;
(*d*) any instrument appointing an agent of a building society or revoking such an appointment; and
(*e*) any other instrument whatsoever which is required or authorised to be given, issued, signed, made or produced in pursuance of this Act or of the rules of a building society.

[(2) No transfer effected by subsection (6) or (7) of section 97 shall give rise to any liability to stamp duty.][1]

Amendments—[1] Sub-s (1) numbered as such, and sub-s (2) inserted, by FA 1988 s 145, Sch 12 para 8.

FINANCE ACT 1987

(1987 Chapter 16)

An Act to grant certain duties, to alter other duties, and to amend the law relating to the National Debt and the Public Revenue, and to make further provision in connection with Finance

[15th May 1987]

PART III
STAMP DUTY AND STAMP DUTY RESERVE TAX

Stamp duty

48 Unit trusts

(*amends* FA 1946 s 57).

49 Contract notes

Amendments—This section repealed by FA 1999 Sch 20 Pt V(2) with effect in relation to instruments executed, or bearer instruments issued, from 1 October 1999, subject to the provisions in FA 1999 Sch 20 Pt V(2) Note 2. Previously the text repealed F(1909–10)A 1910, ss 78, 79 so far as unrepealed.

50 Warrants to purchase Government stock, etc

(1) Where an interest in, a right to an allotment of or to subscribe for, or an option to acquire [or to dispose of][1], exempt securities is transferred to or vested in any person by any instrument, no stamp duty shall be chargeable on the instrument by virtue of [Part I, *or paragraph 16*[6] of Schedule 13 to the Finance Act 1999 ([transfer][5] on sale or otherwise)].[3]

Stamp Taxes

(2) No stamp duty under [Schedule 15 to the Finance Act 1999 (bearer instruments)][2] shall be chargeable—

(*a*) on the issue of an instrument which relates to such an interest, right or option as is mentioned in subsection (1) above, or

(*b*) on the transfer of the interest, right or option constituted by, or transferable by means of, such an instrument.

(3) For the purposes of this section, "exempt securities" means—

(*a*) securities the transfer of which is exempt from all stamp duties,

(*b*) securities constituted by or transferable by means of an instrument the issue of which is [exempt from stamp duty under paragraph 1 of Schedule 15 to the Finance Act 1999 (issue of bearer instrument) by virtue of paragraph 17 of that Schedule (certain non-sterling instruments)][2], or

(*c*) securities the transfer of which is [exempt from stamp duty under that Schedule by virtue of paragraph 17 of that Schedule or section 79(2) of the Finance Act 1986][2];

and "securities" means stock or marketable securities and includes loan capital as defined in section 78(7) of the Finance Act 1986.

(4), (5) …[4]

Note—This section was to be repealed by FA 1990 Sch 19 Pt VI with effect from an appointed day in accordance with FA 1990 ss 107–111. The Treasury order specifying the appointed day for the purposes of FA 1990 ss 107–110 was to coincide with the start of paperless trading under the Stock Exchange's planned TAURUS system (IR press release, 20-3-90). However, on 11-3-93 the London Stock Exchange News Release 6/93 announced that TAURUS had been abandoned.

Amendments—[1] Words in sub-s (1) inserted by F (No 2) A 1987, s 99 (1).

[2] Words in sub-ss (2), (3)(*b*)(*c*) substituted by FA 1999 s 113(3), Sch 16 para 10 with effect in relation to bearer instruments issued after 30 September 1999. For prospective repeal of FA 1999 s 113, Sch 16 para 10 see FA 1999 s 123(3). Previously the text read 'the heading "Bearer Instrument" in Schedule 1 to the Stamp Act 1891', 'by virtue of section 30 of the Finance Act 1967 or section 7 of the Finance Act (Northern Ireland) 1967 [or section 79(2) of the Finance Act 1986] exempt from stamp duty under the heading "Bearer Instrument" in Schedule 1 to the Stamp Act 1891' and 'by virtue of section 30 of the Finance Act 1967 or section 7 of the Finance Act (Northern Ireland) 1967 [or section 79(2) of the Finance Act 1986] from stamp duty under that heading' respectively.

[3] Words in sub-s (1) substituted by FA 1999 s 112(4), Sch 14 para 21 with effect in relation to instruments executed after 30 September 1999. This does not apply to transfers or other instruments relating to units under a unit trust scheme by virtue of FA 1999 s 122. For prospective repeal of FA 1999 Sch 14 para 21 see FA 1999 s 123(3). Previously the text read:

"either of the following headings in Schedule 1 to the Stamp Act 1891—

(*a*) "Conveyance or Transfer on Sale";

(*b*) "Conveyance or Transfer of any kind not hereinbefore described"."

[4] Sub-ss (4) and (5) repealed by FA 1999 Sch 20 Pt V(2) with effect in relation to instruments executed, or bearer instruments issued, from 1 October 1999, subject to the provisions in FA 1999 Sch 20 Pt V(2) Note 2. Previously the text read:

"(4) Subsection (1) above applies to any instrument executed on or after 1st August 1987.

(5) Subsection (2) above applies—

(*a*) to any instrument which falls within section 60(1) of the Finance Act 1963 or section 9(1) (*a*) of the Finance Act (Northern Ireland) 1963, and is issued on or after 1st August 1987, and

(*b*) to any instrument which falls within section 60(2) of the Finance Act 1963 or section 9(1)(*b*) of the Finance Act (Northern Ireland) 1963, if the interest, right or option constituted by or transferable by means of it is transferred on or after 1st August 1987."

[5] The word "transfer" substituted for the words "conveyance or transfer" in enactments relating to stamp duty by FA 2003 Sch 20 para 3.

[6] Words in sub-s (1) repealed by FA 2008 s 99, Sch 32 paras 16, 17 with effect in relation to instruments executed on or after 13 March 2008 and not stamped before 19 March 2008.

51 Bearer instruments relating to stock in foreign currencies

Amendments—This section repealed by FA 1999 Sch 20 Pt V(2) with effect in relation to instruments executed, or bearer instruments issued, from 1 October 1999, subject to the provisions in FA 1999 Sch 20 Pt V(2) Note 2. Previously the text amended FA 1967 s 30 and FA (Northern Ireland) 1967 s 7.

52 Clearance services

(*amended* FA 1986 s 70(6) *and is repealed by* FA 1990 Sch 19 Pt VI *with effect from an appointed day*).

53 Borrowing of stock by market makers

(*amended* FA 1986 s 82(6) *and is repealed by* FA 1990 Sch 19 Pt VI *with effect from an appointed day and by* FA 1997, Sch 18 Pt VII *with effect from a day appointed under* FA 1977 s 98(4)).

54 Shared ownership transactions

(1) (*amends* FA 1980 s 97(3)(*b*)).

(2) Section 97 of the Finance Act 1980 and section 108(5) and (6) of the Finance Act 1981 shall apply to a lease within subsection (3) below as they apply to a lease granted by a body mentioned in section 97(3) of the Finance Act 1980.

(3) A lease is within this subsection if it is granted—

(*a*) by a person against whom the right to buy under Part V of the Housing Act 1985 is exercisable by virtue of section 171A of that Act (preservation of right to buy on disposal to private sector landlord), and

(*b*) to a person who is the qualifying person for the purposes of the preserved right to buy and in relation to whom that dwelling-house is the qualifying dwelling-house.

(4) This section applies to leases granted on or after 1st August 1987.

55 Crown exemption

(1) Where any conveyance, transfer or lease is made or agreed to be made—

[(*a*)][3] to a Minister of the Crown or

[(*b*)][3] to the Solicitor for the affairs of Her Majesty's Treasury, [or

[(*c*)][3] to the Welsh Ministers, the First Minister for Wales, the Counsel General to the Welsh Assembly Government or the National Assembly for Wales Commission][5],][1] [or

(*d*) to the Northern Ireland Assembly Commission,][4]

no stamp duty shall be chargeable [under Part I or II, *or paragraph 16*[6] of Schedule 13 to the Finance Act 1999][2] on the instrument by which the conveyance, transfer or lease, or the agreement for it, is effected.

(2) In this section "Minister of the Crown" has the same meaning as in the Ministers of the Crown Act 1975.

(3) Article 3 (6) of the Secretary of State for the Environment Order 1970 and Article 4 (5) of the Secretary of State for Transport Order 1976 (which exempt transfers by, to or with those Ministers) shall cease to have effect.

(4) This section applies to instruments executed on or after 1st August 1987.

Note—In this section references to a Minister of the Crown shall be read as including the Scottish Ministers, the Lord Advocate and the Parliamentary corporation by virtue of the Scotland Act 1998 with effect from a date to be appointed by Statutory Instrument.

Amendments—[1] Words in sub-s (1) inserted by the Government of Wales Act 1998 Sch 12 para 25 with effect from 1 April 1999 by virtue of the Government of Wales Act 1998 (Commencement No 4) Order, SI 1999/782.

[2] Words in sub-s (1) substituted by FA 1999 s 112(4), Sch 14 para 22 with effect in relation to instruments executed after 30 September 1999. This does not apply to transfers or other instruments relating to units under a unit trust scheme by virtue of FA 1999 s 122. Previously the text read

'by virtue of any of the following headings in Schedule 1 to the Stamp Act 1891—

(*a*) "Conveyance or Transfer on Sale",

(*b*) "Conveyance or Transfer of any kind not herein before described",

(*c*) "Lease or Tack",'

[3] References to "(*a*)", "(*b*)" and "(*c*)" in sub-s (1) inserted by FA 2000 s 132(1), (2) with effect from 28 March 2000.

[4] Sub-s (1)(*d*) and word "or" preceding it inserted by FA 2000 s 132(1), (3), with effect for instruments executed after 27 March 2000.

[5] Words in sub-s (1)(*c*) substituted by the Government of Wales Act 2006 s 160(1), Sch 10 para 20 with effect from 25 May 2007, being the date on which the initial period ended (following the appointment of the First Minister) (Government of Wales Act 2006 ss 46, 161(4), (5)).

[6] Words in sub-s (1) repealed by FA 2008 s 99, Sch 32 paras 16, 18 with effect in relation to instruments executed on or after 13 March 2008 and not stamped before 19 March 2008.

This amendment does not have effect in relation to an instrument effecting a land transaction or a duplicate or counterpart of such an instrument. "Land transaction" has the same meaning as in FA 2003 Part 4, except that it does not include a transfer of an interest in a property-investment partnership (within the meaning of FA 2003 Sch 15) (FA 2008 s 99, Sch 32 para 22).

Stamp duty reserve tax

56 Stamp duty reserve tax

Schedule 7 to this Act (which contains miscellaneous amendments of Part IV of the Finance Act 1986) shall have effect.[1]

Amendments—[1] This section repealed by FA 1990 Sch 19 Pt VII with effect from an appointed day.

PART VI

MISCELLANEOUS AND SUPPLEMENTARY

72 Short title, interpretation, construction and repeals

(1) This Act may be cited as the Finance Act 1987.

(2), (3) (*not relevant to stamp duty*).

(4) Part III of this Act, except section 56 and Schedule 7, shall be construed as one with the Stamp Act 1891.

(5), (6) (*not relevant to stamp duty*).

(7) The enactments specified in Schedule 16 to this Act (which include enactments which are spent or otherwise unnecessary) are hereby repealed to the extent specified in the third column of that Schedule, but subject to any provision at the end of any Part of that Schedule.

SCHEDULE 7

STAMP DUTY RESERVE TAX

Section 56

Note—This Schedule amended FA 1986 ss 87, 88, 89, 90, 92 and is repealed by FA 1990 Sch 19 Pt VII with effect from an appointed day. Sch 7 para (4) is also repealed by FA 1997 Sch 18 Pt VII in relation to an agreement to transfer securities (*a*) in the case of an agreement which is not conditional, if the agreement is made on or after 20 October 1997 (as appointed by SI 1997/2428 under FA 1997 s 102(6)); and (*b*) in the case of a conditional agreement, if the condition is satisfied on or after that date.

FINANCE ACT 1988

(1988 Chapter 39)

An Act to grant certain duties, to alter other duties, and to amend the law relating to the National Debt and the Public Revenue, and to make further provision in connection with Finance.

[29th July 1988]

PART IV

MISCELLANEOUS AND GENERAL

Stamp duty and stamp duty reserve tax

140 Abolition of stamp duty under the heading "Unit Trust Instrument"

Amendments—This section repealed by FA 1999 Sch 20 Pt V(2) with effect in relation to instruments executed, or bearer instruments issued, from 1 October 1999, subject to the provisions in FA 1999 Sch 20 Pt V(2) Note 2. Previously the text read:

"(1) The stamp duty chargeable by virtue of the heading in Schedule 1 to the Stamp Act 1891 "Unit Trust Instrument" is abolished; and accordingly that heading and the following enactments, namely—

(*a*) section 53 of the Finance Act 1946;

(*b*) section 24 of the Finance (No 2) Act (Northern Ireland) 1946;

(*c*) section 30 of the Finance Act 1962; and

(*d*) section 3 of the Finance Act (Northern Ireland) 1962,

shall cease to have effect.

(2) Subsection (1) above shall have effect in relation to—

(*a*) any trust instrument executed on or after 22nd March 1988;

(*b*) any trust instrument executed on or after 16th March 1988 which is not stamped before 22nd March 1988;

(*c*) any property becoming trust property on or after 22nd March 1988; and

(*d*) any property becoming trust property on or after 16th March 1988 in respect of which the trust instrument is not stamped before 22nd March 1988.

(3) For the purposes of section 14 (4) of the Stamp Act 1891 (instruments not to be given in evidence etc unless stamped in accordance with the law in force at the time of execution), the law in force—

(*a*) at the time of execution of a trust instrument falling within subsection (2)(b) above; or

(*b*) on the day on which property falling within subsection (2)(d) above becomes trust property,

shall be deemed to be that as varied in accordance with this section.

(4) In this section "trust instrument" and "trust property" have the meanings given by section 57 of the Finance Act 1946 or section 28 of the Finance (No 2) Act (Northern Ireland) 1946.

(5) This section shall be construed as one with the Stamp Act 1891.

(6) This section shall be deemed to have come into force on 22nd March 1988."

141 Abolition of stamp duty on documents relating to transactions of capital companies

Amendments—This section repealed by FA 1999 Sch 20 Pt V(2) with effect in relation to instruments executed, or bearer instruments issued, from 1 October 1999, subject to the provisions in FA 1999 Sch 20 Pt V(2) Note 2. Previously the text read:

"(1) The stamp duties chargeable by virtue of section 47 of the Finance Act 1973 and Article 8 of the Finance (Miscellaneous Provisions) (Northern Ireland) Order 1973 (stamp duties on documents relating to chargeable transactions of capital companies) are abolished; and accordingly—

(*a*) that section, section 48 of that Act and Schedule 19 to that Act; and

(*b*) that Article, Article 9 of that Order and Schedule 2 to that Order,

shall cease to have effect.

(2) Subsection (1) above shall have effect in relation to—

(*a*) any transaction occurring on or after 22nd March 1988;

(*b*) any transaction occurring on or after 16th March 1988 in respect of which the relevant document is not stamped before 22nd March 1988;

(*c*) any exempt transaction occurring before 22nd March 1988 in respect of which a relevant event occurs on or after 22nd March 1988; and

(*d*) any exempt transaction occurring before 16th March 1988 in respect of which a relevant event occurs on or after 16th March 1988 and the relevant duty is not paid before 22nd March 1988.

(3) For the purposes of section 14(4) of the Stamp Act 1891 (instruments not to be given in evidence etc unless stamped in accordance with the law in force at the time of execution), the law in force—

(*a*) in a case falling within subsection (2)(*b*) above, at the time of execution of the relevant document; or

(*b*) in a case falling within subsection (2)(*d*) above, on the day on which the relevant event occurs,

shall be deemed to be that as varied in accordance with this section.

(4) In this section—

"exempt transaction" means a transaction which is exempt by virtue of paragraph 10(1) of Schedule 19 to the Finance Act 1973;

"relevant document" has the meaning given by section 47 of that Act;

"relevant duty" means the duty payable under paragraph 10(4) of Schedule 19 to that Act;

"relevant event" means such an event as is mentioned in paragraph 10(3) (*a*) or (*b*) of Schedule 19 to that Act,

and any reference in this subsection to section 47 of or Schedule 19 to that Act includes a reference to Article 8 of or Schedule 2 to the Finance (Miscellaneous Provisions) (Northern Ireland) Order 1973.

(5) This section shall be construed as one with the Stamp Act 1891.

(6) This section shall be deemed to have come into force on 22nd March 1988."

142 Stamp duty: housing action trusts

(*amends* FA 1980 s 97; FA 1981 s 107).

143 Stamp duty: paired shares

(1) This section applies where—

(*a*) the articles of association of a company incorporated in the United Kingdom ("the UK company") and the equivalent instruments governing a company which is not so incorporated ("the foreign company") each provide that no share in the company to which they relate may be transferred otherwise than as part of a unit comprising one share in that company and one share in the other; and

(*b*) such units are to be or have been offered for sale to the public in the United Kingdom and, at the same time, [other][1] such units are to be or, as the case may be, have been offered for sale to the public at a broadly equivalent price in the country in which the foreign company is incorporated ("the foreign country").

[(2) In relation to an instrument to which this subsection applies, no duty is chargeable under paragraph 1 of Schedule 15 to the Finance Act 1999 (bearer instruments: charge on issue); but this does not affect the other requirements of that Schedule.][2]

(3) [Subsection (2) above applies][3] to any bearer instrument issued on or after 1st November 1987 which represents shares in the UK company, or a right to an allotment of or to subscribe for such shares, if the purpose of the issue is—

(*a*) to make such shares available for sale (as part of such units as are referred to in subsection (1) above) in pursuance of either of the offers referred to in subsection (1)(*b*) above or of any other offer for sale of such units to the public made at the same time and at a broadly equivalent price in a country other than the United Kingdom or the foreign country; or

(*b*) to give effect to an allotment of such shares (as part of such units) as fully or partly paid bonus shares.

[(4) In relation to an instrument to which this subsection applies—

(*a*) the foreign company shall be treated for the purposes of Schedule 15 to the Finance Act 1999 (stamp duty on bearer instruments) as a UK company, and

(*b*) paragraph 17 of that Schedule (exemption for non-sterling instruments) shall not apply.][4]

(5) [Subsection (4) above applies][3] to any bearer instrument issued on or after 9th December 1987 which represents shares in the foreign company, or a right to an allotment of or to subscribe for such shares, and is not issued for the purpose—

(*a*) of making shares in the foreign company available for sale (as part of such units as are referred to in subsection (1) above) in pursuance of either of the offers referred to in subsection (1)(*b*) above or of any other offer such as is mentioned in subsection (3)(*a*) above; or

(*b*) of giving effect to an allotment of such shares (as part of such units) as fully or partly paid bonus shares.

(6) In relation to any instrument which transfers such units as are referred to in subsection (1) above and is executed on or after the date of the passing of this Act, the foreign company shall be treated for the purposes of sections 67 and 68 (depositary receipts) and 70 and 71 (clearance services) of the Finance Act 1986 as a company incorporated in the United Kingdom.

(7) Section 3 of the Stamp Act 1891 (which requires every instrument written upon the same piece of material as another instrument to be separately stamped) shall not apply in relation to any bearer instrument issued on or after 9th December 1987 which represents shares in the UK company or the foreign company, or a right to an allotment of or to subscribe for such shares.

(8) This section shall be construed as one with the Stamp Act 1891.

(9) Subsections (2) and (3) above, together with subsection (1) above so far as relating to them, shall be deemed to have come into force on 1st November 1987, and subsections (4), (5) and (7) above, together with subsection (1) above so far as relating to them, shall be deemed to have come into force on 9th December 1987.

Cross references—See FA 1990 s 112 (modification of sub-s(1)(*b*) by the substitution of the word "other" for the words "an equal number of" in specified circumstances).

Note—This section was to be repealed by FA 1990 Sch 19 Pt VI with effect from an appointed day in accordance with FA 1990 ss 107–111. The Treasury order specifying the appointed day for the purposes of FA 1990 ss 107–110 was to coincide with the start of paperless trading under the Stock Exchange's planned TAURUS system (IR press release, 20-3-90). However, on 11-3-93 the London Stock Exchange News Release 6/93 announced that TAURUS had been abandoned.

Amendments—[1] Sub-s (1)(*b*) amended by FA 1990 s 112 with effect from 26 July 1990.

[2] Sub-s (2) substituted by FA 1999 s 113(3), Sch 16 para 11 with effect in relation to bearer instruments issued after 30 September 1999. For prospective repeal of FA 1999 s 113, Sch 16 para 11 see FA 1999 s 123(3). Previously the text read:

"(2) In relation to an instrument to which subsection (3) below applies, any duty chargeable on issue under the heading "Bearer Instrument" in Schedule 1 to the Stamp Act 1891 (which, apart from this subsection, would be payable by virtue of section 60 of the Finance Act 1963 or section 9 of the Finance Act (Northern Ireland) 1963) shall not be so payable; but nothing in this subsection shall be taken as affecting the other requirements of that section."

[3] Words in sub-ss (3) and (5) substituted by FA 1999 s 113(3), Sch 16 para 11 with effect in relation to bearer instruments issued after 30 September 1999. For prospective repeal of FA 1999 s 113, Sch 16 para 11 see FA 1999 s 123(3). Previously the text read 'This subsection applies'.

[4] Sub-s (4) substituted by FA 1999 s 113(3), Sch 16 para 11 with effect in relation to bearer instruments issued after 30 September 1999. For prospective repeal of FA 1999 s 113, Sch 16 para 11 see FA 1999 s 123(3). Previously the text read:

"(4) In relation to an instrument to which subsection (5) below applies—

(*a*) the foreign company shall be treated—

(i) for the purposes of sections 59 and 60 of the Finance Act 1963 (which make provision in respect of stamp duty under the heading "Bearer Instrument" in Schedule 1 to the Stamp Act 1891) as a company formed or established in Great Britain; and

(ii) for the purposes of sections 8 and 9 of the Finance Act (Northern Ireland) 1963 (which make corresponding provision for Northern Ireland) as a company formed or established in Northern Ireland; and

(*b*) section 30 of the Finance Act 1967 and section 7 of the Finance Act (Northern Ireland) 1967 (exemption for bearer instruments relating to stock in foreign currencies) shall not apply."

144 Stamp duty reserve tax: paired shares etc

(*amended* FA 1986 s 99 *and sub-s (3) repealed by* FA 1999 Sch 20 Pt V(5) *with effect in relation to instruments executed from 6 February 2000*).

Miscellaneous

147 Interpretation etc

(1) In this Act "the Taxes Act 1970" means the Income and Corporation Taxes Act 1970 and "the Taxes Act 1988" means the Income and Corporation Taxes Act 1988.

(2)–(3) (*not relevant to stamp duty*).

FINANCE ACT 1989

(1989 Chapter 26)

ARRANGEMENT OF SECTIONS

PART III
MISCELLANEOUS AND GENERAL

Stamp duty etc

Interest etc

Miscellaneous

General

An Act to grant certain duties, to alter other duties, and to amend the law relating to the National Debt and the Public Revenue, and to make further provision in connection with Finance.

[27th July 1989]

PART III
MISCELLANEOUS AND GENERAL

Stamp duty etc

173 Insurance: abolition of certain duties

Amendments—This section repealed by FA 1999 Sch 20 Pt V(2) with effect in relation to instruments executed, or bearer instruments issued, from 1 October 1999, subject to the provisions in FA 1999 Sch 20 Pt V(2) Note 2. Previously the text read:

"(1) Stamp duty shall not be chargeable under—

(*a*) the heading "Policy of Life Insurance" in Schedule 1 to the Stamp Act 1891, or

(*b*) paragraph (3) of the heading "Bond, Covenant, or Instrument of any kind whatsoever" in that Schedule (superannuation annuities).

(2) Subject to section 4 of the Stamp Act 1891 (separate charges on instruments containing or relating to several distinct matters) an instrument which, but for subsection (1) above, would be chargeable with stamp duty under paragraph (3) of the heading mentioned in paragraph (*b*) of that subsection shall not be chargeable with stamp duty under any other provision of the Stamp Act 1891.

(3) (*repeals* SA 1891 s 100).

(4) (*repeals* SA 1891, s 118).

(5) (*repeals* FA 1966 s 47(3); FA (Northern Ireland) 1966 s 5(3)).
(6) Subsections (1) and (2) above apply to instruments made after 31st December 1989.
(7) So far as it relates to section 100(1) of the 1891 Act, subsection (3) above applies where a person receives, or takes credit for, a premium or consideration for insurance after 30th November 1989.
(8) So far as it relates to section 100 (2) of the 1891 Act, subsection (3) above applies where the policy is made after 31st December 1989.
(9) Subsection (4) above applies to instruments of assignment made after 31st December 1989.
(10) Subsection (5) above applies where the policy is varied after 31st December 1989 (whenever it was made)."

174 Unit trusts

Amendments—This section repealed by FA 1999 Sch 20 Pt V(5) with effect in relation to instruments executed from 6 February 2000.

175 Stamp duty: stock exchange nominees

(1) The Treasury may by regulations provide that where—

(*a*) circumstances would (apart from the regulations) give rise to a charge to stamp duty under [Part I of Schedule 13 to the Finance Act 1999 ([transfer][2] on sale)][1] and to a charge to stamp duty reserve tax,
(*b*) the circumstances involve a stock exchange nominee, and
(*c*) the circumstances are such as are prescribed,

the charge to stamp duty shall be treated as not arising.

(2) The power to make regulations under this section shall be exercisable by statutory instrument subject to annulment in pursuance of a resolution of the House of Commons.

(3) In this section—

(*a*) "prescribed" means prescribed by the regulations, and
(*b*) "stock exchange nominee" means a person designated for the purposes of section 127 of the Finance Act 1976 as a nominee of The Stock Exchange by an order made by the Secretary of State under subsection (5) of that section.

Notes—This section was to be repealed by FA 1990 Sch 19 Pt VI with effect from an appointed day in accordance with FA 1990 ss 107–111. The Treasury order specifying the appointed day for the purposes of FA 1990 ss 107–110 was to coincide with the start of paperless trading under the Stock Exchange's planned TAURUS system (IR press release, 20-3-90). However, on 11-3-93 the London Stock Exchange News Release 6/93 announced that TAURUS had been abandoned.

Amendments—[1] Words in sub-s (1)(*a*) substituted by FA 1999 s 112(4), Sch 14 para 23 with effect in relation to instruments executed after 30 September 1999. This does not apply to transfers or other instruments relating to units under a unit trust scheme by virtue of FA 1999 s 122. For prospective repeal of FA 1999 Sch 14 para 23 see FA 1999 s 123(3). Previously the text read 'the heading "Conveyance or Transfer on Sale" in Schedule 1 to the Stamp Act 1891'.

[2] The word "transfer" substituted for the words "conveyance or transfer" in enactments relating to stamp duty by FA 2003 Sch 20 para 3.

176 Stamp duty reserve tax: stock exchange nominees

(1) The Treasury may by regulations provide that where—

(*a*) circumstances would (apart from the regulations) give rise to two charges to stamp duty reserve tax,
(*b*) the circumstances involve a stock exchange nominee, and
(*c*) the circumstances are such as are prescribed,

such one of the charges as may be prescribed shall be treated as not arising.

(2) The Treasury may by regulations provide that where—

(*a*) circumstances would (apart from the regulations) give rise to a charge to stamp duty reserve tax and a charge to stamp duty,
(*b*) the circumstances involve a stock exchange nominee, and
(*c*) the circumstances are such as are prescribed,

the charge to stamp duty reserve tax shall be treated as not arising.

(3) The Treasury may by regulations provide that a provision of an Act by virtue of which there is no charge to stamp duty reserve tax shall also apply in circumstances which involve a stock exchange nominee and are such as are prescribed.

(4) The Treasury may by regulations provide that a provision of an Act by virtue of which the rate at which stamp duty reserve tax is charged is less than it would be apart from the provision shall also apply in circumstances which involve a stock exchange nominee and are such as are prescribed.

(5) The power to make regulations under this section shall be exercisable by statutory instrument subject to annulment in pursuance of a resolution of the House of Commons.

(6) In this section—

(*a*) "prescribed" means prescribed by the regulations, and
(*b*) "stock exchange nominee" means a person designated for the purposes of section 127 of the Finance Act 1976 as a nominee of The Stock Exchange by an order made by the Secretary of State under subsection (5) of the section.[1]

Amendments—[1] This section repealed by FA 1990 Sch 19 Pt VII with effect from an appointed day.

177 Stamp duty reserve tax: information

Regulations under section 98(1) of the Finance Act 1986 (administration etc of stamp duty reserve tax) may include—

(*a*) provision that notice which the regulations require to be given to the Commissioners of Inland Revenue shall be given in a manner or form specified by the Commissioners;

(*b*) provision that information which the regulations require to be supplied to the Commissioners shall be supplied in a manner or form specified by the Commissioners.[1]

Amendments—[1] This section repealed by FA 1990 Sch 19 Pt VII with effect from an appointed day.

Interest etc

178 Setting of rates of interest

(1) The rate of interest applicable for the purposes of an enactment to which this section applies shall be the rate which for the purposes of that enactment is provided for by regulations made by the Treasury under this section.

(2) This section applies to—

[(*aa*) section 15A of the Stamp Act 1891;][2]

(*a*)–(*e*) …

(*f*) sections [86, …][1] of the Taxes Management Act 1970,

(*g*)–(*k*) …

(*l*) section 92 of the Finance Act 1986 and

(*m*)–(*o*) …[, and

(*p*) section 110 of the Finance Act 1999.][3]

[(*q*) …

[(*r*) sections 87, 88 and 89 of the Finance Act 2003.][4]

(3) Regulations under this section may—

(*a*) make different provision for different enactments or for different purposes of the same enactment,

(*b*) either themselves specify a rate of interest for the purposes of an enactment or make provision for any such rate to be determined by reference to such rate or the average of such rates as may be referred to in the regulations,

(*c*) provide for rates to be reduced below, or increased above, what they otherwise would be by specified amounts or by reference to specified formulae,

(*d*) provide for rates arrived at by reference to averages to be rounded up or down,

(*e*) provide for circumstances in which alteration of a rate of interest is or is not to take place, and

(*f*) provide that alterations of rates are to have effect for periods beginning on or after a day determined in accordance with the regulations in relation to interest running from before that day as well as from or from after that day.

(4) The power to make regulations under this section shall be exercisable by statutory instrument which shall be subject to annulment in pursuance of a resolution of the House of Commons.

(5) Where—

(*a*) the rate provided for by regulations under this section as the rate applicable for the purposes of any enactment is changed, and

(*b*) the new rate is not specified in the regulations,

the Board shall by order specify the new rate and the day from which it has effect.

(6) …

(7) Subsection (1) shall have effect for periods beginning on or after such day as the Treasury may by order made by statutory instrument appoint and shall have effect in relation to interest running from before that day as well as from or from after that day; and different days may be appointed for different enactments.

Note—For the application of TMA 1970 s 86 (as modified) to stamp duty reserve tax, see Stamp Duty Reserve Tax Regulations, SI 1986/1711 reg 20, Sch Pt II.

Provisions omitted from this section are not relevant to stamp duty.

Cross references—See the Taxes (Interest Rate) Regulations, SI 1989/1297.

Amendments—[1] Sub-s (2)(*f*) amended by FA 1994 ss 196, 199(2), (3), Sch 19 Pt III para 44 (words omitted are not relevant to stamp duty).

[2] Sub-s (2)(*aa*) inserted by FA 1999 s 109(2) with effect in relation to instruments executed after 30 September 1999. This does not apply to transfers or other instruments relating to units under a unit trust scheme by virtue of FA 1999 s 122.

[3] Sub-s (2)(*p*) inserted by FA 1999 s 110(9) with effect in relation to instruments executed after 30 September 1999. This does not apply to transfers or other instruments relating to units under a unit trust scheme by virtue of FA 1999 s 122.

[4] Sub-s (2)(*r*) inserted by FA 2003 s 123(1), Sch 18 para 4 with effect in accordance with FA 2003 s 124, Sch 19.

179 Provisions consequential on section 178

(1)–(3) …

(4) Any amendment made by subsection (1) … above shall have effect in relation to any period for which section 178(1) above has effect for the purposes of the enactment concerned.

(5) …

Note—Sub-s (1)(*f*) amended FA 1986 s 92 with effect from 18 August 1989. The rest of sub-s (1) and sub-ss (2), (3), (5) not relevant to stamp duty.

180 Repayment interest: period of accrual

(1)–(4) ...

(5) (*amends* FA 1986 s 92).

(6) ...

(7) The amendments made by this section shall be deemed always to have had effect.

Note—Sub-ss (1)–(4), (6) not relevant to stamp duty.

Miscellaneous

182 Disclosure of information

(1) A person who discloses any information which he holds or has held in the exercise of tax functions[, tax credit functions][4][, child trust fund functions][8] [or social security functions][3] is guilty of an offence if it is information about any matter relevant, for the purposes of [any of those functions—

(*a*) to tax or duty in the case of any identifiable person,

[(*aa*) to a tax credit in respect of any identifiable person,][4]

[(*ab*) to a child trust fund of any identifiable person,][8]

(*b*) to contributions payable by or in respect of any identifiable person, or

(*c*) to statutory sick pay[, statutory maternity pay, statutory paternity pay or statutory adoption pay][5] in respect of any identifiable person.][3]

(2) In this section "tax functions" means functions relating to tax or duty—

(*a*) of ..., the Board and their officers,

(*b*) of any person carrying out the administrative work of any tribunal mentioned in subsection (3) below, and

(*c*) of any other person providing, or employed in the provision of, services to any person mentioned in paragraph (*a*) or (*b*) above.

[(2ZA) In this section "tax credit functions" means the functions relating to tax credits—

(*a*) of the Board,

(*b*) of any person carrying out the administrative work of the General Commissioners or the Special Commissioners, and

(*c*) of any other person providing, or employed in the provision of, services to the Board or to any person mentioned in paragraph (*b*) above.][4]

[(2ZB) In this section "child trust fund functions" means the functions relating to child trust funds—

(*a*) of the Board and their officers,

(*b*) of any person carrying out the administrative work of the [First-tier Tribunal or an appeal tribunal constituted under Chapter 1 of Part 2 of the Social Security (Northern Ireland) Order 1998][12], or

(*c*) of any person providing, or employed in the provision of, services to the Board or any person mentioned in paragraph (*b*) above.][8]

[(2A) In this section "social security functions" means—

(*a*) the functions relating to contributions, [child benefit, guardian's allowance,][6] statutory sick pay[, statutory maternity pay, statutory paternity pay or statutory adoption pay][5]—

(i) of the Board and their officers,

(ii) of any person carrying out the administrative work of [the First-tier Tribunal or Upper Tribunal][12], and

(iii) of any other person providing, or employed in the provision of, services to any person mentioned in sub-paragraph (i) or (ii) above, and

(*b*) the functions under Part III of the Pension Schemes Act 1993 or Part III of the Pension Schemes (Northern Ireland) Act 1993 of the Board and their officers and any other person providing, or employed in the provision of, services to the Board or their officers.][3]

(3) The tribunals referred to in subsection (2)(*b*) above are—

(*a*) ... the Special Commissioners,

(*b*) ...

(*c*) ...[1]

(*d*) ...

(4) A person who discloses any information which—

(*a*) he holds or has held in the exercise of functions—

(i) of the Comptroller and Auditor General and any member of the staff of the National Audit Office, ...[2]

(ii) of the Parliamentary Commissioner for Administration and his officers,

[(iii) of the Auditor General for Wales and any member of his staff, ...[9]

[(iv) of the Public Services Ombudsman for Wales and any member of his staff, or][11]

(v) of the Scottish Public Services Ombudsman and any member of his staff,][9]

Stamp Taxes

(*b*) is, or is derived from, information which was held by any person in the exercise of tax functions[, tax credit functions][4][, child trust fund functions][8] [or social security functions][3], and

(*c*) is information about any matter relevant, for the purposes of [tax functions[, tax credit functions][4][, child trust fund functions][8] or social security functions—

(i) to tax or duty in the case of any identifiable person,

[(ia) to a tax credit in respect of any identifiable person,][4]

[(ib) to a child trust fund of any identifiable person,][8]

(ii) to contributions payable by or in respect of any identifiable person, or

(iii) to [child benefit, guardian's allowance,][6] statutory sick pay [, statutory maternity pay, statutory paternity pay or statutory adoption pay][5] in respect of any identifiable person.][3]

is guilty of an offence.

(5) Subsections (1) and (4) above do not apply to any disclosure of information—

(*a*) with lawful authority,

(*b*) with the consent of any person in whose case the information is about a matter relevant to tax or duty[, to a tax credit or to a child trust fund][8] [or to contributions …][3], or

(*c*) which has been lawfully made available to the public before the disclosure is made.

(6) For the purposes of this section a disclosure of any information is made with lawful authority if, and only if, it is made—

(*a*) by a Crown servant in accordance with his official duty,

(*b*) by any other person for the purposes of the function in the exercise of which he holds the information and without contravening any restriction duly imposed by the person responsible,

(*c*) to, or in accordance with an authorisation duly given by, the person responsible,

(*d*) in pursuance of any enactment or of any order of a court, or

(*e*) in connection with the institution of or otherwise for the purposes of any proceedings relating to any matter within the general responsibility of … the Board,

and in this subsection "the person responsible" means …, the Board, the Comptroller[, the Parliamentary Commissioner, the Auditor General for Wales[, [the Public Services Ombudsman for Wales][11] or the Scottish Public Services Ombudsman][9],][2] as the case requires.

(7) It is a defence for a person charged with an offence under this section to prove that at the time of the alleged offence—

(*a*) he believed that he had lawful authority to make the disclosure in question and had no reasonable cause to believe otherwise, or

(*b*) he believed that the information in question had been lawfully made available to the public before the disclosure was made and had no reasonable cause to believe otherwise.

(8) A person guilty of an offence under this section is liable—

(*a*) on conviction on indictment, to imprisonment for a term not exceeding two years or a fine or both, and

(*b*) on summary conviction, to imprisonment for a term not exceeding six months or a fine not exceeding the statutory maximum or both.

(9) No prosecution for an offence under this section shall be instituted in England and Wales or in Northern Ireland except—

(*a*) by … the Board, …, or

(*b*) by or with the consent of the Director of Public Prosecutions or, in Northern Ireland, the Director of Public Prosecutions for Northern Ireland.

(10) In this section—

"the Board" means the Commissioners of Inland Revenue,

["child trust fund" has the same meaning as in the Child Trust Funds Act 2004,][8]

…

["contributions" means contributions under Part I of the Social Security Contributions and Benefits Act 1992 or Part I of the Social Security Contributions and Benefits (Northern Ireland) Act 1992;][3]

"Crown servant" has the same meaning as in the Official Secrets Act 1989 and

["tax credit" means a tax credit under the Tax Credits Act 2002,][4] and

"tax or duty" means any tax or duty within the general responsibility of … the Board.

[(10A) In this section, in relation to disclosure of information "identifiable person" means a person whose identity is specified in the disclosure or can be deduced from it.][7]

(11) In this section—

(*a*) references to the Comptroller and Auditor General include the Comptroller and Auditor General for Northern Ireland,

(*b*) references to the National Audit Office include the Northern Ireland Audit Office, and

(*c*) references to the Parliamentary Commissioner for Administration include the Health Service Commissioner for England …[11], …[9] the [Assembly, Ombudsman for Northern Ireland][10] and the Northern Ireland Commissioner for Complaints.

[(11A) In this section, references to statutory paternity pay or statutory adoption pay include statutory pay under Northern Ireland legislation corresponding to Part 12ZA or Part 12ZB of the Social Security Contributions and Benefits Act 1992 (c 4).][5]

(12) This section shall come into force on the repeal of section 2 of the Official Secrets Act 1911.

Amendments—[1] Sub-s (3)(*c*) repealed by Statute Law (Repeals) Act 2004 Sch 1 Part 5 Group 18, with effect from 22 July 2004.

[2] Sub-s (4)(*a*)(iii) inserted and words in sub-s (6) substituted by the Government of Wales Act 1998 Sch 12 para 31 with effect from 1 February 1999 by virtue of the Government of Wales Act 1998 (Commencement No 3) Order, SI 1999.118. Words in sub-s (6) previously read 'or the Parliamentary Commissioner,'.

[3] Words in sub-ss (1), (4)(*b*), (*c*), (5)(*b*) amended, and sub-s (2A) and definition in sub-s (10) inserted, by the Social Security Contributions (Transfer of Functions, etc) Act 1999 s 6, Sch 6 para 9 with effect from 1 April 1999 by virtue of Social Security Contributions (Transfer of Functions, etc) Act 1999 (Commencement No 1 and Transitional Provisions) Order, SI 1999/527.

[4] Words in sub-ss (1), (4), inserted, sub-ss (1)(*aa*), (4)(*c*)(ia) substituted, sub-s (2ZA) substituted for sub-s (2AA), and in sub-s (10), definition of "tax credit" inserted, by TCA 2002 s 59, Sch 5 para 11(1), (2) with effect from 1 August 2002 (by virtue of SI 2002/1727).

[5] Words in sub-ss (1)(*c*), (2A)(*a*) substituted, and sub-s (11A) inserted, by the Employment Act 2002 s 53, Sch 7 para 1 with effect from 8 December 2002 (by virtue of SI 2002/2866).

[6] Words in sub-ss (2A)(*a*), (4)(*c*)(iii) inserted by TCA 2002 s 59, Sch 5 para 11(1), (4) with effect for the purpose of making subordinate legislation, from 26 February 2003, and for remaining purposes, from 1 April 2003 (by virtue of SI 2003/392).

[7] Sub-s (10A) inserted by Commissioners for Revenue and Customs Act 2005 s 50, Sch 4 para 39 with effect from 18 April 2005 by virtue of the Commissioners for Revenue and Customs Act (Commencement) Order, SI 2005/1126, art 2(2).

[8] Words in sub-ss (1), (4)(*b*), (*c*), (10), sub-ss (1)(*ab*), (2ZB), (4)(*c*)(ib) inserted, words in sub-s (5)(*b*) substituted by Child Trust Funds Act 2004 s 18 with effect from 1 January 2005 (by virtue of Child Trust Funds Act 2004 (Commencement No 1) Order, SI 2004/2422, art 2).

[9] Word in sub-s (4)(*a*)(iii), (11)(*c*) repealed, sub-s (4)(*a*)(v) inserted, words in sub-s (6) substituted by Scottish Public Services Ombudsman Act 2002 (Consequential Provisions and Modifications) Order, SI 2004/1823, art 10 with effect from 14 July 2004.

[10] Words substituted by Ombudsman (Northern Ireland) Order, SI 1996/1298 (NI 8) art 21(1), Sch 5.

[11] Sub-s (4)(*a*)(iv) substituted, words in sub-s (6) substituted, and words in sub-s (11)(*c*) repealed, by the Public Services Ombudsman (Wales) Act 2005, s 39(1), Sch 6, para 22 with effect from 1 April 2006, by virtue of the Public Services Ombudsman (Wales) Act 2005 (Commencement No 1 and Transitional Provisions and Savings) Order, SI 2005/2800. For further effect in relation to complaints made or referred to the Ombudsman about a matter relating to events that occurred before or after 1 April 2006, and in relation to estimates for income and expenses in relation to the financial year ending 31 March 2007, see arts 6, 7 thereof.

[12] In sub-s (2ZB)(*b*), words substituted for words "General Commissioners or the Special Commissioners", in sub-s (2A)(*a*)(ii), words substituted for words "the General Commissioners or the Special Commissioners", and sub-s (3) repealed, by the Transfer of Tribunal Functions and Revenue and Customs Appeals Order, SI 2009/56 art 3(1), Sch 1 paras 166, 167 with effect from 1 April 2009.

General

186 Interpretation etc

(1) In this Act "the Taxes Act 1970" means the Income and Corporation Taxes Act 1970 and "the Taxes Act 1988" means the Income and Corporation Taxes Act 1988.

(2), (3) (*not relevant to stamp duty*).

187 Repeals

(1) The enactments specified in Schedule 17 to this Act (which include unnecessary enactments) are hereby repealed to the extent specified in the third column of that Schedule, but subject to any provision at the end of any Part of that Schedule.

(2) (*not relevant to stamp duty*).

188 Short title

This Act may be cited as the Finance Act 1989.

FINANCE ACT 1990

(1990 Chapter 29)

ARRANGEMENT OF SECTIONS

PART III

STAMP DUTY AND STAMP DUTY RESERVE TAX

Repeals

Paired shares

An Act to grant certain duties, to alter other duties, and to amend the law relating to the National Debt and the Public Revenue, and to make further provision in connection with Finance.

[26th July 1990]

PART III

STAMP DUTY AND STAMP DUTY RESERVE TAX

Repeals

[107 Stamp duty to be abolished on bearer instruments][1]

[(1) Stamp duty shall not be chargeable under Schedule 15 to the Finance Act 1999 (bearer instruments).

(2) Subsection (1) above applies in relation to the charge under paragraph 1 of that Schedule (charge on issue) where the instrument is issued on or after the abolition day.

(3) Subsection (1) above applies in relation to the charge under paragraph 2 of that Schedule (charge on transfer of stock) where the stock constituted by or transferable by means of the instrument is transferred on or after the abolition day.][1]

Amendments—[1] This section substituted by FA 1999 s 113(3), Sch 16 para 12 with effect in relation to bearer instruments issued after 30 September 1999.

108 Transfer of securities: abolition of stamp duty

[(1) Stamp duty shall not be chargeable under Schedule 13 to the Finance Act 1999 (transfer of securities) [or section 67(3) or 70(3) of the Finance Act 1986 (stamp duty on certain transfers to depositary receipt systems and clearance systems)][2].][1]

(7) Subject to subsection (8) below, this section applies if the instrument is executed in pursuance of a contract made on or after the abolition day.

(8) In the case of an instrument—

(*a*) which falls within section 67(1) or (9) of the Finance Act 1986 (depositary receipts) or section 70(1) or (9) of that Act (clearance services), or

(*b*) which does not fall within section 67(1) or (9) or section 70(1) or (9) of that Act and is not executed in pursuance of a contract,

this section applies if the instrument is executed on or after the abolition day.

Amendments—[1] Sub-s (1) substituted for sub-ss (1)–(6) by FA 2003 s 125(4), Sch 20 para 5 with effect—

(*a*) in relation to instruments effecting land transactions that—

(i) are SDLT transactions within the meaning of Schedule 19 (stamp duty land tax: commencement and transitional provisions), or

(ii) would be such transactions but for an exemption or relief from stamp duty land tax;

(*b*) in relation to other instruments, if they are executed on or after the implementation date for the purposes of stamp duty land tax.

The implementation date is 1 December 2003 (by virtue of SI 2003/2899).

FA 2003 s 125 and Sch 20 have effect subject to FA 2003 Sch 15 para 13(2), (3).

[2] Words inserted in sub-s (1) by FA 2008 s 99, Sch 32 para 19 with effect in relation to instruments executed on or after 13 March 2008 and not stamped before 19 March 2008.

109 Stamp duty: other repeals

(1) Section 83 of the Stamp Act 1891 (fine for certain acts relating to securities) shall not apply where an instrument of assignment or transfer is executed, or a transfer or negotiation of the stock constituted by or transferable by means of a bearer instrument takes place, on or after the abolition day.

(2) The following provisions (which relate to the cancellation of certain instruments) shall not apply where the stock certificate or other instrument is entered on or after the abolition day—

(*a*) section 109(1) of the Stamp Act 1891,

(*b*) section 5(2) of the Finance Act 1899,

(*c*), (*d*) ...[1]

(3) Section 67 of the Finance Act 1963 (prohibition of circulation of blank transfers) shall not apply where the sale is made on or after the abolition day; and section 16 of the Finance Act (Northern Ireland) 1963 (equivalent provision for Northern Ireland) shall not apply where the sale is made on or after the abolition day.

(4) No person shall be required to notify the Commissioners under section 68(1) or (2) or 71(1) or (2) of the Finance Act 1986 (depositary receipts and clearance services) if he first issues the receipts, provides the services or holds the securities as there mentioned on or after the abolition day.

(5) No company shall be required to notify the Commissioners under section 68(3) or 71(3) of that Act if it first becomes aware as there mentioned on or after the abolition day.

(6) The following provisions shall cease to have effect—

(*a*), (*b*) ...[1]

(*c*) section 33 of the Finance Act 1970 (composition by financial institutions in respect of stamp duty),

(*d*) section 127(7) of the Finance Act 1976 (extension of composition provisions to Northern Ireland), and

(*e*) section 85 of the Finance Act 1986 (provisions about stock, marketable securities, etc).

(7) The provisions mentioned in subsection (6) above shall cease to have effect as provided by the Treasury by order.

(8) An order under subsection (7) above—

(*a*) shall be made by statutory instrument;

(*b*) may make different provision for different provisions or different purposes;

(*c*) may include such supplementary, incidental, consequential or transitional provisions as appear to the Treasury to be necessary or expedient.

(9) ...[1]

Amendments—[1] Sub-ss (2)(*c*)(*d*), (6)(*a*)(*b*) and (9) repealed by FA 1999 Sch 20 Pt V(5) with effect for instruments executed from 6 February 2000.

110 Stamp duty reserve tax: abolition

(1) Stamp duty reserve tax shall cease to be chargeable.

(2) In relation to the charge to tax under section 87 of the Finance Act 1986 subsection (1) above applies where—

(*a*) the agreement to transfer is conditional and the condition is satisfied on or after the abolition day, or

(*b*) the agreement is not conditional and is made on or after the abolition day.

(3) In relation to the charge to tax under section 93(1) of that Act subsection (1) above applies where securities are transferred, issued or appropriated on or after the abolition day (whenever the arrangement was made).

(4) In relation to the charge to tax under section 96(1) of that Act subsection (1) above applies where securities are transferred or issued on or after the abolition day (whenever the arrangement was made).

(5) In relation to the charge to tax under section 93(10) of that Act subsection (1) above applies where securities are issued or transferred on sale, under terms there mentioned, on or after the abolition day.

(6) In relation to the charge to tax under section 96(8) of that Act subsection (1) above applies where securities are issued or transferred on sale, under terms there mentioned, on or after the abolition day.

(7) Where before the abolition day securities are issued or transferred on sale under terms mentioned in section 93(10) of that Act, in construing section 93(10) the effect of subsections (1) and (3) above shall be ignored.

(8) Where before the abolition day securities are issued or transferred on sale under terms mentioned in section 96(8) of that Act, in construing section 96(8) the effect of subsections (1) and (4) above shall be ignored.

111 General

(1) In sections 107 to 110 above "the abolition day" means such day as may be appointed by the Treasury by order made by statutory instrument.

(2) Sections 107 to 109 above shall be construed as one with the Stamp Act 1891.

Paired shares

112 Stamp duty

(1) (*amends* FA 1988 s 143(1)(*b*)).

(2) Subsection (1) above applies where—

(*a*) the offers referred to in section 143(1) are made, or are to be made, on or after the day on which this Act is passed, and

(*b*) before the offers are made, or are to be made, units comprising shares in the two companies concerned were offered (whether before or on or after the day on which this Act is passed) in circumstances where section 143 applied without the amendment made by subsection (1) above.

113 Stamp duty reserve tax

(1) Section 99 of the Finance Act 1986 (stamp duty reserve tax: interpretation) shall be amended as follows.

(2), (3) (*amend* FA 1986 s 99(6A) and *insert* FA 1986 s 99(6B)).

(4) (*amends* FA 1986 s 99(9) *and is repealed by* FA 1999 Sch 20 Pt V(5) *with effect in relation to instruments executed from 6 February 2000*).

(5) Subsection (2) above applies where—

(*a*) the offers referred to in section 99(6A) are made on or after the day on which this Act is passed, and

(*b*) before the offers are made, units comprising shares in the two companies concerned were offered (whether before or on or after the day on which this Act is passed) in circumstances where section 99(6A) applied without the amendment made by subsection (2) above.

(6) Subsections (3) and (4) above apply where—

(*a*) the shares referred to in section 99(6B) are issued on or after the day on which this Act is passed, and

(*b*) before they are issued, units comprising shares in the two companies concerned were offered (whether before or on or after the day on which this Act is passed) in circumstances where section 99(6A) applied without the amendment made by subsection (2) above.

International organisations

114 International organisations

(1) (*inserts* FA 1984 s 126(3)(*d*)).

(2) Where an organisation or body is designated under section 126(1) or (4) before the day on which this Act is passed, subsection (1) above applies in relation to the issue of securities by the organisation or body on or after that day.

(3) Where an organisation or body is designated under section 126(1) or (4) on or after the day on which this Act is passed, subsection (1) above applies in relation to the issue of securities by the organisation or body after the designation.

PART IV
MISCELLANEOUS AND GENERAL

132 Repeals

The enactments specified in Schedule 19 to this Act (which include spent or unnecessary enactments) are hereby repealed to the extent specified in the third column of that Schedule, but subject to any provision at the end of any Part of that Schedule.

133 Short title

This Act may be cited as the Finance Act 1990.

SCHEDULE 19
REPEALS

Section 132

PART VI
STAMP DUTY

Chapter	Short title	Extent of repeal
1891 c 39.	The Stamp Act 1891.	In section 59(1), the words “or stock, or marketable securities,”. Section 83. Section 109(1).

Chapter	Short title	Extent of repeal
		In Schedule 1, the whole of the heading beginning "Bearer Instrument", and paragraph (1) of the general exemptions at the end of the Schedule.
1899 c 9.	The Finance Act 1899.	Section 5(2).
1946 c 64.	The Finance Act 1946.	Section 54(3) and (4). Section 56. Section 57(2) to (4).
1946 c 17 (NI).	The Finance (No 2) Act (Northern Ireland) 1946.	Section 25(3) and (4). Section 27. Section 28(2) to (4).
1947 c 35.	The Finance Act 1947.	Section 57.
1948 c 49.	The Finance Act 1948.	Section 74.
1950 c 32 (NI).	The Finance (No 2) Act (Northern Ireland) 1950.	Section 3(1).
1951 c 43.	The Finance Act 1951.	Section 42.
1963 c 18.	The Stock Transfer Act 1963.	In section 2(3), in paragraph (*a*) the words "and section 56(4) of the Finance Act 1946", and paragraph (*c*) and the word "and" immediately preceding it.
1963 c 25.	The Finance Act 1963.	Section 55(1A). In section 59, subsections (1) to (4). Section 60. Section 61. In section 62, in subsection (1) the words from "and any" to the end, and subsection (4). Section 65(1). Section 67.
1963 c 22 (NI).	The Finance Act (Northern Ireland) 1963.	Section 4(1A). In section 8, subsections (1) to (4). Section 9. Section 10. In section 11, in subsection (1) the words from "and any" to the end, and subsection (3). Section 14(1). Section 16.
1963 c 24 (NI).	The Stock Transfer Act (Northern Ireland) 1963.	In section 2(3), in paragraph (*a*) the words "and section 27(4) of the Finance (No 2) Act (Northern Ireland) 1946", and paragraph (*c*) and the word "and" immediately preceding it.
1967 c 54.	The Finance Act 1967.	Section 30.
1967 c 20 (NI).	The Finance Act (Northern Ireland) 1967.	Section 7.
1970 c 24.	The Finance Act 1970.	Section 33. In Schedule 7, paragraph 6.
1970 c 21 (NI).	The Finance Act (Northern Ireland) 1970.	In Schedule 2, paragraph 6.
1974 c 30.	The Finance Act 1974.	In Schedule 11, paragraphs 2 and 12.
1975 c 80.	The OECD Support Fund Act 1975.	Section 4(2).
1976 c 40.	The Finance Act 1976.	In section 127, subsections (1) and (4) to (7). Section 131(3).
1980 c 48.	The Finance Act 1980.	Section 101.
1984 c 43.	The Finance Act 1984.	Section 126(3)(*c*) and (5).
1985 c 6.	The Companies Act 1985.	In Schedule 14, in paragraph 8 the words from "and, unless" to the end.

Chapter	Short title	Extent of repeal
1985 c 54.	The Finance Act 1985.	Section 81.
1986 c 41.	The Finance Act 1986.	Section 64(1).
		Sections 65 to 72.
		Section 77.
		In section 79, subsections (2) to (8), and in subsection (12) the words "(7), (9),".
		Sections 80 to 85.
SI 1986/1032 (N16).	The Companies (Northern Ireland) Order 1986.	In Schedule 14, in paragraph 7 the words from "and unless" to the end.
1987 c 16.	The Finance Act 1987.	Sections 50 to 53.
1987 c 51.	The Finance (No 2) Act 1987.	Section 99.
1988 c 39.	The Finance Act 1988.	Section 143.
		In Schedule 13, paragraph 19.
1989 c 26.	The Finance Act 1989.	Sections 174 and 175.

1. So far as these repeals relate to bearer instruments, they have effect in accordance with section 107 of this Act.

2. So far as these repeals relate to instruments other than bearer instruments, they have effect in accordance with section 108 of this Act.

3. So far as these repeals relate to—

(*a*) any provision mentioned in subsection (1), (2), (3), (4) or (5) of section 109 of this Act, or
(*b*) any other provision to the extent that it is ancillary to or dependent on any provision so mentioned,

the repeals have effect in accordance with the subsection concerned.

4. So far as these repeals relate to—

(*a*) any provision mentioned in section 109(6) of this Act, or
(*b*) any other provision to the extent that it is ancillary to or dependent on any provision so mentioned,

the repeals have effect in accordance with any order under section 109(7) of this Act.

5. Paragraphs 1 and 2 above have effect subject to paragraphs 3 and 4 above.

PART VII
STAMP DUTY RESERVE TAX

Chapter	Short title	Extent of repeal
1986 c 41.	The Finance Act 1986.	Part IV.
1987 c 16.	The Finance Act 1987.	Section 56.
		Schedule 7.
1987 c 51.	The Finance (No 2) Act 1987.	Section 100.
1988 c 39.	The Finance Act 1988.	Section 144.
		In Schedule 13, paragraph 23.
1989 c 26.	The Finance Act 1989.	Sections 176 and 177.

These repeals have effect in accordance with section 110 of this Act.

FINANCE ACT 1991

(1991 Chapter 31)

An Act to grant certain duties, to alter other duties, and to amend the law relating to the National Debt and the Public Revenue, and to make further provision in connection with Finance.

[25th July 1991]

PART IV
STAMP DUTY

110 Stamp duty abolished in certain cases

[(1) Where apart from this section stamp duty under any of the provisions of Schedule 13 to the Finance Act 1999 would be chargeable on an instrument, stamp duty shall not be so chargeable if the property consists entirely of exempt property.][2]

(2)–(4) …[2]

(5) For the purposes of this section exempt property is property other than—

(*a*) land,

(*b*) …[1]

(*c*) a licence to occupy land.

(6) This section applies to—

(*a*) an instrument executed in pursuance of a contract made on or after the abolition day;

(*b*) an instrument which is not executed in pursuance of a contract and is executed on or after the abolition day.

(7) For the purposes of this section the abolition day is such day as may be appointed under section 111(1) of the Finance Act 1990 (abolition of stamp duty for securities etc).

Amendments—[1] Sub-s (5)(*b*) repealed by the Trusts of Land and Appointment of Trustees Act 1996 s 25(2), Sch 4 with effect from 1 January 1997 (by virtue of SI 1996/2974), subject to savings in s 25(4), (5).

[2] Sub-ss (1)–(4) substituted by sub-s (1) by FA 1999 s 112(4), Sch 14 para 25 with effect in relation to instruments executed after 30 September 1999. This does not apply to transfers or other instruments relating to units under a unit trust scheme by virtue of FA 1999 s 122. Previously the text read:

"(1) This section applies where—

(*a*) apart from this section stamp duty under any of the headings mentioned in subsection (3) below would be chargeable on an instrument to which this section applies, and

(*b*) the condition mentioned in subsection (4) below is fulfilled.

(2) In such a case stamp duty under the heading concerned shall not be chargeable on the instrument.

(3) The headings are the following headings in Schedule 1 to the Stamp Act 1891—

(*a*) the heading "conveyance or transfer on sale";

(*b*) the heading "conveyance or transfer of any kind not hereinbefore described";

(*c*) the heading beginning "declaration of any use or trust";

(*d*) the heading beginning "disposition in Scotland of any property";

(*e*) …;

(*f*) the heading "partition or division";

(*g*) the heading "release or renunciation of any property, or of any right or interest in any property";

(*h*) the heading "surrender".

(4) The condition is that the property concerned consists entirely of exempt property; …"

111 Stamp duty reduced in certain cases

(1) This section applies where—

(*a*) stamp duty under [Part I of Schedule 13 to the Finance Act 1999 ([transfer][2] on sale)][1] is chargeable on an instrument to which this section applies, and

(*b*) part of the property concerned consists of exempt property.

(2) In such a case—

(*a*) the consideration in respect of which duty would be charged (apart from this section) shall be apportioned, on such basis as is just and reasonable, as between the part of the property which consists of exempt property and the part which does not, and

(*b*) the instrument shall be charged only in respect of the consideration attributed to such of the property as is not exempt property.

(3) In this section "exempt property" has the same meaning as in section 110 above.

(4) This section applies to—

(*a*) an instrument executed in pursuance of a contract made on or after the abolition day;

(*b*) an instrument which is not executed in pursuance of a contract and is executed on or after the abolition day.

(5) In this section "the abolition day" has the same meaning as in section 110 above.

Amendments—[1] Words in sub-s (1) substituted by FA 1999 s 112(4), Sch 14 para 26 with effect in relation to instruments executed after 30 September 1999. This does not apply to transfers or other instruments relating to units under a unit trust scheme by virtue of FA 1999 s 122. Previously the text read 'the heading "conveyance or transfer on sale" in Schedule 1 to the Stamp Act 1891'.

[2] The word "transfer" substituted for the words "conveyance or transfer" in enactments relating to stamp duty by FA 2003 Sch 20 para 3.

112 Apportionment of consideration for stamp duty purposes

(1) Subsection (2) below applies where part of the property referred to in section 58(1) of the Stamp Act 1891 (consideration to be apportioned between different instruments as parties think fit) consists of exempt property.

(2) Section 58 (1) shall have effect as if "the parties think fit" read "is just and reasonable".

(3) Subsection (4) below applies where—

(*a*) part of the property referred to in section 58(2) of the Stamp Act 1891 (property contracted to be purchased by two or more persons etc) consists of exempt property, and

(*b*) both or (as the case may be) all the relevant persons are connected with one another.

(4) Section 58(2) shall have effect as if the words from "for distinct parts of the consideration" to the end of the subsection read ", the consideration is to be apportioned in such manner as is just and reasonable, so that a distinct consideration for each separate part or parcel is set forth in the conveyance relating thereto, and such conveyance is to be charged with *ad valorem* duty in respect of such distinct consideration".

(5) In a case where subsection (2) or (4) above applies and the consideration is apportioned in a manner that is not just and reasonable, the enactments relating to stamp duty shall have effect as if—

(*a*) the consideration had been apportioned in a manner that is just and reasonable, and

(*b*) the amount of any distinct consideration set forth in any conveyance relating to a separate part or parcel of property were such amount as is found by a just and reasonable apportionment (and not the amount actually set forth).

(6) In this section "exempt property" has the same meaning as in section 110 above.

(7) For the purposes of subsection (3) above—

(*a*) a person is a relevant person if he is a person by or for whom the property is contracted to be purchased;

(*b*) the question whether persons are connected with one another shall be determined in accordance with section 839 of the Taxes Act 1988.

(8) This section applies where the contract concerned is made on or after the abolition day.

(9) In this section "the abolition day" has the same meaning as in section 110 above.

113 Certification of instruments for stamp duty purposes

[(1) For the purposes of paragraph 6(1) of Schedule 13 to the Finance Act 1999 (meaning of instrument being certified at an amount)—

(*a*) a sale or contract or agreement for the sale of exempt property within the meaning of section 110 above shall be disregarded; and

(*b*) any statement as mentioned in that provision shall be construed as leaving out of account any matter which is to be so disregarded.][1]

(2), (3) …[1]

(4) This section applies to—

(*a*) an instrument executed in pursuance of a contract made on or after the abolition day;

(*b*) an instrument which is not executed in pursuance of a contract and is executed on or after the abolition day.

(5) In this section "the abolition day" has the same meaning as in section 110 above.

Amendments—[1] Sub-ss (1)–(3) substituted by sub-s (1) by FA 1999 s 112(4), Sch 14 para 27 with effect in relation to instruments executed after 30 September 1999. This does not apply to transfers or other instruments relating to units under a unit trust scheme by virtue of FA 1999 s 122. Previously the text read:

"(1) Section 34 of the Finance Act 1958 and section 7 of the Finance Act (Northern Ireland) 1958 shall be amended as mentioned in subsections (2) and (3) below.

(2) In subsection (4) of each of those sections (certification of instrument at a particular amount) the following paragraph shall be substituted for paragraph (a)—

"(*a*) any sale or contract or agreement for the sale of exempt property shall be disregarded; and".

(3) In each of those sections the following subsection shall be inserted after subsection (4)—

'(4A) In subsection (4) above "exempt property" has the same meaning as in section 110 of the Finance Act 1991.'"

114 Acquisition under statute: exempt property

(1)–(3) …[1]

(4) This section applies where the Act mentioned in section 12 of the Finance Act 1895, and by virtue of which property is vested or a person is authorised to purchase property, is passed on or after the abolition day.

(5) In this section "the abolition day" has the same meaning as in section 110 above.

Note—Sub-ss (1)–(3) amend FA 1949 s 36 and FA(NI)1949 s 9.

115 Northern Ireland bank notes: duty abolished

Amendments—This section repealed by FA 1999 Sch 20 Pt V(2) with effect in relation to instruments executed, or bearer instruments issued, from 1 October 1999, subject to the provisions in FA 1999 Sch 20 Pt V(2) Note 2. Previously the text read:

"(1) In its application to Northern Ireland, the Stamp Act 1891 shall have effect with the omission from Schedule 1 of the heading "bank note".

(2) The licences required to be taken out under the Bankers' Composition (Ireland) Act 1828 (licences for bankers in Northern Ireland issuing certain promissory notes) are hereby abolished.
(3) This section takes effect on 1st January 1992."

116 Investment exchanges and clearing houses: stamp duty

(1) The Treasury may make regulations providing as mentioned in this section with regard to any circumstances which—

(*a*) would (apart from the regulations) give rise to a charge to stamp duty,
(*b*) involve a prescribed recognised investment exchange or a prescribed recognised clearing house, or a member or nominee (or member or nominee of a prescribed description) of such an exchange, or a nominee (or nominee of a prescribed description) of such a clearing house, or a nominee (or nominee of a prescribed description) of a member of such an exchange, and
(*c*) are such as are prescribed.

(2) The regulations may provide that the charge to stamp duty shall be treated as not arising or (depending on the terms of the regulations) as reduced.

(3) Regulations under this section—

(*a*) shall be made by statutory instrument subject to annulment in pursuance of a resolution of the House of Commons;
(*b*) may include such supplementary, incidental, consequential or transitional provisions as appear to the Treasury to be necessary or expedient;
(*c*) may make different provision for different circumstances;
(*d*) may make any provision in such way as the Treasury think fit (whether by amending enactments or otherwise).

(4) In this section—

[(*aa*) "the Directive" means Directive 2004/39/EC of the European Parliament and of the Council of 21 April 2004 on markets in financial instruments, as amended from time to time,][2]
(*a*) "prescribed" means prescribed by the regulations,
(*b*) "recognised investment exchange" means a recognised investment exchange within the meaning of the [Financial Services and Markets Act 2000][1][, a regulated market within the meaning of the Directive or a multilateral trading facility within the meaning of the Directive][2] and
(*c*) "recognised clearing house" means a recognised clearing house within the meaning of that Act.

Regulations—See Stamp Duty and Stamp Duty Reserve Tax (Investment Exchanges and Clearing Houses) Regulations, SI 1997/2429 and SI 1999/3263.
Stamp Duty and Stamp Duty Reserve Tax (Investment Exchanges and Clearing Houses) (Jiway Limited) Regulations, SI 2000/2995.
Stamp Duty Reserve Tax (Investment Exchanges and Clearing Houses) (The London Stock Exchange) Regulations, SI 2001/255.
Stamp Duty and Stamp Duty Reserve Tax (Investment Exchanges and Clearing Houses) Regulations, SI 2004/3218.
Stamp Duty and Stamp Duty Reserve Tax (Investment Exchanges and Clearing Houses) (Eurex Clearing AG) Regulations, SI 2007/1097.
Stamp Duty and Stamp Duty Reserve Tax (Investment Exchanges and Clearing Houses) (European Central Counterparty Limited and the Turquoise Multilateral Trading Facility) Regulations, SI 2008/1814.
Stamp Duty and Stamp Duty Reserve Tax (Investment Exchanges and Clearing Houses) Regulations, SI 2008/2777.
Stamp Duty and Stamp Duty Reserve Tax (Investment Exchanges and Clearing Houses) Regulations (No 2), SI 2008/3235.
Stamp Duty and Stamp Duty Reserve Tax (Investment Exchanges and Clearing Houses) Regulations, SI 2009/35.
Stamp Duty and Stamp Duty Reserve Tax (Investment Exchanges and Clearing Houses) Regulations (No 2), SI 2009/194.
Stamp Duty and Stamp Duty Reserve Tax (Investment Exchanges and Clearing Houses) Regulations (No 3), SI 2009/397.
Stamp Duty and Stamp Duty Reserve Tax (Investment Exchanges and Clearing Houses) Regulations (No 4), SI 2009/1115.
Stamp Duty and Stamp Duty Reserve Tax (Investment Exchanges and Clearing Houses) Regulations (No 5), SI 2009/1344.
Stamp Duty and Stamp Duty Reserve Tax (Investment Exchanges and Clearing Houses) Regulations (No 6), SI 2009/1462.
Stamp Duty and Stamp Duty Reserve Tax (Investment Exchanges and Clearing Houses) Regulations (No 7), SI 2009/1601.
Stamp Duty and Stamp Duty Reserve Tax (Investment Exchanges and Clearing Houses) Regulations (No 8), SI 1827.
Stamp Duty and Stamp Duty Reserve Tax (Investment Exchanges and Clearing Houses) Regulations (No 9), SI 2009/1828.
Stamp Duty and Stamp Duty Reserve Tax (Investment Exchanges and Clearing Houses) Regulations (No 10), SI 2009/1831.
Stamp Duty and Stamp Duty Reserve Tax (Investment Exchanges and Clearing Houses) Regulations (No 11), SI 2009/1832.
Amendments—[1] Words substituted by the Financial Services and Markets Act 2000 s 432(1), Sch 20 para 5 with effect from 1 December 2001 (by virtue of SI 2001/3538).
[2] In sub-s (4), para (*aa*) inserted, and words in para (*b*) inserted, by FA 2007 s 73, Sch 21 para 7 with effect from 19 July 2007.

117 Investment exchanges and clearing houses: SDRT

(1) The Treasury may make regulations providing as mentioned in this section with regard to any circumstances which—

(*a*) would (apart from the regulations) give rise to a charge to stamp duty reserve tax,
(*b*) involve a prescribed recognised investment exchange or a prescribed recognised clearing house, or a member or nominee (or member of nominee of a prescribed description) of such an exchange, or a nominee (or nominee of a prescribed description) of such a clearing house, or a nominee (or nominee of a prescribed description) of a member of such an exchange, and
(*c*) are such as are prescribed.

(2) The regulations may provide that the charge to stamp duty reserve tax shall be treated as not arising or (depending on the terms of the regulations) as reduced.

(3) Subsections (3) and (4) of section 116 above shall apply for the purposes of this section as they apply for the purposes of that.

Regulations—See Stamp Duty and Stamp Duty Reserve Tax (Investment Exchanges and Clearing Houses) Regulations, SI 1997/2429 and SI 1999/3263.
Stamp Duty Reserve Tax (virt-x Exchange Ltd) Regulations, SI 1995/2051.
Stamp Duty and Stamp Duty Reserve Tax (Investment Exchanges and Clearing Houses) (Jiway Limited) Regulations, SI 2000/2995.
Stamp Duty Reserve Tax (Investment Exchanges and Clearing Houses) (The London Stock Exchange) Regulations, SI 2001/255.
Stamp Duty and Stamp Duty Reserve Tax (Investment Exchanges and Clearing Houses) Regulations, SI 2004/3218.
Stamp Duty and Stamp Duty Reserve Tax (Investment Exchanges and Clearing Houses) (Eurex Clearing AG) Regulations, SI 2007/1097.
Stamp Duty and Stamp Duty Reserve Tax (Investment Exchanges and Clearing Houses) (European Central Counterparty Limited and the Turquoise Multilateral Trading Facility) Regulations, SI 2008/1814.
Stamp Duty and Stamp Duty Reserve Tax (Investment Exchanges and Clearing Houses) Regulations, SI 2008/2777.
Stamp Duty and Stamp Duty Reserve Tax (Investment Exchanges and Clearing Houses) Regulations, SI 2009/35.
Stamp Duty and Stamp Duty Reserve Tax (Investment Exchanges and Clearing Houses) Regulations (No 2), SI 2009/194.
Stamp Duty and Stamp Duty Reserve Tax (Investment Exchanges and Clearing Houses) Regulations (No 3), SI 2009/397.
Stamp Duty and Stamp Duty Reserve Tax (Investment Exchanges and Clearing Houses) Regulations (No 4), SI 2009/1115.
Stamp Duty and Stamp Duty Reserve Tax (Investment Exchanges and Clearing Houses) Regulations (No 5), SI 2009/1344.
Stamp Duty and Stamp Duty Reserve Tax (Investment Exchanges and Clearing Houses) Regulations (No 6), SI 2009/1462.
Stamp Duty and Stamp Duty Reserve Tax (Investment Exchanges and Clearing Houses) Regulations (No 7), SI 2009/1601.
Stamp Duty and Stamp Duty Reserve Tax (Investment Exchanges and Clearing Houses) Regulations (No 8), SI 1827.
Stamp Duty and Stamp Duty Reserve Tax (Investment Exchanges and Clearing Houses) Regulations (No 9), SI 2009/1828.
Stamp Duty and Stamp Duty Reserve Tax (Investment Exchanges and Clearing Houses) Regulations (No 10), SI 2009/1831.
Stamp Duty and Stamp Duty Reserve Tax (Investment Exchanges and Clearing Houses) Regulations (No 11), SI 2009/1832.

FINANCE (NO 2) ACT 1992

(1992 Chapter 48)

Note—This Act received Royal Assent on 16 July 1992.

SCHEDULE 17

NORTHERN IRELAND ELECTRICITY

Section 77

Interpretation

1— (1) In this Schedule—

"the final accounting period" means the last complete accounting period of NIE ending before the transfer date;

"NIE" means Northern Ireland Electricity;

"the Order" means the Electricity (Northern Ireland) Order 1992;

"successor company" means a company nominated under Article 69(2) of the Order for the purposes of Article 69(1) of the Order;

"transfer date" means the day appointed under Article 69(3) of the Order for the purposes of Article 69(4) of the Order;

"transfer scheme" means a scheme under Article 69(1) of the Order.

(2) This Schedule, so far as it relates to corporation tax on chargeable gains, shall be construed as one with the Capital Gains Tax Act 1979 or, where appropriate, the Taxation of Chargeable Gains Act 1992.

(3) For the purposes of this Schedule a transfer or agreement shall be regarded as made in pursuance of Schedule 10 to the Order if the making of that transfer or agreement is required or authorised by or under paragraph 3 or 5 of that Schedule (allocation of assets and liabilities and variation of transfers by agreement).

Stamp duty reserve tax

9— (1) No agreement made for the purposes of or for purposes connected with the transfer scheme shall give rise to a charge to stamp duty reserve tax.

(2) No agreement which is made in pursuance of Schedule 10 to the Order shall give rise to a charge to stamp duty reserve tax.

(3) This paragraph shall be deemed to have come into force on 1st April 1992.

FINANCE ACT 1993

(1993 Chapter 34)

Note—This Act received Royal Assent on 27 July 1993.

PART V
STAMP DUTY

201 Increase in stamp duty threshold

Amendments—This section repealed by FA 1999 Sch 20 Pt V(2) with effect in relation to instruments executed, or bearer instruments issued, from 1 October 1999, subject to the provisions in FA 1999 Sch 20 Pt V(2) Note 2. Previously the text read:

"(1) (*amends* FA 1963 s 55(1), (2) and FA (Northern Ireland) 1963, s 4(1), (2)).

(2) This section applies to—

(*a*) instruments executed on or after 16th March 1993 and before 23rd March 1993 and not stamped before 23rd March 1993;

(*b*) instruments executed on or after 23rd March 1993.

(3) For the purposes of section 14(4) of the Stamp Act 1891 (instruments not to be given in evidence etc unless stamped in accordance with the law in force at the time of first execution) the law in force at the time of execution of an instrument falling within subsection (2)(*a*) above shall be deemed to be that as varied in accordance with subsection (1) above.

(4) This section shall be deemed to have come into force on 23rd March 1993."

202 Rent to mortgage: England and Wales

(1) Subsection (2) below applies where—

(*a*) a person exercises the right to acquire on rent to mortgage terms under Part V of the Housing Act 1985 and

(*b*) in pursuance of the exercise of that right a conveyance of the freehold is executed in his favour as regards the dwelling-house concerned.

(2) For the purposes of the enactments relating to stamp duty chargeable under [Part I of Schedule 13 to the Finance Act 1999 ([transfer][2] on sale)][1], the consideration for the sale shall be taken to be equal to the price which, by virtue of section 126 of the Housing Act 1985 would be payable for the dwelling-house on a conveyance if the person were exercising the right to buy under Part V of that Act.

(3) Subsection (4) below applies where—

(*a*) a person exercises the right to acquire on rent to mortgage terms under Part V of the Housing Act 1985 and

(*b*) in pursuance of the exercise of that right a lease is executed in his favour as regards the dwelling-house concerned.

(4) In such a case—

(*a*) the lease shall not be chargeable with stamp duty under [Part II of Schedule 13 to the Finance Act 1999 (lease)][2] but shall be chargeable with stamp duty under [Part I of that Schedule ([transfer][3] on sale)][2] as if it were a conveyance on sale;

(*b*) for the purposes of the enactments relating to stamp duty chargeable under [Part I of that Schedule][2] the consideration for the sale mentioned in paragraph (*a*) above shall be taken to be equal to the price which, by virtue of section 126 of the Housing Act 1985 would be payable for the dwelling-house on a grant if the person were exercising the right to buy under Part V of that Act.

(5) This section shall apply where the conveyance or lease is executed after the day on which this Act is passed.

Amendments—[1] Words in sub-s (2) substituted by FA 1999 s 112(4), Sch 14 para 28 with effect in relation to instruments executed after 30 September 1999. This does not apply to transfers or other instruments relating to units under a unit trust scheme by virtue of FA 1999 s 122. Previously the text read 'the heading "Conveyance or Transfer on Sale" in Schedule 1 to the Stamp Act 1891'.

[2] Words in sub-s (4) substituted by FA 1999 s 112(4), Sch 14 para 28 with effect in relation to instruments executed after 30 September 1999. This does not apply to transfers or other instruments relating to units under a unit trust scheme by virtue of FA 1999 s 122. Previously the text read 'the heading "Lease or Tack" in Schedule 1 to the Stamp Act 1891', 'the heading "Conveyance or Transfer on Sale" in that Schedule' and 'the heading "Conveyance or Transfer on Sale" ' respectively.

[3] The word "transfer" substituted for the words "conveyance or transfer" in enactments relating to stamp duty by FA 2003 Sch 20 para 3.

203 Rent to loan: Scotland

(1) Subsection (2) below applies where—

(*a*) a person exercises the right to purchase a house by way of the rent to loan scheme under Part III of the Housing (Scotland) Act 1987 and

(*b*) in pursuance of the exercise of that right a heritable disposition of the house is executed in favour of him.

(2) For the purposes of the enactments relating to stamp duty chargeable under [Part I of Schedule 13 to the Finance Act 1999 ([transfer][2] on sale)][1], the consideration for the sale shall be taken to be equal to the price which, by virtue of section 62 of the Housing (Scotland) Act 1987 would be payable for the house if the person were exercising the right to purchase under section 61 of that Act.

(3) This section shall apply where the disposition is executed after the day on which this Act is passed.

Amendments—[1] Words in sub-s (2) substituted by FA 1999 s 112(4), Sch 14 para 29 with effect in relation to instruments executed after 30 September 1999. This does not apply to transfers or other instruments relating to units under a unit trust scheme by virtue of FA 1999 s 122. Previously the text read 'the heading "Conveyance or Transfer on Sale" in Schedule 1 to the Stamp Act 1891'.

[2] The word "transfer" substituted for the words "conveyance or transfer" in enactments relating to stamp duty by FA 2003 Sch 20 para 3.

204 Method of denoting stamp duty

(1) The Treasury may make regulations as to the method by which stamp duty is to be denoted.

(2) In particular, regulations under this section may—

(*a*) provide for duty to be denoted by impressed stamps or adhesive stamps or by a record printed or made by a machine or implement or by such other method as may be prescribed;
(*b*) provide for one method only to be used, whether generally or in prescribed cases;
(*c*) provide for alternative methods to be available, whether generally or in prescribed cases;
(*d*) make different provision for different cases;

and cases may be designated by reference to the type of instrument concerned, the geographical area involved, or such other factors as the Treasury think fit.

(3) Regulations under this section may provide that where stamp duty is denoted by a method which (in the case of the instrument concerned) is required or permitted by the law in force at the time it is stamped, for the purposes of section 14(4) of the Stamp Act 1891 (instruments not to be given in evidence etc unless stamped in accordance with the law in force at the time of *first*[1] execution) the method shall be treated as being in accordance with the law in force at the time when the instrument was *first*[1] executed.

(4) Regulations under this section may include such supplementary, incidental, consequential or transitional provisions as appear to the Treasury to be necessary or expedient.

(5) Regulations under this section may make provision in such way as the Treasury think fit, and in particular may amend or repeal or modify the effect of any provision of any Act.

(6) In this section "prescribed" means prescribed by regulations under this section.

(7) The power to make regulations under this section shall be exercisable by statutory instrument subject to annulment in pursuance of a resolution of the House of Commons.

Amendments—[1] Words in sub-s (3) repealed by FA 2000 s 156, Sch 40 Pt III with effect from 28 July 2000.

PART VI

MISCELLANEOUS AND GENERAL

Statutory effect of resolutions etc

205 The 1968 Act

(1) The Provisional Collection of Taxes Act 1968 shall be amended as follows.

(2)–(3) (*not relevant to stamp duty*).

(4)–(5) (*amend* PCTA 1968 s 1).

(6) (*not relevant to stamp duty*).

(7) This section shall apply in relation to resolutions passed after the day on which this Act is passed.

207 Stamp duty

(1) (*amends* FA 1973 s 50(2)).

(2) This section shall apply in relation to resolutions passed after the day on which this Act is passed.

FINANCE ACT 1994

(1994 Chapter 9)

An Act to grant certain duties, to alter other duties, and to amend the law relating to the National Debt and the Public Revenue, and to make further provision in connection with Finance.

[3rd May 1994]

PART VI

[STAMP DUTY][1]

Amendments—[1] Part Heading substituted by F(No 2)A 2005 s 48(3), (5) with effect from a date to be appointed. Heading previously read "Stamp duty and stamp duty land tax".

239 Execution of deeds

(1) (*amends* SA 1891, s 122).

(2) (*amends* SDMA 1891, s 27).

(3) This section shall apply to any instrument except one which, on or before 7th December 1993, has been executed for the purposes of the Stamp Act 1891 as that Act has effect before amendment by this section.

[240 Time for presenting agreement for lease][1]

[(1) This section applies if there are presented for stamping at the same time in pursuance of Schedule 13 to the Finance Act 1999—

(*a*) an agreement for a lease, and

(*b*) the lease which gives effect to the agreement,

and the duty (if any) chargeable on the agreement is paid.

(2) Section 15A of that Act (interest payable on late stamping) applies in relation to the agreement as if the reference to the day on which the instrument was executed were to the day on which the lease was executed.

(3) For the purposes of section 15B of that Act (penalty on late stamping) the agreement is treated—

(*a*) as if it had been executed at the same time and place as the lease, and

(*b*) where the lease was executed outside the United Kingdom, as if it had been first received in the United Kingdom at the same time as the lease.

(4) For the purposes of this section a lease gives effect to an agreement if the lease is granted subsequent to the agreement and either is in conformity with the agreement or relates to substantially the same property and term as the agreement.

(5) References in this section to an agreement for a lease include missives of let in Scotland.][1]

Amendments—[1] This section substituted by FA 1999 s 109(3), Sch 12 para 4 with effect in relation to instruments executed after 30 September 1999. This does not apply to transfers or other instruments relating to units under a unit trust scheme by virtue of FA 1999 s 122. Previously the text read:

"240 Time for presenting agreements for leases

(1) If there are presented for stamping at the same time in pursuance of the Stamp Act 1891—

(*a*) an agreement for a lease or tack, and

(*b*) the lease or tack which gives effect to the agreement,

and the duty (if any) chargeable on the agreement is paid, the agreement shall be treated for the purposes of section 15 of that Act (penalty upon stamping instruments after execution) as if it had been first executed when the lease or tack which gives effect to the agreement was first executed.

(2) No lease or tack shall be treated as duly stamped unless—

(*a*) it contains a certificate that there is no agreement to which it gives effect, or

(*b*) it is stamped with a stamp denoting—

(i) that there is an agreement to which it gives effect which is not chargeable with duty, or

(ii) the duty paid on the agreement to which it gives effect.

(3) For the purposes of this section a lease or tack gives effect to an agreement if the lease or tack is granted subsequent to the agreement and either is in conformity with the agreement or relates to substantially the same property and term as the agreement.

(4) Subsection (1) above shall apply to agreements executed on or after 6th May 1994; and subsection (2) above shall apply to any lease or tack executed on or after that day."

[240A Requirements before lease treated as duly stamped][1]

[(1) A lease shall not be treated as duly stamped unless—

(*a*) it contains a certificate that there is no agreement to which it gives effect, or

(*b*) it is stamped with a stamp denoting—

(i) that there is an agreement to which it gives effect which is not chargeable with duty, or

(ii) the duty paid on the agreement to which it gives effect.

(2) For the purposes of this section a lease gives effect to an agreement if the lease is granted subsequent to the agreement and either is in conformity with the agreement or relates to substantially the same property and term as the agreement.

(3) References in this section to a lease do not include, and references in this section to an agreement do include, missives of let in Scotland.][1]

Amendments—[1] This section inserted by FA 1999 s 109(3), Sch 12 para 4 with effect in relation to instruments executed after 30 September 1999. This does not apply to transfers or other instruments relating to units under a unit trust scheme by virtue of FA 1999 s 122.

241 Exchange, partition, etc

(1) Where—

(*a*) the consideration for the transfer or vesting of any estate or interest in land or the grant of any [lease][1] consists of or includes any property, and

(*b*) for the purposes of stamp duty chargeable under or by reference to [Part I of Schedule 13 to the Finance Act 1999 ([transfer][3] on sale)][1] no amount or value is, apart from this section, attributed to that property on that transfer, vesting or grant,

Stamp Taxes

then, for those purposes, the consideration or, as the case may be, the consideration so far as relating to that property shall be taken to be the market value of the property immediately before the instrument in question is executed and accordingly the instrument shall be charged with *ad valorem* duty under that heading.

(2) For the purposes of this section the market value of property at any time is the price which that property might reasonably be expected to fetch on a sale at that time in the open market.

(3)–(5) …[2]

(6) This section shall apply to instruments executed after 7th December 1993, not being instruments executed in pursuance of a contract made before 30th November 1993.

Press releases etc—IR Tax Bulletin August 1995 (general guidance on stamp duty on exchanges of interests in land and buildings).

Amendments—[1] Words in sub-s (1) substituted by FA 1999 s 112(4), Sch 14 para 30 with effect in relation to instruments executed after 30 September 1999. This does not apply to transfers or other instruments relating to units under a unit trust scheme by virtue of FA 1999 s 122. Previously the text read 'lease or tack' and 'the heading "Conveyance or Transfer on Sale" in Schedule 1 to the Stamp Act 1891' respectively.

[2] Sub-ss (3)–(5) repealed by FA 1999 Sch 20 Pt V(2) with effect in relation to instruments executed, or bearer instruments issued, from 1 October 1999, subject to the provisions in FA 1999 Sch 20 Pt V(2) Note 2. Previously the text read:

"(3) Stamp duty shall not be chargeable under the heading "Exchange or Excambion" in Schedule 1 to the Stamp Act 1891, and section 73 of that Act (exchange and partition or division) shall cease to apply to the exchange of property; …

(4), (5) …".

[3] The word "transfer" substituted for the words "conveyance or transfer" in enactments relating to stamp duty by FA 2003 Sch 20 para 3.

242 Where consideration not ascertainable from conveyance or lease

(1) Where, for the purposes of stamp duty chargeable under or by reference to [Part I of Schedule 13 to the Finance Act 1999 ([transfer][3] on sale)][2], the consideration, or any part of the consideration, for—

(*a*) the transfer or vesting of any estate or interest in land, or

(*b*) the grant of any [lease][1],

cannot, apart from this subsection, be ascertained at the time the instrument in question is executed, the consideration for the transfer, vesting or grant shall for those purposes be taken to be the market value immediately before the instrument is executed of the estate or interest transferred or vested or, as the case may be, the [lease][1] granted.

(2) Where, for the purposes of stamp duty chargeable under [paragraph 12 of Schedule 13 to the Finance Act 1999][2], the rent, or any part of the rent, payable under any [lease][1] cannot, apart from this subsection, be ascertained at the time it is executed, the rent shall for those purposes be taken to be the market rent at that time.

(3) For the purposes of this section—

(*a*) the cases where consideration or rent cannot be ascertained at any time do not include cases where the consideration or rent could be ascertained on the assumption that any future event mentioned in the instrument in question were or were not to occur, and

(*b*) the market rent of a [lease][1] at any time is the rent which the [lease][1] might reasonably be expected to fetch at that time in the open market,

and in this section "market value" has the same meaning as in section 241 above.

(4) This section shall apply to instruments executed after 7th December 1993.

Press releases etc—IR Tax Bulletin August 1995 (general guidance on stamp duty where the consideration is unascertainable).

Amendments—[1] "Lease" substituted for the words "lease or tack" throughout the section by FA 1999 s 112(4), Sch 14 para 31 with effect in relation to instruments executed after 30 September 1999. This does not apply to transfers or other instruments relating to units under a unit trust scheme by virtue of FA 1999 s 122.

[2] Words in sub-ss (1) and (2) substituted by FA 1999 s 112(4), Sch 14 para 31 with effect in relation to instruments executed after 30 September 1999. This does not apply to transfers or other instruments relating to units under a unit trust scheme by virtue of FA 1999 s 122. Previously the text read 'the heading "Conveyance or Transfer on Sale" in Schedule 1 to the Stamp Act 1891' and 'paragraph (3) of the heading "Lease or Tack" in Schedule 1 to that Act' respectively.

[3] The word "transfer" substituted for the words "conveyance or transfer" in enactments relating to stamp duty by FA 2003 Sch 20 para 3.

243 Agreements to surrender leases

(1) Where, in pursuance of any agreement, any lease is surrendered (or, in Scotland, renounced) at any time otherwise than by deed, the agreement shall be treated for the purposes of [stamp duty][1] as if it were a deed executed at that time effecting the surrender (or, as the case may be, renunciation).

(2) This section shall apply to any agreement made after 7th December 1993.

Press releases etc—IR Tax Bulletin August 1995 paras 25, 26 (documents which merely record an agreement to surrender may be stampable).

Amendments—[1] Words in sub-s (1) substituted by FA 1999 s 112(4), Sch 14 para 32 with effect in relation to instruments executed after 30 September 1999. This does not apply to transfers or other instruments relating to units under a unit trust scheme by virtue of FA 1999 s 122. Previously the text read 'any duty chargeable under the Stamp Act 1891'.

244 Production of documents on transfer of land in Northern Ireland

(1) Subject to section 245 below, on the occasion of—

(*a*) any transfer on sale of any freehold interest in land in Northern Ireland, or

(*b*) the grant, or any transfer on sale, of any lease of such land,

the transferee, lessee or proposed lessee shall produce to the Commissioners the instrument by means of which the transfer is effected or the lease granted or agreed to be granted, as the case may be.

(2) Any transferee, lessee or proposed lessee required to produce any instrument under subsection (1) above shall produce with it a document (signed by him or by some person on his behalf and showing his address) giving such particulars as may be prescribed.

(3) Any person who, within thirty days—

(*a*) after the execution of an instrument which he is required under subsection (1) above to produce, or

(*b*) in the case of such an instrument executed at a place outside Northern Ireland, after it is first received in Northern Ireland,

fails to comply with that subsection or subsection (2) above shall be liable on summary conviction to a fine not exceeding level 1 on the standard scale.

(4) Where any agreement for any lease of land in Northern Ireland is produced to the Commissioners together with a document (signed as mentioned in subsection (2) above) giving such particulars as may be prescribed—

(*a*) it shall not be necessary to produce to them the instrument granting the lease, or any further such document as is referred to in that subsection, unless that instrument is inconsistent with the agreement, but

(*b*) the Commissioners shall, if any such instrument is produced to them and application is made for that purpose, denote on the instrument that it has been produced to them.

(5) Notwithstanding anything in section 12 of the Stamp Act 1891, no instrument required by this section to be produced to the Commissioners shall be deemed, for the purposes of section 14 of that Act, to be duly stamped unless it is stamped with a stamp denoting that the instrument has been so produced.

Notes—This section came into force on 4 November 1996 by virtue of Finance Act 1994, sections 244 and 245, (Commencement) Order, SI 1996/2316.

Cross references—See Stamp Duty (Production of Documents) (Northern Ireland) Regulations, SI 1996/2348, Reg 3, Sch (particulars to be given in a document produced pursuant to sub-s (2) above).

245 Production of documents: supplementary

(1) Section 244 above shall not apply to any instrument (an "exempt instrument") falling within any prescribed class; but regulations may, in respect of exempt instruments or such descriptions of exempt instruments as may be prescribed, require such a document as is mentioned in subsection (2) of that section to be furnished in accordance with the regulations to the Commissioner of Valuation for Northern Ireland.

[(2) The information contained in any document produced to the Commissioners under section 244(2) above shall be available for use by the Commissioner of Valuation for Northern Ireland.][2]

(3) Any person who fails to comply with any requirement imposed by virtue of subsection (1) above shall be liable on summary conviction to a fine not exceeding level 3 on the standard scale.

(4) Section 244 above shall also not apply to any instrument which relates solely to—

(*a*) incorporeal hereditaments or to a grave or right of burial,...[1]

(*b*) land subject to land purchase annuities which are registered in the Land Registry in Northern Ireland[, or

(*c*) an SDLT transaction within the meaning of paragraph 1(2) of Schedule 19 to the Finance Act 2003.][1]

(5) In this section and section 244 above—

"lease"—

(*a*) includes an underlease or other tenancy and an agreement for a lease, underlease or tenancy, but

(*b*) does not include a mortgage, charge or lien on any property for securing money or money's worth,

and "lessee" and "grant" shall be construed accordingly,

"prescribed" means prescribed by regulations, and

"regulations" means regulations made by the Commissioners under this section.

(6) The power to make regulations under this section shall be exercisable by statutory instrument which shall be subject to annulment in pursuance of a resolution of the House of Commons.

(7) Regulations under this section may make different provision for different cases.

(8) This section and section 244 above shall come into force on such day as the Treasury may by order made by statutory instrument appoint.

Notes—This section came into force on 4 November 1996 by virtue of Finance Act 1994, sections 244 and 245, (Commencement) Order, SI 1996/2316.

Cross references—See Stamp Duty (Production of Documents) (Northern Ireland) Regulations, SI 1996/2348, Reg 4–6, (classes of instruments which are exempt instruments for the purposes of sub-s (1) above and certain documents to be produced to the Registrar of Titles or the Registrar of Deeds and then furnished by the registrar to the Commissioner of Valuation for Northern Ireland under sub-s (2) above).

Amendments—[1] In sub-s (4), word in para (*a*) repealed, word in para (*b*) inserted, and para (*c*) inserted by the Stamp Duty Land Tax (Consequential Amendment of Enactments) Regulations, SI 2003/2867, reg 2, Schedule, para 22 with effect from 1 December 2003.

[2] Sub-s (2) substituted by F(No 2)A 2005 s 48(2), (5) with effect from a date to be appointed. Sub-s (2) previously read as follows—

"(2) The information contained in[—

(*a*)] any document produced to the Commissioners under section 244(2) above[, or]

[(*b*) any return delivered to the Commissioners under Part 4 of the Finance Act 2003 (stamp duty land tax),]

shall be available for use by the Commissioner of Valuation for Northern Ireland.".

PART VIII
MISCELLANEOUS AND GENERAL

General

257 Interpretation and construction

(1), (2) (*not relevant to stamp duty*).

(3) Part VI of this Act shall be construed as one with the Stamp Act 1891.

FINANCE ACT 1995

(1995 Chapter 4)

An Act to grant certain duties, to alter other duties, and to amend the law relating to the National Debt and the Public Revenue, and to make further provision in connection with Finance.

[1st May 1995]

PART V
STAMP DUTY

149 Transfer: associated bodies

(1)–(5) (*amend* FA 1930 s 42).

(6) (*amends* FA 1967 s 27).

(7) This section shall apply in relation to instruments executed on or after the day on which this Act is passed.

151 [Lease][2]: associated bodies

(1) Stamp duty under [Part II of Schedule 13 to the Finance Act 1999 (lease)][1] shall not be chargeable on an instrument which is—

(*a*) a [lease][2],

(*b*) an agreement for a [lease][2], or

(*c*) an agreement with respect to a letting,

as respects which the condition in subsection (2) below is satisfied.

[This subsection is subject to subsection (4A) below.][3]

(2) The condition is that it is shown to the satisfaction of the Commissioners of Inland Revenue that—

(*a*) the lessor is a body corporate and the lessee is another body corporate,

(*b*) those bodies are associated at the time the instrument is executed,

(*c*) in the case of an agreement, the agreement is for the [lease][2] or letting to be granted to the lessee or to a body corporate which is associated with the lessee at the time the instrument is executed, and

(*d*) the instrument is not executed in pursuance of or in connection with an arrangement falling within subsection (3) below.

(3) An arrangement falls within this subsection if it is one under which—

(*a*) the consideration, or any part of the consideration, for the [lease][2] or agreement was to be provided or received (directly or indirectly) by a person other than a body corporate which at the relevant time was associated with either the lessor or the lessee, or

(*b*) the lessor and the lessee were to cease to be associated by reason of the lessor or a third body corporate ceasing to be the lessee's parent;

and the relevant time is the time of the execution of the instrument.

(4) Without prejudice to the generality of paragraph (*a*) of subsection (3) above, an arrangement shall be treated as within that paragraph if it is one under which the lessor or the lessee or a body corporate associated with either at the relevant time was to be enabled to provide any of the consideration, or was to part with any of it, by or in consequence of the carrying out of a transaction which involved (or transactions any of which involved) a payment or other disposition by a person other than a body corporate associated with the lessor or the lessee at the relevant time.

[(4A) An instrument shall not be exempt from stamp duty by virtue of subsection (1) above if at the time the instrument is executed arrangements are in existence by virtue of which at that or some later time any person has or could obtain, or any persons together have or could obtain, control of the lessee but not of the lessor.][3]

(5) An instrument mentioned in subsection (1) above shall not be treated as duly stamped unless—

(*a*) it is duly stamped in accordance with the law that would apply but for that subsection, or
(*b*) it has, in accordance with section 12 of the Stamp Act 1891, been stamped with a particular stamp denoting either that it is not chargeable with any duty or that it is duly stamped.

(6) In this section—

(*a*) references to the lessor are to the person granting the [lease][2] or (in the case of an agreement) agreeing to grant the [lease][2] or letting;
(*b*) references to the lessee are to the person being granted the [lease][2] or (in the case of an agreement) agreeing for the [lease][2] or letting to be granted to him or another.

(7) For the purposes of this section bodies corporate are associated at a particular time if at that time one is the parent of the other or another body corporate is the parent of each.

(8) For the purposes of this section one body corporate is the parent of another at a particular time if at that time the first body—

[(*a*)][3] is beneficial owner of not less than 75 per cent of the ordinary share capital of the second body;
[(*b*) is beneficially entitled to not less than 75 per cent of any profits available for distribution to equity holders of the second body; and
(*c*) would be beneficially entitled to not less than 75 per cent of any assets of the second body available for distribution to its equity holders on a winding-up.][3]

(9) In subsection (8) above "ordinary share capital", in relation to a body corporate, means all the issued share capital (by whatever name called) of the body corporate, other than capital the holders of which have a right to a dividend at a fixed rate but have no other right to share in the profits of the body corporate.

(10) The ownership referred to in [paragraph (*a*) of][3] subsection (8) above is ownership either directly or through another body corporate or other bodies corporate, or partly directly and partly through another body corporate or other bodies corporate; and Part I of Schedule 4 to the Finance Act 1938 (determination of amount of capital held through other bodies corporate) shall apply for the purposes of [that paragraph][4].

[(10A) Schedule 18 to the Income and Corporation Taxes Act 1988 shall apply for the purposes of paragraphs (*b*) and (*c*) of subsection (8) as it applies for the purposes of paragraphs (*a*) and (*b*) of section 413(7) of that Act; but this is subject to subsection (10B).

(10B) In determining for the purposes of this section whether a body corporate is the parent of the lessor, paragraphs 5(3) and 5B to 5E of Schedule 18 to the Income and Corporation Taxes Act 1988 shall not apply for the purposes of paragraph (*b*) or (*c*) of subsection (8) above.

(10C) In this section, "control" shall be construed in accordance with section 840 of the Income and Corporation Taxes Act 1988.][3]

(11) This section shall apply in relation to instruments executed on or after the day on which this Act is passed.

Statement of Practice SP 3/98—Stamp duty—group relief.

Amendments—[1] Words in sub-s (1) substituted by FA 1999 s 112(4), Sch 14 para 33 with effect in relation to instruments executed after 30 September 1999. This does not apply to transfers or other instruments relating to units under a unit trust scheme by virtue of FA 1999 s 122. Previously the text read 'the heading "Lease or Tack" in Schedule 1 to the Stamp Act 1891'.

[2] "Lease" substituted for the words "lease or tack" throughout the section by FA 1999 s 112(4), Sch 14 para 33 with effect in relation to instruments executed after 30 September 1999. This does not apply to transfers or other instruments relating to units under a unit trust scheme by virtue of FA 1999 s 122.

[3] Words in sub-s (1), whole of sub-s (4A), in sub-s (8) reference to "(*a*)" and whole of paras (*b*), (*c*), sub-ss (10A)–(10C) and words in sub-s (10) inserted by FA 2000 s 125(1)–(4), (5)(*a*), (6) with effect for instruments executed after 28 July 2000.

[4] Words in sub-s (10) substituted for "this section" by FA 2000 s 125(5)(*b*), with effect for instruments executed after 28 July 2000.

PART VI

MISCELLANEOUS AND GENERAL

Miscellaneous

152 Open-ended investment companies

(1) The Treasury may, by regulations, make such provision as they consider appropriate for securing that the enactments specified in subsection (2) below have effect in relation to—

(*a*) open-ended investment companies of any such description as may be specified in the regulations,

(*b*) holdings in, and the assets of, such companies, and

(*c*) transactions involving such companies,

in a manner corresponding, subject to such modifications as the Treasury consider appropriate, to the manner in which they have effect in relation to unit trusts, to rights under, and the assets subject to, such trusts and to transactions for purposes connected with such trusts.

(2) The enactments referred to in subsection (1) above are—

(*a*) the Tax Acts and the Taxation of Chargeable Gains Act 1992; and

(*b*) the enactments relating to stamp duty and [stamp duty reserve tax][1].

(3) The power of the Treasury to make regulations under this section in relation to any such enactments shall include power to make provision which does any one or more of the following, that is to say—

(*a*) identifies the payments which are or are not to be treated, for the purposes of any prescribed enactment, as the distributions of open-ended investment companies;

(*b*) modifies the operation of Chapters II, III and VA of Part VI of the Taxes Act 1988 in relation to open-ended investment companies or in relation to payments falling to be treated as the distributions of such companies;

(*c*) applies and adapts any of the provisions of [the enactments relating to stamp duty or stamp duty reserve tax][1] for the purpose of making in relation to transactions involving open-ended investment companies any provision corresponding (with or without modifications) to that which applies under [those enactments][1] in the case of equivalent transactions involving unit trusts;

(*d*) provides for any or all of the provisions of sections 75 to 77 of the Finance Act 1986 to have effect or not to have effect in relation to open-ended investment companies or the undertakings of, or any shares in, such companies;

(*e*) so modifies the operation of any prescribed enactment in relation to any such companies as to secure that arrangements for treating the assets of an open-ended investment company as assets comprised in separate pools are given an effect corresponding, in prescribed respects, to that of equivalent arrangements constituting the separate parts of an umbrella scheme;

(*f*) requires prescribed enactments to have effect in relation to an open-ended investment company as if it were, or were not, a member of the same group of companies as one or more other companies;

(*g*) identifies the holdings in open-ended investment companies which are, or are not, to be treated for the purposes of any prescribed enactment as comprised in the same class of holdings;

(*h*) preserves a continuity of tax treatment where, in connection with any scheme of re-organisation, assets of one or more unit trusts become assets of one or more open-ended investment companies, or vice versa;

(*i*) treats the separate parts of the undertaking of an open-ended investment company in relation to which provision is made by virtue of paragraph (*e*) above as distinct companies for the purposes of any regulations under this section;

(*j*) amends, adapts or applies the provisions of any subordinate legislation made under or by reference to any enactment modified by the regulations.

(4) The power to make regulations under this section shall be exercisable by statutory instrument and shall include power—

(*a*) to make different provision for different cases; and

(*b*) to make such incidental, supplemental, consequential and transitional provision as the Treasury may think fit.

(5) A statutory instrument containing regulations under this section shall be subject to annulment in pursuance of a resolution of the House of Commons.

(6) In this section—

"the enactments relating to stamp duty" means the Stamp Act 1891, and any enactment (including any Northern Ireland legislation) which amends or is required to be construed together with that Act;

["the enactments relating to stamp duty reserve tax" means Part IV of the Finance Act 1986 and any enactment which amends or is required to be construed as one with that Part;][1]

"Northern Ireland legislation" shall have the meaning given by section 24(5) of the Interpretation Act 1978;

"open-ended investment company" has the same meaning as in the Financial Services Act 1986;

"prescribed" means prescribed by regulations under this section;

"subordinate legislation" means any subordinate legislation within the meaning of the Interpretation Act 1978 or any order or regulations made by statutory instrument under Northern Ireland legislation; and

"umbrella scheme" shall have the meaning given by section 468 of the Taxes Act 1988;

and references in this section to the enactments relating to stamp duty, or to any of them, or to Part IV of the Finance Act 1986 shall have effect as including references to enactments repealed by sections 107 to 110 of the Finance Act 1990.

(7) Any reference in this section to unit trusts has effect—

(*a*) for the purposes of so much of this section as confers power in relation to the enactments specified in paragraph (*a*) of subsection (2) above, as a reference to authorised unit trusts (within the meaning of section 468 of the Taxes Act 1988), and

(*b*) for the purposes of so much of this section as confers power in relation to the enactments specified in paragraph (*b*) of that subsection, as a reference to any unit trust scheme (within the meaning given by section 57 of the Finance Act 1946).

(8) For the purposes of this section the enactments which shall be taken to make provision in relation to companies that are members of the same group of companies shall include any enactments which make provision in relation to a case—

(*a*) where one company has, or in relation to another company is, a subsidiary, or a subsidiary of a particular description, or

(*b*) where one company controls another or two or more companies are under the same control.

Regulations—See the Stamp Duty and Stamp Duty Reserve Tax (Definition of Unit Trust Scheme and Open-ended Investment Company) Regulations, SI 2001/964.

Amendments—[1] Words in sub-ss (2)(*b*), (3)(*c*) substituted and in sub-s (6) definition of "the enactments relating to stamp duty reserve tax" inserted by the Finance Act 1999, s 122(4), Sch 19, para 13 with effect from 6 February 2000.

FINANCE ACT 1996

(1996 Chapter 8)

ARRANGEMENT OF SECTIONS

PART VI

STAMP DUTY AND STAMP DUTY RESERVE TAX

Stamp duty

Stamp duty reserve tax

Clearance services

PART VII

MISCELLANEOUS AND SUPPLEMENTAL

Miscellaneous: direct taxation

Miscellaneous: other matters

Supplemental

An Act to grant certain duties, to alter other duties, and to amend the law relating to the National Debt and the Public Revenue, and to make further provision in connection with Finance.

[29th April 1996]

PART VI

STAMP DUTY AND STAMP DUTY RESERVE TAX

Stamp duty

186 Transfers of securities to members of electronic transfer systems etc

(1) Stamp duty shall not be chargeable on an instrument effecting a transfer of securities if the transferee is a member of an electronic transfer system and the instrument is in a form which will, in accordance with the rules of the system, ensure that the securities are changed from being held in certificated form to being held in uncertificated form so that title to them may become transferable by means of the system.

(2) In this section—

"certificated form" has the same meaning as in the relevant regulations;

"electronic transfer system" means a system and procedures which, in accordance with the relevant regulations, enable title to securities to be evidenced and transferred without a written instrument;

"member", in relation to an electronic transfer system, means a person who is permitted by the operator of the system to transfer by means of the system title to securities held by him in uncertificated form;

"operator" means a person approved by the Treasury under the relevant regulations as operator of an electronic transfer system;

"the relevant regulations" means regulations under section [785][1] of the Companies Act [2006][1] (transfer without written instrument);

"securities" means stock or marketable securities;

"uncertificated form" has the same meaning as it has in the relevant regulations.

(3) This section applies in relation to instruments executed on or after 1st July 1996.

(4) This section shall be construed as one with the Stamp Act 1891.

Amendments—This section repealed by Sch 41 Pt VII with effect from an appointed day in accordance with FA 1990 s 108.
Amendments—[1] In sub-s (2), figures substituted for figures "207" and "1989", by the Companies Act 2006 (Consequential Amendments) (Taxes and National Insurance) Order, SI 2009/1890 art 10 with effect from 1 October 2009.

Stamp duty reserve tax

187 Territorial scope of the tax

(1) (*inserts* FA 1986 s 86(4)).

(2) The amendment made by subsection (1) above shall have effect—

(*a*) in relation to an agreement, if—

(i) the agreement is conditional and the condition is satisfied on or after 1st July 1996; or
(ii) the agreement is not conditional and is made on or after that date; and

(*b*) in relation to a transfer, issue or appropriation made or effected on or after that date.

Amendments—This section repealed by FA 1996 Sch 41 Pt VII with effect from an appointed day in accordance with FA 1990 s 110.

188 Removal of the two month period

(1) (*amends* FA 1986 s 87(2)).

(2) …[2]

(3) (*repeals* FA 1986 s 88 (2), (3)).

(4) (*amends* FA 1986 s 92(1)).

(5) *The amendments made by this section shall have effect in relation to an agreement to transfer securities if—*

(*a*) *the agreement is conditional and the condition is satisfied on or after 1st July 1996; or* (*b*) *the agreement is not conditional and is made on or after that date.*[1]

Amendments—[1] This section repealed by Sch 41 Pt VII with effect from an appointed day in accordance with FA 1990 s 110.

[2] Sub-s (2) repealed by FA 1999 Sch 20 Pt V(2) with effect in relation to instruments executed, or bearer instruments issued, from 1 October 1999, subject to the provisions in FA 1999 Sch 20 Pt V(2) Note 2. Previously the text inserted FA 1986 s 88 (1)(*aa*),(*ab*).

189 Transfers to members of electronic transfer systems etc

(1) (*inserts* FA 1986 s 88(1A)).

(2) This section has effect in relation to an agreement to transfer securities if an instrument is executed on or after 1st July 1996 in pursuance of the agreement.

Amendments—This section repealed by Sch 41 Pt VII with effect from an appointed day.

190 Transfers between associated bodies

(1) (*inserts* FA 1986 s 88(1B)).

(2) (*adds* FA 1986 s 88(4)–(6)).

(3) This section has effect where the instrument on which stamp duty is not chargeable by virtue of section 42 of the Finance Act 1930 or section 11 of the Finance Act (Northern Ireland) 1954 is executed on or after 4th January 1996 in pursuance of an agreement to transfer securities made on or after that date.

Amendments—This section repealed by Sch 41 Pt VII with effect from an appointed day in accordance with FA 1990 s 110

191 Stock lending and collateral security arrangements

(1) (*inserts* FA 1986 s 89B).

(2) This section applies in relation to agreements to transfer chargeable securities in pursuance of an arrangement entered into on or after 1st July 1996.

Amendments—This section repealed by Sch 41 Pt VII with effect from an appointed day in accordance with FA 1990 s 110.

192 Repayment or cancellation of tax

(1)–(5) (*repeal* FA 1986 s 87(4), (5), (8), *amend* ss 88(1), (1A), (1B), 92(1), *insert* FA 1986 s 92 (1A), (1B) and *add* s 92(6)).

(6) The amendments made by this section shall have effect in relation to an agreement to transfer securities if—

(*a*) the agreement is conditional and the condition is satisfied on or after 1st July 1996; or

(*b*) the agreement is not conditional and is made on or after that date.

Amendments—This section repealed by Sch 41 Pt VII with effect from an appointed day in accordance with FA 1990 s 110.

193 Depositary receipts

(1)–(3) (*amend* FA 1986 s 93(1), (6)).

(4) This section has effect—

(*a*) so far as relating to the charge to tax under section 93(1) of the Finance Act 1986, where securities are transferred, issued or appropriated on or after 1st July 1996 (whenever the arrangement was made);

(*b*) so far as relating to the charge to tax under section 93(10) of that Act, in relation to instalments payable on or after 1st July 1996.

Amendments—This section repealed by Sch 41 Pt VII with effect from an appointed day in accordance with FA 1990 s 110.

194 Rates of charge expressed as percentages

(1)–(6) (*amend* FA 1986 ss 87(6), 93(4), (5), (10), 96(2), (3), (8), *repeal* ss 94(8), 96(12) and *add* s 99(13)).

(7) Subsections (1) to (5) above have effect in accordance with the following provisions of this subsection, that is to say—

(*a*) in relation to the charge to tax under section 87 of the Finance Act 1986, subsection (1) above applies where—

(i) the agreement to transfer is conditional and the condition is satisfied on or after 1st July 1996; or

(ii) the agreement is not conditional and is made on or after 1st July 1996;

(*b*) in relation to the charge to tax under section 93(1) of that Act, paragraphs (*a*) and (*b*) of subsection (2) above apply where securities are transferred, issued or appropriated on or after 1st July 1996 (whenever the arrangement was made) and subsection (3) above has effect accordingly;

(*c*) in relation to the charge to tax under section 93(10) of that Act, paragraph (*c*) of sub-section (2) above applies in relation to instalments payable on or after 1st July 1996;

(*d*) in relation to the charge to tax under section 96(1) of that Act, paragraphs (*a*) and (*b*) of subsection (4) above apply where securities are transferred or issued on or after 1st July 1996 (whenever the arrangement was made) and subsection (5) above has effect accordingly;

(*e*) in relation to the charge to tax under section 96(8) of that Act, paragraph (*c*) of subsection (4) above applies in relation to instalments payable on or after 1st July 1996.

Amendments—This section repealed by Sch 41 Pt VII with effect from an appointed day in accordance with FA 1990 s 110.

195 Regulations concerning administration: sub-delegation to the Board

(*inserted* FA 1986 s 98(1A)).

Amendments—This section repealed by Sch 41 Pt VII with effect from an appointed day in accordance with FA 1990 s 110.

Clearance services

196 Election by operator for alternative system of charge

(*amended* FA 1986 ss 70(1), 96(1), 99(10), *inserted* s 97A *and repealed* s 97(2)).

Amendments—This section repealed by Sch 41 Pt VII with effect from an appointed day in accordance with FA 1990 s 110.

PART VII

MISCELLANEOUS AND SUPPLEMENTAL

Miscellaneous: direct taxation

201 Enactment of Inland Revenue concessions

Schedule 39 to this Act has effect for the purpose of enacting certain extra-statutory concessions relating to income tax, corporation tax, capital gains tax, and stamp duty.

Miscellaneous: other matters

202 Gilt stripping

(1)–(4) (*not relevant to stamp duty or SDRT*).

(5) The Treasury may by regulations make provision for securing that enactments and subordinate legislation which—

(*a*) apply in relation to government securities or to any description of such securities, or

(*b*) for any other purpose refer (in whatever terms) to such securities or to any description of them,

have effect with such modifications as the Treasury may think appropriate in consequence of the making of any provision or arrangements for, or in connection with, the issue or transfer of strips of government securities or the consolidation of such strips into other securities.

(6) Regulations under subsection (5) above may—

(*a*) impose a charge to income tax, corporation tax, capital gains tax, inheritance tax, stamp duty or stamp duty reserve tax;

(*b*) include provision applying generally to, or to any description of, enactments or subordinate legislation;

(*c*) make different provision for different cases; and

(*d*) contain such incidental, supplemental, consequential and transitional provision as the Treasury think appropriate.

(7) The power to make regulations under subsection (5) above shall be exercisable by statutory instrument subject to annulment in pursuance of a resolution of the House of Commons.

(8) Schedule 40 to this Act (which makes provision in relation to strips for taxation purposes) shall have effect.

(9) The enactments that may be modified by regulations under this section shall include section 95 above and the enactments contained in Schedule 40 to this Act.

(10) In this section—

"government securities" means any securities included in Part I of Schedule 11 to the Finance Act 1942;

"modifications" includes amendments, additions and omissions; and

"subordinate legislation" has the same meaning as in the Interpretation Act 1978;

and expressions used in this section and in section 47 of the Finance Act 1942 have the same meanings in this section as in that section.

Supplemental

205 Repeals

(1) The enactments mentioned in Schedule 41 to this Act (which include spent provisions) are hereby repealed to the extent specified in the third column of that Schedule.

(2) The repeals specified in that Schedule have effect subject to the commencement provisions and savings contained in, or referred to, in the notes set out in that Schedule.

206 Short title

This Act may be cited as the Finance Act 1996.

SCHEDULES

SCHEDULE 39

ENACTMENT OF CERTAIN INLAND REVENUE EXTRA-STATUTORY CONCESSIONS

Section 201

PART III

STAMP DUTY

Lost or spoiled instruments

10— (1) The Stamp Duties Management Act 1891 ("the Management Act") shall be amended as follows.

(2) (*amends* SDMA 1891 s 9(7)(*e*)).

(3) (*inserts* SDMA 1891 s 12A).

(4) Subject to subparagraph (5) below, the amendments made by this paragraph shall have effect from the day on which this Act is passed.

(5) The amendments made by this paragraph shall not apply in relation to an instrument which has been accidentally spoiled if an application for allowance under section 9 of the Management Act was made before the day on which this Act is passed.

SCHEDULE 40

GILT STRIPPING: TAXATION PROVISIONS

Section 202

The Stamp Act 1891 (c 39)

1 (amends SA 1891 s 122(1)).

2 …[1]

Amendments—[1] Para 2 repealed by FA 1999 Sch 20 Pt V(2) with effect in relation to instruments executed, or bearer instruments issued, from 1 October 1999, subject to the provisions in FA 1999 Sch 20 Pt V(2) Note 2. Previously the text read:

"2—(1) (*amends* SA 1891 Sch 1).

(2) Where any day is appointed as the abolition day for the purposes of sections 107 to 110 of the Finance Act 1990, sub-paragraph (1) above shall cease to have effect in accordance with the provisions of that Act for the coming into force of the repeal of the paragraph mentioned in that sub-paragraph."

SCHEDULE 41

REPEALS

Section 205

PART VII

STAMP DUTY AND STAMP DUTY RESERVE TAX

Chapter	Short title	Extent of repeal
…	…	…
1996 c 8.	The Finance Act 1996.	Sections 186 to 196.

1–3 …

4 The repeals in the Finance Act 1996 have effect—

(*a*) so far as relating to stamp duty, in accordance with section 108 of the Finance Act 1990; and

(*b*) so far as relating to stamp duty reserve tax, in accordance with section 110 of the Finance Act 1990.

Note—Details of repeals already in force have not been reproduced.

FINANCE ACT 1997

(1997 Chapter 16)

ARRANGEMENT OF SECTIONS

PART VII

STAMP DUTY AND STAMP DUTY RESERVE TAX

Stamp duty

PART VIII

MISCELLANEOUS AND SUPPLEMENTAL

Supplemental

An Act to grant certain duties, to alter other duties, and to amend the law relating to the National Debt and the Public Revenue, and to make further provision in connection with Finance.

[19th March 1997]

PART VII

STAMP DUTY AND STAMP DUTY RESERVE TAX

Stamp duty

95 Mergers of authorised unit trusts

(1) Stamp duty shall not be chargeable on an instrument transferring any property which is subject to the trusts of an authorised unit trust ("the target trust") to the trustees of another authorised unit trust ("the acquiring trust") if the conditions set out in subsection (2) below are fulfilled.

(2) Those conditions are that—

(*a*) the transfer forms part of an arrangement under which the whole of the available property of the target trust is transferred to the trustees of the acquiring trust;
(*b*) under the arrangement all the units in the target trust are extinguished;
(*c*) the consideration under the arrangement consists of or includes the issue of units ("the consideration units") in the acquiring trust to the persons who held the extinguished units;
(*d*) the consideration units are issued to those persons in proportion to their holdings of the extinguished units; and
(*e*) the consideration under the arrangement does not include anything else, other than the assumption or discharge by the trustees of the acquiring trust of liabilities of the trustees of the target trust.

(3) An instrument on which stamp duty is not chargeable by virtue only of this section shall not be taken to be duly stamped unless it is stamped with the duty to which it would be liable but for this section or it has, in accordance with section 12 of the Stamp Act 1891, been stamped with a particular stamp denoting that it is not chargeable with any duty.

(4) In this section—

"authorised unit trust" means a unit trust scheme in the case of which an order under section [243 of the Financial Services and Markets Act 2000][1] is in force;

"the whole of the available property of the target trust" means the whole of the property subject to the trusts of the target trust, other than any property which is retained for the purpose of discharging liabilities of the trustees of the target trust;

"unit" and "unit trust scheme" have the same meanings as in Part VII of the Finance Act 1946.

(5) Each of the parts of an umbrella scheme (and not the scheme as a whole) shall be regarded for the purposes of this section as an authorised unit trust; and in this section "umbrella scheme" has the same meaning as in section 468 of the Taxes Act 1988 and references to parts of an umbrella scheme shall be construed in accordance with that section.

(6) This section applies to any instrument which is executed—

(*a*) on or after the day on which this Act is passed; but

(*b*) before 1st July 1999.

Amendments—[1] In sub-s (4), words in the definition of "authorised unit trust" substituted by the Financial Services and Markets Act 2000 (Consequential Amendments) (Taxes) Order, SI 2001/3629 arts 97, 99 with effect for any instrument executed after 30 November 2001.

96 Demutualisation of insurance companies

(1) This section applies where there is a relevant transfer, under a scheme, of the whole or any part of the business carried on by a mutual insurance company ("the mutual") to a company which has share capital ("the acquiring company").

(2) Stamp duty shall not be chargeable on an instrument executed for the purposes of or in connection with the transfer if the requirements of subsections (3) and (4) below are satisfied in relation to the shares of a company ("the issuing company") which is either—

(*a*) the acquiring company; or

(*b*) a company of which the acquiring company is a wholly-owned subsidiary.

(3) Shares in the issuing company must be offered, under the scheme, to at least 90 per cent of the persons who immediately before the transfer are members of the mutual.

(4) Under the scheme, all the shares in the issuing company which will be in issue immediately after the transfer has been made, other than shares which are to be or have been issued pursuant to an offer to the public, must be offered to the persons who (at the time of the offer) are—

(*a*) members of the mutual;

(*b*) persons who are entitled to become members of the mutual; or

(*c*) employees, former employees or pensioners of the mutual or of a company which is a wholly-owned subsidiary of the mutual.

(5) An instrument on which stamp duty is not chargeable by virtue only of subsection (2) above shall not be taken to be duly stamped unless it is stamped with the duty to which it would be liable but for that subsection or it has, in accordance with section 12 of the Stamp Act 1891, been stamped with a particular stamp denoting that it is not chargeable with any duty.

(6) For the purposes of this section, a company is a wholly-owned subsidiary of another person ("the parent") if it has no members except the parent and the parent's wholly-owned subsidiaries or persons acting on behalf of the parent or its wholly-owned subsidiaries.

(7) In this section "relevant transfer" means—

[(*a*) a transfer from a company to another person of business consisting of the effecting or carrying out of contracts of insurance which is effected under an insurance business transfer scheme; or

(*b*) a transfer of the whole or any part of the business of a general insurance company carried on through a branch or agency in the United Kingdom which takes place in accordance with any authorisation granted outside the United Kingdom for the purposes of—

[(i) Article 14 of the life assurance consolidation directive, or][2]

(ii) Article 12 of the third non-life insurance directive.][1]

(8) In this section—

["the life assurance consolidation directive" means Directive 2002/83/EC of the European Parliament and of the Council of 5th November 2002 concerning life assurance;][2]

["contract of insurance" has the meaning given by Article 3(1) of the Financial Services and Markets Act 2000 (Regulated Activities) Order 2001;][1]

"employee", in relation to a mutual insurance company or its wholly-owned subsidiary, includes any officer or director of the company or subsidiary and any other person taking part in the management of the affairs of the company or subsidiary;

["general insurance company" means a company which has permission under Part 4 of the Financial Services and Markets Act 2000 or under paragraph 15 of Schedule 3 to that Act (as a result of qualifying for authorisation under paragraph 12(1) of that Schedule) to effect or carry out contracts of insurance;

"insurance business transfer scheme" has the same meaning as in Part 7 of the Financial Services and Markets Act 2000;

"insurance company" means a company which carries on the business of effecting or carrying out contracts of insurance;][1]

"mutual insurance company" means an insurance company carrying on business without having any share capital;

[...][2]

"the third non-life insurance directive" means the Council Directive of 18th June 1992 on the co-ordination of laws, regulations and administrative provisions relating to direct insurance other than life assurance and amending Directives 73/239/EEC and 88/357/EEC (No 92/49/EEC);][1]

"pensioner", in relation to a mutual insurance company or its wholly-owned subsidiary, means a person entitled (whether presently or prospectively) to a pension, lump sum, gratuity or other like benefit referable to the service of any person as an employee of the company or subsidiary.

(9) The Treasury may by regulations amend subsection (3) above by substituting a lower percentage for the percentage there mentioned.

(10) The Treasury may by regulations provide that any or all of the references in subsections (3) and (4) above to members shall be construed as references to members of a class specified in the regulations; and different provision may be made for different cases.

(11) The power to make regulations under this section shall be exercisable by statutory instrument subject to annulment in pursuance of a resolution of the House of Commons.

(12) This section applies in relation to instruments executed on or after the day on which this Act is passed.

Cross references—See FA 1986 s 90(1A)(*c*) (exemption from charge under FA 1986 s 87 for agreement to transfer unit under unit trust scheme).

FA 1999 Sch 19 para 6(5)(*c*) (exclusion, in certain cases of change of ownership, of charge to SDRT on surrender of unit to managers).

Amendments—[1] In sub-s (7), paras (*a*), (*b*) substituted; in sub-s (8), definition of "contract of insurance" inserted, definitions of "general insurance company", "insurance business transfer scheme" and "insurance company" substituted for that of "insurance company"; and definitions of "the third life insurance directive" and "the third non-life insurance directive" inserted by the Financial Services and Markets Act 2000 (Consequential Amendments) (Taxes) Order, SI 2001/3629 arts 97, 100 with effect from 1 December 2001 (immediately after the coming into force of the Financial Services and Markets Act 2000 ss 411, 432(1), Sch 20). SI 2001/3629 art 100 has effect for any instrument executed after 30 November 2001 which effects a transfer—

(*a*) under a scheme falling within the Financial Services and Markets Act 2000 s 105, including an excluded scheme falling within Case 2, 3 or 4 of the Financial Services and Markets Act 2000 s 105(3); or

(*b*) in relation to which the Financial Services and Markets Act 2000 s 116 applies.

[2] Sub-s (7)(*b*)(i) substituted; words in sub-s (8) inserted; and words in sub-s (8) repealed by the Life Assurance Consolidation Directive (Consequential Amendments) Regulations, SI 2004/3379 reg 5 with effect from 11 January 2005.

97 Relief for intermediaries

(1)–(3) (*insert* FA 1986 s 80A, 80B, *repeal* s 81 and *amend* s 88(1B)(*b*)(i)).

(4) Subsections (1) and (2) above apply to instruments executed on or after the commencement day.

(5) Subsection (3) above applies in relation to an agreement to transfer chargeable securities if the securities were acquired in a transaction which was given effect to by an instrument of transfer executed on or after the commencement day.

(6) For the purposes of this section the commencement day is such day as the Treasury may by order made by statutory instrument appoint.

Note—This section given an effective date of 20 October 1997 by virtue of the Finance Act 1997 (Stamp Duty and Stamp Duty Reserve Tax) (Appointed Day) Order, SI 1997/2428.

98 Repurchases and stock lending

(1), (2) (*insert* FA 1986 s 80C and *repeal* s 82).

(3) This section applies to instruments executed on or after the commencement day.

(4) For the purposes of this section the commencement day is such day as the Treasury may by order made by statutory instrument appoint.

Note—This section given an effective date of 20 October 1997 by virtue of the Finance Act 1997 (Stamp Duty and Stamp Duty Reserve Tax) (Appointed Day) Order, SI 1997/2428.

99 Depositary receipts and clearance services

(1)–(4) (*repeal* FA 1986 ss 67 (4), 69(6)–(8), 70(4), 72(4) and *amend* ss 67(3), 70(3)).

(5) This section applies to any instrument executed on or after the day which is the commencement day for the purposes of section 97 above, except an instrument which transfers relevant securities which were acquired by the transferor before that date.

Stamp duty reserve tax

100 Mergers of authorised unit trusts

(1) Section 87 of the Finance Act 1986 shall not apply as regards an agreement to transfer securities which constitute property which is subject to the trusts of an authorised unit trust

("the target trust") to the trustees of another authorised unit trust ("the acquiring trust") if the conditions set out in subsection (2) below are fulfilled.

(2) Those conditions are that—

(*a*) the agreement forms part of an arrangement under which the whole of the available property of the target trust is transferred to the trustees of the acquiring trust;

(*b*) under the arrangement all the units in the target trust are extinguished;

(*c*) the consideration under the arrangement consists of or includes the issue of units ("the consideration units") in the acquiring trust to the persons who held the extinguished units;

(*d*) the consideration units are issued to those persons in proportion to their holdings of the extinguished units; and

(*e*) the consideration under the arrangement does not include anything else, other than the assumption or discharge by the trustees of the acquiring trust of liabilities of the trustees of the target trust.

(3) Where—

(*a*) stamp duty is not chargeable on an instrument by virtue of section 95(1) above, or

(*b*) section 87 of the Finance Act 1986 does not apply as regards an agreement by virtue of subsection (1) above,

section 87 of the Finance Act 1986 shall not apply as regards an agreement, or a deemed agreement, to transfer a unit to the managers of the target trust which is made in order that the unit may be extinguished under the arrangement mentioned in section 95(2)(*a*) or, as the case may be, subsection (2)(*a*) above.

(4) In this section—

"authorised unit trust" means a unit trust scheme in the case of which an order under section [243 of the Financial Services and Markets Act 2000][1] is in force;

"the whole of the available property of the target trust" means the whole of the property subject to the trusts of the target trust, other than any property which is retained for the purpose of discharging liabilities of the trustees of the target trust;

"unit" and "unit trust scheme" have the same meanings as in Part VII of the Finance Act 1946.

(5) Each of the parts of an umbrella scheme (and not the scheme as a whole) shall be regarded for the purposes of this section as an authorised unit trust; and in this section "umbrella scheme" has the same meaning as in section 468 of the Taxes Act 1988 and references to parts of an umbrella scheme shall be construed in accordance with that section.

(6) This section applies—

(*a*) to an agreement which is not conditional, if the agreement is made on or after the day on which this Act is passed but before 1st July 1999; and

(*b*) to a conditional agreement, if the condition is satisfied on or after the day on which this Act is passed but before 1st July 1999.

Amendments—[1] In sub-s (4), words in definition of "authorised unit trust" substituted by the Financial Services and Markets Act 2000 (Consequential Amendments) (Taxes) Order, SI 2001/3629 arts 97, 101 with effect for—

(*a*) an agreement to transfer chargeable securities which is not conditional, if the agreement is made after 30 November 2001;

(*b*) a conditional agreement to transfer such securities, if the condition is satisfied after that date.

101 Direction to hold trust property on other trusts

(1) Where an agreement to transfer securities constituting property subject to the trusts of an authorised unit trust ("the absorbed trust") is made by means of a direction by the holders of units in the absorbed trust ("the sellers") to the trustees of another trust ("the continuing trust") to hold the whole of the available property of the absorbed trust on the trusts of the continuing trust, section 87 of the Finance Act 1986 shall not apply as regards the agreement if the conditions set out in subsection (2) below are fulfilled.

(2) Those conditions are that—

(*a*) the trustees of the absorbed trust are the same persons as the trustees of the continuing trust;

(*b*) the agreement forms part of an arrangement under which all the units in the absorbed trust are extinguished;

(*c*) the consideration for the direction by the sellers consists of or includes the issue of units ("the consideration units") in the continuing trust to the sellers;

(*d*) the consideration units are issued to the sellers in proportion to their holdings of the extinguished units; and

(*e*) the consideration for the direction by the sellers does not include anything else, other than the assumption or discharge by the trustees of the continuing trust of liabilities of the trustees of the absorbed trust.

(3) Where section 87 of the Finance Act 1986 does not apply as regards an agreement by virtue of subsection (1) above, that section shall not apply as regards an agreement, or a deemed agreement, to transfer a unit to the managers of the absorbed trust which is made in order that the unit may be extinguished under the arrangement mentioned in subsection (2)(*b*) above.

(4) In this section—

"authorised unit trust" and "unit" have the same meanings as in section 100 above (and section 100(5) applies for the purposes of this section as it applies for the purposes of section 100);

"the whole of the available property of the absorbed trust" means the whole of the property subject to the trusts of the absorbed trust, other than any property which is retained for the purpose of discharging liabilities of the trustees of the absorbed trust.

(5) This section applies—

(*a*) to an agreement which is not conditional, if the agreement is made on or after the day on which this Act is passed but before 1st July 1999; and

(*b*) to a conditional agreement, if the condition is satisfied on or after the day on which this Act is passed but before 1st July 1999.

102 Relief for intermediaries

(1)–(3) (*insert* FA 1986 s 88A, 88B, *repeal* s 89 and *amend* s 88(1B)(*b*)(ii)).

(4) Subsections (1) and (2) above apply to an agreement to transfer securities—

(*a*) in the case of an agreement which is not conditional, if the agreement is made on or after the commencement day; and

(*b*) in the case of a conditional agreement, if the condition is satisfied on or after the commencement day.

(5) Subsection (3) above applies in relation to property consisting of chargeable securities if the securities were acquired in pursuance of an agreement to which subsections (1) and (2) above apply (by virtue of subsection (4) above).

(6) For the purposes of this section the commencement day is such day as the Treasury may by order made by statutory instrument appoint.

Note—This section given an effective date of 20 October 1997 by virtue of the Finance Act 1997 (Stamp Duty and Stamp Duty Reserve Tax) (Appointed Day) Order, SI 1997/2428.

103 Repurchases and stock lending

(1)–(4) (*insert* FA 1986 ss 88(1C), (1D), 89AA, *repeal* s 89B and *amend* s 88(1B)(*b*)(iia)).

(5) Subsections (1) and (2) above apply to an agreement to transfer securities—

(*a*) in the case of an agreement which is not conditional, if the agreement is made on or after the commencement day; and

(*b*) in the case of a conditional agreement, if the condition is satisfied on or after the commencement day.

(6) Subsection (3) above applies in relation to property consisting of chargeable securities if the securities were acquired in pursuance of an agreement to which subsections (1) and (2) above apply (by virtue of subsection (5) above).

(7) Subsection (4) above applies to instruments executed on or after the commencement day.

(8) For the purposes of this section the commencement day is such day as the Treasury may by order made by statutory instrument appoint.

Note—This section given an effective date of 20 October 1997 by virtue of the Finance Act 1997 (Stamp Duty and Stamp Duty Reserve Tax) (Appointed Day) Order, SI 1997/2428.

104 Depositary receipts and clearance services

(1)–(4) (*repeal* FA 1986 ss 93(5), 94(5)–(7), 96(3), (11) and *amend* ss 93(4), (7)(*a*), 96(2), (5)(*a*)).

(5) This section applies where securities are transferred on or after the day which is the commencement day for the purposes of section 102 above, unless the securities were acquired by the transferor before that day.

105 Inland bearer instruments

(1)–(3) (*repeal* FA 1986 s 90(3)(*b*) and *insert* ss 90(3A)–(3F), (8), (9)).

(4) This section applies to an agreement if the inland bearer instrument in question was issued on or after 26th November 1996 and—

(*a*) in the case of an agreement which is not conditional, the agreement is made on or after 26th November 1996; or

(*b*) in the case of a conditional agreement, the condition is satisfied on or after 26th November 1996.

106 Repayment or cancellation of tax

(1) Section 87 of the Finance Act 1986 (the principal charge) shall be amended in accordance with subsections (2) and (3) below.

(2), (3) (*substitutes* FA 1986 s 87(7A) and *repeal* s 87(7B)).

(4) Section 88 of the Finance Act 1986 (special cases) shall be amended in accordance with subsections (5) to (7) below.

(5) (*amends* FA 1986 s 88(1B)(*a*) and (*b*), *and inserts* s 88(1B)(*b*)(iia)).

(6) (*substitutes* FA 1986 s 88(4) and (5)).
(7) (*substitutes heading in* FA 1986 s 88).
(8) (*inserts* FA 1986 s 92(7)).
(9) The amendments made by subsections (2), (3) and (8) above have effect in relation to an agreement to transfer securities if—
(*a*) the agreement is conditional and the condition is satisfied on or after 4th January 1997; or
(*b*) the agreement is not conditional and is made on or after that date.
(10) The amendments made by subsections (5) and (6) above have effect where the instrument on which stamp duty is not chargeable by virtue of section 42 of the Finance Act 1930 or section 11 of the Finance Act (Northern Ireland) 1954 is executed on or after 4th January 1997 in pursuance of an agreement to transfer securities made on or after that date.

PART VIII
MISCELLANEOUS AND SUPPLEMENTAL

Supplemental

112 Interpretation
In this Act "the Taxes Act 1988" means the Income and Corporation Taxes Act 1988.

113 Repeals
(1) The enactments mentioned in Schedule 18 to this Act (which include spent provisions) are hereby repealed to the extent specified in the third column of that Schedule.
(2) The repeals specified in that Schedule have effect subject to the commencement provisions and savings contained or referred to in the notes set out in that Schedule.

114 Short title
This Act may be cited as the Finance Act 1997.

SCHEDULES

SCHEDULE 18
REPEALS

Section 113

PART VII
STAMP DUTY AND STAMP DUTY RESERVE TAX

Chapter	Short title	Extent of repeal
1986 c 41.	The Finance Act 1986	Section 67(4). Section 69(6) to (8). Section 70(4). Section 72(4). Sections 80A to 80C. Sections 81 and 82. Section 87(7B). In section 88(1B)(*b*), the word "or" at the end of sub-paragraph (ii). Sections 88A and 88B. Section 89. Section 89AA. Section 89B. Section 90(3)(*b*). Section 93(5). Section 94(5) to (7). In section 96(3) and (11).
1987 c 16.	The Finance Act 1987	Section 53. In Schedule 7, paragraph 4.
1988 c 39.	The Finance Act 1988	In Schedule 13, paragraph 23.

Stamp Taxes

Chapter	Short title	Extent of repeal
1996 c 8.	The Finance Act 1996	Section 191. Section 194(2)(*b*) and (4)(*b*).
1997 c 16.	The Finance Act 1997	Sections 97 to 106.

1 The repeals in sections 80A to 80C of the Finance Act 1986 and sections 97 to 99 and of this Act have effect in accordance with section 108 of the Finance Act 1990.

2 The repeals in sections 67, 69, 70 and 72 of the Finance Act 1986 have effect in accordance with section 99 of this Act.

3 The repeal of section 81 of the Finance Act 1986 has effect in accordance with section 97 of this Act.

4 The repeals of section 82 of the Finance Act 1986 and section 53 of the Finance Act 1987 have effect in accordance with section 98 of this Act.

5 The repeals in sections 87 and 88 of the Finance Act 1986 have effect in accordance with section 106 of this Act.

6 The repeals of sections 88A, 88B and 89AA of the Finance Act 1986 and sections 100 to 106 of this Act have effect in accordance with section 110 of the Finance Act 1990.

7 The repeal of section 89 of the Finance Act 1986 and the repeal in Schedule 7 to the Finance Act 1987 have effect in accordance with section 102 of this Act.

8 The repeals of section 89B of the Finance Act 1986 and section 191 of the Finance Act 1996 have effect in accordance with section 103 of this Act.

9 The repeal of section 90(3)(*b*) of the Finance Act 1986 has effect in accordance with section 105 of this Act.

10 The repeals in sections 93, 94 and 96 of the Finance Act 1986, in Schedule 13 to the Finance Act 1988 and in section 194 of the Finance Act 1996 have effect in accordance with section 104 of this Act.

FINANCE (NO 2) ACT 1997

(1997 Chapter 58)

PART IV

MISCELLANEOUS AND SUPPLEMENTARY

Stamp duty

49 Stamp duty on conveyance or transfer on sale

Simon's Tax Cases—*Swallow Hotels Ltd v IRC* [2000] STC 45.

Amendments—This section repealed by FA 1999 Sch 20 Pt V(2) with effect in relation to instruments executed, or bearer instruments issued, from 1 October 1999, subject to the provisions in FA 1999 Sch 20 Pt V(2) Note 2. Previously the text read:

"(1) Section 55 of the Finance Act 1963 and section 4 of the Finance Act (Northern Ireland) 1963 (both of which provide for rates of stamp duty on conveyance and transfer on sale) shall each be amended in accordance with the provisions of subsections (2) to (4) below.
(2) (*substitutes* FA 1963 s 55(1)(*b*)(*c*) and FA (Northern Ireland) 1963 s 4(1)(*b*)(*c*)).
(3) (*amends* FA 1963 s 55(1A)).
(4) (*amends* FA 1963 s 55(2)).
(5) (*amends* FA (Northern Ireland) 1963 s 4).
(6) This section shall apply to instruments executed on or after 8th July 1997, except where the instrument in question is executed in pursuance of a contract made on or before 2nd July 1997.
(7) This section shall be deemed to have come into force on 8th July 1997."

FINANCE ACT 1998

(1998 Chapter 36)

An Act to grant certain duties, to alter other duties, and to amend the law relating to the National Debt and the Public Revenue, and to make further provision in connection with Finance.

[31 July 1998]

PART V
OTHER TAXES

Stamp duty

149 Stamp duty on conveyance or transfer on sale.

Amendments—This section repealed by FA 1999 Sch 20 Pt V(2) with effect in relation to instruments executed, or bearer instruments issued, from 1 October 1999, subject to the provisions in FA 1999 Sch 20 Pt V(2) Note 2. Previously the text read:

"(1) Section 55 of the Finance Act 1963 and section 4 of the Finance Act (Northern Ireland) 1963 (both of which provide for rates of stamp duty on conveyance or transfer on sale) shall each be amended as follows.
(2) In subsection (1)(*d*) (rate of £1.50p for every £100 etc where consideration does not exceed £500,000 and the instrument is certified at that amount) for "£1.50p" there shall be substituted "£2".
(3) In subsection (1)(*e*) (rate of £2 for every £100 etc) for "£2" there shall be substituted "£3".
(4) This section shall apply to instruments executed on or after 24th March 1998, except where the instrument in question is executed in pursuance of a contract made on or before 17th March 1998.
(5) This section shall be deemed to have come into force on 24th March 1998."

150 Relief from double stamp duties etc.

(1) Where an instrument which is chargeable with stamp duty in Great Britain and in Northern Ireland has been stamped in either of those parts of the United Kingdom—

(*a*) the instrument shall, to the extent of the duty it bears, be deemed to be stamped in the other part of the United Kingdom, but

(*b*) if the stamp duty chargeable on the instrument in that other part of the United Kingdom exceeds the stamp duty chargeable on the instrument in the part of the United Kingdom in which it has been stamped, the instrument shall not be deemed to have been duly stamped in that other part of the United Kingdom unless and until stamped in accordance with the law which has effect in that part of the United Kingdom with a stamp denoting an amount equal to the excess.

(2) An instrument which, by virtue of paragraph (*b*) of subsection (1) above, is not deemed to have been duly stamped in a part of the United Kingdom unless and until stamped with a stamp denoting an amount equal to the excess mentioned in that paragraph may, notwithstanding anything in section 15 of the Stamp Act 1891, be stamped with such a stamp without payment of any penalty at any time within 30 days after it has first been received in that part of the United Kingdom.

(3) (*amends* SDMA 1891 s 22).

(4) (*repeals* the Government of Ireland Act 1920 s 29).

(5) The saving in Part I of Schedule 6 to the Northern Ireland Constitution Act 1973 (repeals) for orders made under section 69 of the Government of Ireland Act 1920 shall cease to have effect in relation to Part IV of the Government of Ireland (Adaptation of the S.R. & O. 1922/80.Taxing Acts) Order 1922 (the provisions of which are either spent or re-enacted with modifications in subsections (2) and (3) above).

Stamp duty reserve tax

151 Depositary receipts and clearance services: exchanges of shares.

(1)–(5) (*amend* FA 1986 ss 95(3), 97(4), 99(10) and *insert* ss 95(5)–(7), 97(6), (7)).

(6) This section applies where the issue by company X referred to in section 95(3) or (6) or 97(4) or (7) of the Finance Act 1986 is an issue on or after 1st May 1998.

HUMAN RIGHTS ACT 1998

(1998 Chapter 42)

An Act to give further effect to rights and freedoms guaranteed under the European Convention on Human Rights; to make provision with respect to holders of certain judicial offices who become judges of the European Court of Human Rights; and for connected purposes.

[9th November 1998]

Note—Please see VAT Statutes *ante* for the text of this Act.

FINANCE ACT 1999

(1999 Chapter 16)

ARRANGEMENT OF SECTIONS

PART VI
STAMP DUTY AND STAMP DUTY RESERVE TAX

Stamp duty

Stamp duty reserve tax

Units in unit trusts

Supplementary provisions

PART VIII
MISCELLANEOUS AND SUPPLEMENTAL

Supplemental

SCHEDULES:

Part IV—General definitions.

An Act to grant certain duties, to alter other duties, and to amend the law relating to the National Debt and the Public Revenue, and to make further provision in connection with Finance.

[27 July 1999]

PART VI

STAMP DUTY AND STAMP DUTY RESERVE TAX

Stamp duty

109 Interest and penalties on late stamping

(1) (*substitutes* the Stamp Act 1891 ss 15, 15A, 15B (for original s 15)).

(2) (*amends* FA 1989 s 178(2)).

(3) The consequential amendments in Schedule 12 to this Act have effect.

(4) This section applies to instruments executed on or after 1st October 1999.

110 Interest on repayment of duty overpaid etc

(1) A payment by the Commissioners to which this section applies shall be paid with interest at the rate applicable under section 178 of the Finance Act 1989 for the period between the relevant time (as defined below) and the date on which the order for the payment is issued.

(2) This section applies to any repayment by the Commissioners of duty, or any penalty on late stamping, under the enactments relating to stamp duty.

In that case the relevant time is 30 days after the day on which the instrument in question was executed or, if later, the date on which the payment of duty or penalty was made.

(3) This section applies to a repayment by the Commissioners of an amount lodged with them in respect of the duty payable on stamping an instrument if—

(*a*) the instrument is presented for stamping,

(*b*) the instrument is duly stamped, and

(*c*) the repayment is of an amount then repayable.

In that case the relevant time is 30 days after the day on which the instrument was executed or, if later, the date on which the amount was lodged with the Commissioners.

(4) This section also applies to a money payment made by the Commissioners under section 11 of the Stamp Duties Management Act 1891 (allowances for spoiled or misused stamps).

In that case the relevant time is the date on which the duty was paid for the stamp in respect of which the allowance is made.

(5) A payment by the Commissioners under section 12A(2)(*b*) of that Act (allowances for lost or spoiled instruments) is treated for the purposes of this section as a repayment of the duty or penalty by reference to which it is made.

In that case the relevant time is the date on which the payment of duty or penalty was made.

(6) No interest is payable under this section if the amount of the payment to which this section applies is less than £25.

(7) No interest is payable under this section in respect of a payment made in consequence of an order or judgment of a court having power to allow interest on the payment.

(8) Interest paid to any person under this section is not income of that person for any tax purposes.

(9) (*amends* FA 1989 s 178(2)).

(10) This section applies in relation to instruments executed on or after 1st October 1999.

Cross references—See FA 2000 Sch 33 para 5 (application of this section to repayments of any amount paid by way of stamp duty or penalty on late stamping under FA 2000 Sch 33 para 5).

111 Stamp duty on [transfer][1] on sale

(1)–(3) (*amend* FA 1963 s 55)).

(4) This section applies to instruments executed on or after 16th March 1999, except where the instrument in question is executed in pursuance of a contract made on or before 9th March 1999.

(5) This section shall be deemed to have come into force on 16th March 1999.

Amendments—[1] The word "transfer" substituted for the words "conveyance or transfer" in enactments relating to stamp duty by FA 2003 Sch 20 para 3.

112 General amendment of charging provisions

(1) The amount of any stamp duty chargeable *ad valorem*—

(*a*) shall be a percentage of the amount specified in the relevant charging provision, and

(*b*) shall be rounded up (if necessary) to the nearest multiple of £5.

Stamp Taxes

(2) The amount of every fixed stamp duty shall be £5.

(3) The provisions of Schedule 13 to this Act have effect in place of Schedule 1 to the Stamp Act 1891, and certain related enactments, so far as they relate to the instruments (other than bearer instruments) chargeable to duty and the method of calculation and rates of duty.

(4) The consequential amendments in Schedule 14 to this Act have effect.

(5) The percentage rates specified in Schedule 13 and the enactments amended by Schedule 14 correspond to the rates of duty generally in force at the passing of this Act.

In the case of an instrument in relation to which there was then in force transitional provision in connection with an earlier change in the rate of duty having the effect that a different rate applied, the new or amended provisions have effect as if a reference to a percentage corresponding to that different rate were substituted.

(6) This section has effect in relation to instruments executed on or after 1st October 1999.

113 Bearer instruments

(1) The provisions of Schedule 15 to this Act have effect in place of the heading "Bearer Instruments" in Schedule 1 to the Stamp Act 1891, and certain related enactments, and incorporate amendments in relation to bearer instruments corresponding to those made by—

section 109 (interest and penalties on late stamping),
section 112 (general amendment of charging provisions), and
Part I of Schedule 17 to this Act (amendments of penalties other than on late stamping).

(2) The percentage rates specified in Schedule 15 correspond to the rates of duty generally in force at the passing of this Act.

In the case of an instrument in relation to which there was then in force transitional provision in connection with an earlier change in the rate of duty having the effect that a different rate applied, the new provisions have effect as if a reference to a percentage corresponding to that different rate were substituted.

(3) The consequential amendments specified in Schedule 16 to this Act have effect.

(4) This section applies in relation to bearer instruments issued on or after 1st October 1999.

Prospective amendment—This section to be repealed by FA 1999 s 123(3), Sch 20 Pt V(6) with effect on the abolition day appointed by virtue of FA 1990 ss 107–111.

114 Penalties other than on late stamping

(1) The provisions of Schedule 17 to this Act (stamp duty: penalties other than on late stamping) have effect.

(2) The provisions of that Schedule have effect in relation to penalties in respect of things done or omitted on or after 1st October 1999.

115 Minor amendments and repeal of obsolete provisions

Schedule 18 to this Act (stamp duty: minor amendments and repeal of obsolete provisions) has effect.

Stamp duty reserve tax

116 Non-sterling bearer instruments issued in connection with merger or takeover

(1), (2) (*amend* FA 1986 ss 95, 97)).

(3) This section applies to any instrument issued on or after 30th January 1999, except one giving effect to an agreement for a company merger or takeover entered into in writing by the companies involved before that date.

Prospective amendment—This section to be repealed by FA 1999 s 123(3), Sch 20 Pt V(6) with effect on the appointed day by virtue of FA 1990 s 111(1).

117 Scope of exceptions for certain bearer instruments

(1)–(6) (*amend* FA 1986 ss 95(2), 97(3), *insert* ss 95(2A)–(2D), 97(3A)–(3D) and *substitute* ss 95(6), 97(7)).

(7) Subsections (1) to (6) above apply in relation to any instrument issued on or after 9th March 1999, except one giving effect to an agreement for a company merger or takeover entered into in writing by the companies involved before 30th January 1999.

Prospective amendment—This section to be repealed by FA 1999 s 123(3), Sch 20 Pt V(6) with effect on the appointed day by virtue of FA 1990 s 111(1).

118 Relief in case of certain replacement securities

(1)–(4) (*insert* FA 1996 ss 95A, 97AA and *amend* s 99(10)).

(5) This section applies in relation to securities issued on or after 1st May 1998.

119 Power to exempt UK depositary interests in foreign securities

(1) The Treasury may by regulations make provision excluding from the definition of "chargeable securities" in Part IV of the Finance Act 1986 such rights in or in relation to securities as, in accordance with the regulations, are to be treated as exempt UK depositary interests in foreign securities.

(2) Subject to subsection (3), the regulations may—

(*a*) define "depositary interest", "UK depositary interest" and "foreign securities" for this purpose; and

(*b*) exempt such descriptions of UK depositary interests in foreign securities (as so defined) as may from time to time be specified in the regulations.

(3) The regulations shall not make provision for the exemption of a depositary interest unless the terms of issue of the interest are such that it can only be transferred in accordance with regulations under section [785][1] of the Companies Act [2006][1] (transfer of securities without written instrument) or by means of a transfer within section 186(1) of the Finance Act 1996 (transfer of securities to member of electronic transfer system).

(4) The regulations may contain such incidental, supplementary, consequential and transitional provision as appears to the Treasury to be appropriate.

This may include provision modifying the enactments relating to stamp duty reserve tax for the purpose of giving effect to the exemption conferred by regulations under this section (or, where earlier regulations are varied or revoked, withdrawing an exemption formerly conferred).

(5) Regulations under this section may make different provision for different cases.

(6) Regulations under this section shall be made by statutory instrument which shall be subject to annulment in pursuance of a resolution of the House of Commons.

Amendments—[1] In sub-s (3), figures substituted for figures "207" and "1989", by the Companies Act 2006 (Consequential Amendments) (Taxes and National Insurance) Order, SI 2009/1890 art 11(*a*) with effect from 1 October 2009.

Prospective amendment—This section to be repealed by FA 1999 s 123(3), Sch 20 Pt V(6) with effect on the appointed day by virtue of FA 1990 s 111(1).

120 Minor amendments of exceptions to general charge

(1) Section 90 of the Finance Act 1986 (exceptions from the general charge to stamp duty reserve tax) is amended as follows.

(2) (*amend* FA 1986 s 90(3F)(*c*)).

(3) (*amend* FA 1986 s 90(5), (6)).

(4) Subsection (2) above applies to instruments issued on or after 9th March 1999.

(5) Subsection (3) above applies to agreements to transfer securities made on or after 9th March 1999.

Prospective amendment—This section to be repealed by FA 1999 s 123(3), Sch 20 Pt V(6) with effect on the appointed day by virtue of FA 1990 s 111(1).

121 Power to make regulations with respect to administration, etc

(1) The following provisions have effect with respect to the power conferred on the Treasury by section 98(1) of the Finance Act 1986 (stamp duty reserve tax: regulations with respect to administration, etc).

(2) That power includes power to make provision—

(*a*) applying the provisions of the Taxes Management Act 1970 relating to penalties and the payment of interest on overdue tax, and

(*b*) requiring information to be provided, or books, documents or other records to be made available for inspection, and imposing a penalty for failure to do so.

(3) That power includes, and shall be deemed always to have included, power to make provision requiring specified descriptions of persons to account for and pay tax, and any interest on it, on behalf of the person liable to pay it.

Regulations—See the Stamp Duty and Stamp Duty Reserve Tax (Definition of Unit Trust Scheme and Open-ended Investment Company) Regulations, SI 2001/964.

Prospective amendment—This section to be repealed by FA 1999 s 123(3), Sch 20 Pt V(6) with effect on the appointed day by virtue of FA 1990 s 111(1).

Units in unit trusts

122 Stamp duty and stamp duty reserve tax: unit trusts

(1) The following provisions of this Act (which apply generally to instruments executed on or after 1st October 1999)—

(*a*) section 109 and Schedule 12 (interest and penalties on late stamping),

(*b*) section 110 (interest on duty overpaid, etc), and

(*c*) section 112 and Schedules 13 and 14 (general amendment of charging provisions),

do not apply to transfers or other instruments relating to units under a unit trust scheme.

(2) Subsection (1) does not affect the operation of those provisions in relation to stamp duty—

(*a*) on a [transfer][1] on sale of property other than units under a unit trust scheme in relation to which such units form the whole or part of the consideration, or

(*b*) under Schedule 15 to this Act (bearer instruments).

(3) In subsections (1) and (2) "unit" and "unit trust scheme" have the same meaning as in Part VII of the Finance Act 1946 or Part III of the Finance (No 2) Act (Northern Ireland) 1946.

(4) Schedule 19 to this Act (stamp duty and stamp duty reserve tax: unit trusts) has effect. This subsection and that Schedule come into force on 6th February 2000.

Amendments—[1] The word "transfer" substituted for the words "conveyance or transfer" in enactments relating to stamp duty by FA 2003 Sch 20 para 3.

Supplementary provisions

123 Construction of this Part and other supplementary provisions

(1) This Part—

(*a*) so far as it relates to stamp duty shall be construed as one with the Stamp Act 1891, and

(*b*) so far as it relates to stamp duty reserve tax shall be construed as one with Part IV of the Finance Act 1986.

(2) In this Part—

(*a*) "the enactments relating to stamp duty" means the Stamp Act 1891 and any enactment amending or which is to be construed as one with that Act; and

(*b*) "the enactments relating to stamp duty reserve tax" means Part IV of the Finance Act 1986 and any enactment amending or which is to be construed as one with that Part.

(3) The following provisions of this Part shall cease to have effect on the day appointed under section 111(1) of the Finance Act 1990 (abolition of stamp duty for securities etc):

section 113;

sections 116 to 121;

subsections (1)(*b*) and (2)(*b*) of this section;

in Schedule 13—

paragraph 3,

in paragraph 4 the words "in the case of any other [transfer][1] on sale",

paragraph 7(1)(*b*)(ii) to (iv),

paragraph 24(*a*), (*b*) and (*d*);

in Schedule 14, paragraphs 5, 8, 12, 13, 16 to 21 and 23;

Schedule 15;

in Schedule 16, paragraphs 2 to 11;

in Schedule 17, paragraphs 6 to 8;

Parts I to III of Schedule 19;

in Part IV of that Schedule, the words "and the enactments relating to stamp duty reserve tax" in paragraphs 14(1), 15, 16, 17(1) and 18(1).

(4) The amendment by this Part, or the repeal in consequence of this Part, of any enactment relating to stamp duty does not affect that enactment as applied for any purpose other than stamp duty.

Amendments—[1] The word "transfer substituted for the words "conveyance or transfer" in enactments relating to stamp duty by FA 2003 Sch 20 para 3.

Prospective amendment—Sub-ss (1)(*b*) and (2)(*b*), and the word "and" immediately preceding it, to be repealed by FA 1999 s 123(3), Sch 20 Pt V(6) with effect on the appointed day by virtue of FA 1990 s 111(1).

PART VIII

MISCELLANEOUS AND SUPPLEMENTAL

Supplemental

139 Repeals

(1) The enactments mentioned in Schedule 20 to this Act (which include provisions that are spent or of no practical utility) are hereby repealed to the extent specified in the third column of that Schedule.

(2) The repeals specified in that Schedule have effect subject to the commencement provisions and savings contained or referred to in the notes set out in that Schedule.

140 Short title

This Act may be cited as the Finance Act 1999.

SCHEDULES

SCHEDULE 12

STAMP DUTY: INTEREST AND PENALTIES ON LATE STAMPING

Section 109(3)

Stamp Act 1891 (c 39)

1 (*substitutes* SA 1891 ss 12, 12A for original s 12).

2 (*substitutes* SA 1891 ss 13, 13A, 13B for original s 13).
3 (*amends* SA 1891 s 14).

Finance Act 1994 (c 9)

4 (*substitutes* FA 1994 ss 240, 240A for original s 240).

SCHEDULE 13

STAMP DUTY: INSTRUMENTS CHARGEABLE AND RATES OF DUTY

Section 112(3)

PART I

[TRANSFER][1] ON SALE

Amendments—[1] The word "transfer" substituted for the words "conveyance or transfer" in enactments relating to stamp duty by FA 2003 Sch 20 para 3.

Cross references—See FA 2000 s 118(2), (4) (for the purposes of this Part, in relation to land transferred for consideration of other property, the instrument transferring or vesting the estate or interest shall be taken to be a transfer on sale of the estate or interest).

FA 2000 s 119(2) (for the purposes of this Part, in relation to where an estate or interest in land is transferred to or vested in a company, the instrument transferring or vesting the estate or interest shall be taken to be a transfer on sale of the estate or interest).

FA 2000 s 121(2) (for the purposes of stamp duty chargeable under Part II of this Schedule, in reference to this Part, where a lease is granted to a connected company, the amount or value of consideration for the grant of the lease shall be taken to be the market value, immediately before the instrument granting the lease is executed, of the lease granted, but reduced by the value of so much of any actual consideration as does not consist of property).

FA 2000 s 122(2) (for the purposes of this Part, in relation to where marketable securities are transferred for exempt property, the instrument transferring the marketable securities shall be taken to be a transfer on sale of those securities).

FA 2000 s 130(1) (no stamp duty chargeable under this Part on a conveyance or transfer of an estate or interest in land, or on a lease of land, to registered social landlords etc).

FA 2000 Sch 34 para 2 (stamp duty reduced where part of the property concerned consists of intellectual property).

FA 2001 s 92(1) (no stamp duty chargeable under this Part on a conveyance of land or transfer of an estate or interest in land, or a lease of land, if the land is situated in a disadvantaged area).

FA 2001 Sch 30 para 1(1) (where any land is situated partly in a disadvantaged area and partly outside such an area, liability to stamp duty under this Part I on a conveyance or transfer of an estate or interest in the land, or a lease of the land, shall be determined in accordance with FA 2000 Sch 30 para 1(2))

FA 2003 s 125(1) (stamp duty is chargeable under this Schedule only on instruments relating to stock or marketable securities).

FA 2003 Sch 20 para 1 (application of that paragraph where stamp duty is chargeable under this Part on an instrument that relates partly to stock or marketable securities and partly to property other than stock or marketable securities).

Charge

1— (1) Stamp duty is chargeable on a [transfer][3] on sale.

(2) For this purpose "[transfer on sale]"[2] includes every instrument, and every decree or order of a court or commissioners, by which any property, or any estate or interest in property, is, on being sold, transferred to or vested in the purchaser or another person on behalf of or at the direction of the purchaser.

[(3) Sub-paragraph (1) is subject to sub-paragraphs [(3A)][4] to (6).][1]

[(3A) Stamp duty is not chargeable under sub-paragraph (1) on a transfer of stock or marketable securities where—

(*a*) the amount or value of the consideration for the sale is £1,000 or under, and
(*b*) the instrument is certified at £1,000.][4]

[(4) Where a company acquires any shares in itself by virtue of section [690][6] of the Companies Act [2006][6] (power of company to purchase own shares) or otherwise, sub-paragraph (1) does not apply to any instrument by which the shares are transferred to the company.][1]

[(5) Where a company holds any shares in itself by virtue of section [724][6] of that Act (treasury shares) or otherwise, [sub-paragraph (1) does not apply to any instrument to which sub-paragraph (6) applies.][5]][1]

[(6) This sub-paragraph applies to any instrument for the sale or transfer of any of the shares by the company, other than an instrument which, in the absence of sub-paragraph (5), would be an instrument in relation to which—

(*a*) section 67(2) of the Finance Act 1986 (transfer to person whose business is issuing depositary receipts etc), or
(*b*) section 70(2) of that Act (transfer to person who provides clearance services etc),

applied.][1]

Amendments—[1] Sub-paras (3)–(6) inserted by FA 2003 s 195, Sch 40 para 5 with effect for any acquisition of shares by a company on or after 1 December 2003 (by virtue of SI 2003/3077).

[2] In sub-para (2), words "transfer on sale" substituted for the words "conveyance on sale" by FA 2003 s 125(4), Sch 20 para 6 with effect—

(*a*) in relation to instruments effecting land transactions that—
(i) are SDLT transactions within the meaning of FA 2003 Sch 19, or
(ii) would be such transactions but for an exemption or relief from stamp duty land tax;

(*b*) in relation to other instruments, if they are executed on or after the implementation date for the purposes of stamp duty land tax.

The implementation date is 1 December 2003 (by virtue of SI 2003/2899).

FA 2003 s 125 and Sch 20 have effect subject to FA 2003 Sch 15 para 13(2), (3).

3 The word "transfer" substituted for the words "conveyance or transfer" in enactments relating to stamp duty by FA 2003 Sch 20 para 3.

4 In sub-para (3), reference substituted for reference "(4)", and sub-para (3A) inserted, by FA 2008 s 98(1)–(3), with effect in relation to instruments executed on or after 13 March 2008 and not stamped before 19 March 2008.

5 Words in sub-para (5) substituted, by FA 2008 s 99, Sch 32 para 10(1), (2) with effect in relation to instruments executed on or after 13 March 2008 and not stamped before 19 March 2008.

This amendment does not have effect in relation to an instrument effecting a land transaction or a duplicate or counterpart of such an instrument. "Land transaction" has the same meaning as in FA 2003 Part 4, except that it does not include a transfer of an interest in a property-investment partnership (within the meaning of FA 2003 Sch 15) (FA 2008 s 99, Sch 32 para 22).

Sub-para (5) previously read as follows—

"(5) Where a company holds any shares in itself by virtue of section 162A of that Act (treasury shares) or otherwise, any instrument to which sub-paragraph (6) applies is to be treated for the purposes of this Schedule as a conveyance otherwise than on sale, and paragraph 16 applies accordingly."

6 In sub-para (4), figures substituted for figures "162" and "1985", and in sub-para (5), figure substituted for figure "162A", by the Companies Act 2006 (Consequential Amendments) (Taxes and National Insurance) Order, SI 2009/1890 art 11(*b*), (*c*) with effect from 1 October 2009.

Rates of duty

2 Duty under this Part is chargeable by reference to the amount or value of the consideration for the sale.

3 In the case of a conveyance or transfer of stock or marketable securities the rate is 0.5%.

Notes—The word "transfer" substituted for the words "conveyance or transfer" in enactments relating to stamp duty: FA 2003 Sch 20 para 3.

Prospective amendment—Para 3 to be repealed by FA 1999 s 123(3), Sch 20 Pt V(6) with effect on the appointed day by virtue of FA 1990 s 111(1).

4 In the case of any other [transfer][2] on sale the rates of duty are as follows—

1.	Where the amount or value of the consideration is [£125,000][3] or under and the instrument is certified at [£125,000][3]	Nil
2.	Where the amount or value of the consideration is £250,000 or under and the instrument is certified at £250,000	1%
3.	Where the amount or value of the consideration is £500,000 or under and the instrument is certified at £500,000	[3%][1]
4.	Any other case	[4%][1]

Cross references—See FA 2000 Sch 33 para 3 (power to vary stamp duties not to be used to vary any threshold specified in this paragraph).

Amendments—1 Figures in table substituted by FA 2000 s 114(1) with effect for instruments executed after 27 March 2000, except in relation to an instrument giving effect to a contract made before 22 March 2000, unless—

(*a*) the instrument is made in consequence of the exercise after that date of any option, right of pre-emption or similar right; or

(*b*) the instrument transfers the property in question to, or vests it in, a person other than the purchaser under the contract, because of an assignment (or, in Scotland, assignation) or further contract made after that date.

Previously the figures read "2.5%" and "3.5%" respectively.

2 The word "transfer" substituted for the words "conveyance or transfer" in enactments relating to stamp duty by FA 2003 Sch 20 para 3.

3 "£125,000" substituted for "£120,000" by FA 2006 s 162(3), with effect in relation to instruments executed after 22 March 2006. Previous figure of "£120,000" substituted for "£60,000" by FA 2005 s 95(3), (5) with effect for instruments executed after 16 March 2005.

Prospective amendment—Words "in the case of any other conveyance or transfer on sale" in para 4 to be repealed by FA 1999 s 123(3), Sch 20 Pt V(6) with effect on the appointed day by virtue of FA 1990 s 111(1).

5 The above provisions are subject to any enactment setting a different rate or setting an upper limit on the amount of duty chargeable.

Meaning of instrument being certified at an amount

6— (1) The references in [paragraphs 1(3A) and][2] 4 above to an instrument being certified at a particular amount mean that it contains a statement that the transaction effected by the instrument does not form part of a larger transaction or series of transactions in respect of which the amount or value, or aggregate amount or value, of the consideration exceeds that amount.

(2) For this purpose a sale or contract or agreement for the sale of goods, wares or merchandise shall be disregarded—

(*a*) in the case of an instrument which is not an actual [transfer][1] of the goods, wares or merchandise (with or without other property);

(*b*) in the case of an instrument treated as such a [transfer][1] only by virtue of paragraph 7 (contracts or agreements chargeable as conveyances on sale);

and any statement as mentioned in sub-paragraph (1) shall be construed as leaving out of account any matter which is to be so disregarded.

Cross references—FA 2000 Sch 34 para 6 (intellectual property to be disregarded for the purposes of this paragraph).

FA 2001 Sch 30 para 3 (a transaction which relates (or the extent to which a transaction relates) to an estate or interest in land which is situated in a disadvantaged area to be disregarded for the purposes of this paragraph).

Amendments—[1] The word "transfer" substituted for the words "conveyance or transfer" in enactments relating to stamp duty by FA 2003 Sch 20 para 3.
[2] In sub-para (1), words substituted for word "paragraph" by FA 2008 s 98(4) with effect in relation to instruments executed on or after 13 March 2008 and not stamped before 19 March 2008.

Contracts or agreements chargeable as conveyances on sale

7— (1) A contract or agreement for the sale of—

(*a*) any equitable estate or interest in property, or
(*b*) any estate or interest in property except—
(i) land,
(ii) goods, wares or merchandise,
(iii) stock or marketable securities,
(iv) any ship or vessel, or a part interest, share or property of or in any ship or vessel, or
(v) property of any description situated outside the United Kingdom,

is chargeable with the same *ad valorem* duty, to be paid by the purchaser, as if it were an actual conveyance on sale of the estate, interest or property contracted or agreed to be sold.

(2) Where the purchaser has paid *ad valorem* duty and before having obtained a [transfer][1] of the property enters into a contract or agreement for the sale of the same, the contract or agreement is chargeable, if the consideration for that sale is in excess of the consideration for the original sale, with the *ad valorem* duty payable in respect of the excess consideration but is not otherwise chargeable.

(3) Where duty has been paid in conformity with sub-paragraphs (1) and (2), the [transfer][1] to the purchaser or sub-purchaser, or any other person on his behalf or by his direction, is not chargeable with any duty.

(4) In that case, upon application and upon production of the contract or agreement (or contracts or agreements) duly stamped, the Commissioners shall either—

(*a*) denote the payment of the *ad valorem* duty upon the [transfer][1], or
(*b*) transfer the *ad valorem* duty to the [transfer][1].

Cross references—FA 2003 Sch 19 para 6(1) (where in the case of a contract that, apart from this paragraph, would not be chargeable with stamp duty—
(*a*) a conveyance made in conformity with the contract is effected after the implementation date, and
(*b*) stamp duty land tax is duly paid in respect of that transaction or no tax is chargeable because of an exemption or relief, the contract shall be deemed to be duly stamped).
Prospective amendment—Sub-paras (1)(*b*)(i)–(iv) to be repealed by FA 1999 s 123(3), Sch 20 Pt V(6) with effect on the appointed day by virtue of FA 1990 s 111(1).
Amendments—[1] The word "transfer" substituted for the words "conveyance or transfer" in enactments relating to stamp duty by FA 2003 Sch 20 para 3.

8— (1) Where a contract or agreement would apart from paragraph 7 not be chargeable with any duty and a [transfer][1] made in conformity with the contract or agreement is presented to the Commissioners for stamping with the *ad valorem* duty chargeable on it—

(*a*) within the period of six months after the execution of the contract or agreement, or
(*b*) within such longer period as the Commissioners may think reasonable in the circumstances of the case,

the [transfer][1] shall be stamped accordingly, and both it and the contract or agreement shall be deemed to be duly stamped.

(2) Nothing in this paragraph affects the provisions as to the stamping of a conveyance or transfer after execution.

Amendments—[1] The word "transfer" substituted for the words "conveyance or transfer" in enactments relating to stamp duty: FA 2003 Sch 20 para 3.

9 The *ad valorem* duty paid upon a contract or agreement by virtue of paragraph 7 shall be repaid by the Commissioners if the contract or agreement is afterwards rescinded or annulled or is for any other reason not substantially performed or carried into effect so as to operate as or be followed by a [transfer][1].

Amendments—[1] The word "transfer" substituted for the words "conveyance or transfer" in enactments relating to stamp duty: FA 2003 Sch 20 para 3.

PART II

LEASE

Cross references—See FA 2000 s 121(2) (for the purposes of stamp duty chargeable under this Part, in reference to Part I of the Schedule, where a lease is granted to a connected company, the amount or value of consideration for the grant of the lease shall be taken to be the market value, immediately before the instrument granting the lease is executed, of the lease granted, but reduced by the value of so much of any actual consideration as does not consist of property).
FA 2000 s 130(1) (no stamp duty chargeable under this Part on a conveyance or transfer of an estate or interest in land, or on a lease of land, to registered social landlords etc).
FA 2001 s 92(1) (no stamp duty chargeable under this Part on a conveyance of land or transfer of an estate or interest in land, or a lease of land, if the land is situated in a disadvantaged area).
FA 2001 Sch 30 para 1(1) (where any land is situated partly in a disadvantaged area and partly outside such an area, liability to stamp duty under this Part I on a conveyance or transfer of an estate or interest in the land, or a lease of the land, shall be determined in accordance with FA 2000 Sch 30 para 1(2)).

FA 2003 s 128(1) (no stamp duty is chargeable under this Part on a lease of a dwelling granted by a registered social landlord to one or more individuals in accordance with arrangements to which FA 2003 s 128 applies if the lease is for an indefinite term or is terminable by notice of a month or less).

Charge

10 Stamp duty is chargeable on a lease.

Rates of duty

11 In the case of a lease for a definite term less than a year the duty is as follows—

1.	Lease of furnished dwelling-house or apartments where the rent for the term exceeds [£5,000][1]	£5
2.	Any other lease of land	The same duty as for a lease for a year at the rent reserved for the definite term

Cross references—See FA 2000 Sch 33 para 3 (power to vary stamp duties not to be used to vary any threshold specified in this paragraph in respect of rent or the term of a lease).

Amendments—[1] Sum in table substituted by FA 2000 s 115(1)(*a*) with effect for instruments executed after 27 March 2000.

12— (1) In the case of a lease of land for any other definite term, or for an indefinite term, the duty is determined as follows.

(2) If the consideration or part of the consideration moving to the lessor or to any other person consists of any money, stock, security or other property, the duty in respect of that consideration is the same as that on a conveyance on a sale for the same consideration.

But if—

(*a*) part of the consideration is rent, and

(*b*) that rent exceeds £600 a year,

the duty is calculated as if paragraph 1 of the Table in paragraph 4 of this Schedule were omitted.

(3) If the consideration or part of the consideration is rent, the duty in respect of that consideration is determined by reference to the rate or average rate of the rent (whether reserved as a yearly rent or not), as follows.

1.	Term [not more than 7 years][1] or indefinite—	
	(*a*) if the rent is [£5,000][2] or less	Nil
	(*b*) if the rent is more than [£5,000][2]	1%
2.	Term more than 7 years but not more than 35 years	2%
3.	Term more than 35 years but not more than 100 years	12%
4.	Term more than 100 years	24%

Cross references—See FA 2000 Sch 33 para 3 (power to vary stamp duties not to be used to vary any threshold specified in this paragraph in respect of rent or the term of a lease).

Amendments—[1] Words in table substituted by FA 2000 s 116(1) with effect for instruments executed after 30 September 1999, subject to transitional provisions for instruments executed after 30 September 1999 but before 28 March 2000: see FA 2000 Sch 32 below.

[2] Sums in table substituted by FA 2000 s 115(1)(*b*) with effect for instruments executed after 27 March 2000.

13 Stamp duty of £5 is chargeable on a lease not within paragraph 11 or 12 above.

Agreement for a lease charged as a lease

14— (1) An agreement for a lease is chargeable with the same duty as if it were an actual lease made for the term and consideration mentioned in the agreement.

(2) Where duty has been duly paid on an agreement for a lease and subsequent to that agreement a lease is granted which either—

(*a*) is in conformity with the agreement, or

(*b*) relates to substantially the same property and term as the agreement,

the duty which would otherwise be charged on the lease is reduced by the amount of the duty paid on the agreement.

(3) Sub-paragraph (1) does not apply to missives of let in Scotland that constitute an actual lease.

Subject to that, references in this paragraph to an agreement for a lease include missives of let in Scotland.

Lease for fixed term and then until determined

15— (1) For the purposes of this Part a lease granted for a fixed term and thereafter until determined is treated as a lease for a definite term equal to the fixed term together with such further period as must elapse before the earliest date at which the lease can be determined.

(2) Paragraph 14 (agreement for a lease charged as a lease) shall be construed accordingly.

PART III
OTHER INSTRUMENTS

[Transfer][1] otherwise than on sale[2]

16— *(1) Stamp duty of £5 is chargeable on a [transfer][1] of property otherwise than on sale.*

(2) In sub-paragraph (1) "[transfer][1]" includes every instrument, and every decree or order of a court or commissioners, by which any property is transferred to or vested in any person.[2]

Cross references—See FA 2000 s 130(1) (no stamp duty chargeable under this paragraph on a conveyance or transfer of an estate or interest in land, or on a lease of land, to registered social landlords etc).

FA 2001 s 92(1) (no stamp duty chargeable under this paragraph on a conveyance of land or transfer of an estate or interest in land, or a lease of land, if the land is situated in a disadvantaged area).

FA 2001 Sch 30 para 1(1) (where any land is situated partly in a disadvantaged area and partly outside such an area, liability to stamp duty under this paragraph on a conveyance or transfer of an estate or interest in the land, or a lease of the land, shall be determined in accordance with FA 2001 Sch 30 para 1(2)).

Amendments—[1] The word "transfer" substituted for the words "conveyance or transfer" in enactments relating to stamp duty by FA 2003 Sch 20 para 3.

[2] This para and preceding heading repealed by FA 2008 s 99, Sch 32 paras 9, 10(1), (3) with effect in relation to instruments executed on or after 13 March 2008 and not stamped before 19 March 2008.

This amendment does not have effect in relation to an instrument effecting a land transaction or a duplicate or counterpart of such an instrument. "Land transaction" has the same meaning as in FA 2003 Pt 4, except that it does not include a transfer of an interest in a property-investment partnership (within the meaning of FA 2003 Sch 15) (FA 2008 s 99, Sch 32 para 22).

Declaration of use or trust[2]

17— *(1) Stamp duty of £5 is chargeable on a declaration of any use or trust of or concerning property unless the instrument constitutes a [transfer][1] on sale.*

(2) This does not apply to a will.[2]

Amendments—[1] The word "transfer" substituted for the words "conveyance or transfer" in enactments relating to stamp duty by FA 2003 Sch 20 para 3.

[2] This para and preceding heading repealed by FA 2008 s 99, Sch 32 paras 9, 10(1), (3) with effect in relation to instruments executed on or after 13 March 2008 and not stamped before 19 March 2008.

This amendment does not have effect in relation to an instrument effecting a land transaction or a duplicate or counterpart of such an instrument. "Land transaction" has the same meaning as in FA 2003 Part 4, except that it does not include a transfer of an interest in a property-investment partnership (within the meaning of FA 2003 Sch 15) (FA 2008 s 99, Sch 32 para 22).

Dispositions in Scotland

18— (1) The following are chargeable with duty as a conveyance on sale—

(*a*) a disposition of heritable property in Scotland to singular successors or purchasers;

(*b*) a disposition of heritable property in Scotland to a purchaser containing a clause declaring all or any part of the purchase money a real burden upon, or affecting, the heritable property thereby disponed, or any part of it;

(*c*) …[1]

(2) *A disposition in Scotland of any property, or any right or interest in property, that is not so chargeable is chargeable with stamp duty of £5.[2]*

Amendment—[1] Sub-para (1)(*c*) repealed by the Abolition of Feudal Tenure etc (Scotland) Act 2000 s 76(1), (2), Sch 12 Pt I para 61, Sch 13 Pt 1 with effect from 28 November 2004 (by virtue of SI 2003/456).

[2] Sub-para (2) repealed by FA 2008 s 99, Sch 32 paras 9, 10(1), (3) with effect in relation to instruments executed on or after 13 March 2008 and not stamped before 19 March 2008.

This amendment does not have effect in relation to an instrument effecting a land transaction or a duplicate or counterpart of such an instrument. "Land transaction" has the same meaning as in FA 2003 Pt 4, except that it does not include a transfer of an interest in a property-investment partnership (within the meaning of FA 2003 Sch 15) (FA 2008 s 99, Sch 32 para 22).

Duplicate or counterpart

19— *(1) A duplicate or counterpart of an instrument chargeable with duty is chargeable with duty of £5.[1]*

(2) The duplicate or counterpart of an instrument chargeable with duty is not duly stamped unless—

(*a*) it is stamped as an original instrument, or

(*b*) it appears by some stamp impressed on it that the full and proper duty has been paid on the original instrument of which it is the duplicate or counterpart.

(3) Sub-paragraph (2) does not apply to the counterpart of an instrument chargeable as a lease, if that counterpart is not executed by or on behalf of any lessor or grantor.

Amendments—[1] Sub-para (1) repealed by FA 2008 s 99, Sch 32 paras 9, 10(1), (3) with effect in relation to instruments executed on or after 13 March 2008 and not stamped before 19 March 2008.

This amendment does not have effect in relation to an instrument effecting a land transaction or a duplicate or counterpart of such an instrument. "Land transaction" has the same meaning as in FA 2003 Pt 4, except that it does not include a transfer of an interest in a property-investment partnership (within the meaning of FA 2003 Sch 15) (FA 2008 s 99, Sch 32 para 22).

Instrument increasing rent

20— (1) An instrument (not itself a lease)—

(*a*) by which it is agreed that the rent reserved by a lease should be increased, or

(*b*) which confirms or records any such agreement made otherwise than in writing,

is chargeable with the same duty as if it were a lease in consideration of the additional rent made payable by it.

(2) Sub-paragraph (1) does not apply to an instrument giving effect to provision in the lease for periodic review of the rent reserved by it.

Partition or division

21— (1) Where on the partition or division of an estate or interest in land consideration exceeding £100 in amount or value is paid or given, or agreed to be paid or given, for equality, the principal or only instrument by which the partition or division is effected is chargeable with the same *ad valorem* duty as a conveyance on sale for the consideration, and with that duty only.

(2) Where there are several instruments for completing the title of either party, the principal instrument is to be ascertained, and the other instruments shall be charged with duty, as provided by sections 58(3) and 61 of the Stamp Act 1891 in the case of several instruments of conveyance.

(3) Stamp duty of £5 is chargeable on an instrument effecting a partition or division to which the above provisions do not apply.[1]

Release or renunciation[2]

22 *Stamp duty of £5 is chargeable on a release or renunciation of property unless the instrument constitutes a [transfer]*[1] *on sale.*[2]

Amendments—[1] The word "transfer" substituted for the words "conveyance or transfer" in enactments relating to stamp duty by FA 2003 Sch 20 para 3.

[2] This para and preceding heading repealed by FA 2008 s 99, Sch 32 paras 9, 10(1), (3) with effect in relation to instruments executed on or after 13 March 2008 and not stamped before 19 March 2008.

This amendment does not have effect in relation to an instrument effecting a land transaction or a duplicate or counterpart of such an instrument. "Land transaction" has the same meaning as in FA 2003 Pt 4, except that it does not include a transfer of an interest in a property-investment partnership (within the meaning of FA 2003 Sch 15) (FA 2008 s 99, Sch 32 para 22).

Surrender[2]

23 *Stamp duty of £5 is chargeable on a surrender of property unless the instrument constitutes a [transfer]*[1] *on sale.*[2]

Amendments—[1] The word "transfer" substituted for the words "conveyance or transfer" in enactments relating to stamp duty by FA 2003 Sch 20 para 3.

[2] This para and preceding heading repealed by FA 2008 s 99, Sch 32 paras 9, 10(1), (3) with effect in relation to instruments executed on or after 13 March 2008 and not stamped before 19 March 2008.

This amendment does not have effect in relation to an instrument effecting a land transaction or a duplicate or counterpart of such an instrument. "Land transaction" has the same meaning as in FA 2003 Pt 4, except that it does not include a transfer of an interest in a property-investment partnership (within the meaning of FA 2003 Sch 15) (FA 2008 s 99, Sch 32 para 22).

PART IV

GENERAL EXEMPTIONS

24 The following are exempt from stamp duty under this Schedule—

(*a*) transfers of shares in the government or parliamentary stocks or funds or strips (within the meaning of section 47 of the Finance Act 1942) of such stocks or funds;

(*b*) instruments for the sale, transfer, or other disposition (absolutely or otherwise) of any ship or vessel, or any part, interest, share or property of or in a ship or vessel;

(*c*) testaments, testamentary instruments and dispositions *mortis causa* in Scotland;

(*d*) renounceable letters of allotment, letters of rights or other similar instruments where the rights under the letter or other instrument are renounceable not later than six months after its issue.

Prospective amendment—Sub-paras (*a*), (*b*) and (*d*) to be repealed by FA 1999 s 123(3), Sch 20 Pt V(6) with effect on the appointed day by virtue of FA 1990 s 111(1).

25 Stamp duty is not chargeable under this Schedule on any description of instrument in respect of which duty was abolished by—

(*a*) section 64 of the Finance Act 1971 or section 5 of the Finance Act (Northern Ireland) 1971 (abolition of duty on mortgages, bonds, debentures etc), or

(*b*) section 173 of the Finance Act 1989 (life insurance policies and superannuation annuities).

26 Nothing in this Schedule affects any other enactment conferring exemption or relief from stamp duty.

SCHEDULE 14

STAMP DUTY: AMENDMENTS CONSEQUENTIAL ON SECTION 112

Section 112(4)

General amendments

1— (1) Any reference (express or implied) in any enactment, instrument or other document to any of the headings in Schedule 1 to the Stamp Act 1891 (other than the heading "Bearer Instrument") shall be construed, so far as is required for continuing its effect, as being or, as the case may require, including a reference to the corresponding provision of Schedule 13 to this Act.

(2) Sub-paragraph (1)—

(*a*) has effect subject to any express amendment made by this Act, and

(*b*) is without prejudice to the general application of section 17(2) of the Interpretation Act 1978 (general effect of repeal and re-enactment).

2 In the enactments relating to stamp duty for "lease or tack", wherever occurring, substitute "lease".

Finance Act 1930 (c 28)

3 (*amends* FA 1930 s 42(1)).

Finance Act (Northern Ireland) 1954 (c 23 (NI))

4 (*amends* FA(NI) 1954 s 11(1)).

Finance Act 1970 (c 24)

5 (*amends* FA 1970 s 33(1)).

Prospective amendment—This paragraph to be repealed by FA 1999 s 123(3), Sch 20 Pt V(6) with effect on the appointed day by virtue of FA 1990 s 111(1).

Finance Act 1980 (c 48)

6 (*amends* FA 1980 s 97(1)).

Finance Act 1982 (c 39)

7 (*amends* FA 1982 s 129(1)).

Finance Act 1985 (c 54)

8 (*amends* FA 1985 s 81).

Prospective amendment—This paragraph to be repealed by FA 1999 s 123(3), Sch 20 Pt V(6) with effect on the appointed day by virtue of FA 1990 s 111(1).

9 (*amends* FA 1985 s 82(5): *repealed* by FA 2008 s 100(2) in relation to instruments executed on or after 13 March 2008, other than instruments effecting a land transaction (within the meaning of FA 2008 Sch 32 para 22)).

10 (*amended* FA 1985 s 83: sub-para (*b*) *repealed* by FA 2008 s 99, Sch 32 para 20 with effect in relation to instruments executed on or after 13 March 2008 and not stamped before 19 March 2008. This amendment does not have effect in relation to an instrument effecting a land transaction or a duplicate or counterpart of such an instrument. "Land transaction" has the same meaning as in FA 2003 Pt 4, except that it does not include a transfer of an interest in a property-investment partnership (within the meaning of FA 2003 Sch 15) (FA 2008 s 99, Sch 32 para 22)).

11 (*amends* FA 1985 s 84: sub-para (*b*) *repealed* by FA 2008 s 99, Sch 32 para 20 with effect in relation to instruments executed on or after 13 March 2008 and not stamped before 19 March 2008. This amendment does not have effect in relation to an instrument effecting a land transaction or a duplicate or counterpart of such an instrument. "Land transaction" has the same meaning as in FA 2003 Pt 4, except that it does not include a transfer of an interest in a property-investment partnership (within the meaning of FA 2003 Sch 15) (FA 2008 s 99, Sch 32 para 22)).

Finance Act 1986 (c 41)

12 (*amends* FA 1986 s 67: sub-para (3) *repealed* by FA 2008 s 99, Sch 32 para 20 with effect in relation to instruments executed on or after 13 March 2008 and not stamped before 19 March 2008).

Prospective amendment—This paragraph to be repealed by FA 1999 s 123(3), Sch 20 Pt V(6) with effect on the appointed day by virtue of FA 1990 s 111(1).

13 (*amends* FA 1986 s 70:sub-para (3) *repealed* by FA 2008 s 99, Sch 32 para 20 with effect in relation to instruments executed on or after 13 March 2008 and not stamped before 19 March 2008).

Prospective amendment—This paragraph to be repealed by FA 1999 s 123(3), Sch 20 Pt V(6) with effect on the appointed day by virtue of FA 1990 s 111(1).

14 (*amends* FA 1986 s 75(2)).

15 (*amends* FA 1986 s 76).

16 (*amends* FA 1986 s 77(1)).

Prospective amendment—This paragraph to be repealed by FA 1999 s 123(3), Sch 20 Pt V(6) with effect on the appointed day by virtue of FA 1990 s 111(1).

17 (*amends* FA 1986 s 79).

Prospective amendment—This paragraph to be repealed by FA 1999 s 123(3), Sch 20 Pt V(6) with effect on the appointed day by virtue of FA 1990 s 111(1).

18 (*amends* FA 1986 s 80B(7)).

Prospective amendment—This paragraph to be repealed by FA 1999 s 123(3), Sch 20 Pt V(6) with effect on the appointed day by virtue of FA 1990 s 111(1).

19 (*amends* FA 1986 s 80C(8)).

Prospective amendment—This paragraph to be repealed by FA 1999 s 123(3), Sch 20 Pt V(6) with effect on the appointed day by virtue of FA 1990 s 111(1).

20 (*amends* FA 1986 s 88).

Prospective amendment—This paragraph to be repealed by FA 1999 s 123(3), Sch 20 Pt V(6) with effect on the appointed day by virtue of FA 1990 s 111(1).

Finance Act 1987 (*c 16*)

21 (*amends* FA 1987 s 50(1)).

Prospective amendment—This paragraph to be repealed by FA 1999 s 123(3), Sch 20 Pt V(6) with effect on the appointed day by virtue of FA 1990 s 111(1).

22 (*amends* FA 1987 s 55(1)).

Finance Act 1989 (*c 26*)

23 (*amends* FA 1989 s 175(1)).

Prospective amendment—This paragraph to be repealed by FA 1999 s 123(3), Sch 20 Pt V(6) with effect on the appointed day by virtue of FA 1990 s 111(1).

National Health Service and Community Care Act 1990 (*c 19*)

24 (*amends* the National Health Service and Community Care Act 1990 s 61(3)).

Finance Act 1991 (*c 31*)

25 (*amends* FA 1991 s 110).

26 (*amends* FA 1991 s 111(1)).

27 (*substitutes* FA 1991 s 113(1) (for original sub-ss (1)–(3)).

Finance Act 1993 (*c 34*)

28 (*amends* FA 1993 s 202).

29 (*amends* FA 1993 s 203(2)).

Finance Act 1994 (*c 9*)

30 (*amends* FA 1994 s 241(1)).

31 (*amends* FA 1994 s 242).

32 (*amends* FA 1994 s 243).

Finance Act 1995 (*c 4*)

33 (*amends* FA 1995 s 151).

SCHEDULE 15
STAMP DUTY: BEARER INSTRUMENTS

Section 113(1)

Prospective amendment—This Schedule to be repealed by FA 1999 s 123(3), Sch 20 Pt V(6) with effect on the appointed day by virtue of FA 1990 s 111(1).

PART I

CHARGING PROVISIONS

Charge on issue of instrument

1— (1) Stamp duty is chargeable—

(*a*) on the issue of a bearer instrument in the United Kingdom, and

(*b*) on the issue of a bearer instrument outside the United Kingdom by or on behalf of a UK company.

(2) This is subject to the exemptions in Part II of this Schedule.

Charge on transfer of stock by means of instrument

2 Stamp duty is chargeable on the transfer in the United Kingdom of the stock constituted by or transferable by means of a bearer instrument if duty was not chargeable under paragraph 1 on the issue of the instrument and—

(*a*) duty would be chargeable under Part I of Schedule 13 ([transfer][1] on sale) if the transfer were effected by an instrument other than a bearer instrument, or

(*b*) the stock constituted by or transferable by means of a bearer instrument consists of units under a unit trust scheme.

Amendments—[1] The word "transfer" substituted for the words "conveyance or transfer" in enactments relating to stamp duty by FA 2003 Sch 20 para 3.

Meaning of "bearer instrument"

3 In this Schedule "bearer instrument" means—

(*a*) a marketable security transferable by delivery;

(*b*) a share warrant or stock certificate to bearer or instrument to bearer (by whatever name called) having the like effect as such a warrant or certificate;

(*c*) a deposit certificate to bearer;

(*d*) any other instrument to bearer by means of which stock can be transferred; or

(*e*) an instrument issued by a non-UK company that is a bearer instrument by usage.

Rates of duty

4 The duty chargeable under this Schedule is 1.5% of the market value of the stock constituted by or transferable by means of the instrument, unless paragraph 5 or 6 applies.

5 In the case of—

(*a*) a deposit certificate in respect of stock of a single non-UK company, or

(*b*) an instrument issued by a non-UK company that is a bearer instrument by usage (and is not otherwise within the definition of "bearer instrument" in paragraph 3),

the duty is 0.2% of the market value of the stock constituted by or transferable by means of the instrument.

6 *In the case of an instrument given in substitution for a like instrument stamped ad valorem (whether under this Schedule or not) the duty is £5.*[1]

Amendments—[1] This para repealed by FA 2008 s 99, Sch 32 paras 9, 11(1), (2) with effect in relation to instruments executed on or after 13 March 2008 and not stamped before 19 March 2008.

Ascertainment of market value

7— (1) For the purposes of duty under paragraph 1 (charge on issue of instrument) the market value of the stock constituted by or transferable by means of the instrument is ascertained as follows.

(2) If the stock was offered for public subscription (whether in registered or in bearer form) within twelve months before the issue of the instrument, the market value shall be taken to be the amount subscribed for the stock.

(3) In any other case the market value shall be taken to be—

(*a*) the value of the stock on the first day within one month after the issue of the instrument on which stock of that description is dealt in on a stock exchange in the United Kingdom, or

(*b*) if stock of that description is not so dealt in, the value of the stock immediately after the issue of the instrument.

8— (1) For the purposes of duty under paragraph 2 (charge on transfer of stock by means of instrument) the market value of the stock constituted by or transferable by means of the instrument is ascertained as follows.

(2) In the case of a transfer pursuant to a contract of sale, the market value shall be taken to be the value of the stock on the date when the contract is made.

(3) In any other case, the market value shall be taken to be the value of the stock on the day preceding that on which the instrument is presented to the Commissioners for stamping, or, if it is not so presented, on the date of the transfer.

Meaning of "deposit certificate"

9 In this Schedule a "deposit certificate" means an instrument acknowledging the deposit of stock and entitling the bearer to rights (whether expressed as units or otherwise) in or in relation to the stock deposited or equivalent stock.

Bearer instruments by usage

10— (1) In this Schedule a "bearer instrument by usage" means an instrument—

(*a*) which is used for the purpose of transferring the right to stock, and

(*b*) delivery of which is treated by usage as sufficient for the purposes of a sale on the market, whether that delivery constitutes a legal transfer or not.

(2) A bearer instrument by usage is treated—

(*a*) as transferring the stock on delivery of the instrument, and

(*b*) as issued by the person by whom or on whose behalf it was first issued, whether or not it was then capable of being used for transferring the right to the stock without execution by the holder.

Meaning of "company", "UK company" and "non-UK company"

11 In this Schedule—

"company" includes any body of persons, corporate or unincorporate;

["UK company" means—

(*a*) a company that is formed or established in the United Kingdom (other than an SE which has its registered office outside the United Kingdom following a transfer in accordance with Article 8 of Council Regulation (EC) 2157/2001 on the Statute for a European Company (Societas Europaea)), or

(*b*) an SE which has its registered office in the United Kingdom following a transfer in accordance with Article 8 of that Regulation;][1] and

"non-UK company" means a company that is not a UK company.

Amendments—[1] Definition of "UK company" substituted by F(No 2)A 2005 s 58(3), (4) with effect for the purposes of determining whether or not stamp duty or stamp duty reserve tax is chargeable in respect of anything done on or after 1 April 2005.

That definition previously read as follows—

" 'UK company' means a company that is formed or established in the United Kingdom;".

Meaning of "stock" and "transfer"

12— (1) In this Schedule "stock" includes securities.

(2) References in this Schedule to stock include any interest in, or in any fraction of, stock or in any dividends or other rights arising out of stock and any right to an allotment of or to subscribe for stock.

(3) In this Schedule "transfer" includes negotiation, and "transferable", "transferred" and "transferring" shall be construed accordingly.

PART II
EXEMPTIONS

[Substitute instruments

12A— (1) Stamp duty is not chargeable on a substitute instrument.

(2) A substitute instrument is a bearer instrument given in substitution for a like instrument stamped *ad valorem* (whether under this Schedule or otherwise) ("the original instrument").

(3) The substitute instrument shall not be treated as duly stamped unless it appears by some stamp impressed on it that the full and proper duty has been paid on the original instrument.][1]

Amendments—[1] This para and preceding heading inserted by FA 2008 s 99, Sch 32 paras 9, 11(1), (3) with effect in relation to instruments executed on or after 13 March 2008 and not stamped before 19 March 2008.

Foreign loan securities

13 Stamp duty is not chargeable on a bearer instrument issued outside the United Kingdom in respect of a loan which is expressed in a currency other than sterling and which is not—

(*a*) offered for subscription in the United Kingdom, or

(*b*) offered for subscription with a view to an offer for sale in the United Kingdom of securities in respect of the loan.

Stock exempt from duty on transfer

14 Stamp duty is not chargeable under this Schedule on an instrument constituting, or used for transferring, stock (other than units in a unit trust) that is exempt from all stamp duties on transfer.

Instruments in respect of which duty previously abolished

15 Stamp duty is not chargeable under this Schedule on any description of instrument in respect of which duty was abolished by—

(*a*) section 64 of the Finance Act 1971 or section 5 of the Finance Act (Northern Ireland) 1971 (abolition of duty on mortgages, bonds, debentures etc), or

(*b*) section 173 of the Finance Act 1989 (life insurance policies and superannuation annuities).

Renounceable letters of allotment

16 Stamp duty is not chargeable under this Schedule on renounceable letters of allotment, letters of rights or other similar instruments where the rights under the letter or other instrument are renounceable not later than six months after its issue.

Instruments relating to non-sterling stock

17— (1) Stamp duty is not chargeable under this Schedule on the issue of an instrument which relates to stock expressed—

(*a*) in a currency other than sterling, or

(*b*) in units of account defined by reference to more than one currency (whether or not including sterling),

or on the transfer of the stock constituted by or transferable by means of any such instrument.

(2) Where the stock to which the instrument relates consists of a loan for the repayment of which there is an option between sterling and one or more other currencies, sub-paragraph (1) applies if the option is exercisable only by the holder of the stock and does not apply in any other case.

18 Where the capital stock of a company is not expressed in terms of any currency, it shall be treated for the purposes of paragraph 17 as expressed in the currency of the territory under the law of which the company is formed or established.

19— (1) A unit under a unit trust scheme or a share in a foreign mutual fund shall be treated for the purposes of paragraph 17 as capital stock of a company formed or established in the territory by the law of which the scheme or fund is governed.

(2) A "foreign mutual fund" means a fund administered under arrangements governed by the law of a territory outside the United Kingdom under which subscribers to the fund are entitled to participate in, or receive payments by reference to, profits or income arising to the fund from the acquisition, holding, management or disposal of investments.

(3) In relation to a foreign mutual fund "share" means the right of a subscriber, or of another in his right, to participate in or receive payments by reference to profits or income so arising.

Variation of original terms or conditions

20 Where a bearer instrument issued by or on behalf of a non-UK company in respect of a loan expressed in sterling—

(*a*) has been stamped *ad valorem*, or

[(*b*) has been stamped in accordance with paragraph 12A, or][1]

(*c*) has been stamped with the denoting stamp referred to in paragraph 21(2)(*b*) below,

duty is not chargeable under this Schedule by reason only that the instrument is amended on its face pursuant to an agreement for the variation of any of its original terms or conditions.

Amendments—[1] Para (*b*) substituted by FA 2008 s 99, Sch 32 paras 9, 11(1), (4) with effect in relation to instruments executed on or after 13 March 2008 and not stamped before 19 March 2008. Para (*b*) previously read as follows—

"(*b*) has been stamped with duty under paragraph 6 above (fixed duty on instrument given in substitution for another instrument stamped *ad valorem*), or".

PART III

SUPPLEMENTARY PROVISIONS

Duty chargeable on issue of instrument

21— (1) This paragraph applies where duty is chargeable under paragraph 1 of this Schedule.

(2) The instrument—

(*a*) shall before being issued be produced to the Commissioners, together with such particulars in writing of the instrument as the Commissioners may require, and

(*b*) shall be deemed to be duly stamped if and only if it is stamped with a particular stamp denoting that it has been produced to the Commissioners.

(3) Within six weeks of the date on which the instrument is issued, or such longer time as the Commissioners may allow, a statement in writing containing the date of the issue and such further particulars as the Commissioners may require in respect of the instrument shall be delivered to the Commissioners.

(4) The duty chargeable in respect of the instrument shall be paid to the Commissioners on delivery of that statement or within such longer time as the Commissioners may allow.

22— (1) If default is made in complying with paragraph 21—

(*a*) the person by whom or on whose behalf the instrument is issued, and

(*b*) any person who acts as the agent of that person for the purposes of the issue,

are each liable to a penalty not exceeding the aggregate of £300 and the duty chargeable.

(2) Those persons are also jointly and severally liable to pay to Her Majesty—

(*a*) the duty chargeable, and

(*b*) interest on the unpaid duty from the date of the default until the duty is paid.

Duty chargeable on transfer of stock by means of instrument

23— (1) This paragraph applies where duty is chargeable under paragraph 2 of this Schedule.

(2) Where the instrument is presented to the Commissioners for stamping—

(*a*) the person presenting it, and

(*b*) the owner of the instrument,

shall furnish to the Commissioners such particulars in writing as the Commissioners may require for determining the amount of duty chargeable.

(3) If the instrument is not duly stamped each person who in the United Kingdom—

(*a*) transfers any stock by or by means of the instrument, or

(*b*) is concerned as broker or agent in any such transfer,

is liable to a penalty not exceeding the aggregate of £300 and the amount of duty chargeable.

(4) Those persons are also jointly and severally liable to pay to Her Majesty—

(*a*) the duty chargeable, and

(*b*) interest on the unpaid duty from the date of the transfer in question until the duty is paid.

Supplementary provisions as to interest

24— (1) The following provisions apply to interest under paragraph 22(2) or 23(4).

(2) If an amount is lodged with the Commissioners in respect of the duty, the amount on which interest is payable is reduced by that amount.

(3) Interest is payable at the rate prescribed under section 178 of the Finance Act 1989 for the purposes of section 15A of the Stamp Act 1891 (interest on late stamping).

(4) The amount of interest shall be rounded down (if necessary) to the nearest multiple of £5. No interest is payable if the amount is less than £25.

(5) The interest shall be paid without any deduction of income tax and shall not be taken into account in computing income or profits for any tax purposes.

Penalty for false statement

25 A person who in furnishing particulars under this Part of this Schedule wilfully or negligently furnishes particulars that are false in any material respect is liable to a penalty not exceeding the aggregate of £300 and twice the amount by which the stamp duty chargeable exceeds that paid.

26 An instrument in respect of which duty is chargeable under paragraph 2 of this Schedule which—

(*a*) has been stamped *ad valorem*, …[1]

(*b*) …[1]

shall be treated as duly stamped for all purposes other than paragraph 25.

Amendments—[1] Para (*b*) and the "or" before it repealed by FA 2008 s 99, Sch 32 paras 9, 11(1), (5) with effect in relation to instruments executed on or after 13 March 2008 and not stamped before 19 March 2008. Para (*b*) previously read as follows—

"(*b*) has been stamped with a stamp indicating that it is chargeable with a fixed duty under paragraph 6 (instrument in substitution for one stamped *ad valorem*) and has been stamped under that paragraph,".

SCHEDULE 16

STAMP DUTY: AMENDMENTS CONSEQUENTIAL ON SECTION 113

Section 113(3)

General amendment

1— (1) Any reference (express or implied) in any enactment, instrument or other document to the heading "Bearer Instrument" in Schedule 1 to the Stamp Act 1891 shall be construed, so far as is required for continuing its effect, as being or, as the case may require, including a reference to Schedule 15 to this Act.

(2) Sub-paragraph (1)—

(*a*) has effect subject to any express amendment made by this Act, and

(*b*) is without prejudice to the general application of section 17(2) of the Interpretation Act 1978 (general effect of repeal and re-enactment).

Finance Act 1963 (*c 25*)

2 (*substitutes* FA 1963 s 67(4)).

Prospective amendment—This paragraph to be repealed by FA 1999 s 123(3), Sch 20 Pt V(6) with effect on the appointed day by virtue of FA 1990 s 111(1).

Finance Act 1976 (*c 40*)

3 (*amends* FA 1976 s 131(3)).

Prospective amendment—This paragraph to be repealed by FA 1999 s 123(3), Sch 20 Pt V(6) with effect on the appointed day by virtue of FA 1990 s 111(1).

Finance Act 1984 (*c 43*)

4 (*amends* FA 1984 s 126(3)(*c*), (5)).

Prospective amendment—This paragraph to be repealed by FA 1999 s 123(3), Sch 20 Pt V(6) with effect on the appointed day by virtue of FA 1990 s 111(1).

Finance Act 1986 (*c 41*)

5 (*amends* FA 1986 s 79(2)).

Prospective amendment—This paragraph to be repealed by FA 1999 s 123(3), Sch 20 Pt V(6) with effect on the appointed day by virtue of FA 1990 s 111(1).

6 (*amends* FA 1986 s 90).

Prospective amendment—This paragraph to be repealed by FA 1999 s 123(3), Sch 20 Pt V(6) with effect on the appointed day by virtue of FA 1990 s 111(1).

7— (1) (*substitutes* FA 1986 s 95(2)).

(2) There shall be no charge to tax under section 93 of that Act by virtue of paragraph (*b*) of subsection (2) of section 95 as substituted by sub-paragraph (1) above in the case of an instrument which gives effect to an agreement for a company merger or takeover entered into in writing by the companies involved before 30th January 1999.

Prospective amendment—This paragraph to be repealed by FA 1999 s 123(3), Sch 20 Pt V(6) with effect on the appointed day by virtue of FA 1990 s 111(1).

8— (1) (*substitutes* FA 1986 s 97(3)).

(2) There shall be no charge to tax under section 96 of that Act by virtue of paragraph (*b*) of subsection (3) of section 97 as substituted by sub-paragraph (1) above in the case of an instrument which gives effect to an agreement for a company merger or takeover entered into in writing by the companies involved before 30th January 1999.

Prospective amendment—This paragraph to be repealed by FA 1999 s 123(3), Sch 20 Pt V(6) with effect on the appointed day by virtue of FA 1990 s 111(1).

9 In section 99 of the Finance Act 1986 (interpretation of Part IV), after subsection (1) insert—

"(1A) 'Bearer instrument' has the same meaning as in Schedule 15 to the Finance Act 1999. An instrument is a 'UK bearer instrument' or 'non-UK bearer instrument' according to whether it is issued by or on behalf of a UK company or a non-UK company within the meaning of that Schedule.".

Prospective amendment—This paragraph to be repealed by FA 1999 s 123(3), Sch 20 Pt V(6) with effect on the appointed day by virtue of FA 1990 s 111(1).

Finance Act 1987 (*c 16*)

10 (*amends* FA 1987 s 50).

Prospective amendment—This paragraph to be repealed by FA 1999 s 123(3), Sch 20 Pt V(6) with effect on the appointed day by virtue of FA 1990 s 111(1).

Finance Act 1988 (*c 39*)

11 (*amends* FA 1987 s 143).

Prospective amendment—This paragraph to be repealed by FA 1999 s 123(3), Sch 20 Pt V(6) with effect on the appointed day by virtue of FA 1990 s 111(1).

Finance Act 1990 (*c 29*)

12 (*substitutes* FA 1990 s 107).

SCHEDULE 17

STAMP DUTY: PENALTIES OTHER THAN ON LATE STAMPING

Section 114

PART I

AMENDMENTS OF PENALTIES

Introduction

1 The amendments in this Part of this Schedule—

(*a*) replace administrative fines by penalties;

(*b*) amend provisions imposing a fine or penalty of a specified amount so as to impose a penalty not exceeding a specified amount;
(*c*) increase or modernise in certain cases the maximum penalty.

Stamp Duties Management Act 1891 (*c 38*)

2 (*amends* SDMA 1891 ss 12A, 21).

Stamp Act 1891 (*c 39*)

3 (*amends* SA 1891 ss 5, 9(1), 16, 17, 83).

Finance Act 1946 (*c 64*)

4 (*amends* FA 1946 s 56(3)).

Finance (*No 2*) *Act* (*Northern Ireland*) *1946* (*c 17* (*NI*))

5 (*amends* F(No 2)A (NI) 1946 s 27(3)).

Finance Act 1963 (*c 25*)

6 (*amends* FA 1963 s 67(1)).

Prospective amendment—This paragraph to be repealed by FA 1999 s 123(3), Sch 20 Pt V(6) with effect on the appointed day by virtue of FA 1990 s 111(1).

Finance Act (*Northern Ireland*) *1963* (*c 22* (*NI*))

7 (*amends* FA(NI) 1963 s 16(1)).

Prospective amendment—This paragraph to be repealed by FA 1999 s 123(3), Sch 20 Pt V(6) with effect on the appointed day by virtue of FA 1990 s 111(1).

Finance Act 1986 (*c 41*)

8 (*amends* FA 1986 ss 68(4), (5), 71(4), (5)).

Prospective amendment—This paragraph to be repealed by FA 1999 s 123(3), Sch 20 Pt V(6) with effect on the appointed day by virtue of FA 1990 s 111(1).

PART II

[DETERMINATION OF PENALTY, REVIEWS AND APPEALS][1]

Amendment—[1] Heading substituted by the Transfer of Tribunal Functions and Revenue and Customs Appeals Order, SI 2009/56 art 3, Sch 1 para 279 with effect from 1 April 2009. Text previously read as follows—
"Determination of penalty and appeals".

Introduction

9— (1) This Part of this Schedule applies to penalties under the enactments relating to stamp duty, other than penalties under section 15B of the Stamp Act 1891 (penalty on late stamping).

(2) Nothing in this Part of this Schedule affects criminal proceedings for an offence.

[(3) For the purposes of this Part "tribunal" means the First-tier Tribunal or, where determined by or under Tribunal Procedure Rules, the Upper Tribunal.][1]

Amendment—[1] Sub-para (3) inserted by the Transfer of Tribunal Functions and Revenue and Customs Appeals Order, SI 2009/56 art 3, Sch 1 para 280 with effect from 1 April 2009.

Determination of penalty by officer of Commissioners

10— (1) An officer of the Commissioners authorised by the Commissioners for the purposes of this paragraph may make a determination—

(*a*) imposing the penalty, and
(*b*) setting it at such amount as in the officer's opinion is correct or appropriate.

(2) Notice of the determination must be served on the person liable to the penalty.

The notice must also state—

(*a*) the date on which the notice is issued, and
(*b*) the time within which an appeal against the determination may be made.

(3) After notice of the determination has been served, the determination cannot be altered except—

(*a*) in accordance with sub-paragraph (4),
(*b*) by agreement in writing, or
(*c*) on appeal.

(4) If it is discovered by an officer of the Commissioners authorised by the Commissioners for the purposes of this paragraph that the amount of a penalty determined under this paragraph is or has become insufficient, the officer may make a determination in a further amount so that the penalty is set at the amount which in the officer's opinion is correct or appropriate.

(5) If a person liable to a penalty has died—

(*a*) any determination which could have been made in relation to that person may be made in relation to his personal representatives, and

(*b*) any penalty imposed on them is a debt due from and payable out of the person's estate.

(6) A penalty determined under this paragraph is due and payable at the end of the period of 30 days beginning with the date of the issue of the notice of determination.

11— (1) An appeal [may be made][1] against a determination under paragraph 10.

(2) Notice of appeal must be given in writing to the officer of the Commissioners by whom the determination was made within 30 days of the date of the notice of the determination.

(3) …[1]

[(4) The notice of appeal must specify the grounds of appeal.

[(4A) Sections 49A to 49I of the Taxes Management Act 1970 shall apply to appeals under this paragraph, subject to the modifications in sub-paragraphs (4B) to (4E).

(4B) In the application of section 49C(4) for "contained in an agreement in writing under section 54(1) for the settlement of the matter" there is to be substituted "a written agreement under paragraph 10(3)(b) of Schedule 17 to the Finance Act 1999".

(4C) Section 49C(5) and (6) are not to apply.

(4D) In the application of section 49F(2) for "an agreement in writing under section 54(1) for the settlement of the matter in question" there is to be substituted "a written agreement under paragraph 10(3)(b) of Schedule 17 to the Finance Act 1999",

(4E) Sections 49F(3) and (4) are not to apply.

(4F) References to "the tribunal" are to be taken to be references to the "First-tier Tribunal.][1]

(5) …[1]

(6) On an appeal under this paragraph the [First-tier Tribunal][1] may—

(*a*) if it appears to them that no penalty has been incurred, set the determination aside;

(*b*) if the amount determined appears …[1] to be appropriate, confirm the determination;

(*c*) if the amount determined appears …[1] to be excessive, reduce it to such other amount (including nil) as [the First-tier Tribunal considers][1] appropriate;

(*d*) if the amount determined appears to them to be insufficient, increase it to such amount not exceeding the permitted maximum as [the First-tier Tribunal considers][1] appropriate.

Amendments—[1] In sub-para (1) words substituted for the words "lies to the Special Commissioners"; sub-paras (3), (5) repealed; sub-para (4) substituted; sub-paras (4A)–(4F) inserted; in sub-para (6) words at the beginning substituted for the words "Special Commissioners"; in sub para (6)(*b*), (*c*) words "to them" repealed in both places; in sub-para (6)(*c*), (*d*) words substituted for the words "they consider" in both places by the Transfer of Tribunal Functions and Revenue and Customs Appeals Order, SI 2009/56 art 3, Sch 1 para 281 with effect from 1 April 2009. Sub-paras (3), (4), (5) previously read as follows—

"(3) An appeal may be brought out of time with the consent of the Commissioners or the Special Commissioners.

The Commissioners—

(*a*) shall give that consent if satisfied, on an application for that purpose, that there was a reasonable excuse for not bringing the appeal within the time limit, and

(*b*) if not so satisfied, shall refer the matter for determination by the Special Commissioners.

(4) The notice of appeal must specify the grounds of appeal, but on the hearing of the appeal the Special Commissioners may allow the appellant to put forward a ground not specified in the notice of appeal, and take it into consideration, if satisfied that the omission was not wilful or unreasonable.

(5) The powers conferred by section 46A(1)(*c*) and (2) to (4) and sections 56B to 56D of the Taxes Management Act 1970 (power of Lord Chancellor to make regulations as to jurisdiction, practice and procedure in relation to appeals to Special Commissioners) apply in relation to appeals under this paragraph.'

[11A— (1) This paragraph applies in a case where—

(*a*) notice of appeal may be given to HMRC, but

(*b*) no notice is given before the relevant time limit.

(2) Notice may be given after the relevant time limit if—

(*a*) HMRC agree, or

(*b*) where HMRC do not agree, the tribunal gives permission.

(3) If the following conditions are met, HMRC shall agree to notice being given after the relevant time limit.

(4) Condition A is that the appellant has made a request in writing to HMRC to agree to the notice being given.

(5) Condition B is that HMRC are satisfied that there was reasonable excuse for not giving the notice before the relevant time limit.

(6) Condition C is that HMRC are satisfied that the request under sub-paragraph (4) was made without unreasonable delay after the reasonable excuse ceased.

(7) If a request of the kind referred to in sub-paragraph (4) is made, HMRC must notify the appellant whether or not HMRC agree to the appellant giving notice of appeal after the relevant time limit.

(8) In this paragraph "relevant time limit", in relation to notice of appeal, means the time before which the notice is to be given (but for this paragraph).][1]

Amendment—[1] Paragraph 11A inserted by the Transfer of Tribunal Functions and Revenue and Customs Appeals Order, SI 2009/56 art 3, Sch 1 para 282 with effect from 1 April 2009.

12— (1) ...[1]

[(2) In addition to any right of appeal on a point of law under section 11(2) of the Tribunals, Courts and Enforcement Act 2007, the person liable to the penalty may appeal to the Upper Tribunal against the amount of the penalty which had been determined under paragraph 11(6) above, but not against any decision which falls under section 11(5)(*d*) or (*e*) of that Act and was made in connection with the determination of the amount of the penalty.

(2A) Section 11(3) and (4) of the Tribunals, Courts and Enforcement Act 2007 applies to the right of appeal under sub-paragraph (2) as it applies to the right of appeal under section 11(2) of that Act.

(3) On an appeal under sub-paragraph (2) the [Upper Tribunal][1] has the same powers as are conferred on the [First-tier Tribunal][1] by paragraph 11(6) above.

Amendment—[1] Sub-para (1) repealed; sub-paras (2), (2A) substituted for former sub-para (2); in sub-para (3) words substituted in the first place for the word "court" and in the second place for the words "Special Commissioners" by the Transfer of Tribunal Functions and Revenue and Customs Appeals Order, SI 2009/56 art 3, Sch 1 para 283 with effect from 1 April 2009. Sub-paras (1), (2) previously read as follows—

"(1) Section 56A of the Taxes Management Act 1970 (general right of appeal on point of law) applies in relation to a decision of the Special Commissioners under paragraph 11.

(2) Without prejudice to that right of appeal, an appeal lies against the amount of a penalty determined by the Special Commissioners under paragraph 11, at the instance of the person liable to the penalty—

(*a*) to the High Court, or

(*b*) in Scotland, to the Court of Session sitting as the Court of Exchequer."

Penalty proceedings before the court

13— (1) Where in the opinion of the Commissioners the liability of a person for a penalty arises by reason of his fraud or the fraud of another person, proceedings for the penalty may be brought—

(*a*) in the High Court, or

(*b*) in Scotland, in the Court of Session sitting as the Court of Exchequer.

(2) Proceedings under this paragraph in England and Wales shall be brought—

(*a*) by and in the name of the Commissioners as an authorised department for the purposes of the Crown Proceedings Act 1947, or

(*b*) in the name of the Attorney General.

Any such proceedings shall be deemed to be civil proceedings by the Crown within the meaning of Part II of the Crown Proceedings Act 1947.

(3) Proceedings under this paragraph in Scotland shall be brought in the name of the Advocate General for Scotland.

(4) Proceedings under this paragraph in Northern Ireland shall be brought—

(*a*) by and in the name of the Commissioners as an authorised department for the purposes of the Crown Proceedings Act 1947 as for the time being in force in Northern Ireland, or

(*b*) in the name of the Attorney General for Northern Ireland.

Any such proceedings shall be deemed to be civil proceedings within the meaning of Part II of the Crown Proceedings Act 1947 as for the time being in force in Northern Ireland.

(5) If in proceedings under this paragraph the court does not find that fraud is proved but considers that the person concerned is nevertheless liable to a penalty, the court may determine a penalty notwithstanding that, but for the opinion of the Commissioners as to fraud, the penalty would not have been a matter for the court.

(6) Paragraph 10 above (determination of penalty by officer of Commissioners) does not apply where proceedings are brought under this paragraph.

Supplementary provisions

14— (1) The Commissioners may in their discretion mitigate any penalty, or stay or compound any proceedings for the recovery of a penalty.

(2) They may also, after judgment, further mitigate or entirely remit the penalty.

15 A penalty may be determined under paragraph 10, or proceedings for a penalty brought under paragraph 13, at any time within six years after the date on which the penalty was incurred.

PART III

POWER TO APPLY PROVISIONS AS TO COLLECTION AND RECOVERY ETC

16— (1) The Treasury may make regulations applying in relation to penalties to which Part II of this Schedule applies such provisions of the Taxes Management Act 1970 as they think fit.

(2) The regulations may apply the provisions of that Act with such modifications as the Treasury think fit.

(3) Regulations under this paragraph shall be made by statutory instrument which shall be subject to annulment in pursuance of a resolution of the House of Commons.

17 Without prejudice to the generality of the power conferred by paragraph 16, regulations under that paragraph may apply—

(*a*) any of the provisions of Part VI of the Taxes Management Act 1970 (collection and recovery), and

(*b*) such of the provisions of Part XI of that Act (miscellaneous and supplemental provisions) as appear to the Treasury to be appropriate.

18 Sections 21, 22 and 35 of the Inland Revenue Regulation Act 1890 (proceedings for fines, etc) do not apply in relation to penalties to which Part II of this Schedule applies.

SCHEDULE 18

STAMP DUTY: MINOR AMENDMENTS AND REPEAL OF OBSOLETE PROVISIONS

Section 115

PART I

MINOR AMENDMENTS

Introduction

1 The provisions of this Part of this Schedule have effect for the purposes of the enactments relating to stamp duty.

Payment by cheque

2— (1) Where—

(*a*) any payment to the Commissioners is made by cheque, and

(*b*) the cheque is paid on its first presentation to the banker on whom it is drawn,

the payment is treated as made on the day on which the cheque was first received by the Commissioners.

(2) Sub-paragraph (1) applies where the cheque was first received by the Commissioners on or after 1st October 1999.

[Admissibility of evidence not affected by offer of settlement etc][1]

3— (1) Statements made or documents produced by or on behalf of a person are not inadmissible in any such proceedings as are mentioned in sub-paragraph (2) by reason only that it has been drawn to that person's attention—

[(*a*) that where serious stamp duty fraud has been committed the Board may accept a money settlement and that the Board will accept such a settlement, and will not pursue a criminal prosecution, if he makes a full confession of all stamp duty irregularities, or][1]

[(*b*) that the extent to which he is helpful and volunteers information is a factor that will be taken into account in determining the amount of any penalty,][1]

and that he was or may have been induced thereby to make the statements or produce the documents.

(2) The proceedings mentioned in sub-paragraph (1) are—

(*a*) any criminal proceedings against the person in question for any form of fraudulent conduct in connection with or in relation to stamp duty, and

(*b*) any proceedings against that person for the recovery of any stamp duty or interest on unpaid stamp duty due from him, and

(*c*) any proceedings for a penalty, or on appeal against the determination of a penalty, in connection with or in relation to stamp duty.

Amendments—[1] Sub-para (1)(*a*), (*b*) substituted, and Heading substituted, by FA 2003 s 206(3)–(5) with effect for statements made, or documents produced, after the passing of FA 2003. The Act received Royal Assent on 10 July 2003.

The Heading previously read as follows—

"Evidence in cases of fraudulent conduct, etc".

Sub-para (1)(*a*), (*b*) previously read as follows—

"(*a*) that pecuniary settlements may be accepted instead of a penalty being determined, or proceedings being instituted, or

(*b*) that, though no undertaking can be given as to whether or not the Commissioners will accept such a settlement in the case of any particular person, it is the practice of the Commissioners to be influenced by the fact that a person has made a full confession of any fraudulent conduct to which he had been a party and has given full facilities for investigation,".

References to duration of lease

4 In relation to Scotland, the expression "term", where referring to the duration of a lease, means "period".

PART II

OBSOLETE PROVISIONS

5— (1)–(5) (*amend* SDMA 1891 s 13).

(6) This paragraph has effect in relation to things done or omitted on or after 1st October 1999.

6— (1) (*repeals* SDMA 1891 ss 2–6, 8, 9(2), (3), 12, 17–20, 25 and *amends* s 11).

(2) This paragraph comes into force on 1st October 1999.

SCHEDULE 19

STAMP DUTY AND STAMP DUTY RESERVE TAX: UNIT TRUSTS

Section 122(4)

Prospective amendment—Parts I–III, and the words "and the enactments relating to stamp duty reserve tax" in paras 14(1), 15, 16, 17(1) and 18(1) of Part IV of this Schedule to be repealed by FA 1999 s 123(3), Sch 20 Pt V(6) with effect on the appointed day by virtue of FA 1990 s 111(1).

PART I

ABOLITION OF STAMP DUTY ON TRANSFERS ETC OF UNITS IN UNIT TRUSTS

1— (1) No stamp duty is chargeable on a transfer or other instrument relating to a unit under a unit trust scheme.

(2) Sub-paragraph (1) does not affect any charge to stamp duty—

(*a*) on a [transfer][1] on sale of property other than units under a unit trust scheme in relation to which such units form the whole or part of the consideration, or

(*b*) under Schedule 15 to this Act (bearer instruments).

(3) This paragraph has effect in relation to instruments executed on or after 6th February 2000.

Prospective amendment—This Part to be repealed by FA 1999 s 123(3), Sch 20 Pt V(6) with effect on the appointed day by virtue of FA 1990 s 111(1).

Amendments—[1] The word "transfer" substituted for the words "conveyance or transfer" in enactments relating to stamp duty by FA 2003 Sch 20 para 3.

PART II

STAMP DUTY RESERVE TAX ON DEALINGS WITH UNITS IN UNIT TRUSTS

Cross reference—See FA 2001 s 94(1) (where there are two or more classes of shares in an open-ended investment company and the company's instrument of incorporation—

(*a*) provides that shares of one or more of those classes ("the IPA classes") may only be held within an individual pension account, and

(*b*) does not make such provision in relation to shares of at least one other class,

there is no charge to SDRT under this Part on the surrender of a share of any of the IPA classes with effect for surrenders made or effected after 5 April 2001).

Prospective amendment—This Part to be repealed by FA 1999 s 123(3), Sch 20 Pt V(6) with effect on the appointed day by virtue of FA 1990 s 111(1).

Charge to tax

2— (1) There is a charge to stamp duty reserve tax where—

(*a*) a person authorises or requires the trustees or managers under a unit trust scheme to treat him as no longer interested in a unit under the scheme, or

(*b*) a unit under a unit trust scheme is transferred to the managers of the scheme,

and the unit is a chargeable security.

Those events are referred to in this Part of this Schedule as a "surrender" of the unit to the managers.

(2) The tax is chargeable—

(*a*) whether the surrender is made or effected in the United Kingdom or elsewhere, and

(*b*) whether or not any party is resident or situate in any part of the United Kingdom.

(3) The persons liable for the tax are the trustees of the unit trust.

(4) This paragraph is subject to the exclusions provided for in paragraphs 6[, 6A][1] and 7.

Amendment—[1] Word in sub-para (4) inserted by FA 2001 s 93(2), (6) with effect for surrenders made or effected after 5 April 2001.

Rate of tax

3— (1) Tax under this Part of this Schedule is chargeable at the rate of 0.5% of the market value of the unit.

This is subject to any reduction under paragraph 4 or 5.

(2) The market value of a unit means whichever is higher of—

(*a*) the price the unit might reasonably be expected to fetch on a sale in the open market at the time of surrender, and
(*b*) its cancellation price, or if it is redeemed its redemption price, at that time, calculated in accordance with the trust instrument.

Proportionate reduction of tax by reference to units issued

4— (1) The amount of tax chargeable shall be proportionately reduced if the number of units of the same class as the unit in question that are surrendered to the managers in the relevant two-week period exceeds the number of units of that class issued by the managers in that period.

(2) The "relevant two-week period" in relation to a surrender is the period from the beginning of the week in which the surrender occurs to the end of the following week.

For this purpose a week means a period of seven days beginning with a Sunday.

(3) The reduction is made by applying the following fraction to the amount otherwise chargeable—

$$\frac{I}{S}$$

Where:

I is the number of units of the class issued by the managers in the relevant two-week period, and
S is the number of units of the class surrendered to the managers in that period.

(4) If a consolidation or sub-division of units affects the comparison of the number of units surrendered and the number of units issued, the numbers shall be determined as if the consolidation or sub-division had not taken place.

"Consolidation or sub-division" includes any alteration of the number of units of the class in question otherwise than in consequence of an increase or reduction in the trust property.

(5) This paragraph does not apply if on the surrender of the unit the unit holder receives anything other than money; and for the purposes of this paragraph no account shall be taken of a surrender or issue that is not entirely for money.

[(6) If a certificate is given in accordance with paragraph 6A(1)(*c*) in respect of a period which includes the relevant two-week period in the case of the unit in question in sub-paragraph (1), there shall be left out of account in applying this paragraph in relation to that unit—

(*a*) any issue of a unit which is to be held within an individual pension account, and
(*b*) any surrender of a unit which, immediately before the surrender, was held within an individual pension account.][1]

[(7) "Individual pension account" has the same meaning in sub-paragraph (6) as it has in paragraph 6A.][1]

Modification—This section is modified, in relation to open-ended investment companies, by the Stamp Duty and Stamp Duty Reserve Tax (Open-ended Investment Companies) Regulations, SI 1997/1156, regs 4, 4A(1), (2), as amended by the Stamp Duty and Stamp Duty Reserve Tax (Open-ended Investment Companies) (Amendment No 2) Regulations, SI 1999/3261, reg 5, with effect from 6 February 2000.

Amendments—[1] Sub-paras (6), (7) inserted by FA 2001 s 93(3), (5) with effect where the relevant two-week period mentioned in FA 1999 Sch 19 para 4(1) ends after 6 April 2001.

Proportionate reduction of tax by reference to assets held

5— (1) The amount of tax chargeable after any reduction under paragraph 4 shall be further reduced if in the relevant two-week period the trust property is invested in both exempt and non-exempt investments.

(2) The reduction is made by applying the following fraction to that amount—

$$\frac{N}{N + E}$$

Where—

N is the average market value of the non-exempt investments over the relevant two-week period, and
E is the average market value of the exempt investments over that period.

(3) In this paragraph "exempt investment" has the same meaning as in section 99(5A)(*b*) of the Finance Act 1986; and "non-exempt investment" means any investment that is not an exempt investment.

Exclusion of charge in certain cases of change of ownership

6— (1) This paragraph applies where in pursuance of arrangements between the person entitled to a unit and another person ("the new owner")—

(*a*) the unit is surrendered to the managers, and
(*b*) the person surrendering the unit authorises or requires the managers or trustees to treat the new owner as entitled to it.

(2) There is no charge to tax under this Part of this Schedule if no consideration in money or money's worth is given in connection with the surrender of the unit or the new owner's becoming entitled to it.

(3) There is no charge to tax under this Part of this Schedule if the new owner is—

(*a*) a body of persons established for charitable purposes only, or
(*b*) the trustees of a trust established for those purposes only, or
(*c*) the Trustees of the National Heritage Memorial Fund, or
(*d*) the Historic Buildings and Monuments Commission for England.

(4) There is no charge to tax under this Part of this Schedule if an instrument executed at the time of the surrender—

(*a*) in pursuance of arrangements between the person entitled to the unit and the new owner, and
(*b*) transferring the unit from the one to the other,

would be exempt from stamp duty (if stamp duty were otherwise chargeable) by virtue of any of the provisions mentioned in sub-paragraph (5).

(5) The provisions referred to in sub-paragraph (4) are—

(*a*) section 42 of the Finance Act 1930 or section 11 of the Finance Act (Northern Ireland) 1954 (transfers between associated companies); and
(*b*) regulations under section 87(2) of the Finance Act 1985 (power to exempt instruments from stamp duty of fixed amount)[; and
(*c*) section 96 of the Finance Act 1997 (demutualisation of insurance companies).][2]

(6) Where by virtue of sub-paragraph (2), (3) or (4) there is no charge to tax, both the surrender and the related issue shall be left out of account for the purposes of paragraph 4.

[Exclusion of charge in case of individual pension accounts

6A— (1) There is no charge to tax under this Part of this Schedule on the surrender of the unit if—

(*a*) immediately before the surrender, the unit is held within an individual pension account,
(*b*) not all the units under the unit trust scheme are so held at that time, and
(*c*) a certificate pursuant to sub-paragraph (2) is contained in, or provided with, the relevant monthly tax return.

(2) The certificate must be given by the persons making the relevant monthly tax return and must state—

(*a*) that at all times in the period to which the return relates the trustees or managers were able to identify which of the units under the scheme were held within individual pension accounts, and
(*b*) that at no time in that period have the trustees or managers imposed any charge on, or recovered any amount from, an IPA unit holder which included an amount directly or indirectly attributable to tax payable by the trustees under this Part of this Schedule.

(3) In sub-paragraph (2), "IPA unit holder" means—

(*a*) a person acquiring, or who has acquired, a unit under the unit trust scheme, where the unit is to be held within an individual pension account,
(*b*) a person holding a unit under the scheme, where the unit is held within an individual pension account, or
(*c*) a person surrendering, or who has surrendered, a unit under the scheme, where immediately before the surrender the unit is or was held within an individual pension account.

(4) In this paragraph—

["individual pension account" has the meaning given by regulations made by the Commissioners of Inland Revenue;][3]
"the relevant monthly tax return", in the case of any surrender, means the notice required by regulations under section 98 of the Finance Act 1986 to be given by the managers (or, failing that, the trustees) under the unit trust scheme to the Commissioners of Inland Revenue containing among other things details of all surrenders in the relevant two-week period;
"the relevant two-week period" has the meaning given by paragraph 4(2).][1]

[(5) Regulations under sub-paragraph (4) shall be made by statutory instrument which shall be subject to annulment in pursuance of a resolution of the House of Commons.][3]

Amendment—[1] This paragraph inserted by FA 2001 s 93(4), (6) with effect for surrenders made or effected after 5 April 2001.
[2] Sub-para (5)(*c*) and preceding word "; and" inserted by FA 2005 s 97(4), (6) with effect for surrenders (within the meaning of FA 1999 Sch 19 Pt 2) occurring on or after 7 April 2005.
[3] Definition of "individual pension account" in sub-para (3) substituted, and sub-para (5) inserted, by FA 2004 s 281, Sch 35 para 46, with effect from 6 April 2006, subject to transitional provisions and savings in FA 2004 Sch 36.

Exclusion of charge in case of in specie redemption

7 There is no charge to tax under this Part of this Schedule if on the surrender of the unit the unit holder receives only such part of each description of asset in the trust property as is proportionate to, or as nearly as practicable proportionate to, the unit holder's share.

Interpretation

8— (1) For the purposes of this Part of this Schedule "issue" in the context of the issue of a unit by the managers under a unit trust scheme includes their transferring an existing unit or authorising or requiring the trustees to treat a person as entitled to a unit under the scheme.

(2) References in this Part of this Schedule to the surrender or issue of a unit under a unit trust scheme do not include a surrender or issue effected by means of, or consisting of the issue of, a certificate to bearer.

Transitional provision

9 This Part of this Schedule applies where the surrender of the unit to the managers occurs on or after 6th February 2000.

Prospective amendment—This paragraph to be repealed by FA 1999 s 123(3), Sch 20 Pt V(6) with effect on the appointed day by virtue of FA 1990 s 111(1).

PART III

MINOR AND CONSEQUENTIAL AMENDMENTS

Prospective amendment—This Part to be repealed by FA 1999 s 123(3), Sch 20 Pt V(6) with effect on the appointed day by virtue of FA 1990 s 111(1).

Finance Act 1986 (c 41)

10 (*amend* FA 1986 s 88(1)).

11— (1) Section 90 of the Finance Act 1986 (exceptions from general charge to stamp duty reserve tax) is amended as follows.

(2) (*amend* FA 1986 s 90(1)).

(3) (*insert* FA 1986 s 90(1A)).

(4) (*insert* FA 1986 s 90(1B)).

(5) The amendments in sub-paragraphs (2) and (3) apply where the relevant day for the purposes of section 87 of the Finance Act 1986 falls on or after 6th February 2000.

(6) The amendment in sub-paragraph (4) applies where the surrender (within the meaning of Part II of Schedule 19 to the Finance Act 1999) occurs on or after 6th February 2000.

12 (*amend* FA 1986 s 99).

Finance Act 1995 (c 4)

13 (*amend* FA 1995 s 152).

Prospective amendment—This paragraph to be repealed by FA 1999 s 123(3), Sch 20 Pt V(6) with effect on the appointed day by virtue of FA 1990 s 111(1).

PART IV

GENERAL DEFINITIONS

Meaning of "unit trust scheme" and related expressions

14— (1) The following definitions apply for the purposes of the enactments relating to stamp duty and the enactments relating to stamp duty reserve tax.

(2) "Unit trust scheme" has [the meaning given by section 237(1) of the Financial Services and Markets Act 2000][1], subject to paragraphs 15 to 18.

(3) In relation to a unit trust scheme—

"trust instrument" means the trust deed or other instrument (whether under seal or not) creating or recording the trusts on which the property in question is held;

"trust property" means the property subject to the trusts of the trust instrument;

"unit" means a right or interest (whether described as a unit, as a sub-unit or otherwise) of a beneficiary under the trust instrument;

"unit holder" means a person entitled to a share of the trust property; and

"certificate to bearer", in relation to a unit, means a document by the delivery of which the unit can be transferred.

Modification—This para is modified, in relation to open-ended investment companies, by the Stamp Duty and Stamp Duty Reserve Tax (Open-ended Investment Companies) Regulations, SI 1997/1156, regs 4, 4A(1), (3), as amended by the Stamp Duty and Stamp Duty Reserve Tax (Open-ended Investment Companies) (Amendment No 2) Regulations, SI 1999/3261, reg 5, with effect from 6 February 2000.

Prospective amendment—The words "and the enactments relating to stamp duty reserve tax" in sub-para (1) to be repealed by FA 1999 s 123(3), Sch 20 Pt V(6) with effect on the appointed day by virtue of FA 1990 s 111(1).

Amendments—[1] Words in sub-para (2) substituted by the Financial Services and Markets Act 2000 (Consequential Amendments) (Taxes) Order, SI 2001/3629 art 104 with effect—

(*a*) for the purposes of stamp duty, in relation to any instrument executed after 30 November 2001;

(*b*) for the purposes of stamp duty reserve tax, in relation to—

(i) an agreement to transfer chargeable securities which is not conditional, if the agreement is made after 30 November 2001;

Stamp Taxes

(ii) a conditional agreement to transfer such securities, if the condition is satisfied after that date;
(iii) a surrender (as referred to in FA 1999 Sch 19 Pt 2) which occurs after that date.

Schemes not treated as unit trust schemes

15 References in the enactments relating to stamp duty and the enactments relating to stamp duty reserve tax to a unit trust scheme do not include—

(*a*) a common investment scheme under section 22 of the Charities Act 1960, section 25 of the Charities Act (Northern Ireland) 1964, or section 24 of the Charities Act 1993,

(*b*) a common deposit scheme under section 22A of the Charities Act 1960 or section 25 of the Charities Act 1993, or

(*c*) a unit trust scheme the units in which are under the terms of the trust instrument required to be held only by bodies of persons established for charitable purposes only or trustees of trusts so established.

Prospective amendment—Words "and the enactments relating to stamp duty reserve tax" to be repealed by FA 1999 s 123(3), Sch 20 Pt V(6) with effect on the appointed day by virtue of FA 1990 s 111(1).

16 References in the enactments relating to stamp duty and the enactments relating to stamp duty reserve tax to a unit trust scheme do not include common investment arrangements made by trustees of exempt approved schemes (within the meaning of section 592(1) of the Taxes Act 1988) solely for the purposes of the schemes.

Prospective amendment—The words "and the enactments relating to stamp duty reserve tax" to be repealed by FA 1999 s 123(3), Sch 20 Pt V(6) with effect on the appointed day by virtue of FA 1990 s 111(1).

17— (1) The Treasury may by regulations provide that any scheme of a description specified in the regulations shall be treated as not being a unit trust scheme for the purposes of the enactments relating to stamp duty and the enactments relating to stamp duty reserve tax.

(2) Regulations under this paragraph—

(*a*) may contain such supplementary and transitional provisions as appear to the Treasury to be necessary or expedient, and

(*b*) shall be made by statutory instrument which shall be subject to annulment in pursuance of a resolution of the House of Commons.

(3) This paragraph replaces section 57(1A) and (1B) of the Finance Act 1946 and section 28(1A) and (1B) of the Finance (No2) Act (Northern Ireland) 1946.

(4) Any regulations having effect under those provisions for the purposes of Part VII of the Finance Act 1946 or Part III of the Finance (No2) Act (Northern Ireland) 1946 which are in force immediately before the commencement of this Schedule shall have effect as if made under this paragraph.

Regulations—See the Stamp Duty and Stamp Duty Reserve Tax (Definition of Unit Trust Scheme and Open-ended Investment Company) Regulations, SI 2001/964.
Modification—Sub-para (4) is revoked, in relation to open-ended investment companies, by the Stamp Duty and Stamp Duty Reserve Tax (Open-ended Investment Companies) Regulations, SI 1997/1156, regs 4, 4A(1), (3), as amended by the Stamp Duty and Stamp Duty Reserve Tax (Open-ended Investment Companies) (Amendment No 2) Regulations, SI 1999/3261, reg 5, with effect from 6 February 2000.
Prospective amendment—The words "and the enactments relating to stamp duty reserve tax" in sub-para (1) to be repealed by FA 1999 s 123(3), Sch 20 Pt V(6) with effect on the appointed day by virtue of FA 1990 s 111(1).

Treatment of umbrella schemes

18— (1) For the purposes of the enactments relating to stamp duty and the enactments relating to stamp duty reserve tax each of the parts of an umbrella scheme is regarded as a unit trust scheme and the scheme as a whole is not so regarded.

(2) An "umbrella scheme" means a unit trust scheme—

(*a*) which provides arrangements for separate pooling of the contributions of participants and of the profits or income out of which payments are to be made to them, and

(*b*) under which the participants are entitled to exchange rights in one pool for rights in another;

and a "part of an umbrella scheme" means such of the arrangements as relate to a separate pool.

(3) In relation to a part of an umbrella scheme—

(*a*) any reference to the trust property has effect as a reference to such of the trust property as under the arrangements forms part of the separate pool to which the part of the umbrella scheme relates, and

(*b*) any reference to a unit holder has effect as a reference to a person for the time being having rights in that separate pool.

Prospective amendment—The words "and the enactments relating to stamp duty reserve tax" in sub-para (1) to be repealed by FA 1999 s 123(3), Sch 20 Pt V(6) with effect on the appointed day by virtue of FA 1990 s 111(1).

References to stock in stamp duty enactments include units under unit trust scheme

19 In the enactments relating to stamp duty—

(*a*) any reference to stock includes a unit under a unit trust scheme, and

(*b*) any reference to a stock certificate to bearer includes a certificate to bearer in relation to a unit under a unit trust scheme.

Prospective amendment—The words "and the enactments relating to stamp duty reserve tax" in paras 14(1), 15, 16, 17(1) and 18(1) of Part IV of this Schedule to be repealed by FA 1999 s 123(3), Sch 20 Pt V(6) with effect on the appointed day by virtue of FA 1990 s 111(1).

FINANCIAL SERVICES AND MARKETS ACT 2000

(2000 Chapter 8)

ARRANGEMENT OF SECTIONS

PART XVII
COLLECTIVE INVESTMENT SCHEMES

CHAPTER I
INTERPRETATION

CHAPTER III
AUTHORISED UNIT TRUST SCHEMES

Applications for authorisation

Certificates

PART XVIII
RECOGNISED INVESTMENT EXCHANGES AND CLEARING HOUSES

CHAPTER I
EXEMPTION

General

An Act to make provision about the regulation of financial services and markets; to provide for the transfer of certain statutory functions relating to building societies, friendly societies, industrial and provident societies and certain other mutual societies; and for connected purposes.

[14th June 2000]

PART XVII
COLLECTIVE INVESTMENT SCHEMES

CHAPTER I
INTERPRETATION

235 Collective investment schemes

(1) In this Part "collective investment scheme" means any arrangements with respect to property of any description, including money, the purpose or effect of which is to enable persons taking part in the arrangements (whether by becoming owners of the property or any part of it or otherwise) to participate in or receive profits or income arising from the acquisition, holding, management or disposal of the property or sums paid out of such profits or income.

(2) The arrangements must be such that the persons who are to participate ("participants") do not have day-to-day control over the management of the property, whether or not they have the right to be consulted or to give directions.

(3) The arrangements must also have either or both of the following characteristics—

(*a*) the contributions of the participants and the profits or income out of which payments are to be made to them are pooled;

(*b*) the property is managed as a whole by or on behalf of the operator of the scheme.

(4) If arrangements provide for such pooling as is mentioned in subsection (3)(*a*) in relation to separate parts of the property, the arrangements are not to be regarded as constituting a single collective investment scheme unless the participants are entitled to exchange rights in one part for rights in another.

(5) The Treasury may by order provide that arrangements do not amount to a collective investment scheme—

(*a*) in specified circumstances; or

(*b*) if the arrangements fall within a specified category of arrangement.

236 Open-ended investment companies

(1) In this Part "an open-ended investment company" means a collective investment scheme which satisfies both the property condition and the investment condition.

(2) The property condition is that the property belongs beneficially to, and is managed by or on behalf of, a body corporate ("BC") having as its purpose the investment of its funds with the aim of—

(*a*) spreading investment risk; and

(*b*) giving its members the benefit of the results of the management of those funds by or on behalf of that body.

(3) The investment condition is that, in relation to BC, a reasonable investor would, if he were to participate in the scheme—

(*a*) expect that he would be able to realize, within a period appearing to him to be reasonable, his investment in the scheme (represented, at any given time, by the value of shares in, or securities of, BC held by him as a participant in the scheme); and

(*b*) be satisfied that his investment would be realized on a basis calculated wholly or mainly by reference to the value of property in respect of which the scheme makes arrangements.

(4) In determining whether the investment condition is satisfied, no account is to be taken of any actual or potential redemption or repurchase of shares or securities under—

(*a*) Chapter VII of Part V of the Companies Act 1985;

(*b*) Chapter VII of Part VI of the Companies (Northern Ireland) Order 1986;

(*c*) corresponding provisions in force in another EEA State; or

(*d*) provisions in force in a country or territory other than an EEA state which the Treasury have, by order, designated as corresponding provisions.

(5) The Treasury may by order amend the definition of "an open-ended investment company" for the purposes of this Part.

237 Other definitions

(1) In this Part "unit trust scheme" means a collective investment scheme under which the property is held on trust for the participants.

(2) In this Part—

"trustee", in relation to a unit trust scheme, means the person holding the property in question on trust for the participants;

"depositary", in relation to—

(*a*) a collective investment scheme which is constituted by a body incorporated by virtue of regulations under section 262, or

(*b*) any other collective investment scheme which is not a unit trust scheme,

means any person to whom the property subject to the scheme is entrusted for safekeeping;

"the operator", in relation to a unit trust scheme with a separate trustee, means the manager and in relation to an open-ended investment company, means that company;

"units" means the rights or interests (however described) of the participants in a collective investment scheme.

(3) In this Part—

"an authorised unit trust scheme" means a unit trust scheme which is authorised for the purposes of this Act by an authorisation order in force under section 243;

"an authorised open-ended investment company" means a body incorporated by virtue of regulations under section 262 in respect of which an authorisation order is in force under any provision made in such regulations by virtue of subsection (2)(*l*) of that section;

"a recognised scheme" means a scheme recognised under section 264, 270 or 272.

CHAPTER III

AUTHORISED UNIT TRUST SCHEMES

Applications for authorisation

243 Authorisation orders

(1) If, on an application under section 242 in respect of a unit trust scheme, the Authority—

(*a*) is satisfied that the scheme complies with the requirements set out in this section, (*b*) is satisfied that the scheme complies with the requirements of the trust scheme rules, and

(*c*) has been provided with a copy of the trust deed and a certificate signed by a solicitor to the effect that it complies with such of the requirements of this section or those rules as relate to its contents,

the Authority may make an order declaring the scheme to be an authorised unit trust scheme.

(2) If the Authority makes an order under subsection (1), it must give written notice of the order to the applicant.

(3) In this Chapter "authorisation order" means an order under subsection (1).

(4) The manager and the trustee must be persons who are independent of each other.

(5) The manager and the trustee must each—

(*a*) be a body corporate incorporated in the United Kingdom or another EEA State, and

(*b*) have a place of business in the United Kingdom,

and the affairs of each must be administered in the country in which it is incorporated.

(6) If the manager is incorporated in another EEA State, the scheme must not be one which satisfies the requirements prescribed for the purposes of section 264.

(7) The manager and the trustee must each be an authorised person and the manager must have permission to act as manager and the trustee must have permission to act as trustee.

(8) The name of the scheme must not be undesirable or misleading.

(9) The purposes of the scheme must be reasonably capable of being successfully carried into effect.

(10) The participants must be entitled to have their units redeemed in accordance with the scheme at a price—

(*a*) related to the net value of the property to which the units relate; and

(*b*) determined in accordance with the scheme.

(11) But a scheme is to be treated as complying with subsection (10) if it requires the manager to ensure that a participant is able to sell his units on an investment exchange at a price not significantly different from that mentioned in that subsection.

Certificates

246 Certificates

(1) If the manager or trustee of a unit trust scheme which complies with the conditions necessary for it to enjoy the rights conferred by any relevant Community instrument so requests, the Authority may issue a certificate to the effect that the scheme complies with those conditions.

(2) Such a certificate may be issued on the making of an authorisation order in respect of the scheme or at any subsequent time.

PART XVIII

RECOGNISED INVESTMENT EXCHANGES AND CLEARING HOUSES

CHAPTER I

EXEMPTION

General

285 Exemption for recognised investment exchanges and clearing houses

(1) In this Act—

(*a*) "recognised investment exchange" means an investment exchange in relation to which a recognition order is in force; and

(*b*) "recognised clearing house" means a clearing house in relation to which a recognition order is in force.

(2) A recognised investment exchange is exempt from the general prohibition as respects any regulated activity—

(*a*) which is carried on as a part of the exchange's business as an investment exchange; or

(*b*) which is carried on for the purposes of, or in connection with, the provision of clearing services by the exchange.

(3) A recognised clearing house is exempt from the general prohibition as respects any regulated activity which is carried on for the purposes of, or in connection with, the provision of clearing services by the clearing house.

286 Qualification for recognition

(1) The Treasury may make regulations setting out the requirements—

(*a*) which must be satisfied by an investment exchange or clearing house if it is to qualify as a body in respect of which the Authority may make a recognition order under this Part; and (*b*) which, if a recognition order is made, it must continue to satisfy if it is to remain a recognised body.

(2) But if regulations contain provision as to the default rules of an investment exchange or clearing house, or as to proceedings taken under such rules by such a body, they require the approval of the Secretary of State.

(3) "Default rules" means rules of an investment exchange or clearing house which provide for the taking of action in the event of a person's appearing to be unable, or likely to become unable, to meet his obligations in respect of one or more market contracts connected with the exchange or clearing house.

(4) "Market contract" means—

(*a*) a contract to which Part VII of the Companies Act 1989 applies as a result of section 155 of that Act or a contract to which Part V of the Companies (No 2)(Northern Ireland) Order 1990 applies as a result of Article 80 of that Order; and

(*b*) such other kind of contract as may be prescribed.

(5) Requirements resulting from this section are referred to in this Part as "recognition requirements".

[(6) In the case of an investment exchange, requirements resulting from this section are in addition to requirements which must be satisfied by the exchange as a result of section 290(1A) before the Authority may make a recognition order declaring the exchange to be a recognised investment exchange.][1]

Amendments—[1] Sub-s (6) inserted by the Financial Services and Markets Act 2000 (Markets in Financial Instruments) Regulations, SI 2007/126 reg 3(2), Sch 2 paras 1, 2 with effect for certain purposes from 1 April 2007, and for remaining purposes from 1 November 2007.

LIMITED LIABILITY PARTNERSHIPS ACT 2000

(2000 Chapter 12)

An Act to make provision for limited liability partnerships

[20th July 2000]

12 Stamp duty

(1) Stamp duty shall not be chargeable on an instrument by which property is conveyed or transferred by a person to a limited liability partnership in connection with its incorporation within the period of one year beginning with the date of incorporation if the following two conditions are satisfied.

(2) The first condition is that at the relevant time the person—

(*a*) is a partner in a partnership comprised of all the persons who are or are to be members of the limited liability partnership (and no-one else), or

(*b*) holds the property conveyed or transferred as nominee or bare trustee for one or more of the partners in such a partnership.

(3) The second condition is that—

(*a*) the proportions of the property conveyed or transferred to which the persons mentioned in subsection (2)(*a*) are entitled immediately after the [transfer][1] are the same as those to which they were entitled at the relevant time, or

(*b*) none of the differences in those proportions has arisen as part of a scheme or arrangement of which the main purpose, or one of the main purposes, is avoidance of liability to any duty or tax.

(4) For the purposes of subsection (2) a person holds property as bare trustee for a partner if the partner has the exclusive right (subject only to satisfying any outstanding charge, lien or other right of the trustee to resort to the property for payment of duty, taxes, costs or other outgoings) to direct how the property shall be dealt with.

(5) In this section "the relevant time" means—

(*a*) if the person who conveyed or transferred the property to the limited liability partnership acquired the property after its incorporation, immediately after he acquired the property, and

(*b*) in any other case, immediately before its incorporation.

(6) An instrument in respect of which stamp duty is not chargeable by virtue of subsection (1) shall not be taken to be duly stamped unless—

(*a*) it has, in accordance with section 12 of the Stamp Act 1891, been stamped with a particular stamp denoting that it is not chargeable with any duty or that it is duly stamped, or

(*b*) it is stamped with the duty to which it would be liable apart from that subsection.

Note—This section comes into force on 6 April 2001 (by virtue of SI 2000/3316 art 2).

Amendments—[1] The word "transfer" substituted for the words "conveyance or transfer" in enactments relating to stamp duty by FA 2003 Sch 20 para 3.

FINANCE ACT 2000

(2000 Chapter 17)

ARRANGEMENT OF SECTIONS

PART IV

STAMP DUTY

Stamp duty

An act to grant certain duties, to alter other duties, and to amend the law relating to the National Debt and the Public Revenue, and to make further provision in connection with finance.

[28 July 2000]

PART IV

STAMP DUTY AND STAMP DUTY RESERVE TAX

Stamp duty

114 Rates: [transfer][1] on sale

(1) (*amends* FA 1999 Sch 13 para 4).

(2) This section applies to instruments executed on or after 28th March 2000.

(3) But this section does not apply to an instrument giving effect to a contract made on or before 21st March 2000, unless—

Stamp Taxes

(*a*) the instrument is made in consequence of the exercise after that date of any option, right of pre-emption or similar right; or

(*b*) the instrument transfers the property in question to, or vests it in, a person other than the purchaser under the contract, because of an assignment (or, in Scotland, assignation) or further contract made after that date.

(4) This section shall be deemed to have come into force on 28th March 2000.

Amendments—[1] The word "transfer" substituted for the words "conveyance or transfer" in enactments relating to stamp duty by FA 2003 Sch 20 para 3.

115 Rates: duty on lease chargeable by reference to rent

(1) (*amends* FA 1999 Sch 13 paras 11, 12(3)).

(2) This section has effect in relation to instruments executed on or after 28th March 2000.

(3) This section shall be deemed to have come into force on 28th March 2000.

116 Rate of duty on seven year leases

(1) (*amends* FA 1999 Sch 13 para 12(3)).

(2) This section applies to instruments executed on or after 1st October 1999, subject to Schedule 32 to this Act (which makes transitional provision for instruments executed on or after 1st October 1999 but before 28th March 2000).

(3) This section shall be deemed to have come into force on 28th March 2000.

117 Power to vary stamp duties

Schedule 33 to this Act (power to vary stamp duties) has effect.

118 Land transferred etc for other property

(1) Subsection (2) applies where—

(*a*) an instrument transferring or vesting an estate or interest in land would not, apart from this section, be or fall to be treated as a [transfer][1] on sale for the purposes of stamp duty; but

(*b*) the transfer or vesting of the estate or interest is for consideration; and

(*c*) the consideration is or includes any property ("the other property").

(2) For the purposes of Part I of Schedule 13 to the Finance Act 1999 (stamp duty on [transfer][1] on sale) the instrument transferring or vesting the estate or interest shall be taken to be a transfer on sale of the estate or interest.

(3) If—

(*a*) the other property is or includes one or more estates or interests in land, and

(*b*) *ad valorem* duty is chargeable on the [transfer][1] of all or any of those estates or interests,

the amount of duty that would (apart from this subsection) be chargeable in consequence of subsection (2) on the transfer on sale there mentioned shall be reduced (but not below nil) by the total of the *ad valorem* duty chargeable as mentioned in paragraph (*b*).

(4) If, for the purposes of Part I of Schedule 13 to the Finance Act 1999, the amount or value of the consideration for the transfer on sale mentioned in subsection (2) would (apart from this subsection) exceed the market value of the estate or interest immediately before the execution of the instrument transferring or vesting it, the amount or value of the consideration shall be taken for those purposes to be equal to that market value.

(5) For the purposes of this section, the market value of property at any time is the price which that property might reasonably be expected to fetch on a sale at that time in the open market.

(6) Subsection (2) has effect even though—

(*a*) the transfer or vesting of the estate or interest is the whole or part of the consideration for a sale of the other property; or

(*b*) the transaction is by way of exchange.

(7) Subsection (2) does not affect any charge to stamp duty in respect of the same or any other instrument so far as it relates to the transfer of the other property.

(8) This section is subject to subsection (5) of section 119.

(9) This section shall be construed as one with the Stamp Act 1891.

(10) This section applies to instruments executed on or after 28th March 2000.

(11) But this section does not apply to an instrument giving effect to a contract made on or before 21st March 2000, unless—

(*a*) the instrument is made in consequence of the exercise after that date of any option, right of pre-emption or similar right; or

(*b*) the instrument transfers the property in question to, or vests it in, a person other than the purchaser under the contract, because of an assignment (or, in Scotland, assignation) or further contract made after that date.

(12) This section shall be deemed to have come into force on 28th March 2000.

Amendments—[1] The word "transfer" substituted for the words "conveyance or transfer" in enactments relating to stamp duty by FA 2003 Sch 20 para 3.

119 Transfer of land to connected company

(1) This section applies where an estate or interest in land is transferred to or vested in a company ("A") and—

(*a*) the person transferring or vesting the estate or interest ("B") is connected with A; or

(*b*) some or all of the consideration for the transfer or vesting consists of the issue or transfer of shares in a company with which B is connected.

(2) For the purposes of Part I of Schedule 13 to the Finance Act 1999 (stamp duty on [transfer][1] on sale) an instrument transferring or vesting the estate or interest shall be taken to be a transfer on sale of the estate or interest.

(3) If for those purposes the amount or value of the consideration for the transfer on sale of the estate or interest would, apart from this subsection, be less than the value determined under subsection (4), the consideration shall be taken for those purposes to be the value determined under subsection (4).

(4) That value is—

(*a*) the market value of the estate or interest immediately before the execution of the instrument transferring or vesting it; but

(*b*) reduced by the value of so much of any actual consideration as does not consist of property.

(5) Where—

(*a*) apart from this section, an instrument would be chargeable to stamp duty in accordance with section 118, and

(*b*) apart from that section, the instrument would be chargeable to stamp duty in accordance with this section,

the stamp duty chargeable on the instrument shall be determined in accordance with this section (instead of that section).

(6) This section applies only if, in consequence of its application, the instrument transferring or vesting the estate or interest is chargeable with a greater amount of stamp duty than it would be apart from this section and section 118.

(7) For the purposes of this section, the market value of property at any time is the price which that property might reasonably be expected to fetch on a sale at that time in the open market.

(8) In this section—

"company" means any body corporate;

"shares" includes stock and the reference to shares in a company includes a reference to securities issued by a company.

(9) For the purposes of this section, the question whether any person is connected with another shall be determined in accordance with the provisions of section 839 of the Taxes Act 1988.

(10) This section shall be construed as one with the Stamp Act 1891.

(11) This section applies to instruments executed on or after 28th March 2000.

(12) But this section does not apply to an instrument giving effect to a contract made on or before 21st March 2000, unless—

(*a*) the instrument is made in consequence of the exercise after that date of any option, right of pre-emption or similar right; or

(*b*) the instrument transfers the property in question to, or vests it in, a person other than the purchaser under the contract, because of an assignment (or, in Scotland, assignation) or further contract made after that date.

(13) This section shall be deemed to have come into force on 28th March 2000.

Amendments—[1] The word "transfer" substituted for the words "conveyance or transfer" in enactments relating to stamp duty by FA 2003 Sch 20 para 3.

120 Exceptions from section 119

(1) Section 119 does not apply by virtue of paragraph (*a*) of subsection (1) of that section in any of the following cases (any reference in this section to A or B being taken as a reference to the person referred to as A or B, as the case may be, in that subsection).

(2) Case 1 is where B holds the estate or interest as nominee or bare trustee for A.

(3) Case 2 is where A is to hold the estate or interest as nominee or bare trustee for B.

(4) Case 3 is where B holds the estate or interest as nominee or bare trustee for some other person and A is to hold it as nominee or bare trustee for that other person.

(5) Case 4 is where (in a case not falling within subsection (2) or (4) above)—

(*a*) the transfer or vesting is a [transfer][1] out of a settlement in or towards satisfaction of a beneficiary's interest;

(*b*) the beneficiary's interest is not an interest acquired for money or money's worth; and

(*c*) the [transfer][1] is a distribution of property in accordance with the provisions of the settlement.

(6) Case 5 is where (in a case not falling within subsection (3) above) A—

(*a*) is a person carrying on a business which consists of or includes the management of trusts; and

(*b*) is to hold the estate or interest as trustee acting in the course of that business.

(7) Case 6 is where (in a case not falling within subsection (3) above) A is to hold the estate or interest as trustee and, apart from section 839(3) of the Taxes Act 1988 (trustees as connected persons), would not be connected with B.

(8) Case 7 is where—

(*a*) B is a company;

(*b*) the transfer or vesting is, or is part of, a distribution of assets (whether or not in connection with the winding up of the company); and

(*c*) the estate or interest was acquired by B by virtue of an instrument which is duly stamped.

(9) This section shall be construed as one with the Stamp Act 1891.

(10) This section applies to instruments executed after the day on which this Act is passed.

Amendments—[1] The word "transfer" substituted for the words "conveyance or transfer" in enactments relating to stamp duty by FA 2003 Sch 20 para 3.

121 Grant of lease to connected company

(1) This section applies where a lease is granted to a company ("A") and—

(*a*) the person granting the lease ("B") is connected with A; or

(*b*) some or all of the consideration for the grant of the lease consists of the issue or transfer of shares in a company with which B is connected.

(2) Subsection (3) has effect for the purposes of stamp duty chargeable under Part II of Schedule 13 to the Finance Act 1999 (stamp duty on a lease) by reference to Part I of that Schedule ([transfer][1] on sale).

(3) If, apart from this subsection, the amount or value of the consideration for the grant would be less than the value determined under subsection (4), the consideration shall be taken to be the value determined under subsection (4).

(4) That value is—

(*a*) the market value, immediately before the instrument granting the lease is executed, of the lease granted; but

(*b*) reduced by the value of so much of any actual consideration as does not consist of property.

(5) This section applies only if, in consequence of its application, the lease is chargeable with a greater amount of stamp duty than it would be apart from this section.

(6) For the purposes of this section, the market value of property at any time is the price which that property might reasonably be expected to fetch on a sale at that time in the open market.

(7) In this section—

"company" means any body corporate;

"shares" includes stock and the reference to shares in a company includes a reference to securities issued by a company.

(8) For the purposes of this section, the question whether any person is connected with another shall be determined in accordance with the provisions of section 839 of the Taxes Act 1988.

(9) This section shall be construed as one with the Stamp Act 1891.

(10) This section applies to instruments executed on or after 28th March 2000.

(11) But this section does not apply to an instrument giving effect to a contract made on or before 21st March 2000, unless—

(*a*) the instrument is made in consequence of the exercise after that date of any option, right of pre-emption or similar right; or

(*b*) the instrument transfers the property in question to, or vests it in, a person other than the purchaser under the contract, because of an assignment (or, in Scotland, assignation) or further contract made after that date.

(12) This section shall be deemed to have come into force on 28th March 2000.

Amendments—[1] The word "transfer" substituted for the words "conveyance or transfer" in enactments relating to stamp duty by FA 2003 Sch 20 para 3.

122 Marketable securities transferred etc for exempt property

(1) Subsection (2) applies where—

(*a*) an instrument transferring marketable securities would not, apart from this section, be or fall to be treated as a transfer on sale for the purposes of stamp duty; but

(*b*) the transfer of the marketable securities is for consideration; and

(*c*) the consideration is or includes any qualifying property ("the other property").

(2) For the purposes of Part I of Schedule 13 to the Finance Act 1999 (stamp duty on [transfer][1] on sale) the instrument transferring the marketable securities shall be taken to be a transfer on sale of those securities.

(3) If the amount or value of the consideration for that transfer on sale would (apart from this subsection) exceed the market value of the marketable securities immediately before the execution of the instrument transferring them, the amount or value of the consideration shall be taken to be equal to that market value.

For this purpose the market value of property at any time is the price which that property might reasonably be expected to fetch on a sale at that time in the open market.

(4) Subsection (2) has effect even though—

(*a*) the transfer of the marketable securities is the whole or part of the consideration for a sale of the other property; or

(*b*) the transaction is by way of exchange.

(5) Subsection (2) does not affect any charge to stamp duty in respect of the same or any other instrument so far as it relates to the transfer of the other property.

(6) In this section "qualifying property" means any debt due, stock or securities, to the extent that the debt, stock or securities are not chargeable securities, within the meaning of Part IV of the Finance Act 1986 (stamp duty reserve tax).

(7) This section shall be construed as one with the Stamp Act 1891.

(8) This section applies to instruments executed on or after 28th March 2000.

(9) But this section does not apply to an instrument giving effect to a contract made on or before 21st March 2000, unless—

(*a*) the instrument is made in consequence of the exercise after that date of any option, right of pre-emption or similar right; or

(*b*) the instrument transfers the property in question to, or vests it in, a person other than the purchaser under the contract, because of an assignment (or, in Scotland, assignation) or further contract made after that date.

(10) This section shall be deemed to have come into force on 28th March 2000.

Amendments—[1] The word "transfer" substituted for the words "conveyance or transfer" in enactments relating to stamp duty by FA 2003 Sch 20 para 3.

123 Transfer of property between associated companies: Great Britain

(1) Amend section 42 of the Finance Act 1930 as follows.

(2), (3) (*amend* FA 1930 s 42(2)).

(4) (*amends* FA 1930 s 42(2B)).

(5) (*amends* FA 1930 s 42(3)).

(6) (*adds* FA 1930 s 42(5)–(7)).

(7) This section has effect in relation to instruments executed after the day on which this Act is passed.

124 Transfer of property between associated companies: Northern Ireland

(1) Amend section 11 of the Finance Act (Northern Ireland) 1954 as follows.

(2) After subsection (2) (instruments on which stamp duty not chargeable) insert—

"(2A) But this section does not apply to an instrument by virtue of subsection (2)(*a*) if, at the time the instrument is executed, arrangements are in existence by virtue of which at that or some later time any person has or could obtain, or any persons together have or could obtain, control of the transferee but not of the transferor.".

(3) In subsection (3AA) (body to be parent of another if beneficial owner of 75% of ordinary share capital) after "if at that time the first body" insert "(*a*)" and at the end of the subsection add—

"(*b*) is beneficially entitled to not less than 75 per cent of any profits available for distribution to equity holders of the second body; and

(*c*) would be beneficially entitled to not less than 75 per cent of any assets of the second body available for distribution to its equity holders on a winding-up.".

(4) In subsection (3A)—

(*a*) after "The ownership referred to in" insert "paragraph (*a*) of"; and

(*b*) for "this section" substitute "that paragraph".

(5) At the end of the section add—

"(6) Schedule 18 to the Income and Corporation Taxes Act 1988 shall apply for the purposes of paragraphs (*b*) and (*c*) of subsection (3AA) as it applies for the purposes of paragraphs (*a*) and (*b*) of section 413(7) of that Act; but this is subject to subsection (7).

(7) In determining for the purposes of this section whether a body corporate is the parent of the transferor, paragraphs 5(3) and 5B to 5E of Schedule 18 to the Income and Corporation Taxes Act 1988 shall not apply for the purposes of paragraph (*b*) or (*c*) of subsection (3AA).

(8) In subsection (3AAA), "control" shall be construed in accordance with section 840 of the Income and Corporation Taxes Act 1988.".

(6) This section has effect in relation to instruments executed after the day on which this Act is passed.

125 Grant of leases etc between associated companies

(1) Amend section 151 of the Finance Act 1995 as follows.

(2) (*amends* FA 1995 s 151(1)).

(3) (*inserts* FA 1995 s 151(4A)).

(4) (*amends* FA 1995 s 151(8)).

(5) (*amends* FA 1995 s 151(10)).

(6) (*inserts* FA 1995 s 151(10A)–(10C)).

(7) This section has effect in relation to instruments executed after the day on which this Act is passed.

126 Future issues of stock

(1) Amend section 55 of the Stamp Act 1891 (calculation of ad valorem duty in respect of stock and securities) as follows.

(2) (*inserts* SA 1891 s 55(1A)).

(3) This section has effect in relation to instruments executed on or after the day on which this Act is passed.

127 Company acquisition reliefs: redeemable shares

(1) Amend section 75 of the Finance Act 1986 (acquisitions: reliefs) in accordance with subsections (2) and (3).

(2), (3) (*amend* FA 1986 s 75(4)).

(4) (*amends* FA 1986 s 76(3)(a)).

(5) This section has effect in relation to instruments executed after the day on which this Act is passed.

128 Surrender of leases

(1) Where a lease is or has been surrendered or, in Scotland, renounced at any time, a document evidencing the surrender or renunciation shall be treated for the purposes of stamp duty as if it were a deed executed at that time effecting the surrender or renunciation.

(2) Stamp duty shall be chargeable by virtue of subsection (1) on a document containing a statutory declaration, notwithstanding anything in [land registration rules under the Land Registration Act 2002][1].

(3) Stamp duty shall not be chargeable by virtue of subsection (1) on any lease or agreement for a lease or with respect to any letting if the lease or agreement—

(*a*) is made in consideration of the surrender or renunciation; and

(*b*) relates to the same subject matter as the lease surrendered or renounced.

(4) Stamp duty shall not be chargeable by virtue of subsection (1) on any document if a document falling within subsection (5) has been duly stamped.

(5) The documents that fall within this subsection are—

(*a*) a deed effecting the surrender or renunciation;

(*b*) an agreement which falls to be treated for the purposes of stamp duty as if it were such a deed;

(*c*) any document which falls to be so treated by virtue of subsection (1); and

(*d*) any lease or agreement falling within subsection (3).

(6) A land registrar shall regard a document which by virtue of subsection (4) is not chargeable to stamp duty by virtue of subsection (1) as not duly stamped unless—

(*a*) it is stamped as if it were a deed effecting the surrender or renunciation; or

(*b*) it appears by some stamp impressed on it that the full and proper duty chargeable on such a deed has been paid on another document; or

(*c*) it appears by some stamp impressed on it that a lease or agreement falling within subsection (3) has been duly stamped; or

(*d*) the land registrar is aware of a document falling within subsection (5) which has been duly stamped.

(7) The documents which evidence the surrender or renunciation of a lease shall be taken to include an application, in consequence of the surrender or renunciation of the lease, for—

(*a*) the making in a land register, or

(*b*) the removal from a land register,

of an entry relating to the lease.

(8) In this section—

"land register"—

(*a*) in relation to England and Wales, means the register kept under section 1 of the [Land Registration Act 2002][1];
(*b*) in relation to Scotland, means the Land Register of Scotland or the General Register of Sasines;
(*c*) in relation to Northern Ireland, means the register maintained under section 10 of the Land Registration Act (Northern Ireland) 1970;

"land registrar"—
(*a*) in relation to England and Wales, means the Chief Land Registrar or any other officer of Her Majesty's Land Registry exercising functions of the Chief Land Registrar;
(*b*) in relation to Scotland, means the Keeper of the Registers of Scotland;
(*c*) in relation to Northern Ireland, means the Registrar of Titles or any other official of the Land Registry exercising functions of the Registrar of Titles.

(9) This section shall be construed as one with the Stamp Act 1891.

(10) This section applies to documents relating to the surrender or renunciation of a lease on or after the day on which this Act is passed.

Amendments—[1] Words in sub-ss (2), (8) substituted by the Land Registration Act 2002 ss 133, 136(2), Sch 11 para 39 with effect from 13 October 2003 (by virtue of SI 2003/1725).

129 Abolition of duty on instruments relating to intellectual property

(1) No stamp duty is chargeable on an instrument for the sale, transfer or other disposition of intellectual property.

(2) In subsection (1) "intellectual property" means—
(*a*) any patent, trade mark, registered design, copyright or design right,
(*b*) any plant breeders' rights and rights under section 7 of the Plant Varieties Act 1997,
(*c*) any licence or other right in respect of anything within paragraph (*a*) or (*b*), and
(*d*) any rights under the law of a country or territory outside the United Kingdom that correspond or are similar to those within paragraph (*a*), (*b*) or (*c*).

(3) Schedule 34 to this Act (which contains provisions supplementing this section) has effect.

(4) This section and Schedule 34 shall be construed as one with the Stamp Act 1891.

(5) This section applies to instruments executed on or after 28th March 2000.

(6) This section shall be deemed to have come into force on that date.

130 Transfers to registered social landlords etc

(1) No stamp duty shall be chargeable under Part I or II, or paragraph 16 of Part III, of Schedule 13 to the Finance Act 1999 on a [transfer][1] of an estate or interest in land, or on a lease of land,—
(*a*) to a qualifying landlord controlled by its tenants;
(*b*) to a qualifying landlord by a qualifying transferor; or
(*c*) to a qualifying landlord purchasing the estate or interest, or the grant of the lease, with the assistance of a public subsidy.

(2) For the purposes of this section the cases where a qualifying landlord is controlled by its tenants are those cases where the majority of the board members of the qualifying landlord are tenants occupying properties owned or managed by the qualifying landlord.

(3) For the purposes of subsection (2) a "board member" means—
(*a*) in relation to a qualifying landlord which is a company, a director of the company;
(*b*) in relation to a qualifying landlord which is a body corporate whose affairs are managed by its members, a member;
(*c*) in relation to a qualifying landlord which is a body of trustees, a member of that body of trustees;
(*d*) in relation to a qualifying landlord not falling within any of paragraphs (*a*) to (*c*), a member of the committee of management or other body to which is entrusted the direction of the affairs of the qualifying landlord.

(4) In subsection (3), "company" has the same meaning as in the Companies Act [2006][3] (see section [1][3] of that Act).

(5) In this section "qualifying landlord" means—
(*a*) in relation to England and Wales, any body registered as a social landlord in a register maintained under section 1(1) of the Housing Act 1996;
(*b*) in relation to Scotland—
(i) any housing association registered in the register maintained under section 3(1) of the Housing Associations Act 1985 by Scottish Homes; or
(ii) any body corporate whose objects correspond to those of a housing association and which, pursuant to a contract with Scottish Homes, is registered in a register kept for the purpose by Scottish Homes;
(*c*) in relation to Northern Ireland, any housing association registered in the register maintained under Article 14 of the Housing (Northern Ireland) Order 1992.

(6) In this section "qualifying transferor" means any of the following—

Stamp Taxes

(a) a qualifying landlord;
(b) a housing action trust established under Part III of the Housing Act 1988;
(c) a principal council, within the meaning of the Local Government Act 1972;
(d) the Common Council of the City of London;
(e) a council constituted under section 2 of the Local Government etc (Scotland) Act 1994;
(f) Scottish Homes;
(g) the Department for Social Development in Northern Ireland;
(h) the Northern Ireland Housing Executive.

(7) In this section "public subsidy" means any grant or other financial assistance—

(a) made or given by way of a distribution pursuant to section 25 of the National Lottery etc Act 1993 (application of money by distributing bodies);
(b) under section 18 of the Housing Act 1996 (social housing grants);
(c) under section 126 of the Housing Grants, Construction and Regeneration Act 1996 (financial assistance for regeneration and development);
(d) under section 2 of the Housing (Scotland) Act 1988 (general functions of Scottish Homes); or
(e) under Article 33 [or 33A][2] of the Housing (Northern Ireland) Order 1992 (housing association grants).

(8) Where stamp duty would be chargeable on an instrument but for paragraph (c) of subsection (1), that subsection shall only have effect in relation to the instrument if the instrument is certified to the Board by the qualifying landlord concerned as being an instrument on which stamp duty is by virtue of that paragraph not chargeable.

(9) An instrument on which stamp duty is not chargeable by virtue only of this section shall not be taken to be duly stamped unless—

(a) it is stamped with the duty to which it would be liable but for this section; or
(b) it has, in accordance with section 12 of the Stamp Act 1891, been stamped with a particular stamp denoting that it is not chargeable with any duty.

(10) This section applies to instruments executed after the day on which this Act is passed.

Amendments—[1] The word "transfer" substituted for the words "conveyance or transfer" in enactments relating to stamp duty by FA 2003 Sch 20 para 3.
[2] Words in sub-s (7)(e) inserted by the Housing (Amendment) (Northern Ireland) Order, SI 2006/3337 art 3, Schedule, para 7 with effect from 1 April 2007 (by virtue of SR 2007/37 art 2).
[3] In sub-s (4), words substituted for words "1985" and "735(1)", by the Companies Act 2006 (Consequential Amendments) (Taxes and National Insurance) Order, SI 2009/1890 art 3(4) with effect from 1 October 2009.

131 Relief for certain instruments executed before this Act has effect

(1) This section applies to an instrument of any of the following descriptions executed in the period beginning with 22nd March 2000 and ending with the day on which this Act is passed—

(a) an instrument transferring or vesting an estate or interest in land in such circumstances as are mentioned in section 119 (transfer of land to connected company), in a case specified in section 120 (excepted cases);
(b) a [transfer][1] of an estate or interest in land, or a lease of land, to a qualifying landlord within the meaning of section 130 (transfers to registered social landlords, etc) from a qualifying transferor within subsection (6)(c), (d), (e), (f) or (h) of that section.

(2) If the instrument is not stamped until after the day on which this Act is passed, the law in force at the time of its execution shall be deemed for stamp duty purposes to be that which would have applied if it had been executed after that day.

(3) If the Commissioners are satisfied that—

(a) the instrument was stamped on or before the day on which this Act is passed,
(b) stamp duty was chargeable in respect of it, and
(c) had it been stamped after that day no stamp duty, or less stamp duty, would have been chargeable,

they shall pay to such person as they consider appropriate an amount equal to the duty (and any interest or penalty) that would not have been payable if the law in force at the time of execution of the instrument had been that which would have applied had it been executed after that day.

(4) Any such payment must be claimed before 1st April 2001.

(5) Entitlement to a payment is subject to compliance with such conditions as the Commissioners may determine with respect to the production of the instrument, to its being stamped so as to indicate that it has been produced under this section or to other matters.

(6) For the purposes of section 10 of the Exchequer and Audit Departments Act 1866 (Commissioners to deduct repayments from gross revenues) any amount paid under this section shall be treated as a repayment.

(7) This section shall be construed as one with the Stamp Act 1891.

Amendments—[1] The word "transfer" substituted for the words "conveyance or transfer" in enactments relating to stamp duty by FA 2003 Sch 20 para 3.

132 The Northern Ireland Assembly Commission

(1) Amend section 55 of the Finance Act 1987 (Crown exemption from stamp duty) as follows.

(2), (3) (*amend* FA 1987 s 55(1)).

(4) Subsection (3) has effect in relation to instruments executed on or after 28th March 2000.

(5) This section shall be deemed to have come into force on 28th March 2000.

Stamp duty and Stamp duty reserve tax

133 Loan capital where return bears inverse relationship to results

(1) (*Inserts* FA 1986 s 79(7A)).

(2) For the purposes of stamp duty, subsection (1) above has effect where the instrument is executed on or after 21st March 2000.

(3) For the purposes of stamp duty reserve tax, subsection (1) above has effect—

(*a*) in relation to the charge to tax under section 87 of the Finance Act 1986, where—

(i) the agreement to transfer is conditional and the condition is satisfied on or after 21st March 2000, or

(ii) the agreement is not conditional and is made on or after that date;

(*b*) in relation to the charge to tax under section 93(1) of that Act, where securities are transferred, issued or appropriated on or after 21st March 2000 (whenever the arrangement was made);

(*c*) in relation to the charge to tax under section 96(1) of that Act, where securities are transferred or issued on or after 21st March 2000 (whenever the arrangement was made);

(*d*) in relation to the charge to tax under section 93(10) of that Act, where securities are issued or transferred on sale, under terms there mentioned, on or after 21st March 2000;

(*e*) in relation to the charge to tax under section 96(8) of that Act, where securities are issued or transferred on sale, under terms there mentioned, on or after 21st March 2000.

Amendments—This section repealed by FA 2000 s 156, Sch 40 Pt III with effect—
- for stamp duty on bearer instruments in accordance with FA 1990 s 107;
- for stamp duty purposes on instruments other than bearer instruments in accordance with FA 1990 s 108; and
- for stamp duty reserve tax purposes in accordance with FA 1990 s 110.

134 Transfers between depositary receipt systems and clearance systems

(1) (*inserts* FA 1986 s 72A).

(2) (*inserts* FA 1986 s 97B).

(3) (*amends* FA 1986 ss 67(9), 70(9), 95(1) and 97(1)).

(4) (*adds* FA 1986 s 97A(13)).

(5) The amendments in this section have effect as follows—

(*a*) subsection (1), and subsections (3) and (4) as they apply for stamp duty purposes, apply in relation to instruments executed after the day on which this Act is passed;

(*b*) subsection (2), and subsections (3) and (4) as they apply for the purposes of stamp duty reserve tax, apply where the securities are transferred after that day.

Amendments—This section repealed by FA 2000 s 156, Sch 40 Pt III with effect—
- for stamp duty on bearer instruments in accordance with FA 1990 s 107;
- for stamp duty purposes on instruments other than bearer instruments in accordance with FA 1990 s 108; and
- for stamp duty reserve tax purposes in accordance with FA 1990 s 110.

PART VI
MISCELLANEOUS AND SUPPLEMENTARY PROVISIONS

Supplementary provisions

155 Interpretation

In this Act "the Taxes Act 1988" means the Income and Corporation Taxes Act 1988.

156 Repeals

(1) The enactments mentioned in Schedule 40 to this Act (which include provisions that are spent or of no practical utility) are repealed to the extent specified in the third column of that Schedule.

(2) The repeals specified in that Schedule have effect subject to the commencement provisions and savings contained or referred to in the notes set out in that Schedule.

157 Short title

This Act may be cited as the Finance Act 2000

SCHEDULES

SCHEDULE 8
EMPLOYEE SHARE OWNERSHIP PLANS

Section 47

[Exemptions from stamp duty and stamp duty reserve tax

116A Where, under an approved employee share ownership plan, partnership shares or dividend shares are transferred by the trustees to an employee—

(*a*) no *ad valorem* stamp duty is chargeable on any instrument by which the transfer is made, and

(*b*) no stamp duty reserve tax is chargeable on any agreement by the trustees to make the transfer.][1]

Amendment—[1] This paragraph inserted by FA 2001 s 95 with effect for instruments executed (within the meaning of SA 1891) after 11 May 2001, and agreements to transfer shares made after 11 May 2001. But see ITEPA 2003 s 722, Sch 6, para 257 which substitutes FA 2001 s 95, by virtue of which this paragraph is inserted.

SCHEDULE 32
STAMP DUTY ON SEVEN YEAR LEASES: TRANSITIONAL PROVISIONS

Section 116(2)

Introductory

1 In this Schedule—

"additional duty", in relation to an instrument, means additional stamp duty chargeable on the instrument as a result of section 116;

"the appropriate amount of duty", in relation to an instrument, means the stamp duty that would have been chargeable on the instrument if section 116 had been in force when it was executed; and

"the commencement date" means 28th March 2000.

Instruments to which this Schedule applies

2 The instruments to which this Schedule applies are—

(*a*) leases of land for a term of seven years, and

(*b*) agreements for leases of land for a term of seven years,

executed on or after 1st October 1999 and before the commencement date.

Instruments which remain duly stamped

3 An instrument to which this Schedule applies which is stamped with the appropriate amount of duty is duly stamped, whenever it was executed.

Instruments which cease to be duly stamped

4— (1) An instrument to which this Schedule applies which—

(*a*) immediately before the commencement date was duly stamped, but

(*b*) was stamped with less than the appropriate amount of duty,

ceases to be duly stamped on the commencement date.

(2) Sub-paragraph (1) applies even if the instrument has been stamped in accordance with section 12(5) of the Stamp Act 1891 with a stamp denoting that it is duly stamped.

(3) If an instrument ceases to be duly stamped on the commencement date as a result of sub-paragraph (1)—

(*a*) section 12(6) of the Stamp Act 1891 (adjudicated instruments admissible in evidence) does not apply to it at any time when it is not duly stamped, and

(*b*) section 14(1) of that Act (receipt in evidence of insufficiently stamped instruments if unpaid duty paid to court) does not apply to it at any time when it is not duly stamped, unless the unpaid duty and any interest or penalty is paid in accordance with that subsection.

Stamping following earlier adjudication

5 Section 12A(1) of the Stamp Act 1891 (adjudicated instruments not to be stamped other than in accordance with adjudication decision) does not prevent an instrument to which this Schedule applies which is stamped with less than the appropriate amount of duty from being stamped with additional duty.

Use of instruments in evidence, etc

6 Section 14(4) of the Stamp Act 1891 (instruments not to be used unless duly stamped in accordance with law in force when executed) applies in relation to an instrument to which this Schedule applies as if, as respects any time on or after the commencement date, the reference to the law in force at the time when it was executed were to the law in force on the commencement date.

Adjudication, interest and penalties

7— (1) This paragraph applies for the purpose of applying sections 12 to 13B and 15 to 15B of the Stamp Act 1891 (adjudication by Commissioners and interest and penalties on late stamping) in relation to any additional duty chargeable on an instrument to which this Schedule applies.

(2) Those sections continue to apply without modification as respects any other stamp duty chargeable on the instrument.

(3) Those sections have effect as respects the additional duty as if—

(*a*) the additional duty were the only stamp duty chargeable on the instrument;
(*b*) the instrument had been executed on the commencement date; and
(*c*) in the case of an instrument executed outside the United Kingdom and first received in the United Kingdom before the commencement date, the instrument had been first received in the United Kingdom on the commencement date.

(4) Accordingly, those sections apply as respects additional duty as if—

(*a*) references to duty were to additional duty;
(*b*) references to stamping were to stamping with additional duty;
(*c*) references to an instrument's being stamped were to its being stamped with additional duty;
(*d*) references to an instrument's being duly stamped were to its being stamped with all the additional duty chargeable on it;
(*e*) references to an instrument's being unstamped were to its not being stamped with any additional duty;
(*f*) references to an instrument's being insufficiently stamped were to its being stamped with insufficient additional duty;
(*g*) references to adjudication, or an appeal, under any of those sections were to adjudication or an appeal under the section in question as it has effect as respects additional duty; and
(*h*) references to the maximum penalty were to the maximum penalty as respects additional duty.

Stamp Taxes

SCHEDULE 33

POWER TO VARY STAMP DUTIES

Section 117

Power of Treasury to make provision by regulations

1— (1) The Treasury may if they consider it expedient in the public interest make provision by regulations for the variation of an existing stamp duty.

(2) The power conferred by this paragraph includes, in particular, power to alter the descriptions of document in respect of which an existing stamp duty, or an existing rate or amount of duty, is chargeable.

(3) The power to make regulations under this paragraph is exercisable by statutory instrument.

Regulations—Variation of Stamp Duties Regulations, SI 2001/3746.

Power only to be used for cases involving land or shares etc

2— (1) The power conferred by paragraph 1 does not include power—

(*a*) to vary the amount chargeable by way of stamp duty on an excepted instrument, or
(*b*) to cause stamp duty to become chargeable on an excepted instrument.

(2) For the purposes of this paragraph—

(*a*) an "excepted instrument" is any document that is not a relevant property instrument, and
(*b*) a "relevant property instrument" is a document that (whether or not it also relates to any other transaction) relates to a transaction that to any extent involves—
  (i) land, stock or marketable securities, or
  (ii) any estate or interest in land, stock or marketable securities.

Power not to be used to vary rates or thresholds

3 The power conferred by paragraph 1 does not, except as mentioned in paragraph 1(2), include power to vary—

(*a*) the rate, or rates, of an existing *ad valorem* stamp duty,
(*b*) the amount of an existing fixed stamp duty,

(*c*) any threshold specified in paragraph 4 of Schedule 13 to the Finance Act 1999 (rate bands for [transfer][1] on sale), or

(*d*) any threshold specified in paragraph 11 or 12 of that Schedule (duty on leases) in respect of rent or the term of a lease.

Amendments—[1] The word "transfer" substituted for the words "conveyance or transfer" in enactments relating to stamp duty by FA 2003 Sch 20 para 3.

Approval of regulations by House of Commons

4— (1) An instrument containing regulations under paragraph 1 shall be laid before the House of Commons after being made.

(2) If the regulations are not approved by the House of Commons before the end of the period of 28 days beginning with the day on which they are made, they shall cease to have effect at the end of that period if they have not already ceased to have effect under sub-paragraph (3).

(3) If on any day during that period of 28 days the House of Commons, in proceedings on a motion that (or to the effect that) the regulations be approved, comes to a decision rejecting the regulations, they shall cease to have effect at the end of that day.

(4) Where regulations cease to have effect under sub-paragraph (2) or (3), their ceasing to have effect is without prejudice to anything done in reliance on them.

(5) In reckoning any such period of 28 days take no account of any time during which—

(*a*) Parliament is prorogued or dissolved, or

(*b*) the House of Commons is adjourned for more than four days.

Claim for repayment if regulations not approved

5— (1) Where regulations cease to have effect under paragraph 4(2) or (3), any amount paid by way of stamp duty, or interest or penalty on late stamping, that would not have been payable but for the regulations shall, on a claim, be repaid by the Commissioners.

(2) Section 110 of the Finance Act 1999 (interest on repayment of duty overpaid etc) applies to a repayment under this paragraph of any amount paid by way of stamp duty or penalty on late stamping.

In the case of a repayment under this paragraph, the relevant time for the purposes of that section is 30 days after the day on which the instrument in question was executed or, if later, the date on which the payment of duty or penalty was made.

(3) A claim for repayment must be made within two years after the date of the instrument in question or, if it is not dated, within two years after its execution.

(4) No repayment shall be made on a claim until the instrument in question has been produced to the Commissioners for such cancelling of stamps, and such stamping to denote the making of the repayment or the producing of the instrument under this paragraph, as the Commissioners consider appropriate.

(5) Any repayment shall, subject to any regulations under sub-paragraph (6)(*d*), be made to such person as the Commissioners consider appropriate.

(6) The Commissioners may make provision by regulations—

(*a*) for varying the time limit having effect under sub-paragraph (3);

(*b*) for varying or repealing the condition having effect under sub-paragraph (4);

(*c*) as to any other conditions that must be met before repayment is made;

(*d*) as to the person to whom repayment is to be made.

(7) Regulations under this paragraph shall be made by statutory instrument which shall be subject to annulment in pursuance of a resolution of the House of Commons.

Use in evidence, etc of instruments affected by regulations ceasing to have effect

6— (1) Where regulations cease to have effect under paragraph 4(2) or (3), the following provisions apply to an instrument that—

(*a*) was executed at a time when the regulations were in force, and

(*b*) was at that time chargeable with any amount of stamp duty with which it would not have been chargeable apart from the regulations.

(2) If the instrument was stamped while the regulations were in force, nothing done in pursuance of paragraph 5 (repayment of duty etc) prevents it being treated for any purpose as duly stamped in accordance with the law in force at the time when it was executed.

(3) If the instrument was not stamped while the regulations were in force, the law in force at the time when it was executed shall be deemed to have been what the law would have been apart from the regulations.

Temporary effect of regulations

7— (1) Regulations under paragraph 1 shall not apply in relation to instruments executed after the end of—

(*a*) the period of 18 months beginning with the day on which the regulations were made, or

(*b*) such shorter period as may be specified in the regulations.

(2) This does not affect the power to make further provision by regulations under paragraph 1 to the same or similar effect.

Power to make transitional etc provision

8 Any power to make regulations under this Schedule includes power to make such transitional, supplementary and incidental provision as appears to the authority making the regulations to be necessary or expedient.

Interpretation

9— (1) In relation to a bearer instrument (as defined in paragraph 3 of Schedule 15 to the Finance Act 1999), references in this Schedule to the execution of the instrument shall be read as references to its issue.[1]

(2) This Schedule shall be construed as one with the Stamp Act 1891.

Amendments—[1] Para 9(1) repealed by FA 2000 s 156, Sch 40 Pt III with effect in accordance with FA 1990 s 107.

SCHEDULE 34

ABOLITION OF STAMP DUTY ON INSTRUMENTS RELATING TO INTELLECTUAL PROPERTY: SUPPLEMENTARY PROVISIONS

Section 129

Introduction

1 In this Schedule "intellectual property" has the same meaning as in section 129(1).

Stamp duty reduced in certain other cases

2— (1) This paragraph applies where—

(*a*) stamp duty under Part I of Schedule 13 to the Finance Act 1999 ([transfer][1] on sale) is chargeable on an instrument, and

(*b*) part of the property concerned consists of intellectual property.

(2) In such a case—

(*a*) the consideration in respect of which duty would otherwise be charged shall be apportioned, on such basis as is just and reasonable, as between the part of the property which consists of intellectual property and the part which does not, and

(*b*) the instrument shall be charged only in respect of the consideration attributed to such of the property as is not intellectual property.

(3) This paragraph applies to instruments executed on or after 28th March 2000.

Amendments—[1] The word "transfer" substituted for the words "conveyance or transfer" in enactments relating to stamp duty by FA 2003 Sch 20 para 3.

Apportionment of consideration for stamp duty purposes

3— (1) Where part of the property referred to in section 58(1) of the Stamp Act 1891 (consideration to be apportioned between different instruments as parties think fit) consists of intellectual property, that provision shall have effect as if "the parties think fit" read "is just and reasonable".

(2) Where—

(*a*) part of the property referred to in section 58(2) of the Stamp Act 1891 (property contracted to be purchased by two or more persons etc) consists of intellectual property, and

(*b*) both or (as the case may be) all the relevant persons are connected with one another,

that provision shall have effect as if the words from "for distinct parts of the consideration" to the end of the subsection read ", the consideration is to be apportioned in such manner as is just and reasonable, so that a distinct consideration for each separate part or parcel is set forth in the conveyance relating thereto, and such conveyance is to be charged with *ad valorem* duty in respect of such distinct consideration.".

(3) In a case where sub-paragraph (1) or (2) applies and the consideration is apportioned in a manner that is not just and reasonable, the enactments relating to stamp duty shall have effect as if—

(*a*) the consideration had been apportioned in a manner that is just and reasonable, and

(*b*) the amount of any distinct consideration set forth in any conveyance relating to a separate part or parcel of property were such amount as is found by a just and reasonable apportionment (and not the amount actually set forth).

(4) For the purposes of sub-paragraph (2)—

(*a*) a person is a relevant person if he is a person by or for whom the property is contracted to be purchased;

(*b*) the question whether persons are connected with one another shall be determined in accordance with section 839 of the Taxes Act 1988.

(5) In sub-paragraph (3) "the enactments relating to stamp duty" means the Stamp Act 1891 and any enactment amending or which is to be construed as one with that Act.

(6) This paragraph applies to instruments executed on or after 28th March 2000.

Certification of instruments for stamp duty purposes

4—(1) Intellectual property shall be disregarded for the purposes of paragraph 6 of Schedule 13 to the Finance Act 1999 (certification of instrument as not forming part of transaction or series of transactions exceeding specified amount).

(2) Any statement as mentioned in paragraph 6(1) of that Schedule shall be construed as leaving out of account any matter which is to be so disregarded.

(3) This paragraph applies to instruments executed on or after 28th March 2000.

Acquisition under statute

5—(1) Section 12 of the Finance Act 1895 (property vested by Act or purchased under statutory powers) does not require any person who is authorised to purchase any property as mentioned in that section on or after 28th March 2000 to include any intellectual property in the instrument of conveyance required by that section to be produced to the Commissioners.

(2) If the property consists wholly of intellectual property no instrument of conveyance need be produced to the Commissioners under that section.

(3) This paragraph applies where the Act mentioned in that section, and by virtue of which property is vested or a person is authorised to purchase property, is passed on or after 28th March 2000.

SCHEDULE 40

REPEALS

Section 156

Note—All repeals relevant to stamp duty are already in effect and have therefore been omitted.

FINANCE ACT 2001

(2001 Chapter 9)

An Act to grant certain duties, to alter other duties, and to amend the law relating to the National Debt and the Public Revenue, and to make further provision in connection with Finance.

[11 May 2001]

PART 4

OTHER TAXES

Stamp duty and stamp duty reserve tax

92 Stamp duty: exemption for land in disadvantaged areas

(1) [No *ad valorem* stamp duty shall be chargeable on—][1]

(*a*) a [transfer][2] of an estate or interest in land, or

(*b*) a lease of land,

if the land is situated in a disadvantaged area.

(2) Where stamp duty would be chargeable on an instrument but for subsection (1), that subsection shall have effect in relation to the instrument only if the instrument is certified to the Commissioners as being an instrument on which stamp duty is by virtue of that subsection not chargeable.

(3) No instrument which is certified as mentioned in subsection (2) shall be taken to be duly stamped unless—

(*a*) it is stamped in accordance with section 12 of the Stamp Act 1891 with a particular stamp denoting that it is not chargeable with any duty or that it is duly stamped, or

(*b*) it is stamped with the duty to which it would have been liable but for this section.

(4) For the purposes of this section and Schedule 30 to this Act, a disadvantaged area is an area designated as such by regulations made by the Treasury; and any such regulations may—

(*a*) designate specified areas as disadvantaged areas, or

(*b*) provide for areas of a description specified in the regulations to be designated as disadvantaged areas.

(5) If regulations under subsection (4) so provide, the designation of an area as a disadvantaged area shall have effect for such period as may be specified by or determined in accordance with the regulations.

(6) Schedule 30 to this Act (which makes further provision about land in disadvantaged areas) shall have effect.

[(6A) This section and Schedule 30 to this Act have effect subject to section 92A.][1]

(7) This section and Schedule 30 to this Act shall be construed as one with the Stamp Act 1891.

(8) The provisions of this section and Schedule 30 to this Act shall have effect in relation to instruments executed on or after such date as may be specified by order made by the Treasury.

(9) Regulations under subsection (4)—

(*a*) may make different provision for different cases, and

(*b*) may contain such incidental, supplementary, consequential or transitional provision as appears to the Treasury to be necessary or expedient.

(10) The power to make regulations under subsection (4) shall be exercisable by statutory instrument subject to annulment in pursuance of a resolution of the House of Commons.

(11) The power to make an order under subsection (8) shall be exercisable by statutory instrument.

Regulations—Stamp Duty (Disadvantaged Areas) Regulations, SI 2001/3747.
Finance Act 2001, Section 92(8), (Specified Day) Order, SI 2001/3748 (the day specified for the purposes of sub-s (8) above is 30 November 2001).
Statement of Practice SP 1/03—(Disadvantaged areas relief, Stamp Office approach to borderline cases).
Amendments—[1] Words in sub-s (1) substituted, and sub-s (6A) inserted, by FA 2002 s 110(1), (2) with effect from 24 July 2002.
[2] The word "transfer" substituted for the words "conveyance or transfer" in enactments relating to stamp duty by FA 2003 Sch 20 para 3.

[92A Restriction of exemption in the case of residential property etc

(1) Regulations may provide for an exemption conferred by section 92 or by Schedule 30 to this Act not to apply in cases specified by reference to either or both of the following—

(*a*) whether the land in question is residential property;

(*b*) the amount or value of the consideration.

(2) Regulations may contain provision corresponding to or modifying that made by Schedule 30 to this Act in the case of—

(*a*) a building or land only part of which falls within subsection (1)(*a*) or (*b*) of section 92B (meaning of "residential property"), or

(*b*) an interest in or right over land that subsists only partly as mentioned in subsection (1)(*c*) of that section.

(3) Where by virtue of regulations under this section the availability of an exemption depends on the land in question not being, or not being entirely, residential property, the certification under section 92(2) must include a statement that the land is not residential property or, as the case may be, that it is not residential property to the extent stated.

(4) Where by virtue of regulations under this section the availability of an exemption depends on the amount or value of the consideration not exceeding a specified amount, the instrument in question must be certified at that amount (or at a lower amount).

The reference here to an instrument being certified at an amount shall be construed in accordance with paragraph 6 of Schedule 13 to the Finance Act 1999 (c 16) (as if the reference were contained in paragraph 4 of that Schedule).

(5) The power to make regulations under this section is exercisable by the Treasury.

(6) Regulations under this section—

(*a*) may make different provision for different cases, and

(*b*) may contain such incidental, supplementary, consequential or transitional provision as appears to the Treasury to be necessary or expedient.

(7) Regulations under this section must be made by statutory instrument, which shall be subject to annulment in pursuance of a resolution of the House of Commons.][1]

Definitions—"Residential property", s 92B(1).
Cross reference—FA 2002 s 110(6) (regulations under this section may contain provisions revoking the Variation of Stamp Duties Regulations, SI 2001/3746).
Regulations—Stamp Duty (Disadvantaged Areas) (Application of Exemptions) Regulations, SI 2003/1056.
Statement of Practice SP 1/03—(Disadvantaged areas relief, Stamp Office approach to borderline cases).
Amendments—[1] This section inserted by FA 2002 s 110(3) with effect from 24 July 2002.

[92B Meaning of "residential property"

(1) In section 92A "residential property" means—

(*a*) a building that is used or suitable for use as a dwelling, or is in the process of being constructed or adapted for such use,

(*b*) land that is or forms part of the garden or grounds of a building within paragraph (*a*) (including any building or structure on such land);

Stamp Taxes

(c) an interest in or right over land that subsists for the benefit of a building within paragraph (a) or of land within paragraph (b).

(2) For the purposes of subsection (1) use of a building as—

(a) residential accommodation for school pupils,

(b) residential accommodation for students, other than accommodation falling within subsection (3)(b),

(c) residential accommodation for members of any of the armed forces, or

(d) an institution that is the sole or main residence of at least 90% of its residents and does not fall within any of paragraphs (a) to (f) of subsection (3),

is use of a building as a dwelling.

(3) For the purposes of subsection (1) use of a building as—

(a) a home or other institution providing residential accommodation for children,

(b) a hall of residence for students in further or higher education,

(c) a home or other institution providing residential accommodation with personal care for persons in need of personal care by reason of old age, disablement, past or present dependence on alcohol or drugs or past or present mental disorder,

(d) a hospital or hospice,

(e) a prison or similar establishment, or

(f) a hotel or inn or similar establishment,

is not use of a building as a dwelling.

(4) Where a building is used in a manner specified in subsection (3), no account shall be taken for the purposes of subsection (1)(a) of its suitability for any other use.

(5) Where a building that is not in use is suitable for at least one of the uses specified in subsection (2) and at least one of those specified in subsection (3)—

(a) if there is one such use for which it is most suitable, or if the uses for which it is most suitable are all specified in the same subsection, no account shall be taken for the purposes of subsection (1)(a) of its suitability for any other use,

(b) otherwise, the building shall be treated for those purposes as suitable for use as a dwelling.

(6) Regulations under section 92A may provide that, where there is a single contract for the conveyance, transfer or lease of land comprising or including six or more separate dwellings, none of that land counts as residential property for the purposes of the regulations.

(7) The Treasury may by order amend this section so as to change or clarify the cases where use of a building is, or is not, use of a building as a dwelling for the purposes of subsection (1).

(8) An order under subsection (7) may contain such incidental, supplementary, consequential or transitional provision as appears to the Treasury to be necessary or expedient.

(9) An order under subsection (7) must be made by statutory instrument, which shall be subject to annulment in pursuance of a resolution of the House of Commons.

(10) In this section "building" includes part of a building.][1]

Regulations—Stamp Duty (Disadvantaged Areas) (Application of Exemptions) Regulations, SI 2003/1056.
Statement of Practice SP 1/03—(Disadvantaged areas relief, Stamp Office approach to borderline cases).
Amendments—[1] This section inserted by FA 2002 s 110(3) with effect from 24 July 2002.

93 SDRT: unit trust schemes and individual pension accounts

(1) Schedule 19 to the Finance Act 1999 (which abolishes charges to stamp duty, and introduces a charge to stamp duty reserve tax, in relation to units under a unit trust scheme) is amended as follows.

(2) (*amends* FA 1999 Sch 19 para 2(4)).

(3) (*inserts* FA 1999 Sch 19 para 4(6), (7)).

(4) (*inserts* FA 1999 Sch 19 para 6A).

(5) The amendment made by subsection (3) has effect where the relevant two-week period mentioned in paragraph 4(1) of Schedule 19 to the Finance Act 1999 ends after 6th April 2001.

(6) The other amendments made by this section have effect in relation to surrenders made or effected on or after 6th April 2001.

94 SDRT: open-ended investment companies and individual pension accounts

(1) Where there are two or more classes of shares in an open-ended investment company and the company's instrument of incorporation—

(a) provides that shares of one or more of those classes ("the IPA classes") may only be held within an individual pension account, and

(b) does not make such provision in relation to shares of at least one other class,

there is no charge to stamp duty reserve tax under Part II of Schedule 19 to the Finance Act 1999 on the surrender of a share of any of the IPA classes.

(2) References in this section to provisions of Schedule 19 to the Finance Act 1999 are references to those provisions as they have effect in relation to open-ended investment companies by virtue

of regulations from time to time in force under section 152 of the Finance Act 1995 (as at 6th April 2001, see regulations 3 to 4B of the 1997 Regulations as amended by regulations 4 and 5 of the 1999 (No 2) Regulations).

(3) In this section—

"individual pension account" has the same meaning as it has in regulations from time to time in force under section 638A of the Taxes Act 1988 (as at 6th April 2001, see regulation 4 of the 2001 Regulations);

"open-ended investment company" has the meaning given by paragraph 14(2) of Schedule 19 to the Finance Act 1999;

"surrender", in relation to a share in an open-ended investment company, has the same meaning as it has in Part II of Schedule 19 to the Finance Act 1999.

(4) For the purposes of subsections (2) and (3)—

"the 1997 Regulations" are the Stamp Duty and Stamp Duty Reserve Tax (Open-ended Investment Companies) Regulations 1997;

"the 1999 (No 2) Regulations" are the Stamp Duty and Stamp Duty Reserve Tax (Open-ended Investment Companies) (Amendment No 2) Regulations 1999;

"the 2001 Regulations" are the Personal Pension Schemes (Restriction on Discretion to Approve) (Permitted Investments) Regulations 2001.

(5) This section has effect in relation to surrenders made or effected on or after 6th April 2001.

Stamp Taxes

[95 Exemptions in relation to approved share incentive plans

(1) This section forms part of the SIP code (see section 488 of the Income Tax (Earnings and Pensions) Act 2003 (approved share incentive plans)).

(2) Accordingly, expressions used in this section and contained in the index at the end of Schedule 2 to that Act (approved share incentive plans) have the meaning indicated by that index.

(3) Where, under an approved share incentive plan, partnership shares or dividend shares are transferred by the trustees to an employee—

(*a*) no ad valorem stamp duty is chargeable on any instrument by which the transfer is made, and

(*b*) no stamp duty reserve tax is chargeable on any agreement by the trustees to make the transfer.

(4) But subsection (3) does not apply to—

(*a*) any instrument executed (within the meaning of the Stamp Act 1891) before 6th April 2003, or

(*b*) any agreement to transfer shares made before that date.][1]

Amendments—[1] This section substituted by ITEPA 2003 s 722, Sch 6 para 257 with effect, for income tax purposes, from 2003–04; and for corporation tax purposes, for accounting periods ending after 5 April 2003. For transitional provisions and savings see ITEPA 2003 s 723, Sch 7.

This section previously read as follows—

"95 Exemptions in relation to employee share ownership plans

(1) Schedule 8 to the Finance Act 2000 (employee share ownership plans) is amended as follows.

(2) After paragraph 116 insert—

"Exemptions from stamp duty and stamp duty reserve tax

116A Where, under an approved employee share ownership plan, partnership shares or dividend shares are transferred by the trustees to an employee—

(*a*) no ad valorem stamp duty is chargeable on any instrument by which the transfer is made, and

(*b*) no stamp duty reserve tax is chargeable on any agreement by the trustees to make the transfer.".

(3) This section has effect in relation to—

(*a*) instruments executed (within the meaning of the Stamp Act 1891) after the day on which this Act is passed, and

(*b*) agreements to transfer shares made after the day on which this Act is passed.".

SCHEDULES

SCHEDULE 30

STAMP DUTY: LAND IN DISADVANTAGED AREAS

Section 92

Regulations—Stamp Duty (Disadvantaged Areas) (Application of Exemptions) Regulations, SI 2003/1056.

Stamp duty reduced for land partly in a disadvantaged area

1— (1) Where any land is situated partly in a disadvantaged area and partly outside such an area, liability to [*ad valorem* stamp duty][1] on—

(*a*) a [transfer][2] of an estate or interest in the land, or

(*b*) a lease of the land,

shall be determined in accordance with sub-paragraph (2).

(2) Where liability to stamp duty falls to be determined in accordance with this sub-paragraph—

(*a*) the consideration in respect of which duty would be chargeable, but for the provisions of this paragraph, shall be apportioned, on such basis as is just and reasonable, as between the part of the land which is situated in a disadvantaged area and the part which is not so situated, and

(*b*) the instrument shall be chargeable only in respect of the consideration attributed to such part of the land as is not situated in a disadvantaged area.

(3) Where stamp duty, or a greater amount of stamp duty, would be chargeable on an instrument but for sub-paragraphs (1) and (2), those sub-paragraphs shall have effect in relation to the instrument only if the instrument is certified to the Commissioners as being an instrument in relation to which those sub-paragraphs have effect.

(4) No instrument which is certified as mentioned in sub-paragraph (3) shall be taken to be duly stamped unless—

(*a*) it is stamped in accordance with section 12 of the Stamp Act 1891 with a particular stamp denoting that it is not chargeable with any duty or that it is duly stamped, or

(*b*) it is stamped with the duty to which it would have been liable but for this paragraph.

Amendments—[1] Words in para (1) substituted by FA 2002 s 110(4) with effect from 24 July 2002.
[2] The word "transfer" substituted for the words "conveyance or transfer" in enactments relating to stamp duty by FA 2003 Sch 20 para 3.

Apportionment of consideration for stamp duty purposes

2— (1) Where any part or parcel of the property referred to in section 58(1) of the Stamp Act 1891 (consideration to be apportioned between separate parts or parcels as parties think fit) consists of an estate or interest in land situated wholly or partly in a disadvantaged area, that provision shall have effect—

(*a*) as if "the parties think fit" read "is just and reasonable", and

(*b*) as if "such conveyance is" read "such conveyance is (subject to section 92 of, and Schedule 30 to, the Finance Act 2001)".

(2) Where—

(*a*) any part or parcel of the property referred to in section 58(2) of the Stamp Act 1891 (property contracted to be purchased by two or more persons etc) consists of an estate or interest in land situated wholly or partly in a disadvantaged area, and

(*b*) both or (as the case may be) all the relevant persons are connected with one another,

that provision shall have effect in accordance with sub-paragraph (3).

(3) In a case falling within sub-paragraph (2), section 58(2) of that Act shall have effect as if the words from "for distinct parts of the consideration" to the end of the subsection read ", the consideration is to be apportioned in such manner as is just and reasonable, so that a distinct consideration for each separate part or parcel is set forth in the conveyance relating thereto, and such conveyance is (subject to section 92 of, and Schedule 30 to, the Finance Act 2001) to be charged with *ad valorem* duty in respect of such distinct consideration.".

(4) In a case where sub-paragraph (1) or (3) applies and the consideration is apportioned in a manner that is not just and reasonable, the enactments relating to stamp duty shall have effect as if—

(*a*) the consideration had been apportioned in a manner that is just and reasonable, and

(*b*) the amount of any distinct consideration set forth in any conveyance relating to a separate part or parcel of property were such amount as is found by a just and reasonable apportionment (and not the amount actually set forth).

(5) For the purposes of sub-paragraph (2)—

(*a*) a person is a relevant person if he is a person by or for whom the property is contracted to be purchased; and

(*b*) the question whether persons are connected with one another shall be determined in accordance with section 839 of the Taxes Act 1988.

(6) In sub-paragraph (4) "the enactments relating to stamp duty" means the Stamp Act 1891 and any enactment amending, or which is to be construed as one with, that Act.

Certification of instruments for stamp duty purposes

3— (1) If or to the extent that [a conveyance, transfer or lease is exempted from stamp duty by section 92(1) or paragraph 1 above (read with section 92A) the transaction in question shall be disregarded][1] for the purposes of paragraph 6 of Schedule 13 to the Finance Act 1999 (certification of instrument as not forming part of transaction or series of transactions exceeding specified amount).

[This is without prejudice to section 92A(4) (instrument must be certified where exemption depends on amount or value of consideration).][1]

(2) Any statement as mentioned in paragraph 6(1) of that Schedule shall be construed as leaving out of account any matter which is to be disregarded in accordance with sub-paragraph (1) above.

Amendments—[1] Words in para (1) substituted, and words added, by FA 2002 s 110(5) with effect from 24 July 2002.

FINANCE ACT 2002

(2002 Chapter 23)

An Act to grant certain duties, to alter other duties, and to amend the law relating to the National Debt and the Public Revenue, and to make further provision in connection with finance.

[24 July 2002]

PART 4
STAMP DUTY AND STAMP DUTY RESERVE TAX

Stamp duty

110 Land in disadvantaged areas

(1) (*amends* FA 2001 s 92(1)).

(2) (*inserts* FA 2001 s 92(6A)).

(3) (*inserts* FA 2001 ss 92A, 92B).

(4) (*amends* FA 2001 Sch 30 para 1(1)).

(5) (*amends* FA 2001 Sch 30 para 1(3)).

(6) Regulations under section 92A of the Finance Act 2001 (inserted by subsection (1) above) may contain provision revoking the Variation of Stamp Duties Regulations 2001 (SI 2001/3746) (which provide for section 92(1) of, and paragraph 1 of Schedule 30 to, that Act not to apply in cases where the consideration for the conveyance etc exceeds £150,000).

Regulations—Stamp Duty (Disadvantaged Areas) (Application of Exemptions) Regulations, SI 2003/1056.

111 Withdrawal of group relief

(1) This section applies where—

(*a*) an instrument ("the relevant instrument") transferring land in the United Kingdom from one company ("the transferor company") to another ("the transferee company") has been stamped on the basis that group relief applies,

(*b*) before the end of the period of [three years][1] beginning with the date on which the instrument was executed the transferee company ceases to be a member of the same group as the transferor company, and

(*c*) at the time when [the transferee company ceases][1] to be a member of the same group as the transferor company [it or a relevant associated company holds][1] an estate or interest in land—

(i) that was transferred [to the transferee company][1] by the relevant instrument, or

(ii) that is derived from an estate or interest that was so transferred,

[and that has not subsequently been transferred at market value by a duly stamped instrument on which *ad valorem* duty was paid and in respect of which group relief was not claimed.][1]

(2) In those circumstances—

(*a*) group relief in relation to the relevant instrument, or an appropriate proportion of it, is withdrawn, and

(*b*) the stamp duty that would have been payable on stamping the relevant instrument but for group relief if the estate or interest in land transferred by that instrument had been transferred at market value, or an appropriate proportion of the duty that would have been so paid, is payable by the transferee company within 30 days after that company ceases to be a member of the same group as the transferor company.

(3) In subsection (2)(*a*) and (*b*) "an appropriate proportion" means an appropriate proportion having regard to what was transferred [to the transferee company][1] by the relevant instrument and [what is held by that company or, as the case may be, that company and any relevant associated companies, at the time it or they cease to be members][1] of the same group as the transferor company.

(4) In this section "group relief" means relief under any of the following provisions—

(*a*) section 42 of the Finance Act 1930 (c 28) or section 11 of the Finance Act (Northern Ireland) 1954 (c 23 (NI)) (transfer of property between associated bodies corporate);

(*b*) section 151 of the Finance Act 1995 (c 4) (leases etc between associated bodies corporate.)

[(4A) In this section "relevant associated company", in relation to the transferee company, means a company that—

(*a*) is a member of the same group as the transferee company immediately before that company ceases to be a member of the same group as the transferor company, and

(*b*) ceases to be a member of the same group as the transferor company in consequence of the transferee company so ceasing.][1]

(5) In this section—

(*a*) references to the transfer of land include the grant or surrender of an estate or interest in or over land;

Stamp Taxes

(*b*) "company" includes any body corporate; and

(*c*) references to a company being in the same group as another company are to the companies being associated bodies corporate within the meaning of the relevant group relief provision.

(6) Schedule 34 to this Act contains provisions supplementing this section.

(7) Where the relevant instrument transfers land in the United Kingdom together with other property, the provisions of this section and of Schedule 34 apply as if there were two separate instruments, one relating to land in the United Kingdom and the other relating to other property.

(8) This section applies where the relevant instrument is executed after 23rd April 2002.

(9) But this section does not apply to an instrument giving effect to a contract made on or before 17th April 2002, unless—

(*a*) the instrument is made in consequence of the exercise after that date of any option, right of pre-emption or similar right, or

(*b*) the instrument transfers the property in question to, or vests it in, a person other than the purchaser under the contract because of an assignment (or, in Scotland, assignation) or further contract made after that date.

(10) This section shall be deemed to have come into force on 24th April 2002.

Cross references—FA 2003 Sch 19 para 6(2) (the references in sub-s (1)(*c*) above to a transfer at market value by a duly stamped instrument on which ad valorem duty was paid and in respect of which group relief was not claimed shall be read, on or after the implementation date, as including a reference to a transfer at market value by a chargeable transaction in respect of which relief under FA 2003 Sch 7 Pt 1 was available but was not claimed. For the implementation date, see FA 2003 Sch 19 para 2).

Amendments—[1] In sub-s (1)(*b*), words substituted for the words "two years", in sub-s (1)(*c*), words substituted for the words "it ceases", "it holds", "to it", and "and that was not subsequently transferred to it by a duly stamped instrument for which group relief was not claimed."; in sub-s (3), words inserted, and words substituted for the words "what the transferee company holds at the time it ceases to be a member"; and sub-s (4A) inserted; by FA 2003 s 126(1)–(5), (9)–(11) with effect for instruments executed after 14 April 2003. FA 2003 s 126 is deemed to have come into force on 15 April 2003.

FA 2003 s 126 does not apply to an instrument giving effect to a contract made on or before 9th April 2003, unless—

(*a*) the instrument is made in consequence of the exercise after that date of any option, right of pre-emption or similar right, or

(*b*) the instrument transfers the property in question to, or vests it in, a person other than the purchaser under the contract because of an assignment (or, in Scotland, assignation) or further contract made after that date: FA 2003 s 126(10).

112 Restriction of relief for company acquisitions

(1) Section 76 of the Finance Act 1986 (c 41) (relief where company acquires the whole or part of the undertaking of another company) is amended as follows.

(2) (*amends* FA 1986 s 76(2)).

(3) (*amends* FA 1986 s 76(3)).

(4) (*inserts* FA 1986 s 76(3A), (3B).

(5) (*amends* FA 1986 s 76(5)).

(6) (*inserts* FA 1986 s 76(6A)).

(7) This section applies to instruments executed after 23rd April 2002.

(8) But this section does not apply to an instrument giving effect to a contract made on or before 17th April 2002, unless—

(*a*) the instrument is made in consequence of the exercise after that date of any option, right of pre-emption or similar right, or

(*b*) the instrument transfers the property in question to, or vests it in, a person other than the purchaser under the contract because of an assignment (or, in Scotland, assignation) or further contract made after that date.

(9) This section shall be deemed to have come into force on 24th April 2002.

113 Withdrawal of relief for company acquisitions

(1) This section applies where—

(*a*) an instrument ("the relevant instrument") transferring land in the United Kingdom from one company to another company ("the acquiring company") has been stamped on the basis that relief under section 76 of the Finance Act 1986 (c 41) ("section 76 relief") applies,

(*b*) before the end of the period of [three years][1] beginning with the date on which the instrument was executed control of the acquiring company changes, and

(*c*) at the time control of that company changes the acquiring company [or a relevant associated company][1] holds an estate or interest in land—

(i) that was transferred [to the acquiring company][1] by the relevant instrument, or

(ii) that is derived from an estate or interest so transferred,

[and that has not subsequently been transferred at market value by a duly stamped instrument on which *ad valorem* duty was paid and in respect of which section 76 relief was not claimed][1].

(2) In those circumstances—

(*a*) section 76 relief in relation to the relevant instrument, or an appropriate proportion of it, is withdrawn, and

(*b*) the additional stamp duty that would have been payable on stamping the relevant instrument but for section 76 relief if the estate or interest in land transferred by that instrument had been transferred at market value, or an appropriate proportion of that additional duty, is payable by the acquiring company within 30 days after control of that company changes.

(3) In subsection (2)(*a*) and (*b*) "an appropriate proportion" means an appropriate proportion having regard to what was transferred by the relevant instrument and [what is held by that company or, as the case may be, by that company and any relevant associated companies][1] at the time control of it changes.

[(3A) In this section "relevant associated company", in relation to the acquiring company, means a company—

(*a*) that is controlled by the acquiring company immediately before the control of that company changes, and

(*b*) of which control changes in consequence of the change of control of that company.][1]

(4) In this section—

(*a*) references to the transfer of land include the grant or surrender of an estate or interest in or over land;

(*b*) "control" shall be construed in accordance with section 416 of the Taxes Act 1988; and

(*c*) references to control of a company changing are to the company becoming controlled—

(i) by a different person,

(ii) by a different number of persons, or

(iii) by two or more persons at least one of whom is not the person, or one of the persons, by whom the company was previously controlled.

(5) Schedule 35 to this Act contains provisions supplementing this section.

(6) Where the relevant instrument transfers land in the United Kingdom together with other property, the provisions of this section and of Schedule 35 apply as if there were two separate instruments, one relating to land in the United Kingdom and the other relating to other property.

(7) This section applies where the relevant instrument is executed after 23rd April 2002.

(8) But this section does not apply to an instrument giving effect to a contract made on or before 17th April 2002, unless—

(*a*) the instrument is made in consequence of the exercise after that date of any option, right of pre-emption or similar right, or

(*b*) the instrument transfers the property in question to, or vests it in, a person other than the purchaser under the contract because of an assignment (or, in Scotland, assignation) or further contract made after that date.

(9) This section shall be deemed to have come into force on 24th April 2002.

Cross references—FA 2003 Sch 19 para 6(3) (the references in sub-s (1)(*c*) above to a transfer at market value by a duly stamped instrument on which ad valorem duty was paid and in respect of which section 76 relief was not claimed shall be read, on or after the implementation date, as including a reference to a transfer at market value by a chargeable transaction on which stamp duty land tax was chargeable and in respect of which relief under FA 2003 Sch 7 Pt 2 was available but was not claimed).

Amendments—[1] In sub-s (1)(*b*), words substituted for the words "two years", "to it", and "and that was not subsequently transferred to it by a duly stamped instrument on which *ad valorem* duty was paid and in relation to which section 76 relief was not claimed", and words inserted; in sub-s (3), words substituted for the words "what the acquiring company holds"; and sub-s (3A) inserted, by FA 2003 s 127(1)–(5) with effect for instruments executed after 14 April 2003.

FA 2003 s 127 shall be deemed to have come into force on 15 April 2003.

FA 2003 s 127 does not apply to an instrument giving effect to a contract made on or before 9 April 2003, unless—

(*a*) the instrument is made in consequence of the exercise after that date of any option, right of pre-emption or similar right, or

(*b*) the instrument transfers the property in question to, or vests it in, a person other than the purchaser under the contract because of an assignment (or, in Scotland, assignation) or further contract made after that date: FA 2003 s 127(8).

114 Penalties for late stamping

(1) Section 15B of the Stamp Act 1891 (c 39) (late stamping: penalties) is amended as follows.

(2) (*amends* SA 1891 s 15B(1)).

(3) (*inserts* SA 1891 s 15B(1A)).

(4) This section applies in relation to instruments executed on or after the day on which this Act is passed.

115 Contracts for the sale of an estate or interest in land chargeable as conveyances

(1) This section applies to a contract or agreement for the sale of an estate or interest in land in the United Kingdom where—

(*a*) the amount or value of the consideration exceeds £10 million, or

(*b*) the instrument forms part of a larger transaction or series of transactions in respect of which the amount or value, or aggregate amount or value, of the consideration exceeds £10 million.

(2) If, in the case of such a contract or agreement that is not otherwise chargeable to stamp duty, a [transfer][1] made in conformity with the contract or agreement is not presented to the Commissioners for stamping with the *ad valorem* duty chargeable on it—

(*a*) within the period of 90 days after the execution of the contract or agreement, or

(*b*) within such longer period as the Commissioners may think reasonable in the circumstances of the case,

the contract or agreement shall be chargeable with the same ad valorem duty, to be paid by the purchaser, as if it were an actual conveyance on sale of the estate or interest contracted or agreed to be sold.

(3) The Commissioners—

(*a*) may refuse to allow a longer period unless they are provided with a copy of the contract or agreement and such other evidence as they may reasonably require as to the facts and circumstances relevant to their decision,

(*b*) may allow a longer period subject to compliance with such conditions as they think fit, and

(*c*) shall not allow any longer period if it appears to them that the whole, or substantially the whole, of the intended consideration has been paid or transferred.

(4) Where an instrument to which this section applies is presented for stamping before the end of the period mentioned in subsection (2)—

(*a*) any adjudication to the effect that stamp duty is not chargeable does not affect the operation of this section, and

(*b*) the fact that duty may be chargeable under this section may be denoted on the instrument in such manner as the Commissioners think fit.

(5) Where an instrument is chargeable with duty under this section—

(*a*) section 14(4) of the Stamp Act 1891 (c 39) (inadmissibility of unstamped instruments) does not apply in relation to it until after the end of the period mentioned in subsection (2) above, and

(*b*) sections 15A and 15B of that Act (late stamping: interest and penalties), apply in relation to it as if it had been executed at the end of that period.

(6) The *ad valorem* duty paid upon a contract or agreement under this section shall be repaid by the Commissioners if the contract or agreement is afterwards rescinded or annulled or is for any other reason not substantially performed or carried into effect.

(7) Schedule 36 contains provisions supplementing this section.

(8) This section and that Schedule apply to contracts or agreements executed after the day on which this Act is passed.

Amendments—[1] The word "transfer" substituted for the words "conveyance or transfer" in enactments relating to stamp duty by FA 2003 Sch 20 para 3.

116 Abolition of duty on instruments relating to goodwill

(1) No stamp duty is chargeable on an instrument for the sale, transfer or other disposition of goodwill.

(2) Schedule 37 to this Act contains provisions supplementing this section.

(3) This section and that Schedule shall be construed as one with the Stamp Act 1891 (c 39).

(4) This section applies to instruments executed on or after 23rd April 2002.

(5) This section shall be deemed to have come into force on that date.

Stamp duty and stamp duty reserve tax

117 Power to extend exceptions relating to recognised exchanges

(1) The Treasury may by regulations extend the application of the provisions mentioned in subsection (2) to any market (specified by name or by description) that is not a recognised exchange but is prescribed by order under section 118(3) of the Financial Services and Markets Act 2000 (c 8).

(2) The provisions referred to in subsection (1) are—

sections 80A and 80C of the Finance Act 1986 (c 41) (stamp duty: exceptions for sales to intermediaries and for repurchases and stock lending); and

sections 88A and 89AA of that Act (stamp duty reserve tax: exceptions for intermediaries and for repurchases and stock lending).

(3) In subsection (1) "recognised exchange" means an EEA exchange, a recognised foreign exchange or recognised foreign options exchange within the meaning of the provisions mentioned in subsection (2).

(4) Regulations under this section may provide for the application of the provisions mentioned in subsection (2) subject to any adaptations appearing to the Treasury to be necessary or expedient.

(5) Regulations under this section shall be made by statutory instrument which shall be subject to annulment in pursuance of a resolution of the House of Commons.[1]

Cross reference—Stamp Duty and Stamp Duty Reserve Tax (Extension of Exceptions relating to Recognised Exchanges) Regulations SI 2002/1975 (extension of the provisions in sub-s (2) above to the market known as OFEX).
Stamp Duty and Stamp Duty Reserve Tax (Extension of Exceptions relating to Recognised Exchanges) Regulations 2004/2421 (extension of the provisions in sub-s (2) above to the market known as the Alternative Investment Market established under the rules of the London Stock Exchange plc).
Amendments—[1] This section repealed by F(No 2)A 2005 ss 50(6), 70, Sch 11 Pt 3(2) with effect from 11 August 2005 (by virtue of SI 2005/2007).

PART 6
MISCELLANEOUS AND SUPPLEMENTARY PROVISIONS

Supplementary

143 Short title
This Act may be cited as the Finance Act 2002.

SCHEDULES

SCHEDULE 34
STAMP DUTY: WITHDRAWAL OF GROUP RELIEF: SUPPLEMENTARY PROVISIONS

Section 111

Introduction

1— (1) The provisions of this Schedule supplement section 111 (withdrawal of group relief).

(2) Expressions used in this Schedule that are defined for the purposes of that section have the same meaning in this Schedule.

Relief not withdrawn if transferor company leaves group

2— (1) Section 111 does not apply if the transferee company ceases to be a member of the same group as the transferor company by reason of the latter company leaving the group.

(2) The transferor company is regarded as leaving the group if the companies cease to be members of the same group by reason of a transaction relating to shares in—

(*a*) the transferor company, or
(*b*) another company that as a result of the transaction ceases to be a member of the same group as the transferee company.

Relief not withdrawn in case of winding-up

3— (1) Section 111 does not apply if the transferee company ceases to be a member of the same group as the transferor company by reason of anything done for the purposes of, or in the course of, winding up the transferor company or another company that is above the transferor company in the group structure.

(2) For the purposes of this paragraph a company is "above" the transferor company in the group structure if it is the parent (within the meaning of the relevant group relief provision)—

(*a*) of the transferor company, or
(*b*) of another company that is above the transferor company in the group structure.

Relief not withdrawn in case of exempt acquisition

4— (1) Section 111 does not apply if—

(*a*) the transferee company ceases to be a member of the same group as the transferor company as a result of an acquisition of shares by another company ("the parent company") in relation to which acquisition relief applies, and
(*b*) the transferee company is immediately after that acquisition a member of the same group as the parent company ("the new group").

(2) For this purpose—

(*a*) "acquisition relief" means relief under section 75 of the Finance Act 1986 (c 41); and
(*b*) references to an acquisition in relation to which such relief applies are to an acquisition such that an instrument effecting the transfer of the shares is exempt from stamp duty by virtue of that provision.

(3) But if before the end of the period of two years beginning with the date on which the relevant instrument was executed—

(*a*) the transferee company ceases to be a member of the new group, and
(*b*) at the time when [the transferee company ceases][1] to be a member of the new group [it or a relevant associated company (as defined in sub-paragraph (4) below) holds][1] an estate or interest in land that—

(i) was transferred [to the transferee company][1] by the relevant instrument, or
(ii) is derived from an estate or interest that was so transferred,

[and that has not subsequently been transferred at market value by a duly stamped instrument on which *ad valorem* duty was paid and in respect of which group relief was not claimed,][1] section 11 and the provisions of this Schedule apply [as if the transferee had then ceased to be a member of the same group as the transferor company and had then held the estate or interest referred to in paragraph (*b*).][1].

[(4) In sub-paragraph (3)(*b*) "relevant associated company", in relation to the transferee company, means a company that is in the same group as the transferee company immediately before the transferee company ceases to be a member of the new group and which ceases to be a member of the new group in consequence of the transferee company so ceasing.][1]

Cross references—FA 2003 Sch 19 para 6(2) (the references in sub-para (3) above to a transfer at market value by a duly stamped instrument on which ad valorem duty was paid and in respect of which group relief was not claimed shall be read, on or after the implementation date, as including a reference to a transfer at market value by a chargeable transaction in respect of which relief under FA 2003 Sch 7 Pt 1 was available but was not claimed. For the implementation date, see FA 2003 Sch 19 para 2).

Amendments—[1] In sub-para (3)(*b*), words substituted for the words "it ceases", "it holds", "to it", "and that was not subsequently transferred to it by a duly stamped instrument for which group relief was not claimed,", and "as if the company had then ceased to be a member of the same group as the transferor company."; and sub-para (4) inserted, by FA 2003 s 126(6)–(11) with effect for instruments executed after 14 April 2003.

FA 2003 s 126 shall be deemed to have come into force on 15 April 2003.

FA 2003 s 126 does not apply to an instrument giving effect to a contract made on or before 9th April 2003, unless—

(*a*) the instrument is made in consequence of the exercise after that date of any option, right of pre-emption or similar right, or

(*b*) the instrument transfers the property in question to, or vests it in, a person other than the purchaser under the contract because of an assignment (or, in Scotland, assignation) or further contract made after that date.

Interest

5— (1) If any duty payable under section 111 is not paid within the period of 30 days within which payment is to be made, interest is payable on the amount remaining unpaid.

(2) The provisions of section 15A(3) to (5) of the Stamp Act 1891 (c 39) (rate of interest on unpaid duty, etc) apply in relation to interest under sub-paragraph (1).

Duty of transferee company to notify particulars

6— (1) The transferee company shall, within the period of 30 days mentioned in section 111(2)(*b*) within which payment is to be made, notify the Commissioners of—

(*a*) the date on which it ceased to be a member of the same group as the transferor company,
(*b*) the relevant land held by it at that time,
(*c*) the nature of the relevant instrument, the date on which it was executed, the parties to the instrument and the date on which the instrument was stamped,
(*d*) the market value of the land transferred to it by the relevant instrument at the date on which that instrument was executed, and
(*e*) the amount of duty and interest payable by it under section 111 or this Schedule.

(2) In sub-paragraph (1)(*b*) the "relevant land" held by the transferee company means every estate or interest to in relation to which section 111(1)(*c*) applies.

(3) In section 98(5) of the Taxes Management Act 1970 (c 9) (penalty for failure to provide information), in the second column of the Table, at the appropriate place insert "paragraph 6 of Schedule 34 to the Finance Act 2002".

Determination, collection and recovery of duty and interest

7 The provisions of regulations under section 98 of the Finance Act 1986 (c 41) (stamp duty reserve tax: administration etc), and the provisions of the Taxes Management Act 1970 applied by those regulations, have effect with the necessary modifications in relation to—

(*a*) the determination by the Commissioners of the duty payable under section 111 or the interest payable thereon,
(*b*) appeals against any such determination, and
(*c*) the collection and recovery of any such duty or interest,

as if it were an amount of stamp duty reserve tax.

Recovery of group relief from another group company or controlling director

8— (1) This paragraph applies where—

(*a*) an amount is payable under section 111 or this Schedule by the transferee company,
(*b*) a notice of determination of the amount payable has been issued by the Commissioners, and
(*c*) the whole or part of that amount is unpaid six months after the date on which it became payable.

(2) The following persons may, by notice under paragraph 8, be required to pay the unpaid amount—

(*a*) the transferor company;

(*b*) any company that, at any relevant time, was a member of the same group as the transferee company and was above it in the group structure;

(*c*) any person who at any relevant time was a controlling director of the transferee company or of a company having control of the transferee company.

(3) For the purposes of this paragraph—

(*a*) a "relevant time" means any time between the execution of the relevant instrument and the transferee company ceasing to be a member of the same group as the transferor company

(*b*) a company is "above" another company in a group structure if it is the parent (within the meaning of the relevant group relief provision)—

(i) of that company, or

(ii) of another company that is above that company in the group structure.

(4) In this paragraph—

"director", in relation to a company, has the meaning given by section 168(8) of the Taxes Act 1988 (read with subsection (9) of that section) and includes any person falling within section 417(5) of that Act (read with subsection (6) of that section); and

"controlling director", in relation to a company, means a director of the company who has control of it (construing control in accordance with section 416 of the Taxes Act 1988).

Recovery of group relief from another group company or controlling director: procedure and time limit

9— (1) The Commissioners may serve a notice on a person within paragraph 8(2) requiring him, within 30 days of the service of the notice, to pay the amount that remains unpaid.

(2) Any notice under this paragraph must be served before the end of the period of three years beginning with the date on which the notice of determination mentioned in paragraph 8(1)(*b*) is issued.

(3) The notice must state the amount required to be paid by the person on whom the notice is served.

(4) The notice has effect—

(*a*) for the purposes of the recovery from that person of the amount required to be paid and of interest on that amount, and

(*b*) for the purposes of appeals,

as if it were a notice of determination and that amount were an amount of stamp duty reserve tax due from that person.

(5) A person who has paid an amount in pursuance of a notice under this paragraph may recover that amount from the transferee company.

(6) A payment in pursuance of a notice under this paragraph is not allowed as a deduction in computing any income, profits or losses for any tax purposes.

Power to require information

10— (1) The Commissioners may by notice require any person to furnish them within such time, not being less than 30 days, as may be specified in the notice with such information (including documents or records) as the Commissioners may reasonably require for the purposes of section 111 or this Schedule.

(2) A barrister or solicitor shall not be obliged in pursuance of a notice under this paragraph to disclose, without his client's consent, any information with respect to which a claim to professional privilege could be maintained.

(3) In section 98(5) of the Taxes Management Act 1970 (c 9) (penalty for failure to comply with notice to provide information), in the first column of the Table, at the appropriate place insert "paragraph 10 of Schedule 34 to the Finance Act 2002".

Prospective amendments—In sub-para (2), words "A relevant lawyer" to be substituted for words "A barrister or solicitor", and sub-para (2A) to be inserted, by the Legal Services Act 2007 s 208, Sch 21 paras 134, 135 with effect from a date to be appointed. Sub-s (2A) to read as follows—

"(2A) "Relevant lawyer" means a barrister, advocate, solicitor or other legal representative communications with whom may be the subject of a claim to professional privilege.".

Supplementary

11 Section 111 and this Schedule shall be construed as one with the Stamp Act 1891 (c 39).

SCHEDULE 35

STAMP DUTY: WITHDRAWAL OF RELIEF FOR COMPANY ACQUISITIONS: SUPPLEMENTARY PROVISIONS

Section 113

Introduction

1— (1) The provisions of this Schedule supplement section 113 (withdrawal of relief under section 76 of the Finance Act 1986 (c 41)).

(2) Expressions used in this Schedule that are defined for the purposes of that section have the same meaning in this Schedule.

Change of control due to exempt transfer

2 Section 113 does not apply by reason of control of the acquiring company changing as a result of any of the transactions listed in the Schedule to the Stamp Duty (Exempt Instruments) Regulations 1987 (SI 1987/516).

Change of control due to intra-group transfer

3—(1) Section 113 does not apply by reason of control of the acquiring company changing as a result of a transfer of shares ("the intra-group transfer") in relation to which group relief applies.

(2) In this paragraph—

(*a*) "group relief" means relief under section 42 of the Finance Act 1930 (c 28) or section 11 of the Finance Act (Northern Ireland) 1954 (c 23 (NI)) (transfer of property between associated bodies corporate); and

(*b*) references to a transfer in relation to which group relief applies are to a transfer such that an instrument effecting the transfer is exempt from stamp duty by virtue of either of the group relief provisions.

(3) But if before the end of the period of two years beginning with the date on which the relevant instrument was executed—

(*a*) a company ("company B") holding shares in the acquiring company to which the intra-group share transfer related, or that are derived from shares to which that instrument related, ceases to be a member of the same group as the company referred to in section 76 as the target company ("company C"), and

(*b*) the acquiring company [or a relevant associated company][1], at that time, holds an estate or interest in land—

(i) that was transferred [to the acquiring company][1] by the relevant instrument, or

(ii) that is derived from an estate or interest so transferred,

[and that has not subsequently been transferred at market value by a duly stamped instrument on which *ad valorem* duty was paid and in respect of which section 76 relief was not claimed,][1]

the following provisions apply.

(4) In those circumstances—

(*a*) section 76 relief in relation to the relevant instrument (or an appropriate proportion of that relief) is withdrawn, and

(*b*) the additional stamp duty that would have been paid on stamping the relevant instrument but for that relief if the land in question had been transferred by that instrument at market value, or an appropriate proportion of that amount, is payable by the acquiring company within 30 days after company B ceases to be a member of the same group as company C.

(5) In this paragraph—

(*a*) "company" includes any body corporate; and

(*b*) references to a company being in the same group as another company are to the companies being associated bodies corporate within the meaning of the relevant group relief provision.

Cross references—FA 2003 Sch 19 para 6(3) (the references in sub-para (3) above to a transfer at market value by a duly stamped instrument on which ad valorem duty was paid and in respect of which section 76 relief was not claimed shall be read, on or after the implementation date, as including a reference to a transfer at market value by a chargeable transaction on which stamp duty land tax was chargeable and in respect of which relief under FA 2003 Sch 7 Pt 2 was available but was not claimed).

Amendments—[1] In sub-para (3)(*b*), words inserted, and words substituted for the words "to it" and "and that was not subsequently transferred to it by a duly stamped instrument on which *ad valorem* duty was paid and in relation to which section 76 relief was not claimed,", by FA 2003 s 127(6)–(9) with effect for instruments executed after 14 April 2003. FA 2003 s 127 shall be deemed to have come into force on 15 April 2003.

FA 2003 s 127 does not apply to an instrument giving effect to a contract made on or before 9 April 2003, unless—

(*a*) the instrument is made in consequence of the exercise after that date of any option, right of pre-emption or similar right, or

(*b*) the instrument transfers the property in question to, or vests it in, a person other than the purchaser under the contract because of an assignment (or, in Scotland, assignation) or further contract made after that date: FA 2003 s 127(8).

Change of control due to exempt share acquisition

4—(1) Section 113 does not apply by reason of control of the acquiring company changing as a result of a transfer of shares ("the exempt transfer") to another company ("the parent company") in relation to which share acquisition relief applies.

(2) For this purpose—

(*a*) "share acquisition relief" means relief under section 77 of the Finance Act 1986 (c 41); and

(*b*) references to a transfer in relation to which such relief applies are to a transfer such that an instrument effecting the transfer is exempt from stamp duty by virtue of that provision.

(3) But if before the end of the period of two years beginning with the date on which the relevant instrument was executed—

(*a*) control of the parent company changes at a time when that company holds any shares transferred to it by the exempt transfer, or any shares derived from shares so transferred, and

(*b*) the acquiring company [or a relevant associated company][1], at that time, holds an estate or interest in land—

(i) that was transferred [to the acquiring company][1] by the relevant instrument, or

(ii) that is derived from an estate or interest so transferred,

[and that has not subsequently been transferred at market value by a duly stamped instrument on which *ad valorem* duty was paid and in respect of which section 76 relief was not claimed,][1]

the following provisions apply.

(4) In those circumstances—

(*a*) section 76 relief in relation to the relevant instrument (or an appropriate proportion of that relief) is withdrawn, and

(*b*) the additional stamp duty that would have been paid on stamping the relevant instrument but for that relief if the land in question had been transferred by that instrument at market value, or an appropriate proportion of that additional duty, is payable by the acquiring company within 30 days after control of the parent company changed.

Cross references—FA 2003 Sch 19 para 6(3) (the references in sub-para (3) above to a transfer at market value by a duly stamped instrument on which ad valorem duty was paid and in respect of which section 76 relief was not claimed shall be read, on or after the implementation date, as including a reference to a transfer at market value by a chargeable transaction on which stamp duty land tax was chargeable and in respect of which relief under FA 2003 Sch 7 Pt 2 was available but was not claimed).

Amendments—[1] In sub-para (3)(*b*), words inserted, and words substituted for the words "to it" and "and that was not subsequently transferred to it by a duly stamped instrument on which *ad valorem* duty was paid and in relation to which section 76 relief was not claimed,", by FA 2003 s 127(6)–(9) with effect for instruments executed after 14 April 2003.

FA 2003 s 127 shall be deemed to have come into force on 15 April 2003.

FA 2003 s 127 does not apply to an instrument giving effect to a contract made on or before 9 April 2003, unless—

(*a*) the instrument is made in consequence of the exercise after that date of any option, right of pre-emption or similar right, or

(*b*) the instrument transfers the property in question to, or vests it in, a person other than the purchaser under the contract because of an assignment (or, in Scotland, assignation) or further contract made after that date: FA 2003 s 127(8).

Change of control due to interest of loan creditor

5— (1) Section 113 does not apply by reason of control of the acquiring company changing as a result of a loan creditor becoming, or ceasing to be, treated as having control of the company if the other persons who were previously treated as controlling the company continue to be so treated.

(2) In sub-paragraph (1) "loan creditor" has the meaning given by section 417(7) to (9) of the Taxes Act 1988.

Interest

6— (1) If any duty payable under section 113 or this Schedule is not paid within the period of 30 days within which payment is to be made, interest is payable on the amount remaining unpaid.

(2) The provisions of section 15A(3) to (5) of the Stamp Act 1891 (c 39) (rate of interest on unpaid duty, etc) apply in relation to interest under this paragraph.

Duty of acquiring company to notify particulars

7— (1) The acquiring company shall, within the period of 30 days within which payment is to be made, notify the Commissioners of—

(*a*) the date on which the event occurred by reason of which it is liable to make a payment of duty under section 113 or this Schedule,

(*b*) the relevant land held by it at that time,

(*c*) the nature of the relevant instrument, the date on which it was executed, the parties to the instrument and the date on which the instrument was stamped,

(*d*) the market value of the land transferred to it by the relevant instrument at the date it was executed, and

(*e*) the amount of duty and interest payable by it.

(2) In sub-paragraph (1)(*b*) the "relevant land" held by the acquiring company means every estate or interest to in relation to which section 113(1)(*c*) applies.

(3) In section 98(5) of the Taxes Management Act 1970 (penalty for failure to provide information), in the second column of the Table, at the appropriate place insert "paragraph 6 of Schedule 35 to the Finance Act 2002".

Determination, collection and recovery of duty and interest

8 The provisions of regulations under section 98 of the Finance Act 1986 (c 41) (stamp duty reserve tax: administration etc), and the provisions of the Taxes Management Act 1970 (c 9) applied by those regulations, have effect with the necessary modifications in relation to—

(*a*) the determination by the Commissioners of the duty payable under section 113 or this Schedule, or of the interest payable thereon,

(*b*) appeals against any such determination, and

(*c*) the collection and recovery of any such duty or interest,

as if it were an amount of stamp duty reserve tax.

Recovery of section 76 relief from another group company or controlling director

9— (1) This paragraph applies where—

(*a*) an amount is payable under section 113 or this Schedule by the acquiring company,

(*b*) a notice of determination of the amount payable has been issued by the Inland Revenue, and

(*c*) the whole or part of that amount is unpaid six months after the date on which it became payable.

(2) The following persons may, by notice under paragraph 9, be required to pay the unpaid amount—

(*a*) any company that at any relevant time was a member of the same group as the acquiring company and was above it in the group structure, and

(*b*) any person who at any relevant time was a controlling director of the acquiring company or of a company having control of the acquiring company.

(3) For this purpose a "relevant time" means any time between the execution of the relevant instrument and the change of control by virtue of which the liability to pay the amount arises.

(4) In this paragraph—

(*a*) references to companies being in the same group are to one company having control of the other or both companies being under the control of the same person or persons;

(*b*) a company is "above" another company in a group structure if it controls—

(i) that company, or

(ii) another company that is above that company in the group structure;

(*c*) "director", in relation to a company, has the meaning given by section 168(8) of the Taxes Act 1988 (read with subsection (9) of that section) and includes any person falling within section 417(5) of that Act (read with subsection (6) of that section); and

(*d*) "controlling director", in relation to a company, means a director of the company who has control of it.

Recovery of section 76 relief from another group company or controlling director: procedure and time limit

10— (1) The Commissioners may serve a notice on a person within paragraph 9(2) requiring him, within 30 days of the service of the notice, to pay the amount that remains unpaid.

(2) A notice under this paragraph must be served before the end of the period of three years beginning with the date on the notice of determination mentioned in paragraph 9(1)(*b*) is issued.

(3) The notice must state the amount required to be paid by the person on whom the notice is served.

(4) The notice has effect—

(*a*) for the purposes of the recovery from that person of the amount required to be paid and of interest on that amount, and

(*b*) for the purposes of appeals,

as if it were a notice of determination and that amount were an amount of stamp duty reserve tax due from that person.

(5) A person who has paid an amount in pursuance of a notice under this paragraph may recover that amount from the acquiring company.

(6) A payment in pursuance of a notice under this paragraph is not allowed as a deduction in computing any income, profits or losses for any tax purposes.

Power to require information

11— (1) The Commissioners may by notice require any person to furnish them within such time, not being less than 30 days, as may be specified in the notice with such information (including documents or records) as the Commissioners may reasonably require for the purposes of section 113 or this Schedule.

(2) A barrister or solicitor shall not be obliged in pursuance of a notice under this paragraph to disclose, without his client's consent, any information with respect to which a claim to professional privilege could be maintained.

(3) In section 98(5) of the Taxes Management Act 1970 (c 9) (penalty for failure to comply with notice to provide information), in the first column of the Table, at the appropriate place insert "paragraph 11 of Schedule 35 to the Finance Act 2002".

Prospective amendments—In sub-para (2), words "A relevant lawyer" to be substituted for words "A barrister or solicitor", and sub-para (2A) to be inserted, by the Legal Services Act 2007 s 208, Sch 21 paras 134, 136 with effect from a date to be appointed. Sub-s (2A) to read as follows—

"(2A) "Relevant lawyer" means a barrister, advocate, solicitor or other legal representative communications with whom may be the subject of a claim to professional privilege.".

Supplementary

12 Section 113 and this Schedule shall be construed as one with the Stamp Act 1891 (c 39).

SCHEDULE 36

STAMP DUTY: CONTRACTS CHARGEABLE AS CONVEYANCES: SUPPLEMENTARY PROVISIONS

Section 115(7)

PART 1

SUBSALES

Introduction

1 This Part of this Schedule has effect for affording relief from duty under section 115 (contracts chargeable as conveyances) on a subsale.

Meaning of "subsale"

2 For the purposes of this Schedule there is a subsale—

(*a*) where the purchaser under a contract or agreement for the sale of an estate or interest in land in the United Kingdom ("the original sale"), without having obtained a conveyance of the property contracted to be sold, contracts to sell the whole or part of the property to another person, or

(*b*) where the sub-purchaser under a subsale of an estate or interest in land in the United Kingdom, without having obtained a conveyance of the property contracted to be sold, contracts to sell to another person the whole or part of the property contracted to be sold by the original sale,

so as to entitle that person to call for a conveyance from the original seller.

Relief where duty paid on original sale or earlier subsale

3— (1) Where duty under section 115 has been paid—

(*a*) on the original sale, or

(*b*) on an intervening subsale,

duty under that section on a subsale, or subsequent subsale, is chargeable only in respect of the amount (if any) by which the chargeable consideration on that transaction exceeds the chargeable consideration on the earlier transaction.

(2) If there is more than one such earlier transaction on which duty has been paid, the reference in sub-paragraph (1) to the chargeable consideration on the earlier transaction shall be read as a reference to the higher or highest amount of chargeable consideration on which duty has been paid.

(3) If the subsale does not relate to the whole of the property to which the earlier transaction related, the references in sub-paragraphs (1) and (2) to the chargeable consideration on an earlier transaction shall be read as references to an appropriate proportion of that consideration.

(4) What is an appropriate proportion shall be determined on a just and reasonable basis having regard to the subject matter of the subsale and of the earlier transaction.

(5) For the purposes of this paragraph the chargeable consideration on a transaction is the consideration that falls to be brought into account in determining the duty chargeable on it.

(6) Where under this paragraph duty on a subsale is chargeable in respect of part only of the consideration for the subsale, it is chargeable at the rate that would be applicable if the whole of the chargeable consideration on the subsale were taken into account

PART 2

SUBSEQUENT [TRANSFER][1]

Amendments—[1] The word "transfer" substituted for the words "conveyance or transfer" in enactments relating to stamp duty by FA 2003 Sch 20 para 3.

Introduction

4— (1) This Part of this Schedule has effect for affording relief where *ad valorem* duty is chargeable both—

(*a*) under section 115 on a contract or agreement ("the original sale"), and

(*b*) on a subsequent [transfer][1] by the original seller to the purchaser, or a sub-purchaser, in conformity with that contract or agreement.

Stamp Taxes

(2) References in this Part to the purchaser under the original sale, or a sub-purchaser under a subsale, include a person by whom the rights of the purchaser, or a sub-purchaser, are exercisable by virtue of any assignment (in Scotland, assignation) or agreement (other than a subsale).

Amendments—[1] The word "transfer" substituted for the words "conveyance or transfer" in enactments relating to stamp duty by FA 2003 Sch 20 para 3.

[Transfer][1] of property contracted to be sold

5— (1) Where the original seller conveys the whole of the property contracted to be sold—

(*a*) to the purchaser, or

(*b*) to a sub-purchaser in circumstances in which section 58(4) of the Stamp Act 1891 (c 39) applies (conveyance chargeable only on consideration moving from sub-purchaser),

the [transfer][1] is chargeable with duty only to the extent (if any) that the *ad valorem* duty chargeable on it (apart from this sub-paragraph) exceeds the duty paid under section 115 on the original sale together with the amount of any such duty paid on an intervening subsale.

(2) Where—

(*a*) the original seller conveys the property contracted to be sold to different sub-purchasers in parts or parcels, and

(*b*) section 58(5) of the Stamp Act 1891 applies (conveyance chargeable only on consideration moving from sub-purchaser),

the [transfer][1] of each part or parcel is chargeable with duty only to the extent (if any) that the *ad valorem* duty chargeable on it (apart from this sub-paragraph) exceeds an appropriate proportion of the *ad valorem* duty paid on the original sale together with an appropriate proportion of any such duty paid on an intervening subsale.

(3) What is an appropriate proportion shall be determined on a just and reasonable basis having regard to the subject matter of the [transfer][1] and of the earlier transaction.

(4) Where sub-paragraph (1) or (2) applies to reduce or extinguish the duty payable on a [transfer][1], the Commissioners shall, upon application and upon production of the earlier instrument or instruments, duly stamped, either—

(*a*) denote the payment of the whole of the *ad valorem* duty upon the [transfer][1], or

(*b*) transfer to the [transfer][1] the *ad valorem* duty paid on the earlier instrument or instruments.

Amendments—[1] The word "transfer" substituted for the words "conveyance or transfer" in enactments relating to stamp duty by FA 2003 Sch 20 para 3.

Repayment of duty in certain cases

6— (1) Where—

(*a*) duty is paid under section 115 on the original sale,

(*b*) one or more conveyances or transfers are executed in conformity with that contract or agreement so that the whole of the property contracted to be sold is duly conveyed to a purchaser or to one or more sub-purchasers,

(*c*) those conveyances or transfers are all duly stamped, and

(*d*) the aggregate amount of the duty that would have been paid on those conveyances or transfers but for duty having been previously paid on the original sale is less that the duty paid on the original sale,

the Commissioners shall repay the difference to the person by whom the duty was paid on the original sale.

(2) If duty has been paid under section 115 on one or more intervening subsales, sub-paragraph (1) has effect with the following modifications—

(*a*) the reference to duty having been paid on the original sale shall be read as a reference to duty having been paid either on the original sale or on an intervening subsale;

(*b*) the reference to the amount of duty paid on the original sale shall be read as a reference to the aggregate of the amounts paid on the original sale and any intervening subsales, and

(*c*) any repayment shall be apportioned among the persons by whom those amounts were paid.

(3) The apportionment mentioned in sub-paragraph (2)(*c*) shall be made on a just and reasonable basis having regard to the subject matter of the original sale and of the subsale or subsales in question.

PART 3
GENERAL SUPPLEMENTARY PROVISIONS

Construction of references to duty on transactions

7 Any reference in section 115 or this Schedule to duty chargeable or paid on a transaction is to duty chargeable or paid on the stamping of the instrument by which the transaction is effected.

Transactions relating to land in the UK and to other property

8— (1) Where a transaction relates both to land in the United Kingdom and to other property, section 115 and this Schedule apply as if there were separate transactions.

(2) Similarly, the reference in section 115(1)(*b*) to a series of transactions is to a series of transactions so far as relating to land in the United Kingdom.

(3) If, in a case where a transaction or series of transactions relates partly to land in the United Kingdom and partly to other property, the consideration is not apportioned in a manner that is just and reasonable, section 115 and this Schedule shall have effect as if the consideration had been apportioned in such a manner.

Person claiming relief to establish entitlement

9 It is for a person claiming any relief under this Schedule to prove to the satisfaction of the Commissioners that he is entitled to relief and in what amount.

Construction as one

10 Section 115 and this Schedule shall be construed as one with the Stamp Act 1891 (c 39).

SCHEDULE 37

STAMP DUTY: ABOLITION OF DUTY ON INSTRUMENTS RELATING TO GOODWILL: SUPPLEMENTARY PROVISIONS

Section 116(2)

Reduction of stamp duty where instrument partly relating to goodwill

1— (1) This paragraph applies where stamp duty under Part 1 of Schedule 13 to the Finance Act 1999 (c 16) ([transfer][1] on sale) is chargeable on an instrument that relates partly to goodwill and partly to property other than goodwill.

(2) In such a case—

(*a*) the consideration in respect of which duty would otherwise be charged shall be apportioned, on a just and reasonable basis, as between the goodwill and the other property, and

(*b*) the instrument shall be charged only in respect of the consideration attributed to the other property.

(3) This paragraph applies to instruments executed on or after 23rd April 2002.

Amendments—[1] The word "transfer" substituted for the words "conveyance or transfer" in enactments relating to stamp duty by FA 2003 Sch 20 para 3.

Apportionment of consideration for stamp duty purposes

2— (1) Where part of the property referred to in section 58(1) of the Stamp Act 1891 (c 39) (consideration to be apportioned between different instruments as parties think fit) consists of goodwill, that provision shall have effect as if "the parties think fit" read "is just and reasonable".

(2) Where—

(*a*) part of the property referred to in section 58(2) of the Stamp Act 1891 (property contracted to be purchased by two or more persons etc) consists of goodwill, and

(*b*) both or (as the case may be) all the relevant persons are connected with one another,

that provision shall have effect as if the words from "for distinct parts of the consideration" to the end of the subsection read ", the consideration shall be apportioned in such manner as is just and reasonable, so that a distinct consideration for each separate part or parcel is set forth in the conveyance relating thereto, and such conveyance is to be charged with *ad valorem* duty in respect of such distinct consideration.".

(3) In a case where sub-paragraph (1) or (2) applies and the consideration is apportioned in a manner that is not just and reasonable, the enactments relating to stamp duty shall have effect as if—

(*a*) the consideration had been apportioned in a manner that is just and reasonable, and

(*b*) the amount of any distinct consideration set forth in any conveyance relating to a separate part or parcel of property were such amount as is found by a just and reasonable apportionment (and not the amount actually set forth).

(4) For the purposes of sub-paragraph (2)—

(*a*) a person is a relevant person if he is a person by or for whom the property is contracted to be purchased;

(*b*) the question whether persons are connected with one another shall be determined in accordance with section 839 of the Taxes Act 1988.

(5) This paragraph applies to instruments executed on or after 23rd April 2002.

Certification of instruments for stamp duty purposes

3— (1) Goodwill shall be disregarded for the purposes of paragraph 6 of Schedule 13 to the Finance Act 1999 (c 19) (certification of instrument as not forming part of transaction or series of transactions exceeding specified amount).

(2) Any statement as mentioned in paragraph 6(1) of that Schedule shall be construed as leaving out of account any matter which is to be so disregarded.

(3) This paragraph applies to instruments executed on or after 23rd April 2002.

Acquisition under statute

4— (1) Section 12 of the Finance Act 1895 (c 16) (property vested by Act or purchased under statutory powers) does not require any person who is authorised to purchase any property as mentioned in that section after 23rd April 2002 to include any goodwill in the instrument of conveyance required by that section to be produced to the Commissioners.

(2) If the property consists wholly of goodwill no instrument of conveyance need be produced to the Commissioners under that section.

(3) This paragraph applies where the Act mentioned in that section, and by virtue of which property is vested or a person is authorised to purchase property, is passed after 23rd April 2002.

Interpretation

5 In this Schedule "the enactments relating to stamp duty" means the Stamp Act 1891 (c 39) and any enactment amending that Act or that is to be construed as one with that Act.

FINANCE ACT 2003

(2003 Chapter 14)

ARRANGEMENT OF SECTIONS

PART 4
STAMP DUTY LAND TAX

Supplementary provisions

Interpretation etc

Final provisions

PART 5
STAMP DUTY

PART 9
MISCELLANEOUS AND SUPPLEMENTARY PROVISIONS

Provisions consequential on changes to company law

Administrative matters

Supplementary

SCHEDULES:

Stamp Taxes

An Act to grant certain duties, to alter other duties, and to amend the law relating to the National Debt and the Public Revenue, and to make further provision in connection with finance.
[10 July 2003]

PART 4

STAMP DUTY LAND TAX

Introduction

42 The tax

(1) A tax (to be known as "stamp duty land tax") shall be charged in accordance with this Part on land transactions.

(2) The tax is chargeable—

(*a*) whether or not there is any instrument effecting the transaction,
(*b*) if there is such an instrument, whether or not it is executed in the United Kingdom, and
(*c*) whether or not any party to the transaction is present, or resident, in the United Kingdom.

(3) The tax is under the care and management of the Commissioners of Inland Revenue (referred to in this Part as "the Board").

Land transactions

43 Land transactions

(1) In this Part a "land transaction" means any acquisition of a chargeable interest.

As to the meaning of "chargeable interest" see section 48.

(2) Except as otherwise provided, this Part applies however the acquisition is effected, whether by act of the parties, by order of a court or other authority, by or under any statutory provision or by operation of law.

(3) For the purposes of this Part—

(*a*) the creation of a chargeable interest is—
(i) an acquisition by the person becoming entitled to the interest created, and
(ii) a disposal by the person whose interest or right is subject to the interest created;

(*b*) the surrender or release of a chargeable interest is—

(i) an acquisition of that interest by any person whose interest or right is benefitted or enlarged by the transaction, and

(ii) a disposal by the person ceasing to be entitled to that interest; ...[2]

(*c*) the variation of a chargeable interest [(other than a lease)][1] is—

(i) an acquisition of a chargeable interest by the person benefitting from the variation, and

(ii) a disposal of a chargeable interest by the person whose interest is subject to or limited by the variation.

[(*d*) the variation of a lease is an acquisition and disposal of a chargeable interest only where—

[(i) it takes effect, or is treated for the purposes of this Part, as the grant of a new lease[, or

(ii) paragraph 15A of Schedule 17A (reduction of rent or term) applies][3].][1]

(4) References in this Part to the "purchaser" and "vendor", in relation to a land transaction, are to the person acquiring and the person disposing of the subject-matter of the transaction.

These expressions apply even if there is no consideration given for the transaction.

(5) A person is not treated as a purchaser unless he has given consideration for, or is a party to, the transaction.

(6) References in this Part to the subject-matter of a land transaction are to the chargeable interest acquired (the "main subject-matter"), together with any interest or right appurtenant or pertaining to it that is acquired with it.

HMRC Manuals—Stamp Duty Land Tax Manual SDLTM00260 (definition of "land transaction")
SDLTM00270 (definition of "acquisition")
SDLTM00280 (definition of "chargeable interest")
SDLTM00290 (meaning of "main subject matter")
SDLTM00300 (method of acquisition of chargeable interest in unimportant)
SDLTM07100 (identity of the purchaser – with examples)
SDLTM07200 ("purchaser" includes a tenant where the interest in land is the grant of a lease)

Amendments—[1] In sub-s (3), words in para (*c*) inserted, and para (*d*) inserted, by FA 2004 s 296, Sch 39 paras 1, 2 with effect for any transaction of which the effective date is after 17 March 2004: FA 2004 Sch 39 para 13(3).

[2] Word "and" preceding sub-s (3)(*c*) repealed by FA 2004 s 326, Sch 42 Pt 4(2) with effect in accordance with FA 2004 Sch 39 para 13.

[3] Words in sub-s (3)(*d*) inserted by FA 2004 s 297(1), (2), (9) with effect for any transaction of which the effective date is on or after 22 July 2004.

44 Contract and conveyance

(1) This section applies where a contract for a land transaction is entered into under which the transaction is to be completed by a conveyance.

(2) A person is not regarded as entering into a land transaction by reason of entering into the contract, but the following provisions have effect.

(3) If the transaction is completed without previously having been substantially performed, the contract and the transaction effected on completion are treated as parts of a single land transaction.

In this case the effective date of the transaction is the date of completion.

(4) If the contract is substantially performed without having been completed, the contract is treated as if it were itself the transaction provided for in the contract.

In this case the effective date of the transaction is when the contract is substantially performed.

(5) A contract is "substantially performed" when—

(*a*) the purchaser[, or a person connected with the purchaser,][1] takes possession of the whole, or substantially the whole, of the subject-matter of the contract, or

(*b*) a substantial amount of the consideration is paid or provided.

(6) For the purposes of subsection (5)(*a*)—

[(*a*) possession includes receipt of rents and profits or the right to receive them, and][1]

(*b*) it is immaterial whether [possession is taken][1] under the contract or under a licence or lease of a temporary character.

(7) For the purposes of subsection (5)(*b*) a substantial amount of the consideration is paid or provided—

(*a*) if none of the consideration is rent, where the whole or substantially the whole of the consideration is paid or provided;

(*b*) if the only consideration is rent, when the first payment of rent is made;

(*c*) if the consideration includes both rent and other consideration, when—

(i) the whole or substantially the whole of the consideration other than rent is paid or provided, or

(ii) the first payment of rent is made.

(8) Where subsection (4) applies and the contract is subsequently completed by a conveyance—

(*a*) both the contract and the transaction effected on completion are notifiable transactions, and (*b*) tax is chargeable on the latter transaction to the extent (if any) that the amount of tax chargeable on it is greater than the amount of tax chargeable on the contract.

(9) Where subsection (4) applies and the contract is (to any extent) afterwards rescinded or annulled, or is for any other reason not carried into effect, the tax paid by virtue of that subsection shall (to that extent) be repaid by the Inland Revenue.

Repayment must be claimed by amendment of the land transaction return made in respect of the contract.

[(9A) Where—

(*a*) paragraph 12A of Schedule 17A applies (agreement for lease), or

(*b*) paragraph 19(3) to (6) of Schedule 17A applies (missives of let etc in Scotland),

it applies in place of subsections (4), (8) and (9).][2]

(10) In this section—

(*a*) references to completion are to completion of the land transaction proposed, between the same parties, in substantial conformity with the contract; and

(*b*) "contract" includes any agreement and "conveyance" includes any instrument.

[(11) Section 839 of the Taxes Act 1988 (connected persons) has effect for the purposes of this section.][1]

HMRC Manuals—Stamp Duty Land Tax Manual, SDLTM07700 (contracts, completion and substantial performance)
SDLTM01080 (transfer of rights does not affect operation of s 44 in relation to the original contract)
SDLTM01090a (substantial performance of original contract – examples)
SDLTM07900, 07900a (contract substantially performed when purchaser takes possession – with examples)
SDLTM07950 ("substantially the whole" is usually an amount equal to or greater than 90% of the total consideration due under the contract)

Amendments—[1] Words in sub-s (5)(*a*) inserted, sub-s (6)(*a*) substituted, words in sub-s (6)(*b*) substituted, and sub-s (11) inserted, by FA 2004 s 296, Sch 39 para 15 with effect for any transaction of which the effective date (within the meaning of FA 2003 Pt 4) is on or after 22 July 2004: FA 2004 Sch 39 para 26. These amendments were previously made by the Stamp Duty and Stamp Duty Land Tax (Variation of the Finance Act 2003) (No 2) Regulations, SI 2003/2816 regs 1, 2, Schedule para 1 with effect from 1 December 2003. Those regulations are revoked by FA 2004 Sch 39 para 14(2).

[2] Sub-s (9A) inserted by FA 2004 s 296, Sch 39 paras 1, 3 with effect for any transaction of which the effective date is after 17 March 2004: FA 2004 Sch 39 para 13(3).

[44A Contract providing for conveyance to third party

(1) This section applies where a contract is entered into under which a chargeable interest is to be conveyed by one party to the contract (A) at the direction or request of the other (B)—

(*a*) to a person (C) who is not a party to the contract, or

(*b*) either to such a person or to B.

(2) B is not regarded as entering into a land transaction by reason of entering into the contract, but the following provisions have effect.

(3) If the contract is substantially performed B is treated for the purposes of this Part as acquiring a chargeable interest, and accordingly as entering into a land transaction.

The effective date of the transaction is when the contract is substantially performed.

(4) Where the contract is (to any extent) afterwards rescinded or annulled, or is for any other reason not carried into effect, the tax paid by virtue of subsection (3) shall (to that extent) be repaid by the Inland Revenue.

Repayment must be claimed by amendment of the land transaction return made in respect of the contract.

(5) Subject to subsection (6), section 44 (contract and conveyance) does not apply (except so far as it defines "substantial performance") in relation to the contract.

(6) Where—

(*a*) this section applies by virtue of subsection (1)(*b*), and

(*b*) by reason of B's direction or request, A becomes obliged to convey a chargeable interest to B,

section 44 applies to that obligation as it applies to a contract for a land transaction that is to be completed by a conveyance.

(7) Section 44 applies in relation to any contract between B and C, in respect of the chargeable interest referred to in subsection (1) above, that is to be completed by a conveyance.

References to completion in that section, as it so applies, include references to conveyance by A to C of the subject matter of the contract between B and C.

(8) In this section "contract" includes any agreement and "conveyance" includes any instrument.][1]

Amendments—[1] This section inserted by FA 2004 s 296, Sch 39 paras 1, 4(1) with effect for any contract entered into after 17 March 2004: FA 2004 Sch 39 para 13(1).

45 Contract and conveyance: effect of transfer of rights

(1) This section applies where—

(*a*) a contract for a land transaction ("the original contract") is entered into under which the transaction is to be completed by a conveyance, …[2]

(*b*) there is an assignment, subsale or other transaction (relating to the whole or part of the subject-matter of the original contract) as a result of which a person other than the original purchaser becomes entitled to call for a conveyance to him[, and

(*c*) paragraph 12B of Schedule 17A (assignment of agreement for lease) does not apply.][1]

References in the following provisions of this section to a transfer of rights are to any such assignment, subsale or other transaction[, and references to the transferor and the transferee shall be read accordingly][1].

(2) The transferee is not regarded as entering into a land transaction by reason of the transfer of rights, but section 44 (contract and conveyance) has effect in accordance with the following provisions of this section.

(3) That section applies as if there were a contract for a land transaction (a "secondary contract") under which—

(*a*) the transferee is the purchaser, and

(*b*) the consideration for the transaction is—

(i) so much of the consideration under the original contract as is referable to the subject-matter of the transfer of rights and is to be given (directly or indirectly) by the transferee or a person connected with him, and

(ii) the consideration given for the transfer of rights.

The substantial performance or completion of the original contract at the same time as, and in connection with, the substantial performance or completion of the secondary contract shall be disregarded [except in a case where the secondary contract gives rise to a transaction that is exempt from charge by virtue of subsection (3) of section 73 (alternative property finance: land sold to financial institution and re-sold to individual)][3].

(4) Where there are successive transfers of rights, subsection (3) has effect in relation to each of them.

The substantial performance or completion of the secondary contract arising from an earlier transfer of rights at the same time as, and in connection with, the substantial performance or completion of the secondary contract arising from a subsequent transfer of rights shall be disregarded.

[(5) Where a transfer of rights relates to part only of the subject-matter of the original contract ("the relevant part")—

(*a*) subsection (8)(*b*) of section 44 (restriction of charge to tax on subsequent conveyance) has effect as if the reference to the amount of tax chargeable on that contract were a reference to an appropriate proportion of that amount, and

(*b*) a reference in the second sentence of subsection (3) above to the original contract, or a reference in subsection (4) above to the secondary contract arising from an earlier transfer of rights, is to that contract so far as relating to the relevant part (and that contract so far as not relating to the relevant part shall be treated as a separate contract).][1]

[(5A) In relation to a land transaction treated as taking place by virtue of subsection (3)—

(*a*) references in Schedule 7 (group relief) to the vendor shall be read as references to the vendor under the original contract;

(*b*) other references in this Part to the vendor shall be read, where the context permits, as referring to either the vendor under the original contract or the transferor.][1]

(6) Section 839 of the Taxes Act 1988 (connected persons) applies for the purposes of subsection (3)(*b*)(i).

(7) In this section "contract" includes any agreement and "conveyance" includes any instrument.

HMRC Manuals—Stamp Duty Land Tax Manual, SDLTM01060 (transfer of rights to third party by sub-sale, assignment or other transaction)
SDLTM01060a (assignment or sub-sale – with examples)
SDLTM01090a (substantial performance of original contract – examples)
SDLTM01100a (series of transfers – example)
SDLTM01110 (transfer of part only – apportionment of original price)
SDLTM01110a (transfer of part only – example)

Amendments—[1] Sub-s (1)(*c*) inserted, and words in sub-s (1) inserted; sub-s (5) substituted; and sub-s (5A) inserted; by FA 2004 s 296, Sch 39 para 5(1)–(4) with effect for any transfer of rights occurring after 17 March 2004: FA 2004 Sch 39 para 13(2).

[2] Word "and" preceding sub-s (1)(*b*) repealed by FA 2004 s 326, Sch 42 Pt 4(2) with effect in accordance with FA 2004 Sch 39 para 13.

[3] Words in sub-s (3) inserted by F(No 2)A 2005 s 49, Sch 10 paras 1, 2 with effect in relation to any transaction of which the effective date is after 19 May 2005.

However, this amendment does not have effect—

(*a*) in relation to any transaction which is effected in pursuance of a contract entered into and substantially performed on or before the specified date (ie 16 March 2005), or

(*b*) subject to what follows below, in relation to any other transaction which is effected in pursuance of a contract entered into on or before the specified date (ie 16 March 2005).

The exclusion by para (*b*) above of transactions effected in pursuance of contracts entered into on or before the specified date does not apply—

(*a*) if there is any variation of the contract or assignment of rights under the contract after that date,

(*b*) if the transaction is effected in consequence of the exercise after that date of any option, right of pre-emption or similar right, or

(*c*) if after that date there is an assignment, subsale or other transaction (relating to the whole or part of the subject-matter of the contract) as a result of which a person other than the purchaser under the contract becomes entitled to call for a conveyance to him: F(No 2)A 2005 Sch 10 para 16(5)–(8).

[45A Contract providing for conveyance to third party: effect of transfer of rights

(1) This section applies where—

(*a*) a contract ("the original contract") is entered into under which a chargeable interest is to be conveyed by one party to the contract (A) at the direction or request of the other (B)—

(i) to a person (C) who is not a party to the contract, or

(ii) either to such a person or to B,

and

(*b*) there is an assignment or other transaction (relating to the whole or part of the subject-matter of the original contract) as a result of which a person (D) becomes entitled to exercise any of B's rights under the original contract in place of B.

References in the following provisions of this section to a transfer of rights are to any such assignment or other transaction.

(2) D is not regarded as entering into a land transaction by reason of the transfer of rights, but section 44A (contract providing for conveyance to third party) has effect in accordance with the following provisions of this section.

(3) That section applies as if—

(*a*) D had entered into a contract (a "secondary contract") in the same terms as the original contract except with D as a party instead of B, and

(*b*) the consideration due from D under the secondary contract were—

(i) so much of the consideration under the original contract as is referable to the subject-matter of the transfer of rights and is to be given (directly or indirectly) by D or a person connected with him, and

(ii) the consideration given for the transfer of rights.

(4) The substantial performance of the original contract shall be disregarded if—

(*a*) it occurs at the same time as, and in connection with, the substantial performance of the secondary contract, or

(*b*) it occurs after the transfer of rights.

(5) Where there are successive transfers of rights, subsection (3) has effect in relation to each of them.

(6) The substantial performance of the secondary contract arising from an earlier transfer of rights shall be disregarded if—

(*a*) it occurs at the same time as, and in connection with, the substantial performance of the secondary contract arising from a subsequent transfer of rights, or

(*b*) it occurs after that subsequent transfer.

(7) Where a transfer of rights relates to only part of the subject matter of the original contract, or to only some of the rights under that contract—

(*a*) a reference in subsection (3)(*a*) or (4) to the original contract, or a reference in subsection (6) to the secondary contract arising from an earlier transfer, is to that contract so far as relating to that part or those rights, and

(*b*) that contract so far as not relating to that part or those rights shall be treated as a separate contract.

(8) The effective date of a land transaction treated as entered into by virtue of subsection (3) is not earlier than the date of the transfer of rights.

(9) In relation to a such a transaction—

(*a*) references in Schedule 7 (group relief) to the vendor shall be read as references to A;

(*b*) other references in this Part to the vendor shall be read, where the context permits, as referring to either A or B.

(10) Section 839 of the Taxes Act 1988 (connected persons) applies for the purposes of subsection (3)(*b*).

(11) In this section "contract" includes any agreement.][1]

Amendments—[1] This section inserted by FA 2004 s 296, Sch 39 para 5(1), (5) with effect for any transfer of rights occurring after 17 March 2004: FA 2004 Sch 39 para 13(2).

46 Options and rights of pre-emption

(1) The acquisition of—

(*a*) an option binding the grantor to enter into a land transaction, or

(*b*) a right of pre-emption preventing the grantor from entering into, or restricting the right of the grantor to enter into, a land transaction,

is a land transaction distinct from any land transaction resulting from the exercise of the option or right.

They may be "linked transactions" (see section 108).

(2) The reference in subsection (1)(*a*) to an option binding the grantor to enter into a land transaction includes an option requiring the grantor either to enter into a land transaction or to discharge his obligations under the option in some other way.

(3) The effective date of the transaction in the case of the acquisition of an option or right such as is mentioned in subsection (1) is when the option or right is acquired (as opposed to when it becomes exercisable).

(4) Nothing in this section applies to so much of an option or right of pre-emption as constitutes or forms part of a land transaction apart from this section.

HMRC Manuals—Stamp Duty Land Tax Manual, SDLTM01300 (charge to SDLT arises on acquisition of an option or right of pre-emption)
SDLTM01300a (options and rights of pre-emption – example)

47 Exchanges

(1) Where a land transaction is entered into by the purchaser (alone or jointly) wholly or partly in consideration of another land transaction being entered into by him (alone or jointly) as vendor, this Part applies in relation to each transaction as if each were distinct and separate from the other [(and they are not linked transactions within the meaning of section 108)][3].

(2) A transaction is treated for the purposes of this Part as entered into by the purchaser wholly or partly in consideration of another land transaction being entered into by him as vendor in any case where an obligation to give consideration for a land transaction that a person enters into as purchaser is met wholly or partly by way of that person entering into another transaction as vendor.

(3) As to the amount of the chargeable consideration in the case of exchanges and similar transactions, see—

paragraphs 5 and 6 of Schedule 4 (exchanges, partition etc) …[1]
[paragraph 17 of that Schedule (arrangements involving public or educational bodies), *and*][2]

Amendments—[1] Words ", and section 58 (relief for certain exchanges of residential property)" repealed by FA 2004 s 326, Sch 42 Pt 4(2) with effect in accordance with FA 2004 Sch 39 para 26. This repeal was previously made by the Stamp Duty and Stamp Duty Land Tax (Variation of the Finance Act 2003) (No 2) Regulations, SI 2003/2816 regs 1, 2, Schedule para 3(5) with effect from 1 December 2003. Those regulations have been revoked by FA 2004 Sch 39 para 14(2).
[2] Words inserted by the SDLT (Amendment of Part 4 of the Finance Act 2003) Regulations, SI 2004/1069 regs 2, 3 with effect from 7 April 2004.
[3] Words in sub-s (1) inserted by FA 2007 s 76(1), (3) with effect in relation to a set of land transactions if the effective date of any of them is on or after 19 July 2007.

Chargeable interests, chargeable transactions and chargeable consideration

48 Chargeable interests

(1) In this Part "chargeable interest" means—

(*a*) an estate, interest, right or power in or over land in the United Kingdom, or
(*b*) the benefit of an obligation, restriction or condition affecting the value of any such estate, interest, right or power,

other than an exempt interest.

(2) The following are exempt interests—

(*a*) any security interest;
(*b*) a licence to use or occupy land;
(*c*) in England and Wales or Northern Ireland—
(i) a tenancy at will;
(ii) an advowson, franchise or manor.

(3) In subsection (2)—

(*a*) "security interest" means an interest or right (other than a rentcharge) held for the purpose of securing the payment of money or the performance of any other obligation; and
(*b*) "franchise" means a grant from the Crown such as the right to hold a market or fair, or the right to take tolls.

[(3A) Section 73B makes additional provision about exempt interests in relation to alternative finance arrangements.][3]

(4) In the application of this Part in Scotland the reference in subsection (3)(*a*) to a rentcharge shall be read as a reference to a feu duty or a payment mentioned in section 56(1) of the Abolition of Feudal Tenure etc (Scotland) Act 2000 (asp 5).

(5) The Treasury may by regulations provide that any other description of interest or right in relation to land in the United Kingdom is an exempt interest.

(6) The regulations may contain such supplementary, incidental and transitional provision as appears to the Treasury to be appropriate.

[(7) This section has effect subject to subsection (3) of section 44A (contract and conveyance to third party) [and to paragraph 15A of Schedule 17A (reduction of rent or term of lease)][2].][1]

HMRC Manuals—Stamp Duty Land Tax Manual, SDLTM00280 (definition of "chargeable interest")
SDLTM00320 (certain exempt interests in land)

Amendments—[1] Sub-s (7) inserted by FA 2004 s 296, Sch 39 paras 1, 4(2) with effect for any contract entered into after 17 March 2004: FA 2004 Sch 39 para 13(1).
[2] Words in sub-s (7) inserted by FA 2004 s 297(1), (3), (9) with effect for any transaction of which the effective date is on or after 22 July 2004.
[3] Sub-s (3A) inserted by FA 2007 s 75(2), (4). This amendment—

(*a*) has effect in relation to anything that would, but for the exemption provided by this section, be a land transaction with an effective date on or after 22 March 2007, and
(*b*) applies, in accordance with paragraph (*a*), to interests irrespective of the date of their creation.

49 Chargeable transactions

(1) A land transaction is a chargeable transaction if it is not a transaction that is exempt from charge.

(2) Schedule 3 provides for certain transactions to be exempt from charge.

Other transactions are exempt from charge under other provisions of this Part.

HMRC Manuals—Stamp Duty Land Tax Manual, SDLTM00520 (specific transactions that are exempt from SDLT)

50 Chargeable consideration

(1) Schedule 4 makes provision as to the chargeable consideration for a transaction.

(2) The Treasury may by regulations amend or repeal the provisions of this Part relating to chargeable consideration and make such other provision as appears to them appropriate with respect to—

(*a*) what is to count as chargeable consideration, or
(*b*) the determination of the amount of chargeable consideration.

(3) The regulations may make different provision in relation to different descriptions of transaction or consideration and different circumstances.

HMRC Manuals—Stamp Duty Land Tax Manual, SDLTM03700 (general meaning of chargeable consideration for SDLT purposes)

51 Contingent, uncertain or unascertained consideration

(1) Where the whole or part of the chargeable consideration for a transaction is contingent, the amount or value of the consideration shall be determined for the purposes of this Part on the assumption that the outcome of the contingency will be such that the consideration is payable or, as the case may be, does not cease to be payable.

(2) Where the whole or part of the chargeable consideration for a transaction is uncertain or unascertained, its amount or value shall be determined for the purposes of this Part on the basis of a reasonable estimate.

(3) In this Part—

"contingent", in relation to consideration, means—

(*a*) that it is to be paid or provided only if some uncertain future event occurs, or
(*b*) that it is to cease to be paid or provided if some uncertain future event occurs; and

"uncertain", in relation to consideration, means that its amount or value depends on uncertain future events.

(4) This section has effect subject to—

section 80 (adjustment where contingency ceases or consideration is ascertained), and
section 90 (application to defer payment in case of contingent or uncertain consideration).

[(5) This section applies in relation to chargeable consideration consisting of rent only to the extent that it is applied by paragraph 7 of Schedule 17A.][1]

HMRC Manuals—Stamp Duty Land Tax Manual, SDLTM05010a (contingent consideration calculation – example)
Amendments—[1] Sub-s (5) inserted by FA 2004 s 296, Sch 39 para 22(3) with effect for any transaction of which the effective date (within the meaning of FA 2003 Pt 4) is on or after 22 July 2004: FA 2004 Sch 39 para 26. These amendments were previously made by the Stamp Duty and Stamp Duty Land Tax (Variation of the Finance Act 2003) (No 2) Regulations, SI 2003/2816 regs 1, 2, Schedule para 8(3) with effect from 1 December 2003. Those regulations are revoked by FA 2004 Sch 39 para 14(2).

52 Annuities etc: chargeable consideration limited to twelve years' payments

(1) This section applies to so much of the chargeable consideration for a land transaction as consists of an annuity payable—

(*a*) for life, or
(*b*) in perpetuity, or
(*c*) for an indefinite period, or
(*d*) for a definite period exceeding twelve years.

(2) For the purposes of this Part the consideration to be taken into account is limited to twelve years' annual payments.

(3) Where the amount payable varies, or may vary, from year to year, the twelve highest annual payments shall be taken.

No account shall be taken for the purposes of this Schedule of any provision for adjustment of the amount payable in line with the retail price index.

(4) References in this section to annual payments are to payments in respect of each successive period of twelve months beginning with the effective date of the transaction.

(5) For the purposes of this section the amount or value of any payment shall be determined (if necessary) in accordance with section 51 (contingent, uncertain or unascertained consideration).

(6) References in this section to an annuity include any consideration (other than rent) that falls to be paid or provided periodically.

References to payment shall be read accordingly.

(7) Where this section applies—

(*a*) section 80 (adjustment where contingency ceases or consideration is ascertained) does not apply, and

(*b*) no application may be made under section 90 (application to defer payment in case of contingent or uncertain consideration).

HMRC Manuals—Stamp Duty Land Tax Manual, SDLTM06040 (no deferral or adjustment where chargeable consideration is in the form of an annuity)

53 Deemed market value where transaction involves connected company

[(1) This section applies where the purchaser is a company and—

(*a*) the vendor is connected with the purchaser, or

(*b*) some or all of the consideration for the transaction consists of the issue or transfer of shares in a company with which the vendor is connected.][1]

[(1A) The chargeable consideration for the transaction shall be taken to be not less than—

(*a*) the market value of the subject-matter of the transaction as at the effective date of the transaction, and

(*b*) if the acquisition is the grant of a lease at a rent, that rent.][1]

(2) Section 839 of the Taxes Act 1988 (connected persons) has effect for the purposes of this section.

(3) In this section—

"company" means any body corporate;

"shares" includes stock and the reference to shares in a company includes a reference to securities issued by a company.

(4) Where this section applies paragraph 1 of Schedule 3 (exemption of transactions for which there is no chargeable consideration) does not apply.

But this section has effect subject to any other provision affording exemption or relief from stamp duty land tax.

(5) This section is subject to the exceptions provided for in section 54.

Amendments—[1] Sub-ss (1), (1A) substituted for sub-s (1) by FA 2004 s 297(1), (4), (9) with effect for any transaction of which the effective date is on or after 22 July 2004.

54 Exceptions from deemed market value rule

(1) Section 53 (chargeable consideration: transaction with connected company) does not apply in the following cases.

In the following provisions "the company" means the company that is the purchaser in relation to the transaction in question.

(2) Case 1 is where immediately after the transaction the company holds the property as trustee in the course of a business carried on by it that consists of or includes the management of trusts.

(3) Case 2 is where—

(*a*) immediately after the transaction the company holds the property as trustee, and

(*b*) the vendor is connected with the company only because of section 839(3) of the Taxes Act 1988.

(4) Case 3 is where—

(*a*) the vendor is a company and the transaction is, or is part of, a distribution of the assets of that company (whether or not in connection with its winding up), and

(*b*) it is not the case that—

(i) the subject-matter of the transaction, or

(ii) an interest from which that interest is derived,

has, within the period of three years immediately preceding the effective date of the transaction, been the subject of a transaction in respect of which group relief was claimed by the vendor.

Cross references—FA 2003 Sch 19 para 7(3) (the reference in sub-s (4)(*b*) above to group relief having been claimed in respect of a transaction shall be read in relation to a transaction carried out before the implementation date as a reference to relief having been claimed under FA 1930 s 42, Finance Act (Northern Ireland) 1954 s 11, or FA 1995 s 151 in respect of stamp duty on the instrument by which the transaction was effected. For implementation date, see FA 2003 Sch 19 para 2).

Amount of tax chargeable

55 Amount of tax chargeable: general

(1) The amount of tax chargeable in respect of a chargeable transaction is a percentage of the chargeable consideration for the transaction.

(2) That percentage is determined by reference to whether the relevant land—

(*a*) consists entirely of residential property (in which case Table A below applies), or
(*b*) consists of or includes land that is not residential property (in which case Table B below applies),

and, in either case, by reference to the amount of the relevant consideration.

TABLE A: RESIDENTIAL

Relevant consideration	*Percentage*
Not more than [£125,000][1]	0%
More than [£125,000][1] but not more than £250,000	1%
More than £250,000 but not more than £500,000	3%
More than £500,000	4%

TABLE B: NON-RESIDENTIAL OR MIXED

Relevant consideration	*Percentage*
Not more than £150,000	0%
More than £150,000 but not more than £250,000	1%
More than £250,000 but not more than £500,000	3%
More than £500,000	4%

(3) For the purposes of subsection (2)—
(*a*) the relevant land is the land an interest in which is the main subject-matter of the transaction, and
(*b*) the relevant consideration is the chargeable consideration for the transaction, subject as follows.

(4) If the transaction in question is one of a number of linked transactions—
(*a*) the relevant land is any land an interest in which is the main subject-matter of any of those transactions, and
(*b*) the relevant consideration is the total of the chargeable consideration for all those transactions.

(5) This section has effect subject to—
section 74 ([exercise of collective rights by tenants of flats][2]), and
section 75 (crofting community right to buy),

(which provide for the rate of tax to be determined by reference to a fraction of the relevant consideration).

(6) In the case of a transaction for which the whole or part of the chargeable consideration is rent this section has effect subject to section 56 and Schedule 5 (amount of tax chargeable: rent).

(7) References in this Part to the "rate of tax" are to the percentage determined under this section.

Modification—Stamp Duty Land Tax (Zero-Carbon Homes Relief) Regulations, SI 2007/3437 reg 9 (disapplication of sub-s (4) in relation to the first acquisition of one or more zero-carbon homes where that acquisition is one of a number of linked transactions for the purposes of SI 2007/3437).

Regulations—The Stamp Duty Land Tax (Exemption of Certain Acquisitions of Residential Property) Regulations, SI 2008/2339 (exemption from stamp duty land tax for relevant acquisitions of land for chargeable consideration of not more than £175,000, with effect in relation to acquisitions made on or after 3 September 2008 but before 3 September 2009).

Amendments—[1] £125,000" substituted for "£120,000" by FA 2006 s 162(1), with effect in relation to any transaction of which the effective date (within the meaning of Part 4 of FA 2003) is after 22 March 2006. The figure of "£175,000" is substituted for "£125,000" (in both places) in Table A in relation to transactions with an effective date on or after 22 April 2009 but before 1 January 2010; FA 2009 s 10(1)(*a*).

[2] In sub-s (5), words substituted for words "collective enfranchisement by leaseholders" by FA 2009 s 80(1), (6) with effect in relation to transactions with an effective date on or after 22 April 2009.

56 Amount of tax chargeable: rent

Schedule 5 provides for the calculation of the tax chargeable where the chargeable consideration for a transaction consists of or includes rent.

Reliefs

57 Disadvantaged areas relief

(1) Schedule 6 provides for relief in the case of transactions relating to land in a disadvantaged area.

(2) In that Schedule—
Part 1 defines "disadvantaged area",
Part 2 relates to transactions where the land to which the transaction relates is wholly situated in a disadvantaged area,
Part 3 relates to transactions where the land to which the transaction relates is partly situated in a disadvantaged area, and
Part 4 contains supplementary provisions.

HMRC Manuals—Stamp Duty Land Tax Manual, SDLTM00700 (claims for relief – cases where a land transaction return is required).
SDLTM20050–20100 (general explanation of relief).
Statement of Practice SP 1/04—(Disadvantaged areas relief, Stamp Office approach to borderline cases).

[57A Sale and leaseback arrangements

(1) The leaseback element of a sale and leaseback arrangement is exempt from charge if the qualifying conditions specified below are met.

(2) A "sale and leaseback" arrangement means an arrangement under which—

(*a*) A transfers or grants to B a major interest in land (the "sale"), and
(*b*) out of that interest B grants a lease to A (the "leaseback").

(3) The qualifying conditions are—

(*a*) that the sale transaction is entered into wholly or partly in consideration of the leaseback transaction being entered into,
(*b*) that the only other consideration (if any) for the sale is the payment of money or the assumption, satisfaction or release of a debt (or both),
(*c*) that the sale is not a transfer of rights within the meaning of section 45 (contract and conveyance: effect of transfer of rights) or 45A (contract providing for conveyance to third party: effect of transfer of rights), and
(*d*) where A and B are both bodies corporate at the effective date of the leaseback transaction, that they are not members of the same group for the purposes of group relief (see paragraph 1 of Schedule 7) at that date.

(4) In this section—

"debt" means an obligation, whether certain or contingent, to pay a sum of money either immediately or at a future date; and

"money" means money in sterling or another currency.][1]

HMRC Manuals—Stamp Duty Land Tax Manual, SDLTM00700 (claims for relief – cases where a land transaction return is required)

Amendments—[1] This section inserted by FA 2004 s 296, Sch 39 para 16 with effect for any transaction of which the effective date (within the meaning of FA 2003 Pt 4) is on or after 22 July 2004: FA 2004 Sch 39 para 26. This insertion was previously made by the Stamp Duty and Stamp Duty Land Tax (Variation of the Finance Act 2003) (No 2) Regulations, SI 2003/2816, regs 1, 2, Sch para 2 with effect from 1 December 2003. Those regulations are revoked by FA 2004 Sch 39 para 14(2) with effect for any transaction of which the effective date is on or after 22 July 2004.
FA 2004 Sch 39 para 6 amended the old version of this section (i e that inserted by SI 2003/2816) as follows: in sub-s (3), paras (*aa*), (*b*) are substituted for para (*b*), and paras (*c*), (*d*) are inserted; and sub-s (4) is repealed. These amendments have effect for any transaction of which the effective date is after 17 March 2004 and before 22 July 2004: FA 2004 Sch 39 para 13(3), (5).

[58A Relief for certain acquisitions of residential property

Schedule 6A provides for relief in the case of certain acquisitions of residential property.][1]

HMRC Manuals—Stamp Duty Land Tax Manual SDLTM00700 (claims for relief – cases where a land transaction return is required).
SDLTM21000–21070 (explanation of scope of this relief).

Amendments—[1] This section substituted for sections 58, 59, by FA 2004 s 296, Sch 39 para 17(1) with effect for any transaction of which the effective date (within the meaning of FA 2003 Pt 4) is on or after 22 July 2004: FA 2004 Sch 39 para 26. The substitution was previously made by the Stamp Duty and Stamp Duty Land Tax (Variation of the Finance Act 2003) (No 2) Regulations, SI 2003/2816 regs 1, 2, Schedule para 3(1) with effect from 1 December 2003. Those regulations are revoked by FA 2004 Sch 39 para 14(2).

[58B Relief for new zero-carbon homes

(1) The Treasury may make regulations granting relief on the first acquisition of a dwelling which is a "zero-carbon home".

[(2) For the purposes of this section—

(*a*) a building, or a part of a building, is a dwelling if it is constructed for use as a single dwelling, and
(*b*) "first acquisition", in relation to a dwelling, means its acquisition when it has not previously been occupied.][2]

(3) For the purpose of subsection (2) land occupied or enjoyed with a dwelling as a garden or grounds is part of the dwelling.

(4) The regulations shall define "zero-carbon home" by reference to specified aspects of the energy efficiency of a building; for which purpose "energy efficiency" includes—

(*a*) consumption of energy,
(*b*) conservation of energy, and
(*c*) generation of energy.

(5) The relief may take the form of—

(*a*) exemption from charge, or
(*b*) a reduction in the amount of tax chargeable.

(6) Regulations under this section shall not have effect in relation to acquisitions on or after 1st October 2012.

(7) The Treasury may by order—

(*a*) substitute a later date for the date in subsection (6);

(*b*) make transitional provision, or provide savings, in connection with the effect of subsection (6).][1]

Regulations—Stamp Duty Land Tax (Zero-Carbon Homes Relief) Regulations, SI 2007/3437.

Amendments—[1] Sections 58B, 58C inserted by FA 2007 s 19(1) with effect from 19 July 2007.

[2] Sub-s (2) substituted by FA 2008 s 93(1), (2); this amendment is treated as always having had effect; and provision included in regulations by virtue of this amendment may be made so as to have effect in relation to acquisitions on or after 1 October 2007.

[58C Relief for new zero-carbon homes: supplemental

(1) Regulations under section 58B—

(*a*) shall include provision about the method of claiming relief (including documents or information to be provided), and

(*b*) in particular, shall include provision about the evidence to be adduced to show that a [dwelling][2] satisfies the definition of "zero-carbon home".

(2) Regulations made by virtue of subsection (1)(*b*) may, in particular—

(*a*) refer to a scheme or process established by or for the purposes of an enactment about building;

(*b*) establish or provide for the establishment of a scheme or process of certification;

(*c*) specify, or provide for the approval of, one or more schemes or processes for certifying energy efficiency.

[(*d*) provide for the charging of fees of a reasonable amount in respect of services provided as part of a scheme or process of certification.][3]

(3) In defining "zero-carbon home" regulations under section 58B may include requirements which may be satisfied in relation to [a dwelling][2] either—

(*a*) by features of the [building which, or part of which, constitutes the dwelling][2], or

(*b*) by other installations or utilities.

(4) Regulations under section 58B may modify the effect of section 108, or another provision of this Part about linked transactions, in relation to a set of transactions of which at least one is the first acquisition of a dwelling which is a zero-carbon home.

(5) In determining whether section 116(7) applies, and in the application of section 116(7), a transaction shall be disregarded if or in so far as it involves the first acquisition of a dwelling which is a zero-carbon home.

(6) Regulations under section 58B—

(*a*) may provide for relief to be wholly or partly withdrawn if a dwelling ceases to be a zero-carbon home, and

(*b*) may provide for the reduction or withholding of relief where a person acquires more than one zero-carbon home within a specified period.

(7) Regulations under section 58B may include provision for relief to be granted in respect of acquisitions occurring during a specified period before the regulations come into force.][1]

Regulations—Stamp Duty Land Tax (Zero-Carbon Homes Relief) Regulations, SI 2007/3437.

Amendments—[1] Sections 58B, 58C inserted by FA 2007 s 19(1) with effect from 19 July 2007.

[2] Words in sub-ss (1), (3) substituted by FA 2008 s 93(3), (4), (6); these amendments are treated as always having had effect; and provision included in regulations by virtue of these amendments may be made so as to have effect in relation to acquisitions on or after 1 October 2007.

[3] Sub-s (2)(*d*) inserted by FA 2008 s 93(3), (5) with effect from 21 July 2008.

60 Compulsory purchase facilitating development

(1) A compulsory purchase facilitating development is exempt from charge.

(2) In this section "compulsory purchase facilitating development" means—

(*a*) in relation to England and Wales or Scotland, the acquisition by a person of a chargeable interest in respect of which that person has made a compulsory purchase order for the purpose of facilitating development by another person;

(*b*) in relation to Northern Ireland, the acquisition by a person of a chargeable interest by means of a vesting order made for the purpose of facilitating development by a person other than the person who acquires the interest.

(3) For the purposes of subsection (2)(*a*) it does not matter how the acquisition is effected (so that provision applies where the acquisition is effected by agreement).

(4) In subsection (2)(*b*) a "vesting order" means an order made under any statutory provision to authorise the acquisition of land otherwise than by agreement.

(5) In this section "development"—

(*a*) in relation to England and Wales, has the same meaning as in the Town and Country Planning Act 1990 (c 8) (see section 55 of that Act);

(*b*) in relation to Scotland, has the same meaning as in the Town and Country Planning (Scotland) Act 1997 (c 8) (see section 26 of that Act); and

(*c*) in relation to Northern Ireland, has the same meaning as in the Planning (Northern Ireland) Order 1991 (1991/1220 (NI 11)) (see Article 11 of that Order).

HMRC Manuals—Stamp Duty Land Tax Manual, SDLTM00700 (claims for relief – cases where a land transaction return is required).
SDLTM22000–22020 (explanation of this relief).

61 Compliance with planning obligations

(1) A land transaction that is entered into in order to comply with a planning obligation or a modification of a planning obligation is exempt from charge if—

(*a*) the planning obligation or modification is enforceable against the vendor,
(*b*) the purchaser is a public authority, and
(*c*) the transaction takes place within the period of five years beginning with the date on which the planning obligation was entered into or modified.

(2) In this section—

(*a*) in relation to England and Wales—

"planning obligation" means either of the following—

(*a*) a planning obligation within the meaning of section 106 of the Town and Country Planning Act 1990 that is entered into in accordance with subsection (9) of that section, or

(*b*) a planning obligation within the meaning of section 299A of that Act that is entered into in accordance with subsection (2) of that section; and

"modification" of a planning obligation means modification as mentioned in section 106A(1) of that Act;

(*b*) in relation to Scotland, "planning obligation" means an agreement made under section 75 or section 246 of the Town and Country Planning (Scotland) Act 1997;
(*c*) in relation to Northern Ireland—

"planning obligation" means a planning agreement within the meaning of Article 40 of the Planning (Northern Ireland) Order 1991 (1991/1220 (NI 11)) that is entered into accordance with paragraph (10) of that Article, and
"modification" of a planning obligation means modification as mentioned in Article 40A(1) of that Order.

(3) The following are public authorities for the purposes of subsection (1)(*b*)—

Government

A Minister of the Crown or government department
The Scottish Ministers
A Northern Ireland department
[The Welsh Ministers, the First Minister for Wales and the Counsel General to the Welsh Assembly Government][2]

Local government: England

A county or district council constituted under section 2 of the Local Government Act 1972 (c 70)
The council of a London borough
The Common Council of the City of London
The Greater London Authority
Transport for London
The Council of the Isles of Scilly

Local government: Wales

A county or county borough council constituted under section 21 of the Local Government Act 1972

Local government: Scotland

A council constituted under section 2 of the Local Government etc (Scotland) Act 1994 (c 39)

Local government: Northern Ireland

A district council within the meaning of the Local Government Act (Northern Ireland) 1972 (c 9 (NI))

Health: England and Wales

A Strategic Health Authority [established under section 13 of the National Health Service Act 2006][1]
A Special Health Authority established under [section 28 of that Act or section 22 of the National Health Service (Wales) Act 2006][1]
A Primary Care Trust established under [section 18 of the National Health Service Act 2006][1]
A Local Health Board established under [section 11 of the National Health Service (Wales) Act 2006][1]
A National Health Service Trust established under [section 25 of the National Health Service Act 2006 or section 18 of the National Health Service (Wales) Act 2006][1]

Health: Scotland

The Common Services Agency established under section 10(1) of the National Health Service (Scotland) Act 1978 (c 29)

A Health Board established under section 2(1)(a) of that Act

A National Health Service Trust established under section 12A(1) of that Act

A Special Health Board established under section 2(1)(b) of that Act

Health: Northern Ireland

A Health and Social Services Board established under Article 16 of the Health and Personal Social Services (Northern Ireland) Order 1972 (SI 1972/1265 (NI 14))

A Health and Social Services Trust established under Article 10 of the Health and Personal Social Services (Northern Ireland) Order 1991 (SI 1991/194 (NI 1))

Other planning authorities

Any other authority that—

(*a*) is a local planning authority within the meaning of the Town and Country Planning Act 1990 (c 8), or

(*b*) is the planning authority for any of the purposes of the planning Acts within the meaning of the Town and Country Planning (Scotland) Act 1997 (c 8).

Prescribed persons

A person prescribed for the purposes of this section by Treasury order

HMRC Manuals—Stamp Duty Land Tax Manual, SDLTM00700 (claims for relief – cases where a land transaction return is required).
SDLTM22500–22550 (explanation of this relief).

Amendments—[1] In sub-s (3), in entries beginning "A Strategic Health Authority", "A Special Health Authority", "A Primary Care Trust", "A Local Health Board" and "A National Health Service Trust", words substituted by the National Health Service (Consequential Provisions) Act 2006 s 2, Sch 1 paras 232, 233(*a*)–(*e*) with effect from 1 March 2007 (National Health Service (Consequential Provisions) Act 2006 s 8(2)).

[2] In subs-s (3), entry "The Welsh Ministers, the First Minister for Wales and the Counsel General to the Welsh Assembly Government" substituted by the Government of Wales Act 2006 s 160(1), Sch 10 paras 62, 63 with effect from 25 May 2007, being the date on which the initial period ended (following the appointment of the First Minister) (Government of Wales Act 2006 ss 46, 161(4), (5))

62 Group relief and reconstruction or acquisition relief

(1) Schedule 7 provides for relief from stamp duty land tax.

(2) In that Schedule—

Part 1 makes provision for group relief,

Part 2 makes provision for reconstruction and acquisition reliefs.

(3) Any relief under that Schedule must be claimed in a land transaction return or an amendment of such a return.

HMRC Manuals—Stamp Duty Land Tax Manual SDLTM00700 (claims for relief – cases where a land transaction return is required).
SDLTM23000–23280 (explanation of group, reconstruction or acquisition relief).

63 Demutualisation of insurance company

(1) A land transaction is exempt from charge if it is entered into for the purposes of or in connection with a qualifying transfer of the whole or part of the business of a mutual insurance company ("the mutual") to a company that has share capital ("the acquiring company").

(2) A transfer is a qualifying transfer if—

(*a*) it is a transfer of business consisting of the effecting or carrying out of contracts of insurance and takes place under an insurance business transfer scheme, or

(*b*) it is a transfer of business of a general insurance company carried on through a permanent establishment in the United Kingdom and takes place in accordance with authorisation granted outside the United Kingdom for the purposes of—

(i) Article 14 of the life assurance Directive, or

(ii) Article 12 of the 3rd non-life insurance Directive,

and, in either case, the requirements of subsections (3) and (4) are met in relation to the shares of a company ("the issuing company") which is either the acquiring company or a company of which the acquiring company is a wholly-owned subsidiary.

(3) Shares in the issuing company must be offered, under the scheme, to at least 90% of the persons who are members of the mutual immediately before the transfer.

(4) Under the scheme all of the shares in the issuing company that will be in issue immediately after the transfer has been made, other than shares that are to be or have been issued pursuant to an offer to the public, must be offered to the persons who (at the time of the offer) are—

(*a*) members of the mutual,

(*b*) persons who are entitled to become members of the mutual, or

(*c*) employees, former employees or pensioners of—

(i) the mutual, or

(ii) a wholly-owned subsidiary of the mutual.

(5) The Treasury may by regulations—

(*a*) amend subsection (3) by substituting a lower percentage for the percentage mentioned there;

(*b*) provide that any or all of the references in subsections (3) and (4) to members shall be construed as references to members of a class specified in the regulations.

Regulations under paragraph (*b*) may make different provision for different cases.

(6) For the purposes of this section a company is the wholly-owned subsidiary of another company ("the parent") if the company has no members except the parent and the parent's wholly-owned subsidiaries or persons acting on behalf of the parent or the parent's wholly-owned subsidiaries.

(7) In this section—

"contract of insurance" has the meaning given by Article 3(1) of the Financial Services and Markets Act 2000 (Regulated Activities) Order 2001 (SI 2001/544);

"employee", in relation to a mutual insurance company or its wholly-owned subsidiary, includes any officer or director of the company or subsidiary and any other person taking part in the management of the affairs of the company or subsidiary;

"general insurance company" means a company that has permission under Part 4 of the Financial Services and Markets Act 2000 (c 8), or paragraph 15 of Schedule 3 to that Act (as a result of qualifying for authorisation under paragraph 12(1) of that Schedule), to effect or carry out contracts of insurance;

"insurance company" means a company that carries on the business of effecting or carrying out contracts of insurance;

"insurance business transfer scheme" has the same meaning as in Part 7 of the Financial Services and Markets Act 2000;

"the life assurance Directive" means the Council Directive of 5th November 2002 concerning life assurance (No 2002/83/EC);

"mutual insurance company" means an insurance company carrying on business without having any share capital;

"the 3rd non-life insurance Directive" means the Council Directive of 18th June 1992 on the co-ordination of laws, regulations and administrative provisions relating to direct insurance other than life insurance and amending Directives 73/239/EEC and 88/357/EEC (No 92/49/EEC);

"pensioner", in relation to a mutual insurance company or its wholly-owned subsidiary, means a person entitled (whether presently or prospectively) to a pension, lump sum, gratuity or other like benefit referable to the service of any person as an employee of the company or subsidiary.

HMRC Manuals—Stamp Duty Land Tax Manual, SDLTM00700 (claims for relief – cases where a land transaction return is required).
SDLTM23500–23520 (explanation of this relief).

64 Demutualisation of building society

A land transaction effected by section 97(6) or (7) of the Building Societies Act 1986 (c 53) (transfer of building society's business to a commercial company) is exempt from charge.

HMRC Manuals—Stamp Duty Land Tax Manual, SDLTM00700 (claims for relief – cases where a land transaction return is required).
SDLTM24000 (explanation of this relief).

64A Initial transfer of assets to trustees of unit trust scheme

...[1]

Amendments—[1] Section 64A repealed by FA 2006 s 166(2), s 178, Sch 26 Pt 7(3) with effect in relation to any land transaction of which the effective date is, or is after, 22 March 2006, subject to FA 2006 s 166(5), (6).

65 Incorporation of limited liability partnership

(1) A transaction by which a chargeable interest is transferred by a person ("the transferor") to a limited liability partnership in connection with its incorporation is exempt from charge if the following three conditions are met.

(2) The first condition is that the effective date of the transaction is not more than one year after the date of incorporation of the limited liability partnership.

(3) The second condition is that at the relevant time the transferor—

(*a*) is a partner in a partnership comprised of all the persons who are or are to be members of the limited liability partnership (and no-one else), or

(*b*) holds the interest transferred as nominee or bare trustee for one or more of the partners in such a partnership.

(4) The third condition is that—

(*a*) the proportions of the interest transferred to which the persons mentioned in subsection (3)(*a*) are entitled immediately after the transfer are the same as those to which they were entitled at the relevant time, or (*b*) none of the differences in those proportions has arisen as part of a scheme or arrangement of which the main purpose, or one of the main purposes, is avoidance of liability to any duty or tax.

(5) In this section "the relevant time" means—

(*a*) where the transferor acquired the interest after the incorporation of the limited liability partnership, immediately after he acquired it, and

(*b*) in any other case, immediately before its incorporation.

(6) In this section "limited liability partnership" means a limited liability partnership formed under the Limited Liability Partnerships Act 2000 (c 12) or the Limited Liability Partnerships Act (Northern Ireland) 2002 (c 12 (NI)).

HMRC Manuals—Stamp Duty Land Tax Manual, SDLTM00700 (claims for relief – cases where a land transaction return is required).
SDLTM24500 (explanation of this relief).

66 Transfers involving public bodies

(1) A land transaction entered into on, or in consequence of, or in connection with, a reorganisation effected by or under a statutory provision is exempt from charge if the purchaser and vendor are both public bodies.

(2) The Treasury may by order provide that a land transaction that is not entered into as mentioned in subsection (1) is exempt from charge if—

(*a*) the transaction is effected by or under a prescribed statutory provision, and

(*b*) either the purchaser or the vendor is a public body.

In this subsection "prescribed" means prescribed in an order made under this subsection.

(3) A "reorganisation" means changes involving—

(*a*) the establishment, reform or abolition of one or more public bodies,

(*b*) the creation, alteration or abolition of functions to be discharged or discharged by one or more public bodies, or

(*c*) the transfer of functions from one public body to another.

(4) The following are public bodies for the purposes of this section—

Government, Parliament etc

A Minister of the Crown
The Scottish Ministers
A Northern Ireland department
[The Welsh Ministers, the First Minister for Wales and the Counsel General to the Welsh Assembly Government][2]
The Corporate Officer of the House of Lords
The Corporate Officer of the House of Commons
The Scottish Parliamentary Corporate Body
The Northern Ireland Assembly Commission
[The National Assembly for Wales Commission][2]

Local government: England

A county or district council constituted under section 2 of the Local Government Act 1972 (c 70)
The council of a London borough
The Greater London Authority
The Common Council of the City of London
The Council of the Isles of Scilly

Local government: Wales

A county or county borough council constituted under section 21 of the Local Government Act 1972

Local government: Scotland

A council constituted under section 2 of the Local Government etc (Scotland) Act 1994 (c 39)

Local government: Northern Ireland

A district council within the meaning of the Local Government Act (Northern Ireland) 1972 (c 9 (NI))

Health: England and Wales

A Strategic Health Authority [established under section 13 of the National Health Service Act 2006][3]
A Special Health Authority established under [section 28 of that Act or section 22 of the National Health Service (Wales) Act 2006][3]
A Primary Care Trust established under [section 18 of the National Health Service Act 2006][3]
A Local Health Board established under [section 11 of the National Health Service (Wales) Act 2006][3]

A National Health Service Trust established under [section 25 of the National Health Service Act 2006 or section 18 of the National Health Service (Wales) Act 2006][3]

Health: Scotland

The Common Services Agency established under section 10(1) of the National Health Service (Scotland) Act 1978 (c 29)

A Health Board established under section 2(1)(*a*) of that Act

A National Health Service Trust established under section 12A(1) of that Act

A Special Health Board established under section 2(1)(*b*) of that Act

Health: Northern Ireland

A Health and Social Services Board established under Article 16 of the Health and Personal Social Services (Northern Ireland) Order 1972 (SI 1972/1265 (NI 14))

A Health and Social Services Trust established under Article 10 of the Health and Personal Social Services (Northern Ireland) Order 1991 (SI 1991/194 (NI 1))

Other planning authorities

Any other authority that—

(*a*) is a local planning authority within the meaning of the Town and Country Planning Act 1990 (c 8), or

(*b*) is the planning authority for any of the purposes of the planning Acts within the meaning of the Town and Country Planning (Scotland) Act 1997 (c 8)

Statutory bodies

A body (other than a company) that is established by or under a statutory provision for the purpose of carrying out functions conferred on it by or under a statutory provision

Prescribed persons

A person prescribed for the purposes of this section by Treasury order

(5) In this section references to a public body include—

(*a*) a company in which all the shares are owned by such a body, and

(*b*) a wholly-owned subsidiary of such a company.

[(6) In this section "company" means a company as defined by section [1][4] of the Companies Act [2006][4].][1]

HMRC Manuals—Stamp Duty Land Tax Manual, SDLTM00700 (claims for relief – cases where a land transaction return is required).

SDLTM25000–25030 (explanation of this relief).

Orders—Finance Act 2003, Section 66 (Prescribed Persons) Order, SI 2005/83; Finance Act 2003, Section 66 (Prescribed Transactions) Order, SI 2005/645; Finance Act 2003, Section 66 (Prescribed Statutory Provisions) Order 2007, SI 2007/1385.

Amendments—[1] Sub-s (6) inserted by F(No 2)A 2005 s 49, Sch 10 paras 17, 18 with effect in relation to any transaction of which the effective date is on or after 20 July 2005: F(No 2)A 2005 Sch 10 para 22(1).

[2] In sub-s (4), entry beginning "The Welsh Ministers," substituted, and entry "The National Assembly for Wales Commission" inserted, by the Government of Wales Act 2006 s 160(1), Sch 10 paras 62, 64 with effect from 25 May 2007 being the date on which the initial period ended (following the appointment of the First Minister) (Government of Wales Act 2006 ss 46, 161(4), (5)).

[3] In sub-s (4), in entries beginning "A Strategic Health Authority", "A Special Health Authority", "A Primary Care Trust", "A Local Health Board" and "A National Health Service Trust", words substituted by the National Health Service (Consequential Provisions) Act 2006 s 2, Sch 1, paras 232, 234 with effect from 1 March 2007.

[4] In sub-s (6), word substituted for words "735(1)" and "1985", and words "or Article 3(1) of the Companies (Northern Ireland) Order 1986" repealed, by the Companies Act 2006 (Consequential Amendments) (Taxes and National Insurance) Order, SI 2009/1890 art 3(5)(*a*) with effect from 1 October 2009.

67 Transfer in consequence of reorganisation of parliamentary constituencies

(1) Where—

(*a*) an Order in Council is made under the Parliamentary Constituencies Act 1986 (c 56) (orders specifying new parliamentary constituencies), and

(*b*) an existing local constituency association transfers a chargeable interest to—

(i) a new association that is a successor to the existing association, or

(ii) a related body that as soon as practicable transfers the interest or right to a new association that is a successor to the existing association,

the transfer, or where paragraph (*b*)(ii) applies each of the transfers, is exempt from charge.

(2) In relation to any such order as is mentioned in subsection (1)(*a*)—

(*a*) "the date of the change" means the date on which the order comes into operation;

(*b*) "former parliamentary constituency" means an area that, for the purposes of parliamentary elections, was a constituency immediately before that date but is no longer such a constituency after that date;

(*c*) "new parliamentary constituency" means an area that, for the purposes of parliamentary elections, is such a constituency after that date but was not such a constituency immediately before that date.

(3) In relation to the date of the change—

(*a*) "existing local constituency association" means a local constituency association whose area was the same, or substantially the same, as the area of a former parliamentary constituency or two or more such constituencies, and (*b*) "new association" means a local constituency association whose area is the same, or substantially the same, as that of a new parliamentary constituency or two or more such constituencies.

(4) In this section—

(*a*) "local constituency association" means an unincorporated association (whether described as an association, a branch or otherwise) whose primary purpose is to further the aims of a political party in an area that at any time is or was the same or substantially the same as the area of a parliamentary constituency or two or more parliamentary constituencies, and

(*b*) "related body", in relation to such an association, means a body (whether corporate or unincorporated) that is an organ of the political party concerned.

(5) For the purposes of this section a new association is a successor to an existing association if any part of the existing association's area is comprised in the new association's area.

HMRC Manuals—Stamp Duty Land Tax Manual, SDLTM00700 (claims for relief – cases where a land transaction return is required).
SDLTM25500–25510 (explanation of this relief).

68 Charities relief

(1) Schedule 8 provides for relief from stamp duty land tax for acquisitions by charities.

(2) Any relief under that Schedule must be claimed in a land transaction return or an amendment of such a return.

HMRC Manuals—Stamp Duty Land Tax Manual, SDLTM00700 (claims for relief – cases where a land transaction return is required).
SDLTM26000–26020 (explanation of this relief).

69 Acquisition by bodies established for national purposes

A land transaction is exempt from charge if the purchaser is any of the following—

(*a*) the Historic Buildings and Monuments Commission for England;
(*b*) the National Endowment for Science, Technology and the Arts;
(*c*) the Trustees of the British Museum;
(*d*) the Trustees of the National Heritage Memorial Fund;
(*e*) the Trustees of the Natural History Museum.

HMRC Manuals—Stamp Duty Land Tax Manual, SDLTM00700 (claims for relief – cases where a land transaction return is required).
SDLTM26500 (explanation of this relief).

70 Right to buy transactions, shared ownership leases etc

Schedule 9 makes provision for relief in the case of right to buy transactions, shared ownership leases and certain related transactions.

HMRC Manuals—Stamp Duty Land Tax Manual, SDLTM00700 (claims for relief – cases where a land transaction return is required).
SDLTM27000–27070 (explanation of this relief).

71 Certain acquisitions by registered social landlord

[(A1) A land transaction under which the purchaser is a profit-making registered provider of social housing is exempt from charge if the transaction is funded with the assistance of a public subsidy.][3]

(1) A land transaction under which the purchaser is a registered social landlord is exempt from charge if—

(*a*) the registered social landlord is controlled by its tenants,
(*b*) the vendor is a qualifying body, or
(*c*) the transaction is funded with the assistance of a public subsidy.

(2) The reference in subsection (1)(*a*) to a registered social landlord "controlled by its tenants" is to a registered social landlord the majority of whose board members are tenants occupying properties owned or managed by it.

"Board member", in relation to a registered social landlord, means—

(*a*) if it is a company, a director of the company,
(*b*) if it is a body corporate whose affairs are managed by its members, a member,
(*c*) if it is body of trustees, a trustee,
(*d*) if it is not within paragraphs (*a*) to (*c*), a member of the committee of management or other body to which is entrusted the direction of the affairs of the registered social landlord.

(3) In subsection (1)(*b*) "qualifying body" means—

(*a*) a registered social landlord,
(*b*) a housing action trust established under Part 3 of the Housing Act 1988 (c 50),
(*c*) a principal council within the meaning of the Local Government Act 1972 (c 70),
(*d*) the Common Council of the City of London,
(*e*) the Scottish Ministers,

(*f*) a council constituted under section 2 of the Local Government etc (Scotland) Act 1994 (c 39),
(*g*) Scottish Homes,
(*h*) the Department for Social Development in Northern Ireland, or
(*i*) the Northern Ireland Housing Executive.

(4) In [this section][3] "public subsidy" means any grant or other financial assistance—

(*a*) made or given by way of a distribution pursuant to section 25 of the National Lottery etc Act 1993 (c 39) (application of money by distributing bodies),
(*b*) under section 18 of the Housing Act 1996 (c 52) (social housing grants),
(*c*) under section 126 of the Housing Grants, Construction and Regeneration Act 1996 (c 53) (financial assistance for regeneration and development),
[(*ca*) under section 19 of the Housing and Regeneration Act 2008 (financial assistance by the Homes and Communities Agency),][2]
(*d*) under section 2 of the Housing (Scotland) Act 1988 (c 43) (general functions of the Scottish Ministers), or
(*e*) under Article 33 [or 33A][1] of the Housing (Northern Ireland) Order 1992 (SI 1992/1725 (NI 15)).

HMRC Manuals—Stamp Duty Land Tax Manual, SDLTM00700 (claims for relief – cases where a land transaction return is required).
SDLTM27500 (explanation of this relief).

Amendments—[1] Words in sub-s (4)(*e*) inserted by the Housing (Amendment) (Northern Ireland) Order, SI 2006/3337 art 3, Schedule para 8 with effect from 1 April 2007 (by virtue of SR 2007/37 art 2).
[2] Sub-s (4)(*ca*) inserted by the Housing and Regeneration Act 2008 s 56, Sch 8 para 79 with effect from 1 December 2008 (by virtue of SI 2008/3068, arts 1(2), 2(1)(*w*), (3)).
[3] Sub-s (A1) inserted and in sub-s (4) words substituted for words "subsection (1)(*c*)" by FA 2009 s 81(1)–(4) with effect in relation to transactions with an effective date on or after 21 July 2009.

[71A Alternative property finance: land sold to financial institution and leased to [person][2]

(1) This section applies where arrangements are entered into between [a person][2] and a financial institution under which—

(*a*) the institution purchases a major interest in land or an undivided share of a major interest in land ("the first transaction"),
(*b*) where the interest purchased is an undivided share, the major interest is held on trust for the institution and the [person][2] as beneficial tenants in common,
(*c*) the institution (or the person holding the land on trust as mentioned in paragraph (b)) grants to the [person][2] out of the major interest a lease (if the major interest is freehold) or a sub-lease (if the major interest is leasehold) ("the second transaction"), and
(*d*) the institution and the [person][2] enter into an agreement under which the [person][2] has a right to require the institution or its successor in title to transfer to the [person][2] (in one transaction or a series of transactions) the whole interest purchased by the institution under the first transaction.

(2) The first transaction is exempt from charge if the vendor is—

(*a*) the [person][2], or
(*b*) another financial institution by whom the interest was acquired under arrangements of the kind mentioned in subsection (1) entered into between it and the [person][2].

(3) The second transaction is exempt from charge if the provisions of this Part relating to the first transaction are complied with (including the payment of any tax chargeable).

(4) Any transfer to the [person][2] that results from the exercise of the right mentioned in subsection (1)(*d*) ("a further transaction") is exempt from charge if—

(*a*) the provisions of this Part relating to the first and second transactions are complied with, and
(*b*) at all times between the second transaction and the further transaction—

(i) the interest purchased under the first transaction is held by a financial institution so far as not transferred by a previous further transaction, and
(ii) the lease or sub-lease granted under the second transaction is held by the [person][2].

(5) The agreement mentioned in subsection (1)(*d*) is not to be treated—

(*a*) as substantially performed unless and until the whole interest purchased by the institution under the first transaction has been transferred (and accordingly section 44(5) does not apply), or
(*b*) as a distinct land transaction by virtue of section 46 (options and rights of pre-emption).

(6) …[2]

(7) A further transaction that is exempt from charge by virtue of subsection (4) is not a notifiable transaction unless the transaction involves the transfer to the [person][2] of the whole interest purchased by the institution under the first transaction, so far as not transferred by a previous further transaction.

(8) [In this section "financial institution" has the meaning given by section 46 of the Finance Act 2005 (alternative finance arrangements).][3]

(9) References in this section to [a person][2] shall be read, in relation to times after the death of the [person][2] concerned, as references to his personal representatives.

(10) This section does not apply in relation to land in Scotland.][1]

Amendments—[1] This section inserted by FA 2005 s 94, Sch 8 para 2 with effect in any case where the effective date (within the meaning of Part 4 of FA 2003) of the first transaction (within the meaning of this section) falls on or after 7 April 2005: FA 2005 Sch 8 para 7(1), (3).

[2] Word "person" substituted for word "individual" and words "a person" substituted for words "an individual" throughout the section, sub-s (6) repealed by FA 2006 s 168(1), (2), s 178, Sch 26 Pt 7(4) with effect in relation to arrangements in which the effective date (within the meaning of FA 2003 s 119(1)) of the first transaction (within the meaning of FA 2003 ss 71A–73) is on or after 19 July 2006.

[3] Sub-s (8) substituted by FA 2007 s 75(3), (4). This amendment—

(*a*) has effect in relation to anything that would, but for the exemption provided by this section, be a land transaction with an effective date on or after 22 March 2007, and

(*b*) applies, in accordance with paragraph (*a*), to interests irrespective of the date of their creation.

72 Alternative property finance [in Scotland][1]: land sold to financial institution and leased to [person][2]

(1) This section applies where arrangements are entered into between [a person][2] and a financial institution under which the institution—

(*a*) purchases a major interest in land ("the first transaction"),

(*b*) grants to the [person][2] out of that interest a lease (if the interest acquired is [the interest of the owner][1]) or a sub-lease (if the interest acquired is [the tenant's right over or interest in a property subject to a lease][1]) ("the second transaction"), and

(*c*) enters into an agreement under which the [person][2] has a right to require the institution ...[1] to transfer the major interest purchased by the institution under the first transaction.

(2) The first transaction is exempt from charge if the vendor is—

(*a*) the [person][2], or

(*b*) another financial institution by whom the interest was acquired under arrangements of the kind mentioned in subsection (1) entered into between it and the [person][2].

(3) The second transaction is exempt from charge if the provisions of this Part relating to the first transaction are complied with (including the payment of any tax chargeable).

(4) A transfer to the [person][2] that results from the exercise of the right mentioned in subsection (1)(*c*) ("the third transaction") is exempt from charge if—

(*a*) the provisions of this Part relating to the first and second transactions are complied with, and

(*b*) at all times between the second and third transactions—

(i) the interest purchased under the first transaction is held by a financial institution, and

(ii) the lease or sub-lease granted under the second transaction is held by the [person][2].

(5) The agreement mentioned in subsection (1)(*c*) is not to be treated—

(*a*) as substantially performed unless and until the third transaction is entered into (and accordingly section 44(5) does not apply), or

(*b*) as a distinct land transaction by virtue of section 46 (options and rights of pre-emption).

(6) ...[2]

(7) [In this section "financial institution" has the meaning given by section 46 of the Finance Act 2005 (alternative finance arrangements).][3]

(8) ...[1]

(9) References in this section to [a person][2] shall be read, in relation to times after the death of the [person][2] concerned, as references to his personal representatives.

[(10) This section applies only in relation to land in Scotland.][1]

HMRC Manuals—Stamp Duty Land Tax Manual, SDLTM00700 (claims for relief – cases where a land transaction return is required).

SDLTM28000–28140 (explanation of this relief).

Amendments—[1] In sub-s (1)(*b*), words substituted; in sub-s (1)(*c*) words repealed; sub-s (8) repealed; sub-s (10) inserted; and words in heading inserted by FA 2005 ss 94, 104, Sch 8 para 3 and Sch 11 Pt 3(1) with effect in any case where the effective date (within the meaning of Part 4 of FA 2003) of the first transaction (within the meaning of FA 2003 s 71A) falls on or after 7 April 2005: FA 2005 Sch 8 para 7(1), (3).

[2] Word "person" substituted for word "individual" and words "a person" substituted for words "an individual" throughout the section, sub-s (6) repealed by FA 2006 s 168(1), (2), s 178, Sch 26 Pt 7(4) with effect in relation to arrangements in which the effective date (within the meaning of FA 2003 s 119(1)) of the first transaction (within the meaning of FA 2003 ss 71A–73) is on or after 19 July 2006.

[3] Sub-s (7) substituted by FA 2007 s 75(3), (4). This amendment—

(*a*) has effect in relation to anything that would, but for the exemption provided by this section, be a land transaction with an effective date on or after 22 March 2007, and

(*b*) applies, in accordance with paragraph (*a*), to interests irrespective of the date of their creation.

[72A Alternative property finance in Scotland: land sold to financial institution and [person][2] in common

(1) This section applies where arrangements are entered into between [a person][2] and a financial institution under which—

(*a*) the institution and the [person][2] purchase a major interest in land as owners in common ("the first transaction"),

(*b*) the institution and the [person][2] enter into an agreement under which the [person][2] has a right to occupy the land exclusively ("the second transaction"), and (*c*) the institution and the [person][2] enter into an agreement under which the [person][2] has a right to require the institution to transfer to the [person][2] (in one transaction or a series of transactions) the whole interest purchased under the first transaction.

(2) The first transaction is exempt from charge if the vendor is—

(*a*) the [person][2], or

(*b*) another financial institution by whom the interest was acquired under arrangements of the kind mentioned in subsection (1) entered into between it and the [person][2].

(3) The second transaction is exempt from charge if the provisions of this Part relating to the first transaction are complied with (including the payment of any tax chargeable).

(4) Any transfer to the [person][2] that results from the exercise of the right mentioned in subsection (1)(*c*) ("a further transaction") is exempt from charge if—

(*a*) the provisions of this Part relating to the first transaction are complied with, and

(*b*) at all times between the first and the further transaction—

(i) the interest purchased under the first transaction is held by a financial institution and the [person][2] as owners in common, and

(ii) the land is occupied by the [person][2] under the agreement mentioned in subsection (1)(*b*).

(5) The agreement mentioned in subsection (1)(*c*) is not to be treated—

(*a*) as substantially performed unless and until the whole interest purchased by the institution under the first transaction has been transferred (and accordingly section 44(5) does not apply), or

(*b*) as a distinct land transaction by virtue of section 46 (options and rights of pre-emption).

(6) …[2]

(7) A further transaction that is exempt from charge by virtue of subsection (4) is not a notifiable transaction unless the transaction involves the transfer to the [person][2] of the whole interest purchased by the institution under the first transaction, so far as not transferred by a previous further transaction.

(8) [In this section "financial institution" has the meaning given by section 46 of the Finance Act 2005 (alternative finance arrangements).][3]

(9) References in this section to [a person][2] shall be read, in relation to times after the death of the [person][2] concerned, as references to his personal representatives.

(10) This section applies only in relation to land in Scotland.][1]

Amendments—[1] This section inserted by FA 2005 s 94, Sch 8 para 4 with effect in any case where the effective date (within the meaning of Part 4 of FA 2003) of the first transaction (within the meaning of this section) falls on or after 7 April 2005: FA 2005 Sch 8 para 7(2), (3).

[2] Word "person" substituted for word "individual" and words "a person" substituted for words "an individual" throughout the section, sub-s (6) repealed by FA 2006 s 168(1), (2) with effect in relation to arrangements in which the effective date (within the meaning of FA 2003 s 119(1)) of the first transaction (within the meaning of FA 2003 ss 71A–73) is on or after 19 July 2006.

[3] Sub-s (8) substituted by FA 2007 s 75(3), (4). This amendment—

(*a*) has effect in relation to anything that would, but for the exemption provided by this section, be a land transaction with an effective date on or after 22 March 2007, and

(*b*) applies, in accordance with paragraph (*a*), to interests irrespective of the date of their creation.

73 Alternative property finance: land sold to financial institution and re-sold to [person][2]

(1) This section applies where arrangements are entered into between [a person][2] and a financial institution under which—

(*a*) the institution—

(i) purchases a major interest in land ("the first transaction"), and

(ii) sells that interest to the [person][2] ("the second transaction"), and

(*b*) the [person][2] grants the institution a legal mortgage over that interest.

(2) The first transaction is exempt from charge if the vendor is—

(*a*) the [person][2] concerned, or

(*b*) another financial institution by whom the interest was acquired under other arrangements of the kind mentioned in [section 71A(1), 72(1) or 72A(1)][1] entered into between it and the [person][2].

(3) The second transaction is exempt from charge if the financial institution complies with the provisions of this Part relating to the first transaction (including the payment of any tax chargeable [on a chargeable consideration that is not less than the market value of the interest and, in the case of the grant of a lease at a rent, the rent][2]).

(4) …[2]

(5) In this section—

(*a*) [*In this section* "financial institution" has the meaning given by section 46 of the Finance Act 2005 (alternative finance arrangements).][3];

(*b*) "legal mortgage"—

(i) in relation to land in England or Wales, means a legal mortgage as defined in section 205(1)(*xvi*) of the Law of Property Act 1925 (c 20);

(ii) in relation to land in Scotland, means a standard security;

(iii) in relation to land in Northern Ireland, means a mortgage by conveyance of a legal estate or by demise or sub-demise or a charge by way of legal mortgage.

(6) References in this section to [a person][2] shall be read, in relation to times after the death of the [person][2] concerned, as references to his personal representatives.

Note—Words in italics in sub-s (5)(*a*) above represent duplicate text, due to a drafting error in FA 2007 s 75(3), which amended the sub-section.

HMRC Manuals—Stamp Duty Land Tax Manual, SDLTM00700 (claims for relief – cases where a land transaction return is required).

SDLTM28200–28230 (explanation of this relief).

Amendments—[1] Words substituted by FA 2005 s 94, Sch 8 para 5 with effect in any case where the effective date (within the meaning of Part 4 of FA 2003) of the first transaction (within the meaning of FA 2003 s 71A (so far as relating to that section) or s 72A (so far as relating to that section)) falls on or after 7 April 2005: FA 2005 Sch 8 para 7.

[2] Word "person" substituted for word "individual" and words "a person" substituted for words "an individual" throughout the section, words in sub-s (3) inserted, sub-s (4) repealed by FA 2006 s 168(1)–(3) with effect in relation to arrangements in which the effective date (within the meaning of FA 2003 s 119(1)) of the first transaction (within the meaning of FA 2003 ss 71A–73) is on or after 19 July 2006.

[3] Sub-s (5)(*a*) substituted by FA 2007 s 75(3), (4). This amendment—

(*a*) has effect in relation to anything that would, but for the exemption provided by this section, be a land transaction with an effective date on or after 22 March 2007, and

(*b*) applies, in accordance with paragraph (*a*), to interests irrespective of the date of their creation.

Stamp Taxes

[73A [Sections 71A to 73: relationship with Schedule 7][2]

Sections 71A to 73 do not apply to arrangements in which the first transaction is exempt from charge by virtue of Schedule 7.][1]

Amendments—[1] This section inserted by FA 2006 s 168(4) with effect in relation to arrangements in which the effective date (within the meaning of FA 2003 s 119(1)) of the first transaction (within the meaning of FA 2003 ss 71A–73) is on or after 19 July 2006.

[2] Section heading substituted by FA 2008 s 155(1), (2) with effect in relation to alternative finance arrangements entered into on or after 12 March 2008.

[73AB Sections 71A to 72A: arrangements to transfer control of financial institution

(1) Section 71A, 72 or 72A does not apply to alternative finance arrangements if those arrangements, or any connected arrangements, include arrangements for a person to acquire control of the relevant financial institution.

(2) That includes arrangements for a person to acquire control of the relevant financial institution only if one or more conditions are met (such as the happening of an event or doing of an act).

(3) In this section—

"alternative finance arrangements" means the arrangements referred to in section 71A(1), 72(1) or 72A(1);

"arrangements" includes any agreement, understanding, scheme, transaction or series of transactions (whether or not legally enforceable);

"connected arrangements" means any arrangements entered into in connection with the making of the alternative finance arrangements (including arrangements involving one or more persons who are not parties to the alternative finance arrangements);

"relevant financial institution" means the financial institution which enters into the alternative finance arrangements.

(4) Section 840 of the Taxes Act 1988 applies for the purposes of determining who has control of the relevant financial institution.][1]

Amendments—[1] Section 73AB inserted by FA 2008 s 155(1), (3) with effect in relation to alternative finance arrangements entered into on or after 12 March 2008.

[73B Exempt interests

(1) An interest held by a financial institution as a result of the first transaction within the meaning of section 71A(1)(*a*), 72(1)(*a*) or 72A(1)(*a*) is an exempt interest for the purposes of stamp duty land tax.

(2) That interest ceases to be an exempt interest if—

(*a*) the lease or agreement mentioned in section 71A(1)(*c*), 72(1)(*b*) or 72A(1)(*b*) ceases to have effect, or

(*b*) the right under section 71A(1)(*d*), 72(1)(*c*) or 72A(1)(*c*) ceases to have effect or becomes subject to a restriction.

(3) Subsection (1) does not apply if the first transaction is exempt from charge by virtue of Schedule 7.

(4) Subsection (1) does not make an interest exempt in respect of—

(*a*) the first transaction itself, or

(*b*) a further transaction or third transaction within the meaning of section 71A(4), 72(4) or 72A(4).][1]

Amendments—[1] This section inserted by FA 2007 s 75(1), (4). This amendment—

(*a*) has effect in relation to anything that would, but for the exemption provided by this section, be a land transaction with an effective date on or after 22 March 2007, and

(*b*) applies, in accordance with paragraph (*a*), to interests irrespective of the date of their creation.

[73C Alternative finance investment bonds

Schedule 61 to the Finance Act 2009 makes provision for relief from charge in the case of arrangements falling within section 48A of the Finance Act 2005 (alternative finance investment bonds).][1]

Amendments—[1] This section inserted by FA 2009 s 123, Sch 61 paras 24, 25 with effect from 21 July 2009.

74 [Exercise of collective rights by tenants of flats][1]

[(1) This section applies where a chargeable transaction is entered into by a person or persons nominated or appointed by qualifying tenants of flats contained in premises in exercise of—

(*a*) a right under Part 1 of the Landlord and Tenant Act 1987 (right of first refusal), or

(*b*) a right under Chapter 1 of Part 1 of the Leasehold Reform, Housing and Urban Development Act 1993 (right to collective enfranchisement).][1]

(2) …[1] the rate of tax is determined by reference to the fraction of the relevant consideration produced by dividing the total amount of that consideration by the number of [qualifying flats contained in the premises][1].

(3) The tax chargeable is then determined by applying that rate to the chargeable consideration for the transaction.

[(4) In this section—

"flat" and "qualifying tenant" have the same meaning as in the Chapter or Part of the Act conferring the right being exercised;

"qualifying flat" means a flat that is held by a qualifying tenant who is participating in the exercise of the right.][1]

(5) References in this section to the relevant consideration have the same meaning as in section 55.

HMRC Manuals—Stamp Duty Land Tax Manual, SDLTM00700 (claims for relief – cases where a land transaction return is required).

SDLTM28500–28510 (explanation of this relief).

Simon's Tax Cases—*Elizabeth Court (Bournemouth) Ltd v R&C Comrs* [2009] STC 682.

Amendments—[1] Sub-s (1) substituted, in sub-s (2) words "In that case," repealed and words "flats in respect of which the right of collective enfranchisement is being exercised" substituted, sub-s (4) substituted and the heading substituted by FA 2009 s 80 with effect in relation to transactions with an effective date on or after 22 April 2009. Sub-s (1) previously read as follows—

"(1) This section applies where a chargeable transaction is entered into by an RTE company in pursuance of a right of collective enfranchisement."

Sub-s (4) previously read as follows—

"(4) In this section—

(*a*) "RTE company" has the meaning given by section 4A of the Leasehold Reform, Housing and Urban Development Act 1993 (c 28);

(*b*) "right of collective enfranchisement" means the right exercisable by an RTE company under—

(i) Part 1 of the Landlord and Tenant Act 1987 (c 31), or

(ii) Chapter 1 of Part 1 of the Leasehold Reform, Housing and Urban Development Act 1993 (c 28); and

(*c*) "flat" has the same meaning as in the Act conferring the right of collective enfranchisement."

75 Crofting community right to buy

(1) This section applies where—

(*a*) a chargeable transaction is entered into in pursuance of the crofting community right to buy, and

(*b*) under that transaction two or more crofts are being bought.

(2) In that case, the rate of tax is determined by reference to the fraction of the relevant consideration produced by dividing the total amount of that consideration by the number of crofts being bought.

(3) The tax chargeable is then determined by applying that rate to the amount of the chargeable consideration for the transaction in question.

(4) In this section "crofting community right to buy" means the right exercisable by a crofting community body under Part 3 of the Land Reform (Scotland) Act 2003 (asp 2).

(5) References in this section to the relevant consideration have the same meaning as in section 55.

HMRC Manuals—Stamp Duty Land Tax Manual, SDLTM00700 (claims for relief – cases where a land transaction return is required).

SDLTM29000–29010 (explanation of this relief).

[75A Anti-avoidance

(1) This section applies where—

(*a*) one person (V) disposes of a chargeable interest and another person (P) acquires either it or a chargeable interest deriving from it,

(*b*) a number of transactions (including the disposal and acquisition) are involved in connection with the disposal and acquisition ("the scheme transactions"), and (*c*) the sum of the amounts of stamp duty land tax payable in respect of the scheme transactions is less than the amount that would be payable on a notional land transaction effecting the acquisition of V's chargeable interest by P on its disposal by V.

(2) In subsection (1) "transaction" includes, in particular—

(*a*) a non-land transaction,

(*b*) an agreement, offer or undertaking not to take specified action,

(*c*) any kind of arrangement whether or not it could otherwise be described as a transaction, and

(*d*) a transaction which takes place after the acquisition by P of the chargeable interest.

(3) The scheme transactions may include, for example—

(*a*) the acquisition by P of a lease deriving from a freehold owned or formerly owned by V;

(*b*) a sub-sale to a third person;

(*c*) the grant of a lease to a third person subject to a right to terminate;

(*d*) the exercise of a right to terminate a lease or to take some other action;

(*e*) an agreement not to exercise a right to terminate a lease or to take some other action;

(*f*) the variation of a right to terminate a lease or to take some other action.

(4) Where this section applies—

(*a*) any of the scheme transactions which is a land transaction shall be disregarded for the purposes of this Part, but

(*b*) there shall be a notional land transaction for the purposes of this Part effecting the acquisition of V's chargeable interest by P on its disposal by V.

(5) The chargeable consideration on the notional transaction mentioned in subsections (1)(*c*) and (4)(*b*) is the largest amount (or aggregate amount)—

(*a*) given by or on behalf of any one person by way of consideration for the scheme transactions, or

(*b*) received by or on behalf of V (or a person connected with V within the meaning of section 839 of the Taxes Act 1988) by way of consideration for the scheme transactions.

(6) The effective date of the notional transaction is—

(*a*) the last date of completion for the scheme transactions, or

(*b*) if earlier, the last date on which a contract in respect of the scheme transactions is substantially performed.

(7) This section does not apply where subsection (1)(*c*) is satisfied only by reason of—

(*a*) sections 71A to 73, or

(*b*) a provision of Schedule 9.][1]

Amendments—[1] Sections 75A–75C substituted for section 75A by FA 2007 s 71 with effect in respect of disposals and acquisitions if the disposal mentioned in sub-s (1)(*a*) above takes place on or after 6 December 2006.
However—

(*a*) the transitional provisions of the Stamp Duty Land Tax (Variation of the Finance Act 2003) Regulations, SI 2006/3237 Schedule para 1(2)–(5) continue to have effect in relation to FA 2007 s 71 as in relation to that paragraph, and

(*b*) a provision of FA 2003 s 75C (as inserted by FA 2007 s 71) shall not have effect where the disposal mentioned in sub-s (1)(*a*) above took place before 19 July 2007, if or in so far as the provision would make a person liable for a higher amount of tax than would have been charged in accordance with those regulations.

[75B Anti-avoidance: incidental transactions

(1) In calculating the chargeable consideration on the notional transaction for the purposes of section 75A(5), consideration for a transaction shall be ignored if or in so far as the transaction is merely incidental to the transfer of the chargeable interest from V to P.

(2) A transaction is not incidental to the transfer of the chargeable interest from V to P—

(*a*) if or in so far as it forms part of a process, or series of transactions, by which the transfer is effected,

(*b*) if the transfer of the chargeable interest is conditional on the completion of the transaction, or

(*c*) if it is of a kind specified in section 75A(3).

(3) A transaction may, in particular, be incidental if or in so far as it is undertaken only for a purpose relating to—

(*a*) the construction of a building on property to which the chargeable interest relates,

(*b*) the sale or supply of anything other than land, or

(*c*) a loan to P secured by a mortgage, or any other provision of finance to enable P, or another person, to pay for part of a process, or series of transactions, by which the chargeable interest transfers from V to P.

(4) In subsection (3)—

(*a*) paragraph (*a*) is subject to subsection (2)(*a*) to (*c*),

(*b*) paragraph (*b*) is subject to subsection (2)(*a*) and (*c*), and

(*c*) paragraph (*c*) is subject to subsection (2)(*a*) to (*c*).

(5) The exclusion required by subsection (1) shall be effected by way of just and reasonable apportionment if necessary.

Stamp Taxes

(6) In this section a reference to the transfer of a chargeable interest from V to P includes a reference to a disposal by V of an interest acquired by P.][1]

Amendments—[1] Sections 75A–75C substituted for section 75A by FA 2007 s 71 with effect in respect of disposals and acquisitions if the disposal mentioned in FA 2003 s 75A(1)(*a*) takes place on or after 6 December 2006.
However—
(*a*) the transitional provisions of the Stamp Duty Land Tax (Variation of the Finance Act 2003) Regulations, SI 2006/3237 Schedule para 1(2)–(5) continue to have effect in relation to FA 2007 s 71 as in relation to that paragraph, and
(*b*) a provision of FA 2003 s 75C (as inserted by FA 2007 s 71) shall not have effect where the disposal mentioned in FA 2003 s 75A(1)(*a*) took place before 19 July 2007, if or in so far as the provision would make a person liable for a higher amount of tax than would have been charged in accordance with those regulations.

[75C Anti-avoidance: supplemental

(1) A transfer of shares or securities shall be ignored for the purposes of section 75A if but for this subsection it would be the first of a series of scheme transactions.

(2) The notional transaction under section 75A attracts any relief under this Part which it would attract if it were an actual transaction (subject to the terms and restrictions of the relief).

(3) The notional transaction under section 75A is a land transaction entered into for the purposes of or in connection with the transfer of an undertaking or part for the purposes of paragraphs 7 and 8 of Schedule 7, if any of the scheme transactions is entered into for the purposes of or in connection with the transfer of the undertaking or part.

(4) In the application of section 75A(5) no account shall be taken of any amount paid by way of consideration in respect of a transaction to which any of sections 60, 61, 63, 64, 65, 66, 67, 69, 71, 74 and 75, or a provision of Schedule 6A or 8, applies.

(5) In the application of section 75A(5) an amount given or received partly in respect of the chargeable interest acquired by P and partly in respect of another chargeable interest shall be subjected to just and reasonable apportionment.

(6) Section 53 applies to the notional transaction under section 75A.

(7) Paragraph 5 of Schedule 4 applies to the notional transaction under section 75A.

(8) For the purposes of section 75A—

(*a*) an interest in a property-investment partnership (within the meaning of paragraph 14 of Schedule 15) is a chargeable interest in so far as it concerns land owned by the partnership, and

(*b*) where V or P is a partnership, Part 3 of Schedule 15 applies to the notional transaction as to the transfer of a chargeable interest from or to a partnership.

(9) For the purposes of section 75A a reference to an amount of consideration includes a reference to the value of consideration given as money's worth.

(10) Stamp duty land tax paid in respect of a land transaction which is to be disregarded by virtue of section 75A(4)(*a*) is taken to have been paid in respect of the notional transaction by virtue of section 75A(4)(*b*).

(11) The Treasury may by order provide for section 75A not to apply in specified circumstances.

(12) An order under subsection (11) may include incidental, consequential or transitional provision and may make provision with retrospective effect.][1]

Amendments—[1] Sections 75A–75C substituted for section 75A by FA 2007 s 71 with effect in respect of disposals and acquisitions if the disposal mentioned in FA 2003 s 75A(1)(*a*) takes place on or after 6 December 2006.
However—
(*a*) the transitional provisions of the Stamp Duty Land Tax (Variation of the Finance Act 2003) Regulations, SI 2006/3237 Schedule para 1(2)–(5) continue to have effect in relation to FA 2007 s 71 as in relation to that paragraph, and
(*b*) a provision of FA 2003 s 75C (as inserted by FA 2007 s 71) shall not have effect where the disposal mentioned in FA 2003 s 75A(1)(*a*) took place before 19 July 2007, if or in so far as the provision would make a person liable for a higher amount of tax than would have been charged in accordance with those regulations.

Returns and other administrative matters

76 Duty to deliver land transaction return

(1) In the case of every notifiable transaction the purchaser must deliver a return (a "land transaction return") to the Inland Revenue before the end of the period of 30 days after the effective date of the transaction.

(2) The Inland Revenue may by regulations amend subsection (1) so as to require a land transaction return to be delivered before the end of such shorter period after the effective date of the transaction as may be prescribed or, if the regulations so provide, on that date.

(3) A land transaction return in respect of a chargeable transaction must—

(*a*) include an assessment (a "self-assessment") of the tax that, on the basis of the information contained in the return, is chargeable in respect of the transaction, …[1]

(*b*) …[1]

HMRC Manuals—Stamp Duty Land Tax Manual SDLTM50100 (details of the required forms).
Cross references—FA 2009 Sch 55 (penalty for failure to make returns etc).
Amendments—[1] Sub-s (3)(*b*) and preceding word "and" repealed by FA 2007 ss 80(1), (2), (9)(*a*), 114, Sch 27 Pt 4(4) with effect in relation to land transactions with an effective date on or after 19 July 2007.

[77 Notifiable transactions

(1) A land transaction is notifiable if it is—

(*a*) an acquisition of a major interest in land that does not fall within one or more of the exceptions in section 77A,

(*b*) an acquisition of a chargeable interest other than a major interest in land where there is chargeable consideration in respect of which tax is chargeable at a rate of 1% or higher or would be so chargeable but for a relief,

(*c*) a land transaction that a person is treated as entering into by virtue of section 44A(3), or

(*d*) a notional land transaction under section 75A.

(2) This section has effect subject to—

(*a*) sections 71A(7) and 72A(7), and

(*b*) paragraph 30 of Schedule 15.

(3) In this section "relief" does not include an exemption from charge under Schedule 3.][1]

HMRC Manuals—Stamp Duty Land Tax Manual, SDLTM00310, 00310a (notifiable transaction – with examples) SDLTM00330, 00330a (whether notification is required – with examples)

Amendments—[1] Sections 77, 77A substituted for s 77 by FA 2008 s 94(1), (2) with effect in relation to transactions with an effective date on or after 12 March 2008.

[77A Exceptions for certain acquisitions of major interests in land

(1) The exceptions referred to in section 77(1)(*a*) are as follows.

1. An acquisition which is exempt from charge under Schedule 3 [other than an acquisition which is exempt by virtue of any regulations made under paragraph 5 of that Schedule][2].

2. An acquisition (other than the grant, assignment or surrender of a lease) where the chargeable consideration for that acquisition, together with the chargeable consideration for any linked transactions, is less than £40,000.

3. The grant of a lease for a term of 7 years or more where—

(*a*) any chargeable consideration other than rent is less than £40,000, and

(*b*) the relevant rent is less than £1,000.

4. The assignment or surrender of a lease where—

(*a*) the lease was originally granted for a term of 7 years or more, and

(*b*) the chargeable consideration for the assignment or surrender is less than £40,000.

5. The grant of a lease for a term of less than 7 years where the chargeable consideration does not exceed the zero rate threshold.

6. The assignment or surrender of a lease where—

(*a*) the lease was originally granted for a term of less than 7 years, and

(*b*) the chargeable consideration for the assignment or surrender does not exceed the zero rate threshold.

(2) Chargeable consideration for an acquisition does not exceed the zero rate threshold if it does not consist of or include—

(*a*) any amount in respect of which tax is chargeable at a rate of 1% or higher, or

(*b*) any amount in respect of which tax would be so chargeable but for a relief.

(3) In this section—

"annual rent" has the meaning given in paragraph 9A of Schedule 5,

"relevant rent" means—

(*a*) the annual rent, or

(*b*) in the case of the grant of a lease to which paragraph 11 or 19 of Schedule 15 applies, the relevant chargeable proportion of the annual rent (as calculated in accordance with that paragraph), and

"relief" does not include an exemption from charge under Schedule 3.][1]

Amendments—[1] Sections 77, 77A substituted for s 77 by FA 2008 s 94(1), (2) with effect in relation to transactions with an effective date on or after 12 March 2008.

[2] Words in sub-s (1), item 1, inserted by the Stamp Duty Land Tax (Variation of Part 4 of the Finance Act 2003) Regulations, SI 2008/2338 reg 2 with effect in relation to transactions with an effective date on or after 3 September 2008, and before 3 September 2009.

78 Returns, enquiries, assessments and related matters

(1) Schedule 10 has effect with respect to land transaction returns, assessments and related matters.

(2) In that Schedule—

Part 1 contains general provisions about returns;
Part 2 imposes a duty to keep and preserve records;
Part 3 makes provision for enquiries into returns;
Part 4 provides for a Revenue determination if no return is delivered;
Part 5 provides for Revenue assessments;
Part 6 provides for relief in case of excessive assessment; and
Part 7 provides for appeals against Revenue decisions on tax.

(3) The Treasury may by regulations make such amendments of that Schedule, and such consequential amendments of any other provisions of this Part, as appear to them to be necessary or expedient from time to time.

[78A Disclosure of information contained in land transaction returns

(1) Relevant information contained in land transaction returns delivered under section 76 (whether before or after the commencement of this section) is to be available for use—

(*a*) by listing officers appointed under section 20 of the Local Government Finance Act 1992, for the purpose of facilitating the compilation and maintenance by them of valuation lists in accordance with Chapter 2 of Part 1 of that Act,

(*b*) as evidence in an appeal by virtue of section 24(6) of that Act to a valuation tribunal established under Schedule 11 to the Local Government Finance Act 1988,

(*c*) by the Commissioner of Valuation for Northern Ireland, for the purpose of maintaining a valuation list prepared, and from time to time altered, by him in accordance with Part 3 of the Rates (Northern Ireland) Order 1977, and

(*d*) by such other persons or for such other purposes as the Treasury may by regulations prescribe.

(2) In this section, "relevant information" means any information of the kind mentioned in paragraph 1(4) of Schedule 10 (information corresponding to particulars required under previous legislation).

(3) The Treasury may by regulations amend the definition of relevant information in subsection (2).][1]

Amendments—[1] This section inserted by F(No 2)A 2005 s 48(1), (5) with effect on such day as the Treasury may by order appoint.

Prospective amendments—In sub-s (1)(*b*), words "established under Schedule 11 to the Local Government Finance Act 1988" to be repealed, and sub-s (4) to be inserted, by the Local Government and Public Involvement in Health Act 2007 ss 220, 241, Sch 16 para 9, Sch 18 Pt 17 with effect from a date to be appointed. Sub-s (4) to read as follows—

"(4) In this section "valuation tribunal" means—

(*a*) in relation to England: the Valuation Tribunal for England;

(*b*) in relation to Wales: a valuation tribunal established under paragraph 1 of Schedule 11 to the Local Government Finance Act 1988.".

79 Registration of land transactions etc

(1) A land transaction to which this section applies, or (as the case may be) a document effecting or evidencing a land transaction to which this section applies, shall not be registered, recorded or otherwise reflected in an entry made—

(*a*) in England and Wales, in the register of title maintained by the Chief Land Registrar,

(*b*) in Scotland, in any register maintained by the Keeper of the Registers of Scotland [(other than the Register of Community Interests in Land)][2], or

(*c*) in Northern Ireland, in any register maintained by the Land Registry of Northern Ireland or in the Registry of Deeds for Northern Ireland,

unless there is produced, together with the relevant application, a certificate as to compliance with the requirements of this Part in relation to the transaction [or such information about compliance as the Commissioners for Her Majesty's Revenue and Customs may specify in regulations.][4].

This does not apply where the entry is required to be made without any application or so far as the entry relates to an interest or right other than the chargeable interest acquired by the purchaser under the land transaction that gives rise to the application.

(2) This section applies to every [notifiable][5] land transaction [other than a transaction treated as taking place—

(*a*) under subsection (4) of section 44 (contract and conveyance) or under that section as it applies [by virtue of—

(i) section 45 (contract and conveyance: effect of transfer of rights), or

(ii) paragraph 12B of Schedule 17A (assignment of agreement for lease),][3] or

(*b*) under subsection (3) of section 44A (contract providing for conveyance to third party) or under that section as it applies by virtue of section 45A (contract providing for conveyance to third party: effect of transfer of rights).][1]

[(*c*) under paragraph 12A(2) or 19(3) of Schedule 17A (agreement for lease), or][3]

[(*d*) under paragraph 13 (increase of rent) or 15A (reduction of rent or term) of that Schedule.][3]

In this subsection "contract" includes any agreement and "conveyance" includes any instrument.

[(2A) Subsection (1), so far as relating to the entry of a notice under section 34 of the Land Registration Act 2002 or section 38 of the Land Registration Act (Northern Ireland) 1970 (notice in respect of interest affecting registered land), does not apply where the land transaction in question is the variation of a lease.][3]

(3) The certificate [referred to in subsection (1)][3] must be …[5]—

(*a*) a certificate by the Inland Revenue (a "Revenue certificate") that a land transaction return has been delivered in respect of the transaction, …[5]

(*b*) …[5]

(4) The Inland Revenue may make provision by regulations about Revenue certificates.

The regulations may, in particular—

(*a*) make provision as to the conditions to be met before a certificate is issued;
(*b*) prescribe the form and content of the certificate;
(*c*) make provision about the issue of duplicate certificates if the original is lost or destroyed;
(*d*) provide for the issue of multiple certificates where a return is made relating to more than one transaction.

[(5) Part 2 of Schedule 11 imposes a duty to keep and preserve records in respect of transactions that are not notifiable.][5]

(6) The registrar (in Scotland, the Keeper of the Registers of Scotland)—

(*a*) shall allow the Inland Revenue to inspect any certificates …[5] produced to him under this section and in his possession, and
(*b*) may enter into arrangements for affording the Inland Revenue other information and facilities for verifying that the requirements of this Part have been complied with.

HMRC Manuals—Stamp Duty Land Tax Manual SDLTM50200 (self-certification required for land transactions which are not notifiable transactions under FA 2003 s 77, e g freehold or leasehold transfers for no chargeable consideration; the grant of a lease for no chargeable consideration or a peppercorn rent; and certain transactions in connection with divorce and death).

Amendments—[1] Words in sub-s (2) substituted by FA 2004 s 296, Sch 39 para 7 with effect in accordance with FA 2004 Sch 39 para 13(1), (2).

[2] Words in sub-s (1)(*b*) inserted by FA 2004 s 298(1), (3) with effect from 22 July 2004.

[3] Words in sub-s (2)(*a*) substituted for the words "by virtue of section 45 (contract and conveyance: effect of transfer of rights)," sub-ss (2)(*c*), (*d*), (2A) and words in sub-s (3) inserted, by FA 2004 s 297(1), (5)–(7), (10) with effect for any transaction or deemed transaction of which the effective date is after 16 March 2004.

[4] Words in sub-s (1) inserted by F(No 2)A 2005 s 47(2) with effect from 20 July 2005.

[5] Word in sub-s (2) inserted, words in sub-ss (3), (6)(*a*), and sub-s (3)(*b*), repealed, and sub-s (5) substituted, by FA 2008 s 94(1), (4), Sch 30 paras 1, 2 with effect in relation to transactions with an effective date on or after 12 March 2008.

Stamp Taxes

80 Adjustment where contingency ceases or consideration is ascertained

(1) Where section 51 (contingent, uncertain or unascertained consideration) applies in relation to a transaction and—

(*a*) in the case of contingent consideration, the contingency occurs or it becomes clear that it will not occur, or
(*b*) in the case of uncertain or unascertained consideration, an amount relevant to the calculation of the consideration, or any instalment of consideration, becomes ascertained,

the following provisions have effect to require or permit reconsideration of how this Part applies to the transaction (and to any transaction in relation to which it is a linked transaction).

(2) If the effect of the new information is that a transaction becomes notifiable …[1], or that additional tax is payable in respect of a transaction or that tax is payable where none was payable before—

(*a*) the purchaser must make a return to the Inland Revenue within 30 days,
(*b*) the return must contain a self-assessment of the tax chargeable in respect of the transaction on the basis of the information contained in the return,
(*c*) the tax so chargeable is to be calculated by reference to the rates in force at the effective date of the transaction, and
[(*d*) the tax or additional tax payable must be paid not later than the filing date for the return.][5]

(3) The provisions of Schedule 10 (returns, enquiries, assessments and other matters) apply to a return under this section as they apply to a [return under section 76 (general requirement to make land transaction return), subject to the adaptation that references to the effective date of the transaction shall be read as references to the date of the event as a result of which the return is required][2].

(4) If the effect of the new information is that less tax is payable in respect of a transaction than has already been paid,[—

(*a*) the purchaser may, within the period allowed for amendment of the land transaction return, amend the return accordingly;
(*b*) after the end of that period he may (if the land transaction return is not so amended) make a claim to the Inland Revenue for repayment of the amount overpaid][3]

[(4A) Where the transaction ("the relevant transaction") is the grant or assignment of a lease, no claim may be made under subsection (4)—

(*a*) in respect of the repayment (in whole or part) of any loan or deposit that is treated by paragraph 18A of Schedule 17A as being consideration given for the relevant transaction, or
(*b*) in respect of the refund of any of the consideration given for the relevant transaction, in a case where the refund—

(i) is made under arrangements that were made in connection with the relevant transaction, and
(ii) is contingent on the determination or assignment of the lease or on the grant of a chargeable interest out of the lease.][4]

[(5) This section does not apply so far as the consideration consists of rent (see paragraph 8 of Schedule 17A).][2]

HMRC Manuals—Stamp Duty Land Tax Manual, SDLTM05040a (claim for repayment of SDLT after end of period for amendment – example)

Amendments—[1] In sub-s (2), words "or chargeable" repealed by FA 2004 s 326, Sch 42 Pt 4(2) with effect in accordance with FA 2004 Sch 39 para 26. This repeal was previously made by the Stamp Duty and Stamp Duty Land Tax (Variation of the Finance Act 2003) (No 2) Regulations, SI 2003/2816, regs 1, 2, Schedule para 5(2) with effect from 1 December 2003. Those regulations have been revoked by FA 2004 Sch 39 para 14(2).

[2] In sub-s (3), words substituted for the words "land transaction return", and sub-s (5) inserted, by FA 2004 s 296, Sch 39 para 22(4) with effect for any transaction of which the effective date (within the meaning of FA 2003 Pt 4) is on or after 22 July 2004: FA 2004 Sch 39 para 26. These amendments were previously made by the Stamp Duty and Stamp Duty Land Tax (Variation of the Finance Act 2003) (No 2) Regulations, SI 2003/2816 regs 1, 2, Schedule paras 5(3), 8(5) with effect from 1 December 2003. Those regulations are revoked by FA 2004 Sch 39 para 14(2).

[3] In sub-s (4), words substituted for the words "the amount overpaid shall on a claim by the purchaser be repaid together with interest as from the date of payment." by FA 2004 s 299(1), (4) with effect from 22 July 2004.

[4] Sub-s (4A) inserted by F(No 2)A 2005 s 49, Sch 10 paras 1, 15 with effect in relation to any transaction of which the effective date is after 19 May 2005.

However, this amendment does not have effect—

(*a*) in relation to any transaction which is effected in pursuance of a contract entered into and substantially performed on or before the specified date (i e 16 March 2005), or

(*b*) subject to what follows below, in relation to any other transaction which is effected in pursuance of a contract entered into on or before the specified date (i e 16 March 2005).

The exclusion by para (*b*) above of transactions effected in pursuance of contracts entered into on or before the specified date does not apply—

(*a*) if there is any variation of the contract or assignment of rights under the contract after that date,

(*b*) if the transaction is effected in consequence of the exercise after that date of any option, right of pre-emption or similar right, or

(*c*) if after that date there is an assignment, subsale or other transaction (relating to the whole or part of the subject-matter of the contract) as a result of which a person other than the purchaser under the contract becomes entitled to call for a conveyance to him: F(No 2)A 2005 Sch 10 para 16(5)–(8).

[5] Sub-s (2)(*d*) repealed by FA 2007 s 80(1), (3), (9)(*b*) with effect in relation to returns where the event as a result of which the return is required occurs on or after 19 July 2007.

81 Further return where relief withdrawn

(1) Where relief is withdrawn to any extent under—

[(*za*) paragraph 11 of Schedule 6A (relief for certain acquisitions of residential property),][1]

(*a*) Part 1 of Schedule 7 (group relief),

(*b*) Part 2 of that Schedule (reconstruction or acquisition relief), or

(*c*) Schedule 8 (charities relief),

the purchaser must deliver a further return before the end of the period of 30 days after the date on which the disqualifying event occurred.

(2) The return must—

(*a*) include a self-assessment of the amount of tax chargeable, …[4]

(*b*) …[4]

[(2A) Tax payable must be paid not later than the filing date for the return.][4]

(3) The provisions of Schedule 10 (returns, assessments and other matters) apply to a return under this section as they apply to a [return under section 76 (general requirement to deliver land transaction return)][2], with the following adaptations—

(*a*) references to the transaction to which the return relates shall be read as references to the disqualifying event;

(*b*) references to the effective date of the transaction shall be read as references to the date on which the disqualifying event occurs.

(4) In this section "the disqualifying event" means—

[(*za*) in relation to the withdrawal of relief under Schedule 6A, an event mentioned in paragraph (*a*), (*b*) or (*c*) of paragraph 11(2), (3), (4) or (5) of that Schedule;][1]

(*a*) in relation to the withdrawal of group relief, the purchaser ceasing to be a member of the same group as the vendor within the meaning of Part 1 of Schedule 7;

(*b*) in relation to the withdrawal of reconstruction or acquisition relief, the change of control of the acquiring company mentioned in paragraph 9(1)(*a*) of Schedule 7 or, as the case may be, the event mentioned in paragraph 11(1)(*a*) or (2)(*a*) of that Schedule;

(*c*) in relation to the withdrawal of charities relief, a disqualifying event as defined in paragraph 2(3) [or 3(2)][3] of Schedule 8.

Cross references—FA 2009 Sch 55 (penalty for failure to make returns etc).
FA 2009 Sch 56 (penalty for failure to make payments on time).

Amendments—[1] Sub-ss (1)(*za*), (4)(*za*) inserted by FA 2004 s 296, Sch 39 para 17(3) with effect for any transaction of which the effective date (within the meaning of FA 2003 Pt 4) is on or after 22 July 2004: FA 2004 Sch 39 para 26. The insertions were previously made by the Stamp Duty and Stamp Duty Land Tax (Variation of the Finance Act 2003) (No 2) Regulations, SI 2003/2816 regs 1, 2, Schedule para 3(3) with effect from 1 December 2003. Those regulations are revoked by FA 2004 Sch 39 para 14(2).

[2] Words in sub-s (3) substituted for "land transaction return" by FA 2004 s 296, Sch 39 para 19(2) with effect for any transaction of which the effective date (within the meaning of FA 2003 Pt 4) is on or after 22 July 2004: FA 2004 Sch 39 para 26. This amendment was previously made by SI 2003/2816 regs 1, 2, Schedule para 5(3) with effect from 1 December 2003. Those regulations are revoked by FA 2004 Sch 39 para 14(2).

[3] Words in sub-s (4)(*c*) inserted by FA 2004 s 302(5), (7) with effect for any transaction of which the effective date (within the meaning of FA 2003 Pt 4) is on or after 22 July 2004.

[4] Sub-s (2)(*b*) and preceding word "and" repealed, and sub-s (2A) inserted, by FA 2007 ss 80(1), (4), (9)(*c*), 114, Sch 27 Pt 4(4) with effect in relation to returns where the disqualifying event occurs on or after 19 July 2007.

[81A Return or further return in consequence of later linked transaction

(1) Where the effect of a transaction ("the later transaction") that is linked to an earlier transaction is that the earlier transaction becomes notifiable, or that additional tax is payable in respect of the earlier transaction or that tax is payable in respect of the earlier transaction where none was payable before—

(*a*) the purchaser under the earlier transaction must deliver a return or further return in respect of that transaction before the end of the period of 30 days after the effective date of the later transaction,

(*b*) the return must include a self-assessment of the amount of tax chargeable as a result of the later transaction,

(*c*) the tax so chargeable is to be calculated by reference to the rates in force at the effective date of the earlier transaction, and

[(*d*) the tax or additional tax payable must be paid not later than the filing date for the return.][2]

(2) The provisions of Schedule 10 (returns, enquiries, assessments and other matters) apply to a return under this section as they apply to a return under section 76 (general requirement to deliver land transaction return), with the following adaptations—

(*a*) in paragraph 5 (formal notice to deliver return), the requirement in sub-paragraph (2)(*a*) that the notice specify the transaction to which it relates shall be read as requiring both the earlier and later transactions to be specified;

(*b*) references to the effective date of the transaction to which the return relates shall be read as references to the effective date of the later transaction.

(3) This section does not affect any requirement to make a return under section 76 in respect of the later transaction.][1]

Amendments—[1] Inserted by FA 2004 s 296, Sch 39 para 19(1) with effect for any transaction of which the effective date (within the meaning of FA 2003 Pt 4) is on or after 22 July 2004: FA 2004 Sch 39 para 26. This insertion was previously made by the Stamp Duty and Stamp Duty Land Tax (Variation of the Finance Act 2003) (No 2) Regulations, SI 2003/2816 regs 1, 2, Schedule para 5(1) with effect from 1 December 2003. Those regulations are revoked by FA 2004 Sch 39 para 14(2).

[2] Sub-s (1)(*d*) substituted by FA 2007 s 80(1), (5), (9)(*d*) with effect in relation to returns where the effective date of the later transaction is on or after 19 July 2007.

[81B Declaration by person authorised to act on behalf of individual

(1) This section applies to the declaration mentioned in paragraph 1(1)(*c*) of Schedule 10 …[2] (declaration that return …[2] is correct and complete).

(2) The requirement that an individual make such a declaration (alone or jointly with others) is treated as met if a declaration to that effect is made by a person authorised to act on behalf of that individual in relation to the matters to which the return or certificate relates.

(3) For the purposes of this section a person is not regarded as authorised to act on behalf of an individual unless he is so authorised by a power of attorney in writing, signed by that individual.

In this subsection as it applies in Scotland "power of attorney" includes factory and commission.

(4) Nothing in this section affects the making of a declaration in accordance with—

(*a*) section 100(2) (persons through whom a company acts), or

(*b*) section 106(1) or (2) (person authorised to act on behalf of incapacitated person or minor).][1]

Amendments—[1] Inserted by FA 2004 s 296, Sch 39 para 20 with effect for any transaction of which the effective date (within the meaning of FA 2003 Pt 4) is on or after 22 July 2004: FA 2004 Sch 39 para 26. This insertion was previously made by the Stamp Duty and Stamp Duty Land Tax (Variation of the Finance Act 2003) (No 2) Regulations, SI 2003/2816 regs 1, 2, Schedule para 6 with effect from 1 December 2003. Those regulations are revoked by FA 2004 Sch 39 para 14(2).

[2] Words in sub-s (1) repealed by FA 2008 s 94, Sch 30 paras 1, 3 with effect in relation to transactions with an effective date on or after 12 March 2008.

82 Loss or destruction of, or damage to, return etc

(1) This section applies where—

(*a*) a return delivered to the Inland Revenue, or

(*b*) any other document relating to tax made by or provided to the Inland Revenue,

has been lost or destroyed, or been so defaced or damaged as to be illegible or otherwise useless.

(2) The Inland Revenue may treat the return as not having been delivered or the document as not having been made or provided.

(3) Anything done on that basis shall be as valid and effective for all purposes as it would have been if the return had not been made or the document had not been made or provided.

(4) But if as a result a person is charged with tax and he proves to the satisfaction of the [tribunal][1] having jurisdiction in the case that he has already paid tax in respect of the transaction in question, relief shall be given, by reducing the charge or by repayment as the case may require.

Amendments—[1] In sub-s (4) word substituted for the words "General or Special Commissioners" by the Transfer of Tribunal Functions and Revenue and Customs Appeals Order, SI 2009/56 art 3, Sch 1 para 367 with effect from 1 April 2009.

[82A Claims not included in returns

Schedule 11A has effect with respect to claims not included in returns.][1]

Amendments—[1] This section inserted by FA 2004 s 299(1), (2) with effect from 22 July 2004.

83 Formal requirements as to assessments, penalty determinations etc

(1) An assessment, determination, notice or other document required to be used in assessing, charging, collecting and levying tax or determining a penalty under this Part must be in accordance with the forms prescribed from time to time by the Board and a document in the form so prescribed and supplied or approved by the Board is valid and effective.

(2) Any such assessment, determination, notice or other document purporting to be made under this Part is not ineffective—

(*a*) for want of form, or

(*b*) by reason of any mistake, defect or omission in it,

if it is substantially in conformity with this Part and its intended effect is reasonably ascertainable by the person to whom it is directed.

(3) The validity of an assessment or determination is not affected—

(*a*) by any mistake in it as to—

(i) the name of a person liable, or

(ii) the amount of the tax charged, or

(*b*) by reason of any variance between the notice of assessment or determination and the assessment or determination itself.

84 Delivery and service of documents

(1) A notice or other document to be served under this Part on a person may be delivered to him or left at his usual or last known place of abode.

(2) A notice or other document to be given, served or delivered under this Part may be served by post.

(3) For the purposes of section 7 of the Interpretation Act 1978 (c 30) (general provisions as to service by post) any such notice or other document to be given or delivered to, or served on, any person by the Inland Revenue is properly addressed if it is addressed to that person—

(*a*) in the case of an individual, at his usual or last known place of residence or his place of business;

(*b*) in the case of a company—

(i) at its principal place of business,

(ii) if a liquidator has been appointed, at his address for the purposes of the liquidation, or

(iii) at any place prescribed by regulations made by the Inland Revenue.

Liability for and payment of tax

85 Liability for tax

(1) The purchaser is liable to pay the tax in respect of a chargeable transaction.

(2) As to the liability of purchasers acting jointly see—

section 103(2)(*c*) (joint purchasers);
Part 2 of Schedule 15 (partners); and
paragraph 5 of Schedule 16 (trustees).

86 Payment of tax

(1) Tax payable in respect of a land transaction must be paid [not later than the filing date for the land transaction return relating to the transaction.][1]

(2) Tax payable as a result of the withdrawal of relief under—

(*a*) Part 1 of Schedule 7 (group relief),

(*b*) Part 2 of that Schedule (reconstruction or acquisition relief), or

(*c*) Schedule 8 (charities relief),

must be paid [not later than the filing date for the return relating to the withdrawal][1] (see section 81).

(3) Tax payable as a result of the amendment of a return must be paid forthwith or, if the amendment is made before the filing date for the return, not later than that date.

(4) Tax payable in accordance with a determination or assessment by the Inland Revenue must be paid within 30 days after the determination or assessment is issued.

(5) The above provisions are subject to—

(*a*) section 90 (application to defer payment of tax in case of contingent or uncertain consideration), and

(*b*) paragraphs 39 and 40 of Schedule 10 (postponement of payment pending determination of appeal).

[(5A) The above provisions are also subject to paragraph 7 of Schedule 61 to the Finance Act 2009 (payment of tax where land ceases to qualify for relief in respect of alternative finance investment bonds).][2]

(6) This section does not affect the date from which interest is payable (as to which, see section 87).

Cross references—FA 2009 Sch 56 (penalty for failure to make payments on time).

Amendments—[1] Words in sub-ss (1), (2) substituted by FA 2007 s 80(1), (6), (9)(*e*) with effect in relation to land transactions with an effective date on or after 19 July 2007.

[2] Sub-s (5A) inserted by FA 2009 s 123, Sch 61 paras 24, 26 with effect where the effective date of the first transaction (within the meaning given by FA 2009 Sch 61 para 5(2)) is on or after 21 July 2009.

87 Interest on unpaid tax

(1) Interest is payable on the amount of any unpaid tax from the end of the period of 30 days after the relevant date until the tax is paid.

(2) The Inland Revenue may by regulations amend subsection (1) so as to make interest run from the end of such shorter period after the relevant date as may be prescribed or, if the regulations so provide, from that date.

(3) For the purposes of this section "the relevant date" is—

(*a*) in the case of an amount payable because relief is withdrawn under—

[(ia) Schedule 6A (relief for certain acquisitions of residential property),][1]

(i) Part 1 of Schedule 7 (group relief),

(ii) Part 2 of that Schedule (reconstruction or acquisition relief), or

(iii) Schedule 8 (charities relief),

the date of the disqualifying event;

[(*aa*) in the case of an amount payable under section 81A in respect of an earlier transaction because of the effect of a later linked transaction, the effective date of the later transaction;][2]

[(*ab*) in the case of an amount payable under paragraph 3(3) or 4(3) of Schedule 17A (leases that continue after a fixed term and treatment of leases for an indefinite term), the day on which the lease becomes treated as being for a longer fixed term;][3]

(*b*) in the case of a deferred payment under section 90, the date when the deferred payment is due;

(*c*) in any other case, the effective date of the transaction.

(4) In subsection (3)(*a*) "the disqualifying event" means—

[(*za*) in relation to the withdrawal of relief under Schedule 6A an event mentioned in paragraph (*a*), (*b*) or (*c*) of paragraph 11(2), (3), (4) or (5) of that Schedule;][1]

(*a*) in relation to the withdrawal of group relief, the purchaser ceasing to be a member of the same group as the vendor within the meaning of Part 1 of Schedule 7);

(*b*) in relation to the withdrawal of reconstruction or acquisition relief, the change of control of the acquiring company mentioned in paragraph 9(1)(*a*) of that Schedule or, as the case may be, the event mentioned in paragraph 11(1)(*a*) or (2)(*a*) of that Schedule;

(*c*) in relation to the withdrawal of charities relief, a disqualifying event as defined in paragraph 2(3) [or 3(2)][4] of Schedule 8.

(5) Subsection (3)(*c*) applies in a case within section 51 (contingent, uncertain or unascertained consideration) if payment is not deferred under section 90, with the result that interest on any tax payable under section 80 (adjustment where contingency ceases or consideration is ascertained) runs from the effective date of the transaction.

(6) If an amount is lodged with the Inland Revenue in respect of the tax, the amount on which interest is payable is reduced by that amount.

(7) Interest is calculated at the rate applicable under section 178 of the Finance Act 1989 (c 26) (power of Treasury to prescribe rates of interest).

Amendments—[1] In sub-s (3), para (*a*)(ia) inserted, and sub-s (4)(*za*) inserted by FA 2004 s 296, Sch 39 para 17(4) with effect for any transaction of which the effective date (within the meaning of FA 2003 Pt 4) is on or after 22 July 2004: FA 2004 Sch 39 para 26. These insertions were previously made by the Stamp Duty and Stamp Duty Land Tax (Variation of the Finance Act 2003) (No 2) Regulations, SI 2003/2816 regs 1, 2, Schedule para 3(4) with effect from 1 December 2003. Those regulations are revoked by FA 2004 Sch 39 para 14(2).

[2] Sub-s (3)(*aa*) inserted by FA 2004 s 296, Sch 39 para 19(3) with effect for any transaction of which the effective date (within the meaning of FA 2003 Pt 4) is on or after 22 July 2004: FA 2004 Sch 39 para 26. This insertion was previously made by SI 2003/2816 regs 1, 2, Schedule para 5(4) with effect from 1 December 2003. Those regulations are revoked by FA 2004 Sch 39 para 14(2).

[3] Sub-s (3)(*ab*) inserted by FA 2004 s 296, Sch 39 para 22(5) with effect for any transaction of which the effective date (within the meaning of FA 2003 Pt 4) is on or after 22 July 2004: FA 2004 Sch 39 para 26. This insertion previously made by the Stamp Duty and Stamp Duty Land Tax (Variation of the Finance Act 2003) (No 2) Regulations, SI 2003/2816 regs 1, 2, Schedule para 8(6) with effect from 1 December 2003. Those regulations are revoked by FA 2004 Sch 39 para 14(2).

[4] Words in sub-s (4)(*c*) inserted by FA 2004 s 302(6), (7) with effect for any transaction of which the effective date (within the meaning of FA 2003 Pt 4) is on or after 22 July 2004.

88 Interest on penalties

A penalty under this Part shall carry interest at the rate applicable under section 178 of the Finance Act 1989 from the date it is determined until payment.

89 Interest on repayment of tax overpaid etc

(1) A repayment by the Inland Revenue to which this section applies shall be made with interest at the rate applicable under section 178 of the Finance Act 1989 for the period between the relevant time (as defined below) and the date when the order for repayment is issued.

(2) This section applies to—

(*a*) any repayment of tax, and

(*b*) any repayment of a penalty under this Part.

In that case the relevant time is the date on which the payment of tax or penalty was made.

(3) This section also applies to a repayment by the Inland Revenue of an amount lodged with them in respect of the tax payable in respect of a transaction.

In that case the relevant time is the date on which the amount was lodged with them.

(4) No interest is payable under this section in respect of a payment made in consequence of an order or judgment of a court having power to allow interest on the payment.

(5) Interest paid to any person under this section is not income of that person for any tax purposes.

90 Application to defer payment in case of contingent or uncertain consideration

(1) The purchaser may apply to the Inland Revenue to defer payment of tax in a case where the amount payable depends on the amount or value of chargeable consideration that—

(*a*) at the effective date of the transaction is contingent or uncertain, and

(*b*) falls to be paid or provided on one or more future dates of which at least one falls, or may fall, more than six months after the effective date of the transaction.

(2) The Inland Revenue may make provision by regulations for carrying this section into effect.

(3) The regulations may in particular—

(*a*) specify when an application is to be made;

(*b*) impose requirements as to the form and contents of an application;

(*c*) require the applicant to provide such information as the Inland Revenue may reasonably require for the purposes of determining whether to accept an application;

(*d*) specify the grounds on which an application may be refused;

(*e*) specify the procedure for reaching a decision on an application;

(*f*) make provision for postponing payment of tax when an application has been made;

(*g*) provide for an appeal to the [tribunal][2] against a refusal to accept an application, and make provision in relation to such an appeal corresponding to any provision made in relation to appeals under Part 7 of Schedule 10 (appeals against Revenue decisions on tax);

(*h*) provide for the effect of accepting an application;

(*i*) require the purchaser to make a return or further return, and to make such payments or further payments of tax as may be specified, in such circumstances as may be specified.

(4) The provisions of Schedule 10 (returns, enquiries, assessments and other matters) apply to a return under this section as they apply to a land transaction return.

(5) An application under this section does not affect the purchaser's obligations as regards payment of tax in respect of chargeable consideration that has already been paid or provided or is not contingent and whose amount is ascertained or ascertainable at the time the application is made.

This applies as regards both the time of payment and the calculation of the amount payable.

(6) Regulations under this section may provide that where—

(*a*) a payment is made as mentioned in subsection (5), and

(*b*) an application under this section is accepted in respect of other chargeable consideration taken into account in calculating the amount of that payment,

section 80 (adjustment where contingency ceases or consideration is ascertained) does not apply in relation to the payment and, instead, any necessary adjustment shall be made in accordance with the regulations.

[(7) This section does not apply so far as the consideration consists of rent.][1]

HMRC Manuals—Stamp Duty Land Tax Manual SDLTM50900–52000 (general guidance on making applications under this section, including guidance on pre-transaction and post-transaction rulings).

Amendments—[1] Sub-s (7) inserted by FA 2004 s 296, Sch 39 para 22(6) with effect for any transaction of which the effective date (within the meaning of FA 2003 Pt 4) is on or after 22 July 2004: FA 2004 Sch 39 para 26. This insertion was previously made by the Stamp Duty and Stamp Duty Land Tax (Variation of the Finance Act 2003) (No 2) Regulations, SI 2003/2816 regs 1, 2, Schedule para 8(7) with effect from 1 December 2003. Those regulations are revoked by FA 2004 Sch 39 para 14(2).

[2] In sub-s (3)(*g*) word substituted for the words "General or Special Commissioners" by the Transfer of Tribunal Functions and Revenue and Customs Appeals Order, SI 2009/56 art 3, Sch 1 para 368 with effect from 1 April 2009.

91 Collection and recovery of tax etc

(1) The provisions of Schedule 12 have effect with respect to the collection and recovery of tax.

In that Schedule—

Part 1 contains general provisions, and

Part 2 relates to court proceedings.

(2) The provisions of that Schedule have effect in relation to the collection and recovery of any unpaid amount by way of—
(*a*) penalty under this Part, or
(*b*) interest under this Part (on unpaid tax or penalty),
as if it were an amount of unpaid tax.

92 Payment by cheque

For the purposes of this Part where—
(*a*) payment to the Inland Revenue is made by cheque, and
(*b*) the cheque is paid on its first presentation to the banker on whom it is drawn,
the payment is treated as made on the day on which the cheque was received by the Inland Revenue.

Compliance

93 Information powers

(1) Schedule 13 has effect with respect to the powers of the Inland Revenue to call for documents and information for the purposes of stamp duty land tax.

(2) In that Schedule—
Part 1 confers power on an authorised officer to call for documents or information from the taxpayer;
Part 2 confers power on an authorised officer to call for documents from a third party;
Part 3 confers power on an authorised officer to call for the papers of a tax accountant;
Part 4 imposes restrictions on the powers under Parts 1 to 3;
Part 5 confers powers on the Board to call for documents or information;
Part 6 provides for an order of a judicial authority for the delivery of documents;
Part 7 provides for entry with a warrant to obtain evidence of an offence;
Part 8 relates to falsification etc of documents.

(3) A person who is required by a notice under Part 1, 2 or 3 of Schedule 13 to deliver a document or to provide information, or to make a document available for inspection, and who fails to comply with the notice is liable to a penalty not exceeding £300.

(4) If the failure continues after a penalty has been imposed under subsection (3), he is liable to a further penalty or penalties not exceeding £60 for each day on which the failure continues after the day on which the penalty under that subsection was imposed (but excluding any day for which a penalty under this subsection has already been imposed).

(5) No penalty shall be imposed under subsection (3) or (4) in respect of a failure at any time after the failure has been remedied.

(6) A person who is required by a notice under Part 1, 2 or 3 of Schedule 13 to deliver a document or to provide information, or to make a document available for inspection, and who fraudulently or negligently delivers, provides or makes available any incorrect document or information is liable to a penalty not exceeding £3,000.

94 Power to inspect premises

(1) If for the purposes of this Part the Board authorise an officer of theirs to inspect any property for the purpose of ascertaining its market value, or any other matter relevant for the purposes of this Part, the person having custody or possession of the property shall permit the officer so authorised to inspect it at such reasonable times as the Board may consider necessary.

(2) A person who wilfully delays or obstructs an officer of the Board acting in pursuance of this section commits an offence and is liable on summary conviction to a fine not exceeding level 1 on the standard scale.

95 Offence of fraudulent evasion of tax

(1) A person commits an offence if he is knowingly concerned in the fraudulent evasion of tax by him or any other person.

(2) A person guilty of an offence under this section is liable—
(*a*) on summary conviction to imprisonment for a term not exceeding six months or a fine not exceeding the statutory maximum, or both;
(*b*) on conviction on indictment, to imprisonment for a term not exceeding seven years or a fine, or both.

96 Penalty for assisting in preparation of incorrect return etc

A person who assists in or induces the preparation or delivery of any information, return or other document that—
(*a*) he knows will be, or is likely to be, used for any purpose of tax, and
(*b*) he knows to be incorrect,
is liable to a penalty not exceeding £3,000.

97 Power to allow further time and reasonable excuse for failure

(1) For the purposes of this Part a person shall be deemed not to have failed to do anything required to be done within a limited time if he did it within such further time, if any, as the Inland Revenue may allow.

(2) Where a person had a reasonable excuse for not doing anything required to be done for the purposes of this Part

(*a*) he shall be deemed not to have failed to do it unless the excuse ceased, and

(*b*) after the excuse ceased, he shall be deemed not to have failed to do it if he did it without unreasonable delay after the excuse had ceased.

98 Admissibility of evidence not affected by offer of settlement etc

(1) Statements made or documents produced by or on behalf of a person are not inadmissible in proceedings to which this section applies by reason only that it has been drawn to his attention—

(*a*) that where serious tax fraud has been committed the Board may accept a money settlement and that the Board will accept such a settlement, and will not pursue a criminal prosecution, if he makes a full confession of all tax irregularities, or

(*b*) that the extent to which he is helpful and volunteers information is a factor that will be taken into account in determining the amount of any penalty,

and that he was or may have been induced thereby to make the statements or produce the documents.

(2) The proceedings to which this section applies are—

(*a*) any criminal proceedings against the person in question for any form of fraudulent conduct in connection with or in relation to tax;

(*b*) any proceedings against him for the recovery of any tax due from him;

(*c*) any proceedings for a penalty or on appeal against the determination of a penalty.

99 General provisions about penalties

(1) Schedule 14 has effect with respect to the determination of penalties under this Part and related appeals.

(2) The Board may in their discretion mitigate a penalty under this Part, or stay or compound any proceedings for the recovery of such a penalty.

They may also, after judgment, further mitigate or entirely remit the penalty.

[(2A) Where a person is liable to more than one tax-related penalty in respect of the same land transaction, each penalty after the first shall be reduced so that his liability to such penalties, in total, does not exceed the amount of whichever is (or, but for this subsection, would be) the greatest one.][1]

(3) Nothing in the provisions of this Part relating to penalties affects any criminal proceedings for an offence.

HMRC Manuals—Stamp Duty Land Tax Manual SDLTM86600, 86620 (maximum penalties payable can be reduced or abated by up to 20 per cent (exceptionally 30 per cent where there is spontaneous and complete disclosure and the purchaser has no reason to fear early discovery) for the amount of disclosure by the purchaser; 40 per cent for the amount of co-operation received from the purchaser during the enquiry; 40 per cent for the size and the gravity of the offences).

Amendments—[1] Sub-s (2A) inserted by FA 2004 s 298(1), (4), with effect from 22 July 2004.

Application of provisions

100 Companies

(1) In this Part "company", except as otherwise expressly provided, means any body corporate or unincorporated association, but does not include a partnership.

(2) Everything to be done by a company under this Part shall be done by the company acting through—

(*a*) the proper officer of the company, or

(*b*) another person having for the time being having the express, implied or apparent authority of the company to act on its behalf for the purpose.

Paragraph (*b*) does not apply where a liquidator has been appointed for the company.

(3) Service on a company of any document under or in pursuance of this Part may be effected by serving it on the proper officer.

(4) Tax due from a company that—

(*a*) is not a body corporate, or

(*b*) is incorporated under the law of a country or territory outside the United Kingdom,

may, without prejudice to any other method of recovery, be recovered from the proper officer of the company.

(5) The proper officer may retain out of any money coming into his hands on behalf of the company sufficient sums to pay that tax and, so far as he is not so reimbursed, he is entitled to be indemnified by the company in respect of the liability imposed on him.

(6) For the purposes of this Part—

(*a*) the proper officer of a body corporate is the secretary, or person acting as secretary, of the company, and
(*b*) the proper officer of an unincorporated association, or of a body corporate that does not have a proper officer within paragraph (*a*), is the treasurer, or person acting as treasurer, of the company.

This subsection does not apply if a liquidator or administrator has been appointed for the company.

(7) If a liquidator or administrator has been appointed for the company, then, for the purposes of this Part—

(*a*) the liquidator or, as the case may be, the administrator is the proper officer, and
(*b*) if two or more persons are appointed to act jointly or concurrently as the administrator of the company, the proper officer is—

(i) such one of them as is specified in a notice given to the Inland Revenue by those persons for the purposes of this section, or
(ii) where the Inland Revenue is not so notified, such one or more of those persons as the Inland Revenue may designate as the proper officer for those purposes.

101 Unit trust schemes

(1) This Part (with the exception of the [provision][1] mentioned in subsection (7) below) applies in relation to a unit trust scheme as if—

(*a*) the trustees were a company, and
(*b*) the rights of the unit holders were shares in the company.

(2) Each of the parts of an umbrella scheme is regarded for the purposes of this Part as a separate unit trust scheme and the scheme as a whole is not so regarded.

(3) An "umbrella scheme" means a unit trust scheme—

(*a*) that provides arrangements for separate pooling of the contributions of participants and the profits or income out of which payments are to be made for them, and
(*b*) under which the participants are entitled to exchange rights in one pool for rights in another.

A "part" of an umbrella scheme means such of the arrangements as relate to a separate pool.

(4) In this Part, subject to any regulations under subsection (5)—

"unit trust scheme" has the same meaning as in the Financial Services and Markets Act 2000 (c 8), and
"unit holder" means a person entitled to a share of the investments subject to the trusts of a unit trust scheme.

(5) The Treasury may by regulations provide that a scheme of a description specified in the regulations is to be treated as not being a unit trust scheme for the purposes of this Part.

Any such regulations may contain such supplementary and transitional provisions as appear to the Treasury to be necessary or expedient.

(6) Section 469A of the Taxes Act 1988 (court common investment funds treated as authorised unit trusts) applies for the purposes of this Part as it applies for the purposes of that Act, with the substitution for references to an authorised unit trust of references to a unit trust scheme.

(7) An unit trust scheme is not to be treated as a company for the purposes of—

...[1] Schedule 7 (group relief, reconstruction relief or acquisition relief).

Amendments—[1] Words in sub-s (1) substituted, words in sub-s (7) repealed by FA 2006 s 166(3), s 178, Sch 26 Pt 7(3) with effect in relation to any land transaction of which the effective date is, or is after, 22 March 2006, subject to FA 2006 s 166(5), (6).

102 Open-ended investment companies

(1) The Treasury may by regulations make such provision as they consider appropriate for securing that the provisions of this Part have effect in relation to—

(*a*) open-ended investment companies of such description as may be prescribed in the regulations, and
(*b*) transactions involving such companies,

in a manner corresponding, subject to such modifications as the Treasury consider appropriate, to the manner in which they have effect in relation to unit trust schemes and transactions involving such trusts.

(2) The regulations may, in particular, make provision—

(*a*) modifying the operation of any prescribed provision in relation to open-ended investment companies so as to secure that arrangements for treating the assets of such a company as assets comprised in separate pools are given an effect corresponding to that of equivalent arrangements constituting the separate parts of an umbrella scheme;
(*b*) treating the separate parts of the undertaking of an open-ended investment company in relation to which such provision is made as distinct companies for the purposes of this Part.

(3) Regulations under this section may—

(*a*) make different provision for different cases, and

(*b*) contain such incidental, supplementary, consequential and transitional provision as the Treasury think fit.

(4) In this section—

"open-ended investment company" has the meaning given by section 236 of the Financial Services and Markets Act 2000 (c 8);

"prescribed" means prescribed by regulations under this section; and

"unit trust scheme" and "umbrella scheme" have the same meaning as in section 101.

103 Joint purchasers

(1) This section applies to a land transaction where there are two or more purchasers who are or will be jointly entitled to the interest acquired.

(2) The general rules are that—

(*a*) any obligation of the purchaser under this Part in relation to the transaction is an obligation of the purchasers jointly but may be discharged by any of them,

(*b*) anything required or authorised by this Part to be done in relation to the purchaser must be done by or in relation to all of them, and

(*c*) any liability of the purchaser under this Part in relation to the transaction (in particular, any liability arising by virtue of the failure to fulfil an obligation within paragraph (*a*)), is a joint and several liability of the purchasers.

These rules are subject to the following provisions.

(3) If the transaction is a notifiable transaction, a single land transaction return is required.

(4) The declaration required by paragraph 1(1)(*c*) of Schedule 10 …[1] (declaration that return …[1] is complete and correct) must be made by all the purchasers.

(5) If the Inland Revenue give notice of an enquiry into the return …[1]—

(*a*) the notice must be given to each of the purchasers,

(*b*) the powers of the Inland Revenue as to the production of documents and provision of information for the purposes of the enquiry are exercisable separately (and differently) in relation to each of the purchasers,

(*c*) any of the purchasers may apply for a direction that a closure notice be given (and all of them are entitled to [to be parties to the application][2]), and

(*d*) the closure notice must be given to each of the purchasers.

(6) A Revenue determination or discovery assessment relating to the transaction must be made against all the purchasers and is not effective against any of them unless notice of it is given to each of them whose identity is known to the Inland Revenue.

(7) In the case of an appeal arising from proceedings under this Part relating to the transaction—

(*a*) the appeal may be brought by any of the purchasers,

(*b*) notice of the appeal must be given to any of them by whom it is not brought,

(*c*) the agreement of all the purchasers is required if the appeal is to be settled by agreement,

[(*d*) if it is not settled, and is notified to the tribunal, any of them are entitled to be parties to the appeal, and][2]

[(*e*) the tribunal's decision on the appeal binds all of them.][2]

[(7A) In a case where subsection (7) applies and some (but not all) of the purchasers require HMRC to undertake a review under paragraph 36B or 36C of Schedule 10—

(*a*) notification of the review must be given by HMRC to each of the other purchasers whose identity is known to HMRC,

(*b*) any of the other purchasers may be a party to the review if they notify HMRC in writing,

(*c*) the notice of HMRC's conclusions must be given to each of the other purchasers whose identity is known to HMRC,

(*d*) paragraph 36F of Schedule 10 (effect of conclusions of review) applies in relation to all of the purchasers, and

(*e*) any of the purchasers may notify the appeal to the tribunal under paragraph 36G.][2]

(8) This section has effect subject to—

the provisions of Schedule 15 relating to partnerships, and

the provisions of Schedule 16 relating to trustees.

Amendments—[1] Words in sub-ss (4), (5) repealed by FA 2008 s 94, Sch 30 paras 1, 4 with effect in relation to transactions with an effective date on or after 12 March 2008.

[2] In sub-s (5)(*c*) words substituted for the words "appear and be heard on the application"; sub-s (7)(*d*), (*e*) substituted; sub-s (7A) inserted by the Transfer of Tribunal Functions and Revenue and Customs Appeals Order, SI 2009/56 art 3, Sch 1 para 369 with effect from 1 April 2009. Sub-s (7)(*d*), (*e*) previously read as follows—

"(*d*) if it is not settled, any of them are entitled to appear and be heard, and
(*e*) the decision on the appeal binds all of them.".

104 Partnerships

(1) Schedule 15 has effect with respect to the application of this Part in relation to partnerships.

(2) In that Schedule—

Part 1 defines "partnership" and contains other general provisions, and

Part 2 deals with ordinary partnership transactions, and
Part 3 [makes special provision for certain transactions][1].

Amendments—[1] Words in para (2) substituted for the words "excludes certain transactions from stamp duty land tax "by FA 2004 s 304, Sch 41 paras 2(*a*), 3 with effect for any partnership transaction of which the effective date (within the meaning of FA 2003 Pt 4) is after 22 July 2004. A "partnership transaction" means a transaction mentioned in FA 2003 Sch 15 para 9(1): FA 2004 Sch 41 para 3(2).

105 Trustees

Schedule 16 has effect with respect to the application of this Part in relation to trustees.

106 Persons acting in a representative capacity etc

(1) The person having the direction, management or control of the property of an incapacitated person—

(*a*) is responsible for discharging any obligations under this Part, in relation to a transaction affecting that property, to which the incapacitated person would be subject if he were not incapacitated, and

(*b*) may retain out of money coming into his hands on behalf of the incapacitated person sums sufficient to meet any payment he is liable to make under this Part, and, so far as he is not so reimbursed, is entitled to be indemnified in respect of any such payment.

(2) The parent or guardian of a minor is responsible for discharging any obligations of the minor under this Part that are not discharged by the minor himself.

(3) The personal representatives of a person who is the purchaser under a land transaction—

(*a*) are responsible for discharging the obligations of the purchaser under this Part in relation to the transaction, and

(*b*) may deduct any payment made by them under this Part out of the assets and effects of the deceased person.

(4) A receiver appointed by a court in the United Kingdom having the direction and control of any property is responsible for discharging any obligations under this Part in relation to a transaction affecting that property as if the property were not under the direction and control of the court.

107 Crown application

[(1) This Part binds the Crown, subject to the following provisions of this section.][1]

(2) A land transaction under which the purchaser is any of the following is exempt from charge:

Government

A Minister of the Crown
The Scottish Ministers
A Northern Ireland department
[The Welsh Ministers, the First Minister for Wales and the Counsel General to the Welsh Assembly Government][2]

Parliament etc

The Corporate Officer of the House of Lords
The Corporate Officer of the House of Commons
The Scottish Parliamentary Corporate Body
The Northern Ireland Assembly Commission
[The National Assembly for Wales Commission][2]
The National Assembly for Wales

(3) The powers conferred by Part 7 of Schedule 13 (entry with warrant to obtain information) are not exercisable in relation to premises occupied for the purposes of the Crown.

[(4) Nothing in this section shall be read as making the Crown liable to prosecution for an offence.][1]

Amendments—[1] Sub-s (1) substituted, and sub-s (4) inserted, by FA 2004 s 296, Sch 39 para 21 with effect for any transaction of which the effective date (within the meaning of FA 2003 Pt 4) is on or after 22 July 2004: FA 2004 Sch 39 para 26. These amendments were previously made by the Stamp Duty and Stamp Duty Land Tax (Variation of the Finance Act 2003) (No 2) Regulations, SI 2003/2816 regs 1, 2, Schedule para 7 with effect from 1 December 2003. Those regulations are revoked by FA 2004 Sch 39 para 14(2).

[2] In sub-s (2) entry beginning "The Welsh Ministers," inserted and entry "The National Assembly for Wales Commission" substituted, by the Government of Wales Act 2006 s 160(1), Sch 10 paras 62, 65 with effect from 25 May 2007, being the date on which the initial period ended (following the appointment of the First Minister) (Government of Wales Act 2006 ss 46, 161(4), (5)).

Supplementary provisions

108 Linked transactions

(1) Transactions are "linked" for the purposes of this Part if they form part of a single scheme, arrangement or series of transactions between the same vendor and purchaser or, in either case, persons connected with them.

Section 839 of the Taxes Act 1988 (connected persons) has effect for the purposes of this subsection.

Stamp Taxes

(2) Where there are two or more linked transactions with the same effective date, the purchaser, or all of the purchasers if there is more than one, may make a single land transaction return as if all of those transactions that are notifiable were a single notifiable transaction.

(3) Where two or more purchasers make a single return in respect of linked transactions, section 103 (joint purchasers) applies as if—

(*a*) the transactions in question were a single transaction, and

(*b*) those purchasers were purchasers acting jointly.

[(4) This section is subject to section 47(1).][1]

Amendments—[1] Sub-s (4) inserted by FA 2007 s 76(2), (3) with effect in relation to a set of land transactions if the effective date of any of them is on or after 19 July 2007.

109 General power to vary this Part by regulations

(1) The Treasury may if they consider it expedient in the public interest make provision by regulations for the variation of this Part in its application to land transactions of any description.

(2) The power conferred by this section includes, in particular, power to alter—

(*a*) the descriptions of land transaction that are chargeable or notifiable;

(*b*) the descriptions of land transaction in respect of which tax is chargeable at any existing rate or amount.

(3) The power conferred by this section does not, except as mentioned in subsection (2)(*b*), include power to vary any threshold, rate or amount specified in—

(*a*) section 55 (amount of tax chargeable: general), or

(*b*) Schedule 5 (amount of tax chargeable: rent).

(4) This section has effect subject to section 110 (approval of regulations by House of Commons).

(5) Regulations under this section do not apply in relation to any transaction of which the effective date is after the end of—

(*a*) the period of 18 months beginning with the day on which the regulations were made, or

(*b*) such shorter period as may be specified in the regulations.

This does not affect the power to make further provision by regulations under this section to the same or similar effect.

(6) Regulations under this section may include such supplementary, transitional and incidental provision as appears to the Treasury to be necessary or expedient.

(7) The power conferred by this section may be exercised at any time after the passing of this Act.

110 Approval of regulations under general power

(1) An instrument containing regulations under section 109 (general power to vary this Part by regulations) must be laid before the House of Commons after being made.

(2) If the regulations are not approved by the House of Commons before the end of the period of 28 days beginning with the day on which they are made, they shall cease to have effect at the end of that period (if they have not already ceased to have effect under subsection (3)).

(3) If on any day during that period of 28 days the House of Commons, in proceedings on a motion that (or to the effect that) the regulations be approved, comes to a decision rejecting the regulations, they shall cease to have effect at the end of that day.

(4) In reckoning any such period of 28 days take no account of any time during which—

(*a*) Parliament is prorogued or dissolved, or

(*b*) the House of Commons is adjourned for more than four days.

(5) Where regulations cease to have effect under this section, their ceasing to have effect is without prejudice to anything done in reliance on them.

As to claims for repayment, see section 111.

111 Claim for repayment if regulations under general power not approved

(1) Where regulations cease to have effect under section 110, [a claim may be made to the Inland Revenue for repayment of any tax, interest or penalty that would not have been payable but for the regulations][1].

(2) Section 89 (interest on repayment of tax overpaid etc) applies to a repayment under this section.

(3) A claim for repayment must be made within two years after the effective date of the transaction in question.

(4) The Inland Revenue may make provision by regulations—

(*a*) for varying the time limit for making a claim;

(*b*) as to any other conditions that must be met before repayment is made.

Amendments—[1] In sub-s (1), words substituted for the words "any amount paid by way of tax, or interest or penalty, that would not have been payable but for the regulations shall, on a claim, be repaid by the Inland Revenue" by FA 2004 s 299(1), (5) with effect from 22 July 2004.

112 Power to amend certain provisions before implementation

(1) The Treasury may by regulations amend the following provisions of this Part—

(*a*) Schedule 5 (amount of tax chargeable: rent);

(*b*) subsection (2) of section 55 (amount of tax chargeable: general) so far as relating to the thresholds at which different rates of tax become payable.

(2) The regulations may make such consequential amendments of Schedule 6 (disadvantaged areas relief) as appear to the Treasury to be appropriate.

(3) A statutory instrument containing regulations under this section shall not be made unless a draft of the instrument has been laid before and approved by resolution of the House of Commons.

(4) The power conferred by this section is not exercisable after the implementation date.

113 Functions conferred on "the Inland Revenue"

(1) References in this Part to "the Inland Revenue" are to any officer of the Board, except as otherwise provided.

(2) Any power of the Inland Revenue to make regulations is exercisable only by the Board.

(3) In Schedule 10 (returns, assessments and other administrative matters)—

(*a*) functions of the Inland Revenue under these provisions are exercisable by the Board or an officer of the Board—

(i) paragraph 28 (discovery assessment),

(ii) paragraph 29 (assessment to recover excessive repayment);

(*b*) functions of the Inland Revenue under these provisions are functions of the Board—

(i) paragraph 33 (relief in case of double assessment),

(ii) paragraph 34 (relief in case of mistake in return).

[(3A) The following functions of the Inland Revenue under Schedule 11A (claims not included in returns) are functions of the Board—

(*a*) functions under paragraph 2(1) (form of claims),

(*b*) functions relating to a claim made to the Board.][1]

(4) Nothing in this section affects any provision of this Part that expressly confers functions on the Board, an officer of the Board, a collector or a specific officer of the Board.

Amendments—[1] Sub-s (3A) inserted by FA 2004 s 299(1), (6) with effect from 22 July 2004.

114 Orders and regulations made by the Treasury or the Inland Revenue

(1) Except as otherwise provided, any power of the Treasury or the Inland Revenue to make an order or regulations under this Part, or under any other enactments relating to stamp duty land tax (including enactments passed after this Act), is exercisable by statutory instrument.

(2) Subsection (1) does not apply in relation to the power conferred by—

paragraph 8 of Schedule 5 to this Act (tax chargeable in respect of rent: power to prescribe temporal discount rate),

section 178(5) of the Finance Act 1989 (c 26) (power to prescribe rates of interest).

(3) Except as otherwise provided, a statutory instrument containing any order or regulations made by the Treasury or the Inland Revenue under this Part, or under any other enactments relating to stamp duty land tax (including enactments passed after this Act), shall be subject to annulment in pursuance of a resolution of the House of Commons.

(4) Subsection (3) does not apply to a statutory instrument made under the power conferred by—

section 61(3) (compliance with planning obligations: power to add to list of public authorities);

paragraph 1(3) of Schedule 9 (right to buy transactions: power to add to list of relevant public sector bodies);

paragraph 2(2) of Schedule 19 (commencement and transitional provisions: power to appoint implementation date).

[(5) The first set of regulations under section 58B (new zero-carbon homes) may not be made unless a draft has been laid before and approved by resolution of the House of Commons.][1]

[(6) An order or regulations under this Part—

(*a*) may make provision having effect generally or only in specified cases or circumstances,

(*b*) may make different provision for different cases or circumstances, and

(*c*) may include incidental, consequential or transitional provision or savings.][1]

Cross reference—See F(No 2)A 2005 s 48(6) (disclosure of information contained in land transaction returns: sub-s (3) above does not apply to a Treasury order made under F(No 2)A 2005 s 48(5)).

Amendments—[1] Sub-ss (5), (6) inserted by FA 2007 s 19(2) with effect from 19 July 2007.

Stamp Taxes

[115 General and Special Commissioners, appeals and other proceedings

Schedule 17 makes provision about the General and Special Commissioners, appeals and other proceedings before the Commissioners and related matters.][1]

Amendment—[1] Section 115 repealed by the Transfer of Tribunal Functions and Revenue and Customs Appeals Order, SI 2009/56 art 3, Sch 1 para 370 with effect from 1 April 2009.

Interpretation etc

116 Meaning of "residential property"

(1) In this Part "residential property" means—

(*a*) a building that is used or suitable for use as a dwelling, or is in the process of being constructed or adapted for such use, and

(*b*) land that is or forms part of the garden or grounds of a building within paragraph (*a*) (including any building or structure on such land), or

(*c*) an interest in or right over land that subsists for the benefit of a building within paragraph (*a*) or of land within paragraph (*b*);

and "non-residential property" means any property that is not residential property.

This is subject to the rule in subsection (7) in the case of a transaction involving six or more dwellings.

(2) For the purposes of subsection (1) a building used for any of the following purposes is used as a dwelling—

(*a*) residential accommodation for school pupils;

(*b*) residential accommodation for students, other than accommodation falling with subsection (3)(*b*);

(*c*) residential accommodation for members of the armed forces;

(*d*) an institution that is the sole or main residence of at least 90% of its residents and does not fall within any of paragraphs (*a*) to (*f*) of subsection (3).

(3) For the purposes of subsection (1) a building used for any of the following purposes is not used as a dwelling—

(*a*) a home or other institution providing residential accommodation for children;

(*b*) a hall of residence for students in further or higher education;

(*c*) a home or other institution providing residential accommodation with personal care for persons in need of personal care by reason of old age, disablement, past or present dependence on alcohol or drugs or past or present mental disorder;

(*d*) a hospital or hospice;

(*e*) a prison or similar establishment;

(*f*) a hotel or inn or similar establishment.

(4) Where a building is used for a purpose specified in subsection (3), no account shall be taken for the purposes of subsection (1)(*a*) of its suitability for any other use.

(5) Where a building that is not in use is suitable for use for at least one of the purposes specified in subsection (2) and at least one of those specified in subsection (3)—

(*a*) if there is one such use for which it is most suitable, or if the uses for which it is most suitable are all specified in the same sub-paragraph, no account shall be taken for the purposes of subsection (1)(*a*) of its suitability for any other use,

(*b*) otherwise, the building shall be treated for those purposes as suitable for use as a dwelling.

(6) In this section "building" includes part of a building.

(7) Where six or more separate dwellings are the subject of a single transaction involving the transfer of a major interest in, or the grant of a lease over, them, then, for the purposes of this Part as it applies in relation to that transaction, those dwellings are treated as not being residential property.

(8) The Treasury may by order—

(*a*) amend subsections (2) and (3) so as to change or clarify the cases where use of a building is, or is not to be, use of a building as a dwelling for the purposes of subsection (1);

(*b*) amend or repeal subsection (7) and the reference to that subsection in subsection (1).

Any such order may contain such incidental, supplementary, consequential or transitional provision as appears to the Treasury to be necessary or expedient.

HMRC Manuals—Stamp Duty Land Tax Manual, SDLTM20070 (definition of residential property; HMRC intelligent decision-making tool is available at www.hmrc.gov.uk; non-residential property defined by exclusion from residential property definition)

Statement of Practice SP 1/04—(Disadvantaged areas relief, Stamp Office approach to borderline cases).

117 Meaning of "major interest" in land

(1) References in this Part to a "major interest" in land shall be construed as follows.

(2) In relation to land in England or Wales, the references are to—

(*a*) an estate in fee simple absolute, or

(*b*) a term of years absolute,

whether subsisting at law or in equity.

(3) In relation to land in Scotland, the references are to—

(*a*) the interest of an owner of land, or

(*b*) the tenant's right over or interest in a property subject to a lease.

Until the appointed day for the purposes of the Abolition of Feudal Tenure etc (Scotland) Act 2000 (asp 5), the reference in paragraph (*a*) to the interest of the owner shall be read, in relation to feudal property, as a reference to the estate or interest of the proprietor of the *dominium utile*.

(4) In relation to land in Northern Ireland, the references are to—

(*a*) any freehold estate, or

(*b*) any leasehold estate,

whether subsisting at law or in equity.

118 Meaning of "market value"

For the purposes of this Part "market value" shall be determined as for the purposes of the Taxation of Chargeable Gains Act 1992 (c 12) (see sections 272 to 274 of that Act).

HMRC Manuals—Stamp Duty Land Tax Manual, SDLTM04140 (meaning of market value – consideration by transfer of asset or provision of services)

119 Meaning of "effective date" of a transaction

(1) Except as otherwise provided, the effective date of a land transaction for the purposes of this Part is—

[(*a*) the date of completion, or

(*b*) such alternative date as the Commissioners for Her Majesty's Revenue and Customs may prescribe by regulations.][3].

(2) Other provision as to the effective date of certain descriptions of land transaction is made by—

section 44(4) (contract and conveyance: contract substantially performed without having been completed), …[2]

[section 44A(3) (contract providing for conveyance to third party),][1]

[section 45A(8) (contract providing for conveyance to third party: effect of transfer of rights),][1]

section 46(3) (options and rights of pre-emption)

[paragraph 12A(2) of Schedule 17A (agreement for lease followed by substantial performance),][1]

[paragraph 12B(3) of that Schedule (assignment of agreement for lease occurring after agreement substantially performed), and][1]

[paragraph 19(3) of that Schedule (missives of let etc in Scotland followed by substantial performance).][1]

HMRC Manuals—Stamp Duty Land Tax Manual, SDLTM07750–08050 (substantial performance of contract)

Amendments—[1] Words inserted by FA 2004 s 296, Sch 39 para 8 with effect in accordance with FA 2004 Sch 39 para 13(1), (2).

[2] Word "and" repealed by FA 2004 s 326, Sch 42 Pt 4(2) with effect in accordance with FA 2004 Sch 39 para 13.

[3] In sub-s (1), words substituted for the words "the date of completion" by F(No 2)A 2005 s 47(3) with effect from 20 July 2005.

[120 Further provisions relating to leases

Schedule 17A contains further provisions relating to leases.][1]

Amendments—[1] Substituted by FA 2004 s 296, Sch 39 para 22(1) with effect for any transaction of which the effective date (within the meaning of FA 2003 Pt 4) is on or after 22 July 2004: FA 2004 Sch 39 para 26. These amendments were previously made by the Stamp Duty and Stamp Duty Land Tax (Variation of the Finance Act 2003) (No 2) Regulations, SI 2003/2816 regs 1, 2, Schedule para 8(1) with effect from 1 December 2003. Those regulations are revoked by FA 2004 Sch 39 para 14(2).

121 Minor definitions

In this Part—

"assignment", in Scotland, means assignation;

"completion", in Scotland, means—

(*a*) in relation to a lease, when it is executed by the parties (that is to say, by signing) or constituted by any means;

(*b*) in relation to any other transaction, the settlement of the transaction;

"employee" includes an office-holder and related expressions have a corresponding meaning;

["HMRC" means Her Majesty's Revenue and Customs;][1]

"jointly entitled" means—

(*a*) in England and Wales, beneficially entitled as joint tenants or tenants in common,

(*b*) in Scotland, entitled as joint owners or owners in common,

(*c*) in Northern Ireland, beneficially entitled as joint tenants, tenants in common or coparceners;

"land" includes—

(*a*) buildings and structures, and
(*b*) land covered by water;

"registered social landlord" means—
(*a*) in relation to England and Wales, a body registered as a social landlord in a register maintained under section 1(1) of the Housing Act 1996 (c 52);
(*b*) in relation to Scotland, a body registered in the register maintained under section 57 of the Housing (Scotland) Act 2001 (asp 10);
(*c*) in relation to Northern Ireland, a housing association registered in the register maintained under Article 14 of the Housing (Northern Ireland) Order 1992 (SI 1992/1725 (NI 15));

"standard security" has the meaning given by the Conveyancing and Feudal Reform (Scotland) Act 1970 (c 35);

"statutory provision" means any provision made by or under an Act of Parliament, an Act of the Scottish Parliament or any Northern Ireland legislation;

"surrender", in Scotland, means renunciation;

"tax", unless the context otherwise requires, means tax under this Part.

["tribunal" means the First-tier Tribunal or, where determined by or under Tribunal Procedure Rules, the Upper Tribunal.][1]

Amendments—[1] Definitions inserted by the Transfer of Tribunal Functions and Revenue and Customs Appeals Order, SI 2009/56 art 3, Sch 1 para 371 with effect from 1 April 2009.

122 Index of defined expressions

In this Part the expressions listed below are defined or otherwise explained by the provisions indicated—

acquisition relief	Schedule 7, paragraph 8(1)
assignment (in Scotland)	section 121
bare trust	Schedule 16, paragraph 1(2)
the Board (in relation to the Inland Revenue)	section 42(3)
chargeable consideration	section 50 and Schedule 4
chargeable interest	section 48(1)
chargeable transaction	section 49
charities relief	Schedule 8, paragraph 1(1)
closure notice	Schedule 10, paragraph 23(1) (in relation to a land transaction return); ...[5]
company	section 100 (except as otherwise expressly provided)
completion (in Scotland)	section 121
contingent (in relation to consideration)	section 51(3)
delivery (in relation to a land transaction return)	Schedule 10, paragraph 2(2)
discovery assessment	Schedule 10, paragraph 28(1)
effective date (in relation to a land transaction)	section 119
employee	section 121
exempt interest	section 48(2) to (5)
filing date (in relation to a land transaction return)	Schedule 10, paragraph 2(1)
implementation date	Schedule 19, paragraph 2(2)
the Inland Revenue	section 113
jointly entitled	section 121
land	section 121
land transaction	section 43(1)
land transaction return	section 76(1)
lease (and related expressions)	[Schedule 17A][1]
linked transactions	section 108
main subject-matter (in relation to a land transaction)	section 43(6)
major interest (in relation to land)	section 117
market value	section 118
notice of enquiry	Schedule 10, paragraph 12(1) (in relation to a land transaction return); ...[5]
notifiable (in relation to a land transaction)	section 77 [(see too sections 71A(7) and 72A(7) [and paragraph 30 of Schedule 15][5])][4]
partnership (and related expressions)	Schedule 15, paragraphs 1 to 4
purchaser	section 43(4)
rate of tax	section 55(7)

reconstruction relief	Schedule 7, paragraph 7(1)
registered social landlord	section 121
residential property	section 116
[Revenue certificate	section 79(3)(*a*)][2]
Revenue determination	Schedule 10, paragraph 25(1)
self-assessment	section 76(3)(*a*)
. . .[5]	. . .[5]
settlement	Schedule 16, paragraph 1(1)
standard security	section 121
statutory provision	section 121
subject-matter (in relation to a land transaction)	section 43(6)
substantial performance (in relation to a contract)	section 44(5) to (7)
surrender (in Scotland)	section 121
tax	section 121
[tribunal	section 121][6]
uncertain (in relation to consideration)	section 51(3)
unit holder	section 101(4)
unit trust scheme	section 101(4)
vendor	section 43(4)[(see too sections 45(5A) and 45A(9))][3]

Amendments—[1] In Column 2 of the entry for "lease and related expressions", words substituted for the words "section 120" by FA 2004 s 296, Sch 39 para 22(7) with effect for any transaction of which the effective date (within the meaning of FA 2003 Pt 4) is on or after 22 July 2004: FA 2004 Sch 39 para 26. This substitution was previously made by the Stamp Duty and Stamp Duty Land Tax (Variation of the Finance Act 2003) (No 2) Regulations, SI 2003/2816 regs 1, 2, Schedule para 8(8) with effect from 1 December 2003. Those regulations are revoked by FA 2004 Sch 39 para 14(2).

[2] Entry inserted by FA 2004 s 296, Sch 39 para 25(4) with effect for any transaction of which the effective date (within the meaning of FA 2003 Pt 4) is on or after 22 July 2004: FA 2004 Sch 39 para 26. This insertion was previously made by the Stamp Duty and Stamp Duty Land Tax (Variation of the Finance Act 2003) (No 2) Regulations, SI 2003/2816 regs 1, 2, Schedule para 11(4) with effect from 1 December 2003. Those regulations are revoked by FA 2004 Sch 39 para 14(2).

[3] Words inserted by FA 2004 s 296, Sch 39 para 5(1), (6) with effect for any transfer of rights occurring after 17 March 2004: FA 2004 Sch 39 para 13(2).

[4] Words inserted by FA 2005 s 94, Sch 8 para 6 with effect in any case where the effective date (within the meaning of Part 4 of FA 2003) of the first transaction (within the meaning of FA 2003 s 71A (so far as relating to that section) or s 72A (so far as relating to that section)) falls on or after 7 April 2005: FA 2005 Sch 8 para 7.

[5] Words in definitions of "closure notice" and "notice of enquiry", and whole of definition of "self-certificate", repealed, and words in definition of "notifiable (in relation to a land transaction)" inserted, by FA 2008 s 94, Sch 30 paras 1, 5 with effect in relation to transactions with an effective date on or after 12 March 2008.

[6] Entry inserted by the Transfer of Tribunal Functions and Revenue and Customs Appeals Order, SI 2009/56 art 3, Sch 1 para 372 with effect from 1 April 2009.

Final provisions

123 Consequential amendments

(1) Schedule 18 contains certain amendments consequential on the provisions of this Part.

(2) The Treasury may by regulations make such other amendments and repeals as appear to them appropriate in consequence of the provisions of this Part.

(3) The regulations may, in particular, make such provision as the Treasury think fit for reproducing in relation to stamp duty land tax the effect of enactments providing for exemption from stamp duty.

124 Commencement and transitional provisions

Schedule 19 makes provision for and in connection with the coming into force of the provisions of this Part.

PART 5
STAMP DUTY

125 Abolition of stamp duty except on instruments relating to stock or marketable securities

(1) Stamp duty is chargeable under Schedule 13 of the Finance Act 1999 (c 16) only on instruments relating to stock or marketable securities.

(2) Section 12 of the Finance Act 1895 (c 16) (collection of stamp duty in cases of property vested by Act or purchased under statutory powers) does not apply to property other than stock or marketable securities.

(3) This section shall be construed as one with the Stamp Act 1891 (c 39).

(4) Part 1 of Schedule 20 to this Act contains provisions supplementing this section and Part 2 of that Schedule provides for consequential amendments and repeals.

(5) This section and that Schedule have effect—

(*a*) in relation to an instrument effecting a land transaction [(or any duplicate or counterpart of such an instrument)][1], if the transaction—

(i) is an SDLT transaction within the meaning of Schedule 19 to this Act (stamp duty land tax: commencement and transitional provisions), or

(ii) would be such a transaction but for an exemption or relief from stamp duty land tax;

(*b*) in relation to an instrument effecting a transaction other than a land transaction [(or any duplicate or counterpart of such an instrument)][1], if the instrument is executed on or after the implementation date for the purposes of stamp duty land tax (see paragraph 2(2) of that Schedule).

For this purpose an instrument effecting both a land transaction and a transaction other than a land transaction [(or any duplicate or counterpart of such an instrument)][1] is treated as if it were two instruments to which paragraph (*a*) and paragraph (*b*) above respectively applied.

(6) Where in the case of an instrument effecting both a land transaction and a transaction other than a land transaction the result of applying subsection (5) is that stamp duty is chargeable on either or both of the deemed instruments, the enactments relating to stamp duty have effect as if—

(*a*) there were two instruments as mentioned in the closing words of that subsection,

(*b*) the consideration had been apportioned between them in a just and reasonable manner, and

(*c*) the amount found on that apportionment to be attributable to the chargeable instrument, or (as the case may be) to each of them, had been set forth distinctly in that instrument.

(7) In subsections (5) and (6) "land transaction" has the same meaning as in Part 4 of this Act.

(8) This section and Schedule 20 have effect subject to [paragraph 31][2] of Schedule 15 to this Act (continued application of stamp duty in relation to certain partnership transactions).

Cross references—See FA 2003 Sch 15 para 31(1) (nothing in this section affects the application of enactments relating to stamp duty in relation to an instrument by which a transfer of an interest in a partnership is effected).

Amendments—[1] Words in sub-s (5) inserted by FA 2004 s 296, Sch 39 para 23 with effect for any transaction of which the effective date (within the meaning of FA 2003 Pt 4) is on or 22 July 2004: FA 2004 Sch 39 para 26. These amendments were previously made by the Stamp Duty and Stamp Duty Land Tax (Variation of the Finance Act 2003) (No 2) Regulations, SI 2003/2816 regs 1, 2, Schedule para 9 with effect from 1 December 2003. Those regulations are revoked by FA 2004 Sch 39 para 14(2).

[2] In sub-s (8), words substituted for the words "paragraph 13(2) and (3)" by FA 2004 s 304, Sch 41 paras 2(*b*), 3 with effect for any partnership transaction of which the effective date (within the meaning of FA 2003 Pt 4) is after 22 July 2004. A "partnership transaction" means a transaction mentioned in FA 2003 Sch 15 para 9(1): FA 2004 Sch 41 para 3(2).

126 Circumstances in which group relief withdrawn

(1)–(5) (*amend* FA 2002 s 111(1), (3), *insert* sub-s (4A))

(6)–(8) (*amend* FA 2002 Sch 34 para 4)

(9) This section applies to instruments executed after 14th April 2003.

(10) But this section does not apply to an instrument giving effect to a contract made on or before 9th April 2003, unless—

(*a*) the instrument is made in consequence of the exercise after that date of any option, right of pre-emption or similar right, or

(*b*) the instrument transfers the property in question to, or vests it in, a person other than the purchaser under the contract because of an assignment (or, in Scotland, assignation) or further contract made after that date.

(11) This section shall be deemed to have come into force on 15th April 2003.

127 Circumstances in which relief for company acquisitions withdrawn

(1)–(5) (*amend* FA 2002 s 113(1), (3), *insert* sub-s (3A))

(6) (*amend* FA 2002 Sch 35 paras 3, 4)

(7) This section applies to instruments executed after 14th April 2003.

(8) But this section does not apply to an instrument giving effect to a contract made on or before 9th April 2003, unless—

(*a*) the instrument is made in consequence of the exercise after that date of any option, right of pre-emption or similar right, or

(*b*) the instrument transfers the property in question to, or vests it in, a person other than the purchaser under the contract because of an assignment (or, in Scotland, assignation) or further contract made after that date.

(9) This section shall be deemed to have come into force on 15th April 2003.

128 Exemption of certain leases granted by registered social landlords

(1) No stamp duty is chargeable under Part 2 of Schedule 13 to the Finance Act 1999 (c 16) on a lease of a dwelling granted by a registered social landlord to one or more individuals in accordance with arrangements to which this section applies if the lease is for an indefinite term or is terminable by notice of a month or less.

(2) "Registered social landlord" means—

(*a*) in relation to England and Wales, a body registered in the register maintained under section 1(1) of the Housing Act 1996 (c 52);

(*b*) in relation to Scotland, a body registered in the register maintained under section 57 of the Housing (Scotland) Act 2001 (asp 10);

(*c*) in relation to Northern Ireland, a housing association registered in the register maintained under Article 14 of the Housing (Northern Ireland) Order 1992 (SI 1992/1725 (NI 15)).

(3) This section applies to arrangements between a registered social landlord and a housing authority under which the landlord provides, for individuals nominated by the authority in pursuance of its statutory housing functions, temporary rented accommodation which the landlord itself has obtained on a short-term basis.

The reference above to accommodation obtained by the landlord "on a short-term basis" is to accommodation leased to the landlord for a term of five years or less.

(4) A "housing authority" means—

(*a*) in relation to England and Wales—

(i) a principal council within the meaning of the Local Government Act 1972 (c 70), or

(ii) the Common Council of the City of London;

(*b*) in relation to Scotland, a council constituted under section 2 of the Local Government etc (Scotland) Act 1994 (c 39);

(*c*) in relation to Northern Ireland—

(i) the Department for Social Development in Northern Ireland, or

(ii) the Northern Ireland Housing Executive.

(5) An instrument on which stamp duty is not chargeable by virtue only of this section shall not be taken to be duly stamped unless—

(*a*) it is stamped with the duty to which it would be liable but for this section, or

(*b*) it has, in accordance with section 12 of the Stamp Act 1891 (c 39), been stamped with a particular stamp denoting that it is not chargeable with any duty.

(6) This section shall be construed as one with the Stamp Act 1891.

(7) This section applies to instruments executed after the day on which this Act is passed.

129 Relief for certain leases granted before section 128 has effect

(1) This section applies to instruments that—

(*a*) are executed in the period beginning with 1 January 2000 and ending with the day on which this Act is passed, and

(*b*) are instruments to which section 128 (exemption of certain leases granted by registered social landlords) would have applied if that provision had been in force when the instrument was executed.

(2) If the instrument is not stamped until after the day on which this Act is passed, the law in force at the time of its execution shall be deemed for stamp duty purposes to be what it would have been if section 128 had been in force at that time.

(3) If the Commissioners are satisfied that—

(*a*) the instrument was stamped on or before the day on which this Act is passed,

(*b*) stamp duty was chargeable in respect of it, and

(*c*) had it been stamped after that day stamp duty would, by virtue of section 128, not have been chargeable,

they shall pay to such person as they consider appropriate an amount equal to the duty (and any interest or penalty) that would not have been payable if that section had been in force at the time the instrument was executed.

(4) Any such payment must be claimed before 1st January 2004.

(5) Entitlement to a payment is subject to compliance with such conditions as the Commissioners may determine with respect to the production of the instrument, to its being stamped so as to indicate that it has been produced under this section or to other matters.

(6) For the purposes of [section 44 of the Commissioners for Revenue and Customs Act 2005 (payment into Consolidated Funds)][1] any amount paid under this section is a repayment.

(7) This section shall be construed as one with the Stamp Act 1891.

(8) For the purposes of this section as it applies in relation to instruments executed before the coming into force of section 57 of the Housing (Scotland) Act 2001 (asp 10), the references in section 128 to a registered social landlord shall be read in relation to Scotland as references to—

(*a*) a housing association registered in the register maintained under section 3(1) of the Housing Associations Act 1985 (c 69) by Scottish Homes, or

(*b*) a body corporate whose objects corresponded to those of a housing association and which, pursuant to a contract with Scottish Homes, was registered in a register kept for the purpose by Scottish Homes.

Amendment—[1] Words in sub-s (6) substituted by Commissioners for Revenue and Customs Act 2005 s 50, Sch 4 paras 125, 126 with effect from 18 April 2005 by virtue of the Commissioners for Revenue and Customs Act (Commencement) Order, SI 2005/1126, art 2(2).

130 Registered social landlords: treatment of certain leases granted between 1st January 1990 and 27th March 2000

(1) This section applies to a lease in relation to which the following conditions are met—

(*a*) it is a lease of a dwelling to one or more individuals;
(*b*) it is for an indefinite term or is terminable by notice of a month or less;
(*c*) it was executed on or after 1st January 1990 and before 28th March 2000;
(*d*) at the time it was executed the rate or average rate of the rent (whether reserved as a yearly rent or not) was £5,000 a year or less; and
(*e*) the landlord's interest has at any time before 26th June 2003 been held by a registered social landlord.

(2) A lease to which this section applies (whether or not presented for stamping) shall be treated—

(*a*) for the purposes of section 14 of the Stamp Act 1891 (c 39) (production of instrument in evidence) as it applies in relation to proceedings begun after the day on which this Act is passed, and
(*b*) for the purposes of section 17 of that Act (enrolment etc of instrument) as it applies to any act done after that day,

as if it had been duly stamped in accordance with the law in force at the time when it was executed.

(3) If in the case of a lease to which this section applies the Commissioners are satisfied—

(*a*) that the instrument was stamped on or before the day on which this Act is passed, and
(*b*) that stamp duty was charged in respect of it,

they shall pay to such person as they consider appropriate an amount equal to the duty (and any interest or penalty) so charged.

(4) Any such payment must be claimed before 1st January 2004.

(5) Entitlement to a payment under subsection (3) is subject to compliance with such conditions as the Commissioners may determine with respect to the production of the instrument, to its being stamped so as to indicate that it has been produced under this section or to other matters.

(6) For the purposes of [section 44 of the Commissioners for Revenue and Customs Act 2005 (payment into Consolidated Funds)][1] any amount paid under subsection (3) above is a repayment.

(7) This section shall be construed as one with the Stamp Act 1891.

(8) The reference in subsection (1) above to the landlord's interest being held by a "registered social landlord" is to its being held by a body that—

(*a*) is registered in a register maintained under—

(i) Article 124 of the Housing (Northern Ireland) Order 1981 (SI 1981/156 (NI 3)),
(ii) section 3(1) of the Housing Associations Act 1985 (c 69),
(iii) Article 14 of the Housing (Northern Ireland) Order 1992 (SI 1992/1725 (NI 15)),
(iv) section 1(1) of the Housing Act 1996 (c 52), or
(v) section 57 of the Housing (Scotland) Act 2001 (asp 10), or

(*b*) is a body corporate whose objects correspond to those of a housing association and which, pursuant to a contract with Scottish Homes, is registered in a register kept for the purposes by Scottish Homes.

(9) Section 129 of this Act (relief for certain leases granted on or after 1st January 2000) does not apply to a lease to which this section applies.

Amendment—[1] Words in sub-s (6) substituted by Commissioners for Revenue and Customs Act 2005 s 50, Sch 4 paras 125, 127 with effect from 18 April 2005 by virtue of the Commissioners for Revenue and Customs Act (Commencement) Order, SI 2005/1126, art 2(2).

PART 9

MISCELLANEOUS AND SUPPLEMENTARY PROVISIONS

Provisions consequential on changes to company law

195 Companies acquiring their own shares

(1) This section applies for the purposes of the Taxes Acts and the Inheritance Tax Act 1984 (c 51) where a company acquires any of its own shares (whether by purchase, the issuing of bonus shares or otherwise).

(2) The acquisition of any of those shares by the company is not to be treated as the acquisition of an asset.

(3) The company is not, by virtue of the acquisition or holding of any of those shares or its being entered in the company's register of members in respect of any of them, to be treated as a member of itself.

(4) Subject to subsection (5)—

(*a*) the company's issued share capital is to be treated as if it had been reduced by the nominal value of the shares acquired,

(*b*) such of those shares as are not cancelled on acquisition are to be treated as if they had been so cancelled, and

(*c*) any subsequent cancellation by the company of any of those shares is to be disregarded (and, accordingly, is not the disposal of an asset and does not give rise to an allowable loss within the meaning of the Taxation of Chargeable Gains Act 1992 (c 12)).

(5) Where the shares are issued to the company as bonus shares, subsection (4)(*a*) and (*b*) does not apply and the shares are to be treated as if they had not been issued.

(6) Where, disregarding subsections (2) to (5)—

(*a*) a company holds any of its own shares, and

(*b*) the company issues bonus shares in respect of those shares or any class of those shares ("the existing shares"),

nothing in this section prevents the existing shares being the company's holding of shares for the purposes of the application of section 126 of the Taxation of Chargeable Gains Act 1992 (application of sections 127 to 131 of that Act (company reorganisations etc)).

(7) In subsection (6) the reference to the application of section 126 of the Taxation of Chargeable Gains Act 1992 does not include a reference to the application of that section in a modified form by virtue of any enactment relating to chargeable gains.

(8) Where a company disposes of any of its own shares to a person in circumstances where, but for subsections (2) to (5), it would be regarded as holding the shares immediately before the disposal—

(*a*) subsections (4)(*b*) and (*c*) and (5) cease to apply in relation to the shares disposed of ("the relevant shares"),

(*b*) the relevant shares are to be treated as having been issued as new shares to that person by the company at the time of the disposal (and not as having been disposed of by the company at that time),

(*c*) that person is to be treated as having subscribed for the relevant shares,

(*d*) an amount equal to the amount or value of the consideration (if any) payable for the disposal of the relevant shares is to be treated as the amount subscribed for those shares,

(*e*) if the amount or value of that consideration does not exceed the nominal value of those shares, the share capital of those shares is to be treated for the purposes of Part 6 of the Taxes Act 1988 as if it were an amount equal to the amount or value of that consideration, and

(*f*) if the amount or value of that consideration exceeds their nominal value, the relevant shares are to be treated as if they had been issued at a premium representing that excess.

(9) Where—

(*a*) a company purchases its own shares, and

(*b*) the price payable by a company for the shares is taken into account in computing the profits of the company which are chargeable to tax in accordance with the provisions of the Taxes Act 1988 applicable to Case I or II of Schedule D,

subsections (2) to (7) do not apply and subsection (8) does not apply in relation to any disposal by the company of any of the shares.

(10) Schedule 40 to this Act (which makes amendments relating to the acquisition and disposal by a company of its own shares) has effect.

(11) For the purposes of this section—

(*a*) a company issues "bonus shares" if it issues share capital as paid up otherwise than by the receipt of new consideration (within the meaning of section 254 of the Taxes Act 1988), and

(*b*) "the Taxes Acts" has the same meaning as in the Taxes Management Act 1970 (c 9),

and in this section references to a "company" are to a company with a share capital.

(12) The preceding provisions of this section and the provisions of Schedule 40 to this Act have effect in relation to any acquisition of shares by a company on or after such day as the Treasury may by order made by statutory instrument appoint.

Commentary—*Simon's Taxes* **D5.502; E3.211.**

Regulations—The Finance Act 2003, Section 195 and Schedule 40 (Appointed Day) Order, SI 2003/3077 (s 195 and Sch 40 have effect in relation to any acquisition of shares by a company on or after 1 December 2003).

Administrative matters

206 Admissibility of evidence not affected by offer of settlement etc

...

(3), (4) (*amend* FA 1999 Sch 18 para 3)

(5) The above amendments have effect in relation to statements made, or documents produced, after the passing of this Act.

Commentary—*Simon's Taxes* **A4.165.**

Supplementary

215 Interpretation

In this Act "the Taxes Act 1988" means the Income and Corporation Taxes Act 1988 (c 1).

216 Repeals

(1) The enactments mentioned in Schedule 43 to this Act (which include provisions that are spent or of no practical utility) are repealed to the extent specified.

(2) The repeals specified in that Schedule have effect subject to the commencement provisions and savings contained or referred to in the notes set out in that Schedule.

217 Short title

This Act may be cited as the Finance Act 2003.

SCHEDULES

SCHEDULE 3

STAMP DUTY LAND TAX: TRANSACTIONS EXEMPT FROM CHARGE

Section 49

No chargeable consideration

1 A land transaction is exempt from charge if there is no chargeable consideration for the transaction.

Cross references—FA 2003 Sch 15 para 25 (this paragraph does not apply to cases where FA 2003 Sch 15 paras 10, 14, 17, 18 apply).

Grant of certain leases by registered social landlords

2— (1) The grant of a lease of a dwelling is exempt from charge if the lease—

(*a*) is granted by a registered social landlord to one or more individuals in accordance with arrangements to which this paragraph applies, and

(*b*) is for an indefinite term or is terminable by notice of a month or less.

(2) This paragraph applies to arrangements between a registered social landlord and a housing authority under which the landlord provides, for individuals nominated by the authority in pursuance of its statutory housing functions, temporary rented accommodation which the landlord itself has obtained on a short-term basis.

The reference above to accommodation obtained by the landlord "on a short-term basis" is to accommodation leased to the landlord for a term of five years or less.

(3) A "housing authority" means—

(*a*) in relation to England and Wales—

(i) a principal council within the meaning of the Local Government Act 1972 (c 70), or

(ii) the Common Council of the City of London;

(*b*) in relation to Scotland, a council constituted under section 2 of the Local Government etc (Scotland) Act 1994 (c 39);

(*c*) in relation to Northern Ireland—

(i) the Department for Social Development in Northern Ireland, or

(ii) the Northern Ireland Housing Executive.

Transactions in connection with divorce etc

3 A transaction between one party to a marriage and the other is exempt from charge if it is effected—

(*a*) in pursuance of an order of a court made on granting in respect of the parties a decree of divorce, nullity of marriage or judicial separation;

(*b*) in pursuance of an order of a court made in connection with the dissolution or annulment of the marriage, or the parties' judicial separation, at any time after the granting of such a decree;

(*c*) in pursuance of—

(i) an order of a court made at any time under section 22A, 23A or 24A of the Matrimonial Causes Act 1973 (c 18), or

(ii) an incidental order of a court made under section 8(2) of the Family Law (Scotland) Act 1985 (c 37) by virtue of section 14(1) of that Act;

(*d*) at any time in pursuance of an agreement of the parties made in contemplation or otherwise in connection with the dissolution or annulment of the marriage, their judicial separation or the making of a separation order in respect of them.

[Assents and appropriations by personal representatives

3A— (1) The acquisition of property by a person in or towards satisfaction of his entitlement under or in relation to the will of a deceased person, or on the intestacy of a deceased person, is exempt from charge.

(2) Sub-paragraph (1) does not apply if the person acquiring the property gives any consideration for it, other than the assumption of secured debt.

(3) Where sub-paragraph (1) does not apply because of sub-paragraph (2), the chargeable consideration for the transaction is determined in accordance with paragraph 8A(1) of Schedule 4.

(4) In this paragraph—

"debt" means an obligation, whether certain or contingent, to pay a sum of money either immediately or at a future date, and

"secured debt" means debt that, immediately after the death of the deceased person, is secured on the property.][1]

Amendments—[1] Paragraph 3A inserted by FA 2004 s 300 and deemed always to have had effect.

[Transactions in connection with dissolution of civil partnership etc

3A A transaction between one party to a civil partnership and the other is exempt from charge if it is effected—

(*a*) in pursuance of an order of a court made on granting in respect of the parties an order or decree for the dissolution or annulment of the civil partnership or their judicial separation;

(*b*) in pursuance of an order of a court made in connection with the dissolution or annulment of the civil partnership, or the parties' judicial separation, at any time after the granting of such an order or decree for dissolution, annulment or judicial separation as mentioned in paragraph (*a*);

(*c*) in pursuance of—

(i) an order of a court made at any time under any provision of Schedule 5 to the Civil Partnership Act 2004 that corresponds to section 22A, 23A or 24A of the Matrimonial Causes Act 1973, or

(ii) an incidental order of a court made under any provision of the Civil Partnership Act 2004 that corresponds to section 8(2) of the Family Law (Scotland) Act 1985 by virtue of section 14(1) of that Act of 1985;

(*d*) at any time in pursuance of an agreement of the parties made in contemplation of or otherwise in connection with the dissolution or annulment of the civil partnership, their judicial separation or the making of a separation order in respect of them.][1]

Amendments—[1] Second paragraph 3A inserted by Tax and Civil Partnership Regulations, SI 2005/3229, reg 174, with effect from 5 December 2005 (reg 1(1)).

Variation of testamentary dispositions etc

4— (1) A transaction following a person's death that varies a disposition (whether effected by will, under the law relating to intestacy or otherwise) of property of which the deceased was competent to dispose is exempt from charge if the following conditions are met.

(2) The conditions are—

(*a*) that the transaction is carried out within the period of two years after a person's death, and

(*b*) that no consideration in money or money's worth other than the making of a variation of another such disposition is given for it.

[(2A) Where the condition in sub-paragraph (2)(*b*) is not met, the chargeable consideration for the transaction is determined in accordance with paragraph 8A(2) of Schedule 4.][1]

(3) This paragraph applies whether or not the administration of the estate is complete or the property has been distributed in accordance with the original dispositions.

Amendments—[1] Sub-para (2A) inserted by FA 2004 s 301(1), (7) and deemed always to have had effect.

Power to add further exemptions

5— (1) The Treasury may by regulations provide that any description of land transaction specified in the regulations is exempt from charge.

(2) The regulations may contain such supplementary, incidental and transitional provision as appears to the Treasury to be appropriate.

Regulations—The Stamp Duty Land Tax (Exemption of Certain Acquisitions of Residential Property) Regulations, SI 2008/2339 (exemption from stamp duty land tax for relevant acquisitions of land for chargeable consideration of not more than £175,000, with effect in relation to acquisitions made on or after 3 September 2008 but before 3 September 2009).

SCHEDULE 4

STAMP DUTY LAND TAX: CHARGEABLE CONSIDERATION

Section 50

HMRC Manuals—Stamp Duty Land Tax Manual, SDLTM03700 (general meaning of chargeable consideration for SDLT purposes)

Money or money's worth

1— (1) The chargeable consideration for a transaction is, except as otherwise expressly provided, any consideration in money or money's worth given for the subject-matter of the transaction, directly or indirectly, by the purchaser or a person connected with him.

(2) Section 839 of the Taxes Act 1988 (connected persons) applies for the purposes of sub-paragraph (1).

Value added tax

2 The chargeable consideration for a transaction shall be taken to include any value added tax chargeable in respect of the transaction, other than value added tax chargeable by virtue of an [option to tax any land under Part 1 of Schedule 10][1] to the Value Added Tax Act 1994 (c 23) made after the effective date of the transaction.

Amendments—[1] Words substituted by the Value Added Tax (Buildings and Land) Order, SI 2008/1146, art 6, Sch 1 paras 10, 11 with effect in relation to supplies made on or after 1 June 2008, subject to savings in Sch 2 of the Order.

Postponed consideration

3 The amount or value of the chargeable consideration for a transaction shall be determined without any discount for postponement of the right to receive it or any part of it.

Just and reasonable apportionment

4— (1) For the purposes of this Part consideration attributable—

(*a*) to two or more land transactions, or

(*b*) in part to a land transaction and in part to another matter, or

(*c*) in part to matters making it chargeable consideration and in part to other matters,

shall be apportioned on a just and reasonable basis.

(2) If the consideration is not so apportioned, this Part has effect as if it had been so apportioned.

(3) For the purposes of this paragraph any consideration given for what is in substance one bargain shall be treated as attributable to all the elements of the bargain, even though—

(*a*) separate consideration is, or purports to be, given for different elements of the bargain, or

(*b*) there are, or purport to be, separate transactions in respect of different elements of the bargain.

HMRC Manuals—Stamp Duty Land Tax Manual, SDLTM04010a (just and reasonable apportionment – example)

Exchanges

5— (1) This paragraph applies to determine the chargeable consideration where one or more land transactions are entered into by a person as purchaser (alone or jointly) wholly or partly in consideration of one or more other land transactions being entered into by him (alone or jointly) as vendor.

(2) In this paragraph—

(*a*) "relevant transaction" means any of those transactions, and

(*b*) "relevant acquisition" means a relevant transaction entered into as purchaser and "relevant disposal" means a relevant transaction entered into as vendor.

(3) The following rules apply if the subject-matter of any of the relevant transactions is a major interest in land—

(*a*) where a single relevant acquisition is made, the chargeable consideration for the acquisition is—

(i) the market value of the subject-matter of the acquisition, and

(ii) if the acquisition is the grant of a lease at a rent, that rent;

(*b*) where two or more relevant acquisitions are made, the chargeable consideration for each relevant acquisition is—

(i) the market value of the subject-matter of that acquisition, and

(ii) if the acquisition is the grant of a lease at a rent, that rent.

(4) The following rules apply if the subject-matter of none of the relevant transactions is a major interest in land—

(*a*) where a single relevant acquisition is made in consideration of one or more relevant disposals, the chargeable consideration for the acquisition is the amount or value of any chargeable consideration other than the disposal or disposals that is given for the acquisition;

(*b*) where two or more relevant acquisitions are made in consideration of one or more relevant disposals, the chargeable consideration for each relevant acquisition is the appropriate proportion of the amount or value of any chargeable consideration other than the disposal or disposals that is given for the acquisitions.

(5) For the purposes of sub-paragraph (4)(*b*) the appropriate proportion is—

$$\frac{MV}{TMV}$$

where—

MV is the market value of the subject-matter of the acquisition for which the chargeable consideration is being determined, and

TMV is the total market value of the subject-matter of all the relevant acquisitions.

(6) This paragraph has effect subject to—

paragraph 6 of this Schedule (partition etc: disregard of existing interest) …[1]

…[2]

[(7) This paragraph does not apply in a case to which paragraph 17 applies.][2]

HMRC Manuals—Stamp Duty Land Tax Manual, SDLTM04020a (exchanges and chargeable consideration – examples)
Cross references—FA 2003 Sch 15 para 16(1), (2) (application of this paragraph where an interest in a partnership is acquired in consideration of entering into a land transaction with an existing partner).
Amendments—[1] Words ", and section 58 (relief for certain exchanges of residential property)" repealed by FA 2004 s 326, Sch 42 Pt 4(2) with effect in accordance with FA 2004 Sch 39 para 26. This repeal was previously made by the Stamp Duty and Stamp Duty Land Tax (Variation of the Finance Act 2003) (No 2) Regulations, SI 2003/2816 regs 1, 2, Schedule para 3(5) with effect from 1 December 2003. Those regulations have been revoked by FA 2004 Sch 39 para 14(2).
[2] Words in sub-para (6) repealed, and sub-para (7) inserted, by the SDLT (Amendment of Part 4 of the Finance Act 2003) Regulations, SI 2004/1069 regs 2, 4(1), (2) with effect from 7 April 2004.

Partition etc: disregard of existing interest

6 In the case of a land transaction giving effect to a partition or division of a chargeable interest to which persons are jointly entitled, the share of the interest held by the purchaser immediately before the partition or division does not count as chargeable consideration.

HMRC Manuals—Stamp Duty Land Tax Manual, SDLTM04030a (land partitioned – example)
Cross references—FA 2003 Sch 15 para 16(3) (disapplication of this paragraph where FA 2003 Sch 15 para 16 applies)

Valuation of non-monetary consideration

7 Except as otherwise expressly provided, the value of any chargeable consideration for a land transaction, other than—

(*a*) money (whether in sterling or another currency), or

(*b*) debt as defined for the purposes of paragraph 8 (debt as consideration),

shall be taken to be its market value at the effective date of the transaction.

Debt as consideration

8— (1) Where the chargeable consideration for a land transaction consists in whole or in part of—

(*a*) the satisfaction or release of debt due to the purchaser or owed by the vendor, or

(*b*) the assumption of existing debt by the purchaser,

the amount of debt satisfied, released or assumed shall be taken to be the whole or, as the case may be, part of the chargeable consideration for the transaction.

[(1A) Where—

(*a*) debt is secured on the subject-matter of a land transaction immediately before and immediately after the transaction, and

(*b*) the rights or liabilities in relation to that debt of any party to the transaction are changed as a result of or in connection with the transaction,

then for the purposes of this paragraph there is an assumption of that debt by the purchaser, and that assumption of debt constitutes chargeable consideration for the transaction.][1]

[(1B) Where in a case in which sub-paragraph (1)(*b*) applies—

(*a*) the debt assumed is or includes debt secured on the property forming the subject-matter of the transaction, and

(*b*) immediately before the transaction there were two or more persons each holding an undivided share of that property, or there are two or more such persons immediately afterwards,

the amount of secured debt assumed shall be determined as if the amount of that debt owed by each of those persons at a given time were the proportion of it corresponding to his undivided share of the property at that time.][1]

[(1C) For the purposes of sub-paragraph (1B), in England and Wales and Northern Ireland each joint tenant of property is treated as holding an equal undivided share of it.][1]

Stamp Taxes

(2) If the effect of [this paragraph][1] would be that the amount of the chargeable consideration for the transaction exceeded the market value of the subject-matter of the transaction, the amount of the chargeable consideration is treated as limited to that value.

(3) In this paragraph—

(*a*) "debt" means an obligation, whether certain or contingent, to pay a sum of money either immediately or at a future date,

(*b*) "existing debt", in relation to a transaction, means debt created or arising before the effective date of, and otherwise than in connection with, the transaction, and

(*c*) references to the amount of a debt are to the principal amount payable or, as the case may be, the total of the principal amounts payable, together with the amount of any interest that has accrued due on or before the effective date of the transaction.

HMRC Manuals—Stamp Duty Land Tax Manual, SDLTM04040a (assumption of debt – example).
Cross references—Pension Protection Fund (Tax) Regulations, SI 2006/575 reg 43(1) (Pension Protection Fund: circumstances in which this paragraph does not apply).
Amendments—[1] Sub-paras (1A)–(1C) inserted, and in sub-para (2), words substituted for the words "sub-paragraph (1)" by FA 2004 s 301(2)–(4), (6) with effect for any transaction of which the effective date (within the meaning of FA 2003 Pt 4) is on or after 22 July 2004.

[Cases where conditions for exemption not fully met

8A— (1) Where a land transaction would be exempt from charge under paragraph 3A of Schedule 3 (assents and appropriations by personal representatives) but for sub-paragraph (2) of that paragraph (cases where person acquiring property gives consideration for it), the chargeable consideration for the transaction does not include the amount of any secured debt assumed.

"Secured debt" has the same meaning as in that paragraph.

(2) Where a land transaction would be exempt from charge under paragraph 4 of Schedule 3 (variation of testamentary dispositions etc) but for a failure to meet the condition in sub-paragraph (2)(*b*) of that paragraph (no consideration other than variation of another disposition), the chargeable consideration for the transaction does not include the making of any such variation as is mentioned in that sub-paragraph.][1]

Amendments—[1] This paragraph inserted by FA 2004 s 301(2), (5), (7) and deemed always to have had effect.

Conversion of amounts in foreign currency

9— (1) References in this Part to the amount or value of the consideration for a transaction are to its amount or value in sterling.

(2) For the purposes of this Part the sterling equivalent of an amount expressed in another currency shall be ascertained by reference to the London closing exchange rate on the effective date of the transaction (unless the parties have used a different rate for the purposes of the transaction).

Carrying out of works

10— (1) Where the whole or part of the consideration for a land transaction consists of the carrying out of works of construction, improvement or repair of a building or other works to enhance the value of land, then—

(*a*) to the extent that the conditions specified in sub-paragraph (2) are met, the value of the works does not count as chargeable consideration, and

(*b*) to the extent that those conditions are not met, the value of the works shall be taken into account as chargeable consideration.

(2) The conditions referred to in sub-paragraph (1) are—

(*a*) that the works are carried out after the effective date of the transaction,

(*b*) that the works are carried out on land acquired or to be acquired under the transaction or on other land held by the purchaser or a person connected with him, and

(*c*) that it is not a condition of the transaction that the works are carried out by the vendor or a person connected with him.

[(2A) [Where by virtue of—

(*a*) subsection (8) of section 44 (contract and conveyance),

(*b*) paragraph 12A of Schedule 17A (agreement for lease), or

(*c*) paragraph 19(3) to (6) of Schedule 17A (missives of let etc in Scotland),

there are two notifiable transactions (the first being the contract or agreement and the second being the transaction effected on completion or, as the case may be, the grant or execution of the lease),][3] the condition in sub-paragraph (2)(*a*) is treated as met in relation to the second transaction if it is met in relation to the first.][2]

(3) In this paragraph—

(*a*) references to the acquisition of land are to the acquisition of a major interest in it;

(*b*) the value of the works shall be taken to be the amount that would have to be paid in the open market for the carrying out of the works in question.

(4) Section 839 of the Taxes Act 1988 (connected persons) has effect for the purposes of this paragraph.

[(5) This paragraph is subject to paragraph 17 (arrangements involving public or educational bodies).][1]

HMRC Manuals—Stamp Duty Land Tax Manual, SDLTM04060a (construction works – example)

Amendments—[1] Sub-para (5) inserted by the SDLT (Amendment of Schedule 4 to the Finance Act 2003) Regulations, SI 2003/3293 reg 2(1), (3) with effect from 19 December 2003.

[2] Sub-para (2A) inserted by FA 2004 s 296, Sch 39 para 9(1), (2) with effect for any transaction of which the effective date is after 17 March 2004: FA 2004 Sch 39 para 13(3).

[3] Words in sub-para (2A) substituted for the words "Where subsection (8) of section 44 (contract and conveyance) applies, so that there are two notifiable transactions (the first being the contract and the second being the transaction effected on completion)," by FA 2004 s 297(1), (8), (9) with effect for any transaction of which the effective date is on or after 22 July 2004.

Provision of services

11[— (1)][1] Where the whole or part of the consideration for a land transaction consists of the provision of services (other than the carrying out of works to which paragraph 10 applies), the value of that consideration shall be taken to be the amount that would have to be paid in the open market to obtain those services.

[(2) This paragraph is subject to paragraph 17 (arrangements involving public or educational bodies).][1]

Amendments—[1] Sub-para (1) numbered as such, and sub-para (2) inserted, by the SDLT (Amendment of Schedule 4 to the Finance Act 2003) Regulations, SI 2003/3293 reg 2(1), (4) with effect from 19 December 2003.

Land transaction entered into by reason of employment

12— (1) Where a land transaction is entered into by reason of the purchaser's employment, or that of a person connected with him, then—

(*a*) if the transaction gives rise to a charge to tax under Chapter 5 of Part 3 of the Income Tax (Earnings and Pensions) Act 2003 (c 1) (taxable benefits: living accommodation) and—

(i) no rent is payable by the purchaser, or

(ii) the rent payable by the purchaser is less than the cash equivalent of the benefit calculated under section 105 or 106 of that Act,

there shall be taken to be payable by the purchaser as rent an amount equal to the cash equivalent chargeable under those sections;

(*b*) if the transaction would give rise to a charge under that Chapter but for section 99 of that Act (accommodation provided for performance of duties), the consideration for the transaction is the actual consideration (if any);

(*c*) if neither paragraph (*a*) nor paragraph (*b*) applies, the consideration for the transaction shall be taken to be not less than the market value of the subject-matter of the transaction as at the effective date of the transaction.

(2) Section 839 of the Taxes Act 1988 (connected persons) has effect for the purposes of this paragraph.

13–15

Amendment—Repealed by FA 2004 s 326, Sch 42 Pt 4(2) with effect in accordance with FA 2004 Sch 39 para 26. This repeal was previously made by the Stamp Duty and Stamp Duty Land Tax (Variation of the Finance Act 2003) (No 2) Regulations, SI 2003/2816 regs 1, 2, Schedule para 8(11) with effect from 1 December 2003. Those regulations have been revoked by FA 2004 Sch 39 para 14(2).

Indemnity given by purchaser

16 Where the purchaser agrees to indemnify the vendor in respect of liability to a third party arising from breach of an obligation owed by the vendor in relation to the land that is the subject of the transaction, neither the agreement nor any payment made in pursuance of it counts as chargeable consideration.

[Purchaser bearing inheritance tax liability

16A Where—

(*a*) there is a land transaction that is—

(i) a transfer of value within section 3 of the Inheritance Tax Act 1984 (transfers of value), or

(ii) a disposition, effected by will or under the law of intestacy, of a chargeable interest comprised in the estate of a person immediately before his death,

and

(*b*) the purchaser is or becomes liable to pay, agrees to pay or does in fact pay any inheritance tax due in respect of the transfer or disposition,

his liability, agreement or payment does not count as chargeable consideration for the transaction.][1]

Amendments—[1] Paragraphs 16A–16C inserted by the SDLT (Amendment to the Finance Act 2003) Regulations, SI 2006/875 regs 2, 3. SI 2006/875 came into force on 12 April 2006, and the amendments have effect in relation to land transactions with an effective date on or after that date: SI 2006/875 reg 1.

[Purchaser bearing capital gains tax liability

16B— (1) Where—

(*a*) there is a land transaction under which the chargeable interest in question—

(i) is acquired otherwise than by a bargain made at arm's length, or

(ii) is treated by section 18 of the Taxation of Chargeable Gains Act 1992 (connected persons) as so acquired,

and

(*b*) the purchaser is or becomes liable to pay, or does in fact pay, any capital gains tax due in respect of the corresponding disposal of the chargeable interest,

his liability or payment does not count as chargeable consideration for the transaction.

(2) Sub-paragraph (1) does not apply if there is chargeable consideration for the transaction (disregarding the liability or payment referred to in sub-paragraph (1)(*b*)).][1]

Amendments—[1] Paragraphs 16A–16C inserted by the SDLT (Amendment to the Finance Act 2003) Regulations, SI 2006/875 regs 2, 3. SI 2006/875 came into force on 12 April 2006, and the amendments have effect in relation to land transactions with an effective date on or after that date: SI 2006/875 reg 1.

[Costs of enfranchisement

16C Costs borne by the purchaser under section 9(4) of the Leasehold Reform Act 1967 or section 33 of the Leasehold Reform, Housing and Urban Development Act 1993 (costs of enfranchisement) do not count as chargeable consideration.][1]

Amendments—[1] Paragraphs 16A–16C inserted by the SDLT (Amendment to the Finance Act 2003) Regulations, SI 2006/875 regs 2, 3. SI 2006/875 came into force on 12 April 2006, and the amendments have effect in relation to land transactions with an effective date on or after that date: SI 2006/875 reg 1.

[Arrangements involving public or educational bodies

17— (1) This paragraph applies in any case where arrangements are entered into under which—

[(*a*) there is a transfer, or the grant or assignment of a lease, of land by a qualifying body ("A") to a non-qualifying body ("B") ("the main transfer"),][2]

[(*b*) in consideration (whether in whole or in part) of the main transfer there is a grant by B to A of a lease or under-lease of the whole, or substantially the whole, of that land ("the leaseback"),][3]

(*c*) B undertakes to carry out works or provide services to A, and

(*d*) some or all of the consideration given by A to B for the carrying out of those works or the provision of those services is consideration in money,

[whether or not there is also a transfer, or the grant or assignment of a lease, of any other land by A to B (a "transfer of surplus land").][2]

(2) The following are qualifying bodies—

(*a*) public bodies within section 66,

(*b*) institutions within the further education sector or the higher education sector within the meaning of 91 of the Further and Higher Education Act 1992,

(*c*) further education corporations within the meaning of section 17 of that Act,

(*d*) higher education corporations within the meaning section 90 of that Act,

(*e*) persons who undertake to establish and maintain, and carry on, or provide for the carrying on, of an Academy within the meaning of section 482 of the Education Act 1996, and

(*f*) in Scotland, institutions funded by the Scottish Further Education Funding Council or the Scottish Higher Education Funding Council.

[(3) The following shall not count as chargeable consideration for the main transfer or any transfer of surplus land—

(*a*) the lease-back;

(*b*) the carrying out of building works by B for A; or

(*c*) the provision of services by B to A.][2]

[(4) The chargeable consideration for the lease back does not include—

(*a*) the main transfer;

(*b*) any transfer of surplus land; or

(*c*) the consideration in money paid by A to B for the building works or other services referred to in sub-paragraph (3).][2]

[(4A) Sub-paragraphs (3) and (4) shall be disregarded for the purposes of determining whether the land transaction in question is notifiable.][4]

(5) This paragraph applies to Scotland as if—

(*a*) references to A transferring land to B were references to A transferring the interest of an owner of land to B, and

[(*b*) references in sub-paragraph (1) to assignment were references to assignation.][2]

Until the appointed day for the purposes of the Abolition of Feudal Tenure etc (Scotland) Act 2000 (asp 5), the reference in paragraph (*a*) to the interest of the owner shall be read, in relation to feudal property, as a reference to the estate or interest of the proprietor of the *dominium utile*.

(6) In this paragraph "under-lease" includes a sub-lease.][1]

Amendments—[1] This paragraph inserted by the SDLT (Amendment of Schedule 4 to the Finance Act 2003) Regulations, SI 2003/3293 reg 2(1), (5) with effect from 19 December 2003.

[2] Sub-para (1)(*a*), (*b*) and words at end of sub-para (1) substituted, and sub-paras (3), (4), (5)(*b*) substituted, by the SDLT (Amendment of Part 4 of the Finance Act 2003) Regulations, SI 2004/1069 regs 2, 4 with effect from 7 April 2004.

[3] Sub-para (1)(*b*) substituted by the SDLT (Amendment of Part 4 of the Finance Act 2003) (No 2) Regulations, SI 2004/1206 with effect from 27 April 2004.

[4] Sub-para (4A) inserted by FA 2004 s 296, Sch 39 para 9(1), (3) with effect for any transaction of which the effective date is after 17 March 2004: FA 2004 Sch 39 para 13(3).

SCHEDULE 5

STAMP DUTY LAND TAX: AMOUNT OF TAX CHARGEABLE: RENT

Section 56

Introduction

1 This Schedule provides for calculating the tax chargeable—

(*a*) in respect of a chargeable transaction for which the chargeable consideration consists of or includes rent, or

(*b*) where such a transaction is to be taken into account as a linked transaction.

[Amounts payable in respect of periods before grant of lease

1A For the purposes of this Part "rent" does not include any chargeable consideration for the grant of a lease that is payable in respect of a period before the grant of the lease.][1]

Amendment—[1] This paragraph inserted by FA 2004 s 296, Sch 39 para 10 with effect for any transaction of which the effective date is after 17 March 2004: FA 2004 Sch 39 para 13(3).

Calculation of tax chargeable in respect of rent

2— (1) Tax is chargeable under this Schedule in respect of so much of the chargeable consideration as consists of rent.

[(2) The tax chargeable is the total of the amounts produced by taking the relevant percentage of so much of the relevant rental value as falls within each rate band.][1]

[(3) The relevant percentages and rate bands are determined by reference to whether the relevant land—

(*a*) consists entirely of residential property (in which case Table A below applies), or

(*b*) consists of or includes land that is not residential property (in which case Table B below applies).

TABLE A: RESIDENTIAL

Rate bands	*Percentage*
£0 to [£125,000][2]	0%
Over [£125,000][2]	1%

TABLE B: NON-RESIDENTIAL OR MIXED

Rate bands	*Percentage*
£0 to £150,000	0%
Over £150,000	1%][1]

[(4) For the purposes of sub-paragraphs (2) and (3)—

(*a*) the relevant rental value is the net present value of the rent payable over the term of the lease, and

(*b*) the relevant land is the land that is the subject of the lease.][1]

[(5) If the lease in question is one of a number of linked transactions for which the chargeable consideration consists of or includes rent, the above provisions are modified.][1]

[(6) In that case the tax chargeable is determined as follows.

First, calculate the amount of the tax that would be chargeable if the linked transactions were a single transaction, so that—

(*a*) the relevant rental value is the total of the net present values of the rent payable over the terms of all the leases, and

(*b*) the relevant land is all land that is the subject of any of those leases.

Then, multiply that amount by the fraction:

$$\frac{NPV}{TNPV}$$

where—

NPV is the net present value of the rent payable over the term of the lease in question, and
TNPV is the total of the net present values of the rent payable over the terms of the all the leases.][1]

Note—In sub-para (3) in Table A "£175,000" substituted for "£125,000" (in both places) in relation to transactions with an effective date on or after 22 April 2009 but before 1 January 2010; FA 2009 s 10(1)(*b*).

Modifications—FA 2003 Sch 15 para 11 (modification of this paragraph where there is a transfer of a chargeable interest to a partnership, and the chargeable consideration includes rent).

FA 2003 Sch 15 para 19 (modification of this paragraph where there is a transfer of a chargeable interest from a partnership, and the chargeable consideration includes rent).

Regulations—The Stamp Duty Land Tax (Exemption of Certain Acquisitions of Residential Property) Regulations, SI 2008/2339 (exemption from stamp duty land tax for relevant acquisitions of land for chargeable consideration of not more than £175,000, with effect in relation to acquisitions made on or after 3 September 2008 but before 3 September 2009).

Amendment—[1] Sub-paras (2)–(6) substituted for sub-paras (2)–(5) by the Stamp Duty Land Tax (Amendment of Schedule 5 to the Finance Act 2003) Regulations, SI 2003/2914 reg 2, Schedule para 1 with effect from 1 December 2003.

[2] "£125,000" substituted for "£120,000" by FA 2006 s 162(2), with effect in relation to any transaction of which the effective date (within the meaning of Part 4 of FA 2003) is after 22 March 2006. The figure of "£175,000" is substituted for "£125,000" (in both places) in Table A in relation to transactions with an effective date on or after 22 April 2009 but before 1 January 2010: FA 2009 s 10(1)(*b*).

Net present value of rent payable over term of lease

3 The net present value (v) of the rent payable over the term of a lease is calculated by applying the formula:

$$v = \sum_{i=1}^{n} \frac{r_i}{(1+T)^i}$$

where—

r_i is the rent payable …[1] [in respect of year i][2],
i is the first, second, third, etc year of the term,
n is the term of the lease …[1], and
T is the temporal discount rate (see paragraph 8).

Amendments—[1] Words "(see paragraphs 4 and 5)" and "(see paragraphs 6 and 7)" repealed by FA 2004 s 326, Sch 42 Pt 4(2) with effect in accordance with FA 2004 Sch 39 para 26. This repeal was previously made by the Stamp Duty and Stamp Duty Land Tax (Variation of the Finance Act 2003) (No 2) Regulations, SI 2003/2816 regs 1, 2, Schedule para 8(9) with effect from 1 December 2003. Those regulations have been revoked by FA 2004 Sch 39 para 14(2).

[2] Words substituted for the words "in year i" by FA 2006 s 164(2) with effect in relation to any lease granted or treated as granted on or after 19 July 2006.

4–7

Amendment—Repealed by FA 2004 s 326, Sch 42 Pt 4(2) with effect in accordance with FA 2004 Sch 39 para 26. This repeal was previously made by the Stamp Duty and Stamp Duty Land Tax (Variation of the Finance Act 2003) (No 2) Regulations, SI 2003/2816 regs 1, 2, Schedule para 8(11) with effect from 1 December 2003. Those regulations have been revoked by FA 2004 Sch 39 para 14(2).

Temporal discount rate

8— (1) For the purposes of this Schedule the "temporal discount rate" is 3.5% or such other rate as may be specified by regulations made by the Treasury.

(2) Regulations under this paragraph may make any such provision as is mentioned in subsection (3)(*b*) to (*f*) of section 178 of the Finance Act 1989 (c 26) (power of Treasury to set rates of interest).

(3) Subsection (5) of that section (power of Inland Revenue to specify rate by order in certain circumstances) applies in relation to regulations under this paragraph as it applies in relation to regulations under that section.

Tax chargeable in respect of consideration other than rent[: general][1]

9— (1) Where in the case of a transaction to which this Schedule applies there is chargeable consideration other than rent, the provisions of this Part apply in relation to that consideration as in relation to other chargeable consideration [(but see paragraph 9A)][1].

(2)–(3) …[1]

(4) Tax chargeable under this Schedule is in addition to any tax chargeable under section 55 in respect of consideration other than rent.

(5) Where a transaction to which this Schedule applies falls to be taken into account for the purposes of that section as a linked transaction, no account shall be taken of rent in determining the relevant consideration.

Amendment—[1] Words in sub-para (1) inserted, and whole of sub-paras (2)–(3), repealed, and word in heading inserted, by FA 2008 s 95(1), (2) with effect in relation to transactions with an effective date on or after 12 March 2008.

[Tax chargeable in respect of consideration other than rent: 0% band

9A— (1) This paragraph applies in the case of a transaction to which this Schedule applies where there is chargeable consideration other than rent.

(2) If—

(*a*) the relevant land consists entirely of land that is non-residential property, and

(*b*) the relevant rent is at least £1,000,

the 0% band in Table B in section 55(2) does not apply in relation to the consideration other than rent and any case that would have fallen within that band is treated as falling within the 1% band.

(3) Sub-paragraphs (4) and (5) apply if—

(*a*) the relevant land is partly residential property and partly non-residential property, and

(*b*) the relevant rent attributable, on a just and reasonable apportionment, to the land that is non-residential property is at least £1,000.

(4) For the purpose of determining the amount of tax chargeable under section 55 in relation to the consideration other than rent, the transaction (or, where it is one of a number of linked transactions, that set of transactions) is treated as if it were two separate transactions (or sets of linked transactions), namely—

(*a*) one whose subject-matter consists of all of the interests in land that is residential property, and

(*b*) one whose subject-matter consists of all of the interests in land that is non-residential property.

(5) For that purpose, the chargeable consideration attributable to each of those separate transactions (or sets of linked transactions) is the chargeable consideration so attributable on a just and reasonable apportionment.

(6) In this paragraph "the relevant rent" means—

(*a*) the annual rent in relation to the transaction in question, or

(*b*) if that transaction is one of a number of linked transactions for which the chargeable consideration consists of or includes rent, the total of the annual rents in relation to all of those transactions.

(7) In sub-paragraph (6) the "annual rent" means the average annual rent over the term of the lease or, if—

(*a*) different amounts of rent are payable for different parts of the term, and

(*b*) those amounts (or any of them) are ascertainable at the effective date of the transaction,

the average annual rent over the period for which the highest ascertainable rent is payable.

(8) In this paragraph "relevant land" has the meaning given in section 55(3) and (4).][1]

Amendments—[1] Paragraph 9A inserted by FA 2008 s 95(1), (3) with effect in relation to transactions with an effective date on or after 12 March 2008.

10, 11

Amendment—Repealed by FA 2004 s 326, Sch 42 Pt 4(2) with effect in accordance with FA 2004 Sch 39 para 26. This repeal was previously made by the Stamp Duty and Stamp Duty Land Tax (Variation of the Finance Act 2003) (No 2) Regulations, SI 2003/2816 regs 1, 2, Schedule para 8(11) with effect from 1 December 2003. Those regulations have been revoked by FA 2004 Sch 39 para 14(2).

SCHEDULE 6

STAMP DUTY LAND TAX: DISADVANTAGED AREAS RELIEF

Section 57

HMRC Manuals—Stamp Duty Land Tax Manual SDLTM20050–20100 (general explanation of disadvantaged relief).
Statement of Practice SP 1/04—(Disadvantaged areas relief, Stamp Office approach to borderline cases).
Modifications—FA 2003 Sch 15 para 26 (modification of this Schedule in its application to the transfer of an interest in a partnership that is a chargeable transaction by virtue of FA 2003 Sch 15 para 14 or 17).

PART 1

DISADVANTAGED AREAS

Meaning of "disadvantaged area"

1— (1) For the purposes of this Schedule a "disadvantaged area" means an area designated as a disadvantaged area by regulations made by the Treasury.

(2) The regulations may—

(*a*) designate specified areas as disadvantaged areas, or

(*b*) provide for areas of a description specified in the regulations to be designated as disadvantaged areas.

(3) If the regulations so provide, the designation of an area as a disadvantaged area shall have effect for such period as may be specified by or determined in accordance with the regulations.

(4) The regulations may—

Stamp Taxes

(*a*) make different provision for different cases, and

(*b*) contain such incidental, supplementary, consequential or transitional provision as appears to the Treasury to be necessary or expedient.

Continuation of regulations made for purposes of stamp duty

2 Any regulations made by the Treasury—

(*a*) designating areas as disadvantaged areas for the purposes of section 92 of the Finance Act 2001 (c 9) (stamp duty exemption for land in disadvantaged areas), and

(*b*) in force immediately before the implementation date,

have effect for the purposes of this Schedule as if made under paragraph 1 above and may be varied or revoked accordingly.

PART 2

LAND WHOLLY SITUATED IN A DISADVANTAGED AREA

Introduction

3 This Part of this Schedule applies to a land transaction if—

[(*a*)][1] the subject matter of the transaction is a chargeable interest in relation to land that is wholly situated in a disadvantaged area[, and

(*b*) the land is wholly or partly residential property][1].

Modifications—FA 2003 Sch 15 para 26 (modification of this paragraph in its application to the transfer of an interest in a partnership that is a chargeable transaction by virtue of FA 2003 Sch 15 para 14 or 17).

Amendment—[1] Words inserted by FA 2005 s 96, Sch 9 paras 1(2), 4 with effect, subject to FA 2005 Sch 9 para 4(2), for any transaction of which the effective date (as defined by FA 2005 Sch 9 para 4(4)) is after 16 March 2005.

Land all non-residential

4 ...[1]

Amendment—[1] Paragraph repealed by FA 2005 ss 96, 104, Sch 9 paras 1(3), 4 and Sch 11 Pt 3(2) with effect, subject to FA 2005 Sch 9 para 4(2), for any transaction of which the effective date (as defined by FA 2005 Sch 9 para 4(4)) is after 16 March 2005.

Land all residential

5— (1) This paragraph applies where all the land is residential property.

(2) If—

(*a*) the consideration for the transaction does not include rent and the relevant consideration does not exceed £150,000, or

(*b*) the consideration for the transaction consists only of rent and the relevant rental value does not exceed £150,000,

the transaction is exempt from charge.

(3) If the consideration for the transaction includes rent and the relevant rental value does not exceed £150,000, the rent does not count as chargeable consideration.

(4) If the consideration for the transaction includes consideration other than rent, then—

(*a*) if—

(i) ...[1]

(ii) the relevant consideration does not exceed £150,000,

the consideration other than rent does not count as chargeable consideration;

(*b*) ...[1]

Modifications—FA 2003 Sch 15 para 26 (modification of this paragraph in its application to the transfer of an interest in a partnership that is a chargeable transaction by virtue of FA 2003 Sch 15 para 14 or 17).

HMRC Manuals—Stamp Duty Land Tax Manual, SDLTM20060 (residential property – leases executed between 10.04.03 and 30.10.03, and those from 01.12.03)

Amendments—[1] Sub-para (4)(*a*)(i), (*b*) repealed by FA 2008 s 95(4)(*a*), (5) with effect in relation to transactions with an effective date on or after 12 March 2008.

Land partly non-residential and partly residential

6— (1) [This paragraph applies, where the land is partly non-residential property and partly residential property, in relation to the consideration attributable to land that is residential property.][1]

References in this paragraph to the consideration attributable to ...[1] land that is residential property (or to the rent or annual rent so attributable) are to the consideration (or rent or annual rent) so attributable on a just and reasonable apportionment.

(2) ...[1]

(3) ...[1]

(4) If—

(*a*) the consideration so attributable does not include rent and the relevant consideration does not exceed £150,000, or (*b*) the consideration so attributable consists only of rent and the relevant rental value does not exceed £150,000,

none of the consideration so attributable counts as chargeable consideration.

(5) If the consideration so attributable includes rent and the relevant rental value does not exceed £150,000, the rent so attributable does not count as chargeable consideration.

(6) If the consideration so attributable includes consideration other than rent, then—

(*a*) if—

(i) …[2]

(ii) the relevant consideration does not exceed £150,000,

the consideration other than rent does not count as chargeable consideration;

(*b*) …[2]

HMRC Manuals—Stamp Duty Land Tax Manual SDLTM20080 (apportionment under this paragraph might be on the basis of the percentage areas quoted in planning applications, where appropriate, or alternatively of floor space relating to the respective uses. Other methods of apportionment will be considered.)

Modifications—FA 2003 Sch 15 para 26 (modification of this paragraph in its application to the transfer of an interest in a partnership that is a chargeable transaction by virtue of FA 2003 Sch 15 para 14 or 17).

Amendment—[1] Words in sub-para (1) substituted and repealed; and sub-paras (2), (3) repealed by FA 2005 ss 96, 104, Sch 9 paras 1(4), 4 and Sch 11 Pt 3(2) with effect, subject to FA 2005 Sch 9 para 4(2), for any transaction of which the effective date (as defined by FA 2005 Sch 9 para 4(4)) is after 16 March 2005.

[2] Sub-para (6)(*a*)(i), (*b*) repealed by FA 2008 s 95(4)(*b*), (5) with effect in relation to transactions with an effective date on or after 12 March 2008.

Stamp Taxes

PART 3
LAND PARTLY SITUATED IN A DISADVANTAGED AREA

Introduction

7— (1) This Part of this Schedule applies to a land transaction if—

[(*a*)][1] the subject matter of the transaction is a chargeable interest in relation to land that is partly in a disadvantaged area and partly outside such an area[, and

(*b*) the land situated in a disadvantaged area is wholly or partly residential property][1].

(2) References in this Part to the consideration attributable to land situated in a disadvantaged area and to land not so situated (or to the rent or annual rent so attributable) are to the consideration (or rent or annual rent) so attributable on a just and reasonable apportionment.

Modifications—FA 2003 Sch 15 para 26 (modification of this paragraph in its application to the transfer of an interest in a partnership that is a chargeable transaction by virtue of FA 2003 Sch 15 para 14 or 17).

Amendment—[1] Words inserted by FA 2005 s 96, Sch 9 paras 1(5), 4 with effect, subject to FA 2005 Sch 9 para 4(2), for any transaction of which the effective date (as defined by FA 2005 Sch 9 para 4(4)) is after 16 March 2005.

Land all non-residential

8 …[1]

Amendment—[1] Paragraph repealed by FA 2005 ss 96, 104, Sch 9 paras 1(6), 4 and Sch 11 Pt 3(2) with effect, subject to FA 2005 Sch 9 para 4(2), for any transaction of which the effective date (as defined by FA 2005 Sch 9 para 4(4)) is after 16 March 2005.

Land all residential

9— (1) This paragraph applies where all the land situated in a disadvantaged area is residential property.

(2) If—

(*a*) the consideration attributable to land situated in a disadvantaged area does not include rent and the relevant consideration does not exceed £150,000, or

(*b*) the consideration so attributable consists only of rent and the relevant rental value does not exceed £150,000,

none of the consideration so attributable counts as chargeable consideration.

(3) If the consideration attributable to land situated in a disadvantaged area includes rent and the relevant rental value does not exceed £150,000, the rent so attributable does not count as chargeable consideration.

(4) If the consideration attributable to land in a disadvantaged area includes consideration other than rent ("non-rent consideration"), then—

(*a*) if—

(i) …[1]

(ii) the relevant consideration does not exceed £150,000,

the non-rent consideration so attributable does not count as chargeable consideration;

(*b*) …[1]

Modifications—FA 2003 Sch 15 para 19 (modification of this paragraph in its application to the transfer of a chargeable interest from a partnership: chargeable consideration including rent).

FA 2003 Sch 15 para 26 (modification of this paragraph in its application to the transfer of an interest in a partnership that is a chargeable transaction by virtue of FA 2003 Sch 15 para 14 or 17).

Amendments—[1] Sub-para (4)(*a*)(i), (*b*) repealed by FA 2008 s 95(4)(*c*), (5) with effect in relation to transactions with an effective date on or after 12 March 2008.

Land partly non-residential and partly residential

10— (1) [This paragraph applies, where the land situated in a disadvantaged area is partly non-residential property and partly residential property, in relation to the consideration attributable to land that is residential property.][1]

References in this paragraph to the consideration attributable to …[1] land that is residential property (or to the rent or annual rent so attributable) are to the consideration (or rent or annual rent) attributable to land in a disadvantaged area that is, on a just and reasonable apportionment, so attributable.

(2) …[1]

(3) …[1]

(4) If—

(*a*) the consideration so attributable does not include rent and the relevant consideration does not exceed £150,000, or

(*b*) the consideration so attributable consists only of rent and the relevant rental value does not exceed £150,000,

none of the consideration so attributable counts as chargeable consideration.

(5) If the consideration so attributable includes rent and the relevant rental value does not exceed £150,000, the rent so attributable does not count as chargeable consideration.

(6) If the consideration so attributable includes consideration other than rent, then—

(*a*) if—

(i) …[2]

(ii) the relevant consideration does not exceed £150,000,

the consideration other than rent does not count as chargeable consideration;

(*b*) …[2]

Modifications—FA 2003 Sch 15 para 26 (modification of this paragraph in its application to the transfer of an interest in a partnership that is a chargeable transaction by virtue of FA 2003 Sch 15 para 14 or 17).

Amendment—[1] Words in sub-para (1) substituted and repealed; and sub-paras (2), (3) repealed by FA 2005 ss 96, 104, Sch 9 paras 1(7), 4 and Sch 11 Pt 3(2) with effect, subject to FA 2005 Sch 9 para 4(2), for any transaction of which the effective date (as defined by FA 2005 Sch 9 para 4(4)) is after 16 March 2005.

[2] Sub-para (6)(*a*)(i), (*b*) repealed by FA 2008 s 95(4)(*d*), (5) with effect in relation to transactions with an effective date on or after 12 March 2008.

PART 4

[SUPPLEMENTARY][1]

Amendments—[1] Heading (which previously read "Interpretation") substituted by FA 2004 s 298(1), (5)(*a*) with effect from 22 July 2004.

Relevant consideration and relevant rental value

11— (1) References in this Schedule to the "relevant consideration" in relation to a transaction are to the amount falling to be taken into account for the purposes of section 55(2) in determining the rate of tax chargeable under that section in relation to the transaction apart from any relief under this Schedule (whether in relation to that or any other transaction).

(2) References in this Schedule to the "relevant rental value" in relation to a transaction are to the amount falling to be taken into account for the purposes of paragraph 2(3) of Schedule 5 in determining the rate of tax chargeable under that Schedule in relation to the transaction apart from any relief under this Schedule (whether in relation to that or any other transaction).

Modifications—FA 2003 Sch 15 para 26 (modification of this paragraph in its application to the transfer of an interest in a partnership that is a chargeable transaction by virtue of FA 2003 Sch 15 para 14 or 17).

Rent and annual rent

12 For the purposes of this Schedule "rent" has the same meaning as in Schedule 5 (amount of tax chargeable: rent) and "annual rent" has the same meaning as in paragraph [9A][1] of that Schedule.

Modifications—FA 2003 Sch 15 para 26 (modification of this paragraph in its application to the transfer of an interest in a partnership that is a chargeable transaction by virtue of FA 2003 Sch 15 para 14 or 17).

Amendments—[1] Reference substituted by FA 2008 s 95 (6) with effect in relation to transactions with an effective date on or after 12 March 2008.

[Notification of transactions

13 For the purposes of [sections 77 and 77A (which specify][2] what land transactions are notifiable) no account shall be taken of any provision of this Schedule to the effect that consideration does not count as chargeable consideration.][1]

Amendments—[1] This paragraph inserted by FA 2004 s 298 (1), (5)(*b*) with effect from 22 July 2004.
[2] Words substituted by FA 2008 s 94, Sch 30 para 6 with effect in relation to transactions with an effective date on or after 12 March 2008.

[SCHEDULE 6A

RELIEF FOR CERTAIN ACQUISITIONS OF RESIDENTIAL PROPERTY][1]

Section 58A][1]

HMRC Manuals—Stamp Duty Land Tax Manual SDLTM21000–21070 (explanation of scope of this relief).
Amendments—[1] This Schedule inserted by FA 2004 s 296, Sch 39 para 17(2) with effect for any transaction of which the effective date (within the meaning of FA 2003 Pt 4) is on or after 22 July 2004: FA 2004 Sch 39 para 26. The insertion was previously made by the Stamp Duty and Stamp Duty Land Tax (Variation of the Finance Act 2003) (No 2) Regulations, SI 2003/2816 regs 1, 2, Schedule para 3(2) with effect from 1 December 2003. Those regulations are revoked by FA 2004 Sch 39 para 14(2).

[Acquisition by house-building company from individual acquiring new dwelling

1— (1) Where a dwelling ("the old dwelling") is acquired by a house-building company from an individual (whether alone or with other individuals), the acquisition is exempt from charge if the following conditions are met.

(2) The conditions are—

(*a*) that the individual (whether alone or with other individuals) acquires from the house-building company a new dwelling,

(*b*) that the individual—

(i) occupied the old dwelling as his only or main residence at some time in the period of two years ending with the date of its acquisition, and

(ii) intends to occupy the new dwelling as his only or main residence,

(*c*) that each acquisition is entered into in consideration of the other, and

(*d*) that the area of land acquired by the house-building company does not exceed the permitted area.

(3) Where the conditions in sub-paragraph (2)(*a*) to (*c*) are met but the area of land acquired by the house-building company exceeds the permitted area, the chargeable consideration for the acquisition is taken to be the amount calculated by deducting the market value of the permitted area from the market value of the old dwelling.

(4) A "house-building company" means a company that carries on the business of constructing or adapting buildings or parts of buildings for use as dwellings.

References in this paragraph to such a company include any company connected with it.

(5) In this paragraph—

(*a*) references to the acquisition of the new dwelling are to the acquisition, by way of grant or transfer, of a major interest in the dwelling;

(*b*) references to the acquisition of the old dwelling are to the acquisition, by way of transfer, of a major interest in the dwelling; and

(*c*) references to the market value of the old dwelling and of the permitted area are, respectively, to the market value of that major interest in the dwelling and of that interest so far as it relates to that area.][1]

Amendments—[1] This Schedule inserted by FA 2004 s 296, Sch 39 para 17(2) with effect for any transaction of which the effective date (within the meaning of FA 2003 Pt 4) is on or after 22 July 2004: FA 2004 Sch 39 para 26. The insertion was previously made by the Stamp Duty and Stamp Duty Land Tax (Variation of the Finance Act 2003) (No 2) Regulations, SI 2003/2816 regs 1, 2, Schedule para 3(2) with effect from 1 December 2003. Those regulations are revoked by FA 2004 Sch 39 para 14(2).

[Acquisition by property trader from individual acquiring new dwelling

2— (1) Where a dwelling ("the old dwelling") is acquired by a property trader from an individual (whether alone or with other individuals), the acquisition is exempt from charge if the following conditions are met.

(2) The conditions are—

(*a*) that the acquisition is made in the course of a business that consists of or includes acquiring dwellings from individuals who acquire new dwellings from house-building companies,

(*b*) that the individual (whether alone or with other individuals) acquires a new dwelling from a house-building company,

(*c*) that the individual—

(i) occupied the old dwelling as his only or main residence at some time in the period of two years ending with the date of its acquisition, and

(ii) intends to occupy the new dwelling as his only or main residence,

(*d*) that the property trader does not intend—

(i) to spend more than the permitted amount on refurbishment of the old dwelling, or

(ii) to grant a lease or licence of the old dwelling, or

Stamp Taxes

(iii) to permit any of its principals or employees (or any person connected with any of its principals or employees) to occupy the old dwelling, and

(*e*) that the area of land acquired by the property trader does not exceed the permitted area.

Paragraph (*d*)(ii) does not apply to the grant of lease or licence to the individual for a period of no more than six months.

(3) Where the conditions in sub-paragraph (2)(*a*) to (*d*) are met, but the area of land acquired by the property trader exceeds the permitted area, the chargeable consideration for the acquisition is taken to be the amount calculated by deducting the market value of the permitted area from the market value of the old dwelling.

(4) The provisions of paragraph 1(4) (meaning of "house-building company" etc) also have effect for the purposes of this paragraph.

(5) In this paragraph—

(*a*) references to the acquisition of a new dwelling are to the acquisition, by way of grant or transfer, of a major interest in the dwelling;

(*b*) references to the acquisition of the old dwelling are to the acquisition, by way of transfer, of a major interest in the dwelling; and

(*c*) references to the market value of the old dwelling and of the permitted area are, respectively, to the market value of that major interest in the dwelling and of that interest so far as it relates to that area.][1]

Amendments—[1] This Schedule inserted by FA 2004 s 296, Sch 39 para 17(2) with effect for any transaction of which the effective date (within the meaning of FA 2003 Pt 4) is on or after 22 July 2004: FA 2004 Sch 39 para 26. The insertion was previously made by the Stamp Duty and Stamp Duty Land Tax (Variation of the Finance Act 2003) (No 2) Regulations, SI 2003/2816 regs 1, 2, Schedule para 3(2) with effect from 1 December 2003. Those regulations are revoked by FA 2004 Sch 39 para 14(2).

[Acquisition by property trader from personal representatives

3— (1) Where a dwelling is acquired by a property trader from the personal representatives of a deceased individual, the acquisition is exempt from charge if the following conditions are met.

(2) The conditions are—

(*a*) that the acquisition is made in the course of a business that consists of or includes acquiring dwellings from personal representatives of deceased individuals,

(*b*) that the deceased individual occupied the dwelling as his only or main residence at some time in the period of two years ending with the date of his death,

(*c*) that the property trader does not intend—

(i) to spend more than the permitted amount on refurbishment of the dwelling, or

(ii) to grant a lease or licence of the dwelling, or

(iii) to permit any of its principals or employees (or any person connected with any of its principals or employees) to occupy the dwelling, and

(*d*) that the area of land acquired does not exceed the permitted area.

(3) Where the conditions in sub-paragraph (2)(*a*) to (*c*) are met, but the area of land acquired exceeds the permitted area, the chargeable consideration for the acquisition is taken to be the amount calculated by deducting the market value of the permitted area from the market value of the dwelling.

(4) In this paragraph—

(*a*) references to the acquisition of the dwelling are to the acquisition, by way of transfer, of a major interest in the dwelling; and

(*b*) references to the market value of the dwelling and of the permitted area are, respectively, to the market value of that major interest in the dwelling and of that interest so far as it relates to that area.][1]

Amendments—[1] This Schedule inserted by FA 2004 s 296, Sch 39 para 17(2) with effect for any transaction of which the effective date (within the meaning of FA 2003 Pt 4) is on or after 22 July 2004: FA 2004 Sch 39 para 26. The insertion was previously made by the Stamp Duty and Stamp Duty Land Tax (Variation of the Finance Act 2003) (No 2) Regulations, SI 2003/2816 regs 1, 2, Schedule para 3(2) with effect from 1 December 2003. Those regulations are revoked by FA 2004 Sch 39 para 14(2).

[Acquisition by property trader from individual where chain of transactions breaks down

4— (1) Where a dwelling ("the old dwelling") is acquired by a property trader from an individual (whether alone or with other individuals), the acquisition is exempt from charge if—

(*a*) the individual has made arrangements to sell a dwelling ("the old dwelling") and acquire another dwelling ("the second dwelling"),

(*b*) the arrangements to sell the old dwelling fail, and

(*c*) the acquisition of the old dwelling is made for the purpose of enabling the individual's acquisition of the second dwelling to proceed,

and the following conditions are met.

(2) The conditions are—

(*a*) that the acquisition is made in the course of a business that consists of or includes acquiring dwellings from individuals in those circumstances,

(*b*) that the individual—

(i) occupied the old dwelling as his only or main residence at some time in the period of two years ending with the date of its acquisition, and

(ii) intends to occupy the second dwelling as his only or main residence,

(*c*) that the property trader does not intend—

(i) to spend more than the permitted amount on refurbishment of the old dwelling, or

(ii) to grant a lease or licence of the old dwelling, or

(iii) to permit any of its principals or employees (or any person connected with any of its principals or employees) to occupy the old dwelling, and

(*d*) that the area of land acquired does not exceed the permitted area.

Paragraph (*c*)(ii) does not apply to the grant of a lease or licence to the individual for a period of no more than six months.

(3) Where the conditions in sub-paragraph (2)(*a*) to (*c*) are met, but the area of land acquired exceeds the permitted area, the chargeable consideration for the acquisition is taken to be the amount calculated by deducting the market value of the permitted area from the market value of the old dwelling.

(4) In this paragraph—

(*a*) references to the acquisition of the second dwelling are to the acquisition, by way of grant or transfer, of a major interest in the dwelling;

(*b*) references to the acquisition of the old dwelling are to the acquisition, by way of transfer, of a major interest in the dwelling; and

(*c*) references to the market value of the old dwelling and of the permitted area are, respectively, to the market value of that major interest in the dwelling and of that interest so far as it relates to that area.][1]

Amendments—[1] This Schedule inserted by FA 2004 s 296, Sch 39 para 17(2) with effect for any transaction of which the effective date (within the meaning of FA 2003 Pt 4) is on or after 22 July 2004: FA 2004 Sch 39 para 26. The insertion was previously made by the Stamp Duty and Stamp Duty Land Tax (Variation of the Finance Act 2003) (No 2) Regulations, SI 2003/2816 regs 1, 2, Schedule para 3(2) with effect from 1 December 2003. Those regulations are revoked by FA 2004 Sch 39 para 14(2).

[Acquisition by employer in case of relocation of employment

5— (1) Where a dwelling is acquired from an individual (whether alone or with other individuals) by his employer, the acquisition is exempt from charge if the following conditions are met.

(2) The conditions are—

(*a*) that the individual occupied the dwelling as his only or main residence at some time in the period of two years ending with the date of the acquisition,

(*b*) that the acquisition is made in connection with a change of residence by the individual resulting from relocation of employment,

(*c*) that the consideration for the acquisition does not exceed the market value of the dwelling, and

(*d*) that the area of land acquired does not exceed the permitted area.

(3) Where the conditions in sub-paragraph (2)(*a*) to (*c*) are met but the area of land acquired exceeds the permitted area, the chargeable consideration for the acquisition is taken to be the amount calculated by deducting the market value of the permitted area from the market value of the dwelling.

(4) In this paragraph "relocation of employment" means a change of the individual's place of employment due to—

(*a*) his becoming an employee of the employer,

(*b*) an alteration of the duties of his employment with the employer, or

(*c*) an alteration of the place where he normally performs those duties.

(5) For the purposes of this paragraph a change of residence is one "resulting from" relocation of employment if—

(*a*) the change is made wholly or mainly to allow the individual to have his residence within a reasonable daily travelling distance of his new place of employment, and

(*b*) his former residence is not within a reasonable daily travelling distance of that place.

The individual's "new place of employment" means the place where he normally performs, or is normally to perform, the duties of his employment after the relocation.

(6) In this paragraph—

(*a*) references to the acquisition of the dwelling are to the acquisition, by way of transfer, of a major interest in the dwelling;

(*b*) references to the market value of the dwelling and of the permitted area are, respectively, to the market value of that major interest in the dwelling and of that interest so far as it relates to that area; and

(*c*) references to an individual's employer include a prospective employer.][1]

Amendments—[1] This Schedule inserted by FA 2004 s 296, Sch 39 para 17(2) with effect for any transaction of which the effective date (within the meaning of FA 2003 Pt 4) is on or after 22 July 2004: FA 2004 Sch 39 para 26. The insertion was previously made by the Stamp Duty and Stamp Duty Land Tax (Variation of the Finance Act 2003) (No 2) Regulations, SI 2003/2816 regs 1, 2, Schedule para 3(2) with effect from 1 December 2003. Those regulations are revoked by FA 2004 Sch 39 para 14(2).

[Acquisition by property trader in case of relocation of employment

6— (1) Where a dwelling is acquired by a property trader from an individual (whether alone or with other individuals), the acquisition is exempt from charge if the following conditions are met.

(2) The conditions are—

(*a*) that the acquisition is made in the course of a business that consists of or includes acquiring dwellings from individuals in connection with a change of residence resulting from relocation of employment,

(*b*) that the individual occupied the dwelling as his only or main residence at some time in the period of two years ending with the date of the acquisition,

(*c*) that the acquisition is made in connection with a change of residence by the individual resulting from relocation of employment,

(*d*) that the consideration for the acquisition does not exceed the market value of the dwelling,

(*e*) that the property trader does not intend—

(i) to spend more than the permitted amount on refurbishment of the dwelling, or

(ii) to grant a lease or licence of the dwelling, or

(iii) to permit any of its principals or employees (or any person connected with any of its principals or employees) to occupy the dwelling, and

(*f*) that the area of land acquired does not exceed the permitted area.

Paragraph (*e*)(ii) does not apply to the grant of a lease or licence to the individual for a period of no more than six months.

(3) Where the conditions in sub-paragraph (2)(*a*) to (*e*) are met but the area of land acquired exceeds the permitted area, the chargeable consideration for the acquisition is taken to be the amount calculated by deducting the market value of the permitted area from the market value of the dwelling.

(4) In this paragraph "relocation of employment" means a change of the individual's place of employment due to—

(*a*) his becoming employed by a new employer,

(*b*) an alteration of the duties of his employment, or

(*c*) an alteration of the place where he normally performs those duties.

(5) For the purposes of this paragraph a change of residence is one "resulting from" relocation of employment if—

(*a*) the change is made wholly or mainly to allow the individual to have his residence within a reasonable daily travelling distance of his new place of employment, and

(*b*) his former residence is not within a reasonable daily travelling distance of that place.

An individual's "new place of employment" means the place where he normally performs, or is normally to perform, the duties of his employment after the relocation.

(6) In this paragraph—

(*a*) references to the acquisition of the dwelling are to the acquisition, by way of transfer, of a major interest in the dwelling; and

(*b*) references to the market value of the dwelling and of the permitted area are, respectively, to the market value of that major interest in the dwelling and of that interest so far as it relates to that area.][1]

Amendments—[1] This Schedule inserted by FA 2004 s 296, Sch 39 para 17(2) with effect for any transaction of which the effective date (within the meaning of FA 2003 Pt 4) is on or after 22 July 2004: FA 2004 Sch 39 para 26. The insertion was previously made by the Stamp Duty and Stamp Duty Land Tax (Variation of the Finance Act 2003) (No 2) Regulations, SI 2003/2816 regs 1, 2, Schedule para 3(2) with effect from 1 December 2003. Those regulations are revoked by FA 2004 Sch 39 para 14(2).

[Meaning of "dwelling", "new dwelling" and "the permitted area"

7— (1) "Dwelling" includes land occupied and enjoyed with the dwelling as its garden or grounds.

(2) A building or part of a building is a "new dwelling" if—

(*a*) it has been constructed for use as a single dwelling and has not previously been occupied, or

(*b*) it has been adapted for use as a single dwelling and has not been occupied since its adaptation.

(3) "The permitted area", in relation to a dwelling, means land occupied and enjoyed with the dwelling as its garden or grounds that does not exceed—

(*a*) an area (inclusive of the site of the dwelling) of 0.5 of a hectare, or

(*b*) such larger area as is required for the reasonable enjoyment of the dwelling as a dwelling having regard to its size and character.

(4) Where sub-paragraph (3)(*b*) applies, the permitted area is taken to consist of that part of the land that would be the most suitable for occupation and enjoyment with the dwelling as its garden or grounds if the rest of the land were separately occupied.][1]

Amendments—[1] This Schedule inserted by FA 2004 s 296, Sch 39 para 17(2) with effect for any transaction of which the effective date (within the meaning of FA 2003 Pt 4) is on or after 22 July 2004: FA 2004 Sch 39 para 26. The insertion was previously made by the Stamp Duty and Stamp Duty Land Tax (Variation of the Finance Act 2003) (No 2) Regulations, SI 2003/2816 regs 1, 2, Schedule para 3(2) with effect from 1 December 2003. Those regulations are revoked by FA 2004 Sch 39 para 14(2).

[Meaning of "property trader" and "principal"

8— (1) A "property trader" means—

(*a*) a company,
(*b*) a limited liability partnership, or
(*c*) a partnership whose members are all either companies or limited liability partnerships,

that carries on the business of buying and selling dwellings.

(2) In relation to a property trader a "principal" means—

(*a*) in the case of a company, a director;
(*b*) in the case of a limited liability partnership, a member;
(*c*) in the case of a partnership whose members are all either companies or limited liability partnerships, a member or a person who is a principal of a member.

(3) For the purposes of this Schedule—

(*a*) anything done by or in relation to a company connected with a property trader is treated as done by or in relation to that property trader, and
(*b*) references to the principals or employees of a property trader include the principals or employees of any such company.][1]

Amendments—[1] This Schedule inserted by FA 2004 s 296, Sch 39 para 17(2) with effect for any transaction of which the effective date (within the meaning of FA 2003 Pt 4) is on or after 22 July 2004: FA 2004 Sch 39 para 26. The insertion was previously made by the Stamp Duty and Stamp Duty Land Tax (Variation of the Finance Act 2003) (No 2) Regulations, SI 2003/2816 regs 1, 2, Schedule para 3(2) with effect from 1 December 2003. Those regulations are revoked by FA 2004 Sch 39 para 14(2).

[Meaning of "refurbishment" and "the permitted amount"

9— (1) "Refurbishment" of a dwelling means the carrying out of works that enhance or are intended to enhance the value of the dwelling, but does not include—

(*a*) cleaning the dwelling, or
(*b*) works required solely for the purpose of ensuring that the dwelling meets minimum safety standards.

(2) The "permitted amount", in relation to the refurbishment of a dwelling, is—

(*a*) £10,000, or
(*b*) 5% of the consideration for the acquisition of the dwelling, whichever is the greater, but subject to a maximum of £20,000.][1]

Amendments—[1] This Schedule inserted by FA 2004 s 296, Sch 39 para 17(2) with effect for any transaction of which the effective date (within the meaning of FA 2003 Pt 4) is on or after 22 July 2004: FA 2004 Sch 39 para 26. The insertion was previously made by the Stamp Duty and Stamp Duty Land Tax (Variation of the Finance Act 2003) (No 2) Regulations, SI 2003/2816 regs 1, 2, Schedule para 3(2) with effect from 1 December 2003. Those regulations are revoked by FA 2004 Sch 39 para 14(2).

[Connected companies etc

10 Section 839 of the Taxes Act 1988 (connected persons) has effect for the purposes of this Schedule.][1]

Amendments—[1] This Schedule inserted by FA 2004 s 296, Sch 39 para 17(2) with effect for any transaction of which the effective date (within the meaning of FA 2003 Pt 4) is on or after 22 July 2004: FA 2004 Sch 39 para 26. The insertion was previously made by the Stamp Duty and Stamp Duty Land Tax (Variation of the Finance Act 2003) (No 2) Regulations, SI 2003/2816 regs 1, 2, Schedule para 3(2) with effect from 1 December 2003. Those regulations are revoked by FA 2004 Sch 39 para 14(2).

[Withdrawal of relief under this Schedule

11— (1) Relief under this Schedule is withdrawn in the following circumstances.

(2) Relief under paragraph 2 (acquisition by property trader from individual acquiring new dwelling) is withdrawn if the property trader—

(*a*) spends more than the permitted amount on refurbishment of the old dwelling, or
(*b*) grants a lease or licence of the old dwelling, or
(*c*) permits any of its principals or employees (or any person connected with any of its principals or employees) to occupy the old dwelling.

Paragraph (*b*) does not apply to the grant of lease or licence to the individual for a period of no more than six months.

(3) Relief under paragraph 3 (acquisition by property trader from personal representatives) is withdrawn if the property trader—

(*a*) spends more than the permitted amount on refurbishment of the dwelling, or

(*b*) grants a lease or licence of the dwelling, or
(*c*) permits any of its principals or employees (or any person connected with any of its principals or employees) to occupy the dwelling.

(4) Relief under paragraph 4 (acquisition by property trader from individual where chain of transactions breaks down) is withdrawn if the property trader—

(*a*) spends more than the permitted amount on refurbishment of the old dwelling, or
(*b*) grants a lease or licence of the old dwelling, or
(*c*) permits any of its principals or employees (or any person connected with any of its principals or employees) to occupy the old dwelling.

Paragraph (*b*) does not apply to the grant of lease or licence to the individual for a period of no more than six months.

(5) Relief under paragraph 6 (acquisition by property trader in case of relocation of employment) is withdrawn if the property trader—

(*a*) spends more than the permitted amount on refurbishment of the dwelling, or
(*b*) grants a lease or licence of the dwelling, or
(*c*) permits any of its principals or employees (or any person connected with any of its principals or employees) to occupy the dwelling.

Paragraph (*b*) does not apply to the grant of lease or licence to the individual for a period of no more than six months.

(6) Where relief is withdrawn the amount of tax chargeable is the amount that would have been chargeable in respect of the acquisition but for the relief.][1]

Amendments—[1] This Schedule inserted by FA 2004 s 296, Sch 39 para 17(2) with effect for any transaction of which the effective date (within the meaning of FA 2003 Pt 4) is on or after 22 July 2004: FA 2004 Sch 39 para 26. The insertion was previously made by the Stamp Duty and Stamp Duty Land Tax (Variation of the Finance Act 2003) (No 2) Regulations, SI 2003/2816 regs 1, 2, Schedule para 3(2) with effect from 1 December 2003. Those regulations are revoked by FA 2004 Sch 39 para 14(2).

SCHEDULE 7

STAMP DUTY LAND TAX: GROUP RELIEF AND RECONSTRUCTION AND ACQUISITION RELIEFS

Section 62

HMRC Manuals—Stamp Duty Land Tax Manual SDLTM23000–23280 (explanation of this relief).

PART 1

GROUP RELIEF

Group relief

1— (1) A transaction is exempt from charge if the vendor and purchaser are companies that at the effective date of the transaction are members of the same group.

(2) For the purposes of group relief—

(*a*) "company" means a body corporate, and
(*b*) companies are members of the same group if one is the 75% subsidiary of the other or both are 75% subsidiaries of a third company.

(3) For the purposes of group relief a company ("company A") is the 75% subsidiary of another company ("company B") if company B—

(*a*) is beneficial owner of not less than 75% of the ordinary share capital of company A,
(*b*) is beneficially entitled to not less than 75% of any profits available for distribution to equity holders of company A, and
(*c*) would be beneficially entitled to not less than 75% of any assets of company A available for distribution to its equity holders on a winding-up.

(4) The ownership referred to in sub-paragraph (3)(*a*) is ownership either directly or through another company or companies.

For the purposes of that provision the amount of ordinary share capital of company A owned by company B through another company or companies shall be determined in accordance with section 838(5) to (10) of the Taxes Act 1988.

(5) In sub-paragraphs (3)(*a*) and (4) above "ordinary share capital", in relation to a company, means all the issued share capital (by whatever name called) of the company, other than capital the holders of which have a right to a dividend at a fixed rate but have no other right to share in the profits of the company.

(6) Schedule 18 to the Taxes Act 1988 (equity holders and profits or assets available for distribution) applies for the purposes of subsection (3)(*b*) and (*c*) above as it applies for the purposes of section 413(7)(*a*) and (*b*) of that Act, but with the omission of paragraphs 5(3) and 5B to 5E.

(7) This paragraph is subject to paragraph 2 (restrictions on availability of group relief) and [paragraphs 3 and 4A][1] (withdrawal of group relief).

Modifications—Pension Protection Fund (Tax) Regulations, SI 2006/575 reg 43(2) (this paragraph applies in relation to a group of companies of which the Board of the Pension Protection Fund is a member as if, in the case of each reference to 75 per cent, there were substituted a reference to 50 per cent.).

Amendments—[1] In sub-para (7), words substituted for the words "paragraph 3" by F(No 2)A 2005 s 49, Sch 10 paras 1, 3 with effect where the effective date of the relevant transaction (within the meaning of FA 2003 Sch 7 para 3 or 4A) is after 19 May 2005.

However, this amendment does not have effect—

(*a*) in relation to any transaction which is effected in pursuance of a contract entered into and substantially performed on or before the specified date (ie 16 March 2005), or

(*b*) subject to what follows below, in relation to any other transaction which is effected in pursuance of a contract entered into on or before the specified date (ie 16 March 2005).

The exclusion by para (*b*) above of transactions effected in pursuance of contracts entered into on or before the specified date does not apply—

(*a*) if there is any variation of the contract or assignment of rights under the contract after that date,

(*b*) if the transaction is effected in consequence of the exercise after that date of any option, right of pre-emption or similar right, or

(*c*) if after that date there is an assignment, subsale or other transaction (relating to the whole or part of the subject-matter of the contract) as a result of which a person other than the purchaser under the contract becomes entitled to call for a conveyance to him: F(No 2)A 2005 Sch 10 para 16(1), (6)–(8).

Restrictions on availability of group relief

2— (1) Group relief is not available if at the effective date of the transaction there are arrangements in existence by virtue of which, at that or some later time, a person has or could obtain, or any persons together have or could obtain, control of the purchaser but not of the vendor.

This does not apply to arrangements entered into with a view to an acquisition of shares by a company ("the acquiring company")—

(*a*) in relation to which section 75 of the Finance Act 1986 (c 41) (stamp duty: acquisition relief) will apply,

(*b*) in relation to which the conditions for relief under that section will be met, and

(*c*) as a result of which the purchaser will be a member of the same group as the acquiring company.

[For another exception to this, see sub-paragraph (3A).][2]

(2) Group relief is not available if the transaction is effected in pursuance of, or in connection with, arrangements under which—

(*a*) the consideration, or any part of the consideration, for the transaction is to be provided or received (directly or indirectly) by a person other than a group company, or

(*b*) the vendor and the purchaser are to cease to be members of the same group by reason of the purchaser ceasing to be a 75% subsidiary of the vendor or a third company.

(3) Arrangements are within sub-paragraph (2)(*a*) if under them the vendor or the purchaser, or another group company, is to be enabled to provide any of the consideration, or is to part with any of it, by or in consequence of the carrying out of a transaction or transactions involving, or any of them involving, a payment or other disposition by a person other than a group company.

[(3A) Sub-paragraphs (1) and (2)(*b*) do not apply to arrangements in so far as they are for the purpose of facilitating a transfer of the whole or part of the business of a company to another company in relation to which—

(*a*) section 96 of the Finance Act 1997 is intended to apply (stamp duty relief: demutualisation of insurance companies), and

(*b*) the conditions for relief under that section are intended to be met.][2]

(4) In sub-paragraphs (2)(*a*) and (3) a "group company" means a company that at the effective date of the transaction is a member of the same group as the vendor or the purchaser.

[(4A) Group relief is not available if the transaction—

(*a*) is not effected for bona fide commercial reasons, or

(*b*) forms part of arrangements of which the main purpose, or one of the main purposes, is the avoidance of liability to tax.

"Tax" here means stamp duty, income tax, corporation tax, capital gains tax or tax under this Part.][1]

(5) In this paragraph—

"arrangements" includes any scheme, agreement or understanding, whether or not legally enforceable; and

"control" has the meaning given by section 840 of the Taxes Act 1988.

Amendments—[1] Sub-para (4A) inserted by F(No 2)A 2005 s 49, Sch 10 paras 17, 19 with effect in relation to any transaction of which the effective date is on or after 20 July 2005.

However, this amendment does not have effect—

(*a*) in relation to any transaction which is effected in pursuance of a contract entered into and substantially performed on or before 16 March 2005, or

(*b*) (subject to what follows below) in relation to any other transaction which is effected in pursuance of a contract entered into on or before that date.

The exclusion by para (*b*) above of transactions effected in pursuance of contracts entered into on or before 16 March 2005 does not apply—

(*a*) if there is any variation of the contract or assignment of rights under the contract after that date, (*b*) if the transaction is effected in consequence of the exercise after that date of any option, right of pre-emption or similar right, or

(*c*) if after that date there is an assignment, subsale or other transaction (relating to the whole or part of the subject-matter of the contract) as a result of which a person other than the purchaser under the contract becomes entitled to call for a conveyance to him: F(No 2)A 2005 Sch 10 para 22(1)–(3).

[2] Words at the end of sub-para (1) and the whole of sub-para (3A) inserted by FA 2006 s 167(2), (3) with effect in relation to any transfer which takes place, or is intended to take place, after 22 March 2006.

Withdrawal of group relief

3— (1) Where in the case of a transaction ("the relevant transaction") that is exempt from charge by virtue of paragraph 1 (group relief)—

(*a*) the purchaser ceases to be a member of the same group as the vendor—

(i) before the end of the period of three years beginning with the effective date of the transaction, or

(ii) in pursuance of, or in connection with, arrangements made before the end of that period,

and

(*b*) at the time the purchaser ceases to be a member of the same group as the vendor ("the relevant time"), it or a relevant associated company holds a chargeable interest—

(i) that was acquired by the purchaser under the relevant transaction, or

(ii) that is derived from a chargeable interest so acquired,

and that has not subsequently been acquired at market value under a chargeable transaction for which group relief was available but was not claimed,

group relief in relation to the relevant transaction, or an appropriate proportion of it, is withdrawn and tax is chargeable in accordance with this paragraph.

[(2) The amount chargeable is the tax that would have been chargeable in respect of the relevant transaction but for group relief if the chargeable consideration for that transaction had been an amount equal to—

(*a*) the market value of the subject-matter of the transaction, and

(*b*) if the acquisition was the grant of a lease at a rent, that rent,

or, as the case may be, an appropriate proportion of the tax that would have been so chargeable.][1]

(3) In sub-paragraphs (1) and (2) "an appropriate proportion" means an appropriate proportion having regard to the subject matter of the relevant transaction and what is held at the relevant time by the transferee company or, as the case may be, by that company and its relevant associated companies.

(4) In this paragraph—

"arrangements" includes any scheme, agreement or understanding, whether or not legally enforceable; and

"relevant associated company", in relation to the purchaser, means a company that—

(*a*) is a member of the same group as the purchaser immediately before the purchaser ceases to be a member of the same group as the vendor, and

(*b*) ceases to be a member of the same group as the vendor in consequence of the purchaser so ceasing.

(5) This paragraph has effect subject to [paragraphs 4 and 4ZA][3] (cases in which group relief not withdrawn) [and paragraph 4A (withdrawal of group relief in certain cases involving successive transactions)][2].

Cross references—Pension Protection Fund (Tax) Regulations, SI 2006/575 reg 43(3) (for the purposes of sub-para (1) above, there is no withdrawal of group relief if the vendor is the Board of the Pension Protection Fund).

Modifications—FA 2003 Sch 15 para 27 (modification of this paragraph in its application to the transfer of an interest in a partnership that is a chargeable transaction by virtue of FA 2003 Sch 15 para 17).

Amendments—[1] Sub-para (2) substituted by F(No 2)A 2005 s 49, Sch 10 paras 1, 4(*a*) with effect where the effective date of the relevant transaction (within the meaning of FA 2003 Sch 7 para 3 or 4A) is after 19 May 2005.

However, this amendment does not have effect—

(*a*) in relation to any transaction which is effected in pursuance of a contract entered into and substantially performed on or before the specified date (ie 19 May 2005), or

(*b*) subject to what follows below, in relation to any other transaction which is effected in pursuance of a contract entered into on or before the specified date (ie 19 May 2005).

The exclusion by para (*b*) above of transactions effected in pursuance of contracts entered into on or before the specified date does not apply—

(*a*) if there is any variation of the contract or assignment of rights under the contract after that date,

(*b*) if the transaction is effected in consequence of the exercise after that date of any option, right of pre-emption or similar right, or

(*c*) if after that date there is an assignment, subsale or other transaction (relating to the whole or part of the subject-matter of the contract) as a result of which a person other than the purchaser under the contract becomes entitled to call for a conveyance to him: F(No 2)A 2005 Sch 10 para 16(1), (6)–(8).

[2] Words in sub-para (5) inserted by F(No 2)A 2005 s 49, Sch 10 paras 1, 4(*b*) with effect where the effective date of the relevant transaction (within the meaning of FA 2003 Sch 7 para 3 or 4A) is after 19 May 2005. This amendment is also subject to the qualifications given in note [1] above, save that the "specified date" in this instance is 16 March 2005: F(No 2)A 2005 Sch 10 para 16(1), (6)–(8).

[3] Words in sub-para (5) substituted by FA 2008 s 96(1), (2) with effect in relation to transactions with an effective date on or after 13 March 2008.

Cases in which group relief not withdrawn

4— (1) Group relief is not withdrawn under paragraph 3 in the following cases.

(2), (3) ...[3]

(4) The second case is where the purchaser ceases to be a member of the same group as the vendor by reason of anything done for the purposes of, or in the course of, winding up the vendor or another company that is above the vendor in the group structure.

(5) For [the purposes of [sub-paragraph (4)][3]][1] a company is "above" the vendor in the group structure if the vendor, or another company that is above the vendor in the group structure, is a 75% subsidiary of the company.

(6) The third case is where—

(*a*) the purchaser ceases to be a member of the same group as the vendor as a result of an acquisition of shares by another company ("the acquiring company") in relation to which—

(i) section 75 of the Finance Act 1986 (c 41) applies (stamp duty: acquisition relief), and

(ii) the conditions for relief under that section are met,

and

(*b*) the purchaser is immediately after that acquisition a member of the same group as the acquiring company.

[(6A) The fourth case is where—

(*a*) the purchaser ceases to be a member of the same group as the vendor as a result of the transfer of the whole or part of the vendor's business to another company ("the acquiring company") in relation to which—

(i) section 96 of the Finance Act 1997 applies (stamp duty relief: demutualisation of insurance companies), and

(ii) the conditions for relief under that section are met, and

(*b*) the purchaser is immediately after that transfer a member of the same group as the acquiring company.][2]

(7) But if in a case within sub-paragraph (6) [or (6A)][2]—

(*a*) the purchaser ceases to be a member of the same group as the acquiring company—

(i) before the end of the period of three years beginning with the effective date of the relevant transaction, or

(ii) in pursuance of, or in connection with, arrangements made before the end of that period,

and

(*b*) at the time the purchaser ceases to be a member of the same group as the acquiring company, it or a relevant associated company holds a chargeable interest—

(i) that was acquired by the purchaser under the relevant transaction, or

(ii) that is derived from an interest so acquired,

and that has not subsequently been acquired at market value under a chargeable transaction for which group relief was available but was not claimed,

the provisions of this Part relating to group relief apply as if the purchaser had then ceased to be a member of the same group as the vendor.

(8) In sub-paragraph (7)—

"arrangements" includes any scheme, agreement or understanding, whether or not legally enforceable; and

"relevant associated company", in relation to the purchaser, means a company that is a member of the same group as the purchaser that ceases to be a member of the same group as the acquiring company in consequence of the purchaser so ceasing.

Modifications—FA 2003 Sch 15 para 27 (modification of this paragraph in its application to the transfer of an interest in a partnership that is a chargeable transaction by virtue of FA 2003 Sch 15 para 17).

Amendments—[1] Sub-para (3)(*b*) substituted, and in sub-para (5), words substituted for the words "this purpose" by F(No 2)A 2005 s 49, Sch 10 paras 1, 5 with effect where the effective date of the relevant transaction (within the meaning of FA 2003 Sch 7 para 3 or 4A) is after 19 May 2005.

However, this amendment does not have effect—

(*a*) in relation to any transaction which is effected in pursuance of a contract entered into and substantially performed on or before the specified date (ie 16 March 2005), or

(*b*) subject to what follows below, in relation to any other transaction which is effected in pursuance of a contract entered into on or before the specified date (ie 16 March 2005).

The exclusion by para (*b*) above of transactions effected in pursuance of contracts entered into on or before the specified date does not apply—

(*a*) if there is any variation of the contract or assignment of rights under the contract after that date,

(*b*) if the transaction is effected in consequence of the exercise after that date of any option, right of pre-emption or similar right, or

(*c*) if after that date there is an assignment, subsale or other transaction (relating to the whole or part of the subject-matter of the contract) as a result of which a person other than the purchaser under the contract becomes entitled to call for a conveyance to him: F(No 2)A 2005 Sch 10 para 16(1), (6)–(8).

[2] Sub-para (6A) and words in sub-para (7) inserted by FA 2006 s 167(4) with effect in relation to any transfer which takes place, or is intended to take place, after 22 March 2006.

[3] Sub-paras (2), (3) repealed and words in sub-para (5) substituted, by FA 2008 s 96(1), (3) with effect in relation to transactions with an effective date on or after 13 March 2008.

Stamp Taxes

[Group relief not withdrawn where vendor leaves group

4ZA— (1) Group relief is not withdrawn under paragraph 3 where the purchaser ceases to be a member of the same group as the vendor because the vendor leaves the group.

(2) The vendor is regarded as leaving the group if the companies cease to be members of the same group by reason of a transaction relating to shares in—

(*a*) the vendor, or

(*b*) another company that—

(i) is above the vendor in the group structure, and

(ii) as a result of the transaction ceases to be a member of the same group as the purchaser.

(3) For the purpose of sub-paragraph (2) a company is "above" the vendor in the group structure if the vendor, or another company that is above the vendor in the group structure, is a 75% subsidiary of the company.

(4) But if there is a change in the control of the purchaser after the vendor leaves the group, paragraphs 3, 4(6) and (7), 5 and 6 have effect as if the purchaser had then ceased to be a member of the same group as the vendor (but see sub-paragraph (7)).

(5) For the purposes of this paragraph there is a change in the control of the purchaser if—

(*a*) a person who controls the purchaser (alone or with others) ceases to do so,

(*b*) a person obtains control of the purchaser (alone or with others), or

(*c*) the purchaser is wound up.

(6) For the purposes of sub-paragraph (5) a person does not control, or obtain control of, the purchaser if that person is under the control of another person or other persons.

(7) Sub-paragraph (4) does not apply where—

(*a*) there is a change in the control of the purchaser because a loan creditor (within the meaning of section 417(7) to (9) of the Taxes Act 1988) obtains control of, or ceases to control, the purchaser, and

(*b*) the other persons who controlled the purchaser before that change continue to do so.

(8) In this paragraph references to "control" shall be interpreted in accordance with section 416 of the Taxes Act 1988 (subject to sub-paragraph (6)).][1]

Amendments—[1] Para 4ZA inserted by FA 2008 s 96(1), (4) with effect in relation to transactions with an effective date on or after 13 March 2008.

[Withdrawal of group relief in certain cases involving successive transactions

4A— (1) Where, in the case of a transaction ("the relevant transaction") that is exempt from charge by virtue of paragraph 1 (group relief)—

(*a*) there is a change in the control of the purchaser,

(*b*) that change occurs—

(i) before the end of the period of three years beginning with the effective date of the relevant transaction, or

(ii) in pursuance of, or in connection with, arrangements made before the end of that period,

(*c*) apart from this paragraph, group relief in relation to the relevant transaction would not be withdrawn under paragraph 3, and

(*d*) any previous transaction falls within sub-paragraph (2),

paragraphs 3[, 4 and 4ZA][2] have effect in relation to the relevant transaction as if the vendor in relation to the earliest previous transaction falling within sub-paragraph (2) were the vendor in relation to the relevant transaction.

[(1A) Sub-paragraph (1) has effect subject to sub-paragraph (3A).][2]

(2) A previous transaction falls within this sub-paragraph if—

(*a*) the previous transaction is exempt from charge by virtue of paragraph 1, 7 or 8,

(*b*) the effective date of the previous transaction is less than three years before the date of the event falling within sub-paragraph (1)(*a*),

(*c*) the chargeable interest acquired under the relevant transaction by the purchaser in relation to that transaction is the same as, comprises, forms part of, or is derived from, the chargeable interest acquired under the previous transaction by the purchaser in relation to the previous transaction, and

(*d*) since the previous transaction, the chargeable interest acquired under that transaction has not been acquired by any person under a transaction that is not exempt from charge by virtue of paragraph 1, 7 or 8.

(3) For the purposes of [this paragraph][2] there is a change in the control of a company if—

(*a*) any person who controls the company (alone or with others) ceases to do so,

(*b*) a person obtains control of the company (alone or with others), or

(*c*) the company is wound up.

References to "control" in [this paragraph][2] shall be construed in accordance with section 416 of the Taxes Act 1988.

[(3A) Sub-paragraph (1) does not apply where—

(*a*) there is a change in the control of the purchaser because a loan creditor (within the meaning of section 417(7) to (9) of the Taxes Act 1988) obtains control of, or ceases to control, the purchaser, and

(*b*) the other persons who controlled the purchaser before that change continue to do so.][2]

(4) If two or more transactions effected at the same time are the earliest previous transactions falling within sub-paragraph (2), the reference in sub-paragraph (1) to the vendor in relation to the earliest previous transaction is a reference to the persons who are the vendors in relation to the earliest previous transactions.

(5) In this paragraph "arrangements" includes any scheme, agreement or understanding, whether or not legally enforceable.][1]

Amendments—[1] Paragraph 4A inserted by F(No 2)A 2005 s 49, Sch 10 paras 1, 6 with effect where the effective date of the relevant transaction (within the meaning of FA 2003 Sch 7 para 3 or 4A) is after 19 May 2005.

However, this amendment does not have effect—

(*a*) in relation to any transaction which is effected in pursuance of a contract entered into and substantially performed on or before the specified date (i e 16 March 2005), or

(*b*) subject to what follows below, in relation to any other transaction which is effected in pursuance of a contract entered into on or before the specified date (i e 16 March 2005).

The exclusion by para (*b*) above of transactions effected in pursuance of contracts entered into on or before the specified date does not apply—

(*a*) if there is any variation of the contract or assignment of rights under the contract after that date,

(*b*) if the transaction is effected in consequence of the exercise after that date of any option, right of pre-emption or similar right, or

(*c*) if after that date there is an assignment, subsale or other transaction (relating to the whole or part of the subject-matter of the contract) as a result of which a person other than the purchaser under the contract becomes entitled to call for a conveyance to him: F(No 2)A 2005 Sch 10 para 16(1), (6)–(8).

[2] In sub-paras (1), (3) words substituted, sub-paras (1A), (3A) inserted, by FA 2008 s 96(1), (5) with effect in relation to transactions with an effective date on or after 13 March 2008.

Recovery of group relief from another group company or controlling director

5— (1) This paragraph applies where—

(*a*) tax is chargeable under paragraph 3 (withdrawal of group relief),

(*b*) the amount so chargeable has been finally determined, and

(*c*) the whole or part of the amount so chargeable is unpaid six months after the date on which it became payable.

(2) The following persons may, by notice under paragraph 6, be required to pay the unpaid tax—

(*a*) the vendor;

(*b*) any company that at any relevant time was a member of the same group as the purchaser and was above it in the group structure;

(*c*) any person who at any relevant time was a controlling director of the purchaser or a company having control of the purchaser.

(3) For the purposes of sub-paragraph (2)(*b*)—

(*a*) a "relevant time" means any time between effective date of the relevant transaction and the purchaser ceasing to be a member of the same group as the vendor; and

(*b*) a company ("company A") is "above" another company ("company B") in a group structure if company B, or another company that is above company B in the group structure, is a 75% subsidiary of company A.

(4) In sub-paragraph (2)(*c*)—

"director", in relation to a company, has the meaning given by section 67(1) of the Income Tax (Earnings and Pensions) Act 2003 (c 1) (read with subsection (2) of that section) and includes any person falling within section 417(5) of the Taxes Act 1988 (read with subsection (6) of that section); and

"controlling director", in relation to a company, means a director of the company who has control of it (construing control in accordance with section 416 of the Taxes Act 1988).

Modifications—FA 2003 Sch 15 para 27 (modification of this paragraph in its application to the transfer of an interest in a partnership that is a chargeable transaction by virtue of FA 2003 Sch 15 para 17).

Recovery of group relief: supplementary

6— (1) The Inland Revenue may serve a notice on a person within paragraph 5(2) above requiring him within 30 days of the service of the notice to pay the amount that remains unpaid.

(2) Any such notice must be served before the end of the period of three years beginning with the date of the final determination mentioned in paragraph 5(1)(*b*).

(3) The notice must state the amount required to be paid by the person on whom the notice is served.

(4) The notice has effect—

(*a*) for the purposes of the recovery from that person of the amount required to be paid and of interest on that amount, and

(*b*) for the purposes of appeals,

as if it were a notice of assessment and that amount were an amount of tax due from that person.

(5) A person who has paid an amount in pursuance of a notice under this paragraph may recover that amount from the purchaser.

(6) A payment in pursuance of a notice under this paragraph is not allowed as a deduction in computing any income, profits or losses for any tax purpose.

Modifications—FA 2003 Sch 15 para 27 (modification of this paragraph in its application to the transfer of an interest in a partnership that is a chargeable transaction by virtue of FA 2003 Sch 15 para 17).

PART 2

RECONSTRUCTION AND ACQUISITION RELIEFS

Reconstruction relief

7— (1) Where—

(*a*) a company ("the acquiring company") acquires the whole or part of the undertaking of another company ("the target company") in pursuance of a scheme for the reconstruction of the target company, and

(*b*) the first, second and third conditions specified below are met,

a land transaction entered into for the purposes of or in connection with the transfer of the undertaking or part is exempt from charge.

Relief under this paragraph is referred to in this Part as "reconstruction relief".

(2) The first condition is that the consideration for the acquisition consists wholly or partly of the issue of non-redeemable shares in the acquiring company to all the shareholders of the target company.

"Non-redeemable shares" means shares that are not redeemable shares.

(3) Where the consideration for the acquisition consists partly of the issue of non-redeemable shares as mentioned in the first condition, that condition is met only if the rest of the consideration consists wholly of the assumption or discharge by the acquiring company of liabilities of the target company.

(4) The second condition is that after the acquisition has been made—

(*a*) each shareholder of each of the companies is a shareholder of the other, and

(*b*) the proportion of shares of one of the companies held by any shareholder is the same, or as nearly as may be the same, as the proportion of shares of the other company held by that shareholder.

(5) The third condition is that the acquisition is effected for bona fide commercial reasons and does not form part of a scheme or arrangement of which the main purpose, or one of the main purposes, is the avoidance of liability to tax.

[(5A) If immediately before the acquisition the target company or the acquiring company holds any of its own shares, the shares are to be treated for the purposes of sub-paragraphs (2) and (4) as having been cancelled before the acquisition (and, accordingly, the company is to be treated as if it were not a shareholder of itself).][1]

"Tax" here means stamp duty, income tax, corporation tax, capital gains tax or tax under this Part.

(6) This paragraph is subject to paragraph 9 (withdrawal of reconstruction or acquisition relief).

Amendments—[1] Sub-para (5A) inserted by FA 2007 s 74(3), (5) with effect in relation to any land transaction of which the effective date is on or after 19 July 2007.

Acquisition relief

8— (1) Where—

(*a*) a company ("the acquiring company") acquires the whole or part of the undertaking of another company ("the target company"), and

(*b*) [all the conditions][1] specified below are met,

the rate of tax chargeable on a land transaction entered into for the purposes of or in connection with the transfer of the undertaking or part is limited to 0.5%.

Relief under this section is referred to in this Part as "acquisition relief".

(2) The first condition is that the consideration for the acquisition consists wholly or partly of the issue of non-redeemable shares in the acquiring company to—

(*a*) the target company, or

(*b*) all or any of the target company's shareholders.

"Non-redeemable shares" means shares that are not redeemable shares.

(3) Where the consideration for the acquisition consists partly of the issue of non-redeemable shares as mentioned in the first condition, that condition is met only if the rest of the consideration consists wholly of—

(*a*) cash not exceeding 10% of the nominal value of the non-redeemable shares so issued, or

(*b*) the assumption or discharge by the acquiring company of liabilities of the target company, or

(c) both of those things.

(4) The second condition is that the acquiring company is not associated with another company that is a party to arrangements with the target company relating to shares of the acquiring company issued in connection with the transfer of the undertaking or part.

[(5) For this purpose companies are associated if one has control of the other or both are controlled by the same person or persons.

The reference to control shall be construed in accordance with section 416 of the Taxes Act 1988.][2]

[(5A) The third condition is that the undertaking or part acquired by the acquiring company has as its main activity the carrying on of a trade that does not consist wholly or mainly of dealing in chargeable interests.

In this sub-paragraph "trade" has the same meaning as in the Taxes Act 1988.][1]

[(5B) The fourth condition is that the acquisition is effected for bona fide commercial reasons and does not form part of arrangements of which the main purpose, or one of the main purposes, is the avoidance of liability to tax.

"Tax" here means stamp duty, income tax, corporation tax, capital gains tax or tax under this Part.][2]

[(5C) In this paragraph "arrangements" include any scheme, agreement or understanding, whether or not legally enforceable.][2]

(6) This paragraph is subject to paragraph 9 (withdrawal of reconstruction or acquisition relief).

Amendments—[1] In sub-para (1)(b), words substituted for the words "the first and second conditions", and sub-para (5A) inserted; by F(No 2)A 2005 s 49, Sch 10 paras 1, 8 with effect in relation to any transaction of which the effective date is after 19th May 2005.

However, this amendment does not have effect—

(a) in relation to any transaction which is effected in pursuance of a contract entered into and substantially performed on or before the specified date (ie 16 March 2005), or

(b) subject to what follows below, in relation to any other transaction which is effected in pursuance of a contract entered into on or before the specified date (ie 16 March 2005).

The exclusion by para (b) above of transactions effected in pursuance of contracts entered into on or before the specified date does not apply—

(a) if there is any variation of the contract or assignment of rights under the contract after that date,

(b) if the transaction is effected in consequence of the exercise after that date of any option, right of pre-emption or similar right, or

(c) if after that date there is an assignment, subsale or other transaction (relating to the whole or part of the subject-matter of the contract) as a result of which a person other than the purchaser under the contract becomes entitled to call for a conveyance to him: F(No 2)A 2005 Sch 10 para 16(5)–(8).

[2] Sub-para (5) substituted, and sub-paras (5B), (5C) inserted, by F(No 2)A 2005 s 49, Sch 10 paras 17, 20 with effect in relation to any transaction of which the effective date is on or after the day on which F(No 2)A 2005 is passed.

However, this amendment does not have effect—

(a) in relation to any transaction which is effected in pursuance of a contract entered into and substantially performed on or before 16 March 2005, or

(b) (subject to what follows below) in relation to any other transaction which is effected in pursuance of a contract entered into on or before that date.

The exclusion by para (b) above of transactions effected in pursuance of contracts entered into on or before 16 March 2005 does not apply—

(a) if there is any variation of the contract or assignment of rights under the contract after that date,

(b) if the transaction is effected in consequence of the exercise after that date of any option, right of pre-emption or similar right, or

(c) if after that date there is an assignment, subsale or other transaction (relating to the whole or part of the subject-matter of the contract) as a result of which a person other than the purchaser under the contract becomes entitled to call for a conveyance to him: F(No 2)A 2005 Sch 10 para 22(1)–(3).

Withdrawal of reconstruction or acquisition relief

9—(1) Where in the case of a transaction ("the relevant transaction") that is exempt by virtue of reconstruction relief or is subject to a reduced rate of tax by virtue of acquisition relief—

(a) control of the acquiring company changes—

(i) before the end of the period of three years beginning with the effective date of the transaction, or

(ii) in pursuance of, or in connection with, arrangements made before the end of that period,

and

(b) at the time control of the acquiring company changes ("the relevant time"), it or a relevant associated company holds a chargeable interest—

(i) that was acquired by the acquiring company under the relevant transaction, or

(ii) that is derived from an interest so acquired,

and that has not subsequently been acquired at market value under a chargeable transaction in relation to which reconstruction or acquisition relief was available but was not claimed,

reconstruction or acquisition relief in relation to the relevant transaction, or an appropriate proportion of it, is withdrawn and tax is chargeable in accordance with this paragraph.

[(2) The amount chargeable is the tax that would have been chargeable in respect of the relevant transaction but for reconstruction or acquisition relief if the chargeable consideration for that transaction had been an amount equal to—

(a) the market value of the subject-matter of the transaction, and

Stamp Taxes

(*b*) if the acquisition was the grant of a lease at a rent, that rent,

or, as the case may be, an appropriate proportion of the tax that would have been so chargeable.][1]

(3) In sub-paragraphs (1) and (2) "an appropriate proportion" means an appropriate proportion having regard to the subject-matter of the relevant transaction and what is held at the relevant time by the acquiring company or, as the case may be, by that company and any relevant associated companies.

(4) In this paragraph "relevant associated company", in relation to the acquiring company, means a company—

(*a*) that is controlled by the acquiring company immediately before the control of that company changes, and

(*b*) of which control changes in consequence of the change of control of that company.

(5) In this paragraph—

(*a*) "arrangements" includes any scheme, agreement or understanding, whether or not legally enforceable;

(*b*) "control" shall be construed in accordance with section 416 of the Taxes Act 1988; and

(*c*) references to control of a company changing are to the company becoming controlled—

(i) by a different person,

(ii) by a different number of persons, or

(iii) by two or more persons at least one of whom is not the person, or one of the persons, by whom the company was previously controlled.

(6) This paragraph has effect subject to paragraph 10 (cases in which reconstruction or acquisition relief not withdrawn).

Amendments—[1] Sub-para (2) substituted by F(No 2)A 2005 s 49, Sch 10 paras 1, 9 with effect where the effective date of the relevant transaction (within the meaning of this paragraph) is after 19 May 2005.

However, this amendment does not have effect—

(*a*) in relation to any transaction which is effected in pursuance of a contract entered into and substantially performed on or before the specified date (i e 19 May 2005), or

(*b*) subject to what follows below, in relation to any other transaction which is effected in pursuance of a contract entered into on or before the specified date (i e 19 May 2005).

The exclusion by para (*b*) above of transactions effected in pursuance of contracts entered into on or before the specified date does not apply—

(*a*) if there is any variation of the contract or assignment of rights under the contract after that date,

(*b*) if the transaction is effected in consequence of the exercise after that date of any option, right of pre-emption or similar right, or

(*c*) if after that date there is an assignment, subsale or other transaction (relating to the whole or part of the subject-matter of the contract) as a result of which a person other than the purchaser under the contract becomes entitled to call for a conveyance to him: F(No 2)A 2005 Sch 10 para 16(2), (6)–(8).

Cases in which reconstruction or acquisition relief not withdrawn

10— (1) Reconstruction or acquisition relief is not withdrawn under paragraph 9 in the following cases.

(2) The first case is where control of the acquiring company changes as a result of a share transaction that is effected as mentioned in any of paragraphs (*a*) to (*d*) of paragraph 3 of Schedule 3 (transactions in connection with divorce etc).

(3) The second case is where control of the acquiring company changes as a result of a share transaction that—

(*a*) is effected as mentioned in paragraph 4(1) of Schedule 3, and

(*b*) meets the conditions in paragraph 4(2) of that Schedule (variation of testamentary dispositions etc).

(4) The third case is where control of the acquiring company changes as a result of an exempt intra-group transfer.

An "exempt intra-group transfer" means a transfer of shares effected by an instrument that is exempt from stamp duty by virtue of section 42 of the Finance Act 1930 (c 28) or section 11 of the Finance Act (Northern Ireland) 1954 (c 23 (NI)) (transfers between associated bodies corporate).

But see paragraph 11 (withdrawal of relief in case of subsequent non-exempt transfer).

(5) The fourth case is where control of the acquiring company changes as a result of a transfer of shares to another company in relation to which share acquisition relief applies.

"Share acquisition relief" means relief under section 77 of the Finance Act 1986 (c 41) and a transfer is one in relation to which that relief applies if an instrument effecting the transfer is exempt from stamp duty by virtue of that provision.

But see paragraph 11 (withdrawal in case of subsequent non-exempt transfer).

(6) The fifth case is where—

(*a*) control of the acquiring company changes as a result of a loan creditor becoming, or ceasing to be, treated as having control of the company, and

(*b*) the other persons who were previously treated as controlling the company continue to be so treated.

"Loan creditor" here has the meaning given by section 417(7) to (9) of the Taxes Act 1988.

Withdrawal of reconstruction or acquisition relief on subsequent non-exempt transfer

11— (1) Where paragraph 10(4) (change of control of acquiring company as a result of exempt intra-group transfer) has effect to prevent the withdrawal of reconstruction or acquisition relief on a change of control of the acquiring company, but—

(*a*) a company holding shares in the acquiring company to which the exempt intra-group transfer related, or that are derived from shares to which that transfer related, ceases to be a member of the same group as the target company—

(i) before the end of the period of three years beginning with the effective date of the relevant transaction, or

(ii) in pursuance of or in connection with arrangements made before the end of that period,

and

(*b*) the acquiring company or a relevant associated company, at that time ("the relevant time"), holds a chargeable interest—

(i) that was transferred to the acquiring company by the relevant transaction, or

(ii) that is derived from an interest that was so transferred, and that has not subsequently been transferred at market value by a chargeable transaction in relation to which reconstruction or acquisition relief was available but was not claimed,

reconstruction or acquisition relief in relation to the relevant transaction, or an appropriate proportion of it, is withdrawn and tax is chargeable in accordance with this paragraph.

(2) Where paragraph 10(5) (change of control of acquiring company as a result of a transfer to which share acquisition relief applies) has effect to prevent the withdrawal of reconstruction or acquisition relief on a change of control of the acquiring company, but—

(*a*) control of the other company mentioned in that provision changes—

(i) before the end of the period of three years beginning with the effective date of the relevant transaction, or

(ii) in pursuance of or in connection with arrangements made before the end of that period,

at a time when that company holds any shares transferred to it by the exempt transfer, or any shares derived from shares so transferred, and

(*b*) the acquiring company or a relevant associated company, at that time ("the relevant time"), holds a chargeable interest—

(i) that was transferred to the acquiring company by the relevant transaction, or

(ii) that is derived from an interest that was so transferred,

and that has not subsequently been transferred at market value by a chargeable transaction in relation to which reconstruction or acquisition relief was available but was not claimed,

reconstruction or acquisition relief in relation to the relevant transaction, or an appropriate proportion of it, is withdrawn and tax is chargeable in accordance with this paragraph.

(3) The amount chargeable is the tax that would have been chargeable in respect of the relevant transaction but for reconstruction or acquisition relief if the chargeable consideration for that transaction had been an amount equal to the market value of the subject matter of the transaction or, as the case may be, an appropriate proportion of the tax that would have been so chargeable.

(4) In sub-paragraphs (1), (2) and (3) "an appropriate proportion" means an appropriate proportion having regard to the subject-matter of the relevant transaction and what is held at the relevant time by the acquiring company or, as the case may be, by that company and any relevant associated companies.

(5) In this paragraph "relevant associated company", in relation to the acquiring company, means a company—

(*a*) that is controlled by the acquiring company immediately before the control of that company changes, and

(*b*) of which control changes in consequence of the change of control of that company.

(6) In this paragraph—

(*a*) "arrangements" includes any scheme, agreement or understanding, whether or not legally enforceable;

(*b*) "control" shall be construed in accordance with section 416 of the Taxes Act 1988; and

(*c*) references to control of a company changing are to the company becoming controlled—

(i) by a different person,

(ii) by a different number of persons, or

(iii) by two or more persons at least one of whom is not the person, or one of the persons, by whom the company was previously controlled.

Recovery of reconstruction or acquisition relief from another group company or controlling director

12— (1) This paragraph applies where—

(*a*) tax is chargeable under paragraph 9 or 11 (withdrawal of reconstruction or acquisition relief),

(*b*) the amount so chargeable has been finally determined, and

(*c*) the whole or part of the amount so chargeable is unpaid six months after the date on which it became payable.

(2) The following persons may, by notice under paragraph 13, be required to pay the unpaid tax—

(*a*) any company that at any relevant time was a member of the same group as the acquiring company and was above it in the group structure;

(*b*) any person who at any relevant time was a controlling director of the acquiring company or a company having control of the acquiring company.

(3) For the purposes of sub-paragraph (2) "relevant time" means any time between effective date of the relevant transaction and the change of control by virtue of which tax is chargeable.

(4) For the purposes of sub-paragraph (2)(*a*) a company ("company A") is "above" another company ("company B") in a group structure if company B, or another company that is above company B in the group structure, is a 75% subsidiary of company A.

(5) For the purposes of sub-paragraph (2)(*b*)—

(*a*) "director", in relation to a company, has the meaning given by section 67(1) of the Income Tax (Earnings and Pensions) Act 2003 (c 1) (read with subsection (2) of that section) and includes any person falling within section 417(5) of the Taxes Act 1988 (read with subsection (6) of that section); and

(*b*) "controlling director", in relation to a company, means a director of the company who has control of it (construing control in accordance with section 416 of the Taxes Act 1988).

Recovery of reconstruction or acquisition relief: supplementary

13— (1) The Inland Revenue may serve a notice on a person within paragraph 12(2) above requiring him within 30 days of the service of the notice to pay the amount that remains unpaid.

(2) Any such notice must be served before the end of the period of three years beginning with the date of the final determination mentioned in paragraph 12(1)(*b*).

(3) The notice must state the amount required to be paid by the person on whom the notice is served.

(4) The notice has effect—

(*a*) for the purposes of the recovery from that person of the amount required to be paid and of interest on that amount, and

(*b*) for the purposes of appeals,

as if it were a notice of assessment and that amount were an amount of tax due from that person.

(5) A person who has paid an amount in pursuance of a notice under this paragraph may recover that amount from the acquiring company.

(6) A payment in pursuance of a notice under this paragraph is not allowed as a deduction in computing any income, profits or losses for any tax purpose.

SCHEDULE 8

STAMP DUTY LAND TAX: CHARITIES RELIEF

Section 68

HMRC Manuals—Stamp Duty Land Tax Manual SDLTM26000–26020 (explanation of this relief).

Modifications—FA 2003 Sch 15 para 28 (this Schedule applies to the transfer of an interest in a partnership that is a chargeable transaction by virtue of FA 2003 Sch 15 paras 14 or 17, with the insertion of para 3, and the modification of paras 1, 2).

Charities relief

1— (1) A land transaction is exempt from charge if the purchaser is a charity and the following conditions are met.

Relief under [this Schedule][1] is referred to in this Part as "charities relief".

(2) The first condition is that the purchaser must intend to hold the subject-matter of the transaction for qualifying charitable purposes, that is—

(*a*) for use in furtherance of the charitable purposes of the purchaser or of another charity, or

(*b*) as an investment from which the profits are applied to the charitable purposes of the purchaser.

(3) The second condition is that the transaction must not have not been entered into for the purpose of avoiding tax under this Part (whether by the purchaser or any other person).

(4) In this section a "charity" means a body or trust established for charitable purposes only.

Modifications—FA 2003 Sch 15 para 28 (this Schedule applies to the transfer of an interest in a partnership that is a chargeable transaction by virtue of FA 2003 Sch 15 paras 14 or 17, with the insertion of para 3, and the modification of paras 1, 2).

Amendments—[1] In sub-para (1), words substituted for the words "this paragraph " by FA 2004 s 302(3), (7) with effect for any transaction of which the effective date (within the meaning of FA 2004 Pt 4) is on or after the day 22 July 2004.

Withdrawal of charities relief

2— (1) Where in the case of a transaction ("the relevant transaction") that is exempt by virtue of [this Schedule][1]—

(*a*) a disqualifying event occurs—

(i) before the end of the period of three years beginning with the effective date of the transaction, or

(ii) in pursuance of, or in connection with, arrangements made before the end of that period,

and

(*b*) at the time of the disqualifying event the purchaser holds a chargeable interest—

(i) that was acquired by the purchaser under the relevant transaction, or

(ii) that is derived from an interest so acquired,

charities relief in relation to the relevant transaction, or an appropriate proportion of it, is withdrawn and tax is chargeable in accordance with this paragraph.

(2) The amount chargeable is the amount that would have been chargeable in respect of the relevant transaction but for charities relief or, as the case may be, an appropriate proportion of the tax that would have been so chargeable.

(3) For the purposes of this paragraph a "disqualifying event" means—

(*a*) the purchaser ceasing to be established for charitable purposes only, or

(*b*) the subject-matter of the transaction, or any interest or right derived from it, being used or held by the purchaser otherwise than for qualifying charitable purposes.

(4) In sub-paragraphs (1) and (2) an "appropriate proportion" means an appropriate proportion having regard to—

(*a*) what was acquired by the purchaser under the relevant transaction and what is held by the purchaser at the time of the disqualifying event, and

(*b*) the extent to which what is held by the purchaser at that time becomes used or held for purposes other than qualifying charitable purposes.

(5) In this paragraph "qualifying charitable purposes" has the same meaning as in paragraph 1.

Modifications—FA 2003 Sch 8 para 3 (modification of this paragraph in relation to a transaction that, by virtue of FA 2003 Sch 8 para 3, is a disqualifying event for the purposes of this paragraph).

FA 2003 Sch 15 para 28 (this Schedule applies to the transfer of an interest in a partnership that is a chargeable transaction by virtue of FA 2003 Sch 15 paras 14 or 17, with the insertion of para 3, and the modification of paras 1, 2).

Amendments—[1] In sub-para (1), words substituted for the words "paragraph 1 (charities relief)" by FA 2004 s 302(4), (7) with effect for any transaction of which the effective date (within the meaning of FA 2004 Pt 4) is on or after 22 July 2004.

[Cases where first condition not fully met

3— (1) This paragraph applies where—

(*a*) a land transaction is not exempt from charge under paragraph 1 because the first condition in that paragraph is not met, but

(*b*) the purchaser ("C") intends to hold the greater part of the subject-matter of the transaction for qualifying charitable purposes.

(2) In such a case—

(*a*) the transaction is exempt from charge, but

(*b*) for the purposes of paragraph 2 (withdrawal of charities relief) "disqualifying event" includes—

(i) any transfer by C of a major interest in the whole or any part of the subject-matter of the transaction, or

(ii) any grant by C at a premium of a low-rental lease of the whole or any part of that subject-matter,

that is not made in furtherance of the charitable purposes of C.

(3) For the purposes of sub-paragraph (2)(*b*)(ii)—

(*a*) a lease is granted "at a premium" if there is consideration other than rent, and

(*b*) a lease is a "low-rental" lease if the annual rent (if any) [is less than £1,000][2] a year.

(4) In relation to a transaction that, by virtue of this paragraph, is a disqualifying event for the purposes of paragraph 2—

(*a*) the date of the event for those purposes is the effective date of the transaction;

(*b*) paragraph 2 has effect as if—

(i) in sub-paragraph (1)(*b*), for "at the time of" there were substituted "immediately before",

(ii) in sub-paragraph (4)(*a*), for "at the time of" there were substituted "immediately before and immediately after", and

(iii) sub-paragraph (4)(*b*) were omitted.

(5) In this paragraph—

Stamp Taxes

"qualifying charitable purposes" has the same meaning as in paragraph 1;
"rent" has the same meaning as in Schedule 5 (amount of tax chargeable: rent) and "annual rent" has the same meaning as in paragraph [9A][2] of that Schedule.][1]

Modifications—FA 2003 Sch 15 para 28 (this Schedule applies to the transfer of an interest in a partnership that is a chargeable transaction by virtue of FA 2003 Sch 15 paras 14 or 17, with the insertion of para 3 (headed "Interpretation" as shown in FA 2003 Sch 15 para 28(2)), and the modification of paras 1, 2).

Amendments—[1] This paragraph inserted by FA 2004 s 302(1), (7) with effect for any transaction of which the effective date (within the meaning of FA 2004 Pt 4) is on or after 22 July 2004.

[2] Words in sub-paras (3)(*b*), (5) substituted by FA 2008 s 95(7) with effect in relation to transactions with an effective date on or after 12 March 2008.

[Charitable trusts

4— (1) This Schedule applies in relation to a charitable trust as it applies in relation to a charity.

(2) In this paragraph "charitable trust" means—

(*a*) a trust of which all the beneficiaries are charities, or

(*b*) a unit trust scheme in which all the unit holders are charities, and "charity" has the same meaning as in paragraph 1.

(3) In this Schedule as it applies by virtue of this paragraph—

(*a*) references to the purchaser in paragraphs (*a*) and (*b*) of paragraph 1(2) are to the beneficiaries or unit holders, or any of them;

(*b*) the reference to the purchaser in paragraph 2(3)(*a*) is to any of the beneficiaries or unit holders;

(*c*) the reference in paragraph 3(2)(*b*) to the charitable purposes of C is to those of the beneficiaries or unit holders, or any of them.][1]

Modifications—FA 2003 Sch 15 para 28 (this Schedule applies to the transfer of an interest in a partnership that is a chargeable transaction by virtue of FA 2003 Sch 15 paras 14 or 17, with the insertion of para 3, and the modification of paras 1, 2).

Amendments—[1] This paragraph inserted by FA 2004 s 302(2), (7) with effect for any transaction of which the effective date (within the meaning of FA 2004 Pt 4) is on or after 22 July 2004.

SCHEDULE 9

STAMP DUTY LAND TAX: RIGHT TO BUY, SHARED OWNERSHIP LEASES ETC

Section 70

HMRC Manuals—Stamp Duty Land Tax Manual SDLTM27000–27070 (explanation of this relief).

Right to buy transactions

1— (1) In the case of a right to buy transaction—

(*a*) section 51(1) (contingent consideration to be included in chargeable consideration on assumption that contingency will occur) does not apply, and

(*b*) any consideration that would be payable only if a contingency were to occur, or that is payable only because a contingency has occurred, does not count as chargeable consideration.

(2) A "right to buy transaction" means—

(*a*) the sale of a dwelling at a discount, or the grant of a lease of a dwelling at a discount, by a relevant public sector body, or

(*b*) the sale of a dwelling, or the grant of a lease of a dwelling, in pursuance of the preserved right to buy.

(3) The following are relevant public sector bodies for the purposes of sub-paragraph (2)(*a*):

Government

A Minister of the Crown
The Scottish Ministers
A Northern Ireland department

Local Government

A local housing authority within the meaning of the Housing Act 1985 (c 68)
A county council in England
A council constituted under section 2 of the Local Government etc (Scotland) Act 1994 (c 39), the common good of such a council or any trust under its control
A district council within the meaning of the Local Government Act (Northern Ireland) 1972 (c 9 (NI))

Social housing

The Housing Corporation
Scottish Homes
The Northern Ireland Housing Executive
A registered social landlord
A housing action trust established under Part 3 of the Housing Act 1988 (c 50)

New towns and development corporations [etc][2]

The [Homes and Communities Agency][2]
A development corporation established by an order made, or having effect as if made, under the New Towns Act 1981 (c 64)
A development corporation established by an order made, or having effect as if made, under the New Towns (Scotland) Act 1968 (c 16)
A new town commission established under section 7 of the New Towns Act (Northern Ireland) 1965 (c 13 (NI))
An urban development corporation established by an order made under section 135 of the Local Government, Planning and Land Act 1980 (c 65)
. . .[1]

Police

A police authority within the meaning of section 101(1) of the Police Act 1996 (c 16)
A police authority within the meaning of section 2(1) or 19(9)(*b*) of the Police (Scotland) Act 1967 (c 77)
The Northern Ireland Policing Board

Miscellaneous

An Education and Libraries Board within the meaning of the Education and Libraries (Northern Ireland) Order 1986 (SI1986/594 (NI 3))
The United Kingdom Atomic Energy Authority
Any person mentioned in paragraphs (*g*), (*k*), (*l*) or (*n*) of section 61(11) of the Housing (Scotland) Act 1987 (c 26)
A body prescribed for the purposes of this sub-paragraph by Treasury order.

(4) For the purposes of sub-paragraph (2)(*b*) the transfer of a dwelling, or the grant of a lease of a dwelling, is made in pursuance of the preserved right to buy if—

(*a*) the vendor is—

(i) in England and Wales, a person against whom the right to buy under Part 5 of the Housing Act 1985 (c 68) is exercisable by virtue of section 171A of that Act, or

(ii) in Scotland, a person against whom the right to buy under section 61 of the Housing (Scotland) Act 1987 is exercisable by virtue of section 81A of that Act,

(which provide for the preservation of the right to buy on disposal to a private sector landlord),

(*b*) the purchaser is the qualifying person for the purposes of the preserved right to buy, and

(*c*) the dwelling is the qualifying dwelling-house in relation to the purchaser.

(5) A grant under section 20 or 21 of the Housing Act 1996 (c 52) (purchase grants in respect of disposals at a discount by registered social landlords) does not count as part of the chargeable consideration for a right to buy transaction in relation to which the vendor is a registered social landlord.

Modification—Transfer of Housing Corporation Functions (Modifications and Transitional Provisions) Order, SI 2008/2839 art 3, Schedule (any reference to the Housing Corporation shall be treated as if it were a reference to the Regulator of Social Housing).

Amendments—[1] Words in sub-para (3) omitted, repealed by the Welsh Development Agency (Transfer of Functions to the National Assembly for Wales and Abolition) Order, SI 2005/3226 art 7(1), Sch 2 para 14 with effect from 23 November 2005.

[2] In sub-para (3), word inserted, and words substituted for words "Commission for the New Towns" by the Housing and Regeneration Act 2008 s 56, Sch 8 para 80 with effect from 1 December 2008 (by virtue of SI 2008/3068, arts 1(2), 2(1)(*w*), (3)).

Shared ownership lease: election for market value treatment

2— (1) This paragraph applies where—

(*a*) a lease is granted—

(i) by a qualifying body, or

(ii) in pursuance of the preserved right to buy,

(*b*) the conditions in sub-paragraph (2) are met, and

(*c*) the purchaser elects for tax to be charged in accordance with this paragraph.

(2) The conditions are as follows—

(*a*) the lease must be of a dwelling;

(*b*) the lease must give the lessee or lessees exclusive use of the dwelling;

(*c*) the lease must provide for the lessee or lessees to acquire the reversion;

(*d*) the lease must be granted partly in consideration of rent and partly in consideration of a premium calculated by reference to—

(i) the market value of the dwelling, or

(ii) a sum calculated by reference to that value;

(*e*) the lease must contain a statement of—

(i) the market value of the dwelling, or

(ii) the sum calculated by reference to that value,

by reference to which the premium is calculated.

Stamp Taxes

(3) An election for tax to be charged in accordance with this paragraph must be included in the land transaction return made in respect of the grant of the lease, or in an amendment of that return, and is irrevocable, so that the return may not be amended so as to withdraw the election.

(4) Where this paragraph applies the chargeable consideration for the grant of the lease shall be taken to be the amount stated in the lease in accordance with sub-paragraph (2)(*e*)(i) or (ii).

[(4A) Where this paragraph applies no account shall be taken for the purposes of stamp duty land tax of the rent mentioned in sub-paragraph (2)(*d*).][1]

As to the tax treatment of the acquisition of the reversion in pursuance of the lease, see paragraph 3.

(5) Section 118 (meaning of "market value") does not apply in relation to the reference in sub-paragraph (2)(*e*) above to the market value of the dwelling.

Amendments—[1] Sub-para (4A) inserted by FA 2007 s 78 with effect from 19 July 2007.

Transfer of reversion under shared ownership lease where election made for market value treatment

3 The transfer of the reversion to the lessee or lessees under the terms of a lease to which paragraph 2 applies (shared ownership lease: election for market value treatment) is exempt from charge if—

(*a*) an election was made for tax to be charged in accordance with that paragraph, and
(*b*) any tax chargeable in respect of the grant of the lease has been paid.

Cross references—FA 2003 Sch 19 para 7(2) (in this paragraph as it applies in a case where the original lease was granted before the implementation date—
(*a*) the reference to a lease to which FA 2003 Sch 9 para 2 applies shall be read as a reference to a lease to which FA 1980 s 97 applied), and
(*b*) the reference to an election having been made for tax to be charged under that paragraph shall be read accordingly as a reference to a corresponding election having been in relation to stamp duty under that section.
For the implementation date, see FA 2003 Sch 19 para 2).

Shared ownership lease: election where staircasing allowed

4— (1) This paragraph applies where—

(*a*) a lease is granted by a qualifying body or in pursuance of the preserved right to buy,
(*b*) the conditions in sub-paragraph (2) below are met, and
(*c*) the purchaser elects for tax to be charged in accordance with this paragraph.

(2) The conditions are as follows—

(*a*) the lease must be of a dwelling;
(*b*) the lease must give the lessee or lessees exclusive use of the dwelling;
(*c*) the lease must provide that the lessee or lessees may, on the payment of a sum, require the terms of the lease to be altered so that the rent payable under it is reduced;
(*d*) the lease must be granted partly in consideration of rent and partly in consideration of a premium calculated by reference to—

(i) the premium obtainable on the open market for the grant of a lease containing the same terms as the lease but with the substitution of the minimum rent for the rent payable under the lease, or
(ii) a sum calculated by reference to that premium;

(*e*) the lease must contain a statement of the minimum rent and of—

(i) the premium obtainable on the open market, or
(ii) the sum calculated by reference to that premium,

by reference to which the premium is calculated.

(3) An election for tax to be charged in accordance with this paragraph must be included in the land transaction return made in respect of the grant of the lease, or in an amendment of that return, and is irrevocable, so that the return may not be amended so as to withdraw the election.

(4) Where this paragraph applies—

(*a*) the rent in consideration of which the lease is granted shall be taken to be the minimum rent stated in the lease in accordance with sub-paragraph (2)(*e*), and
(*b*) the chargeable consideration for the grant other than rent shall be taken to be the amount stated in the lease in accordance with sub-paragraph (2)(*e*)(i) or (ii).

(5) In this paragraph the "minimum rent" means the lowest rent which could become payable under the lease if it were altered as mentioned in sub-paragraph (2)(*c*) at the date when the lease is granted.

[Shared ownership lease: treatment of staircasing transaction

4A— (1) This paragraph applies where under a shared ownership lease—

(*a*) the lessee or lessees have the right, on the payment of a sum, to require the terms of the lease to be altered so that the rent payable under it is reduced, and
(*b*) by exercising that right the lessee or lessees acquire an interest, additional to one already held, calculated by reference to the market value of the dwelling and expressed as a percentage of the dwelling or its value (a "share of the dwelling").

(2) Such an acquisition is exempt from charge if—

(*a*) an election was made for tax to be charged in accordance with paragraph 2 or, as the case may be, paragraph 4 and any tax chargeable in respect of the grant of the lease has been paid, or

(*b*) immediately after the acquisition the total share of the dwelling held by the lessee or lessees does not exceed 80%.

(3) In this paragraph "shared ownership lease" means a lease granted—

(*a*) by a qualifying body, or

(*b*) in pursuance of the preserved right to buy,

in relation to which the conditions in paragraph 2(2) or 4(2) are met.

(4) Section 118 (meaning of "market value") does not apply in relation to the references in this paragraph to the market value of the dwelling.][1]

Amendments—[1] This paragraph inserted by FA 2004 s 303(1), (4) with effect for an acquisition after 17 March 2004.

[Shared ownership lease: grant not linked with staircasing transactions etc

4B— (1) For the purpose of determining the rate of tax chargeable on the grant of a shared ownership lease of a dwelling, the grant shall be treated as if it were not linked to—

(*a*) any acquisition of an interest in the dwelling to which paragraph 4A applies, or

(*b*) a transfer of the reversion to the lessee or lessees under the terms of the lease.

(2) In this paragraph "shared ownership lease" has the same meaning as in paragraph 4A.][1]

Amendments—[1] Para 4B inserted by FA 2008 s 95(8) with effect in relation to transactions with an effective date on or after 12 March 2008.

Shared ownership leases: meaning of "qualifying body" and "preserved right to buy"

5— (1) This paragraph has effect for the purposes of paragraphs [2, 4 and 4A][1] (shared ownership leases: election as to basis of taxation).

(2) A "qualifying body" means—

(*a*) a local housing authority within the meaning of the Housing Act 1985 (c 68);

(*b*) a housing association within the meaning of—

(i) the Housing Associations Act 1985 (c 69), or

(ii) Part 2 of the Housing (Northern Ireland) Order 1992 (SI 1992/1725 (NI 15));

(*c*) a housing action trust established under Part 3 of the Housing Act 1988 (c 50);

(*d*) the Northern Ireland Housing Executive;

[(*e*) the Homes and Communities Agency;][2]

(*f*) a development corporation established by an order made, or having effect as if made, under the New Towns Act 1981 (c 64);

[(*g*) a registered provider of social housing that is not within paragraph (*b*) (subject to sub-paragraph (2A)).][3]

[(2A) A registered provider of social housing within sub- paragraph (2)(*g*) ("R") is only a qualifying body in relation to a lease of premises if the following has been funded with the assistance of a grant or other financial assistance under section 19 of the Housing and Regeneration Act 2008—

(*a*) the purchase or construction of the premises by R (or a person connected with R), or

(*b*) the adaptation of the premises by R (or a person connected with R) for use as a dwelling.

(2B) Section 839 of the Taxes Act 1988 (connected persons) has effect for the purposes of sub-paragraph (2A).][3]

(3) A lease is granted "in pursuance of the preserved right to buy" if—

(*a*) the vendor is a person against whom the right to buy under Part 5 of the Housing Act 1985 is exercisable by virtue of section 171A of that Act (preservation of right to buy on disposal to private sector landlord),

(*b*) the lessee is, or lessees are, the qualifying person for the purposes of the preserved right to buy, and

(*c*) the lease is of a dwelling that is the qualifying dwelling-house in relation to the purchaser.

Amendments—[1] References substituted by FA 2004 s 303(2), (4) with effect for an acquisition after 17 March 2004.

[2] Sub-para (2)(*e*) substituted by the Housing and Regeneration Act 2008 s 56, Sch 8 para 81 with effect from 1 December 2008 (by virtue of SI 2008/3068, arts 1(2), 2(1)(*w*), (3)).

[3] Sub-paras (2)(*g*), (2A), (2B) inserted by FA 2009 s 81(1), (5), (6) with effect in relation to transactions with an effective date on or after 21 July 2009.

Rent to mortgage or rent to loan: chargeable consideration

6— (1) The chargeable consideration for a rent to mortgage or rent to loan transaction is determined in accordance with this paragraph.

(2) A "rent to mortgage transaction" means—

(*a*) the transfer of a dwelling to a person, or

(*b*) the grant of a lease of a dwelling to a person,

pursuant to the exercise by that person of the right to acquire on rent to mortgage terms under Part 5 of the Housing Act 1985 (c 68).

(3) The chargeable consideration for such a transaction is equal to the price that, by virtue of section 126 of the Housing Act 1985, would be payable for—

(*a*) a transfer of the dwelling to the person (where the rent to mortgage transaction is a transfer), or

(*b*) the grant of a lease of the dwelling to the person (where the rent to mortgage transaction is the grant of a lease),

if the person were exercising the right to buy under Part 5 of that Act.

(4) A "rent to loan transaction" means the execution of a heritable disposition in favour of a person pursuant to the exercise by that person of the right to purchase a house by way of the rent to loan scheme in Part 3 of the Housing (Scotland) Act 1987 (c 26).

(5) The chargeable consideration for such a transaction is equal to the price that, by virtue of section 62 of the Housing (Scotland) Act 1987 (c 26), would be payable for the house if the person were exercising the right to purchase under section 61 of that Act.

[Shared ownership trust: introduction

7— (1) In this Schedule "shared ownership trust" means a trust of land, within the meaning of section 1 of the Trusts of Land and Appointment of Trustees Act 1996, which satisfies the following conditions.

(2) Condition 1 is that the trust property is—

(*a*) a dwelling, and
(*b*) in England or Wales.

(3) Condition 2 is that one of the beneficiaries ("the social landlord") is a qualifying body …[2].

(4) Condition 3 is that the terms of the trust—

(*a*) provide for one or more of the individual beneficiaries ("the purchaser") to have exclusive use of the trust property as the only or main residence of the purchaser,

(*b*) require the purchaser to make an initial payment to the social landlord ("the initial capital"),

(*c*) require the purchaser to make additional payments to the social landlord by way of compensation under section 13(6)(*a*) of the Trusts of Land and Appointment of Trustees Act 1996, ("rent-equivalent payments"),

(*d*) enable the purchaser to make other additional payments to the social landlord ("equity-acquisition payments"),

(*e*) determine the initial beneficial interests of the social landlord and of the purchaser by reference to the initial capital,

(*f*) specify a sum, equating or relating to the market value of the dwelling, by reference to which the initial capital was calculated, and

(*g*) provide for the purchaser's beneficial interest in the trust property to increase, and the social landlord's to diminish (or to be extinguished), as equity-acquisition payments are made.

(5) Section 118 (meaning of "market value") does not apply to this paragraph.

(6) In Condition 1 "dwelling" includes—

(*a*) a building which is being constructed or adapted for use as a dwelling,
(*b*) land which is to be used for the purpose of the construction of a dwelling, and
(*c*) land which is, or is to become, the garden or grounds of a dwelling.][1]

[(7) In Condition 2 "qualifying body" means—

(*a*) a qualifying body within the meaning of paragraph 5(2)(*a*) to (*f*), or
(*b*) a registered provider of social housing within paragraph 5(2)(*g*) (subject to sub-paragraph (8)).

(8) A registered provider of social housing within paragraph 5(2)(*g*) ("R") is only a qualifying body in relation to a shared ownership trust if the following has been or is being funded with the assistance of a grant or other financial assistance under section 19 of the Housing and Regeneration Act 2008—

(*a*) the purchase or construction of the trust property by R (or a person connected with R), or
(*b*) the adaptation of the trust property by R (or a person connected with R) for use as a dwelling.

(9) Section 839 of the Taxes Act 1988 (connected persons) has effect for the purposes of sub-paragraph (8).][2]

Amendments—[1] Paragraphs 7–11 inserted by FA 2007 s 77 with effect in relation to land transactions with an effective date on or after 19 July 2007.

[2] In sub-para (3) words "(within the meaning of paragraph 5(2))" repealed and sub-paras (7)–(9) inserted by FA 2009 s 81(1), (7) with effect in relation to transactions with an effective date on or after 21 July 2009.

[Shared ownership trust: "purchaser"

8 For the purposes of the application of stamp duty land tax in relation to a shared ownership trust, the person (or persons) identified as the purchaser in accordance with paragraph 7, and not the social landlord or any other beneficiary, is (or are) to be treated as the purchaser of the trust property.][1]

Amendments—[1] Paragraphs 7–11 inserted by FA 2007 s 77 with effect in relation to land transactions with an effective date on or after 19 July 2007.

[Shared ownership trust: election for market value treatment

9— (1) This paragraph applies where—

(*a*) a shared ownership trust is declared, and
(*b*) the purchaser elects for tax to be charged in accordance with this paragraph.

(2) An election must be included in—

(*a*) the land transaction return for the declaration of the shared ownership trust, or
(*b*) an amendment of that return.

(3) An election may not be revoked.

(4) Where this paragraph applies—

(*a*) the chargeable consideration for the declaration of the shared ownership trust shall be taken to be the amount stated in accordance with paragraph 7(4)(*f*), and
(*b*) no account shall be taken for the purposes of stamp duty land tax of rent-equivalent payments.

(5) The transfer to the purchaser of an interest in the trust property upon the termination of the trust is exempt from charge if—

(*a*) an election was made under this paragraph, and
(*b*) any tax chargeable in respect of the declaration of the shared ownership trust has been paid.][1]

Amendments—[1] Paragraphs 7–11 inserted by FA 2007 s 77 with effect in relation to land transactions with an effective date on or after 19 July 2007.

[Shared ownership trust: treatment of staircasing transaction

10— (1) An equity-acquisition …[2] payment under a shared ownership trust, and the consequent increase in the purchaser's beneficial interest, shall be exempt from charge if—

(*a*) an election was made under paragraph 9, and
(*b*) any tax chargeable in respect of the declaration of trust has been paid.

(2) An equity-acquisition …[2] payment under a shared ownership trust, and the consequent increase in the purchaser's beneficial interest, shall also be exempt from charge if following the increase the purchaser's beneficial interest does not exceed 80% of the total beneficial interest in the trust property.][1]

Amendments—[1] Paragraphs 7–11 inserted by FA 2007 s 77 with effect in relation to land transactions with an effective date on or after 19 July 2007.
[2] In sub-paras (1), (2) word repealed by FA 2008 s 95(9) with effect in relation to transactions with an effective date on or after 12 March 2008.

[Shared ownership trust: treatment of additional payments where no election made

11— Where no election has been made under paragraph 9 in respect of a shared ownership trust—

(*a*) the initial capital shall be treated for the purposes of stamp duty land tax as chargeable consideration other than rent, and
(*b*) any rent-equivalent …[2] payment by the purchaser shall be treated for the purposes of stamp duty land tax as a payment of rent.][1]

Amendments—[1] Paragraphs 7–11 inserted by FA 2007 s 77 with effect in relation to land transactions with an effective date on or after 19 July 2007.
[2] In sub-para (*b*) word repealed by FA 2008 s 95(9) with effect in relation to transactions with an effective date on or after 12 March 2008.

[Shared ownership trust: declaration not linked with staircasing transactions etc

12 For the purpose of determining the rate of tax chargeable on the declaration of a shared ownership trust, the declaration shall be treated as if it were not linked to—

(*a*) any equity-acquisition payment under the trust or any consequent increase in the purchaser's beneficial interest in the trust property, or
(*b*) a transfer to the purchaser of an interest in the trust property upon the termination of the trust.][1]

Amendments—[1] Para 12 inserted by FA 2008 s 95(10) with effect in relation to transactions with an effective date on or after 12 March 2008.

[Rent to shared ownership lease: charge to tax

13— (1) The chargeable consideration for transactions forming part of a rent to shared ownership lease scheme is determined in accordance with this paragraph.

(2) A "rent to shared ownership lease scheme" means a scheme or arrangement under which a qualifying body—

(*a*) grants an assured shorthold tenancy of a dwelling to a person ("the tenant") or persons ("the tenants"), and

(*b*) subsequently grants a shared ownership lease of the dwelling or another dwelling to the tenant or one or more of the tenants.

(3) The following transactions are to be treated as if they were not linked to each other—

(*a*) the grant of the assured shorthold tenancy,

(*b*) the grant of the shared ownership lease, and

(*c*) any other land transaction between the qualifying body and the tenant, or any of the tenants, entered into as part of the scheme.

(4) For the purpose of determining the effective date of the grant of the shared ownership lease, the possession of the dwelling by the tenant or tenants pursuant to the assured shorthold tenancy is to be disregarded.

(5) In this paragraph—

"assured shorthold tenancy" has the same meaning as in Part 1 of the Housing Act 1988;

"qualifying body" has the same meaning as in paragraph 5;

"shared ownership lease" has the same meaning as in paragraph 4A.][1]

Amendments—[1] Paras 13 and 14 inserted by FA 2009 s 82(1) with effect in relation to cases in which the effective date of the grant of the shared ownership lease or the declaration of the shared ownership trust is on or after 22 April 2009.

[Rent to shared ownership trust: charge to tax

14— (1) The chargeable consideration for transactions forming part of a rent to shared ownership trust scheme is determined in accordance with this paragraph.

(2) A "rent to shared ownership trust scheme" means a scheme or arrangement under which—

(*a*) a qualifying body grants an assured shorthold tenancy of a dwelling to a person ("the tenant") or persons ("the tenants"), and

(*b*) the tenant, or one or more of tenants, subsequently becomes the purchaser under a shared ownership trust of the dwelling, or another dwelling, under which the qualifying body is the social landlord.

(3) The following transactions are to be treated as if they were not linked to each other—

(*a*) the grant of the assured shorthold tenancy,

(*b*) the declaration of the shared ownership trust, and

(*c*) any other land transaction between the qualifying body and the tenant, or any of the tenants, entered into as part of the scheme.

(4) For the purpose of determining the effective date of the declaration of the shared ownership trust, the possession of the dwelling by the tenant or tenants pursuant to the assured shorthold tenancy is to be disregarded.

(5) In this paragraph—

"assured shorthold tenancy" has the same meaning as in Part 1 of the Housing Act 1988;

"qualifying body" has the same meaning as in paragraph 5;

"social landlord" and "purchaser", in relation to a shared ownership trust, have the same meaning as in paragraph 7.][1]

Amendments—[1] Paras 13 and 14 inserted by FA 2009 s 82(1) with effect in relation to cases in which the effective date of the grant of the shared ownership lease or the declaration of the shared ownership trust is on or after 22 April 2009.

SCHEDULE 10

STAMP DUTY LAND TAX: RETURNS, ENQUIRIES, ASSESSMENTS AND APPEALS

Section 78

PART 1

LAND TRANSACTION RETURNS

Contents of return

1— (1) A land transaction return must—

(*a*) be in the prescribed form,

(*b*) contain the prescribed information, and

(*c*) include a declaration by the purchaser (or each of them) that the return is to the best of his knowledge correct and complete.

[(1A) Sub-paragraph (1)(*c*) is subject to paragraphs 1A and 1B.][1]

(2) In sub-paragraph (1) "prescribed" means prescribed by regulations made by the Inland Revenue.

(3) The regulations may make different provision for different kinds of return.

(4) Regulations under sub-paragraph (1)(*b*) may require the provision of information corresponding to any of the particulars formerly required under—

(*a*) Schedule 2 to the Finance Act 1931 (c 28) (requirement to deliver particulars of land transactions in Great Britain), or

(*b*) section 244 of the Finance Act 1994 (c 9) (corresponding provision for Northern Ireland).

(5) The return is treated as containing any information provided by the purchaser for the purpose of completing the return.

Amendments—[1] Sub-para (1A) inserted by the SDLT (Land Transaction Returns) Regulations, SI 2004/3208 regs 2, 3 with effect from 8 December 2004, in relation to a land transaction the effective date of which is on or after 8 December 2004.

[Declaration by agent

1A— (1) Where—

(*a*) the purchaser (or each of them) authorises an agent to complete a land transaction return,

(*b*) the purchaser (or each of them) makes a declaration that, with the exception of the effective date, the information provided in the return is to the best of his knowledge correct and complete, and

(*c*) the land transaction return includes a declaration by the agent that the effective date provided in the return is to the best of his knowledge correct,

the requirement in paragraph 1(1)(*c*) shall be deemed to be met.

(2) Sub-paragraph (1) applies only where the return is in a form specified by the Inland Revenue for the purposes of that sub-paragraph.

(3) Nothing in this paragraph affects the liability of the purchaser (or each of them) under this Part of this Act.][1]

Amendments—[1] Paragraphs 1A, 1B inserted by the SDLT (Land Transaction Returns) Regulations, SI 2004/3208 regs 2, 3 with effect from 8 December 2004, in relation to a land transaction the effective date of which is on or after 8 December 2004.

[Declaration by the relevant Official Solicitor

1B— (1) Where—

(*a*) the purchaser (or any of them) is a person under a disability,

(*b*) the Official Solicitor is acting for the purchaser (or any of them), and

(*c*) the land transaction return includes a declaration by the Official Solicitor that the return is to the best of his knowledge correct and complete,

the requirement in paragraph 1(1)(c) shall be deemed to be met.

(2) Sub-paragraph (1) applies only where the return is in a form specified by the Inland Revenue for the purposes of that sub-paragraph.

(3) Nothing in this paragraph affects the liability of the purchaser (or each of them) under this Part of this Act.

(4) In this paragraph "the Official Solicitor" means the Official Solicitor to the Supreme Court of England and Wales or the Official Solicitor to the Supreme Court of Northern Ireland (as the case requires).][1]

Amendments—[1] Paragraphs 1A, 1B inserted by the SDLT (Land Transaction Returns) Regulations, SI 2004/3208 regs 2, 3 with effect from 8 December 2004, in relation to a land transaction the effective date of which is on or after 8 December 2004.

Meaning of filing date and delivery of return

2— (1) References in this Part of this Act to the filing date, in relation to a land transaction return, are to the last day of the period within which the return must be delivered.

(2) References in this Part of this Act to the delivery of a land transaction return are to the delivery of a return that—

(*a*) complies with the requirements of paragraph 1(1) (contents of return), …[1]

(*b*) …[1]

Amendments—[1] Sub-para (2)(*b*) and preceding word "and" repealed by FA 2007 ss 80(1), (7), (9)(*f*), 114, Sch 27 Pt 4(4) with effect in relation to land transactions with an effective date on or after 19 July 2007.

Failure to deliver return: flat-rate penalty

3— (1) A person who is required to deliver a land transaction return and fails to do so by the filing date is liable to a flat-rate penalty under this paragraph.

He may also be liable to a tax-related penalty under paragraph 4.

(2) The penalty is—

(*a*) £100 if the return is delivered within three months after the filing date, and

(*b*) £200 in any other case.

Stamp Taxes

Failure to deliver return: tax-related penalty

4— (1) A purchaser who is required to deliver a land transaction return in respect of a chargeable transaction and fails to do so within twelve months after the filing date is liable to a tax-related penalty under this paragraph.

This is in addition to any flat-rate penalty under paragraph 3.

(2) The penalty is an amount not exceeding the amount of tax chargeable in respect of the transaction.

Formal notice to deliver return: daily penalty

5— (1) If it appears to the Inland Revenue—

(*a*) that a purchaser required to deliver a land transaction return in respect of a chargeable transaction has failed to do so, and

(*b*) that the filing date has now passed,

they may issue a notice requiring him to deliver a land transaction return in respect of the transaction.

(2) The notice must specify—

(*a*) the transaction to which it relates, and

(*b*) the period for complying with the notice (which must not be less than 30 days from the date of issue of the notice).

(3) If the purchaser does not comply with the notice within the specified period, the Inland Revenue may apply to the [tribunal][1] for an order imposing a daily penalty.

(4) On such an application the [tribunal][1] may direct that the purchaser shall be liable to a penalty or penalties not exceeding £60 for each day on which the failure continues after the day on which he is notified of the direction.

(5) This paragraph does not affect, and is not affected by, any penalty under paragraph 3 or 4 (flat-rate or tax-related penalty for failure to deliver return).

Amendments—[1] In sub-para(3) word substituted for the words "General or Special Commissioners"; in sub-para (4) word substituted for the word "Commissioners" by the Transfer of Tribunal Functions and Revenue and Customs Appeals Order, SI 2009/56 art 3, Sch 1 para 374 with effect from 1 April 2009.

Amendment of return by purchaser

6— (1) The purchaser may amend a land transaction return given by him by notice to the Inland Revenue.

(2) The notice must be in such form, and contain such information, as the Inland Revenue may require.

[(2A) If the effect of the amendment would be to entitle the purchaser to a repayment of tax, the notice must be accompanied by—

(*a*) the contract for the land transaction; and

(*b*) the instrument (if any) by which that transaction was effected.][1]

(3) Except as otherwise provided, an amendment may not be made more than twelve months after the filing date.

Amendments—[1] Sub-para (2A) inserted by the SDLT (Land Transaction Returns) Regulations, SI 2004/3208 regs 2, 3 with effect from 8 December 2004, in relation to a land transaction the effective date of which is on or after 8 December 2004.

Correction of return by Revenue

7— (1) The Inland Revenue may amend a land transaction return so as to correct obvious errors or omissions in the return (whether errors of principle, arithmetical mistakes or otherwise).

[(1A) The power under sub-paragraph (1) may, in such circumstances as the Commissioners for Her Majesty's Revenue and Customs may specify in regulations, be exercised—

(*a*) in relation to England and Wales, by the Chief Land Registrar;

(*b*) in relation to Scotland, by the Keeper of the Registers of Scotland;

(*c*) in relation to Northern Ireland, by the Registrar of Titles or the registrar of deeds;

(*d*) in any case, by such other persons with functions relating to the registration of land as the regulations may specify.][1]

(2) A correction under this paragraph is made by notice to the purchaser.

(3) No such correction may be made more than nine months after—

(*a*) the day on which the return was delivered, or

(*b*) if the correction is required in consequence of an amendment under paragraph 6, the day on which that amendment was made.

(4) A correction under this paragraph is of no effect if the purchaser—

(*a*) amends the return so as to reject the correction, or

(*b*) after the end of the period within which he may amend the return, but within three months from the date of issue of the notice of correction, gives notice rejecting the correction.

(5) Notice under sub-paragraph (4)(*b*) must be given to the officer of the Board by whom notice of the correction was given.

Amendments—[1] Sub-para (1A) inserted by F(No 2)A 2005 s 47(4) with effect from 20 July 2005.

Penalty for incorrect or uncorrected return

8— (1) A purchaser who—

(a) fraudulently or negligently delivers in respect of a chargeable transaction a land transaction return which is incorrect, or

(b) discovers that a land transaction return delivered by him in respect of a chargeable transaction (neither fraudulently nor negligently) is incorrect and does not remedy the error without unreasonable delay,

is liable to a tax-related penalty.

(2) The penalty is an amount not exceeding the amount of tax understated, that is, the difference between—

(a) the amount of tax chargeable in respect of the transaction, and

(b) the amount that would have been chargeable on the basis of the return delivered.[1]

HMRC Manuals—Stamp Duty Land Tax Manual SDLTM86190–86220 (Revenue practice on penalties under this paragraph).

Cross references—See FA 2004 s 313(4)(*f*) (disclosure of tax avoidance schemes: no liability to a penalty under this paragraph by reason of any failure to include in any return or account any reference number or other information required by virtue of FA 2004 s 313(3)(*a*)).

Amendments—[1] Para 8 repealed by FA 2008 s 122, Sch 40 para 21(*k*) with effect from 1 April 2009 (by virtue of SI 2009/571 art 2).

PART 2

DUTY TO KEEP AND PRESERVE RECORDS

Duty to keep and preserve records

9— (1) A purchaser who is required to deliver a land transaction return must—

(*a*) keep such records as may be needed to enable him to deliver a correct and complete return, and

(*b*) preserve those records in accordance with this paragraph.

(2) The records must be preserved for six years after the effective date of the transaction and until any later date on which—

(*a*) an enquiry into the return is completed, or

(*b*) if there is no enquiry, the Inland Revenue no longer have power to enquire into the return.

(3) The records required to be kept and preserved under this paragraph include—

(*a*) relevant instruments relating to the transaction, in particular, any contract or conveyance, and any supporting maps, plans or similar documents;

(*b*) records of relevant payments, receipts and financial arrangements.

Prospective amendments—In sub-para (2) words "until the end of the later of the relevant day and the" to be substituted for the words "or six years after the effective date of the transaction and until any later", sub-paras (2A), (4)–(6) to be inserted by FA 2009 s 98, Sch 50 paras 3–5 with effect from a date to be appointed. New sub-paras (2A), (4)–(6) to read as follows—

"(2A) "The relevant day" means—

(*a*) the sixth anniversary of the effective date of the transaction, or

(*b*) such earlier day as may be specified in writing by the Commissioners for Her Majesty's Revenue and Customs (and different days may be specified for different cases).".

"(4) The Commissioners for Her Majesty's Revenue and Customs may by regulations—

(*a*) provide that the records required to be kept and preserved under this paragraph include, or do not include, records specified in the regulations, and

(*b*) provide that those records include supporting documents so specified.

(5) Regulations under this paragraph may make provision by reference to things specified in a notice published by the Commissioners for Her Majesty's Revenue and Customs in accordance with the regulations (and not withdrawn by a subsequent notice).

(6) "Supporting documents" includes accounts, books, deeds, contracts, vouchers and receipts.".

Preservation of information instead of original records

10— (1) The duty under paragraph 9 to preserve records may be satisfied by the preservation of the information contained in them.

(2) Where information is so preserved a copy of any document forming part of the records is admissible in evidence in any proceedings before the [tribunal][1] to the same extent as the records themselves.

Amendments—[1] In sub-para (2) word substituted for the word "Commissioners" by the Transfer of Tribunal Functions and Revenue and Customs Appeals Order, SI 2009/56 art 3, Sch 1 para 375 with effect from 1 April 2009.

Prospective amendments—In the heading, word "etc" to be substituted for the words "instead of original records", and para 10 to be substituted, by FA 2009 s 98, Sch 50 paras 6, 7 with effect from a date to be appointed. Para 10, as substituted, to read as follows—

"**10** The duty under paragraph 9 to preserve records may be satisfied—

(*a*) by preserving them in any form and by any means, or

(*b*) by preserving the information contained in them in any form and by any means,

subject to any conditions or exceptions specified in writing by the Commissioners for Her Majesty's Revenue and Customs.".

Stamp Taxes

Penalty for failure to keep and preserve records

11— (1) A person who fails to comply with paragraph 9 in relation to a transaction is liable to a penalty not exceeding £3,000, subject to the following exception.

(2) No penalty is incurred if the Inland Revenue are satisfied that any facts that they reasonably require to be proved, and that would have been proved by the records, are proved by other documentary evidence provided to them.

PART 3

ENQUIRY INTO RETURN

HMRC Manuals—Stamp Duty Land Tax Manual SDLTM80800–81500 (Revenue practice on opening an enquiry). SDLTM81400–81940 (working an enquiry, including guidance on meetings and reassessing the tax payable). SDLTM82400–82970 (concluding an enquiry).

Notice of enquiry

12— (1) The Inland Revenue may enquire into a land transaction return if they give notice of their intention to do so ("notice of enquiry")—

(*a*) to the purchaser,

(*b*) before the end of the enquiry period.

(2) The enquiry period is the period of nine months—

(*a*) after the filing date, if the return was delivered on or before that date;

(*b*) after the date on which the return was delivered, if the return was delivered after the filing date;

(*c*) after the date on which the amendment was made, if the return is amended under paragraph 6 (amendment by purchaser).

[This is subject to the following qualification.][1]

[(2A) If—

(*a*) the Inland Revenue give notice, within the period specified in sub-paragraph (2), of their intention to enquire into a land transaction return delivered under section 80 (adjustment where contingency ceases or consideration is ascertained), 81 (further return where relief withdrawn) or 81A (return or further return in consequence of later linked transaction), and

(*b*) it appears to the Inland Revenue to be necessary to give a notice under this paragraph in respect of an earlier land transaction return in respect of the same land transaction,

a notice may be given notwithstanding that the period referred to in sub-paragraph (2) has elapsed in relation to that earlier land transaction.]

(3) A return that has been the subject of one notice of enquiry may not be the subject of another, except one given in consequence of an amendment (or another amendment) of the return under paragraph 6.

Amendments—[1] Words in sub-para (2) inserted, and sub-para (2A) inserted, by the SDLT (Land Transaction Returns) Regulations, SI 2004/3208 regs 2, 4 with effect from 8 December 2004, in relation to a land transaction the effective date of which is on or after 8 December 2004.

Scope of enquiry

13— (1) An enquiry extends to anything contained in the return, or required to be contained in the return, that relates—

(*a*) to the question whether tax is chargeable in respect of the transaction, or

(*b*) to the amount of tax so chargeable.

This is subject to the following exception.

(2) If the notice of enquiry is given as a result of an amendment of the return under paragraph 6 (amendment by purchaser)—

(*a*) at a time when it is no longer possible to give notice of enquiry under paragraph 12, or

(*b*) after an enquiry into the return has been completed,

the enquiry into the return is limited to matters to which the amendment relates or that are affected by the amendment.

Notice to produce documents etc for purposes of enquiry

14— (1) If the Inland Revenue give notice of enquiry into a land transaction return, they may by notice in writing require the purchaser—

(*a*) to produce to them such documents in his possession or power, and

(*b*) to provide them with such information, in such form,

as they may reasonably require for the purposes of the enquiry.

(2) A notice under this paragraph (which may be given at the same time as the notice of enquiry) must specify the time (which must not be less than 30 days) within which the purchaser is to comply with it.

(3) In complying with a notice under this paragraph copies of documents may be produced instead of originals, but—

(*a*) the copies must be photographic or other facsimiles, and

(*b*) the Inland Revenue may by notice require the original to be produced for inspection.

A notice under paragraph (*b*) must specify the time (which must not be less than 30 days) within which the purchaser is to comply with it.

(4) The Inland Revenue may take copies of, or make extracts from, any documents produced to them under this paragraph.

(5) A notice under this paragraph does not oblige a purchaser to produce documents or provide information relating to the conduct of—

(*a*) any pending appeal by him, or

(*b*) any pending referral to the [tribunal][1] under paragraph 19 to which he is a party.

HMRC Manuals—Stamp Duty Land Tax Manual SDLTM84570–84670 (Revenue guidance on requesting information from purchaser).

Amendments—[1] In sub-para (5)(*b*) word substituted for the words "Special Commissioners" by the Transfer of Tribunal Functions and Revenue and Customs Appeals Order, SI 2009/56 art 3, Sch 1 para 376 with effect from 1 April 2009.

Appeal against notice to produce documents etc

15— (1) An appeal may be brought against a requirement imposed by a notice under paragraph 14 to produce documents or provide information.

(2) Notice of appeal must be given—

(*a*) in writing,

(*b*) within 30 days after the issue of the notice appealed against,

(*c*) to the officer of the Board by whom that notice was given.

(3) An appeal under this paragraph shall be …[1] determined in the same way as an appeal against an assessment.

(4) On an appeal under this paragraph [that is notified to the tribunal, the tribunal][1]—

(*a*) shall set aside the notice so far as it requires the production of documents, or the provision of information, that appears …[1] not reasonably required for the purposes of the enquiry, and

(*b*) shall confirm the notice so far as it requires the production or documents, or the provision of information, that appears …[1] reasonably required for the purposes of the enquiry.

(5) A notice that is confirmed by the [tribunal][1] (or so far as it is confirmed) has effect as if the period specified in it for complying was 30 days from the determination of the appeal.

[(6) Notwithstanding the provisions of sections 11 and 13 of the Tribunals, Courts and Enforcement Act 2007 the decision of the tribunal on an appeal under this paragraph is final.][1]

Amendments—[1] In sub-para (3) words "heard and" repealed; in sub-para (4) words substituted for the words "the Commissioners" and words "to them" repealed in both places; in sub-para (5) word substituted for the word "Commissioners"; sub-para (6) substituted by the Transfer of Tribunal Functions and Revenue and Customs Appeals Order, SI 2009/56 art 3, Sch 1 para 377 with effect from 1 April 2009. Sub-para (6) previously read as follows—

"(6) The decision of the Commissioners on an appeal under this paragraph is final.".

Penalty for failure to produce documents etc

16— (1) A person who fails to comply with a notice under paragraph 14 (notice to produce documents etc for purposes of enquiry) is liable—

(*a*) to a penalty of £50, and

(*b*) if the failure continues after a penalty is imposed under paragraph (*a*) above, to a further penalty or penalties not exceeding the amount specified in sub-paragraph (2) below for each day on which the failure continues.

(2) The amount referred to in sub-paragraph (1)(*b*) is—

(*a*) £30 if the penalty is determined by an officer of the Board, and

(*b*) £150 if the penalty is determined by the court.

(3) No penalty shall be imposed under this paragraph in respect of a failure at any time after the failure has been remedied.

HMRC Manuals—Stamp Duty Land Tax Manual SDLTM86250–86300 (Revenue guidance on penalties under this paragraph).

Amendment of self-assessment during enquiry to prevent loss of tax

17— (1) If at a time when an enquiry is in progress into a land transaction return the Inland Revenue form the opinion—

(*a*) that the amount stated in the self-assessment contained in the return as the amount of tax payable is insufficient, and

(*b*) that unless the assessment is immediately amended there is likely to be a loss of tax to the Crown,

they may by notice in writing to the purchaser amend the assessment to make good the deficiency.

(2) In the case of an enquiry that under paragraph 13(2) is limited to matters arising from an amendment of the return, sub-paragraph (1) above applies only so far as the deficiency is attributable to the amendment.

(3) For the purposes of this paragraph the period during which an enquiry is in progress is the whole of the period—

(*a*) beginning with the day on which notice of enquiry is given, and

(*b*) ending with the day on which the enquiry is completed.

HMRC Manuals—Stamp Duty Land Tax Manual SDLTM81900–81940 (Revenue practice on jeopardy assessments under this paragraph).
SDLTM81920 (circumstances where the Revenue consider making jeopardy assessments).

Amendment of return by taxpayer during enquiry

18— (1) This paragraph applies if a return is amended under paragraph 6 (amendment by purchaser) at a time when an enquiry is in progress into the return.

(2) The amendment does not restrict the scope of the enquiry but may be taken into account (together with any matters arising) in the enquiry.

(3) So far as the amendment affects the amount stated in the self-assessment included in the return as the amount of tax payable, it does not take effect while the enquiry is in progress and—

(*a*) if the Inland Revenue state in the closure notice that they have taken the amendments into account and that—

(i) the amendment has been taken into account in formulating the amendments contained in the notice, or

(ii) their conclusion is that the amendment is incorrect,

the amendment shall not take effect;

(*b*) otherwise, the amendment takes effect when the closure notice is issued.

(4) For the purposes of this paragraph the period during which an enquiry is in progress is the whole of the period—

(*a*) beginning with the day on which notice of enquiry is given, and

(*b*) ending with the day on which the enquiry is completed.

Referral of questions to [the tribunal][1] during enquiry

19— (1) At any time when an enquiry is in progress into a land transaction return any question arising in connection with the subject-matter of the enquiry may be referred [to the tribunal for determination][1].

(2) Notice of referral must be given—

(*a*) jointly by the purchaser and the Inland Revenue,

(*b*) …[1]

(*c*) to the [tribunal][1].

(3) …[1].

(4) More than one notice of referral may be given under this paragraph in relation to an enquiry.

(5) For the purposes of this paragraph the period during which an enquiry is in progress is the whole of the period—

(*a*) beginning with the day on which the notice of enquiry was given, and

(*b*) ending with the day on which the enquiry is completed.

Amendments—[1] In the heading, sub-para (2)(*c*) words substituted for the words "Special Commissioners"; in sub-para (1) words substituted for the words "to the Special Commissioners for their determination"; sub-paras (2)(*b*), (3) repealed; by the Transfer of Tribunal Functions and Revenue and Customs Appeals Order, SI 2009/56 art 3, Sch 1 para 378 with effect from 1 April 2009. Sub-paras (2)(*b*), (3) previously read as follows—

"(*b*) in writing,"

"(3) The notice of referral must specify the question or questions being referred.".

Withdrawal of notice of referral

20— (1) The Inland Revenue or the purchaser may withdraw a notice of referral under paragraph 19 …[1].

(2) …[1]

Amendments—[1] In sub-para (1) words "by notice in accordance with this paragraph" repealed; sub-para (2) repealed by the Transfer of Tribunal Functions and Revenue and Customs Appeals Order, SI 2009/56 art 3, Sch 1 para 379 with effect from 1 April 2009. Sub-para (2) previously read as follows—

"(2) Notice of withdrawal must be given—

(*a*) in writing,

(*b*) to the other party to the referral and to the Special Commissioners,

(*c*) before the first hearing by the Special Commissioners in relation to the referral.".

Effect of referral on enquiry

21— (1) While proceedings on a referral under paragraph 19 are in progress in relation to an enquiry—

(*a*) no closure notice shall be given in relation to the enquiry, and (*b*) no application may be made for a direction to give such a notice.

(2) For the purposes of this paragraph proceedings on a referral are in progress where—

(*a*) notice of referral has been given,
(*b*) the notice has not been withdrawn, and
(*c*) the questions referred have not been finally determined.

(3) For the purposes of sub-paragraph (2)(*c*) a question referred is finally determined when—

(*a*) it has been determined by the [tribunal][1], and
(*b*) there is no further possibility of the determination being varied or set aside (disregarding any power to grant permission to appeal out of time).

Amendments—[1] In sub-para (3)(*a*) word substituted for the words "Special Commissioners" by the Transfer of Tribunal Functions and Revenue and Customs Appeals Order, SI 2009/56 art 3, Sch 1 para 380 with effect from 1 April 2009.

Effect of determination

22— (1) The determination of a question referred to the [tribunal][1] under paragraph 19 is binding on the parties to the referral in the same way, and to the same extent, as a decision on a preliminary issue in an appeal.

(2) The determination shall be taken into account by the Inland Revenue—

(*a*) in reaching their conclusions on the enquiry, and
(*b*) in formulating any amendments of the return required to give effect to those conclusions.

(3) Any right of appeal under paragraph 35 (appeals against assessments) may not be exercised so as to reopen the question determined except to the extent (if any) that it could be reopened if it had been determined as a preliminary issue in that appeal.

Amendments—[1] In sub-para (1) word substituted for the words "Special Commissioners" by the Transfer of Tribunal Functions and Revenue and Customs Appeals Order, SI 2009/56 art 3, Sch 1 para 381 with effect from 1 April 2009.

Completion of enquiry

23— (1) An enquiry under paragraph 12 is completed when the Inland Revenue by notice (a "closure notice") inform the purchaser that they have completed their enquiries and state their conclusions.

(2) A closure notice must either—

(*a*) state that in the opinion of the Inland Revenue no amendment of the return is required, or
(*b*) make the amendments of the return required to give effect to their conclusions.

(3) A closure notice takes effect when it is issued.

Direction to complete enquiry

24— (1) The purchaser may apply to the [tribunal][1] for a direction that the Inland Revenue give a closure notice within a specified period.

[(2) Any such application is to be subject to the relevant provisions of Part 5 of the Taxes Management Act 1970 (see, in particular, section 48(2)(*b*) of that Act).][1]

(3) The [tribunal][1] hearing the application shall give a direction unless …[1] satisfied that the Inland Revenue have reasonable grounds for not giving a closure notice within a specified period.

Amendments—[1] In sub-para (1) word substituted for the words "General or Special Commissioners"; sub-para (2) substituted; in sub-para (3) word substituted for the word "Commissioners" and words "they are" repealed by the Transfer of Tribunal Functions and Revenue and Customs Appeals Order, SI 2009/56 art 3, Sch 1 para 382 with effect from 1 April 2009. Sub-para (2) previously read as follows—

"(2) Any such application shall be heard and determined in the same way as an appeal.".

PART 4

REVENUE DETERMINATION IF NO RETURN DELIVERED

Cross references—Pension Protection Fund (Tax) Regulations, SI 2006/575 reg 43(4) (SI 2006/575 reg 43 to be construed as one with this Part).

Determination of tax chargeable if no return delivered

25— (1) If in the case of a chargeable transaction no land transaction return is delivered by the filing date, the Inland Revenue may make a determination (a "Revenue determination") to the best of their information and belief of the amount of tax chargeable in respect of the transaction.

(2) Notice of the determination must be served on the purchaser, stating the date on which it is issued.

(3) No Revenue determination may be made more than six years after the effective date of the transaction.

Cross references—FA 2009 Sch 56 (penalty for failure to make payments on time).
Prospective amendments—In sub-para (3) words "4 years" to be substituted for the words "six years" by FA 2009 s 99, Sch 51 paras 14, 15(1), (2) with effect from a date to be appointed.

Stamp Taxes

Determination to have effect as a self-assessment

26— (1) A determination under paragraph 25 has effect for enforcement purposes as if were a self-assessment by the purchaser.

(2) In sub-paragraph (1) "for enforcement purposes" means for the purposes of the following provisions of this Part of this Act—

(*a*) the provisions of this Schedule providing for tax-related penalties;
(*b*) section 87 (interest on unpaid tax);
(*c*) section 91 and Schedule 12 (collection and recovery of unpaid tax etc).

(3) Nothing in this paragraph affects any liability of the purchaser to a penalty for failure to deliver a return.

Determination superseded by actual self-assessment

27— (1) If after a Revenue determination has been made the purchaser delivers a land transaction return in respect of the transaction, the self-assessment included in that return supersedes the determination.

(2) Sub-paragraph (1) does not apply to a return delivered—

(*a*) more than six years after the day on which the power to make the determination first became exercisable, or
(*b*) more than twelve months after the date of the determination,

whichever is the later.

(3) Where—

(*a*) proceedings have been begun for the recovery of any tax charged by a Revenue determination, and
(*b*) before the proceedings are concluded the determination is superseded by a self-assessment,

the proceedings may be continued as if they were proceedings for the recovery of so much of the tax charged by the self-assessment as is due and payable and has not been paid.

Prospective amendments—In sub-para (2)(*a*) words "4 years" to be substituted for the words "six years" by FA 2009 s 99, Sch 51 paras 14, 15(1), (3) with effect from a date to be appointed.

PART 5
REVENUE ASSESSMENTS

Assessment where loss of tax discovered

28— (1) If the Inland Revenue discover as regards a chargeable transaction that—

(*a*) an amount of tax that ought to have been assessed has not been assessed, or
(*b*) an assessment to tax is or has become insufficient, or
(*c*) relief has been given that is or has become excessive,

they may make an assessment (a "discovery assessment") in the amount or further amount that ought in their opinion to be charged in order to make good to the Crown the loss of tax.

(2) The power to make a discovery assessment in respect of a transaction for which the purchaser has delivered a return is subject to the restrictions specified in paragraph 30.

Assessment to recover excessive repayment of tax

29— (1) If an amount of tax has been repaid to any person that ought not to have been repaid to him, that amount may be assessed and recovered as if it were unpaid tax.

(2) Where the repayment was made with interest, the amount assessed and recovered may include the amount of interest that ought not to have been paid.

(3) The power to make an assessment under this paragraph in respect of a transaction for which the purchaser has delivered a land transaction return is subject to the restrictions specified in paragraph 30.

Restrictions on assessment where return delivered

30— (1) If the purchaser has delivered a land transaction return in respect of the transaction in question, an assessment under paragraph 28 or 29 in respect of the transaction—

(*a*) may only be made in the two cases specified in sub-paragraph (2) and (3) below, and
(*b*) may not be made in the circumstances specified in sub-paragraph (5) below.

(2) The first case is where the situation mentioned in paragraph 28(1) or 29(1) is attributable to fraudulent or negligent conduct on the part of—

(*a*) the purchaser,
(*b*) a person acting on behalf of the purchaser, or
(*c*) a person who was a partner of the purchaser at the relevant time.

(3) The second case is where the Inland Revenue, at the time they—

(*a*) ceased to be entitled to give a notice of enquiry into the return, or (*b*) completed their enquiries into the return,

could not have been reasonably expected, on the basis of the information made available to them before that time, to be aware of the situation mentioned in paragraph 28(1) or 29(1).

(4) For this purpose information is regarded as made available to the Inland Revenue if—

(*a*) it is contained in a land transaction return made by the purchaser,

(*b*) it is contained in any documents produced or information provided to the Inland Revenue for the purposes of an enquiry into any such return, or

(*c*) it is information the existence of which, and the relevance of which as regards the situation mentioned in paragraph 28(1) or 29(1)—

(i) could reasonably be expected to be inferred by the Inland Revenue from information falling within paragraphs (*a*) or (*b*) above, or

(ii) are notified in writing to the Inland Revenue by the purchaser or a person acting on his behalf.

(5) No assessment may be made if—

(*a*) the situation mentioned in paragraph 28(1) or 29(1) is attributable to a mistake in the return as to the basis on which the tax liability ought to have been computed, and

(*b*) the return was in fact made on the basis or in accordance with the practice generally prevailing at the time it was made.

Stamp Taxes

Time limit for assessment

31— (1) The general rule is that no assessment may be made more than six years after the effective date of the transaction to which it relates.

(2) In a case involving fraud or negligence on the part of—

(*a*) the purchaser, or

(*b*) a person acting on behalf of the purchaser, or

(*c*) a person who was a partner of the purchaser at the relevant time,

an assessment may be made up to 21 years after the effective date of the transaction to which it relates.

(3) An assessment under paragraph 29 (assessment to recover excessive repayment of tax) is not out of time—

(*a*) in a case where notice of enquiry is given into the land transaction return delivered by the person concerned, if it is made before the enquiry is completed;

(*b*) in any case, if it is made within one year after the repayment in question was made.

(4) Where the purchaser has died—

(*a*) any assessment on the personal representatives of the deceased must be made within three years after his death, and

(*b*) an assessment shall not be made by virtue of sub-paragraph (2) in respect of a transaction of which the effective date was more than six years before the death.

(5) Any objection to the making of an assessment on the ground that the time limit for making it has expired can only be made on an appeal against the assessment.

Prospective amendments—In sub-para (1) words "4 years" to be substituted for the words "six years", sub-paras (2), (2A) to be substituted for sub-para (2), in sub-para (4)(*a*) words "4 years" to be substituted for the words "three years", and sub-para (6) to be inserted, by FA 2009 s 99, Sch 51 paras 14, 15(1), (4)–(8) with effect from a date to be appointed. New sub-paras (2), (2A), (6) to read as follows—

"(2) An assessment of a person to tax in a case involving a loss of tax brought about carelessly by the purchaser or a related person may be made at any time not more than 6 years after the effective date of the transaction to which it relates (subject to sub-paragraph (2A)).

(2A) An assessment of a person to tax in a case involving a loss of tax—

(*a*) brought about deliberately by the purchaser or a related person,

(*b*) attributable to a failure by the person to comply with an obligation under section 76(1) or paragraph 3(3)(*a*), 4(3)(*a*) or 8(3)(*a*) of Schedule 17A, or

(*c*) attributable to arrangements in respect of which the person has failed to comply with an obligation under section 309, 310 or 313 of the Finance Act 2004 (obligation of parties to tax avoidance schemes to provide information to Her Majesty's Revenue and Customs),

may be made at any time not more than 20 years after the effective date of the transaction to which it relates.".

"(6) In this paragraph "related person", in relation to a purchaser, means—

(*a*) a person acting on behalf of the purchaser, or

(*b*) a person who was a partner of the purchaser at the relevant time.".

[Losses brought about carelessly or deliberately

31A— (1) This paragraph applies for the purposes of paragraph 31.

(2) A loss of tax is brought about carelessly by a person if the person fails to take reasonable care to avoid bringing about that loss.

(3) Where—

(*a*) information is provided to Her Majesty's Revenue and Customs,

(*b*) the person who provided the information, or the person on whose behalf the information was provided, discovers some time later that the information was inaccurate, and

(*c*) that person fails to take reasonable steps to inform Her Majesty's Revenue and Customs, any loss of tax brought about by the inaccuracy is to be treated as having been brought about carelessly by that person.

(4) References to a loss of tax brought about deliberately by a person include a loss of tax brought about as a result of a deliberate inaccuracy in a document given to Her Majesty's Revenue and Customs by or on behalf of that person.]

Prospective amendments—This para to be inserted by FA 2009 s 99, Sch 51 paras 14, 15(1), (9) with effect from a date to be appointed.

Assessment procedure

32— (1) Notice of an assessment must be served on the purchaser.

(2) The notice must state—

(*a*) the tax due,

(*b*) the date on which the notice is issued, and

(*c*) the time within which any appeal against the assessment must be made.

(3) After notice of the assessment has been served on the purchaser, the assessment may not be altered except in accordance with the express provisions of this Part of this Act.

(4) Where an officer of the Board has decided to make an assessment to tax, and has taken all other decisions needed for arriving at the amount of the assessment, he may entrust to some other officer of the Board responsibility for completing the assessing procedure, whether by means involving the use of a computer or otherwise, including responsibility for serving notice of the assessment.

PART 6

RELIEF IN CASE OF EXCESSIVE ASSESSMENT

Relief in case of double assessment

33— (1) A person who believes he has been assessed to tax more than once in respect of the same matter may make a claim [to the Inland Revenue for relief against any double charge][1].

(2), (3) …[1]

[(4) An appeal may be made against a decision on a claim for relief under this paragraph.][2]

Amendments—[1] Words in sub-para (1) substituted for the words "for relief under this paragraph", and sub-paras (2), (3) repealed, by FA 2004 ss 299(1), (7), 326, Sch 42 Pt 4(2) with effect from 22 July 2004.

[2] Sub-para (4) substituted by the Transfer of Tribunal Functions and Revenue and Customs Appeals Order, SI 2009/56 art 3, Sch 1 para 383 with effect from 1 April 2009. Sub-para (4) previously read as follows—

"(4) An appeal against a decision of the Inland Revenue on a claim for relief under this paragraph may be brought to the Commissioners having jurisdiction to hear an appeal relating to the assessment, or the later of the assessments, to which the claim relates.".

Relief in case of mistake in return

34— (1) A person who believes he has paid tax under an assessment that was excessive by reason of some mistake in a land transaction return may make a claim [to the Inland Revenue for relief against any excessive charge][1].

(2) The claim must be made …[1] not more than six years after the effective date of the transaction.

(3) …[1]

(4) No relief shall be given under this paragraph—

(*a*) in respect of a mistake as to the basis on which the liability of the claimant ought to have been computed when the return was in fact made on the basis or in accordance with the practice generally prevailing at the time when it was made, or

(*b*) in respect of a mistake in a claim or election included in the return.

(5) In determining a claim under this paragraph the Inland Revenue shall have regard to all the relevant circumstances of the case.

They shall, in particular, consider whether the granting of relief would result in amounts being excluded from charge to tax.

(6) On an appeal against the Inland Revenue's decision on the claim, [that is notified to the tribunal, the tribunal shall][2] hear and determine the claim in accordance with the same principles as apply to the determination by the Inland Revenue of claims under this paragraph.

HMRC Manuals—Stamp Duty Land Tax Manual SDLTM52500–52550 (Revenue practice on this relief).

Amendments—[1] Words in sub-para (1) substituted for the words "for relief under this paragraph"; in para (2), words "by notice in writing given to the Inland Revenue" repealed; and sub-para (3) repealed, by FA 2004 ss 299(1), (8), 326, Sch 42 Pt 4(2) with effect from 22 July 2004.

[2] In sub-para (6) words substituted for the words "the Special Commissioners shall" by the Transfer of Tribunal Functions and Revenue and Customs Appeals Order, SI 2009/56 art 3, Sch 1 para 384 with effect from 1 April 2009.

Prospective amendments—In sub-para (2) words "4 years" to be substituted for the words "six years" by FA 2009 s 99, Sch 51 paras 14, 15(1), (10) with effect from a date to be appointed.

PART 7

[REVIEWS AND APPEALS][1]

Amendments—[1] Heading substituted for former heading "Appeals against Revenue decisions on tax" by the Transfer of Tribunal Functions and Revenue and Customs Appeals Order, SI 2009/56 art 3, Sch 1 para 385 with effect from 1 April 2009.

Right of appeal

35— (1) An appeal may be brought against—

(*a*) an amendment of a self-assessment under paragraph 17 (amendment by Revenue during enquiry to prevent loss of tax),

(*b*) a conclusion stated or amendment made by a closure notice,

(*c*) a discovery assessment, ...[1]

(*d*) an assessment under paragraph 29 (assessment to recover excessive repayment)[, or

(*e*) a Revenue determination under paragraph 25 (determination of tax chargeable if no return delivered).][1]

(2) ...[2]

(3) [If][2] an appeal under sub-paragraph (1)(*a*) against an amendment of a self-assessment [is][2] made while an enquiry is in progress [none of the steps mentioned in paragraph 36A(2)(*a*) to (*c*) may be taken in relation to the appeal][2] until the enquiry is completed.

Amendments—[1] Word in sub-para (1)(*c*) repealed, and sub-para (1)(*e*) inserted, by the SDLT (Land Transaction Returns) Regulations, SI 2004/3208 regs 2, 5(1), (2) with effect from 8 December 2004, in relation to a land transaction the effective date of which is on or after 8 December 2004.

[2] Sub-para (2) repealed; in sub-para (3) word in the first and second places inserted and in the third place words substituted for the words "shall not be heard and determined" by the Transfer of Tribunal Functions and Revenue and Customs Appeals Order, SI 2009/56 art 3, Sch 1 para 386 with effect from 1 April 2009. Sub-para (2) previously read as follows—

"(2) The appeal lies to the General or Special Commissioners.".

Notice of appeal

36— (1) Notice of an appeal under paragraph 35 must be given—

(*a*) in writing

(*b*) within 30 days after the specified date,

(*c*) to the relevant officer of the Board.

(2) In relation to an appeal under paragraph 35(1)(*a*)—

(*a*) the specified date is the date on which the notice of amendment was issued, and

(*b*) the relevant officer of the Board is the officer by whom the notice of amendment was given.

(3) In relation to an appeal under paragraph 35(1)(*b*)—

(*a*) the specified date is the date on which the closure notice was issued, and

(*b*) the relevant officer of the Board is the officer by whom the closure notice was given.

(4) In relation to an appeal under paragraph 35(1)(*c*) or (*d*)—

(*a*) the specified date is the date on which the notice of assessment was issued, and

(*b*) the relevant officer of the Board is the officer by whom the notice of assessment was given.

[(4A) In relation to an appeal under paragraph 35(1)(*e*)—

(*a*) the specified date is the date on which the Revenue determination was issued, and

(*b*) the relevant officer of the Board is the officer by whom the determination was made.][1]

(5) The notice of appcal must specify the grounds of appeal.

[(5A) The only grounds on which an appeal lies under paragraph 35(1)(*e*) are that—

(*a*) the purchase to which the determination relates did not take place,

(*b*) the interest in the land to which the determination relates has not been purchased,

(*c*) the contract for the purchase of the interest to which the determination relates has not been substantially performed, or

(*d*) the land transaction is [not notifiable][2] (for example, because the land transaction is exempt from charge under Schedule 3).][1]

(6) ...[3]

Amendments—[1] Sub-paras (4A), (5A) inserted by the SDLT (Land Transaction Returns) Regulations, SI 2004/3208 regs 2, 5(1), (3) with effect from 8 December 2004, in relation to a land transaction the effective date of which is on or after 8 December 2004.

[2] Words in sub-para (5A)(*d*) substituted by FA 2008 s 94, Sch 30 para 7 with effect in relation to transactions with an effective date on or after 12 March 2008.

[3] Sub-para (6) repealed by the Transfer of Tribunal Functions and Revenue and Customs Appeals Order, SI 2009/56 art 3, Sch 1 para 387 with effect from 1 April 2009. Sub-para (6) previously read as follows—

"(6) On the hearing of the appeal the Commissioners may allow the appellant to put forward grounds not specified in the notice, and take them into consideration, if satisfied that the omission was not deliberate or unreasonable.".

[Appeal: HMRC review or determination by tribunal

36A— (1) This paragraph applies if notice of appeal has been given to HMRC.

(2) In such a case—

(a) the appellant may notify HMRC that the appellant requires HMRC to review the matter in question (see paragraph 36B),

(b) HMRC may notify the appellant of an offer to review the matter in question (see paragraph 36C), or

(c) the appellant may notify the appeal to the tribunal (see paragraph 36D).

(3) See paragraphs 36G and 36H for provision about notifying appeals to the tribunal after a review has been required by the appellant or offered by HMRC.

(4) This paragraph does not prevent the matter in question from being dealt with in accordance with paragraph 37(1) (settling of appeals by agreement).][1]

Amendments—[1] Paragraphs 36A–36I inserted by the Transfer of Tribunal Functions and Revenue and Customs Appeals Order, SI 2009/56 art 3, Sch 1 para 388 with effect from 1 April 2009.

[Appellant requires review by HMRC

36B— (1) Sub-paragraphs (2) and (3) apply if the appellant notifies HMRC that the appellant requires HMRC to review the matter in question.

(2) HMRC must, within the relevant period, notify the appellant of HMRC's view of the matter in question.

(3) HMRC must review the matter in question in accordance with paragraph 36E.

(4) The appellant may not notify HMRC that the appellant requires HMRC to review the matter in question and HMRC shall not be required to conduct a review if—

(*a*) the appellant has already given a notification under this paragraph in relation to the matter in question,

(*b*) HMRC have given a notification under paragraph 36C in relation to the matter in question, or

(*c*) the appellant has notified the appeal to the tribunal under paragraph 36D.

(5) In this paragraph "relevant period" means—

(*a*) the period of 30 days beginning with the day on which HMRC receive the notification from the appellant, or

(*b*) such longer period as is reasonable.][1]

Amendments—[1] Paragraphs 36A–36I inserted by the Transfer of Tribunal Functions and Revenue and Customs Appeals Order, SI 2009/56 art 3, Sch 1 para 388 with effect from 1 April 2009.

[HMRC offer review

36C— (1) Sub-paragraphs (2) to (6) apply if HMRC notify the appellant of an offer to review the matter in question.

(2) When HMRC notify the appellant of the offer, HMRC must also notify the appellant of HMRC's view of the matter in question.

(3) If, within the acceptance period, the appellant notifies HMRC of acceptance of the offer, HMRC must review the matter in question in accordance with paragraph 36E.

(4) If the appellant does not give HMRC such a notification within the acceptance period, HMRC's view of the matter in question is to be treated as if it were contained in an agreement in writing under paragraph 37(1) for the settlement of that matter.

(5) The appellant may not give notice under paragraph 37(2) (desire to withdraw from agreement) in a case where sub-paragraph (4) applies.

(6) Sub-paragraph (4) does not apply to the matter in question if, or to the extent that, the appellant notifies the appeal to the tribunal under paragraph 36H.

(7) HMRC may not notify the appellant of an offer to review the matter in question (and, accordingly, HMRC shall not be required to conduct a review) if—

(*a*) HMRC have already given a notification under this paragraph in relation to the matter in question,

(*b*) the appellant has given a notification under paragraph 36B in relation to the matter in question, or

(*c*) the appellant has notified the appeal to the tribunal under paragraph 36D.

(8) In this paragraph "acceptance period" means the period of 30 days beginning with the date of the document by which HMRC notify the appellant of the offer to review the matter in question.][1]

Amendments—[1] Paragraphs 36A–36I inserted by the Transfer of Tribunal Functions and Revenue and Customs Appeals Order, SI 2009/56 art 3, Sch 1 para 388 with effect from 1 April 2009.

[Notifying appeal to the tribunal

36D— (1) This paragraph applies in a case where paragraph 36A applies.

(2) The appellant may notify the appeal to the tribunal.

(3) If the appellant notifies the appeal to the tribunal, the tribunal is to decide the matter in question.

(4) Sub-paragraphs (2) and (3) do not apply in a case where—

(*a*) HMRC have given a notification of their view of the matter in question under paragraph 36B, or

(*b*) HMRC have given a notification under paragraph 36C in relation to the matter in question.

(5) In a case falling within sub-paragraph (4)(a) or (b), the appellant may notify the appeal to the tribunal, but only if permitted to do so by paragraph 36G or 36H.][1]

Amendments—[1] Paragraphs 36A–36I inserted by the Transfer of Tribunal Functions and Revenue and Customs Appeals Order, SI 2009/56 art 3, Sch 1 para 388 with effect from 1 April 2009.

[Nature of review etc

36E— (1) This paragraph applies if HMRC are required by paragraph 36B or 36C to review the matter in question.

(2) The nature and extent of the review are to be such as appear appropriate to HMRC in the circumstances.

(3) For the purpose of sub-paragraph (2), HMRC must, in particular, have regard to steps taken before the beginning of the review—

(*a*) by HMRC in deciding the matter in question, and

(*b*) by any person in seeking to resolve disagreement about the matter in question.

(4) The review must take account of any representations made by the appellant at a stage which gives HMRC a reasonable opportunity to consider them.

(5) The review may conclude that HMRC's view of the matter in question is to be—

(*a*) upheld,

(*b*) varied, or

(*c*) cancelled.

(6) HMRC must notify the appellant of the conclusions of the review and their reasoning within—

(*a*) the period of 45 days beginning with the relevant day, or

(*b*) such other period as may be agreed.

(7) In sub-paragraph (6) "relevant day" means—

(*a*) in a case where the appellant required the review, the day when HMRC notified the appellant of HMRC's view of the matter in question,

(*b*) in a case where HMRC offered the review, the day when HMRC received notification of the appellant's acceptance of the offer.

(8) Where HMRC are required to undertake a review but do not give notice of the conclusions within the period specified in sub-paragraph (6), the review is treated as having concluded that HMRC's view of the matter in question (see paragraphs 36B(2) and 36C(2)) is upheld.

(9) If sub-paragraph (8) applies, HMRC must notify the appellant of the conclusions which the review is treated as having reached.][1]

Amendments—[1] Paragraphs 36A–36I inserted by the Transfer of Tribunal Functions and Revenue and Customs Appeals Order, SI 2009/56 art 3, Sch 1 para 388 with effect from 1 April 2009.

[Effect of conclusions of review

36F— (1) This paragraph applies if HMRC give notice of the conclusions of a review (see paragraph 36E).

(2) The conclusions are to be treated as if they were an agreement in writing under paragraph 37(1) for the settlement of the matter in question.

(3) The appellant may not give notice under paragraph 37(2) (desire to withdraw from agreement) in a case where sub-paragraph (2) applies.

(4) Sub-paragraph (2) does not apply to the matter in question if, or to the extent that, the appellant notifies the appeal to the tribunal under paragraph 36G.][1]

Amendments—[1] Paragraphs 36A–36I inserted by the Transfer of Tribunal Functions and Revenue and Customs Appeals Order, SI 2009/56 art 3, Sch 1 para 388 with effect from 1 April 2009.

[Notifying appeal to tribunal after review concluded

36G— (1) This paragraph applies if—

(*a*) HMRC have given notice of the conclusions of a review in accordance with paragraph 36E, or

(*b*) the period specified in paragraph 36E(6) has ended and HMRC have not given notice of the conclusions of the review.

(2) The appellant may notify the appeal to the tribunal within the post-review period.

(3) If the post-review period has ended, the appellant may notify the appeal to the tribunal only if the tribunal gives permission.

(4) If the appellant notifies the appeal to the tribunal, the tribunal is to determine the matter in question.

(5) In this paragraph "post-review period" means—

(*a*) in a case falling with sub-paragraph (1)(*a*), the period of 30 days beginning with the date of the document in which HMRC give notice of the conclusions of the review in accordance with paragraph 36E(6), or

(*b*) in a case falling within sub-paragraph (1)(*b*), the period that—

(i) begins with the day following the last day of the period specified in paragraph 36E(6), and

(ii) ends 30 days after the date of the document in which HMRC give notice of the conclusions of the review in accordance with paragraph 36E(9).][1]

Amendments—[1] Paragraphs 36A–36I inserted by the Transfer of Tribunal Functions and Revenue and Customs Appeals Order, SI 2009/56 art 3, Sch 1 para 388 with effect from 1 April 2009.

[Notifying appeal to tribunal after review offered but not accepted

36H— (1) This paragraph applies if—

(*a*) HMRC have offered to review the matter in question (see paragraph 36C), and

(*b*) the appellant has not accepted the offer.

(2) The appellant may notify the appeal to the tribunal within the acceptance period.

(3) But if the acceptance period has ended, the appellant may notify the appeal to the tribunal only if the tribunal gives permission.

(4) If the appellant notifies the appeal to the tribunal, the tribunal is to determine the matter in question.

(5) In this paragraph "acceptance period" has the same meaning as in paragraph 36C.][1]

Amendments—[1] Paragraphs 36A–36I inserted by the Transfer of Tribunal Functions and Revenue and Customs Appeals Order, SI 2009/56 art 3, Sch 1 para 388 with effect from 1 April 2009.

[Other interpretation

36I— (1) In paragraphs 36A to 36H—

(*a*) "matter in question" means the matter to which an appeal relates;

(*b*) a reference to a notification is a reference to a notification in writing.

(2) In paragraphs 36A to 36H, a reference to the appellant includes a person acting on behalf of the appellant except in relation to—

(*a*) notification of HMRC's view under paragraph 36B(2),

(*b*) notification by HMRC of an offer of review (and of their view of the matter) under paragraph 36C,

(*c*) notification of the conclusions of a review under paragraph 36E(6), and

(*d*) notification of the conclusions of a review under paragraph 36E(9).

(3) But if a notification falling within any of the sub-paragraphs of paragraph (2) is given to the appellant, a copy of the notification may also be given to a person acting on behalf of the appellant.][1]

Amendments—[1] Paragraphs 36A–36I inserted by the Transfer of Tribunal Functions and Revenue and Customs Appeals Order, SI 2009/56 art 3, Sch 1 para 388 with effect from 1 April 2009.

Settling of appeals by agreement

37— (1) If, before an appeal under paragraph 35 is determined, the appellant and the Inland Revenue agree that the decision appealed against—

(*a*) should be upheld without variation,

(*b*) should be varied in a particular manner, or

(*c*) should be discharged or cancelled,

the same consequences shall follow, for all purposes, as would have followed if, at the time the agreement was come to, the [tribunal][1] had determined the appeal and had upheld the decision without variation, varied it in that manner or discharged or cancelled it, as the case may be.

(2) Sub-paragraph (1) does not apply if, within 30 days from the date when the agreement was come to, the appellant gives notice in writing to the Inland Revenue that he wishes to withdraw from the agreement.

(3) Where the agreement is not in writing—

(*a*) sub-paragraphs (1) and (2) do not apply unless the fact that an agreement was come to, and the terms agreed, are confirmed by notice in writing given by the Inland Revenue to the appellant or by the appellant to the Inland Revenue, and

(*b*) the references in those provisions to the time when the agreement was come to shall be read as references to the time when the notice of confirmation was given.

(4) Where—

(*a*) the appellant notifies the Inland Revenue, orally or in writing, that he does not wish to proceed with the appeal, and

(*b*) the Inland Revenue do not, within 30 days after that notification, give the appellant notice in writing indicating that they are unwilling that the appeal should be withdrawn, the provisions of sub-paragraphs (1) to (3) have effect as if, at the date of the appellant's notification, the appellant and the Inland Revenue had come to an agreement (orally or in writing, as the case may be) that the decision under appeal should be upheld without variation.

(5) References in this paragraph to an agreement being come to with an appellant, and to the giving of notice or notification by or to the appellant, include references to an agreement being come to, or notice or notification being given by or to, a person acting on behalf of the appellant in relation to the appeal.

Amendments—[1] In sub-para (1) word substituted for the word "Commissioners" by the Transfer of Tribunal Functions and Revenue and Customs Appeals Order, SI 2009/56 art 3, Sch 1 para 389 with effect from 1 April 2009.

Recovery of tax not postponed by appeal

38— (1) Where there is an appeal ...[1] under paragraph 35, the tax charged by the amendment or assessment in question remains due and payable as if there had been no appeal.

(2) Sub-paragraph (1) is subject to—

paragraph 39 (direction by [the tribunal][1] postponing payment), and
paragraph 40 (agreement to postpone payment).

Amendments—[1] In sub-para (1) words "to the Commissioners" repealed; in sub-para (2) words substituted for the word "Commissioners" by the Transfer of Tribunal Functions and Revenue and Customs Appeals Order, SI 2009/56 art 3, Sch 1 para 390 with effect from 1 April 2009.

Direction by [the tribunal][1] to postpone payment

39— [(1) If the appellant has grounds for believing that the amendment or assessment overcharges the appellant to tax, or as a result of the conclusion stated in the closure notice the tax charged on the appellant is excessive, the appellant may—

(a) first apply by notice in writing to HMRC within 30 days of the specified date for a determination by them of the amount of tax the payment of which should be postponed pending the determination of the appeal;

(b) where such a determination is not agreed, refer the application for postponement to the tribunal within 30 days from the date of the document notifying HMRC's decision on the amount to be postponed.

An application under sub-paragraph (a) must state the amount believed to be overcharged to tax and the grounds for that belief.][1]

(2) ...[1]

(3) An application may be made more than 30 days after the specified date if there is a change in the circumstances of the case as a result of which the appellant has grounds for believing that he is overcharged to tax by the decision appealed against.

(4) If, after any determination on such an application of the amount of tax the payment of which should be postponed, there is a change in the circumstances of the case as a result of which either party has grounds for believing that the amount so determined has become excessive or, as the case may be, insufficient, he may, [if the parties cannot agree on a revised determination, apply, at any time before the determination of the appeal, to the tribunal for a revised][1] determination of that amount.

[(5) An application under this paragraph is to be subject to the relevant provisions of Part 5 of the Taxes Management Act 1970 (see, in particular, section 48(2)(*b*) of that Act).][1]

The fact that any such application has been heard and determined by any Commissioners does not preclude them from hearing and determining the appeal or any further application under this paragraph.

(6) The amount of tax of which payment is to be postponed pending the determination of the appeal is the amount (if any) by which it appears ...[1] that there are reasonable grounds for believing that the appellant is overcharged.

(7) Where an application is made under this paragraph, the date on which any tax of which payment is not postponed is due and payable shall be determined as if the tax were charged by an amendment or assessment of which notice was issued on the date on which the application was determined and against which there was no appeal.

(8) On the determination of the appeal—

(*a*) the date on which any tax payable in accordance with that determination is due and payable shall, so far as it is tax the payment of which had been postponed, or which would not have been charged by the amendment or assessment if there had been no appeal, be determined as if the tax were charged by an amendment or assessment—

(i) of which notice was issued on the date on which [HMRC][1] issues to the appellant a notice of the total amount payable in accordance with the determination, and

(ii) against which there had been no appeal, and

(*b*) any tax overpaid shall be repaid.

Amendments—[1] In heading, words substituted for the word "Commissioners"; sub-paras (1), (5) substituted; sub-para (2) repealed; in sub-para (4) words substituted for the words "by notice in writing given to the other party at any time before the determination of the appeal, apply to the Commissioners for a further"; in sub-para (6) words "to the Commissioners, having regard to the representations made and any evidence adduced," repealed; in sub-para (8) words substituted for the words "the Inland Revenue" by the Transfer of Tribunal Functions and Revenue and Customs Appeals Order, SI 2009/56 art 3, Sch 1 para 391 with effect from 1 April 2009. Sub-paras (1), (2), (5) previously read as follows—

"(1) If the appellant has grounds for believing that he is overcharged to tax by the decision appealed against, he may by notice in writing apply to the Commissioners for a direction that payment of an amount of tax shall be postponed pending the determination of the appeal.

(2) The notice must—

(*a*) be given to the relevant officer of the Board within 30 days after the specified date, and

(*b*) state the amount by which the appellant believes himself to be overcharged to tax, and his grounds for that belief.

(5) An application under this paragraph shall be heard and determined by the Commissioners in the same way as an appeal.".

Agreement to postpone payment of tax

40— (1) If the appellant and the relevant officer of the Board agree that payment of an amount of tax should be postponed pending the determination of the appeal, the same consequences shall follow, for all purposes, as would have followed if, at the time the agreement was come to, the [tribunal][1] had made a direction to the same effect.

This is without prejudice to the making of a further agreement or of a further direction.

(2) Where the agreement is not in writing—

(*a*) sub-paragraph (1) does not apply unless the fact that an agreement was come to, and the terms agreed, are confirmed by notice in writing given by the relevant officer of the Board to the appellant or by the appellant to that officer, and

(*b*) the reference in that provision to the time when the agreement was come to shall be read as a reference to the time when notice of confirmation was given.

(3) References in this paragraph to an agreement being come to with an appellant, and to the giving of notice to or by the appellant, include references to an agreement being come to, or notice being given to or by, a person acting on behalf of the appellant in relation to the appeal.

Amendments—[1] In sub-para (1) word substituted for the word "Commissioners" by the Transfer of Tribunal Functions and Revenue and Customs Appeals Order, SI 2009/56 art 3, Sch 1 para 392 with effect from 1 April 2009.

[Tribunal determinations

41 The determination of the tribunal in relation to any proceedings under the enactments relating to stamp duty land tax shall be final and conclusive except as otherwise provided in—

(*a*) sections 9 to 14 of the Tribunals, Courts and Enforcement Act 2007,

(*b*) the Taxes Management Act 1970 applied as modified, or

(*c*) the enactments relating to stamp duty land tax.][1]

Amendments—[1] Paragraphs 41–46 inserted by the Transfer of Tribunal Functions and Revenue and Customs Appeals Order, SI 2009/56 art 3, Sch 1 para 393 with effect from 1 April 2009.

[Assessments and self assessments

42— (1) In this paragraph any reference to an appeal means an appeal under paragraphs 33(4) or 35(1).

(2) If, on an appeal notified to the tribunal, the tribunal decides—

(*a*) that the appellant is overcharged by a self-assessment; or

(*b*) that the appellant is overcharged by an assessment other than a self-assessment,

the assessment shall be reduced accordingly, but otherwise the assessment shall stand good.

(3) If, on appeal it appears to the tribunal—

(*a*) that the appellant is undercharged to stamp duty land tax by a self-assessment; or

(*b*) that the appellant is undercharged by an assessment other than a self-assessment,

the assessment shall be increased accordingly.

(4) Where, on an appeal against an assessment other than a self-assessment which—

(*a*) assesses an amount which is chargeable to stamp duty land tax, and

(*b*) charges stamp duty land tax on the amount assessed,

it appears to the tribunal as mentioned in sub-paragraphs (2) or (3), it may, unless the circumstances of the case otherwise require, reduce or increase only the amount assessed; and where an appeal is so determined the stamp duty land tax charged by that assessment shall be taken to have been reduced or increased accordingly.][1]

Amendments—[1] Paragraphs 41–46 inserted by the Transfer of Tribunal Functions and Revenue and Customs Appeals Order, SI 2009/56 art 3, Sch 1 para 393 with effect from 1 April 2009.

[Payment of stamp duty land tax where there is a further appeal

43— (1) Where a party to an appeal to the tribunal under paragraph 35 makes a further appeal, notwithstanding that the further appeal is pending, stamp duty land tax shall nevertheless be payable or repayable in accordance with the determination of the tribunal or court as the case may be.

(2) But if the amount charged by the assessment is altered by the order or judgment of the Upper Tribunal or court—

(*a*) if too much stamp duty land tax has been paid, the amount overpaid shall be refunded with such interest, if any, as may be allowed by that order or judgment; and

(*b*) if too little stamp duty land tax has been charged, the amount undercharged shall be due and payable at the expiration of a period of thirty days beginning with the date on which HMRC issue to the other party a notice of the total amount payable in accordance with the order or judgment.][1]

Amendments—[1] Paragraphs 41–46 inserted by the Transfer of Tribunal Functions and Revenue and Customs Appeals Order, SI 2009/56 art 3, Sch 1 para 393 with effect from 1 April 2009.

[Late notice of appeal

44— (1) This paragraph applies in a case where—

(*a*) notice of appeal may be given to HMRC under this Schedule or any other provision of Part 4 of this Act, but

(*b*) no notice is given before the relevant time limit.

(2) Notice may be given after the relevant time limit if—

(*a*) HMRC agree, or

(*b*) where HMRC do not agree, the tribunal gives permission.

(3) If the following conditions are met, HMRC shall agree to notice being given after the relevant time limit.

(4) Condition A is that the appellant has made a request in writing to HMRC to agree to the notice being given.

(5) Condition B is that HMRC are satisfied that there was reasonable excuse for not giving the notice before the relevant time limit.

(6) Condition C is that HMRC are satisfied that request under sub-paragraph (4) was made without unreasonable delay after the reasonable excuse ceased.

(7) If a request of the kind referred to in sub-paragraph (4) is made, HMRC must notify the appellant whether or not HMRC agree to the appellant giving notice of appeal after the relevant time limit.

(8) In this paragraph "relevant time limit", in relation to notice of appeal, means the time before which the notice is to be given (but for this paragraph).][1]

Amendments—[1] Paragraphs 41–46 inserted by the Transfer of Tribunal Functions and Revenue and Customs Appeals Order, SI 2009/56 art 3, Sch 1 para 393 with effect from 1 April 2009.

[Questions to be determined by the relevant [tribunal][2]

45— (1) Where the question in any dispute on any appeal under paragraphs 34(6) or 35(1) is a question of the market value of the subject matter of the land transaction that question shall be determined on a reference by the relevant [tribunal][2].

(2) In this [paragraph "the relevant tribunal"][2] means—

(*a*) where the land is in England and Wales, the [Upper Tribunal][2];

(*b*) where the land is in Scotland, the Lands Tribunal for Scotland;

(*c*) where the land is in Northern Ireland, the Lands Tribunal for Northern Ireland.][1]

Amendments—[1] Paragraphs 41–46 inserted by the Transfer of Tribunal Functions and Revenue and Customs Appeals Order, SI 2009/56 art 3, Sch 1 para 393 with effect from 1 April 2009.

[2] In heading and sub-para (1), words substituted for words "Lands Tribunal", and in sub-para (2), words substituted for words "regulation 'the relevant Lands Tribunal' " and "Lands Tribunal" by the Transfer of Tribunal Functions (Lands Tribunal and Miscellaneous Amendments) Order, SI 2009/1307 art 5(1), (2), Sch 1 para 270 with effect from 1 June 2009.

[Meaning of HMRC

46 In this Schedule "HMRC" means Her Majesty's Revenue and Customs.][1]

Amendments—[1] Paragraphs 41–46 inserted by the Transfer of Tribunal Functions and Revenue and Customs Appeals Order, SI 2009/56 art 3, Sch 1 para 393 with effect from 1 April 2009.

SCHEDULE 11

STAMP DUTY LAND TAX: [RECORD-KEEPING WHERE TRANSACTION IS NOT NOTIFIABLE][1]

Section 79

Amendment—[1] Words in heading substituted by FA 2008 s 94, Sch 30 para 11 with effect in relation to transactions with an effective date on or after 12 March 2008.

PART 1

GENERAL

Repeal—Part 1 repealed by FA 2008 s 94, Sch 30 para 8 with effect in relation to transactions with an effective date on or after 12 March 2008.

PART 2

DUTY TO KEEP AND PRESERVE RECORDS

Duty to keep and preserve records

4— [(A1) This paragraph applies where a transaction is not notifiable, unless the transaction is a transaction treated as taking place under a provision listed in section 79(2)(*a*) to (*d*).][1]

(1) [The purchaser][1] must—

(*a*) keep such records as may be needed to enable him [to demonstrate that the transaction is not notifiable][1], and

(*b*) preserve those records in accordance with this paragraph.

(2) The records must be preserved for six years after the effective date of the transaction …[1]

(3) The records required to be kept and preserved under this paragraph include—

(*a*) relevant instruments relating to the transaction, in particular, any contract or conveyance, and any supporting maps, plans or similar documents;

(*b*) records of relevant payments, receipts and financial arrangements.

Amendments—[1] Sub-para (A1) inserted, words in sub-para (1) substituted, and words in sub-para (2) repealed, by FA 2008 s 94, Sch 30 para 9 with effect in relation to transactions with an effective date on or after 12 March 2008.

Prospective amendments—In sub-para (2), new paras (*a*), (*b*) and preceding words to be substituted for the words "for six years after the effective date of the transaction", and sub-paras (4)–(6) to be inserted, by FA 2009 s 98, Sch 50 paras 8, 9 with effect from a date to be appointed. New sub-paras (2)(*a*), (*b*), (4)–(6), to read as follows—

"until the end of—

(*a*) the sixth anniversary of the effective date of the transaction, or

(*b*) such earlier day as may be specified in writing by the Commissioners for Her Majesty's Revenue and Customs (and different days may be specified for different cases).".

"(4) The Commissioners for Her Majesty's Revenue and Customs may by regulations—

(*a*) provide that the records required to be kept and preserved under this paragraph include, or do not include, records specified in the regulations, and

(*b*) provide that those records include supporting documents so specified.

(5) Regulations under this paragraph may make provision by reference to things specified in a notice published by the Commissioners for Her Majesty's Revenue and Customs in accordance with the regulations (and not withdrawn by a subsequent notice).

(6) "Supporting documents" includes accounts, books, deeds, contracts, vouchers and receipts.".

Preservation of information instead of original records

5— (1) The duty under paragraph 4 to preserve records may be satisfied by the preservation of the information contained in them.

(2) Where information is so preserved a copy of any document forming part of the records is admissible in evidence in any proceedings before the [tribunal][1] to the same extent as the records themselves.

Amendments—[1] In para (5)(2) word substituted for the word "Commissioners" by the Transfer of Tribunal Functions and Revenue and Customs Appeals Order, SI 2009/56 art 3, Sch 1 para 394 with effect from 1 April 2009.

Prospective amendments—In heading word "etc" to be substituted for the words "instead of original records", and para 5 to be substituted by FA 2009 s 98, Sch 50 paras 8, 10, 11 with effect from a date to be appointed. Para 5, as substituted, to read as follows—

"**5** The duty under paragraph 4 to preserve records may be satisfied—

(*a*) by preserving them in any form and by any means, or

(*b*) by preserving the information contained in them in any form and by any means,

subject to any conditions or exceptions specified in writing by the Commissioners for Her Majesty's Revenue and Customs.".

Penalty for failure to keep and preserve records

6— (1) A person who fails to comply with paragraph 4 in relation to a transaction is liable to a penalty not exceeding £3,000, subject to the following exception.

(2) No penalty is incurred if the Inland Revenue are satisfied that any facts that they reasonably require to be proved, and that would have been proved by the records, are proved by other documentary evidence provided to them.

PART 3

ENQUIRY INTO SELF-CERTIFICATE

Repeal—Part 3 repealed by FA 2008 s 94, Sch 30 para 10 with effect in relation to transactions with an effective date on or after 12 March 2008.

[SCHEDULE 11A

STAMP DUTY LAND TAX: CLAIMS NOT INCLUDED IN RETURNS

Section 82A][1]

Amendments—[1] This Schedule inserted by FA 2004 s 299(1), (3), Sch 40 with effect from 22 July 2004.

[Introductory

1 This Schedule applies to a claim under any provision of this Part other than a claim that is required to be made in, or by amendment to, a return under this Part.

References in this Schedule to a claim shall be read accordingly.][1]

Amendments—[1] This Schedule inserted by FA 2004 s 299(1), (3), Sch 40 with effect from 22 July 2004.

[Making of claims

2— (1) A claim must be made in such form as the Inland Revenue may determine.

(2) The form of claim must provide for a declaration to the effect that all the particulars given in the form are correctly stated to the best of the claimant's information and belief.

(3) The form of claim may require—

(*a*) a statement of the amount of tax that will be required to be discharged or repaid in order to give effect to the claim;

(*b*) such information as is reasonably required for the purpose of determining whether and, if so, the extent to which the claim is correct;

(*c*) the delivery with the claim of such statements and documents, relating to the information contained in the claim, as are reasonably required for the purpose mentioned in paragraph (*b*).

(4) A claim for repayment of tax may not be made unless the claimant has documentary evidence that the tax has been paid.][1]

Amendments—[1] This Schedule inserted by FA 2004 s 299(1), (3), Sch 40 with effect from 22 July 2004.

[Duty to keep and preserve records

3— (1) A person who may wish to make a claim must—

(*a*) keep such records as may be needed to enable him to make a correct and complete claim, and

(*b*) preserve those records in accordance with this paragraph.

(2) The records must be preserved until the latest of the following times—

(*a*) the end of the period of twelve months beginning with day on which the claim was made;

(*b*) where there is an enquiry into the claim, or into an amendment of the claim, the time when the enquiry is completed;

(*c*) where the claim is amended and there is there is no enquiry into the amendment, the time when the Inland Revenue no longer have power to enquire into the amendment.

(3) The duty under this paragraph to preserve records may be satisfied by the preservation of the information contained in them.

(4) Where information is so preserved a copy of any document forming part of the records is admissible in evidence in any proceedings before the [tribunal][2] to the same extent as the records themselves.

(5) A person who fails to comply with this paragraph in relation to a claim that he makes is liable to a penalty not exceeding £3,000, subject to the following exception.

(6) No penalty is incurred if the Inland Revenue are satisfied that any facts that they reasonably require to be proved, and that would have been proved by the records, are proved by other documentary evidence provided to them.][1]

Amendments—[1] This Schedule inserted by FA 2004 s 299(1), (3), Sch 40 with effect from 22 July 2004.

[2] In sub-para (4) word substituted for the word "Commissioners" by the Transfer of Tribunal Functions and Revenue and Customs Appeals Order, SI 2009/56 art 3, Sch 1 para 396 with effect from 1 April 2009.

Prospective amendments—Sub-paras (3), (4) to be repealed, and sub-paras (4A)–(4C) to be inserted, by FA 2009 s 98, Sch 50 paras 12, 13 with effect from a date to be appointed. New sub-paras (4A)–(4C) to read as follows—

"(4A) The Commissioners for Her Majesty's Revenue and Customs may by regulations—

(*a*) provide that the records required to be kept and preserved under this paragraph include, or do not include, records specified in the regulations, and

(*b*) provide that those records include supporting documents so specified.

(4B) Regulations under this paragraph may make provision by reference to things specified in a notice published by the Commissioners for Her Majesty's Revenue and Customs in accordance with the regulations (and not withdrawn by a subsequent notice).

(4C) "Supporting documents" includes accounts, books, deeds, contracts, vouchers and receipts.".

[Preservation of information etc

3A The duty under paragraph 3 to preserve records may be satisfied—

(*a*) by preserving them in any form and by any means, or

(*b*) by preserving the information contained in them in any form and by any means,

subject to any conditions or exceptions specified in writing by the Commissioners for Her Majesty's Revenue and Customs.]

Prospective amendments—Para 3A to be inserted by FA 2009 s 98, Sch 50 paras 12, 14 with effect from a date to be appointed.

Stamp Taxes

[Amendment of claim by claimant

4— (1) The claimant may amend his claim by notice to the Inland Revenue.

(2) No such amendment may be made—

(*a*) more than twelve months after the day on which the claim was made, or

(*b*) if the Inland Revenue give notice under paragraph 7 (notice of enquiry), during the period—

(i) beginning with the day on which notice is given, and

(ii) ending with the day on which the enquiry under that paragraph is completed.][1]

Amendments—[1] This Schedule inserted by FA 2004 s 299(1), (3), Sch 40 with effect from 22 July 2004.

[Correction of claim by Revenue

5— (1) The Inland Revenue may by notice to the claimant amend a claim so as to correct obvious errors or omissions in the claim (whether errors of principle, arithmetical mistakes or otherwise).

(2) No such correction may be made—

(*a*) more than nine months after the day on which the claim was made, or

(*b*) if the Inland Revenue give notice under paragraph 7 (notice of enquiry), during the period—

(i) beginning with the day on which notice is given, and

(ii) ending with the day on which the enquiry under that paragraph is completed.

(3) A correction under this paragraph is of no effect if, within three months from the date of issue of the notice of correction, the claimant gives notice rejecting the correction.

(4) Notice under sub-paragraph (3) must be given to the officer of the Board by whom the notice of correction was given.][1]

Amendments—[1] This Schedule inserted by FA 2004 s 299(1), (3), Sch 40 with effect from 22 July 2004.

[Giving effect to claims and amendments

6— (1) As soon as practicable after a claim is made, or is amended under paragraph 4 or 5, the Inland Revenue shall give effect to the claim or amendment by discharge or repayment of tax.

(2) Where the Inland Revenue enquire into a claim or amendment—

(*a*) sub-paragraph (1) does not apply until a closure notice is given under paragraph 11 (completion of enquiry), and then it applies subject to paragraph 13 (giving effect to amendments under paragraph 11), but

(*b*) the Inland Revenue may at any time before then give effect to the claim or amendment, on a provisional basis, to such extent as they think fit.][1]

Amendments—[1] This Schedule inserted by FA 2004 s 299(1), (3), Sch 40 with effect from 22 July 2004.

[Notice of enquiry

7— (1) The Inland Revenue may enquire into a person's claim or amendment of a claim if they give him notice of their intention to do so ("notice of enquiry") before the end of the period of nine months after the day on which the claim or amendment was made.

(2) A claim or amendment that has been the subject of one notice of enquiry may not be the subject of another.][1]

Amendments—[1] This Schedule inserted by FA 2004 s 299(1), (3), Sch 40 with effect from 22 July 2004.

[Notice to produce documents etc for purposes of enquiry

8— (1) If the Inland Revenue give a person a notice of enquiry, they may by notice in writing require him—

(*a*) to produce to them such documents in his possession or power, and

(*b*) to provide them with such information, in such form, as they may reasonably require for the purposes of the enquiry.

(2) A notice given to a person under this paragraph (which may be given at the same time as the notice of enquiry) must specify the time (which must not be less than 30 days) within which he is to comply with it.

(3) In complying with a notice under this paragraph copies of documents may be produced instead of originals, but—

(*a*) the copies must be photographic or other facsimiles, and

(*b*) the Inland Revenue may by notice require the original to be produced for inspection.

A notice under paragraph (*b*) must specify the time (which must not be less than 30 days) within which the person is to comply with it.

(4) The Inland Revenue may take copies of, or make extracts from, any documents produced to them under this paragraph.

(5) A notice under this paragraph does not oblige a person to produce documents or provide information relating to the conduct of any pending appeal by him.][1]

Amendments—[1] This Schedule inserted by FA 2004 s 299(1), (3), Sch 40 with effect from 22 July 2004.

[Appeal against notice to produce documents etc

9— (1) An appeal may be brought against a requirement imposed by a notice under paragraph 8 to produce documents or provide information.

(2) Notice of appeal must be given—

(*a*) in writing,
(*b*) within 30 days after the issue of the notice appealed against,
(*c*) to the officer of the Board by whom that notice was given.

(3) An appeal under this paragraph shall be ...[2] determined in the same way as an appeal against an assessment.

(4) On an appeal under this paragraph [that is notified to the tribunal, the tribunal][2]—

(*a*) shall set aside the notice so far as it requires the production of documents, or the provision of information, that appears ...[2] not reasonably required for the purposes of the enquiry, and
(*b*) shall confirm the notice so far as it requires the production of documents, or the provision of information, that appears ...[2] reasonably required for the purposes of the enquiry.

(5) A notice that is confirmed by the [tribunal][2] (or so far as it is confirmed) has effect as if the period specified in it for complying was 30 days from the determination of the appeal.

[(6) Notwithstanding the provisions of sections 11 and 13 of the Tribunals, Courts and Enforcement Act 2007, the decision of the tribunal on an appeal under this paragraph is final.][2]][1]

Amendments—[1] This Schedule inserted by FA 2004 s 299(1), (3), Sch 40 with effect from 22 July 2004.
[2] In sub-para (3) words "heard and" repealed; in sub-para (4) words substituted for the words "the Commissioners" and words "to them" repealed in both places; in sub-para (5) word substituted for the word "Commissioners"; sub-para (6) substituted by the Transfer of Tribunal Functions and Revenue and Customs Appeals Order, SI 2009/56 art 3, Sch 1 para 397 with effect from 1 April 2009. Sub-para (6) previously read as follows—

"(6) The decision of the Commissioners on an appeal under this paragraph is final.".

[Penalty for failure to produce documents etc

10— (1) A person who fails to comply with a notice under paragraph 8 (notice to produce documents etc for purposes of enquiry) is liable—

(*a*) to a penalty of £50, and
(*b*) if the failure continues after a penalty is imposed under paragraph (*a*), to a further penalty or penalties not exceeding £30 for each day on which the failure continues.

(2) No penalty shall be imposed under this paragraph in respect of a failure at any time after the failure has been remedied.][1]

Amendments—[1] This Schedule inserted by FA 2004 s 299(1), (3), Sch 40 with effect from 22 July 2004.

[Completion of enquiry

11— (1) An enquiry under paragraph 7 is completed when the Inland Revenue by notice (a "closure notice") inform the purchaser that they have completed their enquiries and state their conclusions.

(2) A closure notice must either—

(*a*) state that in the opinion of the Inland Revenue no amendment of the claim is required, or
(*b*) if in the Inland Revenue's opinion the claim is insufficient or excessive, amend the claim so as to make good or eliminate the deficiency or excess.

In the case of an enquiry into an amendment of a claim, paragraph (*b*) applies only so far as the deficiency or excess is attributable to the amendment.

(3) A closure notice takes effect when it is issued.][1]

Amendments—[1] This Schedule inserted by FA 2004 s 299(1), (3), Sch 40 with effect from 22 July 2004.

[Direction to complete enquiry

12— (1) The claimant may apply to the [tribunal][2] for a direction that the Inland Revenue give a closure notice within a specified period.

[(2) Any such application is to be subject to the relevant provisions of Part 5 of the Taxes Management Act 1970 (see, in particular, section 48(2)(*b*) of that Act).][2]

(3) The [tribunal][2] shall give a direction unless ...[2] satisfied that the Inland Revenue have reasonable grounds for not giving a closure notice within a specified period.][1]

Amendments—[1] This Schedule inserted by FA 2004 s 299(1), (3), Sch 40 with effect from 22 July 2004.
[2] In sub-para (1) words substituted for the words "General or Special Commissioners"; sub-para (2) substituted; in sub-para (3) word substituted for the words "Commissioners hearing the application" and words "they are" repealed by the Transfer of Tribunal Functions and Revenue and Customs Appeals Order, SI 2009/56 art 3, Sch 1 para 397 with effect from 1 April 2009. Sub-para (2) previously read as follows—

"(2) Any such application shall be heard and determined in the same way as an appeal.".

[Giving effect to amendments under paragraph 11

13— (1) Within 30 days after the date of issue of a notice under paragraph 11(2)(*b*) (closure notice that amends claim), the Inland Revenue shall give effect to the amendment by making such adjustment as may be necessary, whether—

(*a*) by way of assessment on the claimant, or

(*b*) by discharge or repayment of tax.

(2) An assessment made under sub-paragraph (1) is not out of time if it is made within the time mentioned in that sub-paragraph.][1]

Amendments—[1] This Schedule inserted by FA 2004 s 299(1), (3), Sch 40 with effect from 22 July 2004.

[Appeals against amendments under paragraph 11

14— (1) An appeal may be brought against a conclusion stated or amendment made by a closure notice.

(2) Notice of the appeal must be given—

(*a*) in writing,

(*b*) within 30 days after the date on which the closure notice was issued,

(*c*) to the officer of the Board by whom the closure notice was given.

(3) The notice of appeal must specify the grounds of appeal.

(4) ...[2]

(5) [Paragraphs 36A to 37 and 44][2] of Schedule 10 (settling of appeals by agreement) applies in relation to an appeal under this paragraph as [they apply][2] in relation to an appeal under paragraph 35 of that Schedule.

(6) On an appeal against an amendment made by a closure notice, the [tribunal][2] may vary the amendment appealed against whether or not the variation is to the advantage of the appellant.

(7) Where any such amendment is varied, whether by the [tribunal][2] or by the order of a court, paragraph 13 (giving effect to amendments under paragraph 11) applies (with the necessary modifications) in relation to the variation as it applied in relation to the amendment.][1]

Amendments—[1] This Schedule inserted by FA 2004 s 299(1), (3), Sch 40 with effect from 22 July 2004.

[2] Sub-para (4) repealed; in sub-para (5) words substituted for the words "Paragraph 37" and for the words "it applies"; in sub-paras (6), (7) word substituted for the word "Commissioners"; by the Transfer of Tribunal Functions and Revenue and Customs Appeals Order, SI 2009/56 art 3, Sch 1 para 399 with effect from 1 April 2009. Sub-para (4) previously read as follows—

"(4) On the hearing of the appeal the Commissioners may allow the appellant to put forward grounds not specified in the notice, and take them into consideration, if satisfied that the omission was not deliberate or unreasonable.".

[Jurisdiction of Commissioners

[15— *(1) An appeal against a conclusion stated or amendment made by a closure notice is to be made to the Special Commissioners if it relates to a claim made to the Board.*

(2) Subject to—

(a) sub-paragraph (1),

(b) paragraph 33(4) of Schedule 10 (appeal against decision on claim for relief in case of double assessment), and

(c) any right to elect to bring an appeal before the Special Commissioners conferred by regulations under Schedule 17 (General and Special Commissioners, appeals and other proceedings),

an appeal under any provision of this Schedule is to be made to the General Commissioners.][2]][1]

Amendments—[1] This Schedule inserted by FA 2004 s 299(1), (3), Sch 40 with effect from 22 July 2004.

[2] Para 15 repealed by the Transfer of Tribunal Functions and Revenue and Customs Appeals Order, SI 2009/56 art 3, Sch 1 para 400 with effect from 1 April 2009.

SCHEDULE 12

STAMP DUTY LAND TAX: COLLECTION AND RECOVERY OF TAX

Section 91

PART 1

GENERAL

Issue of tax demands and receipts

1— (1) Where tax is due and payable, a collector may make demand of the sum charged from the person liable to pay it.

(2) On payment of the tax, the collector shall if so requested give a receipt.

Prospective amendments—Para 1A to be inserted by the Tribunals, Courts and Enforcement Act 2007 s 62(3), Sch 13 para 147(1), (2) with effect from a date to be appointed. Para 1A to read as follows—

"*Recovery of tax by taking control of goods*

1A In England and Wales, if a person neglects or refuses to pay the sum charged, the collector may use the procedure in Schedule 12 to the Tribunals, Courts and Enforcement Act 2007 (taking control of goods) to recover the sum."

Para 1A to be repealed by FA 2008 s 129, Sch 43 para 9 with effect from a date to be appointed.

Recovery of tax by distraint

2— (1) In England and Wales or Northern Ireland, if a person neglects or refuses to pay the sum charged, upon demand made by the collector, the collector may distrain upon the goods and chattels of the person charged ("the person in default").

(2) For the purposes of levying such distress a justice of the peace, on being satisfied by information on oath that there is reasonable ground for believing that a person is neglecting or refusing to pay a sum charged, may issue a warrant in writing authorising a collector to break open, in the daytime, any house or premises, calling to his assistance any constable.

Every such constable shall, when so required, assist the collector in the execution of the warrant and in levying such distress in the house or premises.

(3) A levy or warrant to break open must be executed by, or under the direction of, and in the presence of, the collector.

(4) A distress levied by the collector shall be kept for five days, at the costs and charges of the person in default.

(5) If the person in default does not pay the sum due, together with the costs and charges, the distress shall be appraised by one or more independent persons appointed by the collector, and shall be sold by public auction by the collector for payment of the sum due and all costs and charges.

Any surplus resulting from the distress, after the deduction of the costs and charges and of the sum due, shall be restored to the owner of the goods distrained.

(6) The Treasury may by regulations make provision with respect to—

(*a*) the fees chargeable on or in connection with the levying of distress, and

(*b*) the costs and charges recoverable where distress has been levied.

Recovery of tax by diligence in Scotland

3— (1) In Scotland, where any tax is due and has not been paid, the sheriff, on an application by the collector accompanied by a certificate by the collector—

(*a*) stating that none of the persons specified in the application has paid the tax to him,

(*b*) stating that the collector has demanded payment under paragraph 1 from each such person of the amount due by him,

(*c*) stating that 14 days have elapsed since the date of such demand without payment of that amount, and

(*d*) specifying the amount due and unpaid by each such person,

shall grant a summary warrant in a form prescribed by Act of Sederunt authorising the recovery, by any of the diligences mentioned in sub-paragraph (2), of the amount remaining due and unpaid.

(2) The diligences referred to in sub-paragraph (1) are—

(*a*) an attachment;

(*b*) an earnings arrestment;

(*c*) an arrestment and action of furthcoming or sale.

(3) Subject to sub-paragraph (4), the sheriff officer's fees, together with the outlays necessarily incurred by him, in connection with the execution of a summary warrant are chargeable against the debtor.

(4) No fee is chargeable by the sheriff officer against the debtor for collecting, and accounting to the collector for, sums paid to him by the debtor in respect of the amount owing.

Prospective amendments—Sub-para (2)(*aa*) to be inserted by the Bankruptcy and Diligence etc (Scotland) Act 2007 s 226(1), Sch 5 para 32 with effect from a date to be appointed. Sub-para (2)(*aa*) as inserted, to read—

"(*aa*) a money attachment;".

This para to be repealed by FA 2008 s 129, Sch 43 para 16 with effect from a date to be appointed.

PART 2

COURT PROCEEDINGS

Civil proceedings in magistrates' court or court of summary jurisdiction

4— (1) An amount not exceeding £2,000 due and payable by way of tax is in England and Wales or Northern Ireland recoverable summarily as a civil debt in proceedings brought in the name of the collector.

(2) All or any of the sums recoverable under this paragraph that are—

(*a*) due from any one person, and

(*b*) payable to any one collector,

may be included in the same complaint, summons or other document required to be laid before or issued by justices.

Each such document shall, as respects each such sum, be construed as a separate document and its invalidity as respects any one such sum does not affect its validity as respects any other such sum.

(3) Proceedings under this paragraph in England and Wales may be brought at any time within one year from the time when the matter complained of arose.

(4) In sub-paragraph (1) the expression "recoverable summarily as a civil debt" in relation to proceedings in Northern Ireland means recoverable by proceedings under Article 62 of the Magistrates' Courts (Northern Ireland) Order 1981 (SI 1981/1675 (NI 26)).

(5) The Treasury may by order increase the sum specified in sub-paragraph (1).

Proceedings in county court or sheriff court

5— (1) Tax due and payable may be sued for and recovered from the person charged as a debt due to the Crown by proceedings *brought in the name of a collector*[1]—

(*a*) in a county court, or

(*b*) in a sheriff court.

(2) *An officer of the Board who is authorised by the Board to do so may address the court in any proceedings under this paragraph in England and Wales or Scotland.*[1]

(3) In Northern Ireland—

(*a*) the reference in sub-paragraph (1) to a county court is to a county court held for a division under the County Courts (Northern Ireland) Order 1980 (SI 1980/397 (NI 3));

(*b*) proceedings may not be brought under this paragraph if the amount exceeds the limit specified in Article 10(1) of that Order;

(*c*) Part III of that Order (general civil jurisdiction) applies for the purposes of this paragraph; and

(*d*) sections 21 and 42(2) of the Interpretation Act (Northern Ireland) 1954 (c 33 (NI)) apply as if any reference in those provisions to an enactment included this paragraph.

Amendments—[1] Words in sub-para (1), and whole of sub-para (2), repealed, by FA 2008 s 137(6) with effect from 21 July 2008. These amendments do not affect proceedings commenced or brought in the name of a collector or authorised officer before this date (FA 2008 s 137(7)).

Proceedings in High Court or Court of Session

6 Tax may be sued for and recovered from the person charged—

(*a*) as a debt due to the Crown, or

(*b*) by any other means by which a debt of record or otherwise due to the Crown may be sued for and recovered,

by proceedings in the High Court or, in Scotland, in the Court of Session sitting as the Court of Exchequer.

…[1]

7 …[1]

Amendments—[1] This para and preceding heading repealed by FA 2008 s 138, Sch 44 para 10 with effect from 21 July 2008.

SCHEDULE 13

STAMP DUTY LAND TAX: INFORMATION POWERS

Section 93

PART 1

POWER OF AUTHORISED OFFICER TO CALL FOR DOCUMENTS OR INFORMATION FROM TAXPAYER

Notice requiring taxpayer to deliver documents or provide information

1— (1) An authorised officer of the Board may by notice in writing require a person—

(*a*) to deliver to him such documents as are in that person's possession or power and (in the officer's reasonable opinion) contain, or may contain, information relevant to—

(i) any tax liability to which that person is or may be subject, or

(ii) the amount of any such liability, or

(*b*) to provide him with such information as he may reasonably require as being relevant to, or to the amount of, any such liability.

(2) An "authorised officer of the Board" means an officer of the Board authorised for the purposes of this Part of this Schedule.

(3) Before a person is given a notice under this paragraph he must be given a reasonable opportunity to deliver the documents or provide the information in question.

No application for consent under paragraph 2 shall be made unless he has been given that opportunity.

Requirement of consent of [the tribunal][1]

2— (1) The consent of [the tribunal][1] is required for the giving of a notice under paragraph 1.

(2) Consent shall not be given unless the Commissioner is satisfied that in all the circumstances the officer is justified in proceeding under that paragraph.

(3) …[1]

Amendments—[1] In the heading, words substituted for the words "General or Special Commissioner"; in sub-para (1) words substituted for the words "a General or Special Commissioner"; in sub-para (2) word substituted for the word "Commissioner"; sub-para (3) and the word following, repealed by the Transfer of Tribunal Functions and Revenue and Customs Appeals Order, SI 2009/56 art 3, Sch 1 para 402 with effect from 1 April 2009. Text previously read as follows—

"(3) A Commissioner who has given such consent shall not take part in, or be present at, any proceedings on, or related to, any appeal brought by the person to whom the notice applies if the Commissioner has reason to believe that any of the required information is likely to be adduced in evidence in those proceedings.

The "required information" means any document or information that was the subject of the notice with respect to which the Commissioner gave his consent.".

Contents of notice under this Part

3— (1) A notice under paragraph 1 must—

(*a*) specify or describe the documents or information to which it relates, and

(*b*) require the documents to be delivered, or the information to be provided, within such time as may be specified in the notice.

(2) The period specified for complying with the notice must not be less than 30 days after the date of the notice.

Summary of reasons to be given

4— (1) An officer who gives a notice under paragraph 1 must also give to the person to whom the notice applies a written summary of his reasons for applying for consent to the notice.

(2) This does not require the disclosure of any information—

(*a*) that would, or might, identify any person who has provided the officer with any information which he took into account in deciding whether to apply for consent, or

(*b*) that the [tribunal][1] giving consent under paragraph 2 directs need not be disclosed.

(3) [The tribunal][1] shall not give any such direction unless …[1] satisfied that the officer has reasonable grounds for believing that disclosure of the information in question would prejudice the assessment or collection of tax.

Amendments—[1] In sub-para (2)(*b*) word substituted for the words "General or Special Commissioner"; in sub-para (3) words substituted for the words "A Commissioner" and words "he is" repealed by the Transfer of Tribunal Functions and Revenue and Customs Appeals Order, SI 2009/56 art 3, Sch 1 para 403 with effect from 1 April 2009.

Power to take copies of documents etc

5 The person to whom documents are delivered, or to whom information is provided, in pursuance of a notice under paragraph 1 may take copies of them or of extracts from them.

PART 2
POWER OF AUTHORISED OFFICER TO CALL FOR DOCUMENTS FROM THIRD PARTY

Notice requiring documents to be delivered or made available

6— (1) An authorised officer of the Board may for the purpose of enquiring into the tax liability of any person ("the taxpayer") by notice in writing require any other person—

(*a*) to deliver to the officer, or

(*b*) if the person to whom the notice is given so elects, to make available for inspection by a named officer of the Board,

such documents as are in that person's possession or power and (in the officer's reasonable opinion) contain, or may contain, information relevant to any tax liability to which the taxpayer is or may be, or may have been, subject, or the amount of any such liability.

(2) An "authorised officer of the Board" means an officer of the Board authorised for the purposes of this Part of this Schedule.

(3) Before a person is given a notice under this paragraph he must be given a reasonable opportunity to deliver or make available the documents in question.

No application for consent under paragraph 7 shall be made unless he has been given that opportunity.

(4) The persons who may be treated as "the taxpayer" for the purposes of this paragraph include a company that has ceased to exist and an individual who has died.

But a notice in relation to a taxpayer who has died may not be given more than six years after his death.

Requirement of consent of [the tribunal][1]

7— (1) The consent of [the tribunal][1] is required for the giving of a notice under paragraph 6.

(2) Consent shall not be given unless the [tribunal][1] is satisfied that in all the circumstances the officer is justified in proceeding under that paragraph.

(3) …[1]

Amendments—[1] In the heading words substituted for the words "General or Special Commissioner"; in sub-para (1) words substituted for the words "a General or Special Commissioner"; in sub-para (2) word substituted for the word "Commissioner"; sub-para (3) repealed by the Transfer of Tribunal Functions and Revenue and Customs Appeals Order, SI 2009/56 art 3, Sch 1 para 404 with effect from 1 April 2009. Sub-para (3) previously read as follows—

"(3) A Commissioner who has given such consent shall not take part in, or be present at, any proceedings on, or related to, any appeal brought by the taxpayer concerned if the Commissioner has reason to believe that any of the documents that were the subject of the notice is likely to be adduced in evidence in those proceedings.".

Contents of notice under paragraph 6

8— (1) A notice under paragraph 6 must—

(*a*) specify or describe the documents to which it relates, and

(*b*) require the documents to be delivered or made available within such time as may be specified in the notice.

(2) The period specified for complying with the notice must not be less than 30 days after the date of the notice.

(3) Subject to paragraph 11 (power to give notice in respect of unnamed taxpayer or taxpayers), a notice under this paragraph must name the taxpayer to whom it relates.

Copy of notice to be given to taxpayer

9— (1) Where a notice is given to a person under this paragraph, the officer shall give a copy of the notice to the taxpayer to whom it relates.

(2) This paragraph does not apply if, on application by the officer, [the tribunal][1] directs that it shall not apply.

(3) Such a direction shall only be given if the [tribunal][1] is satisfied that the officer has reasonable grounds for suspecting the taxpayer of fraud.

Amendments—[1] In sub-para (2) words substituted for the words "a General or Special Commissioner"; in sub-para (3) word substituted for the word "Commissioner" by the Transfer of Tribunal Functions and Revenue and Customs Appeals Order, SI 2009/56 art 3, Sch 1 para 405 with effect from 1 April 2009.

Summary of reasons to be given

10— (1) An officer who gives a notice under paragraph 6 must also give to the taxpayer concerned a written summary of his reasons for applying for consent to the notice.

(2) This does not require the disclosure of any information—

(*a*) that would, or might, identify any person who has provided the officer with any information which he took into account in deciding whether to apply for consent, or

(*b*) that the [tribunal][1] giving consent under paragraph 7 directs need not be disclosed.

(3) [The tribunal][1] shall not give such a direction unless …[1] satisfied that the officer has reasonable grounds for believing that disclosure of the information in question would prejudice the assessment or collection of tax.

(4) This paragraph does not apply if under paragraph 9(2) a copy of the notice need not be given to the taxpayer.

Amendments—[1] In sub-para (2)(*b*) word substituted for the words "General or Special Commissioner"; in sub-para (3) words substituted for the words "A Commissioner" and words "he is" repealed by the Transfer of Tribunal Functions and Revenue and Customs Appeals Order, SI 2009/56 art 3, Sch 1 para 406 with effect from 1 April 2009.

Power to give notice relating to unnamed taxpayer or taxpayers

11— (1) If, on an application made by an officer of the Board and authorised by an order of the Board, [the tribunal gives consent][1], the officer may give such a notice as is mentioned in paragraph 6 without naming the taxpayer to whom the notice relates.

(2) Consent shall not be given unless the [tribunal][1] is satisfied—

(*a*) that the notice relates—

(i) to a taxpayer whose identity is not known to the officer, or

(ii) to a class of taxpayers whose individual identities are not so known,

(*b*) that there are reasonable grounds for believing that the taxpayer, or any of the class of taxpayers, to whom the notice relates may have failed or may fail to comply with any provision of this Part of this Act,

(*c*) that any such failure is likely to have led or to lead to serious prejudice to the proper assessment or collection of tax, and (*d*) that the information that is likely to be contained in the documents to which the notice relates is not readily available from another source.

(3) Before a person is given a notice under this paragraph he must be given a reasonable opportunity to deliver or make available the documents in question.

No application for consent under sub-paragraph (1) shall be made unless he has been given that opportunity.

(4) A person to whom there is given a notice under this paragraph may, by notice in writing given to the officer within 30 days after the date of the notice, object to it on the ground that it would be onerous for him to comply with it.

(5) If the matter is not resolved by agreement it shall be referred to the [tribunal][1] who may confirm, vary or cancel the notice.

Amendments—[1] In sub-para (1) words substituted for the words "a Special Commissioner gives his consent"; in sub-para (2) word substituted for the word "Commissioner"; in sub-para (5) word substituted for the words "Special Commissioner" by the Transfer of Tribunal Functions and Revenue and Customs Appeals Order, SI 2009/56 art 3, Sch 1 para 407 with effect from 1 April 2009.

Contents of notice under paragraph 11

12— (1) A notice under paragraph 11 must—

(*a*) specify or describe the documents to which it relates, and

(*b*) require the documents to be delivered or made available within such time as may be specified in the notice.

(2) The period specified for complying with the notice must not be less than 30 days after the date of the notice.

Power to take copies of documents etc

13 The person to whom documents are delivered or made available in pursuance of a notice under this Part of this Schedule may take copies of them or of extracts from them.

PART 3

POWER TO CALL FOR PAPERS OF TAX ACCOUNTANT

Power to call for papers of tax accountant

14— (1) Where a person who has stood in relation to others as a tax accountant—

(*a*) is convicted of an offence in relation to tax by or before a court in the United Kingdom, or

(*b*) has a penalty imposed on him under section 96 (assisting in preparation of incorrect return etc),

an authorised officer of the Board may by notice in writing require that person to deliver to him such documents as are in his possession or power and (in the officer's reasonable opinion) contain information relevant to any tax liability to which any client of his is or has been, or may be or have been, subject, or to the amount of any such liability.

(2) An "authorised officer of the Board" means an officer of the Board authorised for the purposes of this Part of this Schedule.

(3) Before a person is given a notice under this paragraph he must be given a reasonable opportunity to deliver the documents in question.

No application for consent under paragraph 16 shall be made unless he has been given that opportunity.

When notice may be given

15— (1) No notice under paragraph 14 may be given for so long as an appeal is pending against the conviction or penalty.

(2) For the purposes of sub-paragraph (1)—

(*a*) an appeal is treated as pending (where one is competent but has not been brought) until the expiration of the time for bringing it or, in the case of a conviction in Scotland, until the expiration of 28 days from the date of conviction; and

(*b*) references to an appeal include a further appeal, but in relation to the imposition of a penalty do not include an appeal against the amount of the penalty.

(3) No notice may be given under paragraph 14 by reference to a person's conviction or the imposition on him of a penalty after the end of the period of twelve months beginning with the date on which the power to give such a notice was first exercisable in his case by virtue of that conviction or penalty.

Requirement of consent of appropriate judicial authority

16— (1) The consent of the appropriate judicial authority is required for the giving of a notice under paragraph 14.

(2) Consent shall not be given unless that authority is satisfied that in all the circumstances the officer is justified in proceeding under that paragraph.

(3) The appropriate judicial authority is—

(*a*) in England and Wales, a circuit judge;
(*b*) in Scotland, a sheriff;
(*c*) in Northern Ireland, a county court judge.

Contents of notice

17— (1) A notice under paragraph 14 must—

(*a*) specify or describe the documents to which it relates, and
(*b*) require the documents to be delivered within such time as may be specified in the notice.

(2) The period specified for complying with the notice must not be less than 30 days after the date of the notice.

Power to take copies of documents etc

18 The officer to whom documents are delivered in pursuance of a notice under paragraph 14 may take copies of them or of extracts from them.

PART 4

RESTRICTIONS ON POWERS UNDER PARTS 1 TO 3

Introduction

19 The provisions of Parts 1 to 3 of this Schedule have effect subject to the following restrictions.

Personal records or journalistic material

20— (1) Parts 1 to 3 of this Schedule do not apply—

(*a*) to documents that are personal records or journalistic material, or
(*b*) to information contained in any personal records or journalistic material.

(2) In sub-paragraph (1)—

"personal records" means personal records as defined in section 12 of the Police and Criminal Evidence Act 1984 (c 60) or, in Northern Ireland, in Article 14 of the Police and Criminal Evidence (Northern Ireland) Order 1989 (SI 1989/1341 (NI 12)); and

"journalistic material" means journalistic material as defined in section 13 of that Act or, in Northern Ireland, in Article 15 of that Order.

Documents or information relating to pending appeal

21— (1) A notice under Part 1 of this Schedule does not oblige a person to deliver documents or provide information relating to the conduct of any pending appeal by him.

(2) A notice under Part 2 of this Schedule does not oblige a person to deliver or make available documents relating to the conduct of a pending appeal by the taxpayer.

(3) A notice under Part 3 of this Schedule does not oblige a person to deliver documents relating to the conduct of a pending appeal by the client.

(4) An "appeal" here means an appeal relating to tax.

Barristers, advocates and solicitors

22— (1) A notice under Part 2 or 3 of this Schedule may not be given to a barrister, advocate or solicitor by an authorised officer of the Board but only by the Board.

(2) Accordingly, in relation to a barrister, advocate or solicitor, the references in those Parts to an authorised officer of the Board shall be read as references to the Board.

Prospective amendments—In sub-paras (1), (2), words "relevant lawyer" to be substituted for words "barrister, advocate or solicitor", and sub-paras (3), (4) to be inserted, by the Legal Services Act 2007 s 208, Sch 21 para 138 with effect from a date to be appointed. Sub-paras (3), (4) to read as follows—

"(3) "Relevant lawyer" means a barrister, advocate, solicitor or other professional legal adviser communications with whom may be the subject of a claim to legal privilege.

(4) "Legal privilege" here has the same meaning as in paragraph 35 of this Schedule.".

Provision of copies instead of original documents

23— (1) To comply with a notice under Part 1 or 3 of this Schedule, and as an alternative to delivering documents to comply with a notice under Part 2 of this Schedule, copies of documents may be delivered instead of originals.

(2) The copies must be photographic or otherwise by way of facsimile.

(3) If so required by the officer (or, as the case may be, the Board) in the case of any documents specified in the requirement, the originals must be made available for inspection by a named officer of the Board.

(4) Failure to comply with such a requirement counts as failure to comply with the notice.

Documents originating more than six years before date of notice

24— (1) A notice under Part 2 of this Schedule does not oblige a person to deliver or make available a document the whole of which originates more than six years before the date of the notice.

(2) Sub-paragraph (1) does not apply where the notice is so expressed as to exclude the restrictions of that sub-paragraph.

(3) A notice may only be so expressed if—

(*a*) in the case of a notice given by an authorised officer, the [tribunal][1] giving consent to the notice has also given approval to the exclusion;

(*b*) in the case of a notice given by the Board, they have applied to [the tribunal][1] for, and obtained, that approval.

(4) Approval shall only be given if the [tribunal][1] is satisfied, on application by the officer or the Board, that tax has been, or may have been, lost to the Crown owing to the fraud of the taxpayer.

Amendments—[1] In sub-para (3)(*a*) word substituted for the words "General or Special Commissioner"; in sub-para (3)(*b*) words substituted for the words "a General or Special Commissioner"; in sub-para (5) word substituted for the word "Commissioner" by the Transfer of Tribunal Functions and Revenue and Customs Appeals Order, SI 2009/56 art 3, Sch 1 para 408 with effect from 1 April 2009.

Documents subject to legal privilege

25— (1) A notice under Part 2 or 3 of this Schedule does not oblige a barrister, advocate or solicitor to deliver or make available, without his client's consent, any document with respect to which a claim to legal privilege could be maintained.

(2) "Legal privilege" here has the same meaning as in paragraph 35 of this Schedule.

Prospective amendments—Words "relevant lawyer (within the meaning of paragraph 22(3))" to be substituted for words "barrister, advocate or solicitor", by the Legal Services Act 2007 s 208, Sch 21 para 138(*c*) with effect from a date to be appointed.

Documents belonging to auditor or tax adviser

26— (1) A notice under Part 2 of this Schedule—

(*a*) does not oblige a person who has been appointed as auditor for the purposes of any enactment to deliver or make available documents that are his property and were created by him or on his behalf for or in connection with the performance of his functions under that enactment, and

(*b*) does not oblige a tax adviser to deliver or make available documents that are his property and consist of relevant communications (as defined below).

(2) "Relevant communications" means communications between the tax adviser and—

(*a*) a person in relation to whose tax affairs he has been appointed, or

(*b*) any other tax adviser of such a person,

the purpose of which is the giving or obtaining of advice about any of those tax affairs.

(3) In this paragraph "tax adviser" means a person appointed to give advice about the tax affairs of another person (whether appointed directly by that other person or by another tax adviser of his).

(4) This paragraph has effect subject to paragraph 27 (documents belonging to auditor or tax adviser: information to be disclosed).

Documents belonging to auditor or tax adviser: information to be disclosed

27— (1) This paragraph applies where a notice is given under Part 2 of this Schedule relating to a document that falls within paragraph 26 (documents belonging to auditor or tax adviser) but contains—

(*a*) information explaining any information, return or other document that the person to whom the notice is given has, as tax accountant, assisted any client of his in preparing for, or for delivering to, the officer or the Board, or

(*b*) in the case of a notice under paragraph 11 (notice in respect of unnamed taxpayer or taxpayers), information as to the identity or address of any taxpayer to whom the notice relates or any person who has acted on behalf of any such person,

that has not otherwise been made available to the Inland Revenue.

(2) For this purpose information is regarded as having been made available to the Inland Revenue if it is contained in some other document and—

(*a*) that other document, or a copy of it, has been delivered to the officer or the Board, or

(*b*) that other document has been inspected by an officer of the Board.

(3) Where this paragraph applies the person to whom the notice is given must, if he does not deliver the document or make it available for inspection in accordance with the notice—

(*a*) deliver to the officer (or, as the case may be, the Board) a copy (photographic or otherwise by way of facsimile) of any parts of the document that contain such information as is mentioned in sub-paragraph (1), and (*b*) if so required by the officer (or, as the case may be, the Board), make available for inspection by a named officer of the Board such parts of the original document as contain such information.

(4) Failure to comply with any such requirement counts as a failure to comply with the notice.

PART 5

POWERS OF BOARD TO CALL FOR DOCUMENTS OR INFORMATION

Notice requiring delivery of documents or provision of information

28— (1) The Board may by notice in writing require a person—

(*a*) to deliver to a named officer of the Board such documents as are in the person's possession or power and (in the Board's reasonable opinion) contain, or may contain, information relevant to—

(i) any tax liability to which the person is or may be subject, or

(ii) the amount of any such liability, or

(*b*) to provide to a named officer of the Board such information as the Board may reasonably require as being relevant to, or to the amount of, any such liability.

(2) Notice under this paragraph shall not be given unless the Board have reasonable grounds for believing—

(*a*) that the person to whom it relates may have failed, or may fail, to comply with any provision of this Part of this Act, and

(*b*) that any such failure is likely to have led, or to lead, to serious prejudice to the proper assessment or collection of tax.

Contents of notice

29 A notice under paragraph 28 must—

(*a*) specify or describe the documents or information to which it relates, and

(*b*) require the documents to be delivered or the information to be provided within such time as may be specified in the notice.

Power to take copies of documents etc

30 The person to whom documents are delivered, or to whom information is provided, in pursuance of a notice under paragraph 28 may take copies of them or of extracts from them.

Exclusion of personal records or journalistic material

31— (1) This Part of this Schedule does not apply to documents that are personal records or journalistic material.

(2) In sub-paragraph (1)—

"personal records" means personal records as defined in section 12 of the Police and Criminal Evidence Act 1984 (c 60) or, in Northern Ireland, in Article 14 of the Police and Criminal Evidence (Northern Ireland) Order 1989 (SI 1989/1341 (NI 12)); and

"journalistic material" means journalistic material as defined in section 13 of that Act or, in Northern Ireland, in Article 15 of that Order.

PART 6

ORDER OF JUDICIAL AUTHORITY FOR THE DELIVERY OF DOCUMENTS

Order for the delivery of documents

32— (1) The appropriate judicial authority may make an order under this paragraph if satisfied on information on oath given by an authorised officer of the Board—

(*a*) that there is reasonable ground for suspecting that an offence involving serious fraud in connection with, or in relation to, stamp duty land tax has been or is about to be committed, and

(*b*) that documents that may be required as evidence for the purposes of any proceedings in respect of such an offence are or may be in the power or possession of any person.

(2) An order under this paragraph is an order requiring the person who appears to the authority to have in his possession or power the documents specified or described in the order to deliver them to an officer of the Board within—

(*a*) ten working days after the day on which notice of the order is served on him, or

(*b*) such shorter or longer period as may be specified in the order.

For this purpose a "working day" means any day other than a Saturday, Sunday or public holiday.

(3) The appropriate judicial authority is—

(*a*) in England and Wales, a circuit judge;

(*b*) in Scotland, a sheriff;
(*c*) in Northern Ireland, a county court judge.

(4) Where in Scotland the information relates to persons residing or having places of business at addresses situated in different sheriffdoms—

(*a*) an application for an order may be made to the sheriff for the sheriffdom in which any of the addresses is situated, and
(*b*) where the sheriff makes an order in respect of a person residing or having a place of business in his own sheriffdom, he may also make orders in respect of all or any of the other persons to whom the information relates (whether or not they have an address within the sheriffdom).

(5) In sub-paragraph (1) an "authorised officer of the Board" means an officer of the Board authorised by the Board for the purposes of this Part of this Schedule.

(6) The Inland Revenue may make provision by regulations as to—

(*a*) the procedures for approving in any particular case the decision to apply for an order under this Part of this Schedule, and
(*b*) the descriptions of officer by whom such approval may be given.

Notice of application for order

33— (1) A person is entitled—

(*a*) to notice of the intention to apply for an order against him under paragraph 32, and
(*b*) to appear and be heard at the hearing of the application,

unless the appropriate judicial authority is satisfied that this would seriously prejudice the investigation of the offence.

(2) The Inland Revenue may make provision by regulations as to the notice to be given, the contents of the notice and the manner of giving it.

Obligations of person given notice of application

34— (1) A person who has been given notice of intention to apply for an order under paragraph 32 must not—

(*a*) conceal, destroy, alter or dispose of any document to which the application relates, or
(*b*) disclose to any other person information or any other matter likely to prejudice the investigation of the offence to which the application relates.

This is subject to the following qualifications.

(2) Sub-paragraph (1)(*a*) does not prevent anything being done—

(*a*) with the leave of the appropriate judicial authority,
(*b*) with the written permission of an officer of the Board,
(*c*) after the application has been dismissed or abandoned, or
(*d*) after any order made on the application has been complied with.

(3) Sub-paragraph (1)(*b*) does not prevent a professional legal adviser from disclosing any information or other matter—

(*a*) to, or to a representative of, a client of his in connection with the giving by the adviser of legal advice to the client, or
(*b*) to any person—
  (i) in contemplation or, or in connection with, legal proceedings, and
  (ii) for the purposes of those proceedings.

This sub-paragraph does not apply in relation to any information or other matter that is disclosed with a view to furthering a criminal purpose.

(4) A person who fails to comply with the obligation in sub-paragraph (1)(*a*) or (*b*) may be dealt with as if he had failed to comply with an order under paragraph 32.

Exception of items subject to legal privilege

35— (1) This Part of this Schedule does not apply to items subject to legal privilege.

(2) Items "subject to legal privilege" means—

(*a*) communications between a professional legal adviser and his client or any person representing his client made in connection with the giving of legal advice to the client;
(*b*) communications between a professional legal adviser and his client or any person representing his client, or between such an adviser or his client or any such representative and any other person, made in connection with or in contemplation of legal proceedings and for the purposes of such proceedings;
(*c*) items enclosed with or referred to in such communications and made—
  (i) in connection with the giving of legal advice, or
  (ii) in connection with or in contemplation of legal proceedings and for the purposes of such proceedings,

when they are in possession of a person entitled to possession of them.

(3) Items held with the intention of furthering a criminal purpose are not subject to legal privilege.

Resolution of disputes as to legal privilege

36— (1) The Inland Revenue may make provision by regulations for the purposes of this Part of this Schedule for the resolution of disputes as to whether a document, or part of a document, is an item subject to legal privilege.

(2) The regulations may, in particular, make provision as to—

(*a*) the custody of the document whilst its status is being decided,

(*b*) the appointment of an independent, legally qualified person to decide the matter,

(*c*) the procedures to be followed, and

(*d*) who is to meet the costs of the proceedings.

Complying with an order

37— (1) The Inland Revenue may make provision by regulations as to how a person is to comply with an order under paragraph 32.

(2) The regulations may, in particular, make provision as to—

(*a*) the officer of the Board to whom the documents are to be produced,

(*b*) the address to which the documents are to be taken or sent, and

(*c*) the circumstances in which sending documents by post complies with the order.

(3) Where an order relates to a document in electronic or magnetic form, the order shall be taken to require the person to deliver the information recorded in the document in a form in which it is visible and legible.

Document not to be retained if photograph or copy sufficient

38 Where a document delivered to an officer of the Board under this Part of this Schedule is of such a nature that a photograph or copy of it would be sufficient—

(*a*) for use as evidence at a trial for an offence, or

(*b*) for forensic examination or for investigation in connection with an offence,

it shall not be retained longer than is necessary to establish that fact and to obtain the photograph or copy.

Access to or supply of photograph or copy of documents delivered

39— (1) If a request for permission to be granted access to a document that—

(*a*) has been delivered to an officer of the Board under this Part of this Schedule, and

(*b*) is retained by the Board for the purposes of investigating an offence,

is made to the officer in overall charge of the investigation by a person who had custody or control of the document immediately before it was so delivered, or by someone acting on behalf of any such person, the officer shall allow the person who made the request access to it under the supervision of an officer of the Board.

(2) If a request for a photograph or copy of any such document is made to the officer in overall charge of the investigation by a person who had custody or control of the document immediately before it was so delivered, or by someone acting on behalf of any such person, the officer shall—

(*a*) allow the person who made the request access to it under the supervision of an officer of the Board for the purpose of photographing or copying it, or

(*b*) photograph or copy it, or cause it to be photographed or copied.

(3) Where a document is photographed or copied under sub-paragraph (2)(*b*) the photograph or copy shall be supplied to the person who made the request.

(4) The photograph or copy shall be supplied within a reasonable time from the making of the request.

(5) There is no duty under this paragraph to grant access to, or to supply a photograph or copy of, a document if the officer in overall charge of the investigation for the purposes of which it was delivered has reasonable grounds for believing that to do so would prejudice—

(*a*) that investigation,

(*b*) the investigation of an offence other than the offence for the purposes of the investigation of which the document was delivered, or

(*c*) any criminal proceedings that may be brought as a result of—

(i) the investigation of which he is in charge, or

(ii) any such investigation as is mentioned in paragraph (*b*).

(6) The references in this paragraph to the officer in overall charge of the investigation is to the person whose name and address are endorsed on the order concerned as being the officer so in charge.

Sanction for failure to comply with order

40— (1) A person who fails to comply with an order under this Part of this Schedule may be dealt with as if he had committed a contempt of the court.

(2) For this purpose "the court" means—

(*a*) in relation to an order made by a circuit judge, the Crown Court;

(*b*) in relation to an order made by a sheriff, a sheriff court;

(*c*) in relation to an order made by a county court judge in Northern Ireland, a county court in Northern Ireland.

Notice of order, etc

41 The Inland Revenue may make provision by regulations as to the circumstances in which notice of an order under paragraph 32, or of an application for such an order, is to be treated as having been given.

General provisions about regulations

42 Regulations under this Part of this Schedule may contain such incidental, supplementary and transitional provision as appears to the Inland Revenue to be appropriate.

PART 7
ENTRY WITH WARRANT TO OBTAIN EVIDENCE OF OFFENCE

Amendments—Part 7 (paras 43–52) repealed by FA 2007 ss 84(4), 114, Sch 22 paras 3, 16, Sch 27 Pt 5(1) with effect from 1 December 2007 by virtue of SI 2007/3166 art 3.
Note that, although SI 2007/3166 does not specifically commence FA 2007 Sch 22, the relevant Government department has confirmed to the publisher that the commencement of s 84(4) takes with it Sch 22.

Power to issue warrant

43— (1) The appropriate judicial authority, if satisfied on information on oath given by an officer of the Board that—

(a) there is reasonable ground for suspecting that an offence involving serious fraud in connection with, or in relation to, tax is being, has been or is about to be committed and that evidence of it is to be found on premises specified in the information, and

(b) in applying under this paragraph the officer acts with the approval of the Board given in relation to the particular case,

may issue a warrant in writing authorising an officer of the Board to enter the premises, if necessary by force, at any time within 14 days from the time of issue of the warrant, and search them.

(2) The appropriate judicial authority is—

(a) in England and Wales, a circuit judge;

(b) in Scotland, a sheriff;

(c) in Northern Ireland, a county court judge.

(3) Where in Scotland the information relates to premises situated in different sheriffdoms—

(a) petitions for the issue of warrants in respect of all the premises to which the information relates may be made to the sheriff for a sheriffdom in which any of the premises is situated, and

(b) where the sheriff issues a warrant in respect of premises situated in his own sheriffdom, he shall also have jurisdiction to issue warrants in respect of all or any of the other premises to which the information relates.

This does not affect any power or jurisdiction of a sheriff to issue a warrant in respect of an offence committed within his own sheriffdom.

Amendments—Part 7 (paras 43–52) repealed by FA 2007 ss 84(4), 114, Sch 22 paras 3, 16, Sch 27 Pt 5(1) with effect from 1 December 2007 by virtue of SI 2007/3166 art 3.
Note that, although SI 2007/3166 does not specifically commence FA 2007 Sch 22, the relevant Government department has confirmed to the publisher that the commencement of s 84(4) takes with it Sch 22.

Meaning of offence involving serious fraud

44— (1) An offence that involves fraud is for the purposes of this Part of this Schedule an offence involving serious fraud if its commission has led, or is intended or likely to lead, either—

(a) to substantial financial gain to any person, or

(b) to serious prejudice to the proper assessment or collection of tax.

(2) An offence that, if considered alone, would not be regarded as involving serious fraud may nevertheless be so regarded if there is reasonable ground for suspecting that it forms part of a course of conduct that is, or but for its detection would be, likely to result in serious prejudice to the proper assessment or collection of tax.

(3) Sub-paragraphs (1) and (2) are without prejudice to the general concept of serious fraud.

Amendments—Part 7 (paras 43–52) repealed by FA 2007 ss 84(4), 114, Sch 22 paras 3, 16, Sch 27 Pt 5(1) with effect from 1 December 2007 by virtue of SI 2007/3166 art 3.

Note that, although SI 2007/3166 does not specifically commence FA 2007 Sch 22, the relevant Government department has confirmed to the publisher that the commencement of s 84(4) takes with it Sch 22.

Approval of application by Board

45— *(1) The Board shall not approve an application for a warrant under this Part of this Schedule unless they have reasonable grounds for believing that use of the procedure under Part 6 of this Schedule (order for delivery of documents) might seriously prejudice the investigation.*

(2) Section 4A of the Inland Revenue Regulation Act 1890 (c 21) (Board's functions exercisable by an officer acting under their authority) does not apply to the giving of Board approval under this paragraph.

Amendments—Part 7 (paras 43–52) repealed by FA 2007 ss 84(4), 114, Sch 22 paras 3, 16, Sch 27 Pt 5(1) with effect from 1 December 2007 by virtue of SI 2007/3166 art 3.

Note that, although SI 2007/3166 does not specifically commence FA 2007 Sch 22, the relevant Government department has confirmed to the publisher that the commencement of s 84(4) takes with it Sch 22.

Extent of powers conferred by warrant

46 *The powers conferred by a warrant under this Part of this Schedule are not exercisable—*

(a) by more than such number of officers of the Board as may be specified in the warrant,

(b) outside such times of day as may be so specified, and

(c) if the warrant so provides, otherwise than in the presence of a constable in uniform.

Amendments—Part 7 (paras 43–52) repealed by FA 2007 ss 84(4), 114, Sch 22 paras 3, 16, Sch 27 Pt 5(1) with effect from 1 December 2007 by virtue of SI 2007/3166 art 3.

Note that, although SI 2007/3166 does not specifically commence FA 2007 Sch 22, the relevant Government department has confirmed to the publisher that the commencement of s 84(4) takes with it Sch 22.

Exercise of powers conferred by warrant

47— *(1) An officer of the Board seeking to exercise the powers conferred by a warrant under this Part of this Schedule or, if there is more than one such officer, the one who is in charge of the search—*

(a) if the occupier of the premises concerned is present at the time the search is to begin, shall supply a copy of the warrant endorsed with his name to the occupier;

(b) if at that time the occupier is not present but a person who appears to the officer to be in charge of the premises is present, shall supply such a copy to that person; and

(c) if neither paragraph (a) nor paragraph (b) applies, shall leave such a copy in a prominent place on the premises.

(2) An officer who enters the premises under the authority of a warrant under this Part of this Schedule may—

(a) take with him such other persons as appear to him to be necessary,

(b) seize and remove any things whatsoever found there that he has reasonable cause to believe may be required as evidence for the purposes of proceedings in respect of such an offence as is mentioned in paragraph 43(1), and

(c) search or cause to be searched any person found on the premises whom he has reasonable cause to believe to be in possession of such things.

But no person shall be searched except by a person of the same sex.

(3) In the case of information contained in a computer that—

(a) an officer who enters the premises as mentioned in sub-paragraph (2) has reasonable cause to believe may be required as evidence for the purposes mentioned in paragraph (b) of that sub-paragraph, and

(b) is accessible from the premises,

the power of seizure under that sub-paragraph includes a power to require the information to be produced in a form in which it can be taken away and in which it is visible and legible.

Amendments—Part 7 (paras 43–52) repealed by FA 2007 ss 84(4), 114, Sch 22 paras 3, 16, Sch 27 Pt 5(1) with effect from 1 December 2007 by virtue of SI 2007/3166 art 3.

Note that, although SI 2007/3166 does not specifically commence FA 2007 Sch 22, the relevant Government department has confirmed to the publisher that the commencement of s 84(4) takes with it Sch 22.

Items subject to legal privilege

48— *(1) Nothing in this Part of this Schedule authorises the seizure of items subject to legal privilege.*

(2) Items "subject to legal privilege" means—

(a) communications between a professional legal adviser and his client or any person representing his client made in connection with the giving of legal advice to the client;

(b) communications between a professional legal adviser and his client or any person representing his client, or between such an adviser or his client or any such representative and any other person, made in connection with or in contemplation of legal proceedings and for the purposes of such proceedings;

(c) items enclosed with or referred to in such communications and made—

(i) in connection with the giving of legal advice, or

(ii) in connection with or in contemplation of legal proceedings and for the purposes of such proceedings,

when they are in possession of a person entitled to possession of them.

(3) Items held with the intention of furthering a criminal purpose are not subject to legal privilege.

Amendments—Part 7 (paras 43–52) repealed by FA 2007 ss 84(4), 114, Sch 22 paras 3, 16, Sch 27 Pt 5(1) with effect from 1 December 2007 by virtue of SI 2007/3166 art 3.

Note that, although SI 2007/3166 does not specifically commence FA 2007 Sch 22, the relevant Government department has confirmed to the publisher that the commencement of s 84(4) takes with it Sch 22.

Procedure where documents etc are removed

49— (1) An officer of the Board who removes anything in the exercise of the powers conferred by this Part of this Schedule shall, if so requested by a person showing himself—

(a) to be the occupier of the premises from which it was removed, or

(b) to have had custody or control of it immediately before the removal,

provide that person with a record of what he removed.

(2) The officer of the Board shall provide the record within a reasonable time from the making of the request for it.

Amendments—Part 7 (paras 43–52) repealed by FA 2007 ss 84(4), 114, Sch 22 paras 3, 16, Sch 27 Pt 5(1) with effect from 1 December 2007 by virtue of SI 2007/3166 art 3.

Note that, although SI 2007/3166 does not specifically commence FA 2007 Sch 22, the relevant Government department has confirmed to the publisher that the commencement of s 84(4) takes with it Sch 22.

Document not to be retained if photograph or copy sufficient

50 Where anything that has been removed by an officer of the Board as mentioned in paragraph 49 is of such a nature that a photograph or copy of it would be sufficient—

(a) for use as evidence at a trial for an offence, or

(b) for forensic examination or for investigation in connection with an offence,

it shall not be retained longer than is necessary to establish that fact and to obtain the photograph or copy.

Amendments—Part 7 (paras 43–52) repealed by FA 2007 ss 84(4), 114, Sch 22 paras 3, 16, Sch 27 Pt 5(1) with effect from 1 December 2007 by virtue of SI 2007/3166 art 3.

Note that, although SI 2007/3166 does not specifically commence FA 2007 Sch 22, the relevant Government department has confirmed to the publisher that the commencement of s 84(4) takes with it Sch 22.

Access to or supply of photograph or copy of items removed

51 (1) If a request for permission to be granted access to anything that—

(a) has been removed by an officer of the Board, and

(b) is retained by the Board for the purposes of investigating an offence,

is made to the officer in overall charge of the investigation by a person who had custody or control of the thing immediately before it was so removed or by someone acting on behalf of any such person, the officer shall allow the person who made the request access to it under the supervision of an officer of the Board.

(2) If a request for a photograph or copy of any such thing is made to the officer in overall charge of the investigation by a person who has custody or control of the thing immediately before it was so removed, or by someone acting on behalf of any such person, the officer shall—

(a) allow the person who made the request access to it under the supervision of an officer of the Board for the purpose of photographing or copying it, or

(b) photograph or copy it, or cause it to be photographed or copied.

(3) Where anything is photographed or copied under sub-paragraph (2)(b) the photograph or copy shall be supplied to the person who made the request.

(4) The photograph or copy shall be supplied within a reasonable time from the making of the request.

(5) There is no duty under this paragraph to grant access to, or to supply a photograph or copy of, anything if the officer in overall charge of the investigation for the purposes of which it was removed has reasonable grounds for believing that to do so would prejudice—

(a) that investigation,

(b) the investigation of an offence other than the offence for the purposes of the investigation of which the thing was removed, or

(c) any criminal proceedings that may be brought as a result of—

(i) the investigation of which he is in charge, or

(ii) any such investigation as is mentioned in paragraph (b).

(6) The references in this paragraph to the officer in overall charge of the investigation is to the person whose name and address are endorsed on the warrant concerned as being the officer so in charge.

Amendments—Part 7 (paras 43–52) repealed by FA 2007 ss 84(4), 114, Sch 22 paras 3, 16, Sch 27 Pt 5(1) with effect from 1 December 2007 by virtue of SI 2007/3166 art 3.

Stamp Taxes

Note that, although SI 2007/3166 does not specifically commence FA 2007 Sch 22, the relevant Government department has confirmed to the publisher that the commencement of s 84(4) takes with it Sch 22.

Endorsement and custody etc of warrant

52— *(1) Where entry has been made with a warrant under this Part of this Schedule, and the officer making the entry has seized any things under the authority of the warrant, he shall endorse on or attach to the warrant a list of the things seized.*

(2) The following provisions (which relate to return, retention and inspection of warrants), that is—

(a) in England and Wales, section 16(10) to (12) of the Police and Criminal Evidence Act 1984 (c 60), and

(b) in Northern Ireland, Article 18(10) to (12) of the Police and Criminal Evidence (Northern Ireland) Order 1989 (SI 1989/1341 (NI 12)),

apply to a warrant under this Part of this Schedule (together with any list endorsed on or attached to it under sub-paragraph (1)) as they apply to a warrant issued to a constable under any enactment.

Amendments—Part 7 (paras 43–52) repealed by FA 2007 ss 84(4), 114, Sch 22 paras 3, 16, Sch 27 Pt 5(1) with effect from 1 December 2007 by virtue of SI 2007/3166 art 3.

Note that, although SI 2007/3166 does not specifically commence FA 2007 Sch 22, the relevant Government department has confirmed to the publisher that the commencement of s 84(4) takes with it Sch 22.

PART 8
FALSIFICATION ETC OF DOCUMENTS

Falsification etc of documents

53— (1) A person commits an offence if he intentionally—

(*a*) falsifies, conceals, destroys or otherwise disposes of, or

(*b*) causes or permits the falsification, concealment, destruction or disposal of,

a document to which this paragraph applies.

(2) This paragraph applies to any document that the person—

(*a*) has been required by a notice under Part 1, 2, 3 or 5 of this Schedule, or an order under Part 6 of this Schedule, to deliver, or to deliver or make available for inspection, or

(*b*) has been given an opportunity in accordance with paragraph 1(3), 6(3), 11(3) or 14(3) to deliver, or to deliver or make available for inspection.

(3) A person does not commit an offence under this paragraph if he acts—

(*a*) with the written permission of [the tribunal][1] or an officer of the Board,

(*b*) after the document has been delivered or, in a case within Part 2 of this Schedule, inspected, or

(*c*) after a copy has been delivered in accordance with paragraph 23(1) or 27(3) and the original has been inspected.

(4) A person does not commit an offence under this paragraph as it applies by virtue of sub-paragraph (2)(*a*) if he acts after the end of the period of two years beginning with the date on which the notice is given or the order is made, unless before the end of that period an officer of the Board has notified the person, in writing, that the notice or order has not been complied with to his satisfaction.

(5) A person does not commit an offence under this paragraph as it applies by virtue of sub-paragraph (2)(*b*) if he acts—

(*a*) after the end of the period of six months beginning with the date on which an opportunity to deliver the document was given, or

(*b*) after an application for consent to a notice being given in relation to the document has been refused.

(6) A person guilty of an offence under this paragraph is liable—

(*a*) on summary conviction, to a fine not exceeding the statutory maximum;

(*b*) on conviction on indictment, to imprisonment for a term not exceeding two years or a fine or to both.

Amendments—[1] In sub-para (3)(*a*) words substituted for the words "a General or Special Commissioner" by the Transfer of Tribunal Functions and Revenue and Customs Appeals Order, SI 2009/56 art 3, Sch 1 para 409 with effect from 1 April 2009.

SCHEDULE 14
STAMP DUTY LAND TAX: DETERMINATION OF PENALTIES AND RELATED APPEALS

Section 99

HMRC Manuals—Stamp Duty Land Tax Manual SDLTM86530–86640 (Revenue practice on contract settlements and abatement).
SDLTM86710–86740 (determination of penalties under this Schedule).

Determination of penalties and appeals

1 The provisions of this Schedule apply in relation to penalties under this Part of this Act.

Determination of penalty by officer of the Board

2— (1) An officer of the Board authorised for the purposes of this paragraph may make a determination—

(*a*) imposing the penalty, and
(*b*) setting it at such amount as in the officer's opinion is correct or appropriate.

(2) Notice of the determination must be served on the person liable to the penalty.

(3) The notice must also state—

(*a*) the date on which the notice is issued, and
(*b*) the time within which an appeal against the determination may be made.

(4) A penalty determined under this paragraph is due and payable at the end of the period of 30 days beginning with the date of issue of the notice of determination.

(5) Where an officer of the Board has decided to impose a penalty, and has taken all other decisions needed for arriving at the amount of the penalty, he may entrust to any other officer of the Board responsibility for completing the determination procedure, whether by means involving the use of a computer or otherwise, including responsibility for serving notice of the determination.

Alteration of penalty determination

3— (1) After notice has been served of the determination of a penalty, the determination cannot be altered except in accordance with this paragraph or on appeal.

(2) If it is discovered by an authorised officer that the amount of the penalty is or has become insufficient, the officer may make a determination in a further amount so that the penalty is set at the amount which in the officer's opinion is correct or appropriate.

(3) If in the case of a tax-related penalty it is discovered by an authorised officer that the amount taken into account as the amount of tax is or has become excessive, he may revise the determination so that the penalty is set at the amount that is correct.

Where more than the correct amount has already been paid the appropriate amount shall be repaid.

(4) In this paragraph an "authorised officer" means an officer of the Board authorised by the Board for the purposes of this paragraph.

Liability of personal representatives

4 If a person liable to a penalty has died—

(*a*) any determination that could have been made in relation to that person may be made in relation to his personal representatives, and
(*b*) any penalty imposed on them is a debt due from and payable out of the person's estate.

Appeal against penalty determination

5— (1) An appeal [may be made][1] against the determination of a penalty.

(2) Notice of appeal must be given in writing to the officer of the Board by whom the determination was made within 30 days of the date of issue of the notice of determination.

[(3) The notice of appeal must specify the grounds of appeal.][1]

(4) On an appeal under this paragraph [that is notified to the First-tier Tribunal, the tribunal][1] may—

(*a*) if it appears …[1] that no penalty has been incurred, set the determination aside;
(*b*) if the amount determined appears …[1] to be appropriate, confirm the determination;
(*c*) if the amount determined appears to them to be excessive, reduce it to such other amount (including nil) as appears to them to be appropriate;
(*d*) if the amount determined appears to them to be insufficient, increase it to such amount, not exceeding the permitted maximum, [as the First-tier Tribunal considers appropriate][1].

[(5) The provisions of paragraphs 36A to 36I of Schedule 10 apply to appeals under this paragraph.][1]

Amendments—[1] In sub-para (1) words substituted for the words "lies to the General or Special Commissioners"; sub-para (3) substituted; in sub-para (4) words substituted for the words "the Commissioners"; in sub-para (4)(*a*), (*b*) words "to them" repealed in both places; in sub-para (4)(*d*) words substituted for the words "as they consider appropriate"; sub-para (5) inserted by the Transfer of Tribunal Functions and Revenue and Customs Appeals Order, SI 2009/56 art 3, Sch 1 para 411 with effect from 1 April 2009. Sub-para (3) previously read as follows—

"(3) The notice of appeal must specify the grounds of appeal, but on the hearing of the appeal the Commissioners may allow the appellant to put forward a ground not specified in the notice of appeal, and take it into consideration, if satisfied that the omission was not deliberate or unreasonable.".

Further appeal

6— [(1) In addition to any right of appeal on a point of law under section 11(2) of the Tribunals, Courts and Enforcement Act 2007, the person liable to the penalty may appeal to the Upper

Tribunal against the amount of the penalty which has been determined under paragraph (5), but not against any decision which falls under section 11(5)(*d*) or (*e*) of that Act and was made in connection with the determination of the amount of the penalty.

(1A) Section 11(3) and (4) of the Tribunals, Courts and Enforcement Act 2007 applies to the right of appeal under sub-paragraph (1) as it applies to the right of appeal under section 11(2) of that Act.][1]

(2) On an appeal under this paragraph the [Upper Tribunal][1] has the same powers as are conferred on the [First-tier Tribunal][1] by paragraph 5(4) above.

(3) …[1]

Amendments—[1] Sub-paras (1), (1A) substituted for former sub-para (1); in sub-para (2) words in the first place substituted for the word "court" and in the second place substituted for the word "Commissioners"; sub-para (3) repealed by the Transfer of Tribunal Functions and Revenue and Customs Appeals Order, SI 2009/56 art 3, Sch 1 para 4128 with effect from 1 April 2009. Sub-paras (1), (3) previously read as follows—

"(1) An appeal lies against the amount of a penalty determined by the Commissioners on an appeal under paragraph 5, at the instance of the person liable to the penalty—

(*a*) to the High Court, or

(*b*) in Scotland, to the Court of Session sitting as the Court of Exchequer.'

"(3) The right of appeal under this paragraph is in addition to any right of appeal conferred by regulations under paragraph 9 of Schedule 17 (general power to provide for appeals on points of law).".

Penalty proceedings before the court

7— (1) Where in the opinion of the Board the liability of a person for a penalty arises by reason of his fraud, or the fraud of another person, proceedings for the penalty may be brought—

(*a*) in the High Court, or

(*b*) in Scotland, in the Court of Session sitting as the Court of Exchequer.

(2) Proceedings under this paragraph in England and Wales shall be brought—

(*a*) by and in the name of the Board as an authorised department for the purposes of the Crown Proceedings Act 1947 (c 44), or

(*b*) in the name of the Attorney General.

Any such proceedings shall be deemed to be civil proceedings by the Crown within the meaning of Part 2 of the Crown Proceedings Act 1947.

(3) Proceedings under this paragraph in Scotland shall be brought in the name of the Advocate General for Scotland.

(4) Proceedings under this paragraph in Northern Ireland shall be brought—

(*a*) by and in the name of the Board as an authorised department for the purposes of the Crown Proceedings Act 1947 as for the time being in force in Northern Ireland, or

(*b*) in the name of the Advocate General for Northern Ireland.

Any such proceedings shall be deemed to be civil proceedings within the meaning of Part 2 of the Crown Proceedings Act 1947 as for the time being in force in Northern Ireland.

(5) If in proceedings under this paragraph the court does not find that fraud is proved but considers that the person concerned is nevertheless liable to a penalty, the court may determine a penalty notwithstanding that, but for the opinion of the Board as to fraud, the penalty would not have been a matter for the court.

(6) Paragraph 2 (determination of penalty by officer of the Board) does not apply where proceedings are brought under this paragraph.

(7) In relation to any time before the coming into force of section 2(1) of the Justice (Northern Ireland) Act 2002 (c 26), the reference in sub-paragraph (4)(*b*) to the Advocate General for Northern Ireland shall be read as a reference to the Attorney General for Northern Ireland.

Time limit for determination of penalties

8— (1) The following time limits apply in relation to the determination of penalties under this Schedule.

(2) The general rule is that—

(*a*) no penalty may be determined under paragraph 2 (determination by officer of Board), and

(*b*) no proceedings for a penalty may be brought under paragraph 7 (penalty proceedings before the court),

more than six years after the date on which the penalty was incurred or, in the case of a daily penalty, began to be incurred.

This rule is subject to the following provisions of this paragraph.

(3) Where the amount of a penalty is to be ascertained by reference to the tax chargeable in respect of a transaction, a penalty may be determined under paragraph 2, or proceedings for a penalty may be begun under paragraph 7, at any time within three years after the final determination of the amount of tax by reference to which the amount of the penalty is to be determined.

(4) Sub-paragraph (3) does not apply where a person has died and the determination would be made in relation to his personal representatives if the tax was charged in an assessment made more than six years after the effective date of the transaction to which it relates.

(5) A penalty under section 96 (penalty for assisting in preparation of incorrect return) may be determined by an officer of the Board, or proceedings for such a penalty may be commenced before a court, at any time within 20 years after the date on which the penalty was incurred.

Prospective amendments—In sub-para (2) words "4 years" to be substituted for the words "six years" and words "("the relevant date")" to be inserted after the words "began to be incurred", in sub-para (3) words "(subject to any of the following provisions of this paragraph allowing a longer period)" to be inserted at the end, and sub-paras (4A)–(4C) to be inserted, by FA 2009 s 99, Sch 51 paras 14, 16 with effect from a date to be appointed. New sub-paras (4A)–(4C) read as follows—

"(4A) Where a person is liable to a penalty in a case involving a loss of tax brought about carelessly by the person (or by another person acting on that person's behalf), the penalty may be determined, or the proceedings may be brought, at any time not more than 6 years after the relevant date (subject to sub-paragraphs (4B) and (5)).

(4B) Where a person is liable to a penalty in a case involving a loss of tax—

(*a*) brought about deliberately by the person (or by another person acting on that person's behalf),
(*b*) attributable to a failure by the person to comply with an obligation under section 76(1) or paragraph 3(3)(*a*), 4(3)(*a*) or 8(3)(*a*) of Schedule 17A, or
(*c*) attributable to arrangements in respect of which the person has failed to comply with an obligation under section 309, 310 or 313 of the Finance Act 2004 (obligation of parties to tax avoidance schemes to provide information to Her Majesty's Revenue and Customs),

the penalty may be determined, or the proceedings may be brought, at any time not more than 20 years after the relevant date.

(4C) Paragraph 31A of Schedule 10 (losses brought about carelessly or deliberately) applies for the purpose of this paragraph.".

SCHEDULE 15

STAMP DUTY LAND TAX: PARTNERSHIPS

Section 104

PART 1

GENERAL PROVISIONS

Partnerships

1 In this Part of this Act a "partnership" means—

(*a*) a partnership within the Partnership Act 1890 (c 39),
(*b*) a limited partnership registered under the Limited Partnerships Act 1907 (c 24), or
(*c*) a limited liability partnership formed under the Limited Liability Partnerships Act 2000 (c 12) or the Limited Liability Partnerships Act (Northern Ireland) 2002 (c 12 (NI)),

or a firm or entity of a similar character to any of those mentioned above formed under the law of a country or territory outside the United Kingdom.

Legal personality of partnership disregarded

2— (1) For the purposes of this Part of this Act—

(*a*) a chargeable interest held by or on behalf of a partnership is treated as held by or on behalf of the partners, and
(*b*) a land transaction entered into for the purposes of a partnership is treated as entered into by or on behalf of the partners,

and not by or on behalf of the partnership as such.

(2) Sub-paragraph (1) applies notwithstanding that the partnership is regarded as a legal person, or as a body corporate, under the law of the country or territory under which it is formed.

Continuity of partnership

3 For the purposes of this Part of this Act a partnership is treated as the same partnership notwithstanding a change in membership if any person who was a member before the change remains a member after the change.

Partnership not to be regarded as unit trust scheme etc

4 A partnership is not to be regarded for the purposes of this Part of this Act as a unit trust scheme or an open ended investment company.

Stamp Taxes

PART 2
ORDINARY PARTNERSHIP TRANSACTIONS

Introduction

5— (1) This Part of this Schedule applies to transactions entered into as purchaser by or on behalf of the members of a partnership, other than transactions within Part 3 of this Schedule [(transactions to which special provisions apply)][1].

Amendments—[1] Words substituted for the words "(transactions excluded from stamp duty land tax)" by FA 2004 s 304, Sch 41 paras 2(*c*), 3 with effect for any partnership transaction of which the effective date (within the meaning of FA 2003 Pt 4) is after 22 July 2004. A "partnership transaction" means a transaction mentioned in FA 2003 Sch 15 para 9(1): FA 2004 Sch 41 para 3(2).

Responsibility of partners

6— (1) Anything required or authorised to be done under this Part of this Act by or in relation to the purchaser under the transaction is required or authorised to be done by or in relation to all the responsible partners.

(2) The responsible partners in relation to a transaction are—

(*a*) the persons who are partners at the effective date of the transaction, and

(*b*) any person who becomes a member of the partnership after the effective date of the transaction.

(3) This paragraph has effect subject to paragraph 8 (representative partners).

Joint and several liability of responsible partners

7— (1) Where the responsible partners are liable—

(*a*) to make a payment of tax or to interest on unpaid tax,

(*b*) to make a payment in accordance with an assessment under paragraph 29 of Schedule 10 (recovery of excessive repayment), or

(*c*) to a penalty under this Part of this Act or to interest on such a penalty,

the liability is a joint and several liability of those partners.

[(1A) No amount may be recovered by virtue of sub-paragraph (1)(*a*) or (*b*) from a person who did not become a responsible partner until after the effective date of the transaction in respect of which the tax is payable.][1]

(2) No amount may be recovered by virtue of sub-paragraph (1)(*c*) from a person who did not become a responsible partner until after the relevant time.

(3) The relevant time for this purpose is—

(*a*) in relation to so much of a penalty as is payable in respect of any day, or to interest on so much of a penalty as is so payable, the beginning of that day;

(*b*) in relation to any other penalty, or interest on such a penalty, the time when the act or omission occurred that caused the penalty to become payable.

Amendments—[1] Sub-para (1A) inserted by FA 2004 s 305 with effect from 22 July 2004.

Representative partners

8— (1) Anything required or authorised to be done by or in relation to the responsible partners may instead be done by or in relation to any representative partner or partners.

(2) This includes making the declaration required by paragraph 1(1)(*c*) of Schedule 10 …[1] (declaration that return …[1] is complete and correct).

(3) A representative partner means a partner nominated by a majority of the partners to act as the representative of the partnership for the purposes of this Part of this Act.

(4) Any such nomination, or the revocation of such a nomination, has effect only after notice of the nomination, or revocation, has been given to the Inland Revenue.

Amendments—[1] Words in sub-para (2) repealed by FA 2008 s 94, Sch 30 para 12 with effect in relation to transactions with an effective date on or after 12 March 2008.

[PART 3
TRANSACTIONS TO WHICH SPECIAL PROVISIONS APPLY][1]

Amendments—[1] This Part substituted by FA 2004 s 304, Sch 41 paras 1, 3 with effect for any partnership transaction of which the effective date (within the meaning of FA 2003 Pt 4) is after 22 July 2004. A "partnership transaction" means a transaction mentioned in FA 2003 Sch 15 para 9(1): FA 2004 Sch 41 para 3(2).

[Introduction

9— (1) This Part of this Schedule applies to certain transactions involving—

(*a*) the transfer of a chargeable interest to a partnership (paragraph 10),

(*b*) the transfer of an interest in a partnership (paragraphs 14, 17, 31 and 32), or

(*c*) the transfer of a chargeable interest from a partnership (paragraph 18).

(2) References in this Part of this Schedule to the transfer of a chargeable interest include—

(*a*) the grant or creation of a chargeable interest,
(*b*) the variation of a chargeable interest, and
(*c*) the surrender, release or renunciation of a chargeable interest.][1]

Amendments—[1] This Part substituted by FA 2004 s 304, Sch 41 paras 1, 3 with effect for any partnership transaction of which the effective date (within the meaning of FA 2003 Pt 4) is after 22 July 2004. A "partnership transaction" means a transaction mentioned in sub para (1) above: FA 2004 Sch 41 para 3(2).

[Transfer of chargeable interest to a partnership: general

10— (1) This paragraph applies where—
(*a*) a partner transfers a chargeable interest to the partnership, or
(*b*) a person transfers a chargeable interest to a partnership in return for an interest in the partnership, or
(*c*) a person connected with—
(i) a partner, or
(ii) a person who becomes a partner as a result of or in connection with the transfer,
transfers a chargeable interest to the partnership.

It applies whether the transfer is in connection with the formation of the partnership or is a transfer to an existing partnership.

[(2) The chargeable consideration for the transaction shall (subject to paragraph 13) be taken to be equal to—

$$MV \times (100 - SLP)\%$$

where—
MV is the market value of the interest transferred, and
SLP is the sum of the lower proportions.][2]

(5) Paragraph 12 provides for determining the sum of the lower proportions.

(6) Paragraph 11 applies …[2] if the whole or part of the chargeable consideration for the transaction is rent.

(7) Paragraphs 6 to 8 (responsibility of partners) have effect in relation to a transaction to which this paragraph applies, but the responsible partners are—
(*a*) those who were partners immediately before the transfer and who remain partners after the transfer, and
(*b*) any person becoming a partner as a result of, or in connection with, the transfer.

[(8) This paragraph has effect subject to any election under paragraph 12A.][3]][1]

Cross references—See FA 2003 Sch 15 para 23 (sub-paras (2)–(5) above do not apply where there is a transfer of a chargeable interest from a partnership to a partnership, and none of the chargeable consideration is rent).
FA 2008 Sch 31 para 11 (application of sub-para (1)(*a*)–(*c*) to a transfer of a chargeable interest to a partnership where the effective date of the transaction is before 21 July 2008).

Modifications—FA 2003 Sch 15 para 13 (modification of this paragraph where there is a transfer of a chargeable interest to a partnership consisting wholly of bodies corporate).

Amendments—[1] This Part substituted by FA 2004 s 304, Sch 41 paras 1, 3 with effect for any partnership transaction of which the effective date (within the meaning of FA 2003 Pt 4) is after 22 July 2004. A "partnership transaction" means a transaction mentioned in FA 2003 Sch 15 para 9(1): FA 2004 Sch 41 para 3(2).
[2] Sub-para (2) substituted for sub-paras (2)–(4) and in sub-para (6), words "(instead of sub-paragraphs (2) to (5))" repealed by FA 2006 s 162, Sch 24 para 2, s 178, Sch 26 Pt 7(2) with effect in relation to any transfer of which the effective date (within the meaning of FA 2003 Pt 4) is on or after 19 July 2006.
[3] Sub-para (8) inserted by FA 2008 s 97, Sch 31 para 5 with effect from 21 July 2008.

[Transfer of chargeable interest to a partnership: chargeable consideration including rent

11— (1) This paragraph applies in relation to a transaction to which paragraph 10 applies where the whole or part of the chargeable consideration for the transaction is rent.

[(2) Schedule 5 (amount of tax chargeable: rent) has effect with the modifications set out in sub-paragraphs (2A) to (2C).

(2A) In paragraph 2—
(*a*) for "the net present value of the rent payable over the term of the lease" substitute "the relevant chargeable proportion of the net present value of the rent payable over the term of the lease", and
(*b*) for "the net present values of the rent payable over the terms of all the leases" substitute "the relevant chargeable proportions of the net present values of the rent payable over the terms of all the leases".

(2B) In paragraph [9A(6)][3]—
(*a*) for "the annual rent" substitute "the relevant chargeable proportion of the annual rent", and
(*b*) for "the total of the annual rents" substitute "the relevant chargeable proportion of the total of the annual rents".

(2C) For paragraph 9(4) substitute—
"(4) Tax chargeable under this Schedule is in addition to any tax chargeable under section 55 as it has effect by virtue of paragraph 10 of Schedule 15.".

(2D) For the purposes of sub-paragraphs (2A) and (2B) the relevant chargeable proportion is—

(100 – SLP)%

where SLP is the sum of the lower proportions.

…]²

(8) Paragraph 12 provides for determining the sum of the lower proportions.

(9) This paragraph is subject to paragraph 13.]¹

Cross references—See FA 2003 Sch 15 para 23 (this paragraph does not apply where there is transfer of a chargeable interest from a partnership to a partnership, and the whole or part of the chargeable consideration is rent).

Modifications—FA 2003 Sch 15 para 13 (modification of this paragraph where there is a transfer of a chargeable interest to a partnership consisting wholly of bodies corporate).

Amendments—¹ This Part substituted by FA 2004 s 304, Sch 41 paras 1, 3 with effect for any partnership transaction of which the effective date (within the meaning of FA 2003 Pt 4) is after 22 July 2004. A "partnership transaction" means a transaction mentioned in FA 2003 Sch 15 para 9(1): FA 2004 Sch 41 para 3(2).

² Sub-paras (2)–(2D) substituted for former sub-paras (2)–(7) by FA 2006 s 162, Sch 24 para 3 with effect in relation to any transfer of which the effective date (within the meaning of FA 2003 Pt 4) is on or after 19 July 2006.

³ Reference in sub-para (2B) substituted by FA 2008 s 95(11)(*a*) with effect in relation to transactions with an effective date on or after 12 March 2008.

[Transfer of chargeable interest to a partnership: sum of the lower proportions

12— (1) The sum of the lower proportions in relation to a transaction to which paragraph 10 applies is determined as follows:—

Step One

Identify the relevant owner or owners.

A person is a relevant owner if—

(*a*) immediately before the transaction, he was entitled to a proportion of the chargeable interest, and

(*b*) immediately after the transaction, he is a partner or connected with a partner.

Step Two

For each relevant owner, identify the corresponding partner or partners.

A person is a corresponding partner in relation to a relevant owner if, immediately after the transaction—

(*a*) he is a partner, and

(*b*) he is the relevant owner [or is an individual connected with the relevant owner]².

[(If there is no relevant owner with a corresponding partner, the sum of the lower proportions is nil.)]²

Step Three

For each relevant owner, find the proportion of the chargeable interest to which he was entitled immediately before the transaction.

Apportion that proportion between any one or more of the relevant owner's corresponding partners.

Step Four

Find the lower proportion for each person who is a corresponding partner in relation to one or more relevant owners.

The lower proportion is—

(*a*) the proportion of the chargeable interest attributable to the partner, or

(*b*) if lower, the partner's partnership share immediately after the transaction.

The proportion of the chargeable interest attributable to the partner is—

(i) if he is a corresponding partner in relation to only one relevant owner, the proportion (if any) of the chargeable interest apportioned to him (at Step Three) in respect of that owner;

(ii) if he is a corresponding partner in relation to more than one relevant owner, the sum of the proportions (if any) of the chargeable interest apportioned to him (at Step Three) in respect of each of those owners.

Step Five

Add together the lower proportions of each person who is a corresponding partner in relation to one or more relevant owners.

The result is the sum of the lower proportions.

(2) For the purposes of this paragraph persons who are entitled to a chargeable interest as beneficial joint tenants (or, in Scotland, as joint owners) shall be taken to be entitled to the chargeable interest as beneficial tenants in common (or, in Scotland, as owners in common) in equal shares.]¹

[(3) For the purpose of paragraph (*b*) of Step 2 a company is to be treated as an individual connected with the relevant owner in so far as it—

(*a*) holds property as trustee, and

(*b*) is connected with the relevant owner only because of section 839(3) of the Taxes Act 1988.]³

Amendments—[1] This Part substituted by FA 2004 s 304, Sch 41 paras 1, 3 with effect for any partnership transaction of which the effective date (within the meaning of FA 2003 Pt 4) is after 22 July 2004. A "partnership transaction" means a transaction mentioned in FA 2003 Sch 15 para 9(1): FA 2004 Sch 41 para 3(2).

[2] Words in sub-para (1) step two para (*b*) substituted, and words at end of step two para (*b*) inserted, by FA 2007 s 72(1)–(3) with effect in respect of transfers occurring on or after 19 July 2007: FA 2007 s 72(13).

The amendments are to this paragraph as it stood before amendment by the Stamp Duty Land Tax (Variation of the Finance Act 2003) Regulations, SI 2006/3237. The amendments, to the extent provided for by FA 2007 s 72(13)–(15), replace the amendments made by those regulations: see FA 2007 s 72(2), (16). However, the amendments by FA 2007 are subject to transitional provisions as provided by FA 2007 s 72(17).

[3] Sub-para (3) inserted by FA 2007 s 72(1), (2), (4) with effect in respect of transfers occurring on or after 19 July 2007: FA 2007 s 72(13).

[Election by property-investment partnership to disapply paragraph 10

12A— (1) Paragraph 10 does not apply to a transfer of a chargeable interest to a property-investment partnership if the purchaser in relation to the transaction elects for that paragraph not to apply.

(2) Where an election under this paragraph is made in respect of a transaction—

(*a*) paragraph 18 (if relevant) is also disapplied,

(*b*) the chargeable consideration for the transaction shall be taken to be the market value of the chargeable interest transferred, and

(*c*) the transaction falls within Part 2 of this Schedule.

(3) An election under this paragraph must be included in the land transaction return made in respect of the transaction or in an amendment of that return.

(4) Such an election is irrevocable and a land transaction return may not be amended so as to withdraw the election.

(5) Where an election under this paragraph in respect of a transaction (the "main transaction") is made in an amendment of a land transaction return—

(*a*) the election has effect as if it had been made on the date on which the land transaction return was made, and

(*b*) any land transaction return in respect of an affected transaction may be amended (within the period allowed for amendment of that return) to take account of that election.

(6) In sub-paragraph (5) "affected transaction", in relation to the main transaction, means a transaction—

(*a*) to which paragraph 14 applied, and

(*b*) with an effective date on or after the effective date of the main transaction.

(7) In this paragraph "property-investment partnership" has the meaning given in paragraph 14(8).][1]

Amendments—[1] This para inserted by FA 2008 s 97, Sch 31 para 6 with effect from 21 July 2008.

[Transfer of chargeable interest to a partnership consisting wholly of bodies corporate

13 …

Amendment—This paragraph repealed by FA 2007 ss 72(1), (5), 114, Sch 27 Pt 4(1) with effect in respect of transfers occurring on or after 19 July 2007: FA 2007 s 72(13).

The repeal is in relation to this paragraph as it stood before amendment by the Stamp Duty Land Tax (Variation of the Finance Act 2003) Regulations, SI 2006/3237. The repeal, to the extent provided for by FA 2007 s 72(13)–(15), replaces the amendments made by those regulations: see FA 2007 s 72(2), (16). However, the repeal is subject to transitional provisions as provided by FA 2007 s 72(17).

[[Transfer …[3] of interest in property-investment partnership][2]

14— (1) This paragraph applies where—

(*a*) there is a transfer of an interest in a [property-investment][2] partnership;

(*b*) …[3]

(*c*) the relevant partnership property includes a chargeable interest.

(2) The transfer—

(*a*) shall be taken for the purposes of this Part to be a land transaction;

(*b*) is a chargeable transaction.

(3) The purchaser under the transaction is the person who acquires an increased partnership share or, as the case may be, becomes a partner in consequence of the transfer.

[(3A) A transfer to which this paragraph applies is a Type A transfer if it takes the form of arrangements entered into under which—

(*a*) the whole or part of a partner's interest as partner is acquired by another person (who may be an existing partner), and

(*b*) consideration in money or money's worth is given by or on behalf of the person acquiring the interest.

(3B) A transfer to which this paragraph applies is also a Type A transfer if it takes the form of arrangements entered into under which—

(*a*) a person becomes a partner,

(*b*) the interest of an existing partner in the partnership is reduced or an existing partner ceases to be a partner, and

Stamp Taxes

(*c*) there is a withdrawal of money or money's worth from the partnership by the existing partner mentioned in paragraph (*b*) (other than money or money's worth paid from the resources available to the partnership prior to the transfer).

(3C) Any other transfer to which this paragraph applies is a Type B transfer.][4]

(4) ...[3]

(5) The "relevant partnership property", in relation to [a Type A transfer][4] of an interest in a partnership, is every chargeable interest held as partnership property immediately after the transfer, other than—

(*a*) any [chargeable][4] interest that was transferred to the partnership in connection with the transfer;

(*b*) a lease to which paragraph 15 (exclusion of market rent leases) applies[, and

(*c*) any chargeable interest that is not attributable economically to the interest in the partnership that is transferred][4].

[(5A) The "relevant partnership property", in relation to a Type B transfer of an interest in a partnership, is every chargeable interest held as partnership property immediately after the transfer, other than—

(*a*) any chargeable interest that was transferred to the partnership in connection with the transfer,

(*b*) a lease to which paragraph 15 (exclusion of market rent leases) applies,

(*c*) any chargeable interest that is not attributable economically to the interest in the partnership that is transferred,

(*d*) any chargeable interest that was transferred to the partnership on or before 22 July 2004,

(*e*) any chargeable interest in respect of whose transfer to the partnership an election has been made under paragraph 12A, and

(*f*) any other chargeable interest whose transfer to the partnership did not fall within paragraph 10(1)(*a*), (*b*) or (*c*).][4]

(6) The chargeable consideration for the transaction shall be taken to be equal to a proportion of the market value of the relevant partnership property.

(7) That proportion is—

(*a*) if the person acquiring the interest in the partnership was not a partner before the transfer, his partnership share immediately after the transfer;

(*b*) if he was a partner before the transfer, the difference between his partnership share before and after the transfer.][1]

[(8) In this paragraph—

"property-investment partnership" means a partnership whose sole or main activity is investing or dealing in chargeable interests (whether or not that activity involves the carrying out of construction operations on the land in question);

"construction operations" has the same meaning as in Chapter 3 of Part 3 of the Finance Act 2004 (see section 74 of that Act).][2]

[(9) An interest in respect of the transfer of which this paragraph applies shall be treated as a chargeable interest for the purposes of paragraph 3(1) of Schedule 7 to the extent that the relevant partnership property consists of a chargeable interest.][3]

Cross references—See FA 2003 Sch 15 para 30 (a transaction which is a chargeable transaction by virtue of this paragraph is a notifiable transaction if (but only if) the consideration for the transaction exceeds the zero rate threshold).

Amendments—[1] This Part substituted by FA 2004 s 304, Sch 41 paras 1, 3 with effect for any partnership transaction of which the effective date (within the meaning of FA 2003 Pt 4) is after 22 July 2004. A "partnership transaction" means a transaction mentioned in FA 2003 Sch 15 para 9(1): FA 2004 Sch 41 para 3(2).

[2] Heading substituted for former heading "Transfer of partnership interest: consideration given and chargeable interest held", words in sub-para (1)(*a*) and the whole of sub-para (8) inserted by FA 2006 s 163, Sch 24 para 9 with effect in relation to any transfer that has (or, but for the amendment made by FA 2006 Sch 24 para 9, would have) an effective date (within the meaning of FA 2003 Pt 4) which is on or after 19 July 2006.

[3] Sub-paras (1)(*b*), (4), and in Heading, words "for consideration" repealed, and sub-para (9) inserted, by FA 2007 ss 72(1), (2), (6), Sch 27 Pt 4(1) with effect in respect of transfers occurring on or after the day on which FA 2007 is passed: FA 2007 s 72(13).

The amendments are to this paragraph as it stood before amendment by the Stamp Duty Land Tax (Variation of the Finance Act 2003) Regulations, SI 2006/3237. The amendments, to the extent provided for by FA 2007 s 72(13)–(15), replace the amendments made by those regulations: see FA 2007 s 72(2), (16). However, the amendments by FA 2007 are subject to transitional provisions as set out by FA 2007 s 72(17).

But the amendments do not have effect in respect of anything done in respect of a property-investment partnership established before 19 July 2007 if—

(*a*) the partnership does not acquire a chargeable interest on or after that day, and

(*b*) stamp duty land tax was paid in respect of each chargeable interest acquired before that day, by reference to chargeable consideration of not less than the market value: FA 2007 s 72(14).

[4] Sub-paras (3A)–(3C), (5A) inserted, words in sub-para (5) substituted (for words "a transfer") and inserted, and sub-para (5)(*c*) and preceding word "and" inserted, by FA 2008 s 97, Sch 31 para 1. These amendments have effect in respect of transfers occurring on or after 19 July 2007 and are treated as having come into force on that day.

FA 2007 s 72(14), (17) apply in relation to these amendments as they apply in relation to the amendments made by FA 2007 s 72(6), (10).

[Exclusion of market rent leases

15— (1) A lease held as partnership property immediately after a transfer of an interest in the partnership is not relevant partnership property for the purposes of paragraph 14(5) [or (5A)][2] if the following four conditions are met.

(2) The first condition is that—

(*a*) no chargeable consideration other than rent has been given in respect of the grant of the lease, and

(*b*) no arrangements are in place at the time of the transfer for any chargeable consideration other than rent to be given in respect of the grant of the lease.

(3) The second condition is that the rent payable under the lease as granted was a market rent at the time of the grant.

(4) The third condition is that—

(*a*) the term of the lease is 5 years or less, or

(*b*) if the term of the lease is more than 5 years—

(i) the lease provides for the rent payable under it to be reviewed at least once in every 5 years of the term, and

(ii) the rent payable under the lease as a result of a review is required to be a market rent at the review date.

(5) The fourth condition is that there has been no change to the lease since it was granted which is such that, immediately after the change has effect, the rent payable under the lease is less than a market rent.

(6) The market rent of a lease at any time is the rent which the lease might reasonably be expected to fetch at that time in the open market.

(7) A review date is a date from which the rent determined as a result of a rent review is payable.][1]

Amendments—[1] This Part substituted by FA 2004 s 304, Sch 41 paras 1, 3 with effect for any partnership transaction of which the effective date (within the meaning of FA 2003 Pt 4) is after 22 July 2004. A "partnership transaction" means a transaction mentioned in FA 2003 Sch 15 para 9(1): FA 2004 Sch 41 para 3(2).

[2] Words in sub-para (1) inserted by FA 2008 s 97, Sch 31 para 2. This amendment has effect in respect of transfers occurring on or after 19 July 2007 and is treated as having come into force on that day.

FA 2007 s 72(14), (17) apply in relation to this amendment as they apply in relation to the amendments made by s FA 2007 s 72(6), (10).

[Partnership interests: application of provisions about exchanges etc.

16— (1) Where paragraph 5 of Schedule 4 (exchanges) applies to the acquisition of an interest in a partnership in consideration of entering into a land transaction with an existing partner, the interest in the partnership shall be treated as a major interest in land for the purposes of that paragraph if the relevant partnership property includes a major interest in land.

(2) In sub-paragraph (1) "relevant partnership property" has the meaning given by paragraph 14(5) [or (5A) (as appropriate)][2].

(3) The provisions of paragraph 6 of Schedule 4 (partition etc: disregard of existing interest) do not apply where this paragraph applies.][1]

Amendments—[1] This Part substituted by FA 2004 s 304, Sch 41 paras 1, 3 with effect for any partnership transaction of which the effective date (within the meaning of FA 2003 Pt 4) is after 22 July 2004. A "partnership transaction" means a transaction mentioned in FA 2003 Sch 15 para 9(1): FA 2004 Sch 41 para 3(2).

[2] Words in sub-para (2) inserted by FA 2008 s 97, Sch 31 para 3. This amendment has effect in respect of transfers occurring on or after 19 July 2007 and is treated as having come into force on that day.

FA 2007 s 72(14), (17) apply in relation to this amendment as they apply in relation to the amendments made by s FA 2007 s 72(6), (10).

[Transfer of partnership interest pursuant to earlier arrangements

17— (1) This paragraph applies where—

(*a*) there is a transfer of a chargeable interest to a partnership ("the land transfer");

(*b*) the land transfer falls within paragraph (*a*), (*b*) or (*c*) of paragraph 10(1);

(*c*) there is subsequently a transfer of an interest in the partnership ("the partnership transfer");

(*d*) the partnership transfer is made—

(i) if the land transfer falls within paragraph 10(1)(*a*) or (*b*), by the person who makes the land transfer;

(ii) if the land transfer falls within paragraph 10(1)(*c*), by the partner concerned;

(*e*) the partnership transfer is made pursuant to arrangements that were in place at the time of the land transfer;

(*f*) the partnership transfer is not (apart from this paragraph) a chargeable transaction.

(2) The partnership transfer—

(*a*) shall be taken for the purposes of this Part to be a land transaction;

(*b*) is a chargeable transaction.

(3) The partners shall be taken to be the purchasers under the transaction.

(4) The chargeable consideration for the transaction shall be taken to be equal to a proportion of the market value, as at the date of the transaction, of the interest transferred by the land transfer.

(5) That proportion is—

Stamp Taxes

(*a*) if the person making the partnership transfer is not a partner immediately after the transfer, his partnership share immediately before the transfer;

(*b*) if he is a partner immediately after the transfer, the difference between his partnership share before and after the transfer.

(6) The partnership transfer and the land transfer shall be taken to be linked transactions.

(7) Paragraphs 6 to 8 (responsibility of partners) have effect in relation to the partnership transfer, but the responsible partners are—

(*a*) those who were partners immediately before the transfer and who remain partners after the transfer, and

(*b*) any person becoming a partner as a result of, or in connection with, the transfer.][1]

Cross references—See FA 2003 Sch 15 para 30 (a transaction which is a chargeable transaction by virtue of this paragraph is a notifiable transaction if (but only if) the consideration for the transaction exceeds the zero rate threshold).

Amendments—[1] This Part substituted by FA 2004 s 304, Sch 41 paras 1, 3 with effect for any partnership transaction of which the effective date (within the meaning of FA 2003 Pt 4) is after 22 July 2004. A "partnership transaction" means a transaction mentioned in FA 2003 Sch 15 para 9(1): FA 2004 Sch 41 para 3(2).

[Withdrawal of money etc from partnership after transfer of chargeable interest

17A— (1) This paragraph applies where—

(*a*) there is a transfer of a chargeable interest to a partnership ("the land transfer");

(*b*) the land transfer falls within paragraph (*a*), (*b*) or (*c*) of paragraph 10(1);

(*c*) during the period of three years beginning with the date of the land transfer, a qualifying event occurs;

[(*d*) at the time of the qualifying event, an election has not been made in respect of the land transfer under paragraph 12A.][3]

(2) A qualifying event is—

(*a*) a withdrawal from the partnership of money or money's worth which does not represent income profit by the relevant person—

(i) withdrawing capital from his capital account,

(ii) reducing his interest, or

(iii) ceasing to be a partner, or

(*b*) in a case where the relevant person has made a loan to the partnership—

(i) the repayment (to any extent) by the partnership of the loan, or

(ii) a withdrawal by the relevant person from the partnership of money or money's worth which does not represent income profit.

(3) For this purpose the relevant person is—

(*a*) where the land transfer falls within paragraph 10(1)(*a*) or (*b*), the person who makes the land transfer, and

(*b*) where the land transfer falls within paragraph 10(1)(*c*), the partner concerned or a person connected with him.

(4) The qualifying event—

(*a*) shall be taken to be a land transaction, and

(*b*) is a chargeable transaction.

(5) The partners shall be taken to be the purchasers under the transaction.

(6) Paragraphs 6 to 8 (responsibility of partners) have effect in relation to the transaction.

(7) The chargeable consideration for the transaction shall be taken to be—

(*a*) in a case falling within sub-paragraph (2)(*a*), equal to the value of the money or money's worth withdrawn from the partnership, or

(*b*) in a case falling within sub-paragraph (2)(*b*)(i), equal to the amount repaid, and

(*c*) in a case falling within sub-paragraph (2)(*b*)(ii), equal to so much of the value of the money or money's worth withdrawn from the partnership as does not exceed the amount of the loan,

but (in any case) shall not exceed the market value, as at the effective date of the land transfer, of the chargeable interest transferred by the land transfer, reduced by any amount previously chargeable to tax.][1]

[(8) Where—

(*a*) a qualifying event gives rise to a charge under this paragraph, and

(*b*) the same event gives rise to a charge under paragraph 14 (transfer for consideration of interest in property- investment partnership),

the amount of the charge under this paragraph is reduced (but not below nil) by the amount of the charge under that paragraph.][2]

Amendments—[1] This paragraph inserted by F(No 2)A 2005 s 49, Sch 10 paras 1, 10 with effect where the effective date of the transaction transferring the chargeable interest to the partnership is after 19 May 2005.

However, this amendment does not have effect—

(*a*) in relation to any transaction which is effected in pursuance of a contract entered into and substantially performed on or before the specified date (i e 16 March 2005), or

(*b*) subject to what follows below, in relation to any other transaction which is effected in pursuance of a contract entered into on or before the specified date (i e 16 March 2005).

The exclusion by para (*b*) above of transactions effected in pursuance of contracts entered into on or before the specified date does not apply—

(*a*) if there is any variation of the contract or assignment of rights under the contract after that date,

(*b*) if the transaction is effected in consequence of the exercise after that date of any option, right of pre-emption or similar right, or

(*c*) if after that date there is an assignment, subsale or other transaction (relating to the whole or part of the subject-matter of the contract) as a result of which a person other than the purchaser under the contract becomes entitled to call for a conveyance to him: F(No 2)A 2005 Sch 10 para 16(3), (6)–(8).

2 Sub-para (8) inserted by FA 2006 s 163, Sch 24 para 10 with effect in relation to any qualifying event of which the effective date (within the meaning of FA 2003 Pt 4) is on or after 19 July 2006.

3 Sub-para (1)(*d*) inserted by FA 2008 s 97, Sch 31 para 8 with effect from 21 July 2008.

[Transfer of chargeable interest from a partnership: general

18— (1) This paragraph applies where a chargeable interest is transferred—

(*a*) from a partnership to a person who is or has been one of the partners, or

(*b*) from a partnership to a person connected with a person who is or has been one of the partners.

[(2) The chargeable consideration for the transaction shall (subject to paragraph 24) be taken to be equal to—

$$MV \times (100 - SLP)\%$$

where—

MV is the market value of the interest transferred, and

SLP is the sum of the lower proportions.

…][2]

(5) Paragraph 20 provides for determining the sum of the lower proportions.

(6) Paragraph 19 applies …[2] if the whole or part of the chargeable consideration for the transaction is rent.

(7) For the purposes of this paragraph property that was partnership property before the partnership was dissolved or otherwise ceased to exist shall be treated as remaining partnership property until it is distributed.

[(8) This paragraph has effect subject to any election under paragraph 12A.][3]][1]

Cross references—See FA 2003 Sch 15 para 23 (sub-paras (2)–(5) above do not apply where there is a transfer of a chargeable interest from a partnership to a partnership, and none of the chargeable consideration is rent).

Modifications—FA 2003 Sch 15 para 24 (modification of this paragraph in certain circumstances involving a transfer of a chargeable interest from a partnership consisting wholly of bodies corporate).

Amendments—1 This Part substituted by FA 2004 s 304, Sch 41 paras 1, 3 with effect for any partnership transaction of which the effective date (within the meaning of FA 2003 Pt 4) is after 22 July 2004. A "partnership transaction" means a transaction mentioned in FA 2003 Sch 15 para 9(1): FA 2004 Sch 41 para 3(2).

2 Sub-para (2) substituted for former sub-paras (2)–(4) and in sub-para (6) words "(instead of sub-paragraphs (2) to (5))" repealed by FA 2006 s 162, Sch 24 para 5, s 178, Sch 26 Pt 7(2) with effect in relation to any transfer of which the effective date (within the meaning of FA 2003 Pt 4) is on or after 19 July 2006.

3 Sub-para (8) inserted by FA 2008 s 97, Sch 31 para 7 with effect from 21 July 2008.

[Transfer of chargeable interest from a partnership: chargeable consideration including rent

19— (1) This paragraph applies in relation to a transaction to which paragraph 18 applies where the whole or part of the chargeable consideration for the transaction is rent.

[(2) Schedule 5 (amount of tax chargeable: rent) has effect with the modifications set out in sub-paragraphs (2A) to (2C).

(2A) In paragraph 2—

(*a*) for "the net present value of the rent payable over the term of the lease" substitute "the relevant chargeable proportion of the net present value of the rent payable over the term of the lease", and

(*b*) for "the net present values of the rent payable over the terms of all the leases" substitute "the relevant chargeable proportions of the net present values of the rent payable over the terms of all the leases".

(2B) In paragraph [9A(6)][3]—

(*a*) for "the annual rent" substitute "the relevant chargeable proportion of the annual rent", and

(*b*) for "the total of the annual rents" substitute "the relevant chargeable proportion of the total of the annual rents".

(2C) For paragraph 9(4) substitute—

"(4) Tax chargeable under this Schedule is in addition to any tax chargeable under section 55 as it has effect by virtue of paragraph 18 of Schedule 15.".

(2D) For the purposes of sub-paragraphs (2A) and (2B) the relevant chargeable proportion is—

$$(100 - SLP)\%$$

where SLP is the sum of the lower proportions.

…][2]

(8) Paragraph 20 provides for determining the sum of the lower proportions.

(9) This paragraph is subject to paragraph 24.][1]

Stamp Taxes

Cross references—See FA 2003 Sch 15 para 23 (this paragraph does not apply where there is transfer of a chargeable interest from a partnership to a partnership, and the whole or part of the chargeable consideration is rent).
Modifications—FA 2003 Sch 15 para 24 (modification of this paragraph in certain circumstances involving a transfer of a chargeable interest from a partnership consisting wholly of bodies corporate).
Amendments—[1] This Part substituted by FA 2004 s 304, Sch 41 paras 1, 3 with effect for any partnership transaction of which the effective date (within the meaning of FA 2003 Pt 4) is after 22 July 2004. A "partnership transaction" means a transaction mentioned in FA 2003 Sch 15 para 9(1): FA 2004 Sch 41 para 3(2).
[2] Sub-paras (2)–(2D) substituted for former sub-paras (2)–(7) by FA 2006 s 162, Sch 24 para 6 with effect in relation to any transfer of which the effective date (within the meaning of FA 2003 Pt 4) is on or after 19 July 2006.
[3] Reference in sub-para (2B) substituted by FA 2008 s 95(11)(*b*) with effect in relation to transactions with an effective date on or after 12 March 2008.

[Transfer of chargeable interest from a partnership: sum of the lower proportions

20— (1) The sum of the lower proportions in relation to a transaction to which paragraph 18 applies is determined as follows:—

Step One

Identify the relevant owner or owners.

A person is a relevant owner if—

(*a*) immediately after the transaction, he is entitled to a proportion of the chargeable interest, and

(*b*) immediately before the transaction, he was a partner or connected with a partner.

Step Two

For each relevant owner, identify the corresponding partner or partners.

A person is a corresponding partner in relation to a relevant owner if, immediately before the transaction—

(*a*) he was a partner, and

(*b*) he was the relevant owner [or was an individual connected with the relevant owner][2].

[(If there is no relevant owner with a corresponding partner, the sum of the lower proportions is nil.)][2]

Step Three

For each relevant owner, find the proportion of the chargeable interest to which he is entitled immediately after the transaction.

Apportion that proportion between any one or more of the relevant owner's corresponding partners.

Step Four

Find the lower proportion for each person who is a corresponding partner in relation to one or more relevant owners.

The lower proportion is—

(*a*) the proportion of the chargeable interest attributable to the partner, or

(*b*) if lower, the partnership share attributable to the partner.

The proportion of the chargeable interest attributable to the partner is—

(i) if he is a corresponding partner in relation to only one relevant owner, the proportion (if any) of the chargeable interest apportioned to him (at Step Three) in respect of that owner;

(ii) if he is a corresponding partner in relation to more than one relevant owner, the sum of the proportions (if any) of the chargeable interest apportioned to him (at Step Three) in respect of each of those owners.

Paragraph 21 provides for determining the partnership share attributable to the partner.

Step Five

Add together the lower proportions of each person who is a corresponding partner in relation to one or more relevant owners.

The result is the sum of the lower proportions.

(2) For the purposes of this paragraph persons who are entitled to a chargeable interest as beneficial joint tenants (or, in Scotland, as joint owners) shall be taken to be entitled to the chargeable interest as beneficial tenants in common (or, in Scotland, as owners in common) in equal shares.][1]

[(3) For the purpose of paragraph (*b*) of Step 2 a company is to be treated as an individual connected with the relevant owner in so far as it—

(*a*) holds property as trustee, and

(*b*) is connected with the relevant owner only because of section 839(3) of the Taxes Act 1988.][3]

Amendments—[1] This Part substituted by FA 2004 s 304, Sch 41 paras 1, 3 with effect for any partnership transaction of which the effective date (within the meaning of FA 2003 Pt 4) is after 22 July 2004. A "partnership transaction" means a transaction mentioned in FA 2003 Sch 15 para 9(1): FA 2004 Sch 41 para 3(2).
[2] Words in sub-para (1) step two para (*b*) substituted, and words at end of step two inserted, by FA 2007 s 72(1), (2), (7) with effect in respect of transfers occurring on or after 19 July 2007: FA 2007 s 72(13).
The amendments are to this paragraph as it stood before amendment by the Stamp Duty Land Tax (Variation of the Finance Act 2003) Regulations, SI 2006/3237.

The amendments, to the extent provided for by FA 2007 s 72(13)–(15), replace the amendments made by those regulations: see FA 2007 s 72(2), (16). However, the amendments by FA 2007 are subject to transitional provisions as provided by FA 2007 s 72(17).

[3] Sub-para (3) inserted by FA 2007 s 72(1), (2), (8) with effect in respect of transfers occurring on or after 19 July 2007: FA 2007 s 72(13).

[Transfer of chargeable interest from a partnership: partnership share attributable to partner

21— (1) This paragraph provides for determining the partnership share attributable to a partner for the purposes of paragraph 20(1) (see Step Four).

(2) Paragraph 22 applies for determining the partnership share attributable to a partner where—

(*a*) the effective date of the transfer of the relevant chargeable interest to the partnership was before 20th October 2003, or

(*b*) the effective date of the transfer of the relevant chargeable interest to the partnership was on or after that date and—

(i) the instrument by which the transfer was effected has been duly stamped with *ad valorem* stamp duty, or

(ii) any tax payable in respect of the transfer has been duly paid under this Part.

(3) Where the effective date of the transfer of the relevant chargeable interest to the partnership was on or after 20th October 2003 but neither of the conditions in sub-paragraphs (i) and (ii) of sub-paragraph (2)(*b*) is met, the partnership share attributable to the partner is zero.

(4) The relevant chargeable interest is—

(*a*) the chargeable interest which ceases to be partnership property as a result of the transaction to which paragraph 18 applies, or

(*b*) where the transaction to which paragraph 18 applies is the grant or creation of a chargeable interest, the chargeable interest out of which that interest is granted or created.][1]

Amendments—[1] This Part substituted by FA 2004 s 304, Sch 41 paras 1, 3 with effect for any partnership transaction of which the effective date (within the meaning of FA 2003 Pt 4) is after 22 July 2004. A "partnership transaction" means a transaction mentioned in FA 2003 Sch 15 para 9(1): FA 2004 Sch 41 para 3(2).

[22— (1) Where this paragraph applies, the partnership share attributable to the partner is determined as follows:—

Step One

Find the partner's actual partnership share on the relevant date.

In a case falling within paragraph 21(2)(*a*), the relevant date—

(*a*) if the partner was a partner on 19th October 2003, is that date;

(*b*) if the partner became a partner after that date, is the date on which he became a partner.

In a case falling within paragraph 21(2)(*b*), the relevant date

(*a*) if the partner was a partner on the effective date of the transfer of the relevant chargeable interest to the partnership, is that date;

(*b*) if the partner became a partner after that date, is the date on which he became a partner.

Step Two

Add to that partnership share any increases in the partner's partnership share which—

(*a*) occur in the period starting on the day after the relevant date and ending immediately before the transaction to which paragraph 18 applies, and

(*b*) count for this purpose.

The result is the increased partnership share.

An increase counts for the purpose of paragraph (*b*) only if—

(i) where the transfer which resulted in the increase took place on or before the date on which the Finance Act 2004 was passed, the instrument by which the transfer was effected has been duly stamped with *ad valorem* stamp duty under the enactments relating to stamp duty;

(ii) where the transfer which resulted in the increase took place after that date, any tax payable in respect of the transfer has been duly paid under this Part.

Step Three

Deduct from the increased partnership share any decreases in the partner's partnership share which occur in the period starting on the day after the relevant date and ending immediately before the transaction to which paragraph 18 applies.

The result is the partnership share attributable to the partner.

(2) If the effect of applying Step Three would be to reduce the partnership share attributable to the partner below zero, the partnership share attributable to the partner is zero.

(3) In a case falling within paragraph 21(2)(*a*), if the partner ceased to be a partner before 19th October 2003, the partnership share attributable to the partner is zero.

(4) In a case falling within paragraph 21(2)(*b*), if the partner ceased to be a partner before the effective date of the transfer of the relevant chargeable interest to the partnership, the partnership share attributable to the partner is zero.

(5) Paragraph 21(4) (relevant chargeable interest) applies for the purposes of this paragraph.][1]

Amendments—[1] This Part substituted by FA 2004 s 304, Sch 41 paras 1, 3 with effect for any partnership transaction of which the effective date (within the meaning of FA 2003 Pt 4) is after 22 July 2004. A "partnership transaction" means a transaction mentioned in FA 2003 Sch 15 para 9(1): FA 2004 Sch 41 para 3(2).

[Transfer of chargeable interest from a partnership to a partnership

23— (1) This paragraph applies where—

(*a*) there is a transfer of a chargeable interest from a partnership to a partnership, and
(*b*) the transfer is both—

(i) a transaction to which paragraph 10 applies, and
(ii) a transaction to which paragraph 18 applies.

[(2) Paragraphs 10(2) and 18(2) do not apply.

(2A) The chargeable consideration for the transaction shall be taken to be what it would have been if paragraph 10(2) had applied or, if greater, what it would have been if paragraph 18(2) had applied.

(3) Where the whole or part of the chargeable consideration for the transaction is rent—

(*a*) paragraphs 11 and 19 do not apply;
(*b*) the tax chargeable in respect of so much of the chargeable consideration as consists of rent shall be taken to be what it would have been if paragraph 11 had applied or, if greater, what it would have been if paragraph 19 had applied;
(*c*) the disapplication of the 0% band provided for by paragraph [9A][3] of Schedule 5 has effect if—

(i) it would have had effect if paragraph 11(2B) of this Schedule had applied, or
(ii) it would have had effect if paragraph 19(2B) of this Schedule had applied.][2]][1]

Modifications—FA 2003 Sch 15 para 24 (modification of this paragraph in certain circumstances involving a transfer of a chargeable interest from a partnership consisting wholly of bodies corporate).

Amendments—[1] This Part substituted by FA 2004 s 304, Sch 41 paras 1, 3 with effect for any partnership transaction of which the effective date (within the meaning of FA 2003 Pt 4) is after 22 July 2004. A "partnership transaction" means a transaction mentioned in FA 2003 Sch 15 para 9(1): FA 2004 Sch 41 para 3(2).

[2] Sub-paras (2)–(3) substituted for former sub-paras (2), (3) by FA 2006 s 162, Sch 24 para 8 with effect in relation to any transfer of which the effective date (within the meaning of FA 2003 Pt 4) is on or after 19 July 2006.

[3] Reference in sub-para (3)(*c*) substituted by FA 2008 s 95(11)(*c*) with effect in relation to transactions with an effective date on or after 12 March 2008.

[Transfer of chargeable interest from a partnership consisting wholly of bodies corporate

24— (1) This paragraph applies where—

(*a*) there is a transaction to which paragraph 18 applies;
(*b*) immediately before the transaction all the partners are bodies corporate;
(*c*) the sum of the lower proportions is 75 or more.

(2) Paragraphs 18, 19 and 23 have effect with these modifications.

(3) In paragraph 18, for [sub-paragraphs (2) and (5)][2] substitute—

"(2) The chargeable consideration for the transaction shall be taken to be equal to the market value of the interest transferred.".

[(4A) In paragraph 19(2), for "sub-paragraphs (2) to (2C)" substitute "sub-paragraph (2C)".
(5) In paragraph 19, omit sub-paragraphs (2A), (2B), (2D) and (8).
...][2]

(9) Paragraph 20 provides for determining the sum of the lower proportions.][1]

Amendments—[1] This Part substituted by FA 2004 s 304, Sch 41 paras 1, 3 with effect for any partnership transaction of which the effective date (within the meaning of FA 2003 Pt 4) is after 22 July 2004. A "partnership transaction" means a transaction mentioned in FA 2003 Sch 15 para 9(1): FA 2004 Sch 41 para 3(2).

[2] In sub-para (3) words substituted for "sub-paragraphs (2) to (5)" and sub-paras (4A), (5) substituted for former sub-paras (4)–(8) by FA 2006 s 162, Sch 24 para 7 with effect in relation to any transfer of which the effective date (within the meaning of FA 2003 Pt 4) is on or after 19 July 2006.

[Application of exemptions and reliefs

25— (1) Where paragraph 10, 14, 17 or 18 applies, paragraph 1 of Schedule 3 (exemption of transactions for which there is no chargeable consideration) does not apply.

(2) But (subject to paragraphs 26 to 28) this Part of this Schedule has effect subject to any other provision affording exemption or relief from stamp duty land tax.][1]

Amendments—[1] This Part substituted by FA 2004 s 304, Sch 41 paras 1, 3 with effect for any partnership transaction of which the effective date (within the meaning of FA 2003 Pt 4) is after 22 July 2004. A "partnership transaction" means a transaction mentioned in FA 2003 Sch 15 para 9(1): FA 2004 Sch 41 para 3(2).

[Application of disadvantaged areas relief

26— (1) Schedule 6 (disadvantaged areas relief) applies to the transfer of an interest in a partnership that is a chargeable transaction by virtue of paragraph 14 or 17 with these modifications.

(2) For paragraph 3 substitute—

"**3**— (1) This Part of this Schedule applies to a transfer of an interest in a partnership that is a chargeable transaction by virtue of paragraph 14 of Schedule 15 if every chargeable interest comprising the relevant partnership property is a chargeable interest in relation to land that is wholly situated in a disadvantaged area.

(2) This Part of this Schedule applies to a transfer of an interest in a partnership that is a chargeable transaction by virtue of paragraph 17 of Schedule 15 if the subject matter of the land transfer is a chargeable interest in relation to land that is wholly situated in a disadvantaged area.".

(3) In paragraph 5, for sub-paragraphs (2) to (4) substitute—

"(2) If the relevant consideration does not exceed £150,000 the transaction is exempt from charge.".

(4) For paragraph 6 substitute—

"**6**— (1) This paragraph applies where the land is partly non-residential property and partly residential property.

(2) The non-residential proportion of the chargeable consideration for the transaction does not count as chargeable consideration.

(3) The non-residential proportion is the proportion of the market value of the relevant property that, on a just and reasonable apportionment, is attributable to land that is non-residential property.

(4) If the relevant consideration does not exceed £150,000, none of the residential proportion of the chargeable consideration counts as chargeable consideration.

(5) The residential proportion is the proportion of the market value of the relevant property that, on a just and reasonable apportionment, is attributable to land that is residential property.".

(5) For paragraph 7 substitute—

"**7**— (1) This Part of this Schedule applies to a transfer of an interest in a partnership that is a chargeable transaction by virtue of paragraph 14 of Schedule 15 if—

(*a*) some (but not all) of the chargeable interests comprising the relevant partnership property are chargeable interests in relation to land that is wholly situated in a disadvantaged area, or

(*b*) any chargeable interest comprised in the relevant partnership property is a chargeable interest in relation to land that is partly situated in a disadvantaged area and partly situated outside such an area.

(2) This Part of this Schedule applies to a transfer of an interest in a partnership that is a chargeable transaction by virtue of paragraph 17 of Schedule 15 if the subject matter of the land transfer is a chargeable interest in relation to land that is partly situated in a disadvantaged area and partly situated outside such an area.

(3) In this Part—

(*a*) references to the disadvantaged-area proportion are to the proportion of the market value of the relevant property that, on a just and reasonable apportionment, is attributable to land situated in a disadvantaged area;

(*b*) references to the advantaged-area proportion are to the proportion of the market value of the relevant property that, on a just and reasonable apportionment, is attributable to land that is situated outside a disadvantaged area.".

(6) In paragraph 8, for "consideration attributable to the land situated in the disadvantaged area" substitute "disadvantaged-area proportion of the chargeable consideration".

(7) In paragraph 9, for sub-paragraphs (2) to (4) substitute—

"(2) If the relevant consideration does not exceed £150,000 none of the disadvantaged-area proportion of the chargeable consideration counts as chargeable consideration.".

(8) For paragraph 10 substitute—

"**10**— (1) This paragraph applies where the land situated in a disadvantaged area is partly non-residential property and partly residential property.

(2) The non-residential proportion of the disadvantaged-area proportion of the chargeable consideration for the transaction does not count as chargeable consideration [(subject to any election under paragraph 12A)][3].

(3) The non-residential proportion is the proportion of the disadvantaged-area proportion of the market value of the relevant property that, on a just and reasonable apportionment, is attributable to land that is not residential property.

(4) If the relevant consideration does not exceed £150,000, none of the residential proportion of the disadvantaged-area proportion of the chargeable consideration counts as chargeable consideration [(subject to any election under paragraph 12A)][3].

(5) The residential proportion is the proportion of the disadvantaged-area proportion of the market value of the relevant property that, on a just and reasonable apportionment, is attributable to land that is residential property.".

(9) After paragraph 11(1) insert—

"(1A) In this Schedule—

"the land transfer" means the transaction that is the land transfer for the purposes of paragraph 17 of Schedule 15;

"the relevant partnership property" has the meaning given by paragraph 14(5) [or (5A) (as appropriate)][2] of Schedule 15;

"the relevant property"—

(*a*) in the case of a transfer of an interest in a partnership that is a chargeable transaction by virtue of paragraph 14 of Schedule 15, means the relevant partnership property;

(*b*) in the case of a transfer of an interest in a partnership that is a chargeable transaction by virtue of paragraph 17 of Schedule 15, means the subject matter of the land transfer.

(1B) There is a transfer of an interest in a partnership for the purposes of this Schedule if there is such a transfer for the purposes of Part 3 of Schedule 15 (see paragraph 36 of that Schedule).".

(10) Omit paragraphs 11(2) and 12.][1]

Amendments—[1] This Part substituted by FA 2004 s 304, Sch 41 paras 1, 3 with effect for any partnership transaction of which the effective date (within the meaning of FA 2003 Pt 4) is after 22 July 2004. A "partnership transaction" means a transaction mentioned in FA 2003 Sch 15 para 9(1): FA 2004 Sch 41 para 3(2).

[2] In sub-para (9), in the inserted sub-para (1A), words in the definition of "the relevant partnership property" inserted, by FA 2008 s 97, Sch 31 para 4. This amendment has effect in respect of transfers occurring on or after 19 July 2007 and is treated as having come into force on that day.

FA 2007 s 72(14), (17) apply in relation to this amendment as they apply in relation to the amendments made by FA 2007 s 72(6), (10).

[3] Sub-para (8), in substituted para (10)(2), (4) words inserted by FA 2008 s 97, Sch 31 para 9 with effect from 21 July 2008.

[Application of group relief

27— (1) Part 1 of Schedule 7 (group relief) applies to—

(*a*) a transaction to which paragraph 10 applies, and

(*b*) a transaction that is a chargeable transaction by virtue of paragraph 17,

with these modifications.

(2) In paragraph 3(1)(*a*), for "the purchaser" substitute "a partner who was a partner at the effective date of the relevant transaction ("the relevant partner")".

(3) In paragraph 3(1), for paragraph (*b*) substitute—

"(*b*) at the time the relevant partner ceases to be a member of the same group as the vendor ("the relevant time"), a chargeable interest is held by or on behalf of the members of the partnership and that chargeable interest—

(i) was acquired by or on behalf of the partnership under the relevant transaction, or

(ii) is derived from a chargeable interest so acquired, and has not subsequently been acquired at market value under a chargeable transaction for which group relief was available but was not claimed,".

(4) In paragraph 3(3), for the words from "the transferee company" to the end substitute "or on behalf of the partnership and to the proportion in which the relevant partner is entitled at the relevant time to share in the income profits of the partnership.".

(5) In paragraph 3(4), omit the definition of "relevant associated company".

(6) In paragraphs 4 to 6, for "the purchaser" (wherever appearing) substitute "the relevant partner".][1]

Amendments—[1] This Part substituted by FA 2004 s 304, Sch 41 paras 1, 3 with effect for any partnership transaction of which the effective date (within the meaning of FA 2003 Pt 4) is after 22 July 2004. A "partnership transaction" means a transaction mentioned in FA 2003 Sch 15 para 9(1): FA 2004 Sch 41 para 3(2).

[27A— (1) This paragraph applies where in calculating the sum of the lower proportions in relation to a transaction (in accordance with paragraph 12)—

(*a*) a company ("the connected company") would have been a corresponding partner of a relevant owner ("the original owner") but for the fact that paragraph (*b*) of Step Two includes connected persons only if they are individuals, and

(*b*) the connected company and the original owner are members of the same group.

(2) The charge in respect of the transaction shall be reduced to the amount that would have been payable had the connected company been a corresponding partner of the original owner for the purposes of calculating the sum of the lower proportions.

(3) The provisions of Part 1 of Schedule 7 apply to group relief under sub-paragraph (2) above as to group relief under paragraph 1(1) of Schedule 7, but—

(*a*) with the omission of paragraph 2(2)(*a*),

(*b*) with the substitution for "the purchaser" in paragraph 3(1)(*a*) of "a partner who was, at the effective date of the transaction, a partner and a member of the same group as the transferor ("the relevant partner")", and

(*c*) with the other modifications specified in paragraph 27(3) to (6) above.][1]

Amendments—[1] This paragraph inserted by FA 2007 s 72(1), (2), (9) with effect in respect of transfers occurring on or after 19 July 2007: FA 2007 s 72(13).
The insertion, to the extent provided for by FA 2007 s 72(13)–(15), replaces that made by the Stamp Duty Land Tax (Variation of the Finance Act 2003) Regulations, SI 2006/3237: see FA 2007 s 72(2). However, this amendment is subject to transitional provisions as provided by FA 2007 s 72(17).

[Application of charities relief

28— (1) Schedule 8 (charities relief) applies to the transfer of an interest in a partnership that is a chargeable transaction by virtue of paragraph 14 or 17 with these modifications.

(2) In paragraph 1(1), for "A land transaction is exempt from charge if the purchaser is a charity" substitute "A transfer of an interest in a partnership that is a chargeable transaction by virtue of paragraph 14 or 17 of Schedule 15 is exempt from charge if the transferee is a charity".

(3) In paragraph 1(2)—

(*a*) for "the purchaser must intend to hold the subject-matter of the transaction" substitute "every chargeable interest held as partnership property immediately after the transfer must be held";

(*b*) in paragraphs (*a*) and (*b*) for "the purchaser" substitute "the transferee".

(4) In paragraph 1(3) for "the purchaser" substitute "the transferee".

(5) In paragraph 2(1), for paragraph (*b*) substitute—

"(*b*) at the time of the disqualifying event the partnership property includes a chargeable interest—

(i) that was held as partnership property immediately after the relevant transaction, or

(ii) that is derived from an interest held as partnership property at that time,".

(6) In paragraph 2(3)(*a*), for "the purchaser" substitute "the transferee".

(7) In paragraph 2(3), for paragraph (*b*) substitute—

"(*b*) any chargeable interest held as partnership property immediately after the relevant transaction, or any interest or right derived from it, being used or held otherwise than for qualifying charitable purposes.".

(8) For paragraph 2(4) substitute—

"(4) In sub-paragraphs (1) and (2) an "appropriate proportion" means an appropriate proportion having regard to—

(*a*) the chargeable interests held as partnership property immediately after the relevant transaction and the chargeable interests held as partnership property at the time of the disqualifying event, and

(*b*) the extent to which any chargeable interest held as partnership property at that time becomes used or held for purposes other than qualifying charitable purposes.".

(9) After paragraph 2 insert—

"Interpretation

3— (1) There is a transfer of an interest in a partnership for the purposes of this Schedule if there is such a transfer for the purposes of Part 3 of Schedule 15 (see paragraph 36 of that Schedule).

(2) Paragraph 34(1) of Schedule 15 (meaning of references to partnership property) applies for the purposes of this Schedule as it applies for the purposes of Part 3 of that Schedule.".][1]

Amendments—[1] This Part substituted by FA 2004 s 304, Sch 41 paras 1, 3 with effect for any partnership transaction of which the effective date (within the meaning of FA 2003 Pt 4) is after 22 July 2004. A "partnership transaction" means a transaction mentioned in FA 2003 Sch 15 para 9(1): FA 2004 Sch 41 para 3(2).

[Acquisition of interest in partnership not chargeable except as specially provided

29 Except as provided by—

(*a*) paragraph 10 (transfer of chargeable interest to a partnership), or

(*b*) paragraph 14 (transfer of partnership interest: consideration given and chargeable interest held), or

(*c*) paragraph 17 (transfer of partnership interest pursuant to earlier arrangements),

the acquisition of an interest in a partnership is not a chargeable transaction, notwithstanding that the partnership property includes land.][1]

Amendments—[1] This Part substituted by FA 2004 s 304, Sch 41 paras 1, 3 with effect for any partnership transaction of which the effective date (within the meaning of FA 2003 Pt 4) is after 22 July 2004. A "partnership transaction" means a transaction mentioned in FA 2003 Sch 15 para 9(1): FA 2004 Sch 41 para 3(2).

[Transactions that are not notifiable

30— (1) A transaction which is a chargeable transaction by virtue of paragraph 14 or 17 (transfer of partnership interest) is a notifiable transaction if (but only if) the consideration for the transaction exceeds the zero rate threshold.

(2) The consideration for a transaction exceeds the zero rate threshold if either or both of the following conditions are met—

Stamp Taxes

(*a*) the relevant consideration for the purposes of section 55 (amount of tax chargeable: general) is such that the rate of tax chargeable under that section is 1% or higher;

(*b*) the relevant rental value for the purposes of Schedule 5 (amount of tax chargeable: rent) is such that the rate of tax chargeable under that Schedule is 1% or higher.][1]

Amendments—[1] This Part substituted by FA 2004 s 304, Sch 41 paras 1, 3 with effect for any partnership transaction of which the effective date (within the meaning of FA 2003 Pt 4) is after 22 July 2004. A "partnership transaction" means a transaction mentioned in FA 2003 Sch 15 para 9(1): FA 2004 Sch 41 para 3(2).

[Stamp duty on transfers of partnership interests: continued application

31— (1) Nothing in section 125 (abolition of stamp duty except in relation to stock or marketable securities), or in Part 2 of Schedule 20 (amendments and repeals consequential on that section), affects the application of the enactments relating to stamp duty in relation to an instrument by which a transfer of an interest in a partnership is effected.

(2) In Part 1 of Schedule 20 (provisions supplementing section 125) references to stock or marketable securities shall be read as including any property that is the subject-matter of a transaction by which an interest in a partnership is transferred.

(3) In their application in relation to an instrument by which a transfer of an interest in a partnership is effected, the enactments relating to stamp duty have effect subject to paragraphs 32 and 33.][1]

Amendments—[1] This Part substituted by FA 2004 s 304, Sch 41 paras 1, 3 with effect for any partnership transaction of which the effective date (within the meaning of FA 2003 Pt 4) is after 22 July 2004. A "partnership transaction" means a transaction mentioned in FA 2003 Sch 15 para 9(1): FA 2004 Sch 41 para 3(2).

[Stamp duty on transfers of partnership interests: modification

32— (1) This paragraph applies where—

(*a*) stamp duty under Part 1 of Schedule 13 to the Finance Act 1999 (transfer on sale) is chargeable on an instrument effecting a transfer of an interest in a partnership, and

(*b*) the relevant partnership property includes a chargeable interest.

(2) The "relevant partnership property", in relation to a transfer of an interest in a partnership, is every chargeable interest held as partnership property immediately after the transfer, other than any interest that was transferred to the partnership in connection with the transfer.

(3) The consideration for the transaction shall (subject to sub-paragraph (8)) be taken to be equal to the actual consideration for the transaction less the excluded amount.

(4) The excluded amount is a proportion of the net market value of the relevant partnership property immediately after the transfer.

(5) That proportion is—

(*a*) if the person acquiring the interest in the partnership was not a partner before the transfer, his partnership share immediately after the transfer;

(*b*) if he was a partner before the transfer, the difference between his partnership share before and after the transfer.

(6) The net market value of a chargeable interest at a particular date is—

$$MV - SL$$

where—

MV is the market value of the chargeable interest at that date, and

SL is the amount outstanding at that date on any loan secured solely on the chargeable interest.

(7) If, in relation to a chargeable interest, SL is greater than MV, the net market value of the chargeable interest shall be taken to be nil.

(8) If the excluded amount is greater than the actual consideration for the transaction, the consideration for the transaction shall be taken to be nil.

(9) Where this paragraph applies in relation to an instrument, the instrument shall not be regarded as duly stamped unless it has been stamped in accordance with section 12 of the Stamp Act 1891.][1]

Amendments—[1] This Part substituted by FA 2004 s 304, Sch 41 paras 1, 3 with effect for any partnership transaction of which the effective date (within the meaning of FA 2003 Pt 4) is after 22 July 2004. A "partnership transaction" means a transaction mentioned in FA 2003 Sch 15 para 9(1): FA 2004 Sch 41 para 3(2).

[33— [(1) This paragraph applies where stamp duty under Part 1 of Schedule 13 to the Finance Act 1999 (transfer on sale) is, apart from this paragraph, chargeable on an instrument effecting a transfer of an interest in a partnership.][2]

[(1A) If the relevant partnership property does not include any stock or marketable securities, no stamp duty shall (subject to sub-paragraph (8)) be chargeable on the instrument.][2]

(3) [If the relevant partnership property includes stock or marketable securities,][2] the stamp duty chargeable on the instrument shall not exceed the stamp duty that would be chargeable if—

(*a*) the instrument were an instrument effecting a transfer of [that stock and those securities][2], and [(*b*) the consideration for the transfer were equal to the appropriate proportion of the net market value of that stock and those securities immediately after the transfer.][2]

[(3A) The "relevant partnership property", in relation to a transfer of an interest in a partnership, is the partnership property immediately after the transfer, other than any partnership property that was transferred to the partnership in connection with the transfer.][2]

(4) ...[2]

(5) [The appropriate][2] proportion is—

(*a*) if the person acquiring the interest in the partnership was not a partner before the transfer, his partnership share immediately after the transfer;

(*b*) if he was a partner before the transfer, the difference between his partnership share before and after the transfer.

(6) The net market value of stock or securities at a particular date is—

$$MV - SL$$

where—

MV is the market value of the stock or securities at that date, and

SL is the amount outstanding at that date on any loan secured solely on the stock or securities.

(7) If, in relation to any stock or securities, SL is greater than MV, the net market value of the stock or securities shall be taken to be nil.

(8) Where this paragraph applies in relation to an instrument, the instrument shall not be regarded as duly stamped unless it has been stamped in accordance with section 12 of the Stamp Act 1891.

(9) This paragraph shall be construed as one with the Stamp Act 1891.][1]

Amendments—[1] This Part substituted by FA 2004 s 304, Sch 41 paras 1, 3 with effect for any partnership transaction of which the effective date (within the meaning of FA 2003 Pt 4) is after 22 July 2004. A "partnership transaction" means a transaction mentioned in FA 2003 Sch 15 para 9(1): FA 2004 Sch 41 para 3(2).

[2] Sub-paras (1), (1A) substituted for sub-paras (1), (2); in sub-para (3), words inserted, and words substituted for the words "the stock and marketable securities comprised in the relevant partnership property"; sub-para (3)(*b*) substituted; sub-para (3A) inserted; sub-para (4) repealed; and in sub-para (5), words substituted for the word "That"; by F(No 2)A 2005 ss 49, 70, Sch 10 paras 17, 21, Sch 11 Pt 3(1) with effect in relation to any instrument executed on or after the day on which F(No 2)A 2005 is passed: F(No 2)A 2005 Sch 10 para 22.

[Interpretation: partnership property and partnership share

34— (1) Any reference in this Part of this Schedule to partnership property is to an interest or right held by or on behalf of a partnership, or the members of a partnership, for the purposes of the partnership business.

(2) Any reference in this Part of this Schedule to a person's partnership share at any time is to the proportion in which he is entitled at that time to share in the income profits of the partnership.][1]

Amendments—[1] This Part substituted by FA 2004 s 304, Sch 41 paras 1, 3 with effect for any partnership transaction of which the effective date (within the meaning of FA 2003 Pt 4) is after 22 July 2004. A "partnership transaction" means a transaction mentioned in FA 2003 Sch 15 para 9(1): FA 2004 Sch 41 para 3(2).

[Interpretation: transfer of chargeable interest to a partnership

35 For the purposes of this Part of this Schedule, there is a transfer of a chargeable interest to a partnership in any case where a chargeable interest becomes partnership property.][1]

Amendments—[1] This Part substituted by FA 2004 s 304, Sch 41 paras 1, 3 with effect for any partnership transaction of which the effective date (within the meaning of FA 2003 Pt 4) is after 22 July 2004. A "partnership transaction" means a transaction mentioned in FA 2003 Sch 15 para 9(1): FA 2004 Sch 41 para 3(2).

[Interpretation: transfer of interest in a partnership

[**36** For the purposes of this Part of this Schedule, where a person acquires or increases a partnership share there is a transfer of an interest in the partnership (to that partner and from the other partners).][2]][1]

Amendments—[1] This Part substituted by FA 2004 s 304, Sch 41 paras 1, 3 with effect for any partnership transaction of which the effective date (within the meaning of FA 2003 Pt 4) is after 22 July 2004. A "partnership transaction" means a transaction mentioned in FA 2003 Sch 15 para 9(1): FA 2004 Sch 41 para 3(2).

[2] This paragraph substituted by FA 2007 s 72(1), (2), (10) with effect in respect of transfers occurring on or after 19 July 2007: FA 2007 s 72(13).

However, this substitution does not have effect in respect of anything done in respect of a property-investment partnership established before 19 July 2007 if—

(*a*) the partnership does not acquire a chargeable interest on or after that day, and

(*b*) stamp duty land tax was paid in respect of each chargeable interest acquired before that day, by reference to chargeable consideration of not less than the market value: FA 2007 s 72(14).

[Interpretation: transfer of chargeable interest from a partnership

37 For the purposes of this Part of this Schedule, there is a transfer of a chargeable interest from a partnership in any case where—

(*a*) a chargeable interest that was partnership property ceases to be partnership property, or

(*b*) a chargeable interest is granted or created out of partnership property and the interest is not partnership property.][1]

Amendments—[1] This Part substituted by FA 2004 s 304, Sch 41 paras 1, 3 with effect for any partnership transaction of which the effective date (within the meaning of FA 2003 Pt 4) is after 22 July 2004. A "partnership transaction" means a transaction mentioned in FA 2003 Sch 15 para 9(1): FA 2004 Sch 41 para 3(2).

[Interpretation: market value of leases

38— (1) This paragraph applies in relation to a lease for the purposes of this Part of this Schedule if—

(*a*) the grant of the lease is or was a transaction to which paragraph 10 applies or applied (or a transaction to which paragraph 10 would have applied if that paragraph had been in force at the time of the grant), or

(*b*) the grant of the lease is a transaction to which paragraph 18 applies.

(2) In determining the market value of the lease, an obligation of the tenant under the lease is to be taken into account if (but only if)—

(*a*) it is an obligation such as is mentioned in paragraph 10(1) of Schedule 17A, or

(*b*) it is an obligation to make a payment to a person.][1]

Amendments—[1] This Part substituted by FA 2004 s 304, Sch 41 paras 1, 3 with effect for any partnership transaction of which the effective date (within the meaning of FA 2003 Pt 4) is after 22 July 2004. A "partnership transaction" means a transaction mentioned in FA 2003 Sch 15 para 9(1): FA 2004 Sch 41 para 3(2).

[Interpretation: connected persons

39— (1) Section 839 of the Taxes Act 1988 (connected persons) has effect for the purposes of this Part of this Schedule.

(2) As applied by sub-paragraph (1), that section has effect with the omission of subsection (4) (partners connected with each other).][1]

[(3) As applied by sub-paragraph (1) for the purposes of paragraph 12 or 20, that section has effect with the omission of subsection (3)(*c*) (trustee connected with settlement).][2]

Amendments—[1] This Part substituted by FA 2004 s 304, Sch 41 paras 1, 3 with effect for any partnership transaction of which the effective date (within the meaning of FA 2003 Pt 4) is after 22 July 2004. A "partnership transaction" means a transaction mentioned in FA 2003 Sch 15 para 9(1): FA 2004 Sch 41 para 3(2).

[2] Sub-para (3) inserted by FA 2007 s 72(1), (2), (11) with effect in respect of transfers occurring on or after 19 July 2007: FA 2007 s 72(13).

[Interpretation: arrangements

40 In this Part of this Schedule "arrangements" includes any scheme, agreement or understanding, whether or not legally enforceable.][1]

Amendments—[1] This Part substituted by FA 2004 s 304, Sch 41 paras 1, 3 with effect for any partnership transaction of which the effective date (within the meaning of FA 2003 Pt 4) is after 22 July 2004. A "partnership transaction" means a transaction mentioned in FA 2003 Sch 15 para 9(1): FA 2004 Sch 41 para 3(2).

SCHEDULE 16

STAMP DUTY LAND TAX: TRUSTS AND POWERS

Section 105

HMRC Manuals—Stamp Duty Land Tax Manual SDLTM31700–32500 (explanation of this Schedule).

Meaning of "settlement" and "bare trust"

1— (1) In this Part "settlement" means a trust that is not a bare trust.

(2) In this Part a "bare trust" means a trust under which property is held by a person as trustee—

(*a*) for a person who is absolutely entitled as against the trustee, or who would be so entitled but for being a minor or other person under a disability, or

(*b*) for two or more persons who are or would be jointly so entitled,

and includes a case in which a person holds property as nominee for another.

(3) In sub-paragraph (2)(*a*) and (*b*) the references to a person being absolutely entitled to property as against the trustee are references to a case where the person has the exclusive right, subject only to satisfying any outstanding charge, lien or other right of the trustee, to resort to the property for payment of duty, taxes, costs or other outgoings or to direct how the property is to be dealt with.

(4) In sub-paragraph (2) "minor", in relation to Scotland, means a person under legal disability by reason of nonage.

HMRC Manuals—Stamp Duty Land Tax Manual SDLTM31710 (the phrase "absolutely entitled" broadly means that the beneficiary may acquire or receive the trust property either immediately or by giving the requisite notice to the trustees in accordance with the terms of the trust; and the trustees have no power over or right to deal with the trust property without the permission of the beneficiary who enjoys absolute entitlement).
SDLTM31710a (Revenue example).
SDLTM31720 (common examples of settlements).

Interests of beneficiaries under certain trusts

2 Where property is held in trust under the law of Scotland, or of a country or territory outside the United Kingdom, on terms such that, if the trust had effect under the law of England and Wales, a beneficiary would be regarded as having an equitable interest in the trust property—

(*a*) that beneficiary shall be treated for the purposes of this Part as having such an interest notwithstanding that no such interest is recognised by the law of Scotland or, as the case may be, the country or territory outside the United Kingdom, and

(*b*) an acquisition of the interest of a beneficiary under the trust shall accordingly be treated as involving the acquisition of an interest in the trust property.

[Bare trustee

3— (1) Subject to sub-paragraph (2), where a person acquires a chargeable interest [or an interest in a partnership][2] as bare trustee, this Part applies as if the interest were vested in, and the acts of the trustee in relation to it were the acts of, the person or persons for whom he is trustee.

(2) Sub-paragraph (1) does not apply in relation to the grant of a lease.

(3) Where a lease is granted to a person as bare trustee, he is treated for the purposes of this Part, as it applies in relation to the grant of the lease, as purchaser of the whole of the interest acquired.

(4) Where a lease is granted by a person as bare trustee, he is to be treated for the purposes of this Part, as it applies in relation to the grant of the lease, as vendor of the whole of the interest disposed of.][1]

Amendments—[1] This paragraph substituted by F(No 2)A 2005 s 49, Sch 10 paras 1, 11 with effect where the effective date of the land transaction consisting of the grant of the lease is after 19th May 2005.

However, this amendment does not have effect—

(*a*) in relation to any transaction which is effected in pursuance of a contract entered into and substantially performed on or before the specified date (ie 16 March 2005), or

(*b*) subject to what follows below, in relation to any other transaction which is effected in pursuance of a contract entered into on or before the specified date (ie 16 March 2005).

The exclusion by para (*b*) above of transactions effected in pursuance of contracts entered into on or before the specified date does not apply—

(*a*) if there is any variation of the contract or assignment of rights under the contract after that date,

(*b*) if the transaction is effected in consequence of the exercise after that date of any option, right of pre-emption or similar right, or

(*c*) if after that date there is an assignment, subsale or other transaction (relating to the whole or part of the subject-matter of the contract) as a result of which a person other than the purchaser under the contract becomes entitled to call for a conveyance to him: F(No 2)A 2005 Sch 10 para 16(4), (6)–(8).

[2] Words in sub-para (1) inserted by FA 2007 s 72(1), (2), (12)(*a*) with effect in respect of acquisitions occurring on or after 19 July 2007: FA 2007 s 72(15). However, the commencement provision is subject to transitional provisions as set out in FA 2007 s 72(17).

Acquisition by trustees of settlement

4 Where persons acquire a chargeable interest [or an interest in a partnership][1] as trustees of a settlement, they are treated for the purposes of this Part, as it applies in relation to that acquisition, as purchasers of the whole of the interest acquired (including the beneficial interest).

Amendments—[1] Words inserted by FA 2007 s 72(1), (2), (12)(*b*) with effect in respect of acquisitions occurring on or after 19 July 2007: FA 2007 s 72(15). However, the commencement provision is subject to transitional provisions as set out in FA 2007 s 72(17).

Responsibility of trustees of settlement

5— (1) Where the trustees of a settlement are liable—

(*a*) to make a payment of tax or interest on unpaid tax,

(*b*) to make a payment in accordance with an assessment under paragraph 29 of Schedule 10 (recovery of excessive repayment), or

(*c*) to a penalty under this Part or to interest on such a penalty,

the payment, penalty or interest may be recovered (but only once) from any one or more of the responsible trustees.

(2) No amount may be recovered by virtue of sub-paragraph (1)(*c*) from a person who did not become a responsible trustee until after the relevant time.

(3) The responsible trustees, in relation to a land transaction, are the persons who are trustees at the effective date of the transaction and any person who subsequently becomes a trustee.

(4) The relevant time for this purpose is—

(*a*) in relation to so much of a penalty as is payable in respect of any day, or to interest on so much of a penalty as is so payable, the beginning of that day;

(*b*) in relation to any other penalty, or interest on such a penalty, the time when the act or omission occurred that caused the penalty to become payable.

Relevant trustees for purposes of return etc

6— (1) A return …[1] in relation to a land transaction may be made or given by any one or more of the trustees who are the responsible trustees in relation to the transaction.

The trustees by whom such a return or self-certificate is made are referred to below as "the relevant trustees".

(2) The declaration required by paragraph 1(1)(*c*) of Schedule 10 ...[1] (declaration that return ...[1] is complete and correct) must be made by all the relevant trustees.

(3) If the Inland Revenue give notice of an enquiry into the return ...[1]—

(*a*) the notice must be given to each of the relevant trustees,

(*b*) the powers of the Inland Revenue as to the production of documents and provision of information for the purposes of the enquiry are exercisable separately (and differently) in relation to each of the relevant trustees,

(*c*) any of the relevant trustees may apply for a direction that a closure notice be given (and all of them are entitled to appear and be heard on the application), and

(*d*) the closure notice must be given to each of the relevant trustees.

Provided that a notice is not invalidated by virtue of paragraph (*a*) or (*d*) if it is given to each of the relevant trustees whose identity is known to the Inland Revenue.

(4) A Revenue determination or discovery assessment relating to the transaction must be made against all of the relevant trustees and is not effective against any of them unless notice of it is given to each of them whose identity is known to the Inland Revenue.

(5) In the case of an appeal arising from proceedings under this Part relating to the transaction—

(*a*) the appeal may be brought by any of the relevant trustees,

(*b*) notice of the appeal must be given to any of them by whom it is not brought,

(*c*) the agreement of all the relevant trustees is required if the appeal is to be settled by agreement,

(*d*) if it is not settled, any of them are entitled to appear and be heard, and

(*e*) the decision on the appeal binds all of them.

Amendments—[1] Words in sub-paras (1)–(3) repealed by FA 2008 s 94, Sch 30 para 13 with effect in relation to transactions with an effective date on or after 12 March 2008.

Consideration for exercise of power of appointment or discretion

7 Where a chargeable interest is acquired by virtue of—

(*a*) the exercise of a power of appointment, or

(*b*) the exercise of a discretion vested in trustees of a settlement,

there shall be treated as consideration for the acquisition of the interest or right by virtue of the exercise of the power or discretion any consideration given for the person in whose favour the appointment was made or the discretion was exercised becoming an object of the power or discretion.

[Reallocation of trust property as between beneficiaries

8 Where—

(*a*) the trustees of a settlement reallocate trust property in such a way that a beneficiary acquires an interest in certain trust property and ceases to have an interest in other trust property, and

(*b*) the beneficiary consents to ceasing to have an interest in that other property,

the fact that he gives consent does not mean that there is chargeable consideration for the acquisition.][1]

Amendments—[1] This paragraph inserted by FA 2006 s 165 with effect in relation to any acquisition of which the effective date (within the meaning of Part 4 of FA 2003) is on or after 19 July 2006.

[SCHEDULE 17

STAMP DUTY LAND TAX: GENERAL AND SPECIAL COMMISSIONERS, APPEALS AND OTHER PROCEEDINGS][1]

Section 115

Amendments—[1] Schedule 17 repealed by the Transfer of Tribunal Functions and Revenue and Customs Appeals Order, SI 2009/56 art 3, Sch 1 para 413 with effect from 1 April 2009.

General and Special Commissioners: application of general provisions

1 *[Part 1 of the Taxes Management Act 1970 (c 9) (administration) has effect as if this Part of this Act were part of the Taxes Acts.]*[1]

Amendments—[1] Schedule 17 repealed by the Transfer of Tribunal Functions and Revenue and Customs Appeals Order, SI 2009/56 art 3, Sch 1 para 413 with effect from 1 April 2009.

Prescribed matters to be determined by Commissioners or Lands Tribunal

[2— *(1) The Lord Chancellor may make regulations providing that a question, dispute, appeal or other matter that is of a prescribed description and arises in relation to the provisions of this Part is to be determined*—

(*a*) *by the General Commissioners,*
(*b*) *by the Special Commissioners,*
(*c*) *by the General or Special Commissioners, or*
(*d*) *by the relevant Lands Tribunal.*

[(1A) The Lord Chancellor may make regulations under this paragraph only after consulting all of the following—

(*a*) *the Lord Chief Justice of England and Wales;*
(*b*) *the Lord President of the Court of Session;*
(*c*) *the Lord Chief Justice of Northern Ireland.*

(1B) The Lord Chief Justice of England and Wales may nominate a judicial office holder (as defined in section 109(4) of the Constitutional Reform Act 2005) to exercise his functions under this paragraph.

(1C) The Lord President of the Court of Session may nominate a judge of the Court of Session who is a member of the First or Second Division of the Inner House of that Court to exercise his functions under this paragraph.

(1D) The Lord Chief Justice of Northern Ireland may nominate any of the following to exercise his functions under this paragraph—

(*a*) *the holder of one of the offices listed in Schedule 1 to the Justice (Northern Ireland) Act 2002;*
(*b*) *a Lord Justice of Appeal (as defined in section 88 of that Act).]*[1]

(2) In this paragraph—

"prescribed" means prescribed in regulations under this paragraph;
"relevant Lands Tribunal" means—

(*a*) *in relation to land in England and Wales, the Lands Tribunal;*
(*b*) *in relation to land in Scotland, the Lands Tribunal for Scotland;*
(*c*) *in relation to land in Northern Ireland, the Lands Tribunal for Northern Ireland.]*[2]

Amendments—[1] Sub-paras (1A)–(1D) inserted by the Constitutional Reform Act 2005 s 15, Sch 4 para 307(1), (2) with effect from 3 April 2006 (by virtue of SI 2006/1014 art 2(*a*), Sch 1 para 11).
[2] Schedule 17 repealed by the Transfer of Tribunal Functions and Revenue and Customs Appeals Order, SI 2009/56 art 3, Sch 1 para 413 with effect from 1 April 2009.

General or Special Commissioners: jurisdiction

[3— *(1) Where the General or Special Commissioners have jurisdiction in respect of a matter, the Lord Chancellor may make regulations for determining—*

(*a*) *whether the General or Special Commissioners, or both of them, are to have the jurisdiction, and*
(*b*) *if both of them are to have the jurisdiction, how it is to be divided between them.*

(2) Where the General Commissioners have jurisdiction in respect of a matter, the General Commissioners for that division which is determined in accordance with regulations made by the Lord Chancellor under this paragraph are to have the jurisdiction.

(3) The Lord Chancellor may make regulations—

(*a*) *providing that, in certain circumstances, the Special Commissioners are to have jurisdiction in respect of a matter instead of the General Commissioners or the General Commissioners are to have jurisdiction instead of the Special Commissioners;*
(*b*) *providing that, in certain circumstances, the General Commissioners for one division are have to jurisdiction in respect of a matter instead of the General Commissioners for another division.*

[(4) The Lord Chancellor may make regulations under this paragraph only after consulting all of the following—

(*a*) *the Lord Chief Justice of England and Wales;*
(*b*) *the Lord President of the Court of Session;*
(*c*) *the Lord Chief Justice of Northern Ireland.*

(5) The Lord Chief Justice of England and Wales may nominate a judicial office holder (as defined in section 109(4) of the Constitutional Reform Act 2005) to exercise his functions under this paragraph.

(6) The Lord President of the Court of Session may nominate a judge of the Court of Session who is a member of the First or Second Division of the Inner House of that Court to exercise his functions under this paragraph.

(7) The Lord Chief Justice of Northern Ireland may nominate any of the following to exercise his functions under this paragraph—

(*a*) *the holder of one of the offices listed in Schedule 1 to the Justice (Northern Ireland) Act 2002;*
(*b*) *a Lord Justice of Appeal (as defined in section 88 of that Act).*][1]][2]

Amendments—[1] Sub-paras (4)–(7) inserted by the Constitutional Reform Act 2005 s 15, Sch 4 para 307(1), (3) with effect from 3 April 2006 (by virtue of SI 2006/1014 art 2(*a*), Sch 1 para 11).
[2] Schedule 17 repealed by the Transfer of Tribunal Functions and Revenue and Customs Appeals Order, SI 2009/56 art 3, Sch 1 para 413 with effect from 1 April 2009.

Proceedings brought out of time

[4— *(1) An appeal under this Part to the General or Special Commissioners may be brought out of time with the consent in writing of an officer of the Board or the Board.*

(2) Consent shall be given if the officer or, as the case may be, the Board are satisfied—

(a) that there was a reasonable excuse for not bringing the appeal within the time limit, and

(b) that an application for consent was made without unreasonable delay.

(3) If the officer or, as the case may be, the Board are not so satisfied, they shall refer the matter for determination by the Commissioners.

(4) If there is a right to elect to bring the appeal before the Special Commissioners instead of before the General Commissioners, the Commissioners to whom an application under this paragraph is to be referred are the General Commissioners, unless the election has been made before the application is referred.][1]

Amendments—[1] Schedule 17 repealed by the Transfer of Tribunal Functions and Revenue and Customs Appeals Order, SI 2009/56 art 3, Sch 1 para 413 with effect from 1 April 2009.

Quorum etc of the Commissioners

[5 *[(1)][1] The Lord Chancellor may make regulations about the number of General or Special Commissioners required or permitted to perform functions in relation to a relevant matter.*

[(2) The Lord Chancellor may make regulations under this paragraph only after consulting all of the following—

(a) the Lord Chief Justice of England and Wales;

(b) the Lord President of the Court of Session;

(c) the Lord Chief Justice of Northern Ireland.

(3) The Lord Chief Justice of England and Wales may nominate a judicial office holder (as defined in section 109(4) of the Constitutional Reform Act 2005) to exercise his functions under this paragraph.

(4) The Lord President of the Court of Session may nominate a judge of the Court of Session who is a member of the First or Second Division of the Inner House of that Court to exercise his functions under this paragraph.

(5) The Lord Chief Justice of Northern Ireland may nominate any of the following to exercise his functions under this paragraph—

(a) the holder of one of the offices listed in Schedule 1 to the Justice (Northern Ireland) Act 2002;

(b) a Lord Justice of Appeal (as defined in section 88 of that Act).][1]][2]

Amendments—[1] Paragraph renumbered as such, and sub-paras (2)–(5) inserted, by the Constitutional Reform Act 2005 s 15, Sch 4 para 307(1), (4) with effect from 3 April 2006 (by virtue of SI 2006/1014 art 2(*a*), Sch 1 para 11).
[2] Schedule 17 repealed by the Transfer of Tribunal Functions and Revenue and Customs Appeals Order, SI 2009/56 art 3, Sch 1 para 413 with effect from 1 April 2009.

Procedure

[6— *(1) The Lord Chancellor may make regulations about the practice and procedure to be followed in connection with matters in respect of which the Special or General Commissioners have jurisdiction.*

(2) The regulations may, in particular, include provision—

(a) enabling the Commissioners to join as a party to the proceedings a person who would not otherwise be a party;

(b) for requiring a party to the proceedings to provide information and make documents available for inspection by—

(i) the Commissioners,

(ii) any party to the proceedings, or

(iii) an officer of the Board;

(c) for requiring persons to attend the hearing to give evidence and produce documents;

(d) as to evidence generally in relation to proceedings;

(e) enabling the Commissioners to review their decisions;

(f) for the imposition of penalties not exceeding an amount specified in the regulations;

(g) for the determination and recovery of penalties imposed by virtue of paragraph (f) and for appeals against such penalties.][1]

Amendments—[1] Schedule 17 repealed by the Transfer of Tribunal Functions and Revenue and Customs Appeals Order, SI 2009/56 art 3, Sch 1 para 413 with effect from 1 April 2009.

Consequences of determination by the Commissioners

[7 *The Lord Chancellor may make regulations prescribing the consequences of any determination by the General or Special Commissioners in respect of a relevant matter.*][1]

Amendments—[1] Schedule 17 repealed by the Transfer of Tribunal Functions and Revenue and Customs Appeals Order, SI 2009/56 art 3, Sch 1 para 413 with effect from 1 April 2009.

Costs

[**8** *The Lord Chancellor may make regulations about—*

(*a*) *the award by the General or Special Commissioners of the costs of, or incidental to, a determination by them in respect of a relevant matter;*
(*b*) *the recovery of costs so awarded.*][1]

Amendments—[1] Schedule 17 repealed by the Transfer of Tribunal Functions and Revenue and Customs Appeals Order, SI 2009/56 art 3, Sch 1 para 413 with effect from 1 April 2009.

Finality of decisions of the Commissioners

[**9**— *(1) The Lord Chancellor may make regulations about the following matters—*

(*a*) *the circumstances in which—*

(*i*) *a determination by the General or Special Commissioners in respect of a relevant matter, or*
(*ii*) *an award of costs under regulations under paragraph 8,*

may or may not be questioned;

(*b*) *if a determination or award may be questioned, how it may be questioned.*

(2) The regulations may—

(*a*) *authorise or require the Commissioners, in circumstances specified in the regulations, to state a case for the opinion of a court;*
(*b*) *make provision as to the practice and procedure to be followed in connection with cases so stated;*
(*c*) *make provision in relation to cases so stated corresponding to any provision made by section 56 of the Taxes Management Act 1970 (c 9) (statement of case for opinion of High Court) or by that section as modified in its application to Northern Ireland by section 58 of that Act.*

(3) The regulations may—

(*a*) *provide for an appeal to lie to a court on a question of law arising from a decision of the Commissioners;*
(*b*) *make provision as to the practice and procedure to be followed in connection with such appeals;*
(*c*) *make provision in relation to such appeals corresponding to any provision made by section 56A of the Taxes Management Act 1970 (appeals from the Special Commissioners) or by that section as modified in its application to Northern Ireland by section 58 of that Act.*][1]

Amendments—[1] Schedule 17 repealed by the Transfer of Tribunal Functions and Revenue and Customs Appeals Order, SI 2009/56 art 3, Sch 1 para 413 with effect from 1 April 2009.

Publication of reports of decisions

[**10**— *(1) The Lord Chancellor may make regulations authorising the Special Commissioners to publish reports of such of their decisions as they consider appropriate.*

(2) The regulations shall provide that any report published that is not a report of proceedings heard in public must be in a form that so far as possible prevents the identification of any person whose affairs are dealt with in the report.

(3) No obligation of secrecy to which the Special Commissioners are subject prevents their publishing reports of their decisions in accordance with provision made by virtue of this paragraph.][1]

Amendments—[1] Schedule 17 repealed by the Transfer of Tribunal Functions and Revenue and Customs Appeals Order, SI 2009/56 art 3, Sch 1 para 413 with effect from 1 April 2009.

Supplementary provisions

[**11**— *[(1) Any power to make regulations under this Schedule is exercisable—*

(*a*) *only with the consent of the Scottish Ministers;*
(*b*) *subject to any other provision of this Schedule.*][1]

(2) Regulations under this Schedule shall be made by statutory instrument which shall be subject to annulment in pursuance of a resolution of either House of Parliament.

(3) Regulations under this Schedule may—

(*a*) *apply any other enactment, with or without modifications;*
(*b*) *make different provision for different cases or different circumstances;*
(*c*) *contain such supplementary, incidental, consequential and transitional provision as the Lord Chancellor thinks appropriate.*

(4) In this Schedule—

(*a*) *"relevant matter", in relation to the General or Special Commissioners, means a matter in respect of which they have jurisdiction;*
(*b*) *references to the provisions of this Part include any instrument made under such a provision;*
(*c*) *references to the General or Special Commissioners having jurisdiction are to the Commissioners having jurisdiction by virtue of the provisions of this Part;*

Stamp Taxes

(*d*) *references to the General or Special Commissioners having jurisdiction in respect of a matter include cases where a question, dispute, appeal or other matter that arises in relation to the provisions of this Part is to be determined by the Commissioners.*][2]

Amendments—[1] Sub-para (1) substituted by the Constitutional Reform Act 2005 s 15, Sch 4 para 307(1), (5) with effect from 3 April 2006 (by virtue of SI 2006/1014 art 2(*a*), Sch 1 para 11).

[2] Schedule 17 repealed by the Transfer of Tribunal Functions and Revenue and Customs Appeals Order, SI 2009/56 art 3, Sch 1 para 413 with effect from 1 April 2009.

[SCHEDULE 17A
FURTHER PROVISIONS RELATING TO LEASES][1]

Section 120][1]

Amendments—[1] This Schedule inserted by FA 2004 s 296, Sch 39 para 22(2) with effect for any transaction of which the effective date (within the meaning of FA 2003 Pt 4) is on or after 22 July 2004: FA 2004 Sch 39 para 26. This insertion was previously made by the Stamp Duty and Stamp Duty Land Tax (Variation of the Finance Act 2003) (No 2) Regulations, SI 2003/2816 regs 1, 2, Schedule para 8(2) with effect from 1 December 2003. Those regulations are revoked by FA 2004 Sch 39 para 14(2).

[Meaning of "lease"

1 In the application of this Part to England and Wales or Northern Ireland "lease" means—

(*a*) an interest or right in or over land for a term of years (whether fixed or periodic), or

(*b*) a tenancy at will or other interest or right in or over land terminable by notice at any time.][1]

Amendments—[1] This Schedule inserted by FA 2004 s 296, Sch 39 para 22(2) with effect for any transaction of which the effective date (within the meaning of FA 2003 Pt 4) is on or after 22 July 2004: FA 2004 Sch 39 para 26. This insertion was previously made by the Stamp Duty and Stamp Duty Land Tax (Variation of the Finance Act 2003) (No 2) Regulations, SI 2003/2816 regs 1, 2, Schedule para 8(2) with effect from 1 December 2003. Those regulations are revoked by FA 2004 Sch 39 para 14(2).

[Leases for a fixed term

2 In the application of the provisions of this Part to a lease for a fixed term, no account shall be taken of—

(*a*) any contingency as a result of which the lease may determine before the end of the fixed term, or

(*b*) any right of either party to determine the lease or renew it.][1]

Amendments—[1] This Schedule inserted by FA 2004 s 296, Sch 39 para 22(2) with effect for any transaction of which the effective date (within the meaning of FA 2003 Pt 4) is on or after 22 July 2004: FA 2004 Sch 39 para 26. This insertion was previously made by the Stamp Duty and Stamp Duty Land Tax (Variation of the Finance Act 2003) (No 2) Regulations, SI 2003/2816 regs 1, 2, Schedule para 8(2) with effect from 1 December 2003. Those regulations are revoked by FA 2004 Sch 39 para 14(2).

[Leases that continue after a fixed term

3— (1) This paragraph applies to—

(*a*) a lease for a fixed term and thereafter until determined, or

(*b*) a lease for a fixed term that may continue beyond the fixed term by operation of law.

(2) For the purposes of this Part (except [sections 77 and 77A][3] (notifiable transactions)), a lease to which this paragraph applies is treated—

(*a*) in the first instance as if it were a lease for the original fixed term and no longer,

(*b*) if the lease continues after the end of that term, as if it were a lease for a fixed term one year longer than the original fixed term,

(*c*) if the lease continues after the end of the term resulting from the application of paragraph (*b*), as if it were a lease for a fixed term two years longer than the original fixed term,

and so on.

(3) Where the effect of sub-paragraph (2) in relation to the continuation of the lease after the end of a fixed term is that additional tax is payable in respect of a transaction or that tax is payable in respect of a transaction where none was payable before—

(*a*) the purchaser must deliver a return or further return in respect of that transaction before the end of the period of 30 days after the end of that term,

(*b*) the return must include a self-assessment of the amount of tax chargeable in respect of the transaction on the basis of the information contained in the return,

(*c*) the tax so chargeable is to be calculated by reference to the rates in force at the effective date of the transaction, and

[(*d*) the tax or additional tax payable must be paid not later than the filing date for the return.][2]

(4) The provisions of Schedule 10 (returns, enquiries, assessments and other matters) apply to a return under this paragraph as they apply to a return under section 76 (general requirement to deliver land transaction return), with the adaptation that references to the effective date of the transaction shall be read as references to the day on which the lease becomes treated as being for a longer fixed term.

(5) For the purposes of [sections 77 and 77A][3] (notifiable transactions) a lease to which this paragraph applies is a lease for whatever is its fixed term.][1]

Modifications—Pensions Schemes (Taxable Property Provisions) Regulations, SI 2006/1958 reg 7 (application of this paragraph, subject to modifications for the purposes of FA 2004 Sch 29 para 34(2)).
Cross references—FA 2009 Sch 55 (penalty for failure to make returns etc).
Amendments—[1] This Schedule inserted by FA 2004 s 296, Sch 39 para 22(2) with effect for any transaction of which the effective date (within the meaning of FA 2003 Pt 4) is on or after 22 July 2004: FA 2004 Sch 39 para 26. This insertion was previously made by the Stamp Duty and Stamp Duty Land Tax (Variation of the Finance Act 2003) (No 2) Regulations, SI 2003/2816 regs 1, 2, Schedule para 8(2) with effect from 1 December 2003. Those regulations are revoked by FA 2004 Sch 39 para 14(2).
[2] Sub-para (3)(*d*) substituted by FA 2007 s 80(1), (8), (9)(*g*) with effect in respect of requirements to deliver a return or further return which arise on or after 19 July 2007.
[3] Words in sub-paras (2), (5) substituted by FA 2008 s 94, Sch 30 para 14 with effect in relation to transactions with an effective date on or after 12 March 2008.

[Treatment of leases for indefinite term

4— (1) For the purposes of this Part (except [sections 77 and 77A][3] (notifiable transactions))—
(*a*) a lease for an indefinite term is treated in the first instance as if it were a lease for a fixed term of a year,
(*b*) if the lease continues after the end of the term resulting from the application of paragraph (*a*), it is treated as if it were a lease for a fixed term of two years,
(*c*) if the lease continues after the end of the term resulting from the application of paragraph (*b*), it is treated as if it were a lease for a fixed term of three years,
and so on.

(2) No account shall be taken for the purposes of this Part of any other statutory provision in England and Wales or Northern Ireland deeming a lease for an indefinite period to be a lease for a different term.

(3) Where the effect of sub-paragraph (1) in relation to the continuation of the lease after the end of a deemed fixed term is that additional tax is payable in respect of a transaction or that tax is payable in respect of a transaction where none was payable before—
(*a*) the purchaser must deliver a return or further return in respect of that transaction before the end of the period of 30 days after the end of that term,
(*b*) the return must include a self-assessment of the amount of tax chargeable in respect of the transaction on the basis of the information contained in the return,
(*c*) the tax so chargeable is to be calculated by reference to the rates in force at the effective date of the transaction, and
[(*d*) the tax or additional tax payable must be paid not later than the filing date for the return.][2]

(4) The provisions of Schedule 10 (returns, enquiries, assessments and other matters) apply to a return under this paragraph as they apply to a return under section 76 (general requirement to deliver land transaction return), with the adaptation that references to the effective date of the transaction shall be read as references to the day on which the lease becomes treated as being for a longer fixed term.

(4A) For the purposes of [sections 77 and 77A][3] (notifiable transactions) a lease for an indefinite term is a lease for a term of less then seven years.

(5) References in this paragraph to a lease for an indefinite period include—
(*a*) a periodic tenancy or other interest or right terminable by a period of notice,
(*b*) a tenancy at will in England and Wales or Northern Ireland, or
(*c*) any other interest or right terminable by notice at any time.][1]

Modifications—Pensions Schemes (Taxable Property Provisions) Regulations, SI 2006/1958 reg 7 (application of this paragraph, subject to modifications for the purposes of FA 2004 Sch 29 para 34(2)).
Cross references—FA 2009 Sch 55 (penalty for failure to make returns etc).
Amendments—[1] This Schedule inserted by FA 2004 s 296, Sch 39 para 22(2) with effect for any transaction of which the effective date (within the meaning of FA 2003 Pt 4) is on or after 22 July 2004: FA 2004 Sch 39 para 26. This insertion was previously made by the Stamp Duty and Stamp Duty Land Tax (Variation of the Finance Act 2003) (No 2) Regulations, SI 2003/2816 regs 1, 2, Schedule para 8(2) with effect from 1 December 2003. Those regulations are revoked by FA 2004 Sch 39 para 14(2).
[2] Sub-para (3)(*d*) substituted by FA 2007 s 80(1), (8), (9)(*g*) with effect in respect of requirements to deliver a return or further return which arise on or after 19 July 2007.
[3] Words in sub-paras (1), (4A) substituted by FA 2008 s 94, Sch 30 para 14 with effect in relation to transactions with an effective date on or after 12 March 2008.

[Treatment of successive linked leases

5— (1) This paragraph applies where—
(*a*) successive leases are granted or treated as granted (whether at the same time or at different times) of the same or substantially the same premises, and
(*b*) those grants are linked transactions.

(2) This Part applies as if the series of leases were a single lease—
(*a*) granted at the time of the grant of the first lease in the series,
(*b*) for a term equal to the aggregate of the terms of all the leases, and
(*c*) in consideration of the rent payable under all of the leases.

(3) The grant of later leases in the series is accordingly disregarded for the purposes of this Part except section 81A (return or further return in consequence of later linked transaction).][1]

Amendments—[1] This Schedule inserted by FA 2004 s 296, Sch 39 para 22(2) with effect for any transaction of which the effective date (within the meaning of FA 2003 Pt 4) is on or after 22 July 2004: FA 2004 Sch 39 para 26. This insertion was previously made by the Stamp Duty and Stamp Duty Land Tax (Variation of the Finance Act 2003) (No 2) Regulations, SI 2003/2816 regs 1, 2, Schedule para 8(2) with effect from 1 December 2003. Those regulations are revoked by FA 2004 Sch 39 para 14(2).

[Rent

6—(1) For the purposes of this Part a single sum expressed to be payable in respect of rent, or expressed to be payable in respect of rent and other matters but not apportioned, shall be treated as entirely rent.

(2) Sub-paragraph (1) is without prejudice to the application of paragraph 4 of Schedule 4 (chargeable consideration: just and reasonable apportionment) where separate sums are expressed to be payable in respect of rent and other matters.][1]

Amendments—[1] This Schedule inserted by FA 2004 s 296, Sch 39 para 22(2) with effect for any transaction of which the effective date (within the meaning of FA 2003 Pt 4) is on or after 22 July 2004: FA 2004 Sch 39 para 26. This insertion was previously made by the Stamp Duty and Stamp Duty Land Tax (Variation of the Finance Act 2003) (No 2) Regulations, SI 2003/2816 regs 1, 2, Schedule para 8(2) with effect from 1 December 2003. Those regulations are revoked by FA 2004 Sch 39 para 14(2).

[Variable or uncertain rent

7—(1) This paragraph applies to determine the amount of rent payable under a lease where that amount—

(*a*) varies in accordance with provision in the lease, or
(*b*) is contingent, uncertain or unascertained.

(2) As regards rent payable in respect of any period before the end of the fifth year of the term of the lease—

(*a*) the provisions of this Part apply as in relation to other chargeable consideration, and
(*b*) the provisions of section 51(1) and (2) accordingly apply if the amount is contingent, uncertain or unascertained.

(3) As regards rent payable in respect of any period after the end of the fifth year of the term of the lease, the annual amount is assumed for the purposes of this Part to be, in every case, equal to the highest amount of rent payable in respect of any consecutive twelve month period in the first five years of the term.

In determining that amount take into account (if necessary) any amounts determined as mentioned in sub-paragraph (2)(*b*), but disregard [paragraphs 9(2) and 9A(3) (deemed reduction of rent, where further lease granted, for period during which rents overlap)][3].

(4) This paragraph has effect subject to paragraph 8 (adjustment where rent payable ceases to be uncertain).

[(4A) For the purposes of this paragraph and paragraph 8, the cases where the amount of rent payable under a lease is uncertain or unascertained include cases where there is a possibility of that amount being varied under—

(*a*) section 12, 13 or 33 of the Agricultural Holdings Act 1986,
(*b*) Part 2 of the Agricultural Tenancies Act 1995,
(*c*) section 13, 14, 15 or 31 of the Agricultural Holdings (Scotland) Act 1991, or
(*d*) section 9, 10 or 11 of the Agricultural Holdings (Scotland) Act 2003.][2]

(5) No account shall be taken for the purposes of this Part of any provision for rent to be adjusted in line with the retail prices index.][1]

Amendments—[1] This Schedule inserted by FA 2004 s 296, Sch 39 para 22(2) with effect for any transaction of which the effective date (within the meaning of FA 2003 Pt 4) is on or after 22 July 2004: FA 2004 Sch 39 para 26. This insertion was previously made by the Stamp Duty and Stamp Duty Land Tax (Variation of the Finance Act 2003) (No 2) Regulations, SI 2003/2816 regs 1, 2, Schedule para 8(2) with effect from 1 December 2003. Those regulations are revoked by FA 2004 Sch 39 para 14(2).

[2] Sub-para (4A) inserted by FA 2006 s 164, Sch 25 para 2(1) with effect in relation to any lease granted or treated as granted on or after 19 July 2006 by virtue of FA 2006 Sch 25 para 9(6).

[3] Words in sub-para (3) substituted for "paragraph 9(2) (deemed reduction of rent for overlap period in case of grant of further lease)" by FA 2006 s 164, Sch 25 para 3(2) with effect in relation to any case where—

(*a*) the grant of the old lease was chargeable to stamp duty land tax, and
(*b*) the new lease is granted on or after 19 July 2006 by virtue of FA 2006 Sch 25 para 9(6).

"The old lease" and "the new lease" mean the leases referred to in sub-paragraphs (1)(*a*) and (1)(*b*), respectively, of paragraph 9A of Schedule 17A to FA 2003 (inserted by paragraph 3).

[First rent review in final quarter of fifth year

7A Where—

(*a*) a lease contains provision under which the rent may be adjusted,
(*b*) under that provision the first (or only) such adjustment—

(i) is to an amount that (before the adjustment) is uncertain, and
(ii) has effect from a date (the "review date") that is expressed as falling five years after a specified date,

and

(*c*) the specified date falls within the three months before the beginning of the term of the lease,

this Schedule has effect as if references to the first five years of the term of the lease were to the period beginning with the start of the term of the lease and ending with the review date. References to the fifth year of the term of the lease shall be read accordingly.][1]

Amendments—[1] This Schedule inserted by FA 2004 s 296, Sch 39 para 22(2) with effect for any transaction of which the effective date (within the meaning of FA 2003 Pt 4) is on or after 22 July 2004: FA 2004 Sch 39 para 26. This insertion was previously made by the Stamp Duty and Stamp Duty Land Tax (Variation of the Finance Act 2003) (No 2) Regulations, SI 2003/2816 regs 1, 2, Schedule para 8(2) with effect from 1 December 2003. Those regulations are revoked by FA 2004 Sch 39 para 14(2).

This paragraph was however not contained in the original Schedule 17A as inserted by SI 2003/2816. FA 2004 Sch 39 para 11(1), (2) amends that version of the Schedule to insert the above paragraph. That insertion had effect for any transaction of which the effective date was after 17 March 2004 and before 22 July 2004: FA 2004 Sch 39 para 13(3), (5).

[Adjustment where rent ceases to be uncertain

8— (1) Where the provisions of section 51(1) and (2) (contingent, uncertain or unascertained consideration) apply in relation to a transaction by virtue of paragraph 7 (uncertain rent) and—

(*a*) the end of the fifth year of the term of the lease is reached, or

(*b*) the amount of rent payable in respect of the first five years of the term of the lease ceases to be uncertain at an earlier date,

the following provisions have effect to require or permit reconsideration of how this Part applies to the transaction (and to any transaction in relation to which it is a linked transaction).

(2) For the purposes of this paragraph the amount of rent payable ceases to be uncertain when—

(*a*) in the case of contingent rent, the contingency occurs or it becomes clear that it will not occur, and

(*b*) in the case of uncertain or unascertained rent, the amount becomes ascertained.

(3) If the result as regards the rent paid or payable in respect of the first five years of the term of the lease is that a transaction becomes notifiable, or that additional tax is payable in respect of a transaction or that tax is payable where none was payable before—

(*a*) the purchaser must make a return to the Inland Revenue within 30 days of the date referred to in sub-paragraph (1)(*a*) or (*b*),

(*b*) the return must contain a self-assessment of the tax chargeable in respect of the transaction on the basis of the information contained in the return,

(*c*) the tax so chargeable is to be calculated by reference to the rates in force at the effective date of the transaction, and

[(*d*) the tax or additional tax payable must be paid not later than the filing date for the return.][2]

(4) The provisions of Schedule 10 (returns, enquiries, assessment and other matters) apply to a return under this paragraph as they apply to a return under section 76 (general requirement to make land transaction return), subject to the adaptation that references to the effective date of the transaction shall be read as references to the date referred to in sub-paragraph (1)(*a*) or (*b*).

(5) If the result as regards the rent paid or payable in respect of the first five years of the term of the lease is that less tax is payable in respect of the transaction than has already been paid—

(*a*) the purchaser may, within the period allowed for amendment of the land transaction return, amend the return accordingly;

(*b*) after the end of that period he may (if the land transaction return is not so amended) make a claim to the Inland Revenue for repayment of the amount overpaid.][1]

Modifications—Pensions Schemes (Taxable Property Provisions) Regulations, SI 2006/1958 reg 8 (application of this paragraph, subject to modifications for the purposes of FA 2004 Sch 29 para 34(2)).

Cross references—FA 2009 Sch 55 (penalty for failure to make returns etc).

Amendments—[1] This Schedule inserted by FA 2004 s 296, Sch 39 para 22(2) with effect for any transaction of which the effective date (within the meaning of FA 2003 Pt 4) is on or after 22 July 2004: FA 2004 Sch 39 para 26. This insertion was previously made by the Stamp Duty and Stamp Duty Land Tax (Variation of the Finance Act 2003) (No 2) Regulations, SI 2003/2816 regs 1, 2, Schedule para 8(2) with effect from 1 December 2003. Those regulations are revoked by FA 2004 Sch 39 para 14(2).

[2] Sub-para (3)(*d*) substituted by FA 2007 s 80(1), (8), (9)(*g*) with effect in respect of requirements to deliver a return or further return which arise on or after the day on which FA 2007 is passed.

[Rent for overlap period in case of grant of further lease

9— (1) This paragraph applies where—

(*a*) A surrenders an existing lease to B ("the old lease") and in consideration of that surrender B grants a lease to A of the same or substantially the same premises ("the new lease"),

(*b*) the tenant under a lease ("the old lease") of premises to which Part 2 of the Landlord and Tenant Act 1954 or the Business Tenancies (Northern Ireland) Order 1996 applies makes a request for a new tenancy ("the new lease") which is duly executed,

(*c*) on termination of a lease ("the head lease") a sub-tenant is granted a lease ("the new lease") of the same or substantially the same premises as those comprised in his original lease ("the old lease")—

(i) in pursuance of an order of a court on a claim for relief against re-entry or forfeiture, or

Stamp Taxes

(ii) in pursuance of a contractual entitlement arising in the event of the head lease being terminated,

or

(*d*) a person who has guaranteed the obligations of a lessee under a lease that has been terminated ("the old lease") is granted a lease of the same or substantially the same premises ("the new lease") in pursuance of the guarantee.

(2) For the purposes of this Part the rent payable under the new lease in respect of any period falling within the overlap period is treated as reduced by the amount of the rent that would have been payable in respect of that period under the old lease.

(3) The overlap period is the period between the date of grant of the new lease and what would have been the end of the term of the old lease had it not been terminated.

(4) The rent that would have been payable under the old lease shall be taken to be the amount taken into account in determining the stamp duty land tax chargeable in respect of the acquisition of the old lease.

(5) This paragraph does not have effect so as to require the rent payable under the new lease to be treated as a negative amount.][1]

Amendments—[1] This Schedule inserted by FA 2004 s 296, Sch 39 para 22(2) with effect for any transaction of which the effective date (within the meaning of FA 2003 Pt 4) is on or after 22 July 2004: FA 2004 Sch 39 para 26.
This paragraph was first inserted by the Stamp Duty and Stamp Duty Land Tax (Variation of the Finance Act 2003) (No 2) Regulations, SI 2003/2816 regs 1, 2, Schedule para 8(2) with effect from 1 December 2003. (Those regulations are revoked by FA 2004 Sch 39 para 14(2).) That version was amended by FA 2004 Sch 39 para 11(1) with effect for any transaction of which the effective date was after 17 March 2004 and before 22 July 2004: FA 2004 Sch 39 para 13(3), (5).

[Backdated lease granted to tenant holding over

9A— (1) This paragraph applies where—

(*a*) the tenant under a lease continues in occupation after the date on which, under its terms, the lease terminates ("the contractual termination date"),

(*b*) he is granted a new lease of the same or substantially the same premises, and

(*c*) the term of the new lease is expressed to begin on or immediately after the contractual termination date.

(2) The term of the new lease is treated for the purposes of this Part as beginning on the date on which it is expressed to begin.

(3) The rent payable under the new lease in respect of any period falling—

(*a*) after the contractual termination date, and

(*b*) before the date on which the new lease is granted,

is treated for the purposes of this Part as reduced by the amount of taxable rent that is payable in respect of that period otherwise than under the new lease.

(4) For the purposes of sub-paragraph (3) rent is "taxable" if or to the extent that it is taken into account in determining liability to stamp duty land tax.

(5) Sub-paragraph (3) does not have effect so as to require the rent payable under the new lease to be treated as a negative amount.][1]

Amendments—[1] This paragraph inserted by FA 2006 s 164, Sch 25 para 3(1) with effect in relation to any case where—
(*a*) the grant of the old lease was chargeable to stamp duty land tax, and
(*b*) the new lease is granted on or after 19 July 2006 by virtue of FA 2006 Sch 25 para 9(6).
"The old lease" and "the new lease" mean the leases referred to in FA 2003 Sch 17A para 9A(1)(*a*), (*b*), respectively.

[Tenants' obligations etc that do not count as chargeable consideration

10— (1) In the case of the grant of a lease none of the following counts as chargeable consideration—

(*a*) any undertaking by the tenant to repair, maintain or insure the demised premises (in Scotland, the leased premises);

(*b*) any undertaking by the tenant to pay any amount in respect of services, repairs, maintenance or insurance or the landlord's costs of management;

(*c*) any other obligation undertaken by the tenant that is not such as to affect the rent that a tenant would be prepared to pay in the open market;

(*d*) any guarantee of the payment of rent or the performance of any other obligation of the tenant under the lease;

(*e*) any penal rent, or increased rent in the nature of a penal rent, payable in respect of the breach of any obligation of the tenant under the lease;

[(*f*) any liability of the tenant for costs under section 14(2) of the Leasehold Reform Act 1967 or section 60 of the Leasehold Reform, Housing and Urban Development Act 1993 (costs to be borne by person exercising statutory right to be granted lease);][2]

[(*g*) any other obligation of the tenant to bear the landlord's reasonable costs or expenses of or incidental to the grant of a lease;][2]

[(*h*) any obligation under the lease to transfer to the landlord, on the termination of the lease, payment entitlements granted to the tenant under the single payment scheme (that is, the scheme of income support for farmers in pursuance of Title III of Council Regulation (EC) No 1782/2003) in respect of land subject to the lease.][2]

(2) Where sub-paragraph (1) applies in relation to an obligation, a payment made in discharge of the obligation does not count as chargeable consideration.

(3) The release of any such obligation as is mentioned in sub-paragraph (1) does not count as chargeable consideration in relation to the surrender of the lease.][1]

Amendments—[1] This Schedule inserted by FA 2004 s 296, Sch 39 para 22(2) with effect for any transaction of which the effective date (within the meaning of FA 2003 Pt 4) is on or after 22 July 2004: FA 2004 Sch 39 para 26. This insertion was previously made by the Stamp Duty and Stamp Duty Land Tax (Variation of the Finance Act 2003) (No 2) Regulations, SI 2003/2816 regs 1, 2, Schedule para 8(2) with effect from 1 December 2003. Those regulations are revoked by FA 2004 Sch 39 para 14(2).

[2] Sub-paras (1)(*f*)–(*h*) inserted by the SDLT (Amendment to the Finance Act 2003) Regulations, SI 2006/875 regs 2, 4. SI 2006/875 came into force on 12 April 2006, and this amendment has effect in relation to land transactions with an effective date on or after that date: SI 2006/875 reg 1.

[Cases where assignment of lease treated as grant of lease

11— [(1) This paragraph applies where the grant of a lease is exempt from charge by virtue of any of the provisions specified in sub-paragraph (3).][3]

(2) The first assignment of the lease that is not exempt from charge by virtue of any of the provisions specified in sub-paragraph (3), and in relation to which the assignee does not acquire the lease as a bare trustee of the assignor, is treated for the purposes of this Part as if it were the grant of a lease by the assignor—

(*a*) for a term equal to the unexpired term of the lease referred to in sub-paragraph (1), and

(*b*) on the same terms as those on which the assignee holds that lease after the assignment.

(3) The provisions are—

(*a*) section 57A (sale and leaseback arrangements);

(*b*) Part 1 or 2 of Schedule 7 (group relief or reconstruction or acquisition relief);

(*c*) section 66 (transfers involving public bodies);

(*d*) Schedule 8 (charities relief);

(*e*) any such regulations as are mentioned in section 123(3) (regulations reproducing in relation to stamp duty land tax the effect of enactments providing for exemption from stamp duty).

(4) This paragraph does not apply where the relief in question is group relief, reconstruction or acquisition relief or charities relief and is withdrawn as a result of a disqualifying event occurring before the effective date of the assignment.

(5) For the purposes of sub-paragraph (4) "disqualifying event" means—

(*a*) in relation to the withdrawal of group relief, [the event falling within paragraph 3(1)(*a*) of Schedule 7 (purchaser ceasing to be a member of the same group as the vendor), as read with paragraph 4A of that Schedule][2];

(*b*) in relation to the withdrawal of reconstruction or acquisition relief, the change of control of the acquiring company mentioned in paragraph 9(1)(*a*) of that Schedule or, as the case may be, the event mentioned in paragraph 11(1)(*a*) or (2)(*a*) of that Schedule;

(*c*) in relation to the withdrawal of charities relief, a disqualifying event as defined in paragraphs 2(3) or 3(2) of Schedule 8.][1]

Amendments—[1] This Schedule inserted by FA 2004 s 296, Sch 39 para 22(2) with effect for any transaction of which the effective date (within the meaning of FA 2003 Pt 4) is on or after 22 July 2004: FA 2004 Sch 39 para 26. This insertion was previously made by the Stamp Duty and Stamp Duty Land Tax (Variation of the Finance Act 2003) (No 2) Regulations, SI 2003/2816 regs 1, 2, Schedule para 8(2) with effect from 1 December 2003. Those regulations are revoked by FA 2004 Sch 39 para 14(2).

[2] In sub-para (5)(*a*), words substituted for the words "the purchaser ceasing to be a member of the same group as the vendor (within the meaning of Part 1 of Schedule 7);" by F(No 2)A 2005 s 49, Sch 10 paras 1, 7 with effect where the effective date of the relevant transaction (within the meaning of FA 2003 Sch 7 para 3 or 4A) is after 19 May 2005. However, this amendment does not have effect—

(*a*) in relation to any transaction which is effected in pursuance of a contract entered into and substantially performed on or before the specified date (ie 16 March 2005), or

(*b*) subject to what follows below, in relation to any other transaction which is effected in pursuance of a contract entered into on or before the specified date (ie 16 March 2005).

The exclusion by para (*b*) above of transactions effected in pursuance of contracts entered into on or before the specified date does not apply—

(*a*) if there is any variation of the contract or assignment of rights under the contract after that date,

(*b*) if the transaction is effected in consequence of the exercise after that date of any option, right of pre-emption or similar right, or

(*c*) if after that date there is an assignment, subsale or other transaction (relating to the whole or part of the subject-matter of the contract) as a result of which a person other than the purchaser under the contract becomes entitled to call for a conveyance to him: F(No 2)A 2005 Sch 10 para 16(1), (6)–(8).

[3] Sub-para (1) substituted by F(No 2)A 2005 s 49, Sch 10 paras 1, 12 with effect where the effective date of the land transaction consisting of the grant of the lease is after 19 May 2005. However, this amendment is subject to the qualifications detailed in note [2] above: F(No 2)A 2005 Sch 10 para 16(4), (6)–(8).

[Assignment of lease: responsibility of assignee for returns etc

12— (1) Where a lease is assigned, anything that but for the assignment would be required or authorised to be done by or in relation to the assignor under or by virtue of—

(*a*) section 80 (adjustment where contingency ceases or consideration is ascertained),

(*b*) section 81A (return or further return in consequence of later linked transaction),

(*c*) paragraph 3 or 4 of this Schedule (return or further return required where lease for indefinite period continues), or (*d*) paragraph 8 of this Schedule (adjustment where rent ceases to be uncertain),

shall, if the event giving rise to the adjustment or return occurs after the effective date of the assignment, be done instead by or in relation to the assignee.

(2) So far as necessary for giving effect to sub-paragraph (1) anything previously done by or in relation to the assignor shall be treated as if it had been done by or in relation to the assignee.

(3) This paragraph does not apply if the assignment falls to be treated as the grant of a lease by the assignor (see paragraph 11).][1]

Amendments—[1] This Schedule inserted by FA 2004 s 296, Sch 39 para 22(2) with effect for any transaction of which the effective date (within the meaning of FA 2003 Pt 4) is on or after 22 July 2004: FA 2004 Sch 39 para 26. This insertion was previously made by the Stamp Duty and Stamp Duty Land Tax (Variation of the Finance Act 2003) (No 2) Regulations, SI 2003/2816 regs 1, 2, Schedule para 8(2) with effect from 1 December 2003. Those regulations are revoked by FA 2004 Sch 39 para 14(2).

[Agreement for lease

12A— (1) This paragraph applies where in England and Wales or Northern Ireland—

(*a*) an agreement for a lease is entered into, and

(*b*) the agreement is substantially performed without having been completed.

(2) The agreement is treated as if it were the grant of a lease in accordance with the agreement ("the notional lease"), beginning with the date of substantial performance.

The effective date of the transaction is that date.

(3) Where a lease is subsequently granted in pursuance of the agreement—

(*a*) the notional lease is treated as if it were surrendered at that time, and

(*b*) the lease itself is treated for the purposes of paragraph 9 (rent for overlap period in case of grant of further lease) as if it were granted in consideration of that surrender.

[Paragraph 5 does not apply so as to treat the notional lease and the lease itself as a single lease.][2]

(4) Where sub-paragraph (1) applies and the agreement is (to any extent) afterwards rescinded or annulled, or is for any other reason not carried into effect, the tax paid by virtue of that sub-paragraph shall (to that extent) be repaid by the Inland Revenue. Repayment must be claimed by amendment of the land transaction return made in respect of the agreement.

(5) In this paragraph "substantially performed" and "completed" have the same meanings as in section 44 (contract and conveyance).][1]

Amendments—[1] This Schedule inserted by FA 2004 s 296, Sch 39 para 22(2) with effect for any transaction of which the effective date (within the meaning of FA 2003 Pt 4) is on or after 22 July 2004: FA 2004 Sch 39 para 26. This insertion was previously made by the Stamp Duty and Stamp Duty Land Tax (Variation of the Finance Act 2003) (No 2) Regulations, SI 2003/2816 regs 1, 2, Schedule para 8(2) with effect from 1 December 2003. Those regulations are revoked by FA 2004 Sch 39 para 14(2).

Paragraphs 12A and 12B (below) were however not contained in the original Schedule 17A as inserted by SI 2003/2816. FA 2004 Sch 39 para 11(1), (4) amended that version of the Schedule to insert those paragraphs (identical to the paragraphs 12A and 12B as shown) with effect for any transaction of which the effective date is after 17 March 2004 and before 22 July 2004: FA 2004 Sch 39 para 13(3), (5).

[2] Words at the end of sub-para (3) inserted by FA 2006 s 164, Sch 25 para 4 with effect in relation to any agreement that is substantially performed on or after 19 July 2006 by virtue of FA 2006 Sch 25 para 9(6).

[Assignment of agreement for lease

12B— (1) This paragraph applies, in place of section 45 (contract and conveyance: effect of transfer of rights), where in England and Wales or Northern Ireland a person assigns his interest as lessee under an agreement for a lease.

(2) If the assignment occurs without the agreement having been substantially performed, section 44 (contract and conveyance) has effect as if—

(*a*) the contract were with the assignee and not the assignor, and

(*b*) the consideration given by the assignee for entering into the contract included any consideration given by him for the assignment.

(3) If the assignment occurs after the agreement has been substantially performed—

(*a*) the assignment is a separate land transaction, and

(*b*) the effective date of that transaction is the date of the assignment.

(4) Where there are successive assignments, this paragraph has effect in relation to each of them.][1]

Amendments—[1] This Schedule inserted by FA 2004 s 296, Sch 39 para 22(2) with effect for any transaction of which the effective date (within the meaning of FA 2003 Pt 4) is on or after 22 July 2004: FA 2004 Sch 39 para 26. This insertion was previously made by the Stamp Duty and Stamp Duty Land Tax (Variation of the Finance Act 2003) (No 2) Regulations, SI 2003/2816 regs 1, 2, Schedule para 8(2) with effect from 1 December 2003. Those regulations are revoked by FA 2004 Sch 39 para 14(2).

Paragraphs 12A (above) and 12B were however not contained in the original Schedule 17A as inserted by SI 2003/2816. FA 2004 Sch 39 para 11(1), (4) amended that version of the Schedule to insert those paragraphs (identical to the paragraphs 12A and 12B as shown) with effect for any transaction of which the effective date is after 17 March 2004 and before 22 July 2004: FA 2004 Sch 39 para 13(3), (5).

[Increase of rent treated as grant of new lease: variation of lease [in first five years][3]

13— (1) Where a lease is varied so as to increase the amount of the rent [as from a date before the end of the fifth year of the term of the lease][3], the variation is treated for the purposes of this Part as if it were the grant of a lease in consideration of the additional rent made payable by it.

(2) Sub-paragraph (1) does not apply to an increase of rent [in pursuance of—

(*a*) a provision contained in the lease, or

(*b*) a provision mentioned in any of paragraphs (*a*) to (*d*) of paragraph 7(4A)][2].][1]

Amendments—[1] This Schedule inserted by FA 2004 s 296, Sch 39 para 22(2) with effect for any transaction of which the effective date (within the meaning of FA 2003 Pt 4) is on or after 22 July 2004: FA 2004 Sch 39 para 26. This insertion was previously made by the Stamp Duty and Stamp Duty Land Tax (Variation of the Finance Act 2003) (No 2) Regulations, SI 2003/2816 regs 1, 2, Schedule para 8(2) with effect from 1 December 2003. Those regulations are revoked by FA 2004 Sch 39 para 14(2).

[2] In sub-para (2), words substituted for "in pursuance of a provision contained in the lease (but see paragraph 14)" by FA 2006 s 164, Sch 25 para 2(2) with effect in relation to any lease granted or treated as granted on or after 19 July 2006 by virtue of FA 2006 Sch 25 para 9(6).

[3] In heading and sub-para (1), words inserted by FA 2006 s 164, Sch 25 para 6 with effect in relation to any variation of a lease made on or after 19 July 2006 by virtue of FA 2006 Sch 25 para 9(6).

[Increase of rent treated as grant of new lease: abnormal increase after fifth year

14— (1) This paragraph applies if, after the end of the fifth year of the term of a lease—

(*a*) the amount of rent payable increases (or is increased)[, whether in accordance with the provisions of the lease or otherwise][2], and

(*b*) the rent payable as a result ("the new rent") is such that the increase falls to be regarded as abnormal (see paragraph 15).

(2) The increase in rent is treated as if it were the grant of a lease in consideration of the excess rent.

(3) The excess rent is the difference between the new rent and the rent previously taxed.

[(4) Where the provisions of this paragraph have not previously applied to an increase in the rent payable under the lease, the rent previously taxed is—

(*a*) if paragraph (*b*) or (*c*) does not apply, the rent payable under the lease without the increase referred to in sub-paragraph (1);

(*b*) if the amount of rent payable under the lease is determined under paragraph 7 (variable or uncertain rent), the rent that is assumed to be payable after the fifth year of the term of the lease (in accordance with paragraph 7(3));

(*c*) if there has been a variation in the lease falling within paragraph 13 (increase of rent treated as grant of new lease: variation of lease in first five years), the rent payable as a result of the variation (or, if there has been more than one such variation, the most recent one).

(4A) Where the provisions of this paragraph have previously applied to an increase in the rent payable under the lease, the rent previously taxed is the rent payable as a result of the last increase in relation to which the provisions of this paragraph applied.

(4B) In determining the rent previously taxed, disregard paragraphs 9(2) and 9A(3) (deemed reduction of rent, where further lease granted, for period during which rents overlap).][2]

(5) The deemed grant is treated as—

(*a*) made on the date on which the increased rent first became payable, and

(*b*) for a term equal to the unexpired part of the original lease, and as linked with the grant of the original lease (and with any other transaction with which that transaction is linked).

(6) The assumption in paragraph 7(3) (that the rent does not change after the end of the fifth year of the term of a lease) does not apply for the purposes of this paragraph or paragraph 15 except for the purpose of determining the rent previously taxed.][1]

[(7) The reference to a lease in sub-paragraph (1) is to—

(*a*) a lease actually granted on or after the implementation date, or

(*b*) a lease that is treated as existing by reason of a deemed grant under paragraph 12A(2) or 19(3) of which the effective date is on or after the implementation date.][2]

Amendments—[1] This Schedule inserted by FA 2004 s 296, Sch 39 para 22(2) with effect for any transaction of which the effective date (within the meaning of FA 2003 Pt 4) is on or after 22 July 2004: FA 2004 Sch 39 para 26. This insertion was previously made by the Stamp Duty and Stamp Duty Land Tax (Variation of the Finance Act 2003) (No 2) Regulations, SI 2003/2816 regs 1, 2, Schedule para 8(2) with effect from 1 December 2003. Those regulations are revoked by FA 2004 Sch 39 para 14(2).

[2] Words in sub-para (1)(*a*) substituted for "in accordance with the provisions of the lease", sub-paras (4)–(4B) substituted for former sub-para (4), sub-para (7) inserted by FA 2006 s 164, Sch 25 para 7 with effect in relation to any increase of rent that takes effect or after 19 July 2006 by virtue of FA 2006 Sch 25 para 9(6).

[Increase of rent after fifth year: whether regarded as abnormal

15— Whether an increase in rent is to be regarded for the purposes of paragraph 14 as abnormal is determined as follows:—

[Step One

Find the start date.

Where the provisions of paragraph 14 have not previously applied to an increase in the rent payable under the lease, the start date is—

(*a*) if paragraph (*b*) or (*c*) does not apply, the beginning of the term of the lease;

(*b*) if the amount of rent payable under the lease is determined under paragraph 7 (variable or uncertain rent), the beginning of the period by reference to which the rent assumed to be payable after the fifth year of the term of the lease is determined in accordance with paragraph 7(3);

(*c*) if there has been a variation in the lease falling within paragraph 13 (increase of rent treated as grant of new lease: variation of lease in first five years), the date of the variation (or, if there has been more than one such variation, the date of the most recent one).

Where the provisions of paragraph 14 have previously applied to an increase in the rent payable under the lease, the start date is the date of the last increase in relation to which the provisions of that paragraph applied.

Step Two

Find the number of whole years in the period between the start date and the date on which the new rent first becomes payable.

Step Three

The rent increase is regarded as abnormal if the excess rent (see paragraph 14(3)) is greater than:

$$\frac{R \times Y}{5}$$

where—

R is the rent previously taxed (see paragraph 14(4) or (4A)), and

Y is the number of whole years found under Step Two.][2][1]

Amendments—[1] This Schedule inserted by FA 2004 s 296, Sch 39 para 22(2) with effect for any transaction of which the effective date (within the meaning of FA 2003 Pt 4) is on or after 22 July 2004: FA 2004 Sch 39 para 26. This insertion was previously made by the Stamp Duty and Stamp Duty Land Tax (Variation of the Finance Act 2003) (No 2) Regulations, SI 2003/2816 regs 1, 2, Schedule para 8(2) with effect from 1 December 2003. Those regulations are revoked by FA 2004 Sch 39 para 14(2).

[2] Steps One to Three substituted for former Steps One to Six by FA 2006 s 164, Sch 25 para 8 with effect in relation to any increase of rent that takes effect or after 19 July 2006 by virtue of FA 2006 Sch 25 para 9(6).

[[Reduction of rent or term or other variation of lease][2]

15A— (1) Where a lease is varied so as to reduce the amount of the rent, the variation is treated for the purposes of this Part as an acquisition of a chargeable interest by the lessee.

[1A) Where any consideration in money or money's worth (other than an increase in rent) is given by the lessee for any variation of a lease, other than a variation of the amount of the rent or of the term of the lease, the variation is treated for the purposes of this Part as an acquisition of a chargeable interest by the lessee.][2]

(2) Where a lease is varied so as to reduce the term, the variation is treated for the purposes of this Part as an acquisition of a chargeable interest by the lessor.][1]

Amendments—[1] This Schedule inserted by FA 2004 s 296, Sch 39 para 22(2) with effect for any transaction of which the effective date (within the meaning of FA 2003 Pt 4) is on or after 22 July 2004: FA 2004 Sch 39 para 26. This insertion was previously made by the Stamp Duty and Stamp Duty Land Tax (Variation of the Finance Act 2003) (No 2) Regulations, SI 2003/2816 regs 1, 2, Schedule para 8(2) with effect from 1 December 2003. Those regulations are revoked by FA 2004 Sch 39 para 14(2).

[2] Sub-para (1A) inserted, and Heading substituted, by F(No 2)A 2005 s 49, Sch 10 paras 1, 13 with effect in relation to any transaction of which the effective date is after 19 May 2005.

However, this amendment does not have effect—

(*a*) in relation to any transaction which is effected in pursuance of a contract entered into and substantially performed on or before the specified date (ie 16 March 2005), or

(*b*) subject to what follows below, in relation to any other transaction which is effected in pursuance of a contract entered into on or before the specified date (ie 16 March 2005).

The exclusion by para (*b*) above of transactions effected in pursuance of contracts entered into on or before the specified date does not apply—

(*a*) if there is any variation of the contract or assignment of rights under the contract after that date,

(*b*) if the transaction is effected in consequence of the exercise after that date of any option, right of pre-emption or similar right, or

(*c*) if after that date there is an assignment, subsale or other transaction (relating to the whole or part of the subject-matter of the contract) as a result of which a person other than the purchaser under the contract becomes entitled to call for a conveyance to him: F(No 2)A 2005 Sch 10 para 16(5)–(8).

[Surrender of existing lease in return for new lease

16— Where a lease is granted in consideration of the surrender of an existing lease between the same parties—

(*a*) the grant of the new lease does not count as chargeable consideration for the surrender, and

(*b*) the surrender does not count as chargeable consideration for the grant of the new lease.

Paragraph 5 (exchanges) of Schedule 4 (chargeable consideration) does not apply in such a case.][1]

Amendments—[1] This Schedule inserted by FA 2004 s 296 Sch 39 para 22(2) with effect for any transaction of which the effective date (within the meaning of FA 2003 Pt 4) is on or after 22 July 2004: FA 2004 Sch 39 para 26. This insertion was previously made by the Stamp Duty and Stamp Duty Land Tax (Variation of the Finance Act 2003) (No 2) Regulations, SI 2003/2816 regs 1, 2, Schedule para 8(2) with effect from 1 December 2003. Those regulations are revoked by FA 2004 Sch 39 para 14(2).

The final sentence of paragraph 16 above was however not contained in the original Schedule 17A as inserted by SI 2003/2816. FA 2004 Sch 39 para 11(1), (5) amended that version of the Schedule to insert that sentence. That insertion had effect for any transaction of which the effective date was after 17 March 2004 and before 22 July 2004: FA 2004 Sch 39 para 13(3), (5).

[Assignment of lease: assumption of obligations by assignee

17 In the case of an assignment of a lease the assumption by the assignee of the obligation—

(*a*) to pay rent, or

(*b*) to perform or observe any other undertaking of the tenant under the lease,

does not count as chargeable consideration for the assignment.][1]

Amendments—[1] This Schedule inserted by FA 2004 s 296, Sch 39 para 22(2) with effect for any transaction of which the effective date (within the meaning of FA 2003 Pt 4) is on or after 22 July 2004: FA 2004 Sch 39 para 26. This insertion was previously made by the Stamp Duty and Stamp Duty Land Tax (Variation of the Finance Act 2003) (No 2) Regulations, SI 2003/2816 regs 1, 2, Schedule para 8(2) with effect from 1 December 2003. Those regulations are revoked by FA 2004 Sch 39 para 14(2).

[Reverse premium

18— (1) In the case of the grant, assignment or surrender of a lease a reverse premium does not count as chargeable consideration.

(2) A "reverse premium" means—

(*a*) in relation to the grant of a lease, a premium moving from the landlord to the tenant;

(*b*) in relation to the assignment of a lease, a premium moving from the assignor to the assignee;

(*c*) in relation to the surrender of a lease, a premium moving from the tenant to the landlord.][1]

Amendments—[1] This Schedule inserted by FA 2004 s 296, Sch 39 para 22(2) with effect for any transaction of which the effective date is on or after 22 July 2004: FA 2004 Sch 39 para 26. This insertion was previously made by the Stamp Duty and Stamp Duty Land Tax (Variation of the Finance Act 2003) (No 2) Regulations, SI 2003/2816 regs 1, 2, Schedule para 8(2) with effect from 1 December 2003. Those regulations are revoked by FA 2004 Sch 39 para 14(2).

[Loan or deposit in connection with grant or assignment of lease

18A— (1) Where, under arrangements made in connection with the grant of a lease—

(*a*) the lessee, or any person connected with him or acting on his behalf, pays a deposit, or makes a loan, to any person, and

(*b*) the repayment of all or part of the deposit or loan is contingent on anything done or omitted to be done by the lessee or on the death of the lessee,

the amount of the deposit or loan (disregarding any repayment) is to be taken for the purposes of this Part to be consideration other than rent given for the grant of the lease.

(2) Where, under arrangements made in connection with the assignment of a lease—

(*a*) the assignee, or any person connected with him or acting on his behalf, pays a deposit, or makes a loan, to any person, and

(*b*) the repayment of all or part of the deposit or loan is contingent on anything done or omitted to be done by the assignee or on the death of the assignee,

the amount of the deposit or loan (disregarding any repayment) is to be taken for the purposes of this Part to be consideration other than rent given for the assignment of the lease.

(3) Sub-paragraph (1) or (2) does not apply in relation to a deposit if the amount that would otherwise fall within the sub-paragraph in question in relation to the grant or (as the case requires) assignment of the lease is not more than twice the relevant maximum rent.

(4) The relevant maximum rent is—

(*a*) in relation to the grant of a lease, the highest amount of rent payable in respect of any consecutive twelve month period in the first five years of the term;

(*b*) in relation to the assignment of a lease, the highest amount of rent payable in respect of any consecutive twelve month period in the first five years of the term remaining outstanding as at the date of the assignment,

the highest amount of rent being determined (in either case) in the same way as the highest amount of rent mentioned in paragraph 7(3).

(5) Tax is not chargeable by virtue of this paragraph—

(*a*) merely because of paragraph [9A][2] of Schedule 5 (which excludes the 0% band in [Table B][2] in section 55(2) in cases where [the relevant rent attributable to non-residential property is not less than £1,000][2] a year), or

(*b*) merely because of paragraph 5(4)(*b*), 6(6)(*b*), 9(4)(*b*) or 10(6)(*b*) of Schedule 6 (which make similar provision in relation to land which is wholly or partly residential property and is wholly or partly situated in a disadvantaged area).

(6) Section 839 of the Taxes Act 1988 (connected persons) has effect for the purposes of this paragraph.][1]

Amendments—[1] This paragraph inserted by F(No 2)A 2005 s 49, Sch 10 paras 1, 14 with effect in relation to any transaction of which the effective date is after 19 May 2005.

However, this amendment does not have effect—

(*a*) in relation to any transaction which is effected in pursuance of a contract entered into and substantially performed on or before the specified date (i e 16 March 2005), or

(*b*) subject to what follows below, in relation to any other transaction which is effected in pursuance of a contract entered into on or before the specified date (i e 16 March 2005).

The exclusion by para (*b*) above of transactions effected in pursuance of contracts entered into on or before the specified date does not apply—

Stamp Taxes

(*a*) if there is any variation of the contract or assignment of rights under the contract after that date,
(*b*) if the transaction is effected in consequence of the exercise after that date of any option, right of pre-emption or similar right, or
(*c*) if after that date there is an assignment, subsale or other transaction (relating to the whole or part of the subject-matter of the contract) as a result of which a person other than the purchaser under the contract becomes entitled to call for a conveyance to him: F(No 2)A 2005 Sch 10 para 16(5)–(8).

[2] In sub-para (5)(*a*), words substituted by FA 2008 s 95(12) with effect in relation to transactions with an effective date on or after 12 March 2008.

[Provisions relating to leases in Scotland

19— (1) In the application of this Part to Scotland—

(*a*) any reference to the term of a lease is to the period of the lease, and
(*b*) any reference to the reversion on a lease is to the interest of the landlord in the property subject to the lease.

(2) Where in Scotland there is a lease constituted by concluded missives of let ("the first lease") and at some later time a lease is executed ("the second lease")—

(*a*) the first lease is treated as if it were surrendered at that time, and
(*b*) the second lease is treated for the purposes of paragraph 9 (rent for overlap period in case of grant of further lease) as if it were granted in consideration of that surrender.

[Paragraph 5 does not apply so as to treat the first lease and the second lease as a single lease.][2]

(3) Where in Scotland—

(*a*) there is an agreement (including missives of let not constituting a lease) under which a lease is to be executed, and
(*b*) the agreement is substantially performed without a lease having been executed,

the agreement is treated as if it were the grant of a lease in accordance with the agreement ("the notional lease"), beginning with the date of substantial performance.

The effective date of the transaction is when the agreement is substantially performed.

(4) Where sub-paragraph (3) applies and at some later time a lease is executed—

(*a*) the notional lease is treated as if it were surrendered at that time, and
(*b*) the lease itself is treated for the purposes of paragraph 9 as if it were granted in consideration of that surrender.

[Paragraph 5 does not apply so as to treat the notional lease and the lease itself as a single lease.][2]

(5) References in sub-paragraphs (2) to (4) to the execution of a lease are to the execution of a lease that either is in conformity with, or relates to substantially the same property and period as, the missives of let or other agreement.

(6) Where sub-paragraph (3) applies and the agreement is (to any extent) afterwards rescinded or annulled, or is for any other reason not carried into effect, the tax paid by virtue of that sub-paragraph shall (to that extent) be repaid by the Inland Revenue. Repayment must be claimed by amendment of the land transaction return made in respect of the agreement.][1]

Amendments—[1] This Schedule inserted by FA 2004 s 296, Sch 39 para 22(2) with effect for any transaction of which the effective date (within the meaning of FA 2003 Pt 4) is on or after 22 July 2004: FA 2004 Sch 39 para 26. This insertion was previously made by the Stamp Duty and Stamp Duty Land Tax (Variation of the Finance Act 2003) (No 2) Regulations, SI 2003/2816 regs 1, 2, Schedule para 8(2) with effect from 1 December 2003. Those regulations are revoked by FA 2004 Sch 39 para 14(2).

Sub-para (2) above read differently in the original Schedule 17A as inserted by SI 2003/2816. FA 2004 Sch 37 para 11(1), (6) amended that version of the Schedule by substituting sub-paras (2)–(6) for the original sub-para (2). The effect was that it read the same as the new version of the Schedule. That substitution had effect for any transaction of which the effective date was after 17 March 2004 and before 22 July 2004: FA 2004 Sch 39 para 13(3), (5).

[2] Words in sub-paras (2), (4) inserted by FA 2006 s 164, Sch 25 para 5 with effect in relation to any agreement that is substantially performed on or after 19 July 2006 by virtue of FA 2006 Sch 25 para 9(6).

SCHEDULE 18

STAMP DUTY LAND TAX: CONSEQUENTIAL AMENDMENTS

Section 123

Provisional Collection of Taxes Act 1968

1 (*amends* PCTA 1968 s 1(1))

Inheritance Tax Act 1984

2 (*amends* IHTA 1984 s 190(4))

Income and Corporation Taxes Act 1988

3 (*amends* TA 1988 ss 209B, 213, 214, 215, 827)

Finance Act 1989

4 (*amends* FA 1989 s 178(2))

Taxation of Chargeable Gains Act 1992

5 (*amends* TCGA 1992 s 38(2))

Income Tax (Earnings and Pensions) Act 2003

6 (*amends* ITEPA 2003 s 277(3))

SCHEDULE 19

STAMP DUTY LAND TAX: COMMENCEMENT AND TRANSITIONAL PROVISIONS

Section 124

HMRC Manuals—Stamp Duty Land Tax Manual SDLTM49000–49700 (explanation of this Schedule, with examples).

Introduction

1— (1) Subject to the provisions of this Schedule, the provisions of this Part come into force on the passing of this Act.

(2) The following provisions have effect as regards what transactions are SDLT transactions, that is, are chargeable or notifiable or are transactions in relation to which section 79 (registration etc) applies.

(3) Nothing in this Schedule shall be read as meaning that other transactions, whether effected before or after the passing of this Act, are to be disregarded in applying the provisions of this Part.

The implementation date

2— (1) A transaction is not an SDLT transaction unless the effective date of the transaction is on or after the implementation date.

(2) In this Part "the implementation date" means the date appointed by Treasury order as the implementation date for the purposes of stamp duty land tax.

Regulations—Stamp Duty Land Tax (Appointment of the Implementation Date) Order, SI 2003/2899 (appoints 1 December 2003 as the implementation date).

Contract entered into before first relevant date

3— (1) Subject to the following provisions of this paragraph, a transaction is not an SDLT transaction if it is effected in pursuance of a contract entered into before the first relevant date.

(2) The "first relevant date" is the day after the passing of this Act.

(3) The exclusion of transactions effected in pursuance of contracts entered into before the first relevant date does not apply—

(*a*) if there is any variation of the contract or assignment of rights under the contract on or after that date;

(*b*) if the transaction is effected in consequence of the exercise after that date of any option, right of pre-emption or similar right;

[(*c*) if on or after that date there is an assignment, subsale or other transaction (relating to the whole or part of the subject-matter of the contract) as a result of which a person other than the purchaser under the contract becomes entitled to call for a conveyance to him.][1]

Amendments—[1] Sub-para (3)(*c*) substituted by FA 2004 s 296, Sch 39 para 12 with effect for any transaction of which the effective date is after 17 March 2004. However, this amendment does not apply in relation to a contract that was substantially performed before 17 March 2004: FA 2004 Sch 39 para 13(3), (4).

Contract substantially performed before implementation date

4— (1) This paragraph applies where a transaction—

(*a*) is completed on or after the implementation date,

(*b*) is effected in pursuance of a contract entered into and substantially performed before that date, and

(*c*) is not excluded from being an SDLT transaction by paragraph 3.

(2) The transaction is not an SDLT transaction if the contract was substantially performed before the first relevant date.

(3) In any other case, the fact that the contract was substantially performed before the implementation date does not affect the matter.

Accordingly, the effective date of the transaction is the date of completion.

[Contracts substantially performed after implementation date

4A Where—

(*a*) a transaction is effected in pursuance of a contract entered into before the first relevant date, (*b*) the contract is substantially performed, without having been completed, after the implementation date, and

(*c*) there is subsequently an event within paragraph 3(3) by virtue of which the transaction is an SDLT transaction,

the effective date of the transaction shall be taken to be the date of the event referred to in paragraph (*c*) (and not the date of substantial performance).][1]

Amendments—[1] Paragraphs 4A, 4B inserted by FA 2004 s 296, Sch 39 para 24 with effect for any transaction of which the effective date (within the meaning of FA 2003 Pt 4) is on or after 22 July 2004: FA 2004 Sch 39 para 26. This insertion was previously made by the Stamp Duty and Stamp Duty Land Tax (Variation of the Finance Act 2003) (No 2) Regulations, SI 2003/2816 regs 1, 2, Schedule para 10 with effect from 1 December 2003. Those regulations are revoked by FA 2004 Sch 39 para 14(2).

[Application of provisions in case of transfer of rights

4B— (1) This paragraph applies where section 44 (contract and conveyance) has effect in accordance with section 45 (effect of transfer of rights).

(2) Any reference in paragraph 3, 4 or 4A to the date when a contract was entered into (or made) shall be read, in relation to a contract deemed to exist by virtue of section 45(3) (deemed secondary contract with transferee), as a reference to the date of the assignment, subsale or other transaction in question.][1]

Amendments—[1] Paragraphs 4A, 4B inserted by FA 2004 s 296, Sch 39 para 24 with effect for any transaction of which the effective date (within the meaning of FA 2003 Pt 4) is on or after 22 July 2004: FA 2004 Sch 39 para 26. This insertion was previously made by the Stamp Duty and Stamp Duty Land Tax (Variation of the Finance Act 2003) (No 2) Regulations, SI 2003/2816 regs 1, 2, Schedule para 10 with effect from 1 December 2003. Those regulations are revoked by FA 2004 Sch 39 para 14(2).

Credit for ad valorem stamp duty paid

5— (1) Where a transaction chargeable to stamp duty land tax is effected in pursuance of a contract entered into before the implementation date, any *ad valorem* stamp duty paid on the contract shall go to reduce the amount of tax payable (but not so as to give rise to any repayment).

(2) Where the application or operation of any exemption or relief from stamp duty land tax turns on whether tax was paid or payable in respect of an earlier transaction, that requirement is treated as met if *ad valorem* stamp duty was paid or (as the case may be) payable in respect of the instrument by which that transaction was effected.

Effect for stamp duty purposes of stamp duty land tax being paid or chargeable

6— (1) . . .[1]

(2) The references in section 111(1)(*c*) of, and paragraph 4(3) of Schedule 34 to, the Finance Act 2002 (c 23) (which relate to the circumstances in which stamp duty group relief is withdrawn) to a transfer at market value by a duly stamped instrument on which *ad valorem* duty was paid and in respect of which group relief was not claimed shall be read, on or after the implementation date, as including a reference to a transfer at market value by a chargeable transaction in respect of which relief under Part 1 of Schedule 7 to this Act was available but was not claimed.

(3) The references in section 113(1)(*c*) of, and in paragraph 3(3) or 4(3) of Schedule 35 to, the Finance Act 2002 (which relate to the circumstances in which stamp duty company acquisitions relief is withdrawn) to a transfer at market value by a duly stamped instrument on which *ad valorem* duty was paid and in respect of which section 76 relief was not claimed shall be read, on or after the implementation date, as including a reference to a transfer at market value by a chargeable transaction on which stamp duty land tax was chargeable and in respect of which relief under Part 2 of Schedule 7 to this Act was available but was not claimed.

Amendments—[1] Sub-para (1) repealed by FA 2004 s 326, Sch 42 Pt 4(2) with effect in accordance with FA 2004 Sch 39 para 26. This repeal was previously made by the Stamp Duty and Stamp Duty Land Tax (Variation of the Finance Act 2003) (No 2) Regulations, SI 2003/2816 regs 1, 2, Schedule para 11(1) with effect from 1 December 2003. Those regulations have been revoked by FA 2004 Sch 39 para 14(2).

Earlier related transactions under stamp duty

7— (1) In relation to a transaction that is not an SDLT transaction but which is linked to an SDLT transaction and accordingly falls to be taken into account in determining the rate of stamp duty land tax chargeable on the latter transaction, any reference in this Part to the chargeable consideration for the first-mentioned transaction shall be read as a reference to the consideration by reference to which *ad valorem* stamp duty was payable in respect of the instrument by which that transaction was effected.

[(2) In paragraph 3 of Schedule 9 (relief for transfer of reversion under shared ownership lease where election made for market value treatment) and paragraph 4A of that Schedule (shared ownership lease: treatment of staircasing transaction) as they apply in a case where the original lease was granted before the implementation date—

(*a*) a reference to a lease to which paragraph 2 of that Schedule applies shall be read as a reference to a lease to which section 97 of the Finance Act 1980 applied (which made provision for stamp duty corresponding to that paragraph), and (*b*) a reference to an election having been made for tax to be charged in accordance with paragraph 2 or 4 of that Schedule shall be read as a reference to the lease having contained a statement of the parties' intention such as is mentioned in section 97(2)(*d*) of the Finance Act 1980 or, as the case may be, paragraph (*d*) of section 108(5) of the Finance Act 1981 (which made provision for stamp duty corresponding to paragraph 4).][2]

(3) In section 54 (exceptions from deemed market value rule for transactions with connected company) the reference in subsection (4)(*b*) to group relief having been claimed in respect of a transaction shall be read in relation to a transaction carried out before the implementation date as a reference to relief having been claimed under section 42 of the Finance Act 1930 (c 28), section 11 of the Finance Act (Northern Ireland) 1954 (c 23 (NI)) or section 151 of the Finance Act 1995 (c 4) in respect of stamp duty on the instrument by which the transaction was effected.

[(4) For the purposes of paragraph 5 of Schedule 17A (treatment of successive linked leases) no account shall be taken of any transaction that is not an SDLT transaction.][1]

Amendments—[1] Sub-para (4) inserted by FA 2004 s 296, Sch 39 para 22(8) with effect for any transaction of which the effective date (within the meaning of FA 2003 Pt 4) is on or after 22 July 2004: FA 2004 Sch 39 para 26. This insertion was previously made by the Stamp Duty and Stamp Duty Land Tax (Variation of the Finance Act 2003) (No 2) Regulations, SI 2003/2816 regs 1, 2, Schedule para 8(1) with effect from 1 December 2003. Those regulations are revoked by FA 2004 Sch 39 para 14(2).

[2] Sub-para (2) substituted by FA 2004 s 303(3), (5), and deemed to have come into force on 1 December 2003.

[Stamping of contract where transaction on completion subject to stamp duty land tax

7A— (1) This paragraph applies where—

(*a*) a contract that apart from paragraph 7 of Schedule 13 to the Finance Act 1999 (contracts chargeable as conveyances on sale) would not be chargeable with stamp duty is entered into before the implementation date,

(*b*) a conveyance made in conformity with the contract is effected on or after the implementation date, and

(*c*) the transaction effected on completion is an SDLT transaction or would be but for an exemption or relief from stamp duty land tax.

(2) If in those circumstances the contract is presented for stamping together with a Revenue certificate as to compliance with the provisions of this Part of this Act in relation to the transaction effected on completion—

(*a*) the payment of stamp duty land tax on that transaction or, as the case may be, the fact that no such tax was payable shall be denoted on the contract by a particular stamp, and

(*b*) the contract shall be deemed thereupon to be duly stamped.

(3) In this paragraph "conveyance" includes any instrument.][1]

Amendments—[1] Paragraph 7A inserted by FA 2004 s 296, Sch 39 para 25(1) with effect for any transaction of which the effective date (within the meaning of FA 2003 Pt 4) is on or after 22 July 2004: FA 2004 Sch 39 para 26. This insertion was previously made by the Stamp Duty and Stamp Duty Land Tax (Variation of the Finance Act 2003) (No 2) Regulations, SI 2003/2816 regs 1, 2, Schedule para 11(1) with effect from 1 December 2003. Those regulations are revoked by FA 2004 Sch 39 para 14(2).

[Stamping of agreement for lease where grant of lease subject to stamp duty land tax][1]

8— (1) [This paragraph applies where—][1]

(*a*) an agreement for a lease is entered into before the implementation date,

(*b*) a lease giving effect to the agreement is executed on or after that date, and

(*c*) the transaction effected on completion is an SDLT transaction or would be but for an exemption or relief from stamp duty land tax.

[(2) If in those circumstances the agreement is presented for stamping together with a Revenue certificate as to compliance with the provisions of this Part of this Act in relation to the grant of the lease—

(*a*) the payment of stamp duty land tax in respect of the grant of the lease or, as the case may be, the fact that no such tax was payable shall be denoted on the agreement by a particular stamp, and

(*b*) the agreement shall be deemed thereupon to be duly stamped.][1]

(3) For the purposes of this paragraph a lease gives effect to an agreement if the lease either is in conformity with the agreement or relates to substantially the same property and term as the agreement.

(4) References in this paragraph to an agreement for a lease include missives of let in Scotland.

Amendments—[1] Heading and words in sub-para (1) substituted, and sub-para (2) substituted, by FA 2004 s 296, Sch 39 para 25(2), (3) with effect for any transaction of which the effective date (within the meaning of FA 2003 Pt 4) is on or after 22 July 2004: FA 2004 Sch 39 para 26. These amendments were previously made by the Stamp Duty and Stamp Duty Land Tax (Variation of the Finance Act 2003) (No 2) Regulations, SI 2003/2816 regs 1, 2, Schedule para 11(2), (3) with effect from 1 December 2003. Those regulations are revoked by FA 2004 Sch 39 para 14(2).

Exercise of option or right of pre-emption acquired before implementation date

9— (1) This paragraph applies where—

(*a*) an option binding the grantor to enter into a land transaction, or (*b*) a right of pre-emption preventing the grantor from entering into, or restricting the right of the grantor to enter into, a land transaction,

is acquired before the implementation date and exercised on or after that date.

(2) Where the option or right was acquired on or after 17th April 2003, any consideration for the acquisition is treated as part of the chargeable consideration for the transaction resulting from the exercise of the option or right.

(3) Where the option or right was varied on or after 17th April 2003 and before the implementation date, any consideration for the variation is treated as part of the chargeable consideration for the transaction resulting from the exercise of the option or right.

(4) Whether or not sub-paragraph (2) or (3) applies, the acquisition of the option or right and any variation of the option or right is treated as linked with the land transaction resulting from the exercise of the option or right.

But not so as to require the consideration for the acquisition or variation to be counted twice in determining the rate of tax chargeable on the land transaction resulting from the exercise of the option or right.

(5) Where this paragraph applies any *ad valorem* stamp duty paid on the acquisition or variation of the option or right shall go to reduce the amount of tax payable on the transaction resulting from the exercise of the option or right (but not so as to give rise to any repayment).

Supplementary

10 In this Schedule "contract" includes any agreement.

SCHEDULE 20

STAMP DUTY: RESTRICTION TO INSTRUMENTS RELATING TO STOCK OR MARKETABLE SECURITIES

Section 125

PART 1

SUPPLEMENTARY PROVISIONS

Cross references—See FA 2003 Sch 15 para 31(2) (in this Part, references to stock or marketable securities shall be read as including any property that is the subject matter of a transaction by which an interest in a partnership is transferred).

Reduction of stamp duty where instrument partly relating to stock or marketable securities

1— (1) This paragraph applies where stamp duty under Part 1 of Schedule 13 to the Finance Act 1999 (c 16) (transfer on sale) is chargeable on an instrument that relates partly to stock or marketable securities and partly to property other than stock or marketable securities.

(2) In such a case—

(*a*) the consideration in respect of which duty would otherwise be charged shall be apportioned, on a just and reasonable basis, as between the stock or marketable securities and the other property, and

(*b*) the instrument shall be charged only in respect of the consideration attributed to the stock or marketable securities.

Apportionment of consideration for stamp duty purposes

2— (1) Where part of the property referred to in section 58(1) of the Stamp Act 1891 (c 39) (consideration to be apportioned between different instruments as parties think fit) consists of stock or marketable securities, that provision shall have effect as if "the parties think fit" read "is just and reasonable".

(2) Where—

(*a*) part of the property referred to in section 58(2) of the Stamp Act 1891 (c 39) (property contracted to be purchased by two or more persons etc) consists of stock or marketable securities, and

(*b*) both or (as the case may be) all the relevant persons are connected with one another,

that provision shall have effect as if the words from "for distinct parts of the consideration" to the end of the subsection read ", the consideration shall be apportioned in such manner as is just and reasonable, so that a distinct consideration for each part of the property transferred is set forth in the transfer relating to that part, and the transfer shall be charged with *ad valorem* duty in respect of that consideration.".

(3) If in a case where sub-paragraph (1) or (2) applies the consideration is apportioned in a manner that is not just and reasonable, the enactments relating to stamp duty shall have effect as if—

(*a*) the consideration had been apportioned in a manner that is just and reasonable, and (*b*) the amount of any distinct consideration set forth in any transfer relating to a part of the property transferred were such amount as is found by a just and reasonable apportionment (and not the amount actually set forth).

(4) For the purposes of sub-paragraph (2)—

(*a*) a person is a relevant person if he is a person by or for whom the property is contracted to be purchased;

(*b*) the question whether persons are connected with one another shall be determined in accordance with section 839 of the Taxes Act 1988.

PART 2

CONSEQUENTIAL AMENDMENTS AND REPEALS

Cross references—See FA 2003 Sch 15 para 31(1) (nothing in this Part affects the application of enactments relating to stamp duty in relation to an instrument by which a transfer of an interest in a partnership is effected).

Removal of unnecessary references to "conveyance"

3 In the enactments relating to stamp duty for "conveyance or transfer", wherever occurring, substitute "transfer".

Finance Act 1895

4 (*amends* FA 1895 s 12)

Finance Act 1990

5 (*amends* FA 1990 s 108)

Finance Act 1999

6 (*amends* FA 1999 Sch 13 para 1)

Power to make further consequential amendments or repeals

7— (1) The Treasury may by regulations make such other amendments or repeals of enactments relating to stamp duty or stamp duty reserve tax as appear to them appropriate in consequence of the abolition of stamp duty except on instruments relating to stock or marketable securities.

(2) The regulations may include such transitional provisions and savings as appear to the Treasury to be appropriate.

(3) Regulations under this paragraph shall be made by statutory instrument which shall be subject to annulment in pursuance of a resolution of the House of Commons.

SCHEDULE 40

ACQUISITION BY COMPANY OF ITS OWN SHARES

Section 195

Commentary—*Simon's Taxes* **D5.502; E3.211.**

Regulations—The Finance Act 2003, Section 195 and Schedule 40 (Appointed Day) Order, SI 2003/3077 (s 195 and Sch 40 have effect in relation to any acquisition of shares by a company on or after 1st December 2003).

…

Stamp duty and stamp duty reserve tax

2–4 (*amend* FA 1986 ss 66, 90, 92: para 2(*b*) *repealed* by FA 2008 s 99, Sch 32 para 21 with effect in relation to instruments executed on or after 13 March 2008 and not stamped before 19 March 2008.)

5 (*amends* FA 1999 Sch 13 para 1)

FINANCE ACT 2004

(2004 Chapter 12)

ARRANGEMENT OF SECTIONS

PART 6

OTHER TAXES

Stamp duty land tax and stamp duty

Stamp Taxes

An Act to Grant certain duties, to alter other duties, and to amend the law relating to the National Debt and the Public Revenue, and to make further provision in connection with finance.

[22 July 2004]

PART 6
OTHER TAXES

Stamp duty land tax and stamp duty

296 Miscellaneous amendments

Schedule 39 to this Act, which makes amendments to Part 4 (stamp duty land tax) and Part 5 (stamp duty) of the Finance Act 2003 (c 14), has effect.

Stamp duty land tax

297 Leases

(1), (2) (*amends* FA 2003 s 43(3))

(3) (*amends* FA 2003 s 48(7))

(4) (*substitutes* FA 2003 s 53(1))

(5)–(7) (*amends* FA 2003 s 79)

(8) (*amends* FA 2003 Sch 4 para 10(2A))

(9) Subsections (2) to (4) and (8) apply in relation to any transaction of which the effective date is on or after the day on which this Act is passed.

(10) Subsections (5) to (7) apply in relation to any transaction or deemed transaction of which the effective date is on or after 17th March 2004.

(11) In this section "effective date" has the same meaning as in Part 4 of the Finance Act 2003.

298 Notification, registration and penalties

(1) Part 4 of the Finance Act 2003 (c 14) (stamp duty land tax) is amended as follows.

(2) (*amends* FA 2003 s 77)

(3) (*amends* FA 2003 s 79(1))

(4) (*inserts* FA 2003 s 99(2A))

(5) (*amends* heading of FA 2003 Sch 6 Part 4; *inserts* FA 2003 Sch 6 para 13)

299 Claims not included in returns

(1) Part 4 of the Finance Act 2003 (c 14) (stamp duty land tax) is amended as follows.

(2) (*inserts* FA 2003 s 82A)

(3) After Schedule 11 insert the Schedule set out in Schedule 40 to this Act.

(4) (*amends* FA 2003 s 80(4))

(5) (*amends* FA 2003 s 111(1))

(6) (*inserts* FA 2003 s 113(3A))

(7) (*amends* FA 2003 Sch 10 para 33)

(8) (*amends* FA 2003 Sch 10 para 34)

300 Assents and appropriations by personal representatives

(1) (*inserts* FA 2003 Sch 3 para 3A)

(2) The amendment made by this section is deemed always to have had effect.

301 Chargeable consideration

(1) (*inserts* FA 2003 Sch 3 para 4(2A))

(2) Schedule 4 to that Act (stamp duty land tax: chargeable consideration) is amended as follows.

(3), (4) (*amends* FA 2003 Sch 4 para 8)

(5) (*inserts* FA 2003 Sch 4 para 8A)

(6) The amendments made by subsections (3) and (4) apply in relation to any transaction of which the effective date (within the meaning of Part 4 of the Finance Act 2003) is on or after the day on which this act is passed.

(7) The other amendments made by this section are deemed always to have had effect.

302 Charities relief

(1) (*inserts* FA 2003 Sch 8 para 3)

(2) (*inserts* FA 2003 Sch 8 para 4)

(3) (*amends* FA 2003 Sch 8 para 1(1))

(4) (*amends* FA 2003 Sch 8 para 2(1))

(5) (*amends* FA 2003 s 81(4))

(6) (*amends* FA 2003 s 87(4))

(7) This section applies in relation to any transaction of which the effective date (within the meaning of Part 4 of the Finance Act 2003 (c 14)) is on or after the day on which this Act is passed.

303 Shared ownership leases

(1) (*inserts* FA 2003 Sch 9 para 4A)

(2) (*amends* FA 2003 Sch 9 para 5)

(3) (*amends* FA 2003 Sch 19 para 7(2))

(4) Subsections (1) and (2) apply in relation to an acquisition after 17th March 2004.

(5) Subsection (3) is deemed to have come into force on 1st December 2003.

304 Application to certain partnership transactions

Schedule 41 to this Act (which makes provision with respect to the application of stamp duty land tax to certain transactions involving partnerships) has effect.

305 Liability of partners

(*inserts* FA 2003 Sch 15 para 7(1A))

PART 7
DISCLOSURE OF TAX AVOIDANCE SCHEMES

306 Meaning of "notifiable arrangements" and "notifiable proposal"

(1) In this Part "notifiable arrangements" means any arrangements which—

(*a*) fall within any description prescribed by the Treasury by regulations,

(*b*) enable, or might be expected to enable, any person to obtain an advantage in relation to any tax that is so prescribed in relation to arrangements of that description, and

(*c*) are such that the main benefit, or one of the main benefits, that might be expected to arise from the arrangements is the obtaining of that advantage.

(2) In this Part "notifiable proposal" means a proposal for arrangements which, if entered into, would be notifiable arrangements (whether the proposal relates to a particular person or to any person who may seek to take advantage of it).

307 Meaning of "promoter"

(1) For the purposes of this Part a person is a promoter—

(*a*) in relation to a notifiable proposal, if, in the course of a relevant business—

(i) he is to any extent responsible for the design of the proposed arrangements, or

(ii) he makes the notifiable proposal available for implementation by other persons, and

(*b*) in relation to notifiable arrangements, if he is by virtue of paragraph (*a*)(ii) a promoter in relation to a notifiable proposal which is implemented by those arrangements or if, in the course of a relevant business, he is to any extent responsible for—

(i) the design of the arrangements, or

(ii) the organisation or management of the arrangements.

(2) In this section "relevant business" means any trade, profession or business which—

(*a*) involves the provision to other persons of services relating to taxation, or

(*b*) is carried on by a bank, as defined by section 840A of the Taxes Act 1988, or by a securities house, as defined by section 209A(4) of that Act.

(3) For the purposes of this section anything done by a company is to be taken to be done in the course of a relevant business if it is done for the purposes of a relevant business falling within subsection (2)(*b*) carried on by another company which is a member of the same group.

(4) Section 170 of the Taxation of Chargeable Gains Act 1992 has effect for determining for the purposes of subsection (3) whether two companies are members of the same group, but as if in that section—

(*a*) for each of the references to a 75 per cent subsidiary there were substituted a reference to a 51 per cent subsidiary, and

(*b*) subsection (3)(*b*) and subsections (6) to (8) were omitted.

(5) A person is not to be treated as a promoter for the purposes of this Part by reason of anything done in prescribed circumstances.

308 Duties of promoter

(1) The promoter must, within the prescribed period after the relevant date, provide the Board with prescribed information relating to any notifiable proposal.

(2) In subsection (1) "the relevant date" means the earlier of the following—

(*a*) the date on which the promoter makes a notifiable proposal available for implementation by any other person, or

(*b*) the date on which the promoter first becomes aware of any transaction forming part of notifiable arrangements implementing the notifiable proposal.

(3) The promoter must, within the prescribed period after the date on which he first becomes aware of any transaction forming part of any notifiable arrangements, provide the Board with prescribed information relating to those arrangements, unless those arrangements implement a proposal in respect of which notice has been given under subsection (1).

(4) Where two or more persons are promoters in relation to the same notifiable proposal or notifiable arrangements, compliance by any of them with subsection (1) or (3) discharges the duty under either of those subsections of the other or others.

(5) Where a person is a promoter in relation to two or more notifiable proposals or sets of notifiable arrangements which are substantially the same (whether they relate to the same parties or different parties), he need not provide information under subsection (1) or (3) if he has already provided information under either of those subsections in relation to any of the other proposals or arrangements.

Prospective amendments—In sub-s (1), words "A person who is a promoter in relation to a notifiable proposal" to be substituted for words "The promoter", and word "the" to be substituted for word "any"; in sub-s (2)(*a*), word "the" to be substituted for word "a"; in sub-s (3), words "A person who is a promoter in relation to notifiable arrangements" to be substituted for words "The promoter", and words "the notifiable" to be substituted for words "any notifiable"; and sub-s (4) to be substituted; by FA 2008 s 116, Sch 38 paras 1, 2 with effect from 1 November 2008 (by virtue of SI 2008/1935 art 2(1)). However, none of these amendments comes into force for the purposes of stamp duty land tax (SI 2008/1935 art 2(2)). Sub-s (4), as substituted, to read as follows—

"(4) Subsection (4A) applies where a person complies with subsection (1) in relation to a notifiable proposal for arrangements and another person is—

(*a*) also a promoter in relation to the notifiable proposal or is a promoter in relation to a notifiable proposal for arrangements which are substantially the same as the proposed arrangements (whether they relate to the same or different parties), or

(*b*) a promoter in relation to notifiable arrangements implementing the notifiable proposal or notifiable arrangements which are substantially the same as notifiable arrangements implementing the notifiable proposal (whether they relate to the same or different parties).

(4A) Any duty of the other person under subsection (1) or (3) in relation to the notifiable proposal or notifiable arrangements is discharged if—

(*a*) the person who complied with subsection (1) has notified the identity and address of the other person to HMRC or the other person holds the reference number allocated to the proposed notifiable arrangements under section 311, and

(*b*) the other person holds the information provided to HMRC in compliance with subsection (1).

(4B) Subsection (4C) applies where a person complies with subsection (3) in relation to notifiable arrangements and another person is—

(*a*) a promoter in relation to a notifiable proposal for arrangements which are substantially the same as the notifiable arrangements (whether they relate to the same or different parties), or

(*b*) also a promoter in relation to the notifiable arrangements or notifiable arrangements which are substantially the same (whether they relate to the same or different parties).

(4C) Any duty of the other person under subsection (1) or (3) in relation to the notifiable proposal or notifiable arrangements is discharged if—

(*a*) the person who complied with subsection (3) has notified the identity and address of the other person to HMRC or the other person holds the reference number allocated to the notifiable arrangements under section 311, and

(*b*) the other person holds the information provided to HMRC in compliance with subsection (3).".

Stamp Taxes

309 Duty of person dealing with promoter outside United Kingdom

(1) Any person ("the client") who enters into any transaction forming part of any notifiable arrangements in relation to which—

(*a*) a promoter is resident outside the United Kingdom, and
(*b*) no promoter is resident in the United Kingdom,

must, within the prescribed period after doing so, provide the Board with prescribed information relating to the notifiable arrangements.

(2) Compliance with section 308(1) by any promoter in relation to the notifiable arrangements discharges the duty of the client under subsection (1).

310 Duty of parties to notifiable arrangements not involving promoter

Any person who enters into any transaction forming part of notifiable arrangements as respects which neither he nor any other person in the United Kingdom is liable to comply with section 308 (duties of promoter) or section 309 (duty of person dealing with promoter outside the United Kingdom) must at the prescribed time provide the Board with prescribed information relating to the notifiable arrangements.

311 Arrangements to be given reference number

(1) Where a person complies with section 308(1) or (3), 309(1) or 310 in relation to any notifiable proposal or notifiable arrangements, the Board may within 30 days—

(*a*) allocate a reference number to the notifiable arrangements or, in the case of a notifiable proposal, to the proposed notifiable arrangements, and
(*b*) if it does so, notify the person of that number.

(2) The allocation of a reference number to any notifiable arrangements (or proposed notifiable arrangements) is not to be regarded as constituting any indication by the Board that the arrangements could as a matter of law result in the obtaining by any person of a tax advantage.

(3) In this Part "reference number", in relation to any notifiable arrangements, means the reference number allocated under this section.

Prospective amendments—In sub-s (1), words "or purports to comply" to be inserted after word "complies", words "may within 30 days" to be repealed, words "may within 30 days" to be inserted before word "allocate", and words to be substituted for words "notify the person of that number", by FA 2008 s 116, Sch 38 paras 1, 3 with effect from 1 November 2008 (by virtue of SI 2008/1935 art 2(1)). However, none of these amendments comes into force for the purposes of stamp duty land tax (SI 2008/1935 art 2(2)).

Words to be substituted for words "notify the person of that number", to read as follows—

"must notify that number to the person and (where the person is one who has complied or purported to comply with section 308(1) or (3)) to any other person—

(i) who is a promoter in relation to the notifiable proposal (or arrangements implementing the notifiable proposal) or the notifiable arrangements (or proposal implemented by the notifiable arrangements), and
(ii) whose identity and address has been notified to HMRC by the person.".

312 Duty of promoter to notify client of number

(1) Any promoter who is providing services to any person ("the client") in connection with notifiable arrangements must, within 30 days after the relevant date, provide the client with prescribed information relating to any reference number that has been notified to the promoter by the Board—

(*a*) in relation to those arrangements, or

(*b*) in relation to arrangements which are substantially the same as those arrangements (whether made between the same parties or different parties).

(2) In subsection (1) "the relevant date" means—

(*a*) the date on which the promoter first becomes aware of any transaction forming part of the notifiable arrangements, or

(*b*) if later, the date on which the number is notified to the promoter under section 311.

Prospective amendments—Sections 312, 312A to be substituted for this section by FA 2008 s 116, Sch 38 paras 1, 4 with effect from 1 November 2008 (by virtue of SI 2008/1935 art 2(1)). However, none of these amendments comes into force for the purposes of stamp duty land tax (SI 2008/1935 art 2(2)). Those sections, as substituted, to read as follows—

"312 Duty of promoter to notify client of number

(1) This section applies where a person who is a promoter in relation to notifiable arrangements is providing (or has provided) services to any person ("the client") in connection with the notifiable arrangements.

(2) The promoter must, within 30 days after the relevant date, provide the client with prescribed information relating to any reference number (or, if more than one, any one reference number) that has been notified to the promoter (whether by HMRC or any other person) in relation to—

(*a*) the notifiable arrangements, or

(*b*) any arrangements substantially the same as the notifiable arrangements (whether involving the same or different parties).

(3) In subsection (2) "the relevant date" means the later of—

(*a*) the date on which the promoter becomes aware of any transaction which forms part of the notifiable arrangements, and

(*b*) the date on which the reference number is notified to the promoter.

(4) But where the conditions in subsection (5) are met the duty imposed on the promoter under subsection (2) to provide the client with information in relation to notifiable arrangements is discharged.

(5) Those conditions are—

(*a*) that the promoter is also a promoter in relation to a notifiable proposal and provides services to the client in connection with them both,

(*b*) the notifiable proposal and the notifiable arrangements are substantially the same, and

(*c*) the promoter has provided to the client, in a form and manner specified by HMRC, prescribed information relating to the reference number that has been notified to the promoter in relation to the proposed notifiable arrangements.

(6) HMRC may give notice that, in relation to notifiable arrangements specified in the notice, promoters are not under the duty under subsection (2) after the date specified in the notice.

312A Duty of client to notify parties of number

(1) This section applies where a person (a "client") to whom a person who is a promoter in relation to notifiable arrangements or a notifiable proposal is providing (or has provided) services in connection with the notifiable arrangements or notifiable proposal receives prescribed information relating to the reference number allocated to the notifiable arrangements or proposed notifiable arrangements.

(2) The client must, within the prescribed period, provide prescribed information relating to the reference number to any other person—

(*a*) who the client might reasonably be expected to know is or is likely to be a party to the arrangements or proposed arrangements, and

(*b*) who might reasonably be expected to gain a tax advantage in relation to any relevant tax by reason of the arrangements or proposed arrangements.

(3) For the purposes of subsection (1) a tax is a "relevant tax" in relation to arrangements or arrangements proposed in a proposal of any description if it is prescribed in relation to arrangements or proposals of that description by regulations under section 306.

(4) HMRC may give notice that, in relation to notifiable arrangements or a notifiable proposal specified in the notice, persons are not under the duty under subsection (2) after the date specified in the notice.

(5) The duty under subsection (2) does not apply in prescribed circumstances.".

313 Duty of parties to notifiable arrangements to notify Board of number, etc

(1) Any person who is a party to any notifiable arrangements must provide the Board with prescribed information relating to—

(*a*) any reference number notified to him under section 311 by the Board or under section 312 by the promoter, and

(*b*) the time when he obtains or expects to obtain by virtue of the arrangements an advantage in relation to any relevant tax.

(2) For the purposes of subsection (1) a tax is a "relevant tax" in relation to any notifiable arrangements if it is prescribed in relation to arrangements of that description by regulations under section 306.

(3) Regulations under subsection (1) may—

(*a*) in prescribed cases, require the number and other information to be included in any return or account which the person is required by or under any enactment to deliver to the Board, and

(*b*) in prescribed cases, require the number and other information to be provided separately to the Board at the prescribed time or times.

(4) A person is not liable to a penalty under—

(*a*) section 95 of the Taxes Management Act 1970 (c 9) (incorrect return or accounts for income tax or capital gains tax),

(*b*) paragraph 8 of Schedule 2 to the Oil Taxation Act 1975 (c 22) (incorrect returns and accounts for purposes of petroleum revenue tax),

(*c*) section 247 of the Inheritance Tax Act 1984 (c 51) (provision of incorrect information for purposes of inheritance tax),

(*d*) any provision relating to incorrect or uncorrected returns made under section 98 of the Finance Act 1986 (c 41) (administration of stamp duty reserve tax),
(*e*) paragraph 20 of Schedule 18 to the Finance Act 1998 (c 36) (incorrect or uncorrected return for corporation tax),
(*f*) paragraph 8 of Schedule 10 to the Finance Act 2003 (incorrect or uncorrected return for purposes of stamp duty land tax), or
(*g*) any other prescribed provision,

by reason of any failure to include in any return or account any reference number or other information required by virtue of subsection (3)(*a*) (but see section 98C of the Taxes Management Act 1970 for the penalty for failure to comply with this section).

Prospective amendments—In sub-s (1)(*a*), words "under section 311 by the Board or under section 312 by the promoter" to be repealed; in sub-s (3), words "made by HMRC" to be substituted for words "under subsection (1)", in para (*a*), words "information prescribed under subsection (1)", to be substituted for words "number and other information", and in para (*b*), words "information prescribed under subsection (1) and such other information as is prescribed" to be substituted for words "number and other information"; and new sub-s (5) to be inserted; by FA 2008 s 116, Sch 38 paras 1, 5 with effect from 1 November 2008 (by virtue of SI 2008/1935 art 2(1)). However, none of these amendments comes into force for the purposes of stamp duty land tax (SI 2008/1935 art 2(2)).
Sub-s (5), as substituted, to read as follows—

"(5) HMRC may give notice that, in relation to notifiable arrangements specified in the notice, persons are not under the duty under subsection (1) after the date specified in the notice.".

314 Legal professional privilege

(1) Nothing in this Part requires any person to disclose to the Board any privileged information.

(2) In this Part "privileged information" means information with respect to which a claim to legal professional privilege, or, in Scotland, to confidentiality of communications, could be maintained in legal proceedings.

315 Penalties

(1) (*inserts* TMA 1970 s 98C)

(2) (*amends* TMA 1970 s 100(2))

(3) (*inserts* TMA 1970 s 100C(1A))

316 Information to be provided in form and manner specified by Board

The information required by section 308(1) or (3), 309(1), 310, 312(1) or 313(1) must be provided in a form and manner specified by the Board.

Prospective amendments—This section to be substituted by FA 2008 s 116, Sch 38 paras 1, 6 with effect from 1 November 2008 (by virtue of SI 2008/1935 art 2(1)). However, this amendment does not come into force for the purposes of stamp duty land tax (SI 2008/1935 art 2(2)). This section, as substituted, to read as follows—

"316 Information to be provided in form and manner specified by HMRC

(1) HMRC may specify the form and manner in which information required to be provided by any of the information provisions must be provided if the provision is to be complied with.

(2) The "information provisions" are sections 308(1) and (3), 309(1), 310, 312(2), 312A(2) and 313(1) and (3).".

317 Regulations under Part 7

(1) Any power of the Treasury or the Board to make regulations under this Part is exercisable by statutory instrument.

(2) Regulations made by the Treasury or the Board under this Part may contain transitional provisions and savings.

(3) A statutory instrument containing regulations made by the Treasury or the Board under any provision of this Part is subject to annulment in pursuance of a resolution of the House of Commons.

318 Interpretation of Part 7

(1) In this Part—

"advantage", in relation to any tax, means—
(*a*) relief or increased relief from, or repayment or increased repayment of, that tax, or the avoidance or reduction of a charge to that tax or an assessment to that tax or the avoidance of a possible assessment to that tax,
(*b*) the deferral of any payment of tax or the advancement of any repayment of tax, or
(*c*) the avoidance of any obligation to deduct or account for any tax;

"arrangements" includes any scheme, transaction or series of transactions;
"corporation tax" includes any amount which, by virtue of any of the provisions mentioned in paragraph 1 of Schedule 18 to the Finance Act 1998 (c 36) (company tax returns, assessments and related matters) is assessable and chargeable as if it were corporation tax;
"notifiable arrangements" has the meaning given by section 306(1);
"notifiable proposal" has the meaning given by section 306(2);
"prescribed", except in section 306, means prescribed by regulations made by the Board;
"promoter", in relation to notifiable arrangements or a notifiable proposal, has the meaning given by section 307;

Stamp Taxes

"reference number", in relation to notifiable arrangements, has the meaning given by section 311(3);

"tax" means—

(*a*) income tax,
(*b*) capital gains tax,
(*c*) corporation tax,
(*d*) petroleum revenue tax,
(*e*) inheritance tax,
(*f*) stamp duty land tax, or
(*g*) stamp duty reserve tax.

(2) Subject to subsection (1), expressions which are defined in the Taxes Act 1988 for the purposes of the Tax Acts, as defined in section 831(2) of that Act, have the same meaning in this Part.

319 Part 7: commencement and savings

(1) The following provisions of this Part come into force on the passing of this Act—

sections 306 to 315, so far as is necessary for enabling the making of any regulations for which they provide, and

sections 317 and 318 and this section.

(2) Except as provided by subsection (1), the provisions of this Part come into force on 1st August 2004.

(3) Section 308 does not apply to a promoter in the case of—

(*a*) any notifiable proposal as respects which the relevant date, as defined by subsection (2) of that section, fell before 18th March 2004,

(*b*) any notifiable arrangements which implement such a proposal, or

(*c*) any notifiable arrangements which include any transaction entered into before 18th March 2004.

(4) Sections 309 and 310 do not apply in relation to notifiable arrangements which include any transaction entered into before 23rd April 2004.

(5) Section 313 does not apply in relation to any notifiable arrangements in respect of which, by virtue of subsection (3) or (4), none of the duties imposed by sections 308 to 310 arises.

PART 9
SUPPLEMENTARY PROVISIONS

326 Repeals

(1) The enactments mentioned in Schedule 42 to this Act (which include provisions that are spent or of no practical utility) are repealed to the extent specified.

(2) The repeals specified in that Schedule have effect subject to the commencement provisions and savings contained or referred to in the notes set out in that Schedule.

327 Interpretation

In this Act "the Taxes Act 1988" means the Income and Corporation Taxes Act 1988 (c 1).

328 Short title

This Act may be cited as the Finance Act 2004.

SCHEDULES

SCHEDULE 39
STAMP DUTY LAND TAX AND STAMP DUTY

Section 296

PART 1
AMENDMENTS TO PART 4 OF THE FINANCE ACT 2003: GENERAL

Introduction

1 Part 4 of the Finance Act 2003 (c 14) (stamp duty land tax) is amended in accordance with this Part of this Schedule.

Variation of lease

2 (*amends* FA 2003 s 43(3))

Agreement for lease

3 (*inserts* FA 2003 s 44(9A))

Contract providing for conveyance to third party

4— (1) (*inserts* FA 2003 s 44A)

(2) (*inserts* FA 2003 s 48(7))

(3) (*inserts* FA 2003 s 77(5))

Contract and conveyance: effect of transfer of rights

5— (1)–(4) (*amends* FA 2003 s 45)

(5) (*inserts* FA 2003 s 45A)

(6) (*amends* FA 2003 s 122)

Relief for sale and leaseback arrangements

6 …

Amendment—This paragraph repealed by FA 2004 s 326, Sch 42 Pt 4(2) with effect in accordance with FA 2004 Sch 39 para 26.

Registration of land transactions

7 (*amends* FA 2003 s 79(2))

"Effective date" of a transaction

8 (*amends* FA 2003 s 119(2))

Chargeable consideration

9— (1) Schedule 4 (chargeable consideration) is amended as follows.

(2) (*inserts* FA 2003 Sch 4 para 10(2A))

(3) (*inserts* FA 2003 Sch 4 para 17(4A))

Provisions relating to leases

10 (*inserts* FA 2003 Sch 5 para 1A)

11 …

Amendment—This paragraph repealed by FA 2004 s 326, Sch 42 Pt 4(2) with effect in accordance with FA 2004 Sch 39 para 26.

Transfer of rights after 10th July 2003 relating to earlier contract: applicability of SDLT regime

12 (*amends* FA 2003 Sch 19 para 3(3))

Commencement

13— (1) Paragraph 4, and paragraphs 7 and 8 so far as relating to the section 44A inserted by that paragraph, apply in relation to any contract entered into after 17th March 2004.

(2) Paragraph 5, and paragraphs 7 and 8 so far as relating to the section 45A inserted by that paragraph, apply in relation to any transfer of rights occurring after that date.

(3) Subject to sub-paragraphs (4) and (5), the amendments made by the other provisions of this Part of this Schedule apply in relation to any transaction of which the effective date is after 17th March 2004.

(4) Paragraph 12 does not apply in relation to a contract that was substantially performed before 17th March 2004.

(5) Paragraphs 6 and 11 (which contain amendments the effect of which is reproduced in Part 2 of this Schedule) do not apply in relation to any transaction of which the effective date is on or after the day on which this Act is passed.

(6) In this paragraph—

"effective date" and "substantially performed" have the same meaning as in Part 4 of the Finance Act 2003 (as amended by this Part of this Schedule);

"transfer of rights" has the same meaning as in section 45 of that Act or, as the case may require, section 45A of that Act (inserted by paragraph 5(5)).

PART 2
RE-ENACTMENT, WITH CHANGES, OF AMENDMENTS MADE BY SECTION 109 REGULATIONS

Introduction and revocation

14— (1) This Part of this Schedule contains amendments to Parts 4 and 5 of the Finance Act 2003 (c 14) (stamp duty land tax and stamp duty) corresponding, subject to certain changes, to those made by the Stamp Duty and Stamp Duty Land Tax (Variation of the Finance Act 2003) (No. 2) Regulations 2003 (SI 2003/2816) (made under section 109 of that Act).

(2) Those regulations are revoked.

Meaning of taking possession

15— (1)–(4) (*amends* FA 2003 s 44)

Relief for sale and leaseback arrangements

16 (*inserts* FA 2003 s 57A)

Relief for certain acquisitions of residential property

17— (1) (*substitutes* FA 2003 s 58A for FA 2003 ss 58, 59)

(2) (*inserts* FA 2003 Sch 6A)

(3) (*amends* FA 2003 s 81(1), (4))

(4) (*amends* FA 2003 s 87(3), (4))

Initial transfer of assets to trustees of unit trust scheme

18 (*inserted* FA 2003 s 64A and *repealed by* FA 2006 s 178, Sch 26 Pt 7(3).)

Return or further return in consequence of later linked transaction

19— (1) (*inserts* FA 2003 s 81A)

(2) (*amends* FA 2003 s 81(3))

(3) (*amends* FA 2003 s 87(3))

Declaration by person authorised to act on behalf of purchaser

20 (*inserts* FA 2003 s 81B)

Crown application

21— (1)–(3) (*amends* FA 2003 s 107)

Further provision relating to leases

22— (1) (*substitutes* FA 2003 s 120)

(2) (*inserts* FA 2003 Sch 17A)

(3) (*inserts* FA 2003 s 51(5))

(4) (*amends* FA 2003 s 80)

(5) (*amends* FA 2003 s 87(3))

(6) (*inserts* FA 2003 s 90(7))

(7) (*amends* table in FA 2003 s 122)

(8) (*inserts* FA 2003 Sch 19 para 7(4))

Abolition of stamp duty: application to duplicates and counterparts

23 (*amends* FA 2003 s 125(5))

Application of transitional provisions to certain contracts

24 (*inserts* FA 2003 Sch 19 paras 4A, 4B)

Stamping of contract or agreement where transaction on completion or grant of lease subject to stamp duty land tax

25— (1) (*inserts* FA 2003 Sch 19 para 7A)

(2) (*amends* FA 2003 Sch 19 para 8)

(4) (*amends* FA 2003 s 122)

Commencement

26 This Part of this Schedule applies in relation to any transaction of which the effective date (within the meaning of Part 4 of the Finance Act 2003) is on or after the day on which this Act is passed.

SCHEDULE 40

STAMP DUTY LAND TAX: CLAIMS NOT INCLUDED IN RETURNS

Section 299

(*inserts* FA 2003 Sch 11A)

SCHEDULE 41

STAMP DUTY LAND TAX: APPLICATION TO CERTAIN PARTNERSHIP TRANSACTIONS

Section 304

1 (*substitutes* FA 2003 Sch 15 Pt 3)

2 (*amends* FA 2003 ss 104(2), 125(8), Sch 15 para 5)

3— (1) The preceding provisions of this Schedule have effect in relation to any partnership transaction of which the effective date (within the meaning of Part 4 of the Finance Act 2003 (c 14)) is after the day on which this Act is passed.

(2) "Partnership transaction" means a transaction mentioned in paragraph 9(1) of Schedule 15 to the Finance Act 2003 (as substituted by paragraph 1 of this Schedule).

SCHEDULE 42

REPEALS

Section 326

PART 4

OTHER TAXES

(2) Stamp Duty Land Tax

Note—As the repeals are already in force, this table has been omitted.

FINANCE ACT 2005

(2005 Chapter 7)

An Act to Grant certain duties, to alter other duties, and to amend the law relating to the National Debt and the Public Revenue, and to make further provision in connection with finance.

[7 April 2005]

PART 3

STAMP TAXES

Stamp duty land tax

94 Alternative property finance

Schedule 8 (which makes amendments of Part 4 of FA 2003 relating to alternative property finance) has effect.

Stamp duty land tax and stamp duty

95 Raising of thresholds

. . .[1]

Amendments—[1] Section 95 repealed by FA 2006 s 178, Sch 26 Pt 7(1) in relation to any transaction of which the effective date (within the meaning of Part 4 of FA 2003) is after 22 March 2006 and to instruments executed after 22 March 2006, by virtue of FA 2006 s 162(4), (5).

96 Removal of disadvantaged areas relief for non-residential property

Schedule 9 (which provides for the removal, in relation to non-residential property, of relief from stamp duty land tax and stamp duty for land in disadvantaged areas) has effect.

Stamp duty and stamp duty reserve tax

97 Demutualisation of insurance companies

(1) Section 90 of FA 1986 (other exceptions to the principal charge to stamp duty reserve tax under section 87 of that Act) is amended as follows.

(2) (*amends* FA 1986 s 90(1A)).

(3) Schedule 19 to FA 1999 (stamp duty and stamp duty reserve tax: unit trusts) is amended as follows.

(4) (*amends* FA 1986 Sch 19 para 6(5)).

(5) The amendment in subsection (2) applies where the relevant day for the purposes of section 87 of FA 1986 falls on or after the day on which this Act is passed.

(6) The amendment in subsection (4) applies in relation to surrenders (within the meaning of Part 2 of Schedule 19 to FA 1999) occurring on or after the day on which this Act is passed.

PART 7
SUPPLEMENTARY PROVISIONS

104 Repeals

(1) The enactments mentioned in Schedule 11 (which include provisions that are spent or of no practical utility) are repealed to the extent specified.

(2) The repeals specified in that Schedule have effect subject to the commencement provisions and savings contained or referred to in the notes set out in that Schedule.

105 Interpretation

In this Act—

"ALDA 1979" means the Alcoholic Liquor Duties Act 1979 (c 4);
"CAA 2001" means the Capital Allowances Act 2001 (c 2);
"FA", followed by a year, means the Finance Act of that year;
"F(No 2)A", followed by a year, means the Finance (No 2) Act of that year;
"HODA 1979" means the Hydrocarbon Oil Duties Act 1979 (c 5);
"ICTA" means the Income and Corporation Taxes Act 1988 (c 1);
"IHTA 1984" means the Inheritance Tax Act 1984 (c 51);
"ITEPA 2003" means the Income Tax (Earnings and Pensions) Act 2003 (c 1);
"ITTOIA 2005" means the Income Tax (Trading and Other Income) Act 2005 (c 5);
"TCGA 1992" means the Taxation of Chargeable Gains Act 1992 (c 12);
"TMA 1970" means the Taxes Management Act 1970 (c 9);
"VERA 1994" means the Vehicle Excise and Registration Act 1994 (c 22).

106 Short title

This Act may be cited as the Finance Act 2005.

SCHEDULES

SCHEDULE 8
STAMP DUTY LAND TAX: ALTERNATIVE PROPERTY FINANCE

Section 94

Introduction

1 Part 4 of FA 2003 is amended in accordance with this Schedule.

Alternative property finance: England and Wales and Northern Ireland

2 (*inserts* FA 2003 s 71A).

Alternative property finance: Scotland

3— (1) Section 72 (alternative property finance: land sold to financial institution and leased to individual) is amended as follows.

(2) (*amends* FA 2003 s 72(1)).

(3) (*substitutes* FA 2003 s 72(7)).

(4) (*repeals* FA 2003 s 72(8)).

(5) (*inserts* FA 2003 s 72(10)).

(6) (*amends* heading to FA 2003 s 72).

4 (*inserts* FA 2003 s 72A).

Consequential amendments

5— (1) Section 73 (alternative property finance: land sold to individual and re-sold to individual) is amended as follows.

(2) (*amends* FA 2003 s 73(2)(*b*)).

(3) (*amends* FA 2003 s 73(5)(*a*)).

6 (*amends* FA 2003 s 122).

Commencement

7— (1) Paragraphs 2 and 3, and paragraphs 5 and 6 so far as relating to section 71A of FA 2003, have effect in any case where the effective date of the first transaction, within the meaning of section 71A of FA 2003 (as inserted by paragraph 2), falls on or after the day on which this Act is passed.

(2) Paragraph 4, and paragraphs 5 and 6 so far as relating to section 72A of FA 2003, have effect in any case where the effective date of the first transaction, within the meaning of section 72A of FA 2003 (as inserted by paragraph 4), falls on or after the day on which this Act is passed.

(3) In this paragraph "the effective date" has the same meaning as in Part 4 of FA 2003.

SCHEDULE 9

STAMP DUTY LAND TAX AND STAMP DUTY: REMOVAL OF DISADVANTAGED AREAS RELIEF FOR NON-RESIDENTIAL PROPERTY

Section 96

Stamp duty land tax

1— (1) Schedule 6 to FA 2003 (disadvantaged areas relief) is amended as follows.

(2) (*amends* FA 2003 Sch 6 para 3).

(3) (*repeals* FA 2003 Sch 6 para 4).

(4) (*amends* FA 2003 Sch 6 para 6).

(5) (*amends* FA 2003 Sch 6 para 7).

(6) (*repeals* FA 2003 Sch 6 para 8).

(7) (*amends* FA 2003 Sch 6 para 10).

Stamp duty

2— (1) The Stamp Duty (Disadvantaged Areas) (Application of Exemptions) Regulations 2003 (SI 2003/1056) are amended as follows.

(2) (*inserts* SI 2003/1056 reg 2A).

(3) (*inserts* SI 2003/1056 reg 5(3A)).

3 The insertion by paragraph 2 of provisions into the Stamp Duty (Disadvantaged Areas) (Application of Exemptions) Regulations 2003 is without prejudice to the power to amend or revoke those provisions by further regulations under section 92A of FA 2001.

Commencement and transitional provisions

4— (1) Subject to sub-paragraph (2), paragraph 1 applies in relation to any transaction of which the effective date is after 16th March 2005.

(2) That paragraph does not apply—

(*a*) in relation to any transaction that is effected in pursuance of a contract entered into and substantially performed on or before 16th March 2005, or

(*b*) (subject to sub-paragraph (3)) in relation to any other transaction that is effected in pursuance of a contract entered into on or before that date.

(3) The exclusion by sub-paragraph (2)(*b*) of transactions effected in pursuance of contracts entered into on or before 16th March 2005 does not apply—

(*a*) if there is any variation of the contract or assignment of rights under the contract after that date,

(*b*) if the transaction is effected in consequence of the exercise after that date of any option, right of pre-emption or similar right, or

(*c*) if after that date there is an assignment, subsale or other transaction (relating to the whole or part of the subject-matter of the contract) as a result of which a person other than the purchaser under the contract becomes entitled to call for a conveyance to him.

(4) In this paragraph "effective date" and "substantially performed" have the same meaning as in Part 4 of FA 2003.

5— (1) Subject to sub-paragraph (2), paragraph 2 applies in relation to instruments executed after 16th March 2005.

(2) That paragraph does not apply in relation to an instrument giving effect to a contract entered into on or before 16th March 2005, unless—

(*a*) the instrument is made in consequence of the exercise after that date of any option, right of pre-emption or similar right, or

(*b*) the instrument transfers the property in question to, or vests it in, a person other than the purchaser under the contract, because of an assignment (or, in Scotland, assignation) or further contract made after that date.

SCHEDULE 11

REPEALS

Section 104

PART 3

STAMP TAXES

(1) Stamp Duty Land Tax: Alternative Property Finance

Short title and chapter	*Extent of repeal*
Finance Act 2003 (c 14)	In section 72, in subsection (1)(*c*) the words "or its successor in title", and subsection (8).

These repeals have effect in accordance with paragraph 7(1) of Schedule 8 to this Act.

(2) Stamp Duty Land Tax: Disadvantaged Areas Relief

Short title and chapter	*Extent of repeal*
Finance Act 2003 (c 14)	In Schedule 6— (*a*) paragraph 4; (*b*) in the second sentence of paragraph 6(1), the words "land that is non-residential property or"; (*c*) paragraphs 6(2) and 6(3); (*d*) paragraph 8; (*e*) in the second sentence of paragraph 10(1), the words "land that is non-residential property or"; (*f*) paragraphs 10(2) and 10(3).

These repeals have effect in accordance with paragraph 4 of Schedule 9 to this Act.

COMMISSIONERS FOR REVENUE AND CUSTOMS ACT 2005

(2005 Chapter 11)

An Act to make provision for the appointment of Commissioners to exercise functions presently vested in the Commissioners of Inland Revenue and the Commissioners of Customs and Excise; for the establishment of a Revenue and Customs Prosecutions Office; and for connected purposes.

[7 April 2005]

Note—Please see VAT statutes for the text of this Act.

Regulations—See the Revenue and Customs (Inspections) Regulations, SI 2005/1133 (reproduced in the VAT statutory instruments section).

FINANCE (NO 2) ACT 2005

(2005 Chapter 22)

ARRANGEMENT OF SECTIONS

PART 3

STAMP TAXES

Stamp duty land tax

An Act to Grant certain duties, to alter other duties, and to amend the law relating to the National Debt and the Public Revenue, and to make further provision in connection with finance.

[20 July 2005]

PART 3
STAMP TAXES

Stamp duty land tax

47 E-conveyancing

(1) (*amends* Public Finance and Accountability (Scotland) Act 2000 s 9(1)).

(2) (*amends* FA 2003 s 79(1)).

(3) (*substitutes* FA 2003 s 119(1)(*a*), (*b*)).

(4) (*inserts* FA 2003 Sch 10 para 7(1A)).

(5) The Commissioners for Her Majesty's Revenue and Customs—

(*a*) may make regulations conferring administrative functions on a land registrar in connection with stamp duty land tax, and

(*b*) may make payments to land registrars in respect of the exercise of those functions.

(6) In subsection (5) "land registrar" means—

(*a*) in relation to England and Wales, the Chief Land Registrar,

(*b*) in relation to Scotland, the Keeper of the Registers of Scotland,

(*c*) in relation to Northern Ireland, the Registrar of Titles or the registrar of deeds, and

(*d*) in any case, such other persons with functions relating to the registration of land as regulations under subsection (5) may specify.

(7) Regulations under subsection (5)—

(*a*) shall be made by statutory instrument, and

(*b*) shall be subject to annulment in pursuance of a resolution of the House of Commons.

48 Disclosure of information contained in land transaction returns

(1) (*inserts* FA 2003 s 78A).

(2) (*substitutes* FA 1994 s 245(2)).

(3) (*substitutes* heading to FA 1994 Part 6).

(4) (*revokes* Stamp Duty Land Tax (Consequential Amendment of Enactments) Regulations, SI 2005/82, reg 3).

(5) Subsections (1) to (4) come into force on such day as the Treasury may by order appoint.

(6) Section 114(3) of FA 2003 (negative resolution procedure) does not apply to an order made under subsection (5).

49 Miscellaneous amendments

Schedule 10 (which makes miscellaneous amendments of Part 4 of FA 2003) has effect.

Stamp duty and stamp duty reserve tax

50 Power to extend exceptions relating to recognised exchanges

(1) The Treasury may by regulations extend the application of the provisions mentioned in subsection (2) to any market (specified by name or by description) which—

(a) is not a recognised exchange, but

(b) is a multilateral trading facility (or, assuming compliance with the provisions of Title II of the Directive (authorisation and operating conditions), would be such a facility).

(2) The provisions referred to in subsection (1) are—

(a) sections 80A and 80C of FA 1986 (stamp duty: exceptions for sales to intermediaries and for repurchases and stock lending), and

(b) sections 88A and 89AA of that Act (stamp duty reserve tax: exceptions for intermediaries and for repurchases and stock lending).

(3) In this section—

"the Directive" means Directive 2004/39/EC of the European Parliament and of the Council of 21 April 2004 on markets in financial instruments;

"multilateral trading facility" has the same meaning as in the Directive (see Article 4(15));

"recognised exchange" means any of the following—

(a) an EEA exchange,

(b) a recognised foreign exchange,

(c) a recognised foreign options exchange,

within the meaning of the provisions mentioned in subsection (2).

(4) Regulations under this section may provide for the application of the provisions mentioned in subsection (2) subject to any adaptations appearing to the Treasury to be necessary or expedient.

(5) In subsection (1)(b) the words "(or, assuming compliance with the provisions of Title II of the Directive (authorisation and operating conditions), would be such a facility)" shall cease to have effect on such day as the Treasury may by order appoint.

(6) Section 117 of FA 2002 (power to extend the exceptions in subsection (2) to any market prescribed by order under section 118(3) of the Financial Services and Markets Act 2000) shall cease to have effect on such day as the Treasury may by order appoint.

(7) The power to make regulations or an order under this section is exercisable by statutory instrument.

(8) A statutory instrument containing—

(a) regulations under this section, or

(b) an order under subsection (5),

shall be subject to annulment in pursuance of a resolution of the House of Commons.

Regulations—Stamp Duty and Stamp Duty Reserve Tax (Extension of Exceptions relating to Recognised Exchanges) Regulations, SI 2005/1990; Stamp Duty and Stamp Duty Reserve Tax (Extension of Exceptions relating to Recognised Exchanges) Regulations, SI 2006/139.

Amendment—This section repealed by FA 2007 ss 73, 114, Sch 21 para 8, Sch 27 Pt 4(2) with effect from 1 November 2007.

PART 4
EUROPEAN COMPANY STATUTE

57 Stamp duty reserve tax

(1) (*amends* FA 1986 s 99(4)).

(2) Subsection (1) shall have effect for the purposes of determining, in relation to anything occurring on or after 1st April 2005, whether securities (whenever issued or raised) are chargeable securities for the purposes of Part IV of FA 1986.

58 Bearer instruments: stamp duty and stamp duty reserve tax

(1) (*amends* FA 1986 s 90(3C)(*a*)).

(2) (*amends* FA 1986 s 90(3E)(*a*)).

(3) (*amends* FA 1999 Sch 15 para 11).

(4) This section shall have effect for the purposes of determining whether or not stamp duty or stamp duty reserve tax is chargeable in respect of anything done on or after 1st April 2005.

PART 6
SUPPLEMENTARY PROVISIONS

70 Repeals
(1) The enactments mentioned in Schedule 11 (which include provisions that are spent or of no practical utility) are repealed to the extent specified.
(2) The repeals specified in that Schedule have effect subject to the commencement provisions and savings contained or referred to in the notes set out in that Schedule.

71 Interpretation
In this Act—
"CAA 2001" means the Capital Allowances Act 2001 (c 2);
"FA", followed by a year, means the Finance Act of that year;
"ICTA" means the Income and Corporation Taxes Act 1988 (c 1);
"ITEPA 2003" means the Income Tax (Earnings and Pensions) Act 2003 (c 1);
"ITTOIA 2005" means the Income Tax (Trading and Other Income) Act 2005 (c 5);
"TCGA 1992" means the Taxation of Chargeable Gains Act 1992 (c 12);
"VATA 1994" means the Value Added Tax Act 1994 (c 23);
"VERA 1994" means the Vehicle Excise and Registration Act 1994 (c 22).

72 Short title
This Act may be cited as the Finance (No 2) Act 2005.

SCHEDULES

SCHEDULE 10
STAMP DUTY LAND TAX: MISCELLANEOUS AMENDMENTS

Section 49

PART 1
AMENDMENTS COMING INTO FORCE IN ACCORDANCE WITH PARAGRAPH 16

Introduction

1 Part 4 of FA 2003 (stamp duty land tax) is amended in accordance with this Part of this Schedule.

Transfer of rights: exclusion of transaction to which alternative finance provisions apply

2 (*amends* FA 2003 s 45(3)).

Group relief

3 (*amends* FA 2003 Sch 7 para 1(7)).
4 (*amends* FA 2003 Sch 7 para 3).
5 (*amends* FA 2003 Sch 7 para 4).
6 (*inserts* FA 2003 Sch 7 para 4A).
7 (*amends* FA 2003 Sch 17A para 11(5)(*a*)).

Reconstruction and acquisition reliefs

8 (*amends* FA 2003 Sch 7 para 8).
9 (*substitutes* Sch 7 para 9(2)).

Withdrawal of money etc from partnership after transfer of chargeable interest

10 (*inserts* FA 2003 Sch 15 para 17A).

Grant of lease to bare trustee

11 (*substitutes* FA 2003 Sch 16 para 3).
12 (*substitutes* FA 2003 Sch 17A para 11(1)).

Variation of lease

13 (*amends* FA 2003 Sch 17A para 15A).

Loan or deposit in connection with grant or assignment of lease

14 (*inserts* FA 2003 Sch 17A para 18A).

Stamp Taxes

15 (*inserts* FA 2003 s 80(4A)).

Commencement

16— (1) Subject to sub-paragraph (7), paragraphs 3 to 7 have effect where the effective date of the relevant transaction (within the meaning of paragraph 3 or 4A of Schedule 7 to FA 2003) is after 19th May 2005.

(2) Subject to sub-paragraph (7), paragraph 9 has effect where the effective date of the relevant transaction (within the meaning of paragraph 9 of Schedule 7 to FA 2003) is after 19th May 2005.

(3) Subject to sub-paragraph (7), paragraph 10 has effect where the effective date of the transaction transferring the chargeable interest to the partnership is after 19th May 2005.

(4) Subject to sub-paragraph (7), paragraphs 11 and 12 have effect where the effective date of the land transaction consisting of the grant of the lease is after 19th May 2005.

(5) Subject to sub-paragraph (7), the amendments made by the other provisions of this Part of this Schedule have effect in relation to any transaction of which the effective date is after 19th May 2005.

(6) In sub-paragraphs (7) and (8) "the specified date" means—

(*a*) in relation to the amendments made by paragraphs 4(*a*) and 9, 19th May 2005, and

(*b*) in relation to the amendments made by the other provisions of this Part of this Schedule, 16th March 2005.

(7) The amendments made by this Part of this Schedule do not have effect—

(*a*) in relation to any transaction which is effected in pursuance of a contract entered into and substantially performed on or before the specified date, or

(*b*) subject to sub-paragraph (8), in relation to any other transaction which is effected in pursuance of a contract entered into on or before the specified date.

(8) The exclusion by sub-paragraph (7)(*b*) of transactions effected in pursuance of contracts entered into on or before the specified date does not apply—

(*a*) if there is any variation of the contract or assignment of rights under the contract after that date,

(*b*) if the transaction is effected in consequence of the exercise after that date of any option, right of pre-emption or similar right, or

(*c*) if after that date there is an assignment, subsale or other transaction (relating to the whole or part of the subject-matter of the contract) as a result of which a person other than the purchaser under the contract becomes entitled to call for a conveyance to him.

(9) In this paragraph "assignment", "effective date" and "substantially performed" have the same meaning as in Part 4 of FA 2003.

PART 2

AMENDMENTS COMING INTO FORCE IN ACCORDANCE WITH PARAGRAPH 22

Introduction

17 Part 4 of FA 2003 (stamp duty land tax) is amended in accordance with this Part of this Schedule.

Transfers involving public bodies

18 (*inserts* FA 2003 s 66(6)).

Group relief: avoidance arrangements

19 (*inserts* FA 2003 Sch 7 para 2(4A)).

Acquisition relief: avoidance arrangements

20 (*substitutes* FA 2003 Sch 7 para 8(5), and *inserts* para 8(5B), (5C)).

Stamp duty on transfers of partnership interests

21— (1) In Schedule 15 (stamp duty land tax: partnerships), paragraph 33 (which relates to stamp duty on transfers of partnership interests) is amended as follows.

(2) (*substitutes* FA 2003 Sch 15 para 33(1), (1A)).

(3) (*amends* FA 2003 Sch 15 para 33(3)).

(4) (*inserts* FA 2003 Sch 15 para 33(3A)).

(5) (*repeals* FA 2003 Sch 15 para 33(4)).

(6) (*amends* FA 2003 Sch 15 para 33(5)).

Commencement

22— (1) Subject to sub-paragraph (2), paragraphs 18 to 20 have effect in relation to any transaction of which the effective date is on or after the day on which this Act is passed.

(2) Paragraphs 19 and 20 do not have effect—

(*a*) in relation to any transaction which is effected in pursuance of a contract entered into and substantially performed on or before 16th March 2005, or

(*b*) (subject to sub-paragraph (3)) in relation to any other transaction which is effected in pursuance of a contract entered into on or before that date.

(3) The exclusion by sub-paragraph (2)(*b*) of transactions effected in pursuance of contracts entered into on or before 16th March 2005 does not apply—

(*a*) if there is any variation of the contract or assignment of rights under the contract after that date,

(*b*) if the transaction is effected in consequence of the exercise after that date of any option, right of pre-emption or similar right, or

(*c*) if after that date there is an assignment, subsale or other transaction (relating to the whole or part of the subject-matter of the contract) as a result of which a person other than the purchaser under the contract becomes entitled to call for a conveyance to him.

(4) Paragraph 21 has effect in relation to any instrument executed on or after the day on which this Act is passed.

(5) In this paragraph "assignment", "effective date" and "substantially performed" have the same meaning as in Part 4 of FA 2003.

SCHEDULE 11

REPEALS

Section 70

PART 3

STAMP TAXES

(1) Stamp Duty Land Tax: Miscellaneous

Short title and chapter	*Extent of repeal*
Finance Act 2003 (c 14)	In Schedule 15, paragraph 33(4).

This repeal has effect in relation to any instrument executed on or after the day on which this Act is passed.

(2) Stamp Duty and Stamp Duty Reserve Tax: Extension of Exceptions

Short title and chapter	*Extent of repeal*
Finance Act 2002 (c 23)	Section 117.

This repeal has effect in accordance with section 50 of this Act.

FINANCE ACT 2006

(2006 Chapter 25)

ARRANGEMENT OF SECTIONS

PART 8

STAMP TAXES

Stamp duty and stamp duty land tax: thresholds

Stamp duty land tax

An Act to Grant certain duties, to alter other duties, and to amend the law relating to the National Debt and the Public Revenue, and to make further provision in connection with finance.

[19 July 2006]

PART 8
STAMP TAXES

Stamp duty and stamp duty land tax: thresholds

162 Raising of thresholds

(1) (*amends* FA 2003 s 55 Table A)

(2) (*amends* FA 2003 Sch 5 para 2(3) Table A)

(3) (*amends* FA 1999 Sch 13 para 4)

(4) The amendments made by subsections (1) and (2) have effect in relation to any transaction of which the effective date (within the meaning of Part 4 of FA 2003) is after 22nd March 2006.

(5) The amendment made by subsection (3) has effect in relation to instruments executed after 22nd March 2006.

Stamp duty land tax

163 Partnerships

Schedule 24 (amendments of Schedule 15 to FA 2003) has effect.

164 Leases

(1) (*substitutes* FA 2003 s 77(2A))

(2) (*amends* FA 2003 Sch 5 para 3)

(3) Subsection (1) has effect in relation to any assignment of which the effective date (within the meaning of Part 4 of FA 2003) is on or after the day on which this Act is passed.

(4) Subsection (2) has effect in relation to any lease granted or treated as granted on or after that day.

(5) Schedule 25 (amendments of Schedule 17A to FA 2003) has effect.

165 Reallocation of trust property as between beneficiaries

(1) (*inserts* FA 2003 Sch 16 para 8)

(2) Subsection (1) has effect in relation to any acquisition of which the effective date (within the meaning of Part 4 of FA 2003) is on or after the day on which this Act is passed.

166 Unit trust schemes

(1) Part 4 of FA 2003 (stamp duty land tax) is amended as follows.

(2) (*repeals* FA 2003 s 64A)

(3) In section 101 (unit trust schemes)—

(*a*) (*amends* FA 2003 s 101(1))
(*b*) (*amends* FA 2003 s 101(7))

(4) This section has effect in relation to any land transaction of which the effective date is, or is after, 22nd March 2006 (but see subsections (5) and (6)).

(5) This section does not have effect in relation to—

(*a*) any land transaction which is effected in pursuance of a contract entered into and substantially performed before 2 p.m. on 22nd March 2006 ("the relevant time"), or

(*b*) any other land transaction which is effected in pursuance of a contract entered into before the relevant time and which is not an excluded transaction.

(6) For this purpose, a land transaction effected in pursuance of a contract is an excluded transaction if—

(*a*) any provision of the contract has effect by reference to a unit trust scheme and the scheme is not established before the relevant time,

(*b*) at or after the relevant time the contract is varied in a way that significantly affects the land transaction (see subsection (7)),

(*c*) the subject-matter of the land transaction is not identified in the contract in a way that would have enabled its acquisition before the relevant time,

(*d*) rights under the contract are assigned at or after the relevant time,

(*e*) the land transaction is effected in consequence of the exercise, at or after the relevant time, of any option, right of pre-emption or similar right, or

(*f*) at or after the relevant time there is an assignment, subsale or other transaction (relating to the whole or part of the contract's subject-matter) as a result of which a person other than the purchaser under the contract becomes entitled to call for a conveyance to him.

(7) For the purposes of subsection (6)(*b*) the contract is varied in a way that significantly affects the land transaction if (and only if)—

(*a*) it is varied so as to substitute a different purchaser in relation to the land transaction,

(*b*) it is varied so as to alter the subject-matter of the land transaction, or

(*c*) it is varied so as to alter the consideration for the land transaction.

(8) Expressions which are used in Part 4 of FA 2003 and in this section have the same meaning in this section as in that Part.

167 Demutualisation of insurance companies

(1) Schedule 7 to FA 2003 (stamp duty land tax: group relief etc) is amended as follows.

(2) (*amends* FA 2003 Sch 7 para 2)

(3) (*inserts* FA 2003 Sch 7 para 2(3A))

(4) In paragraph 4 (cases in which group relief not withdrawn under paragraph 3)—

(*a*) (*inserts* FA 2003 Sch 7 para 4(6A))

(*b*) (*amends* FA 2003 Sch 7 para 4(7))

(5) The amendments made by this section have effect in relation to any transfer which takes place, or is intended to take place, after 22nd March 2006.

168 Alternative finance

(1) (*amends* FA 2003 ss 71A to 73)

(2) (*repeals* FA 2003 ss 71A(6), 72(6), 72A(6) and 73(4))

(3) (*amends* FA 2003 s 73(3))

(4) (*inserts* FA 2003 s 73A)

(5) This section shall have effect in relation to arrangements in which the effective date of the first transaction (within the meaning of sections 71A to 73 of FA 2003) is on or after the date on which this Act is passed; and section 119(1) of FA 2003 shall have effect for determining the effective date for the purposes of this subsection.

Stamp duty

169 Reliefs for certain company acquisitions

(1) Part 3 of FA 1986 (stamp duty) is amended as follows.

(2) In section 75 (relief for acquisition of target company's undertaking in pursuance of reconstruction scheme)—

(*a*) (*amends* FA 1986 s 75(4))

(*b*) (*amends* FA 1986 s 75(5)(*c*))

(3) (*amends* FA 1986 s 76(3))

(4) In section 77 (relief for acquisition of target company's share capital), in subsection (3) (conditions for relief),—

(*a*) (*repeals* FA 1986 s 77(3)(*a*))

(*b*) (*amends* FA 1986 s 77(3)(*g*))

(*c*) (*amends* FA 1986 s 77(3)(*h*))

(5) The amendments made by this section have effect in relation to instruments executed after the day on which this Act is passed.

PART 10
SUPPLEMENTARY PROVISIONS

178 Repeals

(1) The enactments mentioned in Schedule 26 (which include provisions that are spent or of no practical utility) are repealed to the extent specified.

(2) The repeals specified in that Schedule have effect subject to the commencement provisions and savings contained or referred to in the notes set out in that Schedule.

179 Interpretation

In this Act—

…

"FA", followed by a year, means the Finance Act of that year;

…

SCHEDULES

SCHEDULE 24
STAMP DUTY LAND TAX: AMENDMENTS OF SCHEDULE 15 TO FA 2003

Section 163

Introduction

1 Schedule 15 to FA 2003 (stamp duty land tax: partnerships) is amended as follows.

Transfer of chargeable interest to a partnership

2— (1) (*substitutes* FA 2003 Sch 15 para 10(2))

(2) (*amends* FA 2003 Sch 15 para 10(6))

3 (*substitutes* FA 2003 Sch 15 para 11(2)–(2D))

4— (1) (*amends* FA 2003 Sch 15 para 13(3))

(2) (*substitutes* FA 2003 Sch 15 para 13(4A), (5))

Transfer of chargeable interest from a partnership

5— (1) (*substitutes* FA 2003 Sch 15 para 18(2))

(2) (*amends* FA 2003 Sch 15 para 18(6))

6 (*substitutes* FA 2003 Sch 15 para 19(2)–(2D))

7— (1) (*amends* FA 2003 Sch 15 para 24(3))

(2) (*substitutes* FA 2003 Sch 15 para 24(4A), (5))

Transfer of chargeable interest from a partnership to a partnership

8 (*substitutes* FA 2003 Sch 15 para 23(2)–(3))

Transfer of partnership interest: restriction of charge to property-investment partnerships

9— (1) (*substitutes* FA 2003 Sch 15 para 14 heading)

(2) (*amends* FA 2003 Sch 15 para 14(1)(*a*))

(3) (*inserts* FA 2003 Sch 15 para 14(8))

Prevention of double charge where money etc withdrawn from partnership

10 (*inserts* FA 2003 Sch 15 para 17A(8))

Commencement

11— (1) Paragraphs 2 to 8 have effect in relation to any transfer of which the effective date is on or after the day on which this Act is passed.

(2) Paragraph 9 has effect in relation to any transfer that has (or, but for the amendment made by that paragraph, would have) an effective date which is on or after that day.

(3) Paragraph 10 has effect in relation to any qualifying event of which the effective date is on or after that day.

(4) In this paragraph "effective date" has the same meaning as in Part 4 of FA 2003.

SCHEDULE 25

STAMP DUTY LAND TAX: AMENDMENTS OF SCHEDULE 17A TO FA 2003

Section 164

Introduction

1 Schedule 17A (stamp duty land tax: further provisions relating to leases) is amended as follows.

Agricultural tenancies variable under statutory provisions

2— (1) (*inserts* FA 2003 Sch 17A para 7(4A))

(2) (*substitutes* FA 2003 Sch 17A para 13(2)(*a*), (*b*))

Backdated lease granted to tenant holding over

3— (1) (*inserts* FA 2003 Sch 17A para 9A)

(2) (*amends* FA 2003 Sch 17A para 7(3))

Disapplication of "single lease" treatment where agreement for lease followed by grant

4 (*amends* FA 2003 Sch 17A para 12A(3))

5— (1) (*amends* FA 2003 Sch 17A para 19(2))

(2) (*amends* FA 2003 Sch 17A para 19(4))

Disapplication of "new lease" treatment for certain rent increases after fifth year

6— (1) (*amends* FA 2003 Sch 17A para 13 heading)

(2) (*amends* FA 2003 Sch 17A para 13(1))

Abnormal rent increase after fifth year

7— (1) (*amends* FA 2003 Sch 17A para 14(1)(*a*))

(2) (*substitutes* FA 2003 Sch 17A para 14(4)–(4B))

(3) (*inserts* FA 2003 Sch 17A para 14(7))

8— (1) (*substitutes* FA 2003 Sch 17A para 15 Steps One to Three)

Commencement

9 (1) Paragraph 2 has effect in relation to any lease granted or treated as granted on or after commencement day.

(2) Paragraph 3 has effect in relation to any case where—

(*a*) the grant of the old lease was chargeable to stamp duty land tax, and

(*b*) the new lease is granted on or after commencement day.

"The old lease" and "the new lease" mean the leases referred to in sub-paragraphs (1)(*a*) and (1)(*b*), respectively, of paragraph 9A of Schedule 17A to FA 2003 (inserted by paragraph 3).

(3) Paragraphs 4 and 5 have effect in relation to any agreement that is substantially performed on or after commencement day.

(4) Paragraph 6 has effect in relation to any variation of a lease made on or after commencement day.

(5) Paragraphs 7 and 8 have effect in relation to any increase of rent that takes effect on or after commencement day.

(6) In this paragraph "commencement day" means the day on which this Act is passed.

SCHEDULE 26

REPEALS

Section 178

PART 7

STAMP TAXES

(1) STAMP DUTY AND STAMP DUTY LAND TAX: THRESHOLDS

Short title and chapter	*Extent of repeal*
Finance Act 2005 (c 7)	Section 95.

Stamp Taxes

This repeal has effect in accordance with section 162 of this Act.

(2) Stamp Duty Land Tax: Partnerships

Short title and chapter	Extent of repeal
Finance Act 2003 (c 14)	In Schedule 15— (a) in paragraph 10(6), the words "(instead of sub-paragraphs (2) to (5))"; (b) in paragraph 18(6), the words "(instead of sub-paragraphs (2) to (5))".

These repeals have effect in relation to any transfer of which the effective date (within the meaning of Part 4 of FA 2003) is on or after the day on which this Act is passed.

(3) Stamp Duty Land Tax: Unit Trust Schemes

Short title and chapter	*Extent of repeal*
Finance Act 2003 (c 14)	Section 64A. In section 101(7), the words from "section 53" to "companies), or".
Finance Act 2004 (c 12)	In Schedule 39, paragraph 18.

These repeals have effect in accordance with section 166 of this Act.

(4) Stamp Duty Land Tax: Alternative Finance

Short title and chapter	*Extent of repeal*
Finance Act 2003 (c 14).	Section 71A(6). Section 72(6).

(5) Stamp Duty: Reliefs for Certain Company Acquisitions

Short title and chapter	*Extent of repeal*
Finance Act 1986 (c 41)	In section 75(4), the words "that the registered office of the acquiring company is in the United Kingdom and". In section 76(3), the words "that the registered office of the acquiring company is in the United Kingdom and". Section 77(3)(*a*).

These repeals have effect in accordance with section 169 of this Act.

FINANCE ACT 2007

(2007 Chapter 11)

PART 2
ENVIRONMENT

Energy-saving: houses

19 SDLT relief for new zero-carbon homes

(1) (*inserts* FA 2003 ss 58B, 58C)

(2) (*inserts* FA 2003 s 114(5), (6))

PART 5

SDLT, STAMP DUTY AND SDRT

SDLT: anti-avoidance provisions

71 Anti-avoidance

(1) (*inserts* FA 2003 ss 75A–75C)

(2) The amendment made by subsection (1) has effect in respect of disposals and acquisitions if the disposal mentioned in new section 75A(1)(*a*) (inserted by that subsection) takes place on or after 6th December 2006.

(3) But—

(*a*) the transitional provisions of sub-paragraphs (2) to (5) of paragraph 1 of the Schedule to the Stamp Duty Land Tax (Variation of the Finance Act 2003) Regulations 2006 (SI 2006/3237) continue to have effect in relation to this section as in relation to that paragraph, and

(*b*) a provision of new section 75C (inserted by subsection (1) above) shall not have effect where the disposal mentioned in new section 75A(1)(*a*) took place before the day on which this Act is passed, if or in so far as the provision would make a person liable for a higher amount of tax than would have been charged in accordance with those regulations.

72 Partnerships

(1) Schedule 15 to FA 2003 (stamp duty land tax: partnerships) is amended as follows.

(2) A reference in this section to a provision of that Schedule is to the provision as it had effect before variation by the Stamp Duty Land Tax (Variation of the Finance Act 2003) Regulations 2006.

(3) (*amends* FA 2003 Sch 15 para 12(1) Step Two)

(4) (*inserts* FA 2003 Sch 15 para 12(3))

(5) Omit paragraph 13 (transfer to partnership where all partners are companies).

(6) In paragraph 14 (transfer of interest in property-investment partnership)—

(*a*) (*repeals* FA 2003 Sch 15 para 14(1)(*b*), (4))
(*b*) (*inserts* FA 2003 Sch 15 para 14(9))

(*amends* italic cross-heading before FA 2003 Sch 15 para 14)

(7) (*amends* FA 2003 Sch 15 para 20(1) Step Two)

(8) (*inserts* FA 2003 Sch 15 para 20(3))

(9) (*inserts* FA 2003 Sch 15 para 27A)

(10) (*substitutes* FA 2003 Sch 15 para 36)

(11) (*inserts* FA 2003 Sch 15 para 39(3))

(12) In Schedule 16 to FA 2003 (trusts and powers)—

(*a*) (*amends* FA 2003 Sch 16 para 3(1))
(*b*) (*amends* FA 2003 Sch 16 para 4)

(13) The amendments made by subsections (1) to (11) have effect in respect of transfers occurring on or after the day on which this Act is passed.

(14) But the amendments made by subsections (6) and (10) do not have effect in respect of anything done in respect of a property-investment partnership established before the day on which this Act is passed if—

(a) the partnership does not acquire a chargeable interest on or after that day, and
(b) stamp duty land tax was paid in respect of each chargeable interest acquired before that day, by reference to chargeable consideration of not less than the market value.[1]

(15) The amendment made by subsection (12) has effect in respect of acquisitions occurring on or after the day on which this Act is passed.

(16) An amendment made by this section replaces, to the extent provided for by subsections (13) to (15), any variation made by the Stamp Duty Land Tax (Variation of the Finance Act 2003) Regulations 2006 (SI 2006/3237).

(17) Despite subsections (13) to (16), the transitional provisions of sub-paragraphs (8) to (10) of paragraph 2 of the Schedule to the Stamp Duty Land Tax (Variation of the Finance Act 2003) Regulations 2006 (SI 2006/3237) continue to have effect in relation to the amendments made by this section as in relation to that paragraph.

Amendments—[1] Sub-s (14) repealed by FA 2008 s 97, Sch 31 para 10 with effect from 21 July 2008.

Reliefs in relation to shares etc

73 Exemptions: intermediaries, repurchases etc

Schedule 21 contains provision in relation to exemptions from stamp duty and stamp duty reserve tax in cases involving intermediaries, repurchases, stock lending or recognised investment exchanges.

Prospective amendment—This section to be repealed by FA 2007 s 114, Sch 27 Pt 4(2) with effect in accordance with the provisions of FA 1990 ss 108, 110.

74 Acquisition relief: disregard of company holding own shares

(1) (*inserts* FA 1986 s 75(5A))

(2) (*inserts* FA 1986 s 77(3A))

(3) (*inserts* FA 2003 Sch 7 para 7(5A))

(4) The amendments made by subsections (1) and (2) have effect in relation to any instrument executed on or after the day on which this Act is passed.

(5) The amendment made by subsection (3) has effect in relation to any land transaction of which the effective date is on or after that day.

Other reliefs etc

75 SDLT: alternative finance arrangements

(1) (*inserts* FA 2003 s 73B)

(2) (*inserts* FA 2003 s 48(3A))

(3) (*substitutes* FA 2003 ss 71A(8), 72(7), 72A(8), 73(5)(*a*))

(4) The amendments made by this section—

(*a*) have effect in relation to anything that would, but for the exemption provided by new section 73B inserted by subsection (1) above, be a land transaction with an effective date on or after 22nd March 2007, and

(*b*) apply, in accordance with paragraph (*a*), to interests irrespective of the date of their creation.

76 SDLT: exchanges

(1) (*amends* FA 2003 s 47(1))

(2) (*inserts* FA 2003 s 108(4))

(3) The amendments made by this section have effect in relation to a set of land transactions if the effective date of any of them is on or after the day on which this Act is passed.

77 SDLT: shared ownership trusts

(1) (*inserts* FA 2003 Sch 9 paras 7–11)

(2) The amendment made by subsection (1) has effect in relation to land transactions with an effective date on or after the day on which this Act is passed.

78 SDLT: shared ownership lease

(*inserts* FA 2003 Sch 9 para 2(4A))

79 Certain transfers of school land

(1) In Chapter 7 of Part 2 of the School Standards and Framework Act 1998 (c 31) ("the 1998 Act") (new framework for maintained schools), omit sections 79 and 79A (no stamp duty or SDLT payable in respect of certain transfers).

(2) The repeal of—

(*a*) section 79A of the 1998 Act, and

(*b*) section 79 of that Act as it applies for the purposes of section 79A,

has effect in relation to any land transaction of which the effective date is on or after the day on which this Act is passed.

(3) Subject to that, the repeal of section 79 of the 1998 Act has effect in relation to any instrument executed on or after that day.

SDLT: administration

80 Payment of tax

(1) FA 2003 is amended as follows.

(2) (*repeals* FA 2003 s 76(3)(*b*))

(3) (*substitutes* FA 2003 s 80(2)(*d*))

(4) In section 81 (withdrawal of relief: further return)—

(*a*) (*repeals* FA 2003 s 81(2)(*b*))

(*b*) (*inserts* FA 2003 s 81(2A))

(5) (*substitutes* FA 2003 s 81A(1)(*d*))

(6) (*amends* FA 2003 s 86(1), (2))

(7) (*repeals* FA 2003 Sch 10 para 2(2)(*b*))

(8) (*substitutes* FA 2003 Sch 17A paras 3(3)(*d*), 4(3)(*d*) and 8(3)(*d*))

(9) The amendments made by this section have effect as follows—

(*a*) the amendment made by subsection (2) has effect in relation to land transactions with an effective date on or after the day on which this Act is passed,
(*b*) the amendment made by subsection (3) has effect in relation to returns where the event as a result of which the return is required occurs on or after the day on which this Act is passed,
(*c*) the amendment made by subsection (4) has effect in relation to returns where the disqualifying event occurs on or after the day on which this Act is passed,
(*d*) the amendment made by subsection (5) has effect in relation to returns where the effective date of the later transaction is on or after the day on which this Act is passed,
(*e*) the amendment made by subsection (6) has effect in relation to land transactions with an effective date on or after the day on which this Act is passed,
(*f*) the amendment made by subsection (7) has effect in relation to land transactions with an effective date on or after the day on which this Act is passed, and
(*g*) the amendment made by subsection (8) has effect in respect of requirements to deliver a return or further return which arise on or after the day on which this Act is passed.

81 ...[1]

Amendments—[1] This section repealed by FA 2008 s 94, Sch 30 para 15 with effect in relation to transactions with an effective date on or after 12 March 2008.

PART 7
MISCELLANEOUS

109 Meaning of "recognised stock exchange" etc

Schedule 26 contains—

(*a*) new definitions of "recognised stock exchange" for the purposes of the Tax Acts and TCGA 1992,
(*b*) provision for the valuation for the purposes of TCGA 1992 of certain shares or securities listed on recognised stock exchanges,
(*c*) provision for the valuation for the purposes of Chapter 8 of Part 4 of ITTOIA 2005 of strips and securities exchanged for strips, and
(*d*) minor and consequential amendments in relation to stock exchanges.

110 Mergers Directive: regulations

(1) The Treasury may by regulations make provision about—

(*a*) the tax consequences of a merger to form an SE or SCE,
(*b*) the tax consequences of a merger where—
 (i) each party to the merger is resident in a member State, and
 (ii) the parties are not all resident in the same member State,
(*c*) the tax consequences of a transfer between companies of a business or part of a business, where—
 (i) each party to the transfer is resident in a member State, and
 (ii) the parties are not all resident in the same member State,
(*d*) the tax consequences of a share exchange to which section 135 of TCGA 1992 (exchange of securities) applies where companies A and B are resident in different member States,
(*e*) the residence of an SE or SCE.

(2) Regulations may, in particular, make provision—

(*a*) about the taxation of chargeable gains (including conferring relief from taxation in relation to transfers or mergers which satisfy specified conditions),
(*b*) conferring relief from taxation on a distribution of a company which satisfies specified conditions,
(*c*) about the treatment of securities issued on a transfer or merger,
(*d*) about the treatment of loan relationships,
(*e*) about the treatment of derivative contracts,
(*f*) about the treatment of intangible fixed assets, and
(*g*) about capital allowances.

(3) Regulations may make provision only if the Treasury think it necessary or expedient for the purposes of complying with the United Kingdom's obligations under the Mergers Directive.

(4) In this section—

"the Mergers Directive" means Council Directive 90/434/EEC,
"SCE" means an SCE formed in accordance with Council Regulation (EC) 1435/2003 on the Statute for a European Cooperative Society, and
"SE" means an SE formed in accordance with Council Regulation (EC) 2157/2001 on the Statute for a European Company.

(5) Regulations under this section may—

(*a*) amend the Taxes Acts,
(*b*) make incidental or consequential amendments of enactments other than the Taxes Acts,

(*c*) make provision having retrospective effect,
(*d*) make provision generally or only for specified cases or circumstances,
(*e*) make different provision for different cases or circumstances,
(*f*) make incidental, consequential or transitional provision.

(6) In this section "the Taxes Acts" has the meaning given by section 118(1) of TMA 1970.

112 Updating references to Standing Committees

(1) (*amends* PCTA 1968 s 1(4)(*b*))

(2) (*amends* FA 1973 s 50(2)(*a*))

SCHEDULES

SCHEDULE 21

EXEMPTIONS FROM STAMP DUTY AND SDRT: INTERMEDIARIES, REPURCHASES ETC

Section 73

Prospective amendment—This Schedule to be repealed by FA 2007 s 114, Sch 27 Pt 4(2) with effect in accordance with the provisions of FA 1990 ss 108, 110.

Intermediaries

1— (1) Section 80A of FA 1986 (exemption from stamp duty: sales to intermediaries) is amended as follows.

(2) (*substitutes* FA 1986 s 80A(1)–(2C))

(3) (*amends* FA 1986 s 80A(6))

(4) (*inserts* FA 1986 s 80A(6A))

(5) The amendments made by this paragraph have effect in relation to any instrument executed on or after 1st November 2007.

Prospective amendment—This Schedule to be repealed by FA 2007 s 114, Sch 27 Pt 4(2) with effect in accordance with the provisions of FA 1990 ss 108, 110.

2— (1) Section 80B of FA 1986 (exemption from stamp duty on sales to intermediaries: supplementary) is amended as follows.

(2) In subsection (2)—

(*a*) (*inserts* definition of "the Directive" in FA 1986 s 80B(2))
(*b*) (*repeals* definition of "EEA exchange" in FA 1986 s 80B(2))
(*c*) (*amends* FA 1986 s 80B(2) definition of "EEA State")

(3) (*inserts* FA 1986 s 80B(2A))

(4) (*inserts* FA 1986 s 80B(5A))

(5) (*amends* FA 1986 s 80B(7))

(6) The amendments made by this paragraph have effect in relation to any instrument executed on or after 1st November 2007.

Prospective amendment—This Schedule to be repealed by FA 2007 s 114, Sch 27 Pt 4(2) with effect in accordance with the provisions of FA 1990 ss 108, 110.

3— (1) Section 88A of FA 1986 (exemption from SDRT: sales to intermediaries) is amended as follows.

(2) (*substitutes* FA 1986 s 88A(1)–(2C))

(3) (*amends* FA 1986 s 88A(6))

(4) (*inserts* FA 1986 s 88A(6A))

(5) The amendments made by this paragraph have effect in relation to any agreement to transfer securities—

(*a*) in a case where the agreement is conditional, if the condition is satisfied on or after 1st November 2007, and
(*b*) in any other case, if the agreement is made on or after that date.

Prospective amendment—This Schedule to be repealed by FA 2007 s 114, Sch 27 Pt 4(2) with effect in accordance with the provisions of FA 1990 ss 108, 110.

4— (1) Section 88B of FA 1986 (exemption from SDRT on sales to intermediaries: supplementary) is amended as follows.

(2) In subsection (2)—

(*a*) (*inserts* definition of "the Directive" into FA 1986 s 88B(2))
(*b*) (*repeals* definition of "EEA exchange" in FA 1986 s 88B(2))
(*c*) (*amends* definition of "EEA State" in FA 1986 s 88B(2))

(3) (*inserts* FA 1986 s 88B(2A))

(4) (*inserts* FA 1986 s 88B(3A))

(5) (*amends* FA 1986 s 88B(5))

(6) (*amends* FA 1986 s 88B(7))

(7) The amendments made by this paragraph have effect in relation to any agreement to transfer securities—

(*a*) in a case where the agreement is conditional, if the condition is satisfied on or after 1st November 2007, and
(*b*) in any other case, if the agreement is made on or after that date.

Prospective amendment—This Schedule to be repealed by FA 2007 s 114, Sch 27 Pt 4(2) with effect in accordance with the provisions of FA 1990 ss 108, 110.

Repurchases and stock lending

5— (1) Section 80C of FA 1986 (exemption from stamp duty: repurchases and stock lending) is amended as follows.

(2) (*amends* FA 1986 s 80C(1))

(3) (*inserts* FA 1986 s 80C(2A))

(4) (*amends* FA 1986 s 80C(3))

(5) (*amends* FA 1986 s 80C(6))

(6) In subsection (7)—

(*a*) (*inserts* definitions of "the Directive" and "EEA State")
(*b*) (*repeals* definition of "EEA exchange")

(7) (*inserts* FA 1986 s 80C(7A))

(8) The amendments made by this paragraph have effect in relation to any instrument executed on or after 1st November 2007.

Prospective amendment—This Schedule to be repealed by FA 2007 s 114, Sch 27 Pt 4(2) with effect in accordance with the provisions of FA 1990 ss 108, 110.

6— (1) Section 89AA of FA 1986 (exemption from SDRT: repurchases and stock lending) is amended as follows.

(2) (*amends* FA 1986 s 89AA(1))

(3) (*inserts* FA 1986 s 89AA(2A))

(4) (*amends* FA 1986 s 89AA(3))

(5) (*amends* FA 1986 s 89AA(5))

(6) In subsection (6)—

(*a*) (*inserts* definitions of "the Directive" and "EEA State")
(*b*) (*repeals* definition of "EEA exchange")

(7) (*inserts* FA 1986 s 89AA(6A))

(8) The amendments made by this paragraph have effect in relation to any agreement to transfer securities—

(*a*) in a case where the agreement is conditional, if the condition is satisfied on or after 1st November 2007, and
(*b*) in any other case, if the agreement is made on or after that date.

Prospective amendment—This Schedule to be repealed by FA 2007 s 114, Sch 27 Pt 4(2) with effect in accordance with the provisions of FA 1990 ss 108, 110.

Exemptions from stamp duty and SDRT in cases involving recognised investment exchanges

7— (1) In section 116 of FA 1991 (stamp duty: investment exchanges and clearing houses), subsection (4) is amended as follows.

(2) (*inserts* FA 1991 s 116(4)(*aa*))

(3) (*amends* FA 1991 s 116(4)(*b*))

Prospective amendment—This Schedule to be repealed by FA 2007 s 114, Sch 27 Pt 4(2) with effect in accordance with the provisions of FA 1990 ss 108, 110.

Consequential repeal

8— (1) (*repeals* F(No 2)A 2005 s 50)

(2) This paragraph comes into force on 1st November 2007.

Prospective amendment—This Schedule to be repealed by FA 2007 s 114, Sch 27 Pt 4(2) with effect in accordance with the provisions of FA 1990 ss 108, 110.

SCHEDULE 26

MEANING OF "RECOGNISED STOCK EXCHANGE" ETC

Section 109

Meaning of "recognised stock exchange" etc in Tax Acts and TCGA 1992

1 (*substitutes* ITA 2007 s 1005)

2 (*substitutes* TA 1988 s 841)

3 (*inserts* TCGA 1992 s 288(5A), (5B))

Valuation of shares listed on recognised stock exchange for purposes of TCGA 1992 etc

4— (1) (*substitutes* TCGA 1992 s 272(3), (4))

(2) The amendment made by sub-paragraph (1) has effect where the date of valuation falls on or after such day as may be appointed by the Treasury by order; and different days may be appointed for different purposes.

5— (1) (*substitutes* ITTOIA 2005 s 450)

(2) The amendment made by sub-paragraph (1) has effect where the date of valuation falls on or after such day as may be appointed by the Treasury by order; and different days may be appointed for different purposes.

Minor and consequential amendments

6 (*substitutes* FA 1986 s 90(8)(*b*))

7— (1) ICTA is amended as follows.

(2) (*amends* TA 1988 s 210(4))

(3) (*amends* TA 1988 s 312(1E)(*a*))

(4) (*amends* TA 1988 s 415(1)(*b*))

(5) (*amends* TA 1988 s 576H(2)(*a*))

(6) (*amends* TA 1988 s 587B)

(7) (*amends* TA 1988 s 704)

(8) (*amends* TA 1988 s 828(2))

(9) (*amends* TA 1988 s 842(1)(*c*))

(10) (*amends* TA 1988 Sch 20 para 5)

8— (1) TCGA 1992 is amended as follows.

(2) (*amends* TCGA 1992 s 130(1)(*a*))

(3) (*amends* TCGA 1992 s 144(8)(*a*))

(4) (*amends* TCGA 1992 s 146(4)(*b*))

(5) (*amends* TCGA 1992 s 273(2))

(6) (*repeals* TCGA 1992 s 285)

9 (*amends* FA 2002 Sch 26 para 4(2C)(*b*))

10 (*amends* ITEPA 2003)

11 (*amends* ITTOIA 2005 ss 443(2), 460(3))

12— (1) ITA 2007 is amended as follows.

(2) (*amends* ITA 2007 s 143(2)(*a*))

(3) (*amends* ITA 2007 s 151(2))

(4) (*amends* ITA 2007 s 184(3), (6))

(5) (*amends* ITA 2007 s 257(5))

(6) (*amends* ITA 2007 s 274(2))

(7) (*amends* ITA 2007 s 295(3))

(8) (*amends* ITA 2007 s 382(2))

(9) (*amends* ITA 2007 s 397(6))

(10) (*amends* ITA 2007 s 432)

(11) (*amends* ITA 2007 s 691(1)(*b*))

(12) (*amends* ITA 2007 s 989)

(13) (*repeals* ITA 2007 s 1010)

(14) (*amends* ITA 2007 s 1014(2)(*g*))

(15) (*amends* ITA 2007 Sch 4)

SCHEDULE 27
REPEALS

Section 114

PART 4
SDLT, STAMP DUTY AND SDRT

(1) Anti-avoidance: Partnerships

Short title and chapter	*Extent of repeal*
Finance Act 2003 (c 14)	In Schedule 15— (*a*) paragraphs 13 and 14(1)(*b*) and (4), and (*b*) in the italic cross-heading before paragraph 14 the words "for consideration"

These repeals have effect in accordance with section 72 of this Act.

(2) Exemptions: Intermediaries, Repurchases etc

Short title and chapter	*Extent of repeal*
Finance Act 1986 (c 41)	In section 80B(2), the definition of "EEA exchange". In section 80C(7), the definition of "EEA exchange" (together with the word "and" at the end of it). In section 88B(2), the definition of "EEA exchange". In section 89AA(6), the definition of "EEA exchange".
Finance (No 2) Act 2005 (c 22)	Section 50.
Finance Act 2007 (c.)	Section 73. Schedule 21.

1 Subject to Note 2, these repeals have effect in accordance with Schedule 21 to this Act.

2 The repeals of section 73 of, and Schedule 21 to, this Act have effect in accordance with sections 108 and 110 of FA 1990.

(3) Certain Transfers of School Land

Short title and chapter	*Extent of repeal*
School Standards and Framework Act 1998 (c 31)	Sections 79 and 79A.
Education and Inspections Act 2006 (c 40)	In Part 3 of Schedule 4, paragraph 20.

These repeals have effect in accordance with section 79 of this Act.

(4) Payment of SDLT

Short title and chapter	*Extent of repeal*
Finance Act 2003 (c 14)	In section 76(3), paragraph (*b*) and the word "and" before it. In section 81(2), paragraph (*b*) and the word "and" before it. In Schedule 10, in paragraph 2(2), paragraph (*b*) and the word "and" before it.

These repeals have effect in accordance with section 80 of this Act.

PART 6
MISCELLANEOUS

(5) Meaning of "Recognised Stock Exchange" etc

Short title and chapter	*Extent of repeal*
Income and Corporation Taxes Act 1988 (c 1)	In Schedule 20, in paragraph 5, the words ", or which are dealt in on the Unlisted Securities Market".
Taxation of Chargeable Gains Act 1992 (c 12)	In section 130(1)(*a*), the words "in the United Kingdom or elsewhere". In section 146(4)(*b*), the words "in the United Kingdom or elsewhere". Section 285.
Finance Act 1996 (c 8)	In Schedule 38, paragraphs 7 and 12(1).
Financial Services and Markets Act 2000 (c 8)	In Schedule 20, paragraph 4(6).
Income Tax (Trading and Other Income) Act 2005 (c 5)	Section 443(2)(*g*). In section 460(3), the words "or 451".
Income Tax Act 2007 (c 3)	In section 295(3)(*c*), the words "on the Unlisted Securities Market or dealt in". Section 1010. In Schedule 1, paragraph 227.

FINANCE ACT 2008

(2008 Chapter 9)

CONTENTS

PART 5
STAMP TAXES

Stamp duty land tax

Stamp duty

PART 8
MISCELLANEOUS

Alternative finance arrangements

Schedule 38—Disclosure of tax avoidance schemes

An Act to Grant certain duties, to alter other duties, and to amend the law relating to the National Debt and the Public Revenue, and to make further provision in connection with finance.
[21 July 2008]

PART 5

STAMP TAXES

Stamp duty land tax

93 Zero-carbon homes

(1) Sections 58B and 58C of FA 2003 (relief from SDLT on first acquisition of zero-carbon homes) are amended as follows.

(2) (*substitutes* FA 2003 s 58B(2))

(3) Section 58C is amended as follows.

(4) (*amends* FA 2003 s 58C(1))

(5) (*inserts* FA 2003 s 58C(2)(*d*))

(6) (*amends* FA 2003 s 58C(3))

(7) The amendments made by subsections (2), (4) and (6) are treated as always having had effect; and provision included in regulations by virtue of those amendments may be made so as to have effect in relation to acquisitions on or after 1 October 2007.

Regulations—Stamp Duty Land Tax (Zero-Carbon Homes Relief) (Amendment) Regulations 2008, SI 2008/1932.

94 Notification and registration of transactions

(1) Part 4 of FA 2003 (stamp duty land tax) is amended as follows.

(2) (*substitutes* FA 2003 ss 77, 77A)

(3) (*amends* FA 2003 s 79(2))

(4) Schedule 30 contains consequential provision.

(5) The amendments made by this section and that Schedule have effect in relation to transactions with an effective date on or after 12 March 2008.

95 Charge where consideration includes rent: 0% band

(1) Schedule 5 to FA 2003 (amount of SDLT chargeable: rent) is amended as follows.

(2) (*amends* FA 2003 Sch 5 para 9(1) and heading, *repeals* sub-paras (2)–(3))

(3) (*inserts* FA 2003 Sch 5 para 9A)

(4), (5) (*repeal* FA 2003 Sch 6 paras 5(4)(*a*)(i), (*b*), 6(6))(*a*)(i), (*b*), 9(4))(*a*)(i), (*b*), 10(6))(*a*)(i), (*b*))

(6) (*amends* FA 2003 Sch 6 para 12)

(7) (*amends* FA 2003 Sch 8 para 3(3)(*b*), (5))

(8) (*inserts* FA 2003 Sch 9 para 4B)

(9)) (*amends* FA 2003 Sch 9 paras 10(1), (2), 11(*b*))

(10) (*inserts* FA 2003 Sch 9 para 12)

(11) (*amends* FA 2003 Sch 15 paras 11(2B)(*a*), 19(2B), 23(3)(*c*))

(12) (*amends* FA 2003 Sch 17A para 18A(5)(*a*))

(13) The amendments made by this section have effect in relation to transactions with an effective date on or after 12 March 2008.

96 Withdrawal of group relief

(1) Part 1 of Schedule 7 to FA 2003 (group relief) is amended as follows.

(2) (*amends* FA 2003 Sch 7 para 3(5))

(3) (*repeals* FA 2003 Sch 7 para 4(2), (3), *amends* sub-para (5))

(4) (*inserts* FA 2003 Sch 7 para 4ZA)

(5) (*amends* FA 2003 Sch 7 para 4A(1), (3), *inserts* sub-paras (1A), (3A))

(6) The amendments made by this section have effect in relation to transactions with an effective date on or after 13 March 2008.

97 Transfers of interests in property-investment partnerships

(1) Schedule 31 contains provision relating to stamp duty land tax chargeable on transfers to, and of interests in, property-investment partnerships.

(2) Part 1 of that Schedule (transfer of interest in partnership: "relevant partnership property"), and this section so far as relating to that Part—

(*a*) have effect in respect of transfers occurring on or after 19 July 2007 (subject to subsection (3)), and

(*b*) are treated as having come into force on that day.

(3) Subsections (14) and (17) of section 72 of FA 2007 (partnerships) apply in relation to the amendments made by Part 1 of that Schedule as they apply in relation to the amendments made by subsections (6) and (10) of that section.

Stamp duty

98 Exemption from ad valorem stamp duty for low value transactions

(1) Paragraph 1 of Schedule 13 to FA 1999 (charge to stamp duty on conveyance or transfer on sale) is amended as follows.

(2) (*amends* FA 1999 Sch 13 para 1(3))

(3) (*inserts* FA 1999 Sch 13 para 1(3A))

(4) (*amends* FA 1999 Sch 13 para 6(1))

(5) The amendments made by this section have effect in relation to instruments executed on or after 13 March 2008 and not stamped before 19 March 2008.

(6) For the purposes of section 14(4) of the Stamp Act 1891 (c 39) (instruments not to be given in evidence etc unless stamped in accordance with the law in force at the time of first execution), the law in force at the time of execution of an instrument—

(*a*) executed on or after 13 March 2008 but before 19 March 2008, and

(*b*) not stamped before 19 March 2008,

shall be deemed to be the law as varied in accordance with this section.

99 Abolition of fixed stamp duty on certain instruments

(1) Schedule 32 contains provision abolishing fixed stamp duty on certain instruments.

(2) The amendments and saving made by that Schedule have effect in relation to instruments executed on or after 13 March 2008 and not stamped before 19 March 2008.

(3) For the purposes of section 14(4) of the Stamp Act 1891 (instruments not to be given in evidence etc unless stamped in accordance with the law in force at the time of first execution), the law in force at the time of execution of an instrument—

(*a*) executed on or after 13 March 2008 but before 19 March 2008, and

(*b*) not stamped before 19 March 2008,

shall be deemed to be the law as varied in accordance with Schedule 32.

100 Gifts inter vivos

(1) (*repeals* FA 1985 s 82(5), (9))

(2) (*repeals* FA 1999 Sch 14 para 9)

(3) The amendments made by this section have effect in relation to instruments executed on or after 13 March 2008, other than instruments effecting a land transaction (within the meaning of paragraph 22 of Schedule 32).

(4) For the purposes of section 14(4) of the Stamp Act 1891 (instruments not to be given in evidence etc unless stamped in accordance with the law in force at the time of first execution), the law in force at the time of execution of such an instrument shall be deemed to be the law as varied in accordance with this section.

101 Loan capital

(1) Section 79 of FA 1986 (stamp duty and loan capital) is amended as follows.

(2) (*amends* FA 1986 s 79(6))

(3) (*inserts* FA 1986 s 79(7B))

(4) (*inserts* FA 1986 s 79(13))

(5) The amendments made by this section have effect in relation to any instrument executed on or after the day on which this Act is passed.

PART 8

MISCELLANEOUS

Alternative finance arrangements

154 Stamp duty and stamp duty reserve tax: alternative finance investment bonds

(1) FA 1986 is amended as follows.

(2) (*inserts* FA 1986 s 78(7)(*d*))

(3) Section 79 (loan capital: instruments not chargeable to stamp duty) is amended as follows.

(4) (*inserts* FA 1986 s 79(8A))

(5) (*inserts* FA 1986 s 99(9A))

(6) The amendments made by subsections (2) to (4) have effect in relation to instruments executed on or after the day on which this Act is passed (and for this purpose it does not matter when the arrangements falling within section 48A of FA 2005 [or section 507 of CTA 2009][1] are made).

(7) The amendment made by subsection (5) has effect in relation to—

(*a*) agreements to transfer chargeable securities made on or after the day on which this Act is passed, and

(*b*) the transfer, issue or appropriation of chargeable securities after that day in pursuance of an agreement made after that day;

(and for this purpose it does not matter when the arrangements falling within section 48A of FA 2005 are made).

Amendments—[1] In sub-s (6), words inserted by CTA 2009 s 1322, Sch 1 paras 728, 732. CTA 2009 applies for accounting periods ending on or after 1 April 2009 (for corporation tax purposes) and for tax years 2009–10 onwards (for income and capital gains tax purposes).

155 Alternative property finance: anti-avoidance

(1) FA 2003 is amended as follows.

(2) (*amends* FA 2003 s 73A heading)

(3) (*inserts* FA 2003 s 73AB)

(4) The amendment made by subsection (3) has effect in relation to alternative finance arrangements entered into on or after 12 March 2008.

Stamp Taxes

SCHEDULES

SCHEDULE 30

STAMP DUTY LAND TAX: NOTIFICATION ETC: CONSEQUENTIAL PROVISION

Section 94

FA 2003

1 Part 4 of FA 2003 (stamp duty land tax) is amended as follows.

2— (1) Section 79 (registration of land transactions) is amended as follows.

(2) (*amends* FA 2003 s 79(3))

(3) (*substitutes* FA 2003 s 79(5))

(4) (*amends* FA 2003 s 79(6)(*a*))

3 (*amends* FA 2003 s 81B(1))

4— (1) Section 103 (joint purchasers) is amended as follows.

(2) (*amends* FA 2003 s 103(4))

(3) (*amends* FA 2003 s 103(5))

5— (*amends* FA 2003 s 122)

6 (*amends* FA 2003 Sch 6 para 13)

7 (*amends* FA 2003 Sch 10 para 36(5A)(*d*))

8 (*repeals* FA 2003 Sch 11 Pt 1)

9— (1) In Part 2 of that Schedule (duty to keep and preserve records), paragraph 4 is amended as follows.

(2) (*inserts* FA 2003 Sch 11 para 4(A1))

(3) (*amends* FA 2003 Sch 11 para 4(1))

(4) (*amends* FA 2003 Sch 11 para 4(2))

10 (*repeals* FA 2003 Sch 11 Pt 3)

11 (*amends* FA 2003 Sch 11 heading)

12 (*amends* FA 2003 Sch 15 para 8(2))

13— (1) In Schedule 16 (SDLT: trusts and powers), paragraph 6 is amended as follows.

(2) (*amends* FA 2003 Sch 16 para 6(1), (3))

(3) (*amends* FA 2003 Sch 16 para 6(2))

14 (*amends* FA 2003 Sch 17A paras 3(2), (5) and 4(1), (4A))

FA 2007

15 (*repeals* FA 2007 s 81)

SCHEDULE 31

STAMP DUTY LAND TAX: SPECIAL PROVISIONS FOR PROPERTY-INVESTMENT PARTNERSHIPS

Section 97

PART 1

TRANSFER OF INTEREST IN PARTNERSHIP: "RELEVANT PARTNERSHIP PROPERTY"

Paragraph 14 of Schedule 15 to FA 2003

1— (1) Paragraph 14 of Schedule 15 to FA 2003 (transfer of interest in property-investment partnership) is amended as follows.

(2) (*inserts* FA 2003 Sch 15 para 14(3A)–(3C))

(3) (*amends* FA 2003 Sch 15 para 14(5), *inserts* sub-para (5)(*c*))

(4) (*inserts* FA 2003 Sch 15 para 14(5A))

Consequential provision

2 (*amends* FA 2003 Sch 15 para 15(1))

3 (*amends* FA 2003 Sch 15 para 16(2))

4 (*amends* FA 2003 Sch 15 para 26(9))

PART 2

ELECTIONS IN RESPECT OF INTEREST TRANSFERRED TO PARTNERSHIP

Election when interest transferred to partnership

5 (*amends* FA 2003 Sch 15 para 10)

6 (*inserts* FA 2003 Sch 15 para 12A)

7 (*inserts* FA 2003 Sch 15 para 18(8))

Consequential provision

8 (*inserts* FA 2003 Sch 15 para 17A(1)(*d*))

9 (*amends* FA 2003 Sch 15 para 26(8))

PART 3

TRANSITIONAL PROVISION

10 (*repeals* FA 2007 s 72(14))

11— (1) This paragraph applies in the case of a transfer of a chargeable interest to a partnership falling within paragraph 10(1)(*a*), (*b*) or (*c*) of Schedule 15 to FA 2003 where the effective date of the transaction is before the day on which this Act is passed.

(2) The purchaser in relation to the transaction may at any time before the end of the period of 12 months beginning with that day amend the land transaction return in respect of that transaction so as to make an election under paragraph 12A of Schedule 15 to FA 2003 (inserted by this Schedule).

(3) An election made in reliance on sub-paragraph (2) has effect as if it had been made on the date on which the land transaction return was made, even though paragraph 12A of Schedule 15 to FA 2003 was not in force at that time.

(4) Where an election is made in reliance on sub-paragraph (2), the power under section 12A(5)(*b*) of Schedule 15 to FA 2003 to amend a land transaction return in respect of an affected transaction to take account of that election may be exercised at any time before the end of the period of 12 months beginning with the day on which this Act is passed.

SCHEDULE 32

STAMP DUTY: ABOLITION OF FIXED DUTY ON CERTAIN INSTRUMENTS

Section 99

PART 1

ABOLITION OF FIXED DUTY

FA 1985

1 Part 3 of FA 1985 (stamp duty) is amended as follows.

2 (*repeals* FA 1985 s 83(2))
3 (*repeals* FA 1985 s 83(8), (9), *amends* (11))

FA 1986

4 Part 3 of FA 1986 (stamp duty) is amended as follows.
5 (*repeals* FA 1986 s 66(2A))
6 (*amends* FA 1986 s 67(9))
7 (*amends* FA 1986 s 70(9))
8 (*substitutes* FA 1986 s 72A(1)(*b*))

FA 1999

9 FA 1999 is amended as follows.
10— (1) Schedule 13 (instruments chargeable to stamp duty and rates of duty) is amended as follows.
(2) (*amends* FA 1999 Sch 13 para 1(5))
(3) (*repeals* FA 1999 Sch 13 paras 16, 17, 18(2), 10(1), 21(3), 22, 23)
11— (1) Schedule 15 (stamp duty: bearer instruments) is amended as follows.
(2) (*repeals* FA 1999 Sch 15 para 6)
(3) (*inserts* FA 1999 Sch 15 para 12A)
(4) (*substitutes* FA 1999 Sch 15 para 20(*b*))
(5) (*repeals* FA 1999 Sch 15 para 26(*b*))

PART 2

CONSEQUENTIAL PROVISIONS AND SAVING

FA 1982

12 (*repeals* FA 1982 s 129(1))

FA 1986

13 Part 3 of FA 1986 (stamp duty) is amended as follows.
14— (1) Section 67 (stamp duty on certain transfers to depositary receipt systems) is amended as follows.
(2) (*amends* FA 1986 s 67(1))
(3) (*amends* FA 1986 s 67(3))
(4) (*inserts* FA 1986 s 67(9A))
15— (1) Section 70 (stamp duty on certain transfers to a clearance system) is amended as follows.
(2) (*amends* FA 1986 s 70(1))
(3) (*amends* FA 1986 s 70(3))
(4) (*inserts* FA 1986 s 70(9A))

FA 1987

16 Part 3 of FA 1987 (stamp duty and stamp duty reserve tax) is amended as follows.
17 (*amends* FA 1987 s 50(1))
18 (*amends* FA 1987 s 55(1))

FA 1990

19 (*amends* FA 1990 s 108(1))

FA 1999

20 (*repeals* FA 1999 Sch 14 paras 10(*b*), 11(*b*), 12(3), 13(3))

FA 2003

21 (*repeals* FA 2003 Sch 40 para 2(*b*))

Saving for certain land transactions

22— (1) The following provisions of this Schedule do not have effect in relation to an instrument effecting a land transaction or a duplicate or counterpart of such an instrument—

(*a*) paragraphs 1 to 3,
(*b*) paragraph 10,
(*c*) paragraph 12,
(*d*) paragraph 18, and

(*e*) the repeal of paragraphs 10(*b*) and 11(*b*) of Schedule 14 to FA 1999.

(2) In sub-paragraph (1) "land transaction" has the same meaning as in Part 4 of FA 2003, except that it does not include a transfer of an interest in a property-investment partnership (within the meaning of Schedule 15 of that Act).

Repeals on abolition day

23 If a day is appointed under section 111 of FA 1990 (abolition day), paragraphs 14 and 15 of this Schedule cease to have effect in accordance with section 108 of that Act.

SCHEDULE 38

DISCLOSURE OF TAX AVOIDANCE SCHEMES

Section 116

Orders—The Finance Act 2008, Schedule 38, (Appointed Day) Order, SI 2008/1935 art 2 (1 November 2008 appointed as the day on which the amendments made by this Schedule come into force). Note, however, that these amendments shall not come into force for the purposes of stamp duty land tax (SI 2008/1935 art 2(2)).

Amendments of Part 7 of FA 2004

1 Part 7 of FA 2004 (disclosure of tax avoidance schemes) is amended as follows.

2— (1) Section 308 (duties of promoter) is amended as follows.

(2) (*amends* FA 2004 s 308(1))

(3) (*amends* FA 2004 s 308(2)(*a*))

(4) (*amends* FA 2004 s 308(3))

(5) (*substitutes* FA 2004 s 308(4)–(4C))

3 (*amends* FA 2004 s 311(1))

4 (*substitutes* FA 2004 ss 312, 312A)

5— (1) Section 313 (duty of parties to notifiable arrangements to notify HMRC of number etc) is amended as follows.

(2) (*amends* FA 2004 s 313(1)(*a*))

(3) (*amends* FA 2004 s 313(3))

(4) (*inserts* FA 2004 s 313(5))

6 (*substitutes* FA 2004 s 316)

Amendments of TMA 1970

7— (*amends* TMA 1970 s 98C))

FINANCE ACT 2009

(2009 Chapter 10)

PART 1

CHARGES, RATES, ALLOWANCES, ETC

Stamp duty land tax

PART 3

PENSIONS

PART 5

STAMP TAXES

Stamp duty land tax

An Act to Grant certain duties, to alter other duties, and to amend the law relating to the National Debt and the Public Revenue, and to make further provision in connection with finance.

[21 July 2009]

PART 1

CHARGES, RATES, ALLOWANCES, ETC

Stamp duty land tax

10 Thresholds for residential property

(1) Part 4 of FA 2003 (stamp duty land tax) has effect in relation to transactions with an effective date on or after 22 April 2009 but before 1 January 2010 as if—

(*a*) in section 55(2) (amount of tax chargeable: general), in Table A (bands and percentages for residential property), for "£125,000" (in both places) there were substituted "£175,000", and

(*b*) in paragraph 2(3) of Schedule 5 (amount of tax chargeable: rent), in Table A (bands and percentages for residential property), for "£125,000" (in both places) there were substituted "£175,000".

(2) The following are revoked—

(*a*) the Stamp Duty Land Tax (Variation of Part 4 of the Finance Act 2003) Regulations 2008 (SI 2008/2338), and

(*b*) the Stamp Duty Land Tax (Exemption of Certain Acquisitions of Residential Property) Regulations 2008 (SI 2008/2339).

(3) The revocations made by subsection (2) have effect in relation to transactions with an effective date on or after 22 April 2009.

PART 3
PENSIONS

73 Financial assistance scheme

(1) The Treasury may by regulations make provision for and in connection with—

(*a*) the application of the relevant taxes in relation to the financial assistance scheme, and

(*b*) the application of the relevant taxes in relation to any person in connection with the financial assistance scheme.

(2) "The financial assistance scheme" means the scheme provided for by regulations under section 286 of the Pensions Act 2004.

(3) The provision that may be made by regulations under this section includes provision imposing any of the relevant taxes (as well as provisions for exemptions or reliefs).

(4) The relevant taxes are—

(*a*) income tax,
(*b*) capital gains tax,
(*c*) corporation tax,
(*d*) inheritance tax,
(*e*) value added tax,
(*f*) stamp duty land tax,
(*g*) stamp duty, and
(*h*) stamp duty reserve tax.

(5) Regulations under this section may, in particular, include provision for and in connection with the taxation of payments made by virtue of regulations under section 286 of the Pensions Act 2004.

(6) The exemptions and reliefs that may be given by regulations under this section include, in particular, exemption from charges to income tax, corporation tax or capital gains tax in respect of—

(*a*) income arising from any assets held or managed by, or receipts of, the person who manages the financial assistance scheme ("the scheme manager") and any chargeable gains arising from the disposal of any such assets, and

(*b*) the receipt of fraud compensation payments (within the meaning of Part 2 of the Pensions Act 2004: see section 182(1) of that Act).

(7) Regulations under this section may include provision having effect in relation to any time before they are made if the provision does not increase any person's liability to tax.

(8) The provision made by regulations under this section may be framed as provision applying with appropriate modifications provisions having effect in relation to registered pension schemes; and for this purpose "registered pension scheme" means a pension scheme within the meaning of Part 4 of FA 2004 which is registered under Chapter 2 of that Part of that Act.

(9) Regulations under this section may include—

(*a*) provision amending any enactment or instrument, and
(*b*) consequential, supplementary and transitional provision.

(10) Regulations under this section are to be made by statutory instrument.

(11) A statutory instrument containing regulations under this section is subject to annulment in pursuance of a resolution of the House of Commons.

74 FSCS intervention in relation to insurance in connection with pensions

(1) The Treasury may by regulations make provision for and in connection with the application of the relevant taxes in relation to circumstances in which there is relevant intervention under the FSCS.

(2) "Relevant intervention" means—

(*a*) anything done under, or while seeking to make, arrangements for securing continuity of insurance in connection with registered pension schemes,

(*b*) anything done as part of measures for safeguarding policyholders in connection with registered pension schemes, or

(*c*) the payment of compensation in connection with registered pension schemes.

(3) "The FSCS" means the Financial Services Compensation Scheme (established under Part 15 of the Financial Services and Markets Act 2000).

(4) The provision that may be made by regulations under this section includes provision imposing any of the relevant taxes (as well as provisions for exemptions or reliefs).

(5) The relevant taxes are—

(*a*) income tax,
(*b*) capital gains tax,
(*c*) corporation tax,
(*d*) inheritance tax,
(*e*) stamp duty land tax,

(*f*) stamp duty, and
(*g*) stamp duty reserve tax.

(6) Regulations under this section may include provision having effect in relation to any time before they are made if the provision does not increase any person's liability to tax.

(7) The provision made by regulations under this section may be framed as provision modifying, or applying with appropriate modifications, provisions having effect in relation to registered pension schemes.

(8) Regulations under this section may include—
(*a*) provision amending any enactment or instrument, and
(*b*) consequential, supplementary and transitional provision.

(9) Regulations under this section are to be made by statutory instrument.

(10) A statutory instrument containing regulations under this section is subject to annulment in pursuance of a resolution of the House of Commons.

(11) In this section "registered pension scheme" means a pension scheme within the meaning of Part 4 of FA 2004 which is registered under Chapter 2 of that Part of that Act.

PART 5
STAMP TAXES

Stamp duty land tax

80 Exercise of collective rights by tenants of flats

(1) Section 74 of FA 2003 (collective enfranchisement by leaseholders) is amended as follows.

(2) For subsection (1) substitute—

"(1) This section applies where a chargeable transaction is entered into by a person or persons nominated or appointed by qualifying tenants of flats contained in premises in exercise of—
(*a*) a right under Part 1 of the Landlord and Tenant Act 1987 (right of first refusal), or
(*b*) a right under Chapter 1 of Part 1 of the Leasehold Reform, Housing and Urban Development Act 1993 (right to collective enfranchisement)."

(3) In subsection (2)—
(*a*) omit "In that case,", and
(*b*) for "flats in respect of which the right of collective enfranchisement is being exercised" substitute "qualifying flats contained in the premises".

(4) For subsection (4) substitute—

"(4) In this section—
"flat" and "qualifying tenant" have the same meaning as in the Chapter or Part of the Act conferring the right being exercised;
"qualifying flat" means a flat that is held by a qualifying tenant who is participating in the exercise of the right."

(5) For the heading substitute "Exercise of collective rights by tenants of flats".

(6) Accordingly, in section 55(5) of that Act (amount of tax chargeable), for "collective enfranchisement by leaseholders" substitute "exercise of collective rights by tenants of flats".

(7) The amendments made by this section have effect in relation to transactions with an effective date on or after 22 April 2009.

81 Registered providers of social housing

(1) Part 4 of FA 2003 (stamp duty land tax) is amended as follows.

(2) Section 71 (certain acquisitions by registered social landlord) is amended as follows.

(3) Insert at the beginning—

"(A1) A land transaction under which the purchaser is a profit-making registered provider of social housing is exempt from charge if the transaction is funded with the assistance of a public subsidy."

(4) In subsection (4), for "subsection (1)(*c*)" substitute "this section".

(5) Schedule 9 (right to buy etc) is amended as follows.

(6) In paragraph 5 (shared ownership leases: "qualifying body" etc)—
(*a*) in sub-paragraph (2), insert at the end—
"(*g*) a registered provider of social housing that is not within paragraph (*b*) (subject to sub-paragraph (2A)).", and
(*b*) after that sub-paragraph insert—

"(2A) A registered provider of social housing within sub-paragraph (2)(*g*) ("R") is only a qualifying body in relation to a lease of premises if the following has been funded with the assistance of a grant or other financial assistance under section 19 of the Housing and Regeneration Act 2008—

(*a*) the purchase or construction of the premises by R (or a person connected with R), or

(*b*) the adaptation of the premises by R (or a person connected with R) for use as a dwelling.

(2B) Section 839 of the Taxes Act 1988 (connected persons) has effect for the purposes of sub-paragraph (2A)."

(7) In paragraph 7 (shared ownership trusts: introduction)—

(*a*) in sub-paragraph (3), omit "(within the meaning of paragraph 5(2))", and

(*b*) insert at the end—

"(7) In Condition 2 "qualifying body" means—

(*a*) a qualifying body within the meaning of paragraph 5(2)(*a*) to (*f*), or

(*b*) a registered provider of social housing within paragraph 5(2)(*g*) (subject to sub-paragraph (8)).

(8) A registered provider of social housing within paragraph 5(2)(*g*) ("R") is only a qualifying body in relation to a shared ownership trust if the following has been or is being funded with the assistance of a grant or other financial assistance under section 19 of the Housing and Regeneration Act 2008—

(*a*) the purchase or construction of the trust property by R (or a person connected with R), or

(*b*) the adaptation of the trust property by R (or a person connected with R) for use as a dwelling.

(9) Section 839 of the Taxes Act 1988 (connected persons) has effect for the purposes of sub-paragraph (8)."

(8) The amendments made by this section have effect in relation to transactions with an effective date on or after the day on which this Act is passed.

82 Rent to shared ownership

(1) In Schedule 9 to FA 2003 (stamp duty land tax: right to buy etc), insert at the end—

"Rent to shared ownership lease: charge to tax

13— (1) The chargeable consideration for transactions forming part of a rent to shared ownership lease scheme is determined in accordance with this paragraph.

(2) A "rent to shared ownership lease scheme" means a scheme or arrangement under which a qualifying body—

(*a*) grants an assured shorthold tenancy of a dwelling to a person ("the tenant") or persons ("the tenants"), and

(*b*) subsequently grants a shared ownership lease of the dwelling or another dwelling to the tenant or one or more of the tenants.

(3) The following transactions are to be treated as if they were not linked to each other—

(*a*) the grant of the assured shorthold tenancy,

(*b*) the grant of the shared ownership lease, and

(*c*) any other land transaction between the qualifying body and the tenant, or any of the tenants, entered into as part of the scheme.

(4) For the purpose of determining the effective date of the grant of the shared ownership lease, the possession of the dwelling by the tenant or tenants pursuant to the assured shorthold tenancy is to be disregarded.

(5) In this paragraph—

"assured shorthold tenancy" has the same meaning as in Part 1 of the Housing Act 1988;
"qualifying body" has the same meaning as in paragraph 5;
"shared ownership lease" has the same meaning as in paragraph 4A.

Rent to shared ownership trust: charge to tax

14— (1) The chargeable consideration for transactions forming part of a rent to shared ownership trust scheme is determined in accordance with this paragraph.

(2) A "rent to shared ownership trust scheme" means a scheme or arrangement under which—

(*a*) a qualifying body grants an assured shorthold tenancy of a dwelling to a person ("the tenant") or persons ("the tenants"), and

(*b*) the tenant, or one or more of tenants, subsequently becomes the purchaser under a shared ownership trust of the dwelling, or another dwelling, under which the qualifying body is the social landlord.

(3) The following transactions are to be treated as if they were not linked to each other—

(*a*) the grant of the assured shorthold tenancy,

(*b*) the declaration of the shared ownership trust, and

(*c*) any other land transaction between the qualifying body and the tenant, or any of the tenants, entered into as part of the scheme.

(4) For the purpose of determining the effective date of the declaration of the shared ownership trust, the possession of the dwelling by the tenant or tenants pursuant to the assured shorthold tenancy is to be disregarded.

(5) In this paragraph—

"assured shorthold tenancy" has the same meaning as in Part 1 of the Housing Act 1988;
"qualifying body" has the same meaning as in paragraph 5;
"social landlord" and "purchaser", in relation to a shared ownership trust, have the same meaning as in paragraph 7."

(2) The amendment made by this section has effect in relation to cases in which the effective date of the grant of the shared ownership lease or the declaration of the shared ownership trust is on or after 22 April 2009.

(3) Paragraphs 13(4) and 14(4) of Schedule 9 to FA 2003 (inserted by this section) have effect for the purposes of subsection (2).

Stock lending arrangements

83 Stamp taxes in event of insolvency

(1) Schedule 37 contains provision amending Part 3 (stamp duty) and Part 4 (stamp duty reserve tax) of FA 1986 in respect of repurchase and stock lending arrangements in the event of the insolvency of one of the parties.

(2) The amendments made by that Schedule have effect where the insolvency in question occurs on or after 1 September 2008.

(3) This section and that Schedule cease to have effect—

(*a*) in relation to the amendments made to Part 3 of FA 1986, when the repeal of sections 80 to 85 of that Act (by Part 6 of Schedule 19 to, and in accordance with sections 107 to 109 of, FA 1990) comes into force, and
(*b*) in relation to the amendments made to Part 4 of FA 1986, when the repeal of that Part (by Part 7 of Schedule 19 to, and in accordance with section 110 of, FA 1990) comes into force.

PART 7
ADMINISTRATION

Information etc

96 Extension of information and inspection powers to further taxes

(1) In paragraph 63(1) of Schedule 36 to FA 2008 (information and inspection powers: meaning of "tax"), for paragraph (*e*) (and the "and" before it) substitute—

"(*e*) insurance premium tax,
(*f*) inheritance tax,
(*g*) stamp duty land tax,
(*h*) stamp duty reserve tax,
(*i*) petroleum revenue tax,
(*j*) aggregates levy,
(*k*) climate change levy,
(*l*) landfill tax, and
(*m*) relevant foreign tax,".

(2) Schedule 48 contains further amendments of that Schedule.

(3) The amendments made by this section and Schedule 48 come into force on such day as the Treasury may by order appoint.

(4) An order under subsection (3) may—

(*a*) appoint different days for different purposes, and
(*b*) contain transitional provision and savings.

(5) The Treasury may by order make any incidental, supplemental, consequential, transitional or transitory provision or saving which appears appropriate in consequence of, or otherwise in connection with, this section and Schedule 48.

(6) An order under subsection (5) may—

(*a*) make different provision for different purposes, and
(*b*) make provision amending, repealing or revoking an enactment or instrument (whenever passed or made).

(7) An order under this section is to be made by statutory instrument.

(8) A statutory instrument containing an order under subsection (5) is subject to annulment in pursuance of a resolution of the House of Commons.

98 Record-keeping

(1) Schedule 50 contains provision about obligations to keep records.

(2) The amendments made by that Schedule come into force on such day as the Treasury may by order made by statutory instrument appoint.

Assessments, claims etc

99 Time limits for assessments, claims etc

(1) Schedule 51 contains provision about time limits for assessments, claims etc

(2) The amendments made by that Schedule come into force on such day as the Treasury may by order made by statutory instrument appoint.

(3) An order under subsection (2)—

(*a*) may make different provision for different purposes, and

(*b*) may include transitional provision and savings.

Penalties

106 Penalties for failure to make returns etc

(1) Schedule 55 contains provision for imposing penalties on persons in respect of failures to make returns and other documents relating to liabilities for tax.

(2) That Schedule comes into force on such day as the Treasury may by order appoint.

(3) An order under subsection (2)—

(*a*) may commence a provision generally or only for specified purposes, and

(*b*) may appoint different days for different provisions or for different purposes.

(4) The Treasury may by order make any incidental, supplemental, consequential, transitional, transitory or saving provision which may appear appropriate in consequence of, or otherwise in connection with, Schedule 55.

(5) An order under subsection (4) may include provision amending, repealing or revoking any provision of any Act or subordinate legislation whenever passed or made (including this Act and any Act amended by it).

(6) An order under subsection (4) may make different provision for different purposes.

(7) An order under this section is to be made by statutory instrument.

(8) A statutory instrument containing an order under subsection (4) which includes provision amending or repealing any provision of an Act is subject to annulment in pursuance of a resolution of the House of Commons.

107 Penalties for failure to pay tax

(1) Schedule 56 contains provision for imposing penalties on persons in respect of failures to comply with obligations to pay tax.

(2) That Schedule comes into force on such day as the Treasury may by order appoint.

(3) An order under subsection (2)—

(*a*) may commence a provision generally or only for specified purposes, and

(*b*) may appoint different days for different provisions or for different purposes.

(4) The Treasury may by order make any incidental, supplemental, consequential, transitional, transitory or saving provision which may appear appropriate in consequence of, or otherwise in connection with, Schedule 56.

(5) An order under subsection (4) may include provision amending, repealing or revoking any provision of any Act or subordinate legislation whenever passed or made (including this Act and any Act amended by it).

(6) An order under subsection (4) may make different provision for different purposes.

(7) An order under this section is to be made by statutory instrument.

(8) A statutory instrument containing an order under subsection (4) which includes provision amending or repealing any provision of an Act is subject to annulment in pursuance of a resolution of the House of Commons.

PART 8

MISCELLANEOUS

Other matters

123 Alternative finance investment bonds

Schedule 61 contains provision about the taxation of chargeable gains, stamp duty land tax and capital allowances for and in connection with arrangements falling within section 48A of FA 2005 (alternative finance investment bonds).

124 Mutual societies: tax consequences of transfers of business etc

(1) The Treasury may by regulations make provision for and in connection with—

(*a*) the tax consequences of a transfer of all or part of the business or engagements of a mutual society,
(*b*) the tax consequences of an amalgamation of mutual societies, and
(*c*) the tax consequences of the conversion of a mutual society into a company.

(2) "Mutual society" means—

(*a*) a building society incorporated (or deemed to be incorporated) under the Building Societies Act 1986,
(*b*) a friendly society within the meaning of the Friendly Societies Act 1992, or
(*c*) an industrial and provident society registered (or deemed to be registered) under the Industrial and Provident Societies Act 1965.

(3) Regulations under this section may, in particular, make provision about—

(*a*) relief from tax in respect of losses,
(*b*) capital allowances,
(*c*) the taxation of chargeable gains (including provision conferring relief for specified transfers and amalgamations),
(*d*) the treatment of intangible fixed assets and goodwill,
(*e*) the treatment of loan relationships (and matters treated as loan relationships),
(*f*) the treatment of derivative contracts (and contracts treated as derivative contracts),
(*g*) exemption or other relief from stamp duty, stamp duty reserve tax or stamp duty land tax, and
(*h*) the treatment of arrangements the purpose, or one of the main purposes, of which is to secure a tax advantage.

(4) Regulations under this section may, in particular—

(*a*) modify enactments and instruments relating to tax (whenever passed or made),
(*b*) make different provision for different cases or different purposes, and
(*c*) make incidental, consequential or transitional provision (including provision modifying enactments and instruments, whenever passed or made).

(5) Regulations under this section may include provision having effect in relation to any time before they are made if the provision does not increase any person's liability to tax.

(6) Regulations under this section are to be made by statutory instrument.

(7) A statutory instrument containing regulations under this section is subject to annulment in pursuance of a resolution of the House of Commons.

(8) In this section—

"arrangements" includes any arrangements, scheme or understanding of any kind, whether or not legally enforceable and whether involving a single transaction or two or more transactions;
"company" means a company formed and registered under the Companies Act 2006 (or treated as formed and registered under that Act);
"derivative contract" has the same meaning as in Part 7 of CTA 2009 (see section 576 of that Act);
"goodwill" and "intangible fixed asset" have the same meaning as in Part 8 of CTA 2009 (see sections 713 and 715 of that Act);
"loan relationship" has the same meaning as in the Corporation Tax Acts (see section 302(1) and (2) of CTA 2009);
"modify" includes amend, repeal or revoke;
"tax" includes stamp duty;
"tax advantage" means—

(*a*) a relief from tax (including a tax credit) or increased relief from tax,
(*b*) a repayment of tax or increased repayment of tax,
(*c*) the avoidance, reduction or delay of a charge to tax or an assessment to tax, or
(*d*) the avoidance of a possible assessment to tax.

SCHEDULES

SCHEDULE 37

STOCK LENDING: STAMP TAXES IN THE EVENT OF INSOLVENCY

Section 83

PART 1

STAMP DUTY

1 FA 1986 is amended as follows.

2 In Part 3 (stamp duty), after section 80C insert—

"80D Repurchases and stock lending: replacement stock on insolvency

(1) This section applies where—

(*a*) A and B have entered into an arrangement falling within section 80C(1),
(*b*) the conditions in subsection (2A) or (3) of that section are met,
(*c*) stock is transferred to A or A's nominee, and
(*d*) the conditions in subsection (2) below are met.

(2) The conditions in this subsection are that—

(*a*) A and B are not connected persons within the meaning of section 839 of the Taxes Act 1988,
(*b*) after B has transferred stock under the arrangement, A or B becomes insolvent,
(*c*) it becomes apparent (whether before or after the insolvency occurs) that, as a result of the insolvency, stock will not be transferred to B or B's nominee in accordance with the arrangement,
(*d*) the party who does not become insolvent ("the solvent party") or the solvent party's nominee acquires replacement stock, and
(*e*) the replacement stock is acquired before the end of the period of 30 days beginning with the day on which the insolvency occurs ("the insolvency date").

(3) Where collateral is provided under the arrangement (or under arrangements of which that arrangement forms part), stamp duty is not chargeable on any instrument transferring to the solvent party or the solvent party's nominee—

(*a*) replacement stock acquired using the collateral (whether directly or indirectly), or
(*b*) where the solvent party uses the whole of the value of the collateral to acquire replacement stock, any further replacement stock.

(4) Where no collateral is provided as mentioned in subsection (3), stamp duty is not chargeable on any instrument transferring replacement stock to the solvent party or the solvent party's nominee.

(5) Subsections (3) and (4) may apply as regards more than one instrument (and where those subsections apply as regards more than one instrument, the instruments may be executed by different persons).

(6) But those subsections apply only as regards replacement stock up to the amount of stock which will not be transferred as a result of the insolvency.

(7) An instrument on which stamp duty is not chargeable by virtue only of subsection (3) or (4) is not to be deemed to be duly stamped unless it has been stamped with a stamp denoting that it is not chargeable with any duty.

(8) Despite section 122(1) of the Stamp Act 1891, the stamp mentioned in subsection (7) may be a stamp of such kind as the Commissioners for Her Majesty's Revenue and Customs may prescribe.

(9) For the purposes of this section, a person becomes insolvent—

(*a*) if a company voluntary arrangement takes effect under Part 1 of the Insolvency Act 1986,
(*b*) if an administration application (within the meaning of Schedule B1 to that Act) is made or a receiver or manager, or an administrative receiver, is appointed,
(*c*) on the commencement of a creditor's voluntary winding up (within the meaning of Part 4 of that Act) or a winding up by the court under Chapter 6 of that Part,
(*d*) if an individual voluntary arrangement takes effect under Part 8 of that Act,
(*e*) on the presentation of a bankruptcy petition (within the meaning of Part 9 of that Act),
(*f*) if a compromise or arrangement takes effect under Part 26 of the Companies Act 2006,
(*g*) if a bank insolvency order takes effect under Part 2 of the Banking Act 2009,
(*h*) if a bank administration order takes effect under Part 3 of that Act, or
(*i*) on the occurrence of any corresponding event which has effect under or as a result of the law of Scotland or Northern Ireland or a country or territory outside the United Kingdom.

(10) In this section—

"collateral" means an amount of money or other property which is payable to, or made available for the benefit of, a party to an arrangement or that party's nominee for the purpose of securing the discharge of the requirement to transfer stock to that party or the nominee;
"replacement stock", in the event of a party to an arrangement becoming insolvent, is stock of the same kind as the stock which will not be transferred to the other party or that party's nominee as a result of the insolvency."

3— (1) In consequence of the amendment made by paragraph 2, section 88(1C) (disregard of certain instruments falling within section 80C(1)) is amended as follows.

(2) At the beginning of the words after paragraph (*c*) insert "then, if section 80D does not apply,".

PART 2

STAMP DUTY RESERVE TAX

4 Part 4 of FA 1986 (stamp duty reserve tax) is amended as follows.

5 After section 89AA insert—

"89AB Section 87: exception for repurchases and stock lending in case of insolvency

(1) This section applies where—

(*a*) P and Q have entered into an arrangement falling within section 89AA(1),

(*b*) the only reason that the conditions in subsection (2A) or (3) of that section are not met is that chargeable securities of the same kind and amount as those transferred to P or P's nominee are not transferred to Q or Q's nominee, and

(*c*) the conditions in subsection (2) below are met.

(2) The conditions in this subsection are that—

(*a*) P and Q are not connected persons within the meaning of section 839 of the Taxes Act 1988,

(*b*) after Q has transferred securities under the arrangement, either P or Q becomes insolvent,

(*c*) it becomes apparent (whether before or after the insolvency occurs) that, as a result of the insolvency, securities will not be transferred to Q or Q's nominee in accordance with the arrangement.

(3) Section 87 does not apply as regards an agreement to transfer chargeable securities to P or P's nominee, or Q or Q's nominee, in accordance with the arrangement.

(4) Subsections (5) and (6) apply if—

(*a*) the party who does not become insolvent ("the solvent party") or the solvent party's nominee acquires replacement securities, and

(*b*) the replacement securities are acquired before the end of the period of 30 days beginning with the day on which the insolvency occurs ("the insolvency date").

(5) Where collateral is provided under the arrangement (or under arrangements of which that arrangement forms part), section 87 does not apply as regards any agreement to transfer to the solvent party or the solvent party's nominee—

(*a*) replacement securities acquired using the collateral (whether directly or indirectly), or

(*b*) where the solvent party uses the whole of the value of the collateral to acquire replacement securities, any further replacement securities.

(6) Where no collateral is provided as mentioned in subsection (5), section 87 does not apply as regards any agreement to transfer replacement securities to the solvent party or the solvent party's nominee.

(7) Subsections (5) and (6) may apply as regards more than one agreement (and where those subsections apply as regards more than one agreement, the agreements may be with different persons).

(8) But those subsections apply only as regards replacement securities up to the amount of securities which will not be transferred as a result of the insolvency.

(9) For the purposes of this section, a person becomes insolvent—

(*a*) if a company voluntary arrangement takes effect under Part 1 of the Insolvency Act 1986,

(*b*) if an administration application (within the meaning of Schedule B1 to that Act) is made or a receiver or manager, or an administrative receiver, is appointed,

(*c*) on the commencement of a creditor's voluntary winding up (within the meaning of Part 4 of that Act) or a winding up by the court under Chapter 6 of that Part,

(*d*) if an individual voluntary arrangement takes effect under Part 8 of that Act,

(*e*) on the presentation of a bankruptcy petition (within the meaning of Part 9 of that Act),

(*f*) if a compromise or arrangement takes effect under Part 26 of the Companies Act 2006,

(*g*) if a bank insolvency order takes effect under Part 2 of the Banking Act 2009,

(*h*) if a bank administration order takes effect under Part 3 of that Act, or

(*i*) on the occurrence of any corresponding event which has effect under or as a result of the law of Scotland or Northern Ireland or a country or territory outside the United Kingdom.

(10) In this section—

"collateral" means an amount of money or other property which is payable to, or made available for the benefit of, a party to an arrangement or that party's nominee for the purpose of securing the discharge of the requirement to transfer securities to that party or the nominee;

"replacement securities", in the event of a party to an arrangement becoming insolvent, are chargeable securities of the same kind as the securities which will not be transferred to the other party or that party's nominee as a result of the insolvency."

SCHEDULE 48

EXTENSION OF INFORMATION AND INSPECTION POWERS

Section 96

1 Schedule 36 to FA 2008 (information and inspection powers) is amended as follows.

2 In paragraph 5(4)(*b*) (power to obtain information and documents about persons whose identity is not known), for the words from ", VATA 1994" to the end substitute "or any other enactment relating to UK tax".

3 After paragraph 10 insert—

"Power to inspect business premises etc of involved third parties

10A— (1) An officer of Revenue and Customs may enter business premises of an involved third party (see paragraph 61A) and inspect—

(*a*) the premises,

(*b*) business assets that are on the premises, and

(*c*) relevant documents that are on the premises,

if the inspection is reasonably required by the officer for the purpose of checking the position of any person or class of persons as regards a relevant tax.

(2) The powers under this paragraph may be exercised whether or not the identity of that person is, or the individual identities of those persons are, known to the officer.

(3) The powers under this paragraph do not include power to enter or inspect any part of the premises that is used solely as a dwelling.

(4) In relation to an involved third party, "relevant documents" and "relevant tax" are defined in paragraph 61A."

4— (1) Paragraph 12 (carrying out inspections) is amended as follows.

(2) In sub-paragraph (1), for "this Part of this Schedule" substitute "paragraph 10, 10A or 11".

(3) Accordingly, in the heading, insert at the end "*under paragraph 10, 10A or 11*".

5 After that paragraph insert—

"Powers to inspect property for valuation etc

12A— (1) An officer of Revenue and Customs may enter and inspect premises for the purpose of valuing the premises if the valuation is reasonably required for the purpose of checking any person's position as regards income tax or corporation tax.

(2) An officer of Revenue and Customs may enter premises and inspect—

(*a*) the premises, and

(*b*) any other property on the premises,

for the purpose of valuing, measuring or determining the character of the premises or property.

(3) Sub-paragraph (2) only applies if the valuation, measurement or determination is reasonably required for the purpose of checking any person's position as regards—

(*a*) capital gains tax,

(*b*) corporation tax in respect of chargeable gains,

(*c*) inheritance tax,

(*d*) stamp duty land tax, or

(*e*) stamp duty reserve tax.

(4) A person who the officer considers is needed to assist with the valuation, measurement or determination may enter and inspect the premises or property with the officer.

Carrying out inspections under paragraph 12A

12B— (1) An inspection under paragraph 12A may be carried out only if condition A or B is satisfied.

(2) Condition A is that—

(*a*) the inspection is carried out at a time agreed to by a relevant person, and

(*b*) the relevant person has been given notice in writing of the agreed time of the inspection.

(3) "Relevant person" means—

(*a*) the occupier of the premises, or

(*b*) if the occupier cannot be identified or the premises are vacant, a person who controls the premises.

(4) Condition B is that—

(*a*) the inspection has been approved by the tribunal, and

(*b*) any relevant person specified by the tribunal has been given at least 7 days' notice in writing of the time of the inspection.

(5) A notice under sub-paragraph (4)(*b*) must state the possible consequences of obstructing the officer in the exercise of the power.

(6) If a notice is given under this paragraph in respect of an inspection approved by the tribunal (see paragraph 13), it must state that the inspection has been so approved.

(7) An officer of Revenue and Customs seeking to carry out an inspection under paragraph 12A must produce evidence of authority to carry out the inspection if asked to do so by—

(*a*) the occupier of the premises, or

(*b*) any other person who appears to the officer to be in charge of the premises or property."

6— (1) Paragraph 13 (approval of tribunal) is amended as follows.

(2) In sub-paragraph (1), insert at the end "(and for the effect of obtaining such approval see paragraph 39 (penalties))".

(3) In sub-paragraph (1A) (inserted by Schedule 47), insert at the end "(except as required under sub-paragraph (2A))".

(4) In sub-paragraph (2), after "an inspection" insert "under paragraph 10, 10A or 11".

(5) After that sub-paragraph insert—

"(2A) The tribunal may not approve an inspection under paragraph 12A unless—

(*a*) an application for approval is made by, or with the agreement of, an authorised officer of Revenue and Customs,

(*b*) the person whose tax position is the subject of the proposed inspection has been given a reasonable opportunity to make representations to the officer of Revenue and Customs about that inspection,

(*c*) the occupier of the premises has been given a reasonable opportunity to make such representations,

(*d*) the tribunal has been given a summary of any representations made, and

(*e*) the tribunal is satisfied that, in the circumstances, the inspection is justified.

(2B) Paragraph (*c*) of sub-paragraph (2A) does not apply if the tribunal is satisfied that the occupier of the premises cannot be identified."

7 In paragraph 17(*b*) (power to record information), after "premises," insert "property, goods,".

8— (1) Paragraph 21 (restrictions on giving taxpayer notices) is amended as follows.

(2) In sub-paragraph (7), for "VAT position" substitute "position as regards any tax other than income tax, capital gains tax or corporation tax".

(3) In the heading, insert at the end "*following tax return*".

9 After that paragraph insert—

"Taxpayer notices following land transaction return

21A— (1) Where a person has delivered a land transaction return under section 76 of FA 2003 (returns for purposes of stamp duty land tax) in respect of a transaction, a taxpayer notice may not be given for the purpose of checking that person's stamp duty land tax position in relation to that transaction.

(2) Sub-paragraph (1) does not apply where, or to the extent that, any of conditions A to C is met.

(3) Condition A is that a notice of enquiry has been given in respect of—

(*a*) the return, or

(*b*) a claim (or an amendment of a claim) made by the person in connection with the transaction,

and the enquiry has not been completed.

(4) In sub-paragraph (3) "notice of enquiry" means a notice under paragraph 12 of Schedule 10, or paragraph 7 of Schedule 11A, to FA 2003.

(5) Condition B is that, as regards the person, an officer of Revenue and Customs has reason to suspect that—

(*a*) an amount that ought to have been assessed to stamp duty land tax in respect of the transaction may not have been assessed,

(*b*) an assessment to stamp duty land tax in respect of the transaction may be or have become insufficient, or

(*c*) relief from stamp duty land tax in respect of the transaction may be or have become excessive.

(6) Condition C is that the notice is given for the purpose of obtaining any information or document that is also required for the purpose of checking that person's position as regards a tax other than stamp duty land tax."

10 In paragraph 28 (restrictions on inspection of business documents), and in the heading before that paragraph, omit "*business*".

11 After paragraph 34 insert—

"Involved third parties

34A— (1) This paragraph applies to a third party notice or a notice under paragraph 5 if—

(*a*) it is given to an involved third party (see paragraph 61A),

(*b*) it is given for the purpose of checking the position of a person, or a class of persons, as regards the relevant tax, and

(*c*) it refers only to relevant information or relevant documents.

(2) In relation to such a third party notice—

(*a*) paragraph 3(1) (approval etc of third party notices) does not apply,

(*b*) paragraph 4(1) (copying third party notices to taxpayer) does not apply, and

(*c*) paragraph 30(1) (appeal) has effect as if it permitted an appeal on any grounds.

(3) In relation to such a notice under paragraph 5—

(*a*) sub-paragraphs (3) and (4) of that paragraph (approval of tribunal) have effect as if they permitted, but did not require, an authorised officer of Revenue and Customs to obtain the approval of the tribunal, and

(*b*) paragraph 31 (appeal) has effect as if it permitted an appeal on any grounds.

(4) The involved third party may not appeal against a requirement in the notice to provide any information, or produce any document, that forms part of the involved third party's statutory records.

(5) In relation to an involved third party, "relevant documents", "relevant information" and "relevant tax" are defined in paragraph 61A.

Registered pension schemes etc

34B— (1) This paragraph applies to a third party notice or a notice under paragraph 5 if it refers only to information or documents that relate to any pensions matter.

(2) "Pensions matter" means any matter relating to—

(*a*) a registered pension scheme,

(*b*) an annuity purchased with sums or assets held for the purposes of a registered pension scheme or a pre-2006 pension scheme, or

(*c*) an employer-financed retirement benefits scheme.

(3) In relation to such a third party notice—

(*a*) paragraph 3(1) (approval etc of third party notices) does not apply,

(*b*) paragraph 4(1) (copying third party notices to taxpayer) does not apply, and

(*c*) paragraph 30(1) (appeal) has effect as if it permitted an appeal on any grounds.

(4) In relation to such a notice under paragraph 5—

(*a*) sub-paragraphs (3) and (4) of that paragraph (approval of tribunal) have effect as if they permitted, but did not require, an authorised officer of Revenue and Customs to obtain the approval of the tribunal, and

(*b*) paragraph 31 (appeal) has effect as if it permitted an appeal on any grounds.

(5) A person may not appeal against a requirement in the notice to provide any information, or produce any document, that forms part of any person's statutory records.

(6) Where the notice relates to a matter within sub-paragraph (2)(*a*) or (*b*), the officer of Revenue and Customs who gives the notice must give a copy of the notice to the scheme administrator in relation to the pension scheme.

(7) Where the notice relates to a matter within sub-paragraph (2)(*c*), the officer of Revenue and Customs who gives the notice must give a copy of the notice to the responsible person in relation to the employer-financed retirement benefits scheme.

(8) Sub-paragraphs (6) and (7) do not apply if the notice is given to a person who, in relation to the scheme or annuity to which the notice relates, is a prescribed description of person.

Registered pension schemes etc: interpretation

34C In paragraph 34B—

"employer-financed retirement benefits scheme" has the same meaning as in Chapter 2 of Part 6 of ITEPA 2003 (see sections 393A and 393B of that Act);

"pension scheme" has the same meaning as in Part 4 of FA 2004;

"pre-2006 pension scheme" means a scheme that, at or in respect of any time before 6 April 2006, was—

(*a*) a retirement benefits scheme approved for the purposes of Chapter 1 of Part 14 of ICTA,

(*b*) a former approved superannuation fund (as defined in paragraph 1(3) of Schedule 36 to FA 2004),

(*c*) a relevant statutory scheme (as defined in section 611A of ICTA) or a pension scheme treated as if it were such a scheme, or

(*d*) a personal pension scheme approved under Chapter 4 of Part 14 of ICTA;

"prescribed" means prescribed by regulations made by the Commissioners;

"registered pension scheme" means a pension scheme that is or has been a registered pension scheme within the meaning of Part 4 of FA 2004 or in relation to which an application for registration under that Part of that Act has been made;
"responsible person", in relation to an employer-financed retirement benefits scheme, has the same meaning as in Chapter 2 of Part 6 of ITEPA 2003 (see section 399A of that Act);
"scheme administrator", in relation to a pension scheme, has the same meaning as in Part 4 of FA 2004 (see section 270 of that Act)."

12 In paragraph 35 (special cases: groups of undertakings), in sub-paragraph (4A)(*c*) (inserted by Schedule 47)—

(*a*) for "paragraph 21" substitute "paragraphs 21 and 21A", and
(*b*) for "applies" substitute "apply".

13 In paragraph 37 (special cases: partnerships), after sub-paragraph (2) insert—

"(2A) Where, in respect of a transaction entered into as purchaser by or on behalf of the members of the partnership, any of the partners has—

(*a*) delivered a land transaction return under Part 4 of FA 2003 (stamp duty land tax), or
(*b*) made a claim under that Part of that Act, paragraph 21A (restrictions where taxpayer has delivered land transaction return) has effect as if that return had been delivered, or that claim had been made, by each of the partners."

14 After paragraph 61 insert—

"Involved third parties

61A— (1) In this Schedule, "involved third party" means a person described in the first column of the Table below.

(2) In this Schedule, in relation to an involved third party, "relevant information", "relevant document" and "relevant tax" have the meaning given in the corresponding entries in that Table.

	Involved third party	*Relevant information and relevant documents*	*Relevant tax*
1	A body approved by an officer of Revenue and Customs for the purpose of paying donations within the meaning of Part 12 of ITEPA 2003 (donations to charity: payroll giving) (see section 714 of that Act)	Information and documents relating to the donations	Income tax
2	A plan manager (see section 696 of ITTOIA 2005 (managers of individual investment plans))	Information and documents relating to the plan, including investments which are or have been held under the plan	Income tax
3	An account provider in relation to a child trust fund (as defined in section 3 of the Child Trust Funds Act 2004)	Information and documents relating to the fund, including investments which are or have been held under the fund	Income tax
4	A person who is or has been registered as a managing agent at Lloyd's in relation to a syndicate of underwriting members of Lloyd's	Information and documents relating to, and to the activities of, the syndicate	Income tax Capital gains tax Corporation tax
5	A person involved (in any capacity) in an insurance business (as defined for the purposes of Part 3 of FA 1994)	Information and documents relating to contracts of insurance entered into in the course of the business	Insurance premium tax

	Involved third party	*Relevant information and relevant documents*	*Relevant tax*
6	A person who makes arrangements for persons to enter into contracts of insurance	Information and documents relating to the contracts	Insurance premium tax
7	A person who— (*a*)is concerned in a business that is not an insurance business (as defined for the purposes of Part 3 of FA 1994), and (*b*)has been involved in the entry into a contract of insurance providing cover for any matter associated with that business	Information and documents relating to the contracts	Insurance premium tax
8	A person who, in relation to a charge to stamp duty reserve tax on an agreement, transfer, issue, appropriation or surrender, is an accountable person (as defined in regulation 2 of the Stamp Duty Reserve Tax Regulations SI 1986/1711 (as amended from time to time))	Information and documents relating to the agreement, transfer, issue, appropriation or surrender	Stamp duty reserve tax
9	A responsible person in relation to an oil field (as defined for the purposes of Part 1 of OTA 1975)	Information and documents relating to the oil field	Petroleum revenue tax
10	A person involved (in any capacity) in subjecting aggregate to exploitation in the United Kingdom (as defined for the purposes of Part 2 of FA 2001) or in connected activities	Information and documents relating to matters in which the person is or has been involved	Aggregates levy
11	A person involved (in any capacity) in making or receiving taxable commodities (as defined for the purposes of Schedule 6 to FA 2000) or in connected activities	Information and documents relating to matters in which the person is or has been involved	Climate change levy
12	A person involved (in any capacity) with any landfill disposal (as defined for the purposes of Part 3 of FA 1996)	Information and documents relating to the disposal	Landfill tax".

15— (1) Paragraph 62 (meaning of "statutory records") is amended as follows.

(2) In sub-paragraph (1), for paragraph (*b*) substitute—

"(*b*) any other enactment relating to a tax,".

(3) In sub-paragraph (2)(*b*), for "VATA 1994 or any other enactment relating to value added tax" substitute "any other enactment relating to a tax".

SCHEDULE 50

RECORD-KEEPING

Section 98

Stamp duty land tax

3 Part 4 of FA 2003 (stamp duty land tax) is amended as follows.

4 Schedule 10 (stamp duty land tax: returns, enquiries, assessments and appeals) is amended in accordance with paragraphs 5 to 7.

5— (1) Paragraph 9 (duty to keep and preserve records) is amended as follows.

(2) In sub-paragraph (2), for "for six years after the effective date of the transaction and until any later" substitute "until the end of the later of the relevant day and the".

(3) After that sub-paragraph insert—

"(2A) "The relevant day" means—

(*a*) the sixth anniversary of the effective date of the transaction, or

(*b*) such earlier day as may be specified in writing by the Commissioners for Her Majesty's Revenue and Customs (and different days may be specified for different cases)."

(4) After sub-paragraph (3) insert—

"(4) The Commissioners for Her Majesty's Revenue and Customs may by regulations—

(*a*) provide that the records required to be kept and preserved under this paragraph include, or do not include, records specified in the regulations, and

(*b*) provide that those records include supporting documents so specified.

(5) Regulations under this paragraph may make provision by reference to things specified in a notice published by the Commissioners for Her Majesty's Revenue and Customs in accordance with the regulations (and not withdrawn by a subsequent notice).

(6) "Supporting documents" includes accounts, books, deeds, contracts, vouchers and receipts."

6 For paragraph 10 (preservation of information instead of original records) substitute—

"**10** The duty under paragraph 9 to preserve records may be satisfied—

(*a*) by preserving them in any form and by any means, or

(*b*) by preserving the information contained in them in any form and by any means, subject to any conditions or exceptions specified in writing by the Commissioners for Her Majesty's Revenue and Customs."

7 Accordingly, in the heading before paragraph 10, for "*instead of original records*" substitute "*etc*".

8 Schedule 11 (record-keeping where transaction is not notifiable) is amended in accordance with paragraphs 9 to 11.

9— (1) Paragraph 4 (duty to keep and preserve records) is amended as follows.

(2) In sub-paragraph (2), for "for six years after the effective date of the transaction" substitute "until the end of—

(*a*) the sixth anniversary of the effective date of the transaction, or

(*b*) such earlier day as may be specified in writing by the Commissioners for Her Majesty's Revenue and Customs (and different days may be specified for different cases)."

(3) After sub-paragraph (3) insert—

"(4) The Commissioners for Her Majesty's Revenue and Customs may by regulations—

(*a*) provide that the records required to be kept and preserved under this paragraph include, or do not include, records specified in the regulations, and

(*b*) provide that those records include supporting documents so specified.

(5) Regulations under this paragraph may make provision by reference to things specified in a notice published by the Commissioners for Her Majesty's Revenue and Customs in accordance with the regulations (and not withdrawn by a subsequent notice).

(6) "Supporting documents" includes accounts, books, deeds, contracts, vouchers and receipts."

10 For paragraph 5 (preservation of information instead of original records) substitute—

"**5** The duty under paragraph 4 to preserve records may be satisfied—

(*a*) by preserving them in any form and by any means, or

(*b*) by preserving the information contained in them in any form and by any means, subject to any conditions or exceptions specified in writing by the Commissioners for Her Majesty's Revenue and Customs."

11 Accordingly, in the heading before paragraph 5, for "*instead of original records*" substitute "*etc*".

12 Schedule 11A (claims not included in returns) is amended in accordance with paragraphs 13 and 14.

13— (1) Paragraph 3 (duty to keep and preserve records) is amended as follows.

(2) Omit sub-paragraphs (3) and (4).

(3) After sub-paragraph (4) insert—

"(4A) The Commissioners for Her Majesty's Revenue and Customs may by regulations—

(*a*) provide that the records required to be kept and preserved under this paragraph include, or do not include, records specified in the regulations, and

(*b*) provide that those records include supporting documents so specified.

(4B) Regulations under this paragraph may make provision by reference to things specified in a notice published by the Commissioners for Her Majesty's Revenue and Customs in accordance with the regulations (and not withdrawn by a subsequent notice).

(4C) "Supporting documents" includes accounts, books, deeds, contracts, vouchers and receipts."

14 After that paragraph insert—

"Preservation of information etc

3A The duty under paragraph 3 to preserve records may be satisfied—

(*a*) by preserving them in any form and by any means, or

(*b*) by preserving the information contained in them in any form and by any means, subject to any conditions or exceptions specified in writing by the Commissioners for Her Majesty's Revenue and Customs."

SCHEDULE 51

TIME LIMITS FOR ASSESSMENTS, CLAIMS ETC

Section 99

Stamp duty land tax

14 Part 4 of FA 2003 (stamp duty land tax) is amended as follows.

15— (1) Schedule 10 (returns, enquiries, assessments and appeals) is amended as follows.

(2) In paragraph 25(3) (determination of tax chargeable if no return delivered), for "six years" substitute "4 years".

(3) In paragraph 27(2)(*a*) (determination superseded by actual self-assessment), for "six years" substitute "4 years".

(4) Paragraph 31 (time limit for assessment) is amended in accordance with sub-paragraphs (5) to (8).

(5) In sub-paragraph (1), for "six years" substitute "4 years".

(6) For sub-paragraph (2) substitute—

"(2) An assessment of a person to tax in a case involving a loss of tax brought about carelessly by the purchaser or a related person may be made at any time not more than 6 years after the effective date of the transaction to which it relates (subject to sub-paragraph (2A)).

(2A) An assessment of a person to tax in a case involving a loss of tax—

(*a*) brought about deliberately by the purchaser or a related person,

(*b*) attributable to a failure by the person to comply with an obligation under section 76(1) or paragraph 3(3)(*a*), 4(3)(*a*) or 8(3)(*a*) of Schedule 17A, or

(*c*) attributable to arrangements in respect of which the person has failed to comply with an obligation under section 309, 310 or 313 of the Finance Act 2004 (obligation of parties to tax avoidance schemes to provide information to Her Majesty's Revenue and Customs),

may be made at any time not more than 20 years after the effective date of the transaction to which it relates."

(7) In sub-paragraph (4)(*a*), for "three years" substitute "4 years".

(8) After sub-paragraph (5) insert—

"(6) In this paragraph "related person", in relation to a purchaser, means—

(*a*) a person acting on behalf of the purchaser, or

(*b*) a person who was a partner of the purchaser at the relevant time."

(9) After paragraph 31 insert—

"Losses brought about carelessly or deliberately

31A— (1) This paragraph applies for the purposes of paragraph 31.

(2) A loss of tax is brought about carelessly by a person if the person fails to take reasonable care to avoid bringing about that loss.

(3) Where—

(*a*) information is provided to Her Majesty's Revenue and Customs, (*b*) the person who provided the information, or the person on whose behalf the information was provided, discovers some time later that the information was inaccurate, and

(*c*) that person fails to take reasonable steps to inform Her Majesty's Revenue and Customs,

any loss of tax brought about by the inaccuracy is to be treated as having been brought about carelessly by that person.

(4) References to a loss of tax brought about deliberately by a person include a loss of tax brought about as a result of a deliberate inaccuracy in a document given to Her Majesty's Revenue and Customs by or on behalf of that person."

(10) In paragraph 34(2) (relief in case of mistake in return), for "six years" substitute "4 years".

16— (1) Paragraph 8 of Schedule 14 (time limit for determination of penalties) is amended as follows.

(2) In sub-paragraph (2)—

(*a*) for "six years" substitute "4 years", and

(*b*) after "began to be incurred" insert "("the relevant date")".

(3) In sub-paragraph (3), insert at the end "(subject to any of the following provisions of this paragraph allowing a longer period)".

(4) After sub-paragraph (4) insert—

"(4A) Where a person is liable to a penalty in a case involving a loss of tax brought about carelessly by the person (or by another person acting on that person's behalf), the penalty may be determined, or the proceedings may be brought, at any time not more than 6 years after the relevant date (subject to sub-paragraphs (4B) and (5)).

(4B) Where a person is liable to a penalty in a case involving a loss of tax—

(*a*) brought about deliberately by the person (or by another person acting on that person's behalf),

(*b*) attributable to a failure by the person to comply with an obligation under section 76(1) or paragraph 3(3)(*a*), 4(3)(*a*) or 8(3)(*a*) of Schedule 17A, or

(*c*) attributable to arrangements in respect of which the person has failed to comply with an obligation under section 309, 310 or 313 of the Finance Act 2004 (obligation of parties to tax avoidance schemes to provide information to Her Majesty's Revenue and Customs),

the penalty may be determined, or the proceedings may be brought, at any time not more than 20 years after the relevant date.

(4C) Paragraph 31A of Schedule 10 (losses brought about carelessly or deliberately) applies for the purpose of this paragraph."

Stamp Taxes

SCHEDULE 55

PENALTY FOR FAILURE TO MAKE RETURNS ETC

Section 106

Penalty for failure to make returns etc'

1— (1) A penalty is payable by a person ("P") where P fails to make or deliver a return, or to deliver any other document, specified in the Table below on or before the filing date.

(2) Paragraphs 2 to 13 set out—

(*a*) the circumstances in which a penalty is payable, and

(*b*) subject to paragraphs 14 to 17, the amount of the penalty.

(3) If P's failure falls within more than one paragraph of this Schedule, P is liable to a penalty under each of those paragraphs (but this is subject to paragraph 17(3)).

(4) In this Schedule—

"filing date", in relation to a return or other document, means the date by which it is required to be made or delivered to HMRC;

"penalty date", in relation to a return or other document, means the date on which a penalty is first payable for failing to make or deliver it (that is to say, the day after the filing date).

(5) In the provisions of this Schedule which follow the Table—

(*a*) any reference to a return includes a reference to any other document specified in the Table, and

(*b*) any reference to making a return includes a reference to delivering a return or to delivering any such document.

	Tax to which return etc relates	*Return or other document*
1	Income tax or capital gains tax	(a) Return under section 8(1)(a) of TMA 1970

	Tax to which return etc relates	*Return or other document*
		(b) Accounts, statement or document required under section 8(1)(b) of TMA 1970
2	Income tax or capital gains tax	(a) Return under section 8A(1)(a) of TMA 1970 (b) Accounts, statement or document required under section 8A(1)(b) of TMA 1970
3	Income tax or corporation tax	(a) Return under section 12AA(2)(a) or (3)(a) of TMA 1970 (b) Accounts, statement or document required under section 12AA(2)(b) or (3)(b) of TMA 1970
4	Income tax	(a) Annual return of payments and net tax deducted for the purposes of PAYE regulations (b) Return of revised payments and net tax deducted for those purposes where those amounts are revised after end of tax year
5	Income tax	Return under section 254 of FA 2004 (pension schemes)
6	Deductions on account of tax under Chapter 3 of Part 3 of FA 2004 (construction industry scheme)	Return under regulations under section 70 of FA 2004
7	Corporation tax	Company tax return under paragraph 3 of Schedule 18 to FA 1998
8	Inheritance tax	Account under section 216 or 217 of IHTA 1984
9	Stamp duty land tax	Land transaction return under section 76 of FA 2003 or further return under section 81 of that Act
10	Stamp duty land tax	Return under paragraph 3, 4 or 8 of Schedule 17A to FA 2003
11	Stamp duty reserve tax	Notice of charge to tax under regulations under section 98 of FA 1986
12	Petroleum revenue tax	Return under paragraph 2 of Schedule 2 to OTA 1975
13	Petroleum revenue tax	Statement under section 1(1)(a) of PRTA 1980

Amount of penalty: occasional returns and annual returns

2 Paragraphs 3 to 6 apply in the case of a return falling within any of items 1 to 5 and 7 to 13 in the Table.

3 P is liable to a penalty under this paragraph of £100.

4— (1) P is liable to a penalty under this paragraph if (and only if)—

(*a*) P's failure continues after the end of the period of 3 months beginning with the penalty date,

(*b*) HMRC decide that such a penalty should be payable, and

(*c*) HMRC give notice to P specifying the date from which the penalty is payable.

(2) The penalty under this paragraph is £10 for each day that the failure continues during the period of 90 days beginning with the date specified in the notice given under sub-paragraph (1)(*c*).

(3) The date specified in the notice under sub-paragraph (1)(*c*)—

(*a*) may be earlier than the date on which the notice is given, but

(*b*) may not be earlier than the end of the period mentioned in sub-paragraph (1)(*a*).

5— (1) P is liable to a penalty under this paragraph if (and only if) P's failure continues after the end of the period of 6 months beginning with the penalty date.

(2) The penalty under this paragraph is the greater of—

(*a*) 5% of any liability to tax which would have been shown in the return in question, and

(*b*) £300.

6— (1) P is liable to a penalty under this paragraph if (and only if) P's failure continues after the end of the period of 12 months beginning with the penalty date.

(2) Where, by failing to make the return, P withholds information which would enable or assist HMRC to assess P's liability to tax, the penalty under this paragraph is determined in accordance with sub-paragraphs (3) and (4).

(3) If the withholding of the information is deliberate and concealed, the penalty is the greater of—

(*a*) 100% of any liability to tax which would have been shown in the return in question, and
(*b*) £300.

(4) If the withholding of the information is deliberate but not concealed, the penalty is the greater of—

(*a*) 70% of any liability to tax which would have been shown in the return in question, and
(*b*) £300.

(5) In any other case, the penalty under this paragraph is the greater of—

(*a*) 5% of any liability to tax which would have been shown in the return in question, and
(*b*) £300.

. . .

Reductions for disclosure

14— (1) Paragraph 15 provides for reductions in the penalty under paragraph 6(3) or (4) or 11(3) or (4) where P discloses information which has been withheld by a failure to make a return ("relevant information").

(2) P discloses relevant information by—

(*a*) telling HMRC about it,
(*b*) giving HMRC reasonable help in quantifying any tax unpaid by reason of its having been withheld, and
(*c*) allowing HMRC access to records for the purpose of checking how much tax is so unpaid.

(3) Disclosure of relevant information—

(*a*) is "unprompted" if made at a time when P has no reason to believe that HMRC have discovered or are about to discover the relevant information, and
(*b*) otherwise, is "prompted".

(4) In relation to disclosure "quality" includes timing, nature and extent.

15— (1) Where a person who would otherwise be liable to a 100% penalty has made an unprompted disclosure, HMRC must reduce the 100% to a percentage, not below 30%, which reflects the quality of the disclosure.

(2) Where a person who would otherwise be liable to a 100% penalty has made a prompted disclosure, HMRC must reduce the 100% to a percentage, not below 50%, which reflects the quality of the disclosure.

(3) Where a person who would otherwise be liable to a 70% penalty has made an unprompted disclosure, HMRC must reduce the 70% to a percentage, not below 20%, which reflects the quality of the disclosure.

(4) Where a person who would otherwise be liable to a 70% penalty has made a prompted disclosure, HMRC must reduce the 70% to a percentage, not below 35%, which reflects the quality of the disclosure.

(5) But HMRC must not under this paragraph—

(*a*) reduce a penalty under paragraph 6(3) or (4) below £300, or
(*b*) reduce a penalty under paragraph 11(3) or (4) below the amount set by paragraph 11(3)(*b*) or (4)(*b*) (as the case may be).

Special reduction

16— (1) If HMRC think it right because of special circumstances, they may reduce a penalty under any paragraph of this Schedule.

(2) In sub-paragraph (1) "special circumstances" does not include—

(*a*) ability to pay, or
(*b*) the fact that a potential loss of revenue from one taxpayer is balanced by a potential over-payment by another.

(3) In sub-paragraph (1) the reference to reducing a penalty includes a reference to—

(*a*) staying a penalty, and
(*b*) agreeing a compromise in relation to proceedings for a penalty.

Interaction with other penalties and late payment surcharges

17— (1) Where P is liable for a penalty under any paragraph of this Schedule which is determined by reference to a liability to tax, the amount of that penalty is to be reduced by the amount of any other penalty incurred by P, if the amount of the penalty is determined by reference to the same liability to tax.

(2) In sub-paragraph (1) the reference to "any other penalty" does not include—

(*a*) a penalty under any other paragraph of this Schedule, or (*b*) a penalty under Schedule 56 (penalty for late payment of tax).

(3) Where P is liable for a penalty under more than one paragraph of this Schedule which is determined by reference to a liability to tax, the aggregate of the amounts of those penalties must not exceed 100% of the liability to tax.

Assessment

18— (1) Where P is liable for a penalty under any paragraph of this Schedule HMRC must—

(*a*) assess the penalty,
(*b*) notify P, and
(*c*) state in the notice the period in respect of which the penalty is assessed.

(2) A penalty under any paragraph of this Schedule must be paid before the end of the period of 30 days beginning with the day on which notification of the penalty is issued.

(3) An assessment of a penalty under any paragraph of this Schedule—

(*a*) is to be treated for procedural purposes in the same way as an assessment to tax (except in respect of a matter expressly provided for by this Schedule),
(*b*) may be enforced as if it were an assessment to tax, and
(*c*) may be combined with an assessment to tax.

(4) A supplementary assessment may be made in respect of a penalty if an earlier assessment operated by reference to an underestimate of the liability to tax which would have been shown in a return.

19— (1) An assessment of a penalty under any paragraph of this Schedule in respect of any amount must be made on or before the later of date A and (where it applies) date B.

(2) Date A is the last day of the period of 2 years beginning with the filing date.

(3) Date B is the last day of the period of 12 months beginning with—

(*a*) the end of the appeal period for the assessment of the liability to tax which would have been shown in the return, or
(*b*) if there is no such assessment, the date on which that liability is ascertained or it is ascertained that the liability is nil.

(4) In sub-paragraph (3)(*a*) "appeal period" means the period during which—

(*a*) an appeal could be brought, or
(*b*) an appeal that has been brought has not been determined or withdrawn.

(5) Sub-paragraph (1) does not apply to a re-assessment under paragraph 24(2)(*b*).

Appeal

20— (1) P may appeal against a decision of HMRC that a penalty is payable by P.

(2) P may appeal against a decision of HMRC as to the amount of a penalty payable by P.

21— (1) An appeal under paragraph 20 is to be treated in the same way as an appeal against an assessment to the tax concerned (including by the application of any provision about bringing the appeal by notice to HMRC, about HMRC review of the decision or about determination of the appeal by the First-tier Tribunal or Upper Tribunal).

(2) Sub-paragraph (1) does not apply—

(*a*) so as to require P to pay a penalty before an appeal against the assessment of the penalty is determined, or
(*b*) in respect of any other matter expressly provided for by this Act.

22— (1) On an appeal under paragraph 20(1) that is notified to the tribunal, the tribunal may affirm or cancel HMRC's decision.

(2) On an appeal under paragraph 20(2) that is notified to the tribunal, the tribunal may—

(*a*) affirm HMRC's decision, or
(*b*) substitute for HMRC's decision another decision that HMRC had power to make.

(3) If the tribunal substitutes its decision for HMRC's, the tribunal may rely on paragraph 16—

(*a*) to the same extent as HMRC (which may mean applying the same percentage reduction as HMRC to a different starting point), or
(*b*) to a different extent, but only if the tribunal thinks that HMRC's decision in respect of the application of paragraph 16 was flawed.

(4) In sub-paragraph (3)(*b*) "flawed" means flawed when considered in the light of the principles applicable in proceedings for judicial review.

(5) In this paragraph "tribunal" means the First-tier Tribunal or Upper Tribunal (as appropriate by virtue of paragraph 21(1)).

Reasonable excuse

23— (1) Liability to a penalty under any paragraph of this Schedule does not arise in relation to a failure to make a return if P satisfies HMRC or (on appeal) the First-tier Tribunal or Upper Tribunal that there is a reasonable excuse for the failure.

(2) For the purposes of sub-paragraph (1)—

(*a*) an insufficiency of funds is not a reasonable excuse, unless attributable to events outside P's control,
(*b*) where P relies on any other person to do anything, that is not a reasonable excuse unless P took reasonable care to avoid the failure, and
(*c*) where P had a reasonable excuse for the failure but the excuse has ceased, P is to be treated as having continued to have the excuse if the failure is remedied without unreasonable delay after the excuse ceased.

Determination of penalty geared to tax liability where no return made

24— (1) References to a liability to tax which would have been shown in a return are references to the amount which, if a complete and accurate return had been delivered on the filing date, would have been shown to be due or payable by the taxpayer in respect of the tax concerned for the period to which the return relates.

(2) In the case of a penalty which is assessed at a time before P makes the return to which the penalty relates—
(*a*) HMRC is to determine the amount mentioned in sub-paragraph (1) to the best of HMRC's information and belief, and
(*b*) if P subsequently makes a return, the penalty must be re-assessed by reference to the amount of tax shown to be due and payable in that return (but subject to any amendments or corrections to the return).

(3) In calculating a liability to tax which would have been shown in a return, no account is to be taken of any relief under subsection (4) of section 419 of ICTA (relief in respect of repayment etc of loan) which is deferred under subsection (4A) of that section.

Partnerships

25— (1) This paragraph applies where—
(*a*) the representative partner, or
(*b*) a successor of the representative partner,
fails to make a return falling within item 3 in the Table (partnership returns).

(2) A penalty in respect of the failure is payable by every relevant partner.

(3) In accordance with sub-paragraph (2), any reference in this Schedule to P is to be read as including a reference to a relevant partner.

(4) An appeal under paragraph 20 in connection with a penalty payable by virtue of this paragraph may be brought only by—
(*a*) the representative partner, or
(*b*) a successor of the representative partner.

(5) Where such an appeal is brought in connection with a penalty payable in respect of a failure, the appeal is to treated as if it were an appeal in connection with every penalty payable in respect of that failure.

(6) In this paragraph—
"relevant partner" means a person who was a partner in the partnership to which the return relates at any time during the period in respect of which the return was required;
"representative partner" means a person who has been required by a notice served under or for the purposes of section 12AA(2) or (3) of TMA 1970 to deliver any return;
"successor" has the meaning given by section 12AA(11) of TMA 1970.

Double jeopardy

26 P is not liable to a penalty under any paragraph of this Schedule in respect of a failure or action in respect of which P has been convicted of an offence.

Interpretation

27— (1) This paragraph applies for the construction of this Schedule.

(2) The withholding of information by P is—
(*a*) "deliberate and concealed" if P deliberately withholds the information and makes arrangements to conceal the fact that the information has been withheld, and
(*b*) "deliberate but not concealed" if P deliberately withholds the information but does not make arrangements to conceal the fact that the information has been withheld.

(3) "HMRC" means Her Majesty's Revenue and Customs.

(4) References to a liability to tax, in relation to a return falling within item 6 in the Table (construction industry scheme), are to a liability to make payments in accordance with Chapter 3 of Part 3 of FA 2004.

(5) References to an assessment to tax, in relation to inheritance tax and stamp duty reserve tax, are to a determination.

SCHEDULE 56

PENALTY FOR FAILURE TO MAKE PAYMENTS ON TIME

Section 107

Penalty for failure to pay tax

1— (1) A penalty is payable by a person ("P") where P fails to pay an amount of tax specified in column 3 of the Table below on or before the date specified in column 4.

(2) Paragraphs 3 to 8 set out—

(*a*) the circumstances in which a penalty is payable, and
(*b*) subject to paragraph 9, the amount of the penalty.

(3) If P's failure falls within more than one provision of this Schedule, P is liable to a penalty under each of those provisions.

(4) In the following provisions of this Schedule, the "penalty date", in relation to an amount of tax, means the date on which a penalty is first payable for failing to pay the amount (that is to say, the day after the date specified in or for the purposes of column 4 of the Table).

	Tax to which payment relates	*Amount of tax payable*	*Date after which penalty is incurred*
PRINCIPAL AMOUNTS			
1	Income tax or capital gains tax	Amount payable under section 59B(3) or (4) of TMA 1970	The date falling 30 days after the date specified in section 59B(3) or (4) of TMA 1970 as the date by which the amount must be paid
2	Income tax	Amount payable under PAYE regulations (except an amount falling within item 20)	The date determined by or under PAYE regulations as the date by which the amount must be paid
3	Income tax	Amount shown in return under section 254(1) of FA 2004	The date falling 30 days after the date specified in section 254(5) of FA 2004 as the date by which the amount must be paid
4	Deductions on account of tax under Chapter 3 of Part 3 of FA 2004 (construction industry scheme)	Amount payable under section 62 of FA 2004 (except an amount falling within item 17, 23 or 24)	The date determined by or under regulations under section 62 of FA 2004 as the date by which the amount must be paid
5	Corporation tax	Amount shown in company tax return under paragraph 3 of Schedule 18 to FA 1998	The filing date for the company tax return for the accounting period for which the tax is due (see paragraph 14 of Schedule 18 to FA 1998)
6	Corporation tax	Amount payable under regulations under section 59E of TMA 1970 (except an amount falling within item 17, 23 or 24)	The filing date for the company tax return for the accounting period for which the tax is due (see paragraph 14 of Schedule 18 to FA 1998)
7	Inheritance tax	Amount payable under section 226 of IHTA 1984 (except an amount falling within item 14 or 21)	The filing date (determined under section 216 of IHTA 1984) for the account in respect of the liability for that amount

	Tax to which payment relates	*Amount of tax payable*	*Date after which penalty is incurred*
8	Inheritance tax	Amount payable under section 227 or 229 of IHTA 1984 (except an amount falling within item 14 or 21)	For the first instalment, the filing date (determined under section 216 of IHTA 1984) for the account in respect of the liability for that amount For any later instalment, the date falling 30 days after the date determined under section 227 or 229 of IHTA 1984 as the date by which the instalment must be paid
9	Stamp duty land tax	Amount payable under section 86(1) or (2) of FA 2003	The date falling 30 days after the date specified in section 86(1) or (2) of FA 2003 as the date by which the amount must be paid
10	Stamp duty reserve tax	Amount payable under section 87, 93 or 96 of FA 1986 or Schedule 19 to FA 1999 (except an amount falling within item 17, 23 or 24)	The date falling 30 days after the date determined by or under regulations under section 98 of FA 1986 as the date by which the amount must be paid
11	Petroleum revenue tax	Amount charged in an assessment under paragraph 11(1) of Schedule 2 to OTA 1975	The date falling 30 days after the date determined in accordance with paragraph 13 of Schedule 2 to OTA 1975 as the date by which the amount must be paid
AMOUNTS PAYABLE IN DEFAULT OF A RETURN BEING MADE			
12	Income tax or capital gains tax	Amount payable under section 59B(5A) of TMA 1970	The date falling 30 days after the date specified in section 59B(5A) of TMA 1970 as the date by which the amount must be paid
13	Corporation tax	Amount shown in determination under paragraph 36 or 37 of Schedule 18 to FA 1998	The filing date for the company tax return for the accounting period for which the tax is due (see paragraph 14 of Schedule 18 to FA 1998)
14	Inheritance tax	Amount shown in a determination made by HMRC in the circumstances set out in paragraph 2	The filing date (determined under section 216 of IHTA 1984) for the account in respect of the liability for that amount
15	Stamp duty land tax	Amount shown in determination under paragraph 25 of Schedule 10 to FA 2003 (including that paragraph as applied by section 81(3) of that Act)	The date falling 30 days after the filing date for the return in question
16	Petroleum revenue tax	Amount charged in an assessment made where participator fails to deliver return for a chargeable period	The date falling 6 months and 30 days after the end of the chargeable period

	Tax to which payment relates	*Amount of tax payable*	*Date after which penalty is incurred*
17	Tax falling within any of items 1 to 6, 9 or 10	Amount (not falling within any of items 12 to 15) which is shown in an assessment or determination made by HMRC in the circumstances set out in paragraph 2	The date falling 30 days after the date by which the amount would have been required to be paid if it had been shown in the return in question
AMOUNT SHOWN TO BE DUE IN OTHER ASSESSMENTS, DETERMINATIONS, ETC			
18	Income tax or capital gains tax	Amount payable under section 55 of TMA 1970	The date falling 30 days after the date determined in accordance with section 55(3), (4), (6) or (9) of TMA 1970 as the date by which the amount must be paid
19	Income tax or capital gains tax	Amount payable under section 59B(5) or (6) of TMA 1970	The date falling 30 days after the date specified in section 59B(5) or (6) of TMA 1970 as the date by which the amount must be paid
20	Income tax	Amount shown in determination made by HMRC where it appears that tax payable under PAYE regulations has not been paid	The date determined by or under PAYE regulations as the date by which the amount must be paid
21	Inheritance tax	Amount shown in— (*a*) an amendment or correction of a return showing an amount falling within item 7 or 8, or (*b*) a determination made by HMRC in circumstances other than those set out in paragraph 2	The later of— (*a*) the filing date (determined under section 216 of IHTA 1984) for the account in respect of the liability for that amount, and (*b*) the date falling 30 days after the date on which the amendment, correction, assessment or determination is made
22	Petroleum revenue tax	Amount charged in an assessment, or an amendment of an assessment, made in circumstances other than those set out in items 11 and 16	The date falling 30 days after— (*a*) the date by which the amount must be paid, or (*b*) the date on which the assessment or amendment is made, whichever is later
23	Tax falling within any of items 1 to 6, 9 or 10	Amount (not falling within any of items 18 to 20) shown in an amendment or correction of a return showing an amount falling within any of items 1 to 6, 9 or 10	The date falling 30 days after— (*a*) the date by which the amount must be paid, or (*b*) the date on which the amendment or correction is made,

	Tax to which payment relates	*Amount of tax payable*	*Date after which penalty is incurred*
			whichever is later
24	Tax falling within any of items 1 to 6, 9 or 10	Amount (not falling within any of items 18 to 20) shown in an assessment or determination made by HMRC in circumstances other than those set out in paragraph 2	The date falling 30 days after— (*a*) the date by which the amount must be paid, or (*b*) the date on which the assessment or determination is made, whichever is later

...

Special reduction

9— (1) If HMRC think it right because of special circumstances, they may reduce a penalty under any paragraph of this Schedule.

(2) In sub-paragraph (1) "special circumstances" does not include—

(*a*) ability to pay, or

(*b*) the fact that a potential loss of revenue from one taxpayer is balanced by a potential over-payment by another.

(3) In sub-paragraph (1) the reference to reducing a penalty includes a reference to—

(*a*) staying a penalty, and

(*b*) agreeing a compromise in relation to proceedings for a penalty.

Suspension of penalty during currency of agreement for deferred payment

10— (1) This paragraph applies if—

(*a*) P fails to pay an amount of tax when it becomes due and payable,

(*b*) P makes a request to HMRC that payment of the amount of tax be deferred, and

(*c*) HMRC agrees that payment of that amount may be deferred for a period ("the deferral period").

(2) If P would (apart from this sub-paragraph) become liable, between the date on which P makes the request and the end of the deferral period, to a penalty under any paragraph of this Schedule for failing to pay that amount, P is not liable to that penalty.

(3) But if—

(*a*) P breaks the agreement (see sub-paragraph (4)), and

(*b*) HMRC serves on P a notice specifying any penalty to which P would become liable apart from sub-paragraph (2),

P becomes liable, at the date of the notice, to that penalty.

(4) P breaks an agreement if—

(*a*) P fails to pay the amount of tax in question when the deferral period ends, or

(*b*) the deferral is subject to P complying with a condition (including a condition that part of the amount be paid during the deferral period) and P fails to comply with it.

(5) If the agreement mentioned in sub-paragraph (1)(*c*) is varied at any time by a further agreement between P and HMRC, this paragraph applies from that time to the agreement as varied.

Assessment

11— (1) Where P is liable for a penalty under any paragraph of this Schedule HMRC must—

(*a*) assess the penalty,

(*b*) notify P, and

(*c*) state in the notice the period in respect of which the penalty is assessed.

(2) A penalty under any paragraph of this Schedule must be paid before the end of the period of 30 days beginning with the day on which notice of the assessment of the penalty is issued.

(3) An assessment of a penalty under any paragraph of this Schedule—

(*a*) is to be treated for procedural purposes in the same way as an assessment to tax (except in respect of a matter expressly provided for by this Schedule),

(*b*) may be enforced as if it were an assessment to tax, and

(*c*) may be combined with an assessment to tax.

(4) A supplementary assessment may be made in respect of a penalty if an earlier assessment operated by reference to an underestimate of an amount of unpaid tax.

(5) A supplementary assessment may be made in respect of a penalty under paragraph 6 if—

(*a*) notice of the assessment of the penalty was issued before the end of the tax year, and

(*b*) before the end of the year, P makes a further default (so that the penalty for the earlier default is increased).

12— (1) An assessment of a penalty under any paragraph of this Schedule in respect of any amount must be made on or before the later of date A and (where it applies) date B.

(2) Date A is the last day of the period of 2 years beginning with the date specified in or for the purposes of column 4 of the Table (that is to say, the last date on which payment may be made without incurring a penalty).

(3) Date B is the last day of the period of 12 months beginning with—

(*a*) the end of the appeal period for the assessment of the amount of tax in respect of which the penalty is assessed, or

(*b*) if there is no such assessment, the date on which that amount of tax is ascertained.

(4) In sub-paragraph (3)(*a*) "appeal period" means the period during which—

(*a*) an appeal could be brought, or

(*b*) an appeal that has been brought has not been determined or withdrawn.

Appeal

13— (1) P may appeal against a decision of HMRC that a penalty is payable by P.

(2) P may appeal against a decision of HMRC as to the amount of a penalty payable by P.

14— (1) An appeal under paragraph 13 is to be treated in the same way as an appeal against an assessment to the tax concerned (including by the application of any provision about bringing the appeal by notice to HMRC, about HMRC review of the decision or about determination of the appeal by the First-tier Tribunal or Upper Tribunal).

(2) Sub-paragraph (1) does not apply—

(*a*) so as to require P to pay a penalty before an appeal against the assessment of the penalty is determined, or

(*b*) in respect of any other matter expressly provided for by this Act.

15— (1) On an appeal under paragraph 13(1) that is notified to the tribunal, the tribunal may affirm or cancel HMRC's decision.

(2) On an appeal under paragraph 13(2) that is notified to the tribunal, the tribunal may—

(*a*) affirm HMRC's decision, or

(*b*) substitute for HMRC's decision another decision that HMRC had power to make.

(3) If the tribunal substitutes its decision for HMRC's, the tribunal may rely on paragraph 9—

(*a*) to the same extent as HMRC (which may mean applying the same percentage reduction as HMRC to a different starting point), or

(*b*) to a different extent, but only if the tribunal thinks that HMRC's decision in respect of the application of paragraph 9 was flawed.

(4) In sub-paragraph (3)(*b*) "flawed" means flawed when considered in the light of the principles applicable in proceedings for judicial review.

(5) In this paragraph "tribunal" means the First-tier Tribunal or Upper Tribunal (as appropriate by virtue of paragraph 14(1)).

Reasonable excuse

16— (1) Liability to a penalty under any paragraph of this Schedule does not arise in relation to a failure to make a payment if P satisfies HMRC or (on appeal) the First-tier Tribunal or Upper Tribunal that there is a reasonable excuse for the failure.

(2) For the purposes of sub-paragraph (1)—

(*a*) an insufficiency of funds is not a reasonable excuse unless attributable to events outside P's control,

(*b*) where P relies on any other person to do anything, that is not a reasonable excuse unless P took reasonable care to avoid the failure, and

(*c*) where P had a reasonable excuse for the failure but the excuse has ceased, P is to be treated as having continued to have the excuse if the failure is remedied without unreasonable delay after the excuse ceased.

Double jeopardy

17 P is not liable to a penalty under any paragraph of this Schedule in respect of a failure or action in respect of which P has been convicted of an offence.

Interpretation

18— (1) This paragraph applies for the construction of this Schedule.

(2) "HMRC" means Her Majesty's Revenue and Customs.

(3) References to tax include construction industry deductions under Chapter 3 of Part 3 of FA 2004.

(4) References to a determination, in relation to an amount payable under PAYE regulations or under Chapter 3 of Part 3 of FA 2004, include a certificate.

(5) References to an assessment to tax, in relation to inheritance tax and stamp duty reserve tax, are to a determination.

SCHEDULE 61

ALTERNATIVE FINANCE INVESTMENT BONDS

Section 123

PART 1

INTRODUCTORY

Interpretation

1— (1) In this Schedule—

"alternative finance investment bond" means arrangements within section 48A of FA 2005 (alternative finance investment bond: introduction);

"bond assets", "bond-holder", "bond-issuer" and "capital" have the meaning given by that section;

"HMRC" means Her Majesty's Revenue and Customs;

"prescribed" means prescribed in regulations made by HMRC;

"qualifying interest" means a major interest in land (within the meaning given by section 117 of FA 2003) except that it does not include a lease if the lease is for—

(*a*) a term of years of 21 years or less, or

(*b*) in Scotland, a period of 21 years or less.

(2) Except where the context otherwise requires, any expression which is used in this Schedule and in Part 4 of FA 2003 has the meaning which it has in that Part.

PART 2

ISSUE, TRANSFER AND REDEMPTION OF RIGHTS UNDER ARRANGEMENTS

Issue, transfer and redemption of rights under bond not be treated as chargeable transaction

2 Section 48B(2) of FA 2005 (effect of bond for purposes of tax) applies for the purposes of stamp duty land tax as it applies for the purposes of income tax and capital gains tax.

Relief not available where bond-holder acquires control of underlying asset

3— (1) Paragraph 2 does not apply if control of the underlying asset is acquired by—

(*a*) a bond-holder, or

(*b*) a group of connected bond-holders.

(2) A bond-holder ("BH"), or a group of connected bond-holders, acquires control of the underlying asset if—

(*a*) the rights of bond-holders under an alternative finance investment bond include the right of management and control of the bond assets, and

(*b*) BH, or the group, acquires sufficient rights to enable BH, or the members of the group acting jointly, to exercise the right of management and control of the bond assets to the exclusion of any other bond-holders.

4— (1) But paragraph 3(1) does not apply (and, accordingly, section 48B(2) of FA 2005 applies by virtue of paragraph 2) in either of the following cases.

(2) The first case is where—

(*a*) at the time that the rights were acquired BH (or all of the connected bond-holders) did not know and had no reason to suspect that the acquisition enabled the exercise of the right of management and control of the bond assets to the exclusion of other bond-holders, and

(*b*) as soon as reasonably practicable after BH (or any of the bond-holders) becomes aware that the acquisition enables that exercise, BH transfers (or some or all of the bond-holders transfer) sufficient rights for that exercise no longer to be possible.

(3) The second case is where BH—

(*a*) underwrites a public offer of rights under the bond, and

(*b*) does not exercise the right of management and control of the bond assets.

(4) In this paragraph—

"connected" is to be read in accordance with section 839 of ICTA, and

"underwrite", in relation to an offer of rights under a bond, means to agree to make payments of capital under the bond in the event that other persons do not make those payments.

PART 3

TRANSACTIONS RELATING TO UNDERLYING ASSETS CONSISTING OF LAND

INTRODUCTORY

General conditions for operation of reliefs etc

5— (1) This paragraph defines conditions A to G for the purposes of paragraphs 6 to 18. Paragraphs 20 and 22 set out circumstances in which the reliefs provided by paragraphs 6 to 18 are not available even if conditions A to G are met.

(2) Condition A is that one person ("P") and another ("Q") enter into arrangements under which—

(*a*) P transfers to Q a qualifying interest in land ("the first transaction"), and

(*b*) P and Q agree that when the interest ceases to be held by Q as mentioned in sub-paragraph (3)(*b*), Q will transfer the interest to P.

(3) Condition B is that—

(*a*) Q, as bond-issuer, enters into an alternative finance investment bond (whether before or after entering into the arrangements mentioned in sub-paragraph (2)), and

(*b*) the interest in land to which those arrangements relate is held by Q as a bond asset.

(4) Condition C is that, for the purpose of generating income or gains for the alternative finance investment bond—

(*a*) Q and P enter into a leaseback agreement, or

(*b*) such other condition or conditions as may be specified in regulations made by the Treasury is or are met.

(5) For the purposes of condition C, Q and P enter into a leaseback agreement if Q grants to P, out of the interest transferred to Q,—

(*a*) a lease (if the interest transferred is freehold or, in Scotland, the interest of the owner), or

(*b*) a sub-lease (if the interest transferred is leasehold or, in Scotland, the tenant's right over or interest in a property subject to a lease).

(6) Condition D is that, before the end of the period of 120 days beginning with the effective date of the first transaction, Q provides HMRC with the prescribed evidence that—

(*a*) in England and Wales, a satisfactory legal charge has been entered in the register of title kept under section 1 of the Land Registration Act 2002,

(*b*) in Scotland, a satisfactory standard security has been registered in the Land Register of Scotland, or

(*c*) in Northern Ireland, a satisfactory charge has been entered in the register of titles kept under section 10 of the Land Registration Act (Northern Ireland) 1970.

(7) A charge or security is satisfactory for the purposes of condition D if it—

(*a*) is a first charge on, or a security ranking first granted over, the interest transferred to Q,

(*b*) is in favour of the Commissioners for Her Majesty's Revenue and Customs, and

(*c*) is for the amount mentioned in sub-paragraph (8).

(8) That amount is the total of—

(*a*) the amount of stamp duty land tax which would (apart from paragraph 6(2)) be chargeable on the first transaction if the chargeable consideration for that transaction had been the market value of the interest at that time, and

(*b*) any interest and any penalties which would for the time being be payable on or in respect of that amount of tax, if the tax had been due and payable (but not paid) in respect of the first transaction.

(9) Condition E is that the total of the payments of capital made to Q before the termination of the bond is not less than 60% of the value of the interest in the land at the time of the first transaction.

(10) Condition F is that Q holds the interest in the land as a bond asset until the termination of the bond.

(11) Condition G is that—

(*a*) before the end of the period of 30 days beginning with the date on which the interest in the land ceases to be held as a bond asset, that interest is transferred by Q to P ("the second transaction"), and

(*b*) the second transaction is effected not more than 10 years after the first transaction.

(12) The Treasury may by regulations amend sub-paragraph (11)(*b*) by substituting for the period mentioned there such other period as may be specified.

STAMP DUTY LAND TAX

Relief from stamp duty land tax: first transaction

6— (1) This paragraph applies if—

(*a*) the first transaction relates to an interest in land in the United Kingdom, and (*b*) each of conditions A to C is met before the end of the period of 30 days beginning with the effective date of that transaction.

(2) Where this paragraph applies the first transaction is exempt from charge to stamp duty land tax.

(3) Where the interest in the land is replaced as the bond asset by an interest in other land, this paragraph is subject to paragraph 18.

(4) This paragraph is also subject to paragraph 20.

7— (1) This paragraph applies if—

(*a*) the interest in the land is transferred by Q to P without conditions E and F having been met,

(*b*) the period mentioned in paragraph 5(11)(*b*) expires without each of those conditions having been met, or

(*c*) at any time it becomes apparent for any other reason that any of conditions E to G cannot or will not be met.

(2) This paragraph also applies if condition D is not met.

(3) The relief provided by paragraph 6(2) is withdrawn and stamp duty land tax is chargeable on the first transaction in accordance with this paragraph.

(4) The amount chargeable is the tax that would have been chargeable in respect of the first transaction (but for relief under paragraph 6(2)) if the chargeable consideration for that transaction had been the market value of the interest at the time of that transaction.

(5) Interest is due and payable on the amount of that tax as from the end of the period of 30 days after the effective date of that transaction until the tax is paid.

(6) Q must deliver a further land transaction return before the end of the period of 30 days after the date on which this paragraph first applies.

(7) The return must include a self-assessment of the amount of tax chargeable.

(8) Tax payable must be paid not later than the filing date for the further return.

(9) Schedule 10 to FA 2003 (returns, assessments and other matters) applies to a return under this paragraph as it applies to a return under section 76 of that Act (general requirement to deliver land transaction return), with the following modifications—

(*a*) references to the transaction to which the return relates are to the event by virtue of which this paragraph applies, and

(*b*) references to the effective date of the transaction are to the date on which that event occurs.

Relief from stamp duty land tax: second transaction

8— (1) The second transaction is exempt from charge to stamp duty land tax if—

(*a*) each of conditions A to G is met, and

(*b*) the provisions of Part 4 of FA 2003 relating to the first transaction are complied with.

(2) Where the interest in the land is replaced as the bond asset by an interest in other land, this paragraph is subject to paragraph 18.

(3) This paragraph is also subject to paragraph 20.

Discharge of charge when conditions for relief met

9 If, after the effective date of the second transaction, Q provides HMRC with the prescribed evidence that each of conditions A to C and E to G has been met, the land ceases to be subject to the charge or security registered in pursuance of condition D.

...

Relief not available if purpose of arrangements is improper

22— (1) The reliefs provided by paragraphs 6 to 12 (and paragraph 18 so far as it relates to those paragraphs) are not available if the arrangements mentioned in paragraph 5(2)—

(*a*) are not effected for genuine commercial reasons, or

(*b*) form part of arrangements of which the main purpose, or one of the main purposes, is the avoidance of liability to tax.

(2) In sub-paragraph (1) “tax” means income tax, corporation tax, capital gains tax, stamp duty or stamp duty land tax.

Regulations

23— (1) Regulations under any paragraph of this Schedule—

(*a*) may make provision generally or only for specified purposes, or different provision for different purposes, and

(*b*) may make consequential, supplementary or incidental provision (including amendments of any enactment).

(2) Regulations under any paragraph of this Schedule are to be made by statutory instrument.

(3) A statutory instrument containing regulations under any paragraph of this Schedule is subject to annulment in pursuance of a resolution of the House of Commons.

PART 4
SUPPLEMENTARY

Consequential amendments of FA 2003

24 FA 2003 is amended as follows.

25 After section 73B insert—

> **"73C Alternative finance investment bonds**
>
> Schedule 61 to the Finance Act 2009 makes provision for relief from charge in the case of arrangements falling within section 48A of the Finance Act 2005 (alternative finance investment bonds)."

26 In section 86 (payment of tax), after subsection (5) insert—

> "(5A) The above provisions are also subject to paragraph 7 of Schedule 61 to the Finance Act 2009 (payment of tax where land ceases to qualify for relief in respect of alternative finance investment bonds)."

STAMP TAXES
STATUTORY INSTRUMENTS

LIST OF PRINTED STATUTORY INSTRUMENTS

Year/No	Title
SI 1985/1688	Stamp Duty (Exempt Instruments) Regulations.
SI 1986/1711	Stamp Duty Reserve Tax Regulations.
SI 1987/516	Stamp Duty (Exempt Instruments) Regulations.
SI 1988/268	Stamp Duty and Stamp Duty Reserve Tax (Definitions of Unit Trust Scheme) Regulations.
SI 1989/1297	Taxes (Interest Rate) Regulations.
SI 1992/197	Stamp Duty and Stamp Duty Reserve Tax (Definition of Unit Trust Scheme) Regulations.
SI 1992/232	Electricity (Northern Ireland Consequential Amendments) Order.
SI 1995/2051	Stamp Duty Reserve Tax ([SWX Europe Limited]) Regulations.
SI 1996/1584	Stamp Duty and Stamp Duty Reserve Tax (Pensions Funds Pooling Schemes) Regulations.
SI 1996/2348	Stamp Duty (Production of Documents) (Northern Ireland) Regulations.
SI 1997/1156	Stamp Duty and Stamp Duty Reserve Tax (Open-ended Investment Companies) Regulations.
SI 1997/2428	Finance Act 1997 (Stamp Duty and Stamp Duty Reserve Tax) (Appointed Day) Order 1997
SI 1997/2429	Stamp Duty and Stamp Duty Reserve Tax (Investment Exchanges and Clearing Houses) Regulations 1997
SI 1998/1517	Visiting Forces and Allied Headquarters (Stamp Duties) (Designation) Order 1998
SI 1998/1518	Visiting Forces (Stamp Duties) (Designation) Order 1998
SI 1998/2244	Government of Wales Act 1998 (Commencement No 1) Order 1998
SI 1998/3177	European Single Currency (Taxes) Regulations 1998
SI 1999/118	Government of Wales Act 1998 (Commencement No 3) Order 1999
SI 1999/2383	Stamp Duty Reserve Tax (UK Depositary Interests in Foreign Securities) Regulations 1999
SI 1999/2537	Stamp Duty (Collection and Recovery of Penalties) Regulations 1999
SI 1999/3262	Stamp Duty and Stamp Duty Reserve Tax (Investment Exchanges and Clearing Houses) (OM London Exchange Limited) Regulations 1999
SI 1999/3263	Distraint by Collectors (Fees, Costs and Charges) (Stamp Duty Penalties) Regulations 1999
SI 2000/2995	Stamp Duty and Stamp Duty Reserve Tax (Investment Exchanges and Clearing Houses) (Jiway Limited) Regulations 2000
SI 2001/255	Stamp Duty Reserve Tax (Investment Exchanges and Clearing Houses) (The London Stock Exchange) Regulations 2001
SI 2001/964	Stamp Duty and Stamp Duty Reserve Tax (Definition of Unit Trust Scheme and Open-ended Investment Company) Regulations 2001
SI 2001/3746	*Variation of Stamp Duties Regulations 2001* (revoked)
SI 2001/3747	Stamp Duty (Disadvantaged Areas) Regulations 2001
SI 2002/1975	Stamp Duty and Stamp Duty Reserve Tax (Extension of Exceptions relating to Recognised Exchanges) Regulations 2002
SI 2003/1056	Stamp Duty (Disadvantaged Areas) (Application of Exemptions) Regulations 2003
SI 2003/2837	Stamp Duty Land Tax (Administration) Regulations 2003
SI 2003/2899	Stamp Duty Land Tax (Appointment of the Implementation Date) Order 2003
SI 2004/1363	*Stamp Duty Land Tax (Appeals) Regulations 2004* (revoked)
SI 2004/1864	Tax Avoidance Schemes (Information) Regulations 2004
SI 2004/2421	Stamp Duty and Stamp Duty Reserve Tax (Extension of Exceptions relating to Recognised Exchanges) Regulations 2004
SI 2004/3218	Stamp Duty and Stamp Duty Reserve Tax (Investment Exchanges and Clearing Houses) Regulations 2004
SI 2005/83	Finance Act 2003, Section 66 (Prescribed Persons) Order 2005
SI 2005/645	Finance Act 2003, Section 66 (Prescribed Transactions) Order 2005
SI 2005/844	Stamp Duty Land Tax (Electronic Communications) Regulations 2005
SI 2005/1868	Stamp Duty Land Tax Avoidance Schemes (Prescribed Descriptions of Arrangements) Regulations 2005
SI 2005/1990	Stamp Duty and Stamp Duty Reserve Tax (Extension of Exceptions relating to Recognised Exchanges) Regulations 2005

Year/No	Title
SI 2006/139	Stamp Duty and Stamp Duty Reserve Tax (Extension of Exceptions relating to Recognised Exchanges) Regulations 2006
SI 2006/3237	Stamp Duty Land Tax (Variation of the Finance Act 2003) Regulations 2006
SI 2007/1097	Stamp Duty and Stamp Duty Reserve Tax (Investment Exchanges and Clearing Houses) (Eurex Clearing AG) Regulations 2007
SI 2007/1385	Finance Act 2003, Section 66 (Prescribed Statutory Provisions) Order 2007
SI 2007/3437	Stamp Duty Land Tax (Zero-Carbon Homes Relief) Regulations 2007
SI 2008/52	Stamp Duty Reserve Tax (Investment Exchanges and Clearing Houses) (The London Stock Exchange) Regulations 2008
SI 2008/710	Stamp Duty Land Tax (Open-ended Investment Companies) Regulations 2008
SI 2008/1814	Stamp Duty and Stamp Duty Reserve Tax (Investment Exchanges and Clearing Houses) (European Central Counterparty Limited and the Turquoise Multilateral Trading Facility) Regulations 2008
SI 2008/2339	Stamp Duty Land Tax (Exemption of Certain Acquisitions of Residential Property) Regulations 2008
SI 2008/2777	Stamp Duty and Stamp Duty Reserve Tax (Investment Exchanges and Clearing Houses) Regulations 2008
SI 2008/3235	Stamp Duty and Stamp Duty Reserve Tax (Investment Exchanges and Clearing Houses) Regulations (No 2) 2008
SI 2009/35	Stamp Duty and Stamp Duty Reserve Tax (Investment Exchanges and Clearing Houses) Regulations 2009
SI 2009/194	Stamp Duty and Stamp Duty Reserve Tax (Investment Exchanges and Clearing Houses) Regulations (No 2) 2009
SI 2009/397	Stamp Duty and Stamp Duty Reserve Tax (Investment Exchanges and Clearing Houses) Regulations (No 3) 2009
SI 2009/1115	Stamp Duty and Stamp Duty Reserve Tax (Investment Exchanges and Clearing Houses) Regulations (No 4) 2009
SI 2009/1344	Stamp Duty and Stamp Duty Reserve Tax (Investment Exchanges and Clearing Houses) Regulations (No 5) 2009
SI 2009/1462	Stamp Duty and Stamp Duty Reserve Tax (Investment Exchanges and Clearing Houses) Regulations (No 6) 2009
SI 2009/1601	Stamp Duty and Stamp Duty Reserve Tax (Investment Exchanges and Clearing Houses) Regulations (No 7) 2009
SI 2009/1827	Stamp Duty and Stamp Duty Reserve Tax (Investment Exchanges and Clearing Houses) Regulations (No 8) 2009
SI 2009/1828	Stamp Duty and Stamp Duty Reserve Tax (Investment Exchanges and Clearing Houses) Regulations (No 9) 2009
SI 2009/1831	Stamp Duty and Stamp Duty Reserve Tax (Investment Exchanges and Clearing Houses) Regulations (No 10) 2009
SI 2009/1832	Stamp Duty and Stamp Duty Reserve Tax (Investment Exchanges and Clearing Houses) Regulations (No 11) 2009
SI 2009/2052	Alternative Finance Investment Bonds (Stamp Duty Land Tax) (Prescribed Evidence) Regulations 2009

CHRONOLOGICAL LIST OF STATUTORY INSTRUMENTS

Year/No	Title
SI 1985/1688	Stamp Duty (Exempt Instruments) Regulations.
SI 1986/1711	Stamp Duty Reserve Tax Regulations.
SI 1987/516	Stamp Duty (Exempt Instruments) Regulations.
SI 1988/268	Stamp Duty and Stamp Duty Reserve Tax (Definitions of Unit Trust Scheme) Regulations.
SI 1988/835	*Stamp Duty Reserve Tax (Amendment) Regulations. (amending)*
SI 1989/1297	Taxes (Interest Rate) Regulations.
SI 1989/1301	*Stamp Duty Reserve Tax (Amendment) Regulations.* (amending)
SI 1992/197	Stamp Duty and Stamp Duty Reserve Tax (Definition of Unit Trust Scheme) Regulations.
SI 1992/232	Electricity (Northern Ireland Consequential Amendments) Order.
SI 1992/570	*Stamp Duty and Stamp Duty Reserve Tax (Investment Exchanges and Clearing Houses) Regulations.* (revoked)

Year/No	Title
SI 1992/3286	*FA 1986 (Stamp Duty and Stamp Duty Reserve Tax) (Amendment) Regulations. (amending)*
SI 1992/3287	*Stamp Duty Reserve Tax (Amendment) Regulations. (amending)*
SI 1993/3110	*Stamp Duty Reserve Tax (Amendment) Regulations. (amending)*
SI 1994/1813	*General and Special Commissioners (Amendment of Enactments) Regulations. (amending)*
SI 1995/2051	Stamp Duty Reserve Tax ([SWX Europe Limited]) Regulations.
SI 1996/1584	Stamp Duty and Stamp Duty Reserve Tax (Pensions Funds Pooling Schemes) Regulations.
SI 1996/2348	Stamp Duty (Production of Documents) (Northern Ireland) Regulations.
SI 1996/3187	*Taxes (Interest Rate)(Amendment No 4) Regulations.* (amending)
SI 1997/1156	Stamp Duty and Stamp Duty Reserve Tax (Open-ended Investment Companies) Regulations.
SI 1997/2428	Finance Act 1997 (Stamp Duty and Stamp Duty Reserve Tax) (Appointed Day) Order
SI 1997/2429	Stamp Duty and Stamp Duty Reserve Tax (Investment Exchanges and Clearing Houses) Regulations 1997
SI 1997/2430	*Stamp Duty Reserve Tax (Amendment) Regulations 1997.* (amending)
SI 1997/2708	*Finance Act 1989 Section 178(1) (Appointed Day) Order 1997* (not reproduced)
SI 1998/311	*Finance Act 1989 Section 178(1) (Appointed Day) Order 1998* (not reproduced)
SI 1998/1517	Visiting Forces and Allied Headquarters (Stamp Duties) (Designation) Order 1998
SI 1998/1518	Visiting Forces (Stamp Duties) (Designation) Order 1998
SI 1998/2244	Government of Wales Act 1998 (Commencement No 1) Order 1998
SI 1998/3176	*Taxes (Interest Rate) (Amendment No 2) Regulations 1998* (amending)
SI 1998/3177	European Single Currency (Taxes) Regulations 1998
SI 1999/118	Government of Wales Act 1998 (Commencement No 3) Order 1999
SI 1999/527	Social Security Contributions (Transfer of Functions, etc) Act 1999 (Commencement No 1 and Transitional Provisions) Order 1999 (see *Yellow Tax Handbook* SIs)
SI 1999/679	Transfer of Functions (Lord Advocate and Advocate General for Scotland) Order 1999
SI 1999/782	Government of Wales Act 1998 (Commencement No 4) Order 1999
SI 1999/1467	*Stamp Duty and Stamp Duty Reserve Tax (Open-ended Investment Companies) (Amendment) Regulations 1999* (amending)
SI 1999/2383	*Stamp Duty Reserve Tax (UK Depositary Interests in Foreign Securities) Regulations 1999* (amending)
SI 1999/2536	*Stamp Duty Reserve Tax (Amendment) Regulations 1999* (amending)
SI 1999/2537	Stamp Duty (Collection and Recovery of Penalties) Regulations 1999
SI 1999/2538	*Taxes (Interest Rate) (Amendment No 3) Regulations 1999* (amending)
SI 1999/2539	*Stamp Duty (Exempt Instruments) (Amendment) Regulations 1999* (amending)
SI 1999/3261	*Stamp Duty and Stamp Duty Reserve Tax (Open-ended Investment Companies) (Amendment No 2) Regulations 1999* (amending)
SI 1999/3262	Stamp Duty and Stamp Duty Reserve Tax (Investment Exchanges and Clearing Houses) (OM London Exchange Limited) Regulations 1999
SI 1999/3263	Distraint by Collectors (Fees, Costs and Charges) (Stamp Duty Penalties) Regulations 1999
SI 1999/3264	*Stamp Duty Reserve Tax (Amendment No 2) Regulations 1999* (amending)
SI 2000/1871	*Stamp Duty Reserve Tax (UK Depositary Interests in Foreign Securities) (Amendment) Regulations 2000* (amending)
SI 2000/2549	*Stamp Duty and Stamp Duty Reserve Tax (Definitions of Unit Trust Scheme) (Amendment) Regulations 2000* (amending)
SI 2000/2995	Stamp Duty and Stamp Duty Reserve Tax (Investment Exchanges and Clearing Houses) (Jiway Limited) Regulations 2000
SI 2001/255	Stamp Duty Reserve Tax (Investment Exchanges and Clearing Houses) (The London Stock Exchange) Regulations 2001
SI 2001/964	Stamp Duty and Stamp Duty Reserve Tax (Definition of Unit Trust Scheme and Open-ended Investment Company) Regulations 2001
SI 2001/2267	*Stamp Duty Reserve Tax (Tradepoint) (Amendment) Regulations* (amend SI 1995/2051)

Year/No	Title
SI 2001/3746	Variation of Stamp Duties Regulations 2001
SI 2001/3747	Stamp Duty (Disadvantaged Areas) Regulations 2001
SI 2001/3779	*Stamp Duty Reserve Tax (UK Depositary Interests in Foreign Securities)(Amendment) Regulations 2001* (amend SI 1999/2383)
SI 2002/1971	*European Single Currency (Taxes) (Amendment) Regulations 2002*
SI 2002/1975	Stamp Duty and Stamp Duty Reserve Tax (Extension of Exceptions relating to Recognised Exchanges) Regulations 2002
SI 2003/1056	Stamp Duty (Disadvantaged Areas) (Application of Exemptions) Regulations 2003
SI 2003/2078	*Stamp Duty Reserve Tax (virt-x Exchange Limited) (Amendment) Regulations 2003* (amend SI 1995/2051)
SI 2003/2816	*Stamp Duty and Stamp Duty Land Tax (Variation of the Finance Act 2003) (No 2) Regulations 2003* (revoked)
SI 2003/2837	Stamp Duty Land Tax (Administration) Regulations 2003
SI 2003/2899	Stamp Duty Land Tax (Appointment of the Implementation Date) Order 2003
SI 2003/2914	*Stamp Duty Land Tax (Amendment of Schedule 5 to the Finance Act 2003) Regulations 2003*
SI 2003/3293	*Stamp Duty Land Tax (Amendment of Schedule 4 to the Finance Act 2003) Regulations 2003*
SI 2004/1069	*SDLT (Amendment of Part 4 of the Finance Act 2003) Regulations 2004*
SI 2004/1206	*SDLT (Amendment of Part 4 of the Finance Act 2003) (No 2) Regulations 2004*
SI 2004/1363	*Stamp Duty Land Tax (Appeals) Regulations 2004* (revoked)
SI 2004/1864	Tax Avoidance Schemes (Information) Regulations 2004
SI 2004/2421	Stamp Duty and Stamp Duty Reserve Tax (Extension of Exceptions relating to Recognised Exchanges) Regulations 2004
SI 2004/3124	*Stamp Duty Land Tax (Administration) (Amendment) Regulations 2004* (amending)
SI 2004/3208	*Stamp Duty Land Tax (Land Transaction Returns) Regulations 2004* (amending)
SI 2004/3218	Stamp Duty and Stamp Duty Reserve Tax (Investment Exchanges and Clearing Houses) Regulations 2004
SI 2005/82	*Stamp Duty Land Tax (Consequential Amendment of Enactments) Regulations 2005* (amending)
SI 2005/83	Finance Act 2003, Section 66 (Prescribed Persons) Order 2005
SI 2005/645	Finance Act 2003, Section 66 (Prescribed Transactions) Order 2005
SI 2005/844	Stamp Duty Land Tax (Electronic Communications) Regulations 2005
SI 2005/1132	*Stamp Duty Land Tax (Administration) (Amendment) Regulations 2005 (amending)*
SI 2005/1868	Stamp Duty Land Tax Avoidance Schemes (Prescribed Descriptions of Arrangements) Regulations 2005
SI 2005/1990	Stamp Duty and Stamp Duty Reserve Tax (Extension of Exceptions relating to Recognised Exchanges) Regulations 2005
SI 2005/2007	*Finance Act 2002, Section 117 (Day Appointed for Cessation of Effect) Order 2005*
SI 2005/2462	*Taxes (Interest Rate) (Amendment) Regulations 2005*
SI 2006/139	Stamp Duty and Stamp Duty Reserve Tax (Extension of Exceptions relating to Recognised Exchanges) Regulations 2006
SI 2006/746	*Stamp Duty and Stamp Duty Reserve Tax (Definition of Unit Trust Scheme and Open-ended Investment Company) (Amendment) Regulations 2006* (amend SI 2001/964)
SI 2006/776	*Stamp Duty Land Tax (Administration) (Amendment) Regulations 2006* (amend SI 2003/2837)
SI 2006/875	*Stamp Duty Land Tax (Amendment to the Finance Act 2003) Regulations 2006*
SI 2006/3237	Stamp Duty Land Tax (Variation of the Finance Act 2003) Regulations 2006
SI 2006/3427	*Stamp Duty Land Tax (Electronic Communications) (Amendment) Regulations 2006*
SI 2007/12	*SDRT (UK Depository Interest in Foreign Securities) (Amendment) Regulations 2007*
SI 2007/126	*Financial Services and Markets Act 2000 (Markets in Financial Instruments) Regulations 2007*

Year/No	**Title**
SI 2007/458	*Stamp Duty and Stamp Duty Reserve Tax (Extension of Exceptions relating to Recognised Exchanges) (Amendment) Regulations 2007*
SI 2007/1097	Stamp Duty and Stamp Duty Reserve Tax (Investment Exchanges and Clearing Houses) (Eurex Clearing AG) Regulations 2007
SI 2007/1385	Finance Act 2003, Section 66 (Prescribed Statutory Provisions) Order 2007
SI 2007/3437	Stamp Duty Land Tax (Zero-Carbon Homes Relief) Regulations 2007
SI 2008/52	Stamp Duty Reserve Tax (Investment Exchanges and Clearing Houses) (The London Stock Exchange) Regulations 2008
SI 2008/164	*Stamp Duty and Stamp Duty Reserve Tax (Investment Exchanges and Clearing Houses) (Eurex Clearing AG) (Amendment) Regulations 2008*
SI 2008/710	Stamp Duty Land Tax (Open-ended Investment Companies) Regulations 2008
SI 2008/914	*Stamp Duty Reserve Tax (virt-x Exchange Limited) (Amendment) Regulations 2008*
SI 2008/1814	Stamp Duty and Stamp Duty Reserve Tax (Investment Exchanges and Clearing Houses) (European Central Counterparty Limited and the Turquoise Multilateral Trading Facility) Regulations 2008
SI 2008/1932	*Stamp Duty Land Tax (Zero-Carbon Homes Relief) (Amendment) Regulations 2008*
SI 2008/1935	*Finance Act 2008, Schedule 38, (Appointed Day) Order 2008*
SI 2008/2338	*Stamp Duty Land Tax (Variation of Part 4 of the Finance Act 2003) Regulations 2008* (revoked)
SI 2008/2339	*Stamp Duty Land Tax (Exemption of Certain Acquisitions of Residential Property) Regulations 2008* (revoked)
SI 2008/2777	Stamp Duty and Stamp Duty Reserve Tax (Investment Exchanges and Clearing Houses) Regulations 2008
SI 2008/3234	*Taxes and Duties (Interest Rate) (Amendment) Regulations 2008*
SI 2008/3235	Stamp Duty and Stamp Duty Reserve Tax (Investment Exchanges and Clearing Houses) Regulations (No 2) 2008
SI 2008/3236	*Stamp Duty Reserve Tax (Amendment of section 89AA of the Finance Act 1986) Regulations 2008*
SI 2009/35	Stamp Duty and Stamp Duty Reserve Tax (Investment Exchanges and Clearing Houses) Regulations 2009
SI 2009/56	*Transfer of Tribunal Functions and Revenue and Customs Appeals Order 2009*
SI 2009/194	Stamp Duty and Stamp Duty Reserve Tax (Investment Exchanges and Clearing Houses) Regulations (No 2) 2009
SI 2009/397	Stamp Duty and Stamp Duty Reserve Tax (Investment Exchanges and Clearing Houses) Regulations (No 3) 2009
SI 2009/1115	Stamp Duty and Stamp Duty Reserve Tax (Investment Exchanges and Clearing Houses) Regulations (No 4) 2009
SI 2009/1307	*Transfer of Tribunal Functions (Lands Tribunal and Miscellaneous Amendments) Order 2009*
SI 2009/1344	Stamp Duty and Stamp Duty Reserve Tax (Investment Exchanges and Clearing Houses) Regulations (No 5) 2009
SI 2009/1462	Stamp Duty and Stamp Duty Reserve Tax (Investment Exchanges and Clearing Houses) Regulations (No 6) 2009
SI 2009/1601	Stamp Duty and Stamp Duty Reserve Tax (Investment Exchanges and Clearing Houses) Regulations (No 7) 2009
SI 2009/1827	Stamp Duty and Stamp Duty Reserve Tax (Investment Exchanges and Clearing Houses) Regulations (No 8) 2009
SI 2009/1828	Stamp Duty and Stamp Duty Reserve Tax (Investment Exchanges and Clearing Houses) Regulations (No 9) 2009
SI 2009/1831	Stamp Duty and Stamp Duty Reserve Tax (Investment Exchanges and Clearing Houses) Regulations (No 10) 2009
SI 2009/1832	Stamp Duty and Stamp Duty Reserve Tax (Investment Exchanges and Clearing Houses) Regulations (No 11) 2009
SI 2009/1890	*Companies Act 2006 (Consequential Amendments) (Taxes and National Insurance) Order 2009*
SI 2009/2032	*Taxes and Duties (Interest Rate) (Amendment) Regulations 2009*
SI 2009/2052	Alternative Finance Investment Bonds (Stamp Duty Land Tax) (Prescribed Evidence) Regulations 2009

STATUTORY INSTRUMENTS

1985/1688
Stamp Duty (Exempt Instruments) Regulations 1985

Made by the Commissioners of Inland Revenue under FA 1985 s 89

Made . . . . *4th November 1985*
Laid before the House of Commons . . . . *6th November 1985*
Coming into Operation . . . . *1st January 1986*

1 These regulations may be cited as the Stamp Duty (Exempt Instruments) Regulations 1985 and shall come into operation on 1st January 1986.

2 In these regulations unless the context otherwise requires:

"Her Majesty's Land Registry" and "Chief Land Registrar" have the same meaning as in section 126 (1) of the Land Registration Act 1925 and "Registered land" has the same meaning as in section 3 of that Act.

3 For the purposes of section 89 of the Finance Act 1985 the following class of instrument is prescribed—

Instruments by means of which any transfer on sale within the meaning of paragraphs (*a*) or (*c*) of section 28 (1) of the Finance Act 1931 is effected and in respect of which the following conditions are fulfilled—

(*a*) the instrument is executed on or after the 1st January 1986;

(*b*) the consideration for the sale in question is of an amount or value such that no stamp duty is chargeable and the instrument is certified in accordance with section 34 (4) of the Finance Act 1958; and

(*c*)

(i) the land in question is registered land; or

(ii) in the case of land which is not registered land it is an instrument—

(*a*) to which section 123 of the Land Registration Act 1925 applies, or

(*b*) which effects a transfer in the case of which under rule 72 of the Land Registration Rules 1925 the transferee is deemed to be the applicant for first registration.

4 Where the instrument is of the class of instrument to which regulation 3 above applies it shall be the duty of the applicant to deliver to the proper office of Her Majesty's Land Registry with his application for registration the instrument of transfer and a document signed by the transferee or by some person on his behalf and showing his address giving all the particulars set out in Schedule 2 to the Finance Act 1931.

5 The Chief Land Registrar shall furnish to the Commissioners of Inland Revenue the said particulars given to him under regulation 4 above.

1986/1711
Stamp Duty Reserve Tax Regulations 1986

Made by the Treasury under FA 1986 s 98

Made . . . . *2nd October 1986*
Laid before the House of Commons . . . . *3rd October 1986*
Coming into Operation . . . . *27th October 1986*

ARRANGEMENT OF REGULATIONS

Stamp Taxes

21 Inland Revenue Regulation Act 1890: provisions not to apply.

SCHEDULE

Part I—Table

Part II—Taxes Management Act 1970

Citation and commencement

1 These Regulations may be cited as the Stamp Duty Reserve Tax Regulations 1986 and shall come into operation on 27th October 1986.

Interpretation

2 In these Regulations unless the context otherwise requires—

"Act" means Part IV of the Finance Act 1986;

["accountable date" means—

(*a*) in relation to a relevant transaction—

(i) in connection with which securities are transferred by means of a relevant system operated by the operator of that system, or

(ii) which is reported by means of a relevant system to [the Financial Services Authority][4] or an exchange by the operator of that system in a case where the securities to which the transaction relates are not transferred by means of a relevant system, or

(iii) which is reported, otherwise than by means of a relevant system, to an exchange, in a case where the securities to which the transaction relates are not transferred by means of a relevant system,

the date agreed between the Board and the operator or, if no such date is agreed, the date which is the fourteenth day following the date of the relevant transaction,

(*b*) in relation to interest on overdue tax arising in connection with a relevant transaction which, by virtue of a party to that transaction being a participant in a relevant system, or a member of an exchange, could have been, but was not, reported to [the Financial Services Authority][5] or an exchange by means of that system, or to an exchange otherwise than by means of a relevant system, the date which is the fourteenth day following the date of the relevant transaction, …[3]

(*c*) in relation to a relevant transaction to which neither paragraph (*a*) nor paragraph (*b*) applies, the date which is the seventh day of the month following the month in which the charge to tax occasioned by the relevant transaction is incurred;][2] [and

(*d*) in relation to a surrender, the date which is the fourteenth day of the month following the month in which the relevant two week period ends;][2]

"accountable person" means—

[(*a*) in relation to a charge under section 87 of the Act ("section 87")—

[(i) if the person mentioned as B in section 87(1) is a member of an exchange, or if a member of an exchange is acting as an agent for B who is not such a member, that member, and failing that

(ii) if the person mentioned as A in section 87(1) is a member of an exchange, or if a member of an exchange is acting as an agent for A who is not such a member; that member, and failing that][2]

(iii) if the person mentioned as B in section 87(1) is a qualified dealer, or if a qualified dealer is acting as an agent for B who is not a qualified dealer, the qualified dealer, and failing that

(iv) if the person mentioned as A in section 87(1) is a qualified dealer, or if a qualified dealer is acting as an agent for A who is not a qualified dealer, the qualified dealer, and failing that

(v) the person mentioned as B in section 87(1),][1]

(*b*) in relation to a charge under section 93(1) to (7) of the Act, the person mentioned in section 93(8) thereof:

Provided that if section 93(9) is applicable, then the accountable person means the person to whom the securities are transferred.

(*c*) in relation to a charge under section 93(10) of the Act, the person liable to pay the instalment,

(*d*) in relation to a charge under section 96(1) to (5) of the Act, the person mentioned in subsection (6) thereof:

Provided that if section 96(7) is applicable, then the accountable person means the person to whom the securities are transferred, …[3]

(*e*) in relation to a charge under section 96(8) of the Act, the person liable to pay the instalment; [and

(*f*) in relation to a charge on the surrender of a unit under paragraph 2(1) of Schedule 19 to the Finance Act 1999—

(i) the managers of the unit trust scheme and, failing that,

(ii) the trustees of the unit trust scheme;

(*g*) in relation to a charge on the surrender of a share in an open-ended investment company under paragraph 2(1) of Schedule 19 to the Finance Act 1999—
(i) the authorised corporate director of the company and, failing that,
(ii) the company;][3]

["authorised corporate director" and "open-ended investment company", have the meanings given by regulation 2 of the Stamp Duty and Stamp Duty Reserve Tax (Open-ended Investment Companies) Regulations 1997;][3]

"barrister" includes a member of the Faculty of Advocates;

["the Board" means the Commissioners of Inland Revenue;

"EEA regulated market" means a market of a kind described in paragraphs (*a*) and (*b*) of article 2 of the Financial Services Act 1986 (EEA Regulated Markets)(Exemption) Order 1995;

"exchange" means—
(*a*) a recognised investment exchange within the meaning given by section [285(1)(*a*) of the Financial Services and Markets Act 2000][4], or
(*b*) an EEA regulated market;][2]

. . .[2]

. . .[4]

"General Commissioners" has the same meaning as in the Taxes Management Act 1970;

["HMRC" means Her Majesty's Revenue and Customs;][6]

["investment business" means business which consists of the carrying on of one or more of the activities specified in Articles 14, 21, 25, 37, 40, 45, 51 and 53 and, in so far as it applies to any of those Articles, Article 64 of the Financial Services and Markets Act 2000 (Regulated Activities) Order 2001;][4]

. . .[2]

"notice" means notice in writing;

["operator" means—
(*a*) a person approved by the Treasury under the Treasury Regulations as Operator of a relevant system;
(*b*) subject to paragraph (*c*), where a relevant transaction is reported to an exchange otherwise than by means of a relevant system, the operator of that exchange or, if there is no such operator, that exchange;
(*c*) where a relevant transaction is reported to more than one exchange otherwise than by means of a relevant system, the operator of the exchange of which the party who is the accountable person in relation to that transaction is a member or, if there is no such operator, that exchange;][2]

["qualified dealer" means a person who, not being a [member of an exchange][2]—
[(*a*) a person who has permission under Part 4 of the Financial Services and Markets Act 2000 to carry on investment business, or][4]
[(*c*) is authorised under a legislative provision of the government of a territory outside the United Kingdom to carry on investment business, or
(d) while not required to be authorised to do so, carries on investment business;][2]

. . .[4]

["relevant system" has the meaning given by regulation 2(1) of the Treasury Regulations;][2]

"relevant transaction" means—
(*a*) an agreement falling within section 87(1) of the Act,
(*b*) a transfer, issue or appropriation falling within section 93(1)(*b*) of the Act, or
(*c*) a transfer or issue falling within section 96(1)(*b*) of the Act,

and in respect of which there is a charge to tax;

["relevant two-week period" has the meaning given by paragraph 4(2) of Schedule 19 to the Finance Act 1999;][3]

"Special Commissioners" has the same meaning as in the Taxes Management Act 1970;

["surrender" shall be construed in accordance with paragraph 2(1) of Schedule 19 to the Finance Act 1999 (surrender of units to managers);][3]

"tax" means stamp duty reserve tax.

["the Treasury Regulations" means the [Uncertificated Securities Regulations 2001][5].][2]

["tribunal" has the same meaning as in the Taxes Management Act 1970;][6]

["unit" and "unit trust scheme" have the meanings given by paragraph 14 of Schedule 19 to the Finance Act 1999.][3]

Amendments—[1] Para (*a*) in the definition of "accountable person" substituted by the Stamp Duty Reserve Tax (Amendment) Regulations, SI 1988/835 with effect from 27 May 1988.

[2] Definitions of "broker and dealer" and "market maker" revoked, definition of "accountable date", paras (i), (ii) in the definition of "accountable person", words in definition of "qualified dealer" substituted and definitions of "the Board", "EEA regulated market", "exchange", "operator", "recognised professional body", "relevant system" and "the Treasury Regulations" inserted by the Stamp Duty Reserve Tax (Amendment) Regulations, SI 1997/2430 with effect from 20 October 1997.

[3] In definitions "accountable date" and "accountable person" words revoked, and words inserted, definitions "authorised corporate director" and "open-ended investment company", "relevant two-week period", "surrender" and "unit" and "unit trust scheme" inserted by the Stamp Duty Reserve Tax (Amendment No 2) Regulations, SI 1999/3264, reg 3, with effect from 6 February 2000.

Stamp Taxes

4 Words substituted in the definition of "accountable date", "EEA regulated market", and "exchange"; definition of "European Institution", "recognised professional body" and "recognised self-regulating organisation" revoked, definition of "investment business" substituted, and in definition of "qualified dealer", para (*a*) substituted for paras (*a*), (*b*), by the Financial Services and Markets Act 2000 (Consequential Amendments) (Taxes) Order, SI 2001/3629 arts 112, 113 with effect from 1 December 2001, immediately after the coming into force of the Financial Services and Markets Act 2000 ss 411, 432(1), Sch 20 (and SI 2001/3629 Pts 1 and 2).

5 Words in definition of "the Treasury Regulations" substituted by the Uncertificated Securities Regulations, SI 2001/3755 reg 51, Sch 7 para 18 with effect from 26 November 2001.

6 Definitions of "General Commissioners" and "Special Commissioners" revoked, and definitions of "HMRC" and "tribunal" inserted, by the Transfer of Tribunal Functions and Revenue and Customs Appeals Order, SI 2009/56 art 3, Sch 2 paras 12, 13 with effect from 1 April 2009.

[2A References in these Regulations to any of the provisions of Schedule 19 to the Finance Act 1999 shall be construed as including references to those provisions as modified in relation to open-ended investment companies by the Stamp Duty and Stamp Duty Reserve Tax (Open-ended Investment Companies) Regulations 1997.][1]

Amendments—[1] This regulation inserted by the Stamp Duty Reserve Tax (Amendment No 2) Regulations, SI 1999/3264, reg 4, with effect from 6 February 2000.

Due date for payment

3 Tax charged under the Act[, or under paragraph 2(1) of Schedule 19 to the Finance Act 1999,][1] shall be due and payable on the accountable date.

Amendments—[1] Words inserted by the Stamp Duty Reserve Tax (Amendment No 2) Regulations, SI 1999/3264, reg 5, with effect from 6 February 2000.

Notice of charge and payment

4— (1) [Subject to paragraph (3), an accountable person, except where][1] different arrangements are authorised in writing by the Board, shall on or before the accountable date—

(*a*) give notice of each charge to tax to the Board, and

(*b*) pay the tax due.

(2) A notice under this regulation shall be in such form as the Board may prescribe or authorise and shall contain such information as they may reasonably require for the purposes of the Act.

[(3) This regulation shall not apply where—

(*a*) the tax in question has been accounted for by the operator under regulation 4A, or

(*b*) regulation 4B applies to the accountable person.][1]

Amendments—[1] Words in para (1) substituted, and para (3) inserted, by the Stamp Duty Reserve Tax (Amendment No 2) Regulations, SI 1999/3264, reg 6, with effect from 6 February 2000.

[4A— (1) An operator, except where different arrangements are authorised in writing by the Board, shall on or before the accountable date—

(*a*) give notice to the Board of each charge to tax arising—

(i) in respect of a relevant transaction in connection with which securities are transferred by means of a relevant system operated by him, or

(ii) in respect of a relevant transaction that is reported to [the Financial Services Authority][2] or an exchange by means of a relevant system operated by him, or

(iii) in respect of a relevant transaction that is reported otherwise than by means of a relevant system to an exchange in relation to which he is the operator, or (as the case may be) which itself is the operator, in a case where the securities to which the transaction relates are not transferred by means of a relevant system, and

(*b*) pay the tax due.

(2) A notice under this regulation shall be in such form as the Board may prescribe or authorise and shall contain such information as they may reasonably require for the purposes of the Act.

(3) The Board may, by notification in writing to an operator, impose such requirements, conditions or procedures as they consider necessary for the purposes of these Regulations.][1]

Amendments—[1] This regulation inserted by Stamp Duty Reserve Tax (Amendment) Regulations, SI 1997/2430 with effect from 20 October 1997.

2 Words in sub-para (1)(*a*)(ii) substituted by the Financial Services and Markets Act 2000 (Consequential Amendments) (Taxes) Order, SI 2001/3629 arts 112, 114 with effect from 1 December 2001, immediately after the coming into force of the Financial Services and Markets Act 2000 ss 411, 432(1), Sch 20 (and SI 2001/3629 Pts 1 and 2).

[4B— (1) An accountable person in relation to a charge to tax on a surrender shall on or before the accountable date—

(*a*) give notice to the Board—

(i) detailing all surrenders for which the relevant two-week period ends in the month preceding that in which the accountable date falls, and

(ii) setting out the total of any reductions under paragraphs 4 and 5 of Schedule 19 to the Finance Act 1999 of the amounts of tax chargeable on those surrenders;

(iii) identifying those surrenders to which [paragraph 6A, 6][2] or 7 of Schedule 19 to the Finance Act 1999 applies, and

(iv) stating the total amount of tax due and payable, and

[(*aa*) give to the Board any certificate pursuant to paragraph 6A(2) of Schedule 19 to the Finance Act 1999 to be contained in, or provided with, the notice, and][2]

(*b*) pay the tax due.

(2) A notice under this regulation shall be given—

(*a*) in relation to each unit trust scheme of which the accountable person is the manager or trustee; and

(*b*) in relation to each open-ended investment company of which the accountable person is the authorised corporate director, or in relation to an open-ended investment company which is the accountable person.

(3) A notice under this regulation[, and any certificate pursuant to paragraph 6A(2) of Schedule 19 to the Finance Act 1999 to be contained in, or provided with, such a notice,][2] shall be in such form as the Board may prescribe or authorise and shall contain such information as they may reasonably require for the purposes of the Act and Part II of Schedule 19 to the Finance Act 1999.][1]

Amendments—[1] This regulation inserted by Stamp Duty Reserve Tax (Amendment No 2) Regulations, SI 1999/3264, reg 7, with effect from 6 February 2000.

[2] Words in para (1)(*a*)(iii) substituted, para (1)(*aa*) and words in para (3) inserted by the Stamp Duty and Stamp Duty Reserve Tax (Definition of Unit Trust Scheme and Open-ended Investment Company) Regulations, SI 2001/964 reg 5 with effect from 6 April 2001.

Power to require information

5— (1) The Board may by notice require any person to furnish them within such time, not being less than 30 days, as may be specified in the notice with such information (including documents or records) as the Board may reasonably require for the purposes of the Act.

(2) A barrister or solicitor shall not be obliged in pursuance of a notice under this regulation to disclose, without his client's consent, any information with respect to which a claim to professional privilege could be maintained.

Notice of determination

6— (1) Where it appears to the Board that a relevant transaction [or surrender][2] has taken place or where a claim is made to the Board in connection with a relevant transaction[or surrender][2], the Board may give notice to any person who appears to them in relation to that transaction [or surrender][2] to be the accountable person [or, having regard to regulation 4A(1), the operator][1], or the person liable for any of the tax charged or to the claimant, stating that they have determined the matters specified in the notice.

(2) If it appears to the Board that any such matter specified in a notice of determination is, or may be, material as respects any liability under the Act of two or more persons, they may give notice of the determination to each of those persons.

(3) Any matter that appears to the Board to be relevant for the purposes of the Act may be determined and specified in a notice under this regulation.

(4) A determination for the purposes of a notice under this regulation of any fact relating to a relevant transaction [or surrender][2] —

(*a*) shall, if that fact has been stated in a notice under regulation [4, 4A, or 4B][2] and the Board are satisfied that the notice is correct, be made by the Board in accordance with that notice, but

(*b*) may, in any other case, be made by the Board to the best of their judgment.

(5) A notice under this regulation shall state the time within which and the manner in which an appeal against any determination in it may be made.

(6) Subject to any variation by agreement in writing or on appeal, a determination in a notice under this regulation shall be conclusive for the purposes of the Act[, and, where appropriate, Part II of Schedule 19 to the Finance Act 1999][2] against a person on whom the notice is served.

Amendments—[1] Words in paras (1) inserted by Stamp Duty Reserve Tax (Amendment) Regulations, SI 1997/2430 with effect from 20 October 1997.

[2] In paras (1), (6) words inserted, and in para (4) first words inserted, and second words substituted, by the Stamp Duty Reserve Tax (Amendment No 2) Regulations, SI 1999/3264, reg 8, with effect from 6 February 2000.

Relief from accountability

7 [If on a claim—

(*a*) in relation to a charge under section 87 of the Act, an accountable person or an operator, other than a person liable under section 91 of the Act, or

(*b*) in relation to a charge under paragraph 2(1) of Schedule 19 to the Finance Act 1999, an accountable person, other than a person liable under paragraph 2(3) of that Schedule,][1]

proves to the Board's satisfaction that he has taken without success all reasonable steps, both before and after the date of the agreement, to recover from the person liable tax for which he is accountable under regulation [4, 4A or 4B][1], he shall be relieved of his liability to account for and pay that tax and any interest on that tax.

Amendments—[1] Words substituted by the Stamp Duty Reserve Tax (Amendment No 2) Regulations, SI 1999/3264, reg 9, with effect from 6 February 2000.

Appeals against determination

8— (1) A person on whom a notice under regulation 6 has been served may, within 30 days of the date of the notice, appeal against any determination specified in it by notice given to the Board and specifying the grounds of appeal.

[(2) Sections 49D, 49G and 49H of the Taxes Management Act 1970 provide for notification of the appeal to the tribunal.][3]

(3) Where—

(*a*) it is so agreed between the appellant and the Board, or

(*b*) the High Court, on an application made by the appellant, is satisfied that the matters to be decided on the appeal are likely to be substantially confined to questions of law and gives leave for that purpose,

the appeal may be [notified][3] to the High Court.

[(4) An appeal on any question as to the value of land in the United Kingdom may be [notified][3] to the appropriate …[4] tribunal.][1]

[(4ZA) The appeal may be notified under subsections (3) or (4) only if it could be notified to the tribunal under section 49D, 49G or 49H of the Taxes Management Act 1970.][3]

[(4A) If and so far as the question in dispute on any appeal under this section which has been notified to the tribunal or the High Court is a question as to the value of land in the United Kingdom, the question shall be determined on a reference to the appropriate …[4] tribunal.][3]

[(4B) In this regulation "the [appropriate][4] tribunal" means—

(*a*) where the land is in England or Wales, the [Upper Tribunal][4];

(*b*) where the land is in Scotland, the Lands Tribunal for Scotland;

(*c*) where the land is in Northern Ireland, the Lands Tribunal for Northern Ireland.][1]

[(4C) On the hearing of an appeal before them, the Special Commissioners may allow the appellant to put forward any ground of appeal not specified in the notice of appeal and take it into account if satisfied that the omission was not wilful or unreasonable.[3]

(4D) [On an appeal that is notified to the tribunal, the tribunal shall][3] confirm the determination appealed against unless …[3] satisfied that the determination ought to be varied or quashed.][2]

(5) In the application of this regulation to Scotland, for references to the High Court there shall be substituted references to the Court of Session.

Amendments—[1] Paras (4), (4B) substituted for para (4) by the Stamp Duty Reserve Tax (Amendment) Regulations, SI 1993/3110 regs 1–3 with effect from 1 January 1994.

[2] Paras (4C), (4D) renumbered by Stamp Duty Reserve Tax (Amendment) Regulations, SI 1997/2430 with effect from 20 October 1997. Prior to amendment, these paras were numbered as second paras (4A), (4B) and were inserted by the General and Special Commissioners (Amendment of Enactments) Regulations, SI 1994/1813 Sch 1 para 28, with effect from 1 September 1994.

[3] Para (2) substituted, words in paras (3), (4), inserted, para (4ZA) inserted, para (4A) substituted, para (4C) revoked, in para (4D), words substituted for words "The Special Commissioners shall on an appeal to them" and words "they are" revoked, by the Transfer of Tribunal Functions and Revenue and Customs Appeals Order, SI 2009/56 art 3, Sch 2 paras 12, 14 with effect from 1 April 2009. Paras (2), (4A) previously read as follows—

"(2) Subject to the following provisions of this regulation the appeal shall be to the Special Commissioners.".

"(4A) If and so far as the question in dispute on any appeal under this regulation to the Special Commissioners or the High Court is a question as to the value of land in the United Kingdom, the question shall be determined on a reference to the appropriate tribunal.".

[4] In paras (4), (4A), words "Lands" revoked, and in para (4B), words substituted for words "appropriate Lands" and "Lands Tribunal", by the Transfer of Tribunal Functions (Lands Tribunal and Miscellaneous Amendments) Order, SI 2009/1307 art 5(1), (3), Sch 2 para 25 with effect from 1 June 2009.

[Late notice of appeal

9— (1) This regulation applies in a case where—

(*a*) notice of appeal may be given to HMRC under regulation 8, but

(*b*) no notice is given before the relevant time limit.

(2) Notice may be given after the relevant time limit if—

(*a*) HMRC agree, or

(*b*) where HMRC do not agree, the tribunal gives permission.

(3) If the following conditions are met, HMRC shall agree to notice being given after the relevant time limit.

(4) Condition A is that the appellant has made a request in writing to HMRC to agree to the notice being given.

(5) Condition B is that HMRC are satisfied that there was reasonable excuse for not giving the notice before the relevant time limit.

(6) Condition C is that HMRC are satisfied that the request under paragraph (4) was made without unreasonable delay after the reasonable excuse ceased.

(7) If a request of the kind referred to in paragraph (4) is made, HMRC must notify the appellant whether or not HMRC agree to the appellant giving notice of appeal after the relevant time limit.

(8) In this regulation "relevant time limit", in relation to notice of appeal, means the time before which the notice is to be given (but for this regulation).][1]

Amendments—[1] Reg 9 substituted by the Transfer of Tribunal Functions and Revenue and Customs Appeals Order, SI 2009/56 art 3, Sch 2 paras 12, 15 with effect from 1 April 2009. This reg previously read as follows—

"*Appeal out of time*

9 An appeal under regulation 8 may be brought out of time with the consent of the Board or the Special Commissioners; and the Board—

(*a*) shall give that consent if satisfied, on an application for the purpose, that there was a reasonable excuse for not bringing the appeal within the time limited and that the application was made thereafter without unreasonable delay, and

(*b*) shall, if not so satisfied, refer the application for determination by the Special Commissioners.".

[Appeals from the Special Commissioners

10— (1) Any party to an appeal, if dissatisfied in point of law with the determination of that appeal by the Special Commissioners, may appeal against that determination to the High Court.

(2) The High Court shall hear and determine any question of law arising on an appeal under paragraph (1) above and may reverse, affirm or vary the determination of the Special Commissioners, or remit the matter to the Special Commissioners with the court's opinion on it, or make such other order in relation to the matter as the court thinks fit.

(3) This regulation shall have effect—

(a) in its application to Scotland, with the substitution of references to the Court of Session for references to the High Court; and

(b) in its application to Northern Ireland, with the substitution of references to the Court of Appeal in Northern Ireland for references to the High Court.][1, 2]

Amendments—[1] This regulation substituted by the General and Special Commissioners (Amendments of Enactments) Regulations, SI 1994/1813 Sch 1 para 29, with effect from 1 September 1994.

[2] This regulation revoked by the Transfer of Tribunal Functions and Revenue and Customs Appeals Order, SI 2009/56 art 3, Sch 2 paras 12, 16 with effect from 1 April 2009.

Interest on overpaid tax

11— (1) Where tax repaid under regulation 14 is not less than £25 it shall be repaid with interest on it at the rate which is the [rate applicable under section 178 of the Finance Act 1989][1] for the purposes of section 92(2) of the Act from the time it was paid.

(2) Interest paid under this regulation shall not constitute income for the purposes of income tax or corporation tax.

Note—For the rate applicable under FA 1989 s 178, see SI 1989/1297 *post*.

Amendments—[1] Words in para (1) substituted by the Stamp Duty Reserve Tax (Amendment) Regulations, SI 1989/1301 reg 3 with effect from 18 August 1989.

Recovery of tax

12— (1) The Board shall not exercise any remedy or take any proceedings for the recovery of any amount of tax which is due from any person unless the amount has been agreed in writing between that person and the Board or has been determined and specified in a notice under regulation 6.

(2) Where an amount has been so determined and specified, but an appeal to which this paragraph applies is pending against the determination, the Board shall not exercise any remedy or take any legal proceedings to recover the amount determined except such part of it as may be agreed in writing or determined and specified in a further notice under regulation 6 to be a part not in dispute.

(3) Paragraph (2) applies to any appeal under regulation 8 but not to any further appeal; and regulation 8 shall have effect, in relation to a determination made in pursuance of paragraph (2) of this regulation, as if [paragraphs (4) to (4B)][1] of that regulation were omitted.

Amendments—[1] Words in para (3) substituted by the Stamp Duty Reserve Tax (Amendment) Regulations, SI 1993/3110 regs 1, 2, 4.

Underpayments

13— (1) Subject to paragraphs (2) and (3), where too little tax has been paid in respect of a relevant transaction [or surrender][2] the tax underpaid shall be payable with interest, whether or not the amount that has been paid was that stated as payable in a notice under regulation [4, 4A or 4B][2].

(2) Where tax charged under the Act [or under paragraph 2(1) of Schedule 19 to the Finance Act 1999,][2] is paid in accordance with a notice given to the Board under regulation [4, 4A or 4B][2] and the payment is made and accepted in full satisfaction of the tax so charged, no additional amount of tax shall be determined and specified in a notice under regulation 6 after the end of the period of 6 years beginning with the later of—

(*a*) the date on which the payment was made and accepted, and

(*b*) the relevant accountable date;

and, subject to paragraph (3), at the end of that period any liability for the additional tax shall be extinguished.

Stamp Taxes

(3) In any case of [fraudulent or negligent conduct][1] by or on behalf of any person in connection with or in relation to tax the period mentioned in paragraph (2) shall be the period of 6 years beginning when the [fraudulent or negligent conduct][1] comes to the knowledge of the Board.

Amendments—[1] Words in para (3) substituted by the Stamp Duty Reserve Tax (Amendment) Regulations, SI 1993/3110 regs 1, 2, 5 with effect from 1 January 1994.
[2] In paras (1), (2) first words inserted, and second words substituted, by Stamp Duty Reserve Tax (Amendment) Regulations, SI 1999/3264, reg 10, with effect from 6 February 2000.

Overpayments

14— (1) If on a claim it is proved to the Board's satisfaction that too much tax has been paid in respect of any relevant transaction [or surrender][1] the excess (and any interest paid thereon) shall be repaid by the Board.

(2) A claim under this regulation shall be made within a period of 6 years beginning with the later of—

(*a*) the date on which the payment was made, and
(*b*) the relevant accountable date.

Amendments—[1] Words inserted by the Stamp Duty Reserve Tax (Amendment) Regulations, SI 1999/3264, reg 11, with effect from 6 February 2000.

Inspection of records

15— (1) Every accountable person [or operator][1] shall, whenever [and wherever][1] required to do so, make available for inspection by an officer of the Board authorised for that purpose all books, documents and other records in his possession or under his control containing information relating to any relevant transaction to which he was a party or in connection with which he acted.

(2) Where records are maintained by computer the person required to make them available for inspection shall provide the officer making the inspection with all facilities necessary for obtaining information from them.

Amendments—[1] Words in para (1) inserted by Stamp Duty Reserve Tax (Amendment) Regulations, SI 1997/2430 with effect from 20 October 1997.

Evidence

16— (1) For the purposes of the preceding provisions of these Regulations, a notice under regulation 6 specifying any determination which can no longer be varied or quashed on appeal shall be sufficient evidence of the matters specified.

(2) In any proceedings for the recovery of tax or interest on tax, a certificate by an officer of the Board—

(*a*) that the tax or interest is due, or
(*b*) that, to the best of his knowledge and belief, it has not been paid,

shall be sufficient evidence that the sum mentioned in the certificate is due or, as the case may be, unpaid; and a document purporting to be such a certificate shall be deemed to be such a certificate unless the contrary is proved.

Determination of questions on previous view of the law

17 Where any payment has been made and accepted in satisfaction of any liability for tax and on a view of the law then generally received or adopted in practice, any question whether too little or too much has been paid or what was the right amount of tax payable shall be determined on the same view, notwithstanding that it appears from a subsequent legal decision or otherwise that the view was or may have been wrong.

Recovery of over-repayment of tax, etc

18— (1) Where an amount of tax has been repaid, or interest has been paid, to any person which ought not to have been repaid or paid to him, that amount may be determined and recovered as if it were tax due from him.

(2) Subject to paragraph (3) a determination under this regulation may be made before the expiration of 6 years from the date on which the amount was repaid or paid.

(3) In any case of [fraudulent or negligent conduct][1] the period mentioned in paragraph (2) shall be 6 years from the date on which the [fraudulent or negligent conduct][1] comes to the knowledge of the Board.

(4) In this regulation an amount repaid or paid includes an amount allowed by way of set off.

Amendments—[1] Words in para (3) substituted by the Stamp Duty Reserve Tax (Amendment) Regulations, SI 1993/3110 regs 1, 2, 6 with effect from 1 January 1994.

Service of documents

19 A notice or other document which is to be served on or given to a person under these Regulations may be delivered to him or left at his usual or last known place of residence or served by post, addressed to him at his usual or last known place of residence or place of business or employment.

Taxes Management Act 1970: provisions to apply

20— (1) The provisions of the Taxes Management Act 1970 specified in the first column of the Table in Part I of the Schedule to these Regulations shall apply in relation to the tax as they apply in relation to a tax within the meaning of that Act subject to any modification specified in the second column of that Table.

(2) Any expression to which a meaning is given by the Act or in these Regulations and which is used in a provision of the Taxes Management Act 1970 as applied by this regulation shall in that provision, as so applied, have the same meaning as in the Act or these Regulations.

(3) The provisions of the Taxes Management Act 1970 specified in …[1] Part I of the Schedule (as modified where appropriate) are restated as so modified and applied in Part II of the Schedule.

Amendments—[1] Word revoked by the Stamp Duty Reserve Tax (Amendment) Regulations, SI 1988/835 regs 1, 2, 7 with effect from 27 May 1988.

Inland Revenue Regulation Act 1890: provisions not to apply

21 Sections 21, 22 and 35 of the Inland Revenue Regulation Act 1890 (proceedings for fines, etc) shall not apply in relation to stamp duty reserve tax.

SCHEDULE

Regulation 20

PART I

TABLE

Provision applied	*Modifications*
Section 23(1)	—
(2)	For the words "five shillings" substitute "25 pence".
(3)	For the word ""security"" substitute ""securities""; and for the words "includes shares, stock, debentures and debenture stock" substitute "means chargeable securities".
25(1)	For the words "chargeable gains an inspector" substitute "relevant transactions the Board"; and omit the words "in writing".
(2)	—
(3)	—
[(4)	For the words "stock exchange in the United Kingdom, other than a market maker," substitute "recognised investment exchange or a market of the kind described in [paragraph 36(2) of Part III of the Schedule to the Financial Services and Markets Act 2000 (Exemption) Order 2001][15] ("EEA regulated market")".][1]
(5)	For the words "a stock exchange in the United Kingdom" substitute ["a recognised investment exchange or an EEA regulated market"][2] and omit the words "after 5th April 1968 and".
(8)	—
(9)	For the words ""company"" to the end substitute ""shares or securities" means chargeable securities and "company" shall be construed accordingly".
26(1)	For the words "chargeable gains" substitute "relevant transactions"; omit the words "in writing"; and omit the words "or an inspector".
(2)	For the words "include" to the end substitute "are references to chargeable securities".
[47C	—][16]
[49A(1) to (3)	—][16]
[49B	—][16]
[49C	In subsection (4) from "is to be treated" to the end substitute "is to be treated as conclusive for the purposes of Part IV of the Finance Act 1986, and where appropriate, Part II of Schedule II to the Finance Act 1999 against a person on whom the notice is served."" and "omit subsection (5)][16]
[49D and 49E	—][16]
[49F	In subsection (2) from "are to be treated" to the end substitute "are to be treated as conclusive for the purposes of Part IV of the Finance Act 1986, and where appropriate, Part II of Schedule II to the Finance Act 1999 against a person on whom the notice is served"" and "omit subsection (3)][16]

Provision applied	*Modifications*
[49G, 49H, 49I	—][16]
[46A(1)	*Omit paragraphs (a) and (b) and the words "General Commissioners or" in paragraph (c); and for the words "appeals or other proceedings under the Taxes Acts" substitute "an appeal against a determination".*[16]
(2)	—[16]
(3)	—[16]
(4)	*—.]*[3, 16]
…	…[4, 16]
[53(1)	*Before the word "Commissioners" insert "special"*[16]
(2)	*—]*[5, 16]
[56B(1)	—[16]
(2)	*Before the word "Commissioners" wherever it occurs insert "Special".*[16]
(3)	*Before the word "Commissioners" in both places where it occurs insert "Special".*[16]
(4)	—[16]
(5)	—[16]
(6)	—[16]
56C	—[16]
56D	—[16]
60	—][3]
61	—
[63(1)	—
(2)	—
63A(1)	—
(2)	—][6]
[65(1)	For paragraphs (a) and (b) there shall be substituted "the amount of any tax for the time being due and payable is less than £1,000,".][7]
(4)	—
[66(1)	For the words "any assessment" substitute "the Act".][7]
(2)	—
(2A)	—
(3)	—
(4)	—
67(1)	Omit the words "under any assessment".
(2)	—
68	—
69	For the words "Part IX of this" substitute "the"; omit the words "charged and"; and omit the words "under the assessment" to the end.
71(2)	For the words "chargeable to" substitute "accountable or liable for"; omit the word "income"; for the words "Income Tax Acts" substitute "Act"; and omit the words "for the purpose of the assessment of the body".
(3)	Omit the word "income"; for the words "charged on the body" substitute "for which the body is accountable or liable"; and for the words "Income Tax Acts" substitute "Act".
72(1)	For the words "assessable and chargeable to income" substitute "accountable or liable for"; and for the words "assessed and charged" substitute "accountable or liable".
(2)	For the word "chargeable" substitute "accountable or liable"; for the words "Income Tax Acts" substitute "Act"; and for the words "of assessment and payment of income tax" substitute "thereof".
(3)	For the words "has been charged" substitute "is accountable or liable"; for the words "Income Tax Acts" in both places in which they occur substitute "Act"; and for the word "charged" substitute "for which he is accountable or liable".
73	For the words "chargeable to income" substitute "accountable or liable for".
74(1)	For the words "chargeable to income" substitute "accountable or liable for"; and for the words "chargeable on such deceased person" substitute "for which such deceased person is accountable or liable".
(2)	—

Provision applied	*Modifications*
78(1)	Omit the words from the beginning to "(Schedule A etc)"; omit the words "whether a British subject or not"; for the words "assessable and chargeable to income" substitute "accountable or liable for"; omit the words from "whether the branch" to "or gains or not"; for the words "assessed and charged" substitute "accountable or liable"; and omit the words from "and in the actual receipt" to the end.
83(1)	For the words "in whose name" substitute "who is accountable or liable in respect of"; omit the words "is chargeable"; for the words "Income Tax Acts" substitute "Act"; and for the words "of assessment and payment of income tax" substitute "thereof".
(2)	For the words "has been charged" substitute "is accountable or liable"; for the words "Income Tax Acts" in both places in which they occur substitute "Act"; and for the word "charged" substitute "for which he is accountable or liable".
[86(1)	For the words "The following" to "section 55 or 59B of this Act," substitute "Tax which becomes due and payable"; and for the words "the relevant date" substitute "1st October 1999 or the accountable date, whichever is the later,".
(3)	For the word 'relevant' substitute 'accountable'.][8]
89(1)	…[9]
(3)	…[9]
90	—
[93(1)	For the words "where" to "with the notice" substitute "where any person (the taxpayer) fails to give a notice which he is required to give under regulation [4, 4A or 4B][14] of the Stamp Duty Reserve Tax Regulations 1986".][1]
[(2)	—][7]
(3)	*Omit the words "General or".[16]*
[(5)	For the words "to (4)" substitute "and (3)"; and for the words from "if" to the end substitute "if the failure by the taxpayer to give the notice continues after the end of a period of one year beginning on the last day on which the notice should have been given, he shall be liable to a penalty of an amount not exceeding the amount of the tax which he should have paid by the date by which he should have given the notice"][7].
(6)	—.][1]
[95(1)	In paragraph (a) for the word "delivers" substitute "gives"; and for the words from "return" to "Act)" substitute "notice under regulation [4, 4A or 4B][14] of the Stamp Duty Reserve Tax Regulations 1986"; in paragraph (b) omit the word "return,", for the words "in connection with" substitute "in, or in connection with,"; omit the words "for any allowance, deduction or relief"; and for the words "income tax or capital gains" substitute "stamp duty reserve"; omit paragraph (c) and the word "or" immediately preceding it.][1]
(2)	In paragraph (a) for the words "income tax and capital gains" substitute "stamp duty reserve"; omit the words "for" to "assessment"; and omit the words "including" to "repayable"; in paragraph (b) for the word "return" substitute "notice"; after the word "statement" insert "or"; omit the words "or accounts"; after the word "as" insert "given or"; and omit the words "or substituted".
97(1)	For the word "return" in both places in which it occurs substitute "notice"; after the word "statement" in both places in which it occurs insert "or"; omit the words "or accounts" in both places in which they occur; for the words "sections 95 and 96" substitute "section 95"; for the words "made or submitted" in both places in which they occur substitute "given or made"; and for the words "those sections" substitute "that section".
[98(1)	Omit the words "Subject to the provisions of this section and section 98A below,".
(2)	Omit the words "Subject to section 98A below".
(3)	—
(4)	—
Table	Omit the provisions specified in the first and second columns of the Table and the words at the end of the Table and insert the following provisions— Section 23 of this Act; — The Stamp Duty Reserve Tax Regulations 1986 (other than [regulations [4, 4A and 4B][14]][10]). Section 25(1), (2), (3), (4), (5), (8) and (9) of this Act; — [The Stamp Duty Reserve Tax (UK Depositary Interests in Foreign Securities) Regulations 1999][11]

Stamp Taxes

Provision applied	*Modifications*
	Section 26 of this Act; The Stamp Duty Reserve Tax Regulations 1986.][10]
[99	For the words "preparation or delivery" substitute "giving"; for the words "information, return, accounts or other document" substitute "notice under regulation [4, 4A or 4B][14], or any information under regulation 5, of the Stamp Duty Reserve Tax Regulations 1986"; and omit paragraph (a).][12]
[100(1)	Before the word "Commissioners" insert "Special"; and for the words "the Taxes Acts" substitute "this Act".
(2)	In paragraph (a) for the words "section 93(1) above" onwards substitute "section 93(1)(a) above, or"; omit paragraph (b); in paragraph (c) for the words "section 98(1) above" onwards substitute "section 98(1)(i) above"; omit paragraphs (d) and (e).
(3)	—
(4)	—
(5)	—
100A(1)	—
(2)	—
(3)	Omit the words "in an assessment".
100B(1)	For the words from "this Act" onwards substitute "the Stamp Duty Reserve Tax Regulations 1986 relating to appeals against determinations specified in notices under regulation 6 of those Regulations ("regulation 6 determinations") shall have effect in relation to an appeal against such a determination as they have effect in relation to appeals against regulation 6 determinations".
(2)	Omit the words "section 50(6) to (8) of this Act shall not apply but"; and before the word "Commissioners" in both places where it occurs insert "Special".
(3)	For the words "section 56 of this Act" substitute "regulation 10 of the Stamp Duty Reserve Tax Regulations 1986"; and before the word "Commissioners" in both places where it occurs insert "Special".
[100C	—][16]
(2)	Before the word "Commissioners" insert "Special".
(3)	Before the word "Commissioners" insert "Special"; and omit the words "in an assessment".
(4)	—
(5)	—
100D	—][12]
101	For the word "assessment" substitute "notice under regulation 6 of The Stamp Duty Reserve Tax Regulations 1986"; after the word "varied" insert "or quashed"; *for the word "any" in the second place in which it occurs substitute "the Special"[16];* and for the word "that" to the end substitute "of the matters specified".
102	—
[103(1)	Omit the words "Subject to subsection (2) below" and the words "for any period"; *and before the word "Commissioners" insert "Special"[16]*.
(3)	—
(4)	*Before the word "Commissioners" insert "Special".][7, 16]*
104	For the words "the Taxes Acts" substitute "this Act"; and for the word "misdemeanour" substitute "offence".
105	—
108(1)	For the words "Taxes Acts" in both places in which they occur substitute "Act"; and omit the words "This subsection" to the end.
(2)	For the words from the beginning to "on" substitute "Tax for which"; and after the word "Charter" insert "is accountable or liable".
(3)	—
111(1)	Omit the words "Capital Gains Tax"; the words "1979"; and omit the words "inspector or other" in both places in which they occur.
(2)	Omit the words "inspector or other"; and for the words "£5" substitute "level 1 on the standard scale as defined in section 75 of the Criminal Justice Act 1982.".

Provision applied	*Modifications*
114(1)	For the words ["An assessment or determination"][13] substitute "A notice of determination"; for the words "Taxes Acts" in both places in which they occur substitute "Act"; omit the words "or property charged or"; and the words "charged or".
(2)	For the words ["An assessment or determination"][13] substitute "A notice of determination"; in paragraph (a)(i) omit the word "liable"; in paragraph (a)(ii) for the words "the description of any profits or property" substitute "any matter specified therein"; and omit the word "or"; omit paragraph (a)(iii); omit paragraph (b).
118(1)	Omit the following expressions and the words which occur after them: "the Board" "chargeable gain" "chargeable period" "inspector" "return" "tax" "the Taxes Acts" "trade"; and in the words which occur after the expression "neglect" for the words "Taxes Act" substitute "Act".
(2)	[After][16] the word "deemed" in the second place in which it occurs insert "not to have failed to do it unless the excuse ceased and, after the excuse ceased, he shall be deemed".

Stamp Taxes

Amendments—[1] Sections 25(4), 93(1), 95(1) substituted by the Stamp Duty Reserve Tax (Amendment) Regulations, SI 1997/2430 reg 11(2)(4) in relation to any relevant transaction entered into from 19 October 1997.

[2] Words in s 25(5) substituted in relation to any relevant transaction entered into from 19 October 1997 by SI 1997/2430 reg 11(3).

[3] Sections 46A, 56B–D, 60 inserted by the Stamp Duty Reserve Tax (Amendment) Regulations, SI 1993/3110 reg 7(2), (3) with effect from 1 January 1994.

[4] Sections 50(3)–(6), 51(1), (2), 52(1)–(3) revoked by the General and Special Commissioners (Amendment of Enactments) Regulations, SI 1994/1813 reg 2, Sch 1 para 30(2), Sch 2 Pt II with effect from 1 September 1994.

[5] Section 53 substituted by SI 1994/1813 reg 2(1), Sch 1 para 30(3) with effect from 1 September 1994.

[6] Section 63 substituted by ss 63 and 63A by SI 1993/3110 reg 7(4) with effect from 1 January 1994.

[7] Sections 65(1), 66(1), 93(2), (5), 103 substituted by SI 1993/3110 reg 7(5), (6), (8), (12) with effect from 1 January 1994.

[8] Section 86 substituted by the Stamp Duty Reserve Tax (Amendment) Regulations, SI 1999/2536, reg 3(1), (2) with effect from 1 October 1999.

[9] Section 89(1), (3) revoked by SI 1989/1301 reg 4(*b*) with effect from 18 August 1989.

[10] Section 98 substituted by SI 1993/3110 reg 7(9), words revoked by SI 1994/1813 reg 2, Sch 1 para 30(4), Sch 2 Part II, and words substituted by SI 1997/2430 reg 11(6) in relation to any relevant transaction entered into with effect from after 20 October 1997.

[11] Words inserted by the Stamp Duty Reserve Tax (UK Depositary Interests in Foreign Securities) Regulations, SI 1999/2383 reg 5 with effect from 25 August 1999.

[12] Section 99 substituted by SI 1993/3110 reg 7(10), and words inserted by SI 1997/2430, reg 11(7) in relation to any relevant transaction entered into from 19 October 1997. Section 100 substituted and ss 100A, 100B, 100C and 100D inserted by SI 1993 reg 7(11) with effect from 1 January 1994.

[13] Words in s 114(1), (2) substituted by SI 1993/3110 reg 7(13) with effect from 1 January 1994.

[14] Words substituted by the Stamp Duty Reserve Tax (Amendment) Regulations, SI 1999/3264, reg 12, with effect from 6 February 2000.

[15] Words substituted by the Financial Services and Markets Act 2000 (Consequential Amendments) (Taxes) Order, SI 2001/3629 arts 112,115(1), (2) with effect from 1 December 2001, immediately after the coming into force of the Financial Services and Markets Act 2000 ss 411, 432(1), Sch 20 (and SI 2001/3629 Pts 1 and 2).

[16] Entries inserted, revoked and substituted, by the Transfer of Tribunal Functions and Revenue and Customs Appeals Order, SI 2009/56 art 3, Sch 2 paras 12, 18 with effect from 1 April 2009.

PART II
TAXES MANAGEMENT ACT 1970

Note—This heading refers to Part II of this statutory instrument, i e SI 1986/1711. It restates the provisions of TMA 1970, Pt III below as modified by Part I of this Schedule.

PART III
OTHER RETURNS AND INFORMATION

Note—This heading refers to Part III of TMA 1970. The following text shows the modified provisions of TMA 1970 as introduced by reg 20(3) above.

23 Power to obtain copies of registers of securities

(1) The Board may cause to be served upon any body corporate a notice requiring them to deliver to the Board within a specified time, being not less than twenty-one days, a copy, certified by a duly authorised officer of such body, of the whole of, or any specified class of entries in, any register containing the names of the holders of any securities issued by them.

(2) On delivery of the copy in accordance with the notice payment shall be made therefor at the rate of 25 pence in respect of each one hundred entries.

(3) In this section "securities" means chargeable securities, and "entry" means, in relation to any register, so much thereof as relates to the securities held by any one person.

25 Issuing houses, stockbrokers, etc

(1) For the purpose of obtaining particulars of relevant transactions the Board may by notice require a return under any of the provisions of this section.

(2) An issuing house or other person carrying on a business of effecting public issues of shares or securities in any company, or placings of shares or securities in any company, either on behalf of the company, or on behalf of holders of blocks of shares or securities which have not previously been the subject of a public issue or placing, may be required to make a return of all such public issues or placings effected by that person in the course of the business in the period specified in the notice requiring the return, giving particulars of the persons to or with whom the shares or securities are issued, allotted or placed, and the number or amount of the shares or securities so obtained by them respectively.

(3) A person not carrying on such a business may be required to make a return as regards any such public issue or placing effected by that person and specified in the notice, giving particulars of the persons to or with whom the shares or securities are issued, allotted, or placed and the number or amount of the shares or securities so obtained by them respectively.

[(4) A member of a recognised investment exchange or a market of the kind described in [paragraph 36(2) of Part III of the Schedule to the Financial Services and Markets Act 2000 (Exemption) Order 2001][2] (EEA Regulated Markets) (Exemption) Order 1995 ("EEA regulated market") may be required to make a return giving particulars of any transactions effected by him in the course of his business in the period specified in the notice requiring the return and giving particulars of—

(*a*) the parties to the transactions,

(*b*) the number or amount of the shares or securities dealt with in the respective transactions, and

(*c*) the amount or value of the consideration.

(5) A person (other than a member of a recognised investment exchange or an EEA regulated market) who acts as an agent or broker in the United Kingdom in transactions in shares or securities may be required to make a return giving particulars of any such transactions effected by him in the period specified in the notice, and giving particulars of—

(*a*) the parties to the transactions,

(*b*) the number or amount of the shares or securities dealt with in the respective transactions, and

(*c*) the amount or value of the consideration.][1]

(8) No person shall be required under this section to include in a return particulars of any transaction effected more than three years before the service of the notice requiring him to make the return.

(9) In this section "shares or securities" means chargeable securities and "company" shall be construed accordingly.

Amendments—[1] Sub-ss (4) and (5) substituted by the Stamp Duty Reserve Tax (Amendment) Regulations, SI 1997/2430 reg 12(2) with effect from 20 October 1997.

[2] Words substituted by the Financial Services and Markets Act 2000 (Consequential Amendments) (Taxes) Order, SI 2001/3629 arts 112, 115(1), (3) with effect from 1 December 2001, immediately after the coming into force of the Financial Services and Markets Act 2000 ss 411, 432(1), Sch 20.

26 Nominee shareholders

(1) If, for the purpose of obtaining particulars of relevant transactions, any person in whose name any shares of a company are registered is so required by notice by the Board, he shall state whether or not he is the beneficial owner of those shares and, if not the beneficial owner of those shares or any of them, shall furnish the name and address of the person or persons on whose behalf the shares are registered in his name.

(2) In this section references to shares are references to chargeable securities.

PART V
APPEAL AND OTHER PROCEEDINGS

Amendments—
This Part substituted by the Transfer of Tribunal Functions and Revenue and Customs Appeals Order, SI 2009/56 art 3, Sch 2 paras 12, 19 with effect from 1 April 2009.

[47C Meaning of tribunal

In this Act "tribunal" means the First-tier Tribunal or, where determined by or under Tribunal Procedure Rules, the Upper Tribunal.][1]

Amendments —

[1] This Part substituted by the Transfer of Tribunal Functions and Revenue and Customs Appeals Order, SI 2009/56 art 3, Sch 2 paras 12, 19 with effect from 1 April 2009.

[49A Appeal: HMRC review or determination by tribunal

(1) This section applies if notice of appeal has been given to HMRC.

(2) In such a case—

(*a*) the appellant may notify HMRC that the appellant requires HMRC to review the matter in question (see section 49B),

(*b*) HMRC may notify the appellant of an offer to review the matter in question (see section 49C), or

(*c*) the appellant may notify the appeal to the tribunal (see section 49D).

(3) See sections 49G and 49H for provision about notifying appeals to the tribunal after a review has been required by the appellant or offered by HMRC.][1]

Amendments —

[1] This Part substituted by the Transfer of Tribunal Functions and Revenue and Customs Appeals Order, SI 2009/56 art 3, Sch 2 paras 12, 19 with effect from 1 April 2009.

[49B Appellant requires review by HMRC

(1) Subsections (2) and (3) apply if the appellant notifies HMRC that the appellant requires HMRC to review the matter in question.

(2) HMRC must, within the relevant period, notify the appellant of HMRC's view of the matter in question.

(3) HMRC must review the matter in question in accordance with section 49E.

(4) The appellant may not notify HMRC that the appellant requires HMRC to review the matter in question and HMRC shall not be required to conduct a review if—

(*a*) the appellant has already given a notification under this section in relation to the matter in question,

(*b*) HMRC have given a notification under section 49C in relation to the matter in question, or

(*c*) the appellant has notified the appeal to the tribunal under section 49D.

(5) In this section "relevant period" means—

(*a*) the period of 30 days beginning with the day on which HMRC receive the notification from the appellant, or

(*b*) such longer period as is reasonable.][1]

Amendments —

[1] This Part substituted by the Transfer of Tribunal Functions and Revenue and Customs Appeals Order, SI 2009/56 art 3, Sch 2 paras 12, 19 with effect from 1 April 2009.

[49C HMRC offer review

(1) Subsections (2) to (6) apply if HMRC notify the appellant of an offer to review the matter in question.

(2) When HMRC notify the appellant of the offer, HMRC must also notify the appellant of HMRC's view of the matter in question.

(3) If, within the acceptance period, the appellant notifies HMRC of acceptance of the offer, HMRC must review the matter in question in accordance with section 49E.

(4) If the appellant does not give HMRC such a notification within the acceptance period HMRC's view of the matter in question is to be treated as conclusive for the purposes of Part IV of the Finance Act 1986, and where appropriate, Part II of Schedule II to the Finance Act 1999 against a person on whom the notice is served.

(6) Subsection (4) does not apply to the matter in question if, or to the extent that, the appellant notifies the appeal to the tribunal under section 49H.

(7) HMRC may not notify the appellant of an offer to review the matter in question (and, accordingly, HMRC shall not be required to conduct a review) if—

(*a*) HMRC have already given a notification under this section in relation to the matter in question,

(*b*) the appellant has given a notification under section 49B in relation to the matter in question, or

(*c*) the appellant has notified the appeal to the tribunal under section 49D.

(8) In this section "acceptance period" means the period of 30 days beginning with the date of the document by which HMRC notify the appellant of the offer to review the matter in question.][1]

Amendments —

[1] This Part substituted by the Transfer of Tribunal Functions and Revenue and Customs Appeals Order, SI 2009/56 art 3, Sch 2 paras 12, 19 with effect from 1 April 2009.

[49D Notifying appeal to the tribunal

(1) This section applies if notice of appeal has been given to HMRC.

(2) The appellant may notify the appeal to the tribunal.

(3) If the appellant notifies the appeal to the tribunal, the tribunal is to decide the matter in question.

(4) Subsections (2) and (3) do not apply in a case where—

(*a*) HMRC have given a notification of their view of the matter in question under section 49B, or

(*b*) HMRC have given a notification under section 49C in relation to the matter in question.

(5) In a case falling within subsection (4)(*a*) or (*b*), the appellant may notify the appeal to the tribunal, but only if permitted to do so by section 49G or 49H.][1]

Amendments —

1 This Part substituted by the Transfer of Tribunal Functions and Revenue and Customs Appeals Order, SI 2009/56 art 3, Sch 2 paras 12, 19 with effect from 1 April 2009.

[49E Nature of review etc

(1) This section applies if HMRC are required by section 49B or 49C to review the matter in question.

(2) The nature and extent of the review are to be such as appear appropriate to HMRC in the circumstances.

(3) For the purpose of subsection (2), HMRC must, in particular, have regard to steps taken before the beginning of the review—

(*a*) by HMRC in deciding the matter in question, and

(*b*) by any person in seeking to resolve disagreement about the matter in question.

(4) The review must take account of any representations made by the appellant at a stage which gives HMRC a reasonable opportunity to consider them.

(5) The review may conclude that HMRC's view of the matter in question is to be—

(*a*) upheld,

(*b*) varied, or

(*c*) cancelled.

(6) HMRC must notify the appellant of the conclusions of the review and their reasoning within—

(*a*) the period of 45 days beginning with the relevant day, or

(*b*) such other period as may be agreed.

(7) In subsection (6) "relevant day" means—

(*a*) in a case where the appellant required the review, the day when HMRC notified the appellant of HMRC's view of the matter in question,

(*b*) in a case where HMRC offered the review, the day when HMRC received notification of the appellant's acceptance of the offer.

(8) Where HMRC are required to undertake a review but do not give notice of the conclusions within the time period specified in subsection (6), the conclusion of the review is deemed to be that HMRC's view of the matter in question (see sections 49B(2) and 49C(2)) is upheld.

(9) If subsection (8) applies, HMRC must notify the appellant of the conclusion which the review is treated as having reached.][1]

Amendments —

1 This Part substituted by the Transfer of Tribunal Functions and Revenue and Customs Appeals Order, SI 2009/56 art 3, Sch 2 paras 12, 19 with effect from 1 April 2009.

[49F Effect of conclusions of review

(1) This section applies if HMRC give notice of the conclusions of a review (see section 49E(6) and (9)).

(2) The conclusions are to be treated as conclusive for the purposes of Part IV of the Finance Act 1986, and where appropriate, Part II of Schedule II to the Finance Act 1999 against a person on whom the notice is served.

(4) Subsection (2) does not apply to the matter in question if, or to the extent that, the appellant notifies the appeal to the tribunal under section 49G.][1]

Amendments —

1 This Part substituted by the Transfer of Tribunal Functions and Revenue and Customs Appeals Order, SI 2009/56 art 3, Sch 2 paras 12, 19 with effect from 1 April 2009.

[49G Notifying appeal to tribunal after review concluded

(1) This section applies if—

(*a*) HMRC have given notice of the conclusions of a review in accordance with section 49E, or (*b*) the period specified in section 49E(6) has ended and HMRC have not given notice of the conclusions of the review.

(2) The appellant may notify the appeal to the tribunal within the post-review period.

(3) If the post-review period has ended, the appellant may notify the appeal to the tribunal only if the tribunal gives permission.

(4) If the appellant notifies the appeal to the tribunal, the tribunal is to determine the matter in question.

(5) In this section "post-review period" means—

(*a*) in a case falling within subsection (1)(*a*) the period of 30 days beginning with the date of the document in which HMRC give notice of the conclusions of the review in accordance with section 49E(6), or

(*b*) in a case falling within subsection (1)(*b*), the period that—

(i) begins with the day following the last day of the period specified in section 49E(6), and

(ii) ends 30 days after the date of the document in which HMRC give notice of the conclusions of the review in accordance with section 49E(9).][1]

Amendments —

[1] This Part substituted by the Transfer of Tribunal Functions and Revenue and Customs Appeals Order, SI 2009/56 art 3, Sch 2 paras 12, 19 with effect from 1 April 2009.

[49H Notifying appeal to tribunal after review offered but not accepted

(1) This section applies if—

(*a*) HMRC have offered to review the matter in question (see section 49C), and

(*b*) the appellant has not accepted the offer.

(2) The appellant may notify the appeal to the tribunal within the acceptance period.

(3) But if the acceptance period has ended, the appellant may notify the appeal to the tribunal only if the tribunal gives permission.

(4) If the appellant notifies the appeal to the tribunal, the tribunal is to determine the matter in question.

(5) In this section "acceptance period" has the same meaning as in section 49C.][1]

Amendments —

[1] This Part substituted by the Transfer of Tribunal Functions and Revenue and Customs Appeals Order, SI 2009/56 art 3, Sch 2 paras 12, 19 with effect from 1 April 2009.

[49I Interpretation of sections 49A to 49H

(1) In sections 49A to 49H—

(*a*) "matter in question" means the matter to which an appeal relates;

(*b*) a reference to a notification is a reference to a notification in writing.

(2) In sections 49A to 49H a reference to the appellant includes a person acting on behalf of the appellant except in relation to—

(*a*) notification of HMRC's view under section 49B(2);

(*b*) notification by HMRC of an offer of review (and of their view of the matter) under section 49C;

(*c*) notification of the conclusions of a review under section 49E(6); and

(*d*) notification of the deemed conclusions of a review under section 49E(9).

(3) But if a notification falling within any of the paragraphs of subsection (2) is given to the appellant, a copy of the notification may also be given to a person acting on behalf of the appellant.][1]

Amendments—[1] This Part substituted by the Transfer of Tribunal Functions and Revenue and Customs Appeals Order, SI 2009/56 art 3, Sch 2 paras 12, 19 with effect from 1 April 2009. This Part previously read as follows—

"46A Regulations about jurisdiction

(1) The Lord Chancellor may, with the consent of the Lord Advocate, make regulations—

(*c*) as to the number of Special Commissioners required or permitted to hear, or perform other functions in relation to, an appeal against a determination.

(2) The Regulations may—

(*a*) make different provision for different cases or different circumstances, and

(*b*) contain such supplementary, incidental, consequential and transitional provision as the Lord Chancellor thinks appropriate.

(3) Provision made by virtue of subsection (1) or (2) above may include provision amending this or any other Act or any instrument made under an Act.

(4) Regulations under this section shall be made by statutory instrument subject to annulment in pursuance of a resolution of either House of Parliament.

Procedure before Special Commissioners

53 Appeals against summary determination of penalties

(1) An appeal shall lie to the High Court or, in Scotland, the Court of Session as the Court of Exchequer in Scotland, against the summary determination by the Special Commissioners of any penalty pursuant to regulations under section 56B of this Act.

(2) On any such appeal the court may either confirm or reverse the determination of the Commissioners or reduce or increase the sum determined.

Jurisdiction

56B Regulations about practice and procedure

(1) The Lord Chancellor may, with the consent of the Lord Advocate, make regulations about the practice and procedure to be followed in connection with appeals.

(2) The regulations may in particular include provision—

(*a*) enabling the Special Commissioners to join as a party to an appeal a person who would not otherwise be a party;
(*b*) for requiring any party to an appeal to provide information and make documents available for inspection by the Special Commissioners or by officers of the Board;
(*c*) for requiring persons to attend the hearing of an appeal to give evidence and produce documents;
(*d*) as to evidence generally in relation to appeals;
(*e*) enabling the Special Commissioners to review their decisions;
(*f*) for the imposition of penalties not exceeding an amount specified in the regulations;
(*g*) for the determination and recovery of penalties (imposed by virtue of paragraph (*f*) above or any other enactment) and for appeals against penalties.

(3) The regulations may also include provision—

(*a*) authorising or requiring the Special Commissioners, in circumstances prescribed in the regulations, to state a case for the opinion of a court;
(*b*) for an appeal to lie to a court on a question of law arising from a decision of the Special Commissioners;
(*c*) as to the practice and procedure to be followed in connection with cases so stated or such appeals.

(4) The regulations may—

(*a*) make different provision for different cases or different circumstances, and
(*b*) contain such supplementary, incidental, consequential and transitional provision as the Lord Chancellor thinks appropriate.

(5) Provision made by virtue of any of subsections (1) to (4) above may include provision amending this or any other Act or any instrument made under an Act.

(6) Regulations under this section shall be made by statutory instrument subject to annulment in pursuance of a resolution of either House of Parliament.

56C Power of Special Commissioners to order costs

(1) Regulations made under section 56B above may include provision for—

(*a*) the award by the Special Commissioners of the costs of, or incidental to, appeal hearings before them,
(*b*) the recovery of costs so awarded, and
(*c*) appeals against such awards.

(2) Any provision made by virtue of subsection 1(*a*) above shall provide that the Special Commissioners shall not award costs against a party to an appeal unless they consider that he has acted wholly unreasonably in connection with the hearing in question.

56D Power of Special Commissioners to publish reports of decisions

(1) Regulations made under section 56B above may include provision for the Special Commissioners to publish reports of such of their decisions as they consider appropriate.

(2) Any provision made by virtue of subsection (1) above shall provide that any report published, other than a report of an appeal that was heard in public, shall be in a form that so far as possible prevents the identification of any person whose affairs are dealt with in the report.

(3) No obligation of secrecy to which the Special Commissioners are subject (by virtue of this Act or otherwise) shall prevent their publishing reports of their decisions in accordance with any provision made by virtue of subsection (1) above.".

PART VI
COLLECTION AND RECOVERY

[60 Issue of demand notes and receipts

(1) Every collector shall, when the tax becomes due and payable, make demand of the respective sums given to him in charge to collect, from the persons charged therewith, or at the places of their last abode, or on the premises in respect of which the tax is charged, as the case may require.

(2) On payment of the tax, the collector shall if requested give a receipt.][1]

Amendments—[1] This section inserted by the Stamp Duty Reserve Tax (Amendment) Regulations, SI 1993/3110 regs 1, 2, 8 with effect from 1 January 1994.

Distraint and poinding

61 Distraint by collectors

(1) If a person neglects or refuses to pay the sum charged, upon demand made by the collector, the collector shall, for non-payment thereof, distrain upon the lands, tenements and premises in respect of which the tax is charged, or distrain the person charged by his goods and chattels, and all such other goods and chattels as the collector is hereby authorised to distrain.

(2) For the purpose of levying any such distress, a collector may, after obtaining a warrant for the purpose signed by the General Commissioners, break open, in the daytime, any house or premises, calling to his assistance any constable.

Every such constable shall, when so required, aid and assist the collector in the execution of the warrant and in levying the distress in the house or premises.

(3) A levy or warrant to break open shall be executed by, or under the direction of, and in the presence of, the collector.

(4) A distress levied by the collector shall be kept for five days, at the costs and charges of a person neglecting or refusing to pay.

(5) If the person aforesaid does not pay the sum due, together with the costs and charges within the said five days, the distress shall be appraised by two or more inhabitants of the parish in which the distress is taken, or by other sufficient persons, and shall be sold by public auction by the collector for payment of the sum due and all costs and charges.

The costs and charges of taking, keeping and selling the distress shall be retained by the collector, and any overplus coming by the distress, after the deduction of the costs and charges and of the sum due, shall be restored to the owner of the goods distrained.

[63 Recovery of tax in Scotland

(1) Subject to subsection (3) below, in Scotland, where any tax is due and has not been paid, the sheriff, on an application by the collector accompanied by a certificate by the collector—

(*a*) stating that none of the persons specified in the application has paid the tax due by him;

(*b*) stating that the collector has demanded payment under section 60 of this Act from each such person of the amount due by him;

(*c*) stating that 14 days have elapsed since the date of such demand without payment of the said amount; and

(*d*) specifying the amount due and unpaid by each such person,

shall grant a summary warrant in a form prescribed by Act of Sederunt authorising the recovery, by any of the diligences mentioned in subsection (2) below, of the amount remaining due and unpaid.

(2) The diligences referred to in subsection (1) above are—

[(*a*) an attachment;][2]

(*b*) an earnings arrestment;

(*c*) an arrestment and action of furthcoming or sale.][1]

Amendments—[1] This section substituted by the Stamp Duty Reserve Tax (Amendment) Regulations, SI 1993/3110 regs 1, 2, 7 with effect from 1 January 1994.

[2] Sub-s (2)(*a*) substituted by the Debt Arrangement and Attachment (Scotland) Act 2002 s 61, Sch 3 para 30(1), (2) with effect from 30 December 2002.

[63A Sheriff officer's fees and outlays

(1) Subject to subsection (2) below and without prejudice to [section 39(1) of the Debt Arrangement and Attachment (Scotland) Act 2002 (asp 17) (expenses of attachment)][2], the sheriff officer's fees, together with the outlays necessarily incurred by him, in connection with the execution of a summary warrant shall be chargeable against the debtor.

(2) No fee shall be chargeable by the sheriff officer against the debtor for collecting, and accounting to the collector for, sums paid to him by the debtor in respect of the amount owing.][1]

Amendments—[1] This section inserted by the Stamp Duty Reserve Tax (Amendment) Regulations, SI 1993/3110 regs 1, 2, 8 with effect from 1 January 1994.

[2] Words in sub-s (1) substituted by the Debt Arrangement and Attachment (Scotland) Act 2002 s 61, Sch 3 para 30(1), (3) with effect from 30 December 2002.

Court proceedings

65 Magistrates' courts

[(1) Where the amount of any tax for the time being due and payable is less than £1,000, the tax shall, without prejudice to any other remedy, be recoverable summarily as a civil debt by proceedings commenced in the name of a collector.][1]

(4) It is hereby declared that in subsection (1) above the expression "recoverable summarily as a civil debt" in respect of proceedings in Northern Ireland means recoverable in proceedings under Article 62 of the Magistrates' Courts (Northern Ireland) Order 1981.

Amendments—[1] Sub-s (1) substituted by the Stamp Duty Reserve Tax (Amendment) Regulations, SI 1993/3110 regs 1, 2, 7 with effect from 1 January 1994.

66 County courts

[(1) Tax due and payable under the Act may, in England and Wales, and in Northern Ireland where the amount does not exceed the limit specified in Article 10(1) of the County Courts (Northern Ireland) Order 1980, without prejudice to any other remedy, be sued for and recovered from the person charged therewith as a debt due to the Crown by proceedings in a county court commenced in the name of a collector.][3]

(2) An officer of the Board who is authorised by the Board to do so may address the court in any proceedings under this section in a county court in England and Wales.

(2A) …[1]

[(3) In this section as it applies in Northern Ireland the expression "county court" shall mean a county court held for a division under the County Courts (Northern Ireland) Order 1980.][2]

(4) Sections 21 and 42(2) of the Interpretation Act (Northern Ireland) 1954 shall apply as if any reference in those provisions to any enactment included a reference to this section, and Part III

of the County Courts (Northern Ireland) Order 1980 (general civil jurisdiction) shall apply for the purposes of this section in Northern Ireland.

Amendments—[1] Sub-s (2A) repealed by the High Court and County Courts Jurisdiction Order, SI 1991/724 with effect from 1 July 1991.
[2] Sub-s (3) substituted by the High Court and County Courts Jurisdiction Order, SI 1991/724 with effect from 1 July 1991.
[3] Sub-s (1) substituted by the Stamp Duty Reserve Tax (Amendment) Regulations, SI 1993/3110 regs 1, 2, 7 with effect from 1 January 1994.

67 Inferior courts in Scotland

(1) In Scotland, where the amount of tax for the time being due and payable does not exceed the sum for the time being specified in section 35(1)(*a*) of the Sheriff Courts (Scotland) Act 1971 the tax may, without prejudice to any other remedy, be sued for and recovered from the person charged therewith as a debt due to the Crown by proceedings commenced in the name of a collector in the sheriff court.

(2) Sections 65 and 66 above shall not apply in Scotland.

68 High Court, etc

(1) Any tax may be sued for and recovered from the person charged therewith in the High Court as a debt due to the Crown, or by any other means whereby any debt of record or otherwise due to the Crown can, or may at any time, be sued for and recovered, as well as by the other means specially provided by this Act for levying the tax.

(2) All matters within the jurisdiction of the High Court under this section shall be assigned in Scotland to the Court of Session sitting as the Court of Exchequer.

Supplemental

69 Interest on tax

Interest charged under the Act shall be treated for the purposes—

(*a*) of sections 61, 63 and 65 to 68 above, and

(*b*) of section 35(2)(*g*) (i) of the Crown Proceedings Act 1947 (rules of court to impose restrictions on set-off and counterclaim where the proceedings or set-off or counterclaim relate to taxes) and of any rules of court (including county court rules) for England and Wales or Northern Ireland, which impose such a restriction, and

(*c*) of section 35(2)(*b*) of the said Act of 1947 as set out in section 50 of that Act (which imposes corresponding restrictions in Scotland),

as if it were tax due and payable.

PART VII
PERSONS CHARGEABLE IN A REPRESENTATIVE CAPACITY, ETC

71 Bodies of persons

(2) Subject to section 108 of this Act, the chamberlain or other officer acting as treasurer, auditor or receiver for the time being of any body of persons accountable or liable for tax shall be answerable for doing all such acts as are required to be done under the Act and for payment of the tax.

(3) Every such officer as aforesaid may from time to time retain, out of any money coming into his hands on behalf of the body, so much thereof as is sufficient to pay the tax for which the body is accountable or liable, and shall be indemnified for all such payments made in pursuance of the Act.

72 Trustees, guardians, etc, of incapacitated persons

(1) The trustee, guardian, tutor, curator or committee or any incapacitated person having the direction, control or management of the property or concern of any such person, whether such person resides in the United Kingdom or not, shall be accountable or liable for tax in like manner and to the like amount as that person would be accountable or liable if he were not an incapacitated person.

(2) The person who is accountable or liable in respect of an incapacitated person shall be answerable for all matters required to be done under the Act for the purpose thereof.

(3) Any person who is accountable or liable under the Act in respect of any incapacitated person as aforesaid may retain, out of money coming into his hands on behalf of any such person, so much thereof from time to time as is sufficient to pay the tax for which he is accountable or liable, and shall be indemnified for all such payments made in pursuance of the Act.

73 Further provision as to infants

If a person accountable or liable for tax is an infant, then his parent, guardian or tutor—

(*a*) shall be liable for the tax in default of payment by the infant, and

(*b*) on neglect or refusal of payment, may be proceeded against in like manner as any other defaulter, and (*c*) if he makes such payment, shall be allowed all sums so paid in his accounts.

74 Personal representatives

(1) If a person accountable or liable for tax dies, the executor or administrator of the person deceased shall be liable for the tax for which such deceased person is accountable or liable, and may deduct any payments made under this section out of the assets and effects of the person deceased.

(3) On neglect or refusal of payment, any person liable under this section may be proceeded against in like manner as any other defaulter.

PART VIII
CHARGES ON NON-RESIDENTS

78 Method of charging non-residents

(1) A person not resident in the United Kingdom shall be accountable or liable for tax in the name of any such trustee, guardian, tutor, curator or committee as is mentioned in section 72 of this Act, or of any branch or agent, in like manner and to the like amount as such non-resident person would be accountable or liable if he were resident in the United Kingdom.

83 Responsibilities and indemnification of persons in whose name a non-resident person is chargeable

(1) A person who is accountable or liable in respect of a non-resident person shall be answerable for all matters required to be done under the Act for the purpose thereof.

(2) A person who is accountable or liable under the Act in respect of any non-resident person as aforesaid may retain, out of money coming into his hands on behalf of any such person, so much thereof from time to time as is sufficient to pay the tax for which he is accountable or liable, and shall be indemnified for all such payments made in pursuance of the Act.

PART IX
INTEREST ON OVERDUE TAX

[86 Interest on overdue tax

(1) Tax which becomes due and payable shall carry interest at the rate applicable under section 178 of the Finance Act 1989 from 1st October 1999 or the accountable date, whichever is the later, until payment.

(3) Subsection (1) above applies even if the accountable date is a non-business day within the meaning of section 92 of the Bills of Exchange Act 1882.][1]

Note—For the rate applicable under FA 1989 s 178, see SI 1989/1297 *post*.

Amendments—[1] This section substituted by the Stamp Duty Reserve Tax (Amendment) Regulations, SI 1999/2536, reg 4(1), (2) with effect from 1 October 1999.

89 The prescribed rate of interest

Amendments—This section repealed by the Stamp Duty Reserve Tax (Amendment) Regulations, SI 1989/1301 reg 5(*b*) with effect from 18 August 1989.

90 Disallowance of relief for interest on tax

Interest payable under this Part of this Act shall be paid without any deduction of income tax and shall not be allowed as a deduction in computing any income, profits or losses for any tax purposes.

PART X
PENALTIES, ETC

93 Failure to give notice for stamp duty reserve tax

[(1) This section applies where any person (the taxpayer) fails to give a notice which he is required to give under regulation [4, 4A or 4B][2] of the Stamp Duty Reserve Tax Regulations 1986.

(2) The taxpayer shall be liable to a penalty which shall be £100.

(3) If, on an application made to them by an officer of the Board, the Special Commissioners so direct, the taxpayer shall be liable to a further penalty or penalties not exceeding £60 for each day on which the failure continues after the day on which he is notified of the direction (but excluding any day for which a penalty under this subsection has already been imposed).[3]

(5) Without prejudice to any penalties under subsections (2) and (3) above, if the failure by the taxpayer to give the notice continues after the end of a period of one year beginning on the last day on which the notice should have been given, he shall be liable to a penalty of an amount not exceeding the amount of the tax which he should have paid by the date by which he should have given the notice.

Stamp Taxes

(6) No penalty shall be imposed under subsection (3) above in respect of a failure at any time after the failure has been remedied.][1]

Amendments—[1] This section substituted by the Stamp Duty Reserve Tax (Amendment) Regulations, SI 1997/2430 reg 12(3) with effect from 20 October 1997.
[2] Words substituted by the Stamp Duty Reserve Tax (Amendment) Regulations, SI 1999/3264, reg 13, with effect from 6 February 2000.
[3] Sub-s (3) repealed by the Transfer of Tribunal Functions and Revenue and Customs Appeals Order, SI 2009/56 art 3, Sch 2 paras 12, 20 with effect from 1 April 2009.

95 Incorrect notice, etc for stamp duty reserve tax

[(1) Where a person fraudulently or negligently—

(*a*) gives any incorrect notice under regulation [4, 4A or 4B][2] of the Stamp Duty Reserve Tax Regulations 1986, or

(*b*) makes any incorrect statement or declaration in, or in connection with, any claim in respect of stamp duty reserve tax,

he shall be liable to a penalty not exceeding the amount of the difference specified in subsection (2) below.][1]

(2) The difference is that between—

(*a*) the amount of stamp duty reserve tax payable by the said person, and

(*b*) the amount which would have been the amount so payable if the notice, statement or declaration as given or made by him had been correct.

Amendments—[1] Sub-s (1) substituted by the Stamp Duty Reserve Tax (Amendment) Regulations, SI 1997/2430 reg 12(4) with effect from 20 October 1997.
[2] Words substituted by the Stamp Duty Reserve Tax (Amendment) Regulations, SI 1999/3264, reg 13, with effect from 6 February 2000.

97 Incorrect notice; supplemental

(1) Where any such notice, statement or declaration as are mentioned in section 95 above were given or made by any person neither fraudulently nor negligently and it comes to his notice (or, if he has died, to the notice of his personal representatives) that they were incorrect, then, unless the error is remedied without unreasonable delay, the notice, statement or declaration shall be treated for the purposes of that section as having been negligently given or made by him.

[98 Special returns, etc

(1) Where any person—

(*a*) has been required, by a notice served under or for the purposes of any of the provisions specified in the first column of the Table below, to deliver any return or other document, to furnish any particulars, to produce any document, or to make anything available for inspection, and he fails to comply with the notice, or

(*b*) fails to furnish any information, give any certificate or produce any document or record in accordance with any of the provisions specified in the second column of the Table below,

he shall be liable, subject to subsections (3) and (4) below—

(i) to a penalty not exceeding £300, and

(ii) if the failure continues after a penalty is imposed under paragraph (i) above, to a further penalty or penalties not exceeding £60 for each day on which the failure continues after the day on which the penalty under paragraph (i) above was imposed (but excluding any day for which a penalty under this paragraph has already been imposed).

(2) Where a person fraudulently or negligently furnishes, gives, produces or makes any incorrect information, certificate, document, record or declaration of a kind mentioned in any of the provisions specified in either column of the Table below, he shall be liable to a penalty not exceeding £3,000.

(3) No penalty shall be imposed under subsection (1) above in respect of a failure within paragraph (*a*) of that subsection at any time after the failure has been remedied.

(4) No penalty shall be imposed under paragraph (ii) of subsection (1) above in respect of a failure within paragraph (*b*) of that subsection at any time after the failure has been remedied.

[TABLE

1	2
Section 23 of this Act;	The Stamp Duty Reserve Tax Regulations 1986 (other than [regulations [4, 4A and 4B][5]][3]).
Section 25 (1), (2), (3), (4), (5), (8) and (9) of this Act;	[The Stamp Duty Reserve Tax (UK Depositary Interests in Foreign Securities) Regulations 1999][4]
Section 26 of this Act;	

1	2
The Stamp Duty Reserve Tax Regulations 1986.][2]][1]	

Amendments—[1] This section substituted by the Stamp Duty Reserve Tax (Amendment) Regulations, SI 1993/3110 regs 1, 2, 7 with effect from 1 January 1994.
[2] Table substituted by the General and Special Commissioners (Amendment of Enactments) Regulations, SI 1994/1813 Sch 1 para 31(4) with effect from 1 September 1994.
[3] Words in Table substituted by the Stamp Duty Reserve Tax (Amendment) Regulations, SI 1997/2430 reg 12(5) with effect from 20 October 1997.
[4] Words inserted by the Stamp Duty Reserve Tax (UK Depositary Interests in Foreign Securities) Regulations, SI 1999/2383 reg 5 with effect from 25 August 1999.
[5] Words substituted by the Stamp Duty Reserve Tax (Amendment) Regulations, SI 1999/3264, reg 13, with effect from 6 February 2000.

[99 Assisting in giving incorrect notice, etc

Any person who assists in or induces the giving of any notice under regulation [4, 4A or 4B][2], or any information under regulation 5, of the Stamp Duty Reserve Tax Regulations 1986 which he knows to be incorrect shall be liable to a penalty not exceeding £3,000.][1]

Amendments—[1] This section substituted by the Stamp Duty Reserve Tax (Amendment) Regulations, SI 1993/3110 regs 1, 2, 7 with effect from 1 January 1994.
[2] Words substituted by the Stamp Duty Reserve Tax (Amendment) Regulations, SI 1999/3264, reg 13, with effect from 6 February 2000.

[100 Determination of penalties by officer of Board

(1) Subject to subsection (2) below and except where proceedings for a penalty have been instituted under section 100D below or a penalty has been imposed by the Special Commissioners under section 53 of this Act, an officer of the Board authorised by the Board for the purposes of this section may make a determination imposing a penalty under any provision of this Act and setting it at such amount as, in his opinion, is correct or appropriate.

(2) Subsection (1) above does not apply where the penalty is a penalty under—

(*a*) section 93(1)(*a*) above, or
(*c*) section 98(1)(i) above.

(3) Notice of a determination of a penalty under this section shall be served on the person liable to the penalty and shall state the date on which it is issued and the time within which an appeal against the determination may be made.

(4) After the notice of a determination under this section has been served the determination shall not be altered except in accordance with this section or on appeal.

(5) If it is discovered by an officer of the Board authorised by the Board for the purposes of this section that the amount of a penalty determined under this section is or has become insufficient the officer may make a determination in a further amount so that the penalty is set at the amount which, in his opinion, is correct or appropriate.][1]

Amendments—[1] Sections 100, 100A–100D substituted for s 100 by the Stamp Duty Reserve Tax (Amendment) Regulations, SI 1993/3110 regs 1, 2, 7 with effect from 1 January 1994.

[100A Provisions supplementary to section 100

(1) Where a person who has incurred a penalty has died, a determination under section 100 above which could have been made in relation to him may be made in relation to his personal representatives, and any penalty imposed on personal representatives by virtue of this subsection shall be a debt due from and payable out of his estate.

(2) A penalty determined under section 100 above shall be due and payable at the end of the period of thirty days beginning with the date of the issue of the notice of determination.

(3) A penalty determined under section 100 above shall for all purposes be treated as if it were tax charged and due and payable.][1]

Amendments—[1] Sections 100, 100A–100D substituted for s 100 by the Stamp Duty Reserve Tax (Amendment) Regulations, SI 1993/3110 regs 1, 2, 7 with effect from 1 January 1994.

[100B Appeals against penalty determinations

(1) An appeal may be brought against the determination of a penalty under section 100 above and, subject to the following provisions of this section, the provisions of the Stamp Duty Reserve Tax Regulations 1986 relating to appeals against determinations specified in notices under regulation 6 of those Regulations ("regulation 6 determinations") shall have effect in relation to an appeal against such a determination as they have effect in relation to appeals against regulation 6 determinations.

(2) On an appeal against the determination of a penalty under section 100 above—

(*a*) in the case of a penalty which is required to be of a particular amount, the [First-tier Tribunal][2] may—

(i) if it appears ...[2] that no penalty has been incurred, set the determination aside,
(ii) if the amount determined appears ...[2] to be correct, confirm the determination, or
(iii) if the amount determined appears ...[2] to be incorrect, increase or reduce it to the correct amount,

(*b*) in the case of any other penalty, the [First-tier Tribunal][2] may—

(i) if it appears ...[2] that no penalty has been incurred, set the determination aside,
(ii) if the amount determined appears ...[2] to be appropriate, confirm the determination,
(iii) if the amount determined appears ...[2] to be excessive, reduce it to such other amount (including nil) [as it considers][2] appropriate, or
(iv) if the amount determined appears ...[2] to be insufficient, increase it to such amount not exceeding the permitted maximum [as it considers][2] appropriate.

[(3) In addition to any right of appeal on a point of law under section 11(2) of the TCEA 2007, the person liable to the penalty may appeal to the Upper Tribunal against the amount of the penalty which had been determined under subsection (2), but not against any decision which falls under section 11(5)(*d*) or (*e*) of that Act and was made in connection with the determination of the amount of the penalty.

(3A) Section 11(3) and (4) of the TCEA 2007 applies to the right of appeal under subsection (3) as it applies to the right of appeal under section 11(2) of that Act.

(3B) On an appeal under this section the Upper Tribunal has the same powers as are conferred on the First-tier Tribunal by virtue of this section.][2]][1]

Amendments—[1] Sections 100, 100A–100D substituted for s 100 by the Stamp Duty Reserve Tax (Amendment) Regulations, SI 1993/3110 regs 1, 2, 7 with effect from 1 January 1994.
[2] In sub-s (2), words substituted for words "Special Commissioners" in each place and "as they consider" in both places, words "to them" repealed in each place, and sub-ss (3)–(3B) substituted for previous sub-s (3), by the Transfer of Tribunal Functions and Revenue and Customs Appeals Order, SI 2009/56 art 3, Sch 2 paras 12, 20(1), (3) with effect from 1 April 2009. Sub-s (3) previously read as follows—

"(3) Without prejudice to regulation 10 of the Stamp Duty Reserve Tax Regulations 1986, an appeal from a decision of the Special Commissioners against the amount of a penalty which has been determined under section 100 above or this section shall lie, at the instance of the person liable to the penalty, to the High Court or, in Scotland, to the Court of Session as the Court of Exchequer in Scotland; and on that appeal the court shall have the like jurisdiction as is conferred on the Special Commissioners by virtue of this section.".

[100C Penalty proceedings before [First-tier Tribunal][2]

(1) An officer of the Board authorised by the Board for the purposes of this section may commence proceedings before the [First-tier Tribunal][2] for any penalty to which subsection (1) of section 100 above does not apply by virtue of subsection (2) of that section.

[(2) the person liable to the penalty shall be a party to the proceedings.][2]

(3) Any penalty determined by the [First-tier Tribunal][2] in proceedings under this section shall for all purposes be treated as if it were tax charged and due and payable.

[(4) In addition to any right of appeal on a point of law under section 11(2) of the TCEA 2007, the person liable to the penalty may appeal to the Upper Tribunal against the amount of the penalty which had been determined under subsection (1), but not against any decision which falls under section 11(5)(d) or (e) of that Act and was made in connection with the determination of the amount of the penalty.

(4A) section 11(3) and (4) of the TCEA 2007 applies to the right of appeal under subsection (4) as it applies to the right of appeal under section 11(2) of that Act.][2]

(5) On any such appeal the [Upper Tribunal][2] may—

(*a*) if it appears that no penalty has been incurred, set the determination aside,
(*b*) if the amount determined appears to be appropriate, confirm the determination,
(*c*) if the amount determined appears to be excessive, reduce it to such other amount (including nil) as the [Upper Tribunal][2] considers appropriate, or
(*d*) if the amount determined appears to be insufficient, increase it to such amount not exceeding the permitted maximum as the [Upper Tribunal][2] considers appropriate.][1]

Amendments—[1] Sections 100, 100A–100D substituted for s 100 by the Stamp Duty Reserve Tax (Amendment) Regulations, SI 1993/3110 regs 1, 2, 7 with effect from 1 January 1994.
[2] In heading, words substituted for words "Commissioners", in sub-ss (1), (3) words substituted for words "Special Commissioners", sub-s (2) substituted, sub-ss (4), (4A) substituted for previous sub-s (4), in sub-s (5), words substituted for words "court" in each place, by the Transfer of Tribunal Functions and Revenue and Customs Appeals Order, SI 2009/56 art 3, Sch 2 paras 12, 20(1), (4) with effect from 1 April 2009. Sub-ss (2), (4) previously read as follows—

"(2) Proceedings under this section shall be by way of information in writing, made to the Special Commissioners, and upon summons issued by them to the defendant (or defender) to appear before them at a time and place stated in the summons; and they shall hear and decide each case in a summary way.".

"(4) An appeal against the determination of a penalty in proceedings under this section shall lie to the High Court or, in Scotland, the Court of Session as the Court of Exchequer in Scotland—
(*a*) by any party on a question of law, and
(*b*) by the defendant (or, in Scotland, the defender) against the amount of the penalty.".

[100D Penalty proceedings before court

(1) Where in the opinion of the Board the liability of any person for a penalty arises by reason of the fraud of that or any other person, proceedings for the penalty may be instituted before the High Court or, in Scotland, the Court of Session as the Court of Exchequer in Scotland.

(2) Proceedings under this section which are not instituted (in England, Wales or Northern Ireland) under the Crown Proceedings Act 1947 by and in the name of the Board as an authorised department for the purposes of that Act shall be instituted—

(*a*) in England and Wales, in the name of the Attorney General,
(*b*) in Scotland, in the name of the Lord Advocate, and
(*c*) in Northern Ireland, in the name of the Attorney General for Northern Ireland.

(3) Any proceedings under this section instituted in England and Wales shall be deemed to be civil proceedings by the Crown within the meaning of Part II of the Crown Proceedings Act 1947 and any such proceedings instituted in Northern Ireland shall be deemed to be civil proceedings within the meaning of that Part of that Act as for the time being in force in Northern Ireland.

(4) If in proceedings under this section the court does not find that fraud is proved but consider that the person concerned is nevertheless liable to a penalty, the court may determine a penalty notwithstanding that, but for the opinion of the Board as to fraud, the penalty would not have been a matter for the court.][1]

Amendments—[1] Sections 100, 100A–100D substituted for s 100 by the Stamp Duty Reserve Tax (Amendment) Regulations, SI 1993/3110 regs 1, 2, 7 with effect from 1 January 1994.

Stamp Taxes

101 Evidence for purposes of preceding provisions of Part X

For the purposes of the preceding provisions of this Part of this Act, any notice under regulation 6 of The Stamp Duty Reserve Tax Regulations 1986 which can no longer be varied or quashed by [a tribunal on an appeal notified to it][1] or by order of any court shall be sufficient evidence of the matters specified.

Amendments—[1] Words substituted for words "the Special Commissioners on appeal", by the Transfer of Tribunal Functions and Revenue and Customs Appeals Order, SI 2009/56 art 3, Sch 2 paras 12, 20(1), (5) with effect from 1 April 2009.

102 Mitigation of penalties

The Board may in their discretion mitigate any penalty, or stay or compound any proceedings for recovery thereof, and may also, after judgment, further mitigate or entirely remit the penalty.

[103 Time limits for penalties

(1) Where the amount of a penalty is to be ascertained by reference to tax payable by a person, the penalty may be determined by an officer of the Board, or proceedings for the penalty may be commenced before the [tribunal][2] or a court—

(*a*) at any time within six years after the date on which the penalty was incurred, or
(*b*) at any later time within three years after the final determination of the amount of tax by reference to which the amount of the penalty is to be ascertained.

(3) A penalty under section 99 of this Act may be determined by an officer of the Board, or proceedings for such a penalty may be commenced before a court, at any time within twenty years after the date on which the penalty was incurred.

(4) A penalty to which neither subsection (1) nor subsection (3) above applies may be so determined, or proceedings for such a penalty may be commenced before the [tribunal][2] or a court, at any time within six years after the date on which the penalty was incurred or began to be incurred.][1]

Amendments—[1] This section substituted by the Stamp Duty Reserve Tax (Amendment) Regulations, SI 1993/3110 regs 1, 2, 7 with effect from 1 January 1994.
[2] In sub-ss (1), (4), words substituted for words "Special Commissioners", by the Transfer of Tribunal Functions and Revenue and Customs Appeals Order, SI 2009/56 art 3, Sch 2 paras 12, 20(1), (6) with effect from 1 April 2009.

104 Saving for criminal proceedings

The provisions of this Act shall not, save so far as is otherwise provided, affect any criminal proceedings for any offence.

105 Evidence in cases of fraud or wilful default

(1) Statements made or documents produced by or on behalf of a person shall not be inadmissible in any such proceedings as are mentioned in subsection (2) below by reason only that it has been drawn to his attention that—

(*a*) in relation to tax, the Board may accept pecuniary settlements instead of instituting proceedings, and
(*b*) though no undertaking can be given as to whether or not the Board will accept such a settlement in the case of any particular person, it is the practice of the Board to be influenced by the fact that a person has made a full confession of any fraud or default to which he had been a party and has given full facilities for investigation,

and that he was or may have been induced thereby to make the statements or produce the documents.

(2) The proceedings mentioned in subsection (1) above are—

(*a*) any criminal proceedings against the person in question for any form of fraud or wilful default in connection with or in relation to tax, and

(*b*) any proceedings against him for the recovery of any sum due from him, whether by way of tax or penalty, in connection with or in relation to tax.

PART XI
MISCELLANEOUS AND SUPPLEMENTAL

Companies

108 Responsibility of company officers

(1) Everything to be done by a company under the Act shall be done by the company acting through the proper officer of the company, and service on a company of any document under or in pursuance of the Act may be effected by serving it on the proper officer.

(2) Tax for which a company which is not a body corporate, or which is a body corporate not incorporated under [any][1] enactment forming part of the law of the United Kingdom, or by Charter, is accountable or liable, may, at any time after the tax becomes due, and without prejudice to any other method of recovery, be recovered from the proper officer of the company, and that officer may retain out of any money coming into his hands on behalf of the company sufficient sums to pay that tax, and, so far as he is not so reimbursed, shall be entitled to be indemnified by the company in respect of the liability so imposed on him.

(3) For the purposes of this section—

(*a*) the proper officer of a company which is a body corporate shall be the secretary or person acting as secretary of the company, except that if a liquidator has been appointed for the company the liquidator shall be the proper officer,

(*b*) the proper officer of a company which is not a body corporate or for which there is no proper officer within paragraph (*a*) above, shall be the treasurer or the person acting as treasurer, of the company.

Amendments—[1] In sub-s (2), word substituted for words "the Companies Act 1985 or any other", by the Companies Act 2006 (Consequential Amendments) (Taxes and National Insurance) Order, SI 2009/1890 art 3(3)(*a*) with effect from 1 October 2009.

Valuation

111 Valuation of assets: power to inspect

(1) If for the purposes of the Act the Board authorise an officer of the Board to inspect any property for the purpose of ascertaining its market value the person having the custody or possession of that property shall permit the officer so authorised to inspect it at such reasonable times as the Board may consider necessary.

(2) If any person wilfully delays or obstructs an officer of the Board acting in pursuance of this section he shall be liable on summary conviction to a fine not exceeding level 1 on the standard scale as defined in section 75 of the Criminal Justice Act 1982.

Documents

114 Want of form or errors not to invalidate notice of determination, etc

(1) A notice of determination, warrant or other proceeding which purports to be made in pursuance of any provision of the Act shall not be quashed, or deemed to be void or voidable, for want of form, or be affected by reason of a mistake, defect or omission therein, if the same is in substance and effect in conformity with or according to the intent and meaning of the Act, and if the person intended to be affected thereby is designated therein according to common intent and understanding.

(2) A notice of determination shall not be impeached or affected—

(*a*) by reason of a mistake therein as to—

(i) the name or surname of a person, or

(ii) any matter specified therein.

Interpretation

118 Interpretation

(1) In this Act, unless the context otherwise requires—

"Act" includes an Act of the Parliament of Northern Ireland and "enactment" shall be construed accordingly,

"body of persons" means any body politic, corporate or collegiate, and any company, fraternity, fellowship and society of persons, whether corporate or not corporate,

"branch or agency" means any factorship, agency, receivership, branch or management, and "branch or agent" shall be construed accordingly,

"collector" means any collector of taxes,

"company" has the meaning given by section [832(1)][1] of the principal Act (with section [468][1] of that Act),

["HMRC" means "Her Majesty's Revenue and Customs;][2]
"incapacitated person" means any infant, person of unsound mind, lunatic, idiot or insane person,
"neglect" means negligence or a failure to give any notice, make any return or to produce or furnish any document or other information required by or under the Act,
"the principal Act" means the Income and Corporation Taxes Act [1988][1]
["the TCEA 2007" means the Tribunals, Courts and Enforcement Act 2007;][2]
["tribunal" is to be read in accordance with section 47C][2].

(2) For the purposes of this Act, a person shall be deemed not to have failed to do anything required to be done within a limited time if he did it within such further time, if any, as the Board or the [tribunal][2] or officer concerned may have allowed; and where a person had a reasonable excuse for not doing anything required to be done he shall be deemed not to have failed to do it unless the excuse ceased and, after the excuse ceased, he shall be deemed not to have failed to do it if he did it without unreasonable delay after the excuse had ceased.

Amendments—[1] Numbers and year in sub-s (1) substituted by TA 1988 Sch 29 para 32 Table.
[2] In sub-s (1), definitions of "HMRC", "the TCEA 2007" and "tribunal" inserted, and in sub-s (2), word substituted for words "Special Commissioners", by the Transfer of Tribunal Functions and Revenue and Customs Appeals Order, SI 2009/56 art 3, Sch 2 paras 12, 21 with effect from 1 April 2009.

1987/516
Stamp Duty (Exempt Instruments) Regulations 1987

Made by the Treasury under FA 1985 s 87(2)

Made . . . . 24th March 1987
Laid before the House of Commons . . . . . . 26th March 1987
Coming into Force . . . . 1st May 1987

Statement of Practice SP 6/90—Conveyances and transfers of property subject to a debt: express covenants.

1 These regulations may be cited as the Stamp Duty (Exempt Instruments) Regulations 1987 and shall come into force on 1st May 1987.

[1A In these Regulations "life policy" means—
(*a*) any policy of insurance on a human life, or on the happening of a contingency dependent upon a human life, except a policy of insurance for a payment only upon the death of a person otherwise than from a natural cause, or
(*b*) a grant or contract for the payment of an annuity upon a human life.][1]

Amendments—[1] This regulation inserted by the Stamp Duty (Exempt Instruments)(Amendment) Regulations, SI 1999/2539 reg 3 with effect from 1 October 1999.

2— (1) An instrument which—
(*a*) is executed on or after 1st May 1987,
(*b*) is a kind specified in the Schedule hereto for the purposes of this regulation, and
(*c*) is certified by a certificate which fulfils the conditions of regulation 3 to be an instrument of that kind,
shall be exempt from duty under the provisions specified in paragraph (2) of this regulation.

(2) The provisions specified are—
[(*a*) the following paragraphs of Part III of Schedule 13 to the Finance Act 1999—
(i) paragraph 16 (conveyance or transfer otherwise than on sale),
(ii) paragraph 17 (declaration of use or trust),
(iii) paragraph 18 (dispositions in Scotland);][1]
(*b*) sections 83(2) and 84 (8) of the Finance Act 1985.

Amendments—[1] Para (2)(*a*) substituted by the Stamp Duty (Exempt Instruments) (Amendment) Regulations, SI 1999/2539 reg 4 with effect from 1 October 1999.

3 The certificate—
(*a*) shall be in writing and—
(i) be included as part of the instrument, or
(ii) be endorsed upon or, where separate, be physically attached to the instrument concerned;
(*b*) shall contain a sufficient description of—
(i) the instrument concerned where the certificate is separate but physically attached to the instrument, and
(ii) the category in the Schedule hereto into which the instrument falls;
(*c*)
(i) shall be signed by the transferor or grantor or by his solicitor or duly authorised agent, and
(ii) where it is not signed by the transferor or grantor or by his solicitor, it shall contain a statement by the signatory of the capacity in which he signs, that he is authorised so to sign and that he gives the certificate from his own knowledge of the facts stated in it.

Stamp Taxes

Modification—The term "solicitor" to be construed as including reference to recognised bodies within the meaning of the Administration of Justice Act 1985 s 9, see the Solicitors' Incorporated Practices Order, SI 1991/2684.

4 The Schedule to these regulations shall have effect for the specification of instruments for the purposes of regulation 2.

5 An instrument which is certified in accordance with these regulations shall not be required under section 82(5) or section 84(9) of the Finance Act 1985 to be stamped in accordance with section 12 of the Stamp Act 1891 with a particular stamp denoting that it is duly stamped or that it is not chargeable with any duty.

SCHEDULE

Regulation 4

An instrument which effects any one or more of the following transactions only is an instrument specified for the purposes of regulation 2—

A. The vesting of property subject to a trust in the trustees of the trust on the appointment of a new trustee, or in the continuing trustees on the retirement of a trustee.

B. The conveyance or transfer of property the subject of a specific devise or legacy to the beneficiary named in the will (or his nominee).

C. The conveyance or transfer of property which forms part of an intestate's estate to the person entitled on intestacy (or his nominee).

D. The appropriation of property within section 84(4) of the Finance Act 1985 (death: appropriation in satisfaction of a general legacy of money) or section 84(5) or (7) of that Act (death: appropriation in satisfaction of any interest of surviving spouse [or civil partner][2] and in Scotland also of any interest of issue).

E. The conveyance or transfer of property which forms part of the residuary estate of a testator to a beneficiary (or his nominee) entitled solely by virtue of his entitlement under the will.

F. The conveyance or transfer of property out of a settlement in or towards satisfaction of a beneficiary's interest, not being an interest acquired for money or money's worth, being a conveyance or transfer constituting a distribution of property in accordance with the provisions of the settlement.

G. The conveyance or transfer of property on and in consideration only of marriage to a party to the marriage (or his nominee) or to trustees to be held on the terms of a settlement made in consideration only of the marriage.

[GG. The conveyance or transfer of property on and in consideration only of the formation of a civil partnership to a party to the civil partnership (or his nominee) or to trustees to be held on the terms of a settlement made in consideration only of the civil partnership.][2]

H. The conveyance or transfer of property within section 83(1) [or (1A)][2] of the Finance Act 1985 (transfers in connection with divorce [or dissolution of civil partnership][2] etc).

I. The conveyance or transfer by the liquidator of property which formed part of the assets of the company in liquidation to a shareholder of that company (or his nominee) in or towards satisfaction of the shareholder's rights on a winding-up.

J. The grant in fee simple of an easement in or over land for no consideration in money or money's worth.

K. The grant of a servitude for no consideration in money or money's worth.

L. The conveyance or transfer of property operating as a voluntary disposition inter vivos for no consideration in money or money's worth nor any consideration referred to in section 57 of the Stamp Act 1891 (conveyance in consideration of a debt etc).

M. The conveyance or transfer of property by an instrument within section 84(1) of the Finance Act 1985 (death: varying disposition).

[N. The declaration of any use or trust of or concerning a life policy, or property representing, or benefits arising under, a life policy.][1]

Amendments—[1] Entry N inserted by the Stamp Duty (Exempt Instruments) (Amendment) Regulations, SI 1999/2539 reg 5 with effect from 1 October 1999.

[2] Words inserted by Tax and Civil Partnership (No 2) Regulations, SI 2005/3230 reg 2, with effect from 5 December 2005 (reg 1).

1988/268

Stamp Duty and Stamp Duty Reserve Tax (Definitions of Unit Trust Scheme) Regulations 1988

Made by the Treasury under FA 1946 s 57 and F(No 2)A (NI) 1946 s 28

Made . . . . *18th February 1988*
Laid before the House of Commons . . . . . . *18th February 1988*
Coming into Force . . . . *11th March 1988*

Citation and commencement

1 These Regulations may be cited as the Stamp Duty and Stamp Duty Reserve Tax (Definitions of Unit Trust Scheme) Regulations 1988 and shall come into force on 11th March 1988.

Interpretation

2 In these Regulations unless the context otherwise requires—

"limited partnership" means a limited partnership registered under the Limited Partnerships Act 1907 and "general partner" and "limited partner" have the same meanings as in that Act;

"limited partnership scheme" means a unit trust scheme of the description specified in regulation 4;

"Part III" means Part III of the Finance (No 2) Act (Northern Ireland) 1946;

"Part VII" means Part VII of the Finance Act 1946;

["participant", in relation to a unit trust scheme, shall be construed in accordance with section 235 of the Financial Services and Markets Act 2000;][1]

"scheme property" means, in relation to a unit trust scheme, property of any description, including money, which is held on trust for the participants in the scheme;

"unit trust scheme" means a scheme which, apart from these Regulations, is a unit trust scheme for the purposes of Part VII or Part III as the case may be.

Amendments—[1] Definition of "participant" substituted by the Financial Services and Markets Act 2000 (Consequential Amendments) (Taxes) Order, SI 2001/3629 art 118 with effect from 1 December 2001, immediately after the coming into force of the Financial Services and Markets Act 2000 ss 411, 432(1), Sch 20 (and SI 2001/3629 Pts 1 and 2).

Exception of certain unit trust schemes from Part VII and Part III

3 A unit trust scheme which is—

(*a*) a limited partnership scheme, or

(*b*) a profit sharing scheme which has been approved in accordance with Part I of Schedule 9 to the Finance Act 1978 [or

(*c*) an employee share ownership plan approved under Schedule 8 to the Finance Act 2000,][1];

shall be treated as not being a unit trust scheme for the purposes of Part VII or Part III as the case may be.

Amendments—[1] Words inserted by the Stamp Duty and Stamp Duty Reserve Tax (Definitions of Unit Trust Scheme) (Amendment) Regulations, SI 2000/2549 with effect from 11 October 2000.

Description of a limited partnership scheme

4 A unit trust scheme is a limited partnership scheme when the scheme property is held on trust for the general partners and the limited partners in a limited partnership.

1989/1297

Taxes (Interest Rate) Regulations 1989

Made by the Treasury under FA 1989 s 178

Made . . . . *27th July 1989*
Laid before the House of Commons . . . . *28th July 1989*
Coming into force . . . . *18th August 1989*

Citation and commencement

1 These Regulations may be cited as the Taxes (Interest Rate) Regulations 1989 and shall come into force on 18th August 1989.

Interpretation

2— (1) In these Regulations unless the context otherwise requires—

["the 1998 Regulations" means the Corporation Tax (Instalment Payments Regulations 1998;][1]

"established rate" means—

(*a*) on the coming into force of these Regulations, 14 per cent per annum; and

(*b*) in relation to any date after the first reference date after the coming into force of these Regulations, the reference rate found on the immediately preceding reference date;

["operative date" means—

(*a*) the [twelfth][3] working day after the reference date, or

(*b*) where regulation 3ZA or 3BA applies—

(i) where the reference date is the first Tuesday, the day which is the Monday next following the first Tuesday, or

(ii) where the reference date is the second Tuesday, the day which is the Monday next following the second Tuesday;][2]

["reference date" means—

(*a*) the …[3] working day following the day on which the most recent meeting of the Monetary Policy Committee of the Bank of England took place, or

(*b*) where regulation 3ZA or 3BA applies—

(i) the day which is the Tuesday next following the day on which that meeting took place ("the first Tuesday"), and

Stamp Taxes

(ii) the day which is the Tuesday ("the second Tuesday") occurring two weeks after the first Tuesday;][2]

"section 178" means section 178 of the Finance Act 1989;

"working day" means any day other than a non-business day within the meaning of section 92 of the Bills of Exchange Act 1882.

[(2) In these Regulations the reference rate found on a reference date is the official bank rate determined by the most recent meeting of the Monetary Policy Committee of the Bank of England.][3]

Amendments—[1] Words in para (1) inserted by the Taxes (Interest Rate) (Amendment No 2) Regulations, SI 1998/3176 reg 3 with effect for accounting periods ending on or after 1 July 1999 by virtue of the Finance Act 1994, Section 199 (Appointed Day) Order, SI 1998/3173 art 2.

[2] In para (1), definitions of "operative date" and "reference date" substituted by the Taxes and Duties (Interest Rate) (Amendment) Regulations, SI 2008/3234 reg 2 with effect from 7 January 2009.

[3] In definition of "operative date" word substituted for word "eleventh", in definition of "reference date" word "second" revoked, and para (2) substituted, by the Taxes and Duties (Interest Rate) (Amendment) Regulations, SI 2009/2032 regs 2, 3 with effect from 12 August 2009. Para (2) previously read as follows—

"(2) In these Regulations the reference rate found on a reference date is the percentage per annum found by averaging the base lending rates at close of business on that date of—

(*a*) Bank of Scotland,
(*b*) Barclays Bank plc,
(*c*) Lloyds Bank plc,
(*d*) Midland Bank plc,
(*e*) National Westminster Bank plc, and
(*f*) The Royal Bank of Scotland plc,

and—

(i) where regulation 3ZA applies, if the result is not a multiple of one-quarter, rounding the result up to the nearest amount which is such a multiple,
(ii) where regulation 3BA applies, if the result is not a multiple of one-quarter, rounding the result down to the nearest amount which is such a multiple,
(iii) in any other case, if the result is not a whole number, rounding the result to the nearest such number, with any result midway between two whole numbers rounded down.".

[Applicable rate of interest equal to zero

2A *In determining the rate of interest applicable under section 178 for any purposes mentioned in these Regulations, if the result is less than zero the rate shall be treated as zero for those purposes.]*[1]

Amendments—[1] This reg inserted by the Taxes and Duties (Interest Rate) (Amendment) Regulations, SI 2008/3234 reg 2 with effect from 7 January 2009, and revoked by the Taxes and Duties (Interest Rate) (Amendment) Regulations, SI 2009/2032 regs 2, 4 with effect from 12 August 2009.

[Applicable rates of interest on unpaid tax, tax repaid and repayment supplement][1]

[3— (1) For the purposes of—

(*a*)–(*c*) …

(*d*) section 15A of the Stamp Act 1891,][2][; and][3]

[(*e*) sections 87 and 88 of the Finance Act 2003.][3]

the rate applicable under section 178 shall, subject to paragraph (2), be 8·5 per cent per annum.

(2) Where, on a reference date after 1st January 1997, the reference rate found on that date differs from the established rate, the rate applicable under section 178 for the purposes of the enactments referred to in paragraph (1) shall, on and after the next operative date, be the percentage per annum found by applying the formula specified in paragraph (3).

(3) The formula specified in this paragraph is—

RR + 2·5,

where RR is the reference rate referred to in paragraph (2).][1]

Note—Text not relevant to stamp duty has been omitted.

The rate of interest under this Regulation changes periodically in accordance with the specified formula. Changes are announced by HMRC press release. The rate applicable at any given time can be obtained from *Simon's Taxes*, Binder 1 and from *Simon's Weekly Tax Intelligence*.

Amendments—[1] This regulation substituted by the Taxes (Interest Rate) (Amendment No 4) Regulations, SI 1996/3187, with effect from 31 January 1997.

[2] In para (1), word revoked from sub-para (*b*), word "and" in sub-para (*c*), and the whole of sub-para (*d*) inserted by the Taxes (Interest Rate) (Amendment No 3) Regulations, SI 1999/2538 reg 3 with effect from 1 October 1999.

[3] Para (1)(*e*) inserted by the Taxes (Interest Rate) (Amendment) Regulations, SI 2005/2642 regs 2, 3 with effect from 26 September 2005.

3AA …

Note—This regulation is not relevant to stamp duty.

[3AB— (1) For the purposes of—

(*a*) section 824 of the Income and Corporation Taxes Act 1988,

(*b*) paragraph 6(2)(*b*) of Schedule 1 to the Social Security Contributions and Benefits Act 1992, …[2]

(*c*) section 283 of the Taxation of Chargeable Gains Act 1992.

[(*d*) section 92 of the Finance Act 1986, …[3]

(*e*) section 110 of the Finance Act 1999,][2] [; and][3]

[(*f*) section 89 of the Finance Act 2003.][3]

the rate applicable under section 178 shall, subject to paragraph (2), be 4 per cent per annum.

(2) Where, on a reference date after 1st January 1997, the reference rate found on that date differs from the established rate, the rate applicable under section 178 for the purposes of the enactments referred to in paragraph (1) shall, on and after the next operative date, be the [higher of—

(*a*) 0.5% per annum, and

(*b*) the percentage per annum found by applying the formula specified in paragraph (3).][4]

[(3) The formula specified in this paragraph is—

RR – 1,

where RR is the reference rate referred to in paragraph (2).][4]][1]

Note—The rate of interest under this Regulation changes periodically in accordance with the specified formula. Changes are announced by HMRC press release. The rate applicable at any given time can be obtained from *Simon's Taxes*, Binder 1 and from *Simon's Weekly Tax Intelligence*.

Amendments—[1] This regulation inserted by the Taxes (Interest Rate) (Amendment No 4) Regulations, SI 1996/3187, with effect from 31 January 1997.

[2] Word "and" in sub-para (1)(*b*) revoked, and sub-paras (1)(*d*), (*e*) inserted, by the Taxes (Interest Rate) (Amendment No 3) Regulations, SI 1999/2538 reg 5 with effect from 1 October 1999.

[3] In para (1), word in sub-para (*d*) revoked, word in sub-para (*e*) inserted, and sub-para (*f*) inserted, by the Taxes (Interest Rate) (Amendment) Regulations, SI 2005/2462 regs 2, 4 with effect from 26 September 2005.

[4] In para (2), words substituted, and para (3) substituted, by the Taxes and Duties (Interest Rate) (Amendment) Regulations, SI 2009/2032 regs 2, 7 with effect from 12 August 2009. Substituted words in para (2) previously read as follows—

"percentage per annum found by applying the formula specified in paragraph (3) and, if the result is not a multiple of one-quarter, rounding the result down to the nearest amount which is such a multiple.".

Para (3) previously read as follows—

"(3) The formula specified in this paragraph is—

(RR – 1) × ((100 – BR)/100)

where RR is the reference rate referred to in paragraph (2) and [BR is the percentage at which income tax at the basic rate is charged for the year of assessment in which the reference date referred to in that paragraph falls.".

3AC ...

Note—This regulation is not relevant to stamp duty.

[Applicable rate of interest on overdue corporation tax]

[3A, 3ZA, 3ZB ...]

Note—These regulations are not relevant to stamp duty.

[Applicable rate of interest on tax overpaid]

[3B, 3BA, 3BB ...]

Note—These regulations are not relevant to stamp duty.

Applicable rate of interest on unpaid inheritance tax, capital transfer tax and estate duty

4 ...

Note—This regulation is not relevant to stamp duty.

Applicable rate of official rate of interest

5 ...

Note—This regulation is not relevant to stamp duty.

Effect of change in applicable rate

6 Where the rate applicable under section 178 for the purpose of any of the enactments referred to in [these Regulations][1] changes on an operative date by virtue of these Regulations, that change shall have effect for periods beginning on or after the operative date in relation to interest running from before that date as well as from or from after that date.

Amendments—[1] Words substituted for words "regulation 3(1) or 4(1)", by the Taxes and Duties (Interest Rate) (Amendment) Regulations, SI 2009/2032 regs 2, 14 with effect from 12 August 2009.

1992/197
Stamp Duty and Stamp Duty Reserve Tax (Definition of Unit Trust Scheme) Regulations 1992

Made by the Treasury under FA 1946 s 57(1A), (1B)

Made . . . . . . *6th February 1992*
Laid before the House of Commons . . . . *7th February 1992*
Coming into force . . . . *1st March 1992*

1 These Regulations may be cited as the Stamp Duty and Stamp Duty Reserve Tax (Definition of Unit Trust Scheme) Regulations 1992 and shall come into force on 1st March 1992.

2 A scheme made by the Lord Chancellor in exercise of the powers conferred on him by section 42(1) of the Administration of Justice Act 1982 shall be treated as not being a unit trust scheme for the purposes of Part VII of the Finance Act 1946.

1992/232
Electricity (Northern Ireland Consequential Amendments) Order 1992

Made under the Northern Ireland Constitution Act 1973 s 38(2) 1973 as extended by paragraph 1(7) of Schedule 1 to the Northern Ireland Act 1974

Made . . . . 11th February 1992
Coming into operation in accordance with Article 1(2)

Title, commencement and extent

1— (1) This Order may be cited as the Electricity (Northern Ireland Consequential Amendments) Order 1992.

(2) This Order comes into force on such day or days as may be appointed by order made under Article 1(2) of the Electricity (Northern Ireland) Order 1992.

(3) Article 2 extends to Northern Ireland only, …

Stamp duty exemption for certain contracts

2 Electricity shall be treated as goods for the purposes of section 59 of the Stamp Act 1891 (certain contracts chargeable as conveyances on sale).

3–5 …

Note—Articles 3–5 and words omitted from art 1(3) are not relevant for stamp duty.

1995/2051
Stamp Duty Reserve Tax ([SWX Europe Limited]) Regulations 1995

Made by the Treasury under FA 1991 ss 116(3), (4) and 117

Made . . . . 1st August 1995
Laid before the House of Commons . . . . 4th August 1995
Coming into force . . . . 25th August 1995

Citation and commencement

1 These Regulations may be cited as the Stamp Duty Reserve Tax ([SWX Europe Limited][1]) Regulations 1995 and shall come into force on 25th August 1995.

Amendment—[1] Words substituted by the Stamp Duty Reserve Tax (virt-x Exchange Limited) (Amendment) Regulations, SI 2008/914 reg 2 with effect from 18 April 2008.

Interpretation

2 In these Regulations unless the context otherwise requires—

"Board of directors" means the Board of directors of [SWX Europe Limited][3];

"clearing participant" means a member (as defined by this regulation) who is also a member of [a relevant clearing service][2] and who as such is permitted by the Board of directors and [the relevant clearing service][2] to clear transactions made on the Exchange for a traded security;

"client" means a person who gives instructions to a participant for equity securities to be purchased or, as the case may be, sold on the Exchange;

"equity securities" means stocks and shares which are issued or raised by a company but does not include stocks and shares issued or raised by a company not incorporated in the United Kingdom unless—

(*a*) they are registered in a register kept in the United Kingdom by or on behalf of the company, or

(*b*) in the case of shares, they are paired, within the meaning of section 99(6A) of the Finance Act 1986, with shares issued by a company incorporated in the United Kingdom;

"the Exchange" means [the exchange operated by [SWX Europe Limited][3]][1];

"member" in relation to [SWX Europe Limited][3] means a person approved by the Board of directors as a participant;

"nominee" means a person whose business is or includes holding equity securities as a nominee for [a relevant clearing service][2] acting in its capacity as a person providing clearing services in connection with a transaction made on the Exchange, or as a nominee for a clearing participant (as the case may be);

"non-clearing participant" means a participant other than a clearing participant;

"participant" means a participant in the Exchange;

["relevant clearing service" means—

(*a*) The London Clearing House Limited; or

(*b*) SIS x-clear Aktiengesellschaft for as long as it is a member (as defined by this regulation);][2]

"section 117" means section 117 of the Finance Act 1991;

...[1]

Amendments—[1] Words in the definition "member" substituted, and the definition of "Tradepoint" repealed by the Stamp Duty Reserve Tax (Tradepoint) (Amendment) Regulations, SI 2001/2267 reg 2(3) with effect from 25 June 2001.

[2] Words substituted in the definitions of "clearing participant" and "nominee", and the definition of "relevant clearing service" inserted; by the Stamp Duty Reserve Tax (virt-x Exchange Limited) (Amendment) Regulations, SI 2003/2078 regs 2, 3 with effect from 17 November 2003.

[3] Words in definitions of "Board of directors", "the Exchange" and "member" substituted by the Stamp Duty Reserve Tax (virt-x Exchange Limited) (Amendment) Regulations, SI 2008/914 reg 3 with effect from 18 April 2008.

Prescribed persons for the purposes of section 117

3 For the purposes of section 117—

(*a*) The London Clearing House Limited is a recognised clearing house which is prescribed;

(*b*) [SWX Europe Limited][1] is a recognised investment exchange which is prescribed and, in relation to that exchange, a member who is a clearing participant is prescribed as a description of member of that exchange.

Amendment—[1] Words in reg (3)(*b*) substituted by the Stamp Duty Reserve Tax (virt-x Exchange Limited) (Amendment) Regulations, SI 2008/914 reg 4 with effect from 18 April 2008.

Prescribed circumstances for the purposes of section 117

4— (1) In the circumstances prescribed by paragraph (2) below, a charge to stamp duty reserve tax shall be treated as not arising.

(2) The circumstances prescribed are where, in connection with a transaction made on the Exchange—

(*a*) equity securities of a particular kind are agreed to be transferred—

(i) from a clearing participant or a nominee of a clearing participant to another clearing participant or nominee, or

(ii) from a non-clearing participant or a client to a clearing participant or a nominee of a clearing participant, or

(iii) from a clearing participant or a nominee of a clearing participant to [a relevant clearing service][1] or to a nominee of [a relevant clearing service][1], or

(iv) from a person other than a clearing participant to [a relevant clearing service][1] or to a nominee of [a relevant clearing service][1], as a result of a failure by a clearing participant to fulfil his obligations in respect of the transaction concerned to transfer equity securities to [the relevant clearing service][1] or to a nominee of [the relevant clearing service][1], or

(v) from [a relevant clearing service][1] or a nominee of [a relevant clearing service][1] a clearing participant or a nominee of a clearing participant; and

(*b*) the person to whom those securities are agreed to be transferred under any of the agreements specified in sub-paragraph (*a*) above ("the relevant agreement") is required on receipt of those shares to transfer equity securities under a matching agreement to another person or, in the case of an agreement falling within paragraph (iv) of that sub-paragraph, would have been so required if the failure referred to in that paragraph had not occurred.

(3) In paragraph (2) above—

(*a*) "matching agreement" means an agreement under which—

(i) the equity securities agreed to be transferred are of the same kind as the equity securities agreed to be transferred under the relevant agreement, and

(ii) the number and transfer price of the equity securities agreed to be transferred are identical to the number and transfer price of the equity securities agreed to be transferred under the relevant agreement;

(*b*) references to [a relevant clearing service][1] are references to [a relevant clearing service][1] in its capacity as a person providing clearing services in connection with a transaction made on the Exchange;

(*c*) references to a clearing participant are references to a clearing participant in his capacity as such.

Press releases etc—Inland Revenue 4-8-95 (exemption from stamp duty reserve tax of Tradepoint).

Amendments—[1] Words in paras (2)(*a*), (3)(*b*) substituted by the Stamp Duty Reserve Tax (virt-x Exchange Limited) (Amendment) Regulations, SI 2003/2078 regs 2, 4 with effect from 17 November 2003.

Consequential provision

5— (1) Equity securities which are the subject of an agreement specified in regulation 4(2)(*a*) shall be dealt with by a clearing participant who is a party to the agreement in a separate designated account, and not otherwise.

(2) In paragraph (1) above "designated account" means an account designated by [the relevant clearing service of which the clearing participant is a member][1] for a clearing participant in connection with the equity securities concerned.

Amendments—[1] Words in para (2) substituted by the Stamp Duty Reserve Tax (virt-x Exchange Limited) (Amendment) Regulations, SI 2003/2078 regs 2, 5 with effect from 17 November 2003.

1996/1584
Stamp Duty and Stamp Duty Reserve Tax (Pension Funds Pooling Schemes) Regulations 1996

Made by the Treasury under FA 1946 s 57(1A) and F(No 2)A (NI) 1946 s 28

Made . . . . 19th June 1996
Laid before the House of Commons . . . . . . 19th June 1996
Coming into force . . . . 11th July 1996

1 These Regulations may be cited as the Stamp Duty and Stamp Duty Reserve Tax (Pension Funds Pooling Schemes) Regulations 1996 and shall come into force on 11th July 1996.

2 In these Regulations—

"pension funds pooling scheme" means a unit trust scheme of the description specified in regulation 4 of the Income Tax (Pension Funds Pooling Schemes) Regulations 1996;

"unit trust scheme" has the meaning given by section [237(1) of the Financial Services and Markets Act 2000][1].

Amendments—[1] Words substituted by the Financial Services and Markets Act 2000 (Consequential Amendments) (Taxes) Order, SI 2001/3629 art 144 with effect from 1 December 2001, immediately after the coming into force of the Financial Services and Markets Act 2000 ss 411, 432(1), Sch 20 (and SI 2001/3629 Pts 1, 2).

3 A unit trust scheme which is a pension funds pooling scheme shall be treated as not being a unit trust scheme for the purposes of Part VII of the Finance Act 1946 or Part III of the Finance (No 2) Act (Northern Ireland) 1946 as the case may be.

1996/2348
Stamp Duty (Production of Documents) (Northern Ireland) Regulations 1996

Made by the Commissioners of Inland Revenue under FA 1994 ss 244(2) and 245(1), (5), (7)

Made . . . . 9th September 1996
Laid before the House of Commons . . . . . 11th September 1996
Coming into force . . . . 4th November 1996

Citation and commencement

1 These Regulations may be cited as the Stamp Duty (Production of Documents) (Northern Ireland) Regulations 1996 and shall come into force on 4th November 1996.

Interpretation

2 In these Regulations unless the context otherwise requires—

"exempt instrument" shall be construed in accordance with regulation 4(1);

"grant", "lease" and "lessee" shall be construed in accordance with section 245(2) of the Finance Act 1994;

"long leasehold interest", in relation to a transaction, means a leasehold interest which, at the time of that transaction, was for a term of 25 years or more before expiry;

"registered land" has the meaning given by section 45(1) of the Interpretation Act (Northern Ireland) 1954;

"relevant instrument" means an instrument which a transferee, lessee or proposed lessee is required to produce to the Commissioners of Inland Revenue under subsection (1) of section 244;

"section 244" means section 244 of the Finance Act 1994;

"short leasehold interest", in relation to a transaction, means a leasehold interest which, at the time of that transaction, was for a term of less than 25 years before expiry.

Prescribed particulars

3 The particulars to be given in a document produced pursuant to subsection (2) of section 244 are those prescribed by the Schedule to these Regulations.

Classes of exempt instrument

4— (1) Paragraphs (2) and (3) prescribe classes of instrument which are exempt instruments for the purposes of section 245(1) of the Finance Act 1994.

(2) The class of instrument prescribed by this paragraph is any instrument effecting any transfer on sale of any freehold interest in land in Northern Ireland where the instrument has the characteristics specified in paragraph (4).

(3) The class of instrument prescribed by this paragraph is any instrument effecting any transfer on sale of any lease of land in Northern Ireland where the instrument has the characteristics specified in paragraph (4).

(4) The characteristics specified are that—

(*a*) the instrument is executed on or after 4th November 1996;

(*b*) by reason of the amount or value of the consideration for the transfer effected by the instrument, no stamp duty is chargeable on the instrument; and (*c*) the instrument is certified in accordance with section 7(4) of the Finance Act (Northern Ireland), 1958.

Furnishing of documents relating to registered land

5— (1) This regulation applies in the case of an exempt instrument which effects a transfer—

(*a*) of land which is registered land, or

(*b*) of land which is not registered land, and the case is one in which, as a result of the transfer, the first registration of the ownership of the land becomes compulsory by virtue of section 24 of the Land Registration Act (Northern Ireland) 1970.

(2) The transferee shall produce to the Registrar of Titles with the exempt instrument such a document as is mentioned in subsection (2) of section 244 and contains the particulars prescribed by the Schedule to these Regulations; and the Registrar of Titles shall furnish that document to the Commissioner of Valuation for Northern Ireland.

(3) In paragraph (2) "the Registrar of Titles" shall be construed in accordance with section 1(4) of the Land Registration Act (Northern Ireland) 1970.

Furnishing of documents relating to unregistered land

6— (1) This regulation applies in the case of an exempt instrument which effects a transfer of land which is not registered land, and the case is one in which, as a result of the transfer, the first registration of the ownership of that land does not become compulsory by virtue of section 24 of the Land Registration Act (Northern Ireland) 1970.

(2) The transferee shall produce to the Registrar of Deeds with the exempt instrument such a document as is mentioned in subsection (2) of section 244 and contains the particulars prescribed by the Schedule to these Regulations; and the Registrar of Deeds shall furnish that document to the Commissioner of Valuation for Northern Ireland.

(3) In paragraph (2) "the Registrar of Deeds" means the officer having the control and management of the registry of deeds; and "the registry of deeds" has the meaning given by section 46(2) of the Interpretation Act (Northern Ireland) 1954.

SCHEDULE

PRESCRIBED PARTICULARS TO BE GIVEN IN A DOCUMENT PRODUCED PURSUANT TO SUBSECTION (2) OF SECTION 244 OR REGULATION 5(2) OR 6(2)

Regulations 3, 5(2), 6(2)

The particulars prescribed are particulars—

(1) of the description of the relevant instrument;

(2) of the date of the relevant instrument;

(3) of the names and addresses of the transferor and the transferee or the lessor and the lessee;

(4) of the situation and postal address of the land to which the transaction relates, including—

(*a*) in any case relating to registered land, the Folio Number, County, Townland and Area,

(*b*) in any case relating to unregistered land or land which is part of a Folio, the Folio Number and Townland, and

(*c*) if necessary for the identification of the land, a photocopy of a plan indicating boundaries and areas, and stating the size of the areas and whether those areas are measured in acres or hectares;

(5) showing whether the interest transferred or granted by the transaction is a freehold interest, a long leasehold interest or a short leasehold interest;

(6) showing whether the transfer or grant relates to—

(*a*) a dwelling house,

(*b*) commercial property,

(*c*) development land,

(*d*) farmland, or

(*e*) other land,

and, in the case of a transfer or grant which relates to other land, specifying the nature of that other land;

(7) in any case where the transfer or grant relates to commercial property, showing whether that transfer or grant relates to a single plot of land for the construction of a dwelling;

(8) in any case where the interest transferred or granted is a freehold interest or a long leasehold interest, specifying the amount of the consideration, and in any case where that amount relates to a number of separate items, the allocation of that amount among those items;

(9) showing whether the consideration for the transaction includes value added tax, and if so the amount of that value added tax;

(10) in any case where the interest transferred or granted is a short leasehold interest, specifying—

(*a*) the term of the lease,
(*b*) the date of commencement of the term,
(*c*) the rent reserved,
(*d*) the dates on which the rent is payable,
(*e*) any capital payment made in connection with the transfer or grant of the lease,
(*f*) whether the lease makes provision for rent reviews, and if so the dates of those rent reviews,
(*g*) whether the lessee is responsible for repairs and insurance,
(*h*) whether the lessee is responsible for any other matters and, if so, specifying those other matters, and
(*i*) any other covenants affecting the value of the lease;

(11) of any debt released by the transaction, the amount of that debt and the person to whom that debt was owed;
(12) of the name and address of any selling or letting agent;
(13) of the name of the solicitor for the transferor or lessor;
(14) in a case where the document is signed by an individual who is not the transferee, lessee or proposed lessee, of the name, address and telephone number of that individual.

1997/1156
Stamp Duty and Stamp Duty Reserve Tax (Open-ended Investment Companies) Regulations 1997

Made by the Treasury under FA 1995 s 152

Made . . . . . . 3rd April 1997
Laid before the House of Commons . . . . 7th April 1997
Coming into force . . . . 28th April 1997

Citation and commencement

1 These Regulations may be cited as the Stamp Duty and Stamp Duty Reserve Tax (Open-ended Investment Companies) Regulations 1997 and shall come into force on 28th April 1997.

Interpretation

2 In these Regulations—

["authorised corporate director", "open-ended investment company", "owner of shares" and "scheme property" have the meanings given by subsection (10) of section 468 of the Income and Corporation Taxes Act 1988, read with subsections (11) to (18) of that section, as those subsections are added in relation to open-ended investment companies by regulation 10(4) of the Open-ended Investment Companies (Tax) Regulations 1997; and accordingly references in subsections (11) to (16) of that section to the "Tax Acts" shall be construed as if they included references both to the enactments relating to stamp duty and to the enactments relating to stamp duty reserve tax;][1]

"authorised unit trust" means a unit trust scheme in the case of which an order under section [243 of the Financial Services and Markets Act 2000][2] is in force;

. . .

["the enactments relating to stamp duty" and "the enactments relating to stamp duty reserve tax" have the meanings given by section 152(6) of the Finance Act 1995;

"the relevant enactments relating to stamp duty or stamp duty reserve tax" means—

(*a*) sections 88(1), 90(1) to (1B), 99(5A) and (5B) of the Finance Act 1986, and
(*b*) section 122(1) and (2) of, and paragraphs 1 to 9, 14 and 17 of Schedule 19 to, the Finance Act 1999;][1]

. . .[1]

["trust instrument", "trust property", "unit", "unit holder" and "unit trust scheme" have the meanings given by paragraph 14 of Schedule 19 to the Finance Act 1999.][1]

Amendments—[1] Definitions of "the Board", "open-ended investment company" and "authorised corporate director", and "the Taxes Act" revoked, definitions "authorised corporate director", "open-ended investment company", "owner of shares" and "scheme property", and "the enactments relating to stamp duty" and "the enactments relating to stamp duty reserve tax" and "the relevant enactments relating to stamp duty or stamp duty reserve tax" inserted, and definitions of "trust instrument", "trust property", "unit", "unit holder" and "unit trust scheme" substituted for original definition "unit" and "unit trust scheme", by the Stamp Duty and Stamp Duty Reserve Tax (Open-ended Investment Companies) (Amendment No 2) Regulations, SI 1999/3261, reg 3, with effect from 6 February 2000.

[2] Words in definition of "authorised unit trust" substituted by the Financial Services and Markets Act 2000 (Consequential Amendments) (Taxes) Order, SI 2001/3629 art 167 with effect from 1 December 2001, immediately after the coming into force of the Financial Services and Markets Act 2000 ss 411, 432(1), Sch 20 (and SI 2001/3629 Pts 1 and 2).

[Stamp duty and stamp duty reserve tax treatment of open-ended investment companies

3 Subject to the modifications set out in regulations 4 to 4B, the relevant enactments relating to stamp duty or stamp duty reserve tax shall have effect in relation to open-ended investment companies in a manner corresponding to that in which they have effect in relation to unit trust schemes.][1]

Amendments—[1] This regulation substituted by the Stamp Duty and Stamp Duty Reserve Tax (Open-ended Investment Companies) (Amendment No 2) Regulations, SI 1999/3261, reg 4, with effect from 6 February 2000.

[General modifications of the relevant enactments relating to stamp duty or stamp duty reserve tax

4— (1) Subject to the modifications specified in regulations 4A and 4B, the relevant enactments relating to stamp duty or stamp duty reserve tax shall be modified as follows in relation to open-ended investment companies.

(2) References, however expressed, to—

(*a*) a unit trust scheme, or
(*b*) the trustees of a unit trust scheme,

shall have effect as if they were references to an open-ended investment company.

(3) References, however expressed, to the managers of a unit trust scheme shall have effect as if they were references to the authorised corporate director of an open-ended investment company.

(4) References, however expressed, to—

(*a*) a unit under a unit trust scheme, or
(*b*) an entitlement to a share of the trust property,

shall have effect as if they were references to a share in an open-ended investment company.

(5) References, however expressed, to—

(*a*) a unit holder, or
(*b*) a person entitled to a unit,

shall have effect as if they were references to the owner of a share in an open-ended investment company.

(6) References, however expressed, to trust property shall have effect as if they were references to scheme property.

(7) References, however expressed, to a trust instrument shall have effect as if they were references to an instrument incorporating an open-ended investment company.][1]

Amendments—[1] This regulation substituted, together with regs 4A, 4B, for original reg 4, by the Stamp Duty and Stamp Duty Reserve Tax (Open-ended Investment Companies) (Amendment No 2) Regulations, SI 1999/3261, reg 5, with effect from 6 February 2000.

[Modifications of Schedule 19 to the Finance Act 1999

4A— (1) Schedule 19 to the Finance Act 1999 shall be modified as follows in relation to open-ended investment companies.

(2) In paragraph 4—

(*a*) in sub-paragraph (1)—

(i) for the words "units of the same class as the unit in question" there shall be substituted the word "shares", and
(ii) for the words "units of that class" there shall be substituted the word "shares";

(*b*) in sub-paragraph (3) for the words "units of the class" in both places where they occur there shall be substituted the word "shares";
(*c*) in sub-paragraph (4) for the words "units of the class in question" there shall be substituted the word "shares";
(*d*) after sub-paragraph (5) there shall be added the following sub-paragraph—

"(6) Where there is more than one class of shares in an open-ended investment company, the proportionate reduction of tax under this paragraph shall be calculated as if all the shares in the company had been converted into shares of a single class."

(3) In paragraph 14—

(*a*) for sub-paragraph (2) there shall be substituted the following sub-paragraph—

"(2) 'Open-ended investment company' has, subject to paragraph 17, the meaning given by subsection (10) of section 468 of the Income and Corporation Taxes Act 1988, read with subsections (11) to (18) of that section, as those subsections are added in relation to open-ended investment companies by regulation 10(4) of the Open-ended Investment Companies (Tax) Regulations 1997; and accordingly references in subsection (11) to (16) of that section to the 'Tax Acts' shall be construed as if they included references both to the enactments relating to stamp duty and to the enactments relating to stamp duty reserve tax; and those enactments shall have effect accordingly."

(*b*) in sub-paragraph (3) the definitions of "trust instrument", "trust property", "unit" and "unit holder" shall be omitted.

(4) In paragraph 17 sub-paragraph (4) shall be omitted.][1]

Amendments—[1] This regulation substituted, together with regs 4, 4B, for original reg 4, by the Stamp Duty and Stamp Duty Reserve Tax (Open-ended Investment Companies) (Amendment No 2) Regulations, SI 1999/3261, reg 5, with effect from 6 February 2000.

[Modifications of the Finance Act 1986

4B— (1) Section 99 of the Finance Act 1986 (general interpretation provisions) shall be modified as follows in relation to open-ended investment companies.

(2) In subsection (5A) paragraph (*a*) and the word 'or' following it shall be omitted.][1]

[(3) After subsection (5B) insert—

"(5C) "Chargeable securities" does not include shares in a company which is treated as not being an open-ended investment company by regulations made under paragraph 17 of Schedule 19 to the Finance Act 1999 ("paragraph 17").

In this subsection the reference to paragraph 17 is a reference to that paragraph as it has effect in relation to open-ended investment companies by virtue of regulations 3 to 4A of the Stamp Duty and Stamp Duty Reserve Tax (Open-ended Investment Companies) Regulations 1997."][2]

Amendments—[1] This regulation substituted, together with regs 4, 4A, for original reg 4, by the Stamp Duty and Stamp Duty Reserve Tax (Open-ended Investment Companies) (Amendment No 2) Regulations, SI 1999/3261, reg 5, with effect from 6 February 2000.

[2] Para (3) inserted by the Stamp Duty and Stamp Duty Reserve Tax (Definition of Unit Trust Scheme and Open-ended Investment Company) Regulations, SI 2001/964 with effect from 6 April 2001.

Bearer securities issued by an open-ended investment company in a foreign currency

5 Bearer securities issued by an open-ended investment company in a currency other than sterling shall be treated, for the purposes of the enactments relating to stamp duty and[the enactments relating to stamp duty reserve tax][1], as if the securities had been issued in sterling.

Amendments—[1] Words substituted by the Stamp Duty and Stamp Duty Reserve Tax (Open-ended Investment Companies) (Amendment No 2) Regulations, SI 1999/3261, reg 6, with effect from 6 February 2000.

Shares in open-ended investment companies dealing in interest-bearing investments

6...

Amendments—This regulation revoked by the Stamp Duty and Stamp Duty Reserve Tax (Open-ended Investment Companies) (Amendment No 2) Regulations, SI 1999/3261, reg 7, with effect from 6 February 2000.

Conversion of an authorised unit trust to an open-ended investment company—exemption from stamp duty charge

7— (1) Stamp duty shall not be chargeable on an instrument transferring any property which is subject to the trusts of an authorised unit trust ("the target trust") to an open-ended investment company ("the acquiring company") if the conditions set out in paragraph (2) are fulfilled.

(2) Those conditions are that—

(*a*) the transfer forms part of an arrangement for the conversion of an authorised unit trust to an open-ended investment company, whereby the whole of the available property of the target trust becomes the whole of the property of the acquiring company;

(*b*) under the arrangement all the units in the target trust are extinguished;

(*c*) the consideration under the arrangement consists of or includes the issue of shares ("the consideration shares") in the acquiring company to the persons who held the extinguished units;

(*d*) the consideration shares are issued to those persons in proportion to their holdings of the extinguished units; and

(*e*) the consideration under the arrangement does not include anything else other than the assumption or discharge by the acquiring company of liabilities of the trustees of the target trust.

(3) An instrument on which stamp duty is not chargeable by virtue only of this regulation shall not be taken to be duly stamped unless it is stamped with the duty to which it would be liable but for this regulation or it has, in accordance with section 12 of the Stamp Act 1891, been stamped with a particular stamp denoting that it is not chargeable with any duty.

(4) In this regulation and in regulations 8 to 10 "the whole of the available property of the target trust" means the whole of the property subject to the trusts of the target trust, other than any property which is retained for the purpose of discharging liabilities of the trustees of the target trust.

(5) For the purposes of this regulation and regulations 8 to 10 each of the parts of an umbrella scheme (and not the scheme as a whole) shall be regarded as an authorised unit trust; and "umbrella scheme" has the same meaning as in section 468 of the Income and Corporation Taxes Act 1988.

Conversion of an authorised unit trust to an open-ended investment company—exemption from stamp duty reserve tax charge

8— (1) Section 87 of the Finance Act 1986 shall not apply as regards an agreement to transfer securities which constitute property which is subject to the trusts of an authorised unit trust ("the target trust") to an open-ended investment company ("the acquiring company") if the conditions set out in paragraph (2) are fulfilled.

(2) Those conditions are that—

(*a*) the agreement forms part of an arrangement for the conversion of an authorised unit trust to an open-ended investment company, whereby the whole of the available property of the target trust becomes the whole of the property of the acquiring company;

(*b*) under the arrangement all the units in the target trust are extinguished;

(*c*) the consideration under the arrangement consists of or includes the issue of shares ("the consideration shares") in the acquiring company to the persons who held the extinguished units;

(*d*) the consideration shares are issued to those persons in proportion to their holdings of the extinguished units; and

(*e*) the consideration under the arrangement does not include anything else other than the assumption or discharge by the acquiring company of liabilities of the trustees of the target trust.

(3) Where—

(*a*) stamp duty is not chargeable on an instrument by virtue of regulation 7(1), or

(*b*) section 87 of the Finance Act 1986 does not apply as regards an agreement by virtue of paragraph (1) of this regulation,

section 87 of the Finance Act 1986 shall not apply as regards an agreement, or a deemed agreement, to transfer a unit to the managers of the target trust which is made in order that the unit may be extinguished under the arrangement mentioned in regulation 7(2)(*b*) or, as the case may be, paragraph (2)(*b*) of this regulation.

Amalgamation of an authorised unit trust with an open-ended investment company—exemption from stamp duty charge

9— (1) Stamp duty shall not be chargeable on an instrument transferring any property which is subject to the trusts of an authorised unit trust ("the target trust") to an open-ended investment company ("the acquiring company") if the conditions set out in paragraph (2) are fulfilled.

(2) Those conditions are that—

(*a*) the transfer forms part of an arrangement for the amalgamation of an authorised unit trust with an open-ended investment company, whereby the whole of the available property of the target trust becomes part (but not the whole) of the property of the acquiring company;

(*b*) under the arrangement all the units in the target trust are extinguished;

(*c*) the consideration under the arrangement consists of or includes the issue of shares ("the consideration shares") in the acquiring company to the persons who held the extinguished units;

(*d*) the consideration shares are issued to those persons in proportion to their holdings of the extinguished units; and

(*e*) the consideration under the arrangement does not include anything else other than the assumption or discharge by the acquiring company of liabilities of the trustees of the target trust.

(3) An instrument on which stamp duty is not chargeable by virtue only of this section shall not be taken to be duly stamped unless it is stamped with the duty to which it would be liable but for this regulation or it has, in accordance with section 12 of the Stamp Act 1891, been stamped with a particular stamp denoting that it is not chargeable with any duty.

(4) This regulation applies to any instrument which is executed—

(*a*) on or after the date of coming into force of these Regulations; ...[1]

(*b*) ...[1]

Amendments—[1] Word "but" in sub-para (4)(*a*) and sub-para (4)(*b*) omitted by Stamp Duty and Stamp Duty Reserve Tax (Open-ended Investment Companies) (Amendment) Regulations, SI 1999/1467 with effect from 16 June 1999.

Amalgamation of an authorised unit trust with an open-ended investment company—exemption from stamp duty reserve tax charge

10— (1) Section 87 of the Finance Act 1986 shall not apply as regards an agreement to transfer securities which constitute property which is subject to the trusts of an authorised unit trust ("the target trust") to an open-ended investment company ("the acquiring company") if the conditions set out in paragraph (2) are fulfilled.

(2) Those conditions are that—

(*a*) the agreement forms part of an arrangement for the amalgamation of an authorised unit trust with an open-ended investment company, whereby the whole of the available property of the target trust becomes part (but not the whole) of the property of the acquiring company;

(*b*) under the arrangement all the units in the target trust are extinguished;

(*c*) the consideration under the arrangement consists of or includes the issue of shares ("the consideration shares") in the acquiring company to the persons who held the extinguished units;

(*d*) the consideration shares are issued to those persons in proportion to their holdings of the extinguished units; and

(*e*) the consideration under the arrangement does not include anything else other than the assumption or discharge by the acquiring company of liabilities of the trustees of the target trust.

(3) Where—

(*a*) stamp duty is not chargeable on an instrument by virtue of regulation 9(1), or

(*b*) section 87 of the Finance Act 1986 does not apply as regards an agreement by virtue of paragraph (1) of this regulation,

section 87 of the Finance Act 1986 shall not apply as regards an agreement, or a deemed agreement, to transfer a unit to the managers of the target trust which is made in order that the unit may be extinguished under the arrangement mentioned in regulation 9(2)(*b*) or, as the case may be, paragraph (2)(*b*) of this regulation.

(4) This regulation applies—

(*a*) to an agreement which is not conditional, if the agreement is made on or after the date of coming into force of these Regulations …[1]; and

(*b*) to a conditional agreement, if the condition is satisfied on or after the date of coming into force of these Regulations …[1].

Amendments—[1] Words "but before 1st July 1999" in sub-paras (4)(*a*)(*b*) revoked by Stamp Duty and Stamp Duty Reserve Tax (Open-ended Investment Companies) (Amendment) Regulations, SI 1999/1467 with effect from 16 June 1999.

Disapplication of section 42 of the Finance Act 1930

11 Section 42 of the Finance Act 1930 (relief from transfer stamp duty in case of transfer of property as between associated companies) shall not apply as regards any beneficial interest in property that is conveyed or transferred to or from an open-ended investment company.

Disapplication of sections 75 to 77 of the Finance Act 1986

12 Sections 75 to 77 of the Finance Act 1986 (acquisition by a company of another company's undertaking) shall not apply as regards open-ended investment companies.

1997/2428
Finance Act 1997 (Stamp Duty and Stamp Duty Reserve Tax) (Appointed Day) Order 1997

Made by the Treasury under FA 1997 ss 97(6), 98(4), 102(6) and 103(8)

Made . . . . *8th October 1997*

1 This Order may be cited as the Finance Act 1997 (Stamp Duty and Stamp Duty Reserve Tax) (Appointed Day) Order 1997.

2— (1) The day appointed for the purposes of each of the enactments specified in paragraph (2) is 20th October 1997.

(2) The enactments specified are sections 97, 98, 102 and 103 of the Finance Act 1997.

1997/2429
Stamp Duty and Stamp Duty Reserve Tax (Investment Exchanges and Clearing Houses) Regulations 1997

Made by the Treasury under FA 1991 ss 116 and 117

Made . . . . *8th October 1997*

Citation, commencement and effect

1— (1) These Regulations may be cited as the Stamp Duty and Stamp Duty Reserve Tax (Investment Exchanges and Clearing Houses) Regulations 1997 and shall come into force on 20th October 1997.

(2) These Regulations shall have effect—

(*a*) as respects the charge to stamp duty, in relation to instruments executed on or after 20th October 1997;

(*b*) as respects the charge to stamp duty reserve tax—

(i) in the case of an agreement to transfer equity securities which is not conditional, where the agreement is made on or after 20th October 1997;

(ii) in the case of an agreement to transfer equity securities which is conditional, where the condition is satisfied on or after that date.

Interpretation

2 In these Regulations unless the context otherwise requires—

"the Board of directors" means the Board of directors of LIFFE (A & M);

"clearing member" means a member (as defined by this regulation) who is also a member of The London Clearing House Limited and who as such is permitted by the Board of directors and that clearing house to clear transactions made on LIFFE for an equity security;

"equity securities" means stocks and shares which are issued or raised by a company but does not include stocks and shares issued or raised by a company not incorporated in the United Kingdom unless—

(*a*) they are registered in a register kept in the United Kingdom by or on behalf of the company, or

(*b*) in the case of shares, they are paired, within the meaning of section 99(6A) of the Finance Act 1986, with shares issued by a company incorporated in the United Kingdom;

"LIFFE" means The London International Financial Futures and Options Exchange;

"LIFFE (A & M)" means LIFFE Administration and Management;

"member" means a member of LIFFE (A & M) who is recognised as such by the Board of directors;

"non-clearing member" means a member other than a clearing member;

"option" means an option to buy or sell securities which is listed by and traded on LIFFE.

Prescription of recognised investment exchange and recognised clearing house

3 For the purposes of sections 116 and 117 of the Finance Act 1991—

(*a*) LIFFE (A & M) is a recognised investment exchange which is prescribed;

(*b*) The London Clearing House Limited is a recognised clearing house which is prescribed.

Transfers of securities to The London Clearing House Limited—prescribed circumstances

4— (1) In the circumstances prescribed by paragraph (2), a charge to stamp duty or to stamp duty reserve tax shall be treated as not arising.

(2) The circumstances prescribed are where, as a result of the exercise of options, equity securities of a particular kind are transferred or issued or agreed to be transferred or issued—

(*a*) to The London Clearing House Limited; or

(*b*) to a person whose business is or includes holding such securities as a nominee for The London Clearing House Limited.

(3) References in this regulation and in regulation 5 to The London Clearing House Limited are references to that clearing house in its capacity as a person providing clearing services in connection with a transaction made on LIFFE.

Transfers of securities to or from members of LIFFE—prescribed circumstances

5— (1) In the circumstances prescribed by paragraph (2), a charge to stamp duty or to stamp duty reserve tax shall be treated as not arising.

(2) The circumstances prescribed are where, in order to meet an obligation to receive securities resulting from the exercise of options, equity securities of a particular kind are transferred or agreed to be transferred—

(*a*) from a non-clearing member or a nominee of a non-clearing member to a clearing member or a nominee of a clearing member; or

(*b*) from The London Clearing House Limited or a nominee of that clearing house to a clearing member or a nominee of a clearing member.

(3) References in paragraph (2) to a clearing member are references to a clearing member in his capacity as such.

Revocation of the Stamp Duty and Stamp Duty Reserve Tax (Investment Exchanges and Clearing Houses) Regulations 1992

6 The Stamp Duty and Stamp Duty Reserve Tax (Investment Exchanges and Clearing Houses) Regulations 1992 are hereby revoked as respects instruments and agreements referred to in regulation 1(2).

Note—This Statutory Instrument revokes the Stamp Duty and Stamp Duty Reserve Tax (Investment Exchanges and Clearing Houses) Regulations, SI 1992/570, in relation to the charge to stamp duty for instruments executed on or after 20 October 1997, and in relation to the charge to stamp duty reserve tax for the transfer of equity securities which are not conditional made on or after 20 October 1997 and for conditional transfers where the condition is satisfied on or after 20 October 1997.

1998/1517

Visiting Forces and Allied Headquarters (Stamp Duties) (Designation) Order 1998

Made under FA 1960 s 74

Made . . . . 24 June 1998
Coming into force . . . . 24 June 1998

1 This Order may be cited as the Visiting Forces and Allied Headquarters (Stamp Duties) (Designation) Order 1998 and shall come into force on 24th June 1998.

2 Each of the countries specified in the First Schedule to this Order and each of the allied headquarters specified in the Second Schedule to this Order is hereby designated for the purposes of section 74 of the Finance Act 1960.

FIRST SCHEDULE

Albania, Bulgaria, the Czech Republic, Estonia, Hungary, Latvia, Lithuania, Poland, Romania, the Slovak Republic, Slovenia, Spain and Sweden.

SECOND SCHEDULE

Headquarters of the Supreme Allied Commander Atlantic (SACLANT).
Headquarters Eastern Atlantic (EASTLANT).
Headquarters Maritime Air Eastern Atlantic (MARAIREASTLANT).
Headquarters Submarine Forces Eastern Atlantic (SUBEASTLANT).
Headquarters Allied Forces North Western Europe (AFNORTHWEST).
Headquarters Allied Naval Forces North Western Europe (NAVNORTHWEST).
Headquarters Allied Air Forces North Western Europe (AIRNORTHWEST).
NATO Airborne Early Warning Force Headquarters and NATO E-3A Component.

1998/1518
Visiting Forces (Stamp Duties) (Designation) Order 1998

Made under FA 1960 s 74

Made . . . . *24 June 1998*
Coming into force in relation to each country specified in article 2, the date determined in accordance with article 1(2)

1— (1) This Order may be cited as the Visiting Forces (Stamp Duties) (Designation) Order 1998 and shall come into force in accordance with the following provisions of this article.

(2) This Order shall come into force, in relation to each of the countries specified in article 2, on whichever is the later of the following dates—

(*a*) the date on which its Government becomes a party to the Agreement among the States Parties to the North Atlantic Treaty and the Other States Participating in the Partnership for Peace regarding the Status of their Forces dated 19th June 1995; and
(*b*) the day after the date on which this Order is made.

(3) The date on which this Order comes into force in relation to each of the countries specified in article 2 shall be notified in the London, Edinburgh and Belfast Gazettes.

2 The following countries are hereby designated for the purposes of section 74 of the Finance Act 1960—

Armenia, Austria, Azerbaijan, Belarus, Finland, Georgia, Kazakhstan, Kyrgyzstan, the Former Yugoslav Republic of Macedonia, Moldova, Russia, Switzerland, Turkmenistan, Ukraine, and Uzbekistan.

1998/2244
Government of Wales Act 1998 (Commencement No 1) Order 1998

Made by the Secretary of State for Wales under the Government of Wales Act 1998 s 158

Made . . . . *1st September 1998*

1 This Order may be cited as the Government of Wales Act 1998 (Commencement No 1) Order 1998.

2 In this Order, references to "the Act" are to the Government of Wales Act 1998.

3 The date of 2nd September 1998 is appointed for the coming into force of the following provisions of the Act—

Section 130(4) and (5) (transfer of Development Board for Rural Wales staff).
Section 132(1) and (6) (preparatory work for winding-down of Development Board for Rural Wales).
Section 133(3) and (4) (Development Board for Rural Wales—consequential etc provisions).
Section 136(4) and (5) (transfer of Land Authority for Wales Staff).
Section 138(1) and (6) (preparatory work for winding-down of Land Authority for Wales).
Section 139(3) and (4) (Land Authority for Wales—consequential etc provisions).
Section 140(5) and (6) (transfer of Housing for Wales staff).
Section 142(1), (7) and (8) (preparatory work for winding-down of Housing for Wales).
Section 143(3) and (4) (Housing for Wales—consequential etc provisions).
Section 150 (abolition of Residuary Body for Wales).
Schedule 18 Part VII and section 152 so far as relating thereto (repeals relating to Residuary Body for Wales).

4 The date of 1st October 1998 is appointed for the coming into force of the following provisions of the Act—

Sections 126 to 128 including all provisions of Schedules 13 and 14 (extension of functions of Welsh Development Agency).

Section 129 including all provisions of Schedule 15, and section 130(1) to (3) (cessation of functions and transfer of property etc of Development Board for Rural Wales).
Section 131 (Development Board for Rural Wales—transitional provisions).
Section 132(2) to (5) and (7) (winding-down of Development Board for Rural Wales).
Section 133(1) and (2) (abolition of Development Board for Rural Wales).
Section 134, 135 and 136(1) to (3) (Land Authority for Wales—cessation of functions, consequential amendment and transfer of property etc).
Section 137 (Land Authority for Wales—transitional provisions).
Section 138(2) to (5) and (7) (winding-down of Land Authority for Wales).
Section 139(1) and (2) (abolition of Land Authority for Wales).
Schedule 18 Parts III to V and section 152 so far as relating thereto (repeals relating to Welsh Development Agency, Development Board for Rural Wales and Land Authority for Wales).

5 The date of 1st November 1998 is appointed for the coming into force of the following provisions of the Act—

Section 140(1) to (4) including all provisions of Schedule 16, and section 141 (Housing for Wales—transfer of functions and transitional provisions).
Section 142(2) to (6) (winding-down of Housing for Wales).
Section 143(1) and (2) (abolition of Housing for Wales).
Schedule 18 Part VI and section 152 so far as relating thereto (repeals relating to Housing for Wales).

Stamp Taxes

1998/3177

European Single Currency (Taxes) Regulations 1998

Made	*17th December 1998*
Laid before the House of Commons	*17th December 1998*
Coming into force	*1st January 1999*

ARRANGEMENT OF REGULATIONS

PART I
INTRODUCTORY

PART VI
REPURCHASES AND STOCK LENDING—STAMP DUTY AND STAMP DUTY RESERVE TAX

PART I
INTRODUCTORY

Citation and commencement

1 These Regulations may be cited as the European Single Currency (Taxes) Regulations 1998 and shall come into force on 1st January 1999.

Interpretation

2— (1) In these Regulations unless the context otherwise requires—

"commodity or financial futures" has the meaning given by subsection (2)(*a*) of section 143 of the 1992 Act, and references in these Regulations to commodity or financial futures include references to a commodity or financial futures contract referred to in subsection (7)(*a*) or (*b*);

"debt", other than a debt on a security, includes a debt owed by a bank which is not in sterling and which is represented by a sum standing to the credit of a person in an account in the bank;

"derivative" means any commodity or financial futures or an option;

"ecu" shall be construed in accordance with section 95(5) of the Finance Act 1993;
"euro" means the single currency adopted or proposed to be adopted as its currency by a member State in accordance with the Treaty establishing the European Community;
"euroconversion" has the meaning given by regulation 3;
...[1]
"member State" means a member State other than the United Kingdom;
"participating member State" means a member State that adopts the euro as its currency;
...[1]
"reconventioning" in relation to a relevant asset means a change, consequent on simple redenomination, in the terms of the asset as a result of which the new terms become aligned to the prevailing terms of equivalent marketable relevant assets denominated in euro;
"relevant asset" means a debt (whether or not a debt on a security), [an option][1] or any commodity or financial futures;
"renominalisation" in relation to a relevant asset means a change, consequent on simple redenomination, in the minimum nominal amount in which the asset can be held or traded to a new round amount;
"security" has the meaning given by section 132(3)(*b*) of the 1992 Act;
"simple redenomination" means the conversion of the currency in which an asset, liability, contract or instrument is expressed from the currency of a participating member State into euro, and any rounding of the resulting amount to the nearest euro cent;
"the Taxes Act" means the Income and Corporation Taxes Act 1988;
"the 1992 Act" means the Taxation of Chargeable Gains Act 1992.

(2) In these Regulations references to an option, without more, are references to an option to which section 144 or 144A of the 1992 Act applies.

Amendments—[1] Definitions of "long-term capital asset" and "long-term capital liability", and "qualifying contract" revoked, and words in definition of "relevant asset" substituted, by the European Single Currency (Taxes) (Amendment) Regulations, SI 2002/1971 regs 2, 3 with effect for accounting periods beginning after 30 September 2002.

Definition of euroconversion

3— (1) "Euroconversion" means—

(*a*) in relation to any currency, or an amount expressed in any currency, of a participating member State, the conversion or restating of that currency or that amount into euro and any rounding of the resulting amount within a euro;

(*b*) in relation to any asset, liability, contract or instrument—

(i) the simple redenomination of that asset, liability, contract or instrument, or

(ii) in the case of a relevant asset, the simple redenomination of that asset accompanied by either or both of renominalisation and reconventioning, or

(iii) the substitution (whether by way of exchange, conversion, replacement or otherwise) for the asset, liability, contract or instrument of an equivalent replacement asset, liability, contract or instrument.

(2) An equivalent replacement asset, liability, contract or instrument means an asset, liability, contract or instrument whose amount, terms and conditions are identical to what is reasonable to assume would be the amount, terms and conditions of the original asset, liability, contract or instrument were it to undergo a simple redenomination, or (in the case of a relevant asset) a simple redenomination accompanied by either or both of renominalisation and reconventioning.

(3) For the purposes of paragraphs (1) and (2) a simple redenomination is accompanied (in the case of a relevant asset) by renominalisation or reconventioning if either—

(*a*) the renominalisation or reconventioning is effected simultaneously, or

(*b*) it is effected within a period of time following the simple redenomination which is such as to enable it reasonably to be inferred that the renominalisation or reconventioning is associated with the simple redenomination.

...

PART VI
REPURCHASES AND STOCK LENDING—STAMP DUTY AND STAMP DUTY RESERVE TAX

Interpretation

24 In this Part of these Regulations "capital payment" means any payment on the euroconversion of securities other than any interest, dividend or other annual payment payable in respect of the securities.

Replacement of stock in a euroconversion

25— (1) This regulation applies in a case where—

(*a*) there is an arrangement involving the transfer of stock to which subsection (1)(*a*) of section 80C of the Finance Act 1986 (repurchases and stock lending—exemption from stamp duty) applies, and (*b*) there is a euroconversion of that stock ("the old stock"), effected wholly or in part by the issue of new stock to replace the old stock.

(2) The new stock shall be regarded, for the purposes of section 80C of the Finance Act 1986, as stock of the same kind and amount as the old stock.

Replacement of chargeable securities in a euroconversion

26— (1) This regulation applies in a case where—

(*a*) there is an arrangement involving the transfer of chargeable securities to which subsection (1)(*a*) of section 89AA of the Finance Act 1986 (repurchases and stock lending—exemption from stamp duty reserve tax) applies, and

(*b*) there is a euroconversion of those chargeable securities ("the old chargeable securities"), effected wholly or partly by the issue of new chargeable securities to replace the old chargeable securities.

(3) The new chargeable securities shall be regarded, for the purposes of section 89AA of the Finance Act 1986, as chargeable securities of the same kind and amount as the old chargeable securities.

Payment or benefit received by transferee on euroconversion

27— (1) This regulation applies in a case where—

(*a*) there is an arrangement involving the transfer of stock to which subsection (1) of section 80C of the Finance Act 1986 applies,

(*b*) a capital payment would, but for the arrangement, be received by the person referred to as B in that section or by his nominee on the euroconversion of that stock,

(*c*) neither the person referred to as A in that section nor his nominee is required under the arrangement to pay to B or to B's nominee an amount equivalent to the amount of that capital payment, and an amount equivalent to the amount of that capital payment is not required under the arrangement to be taken into account in computing the price of stock to be transferred to B or his nominee under the arrangement, and

(*d*) the amount of the capital payment would not exceed 500 euros.

(2) A shall not be regarded, for the purposes of section 80C of the Finance Act 1986, as a person to whom a benefit consisting of an amount equal to the capital payment referred to in paragraph (1) accrues as mentioned in subsection (4)(*b*) of that section.

Payment or benefit received by transferee of chargeable securities on euroconversion

28— (1) This regulation applies in a case where—

(*a*) there is an arrangement involving the transfer of chargeable securities to which subsection (1) of section 89AA of the Finance Act 1986 applies,

(*b*) a capital payment would, but for the arrangement, be received by the person referred to as Q in that section or by his nominee on the euroconversion of those chargeable securities,

(*c*) neither the person referred to as P in that section nor his nominee is required under the arrangement to pay to Q or to Q's nominee an amount equivalent to the amount of that capital payment, and an amount equivalent to the amount of that capital payment is not required under the arrangement to be taken into account in computing the price of the chargeable securities to be transferred to Q or his nominee under the arrangement, and

(*d*) the amount of the capital payment would not exceed 500 euros.

(2) P shall not be regarded, for the purposes of section 89AA of the Finance Act 1986, as a person to whom a benefit consisting of an amount equal to thc capital payment referred to in paragraph (1) accrues as mentioned in subsection (4)(*b*) of that section.

Renominalisation resulting in new minimum denomination in which stock can be held or traded

29— (1) This regulation applies in a case where—

(*a*) there is an arrangement involving the transfer of stock to which subsection (1) of section 80C of the Finance Act 1986 applies,

(*b*) there is a euroconversion of that stock prior to the transfer of stock under the arrangement by A or his nominee to B or his nominee as mentioned in subsection (1)(*b*) of that section,

(*c*) the aggregate nominal value (expressed in euros) of the stock transferred by B to A or his nominee as mentioned in subsection (1)(*a*) of that section, or of stock issued to replace that stock in a euroconversion is, as a result of renominalisation, not a whole multiple of the new minimum denomination in which that stock can be traded at the time of the transfer of stock referred to in sub-paragraph (*b*),

(*d*) stock the aggregate nominal value of which is equal to the largest whole multiple of the new minimum denomination which does not exceed the aggregate nominal value referred to in sub-paragraph (*c*) is required under the arrangement to be transferred by A or his nominee to B or his nominee, and

(*e*) A or his nominee is required under the arrangement to pay to B or his nominee an amount which either—

(i) is equal to the amount of what would, but for the arrangement, have been the proceeds of disposal of the remainder of the stock on the renominalisation received by B, or

(ii) is equal to the value, at the time of the transfer of stock referred to in sub-paragraph (*b*), of the remainder of the stock if the remainder could still be held at that time though not traded.

(2) Where this regulation applies, the requirement for payment of the amount specified in paragraph (1)(*e*) is to be regarded, for the purposes of section 80C of the Finance Act 1986, as equivalent to a requirement for the remainder of the stock to be transferred by A or his nominee to B or his nominee.

(3) the value referred to in paragraph (1)(*e*)(ii) is the appropriate proportion (based on nominal value) of the market value of the minimum amount of the original stock that, at the time of the transfer of stock referred to in sub-paragraph (*b*), could be traded.

(4) Where the amount calculated in accordance with sub-paragraph (*e*) of paragraph (1) does not exceed 500 euros, and the arrangement does not require payment of a sum equal to this amount, this regulation shall have effect as if the amount calculated in accordance with that sub-paragraph were nil and the requirement specified in that sub-paragraph were satisfied.

Renominalisation resulting in new minimum denomination in which chargeable securities can be held or traded

30— (1) This regulation applies in a case where—

(*a*) there is an arrangement involving the transfer of chargeable securities to which subsection (1) of section 89AA of the Finance Act 1986 applies,

(*b*) there is a euroconversion of those chargeable securities prior to the transfer of chargeable securities under the arrangement by P or his nominee to Q to his nominee as mentioned in subsection (1)(*b*) of that section,

(*c*) the aggregate nominal value (expressed in euros) of the chargeable securities transferred by Q to P or his nominee as mentioned in subsection (1)(*a*) of that section, or of chargeable securities issued to replace those chargeable securities in a euroconversion is, as a result of renominalisation, not a whole multiple of the new minimum denomination in which those chargeable securities can be traded at the time of the transfer of chargeable securities referred to sub-paragraph (*b*),

(*d*) chargeable securities the aggregate nominal value of which is equal to the largest whole multiple of the new minimum denomination which does not exceed the aggregate nominal value referred to in sub-paragraph (*c*) are required under the arrangement to be transferred by P or his nominee to Q or his nominee, and

(*e*) P or his nominee is required under the arrangement to pay to Q or his nominee an amount which either—

(i) is equal to the amount of what would, but for the arrangement, have been the proceeds of disposal of the remainder of the chargeable securities on the renominalisation received by Q, or

(ii) is equal to the value, at the time of the transfer of chargeable securities referred to in sub-paragraph (*b*), of the remainder of the chargeable securities if the remainder could still be held at that time though not traded.

(2) Where this regulation applies, the requirement for payment of the amount specified in paragraph (1)(*e*) is to be regarded, for the purposes of section 89AA of the Finance Act 1986, as equivalent to a requirement for the remainder of the chargeable securities to be transferred by P or his nominee to Q or his nominee.

(3) The value referred to in paragraph (1)(*e*)(ii) is the appropriate proportion (based on nominal value) of the market value of the minimum amount of the original chargeable securities that, at the time of the transfer of chargeable securities referred to in paragraph (1)(*b*), could be traded.

(4) Where the amount calculated in accordance with sub-paragraph (*e*) of paragraph (1) does not exceed 500 euros, and the arrangement does not require payment of a sum equal to this amount, this regulation shall have effect as if the amount calculated in accordance with that sub-paragraph were nil and the requirement specified in that sub-paragraph were satisfied.

1999/118

Government of Wales Act 1998 (Commencement No 3) Order 1999

Made by the Secretary of State for Wales under the Government of Wales Act 1998 s 158

Made . . . . *11th January 1999*

1 This Order may be cited as the Government of Wales Act 1998 (Commencement No 3) Order 1999.

2 The date of 1st February 1999 is appointed for the coming into force of the following provisions of the Government of Wales Act 1998—

Section 111(1). (Welsh Administration Ombudsman).

Schedule 9 Part I and section 111(2) so far as relating thereto. (Welsh Administration Ombudsman—appointment, staff etc.).

Schedule 12 paragraphs 1, 18, 19, 31 and 32, and section 125 so far as relating thereto. (Minor and consequential amendments).
Schedule 18 Part I in respect of the repeal in the Finance Act 1989, and section 152 so far as relating thereto. (Repeals—Welsh Administration Ombudsman and Health Service Commissioner for Wales).

1999/2383
Stamp Duty Reserve Tax (UK Depositary Interests in Foreign Securities) Regulations 1999

Made by the Treasury under FA 1986 s 98 and FA 1999 ss 119, 121

Made . . . . *24th August 1999*
Laid before the House of Commons . . . . *24th August 1999*
Coming into force . . . . *25th August 1999*

Citation and commencement

1 These Regulations may be cited as the Stamp Duty Reserve Tax (UK Depositary Interests in Foreign Securities) Regulations 1999 and shall come into force on 25 August 1999.

Interpretation

2 In these Regulations—

"the Board" means the Commissioners of Inland Revenue;

. . .[3]

"depositary interest" means a security which—

(*a*) consists of the rights of a person in or relating to securities of a particular kind which, or entitlements to which, are held on trust for the benefit of that person by another person, and

(*b*) under the terms of its issue, can only be transferred in accordance with regulations under [section 785 of the Companies Act 2006 (provision enabling procedures for evidencing and transferring title)][4] or by means of a transfer within section 186(1) of the Finance Act 1996 (transfer of securities to member of electronic transfer system);

"foreign securities" means securities falling within the definition of "securities" in regulation 3(1) of the Uncertificated Securities Regulations 1995 which—

(*a*) are issued or raised by a body corporate that is not incorporated, and whose central management and control is not exercised, in the United Kingdom;

(*b*) are not registered in a register kept in the United Kingdom by or on behalf of the body corporate by which they are issued or raised;

(*c*) . . .[3]

(*d*) are of the same class in the body corporate as securities which [—

(i) are listed on a recognised stock exchange, or

(ii) are of a type which would have been treated as so listed immediately before 28th November 2001;][2] . . .[1];

"the Management Act" means the Taxes Management Act 1970;

"operator" has the meaning given by regulation 2 of the principal Regulations;

["recognised stock exchange" has the meaning given by section 841 of the Income and Corporation Taxes Act 1988;][1]

"the principal Regulations" means the Stamp Duty Reserve Tax Regulations 1986;

"relevant day" has the meaning given by section 87(3) of the Finance Act 1986;

"the Schedule" means the Schedule to the principal Regulations;

"UK depositary interest" means a depositary interest which is issued in the United Kingdom or registered on a register kept in the United Kingdom.

Amendments—[1] Words in definition "foreign securities" repealed and definition of "recognised stock exchange" substituted for original definition of "recognised stock exchange overseas" by the SDRT (UK Depositary Interests in Foreign Securities) (Amendment) Regulations, SI 2000/1871 regs 3, 4 with effect from 7 August 2000.

[2] In definition of "foreign securities", in para (*d*) words substituted by the SDRT (UK Depositary Interests in Foreign Securities) (Amendment) Regulations, SI 2001/3779 reg 2 with effect from 19 December 2001.

[3] Definition of "collective investment scheme", and para (*c*) in definition of "foreign securities", revoked by the SDRT (UK Depository Interest in Foreign Securities) (Amendment) Regulations, SI 2007/12 reg 2 with effect from 1 February 2007.

[4] Words in definition of "depository interest" substituted by the Companies Act 2006 (Consequential Amendments) (Taxes and National Insurance) Order, SI 2008/954 art 48 with effect from 6 April 2008.

Exclusion of a UK depositary interest in foreign securities from the definition of "chargeable securities" in Part IV of the Finance Act 1986

3— (1) Subject to paragraph (2), a UK depositary interest in foreign securities is not a chargeable security for the purposes of Part IV of the Finance Act 1986.

(2) Paragraph (1) does not apply to an agreement to transfer a security where the security ceases to be a UK depositary interest in foreign securities on or before the relevant day.

Notice relating to UK depositary interests in foreign securities

4— (1) This regulation applies to an operator in circumstances where, for the first time, a depositary interest in a particular foreign security is issued and the operator intends to treat the depositary interest as one to which regulation 3(1) applies.

(2) An operator shall, on or before the date which is the fourteenth day following the date of issue, give notice to the Board of—

(*a*) the date of issue, and
(*b*) the depositary interest issued.

(3) A notice under this regulation shall be in such form as the Board may prescribe or authorise and shall contain such information as they may reasonably require for the purposes of the Finance Act 1986.

5, 6 (*Amend SI 1986/1711, Schedule.*)

1999/2537
Stamp Duty (Collection and Recovery of Penalties) Regulations 1999

Made by the Treasury under FA 1999 Sch 17 paras 16 and 17

Made . . . . *9th September 1999*
Laid before the House of Commons . . . . . . *9th September 1999*
Coming into force . . . . *1st October 1999*

Citation, commencement and effect

1— (1) These Regulations may be cited as the Stamp Duty (Collection and Recovery of Penalties) Regulations 1999 and shall come into force on 1st October 1999.

(2) These Regulations have effect in relation to penalties in respect of things done or omitted on or after 1st October 1999.

Interpretation

2 In these Regulations—

"the enactments relating to stamp duty" means the Stamp Act 1891 and any enactment amending, or which is to be construed as one with, that Act;
"the Management Act" means the Taxes Management Act 1970;
"stamp duty penalty" means a penalty under the enactments relating to stamp duty, other than a penalty under section 15B of the Stamp Act 1891.

The Management Act: provisions to apply

3— (1) The provisions of the Management Act specified in the first column of the Table in Part I of the Schedule to these Regulations shall apply in relation to stamp duty penalties as they apply in relation to taxes within the meaning of that Act subject to any modification specified in the second column of that Table.

(2) Any expression which is used in a provision of the Management Act as applied by this regulation, and to which a meaning is not given by that Act as so applied, shall in that provision have the same meaning as in the enactments relating to stamp duty or these Regulations.

(3) The provisions of the Management Act which are applied subject to modifications by this regulation are restated (as modified where appropriate) in Part II of the Schedule to these Regulations.

SCHEDULE

Regulation 3

PART I—TABLE

Provision applied	*Modifications*
Section 60(1)	For the words "the tax" in the first place where they occur substitute "a stamp duty penalty"; and omit the words "or on the premises in respect of which the tax is charged,".
(2)	For the word "tax" substitute "penalty".
61	—
63	For the side-note to the section substitute "Recovery of stamp duty penalties in Scotland".
(1)	Omit the words "Subject to subsection (3) below,"; for the word "tax" in the first place where it occurs substitute "stamp duty penalty"; and in paragraph (*a*) for the word "tax" substitute "penalty".

Provision applied	*Modifications*
(2)	—
63A	—
65(1)	For the words "income tax, capital gains tax or corporation tax" substitute "a stamp duty penalty".
(2)	For the word "tax" substitute "stamp duty penalties"; and for the words "under one assessment" substitute "in respect of the same act or omission".
(3)	—
(4)	—
(5)	—
66(1)	For the word "Tax" substitute "A stamp duty penalty"; and omit the words "under any assessment".
(2)	—
(3)	—
(4)	—
67(1)	For the word "tax" substitute "a stamp duty penalty"; and omit the words "under any assessment".
(1A)	—
(2)	—
68(1)	For the word "tax" in the first place where it occurs substitute "stamp duty penalty"; and for the word "tax" in the second place where it occurs substitute "penalty".
(2)	—
69	For the side-note to the section substitute "Interest on stamp duty penalties". For the words from "A penalty" to "as if it were interest so charged" substitute "Interest charged under section 103A of this Act on a stamp duty penalty"; and for the words from "as if it were tax" in the first place where they occur to the end substitute "as if it were a stamp duty penalty due and payable in respect of the same act or omission as that to which the stamp duty penalty on which the interest is charged relates".
70(2)	In paragraph (*a*) before the word "penalty" insert "stamp duty"; and omit the words from "under Part II, VA or X" to "under Part IX of this Act"; in paragraph (*b*) omit the words ", surcharge or interest".
103A	For the side-note to the section substitute "Interest on stamp duty penalties". For the words from "penalty" to "Finance Act 1998," substitute "stamp duty penalty"; and after the words "Finance Act 1989" insert "for the purpose of section 15A of the Stamp Act 1891".
107A	For the side-note to the section substitute "Trustees".
(2)	Omit the word "relevant"; for the words from "liable" to "section 86 of this Act" substitute "liable to a stamp duty penalty, or to interest under section 103A of this Act on such a penalty,"; and for the words ", interest, payment or surcharge" substitute "or interest".
(3)	Omit "(*a*) or (*c*)"; for the words "a relevant trustee" substitute "a trustee"; and for the words from "the relevant time" to the end substitute "the time when the act or omission which caused the penalty to become payable occurred".
108(1)	For the words "Taxes Acts" in both places where they occur substitute "relevant enactments relating to stamp duty"; and omit the words from "This subsection" to the end.
(2)	For the words from the beginning to "Corporation Tax Acts on" substitute "A stamp duty penalty for which"; after the word "Charter," insert "is liable,"; for the words "the tax becomes due" substitute "the penalty becomes due"; and for the words "that tax" substitute "that penalty".
(3)	—
112	For the side-note to the section substitute "Loss, destruction or damage to notices of determination, etc".

Provision applied	*Modifications*
(1)	For the words from "assessment to tax" to "or any return" substitute "notice of determination,"; for the words "relating to tax" substitute "relating to a stamp duty penalty"; ...[1]; for the words "in relation to tax" substitute "in relation to the penalty"; for the words "assessment or duplicate of assessment" substitute "notice of determination"; for the words "the return or" substitute "the"; omit the words "made or" in both places where they occur; for the words "charged with tax" substitute "charged with a stamp duty penalty"; and for the words from "any tax for the same chargeable period" to "so charged" substitute "an amount in respect of that same penalty".
(2)	*Omit the words "General or"; and omit the word "concerned".*[1]
113	For the side-note to the section substitute "Form of determinations and other documents".
(1D)	For the words "a penalty under section 100 of this Act" substitute "a stamp duty penalty".
(3)	For the words from "Every assessment" to "of determination" substitute "Every determination, warrant, notice of determination"; omit the word "assessing,"; and for the words "and levying tax or determining a penalty" substitute ", levying or determining a stamp duty penalty".
114	For the side-note to the section substitute "Want of form or errors not to invalidate determinations, etc".
(1)	For the words "An assessment or determination" substitute "A determination"; after the word "proceeding" insert "in relation to a stamp duty penalty"; for the words "the Taxes Acts" in both places where they occur substitute "the relevant enactments relating to stamp duty"; and omit the words "or property".
(2)	For the words "An assessment or determination" substitute "A determination"; in paragraph (*a*)(ii) for the words "the description of any profits or property" substitute "the amount of the penalty"; in paragraph (*a*)(iii) for the words "the amount of the tax charged" substitute "any other matter specified therein"; and in paragraph (*b*) omit the words "assessment or".
115(1)	For the word "form" substitute "other document"; and for the words "the Taxes Acts" substitute "the relevant enactments relating to stamp duty".
(2)	For the words "the Taxes Acts" substitute "the relevant enactments relating to stamp duty"; before the words "by any officer of the Board" insert "or"; omit the words "or by or on behalf of any body of Commissioners"; in paragraph (*b*) omit the words "in the case of a company, at any other prescribed place, and"; omit the words "or any other prescribed place".
(5)	*Omit the words "the General Commissioners Regulations or".*[1]
118(1)	Omit the following definitions— "Act" "branch or agency" "chargeable gain" "chargeable period" *"the General Commissioners Regulations"*[1] "incapacitated person" "infant" "inspector" "the relevant trustees" "return" "successor" "tax" "the Taxes Acts" "the 1992 Act" "trade"; and after the definition of "the principal Act" insert the following definition— " 'the relevant enactments relating to stamp duty' means this Act and— (a) Part II of Schedule 17 to the Finance Act 1999, and (b) the Stamp Duty (Collection and Recovery of Penalties) Regulations 1999,".

Amendments—[1] In table, in entry for s 112(1), words "omit the word "inspectors,"" revoked, entries for ss 112(2), 115(5), and in entry for s 118 words "the General Commissioners Regulations", revoked, by the Transfer of Tribunal Functions and Revenue and Customs Appeals Order, SI 2009/56 art 3, Sch 2 paras 68–70 with effect from 1 April 2009.

PART II
TAXES MANAGEMENT ACT 1970

Note—This Part restates the provisions of TMA 1970, Pt VI as modified by Part I of this Schedule.

PART VI
COLLECTION AND RECOVERY

60 Issue of demand notes and receipts

(1) Every collector shall, when a stamp duty penalty becomes due and payable, make demand of the respective sums given to him in charge to collect, from the persons charged therewith, or at the places of their last abode, as the case may require.

(2) On payment of the penalty, the collector shall if so requested give a receipt.

Distraint and poinding

61 Distraint by collectors

(1) If a person neglects or refuses to pay the sum charged, upon demand made by the collector, the collector may distrain upon the goods and chattels of the person charged (in this section referred to as "the person in default").

(2) For the purpose of levying any such distress, a justice of the peace, on being satisfied by information on oath that there is reasonable ground for believing that a person is neglecting or refusing to pay a sum charged, may issue a warrant in writing authorising a collector to break open, in the daytime, any house or premises, calling to his assistance any constable.

Every such constable shall, when so required, aid and assist the collector in the execution of the warrant and in levying the distress in the house or premises.

(3) A levy or warrant to break open shall be executed by, or under the direction of, and in the presence of, the collector.

(4) A distress levied by the collector shall be kept for five days, at the costs and charges of the person in default.

(5) If the person in default does not pay the sum due, together with the costs and charges, the distress shall be appraised by one or more independent persons appointed by the collector, and shall be sold by public auction by the collector for payment of the sum due and all costs and charges.

Any overplus coming by the distress, after the deduction of the costs and charges and of the sum due, shall be restored to the owner of the goods distrained.

(6) The Treasury may by regulations make provision with respect to—

(*a*) the fees chargeable on or in connection with the levying of distress, and

(*b*) the costs and charges recoverable where distress has been levied;

and any such regulations shall be made by statutory instrument which shall be subject to annulment in pursuance of a resolution of the House of Commons.

63 Recovery of stamp duty penalties in Scotland

(1) In Scotland, where any stamp duty penalty is due and has not been paid, the sheriff, on an application by the collector accompanied by a certificate by the collector—

(*a*) stating that none of the persons specified in the application has paid the penalty due by him;

(*b*) stating that the collector has demanded payment under section 60 of this Act from each such person of the amount due by him;

(*c*) stating that 14 days have elapsed since the date of such demand without payment of the said amount; and

(*d*) specifying the amount due and unpaid by each such person,

shall grant a summary warrant in a form prescribed by Act of Sederunt authorising the recovery, by any of the diligences mentioned in subsection (2) below, of the amount remaining due and unpaid.

(2) The diligences referred to in subsection (1) above are—

[(*a*) an attachment;][1]

(*b*) an earnings arrestment;

(*c*) an arrestment and action of furthcoming or sale.

Amendments—[1] Sub-s (2)(*a*) substituted by the Debt Arrangement and Attachment (Scotland) Act 2002 s 61, Sch 3 para 37(1), (2) with effect from 30 December 2002.

Stamp Taxes

63A Sheriff officer's fees and outlays

(1) Subject to subsection (2) below and without prejudice to [section 39(1) of the Debt Arrangement and Attachment (Scotland) Act 2002 (asp 17) (expenses of attachment)][1], the sheriff officer's fees, together with the outlays necessarily incurred by him, in connection with the execution of a summary warrant shall be chargeable against the debtor.

(2) No fee shall be chargeable by the sheriff officer against the debtor for collecting, and accounting to the collector for, sums paid to him by the debtor in respect of the amount owing.

Amendments—[1] In sub-s (1), words substituted by the Debt Arrangement and Attachment (Scotland) Act 2002 s 61, Sch 3 para 37(1), (3) with effect from 30 December 2002.

Court proceedings

65 Magistrates' courts

(1) Any amount due and payable by way of a stamp duty penalty which does not exceed £2,000 shall, without prejudice to any other remedy, be recoverable summarily as a civil debt by proceedings commenced in the name of the collector.

(2) All or any of the sums due in respect of stamp duty penalties from any one person and payable to any one collector (being sums which are by law recoverable summarily) may, whether or not they are due in respect of the same act or omission, be included in the same complaint, summons, order, warrant or other document required by law to be laid before justices or to be issued by justices, and every such document as aforesaid shall, as respects each such sum, be construed as a separate document and its invalidity as respects any one such sum shall not affect its validity as respects any other such sum.

(3) Proceedings under this section may be brought in England and Wales at any time within one year from the time when the matter complained of arose.

(4) It is hereby declared that in subsection (1) above the expression "recoverable summarily as a civil debt" in respect of proceedings in Northern Ireland means recoverable in proceedings under Article 62 of the Magistrates' Courts (Northern Ireland) Order 1981.

(5) The Treasury may by order made by statutory instrument increase the sum specified in subsection (1) above; and any such statutory instrument shall be subject to annulment in pursuance of a resolution of the Commons House of Parliament.

66 County courts

(1) A stamp duty penalty due and payable may, in England and Wales, and in Northern Ireland where the amount does not exceed the limit specified in Article 10(1) of the County Courts (Northern Ireland) Order 1980, without prejudice to any other remedy, be sued for and recovered from the person charged therewith as a debt due to the Crown by proceedings in a county court commenced in the name of a collector.

(2) An officer of the Board who is authorised by the Board to do so may address the court in proceedings under this section in a county court in England and Wales.

(3) In this section as it applies in Northern Ireland the expression "county court" shall mean a county court held for a division under the County Courts (Northern Ireland) Order 1980.

(4) Sections 21 and 42(2) of the Interpretation Act (Northern Ireland) 1954 shall apply as if any reference in those provisions to any enactment included a reference to this section, and Part III of the County Courts (Northern Ireland) Order 1980 (general civil jurisdiction) shall apply for the purposes of this section in Northern Ireland.

67 Inferior courts in Scotland

(1) In Scotland, a stamp duty penalty due and payable may, without prejudice to any other remedy, be sued for and recovered from the person charged therewith as a debt due to the Crown by proceedings commenced in the name of a collector in the sheriff court.

(1A) An officer of the Board who is authorised by the Board to do so may address the court in any proceedings under this section.

(2) Sections 65 and 66 above shall not apply in Scotland.

68 High Court, etc

(1) Any stamp duty penalty may be sued for and recovered from the person charged therewith in the High Court as a debt due to the Crown, or by any other means whereby any debt of record or otherwise due to the Crown can, or may at any time, be sued for and recovered, as well as by the other means specially provided by this Act for levying the penalty.

(2) All matters within the jurisdiction of the High Court under this section shall be assigned in Scotland to the Court of Session sitting as the Court of Exchequer.

Supplemental

69 Interest on stamp duty penalties

Interest charged under section 103A of this Act on a stamp duty penalty shall be treated for the purposes—

(*a*) of sections 61, 63 and 65 to 68 above, and

(*b*) of section 35(2)(*g*)(i) of the Crown Proceedings Act 1947 (rules of court to impose restrictions on set-off and counterclaim where the proceedings or set-off or counterclaim relate to taxes) and of any rules of court (including county court rules) for England and Wales or Northern Ireland, which impose such a restriction, and

(*c*) of section 35(2)(*b*) of the said Act of 1947 as set out in section 50 of that Act (which imposes corresponding restrictions in Scotland),

as if it were a stamp duty penalty due and payable in respect of the same act or omission as that to which the stamp duty penalty on which the interest is charged relates.

70 Evidence

(2) A certificate of a collector—

(*a*) that a stamp duty penalty is payable, and

(*b*) that payment of the penalty has not been made to him or, to the best of his knowledge and belief, to any other collector or to any person acting on his behalf or on behalf of another collector,

shall be sufficient evidence that the sum mentioned in the certificate is unpaid and is due to the Crown, and any document purporting to be such a certificate as is mentioned in this subsection shall be deemed to be such a certificate unless the contrary is proved.

PART X
PENALTIES, ETC

103A Interest on stamp duty penalties

A stamp duty penalty shall carry interest at the rate applicable under section 178 of the Finance Act 1989 for the purpose of section 15A of the Stamp Act 1891 from the date on which it becomes due and payable until payment.

PART XI
MISCELLANEOUS AND SUPPLEMENTAL

Settlements

107A Trustees

(2) Subject to subsection (3) below, where the trustees of a settlement are liable to a stamp duty penalty, or to interest under section 103A of this Act on such a penalty, the penalty or interest may be recovered (but only once) from any one or more of those trustees.

(3) No amount may be recovered by virtue of subsection (2) above from a person who did not become a trustee until after the time when the act or omission which caused the penalty to become payable occurred.

Companies

108 Responsibility of company officers

(1) Everything to be done by a company under the relevant enactments relating to stamp duty shall be done by the company acting through the proper officer of the company, or, except where a liquidator has been appointed for the company, through such other person as may for the time being have the express, implied or apparent authority of the company to act on its behalf for the purpose, and service on a company of any document under or in pursuance of the relevant enactments relating to stamp duty may be effected by serving it on the proper officer.

(2) A stamp duty penalty for which a company which is not a body corporate, or which is a body corporate not incorporated under [any][1] enactment forming part of the law of the United Kingdom, or by Charter, is liable, may, at any time after the penalty becomes due, and without prejudice to any other method of recovery, be recovered from the proper officer of the company, and that officer may retain out of any money coming into his hands on behalf of the company sufficient sums to pay that penalty, and, so far as he is not so reimbursed, shall be entitled to be indemnified by the company in respect of the liability so imposed on him.

(3) For the purposes of this section—

(*a*) the proper officer of a company which is a body corporate shall be the secretary or person acting as secretary of the company, except that if a liquidator has been appointed for the company the liquidator shall be the proper officer,

(*b*) the proper officer of a company which is not a body corporate or for which there is no proper officer within paragraph (*a*) above, shall be the treasurer or the person acting as treasurer, of the company.

Amendments—[1] In sub-s (2), word substituted for words "the Companies Act 1985 or any other", by the Companies Act 2006 (Consequential Amendments) (Taxes and National Insurance) Order, SI 2009/1890 art 3(3)(*a*) with effect from 1 October 2009.

112 Loss, destruction or damage to notices of determination, etc

(1) Where any notice of determination, or other document relating to a stamp duty penalty, has been lost or destroyed, or been so defaced or damaged as to be illegible or otherwise useless, [HMRC][1] may, notwithstanding anything in any enactment to the contrary, do all such acts and things as they might have done, and all acts and things done under or in pursuance of this section shall be as valid and effectual for all purposes as they would have been, if the notice of determination had not been made, or the other document had not been furnished or required to be furnished:

Provided that, where any person who is charged with a stamp duty penalty in consequence or by virtue of any act or thing done under or in pursuance of this section proves to the satisfaction of [tribunal][1] that he has already paid an amount in respect of that same penalty, relief shall be given to the extent to which the liability of that person has been discharged by the payment so made either by abatement from the charge or by repayment, as the case may require.

(2) *In this section, "the Commissioners" means, as the case may require, either the Board or the Special Commissioners.*[1]

Amendments—[1] In sub-s (1), words substituted for words "the Commissioners, collectors and other officers having powers in relation to the penalty" and "the Commissioners having jurisdiction in the case", and sub-s (2) revoked, by the Transfer of Tribunal Functions and Revenue and Customs Appeals Order, SI 2009/56 art 3, Sch 2 paras 68, 71(1), (2) with effect from 1 April 2009.

113 Form of determinations and other documents

(1D) Where an officer of the Board has decided to impose a stamp duty penalty and has taken all other decisions needed for arriving at the amount of the penalty, he may entrust to any other officer of the Board responsibility for completing the determination procedure, whether by means involving the use of a computer or otherwise, including responsibility for serving notice of the determination on the person liable to the penalty.

(3) Every determination, warrant, notice of determination or of demand, or other document required to be used in charging, collecting, levying or determining a stamp duty penalty shall be in accordance with the forms prescribed from time to time in that behalf by the Board, and a document in the form prescribed and supplied or approved by them shall be valid and effectual.

114 Want of form or errors not to invalidate determinations, etc

(1) A determination, warrant or other proceeding in relation to a stamp duty penalty which purports to be made in pursuance of any provision of the relevant enactments relating to stamp duty shall not be quashed, or deemed to be void or voidable, for want of form, or be affected by reason of a mistake, defect or omission therein, if the same is in substance and effect in conformity with or according to the intent and meaning of the relevant enactments relating to stamp duty, and if the person charged or intended to be charged or affected thereby is designated therein according to common intent and understanding.

(2) A determination shall not be impeached or affected—

(*a*) by reason of a mistake therein as to—

(i) the name or surname of a person liable, or

(ii) the amount of the penalty, or

(iii) any other matter specified therein, or

(*b*) by reason of any variance between the notice and the determination.

115 Delivery and service of documents

(1) A notice or other document which is to be served under the relevant enactments relating to stamp duty on a person may be either delivered to him or left at his usual or last known place of residence.

(2) Any notice or other document to be given, sent, served, or delivered under the relevant enactments relating to stamp duty may be served by post, and, if to be given, sent, served or delivered to or on any person by the Board, or by any officer of the Board, may be so served addressed to that person—

(*a*) at his usual or last known place of residence, or his place of business or employment, or

(*b*) in the case of a liquidator of a company, at his address for the purposes of the liquidation.

(5) *Nothing in this section applies to any notice or other document required or authorised by the Special Commissioners Regulations to be sent or delivered to, or served on, any person.*[1]

Amendments—[1] Sub-s (5) revoked by the Transfer of Tribunal Functions and Revenue and Customs Appeals Order, SI 2009/56 art 3, Sch 2 paras 68, 71(1), (3) with effect from 1 April 2009.

118 Interpretation

(1) In this Act, unless the context otherwise requires—

"the Board" means the Commissioners of Inland Revenue,

"body of persons" means any body politic, corporate or collegiate, and any company, fraternity, fellowship and society of persons, whether corporate or not corporate,

"collector" means any collector of taxes,

"company" has the meaning given by section 832(1) of the principal Act (with section 468 of that Act),

"the principal Act" means the Income and Corporation Taxes Act 1988,

"the relevant enactments relating to stamp duty" means this Act and—

(*a*) Part II of Schedule 17 to the Finance Act 1999, and

(*b*) the Stamp Duty (Collection and Recovery of Penalties) Regulations 1999,

"the Special Commissioners Regulations" means the Special Commissioners (Jurisdiction and Procedure) Regulations 1994.[1]

Amendments—[1] Entry for "the Special Commissioners Regulations" revoked by the Transfer of Tribunal Functions and Revenue and Customs Appeals Order, SI 2009/56 art 3, Sch 2 paras 68, 71(1), (4) with effect from 1 April 2009.

1999/3262
Stamp Duty and Stamp Duty Reserve Tax (Investment Exchanges and Clearing Houses) (OM London Exchange Limited) Regulations 1999

Made by the Treasury under FA 1991 ss 116, 117

Made . . . . *7th December 1999*
Laid before the House of Commons . . . . . . *8th December 1999*
Coming into force . . . . *29th December 1999*

Citation, commencement and effect

1— (1) These Regulations may be cited as the Stamp Duty and Stamp Duty Reserve Tax (Investment Exchanges and Clearing Houses) (OM London Exchange Limited) Regulations 1999 and shall come into force on 29th December 1999.

(2) These Regulations shall have effect—

(*a*) as respects the charge to stamp duty, in relation to instruments executed on or after 29th December 1999;

(*b*) as respects the charge to stamp duty reserve tax—

(i) in the case of an agreement to transfer equity securities which is not conditional, where the agreement is made on or after 29th December 1999;

(ii) in the case of an agreement to transfer equity securities which is conditional, where the condition is satisfied on or after that date.

Interpretation

2 In these Regulations—

"clearing member" means a member who is permitted by the rules of OM London Exchange Limited to clear transactions made on that exchange for an equity security;

"equity securities" means stocks and shares which are issued or raised by a company but does not include stocks and shares issued by a company not incorporated in the United Kingdom unless—

(*a*) they are registered in a register kept in the United Kingdom by or on behalf of the company, or

(*b*) in the case of shares, they are paired, within the meaning of section 99(6A) of the Finance Act 1986, with shares issued by a company incorporated in the United Kingdom;

"member" means a member of OM London Exchange Limited who is recognised as such by the rules of that exchange;

"non-clearing member" means a member other than a clearing member;

"option" means an option to buy or sell securities which is listed by and traded on OM London Exchange Limited;

"futures contract" means a futures, or a forward, contract conferring rights and obligations to buy or sell securities which is listed by and traded on OM London Exchange Limited.

Prescription of recognised investment exchange

3 For the purposes of sections 116 and 117 of the Finance Act 1991 OM London Exchange Limited is a recognised investment exchange which is prescribed.

Transfers and issues of securities to OM London Exchange Limited—prescribed circumstances

4— (1) In the circumstances prescribed by paragraph (2), a charge to stamp duty or to stamp duty reserve tax shall be treated as not arising.

(2) The circumstances prescribed are where, as a result of the exercise of options, or under futures contracts, equity securities of a particular kind are transferred or issued or agreed to be transferred or issued—

(*a*) to OM London Exchange Limited; or

(*b*) to a person whose business is or includes holding such securities as a nominee for OM London Exchange Limited.

Stamp Taxes

(3) References in this regulation and in regulation 5 to OM London Exchange Limited are references to that exchange in its capacity as a person providing clearing services in connection with a transaction made on that exchange.

Transfers of securities to or from members of OM London Exchange Limited—prescribed circumstances

5— (1) In the circumstances prescribed by paragraph (2), a charge to stamp duty or to stamp duty reserve tax shall be treated as not arising.

(2) The circumstances prescribed are where, in order to meet an obligation to receive securities resulting from the exercise of options, or under futures contracts, equity securities of a particular kind are transferred or agreed to be transferred—

(*a*) from a non-clearing member or a nominee of a non-clearing member to a clearing member or the nominee of a clearing member; or

(*b*) from OM London Exchange Limited or a nominee of OM London Exchange Limited to a clearing member or a nominee of a clearing member.

(3) In paragraph (2) references to a clearing member are references to a clearing member in his capacity as such.

1999/3263

Distraint by Collectors (Fees, Costs and Charges) (Stamp Duty Penalties) Regulations 1999

Made by the Treasury under TMA 1970 s 61(6)

Made . . . . *7th December 1999*
Laid before the House of Commons . . . . . . *8th December 1999*
Coming into force . . . . *29th December 1999*

Citation, commencement and effect

1— (1) These Regulations may be cited as the Distraint by Collectors (Fees, Costs and Charges) (Stamp Duty Penalties) Regulations 1999 and shall come into force on 29th December 1999.

(2) These Regulations have effect in relation to the levying of distress under section 61 of the Taxes Management Act 1970 where, upon demand made by a collector, a person has neglected or refused to pay a sum in respect of a stamp duty penalty.

Interpretation

2 In these Regulations—

"close possession" means physical possession by the distrainor or a person acting on his behalf of the goods and chattels distrained;

"the enactments relating to stamp duty" means the Stamp Act 1891 and any enactment amending, or which is to be construed as one with, that Act;

"stamp duty penalty" means a penalty under the enactments relating to stamp duty, other than a penalty under section 15B of the Stamp Act 1891;

"walking possession" means possession in accordance with an agreement between the distrainor and the distrainee whereby, in consideration of the distrainor not remaining in close possession, the distrainor undertakes not to dispose of the goods distrained or any part thereof, or permit their removal by any person not authorised by the distrainor to remove them.

Ascertainment of fees, costs and charges

3 The fees chargeable on or in connection with the levying of distress and the costs recoverable where the distress has been levied shall be those specified in the Schedule to these Regulations, but subject to any provision of that Schedule.

Deduction of fees, costs and charges by the collector

4 The fees, costs and charges specified in the Schedule to these Regulations shall be deducted by the collector from the sums received on or in connection with the levying of distress or where distress has been levied.

Disputes as to fees, costs and charges

5— (1) In the case of dispute as to any fees chargeable, or costs and charges recoverable under the Schedule to these Regulations, the amount of those fees, costs and charges shall be taxed.

(2) Such a taxation shall be carried out by the district judge of the county court for the district in which the distress is or is intended to be levied, and he may give such directions as to the costs of taxation as he thinks fit.

(3) In the application of paragraph (2) to Northern Ireland, there shall be substituted for the words "by the district judge of the county court for the district in which the distress is or is intended to be levied" the words "by the Master (Taxing Office)".

SCHEDULE

Regulation 3

Action taken	*Fees, costs and charges*
On or in connection with the levying of distress	Fees
For making a visit to premises with a view to levying distress (whether the levy is made or not).	A sum not exceeding £12·50.
Levying distress where the total sum charged is £100 or less.	£12·50
Levying distress where the total sum charged is more than £100.	12½ per cent on the first £100 of the amount to be recovered; 4 per cent on the next £400; 2½ per cent on the next £1,500; 1 per cent on the next £8,000; ¼ per cent on any additional sum.
Where distress has been levied	*Costs and Charges*
1 Taking possession	
Where close possession is taken.	£4·50 for the day of levy only.
Where walking possession is taken.	45p per day, payable for the day the distress is levied and up to 14 days thereafter.
2 Removal and storage of goods	The reasonable costs and charges of removal and storage.
3 Appraisement	The reasonable fees, charges and expenses of the person appraising.
4 Sale	
Where the sale is held on the auctioneer's premises, for the auctioneer's commission (to include all out-of-pocket expenses other than charges for advertising, removal and storage).	15 per cent on the sum realised plus the reasonable cost of advertising, removal and storage.
Where the sale is held on the debtor's premises, for the auctioneer's commission (not to include out-of-pocket expenses or charges for advertising).	7½ per cent on the sum realised plus out-of-pocket expenses actually and reasonably incurred and the reasonable costs of advertising.

1 In any case where close possession is taken, an individual left in possession must provide his own board.

2 For the purpose of calculating any percentage fees, costs and charges, a fraction of £1 is to be reckoned as £1, but any fraction of a penny in the total amount so calculated is to be disregarded.

3 In addition to any amount authorised by this Schedule in respect of the supply of goods or services on which value added tax is chargeable there may be added a sum equivalent to value added tax at the appropriate rate on that amount.

2000/2995
Stamp Duty and Stamp Duty Reserve Tax (Investment Exchanges and Clearing Houses) (Jiway Limited) Regulations 2000

Made by the Treasury under FA 1991, ss 116 and 117

Made . . . . *8 November 2000*
Laid before the House of Commons . . . . *9 November 2000*
Coming into force . . . . *10 November 2000*

Citation and commencement

1 These Regulations may be cited as the Stamp Duty and Stamp Duty Reserve Tax (Investment Exchanges and Clearing Houses) (Jiway Limited) Regulations 2000 and shall come into force on 10th November 2000.

Interpretation

2 In these Regulations, "equity securities" means stocks and shares which are issued or raised by a company but does not include stocks and shares issued by a company not incorporated in the United Kingdom unless—

(*a*) they are registered in a register kept in the United Kingdom by or on behalf of the company, or

(*b*) in the case of shares, they are paired, within the meaning of section 99(6A) of the Finance Act 1986, with shares issued by a company incorporated in the United Kingdom.

Prescription of recognised investment exchange

3 For the purposes of sections 116 and 117 of the Finance Act 1991, Jiway Limited is a recognised investment exchange which is prescribed.

Transfers of securities to Jiway Limited—prescribed circumstances

4— (1) In the circumstances prescribed by paragraph (2), a charge to stamp duty or to stamp duty reserve tax shall be treated as not arising.

(2) The circumstances prescribed by this paragraph are where, in connection with a transaction or transactions made or to be made on the exchange operated by Jiway Limited, equity securities are transferred or agreed to be transferred—

(*a*) to Jiway Limited; or

(*b*) to a person whose business is or includes holding equity securities as a nominee of Jiway Limited.

(3) In paragraph (2), references to Jiway Limited are references to that company in its capacity as a person providing clearing services in connection with transactions made on the exchange which it operates.

2001/255
Stamp Duty Reserve Tax (Investment Exchanges and Clearing Houses) (The London Stock Exchange) Regulations 2001

Made by the Treasury under ss 116(3), (4) and 117 of FA 1991

Made	*1 February 2001*
Laid before the House of Commons	*2 February 2001*
Coming into force	*26 February 2001*

Citation and commencement

1 These Regulations may be cited as the Stamp Duty Reserve Tax (Investment Exchanges and Clearing Houses) (The London Stock Exchange) Regulations 2001 and shall come into force on 26th February 2001.

Interpretation

2 In these Regulations unless the context otherwise requires—

"Board of directors" means the Board of directors of London Stock Exchange plc;

"clearing participant" means a member (as defined by this regulation) who is also a member of The London Clearing House Limited and who as such is permitted by the Board of directors and that clearing house to clear transactions made on the Exchange for a traded security;

"client" means a person who gives instructions to a participant for equity securities to be purchased or, as the case may be, sold on the Exchange;

"equity securities" means stocks and shares which are issued or raised by a company but does not include stocks and shares issued or raised by a company not incorporated in the United Kingdom unless—

(*a*) they are registered in a register kept in the United Kingdom by or on behalf of the company, or

(*b*) in the case of shares, they are paired, within the meaning of section 99(6A) of the Finance Act 1986, with shares issued by a company incorporated in the United Kingdom;

"the Exchange" means the London Stock Exchange;

"member" in relation to London Stock Exchange plc means a person approved by the Board of directors as a participant;

"nominee" means a person whose business is or includes holding equity securities as a nominee for The London Clearing House Limited acting in its capacity as a person providing clearing services in connection with a transaction made on the Exchange, or as a nominee for a clearing participant (as the case may be);

"non-clearing participant" means a participant other than a clearing participant;

"participant" means a participant in the Exchange;

"section 117" means section 117 of the Finance Act 1991.

Prescribed persons for the purposes of section 117

3 For the purposes of section 117—

(*a*) The London Clearing House Limited is a recognised clearing house which is prescribed;

(*b*) London Stock Exchange plc is a recognised investment exchange which is prescribed and, in relation to that exchange, a member who is a clearing participant is prescribed as a description of member of that exchange.

Prescribed circumstances for the purposes of section 117

4— (1) In the circumstances prescribed by paragraph (2) below, a charge to stamp duty reserve tax shall be treated as not arising.

(2) The circumstances prescribed are where, in connection with a transaction made on the Exchange—

(*a*) equity securities of a particular kind are agreed to be transferred—

(i) from a clearing participant or a nominee of a clearing participant to another clearing participant or nominee, or

(ii) from a non-clearing participant or a client to a clearing participant or a nominee of a clearing participant, or

(iii) from a clearing participant or a nominee of a clearing participant to The London Clearing House Limited or to a nominee of that clearing house, or

(iv) from a person other than a clearing participant to The London Clearing House Limited or to a nominee of that clearing house, as a result of a failure by a clearing participant to fulfil his obligations in respect of the transaction concerned to transfer equity securities to The London Clearing House Limited or to a nominee of that clearing house, or

(v) from The London Clearing House Limited or a nominee of that clearing house to a clearing participant or a nominee of a clearing participant; and

(*b*) the person to whom those securities are agreed to be transferred under any of the agreements specified in sub-paragraph (*a*) above ("the relevant agreement") is required on receipt of those shares to transfer equity securities under a matching agreement to another person or, in the case of an agreement falling within paragraph (iv) of that sub-paragraph, would have been so required if the failure referred to in that paragraph had not occurred.

(3) In paragraph (2) above—

(*a*) "matching agreement" means an agreement under which—

(i) the equity securities agreed to be transferred are of the same kind as the equity securities agreed to be transferred under the relevant agreement, and

(ii) the number and transfer price of the equity securities agreed to be transferred are identical to the number and transfer price of the equity securities agreed to be transferred under the relevant agreement;

(*b*) references to The London Clearing House Limited are references to that clearing house in its capacity as a person providing clearing services in connection with a transaction made on the Exchange;

(*c*) references to a clearing participant are references to a clearing participant in his capacity as such.

Consequential provision

5— (1) Equity securities which are the subject of an agreement specified in regulation 4(2)(*a*) shall be dealt with by a clearing participant who is a party to the agreement in a separate designated account, and not otherwise.

(2) In paragraph (1) above "designated account" means an account designated by The London Clearing House Limited for a clearing participant in connection with the equity securities concerned.

2001/964

Stamp Duty and Stamp Duty Reserve Tax (Definition of Unit Trust Scheme and Open-ended Investment Company) Regulations 2001

Made by the Treasury under FA 1986 s 98, FA 1995 s 152, and FA 1999 s 121, Sch 19 para 17

Made . . . . *14 March 2001*
Laid before the House of Commons . . . . *14 March 2001*
Coming into force . . . . *6 April 2001*

Citation and commencement

1 These Regulations may be cited as the Stamp Duty and Stamp Duty Reserve Tax (Definition of Unit Trust Scheme and Open-ended Investment Company) Regulations 2001 and shall come into force on 6th April 2001.

Interpretation

[2— (1) In these Regulations—

"feeder fund" means a feeder fund within the meaning of (and complying with the requirements) of paragraph 2 of Part 1 of Schedule 1 to the Personal Pension Schemes (Appropriate Schemes) Regulations 1997 (including a constituent part of an umbrella registered pension unit trust which is regarded as a feeder fund for the purposes of those Regulations);

"open-ended investment company" has the meaning given in section 236 of the Financial Services and Markets Act 2000;

"qualifying EEA investment company" means a company—

(a) which is formed under the law of an EEA State and complies with the requirements specified in [section 833(2) of the Companies Act 2006][2],

(*b*) which may lawfully offer its shares to the public in an EEA State, and

(*c*) in relation to which, on the basis of its last published annual accounts, the ratio between the company's loan capital and the value of its ordinary shares is 50% per cent or less;

"qualifying EEA open-ended investment company" means an open-ended investment company within the meaning given by section 236 of the Financial Services and Markets Act 2000 which—

(*a*) is formed under the law of an EEA state,

(*b*) is not a UCITS, and

(*c*) may lawfully offer its shares to the public in an EEA State;

"recognised scheme" has the meaning given in section 264 of the Financial Services and Markets Act 2000;

"registered pension scheme" has the meaning given in section 150(2) of the Finance Act 2004;

"registered pension unit trust" means a registered pension scheme which is an authorised unit trust scheme of a kind mentioned in Part 1 of Schedule 1 to the Personal Pension Schemes (Appropriate Schemes) Regulations 1997;

"trust instrument" has the meaning given by paragraph 14 of Schedule 19 to the Finance Act 1999;

"UCITS" means an undertaking for collective investment in transferable securities within the meaning of Article 1 of Council Directive 85/611/EEC, as last amended by European Parliament and Council Directive 2001/108/EC;

"umbrella registered pension unit trust" means a registered pension unit trust which is constituted as an umbrella fund within the meaning of the Financial Services (Regulated Scheme) Regulations 1991;

"units" and "unit trust scheme" have the meanings given by section 237 of the Financial Services and Markets Act 2000.

(2) In these Regulations "individual pension account" means an account within which investments may be held and which satisfies the following conditions:

Condition 1

The funds of the account consist only of—

(*a*) monies received from the trustees, managers or administrators of registered pension schemes, or monies held for the purposes of registered pension schemes that are designated to be held within the account, and

(*b*) income and gains arising from those monies when held as funds of the account.

Condition 2

Any monies received in accordance with Condition 1 consist of one or more of the following—

(*a*) contributions to a registered pension scheme by a member, or the employer of a member, of that registered pension scheme,

(*b*) amounts transferred to a registered pension scheme from another registered pension scheme,

(*c*) minimum contributions referred to in section 188(3)(*c*) of the Finance Act 2004,

(*d*) minimum payments within the meaning given by section 8(2) of the Pension Schemes Act 1993.

Condition 3

The funds and other assets of the account—

(*a*) are held—

(i) by the trustees, managers or administrators of the registered pension schemes whose members subscribe to the account as account holders, and

(ii) on behalf of the individual account holders as beneficial owners subject to the account rules, or

(*b*) in the case of assets consisting of units in a registered pension unit trust or, where the registered pension unit trust is an umbrella registered pension unit trust, in the respective parts of the umbrella registered pension unit trust—

(i) are registered in the names of the individual account holders, and

(ii) are issued subject to the terms of the trust deed and the rules constituting the registered pension unit trust.

Condition 4

The funds and other assets of the account are used only to provide benefits in respect of individual account holders under registered pension schemes and subject to the limits and rules of those registered pension schemes.

Condition 5

The assets of the account, other than cash awaiting investment, consist of one or more of the following investments—

(*a*) units in an authorised unit trust scheme or in a unit trust scheme that is a recognised scheme,
(*b*) shares in a qualifying EEA open-ended investment company,
(*c*) units in a UCITS formed under the laws of a member state other than the United Kingdom which has been authorised by the competent authorities of that member state and is a recognised scheme,
(*d*) shares in a body corporate which is a qualifying UK investment company,
(*e*) shares in a body corporate which is a qualifying EEA investment company,
(*f*) shares in an investment company with variable capital, and
(*g*) investments falling within paragraph 13 of Part 2 of Schedule 2 to the Financial Services and Markets Act 2000 (government and public securities).

The reference in head (*a*) to units in an authorised unit trust scheme, where the authorised unit trust scheme is an umbrella registered pension unit trust that is constituted as a feeder fund or comprises feeder funds, comprises both the units in the feeder fund or feeder funds that are issued to the individual account holder and the underlying units held by the feeder fund or feeder funds.

Condition 6

If monies are received by the account that comprise an individual's investment in more than one registered pension scheme the amount relating to each registered pension scheme is separately identified by the administrator of the account.

Condition 7

Whenever required to do so by an officer of Revenue and Customs, the administrator of the account has provided to that officer the following information—

(*a*) the names of individuals who are the account holders,
(*b*) details of the registered pension schemes of which those individuals are members,
(*c*) the amount of the funds, and the description and value of the assets, held on behalf of each account holder,
(*d*) the amount of income and gains accruing to each account holder from funds and assets held on that individual's behalf,
(*e*) transfers of funds to another individual pension account on behalf of an account holder.

Condition 8

Whenever required to do so by an officer of Revenue and Customs, the administrator of the account has enabled that officer to audit and inspect all aspects of the management and administration of the account, including records and systems relating to the management or administration of the account.][1]

Amendments—[1] Regulation 2 substituted by the Stamp Duty and Stamp Duty Reserve Tax (Definition of Unit Trust Scheme and Open-ended Investment Company) (Amendment) Regulations, SI 2006/746 with effect from 6 April 2006.
[2] In para (1), words in definition of "qualifying EEA investment company" substituted by the Companies Act 2006 (Consequential Amendments) (Taxes and National Insurance) Order, SI 2008/954 art 49 with effect from 6 April 2008.

Schemes to be treated as not being unit trust schemes

3— (1) A scheme of the description specified in paragraph (2) shall be treated as not being a unit trust scheme for the purposes of the enactments relating to stamp duty and the enactments relating to stamp duty reserve tax.

(2) The description of scheme specified in this paragraph is a unit trust scheme the units under which are required by the terms of the trust instrument to be held only within individual pension accounts.

Companies to be treated as not being open-ended investment companies

4— (1) A company of the description specified in paragraph (2) shall be treated as not being an open-ended investment company for the purposes of the enactments relating to stamp duty and the enactments relating to stamp duty reserve tax.

(2) The description of company specified in this paragraph is an open-ended investment company the shares in which are required by the terms of the instrument incorporating the company to be held only within individual pension accounts.

Amendments to the Stamp Duty Reserve Tax Regulations 1986

5 (*amends* the Stamp Duty Reserve Tax Regulations, SI 1986/1711).

Amendment to the Stamp Duty and Stamp Duty Reserve Tax (Open-ended Investment Companies) Regulations 1997

6 (*amends* the Stamp Duty and Stamp Duty Reserve Tax (Open-ended Investment Companies) Regulations, SI 1997/1156).

2001/3746
Variation of Stamp Duties Regulations 2001

Made by the Treasury under FA 2000 Sch 33 para 1

Amendments—These regulations revoked by the Stamp Duty (Disadvantaged Areas) (Application of Exemptions) Regulations, SI 2003/1056 reg 8 with effect for instruments executed after 9 April 2003.

Made . . . . 27 November 2001
Laid before the House of Commons . . . . . . 27 November 2001
Coming into force . . . . 28 November 2001

Citation and commencement

1 *These Regulations may be cited as the Variation of Stamp Duties Regulations 2001 and shall come into force on 28th November 2001.*

Interpretation

2 *In these Regulations—*

"lease of land" has the same meaning as in Part 2 of Schedule 13 to the Finance Act 1999;

"qualifying premium", in relation to a lease of land, means the consideration in respect of which, under paragraph 12(2) of Schedule 13 to the Finance Act 1999, the duty is the same as that on a conveyance on sale for the same consideration;

"section 92(1)" means section 92(1) of the Finance Act 2001 (exemption from stamp duty in a disadvantaged area);

"Schedule 30" means Schedule 30 to the Finance Act 2001 (stamp duty—exemption for land in disadvantaged areas).

Instruments to which regulation 4 applies

3— *(1) Regulation 4 applies to an instrument if it is—*

(a) a conveyance or transfer on sale of an estate or interest in land, or

(b) a lease of land,

and the condition in paragraph (2) is satisfied in the case of the instrument.

(2) The condition in this paragraph is satisfied in the case of an instrument if, apart from section 92(1) and paragraphs 1 and 3 of Schedule 30—

(a) the amount or value of the relevant consideration exceeds £150,000; or

(b) the instrument could not be certified under paragraph 4 of Schedule 13 to the Finance Act 1999 at £150,000 or under if that threshold were specified in the Table in that paragraph.

(3) In paragraph (2)(a) "the relevant consideration" means—

(a) in the case of a conveyance or transfer on sale, the consideration for the sale; and

(b) in the case of a lease of land, any qualifying premium.

(4) In this regulation "conveyance on sale" has the same meaning as in Part 1 of Schedule 13 to the Finance Act 1999 (see paragraph 1(2) of that Schedule).

Variation of stamp duty on such instruments

4— *(1) Neither—*

(a) section 92(1), nor

(b) paragraph 1 of Schedule 30 (duty where land partly in disadvantaged area),

shall apply to an instrument to which this regulation applies.

(2) Paragraph 3 of Schedule 30 (exclusion of land in such an area for the purposes of certification at a value) shall not apply where the transaction mentioned in sub-paragraph (1) of that paragraph is one effected by an instrument to which this regulation applies.

Restriction of amount of relief in the case of leases of land

5 *Where section 92(1) or paragraph 1 of Schedule 30 applies in relation to a lease of land, it shall have effect only in relation to duty in respect of the amount or value of any qualifying premium (and, accordingly, does not affect the amount of duty chargeable under paragraph 12(3) of Schedule 13 to the Finance Act 1999 in respect of rent).*

No relief from fixed duties

6 *Neither section 92(1) nor paragraph 1 of Schedule 30 shall have effect in relation to stamp duty chargeable under—*

(a) paragraph 1 of the Table in paragraph 11 of Part 2 of Schedule 13 to the Finance Act 1999 (lease of furnished dwelling etc for less than a year at a rent exceeding £5,000);

(b) paragraph 13 of that Part of that Schedule (leases not within paragraph 11 or 12); or

(c) paragraph 16 of Part 3 of that Schedule (conveyance or transfer of property otherwise than on sale).

Contracts for sale and agreements for leases

7— *(1) The following provisions of Schedule 13 to the Finance Act 1999, namely—*

(a) paragraphs 7 to 9 of Part 1 (contracts or agreements chargeable as conveyances on sale), and

(b) paragraphs 14 and 15 of Part 2 (agreement for a lease and lease for a fixed term and then until determined),

have effect in accordance with the preceding provisions of these Regulations.

(2) Any other provision for stamp duty to be determined by reference to provisions of Part 1 or Part 2, or paragraph 16 of Part 3, of Schedule 13 to the Finance Act 1999 also has effect in accordance with the preceding provisions of these Regulations.

2001/3747
Stamp Duty (Disadvantaged Areas) Regulations 2001

Made by the Treasury under FA 2001 s 92(4) and (9)

Made . . . . *29 November 2001*
Laid before the House of Commons . . . . . . *29 November 2001*
Coming into force . . . . *30 November 2001*

Stamp Taxes

Citation and commencement

1 These Regulations may be cited as the Stamp Duty (Disadvantaged Areas) Regulations 2001 and shall come into force on 30th November 2001.

Designation of disadvantaged areas

2 The following are designated as disadvantaged areas for the purposes of section 92 of, and Schedule 30 to, the Finance Act 2001—

(*a*) the areas in England specified in Schedule 1 to these Regulations;
(*b*) the areas in Wales specified in Schedule 2 to these Regulations;
(*c*) the areas in Scotland specified in Schedule 3 to these Regulations;
(*d*) the areas in Northern Ireland specified in Schedule 4 to these Regulations.

TABLE A—ENGLAND—EAST MIDLANDS
TABLE B—EASTERN ENGLAND
TABLE C—ENGLAND—LONDON
TABLE D—NORTH EASTERN ENGLAND
TABLE E—NORTH WESTERN ENGLAND
TABLE F—SOUTH EASTERN ENGLAND
TABLE G—SOUTH WESTERN ENGLAND
TABLE H—ENGLAND—WEST MIDLANDS
TABLE I—ENGLAND—YORKSHIRE AND HUMBERSIDE
TABLE J—WALES
TABLE K—SCOTLAND
TABLE L—NORTHERN IRELAND

SCHEDULE 1

Regulation 2

AREAS IN ENGLAND DESIGNATED AS DISADVANTAGED AREAS

The areas in England specified in this Schedule are—

(*a*) the wards and electoral divisions, as at 7th May 1998, which are—

(i) listed as wards in the Index of Multiple Deprivation 2000 published by the Department of the Environment, Transport and the Regions, and

(ii) listed in Tables A to I below; and

(*b*) any land which—

(i) as at 7th May 1998, did not fall within any of the wards and electoral divisions mentioned in paragraph (*a*), but

(ii) as at 27th November 2001, had a postcode which was identical to the full postcode of land which, as at 7th May 1998, did fall within one of those wards and electoral divisions.

TABLE A—ENGLAND—EAST MIDLANDS

Local authority	*Ward*
Amber Valley	Aldercar
	Alfreton West

Local authority	*Ward*
Ashfield	Kirkby in Ashfield East
	Sutton in Ashfield East
	Sutton in Ashfield Central
	Kirkby in Ashfield West
	Kirkby in Ashfield Central
	Sutton in Ashfield West
Bassetlaw	Worksop South East
	Rampton
	Hodsock
	Harworth East
	Harworth West
	East Retford North
Bolsover	Shirebrook North-West
	Scarcliffe North
	Shirebrook South
	Shirebrook North
	Shirebrook East
	Elmton-with-Creswell
	Bolsover Central
	Scarcliffe East
	Shirebrook South-West
	Pleasley
	Bolsover North
	Bolsover West
	Ault Hucknall
	Whitwell
Boston	Fenside
	Holland Fen
Broxtowe	Eastwood South
Chesterfield	Markham
	Rother
	Middlecroft
	St. Helen's
	Barrow Hill and Hollingwood
	Lowgates and Woodthorpe
	Dunston
	Old Whittington
Corby	Kingswood
	Hazelwood
Derby	Litchurch
	Osmaston
	Babington
	Derwent
	Normanton
	Sinfin
East Lindsey	Ingoldmells
	Mablethorpe
	Sutton and Trusthorpe
	Winthorpe
	Scarbrough
	Trinity
	St. Clements
	New Leake
	Chapel St. Leonards
	Theddlethorpe St. Helen
Erewash	Ilkeston North
Gedling	Oxclose
High Peak	Gamesley
Leicester	North Braunstone
	Wycliffe

Local authority	*Ward*
	Spinney Hill
	Saffron
	New Parks
	West Humberstone
	Mowmacre
	Belgrave
	Eyres Monsell
	Coleman
	Beaumont Leys
	Latimer
	Charnwood
	Thurncourt
Lincoln	Tritton
	Minster
	Abbey
	Castle
	Longdales
Mansfield	Northfield
	Pleasleyhill
	Meden
	Cumberlands
	Titchfield
	Ladybrook
	Birklands
	Sherwood
	Ravensdale
	Broomhill
	Oak Tree
Newark and Sherwood	Devon
	Clipstone
	Ollerton North
	Bilsthorpe
	Boughton
	Blidworth
North East Derbyshire	Holmewood and Heath
	Hasland
	Clay Cross South
North West Leicestershire	Greenhill
Northampton	Dallington and Kings Heath
	St. Crispin
	Castle
Nottingham	Strelley
	Manvers
	Radford
	Trent
	Aspley
	St. Ann's
	Bulwell West
	Bridge
	Bestwood Park
	Lenton
	Forest
	Beechdale
	Bulwell East
	Byron
	Bilborough
	Robin Hood
	Clifton East
	Basford
	Portland

Stamp Taxes

Local authority	Ward
	Greenwood
South Kesteven	Earlesfield
Wellingborough	Queensway
	Croyland
West Lindsey	Gainsborough East
	Gainsborough South-West

TABLE B—EASTERN ENGLAND

Local Authority	Ward
Basildon	Vange
	Fryerns East
	Pitsea West
	Fryerns Central
Bedford	Kingsbrook
	Cauldwell
	Queens Park
Breckland	Thetford-Abbey
Colchester	St. Andrew's
Fenland	Wisbech North
Great Yarmouth	Regent
	Nelson
	Northgate
	Lichfield and Cobholm
	Magdalen West
	Magdalen East
	Claydon
	Yarmouth North
Harlow	Hare Street and Town Centre
Ipswich	Gainsborough
	Town
	Chantry
King's Lynn and West Norfolk	Lynn North
	St. Margarets
	Gaywood South
	Lynn South West
	Lynn Central
Luton	Dallow
	Biscot
Norwich	Mile Cross
	Mancroft
	Catton Grove
	Bowthorpe
	Lakenham
Peterborough	Central
	Dogsthorpe
	Ravensthorpe
	East
	North
St. Edmundsbury	Clements
Tendring	Golf Green
	St. James
	Rush Green
	St. Marys
	Harwich East
Thurrock	Tilbury Riverside
	Tilbury St. Chads
	Belhus
	Chadwell St. Mary
	West Thurrock

Local Authority	*Ward*
Waveney	Harbour
	Kirkley
	Normanston
	St. Margarets
	Whitton

TABLE C—ENGLAND—LONDON

Local authority	*Ward*
Barking and Dagenham	Gascoigne
	Fanshawe
	Abbey
	Manor
	Alibon
	Marks Gate
	Village
	Thames
	Heath
	Becontree
	Parsloes
	Triptons
	Goresbrook
	Cambell
Bexley	Thamesmead East
Brent	Carlton
	Stonebridge
	St. Raphael's
	Roundwood
	Harlesden
	Church End
	St. Andrew's
	Willesden Green
Bromley	Anerley
	Penge
Camden	St. Pancras
	Somers Town
	Castlehaven
	Grafton
	Caversham
	Gospel Oak
	Priory
	King's Cross
	Holborn
	Regent's Park
	Camden
	Kilburn
Croydon	Fieldway
	New Addington
Ealing	Dormers Wells
	Northcote
	Glebe
	Heathfield
Enfield	Angel Road
	Craig Park
	Latymer
	St. Peters
	Weir Hall
	Ponders End
	St. Alphege
Greenwich	St. Mary's

Local authority	*Ward*
	Arsenal
	Glyndon
	Nightingale
	Middle Park
	Sherard
	Eynsham
	Ferrier
	Hornfair
	West
	Woolwich Common
	Herbert
	Burrage
	Rectory Field
	Lakedale
	Kidbrooke
	Charlton
	Thamesmead Moorings
	Plumstead Common
Hackney	Queensbridge
	Wenlock
	Chatham
	Haggerston
	Westdown
	Eastdown
	Northfield
	New River
	Leabridge
	Dalston
	Springfield
	Kings Park
	Rectory
	Moorfields
	Homerton
	Northwold
	De Beauvoir
	Brownswood
	Victoria
	Clissold
	Wick
	South Defoe
	North Defoe
Hammersmith and Fulham	White City and Shepherds Bush
	College Park and Old Oak
	Broadway
	Wormholt
	Coningham
Haringey	Coleraine
	White Hart Lane
	Park
	Tottenham Central
	Bruce Grove
	High Cross
	South Tottenham
	Seven Sisters
	Noel Park
	West Green
	Green Lanes
	Woodside
	Harringay
	South Hornsey

Local authority	*Ward*
Havering	Hilldene
Hounslow	Hanworth
Islington	Hillmarton
	Sussex
	Tollington
	Junction
	Highview
	Thornhill
	Bunhill
	Holloway
	Canonbury West
	Canonbury East
	Highbury
	Mildmay
	Quadrant
	Barnsbury
	Clerkenwell
	St. Peter
	Hillrise
	St. George's
Kensington and Chelsea	Golborne
	St. Charles
	Avondale
Lambeth	Angell
	Vassall
	Gipsy Hill
	Larkhall
	Bishop's
	Stockwell
	Ferndale
	St. Martin's
	Tulse Hill
	Prince's
	Oval
	Knight's Hill
	Town Hall
Lewisham	Evelyn
	Grinling Gibbons
	Bellingham
	Downham
	Churchdown
	Whitefoot
	Marlowe
	Grove Park
	Rushey Green
	Sydenham West
	Drake
	Hither Green
Newham	Ordnance
	Beckton
	Canning Town and Grange
	St. Stephens
	Stratford
	Park
	Little Ilford
	Plaistow
	Manor Park
	Plashet
	West Ham
	Hudsons

Local authority	*Ward*
	Upton
	Custom House and Silvertown
	Kensington
	Castle
	Monega
	New Town
	Wall End
	Forest Gate
	South
	Central
	Bemersyde
	Greatfield
Redbridge	Loxford
Southwark	Friary
	Consort
	Liddle
	Brunswick
	Rotherhithe
	Chaucer
	Barset
	The Lane
	Burgess
	St. Giles
	Cathedral
	Browning
	Faraday
	Abbey
	Newington
	Waverley
	Bellenden
	Bricklayers
Tower Hamlets	Spitalfields
	Lansbury
	Weavers
	Blackwall
	Limehouse
	Redcoat
	East India
	St. Dunstan's
	St. James'
	Park
	Holy Trinity
	Bromley
	Shadwell
	St. Peter's
	Bow
	St. Mary's
	St. Katherine's
	Millwall
Waltham Forest	Leyton
	Higham Hill
	Cathall
	Cann Hall
	Lea Bridge
	Hoe Street
	St. James Street
Wandsworth	Latchmere
	Roehampton
Westminster	Queen's Park
	Church Street

Local authority	*Ward*
	Westbourne
	Harrow Road

TABLE D—NORTH EASTERN ENGLAND

Local Authority	*Ward*
Alnwick	Alnwick Clayport
Berwick-upon-Tweed	Tower
Blyth Valley	Cowpen
	Croft
	Hartford and West Cramlington
	Kitty Brewster
	Plessey
	Cramlington East
	Isabella
Castle Morpeth	Lynemouth
	Chevington
Chester-le-Street	Chester West
	Grange Villa
	Edmondsley
	Pelton Fell
Darlington	Central
	Eastbourne South
	Cockerton West
	Eastbourne North
	Park East
	Lascelles
	Northgate South
	Bank Top
	Northgate North
Derwentside	South Stanley
	Craghead
	Consett South
	South Moor
	Catchgate
	Delves Lane
	Burnhope
	Stanley Hall
	Leadgate
	Dipton Annfield Plain
Durham	Pelaw
	New Brancepeth
	Shadforth
	Bearpark
Easington	Eden Hill
	Deneside
	Dawdon
	Shotton
	Easington Colliery
	Acre Rigg
	Haswell
	Wheatley Hill
	Horden North
	Horden South
	Wingate
	Dene House
	High Colliery
	Thornley
	Blackhalls
	Howletch

Stamp Taxes

Local Authority	*Ward*
	South
	Hutton Henry
	Murton West
	South Hetton
	Deaf Hill
	Passfield
Gateshead	Bede
	Felling
	Bensham
	High Fell
	Teams
	Deckham
	Saltwell
	Leam
	Lamesley
	Blaydon
Hartlepool	Owton
	Dyke House
	Stranton
	St. Hilda
	Brus
	Jackson
	Rossmere
	Brinkburn
	Park
	Fens
Middlesbrough	Thorntree
	Pallister
	St. Hilda's
	Park End
	Beckfield
	Beechwood
	Berwick Hills
	North Ormesby
	Westbourne
	Grove Hill
	Easterside
	Southfield
	Ayresome
	Gresham
	Stainton and Thornton
	Hemlington
Newcastle upon Tyne	Walker
	Monkchester
	Elswick
	West City
	Byker
	Scotswood
	Benwell
	Woolsington
	Moorside
	Fawdon
	Blakelaw
	Kenton
	Wingrove
	Fenham
	Newburn
	Walkergate
	Denton
North Tyneside	Chirton

Local Authority	*Ward*
	Riverside
	Collingwood
	Longbenton
	Howdon
	Wallsend
	Valley
Redcar and Cleveland	Grangetown
	South Bank
	Kirkleatham
	Coatham
	Newcomen
	Dormanstown
	Eston
	Lockwood and Skinningrove
	Loftus
Sedgefield	West
	Thickley
	Cornforth
	Old Trimdon
	Sunnydale
	New Trimdon and Trimdon Grange
	Chilton
	Broom
	Fishburn
	Tudhoe
	Ferryhill
South Tyneside	Rekendyke
	Bede
	Cleadon Park
	Tyne Dock and Simonside
	Biddick Hall
	Primrose
	Beacon and Bents
	All Saints
	Hebburn South
	Harton
	Whiteleas
	Monkton
	Fellgate and Hedworth
	Horsley Hill
	Hebburn Quay
	Whitburn and Marsden
Stockton-on-Tees	Portrack and Tilery
	Hardwick
	Parkfield
	Newtown
	Roseworth
	Mile House
	Blue Hall
	Victoria
	Charltons
	Mandale
	Grange
	Stainsby
	St. Aidan's
Sunderland	Southwick
	Town End Farm
	Thorney Close
	South Hylton
	Grindon

Local Authority	*Ward*
	Castletown
	Colliery
	Hendon
	Washington North
	Central
	Hetton
	Houghton
	Eppleton
	Thornholme
	Ryhope
	Pallion
Teesdale	Evenwood with Ramshaw
	Cockfield
Tynedale	Prudhoe North
Wansbeck	Hirst
	Newbiggin East
	Choppington
	Central
	Park
	College
	Sleekburn
	Newbiggin West
Wear Valley	Woodhouse Close
	St. Helen's
	Coundon
	Henknowle
	Stanley
	Willington East
	Wheatbottom and Helmington Row
	Coundon Grange
	Tow Law
	Willington West
	West Auckland

TABLE E—NORTH WESTERN ENGLAND

Local Authority	*Ward*
Allerdale	Salterbeck
	Ewanrigg
	Westfield
	Northside
	Moorclose
	Ellenborough
	Clifton
	Netherhall
Barrow-in-Furness	Central
	Risedale
	Hindpool
	Barrow Island
	Ormsgill
	Walney North
Blackburn with Darwen	Audley
	Shadsworth
	Higher Croft
	Wensley Fold
	Shear Brow
	Queen's Park
	Bastwell
	Little Harwood with Whitebirk
	Mill Hill

Local Authority	*Ward*
	Sudell
	Meadowhead
	Corporation Park
Blackpool	Park
	Alexandra
	Claremont
	Talbot
	Foxhall
	Clifton
	Brunswick
	Victoria
	Tyldesley
	Warbreck
	Waterloo
Bolton	Central
	Derby
	Farnworth
	Tonge
	Halliwell
	Burnden
	Harper Green
	Breightmet
Burnley	Daneshouse
	Bank Hall
	Barclay
	Trinity
	Fulledge
	Brunshaw
	Coal Clough with Deerplay
Bury	Redvales
	East
	Besses
Carlisle	Upperby
	Botcherby
	Morton
Chester	Blacon Hall
	Dee Point
Chorley	Chorley East
Copeland	Mirehouse West
	Sandwith
	Cleator Moor South
	Mirehouse East
	Distington
	Frizington
	Harbour
	Cleator Moor North
	Hensingham
Crewe & Nantwich	Maw Green
Ellesmere Port and Neston	Westminster
	Stanlow
	Grange
	Central
	Wolverham
	Rivacre
Halton	Castlefields
	Riverside
	Kingsway
	Murdishaw
	Palace Field
	Grange

Stamp Taxes

Local Authority	*Ward*
	Brookvale
	Halton Brook
	Norton
	Mersey
	Broadheath
	Hough Green
	Ditton
Hyndburn	Central
	Church
	Spring Hill
	Barnfield
Knowsley	Princess
	Longview
	Cherryfield
	Kirkby Central
	Northwood
	Cantril Farm
	Tower Hill
	Knowsley Park
	St. Michaels
	St. Gabriels
	Halewood South
	Whitefield
	Page Moss
	Park
	Halewood West
	Prescot East
	Whiston South
	Whiston North
Lancaster	Alexandra
	Poulton
	Skerton Central
	Skerton East
Liverpool	Speke
	Everton
	Vauxhall
	Granby
	Pirrie
	Breckfield
	Melrose
	Clubmoor
	Smithdown
	Dovecot
	Netherley
	Kensington
	St. Mary's
	Valley
	Abercromby
	County
	Dingle
	Tuebrook
	Fazakerley
	Anfield
	Broadgreen
	Picton
	Old Swan
	Gillmoss
	Warbreck
	Arundel
	Croxteth

Local Authority	*Ward*
	Allerton
Manchester	Benchill
	Harpurhey
	Beswick and Clayton
	Bradford
	Ardwick
	Central
	Newton Heath
	Gorton South
	Woodhouse Park
	Moss Side
	Longsight
	Hulme
	Cheetham
	Lightbowne
	Baguley
	Blackley
	Sharston
	Gorton North
	Charlestown
	Brooklands
	Burnage
	Moston
	Crumpsall
	Northenden
	Rusholme
	Fallowfield
	Whalley Range
	Levenshulme
	Barlow Moor
	Old Moat
Oldham	Coldhurst
	Werneth
	Alexandra
	St. Marys
	Hollinwood
	St. James
	Lees
	St. Pauls
	Chadderton South
Pendle	Whitefield
	Bradley
	Waterside
	Walverden
	Southfield
	Brierfield
	Marsden
	Vivary Bridge
Preston	Fishwick
	Ribbleton
	Deepdale
	St. Matthew's
	Brookfield
	Avenham
	Central
Rochdale	Central and Falinge
	Middleton West
	Smallbridge and Wardleworth
	Newbold
	Middleton Central

Local Authority	*Ward*
	Brimrod and Deeplish
	Balderstone
	Heywood West
Rossendale	Worsley
	Greensclough
	Stacksteads
	Longholme
Salford	Broughton
	Little Hulton
	Blackfriars
	Ordsall
	Pendleton
	Langworthy
	Winton
	Weaste and Seedley
	Barton
	Walkden North
	Pendlebury
Sefton	Linacre
	Orrell
	Derby
	Netherton
	Ford
	Litherland
	St. Oswald
	Church
South Ribble	Seven Stars
St. Helens	Parr and Hardshaw
	Broad Oak
	West Sutton
	Marshalls Cross
	Queen's Park
	Thatto Heath
	Grange Park
	Newton West
	Sutton and Bold
	Haydock
Stockport	Brinnington
Tameside	Ashton St. Peters'
	Hyde
	Godley
	Longdendale Denton South
	Ashton St. Michael's
	Hyde Newton
Trafford	Clifford
	Bucklow
	Talbot
Vale Royal	Over Two
	Wharton
	Vale Royal
Warrington	Westy
	Bewsey and Whitecross
	Orford
	Hulme
	Poplars
West Lancashire	Tanhouse
	Digmoor
	Moorside
	Birch Green
	Skelmersdale North

Local Authority	*Ward*
Wigan	Norley
	Ince
	Newtown
	Abram
	Leigh Central
	Atherton
	Whelley
	Hindley
Wirral	Bidston
	Birkenhead
	Tranmere
	Seacombe
	Leasowe
	Egerton
	Liscard
	New Brighton
	Claughton
	Bromborough
Wyre	Pharos
	Park
	Mount

TABLE F—SOUTH EASTERN ENGLAND

Local authority	*Ward/Electoral division*
Arun	Littlehampton River
	Littlehampton Ham
Ashford	Stanhope
	Ashford Brookfield
	Ashford Hampden
Brighton and Hove	Marine
	Moulsecoomb
	Queen's Park
Dartford	Joyce Green
Dover	Buckland
	St. Radigunds
	Town and Pier
	Castle
	Tower Hamlets
Gravesham	Riverside
Hastings	Central St. Leonards
	Castle
	Gensing
	Hollington
	Broomgrove
	Mount Pleasant
	Maze Hill
	Ore
	Braybrooke
	Wishing Tree
Havant	Warren Park
	Barncroft
	Bondfields
	Battins
Isle of Wight	St. Johns -1
	Pan
	Ryde North East
	Ventnor-1
Maidstone	Shepway West
	Park Wood

Stamp Taxes

Local authority	*Ward/Electoral division*
Medway	Twydall
Milton Keynes	Woughton
	Eaton Manor
Oxford	Blackbird Leys
Portsmouth	Charles Dickens
	Paulsgrove
Reading	Whitley
Shepway	Folkestone Central
	St. Mary in the Marsh
	Folkestone East
	Folkestone Harbour
Southampton	Redbridge
	Bargate
Swale	Sheerness West
	Eastern
	Sheerness East
Thanet	Pier
	Ethelbert
	Newington
	Northdown Park
	Cecil
	Marine
	Central Eastcliff
	Northwood
	Central Westcliff

TABLE G—SOUTH WESTERN ENGLAND

Local authority	*Ward*
Bath and North East Somerset	Twerton
Bournemouth	Boscombe West
	Wallisdown
Bristol, City of	Lawrence Hill
	Filwood
	Southmead
	Knowle
	Ashley
	Whitchurch Park
	Bishopsworth
	Hartcliffe
	Easton
	Lockleaze
	Kingsweston
Carrick	Penwerris
Exeter	Wonford
Gloucester	Barton
	Westgate
	Matson
Kerrier	Illogan South
	Camborne North
	Camborne West
	Redruth North
	Camborne South
North Devon	Trinity
	Ilfracombe Central
	St. Mary's
	Ilfracombe East
North Somerset	Weston-Super-Mare South
	Weston-Super-Mare Ellenborough
Penwith	Penzance East

Local authority	*Ward*
	Penzance West
	Hayle-Gwithian
	Marazion
	St. Ives North
	St. Just
	Hayle-Gwinear
Plymouth	St. Peter
	Ham
	Budshead
	Honicknowle
	Sutton
	St. Budeaux
	Keyham
Swindon	Whitworth
	Park
Taunton Deane	Taunton Halcon
	Taunton Lyngford
Torbay	Tormohun
	Torwood
	Blatchcombe
	Coverdale
Torridge	Westward Hol
West Somerset	Williton
Weymouth and Portland	Melcombe Regis

TABLE H—ENGLAND—WEST MIDLANDS

Local authority	*Ward*
Birmingham	Aston
	Sparkbrook
	Small Heath
	Nechells
	Soho
	Washwood Heath
	Handsworth
	Sparkhill
	Ladywood
	Shard End
	Kingstanding
	Bartley Green
	Fox Hollies
	Longbridge
	Kingsbury
	King's Norton
	Stockland Green
	Weoley
	Yardley
	Sandwell
	Hodge Hill
	Acock's Green
	Billesley
Cannock Chase	Broomhill
County of Herefordshire	Belmont
Coventry	Foleshill
	St. Michael's
	Longford
	Henley
	Binley and Willenhall
	Radford
	Holbrook

Local authority	*Ward*
	Upper Stoke
Dudley	Castle and Priory
	St. Thomas's
	Netherton and Woodside
	Brockmoor & Pensett
	Brierley Hill
	Lye and Wollescote
East Staffordshire	Victoria
	Waterside
	Uxbridge
	Burton
	Broadway
	Eton
Newcastle-under-Lyme	Holditch
	Cross Heath
	Silverdale
Nuneaton & Bedworth	Camp Hill
Redditch	Batchley
Sandwell	Soho and Victoria
	St. Pauls
	Greets Green and Lyng
	Friar Park
	Smethwick
	West Bromwich Central
	Hateley Heath
	Princes End
	Great Bridge
	Oldbury
	Tipton Green
	Wednesbury North
	Wednesbury South
	Bristnall
	Rowley
Solihull	Chelmsley Wood
	Fordbridge
	Smith's Wood
	Kingshurst
South Staffordshire	Huntington
Staffordshire Moorlands	Biddulph East
Stoke-on-Trent	Brookhouse
	Blurton
	Burslem Grange
	Longton South
	Tunstall North
	Great Fenton
	Chell
	Shelton
	Burslem Central
	Berryhill
	Abbey
	Norton and Bradeley
	Meir Park
	Fenton Green
Tamworth	Glascote
Telford & Wrekin	Woodside
	Malinslee and Langley
	Cuckoo Oak
	Brookside
	Donnington
	Arleston

Local authority	*Ward*
Walsall	Blakenall
	St. Matthew's
	Birchills Leamore
	Pleck
	Darlaston South
	Bentley and Darlaston Nth
	Palfrey
	Bloxwich East
	Willenhall South
	Bloxwich West
	Brownhills
Wolverhampton	Low Hill
	East Park
	St. Peter's
	Heath Town
	Ettingshall
	Bilston East
	Blakenhall
	Bilston North
	Graiseley
	Bushbury
	Fallings Park
Worcester	St. Barnabas
Wyre Forest	Oldington and Foley Park

TABLE I—ENGLAND—YORKSHIRE AND HUMBERSIDE

Local authority	*Ward*
Barnsley	Dearne Thurnscoe
	Athersley
	Monk Bretton
	Brierley
	Dearne South
	Ardsley
	Worsbrough
	Cudworth
	Park
	Hoyland West
	North West
	Darfield
	Royston
	Hoyland East
Bradford	Little Horton
	Bradford Moor
	University
	Bowling
	Toller
	Tong
	Undercliffe
	Keighley South
	Heaton
	Eccleshill
	Shipley East
	Odsal
	Keighley West
	Great Horton
Calderdale	St. John's
	Ovenden
	Mixenden
Doncaster	Conisbrough

Local authority	*Ward*
	Central
	Bentley Central
	Thorne
	Mexborough
	Adwick
	Balby
	Askern
	Town Field
	Intake
	Wheatley
	Rossington
	Stainforth
East Riding of Yorkshire	Bridlington South
Kingston upon Hull, City of	Noddle Hill
	Orchard Park
	Myton
	Marfleet
	St. Andrews
	University
	Newington
	Longhill
	Pickering
	Southcoates
	Ings
	Stoneferry
Kirklees	Deighton
	Thornhill
	Dewsbury West
	Crosland Moor
	Newsome
	Batley West
	Batley East
	Dewsbury East
Leeds	City and Holbeck
	Seacroft
	Harehills
	Burmantofts
	Richmond Hill
	Hunslet
	University
	Chapel Allerton
	Beeston
North East Lincolnshire	North East
	South
	Marsh
	Park (Cleethorpes)
	Croft Baker
North Lincolnshire	Brumby
	Frodingham and Town
Rotherham	Central
	Herringthorpe
	Park
	Dalton, Hooton Roberts and Thrybergh
	Brampton, Melton and Wentworth
	Greasbrough
	Rawmarsh West
	Maltby
	Rawmarsh East
	Boston
	Swinton

Local authority	*Ward*
	Wath
	Thurcroft and Whiston
Scarborough	Castle
	Eastfield
	Falsgrave
Selby	Selby South
	Selby North
Sheffield	Southey Green
	Burngreave
	Manor
	Park
	Firth Park
	Castle
	Nether Shire
	Darnall
	Owlerton
	Brightside
	Sharrow
	Norton
Wakefield	Hemsworth
	Castleford Ferry Fryston
	South Kirkby
	Wakefield East
	South Elmsall
	Wakefield Central
	Normanton and Sharlston
	Castleford Whitwood
	Knottingley
	Featherstone
	Wakefield North
	Castleford Glasshoughton

SCHEDULE 2

Regulation 2

AREAS IN WALES DESIGNATED AS DISADVANTAGED AREAS

The areas in Wales specified in this Schedule are—

(*a*) the electoral divisions, as at 1st April 1998, which are—

(i) contained in the Welsh Index of Multiple Deprivation 2000 published by the National Assembly for Wales, and

(ii) listed in Table J below; and

(*b*) any land which—

(i) as at 1st April 1998, did not fall within any of the electoral divisions mentioned in paragraph (*a*), but

(ii) as at 27th November 2001, had a postcode which was identical to the full postcode of land which, as at 1st April 1998, did fall within one of those electoral divisions.

TABLE J—WALES

Unitary authority	*Electoral division*
Blaenau Gwent	Nantyglo
	Tredegar Central and West
	Llanhilleth
	Sirhowy
	Rassau
	Cwmtillery
	Blaina
	Cwm
	Ebbw Vale South
	Ebbw Vale North

Stamp Taxes

Unitary authority	*Electoral division*
	Brynmawr
	Six Bells
	Abertillery
	Beaufort
	Georgetown
	Badminton
Bridgend	Caerau
	Bettws
	Blackmill
	Llangeinor
	Blaengarw
	Cornelly
	Maesteg West
	Morfa
	Nantyffyllon
	St. Bride's Minor
	Pontycymmer
	Nant-y-moel
	Pyle
	Maesteg East
	Ogmore Vale
	Cefn Cribwr
Caerphilly	New Tredegar
	Aberbargoed
	Darran Valley
	Twyn
	Carno
	Tir-Phil
	Pontlottyn
	Bargoed
	Moriah
	Argoed
	Hengoed
	Aber Valley
	Gilfach
	Abertysswg
	St. Cattwg
	Cefn Fforest
	St. James
	Machen
	Bedwas and Trethomas
	Crumlin
	Pengam
	Ynysddu
	Newbridge
	Penyrheol
	Pontllanfraith
	Abercarn
	Nelson
	Crosskeys
Cardiff	Butetown
	Ely
	Caerau
	Splott
	Adamsdown
	Llanrumney
	Trowbridge
	Grangetown
	Llandaff North
	Fairwater

Unitary authority	*Electoral division*
	Riverside
Carmarthenshire	Glanymor
	Llwynhendy
	Felinfoel
	Tyisha
	Pantyffynnon
	Glanamman
	Bigyn
	Bynea
	Garnant
	Kidwelly
	Burry Port
	Trimsaran
	Dafen
	Pembrey
	Quarter Bach Llynfell
	Brynamman
	Elli
	Ammanford
	Llangyndeyrn
	Tumble
	Saron
	Cross Hands
	Myddynfych
	Lliedi
	Hengoed
	Pontyberem
	Betws
	Penygroes
	Glyn
	Llangeler
	Llandybie and Heolddu
	Llangennech
Ceredigion	Aberystwyth South
	Llangeitho
	Cardigan
	Llandyfriog
	Llandysul Town
	Llanarth
	Lledrod
	Troedyraur
	Llangybi
	Penbryn
	Capel Dewi
	Llanfihangel Ystrad
	Tregaron
	New Quay
Conwy	Pant-yr-afon/Penmaenan
	Tudno
	Bryn
	Glyn
	Towyn
	Kinmel Bay
	Pentre Mawr
	Llysfaen
	Gogarth
	Mostyn
Denbighshire	Rhyl West
	Rhyl South West
	Meliden

Unitary authority	*Electoral division*
	Denbigh Upper/Henllan
	Rhyl East
	Bodelwyddan
	Denbigh Central
	Prestatyn North
Flintshire	Flint Castle
	Ffynnongroyw
	Mold West
	Bagillt West
	Higher and East Shotton
	Mostyn
	Holywell West
	Sealand
	Greenfield
	Gronant
	Holywell East
	Connah's Quay Central
	Flint
	Oakenholt
	Queensferry
	Saltney
Gwynedd	Peblig
	Marchog
	Talysarn
	Bowydd and Rhiw
	Barmouth
	Pwllheli South
	Rachub
	Cadnant
	Ogwen
	Deiniolen
	Penygroes
	Conglywal and Maenofferen
	Llanaelhaearn/Pistyll
	Pwllheli North
	Corris/Mawddwy
	Aberdaron
	Arthog
	Seiont
	Llanllyfni
	Hirael
	Gerlan
	Hendre
	Cynfal and Teigl
	Clynnog
	Tudweiliog
	Botwnnog
	Deiniol
	Trawsfynydd
	Penisarwaun
	Llanberis
	Llanbedrog
	Llanrug
	Abersoch
Isle of Anglesey	Morawelon
	Holyhead Town
	Tudur
	Maeshyfryd
	Amlwch Port
	Porthyfelin

Unitary authority	*Electoral division*
	Llannerch-y-medd
	Aberffraw
	Rhosneigr
	Kingsland
	London Road
	Bryngwran
	Llanbadrig
	Moelfre
	Mechell
	Amlwch Rural
	Llanfaethlu
	Bodorgan
	Llaneilian
	Rhosyr
	Parc a'r Mynydd
	Llanidan
Merthyr Tydfil	Gurnos
	Penydarren
	Dowlais
	Merthyr Vale
	Bedlinog
	Cyfarthfa
	Vaynor
	Plymouth
	Town
	Park
	Treharris
Monmouthshire	Lansdown
Neath Port Talbot	Cymmer
	Gwynfi
	Sandfields West
	Glyncorrwg
	Onllwyn
	Sandfields East
	Ystalyfera
	Briton Ferry West
	Neath East
	Lower Brynamman
	Pelenna
	Seven Sisters
	Godre'r graig
	Gwaun-Cae-Gurwen
	Aberdulais
	Aberavon
	Neath South
	Cwmllynfell
	Blaengwrach
	Bryn and Cwmavon
	Glynneath
	Dyffryn
	Crynant
	Trebanos
	Taibach
	Neath North
	Resolven
	Margam
	Pontardawe
	Coedffranc Central
	Port Talbot
	Briton Ferry East

Unitary authority	*Electoral division*
Newport	Pillgwenlly
	Tredegar Park
	Bettws
	Ringland
	Alway
	Victoria
	Stow Hill
	Gaer
	Shaftesbury
Pembrokeshire	Pembroke—Monkton
	Pembroke Dock—Llanion
	Pembroke Dock—Central
	Pembroke—St. Mary
	Neyland West
	Garth
	Milford North and West
	Pembroke Dock—Market
	Hakin
	Pembroke Dock—Pennar
	Goodwick
	Neyland East
	Castle
	Milford Central and East
	Merlin's Bridge
	Maenclochog
	St. Dogmaels
Powys	Ystradgynlais
	Tawe-Uchaf/Ystradfellte
	Aber-craf
	Newtown South
	Cwm-twrch
	Newtown Central
	Ynyscedwyn
	Welshpool Castle
Rhondda, Cynon, Taff	Pen-y-waun
	Maerdy
	Tylorstown
	Glyncoch
	Llwyn-y-pia
	Penrhiwceiber
	Treherbert
	Cwm Clydach
	Rhydfelen Central/Ilan
	Gilfach Goch
	Mountain Ash West
	Cymmer
	Ynyshir
	Trealaw
	Aberaman South
	Tonyrefail West
	Pen-y-graig
	Ystrad
	Cwmbach
	Ferndale
	Tonypandy
	Abercynon
	Tonyrefail East
	Aberaman North
	Hirwaun
	Pentre

Unitary authority	*Electoral division*
	Rhigos
	Rhydfelen Lower
	Porth
	Llanharry
	Treorchy
	Mountain Ash East
	Cilfynydd
	Aberdare East
	Graig
	Ynysybwl
	Tyn-y-nant
	Rhondda
	Aberdare West/Llwydcoed
Swansea	Townhill
	Penderry
	Graigfelen
	Castle
	Bonymaen
	Landore
	Gorseinon East
	St. Thomas
	Dulais East
	Cockett
	Penllergaer
	Mynyddbach
	Lower Loughor
The Vale of Glamorgan	Castleland
	Gibbonsdown
	Court
	Cadoc
	Buttrills
Torfaen	Trevethin
	St. Cadocs and Penygarn
	Cwmyniscoy
	Abersychan
	Upper Cwmbran
	Brynwern
	St. Dials
	Snatchwood
	Greenmeadow
	Blaenavon
	Pontnewynydd
Wrexham	Plas Madoc
	Queensway
	Caia Park
	Gwenfro
	Pant
	Penycae
	Brymbo
	Cefn
	Gwersyllt North
	Whitegate
	Ruabon
	Maesydre
	Ponciau
	Acton

SCHEDULE 3

Regulation 2

AREAS IN SCOTLAND DESIGNATED AS DISADVANTAGED AREAS

The areas in Scotland specified in this Schedule are—

(*a*) the areas which, as at 21st April 1991, had any of the postcodes which are-

(i) contained in Revising the Scottish Area Deprivation Index published by the Scottish Executive, and

(ii) listed in Table K below; and

(*b*) any land which—

(i) as at 21st April 1991, did not fall within any of the areas mentioned in paragraph (*a*), but

(ii) as at 27th November 2001, had a postcode which was identical to the full postcode of land which, as at 21st April 1991, did fall within one of those areas.

TABLE K—SCOTLAND

Postcode	*Local authority*
AB1 3	Aberdeen
AB2 1	Aberdeen
AB2 2	Aberdeen
DD1 5	Dundee
DD11 1	Dundee
DD2 3	Dundee
DD2 4	Dundee
DD3 0	Dundee
DD3 7	Dundee
DD4 0	Dundee/Angus
DD4 6	Dundee
DD4 8	Dundee
DD4 9	Dundee
DG1 2	Dumfries and Galloway
DG9 7	Dumfries and Galloway
EH11 3	Edinburgh
EH14 2	Edinburgh
EH16 4	Edinburgh
EH3 8	Edinburgh
EH4 4	Edinburgh
EH5 1	Edinburgh
EH54 5	West Lothian
EH6 6	Edinburgh
EH8 8	Edinburgh
FK2 7	Falkirk
FK8 1	Stirling
FK10 1	Clackmannanshire
G1 5	Glasgow
G11 6	Glasgow
G13 2	Glasgow
G13 3	Glasgow
G13 4	Glasgow
G14 0	Glasgow
G15 7	Glasgow
G15 8	Glasgow
G20 0	Glasgow
G20 7	Glasgow
G20 8	Glasgow
G20 9	Glasgow
G21 1	Glasgow
G21 2	Glasgow
G21 3	Glasgow
G21 4	Glasgow

Postcode	*Local authority*
G22 5	Glasgow
G22 6	Glasgow
G22 7	Glasgow
G23 5	Glasgow
G3 8	Glasgow
G31 1	Glasgow
G31 2	Glasgow
G31 3	Glasgow
G31 4	Glasgow
G31 5	Glasgow
G32 6	Glasgow
G32 7	Glasgow
G32 8	Glasgow
G33 1	Glasgow
G33 3	Glasgow
G33 4	Glasgow
G33 5	Glasgow
G34 0	Glasgow
G34 9	Glasgow
G4 0	Glasgow
G40 1	Glasgow
G40 2	Glasgow
G40 3	Glasgow
G40 4	Glasgow
G41 1	Glasgow
G42 0	Glasgow
G42 7	Glasgow
G42 8	Glasgow
G42 9	Glasgow
G43 1	Glasgow
G45 0	Glasgow
G45 9	Glasgow
G46 8	Glasgow/East Renfrewshire
G5 0	Glasgow
G5 9	Glasgow
G51 1	Glasgow
G51 2	Glasgow
G51 3	Glasgow
G51 4	Glasgow
G52 1	Glasgow
G52 4	Glasgow
G53 5	Glasgow
G53 6	Glasgow
G53 7	Glasgow/East Renfrewshire
G66 2	East Dunbartonshire
G71 5	North Lanarkshire
G72 0	South Lanarkshire
G72 7	South Lanarkshire
G73 1	South Lanarkshire
G81 1	West Dunbartonshire
G81 2	West Dunbartonshire
G81 4	West Dunbartonshire
G81 5	West Dunbartonshire
KA1 4	East Ayrshire
KA18 3	East Ayrshire
KA18 4	East Ayrshire
KA3 1	East Ayrshire
KA3 2	East Ayrshire/North Ayrshire
KA6 7	East Ayrshire
KA7 1	South Ayrshire

Postcode	*Local authority*
KA8 0	South Ayrshire
KA8 9	South Ayrshire
KY1 2	Fife
KY1 3	Fife
KY5 8	Fife
KY8 2	Fife
KY8 3	Fife
ML1 4	North Lanarkshire
ML2 0	North Lanarkshire
ML2 7	North Lanarkshire
ML2 9	North Lanarkshire
ML3 0	South Lanarkshire
ML4 2	North Lanarkshire
ML5 2	North Lanarkshire
ML5 4	North Lanarkshire
ML5 5	North Lanarkshire
ML6 0	North Lanarkshire
ML6 6	North Lanarkshire
ML6 7	North Lanarkshire
PA1 1	Renfrewshire
PA1 2	Renfrewshire
PA14 6	Inverclyde/Renfrewshire
PA15 2	Inverclyde
PA15 3	Inverclyde
PA15 4	Inverclyde
PA16 0	Inverclyde
PA2 0	Renfrewshire
PA3 1	Renfrewshire
PA3 2	Renfrewshire
PA3 4	Renfrewshire
PA4 8	Renfrewshire
PH1 5	Perth & Kinross

SCHEDULE 4

Regulation 2

AREAS IN NORTHERN IRELAND DESIGNATED AS DISADVANTAGED AREAS

The areas in Northern Ireland specified in this Schedule are—

(*a*) the wards, as at 21st April 1991, which are—

(i) contained in Measures of Deprivation in Northern Ireland 2001 published by the Northern Ireland Statistics and Research Agency, and

(ii) listed in Table L below; and

(*b*) any land which—

(i) as at 21st April 1991, did not fall within any of those wards, but

(ii) as at 27th November 2001, had a postcode which was identical to the full postcode of land which, as at 21st April 1991, did fall within one of those wards.

TABLE L—NORTHERN IRELAND

Local government district	*Ward*
Antrim	Rathenraw
	Fountain Hill
	New Park
Ards	West Winds
	Central
Armagh	Callan Bridge
	Abbey Park
	Downs

Local government district	*Ward*
	Keady
	Carrigatuke
Ballymena	Ballykeel
	Ballee
	Fair Green
	Moat
	Dunclug
	Castle Demesne
Ballymoney	Newhill
	Ballyhoe & Corkey
	Benvardin
	Stranocum
	Route
	Killoquin Lower
	Carnany
Banbridge	Edenderry
	Gilford
Belfast	Crumlin
	Falls
	Whiterock
	St. Annes
	Ballymacarrett
	Woodvale
	New Lodge
	The Mount
	Shankill
	Upper Springfield
	Ardoyne
	Shaftesbury
	Water Works
	Duncairn
	Clonard
	Woodstock
	Beechmount
	Blackstaff
	Glencairn
	Island
	Glencolin
	Glen Road
	Highfield
	Botanic
	Ballysillan
	Legoniel
	Falls Park
	Andersonstown
	Cliftonville
	Bloomfield
	Ladybrook
	Bellevue
	Sydenham
	Chichester Park
Carrickfergus	Northland
	Gortalee
	Sunnylands
	Killycrot
	Love Lane
	Clipperstown
Castlereagh	Tullycarnet
	Enler
	Cregagh

Local government district	*Ward*
	Minnowburn
Coleraine	Ballysally
	Churchland
	Cross Glebe
	Royal Portrush
	Central
	Kilrea
Cookstown	Ardboe
	Pomeroy
	Dunnamore
	Killycolpy
	Killymoon
	Newbuildings
	Gortalowry
	Stewartstown
	The Loop
	Moneymore
Craigavon	Court
	Drumgask
	Drumgor
	Corcrain
	Church
	Tullygally
	Drumnamoe
	Ballybay
	Taghnevan
	Tavanagh
	Ballyoran
Derry	Brandywell
	Creggan South
	The Diamond
	St. Peter's
	Victoria
	Creggan Central
	Shantallow East
	Shantallow West
	Westland
	Glen
	Rosemount
	Carn Hill
	Beechwood
	Corrody
	Strand
	Caw
	Clondermot
	Enagh
	Culmore
	Crevagh & Springtown
	Ebrington
	Banagher
	Claudy
	Faughan
Down	Flying Horse
	Cathedral
	Murlough
	Killyleagh
	Castlewellan
	Ardglass
Dungannon	Ballysaggart
	Coalisland South

Local government district	*Ward*
	Altmore
	Fivemiletown
	Clogher
	Ballygawley
	Mullaghmore
	Washing Bay
	Drumglass
	Augher
	Coalisland West & Newmil
	Coalisland North
	Donaghmore
Fermanagh	Newtownbutler
	Devenish
	Lisnaskea
	Irvinestown
	Rosslea
	Brookeborough
	Belleek & Boa
	Ederny & Lack
	Erne
Larne	Central
	Ballyloran
	Craigy Hill
	Blackcave
	Carnlough
Limavady	Binevenagh
	Coolessan
	Feeny
	Magilligan
	Glack
	Dungiven
	The Highlands
	Upper Glenshane
	Enagh
Lisburn	Twinbrook
	Collin Glen
	Kilwee
	Old Warren
	Knockmore
Magherafelt	Maghera
	Town Parks East
	Upperlands
	Castledawson
	Draperstown
Moyle	Glentaisie
	Bushmills
	Armoy
	Knocklayd
	Bonamargy & Rathlin
	Kinbane
	Glendun
Newry and Mourne	Daisy Hill
	Ballybot
	Crossmaglen
	St. Patrick's
	Creggan
	Derrymore
	Drumgullion
	Camlough
	St. Mary's

Local government district	*Ward*
	Newtownhamilton
	Silver Bridge
	Beesbrook
	Spelga
	Rathfriland
	Forkhill
	Kilkeel South
	Clonallan
	Kilkeel Central
	Lisnascree
	Fathom
Newtownabbey	Braden
	Dunanney
	Coole
	Whitehouse
	Valley
	Monkstown
North Down	Dufferin
	Whitehill
	Conlig
	Harbour
Omagh	Termon
	Fintona
	Owenkillew
	Sixmilecross
	Dromore
	Drumquin
	Gortrush
	Lisanelly
	Drumnakilly
	Camowen
	Newtownsaville
	Trillick
	Dergmoney
Strabane	East
	Castlederg
	Glenderg
	Clare
	Newtownstewart
	Sion Mills
	Dunnamanagh
	West
	Plumbridge
	Victoria Bridge
	South
	Artigarvan
	Slievekirk
	Finn
	North

2002/1975
Stamp Duty and Stamp Duty Reserve Tax (Extension of Exceptions relating to Recognised Exchanges) Regulations 2002

Made by the Treasury under FA 2002 s 117(1)

Made . . . . *25 July 2002*
Laid before the House of Commons . . . . *25 July 2002*
Coming into force . . . . *26 July 2002*

1 These Regulations may be cited as the Stamp Duty and Stamp Duty Reserve Tax (Extension of Exceptions relating to Recognised Exchanges) Regulations 2002 and shall come into force on 26th July 2002.

2 The application of the provisions specified in section 117(2) of the Finance Act 2002 is extended to the market known as OFEX.

2003/1056

Stamp Duty (Disadvantaged Areas) (Application of Exemptions) Regulations 2003

Made by the Treasury under FA 2001 ss 92A, 92B(6), FA 2002 s 110(6)

Made . . . . *9th April 2003*
Laid before the House of Commons . . . . *9th April 2003*
Coming into force . . . . *10th April 2003*

Citation, commencement and effect

1— (1) These Regulations may be cited as the Stamp Duty (Disadvantaged Areas) (Application of Exemptions) Regulations 2003 and shall come into force on 10th April 2003.

(2) These Regulations have effect in relation to instruments executed on or after 10th April 2003.

Interpretation

2— (1) In these Regulations—

"conveyance on sale" has the same meaning as in Part 1 of Schedule 13 to the Finance Act 1999 (see paragraph 1(2) of that Schedule);

"instrument" and "executed" have the meanings given by section 122(1) of the Stamp Act 1891;

"lease of land" has the same meaning as in Part 2 of Schedule 13 to the Finance Act 1999;

"the rate or average rate of rent" means the rate of rent by reference to which stamp duty is determined under paragraph 12(3) of Schedule 13 to the Finance Act 1999;

"relevant consideration" means—

(*a*) in the case of a conveyance or transfer on sale, the consideration for the sale;

(*b*) in the case of a lease of land, the consideration in respect of which, under paragraph 12(2) of Schedule 13 to the Finance Act 1999, the stamp duty is the same as that on a conveyance on a sale for the same consideration;

"residential property" has the meaning given by section 92B read together with regulation 7.

(2) In these Regulations—

(*a*) unless the context otherwise requires, any reference to a numbered section is a reference to the section of the Finance Act 2001 bearing that number; and

(*b*) any reference to "Schedule 30" is a reference to Schedule 30 to that Act.

[Disapplication of exemptions conferred by section 92 or by Schedule 30 where all of land is non-residential property

2A An exemption conferred by section 92 or by Schedule 30 shall not apply where none of the land in question is residential property.][1]

Amendments—[1] Regulation inserted by FA 2005 s 96, Sch 9 paras 2(2), 5 with effect, subject to FA 2005 Sch 9 para 5(2), for instruments executed after 16 March 2005. This insertion is without prejudice to the power to amend or revoke these provisions by further regulations under FA 2001 s 92A: FA 2005 Sch 9 para 3.

Application of exemptions conferred by section 92 or by Schedule 30 where all the land is residential property

3— (1) Subject to paragraph (3), an exemption conferred by section 92 or by Schedule 30 shall not apply in the cases specified by paragraph (2) below.

(2) The cases specified by this paragraph are cases where—

(*a*) all the land in question is residential property, and

(*b*) subject to regulation 6, the amount or value of relevant consideration is more than £150,000.

(3) Where the instrument in question is a lease of land, nothing in this regulation affects the application of an exemption conferred by section 92 or by Schedule 30 in relation to stamp duty chargeable in respect of the rate or average rate of rent.

Leases of land: further provision as to the application of exemptions conferred by section 92 or by Schedule 30

4— (1) This regulation applies where the instrument in question is a lease of land.

(2) Subject to paragraph (4), an exemption conferred by section 92 or by Schedule 30 shall not apply in the cases specified by paragraph (3) below.

(3) The cases specified by this paragraph are cases where—

(*a*) all the land in question is residential property, and

(*b*) subject to regulation 6, the rate or average rate of rent is more than £15,000.

(4) Nothing in this regulation affects the application of an exemption conferred by section 92 or by Schedule 30 in relation to stamp duty chargeable in respect of the amount or value of relevant consideration.

Application of exemptions conferred by section 92 or by Schedule 30 where land only partly residential property

5— (1) This regulation (which includes provisions corresponding to those contained in Schedule 30) applies where the land in question is—

(*a*) a building or land part of which falls within subsection (1)(*a*) or (*b*) of section 92B (meaning of "residential property"), or

(*b*) an interest in or right over land that subsists only partly as mentioned in subsection (1)(c) of that section.

(2) Where the land in question falls wholly or partly within a disadvantaged area, liability to stamp duty under Part 1 or 2 of Schedule 13 to the Finance Act 1999 on—

(*a*) a conveyance or transfer on sale of an estate or interest in land, or

(*b*) a lease of land, shall be determined in accordance with the following paragraphs of this regulation.

(3) Subject to regulation 6, the consideration in respect of which duty would be chargeable, but for the provisions of section 92 or paragraphs 1 and 3 of Schedule 30, shall be apportioned, on such basis as is just and reasonable, as between the land in question to the extent that it is residential property and the land in question to the extent that it is not.

[(3A) An exemption conferred by section 92 or by Schedule 30 shall not apply in relation to any duty chargeable in respect of relevant consideration, or the rate or average rate of rent, attributed to the land in question to the extent that it is not residential property.][1]

(4) An exemption conferred by section 92 or by Schedule 30 shall have effect in relation to any duty otherwise chargeable in respect of relevant consideration attributed to the land in question to the extent that it is residential property only where the amount or value of the consideration so attributed is £150,000 or less.

(5) An exemption conferred by section 92 or by Schedule 30 shall have effect in relation to any duty otherwise chargeable in respect of the rate or average rate of rent attributed to the land in question to the extent that it is residential property only where the rate or average rate so attributed is £15,000 or less.

Determination of consideration for the purposes of regulations 3, 4 and 5: land situated partly in a disadvantaged area and partly outside such an area

Amendments—[1] Para (3A) inserted by FA 2005 s 96, Sch 9 paras 2(3), 5 with effect, subject to FA 2005 Sch 9 para 5(2), for instruments executed after 16 March 2005. This insertion is without prejudice to the power to amend or revoke these provisions by further regulations under FA 2001 s 92A: FA 2005 Sch 9 para 3.

6— (1) In determining the amount of any consideration for the purposes of regulation 3, 4 or 5, the provisions of section 92 and paragraphs 1 and 3 of Schedule 30 shall be disregarded save to the extent mentioned in the following paragraphs of this regulation.

(2) Paragraphs (3) and (4) apply where the land in question is situated partly in a disadvantaged area and partly outside such an area.

(3) For the purposes of regulations 3(2)(*b*) and 4(3)(*b*), the consideration shall be treated as being the attributed consideration.

(4) For the purposes of regulation 5(3), the consideration to be apportioned shall be treated as being the attributed consideration and the apportionment shall be made as between—

(*a*) the land in question to the extent that it is situated in a disadvantaged area and is residential property; and

(*b*) the land in question to the extent that it is it is situated in a disadvantaged area and is not residential property.

(5) "The attributed consideration" means the consideration which would be attributed under paragraph 1(2) of Schedule 30 to such part of the land as is situated in the disadvantaged area.

Land comprising or including six or more separate dwellings

7 Where there is a single contract for the conveyance, transfer or lease of land comprising or including six or more separate dwellings, none of that land counts as residential property for the purposes of these Regulations.

Revocation of the Variation of Stamp Duties Regulations 2001

8 The Variation of Stamp Duties Regulations 2001 are hereby revoked.

2003/2837
Stamp Duty Land Tax (Administration) Regulations 2003

Made by the Commissioners of Inland Revenue under FA 2003 ss 79(4), 90(2), (3), (6) and 113(2), Sch 10 para 1, Sch 11 para 2, and Sch 13 paras 33(2), 36, 37(1) and (2), 41 and 42, and the Treasury, in exercise of the powers conferred upon them by FA 2003 Sch 12 para 2(6)

Made . . . . *7 November 2003*
Laid before the House of Commons . . . . . . *10 November 2003*
Coming into force . . . . *1 December 2003*

ARRANGEMENT OF REGULATIONS

Stamp Taxes

PART 1
GENERAL

Citation and commencement

1— (1) These Regulations may be cited as the Stamp Duty Land Tax (Administration) Regulations 2003 and shall come into force on 1st December 2003.

Interpretation

2— (1) In these Regulations—

"the 2003 Act" means the Finance Act 2003;
"the Board" means the Commissioners of Inland Revenue;
["HMRC" means Her Majesty's Revenue and Customs;][1]
"land transaction return" has the meaning given by section 76(1).

(2) In these Regulations, a reference to a numbered section without more is a reference to the section of the 2003 Act bearing that number.

Amendments—[1] Definition of "HMRC" inserted by the Transfer of Tribunal Functions and Revenue and Customs Appeals Order, SI 2009/56 art 3, Sch 2 paras 112, 113 with effect from 1 April 2009.

PART 2
REVENUE CERTIFICATES AND SELF-CERTIFICATES

Interpretation of Part 2

3 In this Part—

"the Inland Revenue" means any officer of the Board;
"Revenue certificate" has the meaning given by section 79(3)(*a*);
"purchaser" has the meaning given by section 43(4);
"self-certificate" has the meaning given by section 79(3)(*b*);
"vendor" has the meaning given by section 43(4).

Conditions to be met before a Revenue certificate is issued

4— (1) The conditions specified in paragraphs (2) to (5) must be met before a Revenue certificate is issued.

(2) The first condition is that a land transaction return in respect of the transaction must have been received by the Inland Revenue.

(3) The second condition is that the return (together with any other returns that are required)—

(*a*) has been completed; and
(*b*) includes any declaration required by paragraph 1(1)(*c*) of Schedule 10 to the 2003 Act.

(4) The third condition is that—

(*a*) as required by section 76(3)(*a*), a self-assessment is included in the return; and
(*b*) on the basis of the information contained in the return, the self-assessment appears to be correct.

(5) The fourth condition is that, as required by section 76(3)(*b*), payment of the amount of tax chargeable in respect of the transaction accompanies the return.

Form and contents of Revenue certificates

5— (1) A Revenue certificate must be in writing and must contain the information prescribed by paragraphs (2) to (7).

(2) The information prescribed by this paragraph is the address of the land to which the transaction relates.

(3) The information prescribed by this paragraph is any number recorded—

(*a*) as the title number of the land—

(i) for England and Wales, in the register of title maintained by the Chief Land Registrar;

(ii) for Scotland, in the Land Register of Scotland maintained by the Keeper of the Registers of Scotland;

(*b*) for Northern Ireland, as the folio number of the land in any registry maintained by the Land Registry of Northern Ireland.

(4) The information prescribed by this paragraph is any National Land and Property Gazetteer Unique Property Reference Number.

(5) The information prescribed by this paragraph is a description of the transaction.

(6) The information prescribed by this paragraph is the effective date in relation to the transaction (within the meaning given by section 119).

(7) The information prescribed by this paragraph is—

(*a*) the name of the purchaser; and

(*b*) the name of the vendor.

Duplicate Revenue certificates

6— (1) If the Inland Revenue are satisfied that a Revenue certificate has been lost or destroyed ("the original certificate"), a duplicate Revenue certificate may be issued.

(2) The duplicate Revenue certificate may be issued in the form of—

(*a*) a Revenue certificate equivalent to, and replacing, the original certificate; or

(*b*) a new Revenue certificate superseding the original certificate.

Multiple Revenue certificates

7— (1) This regulation applies where a land transaction return is made relating to more than one transaction.

(2) Subject to paragraph (3), the Inland Revenue shall issue one Revenue certificate in respect of the transactions to which the return relates.

(3) If the purchaser requests on the return that separate Revenue certificates be issued in respect of each of the transactions to which the return relates, the Inland Revenue may provide separate certificates in respect of any of those transactions.

Form and contents of self-certificate

8— (1) A self-certificate must be in writing and—

(*a*) on the form prescribed by Schedule 1; or

(*b*) in a form that has been approved by the Board.

(2) A self-certificate must contain the information required by the form prescribed by Schedule 1.

PART 3
LAND TRANSACTION RETURNS

Form and contents of land transaction return

9— (1) A land transaction return must be in writing and completed in black ink.

(2) A land transaction return must be—

(*a*) on the form prescribed by Part 1 of Schedule 2 together with any of the forms prescribed by Parts 2 to 4 of that Schedule which are relevant; or

(*b*) in a form that has been approved by the Board.

(3) A land transaction return must contain the information required by the forms prescribed by Schedule 2.

PART 4
DEFERRED PAYMENTS

Interpretation of this Part

10— (1) In this Part—

"application" means an application under section 90;

"the Inland Revenue" means any officer of the Board;

"relevant events" has the meaning given by regulation 12(2)(*c*).

When application to be made

11 An application must be made on or before the last day of the period within which the land transaction return relating to the transaction in question must be delivered.

Form and contents of application

12— (1) An application must be in writing.

Stamp Taxes

(2) An application must set out all the facts and circumstances relevant to it and, in particular, must specify—

(*a*) the consideration to which it relates;

(*b*) the respects in which that consideration is contingent or uncertain; and

(*c*) the events ("relevant events") on the occurrence of which the whole or any part of that consideration will—

(i) cease to be contingent, or

(ii) become ascertained.

Additional contents of application where consideration consists of works or services

13— (1) This regulation applies where the consideration to which an application relates, or any element of that consideration, consists of—

(*a*) the carrying out of works of construction, improvement or repair of a building or other works to enhance the value of land; or

(*b*) the provision of services (other than the carrying out of such works).

(2) The application must contain a scheme for payment of tax which must include—

(*a*) a proposal for the payment of tax in respect of the consideration, or element of the consideration, consisting of the carrying out of such works or the provision of such services within 30 days after the carrying out or provision is substantially completed;

(*b*) if the carrying out of such works or the provision of such services is expected to last for more than 6 months, proposals for a scheme of payment of tax at intervals of not more than 6 months.

Provision of information

14— (1) The Inland Revenue may by notice in writing require a person by whom an application is made to provide such information as they may reasonably require for the purposes of determining whether to accept the application.

(2) A notice given under this regulation must specify the time (which must not be less than 30 days from the date of issue of the notice) within which the applicant must comply with it.

Recovery of tax not postponed by application

15— (1) This regulation applies where an application has been made but has not been accepted by the Inland Revenue (including where there is an appeal under regulation 19 against the refusal of the application).

(2) The tax in respect of the chargeable consideration to which the application relates remains due and payable as if there had been no application (and, if relevant, no appeal).

This is subject to—

(*a*) the following paragraphs of this regulation;

(*b*) regulation 22 (direction by [tribunal][1] postponing payment); and

(*c*) regulation 23 (agreement to postpone payment).

(3) Payment of an amount of such tax as would not be due and payable if the application were accepted shall be postponed pending the reaching of a decision on the application.

(4) If an application is refused by the Inland Revenue, and there is no appeal under regulation 19 against the refusal of the application, the date on which any tax the payment of which had been postponed under paragraph (3) is due and payable shall be determined as if it were charged by an assessment of which notice was issued on the date on which the Inland Revenue issues to the applicant a notice of the total amount payable in consequence of the refusal of the application.

This is subject to—

(*a*) regulation 22 (direction by [tribunal][1] postponing payment); and

(*b*) regulation 23 (agreement to postpone payment).

Amendments—[1] Word substituted for word "Commissioners", in both places, by the Transfer of Tribunal Functions and Revenue and Customs Appeals Order, SI 2009/56 art 3, Sch 2 paras 112, 114 with effect from 1 April 2009.

Notice of decision on an application

16— (1) The Inland Revenue must give notice in writing to the person by whom the application was made of their decision whether to accept or refuse an application.

(2) Where the Inland Revenue accept an application, the notice must set out the terms on which the application has been accepted and, in particular, must—

(*a*) specify—

(i) any tax payable in accordance with a land transaction return relating to the transaction in question;

(ii) the nature of any relevant events; and

(iii) the dates of any relevant events (if known); and

(*b*) state that tax is payable within 30 days after the occurrence of a relevant event and in accordance with Part 4 of these Regulations.

(3) Where the Inland Revenue refuse an application, the notice must set out—

(*a*) the grounds for the refusal; and
(*b*) the total amount of tax payable in consequence of the refusal.

Grounds on which application may be refused

17— An application may be refused by the Inland Revenue if—

(*a*) the conditions for making an application specified in section 90(1) are not met;
(*b*) the application does not comply with the requirements of regulation 12 or 14;
(*c*) there are tax avoidance arrangements in relation to the transaction in question (see regulation 18);
(*d*) the application, or information provided in connection with it, is incorrect; or
(*e*) information required to be provided under regulation 14 is not provided within such time as the Inland Revenue reasonably required.

Tax avoidance arrangements

18— (1) For the purposes of regulation 17(*c*), arrangements are tax avoidance arrangements in relation to a transaction if their main object or one of their main objects is—

(*a*) to enable payment of the tax payable in respect of the transaction to be deferred; or
(*b*) to avoid the amount or value of the whole or part of the chargeable consideration for the transaction being determined for the purposes of Part 4 of the Finance Act 2003 in accordance with section 51(1).

(2) In this regulation, "arrangements" includes any scheme, agreement or understanding, whether or not legally enforceable.

Right of appeal

19— (1) An appeal may be brought against a refusal by the Inland Revenue to accept an application.

(2) The appeal lies to the General or Special Commissioners ("the Commissioners").[1]

Amendments—[1] Para (2) revoked by the Transfer of Tribunal Functions and Revenue and Customs Appeals Order, SI 2009/56 art 3, Sch 2 paras 112, 115 with effect from 1 April 2009.

Notice of appeal

20— (1) Notice of an appeal under regulation 19 must be given—

(*a*) in writing;
(*b*) within 30 days after the date on which the notice of the decision to refuse the application was issued; and
(*c*) to the officer of the Board by whom that notice was given.

(2) The notice of appeal must specify the grounds of appeal.

[(3) The provisions of paragraphs 36A to 36I of Schedule 10 to the 2003 Act apply to appeals under this regulation.][1]

Amendments—[1] Para (3) substituted by the Transfer of Tribunal Functions and Revenue and Customs Appeals Order, SI 2009/56 art 3, Sch 2 paras 112, 116 with effect from 1 April 2009. Para (3) previously read as follows—

"(3) On the hearing of the appeal the Commissioners may allow the appellant to put forward grounds not specified in the notice, and take them into consideration, if satisfied that the omission was not deliberate or unreasonable.".

Settling of appeals by agreement

21— (1) If before an appeal under regulation 19 is determined, the appellant and the Inland Revenue agree that the decision appealed against—

(*a*) should be upheld without variation,
(*b*) should be varied in a particular manner, or
(*c*) should be discharged or cancelled,

the same consequences shall follow, for all purposes, as would have followed if, at the time the agreement was come to, the [tribunal][1] had determined the appeal and had upheld the decision without variation, varied it in that manner or discharged or cancelled it, as the case may be.

(2) Paragraph (1) does not apply if, within 30 days from the date when the agreement was come to, the appellant gives notice in writing to the Inland Revenue that he wishes to withdraw from the agreement.

(3) Where the agreement is not in writing—

(*a*) paragraphs (1) and (2) do not apply unless the fact that an agreement was come to, and the terms agreed, are confirmed by notice in writing given by the Inland Revenue to the appellant or by the appellant to the Inland Revenue; and
(*b*) the references in those paragraphs to the time when agreement was come to shall be read as references to the time when the notice of confirmation was given.

(4) Where—

(*a*) the appellant notifies the Inland Revenue, orally or in writing, that he does not wish to proceed with the appeal, and
(*b*) the Inland Revenue do not, within 30 days after that notification, give the appellant notice in writing indicating that they are unwilling that the appeal should be withdrawn,

paragraphs (1) to (3) have effect as if, at the date of the appellant's notification, the appellant and the Inland Revenue had come to an agreement (orally or in writing, as the case may be) that the decision under appeal should be upheld without variation.

(5) References in this regulation to an agreement being come to with an appellant, and to the giving of notice or notification by or to the appellant, include references to an agreement being come to, or notice or notification being given by or to, a person acting on behalf of the appellant in relation to the appeal.

Amendments—[1] In para (1), words substituted for word "Commissioners", by the Transfer of Tribunal Functions and Revenue and Customs Appeals Order, SI 2009/56 art 3, Sch 2 paras 112, 117 with effect from 1 April 2009.

Direction by [the tribunal][1] postponing payment

22— [(1) If the appellant has grounds for believing that the amendment or assessment overcharges the appellant to tax, or as a result of the conclusion stated in the closure notice the tax charged on the appellant is excessive, the appellant may—

(*a*) first apply by notice in writing to HMRC within 30 days of the specified date for a determination by them of the amount of tax the payment of which should be postponed pending the determination of the appeal;

(*b*) where such a determination is not agreed, refer the application for postponement to the tribunal within 30 days from the date of the document notifying HMRC's decision on the amount to be postponed;

an application under sub-paragraph (*a*) must state the amount believed to be overcharged to tax and the grounds for that belief.][1]

(2) *The notice must—*

(*a*) *be given within 30 days after the date on which the notice of the decision to refuse the application was issued and to the officer of the Board by whom that notice was given; and*

(*b*) *state the amount of tax to be postponed.*[1]

(3) If, after any determination on such an application of the amount of tax payment of which should be postponed, there is a change in the circumstances of the case as a result of which either party has grounds for believing that the amount so determined has become excessive or, as the case may be, insufficient, he may, [if the parties cannot agree on a revised determination, apply, at any time before the determination of the appeal, to the tribunal for a revised][1] determination of that amount.

[(4) Any such application is to be subject to the relevant provisions of Part 5 of the Taxes Management Act 1970 (see, in particular, section 48(2)(*b*) of that Act).][1]

(5) The amount of tax of which payment is to be postponed pending the determination of the appeal is the amount (if any) which appears …[1] to be appropriate.

(6) Where an application is made under this regulation, the date on which any tax of which payment is not postponed is due and payable shall be determined as if the tax were charged by an assessment of which notice was issued on the date on which the application was determined.

(7) On the determination of the appeal—

(*a*) the date on which any tax payable in accordance with that determination is due and payable shall, so far as it is tax the payment of which had been postponed, be determined as if the tax were charged by an assessment of which notice was issued on the date on which [HMRC][1] issues to the appellant a notice of the total amount payable in accordance with the determination; and

(*b*) any tax overpaid shall be repaid.

Amendments—[1] In heading, words substituted for word "Commissioners", paras (1), (4) substituted, para (2) revoked, in para (3), words substituted for words "by notice in writing given to the other party at any time before the determination of the appeal, apply to the Commissioners for a further", in para (5), words "to the Commissioners, having regard to the representations made and any evidence adduced," revoked, and in para (7)(*a*), word substituted for words "the Inland Revenue", by the Transfer of Tribunal Functions and Revenue and Customs Appeals Order, SI 2009/56 art 3, Sch 2 paras 112, 118 with effect from 1 April 2009. Paras (1), (4) previously read as follows—

"(1) An appellant may by notice in writing apply to the Commissioners for a direction that payment of an amount of tax—

(*a*) in respect of the chargeable consideration to which the application relates, and

(*b*) which would not have been due and payable had the application been accepted,

shall be postponed pending the determination of the appeal.".

"(4) An application under this regulation shall be heard and determined by the Commissioners in the same way as an appeal.

The fact that any such application has been heard and determined by any Commissioners does not preclude them from hearing and determining the appeal or any further application under this regulation.".

Agreement to postpone payment

23— (1) If the appellant and the officer of the Board by whom the notice of the decision to refuse the application was given agree that payment of an amount of tax should be postponed pending the determination of the appeal, the same consequences shall follow, for all purposes, as would have followed if, at the time the agreement was come to, the [tribunal][1] had made a direction to the same effect.

This is without prejudice to the making of a further agreement or of a further direction.

(2) Where the agreement is not in writing—

(*a*) paragraph (1) does not apply unless the fact that an agreement was come to, and the terms agreed, are confirmed by notice in writing given by the officer of the Board in question to the appellant or by the appellant to that officer; and

(*b*) the reference in that paragraph to the time when the agreement was come to shall be read as a reference to the time when notice of confirmation was given.

(3) References in this regulation to an agreement being come to with an appellant, and to the giving of notice to or by the appellant, include references to an agreement being come to, or notice being given to or by a person acting on behalf of the appellant in relation to the appeal.

Amendments—[1] In para (1), word substituted for word "Commissioners" by the Transfer of Tribunal Functions and Revenue and Customs Appeals Order, SI 2009/56 art 3, Sch 2 paras 112, 119 with effect from 1 April 2009.

Payments and returns

24— (1) This regulation applies where the Inland Revenue accepts an application.

(2) If the application relates to deferring the payment of tax that has already been paid, the amount already paid shall be repaid together with interest as from the date of payment.

(3) The purchaser must make a return or further return ("the return") to the Inland Revenue—

(*a*) within 30 days after the occurrence of a relevant event;

(*b*) if relevant—

(i) within the period of 30 days mentioned in regulation 13(2)(*a*);

(ii) subject to regulation 27, in accordance with the scheme for payment mentioned in regulation 13(2)(*b*); or

(iii) after the final payment has been made in accordance with that scheme, within 30 days after the purchaser obtains new information the effect of which is that additional tax or less tax is payable in respect of the transaction than has already been paid.

(4) The return must be accompanied by payment of any tax or additional tax payable.

(5) If the effect of the return is that less tax is payable in respect of a transaction than has already been paid, the amount overpaid shall on a claim by the purchaser be repaid together with interest as from the date of payment.

Form and contents of returns

25— (1) A return under regulation 24(3) must be in writing and must contain the following information—

(*a*) a self-assessment of the amount of tax chargeable in respect of the transaction as a whole on the basis of information contained in the return;

(*b*) a statement of the amount of tax payable in respect of so much of the chargeable consideration for the transaction as is not, or is no longer, contingent or uncertain.

(2) The amounts mentioned in paragraph (1) must be calculated by reference to the rates in force at the effective date of the transaction.

Adjustment of payments made as mentioned in section 90(5)

26 Where—

(*a*) a payment is made as mentioned in section 90(5), and

(*b*) an application is accepted in respect of other chargeable consideration taken into account in calculating the amount of payment,

section 80 (adjustment where contingency ceases or consideration is ascertained) does not apply in relation to the payment and, instead, any necessary adjustment shall be made in accordance with these Regulations.

Returns and payments where consideration consists of works or services

27— (1) This regulation applies where a return or further return is required to be made in accordance with regulation 24(3)(*b*)(ii) and the carrying out of the works or provision of the services in question is expected to be substantially completed within a period of less than 6 months after the date on which the return or further return is required.

(2) Where this regulation applies, the applicant and the Inland Revenue may agree that the scheme of payment mentioned in regulation 13(2)(*b*) should be varied so that the next return or further return due to be made in respect of the consideration, or element of the consideration, consisting of the carrying out of such works or the provision of such services may be made within 30 days after the substantial completion of the carrying out of the works or the provision of the services.

(3) If the carrying out of the works or provision of the services in question is not substantially completed within a period of less than 6 months after the date on which, apart from the variation of the scheme of payment, the return or further return would have been required—

(*a*) the variation shall cease to have effect; and

(*b*) returns or further returns must continue to be made in accordance with regulation 24(3)(*b*)(ii).

Applications accepted by the Inland Revenue having no effect

28— For the purposes of Part 4 of the Finance Act 2003 and these Regulations, an application which has been accepted by the Inland Revenue—

(*a*) shall have no effect if—

(i) it contains false or misleading information; or

(ii) any facts or circumstances relevant to it are not disclosed to the Inland Revenue; and

(*b*) shall cease to have any effect if the facts and circumstances relevant to it materially change.

PART 5
DISTRAINT BY COLLECTORS: FEES, COSTS AND CHARGES

Interpretation of Part 4

29 In this Part—

"close possession" means physical possession by a distrainor or a person acting on his behalf of the goods and chattels distrained;

"walking possession" means possession in accordance with an agreement between a distrainor and a distrainee by which, in consideration of the distrainor not remaining in close possession, the distrainee undertakes neither—

(*a*) to dispose of any of the goods and chattels distrained; nor

(*b*) to permit their removal by any person not authorised by the distrainor to remove them.

Ascertainment of fees, costs and charges

30— (1) The fees chargeable on or in connection with the levying of distress under paragraph 2 of Schedule 12 to the 2003 Act are those specified in the Table in Part 1 of Schedule 3.

(2) The costs and charges recoverable where such distress has been levied are those specified in the Table in Part 2 of that Schedule.

(3) This is subject to the provisions of Part 3 of that Schedule.

Deduction of fees, costs and charges by the collector

31 The fees, costs and charges specified in Schedule 3 shall be deducted by the collector from the sums received on or in connection with the levying of distress or where distress has been levied.

Disputes as to fees, costs and charges

32— (1) In any case of dispute as to the fees chargeable, or costs and charges recoverable, under Schedule 3, the amount of those fees, costs and charges shall be assessed in accordance with this regulation.

(2) The relevant authority shall carry out any such assessment and may give such directions as to the costs of the assessment as he thinks fit.

(3) In paragraph (2), "the relevant authority" means—

(*a*) in England and Wales, the district judge of the county court for the district in which the distress is, or is intended to be, levied;

(*b*) in Northern Ireland, the Master (Taxing Office).

PART 6
INTERPRETATION OF PART 5

33 In this Part—

"the appropriate judicial authority" has the meaning given by paragraph 32(3) of Schedule 13 to the 2003 Act;

"the court" has the meaning given by paragraph 40(2) of Schedule 13 to the 2003 Act;

"items subject to legal privilege" has the meaning given by paragraph 35(2) of Schedule 13 to the 2003 Act;

"notice of application" means the notice of intention to apply for an order to which a person is entitled under paragraph 33(1) of Schedule 13 to the 2003 Act;

"order" means an order under paragraph 32 of Schedule 13 to the 2003 Act;

"working day" means any day other than a Saturday, Sunday or public holiday.

Approval of decision to apply for an order

34— Before the hearing of an application for an order, an officer of [Revenue and Customs][1] who is a member of the Senior Civil Service in—

(*a*) [the Cross-Cutting Policy branch of Her Majesty's Revenue and Customs][1], or

(*b*) [the Special Compliance Office of Her Majesty's Revenue and Customs][1],

must approve in writing the decision to apply for that order.

Amendment—[1] Words substituted by the SDLT (Administration) (Amendment) Regulations, SI 2005/1132 reg 2(1), (2) with effect from 18 April 2005.

Notice of application

35— (1) Notice of application must be given in writing and must contain the following details—

(*a*) the date, time and place of the hearing of the application;

(*b*) the specifications or descriptions of documents which are the subject of the application;

(*c*) a description of the suspected offence to which the application relates; and

(*d*) the name of the person suspected of committing, having committed or being about to commit the suspected offence.

(2) Notice of application must be given to the person entitled to it not less than five working days before the hearing of the application.

Notice of an order, or notice of an application, treated as having been given

36— (1) Where notice of an order, or notice of application, is delivered to a person, or left at his proper address, notice shall be treated as having been given to that person on the day on which it is delivered or left or, where that day is not a working day, on the next working day.

(2) Where notice of application, or notice of an order, is sent to a person's proper address by facsimile transmission or other similar means which produce a document containing a text of the communication, notice shall be treated as given when the text is received in a legible form.

(3) For the purposes of this regulation, a person's proper address is—

(*a*) the usual or last known place of residence, or the place of business or employment, of that person; or

(*b*) in the case of a company, the address of the company's registered office; or

(*c*) in the case of a liquidator of a company, the liquidator's address for the purposes of the liquidation.

Complying with an order

37— (1) A person complies with an order by producing the documents specified or described in the order to the officer of [Revenue and Customs][1] specified in the order within—

(*a*) the period mentioned in paragraph 32(2) of Schedule 13 to the 2003 Act; or

(*b*) such further period, if any, as is agreed with that officer.

(2) For the purposes of paragraph (1), documents are produced to an officer of [Revenue and Customs][1] if they are either—

(*a*) delivered to the officer; or

(*b*) left for the officer at an address specified in the relevant order.

(3) Where documents are sent to an officer of [Revenue and Customs][1] at the address specified in the relevant order by post, they shall be treated, unless the contrary is proved, as having been produced to the officer—

(*a*) if first class post is used, on the second working day after posting;

(*b*) if second class post is used, on the fourth working day after posting.

Amendment—[1] Words substituted by the SDLT (Administration) (Amendment) Regulations, SI 2005/1132 reg 2(1), (3) with effect from 18 April 2005.

Resolution of disputes as to legal privilege

38— (1) This regulation applies where there is a dispute between [the Commissioners for Her Majesty's Revenue and Customs][1] and a person against whom an order has been made as to whether a document, or part of a document, is an item subject to legal privilege.

(2) The person against whom an order has been made may apply to the appropriate judicial authority to resolve the dispute.

(3) All the documents to which an application under paragraph (2) relates must be lodged in the court at the same time as the application is made and shall be held by the court until the appropriate judicial authority resolves the dispute.

(4) The court shall give [the Commissioners for Her Majesty's Revenue and Customs][1] notice of an application made under paragraph (2) not less than five working days before the hearing of the application, and [the Commissioners for Her Majesty's Revenue and Customs][1] shall be entitled to appear and be heard at that hearing in addition to the person making the application.

(5) On the hearing of an application made under paragraph (2), the appropriate judicial authority shall—

(*a*) resolve the dispute by confirming whether the document, or part of the document, is or is not an item subject to legal privilege; and

(*b*) order the costs of the application to be met by [the Commissioners for Her Majesty's Revenue and Customs][1] except where it holds that no document, or no part of any document, to which the application relates is an item subject to legal privilege.

(6) Where a person makes an application under paragraph (2) within the period mentioned in regulation 37(1), he shall be treated as having complied with the order in relation to the documents to which the application relates until the appropriate judicial authority resolves the dispute.

(7) A dispute may be resolved at any time by [the Commissioners for Her Majesty's Revenue and Customs][1] and the person against whom an order has been made reaching an agreement, whether in writing or otherwise, and, for all purposes, the consequences of such an agreement shall be the same as those which would have ensued if, at the time when the agreement was reached, the appropriate judicial authority had resolved the dispute.

Amendment—[1] Words substituted by the SDLT (Administration) (Amendment) Regulations, SI 2005/1132 reg 2(1), (4) with effect from 18 April 2005.

SCHEDULE 1

SELF-CERTIFICATE

Regulation 8

Stamp duty land tax

Certification that no Land Transaction Return is required for a land transaction

This is a self-certificate under Section 79(3) of Finance Act 2003

Effective date of transaction

/ /

Title number/folio number

Property or land address

Name and address of purchaser's solicitor/agent

Name(s) and address of purchaser

Name(s) and address of vendor

Please turn over

SDLT 60 **(Substitute)(LexisNexis Butterworths)**

Stamp Taxes

Reason no Land Transaction Return is required

✓

☐ Transfer or conveyance of a freehold interest in land for no chargeable consideration.

☐ Grant of a lease in England & Wales or Northern Ireland for a term of seven years or more and for no chargeable consideration (that is, no premium and no rent of any monetary value).

☐ Transfer or assignment of a lease for no chargeable consideration.

☐ Grant of a lease where all the following are satisfied:
- the term of the lease is less than seven years, and
- the amount of any premium is not such as to attract a charge to SDLT at a rate of 1% or higher (ignoring the availability of any relief), and
- the amount of any rent is not such as to attract a charge to SDLT at a rate of 1% or higher (ignoring the availability of any relief).

☐ Transfer or assignment of a lease where both the following are satisfied:
- the term of the lease when granted was less than seven years, and
- the amount of any consideration for the assignment is not such as to attract a charge to SDLT at a rate of 1% or higher (ignoring the availability of any relief).

☐ Land transaction (other than the transfer of a freehold interest in land, or grant or assignment of a lease) where the amount of the consideration is not such as to attract a charge to SDLT at a rate of 1% or higher (ignoring the availability of any relief).

☐ Land transaction exempt from SDLT under Schedule 3 paragraph 3 Finance Act 2003 (transactions in connection with divorce or dissolution of a civil partnership formed under the Civil Partnership Act 2004).

☐ Land transaction exempt from SDLT under Schedule 3 paragraph 4 Finance Act 2003 (variation of testamentary dispositions).

☐ Transfer or conveyance of a freehold interest in land consisting entirely of residential property where the chargeable consideration, together with that of any linked transaction(s), is less than £1,000.

☐ Acquisition by a beneficiary entitled under a will or on intestacy, where the only consideration given is the assumption of 'secured debt' as defined in paragraph 3A of Schedule 3 Finance Act 2003.

☐ Transfer of interest in a partnership for chargeable consideration not exceeding the zero rate threshold.

Note: in Scotland

- for 'a freehold interest in land' read 'ownership of land'
- 'a lease' includes missives of let constituting a lease
- for 'assignment of a lease' read 'assignation of a tenant's interest under a lease (including missives of let constituting a lease)'

Declaration

This certificate must be signed by the person acquiring the interest. Signature by an agent is not acceptable. Where there is more than one transferee all of them must sign the certificate, except in certain circumstances (please refer to guidance notes).

I certify that for the reason given (as ticked) I do not need to submit a Land Transaction Return to HM Revenue & Customs.

If you give false information in this certificate you may face financial penalties and prosecution.

I declare that the information I have given in this form is true and complete to the best of my knowledge and belief.

Signature of purchaser(s)

Name (printed)

Capacity in which signing

Date

/ /

Amendments—Form substituted by the SDLT (Administration) (Amendment) Regulations, SI 2006/776 with effect from 17 April 2006. However, in relation to forms delivered before 16 April 2007, the requirement to deliver a self certificate in the form prescribed by this Schedule containing the information required by that form, is satisfied by delivering a certificate—

(*a*) on the form prescribed in this Schedule containing the information required by that form, or

(*b*) on the form formerly prescribed by this Schedule containing the information required by that form.

SCHEDULE 2
LAND TRANSACTION RETURN

Regulation 9

PART 1
MAIN FORM

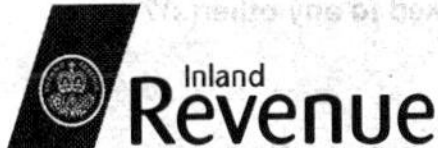

Land Transaction Return

For official use only

Stamp Taxes

Your transaction return

How to fill in this return

The land transaction return guidance notes (SDLT6), available from the Orderline on **0845 302 1472**, will help in completion of this return

- A unique reference number **must** be entered on the return, this is the number shown on the separate payslip in the 'Reference' box. Payslips are available from the Orderline.
- Show amounts in whole pounds only, rounded down to the nearest pound.
- Leave blank any boxes that do not apply
- The completed return should be printed off and then signed
- Do not fold the return.

If you need help with any part of this return or with anything in the guidance notes, please phone the Stamp Taxes enquiry line on **0845 603 0135**, open 8:30am to 5:00pm Monday to Friday, except Bank Holidays. Calls are charged at local rates.

SPECIMEN

Starting your return

ABOUT THE TRANSACTION

1 **Type of property**

Enter code from the guidance notes

2 **Description of transaction**

Enter code from the guidance notes

3 **Interest transferred or created**

Enter code from the guidance notes

4 **Effective date of transaction**

5 **Any restrictions, covenants or conditions affecting the value of the interest transferred or granted?** Put 'X' in one box

Yes No

If 'yes' please provide details

6 **Date of contract or conclusion of missives**

7 **Is any land exchanged or part-exchanged?** Put 'X' in one box

Yes No

If 'yes' please complete address of location

Postcode

House or building number

Rest of address, including house name, building name or flat number

8 **Is the transaction pursuant to a previous option agreement?** Put 'X' in one box

Yes No

ABOUT THE TAX CALCULATION

9 Are you claiming relief? Put 'X' in one box

Yes No

If 'yes' please show the reason

Enter code from the guidance notes

Enter the charity's registered number, if available, or the company's CIS number

For relief claimed on part of the property only, please enter the amount remaining chargeable

£ · 0 0

10 What is the total consideration in money or money 's worth, including any VAT actually payable for the transaction notified?

£ · 0 0

11 If the total consideration for the transaction includes VAT please state the amount

£ · 0 0

12 What form does the consideration take?
Enter the relevant codes from the guidance notes

13 Is this transaction linked to any other(s)?
Put 'X' in one box

Yes No

Total consideration or value in money or money 's worth, including VAT paid for all of the linked transactions

£ · 0 0

14 Total amount of tax due for this transaction

£ · 0 0

15 Total amount paid or enclosed with this notification

£ · 0 0

Does the amount paid include payment of any penalties and any interest due? Put 'X' in one box

Yes No

ABOUT NEW LEASES

If this doesn't apply, go straight to box 26 on page 3.

16 Type of lease

Enter code from the guidance notes

17 Start date as specified in lease

18 End date as specified in lease

19 Rent-free period
Number of months

20 Annual starting rent inclusive of VAT (actually) payable

£ · 0 0

End date for starting rent

Later rent known? Put 'X' in one box

Yes No

21 What is the amount of VAT, if any?

£ · 0 0

22 Total premium payable

£ · 0 0

23 Net present value upon which tax is calculated

£ · 0 0

24 Total amount of tax due – premium

£ · 0 0

25 Total amount of tax due – NPV

£ · 0 0

Check the guidance notes to see if you will need to complete supplementary return 'Additional details about the transaction, including leases', SDLT4.

ABOUT THE LAND including buildings

Where more than one piece of land is being sold or you cannot complete the address field in the space provided, please complete the supplementary return 'Additional details about the land', SDLT3.

26 Number of properties included

27 Where more than one property is involved, do you want a certificate for each property? Put 'X' in one box

Yes No

28 Address or situation of land

Postcode

House or building number

Rest of address, including house name, building name or flat number

Is the rest of the address on the supplementary return 'Additional details about the land', SDLT3?
Put 'X' in one box

Yes No

29 Local authority number

30 Title number, if any

31 NLPG UPRN

32 If agricultural or development land, what is the area (if known)? Put 'X' in one box

Hectares Square metres

Area

.

33 Is a plan attached? Please note that the form reference number should be written/displayed on map. Put 'X' in one box

Yes No

SPECIMEN

ABOUT THE VENDOR including transferor, lessor

34 Number of vendors included (Note: if more than one vendor, complete boxes 45 to 48)

35 Title Enter MR, MRS, MISS, MS or other title
Note: only complete for an individual

36 Vendor (1) surname or company name

37 Vendor (1) first name(s) Note: only complete for an individual

38 Vendor (1) address

Postcode

House or building number

Rest of address, including house name, building name or flat number

Stamp Taxes

ABOUT THE VENDOR CONTINUED

39 **Agent's name**

40 **Agent's address**
Postcode

Building number

Rest of address, including building name

41 **Agent's DX number**

42 **Agent's e-mail address**

43 **Agent's reference**

44 **Agent's telephone number**

ADDITIONAL VENDOR

Details of other people involved (including transferor, lessor), other than vendor (1). If more than one additional vendor please complete supplementary return 'Land Transaction Return – Additional vendor/purchaser details', SDLT2.

45 **Title** Enter MR, MRS, MISS, MS or other title
Note: only complete for an individual

46 **Vendor (2) surname or company name**

47 **Vendor (2) first name(s)**
Note: only complete for an individual

48 **Vendor (2) address**

Put 'X' in this box if the same as box 38.

If not, please give address below
Postcode

House or building number

Rest of address, including house name, building name or flat number

ABOUT THE PURCHASER including transferee, lessee

49 **Number of purchasers included** (Note: if more than one purchaser is involved, complete boxes 65 to 69)

50 **National Insurance number (purchaser 1), if you have one.** Note: only complete for an individual

51 **Title** Enter MR, MRS, MISS, MS or other title
Note: only complete for an individual

52 **Purchaser (1) surname or company name**

53 **Purchaser (1) first name(s)**
Note: only complete for an individual

54 **Purchaser (1) address**

Put 'X' in this box if the same address as box 28.

If not, please give address below
Postcode

House or building number

Rest of address, including house name, building name or flat number

55 **Is the purchaser acting as a trustee?** Put 'X' in one box

Yes No

56 **Please give a daytime telephone number** – this will help us if we need to contact you about your return

57 **Are the purchaser and vendor connected?**
Put 'X' in one box

Yes No

58 **To which address shall we send the certificate?**
Put 'X' in one box

Property (box 28) Purchaser's (box 54)

Agent's (box 61)

59 **I authorise my agent to handle correspondence on my behalf.** Put 'X' in one box

Yes No

60 **Agent's name**

61 **Agent's address**
Postcode

Building number

Rest of address, including building name

62 **Agent's DX number**

63 **Agent's reference**

64 **Agent's telephone number**

Stamp Taxes

ADDITIONAL PURCHASER

Details of other people involved (including transferee, lessee), other than purchaser (1). If more than one additional purchaser, please complete supplementary return 'Land Transaction Return – Additional vendor/purchaser details', SDLT2.

65 **Title** Enter MR, MRS, MISS, MS or other title
Note: only complete for an individual

66 **Purchaser (2) surname or company name**

67 **Purchaser (2) first name(s)**
Note: only complete for an individual

68 **Purchaser (2) address**

Put 'X' in this box if the same as purchaser (1) (box 54).

If not, please give address below
Postcode

House or building number

Rest of address, including house name, building name or flat number

69 **Is the purchaser acting as a trustee?** Put 'X' in one box

Yes No

ADDITIONAL SUPPLEMENTARY RETURNS

70 **How many supplementary returns have you enclosed with this return?** Write the number in each box. If none, please put '0'.

Additional vendor/purchaser details, SDLT2

Additional details about the land, SDLT3

Additional details about the transaction, including leases, SDLT4

DECLARATION

71 **The purchaser (s) must sign this return.** Read the notes in Section 1 of the guidance notes, SDLT6, 'Who should complete the Land Transaction Return?'.

If you give false information, you may face financial penalties and prosecution.
The information I have given on this return is correct and complete to the best of my knowledge and belief.

Signature of purchaser 1

Signature of purchaser 2

Please keep a copy of this return and a note of the unique transaction reference number, which is in the 'Reference' box on the payslip.

Finally, please send your completed return to:
Inland Revenue, Stamp Taxes/SDLT, Comben House, Farriers Way, NETHERTON, Merseyside, Great Britain, L30 4RN, or the DX address is: Rapid Data Capture Centre, DX725593, Bootle 9

Please don't fold it – keep it flat. Fill out the separate payslip, from which the unique reference number was taken, and pay in accordance with the 'How to pay' instructions.

PART 2
ADDITIONAL VENDOR/PURCHASER DETAILS

Land Transaction Return

Additional vendor/purchaser details

When to fill in this return

You must fill in this return for each additional vendor and/or purchaser. The guidance notes will help you answer the questions.

If you need help with any part of this return or with anything in the guidance notes, please phone the Stamp Taxes enquiry line on **0845 603 0135**, open 8:30am to 5:00pm Monday to Friday, except Bank Holidays. Calls are charged at local rates. You can get further copies of this return from the Orderline on **0845 302 1472.**

For official use only

Stamp Taxes

VENDOR OR PURCHASER

1 **Please indicate if this return is for an additional vendor or an additional purchaser.** Put 'X' in one box

Vendor Complete section below only

Purchaser Complete section below and the section over the page

COMPLETE IN ALL CASES

2 **Title** Enter MR, MRS, MISS, MS or other title
Note: only complete for an individual

3 **Surname or company name**

4 **First name(s)**
Note: only complete for an individual

5 **Address**
Postcode

House or building number

Rest of address, including house name, building name or flat number

Please turn over for additional purchaser details.

ADDITIONAL PURCHASER DETAILS

Only complete this section if this return is for an additional purchaser.

6 **Are the purchaser and vendor connected?**
Put 'X' in one box

☐ Yes ☐ No

7 **Is the purchaser acting as a trustee?** Put 'X' in one box

☐ Yes ☐ No

8 **Declaration**

The purchaser(s) must sign this return
Read the notes in Section 1 of the guidance notes, SDLT6 'Who should complete the Land Transction Return?'

If you give false information, you may face financial penalties and prosecution.

The information I have given on this form is correct and complete to the best of my knowledge and belief.
Signature of purchaser.

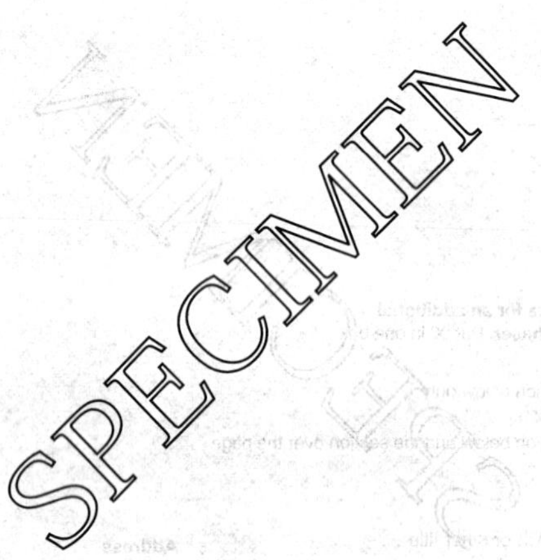

SDLT 2 PG 2

PART 3
ADDITIONAL DETAILS ABOUT THE LAND

Land Transaction Return

Additional details about the land

When to fill in this return

Fill in this return when you cannot fit all the details in the main Land Transaction Return, SDLT1. The guidance notes will help you answer the questions.

If you need help with any part of this return or with anything in the guidance notes, please phone the Stamp Taxes enquiry line on **0845 603 0135**, open 8:30am to 5:00pm Monday to Friday, except Bank Holidays. Calls are charged at local rates. You can get further copies of this return from the Orderline on **0845 302 1472.**

For official use only

Stamp Taxes

ABOUT THE LAND

1 **Type of property**

Enter code from the guidance notes

2 **Local authority number**

3 **Title number, if any**

4 **NLPG UPRN**

5 **Address or situation of land**

Postcode

House or building number

Rest of address, including house name, building name, flat number or continuation from the SDLT1

Please turn over

ABOUT THE LAND CONTINUED

6 **If agricultural or development land, what is the area (if known)?**

☐ Hectares ☐ Square metres

Area

☐☐☐☐☐☐☐☐☐☐ · ☐☐☐

7 **If there are any minerals or mineral rights reserved enter the code below**

☐☐ Enter code from the guidance notes

8 **Is a plan attached?** Please note that the form reference number should be written/displayed on map. Put 'X' in one box

☐ Yes ☐ No

9 **Interest transferred or created**

☐☐ Enter code from the guidance notes

PART 4
ADDITIONAL DETAILS ABOUT THE TRANSACTION, INCLUDING LEASES

Land Transaction Return

Additional details about the transaction, including leases

Stamp Taxes

When to fill in this return

You must fill in this return where additional information about the transaction and/or lease can be provided. The guidance notes will help you answer the questions.

If you need help with any part of this return or with anything in the guidance notes, please phone the Stamp Taxes enquiry line on **0845 603 0135**, open 8:30am to 5:00pm Monday to Friday, except Bank Holidays. Calls are charged at local rates. You can get further copies of this return from the Orderline on **0845 302 1472**.

REFERENCE

Insert the reference number from the payslip on page 7 of the Land Transaction Return, SDLT1, here.

For official use only

ABOUT THE TRANSACTION

1 **If this transaction is part of the sale of business, please say if the sale includes** Put 'X' in relevant boxes

Stock
Goodwill
Other
Chattels and moveables

What is the total amount of the consideration for the sale of the business apportioned to these items?

£ . 00

2 **If the property is for commercial use, what is it?** Put 'X' in the appropriate box(es)

Office
Hotel
Shop
Warehouse
Factory
Other
Other industrial unit

3 **Have you applied for and received a post transaction ruling in accordance with Code of Practice 10, or asked us for advice on the application of the law to this transaction?** Put 'X' in one box

Yes
No

If 'yes' have you followed it when completing this return? Put 'X' in one box

Yes
No
Ruling not received

4 **Is any part of the consideration contingent or dependent on uncertain future events?**

Yes
No

5 **Have you agreed with the Inland Revenue that you will pay on a deferred basis?**

Yes
No

6 **If there are any minerals or mineral rights reserved enter the code below**

Enter code from the guidance notes

7 **If the purchaser is VAT registered, give their VAT reference number**

8 **If the purchaser is a company please give the following details**

Tax reference number

Company registration number

If registered abroad, give its place of registration

ABOUT THE TRANSACTION CONTINUED

9 **Give a description of the purchaser**
Enter code from the guidance notes

ABOUT LEASES

Complete if the transaction notified on SDLT1 is for the grant of more than one lease

10 **Type of property**
Enter code from the guidance notes

11 **Address or situation of land**
Put 'X' in this box if the same as box 28 on SDLT1
If not, please give address below
Postcode

House or building number

Rest of address, including house name, building name, flat number or continuation from the SDLT1

continued at the top of the next column

12 **Local authority number**

13 **Title number, if any**

14 **NLPG UPRN**

15 **If the transaction is for land, what is the unit and area of measurement?** Put 'X' in one box
Hectares Square metres
Area

16 **Is a plan attached? Please note that the form reference number should be written/displayed on the map.**
Put X in one box
Yes No

17 **Interest transferred or created**
Enter code from the guidance notes

18 **Type of lease**
Enter code from the guidance notes

ABOUT LEASES CONTINUED

19 Start date as specified in lease

20 End date as specified in lease

21 Rent free period
Number of months

22 Annual starting rent inclusive of VAT (actually) payable
£ . 0 0
End date for starting rent
Later rent known? Put 'X' in one box
Yes No

23 What is the amount of VAT, if any?
£ . 0 0

24 Total premium payable
£ . 0 0

25 Net present value upon which tax is calculated
£ . 0 0

26 Total amount of tax due - premium
£ . 0 0

27 Total amount of tax due - NPV
£ . 0 0

28 Any terms surrendered

29 Break clause type Put 'X' in one box
Landlord Tenant only
Either

30 What is the date of the break clause?

31 Which of the following relate to this lease?
Put 'X' in relevant boxes. If none, leave blank
Option
Market rent
Turnover rent
Unascertainable rent
Contingent reserved rent

32 Rent review frequency

33 Date of first review

34 Rent review clause (type) Put 'X' in one box
Open market RPI
Other

35 If Schedule 17A para 7FA 2003 has been used in calculating the NPV, what is the date of the rent change?

Please turn over

Stamp Taxes

ABOUT LEASES CONTINUED

36 **Service charge amount if known**

£ . 0 0

37 **Service charge frequency** Put 'X' in one box

Monthly

Annually

Quarterly

Other

38 **Other consideration – tenant to landlord**

(for example, services, building works)

Enter the relevant codes from the guidance notes

39 **Other consideration – landlord to tenant**

(for example, services, building works)

Enter the relevant codes from the guidance notes

SDLT 4 V3 PG 4

Amendments—Form substituted by the SDLT (Administration) (Amendment) Regulations, SI 2004/3124 with effect from 6 December 2004. However, in relation to forms delivered before 1 April 2005, the requirement to make a land transaction return on the form prescribed by this Part containing the information required by that form, is satisfied by making a return—

(*a*) on the prescribed substituted form containing the information required by that form, or
(*b*) on the form formerly prescribed by this Part containing the information required by that form.

SCHEDULE 3
FEES, COSTS AND CHARGES
Regulation 30

PART 1
FEES CHARGEABLE ON OR IN CONNECTION WITH THE LEVYING OF DISTRESS

Action taken in connection with the levying of distress	*Fees*
For making a visit to premises with a view to levying distress (whether the levy is made or not)	A sum not exceeding £12.50.
Levying distress where the total sum charged is £100 or less.	£12.50
Levying distress where the total sum charged is more than £100.	12½ per cent on the first £100 of the amount to be recovered; 4 per cent on the next £400; 2½ per cent on the next £1500; 1 per cent on the next £8000; ¼ per cent on any additional sum.

PART 2
COSTS AND CHARGES RECOVERABLE WHERE DISTRESS HAS BEEN LEVIED

Action taken where distress has been levied	*Costs and charges*
1. Taking possession	
Where close possession is taken.	£4.50 for the day of levy only.
Where walking possession is taken.	45p per day, payable for the day the distress is levied and up to 14 days thereafter.
2. Removal and storage of goods.	The reasonable costs and charges of removal and storage.
3.Appraisement.	The reasonable fees, charges and expenses of the person appraising.
4.Sale.	
Where the sale is held on the auctioneer's premises, for the reasonable cost of advertising, auctioneer's commission (to include all out of pocket expenses other than charges for advertising, removal and storage).	15 per cent on the sum realised plus the reasonable cost of advertising, removal and storage.
Where the sale is held on the debtor's premises, for the auctioneer's commission (not to include out-of-pocket expenses or charges for advertising).	7½ per cent on the sum realised plus out-of-pocket expenses actually and reasonably incurred and the reasonable costs of advertising.

PART 3
MISCELLANEOUS PROVISIONS RELATING TO FEES, COSTS AND CHARGES

1 In any case where close possession is taken, an individual left in possession must provide his own board.

2 For the purpose of calculating any percentage fees, costs and charges, a fraction of £1 is to be reckoned as £1, but any fraction of a penny in the total amount so calculated is to be disregarded.

3 In addition to any amount authorised by this Schedule in respect of the supply of goods or services on which value added tax is chargeable there may be added a sum equivalent to value added tax at the appropriate rate on that amount.

2003/2899
Stamp Duty Land Tax (Appointment of the Implementation Date) Order 2003

Made by the Treasury under FA 2003 Sch 19 para 2(2)

Made . . . . *12th November 2003*

Citation

1 This Order may be cited as the Stamp Duty Land Tax (Appointment of the Implementation Date) Order 2003.

Implementation date

2 The date appointed as the implementation date for the purposes of stamp duty land tax is 1st December 2003.

2004/1363
Stamp Duty Land Tax (Appeals) Regulations 2004

Revocation—These Regulations revoked by the Transfer of Tribunal Functions and Revenue and Customs Appeals Order, SI 2009/56 art 3, Sch 2 para 187(*r*) with effect from 1 April 2009.

2004/1864
Tax Avoidance Schemes (Information) Regulations 2004

Made by the Treasury under FA 1999 s 132, FA 2002 s 135, FA 2004 ss 308(1), (3), 309(1), 310, 312, 313(1), (3), (4)(*g*), 317(2), 318(1)

Made . . . . *22 July 2004*
Laid before the House of Commons . . . . *22 July 2004*
Coming into force . . . . *1 August 2004*

Citation, commencement and effect

1— (1) These Regulations may be cited as the Tax Avoidance Schemes (Information) Regulations 2004 and shall come into force on 1st August 2004.

(2) These Regulations do not have effect in respect of proposals or arrangements (as the case may be) which are notifiable by virtue of any of the provisions of Part 2 of the Schedule to the Arrangements Regulations—

(*a*) for the purposes of section 308(1), if the relevant date in relation to a proposal falls before 22nd June 2004;
(*b*) for the purposes of section 308(3), if the date on which the promoter first becomes aware of any transaction forming part of arrangements falls before that date;
(*c*) for the purposes of sections 309 and 310, if the date on which any transaction forming part of arrangements is entered into falls before that date.

Interpretation

2 In the Regulations—

"the Act" means the Finance Act 2004, and a reference to a numbered section (without more) is a reference to the section of the Act which is so numbered;
"the Arrangements Regulations" means the Tax Avoidance Schemes (Prescribed Descriptions of Arrangements) Regulations 2004;
["the SDLT Arrangements Regulations" means the Stamp Duty Land Tax Avoidance Schemes (Prescribed Descriptions of Arrangements) Regulations 2005;][1]
"corporation tax" shall be construed in accordance with section 318(1);
"employment" has the same meaning as it has for the purposes of the employment income Parts of the Income Tax (Earnings and Pensions) Act 2003 (see section 4 of that Act) and includes offices to which the provisions of those Parts that are expressed to apply to employments apply equally (see section 5 of that Act); and "employee" and "employer" have corresponding meanings;
"notifiable arrangements" has the meaning given by section 306(1);
"notifiable proposal" has the meaning given by section 306(2);
"promoter" has the meaning given by section 307;
"the prescribed taxes" means capital gains tax, corporation tax[, income tax and stamp duty land tax][1];
"the relevant date" has the meaning given by section 308(2).

Amendments—[1] Definition of "the SDLT Arrangements Regulations" inserted, and words in the definition of "the prescribed taxes" substituted, by the Tax Avoidance Schemes (Information) (Amendment) Regulations, SI 2005/1869 regs 2, 3 with effect from 1 August 2005.
However, these amendments do not have effect in respect of proposals or arrangements (as the case may be) which are notifiable by virtue of the Stamp Duty Land Tax Avoidance Schemes (Prescribed Descriptions of Arrangements) Regulations, SI 2005/1868—
(*a*) for the purposes of FA 2004 s 308(1), if the relevant date in relation to a proposal falls before 1 August 2005;
(*b*) for the purposes of FA 2004 s 308(3), if the date on which the promoter first becomes aware of any transaction forming part of the arrangements falls before that date;

(*c*) for the purposes of FA 2004 s 309 or 310, the date on which any transaction forming part of the arrangements is entered into falls before that date: SI 2005/1869 reg 1.

Prescribed information in respect of notifiable proposals and arrangements

3— (1) The information which must be provided to the Board by a promoter under section 308(1) in respect of a notifiable proposal is sufficient information as might reasonably be expected to enable an officer of the Board to comprehend the manner in which the proposal is intended to operate, including—

(*a*) the promoter's name and address;
(*b*) details of the provision of the Arrangements Regulations [or the SDLT Arrangement Regulations][1] by virtue of which the proposal is notifiable;
(*c*) a summary of the proposal and the name (if any) by which it is known;
(*d*) information explaining each element of the proposed arrangements (including the way in which they are structured) from which the tax advantage expected to be obtained under those arrangements arises; and
(*e*) the statutory provisions, relating to any of the prescribed taxes, on which that tax advantage is based.

(2) The information which must be provided to the Board by a promoter under section 308(3) in respect of notifiable arrangements is sufficient information as might reasonably be expected to enable an officer of the Board to comprehend the manner in which the arrangements are intended to operate, including—

(*a*) the promoter's name and address;
(*b*) details of the provision of the Arrangements Regulations [or the SDLT Arrangement Regulations][1] by virtue of which the arrangements are notifiable;
(*c*) a summary of the arrangements and the name (if any) by which they are known;
(*d*) information explaining each element of the arrangements (including the way in which they are structured) from which the tax advantage expected to be obtained under the arrangements arises; and
(*e*) the statutory provisions, relating to any of the prescribed taxes, on which that tax advantage is based.

(3) The information which must be provided to the Board by a client under section 309 (duty of person dealing with promoter outside the United Kingdom) in respect of notifiable arrangements is sufficient information as might reasonably be expected to enable an officer of the Board to comprehend the manner in which the arrangements are intended to operate, including—

(*a*) the client's name and address;
(*b*) the name and address of the promoter;
(*c*) details of the provision of the Arrangements Regulations [or the SDLT Arrangement Regulations][1] by virtue of which the arrangements are notifiable;
(*d*) a summary of the arrangements, and the name (if any) by which they are known;
(*e*) information explaining each element of the arrangements (including the way in which they are structured) from which the tax advantage expected to be obtained under the arrangements arises; and
(*f*) the statutory provisions, relating to any of the prescribed taxes, on which that tax advantage is based.

(4) The information which must be provided to the Board by a person obliged to do so by section 310 (duty of parties to notifiable arrangements not involving promoter) is sufficient information as might reasonably be expected to enable an officer of the Board to comprehend the manner in which the arrangements of which that transaction forms part are intended to operate, including—

(*a*) the name and address of the person entering into the transaction;
(*b*) details of the provision of the Arrangements Regulations [or the SDLT Arrangement Regulations][1] by virtue of which the arrangements are notifiable;
(*c*) a summary of the arrangements and the name (if any) by which they are known;
(*d*) information explaining each element of the arrangements (including the way in which they are structured) from which the tax advantage expected to be obtained under the arrangements arises; and
(*e*) the statutory provisions, relating to any of the prescribed taxes, on which that tax advantage is based.

[(5) If, but for this paragraph—

(*a*) a person would be obliged to provide information in relation to two or more notifiable arrangements,
(*b*) those arrangements are substantially the same (whether they relate to the same parties or different parties), and
(*c*) he has already provided information under paragraph (4) in relation to any of the other arrangements, he need not provide further information under paragraph (4).][1]

Commentary—*Simon's Taxes* **A7.230, A7.232.**

Amendments—[1] Words inserted, and para (5) inserted, by the Tax Avoidance Schemes (Information) (Amendment) Regulations, SI 2005/1869 regs 2, 4 with effect from 1 August 2005.

However, these amendments do not have effect in respect of proposals or arrangements (as the case may be) which are notifiable by virtue of the Stamp Duty Land Tax Avoidance Schemes (Prescribed Descriptions of Arrangements) Regulations, SI 2005/1868—

(*a*) for the purposes of FA 2004 s 308(1), if the relevant date in relation to a proposal falls before 1 August 2005;

(*b*) for the purposes of FA 2004 s 308(3), if the date on which the promoter first becomes aware of any transaction forming part of the arrangements falls before that date;

(*c*) for the purposes of FA 2004 s 309 or 310, the date on which any transaction forming part of the arrangements is entered into falls before that date: SI 2005/1869 reg 1.

Time for providing information under section 308, 309 or 310

4— (1) The period or time (as the case may be) within which the prescribed information under section 308, 309 or 310 must be provided to the Board is found in accordance with the following paragraphs of this regulation.

(2) In the case of a notification under section 308(1), the prescribed period is the period of 5 days beginning with the day after the relevant date.

(3) In the case of a notification under section 308(3), the prescribed period is the period of 5 days beginning with the day after that on which the promoter first becomes aware of any transaction forming part of arrangements to which that subsection applies.

(4) In the case of a notification under section 309(1), the prescribed period is the period of 5 days beginning with the day after that on which the client enters into the first transaction forming part of notifiable arrangements to which that subsection applies.

(5) In the case of a notification under section 310 the prescribed time is any time during the period—

(*a*) beginning with the day after that on which the person enters into the first transaction forming part of the notifiable arrangements; and

(*b*) ending with the latest time at which he would first have had to provide the Board with information under section 313 in accordance with regulation 8.

[This is subject to [paragraphs (5ZA) and (5A)][2].][1]

[(5ZA) In the case of a notification under section 310 in relation to stamp duty land tax, the prescribed time is any time during the period of 30 days beginning with the day after the day on which the person enters into the first transaction forming part of the notifiable arrangements.][2]

[(5A) In the case of a notification under section 310 which arises by virtue of the application of regulation 6 of the Tax Avoidance Schemes (Promoters and Prescribed Circumstances) Regulations 2004 (persons not to be treated as promoters: legal professional privilege), the prescribed time is any time during the period of 5 days beginning with the day after the day on which the person enters into the first transaction forming part of the notifiable arrangements.][1]

(6) In reckoning any period under this regulation or regulation 5 any day which is a non-business day within the meaning of section 92 of the Bills of Exchange Act 1882 shall be disregarded.

(7) Where paragraph (2), (3) or (4) applies, if the prescribed period referred to in that paragraph would otherwise end before 30th September 2004, it shall instead end upon that date.

(8) This regulation is subject to regulations 5 (statutory clearances) and 6 (transitional provisions).

Commentary—*Simon's Taxes* **A7.213, A7.231**.

Amendments—[1] Words in para (5) inserted, and para (5A) inserted, by the Tax Avoidance Schemes (Promoters, Prescribed Circumstances and Information) (Amendment) Regulations, SI 2004/2613 reg 3 with effect from 14 October 2004. However, in any case where the latest time at which a person would by virtue of para (5A) above, be required to provide information to the Board under FA 2004 s 310 would be earlier than 19 November 2004, the latest time at which that information shall be required to be provided shall instead be 19 November 2004: SI 2004/2613 reg 1.

[2] Words in para (5) substituted, and para (5ZA) inserted, by the Tax Avoidance Schemes (Information) (Amendment) Regulations, SI 2005/1869 regs 2, 5 with effect from 1 August 2005.

However, these amendments do not have effect in respect of proposals or arrangements (as the case may be) which are notifiable by virtue of the Stamp Duty Land Tax Avoidance Schemes (Prescribed Descriptions of Arrangements) Regulations, SI 2005/1868—

(*a*) for the purposes of FA 2004 s 308(1), if the relevant date in relation to a proposal falls before 1 August 2005;

(*b*) for the purposes of FA 2004 s 308(3), if the date on which the promoter first becomes aware of any transaction forming part of the arrangements falls before that date;

(*c*) for the purposes of FA 2004 s 309 or 310, the date on which any transaction forming part of the arrangements is entered into falls before that date: SI 2005/1869 reg 1.

Statutory clearances

5— (1) If—

(*a*) a promoter must provide information under subsection (1) of section 308;

(*b*) the relevant date by reference to which he must provide that information is that referred to in subsection (2)(*a*) of that section; and

(*c*) he reasonably expects to make an application on behalf of a client under any of the provisions listed in paragraph (3) ("a clearance application");

the prescribed period is that beginning with the day after the relevant date and ending with the applicable date.

(2) The applicable date is—

(*a*) the date on which the first transaction occurs in pursuance of the arrangements, or

(*b*) if the promoter ceases to hold the reasonable expectation referred to in paragraph (1)(*c*) 5 days after he ceases to hold it.

(3) The provisions are—

(*a*) sections 215, 225, 444A and 707 of the Income and Corporation Taxes Act 1988; and

(*b*) sections 138, 139, 140B and 140D of the Taxation of Chargeable Gains Act 1992.

Commentary—*Simon's Taxes* **A7.231**.

Time for providing information under section 308, 309 or 310: transitional provisions

6— (1) Where paragraph (2) or (3) applies, the prescribed period or time (as the case may be) to be found in accordance with regulation 4 shall end upon 31st October 2004 instead of the day on which it would end by virtue of that regulation.

(2) This paragraph applies in respect of proposals or arrangements (as the case may be) that are notifiable by virtue of any of the provisions of Part 1 of the Schedule to the Arrangements Regulations—

(*a*) for the purposes of section 308(1), if the relevant date in relation to a proposal falls within the period beginning with 18th March 2004 and ending with 31st July 2004;

(*b*) for the purposes of section 308(3), if the date on which the promoter first becomes aware of any transaction forming part of arrangements falls within the period beginning with 18th March 2004 and ending with 31st July 2004;

(*c*) for the purposes of sections 309 and 310, if the date on which any transaction forming part of arrangements is entered into falls within the period beginning with 23rd April 2004 and ending with 31st July 2004.

(3) This paragraph applies in relation to proposals or arrangements that are notifiable by virtue of any of the provisions of Part 2 of the Schedule to the Arrangements Regulations—

(*a*) for the purposes of section 308(1), if the relevant date in relation to a proposal falls within the period beginning with 22nd June 2004 and ending with 31st July 2004;

(*b*) for the purposes of section 308(3), if the date on which the promoter first becomes aware of any transaction forming part of arrangements falls within the period beginning with 22nd June 2004 and ending with 31st July 2004;

(*c*) for the purposes of sections 309 and 310, if the date on which any transaction forming part of arrangements is entered into falls within the period beginning with 22nd June 2004 and ending with 31st July 2004.

Commentary—*Simon's Taxes* **A7.228**.

Prescribed information under section 312

7 For the purposes of section 312 (duty of promoter to notify client of number), the prescribed information is the reference number referred to in subsection (1) of that section.

Commentary—*Simon's Taxes* **A7.233**.

Prescribed information under section 313: timing and manner of delivery

8— (1) For the purposes of section 313 (duty of parties to notifiable arrangements to notify the Board of number, etc)—

(*a*) the prescribed information is—

(i) the reference number allocated by the Board under section 311 to the notifiable arrangements or proposed notifiable arrangements; and

(ii) the year of assessment, tax year or accounting period (as the case may be) in which, or the date on which, the person making the notification expects a tax advantage to be obtained; and

(*b*) the prescribed times at which a person who is a party to notifiable arrangements must provide the Board with information under that section are those specified in whichever of paragraphs (2) to (6) are applicable in his case.

(2) In the case of a person who—

(*a*) expects an advantage to arise in respect of his liability to pay, entitlement to a repayment of, or to a deferment of his liability to pay, income tax or capital gains tax as a result of notifiable arrangements; and

(*b*) is required to make a return to the Board by a notice under section 8 or 8A of the Taxes Management Act 1970 (income tax and capital gains tax: personal return and trustee's return), in respect of income tax or capital gains tax,

the prescribed information shall be included in the return under that section which relates to the year of assessment in which he is notified of the reference number under section 311 or 312 (as the case may be), or in which the advantage is expected to arise if earlier; and (in any case) in the return for each subsequent year of assessment until the advantage ceases to apply to him.

This paragraph does not apply if the advantage arises in respect of a partner's share of partnership profits or gains, and is subject to the qualifications in paragraph (6).

(3) In the case of a partnership—

(*a*) which expects an advantage to arise in respect of a partner's liability to pay, entitlement to a repayment of, or to a deferment of the partner's liability to pay any of the prescribed taxes in respect of partnership profits or gains as a result of notifiable arrangements; and (*b*) in respect of which a return is required to be made to the Board by virtue of a notice under section 12AA of the Taxes Management Act 1970 (partnership return) in respect of any of the prescribed taxes,

the prescribed information shall be included in the returns specified in paragraph (4) covering the period in which the person required to make the return in question is notified of the reference number under section 311 or 312 (as the case may be), or in which the advantage is expected to arise, if earlier; and (in any case) in the return covering each such period until the advantage ceases to apply to the partner in question.

(4) The returns referred to in paragraph (3) are—

(*a*) the partnership's return under section 12AA of the Taxes Management Act 1970, and

(*b*) the return under section 8 or 8A of that Act, or under paragraph 3 of Schedule 18 to the Finance Act 1998, of the partner in respect of whom an advantage is expected.

(5) In the case of a company which—

(*a*) expects a tax advantage to arise in respect of its liability to pay, entitlement to a repayment of, or to a deferment of its liability to pay, corporation tax as a result of notifiable arrangements; and

(*b*) is required to make a return to the Board by a notice under paragraph 3 of Schedule 18 to the Finance Act 1998 (company tax return), in respect of corporation tax,

the prescribed information shall be notified to the Board in the return under that paragraph covering the period in which the company is notified of the reference number under section 311 or 312 (as the case may be), or in which the advantage is expected to arise if earlier; and (in any case) in the return covering each subsequent period until the tax advantage ceases to apply to the company.

This paragraph does not apply if the advantage arises in respect of a partner's share of partnership profits or gains, and is subject to the qualifications in paragraph (6).

(6) In the case of a person who is the employer of an employee, by reason of whose employment a tax advantage is expected to arise to any person in respect of income tax, corporation tax or capital gains tax as a result of notifiable arrangements falling within Part 1 of the Schedule to the Arrangements Regulations, the prescribed information shall be notified to the Board—

(*a*) in the return required under regulation 73 of the Income Tax (Pay As You Earn) Regulations 2003 which relates to the tax year in which—

(i) the employer is notified under section 311 or 312 (as the case may be) of the reference number allocated by the Board under section 311, or

(ii) if earlier in the tax year in which the tax advantage is first expected to arise; and

(*b*) in the return required under that regulation for each subsequent tax year until the tax advantage ceases to apply.

(7) In the case of a person who would be obliged to comply with paragraph (2), (3), (5) or (6), but is not otherwise required, in respect of a year of assessment, accounting period or tax year—

(*a*) in the case of notifiable arrangements to which paragraph (2) applies, to make a return under any of the provisions mentioned in paragraph (2)(*b*),

(*b*) in the case of notifiable arrangements to which paragraph (3) applies, to make a return under any of the provisions referred to in paragraph (4),

(*c*) in the case of notifiable arrangements to which paragraph (5) applies, to make the return mentioned in that paragraph, or

(*d*) in a case to which paragraph (6) applies, to make the return mentioned in that paragraph,

the person must provide the information specified in paragraph (8) to the Board by the appropriate date.

(8) The information specified in this paragraph is—

(*a*) the name and address of the person providing it;

(*b*) any National Insurance number, tax reference number, PAYE reference number or other personal identifier allocated by the Board to the person to whom the information relates;

(*c*) the reference number allocated to the scheme by the Board under section 311;

(*d*) the year of assessment, accounting period or tax year in which, or the date on which, the person providing the information expects to obtain a tax advantage by virtue of the notifiable arrangements;

(*e*) the name of the person providing the declaration as to the accuracy and completeness of the notification;

(*f*) the capacity in which the person mentioned in sub-paragraph (*e*) is acting.

(9) For the purposes of paragraph (7) "the appropriate date" is—

(*a*) in a case falling within sub-paragraph (*a*), 31st January next following the end of the tax year in question;

(*b*) in a case falling within sub-paragraph (*b*), the earliest date by which the person in question could be required to file a return under section 12AA of the Taxes Management Act 1970, determined in accordance with whichever of subsections (4) and (5) of that section applies to him;

(*c*) in a case falling within sub-paragraph (*c*), the date defined as the filing date for the purposes of paragraph 14 of Schedule 18 to the Finance Act 1998 in respect of the period of account in question; and

(*d*) in a case falling within sub-paragraph (*d*), the date by which the return under regulation 73 of the Income Tax (Pay As You Earn) Regulations 2003 would be due in respect of the tax year in question.

(10) References in this regulation to information being included in a return include that information being so included by way of an amendment to the return.

[(11) This regulation does not apply to information provided in respect of the SDLT Arrangement Regulations.][1]

Commentary—*Simon's Taxes* **A7.233**.

Amendments—[1] Para (11) inserted by the Tax Avoidance Schemes (Information) (Amendment) Regulations, SI 2005/1869 regs 2, 6 with effect from 1 August 2005.

However, this amendment does not have effect in respect of proposals or arrangements (as the case may be) which are notifiable by virtue of the Stamp Duty Land Tax Avoidance Schemes (Prescribed Descriptions of Arrangements) Regulations, SI 2005/1868—

(*a*) for the purposes of FA 2004 s 308(1), if the relevant date in relation to a proposal falls before 1 August 2005;

(*b*) for the purposes of FA 2004 s 308(3), if the date on which the promoter first becomes aware of any transaction forming part of the arrangements falls before that date;

(*c*) for the purposes of FA 2004 s 309 or 310, the date on which any transaction forming part of the arrangements is entered into falls before that date: SI 2005/1869 reg 1.

Exemption from liability for penalty

9 For the purposes of section 313(4)(*g*) (exemption from liability to penalty under other provisions about returns in respect of duty to notify Board of reference number for notifiable arrangements) section 98A(4) of the Taxes Management Act 1970 is prescribed.

Electronic delivery of information

10— (1) Information required to be delivered to the Board or to any other person by virtue of these Regulations may be delivered in such form and by such means of electronic communications as are for the time being authorised for that purpose.

(2) The use of a particular means of electronic communications is authorised for the purposes of paragraph (1) only if—

(*a*) it is authorised by directions given by the Board under section 132(5) of the Finance Act 1999 (voluntary filing by electronic means of returns and other documents); and

(*b*) the user complies with any conditions imposed by the Board under that section.

(3) Nothing in this regulation prevents the delivery of information by electronic communications if the information is contained in a return which is—

(*a*) authorised to be delivered electronically by virtue of regulations under section 132 of the Finance Act 1999; or

(*b*) required to be so delivered by virtue of regulations under section 135 of the Finance Act 2002 (mandatory e-filing).

2004/2421

Stamp Duty and Stamp Duty Reserve Tax (Extension of Exceptions relating to Recognised Exchanges) Regulations 2004

Made . . . . *15 September 2004*
Laid before the House of Commons . . . . . . *16 September 2004*
Coming into force . . . . *12 October 2004*

Made by the Treasury under Finance Act 2002 s 117(1)

Citation and commencement

1 These Regulations may be cited as the Stamp Duty and Stamp Duty Reserve Tax (Extension of Exceptions relating to Recognised Exchanges) Regulations 2004 and shall come into force on 12th October 2004.

Extended application of provisions specified in section 117(2) of the Finance Act 2002

2 The application of the provisions specified in section 117(2) of the Finance Act 2002 is extended to the market known as the Alternative Investment Market established under the rules of the London Stock Exchange plc.

2004/3218

Stamp Duty and Stamp Duty Reserve Tax (Investment Exchanges and Clearing Houses) Regulations 2004

Made by the Treasury under FA 1991 ss 116, 117

Made . . . . *8 December 2004*
Laid before the House of Commons . . . . *8 December 2004*
Coming into force . . . . *1 February 2005*

Citation, commencement and effect

1— (1) These regulations may be cited as the Stamp Duty and Stamp Duty Reserve Tax (Investment Exchanges and Clearing Houses) Regulations 2004 and shall come into force on 1st February 2005.

(2) These Regulations have effect—

(*a*) for the purposes of stamp duty, in relation to instruments executed on or after 1st February 2005;

(*b*) for the purposes of stamp duty reserve tax—

(i) in the case of an agreement to transfer equities which is not conditional, where the agreement is made on or after 1st February 2005;

(ii) in the case of an agreement to transfer equities which is conditional, where the condition is satisfied on or after that date.

Interpretation

2 In these Regulations, except where otherwise provided—

"clearing member" means a member of EDX London who is also a member of LCH.Clearnet and who as such is permitted by EDX London and that clearing house to clear futures and options contracts registered by LCH.Clearnet resulting from transactions relating to equities executed on EDX London or reported to it under the rules of EDX London;

"EDX London" means EDX London Limited, a company registered in England and Wales (registered number 4567917) which is a recognised investment exchange under the Financial Services and Markets Act 2000;

"equities" means stocks and shares which are issued or raised by a company but does not include stocks and shares issued or raised by a company not incorporated in the United Kingdom unless—

(*a*) they are registered in a register kept in the United Kingdom by or on behalf of the company; or

(*b*) in the case of shares, they are paired, within the meaning of section 99(6A) of the Finance Act 1986, with shares issued by a company incorporated in the United Kingdom;

"futures contract" means a futures contract or a forward contract conferring rights and obligations to buy or sell equities which is listed by or traded on EDX London or which may be reported to EDX London under the rules of EDX London;

"LCH.Clearnet" means LCH.Clearnet Limited, a company registered in England and Wales (registered number 4743602) which is a recognised clearing house under the Financial Services and Markets Act 2000;

"member" means a member of EDX London;

"non-clearing member" means a member who is not a clearing member;

"option" means an option, to buy or sell securities, which is listed by and traded on EDX London or which may be reported to EDX under the rules of EDX London.

Prescription of recognised investment exchange and recognised clearing house

3 For the purposes of sections 116 and 117 of the Finance Act 1991—

(*a*) EDX London is a prescribed recognised investment exchange;

(*b*) LCH.Clearnet is a prescribed recognised clearing house.

Transfers of securities to LCH.Clearnet — prescribed circumstances

4 No charge to stamp duty or to stamp duty reserve tax arises where, as a result of the exercise of options or the expiration of a futures contract, equities of a particular kind are transferred or issued or agreed to be transferred or issued to—

(*a*) LCH.Clearnet; or

(*b*) a person whose business is or includes holding such securities as a nominee for LCH-.Clearnet.

Here, and in regulation 5, references to LCH.Clearnet are references to that clearing house in its capacity as a person providing clearing services in connection with a transaction made on EDX London or reported to EDX London pursuant to the rules of EDX London.

Transfers of securities to or from members of EDX London — prescribed circumstances

5 No charge to stamp duty or to stamp duty reserve tax arises where, in order to meet an obligation to receive securities resulting from the exercise of options or the expiration of a futures contract, equity securities of a particular kind are transferred or agreed to be transferred from—

(*a*) a non-clearing member or a nominee of a non-clearing member to a clearing member or a nominee of a clearing member; or

(*b*) LCH.Clearnet or a nominee for LCH.Clearnet to a clearing member or a nominee of a clearing member.

Here, references to a clearing member are references to a clearing member in his capacity as such.

2005/83

Finance Act 2003, Section 66 (Prescribed Persons) Order 2005

Made . . . . *20 January 2005*
Laid before the House of Commons . . . . *21 January 2005*
Coming into force . . . . *11 February 2005*

Made by the Treasury under FA 2003 s 66(4)

Citation and commencement

1 This Order may be cited as the Finance Act 2003, Section 66 (Prescribed Persons) Order 2005 and shall come into force on 11th February 2005.

NHS foundation trusts prescribed for purposes of s.66 of Finance Act 2003

2 For the purposes of section 66 of the Finance Act 2003 (stamp duty land tax: public bodies), NHS foundation trusts constituted in accordance with Schedule 1 to the Health and Social Care (Community Health and Standards) Act 2003, are prescribed.

2005/645

Finance Act 2003, Section 66 (Prescribed Transactions) Order 2005

Made . . . . *10 March 2005*
Laid before the House of Commons . . . . *10 March 2005*
Coming into force . . . . *1 April 2005*

Made by the Treasury under Finance Act 2003 s 66(2)

Citation and commencement

1 This Order may be cited as the Finance Act 2003, Section 66 (Prescribed Transactions) Order 2005 and shall come into force on 1st April 2005.

Prescribed transactions

2 Any land transaction is exempt from stamp duty land tax if—

(a) it is effected under section 38 of the Energy Act 2004 (nuclear transfer schemes), and
(b) either the purchaser or the vendor is a public body.

2005/844

Stamp Duty Land Tax (Electronic Communications) Regulations 2005

Made . . . . *21 March 2005*
Laid before the House of Commons . . . . *21 March 2005*
Coming into force . . . . *11 April 2005*

Made by the Commissioners of Inland Revenue under Finance Act 1999 ss 132, 133(2)

PART 1
INTRODUCTION

Citation, commencement and interpretation

1— (1) These Regulations may be cited as the Stamp Duty Land Tax (Electronic Communications) Regulations 2005 and shall come into force on 11th April 2005.

(2) In these Regulations—

["ARTL System" has the meaning given by section 12(1) of the Requirements of Writing (Scotland) Act 1995;][1]

["the Board" means the Commissioners for Her Majesty's Revenue and Customs;][1]

["the Keeper" means the Keeper of the Registers of Scotland;][1]

"land transaction return" means a return complying with the requirements imposed by Part 1 of Schedule 10 to the Finance Act 2003 (stamp duty land tax: land transaction returns) and regulations under that Part; and

"official computer system" means a computer system maintained by or on behalf of the Board—

(*a*) to send or receive information or payments, or
(*b*) to process or store information.

(3) References in these Regulations to information and to the delivery of information shall be construed in accordance with section 132(8) of the Finance Act 1999.

Amendment—[1] Definitions "ARTL System" and "the Keeper" inserted, and definition "the Board" substituted, by the SDLT (Electronic Communications) (Amendment) Regulations, SI 2006/3427 arts 2, 3 with effect from 31 January 2007.

Scope of these Regulations

2— [(1)][1] These Regulations [apply to][1]—

[(*a*) the delivery of a land transaction return to the Board;

(*ab*) the delivery of a land transaction return, by means of the ARTL System, to the Keeper; and][1]

(*b*) the making of any payment or repayment of tax or other sums in connection with the delivery of such a return.

[(2) Part 2 sets out general provisions as to the use of electronic communications in connection with the delivery to the Board of information and payments in relation to stamp duty land tax.

(3) Part 2 does not apply to stamp duty land tax in connection with a land transaction which—

(*a*) falls to be registered in the Land Register of Scotland; and

(*b*) is to be registered by means of the ARTL System.

Instead Part 2A applies to stamp duty land tax, and any land transaction return, in respect of such a land transaction, and in these Regulations—

"an ARTL transaction" means such a land transaction; and

"an ARTL application" means an application for the registration of such a land transaction.

(4) Part 3 contains provisions about evidence in connection with the use of electronic communications in respect of payments of stamp duty land tax and the delivery of land transaction returns.][1]

Amendment—[1] Para (1) numbered as such; words in para (1), and para (1)(*a*), substituted; para (1)(*ab*), and paras (2)–(4) inserted, by the SDLT (Electronic Communications) (Amendment) Regulations, SI 2006/3427 arts 2, 4 with effect from 31 January 2007.

PART 2
ELECTRONIC COMMUNICATIONS—GENERAL PROVISIONS

Restriction on the use of electronic communications

3— (1) The Board may only use electronic communications in connection with the matters referred to in [regulation 2(1)][1] if—

(*a*) the recipient has indicated that he consents to the Board using electronic communications in connection with those matters; and

(*b*) the Board have not been informed that that consent has been withdrawn.

(2) A person other than the Board may only use electronic communications in connection with the matters referred to in [regulation 2(1)][1] if the conditions specified in paragraphs (3) to (6) are satisfied.

(3) The first condition is that the person is for the time being permitted to use electronic communications for the purpose in question by an authorisation given by means of a direction of the Board.

(4) The second condition is that the person uses—

(*a*) an approved method for authenticating the identity of the sender of the communication;

(*b*) an approved method of electronic communications; and

(*c*) an approved method for authenticating any information delivered by means of electronic communications.

(5) The third condition is that any information or payment sent by means of electronic communications is in a form approved for the purpose of these Regulations.

Here "form" includes the manner in which the information is presented.

(6) The fourth condition is that the person maintains such records in written or electronic form as may be specified in a general or specific direction of the Board.

(7) In this regulation "approved" means approved, for the purposes of these Regulations and for the time being, by means of a general or specific direction of the Board.

Note—*Directions under Reg 3 of the SDLT (Electronic Communications) Regulations,* SI 2005/844

Returns under Part 1 of Schedule 10 to the Finance Act 2003

The Commissioners for Her Majesty's Revenue and Customs ("the Commissioners") direct that, on and after 13 July 2005, a person who is required to deliver a land transaction return under Part 1 of Schedule 10 to the Finance Act 2003 ("the relevant information") is authorised to do so over the Internet.

The Commissioners further direct that —

(*a*) the methods approved by them for —

(i) authenticating the identity of the person sending the relevant information,

(ii) delivery of the relevant information, and

(iii) authenticating the relevant information; and

(*b*) the form approved by them in which the relevant information is to be delivered; are the methods and form set out, at the time of, and for the purposes of, the delivery of the relevant information, in the terms and conditions for use of the Stamp Taxes Online Land Transaction Return on the website of Her Majesty's Revenue and Customs (www.hmrc.gov.uk).

Agents acting on behalf of purchasers – returns under Part 1 of Schedule 10 to the Finance Act 2003

The Commissioners for Her Majesty's Revenue and Customs further direct that, on and after 13 July 2005, an agent who delivers information on behalf of a person who is required to deliver the relevant information is authorised to do so over the Internet provided that the following conditions are met.

The first condition is that —

(*a*) the agent makes a copy of the relevant information before it is sent; and

(*b*) the person, who is required to deliver the land transaction return, makes a declaration to the agent, before the return is sent, that either

(i) the relevant information contained is correct to the best of his knowledge and belief, or

(ii) the relevant information, with the exception of the effective date, is correct to the best of his knowledge and belief.

The second condition is that the agent completes the appropriate declaration within the Stamp Taxes Online computer application.

The Commissioners further direct that —

(*a*) the methods approved by them for —

(i) authenticating the identity of the person sending the relevant information,

(ii) delivery of the relevant information, and

(iii) authenticating the relevant information; and

(*b*) the form approved by them in which the relevant information is to be delivered; are the methods and form set out, at the time of, and for the purposes of, the delivery of the relevant information, in the terms and conditions for use of the Stamp Taxes Online Land Transaction Return on the Inland Revenue website (www.hmrc.gov.uk).

Amendment—[1] Words in paras (1), (2) substituted by the SDLT (Electronic Communications) (Amendment) Regulations, SI 2006/3427 arts 2, 5 with effect from 31 January 2007.

Use of intermediaries

4 The Board may use intermediaries in connection with—

(*a*) the delivery of information or the making of payments or repayments by means of electronic communications in connection with the matters referred to in regulation 2(1), and

(*b*) the authentication or security of anything transmitted by such means,

and may require other persons to use intermediaries in connection with those matters.

[PART 2A
ELECTRONIC COMMUNICATIONS AND THE ARTL SYSTEM

Administrative functions of Keeper

4A— (1) The Keeper shall have the following functions in respect of stamp duty land tax—

(*a*) receiving, on behalf of the Board, land transaction returns in respect of ARTL transactions;

(*b*) receiving, on behalf of the Board, payments of any stamp duty land tax in respect of ARTL transactions; and

(*c*) transmitting to the Board those land transaction returns and any payment of stamp duty land tax in respect of the ARTL transactions to which they relate.

(2) The Keeper is the intermediary of the Board in respect of the matters mentioned in sub-paragraphs (*a*) and (*b*) of paragraph (1).][1]

Amendment—[1] Part 2A inserted by the SDLT (Electronic Communications) (Amendment) Regulations, SI 2006/3427 arts 2, 6 with effect from 31 January 2007.

Information to be delivered about compliance with Part 4 of the Finance Act 2003

4B— (1) If a land transaction return is delivered to the Keeper in connection with an ARTL transaction by means of the ARTL system, it must be accompanied by the following information as to compliance—

(*a*) a declaration by the person completing the return ("the responsible person") that the information which it contains has been approved by the purchaser; and

(*b*) a digital signature identifying the responsible person which is included in, or logically associated with, the communication containing the land transaction return.

(2) In this regulation—

"digital signature" means data in electronic form which serves as a method of authentication and which is—

(*a*) uniquely linked to the signatory;

(*b*) capable of identifying the signatory;

(*c*) created using a signature-creation device that the signatory can maintain under the signatory's sole control; and

(*d*) linked to the data to which it relates in such a manner that any subsequent change of data is detectable;

"signature-creation data" means unique data (including, but not limited to, codes or private cryptographic keys) which are used by the signatory to create an electronic signature; and

"signature-creation device" means configured software or hardware used to implement the signature-creation data.][1]

Amendment—[1] Part 2A inserted by the SDLT (Electronic Communications) (Amendment) Regulations, SI 2006/3427 arts 2, 6 with effect from 31 January 2007.

PART 3
ELECTRONIC COMMUNICATIONS—EVIDENTIAL PROVISIONS

Effect of delivering information by means of electronic communications

5— (1) Information to which these Regulations apply, and which is delivered by means of electronic communications, shall be treated as having been delivered, in the manner or form required by Part 4 of the Finance Act 2003 and the Stamp Duty Land Tax (Land Transaction Returns) Regulations 2003 if, but only if, all the conditions imposed by—

(*a*) these Regulations,

Stamp Taxes

(*b*) any other applicable enactment (except to the extent that the condition thereby imposed is incompatible with these Regulations), and

(*c*) any specific or general direction given by the Board,

are satisfied.

(2) Information delivered by means of electronic communications shall be treated as having been delivered on the day on which the last of the conditions imposed as mentioned in paragraph (1) is satisfied.

This is subject to [paragraphs (2A), (3) and (4)][1].

[(2A) Information contained in a land transaction return delivered by electronic communications through the ARTL System to the Keeper in connection with an ARTL application shall be treated as delivered to the Board on the date on which it is delivered to the Keeper.

This is subject to paragraphs (3) and (4).][1]

(3) The Board may by a general or specific direction provide for information to be treated as delivered upon a different date (whether earlier or later) than that given by paragraph (2).

(4) Information shall not be taken to have been delivered to an official computer system [or the ARTL System][1] by means of electronic communications unless it is accepted by the system to which it is delivered.

Amendment—[1] Words in para (2) substituted; para (2A), and words in para (4), inserted; by the SDLT (Electronic Communications) (Amendment) Regulations, SI 2006/3427 arts 2, 7 with effect from 31 January 2007.

Proof of content

6— (1) A document certified by an officer of the Board to be a printed-out version of any information delivered by means of electronic communications under these Regulations on any occasion shall be evidence, unless the contrary is proved, that that information—

(*a*) was delivered by means of electronic communications on that occasion; and

(*b*) constitutes the entirety of what was delivered on that occasion.

[This paragraph does not apply to information delivered by means of electronic communications to the Keeper through the ARTL System.][1]

[(1A) A document certified by the Keeper to be a printed-out version of any information delivered by means of electronic communications through the ARTL System in connection with stamp duty land tax on any occasion shall be evidence, unless the contrary is proved that that information—

(*a*) was delivered by means of electronic communications on that occasion; and

(*b*) constitutes the entirety of what was delivered in that connection on that occasion.][1]

(2) A document purporting to be a certificate given in accordance with paragraph (1) [or (1A)][1] shall be presumed to be such a certificate unless the contrary is proved.

Amendment—[1] Words in para (1), para (1A), and words in para (2), inserted by the Stamp Duty Land Tax (Electronic Communications) (Amendment) Regulations, SI 2006/3427 arts 2, 8 with effect from 31 January 2007.

Proof of sender or recipient

7— [(1)][1] The identity of—

(*a*) the sender of any information delivered to an official computer system by means of electronic communications under these Regulations, or

(*b*) the recipient of any information delivered by means of electronic communications from an official computer system,

shall be presumed, unless the contrary is proved, to be the person recorded as such on an official computer system.

[This paragraph does not apply to information delivered by means of electronic communications to the Keeper through the ARTL System.][1]

[(2) The sender of any information delivered to the Keeper through the ARTL System in connection with stamp duty land tax shall be presumed, unless the contrary is proved, to be the person recorded as such on that system.][1]

Amendment—[1] Para (1) numbered as such, words at end of para (1), and para (2), inserted, by the SDLT (Electronic Communications) (Amendment) Regulations, SI 2006/3427 arts 2, 9 with effect from 31 January 2007.

Information delivered electronically on another's behalf

8 Any information delivered by an approved method of electronic communications on behalf of any person shall be deemed to have been delivered by him unless he proves that it was delivered without his knowledge or connivance.

Proof of delivery of information and payments

9— (1) The use of an authorised method of electronic communications shall be presumed, unless the contrary is proved, to have resulted in the making of a payment or the delivery of information—

(*a*) in the case of information falling to be delivered, or a payment falling to be made, to the Board, if the making of the payment or the delivery of the information has been recorded on an official computer system; and

(*b*) in the case of information falling to be delivered, or a payment falling to be made, by the Board, if the despatch of that payment or information has been recorded on an official computer system.

(2) The use of an authorised method of electronic communications shall be presumed, unless the contrary is proved, not to have resulted in the making of a payment, or the delivery of information—

(*a*) in the case of information falling to be delivered, or a payment falling to be made, to the Board, if the making of the payment or the delivery of the information has not been recorded on an official computer system; and

(*b*) in the case of information falling to be delivered, or a payment falling to be made, by the Board, if the despatch of that payment or information has not been recorded on an official computer system.

(3) The time of receipt of any information or payment sent by an authorised means of electronic communications shall be presumed, unless the contrary is proved, to be that recorded on an official computer system.

[(4) Nothing in this regulation applies to information or a payment delivered by means of electronic communications to the Keeper through the ARTL System in connection with stamp duty land tax.][1]

Amendment—[1] Para (4) inserted by the SDLT (Electronic Communications) (Amendment) Regulations, SI 2006/3427 arts 2, 10 with effect from 31 January 2007.

Use of unauthorised means of electronic communications

10— (1) Paragraph (2) applies to information which is required to be delivered to the Board in connection with the matters mentioned in regulation 2.

(2) The use of a means of electronic communications, for the purpose of delivering any information to which this paragraph applies, shall be conclusively presumed not to have resulted in the delivery of that information, unless—

(*a*) that means of electronic communications is for the time being approved for delivery of information of that kind; and

(*b*) the sender is approved for the use of that means of electronic communications in relation to information of that kind.

2005/1868
Stamp Duty Land Tax Avoidance Schemes (Prescribed Descriptions of Arrangements) Regulations 2005

Made . . . . *11 July 2005*
Laid before the House of Commons . . . . *11 July 2005*
Coming into force . . . . *1 August 2005*

Made by the Treasury under Finance Act 2004 ss 306(1)(a), (b) and 318

Citation, commencement and interpretation

1— (1) These Regulations may be cited as the Stamp Duty Land Tax Avoidance Schemes (Prescribed Descriptions of Arrangements) Regulations 2005 and shall come into force on 1st August 2005.

(2) In these Regulations—

"chargeable interests" has the meaning given by section 48 of the Finance Act 2003;

"residential" and "non-residential property" have the meanings given in section 116 of the Finance Act 2003; and

a reference (without more) to a numbered section is a reference to the section of the Finance Act 2004 which is so numbered.

(3) For the purposes of these Regulations, section 839 of the Income and Corporation Taxes Act 1988 applies to determine whether persons are connected.

Prescribed description of arrangements in relation to stamp duty land tax

2— (1) For the purposes of Part 7 (disclosure of tax avoidance schemes) the arrangements specified in paragraph (3) are prescribed in relation to stamp duty land tax.

(2) In this regulation—

"the applicable value" means the aggregate market value of all of the chargeable interests in non-residential property subject to the arrangements;

"the Commissioners" means the Commissioners for Her Majesty's Revenue and Customs (see section 1 of the Commissioners for Revenue and Customs Act 2005); and

"market value" shall be construed in accordance with section 118 of the Finance Act 2003, and for the purposes of ascertaining that value, all chargeable interests held by the same person or connected persons shall be taken into account.

(3) The arrangements are those—

(*a*) whose subject matter does not consist wholly of residential property;

(*b*) in respect of which the applicable value is at least £5,000,000 at the time any requirement to notify would (but for this sub-paragraph) arise under section 308, 309 or 310 (as the case may be), and

(*c*) are not excluded by virtue of the provisions of the Schedule to these Regulations.

(4) If a promoter does not know whether proposals will result in arrangements, the subject matter of which will consist at least in part of non-residential property, it shall be assumed, for the purposes of these Regulations, that the subject matter of any resulting arrangements will so consist.

(5) If a promoter makes a notifiable proposal available generally, it shall be assumed that the applicable value is £5,000,000 or more.

(6) In any case where—

(*a*) a promoter makes available a proposal for arrangements in circumstances where he knows the identity of at least one of the persons who it is proposed should be a party to the arrangements;

(*b*) a promoter becomes aware of a transaction entered into in pursuance of arrangements of the kind described in sub-paragraph (*a*); or

(*c*) a person becomes a party to any transaction forming part of notifiable arrangements; and liable to comply with—

(i) section 309 (duty of person dealing with promoter outside the United Kingdom); or

(ii)section 310 (duty of parties to notifiable arrangements not involving promoter);

if the person under a duty to provide the Commissioners with prescribed information does not know the applicable value, it shall be assumed to be at least £5,000,000.

SCHEDULE

Regulation 2(3)(c)

Excluded Arrangements

Arrangements are excluded from being prescribed arrangements for the purposes of these Regulations if they—

(*a*) comprise one or more of steps A to F listed below (subject to Rules 1 and 2 which specify arrangements involving combinations of those steps which are not excluded arrangements); but

(*b*) do not include any step, which is necessary for the purpose of securing a tax advantage, other than one listed below.

Rule 1

Arrangements involving Steps B, D, E and F are excluded arrangements unless rule 2 applies.

Rule 2

Arrangements are not excluded arrangements if they—

(*a*) include all, or at least two of, steps A, C and D; or

(*b*) involve more than one instance of step A, C or D.

The steps are as follows.

Step A: Acquisition of a chargeable interest by special purpose vehicle

The acquisition of a chargeable interest in land by a company created for that purpose ("a special purpose vehicle").

Step B: Claims to relief

Making—

(*a*) a single claim to relief under any of the following provisions of the Finance Act 2003—

(i) section 57A (sale and leaseback arrangements);

(ii) section 60 (compulsory purchase facilitating development);

(iii) section 61 (compliance with planning obligation);

(iv) section 64 (demutualisation of building society);

(v) section 64A (initial transfer of assets to trustees of unit trust scheme);

(vi) section 65 (incorporation of limited liability partnership);

(vii) section 66 (transfers involving public bodies);

(viii) section 67 (transfer in consequence of reorganisation of parliamentary constituencies);

(ix) section 69 (acquisition by bodies established for national purposes);

(x) section 71 (certain acquisitions by registered social landlords);

(xi) section 74 (collective enfranchisement by leaseholders);

(xii) section 75 (crofting community right to buy);

(xiii) Schedule 6 (disadvantaged areas relief);

(xiv) Schedule 6A (relief for certain acquisitions of residential property);

(xv) Schedule 7 (group relief and reconstruction acquisition reliefs);

(xvi) Schedule 8 (charities relief); or
(xvii) Schedule 9 (right to buy, shared ownership leases etc.);

(*b*) one or more claims to relief under any one of the following provisions of the Finance Act 2003—

(i) section 71A (alternative property finance: land sold to financial institution and leased to individual);
(ii) section 72 (alternative property finance in Scotland: land sold to financial institution and leased to individual);
(iii) section 72A (alternative property finance in Scotland: land sold to financial institution and individual in common); or
(iv) section 73 (alternative property finance: land sold to financial institution and resold to individual).

Step C: Sale of shares in special purpose vehicle

The sale of shares in a special purpose vehicle, which holds a chargeable interest in land, to a person with whom neither the special purpose vehicle, nor the vendor, is connected.

Step D: Not exercising election to waive exemption from VAT

No election is made to waive exemption from value added tax contained in paragraph 2 of Schedule 10 to the Value Added Tax Act 1994 (treatment of buildings and land for value added tax purposes).

Step E: Transfer of a business as a going concern

Arranging the transfer of a business, connected with the land which is the subject of the arrangements, in such a way that it is treated for the purposes of value added tax as the transfer of a going concern.

Step F: Undertaking a joint venture

The creation of a partnership (within the meaning of paragraph 1 of Schedule 15 to the Finance Act 2003) to which the property which subject to a land transaction is to be transferred.

2005/1990
Stamp Duty and Stamp Duty Reserve Tax (Extension of Exceptions relating to Recognised Exchanges) Regulations 2005

Made . . . . *20 July 2005*
Laid before the House of Commons . . . . *21 July 2005*
Coming into force . . . . *11 August 2005*

The Treasury, in exercise of the powers conferred upon them by section 50(1) and (4) of the Finance (No.2) Act 2005, make the following Regulations;

Citation and commencement

1 These Regulations may be cited as the Stamp Duty and Stamp Duty Reserve Tax (Extension of Exceptions relating to Recognised Exchanges) Regulations 2005 and shall come into force on 11th August 2005.

Extended application of provisions specified in section 50(2) of the Finance (No 2) Act 2005

2 The application of the provisions specified in section 50(2) of the Finance (No 2) Act 2005 ("the relevant provisions") is extended to the following markets, which are multilateral trading facilities (or, assuming compliance with the provisions of Title II of the Directive (authorisation and operating conditions), would be such facilities), namely—

(*a*) the market known as AIM established under the rules of London Stock Exchange plc;
(*b*) the market known as OFEX;
(*c*) the market known as POSIT and operated by Investment Technology Group Limited. The markets specified in sub-paragraphs (*a*) to (*c*) are referred to in these Regulations as "prescribed multilateral trading facilities".

Application of the relevant provisions to prescribed multilateral trading facilities

3 (1) In their application to prescribed multilateral trading facilities, the relevant provisions as adapted as follows.

(2) In the following provisions of these Regulations a reference to a numbered section is a reference to the section of the Finance Act 1986 bearing that number.

Adaptation of section 80A

4 (1) Section 80A (stamp duty—exceptions for sales to intermediaries) is adapted as follows.

(2) In subsection (1)—

(*a*) in paragraph (*a*) for "an EEA exchange, or a recognised foreign exchange," substitute "a prescribed multilateral trading facility"; and
(*b*) in paragraphs (*b*) and (*c*) for "the exchange" substitute "the facility".

(3) In subsection (2)—

Stamp Taxes

(*a*) in paragraph (*a*) for "an EEA exchange, or a recognised foreign options exchange," substitute "a prescribed multilateral trading facility";
(*b*) in paragraph (*b*) for "that exchange" substitute "that facility" (in both places);
(*c*) in paragraph (*c*) for "that exchange" substitute "that facility"; and
(*d*) in paragraph (*d*)—
(i) for "exchange, or a" substitute "exchange, a"; and
(ii) after "foreign exchange" insert "or a prescribed multilateral trading facility".

(4) In subsection (3)—
(*a*) in paragraph (*a*) for "an EEA exchange, or a recognised foreign options exchange," substitute "a prescribed multilateral trading facility"; and
(*b*) in paragraph (*b*) for "that exchange" substitute "that facility" (in both places).

(5) In subsection (6)—
(*a*) in the words before paragraph (*a*) for "an exchange" substitute "a prescribed multilateral trading facility"; and
(*b*) in paragraphs (*a*) and (*b*) for "the exchange" (in each place) substitute "the facility".

(6) At the end of the section add—
"(8) In this section 'prescribed multilateral trading facility' has the meaning given by regulation 2 of the Stamp Duty and Stamp Duty Reserve Tax (Extension of Exceptions relating to Recognised Exchanges) Regulations 2005 (SI 2005/1990).".

Adaptation of section 80C

5 (1) Section 80C (stamp duty—exceptions for repurchases and stock lending) is adapted as follows.

(2) In subsection (3)—
(*a*) in paragraph (*a*) for "an EEA exchange or a recognised foreign exchange" substitute "a prescribed multilateral trading facility";
(*b*) in paragraph (*b*) for "that exchange" substitute "that facility".

(3) In subsection (6)—
(*a*) in the words before paragraph (*a*) for "an exchange" substitute "a prescribed multilateral trading facility"; and
(*b*) in paragraphs (*a*) and (*b*) for "the exchange" (in each place) substitute "the facility".

(4) For subsection (7) substitute—
"(7) In this section 'prescribed multilateral trading facility' has the meaning given by regulation 2 of the Stamp Duty and Stamp Duty Reserve Tax (Extension of Exceptions relating to Recognised Exchanges) Regulations 2005.".

Adaptation of section 88A

6 (1) Section 88A (stamp duty reserve tax—exceptions from the principal charge for transactions involving intermediaries) is adapted as follows.

(2) In subsection (1)—
(*a*) in paragraph (*a*) for "an EEA exchange, or a recognised foreign exchange" substitute "a prescribed multilateral trading facility";
(*b*) in paragraphs (*b*) and (*c*) for "the exchange" (in each place) substitute "the facility".

(3) In subsection (2)—
(*a*) in paragraph (*a*) for "an EEA exchange or a recognised foreign options exchange" substitute "a prescribed multilateral trading facility";
(*b*) in paragraphs (*b*) and (*c*) for "that exchange" (in each place) substitute "that facility";
(*c*) in paragraph (*d*)—
(i) for "exchange, or a" substitute "exchange, a"; and
(ii) after "foreign exchange" insert ", or a prescribed multilateral trading facility".

(4) In subsection (3)—
(*a*) in paragraph (*a*) for "an EEA exchange, or a recognised foreign options exchange" substitute "a prescribed multilateral trading facility"
(*b*) in paragraph (*b*) for "that exchange" (in each place) substitute "that facility".

(5) In subsection (6)—
(*a*) in the words preceding paragraph (*a*) for "an exchange" substitute "a facility"; and
(*b*) in paragraphs (*a*) and (*b*) (in each place) for "the exchange" substitute "the facility".

(6) At the end of the section add—
"(7) In this section 'prescribed multilateral trading facility' has the meaning given by regulation 2 of the Stamp Duty and Stamp Duty Reserve Tax (Extension of Exceptions relating to Recognised Exchanges) Regulations 2005.".

Adaptation of section 89AA

7 (1) Section 89AA (stamp duty reserve tax—exceptions from the principal charge for transactions involving repurchase and stock lending) is adapted as follows.

(2) In subsection (3)—

(*a*) in paragraph (*a*)for "on an EEA exchange or a recognised foreign exchange" substitute "a prescribed multilateral trading facility"; and

(*b*) in paragraph (*b*) for "that exchange" substitute "that facility".

(3) In subsection (5)—

(*a*) in the words preceding paragraph (*a*) for "an exchange" substitute "a facility"; and

(*b*) in paragraphs (*a*) and (*b*) for "the exchange" (in each place) substitute "the facility".

(4) For subsection (6) substitute—

"(6) In this section 'prescribed multilateral trading facility' has the meaning given by regulation 2 of the Stamp Duty and Stamp Duty Reserve Tax (Extension of Exceptions relating to Recognised Exchanges) Regulations 2005.".

2006/139
Stamp Duty and Stamp Duty Reserve Tax (Extension of Exceptions relating to Recognised Exchanges) Regulations 2006

Made by the Treasury under F(No 2)A 2005 s 50(1), (4)

Made . . . . 25 January 2006
Laid before the House of Commons . . . . . 26 January 2006
Coming into force . . . . 16 February 2006

Commentary—*Sergeant and Sims on Stamp Duties* **A16.3.**

Citation and commencement

1 These Regulations may be cited as the Stamp Duty and Stamp Duty Reserve Tax (Extension of Exceptions relating to Recognised Exchanges) Regulations 2006 and shall come into force on 16th February 2006.

Extended application of provisions specified in section 50(2) of the Finance (No 2) Act 2005

2— (1) The application of the provisions specified in section 50(2) of the Finance (No 2) Act 2005 ("the relevant provisions") is extended to the following market, which is a multilateral trading facility (or, assuming compliance with the provisions of Title II of the Directive (authorisation and operating conditions), would be such a facility), namely the market known as [Instinet Chi-X and operated by Instinet Chi-X Limited][1].

(2) Regulations 3 to 7 of the Stamp Duty Reserve Tax (Extension of Exceptions relating to Recognised Exchanges) Regulations 2005 apply to the market mentioned in paragraph (1) as they apply to the multilateral trading facilities listed in paragraphs (*a*) to (*c*) of regulation 2 of those Regulations.

Amendments—[1] Words in para (1) substituted by the Stamp Duty and Stamp Duty Reserve Tax (Extension of Exceptions relating to Recognised Exchanges) (Amendment) Regulations, SI 2007/458 reg 2 with effect from 13 March 2007.

2006/3237
Stamp Duty Land Tax (Variation of the Finance Act 2003) Regulations 2006

Made . . . . 11.00 am on 6th December 2006
Laid before the House of Commons . . 2.00 pm on 6th December 2006
Coming into force . . . . 2.00 pm on 6th December 2006

The Treasury consider it expedient in the public interest to make the provision made by these Regulations.

Accordingly, the Treasury, in exercise of the power conferred upon them by section 109 of the Finance Act 2003, make the following Regulations.

1 Citation and commencement

These Regulations may be cited as The Stamp Duty Land Tax (Variation of the Finance Act 2003) Regulations 2006 and shall come into force at 2 pm on 6th December 2006.

2 Variation of the Finance Act 2003

(1) Part 4 of the Finance Act 2003 is varied—

(*a*) in its application to land transactions which are scheme transactions, within the meaning of the new section 75A set out in paragraph 1 of the Schedule to these Regulations, in accordance with that paragraph (which inserts new section 75A and provides for the charge in respect of those transactions to be computed by reference to a notional land transaction), and

(*b*) in its application to land transactions involving a partnership, in accordance with paragraph 2 of the Schedule to these Regulations.

(2) In these Regulations—

(*a*) expressions which are used in Part 4 of the Finance Act 2003 have the same meaning in the Schedule as in that Part; and

(*b*) "the relevant time" means 2 pm on 6th December 2006.

SCHEDULE

AMENDMENT OF PART 4 OF THE FINANCE ACT 2003

Regulation 2

Stamp Duty Land Tax: anti-avoidance

1— (1) After section 75 of the Finance Act 2003 (stamp duty land tax: crofting) insert—

"75A Anti-avoidance

(1) This section applies where—

(*a*) one person (V) disposes of a chargeable interest and another person (P) acquires either it or a chargeable interest deriving from it,

(*b*) a number of transactions are involved in connection with the disposal and acquisition ("the scheme transactions"), and

(*c*) the sum of the amounts of stamp duty land tax payable in respect of the scheme transactions is less than would be payable on a notional land transaction effecting the acquisition of V's chargeable interest by P on its disposal by V.

(2) In subsection (1) "transaction" includes in particular—

(*a*) a non-land transaction,

(*b*) an agreement, offer or undertaking not to take specified action,

(*c*) any kind of arrangement whether or not it could otherwise be described as a transaction, and

(*d*) a transaction which takes place after the acquisition by P of the chargeable interest.

(3) The scheme transactions may include, for example—

(*a*) the acquisition by P of a lease deriving from a freehold owned or formerly owned by V;

(*b*) a sub-sale to a third person;

(*c*) the grant of a lease to a third person subject to a right to terminate;

(*d*) the exercise of a right to terminate a lease or to take some other action;

(*e*) an agreement not to exercise a right to terminate a lease of to take some other action;

(*f*) the variation of a right to terminate a lease or to take some other action,

(4) Where this section applies—

(*a*) any of the scheme transactions which is a land transaction shall be disregarded for the purposes of this Part, but

(*b*) there shall be a notional land transaction for the purposes of this Part effecting the acquisition of V's chargeable interest by P on its disposal by V.

(5) The chargeable consideration on the notional land transaction mentioned in subsections (1)(*c*) and (4)(*b*) is the largest amount (or aggregate amount) given or received by or on behalf of any one person in respect of the scheme transactions.

(6) The effective date of the notional land transaction is—

(*a*) the last date of completion for the scheme transactions, or

(*b*) if earlier, the date on which a contract in respect of the scheme transactions is substantially performed.

(7) The notional transaction attracts any relief under this Part which it would attract if it were an actual transaction.

(8) This section does not apply where subsection (1)(*c*) is satisfied only by reason of—

(*a*) sections 71A to 73, or

(*b*) a provision of Schedule 9.

(9) For the purposes of this section an interest in a partnership is a chargeable interest in so far as it concerns land owned by the partnership.".

(2) This paragraph has effect in respect of disposals and acquisitions if—

(*a*) the disposal mentioned in the new section 75A(1)(*a*) (inserted by sub-paragraph (1) above) takes place after the relevant time, and

(*b*) all the scheme transactions (within the meaning of the new section 75A(1)(*b*)) take place after that time.

(3) This paragraph does not have effect in relation to—

(*a*) any scheme transaction which is effected in pursuance of a contract entered into and substantially performed before the relevant time.

(*b*) any other scheme transaction which is effected in pursuance of a contract entered into before the relevant time and which is not an excluded transaction.

(4) For this purpose, a scheme transaction effected in pursuance of a contract is an excluded transaction if—

(*a*) at or after the relevant time the contract is varied in a way that significantly affects the scheme transaction (see sub-paragraph (5)),

(*b*) the subject-matter of the scheme transaction is not identified in the contract in a way that would have enabled its acquisition before the relevant time,

(*c*) rights under the contract are assigned at or after the relevant time,
(*d*) the scheme transaction is effected in consequence of the exercise, at or after the relevant time, of any option, right of pre-emption or similar right, or
(*e*) at or after the relevant time there is an assignment, sub-sale or other transaction (relating to the whole or part of the contract's subject-matter) as a result of which a person other than the purchaser under the contract becomes entitled to call for a conveyance to him.

(5) For the purposes of sub-paragraph (4)(*a*) the contract is varied in a way that significantly affects the scheme transaction if (and only if)—

(*a*) it is varied so as to substitute a different purchaser in relation to the scheme transaction,
(*b*) it is varied so as to alter the subject-matter of the scheme transaction, or
(*c*) it is varied so as to alter the consideration for the scheme transaction.

Stamp Duty Land Tax: partnerships

2— (1) Schedule 15 to the Finance Act 2003 (stamp duty land tax: partnerships) is amended as follows.

(2) In Step Two of paragraph 12(1) (transfer to partnership: how to calculate the "sum of the lower proportions")—

(*a*) in paragraph (*b*) for "or is connected with the relevant owner" substitute "or is an individual connected with the relevant owner", and
(*b*) at the end add—
"(If there is no relevant owner with a corresponding partner, the sum of the lower proportions is nil.)".

(3) Omit paragraph 13 (transfer of partnership where all partners are companies).

(4) In paragraph 14 (transfer of interest in property-investment partnership)—

(*a*) for sub-paragraph (1)(*b*) substitute—
"(*b*) either—
(i) the transferee is a person, other than an individual, connected with the transferor, or
(ii) consideration is given for the transfer,",
(*b*) at the end add—
"(9) An interest in respect of the transfer to which this paragraph applies shall be treated as a chargeable interest for the purposes of paragraph 3(1) of Schedule 7 to the extent that the relevant partnership property consists of a chargeable interest.", and
(*c*) in the italic cross-heading omit "for consideration".

(5) In Step Two of paragraph 20(1) (transfer from partnership: how to calculate the "sum of the lower proportions")—

(*a*) in paragraph (*b*) for "or was connected with the relevant owner" substitute "or was an individual connected with the relevant owner", and
(*b*) at the end add—
"(If there is no relevant owner with a corresponding partner, the sum of the lower proportions is nil.)".

(6) After paragraph 27 (application of group relief) insert—

"**27A**— (1) This paragraph applies where in calculating the sum of the lower proportions in relation to a transaction (in accordance with paragraph 12)—

(*a*) a company ("the connected company") would have been a corresponding partner of a relevant owner ("the original owner") but for the fact that paragraph (*b*) of Step Two includes connected persons only if they are individuals, and
(*b*) the connected company and the original owner are members of the same group.

(2) The charge in respect of the transaction shall be reduced to the amount that would have been payable had the connected company been a corresponding partner of the original owner for the purposes of calculating the sum of the lower proportions.

(3) The provisions of Part 1 of Schedule 7 apply to group relief under sub-paragraph (2) above as to group relief under paragraph 1(1) of Schedule 7 but—

(*a*) with the omission of paragraph 2(2)(*a*),
(*b*) with the substitution for "the purchaser" in paragraph 3(1)(*a*) of "a partner who was, at the effective date of the transaction, a partner and a member of the same group as the transferor ("the relevant partner"); and
(*c*) with the other modifications specified in paragraph 27(3) to (6) above.".

(7) This paragraph has effect in relation to any land transaction of which the effective date is, or is after, 6th December 2006 (but see sub-paragraph (8)).

(8) This paragraph does not have effect in relation to—

(*a*) any land transaction which is effected in pursuance of a contract entered into and substantially performed before the relevant time, or
(*b*) any other land transaction which is effected in pursuance of a contract entered into before the relevant time and which is not an excluded transaction.

(9) For this purpose, a land transaction effected in pursuance of a contract is an excluded transaction if—

(*a*) at or after the relevant time the contract is varied in a way that significantly affects the land transaction (see sub-paragraph (10)),

(*b*) the subject-matter of the land transaction is not identified in the contract in a way that would have enabled its acquisition before the relevant time,

(*c*) rights under the contract are assigned at or after the relevant time,

(*d*) the land transaction is effected in consequence of the exercise, at or after the relevant time, of any option, right of pre-emption or similar right, or

(*e*) at or after the relevant time there is an assignment, sub-sale or other transaction (relating to the whole or part of the contract's subject-matter) as a result of which a person other than the purchaser under the contract becomes entitled to call for a conveyance to him.

(10) For the purposes of sub-section (9)(*a*) the contract is varied in a way that significantly affects the land transaction if (and only if)—

(*a*) it is varied so as to substitute a different purchaser in relation to the land transaction,

(*b*) it is varied so as to alter the subject-matter of the land transaction, or

(*c*) it is varied so as to alter the consideration for the land transaction.

2007/1097

Stamp Duty and Stamp Duty Reserve Tax (Investment Exchanges and Clearing Houses) (Eurex Clearing AG) Regulations 2007

Made by the Treasury under FA 1991 ss 116 and 117

Made . . . . *29th March 2007*
Laid before the House of Commons . . . . *30th March 2007*
Coming into force . . . . *23rd April 2007*

1 Citation, commencement and effect

(1) These Regulations may be cited as the Stamp Duty and Stamp Duty Reserve Tax (Investment Exchanges and Clearing Houses) (Eurex Clearing AG) Regulations 2007 and shall come into force on 23rd April 2007.

(2) These Regulations shall have effect—

(*a*) for the purposes of the charge to stamp duty, in relation to instruments executed on or after 23rd April 2007;

(*b*) for the purposes of the charge to stamp duty reserve tax—

(i) in the case of agreements to transfer equities which are not conditional, in relation to agreements made on or after 23rd April 2007;

(ii) in the case of agreements to transfer equities which are conditional, in relation to agreements where the condition is satisfied on or after that date.

2 Interpretation

(1) In these Regulations—

"clearing member" means—

(*a*) a member of Eurex Clearing AG who—

(i) is also a member of the Eurex exchange (as defined by this regulation); and

(ii) is permitted by that exchange and that clearing house to clear options contracts; or

(*b*) a member of Eurex Clearing AG who—

(i) is not a member of the Eurex exchange; and

(ii) is permitted by that clearing house to clear options contracts on behalf of [a non-clearing member][1] (as defined by this regulation),

in his capacity as such a member;

"equities" means stocks and shares which are issued or raised by a company but does not include stocks and shares issued or raised by a company not incorporated in the United Kingdom unless—

(*a*) they are registered in a register kept in the United Kingdom by or on behalf of the company; or

(*b*) in the case of shares, they are paired, within the meaning of section 99(6A) of the Finance Act 1986, with shares issued by a company incorporated in the United Kingdom;

"Eurex Clearing AG" means Eurex Clearing Aktiengesellschaft, a company registered in Germany which is a recognised clearing house under the Financial Services and Markets Act 2000 …[1];

"the Eurex exchange" means either one of the investment exchanges known as Eurex Deutschland and Eurex Zurich;

["non-clearing member" means a member of the Eurex exchange who is not a clearing member, in his capacity as such or in his capacity as a person who is a party to a transaction with a clearing member which is otherwise permitted to be cleared by the rules of Eurex Clearing AG;][1]

"option" means an option, to buy or sell equities, which—

(*a*) is listed by and traded on the Eurex exchange (as defined by this regulation); or

(*b*) is otherwise permitted to be cleared by the rules of Eurex Clearing AG.

Amendments—[1] Words in definition of "clearing member" substituted, words in definition of "Eurex Clearing AG" revoked, and definition of "non-clearing member" inserted, by the Stamp Duty and Stamp Duty Reserve Tax (Investment Exchanges and Clearing Houses) (Eurex Clearing AG) (Amendment) Regulations, SI 2008/164 regs 3, 4 with effect as follows—

– for the purposes of the charge to stamp duty, in relation to instruments executed on or after 19 February 2008;

– for the purposes of the charge to stamp duty reserve tax—

(i) in the case of agreements to transfer equities which are not conditional, in relation to agreements made on or after 19 February 2008;

(ii) in the case of agreements to transfer equities which are conditional, in relation to agreements where the condition is satisfied on or after 19 January 2008.

[3 Prescription of recognised investment exchanges and recognised clearing house

For the purposes of sections 116 and 117 of the Finance Act 1991—

(*a*) Eurex Deutschland is prescribed as a recognised investment exchange;

(*b*) Eurex Zurich is prescribed as a recognised investment exchange; and

(*c*) Eurex Clearing AG is prescribed as a recognised clearing house.][1]

Amendments—[1] Regulation 3 substituted by the Stamp Duty and Stamp Duty Reserve Tax (Investment Exchanges and Clearing Houses) (Eurex Clearing AG) (Amendment) Regulations, SI 2008/164 regs 3, 5 with effect as follows—

– for the purposes of the charge to stamp duty, in relation to instruments executed on or after 19 February 2008;

– for the purposes of the charge to stamp duty reserve tax—

(i) in the case of agreements to transfer equities which are not conditional, in relation to agreements made on or after 19 February 2008;

(ii) in the case of agreements to transfer equities which are conditional, in relation to agreements where the condition is satisfied on or after 19 January 2008.

4 Transfers of securities to Eurex Clearing AG—prescribed circumstances

A charge to stamp duty or to stamp duty reserve tax shall be treated as not arising where, as a result of the exercise of an option, equities are transferred or issued, or agreed to be transferred or issued, to—

(*a*) Eurex Clearing AG, or

(*b*) a person whose business is or includes holding such equities as a nominee for Eurex Clearing AG.

[Here, and in regulation 5, references to Eurex Clearing AG are references to that clearing house in its capacity as a person providing clearing services in connection with a transaction made on the Eurex exchange or otherwise permitted to be cleared by the rules of that clearing house.][1]

Amendments—[1] Words inserted by the Stamp Duty and Stamp Duty Reserve Tax (Investment Exchanges and Clearing Houses) (Eurex Clearing AG) (Amendment) Regulations, SI 2008/164 regs 3, 6 with effect as follows—

– for the purposes of the charge to stamp duty, in relation to instruments executed on or after 19 February 2008;

– for the purposes of the charge to stamp duty reserve tax—

(i) in the case of agreements to transfer equities which are not conditional, in relation to agreements made on or after 19 February 2008;

(ii) in the case of agreements to transfer equities which are conditional, in relation to agreements where the condition is satisfied on or after 19 January 2008.

5 Transfers of securities from Eurex Clearing AG [or a non-clearing member][1]—prescribed circumstances

A charge to stamp duty or to stamp duty reserve tax shall be treated as not arising where, in order to meet an obligation to receive equities resulting from the exercise of an option, equities are transferred, or agreed to be transferred, from—

(*a*) Eurex Clearing AG, …[1]

(*b*) a person whose business is or includes holding such equities as a nominee for Eurex Clearing AG,

(*c*) a non-clearing member, or

(*d*) a person whose business is or includes holding such equities as a nominee for a non-clearing member,][1]

to a clearing member or a nominee of a clearing member.

Amendments—[1] Word "or" in para (*a*) revoked, paras (*c*), (*d*), and words in heading, inserted, by the Stamp Duty and Stamp Duty Reserve Tax (Investment Exchanges and Clearing Houses) (Eurex Clearing AG) (Amendment) Regulations, SI 2008/164 regs 3, 7 with effect as follows—

– for the purposes of the charge to stamp duty, in relation to instruments executed on or after 19 February 2008;

– for the purposes of the charge to stamp duty reserve tax—

(i) in the case of agreements to transfer equities which are not conditional, in relation to agreements made on or after 19 February 2008;

(ii) in the case of agreements to transfer equities which are conditional, in relation to agreements where the condition is satisfied on or after 19 January 2008.

2007/1385
Finance Act 2003, Section 66 (Prescribed Statutory Provisions) Order 2007

Made by the Treasury under FA 2003 s 66(2)

Made . . . . *2nd May 2007*
Laid before the House of Commons . . . . *3rd May 2007*
Coming into force . . . . *25th May 2007*

1 Citation and commencement

This Order may be cited as the Finance Act 2003, Section 66 (Prescribed Statutory Provisions) Order 2007 and shall come into force on 25th May 2007.

2 Prescribed Statutory Provisions

A land transaction that is not entered into as mentioned in section 66(1) of the Finance Act 2003 is exempt from charge to stamp duty land tax if—

(*a*) the transaction is effected—

(i) under paragraph A23(2), 4(2), 5(4B) or 8(2)(*b*) of Schedule 22 to the School Standards and Framework Act 1998 (transfer of land to local education authority), or

(ii) by a transfer required by virtue of regulations made under section 27(2)(*b*) of the Education and Inspections Act 2006 (transfer of land on removal of foundation or reduction in foundation governors), and

(*b*) either the purchaser or the vendor is a public body.

2007/3437
Stamp Duty Land Tax (Zero-Carbon Homes Relief) Regulations 2007

Made by the Treasury under FA 2003 ss 58B and 58C and approved by a resolution of the House of Commons under FA 2003 s 114(5)

Made . . . . *6 December 2007*
Coming into force . . . . *7 December 2007*

1 Citation, commencement and effect

(1) These Regulations may be cited as the Stamp Duty Land Tax (Zero-Carbon Homes Relief) Regulations 2007 and shall come into force on the day after the day on which they are made.

(2) These Regulations shall have effect in relation to acquisitions—

(*a*) made on or after 1st October 2007, and
(*b*) before 1st October 2012.

2 Interpretation

In these Regulations—

"accredited assessor" means—

(*a*) in England or Wales, either—

(i) a person who is a member of an accreditation scheme approved by the Secretary of State in relation to newly erected dwellings for the purposes of regulation 17F (1) to (3) of the Building Regulations 2000, or

(ii) where no accreditation scheme as described in paragraph (i) has yet been approved, a person who is authorised to issue ratings calculated by the Government's Standard Assessment Procedure for Energy Rating of Dwellings ("the SAP") by the holder of a licence granted by the Department for Environment, Food and Rural Affairs to certify that the ratings assessed under the SAP have been issued by a body authorised by the Secretary of State;

(*b*) in Scotland, the Scottish Ministers or a person who is approved by the Scottish Ministers to issue certificates for the purposes of these Regulations; and

(*c*) in Northern Ireland, a person who is a member of an accreditation scheme approved by the Department of Finance and Personnel or the Department for Social Development for the purpose of assessing the energy performance of dwellings by reference to the approved methodology;

"the approved methodology" means—

(*a*) the methodology for the calculation of the energy performance of buildings approved by the Secretary of State for the purposes of regulation 17A of the Building Regulations 2000; and

(*b*) any further methodology for the calculation of energy performance of buildings approved by the Secretary of State under regulation 7;

"zero-carbon home" has the meaning given in regulation 5; and

"zero-carbon home certificate" means a certificate issued under regulation 6(1).

3 Scope of Regulations

These Regulations apply to a land transaction which is the first acquisition of a dwelling which is a zero-carbon home.

4 Relief

(1) Relief from charge to stamp duty land tax shall be granted in relation to a land transaction to which these Regulations apply as follows.

This is subject to paragraph (5).

(2) Where the chargeable consideration is not more than £500,000 and does not consist of or include rent, the transaction is exempt from charge.

(3) Where the chargeable consideration includes rent and consideration other than rent and the consideration other than rent is not more than £500,000, no tax shall be chargeable in respect of the consideration other than rent.

(4) Where the chargeable consideration does not include rent and is more than £500,000, or the consideration other than rent is more than £500,000, the amount of tax chargeable shall be reduced by £15,000.

(5) Her Majesty's Revenue and Customs may refuse relief if they have reasonable grounds to think that a dwelling is not a zero-carbon home within the meaning of these Regulations, notwithstanding that a zero-carbon home certificate has been issued in relation to that dwelling.

5 Zero-Carbon Home

(1) "Zero-carbon home" means a dwelling that is energy efficient in relation to the aspects of energy efficiency in column 1 of the table.

(2) The evidence to be adduced to show that a dwelling satisfies each relevant aspect of energy efficiency is set out in column 2 of the table.

(3) Whether the requirements in column 2 are met shall be determined by an assessment of the dwelling by an accredited assessor.

1 Aspects of energy efficiency	*2 Evidence*
Heat loss parameter ("HLP").	The HLP of the dwelling calculated in accordance with the approved methodology must be no more than 0.8 Watts per square metre Kelvin (W/m^2K).
Dwelling CO_2 emission rate ("DER").	The DER over the course of a year calculated in accordance with the approved methodology must be no more than zero kilograms per square metre (kg/m^2/year).
Net CO_2 emissions.	The net CO_2 emissions from the dwelling over the course of a year calculated in accordance with the approved methodology must be no more than zero kilograms per square metre (kg/m^2/year).

(4) In this regulation—

"dwelling CO_2 emission rate" means the annual CO_2 emissions per unit floor area for space heating, water heating, ventilation and lighting, less the emissions saved by energy generation technologies in or on the dwelling;

"heat loss parameter" means the heat loss per unit of temperature difference per unit floor area determined by the internal dimensions of surfaces bounding the dwelling, the thermal performance of the materials used in construction and the air permeability of the dwelling envelope;

"net CO_2 emissions" means—

(*a*) the annual CO_2 emissions per unit floor area for space heating, water heating, ventilation and lighting, and those associated with appliances and cooking, less

(*b*) the emissions saved by the use of energy generation technologies in or on the dwelling and additional allowable electricity.

(5) For the purposes of the definition of "net CO_2 emissions"—

"allowable electricity" means electricity generated from a zero-carbon energy source designed to serve the dwelling and which is conveyed to the dwelling, or to a sub-station connected directly to the dwelling, by cables used exclusively for the conveyance of electricity from that source;

"zero-carbon energy source" includes wind, photovoltaic and hydro-electric power.

6 Certification

(1) If the dwelling satisfies the definition of zero-carbon home the accredited assessor who carried out the assessment in accordance with regulation 5(3) shall issue a zero-carbon home certificate.

[(1A) The accredited assessor may charge a reasonable fee in respect of the assessment of the dwelling in accordance with regulation 5(3) and production of a zero-carbon home certificate.][1]

(2) A zero-carbon home certificate must state—

(*a*) in relation to the dwelling—

(i) the address ...[1], including postcode,

(ii) that the dwelling is a zero-carbon home within the meaning of these Regulations, and

(iii) in relation to dwellings in England and Wales only, the unique identifying number from the energy performance certificate if an energy performance certificate has been produced;

(*b*) in relation to the accredited assessor issuing the certificate—

(i) the accredited assessor's full name,

(ii) the name and address of the accredited assessor's employer, or if he is self-employed, the name under which he trades and his address, and

(iii) in relation to dwellings in England and Wales only, the accreditation scheme, if any, to which the accredited assessor belongs;

(*c*) the date on which it was issued.

(3) Within the relevant time, the vendor shall

(*a*) obtain a zero-carbon home certificate from an accredited assessor, and

(*b*) give that certificate to the purchaser.

(4) In this regulation—

"energy performance certificate" has the meaning given in regulation 2 of the Energy Performance of Buildings (Certificates and Inspections) (England and Wales) Regulations 2007;

"relevant time" means—

(*a*) in respect of a first acquisition of a zero-carbon home occurring after the coming into force of these Regulations on or before the acquisition, ...[1]

(*b*) in respect of a first acquisition of a zero-carbon home occurring before the coming into force of these Regulations but to which these Regulations apply, as soon as practicable following the coming into force of these Regulations[, and

(*c*) in respect of a first acquisition of a zero-carbon home, which is part of a building constructed for use as a single dwelling, occurring before 13 August 2008, as soon as practicable following that date.][1]

Amendments—[1] Para (1A) inserted, in para (2)(*a*)(i) words "of the building" revoked, in para (4), in the definition of "relevant time", in para (*a*) word "and" revoked and para (*c*) and preceding word "and" inserted, by the Stamp Duty Land Tax (Zero-Carbon Homes Relief) (Amendment) Regulations, SI 2008/1932 reg 2 with effect as follows—
– the insertion of para (1A), and amendment to para (2)(*a*)(i), from 13 August 2008; and
– the amendments to para (4), in relation to acquisitions made on or after 1 October 2007 and before 1 October 2012.

7 Approval of methodology

The Secretary of State may approve a methodology for the calculation of the energy performance of dwellings for the purposes of these Regulations.

8 Claiming Relief

Any relief under these Regulations must be claimed in a land transaction return or an amendment of such a return.

9 Linked transactions including the first acquisition of a zero-carbon home

Where the first acquisition of one or more zero-carbon homes is one of a number of linked transactions—

(*a*) section 55(4) of the Finance Act 2003 shall not apply to that acquisition for the purpose of these Regulations; but

(*b*) that acquisition shall continue to form part of the set of transactions for other purposes.

2008/52

Stamp Duty Reserve Tax (Investment Exchanges and Clearing Houses) (The London Stock Exchange) Regulations 2008

Made by the Treasury under FA 1991 ss 116(3) and (4) and 117

Made . . . . 14 *January* 2008
Laid before the House of Commons . . . . 14 *January* 2008
Coming into force . . . . 4 *February* 2008

1 Citation, commencement and effect

(1) These Regulations may be cited as the Stamp Duty Reserve Tax (Investment Exchanges and Clearing Houses) (The London Stock Exchange) Regulations 2008 and shall come into force on 4th February 2008.

(2) These Regulations shall have effect—

(*a*) in the case of agreements to transfer equities which are not conditional, in relation to agreements made on or after 4th February 2008;

(*b*) in the case of agreements to transfer equities which are conditional, in relation to agreements where the condition is satisfied on or after that date.

2 Interpretation

(1) In these Regulations—

"Board of directors" means the Board of directors of London Stock Exchange plc;

"clearing participant" means a member (as defined by this regulation) who is also a member of x-clear and who as such is permitted by the Board of directors and that clearing house to clear transactions made on the Exchange for a traded security;

"client" means a person who gives instructions to a participant for equity securities to be purchased or, as the case may be, sold on the Exchange;

"equity securities" means stocks and shares which are issued or raised by a company but does not include stocks and shares issued by a company not incorporated in the United Kingdom unless—

(*a*) they are registered in a register kept in the United Kingdom by or on behalf of the company; or

(*b*) in the case of shares, they are paired, within the meaning of section 99(6A) of the Finance Act 1986, with shares issued by a company incorporated in the United Kingdom;

"the Exchange" means the London Stock Exchange;

"member" in relation to London Stock Exchange plc means a person approved by the Board of directors as a participant;

"nominee" means a person whose business is or includes holding equity securities as a nominee for x-clear acting in its capacity as a person providing clearing services in connection with a transaction made on the Exchange, or as a nominee for a clearing participant (as the case may be);

"non-clearing participant" means a participant other than a clearing participant;

"participant" means a participant in the Exchange;

"section 117" means section 117 of the Finance Act 1991;

"x-clear" means SIS x-clear *Aktiengesellschaft*, a company registered in Switzerland which is a recognised clearing house under the Financial Services and Markets Act 2000.

3 Prescription of recognised clearing house

For the purposes of section 117 x-clear is a recognised clearing house which is prescribed.

4 Prescribed circumstances for the purposes of section 117

(1) In the circumstances prescribed by paragraph (2) below, a charge to stamp duty reserve tax shall be treated as not arising.

(2) The circumstances prescribed are where, in connection with a transaction made on the Exchange—

(*a*) equity securities of a particular kind are agreed to be transferred from—

(i) a clearing participant or a nominee of a clearing participant to another clearing participant or nominee, or

(ii) a non-clearing participant or a client to a clearing participant or a nominee of a clearing participant, or

(iii) a clearing participant or a nominee of a clearing participant to x-clear or to a nominee of that clearing house, or

(iv) a person other than a clearing participant to x-clear or to a nominee of that clearing house, as a result of a failure by a clearing participant to fulfil his obligations in respect of the transaction concerned to transfer equity securities to x-clear or to a nominee of that clearing house, or

(v) The London Clearing House Limited or a nominee of that clearing house to x-clear or a nominee of that clearing house, or

(vi) x-clear or a nominee of that clearing house to The London Clearing House Limited or a nominee of that clearing house, or

(vii) x-clear or a nominee of that clearing house to a clearing participant or a nominee of a clearing participant; and

(*b*) the person to whom those securities are agreed to be transferred under any of the agreements specified in sub-paragraph (*a*) above ("the relevant agreement") is required on receipt of those shares to transfer equity securities under a matching agreement to another person or, in the case of an agreement falling within paragraph (iv) of that sub-paragraph, would have been so required if the failure referred to in that paragraph had not occurred.

(3) In paragraph (2) above—

(*a*) "matching agreement" means an agreement under which—

(i) the equity securities agreed to be transferred are of the same kind as the equity securities agreed to be transferred under the relevant agreement, and

Stamp Taxes

(ii) the number and transfer price of the equity securities agreed to be transferred are identical to the number and transfer price of the equity securities agreed to be transferred under the relevant agreement;

(*b*) references to x-clear and to The London Clearing House Limited are references to those clearing houses in their capacity as persons providing clearing services in connection with a transaction made on the Exchange;

(*c*) references to a clearing participant are references to a clearing participant in his capacity as such.

5 Consequential provision

(1) Equity securities which are the subject of an agreement specified in regulation 4(2)(*a*) shall be dealt with by a clearing participant who is a party to the agreement in a separate designated account, and not otherwise.

(2) In paragraph (1) above "designated account" means an account designated by x-clear for a clearing participant in connection with the equity securities concerned.

2008/710
Stamp Duty Land Tax (Open-ended Investment Companies) Regulations 2008

Made by the Treasury under FA 2003 ss 102 and 123(2), (3)

Made . . . . *12 March 2008*
Laid before the House of Commons . . . . *12 March 2008*
Coming into force . . . . *6 April 2008*

1 Citation and commencement

These Regulations may be cited as the Stamp Duty Land Tax (Open-ended Investment Companies) Regulations 2008 and shall come into force on 6th April 2008.

2 Interpretation

In these Regulations—

"authorised unit trust" means a unit trust scheme in the case of which an order under section 243 of the Financial Services and Markets Act 2000 is in force;
"land transaction" has the meaning given by section 43(1) of the Finance Act 2003; and
"land transaction return" has the meaning given by section 76(1) of that Act.

3 Conversion of an authorised unit trust to an open-ended investment company—exemption from stamp duty land tax charge

(1) A land transaction transferring any property which is subject to the trusts of an authorised unit trust ("the target trust") to an open-ended investment company ("the acquiring company") is exempt from charge to stamp duty land tax if the conditions set out in paragraph (2) are fulfilled.

(2) Those conditions are that—

(*a*) the transfer forms part of an arrangement for the conversion of an authorised unit trust to an open-ended investment company, whereby the whole of the available property of the target trust becomes the whole of the property of the acquiring company;

(*b*) under the arrangement all the units in the target trust are extinguished;

(*c*) the consideration under the arrangement consists of or includes the issue of shares ("the consideration shares") in the acquiring company to the persons who held the extinguished units;

(*d*) the consideration shares are issued to those persons in proportion to their holdings of the extinguished units; and

(*e*) the consideration under the arrangement does not include anything else, other than the assumption or discharge by the acquiring company of liabilities of the trustees of the target trust.

(3) Relief under this regulation must be claimed in a land transaction return or an amendment of such a return.

(4) In this regulation and in regulation 4 "the whole of the available property of the target trust" means the whole of the property subject to the trusts of the target trust, other than any property which is retained for the purpose of discharging liabilities of the trustees of the target trust.

(5) For the purposes of this regulation and regulation 4, each of the parts of an umbrella scheme (and not the scheme as a whole) shall be regarded as an authorised unit trust, and "umbrella scheme" has the same meaning as in section 468 of the Income and Corporation Taxes Act 1988.

4 Amalgamation of an authorised unit trust with an open-ended investment company—exemption from stamp duty land tax charge

(1) A land transaction transferring any property which is subject to the trusts of an authorised unit trust ("the target trust") to an open-ended investment company ("the acquiring company") is exempt from charge to stamp duty land tax if the conditions set out in paragraph (2) are fulfilled.

(2) Those conditions are that—

(*a*) the transfer forms part of an arrangement for the amalgamation of an authorised unit trust with an open-ended investment company, whereby the whole of the available property of the target trust becomes part (but not the whole) of the property of the acquiring company;

(*b*) under the arrangement all the units in the target trust are extinguished;

(*c*) the consideration under the arrangement consists of or includes the issue of shares ("the consideration shares") in the acquiring company to the persons who held the extinguished units;

(*d*) the consideration shares are issued to those persons in proportion to their holdings of the extinguished units; and

(*e*) the consideration under the arrangement does not include anything else, other than the assumption or discharge by the acquiring company of liabilities of the trustees of the target trust.

(3) Relief under this regulation must be claimed in a land transaction return or an amendment of such a return.

2008/1814

Stamp Duty and Stamp Duty Reserve Tax (Investment Exchanges and Clearing Houses) (European Central Counterparty Limited and the Turquoise Multilateral Trading Facility) Regulations 2008

Made by the Treasury under FA 1991 ss 116, 117

Made . . . . 8 *July 2008*
Laid before the House of Commons . . . . 9 *July 2008*
Coming into force . . . . 30 *July 2008*

1 Citation, commencement and effect

(1) These Regulations may be cited as the Stamp Duty and Stamp Duty Reserve Tax (Investment Exchanges and Clearing Houses) (European Central Counterparty Limited and the Turquoise Multilateral Trading Facility) Regulations 2008 and shall come into force on 30th July 2008.

(2) These Regulations shall have effect—

(*a*) for the purposes of the charge to stamp duty, in relation to instruments executed on or after 30th July 2008;

(*b*) for the purposes of the charge to stamp duty reserve tax—

(i) in the case of agreements to transfer traded securities which are not conditional, in relation to agreements made on or after 30th July 2008;

(ii) in the case of agreements to transfer traded securities which are conditional, in relation to agreements where the condition is satisfied on or after that date.

2 Interpretation

(1) In these Regulations—

"clearing participant" means a member of EuroCCP who as such is permitted by the Rules of EuroCCP to clear transactions made on the Facility for a traded security and who may or may not also be a participant in the Facility;

"client" means a person who gives instructions to a non-clearing firm for traded securities to be sold on the Facility;

"EuroCCP" means European Central Counterparty Limited, a company which is a recognised clearing house under the Financial Services and Markets Act 2000;

"the Facility" means the multilateral trading facility operated by Turquoise Services Limited, a company which is permitted to operate a multilateral trading facility for the purposes of Part IV of the Financial Services and Markets Act 2000;

"nominee" means a person whose business is or includes holding traded securities as a nominee for EuroCCP acting in its capacity as a person providing clearing services in connection with a transaction made on the Facility, or as a nominee for a clearing participant (as the case may be);

"non-clearing firm" means a participant in the Facility other than a clearing participant;

"traded securities" means stocks and shares which are issued or raised by a company but does not include stocks and shares issued by a company not incorporated in the United Kingdom unless—

(*a*) they are registered in a register kept in the United Kingdom by or on behalf of the company; or

(b) in the case of shares, they are paired, within the meaning of section 99(6A) of the Finance Act 1986, with shares issued by a company incorporated in the United Kingdom.

3 Prescription of recognised clearing house

For the purposes of sections 116 and 117 of the Finance Act 1991—

(a) Turquoise Multilateral Trading Facility ("the Facility") is prescribed as a recognised investment exchange; and

(b) EuroCCP is prescribed as a recognised clearing house.

4 Prescribed circumstances for the purposes of sections 116 and 117

(1) In the circumstances prescribed by paragraph (2) below, a charge to stamp duty or stamp duty reserve tax shall be treated as not arising.

(2) The circumstances prescribed are where, in connection with a transaction made on the Facility—

(a) traded securities of a particular kind are transferred, or agreed to be transferred, from—

(i) a clearing participant or a nominee of a clearing participant to another clearing participant or nominee, or

(ii) a non-clearing firm or its client to a clearing participant or a nominee of a clearing participant, or

(iii) a clearing participant or a nominee of a clearing participant to EuroCCP or to a nominee of that clearing house, or

(iv) a person other than a clearing participant to EuroCCP or to a nominee of that clearing house, as a result of a failure by a clearing participant to fulfil his obligations in respect of the transaction concerned to transfer traded securities to EuroCCP or to a nominee of that clearing house, or

(v) EuroCCP or a nominee of that clearing house to a clearing participant or a nominee of a clearing participant; and

(b) the person to whom those securities are agreed to be transferred under any of the agreements specified in sub-paragraph (a) above ("the relevant agreement") is required on receipt of those securities to transfer traded securities under a matching agreement to another person or, in the case of an agreement falling within paragraph (iv) of that sub-paragraph, would have been so required if the failure referred to in that paragraph had not occurred.

(3) In paragraph (2) above—

(a) "matching agreement" means an agreement under which—

(i) the traded securities agreed to be transferred are of the same kind as the traded securities agreed to be transferred under the relevant agreement, and

(ii) the number and transfer price of the traded securities agreed to be transferred are identical to the number and transfer price of the traded securities agreed to be transferred under the relevant agreement;

(b) references to EuroCCP are references to that clearing houses in its capacity as a person providing clearing services in connection with a transaction made on the Facility;

(c) references to a clearing participant are references to a clearing participant in his capacity as such.

5 Consequential provision

(1) Traded securities which are the subject of an agreement specified in regulation 4(2)(a) shall be dealt with by a clearing participant who is a party to the agreement in a separate designated account, and not otherwise.

(2) In paragraph (1) above "designated account" means an account designated by EuroCCP for a clearing participant in connection with the traded securities concerned.

2008/2339
Stamp Duty Land Tax (Exemption of Certain Acquisitions of Residential Property) Regulations 2008

Made by the Treasury under FA 2003 Sch 3 para 5

Made . . . . *2 September 2008*
Laid before the House of Commons . . . . *2 September 2008*
Coming into force . . . . *3 September 2008*

Amendments—These regulations revoked by FA 2009 s 10(2) with effect in relation to transactions with an effective date on or after 22 April 2009.

1 Citation, commencement and effect

(1) These Regulations may be cited as the Stamp Duty Land Tax (Exemption of Certain Acquisitions of Residential Property) Regulations 2008 and shall come into force on 3rd September 2008.

(2) These Regulations shall have effect in relation to transactions with an effective date—

(*a*) *on or after 3rd September 2008, and*
(*b*) *before 3rd September 2009.*

2 Interpretation

In these Regulations expressions which are used in Part 4 of the Finance Act 2003 have the same meaning as in that Part.

3 Exemption for acquisitions of residential property at not more than £175,000

(1) A land transaction is exempt from the charge to stamp duty land tax if—

(*a*) *it is a relevant acquisition of land which consists entirely of residential property, and*
(*b*) *the relevant chargeable consideration for the transaction is not more than £175,000.*

(2) In paragraph (1)(a) a "relevant acquisition of land" means an acquisition of a major interest in land other than—

(*a*) *the grant of a lease for a term of less than 21 years, or*
(*b*) *the assignment of a lease which has less than 21 years to run.*

(3) In paragraph (1)(b) the "relevant chargeable consideration for the transaction" means—

(*a*) *the chargeable consideration for the transaction, or*
(*b*) *where the transaction is one of a number of linked transactions, the total of the chargeable consideration for all those transactions.*

2008/2777

Stamp Duty and Stamp Duty Reserve Tax (Investment Exchanges and Clearing Houses) Regulations 2008

Made by the Treasury under FA 1991 ss 116, 117

Made	*22 October 2008*
Laid before the House of Commons	*23 October 2008*
Coming into force	*13 November 2008*

1 Citation and commencement

(1) These Regulations may be cited as the Stamp Duty and Stamp Duty Reserve Tax (Investment Exchanges and Clearing Houses) Regulations 2008 and shall come into force on 13th November 2008.

(2) These Regulations shall have effect—

(*a*) for the purposes of the charge to stamp duty, in relation to instruments executed on or after 13th November 2008;
(*b*) for the purposes of the charge to stamp duty reserve tax—
(i) in the case of agreements to transfer traded securities which are not conditional, in relation to agreements made on or after 13th November 2008;
(ii) in the case of agreements to transfer traded securities which are conditional, in relation to agreements where the condition is satisfied on or after that date.

2 Interpretation

(1) In these Regulations—

"clearing participant" means a member of LCH Clearnet Limited who as such is permitted by the Rules of LCH Clearnet Limited to clear transactions made on the Facility for a traded security and who may or may not also be a participant in the Facility;

"client" means a person who gives instructions to a non-clearing firm for traded securities to be sold on the Facility;

"LCH Clearnet Limited" is a company which is a recognised clearing house under the Financial Services and Markets Act 2000;

"Equiduct Trading" is the electronic trading system used by Borse Berlin AG;

"the Facility" means Equiduct Trading operated by Borse Berlin AG, a business which is permitted to operate a trading facility under Article 36 of the Directive;

"nominee" means a person whose business is or includes holding trading securities as a nominee for LCH Clearnet Limited acting in its capacity as a person providing clearing services in connection with a transaction made on the Facility, or as a nominee for a clearing participant (as the case may be);

"non-clearing firm" means a participant in the Facility other than a clearing participant;

"traded securities" means stocks and shares which are issued or raised by a company but does not include stocks and shares issued by a company not incorporated in the United Kingdom unless—

(*a*) the stocks and shares are registered in a register kept in the United Kingdom by or on behalf of the company; or
(*b*) in the case of shares, they are paired, within the meaning of section 99(6A) of the Finance Act 1986, with shares issued by a company incorporated in the United Kingdom.

Stamp Taxes

3 Prescription of recognised investment exchanges and recognised clearing houses

For the purpose of sections 116 and 117 of the Finance Act 1991—

(*a*) Borse Berlin AG is prescribed as a recognised investment exchange; and
(*b*) LCH Clearnet Limited is prescribed as a recognised clearing house.

4 Prescribed circumstances for the purposes of sections 116 and 117

(1) In the circumstances prescribed in this regulation, a charge to stamp duty or stamp duty reserve tax shall be treated as not arising.

(2) The circumstances prescribed are where, in connection with a transaction made on the Facility conditions A and B are met.

(3) Condition A is that traded securities of a particular kind are transferred, or agreed to be transferred, from—

(*a*) a clearing participant or a nominee of a clearing participant to another clearing participant or nominee,
(*b*) a non-clearing firm or its client to a clearing participant or a nominee of a clearing participant,
(*c*) a clearing participant or a nominee of a clearing participant to LCH Clearnet Limited or to a nominee of that clearing house,
(*d*) a person other than a clearing participant to LCH Clearnet Limited or to a nominee of that clearing house, as a result of a failure by a clearing participant to fulfil his obligations in respect of the transaction concerned to transfer traded securities to LCH Clearnet Limited or to a nominee of that clearing house, or
(*e*) LCH Clearnet Limited or a nominee of that clearing house to a clearing participant or a nominee of a clearing participant.

(4) Condition B is that the person to whom those securities are agreed to be transferred under any of the agreements specified in paragraph (3) ("the relevant agreement") is required on receipt of those securities to transfer traded securities under a matching agreement to another person or, in the case of an agreement falling within paragraph (3)(*d*), would have been so required if the failure referred to in that paragraph had not occurred.

(5) In paragraph (4)—

(*a*) a "matching agreement" means an agreement under which—
(i) the traded securities agreed to be transferred are of the same kind as the traded securities agreed to be transferred under the relevant agreement, and
(ii) the number and transfer price of the traded securities agreed to be transferred are identical to the number and transfer price of the traded securities agreed to be transferred under the relevant agreement;
(*b*) references to LCH Clearnet Limited are references to that clearing house in its capacity as a person providing clearing services in connection with a transaction made on the Facility;
(*c*) references to a clearing participant are references to a clearing participant in his capacity as such.

5 Consequential provision

(1) Traded securities which are the subject of an agreement specified in regulation 4(3) shall be dealt with by a clearing participant who is party to the agreement in a separate designated account, and not otherwise.

(2) In paragraph (1) "designated account" means an account designated by LCH Clearnet Limited for a clearing participant in connection with the traded securities concerned.

2008/3235

Stamp Duty and Stamp Duty Reserve Tax (Investment Exchanges and Clearing Houses) Regulations (No 2) 2008

Made by the Treasury under FA 1991 ss 116 and 117

Made . . . . *16 December 2008*
Laid before the House of Commons . . . . . *17 December 2008*
Coming into force . . . . *7 January 2009*

1 Citation and commencement

(1) These Regulations may be cited as the Stamp Duty and Stamp Duty Reserve Tax (Investment Exchanges and Clearing Houses) Regulations (No 2) 2008 and shall come into force on 7th January 2009.

(2) These Regulations shall have effect—

(*a*) for the purposes of the charge to stamp duty, in relation to instruments executed on or after 7th January 2009;
(*b*) for the purposes of the charge to stamp duty reserve tax—

(i) in the case of agreements to transfer traded securities which are not conditional, in relation to agreements made on or after 7th January 2009;

(ii) in the case of agreements to transfer traded securities which are conditional, in relation to agreements where the condition is satisfied on or after that date.

2 Interpretation

(1) In these Regulations—

"clearing participant" means a member of LCH Clearnet Limited who as such is permitted by the Rules of LCH Clearnet Limited to clear transactions made on the Facility for a traded security and who may or may not also be a participant in the Facility;

"client" means a person who gives instructions to a non-clearing firm for traded securities to be sold on the Facility;

"LCH Clearnet Limited" is a company which is a recognised clearing house under the Financial Services and Markets Act 2000;

"the Facility" means the investment exchange operated by PLUS Markets plc, a company which is permitted to operate as an investment exchange under the Financial Services and Markets Act 2000;

"nominee" means a person whose business is or includes holding trading securities as a nominee for LCH Clearnet Limited acting in its capacity as a person providing clearing services in connection with a transaction made on the Facility, or as a nominee for a clearing participant (as the case may be);

"non-clearing firm" means a participant in the Facility other than a clearing participant;

"traded securities" means stocks and shares which are issued or raised by a company but does not include stocks and shares issued by a company not incorporated in the United Kingdom unless—

(*a*) the stocks and shares are registered in a register kept in the United Kingdom by or on behalf of the company; or

(*b*) in the case of shares, they are paired, within the meaning of section 99(6A) of the Finance Act 1986, with shares issued by a company incorporated in the United Kingdom.

3 Prescription of recognised investment exchanges and recognised clearing houses

For the purpose of sections 116 and 117 of the Finance Act 1991—

(*a*) PLUS Markets plc is prescribed as a recognised investment exchange; and

(*b*) LCH Clearnet Limited is prescribed as a recognised clearing house.

4 Prescribed circumstances for the purposes of sections 116 and 117

(1) In the circumstances prescribed in this regulation, a charge to stamp duty or stamp duty reserve tax shall be treated as not arising.

(2) The circumstances prescribed are where, in connection with a transaction made on the Facility conditions A and B are met.

(3) Condition A is that traded securities of a particular kind are transferred, or agreed to be transferred, from—

(*a*) a clearing participant or a nominee of a clearing participant to another clearing participant or nominee,

(*b*) a non-clearing firm or its client to a clearing participant or a nominee of a clearing participant,

(*c*) a clearing participant or a nominee of a clearing participant to LCH Clearnet Limited or to a nominee of that clearing house,

(*d*) a person other than a clearing participant to LCH Clearnet Limited or to a nominee of that clearing house, as a result of a failure by a clearing participant to fulfil his obligations in respect of the transaction concerned to transfer traded securities to LCH Clearnet Limited or to a nominee of that clearing house, or

(*e*) LCH Clearnet Limited or a nominee of that clearing house to a clearing participant or a nominee of a clearing participant.

(4) Condition B is that the person to whom those securities are agreed to be transferred under any of the agreements specified in paragraph (3) ("the relevant agreement") is required on receipt of those securities to transfer traded securities under a matching agreement to another person or, in the case of an agreement falling within paragraph (3)(*d*), would have been so required if the failure referred to in that paragraph had not occurred.

(5) In paragraph (4)—

(*a*) a "matching agreement" means an agreement under which—

(i) the traded securities agreed to be transferred are of the same kind as the traded securities agreed to be transferred under the relevant agreement, and

(ii) the number and transfer price of the traded securities agreed to be transferred are identical to the number and transfer price of the traded securities agreed to be transferred under the relevant agreement;

(*b*) references to LCH Clearnet Limited are references to that clearing house in its capacity as a person providing clearing services in connection with a transaction made on the Facility;

(*c*) references to a clearing participant are references to a clearing participant in his capacity as such.

5 Consequential provision

(1) Traded securities which are the subject of an agreement specified in regulation 4(3) shall be dealt with by a clearing participant who is party to the agreement in a separate designated account, and not otherwise.

(2) In paragraph (1) "designated account" means an account designated by LCH Clearnet Limited for a clearing participant in connection with the traded securities concerned.

2009/35
Stamp Duty and Stamp Duty Reserve Tax (Investment Exchanges and Clearing Houses) Regulations 2009

Made by the Treasury under FA 1991 ss 116, 117

Made . . . . *15 January 2009*
Laid before the House of Commons . . . . *16 January 2009*
Coming into force . . . . *9 February 2009*

1 Citation and commencement

(1) These Regulations may be cited as the Stamp Duty and Stamp Duty Reserve Tax (Investment Exchanges and Clearing Houses) Regulations 2009 and shall come into force on 9th February 2009.

(2) These Regulations shall have effect—

(*a*) for the purposes of the charge to stamp duty, in relation to instruments executed on or after 9th February 2009;

(*b*) for the purposes of the charge to stamp duty reserve tax—

(i) in the case of agreements to transfer traded securities which are not conditional, in relation to agreements made on or after 9th February 2009;

(ii) in the case of agreements to transfer traded securities which are conditional, in relation to agreements where the condition is satisfied on or after that date.

2 Interpretation

(1) In these Regulations—

"clearing participant" means a member of X-Clear who as such is permitted by the Rules of X-CLEAR to clear transactions made on the Facility for a traded security and who may or may not also be a participant in the Facility;

"client" means a person who gives instructions to a non-clearing firm for traded securities to be sold on the Facility;

"X-Clear" means SIX X-Clear AG, a company which is a recognised clearing house under the Financial Services and Markets Act 2000;

"the Facility" means the multilateral trading facility Euro Millennium, operated by NYFIX International Limited, a company which is authorised to operate a multilateral trading facility for the purposes of Part IV of the Financial Services and Markets Act 2000;

"nominee" means a person whose business is or includes holding trading securities as a nominee for X-CLEAR acting in its capacity as a person providing clearing services in connection with a transaction made on the Facility, or as a nominee for a clearing participant (as the case may be);

"non-clearing firm" means a participant in the Facility other than a clearing participant;

"traded securities" means stocks and shares which are issued or raised by a company but does not include stocks and shares issued by a company not incorporated in the United Kingdom unless—

(*a*) the stocks and shares are registered in a register kept in the United Kingdom by or on behalf of the company; or

(*b*) in the case of shares, they are paired, within the meaning of section 99(6A) of the Finance Act 1986, with shares issued by a company incorporated in the United Kingdom.

3 Prescription of recognised investment exchanges and recognised clearing houses

For the purpose of sections 116 and 117 of the Finance Act 1991—

(*a*) Euro Millennium Multilateral Trading Facility ("the Facility") is prescribed as a recognised investment exchange; and

(*b*) SIX X-CLEAR AG is prescribed as a recognised clearing house.

4 Prescribed circumstances for the purposes of sections 116 and 117

(1) In the circumstances prescribed in this regulation, a charge to stamp duty or stamp duty reserve tax shall be treated as not arising.

(2) The circumstances prescribed are where, in connection with a transaction made on the Facility conditions A and B are met.

(3) Condition A is that traded securities of a particular kind are transferred, or agreed to be transferred, from—

(*a*) a clearing participant or a nominee of a clearing participant to another clearing participant or nominee,

(*b*) a non-clearing firm or its client to a clearing participant or a nominee of a clearing participant,

(*c*) a clearing participant or a nominee of a clearing participant to X-CLEAR or to a nominee of that clearing house,

(*d*) a person other than a clearing participant to X-CLEAR or to a nominee of that clearing house, as a result of a failure by a clearing participant to fulfil his obligations in respect of the transaction concerned to transfer traded securities to X-CLEAR or to a nominee of that clearing house, or

(*e*) X-CLEAR or a nominee of that clearing house to a clearing participant or a nominee of a clearing participant.

(4) Condition B is that the person to whom those securities are agreed to be transferred under any of the agreements specified in paragraph (3) ("the relevant agreement") is required on receipt of those securities to transfer traded securities under a matching agreement to another person or, in the case of an agreement falling within paragraph (3)(*d*), would have been so required if the failure referred to in that paragraph had not occurred.

(5) In paragraph (4)—

(*a*) a "matching agreement" means an agreement under which—

(i) the traded securities agreed to be transferred are of the same kind as the traded securities agreed to be transferred under the relevant agreement, and

(ii) the number and transfer price of the traded securities agreed to be transferred are identical to the number and transfer price of the traded securities agreed to be transferred under the relevant agreement;

(*b*) references to X-CLEAR are references to that clearing house in its capacity as a person providing clearing services in connection with a transaction made on the Facility;

(*c*) references to a clearing participant are references to a clearing participant in his capacity as such.

5 Consequential provision

(1) Traded securities which are the subject of an agreement specified in regulation 4(3) shall be dealt with by a clearing participant who is party to the agreement in a separate designated account, and not otherwise.

(2) In paragraph (1) "designated account" means an account designated by X-CLEAR for a clearing participant in connection with the traded securities concerned.

2009/194
Stamp Duty and Stamp Duty Reserve Tax (Investment Exchanges and Clearing Houses) Regulations (No 2) 2009

Made by the Treasury under FA 1991 ss 116, 117

Made . . . . *4 February 2009*
Laid before the House of Commons . . . . *4 February 2009*
Coming into force . . . . *23 February 2009*

1 Citation, commencement and effect

(1) These Regulations may be cited as the Stamp Duty and Stamp Duty Reserve Tax (Investment Exchanges and Clearing Houses) Regulations (No 2) 2009 and shall come into force on 23rd February 2009.

(2) These Regulations shall have effect—

(*a*) for the purposes of the charge to stamp duty, in relation to instruments executed on or after 23rd February 2009;

(*b*) for the purposes of the charge to stamp duty reserve tax—

(i) in the case of agreements to transfer traded securities which are not conditional, in relation to agreements made on or after 23rd February 2009;

(ii) in the case of agreements to transfer traded securities which are conditional, in relation to agreements where the condition is satisfied on or after that date.

2 Interpretation

In these Regulations—

"clearing participant" means a member of EuroCCP who as such is permitted by the Rules of EuroCCP to clear transactions made on the Facility for a traded security and who may or may not also be a participant in the Facility;

"client" means a person who gives instructions to a non-clearing firm for traded securities to be sold on the Facility;
"EuroCCP" means European Central Counterparty Limited, a body corporate which is a recognised clearing house under the Financial Services and Markets Act 2000;
"the Facility" means the multilateral trading facility operated by Smartpool Trading Limited, a body corporate which is permitted to operate a multilateral trading facility for the purposes of Part 4 of the Financial Services and Markets Act 2000;
"nominee" means a person whose business is or includes holding traded securities as a nominee for EuroCCP acting in its capacity as a person providing clearing services in connection with a transaction made on the Facility, or as a nominee for a clearing participant (as the case may be);
"non-clearing firm" means a participant in the Facility other than a clearing participant;
"traded securities" means stocks and shares which are issued or raised by a body corporate but does not include stocks and shares issued by a body corporate not incorporated in the United Kingdom unless—

(*a*) the stocks and shares are registered in a register kept in the United Kingdom by or on behalf of the body corporate; or
(*b*) in the case of shares, they are paired, within the meaning of section 99(6A) of the Finance Act 1986, with shares issued by a body corporate incorporated in the United Kingdom.

3 Prescription of recognised investment exchange and recognised clearing house

For the purposes of sections 116 and 117 of the Finance Act 1991—

(*a*) the SmartPool Multilateral Trading Facility ("the Facility") is prescribed as a recognised investment exchange; and
(*b*) EuroCCP is prescribed as a recognised clearing house.

4 Prescribed circumstances for the purposes of sections 116 and 117

(1) In the circumstances prescribed by paragraph (2) below, the charge to stamp duty and the charge to stamp duty reserve tax shall be treated as not arising.

(2) The circumstances prescribed are where, in connection with a transaction made on the Facility conditions A and B are met.

(3) Condition A is that traded securities of a particular kind are transferred, or agreed to be transferred, from—

(*a*) a clearing participant or a nominee of a clearing participant to another clearing participant or nominee, or
(*b*) a non-clearing firm or its client to a clearing participant or a nominee of a clearing participant, or
(*c*) a clearing participant or a nominee of a clearing participant to EuroCCP or to a nominee of that clearing house, or
(*d*) a person other than a clearing participant to EuroCCP or to a nominee of that clearing house, as a result of a failure by a clearing participant to fulfil his obligations in respect of the transaction concerned to transfer traded securities to EuroCCP or to a nominee of that clearing house, or
(*e*) EuroCCP or a nominee of that clearing house to a clearing participant or a nominee of a clearing participant.

(4) Condition B is that the person to whom those securities are agreed to be transferred under any of the agreements specified in paragraph (3) above ("the relevant agreement") is required on receipt of those securities to transfer traded securities under a matching agreement to another person or, in the case of an agreement falling within sub-paragraph (*d*), would have been so required if the failure referred to in that sub-paragraph had not occurred.

(5) In paragraph (4)—

(*a*) "matching agreement" means an agreement under which—

(i) the traded securities agreed to be transferred are of the same kind as the traded securities agreed to be transferred under the relevant agreement, and
(ii) the number and transfer price of the traded securities agreed to be transferred are identical to the number and transfer price of the traded securities agreed to be transferred under the relevant agreement;

(*b*) references to EuroCCP are references to that clearing houses in its capacity as a person providing clearing services in connection with a transaction made on the Facility;
(*c*) references to a clearing participant are references to a clearing participant in his capacity as such.

5 Consequential provision

(1) Traded securities which are the subject of an agreement specified in regulation 4(3) shall be dealt with by a clearing participant who is a party to the agreement in a separate designated account, and not otherwise.

(2) In paragraph (1) "designated account" means an account designated by EuroCCP for a clearing participant in connection with the traded securities concerned.

2009/397
Stamp Duty and Stamp Duty Reserve Tax (Investment Exchanges and Clearing Houses) Regulations (No 3) 2009

Made by the Treasury under FA 1991 ss 116, 117

Made . . . . *26 February 2009*
Laid before the House of Commons . . . . *2 March 2009*
Coming into force . . . . *23 March 2009*

1 Citation and commencement

(1) These Regulations may be cited as the Stamp Duty and Stamp Duty Reserve Tax (Investment Exchanges and Clearing Houses) Regulations (No 3) 2009 and shall come into force on 23rd March 2009.

(2) These Regulations shall have effect—

(*a*) for the purposes of the charge to stamp duty, in relation to instruments executed on or after 23rd March 2009;

(*b*) for the purposes of the charge to stamp duty reserve tax—

(i) in the case of agreements to transfer traded securities which are not conditional, in relation to agreements made on or after 23rd March 2009;

(ii) in the case of agreements to transfer traded securities which are conditional, in relation to agreements where the condition is satisfied on or after that date.

2 Interpretation

(1) In these Regulations—

"clearing participant" means a member of EuroCCP who as such is permitted by the Rules of EuroCCP to clear transactions made on the Facility for a traded security and who may or may not also be a participant in the Facility;

"client" means a person who gives instructions to a non-clearing firm for traded securities to be sold on the Facility;

"EuroCCP" means European Central Counterparty Limited, a company which is a recognised clearing house under the Financial Services and Markets Act 2000;

"NYSE Arca Europe" or "the Facility" means the multilateral trading facility operated by Euronext Amsterdam NV, a market operator which is permitted to operate a trading facility pursuant to the Directive;

"nominee" means a person whose business is or includes holding traded securities as a nominee for EuroCCP acting in its capacity as a person providing clearing services in connection with a transaction made on the Facility, or as a nominee for a clearing participant (as the case may be);

"non-clearing firm" means a participant in the Facility other than a clearing participant;

"traded securities" means stocks and shares which are issued or raised by a body corporate but does not include stocks and shares issued by a body corporate not incorporated in the United Kingdom unless—

(*a*) the stocks and shares are registered in a register kept in the United Kingdom by or on behalf of the body corporate; or

(*b*) in the case of shares, they are paired, within the meaning of section 99(6A) of the Finance Act 1986, with shares issued by a body corporate incorporated in the United Kingdom.

3 Prescription of recognised investment exchanges and recognised clearing houses

For the purpose of sections 116 and 117 of the Finance Act 1991—

(*a*) NYSE Arca Europe is prescribed as a recognised investment exchange; and

(*b*) EuroCCP is prescribed as a recognised clearing house.

4 Prescribed circumstances for the purposes of sections 116 and 117

(1) In the circumstances prescribed in this regulation, a charge to stamp duty and the charge to stamp duty reserve tax shall be treated as not arising.

(2) The circumstances prescribed are where, in connection with a transaction made on the Facility conditions A and B are met.

(3) Condition A is that traded securities of a particular kind are transferred, or agreed to be transferred, from—

(*a*) a clearing participant or a nominee of a clearing participant to another clearing participant or nominee,

(*b*) a non-clearing firm or its client (or a nominee of a non-clearing firm or of a client of a non-clearing firm) to a clearing participant or a nominee of a clearing participant, (*c*) a clearing participant or a nominee of a clearing participant to EuroCCP or to a nominee of that clearing house,

(*d*) a person other than a clearing participant to EuroCCP or to a nominee of that clearing house, as a result of a failure by a clearing participant to fulfil his obligations in respect of the transaction concerned to transfer traded securities to EuroCCP or to a nominee of that clearing house, or

(*e*) EuroCCP or a nominee of that clearing house to a clearing participant or a nominee of a clearing participant.

(4) Condition B is that the person to whom those securities are agreed to be transferred under any of the agreements specified in paragraph (3) ("the relevant agreement") is required on receipt of those securities to transfer traded securities under a matching agreement to another person or, in the case of an agreement falling within paragraph (3)(*d*), would have been so required if the failure referred to in that paragraph had not occurred.

(5) In paragraph (4)—

(*a*) a "matching agreement" means an agreement under which—

(i) the traded securities agreed to be transferred are of the same kind as the traded securities agreed to be transferred under the relevant agreement, and

(ii) the number and transfer price of the traded securities agreed to be transferred are identical to the number and transfer price of the traded securities agreed to be transferred under the relevant agreement;

(*b*) references to EuroCCP are references to that clearing house in its capacity as a person providing clearing services in connection with a transaction made on the Facility;

(*c*) references to a clearing participant are references to a clearing participant in his capacity as such.

5 Consequential provision

(1) Traded securities which are the subject of an agreement specified in regulation 4(3) shall be dealt with by a clearing participant who is party to the agreement in a separate designated account, and not otherwise.

(2) In paragraph (1) "designated account" means an account designated by EuroCCP for a clearing participant in connection with the traded securities concerned.

2009/1115
Stamp Duty and Stamp Duty Reserve Tax (Investment Exchanges and Clearing Houses) Regulations (No 4) 2009

Made by the Treasury under FA 1991 ss 116, 117

Made . . . . *30 April 2009*
Laid before the House of Commons . . . . . . *1 May 2009*
Coming into force . . . . *22 May 2009*

1 Citation, commencement and effect

(1) These Regulations may be cited as the Stamp Duty and Stamp Duty Reserve Tax (Investment Exchanges and Clearing Houses) Regulations (No 4) 2009 and shall come into force on 22nd May 2009.

(2) These Regulations shall have effect—

(*a*) for the purposes of the charge to stamp duty, in relation to instruments executed on or after 22nd May 2009;

(*b*) for the purposes of the charge to stamp duty reserve tax—

(i) in the case of agreements to transfer traded securities which are not conditional, in relation to agreements made on or after 22nd May 2009;

(ii) in the case of agreements to transfer traded securities which are conditional, in relation to agreements where the condition is satisfied on or after that date.

2 Interpretation

In these Regulations—

"clearing participant" means a member of EuroCCP who as such is permitted by the Rules of EuroCCP to clear transactions made on the Facility for a traded security and who may or may not also be a participant in the Facility;

"client" means a person who gives instructions to a non-clearing firm for traded securities to be sold on the Facility;

"EuroCCP" means European Central Counterparty Limited, a body corporate which is a recognised clearing house under the Financial Services and Markets Act 2000;

"the Facility" means "Block Board" the multilateral trading facility operated by Pipeline Financial Group Limited, a body corporate which is permitted to operate a multilateral trading facility for the purposes of Part 4 of the Financial Services and Markets Act 2000;

"nominee" means a person whose business is or includes holding traded securities as a nominee for EuroCCP acting in its capacity as a person providing clearing services in connection with a transaction made on the Facility, or as a nominee for a clearing participant (as the case may be);

"non-clearing firm" means a participant in the Facility other than a clearing participant;

"traded securities" means stocks and shares which are issued or raised by a body corporate but does not include stocks and shares issued by a body corporate not incorporated in the United Kingdom unless—

(*a*) the stocks and shares are registered in a register kept in the United Kingdom by or on behalf of the body corporate; or

(*b*) in the case of shares, they are paired, within the meaning of section 99(6A) of the Finance Act 1986, with shares issued by a body corporate incorporated in the United Kingdom.

3 Prescription of recognised investment exchange and recognised clearing house

For the purposes of sections 116 and 117 of the Finance Act 1991—

(*a*) "Block Board" is prescribed as a recognised investment exchange; and

(*b*) EuroCCP is prescribed as a recognised clearing house.

4 Prescribed circumstances for the purposes of sections 116 and 117

(1) In the circumstances prescribed by paragraph (2) below, the charge to stamp duty and the charge to stamp duty reserve tax shall be treated as not arising.

(2) The circumstances prescribed are where, in connection with a transaction made on the Facility, conditions A and B are met.

(3) Condition A is that traded securities of a particular kind are transferred, or agreed to be transferred, from—

(*a*) a clearing participant or a nominee of a clearing participant to another clearing participant or nominee, or

(*b*) a non-clearing firm or its client (or a nominee of a non-clearing firm or of a client of a non-clearing firm) to a clearing participant or a nominee of a clearing participant, or

(*c*) a clearing participant or a nominee of a clearing participant to EuroCCP or to a nominee of that clearing house, or

(*d*) a person other than a clearing participant to EuroCCP or to a nominee of that clearing house, as a result of a failure by a clearing participant to fulfil his obligations in respect of the transaction concerned to transfer traded securities to EuroCCP or to a nominee of that clearing house, or

(*e*) EuroCCP or a nominee of that clearing house to a clearing participant or a nominee of a clearing participant.

(4) Condition B is that the person to whom those securities are agreed to be transferred under any of the agreements specified in paragraph (3) above ("the relevant agreement") is required on receipt of those securities to transfer traded securities under a matching agreement to another person or, in the case of an agreement falling within sub-paragraph (3) (*d*), would have been so required if the failure referred to in that sub-paragraph had not occurred.

(5) In paragraph (4)—

(*a*) "matching agreement" means an agreement under which—

(i) the traded securities agreed to be transferred are of the same kind as the traded securities agreed to be transferred under the relevant agreement, and

(ii) the number and transfer price of the traded securities agreed to be transferred are identical to the number and transfer price of the traded securities agreed to be transferred under the relevant agreement;

(*b*) references to EuroCCP are references to that clearing houses in its capacity as a person providing clearing services in connection with a transaction made on the Facility;

(*c*) references to a clearing participant are references to a clearing participant in his capacity as such.

5 Consequential provision

(1) Traded securities which are the subject of an agreement specified in regulation 4(3) shall be dealt with by a clearing participant who is a party to the agreement in a separate designated account, and not otherwise.

(2) In paragraph (1) "designated account" means an account designated by EuroCCP for a clearing participant in connection with the traded securities concerned.

2009/1344
Stamp Duty and Stamp Duty Reserve Tax (Investment Exchanges and Clearing Houses) Regulations (No 5) 2009

Made by the Treasury under FA 1991 ss 116, 117

Made . . . . *1 June 2009*
Laid before the House of Commons . . . . *2 June 2009*
Coming into force . . . . *30 June 2009*

1 Citation and commencement

(1) These Regulations may be cited as the Stamp Duty and Stamp Duty Reserve Tax (Investment Exchanges and Clearing Houses) Regulations (No 5) 2009 and shall come into force on 30th June 2009.

(2) These Regulations shall have effect—

(*a*) for the purposes of the charge to stamp duty, in relation to instruments executed on or after 30th June 2009;

(*b*) for the purposes of the charge to stamp duty reserve tax—

(i) in the case of agreements to transfer traded securities which are not conditional, in relation to agreements made on or after 30th June 2009;

(ii) in the case of agreements to transfer traded securities which are conditional, in relation to agreements where the condition is satisfied on or after that date.

2 Interpretation

(1) In these Regulations—

"clearing participant" means a member of X-CLEAR who as such is permitted by the Rules of X-CLEAR to clear transactions made on the Facility for a traded security and who may or may not also be a participant in the Facility;

"client" means a person who gives instructions to a non-clearing firm for traded securities to be sold on the Facility;

"X-CLEAR" means SIX X-CLEAR AG, a company which is a recognised clearing house under the Financial Services and Markets Act 2000;

"the Facility" means the Liquidnet H2O multilateral trading facility, operated by Liquidnet Europe Limited, a company which is authorised to operate a multilateral trading facility for the purposes of Part IV of the Financial Services and Markets Act 2000;

"nominee" means a person whose business is or includes holding traded securities as a nominee for X-CLEAR acting in its capacity as a person providing clearing services in connection with a transaction made on the Facility, or as a nominee for a clearing participant (as the case may be);

"non-clearing firm" means a participant in the Facility other than a clearing participant;

"traded securities" means stocks and shares which are issued or raised by a company but does not include stocks and shares issued by a company not incorporated in the United Kingdom unless—

(*a*) the stocks and shares are registered in a register kept in the United Kingdom by or on behalf of the company; or

(*b*) in the case of shares, they are paired, within the meaning of section 99(6A) of the Finance Act 1986, with shares issued by a company incorporated in the United Kingdom.

3 Prescription of recognised investment exchanges and recognised clearing houses

For the purpose of sections 116 and 117 of the Finance Act 1991—

(*a*) Liquidnet H2O Multilateral Trading Facility ("the Facility") is prescribed as a recognised investment exchange; and

(*b*) SIX X-CLEAR AG is prescribed as a recognised clearing house.

4 Prescribed circumstances for the purposes of sections 116 and 117

(1) In the circumstances prescribed in this regulation, a charge to stamp duty or stamp duty reserve tax shall be treated as not arising.

(2) The circumstances prescribed are where, in connection with a transaction made on the Facility conditions A and B are met.

(3) Condition A is that traded securities of a particular kind are transferred, or agreed to be transferred, from—

(*a*) a clearing participant or a nominee of a clearing participant to another clearing participant or nominee,

(*b*) a non-clearing firm or its client to a clearing participant or a nominee of a clearing participant,

(*c*) a clearing participant or a nominee of a clearing participant to X-CLEAR or to a nominee of that clearing house, (*d*) a person other than a clearing participant to X-CLEAR or to a nominee of that clearing house, as a result of a failure by a clearing participant to fulfil his obligations in respect of the transaction concerned to transfer traded securities to X-CLEAR or to a nominee of that clearing house, or

(*e*) X-CLEAR or a nominee of that clearing house to a clearing participant or a nominee of a clearing participant.

(4) Condition B is that the person to whom those securities are agreed to be transferred under any of the agreements specified in paragraph (3) ("the relevant agreement") is required on receipt of those securities to transfer traded securities under a matching agreement to another person or, in the case of an agreement falling within paragraph (3)(*d*), would have been so required if the failure referred to in that paragraph had not occurred.

(5) In paragraph (4)—

(*a*) a "matching agreement" means an agreement under which—

(i) the traded securities agreed to be transferred are of the same kind as the traded securities agreed to be transferred under the relevant agreement, and

(ii) the number and transfer price of the traded securities agreed to be transferred are identical to the number and transfer price of the traded securities agreed to be transferred under the relevant agreement;

(*b*) references to X-CLEAR are references to that clearing house in its capacity as a person providing clearing services in connection with a transaction made on the Facility;

(*c*) references to a clearing participant are references to a clearing participant in his capacity as such.

Stamp Taxes

5 Consequential provision

(1) Traded securities which are the subject of an agreement specified in regulation 4(3) shall be dealt with by a clearing participant who is party to the agreement in a separate designated account, and not otherwise.

(2) In paragraph (1) "designated account" means an account designated by X-CLEAR for a clearing participant in connection with the traded securities concerned.

2009/1462

Stamp Duty and Stamp Duty Reserve Tax (Investment Exchanges and Clearing Houses) Regulations (No 6) 2009

Made by the Treasury under FA 1991 ss 116 and 117

Made . . . . 11 June 2009
Laid before the House of Commons . . . . 12 June 2009
Coming into force . . . . 5 July 2009

1 Citation and commencement

(1) These Regulations may be cited as the Stamp Duty and Stamp Duty Reserve Tax (Investment Exchanges and Clearing Houses) Regulations (No 6) 2009 and shall come into force on 5th July 2009.

(2) These Regulations shall have effect—

(*a*) for the purposes of the charge to stamp duty, in relation to instruments executed on or after 5th July 2009;

(*b*) for the purposes of the charge to stamp duty reserve tax—

(i) in the case of agreements to transfer traded securities which are not conditional, in relation to agreements made on or after 5th July 2009;

(ii) in the case of agreements to transfer traded securities which are conditional, in relation to agreements where the condition is satisfied on or after that date.

2 Interpretation

(1) In these Regulations—

"clearing participant" means a member of (*a*) LCH Clearnet Limited who as such is permitted by the Rules of LCH Clearnet Limited or (*b*) X-CLEAR who as such is permitted by the Rules of X-CLEAR or (*c*) European Multilateral Clearing Facility NV (EMCF) who as such is permitted by the Rules of EMCF to clear transactions made on the Facility for a traded security and who may or may not also be a participant in the Facility;

"client" means a person who gives instructions to a non-clearing firm for traded securities to be sold on the Facility;

"LCH Clearnet Limited" is a company which is a recognised clearing house under the Financial Services and Markets Act 2000;

"X-CLEAR" means SIX X-CLEAR AG, a company which is a recognised clearing house under the Financial Services and Markets Act 2000

"EMCF" means European Multilateral Clearing Facility NV, a company which is a recognised clearing house under the Financial Services and Markets Act 2000 "the Facility" means the multilateral trading facility operated by BATS Trading Limited, a company which is authorised to operate a multilateral trading facility for the purposes of Part IV of the Financial Services and Markets Act 2000;

"nominee" means a person whose business is or includes holding traded securities as a nominee for LCH Clearnet Limited or X-CLEAR or EMCF acting in its capacity as a person providing clearing services in connection with a transaction made on the Facility, or as a nominee for a clearing participant (as the case may be);

"non-clearing firm" means a participant in the Facility other than a clearing participant;

"traded securities" means stocks and shares which are issued or raised by a company but does not include stocks and shares issued by a company not incorporated in the United Kingdom unless—

(*a*) the stocks and shares are registered in a register kept in the United Kingdom by or on behalf of the company; or

(*b*) in the case of shares, they are paired, within the meaning of section 99(6A) of the Finance Act 1986, with shares issued by a company incorporated in the United Kingdom.

3 Prescription of recognised investment exchanges and recognised clearing houses

For the purpose of sections 116 and 117 of the Finance Act 1991—

(*a*) BATS Trading Limited multilateral trading facility ("the Facility") is prescribed as a recognised investment exchange; and

(*b*) LCH Clearnet Limited is prescribed as a recognised clearing house; and

(*c*) SIX X-CLEAR AG is prescribed as a recognised clearing house; and

(*d*) European Multilateral Clearing Facility NV is prescribed as a recognised clearing house.

4 Prescribed circumstances for the purposes of sections 116 and 117

(1) In the circumstances prescribed in this regulation, a charge to stamp duty or stamp duty reserve tax shall be treated as not arising.

(2) The circumstances prescribed are where, in connection with a transaction made on the Facility conditions A and B are met.

(3) Condition A is that traded securities of a particular kind are issued or transferred, or agreed to be issued or transferred, from—

(*a*) a clearing participant or a nominee of a clearing participant to another clearing participant or nominee,

(*b*) a non-clearing firm or its client to a clearing participant or a nominee of a clearing participant,

(*c*) a clearing participant or a nominee of a clearing participant to LCH Clearnet Limited, X-CLEAR or EMCF, or to a nominee of either LCH Clearnet Limited, X-CLEAR or EMCF.

(*d*) a person other than a clearing participant to LCH Clearnet Limited, X-CLEAR or EMCF or to a nominee of either LCH Clearnet Limited, X-CLEAR or EMCF as a result of a failure by a clearing participant to fulfil his obligations in respect of the transaction concerned to transfer traded securities to LCH Clearnet Limited, X-CLEAR or EMCF, or to a nominee of either LCH Clearnet Limited, X-CLEAR or EMCF, or

(*e*) LCH Clearnet Limited, X-CLEAR or EMCF, or a nominee of either LCH Clearnet Limited, X-CLEAR or EMCF to a clearing participant or a nominee of a clearing participant.

(*f*) LCH Clearnet Limited or a nominee of that clearing house to X-CLEAR or EMCF or a nominee of that clearing house, or

(*g*) X-CLEAR or a nominee of that clearing house to LCH Clearnet Limited or EMCF or a nominee of that clearing house.

(*h*) EMCF or a nominee of that clearing house to LCH Clearnet Limited or X-CLEAR or a nominee of that clearing house.

(4) Condition B is that the person to whom those securities are agreed to be transferred under any of the agreements specified in paragraph (3) ("the relevant agreement") is required on receipt of those securities to transfer traded securities under a matching agreement to another person or, in the case of an agreement falling within paragraph (3)(*d*), would have been so required if the failure referred to in that paragraph had not occurred.

(5) In paragraph (4)—

(*a*) a "matching agreement" means an agreement under which—

(i) the traded securities agreed to be transferred are of the same kind as the traded securities agreed to be transferred under the relevant agreement, and

(ii) the number and transfer price of the traded securities agreed to be transferred are identical to the number and transfer price of the traded securities agreed to be transferred under the relevant agreement;

(*b*) references to LCH Clearnet Limited, X-CLEAR or EMCF are references to that clearing house in its capacity as a person providing clearing services in connection with a transaction made on the Facility;

(*c*) references to a clearing participant are references to a clearing participant in its capacity as such.

5 Consequential provision

(1) Traded securities which are the subject of an agreement specified in regulation 4(3) shall be dealt with by a clearing participant who is party to the agreement in a separate designated account, and not otherwise.

(2) In paragraph (1) "designated account" means an account designated by LCH Clearnet Limited, X-CLEAR or EMCF for a clearing participant in connection with the traded securities concerned.

2009/1601
Stamp Duty and Stamp Duty Reserve Tax (Investment Exchanges and Clearing Houses) Regulations (No 7) 2009

Made by the Treasury under FA 1991 ss 116, 117

Made . . . . *1 July 2009*
Laid before the House of Commons . . . . *2 July 2009*
Coming into force . . . . *3 August 2009*

1 Citation and commencement

(1) These Regulations may be cited as the Stamp Duty and Stamp Duty Reserve Tax (Investment Exchanges and Clearing Houses) Regulations (No 7) 2009 and shall come into force on 3rd August 2009.

(2) These Regulations shall have effect—

(*a*) for the purposes of the charge to stamp duty, in relation to instruments executed on or after 3rd August 2009;

(*b*) for the purposes of the charge to stamp duty reserve tax—

(i) in the case of agreements to transfer traded securities which are not conditional, in relation to agreements made on or after 3rd August 2009;

(ii) in the case of agreements to transfer traded securities which are conditional, in relation to agreements where the condition is satisfied on or after that date.

2 Interpretation

(1) In these Regulations—

"clearing participant" means a member of (*a*) LCH.Clearnet Limited who as such is permitted by the Rules of LCH.Clearnet Limited or (*b*) X-CLEAR who as such is permitted by the Rules of X-CLEAR or (*c*) European Multilateral Clearing Facility NV (EMCF) who as such is permitted by the Rules of EMCF to clear transactions made on the Facility for a traded security and who may or may not also be a participant in the Facility;

"client" means a person who gives instructions to a non-clearing firm for traded securities to be sold on the Facility;

"LCH.Clearnet Limited" is a company which is a recognised clearing house under the Financial Services and Markets Act 2000;

"X-CLEAR" means SIX X-CLEAR AG, a company which is a recognised clearing house under the Financial Services and Markets Act 2000;

"EMCF" means European Multilateral Clearing Facility NV, a company which is a recognised clearing house under the Financial Services and Markets Act 2000;

"the Facility" means the multilateral trading facility operated by Chi-X Europe Limited, a company which is authorised to operate a multilateral trading facility for the purposes of Part IV of the Financial Services and Markets Act 2000;

"nominee" means a person whose business is or includes holding traded securities as a nominee for LCH.Clearnet Limited or X-CLEAR or EMCF acting in its capacity as a person providing clearing services in connection with a transaction made on the Facility, or as a nominee for a clearing participant (as the case may be);

"non-clearing firm" means a participant in the Facility other than a clearing participant;

"traded securities" means stocks and shares which are issued or raised by a company but does not include stocks and shares issued by a company not incorporated in the United Kingdom unless—

(*a*) the stocks and shares are registered in a register kept in the United Kingdom by or on behalf of the company; or

(*b*) in the case of shares, they are paired, within the meaning of section 99(6A) of the Finance Act 1986, with shares issued by a company incorporated in the United Kingdom.

3 Prescription of recognised investment exchanges and recognised clearing houses

For the purpose of sections 116 and 117 of the Finance Act 1991—

(*a*) Chi-X Europe Limited ("the Facility") is prescribed as a recognised investment exchange; and

Stamp Taxes

(*b*) LCH.Clearnet Limited is prescribed as a recognised clearing house; and
(*c*) SIX X-CLEAR AG is prescribed as a recognised clearing house; and
(*d*) European Multilateral Clearing Facility NV is prescribed as a recognised clearing house.

4 Prescribed circumstances for the purposes of sections 116 and 117

(1) In the circumstances prescribed in this regulation, a charge to stamp duty or stamp duty reserve tax shall be treated as not arising.

(2) The circumstances prescribed are where, in connection with a transaction made on the Facility conditions A and B are met.

(3) Condition A is that traded securities of a particular kind are issued or transferred, or agreed to be issued or transferred, from—

(*a*) a clearing participant or a nominee of a clearing participant to another clearing participant or nominee,

(*b*) a non-clearing firm or its client to a clearing participant or a nominee of a clearing participant,

(*c*) a clearing participant or a nominee of a clearing participant to LCH.Clearnet Limited, X-CLEAR or EMCF, or to a nominee of either LCH.Clearnet Limited, X-CLEAR or EMCF.

(*d*) a person other than a clearing participant to LCH.Clearnet Limited, X-CLEAR or EMCF or to a nominee of either LCH.Clearnet Limited, X-CLEAR or EMCF as a result of a failure by a clearing participant to fulfil his obligations in respect of the transaction concerned to transfer traded securities to LCH.Clearnet Limited, X-CLEAR or EMCF, or to a nominee of either LCH.Clearnet Limited, X-CLEAR or EMCF, or

(*e*) LCH.Clearnet Limited, X-CLEAR or EMCF, or a nominee of either LCH.Clearnet Limited, X-CLEAR or EMCF to a clearing participant or a nominee of a clearing participant.

(*f*) LCH.Clearnet Limited or a nominee of that clearing house to X-CLEAR or EMCF or a nominee of that clearing house, or

(*g*) X-CLEAR or a nominee of that clearing house to LCH.Clearnet Limited or EMCF or a nominee of that clearing house.

(*h*) EMCF or a nominee of that clearing house to LCH.Clearnet Limited or X-CLEAR or a nominee of that clearing house.

(4) Condition B is that the person to whom those securities are agreed to be transferred under any of the agreements specified in paragraph (3) ("the relevant agreement") is required on receipt of those securities to transfer traded securities under a matching agreement to another person or, in the case of an agreement falling within paragraph (3)(*d*), would have been so required if the failure referred to in that paragraph had not occurred.

(5) In paragraph (4)—

(*a*) a "matching agreement" means an agreement under which—

(i) the traded securities agreed to be transferred are of the same kind as the traded securities agreed to be transferred under the relevant agreement, and

(ii) the number and transfer price of the traded securities agreed to be transferred are identical to the number and transfer price of the traded securities agreed to be transferred under the relevant agreement;

(*b*) references to LCH.Clearnet Limited, X-CLEAR or EMCF are references to that clearing house in its capacity as a person providing clearing services in connection with a transaction made on the Facility;

(*c*) references to a clearing participant are references to a clearing participant in its capacity as such.

5 Consequential provision

(1) Traded securities which are the subject of an agreement specified in regulation 4(3) shall be dealt with by a clearing participant who is party to the agreement in a separate designated account, and not otherwise.

(2) In paragraph (1) "designated account" means an account designated by LCH.Clearnet Limited, X-CLEAR or EMCF for a clearing participant in connection with the traded securities concerned.

2009/1827

Stamp Duty and Stamp Duty Reserve Tax (Investment Exchanges and Clearing Houses) Regulations (No 8) 2009

Made by the Treasury under FA 1991 ss 116, 117

Made . . . . *8 July 2009*
Laid before the House of Commons . . . . *9 July 2009*
Coming into force . . . . *4 August 2009*

1 Citation and commencement

(1) These Regulations may be cited as the Stamp Duty and Stamp Duty Reserve Tax (Investment Exchanges and Clearing Houses) Regulations (No 8) 2009 and shall come into force on 4th August 2009.

(2) These Regulations shall have effect—

(*a*) for the purposes of the charge to stamp duty, in relation to instruments executed on or after 4th August 2009;

(*b*) for the purposes of the charge to stamp duty reserve tax—

(i) in the case of agreements to transfer traded securities which are not conditional, in relation to agreements made on or after 4th August 2009;

(ii) in the case of agreements to transfer traded securities which are conditional, in relation to agreements where the condition is satisfied on or after that date.

2 Interpretation

(1) In these Regulations—

"clearing participant" means a member of (*a*) EuroCCP who as such is permitted by the Rules of EuroCCP or (*b*) LCH.Clearnet Limited who as such is permitted by the Rules of LCH.Clearnet Limited or (*c*) X-CLEAR who as such is permitted by the Rules of X-CLEAR to clear transactions made on the Facility for a traded security and who may or may not also be a participant in the Facility;

"client" means a person who gives instructions to a non-clearing firm for traded securities to be sold on the Facility;

"EuroCCP" means European Central Counterparty Limited, a company which is a recognised clearing house under the Financial Services and Markets Act 2000;

"LCH.Clearnet Limited" is a company which is a recognised clearing house under the Financial Services and Markets Act 2000;

"X-CLEAR" means SIX X-CLEAR AG, a company which is a recognised clearing house under the Financial Services and Markets Act 2000;

"Facility" means the multilateral trading facility operated by Turquoise Services Limited, a company which is authorised to operate a multilateral trading facility for the purposes of Part IV of the Financial Services and Markets Act 2000;

"nominee" means a person whose business is or includes holding traded securities as a nominee for EuroCCP or LCH.Clearnet Limited or X-CLEAR acting in its capacity as a person providing clearing services in connection with a transaction made on the Facility, or as a nominee for a clearing participant (as the case may be);

"non-clearing firm" means a participant in the Facility other than a clearing participant;

"traded securities" means stocks and shares which are issued or raised by a company but does not include stocks and shares issued by a company not incorporated in the United Kingdom unless—

(*a*) the stocks and shares are registered in a register kept in the United Kingdom by or on behalf of the company; or

(*b*) in the case of shares, they are paired, within the meaning of section 99(6A) of the Finance Act 1986, with shares issued by a company incorporated in the United Kingdom.

3 Prescription of recognised investment exchange and recognised clearing houses

For the purposes of sections 116 and 117 of the Finance Act 1991—

(*a*) Turquoise Services Limited is prescribed as a recognised investment exchange; and

(*b*) EuroCCP is prescribed as a recognised clearing house,

(*c*) LCH.Clearnet Limited is prescribed as a recognised clearing house, and,

(*d*) X-CLEAR is prescribed as a recognised clearing house.

4 Prescribed circumstances for the purposes of sections 116 and 117

(1) In the circumstances prescribed by paragraph (2), a charge to stamp duty or stamp duty reserve tax shall be treated as not arising.

(2) The circumstances prescribed are where, in connection with a transaction made on the Facility, conditions A and B are met.

(3) Condition A is that traded securities of a particular kind are issued or transferred, or agreed to be issued or transferred, from—

(*a*) a clearing participant or a nominee of a clearing participant to another clearing participant or nominee,

(*b*) a non-clearing firm or its client to a clearing participant or a nominee of a clearing participant,.

(*c*) a clearing participant or a nominee of a clearing participant to EuroCCP, LCH.Clearnet Limited or X-CLEAR, or to a nominee of either EuroCCP, LCH.Clearnet Limited or X-CLEAR.

(*d*) a person other than a clearing participant to EuroCCP, LCH.Clearnet Limited or X-CLEAR or to a nominee of either EuroCCP, LCH.Clearnet Limited or X-CLEAR as a result of a failure by a clearing participant to fulfil his obligations in respect of the transaction concerned to transfer traded securities to EuroCCP, LCH.Clearnet Limited or X-CLEAR, or to a nominee of either EuroCCP, LCH.Clearnet Limited or X-CLEAR, or (*e*) EuroCCP, LCH.Clearnet Limited or X-CLEAR, or a nominee of either EuroCCP, LCH.Clearnet Limited or X-CLEAR to a clearing participant or a nominee of a clearing participant.

(*f*) EuroCCP or a nominee of that clearing house to LCH.Clearnet Limited or X-CLEAR or a nominee of either clearing house, or

(*g*) LCH.Clearnet Limited or a nominee of that clearing house to EuroCCP or X-CLEAR or a nominee of either clearing house.

(*h*) X-CLEAR or a nominee of that clearing house to EuroCCP or LCH.Clearnet Limited or a nominee of either clearing house.

(4) Condition B is that the person to whom those securities are agreed to be transferred under any of the agreements specified in paragraph (3) above ("the relevant agreement") is required on receipt of those securities to transfer traded securities under a matching agreement to another person or, in the case of an agreement falling within sub-paragraph (3)(*d*), would have been so required if the failure referred to in that paragraph had not occurred.

(5) In paragraph (4)—

(*a*) "matching agreement" means an agreement under which—

(i) the traded securities agreed to be transferred are of the same kind as the traded securities agreed to be transferred under the relevant agreement, and

(ii) the number and transfer price of the traded securities agreed to be transferred are identical to the number and transfer price of the traded securities agreed to be transferred under the relevant agreement;

(*b*) references to EuroCCP, LCH.Clearnet Limited or X-CLEAR are references to that clearing house in its capacity as a person providing clearing services in connection with a transaction made on the Facility;

(*c*) references to a clearing participant are references to a clearing participant in its capacity as such.

5 Consequential provision

(1) Traded securities which are the subject of an agreement specified in regulation 4(3) shall be dealt with by a clearing participant who is a party to the agreement in a separate designated account, and not otherwise.

(2) In paragraph (1) "designated account" means an account designated by EuroCCP, LCH-.Clearnet Limited or X-CLEAR for a clearing participant in connection with the traded securities concerned.

6 Revocation of the Stamp and Stamp Duty Reserve Tax (Investment Exchanges and Clearing Houses) (European Central Counterparty Limited and the Turquoise Multilateral Trading Facility) Regulations 2008 (SI 2008/1814)

The Stamp Duty and Stamp Duty Reserve Tax (Investment Exchanges and Clearing Houses) (European Central Counterparty Limited and the Turquoise Multilateral Trading Facility) Regulations 2008 (SI 2008/1814) are hereby revoked as respects instruments and agreements referred to in regulation 1(2).

2009/1828
Stamp Duty and Stamp Duty Reserve Tax (Investment Exchanges and Clearing Houses) Regulations (No 9) 2009

Made by the Treasury under FA 1991 ss 116, 117

Made	*8 July 2009*
Laid before the House of Commons	*9 July 2009*
Coming into force	*30 July 2009*

1 Citation and commencement

(1) These Regulations may be cited as the Stamp Duty and Stamp Duty Reserve Tax (Investment Exchanges and Clearing Houses) Regulations (No 9) 2009 and shall come into force on 30th July 2009.

(2) These Regulations shall have effect—

(*a*) for the purposes of the charge to stamp duty, in relation to instruments executed on or after 30th July 2009;

(*b*) for the purposes of the charge to stamp duty reserve tax—

(i) in the case of agreements to transfer traded securities which are not conditional, in relation to agreements made on or after 30th July 2009;

(ii) in the case of agreements to transfer traded securities which are conditional, in relation to agreements where the condition is satisfied on or after that date.

2 Interpretation

(1) In these Regulations—

"clearing participant" means (*a*) a member of LIFFE who as such is permitted by the Rules of LIFFE to clear transactions made on the Exchange of traded securities or (*b*) LCH.Clearnet Limited, when required by the applicable Rules of LIFFE to clear transactions made on the Exchange;

"the Exchange" means the London International Financial Futures and Options Exchange ("LIFFE") which is operated by LIFFE A&M;

"LCH.Clearnet Limited" is a company which is a recognised clearing house under the Financial Services and Markets Act 2000;

"LIFFE A&M" means LIFFE Administration and Management, an unlimited company having a share capital, which is a recognised investment exchange authorised to provide clearing services under the Financial Services and Markets Act 2000;

"nominee" means a person whose business is or includes holding traded securities as a nominee for LCH.Clearnet Limited or LIFFE A&M, in each case acting in its capacity as a person providing clearing services in connection with a transaction made on the Exchange, or as a nominee for a clearing participant, or as a nominee for a non-clearing firm (as the case may be);

"non-clearing firm" means a member of LIFFE other than a clearing participant;

"option" means an option to buy or sell traded securities where such option is listed by and made on or under the Rules of LIFFE.

"traded securities" means options, stocks, shares or loan capital, or interests in stocks, shares or loan capital, issued or raised by a body corporate but does not include stocks and shares issued by a body corporate not incorporated in the United Kingdom unless—

(*a*) the stocks and shares are registered in a register kept in the United Kingdom by or on behalf of the body corporate; or

(*b*) in the case of shares, they are paired, within the meaning of section 99(6A) of the Finance Act 1986, with shares issued by a body corporate incorporated in the United Kingdom;

3 Prescription of recognised investment exchanges and recognised clearing houses

For the purpose of sections 116 and 117 of the Finance Act 1991—

(*a*) LIFFE A&M is prescribed as a recognised investment exchange; and

(*b*) LCH.Clearnet Limited is prescribed as a recognised clearing house.

4 Prescribed circumstances for the purposes of sections 116 and 117

(1) In the circumstances prescribed in this regulation, the charge to stamp duty and the charge to stamp duty reserve tax shall be treated as not arising.

(2) The circumstances prescribed are where, in connection with a transaction made on the Exchange conditions A and B are met.

(3) Condition A is that traded securities of a particular kind are issued or transferred, or agreed to be issued or transferred, from—

(*a*) a clearing participant or a nominee of a clearing participant to another clearing participant or nominee,

(*b*) a non-clearing firm or a nominee of a non-clearing firm to a clearing participant or a nominee of a clearing participant,

(*c*) a clearing participant or a nominee of a clearing participant to LIFFE A&M, or to LCH.Clearnet Limited, or to a nominee of either LIFFE A&M or LCH.Clearnet Limited,

(*d*) a person other than a clearing participant to LIFFE A&M, or to LCH.Clearnet Limited, or to a nominee of either LIFFE A&M or LCH.Clearnet Limited, as a result of a failure by a clearing participant to fulfil his obligations in respect of the transaction concerned to transfer traded securities to LIFFE A&M, or to LCH.Clearnet Limited, or to a nominee of either LIFFE A&M or LCH.Clearnet Limited, or

(*e*) LIFFE A&M, or LCH.Clearnet Limited, or a nominee of either LIFFE A&M or LCH.Clearnet Limited to a clearing participant or a nominee of a clearing participant.

(4) Condition B is that the person to whom those securities are agreed to be issued or transferred under any of the agreements specified in paragraph (3) ("the relevant agreement") is required on receipt of those securities to transfer traded securities under a matching agreement to another person or, in the case of an agreement falling within paragraph (3)(*d*), would have been so required if the failure referred to in that paragraph had not occurred.

(5) In paragraph (4)—

(*a*) a "matching agreement" means an agreement under which—

(i) the traded securities agreed to be transferred are of the same kind as the traded securities agreed to be transferred under the relevant agreement, and

(ii) the number and transfer price of the traded securities agreed to be transferred are identical to the number and transfer price of the traded securities agreed to be transferred under the relevant agreement;

(*b*) references to LCH.Clearnet Limited are references to that clearing house in its capacity as a person providing clearing services in connection with a transaction made on the Exchange;

(*c*) references to LIFFE A&M are references to LIFFE A&M acting in its capacity as a self-clearing recognised investment exchange providing clearing services in connection with a transaction made on the Exchange;

(*d*) references to a clearing participant are references to a clearing participant in its capacity as such.

5 Consequential provision

(1) Traded securities which are the subject of an agreement specified in regulation 4(3) shall be dealt with by a clearing participant who is party to the agreement in a separate designated account, and not otherwise.

(2) In paragraph (1) "designated account" means an account designated by LIFFE A&M, acting in its capacity as a self-clearing recognised investment exchange in connection with the traded securities concerned.

6 Revocation of the Stamp and Stamp Duty Reserve Tax (Investment Exchanges and Clearing Houses) Regulation 1997/2429

The Stamp Duty and Stamp Duty Reserve Tax (Investment Exchanges and Clearing Houses) Regulations 1997/2429 are hereby revoked as respects instruments and agreements referred to in regulation 1(2).

2009/1831
Stamp Duty and Stamp Duty Reserve Tax (Investment Exchanges and Clearing Houses) Regulations (No 10) 2009

Made by the Treasury under FA 1991 ss 116, 117

Made . . . . *9 July 2009*
Laid before the House of Commons . . . . *9 July 2009*
Coming into force . . . . *3 August 2009*

1 Citation and commencement

(1) These Regulations may be cited as the Stamp Duty and Stamp Duty Reserve Tax (Investment Exchanges and Clearing Houses) Regulations (No 10) 2009 and shall come into force on 3rd August 2009.

(2) These Regulations shall have effect—

(*a*) for the purposes of the charge to stamp duty, in relation to instruments executed on or after 3rd August 2009;

(*b*) for the purposes of the charge to stamp duty reserve tax—

(i) in the case of agreements to transfer traded securities which are not conditional, in relation to agreements made on or after 3rd August 2009;

(ii) in the case of agreements to transfer traded securities which are conditional, in relation to agreements where the condition is satisfied on or after that date.

2 Interpretation

(1) In these Regulations—

"clearing participant" means a member of (*a*) European Multilateral Clearing Facility NV (EMCF) who as such is permitted by the Rules of EMCF or (*b*) X-CLEAR who as such is permitted by the Rules of X-CLEAR to clear transactions made on the Facility for a traded security and who may or may not also be a participant in the Facility;

"client" means a person who gives instructions to a non-clearing firm for traded securities to be sold on the Facility;

"EMCF" means European Multilateral Clearing Facility NV, a company which is a recognised clearing house under the Financial Services and Markets Act 2000;

"X-CLEAR" means SIX X-CLEAR AG, a company which is a recognised clearing house under the Financial Services and Markets Act 2000;

"the Facility" means the multilateral trading facility operated by NASDAQ OMX Europe Limited, a company which is authorised to operate a multilateral trading facility for the purposes of Part IV of the Financial Services and Markets Act 2000;

"nominee" means a person whose business is or includes holding traded securities as a nominee for EMCF or X-CLEAR acting in its capacity as a person providing clearing services in connection with a transaction made on the Facility, or as a nominee for a clearing participant (as the case may be);

"non-clearing firm" means a participant in the Facility other than a clearing participant;

"traded securities" means stocks and shares which are issued or raised by a company but does not include stocks and shares issued by a company not incorporated in the United Kingdom unless—

(*a*) the stocks and shares are registered in a register kept in the United Kingdom by or on behalf of the company; or (*b*) in the case of shares, they are paired, within the meaning of section 99(6A) of the Finance Act 1986, with shares issued by a company incorporated in the United Kingdom.

3 Prescription of recognised investment exchanges and recognised clearing houses

For the purpose of sections 116 and 117 of the Finance Act 1991—

(*a*) NASDAQ OMX Europe Limited ("the Facility") is prescribed as a recognised investment exchange; and

(*b*) European Multilateral Clearing Facility NV is prescribed as a recognised clearing house; and

(*c*) SIX X-CLEAR AG is prescribed as a recognised clearing house.

4 Prescribed circumstances for the purposes of sections 116 and 117

(1) In the circumstances prescribed in this regulation, a charge to stamp duty or stamp duty reserve tax shall be treated as not arising.

(2) The circumstances prescribed are where, in connection with a transaction made on the Facility conditions A and B are met.

(3) Condition A is that traded securities of a particular kind are issued or transferred, or agreed to be issued or transferred, from—

(*a*) a clearing participant or a nominee of a clearing participant to another clearing participant or nominee,

(*b*) a non-clearing firm or its client to a clearing participant or a nominee of a clearing participant,

(*c*) a clearing participant or a nominee of a clearing participant to EMCF or X-CLEAR, or to a nominee of either EMCF or X-CLEAR.

(*d*) a person other than a clearing participant to EMCF or X-CLEAR, or to a nominee of EMCF or X-CLEAR, as a result of a failure by a clearing participant to fulfil his obligations in respect of the transaction concerned to transfer traded securities to EMCF or X-CLEAR, or to a nominee of either EMCF or X-CLEAR, or

(*e*) X-CLEAR or EMCF, or a nominee of either X-CLEAR or EMCF to a clearing participant or a nominee of a clearing participant.

(*f*) X-CLEAR or a nominee of that clearing house to EMCF or a nominee of that clearing house.

(*g*) EMCF or a nominee of that clearing house to X-CLEAR or a nominee of that clearing house.

(4) Condition B is that the person to whom those securities are agreed to be transferred under any of the agreements specified in paragraph (3) ("the relevant agreement") is required on receipt of those securities to transfer traded securities under a matching agreement to another person or, in the case of an agreement falling within paragraph (3)(*d*), would have been so required if the failure referred to in that paragraph had not occurred.

(5) In paragraph (4)—

(*a*) a "matching agreement" means an agreement under which—

(i) the traded securities agreed to be transferred are of the same kind as the traded securities agreed to be transferred under the relevant agreement, and

(ii) the number and transfer price of the traded securities agreed to be transferred are identical to the number and transfer price of the traded securities agreed to be transferred under the relevant agreement;

(*b*) references to X-CLEAR or EMCF are references to that clearing house in its capacity as a person providing clearing services in connection with a transaction made on the Facility;

(*c*) references to a clearing participant are references to a clearing participant in its capacity as such.

5 Consequential provision

(1) Traded securities which are the subject of an agreement specified in regulation 4(3) shall be dealt with by a clearing participant who is party to the agreement in a separate designated account, and not otherwise.

(2) In paragraph (1) "designated account" means an account designated by X-CLEAR or EMCF for a clearing participant in connection with the traded securities concerned.

2009/1832

Stamp Duty and Stamp Duty Reserve Tax (Investment Exchanges and Clearing Houses) Regulations (No 11) 2009

Made by the Treasury under FA 1991 ss 116, 117

Made	*9 July 2009*
Laid before the House of Commons	*9 July 2009*
Coming into force	*3 August 2009*

1 Citation and commencement

(1) These Regulations may be cited as the Stamp Duty and Stamp Duty Reserve Tax (Investment Exchanges and Clearing Houses) Regulations (No 11) 2009 and shall come into force on 3rd August 2009.

Stamp Taxes

(2) These Regulations shall have effect—

(*a*) for the purposes of the charge to stamp duty, in relation to instruments executed on or after 3rd August 2009;

(*b*) for the purposes of the charge to stamp duty reserve tax—

(i) in the case of agreements to transfer traded securities which are not conditional, in relation to agreements made on or after 3rd August 2009;

(ii) in the case of agreements to transfer traded securities which are conditional, in relation to agreements where the condition is satisfied on or after that date.

2 Interpretation

(1) In these Regulations—

"clearing participant" means a member of either (*a*) CC&G who as such is permitted by the Rules of CC&G or (*b*) EMCF who as such is permitted by the Rules of EMCF, to clear transactions made on the Facility for a traded security and who may or may not also be a participant in the Facility;

"client" means a person who gives instructions to a non-clearing firm for traded securities to be sold on the Facility;

"CC&G" means Cassa di Compensazione e Garanzia SpA, a company which is a recognised clearing house under the Financial Services and Markets Act 2000;

"EMCF" means European Multilateral Clearing Facility NV, a company which is a recognised clearing house under the Financial Services and Markets Act 2000;

"the Facility" means the multilateral trading facility operated by Baikal Global Limited, a company which is permitted to operate a multilateral trading facility for the purposes of Part IV of the Financial Services and Markets Act 2000;

"nominee" means a person whose business is or includes holding traded securities as a nominee for either CC&G or EMCF acting in their capacity as a person providing clearing services in connection with a transaction made on the Facility, or as a nominee for a clearing participant (as the case may be);

"non-clearing firm" means a participant in the Facility other than a clearing participant; and

"traded securities" means stocks and shares which are issued or raised by a company but does not include stocks and shares issued by a company not incorporated in the United Kingdom unless—

(*a*) the stocks and shares are registered in a register kept in the United Kingdom by or on behalf of the company; or

(*b*) in the case of shares, they are paired, within the meaning of section 99(6A) of the Finance Act 1986, with shares issued by a company incorporated in the United Kingdom.

3 Prescription of recognised investment exchanges and recognised clearing houses

For the purpose of sections 116 and 117 of the Finance Act 1991—

(*a*) The Facility is prescribed as a recognised investment exchange;

(*b*) CC&G is prescribed as a recognised clearing house; and

(*c*) EMCF is prescribed as a recognised clearing house.

4 Prescribed circumstances for the purposes of sections 116 and 117

(1) In the circumstances prescribed in this regulation, a charge to stamp duty or stamp duty reserve tax shall be treated as not arising.

(2) The circumstances prescribed are where, in connection with a transaction made on the Facility, conditions A and B below are met.

(3) Condition A is that traded securities of a particular kind are issued or transferred, or agreed to be issued or transferred, from—

(*a*) a clearing participant or a nominee of a clearing participant to another clearing participant or a nominee of another clearing participant;

(*b*) a non-clearing firm or its client to a clearing participant or a nominee of a clearing participant;

(*c*) a clearing participant or a nominee of a clearing participant to CC&G or EMCF, or to a nominee of either CC&G or EMCF;

(*d*) a person other than a clearing participant to CC&G or EMCF, or to a nominee of CC&G or EMCF, as a result of a failure by a clearing participant to fulfil his obligations in respect of the transaction concerned to transfer traded securities to CC&G or EMCF, or to a nominee of either CC&G or EMCF;

(*e*) CC&G or EMCF, or a nominee of either CC&G or EMCF, to a clearing participant or a nominee of a clearing participant;

(*f*) CC&G or a nominee of CC&G to EMCF or a nominee of EMCF; or

(*g*) EMCF or a nominee of EMCF to CC&G or a nominee of CC&G.

(4) Condition B is that the person to whom those securities are agreed to be transferred under any of the agreements specified in paragraph (3) ("the relevant agreement") is required on receipt of those securities to transfer traded securities under a matching agreement to another

person or, in the case of an agreement falling within paragraph (3)(*d*), would have been so required if the failure referred to in that paragraph had not occurred.

(5) In paragraph (4)—

(*a*) a "matching agreement" means an agreement under which—

(i) the traded securities agreed to be transferred are of the same kind as the traded securities agreed to be transferred under the relevant agreement, and

(ii) the number and transfer price of the traded securities agreed to be transferred are identical to the number and transfer price of the traded securities agreed to be transferred under the relevant agreement;

(*b*) references to CC&G or EMCF are references to that clearing house in its capacity as a person providing clearing services in connection with a transaction made on the Facility;

(*c*) references to a clearing participant are references to a clearing participant in its capacity as such.

5 Consequential provision

(1) Traded securities which are the subject of an agreement specified in regulation 4(3) shall be dealt with by a clearing participant who is party to the agreement in a separate designated account, and not otherwise.

(2) In paragraph (1) "designated account" means an account designated by CC&G or EMCF for a clearing participant in connection with the traded securities concerned.

2009/2052
Alternative Finance Investment Bonds (Stamp Duty Land Tax) (Prescribed Evidence) Regulations 2009

Made by the Commissioners for HMRC under FA 2009 Sch 61 paras 5(6), 9, 18(5), 18(6) and 23(1)

Made	*23 July 2009*
Laid before the House of Commons	*23 July 2009*
Coming into force	*13 August 2009*

1 Citation and commencement

These Regulations may be cited as the Alternative Finance Investment Bonds (Stamp Duty Land Tax) (Prescribed Evidence) Regulations 2009 and shall come into force on 13th August 2009.

2 Interpretation

(1) In these Regulations—

"Schedule 61" means Schedule 61 to the Finance Act 2009,

"SDLT" means Stamp Duty Land Tax,

"The original owner" is "P" as provided for by paragraph 5(2) of Schedule 61,

"UTRN" means the unique transaction reference number allocated by HMRC to a land transaction for the purposes of stamp duty land tax.

(2) In these Regulations the relevant Land Registry is defined as—

(*a*) in relation to land in England and Wales—Her Majesty's Land Registry,

(*b*) in relation to land in Scotland—Registrars of Scotland,

(*c*) in relation to land in Northern Ireland—The Land Registry of Northern Ireland.

3 Prescribed evidence for the purpose of paragraph 5(6) of Schedule 61

For the purpose of paragraph 5(6) of Schedule 61 (condition D for operation of reliefs) the prescribed evidence is all of the following—

(*a*) any document provided by the relevant Land Registry confirming the creation and registration of a legal charge or standard security in favour of the Commissioners for Her Majesty's Revenue and Customs in relation to that land, and

(*b*) the UTRN for the SDLT land transaction return on which relief from the tax was claimed on the transfer of the land from the original owner to the bond-issuer.

4 Prescribed evidence for the purpose of paragraph 9 of Schedule 61

For the purpose of paragraph 9 of Schedule 61 (discharge of charge when conditions for relief met) the prescribed evidence is all of the following—

(*a*) a statement from the bond-issuer, or a person authorised to act on behalf of the bond-issuer, that all conditions A to C and E to G in Part 3 of Schedule 61 have been met,

(*b*) the UTRN for the SDLT land transaction return on which relief from the tax was claimed on the transfer of the land from the original owner to the bond-issuer,

(*c*) the UTRN for the SDLT land transaction return on which relief from the tax was claimed on the transfer of the land from the bond-issuer to the original owner, and (*d*) any document as provided by the relevant Land Registry confirming that the land has been registered in the name of the original owner.

5 Prescribed evidence for the purpose of paragraph 18(5) of Schedule 61

For the purposes of paragraph 18(5) of Schedule 61 (Substitution of asset) the prescribed evidence is all of the following—

(*a*) the UTRN for the SDLT land transaction return on which relief from the tax was claimed on the transfer of the land from the original owner to the bond-issuer,

(*b*) the UTRN for the SDLT land transaction return on which relief from the tax was claimed on the transfer of the land from the bond-issuer to the original owner, and

(*c*) any document as provided by the relevant Land Registry confirming that the land has been registered in the name of the original owner.

6 Prescribed evidence for the purpose of paragraph 18(6) of Schedule 61

For the purposes of paragraph 18(6) of Schedule 61 (Substitution of asset) the prescribed evidence is all of the following—

(*a*) the UTRN for the SDLT land transaction return on which relief from the tax was claimed on the transfer of the land from the original owner to the bond-issuer,

(*b*) the UTRN for the SDLT land transaction return on which relief from the tax was claimed on the transfer of the land from the bond-issuer to the original owner,

(*c*) any document that confirms that the replacement land is not in the United Kingdom and that conditions A to C in Part 3 of Schedule 61 have been met in relation to that land, and;

(*d*) any document as provided by the relevant Land Registry confirming that the land has been registered in the name of the original owner.

STAMP TAXES
EXTRA-STATUTORY CONCESSIONS

CONTENTS

CONCESSIONS

G1 Stamp allowance on lost documents

Note—This Concession has been classified as obsolete. See now SDMA 1891, s 12A.

G2 Stamping of replicas of documents which have been spoilt or lost

Note—This Concession has been classified as obsolete. See now SDMA 1891, s 12A.

G3 Group life and pension policies

Note—This Concession has been classified as obsolete: see FA 1989 s 173.

G4 Repayment of duty on cancelled policies

Note—This Concession has been classified as obsolete: see FA 1989 s 173.

G5 Transfer of stock from persons to themselves operating as an executor's assent

Stamp duty is not claimed on transfer of stock in a company registered in England, Wales or Northern Ireland from a person to himself (or from two or more persons to themselves) which operates as an executor's assent. The point does not arise in relation to companies registered in Scotland.

G6 Transfers of assets between non-profit making bodies with similar objects

When the reconstruction of a non-profit making body with objects in a field of public interest such as education, community work or scientific research, or the amalgamation of two or more such bodies involves a transfer to the successor body of assets for which there passes no consideration in money or money's worth, the instruments of transfer are treated as exempt from ad valorem stamp duty and charged to £5 fixed duty only. There must be sufficient identity between the members of the transferor and transferee bodies and the rules of both must prohibit the distribution of assets to members and provide that on a winding-up the assets can only be transferred to a similar body subject to like restrictions.

Note—This text of this Concession is as reproduced in IR 1 (August 2002).

G7 Transfers of stock into SEPON

Note—This Concession was replaced by FA 1996 s 191.

G8 Stock loan returns

Note—This Concession was replaced by FA 1996 s 191.

G9 Transfers of collateral

Note—This Concession was replaced by FA 1996 s 191.

STAMP TAXES
STATEMENTS OF PRACTICE

CONTENTS

Notes—Statements of Practice which are obsolete or obsolescent or are not applicable in the current year are listed in italics, but not printed.

Before 18 July 1978 information on administrative practice was issued in various forms including Parliamentary statements and written answers, and letters to professional bodies and journals. An index of those statements issued before 18 July 1978 which remained valid was published in a Revenue Press Release on 18 June 1979 and revised by further Press Releases dated 29 October 1980 and 23 March 1982.

These statements have no binding force and do not affect a taxpayer's right of appeal on points concerning his liability to tax.

HMRC note—The Civil Partnership Act (CPA) received Royal Assent on 18/11/2004 and became effective from 5 December 2005. The Government's commitment is that, for all tax purposes, same-sex couples who form a civil partnership will be treated the same as married couples.

As part of this commitment to tax parity, from 5 December 2005 all Statements of Practice should be taken as extended to apply equally to civil partners and married couples.

Currency—These Statements were updated by HMRC in August 2005. Please note that references to the 'Inland Revenue' should now be considered as referring to 'HM Revenue and Customs' and references to the 'Board of the Inland Revenue' should be read as the 'Commissioners for HM Revenue and Customs'.

SP 5/78 Conveyance in consideration of a debt (8 November 1978)

Note—This Statement was classified as obsolete by IR 131 (August 2002).

SP 3/84 Stamp duty: convertible loan stock (13 March 1984)

Transfers of certain loan capital are exempted from stamp duty by FA 1986 s 79. [Subsection (5)] provides that the exemption is not available where the loan capital carries an unexpired right of conversion into shares or other securities or to the acquisition of shares or other securities, including loan capital of the same description. The Commissioners for HMRC are advised that [subsection (5)] does not exclude from the exemption loan capital which carries an unexpired right of conversion into or acquisition of loan capital which itself comes within terms of the exemption.

Note—This statement was revised in Booklet IR 131 Supp (November 2000).

SP 9/84 Stamp duty: treatment of securities dealt in on the Stock Exchange Unlisted Securities Market

Note—This Statement was classified as obsolete by IR 131 (August 2002).

SP 10/87 Stamp duty: conveyances and leases of building plots (22 December 1987)

Note—This statement is superseded by SP 8/93.

SP 6/90 Conveyances and transfers of property subject to a debt: SA 1891 s 57 (27 April 1990)

INTRODUCTION

1 Since the abolition of the duty on voluntary dispositions in 1985, many enquiries have been received about the stamp duty chargeable on conveyances etc subject to a debt where *no* chargeable consideration (*eg* money or stock) unrelated to the debt is given by the transferee. This Statement of Practice sets out the Commissioners for HMRC's view of the correct stamp duty treatment of such conveyances.

2 For the sake of completeness it should be noted that where chargeable consideration unrelated to debt *is* given by the transferee, s 57 renders the conveyance liable to ad valorem duty on the aggregate of that consideration and the debt whether the transferee assumes liability for the debt or not (*IRC v City of Glasgow Bank* (1881) 8 R (Ct of Sess) 389, 18 SLR 242).

SA 1891 S 57

3 The most commonly misunderstood applications of s 57 arise where:

- a mortgaged property held in the name of one spouse is transferred into the joint names of both spouses;
- a mortgaged property held in the name of one spouse or in their joint names is transferred into the sole name of the other;
- a mortgaged business property, frequently farmland, is conveyed from a sole proprietor to a family partnership or from a family partnership to a fresh partnership bringing in other members of the family.

4 The critical question is whether the transaction to which the conveyance gives effect is or is not a sale. If it is, s 57 will apply and the conveyance will be chargeable to ad valorem duty on the amount of the debt assumed. If it is not, then s 57 will not apply and ad valorem duty will not be payable.

EXPRESS COVENANTS

5 Where property is transferred subject to a debt, the transferee may covenant, either in the instrument or by means of a separate written undertaking, to pay the debt or indemnify the transferor against his personal liability to the lender. Such a covenant or undertaking constitutes valuable consideration and, in view of s 57, establishes the transaction as a sale for stamp duty purposes.

6 Where the transferor covenants to pay the debt and the transferee does not assume any liability for it, no chargeable consideration has been given and there is no sale. The transfer would then be a voluntary disposition—i e an unencumbered gift capable of being certified as Category L under the Stamp Duty (Exempt Instruments) Regulations 1987 (SI 1987/516)—and so exempt from the 50p charge that would otherwise arise.

IMPLIED COVENANTS

7 Where no express covenant or undertaking is given by the transferee, the Commissioners for HMRC are advised that, except in Scotland, a covenant by the transferee may be implied. That makes the transaction a sale, as in para 4 above.

8 Such an implied covenant may be negated if there is evidence that it was the intention of the parties at the time of the transfer that the transferor should continue to be liable for the whole of the mortgage debt. Where evidence of such a contrary intention exists, the transfer would again be treated for stamp duty purposes as a voluntary disposition.

9 Where property in joint names subject to a debt is transferred to one of the joint holders (though with no cash passing), a covenant by the transferee to indemnify the transferor may be implied even where both parties were jointly liable on the mortgage.

AMOUNT CHARGEABLE

10 Where a conveyance of property subject to a debt is chargeable to ad valorem duty and the express or implied covenant by the transferee relates only to part of the debt, only the amount of that part is treated as chargeable consideration within s 57. A certificate of value under [FA 1999 Sch 13 para 6] may, where appropriate, be included in the conveyance where the relevant amount of the debt does not exceed the amount certified.

OTHER PROVISIONS

11 The foregoing does not affect any statutory exemption from duty that may apply, *eg* that for transfers to a charity (FA 1982 s 129) and that available for certain transfers of property from one party to a marriage to the other in connection with their divorce or separation (FA 1985 s 83(1) and Stamp Duty (Exempt Instruments) Regulations 1987, Category H).

PROCEDURE

12 Where the applicant is satisfied that the conveyance or transfer is made on sale, it may be sent or taken for stamping with a remittance for the duty payable. If the transfer contains an appropriate certificate of value—see para 10 above—it may be sent direct to the Land Registry in the usual way if appropriate. In either case, if the amount of the debt outstanding is not given in the conveyance or transfer the amount should be stated in a covering letter.

13 Where the conveyance or transfer contains a covenant by the transferor to pay the debt (see para 6) and is certified as within the Stamp Duty (Exempt Instruments) Regulations 1987, Category L it should also be sent direct to the Land Registry if appropriate.

14 In any other case where the applicant believes that the conveyance or transfer effects a voluntary disposition—see para 8 above—it should be presented for adjudication accompanied by a statement of the facts and any supporting evidence.

Note—This statement was revised in Booklet IR 131 Supp (November 2000).

SP 6/91 Stamp duty and value added tax (VAT): interaction (22 July 1991)

Note—Superseded by SP 11/91.

SP 11/91 Stamp duty and VAT—interaction (12 September 1991)

1 This statement is a revised version of the statement about stamp duty and VAT issued on 22 July 1991, SP 6/91, and replaces it.

INTRODUCTION

2 To comply with a judgment of the European Court of Justice in June 1988, standard rate UK VAT has been applied to non-residential construction with effect from 1 April 1989 (FA 1989 s 18). VAT is compulsory on sales of buildings treated as new for this purpose, which are mainly buildings under three years old that have been completed after March 1989. And owners of non-residential property were given the option from 1 August 1989 of charging VAT on sales of old buildings and on leases.

3 These new charges have prompted a number of enquiries about the relationship between stamp duty and VAT where both taxes arise on a sale or lease of commercial property or, occasionally, other assets.

SALES OF NEW NON-DOMESTIC BUILDINGS

4 The Commissioners for HMRC are advised that for stamp duty purposes the amount or value of the consideration for a sale is the gross amount inclusive of VAT. Therefore where VAT is payable on the sale of new non-residential property, stamp duty is calculated on the VAT-inclusive consideration.

OTHER NON-DOMESTIC TRANSACTIONS

5 Transactions in non-residential property other than sales of new buildings are exempt from VAT. These include—

- sales of old buildings
- the assignment of existing leases, or the creation of new leases, in old or new property.

However, the vendor or lessor can elect to waive the exemption.

6 The Commissioners for HMRC have received legal advice that—

- where the election has already been exercised at the time of the transaction, stamp duty is chargeable on the purchase price, premium or rent including VAT;
- where the election has not been exercised at that time, VAT should similarly be included in any payments to which an election could still apply (which will depend on the facts of each case).

7 The Commissioners for HMRC propose to follow this advice, which will result in a change of practice: in the past, the Stamp Office did not seek to include the VAT element in the stamp duty charge in cases where an election to waive the exemption from VAT had not yet been exercised. The new practice applies to documents executed on or after 1 August 1991.

8 Neither a formal notice of election made to HM Customs & Excise, nor any notification to the purchaser or lessee that such an election has been made, will attract stamp duty.

RENT

9 Where VAT is charged on the rent under a lease, and is itself treated as rent under the lease, stamp duty at the appropriate rate according to the length of the term will be charged on the VAT-inclusive figure. If the lease provides for payment of VAT on the rent otherwise than as rent, duty will be charged on the VAT element as consideration payable periodically (Stamp Act 1891 s 56). In either case the rate of VAT in force at the date of execution of the lease will be used in the calculation.

10 In the case of a formal Deed of Variation or similar document varying the terms of the original lease so as to provide for payment of VAT by way of additional rent, further stamp duty may be payable (Stamp Act 1891 s 77(5)).

AGREEMENTS FOR LEASES

11 Paragraphs 5 to 10 above also apply to an agreement for lease if that is the instrument to be stamped [FA 1999 Sch 13 para 14].

PROCEDURE

12 Applicants for stamping are requested to make clear, either in the conveyance or lease document itself, or in a covering letter to the Stamp Office, whether the property is commercial or residential.

13 Deeds of Variation etc (para 10 above) should be presented for adjudication together with a copy of the original lease.

NO VAT ON STAMP DUTY

14 It is sometimes suggested that stamp duty might itself attract a charge to VAT. This is not the case. The value for VAT depends on the amount (consideration) obtained by the supplier from the purchaser, less the included VAT itself. Stamp duty is paid by the purchaser/lessee of property direct to HMRC and not to the supplier; it does not therefore form part of the consideration for VAT purposes.

Note—This statement was revised in Booklet IR 131 Supp (November 2000).

SP 8/93 Stamp duty: new buildings (12 July 1993)

This statement sets out the practice the Commissioners for HMRC will apply in relation to the stamp duty chargeable in certain circumstances on the conveyance or lease of a new or partly constructed building. It affects transactions where, at the date of the contract for sale or lease of a building plot, building work has not commenced or has been only partially completed on that site but where that work has started or has been completed at the time the conveyance or lease is executed.

This statement reflects the advice the Commissioners for HMRC have received on this subject in the light of the decision in the case of *Prudential Assurance Company Ltd v IRC* ([1992] STC 863; [1993] 1 WLR 211). The statement does not apply to the common situation where the parties have entered into a contract for the sale of a new house and that contract is implemented by a conveyance of the whole property. This statement replaces the statements of practice issued in 1957 and 1987 (SP 10/87) on this subject which are now withdrawn.

The Commissioners for HMRC are advised that, whilst each case will clearly depend on its own facts, the law is as follows—

1 TWO TRANSACTIONS/TWO CONTRACTS

Where the purchaser or lessee is entitled under the terms of a contract to a conveyance or lease of land alone in consideration of the purchase price or rent of the site and a second genuine contract for building works is entered into as a separate transaction, the *ad valorem* duty on the conveyance or lease will be determined by the amount of the purchase price or rent which the purchaser or lessee is obliged to pay under the terms of the first contract. In these circumstances it does not matter whether any building work has commenced at the date of the conveyance or lease. The consideration chargeable to *ad valorem* duty will still be only that passing for the land.

2 ONE TRANSACTION/TWO CONTRACTS

Where there is one transaction between the parties but this is implemented by two contracts, one for the sale or lease of the building plot and one for the building works themselves, the amount of ad valorem duty charged on the instrument will depend on the amount of the consideration, which in turn will depend on whether those contracts can be shown to be genuinely independent of each other.

(i) if the two contracts are so interlocked that they cannot be said to be genuinely capable of independent completion (and in particular where if default occurs on either contract, the other is then not enforceable) ad valorem duty will be charged on the total consideration for the land and buildings, whether completed or not, as if the parties had entered into only one contract.

(ii) if the two contracts are shown to be genuinely independent of each other, ad valorem duty will be charged by reference to the consideration paid or payable for the land and any building works on that land at the date of execution of the instrument. It follows that, where the instrument is executed after the building works are completed, ad valorem duty will be charged on the consideration for the land and the completed building(s).

3 SHAM OR ARTIFICIAL TRANSACTIONS

This statement does not apply to cases where the transaction concerned, or any part of it, involves a sham or artificial transaction.

CONTRACTS ALREADY ENTERED INTO

Where unconditional contracts have been entered into before or within 28 days of the date of this Statement and the duty payable on the resulting conveyance or lease would have been less under the earlier Statements of Practice, the Stamp Office will accept duty in the lesser amount. In such cases the instrument should be submitted together with all the evidence to support the claim that unconditional contracts were entered into within this transitional period.

PROCEDURE FOR SUBMITTING DOCUMENTS

Where a person accepts that a conveyance or lease of a building plot is chargeable on the total price paid or payable for the land and the completed building, it should be submitted for stamping in the usual way together with a covering letter giving the aggregate price and a payment for the duty appropriate to that price.

Where the total price does not exceed the amount up to which the instrument is liable to nil duty (currently £60,000) and a certificate of value is included in the instrument, a conveyance may be sent direct to the Land Registry in England and Wales or, in Scotland, to the Keeper of the Registers of Scotland. A lease will need to be stamped in respect of the rent.

Where the total price exceeds the threshold at which duty becomes payable but the taxpayer takes the view that duty is payable on some smaller sum, the instrument should be submitted to the Stamp Office. This applies even where the taxpayer believes that the amount potentially chargeable to *ad valorem* duty is below the threshold and a certificate of value is included in the instrument. The instrument should be accompanied by a copy of the agreement(s) for sale etc and a letter stating the amount which the taxpayer regards as chargeable consideration, identifying separately any amount attributable to building work. Details of any contractual arrangements not covered by the agreement(s) should also be given in the covering letter.

Note—This statement was revised in Booklet IR 131 (August 2002).

SP 3/98 Stamp duty—group relief (13 October 1998)

1 FA 1930 s 42 gives relief from stamp duty for transfers of property between members of the same group of companies. FA 1995 s 151 similarly gives relief from duty on the grant of a lease between members of the same group.

2 FA 1967 s 27(3) and FA 1995 s 151(3) are designed to prevent the use of group relief to avoid stamp duty when property, or an economic interest in it, passes out of the group.

3 This statement sets out the Stamp Office's current general practice in order to assist practitioners in determining whether claims to relief might qualify. The treatment of a particular case will of course depend on the precise facts. This statement is for general guidance only; and the facts of a particular transaction may, exceptionally, place it outside the guidelines. It applies also to the equivalent Northern Ireland legislation.

GENERAL

4 Broadly, s 27(3) and the corresponding provisions in s 151, provide that relief is not to be given if the transfer was made in pursuance of, or in connection with, an arrangement under which—

(a) all or part of the consideration for the transfer was to be provided or received, directly or indirectly, by a person outside the group; or
(b) the interest being transferred was previously transferred by a person outside the group; or
(c) the transferor and transferee were no longer to be part of the same group.

5 The person claiming the relief when the relevant instrument is adjudicated has the onus of satisfying the Stamp Office that the intra-group transaction is not carried out in pursuance of, or in connection with, an arrangement of a kind which disqualifies the transaction from relief—*Escoigne Properties Ltd v IRC* [1958] AC 549, 564.

"ARRANGEMENT"

6 In this context, arrangement means the plan or scheme in pursuance of which the things identified in ss 27(3), 151(3) have been or are to be done—*Shop and Store Developments Ltd v IRC* [1967] 1 AC 472, 493, 494. The arrangement need not be based in contract. It is sufficient if the intra-group transaction is made in connection with that plan or scheme. The intra-group transaction may be the first bi-lateral step by which legal rights and obligations are created in pursuance of the arrangement. If there is an expectation that a disqualifying event will happen in accordance with the arrangement and no likelihood in practice that it will not, relief will be refused.

7 The words "in connection with" are very broad. In *Escoigne*, there was a gap of four years between the two steps in issue.

PROVISION OR RECEIPT OF CONSIDERATION BY A PERSON OUTSIDE THE GROUP—FA 1967 S 27(3)(A); FA 1995 S 151(3)(A), (4)

8 Section 27(3)(*a*) denies relief where the instrument was executed in pursuance of or in connection with an arrangement under which any of the consideration is to be provided or received, directly or indirectly, by a person outside the group. It also denies relief if the arrangement is one under which the transferor or transferee (or a member of the same group as either of them) is to be enabled to provide any of the consideration, or is to part with it, in consequence of a transaction involving a payment or other disposition by a person outside the group. Section 151 lays down similar rules for leases.

9 In some cases, the question arises whether loan finance for the purchase or lease will disqualify an intra-group transaction from relief. It is necessary to look at all the facts of the individual case, but the Stamp Office will interpret the provisions in the light of their general purpose of denying relief where the intra-group transaction is a means of saving stamp duty when the property, or an interest in it, moves out of the group. Accordingly, the Stamp Office are likely to be satisfied that relief is due if the intra-group transaction is not to be followed by a sale of the property transferred, or an underlease, to a person outside the group. If the intra-group transaction is to be followed by a sale or underlease to a person outside the group, but the claimant can demonstrate that stamp duty will be paid in respect of that transaction in approximately the same amount as would have been payable if the intra-group transferor or lessor had itself sold the property or granted the underlease, the Stamp Office are likely to be satisfied that the intra-group transaction and the transfer or lease out are independent for stamp duty purposes and grant the relief sought.

10 A transaction is not disqualified merely because the transferee within the group obtains a specific loan for the purchase of the asset; or the loan is secured on the asset; or arrangements are made to replace or novate an existing charge on the property transferred. It will be necessary to consider the facts as a whole, especially if the loan finance is not straightforward finance on ordinary commercial terms.

11 Intra-group transactions will be very carefully scrutinised, and relief may be refused, where, for example, the intra-group transaction involves or is to be followed by—

– the creation or transfer of loan stock or equity capital;

- a capital reorganisation of the transferee;
- a guarantee by a third party not associated with the group;
- the creation of a new charge or financial arrangement whereby title to the property is, or may be, vested in the lender otherwise than in satisfaction of all or part of the debt; or
- the assignment of the freehold reversion or the intra-group lease to a person outside the group.

12 Similarly transactions will be very carefully scrutinised where—

- all or part of the consideration for the transaction is to remain outstanding or is represented by intra-group debt, (as the aim and effect may be to reduce the value of the transferee company on a possible future sale outside the group); or
- the existing shareholders of the transferee include shareholders outside the group and the transaction is to be followed by the declaration of a dividend in *specie*, or by the liquidation of the transferee.

13 Further assurances by way of statutory declaration—the document in which the claim is made to the Stamp Office—will be required in any case in which the property transferred or vested intra-group is the only, or only substantial, asset of the transferee. Information to that effect should be provided in the statutory declaration submitted with the documents.

14 Where group member A has granted a lease to a person outside the group, and subsequently grants an underlease to its fellow group member B, so that the rent already payable by the lessee becomes payable to B rather than A, relief is likely to be given for the intra-group underlease, provided there are no other factors which suggest that relief should be denied.

PROPERTY PREVIOUSLY CONVEYED BY A PERSON OUTSIDE THE GROUP—FA 1967 S 27(3)(B)

15 Section 27(3)(*b*) was intended to prevent the avoidance of duty on the transfer of property into a group by means of a sub-sale, so as to take advantage of the Stamp Act 1891 s 58(4). For example, suppose the property is sold to a group member by a vendor outside the group, but the sale rests in contract without a transfer of the legal title. The group member then sells the property to another member of its own group, and directs the vendor to transfer the legal title to that other member. In accordance with s 58(4) the transfer completing the sale and the sub-sale is chargeable to duty only in relation to the sub-sale (thus relieving the effect of s 4 of the Stamp Act). However, s 27(3)(*b*) would deny group relief for that transfer.

16 The Stamp Office will continue to apply s 27(3)(*b*) to schemes of this type and to any other scheme where an attempt has been made to avoid the duty payable on the acquisition by the group. However, where an outside vendor sells a property to a member of the group, the sale is completed by a transfer and stamp duty is paid on that transfer, the Stamp Office will normally regard any subsequent intra-group transfer as independent, and grant relief for the transfer within the purchaser's group.

DISSOCIATION OR DEMERGER OF TRANSFEREE—FA 1967 S 27(3)(C): FA 1995 S 151(3)(B)

17 Before the introduction of s 27(3), almost all the avoidance devices encountered in this area involved the transfer of property to a subsidiary, often created solely as a vehicle for that property, followed by the transfer of the shares in the subsidiary out of the group. Compared with a transfer of the property out of the group, a substantial amount of duty could be avoided even where the subsidiary paid for the property from its own resources. If the consideration for the intra-group transaction remained outstanding or was represented by debt, duty could be reduced further by reducing the value of the shares—hence s 27(3)(*a*).

18 Section 27(3)(*c*) was introduced to counter this avoidance in relation to conveyances and transfers on sale. Section 151(3)(*b*) deals with leases on similar lines.

19 In cases of this kind, the Stamp Office will need to be satisfied that the intra-group transfer or lease is not a step in pursuance of an arrangement to demerge the transferee. The existence of such an arrangement may be apparent from company documents, correspondence and other dealings between members of the group and professional advisers, or from discussions or negotiations with the potential purchasers, underwriters or minority shareholders.

20 In practice, the Stamp Office will apply these provisions so as to preclude group relief if there is evidence of a plan or scheme to dispose of the subsidiary and there is no practical likelihood that the scheme will not be carried through. It will not be regarded as sufficient for the claimant to contend that such an arrangement which is less than contractual may possibly be frustrated by unforeseen events or unlikely occurrences. Even a contract may be frustrated.

21 As the liability of the relevant instrument must, as a matter of general principle, be determined as at the date of the instrument, the question whether an arrangement of the relevant kind exists must also be determined at that time, although the Stamp Office may have regard to what is said and done thereafter to establish the true position (*Wm Cory and Son Ltd v IRC* [1965] AC 1088). For the purposes of stamp duty, it is therefore the existence of the scheme or plan to which these provisions direct attention, not the ultimate outcome of steps, which may be taken to implement that scheme. Accordingly, statements of practice in relation to other taxes have no application in this context.

SP 1/03 Stamp duty—Disadvantaged Areas Relief (April 2003)

This Statement of Practice is intended as guidance for those claiming exemption from stamp duty in respect of transfers of property situated in designated areas ("Disadvantaged Areas Relief") and explains how Inland Revenue Stamp Taxes will interpret the extension to the relief introduced with effect from 10 April 2003.

The relief is one of a number of measures set out in the Government's Urban White Paper "*Our Towns and Cities—The Future—Delivering an Urban Renaissance*" published in November 2000. The measure is designed to stimulate the physical, economic and social regeneration of the UK's most disadvantaged areas by attracting development and by encouraging the purchase of residential and commercial property by individuals and businesses. The areas eligible for relief were designated "Enterprise Areas" by the Chancellor in his 2002 Pre-Budget Report. In addition to the relief, a range of other Government policies designed to support enterprise and economic regeneration, including the Community Investment Tax Relief, will benefit these areas, helping to support the development of new and existing businesses.

INTRODUCTION

1 Disadvantaged Areas Relief (provided for by section 92 of, and Schedule 30 to, the Finance Act 2001) was introduced on 30 November 2001 and was initially only available for conveyances or transfers on sale (of both residential and commercial property) for which the consideration did not exceed £150,000. Stamp duty in respect of conveyances or transfers of commercial property in disadvantaged areas was abolished in consequence of the Stamp Duty (Disadvantaged Areas) (Application of Exemptions) Regulations 2003 ("the Regulations"), which have effect in relation to instruments executed on or after 10 April 2003. Thereafter the £150,000 limit applies only in relation to residential property.

2 Finance Act 2002 inserted the following provisions in Finance Act 2001 to distinguish residential from other property and to provide for differing stamp duty exemptions—

- Section 92A which enables stamp duty relief in designated disadvantaged areas in respect of all properties to be varied depending on whether or not the property is "residential";
- Section 92B which defines "residential property" for the purposes of the relief. Non-residential property, in respect of which unlimited relief is available, is therefore defined in the Act by exclusion. The section also sets out particular building uses that are specifically included within, or specifically excluded from, the definition.

3 In most cases there will be no difficulty in practice in establishing whether or not a property is "residential". This statement sets out in more detail the Stamp Office's approach to borderline cases and gives guidance on the practical application of the legislation. The annexed flowchart provides a quick guide for simpler cases as to whether property constitutes "residential property".

CERTIFICATION

4 Claims for unlimited relief must be accompanied by a certificate stating either that none of the land in question is residential property or, if part is residential, the proportion that is non-residential (together with the usual certificate of value for the remainder).

- Residential property—Section 92A(4) of Finance Act 2001, together with the Regulations, provides that the exemption will only apply if the document is certified to the effect that the amount or value of the consideration does not exceed £150,000.
- Non-residential property—Subsection (2) of section 92 of Finance Act 2001 provides that the exemption will only apply if the document is certified to the Commissioners as being an instrument on which stamp duty is not chargeable by virtue of subsection (1) of that section.

5 The following are suggested forms of words for particular certificates—

- Residential Property— "I/We hereby certify that the transaction effected by this instrument does not form part of a larger transaction or series of transactions in respect of which the amount or value of the consideration exceeds £150,000 and that stamp duty is not chargeable thereon by virtue of the provisions of sections 92 and 92A of the Finance Act 2001."
- Non-residential Property— "I/We hereby certify that this is an instrument in respect of non-residential property on which stamp duty is not chargeable by virtue of the provisions of section 92 of the Finance Act 2001."
- Mixed Use Property— "I/We hereby certify that the transaction effected by this instrument is in respect of property part of which is residential property, and which does not form part of a larger transaction or series of transactions in respect of which the amount or value of the consideration relating to the residential part exceeds £150,000 so that stamp duty is not chargeable by virtue of sections 92 and 92A of the Finance Act 2001, and part of which is

non-residential property on which stamp duty is not chargeable by virtue of the provisions of section 92 of the Finance Act 2001. The basis upon which the allocation between residential and non-residential parts has been made is as follows:...."

6 While the legislation does not specifically require the certificate to be included as part of the document, it is suggested that it should be so included. If the person submitting the document for stamping does not provide a certificate, either in the document or separately in writing, exemption will not be granted.

7 Appropriate contemporaneous evidence should be retained to support any certificate provided. Estate agents' specifications, site plans, planning applications or permissions, marketing material and photographs may all provide relevant information.

8 Anyone falsely certifying a document with a view to obtaining relief that is not due will be committing a stamp duty fraud.

THE MEANING OF RESIDENTIAL PROPERTY

9 Section 92B defines "residential property" as a building which—

- is used as a dwelling, **or**
- is suitable for use as a dwelling, or
- is in the process of being constructed or adapted for such use.

If a property meets any one of these separate tests it will be treated as residential property and be subject to the £150,000 limit for relief, as will any garden or grounds belonging to it or any interests or rights attaching to it. Each element of the definition is considered in turn below.

The question of whether and to what extent a building and grounds are defined as residential property for stamp duty purposes may also have implications for its treatment for capital gains tax and local authority rates.

USE AS A DWELLING

10 Where a building is in use at the date of execution of the relevant instrument, it will be a question of fact whether and to what extent it is used as a dwelling. Use at the date the instrument is executed overrides any past or intended future uses for this purpose.

11 Where the property in question is in use as a dwelling at the date of execution, it is residential property for the purposes of the relief unless it is part of a multiple transaction qualifying for relief under the Regulations (see paragraphs 35 to 39 below).

12 For the treatment of buildings put to both residential and non-residential use, see paragraphs 17 and 18 below.

SUITABLE FOR USE AS A DWELLING

13 The suitability test applies to the state of the building at the time the instrument is executed, having regard to the facilities available and any history of use. For example, HMRC will not regard an office block as "suitable for use as a dwelling", but a house which has been used as an office without particular adaptation may well be so.

14 If a building is not in use at the date of execution but its last use was as a dwelling, it will be taken to be 'suitable for use as a dwelling' and treated as residential property for the purposes of the relief, unless evidence is produced to the contrary (see paragraph 15).

15 Whether a building is suitable for use as a dwelling will depend upon the precise facts and circumstances. The simple removal of, for example, a bathroom suite or kitchen facilities will not be regarded as rendering a building unsuitable for use as a dwelling. Where it is claimed that a previously residential property is no longer suitable for use as a dwelling, perhaps because it is derelict or has been substantially altered, the claimant will need to provide evidence that this is the case. See also paragraph 29.

16 Where a building has been used partly for residential purposes and partly for another purpose, its overall suitability for use as a dwelling will be judged from the facilities available at the date of execution of the relevant document. For example, if two rooms of a house were in use as a dentist's surgery and waiting room at the date of execution, HMRC would nevertheless normally consider this property suitable for use as a dwelling unless the claimant provided evidence to the contrary. In other words, the interaction of the Regulations with section 92B(1) enables a building that is used only partly as a dwelling to be nevertheless suitable for use wholly as a dwelling, with the effect that the £150,000 limit applies to the whole of the consideration. Where only a distinct part of the building is used and suitable for use as a dwelling, that part will be residential property for the purposes of the relief and the mixed use provisions will apply (paragraphs 17 and 18 below).

MIXED USE

17 Where only part of a building (and land or interest relating to it) is "residential property" within section 92B(1), the consideration "shall be apportioned on such basis as is just and reasonable" between the residential and non-residential elements. The £150,000 limit is then applied only to the residential portion, in accordance with the appropriate certification (regulation 5 of the Regulations). For example—

A property situated wholly within a disadvantaged area is bought for:

(a) £200,000
(b) £400,000

50% of the property is "residential property" on the basis of a just and reasonable apportionment.

Relief is conferred by FA 2001 s 92, applied in conjunction with regulation 5 of the Regulations. Paragraph (3) of regulation 5 calls for an apportionment of the total consideration between residential and non-residential elements. Paragraph (4) confirms that relief applies to the residential property element only where the consideration attributed to it does not exceed £150,000. In these examples—

(a) £100,000 is attributed to the residential property element, so relief is due. The part of the land that is not residential property is also exempt under the normal operation of FA 2001 s 92. So no duty is payable.
(b) the £200,000 attributed to the residential property element is not exempt, because of regulation 5(4), but attracts duty at the rate of 1% (stamp duty payable £2,000). The non-residential property element is exempt as above.

18 The "just and reasonable" test is necessarily subjective, and each case will be considered on its merits. Apportionment might be on the basis of the percentage areas quoted in planning applications, where appropriate, or alternatively of floor space relating to the respective uses. Other methods of apportionment will be considered as part of a claim.

SPECIFIC CASES

19 Some types of communal or institutional building are used neither as dwellings nor for commercial purposes. The legislation therefore outlines how these are classified for the purposes of relief, specifically *including* some such buildings within the definition of "dwelling" (section 92B(2)) and specifically *excluding* others (section 92B(3)). If they do not fall within any of the specific categories of section 92B(3), most residential institutions will come within section 92B(2)(*d*) and will be treated as dwellings by default.

20 Categories of building use specifically included within the definition of "use as a dwelling" (so that transfers of such buildings only qualify for relief if the consideration does not exceed £150,000) (section 92B(2)) are—

(a) residential accommodation for school pupils, for example accommodation blocks in boarding schools;
(b) residential accommodation for students, other than that within section 92B(3)(*b*). Student accommodation provided by private landlords is 'a dwelling', as is accommodation leased to students by universities or colleges in flats or houses rather than in halls of residence (see section 92B(3)(*b*));
(c) residential accommodation for members of any of the armed forces, including accommodation for their families (section 92B(2)(*c*));
(d) an institution that is the sole or main residence of at least 90% of its residents and does not fall within any of the categories referred to in section 92B(3) (see section 92B(2)(*d*) and also paragraph 21 below). This would include, for example,
    - sheltered accommodation for the elderly where no nursing or personal care is provided
    - accommodation for religious communities (subject to the rules regarding mixed use; see paragraphs 17 and 18).

21 Categories of building use specifically excluded from the definition of 'use as a dwelling' (so that transfers of such buildings in a disadvantaged area will qualify for unlimited relief) (section 92B(3)) are—

(a) a home or other institution providing residential accommodation for children;
(b) a hall of residence for students in further or higher education. This is not defined in the legislation but in practice property provided by a university or similar establishment will be judged on the facts (number of inhabitants, type of facilities, availability of communal areas);
(c) a home or other institution providing residential accommodation with personal care for persons in need of personal care by reason of old age, disablement, past or present dependence on alcohol or drugs or past or present mental disorder;
(d) a hospital or hospice;
(e) a prison or similar establishment, or
(f) a hotel or inn or similar establishment.

22 The specific inclusions and exclusions set out in paragraphs 20 and 21 above apply not only to a building's actual use at the date of the transfer, but to the uses for which it is suitable at that date. Where, however, a building is being put to one of the non-residential uses specified in section 92B(3), this overrides any suitability for another use (section 92B(4)). For example, a

Stamp Taxes

building used as a children's home may also be suitable for use as a school boarding house, but this will not preclude a claim to unlimited relief.

23 Where a vacant building is suitable for at least one of the uses specified in section 92B(2) and at least one specified in section 92B(3), the tiebreaker in section 92B(5) determines, for the purposes of the relief, the use for which it is "most suitable". Whether or not a vacant building has one or more uses for which it is most suitable is a question of fact. Evidence supporting such uses should be provided with the claim for relief.

24 Where there is a single use for which a building is most suitable, the fact that it is also suitable for another use will be discounted.

25 If there are a number of uses for which a building is most suitable and they all come within either of the two subsections, any other use for which the building is suitable will be discounted.

26 Where no most suitable use can be shown, the default will be to classify the building as residential property and apply the £150,000 limit.

27 Land and buildings that are not suitable for any use at the date of execution will be treated as residential property if they are "in the process of being constructed or adapted for such use"- see paragraphs 28 and 29 below.

PROCESS OF BEING CONSTRUCTED OR ADAPTED FOR USE AS A DWELLING

28 Undeveloped land is in essence non-residential, but land may be "residential property" for the purposes of disadvantaged areas relief if a residential building is being built on it at the date the instrument is executed. The process of construction is taken as commencing when the builders first start work. A development of six or more dwellings is deemed to be non-residential under regulation 6 of the Regulations, even if in the process of construction at the date of the instrument (see paragraph 35 below).

29 Where (at the date the relevant instrument is executed) an existing building is being adapted for, or restored to, domestic use, it is "residential property" for the purposes of the relief. This may apply, for example, where a derelict building is being made fit for habitation, or where a previously non-residential building is being converted to a dwelling. Again, the process is taken as commencing when the builders start work.

THE GARDEN OR GROUNDS OF A BUILDING USED ETC. AS A DWELLING

30 Section 92B(1)(*b*) includes within the definition of residential property "land that is or forms part of the garden or grounds of a building within paragraph (*a*) (including any building or structure on such land)". The test HMRC will apply is similar to that applied for the purposes of the capital gains tax relief for main residences (section 222(3) of the Taxation of Chargeable Gains Act 1992). The land will include that which is needed for the reasonable enjoyment of the dwelling having regard to the size and nature of the dwelling.

31 A caravan or houseboat is not a "building" for this purpose.

32 Commercial farmland is not within the definition of residential property. A farmhouse situated on agricultural land would be dealt with under the mixed use provisions (paragraphs 17 and 18 above).

33 Outhouses on land within the section 92B(1)(*b*) definition will also be "residential property" unless it can be demonstrated that they have a specific non-residential purpose. Where a distinct non-residential use can be demonstrated, the mixed use provisions will apply.

INTEREST IN OR RIGHTS OVER RESIDENTIAL PROPERTY

34 The treatment of interests in, or rights over, land or buildings for the purposes of disadvantaged areas relief will follow that of the land or buildings to which they relate.

SIX OR MORE SEPARATE DWELLINGS TRANSFERRED BY SINGLE CONTRACT

35 The Regulations provide that "where there is a single contract for the conveyance, transfer or lease of land comprising or including six or more separate dwellings, none of that land counts as residential property ..." Accordingly the transaction will qualify for unlimited relief. This recognises that commercial developers and institutional landlords, for example, frequently deal in numerous properties at one time. The fact that those properties may individually be "residential property" does not detract from the inherently commercial nature of the transaction itself.

36 To qualify as "separate", the dwellings must be self-contained. So for example, flats within a block, sharing some common areas but each with their own amenities, will qualify as separate dwellings. Rooms let within a house will not constitute separate dwellings if tenants share amenities such as a kitchen and bathroom.

37 A transaction in respect of six or more such dwellings must be carried out by means of a single contract in order to qualify for relief. Several instruments may however be presented for stamping if the properties are held under separate title.

38 Qualifying multiple transactions will be treated as non-residential property for the purposes of relief, even where the proportionate consideration for individual dwellings exceeds the £150,000 limit for residential property. It is not a condition of relief that multiple transactions comprise only dwellings.

39 The fact that some of the six or more dwellings within the single contract are outside a designated disadvantaged area will not prevent them from constituting a non-residential transaction. However relief will only be available for the portion of the land situated within the disadvantaged area.

PROPERTY ONLY PARTLY WITHIN A DISADVANTAGED AREA

40 Schedule 30 to Finance Act 2001, together with the Regulations, determines how property situated partly within and partly outside a designated disadvantaged area is to be treated for the purposes of the relief. Such cases are relatively rare in practice. Queries may be referred to Inland Revenue (Stamp Taxes) for guidance.

LEASE DUTY

41 Relief is also available from duty on the rental element of new leases executed on or after 10 April 2003. Rental leases of residential property shall be eligible for relief where the average annual rent is no more than £15,000 and/ or where any premium does not exceed £150,000. For non- residential property, full relief is available for the rental element of leases as well as for any premium.

OTHER ISSUES

42 The extended relief applies to documents executed on or after 10 April 2003, irrespective of whether the contract was entered into before or after that date. There is no scope to reclaim stamp duty already paid in respect of transfers executed on or before 9 April 2003.

FLOW CHART TO DETERMINE WHETHER PROPERTY IS OR IS NOT 'RESIDENTIAL PROPERTY'

Is the subject of the conveyance/transfer/lease …

(A)

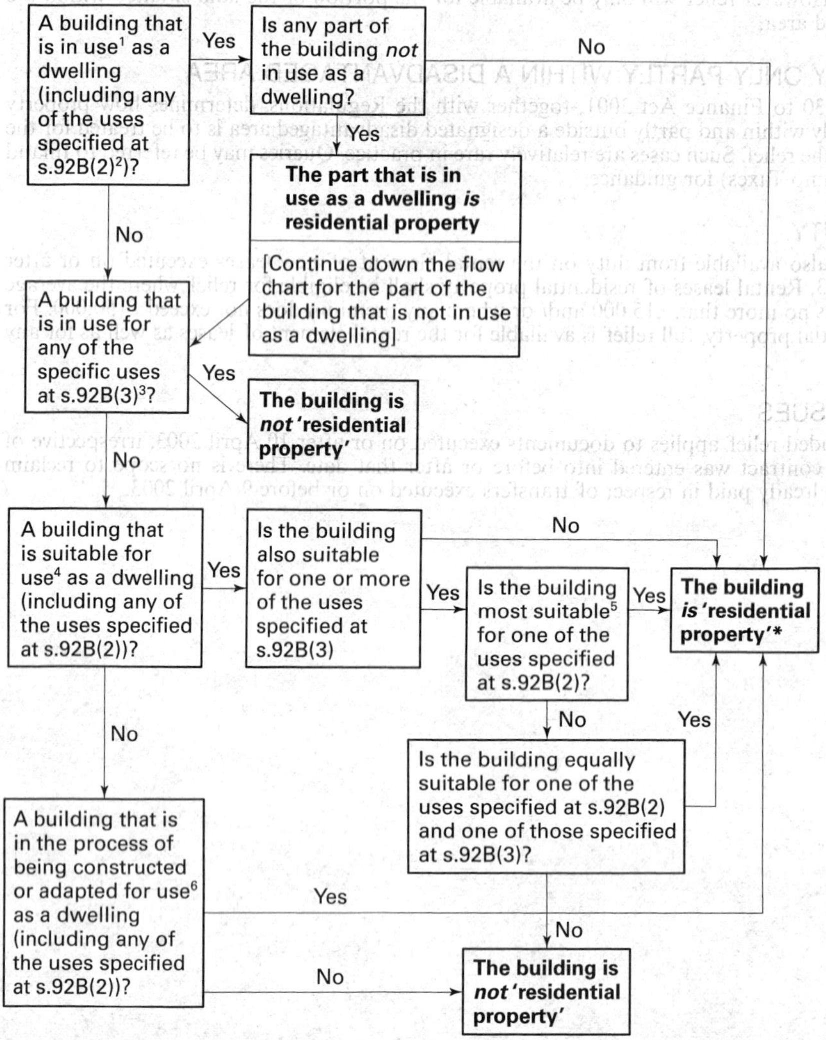

A building that is in use[1] as a dwelling (including any of the uses specified at s.92B(2)[2])?

- Yes → Is any part of the building *not* in use as a dwelling?
  - Yes → **The part that is in use as a dwelling *is* residential property**

    [Continue down the flow chart for the part of the building that is not in use as a dwelling]
  - No → **The building *is* 'residential property'***
- No → A building that is in use for any of the specific uses at s.92B(3)[3]?
  - Yes → **The building is *not* 'residential property'**
  - No → A building that is suitable for use[4] as a dwelling (including any of the uses specified at s.92B(2))?
    - Yes → Is the building also suitable for one or more of the uses specified at s.92B(3)
      - No → **The building *is* 'residential property'***
      - Yes → Is the building most suitable[5] for one of the uses specified at s.92B(2)?
        - Yes → **The building *is* 'residential property'***
        - No → Is the building equally suitable for one of the uses specified at s.92B(2) and one of those specified at s.92B(3)?
          - Yes → **The building *is* 'residential property'***
          - No → **The building is *not* 'residential property'**
    - No → A building that is in the process of being constructed or adapted for use[6] as a dwelling (including any of the uses specified at s.92B(2))?
      - Yes → **The building *is* 'residential property'***
      - No → **The building is *not* 'residential property'**

*unless the conveyance, transfer or lease comprises or includes six or more separate dwellings[7] made persuant to a single contract, in which circumstances none of the land will be 'residential property'

Is the subject of the conveyance/transfer/lease …

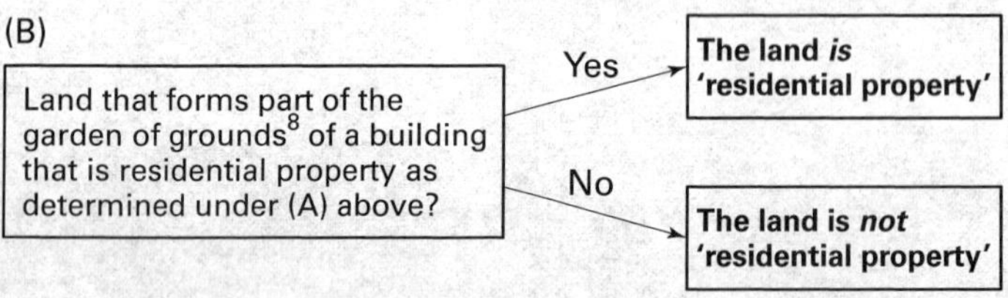

(C)

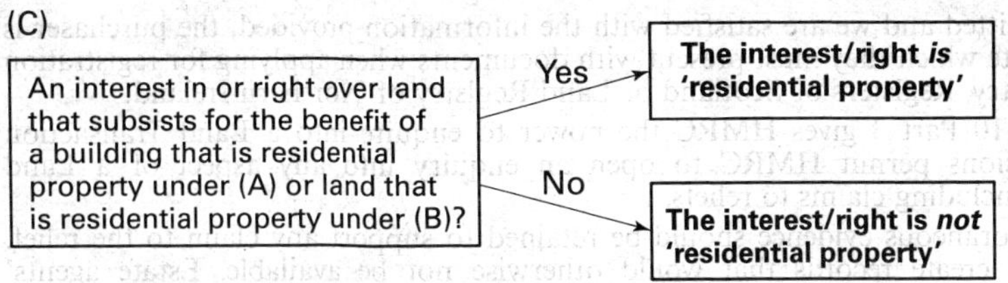
An interest in or right over land that subsists for the benefit of a building that is residential property under (A) or land that is residential property under (B)?
Yes
The interest/right *is* 'residential property'
No
The interest/right is *not* 'residential property'

Footnotes—[1] See paragraph [10] to [12] of SP.
[2] See paragraph [20] of SP.
[3] See paragraph [21] of SP.
[4] See paragraph [13] to [16] of SP.
[5] See paragraph [23] of SP.
[6] See paragraph [28] to [29] of SP.
[7] See paragraph [35] to [39] of SP.
[8] See paragraph [30] of SP.

SP 1/04 Stamp duty land tax—disadvantaged area relief

This Statement of Practice is intended as guidance for those claiming exemption from Stamp Duty Land Tax in respect of transfers of property situated in designated areas ("Disadvantaged Area Relief").

The relief is one of a number of measures set out in the Government's Urban White Paper "Our Towns and Cities: The Future: Delivering an Urban Renaissance" published in November 2000. The measure is designed to stimulate the physical, economic and social regeneration of the UK's most disadvantaged areas by attracting development and by encouraging the purchase of residential and commercial property by individuals and businesses. The areas eligible for relief were designated "Enterprise Areas" by the Chancellor in his 2002 Pre-Budget Report. In addition to the relief, a range of other Government policies designed to support enterprise and economic regeneration, including the Community Investment Tax Relief, will benefit these areas, helping to support the development of new and existing businesses.

BACKGROUND

1 Disadvantaged Area Relief (provided for by section 92 of, and Schedule 30 to, the Finance Act 2001) was introduced on 30 November 2001 and was initially available for conveyances or transfers on sale (of both residential and commercial property) for which the consideration did not exceed £150,000. Stamp duty in respect of conveyances or transfers of commercial property in disadvantaged areas was abolished in consequence of the Stamp Duty (Disadvantaged Areas) (Application of Exemptions) Regulations 2003 ("the Regulations"), which have effect in relation to instruments executed on or after 10 April 2003. Thereafter the £150,000 limit applies only in relation to residential property.

2 Finance Act 2002 inserted the following provisions in Finance Act 2001 to distinguish residential from other property and to provide for differing Stamp Duty Land Tax exemptions—

– FA 2001 Section 92A which enables stamp duty relief in designated disadvantaged areas in respect of all properties to be varied depending on whether or not the property is "residential".

DISADVANTAGED AREA RELIEF UNDER STAMP DUTY LAND TAX

3 Section 57 and Schedule 6 Finance act 2003 provides for Disadvantaged Area Relief under Stamp Duty Land Tax.

4 The definition of residential property under Stamp Duty Land Tax is provided at section 116 FA 2003. Non-residential property is therefore defined in the Act by exclusion. Section 116 also sets out particular building uses that are specifically included within, or specifically excluded from, the definition.

5 In most cases there will be no difficulty in practice in establishing whether or not a property is "residential". This statement sets out in more detail the Stamp Office's approach to borderline cases and gives guidance on the practical application of the legislation. The annexed flowchart provides a quick guide for simpler cases as to whether property constitutes "residential property".

CLAIMING THE RELIEF

6 The way in which relief is claimed is different under Stamp Duty Land Tax.

FA 2003 Section 76 requires that most land transactions, including those that qualify for Disadvantaged Area Relief, must be notified to HMRC on a Land Transaction Return Form (SDLT 1).

7 Relief is claimed by simply completing a box within this form. Certificates of Value are no longer required and no supporting evidence or documentation is required at this point. Once the return has been submitted and we are satisfied with the information provided, the purchaser is issued with a certificate which they must present with documents when applying for registration of title at Land Registry, Registers of Scotland or Land Registry of Northern Ireland.

8 FA 2003 Schedule 10 Part 3 gives HMRC the power to enquire into a Land Transaction Return. These provisions permit HMRC to open an enquiry into any aspect of a Land Transaction Return, including claims to reliefs.

Appropriate contemporaneous evidence should be retained to support any claim to the relief. There is no need to create records that would otherwise not be available. Estate agents' specifications, site plans, planning applications or permissions, marketing material, photographs and print outs of an internet post code search may all provide relevant information should there be an enquiry into a land tax return.

9 As with all claims the onus is on the purchaser to check whether or not the relief is due.

THE MEANING OF RESIDENTIAL PROPERTY

10 FA 2003 Section 116(1) defines "residential property" as a building which:

- is used as a dwelling,
- or is suitable for use as a dwelling,
- or is in the process of being constructed or adapted for such use.

If a property meets any one of these separate tests it will be treated as residential property and be subject to the £150,000 limit for relief, as will any garden or grounds belonging to it or any interests or rights attaching to it. Each element of the definition is considered in turn below. The question of whether and to what extent a building and grounds are defined as residential property for stamp duty purposes may also have implications for its treatment for capital gains tax and local authority rates.

USE AS A DWELLING

11 Where a building is in use at the effective date of the transaction it will be a question of fact whether and to what extent it is used as a dwelling.

Use at the effective date overrides any past or intended future uses for this purpose. For example, a purchaser is buying a house with the intention to refurbish it to create, in its place, an alternative therapy treatment centre. For the purposes of the relief the house in considered to be a dwelling because it was suitable for that use at the effective date of the transaction. (For another example see paragraph 34)

12 Where the property in question is in use as a dwelling at the effective date of the transaction, it is residential property for the purposes of the relief unless it is part of a multiple transaction qualifying for relief under FA 2003 s 116(7) (see paragraphs 40 to 44 below).

13 There is no motive test applicable to the usage of land or buildings, so where a residential property is purchased with the owner intending to use it as a non-residential business the building is considered residential, under the suitability test, for the purposes of the relief.

14 For the treatment of buildings put to both residential and non-residential use, see paragraphs 19 and 20 below.

SUITABLE FOR USE AS A DWELLING

15 The suitability test applies to the state of the building at the effective date of the transaction, having regard to the facilities available and any history of use. For example, HMRC will not regard an office block as "suitable for use as a dwelling", but a house which has been used as an office without particular adaptation may well be so.

16 If a building is not in use at the effective date of the transaction but its last use was as a dwelling, it will be taken to be "suitable for use as a dwelling" and treated as residential property for the purposes of the relief, unless evidence is produced to the contrary (see paragraph 17).

17 Whether a building is suitable for use as a dwelling will depend upon the precise facts and circumstances. The simple removal of, for example, a bathroom suite or kitchen facilities will not be regarded as rendering a building unsuitable for use as a dwelling. Where it is claimed that a previously residential property is no longer suitable for use as a dwelling, perhaps because it is derelict or has been substantially altered, the claimant will need to provide evidence that this is the case. See also paragraph 34.

18 Where a building has been used partly for residential purposes and partly for another purpose, its overall suitability for use as a dwelling will be judged from the facilities available at the effective date of the transaction. For example, if two rooms of a house were in use as a dentist's surgery and waiting room at the effective date of the transaction, HMRC would nevertheless normally consider this property suitable for use as a dwelling unless the claimant provided evidence to the contrary. A building that is used only partly as a dwelling may nevertheless be suitable for use wholly as a dwelling, with the effect that the £150,000 limit applies to the whole of the consideration. Where only a distinct part of the building is used and suitable for use as a dwelling, that part will be residential property for the purposes of the relief and the mixed use provisions will apply (See paragraphs 19 and 20 below).

MIXED USE

19 Where only part of a building (and land or interest relating to it) is "residential property" within section 116(1), the consideration "shall be apportioned on such basis as is just and reasonable" between the residential and non-residential elements. The £150,000 limit is then applied only to the residential portion (Schedule 6 FA 2003). For example:

A property situated wholly within a disadvantaged area is bought for:

(a) £200,000
(b) £400,000

50% of the property is "residential property" on the basis of a just and reasonable apportionment.

In these examples:

(a) £100,000 is attributed to the residential property element, so relief is due. The part of the land that is not residential property is also exempt. So no duty is payable.
(b) the £200,000 attributed to the residential property element is not exempt, because of Schedule 6 paragraph 6, but attracts duty at the rate of 1% (Stamp Duty Land Tax payable £2,000). The non-residential property element is exempt as above.

Where a transaction involves six or more mixed use properties, under S116(7) FA 2003, providing certain conditions are met, the residential element is exempt and no Stamp Duty Land Tax is payable. See paragraphs 40 to 44.

20 The "just and reasonable" test is necessarily subjective, and each case will be considered on its merits. Apportionment might be on the basis of the percentage areas quoted in planning applications, where appropriate, or alternatively of floor space relating to the respective uses. Other methods of apportionment will be considered as part of a claim.

SPECIFIC CASES

21 Some types of communal or institutional building are used neither as dwellings nor for commercial purposes. The legislation therefore outlines how these are classified for the purposes of relief, specifically including some such buildings within the definition of "dwelling" (section 116(2)) and specifically excluding others (section 116(3)). If they do not fall within any of the specific categories of section 116(3), most residential institutions will come within section 116(2)(d) and will be treated as dwellings by default.

22 Categories of building use specifically included within the definition of "use as a dwelling" (so that transfers of such buildings only qualify for relief if the consideration does not exceed £150,000) (section 116(2)) are:

(a) residential accommodation for school pupils, for example accommodation blocks in board ing schools;
(b) residential accommodation for students, other than that within section 116(3)(b). Student accommodation provided by private landlords is "a dwelling", as is accommodation leased to students by universities or colleges in flats or houses rather than in halls of residence (see section 116(3)(b));
(c) residential accommodation for members of any of the armed forces, including accommodation for their families (section 116(2)(c));
(d) an institution that is the sole or main residence of at least 90% of its residents and does not fall within any of the categories referred to in section 116(3) (see section 116(2)(d) and also paragraph 23 below).

This would include, for example:

- sheltered accommodation for the elderly where no nursing or personal care is provided. An example of this would be where an elderly person purchases a home on a warden-assisted housing development.
- accommodation for religious communities (subject to the rules regarding mixed use; see paragraphs 19 and 20).

23 Categories of building use specifically excluded from the definition of "use as a dwelling" (so that transfers of such buildings in a disadvantaged area will qualify for unlimited relief) (section 116(3)) are:

(a) a home or other institution providing residential accommodation for children;
(b) a hall of residence for students in further or higher education. This is not defined in the legislation but in practice property provided by a university or similar establishment will be judged on the facts (number of inhabitants, type of facilities, availability of communal areas);
(c) a home or other institution providing residential accommodation with personal care for persons in need of personal care by reason of old age, disablement, past or present dependence on alcohol or drugs or past or present mental disorder (for example, an institution that provides accommodation as part of a wider care service such as residential care homes or residential drug treatment centres);
(d) a hospital or hospice;
(e) a prison or similar establishment, or
(f) a hotel or inn or similar establishment.

BED AND BREAKFASTS/GUEST HOUSES

24 Each case will be taken on its merits, however, paragraph 25 below provides general examples of the treatment of B&Bs/guest houses.

25 A property providing a Bed and Breakfast (B&B) service, which has amenities installed in each room such as bathing facilities, telephone lines etc and is available all year round as the rooms do not need any further adaptation, would be considered non residential for the purposes of the relief. Example—

- Mr and Mrs Boyd run a bed and breakfast in a disadvantaged area of Blackpool. They live on the premises and it is open all year round but trade declines during the winter months. Under section 116(3) FA 2003, the Boyd's B&B is a "hotel or inn or similar establishment" and is therefore not used as a dwelling.
- Mrs Leaver lives in Southwest London and lets out two spare rooms on a B&B basis during the fortnight of the Wimbledon tennis tournament. She doesn't make any adaptations to the rooms other than the removal of some of her personal items. For the purposes of the relief Mrs Leaver's property is, at all times, considered to be in use as and suitable for use as a dwelling.

26 Buy-to-let properties suitable for use as a dwelling are residential unless they are a development of six or more dwellings whereby they would be non-residential under S116(7).

27 The specific inclusions and exclusions set out in paragraphs 22 and 23 above apply not only to a building's actual use at the effective date of the transaction, but to the uses for which it is suitable at that date. Where, however, a building is being put to one of the non-residential uses specified in section 116(3), this overrides any suitability for another use (section 116(4)). For example, a building used as a children's home may also be suitable for use as a school boarding house, but this will not preclude a claim to unlimited relief.

28 Where a vacant building is suitable for at least one of the uses specified in section 116(2) and at least one specified in section 116(3), section 116(5) determines, for the purposes of the relief, the use for which it is "most suitable". Whether or not a vacant building has one or more uses for which it is most suitable is a question of fact. Evidence supporting such uses should be retained.

29 Where there is a single use for which a building is most suitable, the fact that it is also suitable for another use will be discounted.

30 If there are a number of uses for which a building is most suitable and they all come within either of the two subsections, any other use for which the building is suitable will be discounted.

31 Where no most suitable use can be shown, the default will be to classify the building as residential property and apply the £150,000 limit.

32 Land and buildings that are not suitable for any use at the effective date of the transaction will be treated as residential property if they are "in the process of being constructed or adapted for such use"—see paragraphs 33 and 34 below.

PROCESS OF BEING CONSTRUCTED OR ADAPTED FOR USE AS A DWELLING

33 Undeveloped land is in essence non-residential, but land may be "residential property" for the purposes of Disadvantaged Area Relief if a residential building is being built on it at the effective date of the transaction. A development of six or more dwellings is deemed to be non-residential under S116(7), even if in the process of construction or marketing has not at the effective date of the transaction (see paragraph 40).

34 Where (at the effective date of the transaction) an existing building is being adapted for, marketed for, or restored to, domestic use, it is residential for the purposes of the relief. The process is taken as commencing when the developer begins marketing the properties for sale or starts physical work on the site which ever is earlier.

This may apply, for example, where a derelict building is being made fit for habitation, or where a previously non-residential building is being converted to a dwelling. For example:

> Kristian is buying an apartment, in what will be a converted church, off-plan. The sale is completed on 15th March 2004, the properties were marketed for sale on 3 January 2004 and work on converting the church commenced on 2nd February 2004. For the purposes of this transaction the church is considered to be a dwelling, even though it has yet to be fully converted, from 3rd January. If the consideration is greater than £150,000 Kristian will have to pay the appropriate rate of Stamp Duty Land Tax.

In the above example the developer that initially purchased the church will have bought it as a non-residential property regardless of the intention to turn the building into residential units.

THE GARDEN OR GROUNDS OF A BUILDING USED ETC AS A DWELLING

35 Section 116(1)(*b*) includes within the definition of residential property "land that is or forms part of the garden or grounds of a building within paragraph (*a*) (including any building or structure on such land)". The test HMRC will apply is similar to that applied for the purposes of the capital gains tax relief for main residences (section 222(3) of the Taxation of Chargeable

Gains Act 1992). The land will include that which is needed for the reasonable enjoyment of the dwelling having regard to the size and nature of the dwelling.

36 A caravan or houseboat is not a "building" for this purpose.

37 Commercial farmland is not within the definition of residential property. A farmhouse situated on agricultural land would be dealt with under the mixed use provisions (paragraphs 19 and 20 above).

It may often be the case that farmhouses will occupy only a small fraction of the total land and will therefore, when apportioned, fall below the £150,000 consideration limit thus attracting the residential relief.

38 Outhouses on land within the section 116(1)(b) definition will also be "residential property" unless it can be demonstrated that they have a specific non-residential purpose. Where a distinct non-residential use can be demonstrated, the mixed use provisions will apply.

INTEREST IN OR RIGHTS OVER RESIDENTIAL PROPERTY

39 The treatment of interests in, or rights over, land or buildings for the purposes of Disadvantaged Area Relief will follow that of the land or buildings to which they relate.

SIX OR MORE SEPARATE DWELLINGS TRANSFERRED BY A SINGLE TRANSACTION

40 Section 116(7) FA 2003 provides that "where six or more separate dwellings are the subject of a single transaction involving the transfer of a major interest in, or the grant of a lease over, them, then … those dwellings are treated as not being residential property". This recognises that commercial developers and institutional landlords, for example, frequently deal in numerous properties at one time. The fact that those properties may individually be "residential property" does not detract from the inherently commercial nature of the transaction itself.

41 To qualify as "separate", the dwellings must be self-contained. So for example, flats within a block, sharing some common areas but each with their own amenities will qualify as separate dwellings. Rooms let within a house will not constitute separate dwellings if tenants share amenities such as a kitchen and bathroom.

42 A transaction in respect of six or more such dwellings must be carried out by means of a single transaction in order to qualify for relief.

43 Qualifying multiple transactions will be treated as non-residential property for the purposes of relief, even where the proportionate consideration for individual dwellings exceeds the £150,000 limit for residential property. It is not a condition of relief that multiple transactions comprise only dwellings. One example of this would be where a purchaser is buying eight houses and four shops. Mixed use properties, such as pubs with self-contained residential accommodation, are also treated as non-residential.

44 The fact that some of the six or more dwellings within the single transaction are outside a designated disadvantaged area will not prevent them from constituting a non-residential transaction. However relief will only be available for the portion of the land situated within the disadvantaged area.

PROPERTY ONLY PARTLY WITHIN A DISADVANTAGED AREA

45 Schedule 6, Part 3, FA 2003 determines how property situated partly within and partly outside a designated disadvantaged area is to be treated for the purposes of the relief. Such cases are relatively rare in practice. Queries may be referred to Inland Revenue (Stamp Taxes) for guidance.

GRANTS OF NEW LEASES

46 FA 2003 Schedule 6 Part 2 deals with the charge to Stamp Duty Land Tax on the grant of a new lease.

Land all non-residential

47 If all of the land is non-residential it is exempt from any charge to Stamp Duty Land Tax.

Land all residential

48 The general rule is that:

(a) if the premium (and any other consideration than rent) does not exceed £150,000 then this is exempt from Stamp Duty Land Tax, and

(b) if the "net present value" of the rental payments does not exceed £150,000 then this is exempt from Stamp Duty Land Tax.

"Net present value" is, broadly speaking, the total rental payments due under the lease, discounted to reflect the fact that future rental payments are of less value than current rental payments. There is a tool for calculating net present value on the HMRC website. There is a special rule where the average annual rent exceeds £600. In such a case there is no relief or exemption for any premium. Any premium, however small, will be charged at 1% (or at higher rates if it exceeds £250,000).

49 Where there is mixed use apportionment is applied. The non-residential portion is exempt from lease duty.

If the consideration includes rent and the relevant rental value does not exceed £150,000, the rent does not count as chargeable consideration.

50 If the consideration includes consideration other than rent then:

(a) If the annual rent does not exceed £600 and the relevant consideration does not exceed £150,000, the consideration other than rent does not count as chargeable consideration

(b) If the annual rent exceeds £600, the consideration other than rent is counted as chargeable consideration

The "annual rent" is the average annual rent over the term of the lease.

FURTHER RESOURCES

Information can be found on our website, which also contains:

- A postcode search tool [www.hmrc.gov.uk/so/dar/dar-search.htm] to help identify whether a property falls within a disadvantaged area, and
- an intelligent decision-maker [www.hmrc.gov.uk/so/decisionmaker2.pdf] to help you decide whether a property is residential or non-residential.
- a lease duty calculator [http://ldcalculator.inlandrevenue.gov.uk/] which provides the amount of Stamp Duty Land Tax payable on a lease transaction.

STAMP TAXES
HMRC INTERPRETATIONS

Note—This Interpretation was published in HMRC's *Tax Bulletin*. HMRC state that the Interpretations will normally be applied in relevant cases, but that this is subject to a number of qualifications. Particular cases may turn on their own facts or context and there may be circumstances in which an Interpretation will not apply. There may also be circumstances in which the Board would find it necessary to argue for a different Interpretation in appeal proceedings.

The number before the interpretation (ie RI 174) does not appear in the Tax Bulletin. It has been added by the publishers to facilitate identification for the purpose of cross references.

Please note that references to the 'Inland Revenue' should now be considered as referring to 'HM Revenue and Customs' and references to the 'Board of the Inland Revenue' should be read as the 'Commissioners for HM Revenue and Customs'.

RI 174 (*August 1997*) Stamp duty litigation

PARINV (HATFIELD) LTD V IRC [1996] STC 933—OFF-SHORE DECLARATION OF TRUST INEFFECTIVE TO AVOID AD VALOREM DUTY ON SUBSEQUENT TRANSFERS

This case concerned the effectiveness of an off-shore declaration of trust in avoiding ad valorem stamp duty on subsequent transfers. The High Court held that the device was ineffective. The taxpayer has lodged an appeal. In the meantime, the Stamp Office will continue to apply the law on the basis of the High Court's decision.

In the Parinv case, the taxpayer sought to rely on a copy of an unstamped overseas document to argue that the Stamp Office should stamp a transfer of property to a purchaser at 50p rather than 1%, on the basis that the transfer transferred only bare legal title and that the equitable interest in the property was transferred by the unstamped document. This argument was rejected by the Court on the grounds that the unstamped document was not admissible as evidence, in view of the Stamp Act 1891 s 14(4).

UNSTAMPED DOCUMENTS—INLAND REVENUE PRACTICE

Following enquiries from customers, the Revenue has decided to publicise its current practice with regard to unstamped documents. Under the terms of Stamp Act 1891 s 14(4)—

> "an instrument executed in any part of the United Kingdom, or relating wheresoever executed, to any property situate, or to any matter or thing done or to be done, in any part of the United Kingdom, shall not, except in criminal proceedings, be given in evidence, or be available for any purpose whatever, unless it is duly stamped in accordance with the law in force at the time when it was first executed".

It has been the Revenue's view that an unstamped document cannot be offered in evidence in any legal proceedings other than criminal proceedings, and that this includes hearings before the Special or General Commissioners. Following the case of *Parinv (Hatfield) Ltd v IRC*, the Revenue's current practice will be as follows.

In the *Parinv* case, the Revenue argued that an unstamped instrument was itself excluded from being used in civil proceedings, a view accepted by Lindsay J. Furthermore he took the view that a true copy, sometimes called a conformed copy, of an original unstamped document cannot be used to provide information or material or evidence of the original to the court.

The court then went on to consider the Revenue's position in connection with copy documents. In his analysis of Stamp Act 1891 s 14(4) Lindsay J considered the words "shall not … be available for any purpose whatever". He indicated that these words were not an absolute prohibition because this would prevent an unstamped document being examined even in order to determine what should be the appropriate stamp. The Court referred to a judgement in an earlier case and endorsed the view that the words mean that one person cannot compel another person to rely on and accept an unstamped document.

The Revenue in addition, argued that it was able to look at the copy document with the purpose of establishing the liability to duty of another document. The Court held that because the taxpayer is obliged by s 5 of the Act to provide all facts and circumstances affecting the liability to duty of a document including all such evidence deemed necessary by the Board to form a view if adjudication or assessment is required, the Revenue was not obliged by the Act to exclude from its consideration the contents of a copy of an unstamped document which had been supplied to it in order to meet that obligation. It was unlikely that Parliament would have imposed a fine for non-disclosure (ie a fraudulent act) and yet required the Revenue to ignore the disclosure. So the Revenue can have regard to a document for the purpose of an assessment of duty. But that does not compel the Revenue to go any further.

The Revenue is aware that documents executed overseas are frequently retained there with a view to deferral or avoidance of payment of stamp duty. It will not be the Revenue's practice to request sight of original documents in these or other circumstances, merely to check whether they have been duly stamped or not. However, if the documents are to be relied on by a person in support of any claim to relief, or otherwise used in evidence in relation to any liability to tax, or the amount thereof, that person should be aware that the Revenue cannot be compelled to accept in support of such claim or as evidence unstamped original or conformed unstamped copies of documents.

PENALTY FOR FRAUD

Stamp Act 1891 s 5 requires that all the facts and circumstances affecting the liability of an instrument to duty, or the amount of the duty chargeable, shall be fully and truly set forth in the instrument, and that any failure to do so by the parties or their advisers with intent to defraud the Crown, shall attract a fine. The Stamp Office takes the view that a failure to disclose the fact that the parties are attempting to rely on an unstamped instrument, contrary to Stamp Act 1891 s 14(4) in executing a transfer which purports to convey the bare legal estate, will constitute a breach of s 5, and appropriate action will be taken.

The Stamp Office also takes the view that any attempt by the parties to an instrument containing a certificate under the exempt instruments legislation which relied on another instrument executed overseas which was not duly stamped, would constitute a breach of s 5.

LM TENANCIES 1 PLC V IRC [1996] STC 880—CONSIDERATION CALCULATED IN ACCORDANCE WITH A FORMULA ASCERTAINED BY APPLICATION OF CONTINGENCY PRINCIPLE

This case concerned the application of the contingency principle. The High Court held that where the calculation of duty relied on a future value, (the price of a gilt some time after execution of the document) the Stamp Office could rely on the last published figure.

The taxpayer has lodged an appeal against this decision. In the meantime the Stamp Office will apply the law on the basis of the Court's decision, subject to the normal right of appeal in any individual case. On that basis, duty is payable on an ascertainable amount where the contingency principle can be applied in the way outlined above.

The Stamp Office is of the view that the contingency principle, as it was held to apply in this case, will apply to other reference values which are unknown at the date of execution. An example is the practice of making future rent increases subject to an increase in an index, typically the RPI. The Stamp Office will apply the published increase in RPI over the twelve months prior to execution of the lease or agreement for lease to calculate the average annual rent.

Where the contingency principle does not apply, FA 1994 s 242 now provides that where the consideration for an interest in land is unascertainable, ad valorem stamp duty is chargeable on the basis of the value of the property conveyed.

Commentary—*Simon's Taxes* **I3.602**.

STAMP TAXES
PRESS RELEASES ETC

CONTENTS

2 January 1963 Controller of Stamps	Stamp duty on leases
28 February 1978 Practice Direction of the Principal Registry of the Family Division	Grants of representation
1 May 1984 IR	Stamp duty: purchase by a company of its own shares
20 March 1990 IR	Stamp duty on shares to be abolished
18 July 1990 The Law Society	Stamp duty adjudication
19 March 1991 IR	Stamp duty: charges to be abolished
29 May 1991 The Law Society	Stamp duty—mitigation of penalties
14 June 1991 IR	Finance Bill: stamp duty: abolition of charges
18 October 1991 IR	Proposed merger of LIFFE and LTOM: new tax rules
4 March 1992 Law Society	Stamp duty and VAT
9 June 1993 Law Society	Stamp duty—mitigation of penalties
12 July 1993 IR	Stamp duty—new buildings
17 March 1994 Hansard	Stamp duty (clause 226)
5 April 1994 HM Land Registry	Land Registry announces change in stamp duty adjudication procedures
18 April 1994 IR	Stamp duty—property transactions
29 November 1994 IR	Stamp duty: group relief
3 August 1995 IR Tax Bulletin	Stamp duty: FA 1994
4 August 1995 IR	Tradepoint—Tax and stamp duty reserve tax reliefs
2 October 1995 IR	Stock lending: stamp duty reserve tax
28 November 1995 IR	Stamp duty on shares
27 February 1996 Hansard	Transfer of securities to members of electronic transfer systems etc [FA 1996 s 186]
27 February 1996. Hansard	Stock lending and collateral security arrangements [FA 1996 s 191]
9 May 1996 IR	Open-ended investment companies and authorised unit trusts—stamp duty
26 November 1996 IR	Stamp duty—unit trusts and open-ended investment companies
8 January 1997 Law Society's Gazette	Stamp duty on leases
16 January 1997 Tax Journal. Letter from Macfarlanes with extract from IR letter	SDRT on UK Share Transfers
16 September 1998 Law Society Gazette	Stamp duty and VAT—business transferred as a going concern: change of practice (as amended 15 January 1999)
14 May 1999 IR	Stamp duty—new leases with indexed rent levels.
25 August 1999 IR	Stamp duty reserve tax—depositary interests in foreign securities
17 September 1999 IR	Stamp duty—seven year leases
August 2001 IR Stamp Taxes Bulletin	When is a fixture not a fixture?
February 2002 IR Stamp Taxes Bulletin	Disadvantaged areas—Stamp duty exemption
October 2002 IR Stamp Taxes Bulletin	Options—a response to press articles
March 2003 IR Stamp Taxes Bulletin	Disadvantaged areas—Q & As
June 2003 SDLT Newsletter, Issue 1	The switch to 'stamp duty land tax' planned to take place on 1 December 2003
July 2003. SDLT Newsletter, Issue 2	The switch to stamp duty land tax planned to take place on 1 December 2003
August 2003 SDLT Newsletter, Issue 3	The switch to stamp duty land tax planned to take place on 1 December 2003
September 2003. Stamp Duty Information Bulletin—Issue 4	New process for SDLT that will apply for the majority of transactions completed on or after 1 December 2003
20 October 2003. IR News Release	Modernising stamp duty on land transactions
20 October 2003. IR Technical Note	Stamp duty land tax: Technical Note
20 October 2003. Ministerial Statement	Written Ministerial Statement by the Financial Secretary
November 2003.	SDLT—Guidance notes on self-certification

December 2003. Stamp Taxes Bulletin No 6	Special arrangements for administration of SDLT from 1 December 2003
19 December 2003. IR press release 102/03	Stamp duty land tax: treatment of private finance initiative projects
April 2004. Tax Bulletin article	Stamp duty land tax: group relief
April 2004. Inland Revenue statement.	SDLT—sale of land with associated construction, &c, contract
12 November 2004. Inland Revenue Guidance Note.	Stamp duty land tax and nil-rate band discretionary trusts
14 April 2005. Inland Revenue Notice.	Budget 2005 provisions on stamp duty land tax
14 December 2007. HMRC Guidance Note	Intermediary and Stock Lending Reliefs—FA 2007, Sch 21
4 February 2008. HMRC Note	Stamp Taxes Online—transactions with more than 100 properties
31 March 2008. HMRC Information Sheet	Stamp Duty on Shared Ownership Homes
17 April 2008. HMRC Notice	SDLT—Budget changes to notification requirements
2 September 2008. HM Treasury	Stamp duty exemption for residential property

2 January 1963. Controller of Stamps

Stamp duty on leases

THE BASIS OF ASSESSMENT

The Revenue have recently given consideration to the basis of assessment of duty on leases which contain one or more of the following provisions:

(*a*) a known rent not exceeding £100 pa and a further unascertainable rent;

(*b*) a term commencing from a date prior to the date of execution;

(*c*) a rent or rents fixed for part only of the term, the rent for the remainder of the term to be agreed subsequently.

The question under consideration in regard to leases of type (*a*)...[NB This question was rendered obsolete by FA 1963, which repealed FA 1947 s 54(2).]

In regard to leases of type (*b*) the Board's view is that, in computing the length of the term, any period prior to the date of the lease is to be left out of account on the authority of *Shaw v Kay* (1847) 1 Ex 412, *Cadogan v Guiness* (1936) Ch 515, and *Colton v Becollda Property Investments Ltd* [1950] 1 KB 216. These cases do not, however, provide any authority as to the treatment of rent payable in respect of a period prior to the date of the lease: for the sake of consistency and simplicity, the Board have decided that such rent shall be left out of account, so that the treatment approved by the courts in relation to the term will in practice also be applied to the rent. This means, in effect, a continuation of existing practice, although this practice may not have been applied consistently in individual cases in the past.

Leases of type (*c*)...

Note—The treatment of leases of type (c) no longer applies: see Revenue Bulletin (August 1995).

Stamp Taxes

28 February 1978. Practice Direction of the Principal Registry of the Family Division

Grants of representation

1 Where, for the purposes of applying for a grant of representation, it is necessary for the applicant to produce to the Principal or a District Probate Registry an original deed or other instrument, it is the practice of the Registry to examine the instrument to ensure that it has been properly executed and duly stamped under SA 1891 before proceeding with the application. Where there is any doubt whether the instrument is duly stamped, the applicant will be asked to present the instrument to the Controller of Stamps (Inland Revenue) for adjudication before the issue of the grant.

2 To avoid delay in the issue of the grant in such cases, the Commissioners of Inland Revenue have agreed that the applicant may, if so desired, submit the original instrument to the Adjudication Section of the Office of the Controller of Stamps for preliminary noting, endorsement and return, providing that a written undertaking is at the same time given to the Controller by the solicitor applying for the grant of representation that he will, on or immediately after the issue of the grant, re-submit the original instrument to the Controller for formal adjudication and pay the stamp duty (if any) to which the instrument is adjudged liable.

3 In every case on the application for a grant, the original instrument (after inspection) will be returned as soon as practicable to the applicant, or his solicitor, by the probate registry. Practitioners are reminded, however, that where the application is for a grant to an assignee or assignees under the Non-Contentious Probate Rules 1954 Rule 22, a copy of the original instrument of assignment must be lodged in the registry (see Rule 22(3)).

1 May 1984. Inland Revenue

Stamp duty: purchase by a company of its own shares

In reply to a Parliamentary Question the Financial Secretary to the Treasury gave the following Written Answer yesterday:

> "The Companies Act 1981 enables companies to purchase their own shares. A specific exemption from *ad valorem* stamp duty was not provided although it was intended that s 52 of the Act (Disclosure of Particulars of Purchase and Authorised Contracts) should effectively provide for this. Doubts have arisen as to whether s 52 achieved this objective.
>
> *Ad valorem* duty is payable on any conveyance or transfer on sale and SA 1891 s 54, provides that the expression 'conveyance on sale' includes every instrument whereby any property sold is transferred or vested in the purchaser. The Revenue are advised that although the matter is not free from doubt there are grounds for holding that this section does not apply when a company purchases its own shares. This is the view that the Board proposes to adopt. A Secretary or Registrar of a company may accordingly amend the register without requiring that any delivery statement is stamped with *ad valorem* duty.

The Companies Act 1981 provides an exemption from capital duty for future re-issues of the repurchased shares."

NOTE

The Financial Secretary has clarified the stamp duty treatment on the purchase by a company of its own shares.

The Companies Act 1981 enabled companies to purchase their own shares. An exemption from capital duty was provided to cover any future issues of the cancelled shares but nothing was said in the Act about transfer duty. The Bill however was amended to remove the need for a document which would attract stamp duty. Doubts have arisen as to whether the amendments achieved their objective. The Financial Secretary has informed the House that the Revenue has been advised that although the position is not free from doubt there are grounds for holding that *ad valorem* duty is not payable. This is the view that the Revenue proposes to adopt.

[NB The Companies Act 1981 s 52 is now reproduced as the Companies Act 1985 s 169. Note that Form 169 is itself chargeable under FA 1986 s 66.]

20 March 1990. Inland Revenue

Stamp duty on shares to be abolished

The Chancellor proposes in his Budget to abolish all stamp duties on transactions in shares from a date late in 1991–92 to coincide as far as possible with the introduction of paperless dealing under the Stock Exchange's new share transfer system ("TAURUS").

Abolition of these duties will also:

(*a*) enhance London's competitiveness as an international centre for equity trading;
(*b*) boost wider share ownership by reducing transaction costs and benefit savers.

This is the sixth major tax to be abolished since 1983. It makes a significant contribution to the overall simplification of the tax system and the reduction of compliance burdens on taxpayers.

DETAILS

Stamp duties on shares: main duties

1 The main duties to be abolished are:

(*a*) stamp duty on individual share transfers, which is levied on UK securities at a rate since 1986 of, broadly, 0·5 per cent of the price paid;
(*b*) stamp duty of 1·5 per cent, which is payable where UK shares are converted into depositary receipts ("ADRs") or transferred into clearance services;
(*c*) stamp duty reserve tax, which applies, at the same rates as stamp duty, to some share transactions which are outside the stamp duty net.

Stamp duties on shares: associated charges

2 Also to be abolished are:

(*a*) the stamp duty charges on bearer shares;
(*b*) the 50p fixed duty on share transfers other than sales;
(*c*) stamp duty on all transfers of units under a unit trust scheme.

Timing

3 Legislation to abolish these duties will be in the 1990 Finance Bill. The Chancellor proposes that abolition should be triggered by Treasury Order in due course. He has indicated that this Order will broadly coincide with the start of paperless trading under the Stock Exchange's planned TAURUS system—*ie* towards the end of 1991–92 on the current timetable [but see the Revenue Press Release of 19 December 1991]. Until then, duty continues to apply at the existing rates.

Effects of abolition

4 The Government believes abolition of these taxes will:

(*a*) smooth the path for cheaper and more efficient paperless share dealing, by removing the need for the systems involved to take account of stamp duty;
(*b*) increase the liquidity and efficiency of the London equity market, and maintain its competitiveness in the face of planned tax reductions in other financial centres;
(*c*) encourage investment in UK equities and so foster wider share ownership;
(*d*) benefit savers, including beneficiaries of pension funds and life policies;
(*e*) further simplify the tax system and ease the compliance burden on individual shareholders, the equity market and company registrars.

Cost

5 The timing means that no cost will arise until late in 1991–92. The cost that year will depend on precisely when the duty is abolished; a 1 January 1992 start would for example produce a 1991–92 cost of £120 million. The full year cost will be around £800 million.

Stamp duty on property

6 The Chancellor is not proposing to make any changes to the stamp duty on the transfer of land and property (including houses).

NOTES

Abolition of duties

1 This Government has already abolished
(*a*) In vestment income surcharge (1984);
(*b*) National insurance surcharge (1984);
(*c*) Development land tax (1985);
(*d*) the tax on lifetime gifts (1986);
(*e*) capital duty and the associated unit trust instrument duty (1988)
as well as a number of minor duties. Abolition of stamp duty on shares carries this process forward, making a significant contribution to the overall simplification of the tax system.

Stamp duty on shares

2 The *ad valorem* stamp duty on individual transfers of UK companies' shares is currently charged at 50p per £100 or part thereof, *ie* broadly at 0·5 per cent. There are exemptions for purchases by market-makers and charities. Government stock and most commercial loan capital are outside the scope of the charge.

3 Conversion of UK shares into depositary receipts ("ADRs") or their transfer into a clearance service attracts a 1·5 per cent "season ticket" charge—see para 8 below.

4 Bearer instruments are normally charged at 15 per cent on a once-and-for-all basis, either on issue (for instruments issued in the UK) or on their first transfer in Great Britain.

5 Certain transfers of shares otherwise than on sale can give rise to a fixed 50p charge—for example transfers where there is no change of beneficial ownership.

Stamp duty reserve tax

6 This tax was introduced in 1986 in order to broaden the base of stamp duty on shares, by charging a wider range of transactions. Stamp duty is a tax on *documents*, but stamp duty reserve tax applies to most *agreements* to sell UK securities. It therefore brings within the scope of the charge:
(*a*) the purchase and resale of a security within the same Stock Exchange account;
(*b*) the purchase of renounceable letters of allotment or acceptance;
(*c*) the purchase of shares registered in the name of a nominee acting for seller and purchaser;
(*d*) the purchase of shares which are resold before they are taken into the purchaser's name.

7 Stamp duty reserve tax on individual share transfers is charged at the same rate, 0·5 per cent, as stamp duty on shares. For conversion into ADR form etc there is again a 1·5 per cent charge to parallel the higher rate of stamp duty—see 8 below.

Depositary receipts and clearance services—the higher rate charges

8 Where shares are transferred into depositary receipt form or into a clearance service, the higher rate of 1·5 per cent stamp duty or stamp duty reserve tax applies on the initial transfer. This charge is in the nature of a "season ticket"—subsequent transfers of depositary receipts, or of shares within a clearance service, then take place free of stamp duty or stamp duty reserve tax.

Unit trusts

9 Stamp duty arises on the purchase of units by one unit holder from another, and in the more common situation of a surrender for cash of units to the managers. The rates are broadly the same as the *ad valorem* charge on shares, but special reliefs apply.

18 July 1990. The Law Society

Stamp duty adjudication

The Stamp Office has announced a change in its adjudication procedures. Following examination of an instrument for adjudication, the Stamp Office's practice is to notify the applicant of the amount of duty estimated to be payable.

It will continue to allow 28 days for applicants to respond to estimates of duty payable. If no response has been received after the 28 days, only one reminder will be issued. The office will consider the request for adjudication as having been withdrawn once a further 14 days have elapsed after the issue of the reminder, and will then return the instrument unstamped to the applicant.

This will not prevent the applicant from re-presenting the instrument for adjudication. However, SA 1891 ss 14(4) (instrument not duly stamped not to be given in evidence), 15 (penalty upon stamping instruments after execution) might apply in the event of delay [*Law Society's Gazette*, 18 July 1990, p 13].

19 March 1991. Inland Revenue

Stamp duty: charges to be abolished

The Chancellor proposes in his Budget to abolish stamp duty charges on property other than land and buildings. The intention is to abolish these charges at the same time as the duty on shares (likely to be late in 1991–92).

The stamp duty on Northern Ireland bank notes will be abolished from 1 January 1992.

Abolition of these charges will:

(*a*) relieve from stamp duty a variety of types of property, such as patents, goodwill and debt, including sovereign debt;

(*b*) further simplify the tax system, and reduce the compliance burden on taxpayers.

DETAILS

1 At present stamp duty is charged on transactions in various types of property. FA 1990 included provisions abolishing all the stamp duty charges (including stamp duty reserve tax) on transactions in shares, from a date to be fixed by Treasury order. The date will be fixed to coincide as closely as possible with the introduction of paperless share dealing under the Stock Exchange's automated share transfer system ("TAURUS").

2 The new proposals will remove the 1 per cent and fixed (mainly 50p) stamp duty charges on documents relating to all other types of property except land and buildings (including houses).

3 The only charges that will remain are the 1 per cent sale duty on land and buildings, and the associated fixed charges; and the charge on the premium and rent of new leases, known as lease duty. The Chancellor is not proposing changes to these duties.

4 The Government intend to introduce the legislation at the Committee Stage of the Finance Bill.

5 The full-year cost will be £15 million.

NOTES

Existing stamp duties

1 Stamp duty is a tax on documents. There are a number of separate duties, under different heads of charge.

2 The main stamp duty is a charge at 1 per cent of the price paid on a conveyance or transfer of property by means of a document. In addition, fixed (generally 50p) duties arise on certain deeds where no money usually changes hands—for example, declarations of trust and exchanges.

Stamp duty reforms

3 In addition to the FA 1990 provisions to abolish the duties on shares, this Government has already abolished:

- stamp duty on gifts (1985);
- capital duty (1988);
- unit trust instrument duty (1988);
- life assurance policy duty (1989);

and a number of the fixed duties have been removed.

4 Since 1979 the rate of duty on land and buildings has been reduced, and the threshold below which no stamp duty is payable on land and buildings raised three times. The current threshold is £30,000.

Stamp duty on Northern Ireland bank notes

5 Northern Ireland bank notes, unlike those issued in Great Britain, attract stamp duty under the "Bank Note" head of charge in SA 1891 Sch 1. The duty is charged, at 50p per £100, on the average value of notes in circulation each half year. The duty on bank notes in Great Britain was abolished in 1972.

Cross-reference—Revenue press release 20-3-90 (abolition of stamp duty on shares).

29 May 1991. The Law Society

Stamp duty—mitigation of penalties

A letter from the Inland Revenue Stamp Office (published in the *Law Society's Gazette*, 29 May 1991) sets out the Revenue practice as regards mitigation of the statutory penalties (SA 1891 s 15(2)(*c*)) for late presentation of documents liable to stamp duty as follows:

> "In addition to the duty payable, the price to be paid for late stamping is—
>
> – £10 (SA 1891 s 15(1)), plus
>
> – interest at 5 per cent per annum on the duty outstanding where this is more than £10 (SA 1891 s 15(1)), plus
>
> – a sum equal to the amount of duty outstanding (SA 1891 s 15(2)(*c*)).
>
> In all but those cases of deliberate withholding of duty, avoidance or extreme delay (over one year late), this could be said to be a disproportionately high price to pay. We would not dissent from this view and our practice will be to invoke the authority provided by SA 1891 s 15(3)(*b*) and mitigate the penalty. The degree of mitigation will be influenced by the reasons for and length of delay. However the minimum level to which a penalty can be expected to be mitigated will reflect interest rates prevailing during the period of delay.
>
> Our offices are instructed in general to mitigate penalties to a level equivalent to an interest rate charge of 12 per cent to 15 per cent per annum for a delay of up to three months, 15 per cent to 20 per cent per annum for three to six months delay, and 20 per cent to 25 per cent for six to 12 months."

[See further the letter published in the Law Society's Gazette on 9 June 1993, referred to below.]

14 June 1991. Inland Revenue

Finance Bill: stamp duty: abolition of charges

The Government has tabled six new clauses to the Finance Bill containing its proposals for abolishing stamp duty charges on all property other than land and buildings, as announced in the Chancellor's Budget.

DETAILS

1 Under the new proposals all stamp duty charges will be abolished except where the property being transferred is:

(*a*) land;

(*b*) an interest in the proceeds of sale of land held on trust for sale; or

(*c*) a licence to occupy land.

2 "Land" includes buildings.

3 The property to be exempted includes goodwill, patents and debt, including sovereign debt. The charges to be abolished are the 1 per cent duty on sales of such property, and the fixed (mainly 50p) charges on certain other transactions where none of the property being transferred is land.

4 No change is proposed to the duties on land. So the 1 per cent sale duty on houses and land where the price is above £30,000 [but see FA 1963 s 55, and the Stamp Duty (Temporary Provisions) Act 1992], and the charges on the premium and rent of new leases, remain the same.

5 The rules for cases where property is transferred subject to a debt, or in consideration of a debt, will also remain unchanged.

6 The new clauses provide that, where land and exempt property are transferred together, the purchase price is to be apportioned fairly between them. For example, a business may be transferred at a price which includes both the business premises and goodwill. The provisions will ensure that the chargeable property does not attract either too much or too little stamp duty.

7 With one exception the changes will come into effect at the same time as the abolition of stamp duties on shares, which will be fixed to coincide as closely as possible with the introduction of paperless share dealing ("TAURUS"). The exception is the duty on Northern Ireland banknotes, which will be abolished from 1 January 1992. The TAURUS system is expected to be introduced in May 1992.

Notes

1 The Chancellor's Budget proposals for stamp duty were set out in a press release "Stamp duty: Charges to be abolished" issued on Budget Day, 19 March 1991.

2 Under FA 1990 the abolition date of stamp duties on shares is to be fixed by Treasury Order.

Cross-reference—Revenue press release 20-3-90 (abolition of stamp duty on shares).

18 October 1991. Inland Revenue

Proposed merger of LIFFE and LTOM: new tax rules

The Financial Secretary to the Treasury, Francis Maude, announced yesterday proposed new tax and stamp duty rules for the new market formed from the merger of the London International Financial Futures Exchange (LIFFE) and the London Traded Options Market (LTOM).

In a written reply to a Parliamentary Question (HC Written Answer, 17 October 1991, Vol 196, col 214), the Financial Secretary said—

> "The rules for certain tax reliefs which are available at present to market-makers in traded options assume that the London Traded Options Market is part of the Stock Exchange. When the proposed merger of the London Traded Options Market with the London International Financial Futures Exchange takes place, this will no longer be so. New regulations will be made to adapt the present reliefs accordingly, and to widen them in some respects to take account of the structure of the new market, once the arrangements for the merger have been finalised.
>
> The new regulations will provide stamp duty and stamp duty reserve tax reliefs for members of the new merged market acting as principal traders in equity options. The reliefs will apply, within certain prescribed limits, to transactions in equities which are necessary to hedge positions in options to buy or sell securities which members enter into on their own account and not on behalf of clients.
>
> Stock lending reliefs, and exemption in certain circumstances from the anti-bond-washing legislation, will also apply to such transactions and to transactions where stock is borrowed or purchased to meet a delivery obligation arising from the exercise or assignment of an option, again within certain prescribed limits.
>
> For members of the merged market acting as principal traders in option contracts, regulations will be made to place them on a comparable basis to Stock Exchange market-makers when required to manufacture a dividend."

DETAILS

Stamp duty/SDRT

1 Currently, market-makers in options to buy or sell securities get relief from stamp duty reserve tax (SDRT) on agreements to purchase securities in the ordinary course of their market-making business, provided the options—

(*a*) are quoted on the Stock Exchange; and

(*b*) relate to the same securities as the securities purchased.

This relief—which does not extend to other options dealers—mirrors the SDRT relief for market-makers in shares quoted on the Stock Exchange.

2 The merger of the markets will mean that the traded options market will no longer be part of the Stock Exchange. The regulations will adapt the current stamp duty and SDRT provisions to cater for the merged market. By giving a relief to principal traders on the new market (subject to a more restrictive limitation than market-makers) they will broaden the scope of the present exemption.

3 The regulations will make other provisions about stamp duty and SDRT arising out of the merger. For example, they will ensure that the stamp duty relief for stock-borrowing transactions is extended to members of the merged market subject to the relevant limits; and that delivery of stock on the exercise of an option under the new arrangements does not lead to multiple charges to SDRT.

Stock lending

4 Stock lending is a long established practice that enables securities dealers, in return for a fee, to "borrow" securities (including shares) from institutions such as insurance companies or pension funds when they need them in order to deliver on sales. The dealer undertakes to replace the borrowed stock at a later date with securities of the same kind and amount.

5 Although termed "stock lending" the process involves the transfer of ownership of the securities. Under present law, if securities are borrowed under an approved stock lending arrangement by a market-maker in those securities, both borrower and lender are exempt from tax charges which would otherwise arise when the securities were transferred. These exemptions currently apply only where the borrower is a market maker. This is because such market-makers provide liquidity, and so assist the efficiency of the market, by taking on an obligation to deal at all times at the prices they quote. This may involve selling securities which they do not have, so they may need to borrow securities to enable them to meet their obligations to deliver on the sale.

6 Traded options dealers, whether or not they are market-makers, may be faced with an obligation to deliver securities on which they have entered into options contracts. In the new traded options market it is envisaged that dealers who are not market-makers will play an important role in providing liquidity. The Government has therefore decided to allow tax relief on stock borrowed to hedge positions they have taken in options. Limitations will be prescribed to ensure that the reliefs are restricted to genuine hedging transactions or transactions entered into to enable a delivery obligation to be fulfilled. These limitations will be more restricted for non-market-making principal traders (who can choose whether or not to deal in a particular option) than for market-makers (who have to deal and who therefore require a more flexible regime). Nevertheless the limitations will in each case recognise the need to hedge, and to maintain a hedge, against options positions.

Manufactured dividends

7 Where stock is lent, payments made by the borrower to the lender to compensate the lender for the dividends that would have been received had the securities not been lent are known as "manufactured dividends". The rules for accounting for tax on manufactured dividends include provisions to prevent relief for the tax in respect of manufactured dividends paid outside approved procedures. These rules will apply to members of the new merged market who borrow stock in the same way as they currently apply to equivalent market makers on the Stock Exchange.

Bond-washing

8 Bond-washing is the practice whereby shares are sold with an accrued dividend and bought back immediately after the shares have gone ex dividend so that the payment for the accrued dividend is treated as a capital gain rather than as income and so receives more favourable tax treatment. TA 1988 s 732 discourages securities dealers from entering into such transactions by reducing the amount which they can deduct for tax purposes in respect of the accrued dividend.

9 At present market-makers in securities are exempted from the anti-bond-washing provisions of TA 1988 s 732. This is because a market-maker's business involves buying and selling securities at all times, regardless of whether they are cum or ex dividend.

10 The exemption for market-makers reflects the existing market structure of the Stock Exchange (of which LTOM is presently part). The options and futures market to be formed from the merger of LIFFE and LTOM, however, will rely for its liquidity on a wider category of principal traders than just market-makers, and it has therefore been decided that they too should benefit from the exemption. As with the stock lending reliefs, there will be prescribed limitations to restrict the exemption to hedging transactions, and transactions entered into, to enable a delivery obligation to be fulfilled.

NOTES

Stamp duty/SDRT

1 The regulations will be made under the powers in FA 1991 ss 116, 117.

2 The existing exemption from SDRT for market-makers in options is in FA 1986 s 89(1A).

3 Stamp duty on shares and SDRT are due to be abolished under legislation in FA 1990. The abolition date will be fixed by Treasury Order.

Stock lending

4 The regulations will be made under the powers contained in TA 1988 s 129(4).

5 The existing arrangements for the approval of stock lending arrangements are set out in TA 1988 s 129 and SI 1989/1299 (as amended by SI 1990/2552).

Manufactured dividends

6 The regulations will be made under the powers contained in TA 1988 Sch 23A.

Bondwashing

7 The regulations will be made under TA 1988 s 732 as amended by FA 1991 s 56.

4 March 1992. Law Society

Stamp duty and VAT

Following the publication of Statement of Practice SP 11/91 on the interaction between stamp duty and VAT, the Law Society's revenue law committee raised a number of points of uncertainty in correspondence with the Inland Revenue. The Revenue's views on the points raised are noted below.

Stamp Taxes

[AMOUNT ON WHICH STAMP DUTY IS PAYABLE]

It has emerged from [the correspondence that the Revenue's] view, as a result of the legal advice it has received, and in the light of which SP 11/91 was published, is first that the contingency principle will apply to any transaction in respect of a property which could be affected by an election to waive exemption from VAT, where the election has not been exercised by a landlord at the time that a lease is entered into (and there is no contemporaneous or binding agreement between the parties to the lease that the election will not be exercised). Accordingly in calculating the duty payable VAT should therefore in the Revenue's view be added to any payments to be made by the purchaser or lessee to which an election could still apply.

Secondly, in the cases which deal with the so-called contingency principle it was held that stamp duty is chargeable on a *prima facie* sum regardless of whether that sum might increase or decrease depending on the occurrence of some contingency.

The Revenue considers that the calculation should be based on current rates of VAT, notwithstanding that there may be a fluctuation in the rate of VAT in the period which elapses between the date when the lease is granted and when any election is made.

Apart from the correspondence on the quantum of duty [the Law Society's revenue law committee reports that the correspondence to date has also established the Revenue's views on the following points].

[AGREEMENT BY LESSOR NOT TO ELECT TO WAIVE EXEMPTION]

If, having entered into an agreement for a lease which made no reference to the intending lessor making an election to waive exemption from VAT, the intending lessor subsequently agreed that he or she would not make the election, on what basis would the agreement for lease be stamped, i e what would be the value of the consideration?

[Revenue view] A binding undertaking by a lessor, after an agreement for lease is entered into but before it is stamped, not to exercise an option to charge VAT, would be effective to exclude any stamp duty on VAT that might otherwise be charged on that agreement.

[TRANSFER OF BUSINESS AS A GOING CONCERN]

[The revenue law committee] assume that where the transferor has elected to charge VAT in relation to land (so it will be necessary for the transferee to make a similar election), if the transfer is to be treated as a supply of neither goods nor services for VAT purposes, then conveyances or transfers will be stamped as if no VAT is due, provided the agreement itself or any covering letter to the local stamp office makes it clear that the parties expect such treatment to be available or can confirm that Customs & Excise will apply the transfers of going concerns provisions to the transaction. This would save having to delay submission of documents until it is clear (or has been confirmed post-transfer) that such treatment will apply. Could the Stamp Office confirm that this procedure would be adopted?

[Revenue view] Yes. Such documents can be dealt with at any stamp office and do not need to be sent for adjudication on those grounds alone.

[GROUPS OF COMPANIES]

Where a lease is made between two companies in a VAT group registration (and so the supply is to be ignored for VAT purposes) will the possibility of an election being made at a later date be ignored?

[Revenue view] Yes.

[SUB-SALES]

With sub-sales, is the additional amount that would be payable, had an election to charge VAT been made prior to A agreeing to transfer land to B, ignored in determining whether the consideration provided by C to B upon a sub-sale of the property was less than its value (Stamp Act 1891 s 58(4)(*a*), (7))?

[Revenue view] Yes.

Law Society's Gazette, 4 March 1992, p 16.

9 June 1993. Law Society

Stamp duty—mitigation of penalties

[The following statutory penalties may be imposed for the late presentation of documents liable to stamp duty—

- £10 (Stamp Act 1891 s 15(1)), plus
- interest at 5 per cent per annum on the duty outstanding where this is more than £10 (Stamp Act 1891 s 15(1)), plus
- a sum equal to the amount of duty outstanding (Stamp Act 1891 s 15(2)(*c*)).

In practice, except in cases of deliberate withholding of duty, avoidance or delays exceeding one year, the Revenue exercises its authority to mitigate penalties (Stamp Act 1891 s 15(3)(*b*)).]

In the *Law Society's Gazette* of 29 May 1991, a letter from the Controller of Stamps, Keith Hodgson, was published, which gave details of the scale of charges which the Stamp Office would apply where instruments were not presented for stamping at the proper time.

Since then, there has been a reduction in the level of interest charged, to reflect the general reduction in interest rates, and Stamp Offices are now instructed to mitigate penalties to a level equivalent to an interest rate charge of around 10 per cent per annum for delays of up to three months, and 10 per cent to 15 per cent for three to 12 months: *Law Society's Gazette*, 9 June 1993 p 32.

12 July 1993. Inland Revenue

Stamp duty—new buildings

The Inland Revenue have today published a statement of practice (SP 8/93) setting out their view of how the law on stamp duty applies to certain transactions involving new buildings. The transactions concerned are where there purport to be separate contracts for the construction of the buildings and the purchase of the land on which they are to stand. The statement does not affect the common situation where a contract for the sale of a new house on a plot of land is subsequently given effect by a conveyance of the whole property, in the same way as most ordinary sales of new houses. A copy of the statement is reproduced in Appendix 2.

The statement reflects legal advice given to the Board following the High Court decision in the case of the *Prudential Assurance Company Ltd v IRC* ([1992] STC 863; [1993] 1 WLR 211). It replaces previous statements on this subject published in 1957 and 1987 (SP 10/87).

DETAILS

1 The statement applies only where—

- there is a contract for the sale or lease of a building plot and the builder or developer is to construct buildings on the site for the purchaser; and
- at the date of the contract, building work on the plot has either not been started or is incomplete; and
- at the time the conveyance or lease is executed, building work on the plot has begun (and perhaps been completed).

2 The statement sets out the stamp duty consequences of a number of different arrangements. The stamp duty treatment in a particular case will depend on the precise facts of the case. But in broad terms—

(i) where there is a contract for a conveyance or lease of land and, as a separate transaction, a further contract for building works, stamp duty on the conveyance or lease will be calculated without regard to the further contract.

(ii) where within a single transaction there are separate contracts for the sale or lease of a building plot, and for building works on that plot, the stamp duty charge depends on whether the contracts are genuinely independent. If the contracts are independent, duty will be charged on the price paid or payable for both the land itself and for any building that is on the land at the time the instrument is executed, including partly completed buildings. If the contracts are not independent, stamp duty will be charged on the total price for the land and completed buildings.

3 The statement does not apply where there is evidence of a sham or artificial transaction.

Transitional arrangements

4 Stamp duty can be paid on the basis which applied before this Statement, where that is more beneficial, if unconditional contracts have been entered into either before the Statement or within 28 days after it.

Procedure

5 If stamp duty is offered on the total price paid for a building plot and the completed building, the documents should be submitted to the Stamp Office in the usual way.

6 If the total price does not exceed the stamp duty threshold (£60,000 for documents executed on or after 16 March) the documents (except for new leases) can be submitted direct to the Land Registry (in Scotland, the Keeper of the Registers) provided the usual certificate can be included. New leases will need to be stamped in respect of the rent.

7 If the total price paid exceeds the threshold but duty is offered on a lesser amount, the documents should be sent to the Stamp Office together with a full explanation.

17 March 1994. Hansard

Stamp duty (clause 226)

Mr Andrew Smith: Would not it have been better if the Government had structured the law so that there was equity between the different ways of organising transactions, rather than leaving it to members of the public to organise their affairs so that they can structure the transaction in a way that takes advantage of the ambiguous position of that important aspect of the law?

…

Mr Nelson: I think and hope that the Government have got it right, but to be fair to the Hon Gentleman, I asked the same question when I examined the original proposals. The answer is that stamp duty is a tax on documents, and it is important to consider the substance of the documents involved. Of course, one seeks and hopes for clarity in the imposition of tax so that those who construct documents know exactly what their liabilities are. One cannot, however, avoid considering the nature of the document to ascertain whether duty will arise.

To clarify matters for my Hon Friend the Member for Slough, under the new rules, where a property worth £100,000 is exchanged for another worth £70,000 plus £30,000 cash, it is true that stamp duty will fall on the full £100,000 value on both sides of that exchange. There is no need, however, for that to happen where a cash equality sum is involved, and it can be obviated in two ways. One way is that the exchange contract should have a clause apportioning an amount of £70,000, as in the example, which relates to the value. So it could be said that in exchange for a property worth £100,000, the other party will hand over another which is assumed to have a notional value of £70,000 of the total. Where the value of the property is apportioned in that exchange, I understand that that is the only amount that is liable to stamp duty.

That is not necessarily the only way of getting round a problem that might arise where there is a cash equality sum and stamp duty might otherwise be liable. The better way is for there to be a contract of sale. There is little difference between the effect of a contract of exchange and a contract of sale, but the latter would essentially say, "I sell to you this property worth £100,000 and you will pay me a property worth £70,000 and cash of £30,000." Where it is a sale document, the stamp duty will apply on only one side of that and it would not be necessary to pay full stamp duty the other way round.

House developers and others who take properties in part exchange will be able to do that, only with the imposition of the nominal 50p stamp duty, and then they can sell them. When a part exchange property was sold, its purchaser would have to pay stamp duty in the normal way. That is what would happen if it involved three parties instead of two.

…

Mr Nelson:… The stamp duty office is willing to advise practitioners, or others who are in doubt, about how to structure a contract to ensure that it is effective and that people do not have to pay stamp duty on a value over and above that of the property which is being transferred. That is the right way to proceed.

…

Mr Butterfill: Does my Hon Friend agree that it is almost inconceivable that a house builder of any substance who was operating a part-exchange scheme would fail to point out to a purchaser the way in which the matter should be structured so as to minimise the liability?

Mr Nelson: My Hon Friend is right. I can tell him and the Hon Member for Christchurch (Mrs Maddock), who rightly referred to the propensity of people to part exchange their properties, that the House Builders Federation made representations and explained its concern about the impact that the measure would have on its marketing and on the form of part-exchange deals that are such an essential part of the marketplace. The Government clarified that that would be permitted. I believe that that was broadly welcome by the House Builders Federation.

Mr Andrew Smith: I beg to move amendment No 361, in page 194, line 40 [clause 226(5)], at end insert—

> "(5A) For the purposes of section 34(4) of the Finance Act 1958 (certificates of value) a transaction shall not be regarded as forming part of a larger transaction solely because it is or comprises part of the consideration for the transfer or vesting of another estate or interest in land or the grant of any lease or tack.".

The amendment would make it clear that the £60,000 threshold below which duty is payable applies to both legs of the transaction or exchange. I understand that once again conflicting advice has been issued by different stamp offices on the application of the threshold to exchange transactions following the Budget. Some have said that the threshold will apply to the combined value of the two properties, others that it will apply to each property individually.

…

The treatment of a particular case will depend on all the facts, but where one property is exchanged for another, the stamp office would apply the thresholds to each separately. For example, if a property worth £50,000 was being exchanged for a house worth £50,000, the threshold would apply separately to each property and neither would be liable for duty. Therefore, the amendment is unnecessary.

Mr Smith: I am grateful to the Minister for clarifying that he understands that that is the case. Would any compensation be payable to people who have been advised differently by the Stamp Office on that matter?

...

Mr Nelson:... People can claim repayment if the stamp office has charged them incorrectly. I hope and believe that they have not.

HC Official Report, Standing Committee A (Thirteenth Sitting), cols 714, 715, 718–722.

Note—This has been superseded by Tax Bulletin 18 (August 1995).

5 April 1994. HM Land Registry

Land Registry announces change in stamp duty adjudication procedures

As a means of improving customer service and after discussion with the Stamp Office, the Chief Land Registrar has decided to revise the practice under which an original instrument requiring adjudication must, to gain priority, be lodged at the Land Registry prior to its submission to the Stamp Office.

With effect from 5 April 1994, it will no longer be a requirement for an applicant to lodge the original instrument with an application for registration when that instrument requires adjudication by the Stamp Office.

Instead, a certified copy of the instrument may be lodged with the application, together with a letter to the Land Registry explaining the position and confirming that the original instrument will be lodged with the Land Registry promptly on its return from the Stamp Office.

When the original instrument has been stamped, it must be sent without delay to the district land registry where the application was lodged, with a covering letter of explanation.

18 April 1994. Inland Revenue

Stamp duty—property transactions

This Press Release gives guidance, in response to enquiries and representations, about some aspects of the stamp duty changes introduced by the 1994 Finance Bill [clauses 237–243 of the 1994 Finance Bill as amended]. They are—

(*a*) the calculation of duty on an exchange of properties, particularly where the properties are of unequal value and a payment of money (known as equality money) is also made;

(*b*) the application of the £60,000 threshold to exchanges;

(*c*) the treatment of sales where one property is sold and another property is given in part payment of the sale price. The guidance makes clear that in these circumstances duty at 1 per cent. is charged (subject to the threshold) on the consideration for the property being sold; the transfer of the other property which is given in part payment is liable only to the fixed duty of 50p.

DETAILS

Exchanges

1 Clause 239 of the 1994 Finance Bill [as amended] (originally clause 226) introduces new rules for stamp duty on exchanges of interests in land or buildings. Under the new rules duty is charged on each transfer. The duty in each case is calculated by reference to the "consideration" (*ie* the value) given for the transfer; where the consideration consists of property, its open market value will be taken. For example, if one house worth £100,000 is exchanged for another house worth £100,000, duty of £1,000 (1 per cent of £100,000) is charged on each transfer. The £60,000 threshold is applied separately to each side of the exchange. For example, if there is a straightforward exchange of one house worth £50,000 for another worth £50,000, both transfers are within the threshold and so no duty would be payable on either (see para 10 below).

2 Where the market values of the two properties being exchanged are not equal, a payment of money (or some other consideration) may often be given with the lower value property, so as to equalise the bargain. The treatment of such cases for stamp duty purposes will depend on the facts and the effect of the relevant documents.

Examples

3 For example, where one house worth £100,000 is exchanged for another worth £80,000 plus £20,000 money, the conveyance for the transfer of the £100,000 house will normally say that the consideration for the transfer consists of the £80,000 house and the £20,000 money; and the conveyance will be stamped accordingly with duty on £100,000.

4 On the conveyance of the £80,000 house, the Stamp Office have charged duty under the new rules by reference to the consideration expressed in the conveyance—

(*a*) where the conveyance provides that the consideration for the transfer of the cheaper property is the appropriate proportion of the value of the more expensive property, stamp duty is applied accordingly. Thus if the conveyance provides that the consideration for the £80,000 house is the appropriate proportion of the £100,000 house, the amount charged to duty on the transfer of the £80,000 house is limited to £80,000;

(*b*) more commonly the conveyance may say simply that the consideration for the transfer of the £80,000 house consists of the £100,000 house. In these circumstances, the Stamp Office will have charged duty by reference to the value of the £100,000 house.

Representations

5 Representations have been made that in many cases the wording of the conveyance of the cheaper property may not fully reflect the consideration expressed in the initial contract or agreement. It has been suggested that where the contract provides for an exchange and also provides for money to be paid as equality money by one party to the other, the equality money should be taken into account in deciding how much of the more expensive property is regarded as consideration for the cheaper property (even though the equality money has not been mentioned in the conveyance of the cheaper property).

Revised practice

6 The Revenue have taken legal advice on this. The conclusion is that where it is clear from the contract that the intention of the parties to the transaction is that the cheaper property should be transferred for the more expensive property *less* the equality money, the Stamp Office will limit the charge to duty accordingly. For example, if the initial contract provided for an £80,000 house to be exchanged for a £100,000 house, and for £20,000 to be paid as equality money, the amount charged to duty on the transfer of the £80,000 property would be limited to £80,000. The result in an individual case will depend on the facts of the case and the relevant documents. The Stamp Office will need to see the relevant contract with the conveyance which is to be stamped.

7 Where there is a multiple exchange of properties, an apportionment on similar lines may be made to determine how much of the consideration is attributable to each of the transfers. For example, two or more properties may be exchanged for one larger property, with or without a payment of equality money. Here again, the precise result will depend on the facts of the case.

Past cases

8 Where the transfer of a cheaper property has already been stamped by reference to the full value of a more expensive property, but the person who has paid the duty thinks that the duty would be reduced on the basis explained in paras 6 or 7 above, the Stamp Office will be prepared to review the case. Applicants should resubmit the relevant conveyance, and the contract (or a certified copy of the contract). (If it is not possible to obtain the original stamped document from the relevant Registrar, the Stamp Office should be consulted about alternative arrangements.) Where appropriate, excess duty will be repaid provided the claim is made within the two-year time limit laid down by the Stamp Duties Management Act 1891 s 10.

9 Claims for repayment should be made to the Stamp Office at Worthing (for England, Wales and Northern Ireland), or Edinburgh (for Scotland).

Application of £60,000 threshold

10 Sales of property (other than shares) for a price not exceeding the £60,000 threshold are exempted from duty, provided that a "certificate of value" is given stating that the transfer is not part of a larger transaction, or a series of transactions, for a total price of more than £60,000. The threshold is applied separately to each side of an exchange of properties. If in a particular case the threshold has not been applied separately to each side of an exchange (or to two sales where the purchase prices have been set off against each other), and the person who paid the duty believes that too much duty was paid, the documents (with the certificate of value) may be returned for reconsideration to the Stamp Office on the same basis as in paras 8 and 9 above.

11 Where there is a multiple exchange—for example, properties A and B are exchanged for property C—the transfers of properties A and B would be regarded as parts of a larger transaction, and the threshold would not apply to either of them if the total consideration for both was more than £60,000. The threshold would be applied separately to the transfer of property C.

Sales

12 In many cases, transactions which in the past have been structured and documented as exchanges could equally well be carried out as sales for a price which may be partly satisfied in kind. For example, when a builder offers a property for sale, he may receive the price from the buyer in the form either of money, or partly of money and partly of the buyer's old house. Such a transaction can be carried out and documented (commencing with the initial contract) as a sale. Stamp duty is charged on the consideration for the sale. So if, for example, the buyer is buying a new house for £100,000, and pays for it with £30,000 in cash plus his old house worth £70,000, duty of £1,000 (1 per cent of £100,000) would be charged on the transfer of the £100,000 house. The house which the builder accepts as part payment for the sale would not be regarded as a separate sale for stamp duty purposes. It would be charged only to the fixed duty of 50p. The threshold would not be of relevance to this transfer as it is not a conveyance on sale.

General

13 In cases of doubt about how a particular document of the types mentioned above would be treated by the Stamp Office for stamp duty purposes, the Technical Section, The Stamp Office, Ridgeworth House, Liverpool Gardens, Worthing BN11 1XP, will be willing to help.

Note—This has been superseded by Tax Bulletin 18 (August 1995).

29 November 1994. Inland Revenue

Stamp duty: group relief

The Chancellor proposes in his Budget to make two changes to the stamp duty relief for transfers between companies in the same group. Under these measures,

- companies within a group will, subject to conditions, be able to grant new leases to each other free from stamp duty;
- the test for group membership for the purpose of the relief will be changed from 90 per cent ownership of issued share capital to 75 per cent ownership of ordinary share capital.

The changes will apply to documents executed on or after the day on which the Finance Bill receives Royal Assent.

The Chancellor's intention is to extend stamp duty group relief to new leases, in line with representations; and to bring the group control test for this relief closer to the test for corporation tax purposes.

DETAILS

New leases

1 Sales of land or shares by one company to another company in the same group are exempt from stamp duty, subject to anti-avoidance provisions designed to discourage exploitation of the relief. Assignments of existing leases are similarly exempt. But grants of new leases are outside the scope of these provisions. A number of representations have been received for the relief to be extended to grants of new leases.

2 Under the new rules, new leases will qualify for group relief in the same way as sales and assignments of existing leases. Agreements for lease will similarly qualify (provided they are executed on or after the date of Royal Assent).

Test for group membership

3 Under the present rules, companies are associated for the purpose of the stamp duty group relief if either one company owns 90 per cent of the other, or both are 90 per cent owned by a third company. Ownership is measured by reference to issued share capital.

4 The new rules will be different in two respects. The requirement of 90 per cent ownership will be changed to 75 per cent ownership; and only ordinary shares will be taken into account, instead of the whole of the issued share capital.

5 These changes will broadly align the group control test for stamp duty with that for corporation tax. More transfers between companies will be exempt from stamp duty. In a few cases, the new rules will preclude relief where it would currently be available.

3 August 1995. Tax Bulletin 18

Stamp duty: FA 1994

1 We have received a number of enquiries about the stamp duty provisions in FA 1994 ss 240–243. This article aims to give some general guidance on these points. The precise treatment of a particular document will, of course, depend on all the facts of the case and the legal effect of the document.

EXCHANGES ETC—FA 1994 S 241

2 Section 241 introduced new rules of stamp duty on exchanges of interest in land or buildings. Section 241 operates in a similar manner to SA 1891 ss 6, 55 and 57. These provisions impose a charge on instruments which implement transactions which would not be characterised as a sale at common law because the consideration is something other than a price in money paid or promised. Pursuant to these provisions, certain kinds of consideration are to be treated for the purposes of the charge as equivalent to a money price, the charge being imposed by reference to the value of the consideration to be given. (In relation to s 57, Statement of Practice SP 6/90 remains effective).

3 For the purposes of the charge to duty under the "conveyance or transfer on sale" heading in SA 1891 s 241(1) attributes a value to the consideration and states that "the instrument shall be charged with *ad valorem* duty under that heading" where a charge is not imposed in respect of that consideration by virtue of any other provision.

4 As stamp duty is charged on instruments, rather than transactions, s 241(1) falls to be applied to each instrument which satisfies the terms of the provision. Accordingly, if, for example, the consideration for the transfer of an interest in land is the transfer of an interest in land, each transfer is chargeable by reference to the market value of the interest transferred by the other.

THE £60,000 THRESHOLD

5 The £60,000 threshold is applied separately to each side of the exchange. For example, if there is a straightforward exchange of one house worth £50,000 for another worth £50,000, both transfers are within the threshold and no duty would be payable on either provided each is certified in accordance with FA 1958 s 34(4).

6 Where there is a multiple exchange—for example, properties A and B are exchanged for property C—the transfers of properties A and B would be regarded as parts of a larger transaction (under FA 1958 s 34(4)). The threshold would not apply to either of them if the total consideration for both was more than £60,000, but would be applied separately to the transfer of property C.

EQUALITY MONEY

7 Where the market values of two properties being exchanged are not equal, a payment of money (or some other consideration) is often given with the lower value property, so as to equalise the bargain. In many cases the wording of the conveyance of the lower value property may not fully reflect the consideration expressed in the original contract or agreement. Where it is clear from the contract that the lower value property has been transferred for the higher value property less the equality money, the Stamp Office will limit the charge to duty accordingly. For example, if the initial contract provided for an £80,000 house to be exchanged for a £100,000 house, and for £20,000 to be paid as equality money, the amount charged to duty on the transfer of the £80,000 house would be limited to £80,000. In these cases the Stamp Office needs to see the relevant contract as well as the conveyance.

8 Where there is a multiple exchange of properties, an apportionment on similar lines may be made to determine how much of the consideration is attributable to each of the transfers. For example, two or more properties may be exchanged for one larger property, with or without a payment of equality money.

SALES

9 In many cases, transactions which in the past have been structured and documented as an exchange could equally well be carried out as a sale for a price which may be partly satisfied in kind. For example, when a person offers a property for sale, he may receive the price from the buyer in the form either of money, or partly of money and partly of the buyer's existing house. Such a transaction can be carried out and documented (commencing with the initial contract) as a sale. Section 241 does not apply where duty is already imposed under the conveyance on sale head of charge. Accordingly, if the transaction is within the common law concept of "sale", s 241 is excluded and duty is simply charged by reference to the price of the sale.

10 Although a sale ordinarily involves a price in money paid or promised (*Littlewoods Mail Order Stores Limited v IRC* [1963] AC 135 at page 152), the Courts have held that the transaction is still a "sale" if property is taken in satisfaction of part of the purchase price: *Simpson v Connolly* [1953] 2 All ER 474 p 477; *Connell Estate Agents v Begej* [1993] 2 EGLR 35. In the Connell case, the purchaser had agreed to purchase land for £109,000. In satisfaction of this price the vendor was "to receive ownership of 10 Milner Road, Finedon, plus balance of £53,000". The Court of Appeal held that the transaction was a sale of the more valuable property for the price of £109,000 and that the purchaser's property was part of that price. The Court confirmed however, that a transaction cannot be characterised as a sale unless some money is paid by the purchaser to the vendor and the cash element is more than merely nominal. So if, for example, the buyer is buying a house for £100,000, and pays for it with £30,000 in cash plus his existing house worth £70,000, duty of £1,000 (1 per cent of £100,000) would be charged on the transfer of the £100,000 house.

11 The house which the vendor accepts as part payment for the sale would not be regarded as a separate sale for stamp duty purposes. The consideration for the purchaser's property is not the vendor's property but merely the discharge of a potential obligation to pay part of the purchase price on completion. Accordingly, s 241 does not apply to the transfer of the purchaser's property. SA 1891 s 57 does not apply to the transfer of the purchaser's property because the purchaser's property is not conveyed to the vendor in consideration, wholly or in part, of any "debt due" to the vendor. The word "due" when used in relation to a debt means due and payable (*Re European Life Assurance* [1869] LR 9 Eq 122, and the other cases cited in Stroud's Judicial Dictionary 5th Ed Vol 2 pp 781–783). As the purchase price is not payable until completion, a transfer of property by the purchaser on or before completion cannot be said to be in consideration of a debt due. Ordinarily, on completion, the transfer of the purchaser's property will be handed to the vendor's solicitor, together with a cheque or other means of payment, at the same time as the vendor's solicitor hands over the transfer of the vendor's property. For there to be a debt due to the vendor, the purchaser would have to be put in the position of having taken a transfer of the vendor's property without having paid for it.

12 On the basis that there is a sale for cash to be satisfied in part by the transfer of another property, *ad valorem* stamp duty is charged on the consideration for the sale, but not on the transfer of the other property. That transfer would only be charged to the fixed duty of 50 pence. The threshold would not be relevant to this transfer as it is not a conveyance on sale.

SURRENDER AND REGRANT OF LEASES

13 Where a lease is granted in consideration only of the surrender or abandonment of an existing lease of the same property, SA 1891 s 77(1) provides exemption from duty. If the new lease is granted in consideration of a premium and/or rent as well as the surrender of the existing lease, there is a grant of a lease which is partly exempt (the surrender) and partly chargeable to duty (the premium and/or rent). The Stamp Office would not seek to refuse exemption under SA 1891 s 77(1) merely on the grounds that there were some minor changes in the property subject to the lease, provided that these could be regarded as de minimis. The same treatment would apply where a variation of a lease takes effect in law as a surrender and regrant.

14 Where the lease on one property is being replaced by a lease on another property, the stamp duty treatment will depend on the facts of the case and the effect of the document. But if, for example, the document granted a new lease on one property and the consideration was the surrender of a lease on another property, duty would be charged on the grant of the new lease, by reference to the market value of the lease surrendered (as premium/consideration) and any other payment by way of premium or rent.

15 The stamp duty treatment of the surrender of the old lease will similarly depend on the facts and the documents. In most cases where there is a surrender and regrant, the Stamp Office's experience is that no deed of surrender is submitted for stamping, either because the new lease simply supersedes the old one by operation of law and there is no surrender document, or possibly because any surrender document is not submitted for stamping.

SALE AND LEASEBACK

16 Where there is a sale and leaseback, the Stamp Office normally sees a contract of sale for a price, and an agreement for lease (followed by the grant of a lease), rather than an exchange of one for the other. In that case, the sale would be liable to duty in the normal way by reference to the price and the agreement for lease would be charged by reference to any premium and rent.

17 If, however, the property is transferred in consideration of a leaseback of the same property, alone or together with a sum of money, duty would be assessed on the transfer by reference to the value (if any) of the lease plus any cash element. Duty would also be assessed on the lease by reference to any amount by which the value of the property transferred exceeded the cash consideration.

UNASCERTAINABLE CONSIDERATION—FA 1994 S 242

18 Section 242 deals with sales of land or buildings where the price is not ascertainable at the time the relevant document is executed. In these circumstances, the open market value of the property is to be taken as the consideration for stamp duty purposes. Similarly, where the rent under a new lease is not ascertainable the open market rent is to be taken.

19 That rule does not, however, apply where the amount of the consideration can already be determined by reference to the "contingency principle"—s 242(3)(*a*). Under this principle, if the consideration agreed between the parties and specified in the instrument is subject to possible future variation, the specified figure would be taken for stamp duty purposes (*Independent Television Authority v IR Comrs* [1961] AC 427 p 443). Thus if the consideration is 25 per cent of profits over 5 years, but not to be less than £100,000, the consideration for stamp duty purposes would be £100,000. The existence of additional but unascertainable consideration would bring the transaction within s 242.

20 The ascertainable figure produced by the contingency principle may be a maximum or minimum, or a basic sum which is subject to future variation. But a minimum figure which was merely a nominal figure inserted in a lease to avoid s 242, or which did not represent the agreed

Stamp Taxes

consideration or rent, would not satisfy s 242(3)(*a*) as it would not be a minimum rent for the purpose of the contingency principle as formulated by Lord Radcliffe in the Independent Television Authority case. We consider that for this purpose a minimum rent must be an amount genuinely agreed between the parties as such, ie, as an amount which is contemplated by the parties and accepted by the landlord as compensation for the use and occupation of the premises by the tenant(s). It is therefore necessary to consider all the facts in order to ascertain the true nature and intended purpose of the instrument (*Oughtred v IR Comrs* [1958] Ch 678 page 688; [1960] AC 206).

21 The market value rule applies where part of the consideration or rent is unascertainable. Duty would then be charged on the market value or rent (but not the market value or rent **plus** the ascertainable consideration). Where the rent under a lease is unascertainable for only part of the term, the market rent will be taken for the whole term in order to calculate the average annual rent. In establishing the market rent, all the terms and conditions of the actual lease will be taken into account under normal valuation principles, s 242(3)(*b*). It is the market rent for the particular **lease** and not merely the market rent for the land at a particular time which must be established for the purposes of s 242(2).

22 It has been suggested to us that s 242 is ineffective on the grounds that if there is a valid contract, the consideration will be ascertainable, even though it may not be immediately quantifiable. For a contract to be valid, it is sufficient that the consideration is ascertainable either at the time of the contract or subsequently. Section 242 by contrast applies where the consideration is not ascertainable at the time the document is executed. The section has to be read in conjunction with FA 1963 s 55, which refers to the amount or value of the consideration, and the words "cannot ...be ascertained" clearly mean "cannot be ascertained for the purpose of the charge", rather than "cannot be ascertained as a matter of contract law". Our view is that the wording of s 242(1) is apt to cover the case where the amount or value of the consideration cannot be ascertained at the relevant time for the purposes of stamp duty chargeable under the conveyance on sale head of charge.

23 It has also been suggested that some transactions could come within both s 241 and s 242, on the grounds that where the amount or value of the consideration is not ascertainable, the right to it might be "property" within s 241(1). In general, the two sections deal with distinct types of cases. There may be some cases which could fall within both sections, but the precise treatment will depend on the facts of the case. In practice, where the transfer is for full value, it should make little or no difference to the amount of duty whether s 241 or s 242 applies. Where there is a difference, duty would be charged under the provision which produces the higher amount of duty (following the principle in *Speyer Bros v IR Comrs* [1908] AC 92).

24 The treatment of split-term leases set out in our letter of 2 January 1963 to the Law Society's Gazette (where they are described as leases of type (*c*)) no longer applies. The annex on page 237 reproduces the relevant part of the 1963 letter.

SURRENDERS—FA 1994 S 243

25 Section 243 provides that where, in pursuance of an agreement, a lease is surrendered or renounced without a deed of surrender, the agreement is liable to duty as if it were a deed.

26 We have been asked what particular types of document would be regarded as an "agreement". In an individual case, it would of course be necessary to consider the facts and the terms of the relevant document. The case of *Fleetwood-Hesketh v IR Comrs* [1936] 1 KB 351 shows that a document recording or implementing an agreement may itself be treated as an agreement for stamp duty purposes whether there is a previous oral agreement or an oral agreement contemporaneous with the written agreement. Where such a document satisfies the requirements of the Law of Property (Miscellaneous Provisions) Act 1989 s 2, it will be an agreement within s 243.

VALUATIONS

27 Although the stamp duty legislation does not provide for appeals on valuation to go to the Lands Tribunal, a reference by consent could be made to the Tribunal under the Lands Tribunal Act 1949 s 1(5) on a question of land valuation. We would normally consent. However, where questions of both law and valuation arise in relation to an appeal relating to liability and quantum respectively, we would wish to resolve the legal issue in the High Court prior to any determination of value by the Lands Tribunal. In contrast, a valuation issue would after appeal go to the Lands Tribunal.

AGREEMENT FOR LEASE—FA 1994 S 240

28 Section 240 provides that if an agreement for lease and the lease which gives effect to the agreement, are presented for stamping at the same time, and any duty chargeable on the agreement is paid, the agreement shall be treated as having been executed at the same time as the lease for the purposes of the provisions relating to penalties for late stamping. We have been asked whether FA 1931 s 28 means that the agreement must nevertheless be produced to the

Stamp Office within 30 days of execution. Presentation of the agreement with the lease, within 30 days after the execution of the lease, will be accepted as satisfying the requirement under s 28 to produce the agreement.

GENERAL

29 This article supersedes the relevant parts of the Press Releases of 30 November 1993 and 18 April 1994 and the Stamp Office guidance notes issued in December 1993.

Extract from the Controller of Stamps' letter of 2 January 1963 to the Law Society's Gazette

> "The Board of Inland Revenue have recently given consideration to the basis of assessment of duty on leases which contain one or more of the following provisions:
>
> …
>
> (*c*) a rent or rents fixed for part only of the term, the rent for the remainder of the term to be agreed subsequently.
>
> Leases of type (*c*) present great difficulty and the Board are advised that in the absence of authority, it cannot be said with certainty how the provisions of the lease head of charge should properly be applied. In the absence of such authority and with the object of securing a consistent practice, hitherto lacking, and to bring the assessment of duty as far as possible into line with the facts, the Board have decided that such leases shall be assessed by treating separately the part of the term in respect of which the rent is known from that in respect of which it is unknown; *ad valorem* duty under 'Lease (3)' will be assessed in respect of the former part as if it were a lease at the known rate or average rate of rent for a term of that length, and fixed duty under 'Lease (4)' will be assessed in respect of the latter part.
>
> The practice explained above in relation to leases of type (*c*) will not affect the basis of assessment of leases where there is a rent of one description (eg a ground rent) of known amount for the whole of the term and a further rent of another description (eg a service rent) ascertainable for part only of the term. In such cases the basis of assessment will continue to be *ad valorem* duty under 'Lease (3)' on the average ascertainable annual rent payable throughout the term and fixed duty under 'Lease (4)' on the further uncertain rent."

4 August 1995. Inland Revenue

Tradepoint—Tax and stamp duty reserve tax reliefs

Regulations have been laid today to remove the tax obstacles which might otherwise have prevented effective trading by Tradepoint (a new screen-based market for dealing in equities).

DETAILS

1 These regulations are the Income Tax (Dealers in Securities) (Tradepoint) Regulations 1995, the Income Tax (Manufactured Dividends) (Tradepoint) Regulations 1995 and the Stamp Duty Reserve Tax (Tradepoint) Regulations 1995. They will allow the London Clearing House in its capacity as the clearing house for Tradepoint to be exempt from Stamp Duty Reserve Tax (SDRT) and the anti-bondwashing legislation. They will also allow favourable treatment in respect of manufactured dividends. These three benefits will also apply to certain members of Tradepoint in particular circumstances. Copies of the regulations will be available shortly from Her Majesty's Stationery Office.

2 Bond washing is a device for turning income into capital gains and so, in certain cases, avoiding tax. This is countered by legislation which does not apply to Stock Exchange market makers acting in the ordinary course of market making business. It would also be inappropriate for it to apply to the London Clearing House and to certain members of Tradepoint where they are taking no proprietary interest in Tradepoint transactions but are simply involved as part of Tradepoint's clearing process. These regulations ensure this.

3 Manufactured dividends are paid to compensate recipients for real dividends that are not received. They can be paid when stock is lent over a period which straddles a dividend date or where sales of cum-dividend stock are satisfied by delivery of ex-dividend stock. Unless such payments are approved, the payer is penalised for tax purposes. When made by Stock Exchange market makers such payments are normally treated as approved. These regulations will ensure that the same applies for the London Clearing House and for members of Tradepoint when they are involved only as part of Tradepoint's clearing process.

4 SDRT is a tax on certain agreements to transfer securities, which supplements the stamp duty on shares. Stamp duty applies only where there is a transfer document. Without these regulations, Tradepoint's clearing arrangements could result in more than one charge to stamp duty/SDRT for a single purchase by a Tradepoint client. The regulations ensure that extra charges to SDRT under such arrangements will not arise. In line with transactions on other exchanges, a single charge to stamp duty or SDRT will occur on the transfer of the shares to the purchaser.

Note—Tradepoint received recognition as an investment exchange from the Securities and Investment Board on 7 June 1995.

2 October 1995. Inland Revenue

Stock lending: stamp duty reserve tax

The Inland Revenue have today published three Concessions giving relief from stamp duty reserve tax on certain stock lending transactions [see Concessions G7, G8 and G9 *ante*].

DETAILS

1 In the ordinary course of their business Stock Exchange market makers borrow shares from institutions for the purpose of their market making operations. In return, the lender is given security. These transactions are carried out under standard agreements substantially in a form approved by the Stock Exchange and the Inland Revenue.

2 The Stock Exchange propose to introduce a new Dematerialised Stock Lending Service on 2 October. Stock lenders will be permitted to hold their stock in SEPON (the Stock Exchange's nominee company), so that stock loans (and returns of borrowed stock) can be carried out by electronic transfer within SEPON rather than by paper transfers. Under the new service, the Stock Exchange will collect stamp duty reserve tax (SDRT) on transfers within SEPON where appropriate.

3 The first two concessions relate to the SDRT treatment of the new service.

4 The first concession is concerned with the transfers of stock by lenders into SEPON for the purpose of the new service. Under present legislation transfers into SEPON are exempt from stamp duty but are liable to SDRT at 0·5 per cent, unless they qualify for a specific exemption. Thus if a lender transferred his existing holding of shares into SEPON, the transfer would be liable to 0·5 per cent SDRT. The concession will reduce the SDRT in those circumstances to 50p (in line with the stamp duty charge on a transfer to a nominee in similar circumstances).

5 The second concession is concerned with the return of stock from the market maker to the lender at the end of the loan. Present legislation limits the stamp duty charge on the transfer to 50p. But under the dematerialised service, the return will no longer be a paper transfer. It would therefore be liable to SDRT rather than stamp duty, but there is at present no corresponding SDRT relief limiting the charge to 50p. The concession will limit the SDRT charge to 50p in circumstances where stamp duty would have been limited to 50p if there had been a paper transfer.

6 The third concession stems from changes made in December 1990 to the terms of the standard stock lending agreements to strengthen the security given to stock lenders. These were technical changes but would strictly result in a liability to SDRT in certain circumstances where no stamp duty or SDRT was charged under the previous agreements. The concession, which is already in operation, gives relief from these extra charges.

Note—The concessions will be superseded when the FA 1997 reform of the repurchase and stock lending regime is brought into effect (due to be in 1997–98).

28 November 1995. Inland Revenue

Stamp duty on shares

Changes to the present rules for stamp duty on shares and stamp duty reserve tax (SDRT) were announced by the Chancellor today. Under the proposals:

– the present rules will be adapted to cater for the introduction of paperless share transfers under the CREST system, due to start in July 1996;
– an optional alternative to the present regime for clearance services will be provided.

The changes will apply from 1 July 1996.

DETAILS

1 Stamp duty is charged on documents transferring shares. A company registrar cannot register the transfer of ownership unless the transfer document has been stamped with the appropriate duty (or has been certified as exempt from duty). The Stock Exchange collect duty on transactions involving Stock Exchange members. SDRT is charged on certain agreements to transfer securities, where there is no transfer document and so no liability to stamp duty.

2 The Treasury have laid draft regulations before Parliament to amend company law to permit shares to be held in uncertificated form and to be transferred through an approved paperless transfer system. The proposed CREST system for paperless share transfers is expected to start in July 1996. Paperless transfers will be liable to SDRT rather than stamp duty, and the present stamp duty and SDRT rules need some amendment to cater for them. CREST (and any other system approved under the Treasury regulations) will be required by the tax rules to collect SDRT on relevant transactions settled within the system or reported through it for regulatory purposes.

3 Legislation will be included in the Finance Bill to make a number of changes:

(i) as the law stands, a transfer which is not on sale is liable to 50p stamp duty. There is no corresponding 50p rate of SDRT, and a 50p rate is not being introduced. Deposits of certificated shares into CREST will be exempted from the 50p stamp duty charge. They will not be liable to SDRT unless the 0·5 per cent or 1·5 per cent SDRT charge applies—for example because they are transfers for consideration in money or money's worth;

(ii) at present, a charge to SDRT does not arise until two months after the agreement to transfer the shares. This allows time for a transfer document to be produced and stamped, as will normally happen under the present system. The stamp duty then franks the SDRT liability. With paperless transfers, there will generally be no stamped document, and the two-month delay will no longer be appropriate. The two-month gap will be removed to avoid a cash-flow loss to the Exchequer. Where there is still a stamped transfer document, the stamp duty paid on it will cancel the SDRT charge;

(iii) at present, the rates of SDRT round the tax up to the next 50p—e g 50p per £100 or part of £100. To simplify the calculations, the rates will be changed to a flat percentage—e g 0·5 per cent. (The stamp duty rates will however remain unchanged; the machines used to stamp documents are designed to cater for the present form of rates);

(iv) the territorial scope of SDRT will be clarified. The practice up to now has been to regard agreements made overseas between persons not resident in the United Kingdom (UK) as outside the scope of the tax. Recent legal advice, however, suggests that these agreements are chargeable to SDRT. The legislation will be amended to confirm that. Thus, transfers between non-residents which are settled through CREST will be liable to SDRT (just as they are liable to stamp duty at present where there is a paper transfer). The present practice will however continue to be operated in relation to unconditional agreements which are made before 1 July 1996;

(v) where stock is borrowed by a Stock Exchange market-maker, the stamp duty charge on a transfer of borrowed stock back to the lender is limited to 50p. In the case of dematerialised stock lending, the SDRT charge on the return of stock to the lender is limited to 50p by extra-statutory concession (Inland Revenue Press Release, 2 October). These stock loan returns will be exempted from SDRT from 1 July 1996. The legislation will also provide in statutory form the SDRT relief given at present by extra-statutory concession for transfers of collateral under stock lending arrangements;

(vi) stamp duty and SDRT are charged at 1·5 per cent on transfers of shares into "clearance services"—i e broadly, systems where the shares are held indefinitely by a nominee and rights are bought and sold by book entry transfer without a transfer of the shares themselves. An option will be introduced to enable clearance services to opt for the normal SDRT charges to apply to transactions within the service, instead of the 1·5 per cent charge on transfers into the service. It will be a condition of the option that satisfactory arrangements are made by the clearance service operator for the collection of SDRT and for compliance with the requirements of the SDRT legislation. Where the clearance service has no UK presence, the appointment of a UK tax representative may be required as a condition of the option, unless satisfactory alternative arrangements are made;

(vii) the present rules for the 1·5 per cent SDRT charge on transfers of shares into depositary receipt schemes assume that the shares will be held by a nominee rather than by the issuer of depositary receipts. The legislation will be amended so as to apply also where the shares are held by the issuer of the depositary receipts itself.

4 CREST (and any other paperless system approved under the Treasury regulations) will have a statutory obligation to collect SDRT on relevant transactions carried out within its system or reported through it for regulatory purposes. Firms which are market-makers, brokers and dealers or "qualified dealers" for the purpose of the SDRT regulations—i e broadly firms which are regulated—will be able to obtain any reliefs to which they (or their clients) are entitled, by identifying the relevant transactions in CREST rather than by claiming repayment from the Stamp Office. The present regulations governing the assessment and collection of SDRT are being reviewed and will be amended in due course to make any changes needed to take account of the introduction of paperless share transfers.

27 February 1996. Hansard.

Transfer of securities to members of electronic transfer systems etc [FA 1996 s 186]

Ms Dawn Primarolo: There are issues to be considered when UK shares are traded on foreign stock exchanges. However, there are exemptions where shares are traded abroad—in New York, for instance—in depository form or where settlement is within a clearance system to which a

1·5 per cent clearance system charge applies. Those exemptions will not necessarily cover every case. In some circumstances, the beneficial ownership of shares changes and the stamp duty-related tax that arises from that will not be covered by the exemptions.

Mrs Angela Knight: The variation is that although the 1·5 per cent remains for depository receipts, an alternative is provided for the clearance system. In future, a clearance system can either charge 1·5 per cent on shares that go into the clearance system and then have the transactions take place free of duty, or it will be able to elect, if it so wishes, to pay no charge as shares go into the clearance system but it then pays 0·5 per cent as the shares are transferred.

HC Official Report, Standing Committee E (seventeenth sitting), cols 558, 559, 561, 562

27 February 1996. Hansard.

Stock lending and collateral security arrangements [FA 1996 s 191]

Ms Primarolo: Could the Minister explain what happens if the stock exchange has got it wrong and the CREST system does not operate properly even with the new clause?

....

Mrs Knight: If CREST did not go ahead, the current system would continue to operate. Therefore, we would have the stock-lending process that we have now. On the other hand, if the stock exchange decided that it would not remove the requirement for a broker-dealer—the middle man, an intermediary—but would retain an individual who had to be part of the stock-lending process, the new clause covers that. If the stock exchange decided that, following the implementation of CREST, there would never again be any requirement for an intermediary, the clause covers that as well. Therefore, all rule-change eventualities are covered.

HC Official Report, Standing Committee E (seventeenth sitting), col 564

9 May 1996. Inland Revenue

Open-ended investment companies and authorised unit trusts—stamp duty

The Economic Secretary to the Treasury, Mrs Angela Knight MP, today announced proposals to relax the stamp duty and stamp duty reserve tax rules for authorised unit trusts converting into open-ended investment companies, and for mergers between authorised unit trusts. The proposals will facilitate the introduction of OEICs and at the same time will provide a window of opportunity for rationalisation in the unit trust industry. In reply to a Parliamentary Question, she said:—

> "In response to the consultative document which the Treasury published last year with draft regulations to permit the creation of open-ended investment companies (OEICs), the Treasury have received a number of representations that conversions of authorised unit trusts into OEICs should be exempted from stamp duty and stamp duty reserve tax (SDRT), including conversions of two or more trusts into a single OEIC.
>
> When regulations are made to deal with the stamp duty and SDRT treatment of OEICs, I intend to include in them an exemption for conversions of an authorised unit trust into an OEIC or a single sub-fund of an umbrella OEIC. The regulations will also contain an exemption from stamp duty and SDRT, for a period of some two years, for conversions which involve a merger (such as the conversion of two or more authorised unit trusts into a single OEIC or sub-fund, or the merger of an authorised unit trust with an OEIC).
>
> We also intend to introduce legislation in the next Finance Bill to exempt mergers between authorised unit trusts from stamp duty and SDRT if the merger is carried out after the Bill becomes law and within a period of some two years thereafter.
>
> These measures will give unit trust groups a unique opportunity to rationalise their range of authorised unit trusts, and to convert some or all of them into OEICs if they wish. At the same time, the introduction of OEICs will continue to widen the opportunities for share ownership for the investing public."

DETAILS

1 Open-ended investment companies (OEICs) cannot currently be formed under UK company law. Last year the Treasury issued for consultation a draft of regulations which would permit OEICs to be set up, and the Securities and Investments Board issued draft product regulations for consultation. FA 1995 included powers to make regulations for the tax treatment of OEICs.

2 When an authorised unit trust (AUT) is converted into an OEIC, the transfer of the trust's investments to the OEIC would, as the law stands, generally be liable to stamp duty or stamp duty reserve tax (SDRT). When regulations are made later this year, they will include an exemption from stamp duty and SDRT for the conversion of an AUT into an OEIC, or into a sub-fund of an umbrella OEIC. They will also include an exemption, for a period of some two years, for a merger of two or more AUTs into an OEIC (or a sub-fund of an umbrella OEIC).

3 The Chancellor also proposes to introduce legislation in the next Finance Bill to exempt mergers between authorised unit trusts from stamp duty and SDRT if the merger is carried out after the Bill becomes law and within a period of some two years thereafter.

Notes

Open-ended investment companies are open-ended in the sense that their shares will be continually created or redeemed depending on the net demand by investors to acquire shares or to redeem their existing holdings. As with existing authorised unit trusts, these transactions will be undertaken at a price derived from the net asset value of the OEIC's underlying investments. An OEIC may take "umbrella" form, ie incorporating a number of subfunds in which shareholders can invest separately.

26 November 1996. Inland Revenue

Stamp duty—unit trusts and open-ended investment companies

The temporary stamp duty exemption announced in May for mergers between authorised unit trusts, and mergers of authorised unit trusts into open-ended investment companies (OEICs), is to run until 30 June 1999, under the Chancellor's proposals today. The Government also wishes to simplify the present stamp duty regime for repurchases of units by unit trust managers.

DETAILS

Conversions and mergers

1 The Economic Secretary to the Treasury, Angela Knight MP, announced in May that—

- when regulations were made in due course to deal with the stamp duty and stamp duty reserve tax (SDRT) treatment of OEICs, she intended to include in them an exemption for conversions of an authorised unit trust into an OEIC (or a single sub-fund of an umbrella OEIC);
- the regulations would also provide an exemption, for a period of some two years, for conversions which involve a merger (such as a conversion of two or more authorised unit trusts into a single OEIC);
- legislation would be introduced in the next Finance Bill to exempt mergers between unit trusts if the merger was carried out after the bill became law and within a period of some two years thereafter (Inland Revenue Press Release, 9 May 1996 [see above]).

2 The temporary exemptions will run until 30 June 1999. This will help to facilitate the introduction of OEICs, and will also provide an opportunity for rationalisation in the unit trust industry.

Repurchase of units

3 Under the present stamp duty rules for unit trusts, there is 0.5 per cent charge on the repurchase of units by the manager from investors, but the duty can be repaid if the units are cancelled within the next two months and the underlying investments are sold. This is, however, complex to operate, and is unlikely to fit easily with single pricing of units. It may be uncertain at the time of the repurchase whether the units will in due course be cancelled and the duty repaid.

4 The Government therefore intends to introduce a simpler regime which will apply both for units in unit trusts (whether authorised or unauthorised) and for shares in OEICs. They have in mind to replace the present rule by a lower charge on repurchases, but with no repayment when units (or shares I OEICs) are cancelled. The details are under discussion with representative of the industry, and a further announcement will be made in the near future.

Notes

1 Open-ended investment companies are open-ended in the sense that their shares can be continually created or redeemed depending on the net demand by investors to acquire shares or redeem their existing holdings. As with authorised unit trusts, these transactions will be undertaken at a price derived from the net asset value of the OEIC's underlying investments. An OEIC may take "umbrella" form, with a number of sub-funds with different investment objectives.

2 OEICs cannot currently be formed under UK company law, but the Treasury have made regulations to permit OEICs to be set up (The Open-Ended Investment Companies (Investment Companies with Variable Capital) Regulations 1996 SI 1996/2827). The regulations will come into effect on 6 January 1997. The Securities and Investments Board have issued a final draft of product regulations for OEICs. These are also expected to take effect in January 1997. Regulations for the tax treatment of OEICs will keep in step with that timetable.

3 When an authorised unit trust is converted into an OEIC, the transfer of the trust's investment to the OEIC, would as the law stands, generally be liable to stamp duty or SDRT. Similarly there would be a stamp duty or SDRT liability when unit trusts merge with each other.

8 January 1997. Law Society's Gazette

Stamp duty on leases

A change in practice by the Stamp Office in its approach to calculation of stamp duty on new leases which contain provision for future rent increases in line with RPI (retail price index) changes has resulted in the Law Society's revenue law committee receiving a number of inquiries from solicitors.

The Stamp Office is relying upon the decision in *LM Tenancies plc v IR Comrs* [1996] STC 880 to apply the contingency principle to rent reserved under a lease so that stamp duty is calculated by reference to RPI changes in the year ending with the date of execution of the lease. This approach has led to some excessive estimates of liability.

The revenue law committee has taken up the issue wit the Stamp Office and has made two main points. Firstly, it does not consider that the new approach is justified. *L M Tenancies* was concerned with stamp duty avoidance; to apply the decision in that case across the board to any lease with a rent review clause linked to the RPI is unjustified. Secondly, this is an extremely important change in practice which the Stamp Office has not apparently published effectively.

In response, the Stamp Office has assured the committee that it will examine the facts of each case and give careful consideration to the application of the *LM Tenancies* decision.

The Stamp Office points out that a public announcement of the new practice was made in *Hansard* in a reply given by the Economic Secretary to the Treasury to a parliamentary written question asked by a Conservative MP. It followed representations from the House Builders Federation, the Manufacturing and Construction Industries Alliance and individual property owners.

This reply states:

> "Stamp duty is charges on the grant of a new lease of property by reference to the premium paid for the lease and the average annual rent. Duty on the premium is charged at 1 per cent but there is no charge on the premium where the premium is £60,000 or less and the average annual rent is £6,000 or less. Duty is charged on the average annual rent by reference to a sliding scale of rates which depend on the length of the lease. For example, for a lease of over 100 years, the rate is 24 per cent (£12 per £50 or part of £50 of the average annual rent.)
>
> Where an existing lease is sold by the leaseholder to someone else, duty is charged at 1 per cent on the price paid, in the same way as with the sale of a freehold. No duty is charged on the rent. I have received representations from the House Builders Federation, the Manufacturing and Construction Industries Alliance, and McCarthy and Stone about the treatment of a grant of a new lease under which the rent is to be adjusted in future in line with RPI changes.
>
> Where the terms of a lease lay down specific figures for future rent payments, or provide for the rent to be increased by a fixed percentage each year, there is no difficulty in calculating what the average annual rent is for the purpose of the stamp duty charge. The calculation is more difficult where the rent is to depend on the future movement of an index such as the RPI. Decisions of the courts, including the recent case *L M Tenancies plc v IR Comrs*, have given some guidance on the calculation of the charge to duty where an element is not ascertainable at the outset.
>
> The Inland Revenue has reviewed its practice on the stamp duty treatment of leases of this type then in light of representations that have been made. It accepts that in some cases the calculations made by Stamp Offices produce too high a figure. In the *LM Tenancies* case, the premium paid for a lease was to be calculated by reference to the market price of a Treasury loan stock 25 days after the execution of the lease. The Court decided that duty should be calculated by reference to the value of the stock at the date of execution of the lease.
>
> The Inland Revenue's view, in the light of the court's decision in *LM Tenancies*, is that where the rent under a lease is to be adjusted by reference to RPI changes the duty should be calculated by reference to the change in the year ending with the date of execution of the lease. The precise method of adjustment may depend on the terms of the lease and on the way they provide for the calculation to be made. For example, whether the rent is to be increased annually or only at longer intervals. Generally, where the adjustment is to be made by comparing the value of the RPI at different dates, the difference between the two values over the latest year will be used to measure the rent increase for stamp duty purposes.
>
> For example, if the initial rent is £300 a year and is to be adjusted annually, and the RPI has gone up from 150 to 153, equivalent to 2 per cent over the relevant 12 month period, it would be assumed that the rent would go up by £6 (2 per cent of £300) each year. Thus, the

rent would be taken as £306 in the second year, £312 in the third year, and so on, in order to calculate the average annual rent under the lease.

The Inland Revenue is issuing instructions to Stamp Offices accordingly, to ensure that individual cases are dealt with on a consistent basis. A taxpayer who disagrees with the Stamp Office's calculation of the duty in a particular case will, of course, have the normal rights of appeal."

One firm of solicitors has already obtained counsel's opinion on this issue, to the effect that the Stamp Office's approach is "not sustainable". If there are any changes in this area the revenue law committee will ensure they are reported as soon as possible.

This note was written by Jill Hallpike, the secretary to the Law Society's revenue law committee.

16 January 1997. Tax Journal. Letter from Macfarlanes with extract from Inland Revenue letter

SDRT on UK Share Transfers

... the FA 1996 changes to the stamp duty reserve tax (SDRT) regime. Most of these were designed to deal with the charging and collection of SDRT within CREST. Some of the changes, however, have implications for all transfers of shares in UK companies.

If we ignore, for present purposes, the changes made (in FA 1996 s 187(1)) to the territorial scope of SDRT, the principal changes are as follows—

- The two month delay before the charge to SDRT arises has been repealed and SDRT charge arises immediately when the agreement to transfer shares is entered into or, in the case of a conditional agreement, when that agreement becomes unconditional (see the amendments made to FA 1986 s 87(2) by FA 1996 s 88(1). The accountable date for SDR is therefore correspondingly earlier.
- The SDRT charge is not automatically cancelled until a stock transfer form is executed. If the charge is to be cancelled, it must be shown "to the Board's satisfaction" that two conditions have been fulfilled. Those two conditions are (i) that a stock transfer form (or other transfer document) has been executed and (ii) that the stock transfer form has been properly stamped. Until it is so proved, the duty to notify the inland Revenue of the charge and to pay the SDRT will continue to exist.

Those changes took effect on 1 July 1996.

In correspondence with the Inland Revenue, we have raised the question of how these provisions will affect Stamp Office practice. We referred in particular to cases in which it was not possible to stamp a stock transfer form before the accountable date (and therefore it is not possible to apply for the SDRT charge to be cancelled within that timescale).

This position could, of course, occur in several situations but, in our correspondence, we specifically raised the following circumstances.

The first set of circumstances was where the stock transfer form has been submitted for adjudication and the adjudication has not been completed by the accountable date for SDRT. This might occur (i) where an exemption is being claimed (eg, intra group relief under FA 1930 s 42 or relief for transfers in a reconstruction or amalgamation under FA 1986 s 75) or (ii) where the amount of the consideration is not ascertained or has to be valued (eg, completion accounts being drawn up or the consideration is not in cash).

The accountable date might also be passed without a stampable document being created where completion of the agreement is deferred.

The Inland Revenue's response goes some way to clarifying the practice which the Inland Revenue will adapt in relation to the FA 1996 changes. The Inland Revenue has agreed to the publication of the following extracts from its letter.

> "The revisions introduced by the Finance Act 1996 mean that unless an agreement to transfer chargeable securities for money or money's worth is conditional, the charge to SDRT will arise immediately and will not be cancelled until 'it is proved to the Board's satisfaction' that instruments of transfer have been executed and correctly stamped—FA 1986 s 92 (as amended).
>
> In practice it is likely that, in most cases, the relevant transfer document will have been stamped before the SDRT accountable date is reached. In these cases, the Inland Revenue will not expect a separate application for cancellation of SDRT to be made and will accept that stamping itself is sufficient to cancel the SDRT charge, although it may be necessary at a later date to check on selected cases to ensure that documents have been correctly stamped.
>
> There are no provisions in the legislation for postponing or waiving the payment of SDRT where documents have not been stamped by the accountable date. Late payments will incur interest and penalties can be imposed where the tax is over one year late (TMA 1970 ss 86, 93 and 95). The correct procedure is to pay the SDRT by the accountable date. This will be refunded with interest if documents are subsequently stamped. A refund of penalties cannot, however, be guaranteed.

In your letter, you referred to circumstances in which a document cannot be stamped by the accountable date either because it is subject to adjudication or because completion is deferred. The scenarios outlined in your letter fall into two distinct categories:

(i) those where the consideration is not ascertainable by the accountable date or completion will not be possible by this date, although full *ad valorem* stamp duty will eventually be paid; and

(ii) those where the stamp duty is likely to be nominal or nil (eg, because an exemption is being claimed) but the adjudication process will not be concluded by the accountable date.

In the first scenario, SDRT should be paid on the basis of a reasonable estimate of the likely sum of consideration to be paid; it will not be acceptable to estimate the SDRT as nil simply on the basis that stamp duty will eventually be paid and the SDRT cancelled. Once the consideration has been ascertained and the documents are ready for stamping, provided that the SDRT and accrued interest is not less than the sum required to conclude the stamping process, we would be prepared to transfer the sum paid as SDRT (with interest) to the stamp duty account to facilitate stamping. This will remove the need to pay separately for stamp duty and later claim a refund of SDRT. Please note that once out of the SDRT account, the sum would cease to earn interest. Any overpayment would be refunded by your local stamp office.

Where the sum paid as SDRT and accrued interest is less than the sum required for stamping, there will be no facility for transferring funds internally and accountable persons will be required to produce stamped documents before SDRT can be refunded.

We do not envisage many cases falling into the second scenario because the Stamp Office is usually able to respond quickly to routine applications. If these are made in good time, documents are likely to be stamped before the SDRT accountable date. To the extent that this is not possible, we will be prepared to wait for the documents to be adjudicated on the following conditions—

- The accountable person acknowledges in writing liability for the SDRT due and recognises that the Inland Revenue can pursue him for payment with interest at any time subject to any future production of stamped documents or pending stamping.
- The Shares Unit must be given the adjudication case reference number so that the progress of the case can be monitored.
- If the documents are not stamped within three months of the accountable date , the SDRT should be paid in full with interest.
- If the claim for exemption or nominal stamp fails before the end of three months, SDRT should be paid immediately with any interest due.

The Inland Revenue does not waive its right to impose penalties.

Applications will be considered on a case by case basis and the Inland Revenue reserves the right to exclude any case from the above arrangement.

Subject to agreement with these conditions, SDRT does not need to be paid on the accountable date."

February 1998. Inland Revenue Stamp Office

Stamp Duty Reserve Tax Notes for Guidance

Note—The Guidance Notes were superseded by the Stamp Office Manual, published April 2000. SDRT is covered in Chapters 10–15 of the Manual.

16 September 1998. Law Society Gazette. Article reproduced from Stamp Office Customer News Letter and later amended, 15 January 1999.

Change in practice: value for stamp duty when business transferred as a going concern and action if VAT becomes payable.

The Stamp Office is publicising a change in practice on the sale of a business as a going concern on behalf of HM Customs and Excise. The following is reproduced from the Stamp Office Customer Newsletter.

BUSINESS SALES AND VAT

Sales of businesses often involve the payment of VAT, and we will charge stamp duty on the consideration including that VAT.

If the sale relates to a going concern this is exempt from VAT, which means stamp duty is payable only on the consideration without the addition of VAT.

When you present a business sale document to us, we need to find out whether VAT is payable or not, and whether Custom & Excise accepts that the business qualifies for VAT relief as a transfer of a going concern.

In the past this has often taken the form of advance clearance from Customs & Excise confirming the position.

NEW ARRANGEMENTS

Most Customs & Excise offices will no longer issue these letters, but will instead refer you to the guidance in Public Notice 700/9 (November 1996). Clearance will generally only now be given after the sale has taken place.

DOES THIS MEAN STAMP DUTY WILL BE CHARGED ON THE CONSIDERATION PLUS VAT?

No. Provided that the document does relates to a going concern and there in no clause which allows VAT to be charged at a later date, then duty is payable on the consideration exclusive of VAT.

WHAT IF VAT CAN BE CHARGED?

If the document allows for VAT to be charged later on, for instance, if Customs & Excise refuse clearance, then we will stamp the document on the initial consideration stated and ask you to confirm that—

- the transaction is believed to involve the transfer of a going concern and consequently no VAT has been added to the consideration stated in the document;
- you have advised your client that they are obliged to tell the Stamp Office if that position changes, in line with their obligations under s 5 of the Stamp Act 1891; and
- that the client undertakes to arrange for the document to be returned to the Stamp Office and to pay the extra duty due if VAT does become payable.

A written undertaking from the client to that effect should be enclosed with your letter. The Stamp Office has special arrangements with the Land Registry for the release of documents direct to the Stamp Office where they are held by the Registry but are required for adjustment of the stamp duty they bear.

WHAT CERTIFICATE OF VALUE DO I INCLUDE?

Documents should be certified in respect of the initial consideration paid which is exclusive of VAT.

If a subsequent charge to VAT increases the total amount paid so that the threshold is exceeded, duty will be payable on the VAT-inclusive sum at the higher rate.

14 May 1999.

Stamp duty—new leases with indexed rent levels

The Economic Secretary to the Treasury, Patricia Hewitt, today announced that the Inland Revenue have reviewed their practice in relation to the stamp duty treatment of new leases under which future rent levels are expressed to be dependent on future movements in an index such as the retail prices index (RPI).

The change in practice, based on recent legal advice, means that in general less stamp duty will be payable in these cases. Many people who have paid stamp duty on such leases under the current basis will be entitled to a repayment. The new basis takes effect from today.

In a reply to a Parliamentary Question, Mrs Hewitt said—

> "In the light of recent legal advice given to the Inland Revenue the treatment of these leases for stamp duty is to be changed.
>
> When a new lease is taken out, stamp duty is charged by reference to both the premium and the rent under the lease. The premium attracts duty at the same rates as the selling price on the sale of a freehold interest. The premium gets the benefit of the £60,000 nil rate band provided that the rent does not exceed a ceiling, currently £600 per annum. The average annual rent is charged at rates of between 1% and 24%, depending on the length of the lease.
>
> Many leases provide that the rent is to increase by a fixed percentage at annual or other intervals, or they lay down the actual amounts of the increases. The average annual rent, and therefore the stamp duty, is straightforward to calculate in these cases. But if future rent levels are expressed in terms of future movements in a index, like the RPI, it is less clear how a figure for the average annual rent can be calculated at the time the lease is taken out. In the light of representations, on 6 November 1996 the then Economic Secretary made a statement to this House by way of Written Answer, setting out how the Stamp Office would apply stamp duty in such cases for the future, on the basis of legal advice (HC Written Answer, Vol 284 cols 541–543).

Broadly, where the rent under a lease was to be adjusted by reference to future changes in an index, stamp duty would be calculated by reference to changes in that index during the year ending with the date of execution of the lease.

However, the legal validity of this approach has been challenged. Further legal advice given to the Inland Revenue is that the current system of applying a formula to allow for increases in an index number after the date of execution of a lease is not appropriate. So this practice will cease.

In future, where there is a formula expressed in the lease for rent reviews based on the RPI, only any change in the RPI up to the date of its execution will be taken into account for stamp duty purposes. This is expected to result, in most cases, in the average rent being little more than the initial rent.

This change means that people who have paid stamp duty on this type of lease may have paid more duty than they should have done. The Inland Revenue will invite those who paid duty on a lease of this kind to contact the Stamp Office and claim any repayment due to them. Details of the arrangements for repayments are set out in an Inland Revenue press release and on the Inland Revenue web-site."

DETAILS

The Inland Revenue will make repayments of excess stamp duty paid under the practice announced in 1996 as follows—

- repayments will be made to those who made appeals against the assessment of stamp duty pending the outcome of litigation challenging the Stamp Office's practice;
- repayments will also be made to those affected who present a claim to the Stamp Office within the two years of execution of the relevant lease provided for under the Stamp Duties Management Act 1891; and
- in the exceptional circumstances of this change of practice, the Stamp Office will also consider claims in respect of similar leases executed on or after 25 February 1995, provided that such claims are made within one year of the date of this press release.

NOTES

1 Stamp duty on a new lease is based on two elements of payment—the initial payment (premium) and the rent. Any premium is treated like a sale price and attracts duty at the standard scale if it is over £60,000 (1%, 2% and 3% in 1998–99). And the average annual rent bears duty at between 1% and 24%, depending on the terms of the lease.

2 If the annual rent exceeds £600 then the premium loses the advantage of the £60,000 threshold. This is in order to discourage artificial fragmentation of property deals which are close to the threshold.

3 When a fixed cash sum for instance is stated as the rent to be paid over the term of the lease then there is no difficulty in determining the average rent over the life of the lease. But if the lease specifies that the rent for future years will increase in line with an external index such as the retail price index the mechanism for uprating the rent with respect to that index was not as clear as it should be. Hence today's change.

4 In future where rent reviews are to be based on an external index such as the RPI only any change in the RPI up to the date of the execution of the lease will be taken into account for stamp duty.

5 In most cases this will result in the average rent being little more than the initial rent.

6 Under stamp duty law, repayments of excess duty are made by adjusting the stamps impressed on the document, so as to reflect the correct amount due.

7 Applicants for repayments should contact the Stamp Office at the following address—Stamp Allowance Claims Section, Manchester Stamp Office, Alexandra House, Parsonage, Manchester M60 9BT. DX 14430 Manchester 2.

Applications should where possible be accompanied by the original stamped document. If that is not in the applicant's possession, for example because it is held by a solicitor, building society or land registry, the Stamp Office should be consulted as to alternative arrangements. Duplicate and copy documents are not acceptable.

25 August 1999.

Stamp duty reserve tax—depositary interests in foreign securities

UK depositary interests in foreign securities will be exempt from stamp duty reserve tax (SDRT) following Treasury regulations laid yesterday.

This will allow the operator of an electronic settlement system, which is approved under the Uncertificated Securities Regulations 1995, to provide a settlement service in foreign shares, without purchasers incurring a liability to SDRT.

When UK securities are transferred within such an electronic settlement service, SDRT is charged to match the stamp duty charge on equivalent transfers in paper form. FA 1999 s 119, which provides for these regulations to be made, allows a new kind of security—known as a UK depositary interest in foreign securities—to be transferred within such an electronic settlement service free of SDRT.

Rather than the foreign shares being traded, depositary interests will be issued and traded.

The regulations define the precise scope of these UK depositary interests and ensure that the underlying securities are—

- shares in a foreign company—that is, a company which is neither incorporated in the UK nor centrally managed and controlled in the UK;
- not held on a register in the UK;
- of the same class in the company concerned, as shares that are listed on a stock exchange outside the UK and recognised under TA 1988 s 841;
- not units or shares in a collective investment scheme.

DETAILS

1 The new regulations are the Stamp Duty Reserve Tax (UK Depositary Interests in Foreign Securities) Regulations, SI 1999/2383.

2 The Uncertificated Securities Regulations, SI 1995/3272, made under the Companies Act 1989 s 207, allow relevant securities to be evidenced otherwise than by certificate and transferred by an approved operator within an electronic settlement service, without the use of written instruments.

3 The new regulations, which enable UK depositary interests in foreign securities to be settled within such an electronic settlement service free of SDRT, come into force today.

17 September 1999.

Stamp duty—seven year leases

The rate of stamp duty applying to the rental element of new leases for exactly seven years is to be confirmed in the Finance Bill 2000.

This will reaffirm the Government's intention of ensuring that new leases of exactly seven years are subject to stamp duty on the rent paid under the lease, and will correct a technical omission in FA 1999, putting an end to any uncertainty.

Annual revenue from stamp duty on the rental element of leases of seven years and below is about £1 million.

DETAILS

1 FA 1999 s 112 and Sch 13 re-state the schedule of rates of stamp duty in percentage terms to correspond to the rates of duty generally in force. This is done to introduce a standardised provision for rounding up amounts of duty to multiples of £5 to streamline administration, with effect from 1 October 1999. The stamp duty rates on leases for periods of less than seven years and those for more than seven years are set at percentages of the rental which correspond to the current rates of duty. But there is no explicit reference to the rate of duty for new leases for a period of exactly seven years, although the current legislation sets the stamp duty for the rental element of such leases at 50p for each £50 or part thereof (or zero in the case of annual rents of no more than £500).

2 The effect of this would be that from 1 October 1999 leases for exactly seven years would not be subject to stamp duty on the rent paid under the lease instead of being liable to the current 1% of the average annual rent—though the duty on any premium paid for the lease would not be reduced.

3 A measure will be brought forward in next year's Finance Bill, effective from 1 October 1999, to ensure that the Government's intention (which was set out in the published explanatory notes to FA 1999) is met. This will again put leases for exactly seven years onto the same footing as those for under seven years.

4 There will be two possibilities for relevant documents for seven year leases executed on or after 1 October 1999 arising in the interim—

(*a*) They may be presented for stamping in accordance with the lower amounts of duty specified in FA 1999. In such cases—

- the document will be considered to be "duly stamped" for legal purposes until the new measures take effect (after the vote on Resolutions is taken at the end of next year's Budget debates);
- at this point the document will cease to be duly stamped until it is again presented for stamping so that the duty is topped up to the intended 1%;

– interest and penalties for late stamping will apply to the second stamping only if, and to the extent that, the extra duty is paid or a document is presented (again) more than 30 days after the new measures take effect.

(*b*) Taxpayers may, if they wish, have their documents stamped in the first place at the full 1% to ensure that the documents concerned will remain duly stamped after the new measures take effect. This entirely voluntary procedure will avoid the need for a second presentation for stamping.

NOTES

FA 1999 s 112(3) and Sch 13 include a restatement in percentage terms of the rates of stamp duty in the first schedule to the Stamp Act 1891. An Inland Revenue Budget Day Press Release describes the change to the rounding provisions for stamp duty. The rental element of new leases is charged to stamp duty at a percentage of the average annual rent depending on the length of the lease. Under current legislation, leases for periods not exceeding seven years are charged at 1% and those for between seven and thirty-five years are charged at 2%.

August 2001. Stamp Taxes Bulletin

When is a fixture not a fixture?

DEDUCTIONS FOR CHATTELS (OR MOVEABLES IN SCOTLAND)

Where the consideration for the conveyance or transfer on sale of a property includes an amount attributed by the parties to chattels (or moveables in Scotland), that amount will not normally be charged to stamp duty provided the chattels pass by delivery and are not conveyed in the document.

Case law provides that where assets of different character are agreed to be sold for one consideration for the whole, an apportionment between the chargeable and non-chargeable property must be a bona fide one. This is taken to mean that it must be based on the commercial value of the property concerned. A contract for sale based on a false apportionment may be unenforceable because of its improper intent and can therefore have more far-reaching consequences.

Over the last year or so, Stamp Taxes has seen a steady increase in the number of cases where the amount of consideration attributed to items claimed to be chattels is more than a small percentage of the total consideration. This is especially the case where this brings the chargeable amount just below the £250,000 or £500,000 thresholds.

Customers should note that in cases where it appears that an excessive amount of the consideration has been artificially attributed to non-chargeable items a full inventory and breakdown of the consideration will be requested by Stamp Taxes. This is to ensure that all the items claimed as chattels are properly within that description and that the allocation of the consideration is bona fide and not in breach of Section 5 of the Stamp Act 1891.

Stamp Taxes does not provide a comprehensive list of items which are accepted as chattels or moveables since many cases need to be considered on their own merits and case law is evolving in this area all the time. However items which will generally be accepted as chattels or moveables include—carpets, curtains, light shades, pot plants, free-standing kitchen white goods and portable electric or gas fires.

Items which are generally unacceptable as chattels are—fitted kitchen cabinets and cupboards, fitted kitchen white goods, fitted bathroom sanitary ware, central heating systems, plants growing in the soil, central heating systems and gas fires connected to a piped gas supply.

LOOSE PLANT AND MACHINERY

Plant and machinery may in certain circumstances be treated as "goods, wares and merchandise" and will then fall within the exception to the charge to stamp duty under Paragraph 7, Sch 13, Finance Act 1999.

The requirement for plant and machinery to be in an actual state of severance at the date of the agreement for sale for it to fall within the "goods, wares and merchandise" description is an historical one. It stems from case law based on circumstances involving mortgagees in possession. The two main tests as to whether plant and machinery constitutes goods, wares and merchandise are essentially the same as for chattels, namely (1) the degree of annexation to the building or land and (2) the purpose or object of annexation. Stamp Taxes has for many years required customers to certify that plant and machinery claimed as loose plant must be in an actual state of severance if it is to be considered as goods and therefore outside the charge to duty on an agreement for sale. We will no longer insist upon this certification being given.

Where it would be possible for plant and machinery to be relatively easily severed from the property to which it is fixed, say for example by the simple expedient of removing some bolts securing it to the floor or walls, we will no longer insist that this is actually done before it will be considered to be 'loose plant and machinery'.

The position in law has not changed nor does this mean that all plant and machinery suddenly falls within the exception. As in the past, the consideration attributed to fixed plant will be chargeable to stamp duty on the agreement for sale document [Editor's Note: the consideration is actually chargeable to stamp duty at the conveyance stage]. Heavy plant and machinery which is integral to a building and plant where its removal would damage the building or land will still be considered fixed plant. This will be particularly relevant in respect of plant such as, for example, escalators and elevators, boilers, furnaces, walk-in refrigerators and restaurant cooking stations, none of which would be likely to be classed as loose plant for stamp duty purposes. Each case will be considered on its own merits. The Stamp Taxes form Stamps 22 will be amended to reflect this new treatment. The equivalent forms used in Scotland and Northern Ireland do not require amendment since they did not previously include the certification requirement.

Archie Brown—Technical Adviser

Note—This article was published in the Stamp Taxes Bulletin (Issue 1, August 2001).

February 2002. Stamp Taxes Bulletin

Disadvantaged areas—stamp duty exemption

On 30 November 2001, the Government introduced the first phase of a stamp duty exemption for property transactions in designated disadvantaged areas. The exemption applies to all transfers, conveyances and leases of land, or interests in land, executed on or after 30 November 2001, where the consideration or premium does not exceed £150,000.

BACKGROUND

In the Pre-Budget Report in November 2000 the Chancellor announced that a stamp duty exemption for land transactions in disadvantaged areas would form part of a fiscal package, worth £1 billion over five years, designed to encourage investment and stimulate regeneration in deprived areas. The primary legislation to implement this relief was enacted as Section 92 and Schedule 30 Finance Act 2001. The effect of this legislation was restricted to transactions up to £150,000 by regulations made on 28 November (SI 2001/3746), immediately following the 2001 Pre-Budget Report. The regulations to specify the qualifying areas (SI 2001/3747) and to confirm the date of commencement of the relief (SI 2001/3748) were made on 29 November 2001. This package of regulations reflects the fact that the relief is being implemented in two stages. The next phase, which is subject to approval as state aid by the European Union, is to increase substantially or remove the limit for non-residential property transactions. Before this can be done it is necessary to introduce a definition of residential property in the next Finance Bill.

THE QUALIFYING AREAS: WHERE ARE THEY AND HOW WERE THEY SELECTED?

The areas that qualify for the relief are the most deprived, as determined by the indices of deprivation in each of the four nations that comprise the United Kingdom. In England and Scotland the poorest 15% of wards and postcodes qualify. In Wales and Northern Ireland the poorest 42% of wards are designated as disadvantaged.

In England, Wales and Northern Ireland, the indices refer to electoral wards or divisions. In Scotland the index uses postcode areas. The regulations use wards and postcode areas accordingly.

We have published the qualifying wards and postcode areas in Scotland on our website at www.inlandrevenue.gov.uk/so. In total there are nearly 2,000 qualifying areas.

WHAT HAPPENS IF THE ELECTORAL WARD OR POSTCODE AREA HAS BEEN ABOLISHED OR CHANGED?

From time to time, reorganisations of local government can result in changes to ward boundaries. Postcode areas can also be subject to revision. The ward and postcode areas specified in the regulations match the ward boundaries and postcodes used in each country's most recent index of deprivation. In England and Wales the indices were compiled in 1998, using the wards and electoral divisions that existed at that time. In Northern Ireland the index of deprivation was compiled in 2001 using the electoral boundaries that existed in 1991.

The Scottish index was updated in 1998, using 1991 postcodes. The question of whether a particular property falls within an area that qualifies for relief therefore depends on whether the property is situated in a qualifying area as determined by boundaries current at:

- 7 May 1998 for England
- 1 April 1998 for Wales
- 21 April 1991 for Scotland & Northern Ireland.

HOW SHOULD CLAIMS FOR THE RELIEF BE MADE?

When you are satisfied that a property falls within an area that qualifies for relief from stamp duty, you should submit a claim to one of our offices. The London office offers a counter service for personal callers and cannot accept postal applications. The exemption is an adjudicated relief and documents on which the relief is claimed must be presented for formal adjudication. To assist us in dealing with claims it would help if the following are provided at the time the document is presented for stamping—

– **a certificate confirming that it is a document on which duty is not chargeable by virtue of Section 92 Finance Act 2001.**

The certificate may be within the document itself or in an accompanying letter. Section 92 (2) Finance Act 2002 provides that the exemption will only apply if the document is so certified.

– **the full postcode for the property on which the relief is claimed**

Reference to the postcode is the quickest way for us to confirm that the property is in a qualifying area. The Royal Mail Postcode Enquiry Line 08457 111 222 will supply the postcode for any postal address. For properties that are newly constructed, or for land on which no buildings have been erected, there will be a recently allocated postcode or no postcode at all. We will not in these circumstances, be able to confirm that the property is in a qualifying area. Claims for relief in such cases should be made naming the ward in which the property was located at the qualifying date. A map showing the location of the property and the ward boundaries should be supplied. If this is not possible we will accept a map showing the location of the property in relation to established adjacent properties. The status of the surrounding properties will enable us to confirm that the property, on which relief is claimed, falls within a qualifying area.

– **a completed form L(A)451**
– **a photocopy of the document**
– **a copy of the relevant contract**
– **a certificate of value for £250,000 (not £150,000)**

It was not possible to use the regulations that limit the effect of Section 92 Finance Act 2001 (SI 2001/3746) to alter the various levels of certificates of value, as set out in the Finance Act 1999. Instead the regulations provide that relief only applies if the document could have included a £150,000 certificate of value if that had been one of the levels of certificate in the 1999 Finance Act. Thus the requirement to provide a certificate of value for £250,000 still holds good.

– **the duty payable on the rental element, if the document is a lease and/or agreement for lease.**

The exemption applies only to lease premiums up to £150,000 and duty is payable on ground rents at usual rates.

– **a note of whether the property is residential or non-residential.**

We need this for statistical and evaluation purposes.

You are reminded that if an examination of your claim results in a decision that relief under Section 92 Finance Act 2001 is not due, and as a consequence, stamp duty is paid after the due date for payment, an interest charge may be incurred.

WHAT IS HAPPENING ABOUT THE NEXT PHASE?

The Government announced an intention to raise significantly, or abolish entirely, the £150,000 limit for transactions in "non-residential" property, probably during this year, subject to approval from the European Union as state aid. The current limit will remain in force for "residential" properties.

Before this second phase can be implemented it is necessary to distinguish "residential" and "non-residential" property in the statute.

On 21 December 2001 we issued a consultation document setting out a draft clause for inclusion in the Finance Bill 2002 to define "residential property" for the purposes of the second phase of the stamp duty exemption for land transactions in disadvantaged areas. Comments on the draft clause are invited by 22 February 2002.

Copies of the press release and consultation document are available in paper form from the Visitor Centre, South West Wing, Bush House, Strand, London WC2B 4QN. An electronic version of the consultation document can be obtained at our web site: www.inlandrevenue.gov.uk/so.

FURTHER INFORMATION

If any further information is needed we have published a detailed customer newsletter, which is available from any of our offices. If your question has not been answered in this article, nor in the newsletter, a member of our telephone helpline staff on 0845 603 0135 (Monday to Friday 08.30–17.00) will be pleased to assist you.

Note—This article was published in the Stamp Taxes Bulletin (Issue 2, February 2002).

October 2002. Stamp Taxes Bulletin.

Options—a response to press articles

Stamp Offices have received a significant number of telephone enquiries following the publication of certain newspaper articles that promoted the use of options as a stamp duty saving scheme. Callers have been asking us to confirm that the scheme works in the manner described in the articles.

The Inland Revenue considers that these articles contain serious errors in stamp duty law. We are therefore publishing this item to clarify the issues.

The articles suggested that stamp duty on a purchase of a property at a price of £700,000 could be reduced by structuring the transaction so that the purchaser paid a price of £210,000 for an option to acquire the property at a price of £490,000. It was suggested that by doing so the duty of £28,000 that would apply to a purchase at £700,000 would be reduced to £14,700 (ie duty at 3 per cent on the consideration of £490,000 only).

Under Stamp Act 1891 s 5, all relevant facts and circumstances affecting the liability of an instrument to duty or the amount of that duty must be "fully and truly set forth in the instrument". To comply with Section 5 it would therefore be necessary when presenting a transfer document reciting a purchase price of £490,000, to produce the Option Agreement for stamping. An Agreement granting an option to purchase property made for consideration, is a document liable to ad valorem conveyance on sale duty (*George Wimpey & Co Ltd v IRC* [1975] 2 All ER 45).

The transfer of the property at a price of £490,000 would not be stampable at the 3 per cent rate as suggested in the press articles. Since it stems from the Option Agreement, it forms part of a larger series of transactions at an aggregate value exceeding £500,000. A certificate of value for £500,000 could not be validly inserted in the transfer document and duty would, accordingly, be payable at 4 per cent.

The question also arises as to the rate of duty that should apply to the stamping of the option agreement. In any transaction structured in the manner set out in the articles the Stamp Office will require full disclosure of all correspondence surrounding the negotiations and the manner in which the purchase money or monies was paid. Each case will be treated on its merits, but it should be borne in mind that, in some cases, the Stamp Office are likely to contend that the Option Agreement is itself part of a series of transactions, so that any certificate of value to be included in it must take into account the price to be paid upon exercise of the option.

Note—This article was published in the Stamp Taxes Bulletin (Issue 3, October 2002).
Commentary—*Sergeant and Sims on Stamp Duties* **A4.9**.

13 March 2003. Stamp Taxes Bulletin (extract).

Disadvantaged areas—FA 2001 s 92

Since the postcode search tool has been available on our website we have received a number of follow up telephone calls from customers seeking further advice about this exemption.

In response to this we have compiled a list of frequently asked questions (FAQs) and the answers to these questions that we hope you find helpful.

DO I HAVE TO CLAIM THIS RELIEF FROM STAMP DUTY?

Yes as an adjudicated relief the onus is on the customer to make a claim for exemption from stamp duty.

Once you are satisfied that you meet all the qualifying criteria you should submit all the relevant information and documentation to your local stamp office. You should not submit any payments.

WHAT HAPPENS IF I MAKE A CLAIM FOR RELIEF AND IT FAILS?

In the event that you fail to meet all the qualifying criteria your claim for exemption will fail and we will request payment of the stamp duty together with any interest that may be due.

WHAT HAPPENS IF I HAVE PAID THE STAMP DUTY AND LATER FIND OUT THAT THE PROPERTY QUALIFIES FOR EXEMPTION FROM STAMP DUTY?

Providing that you find this out within two years from the date of the document you will be able to claim back any stamp duty paid in error. If we agree with your claim we will add interest to any monies that we repay. You should in the first instance contact the office that dealt with the stamping of your document.

WHAT HAPPENS IF THE RESULT OF MY POSTCODE SEARCH IS NEGATIVE AND THE MESSAGE SAYS THAT THE POSTCODE HAS NOT BEEN "FOUND"?

The result of your postcode search may be negative because your property/land—

- is part of a new development and/or has been allocated a postcode recently which does not appear on our postcode database yet
- has yet to be allocated a postcode

In cases such as this if you are claiming exemption from stamp duty you should tell us that the postcode has not been found or no postcode is available.

You should name the ward in which the property was located as at the qualifying date.

A map showing the location of the property and the ward boundaries should be supplied. If this is not possible we will accept a map showing the location of the property, in relation to established adjacent properties. The status of the surrounding properties will enable us to confirm that the property, on which relief is claimed, falls within a qualifying area.

A list of the qualifying wards (postcode areas in Scotland) as at the qualifying dates is available on our website).

WHAT ARE THE CURRENT RATES OF INTEREST?

The current rates of interest which came into effect from 6 November 2001 are 6.5 per cent on duty that has been paid late and 2.5 per cent on any monies that is due for repayment.

Commentary—*Sergeant and Sims on Stamp Duties* **A1.1, A17.5.**

June 2003. SDLT Customer Newsletter—Issue 1

The switch to "stamp duty land tax" planned to take place on 1 December 2003

Welcome to the first of a series of newsletters designed to provide guidance on the introduction of stamp duty land tax later this year.

BACKGROUND

In Budget 2002, the Government announced its intention to modernise the stamp duty charge on UK land and buildings. Current legislation was considered outdated, incompatible with modern commercial practice and the move to e-business. A modernised regime is needed to support the automated electronic systems that the land registries intend to introduce in the next 3–8 years. There has also been increasing evidence of widespread avoidance of duty in large commercial transactions.

In April 2002 a consultative document was published outlining proposals of how the duty might be modernised. A number of consultative committees were established and met regularly through the summer and autumn of last year. The responses to the Consultative Document and the contributions of the various committees informed the next stage of the modernisation project. In November 2002 we published draft legislation to stimulate further debate.

Following from this, the publication of the Finance Bill 2003 on 16 April sets out the statutory framework for the modernised tax, which the Chancellor has announced is planned for introduction from 1 December 2003.

Not all aspects of the tax have been finalised and there is to be a further round of consultation about how it will apply in a number of complex commercial areas. But the basic fundamentals that will apply to the vast majority of transactions are set out in the primary legislation. This newsletter provides information about them and how the changes will affect our customers.

THE KEY CHANGES

Stamp duty has always been a tax on documents. But stamp duty land tax will be a tax on transactions involving interests in land in the UK. The tax will not be triggered by the execution of a document. Instead, tax will become payable automatically on the due date, which will be 30 days after the effective date of the transaction. The effective date is generally the date that the purchaser acquires the subject matter of the transaction, which may be in advance of legal completion of the transfer.

Another major change is that the tax will become mandatory. Stamp duty has sometimes been regarded as a "voluntary tax" because it was not directly enforceable against any person and the Stamp Office could not compel payment of it. Payment of duty has traditionally been made as a result of the pressures that stem from having an unstamped document, the chief ones being the inadmissibility of such documents in court in civil proceedings and the fact that registrars, particularly the land registries, cannot register stampable documents that have not been stamped. The legislation introducing the tax will provide that the purchaser, or person acquiring the subject-matter of the transaction must notify the Stamp Office of the transaction by making a land transaction return together with a self-assessment of the tax due. For this purpose "purchaser" includes a lessee where the transaction in question is the grant or assignment of a lease.

HOW WILL THE PROCESS WORK IN PRACTICE?

There are specific transitional rules that will apply to contracts entered into prior to the implementation date but which are completed after it. These will be covered in a separate newsletter. But generally from 1 December 2003, the purchaser will be required to deliver a land transaction return, giving particulars of the transaction and paying the tax that is due. The Land Transaction Return and payment should be sent to our Processing Centre at Netherton. It will not be necessary to send any supporting documentation such as the contract or the actual transfer. The return can also be submitted to local stamp offices, but this will result in a slower service, as the return has to be processed in the central location. The Processing Centre will process the return and issue a stamp duty land tax certificate. The certificate will be required by the land registries before they will accept documents as evidencing a change of ownership. In effect therefore, the certificate replaces the traditional duty stamps that are currently impressed on documents.

The issuing of the stamp duty land tax certificate does not necessarily mean that the matter is finalised. We will be operating a 'process now, check later system'. We can open an enquiry into a transaction notified to us at any time within nine months of the date that the return is due, or is actually notified to us, if later, (the 'filing date').

As now, some transactions will not be liable to the tax either because they are below the threshold or because the transaction qualifies for a relief. These will still have to be notified to us on a land transaction return if chargeable consideration has been provided and the transaction is the transfer of a freehold, the assignment or transfer of an existing lease or the grant of a new lease for a term of seven years or more. By contrast, certain transactions will not require notification and documents can be self certified as being exempt from the tax and sent direct to the land registries. These will be subject to audits and the same enquiry process. Further guidance will be issued on this in a later newsletter.

Eventually we plan to streamline the system further. The introduction of electronic conveyancing and land registration systems should allow the tax to be paid at the time of registration.

ARE THERE ANY CHANGES TO THE RATES OF DUTY?

For conveyances and transfers of land, tax will continue to be charged as a percentage of the "chargeable consideration". The definition of chargeable consideration has been widened so that it is now defined as "money or money's worth". The present rates of stamp duty will continue to apply to purchases of residential property and the threshold remains at £60,000. But for transactions in non-residential and mixed- use properties the threshold will be increased to £150,000 from the implementation of stamp duty land tax.

For leases, tax on premiums will be calculated in exactly the same way as now, that is as a percentage of the amount paid. Again the threshold for non-residential and mixed-use properties will be increased to £150,000. But the Finance Bill includes legislation that provides for an entirely different method of calculating tax on new lease rents. The new charge will be levied at 1% of the net present value of rental payments payable under the terms of the lease. However, the Government has stated that it will consult further on this proposal and will not implement it if an acceptable alternative basis can be found.

LATE NOTIFICATION OF TRANSACTIONS AND LATE PAYMENT OF TAX

A land transaction return must be delivered and payment of the tax must be made within 30 days of the effective date of the transaction. Penalties are payable if the transaction is notified late and interest is payable on tax paid late.

FURTHER INFORMATION

More information will be provided in later customer newsletters. We recognise that the changes represent a major reform of part of the conveyancing system and that our customers need to be fully informed. For this reason we have developed a customer education programme that was launched in Somerset House on 16 May. We will follow this up with further customer newsletters, information bulletins and articles in Solicitors' and Conveyancers' journals and magazines. We will be enhancing our Internet site and publishing revised leaflets.

In addition, we are planning a series of regional training events for the legal profession in partnership with the Law Societies of England & Wales, Scotland and Northern Ireland.

In the meantime, you may like to consult our website at www.inlandrevenue.gov.uk/so/index.htm for the details published on Budget Day and when the Finance Bill was issued.

TRANSACTIONS IN SHARES

It is stressed that the information in this leaflet applies only to interests in UK land. Transactions in shares are not affected by the changes and they will continue to be liable to stamp duty or stamp duty Reserve Tax exactly as they are now.

July 2003. SDLT Customer Newsletter—Issue 2

The switch to "stamp duty land tax" planned to take place on 1 December 2003

Welcome to the second of our newsletters designed to provide guidance on the introduction of stamp duty land tax later this year. This issue focuses on customer awareness and customer education issues.

We are committed to helping to make the changeover as smooth as possible. We will be keeping our customers informed of developments throughout the next few months using a variety of methods, which will be explained later in this newsletter.

WHAT CAN YOU DO NOW?

It is important that our customers are prepared for the changes. Practitioners can do this by ensuring that they consider the legal and practical implications for both themselves and their clients.

CURRENT AWARENESS OF MODERNISATION OF STAMP DUTY

We recently commissioned a study conducted by the British Market Research Bureau to ascertain current awareness levels of the modernisation of stamp duty. 1100 telephone interviews were conducted with a range of solicitors and Licensed Conveyancers from both large and small firms.

The overall level of awareness was 45% but a more detailed breakdown showed that London practitioners were slightly more aware of the changes than those elsewhere—49% compared to 44%. And the more employees in the firm, the greater the level of awareness.

The 493 respondents who were aware of the changes, were asked how they became aware of modernisation. The main sources were the law societies and industry journals at 44% and 42% respectively.

Respondents were then asked whether they felt they had received enough information and a fairly significant 72% said that they hadn't.

In order to assist in the development of an awareness campaign, respondents were asked about their preferred method of receiving information. Leaflets came out well on top at 53%.

HOW WE WILL HELP YOU PREPARE FOR THE CHANGES

On 16 May we hosted an open morning for solicitors, accountants and representatives from various groups affected by the changes to mark the launch of our customer education campaign. The event featured an overview of the new processes and their impact on customers together with a presentation on preparing customers for the changes. The event was very well attended and well received. We intend to hold similar presentations over the next few months. Details and invitations will appear on our website.

The first two issues in a series of **Information Bulletins** have been produced and mailed to around 10,000 firms of solicitors who have had contact with us in the past. These bulletins will continue to be produced in the run up to the commencement of the changes. If people want to be added to the list they should contact Des Newman on 020 7438 7762. The aim of these bulletins is to keep customers informed of developments on an ongoing basis. They will be produced every 4 to 6 weeks.

This series of **Customer Newsletters** will contain more detailed information about technical changes. Again they will be produced every 4 to 6 weeks and will be enclosed when documents are returned from Stamp Offices to Conveyancers.

Eight weeks prior to implementation of the changes, **flyers** will be enclosed with all returned documents reminding Conveyancers about what they need to do from 1 December. This message will focus on a different issue each week.

The above documents will also be available on the Stamp Taxes website.

The market research demonstrated that **industry journals** were one of the key ways in which people obtained information and therefore we will be proactively contacting various magazines and journals with a view to having articles placed.

An exhibition stand has been produced which we are willing to take to any relevant exhibitions and events.

TRAINING

Actual training for solicitors will be delivered by ourselves working in partnership with the three law societies (England & Wales, Scotland and Northern Ireland). Training will be rolled out from September onwards and dates and venues are available from the respective law societies.

The events will be organised by the law societies who will be responsible for the administration and advertising. The actual training material will be produced by us and we will provide the speakers at the sessions which will last around two hours.

The training will cover—

- an overview of the main legislative changes
- details of the enquiry process from opening through to closure
- completion of the new Land Transaction Return
- the various ways in which customers can obtain advice and guidance.

CUSTOMER ASSISTANCE

Customers will be helped with their obligations both before and after go live in a variety of ways.

The existing stamp duty **leaflets** are being reviewed and it is likely that there will be one main SDLT leaflet covering all aspects which will be available only on the Internet. There will then be a simple quick reference guide to SDLT aimed at the public but this will be available in hard copy as well.

In line with other taxes, there will be a **Code of Practice** to support the enquiry process. This will automatically be enclosed when a letter is issued to notify the customer that an enquiry is to take place.

A number of **calculation tools for the Internet** are being developed. An SDLT calculator will allow users to input the price, the date of their purchase in order to obtain the amount of SDLT due (including SDLT on leases). In addition a digital mapping tool for disadvantaged areas is being developed which will allow users to search for, and identify, land and property that qualifies for disadvantaged area relief.

The introduction of SDLT will bring with it a requirement for new **guidance** and an SDLT Manual will be produced covering three areas—technical, procedural and compliance. In accordance with the Code of Practice on Access to Government information the manual will be published on the Internet.

WHERE CAN I FIND FURTHER INFORMATION?

The **Enquiry Line** has already been expanded and there is the capacity to add additional resources should they be required. The Enquiry Line is open from Monday to Friday from 8.30am to 5pm and the number is 0845 6030135. All calls are charged at local rates.

Further information can be found on the Stamp Taxes website.

Additional details are available in the Finance Bill 2003 press notice (REV 55) and the budget day press notice, PN05—Modernising the taxation of property. These can also be found on our website.

August 2003. SDLT Customer Newsletter—Issue 3

The switch to stamp duty land tax planned to take place on 1 December 2003

COMMENCEMENT AND TRANSITIONAL PROVISIONS

This issue of the newsletter is concerned with the introduction of stamp duty land tax on 1 December 2003. It provides guidance on whether transactions that may have been entered into prior to that date but which are completed at a later date are within the existing stamp duty regime, or come within the scope of stamp duty land tax.

In this article we focus on general principles and the main points that are likely to arise. It is not possible to cover every possible scenario. We have already published on our web site a flow chart that can be used to determine whether or not a transaction is a stamp duty or stamp duty land tax matter [reproduced in the Annex below].

More detailed guidance will be available in the new stamp duty land tax manual that will be published in electronic form. A draft version of the manual will be published on the Internet in the beginning of October 2003. We would welcome comments on the content of the manual. Please send comments by post to—

Vivienne Scrimshire , Room 116 , New Wing , Somerset House , London WC2B 1 LR, or alternatively these may be e-mailed to Vivienne.Scrimshire@ir.gsi.gov.uk

The legislation dealing with the commencement and transitional provisions is contained in Finance Act 2003 Sch 19. The Finance Act 2003 received Royal Assent on **10 July 2003** and this is an important date in considering whether or not a transaction is to be subject to stamp duty or stamp duty land tax.

THE BASIC CHARGE TO STAMP DUTY LAND TAX

As a general rule, a land transaction falls within the scope of stamp duty land tax if the "effective date" of the transaction is on or after "implementation date". The "effective date" of a transaction is the earlier of the transaction being completed by a conveyance, or the date that the contract is "substantially performed". Substantial performance of a contract occurs when—

- the purchaser (which includes a lessee under the terms of a lease) has paid any rent, or
- the purchaser has paid the whole or substantially the whole (not normally less than 90%) of any consideration other than rent, or
- the purchaser has taken possession, or become entitled to possession of the property. This includes receipt of, or entitlement to receipt of, rents and profits.

Implementation date means 1 December 2003.

Example 1

A contracts to sell a property to B on 15 December 2003. The transaction is completed by the purchase price being paid in full on 15 January 2004 and a transfer is executed the same day. This is a stamp duty land tax transaction as the effective date of the transaction is after "implementation date", 1 December 2003.

Accordingly the transaction will be notifiable as a stamp duty land tax transaction on a Land Transaction Return. (For guidance on this please refer to Customer Newsletter 1 [reproduced above]).

In example 1 both the contract and the effective date of the transaction were after implementation date. It is not necessary however for the contract to have been entered into after 1 December 2003 for a transaction to be subject to stamp duty land tax. Contracts entered into prior to 1 December 2003 may give rise to a stamp duty land tax charge (see example 2).

Example 2

A contracts to sell a property to B on 18 September 2003. The transaction is completed by the purchase price being paid on 7 December 2003 and a transfer is executed the same day. As the effective date of the transaction is after "implementation date", the transaction is a stamp duty land tax transaction.

CONTRACTS ENTERED INTO ON OR BEFORE 10 JULY 2003

There are however, special rules that apply for land transactions that implement contracts entered into on or before 10 July 2003. The key points are as follows—

- Contracts that are substantially performed on or before 10 July 2003 are not stamp duty land tax transactions (see example 3).
- Contracts that are not substantially performed on or before 10 July 2003 are not stamp duty land tax transactions (see example 4) unless—
  (*a*) there is any variation of the contract or assignment of rights under the contract after 10 July 2003; or
  (*b*) the transaction is effected in consequence of the exercise after 10 July 2003 of any option, right of pre-emption or similar right; or
  (*c*) the purchaser under the transaction is a person other than the purchaser under the contract because of a further contract (for example a sub-sale contract) made after 10 July 2003.

A variation of a contract under (*a*) does not include minor matters peripheral to the contract such as changes to colour schemes or pets being permitted on premises. It does however, include any changes to the following; the parties to the transaction, the subject matter of the sale, the contractual consideration or in an agreement for lease, the length of the term.

Example 3

On 1 May 2003, A contracted to sell a property to B. On 1 June 2003, B paid the purchase price in full (an act of substantial performance). The contract is completed by a conveyance dated 1 March 2004. This is not a stamp duty land tax transaction because it was substantially performed on or before 10 July 2003. The conveyance is liable to stamp duty.

Example 4

A contracts to sell a property to B on 1 July 2003. The contract is not substantially performed in advance of completion and none of the exceptions listed at (*a*) to (*c*) above apply. A conveyance of the property is made to the contracting purchaser, B, on 7 March 2004. This is not a stamp duty land tax transaction but the conveyance is liable to stamp duty.

VARIATIONS AND CONTRACTS ENTERED INTO ON OR AFTER 10 JULY 2003

Finance Act 2003 Sch 19 para 4(3) makes special provisions for contracts entered into prior to implementation date. These include a contract made on or before 10 July 2003 which has not been substantially performed before 10 July 2003, a similar contract that has been varied after that date, or where the contracting purchaser has sub-sold or transferred his rights after that date. It also makes provision for contracts entered into in the period between 10 July 2003 and 1 December 2003.

The substantial performance of such contracts before implementation is disregarded. Consequently a charge to stamp duty land tax can only arise on completion. The following examples illustrate this.

Example 5

A contracts to sell a property to B on 1 October 2003. Substantial performance of the contract takes place on 20 November 2003 when B pays the purchase price in full. The contract is completed by the conveyance of the property to B on 1 July 2006. A charge to stamp duty land tax arises on 1 July 2006.

Example 6

A contracts to sell a property to B on 1 September 2003 and substantial performance occurs on 15 October 2003 when B pays the purchase price in full. On 1 November 2003 B contracts to sell the property to C. The contract is completed on 1 February 2004, when A transfers the property direct to C. There is no charge to stamp duty Land tax on B because the conveyance to the ultimate purchaser does not trigger a stamp duty land tax charge. C incurs a stamp duty land tax liability on 1 February 2004.

In the example above, B has been able to benefit from the availability of a modified form of sub-sale relief. But it should be borne in mind that this relief was available only because substantial performance of the A-B contract occurred before 1 December 2003. Sub-sale relief will only be available in respect of contracts entered into after 10 July 2003 in very limited circumstances. More guidance on sub-sales will be provided in a later Newsletter.

Example 7

A contracts to sell a property to B on 1 November 2003, which is substantially performed (for the first time) on 1 March 2004 in advance of completion when B pays the purchase price. As substantial performance occurred after 1 December 2003 a stamp duty land tax charge arises on B, on 1 March 2004.

STAMP DUTY CREDIT AVAILABLE TO OFFSET AGAINST STAMP DUTY LAND TAX CHARGE

Where a stamp duty land tax transaction is effected pursuant to a contract entered into before 1 December 2003 any ad valorem stamp duty paid on the contract is available for crediting against the stamp duty land tax liability that arises when the transaction is substantially performed or completed. There is however, no entitlement to a refund if it transpires that the stamp duty liability exceeds the stamp duty Land tax charge.

Examples of contracts liable to ad valorem stamp duty are pre-implementation date—

- Agreements for Lease, and
- Contracts for sale chargeable under FA 2002 s115 (consideration exceeding £10 million).

STAMP DUTY PROVISIONS AFFECTING LAND TRANSACTIONS.

- An instrument effecting a land transaction is not subject to stamp duty if the transaction is a stamp duty land tax transaction (FA 2003 s125 (5)(*a*))—See example 2 above.
- If a conveyance is within the charge to stamp duty there is no charge to stamp duty land tax—See example 4 above.
- Sch 19 para 8 makes special provisions that broadly replicate the provisions of FA 1994 s 240 as amended, relating to Agreements for Lease and leases. The following is an example of this.

Example 8

An agreement for lease is entered into on 1 October 2003,which is completed when the lease is executed on 1 March 2004. The Agreement for Lease is a stamp duty transaction because at the time that it was executed it did not effect a stamp duty land tax transaction. It is liable to stamp duty under FA 1999 Sch 13 para 14. Under the provisions of FA 1994 s 240 as amended, stamping of the Agreement can be deferred until 30 days after the execution of the lease without the penalty or interest provisions applying.

In these circumstances the delivery of a stamp duty land tax Return, the Agreement for Lease and payment within 30 days of 1 March 2004 will not give rise to the Agreement incurring a stamp duty penalty or interest charge. Procedural guidance will be issued at a later date regarding the manner that the Return and the Agreement should be presented to Stamp Taxes.

If the Agreement for Lease had been stamped prior to the lease being granted, the duty paid on the Agreement would be credited against the stamp duty land tax charge. Again further guidance will be provided at a later date regarding the procedural arrangements.

An important point to note is that the timing differences of the Agreement for Lease and lease, which straddle the "implementation date", means that an entirely different basis of calculation is used to determine the amount of stamp duty payable on the Agreement, and the amount of stamp duty land tax payable when the lease is granted. This is because lease rents are charged to stamp duty on the average annual rent, whereas stamp duty land tax calculates tax on the net present value of the lease rents over the term. Additional information will be provided on how stamp duty land tax on lease rents is calculated in a later newsletter.

ADDITIONAL MISCELLANEOUS PROVISIONS

In this newsletter we have attempted to concentrate on the main issues that are likely to arise on the more routine transactions. It is not proposed to comment in greater detail on the following, which are, nevertheless, listed for information.

- Contracts liable to stamp duty under FA 1999 Sch 13 para 7 (equitable interests) are deemed to have been duly stamped if they are completed by a stamp duty land tax transaction (FA 2003 Sch 19 para 6(1)).
- Transitional provisions that apply in relation to group relief and acquisition relief are provided at FA 2003 Sch 19 paras 6(2) and 6(3).
- FA 2003 Sch 19 para 7 makes provisions for transactions which are not themselves stamp duty land tax transactions but are "linked" to stamp duty land tax transactions.
- FA 2003 Sch 19 para 9 makes provisions for options and rights of pre-emption acquired before implementation date but exercised on or after implementation date.

In addition to the further Newsletters that will be published in the run up to implementation further guidance will be given at a number of regional training events. For further information on these please refer to Newsletter issue 2 [reproduced above].

ANNEX

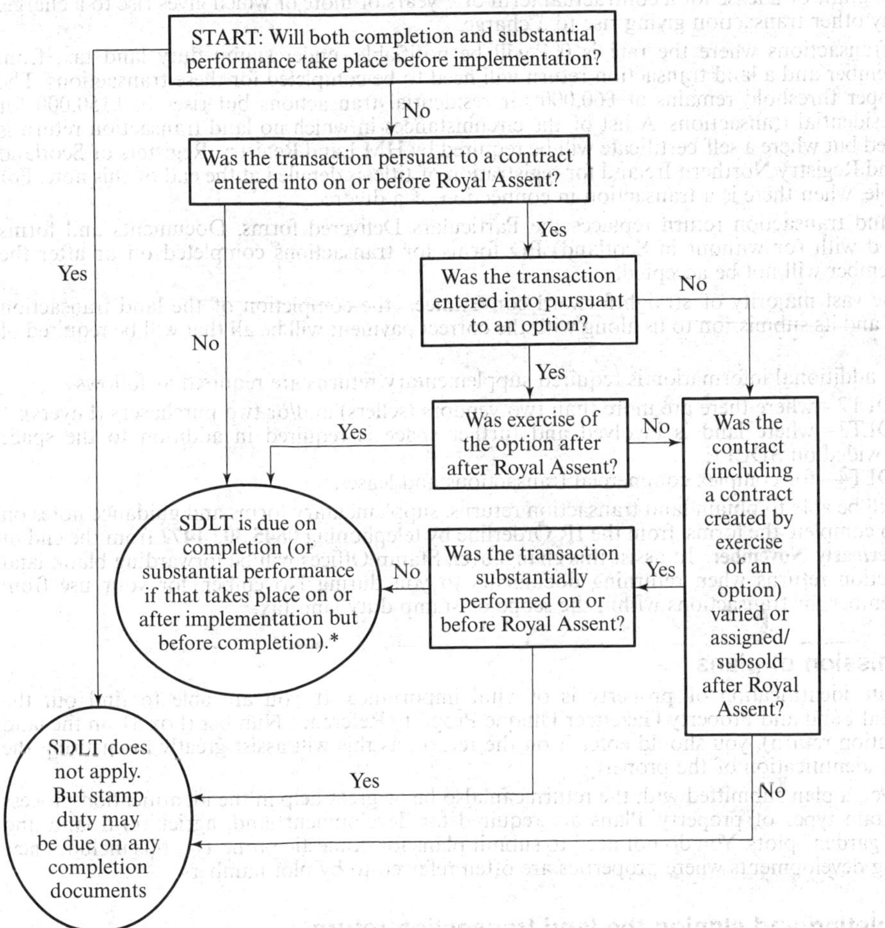

* Stamp duty may still be due on an agreement for lease or contract for over £10 million entered into before implementation. Credit is available against the SDLT due on subsequent completion or substantial performance.

September 2003. Stamp Duty Information Bulletin—Issue 4

New process for SDLT that will apply for the majority of transactions completed on or after 1 December 2003

This issue covers the new process for stamp duty land tax that will apply for the majority of transactions completed on or after 1 December 2003 and answer some frequently asked questions to help you to understand the changes that are taking place. Further information on stamp duty land tax is available on [the Inland Revenue website: http://www.inlandrevenue.gov.uk/so/land_tax_changes.htm].

More detailed guidance will be available in the new stamp duty land tax manual that will be published in electronic form. A draft version of the manual [was] published in the week commencing 22 September 2003 and may be accessed from our website. We would welcome comments on the content of the manual. Please send comments by post to Vivienne Scrimshire, Room 116, New Wing, Somerset House, London WC2B 1LR; or alternatively these may be e-mailed to—Vivienne.Scrimshire@ir.gsi.gov.uk.

THE NEW PROCESS FROM 1 DECEMBER 2003

Stamp duty land tax is a tax on transactions, not documents. For transactions in land and buildings in the UK, completed on or after 1 December 2003 you will no longer need to send in documents for stamping but will be required instead to complete and send in a land transaction return to our data capture centre. The land transaction return should be submitted to notify—

- any transfer of a freehold or assignment or assignation of a lease for consideration, whether or not giving rise to a charge;
- any transaction for which relief is being claimed;
- the grant of a lease for a contractual term of 7 years or more or which gives rise to a charge;
- any other transaction giving rise to a charge.

NB: Transactions where the rate is 0% will be notifiable, under stamp duty land tax, from 1 December and a land transaction return will need to be completed for these transactions. The 0% upper threshold remains at £60,000 for residential transactions but rises to £150,000 for non-residential transactions. A list of the circumstances in which no land transaction return is required but where a self certificate will be required by HM Land Registry, Registers of Scotland or Land Registry Northern Ireland for registration of title, is detailed at the end of this note. For example, when there is a transaction in connection of a divorce.

The land transaction return replaces the Particulars Delivered forms. Documents and forms received with (or without in Scotland) PD forms for transactions completed on or after the 1 December will not be accepted.

For the vast majority of straightforward conveyances, the completion of the land transaction return and its submission to us along with the correct payment will be all that will be required of you.

Where additional information is required supplementary returns are required as follows—

- SDLT2—where there are more than two vendors (sellers) and/or two purchasers (buyers);
- SDLT3—where land is involved and further space is required in addition to the space provided on SDLT1;
- SDLT4—for complex commercial transactions and leases.

You will be able to obtain land transaction returns, supplementary forms and guidance notes on how to complete the forms, from the IR Orderline by telephoning **0845 302 1472** from the end of **October/early November**. To assist this changeover, Stamp Offices will be forwarding blank land transaction returns when returning documents to you during November, for your use from 1 December for transactions within the scope of stamp duty land tax.

Submission of plans

Accurate identification of property is of vital importance. If you are able to find out the National Land and Property Gazetteer Unique Property Reference Number (box 31 on the land transaction return), you should enter it on the return, as this will assist greatly in ensuring the correct identification of the property.

However, a plan submitted with the return can also be of great help in the identification process for certain types of property. Plans are required for development land, agricultural land and small "garden" plots. You do not need to submit plans for domestic property—this includes new housing developments where properties are often referred to by plot numbers.

Completing and signing the land transaction return

The detailed guidance notes should be used when completing the form which must be completed in ***black ink.*** The completed land transaction return **must legally be signed by the purchaser (buyer). If there is more than one purchaser it must be signed by all purchasers.** The return **may not** be signed by the purchaser's solicitor or agent. It is the purchaser's responsibility to ensure that the information contained in the land transaction return is correct and complete. The purchaser may request that their agent be authorised to handle correspondence on their behalf, by completing box 59 of the land transaction return, however the purchaser remains responsible for the return and the payment of the stamp duty land tax

Each form has a unique reference number, so photocopies may not be used.

Where to send the land transaction return

The land transaction return must be sent to the Inland Revenue's rapid data capture centre within 30 days of the effective date of the transaction. The full address is: Inland Revenue, Stamp Taxes, Comben House, Farriers Way, Netherton, Merseyside , L30 4RN.

It is important not to send the returns to local Stamp Offices as this will delay the issue of a certificate. Local offices will not be able to process land transaction returns and will re-direct them to the data capture centre. You should send payment of stamp duty land tax at the same time as you submit the land transaction return. Payment may be made by—

- Cheque, enclosed with the return;
- electronic payment (BACS, CHAPS etc);
- at your bank, Post Office or by Alliance and Leicester/Giro account using the payslip.

The certificate will be based solely on information contained on the land transaction return (and where appropriate supplementary forms). Any additional information provided by way of covering letter or documents will not be considered. Therefore no covering letter, other information or documents should be submitted with the return unless you are submitting a plan because the land is for development, is agricultural or is a small "garden" plot.

Envelopes will be available, via the Orderline, with the Netherton DX (Document exchange) number provided for those firms that have this postal service.

What happens at the rapid data capture centre?

The completed land transaction return is scanned and the data optically- captured The return will only be processed if it contains—

- a unique reference number;
- the liable person's name and address (the liable person is generally the purchaser);
- a signed declaration, signed by all purchasers;
- the effective date of the transaction (an explanation of what is an effective date is described in the frequently asked questions).

Land transaction returns that do not meet these basic requirements cannot be processed and so will be returned to customers. If other areas of the form are not completed, although we may be able to accept the form for processing we will seek that additional information through a follow up letter. To assist us in providing you with a quality service, we would urge you to complete the return as fully as possible to avoid delays.

Land transaction return certificate

A certificate will be issued once the land transaction return has been processed at our data capture centre if—

- all relevant information is provided;
- our own system check verifies the calculation of stamp duty land tax due;
- payment is enclosed.

The certificate replaces the impressed stamp and provides you with valid proof that stamp duty land tax has been paid. The certificate must be presented to HM Land Registry, Registers of Scotland or Land Registry Northern Ireland when applying for registration of title.

Late returns

The Finance Act 2003 introduced a penalty for late notification and payment of stamp duty land tax. Where the land transaction return and/or payment is not received within 30 days of the effective date of the transaction (the filing date) but within three months of the 30 day limit, a penalty of £100 will be charged automatically. A penalty of £200 will be automatically charged in all other cases. Any late payment will also give rise to an interest charge.

Amended returns

Where customers wish to query or amend information captured, they should write to a local Stamp Office who will have a facility to amend the original notification. An amendment may not be made more than 12 months after the filing date.

Circumstances when no land transaction return is required

The following transactions do not need to be notified for stamp duty land tax purposes. However, you will need to certify that the transaction is exempt and submit, as now, that self-certificate to HM Land Registry, Registers of Scotland or Land Registry Northern Ireland when applying for registration of title. We have provided a special form for this purpose which is available from the Orderline.

(1) transfer or conveyance of a freehold interest in land (in Scotland, ownership of land or the interest of the proprietor of the *dominium utile* of land) for no chargeable consideration;

(2) transfer or assignment of a leasehold interest in land (in Scotland, assignation of a tenant's interest under a lease of land) for no chargeable consideration;

(3) grant of lease (in Scotland, exchange of missives of let) where all the following are satisfied—

- the term of the lease is less than seven years;
- the amount of any premium is not such as to attract a charge to stamp duty land tax at a rate of 1% or more (ignoring the availability of any relief);
- the amount of any rent is not such as to attract a charge to stamp duty land tax at a rate of 1% or higher (ignoring the availability of any relief);

(4) other land transaction (for example, the grant of an easement or servitude) where the chargeable consideration is not such as to attract a charge to stamp duty land tax at a rate of 1% or higher (ignoring the availability of any relief);

(5) land transaction exempt from stamp duty land tax under Schedule 3 paragraph 3 Finance Act 2003 (transactions in connection with divorce);

(6) land transaction exempt from stamp duty land tax under Schedule 3 paragraph 4 Finance Act 2003 (variation of testamentary dispositions).

Self-certificate forms will be available from the IR Orderline and HM Land Registry, Registers of Scotland and Land Registry of Northern Ireland from 1 December. You can use photocopies of this form.

FREQUENTLY ASKED QUESTIONS

1. Why do I have to send the form to Netherton?

The Inland Revenue's rapid data capture centre in Netherton, near Liverpool, is one of the sites used for scanning a variety of Inland Revenue forms. This is where completed land transaction returns will be scanned in order to produce a stamp duty land tax certificate, the equivalent of the stamping process undertaken now. This certificate is the document you submit to HM Land Registry, the Registers of Scotland or the Land Registers of Northern Ireland in order to apply for registration of title. Centralising and automating the process in this way will streamline the capture of your property information data and the production of the certificate with the aim of providing rapid and consistent turnaround times for you throughout the year. It is worth noting that our local Stamp Offices will not have this scanning facility so will be unable to offer an alternative service to that provided by the Netherton centre.

2. Why does the form need to be signed by the purchaser(s)?

Unlike the current stamp duty regime, Stamp duty Land Tax introduces a clearly identifiable liable person—usually the purchaser or lessee. This person is legally responsible, for notification and payment of stamp duty land tax. They will also be liable to pay any additional tax, interest or penalties arising as a result of a formal enquiry into the return. It is therefore important that the liable person satisfies him/herself that the information being provided on the land transaction return is complete and correct to the best of their knowledge. Following precedents in other taxes where there is a liable person, the best way for a liable person to confirm to Inland Revenue that they are satisfied with the information being provided is by way of signature on the return. This is a statutory requirement under stamp duty land tax and returns which are not signed will not be accepted.

3. Why is the land transaction return (SDLT1) longer than the LA451 ("Particulars Delivered")?

The new form replaces the information included on the LA451 and the supporting documents provided with it, which can be scrutinised by the Stamp Office. Although there are six pages to the new form, for most straightforward transactions (eg simple residential conveyances), less than half the boxes will need to be completed. The information requested is necessary for the correct liability to be established and for the tax to be properly and fairly administered. Comprehensive and accurate data supplied to us will be invaluable in building up a detailed picture of the property market and will help inform possible future policy and operational decisions on Stamp duty Land Tax.

4. Why do I have to supply National Insurance numbers?

The purchaser's National Insurance number is only required where the purchaser, or one of the purchaser's, is an individual. The Inland Revenue's main record system uses National Insurance numbers and as part of our modernisation programme we are linking into this system. This will allow stamp duty land tax to be administered more efficiently and fairly in line with our other mainstream taxes. We do however appreciate that not all individual purchasers may have a National Insurance number for example if the purchaser is a non-UK national. Our guidance notes to the form cover what you need to do in these circumstances.

5. Why can't I send in documents as previously?

In the vast majority of cases all the necessary data will have been provided on the form so it will no longer be necessary to send in documents as well. This will reduce the amount of paper to be sent through the post to us and should avoid any chance of valuable original documents going astray. The new process also represents a first step towards more streamlined ways of submitting data to us and helps prepare the way for possible future changes, such as the plans for an electronic conveyancing system to co-ordinate the electronic delivery of various aspects of the conveyancing process.

6. Can I complete the form electronically?

We are currently looking at a number of ways to allow the form to be completed on-screen and are working closely with representative bodies and others. We'll keep you informed of our progress as we appreciate that many of you would welcome the opportunity to complete the form this way. Please look out for information about this in future bulletins and on our website.

7. What are the transitional provisions for land and property transactions that take place around the December 2003 changeover date?

The transitional provisions are contained in Schedule 19 Finance Act 2003. This Schedule provides the rules for determining whether a transaction, entered into prior to 1 December 2003, which is completed after 1 December, is chargeable to stamp duty or stamp duty land tax.

A flowchart is available to help you decide if the transaction is subject to stamp duty land tax on our website at—www.inlandrevenue.gov.uk/so/sdlt_flowchart.pdf. Also, information and examples our provided in our Customer Newsletter Issue 3 available at: www.inlandrevenue.gov.uk/so/newsletter3.pdf.

8. What is the effective date of a transaction?

For the majority of transactions the effective date is the date of completion of the transaction, whether or not this is evidenced by a document. However if a contract is substantially performed before completion, the date on which substantial performance takes place is the effective date. Broadly substantial performance is the point at which—

- payment of a substantial amount of the consideration (generally 90% of the total amount) is made;
- the purchaser is entitled to possession of the property;
- the first payment of rent is made);
- option or right of pre-emption—is when the option or right is acquired.

9. What records covering transactions need to be retained and for how long?

The new arrangements for stamp duty land tax are built on the basis of a "process now—check later" system. This is again in line with the way that the Inland Revenue administers other taxes. In order to undertake the "check later" part of this, we will select a small number of transactions for enquiry. In those cases we will ask for supporting evidence concerning the particular property transaction. All records supporting transactions should be kept for six financial years. It is the responsibility of the purchaser to ensure records are kept. Examples of the types of records that need to be retained are detailed below but the list is not exhaustive—

- a contract/agreement for sale and any related papers;
- professional valuations of both the land and any apportionments of fixed fixtures and loose fittings, if such valuations were obtained at the time;
- relevant instruments relating to the transaction, in particular any contract or conveyance, and any supporting maps, plans or similar documents.

10. How do I find out if the property is in a disadvantaged area and qualifies relief?

There is an on-line "postcode tool" on our website at—http://inlandrevenue.gov.uk/so/pcode_search.htm.

This will enable you to determine whether a property is in a disadvantaged area from the postcode. Where exceptionally the answer cannot be found, for example for a new property that has only just received a postcode, you can gain further guidance from our Enquiry Line by telephoning 0845 603 0135.

We are looking at other ways of improving how this information is provided to you. Full details will be provided on our website.

Note

We would also like to clarify a point arising from an overview of the changes that we made in issue 3.

In the previous bulletin where an overview of some of the changes to stamp duty was provided including the point that for transactions completed on or after 1 December 2003, legal practitioners will no longer need to submit documents, on behalf of purchasers, to the Inland Revenue for stamping. Instead they will have to notify liability to tax using the new land transaction return. Payment should be sent at the same time as the return to the Inland Revenue processing centre in Netherton. Provided information and payment are submitted in full, the Inland Revenue will issue a stamp duty land certificate which they or their agents will need to submit to land registries in order to register ownership of land or to record a deed, as appropriate. The certificate replaces the current stamped impressions, which are made onto documents.

We would like to clarify that this is subject to transitional provisions under which certain transactions effected in pursuance of contracts entered into on or before Royal Assent of the Finance Act (10 July 2003) remain subject to stamp duty.

20 October 2003. IR News Release

Modernising stamp duty on land transactions

The Government today announced the next steps in the process of modernising stamp duty on land transactions, following the announcement of the main proposals in Budget 2003.

Stamp Taxes

These include—

- A significant change to the proposed charge on the rental element when a new lease is granted ("lease duty"), reducing tax bills by £1500 per lease on commercial transactions (£600 per lease on residential transactions), which will be of special benefit to smaller businesses.
- A new relief for businesses raising finance through the sale and leaseback of their land and buildings and relief for "chain-breaking" and similar companies which help to ensure an active housing market
- Further consultation on how the new regime might apply to partnerships. The announcement follows extensive consultation on the process throughout the earlier part of this year.

Ruth Kelly MP, Financial Secretary to the Treasury, said—

> "Stamp duty land tax is on course for implementation on 1 December 2003. The proposals announced today, along with those announced in Budget 2003, will help to achieve the Government's aim of a modern, efficient, system of taxing land transactions which promotes fairness between taxpayers, reduces distortions and prevents avoidance. I am also pleased that our proposals, which follow extensive and valuable consultation with interested parties, will be of particular help to small and medium-sized enterprises and business start-ups."

The Government will shortly be laying regulations before the House of Commons to give effect to the changes to lease duty, sale and leaseback, chain-breaking and other reliefs. The regulations will also make some technical corrections and clarifications which are set out in the attached Technical Note. The Government has today published draft clauses for consultation on partnerships.

DETAILS

The story so far

1 In his Budget Statement on 9 April 2003 the Chancellor of the Exchequer announced that a modernised system of stamp duty, renamed "stamp duty land tax", would apply to most land transactions on or after 1 December 2003. This system will replace the current archaic system of impressing a physical stamp on documents with a regime in line with that for other taxes. People acquiring interests in land will be required to submit a "land transaction return" to the Inland Revenue along with payment of the duty. This will substantially reduce the scope for avoidance since liability will depend on the nature of the transaction and not on the technicality of which particular document was used.

2 The Chancellor also announced that on or after 1 December 2003 the threshold below which no stamp duty is payable would be raised, for commercial transactions, to £150,000 from the current £60,000. Furthermore, as an aid to regeneration, commercial transactions in designated disadvantaged areas would be entirely exempt from stamp duty.

3 Stamp duty land tax is on course for implementation on 1 December 2003. The Inland Revenue has launched a substantial customer education programme aimed at ensuring in particular that solicitors, licensed conveyancers and other professional advisers are aware of the significance of the change for their practices.

4 The announcements made today cover stamp duty land tax on the rental element of newly granted leases ("lease duty"), further reliefs for particular commercial transactions and stamp duty land tax on partnership transactions.

Lease duty

5 In his Budget Statement the Chancellor announced his decision that a new structure for lease duty should come into force on 1 December. The current structure, with its arbitrary "cliff edges" and reliance on average annual rent, created distortions, encouraged decisions which were tax-driven rather than business-driven, and gave opportunities for avoidance.

6 The Government is keen that any new structure should—

- minimise potential scope for avoidance,
- reduce the distortions inherent in the current system to achieve greater fairness in the treatment of different transactions,
- better reflect modern commercial practice,
- be based on clear economic principles and in line with modern valuation and accounting principles, and
- be more in line with the charge on freehold transfers (transfers of ownership).

7 A structure which in the Government's view achieves these aims was accordingly included in Finance Act 2003. However the Chancellor made it clear that consultation on a new structure would continue and that changes might be made before implementation of the new structure on 1 December 2003.

8 The Government is extremely grateful to all who participated in the consultation process. A good deal of valuable information and data was provided by participants and some important work was done in partnership. Throughout the consultation process the Government has been particularly keen to have regard to the effect of any new structure on small and medium-sized enterprises and business start-ups.

9 Having considered all the contributions made the Government now proposes to modify the structure contained in Finance Act 2003 as follows—

- The Finance Act charges stamp duty land tax on the "Net Present Value" ("NPV") of rent payable under a lease. NPV sums the discounted values of the rents. This discount recognises that future rent payments will be of less value. The Government believes that NPV represents a fair way of assessing the amount on which stamp duty land tax should be charged and proposes to retain it.
- The Finance Act sets a threshold of £150,000 for commercial leases, £60,000 for residential leases. If the NPV does not exceed the threshold no stamp duty land tax is charged on the rental element. These thresholds mean that 60% of commercial leases and 93% of residential leases will pay no stamp duty land tax on the rental element. The Government believes these thresholds are fair and intend to retain them.
- The Finance Act provides that once the threshold is exceeded stamp duty land tax is charged at 1% of the full amount of the NPV. The Government proposes to modify this so that stamp duty land tax is charged at 1% of the excess over the threshold. This means that on any commercial lease chargeable to stamp duty land tax the tax payable on the rental element will be £1,500 less than under the Finance Act provisions. Similarly for residential leases, the stamp duty land tax payable on the rental element will be £600 less.

Example

A lease of commercial property for 18 years at an annual rent of £15,000 will have an NPV of £197,845. Under the Finance Act provisions stamp duty land tax of £1,978 would be payable. Under the Government's proposals only £478 will be payable.

10 The Government also proposes to clarify the stamp duty land tax treatment of leases with uncertain rents, so as to avoid an undue compliance burden on tenants, and to provide that rent increases more than five years after the start of a lease are ignored (subject to anti-avoidance provisions). Details are set out in the attached Technical Note.

11 The changes to lease duty are estimated to reduce the expected yield from stamp duty land tax by £20 million in a full year.

Other reliefs

12 The Finance Act already provides for many reliefs from stamp duty land tax, for example for property acquired by charities or let by registered social landlords. There are reliefs for house-builders who take houses in part exchange (which benefits in particular those providing retirement homes) and companies which assist in employee relocation.

13 The Government proposes, in line with commitments given by the Chief Secretary to the Treasury, the right Hon Paul Boateng MP, during the passage of Finance Bill 2003 through Parliament, to widen these reliefs to include companies who help to ensure an active housing market, by "chain-breaking" (buying property when a prospective sale falls through) and by buying houses from the personal representatives of people who have died. Details are set out in the attached Technical Note.

14 The Government also proposes to give relief for sale and lease-back transactions (where a company raises finance by selling a property for a capital sum and leasing it back at an annual rent). Provided certain conditions are met the "lease-back" leg of the transaction will not be charged to stamp duty land tax.

15 The cost of and yield from these reliefs is expected to be negligible.

Technical corrections and clarifications

16 The attached Technical Note sets out a number of technical corrections and clarifications. The Government is grateful to all those who made representations on these issues. The cost of and yield from these changes is expected to be negligible.

Partnerships

17 In his Budget statement the Chancellor announced that certain transactions involving partnerships would remain within the existing stamp duty regime until at least 2004 to give time for further consultation. These are: transactions between a partnership and a partner or an incoming partner, changes in partnership interests and transactions between a partnership and a departing partner.

18 The Government is today publishing draft clauses which bring these transactions, so far as they involve dealings in land, within the scope of stamp duty land tax. As with the Government's other proposals the aim is to give fairness between taxpayers, reduce distortions and prevent avoidance.

19 The Government will be meeting interested parties to discuss these proposals but would welcome comments from others. The Government's intention is that the clauses will be included in Finance Bill 2004 and will take effect from the date of Royal Assent to Finance Bill 2004.

NOTES

1 Stamp duty land tax applies (subject to some transitional provisions) to all "land transactions" completed on or after 1 December 2003. "Land transaction" includes the conveyance or transfer of a freehold (in Scotland, transfer of ownership), the assignment or assignation of an existing lease and the grant of a new lease. It replaces stamp duty, which is abolished except for instruments relating to stock and marketable securities, and for instruments relating to some partnership transactions.

2 Where a land transaction takes place the purchaser (including a new tenant) must submit a "land transaction return" to the Inland Revenue (there are exceptions for some transactions which do not have to be notified, for example where there is no consideration in any form chargeable to tax). This replaces the current procedure whereby documents are presented to the Inland Revenue for stamping.

3 The rates and thresholds for stamp duty land tax are the same as they currently are under stamp duty, except that—

(a) Under stamp duty the rate is nil for land transactions where the purchase price does not exceed £60,000. For non-residential transactions this threshold will be raised to £150,000 under stamp duty land tax

(b) There will be a new regime for charging stamp duty land tax on the rental element of new leases ("lease duty") as described above.

4 The current rates of lease duty under stamp duty are based on Average Annual Rent ("AAR") and on the term of the lease. They are—

1 Term not more than 7 years (including indefinite leases and periodic tenancies)—
 (a) if the rent is £5,000 or less Nil,
 (b) if the rent is more than £5,000 1%.

2 Term more than 7 years but not more than 35 years 2%.

3 Term more than 35 years but not more than 100 years 12%.

4 Term more than 100 years 24%.

20 October 2003. IR Technical Note

Stamp duty land tax: Technical Note

1 This Note supplements the News Release of 20 October 2003 [reproduced above]. It gives further details of—

- The technical changes to stamp duty land tax on the rental element of leases ("lease duty").
- The reliefs being given for sale and lease-back transactions and acquisitions by "chain-breaking" and similar companies.
- Other technical corrections and clarifications.

2 These changes will be effected by way of regulations made under FA 2003 s 109. The regulations require approval by the House of Commons.

STAMP DUTY LAND TAX ON LEASES

3 The News Release gives details of the main change proposed for the charging structure. The changes set out below supplement this in order to—

- remove uncertainty in the treatment of some leases;
- keep the compliance burden to a minimum; and
- ensure that taxpayers know what duty they will have to pay.

4 The amendments are as follows.

POST 5 YEAR RENT CHANGES

5 Currently, where rent changes are known and included in the terms of a lease from the outset, they are fully taken into account in calculating the Net Present Value ("NPV") of the lease (unless they are increases only to reflect RPI). However, where rent changes are made, after two years, to reflect market rents, these changes are ignored for the purposes of calculating the NPV.

6 The proposed changes remove this disparity of treatment. They provide that all rent changes after 5 years are ignored for the purposes of the NPV calculation and, for rental due after 5 years, the highest rent paid in any previous period of 12 months is substituted and used in the calculation. This will provide comparability of treatment for these types of lease.

LEASES WITH UNCERTAIN RENT

7 Where rent is expressed as relating to turnover, or where there are rent sharing or similar measures in place, the lessee is required to make a reasonable estimate of the rent due and include this estimate in their land transaction return. When any part of this estimated rent is determined, they must make an amended return including that part of the rent which is now determined. Representations have been received that this could place a severe compliance burden on many small businesses whose rent is determined by monthly turnover.

8 To simplify this area, it is proposed to amend Finance Act 2003 so that, where a lease has a rent which is still uncertain after five years (eg a turnover based lease for 15 years), *one and only one additional return* is required at the five year point. This return will base the NPV on the actual rent paid in the first five years and (for any post five year rent due) will apply the amendment at paragraph 6 above ie the highest rent paid in any 12 month period over the previous five years will be used in the NPV calculation.

9 Where all the uncertainty in the rental of a lease is determined before five years, *one and only one* additionally return is required at that point.

10 These measures will provide certainty and substantially reduce the compliance burden for small businesses.

CONTINGENCIES

11 Amendments will be made to clarify that break and forfeiture clauses in a lease do not operate to artificially shorten the term of a lease in the NPV calculation. Similarly, options to renew, contained in the lease, will not be treated as a contingency extending the term of a lease.

EXTENSIONS TO LEASES DURING THEIR TERM

12 An amendment will be introduced so that where a lease is extended during the currency of its term, this extension is treated as the grant of a new lease for the period by which the term of the lease is extended. This will be treated as a transaction linked with the original grant and, if not already notifiable, should the total term then extend to seven or more years, the whole transaction will be notifiable.

CONTINUATION OF LEASES AND LEASES FOR AN INDEFINITE TERM

13 Currently, where there is a lease for a fixed term and thereafter, this term is defined as the term plus such further period as must elapse before the earliest date at which the lease can be determined. This will be amended so that the term is defined as the term specified in the lease.

14 Where a lease comes to the end of its term but the landlord does not require possession of the property, this extension is treated, in England and Wales, as a periodic tenancy which extends the term of the lease. In Scotland, there is a similar treatment called tacit relocation. Currently, the treatment of this extension is unclear and an amendment will be introduced to clarify the situation. Where a lease continues after the end of its term, this extension will be deemed to be the grant of a new lease for the period of 12 months (or the original term of the previous lease if shorter). Should this continue past this period, it will be deemed to be another lease of similar length and so on. These leases will be linked transactions. This will also apply in Scotland, where the lease is for an unspecified period at the outset. The original period of such a lease will be deemed to be 12 months.

15 Where a lease is granted for an indefinite term, for example if it is for life of until repayment of a debt, the term of these leases will be deemed to be for a period of 12 months. As above, should the lease continue after this period, the continuation will be deemed as the grant of another lease for 12 months and so on with each deemed grant being treated as a linked transaction with those previously.

16 For all these leases and deemed leases, treated as linked transactions, there will be notification requirements, so that, whenever the total NPV of the rents means that stamp duty land tax is due or where the total term of the leases is seven years or more, the series of deemed leases will be notifiable transactions.

ANTI-AVOIDANCE

17 To prevent avoidance of stamp duty land tax using these amendments, it is proposed that, after the five year point when rent changes are not taken into account in the NPV, if the rent rises by more than 5% + RPI annually, this rent increase is deemed to be the grant of a new lease in a similar way to the way Paragraph 10 Schedule 5 already treats rent increases not included in the terms of a lease.

18 Currently, assignments or assignations of leases where the payment of a premium is not involved are stamp duty land tax transactions but the assumption of the obligation to pay rent is not treated as consideration. Therefore, no duty is paid on these type of assignments or assignations. It is proposed to change this treatment in a limited variety of circumstances. Where the lease, at the previous transaction, benefited from a relief, so that the duty payable was reduced or eliminated, assignment or assignation of such a lease will be deemed to be the grant of a lease by the assignor to the assignee. This will prevent the use of reliefs to avoid stamp duty land tax.

OTHER RELIEFS

19 In accordance with commitments made by the Chief Secretary to the Treasury during Standing Committee debates on Finance Bill 2003, the Government has consulted with interested parties with a view to widening the scope of the relief package to include full or partial reliefs from stamp duty land tax for sale and leaseback transactions, certain types of exchange transactions involving house-building companies and for purchases of residential property by "chain-breaking" companies. The following additional reliefs are now proposed:

SALES AND LEASEBACKS

20. Partial relief will be given for the leaseback element of a sale and leaseback of commercial property. These transactions take the form of a sale of premises (or the assignment or assignation of an existing lease of premises) followed by a leaseback of those premises by the purchaser to the vendor. They are commonly entered into as a means of raising finance by companies or other commercial entities. The leaseback element of the transaction will be relieved from a charge to stamp duty land tax, provided that certain conditions are met. These are that the sale and leaseback arrangement does not involve residential property, that the leaseback is of the same premises that were the subject of the sale or assignment (or assignation) and that the consideration for the sale or assignment (or assignation) element of the transaction consists only of cash or the release or assumption of a liability.

EXCHANGE TRANSACTIONS INVOLVING HOUSE-BUILDING COMPANIES

21 Finance Act 2003 s 58 provides for relief where a house-building company acquires a dwelling from individuals in consideration of their agreeing to purchase a new dwelling from the house-building company. However, if the house-building company uses an unconnected company to acquire the individuals' former dwelling, no relief from stamp duty land tax exists in respect of that acquisition. Such an arrangement may commonly occur where the selling individuals are seeking to move to a retirement home. Relief will be introduced in these circumstances where the unconnected company acquires the individuals' former dwelling in the course of carrying on a trade as a property trader, does not spend more than a permitted amount on refurbishments, does not grant a lease or licence over the acquired property and does not permit any officer or employee to occupy the property. If these conditions are met, it is right that the role of the property trading company in providing liquidity to the housing market should not suffer a charge to stamp duty land tax. A charge to tax as provided for under stamp duty land tax legislation enacted in Finance Act 2003 will arise when the property trading company on-sells the property.

22 A similar relief will be provided for companies who specialise in purchasing residential properties from personal representatives of deceased individuals and then on-sell the property. These companies provide liquidity to the residential housing market and, subject to conditions, relief from stamp duty land tax will be given on the acquisition.

CHAIN-BREAKING COMPANIES

23 Relief from stamp duty land tax will be introduced for companies part or all of whose trade consists of buying residential property in order to keep a chain of residential transactions from failing. Individuals looking to move house are often dependent on selling their own house before buying their target home. If their prospective purchaser pulls out, then their own purchase cannot go ahead. In these circumstances, a chain-breaking company would acquire the individuals' current property so that the move can still take place. The chain-breaking company purchases the property and then sells on in a short space of time. The purchase by the chain-breaking company will relieved from stamp duty land tax, provided that it is acting in the course of a trade of buying properties in these circumstances, does not spend more than a permitted amount on refurbishments, does not grant a lease or licence over the acquired property and does not permit any officer or employee to occupy the property. stamp duty land tax will be paid on the eventual sale by the chain-breaking company.

SURRENDERS AND REGRANTS

24 The law will be clarified so that the surrender of any lease will not be consideration for the grant of another and the grant will not be consideration for the surrender. When a new lease is granted the charge to stamp duty land tax will be on the premium and rent due and not on the value of any interest surrendered. Where a lease is surrendered to the landlord, then as long as the surrendered lease is for a fixed rent credit will be given in computing the stamp duty land tax due on the new lease for the amount of rent that was due for the surrendered years. This will help many commercial arrangements for surrenders and regrants.

Example

A commercial lease ("lease 1") is granted for 10 years, rent £100,000 per year. The NPV is £831,660 so stamp duty land tax of £6,816 is chargeable. After 5 years it is surrendered and a new lease ("lease 2") of 10 years with rent of £150,000 per year is granted. Without any relief the NPV of lease 2 would be £1,247,490 and so stamp duty land tax of £10,794 would be chargeable. The relief recognises that rent paid for the first five years of lease 2 has already been partially taken into account in taxing lease 1. So the rent payable under lease 2 is taken to be £50,000 per year for the first five years and £150,000 per year thereafter. This reduces the NPV to £795,985 and the stamp duty land tax chargeable to £6,459.

TECHNICAL CORRECTIONS AND CLARIFICATIONS

25 These are—

(a) Clarification of the interpretation of "taking possession" in section 44, and provision that this includes possession by a person connected with the purchaser;

(b) Clarification that fixed duty is abolished on duplicates and counterparts of instruments that effect a land transaction which is an stamp duty land tax transaction;

(c) Clarification as to the operation of the transitional provisions where a contract is entered into on or before 10 July 2003 in two respects—

- Where a contract is entered into on or before 10 July 2003 but the contracting purchaser sub-sells or assigns his rights after that date the proposed changes make it clear that the sub-sale or assignment (or assignation), if completed or substantially performed on or after 1 December 2003, is an stamp duty land tax transaction.
- Where the transaction provided for in the contract becomes an stamp duty land tax transaction by virtue of FA 2003 Sch 19 para 3(3) the "effective date" is the date of that event if it is later than the date the contract is substantially performed. There are examples of the operation of the transitional provisions at the end of this Note.

(d) Confirmation that the holder of a Power of Attorney can sign a land transaction return

(e) Clarification of the obligation to submit a further land transaction return when stamp duty land tax becomes chargeable, or chargeable at a higher rate, as a result of a later "linked transaction". The purchaser will need to submit a further land transaction return in respect of the earlier transaction(s) and for this purpose the "effective date" will be the date of the later transaction.

(f) Clarification that stamp duty land tax applies to the Crown in the same way as stamp duty does, but subject to the specific exemptions for Government departments and similar bodies (FA 2003 s 107(2)) and for certain transactions by other public bodies (FA 2003 s 66).

(g) A change to the way in which agreements for leases entered into before 1 December 2003 are dealt with for stamp duty purposes if the execution of the lease is an stamp duty land tax transaction. FA 2003 Sch 19 paragraph 8 provides that the agreement for lease can be presented for stamping and the stamp duty is then credited against stamp duty land tax due on the execution of the lease. It has been pointed out to us that this causes delay in being able to deliver the land transaction return. We propose to reverse the procedure so that the stamp duty land tax is paid first and the agreement for lease can then be stamped with a "denoted" stamp.

TRANSITIONAL PROVISIONS: EXAMPLES

Examples 1–5 show the current operation of the transitional provisions and no change is proposed. Example 6 relates to the proposed new provision.

1 A enters into a contract with B on 1 January 2003. The contract is completed on 1 January 2004 without any paragraph 3(3) event having occurred. This is not an stamp duty land tax transaction and the conveyance is chargeable to stamp duty.

2 A enters into a contract with B on 1 January 2003. The contract is varied on 1 September 2003 and completed on 1 January 2004 without having first been substantially performed. The variation is a paragraph 3(3) event and accordingly this is an stamp duty land tax transaction. The effective date is the date of completion.

3 A enters into a contract with B on 1 January 2003. The contract is varied on 1 September 2003, substantially performed on 1 October 2003 and completed on 1 January 2004. The variation is a paragraph 3(3) event and accordingly this is an stamp duty land tax transaction. The effective date is the date of completion because substantial performance pre-implementation is disregarded (FA 2003 Sch 19 para 4(3)).

4 A enters into a contract with B on 1 January 2003. The contract is varied on 1 September 2003, substantially performed on 1 January 2004 and completed on 1 February 2004. The variation is a paragraph 3(3) event and accordingly this is an stamp duty land tax transaction. The effective date is the date of substantial performance (FA 2003 s 44(4)).

5 A enters into a contract with B on 1 January 2003. The contract is substantially performed on 1 November 2003, varied on 1 July 2004 and completed on 1 December 2004. The variation is a paragraph 3(3) event and accordingly this is an stamp duty land tax transaction. The effective date is the date of completion because substantial performance pre-implementation is disregarded (FA 2003 Sch 19 para 4(3)).

6 A enters into a contract with B on 1 January 2003. The contract is substantially performed on 1 January 2004, varied on 1 July 2004 and completed on 1 December 2004. The variation is a paragraph 3(3) event and accordingly this is an stamp duty land tax transaction. By virtue of the changes now being proposed the effective date will be 1 July 2004.

20 October 2003. Ministerial Statement.

Written Ministerial Statement by the Financial Secretary

STAMP DUTY LAND TAX

I am pleased to announce the next steps in the process of modernising stamp duty on land transactions. These include—

- A significant change to the proposed charge on the rental element when a new lease is granted ("lease duty"), reducing tax bills by £1500 per lease on commercial transactions (£600 per lease on residential transactions), which will be of significant benefit to smaller businesses
- A new relief for businesses raising finance through the sale and leaseback of their land and buildings and relief for "chain-breaking" and similar companies which help to ensure an active housing market

Further consultation on how the new regime might apply to partnerships. The announcement follows extensive consultation on the process throughout the earlier part of this year. Theses proposals along with those announced in Budget 2003, will help to achieve the Government's aim of a modern, efficient, system of taxing land transactions which promotes fairness between taxpayers, reduces distortions and prevents avoidance. I am also pleased that our proposals, which follow extensive and valuable consultation with interested parties, will be of particular help to small and medium-sized enterprises and business start-ups. The Inland Revenue is today publishing a News Release, supplemented by a Technical Note [reproduced above], giving details of the proposed changes. I will be laying regulations to give effect to the changes before the House shortly. The Inland Revenue is also publishing for consultation draft clauses on the Stamp Duty Land tax treatment of partnership transactions. The Government's proposals on lease duty follow extensive consultation over the last 18 months. I am extremely grateful to all who participated in the consultation process. A good deal of valuable information and data was provided by participants and some important work was done in partnership. Throughout the consultation process the Government has been particularly keen to have regard to the effect of any new structure on small and medium-sized enterprises and business start-ups.

Having considered all the contributions made I now propose to modify the structure contained in Finance Act 2003, by way of regulations under section 112 of that Act, as follows:

- The Finance Act charges stamp duty land tax on the "Net Present Value" ("NPV") of rent payable under a lease. NPV sums the discounted values of the rents. This discount recognises that future rent payments will be of less value. The Government believes that NPV represents a fair way of assessing the amount on which stamp duty land tax should be charged and proposes to retain it.
- The Finance Act sets a threshold of £150,000 for commercial leases, £60,000 for residential leases. If the NPV does not exceed the threshold no stamp duty land tax is charged on the rental element. These thresholds mean that 60% of commercial leases and 90% of residential leases will pay no stamp duty land tax on the rental element. The Government believes these thresholds are fair and intend to retain them.
- The Finance Act provides that once the threshold is exceeded stamp duty land tax is charged at 1% of the full amount of the NPV. The Government proposes to modify this so that stamp duty land tax is charged at 1% of the excess over the threshold. This means that on any commercial lease chargeable to stamp duty land tax the tax payable will be £1,500 less than under the Finance Act provisions.

Example

A lease for 18 years at an annual rent of £15000 will have an NPV of £197,845. Under the Finance Act provisions stamp duty land tax of £1,978 would be payable. Under the Government's proposals only £478 will be payable.

I also propose to clarify the stamp duty land tax treatment of leases with uncertain rents, so as to avoid an undue compliance burden on tenants, and to provide that rent increases more than five years after the start of a lease are ignored. I also propose (by way of regulations made under section 109 Finance Act 2003) to widen the reliefs in sections 58 and 59 of that Act to include companies who help to ensure an active housing market, by "chain-breaking" (buying property when a prospective sale falls through) and by buying houses from the personal representatives of people who have died. I also propose to give relief for sale and lease-back transactions (where a company raises finance by selling a property for a capital sum and leasing it back at an annual rent).

In his Budget statement my Right Hon Friend the Chancellor of the Exchequer announced that certain transactions involving partnerships would remain within the existing stamp duty regime until at least 2004 to give time for further consultation. These are: transactions between a partnership and an incoming partner, changes in partnership interests and transactions between a partnership and a departing partner.

The Inland Revenue is today publishing draft clauses [see below] which bring these transactions, so far as they involve dealings in land, within the scope of stamp duty land tax. As with the Government's other proposals the aim is to give fairness between taxpayers, reduce distortions and prevent avoidance. My officials will be meeting interested parties to discuss these proposals but would welcome comments from others. The Government's intention is that the clauses will be included in Finance Bill 2004 and will take effect from the date of royal assent to Finance Bill 2004.

HM TREASURY
20 October 2003

November 2003.

SDLT—Guidance notes on self-certification

Form SDLT60 (Certification that no Land Transaction Return is required for a land transaction) is available at http://www.inlandrevenue.gov.uk/so/sdlt60-self-certificate.pdf.

WHAT IS "SELF-CERTIFICATION"?

Most land transactions, including all transactions where a payment of stamp duty land tax is required, must be notified to the Inland Revenue on a Land Transaction Return form (Form SDLT 1). On receipt of the return the Inland Revenue will issue a certificate. The certificate must accompany any application for registration of the transaction (or of a document) at the appropriate land registry.

Some land transactions, however, where no stamp duty land tax is payable do not have to be notified to the Inland Revenue. For such transactions the purchaser can give a "self-certificate" to the appropriate land registry.

For the purposes of SDLT, "purchaser" is defined as the person acquiring the interest even if no consideration is paid.

WHAT LAND TRANSACTIONS MUST BE NOTIFIED TO THE INLAND REVENUE ON A FORM SDLT 1?

These transactions cannot be self-certified and an Inland Revenue certificate must accompany any application for registration.

- The acquisition of a freehold or leasehold interest in land (in Scotland, the acquisition of ownership of land, including the interest of the proprietor of the *dominium utile*, or of the tenant's interest in property subject to a lease) where there is chargeable consideration, **whether or not any stamp duty land tax is payable**. In particular such acquisitions must be notified even if the chargeable consideration is £60,000 or less (£150,000 or less for non-residential property) so that stamp duty land tax is chargeable at 0%. The only exceptions are for some transactions in connection with divorce and some variations of testamentary dispositions (see below).
- The grant of a lease (including, in Scotland, exchange of missives of let) for a term of seven years or more, **whether or not any stamp duty land tax is payable**.
- Any other land transaction which attracts a charge to stamp duty land tax at a rate of 1% or more, or would do so but for some relief.

WHAT LAND TRANSACTIONS DO NOT HAVE TO BE NOTIFIED TO THE INLAND REVENUE, AND SO CAN BE SELF-CERTIFIED?

- The acquisition of a freehold or leasehold interest in land (in Scotland, the acquisition of ownership of land, including the interest of the proprietor of the *dominium utile*, or of the tenant's interest in property subject to a lease) where there is **no chargeable consideration** (see below on what constitutes chargeable consideration).
- The grant of a lease (including, in Scotland, the exchange of missives of let) where **all** the following conditions are satisfied:
  - The term of the lease is less than seven years.
  - The amount of any premium (in Scotland, grassum) is not such as to attract a charge to stamp duty land tax at a rate of 1% or more, ignoring the availability of any relief.
  - The amount of any rent is not such as to attract a charge to stamp duty land tax at a rate of 1% or more, ignoring the availability of any relief.
- Any other acquisition of an interest in land (for example, the acquisition of an easement or servitude) where the chargeable consideration is not such as to attract a charge to stamp duty land tax at a rate of 1% or more, ignoring the availability of any relief.
- Transactions exempt from charge under Finance Act 2003 Schedule 3 paragraph 3 (transactions in connection with divorce).

– Transactions exempt from charge under Finance Act 2003 Schedule 3 paragraph 4 (variations of testamentary dispositions).

WHAT IS CHARGEABLE CONSIDERATION?

The basic rule is that anything given in money or money's worth for the subject-matter of a land transaction is chargeable consideration. There are three special cases (in each case "property" means the subject-matter of a land transaction):

- There is chargeable consideration where a property is transferred subject to an existing debt such as a mortgage (but, in Scotland, only where the transferee assumes liability for the obligation). So a "gift" of property subject to a mortgage is a notifiable transaction and cannot be self-certified.
- There are special rules when one property is exchanged for another which mean that there will normally be chargeable consideration on both transactions.
- There are special rules when property is transferred to a company wholly or partly in exchange for shares which mean that there will normally be chargeable consideration.

There is more detail on chargeable consideration and the special rules in the Guidance Notes for the Land Transaction Return. You can obtain a copy from the Orderline.

WHO CAN SIGN THE SELF-CERTIFICATE?

The purchaser or transferee must sign. If there is more than one purchaser or transferee then all must sign. Signature by an agent such as a solicitor, licensed conveyancer or accountant is not acceptable unless the purchaser has been recognised by a Court as mentally incapable of understanding their affairs. A parent or guardian may sign on behalf of a minor.

Where the purchaser or transferee is a company the Company Secretary or any person having express, implied or apparent authority to act on behalf of the company may sign. However where the company is in liquidation the liquidator must sign.

Where the purchaser or transferee is a partnership the self-certificate may be signed by one or more nominated partners.

Where the purchasers or transferees enter into the transaction as trustees (other than bare trustees as defined in Finance Act 2003 Schedule 16) then any one or more of them may sign.

12 November 2003. Stamp Duty Information Bulletin—Issue 6.

Special arrangements for administration of SDLT from 1 December 2003

INTRODUCTION

From 1 December 2003, stamp duty land tax (SDLT) replaces existing stamp duty for UK land and buildings transactions. In line with other taxes, SDLT will introduce a "process now, check later" system, as well as introducing the new concept of a "liable person".

A key aspect of the new system will be the clear requirement to notify relevant transactions by completing a Land Transaction Return (LTR) within 30 days of the effective date of the transaction. In response, the Stamp Office will issue an SDLT certificate that can be presented to a Land Registry (replacing the current need to get documents stamped).

As with all significant changes, it may take practitioners and their clients some time to get used to the new guidelines, processes and forms. So, after consultation with the Law Society, the Law Society for Scotland and the Law Society for Northern Ireland and other key interested parties, we have put special arrangements in place to help the transition in the first few months.

DETAILS

In the early days of any new system, there can sometimes be failures by practitioners on behalf of their clients that are not deliberate; rather they result from misunderstanding, error or lack of familiarity with the new rules and guidance. Therefore, for a short period **we will:**

- Look wherever possible to process and issue SDLT certificates even if the Land Transaction Returns (LTRs) have been completed unsatisfactorily and contain some omissions or errors.
- Forego late filing penalties for LTRs that have been submitted more than 30 days but not more than 40 days after the effective date of the transaction. Wherever possible, in these instances the LTR will be processed as normal and a SDLT certificate issued.

Nevertheless, forms that contain critical errors or omissions will not receive a certificate. Instead, they will be sent back, with a letter identifying the boxes on the LTR that need to be corrected and re-submitted (see below).

WHAT WILL BE SENT BACK?

LTRs will be sent back where the basic information is missing, such as—

- The correct payment of tax is not enclosed (or paid via the other payment options, as described on the payslip)
- Where it has not been signed by the purchaser or person holding a purchaser's power of attorney
- Key pieces of data including the name of the purchaser(s) or the address of the property being bought which mean a certificate simply cannot be issued.

Where returns are sent back (primarily to practitioners), we will aim to return them immediately and ask that they are remedied and re-submitted quickly. We will also issue a letter with the rejected LTR detailing the omitted item(s) that are required under law. The aim is to help to identify any misunderstandings and avoid future occurrences.

FUTURE DEVELOPMENTS

This "light touch" approach will be constantly monitored and evaluated commencing on 1 December 2003. It is hoped that within a short period of time, the majority of errors and omissions will be reduced and a high proportion of the LTRs will be submitted accurately.

Comprehensive guidance on stamp duty land tax is available on our website at http://www.inlandrevenue.gov.uk/so/. Alternatively our customer service office in Worthing and our enquiry line staff are available to help customers understand the requirements of the new legislation. The telephone number is 0845 6030135.

Even though a LTR may have qualified for a certificate under this relaxed period it should be stressed that the issue of a certificate (and the non-rejection of the LTR), does not mean that we have "accepted" that the tax payable on the LTR is the correct amount. We will not have prejudiced our right to enquire into the transaction within the time limit allowed by the legislation.

A formal announcement will be made (at least 4 weeks) in advance of the date on which this concession is brought to a close.

FIXTURES AND CHATTELS—STAMP DUTY LAND TAX

The same general legal principles which apply to deductions for chattels for stamp duty will also apply to stamp duty land tax.

Stamp duty land tax differs from stamp duty in that it is a tax on the transaction and not on the document that implements it. Stamp duty land tax is charged on transactions.

For an item to be regarded as a fixture or part of the land (chargeable to tax), as opposed to a chattel or moveable in Scotland, (not chargeable) the item must, as a starting point, be annexed to the property. The issue then turns on the degree and purpose of the annexation, with greater emphasis being placed (in the more recent cases) to purpose. Where a purchaser agrees to buy a property for a price that includes an amount properly attributed to chattels or moveables, that amount will not be charged to stamp duty land tax.

In recent times, IR Stamp Taxes has seen an increasing number of cases in which the amount of consideration attributed to chattels is more than a small percentage of the total consideration. This has been particularly noticeable where, as a result of the apportionment, the chargeable consideration is brought just below the £250,000 or £500,000 stamp duty thresholds.

Under the stamp duty land tax regime the purchaser is responsible for the accurate completion of the Land Transaction Return, including the entry in Box 10 of form SDLT 1 of the consideration for the land transaction. Under paragraph (4) of Schedule 4 Finance Act 2003, a "just and reasonable apportionment" is required where a price is paid partly for a land transaction and partly for a non-land transaction such as the purchase of chattels. It does not matter that the parties to a transaction may agree a particular apportionment, which is then documented in the contract. The apportionment will not be correct unless it was arrived at on a "just and reasonable" basis.

We have the right to make enquiries into the accuracy of a Land Transaction Return and the apportionment of the purchase price may well be one of the aspects on which we will make enquiries. Similarly it is quite possible that we will also undertake enquiries into cases where a deduction has been made for chattels to confirm that those items properly fall within the definition of chattels.

We are unable to provide a comprehensive list of items that we accept as chattels or moveables. This is because each case must be considered on its own merits and because this is an area of the law that continues to evolve.

The following are, however, confirmed as being items that will normally fall to be regarded as chattels—

- Carpets (fitted or otherwise);
- Curtains and blinds;
- Free standing furniture;
- Kitchen white goods;
- Electric and gas fires (provided that they can be removed by disconnection from the power supply without causing damage to the property);
- Light shades and fittings (unless recessed).

On the other hand, the following will not normally be regarded as chattels—

- Fitted kitchen units, cupboards and sinks;
- Agas and wall mounted ovens;
- Fitted bathroom sanitary ware;
- Central heating systems;
- Intruder alarm systems.

Externally any plants, shrubs or trees growing in the soil form part of the land and are not regarded as chattels. A deduction would, however, be possible for amounts properly apportioned to any plants growing in pots or containers.

The above guidance is written primarily in the context of sales of residential property. The same principles apply when considering the purchase of industrial or commercial property in which the sale may also involve the acquisition of plant, machinery or equipment.

Further information is available on our website at www.inlandrevenue.gov.uk/so/sdlt_index.htm. The SDLT Manual also available on our website will be updated shortly.

CALCULATION OF STAMP DUTY LAND TAX ON LEASES

When a lease is entered into, the stamp duty land tax (SDLT) due on that lease depends on the premium payable (if any), the rent due under the lease and the term (period) of the lease. SDLT is payable by the lessee (tenant) and **not** by the landlord.

Notifiable lease transactions

A lease transaction is notifiable if—

- the lease is for a term of seven years or more (or treated as being for a term of seven years or more); **or**
- SDLT is due (at more than 0%) on either the premium element or rental element or both of the lease;

If a lease transaction is notifiable, a land transaction return **must** be completed by the tenant and sent into the processing centre at Netherton.

Calculation of the SDLT due

The SDLT due on a lease transaction (if any) depends on the premium payable, the rent due under the lease and the term of the lease. The SDLT is calculated in two separate parts, the SDLT due on the premium and the SDLT due on the rental element. These are added together and entered onto the land transaction return as a total figure of these two elements.

A) SDLT due on the premium

SDLT is due on the premium part of a lease if the premium payable is more than the relevant threshold. The relevant threshold depends on whether the **average annual rent** is more than £600 per year.

Average annual rent is determined by the **ascertainable** rent each year. Rent is ascertainable if you know you are going to have to pay at least this amount for the year. For example—

i) if the rent you have to pay depends **entirely** on the turnover of your business, that is there is no minimum amount of rent you have to pay, then there is no **ascertainable** rent as there is no amount you know you will have to pay;

ii) if the rent you have to pay depends on the turnover of your business and you have a minimum amount you have to pay, whether or not your turnover meets a certain figure, the minimum rent due is the **ascertainable** rent;

iii) if the rent you have to pay is a fixed amount plus an amount based on percentage of turnover, the **ascertainable** rent is the fixed amount you have to pay, excluding any percentage amount;

iv) if your rent is fixed, or any increases in the rent are known from the outset, the **ascertainable** rent is the amount known from the outset.

Average annual rent is calculated by adding all the **ascertainable** rent together and dividing it by the term (period) of the lease.

If the average annual rent is **less than or equal** to £600, the relevant thresholds are—

Residential leases	*Commercial or mixed-use leases*
£60,000	£150,000

If the average annual rent is **more than** £600, the relevant threshold is £0, that is, all the premium is taxable.

If the premium is taxable, the **rate** of tax depends on the amount of premium as follows—

Up to (and including) threshold	0%
From threshold to £250,000	1%
From £250,001 to £500,000	3%
From £500,001	4%

B) SDLT due on the rental element

SDLT is **also** due on the rental element of a lease and is charged at a flat rate of 1% of the **Net Present Value** (NPV) of the rental stream over the term (period) of the lease. NPV depends on the term (period) of the lease and the amount of rent payable in the first five years.

To calculate the NPV, determine what the amount of rent payable for each of the first five years of the term (period) of the lease is. If this cannot be determined, for example, if it depends fully or to some extent on turnover, or some other unknown amount, you should make a reasonable estimate of what you expect the rent to be each year. Once you have determined what the rental payments in the first five years are (or are likely to be) you need to determine what the highest rent payable in any continuous twelve-month period is (this will usually, but not always, be the highest annual rent payable). This amount should be used in the calculation for all years after the first five.

The tables in Annex 1 give factors to apply for all years from 1 to 99 for leases of up to 99 years. There are two columns: individual year factor and cumulative factor.

The column called **individual year factor** should be used where the rent payable in the first five years varies, that is, the yearly rent is not the same in the first five years of the lease.

The column called **cumulative factor** should be used where the rent does not vary in the first five years, that is, the same amount of rent is payable for each of the first five years of the lease.

How to use the column called individual year factor

1) Determine the rental payable for each of the first five years—
   i) Apply year one factor (0.966183575) to the rent for year one. So, for example, if the rent payable in year one was £20,000 the figure to use would be £20,000 × 0.966183575 = £19323.71;
   ii) Apply year two factor (0.9335107) to the rent for year two. So for example, if the rent payable in year two was £25,000 the figures to use would be £25,000 × 0.9335107 = £23,337.76;
   iii) Continue similarly until year six is reached.
2) For years six onwards only one calculation is needed—
   – The **rent used for year six** should be the highest rent payable in any continuous twelve-month period in the first five years. This will normally (but not always) be the highest rent payable in any of the first five years. This rent applies for all subsequent years. The factor to apply to this rent depends on the term (period) of the lease. If you have a six-year lease, apply the factor for year six (0.81350064) to the **rent used for year six** So, for example, if the **rent used for year six** was £32,500, the figure to use would be £32,500 × 0.81350064 = £26,438.77 If you have a twenty-year lease, apply the factor for year twenty (9.69735093) to the **rent used for year six.** So, for example, if the **rent used for year six** was £32,500, the figure to use would be £315,163.90.
3) Calculate the NPV—
   – Add together the figures obtained for years one to five (five figures) and the figure obtained for year six onwards. **This will be a maximum of six figures to add together.** This total is the NPV of the rent.
4) Calculate the SDLT due on the NPV—
   – If the NPV (calculated at step (3) above) is greater than the relevant threshold (£60,000 for residential leases and £150,000 for commercial and mixed-use leases), SDLT is due at 1% of the **excess** of the NPV above the relevant threshold. For example, if a residential lease has an NPV of £72,500 (the residential threshold being £60,000) tax would be due on £72,500 – £60,000 = £15,000 × 1% = £150. **Go to step C.**

How to use the column called cumulative factor

This column should **only** be used where the rent doesn't vary during the first five years, that is, it is the same amount for each of the first five years of the lease.

Use the factor for the term (period) of the lease with the rent payable in year one. For example, if you have a six-year lease, the factor is 5.32855302. The NPV of a lease paying a rent of £30,000 for six years is, therefore, £159,856. If the lease was for twenty years, the factor is 9.697350926 and the NPV is £426,372.

C) Calculate the SDLT due

Add the SDLT calculated on the premium (Step A) to the SDLT calculated on the rent (Step B). This is the total SDLT due for the lease.

Quick guide

The table below gives a guide as to whether SDLT will be due on the premium (if any) and/or the rental element of a lease. This is for guidance only and cannot be relied upon t give accurate amounts due. If the entry is in bold, it is probable that SDLT is due on that element of the payment for the lease.

QUICK GUIDE TABLE

Premium	*NPV**	*AAR***	*Tax on*
Below threshold	Below threshold	Below or equal to £600	—
Below threshold	Below threshold	Greater than £600	Premium
Below threshold	Above threshold	Below or equal to £600	NPV
Below threshold	Above threshold	Greater than £600	Premium/NPV
Above threshold	Below threshold	Below or equal to £600	Premium
Above threshold	Below threshold	Greater than £600	Premium
Above threshold	Above threshold	Below or equal to £600	Premium/NPV
Above threshold	Above threshold	Greater than £600	Premium/NPV

* NPV = Net Present Value
**AAR = Average Annual Rent

Examples

1) A residential lease for 99 years with a premium of £50,000 and an annual rent of £200 for the first 25 years, £400 for the next 25 years and £800 thereafter.

A) The average annual rent is £547 and so the premium thresholds aren't affected. The premium is below the residential threshold and so no SDLT is due on the premium.

B) As the rent doesn't change in the first five years, use the cumulative table. The factor for 99 years is 27.62336529 and the rent to be used for year six is £200. The NPV is, therefore, £5,524. As this is below the residential threshold, no SDLT is due on the rental element.

C) The total SDLT due is nil. However, a land transaction return is still required as the term of the lease is for seven years or more.

2) A residential lease for 25 years with a premium of £50,000 and an annual rent of £1,000 reviewable after five years

A) The average annual rent is £1,000 (which is more than £600) and so the premium threshold becomes £0. SDLT is due on the premium at a rate of 1% (as the premium is not more than £250,000). The SDLT due is £500.

B) As the rent doesn't change in the first five years, use the cumulative table. The factor for 25 years is 16.48151459 and the rent to be used for year six is £1,000. The NPV is, therefore, £16,481. As this is below the residential threshold, no SDLT is due on the rental element.

C) The total SDLT due is £500. This should be included on a land transaction return.

3) A commercial lease for 20 years with a premium of £50,000 and an annual rent of 10% of turnover. There is no minimum rent. Rent payable in the first five years is estimated to be £100,000 each year.

A) The average annual rent is £0 (as there is no ascertainable rent) and so the premium thresholds aren't affected. The premium is below the commercial threshold and so no SDLT is due on the premium.

B) As the rent doesn't change in the first five years, use the cumulative table. The factor for 20 years is 14.2124033 and the rent to be used for year six is £100,000. The NPV is, therefore, £1,421,240. This is above the commercial threshold and SDLT is due on the excess of (£1,421,240 – £150,000 = £1,271,240) at 1%, that is SDLT of £12,712.40 is due.

C) The total SDLT due is £12,712.40 (rounded down to £12,712). This should be included on a land transaction return.

4) A commercial lease for 35 years with a premium of £125,000 and an annual rent based on 10 % of turnover or £38,000, whichever is the greater. Rent payable in the first five years is estimated to be £38,000 for years one and two £40,000 for year three and £45,000 for years four and five.

A) The average annual rent is £38,000 (as this is the ascertainable rent) and so the premium threshold becomes £0. SDLT is due on the premium at a rate of 1% (as the premium is not more than £250,000). The SDLT due is £1,250.

B) As the rent changes in the first five years, use the Individual year table. The factor for year one is 0.96618357 and the NPV for this year is £38,000 × 0.96618357 = £36,714.97. The factor for year two is 0.9335107 and the NPV for this year is £38,000 × 0.9335107 = £35,473.40. The factor for year three is 0.90194271 and the NPV for this year is £40,000 × 0.90194271 = £36,077.70. The factor for year four is 0.87144223 and the NPV for this year is £45,000 × 0.87144223 = £39,214.90. The factor for year five is 0.84197317 and the NPV for this year is £45,000 × 0.84197317 = £37,888.79. The highest rent payable in any twelve month period is £45,000 and this is used as the rent for year six onwards. The factor for a thirty-five year lease is 15.48560872 and the NPV for the balance of the term of the lease is £45,000 × 15.48560872 = £696,852.39. The total NPV is, therefore,

£36,714.97 + £35,473.40 + £36,077.70 + £39,214,.90 + £37,888.79 + £696,852.39 = £882222.15. This is above the commercial threshold and SDLT is due on the excess of (£882,222–£150,000 = £732,222) at 1%, that is SDLT of £7,322.22 is due.

C) The total SDLT due is £1,250.00 + £7,322.22 = £8,572.22 (rounded down to £8,572). This should be included on a land transaction return.

TABLES OF INDIVIDUAL YEAR FACTORS AND CUMULATIVE FACTORS

Year	*Individual year factor*	*Cumulative factor*
1	0.96618357	0.96618357
2	0.93351070	1.89969428
3	0.90194271	2.80163698
4	0.87144223	3.67307921
5	0.84197317	4.51505238
6	0.81350064	5.32855302
7	1.59949160	6.11454398
8	2.35890316	6.87395554
9	3.09263413	7.60768651
10	3.80155295	8.31660532
11	4.48649866	9.00155104
12	5.14828196	9.66333433
13	5.78768611	10.30273849
14	6.40546790	10.92052028
15	7.00235852	11.51741090
16	7.57906443	12.09411681
17	8.13626821	12.65132059
18	8.67462935	13.18968173
19	9.19478504	13.70983742
20	9.69735093	14.21240330
21	10.18292183	14.69797420
22	10.65207246	15.16712484
23	11.10535809	15.62041047
24	11.54331523	16.05836760
25	11.96646222	16.48151459
26	12.37529989	16.89035226
27	12.77031213	17.28536451
28	13.15196647	17.66701885
29	13.52071463	18.03576700
30	13.87699304	18.39204541
31	14.22122338	18.73627576
32	14.55381309	19.06886547
33	14.87515581	19.39020818
34	15.18563186	19.70068423
35	15.48560872	20.00066110
36	15.77544144	20.29049381
37	16.05547305	20.57052542
38	16.32603499	20.84108736
39	16.58744749	21.10249987
40	16.84001996	21.35507234
41	17.08405133	21.59910371
42	17.31983043	21.83488281
43	17.54763633	22.06268870
44	17.76773864	22.28279102
45	17.98039788	22.49545026
46	18.18586575	22.70091813
47	18.38438543	22.89943780
48	18.57619188	23.09124425
49	18.76151212	23.27656450
50	18.94056550	23.45561787
51	19.11356392	23.62861630
52	19.28071217	23.79576454
53	19.44220805	23.95726043

Stamp Taxes

Year	Individual year factor	Cumulative factor
54	19.59824272	24.11329510
55	19.74900086	24.26405323
56	19.89466089	24.40971327
57	20.03539523	24.55044760
58	20.17137043	24.68642281
59	20.30274744	24.81779981
60	20.42968174	24.94473412
61	20.55232358	25.06737596
62	20.67081812	25.18587049
63	20.78530559	25.30035796
64	20.89592150	25.41097388
65	21.00279678	25.51784916
66	21.10605792	25.62111030
67	21.20582714	25.72087951
68	21.30222252	25.81727489
69	21.39535815	25.91041052
70	21.48534427	26.00039664
71	21.57228738	26.08733975
72	21.65629038	26.17134275
73	21.73745270	26.25250508
74	21.81587040	26.33092278
75	21.89163630	26.40668868
76	21.96484006	26.47989244
77	22.03556834	26.55062072
78	22.10390484	26.61895721
79	22.16993044	26.68498281
80	22.23372329	26.74877567
81	22.29535890	26.81041127
82	22.35491021	26.86996258
83	22.41244770	26.92750008
84	22.46803949	26.98309186
85	22.52175136	27.03680373
86	22.57364688	27.08869926
87	22.62378749	27.13883986
88	22.67223252	27.18728489
89	22.71903931	27.23409168
90	22.76426326	27.27931564
91	22.80795790	27.32301028
92	22.85017494	27.36522732
93	22.89096436	27.40601673
94	22.93037442	27.44542680
95	22.96845178	27.48350415
96	23.00524149	27.52029387
97	23.04078711	27.55583948
98	23.07513070	27.59018308
99	23.10831292	27.62336529

Previous issues of the Information Bulletin are available from our website at www.inlandrevenue.gov.uk/so/bull_news_flyers_sdlt.htm.

19 December 2003. IR press release 102/03

Stamp duty land tax: treatment of private finance initiative projects

The Government has today made Regulations clarifying the stamp duty land tax treatment of land transactions forming part of a Private Finance Initiative (PFI) project. These Regulations will take effect from 19 December 2003.

Ruth Kelly MP, Financial Secretary to the Treasury, said: "The Government recognises the importance of PFI transactions and the economic benefits which they bring. Having consulted at length with interested parties, our proposals will ensure that the treatment of these transactions under current stamp duty will be continued for the present under stamp duty land tax".

DETAILS

1 The Regulations are The Stamp Duty Land Tax (Amendment of Schedule 4 to the Finance Act 2003) Regulations 2003 (SI 2003/3923).

2 The Regulations clarify the stamp duty land tax treatment of certain land transactions in PFI projects. The Regulations apply to "qualifying transactions", defined as transactions between certain public and educational bodies ("qualifying bodies") and a private sector supplier under a global agreement which provides for—

- the provision of services or the carrying out of works by the private sector supplier;
- payment for those services by the qualifying body;
- the transfer of land or the grant (or assignment) of a lease by the qualifying body;
- the grant of a lease back to the qualifying body; and
- in some cases, the transfer of land (sometimes termed "Surplus Land") by the qualifying body.

3 The Regulations provide that where a transaction is a qualifying transaction—

- neither the lease back to the public body nor the carrying out of works nor the provision of services is chargeable consideration for the transfer or grant of the lease by the qualifying body, or for the transfer of the Surplus Land (in other words tax will generally be charged only on any cash premium or rent paid by the private sector supplier);
- there is no chargeable consideration for the lease back (in other words there is no charge on the qualifying body); and
- the stamp duty land tax provisions relating to exchanges (which normally charge tax on the market value of the property) do not apply to qualifying transactions.

NOTES

1 Stamp duty land tax applies (subject to some transitional provisions) to all "land transactions" completed on or after 1 December 2003. "Land transaction" includes the conveyance or transfer of a freehold (in Scotland, transfer of ownership), the assignment or assignation of an existing lease and the grant of a new lease. It replaces stamp duty, which is abolished except for instruments relating to stock and marketable securities, and for instruments relating to some partnership transactions.

2 Stamp duty land tax is charged on the "chargeable consideration" given for the transaction. It does not matter whether the consideration is in the form of money or some other form.

3 A PFI transaction is an agreement under which a private sector supplier performs services for a public sector or educational body such as—

(i) the design and construction of a building or complex of buildings (eg a hospital, school, university accommodation, army garrison, bus station, leisure centre, care homes and other buildings or facilities that may be publicly owned);

(ii) the financing of the design and construction of the buildings in (a) above;

(iii) the management and delivery of various services within or related to the buildings constructed at (i) above on a continuous basis.

4 The treatment of PFI transactions under the old stamp duty regime was set out in Tax Bulletin 43C (parts 1–6) published by the Inland Revenue in October 1999.

April 2004. Inland Revenue Tax Bulletin Issue 70

Stamp duty land tax: group relief

1. This article gives practical and technical guidance on claims for group relief in stamp duty land tax under Schedule 7 to the Finance Act 2003. It deals with material which was previously covered by the Statement of Practice issued for stamp duty group relief, SP3/98 published on 13 October 1998. That Statement does not apply to stamp duty land tax but will continue to apply to stamp duty.

How to claim group relief in stamp duty land tax

2. In contrast to stamp duty, documents must not be submitted with a claim. The claim should be made on form SDLT1 by putting a cross at box 9 and inserting code 12.

3. Following procedures for other returns within stamp duty land tax, the certificate that enables title to be registered will be issued provided that the return is complete. Certificates will not be delayed simply because the Inland Revenue may wish to enquire into particular aspects of the return including a claim to group relief.

4. The relief is self-assessed and will be dealt with on a 'process now/check later' basis along with all other stamp duty land tax matters. Under stamp duty land tax the Inland Revenue does not require the preparation and submission of the letter of claim (see paragraph 6.641 of the Inland Revenue Stamp Taxes manual).

5. This means that companies must judge the admissibility of the claim themselves. Under stamp duty land tax the Inland Revenue has the power to assess and collect under-declared tax and seek penalties in cases where errors in returns (including errors in group relief claims) are the result of negligence or fraud.

Enquiries involving group relief claims

6. If the decision is taken to enquire into a return where the transaction is subject to a group relief claim, the Inland Revenue will open an enquiry under paragraph 12 of Schedule 10 FA 2003. The enquiry must be made within 9 months of the filing date. Enquiries may cover all aspects of the return and will not necessarily be limited to the group relief claim itself.

7. The decision to enquire into a transaction will be made after the certificate (form SDLT5) is issued and will not therefore delay registration of title. But the issue of the certificate should not be taken as an indication that the Inland Revenue either accepts the validity of a group relief claim or has chosen not to enquire into that return.

8. Enquiries will consider all aspects of the transaction, including the group relief claim. Documents may be called for and these may include the instruments of transfer and related documents. The Inland Revenue may also ask for more information about the claim. In particular, evidence may be sought to show that the tests in paragraphs 1 and 2 of Schedule 7 were met.

9. If the evidence presented does not support the claim the self assessment will be amended to remove the relief.

Paragraph 1 of Schedule 7

10. Paragraph 1 of Schedule 7 to FA 2003 provides exemption from stamp duty land tax where, at the effective date of the transaction, the companies are members of the same group. Exemption extends to the grant of leases between group companies.

Meaning of company

11. Relief is extended to any 'body corporate' through the definition of 'company' in section 100(1) FA 2003. To determine whether an entity qualifies as a body corporate the Inland Revenue will follow the guidelines for stamp duty set out at paragraph 6.124 of the Stamp Taxes Manual.

Meaning of subsidiary

12. Paragraph 1(2)(b) requires that the companies claiming relief must be 75% subsidiaries of one another or 75% subsidiaries of a third company.

13. Paragraph 1(3) provides that for a company (A) to be a 75% subsidiary of another company (B) if:

- company B is the beneficial owner of at least 75% of the ordinary share capital of company A;
- it is beneficially entitled to not less than 75% of profits available for distribution to equity holders; and
- it would be entitled to not less than 75% of any assets of A available for distribution to equity holders on winding up.

14. Paragraph 1(4) provides that 'ownership' for these purposes is either directly or indirectly through another company or group of companies. The rules in section 838(5) to (10) ICTA 1988 apply to determine the amount of ordinary share capital. Paragraph 1(5) defines 'ordinary share capital'.

15. Paragraph 1(6) applies Schedule 18 ICTA 1988 which defines 'equity holder'.

16. The meaning of subsidiary is also relevant to the arrangements test in paragraph 2(2)(b) of Schedule 7 (see 19 below).

17. The tests in paragraph 1 of Schedule 7 apply independently of the tests in paragraph 2 and claims are not allowable if these tests are not met.

Paragraph 2 of Schedule 7

18. Paragraph 2 provides anti-avoidance rules which restrict the availability of group relief. It will prevent relief being allowable in circumstances where certain 'arrangements' are in place.

Meaning of arrangements

19. 'Arrangements is defined generally for the purposes of paragraph 2 in paragraph 2(5) to include any scheme, arrangement or understanding, whether or not legally enforceable'. This definition is used in section 76(6A)(b) FA 1986 (inserted by section 112(6) FA 2002) but 'arrangements' was not defined for the equivalent stamp duty provisions in section 42(2) FA 1930 or section 27(2) FA 1967. Under this new definition, 'arrangements' will include schemes, arrangements or understandings not in writing and the existence of arrangements in a particular claim will depend on a consideration of all of the facts relating to the claim and the surrounding circumstances.

20. In considering whether arrangements exist that might disqualify the claim, the Inland Revenue will seek to establish whether there was any scheme arrangement or understanding.

Paragraph 2(1): Arrangements for change of control of purchaser

21. Paragraph 2(1) prevents a claim to group relief if arrangements are in existence at the time of the claim for a person (or persons together) to obtain control of the purchaser but not the vendor. Arrangements under paragraph 2(1) have to be in existence at the effective date of the transaction.

22. Where there is a change of control, paragraph 2(1) is intended to prevent avoidance of stamp duty land tax by passing property, or an economic interest in it, out of the group.

23. The statements of the Economic Secretary during debate in Parliament on the equivalent stamp duty provision in Finance Act 2000 are still relevant. The Economic Secretary said:

> 'I have received representations expressing concern about the blocking of relief for transfers from the company about to leave the group to another group member—in other words, when the company leaving the group is the transferor. I am persuaded that there are commercial situations in which an asset is transferred to another group company after arrangements are in place for the transferor company to leave the group. In a sense, therefore, the asset never leaves the original group. I am willing to make a concession for such cases, which will be useful to businesses, as their legal advisers have suggested.
>
> I have some worry that it might be possible to construct avoidance devices from the concession, so I have asked the Stamp Office to monitor carefully the use of the relief. If the concession is abused, the Government will not hesitate to act swiftly.'

(See Hansard 18 July 2000, column 253.)

24. The Inland Revenue will not argue that paragraph 2(1) denies group relief in cases where the transferor is to leave the group having transferred the land to other group members.

25. Furthermore, paragraph 2(1) does not apply if the arrangements that are in place are those for the acquisition of shares by a company under a reconstruction as long as the conditions in paragraph 2(1)(a), (b) and (c) are met. These are:

- that section 75 FA 1986 will apply to the acquisition and the conditions for relief under that section will be met;
- that after the acquisition the purchaser will be a member of the same group as the acquiring company.

Paragraph 2(2) of Schedule 7

26. Paragraph 2(2)(a) denies relief where there are arrangements under which consideration is to be provided or received (directly or indirectly) by a person other than a group company.

27. Where group relief is claimed the Inland Revenue will consider all of the facts and interpret paragraph 2(2)(a) as not denying relief unless the loan finance is provided as part of a scheme to save stamp duty land tax when the property or an interest in it leaves the group.

28. For example, it is unlikely that there will be arrangements within paragraph 2(2)(a) if:

- the claim is not to be followed by a sale or underlease outside the group; or
- the claim is followed by a sale or underlease outside the group but stamp duty land tax is to be paid by the purchaser outside the group on consideration close to market value (or is deemed to be a grant of a lease under paragraph 11 of Schedule 17A FA 2003), then again it is unlikely that relief will be prevented by paragraph 2(2)(a).

29. Loans from commercial lenders on ordinary commercial terms to facilitate the transfer between group members will also not normally disqualify a claim for the purposes of the arrangements test in paragraph 2(2)(a). For example, a claim can be accepted if:

- a specific loan is taken for the purchase of the asset; or
- the loan is secured on the asset; or
- arrangements are made to replace or novate an existing charge on the property transferred.

30. Paragraphs 27 to 29 above are limited to paragraph 2(2)(a) of Schedule 7. They do not mean that if other tests in paragraphs 1 and 2 of Schedule 7 are not met the claim is acceptable.

31. When an enquiry is opened the case will be considered on their particular facts. Some examples of the type of circumstances which the Inland Revenue might want to examine in more detail during an enquiry are where the claim is part of (or is to be followed by):

the creation or transfer of loan stock or equity capital;

- a capital reorganisation of the transferee;
- a guarantee by a third party not associated with the group;
- the creation of a new charge or financial arrangement whereby title to the property is, or may be, vested in the lender otherwise than in satisfaction of all or part of the debt; or
- the assignment of the freehold reversion or the intra-group lease to a person outside the group.

32. Other circumstances which can indicate that the claim is not admissible include where:

- all or part of the consideration for the transaction is to remain outstanding or is represented by intra-group debt, (as the aim and effect may be to reduce the value of the transferee company on a possible future sale outside the group); or

– the existing shareholders of the transferee include shareholders outside the group and the transaction is to be followed by the declaration of a dividend in specie, or by the liquidation of the transferee.

Subsales and group relief in stamp duty land tax

33. Paragraph 2(2) provides rules for stamp duty land tax based on those for stamp duty in section 27(3) FA 1967. Section 27(3)(b) FA 1967 (intended to prevent acquisitions of land from outside the group without stamp duty being paid) is not included in Schedule 7 and this is because the problem it seeks to address, resting on contracts, is not relevant to stamp duty land tax. It is not possible to 'rest on contract' to avoid stamp duty land tax because of the 'substantial' performance rule in section 44 FA 2003.

Paragraph 2(2)(b): arrangements for the purchaser to cease to be a member of the same group

34. A claim for relief is not appropriate if there are arrangements for the purchaser to cease to be a 75% subsidiary of the vendor or a third company. In deciding whether there are any such arrangements, the practical likelihood of the scheme being carried through is not in itself relevant.

35. But the Inland Revenue will not take the view that just because land is transferred to a group company which does nothing other than hold property it follows that there are arrangements for the purchaser to leave the group. We recognise that there are many commercial reasons why groups may transfer property internally. It is necessary to consider the full circumstances of the case to decide whether such arrangements are in place.

36. Whether such arrangements were or were not in place must be decided at the time of the return and Inland Revenue enquiries will seek to establish the facts at the effective date of the transaction.

Relevance of arrangements under paragraph 2 to a recovery of tax under paragraph 3 ('clawback')

37. Paragraph 3 of Schedule 7 is independent of paragraph 2. When an enquiry is made into a claim the question will be the admissibility of the claim itself in accordance with the statutory provisions. The fact that the arrangements, if carried out as planned, could lead to a recovery or will be exempt from a recovery will not mean that claim itself is allowable except as provided in paragraph 2.

Paragraph 3(1)(a)(ii): Arrangements during the three year recovery period

38. Paragraph 3 imposes a requirement to make a return (under section 81 FA 2003) for the withdrawal of relief when the purchaser ceases to be a member of the same group within three years of the effective date of the transaction.

39. Paragraph 3(1)(a) deals with the recovery period. Paragraph 3(1)(a)(ii) provides that group relief will be recovered if the transfer outside the group after the end of the period is under arrangements made before the end of the period.

40. 'Arrangements' is defined in paragraph 3(4) with the same definition as in paragraph 2.

41. When there is a transfer outside the group, companies will need to decide whether to make a return under section 81. If the transfer outside the group is after the end of the three year period, companies will still need to consider whether there were arrangements in place for the transfer during the three year period. To make this decision a proper consideration of all of the circumstances will be required.

42. The Inland Revenue will not assume that just because a company is transferred outside the group shortly after the end of the three year period it will be in accordance with arrangements made within the three year period. We will only seek to argue that there should have been a recovery return if the facts of the case point to there having been such arrangements.

Section 54(4) FA 2003: exception from the connected company charge on a winding up

43. Section 54(4) FA 2003 provides the third case of exception from the deemed market value rule in section 53 FA 2003. The exception applies to the distribution of assets on the winding up of a company, as long as the subject matter of the transaction or an interest from which that interest is derived, has not been the subject of a transaction in respect of which a claim to group relief was made by the vendor. But it is not the Inland Revenue's intention that section 54(4)

should be prevented from applying where a group relief claim was made by the vendor but recovered under paragraph 3 of Schedule 7 either at the time of or before the effective date of the transaction.

April 2004. Inland Revenue statement.

SDLT—sale of land with associated construction, &c, contract

We have been asked how to determine the chargeable consideration for stamp duty land tax purposes where V agrees to sell land to P and V also agrees to carry out work (commonly works of construction, improvement or repair) on the land sold. Our view is that the decision in *Prudential Assurance Co Ltd v IRC* [1992] STC 863 applies for the purposes of stamp duty land tax as it does for stamp duty. This is because the basis of the decision was the identification of the subject matter of the transaction and this is as relevant for stamp duty land tax as it is for stamp duty.

It follows that SP 8/93 will be applied for stamp duty land tax as it was for stamp duty. The paragraphs on "contracts already entered into" and "procedure for submitting documents" are, however, not relevant to stamp duty land tax.

Where, however, the sale of land and the construction, &c, contract are in substance one bargain (as they were in the Prudential case) there must be a just and reasonable apportionment of the total consideration given for all elements of the bargain in order to arrive at the chargeable consideration for stamp duty land tax purposes.

The SDLT Manual will be amended in due course to reflect this.

12 November 2004. Inland Revenue Guidance Note.

Stamp duty land tax and nil-rate band discretionary trusts

1 We have received a number of enquiries about the interaction between stamp duty land tax and 'nil-rate band discretionary trusts' ('NRB Trusts'). This note should enable taxpayers and their advisers to decide on the stamp duty land tax consequences of transactions with NRB Trusts. This note does not cover any taxes other than stamp duty land tax. Neither does it cover the powers or fiduciary responsibilities of trustees of NRB Trusts, or of personal representatives, under general law. Trustees and personal representatives may wish to take independent legal advice on those aspects.

2 An NRB Trust is commonly established under the Will of a deceased person. The typical form is a pecuniary legacy, not exceeding the nil-rate band for inheritance tax, to be held by the trustees of the NRB Trust ('the NRB trustees') on discretionary trusts for a specified class of beneficiaries. The residue of the estate, often including the matrimonial home, commonly passes to the surviving spouse, although it may pass to residuary trustees.

3 Where the personal representatives discharge the pecuniary legacy by payment of the specified sum to the trustees no stamp duty land tax issue arises. However in many cases the personal representatives satisfy the legacy otherwise than by payment of the specified sum. It is in these cases that a stamp duty land tax liability may arise on the transfer of the matrimonial home or other land to the surviving spouse or residuary trustees.

4 The transfer of an interest in land, whether to a residuary beneficiary or to any other person, and whether in satisfaction of an entitlement under a Will or not, is a land transaction for stamp duty land tax purposes. The question is whether the transferee gives any chargeable consideration for the transfer. Very often a beneficiary gives no chargeable consideration for the transfer of land under a Will. However transactions in connection with NRB Trusts may result in the beneficiary giving chargeable consideration.

5 The commonest examples of such transactions, and their stamp duty land tax consequences, are as follows:

- The NRB trustees accept the surviving spouse's promise to pay in satisfaction of the pecuniary legacy and in consideration of that promise land is transferred to the surviving spouse. The promise to pay is chargeable consideration for stamp duty land tax purposes.
- The NRB trustees accept the personal representatives' promise to pay in satisfaction of the pecuniary legacy and land is transferred to the surviving spouse in consideration of the spouse accepting liability for the promise. The acceptance of liability for the promise is chargeable consideration for stamp duty land tax purposes. The amount of chargeable consideration is the amount promised (not exceeding the market value of the land transferred)
- Land is transferred to the surviving spouse and the spouse charges the property with payment of the amount of the pecuniary legacy. The NRB trustees accept this charge in satisfaction of the pecuniary legacy. The charge is money's worth and so is chargeable consideration for stamp duty land tax purposes
- The personal representatives charge land with the payment of the pecuniary legacy. The personal representatives and NRB trustees also agree that the trustees have no right to

Stamp Taxes

enforce payment of the amount of the legacy personally against the owner of the land for the time being. The NRB trustees accept this charge in satisfaction of the legacy. The property is transferred to the surviving spouse subject to the charge. There is no chargeable consideration for stamp duty land tax purpose provided that there is no change in the rights or liabilities of any person in relation to the debt secured by the charge.

6 We have also been asked about the consequences for stamp duty land tax purposes of a Deed of Variation made by beneficiaries after the death of the deceased person. A Deed of Variation may effect a land transaction if it alters the beneficial interests in land, for example by settling land in trust. However, placing a charge on land is not in itself a land transaction. In addition paragraph 4 of Schedule 3 FA 2003 provides that under certain conditions a land transaction effected by a Deed of Variation is exempt from charge.

14 April 2005. Inland Revenue Notice.

Budget 2005 provisions on stamp duty land tax

THE BUDGET 2005 PROVISIONS

1 A number of stamp duty land tax measures were announced on Budget Day, 16 March 2005. This note summarises the effect that subsequent developments have had on these measures. In particular it explains that in some circumstances a repayment may be due to purchasers who have paid tax on the basis of measures announced in the Budget (see paragraph 8 below).

2 All the Budget measures were included in the Finance Bill published on 22 March 2005. However that Bill has now been withdrawn. Instead the Finance (No 2) Bill, containing some but not all of the provisions in the original Finance Bill, was passed by the House of Commons on 6 April and received Royal Assent as Finance Act 2005 on 7 April 2005.

Increase in the threshold for residential transactions from £60,000 to £120,000

3 This measure has been included in Finance Act 2005 (as section 95) and will have effect as announced, that is, for land transactions the effective date of which was on or after 17 March 2005.

Withdrawal of disadvantaged areas relief on non-residential transactions

4 This measure has been included in Finance Act 2005 (as section 96 and Schedule 9) and will have effect as announced, that is, for land transactions the effective date of which was on or after 17 March 2005, subject to transitional provisions for some contracts entered into on or before 16 March 2005.

Extension of reliefs for alternative property finance

5 This measure has been included in Finance Act 2005 (as section 94 and Schedule 8) and will have effect for land transactions where the effective date of the 'first transaction' is on or after 7 April 2005.

Miscellaneous amendments

6 Budget Resolution 46 gave provisional statutory effect under the Provisional Collection of Taxes Act 1968 ('the 1968 Act') to a number of miscellaneous amendments to the legislation governing stamp duty land tax. These amendments were summarised in a Technical Note published by the Inland Revenue on 16 March 2005. Broadly speaking the Resolution had effect for transactions the effective date of which was on or after 17 March 2005.

7 Provisions giving effect to Budget Resolution 46 were included (as Part 1 of Schedule 17) in the original Finance Bill, now withdrawn. However Finance Act 2005 does not contain any provisions giving effect to Budget Resolution 46. It follows that by virtue of section 1(5) of the 1968 Act the Resolution ceased to have statutory effect when Parliament was prorogued on 7 April 2005.

8 If you have paid tax which would not have been payable but for the provisional statutory effect of Budget Resolution 46 a repayment is due to you. Any requests for repayment should be sent, along with an explanation of why you think a repayment is due to you, to:

Complex Transactions Unit
Manchester Stamp Office
Upper 5th Floor
Royal Exchange
Exchange Street
MANCHESTER
M2 7EB

If you are in doubt as to whether a repayment is due please contact the Complex Transactions Unit with an explanation of the circumstances.

STATEMENTS MADE DURING THE DEBATE ON THE FINANCE (NO 2) BILL

9 Purchasers and their advisers will wish to be aware of the statements made by the front-bench spokesmen during debate on the Finance (No 2) Bill, which concern measures in the original Bill which were not included in Finance Act 2005, including the measures in Budget Resolution 46:

Paul Boateng MP (Labour): 'It is therefore our full intention to introduce a second Finance Bill after the election – should it be the wish of the British people – in which the measures not included in this revised version will be brought back. We will, of course, aim to ensure that the statutory dates for these measures will continue to apply, as announced in the Budget.' (Hansard, 6 April 2005, col. 1432)

George Osborne MP (Conservative): 'We agree with the Government about the need to tackle tax avoidance and we agree on principle with the many measures that they have introduced to close tax loopholes. However, the detail of such measures requires the closest possible examination, to ensure that we do not inadvertently damage the competitiveness of UK industry and further increase burdens on business. Indeed, many anti-tax avoidance measures are retrospective, as they would come into force on the day on which they were announced. There would therefore be no revenue implications if we considered them after the election in a Conservative Finance Bill or, in the unlikely event that Labour wins, a Labour one.' (Hansard, 6 April 2005, col 1444)

Dr Vincent Cable MP (Liberal Democrat): 'On the major change, the anti-avoidance measures, we need a great deal more time for reflection. We are all committed to such measures where they are effective, but they are at the core of the Government's budgetary arithmetic, as the Chief Secretary knows. They propose to raise £3 billion over three years, so the ability to make the measures stick is central to the Budget's credibility. For the reasons that have partly been given, it is right that we be given further time for reflection.' (Hansard, 6 April 2005, col 1448)

14 December 2007. HMRC Guidance Note.

Intermediary and Stock Lending Reliefs—FA 2007, Sch 21

Transaction reporting to a Multilateral Trading Facility, Recognised Foreign Exchange or Recognised Foreign Options Exchange.

HM Revenue and Customs (HMRC) has been asked to clarify the operation of the stamp duty and stamp duty reserve tax rules for intermediary and stock lending relief, as amended with effect from 1 November 2007, in respect of transactions involving stocks other than those that are regularly traded on a regulated market.

The intermediary relief legislation covering stocks regularly traded on a multilateral trading facility (MTF), recognised foreign exchange (RFE) or recognised foreign options exchange (RFOE) provides that relief is only available where the transaction is subject to the rules of the particular MTF/exchange and is reported to the MTF/exchange in accordance with those rules (see sections 80A(6) and 88A(6) FA 1986). The stock lending relief provisions contain a similar requirement (see sections 80C(6) and 89AA(5) FA 1986).

HMRC understands that the rules of some MTFs/exchanges may, following the implementation of the Directive on Markets in Financial Instruments (MiFID), no longer contain a requirement to report a transaction to the MTF/exchange. This means that members of those organisations are strictly unable to fulfil the requirement in the legislation that transactions must be reported to the MTF/exchange.

HMRC recognises that a strict reading of the legislation would result in intermediary or stock lending relief not being granted. It therefore intends to amend the legislation to address this at the earliest opportunity. In the meantime, HMRC will not refuse relief where the rules of an MTF/exchange are either silent about the need to report transactions or specifically state that a report is not required. Nor will stock lending relief be denied if the stock loan is reported to CREST for settlement and the Trade System of Origin (TSO) field completed in accordance with the rules of the market/MTF/exchange.

For trading transactions on the Alternative Investment Market (AIM) of the London Stock Exchange (LSE), the trade report that AIM members are required to make to the LSE will be regarded as satisfying the reporting condition for the purposes of section 80A(6) and 88A(6).

4 February 2008. HMRC Notice.

Stamp Taxes Online—transactions with more than 100 properties

The online service can accept transactions of up to 100 properties. We want to extend this, but know that an IT solution is at least 12 months away. In the meantime, we're introducing a new process which we hope will encourage even more people to use online filing.

Currently, if transactions have more than 100 properties, paper returns must be sent to Birmingham Stamp Office, where hand-written certificates are produced for practitioners to submit for registration purposes. The new process will still have a manual element, but should make life easier.

From 1 February 2008 the process will be:

- complete the online return for the first 100 properties
- submit a schedule to Birmingham Stamp Office, by email to: Shujina Bibi for only the properties that exceed 100.

There is no "template" for this schedule. You should simply ensure that all the relevant information is given (see below).

For example:

- If the transaction includes 150 properties, the schedule submitted to Birmingham should include the last 50 properties.
- Birmingham will save the schedule and allocate a reference number in SDLTMP-9999999 format. They will keep a record of the reference number and email this to you, with the agent reference.
- Complete the return online and enter the allocated reference number in the 'Property Address' field, at the end of the address details for the first property.
- Add the remaining 99 properties not included in the schedule and submit the return.
- Send the online certificate(s) and/or the 99 PDFs (if appropriate to the online product being used) together with a copy of the schedule to the appropriate land registry. The reference number allocated by Birmingham will appear on the certificate, under the first property address.

Information required on the schedule for each property is:

- Property address
- Title number
- NLPG UPRN (National Land Property Gazette Unique Property Registration Number)

The schedule must also include:

- First purchaser name
- Description of transaction
- Effective date
- Agents reference

Before the schedule is passed onto the appropriate land registry, you should add:

- Reference number issued by Birmingham
- UTRN

31 March 2008. HMRC Information Sheet.

Stamp Duty on Shared Ownership Homes

BACKGROUND

Shared ownership purchasers acquire a lease, for which they pay a premium representing a percentage of the market value of the property, and rent in respect of the remainder. They may be able to make further capital payments (which will increase their share and reduce the rent payable) and ultimately to acquire the freehold. This is known as 'staircasing'.

SDLT AND SHARED OWNERSHIP

- Shared ownership purchasers can elect to pay SDLT at the outset on the market value of the property. In this case there will be no further SDLT charges at any stage.
- If no election is made, SDLT will be charged on the initial purchase in the normal way – that is, on the premium and the net present value of the rent payable under the lease. (In practice it is very unlikely that any tax will be due on the rent.)
- There is then a special SDLT relief which means staircasing payments are not charged to SDLT until an 80 percent share of the property is reached.
- Any further 'staircasing' payments which take the purchaser above this level – including the acquisition of the freehold, will attract SDLT

BUDGET MEASURE

- The measure announced in the Budget abolishes, from Budget Day, the so called "£600 rule" for residential leases. This rule meant that, where the annual rent under the lease (not the NPV) exceeded £600, SDLT applied at 1 per cent on the premium even where this was below the SDLT threshold (£125,000, or £150,000 in a disadvantaged area).
- The special rules for shared ownership purchasers have not changed, but in practice these purchasers were often hit by the £600 rule because their initial payment was below the threshold but their annual rent was more than £600.

EFFECT OF THE MEASURE FOR SHARED OWNERSHIP PURCHASERS

- Where a market value election is not made, no SDLT will be payable on the premium where this does not exceed the SDLT threshold (£125,000, or £150,000 in a disadvantaged area), whatever the annual rent paid. If the premium is more than this, SDLT will still be charged on the whole premium at 1 per cent (and at higher rates in the unlikely event that the premium exceeds £250,000).

- No tax will be payable on "staircasing" payments which do not take the purchaser above an 80 per cent share of the property.
- Any further "staircasing" payments which take the purchaser above this level – including the acquisition of the freehold, will attract SDLT. Tax will be payable on the amount actually paid at the appropriate rate in force at the time the payment is made.
- The rate of tax charged on these further "staircasing" payments will be based on the total capital payments made to date – that is, on the initial premium and all "staircasing" payments, regardless of whether any tax has previously been paid on them. This is because the various payments are treated as "linked transactions" for SDLT purposes.

Example 1

Market value of the property is £220,000.

Initial lease premium is £110,000, representing a 50 per cent share of the property. SDLT payable is nil (because this amount is below the SDLT threshold).

First "staircasing" payment is £55,000, taking the purchaser's share to 75 per cent. SDLT payable is nil (this payment attracts relief as it doesn't take the purchaser's share over 80 per cent).

Final "staircasing" payment is £55,000, taking the purchaser's share to 100 per cent including acquisition of the freehold. SDLT is payable at 1 per cent on £55,000 (because the rate of SDLT is determined by the total of all payments made, that is £220,000).

Example 2

Market value of the property is £220,000.

Initial lease premium is £165,000, representing a 75 per cent share of the property. SDLT is payable at 1 per cent on £165,000 (because this amount is above the SDLT threshold).

Final staircasing payment is £55,000, taking the purchaser's share to 100 per cent including acquisition of the freehold. SDLT is payable at 1 per cent on £55,000 (because the rate of SDLT is determined by the total of all payments made, that is £220,000).

17 April 2008. HMRC Notice

SDLT—Budget changes to notification requirements

Following on from the announcement of changes in the Stamp Duty Land Tax (SDLT) notification thresholds in Budget 2008 [BN57 and Finance Bill clause 91], the various Land Registries and HM Revenue & Customs (HMRC) have agreed to produce this note which conveyancers and others involved in land transactions may find helpful in explaining how these changes will work in practice.

As you know, Budget 2008 announced changes in requirements for notification of land transactions to HMRC. These changes will have effect for transactions with an effective date on and after 12 March 2008.

The changes raise the threshold for notification of non-leasehold transactions involving major interests in land from a chargeable consideration of £1,000 to £40,000. The changes also affect transactions involving leases for a term of seven years or more, which will now only have to be notified where any chargeable consideration other than rent is equal to or more than £40,000 or where any rent is equal to or more than £1,000.

As a result of these changes it will no longer be necessary to complete either form SDLT 1 Land Transaction Return or form SDLT 60 Self certificate if the transaction is below the new notification threshold.

The new notification system is we hope, much simpler and easier to understand for customers.

Some people have asked whether there are any circumstances in which a certificate that no SDLT is due (form SDLT 60) is now required. We are happy to confirm that there are now no circumstances in which an SDLT 60 is required in order for documents to be registered. Indeed, the current Finance Bill legislates to remove all reference to this form. Subject to Parliamentary approval, these consequential amendments will become law when the Bill receives Royal assent later this summer.

It may also help to mention that the acquisition of a chargeable interest other than a major interest in land remains notifiable only where there is chargeable consideration for which SDLT is due at a rate of 1 per cent or more. The acquisition of an easement, for example, is an acquisition of a chargeable interest other than a major interest in land. So, if the chargeable consideration on it was at the rate of 1 per cent or higher, the transaction would be notifiable.

It will be noted that the new notification threshold differs in two major respects from the previous rules. First, the threshold for notification in relation to major interests in residential property has risen from £1,000 to £40,000. Second, there is now a threshold for mixed and non-residential property, where none previously existed.

HMRC and the land registries will be working together over the coming months to update published guidance and will be happy to advise on any queries you might have.

2 September 2008. HM Treasury

Stamp duty exemption for residential property

The Chancellor of the Exchequer has today announced that stamp duty land tax will not apply to purchases of residential property of £175,000 or less.

This will provide an exemption from stamp duty land tax for land transactions consisting entirely of residential property where the chargeable consideration is not more than £175,000.

This relief will apply to transactions with an effective date on or after 3rd September 2008 and before 3rd September 2009.

Note—See also FA 2009 s 10 (extended zero-rate threshold continues to apply in relation to transactions with an effective date on or after 22 April 2009 but before 1 January 2010).

STAMP TAXES INDEX

Defined words and phrases are listed separately at the end.

ACQUISITION
company, of. *See* COMPANY RECONSTRUCTION
AD VALOREM DUTY
amount of, FA 1999 s 112(1)
debt, consideration consisting of, SA 1891 s 57, FA 1980 s 102, SP 6/90
foreclosure order, on, FA 1898 s 6
foreign currency, in respect of, calculation, SA 1891 s 6, FA 1985 s 88
land. *See* LAND
late stamped instruments, SA 1891 s 15, FA 1994 s 240(1)
lease. *See* LEASE OR TACK
periodical payments, consideration in, SA 1891 s 56
principal instrument, determination for, SA 1891 s 61
property conveyed in parts by separate instruments, SA 1891 s 58, FA 1991 s 112
security, in respect of, calculation, SA 1891 ss 6, 55
stock, in respect of, calculation, SA 1891 ss 6, 55
ADJUDICATION
Commissioners, by—
allotment of shares, in respect of, CA 1985 s 88(4)
appeal against. *See* APPEAL
conveyance in contemplation of sale, FA 1965 s 90(3)
persons entitled to request, SA 1891 s 12(1)
procedure, SA 1891 s 12, PR 18/7/90
stamping of document in accordance with, SA 1891 ss 12(4)–(6), 12A
statutory declaration for purposes of, SA 1891 s 12A(3), (4)
High Court, by, SA 1891 ss 13(5), 13B
AFFIDAVIT
manner of making, SDMA 1891 s 24; RA 1898 s 7(6)
AGREEMENT
liability for insufficient stamp duty, as to, void, SA 1891 s 117
ALLIED HEADQUARTERS
building etc contracts, exemption, FA 1960, s 74
meaning, FA 1960, s 74(6)(*a*)
ALLOTMENT OF SHARES
assessment by Commissioners of duty payable, CA 1985 s 88(4)
non-compliance with reporting requirements, penalty, CA 1985 s 88(5), (6)
oral contract for, CA 1985 s 88(3)
return of, CA 1985 s 88(2)
ALLOWANCE
lost documents, for, SDMA 1891 s 12A, ESC G1, ESC G2
misused stamps, for, SDMA 1891 ss 10, 11
spoiled documents, for, ESC G2
spoiled instruments, SDMA 1891 s 12A
spoiled stamps, for, SDMA 1891 ss 9, 11
ANNUITY
sale of, SA 1891 s 60
APPEAL
First-tier Tribunal, to, SA 1891 s 13A
stamp duties, against adjudication by Commissioners—
assessment by High Court of duty chargeable, SA 1891 ss 13(5), 13B
payment of duty assessed, condition for, SA 1891 s 13(3)
statement of case, SA 1891 s 13B
time limit for, SA 1891 s 13(2)
stamp duty land tax—
agreement, settling by, FA 2003 Sch 10 para 37
assessments and self-assessments, as to, SI 2004/1363 reg 22
definitions, SI 2004/1363 regs 2, 8
General Commissioners, to, SI 2004/1363 regs 3, 7
agreement, assignment by, SI 2004/1363 reg 12
determinations of, SI 2004/1363 regs 18, 21
directions by Board, SI 2004/1363 reg 15
election for, SI 2004/1363 reg 8
further returns, SI 2004/1363 reg 11
Inland Revenue, proceedings commenced by, SI 2004/1363 reg 13
jurisdiction and procedure, SI 2004/1363 reg 23
linked transactions, purchaser's election in, SI 2004/1363 reg 9
notice of election, SI 2004/1363 reg 14
one transaction and more than one division, purchaser's election, SI 2004/1363 reg 10
quorum, SI 2004/1363 reg 20
Taxes Management Act, application of provisions of, SI 2004/1363 reg 25
Lands Tribunal, questions to be determined by, SI 2004/1363 reg 6
notice of, FA 2003 Sch 10 para 36
recovery of tax not postponed by, FA 2003 Sch 10 para 38
right of, FA 2003 Sch 10 para 35
right of election, transfer in case of, SI 2004/1363 reg 16
Special Commissioners, to, SI 2004/1363 regs 4, 5
complex or lengthy, transfer of, SI 2004/1363 reg 17
jurisdiction and procedure, SI 2004/1363 reg 24
shares or securities valuations, SI 2004/1363 reg 19
Taxes Management Act, application of provisions of, SI 2004/1363 regs 25, 26
stamp duty reserve tax—
determination, against—
High Court or Court of Session, to, SI 1986/1711 regs 8(3), 10

Stamp Taxes

APPEAL – *contd*
stamp duty reserve tax – *contd*
determination, against – *contd*
Lands Tribunal, to, SI 1986/1711 reg 8(4)–(4B)
Special Commissioners, to, SI 1986/1711 regs 8, 9, Sch paras 46A, 56B–56D
penalties, against, SI 1986/1711 Sch paras 53, 100B
notification to tribunal, SI 1986/1711 Sch paras 49D, 49G, 49H
reviews, SI 1986/1711 Sch paras 49A–49I
APPRENTICESHIP
instrument of, meaning, SA 1891 s 25
ARMED FORCES
allied headquarters, building etc contracts, exemption, FA 1960 s 74
NATO establishments, building etc contracts, exemption, FA 1960 s 74
visiting forces, building etc contracts, exemption, FA 1960 s 74
ASSESSMENT
liability of instrument for stamp duty, of. *See* ADJUDICATION
ATOMIC ENERGY AUTHORITY
sale of houses at discount, FA 1981 s 107
AUTHORISED UNIT TRUST
See UNIT TRUST SCHEME

BEARER INSTRUMENT
abolition of charge, FA 1990 s 107, 111, PR 20/3/90
by usage, meaning, FA 1999 Sch 15 para 10
clearance system, entry into, FA 1986 s 97(3A)–(3D)
collection and recovery of tax, FA 1999 Sch 17 paras 16–18
company, meaning, FA 1999 Sch 15 para 11
deposit certificate, meaning, FA 1999 Sch 15 para 9
depositary receipt system, entry into, FA 1986 s 95(2)–(2D)
duty on, charge to, FA 1973 Sch 7 para 6 (4)
exemptions—
duty previously abolished, instruments in respect of, FA 1999 Sch 15 para 14
foreign currency stock, instruments issued for, FA 1986 s 90(3C), (3D), (8), (9), FA 1999 Sch 15 para 17
foreign loan securities, FA 1999 Sch 15 para 13
Inter-American Development Bank instruments, FA 1976 s 131(3)
international organisations, instruments issued by, FA 1984 s 126(3)
non-sterling stock, instruments relating to, FA 1999 Sch 15 paras 17–19
original terms or conditions, variation of, FA 1999 Sch 15 para 20
renounceable letters of allotment, FA 1999 Sch 15 para 16
stock exempt from duty on transfer, FA 1999 Sch 15 para 15
substitute instrument, FA 1999 Sch 15 para 12A
false statement, penalty for, FA 1999 Sch 15 paras 25, 26
foreign currency stock, for—
general exemption, FA 1999 Sch 15 para 17
paired shares, FA 1988 s 143(4), (5)

BEARER INSTRUMENT – *contd*
inland—
stamp duty reserve tax exemption, FA 1986 ss 90(3A), 95(2), 97(3)
interest, FA 1999 Sch 13 para 24
issue, charge on, FA 1999 Sch 15 paras 1, 21, 22
loan capital, relating to, exemption, FA 1986 ss 79(2), 90(3E), (3F), (8), (9)
market value of stock transferred by, FA 1999 Sch 15 paras 7, 8
meaning, FA 1999 Sch 15 para 3
overseas—
stamp duty reserve tax exemption, FA 1986 s 90(3)
paired shares, in respect of, FA 1988 s 143
penalties for non-compliance—
amendments, FA 1999 Sch 17 paras 1–8
court proceedings, FA 1999 Sch 17 para 13
determination by officer of Commissioners, FA 1999 Sch 17 paras 10–12
false information provided, FA 1999 Sch 15 paras 25, 26
mitigation or compounding, FA 1999 Sch 17 para 14
rates of duty, FA 1999 Sch 15 paras 4–6, 21–23
transfer of stock by means on, charge on, FA 1999 Sch 15 paras 2, 23
BED AND BREAKFAST TRANSACTIONS
stamp duty reserve tax
BILL OF SALE
conditions of registration, SA 1891 s 41
BODIES CORPORATE
associated, transfers of property between, exemption, FA 1930 s 42, FA 1967 s 27
residence—
change of, compliance requirements, SP 2/90
place of, SP 1/90
stamp duty reserve tax, accountable person, SI 1986/1711 Sch para 108
subsidiaries, identification for national defence contribution, FA 1938 s 42, Sch 4 Part I
BROKER
agreements in ordinary course of business, stamp duty reserve tax exemption, FA 1986 s 89(2), (4), (6)–(8)
BUILDING. ***See also*** LAND
new, separate contracts for land and construction work, SP 8/93, PR 12/7/93
sale of lease subject to VAT. *See* VAT
BUILDING SOCIETY
demutualisation, stamp duty land tax relief, FA 2003 s 64
stamp duty exemption, BSA 1986 s 109
BUSINESS
transfer as going concern, VAT on land, PR 4/3/92

CAPITAL DUTY
companies subject to (before abolition), FA 1973 s 47(1)
exempt transactions, FA 1973 Sch 19 para 10
penalty for late payment of duty, FA 1973 s 47(7)
rate of duty, FA 1973 s 47(5)

CAPITAL DUTY – *contd*
stamping of documents relating to exempt transactions, FA 1973 s 47(6)
statement of chargeable transaction—
excepted transactions, FA 1973 s 47(2)
requirement for, FA 1973 s 47(1)
CERTIFICATE
type of instrument, specifying, FA 1985 s 87, SI 1987/516
CHARITABLE UNIT TRUST
exclusion from treatment as unit trust scheme, FA 1999 Sch 19 para 15(c)
CHARITY
agreement to transfer securities to, stamp duty reserve tax exemption, FA 1986 s 90(7)
stamp duty land tax relief, FA 2003 Sch 8 para 1
withdrawal of, FA 2003 Sch 8 para 2
transfers and leases to, exemption, FA 1982 s 129, FA 1983 s 46
CHARTER-PARTY
meaning, SA 1891, s 49
CHEQUE
payment of duty by, FA 1999 Sch 18 para 2
CHILD
stamp duty reserve tax liability, person accountable for, SI 1986/1711 Sch para 73
CLEARANCE SERVICE
stamp duties—
abolition of charge on instruments of transfer, FA 1990 ss 108(8), 111, PR 20/3/90
alternative system of charge, election for, FA 1986 s 97A
depositary receipt system, transfers to and from, FA 1986 s 72A
nominee companies, transfers to, FA 1986 s 97(1), PR 24/10/86, PR 16/4/87, PR 16/2/89, PR 25/2/94
notification to Commissioners—
abolition of requirement for, FA 1990 ss 109(4), (5), 111, PR 20/3/90
company issuing shares, by, FA 1986 s 71(3), (5)
person having business of holding relevant securities, by, FA 1986 s 71(2), (4)
person providing clearance service, by, FA 1986 s 71(1), (4)
penalties for non-compliance with notification requirements, FA 1986 s 71(4), (5)
relevant securities, meaning, FA 1986 s 72(2)
rates of duty on instrument of transfer, FA 1986 s 70(2)–(5), (9), 72(2)–(4)
transferee, conditions as to, FA 1986 s 70(6)–(8)
stamp duty reserve tax—
abolition of charge to, FA 1990 ss 110, 111, PR 20/3/90
accountable date, meaning, SI 1986/1711 reg 2
accountable person, meaning, SI 1986/1711 reg 2,
agreements subject to, FA 1986 s 96(1)
alternative system of charge, election for, FA 1986 s 97A
chargeable securities, meaning, FA 1986 s 99(3)–(6), (6A), (10)–(12)
credit for stamp duty, FA 1986 s 96(5)
depositary receipt system, transfers to and from, FA 1986 s 97B
CLEARANCE SERVICE – *contd*
stamp duty reserve tax – *contd*
exceptions—
inland bearer instruments, transactions concerning, FA 1986 s 97(3)
nominees of persons providing clearance services, transfers between, FA 1986 s 97(1), PR 24/10/86, PR 16/4/87, PR 16/2/89, PR 25/2/94
replacement securities, FA 1986 s 97AA
share exchanges, FA 1986 s 97(4), (5)
exchanges of shares, FA 1998 s 151
instalment arrangements
person liable for, FA 1986 s 96(6)–(8)
prescription of recognised clearing house, SI 1997/2429 reg 3
qualified dealer, relief for, FA 1986 s 96(3)
rates of charge, FA 1986 ss 96(2)–(5), (8)–(12)
relevant transaction, meaning, SI 1986/1711 reg 2
transfers of securities to or from members of LIFFE, SI 1997/2429 reg 5
transfers of securities to The London Clearing House, SI 1997/2429 reg 4
CLEARING HOUSE
See RECOGNISED CLEARING HOUSE
COLLECTIVE INVESTMENT SCHEME
interpretation, FSMA 2000 s 235
COMMISSION FOR THE NEW TOWNS
lease of house with right to buy, FA 1980 s 97, FA 1981 s 108
sale of house at discount, FA 1981 s 107
COMMISSIONERS OF INLAND REVENUE
adjudication powers. *See* ADJUDICATION
management of stamp duties, responsibility for, SDMA 1891 s 1
management of stamp duty reserve tax, responsibility for, FA 1986 s 86(2)
COMMON DEPOSIT SCHEME
exclusion from treatment as unit trust scheme, FA 1999 Sch 19 para 15(b)
COMMON INVESTMENT SCHEME
exclusion from treatment as unit trust scheme, FA 1999 Sch 19 para 15(a)
COMPANIES
associated, transfer of property between, exemption, FA 1930, s 42, FA 1967 s 27
connected—
grant of lease to, FA 2000 s 121
transfer of property to, FA 2000 s 119
reconstructions. *See* COMPANY RECONSTRUCTION
residence—
change of, compliance requirements, SP 2/90
place of, SP 1/90
stamp duty reserve tax, accountable person, SI 1986/1711 Sch para 108
subsidiaries, identification for national defence contribution, FA 1938 s 42, Sch 4 Part I
COMPANY RECONSTRUCTION
acquisition by one company of another—
relief from duty—
conditions for, FA 1986 ss 75(4), (5), 76(3), 77(1)
extent of, FA 1986 ss 75(2), 76(2), (4)–(6), 77(3)
open-ended investment companies, no relief, SI 1997/1156 reg 12

Stamp Taxes

COMPANY RECONSTRUCTION – *contd*
acquisition by one company of another – *contd*
relief from duty – *contd*
restriction of, FA 2002 s 112
withdrawal, FA 2002 s 113, Sch 35
relief from stamp duty reserve tax, FA 1986 ss 95(3), (4), 97(4), (5)

COMPULSORY PURCHASE
statutory powers, under—
collection of duty, FA 1895 s 12, FA 1949 s 36(4), FA 1991 s 114
harbour reorganisation schemes, FA 1966 s 45
transfers to local authority joint boards etc, exemption, FA 1952 s 74

CONSIDERATION
debt, ad valorem duty, SA 1891 s 57, FA 1980 s 102, SP 6/90
land—
exchange of other property for, FA 1994 s 241, PR 17/3/94, PR 18/4/94
not ascertainable from conveyance or lease, FA 1994 s 242
periodical payments, in, ad valorem duty, SA 1891 s 56
property conveyed in parts by separate instruments, ad valorem duty, SA 1891 s 58, FA 1991 s 112
securities, in, ad valorem duty, SA 1891 ss 6, 55
stock, in, ad valorem duty, SA 1891 ss 6, 55

CONSTITUENCY
reorganisation of, exemption for transfers on, F(No 2)A 1983 s 15

CONVEYANCE. ***See also*** **CONVEYANCE OR TRANSFER ON SALE**
other than on sale or mortgage—
charge of duty on, FA 1999 Sch 13 para 16
meaning, FA 1999 Sch 13 para 16

CONVEYANCE OR TRANSFER ON SALE
abolition of charge for property other than land, FA 1991 s 110, PR 19/3/91, PR 14/6/91
annuity, sale of, SA 1891, s 60
apportionment of charge for partially exempt transfers, FA 1991 s 111
certification of instrument at a particular amount, FA 1991 s 113
charge of stamp duty on, FA 1999 Sch 13 para 1
connected company, transfer to, FA 2000 s 119
consideration exceeding £10 million, FA 2002 s 115, Sch 36
subsales, FA 2002 Sch 36 paras 1–3
subsequent conveyance or transfer, FA 2002 Sch 36 paras 4–6
contracts or agreements chargeable as, FA 1999 Sch 13 paras 7–9
conveyance in contemplation of sale—
annuity reserved out of property, FA 1965 s 90(5)
assessment by Commissioners, requirement for, FA 1965 s 90(3)
instrument having dual purpose, FA 1965 s 90(4)
repayment of duty if sale aborted, FA 1965 s 90(2)
revesting of part of property in original owner, FA 1965 s 90(5)
treatment as conveyance on sale, FA 1965 s 90(1)
valuation of property conveyed, FA 1965 s 90(5)

CONVEYANCE OR TRANSFER ON SALE – *contd*
covenant by purchaser to make additions or improvement to property, FA 1900 s 10
debt, subject to. *See* DEBT
disadvantaged area, land situated in, FA 2001 ss 92, 92A, SI 2003/1056, PR 2/02, PR 13/3/03, SP 1/03
exchange of interests in land, treatment as, FA 1994 s 241, PR 17/3/94, PR 18/4/94
fixture, meaning, PR 8/02
foreclosure order treated as, FA 1898 s 6
government body, to, exemption, FA 1987 s 55
instrument certified at an amount, meaning, FA 1999 Sch 13 para 6
land. *See* LAND
meaning, FA 1999 Sch 13 para 1(2)
mortgaged property transferred for no consideration, SP 6/90
other property, consideration being or including, FA 2000 s 118
partially exempt transfers, apportionment of charge, FA 1991 s 111
penalty for late stamping, person liable for, SA 1891 s 15B
rates of duty on, FA 1997 s 49, FA 1998 ss 147, 149, FA 1999 Sch 13 paras 2–5
rents to mortgage mortgages scheme, FA 1993 s 202
rents to loans scheme (Scotland), FA 1993 s 203
Scotland, dispositions in, FA 1999 Sch 13 para 18
sub-sales, SA 1891 s 58

COUNCIL HOUSE. ***See*** **HOUSE**

COUNTERPART INSTRUMENT
rate of duty on, FA 1999 Sch 13 para 19

COUNTY COURT
proceedings for recovery of duty—
stamp duty land tax, FA 2003 Sch 12 para 5
stamp duty reserve tax, SI 1986/1711 Sch para 66

COURT OF SESSION
stamp duties—
appeal against Commissioners' assessment, SA 1891 ss 13, 122(2)
assessment by, SA 1891 ss 13(3), 122(2)
proceedings to recover duty from payee, SDMA 1891 s 2
stamp duty land tax, recovery of, FA 2003 Sch 12 para 6
stamp duty reserve tax—
determinations, appeals against, SI 1986/1711 reg 8(3), 10
penalties—
determination of, SI 1986/1711 Sch para 100D
hearing of appeals against, SI 1986/1711 Sch para 53
unpaid, proceedings for recovery, SI 1986/1711 Sch para 68(2)

CROWN
lease or conveyance to, exemption, FA 1987 s 55
property of, application of stamp duties, SA 1891 s 119
stamp duty land tax provisions, application of, FA 2003 s 106

DEALING IN STAMPS
forged, SDMA 1891 ss 13–19

DEATH
appropriation of property to satisfy legacies, FA 1985 s 84(4), (8), (9), SI 1987/516 Sch
intestacy, appropriations on, FA 1985 s 84(5)–(9), SI 1987/516 Sch
variation of dispositions on, exemption, FA 1985 s 84(1)–(3), SI 1987/516 Sch
DEBENTURE. *See also* SECURITIES; STOCK
abolition of duties, FA 1990 ss 108, 111, PR 20/3/90
DEBT
consideration, as, calculation of duty, SA 1891 s 57, FA 1980 s 102, SP 6/90
mortgaged properties, conveyance of, SP 6/90
DECLARATION
adjudication by Commissioners, for, SA 1891 s 12A(3)(4)
statutory, manner of making, SDMA 1891 s 24
DECLARATION OF TRUST
rate of duty on, FA 1999 Sch 13 para 17
DEPOSITARY RECEIPTS
meaning, FA 1986 ss 69(1), (2), 94(1), (2), 99(7), (8)
stamp duties—
abolition of charge on instruments of transfer, FA 1990 ss 108(8), 111, PR 20/3/90
clearance system, transfers to and from, FA 1986 s 72A
nominee companies, transfers to, PR 24/10/86, PR 14/6/89, PR 25/2/94
notification to Commissioners—
abolition of requirement for, FA 1990 ss 109(4), (5), 111, PR 20/3/90
company issuing shares, by, FA 1986 s 68(3), (5)
person having business of holding relevant securities, by, FA 1986 s 68(2), (4)
person issuing depositary receipts, by, FA 1986 s 68(1), (4)
penalties for non-compliance with notification requirements, FA 1986 s 68(4), (5)
relevant securities, meaning, FA 1986 s 69(3)
rates of duty on instrument of transfer, FA 1986 s 67(2)–(5), (9), 69(4)–(8)
transferee, conditions as to, FA 1986 s 67(6)–(8)
stamp duty reserve tax—
abolition of charge to, FA 1990 ss 110, 111, PR 20/3/90
accountable date, meaning, SI 1986/1711 reg 2
accountable person, meaning, SI 1986/1711 reg 2
agreements subject to, FA 1986 s 93(1)–(3)
chargeable securities, meaning, FA 1986 s 99(3)–(6), (6A), (10)–(12)
clearance system, transfers to and from, FA 1986 s 97A
credit for stamp duty, FA 1986 s 93(7)
exceptions—
inland bearer instruments, transactions concerning, FA 1986 s 95(2)
replacement securities, FA 1986 s 95A
share exchanges, FA 1986 s 95(3), (4)
DEPOSITARY RECEIPTS – *contd*
stamp duty reserve tax – *contd*
exceptions – *contd*
transfers between nominees of persons issuing depositary receipts, FA 1986 s 95(1), PR 24/10/86, PR 14/6/89, PR 25/2/94
exchanges of shares, FA 1998 s 151
person liable for, FA 1986 s 93(8)–(10)
qualified dealers, relief for, FA 1986 s 93(5)
rates of charge, FA 1986 ss 93(4)–(7), (10), 94(3)–(9)
relevant transaction, meaning, SI 1986/1711 reg 2.
DETERMINATION
stamp duty reserve tax, of, by Board—
appeals against, SI 1986/1711 reg 8
evidence, status as, SI 1986/1711 reg 16(1)
notice of, SI 1986/1711 reg 6, Sch para 114
penalty, amount of, SI 1986/1711 reg Sch paras 100, 100A
DEVELOPMENT BOARD FOR RURAL WALES
lease of house with right to buy, FA 1980 s 97
DEVELOPMENT CORPORATION
lease of house with right to buy, FA 1980 s 97, FA 1981 s 108
sale of house at discount, FA 1981 s 107
DIE
discontinuance of, SDMA 1891 s 22, RA 1898 s 10
fraud and forgery offences—
penalty, SDMA 1891 s 13
search powers, SDMA 1891 s 16, RA 1898 s 12
specific offences, SDMA 1891 s 13
meaning of, SDMA 1891 s 27
DILIGENCE
Scotland, recovery of unpaid duty
stamp duty land tax, FA 2003 Sch 12 para 3
stamp duty reserve tax, SI 1986/1711 Sch paras 63, 64
DISADVANTAGED AREAS
stamp duty exemption, FA 2001 s 92, SI 2003/1056, PR 2/02, PR 13/3/03, SP 1/03
non-residential property, removal of exemption for, FA 2004 s 96, Sch 9
residential property, restriction of exemption for, FA 2001 ss 92A, 92B
stamp duty land tax provisions—
annual rent, meaning, FA 2003 Sch 6 para 12
land partly in, FA 2003 Sch 6 paras 7–10
land wholly in, FA 2003 Sch 6 paras 3–6
meaning, FA 2003 Sch 6 para 1
relevant consideration, FA 2003 Sch 6 para 11(1)
relevant rental value, FA 2003 Sch 6 para 11(2)
relief for, FA 2003 s 57, SP 1/04
rent, meaning, FA 2003 Sch 6 para 12
sale and leaseback arrangements, FA 2003 s 57A
stamp duty regulations, continuation of, FA 2003 Sch 6 para 2
DISPOSITION
Scotland, in,—
mortis causa, exemption, FA 1999 Sch 13 para 24(c)

DISPOSITION – *contd*
Scotland, in, – *contd*
rate of duty on, FA 1999 Sch 13 para 18
DISTRAINT
fees, costs and charges, SI 1999/3263
recovery of unpaid duty, for—
stamp duty land tax, FA 2003 Sch 12 para 2
stamp duty reserve tax, SI 1986/1711 Sch para 61
DIVISION OF PROPERTY
land—
charge on, FA 1994 s 241, FA 1999 Sch 13 para 21 PR 17/3/94, PR 18/4/94
rate of duty—
equality money exceeding £100, FA 1999 Sch 13 para 21(1)
property other than land, abolition of charge, FA 1991 s 110, PR 19/3/91, PR 14/6/91
DIVORCE
transfers in connection with, exemption, FA 1985 s 83 SI 1987/516 Sch
DOCUMENT. *See* INSTRUMENT
DOUBLE STAMP DUTY
relief from, FA 1998 s 150
DUPLICATE INSTRUMENT
rate of duty on, FA 1999 Sch 13 para 19
DUTY
conveyance or transfer on sale, rate of, FA 1997 s 49
meaning, SDMA 1891 s 27
DWELLING. *See* HOUSE

EDUCATIONAL INSTITUTIONS
amalgamation etc, rate of duty, ESC G4
ELECTRICITY
privatisation, transfers on, exemptions—
Northern Ireland, F(No 2)A 1992 Sch 17 paras 1, 9, SI 1992/232
ELECTRONIC TRANSFER SYSTEM
transfer of securities to members of, FA 1986 s 88(1A), FA 1996 s 172
EMPLOYEE SHARE OWNERSHIP PLAN
exemptions from duty, FA 2000 Sch 8 para 116A
EUROPEAN INVESTMENT BANK
exemption for instruments issued and stock transfers, FA 1984 s 126, FA 1985 s 96
EUROPEAN SINGLE CURRENCY
Euroconversion—
capital payment on, SI 1998/3177 reg 24
chargeable securities, replacement of, SI 1998/3177 reg 26
definition, SI 1998/3177 reg 3
stock, replacement of, SI 1998/3177 reg 25
transferee, payment or benefit received by, SI 1998/3177 regs 27, 28
renominalisation—
new minimum denomination, resulting in, SI 1998/3177 reg 29
chargeable securities held or traded in, SI 1998/3177 reg 30
EVIDENCE
stamp duties—
documents not properly stamped, admissibility, SA 1891 s 14
fraudulent conduct, in case of, FA 1999 Sch 18 para 3
insurance contract under Merchant Shipping Act 1894 s 506, admissibility, FA 1959 s 30(6)
EVIDENCE – *contd*
stamp duty reserve tax—
determination, notice of, SI 1986/1711 reg 16(1)
penalties, for, SI 1986/1711 Sch paras 101, 105
EXCISE DUTIES
labels, offences relating to, SDMA 1891 s 23
EXCISE LICENCES
frauds in manufacture of paper SDMA 1891 s 16, RA 1898 s 12
EXEMPT INSTRUMENT
certification of, FA 1985 s 87, SI 1987/516
types of, SI 1985/1688, SI 1987/516 Sch
EXEMPTIONS
allied headquarters, building etc contracts, FA 1960 s 74
associated companies, transfers of property between FA 1930 s 42, FA 1967 s 27
authorised unit trusts—
direction to hold property on other trusts, transfer by means of, FA 1997 s 101
bodies corporate, associated, transfers of property between, FA 1930 s 42, FA 1967 s 27
building society instruments, BSA 1896 s 109
charity, transfer or lease to, FA 1982 s 129
constituency reorganisation, transfers on, F(No 2)A 1983 s 15
death, variation of dispositions on, FA 1985 s 84, SI 1987/516 Sch
disadvantaged areas, FA 2001 s 92, SI 2003/1056, SP 1/03, PR 2/02, PR 13/3/03
stamp duty land tax relief, FA 2003 s 57, Sch 6
dispositions mortis causa (Scotland), FA 1999 Sch 13 para 24(c)
divorce or separation, transfers on, FA 1985 s 83, SI 1987/516 Sch
electricity, transfers on privatisation, F(No 2)A 1992 Sch 17 paras 1, 9, SI 1992/232
European Investment Bank, instruments issued and stock transfers, FA 1984 s 126, FA 1985 s 96
gifts during lifetime, FA 1985 s 82, SI 1987/516 Sch
government body, lease or conveyance to, FA 1987 s 55
government stocks, transfer of, FA 1999 Sch 13 para 24(a)
harbour reorganisation schemes, FA 1966 s 45
hire purchase agreements, FA 1907 s 7
Historic Buildings and Monuments Commission, transfers to, FA 1983 s 46
insurance companies, instrument executed for demutualisation purposes, FA 1997 s 96
Inter-American Development Bank, instruments relating to, FA 1976 s 131, FA 1986 s 79(3)
International Bank for Reconstruction and Development, stock of, FA 1951 s 42
international organisation, instruments issued and stock transfers, FA 1984 s 111, FA 1984 s 126, FA 1985 s 96, FA 1986 s 79(3)
legal aid applications, FA 1963 s 65 (3)
lighthouses, instruments relating to, MSA 1894 s 731

EXEMPTIONS – *contd*
liquidation, conveyance to shareholders on, SI 1987/516 Sch
loan capital, certain instruments relating to, FA 1986, ss 79, 90(3E), (3F), (8), (9)
local authority, joint board etc, transfers to, FA 1952 s 74
maintenance fund for historic buildings, transfer to, FA 1980 s 98
market maker, transactions in ordinary course of business, FA 1986 ss 81, 82, 89
Merchant Shipping Act 1894, instruments under, MSA 1894 s 721
National Debt Commissioners, gift to, FA 1928 s 30(4)
national heritage bodies, transfers to, FA 1982 s 129
National Savings Committee, bonds etc of affiliated bodies, FA 1953 s 31
nationalisation schemes—
documents connected with, FA 1946 s 52
transfer of stocks etc under, FA 1948 s 74
NATO military establishments, buildings etc contracts, FA 1960 s 74
OECD support fund, FA 1986 s 79(3)
parliamentary stocks, transfer of, FA 1999 Sch 13 para 24(a)
renounceable letters of allotment, FA 1986 s 90(3B), FA 1999 Sch 13 para 24(*d*)
repurchases, FA 1986 ss 80C, 88(1C), (1D), 89AA
sale and leaseback arrangement, FA 2003 s 57A
Scottish Savings Committee, bonds etc of affiliated bodies, FA 1953 s 31
seamen's wages, assignments to representative bodies, FA 1944 s 45
shares registered in overseas branch register, CA 1985 Sch 14 para 8
ship, instruments for sale or transfer, FA 1999 Sch 13 para 24(*b*)
stock exchange nominees, transfers to, FA 1976 s 127, FA 1986 s 88(1), FA 1989 s 175
stock lending, FA 1986 ss 80C, 88(1C), (1D), 89AA
stock transfers—
executor's assent, transfer by person to himself, ESC G3
government, FA 1999 Sch 13 para 24(a)
guaranteed by Treasury, FA 1947 s 57
International Bank for Reconstruction and Development, FA 1951 s 42
intermediary, to, FA 1986 ss 80A, 80B, 88A, 88B
nationalisation scheme, under, FA 1948 s 74
parliamentary, FA 1999 Sch 13 para 24(a)
recognised clearing house, to, FA 1986 ss 84(3), 88(1)
recognised investment exchange, to, FA 1986 ss 84(2), 88(1)
repurchases, FA 1986 ss 80C, 88(1C), (1D), 89AA
stock lending, FA 1986 ss 80C, 88(1C), (1D), 89AA
testaments, FA 1999 Sch 13 para 24(c)
transfer of property subject to trusts of authorised unit trust, FA 1997 s 101
trust, transfer of property to, FA 1928 s 30(4)

EXEMPTIONS – *contd*
unit trusts, mergers of authorised, FA 1997 ss 95, 100, PR 9/5/96, PR 26/11/96
visiting forces, building etc contracts, FA 1960 s 74

FINES. *See* PENALTIES
FORECLOSURE
order for—
ad valorem duty on, FA 1898 s 6
conveyance on sale, FA 1898 s 6
FOREIGN CURRENCY
ad valorem duty on instrument in respect of, calculation, SA 1891 s 6, FA 1985 s 88
bearer instruments for stock in, exemption, FA 1987 s 50(1), (3), FA 1999 Sch 15 para 17
FORGERY
meaning, SDMA 1891 s 27
stamps, in connection with—
offences, SDMA 1891 s 13
penalties, SDMA 1891 s 13
search powers in relation to, SDMA 1891 ss 16, 18, RA 1898 s 12
seizure powers in relation to, SDMA 1891 ss 17, 19
FRAUD
alteration, printing or removal of stamps, SDMA 1891 ss 13–19, SA 1891 s 9, RA 1898 s 7(5)
duties, in relation to, SDMA 1891 s 21
excise licences, in relation to, SDMA 1891 s 16, RA 1898 s 12

GIFT
lifetime, exemption, FA 1985 s 82, SI 1987/516 Sch
GILT STRIPPING
power to make regulations, FA 1996 s 202
GOODWILL
abolition of duty on instruments relating to, FA 2002 s 116, Sch 37
GOVERNMENT BODY
lease or conveyance to, exemption, FA 1987 s 55
GOVERNMENT STOCK
transfer of, exemption, FA 1987 s 50, FA 1999 Sch 13 para 24(*a*)
GRANT OF REPRESENTATION
application for, examination of original documents, PR 28/2/78
GROUP OF COMPANIES
lease between members of—
relief from duty, PR 29/11/94
VAT, potentially subject to, PR 4/3/92
transfer of property between members, relief for, SP 3/98
determination, collection and recovery of duty and interest, FA 2002 Sch 34 para 7
exempt acquisition, FA 2002 Sch 34 para 4
information, power to require, FA 2002 Sch 34 para 10
interest on duty, FA 2002 Sch 34 para 5
recovery from another group company or controlling director, FA 2002 Sch 34 paras 8, 9
transferee company, notification of particulars by, FA 2002 Sch 34 para 6
transferor company leaving group, FA 2002 Sch 34 para 2
winding-up, FA 2002 Sch 34 para 3
withdrawal, FA 2002 s 111, Sch 34

GUARDIAN
child or incapacitated person, of, accountability for stamp duty reserve tax, SI 1986/1711 Sch paras 72, 73

HARBOUR REORGANISATION SCHEMES
stamp duties—
proceedings to recover duty from payee, SDMA 1891 s 2
stamp duty reserve tax—
determinations, appeals against, SI 1986/1711 regs 8(3), 10
penalties—
determination of, SI 1986/1711 Sch para 100D
hearing of appeals against, SI 1986/1711 Sch para 53
unpaid, proceedings for recovery, SI 1986/1711 Sch para 68

HIRE PURCHASE AGREEMENT
exemption, FA 1907 s 7

HISTORIC BUILDINGS AND MONUMENTS COMMISSION
agreement to transfer securities to, stamp duty reserve tax exemption, FA 1986 s 90(7)
exempt transfers to, FA 1982 s 129, FA 1983 s 46

HOUSE
lease with right to buy—
housing authority etc, grant by, FA 1980 s 97, FA 1981 s 108, FA 1993 ss 202, 203
private sector landlord, grant by, FA 1987 s 54
sale at discount by housing authority etc, FA 1981 s 107

HOUSE OF COMMONS RESOLUTION
temporary statutory effect—
stamp duties, FA 1973 s 50, F(No 2)A 1975 s 72
stamp duty reserve tax, PCTA 1968 s 1

HOUSING ACTION TRUST
lease of house with right to buy, FA 1980 s 97, FA 1981 s 108
sale of house at discount, FA 1981 s 107

HOUSING ASSOCIATION
lease of house with right to buy, FA 1980 s 97 FA 1981 s 108
sale of house at discount, FA 1981 s 107

HOUSING CORPORATION
sale of house at discount, FA 1981 s 107

HOUSING FOR WALES
sale of house at discount, FA 1981 s 107

INDEMNITY
stamp duty liability, as to, void, SA 1891 s 117

INFORMATION
disclosure by Revenue—
other persons, to, FA 1989 s 182
unlawful, FA 1989 s 182
Revenue powers to require, stamp duty reserve tax—
generally, FA 1989 s 177, SI 1986/1711 reg 5
issuing houses, returns by, SI 1986/1711 Sch para 25
nominee shareholders, from, SI 1986/1711 Sch para 26
registers of securities, SI 1986/1711 Sch para 23
stockbrokers, returns by, SI 1986/1711 Sch para 25

INSPECTION
records held by public officers, Commissioners' powers of—
generally, SA 1891 s 16
stamp duty reserve tax, Revenue powers, SI 1986/1711 reg 15, Sch para 111

INSTRUMENT
apprenticeship, of, meaning, SA 1891 s 25
certification as being of a particular kind, FA 1985 s 87, SI 1987/516
circumstances affecting liability to be set out in, SA 1891 s 5
counterpart, duty on, FA 1999 Sch 13 para 19
denoting of duty paid—
method of, FA 1993 s 204
related instrument, on, SA 1891 s 11
duplicate, duty on, FA 1999 Sch 13 para 19
late stamping of—
interest charge, SA 1891 s 15A, FA 1994 s 240(2); SI 1986/1297 reg 3
penalty, SA 1891 s 15B, FA 1994 s 240(3)
lost, allowance for stamp duty, SDMA 1891 s 12A, ESC G1, ESC G2
meaning, SDMA 1891 s 27
Northern Ireland, production of documents in, SI 1996/2348
not properly stamped, admissibility as evidence, SA 1891 s 14
principal, determination of, SA 1891 s 61
several matters, relating to, separate charge for each matter, SA 1891 s 4
spoiled, allowance for stamp duty, SDMA 1891 s 12A, ESC G2
stamping, manner of—
generally, SA 1891 s 3, FA 1993 s 204
instruments representing paired shares, FA 1988 s 143(9)

INSURANCE COMPANY
demutualisation, FA 1997 s 96
stamp duty land tax exemption, FA 2003 s 63

INSURANCE POLICY
contract under Merchant Shipping Act 1894 s 506, admissibility in evidence, FA 1959 s 30(6)

INTELLECTUAL PROPERTY
instruments relating to, abolition of stamp duty, FA 2000 s 129, Sch 34

INTER-AMERICAN DEVELOPMENT BANK
instruments relating to, exemption, FA 1976 s 131, FA 1986 s 79(3)

INTEREST ON TAX REPAID
payments of, FA 1999 s 110
stamp duties, following appeal, FA 1965, s 91
stamp duty land tax, FA 2003 s 89
stamp duty reserve tax, FA 1989 s 178, SI 1986/1711 reg 11, SI 1989/1297

INTEREST ON UNPAID TAX
stamp duties, rate of, SA 1891 s 15A; SI 1986/1297 reg 3
stamp duty land tax, FA 2003 s 87
stamp duty reserve tax—
disallowance of relief for, SI 1986/1711 Sch para 90
rate of, SI 1986/1711 Sch para 86, SI 1989/1297
recovery of, SI 1986/1711 Sch para 69

INTERMEDIARY
transfer of stock to, stamp duty exemption, FA 1986 ss 80A, 80B, 88A, 88B

INTERNATIONAL BANK FOR RECONSTRUCTION AND DEVELOPMENT
transfers of stock of, exemption, FA 1951 s 42
INTERNATIONAL ORGANISATION
exemption for instruments issued and stock transfers, FA 1984 s 126, FA 1985 s 96, FA 1986 s 79(3)
INTESTACY
appropriations on, exempt instruments, FA 1985 s 84(5)–(9), SI 1987/516 Sch
INVESTMENT COMPANY
open-ended. *See* OPEN-ENDED INVESTMENT COMPANIES
INVESTMENT EXCHANGE *See* RECOGNISED INVESTMENT EXCHANGE

LAND
consideration for—
not ascertainable from conveyance or lease, FA 1994 s 242
other property, in, FA 1994 s 241, PR 17/3/94, PR 18/4/94
VAT, inclusive of, SP 11/91, PR 4/3/92
division of, FA 1994 s 241, FA 1999 Sch 13 para 21, PR 17/3/94, PR 18/4/94
easement granted for no consideration, exempt instrument, SI 1987/516 Sch
exchange of other property for, FA 1994 s 241, PR 17/3/94, PR 18/4/94
lease of. *See* LEASE OR TACK
new building on, separate contracts for land and construction work, SP 8/93, PR 12/7/93
partition of, FA 1994 s 241, FA 1999 Sch 13 para 21, PR 17/3/94, PR 18/4/94
release or renunciation of, FA 1999 Sch 13 para 22
sale of—
documents, production in Northern Ireland, SI 1996/2348
information requirements on transferee—
information to be provided, FA 1931 Sch 2
instrument of transfer to be produced to Commissioners, FA 1931 s 28
instruments exempted from requirements, FA 1985 s 89, SI 1985/1688, SI 1987/516
Northern Ireland, FA 1994 ss 244, 245, SI 1996/2348
surrender, FA 1999 Sch 13 para 23
VAT on, consideration for stamp duty purposes. *See* VAT
LANDS TRIBUNAL
stamp duty land tax, matters determined as to, FA 2003 Sch 17 para 2
stamp duty reserve tax appeals, SI 1986/1711 reg 8(4)–(4B)
LEASE OR TACK
abandonment of, penal rent for, SA 1891 s 77(1)
agreement for—
lease, charged as, FA 1999 Sch 13 para 14
lease giving effect to, FA 1994 s 240A(2)
stamping, requirements for, FA 1994 s 240
subsequent grant of lease, FA 1984 s 111

LEASE OR TACK – *contd*
agreement for – *contd*
term exceeding 35 years, duty to be noted on actual lease, FA 1984 s 111
treatment as actual lease, FA 1891 s 75(1)
assignment, FA 2003 Sch 17A paras 11, 12, 17
loan or deposit in connection with, FA 2003 Sch 17A para 18A
basis of assessment of duty, Extract from Controller of Stamps' letter (2/1/63)
charge of stamp duty on, FA 1999 Sch 13 para 10
commencing prior to execution date, PR 2/1/63
connected company, grant to, FA 2000 s 121
consideration for—
not ascertainable from conveyance or lease, FA 1994 s 242
other property, in, FA 1994, s 241, PR 17/3/94, PR 18/4/94
VAT inclusive of, SP 11/91, PR 4/3/92
covenant by lessee to make improvements or additions to property, SA 1891 s 77(2), RA 1909 s 8
disadvantaged area, land situated in, FA 2001 s 92, SI 2003/1056, SP 1/03, PR 2/02, PR 13/3/03
residential property, restriction of exemption for, FA 2001 ss 92A, 92B
duly stamped, treatment as, FA 1994 s 240A
duration, reference to, AF 1999 Sch 18 para 4
exactly seven years, for, stamp duty on rental element, PR 17/9/99
exchange of other property for, FA 1994 s 241, PR 17/3/94, PR 18/4/94
fixed term, for, FA 2003 Sch 17A para 2
fixed term and then until determined, charge on, FA 1999 Sch 13 para 15
future rent increases in line with RPI, clause in lease as to, effect on duty, PR 8/1/97
government body, to, exemption, FA 1987 s 55
grant of—
information requirements on lessee—
information to be provided, FA 1931 Sch 2
instrument granting lease to be produced to Commissioners, FA 1931 s 28
instruments exempted from requirements, FA 1985 s 89, SI 1987/516
Northern Ireland, FA 1994 ss 244, 245, SI 1996/2348
loan or deposit in connection with, FA 2003 Sch 17A para 18A
indexed rent levels, with, PR 14/5/99
group companies, between—
relief from duty, PR 29/11/94
VAT, potentially subject to, PR 4/3/92
house, of, with right to buy, FA 1980 s 97, FA 1981 s 108, FA 1987 s 54, FA 1993 ss 202, 203
indefinite term, for, FA 2003 Sch 17A para 4
meaning, FA 2003 s 120, Sch 17A para 1
penal rent for, FA 1891 s 77(1)
penalty for late stamping—
agreement and lease presented simultaneously, FA 1994 s 240(1)
premium on. *See* PREMIUM

Stamp Taxes

LEASE OR TACK – *contd*
rates of duty on, FA 1999 Sch 13 paras 11–14
premium, SA 1891 s 56,
rent, FA 2003 Sch 17A paras 6–9, 13–15
rent not fixed for whole term, PR 2/1/63, PR 8/1/97
reverse premium, FA 2003 Sch 17A para 18
sale of lease for seven years or more, requirements on lessee—
information to be provided, FA 1931 Sch 2
instrument of transfer to be produced to Commissioners, FA 1931 s 28
instruments exempted from requirements, FA 1985 s 89
transitional provisions, FA 2000 Sch 32
Scotland, in, FA 2003 Sch 17A para 19
SDLT treatment of, FA 2003 Sch 17A
stamping, requirements for, FA 1994 s 240
successive linked, FA 2003 Sch 17A para 5
surrender of—
agreement for, FA 1994 s 243
new lease, in return for, FA 2003 Sch 17A para 16
penal rent for, SA 1891 s 77(1)
Scotland, in, FA 2000 s 128
tenant's obligations, FA 2003 Sch 17A para 10
variation of duty, SI 2001/3746
VAT on, consideration for stamp duty purposes. *See* VAT

LEGAL AID
application for, exemption, FA 1963 s 65 (3)

LEGAL PROCEEDINGS
recovery of stamp duty, for, SDMA 1891 s 2

LIGHTHOUSE
instruments relating to, exemption, MSA 1894 s 731

LIMITED LIABILITY PARTNERSHIP
incorporation, stamp duty exemption, LLA 2000 s 12
incorporation, stamp duty land tax exemption, FA 2003 s 65

LIMITED PARTNERSHIP SCHEME
exclusion from definition of unit trust scheme, SI 1988/268
meaning, SI 1988/268 reg 2

LIQUIDATION
conveyance of company's assets to shareholder, exempt instrument, SI 1987/516 Sch

LOAN CAPITAL
abolition of charge on instruments of transfer, FA 1990 ss 108, 111, PR 20/3/90
convertible loan stock, duty on transfer, SP 3/84
exemptions for instruments relating to, FA 1986 ss 79, 90(3E), (3F), (8), (9)

LOCAL AUTHORITY
transfer of property to joint committee or joint board of, exemption, FA 1952 s 74

LOCAL HOUSING AUTHORITY
lease of house with right to buy, FA 1980 s 97, FA 1981 s 108, FA 1993 ss 202, 203
sale of house at discount, FA 1981 s 107

LONDON CLEARING HOUSE
stamp duty and stamp duty reserve tax reliefs—
agreements to make transfers, SI 1992/570 regs 7–9
authority for, FA 1991 ss 116, 117

LONDON CLEARING HOUSE – *contd*
stamp duty and stamp duty reserve tax reliefs – *contd*
prescription as recognised clearing house for, SI 1992/570 reg 3
transfers of securities, SI 1997/2429 reg 4
transfers to, SI 1992/570 reg 4

LONDON INTERNATIONAL FINANCIAL FUTURES AND OPTIONS EXCHANGE
formation from merger with London Traded Options Market, PR 18/10/91
stamp duty and stamp duty reserve tax reliefs—
agreements to make transfers, SI 1992/570 regs 7–9, PR 18/10/91
authority for, FA 1991 ss 116, 117
borrowings by, SI 1992/570 regs 6, PR 18/10/91
LIFFE (A & M), prescription as recognised investment exchange for, SI 1992/570 reg 3, PR 18/10/91
transfers of securities to or from members, SI 1997/2429 reg 5
transfers to, SI 1992/570 regs 5, 8, 9, PR 18/10/91

MAGISTRATES COURT
proceedings for recovery of unpaid stamp duty reserve tax, SI 1986/1711 Sch para 65

MAINTENANCE FUND FOR HISTORIC BUILDING
instrument transferring property to, exemption, FA 1980 s 98

MARKET MAKER
stamp duties exemptions—
sale transactions in ordinary course of business, FA 1986 s 81
stock lending transactions in ordinary course of business, FA 1986 s 82
stamp duty reserve tax exemption, agreements in ordinary course of business, FA 1986 s 89(1), (1A), (3), (5)

MARRIAGE. *See also* DIVORCE, SEPARATION OF SPOUSES
conveyance of property in consideration of, exempt instrument, SI 1987/516 Sch

MERCHANT SHIPPING ACT 1894
instruments under, exemption, MSA 1894 s 721
insurance contract under, admissibility as evidence, FA 1959 s 30 (6)

MORTGAGE
transfer of properties subject to—
sale, on, SA 1891 s 57, FA 1980 s 102, SP 6/90
without consideration, SP 6/90

NATIONAL DEBT COMMISSIONERS
instrument conveying gift of property to, exemption, FA 1928 s 30 (4)

NATIONAL DEFENCE CONTRIBUTION
subsidiaries, identification for purposes of, FA 1938 s 42, Sch 4 Part I

NATIONAL HERITAGE MEMORIAL FUND
agreement to transfer securities to, stamp duty reserve tax exemption, FA 1986 s 90(7)
exempt transfers, FA 1982 s 129, FA 1983 s 46

NATIONAL SAVINGS COMMITTEE
instruments made for purposes of affiliated bodies, exemption, FA 1953 s 31
NATIONALISATION SCHEME
documents connected with, exemption, FA 1946 s 52
transfers of stocks etc under, exemption, FA 1948 s 74
NATO. *See* NORTH ATLANTIC TREATY ORGANISATION
NAVY
wages, assignments to representative bodies, exemption, FA 1944 s 45
NEW TOWN COMMISSION
lease of house with right to buy, FA 1980 s 97, FA 1981 s 108
sale of house at discount, FA 1981 s 107
NON-PROFIT-MAKING BODIES
reconstruction or amalgamation, rate of duty, ESC G4
transfer of assets between, ESC G6
NON-RESIDENT
company—
compliance requirements on becoming, SP 2/90
test of, SP 1/90
stamp duty reserve tax liability, person accountable for, SI 1986/1711 Sch paras 78, 83
NORTH ATLANTIC TREATY ORGANISATION
military establishments, building etc contracts, exemption, FA 1960 s 74
NORTHERN IRELAND HOUSING EXECUTIVE
lease of house with right to buy, FA 1980 s 97, FA 1981 s 108
sale of house at discount, FA 1981 s 107
NULLITY OF MARRIAGE
transfers in connection with, exemption, FA 1985 s 83, SI 1987/516 Sch

OATH
manner of making, SDMA 1891 s 24, RA 1898 s 7(6)
OECD. *See* ORGANISATION FOR ECONOMIC CO-OPERATION AND DEVELOPMENT
OFF-SHORE TRUSTS
stamp duty, RI 174
OFFENCES
fraud in connection with duties, SDMA 1891 s 21
fraudulent printing of stamps, SDMA 1891 s 13(3)
fraudulent removal of stamps, SDMA 1891 s 13(4)
fraudulently altered, printed or removed stamps—
search powers in relation to, SDMA 1891 s 16, RA 1898 s 12
specific offences, SDMA 1891 s 13, SA 1891 s 9
omission of relevant facts from instrument, SA 1891 s 5
penalties for. *See* PENALTIES
public officers—
refusal to allow inspection of documents, SA 1891 s 16
registration etc of instrument not duly stamped, SA 1891 s 17
sale of fraudulently printed stamps, SDMA 1891 s 13(8)
OPEN-ENDED INVESTMENT COMPANIES
bearer shares issued in foreign currency, SI 1997/1156 reg 5
enactments applying to, FA 1995 s 152
OPEN-ENDED INVESTMENT COMPANIES – *contd*
exemption from stamp duty, SI 1997/1156 regs 7–9
exemption from stamp duty reserve tax, SI 1997/1156 regs 8, 10
modification of enactments relating to, SI 1997/1156 regs 4–4B
regulations, FA 1995 s 152
relaxation of tax rules following conversion from authorised unit trusts, PR 9/5/96, PR 26/11/96
shares held only within individual pension accounts—
stamp duty reserve tax, exclusion from charge, FA 2001 s 94
exclusion of company from description, SI 2001/964 reg 4
stamp duty land tax provisions applied to, FA 2003 s 102
transfer of property, SI 1997/1156 reg 11
unit trust schemes, SI 1997/1156 reg 3
amalgamation with, SI 2008/710 reg 4
conversion from, SI 2008/710 reg 3
mergers, PR 24/5/04
OPTIONS
saving device, use as, PR 10/02
ORGANISATION FOR ECONOMIC CO-OPERATION AND DEVELOPMENT
support fund, exemptions, FA 1986 s 79(3)

PAIRED SHARES
treatment for stamp duty and stamp duty reserve tax, FA 1986 s 99(6A), FA 1988 s 143
PARLIAMENTARY STOCK
transfer of, exemption, FA 1999 Sch 13 para 24(a)
PARTITION OF PROPERTY
land—
charge on, FA 1994 s 241, FA 1999 Sch 13 para 21 PR 17/3/94, PR 18/4/94
rate of duty—
equality money exceeding £100, FA 1999 Sch 13 para 21(1)
property other than land, abolition of charge, FA 1991 s 110, PR 19/3/91, PR 14/6/91
PARTNERSHIP
connected persons, meaning, FA 2003 Sch 15 para 39
lease, market value of, FA 2003 Sch 15 para 38
meaning, FA 2003 Sch 15 para 1
property, meaning, FA 2003 Sch 15 para 34
share, meaning, FA 2003 Sch 15 para 34
stamp duty land tax. *See* STAMP DUTY LAND TAX
transfer of chargeable interest, meaning, FA 2003 Sch 15 paras 35, 37
transfers of interests—
meaning, FA 2003 Sch 15 para 36
stamp duty on, FA 2003 Sch 15 paras 31, 32
withdrawal of money following, FA 2003 Sch 15 para 17A
PENALTIES
stamp duties—
allotment of shares, non-compliance with reporting requirements, CA 1985 s 88(5), (6)
bearer instruments—
amendments, FA 1999 Sch 17 paras 1–8

Stamp Taxes

PENALTIES – *contd*
stamp duties – *contd*
bearer instruments – *contd*
court proceedings, FA 1999 Sch 17 para 13
determination by officer of Commissioners, FA 1999 Sch 17 paras 10–12
false information provided, FA 1999 Sch 15 paras 25, 26
mitigation or compounding, FA 1999 Sch 17 para 14
blank transfers of stock, FA 1963 s 67(1), FA 1990 ss 109(3), 111
collection and recovery, SI 1999/2537
distraint, fees, costs and charges, SI 1999/3263
foreign securities, assignment etc unstamped, SA 1891 s 83, FA 1990 ss 109(1), 111
fraud in connection with duties, SDMA 1891 s 21
fraudulently printed, altered or removed stamps, SDMA 1891 s 13, SA 1891 s 9, RA 1898 s 7(5)
land, sale of, failure to provide information, FA 1931 s 28(1)
late stamping of instrument, for—
amount of, SA 1891 s 15B
instruments executed outside UK, SA 1891 s 15(3)(*a*)
mitigation of, SA 1891 s 15(3)(*b*), PR 29/5/91, PR 9/6/93
remission of, SA 1891 s 15B(4)
lease over seven years, failure to provide information, FA 1931 s 28(1)
omission of relevant facts from instrument, SA 1891 s 5
possession of fraudulently printed or altered stamps, SDMA 1891 s 13(9)
public officers—
refusal to allow inspection of documents, SA 1891 s 16
registration etc of instrument not duly stamped, SA 1891 s 17
recognised clearing house, failure to deliver accounts, FA 1970 s 33(5)
recognised investment exchange, failure to deliver accounts, FA 1970 s 33(5)
recovery of, FA 1999 Sch 17 paras 16–18
removal and reuse of adhesive stamps, SDMA 1891 s 13, SA 1891 s 9, RA 1898 s 7(5)
stock certificate unstamped, FA 1899 s 5, FA 1990 ss 109(2), 111
Taxes Management Act, provisions applying, SI 1999/2537
stamp duty land tax—
determinations, FA 2003 s 83, Sch 14
fraud or negligence as to self-certificate, for, FA 2003 Sch 11 para 3
general provisions, FA 2003 s 99
incorrect return—
assisting in preparation of, FA 2003 s 96
delivery of, FA 2003 Sch 10 para 8
interest on, FA 2003 s 88
records, failure to keep and preserve, FA 2003 Sch 10 para 11, Sch 11 para 6
return—
failure to deliver, FA 2003 Sch 10 paras 7–9
incorrect or uncorrected, delivery of, FA 2003 Sch 10 para 8

PENALTIES – *contd*
stamp duty reserve tax—
appeal against, SI 1986/1711 Sch paras 53, 100B
criminal proceedings, SI 1986/1711 Sch para 104
determination—
High Court, by, SI 1986/1711 Sch para 100D
Revenue, by, SI 1986/1711 Sch paras 100, 100A
Special Commissioners, by, SI 1986/1711 Sch para 100C
evidence for, SI 1986/1711 Sch paras 101, 105
mitigation of, SI 1986/1711 Sch para 102
notice for—
failure to give, SI 1986/1711 Sch para 93
incorrect, SI 1986/1711 Sch paras 95, 97
returns—
failure to make, SI 1986/1711 reg Sch para 98(1), (3), (4)
incorrect, SI 1986/1711 Sch para 98(2)
time limit for, SI 1986/1711 Sch para 103

PERSONAL REPRESENTATIVE
assent by, exemption, FA 2003 Sch 3 para 3A
grant of representation, application for, PR 28/2/78
stamp duty reserve tax, accountability for, SI 1986/1711 Sch para 74

POLICE AUTHORITY
sale of house at discount, FA 1981 s 107

POSTAL PACKET
stamps, fraudulently removed from, SA 1891 s 9, RA 1898 s 7(4)

PREMIUM
lease on—
lump sum—
periodical payments, rate of duty, SA 1891 s 56

PRIVATE FINANCE INITIATIVE PROJECTS
stamp duty land tax treatment, PR 19/12/03

PROVISIONAL COLLECTION OF TAXES
stamp duties, FA 1973 s 50, F(No 2)A 1975 s 72
stamp duty reserve tax, PCTA 1968 s 1

RATES OF DUTY
bearer instruments, FA 1999 Sch 15 paras 4–6
bonds, covenants etc increasing rent reserved by another instrument, FA 1999 Sch 13 para 20
conveyance or transfer on sale, FA 1999 Sch 13 paras 2–5
declaration of trust, FA 1999 Sch 13 para 17
duplicate or counterpart of instrument, FA 1999 Sch 13 para 19
lease, FA 1999 Sch 13 paras 11–13
premium, SA 1891 s 56,
partition or division of land—
equality money exceeding £100, SA 1891 s 7, FA 1999 Sch 13 para 21(1)
several instruments for, FA 1999 Sch 13 para 21(2)

RECOGNISED CLEARING HOUSE
agreement with Commissioners for composition of duty—
abolition of provisions for, FA 1990 ss 109(6), 111, PR 20/3/90
accounts required, FA 1970 s 33(2)(*c*)
certificates to be issued, FA 1970 s 33(2)(*b*)
penalty for late delivery of account, FA 1970 s 33(5)
remittance of duty to Commissioners, FA 1970 s 33(2)(*d*)
CC&G, prescription of, SI 2009/1832
clearance service. *See* CLEARANCE SERVICE
EuroCCP, prescription of, SI 2009/194, SI 2009/397, SI 2009/1115, SI 2009/1827
European Multilateral Clearing Facility NV, prescription of, SI 2009/1462, SI 2009/1601, SI 2009/1831, SI 2009/1832
LCH Clearnet Limited, prescription of, SI 2008/2777, SI 2008/3235, SI 2009/1462, SI 2009/1601, SI 2009/1827, SI 2009/1828
London Clearing House, prescription as, SI 1992/570 reg 3
meaning, FA 1970 s 33(1)
OM London Exchange Limited, prescription as, SI 1999/3262
reliefs for prescribed transactions by prescribed clearing houses—
agreements to make transfers, SI 1992/570 regs 7–9
authority for, FA 1991 ss 116, 117
London Clearing House, prescription for, SI 1992/570 reg 3
transfers to, SI 1992/570 reg 4
SIX X-CLEAR AG, prescription of, SI 2009/35, SI 2009/1344, SI 2009/1462, SI 2009/1601, SI 2009/1827, SI 2009/1831
transfers of stock to, exemption, FA 1986 ss 84(3), 88(1)
x-clear, SI 2008/52 reg 3

RECOGNISED INVESTMENT EXCHANGE
agreement with Commissioners for composition of duty—
abolition of provisions for, FA 1990 ss 109(6), 111, PR 20/3/90
accounts required, FA 1970 s 33(2)(*c*)
certificates to be issued, FA 1970 s 33(2)(*b*)
penalty for late delivery of account, FA 1970 s 33(5)
remittance of duty to Commissioners, FA 1970 s 33(2)(*d*)
Baikal Global Limited multilateral trading facility, prescription of, SI 2009/1832
BATS Trading Limited, prescription of, SI 2009/1462
Block Board, prescription of, SI 2009/1115
Borse Berlin AG, prescription of, SI 2008/2777
Chi-X Europe, prescription of, SI 2009/1601
Euro Millennium Multilateral Trading Facility, prescription of, SI 2009/35
extension of exceptions, FA 2002 s 117
Jiway Ltd, prescription as, SI 2000/2995
LIFFE (A & M), prescription as, SI 1992/570, SI 2009/1828
Liquidnet H2O Multilateral Trading Facility, prescription of, SI 2009/1344
meaning, FA 1970 s 33(1)

RECOGNISED INVESTMENT EXCHANGE – *contd*
NASDAQ OMX Europe Limited, prescription of, SI 2009/1831
NYSE Arca Europe, prescription of, SI 2009/397
OFEX, prescription as, SI 2002/1975
OM London Exchange Limited, prescription as, SI 1999/3262
PLUS Markets plc, prescription of, SI 2008/3235
prescription of, SI 1997/2429 reg 3
reliefs for prescribed transactions by prescribed exchanges—
agreements to make transfers, SI 1992/570, regs 7–9, PR 18/10/91
authority for, FA 1991 ss 116, 117
borrowings by, SI 1992/570, regs 6, PR 18/10/91
LIFFE (A & M), prescription as, SI 1992/570 reg 3, PR 18/10/91
transfers to, SI 1992/570 regs 5, 8, 9, PR 18/10/91
SmartPool Multilateral Trading Facility, prescription of, SI 2009/194
transfers of stock to, exemption, FA 1986 ss 84(2), 88(1)
Turquoise Services Limited, prescription of, SI 2009/1827

RECONSTRUCTION. *See* COMPANY RECONSTRUCTION

RECOVERY OF TAX
stamp duties—
payee, from, legal proceedings, SDMA 1891 s 2
penalties, FA 1999 Sch 17 paras 16–18
stamp duty land tax—
county court proceedings, FA 2003 Sch 12 para 5
Court of Session proceedings, FA 2003 Sch 12 para 6
court of summary jurisdiction, proceedings in, FA 2003 Sch 12 para 4
diligence, FA 2003 Sch 12 para 3
distraint, FA 2003 Sch 12 para 2
High Court proceedings, FA 2003 Sch 12 para 6
magistrates' court proceedings, FA 2003 Sch 12 para 4
sheriff court proceedings, FA 2003 Sch 12 para 5
tax demands and receipts, issue of, FA 2003 Sch 12 para 1
unpaid tax, evidence of, FA 2003 Sch 12 para 7
stamp duty reserve tax—
amounts determined but unpaid, SI 1986/1711 reg 12
county court proceedings, SI 1986/1711 Sch para 66
demand note for, SI 1986/1711 Sch para 60
diligence, Scotland, SI 1986/1711 Sch paras 63, 64
distraint, SI 1986/1711 Sch para 61
High Court proceedings, SI 1986/1711 Sch para 68
magistrates' court proceedings, SI 1986/1711 Sch para 65
over-repayments, SI 1986/1711 reg 18
Scottish court proceedings, SI 1986/1711 Sch paras 67, 68(2)
underpaid, SI 1986/1711 reg 13

REGISTERED SOCIAL LANDLORD
acquisitions by, stamp duty land tax relief, FA 2003 s 71

REGISTERED SOCIAL LANDLORD – *contd*
leases, exemption of certain, FA 2003 s 128
granted before s 128 takes effect, FA 2003 s 129
granted between 1 January 1990 and 27 March 2000, FA 2003 s 130
land tax, from, FA 2003 Sch 3 para 2
meaning, FA 2003 ss 121, 128(2)
sale of house at discount by, FA 1981 s 107
transfers to, FA 2000 s 130
RELIEFS
double stamp duty, FA 1998 s 150
RENT
instrument increasing, duty on, FA 1999 Sch 13 para 20
lease, under—
not fixed for whole term, PR 2/1/63
rate of duty, FA 1999 Sch 13 para 12
VAT on, SP 11/91 paras 9, 10, PR 18/2/92
RENTS TO LOANS SCHEME
purchase of residential property under (Scotland), FA 1993 s 203
RENTS TO MORTGAGES SCHEME
purchase of residential property under, FA 1993 s 202
REPAYMENT
stamp duty reserve tax—
conditions for, FA 1986 s 92
interest on, FA 1989 s 178, SI 1986/1711 reg 11
overpayment, following, SI 1986/1711 reg 14
over-repayment, recovery of, SI 1986/1711 reg 18
RESIDENCE
company—
change of, compliance requirements, SP 2/90
place of, tests determining, SP 1/90

SCOTTISH HOMES
sale of house at discount, FA 1981 s 107
SCOTTISH SAVINGS COMMITTEE
instruments made for purposes of affiliated bodies, exemption, FA 1953 s 31
SEAFARERS. *See* MERCHANT SHIPPING ACT 1894; NAVY
SEARCH POWERS
fraud and forgery offences in relation to, SDMA 1891 ss 16, 18, RA 1898 s 12
SECURITIES. *See also* SHARES; STOCK
abolition of charge on instruments of transfer, FA 1990 ss 108, 111, PR 20iiiincidental transactions, FA 2003 s 75B/3/90
clearance service. *See* CLEARANCE SERVICE
consideration in, calculation of ad valorem duty, SA 1891 ss 6, 55
depositary receipts. *See* DEPOSITARY RECEIPTS
foreign—
assignments etc of, failure to stamp, SA 1891 s 83, FA 1990 ss 109(1), 111
UK depositary interests in, FA 1999 s 119
marketable, charge to duty, FA 2003 s 125, Sch 20
meaning (simplified transfers), STA 1963 s 4(1)
nationalisation schemes, transfers under, exemption, FA 1948 s 74
registered, meaning (simplified transfers), STA 1963 s 1(4), 4(1)
SECURITIES – *contd*
simplified transfers. *See* STOCK
transfer. *See* TRANSFER OF SECURITIES
SEIZURE POWERS
stolen or fraudulently obtained stamps, SDMA 1891 ss 17, 19
SEPARATION OF SPOUSES
transfers in connection with, exemption, FA 1985 s 83, SI 1987/516 Sch
SERVICE OF DOCUMENTS
stamp duty reserve tax, SI 1986/1711 reg 19
SETTLEMENT
conveyance of property to satisfy beneficiary's interest, exempt instrument SI 1987/516 Sch
meaning, FA 2003 Sch 16 para 1
power of appointment, exercise of, FA 2003 Sch 16 para 7
trustees—
acquisitions by, FA 2003 Sch 16 para 4
discretion, exercise of, FA 2003 Sch 16 para 7
relevant, FA 2003 Sch 16 para 6
responsibility of, FA 2003 Sch 16 para 5
SHARES. *See also* SECURITIES; STOCK
abolition of charge on instruments of transfer, FA 1990 ss 108, 111, PR 20/3/90
allotment of—
assessment by Commissioners of duty payable, CA 1985 s 88(4)
non-compliance with reporting requirements, CA 1985 s 88(5), (6)
oral contract for, CA 1985 s 88(3)
return of, CA 1985 s 88(2)
clearance service. *See* CLEARANCE SERVICE
depositary receipts. *See* DEPOSITARY RECEIPTS
overseas branch register, in, deemed to be situated outside UK, CA 1985 Sch 14 para 8
paired, FA 1986 s 99(6A), FA 1988 s 143
purchase of own, by company, FA 1986 s 66
stamp duty on, PR 28/11/95
transfer—
accountable date, failure to stamp stock transfer form before, PR 16/1/97
adjudication of documents by Stamp Office, PR 16/1/97
overpayment of tax, refund of, PR 16/1/97
stamp duty reserve tax on, PR 16/1/97
unquoted, valuation, PR 4/10/78
SHIP
sale or transfer, exemption, SA 1891, Sch 1, FA 1999 Sch 13 para 24(b)
SPECIAL COMMISSIONERS
stamp duty land tax appeals. *See* APPEALS; STAMP DUTY LAND TAX
stamp duty reserve tax—
appeal hearings—
costs, award of, SI 1986/1711 Sch para 56C
jurisdiction, SI 1986/1711 Sch para 46A
out of time SI 1986/1711 reg 9
penalty, against, SI 1986/1711 Sch para 100B
procedure SI 1986/1711 reg 8, Sch para 56B
reports of decisions, SI 1986/1711 Sch para 56D

SPECIAL COMMISSIONERS – *contd*
stamp duty reserve tax – *contd*
penalties, determination of, SI 1986/1711 Sch para 100C
STAMP
adhesive—
removal and reuse, SA 1891 s 9
alternative methods of denoting duty, FA 1993 s 204
amount of, FA 1999 s 112(2)
denoting payment of duty on another instrument, SA 1891 s 11
excise labels, offences relating to, SDMA 1891 s 23
fraudulently altered, printed or removed—
offence, SDMA 1891 s 13, SA 1891 s 9
penalty, SDMA 1891 s 13, SA 1891 s 9, RA 1898 s 7(5)
search powers in relation to, SDMA 1891 s 16 RA 1898 s 12
meaning, SDMA 1891 s 27
misused, allowance for, SDMA 1891 ss 9, 11
spoiled, allowance for, SDMA 1891 ss 9, 11
STAMP DUTY
contingency principle, RI 174
conveyance or transfer on sale, FA 1998 ss 147, 149
method of denoting, provision for, FA 1993 s 204
off-shore declaration of trust, RI 174
power to vary, FA 2000 Sch 33, SI 2001/3746
provisions in FA 1994 ss 240–243, PR 8/95
stock or marketable securities, only chargeable on, FA 2003 s 125, Sch 20
unstamped documents, RI 174
STAMP DUTY LAND TAX
administration of, FA 2003 s 42(3)
regulations, SI 2003/2837
special arrangements, PR 12/11/03
amendment of provisions before implementation, FA 2003 s 112
amount of, FA 2003 s 55
rent, on, FA 2003 Sch 5
anti-avoidance—
incidental transactions, FA 2003 s 75B
notional transactions, FA 2003 s 75C
scheme transactions, FA 2003 s 75A
appeals. *See* APPEALS
assessment, FA 2003 s 83
appeals and reviews, FA 2003 Sch 10 paras 35–46
excessive, relief in case of, FA 2003 Sch 10 paras 33, 34
Revenue, FA 2003 Sch 10 paras 28–32
building society demutualisation, exemption, FA 2003 s 64
charge to, FA 2003 s 42
chargeable consideration, FA 2003 s 50
annuities, FA 2003 s 52
contingent, FA 2003 s 51(1), (3)
application to defer payment, FA 2003 s 90
cessation, adjustment on, FA 2003 s 80
debt as, FA 2003 Sch 4 para 8
employment, transaction by reason of, FA 2003 Sch 4 para 12
exchanges, for, FA 2003 Sch 4 para 5
foreign currency, in, FA 2003 Sch 4 para 9
indemnity by purchaser, FA 2003 Sch 4 para 16
just and reasonable apportionment, FA 2003 Sch 4 para 4

STAMP DUTY LAND TAX – *contd*
chargeable consideration, FA 2003 s 50 – *contd*
money or money's worth, FA 2003 Sch 4 para 1
non-monetary, valuation of, FA 2003 Sch 4 para 7
obligations under lease, excluded, FA 2003 Sch 4 para 13
partition or division, on, FA 2003 Sch 4 para 6
postponed, FA 2003 Sch 4 para 3
public or educational bodies, arrangements involving, FA 2003 Sch 4 para 17
rent to mortgage or rent to loan, FA 2003 Sch 9 para 6
rent to shared ownership lease, FA 2003 Sch 9 para 13
rent to shared ownership trust, FA 2003 Sch 9 para 14
reverse premium, FA 2003 Sch 4 para 15
services, provision of, FA 2003 Sch 4 para 11
surrender of lease in return for new lease, FA 2003 Sch 4 para 14
twelve years' payments, limited to, FA 2003 s 52
uncertain or unascertained, FA 2003 s 51(2)(3)
application to defer payment, FA 2003 s 90
ascertainment, adjustment on, FA 2003 s 80
value added tax, including, FA 2003 Sch 4 para 2
works, carrying out, FA 2003 Sch 4 para 10
chargeable interest—
creation, surrender, release or variation of, FA 2003 s 43(3)
exempt, FA 2003 s 48(2)
meaning, FA 2003 s 48(1)
claims not included in returns, FA 2003 Sch 11A
collection and recovery of, FA 2003 s 91
collective enfranchisement by leaseholders, on, FA 2003 s 74
commencement of provisions, FA 2003 Sch 19
company, provisions applied to, FA 2003 s 100
compulsory purchase facilitating development, exemption, FA 2003 s 60
consequential amendments, FA 2003 Sch 18
criminal proceedings, effect of offer of settlement, FA 2003 s 98
crofting community right to buy, on, FA 2003 s 75
Crown, application to, FA 2003 s 107
definitions, FA 2003 ss 121, 122
disadvantaged areas—
annual rent, meaning, FA 2003 Sch 6 para 12
land partly in, FA 2003 Sch 6 paras 7–10
land wholly in, FA 2003 Sch 6 paras 3–6
meaning, FA 2003 Sch 6 para 1
relevant consideration, FA 2003 Sch 6 para 11(1)
relevant rental value, FA 2003 Sch 6 para 11(2)
relief for, FA 2003 s 57, SP 1/04
rent, meaning, FA 2003 Sch 6 para 12
sale and leaseback arrangements, FA 2003 s 57A

STAMP DUTY LAND TAX – *contd*
land transaction returns, FA 2003 s 76 – *contd*
determination in default of, FA 2003 Sch 10 paras 25–27
disclosure of information contained in, FA 2003 s 78A
enquiry into, FA 2003 Sch 10 paras 12–24
failure to deliver, FA 2003 Sch 10 paras 3–5
filing date, FA 2003 Sch 10 para 2
form and content, SI 2003/2837 reg 9, Sch 2
incorrect—
assisting in preparation of, FA 2003 s 96
penalty for, FA 2003 Sch 10 para 8
later linked transaction, in consequence of, FA 2003 s 81A
loss, damage or destruction of, FA 2003 s 82
purchaser, amendment by, FA 2003 Sch 10 para 6
records, FA 2003 Sch 10 paras 9–11
Revenue, correction by, FA 2003 Sch 10 para 7
uncorrected, penalty for, FA 2003 Sch 10 para 8
land transactions—
application of provisions, FA 2003 s 43(2)
bodies established for national purposes, exemption, FA 2003 s 69
chargeable, FA 2003 s 49
chargeable interest, creation, surrender, release or variation of, FA 2003 s 43(3)
compliance with planning obligations, entered into for, FA 2003 s 61
connected party, deemed market value in case of, FA 2003 s 53
exceptions from rule, FA 2003 s 54
contract and conveyance for, FA 2003 s 44
secondary contract, FA 2003 s 45(3)
third party, to, FA 2003 ss 44A, 45A
transfer of rights, effect of, FA 2003 ss 45, 45A
demutualisation of insurance company, for purposes of, FA 2003 s 63
effective date of, FA 2003 s 119
exchanges, FA 2003 s 47
exemptions. *See* exemptions, *above*
individual and financial institution, alternative property arrangements between, FA 2003 ss 71A, 72, 72A, 73
exempt interests, FA 2003 s 73B
joint purchasers, involving, FA 2003 s 103
linked, FA 2003 ss 55(4), 81A, 108
meaning, FA 2003 s 43(1)
modernisation, PR 20/10/03
notifiable, FA 2003 ss 77, 77A
options, FA 2003 s 46
pre-emption rights, FA 2003 s 46
public bodies, involving, FA 2003 s 66
purchaser and vendor, FA 2003 s 43(4)
registered social landlords, acquisitions by, FA 2003 s 71
registration, FA 2003 s 79
return. *See* land transaction returns, *above*
subject-matter of, FA 2003 s 43(6)
Lands Tribunal, matters to be determined by, FA 2003 Sch 17 para 2
lease—
agreement for, FA 2003 Sch 17A paras 12A, 12B

STAMP DUTY LAND TAX – *contd*
lease – *contd*
assignment, FA 2003 Sch 17A paras 11, 12, 17
fixed term, for, FA 2003 Sch 17A para 2
indefinite term, for, FA 2003 Sch 17A para 4
meaning, FA 2003 s 120, Sch 17A para 1
rent, FA 2003 Sch 17A paras 6–9, 13–15
reverse premium, FA 2003 Sch 17A para 18
Scotland, in, FA 2003 Sch 17A para 19
successive linked, FA 2003 Sch 17A para 5
surrender in return for new lease, FA 2003 Sch 17A para 16
technical changes, PR 20/10/03
tenant's obligations, FA 2003 Sch 17A para 10
treatment of, FA 2003 Sch 17A
liability to pay, FA 2003 s 85
limited liability partnership incorporation, exemption, FA 2003 s 65
major interest in land, meaning, FA 2003 s 117
market value, meaning, FA 2003 s 118
new zero-carbon homes, relief for, FA 2003 ss 58B, 58C, SI 2007/3437
open-ended investment schemes, provisions applied to, FA 2003 s 102
overpaid, interest on repayment of, FA 2003 s 89
parliamentary constituencies, transfers in consequence of reorganisation of, FA 2003 s 67
partnership—
acquisition of interest in, FA 2003 Sch 15 para 29
charities relief, application of, FA 2003 Sch 15 para 28
continuity, FA 2003 Sch 15 para 3
disadvantaged areas relief, application of, FA 2003 Sch 15 para 26
excluded transactions, FA 2003 Sch 15 paras 9–14
exemptions and reliefs, FA 2003 Sch 15 para 25
group relief, application of, FA 2003 Sch 15 para 27
interest, transfer of, FA 2003 Sch 15 paras 14–17
legal personality, disregarding, FA 2003 Sch 15 para 2
market rent leases, FA 2003 Sch 15 para 15
meaning, FA 2003 Sch 15 para 1
non-notifiable transactions, FA 2003 Sch 15 para 30
ordinary transactions, FA 2003 Sch 15 paras 5–8
property-investment, election by, FA 2003 Sch 15 para 12A
property, references to, FA 2003 Sch 15 para 14
special provisions, application of, FA 2003 Sch 15 paras 9–40
transfer of chargeable interest from, FA 2003 Sch 15 paras 18–24
transfer of chargeable interest to, FA 2003 Sch 15 paras 10–13
unit trust scheme or open-ended investment company, not regarded as, FA 2003 Sch 15 para 4

Stamp Taxes

STAMP DUTY LAND TAX – *contd*
partnership – *contd*
withdrawal of money after transfer of chargeable interest, FA 2003 Sch 15 para 17A
payment of, FA 2003 s 86
agreement to postpone, FA 2003 Sch 10 para 40; SI 2003/2837 reg 23
cheque, by, FA 2003 s 92
deferred, SI 2003/2837 regs 10–28
direction to postpone, FA 2003 Sch 10 para 39
postponement, direction for, SI 2003/2837 reg 22
tax avoidance arrangements, SI 2003/2837 reg 18
penalties—
determinations, FA 2003 s 83, Sch 14
fraud or negligence as to self-certificate, for, FA 2003 Sch 11 para 3
general provisions, FA 2003 s 99
incorrect return—
assisting in preparation of, FA 2003 s 96
delivery of, FA 2003 Sch 10 para 8
interest on, FA 2003 s 88
records, failure to keep and preserve, FA 2003 Sch 10 para 11, Sch 11 para 6
return—
failure to deliver, FA 2003 Sch 10 paras 7–9
incorrect or uncorrected, delivery of, FA 2003 Sch 10 para 8
persons acting in representative capacity, responsibility of, FA 2003 s 106
private finance initiative projects, treatment of, PR 19/12/03
recovery of—
county court proceedings, FA 2003 Sch 12 para 5
Court of Session proceedings, FA 2003 Sch 12 para 6
court of summary jurisdiction, proceedings in, FA 2003 Sch 12 para 4
diligence, FA 2003 Sch 12 para 3
distraint, FA 2003 Sch 12 para 2
High Court proceedings, FA 2003 Sch 12 para 6
magistrates' court proceedings, FA 2003 Sch 12 para 4
sheriff court proceedings, FA 2003 Sch 12 para 5
tax demands and receipts, issue of, FA 2003 Sch 12 para 1
unpaid tax, evidence of, FA 2003 Sch 12 para 7
regulations—
approval of, FA 2003 s 110
claim for repayment in default of approval, FA 2003 s 111
power to vary provisions by, FA 2003 s 109
Treasury or Inland Revenue, by, FA 2003 s 114
relocation relief, FA 2003 s 59
residential property—
acquisitions of, FA 2003 Sch 6A
exchanges, relief of, FA 2003 Sch 6A
meaning, FA 2003 s 116
right to buy transactions, on, FA 2003 Sch 9 para 1
self-certificates—
enquiry into, FA 2003 Sch 11 paras 7–17
form and contents of, FA 2003 Sch 11 para 2; SI 2003/2837 reg 5, Sch 1

STAMP DUTY LAND TAX – *contd*
self-certificates – *contd*
fraud or negligence, tax-related penalty for, FA 2003 Sch 11 para 3
records, duty to keep and preserve, FA 2003 Sch 11 paras 4–6
reference to, FA 2003 Sch 11 para 1
settlement—
meaning, FA 2003 Sch 16 para 1
power of appointment, exercise of, FA 2003 Sch 16 para 7
trustees—
acquisitions by, FA 2003 Sch 16 para 4
discretion, exercise of, FA 2003 Sch 16 para 7
relevant, FA 2003 Sch 16 para 6
responsibility of, FA 2003 Sch 16 para 5
shared ownership lease—
market value treatment, election for, FA 2003 Sch 9 para 2
preserved right to buy, meaning, FA 2003 Sch 9 para 5
qualifying body, meaning, FA 2003 Sch 9 para 5
reversion, treatment of, FA 2003 Sch 9 para 3
staircasing—
election where allowed, FA 2003 Sch 9 para 4
declaration of trust not linked with, FA 2003 Sch 9 para 4C
grant not linked with, FA 2003 Sch 9 para 4B
treatment of transaction, FA 2003 Sch 9 para 4A
shared ownership trusts, FA 2003 Sch 9 para 7
switch to, PR 6/03, PR 7/03, PR 8/03
transitional provisions, FA 2003 Sch 19
trust—
bare, meaning, FA 2003 Sch 16 para 1
beneficial owner, acquisition by bare trustee attributed to, FA 2003 Sch 16 para 3
beneficiaries, interests of, FA 2003 Sch 16 para 2
unit trust schemes, application of provisions to, FA 2003 s 101
unpaid, interest on, FA 2003 s 87
withdrawal of relief, further relief on, FA 2003 s 81
STAMP DUTY RESERVE TAX
abolition of, FA 1990 ss 110, 111, PR 20/3/90
accountable date—
meaning, SI 1986/1711 reg 2
accountable person—
bodies of persons, SI 1986/1711 Sch para 71
child, for, SI 1986/1711 Sch para 73
company, SI 1986/1711 Sch para 108
incapacitated person, for, SI 1986/1711 Sch para 72
meaning, SI 1986/1711 reg 2
non-resident, for, SI 1986/1711 Sch paras 78, 83
payment by, SI 1986/1711 regs 4–4B
personal representative, SI 1986/1711 Sch para 74
relief where unable to recover tax from liable person, SI 1986/1711 reg 7
reporting requirement, SI 1986/1711 reg 4
administration, FA 1999 s 121
agreement covering chargeable and exempt securities, FA 1986 ss 87(7A), 88(5), 92
appeals. *See* APPEAL

STAMP DUTY RESERVE TAX – *contd*
barrister, meaning, SI 1986/1711 reg 2
broker-dealer, meaning, FA 1986 s 89, SI 1986/1711 reg 2
cancellation of charge where instrument executed and duty paid, FA 1986 s 92
certificate of tax due, evidential status, SI 1986/1711 reg 16(2)
change in law, effect on determination of questions, SI 1986/1711 reg 17
chargeable, when, FA 1986 s 86(4)
chargeable securities, meaning, FA 1986 s 99(3)–(6), (6A), (10)–(12)
clearance service. *See* CLEARANCE SERVICE
conditions for principal charge—
  agreement to transfer securities for consideration, FA 1986 s 87(1), 101
depositary receipts. *See* DEPOSITARY RECEIPTS
determination by Board—
  appeal against, SI 1986/1711 reg 8–10, Sch paras 46A, 56B–56D
  evidence, status as, SI 1986/1711 reg 16(1)
  notice of, SI 1986/1711 reg 6, Sch para 114
due date for payment, FA 1986 s 87(2), (3), SI 1986/1711 reg 3
European institution, meaning, SI 1986/1711 reg 2
exceptions from principal charge—
  associated bodies, transfers between, FA 1986 s 88(1B), (4)–(6)
  broker-dealer, agreements in ordinary course of business, FA 1986 s 89(2), (4), (6)–(8)
  charity, agreement to transfer securities to, FA 1986 s 90(7)
  clearance service nominee holding securities, FA 1986 s 90(5), (6)
  collateral security arrangements, FA 1986 s 89B
  electricity industry, transfers on privatisation, F(No 2)A 1992 Sch 17 paras 1, 9
  electronic transfer system etc, transfer to members of, FA 1986 s 88(1A), FA 1996 s 172
  equity securities transferred on Exchange, SI 2008/52 reg 4
  execution and stamping of instrument in pursuance of agreement, FA 1986 s 88(1)
  Historic Buildings and Monuments Commission, agreement to transfer securities to, FA 1986 s 90(7)
  inland bearer instrument, securities transferable by, FA 1986 s 90(3A)
  insolvency, in case of, FA 1986 s 89AB
  market maker, agreements in ordinary course of business, FA 1986 s 89(1), (1A), (3), (5)
  National Heritage Memorial Fund, agreement to transfer securities to, FA 1986 s 90(7)
  overseas bearer instrument, securities transferable by, FA 1986 s 90(3)
  public offers of securities, FA 1986 s 89A
  recognised clearing house, transactions involving. *See* RECOGNISED CLEARING HOUSE
  recognised investment exchange, transactions involving. *See* RECOGNISED INVESTMENT EXCHANGE

STAMP DUTY RESERVE TAX – *contd*
exceptions from principal charge – *contd*
  repurchases, FA 1986 ss 89AA, 89AB
  stock lending, FA 1986 ss 89AA, 89AB, 89B
  units in unit trust scheme—
    transfer to manager, agreement for, FA 1986 s 90(1)
foreign securities, depositary interests in, SI 1999/2383; PR 25/8/99
House of Commons resolutions, temporary statutory effect, PCTA 1968 s 1, FA 1986 s 86(3)
information powers of Revenue—
  generally, FA 1989 s 177, SI 1986/1711 reg 5
  issuing houses, returns by, SI 1986/1711 Sch para 25
  nominee shareholders, from, SI 1986/1711 Sch para 26
  registers of securities, SI 1986/1711 Sch para 23
  stockbrokers, returns by, SI 1986/1711 Sch para 25
inspection powers of Revenue, SI 1986/1711 reg 15, Sch para 111
investment business, meaning, SI 1986/1711 reg 2
investment exchanges. *See* RECOGNISED INVESTMENT EXCHANGE
market maker, meaning, FA 1986 s 89, SI 1986/1711 reg 2
notice of charge by accountable person, SI 1986/1711 reg 4
overpaid, repayment of, SI 1986/1711 reg 14
payment of, SI 1986/1711 reg 4
penalties. *See* PENALTIES
person liable for, FA 1986 s 91, SI 1986/1711 Sch paras 71–74, 78, 83
qualified dealer, meaning, SI 1986/1711 reg 2
rate of charge, FA 1986 s 87(6), (7)
recovery. *See* RECOVERY OF TAX
relevant day, meaning, FA 1986 s 87(3)
relevant transaction, meaning, SI 1986/1711 reg 2
repayment of—
  conditions for, FA 1986 s 92
  interest on, FA 1989 s 178, SI 1986/1711 reg 11
  overpayment, following, SI 1986/1711 reg 14
  over-repayment, recovery of, SI 1986/1711 reg 18
service of documents, SI 1986/1711 reg 19
shares, payable on transfer of, PR 16/1/97
stock exchange nominee, transactions involving, FA 1989 s 176
taxes management provisions, application to, FA 1986 s 98, FA 1989 s 177, SI 1986/1711 reg 20
territorial scope of tax, FA 1986 s 86
time when charge arises, FA 1986 s 87(2), (3)
units in unit trusts, on dealings with—
  change of ownership, exclusion of charge on, FA 1999 Sch 19 para 6
  charge to tax, FA 1999 Sch 19 para 2
  in specie redemption, exclusion of charge in case of, FA 1999 Sch 19 para 7
  individual pensions accounts, exclusion of charge in case of, FA 1999 Sch 19 para 6A
  issue, meaning, FA 1999 Sch 19 para 8
  proportionate reduction of tax, FA 1999 Sch 19 paras 4, 5
  rate of, FA 1999 Sch 19 para 3

STAMP DUTY RESERVE TAX – *contd*
units in unit trusts, on dealings with – *contd*
transitional provisions, FA 1999 Sch 19 para 9
unpaid—
interest on. *See* INTEREST ON UNPAID TAX
recovery of. *See* RECOVERY OF TAX
STAMP OFFICE
relocation of, PR 7/91
STATUTORY POWERS
harbour reorganisation schemes, FA 1966 s 45
purchase of property under, collection of duty, FA 1895 s 12, FA 1949 s 36(4), FA 1991 s 114
transfer of property to local authority joint board etc under, exemption, FA 1952 s 74
vesting of property in any person under, collection of duty, FA 1895 s 12, FA 1949 s 36(4), FA 1991 s 114
STOCK
abolition of charge on instruments of transfer, FA 1990 ss 108, 111, PR 20/3/90
bearer instrument of transfer, exemption, FA 1987 s 50(1), (3), FA 1999 Sch 15 para 14
blank transfers—
meaning, FA 1963 s 67(2)
penalty for, FA 1963 s 67(1)
prohibition of, FA 1963 s 67, FA 1990 ss 109(3), 111
certificate—
cancellation after entry of holder's name in register, SA 1891 s 109, FA 1990 ss 109(2), 111
unstamped, SA 1891 s 109, FA 1990 ss 109(2), 111
charge to duty, FA 2003 s 125, Sch 20
clearance service. *See* CLEARANCE SERVICE
consideration in, calculation of ad valorem duty, SA 1891 ss 6, 55
depositary receipts. *See* DEPOSITORY RECEIPTS
executor's assent, transfer by person to himself, ESC G5
foreign currency, bearer instrument for—
general exemption, FA 1999 Sch 15 para 17
paired shares, FA 1988 s 143(4), (5)
government, transfers of, exemption, FA 1999 Sch 13 para 24(*a*)
guaranteed by Treasury, exemption for transfers, FA 1947 s 57
International Bank for Reconstruction and Development, of, exemption, FA 1951 s 42
nationalisation schemes, transfers under, exemption, FA 1948 s 74
paired shares, FA 1986 s 99(6A), FA 1988 s 143
parliamentary, transfers of, exemption, FA 1999 Sch 13 para 24(a)
recognised clearing house, transfer to, exemption, FA 1986 ss 84(3), FA 1986 s 88(1)
recognised investment exchange, transfer to, exemption, FA 1986 ss 84(2), 88(1)
repurchases, exemption for, FA 1986 ss 80C, 88(1C), (1D), 89AA
SEPON, transfers into, ESC G7
simplified transfers—
companies, regulation of transfers by, STA 1963 s 2(1)
execution of, STA 1963 s 1(2)
forms for, STA 1963 s 3
STOCK – *contd*
simplified transfers – *contd*
instrument for, STA 1963 s 1(1)
refusal to register person as holder, STA 1963 s 2(1)
registered securities, meaning, STA 1963 ss 1(4), 4(1)
securities eligible for, STA 1963 s 1(4)
securities, meaning, STA 1963 s 4(1)
stock exchange, meaning, STA 1963 s 4(1)
stock exchange transaction, meaning, STA 1963 s 4(1)
unit trust scheme unit, treatment as, FA 1999 Sch 19 para 19
STOCK EXCHANGE. ***See also*** RECOGNISED CLEARING HOUSE; RECOGNISED INVESTMENT EXCHANGE
EEA exchange—
meaning, FA 1986 ss 80B(2), 88B(2)
sale to intermediary member of, FA 1986 ss 80A, 80B, 88B
equity securities, transfer not subject to stamp duty reserve tax, SI 2008/52 reg 4
market maker, transactions in ordinary course of business—
stamp duties exemption, FA 1986 s 81
stamp duty reserve tax exemption, FA 1986 s 89(1), (1A), (3), (5)
stock lending, stamp duties exemption, FA 1986 s 82
meaning (simplified transfers of stock), STA 1963 s 4(1)
member of, construction of references to, FA 1973 s 54
nominee—
meaning, FA 1976 s 127(5)
transfer to—
stamp duties, exempt transactions, FA 1976 s 127, FA 1986 ss 80C, 88(1C), (1D), FA 1989 ss 175
stamp duty reserve tax, avoidance of double charge, FA 1989 s 176
quotation on, construction of references to, FA 1973 s 54
recognised foreign exchange, sale to intermediary member of, FA 1986 ss 80A, 80B, 88A, 88B
references to, construction of, FA 1973 s 54
STOCK LENDING
exceptions for, FA 1986 ss 80C, 88(1C), (1D), 89B
returns, ESC G8
stamp duty reserve tax, PR 2/10/95
transfers of collateral, ESC G9
transactions by market maker in ordinary course of business, exemption, FA 1986 s 82

TACK. *See* LEASE OR TACK
TESTAMENTS
exemption, FA 1999 Sch 13 para 24(c)
TRADEPOINT
regulations, SI 1995/2051
tax reliefs, PR 4/8/95
TRANSFER OF SECURITIES
associated bodies, between, FA 1986 s 88(1B), (4)–(6)
electronic transfer systems etc, to members of, FA 1986 s 88(1A), FA 1996 s 172
exempt property, for, FA 2000 s 122
simplified transfers of stock. *See under* STOCK
trust property, direction to hold on other trusts, FA 1997 s 101

TRANSFER ON SALE. *See also* CONVEYANCE OR TRANSFER ON SALE
securities, of. *See* TRANSFER OF SECURITIES
TRUST
bare, meaning, FA 2003 Sch 16 para 1
beneficial owner, acquisition by bare trustee attributed to, FA 2003 Sch 16 para 3
beneficiaries, interests of, FA 2003 Sch 16 para 2
declaration of, duty on, FA 1999 Sch 13 para 17
direction to hold trust property on other trusts, transfer of securities by, FA 1997 s 101
instrument transferring property to, exemption, FA 1928 s 30(4)
TRUSTEES
change in, instrument vesting property following, exemption, SI 1987/516 Sch
incapacitated person, of, accountability for stamp duty reserve tax, SI 1986/1711 Sch para 72

UNIT TRUST SCHEME
abolition of charge on instruments transferring units, FA 1990 s 108, 109(6), 111
authorised—
mergers between, FA 1997 ss 95, 100, PR 9/5/96, PR 26/11/96
open-ended investment company, relaxation of tax rules on conversion into, PR 9/5/96, PR 26/11/96, SI 1997/1156, SI 2008/710
certificates to bearer—
meaning, FA 1999 Sch 19 para 14(3)
meaning, FA 1999 Sch 19 para 14
open-ended investment companies, SI 1997/1156, SI 2008/710
mergers, PR 24/5/04
schemes excluded from being—
charitable schemes, FA 1999 Sch 19 para 15(*c*)
common deposit schemes, FA 1999 Sch 19 para 15(*b*)
common investment schemes, FA 1999 Sch 19 para 15(*a*)
individual pension accounts, units held within, SI 2001/964 reg 3
limited partnership scheme, SI 1988/268
pension funds pooling scheme, SI 1996/1584
schemes under Administration of Justice Act 1982 s 42, SI 1992/197
statutory power to exclude schemes, FA 1999 Sch 19 para 17, SI 1996/1584
stamp duty land tax provisions applied, FA 2003 s 101
stamp duty reserve tax exemptions—
manager, agreement to transfer units to, FA 1986 s 90(1)
transfer of property subject to trusts of authorised unit trust, FA 1997 s 101
trust instrument—
meaning, FA 1999 Sch 19 para 14(3)
penalty for late stamping, SA 1891 s 15B
trust property—
direction to hold on other trusts, FA 1997 s 101
meaning, FA 1999 Sch 19 para 14(3)

UNIT TRUST SCHEME – *contd*
umbrella schemes, treatment of, FA 1999 Sch 19 para 18
units—
abolition of charge on instruments of transfer, FA 1990 ss 108, 109(6), 111, FA 1999 Sch 19 para 1, PR 20/3/90
holder, meaning, FA 1999 Sch 19 para 14(3)
meaning, FA 1999 Sch 19 para 14(3)
mergers between authorised unit trusts, FA 1997 ss 95, 100, PR 9/5/96, PR 26/11/96
provisions not applying to, FA 1999 s 122
reference to stock including, FA 1999 Sch 19 para 19
stamp duty reserve tax on dealings—
change of ownership, exclusion of charge on, FA 1999 Sch 19 para 6
charge to tax, FA 1999 Sch 19 para 2
in specie redemption, exclusion of charge in case of, FA 1999 Sch 19 para 7
issue, meaning, FA 1999 Sch 19 para 8
proportionate reduction of tax, FA 1999 Sch 19 paras 4, 5
rate of, FA 1999 Sch 19 para 3
transitional provisions, FA 1999 Sch 19 para 9
transfer by manager of scheme, FA 1946 ss 54(3), (4), 56(4), 57(4)
transfer to manager of scheme, agreement for, stamp duty reserve tax exemption, FA 1986 s 90(1)
UNQUOTED SHARES
valuation, PR 4/10/78
UNSTAMPED DOCUMENTS
excluded from use as evidence, RI 174

VAT
interaction with stamp duties—
agreement for lease, SP 11/91 para 11
business transferred as going concern, PR 4/3/92
commercial property, sale or lease—
agreement not to waive VAT exemption, PR 4/3/92
new building, sale of, SP 11/91 para 4
potential election to waive VAT exemption, PR 4/3/92
waiver of VAT exemption, SP 11/91 paras 5–7
group companies, lease between, PR 4/3/92
rent, SP 11/91 paras 9, 10, PR 18/2/92
sub-sales, PR 4/3/92
not charged on stamp duty, SP 11/91 para 14
VISITING FORCES. *See also* ARMED FORCES
building etc contracts, exemption, FA 1960 s 74
meaning, FA 1960 s 74(6)(*c*)
VOLUNTARY DISPOSITIONS. *See* GIFT

WALES
Government of Wales Act, commencement, SI 1998/2244
WARRANT FOR GOODS
meaning, SA 1891 s 111
WILL
conveyance of property pursuant to, exempt instrument, SI 1987/516 Sch

Stamp Taxes

Stamp Taxes

WORDS AND PHRASES

Words in brackets indicate the context in which the word or phrase is used.

accountable date (stamp duty reserve tax), SI 1986/1711 reg 2
accountable person (stamp duty reserve tax), SI 1986/1711 reg 2
accredited assessor, SI 2007/3437 reg 2
allied headquarters, FA 1960 s 74(6)(*aa*)
appeal, SI 2004/1363 reg 2
approved methodology, SI 2007/3437 reg 2
assignment, FA 2003 s 121
associated (bodies corporate), FA 1930 s 42(2A), FA 1967 s 27(2)
authorised corporate director, SI 1997/1156 reg 2
authorised unit trust, SI 2008/710 reg 2

bare trust, FA 2003 Sch 15 para 1
barrister (stamp duty reserve tax), SI 1986/1711 reg 2
bearer instrument, FA 1999 Sch 15 para 3
bearer instrument by usage, FA 1999 Sch 15 para 10
body of persons (stamp duty reserve tax), SI 1986/1711 Sch para 118
branch or agency (stamp duty reserve tax), SI 1986/1711 Sch para 118
broker and dealer (stamp duty reserve tax), FA 1986 s 89, SI 1986/1711 reg 2

capital market instrument, FA 1996 s 79(13)
capital payment, SI 1998/3177 reg 24
CC&G, SI 2009/1832 reg 2(1)
certificate to bearer (unit trust scheme), FA 1999 Sch 19 para 14(3)
chargeable interest, FA 2003 s 48(1)
chargeable securities (stamp duty reserve tax), FA 1986 s 99 (3)–(6), (6A), (10)–(12)
charter-party, SA 1891 s 49
chief office, SDMA 1891 s 27
clearing member, SI 1999/3262 reg 2
clearing participant, SI 1995/2051 regs 2, 4(3)(*cc*), SI 2008/52 reg 2(1), SI 2008/2777 reg 2(1), SI 2008/3235 reg 2(1), SI 2009/35 reg 2(1), SI 2009/194 reg 2(1), SI 2009/397 reg 2(1), SI 2009/115 reg 2(1), SI 2009/1344 reg 2(1), , SI 2009/1462 reg 2(1), SI 2009/1601 reg 2(1), SI 2009/1827 reg 2(1), SI 2009/1828 reg 2(1), SI 2009/1831 reg 2(1), SI 2009/1832 reg 2(1)
close possession, SI 1999/3263 reg 2; SI 2003/2837 reg 29
collective investment scheme, FA 1986 ss 80B(2), 88B(2); FSMA 2000 s 235
collector (stamp duty reserve tax), SI 1986/1711 Sch para 118
Commissioners, SDMA 1891 s 27, SA 1891 s 122(1)
commodity or financial futures, SI 1998/3177 reg 2(1)
company (bearer instrument), FA 1999 Sch 15 para 11
company (stamp duty reserve tax), SI 1986/1711 Sch para 118
company's place of business, SI 2004/1363 reg 8
completion, FA 2003 s 121
compulsory purchase facilitating development, FA 2003 s 60
contingent consideration, FA 2003 s 51(3)
contract of insurance, FA 1997 s 96(8)
conveyance on sale, FA 1999 Sch 13 para 1(2)
conveyance or transfer other than on sale, FA 1999 Sch 13 para 16

day of The Stock Exchange reforms, FA 1986 s 85(5)(*aa*)
debt, SI 1998/3177 reg 2(1)
Delta number, SI 1992/570 reg 2
Deltapluslong limit, SI 1992/570 reg 9(1)
Deltaplusshort limit, SI 1992/570 reg 9(2)
deposit certificate (bearer instrument), FA 1999 Sch 15 para 9
depositary interest, SI 1999/2383 reg 2
depositary receipt, FA 1986 ss 69(1), (2), 94(1), (2), 99(7), (8)
derivative, SI 1998/3177 reg 2(1)
die, SDMA 1891 s 27
disadvantaged area, FA 2003 Sch 6 para 1
duty, SDMA 1891 s 27
dwelling, FA 2003 Sch 6A para 7(1)
dwelling CO_2 emission rate, SI 2007/3437 reg 5(4)

ecu, SI 1998/3177 reg 2(1)
EEA State, FA 1986 ss 80B(2), 88B(2)
EMCF, SI 2009/1462 reg 2(1), SI 2009/1601 reg 2(1), SI 2009/1831 reg 2(1), SI 2009/1832 reg 2(1)
employee, FA 2003 s 121
enactments relating to stamp duty, FA 1995 s 152(6); SI 1999/3263 reg 2
Equiduct Trading, SI 2008/2777 reg 2(1)
equity securities, SI 1992/570 reg 2, SI 1995/2051 reg 2, SI 1999/3262 reg 2; SI 2000/2995 reg 2; SI 2008/52 reg 2(1)
euro, SI 1998/3177 reg 2(1)
EuroCCP, SI 2009/194 reg 2(1), SI 2009/397 reg 2(1), SI 2009/1115 reg 2(1), SI 2009/1827 reg 2(1)
Euroconversion, SI 1998/3177 reg 3(1)
European institutions (stamp duty reserve tax), SI 1986/1711 reg 2
executed, SA 1891 s 122(1), (1A)
execution, SA 1891 s 122(1), (1A)
existing local constituency association, FA 2003 s 67(3)

Facility, The, SI 2008/2777 reg 2(1), SI 2008/3235 reg 2(1), SI 2009/35 reg 2(1), SI 2009/194 reg 2(1), SI 2009/397 reg 2(1), SI 2009/115 reg 2(1), SI 2009/1344 reg 2(1), , SI 2009/1462 reg 2(1), SI 2009/1601 reg 2(1), SI 2009/1827 reg 2(1), SI 2009/1828 reg 2(1), SI 2009/1831 reg 2(1), SI 2009/1832 reg 2(1)
financial institution, FA 2003 s 72(7)
foreign mutual fund, FA 1967 s 30(5)
foreign securities, SI 1999/2383 reg 2
forged, SDMA 1891 s 27

Stamp Taxes

former parliamentary constituency, FA 2003 s 67(2)
franchise, FA 2003 s 48(3)
futures contract, SI 1999/3262 reg 2

General Commissioners, SI 1986/1711 reg 2
general insurance company, FA 1997 s 96(8), FA 2003 s 63(7)

harbour reorganisation scheme, FA 1966 s 45(6)
head offices, SDMA 1891 s 27
heat loss parameters, SI 2007/3437 reg 5(4)
housing authority, FA 2003 s 128(4), Sch 3 para 2(3)

incapacitated person (stamp duty reserve tax), SI 1986/1711 Sch para 118
instrument, SDMA 1891 s 27, SA 1891 s 122 (1)
instrument certified at an amount, FA 1999 Sch 13 para 6
instrument of apprenticeship, SA 1891 s 25
insurance business, FA 1986 ss 80B(2), 88B(2)
insurance company, FA 1997 s 96(8), FA 2003 s 63(7)
investment business (stamp duty reserve tax), SI 1986/1711 reg 2
issue (units in unit trust scheme), FA 1999 Sch 19 para 8

jointly entitled, FA 2003 s 121
justice, SDMA 1891 s 27

land, FA 2003 s 121
land registrar, F(No 2)A 2005 s 47(6)
land transactions, FA 2003 s 43(1)
LCH Clearnet Limited, SI 2008/2777 reg 2(1), SI 2008/3235 reg 2(1), SI 2009/1462 reg 2(1), SI 2009/1601 reg 2(1), SI 2009/1827 reg 2(1), SI 2009/1828 reg 2(1)
lease, FA 2003 s 120, Sch 17A para 1
legal mortgage, FA 2003 s 73(5)
life policy, SI 1987/516 reg 1A
LIFFE, SI 1992/570 reg 2
LIFFE (A & M), SI 1992/570 reg 2, SI 2009/1828 reg 2(1)
limited liability partnership, FA 2003 s 65
limited partnership, SI 1988/268 reg 2
limited partnership scheme, SI 1988/268 reg 2
loan capital, FA 1990 s 108(3)
local authority—
  joint boards etc, transfers to, FA 1952 s 74(4)
  simplified transfers of securities, STA 1963 s 4(1)
  transfers of land and leases, FA 1931 s 28(6)
local constituency association, FA 2003 s 67(4)
London Clearing House Ltd, SI 1995/2051 reg 4(3)(*bb*)
long-term capital asset, SI 1998/3177 reg 2(1)
long-term capital liability, SI 1998/3177 reg 2(1)

major interest in land, FA 2003 s 117
market maker (stamp duty reserve tax), FA 1986 s 89, SI 1986/1711 reg 2
market value, FA 2003 s 118
marketable security, SA 1891 s 122 (1)
matching agreement, SI 1995/2051 reg 4(3)(*aa*), SI 2008/52 reg 4(3)
material, SDMA 1891 s 27, SA 1891 s 122(1)
Maxlong limit, SI 1992/570 reg 8(1)
Maxshort limit, SI 1992/570 reg 8(2)
member (OM London Exchange Limited), SI 1999/3262 reg 2
member State, SI 1998/3177 reg 2(1)
money, SA 1891 s 122 (1)
mutual insurance company, FA 1997 s 96(8), FA 2003 s 63(7)

neglect (stamp duty reserve tax), SI 1986/1711 Sch para 118
net CO_2 emission rate, SI 2007/3437 reg 5(4)
new dwelling, FA 2003 Sch 6A para 7(2)
new parliamentary constituency, FA 2003 s 67(2)
non-clearing member (OM London Exchange Limited), SI 1999/3262 reg 2
non-UK company, FA 1999 Sch 15 para 11
notice (stamp duty reserve tax), SI 1986/1711 reg 2
NYSE Arca Europe, SI 2009/397 reg 2(1)

officer, SDMA 1891 s 27
open-ended investment company, FSMA 2000 s 236, SI 1997/1156 reg 2
operator, (collective investment scheme), FA 1986 ss 80B(2), 88B(2)
option, SI 1992/570 reg 2, SI 1999/3262 reg 2
options market maker, SI 1992/570 reg 2
options principal trader, SI 1992/570 reg 2
ordinary share capital, FA 1930 s 42(4), FA 1938 s 42(3)

paired shares, FA 1986 s 99(6A), FA 1988 s 143
parent (body corporate), FA 1930 s 42(2B)
participating member State, SI 1998/3177 reg 2(1)
partnership, FA 2003 Sch 15 para 1
partnership property, FA 2003 Sch 15 para 34
partnership share, FA 2003 Sch 15 para 35
partnership's place of business, SI 2004/1363 reg 8
place of business, SI 2004/1363 reg 8
place of residence, SI 2004/1363 reg 8
planning obligation, FA 2003 s 61(2)
property trader, FA 2003 Sch 6A para 8(1)
public subsidy, FA 2003 s 71(4)

qualified dealer (stamp duty reserve tax), SI 1986/1711 reg 2
qualifying contract, SI 1998/3177 reg 2(1)
qualifying premium, SI 2001/3746 reg 2
quoted or listed options, FA 1986 ss 80B(2), 88B(2)

rate or average rate of rent, SI 2003/1056 reg 2(1)
recognised clearing house, FA 1970 s 33(1)
recognised exchange, FA 2002 s 117(3)
recognised foreign exchange, FA 1986 ss 80B(3), 88B(2)
recognised investment exchange, FA 1970 s 33(1)
recognised stock exchange overseas, SI 1999/2383 reg 2
reconventioning, SI 1998/3177 reg 2(1)
refurbishment, FA 2003 Sch 6A para 9(1)
registered securities (simplified transfers), STA 1963 ss 1(4), 4(1)
registered social landlord, FA 2003 ss 121, 128(2)
relevant asset, SI 1998/3177 reg 2(1)

relevant debts (company reconstructions), FA 1986 s 76(6)
relevant securities (stamp duty reserve tax)—
clearance services, FA 1986 s 72(1)
depositary receipts, FA 1986 s 69(3)
relevant transactions (stamp duty reserve tax), SI 1986/1711 reg 2
relocation company, FA 2003 s 59(5)
relocation of employment, FA 2003 s 59(3), Sch 6A para 5(4), 6(A)
renominalisation, SI 1998/3177 reg 2(1)
rent to shared ownership lease scheme, FA 2003 Sch 9 para 13
rent to shared ownership trust scheme, FA 2003 Sch 9 para 14
residential property, FA 2001 s 92B, FA 2003 s 116

scheme transaction, FA 2003 s 75A
securities (simplified transfers), STA 1963 ss 1(4), 4(1)
security interest, FA 2003 s 48(3)
settlement, FA 2003 Sch 16 para 1
shared ownership trust, FA 2003 Sch 9 para 7
simple redenomination, SI 1998/3177 reg 2(1)
Special Commissioners, SI 1986/1711 reg 2
stamp, SDMA 1891 s 27, SA 1891 s 122(1)
stamp duty penalty, SI 1999/2537 reg 2; SI 1999/3263 reg 2
stamped, SDMA 1891 s 27, SA 1891 s 122(1)
steward, SA 1891 s 122(1)
stock, SA 1891 s 122(1), FA 1986 ss 85(5)(*dd*), FA 1999 Sch 15 para 12(1)
stock exchange (simplified transfers), STA 1963 s 4(1)
stock exchange nominee, FA 1976 s 127(5)
stock exchange transaction (simplified transfers), STA 1963 s 4(1)
subsidiary (national defence contribution), FA 1938 s 42, Sch 4 Part I
surrender, FA 2003 s 121

third life insurance directive, FA 1997 s 96(8)
third non-life insurance directive, FA 1997 s 96(8)
traded securities, SI 2008/2777 reg 2(1), SI 2008/3235 reg 2(1), SI 2009/35 reg 2(1), SI 2009/194 reg 2(1), SI 2009/397 reg 2(1), SI 2009/115 reg 2(1), SI 2009/1344 reg 2(1), , SI 2009/1462 reg 2(1), SI 2009/1601 reg 2(1), SI 2009/1827 reg 2(1), SI 2009/1828 reg 2(1), SI 2009/1831 reg 2(1), SI 2009/1832 reg 2(1)
transfer, FA 1999 Sch 13 para 12(3), SI 2009/35 reg 2(1)
transfer in blank (stock transfer), FA 1963 s 67(2)
transfer of chargeable interest from partnership, FA 2003 Sch 15 para 37
transfer of chargeable interest to partnership, FA 2003 Sch 15 para 35
transfer of interest in partnership, FA 2003 Sch 15 para 36
trust instrument (unit trust scheme), FA 1999 Sch 19 para 14(3)
trust property (unit trust scheme), FA 1999 Sch 19 para 14(3)
trustee (collective investment scheme), FA 1986 ss 80B(2), 88B(2)

UK company, FA 1999 Sch 15 para 11
UK depositary interest, SI 1999/2383 reg 3
umbrella scheme, FA 1999 Sch 19 para 18(2)
uncertain consideration, FA 2003 s 51(3)
unit trust scheme, FA 1999 Sch 19 para 14
unit (unit trust scheme), FA 1999 Sch 19 para 14(3)

visiting forces, FA 1960 s 74(6)(*aa*)

walking possession, SI 1999/3263 reg 2, SI 2003/2837 reg 29
warrant for goods, SA 1891 s 111

X-Clear, SI 2009/35 reg 2(1), SI 2009/1344 reg 2(1), SI 2009/1462 reg 2(1), SI 2009/1601 reg 2(1), SI 2009/1827 reg 2(1), SI 2009/1831 reg 2(1)

zero-carbon home, FA 2003 s 58B, SI 2007/3437 reg 5

INSURANCE PREMIUM TAX

CONTENTS

PROVISIONAL COLLECTION OF TAXES ACT 1968

(1968 Chapter 2)

1 Temporary statutory effect of House of Commons resolutions affecting …, [insurance premium tax][2], …

(1) This section applies only to …, [insurance premium tax][2], …

(2) Subject to that, and to the provisions of subsections (4) to (8) below, where the House of Commons passes a resolution which—

(*a*) provides for the renewal for a further period of any tax in force or imposed during the previous financial year (whether at the same or a different rate, and whether with or without modifications) or for the variation or abolition of any existing tax, and

(*b*) contains a declaration that it is expedient in the public interest that the resolution should have statutory effect under the provisions of this Act,

the resolution shall, for the period specified in the next following subsection, have statutory effect as if contained in an Act of Parliament and, where the resolution provides for the renewal of a tax, all enactments which were in force with reference to that tax as last imposed by Act of Parliament shall during that period have full force and effect with respect to the tax as renewed by the resolution.

In this section references to the renewal of a tax include references to its reimposition, and references to the abolition of a tax include references to its repeal.

(3) The said period is—

(*a*) in the case of a resolution passed in [November or December][3] in any year, one expiring with [5th May in the next calendar year][3];

[(*aa*) in the case of a resolution passed in February or March in any year, one expiring with 5th August in the same calendar year; and][5]

(*b*) in the case of any other resolution, one expiring at the end of four months after the date on which it is expressed to take effect or, if no such date is expressed, after the date on which it is passed.

(4) A resolution shall cease to have statutory effect under this section unless within the next [thirty][4] days on which the House of Commons sits after the day on which the resolution is passed—

(*a*) a Bill renewing, varying or, as the case may be, abolishing the tax is read a second time by the House, or

(*b*) a Bill is amended by the House [in Committee or on Report, or by any [Public Bill Committee][6] of the House][1] so as to include provision for the renewal, variation or, as the case may be, abolition of the tax.

(5) A resolution shall also cease to have statutory effect under this section if—

(*a*) the provisions giving effect to it are rejected during the passage of the Bill containing them through the House, or

(*b*) an Act comes into operation renewing, varying or, as the case may be, abolishing the tax, or

(*c*) Parliament is dissolved or prorogued.

(6) Where, in the case of a resolution providing for the renewal or variation of a tax, the resolution ceases to have statutory effect by virtue of subsection (4) or (5) above, or the period specified in subsection (3) above terminates, before an Act comes into operation renewing or varying the tax, any money paid in pursuance of the resolution shall be repaid or made good, and any deduction made in pursuance of the resolution shall be deemed to be an unauthorised deduction.

(7) Where any tax as renewed or varied by a resolution is modified by the Act renewing or varying the tax, any money paid in pursuance of the resolution which would not have been payable under the new conditions affecting the tax shall be repaid or made good, and any deduction made in pursuance of the resolution shall, so far as it would not have been authorised under the new conditions affecting the tax, be deemed to be an unauthorised deduction.

(8) When during any session a resolution has had statutory effect under this section, statutory effect shall not be again given under this section in the same session to the same resolution or to a resolution having the same effect.

Note—Words and any subsection not relevant for the purposes of IPT have been omitted.

Cross reference—See FA 1994 Sch 7 para 34 (insurance premium tax paid by virtue of a resolution under this Act becoming repayable under sub-s (6) or (7) above).

Amendments—[1] Words in sub-s (4)(*b*) added by FA 1968 s 60.

[2] Words in the heading and in sub-s (1) added by virtue of FA 1994 Sch 7 para 33.

[3] Words in sub-s (3)(*a*) substituted by FA 1993 s 205 in relation to resolutions passed after 27 July 1993.

[4] Word in sub-s (4) substituted by FA 1993 s 205 in relation to resolutions passed after 27 July 1993.

[5] Words in sub-s (3) inserted by F(No 2)A 1997 s 50 in relation to resolutions passed after 31 July 1997.

[6] Words in sub-s (4)(*b*) substituted by FA 2007 s 112(1) with effect from 19 July 2007.

IPT

5 House of Commons resolution giving provisional effect to motions affecting taxation

(1) This section shall apply if the House of Commons resolves that provisional statutory effect shall be given to one or more motions to be moved by the Chancellor of the Exchequer, or some other Minister, and which, if agreed to by the House, would be resolutions—

(*a*) to which statutory effect could be given under section 1 of this Act, or

(*b*), (c) …

(2) Subject to subsection (3) below, on the passing of the resolution under subsection (1) above, sections 1 … of this Act, … shall apply as if each motion to which the resolution applies had then been agreed to by a resolution of the House.

(3) Subsection (2) above shall cease to apply to a motion if that motion, or a motion containing the same proposals with modifications, is not agreed to by a resolution of the House (in this section referred to as "a confirmatory resolution") within the next ten days on which the House sits after the resolution under subsection (1) above is passed, and, if it ceases to apply, all such adjustments, whether by way of discharge or repayment of tax, or discharge of security, or otherwise, shall be made as may be necessary to restore the position to what it would have been if subsection (2) above had never applied to that motion, and to make good any deductions which have become unauthorised deductions.

(4) …

Note—Sub-ss (1)(*b*), (4) and words omitted from sub-s (2) are not relevant to insurance premium tax; sub-s (1)(*c*) is repealed.

Cross reference—See FA 1994 Sch 7 para 34 (insurance premium tax paid by virtue of a resolution under this Act becoming repayable under sub-s (3) above).

6 Short title, repeals and saving as respects Northern Ireland

(1) This Act may be cited as the Provisional Collection of Taxes Act 1968.

(2) …

(3) …[1]

Note—Sub-s (2) repeals enactments specified in Schedule.

Amendments—[1] Sub-s (3) repealed by Northern Ireland Constitution Act 1973 s 41(1)(*a*) and Sch 6 Pt I, with effect from 18 July 1973.

INTERPRETATION ACT 1978

(1978 Chapter 30)

Note—See VAT Statutes, *ante*.

INCOME AND CORPORATION TAXES ACT 1988

(1988 Chapter 1)

PART XIX
SUPPLEMENTAL

Miscellaneous

827 VAT penalties etc

(1), (1A) …

[(1B) Where a person is liable to make a payment by way of—

(a) penalty under any of paragraphs 12 to 19 of Schedule 7 to the Finance Act 1994 (insurance premium tax), or

(b) interest under paragraph 21 of that Schedule,

the payment shall not be allowed as a deduction in computing any income, profits or losses [[for any corporation tax purposes (but see also subsection (3)(a) below)][2].][1]

(1C)–(1F), (2), (3) …[3]

Note—Words omitted are not relevant for the purposes of IPT.

Amendments—[1] Sub-s (1B) inserted by FA 1994 s 64, Sch 7 Pt VI, para 31 and applies when IPT is charged on the receipt of a premium by an insurer under a taxable insurance contract after 30 September 1994; see FA 1994 ss 48, 49.

[2] Words in sub-s (1B) substituted by the Income Tax (Trading and Other Income) Act 2005, s 882(1), Sch 1, Pt 1, paras 1, 332(*a*) with effect, for the purposes of income tax for the year 2005–06 and subsequent tax years, and for the purposes of corporation tax for accounting periods ending after 5 April 2005.

[3] This section repealed by CTA 2009 ss 1322, 1326, Sch 1 paras 1, 268, Sch 3 Part 1. CTA 2009 applies for accounting periods ending on or after 1 April 2009 (for corporation tax purposes) and for tax years 2009–10 onwards (for income and capital gains tax purposes).

FINANCE ACT 1994

(1994 Chapter 9)

ARRANGEMENT OF SECTIONS

PART III

INSURANCE PREMIUM TAX

The basic provisions

Administration

Tax representatives

Review and appeal

Miscellaneous

Supplementary

IPT

SCHEDULES:

Schedule 6A—Premiums liable to tax at the higher rate.
Schedule 7—Insurance premium tax.
Schedule 7A—Insurance premium tax: contracts that are not taxable.

An Act to grant certain duties, to alter other duties, and to amend the law relating to the National Debt and the Public Revenue, and to make further provision in connection with Finance.

[3rd May 1994]

PART III
INSURANCE PREMIUM TAX

The basic provisions

48 Insurance premium tax

(1) A tax, to be known as insurance premium tax, shall be charged in accordance with this Part.

(2) The tax shall be under the care and management of the Commissioners of Customs and Excise.

49 Charge to tax

Tax shall be charged on the receipt of a premium by an insurer if the premium is received—

(*a*) under a taxable insurance contract, and
(*b*) on or after 1st October 1994.

50 Chargeable amount

(1) Tax shall be charged by reference to the chargeable amount.

(2) For the purposes of this Part, the chargeable amount is such amount as, with the addition of the tax chargeable, is equal to the amount of the premium.

(3) [Subsections (1) and (2)][1] above shall have effect subject to section 69 below.

Commentary—*De Voil Indirect Tax Service* **V18.101**.
Amendments—[1] Words substituted by FA 1997 s 23(2) with effect as provided by FA 1997, s 24.

[51 Rate of tax

(1) Tax shall be charged—

(*a*) at the higher rate, in the case of a premium which is liable to tax at that rate; and
(*b*) at the standard rate, in any other case.

(2) For the purposes of this Part—

(*a*) for the higher rate is 17.5 per cent; and
(*b*) the standard rate is [5 per cent][2].][1]

Commentary—*De Voil Indirect Tax Service* **V18.111**.
Press releases etc—C & E News Release 4/97 6-2-97 (by concession, the higher rate will not apply to ordinary motor insurance sold by car or motor cycle dealers or to home contents insurance when sold by retailers).
Amendments—[1] This section substituted by FA 1997 s 21(1) with effect as provided by FA 1997 s 24.
[2] Words in sub-s (2)(*b*) substituted by FA 1999 s 125(1) with effect in relation to a premium which falls to be regarded for the purposes of FA 1994 Pt III (insurance premium tax) as received under a taxable insurance contract by an insurer from 1 July 1999, subject to the provisions of FA 1999 s 125(3) and (4).

[51A Premiums liable to tax at the higher rate

(1) A premium received under a taxable insurance contract by an insurer is liable to tax at the higher rate if it falls within one or more of the paragraphs of Part II of Schedule 6A to this Act.

(2) Part I of Schedule 6A to this Act shall have effect with respect to the interpretation of that Schedule.

(3) Provision may be made by order amending Schedule 6A as it has effect for the time being.

(4) This section is subject to section 69 below.]

Commentary—*De Voil Indirect Tax Service* **V18.112**.
Amendments—This section inserted by FA 1997 s 22(1) with effect as provided by FA 1997 s 24.
Simon's Tax Cases—*R v C&E Comrs, ex p Lunn Poly Ltd* [1999] STC 350.

52 Liability to pay tax

(1) Tax shall be payable by the person who is the insurer in relation to the contract under which the premium is received.

(2) Subsection (1) above shall have effect subject to any regulations made under section 65 below.

Commentary—*De Voil Indirect Tax Service* **V18.126, 127**.

[52A Certain fees to be treated as premiums under higher rate contracts

(1) This section applies where—

(*a*) at or about the time when a higher rate contract is effected, and

(*b*) in connection with that contract,

a fee in respect of an insurance-related service is charged by a taxable intermediary to a person who is or becomes the insured (or one of the insured) under the contract or to a person who acts for or on behalf of such a person.

(2) Where this section applies—

(*a*) a payment in respect of the fee shall be treated for the purposes of this Part as a premium received under a taxable insurance contract by an insurer, and

(*b*) that premium—

(i) shall be treated for the purposes of this Part as so received at the time when the payment is made, and

(ii) shall be chargeable to tax at the higher rate.

(3) Tax charged by virtue of subsection (2) above shall be payable by the taxable intermediary as if he were the insurer under the contract mentioned in paragraph (*a*) of that subsection.

(4) For the purposes of this section, a contract of insurance is a "higher rate contract" if—

(*a*) it is a taxable insurance contract; and

(*b*) the whole or any part of a premium received under the contract by the insurer is (apart from this section) liable to tax at the higher rate.

(5) For the purposes of this Part a "taxable intermediary" is a person falling within subsection (6) [or (6A)][2] below who—

(*a*) at or about the time when a higher rate contract is effected, and

(*b*) in connection with that contract,

charges a fee in respect of an insurance-related service to a person who is or becomes the insured (or one of the insured) under the contract or to a person who acts for or on behalf of such a person.

[(6) A person falls within this subsection if the higher rate contract mentioned in subsection (1) above falls within paragraph 2 or 3 of Schedule 6A to this Act (motor cars or motor cycles, or relevant goods) and the person is—

(*a*) within the meaning of the paragraph in question, a supplier of motor cars or motor cycles or, as the case may be, of relevant goods; or

(*b*) a person connected with a person falling within paragraph (*a*) above; or

(*c*) a person who in the course of his business pays—

(i) the whole or any part of the premium received under that contract, or

(ii) a fee connected with the arranging of that contract,

to a person falling within paragraph (*a*) or (*b*) above.

(6A) A person falls within this subsection if the higher rate contract mentioned in subsection (1) above falls within paragraph 4 of Schedule 6A to this Act (travel insurance) and the person is—

(*a*) the insurer under that contract; or

(*b*) a person through whom that contract is arranged in the course of his business; or

(*c*) a person connected with the insurer under that contract; or

(*d*) a person connected with a person falling within paragraph (*b*) above; or

(*e*) a person who in the course of his business pays—

(i) the whole or any part of the premium received under that contract, or

(ii) a fee connected with the arranging of that contract,

to a person falling within any of paragraphs (*a*) to (*d*) above.][3]

(7) …[3]

(8) For the purposes of this section, any question whether a person is connected with another shall be determined in accordance with section 839 of the Taxes Act 1988.

(9) In this section—

"insurance-related service" means any service which is related to, or connected with, insurance;

…[4]][1]

Commentary—*De Voil Indirect Tax Service* **V18.114**.

Amendments—[1] This section inserted by FA 1997 s 25 in relation to payments in respect of fees charged after 18 March 1997.

[2] Words in sub-s (5) inserted by FA 1998 s 147(2) in relation to payments in respect of fees charged on or after 1 August 1998.

[3] Sub-ss (6), (6A) substituted for sub-ss (6), (7) by FA 1998 s 147(3) in relation to payments in respect of fees charged on or after 1 August 1998. Previously the text read:

"(6) A person falls within this subsection if—

(*a*) he is a supplier of goods or services falling within subsection (7) below; or

(*b*) he is connected with a supplier of goods or services falling within that subsection; or

(*c*) he is a person who pays—

(i) the whole or any part of the premium received under that contract, or

(ii) a fee connected with the arranging of that contract,

to a supplier of goods or services falling within subsection (7) below or to a person who is connected with a supplier of goods or services falling within that subsection.

(7) A person is a supplier of goods or services falling within this subsection if—

(*a*) he is a supplier of motor cars or motor cycles, within the meaning of paragraph 2 of Schedule 6A to this Act;

(*b*) he is a supplier of relevant goods, within the meaning of paragraph 3 of that Schedule; or

(*c*) he is a tour operator or travel agent."

[4] In sub-s (9) the words "tour operator" and "travel agent" omitted by FA 1998 s 147(4) in relation to payments in respect of fees charged on or after 1 August 1998. Previously the text read:

" 'tour operator' and "travel agent" have the same meaning as in paragraph 4 of Schedule 6A to this Act."

Administration

53 Registration of insurers

(1) A person who—

(*a*) receives, as insurer, premiums in the course of a taxable business, and

(*b*) is not registered,

is liable to be registered.

[(1A) The register kept under this section may contain such information as the Commissioners think is required for the purposes of the care and management of the tax.][1]

(2) A person who—

(*a*) at any time forms the intention of receiving, as insurer, premiums in the course of a taxable business, and

(*b*) is not already receiving, as insurer, premiums in the course of another taxable business,

shall notify the Commissioners of those facts.

(3) A person who at any time—

(*a*) ceases to have the intention of receiving, as insurer, premiums in the course of a taxable business, and

(*b*) has no intention of receiving, as insurer, premiums in the course of another taxable business,

shall notify the Commissioners of those facts.

(4) Where a person is liable to be registered by virtue of subsection (1) above the Commissioners shall register him with effect from the time when he begins to receive premiums in the course of the business concerned; and it is immaterial whether or not he notifies the Commissioners under subsection (2) above.

(5) Where a person—

(*a*) notifies the Commissioners under subsection (3) above, [and][2]

(*b*) satisfies them of the facts there mentioned, ...[3]

(*c*) ...[3]

the Commissioners shall cancel his registration with effect from the earliest practicable time after he ceases to receive, as insurer, premiums in the course of any taxable business.

[(5A) In a case where—

(*a*) the Commissioners are satisfied that a person has ceased to receive, as insurer, premiums in the course of any taxable business, but

(*b*) he has not notified them under subsection (3) above,

they may cancel his registration with effect from the earliest practicable time after he so ceased.][4]

(6) For the purposes of this section regulations may make provision—

(*a*) as to the time within which a notification is to be made;

(*b*) as to the circumstances in which premiums are to be taken to be received in the course of a taxable business;

(*c*) as to the form and manner in which any notification is to be made and as to the information to be contained in or provided with it;

(*d*) requiring a person who has made a notification to notify the Commissioners if any information contained in or provided in connection with it is or becomes inaccurate;

(*e*) as to the correction of entries in the register.

(7) References in this section to receiving premiums are to receiving premiums on or after 1st October 1994.

Commentary—*De Voil Indirect Tax Service* **V18.131, 136**.
Regulations—Insurance Premium Tax Regulations, SI 1994/1774.
Cross references—See Insurance Premium Tax Regulations, SI 1994/1774 reg 4(1) (notification of liability to register),
SI 1994/1774 reg 6 (notification of liability to be de-registered),
SI 1994/1774 reg 7 (transfer of a going concern),
SI 1994/1774 reg 11 (death, bankruptcy or incapacity of registrable persons),
SI 1994/1774 reg 19(2) (claim for credit following cancellation of registration).
Amendments—[1] Sub-s (1A) inserted by FA 1995 s 34, Sch 5 para 3.
[2] Word "and" at end of sub-s (5)(*a*) inserted by FA 1995 s 34, Sch 5 para 2(2), (4) with effect for notifications under sub-s (3) made on or after 1 May 1995.
[3] Word "and" at end of sub-s (5)(*b*), and sub-s (5)(*c*), repealed by FA 1995 s 34, Sch 5 para 2(2), (4), Sch 29 Pt VII with effect for notifications under sub-s (3) made after 30 April 1995.
[4] Sub-s (5A) inserted by FA 1995 s 34, Sch 5 para 3.

[53AA Registration of taxable intermediaries

(1) A person who—

(*a*) is a taxable intermediary, and

(*b*) is not registered,

is liable to be registered.

(2) The register kept under this section may contain such information as the Commissioners think is required for the purposes of the care and management of the tax.

(3) A person who—

(*a*) at any time forms the intention of charging taxable intermediary's fees, and

(*b*) is not already charging such fees in the course of another business,

shall notify the Commissioners of those facts.

(4) A person who at any time—

(*a*) ceases to have the intention of charging taxable intermediary's fees in the course of his business, and

(*b*) has no intention of charging such fees in the course of another business of his,

shall notify the Commissioners of those facts.

(5) Where a person is liable to be registered by virtue of subsection (1) above, the Commissioners shall register him with effect from the time when he begins to charge taxable intermediary's fees in the course of the business concerned; and it is immaterial whether or not he notifies the Commissioners under subsection (3) above.

(6) Where a person—

(*a*) notifies the Commissioners under subsection (4) above, and

(*b*) satisfies them of the facts there mentioned,

the Commissioners shall cancel his registration with effect from the earliest practicable time after he ceases to charge taxable intermediary's fees in the course of any business of his.

(7) In a case where—

(*a*) the Commissioners are satisfied that a person has ceased to charge taxable intermediary's fees in the course of any business of his, but

(*b*) he has not notified them under subsection (4) above,

they may cancel his registration with effect from the earliest practicable time after he so ceased.

(8) For the purposes of this section regulations may make provision—

(*a*) as to the time within which a notification is to be made;

(*b*) as to the form and manner in which any notification is to be made and as to the information to be contained in or provided with it;

(*c*) requiring a person who has made a notification to notify the Commissioners if any information contained in or provided in connection with it is or becomes inaccurate;

(*d*) as to the correction of entries in the register.

(9) In this Part "taxable intermediary's fees" means fees which, to the extent of any payment in respect of them, are chargeable to tax by virtue of section 52A above.]

Commentary—*De Voil Indirect Tax Service* **V18.135, 137**.
Amendments—This section inserted by FA 1997 s 26 with effect from 19 March 1997.

[53A Information required to keep register up to date

(1) Regulations may make provision requiring a registrable person to notify the Commissioners of particulars which—

(*a*) are of changes in circumstances relating to the registrable person or any business carried on by him,

(*b*) appear to the Commissioners to be required for the purpose of keeping the register kept under section 53 [or 53AA][2] above up to date, and

(*c*) are of a prescribed description.

(2) Regulations may make provision—

(*a*) as to the time within which a notification is to be made;

(*b*) as to the form and manner in which a notification is to be made;

(*c*) requiring a person who has made a notification to notify the Commissioners if any information contained in it is inaccurate.][1]

Amendments—[1] This section inserted by FA 1995 s 34, Sch 5 para 4.
[2] Words in sub-s(1)(*b*) inserted by FA 1997 s 27(2) with effect from 19 March 1997.

54 Accounting for tax and time for payment

Regulations may provide that a registrable person shall—

(*a*) account for tax by reference to such periods (accounting periods) as may be determined by or under the regulations;

(*b*) make, in relation to accounting periods, returns in such form as may be prescribed and at such times as may be so determined;

(*c*) pay tax at such times and in such manner as may be so determined.

Commentary—*De Voil Indirect Tax Service* **V18.146**.
Regulations—Insurance Premium Tax Regulations, SI 1994/1774.

55 Credit

(1) Regulations may provide that where an insurer [or taxable intermediary][1] has paid tax and all or part of the premium [or taxable intermediary's fee (as the case may be)][1] is repaid, the insurer [or taxable intermediary][1] shall be entitled to credit of such an amount as is found in accordance with prescribed rules.

(2) Regulations may provide that where—

(*a*) by virtue of regulations made under section 68 below tax is charged in relation to a premium which is shown in the accounts of an insurer as due to him,
(*b*) that tax is paid, and
(*c*) it is shown to the satisfaction of the Commissioners that the premium, or part of it, will never actually be received by or on behalf of the insurer,

the insurer shall be entitled to credit of such an amount as is found in accordance with prescribed rules.

(3) Regulations may make provision as to the manner in which an insurer [or taxable intermediary][1] is to benefit from credit, and in particular may make provision—

(*a*) that an insurer [or taxable intermediary][1] shall be entitled to credit by reference to accounting periods;
(*b*) that an insurer [or taxable intermediary][1] shall be entitled to deduct an amount equal to his total credit for an accounting period from the total amount of tax due from him for the period;
(*c*) that if no tax is due from an insurer [or taxable intermediary][1] for an accounting period but he is entitled to credit for the period, the amount of the credit shall be paid to him by the Commissioners;
(*d*) that if the amount of credit to which an insurer [or taxable intermediary][1] is entitled for an accounting period exceeds the amount of tax due from him for the period, an amount equal to the excess shall be paid to him by the Commissioners;
(*e*) for the whole or part of any credit to be held over to be credited for a subsequent accounting period;
(*f*) as to the manner in which a person who has ceased to be registrable [(whether under section 53 or section 53AA)][1] is to benefit from credit.

(4) Regulations under subsection (3)(*c*) or (*d*) above may provide that where at the end of an accounting period an amount is due to an insurer [or taxable intermediary][1] who has failed to submit returns for an earlier period as required by this Part, the Commissioners may withhold payment of the amount until he has complied with that requirement.

(5) Regulations under subsection (3)(*e*) above may provide for credit to be held over either on the insurer's [or taxable intermediary's][1] application or in accordance with general or special directions given by the Commissioners from time to time.

(6) Regulations may provide that—

(*a*) no deduction or payment shall be made in respect of credit except on a claim made in such manner and at such time as may be determined by or under regulations;
(*b*) payment in respect of credit shall be made subject to such conditions (if any) as the Commissioners think fit to impose, including conditions as to repayment in specified circumstances;
(*c*) deduction in respect of credit shall be made subject to such conditions (if any) as the Commissioners think fit to impose, including conditions as to the payment to the Commissioners, in specified circumstances, of an amount representing the whole or part of the amount deducted.

(7) Regulations may require a claim by an insurer [or taxable intermediary][1] to be made in a return required by provision made under section 54 above.

(8) Regulations may provide that where—

(*a*) all or any of the tax payable in respect of a premium [or taxable intermediary's fee][1] has not been paid, and
(*b*) the circumstances are such that a person would be entitled to credit if the tax had been paid,

prescribed adjustments shall be made as regards any amount of tax due from any person.

Commentary—*De Voil Indirect Tax Service* **V18.121**.
Regulations—Insurance Premium Tax Regulations, SI 1994/1774.
Cross references—See Insurance Premium Tax Regulations, SI 1994/1774 reg 18(3) (claims for credit: directions under sub-s (5) of this section).
Amendments—[1] Words inserted by FA 1997 s 27(3) with effect from 19 March 1997.

56–58

Amendment—Repealed by FA 2008 s 142 with effect from 21 July 2008.

Review and appeal

59 [Appeals][4]

(1) [Subject to section 60, an appeal shall lie to an appeal tribunal from any person who is or will be affected by any decision of HMRC with respect to the any of the following matters—][4]

(*a*) the registration or cancellation of registration of any person under this Part;

(*b*) whether tax is chargeable in respect of a premium or how much tax is chargeable;

[(*bb*) whether a payment falls to be treated under section 52A(2) above as a premium received under a taxable insurance contract by an insurer and chargeable to tax at the higher rate;][3]

(*c*) whether a person is entitled to credit by virtue of regulations under section 55 above or how much credit a person is entitled to or the manner in which he is to benefit from credit;

(*d*) an assessment [falling within subsection (1A) below][1] or the amount of such an assessment;

(*e*) any refusal of an application under section 63 below;

(*f*) whether a notice may be served on a person by virtue of regulations made under section 65 below;

(*g*) an assessment under regulations made under section 65 below or the amount of such an assessment;

(*h*) whether a scheme established by regulations under section 68 below applies to an insurer as regards an accounting period;

(*i*) the requirement of any security under paragraph 24 of Schedule 7 to this Act or its amount;

(*j*) any liability to a penalty under paragraphs 12 to 19 of Schedule 7 to this Act;

(*k*) the amount of any penalty or interest specified in an assessment under paragraph 25 of Schedule 7 to this Act;

(*l*) a claim for the repayment of an amount under paragraph 8 of Schedule 7 to this Act;

(*m*) any liability of the Commissioners to pay interest under paragraph 22 of Schedule 7 to this Act or the amount of the interest payable.

[(1A) An assessment falls within this subsection if it is an assessment under section 56 above in respect of an accounting period in relation to which a return required to be made by virtue of regulations under section 54 above has been made.][2]

(2) Any person who is or will be affected by any decision to which this section applies may by notice in writing to the Commissioners require them to review the decision.

(3) The Commissioners shall not be required under this section to review any decision unless the notice requiring the review is given before the end of the period of 45 days beginning with the day on which written notification of the decision, or of the assessment containing the decision, was first given to the person requiring the review.

(4) For the purposes of subsection (3) above it shall be the duty of the Commissioners to give written notification of any decision to which this section applies to any person who—

(a) requests such a notification,

(b) has not previously been given written notification of that decision, and

(c) if given such a notification, will be entitled to require a review of the decision under this section.

(5) A person shall be entitled to give a notice under this section requiring a decision to be reviewed for a second or subsequent time only if—

(a) the grounds on which he requires the further review are that the Commissioners did not, on any previous review, have the opportunity to consider certain facts or other matters, and

(b) he does not, on the further review, require the Commissioners to consider any facts or matters which were considered on a previous review except in so far as they are relevant to any issue not previously considered.

(6) Where the Commissioners are required in accordance with this section to review any decision, it shall be their duty to do so; and on the review they may withdraw, vary or confirm the decision.

(7) In a case where—

(a) it is the duty under this section of the Commissioners to review any decision, and

(b) they do not, within the period of 45 days beginning with the day on which the review was required, give notice to the person requiring it of their determination on the review,

they shall be assumed for the purposes of this Part to have confirmed the decision.

(8) The Commissioners shall not by virtue of any requirement under this section to review a decision have any power, apart from their power in pursuance of paragraph 13 of Schedule 7 to this Act, to mitigate the amount of any penalty imposed under this Part.]

Commentary—*De Voil Indirect Tax Service* **V18.152, 153**.

Note—This section was brought into force on 1 October 1994, by virtue of the FA 1994 (Appointed Day) Order, SI 1994/1773.

Cross references—See Insurance Premium Tax Regulations, SI 1994/1774 reg 42 (distress), SI 1994/1774 reg 43 (diligence).

FA 1997 Sch 5 para 19(2) (review of decision contained in an assessment under FA 1997 Sch 5 para 14, 15 or 17).

Simon's Tax Cases—59(1)(*b*), (*l*), (2), *C&E Comrs v Cresta Holidays Ltd and others* [2001] STC 386.

Amendments—[1] Words in sub-s (1)(*d*) substituted by FA 1995 s 34, Sch 5 para 5(2), (4) with effect for assessments made after 30 April 1995.

[2] Sub-s (1A) inserted by FA 1995 s 34, Sch 5 para 5(3), (4) with effect for assessments made after 30 April 1995.

IPT

[3] Sub-s (1)(*bb*) inserted by FA 1997 s 27(6) with effect from 19 March 1997.
[4] Heading substituted for the former heading "Review of Commissioners' decisions"; words in sub-s (1) first paragraph substituted for the words "This section applies to any decision of the Commissioners with respect to any of the following matters—"; sub-ss (2)–(8) repealed by the Transfer of Tribunal Functions and Revenue and Customs Appeals Order, SI 2009/56 art 3, Sch 1 para 205(3), (4) with effect from 1 April 2009, subject to transitional and savings provisions in Sch 3 paras 2, 3, 9.

[59A Offer of review

(1) HMRC must offer a person (P) a review of a decision that has been notified to P if an appeal lies under section 59 in respect of the decision.

(2) The offer of the review must be made by notice given to P at the same time as the decision is notified to P.

(3) This section does not apply to the notification of the conclusions of a review.][1]

Amendments—[1] Sections 59A–59G inserted by the Transfer of Tribunal Functions and Revenue and Customs Appeals Order, SI 2009/56 art 3, Sch 1 para 206 with effect from 1 April 2009.

[59B Right to require review

(1) Any person (other than P) who has the right of appeal under section 59 against a decision may require HMRC to review that decision if that person has not appealed to the appeal tribunal under section 59G.

(2) A notification that such a person requires a review must be made within 30 days of that person becoming aware of the decision.][1]

Amendments—[1] Sections 59A–59G inserted by the Transfer of Tribunal Functions and Revenue and Customs Appeals Order, SI 2009/56 art 3, Sch 1 para 206 with effect from 1 April 2009.

[59C Review by HMRC

(1) HMRC must review a decision if—

(a) they have offered a review of the decision under section 59A, and

(b) P notifies HMRC accepting the offer within 30 days from the date of the document containing the notification of the offer.

(2) But P may not notify acceptance of the offer if P has already appealed to the appeal tribunal under section 59G.

(3) HMRC must review a decision if a person other than P notifies them under section 59B.

(4) HMRC shall not review a decision if P, or another person, has appealed to the appeal tribunal under section 59G in respect of the decision.][1]

Amendments—[1] Sections 59A–59G inserted by the Transfer of Tribunal Functions and Revenue and Customs Appeals Order, SI 2009/56 art 3, Sch 1 para 206 with effect from 1 April 2009.

[59D Extensions of time

(1) If under section 59A HMRC have offered P a review of a decision, HMRC may within the relevant period notify P that the relevant period is extended.

(2) If under section 59B another person may require HMRC to review a matter, HMRC may within the relevant period notify the other person that the relevant period is extended.

(3) If notice is given the relevant period is extended to the end of 30 days from—

(*a*) the date of the notice, or

(*b*) any other date set out in the notice or a further notice.

(4) In this section "relevant period" means—

(*a*) the period of 30 days referred to in—

(i) section 59C(1)(*b*) (in a case falling within subsection (1)), or

(ii) section 59B(2) (in a case falling within subsection (2)), or

(*b*) if notice has been given under subsection (1) or (2), that period as extended (or as most recently extended) in accordance with subsection (3).][1]

Amendments—[1] Sections 59A–59G inserted by the Transfer of Tribunal Functions and Revenue and Customs Appeals Order, SI 2009/56 art 3, Sch 1 para 206 with effect from 1 April 2009.

[59E Review out of time

(1) This section applies if—

(*a*) HMRC have offered a review of a decision under section 59A and P does not accept the offer within the time allowed under section 59C(1)(*b*) or 59D(3); or

(*b*) a person who requires a review under section 59B does not notify HMRC within the time allowed under that section or section 59D(3).

(2) HMRC must review the decision under section 59C if—

(*a*) after the time allowed, P, or the other person, notifies HMRC in writing requesting a review out of time,

(*b*) HMRC are satisfied that P, or the other person, had a reasonable excuse for not accepting the offer or requiring review within the time allowed, and (*c*) HMRC are satisfied that P, or the other person, made the request without unreasonable delay after the excuse had ceased to apply.

(3) HMRC shall not review a decision if P, or another person, has appealed to the appeal tribunal under section 59G in respect of the decision.][1]

Amendments—[1] Sections 59A–59G inserted by the Transfer of Tribunal Functions and Revenue and Customs Appeals Order, SI 2009/56 art 3, Sch 1 para 206 with effect from 1 April 2009.

[59F Nature of review etc

(1) This section applies if HMRC are required to undertake a review under section 59C or 59E.

(2) The nature and extent of the review are to be such as appear appropriate to HMRC in the circumstances.

(3) For the purpose of subsection (2), HMRC must, in particular, have regard to steps taken before the beginning of the review—

(*a*) by HMRC in reaching the decision, and

(*b*) by any person in seeking to resolve disagreement about the decision.

(4) The review must take account of any representations made by P, or the other person, at a stage which gives HMRC a reasonable opportunity to consider them.

(5) The review may conclude that the decision is to be—

(*a*) upheld,

(*b*) varied, or

(*c*) cancelled.

(6) HMRC must give P, or the other person, notice of the conclusions of the review and their reasoning within—

(*a*) a period of 45 days beginning with the relevant date, or

(*b*) such other period as HMRC and P, or the other person, may agree.

(7) In subsection (6) "relevant date" means—

(*a*) the date HMRC received P's notification accepting the offer of a review (in a case falling within section 59A), or

(*b*) the date HMRC received notification from another person requiring review (in a case falling within section 59B), or

(*c*) the date on which HMRC decided to undertake the review (in a case falling within section 59E).

(8) Where HMRC are required to undertake a review but do not give notice of the conclusions within the time period specified in subsection (6), the review is to be treated as having concluded that the decision is upheld.

(9) If subsection (8) applies, HMRC must notify P or the other person of the conclusion which the review is treated as having reached.][1]

Amendments—[1] Sections 59A–59G inserted by the Transfer of Tribunal Functions and Revenue and Customs Appeals Order, SI 2009/56 art 3, Sch 1 para 206 with effect from 1 April 2009.

[59G Bringing of appeals

(1) An appeal under section 59 is to be made to the appeal tribunal before—

(*a*) the end of the period of 30 days beginning with—

(i) in a case where P is the appellant, the date of the document notifying the decision to which the appeal relates, or

(ii) in a case where a person other than P is the appellant, the date that person becomes aware of the decision, or

(*b*) if later, the end of the relevant period (within the meaning of section 59D).

(2) But that is subject to subsections (3) to (5).

(3) In a case where HMRC are required to undertake a review under section 59C—

(*a*) an appeal may not be made until the conclusion date, and

(*b*) any appeal is to be made within the period of 30 days beginning with the conclusion date.

(4) In a case where HMRC are requested to undertake a review by virtue of section 59E—

(*a*) an appeal may not be made—

(i) unless HMRC have decided whether or not to undertake a review, and

(ii) if HMRC decide to undertake a review, until the conclusion date; and

(*b*) any appeal is to be made within the period of 30 days beginning with—

(i) the conclusion date (if HMRC decide to undertake a review), or

(ii) the date on which HMRC decide not to undertake a review.

(5) In a case where section 59F(8) applies, an appeal may be made at any time from the end of the period specified in section 59F(6) to the date 30 days after the conclusion date.

(6) An appeal may be made after the end of the period specified in subsection (1), (3)(*b*), (4)(*b*) or (5) if the appeal tribunal gives permission to do so.

(7) In this section "conclusion date" means the date of the document notifying the conclusion of the review.][1]

Amendments—[1] Sections 59A–59G inserted by the Transfer of Tribunal Functions and Revenue and Customs Appeals Order, SI 2009/56 art 3, Sch 1 para 206 with effect from 1 April 2009.

60 [Further provisions relating to appeals][1]

(1) …[1]

(2) Without prejudice to paragraph 13 of Schedule 7 to this Act, nothing in [section 59][1] above shall be taken to confer on a tribunal any power to vary an amount assessed by way of penalty or interest except in so far as it is necessary to reduce it to the amount which is appropriate under paragraphs 12 to 21 of that Schedule.

(3) …[1]

[(4) Subject to subsections (4A) and (4B), where the appeal is against the decisions with respect to any of the matters mentioned in section 59(1)(*b*) and (*d*), it shall not be entertained unless the amount which HMRC have determined to be payable as tax has been paid or deposited with them.

(4A) In a case where the amount determined to be payable as tax has not been paid or deposited an appeal shall be entertained if—

(*a*) HMRC are satisfied (on the application of the appellant), or

(*b*) the appeal tribunal decides (HMRC not being so satisfied and on the application of the appellant),

that the requirement to pay or deposit the amount determined would cause the appellant to suffer hardship.

(4B) Notwithstanding the provisions of sections 11 and 13 of the Tribunals, Courts and Enforcement Act 2007, the decision of the appeal tribunal as to the issue of hardship is final.][1]

(5) Where on an appeal against a decision with respect to any of the matters mentioned in section 59(1)(*d*) above—

(*a*) it is found that the amount specified in the assessment is less than it ought to have been, and

(*b*) the tribunal gives a direction specifying the correct amount,

the assessment shall have effect as an assessment of the amount specified in the direction and that amount shall be deemed to have been notified to the appellant.

(6) Where on an appeal under this section it is found that the whole or part of any amount paid or deposited in pursuance of subsection (4) above is not due, so much of that amount as is found not to be due shall be repaid with interest [at the rate applicable under section 197 of the Finance Act 1996][1].

(7) Where on an appeal under this section it is found that the whole or part of any amount due to the appellant by virtue of regulations under section 55(3)(*c*) or (*d*) or (*f*) above has not been paid, so much of that amount as is found not to have been paid shall be paid with interest [at the rate applicable under section 197 of the Finance Act 1996][1].

(8) Where an appeal under this section has been entertained notwithstanding that an amount determined by [HMRC][1] to be payable as tax has not been paid or deposited and it is found on the appeal that that amount is due [it shall be paid with interest at the rate applicable under section 197 of the Finance Act 1996][1]

[(8A) Interest under subsection (8) shall be paid without any deduction of income tax.][1]

(9) On an appeal against an assessment to a penalty under paragraph 12 of Schedule 7 to this Act, the burden of proof as to the matters specified in paragraphs (*a*) and (*b*) of sub-paragraph (1) of paragraph 12 shall lie upon [HMRC][1].

[(10) Sections 85 and 85B of the Value Added Tax Act 1994 (settling of appeals by agreement and payment of tax where there is a further appeal) shall have effect as if—

(*a*) the references to section 83 of that Act included references to section 59 above, and

(*b*) the references to value added tax included references to insurance premium tax.][1]

Commentary—*De Voil Indirect Tax Service* **V18.152**.

Notes—This section was brought into force on 1 October 1994, by virtue of the FA 1994 (Appointed Day) Order, SI 1994/1773.

FA 1985 ss 25, 29 have been consolidated as VATA 1994 ss 85, 87.

VATA 1983 s 40 has been consolidated as VATA 1994 ss 83, 84.

Cross references—See FA 1997 Sch 5 para 19(2) (appeal following decision by Commissioners contained in an assessment under FA 1997 Sch 5 para 14, 15 or 17).

Amendments—[1] The following amendments made by the Transfer of Tribunal Functions and Revenue and Customs Appeals Order, SI 2009/56 art 3, Sch 1 para 207 with effect from 1 April 2009, subject to transitional and savings provisions in Sch 3 paras 2, 3, 9—

- heading substituted for former heading "Appeals";
- sub-ss (1), (3) repealed;
- in sub-s (2) words substituted for the words "subsection (1)";
- sub-ss (4)–(4B) substituted for former sub-s (4);
- words in sub-ss (6), (7) substituted on both places for the words "at such rate as the tribunal may determine";
- in sub-s (8) word substituted for the words "the Commissioners" and words in the second place substituted for the words "the tribunal may, if it thinks fit, direct that that amount shall be paid with interest at such rate as may be specified in the direction";

– sub-s (8A) inserted;
– in sub-s (9) word substituted for the words "the Commissioners";
– sub-s 10 substituted.

Sub-ss (1), (3), (4), 10 previously read as follows—

(1) Subject to the following provisions of this section, an appeal shall lie to an appeal tribunal with respect to any of the following decisions—

(*a*) any decision by the Commissioners on a review under section 59 above (including a deemed confirmation under subsection (7) of that section);

(*b*) any decision by the Commissioners on such review of a decision referred to in section 59(1) above as the Commissioners have agreed to undertake in consequence of a request made after the end of the period mentioned in section 59(3) above.

(3) Where an appeal is made under this section by a person who is required to make returns by virtue of regulations under section 54 above, the appeal shall not be entertained unless the appellant—

(*a*) has made all the returns which he is required to make by virtue of those regulations, and

(*b*) has paid the amounts shown in those returns as payable by him;

but the restriction in paragraph (*b*) above shall not apply in the case of an appeal against a decision with respect to the matter mentioned in section 59(1)(*i*) above.

(4) Where the appeal is against a decision with respect to any of the matters mentioned in paragraphs (*b*) and (*d*) of section 59(1) above it shall not be entertained unless—

(*a*) the amount which the Commissioners have determined to be payable as tax has been paid or deposited with them, or

(*b*) on being satisfied that the appellant would otherwise suffer hardship the Commissioners agree or the tribunal decides that it should be entertained notwithstanding that that amount has not been so paid or deposited.

(10) Sections 25 and 29 of the Finance Act 1985 (settling of appeals by agreement and enforcement of certain decisions of tribunal) shall have effect as if—

(*a*) the references to section 40 of the Value Added Tax Act 1983 included references to this section, and

(*b*) the references to value added tax included references to insurance premium tax.

61 Review and appeal: commencement

Sections 59 and 60 above shall come into force on such day as may be appointed by order.

Miscellaneous

62 Partnership, bankruptcy, transfer of business, etc

(1) Regulations may make provision for determining by what persons anything required by this Part to be done by an insurer [or taxable intermediary][1] is to be done where the business concerned is carried on in partnership or by another unincorporated body.

(2) The registration under this Part of an unincorporated body other than a partnership may be in the name of the body concerned; and in determining whether premiums are received by such a body no account shall be taken of any change in its members.

(3) Regulations may make provision for determining by what person anything required by this Part to be done by an insurer is to be done in a case where insurance business is carried on by persons who are underwriting members of Lloyd's and are members of a syndicate of such underwriting members.

(4) Regulations may—

(*a*) make provision for the registration for the purposes of this Part of a syndicate of underwriting members of Lloyd's;

(*b*) provide that for purposes prescribed by the regulations no account shall be taken of any change in the members of such a syndicate;

and regulations under paragraph (*a*) above may modify section 53 above.

(5) As regards any case where a person carries on a business of an insurer [or taxable intermediary][1] who has died or become bankrupt or incapacitated or been sequestrated, or of an insurer [or taxable intermediary][1] which is in liquidation or receivership or [administration][2], regulations may—

(*a*) require the person to inform the Commissioners of the fact that he is carrying on the business and of the event that has led to his carrying it on;

(*b*) make provision allowing the person to be treated for a limited time as if he were the insurer [or taxable intermediary][1];

(*c*) make provision for securing continuity in the application of this Part where a person is so treated.

(6) Regulations may make provision for securing continuity in the application of this Part in cases where a business carried on by a person is transferred to another person as a going concern.

(7) Regulations under subsection (6) above may in particular provide—

(*a*) for liabilities and duties under this Part of the transferor to become, to such extent as may be provided by the regulations, liabilities and duties of the transferee;

(*b*) for any right of either of them to repayment or credit in respect of tax to be satisfied by making a repayment or allowing a credit to the other;

but the regulations may provide that no such provision as is mentioned in paragraph (*a*) or (*b*) of this subsection shall have effect in relation to any transferor and transferee unless an application in that behalf has been made by them under the regulations.

Commentary—*De Voil Indirect Tax Service* **V18.134**.

Regulations—Insurance Premium Tax Regulations, SI 1994/1774.
Amendments—[1] Words in sub-s (1) and (5) inserted by FA 1997 s 27(7) with effect from 19 March 1997.
[2] Words in sub-s (5) substituted by the Enterprise Act 2002 (Insolvency) Order, SI 2003/2096 art 4, Schedule para 23 with effect from 15 September 2003. However, this amendment does not apply in relation to any case where a petition for an administration order was presented before that date: SI 2003/2096 arts 1(1), 6.

63 Groups of companies

(1) Where under the following provisions of this section any bodies corporate are treated as members of a group, for the purposes of this Part—

(*a*) any taxable business carried on by a member of the group shall be treated as carried on by the representative member,

[(*aa*) any business carried on by a member of the group who is a taxable intermediary shall be treated as carried on by the representative member,][1]

(*b*) the representative member shall be taken to be the insurer in relation to any taxable insurance contract as regards which a member of the group is the actual insurer,

[(*bb*) the representative member shall be taken to be the taxable intermediary in relation to any taxable intermediary's fees as regards which a member of the group is the actual taxable intermediary,] [1]

(*c*) any receipt by a member of the group of a premium under a taxable insurance contract shall be taken to be a receipt by the representative member, and

(*d*) all members of the group shall be jointly and severally liable for any tax due from the representative member.

(2) Two or more bodies corporate are eligible to be treated as members of a group if each of them falls within subsection (3) below and—

(*a*) one of them controls each of the others,

(*b*) one person (whether a body corporate or an individual) controls all of them, or

(*c*) two or more individuals carrying on a business in partnership control all of them.

(3) A body falls within this subsection if it is resident in the United Kingdom or it has an established place of business in the United Kingdom.

(4) Where an application to that effect is made to the Commissioners with respect to two or more bodies corporate eligible to be treated as members of a group, then—

(*a*) from the beginning of an accounting period they shall be so treated, and

(*b*) one of them shall be the representative member,

unless the Commissioners refuse the application; and the Commissioners shall not refuse the application unless it appears to them necessary to do so for the protection of the revenue.

(5) Where any bodies corporate are treated as members of a group and an application to that effect is made to the Commissioners, then, from the beginning of an accounting period—

(*a*) a further body eligible to be so treated shall be included among the bodies so treated,

(*b*) a body corporate shall be excluded from the bodies so treated,

(*c*) another member of the group shall be substituted as the representative member, or

(*d*) the bodies corporate shall no longer be treated as members of a group,

unless the application is to the effect mentioned in paragraph (*a*) or (*c*) above and the Commissioners refuse the application.

(6) The Commissioners may refuse an application under subsection (5)(*a*) or (*c*) above only if it appears to them necessary to do so for the protection of the revenue.

(7) Where a body corporate is treated as a member of a group as being controlled by any person and it appears to the Commissioners that it has ceased to be so controlled, they shall, by notice given to that person, terminate that treatment from such date as may be specified in the notice.

(8) An application under this section with respect to any bodies corporate must be made by one of those bodies or by the person controlling them and must be made not less than 90 days before the date from which it is to take effect, or at such later time as the Commissioners may allow.

(9) For the purposes of this section a body corporate shall be taken to control another body corporate if it is empowered by statute to control that body's activities or if it is that body's holding company within the meaning of section [1159 of and Schedule 6 to][2] the Companies Act [2006][2]; and an individual or individuals shall be taken to control a body corporate if he or they, were he or they a company, would be that body's holding company within the meaning of [those sections][2].

Commentary—*De Voil Indirect Tax Service* **V18.140**.
Amendments—[1] Sub-s (1)(*aa*) and (*bb*) inserted by FA 1997 s 27(8) with effect from 19 March 1997.
[2] In para (9), words substituted for words "736 of", "1985" and "that section", by the Companies Act 2006 (Consequential Amendments) (Taxes and National Insurance) Order, SI 2009/1890 art 4(1)(*b*) with effect from 1 October 2009.

64 Information, powers, penalties, etc

Schedule 7 to this Act (which contains provisions relating to information, powers, penalties and other matters) shall have effect.

65 Liability of insured in certain cases

(1) Regulations may make provision under this section with regard to any case where at any time [the insurer—

(*a*) does not have any business establishment or other fixed establishment in the United Kingdom, and

(*b*) is established in a country or territory in respect of which it appears to the Commissioners that the condition in subsection (1A) below is met.][1]

[(1A) The condition mentioned in subsection (1)(*b*) above is that—

(*a*) the country or territory is neither a member State nor a part of a member State, and

(*b*) there is no provision for mutual assistance between the United Kingdom and the country or territory similar in scope to the assistance provided for between the United Kingdom and each other member State by the mutual assistance provisions.

(1B) In subsection (1A) above "the mutual assistance provisions" means—

(*a*) section 134 of, and Schedule 39 to, the Finance Act 2002 (recovery of taxes etc due in other member States), and

(*b*) section 197 of the Finance Act 2003 (exchange of information between tax authorities of member States).][1]

(2) Regulations may make provision allowing notice to be served in accordance with the regulations on—

(*a*) the person who is insured under a taxable insurance contract, if there is one insured person, or

(*b*) one or more of the persons who are insured under a taxable insurance contract, if there are two or more insured persons;

and a notice so served is referred to in this section as a liability notice.

(3) Regulations may provide that if a liability notice has been served in accordance with the regulations—

(*a*) the Commissioners may assess to the best of their judgment the amount of any tax due in respect of premiums received by the insurer under the contract concerned after the material date and before the date of the assessment, and

(*b*) that amount shall be deemed to be the amount of tax so due.

(4) The material date is—

(*a*) where there is one person on whom a liability notice has been served in respect of the contract, the date when the notice was served or such later date as may be specified in the notice;

(*b*) where there are two or more persons on whom liability notices have been served in respect of the contract, the date when the last of the notices was served or such later date as may be specified in the notices.

(5) Regulations may provide that where—

(*a*) an assessment is made in respect of a contract under provision included in the regulations by virtue of subsection (3) above, and

(*b*) the assessment is notified to the person, or each of the persons, on whom a liability notice in respect of the contract has been served,

the persons mentioned in subsection (6) below shall be jointly and severally liable to pay the tax assessed, and that tax shall be recoverable accordingly.

(6) The persons are—

(*a*) the person or persons mentioned in subsection (5)(*b*) above, and

(*b*) the insurer.

(7) Where regulations make provision under subsection (5) above they must also provide that any provision made under that subsection shall not apply if, or to the extent that, the assessment has subsequently been withdrawn or reduced.

(8) Regulations may make provision as to the time within which, and the manner in which, tax which has been assessed is to be paid.

(9) Where any amount is recovered from an insured person by virtue of regulations made under this section, the insurer shall be liable to pay to the insured person an amount equal to the amount recovered; and regulations may make provision requiring an insurer to pay interest where this subsection applies.

(10) Regulations may make provision for adjustments to be made of a person's liability in any case where—

(*a*) an assessment is made under section 56 above in relation to the insurer, and

(*b*) an assessment made by virtue of regulations under this section relates to premiums received (or assumed for the purposes of the assessment to be received) within a period which corresponds to any extent with the accounting period to which the assessment under section 56 relates.

(11) Regulations may make provision as regards a case where—

(*a*) an assessment made in respect of a contract by virtue of regulations under this section relates to premiums received (or assumed for the purposes of the assessment to be received) within a given period, and

(*b*) an amount of tax is paid by the insurer in respect of an accounting period which corresponds to any extent with that period;

and the regulations may include provision for determining whether, or how much of, any of the tax paid as mentioned in paragraph (*b*) above is attributable to premiums received under the contract in the period mentioned in paragraph (*a*) above.

(12) Regulations may—

(*a*) make provision requiring the Commissioners, in prescribed circumstances, to furnish prescribed information to an insured person;

(*b*) make provision requiring any person on whom a liability notice has been served to keep records, to furnish information, or to produce documents for inspection or cause documents to be produced for inspection;

(*c*) make such provision as the Commissioners think is reasonable for the purpose of facilitating the recovery of tax from the persons having joint and several liability (rather than from the insurer alone);

(*d*) modify the effect of any provision of this Part.

(13) Regulations may provide for an insured person to be liable to pay tax assessed by virtue of the regulations notwithstanding that he has already paid an amount representing tax as part of a premium.

Commentary—*De Voil Indirect Tax Service* **V18.128.**
Regulations—Insurance Premium Tax Regulations, SI 1994/1774.
Cross reference—See Insurance Premium Tax Regulations, SI 1994/1774 reg 39(1) (interest on reimbursements under sub-s (9) of this section).
Amendments—[1] Sub-s (1)(*a*), (*b*) (which was repealed by FA 2008 s 142 with effect from 21 July 2008) substituted, and sub-ss (1A), (1B) inserted, by FA 2008 s 143 with effect from 21 July 2008.

66 Directions as to amounts of premiums

(1) This section applies where—

(*a*) anything is received by way of premium under a taxable insurance contract, and

(*b*) the amount of the premium is less than it would be if it were received under the contract in open market conditions.

(2) The Commissioners may direct that the amount of the premium shall be taken for the purposes of this Part to be such amount as it would be if it were received under the contract in open market conditions.

(3) A direction under subsection (2) above shall be given by notice in writing to the insurer, and no direction may be given more than three years after the time of the receipt.

(4) Where the Commissioners make a direction under subsection (2) above in the case of a contract they may also direct that if—

(*a*) anything is received by way of premium under the contract after the giving of the notice or after such later date as may be specified in the notice, and

(*b*) the amount of the premium is less than it would be if it were received under the contract in open market conditions,

the amount of the premium shall be taken for the purposes of this Part to be such amount as it would be if it were received under the contract in open market conditions.

(5) For the purposes of this section a premium is received in open market conditions if it is received—

(*a*) by an insurer standing in no such relationship with the insured person as would affect the premium, and

(*b*) in circumstances where there is no other contract or arrangement affecting the parties.

(6) For the purpose of this section it is immaterial whether what is received by way of premium is money or something other than money or both.

Commentary—*De Voil Indirect Tax Service* **V18.106.**

67 Deemed date of receipt of certain premiums

(1) In a case where—

(*a*) a premium under a contract of insurance is received by the insurer after 30th November 1993 and before 1st October 1994, and

(*b*) the period of cover for the risk begins on or after 1st October 1994,

for the purposes of this Part the premium shall be taken to be received on 1st October 1994.

(2) Subsection (3) below applies where—

(*a*) a premium under a contract of insurance is received by the insurer after 30th November 1993 and before 1st October 1994,

(*b*) the period of cover for the risk begins before 1st October 1994 and ends after 30th September 1995, and (*c*) the premium, or any part of it, is attributable to such of the period of cover as falls after 30th September 1995.

(3) For the purposes of this Part—

(*a*) so much of the premium as is attributable to such of the period of cover as falls after 30th September 1995 shall be taken to be received on 1st October 1994;

(*b*) so much as is so attributable shall be taken to be a separate premium.

(4) If a contract relates to more than one risk subsection (1) above shall have effect as if the reference in paragraph (*b*) to the risk were to any given risk.

(5) If a contract relates to more than one risk, subsections (2) and (3) above shall apply as follows—

(*a*) so much of the premium as is attributable to any given risk shall be deemed for the purposes of those subsections to be a separate premium relating to that risk;

(*b*) those subsections shall then apply separately in the case of each given risk and the separate premium relating to it;

and any further attribution required by those subsections shall be made accordingly.

(6) Subsections (1) and (4) above do not apply in relation to a contract if the contract belongs to a class of contract as regards which the normal practice is for a premium to be received by or on behalf of the insurer before the date when cover begins.

(7) Subsections (2), (3) and (5) above do not apply in relation to a contract if the contract belongs to a class of contract as regards which the normal practice is for cover to be provided for a period exceeding twelve months.

(8) Any attribution under this section shall be made on such basis as is just and reasonable.

Commentary—*De Voil Indirect Tax Service* **V18.106**.
Cross reference—See Insurance Premium Tax Regulations, SI 1994/1774 reg 23 (deemed date of receipt of certain premiums).

[67A Announced increase in rate of tax: certain premiums treated as received on date of increase

(1) This section applies in any case where a proposed increase is announced by a Minister of the Crown in the rate at which tax is to be charged on a premium if it is received by the insurer on or after a date specified in the announcement ("the date of the change").

(2) In a case where—

(*a*) a premium under a contract of insurance is received by the insurer on or after the date of the announcement but before the date of the change, and

(*b*) the period of cover for the risk begins on or after the date of the change,

for the purposes of this Part the premium shall be taken to be received on the date of the change.

(3) Subsection (4) below applies where—

(*a*) a premium under a contract of insurance is received by the insurer on or after the date of the announcement but before the date of the change;

(*b*) the period of cover for the risk begins before the date of the change and ends on or after the first anniversary of the date of the change; and

(*c*) the premium, or any part of it, is attributable to such of the period of cover as falls on or after the first anniversary of the date of the change.

(4) For the purposes of this Part—

(*a*) so much of the premium as is attributable to such of the period of cover as falls on or after the first anniversary of the date of the change shall be taken to be received on the date of the change; and

(*b*) so much as is so attributable shall be taken to be a separate premium.

(5) In determining whether the condition in subsection (2)(*a*) or (3)(*a*) above is satisfied, the provisions of regulations made by virtue of subsection (3) or (7) of section 68 below apply as they would apart from this section; but, subject to that, where subsection (2) or (4) above applies—

(*a*) that subsection shall have effect notwithstanding anything in section 68 below or regulations made under that section; and

(*b*) any regulations made under that section shall have effect as if the entry made in the accounts of the insurer showing the premium as due to him had been made as at the date of the change.

(6) Any attribution under this section shall be made on such basis as is just and reasonable.

(7) In this section—

"increase", in relation to the rate of tax, includes the imposition of a charge to tax by adding to the descriptions of contract which are taxable insurance contracts;

"Minister of the Crown" has the same meaning as in the Ministers of the Crown Act 1975.][1]

Commentary—*De Voil Indirect Tax Service* **V18.116**.
Cross references—See FA 1998 s 146(5) (application of section in relation to increases in insurance premium tax effected in FA 1998 Part V).
See FA 1999 s 125(5) (application of section in relation to increases in insurance premium tax effected in FA 1999 Part VII).
Amendments—[1] This section inserted by FA 1997 s 29(1) with effect from 26 November 1996.

[67B Announced increase in rate of tax: certain contracts treated as made on date of increase

(1) This section applies in any case where—

(*a*) an announcement falling within section 67A(1) above is made; but

(*b*) a proposed exception from the increase in question is also announced by a Minister of the Crown; and

(*c*) the proposed exception is to apply in relation to a premium only if the conditions described in subsection (2) below are satisfied in respect of the premium.

(2) Those conditions are—

(*a*) that the premium is in respect of a contract made before the date of the change;

(*b*) that the premium falls, by virtue of regulations under section 68 below, to be regarded for the purposes of this Part as received under the contract by the insurer before such date ("the concessionary date") as is specified for the purpose in the announcement.

(3) In a case where—

(*a*) a premium under a contract of insurance is received by the insurer on or after the date of the announcement but before the concessionary date, and

(*b*) the period of cover for the risk begins on or after the date of the change,

the rate of tax applicable in relation to the premium shall be determined as if the contract had been made on the date of the change.

(4) Subsection (5) below applies where—

(*a*) a premium under a contract of insurance is received by the insurer on or after the date of the announcement but before the concessionary date;

(*b*) the period of cover for the risk begins before the date of the change and ends on or after the first anniversary of the date of the change; and

(*c*) the premium, or any part of it, is attributable to such of the period of cover as falls on or after the first anniversary of the date of the change.

(5) Where this subsection applies—

(*a*) the rate of tax applicable in relation to so much of the premium as is attributable to such of the period of cover as falls on or after the first anniversary of the date of the change shall be determined as if the contract had been made on the date of the change; and

(*b*) so much of the premium as is so attributable shall be taken to be a separate premium.

(6) Any attribution under this section shall be made on such basis as is just and reasonable.

(7) In this section—

"the date of the change" has the same meaning as in section 67A above;

"Minister of the Crown" has the same meaning as in section 67A above.][1]

Commentary—*De Voil Indirect Tax Service* **V18.116**.

Cross reference—See FA 1998 s 146(5) (application of section in relation to increases in insurance premium tax effected in FA 1998 Part V).

See FA 1999 s 125(5) (application of section in relation to increases in insurance premium tax effected in FA 1999 Part VII).

Amendments—[1] This section inserted by FA 1997 s 29(1) with effect from 26 November 1996.

[67C Announced increase in rate of tax: exceptions and apportionments

(1) Sections 67A(2) and 67B(3) above do not apply in relation to a premium if the risk to which that premium relates belongs to a class of risk as regards which the normal practice is for a premium to be received by or on behalf of the insurer before the date when cover begins.

(2) Sections 67A(3) and (4) and 67B(4) and (5) above do not apply in relation to a premium if the risk to which that premium relates belongs to a class of risk as regards which the normal practice is for cover to be provided for a period exceeding twelve months.

(3) If a contract relates to more than one risk, then, in the application of section 67A(2), 67A(3) and (4), 67B(3) or 67B(4) and (5) above—

(*a*) the reference in section 67A(2)(*b*) or (3)(*b*) or 67B(3)(*b*) or (4)(*b*), as the case may be, to the risk shall be taken as a reference to any given risk,

(*b*) so much of the premium as is attributable to any given risk shall be taken for the purposes of section 67A(2), 67A(3) and (4), 67B(3) or 67B(4) and (5) above, as the case may be, to be a separate premium relating to that risk,

(*c*) those provisions shall then apply separately in the case of each given risk and the separate premium relating to it, and

(*d*) any further attribution required by section 67A(3) and (4) or 67B(4) and (5) above shall be made accordingly,

and subsections (1) and (2) above shall apply accordingly.

(4) Any attribution under this section shall be made on such basis as is just and reasonable.][1]

Commentary—*De Voil Indirect Tax Service* **V18.116**.

Cross reference—See FA 1998 s 146(5) (application of section in relation to increases in insurance premium tax effected in FA 1998 Part V.

See FA 1999 s 125(5) (application of section in relation to increases in insurance premium tax effected in FA 1999 Part VII).

Amendments—[1] This section inserted by FA 1997 s 29(1) with effect from 26 November 1996.

68 Special accounting schemes

(1) Regulations may make provision establishing a scheme in accordance with the following provisions of this section; and in this section "a relevant accounting period", in relation to an insurer, means an accounting period as regards which the scheme applies to the insurer.

(2) Regulations may provide that if an insurer notifies the Commissioners that the scheme should apply to him as regards accounting periods beginning on or after a date specified in the notification and prescribed conditions are fulfilled, then, subject to any provision made under subsection (9) below, the scheme shall apply to the insurer as regards accounting periods beginning on or after that date.

(3) Regulations may provide that where—

(*a*) an entry is made in the accounts of an insurer showing a premium under a taxable insurance contract as due to him, and

(*b*) the entry is made as at a particular date which falls within a relevant accounting period,

then (whether or not that date is one on which the premium is actually received by the insurer or on which the premium would otherwise be treated for the purposes of this Part as received by him) the premium shall for the purposes of this Part be taken to be received by the insurer on that date or, in prescribed circumstances, to be received by him on a different date determined in accordance with the regulations.

(4) Where regulations make provision under subsection (3) above they may also provide that, for the purposes of this Part, the amount of the premium shall be taken to be the amount which the entry in the accounts treats as its amount.

(5) Regulations may provide that provision made under subsections (3) and (4) above shall apply even if the premium, or part of it, is never actually received by the insurer or on his behalf; and the regulations may include provision that, where the premium is never actually received because the contract under which it would have been received is never entered into or is terminated, the premium is nonetheless to be taken for the purposes of this Part to be received under a taxable insurance contract.

(6) Regulations may provide that any provision made under subsection (4) above shall be subject to any directions made under section 66 above.

(7) Regulations may provide that where a premium is treated as received on a particular date by virtue of provision made under subsection (3) above and there is another date on which the premium—

(*a*) is actually received by the insurer, or

(*b*) would, apart from the regulations, be treated for the purposes of this Part as received by him,

the premium shall be taken for the purposes of this Part not to be received by him on that other date.

(8) Regulations may provide that provision made under subsection (7) above shall apply only to the extent that there is no excess of the actual amount of the premium over the amount which, by virtue of regulations under this section or of a direction under section 66 above, is to be taken for the purposes of this Part to be its amount; and the regulations may include provision that where there is such an excess, the excess amount shall be taken for the purposes of this Part to be a separate premium and to be received by the insurer on a date determined in accordance with the regulations.

(9) Regulations may provide that if a notification has given in accordance with provision made under subsection (2) above and subsequently—

(*a*) the insurer gives notice to the Commissioners that the scheme should not apply to him as regards accounting periods beginning on or after a date specified in the notice, or

(*b*) the Commissioners give notice to the insurer that the scheme is not to apply to him as regards accounting periods beginning on or after a date specified in the notice,

then, if prescribed conditions are fulfilled, the scheme shall not apply to the insurer as regards an accounting period beginning on or after the date specified in the notice mentioned in paragraph (*a*) or (*b*) above unless the circumstances are such as may be prescribed.

(10) Regulations may include provision—

(*a*) enabling an insurer to whom the scheme applies as regards an accounting period to account for tax due in respect of that period on the assumption that the scheme will apply to him as regards subsequent accounting periods;

(*b*) designed to secure that, where the scheme ceases to apply to an insurer, any tax which by virtue of provision made under paragraph (*a*) above has not been accounted for is accounted for and paid.

(11) Regulations may provide that where—

(*a*) an entry in the accounts of an insurer shows a premium as due to him,

(*b*) the entry is made as at a date falling before 1st October 1994,

(*c*) tax in respect of the receipt of the premium would, apart from the regulations, be charged by reference to a date (whether or not the date on which the premium is actually received by the insurer) falling on or after 1st October 1994,

IPT

(*d*) the date by reference to which tax would be charged falls within a relevant accounting period, and

(*e*) prescribed conditions are fulfilled,

the premium, or such part of it as may be found in accordance with prescribed rules, shall be taken for the purposes of this Part to have been received by the insurer before 1st October 1994.

(12) Without prejudice to subsection (13) below, regulations may include provision modifying any provision made under this section so as to secure the effective operation of the provision in a case where a premium consists wholly or partly of anything other than money.

(13) Regulations may modify the effect of any provision of this Part.

(14) The reference in subsection (3)(*a*) above to a premium under a taxable insurance contract includes a reference to anything that, although not actually received by or on behalf of the insurer, would be such a premium if it were so received.

Commentary—*De Voil Indirect Tax Service* **V18.127**.
Regulations—Insurance Premium Tax Regulations, SI 1994/1774.
Concession ESC 4.1—Special accounting scheme—introductory provisions.

[69 Charge to tax where different rates apply

(1) This section applies for the purpose of determining the chargeable amount in a case where a contract provides cover falling within any one of the following paragraphs, that is to say—

(*a*) cover for one or more exempt matters,

(*b*) cover for one or more standard rate matters, or

(*c*) cover for one or more higher rate matters,

and also provides cover falling within another of those paragraphs.

(2) In the following provisions of this section "the non-exempt premium" means the difference between—

(*a*) the amount of the premium; and

(*b*) such part of the premium as is attributable to any exempt matter or matters or, if no part is so attributable, nil.

(3) If the contract provides cover for one or more exempt matters and also provides cover for either—

(*a*) one or more standard rate matters, or

(*b*) one or more higher rate matters,

the chargeable amount is such amount as, with the addition of the tax chargeable at the standard rate or (as the case may be) the higher rate, is equal to the non-exempt premium.

(4) If the contract provides cover for both—

(*a*) one or more standard rate matters, and

(*b*) one or more higher rate matters,

the higher rate element and the standard rate element shall be found in accordance with the following provisions of this section.

(5) For the purposes of this section—

(*a*) "the higher rate element" is such portion of the non-exempt premium as is attributable to the higher rate matters (including tax at the higher rate); and

(*b*) "the standard rate element" is the difference between—

(i) the non-exempt premium; and

(ii) the higher rate element.

(6) In a case falling within subsection (4) above, tax shall be charged separately—

(*a*) at the standard rate, by reference to the standard rate chargeable amount, and

(*b*) at the higher rate, by reference to the higher rate chargeable amount,

and the tax chargeable in respect of the premium is the aggregate of those amounts of tax.

(7) For the purposes of this section—

"the higher rate chargeable amount" is such amount as, with the addition of the tax chargeable at the higher rate, is equal to the higher rate element;

"the standard rate chargeable amount" is such amount as, with the addition of the tax chargeable at the standard rate, is equal to the standard rate element.

(8) References in this Part to the chargeable amount shall, in a case falling within subsection (4) above, be taken as referring separately to the standard rate chargeable amount and the higher rate chargeable amount.

(9) In applying subsection (2)(*b*) above, any amount that is included in the premium as being referable to tax (whether or not the amount corresponds to the actual amount of tax payable in respect of the premium) shall be taken to be wholly attributable to the non-exempt matter or matters.

(10) In applying subsection (5)(*a*) above, any amount that is included in the premium as being referable to tax at the higher rate (whether or not the amount corresponds to the actual amount of tax payable at that rate in respect of the premium) shall be taken to be wholly attributable to the higher rate element.

(11) Subject to subsections (9) and (10) above, any attribution under subsection (2)(*b*) or (5)(*a*) above shall be made on such basis as is just and reasonable.

(12) For the purposes of this section—

(*a*) an "exempt matter" is any matter such that, if it were the only matter for which the contract provided cover, the contract would not be a taxable insurance contract;

(*b*) a "non-exempt matter" is a matter which is not an exempt matter;

(*c*) a "standard rate matter" is any matter such that, if it were the only matter for which the contract provided cover, tax at the standard rate would be chargeable on the chargeable amount;

(*d*) a "higher rate matter" is any matter such that, if it were the only matter for which the contract provided cover, tax at the higher rate would be chargeable on the chargeable amount.

(13) If the contract relates to a lifeboat and lifeboat equipment, the lifeboat and the equipment shall be taken together in applying this section.

(14) For the purposes of this section "lifeboat" and "lifeboat equipment" have the same meaning as in paragraph 6 of Schedule 7A to this Act.][1]

Commentary—*De Voil Indirect Tax Service* **V18.105**.
Simon's Tax Cases—*Manchester and Salford Hospital Saturday Fund v C&E Comrs* [1999] STC 649.
Amendments—[1] This section substituted by FA 1997 s 23(1) with effect as provided by FA 1997 s 24.

Supplementary

70 Interpretation: taxable insurance contracts

(1) Subject to [subsection (1A) below][1], any contract of insurance is a taxable insurance contract.

[(1A) A contract is not a taxable insurance contract if it falls within one or more of the paragraphs of Part I of Schedule 7A to this Act.][2]

[(1B) Part II of Schedule 7A to this Act (interpretation of certain provisions of Part I) shall have effect.][2]

(2)–(10) …[3]

(11) This section has effect subject to section 71 below.

(12) This section and section 71 below have effect for the purposes of this Part.

Commentary—*De Voil Indirect Tax Service* **V18.103**.
Amendments—[1] Words in sub-s (1) substituted by the Insurance Premium Tax (Taxable Insurance Contracts) Order, SI 1994/1698 arts 1, 4 with effect from 1 October 1994.
[2] Sub-ss (1A), (1B) inserted by the Insurance Premium Tax (Taxable Insurance Contracts) Order, SI 1994/1698, arts 1, 4 with effect from 1 October 1994.
[3] Sub-ss (2)–(10) repealed by the Insurance Premium Tax (Taxable Insurance Contracts) Order, SI 1994/1698, arts 1, 4 with effect from 1 October 1994.

71 Taxable insurance contracts: power to change definition

(1) Provision may be made by order that—

(*a*) a contract of insurance that would otherwise not be a taxable insurance contract shall be a taxable insurance contract if it falls within a particular description;

(*b*) a contract of insurance that would otherwise be a taxable insurance contract shall not be a taxable insurance contract if it falls within a particular description.

(2) A description referred to in subsection (1) above may be by reference to the nature of the insured or by reference to such other factors as the Treasury think fit.

(3) Provision under this section may be made in such way as the Treasury think fit, and in particular may be made by amending this Part.

(4) An order under this section may amend or modify the effect of section 69 above in such way as the Treasury think fit.

Commentary—*De Voil Indirect Tax Service* **V18.104**.

72 Interpretation: premium

(1) In relation to a taxable insurance contract, a premium is any payment received under the contract by the insurer, and in particular includes any payment wholly or partly referable to—

(*a*) any risk,
(*b*) costs of administration,
(*c*) commission,
(*d*) any facility for paying in instalments or making deferred payment (whether or not payment for the facility is called interest), or
(*e*) tax.

[(1A) Where an amount is charged to the insured by any person in connection with a taxable insurance contract, any payment in respect of that amount is to be regarded as a payment received under that contract by the insurer unless—

(*a*) the payment is chargeable to tax at the higher rate by virtue of section 52A above; or

(*b*) the amount is charged under a separate contract and is identified in writing to the insured as a separate amount so charged.][1]

IPT

[(1B) Where—

(*a*) an amount is charged (to the insured or any other person) in respect of the acquisition of a right (whether of the insured or any other person) to require the insurer to provide, or offer to provide, any of the cover included in a taxable insurance contract, and

(*b*) any payment in respect of that amount is not regarded as a payment received under that contract by the insurer by virtue of subsection (1A) above,

the payment is to be regarded as a payment received under that contract by the insurer unless it is chargeable to tax at the higher rate by virtue of section 52A above.][3]

(2) A premium may consist wholly or partly of anything other than money, and references to payment in subsection (1) above shall be construed accordingly.

(3) Where a premium is to any extent received in a form other than money, its amount shall be taken to be—

(*a*) an amount equal to the value of whatever is received in a form other than money, or

(*b*) if money is also received, the aggregate of the amount found under paragraph (*a*) above and the amount received in the form of money.

(4) The value to be taken for the purposes of subsection (3) above is open market value at the time of the receipt by the insurer.

(5) The open market value of anything at any time shall be taken to be an amount equal to such consideration in money as would be payable on a sale of it at that time to a person standing in no such relationship with any person as would affect that consideration.

(6) Where (apart from this subsection) anything received under a contract by the insurer would be taken to be an instalment of a premium, it shall be taken to be a separate premium.

(7) Where anything is received by any person on behalf of the insurer—

(*a*) it shall be treated as received by the insurer when it is received by the other person, and

(*b*) the later receipt of the whole or any part of it by the insurer shall be disregarded.

[(7A) Where any person is authorised by or on behalf of an employee to deduct from anything due to the employee under his contract of employment an amount in respect of a payment due under a taxable insurance contract, subsection (7) above shall not apply to the receipt on behalf of the insurer by the person so authorised of the amount deducted.][2]

(8) In a case where—

(*a*) a payment under a taxable insurance contract is made to a person (the intermediary) by or on behalf of the insured, and

(*b*) the whole or part of the payment is referable to commission to which the intermediary is entitled,

in determining for the purposes of subsection (7) above whether, or how much of, the payment is received by the intermediary on behalf of the insurer any of the payment that is referable to that commission shall be regarded as received by the intermediary on behalf of the insurer notwithstanding the intermediary's entitlement.

[(8A) Where, by virtue of subsection (7A) above, subsection (7) above does not apply to the receipt of an amount by a person and the whole or part of the amount is referable to commission to which he is entitled—

(*a*) if the whole of the amount is so referable, the amount shall be treated as received by the insurer when it is deducted by that person; and

(*b*) otherwise, the part of the amount that is so referable shall be treated as received by the insurer when the remainder of the payment concerned is or is treated as received by him.][2]

(9) References in subsection (8) above to a payment include references to a payment in a form other than money.

(10) This section has effect for the purposes of this Part.

Commentary—*De Voil Indirect Tax Service* **V18.101**.

Amendments—[1] Sub-s (1A) inserted by FA 1997 s 28(1) in relation to payments received in respect of amounts charged on or after 1 April 1997.

[2] Sub-ss (7A) and (8A) inserted by FA 1997 s 30 in relation to amounts deducted on or after 19 March 1997.

[3] Sub-s (1B) inserted by FA 2007 s 101 with effect in relation to amounts charged on or after 22 March 2007.

73 Interpretation: other provisions

(1) Unless the context otherwise requires—

"accounting period" shall be construed in accordance with section 54 above;

"appeal tribunal" means [the First-tier Tribunal or, where determined by or under Tribunal Procedure Rules, the Upper Tribunal][8];

"authorised person" means any person acting under the authority of the Commissioners;

"the Commissioners" means the Commissioners of Customs and Excise;

"conduct" includes any act, omission or statement;

["the higher rate" shall be construed in accordance with section 51 above;][3]

["HMRC" means Her Majesty's Revenue and Customs;][8]

["insurance business" means a business which consists of or includes the provision of insurance;][2]

"insurer" means a person or body of persons (whether incorporated or not) carrying on insurance business;

"legislation relating to insurance premium tax" means this Part (as defined by subsection (9) below), any other enactment (whenever passed) relating to insurance premium tax, and any subordinate legislation made under any such enactment;

"prescribed" means prescribed by an order or regulations under this Part;

["the standard rate" shall be construed in accordance with section 51 above;][3]

"tax" means insurance premium tax;

["tax representative" shall be construed in accordance with section 57 above;][7]

"taxable business" means a business which consists of or includes the provision of insurance under taxable insurance contracts;

"taxable insurance contract" shall be construed in accordance with section 70 above;

["taxable intermediary" shall be construed in accordance with section 52A above;][4]

["taxable intermediary's fees" has the meaning given by section 53AA(9) above.][4]

(2) …[1]

(3) [subject to subsection (3A) below,][5] a registrable person is a person who—

(*a*) is registered under section 53 above, or

(*b*) is liable to be registered under that section.

[(3A) Reference in sections 53A and 54 above and paragraphs 1,9 and 12 of Schedule 7 to this Act to a registrable person include a reference to a person who—

(*a*) is registered under section 53AA above; or

(*b*) is liable to be registered under that section.][6]

(4)–(8) …[1]

(9) A reference to this Part includes a reference to any order or regulations made under it and a reference to a provision of this Part includes a reference to any order or regulations made under the provision, unless otherwise required by the context or any order or regulations.

(10) This section has effect for the purposes of this Part.

Commentary—*De Voil Indirect Tax Service* **V18.131, 181**.

Amendments—[1] Sub-ss (2) and (4)–(8) repealed by the Insurance Premium Tax (Taxable Insurance Contracts) Order, SI 1994/1698 arts 1, 6 with effect from 1 October 1994.

[2] Definition of "insurance business" inserted by FA 1995 s 34, Sch 5 para 6.

[3] Definitions of "the higher rate" and "the standard rate" inserted by FA 1997 s 21(2) with effect as provided by FA 1997 s 24.

[4] Definitions of "taxable intermediary" and "taxable intermediary's fees" inserted by FA 1997 s 27(9) with effect from 19 March 1997.

[5] Words in sub-s (3) inserted by FA 1997 s 27 (10) with effect from 19 March 1997.

[6] Sub-s (3A) inserted by FA 1997 s 27(10) with effect from 19 March 1997.

[7] The definition of "tax representative" repealed by FA 2008 s 142 with effect from 21 July 2008.

[8] In sub-s (1) words in definition of "appeal tribunal" substituted for the words "a VAT and duties tribunal"; definition of "HMRC" inserted; by the Transfer of Tribunal Functions and Revenue and Customs Appeals Order, SI 2009/56 art 3, Sch 1 para 208 with effect from 1 April 2009.

74 Orders and regulations

(1) The power to make an order under section 61 above shall be exercisable by the Commissioners, and the power to make an order under any other provision of this Part shall be exercisable by the Treasury.

(2) Any power to make regulations under this Part shall be exercisable by the Commissioners.

(3) Any power to make an order or regulations under this Part shall be exercisable by statutory instrument.

(4) An order under section [51A or][1] 71 above shall be laid before the House of Commons; and unless it is approved by that House before the expiration of a period of 28 days beginning with the date on which it was made it shall cease to have effect on the expiration of that period, but without prejudice to anything previously done under the order or to the making of a new order.

(5) In reckoning any such period as is mentioned in subsection (4) above no account shall be taken of any time during which Parliament is dissolved or prorogued or during which the House of Commons is adjourned for more than four days.

(6) A statutory instrument containing an order or regulations under this Part (other than an order under section [51A or][1] 71 above) shall be subject to annulment in pursuance of a resolution of the House of Commons.

(7) Any power to make an order or regulations under this Part—

(*a*) may be exercised as regards prescribed cases or descriptions of case;

(*b*) may be exercised differently in relation to different cases or descriptions of case.

(8) An order or regulations under this Part may include such supplementary, incidental, consequential or transitional provisions as appear to the Treasury or the Commissioners (as the case may be) to be necessary or expedient.

(9) No specific provision of this Part about an order or regulations shall prejudice the generality of subsections (7) and (8) above.

Order—Insurance Premium Tax (Prescribed Rates of Interest) Order, SI 1994/1819.

Regulations—Insurance Premium Tax Regulations, SI 1994/1774.

IPT

Amendments—[1] Words in sub-s (4), (6) inserted by FA 1997 s 22(2) with effect as provided by FA 1997, s 24.

[SCHEDULE 6A
PREMIUMS LIABLE TO TAX AT THE HIGHER RATE][1]

Section 51A

Commentary—*De Voil Indirect Tax Service* **V18.112.**
Amendments—[1] This Schedule inserted by FA 1997 s 22(3), Sch 4 with effect as provided by FA 1997 s 24.

[PART I
INTERPRETATION

[1— (1) In this Schedule—

"insurance-related service" means any service which is related to, or connected with, insurance;

"supply" includes all forms of supply; and "supplier" shall be construed accordingly.

(2) For the purposes of this Schedule, any question whether a person is connected with another shall be determined in accordance with section 839 of the Taxes Act 1988.]][1]

Amendments—[1] This Schedule inserted by FA 1997 s 22(3), Sch 4 with effect as provided by FA 1997 s 24.

[PART II
DESCRIPTIONS OF PREMIUM

Insurance relating to motor cars or motor cycles

[2— (1) A premium under a taxable insurance contract relating to a motor car or motor cycle falls within this paragraph if—

(*a*) the contract is arranged through a person falling within sub-paragraph (2) below, or

(*b*) the insurer under the contract is a person falling within that sub-paragraph,

unless the insurance is provided to the insured free of charge.

(2) A person falls within this sub-paragraph if—

(*a*) he is a supplier of motor cars or motor cycles;

(*b*) he is connected with a supplier of motor cars or motor cycles; or

(*c*) he pays—

(i) the whole or any part of the premium received under the taxable insurance contract, or

(ii) a fee connected with the arranging of that contract,

to a supplier of motor cars or motor cycles or to a person who is connected with a supplier of motor cars or motor cycles.

[(2A) A premium does not fall within this paragraph if it is—

(*a*) payable under a taxable insurance contract relating to a motor car or motor cycle which is supplied by way of sale, and

(*b*) attributable to cover of the kind generally known as—

(i) fully comprehensive,

(ii) third party, fire and theft, or

(iii) third party.][2]

(3) Where a taxable insurance contract relating to a motor car or motor cycle is arranged through a person who is connected with a supplier of motor cars or motor cycles, the premium does not fall within this paragraph by virtue only of sub-paragraph (2)(*b*) above except to the extent that the premium is attributable to cover for a risk which relates to a motor car or motor cycle supplied by a supplier of motor cars or motor cycles with whom that person is connected.

(4) Where the insurer under a taxable insurance contract relating to a motor car or motor cycle is connected with a supplier of motor cars or motor cycles, the premium does not fall within this paragraph by virtue only of sub-paragraph (2)(*b*) above except to the extent that the premium is attributable to cover for a risk which relates to a motor car or motor cycle supplied by a supplier of motor cars or motor cycles with whom the insurer is connected.

(5) For the purposes of this paragraph, the cases where insurance is provided to the insured free of charge are those cases where no charge (whether by way of premium or otherwise) is made—

(*a*) in respect of the taxable insurance contract, or

(*b*) at or about the time when the taxable insurance contract is made and in connection with that contract, in respect of any insurance-related service,

by any person falling within sub-paragraph (2) above to any person who is or becomes the insured (or one of the insured) under the contract or to any person who acts, otherwise than in the course of a business, for or on behalf of such a person.

(6) In this paragraph—

"motor car" and "motor cycle" have the meaning given—

(*a*) by section 185(1) of the Road Traffic Act 1988; or

(*b*) in Northern Ireland, by Article 3(1) of the Road Traffic (Northern Ireland) Order 1995;

["sale", in relation to a motor car or motor cycle, means—

(*a*) a sale under which title to the motor car or motor cycle passes to the purchaser immediately on purchase, or

(*b*) a sale pursuant to a hire purchase agreement (within the meaning of the Consumer Credit Act 1974) under which it is intended at the outset of the agreement that the title to the motor car or motor cycle is to pass to the purchaser, whether on conclusion of the agreement or at the end of a period specified in the agreement.][2]

"supplier" does not include an insurer who supplies a car or motor cycle as a means of discharging liabilities arising by reason of a claim under an insurance contract.][1]

Amendments—[1] This Schedule inserted by FA 1997 s 22(3), Sch 4 with effect as provided by FA 1997 s 24.
[2] Sub-para (2A), and in sub-para (6) definition of "sale", inserted, by the Insurance Premium Tax (Amendment of Schedule 6A to the Finance Act 1994) Order, SI 2009/219 art 2 with effect in relation to taxable insurance contracts made or coming into operation on or after 1 April 2009.
Press releases etc—C & E News release 4/97 6-2-97 (by concession, the higher rate will not apply to ordinary motor insurance sold by car or motor cycle dealers).

Insurance relating to domestic appliances etc

[3— (1) A premium under a taxable insurance contract relating to relevant goods falls within this paragraph if—

(*a*) the contract is arranged through a person falling within sub-paragraph (2) below, or

(*b*) the insurer under the contract is a person falling within that sub-paragraph,

unless the insurance is provided to the insured free of charge.

(2) A person falls within this sub-paragraph if—

(*a*) he is a supplier of relevant goods;

(*b*) he is connected with a supplier of relevant goods; or

(*c*) he pays—

(i) the whole or any part of the premium received under the taxable insurance contract, or

(ii) a fee connected with the arranging of that contract,

to a supplier of relevant goods or to a person who is connected with a supplier of relevant goods.

(3) Where a taxable insurance contract relating to relevant goods is arranged through a person who is connected with a supplier of relevant goods, the premium does not fall within this paragraph by virtue only of sub-paragraph (2)(*b*) above except to the extent that the premium is attributable to cover for a risk which relates to relevant goods supplied by a supplier of relevant goods with whom that person is connected.

(4) Where the insurer under a taxable insurance contract relating to relevant goods is connected with a supplier of relevant goods, the premium does not fall within this paragraph by virtue only of sub-paragraph (2)(*b*) above except to the extent that the premium is attributable to cover for a risk which relates to relevant goods supplied by a supplier of relevant goods with whom the insurer is connected.

(5) For the purposes of this paragraph, the cases where insurance is provided to the insured free of charge are those cases where no charge (whether by way of premium or otherwise) is made—

(*a*) in respect of the taxable insurance contract, or

(*b*) at or about the time when the taxable insurance contract is made and in connection with that contract, in respect of any insurance-related service,

by any person falling within sub-paragraph (2) above to any person who is or becomes the insured (or one of the insured) under the contract or to any person who acts, otherwise than in the course of a business, for or on behalf of such a person.

(6) In this paragraph—

"relevant goods" means any electrical or mechanical appliance of a kind—

(*a*) which is ordinarily used in or about the home; or

(*b*) which is ordinarily owned by private individuals and used by them for the purposes of leisure, amusement or entertainment;

"supplier" does not include an insurer who supplies relevant goods as a means of discharging liabilities arising by reason of a claim under an insurance contract.

(7) In sub-paragraph (6) above—

"appliance" includes any device, equipment or apparatus;

"the home" includes any private garden and any private garage or private workshop appurtenant to a dwelling.][1]

Amendments—[1] This Schedule inserted by FA 1997 s 22(3), Sch 4 with effect as provided by FA 1997 s 24.
Press releases etc—C & E News release 4/97 6-2-97 (by concession, the higher rate will not apply to home contents insurance when sold by retailers).

[Insurance provided by divided company

3A— (1) A premium under a taxable insurance contract relating to a motor car or motor cycle also falls within paragraph 2 above if—

(*a*) the insurance to be provided under the contract is provided by a divided company, and

(*b*) any division of that company would, if it were a separate company, be a person connected with a supplier of motor cars or motor cycles.

(2) A premium under a taxable insurance contract relating to relevant goods also falls within paragraph 3 above if—

(*a*) the insurance to be provided under the contract is provided by a divided company, and

(*b*) any division of that company would, if it were a separate company, be a person connected with a supplier of relevant goods.

(3) Sub-paragraph (1) or (2) above does not apply if the insurance is provided to the insured free of charge.

(4) A premium falls within paragraph 2 above by virtue of this paragraph only to the extent that it is attributable to cover for a risk which relates to a motor car or motor cycle supplied by a supplier of motor cars or motor cycles with whom the division in question would, if it were a separate company, be connected.

(5) A premium falls within paragraph 3 above by virtue of this paragraph only to the extent that it is attributable to cover for a risk which relates to relevant goods supplied by a supplier of relevant goods with whom the division would, if it were a separate company, be connected.

(6) For the purposes of this paragraph—

(*a*) a company is a "divided company" if under the law under which the company is formed, under the company's constitution or under arrangements entered into by or in relation to the company—

(i) some or all of the assets of the company are available primarily, or only, to meet particular liabilities of the company, and

(ii) some or all of the members of the company, and some or all of its creditors, have rights primarily, or only, in relation to particular assets of the company;

(*b*) a "division" of such a company means an identifiable part of it (by whatever name known) that carries on distinct business activities and to which particular assets and liabilities of the company are primarily or wholly attributable.

(7) In this paragraph "provided to the insured free of charge" has the meaning given by sub-paragraph (5) of paragraph 2 or 3 above.

In determining for this purpose whether a divided company by whom insurance is provided is a person falling within sub-paragraph (2) of paragraph 2 or 3 above, the company shall be treated as connected with any person with whom a division of that company would be connected if it were a separate company.

(8) Other expressions defined for the purposes of paragraph 2 or 3 above have the same meaning in this paragraph.][1]

Amendments—[1] This paragraph inserted by FA 2003 s 194 with effect for a premium that falls to be regarded for the purposes of FA 1994 Pt 3 as received under a taxable insurance contract by an insurer after 9 July 2003.

Travel insurance

[4— (1) A premium under a taxable insurance contract falls within this paragraph if it is in respect of the provision of cover against travel risks for a person travelling.

(2) Where—

(*a*) a contract of insurance provides cover against both travel risks and risks other than travel risks,

(*b*) the premium attributable to the cover against travel risks does not exceed 10 per cent of the total premium payable under the contract, and

(*c*) the contract does not provide cover for a person travelling against travel risks falling within two or more of the paragraphs of sub-paragraph (3) below,

the premium, so far as attributable to the cover against travel risks, does not fall within this paragraph by virtue of sub-paragraph (1) above.

(3) The travel risks mentioned in sub-paragraph (2)(*c*) above are—

(*a*) liability in respect of cancellation of travel or of accommodation arranged in connection with travel;

(*b*) delayed or missed departure;

(*c*) curtailment of travel or of the use of accommodation arranged in connection with travel;

(*d*) loss or delayed arrival of baggage;

(*e*) personal injury or illness or expenses of repatriation.

(4) A premium does not fall within this paragraph by virtue of sub-paragraph (1) above if it is payable under a taxable insurance contract relating to a motor vehicle and is attributable to cover of the kind generally known as—

(*a*) fully comprehensive,

(*b*) third party, fire and theft,

(*c*) third party, or
(*d*) roadside assistance,

or if it is payable under a taxable insurance contract relating to a caravan, boat or aircraft and is attributable to cover of a description broadly corresponding to any of those set out in paragraphs (*a*) to (*d*) above (so far as applicable) provided in respect of the caravan, boat or aircraft for a period of at least one month for the person travelling.

(5) In this paragraph—

"person travelling" includes a person intending to travel;

"travel risks" means risks associated with, or related to, travel or intended travel—

(*a*) outside the United Kingdom,
(*b*) by air within the United Kingdom,
(*c*) within the United Kingdom in connection with travel falling within paragraph (*a*) or (*b*) above, or
(*d*) which involves absence from home for at least one night,

or risks to which a person travelling may be exposed during, or at any place at which he may be in the course of, any such travel.][1]

Press releases etc—Hansard 6-2-97 (Standing Committee B (Sixth sitting): Finance Bill debate) ("The definition of travel agents and tour operators is deliberately drafted to include hotels and caravan sites because we have seen that there is already the potential to value shift …Insurance products are sometimes linked with hotel products and there is a potential for growth in value shifting, which we want to stamp out.")

Hansard 11-2-97 (Standing Committee B (Seventh sitting): Finance Bill debate) (in a situation in which a travel agent sells a package of different holidays, one of which he offers directly as a tour operator while the other is offered by another tour operator on whose behalf he sells the insurance, so long as there is a margin on that sale to the travel agent, the insurance premium tax would be at full rate).

Simon's Tax Cases—*R v C&E Comrs, ex p Lunn Poly Ltd* [1999] STC 350.

Amendments—[1] This Schedule originally inserted by FA 1997 s 22(3), Sch 4 with effect as provided by FA 1997 s 24. Para 4 substituted by FA 1998 s 146(2) in relation to a premium which falls to be regarded as received under a taxable insurance contract by an insurer on or after 1 August 1998.

SCHEDULE 7
INSURANCE PREMIUM TAX

Section 64

PART I
INFORMATION

Commentary—*De Voil Indirect Tax Service* **V18.176, V18.177.**

Records

1— (1) Regulations may require registrable persons to keep records.

(2) Regulations under sub-paragraph (1) above may be framed by reference to such records as may be specified in any notice published by the Commissioners in pursuance of the regulations and not withdrawn by a further notice.

(3) Regulations may require any records kept in pursuance of the regulations to be preserved for such period not exceeding six years as may be specified in the regulations.

(4) Any duty under regulations to preserve records may be discharged by the preservation of the information contained in them by such means as the Commissioners may approve; and where that information is so preserved a copy of any document forming part of the records shall (subject to the following provisions of this paragraph) be admissible in evidence in any proceedings, whether civil or criminal, to the same extent as the records themselves.

(5) The Commissioners may, as a condition of approving under sub-paragraph (4) above any means of preserving information contained in any records, impose such reasonable requirements as appear to them necessary for securing that the information will be as readily available to them as if the records themselves had been preserved.

(6) A statement contained in a document produced by a computer shall not by virtue of sub-paragraph (4) above be admissible in evidence—

(*a*) …[1]
(*b*) …[4]
(*c*) in civil proceedings in Scotland, except in accordance with sections 5 and 6 of the Civil Evidence (Scotland) Act 1988;
(*d*) in criminal proceedings in Scotland, except in accordance with [Schedule 8 to the Criminal Procedure (Scotland) Act 1995][2];
(*e*) …[3]
(*f*) …[5]

Regulations—Insurance Premium Tax Regulations, SI 1994/1774.

Amendments—[1] Para (6)(*a*) repealed by the Civil Evidence Act 1995 s 15(2), Sch 2, with effect from 31 January 1997 (See SI 1996/3217).

[2] Words in para (6)(*d*) substituted by the Criminal Procedure (Consequential Provisions) (Scotland) Act 1995, s 5, Sch 4, para 89(4)(*a*), with effect from 1 April 1996.
[3] Para (6)(*e*) repealed by the Civil Evidence (Northern Ireland) Order, SI 1997/2983 (NI 21) art 13(2) Sch 2, with effect from 6 September 1999 (by virtue of SR 1999/339).
[4] Sub-para (6)(*b*) repealed by the Criminal Justice Act 2003 s 332, 336(3), Sch 37 Pt 6 with effect from 4 April 2005 (by virtue of SI 2005/950).
[5] Sub-para (6)(*f*) repealed by the Criminal Justice (Evidence) (Northern Ireland) Order, SI 2004/1501, art 46(2), Sch 2, with effect from 3 April 2006 (by virtue of SR 2006/63, art 2).

Prospective amendments—In sub-para (3) words "—(*a*) ", to be inserted after the words "may" and paras (*b*), (*c*) and the preceding word "and" to be inserted at the end, sub-paras (4)–(6) to be substituted by new sub-para (4) by FA 2009 s 98, Sch 50 para (1) with effect from a date to be appointed. New sub-paras (3)(*b*), (*c*) and (4) to read as follows—

"(*b*) authorise the Commissioners to direct that any such records need only be preserved for a shorter period than that specified in the regulations, and

(*c*) authorise a direction to be made so as to apply generally or in such cases as the Commissioners may stipulate.

(4) A duty under the regulations to preserve records may be discharged—

(*a*) by preserving them in any form and by any means, or

(*b*) by preserving the information contained in them in any form and by any means,

subject to any conditions or exceptions specified in writing by the Commissioners."

Other provisions

2— (1) Every person who is concerned (in whatever capacity) in [an insurance business][1] shall furnish to the Commissioners such information relating to [contracts of insurance][2] entered into in the course of the business as the Commissioners may reasonably require.

(2) Every person who makes arrangements for other persons to enter into any [contract of insurance][3] shall furnish to the Commissioners such information relating to that contract as the Commissioners may reasonably require.

(3) Every person who—

(*a*) is concerned in a business that is not [an insurance business][1], and

(*b*) has been involved in the entry into any [contract of insurance][3] providing cover for any matter associated with the business,

shall furnish to the Commissioners such information relating to that contract as the Commissioners may reasonably require.

(4) The information mentioned in sub-paragraph (1), (2) or (3) above shall be furnished within such time and in such form as the Commissioners may reasonably require.

Amendments—[1] Words in sub-paras (1), (3)(*a*) substituted by FA 1995 s 34, Sch 5 para 7 with effect for contracts entered into both before and after the passing of FA 1995 (1 May 1995).
[2] Words in sub-para (1) substituted by FA 1995 s 34, Sch 5 para 7.
[3] Words in sub-paras (2), (3)(*b*) substituted by FA 1995 s 34, Sch 5 para 7.

3— (1) Every person who is concerned (in whatever capacity) in [an insurance business][1] shall upon demand made by an authorised person produce or cause to be produced for inspection by that person any documents relating to [contracts of insurance][2] entered into in the course of the business.

(2) Every person who makes arrangements for other persons to enter into any [contract of insurance][3] shall upon demand made by an authorised person produce or cause to be produced for inspection by that person any documents relating to that contract.

(3) Every person who—

(*a*) is concerned in a business that is not [an insurance business][1], and

(*b*) has been involved in the entry into any [contract of insurance][3] providing cover for any matter associated with the business,

shall upon demand made by an authorised person produce or cause to be produced for inspection by that person any documents relating to that contract.

(4) Where, by virtue of any of sub-paragraphs (1) to (3) above, an authorised person has power to require the production of any documents from any person, he shall have the like power to require production of the documents concerned from any other person who appears to the authorised person to be in possession of them; but where any such other person claims a lien on any document produced by him, the production shall be without prejudice to the lien.

(5) The documents mentioned in sub-paragraphs (1) to (4) above shall be produced—

(*a*) at the principal place of business of the person on whom the demand is made or at such other place as the authorised person may reasonably require, and

(*b*) at such time as the authorised person may reasonably require.

(6) An authorised person may take copies of, or make extracts from, any document produced under any of sub-paragraphs (1) to (4) above.

(7) If it appears to him to be necessary to do so, an authorised person may, at a reasonable time and for a reasonable period, remove any document produced under any of sub-paragraphs (1) to (4) above and shall, on request, provide a receipt for any document so removed; and where a lien is claimed on a document produced under sub-paragraph (4) above the removal of the document under this sub-paragraph shall not be regarded as breaking the lien.

(8) Where a document removed by an authorised person under sub-paragraph (7) above is reasonably required for the proper conduct of a business he shall, as soon as practicable, provide a copy of the document, free of charge, to the person by whom it was produced or caused to be produced.

(9) Where any documents removed under the powers conferred by this paragraph are lost or damaged the Commissioners shall be liable to compensate their owner for any expenses reasonably incurred by him in replacing or repairing the documents.

Amendments—[1] Words in sub-paras (1), (3)(*a*) substituted by FA 1995 s 34, Sch 5 para 7 with effect for contracts entered into both before and after the passing of FA 1995 (1 May 1995).
[2] Words in sub-para (1) substituted by FA 1995 s 34, Sch 5 para 7.
[3] Words in sub-paras (2), (3)(*b*) substituted by FA 1995 s 34, Sch 5 para 7.

PART II
POWERS

Commentary—*De Voil Indirect Tax Service* **V18.181–185.**

Entry, arrest, etc

4— (1) For the purpose of exercising any powers under this Part of this Act an authorised person may at any reasonable time enter premises used in connection with the carrying on of a business.

(2)–(7) ...[1]

Cross references—Criminal Justice and Police Act 2001 s 50, Sch 1 Pt 1 (s 50 of that Act which provides additional powers of seizure from premises applies to the power of seizure conferred under sub-para (3) above; for the relevant provisions of the Criminal Justice and Police Act 2001, see the *VAT* section of this publication ante).

Amendments—[1] Sub-paras (2)–(7) repealed by FA 2007 ss 84, 114, Sch 22 paras 3, 9, Sch 27 Pt 5(1) with effect from 1 December 2007 (by virtue of SI 2007/3166 art 3(*a*)).

[Order for access to recorded information etc

4A— (1) Where, on an application by an authorised person, a justice of the peace or, in Scotland, a justice (within the meaning of section 462 of the Criminal Procedure (Scotland) Act 1975) is satisfied that there are reasonable grounds for believing—

(*a*) that an offence in connection with tax is being, has been or is about to be committed, and

(*b*) that any recorded information (including any document of any nature whatsoever) which may be required as evidence for the purpose of any proceedings in respect of such an offence is in the possession of any person,

he may make an order under this paragraph.

(2) An order under this paragraph is an order that the person who appears to the justice to be in possession of the recorded information to which the application relates shall—

(*a*) give an authorised person access to it, and

(*b*) permit an authorised person to remove and take away any of it which he reasonably considers necessary,

not later than the end of the period of 7 days beginning on the date of the order or the end of such longer period as the order may specify.

(3) The reference in sub-paragraph (2)(*a*) above to giving an authorised person access to the recorded information to which the application relates includes a reference to permitting the authorised person to take copies of it or to make extracts from it.

(4) Where the recorded information consists of information [stored in any electronic form][2], an order under this paragraph shall have effect as an order to produce the information in a form in which it is visible and legible [or from which it can readily be produced in a visible and legible form][2] and, if the authorised person wishes to remove it, in a form in which it can be removed.

(5) This paragraph is without prejudice to paragraphs 3 and 4 above.][1]

Amendments—[1] This para inserted by FA 1995 s 34, Sch 5 para 8(1).
[2] Words in sub-para (4) substituted and inserted by the Criminal Justice and Police Act 2001 ss 70, 138, Sch 2 Pt 2 para 13 with effect from 1 April 2003 (by virtue of SI 2003/708).

Removal of documents etc

5— (1) An authorised person who removes anything in the exercise of a power conferred by or under paragraph 4 [or 4A][1] above shall, if so requested by a person showing himself—

(*a*) to be the occupier of premises from which it was removed, or

(*b*) to have had custody or control of it immediately before the removal,

provide that person with a record of what he removed.

(2) The authorised person shall provide the record within a reasonable time from the making of the request for it.

(3) Subject to sub-paragraph (7) below, if a request for permission to be allowed access to anything which—

(*a*) has been removed by an authorised person, and

IPT

(*b*) is retained by the Commissioners for the purposes of investigating an offence,

is made to the officer in overall charge of the investigation by a person who had custody or control of the thing immediately before it was so removed or by someone acting on behalf of such a person, the officer shall allow the person who made the request access to it under the supervision of an authorised person.

(4) Subject to sub-paragraph (7) below, if a request for a photograph or copy of any such thing is made to the officer in overall charge of the investigation by a person who had custody or control of the thing immediately before it was so removed, or by someone acting on behalf of such a person, the officer shall—

(*a*) allow the person who made the request access to it under the supervision of an authorised person for the purpose of photographing it or copying it, or

(*b*) photograph or copy it, or cause it to be photographed or copied.

(5) Subject to sub-paragraph (7) below, where anything is photographed or copied under sub-paragraph (4)(*b*) above the officer shall supply the photograph or copy, or cause it to be supplied, to the person who made the request.

(6) The photograph or copy shall be supplied within a reasonable time from the making of the request.

(7) There is no duty under this paragraph to allow access to, or to supply a photograph or copy of, anything if the officer in overall charge of the investigation for the purposes of which it was removed has reasonable grounds for believing that to do so would prejudice—

(*a*) that investigation,

(*b*) the investigation of an offence other than the offence for the purposes of the investigation of which the thing was removed, or

(*c*) any criminal proceedings which may be brought as a result of the investigation of which he is in charge or any such investigation as is mentioned in paragraph (*b*) above.

(8) Any reference in this paragraph to the officer in overall charge of the investigation is a reference to the person whose name and address are endorsed on the warrant concerned as being the officer so in charge.

Amendments—[1] Words in sub-para (1) inserted by FA 1995 s 34, Sch 5 para 8(2).

6— (1) Where, on an application made as mentioned in sub-paragraph (2) below, the appropriate judicial authority is satisfied that a person has failed to comply with a requirement imposed by paragraph 5 above, the authority may order that person to comply with the requirement within such time and in such manner as may be specified in the order.

(2) An application under sub-paragraph (1) above shall be made—

(*a*) in the case of a failure to comply with any of the requirements imposed by sub-paragraphs (1) and (2) of paragraph 5 above, by the occupier of the premises from which the thing in question was removed or by the person who had custody or control of it immediately before it was so removed, and

(*b*) in any other case, by the person who had such custody or control.

(3) In this paragraph "the appropriate judicial authority" means—

(*a*) in England and Wales, a magistrates' court;

(*b*) in Scotland, the sheriff;

(*c*) in Northern Ireland, a court of summary jurisdiction, as defined in Article 2(2)(*a*) of the Magistrates' Court (Northern Ireland) Order 1981.

(4) In England and Wales and Northern Ireland, an application for an order under this paragraph shall be made by way of complaint; and sections 21 and 42(2) of the Interpretation Act (Northern Ireland) 1954 shall apply as if any reference in those provisions to any enactment included a reference to this paragraph.

PART III

RECOVERY

Commentary—*De Voil Indirect Tax Service* **V18.174**.

Recovery of tax etc

7— (1) Tax due from any person shall be recoverable as a debt due to the Crown.

(2) (*Amends* Insolvency Act 1986 s 386(1) and *inserts* Insolvency Act 1986 Sch 6 para 3A).

(3) In the Bankruptcy (Scotland) Act 1985 Schedule 3 (preferred debts) shall be amended as mentioned in sub-paragraphs (4) and (5) below.

(4) (*Inserts* Bankruptcy (Scotland) Act 1985 Sch 3 para 2(1A)).

(5) (*Inserts* Bankruptcy (Scotland) Act 1985 Sch 3 para 8A).

(6) (*Amends* Insolvency (Northern Ireland) Order, SI 1989/2405 art 346(1) and *inserts* Insolvency (Northern Ireland) Order, SI 1989/2405 Sch 4 para 3A).

(7)–(12) …[1]

Amendments—[1] Sub-paras (7)–(12) repealed by FA 1997 Sch 18 Part V(2) with effect from 1 July 1997 (See SI 1997/1433). Sub-paras (8)–(12) were previously substituted for sub-para (8) by FA 1995 s 34, Sch 5 para 9.

Recovery of overpaid tax

8— (1) Where a person has paid an amount to the Commissioners by way of tax which was not tax due to them, they shall be liable to repay the amount to him.

(2) The Commissioners shall only be liable to repay an amount under this paragraph on a claim being made for the purpose.

(3) It shall be a defence, in relation to a claim under this paragraph, that repayment of an amount would unjustly enrich the claimant.

[(4) The Commissioners shall not be liable, on a claim made under this paragraph, to repay any amount paid to them more than three years before the making of the claim.]

(5) …

(6) A claim under this paragraph shall be made in such form and manner and shall be supported by such documentary evidence as may be prescribed by regulations.

(7) Except as provided by this paragraph, the Commissioners shall not be liable to repay an amount paid to them by way of tax by virtue of the fact that it was not tax due to them.

Regulations—Insurance Premium Tax Regulations, SI 1994/1774.
Cross reference—See Insurance Premium Tax Regulations, SI 1994/1774 reg 14 (claims for overpaid tax: form of claim).
FA 1997 Sch 5 Part I (unjust enrichment).
FA 1997 Sch 5 para 14 (assessment of excessive repayment).
Amendments—Sub para (4) substituted for sub-paras (4) and (5) by FA 1997 s 50, Sch para 5(2) with effect from 19 March 1997.
Prospective amendments—In sub-para (4) words “4 years” to be substituted for the words “three years” by FA 2009 s 99, Sch 51 para 2 with effect from a date to be appointed.

PART IV
PENALTIES

Commentary—*De Voil Indirect Tax Service* **V18.161–165.**

Criminal offences

9— (1) A person is guilty of an offence if—

(*a*) being a registrable person, he is knowingly concerned in, or in the taking of steps with a view to, the fraudulent evasion of tax by him or another registrable person, or

(*b*) not being a registrable person, he is knowingly concerned in, or in the taking of steps with a view to, the fraudulent evasion of tax by a registrable person.

(2) Any reference in sub-paragraph (1) above to the evasion of tax includes a reference to the obtaining of a payment under regulations under section 55(3)(*c*) or (*d*) or (*f*) of this Act.

(3) A person is guilty of an offence if with the requisite intent—

(*a*) he produces, furnishes or sends, or causes to be produced, furnished or sent, for the purposes of this Part of this Act any document which is false in a material particular, or

(*b*) he otherwise makes use for those purposes of such a document;

and the requisite intent is intent to deceive or to secure that a machine will respond to the document as if it were a true document.

(4) A person is guilty of an offence if in furnishing any information for the purposes of this Part of this Act he makes a statement which he knows to be false in a material particular or recklessly makes a statement which is false in a material particular.

(5) A person is guilty of an offence by virtue of this sub-paragraph if his conduct during any specified period must have involved the commission by him of one or more offences under the preceding provisions of this paragraph; and the preceding provisions of this sub-paragraph apply whether or not the particulars of that offence or those offences are known.

(6) A person is guilty of an offence if—

(*a*) he enters into a taxable insurance contract, or

(*b*) he makes arrangements for other persons to enter into a taxable insurance contract,

with reason to believe that tax in respect of the contract will be evaded.

(7) A person is guilty of an offence if he enters into taxable insurance contracts without giving security (or further security) he has been required to give under paragraph 24 below.

Criminal penalties

10— (1) A person guilty of an offence under paragraph 9(1) above shall be liable—

(*a*) on summary conviction, to a penalty of the statutory maximum or of three times the amount of the tax, whichever is the greater, or to imprisonment for a term not exceeding six months or to both;

(*b*) on conviction on indictment, to a penalty of any amount or to imprisonment for a term not exceeding seven years or to both.

(2) The reference in sub-paragraph (1) above to the amount of the tax shall be construed, in relation to tax itself or a payment falling within paragraph 9(2) above, as a reference to the aggregate of—

(*a*) the amount (if any) falsely claimed by way of credit, and

(*b*) the amount (if any) by which the gross amount of tax was falsely understated.

(3) A person guilty of an offence under paragraph 9(3) or (4) above shall be liable—

(*a*) on summary conviction, to a penalty of the statutory maximum or, where sub-paragraph (4) below applies, to the alternative penalty there specified if it is greater, or to imprisonment for a term not exceeding six months or to both;

(*b*) on conviction on indictment, to a penalty of any amount or to imprisonment for a term not exceeding seven years or to both.

(4) In a case where—

(*a*) the document referred to in paragraph 9(3) above is a return required under this Part of this Act, or

(*b*) the information referred to in paragraph 9(4) above is contained in or otherwise relevant to such a return,

the alternative penalty is a penalty equal to three times the aggregate of the amount (if any) falsely claimed by way of credit and the amount (if any) by which the gross amount of tax was understated.

(5) A person guilty of an offence under paragraph 9(5) above shall be liable—

(*a*) on summary conviction, to a penalty of the statutory maximum or (if greater) three times the amount of any tax that was or was intended to be evaded by his conduct, or to imprisonment for a term not exceeding six months or to both;

(*b*) on conviction on indictment, to a penalty of any amount or to imprisonment for a term not exceeding seven years or to both;

and paragraph 9(2) and sub-paragraph (2) above shall apply for the purposes of this sub-paragraph as they apply respectively for the purposes of paragraph 9(1) and sub-paragraph (1) above.

(6) A person guilty of an offence under paragraph 9(6) above shall be liable on summary conviction to a penalty of level 5 on the standard scale or three times the amount of the tax, whichever is the greater.

(7) A person guilty of an offence under paragraph 9(7) above shall be liable on summary conviction to a penalty of level 5 on the standard scale.

(8) In this paragraph—

(*a*) "credit" means credit for which provision is made by regulations under section 55 of this Act;

(*b*) "the gross amount of tax" means the total amount of tax due before taking into account any deduction for which provision is made by regulations under section 55(3) of this Act.

Criminal proceedings etc

11 Sections 145 to 155 of the Customs and Excise Management Act 1979 (proceedings for offences, mitigation of penalties and certain other matters) shall apply in relation to offences under paragraph 9 above and penalties imposed under paragraph 10 above as they apply in relation to offences and penalties under the customs and excise Acts as defined in that Act.

Notes—For CEMA 1979 ss 145–155, see VAT division.
Level 5 on the standard scale, and the statutory maximum is £5,000, with effect from 1 October 1992.

Civil penalties

12— *(1) In a case where—*

(a) for the purpose of evading tax, a registrable person does any act or omits to take any action, and

(b) his conduct involves dishonesty (whether or not it is such as to give rise to criminal liability),

he shall be liable to a penalty equal to the amount of tax evaded, or (as the case may be) sought to be evaded, by his conduct; but this is subject to sub-paragraph (7) below.

(2) The reference in sub-paragraph (1)(a) above to evading tax includes a reference to obtaining a payment under regulations under section 55(3)(c) or (d) or (f) of this Act in circumstances where the person concerned is not entitled to the sum.

(3) The reference in sub-paragraph (1) above to the amount of tax evaded or sought to be evaded is a reference to the aggregate of—

(a) the amount (if any) falsely claimed by way of credit, and

(b) the amount (if any) by which the gross amount of tax was falsely understated.

(4) In this paragraph—

(a) "credit" means credit for which provision is made by regulations under section 55 of this Act;

(b) "the gross amount of tax" means the total amount of tax due before taking into account any deduction for which provision is made by regulations under section 55(3) of this Act.

(5) Statements made or documents produced by or on behalf of a person shall not be inadmissible in any such proceedings as are mentioned in sub-paragraph (6) below by reason only that it has been drawn to his attention—

(a) that, in relation to tax, the Commissioners may assess an amount due by way of a civil penalty instead of instituting criminal proceedings and, though no undertaking can be given as to whether the Commissioners will make such an assessment in the case of any person, it is their practice to be influenced by the fact that a person has made a full confession of any dishonest conduct to which he has been a party and has given full facilities for investigation, and

(b) that the Commissioners or, on appeal, an appeal tribunal have power under paragraph 13 below to reduce a penalty under this paragraph,

and that he was or may have been induced thereby to make the statements or produce the documents.

(6) The proceedings referred to in sub-paragraph (5) above are—

(a) any criminal proceedings against the person concerned in respect of any offence in connection with or in relation to tax, and

(b) any proceedings against him for the recovery of any sum due from him in connection with or in relation to tax.

(7) Where, by reason of conduct falling within sub-paragraph (1) above, a person is convicted of an offence (whether under this Part of this Act or otherwise) that conduct shall not also give rise to liability to a penalty under this paragraph.[1]

Amendments—[1] This para repealed by FA 2008 s 122, Sch 40 para 21(*d*) with effect from 1 April 2009 (by virtue of SI 2009/571 art 2).

This para repealed only in so far as it relates to conduct involving dishonesty which relates to—

(a) an inaccuracy in a document, or

(b) a failure to notify HMRC of an under-assessment by HMRC (SI 2009/571 art 6).

13— (1) Where a person is liable to a penalty under paragraph 12 above the Commissioners or, on appeal, an appeal tribunal may reduce the penalty to such amount (including nil) as they think proper.

(2) In the case of a penalty reduced by the Commissioners under sub-paragraph (1) above an appeal tribunal, on an appeal relating to the penalty, may cancel the whole or any part of the reduction made by the Commissioners.

(3) None of the matters specified in sub-paragraph (4) below shall be matters which the Commissioners or any appeal tribunal shall be entitled to take into account in exercising their powers under this paragraph.

(4) Those matters are—

(a) the insufficiency of the funds available to any person for paying any tax due or for paying the amount of the penalty;

(b) the fact that there has, in the case in question or in that case taken with any other cases, been no or no significant loss of tax.[1]

Amendments—[1] This para repealed by FA 2008 s 122, Sch 40 para 21(*d*) with effect from 1 April 2009 (by virtue of SI 2009/571 art 2).

This para repealed only in so far as it relates to conduct involving dishonesty which relates to—

(a) an inaccuracy in a document, or

(b) a failure to notify HMRC of an under-assessment by HMRC (SI 2009/517 art 6).

14— (1) A person who fails to comply with section 53(2) [or 53AA (3)] [1] of this Act shall be liable to a penalty equal to 5 per cent of the relevant tax or, if it is greater or the circumstances are such that there is no relevant tax, to a penalty of £250; but this is subject to sub-paragraphs (3) and (4) below.

(2) In sub-paragraph (1) above "relevant tax" means the tax (if any) for which the person concerned is liable for the period which—

(*a*) begins on the date with effect from which he is, in accordance with section 53 [or, as the case may be, section 53AA] [2] of this Act, required to be registered, and

(*b*) ends on the date on which the Commissioners received notification of his liability to be registered.

(3) Conduct falling within sub-paragraph (1) above shall not give rise to liability to a penalty under this paragraph if the person concerned satisfies the Commissioners or, on appeal, an appeal tribunal that there is a reasonable excuse for his conduct.

(4) Where, by reason of conduct falling within sub-paragraph (1) above—

(*a*) a person is convicted of an offence (whether under this Part of this Act or otherwise), or

(*b*) a person is assessed to a penalty under paragraph 12 above [or to a penalty for a deliberate inaccuracy under Schedule 24 to the Finance Act 2007 (penalties for errors)][3],

that conduct shall not also give rise to liability to a penalty under this paragraph.

(5) If it appears to the Treasury that there has been a change in the value of money since the passing of this Act or, as the case may be, the last occasion when the power conferred by this

IPT

sub-paragraph was exercised, they may by order substitute for the sum for the time being specified in sub-paragraph (1) above such other sum as appears to them to be justified by the change.

(6) An order under sub-paragraph (5) above shall not apply in relation to a failure which ended on or before the date on which the order comes into force.

Amendments—[1] Words in sub-s (1) inserted by FA 1997 s 27 (11).
[2] Words in sub-s (2)(*a*) inserted by FA 1997 s 27 (11) with effect from 19 March 1997.
[3] Words in sub-s (4)(*b*) inserted by the Finance Act 2008, Schedule 40 (Appointed Day, Transitional Provisions and Consequential Amendments) Order, SI 2009/571 art 8, Sch 1 para 21(1), (2) with effect from 1 April 2009.
Prospective amendments—This para to be repealed by FA 2008 s 123, Sch 41 para 25 with effect from 1 April 2010 (by virtue of SI 2009/511 art 2).

15— (1) This paragraph applies if a person fails to comply with—

(*a*) a requirement imposed by regulations made under section 54 of this Act to pay the tax due in respect of any period within the time required by the regulations, or

(*b*) a requirement imposed by regulations made under that section to furnish a return in respect of any period within the time required by the regulations;

and sub-paragraphs (2) and (3) below shall have effect subject to sub-paragraphs (5) and (6) below and paragraph 25(7) below.

(2) The person shall be liable to a penalty equal to 5 per cent of the tax due or, if it is greater, to a penalty of £250.

(3) The person—

(*a*) shall be liable, in addition to an initial penalty under sub-paragraph (2) above, to a penalty of £20 for every relevant day when he fails to pay the tax or furnish the return, but

(*b*) shall not in respect of the continuation of the failure be liable to further penalties under sub-paragraph (2) above;

and a relevant day is any day falling after the time within which the tax is required to be paid or the return is required to be furnished.

(4) For the purposes of sub-paragraph (2) above the tax due—

(*a*) shall, if the person concerned has furnished a return, be taken to be the tax shown in the return as that for which he is accountable in respect of the period in question, and

(*b*) shall, in any other case, be taken to be such tax as has been assessed for that period and notified to him under section 56(1) of this Act.

(5) A failure falling within sub-paragraph (1) or (3) above shall not give rise to liability to a penalty under this paragraph if the person concerned satisfies the Commissioners or, on appeal, an appeal tribunal that there is a reasonable excuse for the failure.

(6) Where, by reason of a failure falling within sub-paragraph (1) or (3) above—

(*a*) a person is convicted of an offence (whether under this Part of this Act or otherwise), or

(*b*) a person is assessed to a penalty under paragraph 12 above [or to a penalty for a deliberate inaccuracy under Schedule 24 to the Finance Act 2007 (penalties for errors)][1],

that failure shall not also give rise to liability to a penalty under this paragraph.

(7) If it appears to the Treasury that there has been a change in the value of money since the passing of this Act or, as the case may be, the last occasion when the power conferred by this sub-paragraph was exercised, they may by order substitute for the sums for the time being specified in sub-paragraphs (2) and (3) above such other sums as appear to them to be justified by the change.

(8) An order under sub-paragraph (7) above shall not apply in relation to a failure which began before the date on which the order comes into force.

Cross reference—FA 2009 s 108 (suspension of penalties during currency of agreement for deferred payment).
Amendments—[1] Words in sub-s (6)(*b*) inserted by the Finance Act 2008, Schedule 40 (Appointed Day, Transitional Provisions and Consequential Amendments) Order, SI 2009/571 art 8, Sch 1 para 21(1), (3) with effect from 1 April 2009.

16— (1) This paragraph applies where—

(*a*) by virtue of regulations made under section 65 of this Act a liability notice (within the meaning of that section) is served on an insured person,

(*b*) by virtue of such regulations that person is liable to pay an amount of tax which has been assessed in accordance with the regulations, and

(*c*) that tax is not paid within the time required by the regulations;

and sub-paragraphs (2) and (3) below shall have effect subject to sub-paragraphs (4) and (5) below and paragraph 25(7) below.

(2) The person shall be liable to a penalty equal to 5 per cent of the tax assessed as mentioned in sub-paragraph (1) above or, if it is greater, to a penalty of £250.

(3) The person—

(*a*) shall be liable, in addition to an initial penalty under sub-paragraph (2) above, to a penalty of £20 for every relevant day when the tax is unpaid, but

(*b*) shall not in respect of the continuation of the non-payment of the tax be liable to further penalties under sub-paragraph (2) above;

and a relevant day is any day falling after the time within which the tax is required to be paid.

(4) A person shall not be liable to a penalty by virtue of this paragraph if he satisfies the Commissioners or, on appeal, an appeal tribunal that he took all reasonable steps to ensure that the tax mentioned in sub-paragraph (1)(*b*) above was paid within the time required by the regulations.

(5) Where, by reason of a failure to pay tax, a person is convicted of an offence (whether under this Part of this Act or otherwise), that failure shall not also give rise to liability to a penalty under this paragraph.

(6) If it appears to the Treasury that there has been a change in the value of money since the passing of this Act or, as the case may be, the last occasion when the power conferred by this sub-paragraph was exercised, they may by order substitute for the sums for the time being specified in sub-paragraphs (2) and (3) above such other sums as appear to them to be justified by the change.

(7) An order under sub-paragraph (6) above shall not apply in relation to any failure to pay tax that was required to be paid before the date on which the order comes into force.

17— (1) If a person fails to comply with—

(*a*) section 53(3) of this Act,

(*b*) any provision of paragraph 2 or 3 above, or

(*c*) a requirement imposed by any regulations made under this Part of this Act, other than a requirement falling within sub-paragraph (2) below,

he shall be liable to a penalty of £250; but this is subject to sub-paragraphs (3) and (4) below.

(2) A requirement falls within this sub-paragraph if it is—

(*a*) a requirement imposed by regulations made under section 54 of this Act to pay the tax due in respect of any period within the time required by the regulations,

(*b*) a requirement imposed by regulations made under that section to furnish a return in respect of any period within the time required by the regulations,

(*c*) a requirement imposed by regulations made under section 65 of this Act to pay tax within the time required by the regulations, or

(*d*) a requirement specified for the purposes of this sub-paragraph by regulations.

(3) A failure falling within sub-paragraph (1) above shall not give rise to liability to a penalty under this paragraph if the person concerned satisfies the Commissioners or, on appeal, an appeal tribunal that there is a reasonable excuse for the failure.

(4) Where by reason of a failure falling within sub-paragraph (1) above—

(*a*) a person is convicted of an offence (whether under this Part of this Act or otherwise), or

(*b*) a person is assessed to a penalty under paragraph 12 above [or to a penalty for a deliberate inaccuracy under Schedule 24 to the Finance Act 2007 (penalties for errors)][1],

that failure shall not also give rise to liability to a penalty under this paragraph.

(5) If it appears to the Treasury that there has been a change in the value of money since the passing of this Act or, as the case may be, the last occasion when the power conferred by this sub-paragraph was exercised, they may by order substitute for the sum for the time being specified in sub-paragraph (1) above such other sum as appears to them to be justified by the change.

(6) An order under sub-paragraph (5) above shall not apply in relation to a failure which began before the date on which the order comes into force.

Amendments—[1] Words in sub-s (4)(*b*) inserted by the Finance Act 2008, Schedule 40 (Appointed Day, Transitional Provisions and Consequential Amendments) Order, SI 2009/571 art 8, Sch 1 para 21(1), (3) with effect from 1 April 2009.

18 …[1]

Amendments—[1] Para 18 repealed by FA 2008 s 142 with effect from 21 July 2008.

Prospective amendments—Para 18A to be inserted by the Tribunals, Courts and Enforcement Act 2007 s 62(3), Sch 13 paras 113, 116(1), (2) with effect from a date to be appointed. Para 18A to be repealed by FA 2008 s 129, Sch 43 para 3 with effect from such day as the Commissioners may by statutory instrument appoint.

Para 18A as inserted to read—

"18A—(1) This paragraph applies where an enforcement agent acting under the power conferred by section 51(A1) of the Finance Act 1997 (power to use the procedure in Schedule 12 to the Tribunals, Courts and Enforcement Act 2007) has entered into a controlled goods agreement with the person against whom the power is exercisable ("the person in default").

(2) In this paragraph, "controlled goods agreement" has the meaning given by paragraph 13(4) of that Schedule.

(3) Subject to sub-paragraph (4) below, if the person in default removes or disposes of goods (or permits their removal or disposal) in breach of the controlled goods agreement, he is liable to a penalty equal to half of the tax or other amount recoverable under section 51(A1) of the Finance Act 1997.

(4) The person in default shall not be liable to a penalty under subparagraph (3) above if he satisfies the Commissioners or, on appeal, an appeal tribunal, that there is a reasonable excuse for the breach in question.

(5) This paragraph extends only to England and Wales."

19— (1) This paragraph applies where—

(*a*) in accordance with regulations under [section 51 of the Finance Act 1997 (enforcement by distress)][1] above a distress is authorised to be levied on the goods and chattels of a person (a person in default) who has refused or neglected to pay any tax due from him or any amount recoverable as if it were tax due from him, and

IPT

(*b*) the person levying the distress and the person in default have entered into a walking possession agreement.

(2) For the purposes of this paragraph a walking possession agreement is an agreement under which, in consideration of the property distrained upon being allowed to remain in the custody of the person in default and of the delaying of its sale, the person in default—

(*a*) acknowledges that the property specified in the agreement is under distraint and held in walking possession, and

(*b*) undertakes that, except with the consent of the Commissioners and subject to such conditions as they may impose, he will not remove or allow the removal of any of the specified property from the premises named in the agreement.

(3) Subject to sub-paragraph (4) below, if the person in default is in breach of the undertaking contained in a walking possession agreement, he shall be liable to a penalty equal to half of the tax or other amount referred to in sub-paragraph (1)(*a*) above.

(4) The person in default shall not be liable to a penalty under sub-paragraph (3) above if he satisfies the Commissioners or, on appeal, an appeal tribunal that there is a reasonable excuse for the breach in question.

(5) This paragraph does not extend to Scotland.

Amendments—[1] The words in sub-s (1)(*a*) substituted for the words "paragraph 7(7) above" by FA 1997 s 53(5) with effect from 1 July 1997 (see SI 1997/1432).

Prospective amendments—Sub-para (5) to be substituted by the Tribunals, Courts and Enforcement Act 2007 s 50, Sch 10 para 116(1), (3) with effect from a date to be appointed. Sub-para (5) as substituted to read—
"(5) This paragraph extends only to Northern Ireland.".

20 For the purposes of paragraphs 14(3), 15(5), 17(3) …[1] and 19(4) above—

(*a*) an insufficiency of funds available for paying any amount is not a reasonable excuse, and

(*b*) where reliance is placed on any other person to perform any task, neither the fact of that reliance nor any conduct of the person relied upon is a reasonable excuse.

Amendments—[1] Words ", 18(2)" in para 20 repealed by FA 2008 s 142 with effect from 21 July 2008.

PART V
INTEREST

Commentary—*De Voil Indirect Tax Service* **V18.171–173**.

Interest on tax etc

21— (1) Where an assessment is made under any provision of section 56 of this Act, the whole of the amount assessed shall carry interest at [the rate applicable under section 197 of the Finance Act 1996][1] from the reckonable date until payment; but this is subject to sub-paragraph (2) and paragraph 25(7) below.

(2) Sub-paragraph (1) above shall not apply in relation to an assessment under section 56(1) of this Act unless at least one of the following conditions is fulfilled, namely—

(*a*) that the assessment relates to an accounting period in respect of which either a return has previously been made, or an earlier assessment has already been notified to the person concerned;

(*b*) that the assessment relates to an accounting period which exceeds three months and begins on the date with effect from which the person was, or was required to be, registered under this Part of this Act.

(3) In a case where—

(*a*) the circumstances are such that a relevant assessment could have been made, but

(*b*) before such an assessment was made the tax due or other amount concerned was paid (so that no such assessment was necessary),

the whole of the amount paid shall carry interest at [the rate applicable under section 197 of the Finance Act 1996][1] from the reckonable date until the date on which it was paid; and for the purposes of this sub-paragraph a relevant assessment is an assessment in relation to which sub-paragraph (1) above would have applied if the assessment had been made.

(4) The references in sub-paragraphs (1) and (3) above to the reckonable date shall be construed as follows—

(*a*) where the amount assessed or paid is such an amount as is referred to in subsection (2) of section 56 of this Act, the reckonable date is the seventh day after the day on which a written instruction was issued by the Commissioners directing the making of the payment of the amount which ought not to have been paid to the person concerned;

(*b*) in all other cases the reckonable date is the latest date on which (in accordance with regulations under this Part of this Act) a return is required to be made for the accounting period to which the amount assessed or paid relates;

and interest under this paragraph shall run from the reckonable date even if that date is a non-business day, within the meaning of section 92 of the Bills of Exchange Act 1882.

(5) …[2]

(6) Interest under this paragraph shall be paid without any deduction of income tax.

Note—The rate of interest for the purposes of this section has been prescribed as follows—

Commencement date	*Rate*	*SI No*
1 October 1994	5.5%	1994/1819
6 February 1996	6.25%	1996/166, 1997/1016
6 July 1998	9.5%	1998/1461

Amendments—[1] Words in sub-paras (1) and (3) substituted for words "the prescribed rate" by FA 1996 s 197(6)(*b*), (7) with effect for periods beginning on or after 1 April 1997 (see SI 1997/1015). This para has effect in relation to interest running from before that day, as well as in relation to interest running from, or from after, that day.

[2] Sub-s (5) repealed by FA 1996 Sch 41 Pt VIII(1) with effect for periods beginning on or after 1 April 1997 (see SI 1997/1105).

Interest payable by Commissioners

22— (1) Where, due to an error on the part of the Commissioners, a person—

(*a*) has paid to them by way of tax an amount which was not tax due and which they are in consequence liable to repay to him,

(*b*) has failed to claim payment of an amount to the payment of which he was entitled in pursuance of provision made under section 55(3)(*c*), (*d*) or (*f*) of this Act, or

(*c*) has suffered delay in receiving payment of an amount due to him from them in connection with tax,

then, if and to the extent that they would not be liable to do so apart from this paragraph, they shall (subject to the following provisions of this paragraph) pay interest to him on that amount for the applicable period.

[(1A) In sub-paragraph (1) above—

(*a*) the reference in paragraph (*a*) to an amount which the Commissioners are liable to repay in consequence of the making of a payment that was not due is a reference to only so much of that amount as is the subject of a claim that the Commissioners are required to satisfy or have satisfied; and

(*b*) the amounts referred to in paragraph (*c*) do not include any amount payable under this paragraph.][2]

(2) Interest under this paragraph shall be payable at [the rate applicable under section 197 of the Finance Act 1996][1].

(3) The applicable period, in a case falling within sub-paragraph (1)(*a*) above, is the period—

(*a*) beginning with the date on which the payment is received by the Commissioners, and

(*b*) ending with the date on which they authorise payment of the amount on which the interest is payable.

(4) The applicable period, in a case falling within sub-paragraph (1)(*b*) or (*c*) above, is the period—

(*a*) beginning with the date on which, apart from the error, the Commissioners might reasonably have been expected to authorise payment of the amount on which the interest is payable, and

(*b*) ending with the date on which they in fact authorise payment of that amount.

[(5) In determining the applicable period for the purposes of this paragraph there shall be left out of account any period by which the Commissioner's' authorisation of the payment of interest is delayed by the conduct of the person who claims the interest.][4]

[(5A) The reference in sub-paragraph (5) above to a period by which the Commissioner's' authorisation of the payment of interest is delayed by the conduct of the person who claims it includes, in particular, any period which is referable to—

(*a*) any unreasonable delay in the making of the claim for interest or in the making of any claim for the payment or repayment of the amount on which interest is claimed;

(*b*) any failure by that person or a person acting on his behalf or under his influence to provide the Commissioners—

(i) at or before the time of the making of a claim, or

(ii) subsequently in response to a request for information by the Commissioners,

with all the information required by them to enable the existence and amount of the claimant's entitlement to a payment or repayment, and to interest on that payment or repayment, to be determined; and

(*c*) the making, as part of or in association with either—

(i) the claim for interest, or

(ii) any claim for the payment or repayment of the amount on which interest is claimed,

of a claim to anything to which the claimant was not entitled.][4]

(6) In determining for the purposes of sub-paragraph (5A) above whether any period of delay is referable to a failure by any person to provide information in response to a request by the Commissioners, there shall be taken to be so referable, except so far as may be provided for by regulation, any period which—

(*a*) begins with the date on which the Commissioners require that person to provide information which they reasonably consider relevant to the matter to be determined; and (*b*) ends with the earliest date on which it would be reasonable for the Commissioners to conclude—

(i) that they have received a completed answer to their request for information;

(ii) that they have received all that they need in answer to that request; or

(iii) that it is unnecessary for them to be provided with any new information in answer to that request.][4]

(7) …[4]

(8) The Commissioners shall only be liable to pay interest under this paragraph on a claim made in writing for that purpose.

[(9) A claim under this paragraph shall not be made more than three years after the end of the applicable period to which it relates.][3]

[(10) References in this paragraph to the authorisation by the Commissioners of the payment of any amount include references to the discharge by way of set-off the Commissioners' liability to pay that amount.][3]

Note—The rate of interest for the purposes of this section has been prescribed as follows—

Commencement date	*Rate*	*SI No*
1 October 1994	8%	1994/1819
1 April 1997	6%	1997/1016, 1998/1461

Cross references—See FA 1997 Sch 5 para 15 (assessments of overpayment of interest).

Amendments—[1] Words in para (2) substituted for words "such rate as may from time to time be prescribed by order, and—

(*a*) any such order may prescribe different rates for different purposes;

(*b*) any such order shall apply to interest for periods beginning on or after the date on which the order is expressed to come into force, whether or not interest runs from before that date.",

by FA 1996 s 197(6)(*c*), (7) with effect for periods beginning on or after 1 April 1997 (see SI 1997/1015) and has effect in relation to interest running from before that day as well as in relation to interest running from, or from after, that day.

[2] Sub-para (1A) inserted by FA 1997 s 50, Sch 5 para 9(2) and deemed always to have had effect.

[3] Sub-paras (9) and (10) substituted by FA 1997 s 50, Sch 5 para 9(3), (4) and deemed always to have had effect.

[4] Sub-paras (5), (5A) and (6) substituted for sub-paras (5) to (7) by FA 1997 s 50, Sch 5 para 10 for the purposes of determining whether any period beginning on or after 19 March 1997 is left out of account.

Prospective amendments—In sub-para (4) words "4 years" to be substituted for the words "three years" by FA 2009 s 99, Sch 51 para 2 with effect from a date to be appointed.

23— (1) In a case where—

(*a*) any interest is payable by the Commissioners to a person on a sum due to him under this Part of this Act, and

(*b*) he is a person to whom regulations under section 55 of this Act apply,

the interest shall be treated as an amount to which he is entitled by way of credit in pursuance of the regulations.

(2) Sub-paragraph (1) above shall be disregarded for the purpose of determining a person's entitlement to interest or the amount of interest to which he is entitled.

PART VI

MISCELLANEOUS

Security for tax

24 Where it appears to the Commissioners requisite to do so for the protection of the revenue they may require a registrable person, as a condition of his entering into taxable insurance contracts, to give security (or further security) of such amount and in such manner as they may determine for the payment of any tax which is or may become due from him.

Assessments to penalties etc

25— (1) Where a person is liable—

(*a*) to a penalty under any of paragraphs 12 to 19 above, or

(*b*) for interest under paragraph 21 above,

the Commissioners may, subject to sub-paragraph (2) below, assess the amount due by way of penalty or interest (as the case may be) and notify it to him accordingly; and the fact that any conduct giving rise to a penalty under any of paragraphs 12 to 19 above may have ceased before an assessment is made under this paragraph shall not affect the power of the Commissioners to make such an assessment.

(2) In the case of the penalties and interest referred to in the following paragraphs of this sub-paragraph, the assessment under this paragraph shall be of an amount due in respect of the accounting period which in the paragraph concerned is referred to as the relevant period—

(*a*) in the case of a penalty under paragraph 12 above relating to the evasion of tax, the relevant period is the accounting period for which the tax evaded was due;

(*b*) in the case of a penalty under paragraph 12 above relating to the obtaining of a payment under regulations under section 55(3)(*c*) or (*d*) or (*f*) of this Act, the relevant period is the accounting period in respect of which the payment was obtained;

(*c*) in the case of interest under paragraph 21 above, the relevant period is the accounting period in respect of which the tax (or amount assessed as tax) was due.

(3) In a case where the amount of any penalty or interest falls to be calculated by reference to tax which was not paid at the time it should have been and that tax cannot be readily attributed to any one or more accounting periods, it shall be treated for the purposes of this Part of this Act as tax due for such period or periods as the Commissioners may determine to the best of their judgment and notify to the person liable for the tax and penalty or interest.

(4) Where a person is assessed under this paragraph to an amount due by way of any penalty or interest falling within sub-paragraph (2) above and is also assessed under subsection (1) or (2) of section 56 of this Act for the accounting period which is the relevant period under sub-paragraph (2) above, the assessments may be combined and notified to him as one assessment, but the amount of the penalty or interest shall be separately identified in the notice.

(5) Sub-paragraph (6) below applies in the case of—

(*a*) an amount due by way of penalty under paragraph 15 or 16 above;

(*b*) an amount due by way of interest under paragraph 21 above.

(6) Where this sub-paragraph applies in the case of an amount—

(*a*) a notice of assessment under this paragraph shall specify a date, being not later than the date of the notice, to which the aggregate amount of the penalty or, as the case may be, the amount of interest which is assessed is calculated, and

(*b*) if the penalty or interest continues to accrue after that date, a further assessment or further assessments may be made under this paragraph in respect of amounts which so accrue.

(7) If, within such period as may be notified by the Commissioners to the person liable to the penalty under paragraph 15 or 16 above or for the interest under paragraph 21 above—

(*a*) a failure falling within paragraph 15(3) above is remedied,

(*b*) the tax referred to in paragraph 16(1) above is paid, or

(*c*) the amount referred to in paragraph 21(1) above is paid,

it shall be treated for the purposes of paragraph 15, 16 or 21 above (as the case may be) as remedied or paid on the date specified as mentioned in sub-paragraph (6)(*a*) above.

(8) Where an amount has been assessed and notified to any person under this paragraph it shall be recoverable as if it were tax due from him unless, or except to the extent that, the assessment has subsequently been withdrawn or reduced.

(9) Subsection (8) of section 56 of this Act shall apply for the purposes of this paragraph as it applies for the purposes of that section.

Cross references—See the Recovery of Duties and Taxes Etc Due in Other Member States (Corresponding UK Claims, Procedure and Supplementary) Regulations, SI 2004/674 Sch 2 para 4 (modification of the application of this paragraph in respect of recovery of insurance premium tax interest).

IPT

Assessments: time limits

26— (1) Subject to the following provisions of this paragraph, an assessment under—

(*a*) any provision of section 56 of this Act, or

(*b*) paragraph 25 above,

shall not be made more than [three years][1] after the end of the accounting period concerned or, in the case of an assessment under paragraph 25 above of an amount due by way of a penalty which is not a penalty referred to in sub-paragraph (2) of that paragraph, [three][1] years after the event giving rise to the penalty.

(2) An assessment under paragraph 25 above of—

(*a*) an amount due by way of any penalty referred to in sub-paragraph (2) of that paragraph, or

(*b*) an amount duc by way of interest,

may be made at any time before the expiry of the period of two years beginning with the time when the amount of tax due for the accounting period concerned has been finally determined.

(3) In relation to an assessment under paragraph 25 above, any reference in sub-paragraph (1) or (2) above to the accounting period concerned is a reference to that period which, in the case of the penalty or interest concerned, is the relevant period referred to in sub-paragraph (2) of that paragraph.

(4) If tax has been lost—

(*a*) as a result of conduct falling within paragraph 12(1) above or for which a person has been convicted of fraud, or

(*b*) in circumstances giving rise to liability to a penalty under paragraph 14 above,

an assessment may be made as if, in sub-paragraph (1) above, each reference to [three years][1] were a reference to twenty years.

Amendments—[1] Words in sub-paras (1) and (4) substituted for words "six years" by FA 1997 s 50, Sch 5 para 6 with effect from 19 March 1997.

Prospective amendments—In sub-para (1) words "4 years after the relevant event" to be substituted for the words "three years after" in the first place, sub-s (1A) to be inserted, in sub-para (3) words "sub-paragraph (1A)" to be substituted for the words "sub-paragraph (1)", new sub-paras (4), (5) to be substituted for sub-para (4) by FA 2009 s 99, Sch 51 para 4 with effect from a date to be appointed. New sub-paras (1A), (4), (5) to read as follows—

"(1A) In this paragraph "the relevant event", in relation to an assessment, means—

(*a*) the end of the accounting period concerned, or

(*b*) in the case of an assessment under paragraph 25 of an amount due by way of a penalty other than a penalty referred to in paragraph 25(2), the event giving rise to the penalty."

"(4) An assessment of an amount due from a person in a case involving a loss of tax—

(*a*) brought about deliberately by the person (or by another person acting on that person's behalf), or

(*b*) attributable to a failure by the person to comply with an obligation under section 53(1) or (2) or 53AA(1) or (3),

may be made at any time not more than 20 years after the relevant event.

(5) In sub-paragraph (4)(*a*) the reference to a loss brought about deliberately by the person includes a loss brought about as a result of a deliberate inaccuracy in a document given to Her Majesty's Revenue and Customs by or on behalf of that person."

Supplementary assessments

27 If, otherwise than in circumstances falling within subsection (5)(*b*) of section 56 of this Act, it appears to the Commissioners that the amount which ought to have been assessed in an assessment under any provision of that section or under paragraph 25 above exceeds the amount which was so assessed, then—

(*a*) under the like provision as that assessment was made, and

(*b*) on or before the last day on which that assessment could have been made,

the Commissioners may make a supplementary assessment of the amount of the excess and shall notify the person concerned accordingly.

Disclosure of information

28— (1) Notwithstanding any obligation not to disclose information that would otherwise apply, the Commissioners may disclose information—

(*a*) to the Secretary of State, or

(*b*) to an authorised officer of the Secretary of State,

for the purpose of assisting the Secretary of State in the performance of his duties.

(2) Notwithstanding any such obligation as is mentioned in sub-paragraph (1) above—

(*a*) the Secretary of State, or

(*b*) an authorised officer of the Secretary of State,

may disclose information to the Commissioners or to an authorised officer of the Commissioners for the purpose of assisting the Commissioners in the performance of duties in relation to tax.

(3) Information that has been disclosed to a person by virtue of this paragraph shall not be disclosed by him except—

(*a*) to another person to whom (instead of him) disclosure could by virtue of this paragraph have been made, or

(*b*) for the purpose of any proceedings connected with the operation of any provision of, or made under, any enactment in relation to insurance or to tax.

(4) References in the preceding provisions of this paragraph to an authorised officer of the Secretary of State are to any person who has been designated by the Secretary of State as a person to and by whom information may be disclosed under this paragraph.

(5) The Secretary of State shall notify the Commissioners in writing of the name of any person designated under sub-paragraph (4) above.

[28A— (1)Notwithstanding any obligation not to disclose information that would otherwise apply, the Commissioners may disclose information—

(*a*) to the Treasury, or

(*b*) to an authorised officer of the Treasury,

for the purpose of assisting the Treasury in the performance of their duties.

(2) Notwithstanding any such obligation as is mentioned in sub-paragraph (1) above—

(*a*) the Treasury, or

(*b*) an authorised officer of the Treasury,

may disclose information to the Commissioners or to an authorised officer of the Commissioners for the purpose of assisting the Commissioners in the performance of duties in relation to tax.

(3) Information that has been disclosed to a person by virtue of this paragraph shall not be disclosed by him except—

(*a*) to another person to whom (instead of him) disclosure could by virtue of this paragraph have been made, or

(*b*) for the purpose of any proceedings connected with the operation of any provision of, or made under, any enactment in relation to insurance or to tax.

(4) References in the preceding provisions of this paragraph to an authorised officer of the Treasury are to any person who has been designated by the Treasury as a person to and by whom information may be disclosed under this paragraph.

(5) The Treasury shall notify the Commissioners in writing of the name of any person designated under sub-paragraph (4) above.][1]

Amendments—[1] Inserted by SI 1997/2781 with effect from 5 January 1998.

[28B (1) Notwithstanding any obligation not to disclose information that would otherwise apply, the Commissioners may disclose information to the Financial Services Authority ("the Authority") for the purpose of assisting the Authority in the performance of its functions.

(2) Information that has been disclosed to the Authority pursuant to this paragraph shall not be disclosed by the Authority except for the purpose of any proceedings connected with the operation of any provision of, or made under, any enactment in relation to insurance or to tax.][1]

Amendments—[1] This paragraph inserted by the Financial Services and Markets Act 2000 (Consequential Amendments) Order, SI 2004/355 art 4 with effect from 4 March 2004.

Evidence by certificate

29— (1) A certificate of the Commissioners—

(*a*) that a person was or was not at any time registered under section 53 of this Act, [or][1]

(*b*) that any return required by regulations under section 54 of this Act has not been made or had not been made at any time, …[1]

(*c*) …[1]

shall be sufficient evidence of that fact until the contrary is proved.

(2) Any document purporting to be a certificate under sub-paragraph (1) above shall be taken to be such a certificate until the contrary is proved.

Amendments—[1] Words inserted and repealed by FA 2008 s 138, Sch 44 para 5 with effect from 21 July 2008. Para (*c*) previously read as follows—

"(*c*) that any tax shown as due in a return made in pursuance of regulations made under section 54 of this Act, or in an assessment made under section 56 of this Act, has not been paid,".

Service of notices etc

30 Any notice, notification or requirement to be served on, given to or made of any person for the purposes of this Part of this Act may be served, given or made by sending it by post in a letter addressed to that person or his tax representative at the last or usual residence or place of business of that person or representative.

No deduction of penalties or interest

31 (*inserts* TA 1988 s 827(1B)).

Destination of receipts

32 *All money and securities for money collected or received for or on account of the tax shall*—

(a) if collected or received in Great Britain, be placed to the general account of the Commissioners kept at the Bank of England under section 17 of the Customs and Excise Management Act 1979;

(b) if collected or received in Northern Ireland, be paid into the Consolidated Fund of the United Kingdom in such manner as the Treasury may direct.

Amendment—Paragraph repealed by the Commissioners for Revenue and Customs Act 2005 ss 50, 52, Sch 4 para 53 and Sch 5 with effect from 18 April 2005 by virtue of the Commissioners for Revenue and Customs Act (Commencement) Order, SI 2005/1126, art 2(2).

Provisional collection of tax

33 (*amends* PCTA 1968 s 1(1)).

34— (1) In a case where—

(*a*) by virtue of a resolution having effect under the Provisional Collection of Taxes Act 1968 tax has been paid at a rate specified in the resolution, and

(*b*) by virtue of section 1(6) or (7) or 5(3) of that Act any of that tax is repayable in consequence of the restoration in relation to the premium concerned of a lower rate,

the amount repayable shall be the difference between the tax paid by reference to the actual chargeable amount at the rate specified in the resolution and the tax that would have been payable by reference to the actual chargeable amount at the lower rate.

(2) In sub-paragraph (1) above the "actual chargeable amount" means the chargeable amount by reference to which tax was paid.

(3) In a case where—

(*a*) by virtue of a resolution having effect under the Provisional Collection of Taxes Act 1968 tax is chargeable at a rate specified in the resolution, but

(*b*) before the tax is paid it ceases to be chargeable at that rate in consequence of the restoration in relation to the premium concerned of a lower rate,

the tax chargeable at the lower rate shall be charged by reference to the same chargeable amount as that by reference to which tax would have been chargeable at the rate specified in the resolution.

Adjustment of contracts

35— (1) Where, after the making of a contract of insurance and before a given premium is received by the insurer under the contract, there is a change in the tax chargeable on the receipt

IPT

of the premium, then, unless the contract otherwise provided, there shall be added to or deducted from the amount payable as the premium an amount equal to the difference between—

(*a*) the tax chargeable had the change not been made, and

(*b*) the tax in fact chargeable.

(2) References in sub-paragraph (1) above to a change in the tax chargeable include references to a change to or from no tax being chargeable.

(3) Where this paragraph applies, the amount of the premium shall not be treated as altered for the purposes of calculating tax.

[SCHEDULE 7A
INSURANCE PREMIUM TAX: CONTRACTS THAT ARE NOT TAXABLE][1]

Section 70

Commentary—*De Voil Indirect Tax Service* **V18.103.**

Amendments—This Schedule inserted by the Insurance Premium Tax (Taxable Insurance Contracts) Order, SI 1994/1698 arts 1, 5 with effect from 1 October 1994.

PART I
DESCRIPTIONS OF CONTRACT

Contracts of reinsurance

1 A contract falls within this paragraph if it is a contract of reinsurance

Contracts constituting long term business

2— (1) [Subject to sub-paragraph (3) below][1] a contract falls within this paragraph [if it is exclusively a contract of long-term insurance.][2]

[(2) In deciding whether a contract is exclusively a contract of long-term insurance, as is mentioned in sub-paragraph (1) above, where—

(*a*) the contract includes cover for risks relating to accident or sickness;

(*b*) the contract contains related and subsidiary provisions such that it might also be regarded as a contract of general insurance, but is treated as a contract of long-term insurance for the purposes of any relevant order made under section 22 of the Financial Services and Markets Act 2000; and

(*c*) the contract was not entered into after 30th November 1993,

the inclusion of such cover shall be ignored.][2]

[(3) A contract which would otherwise fall within this paragraph does not do so if it is for medical insurance.

(4) Subject to sub-paragraph (5) below, for the purposes of this paragraph a contract is a contract for medical insurance if it provides one or more of the following benefits, whether or not their provision is subject to conditions or limitations—

(*a*) medical, dental or optical, consultation, diagnosis or treatment;

(*b*) alternative or complementary medical treatment or therapy;

(*c*) convalescent care;

(*d*) goods or services related to any of the above;

(*e*) payment or reimbursement of, or a grant towards, the whole or part of the cost of any of the above;

(*f*) payment of a specified sum for optical, dental or medical appointments;

(*g*) payment of a specified sum for each specified period of treatment as a hospital in-patient;

(*h*) payment of a specified sum for each specified period of convalescent care; or

(*i*) payment of a specified sum, except one to which sub-paragraph (6) below applies, when a person is diagnosed as requiring or has undergone a specified medical procedure.

(5) A benefit which would apart from this sub-paragraph fall within sub-paragraph (4) above shall not do so if, before he can become entitled to the benefit, the insured is required—

(*a*) to be suffering from a disability which so impairs his ability to carry out normal activities of daily living that he requires long term care, supervision or assistance; and

(*b*) to have been suffering from the disability for a continuous period of not less than 4 weeks.

(6) This sub-paragraph applies to a payment of a specified sum if the contract under which it is payable provides that only one such payment in relation to each specified medical procedure will be made in respect of each person in relation to whom benefit is payable under the contract.][1]

Amendments—[1] Words in sub-para (1) above and sub-paras (3)–(6) above inserted by the Insurance Premium Tax (Taxable Insurance Contracts) Order, SI 1997/1627 in relation to premiums received or treated as received on or after 1 October 1997.

[2] Words in sub-para (1) substituted, and sub-para (2) substituted, by the Financial Services and Markets Act 2000 (Consequential Amendments and Repeals) Order, SI 2001/3649 art 346(1)–(3) with effect from 1 December 2001.

Contracts relating to motor vehicles for use by handicapped persons

3— (1) A contract falls within this paragraph if it relates only to a motor vehicle and the conditions mentioned in sub-paragraph (2) below are satisfied.

(2) The conditions referred to in sub-paragraph (1) above are that—

(*a*) the vehicle is used, or intended for use, by a handicapped person in receipt of a disability living allowance by virtue of entitlement to the mobility component or of a mobility supplement;

(*b*) the insured lets such vehicles on hire to such persons in the course of a business consisting predominantly of the provision of motor vehicles to such persons; and

(*c*) the insured does not in the course of the business let such vehicles on hire to such persons on terms other than qualifying terms.

(3) For the purposes of sub-paragraph (2)(*c*) above a vehicle is let on qualifying terms to a person (the lessee) if the consideration for the letting consists wholly or partly of sums paid to the insured by—

[(*a*) the Department for Work and Pensions;][1]

(*b*) the Department of Health and Social Services for Northern Ireland; or

(*c*) the Ministry of Defence,

on behalf of the lessee in respect of the disability living allowance or mobility supplement to which the lessee is entitled.

(4) For the purposes of this paragraph—

(*a*) "handicapped" means chronically sick or disabled;

(*b*) "disability living allowance" means a disability living allowance within the meaning of section 71 of the Social Security Contributions and Benefits Act 1992 or section 71 of the Social Security Contributions and Benefits (Northern Ireland) Act 1992;

(*c*) "mobility supplement" means a mobility supplement within the meaning of article 26A of the Naval, Military and Air Forces etc (Disablement and Death) Service Pensions Order 1983, article 25A of the Personal Injuries (Civilians) Scheme 1983, article 3 of the Motor Vehicles (Exemption from Vehicles Excise Duty) Order 1985 or article 3 of the Motor Vehicles (Exemption from Vehicles Excise Duty) (Northern Ireland) Order 1985.

Amendments—[1] Sub-para (3)(*a*) substituted by the Secretaries of State for Education and Skills and for Work and Pensions Order, SI 2002/1397 art 12, Schedule para 10 with effect from 27 June 2002.

Contracts relating to commercial ships

4— (1) A contract falls within this paragraph if it relates only to a commercial ship and is [a contract of general insurance of a relevant class.][1]

[(2) For the purposes of this paragraph, a contract of general insurance is of a relevant class if it insures against risks arising from or in relation to—

(*a*) accidents,

(*b*) ships, or

(*c*) liabilities of ships,

(and no other risks).][1]

(3) For the purposes of this paragraph a commercial ship is a ship which is—

(*a*) of a gross tonnage of 15 tons or more; and

(*b*) not designed or adapted for use for recreation or pleasure.

Amendments—[1] Words in sub-para (1) substituted, and sub-para (2) substituted, by the Financial Services and Markets Act 2000 (Consequential Amendments and Repeals) Order, SI 2001/3649 art 346(4) with effect from 1 December 2001.

Contracts relating to lifeboats and lifeboat equipment

5— (1) A contract falls within this paragraph if it relates only to a lifeboat and is [a contract of general insurance of a relevant class.][1]

[(2) For the purposes of this paragraph, a contract of general insurance is of a relevant class if it insures against risks arising from or in relation to—

(*a*) accidents,

(*b*) ships, or

(*c*) liabilities of ships,

(and no other risks).][1]

(3) For the purposes of this paragraph, a lifeboat is a vessel used or to be used solely for rescue or assistance at sea.

Amendments—[1] Words in sub-para (1) substituted, and sub-para (2) substituted, by the Financial Services and Markets Act 2000 (Consequential Amendments and Repeals) Order, SI 2001/3649 art 346(5) with effect from 1 December 2001.

6— (1) A contract falls within this paragraph if it relates only to a lifeboat and lifeboat equipment and is such that, if it related only to a lifeboat, it would fall within paragraph 5 above.

(2) In deciding whether a contract relates to lifeboat equipment the nature of the risks concerned is immaterial, and they may (for example) be risks of dying or sustaining injury or of loss or damage.

(3) For the purposes of this paragraph—

(*a*) "lifeboat" has the meaning given by paragraph 5(3) above; and

(*b*) "lifeboat equipment" means anything used or to be used solely in connection with a lifeboat.

Contracts relating to commercial aircraft

7— (1) A contract falls within this paragraph if it relates only to a commercial aircraft and is [a contract of general insurance of a relevant class.][1]

[(2) For the purposes of this paragraph, a contract of general insurance is of a relevant class if it insures against risks arising from or in relation to—

(*a*) accidents,

(*b*) aircraft, or

(*c*) aircraft liability,

(and no other risks).][1]

(3) For the purposes of this paragraph a commercial aircraft is an aircraft which is—

(*a*) of a weight of 8,000 kilograms or more; and

(*b*) not designed or adapted for use for recreation or pleasure.

Amendments—[1] Words in sub-para (1) substituted, and sub-para (2) substituted, by the Financial Services and Markets Act 2000 (Consequential Amendments and Repeals) Order, SI 2001/3649 art 346(6) with effect from 1 December 2001.

Contracts relating to risks outside the United Kingdom

8— (1) A contract falls within this paragraph if it relates only to a risk which is situated outside the United Kingdom.

[(2) The question of whether a risk is situated in the United Kingdom shall be determined in accordance with regulations made under section 424(3) of the Financial Services and Markets Act 2000; but in determining that question as respects a contract which relates to a building it shall be irrelevant whether or not the contract also covers the contents of the building.][1]

Amendments—[1] Sub-para (2) substituted, by the Financial Services and Markets Act 2000 (Consequential Amendments and Repeals) Order, SI 2001/3649 art 346(7) with effect from 1 December 2001.

Contracts relating to foreign or international railway rolling stock

9— (1) A contract falls within this paragraph if it relates only to foreign or international railway rolling stock and is [a contract of general insurance of a relevant class.][1]

[(2) For the purposes of this paragraph, a contract of general insurance is of a relevant class if it insures against risks arising from or in relation to—

(*a*) railway rolling stock, or

(*b*) general liability to third parties,

(and no other risks).][1]

(3) For the purposes of this paragraph foreign or international railway rolling stock is railway rolling stock used principally for journeys taking place wholly or partly outside the United Kingdom.

Amendments—[1] Words in sub-para (1) substituted, and sub-para (2) substituted, by the Financial Services and Markets Act 2000 (Consequential Amendments and Repeals) Order, SI 2001/3649 art 346(8) with effect from 1 December 2001.

Contracts relating to the Channel tunnel

10— (1) A contract falls within this paragraph if it relates only to the Channel tunnel system and is [a contract of general insurance of a relevant class.][1]

[(2) For the purposes of this paragraph, a contract of general insurance is of a relevant class if it insures against risks arising from or in relation to—

(*a*) fire or natural forces,

(*b*) damage to property, or

(*c*) general liability to third parties,

(and no other risks).][1]

(3) For the purposes of this paragraph "the Channel tunnel system" means—

(*a*) the tunnels described in section 1(7)(*a*) of the Channel Tunnel Act 1987;

(*b*) the control towers situated in the terminal areas described in section 1(7)(*b*) of that Act; and

(*c*) the shuttle crossovers, wherever situated.

Amendments—[1] Words in sub-para (1) substituted, and sub-para (2) substituted, by the Financial Services and Markets Act 2000 (Consequential Amendments and Repeals) Order, SI 2001/3649 art 346(9) with effect from 1 December 2001.

11— (1) A contract falls within this paragraph if it relates only to relevant Channel tunnel equipment and is [a contract of general insurance of a relevant class.][1]

[(2) For the purposes of this paragraph, a contract of general insurance is of a relevant class if it insures against risks arising from or in relation to—

(*a*) fire or natural forces,

(*b*) damage to property, or

(*c*) general liability to third parties,

(and no other risks).][1]

(3) For the purposes of this paragraph "the Channel tunnel system" has the meaning given by paragraph 10(3) above.

(4) For the purposes of this paragraph "relevant Channel tunnel equipment" means, subject to sub-paragraph (5) below, the fixed or movable equipment needed for the operation of the Channel tunnel system or for the operation of trains through any tunnel forming part of it and in particular includes—

(*a*) any ventilation, cooling or electrical plant used or to be used in connection with any such operation; and

(*b*) any safety, signalling and control equipment which is or is to be so used.

(5) Equipment which consists of or forms part of—

(*a*) roads, bridges, platforms, ticket offices and other facilities for the use of passengers or motor vehicles;

(*b*) administrative buildings and maintenance facilities; and

(*c*) railway track or signalling equipment which is not situated in any part of the Channel tunnel system,

is not relevant Channel tunnel equipment for the purposes of this paragraph.

Amendments—[1] Words in sub-para (1) substituted, and sub-para (2) substituted, by the Financial Services and Markets Act 2000 (Consequential Amendments and Repeals) Order, SI 2001/3649 art 346(10) with effect from 1 December 2001.

Contracts relating to goods in foreign or international transit

12—(1) A contract falls within this paragraph if it relates only to loss of or damage to goods in foreign or international transit and the insured enters into the contract in the course of a business carried on by him.

(2) For the purposes of this paragraph goods in foreign or international transit are goods in transit, and any container in which they are carried, where their carriage—

(*a*) begins and ends outside the United Kingdom;

(*b*) begins outside but ends in the United Kingdom; or

(*c*) ends outside but begins in the United Kingdom.

(3) For the purposes of sub-paragraph (2) above "container" has the same meaning as in regulation 38(3) of the Value Added Tax (General) Regulations 1985.

Contracts relating to credit

13— (1) A contract falls within this paragraph if it relates only to credit granted in relation to goods or services supplied under a relevant contract by a person carrying on business in the United Kingdom.

(2) For the purposes of this paragraph a relevant contract is—

(*a*) a contract to make a relevant supply of goods, or a supply of services, or both, to an overseas customer;

(*b*) a contract to supply goods to a person who is to—

(i) export those goods; or

(ii) incorporate those goods in other goods which he is to export,

where the condition mentioned in sub-paragraph (3) below is satisfied;

(*c*) a contract to supply to a person who is to export goods services consisting of the valuation or testing of, or other work carried out on, those goods where the condition mentioned in sub-paragraph (3) below is satisfied;

(*d*) a contract to supply services to a person in order that he may comply with a legally binding obligation to make a supply of services to an overseas customer.

(3) The condition referred to in sub-paragraph (2)(*b*) and (*c*) above is that the goods to be exported are to be exported in order that the person exporting them may comply with a legally binding obligation to make a relevant supply of goods to an overseas customer.

(4) For the purposes of this paragraph—

(*a*) "export" means export from the United Kingdom and cognate expressions shall be construed accordingly; and

(*b*) any reference to a person who is to export goods shall be taken as including a reference to a person at whose direction the insured is to export them and the reference in sub-paragraph (3) above to the person exporting goods shall be construed accordingly.

(5) Where a contract relates to—

(*a*) credit of the description in sub-paragraph (1) above; and

(*b*) loss resulting from the insured or any third party being required to pay the amount of any bond or guarantee against non-performance by the insured of the contract which involves him making the supply,

the contract shall be treated for the purposes of sub-paragraph (1) above as if it did not relate to loss of the description in paragraph (*b*) above.

Contracts relating to exchange losses

14— (1) A contract falls within this paragraph if—

(*a*) it relates only to loss resulting from a change in the rate at which the price for a supply which is or may be made by the insured may be exchanged for another currency; and

(*b*) the conditions mentioned in sub-paragraph (2) below are satisfied.

(2) The conditions referred to in sub-paragraph (1) above are that—

(*a*) the insured is a person carrying on business in the United Kingdom;

(*b*) the contract of insurance concerns a contract to make a relevant supply of goods, or a supply of services, or both, to an overseas customer (whether or not the contract to make the supply is one into which the insured has entered, or one for which he has tendered or intends to tender); and

(*c*) the period of cover for the risk expires no later than the date by which the whole of the price for the supply is to be paid or, where the contract has not been entered into, would be required to be paid.

(3) Where the contract relates to—

(*a*) loss of the description in sub-paragraph (1)(*a*) above; and

(*b*) loss relating from a change in the rate at which the price of goods which the insured imports into the United Kingdom for the purpose of enabling him to make the supply concerned may be exchanged for another currency,

the contract shall be treated for the purposes of sub-paragraphs (1) and (2) above as if it did not relate to loss of the description in paragraph (*b*) above.

Contracts relating to the provision of financial facilities

15— (1) A contract falls within this paragraph if it relates only to the provision of a relevant financial facility and the conditions mentioned in sub-paragraph (2) below are satisfied.

(2) The conditions referred to in sub-paragraph (1) above are that—

(*a*) the person to whom the relevant financial facility is provided is an overseas customer;

(*b*) it is provided in order that he may comply with a legally binding obligation to receive a relevant supply of goods, or a supply of services, or both, from a person carrying on business ...[1]; and

[(*c*) the contract of insurance insures against risks arising from or in relation to either or both—

(i) credit,

(ii) suretyship.][2]

(3) For the purposes of this paragraph a relevant financial facility is—

(*a*) the making of an advance;

(*b*) the issue of a letter of credit or acceptance of a bill of exchange;

(*c*) the giving of a guarantee or bond; or

(*d*) any other similar transaction entered into in order to provide a customer with the means to pay, or a supplier with the right to call upon a third party for, the consideration for goods or services.

Amendments—[1] Words in sub-para (2)(*b*) deleted by Insurance Premium Tax (Taxable Insurance Contracts) Order, SI 1996/2955, Art 2 with effect from 1 January 1997.

[2] Sub-para (2)(*c*) substituted by the Financial Services and Markets Act 2000 (Consequential Amendments and Repeals) Order, SI 2001/3649 art 346(11) with effect from 1 December 2001.

PART II

INTERPRETATION

16— (1) This Part of this Schedule applies for the purposes of Part I of this Schedule.

(2) A relevant supply of goods is any supply of goods where the supply is to be made outside the United Kingdom or where the goods are to be exported from the United Kingdom.

(3) An overseas customer, in relation to a supply of goods or services, is a person who—

(*a*) does not have any business establishment in the United Kingdom but has such an establishment elsewhere;

(*b*) has such establishments both in the United Kingdom and elsewhere, provided that the establishment at which, or for the purposes of which, the goods or services which are to be supplied to him are most directly to be used is not in the United Kingdom; or

(*c*) has no such establishment in any place and does not have his usual place of residence in the United Kingdom.

[16A Paragraphs 2, 4, 5, 7, 10, 11 and 15 must be read with—

(*a*) section 22 of the Financial Services and Markets Act 2000;

(*b*) any relevant order under that section; and

(*c*) Schedule 2 to that Act.][1]

Amendments—[1] Para 16A added by the Financial Services and Markets Act 2000 (Consequential Amendments and Repeals) Order, SI 2001/3649 art 346(12) with effect from 1 December 2001.

FINANCE ACT 1996

(1996 Chapter 8)

An Act to grant certain duties, to alter other duties, and to amend the law relating to the National Debt and the Public Revenue, and to make further provision in connection with Finance.

[29th April 1996]

PART VII

MISCELLANEOUS AND SUPPLEMENTAL

Miscellaneous: indirect taxation

197 Setting of rates of interest

(1) The rate of interest applicable for the purposes of an enactment to which this section applies shall be the rate which for the purposes of that enactment is provided for by regulations made by the Treasury under this section.

(2) This section applies to—

(*a*) …
(*b*) paragraphs 21 and 22 of Schedule 7 to that Act (interest on amounts of insurance premium tax and on amounts payable by the Commissioners in respect of that tax);
(*c*), (*d*) …
(*e*) paragraph 17 of Schedule 5 to the Finance Act 1997 (interest on amounts repayable in respect of overpayments by the Commissioners in connection with … insurance premium tax …).][1]
(*f*)–(*i*) …

(3) Regulations under this section may—

(*a*) make different provision for different enactments or for different purposes of the same enactment,
(*b*) either themselves specify a rate of interest for the purposes of an enactment or make provision for any such rate to be determined, and to change from time to time, by reference to such rate or the average of such rates as may be referred to in the regulations,
(*c*) provide for rates to be reduced below, or increased above, what they otherwise would be by specified amounts or by reference to specified formulae,
(*d*) provide for rates arrived at by reference to averages or formulae to be rounded up or down,
(*e*) provide for circumstances in which changes of rates of interest are or are not to take place, and
(*f*) provide that changes of rates are to have effect for periods beginning on or after a day determined in accordance with the regulations in relation to interest running from before that day, as well as in relation to interest running from, or from after, that day.

(4) The power to make regulations under this section shall be exercisable by statutory instrument subject to annulment in pursuance of a resolution of the House of Commons.

(5) Where—

(a) regulations under this section provide, without specifying the rate determined in accordance with the regulations, for a new method of determining the rate applicable for the purposes of any enactment, or
(b) the rate which, in accordance with regulations under this section, is the rate applicable for the purposes of any enactment changes otherwise than by virtue of the making of regulations specifying a new rate,[2]

the Commissioners of Customs and Excise shall make an order specifying the new rate and the day from which, in accordance with the regulations, it has effect.

(6) The words "the rate applicable under section 197 of the Finance Act 1996" shall be substituted—

(*a*) …
(*b*) for the words "the prescribed rate" in each of sub-paragraphs (1) and (3) of paragraph 21 of Schedule 7 to that Act (insurance premium tax);
(*c*) for the words from "such rate" onwards in sub-paragraph (2) of paragraph 22 of that Schedule; and
(*d*) …

(7) Subsections (1) and (6) above shall have effect for periods beginning on or after such day as the Treasury may by order made by statutory instrument appoint and shall have effect in relation to interest running from before that day, as well as in relation to interest running from, or from after, that day; and different days may be appointed under this subsection for different purposes.

Note—Sub-ss (2)(*a*), (*c*), (*d*), (*f*), (*g*)–(*i*), (6)(*a*), (*d*) are not relevant to IPT.
Reference to "that Act" in sub-s s (2), (6) are to FA 1994.

Sub-ss (1), (6) have effect for periods beginning on or after 1 April 1997 (see FA 1996 s 197 (Appointed Day) Order, SI 1997/1015).

Amendments—[1] Inserted by FA 1997 s 50, Sch 5 para 21 with effect from 19 March 1997.
[2] Sub-s (5) repealed by FA 2009 s 105(6)(*b*) with effect from 21 July 2009.

Supplemental

205 Repeals

(1) The enactments mentioned in Schedule 41 to this Act (which include spent provisions) are hereby repealed to the extent specified in the third column of that Schedule.

(2) The repeals specified in that Schedule have effect subject to the commencement provisions and savings contained in, or referred to, in the notes set out in that Schedule.

FINANCE ACT 1997

(1997 Chapter 16)

ARRANGEMENT OF SECTIONS

An Act to grant certain duties, to alter other duties, and to amend the law relating to the National Debt and the Public Revenue, and to make further provision in connection with Finance.
[19th March 1997]

PART II

INSURANCE PREMIUM TAX

New rates of tax

21 Rate of tax

(1) (*substitutes* FA 1994, s 51).

(2) (*amends* FA 1994 s 73(1)).

22 Premiums liable to tax at the higher rate

(1) (*inserts* FA 1994 s 51A).

(2) (*amends* FA 1994 s 74).

(3) (*inserts* FA 1994 Sch 6A).

23 Charge to tax where different rates apply

(1) (*substitutes* FA 1994 s 69).

(2) (*amends* FA 1994 s 50).

24 Commencement of sections 21 to 23

(1) Except as provided by subsection (2) below, sections 21 to 23 above have effect in relation to a premium which falls to be regarded for the purposes of Part III of the Finance Act 1994 as received under a taxable insurance contract by an insurer on or after 1st April 1997.

(2) Sections 21 to 23 above do not have effect in relation to a premium if the premium—

(*a*) is in respect of a contract made before 1st April 1997; and

(*b*) falls, by virtue of regulations under section 68 of the Finance Act 1994 (special accounting scheme), to be regarded for the purposes of Part III of that Act as received under the contract by the insurer on a date before 1st August 1997.

(3) Subsection (2) above does not apply in relation to a premium if the premium—

(*a*) is an additional premium under the contract;

(*b*) falls as mentioned in subsection (2)(*b*) above to be regarded as received under the contract by the insurer on or after 1st April 1997; and

(*c*) is in respect of a risk which was not covered by the contract before 1st April 1997.

(4) Without prejudice to the generality of subsections (1) to (3) above, those subsections shall be construed in accordance with sections 67A to 67C of the Finance Act 1994 (which are inserted by section 29 below).

Taxable intermediaries and their fees

25 Certain fees to be treated as premiums under higher rate contracts

(1) (*inserts* FA 1994 s 52A).

(2) The amendment made by subsection (1) above has effect in relation to payments in respect of fees charged on or after the day on which this Act is passed.

26 Registration of taxable intermediaries

(*inserts* FA 1994 s 53AA).

27 Supplementary provisions

(*amends* FA 1994 ss 53A(1)(*b*), 55, 57, 58, 59(*bb*), 62, 63(1)(*aa*), (*bb*), 73(1), (3), Sch 7 para 14 and *inserts* s 73(1A).

Prospective amendments—Sub-s (11) to be repealed by FA 2008 s 123, Sch 41 para 25 with effect from 1 April 2010 (by virtue of SI 2009/511 art 2).

Miscellaneous

28 Amounts charged by other intermediaries

(1) (*inserts* FA 1994 s 72(1A)).

(2) The amendment made by subsection (1) above has effect in relation to payments received in respect of amounts charged on or after 1st April 1997.

29 Prevention of pre-emption

(1) (*inserts* FA 1994 ss 67A, 67B and 67C).

IPT

(2) In the application of sections 67A to 67C of the Finance Act 1994 in relation to the increases in insurance premium tax effected by this Part and the exceptions from those increases—

(*a*) the announcement relating to those increases, as described in section 67A(1), and to those exceptions, as described in section 67B(1), shall be taken to have been made on 26th November 1996;

(*b*) "the date of the change" is 1st April 1997; and

(*c*) "the concessionary date" is 1st August 1997.

(3) The amendment made by subsection (1) above has effect on and after 26th November 1996.

30 Tax point for payroll deductions

(1), (2) (*insert* FA 1994 s 72(7A), (8A)).

(3) This section applies in relation to amounts deducted on or after the day on which this Act is passed.

PART IV

PAYMENTS AND OVERPAYMENTS IN RESPECT OF INDIRECT TAXES

Excise duties and other indirect taxes

50 Overpayments, interest, assessments, etc

(1) Schedule 5 to this Act (which makes provision in relation to excise duties, insurance premium tax and landfill tax which corresponds to that made for VAT by sections 44 to 48 above) shall have effect.

(2) (*not relevant to IPT*).

Enforcement of payment

51 Enforcement by distress

(1) The Commissioners may by regulations make provision—

(*a*) for authorising distress to be levied on the goods and chattels of any person refusing or neglecting to pay—

(i) any amount of relevant tax due from him, or

(ii) any amount recoverable as if it were relevant tax due from him;

(*b*) for the disposal of any goods or chattels on which distress is levied in pursuance of the regulations; and

(*c*) for the imposition and recovery of costs, charges, expenses and fees in connection with anything done under the regulations.

(2) The provision that may be contained in regulations under this section shall include, in particular—

(*a*) provision for the levying of distress, by any person authorised to do so under the regulations, on goods or chattels located at any place whatever (including on a public highway); and

(*b*) provision authorising distress to be levied at any such time of the day or night, and on any such day of the week, as may be specified or described in the regulations.

(3) Regulations under this section may—

(*a*) make different provision for different cases, and

(*b*) contain any such incidental, supplemental, consequential or transitional provision as the Commissioners think fit;

and the transitional provision that may be contained in regulations under this section shall include transitional provision in connection with the coming into force of the repeal by this Act of any other power by regulations to make provision for or in connection with the levying of distress.

(4) The power to make regulations under this section shall be exercisable by statutory instrument subject to annulment in pursuance of a resolution of the House of Commons.

(5) The following are relevant taxes for the purposes of this section, that is to say—

(*a*), (*b*) …

(*c*) insurance premium tax;

(*d*)–(*f*) …

(6) In this section "the Commissioners" means the Commissioners of Customs and Excise.

(7) Regulations made under this section shall not have effect in Scotland.

Notes—Sub-ss (5)(*a*), (*b*), (*d*)–(*f*) are not relevant to IPT.

Prospective amendments—Sub-s (A1) to be inserted, in sub-s (1) words "not having effect in England and Wales or Scotland" to be inserted after words "by regulations", and sub-s (7) to be repealed, by the Tribunals, Courts and Enforcement Act 2007 ss 62(3), 146, Sch 13 para 126, Sch 23 Pt 3, with effect from a date to be appointed. Sub-s (A1) to read as follows—

"(A1) The Commissioners may, in England and Wales, use the procedure in Schedule 12 to the Tribunals, Courts and Enforcement Act 2007 (taking control of goods) to recover any of these that a person refuses or neglects to pay—

(*a*) any amount of relevant tax due from him;
(*b*) any amount recoverable as if it were relevant tax due from him.".

52 Enforcement by diligence

(1) Where any amount of relevant tax or any amount recoverable as if it were relevant tax is due and has not been paid, the sheriff, on an application by the Commissioners accompanied by a certificate by them—

(*a*) stating that none of the persons specified in the application has paid the amount due from him;
(*b*) stating that payment of the amount due from each such person has been demanded from him; and
(*c*) specifying the amount due from and unpaid by each such person,

shall grant a summary warrant in a form prescribed by Act of Sederunt authorising the recovery, by any of the diligences mentioned in subsection (2) below, of the amount remaining due and unpaid.

(2) The diligences referred to in subsection (1) above are—

[(*a*) an attachment][1];
(*b*) an earnings arrestment;
(*c*) an arrestment and action of forthcoming or sale.

(3) Subject to subsection (4) below and without prejudice to [section 39(1) of the Debt Arrangement and Attachment (Scotland) Act 2002 (asp 17) (expenses of attachment)][2] the sheriff officer's fees, together with the outlays necessarily incurred by him, in connection with the execution of a summary warrant shall be chargeable against the debtor.

(4) No fees shall be chargeable by the sheriff officer against the debtor for collecting, and accounting to the Commissioners for, sums paid to him by the debtor in respect of the amount owing.

(5) The following are relevant taxes for the purposes of this section, that is to say—

(*a*), (*b*) …
(*c*) insurance premium tax;
(*d*)–(*f*) …

(6) In this section "the Commissioners" means the Commissioners of Customs and Excise.

(7) This section shall come into force on such day as the Commissioners of Customs and Excise may by order made by statutory instrument appoint, and different days may be appointed under this subsection for different purposes.

(8) This section extends only to Scotland.

Notes—Sub-ss (5)(*a*), (*b*), (*d*)–(*f*) are not relevant to IPT.
The appointed day under sub-s (7) above is 1 July 1997 (see SI 1997/1432).

Amendments—[1] Sub-s (2)(*a*) substituted by the Debt Arrangement and Attachment (Scotland) Act 2002, s 61, Sch 3, Pt 1, para 26(*a*) with effect from 30 December 2002; see the Debt Arrangement and Attachment (Scotland) Act 2002, s 64(2).
[2] Words in sub-s (3) substituted by the Debt Arrangement and Attachment (Scotland) Act 2002, s 61, Sch 3, Pt 1, para 26(*b*) with effect from 30 December 2002; see the Debt Arrangement and Attachment (Scotland) Act 2002, s 64(2).

Prospective amendments—Sub-s (2)(*aa*), and words "and section 196(1) of the Bankruptcy and Diligence etc (Scotland) Act 2007 (asp 3) (expenses of money attachment)" in sub-s (3), to be inserted by the Bankruptcy and Diligence etc (Scotland) Act 2007 s 226(1), Sch 5 para 24 with effect from a date to be appointed. Sub-s (2)(*aa*) as inserted, to read—
"(*aa*) a money attachment;".

As part of the ongoing reform of the penalty regime, s 52 to be repealed from such day as the Commissioners may by statutory instrument appoint: FA 2008 s 129, Sch 43 para 15.

53 Amendments consequential on sections 51 and 52

…

(5) (Amends FA 1994 Sch 7 para 19(1)(*a*)).

…

(9) This section shall come into force on such day as the Commissioners of Customs and Excise may by order made by statutory instrument appoint, and different days may be appointed under this subsection for different purposes.

Notes—Words omitted are not relevant for the purposes of IPT.
The appointed day under sub-s (9) above is 1 July 1997 (see SI 1997/1432).

SCHEDULES

SCHEDULE 4

INSURANCE PREMIUM TAX: THE HIGHER RATE

Section 22

(*inserts* FA 1994 Sch 6A).

SCHEDULE 5
INDIRECT TAXES: OVERPAYMENTS ETC

Section 50

PART I
UNJUST ENRICHMENT

Application of Part I

1— (1) This Part of this Schedule has effect for the purposes of the following provisions (which make it a defence to a claim for repayment that the repayment would unjustly enrich the claimant), namely—

(*a*) section 137A(3) of the Customs and Excise Management Act 1979 (excise duties);
(*b*) paragraph 8(3) of Schedule 7 to the Finance Act 1994 (insurance premium tax); and
(*c*) paragraph 14(3) of Schedule 5 to the Finance Act 1996 (landfill tax).

(2) Those provisions are referred to in this Part of this Schedule as unjust enrichment provisions.

(3) In this Part of this Schedule—

"the Commissioners" means the Commissioners of Customs and Excise;
"relevant repayment provision" means—

(*a*) section 137A of the Customs and Excise Management Act 1979 (recovery of overpaid excise duty);
(*b*) paragraph 8 of Schedule 7 to the Finance Act 1994 (recovery of overpaid insurance premium tax); or
(*c*) paragraph 14 of Schedule 5 to the Finance Act 1996 (recovery of overpaid landfill tax);

"relevant tax" means any duty of excise, insurance premium tax or landfill tax; and
"subordinate legislation" has the same meaning as in the Interpretation Act 1978.

Disregard of business losses

2— (1) This paragraph applies where—

(*a*) there is an amount paid by way of relevant tax which (apart from an unjust enrichment provision) would fall to be repaid under a relevant repayment provision to any person ("the taxpayer"), and
(*b*) the whole or a part of the cost of the payment of that amount to the Commissioners has, for practical purposes, been borne by a person other than the taxpayer.

(2) Where, in a case to which this paragraph applies, loss or damage has been or may be incurred by the taxpayer as a result of mistaken assumptions made in his case about the operation of any provisions relating to a relevant tax, that loss or damage shall be disregarded, except to the extent of the quantified amount, in the making of any determination—

(*a*) of whether or to what extent the repayment of an amount to the taxpayer would enrich him; or
(*b*) of whether or to what extent any enrichment of the taxpayer would be unjust.

(3) In sub-paragraph (2) above "the quantified amount" means the amount (if any) which is shown by the taxpayer to constitute the amount that would appropriately compensate him for loss or damage shown by him to have resulted, for any business carried on by him, from the making of the mistaken assumptions.

(4) The reference in sub-paragraph (2) above to provisions relating to a relevant tax is a reference to any provisions of—

(*a*) any enactment, subordinate legislation or Community legislation (whether or not still in force) which relates to that tax or to any matter connected with it; or
(*b*) any notice published by the Commissioners under or for the purposes of any such enactment or subordinate legislation.

(5) This paragraph has effect for the purposes of making any repayment on or after the day on which this Act is passed, even if the claim for that repayment was made before that day.

Reimbursement arrangements

3— (1) The Commissioners may by regulations make provision for reimbursement arrangements made by any person to be disregarded for the purposes of any or all of the unjust enrichment provisions except where the arrangements—

(*a*) contain such provision as may be required by the regulations; and
(*b*) are supported by such undertakings to comply with the provisions of the arrangements as may be required by the regulations to be given to the Commissioners.

(2) In this paragraph "reimbursement arrangements" means any arrangements for the purposes of a claim under a relevant repayment provision which—

(*a*) are made by any person for the purpose of securing that he is not unjustly enriched by the repayment of any amount in pursuance of the claim; and (*b*) provide for the reimbursement of persons who have for practical purposes borne the whole or any part of the cost of the original payment of that amount to the Commissioners.

(3) Without prejudice to the generality of sub-paragraph (1) above, the provision that may be required by regulations under this paragraph to be contained in reimbursement arrangements includes—

(*a*) provision requiring a reimbursement for which the arrangements provide to be made within such period after the repayment to which it relates as may be specified in the regulations;

(*b*) provision for the repayment of amounts to the Commissioners where those amounts are not reimbursed in accordance with the arrangements;

(*c*) provision requiring interest paid by the Commissioners on any amount repaid by them to be treated in the same way as that amount for the purposes of any requirement under the arrangements to make reimbursement or to repay the Commissioners;

(*d*) provision requiring such records relating to the carrying out of the arrangements as may be described in the regulations to be kept and produced to the Commissioners, or to an officer of theirs.

(4) Regulations under this paragraph may impose obligations on such persons as may be specified in the regulations—

(*a*) to make the repayments to the Commissioners that they are required to make in pursuance of any provisions contained in any reimbursement arrangements by virtue of sub-paragraph (3)(*b*) or (*c*) above;

(*b*) to comply with any requirements contained in any such arrangements by virtue of sub-paragraph (3)(*d*) above.

(5) Regulations under this paragraph may make provision for the form and manner in which, and the times at which, undertakings are to be given to the Commissioners in accordance with the regulations; and any such provision may allow for those matters to be determined by the Commissioners in accordance with the regulations.

(6) Regulations under this paragraph may—

(*a*) contain any such incidental, supplementary, consequential or transitional provision as appears to the Commissioners to be necessary or expedient; and

(*b*) make different provision for different circumstances.

(7) Regulations under this paragraph may have effect (irrespective of when the claim for repayment was made) for the purposes of the making of any repayment by the Commissioners after the time when the regulations are made; and, accordingly, such regulations may apply to arrangements made before that time.

(8) Regulations under this paragraph shall be made by statutory instrument subject to annulment in pursuance of a resolution of the House of Commons.

Contravention of requirement to repay Commissioners

4— (1) Where any obligation is imposed by regulations made by virtue of paragraph 3(4) above, a contravention or failure to comply with that obligation shall, to the extent that it relates to amounts repaid under section 137A of the Customs and Excise Management Act 1979, attract a penalty under section 9 of the Finance Act 1994 (penalties in connection with excise duties).

(2) For the purposes of Schedule 7 to the Finance Act 1994 (insurance premium tax), a contravention or failure to comply with an obligation imposed by regulations made by virtue of paragraph 3(4) above shall be deemed, to the extent that it relates to amounts repaid under paragraph 8 of that Schedule (recovery of overpaid insurance premium tax), to be a failure to comply with a requirement falling within paragraph 17(1)(*c*) of that Schedule (breach of regulations).

(3) Paragraph 23 of Schedule 5 to the Finance Act 1996 (power to provide for penalty) shall have effect as if an obligation imposed by regulations made by virtue of paragraph 3(4) above were, to the extent that it relates to amounts repaid under paragraph 14 of that Schedule (recovery of overpaid landfill tax), a requirement imposed by regulations under Part III of that Act; and the provisions of that Schedule in relation to penalties under Part V of that Schedule shall have effect accordingly.

PART II

TIME LIMITS

Repayments

5— (1) (*not relevant to IPT*)

(2) (*Substitutes* FA 1994 Sch 7 para 8(4), (5)).

(3) (*not relevant to IPT*)

Assessments

6— (1) In each of the enactments specified in sub-paragraph (2) below (which provide for the time limits applying to the making of assessments), for the words "six years", wherever they occur, there shall be substituted the words "three years".

(2) Those enactments are—

(*a*) (*amends* FA 1994 s 12(4)(*a*), (5)).
(*b*) (*amends* FA 1994 Sch 7 para 26(1), (4)).
(*c*) (*amends* FA 1996 Sch 5 para 33(1), (4)).

Prospective amendments—Sub-paras (2)(*b*), (*c*) to be repealed by FA 2009 s 99, Sch 51 para 43(*b*) with effect from a date to be appointed.

PART III

INTEREST

Interest on overpaid insurance premium tax

9— (1) Paragraph 22 of Schedule 7 to the Finance Act 1994 (interest payable by the Commissioners in connection with insurance premium tax) shall have effect, and be deemed always to have had effect, with the amendments for which this paragraph provides.

(2) (*inserts* FA 1994 Sch 7 para 22(1A)).

(3) (*substitutes* FA 1994 Sch 7 para 22(9)).

(4) (*substitutes* FA 1994 Sch 7 para 22(10)).

10— (1) (*substitutes* FA 1994 Sch 7 para 22 (5) to (7)).

(2) Sub-paragraph (1) above shall have effect for the purposes of determining whether any period beginning on or after the day on which this Act is passed is left out of account.

PART V

RECOVERY OF EXCESS PAYMENTS BY THE COMMISSIONERS

Assessment for excessive repayment

14— (1) Where—

(*a*) any amount has been paid at any time to any person by way of a repayment under a relevant repayment provision, and

(*b*) the amount paid exceeded the amount which the Commissioners were liable at that time to repay to that person,

the Commissioners may, to the best of their judgement, assess the excess paid to that person and notify it to him.

(2) Where any person is liable to pay any amount to the Commissioners in pursuance of an obligation imposed by virtue of paragraph 3(4)(*a*) above, the Commissioners may, to the best of their judgement, assess the amount due from that person and notify it to him.

(3) In this paragraph "relevant repayment provision" means—

(*a*) section 137A of the Customs and Excise Management Act 1979 (recovery of overpaid excise duty);

(*b*) paragraph 8 of Schedule 7 to the Finance Act 1994 (recovery of overpaid insurance premium tax); …[1]

(*c*) paragraph 14 of Schedule 5 to the Finance Act 1996 (recovery of overpaid landfill tax) [or

(*d*) Part I of Schedule 3 to the Finance Act 2001 (payments made and rebates disallowed in error)][1].

Amendments—[1] Words in sub-para (3)(*b*) repealed, and sub-para (3)(*d*) inserted, by FA 2001 ss 15, 110, Sch 3, Pt 4, para 19(1), (2), Sch 33 Pt 1(4) with effect from 1 November 2001 (by virtue of SI 2001/3300).

Assessment for overpayments of interest

15— (1) Where—

(*a*) any amount has been paid to any person by way of interest under a relevant interest provision, but

(*b*) that person was not entitled to that amount under that provision,

the Commissioners may, to the best of their judgement, assess the amount so paid to which that person was not entitled and notify it to him.

(2) In this paragraph "relevant interest provision" means—

(*a*) …[1]

(*b*) paragraph 22 of Schedule 7 to that Act (interest payable by the Commissioners on overpayments etc of insurance premium tax); …[1]

(*c*) paragraph 29 of Schedule 5 to the Finance Act 1996 (interest payable by the Commissioners on overpayments etc of landfill tax) [or

(*d*) Part II of Schedule 3 to the Finance Act 2001 (interest)][1].

Amendments—[1] Sub-para (2)(*a*) and words in sub-para (2(*b*) repealed, and sub-para (2)(*d*) inserted, by FA 2001 ss 15, 110, Sch 3, Pt 4, para 19(1), (3), Sch 33 Pt 1(4) with effect from1 November 2001 (by virtue of SI 2001/3300).

Assessments under paragraphs 14 and 15

16— (1) An assessment under paragraph 14 or 15 above shall not be made more than two years after the time when evidence of facts sufficient in the opinion of the Commissioners to justify the making of the assessment comes to the knowledge of the Commissioners.

(2) Where an amount has been assessed and notified to any person under paragraph 14 or 15 above, it shall be recoverable (subject to any provision having effect in accordance with paragraph 19 below) as if it were relevant tax due from him.

(3) Sub-paragraph (2) above does not have effect if, or to the extent that, the assessment in question has been withdrawn or reduced.

Interest on amounts assessed

17— (1) Where an assessment is made under paragraph 14 or 15 above, the whole of the amount assessed shall carry interest at the rate applicable under section 197 of the Finance Act 1996 from the date on which the assessment is notified until payment.

(2) Where any person is liable to interest under sub-paragraph (1) above the Commissioners may assess the amount due by way of interest and notify it to him.

(3) Without prejudice to the power to make assessments under this paragraph for later periods, the interest to which an assessment under this paragraph may relate shall be confined to interest for a period of no more than two years ending with the time when the assessment under this paragraph is made.

(4) Interest under this paragraph shall be paid without any deduction of income tax.

(5) A notice of assessment under this paragraph shall specify a date, being not later than the date of the notice, to which the amount of interest is calculated; and, if the interest continues to accrue after that date, a further assessment or assessments may be made under this paragraph in respect of amounts which so accrue.

(6) If, within such period as may be notified by the Commissioners to the person liable for interest under sub-paragraph (1) above, the amount referred to in that sub-paragraph is paid, it shall be treated for the purposes of that sub-paragraph as paid on the date specified as mentioned in sub-paragraph (5) above.

(7) Where an amount has been assessed and notified to any person under this paragraph it shall be recoverable as if it were relevant tax due from him.

(8) Sub-paragraph (7) above does not have effect if, or to the extent that, the assessment in question has been withdrawn or reduced.

Supplementary assessments

18 If it appears to the Commissioners that the amount which ought to have been assessed in an assessment under paragraph 14, 15 or 17 above exceeds the amount which was so assessed, then—

(*a*) under the same paragraph as that assessment was made, and
(*b*) on or before the last day on which that assessment could have been made,

the Commissioners may make a supplementary assessment of the amount of the excess and shall notify the person concerned accordingly.

Review of decisions and appeals

19— …

(2) Sections [59 to 60][1] of that Act of 1994 (review and appeal in the case of insurance premium tax) shall have effect in relation to any decision which—

(*a*) is contained in an assessment under paragraph 14, 15 or 17 above,
(*b*) is a decision about whether any amount is due to the Commissioners or about how much is due, and
(*c*) is made in a case in which the relevant repayment provision is paragraph 8 of Schedule 7 to that Act or the relevant interest provision is paragraph 22 of that Schedule,

as if that decision were a decision to which section 59 of that Act applies.

…

Amendments—[1] In sub-para (2) words substituted for words "59 and 60" by the Transfer of Tribunal Functions and Revenue and Customs Appeals Order, SI 2009/56, art 3(1), Sch 1 paras 241, 244(1), (3) with effect from 1 April 2009.

Interpretation of Part V

20— (1) In this Part of this Schedule "the Commissioners" means the Commissioners of Customs and Excise.

(2) In this Part of this Schedule "relevant tax", in relation to any assessment, means—

(*a*) a duty of excise if the assessment relates to—
(i) a repayment of an amount paid by way of such a duty,

IPT

(ii) an overpayment of interest under [Part II of Schedule 3 to the Finance Act 2001][1], or
(iii) interest on an amount specified in an assessment in relation to which the relevant tax is a duty of excise;

(*b*) insurance premium tax if the assessment relates to—
(i) a repayment of an amount paid by way of such tax,
(ii) an overpayment of interest under paragraph 22 of Schedule 7 to the Finance Act 1994, or
(iii) interest on an amount specified in an assessment in relation to which the relevant tax is insurance premium tax;

and

(*c*) landfill tax if the assessment relates to—
(i) a repayment of an amount paid by way of such tax,
(ii) an overpayment of interest under paragraph 29 of Schedule 5 to the Finance Act 1996, or
(iii) interest on an amount specified in an assessment in relation to which the relevant tax is landfill tax.

(3) For the purposes of this Part of this Schedule notification to a personal representative, trustee in bankruptcy, interim or permanent trustee, receiver, liquidator or person otherwise acting in a representative capacity in relation to another shall be treated as notification to the person in relation to whom he so acts.

Amendments—[1] Words in sub-para (2)(*a*)(ii) substituted by FA 2001 s 15, Sch 3, Pt 4, para 19(1), (5) with effect from1 November 2001 (by virtue of SI 2001/3300).

Consequential amendment

21 (*inserts* FA 1996 s 197(2)(*e*)).

SCHEDULE 18

REPEALS

Section 113

PART V

INDIRECT TAXES

Note—Details of repeals already in effect have been omitted from this Schedule.

FINANCE ACT 1998

(1998 Chapter 36)

An Act to grant certain duties, to alter other duties, and to amend the law relating to the National Debt and the Public Revenue, and to make further provision in connection with Finance.

[31 July 1998]

PART V

OTHER TAXES

Insurance premium tax

146 Travel insurance: higher rate tax

(1) Schedule 6A to the Finance Act 1994 (premiums liable to tax at the higher rate) shall be amended as follows.

(2) (*substitutes* FA 1994 Sch 6A para 4).

(3) Except as provided by subsection (4) below, subsections (1) and (2) above have effect in relation to a premium which falls to be regarded for the purposes of Part III of the Finance Act 1994 as received under a taxable insurance contract by an insurer on or after 1st August 1998.

(4) Subsections (1) and (2) above do not have effect in relation to a premium if the premium—
(*a*) is in respect of a contract made before 1st August 1998; and
(*b*) falls, by virtue of regulations under section 68 of the Finance Act 1994 (special accounting scheme), to be regarded for the purposes of Part III of that Act as received under the contract by the insurer on a date before 1st February 1999.

(5) In the application of sections 67A to 67C of the Finance Act 1994 in relation to the increase in insurance premium tax effected by this section and the exception from that increase—

(*a*) the announcement relating to that increase, as described in section 67A(1), and to that exception, as described in section 67B(1), shall be taken to have been made on 17th March 1998;

(*b*) "the date of the change" is 1st August 1998; and

(*c*) "the concessionary date" is 1st February 1999.

147 Taxable intermediaries

(1) Section 52A of the Finance Act 1994 (certain fees to be treated as premiums under higher rate contracts) shall be amended as follows.

(2) (*amends* FA 1994 s 52A(5)).

(3) (*substitutes* FA 1994 s 52A(6)(7)).

(4) (*amends* FA 1994 s 52A(9)).

(5) The amendments made by this section have effect in relation to payments in respect of fees charged on or after 1st August 1998.

PART VI
MISCELLANEOUS AND SUPPLEMENTAL

Supplemental

165 Repeals

(1) The enactments mentioned in Schedule 27 to this Act (which include spent provisions) are hereby repealed to the extent specified in the third column of that Schedule.

(2) The repeals specified in that Schedule have effect subject to the commencement provisions and savings contained or referred to in the notes set out in that Schedule.

SCHEDULE 27
REPEALS
PART V
OTHER TAXES

INSURANCE PREMIUM TAX

Note—This repeal is already in force and has therefore been omitted.

IPT

HUMAN RIGHTS ACT 1998

(1998 Chapter 42)

An Act to give further effect to rights and freedoms guaranteed under the European Convention on Human Rights; to make provision with respect to holders of certain judicial offices who become judges of the European Court of Human Rights; and for connected purposes.

[9th November 1998]

Note—Please see VAT Statutes *ante* for the text of this Act.

FINANCE ACT 1999

(1999 Chapter 16)

An Act to grant certain duties, to alter other duties, and to amend the law relating to the National Debt and the Public Revenue, and to make further provision in connection with Finance.

[27 July 1999]

PART VII
OTHER TAXES

Insurance premium tax

125 Rate of insurance premium tax

(1) In section 51(2)(*b*) of the Finance Act 1994 (4 per cent standard rate of insurance premium tax), for "4 per cent" there shall be substituted "5 per cent".

(2) Subsection (1) above has effect in relation to a premium which falls to be regarded for the purposes of Part III of the Finance Act 1994 (insurance premium tax) as received under a taxable insurance contract by an insurer on or after 1st July 1999.

(3) Subsection (1) above does not have effect in relation to a premium which—

(*a*) is in respect of a contract made before 1st July 1999, and

(*b*) falls to be regarded for the purposes of Part III of that Act as received under the contract by the insurer on a date before 1st January 2000, by virtue of regulations under section 68 of that Act (special accounting schemes).

(4) Subsection (3) above does not apply in relation to a premium which—

(*a*) is an additional premium under a contract,

(*b*) falls to be regarded for the purposes of Part III of that Act as received under the contract by the insurer on or after 1st July 1999, by virtue of regulations under section 68 of that Act, and

(*c*) is in respect of a risk which was not covered by the contract before 1st July 1999.

(5) In the application of sections 67A to 67C of that Act (announced increase in rate of insurance premium tax) in relation to the increase under subsection (1) above and the exception under subsection (3) above—

(*a*) the announcement for the purpose of sections 67A(1) and 67B(1) shall be taken to have been made on 9th March 1999,

(*b*) the date of the change is 1st July 1999, and

(*c*) the concessionary date is 1st January 2000.

FINANCIAL SERVICES AND MARKETS ACT 2000

(2000 Chapter 8)

An Act to make provision about the regulation of financial services and markets; to provide for the transfer of certain statutory functions relating to building societies, friendly societies, industrial and provident societies and certain other mutual societies; and for connected purposes.

[14 June 2000]

PART II

REGULATED AND PROHIBITED ACTIVITIES

Regulated activities

22 The classes of activity and categories of investment

(1) An activity is a regulated activity for the purposes of this Act if it is an activity of a specified kind which is carried on by way of business and—

(*a*) relates to an investment of a specified kind; or

(*b*) in the case of an activity of a kind which is also specified for the purposes of this paragraph, is carried on in relation to property of any kind.

(2) Schedule 2 makes provision supplementing this section.

(3) Nothing in Schedule 2 limits the powers conferred by subsection (1).

(4) "Investment" includes any asset, right or interest.

(5) "Specified" means specified in an order made by the Treasury.

Note—This section came into force on 25 February 2001 (by virtue of SI 2001/516).
Regulations—Financial Services and Markets Act 2000 (Regulated Activities) Order, SI 2001/544 (as amended).
Financial Services and Markets Act 2000 (Financial Promotion and Miscellaneous Amendments) Order, SI 2002/1310.

PART XXX
SUPPLEMENTAL

433 Short title

This Act may be cited as the Financial Services and Markets Act 2000.

SCHEDULE 2
REGULATED ACTIVITIES

Section 22(2)

Note—This Schedule came into force on 25 February 2001 (by virtue of SI 2001/516).

Regulations—Financial Services and Markets Act 2000 (Regulated Activities) Order, SI 2001/544 (as amended by SI 2001/3544).

PART I

REGULATED ACTIVITIES

General

1 The matters with respect to which provision may be made under section 22(1) in respect of activities include, in particular, those described in general terms in this Part of this Schedule.

Dealing in investments

2— (1) Buying, selling, subscribing for or underwriting investments or offering or agreeing to do so, either as a principal or as an agent.

(2) In the case of an investment which is a contract of insurance, that includes carrying out the contract.

Arranging deals in investments

3 Making, or offering or agreeing to make—

(*a*) arrangements with a view to another person buying, selling, subscribing for or underwriting a particular investment;

(*b*) arrangements with a view to a person who participates in the arrangements buying, selling, subscribing for or underwriting investments.

Deposit taking

4 Accepting deposits.

Safekeeping and administration of assets

5— (1) Safeguarding and administering assets belonging to another which consist of or include investments or offering or agreeing to do so.

(2) Arranging for the safeguarding and administration of assets belonging to another, or offering or agreeing to do so.

Managing investments

6 Managing, or offering or agreeing to manage, assets belonging to another person where—

(*a*) the assets consist of or include investments; or

(*b*) the arrangements for their management are such that the assets may consist of or include investments at the discretion of the person managing or offering or agreeing to manage them.

Investment advice

7 Giving or offering or agreeing to give advice to persons on—

(*a*) buying, selling, subscribing for or underwriting an investment; or

(*b*) exercising any right conferred by an investment to acquire, dispose of, underwrite or convert an investment.

Establishing collective investment schemes

8 Establishing, operating or winding up a collective investment scheme, including acting as—

(*a*) trustee of a unit trust scheme;

(*b*) depositary of a collective investment scheme other than a unit trust scheme; or

(*c*) sole director of a body incorporated by virtue of regulations under section 262.

Using computer-based systems for giving investment instructions

9— (1) Sending on behalf of another person instructions relating to an investment by means of a computer-based system which enables investments to be transferred without a written instrument.

(2) Offering or agreeing to send such instructions by such means on behalf of another person.

(3) Causing such instructions to be sent by such means on behalf of another person.

(4) Offering or agreeing to cause such instructions to be sent by such means on behalf of another person.

[PART 1A

REGULATED ACTIVITIES: RECLAIM FUNDS]

Activities of reclaim funds

9A— (1) The matters with respect to which provision may be made under section 22(1) in respect of activities include, in particular, any of the activities of a reclaim fund.

IPT

(2) "Reclaim fund" has the meaning given by section 5(1) of the Dormant Bank and Building Society Accounts Act 2008.][1]

Amendments—[1] This Part inserted by the Dormant Bank and Building Society Accounts Act 2008 s 15, Sch 2 para 1(1), (3) with effect from 12 March 2009 (by virtue of SI 2009/490 art 2).

PART II

INVESTMENTS

General

10 The matters with respect to which provision may be made under section 22(1) in respect of investments include, in particular, those described in general terms in this Part of this Schedule.

Securities

11— (1) Shares or stock in the share capital of a company.

(2) "Company" includes—

(*a*) any body corporate (wherever incorporated), and

(*b*) any unincorporated body constituted under the law of a country or territory outside the United Kingdom,

other than an open-ended investment company.

Instruments creating or acknowledging indebtedness

12 Any of the following—

(*a*) debentures;

(*b*) debenture stock;

(*c*) loan stock;

(*d*) bonds;

(*e*) certificates of deposit;

(*f*) any other instruments creating or acknowledging a present or future indebtedness.

Government and public securities

13— (1) Loan stock, bonds and other instruments—

(*a*) creating or acknowledging indebtedness; and

(*b*) issued by or on behalf of a government, local authority or public authority.

(2) "Government, local authority or public authority" means—

(*a*) the government of the United Kingdom, of Northern Ireland, or of any country or territory outside the United Kingdom;

(*b*) a local authority in the United Kingdom or elsewhere;

(*c*) any international organisation the members of which include the United Kingdom or another member State.

Instruments giving entitlement to investments

14— (1) Warrants or other instruments entitling the holder to subscribe for any investment.

(2) It is immaterial whether the investment is in existence or identifiable.

Certificates representing securities

15 Certificates or other instruments which confer contractual or property rights—

(*a*) in respect of any investment held by someone other than the person on whom the rights are conferred by the certificate or other instrument; and

(*b*) the transfer of which may be effected without requiring the consent of that person.

Units in collective investment schemes

16— (1) Shares in or securities of an open-ended investment company.

(2) Any right to participate in a collective investment scheme.

Options

17 Options to acquire or dispose of property.

Futures

18 Rights under a contract for the sale of a commodity or property of any other description under which delivery is to be made at a future date.

Contracts for differences

19 Rights under—

(*a*) a contract for differences; or

(*b*) any other contract the purpose or pretended purpose of which is to secure a profit or avoid a loss by reference to fluctuations in—

(i) the value or price of property of any description; or

(ii) an index or other factor designated for that purpose in the contract.

Contracts of insurance

20 Rights under a contract of insurance, including rights under contracts falling within head C of Schedule 2 to the Friendly Societies Act 1992.

Participation in Lloyd's syndicates

21— (1) The underwriting capacity of a Lloyd's syndicate.

(2) A person's membership (or prospective membership) of a Lloyd's syndicate.

Deposits

22 Rights under any contract under which a sum of money (whether or not denominated in a currency) is paid on terms under which it will be repaid, with or without interest or a premium, and either on demand or at a time or in circumstances agreed by or on behalf of the person making the payment and the person receiving it.

Loans secured on land

23— (1) Rights under any contract under which—

(*a*) one person provides another with credit; and

(*b*) the obligation of the borrower to repay is secured on land.

(2) "Credit" includes any cash loan or other financial accommodation.

(3) "Cash" includes money in any form.

[Other finance arrangements involving land

23A— (1) Rights under any arrangement for the provision of finance under which the person providing the finance either—

(*a*) acquires a major interest in land from the person to whom the finance is provided, or

(*b*) disposes of a major interest in land to that person,

as part of the arrangement.

(2) References in sub-paragraph (1) to a "major interest" in land are to—

(*a*) in relation to land in England or Wales—

(i) an estate in fee simple absolute, or

(ii) a term of years absolute,

whether subsisting at law or in equity;

(*b*) in relation to land in Scotland—

(i) the interest of an owner of land, or

(ii) the tenant's right over or interest in a property subject to a lease;

(*c*) in relation to land in Northern Ireland—

(i) any freehold estate, or

(ii) any leasehold estate,

whether subsisting at law or in equity.

(3) It is immaterial for the purposes of sub-paragraph (1) whether either party acquires or (as the case may be) disposes of the interest in land—

(*a*) directly, or

(*b*) indirectly.][1]

Amendments—[1] Para 23A inserted by the Regulation of Financial Services (Land Transactions) Act 2005 s 1 with effect from 19 February 2006 (Regulation of Financial Services (Land Transactions) Act 2005 s 2(2)).

Rights in investments

24 Any right or interest in anything which is an investment as a result of any other provision made under section 22(1).

PART III

SUPPLEMENTAL PROVISIONS

The order-making power

25— (1) An order under section 22(1) may—

(*a*) provide for exemptions;

(*b*) confer powers on the Treasury or the Authority;

(*c*) authorise the making of regulations or other instruments by the Treasury for purposes of, or connected with, any relevant provision;

(*d*) authorise the making of rules or other instruments by the Authority for purposes of, or connected with, any relevant provision;

(*e*) make provision in respect of any information or document which, in the opinion of the Treasury or the Authority, is relevant for purposes of, or connected with, any relevant provision;

(*f*) make such consequential, transitional or supplemental provision as the Treasury consider appropriate for purposes of, or connected with, any relevant provision.

(2) Provision made as a result of sub-paragraph (1)(f) may amend any primary or subordinate legislation, including any provision of, or made under, this Act.

(3) "Relevant provision" means any provision—

(*a*) of section 22 or this Schedule; or

(*b*) made under that section or this Schedule.

Parliamentary control

26— (1) This paragraph applies to the first order made under section 22(1).

(2) This paragraph also applies to any subsequent order made under section 22(1) which contains a statement by the Treasury that, in their opinion, the effect (or one of the effects) of the proposed order would be that an activity which is not a regulated activity would become a regulated activity.

(3) An order to which this paragraph applies—

(*a*) must be laid before Parliament after being made; and

(*b*) ceases to have effect at the end of the relevant period unless before the end of that period the order is approved by a resolution of each House of Parliament (but without that affecting anything done under the order or the power to make a new order).

(4) "Relevant period" means a period of twenty-eight days beginning with the day on which the order is made.

(5) In calculating the relevant period no account is to be taken of any time during which Parliament is dissolved or prorogued or during which both Houses are adjourned for more than four days.

Interpretation

27— (1) In this Schedule—

"buying" includes acquiring for valuable consideration;

"offering" includes inviting to treat;

"property" includes currency of the United Kingdom or any other country or territory; and

"selling" includes disposing for valuable consideration.

(2) In sub-paragraph (1) "disposing" includes—

(*a*) in the case of an investment consisting of rights under a contract—

(i) surrendering, assigning or converting those rights; or

(ii) assuming the corresponding liabilities under the contract;

(*b*) in the case of an investment consisting of rights under other arrangements, assuming the corresponding liabilities under the contract or arrangements;

(*c*) in the case of any other investment, issuing or creating the investment or granting the rights or interests of which it consists.

(3) In this Schedule references to an instrument include references to any record (whether or not in the form of a document).

FINANCE ACT 2003

(2003 Chapter 14)

An Act to grant certain duties, to alter other duties, and to amend the law relating to the National Debt and the Public Revenue, and to make further provision in connection with finance.

[10 July 2003]

PART 8
OTHER TAXES

Insurance premium tax

194 Higher rate of tax: divided companies

(1) (*inserts* FA 1994 Sch 6A para 3A)

(2) Subsection (1) applies in relation to a premium that falls to be regarded for the purposes of Part 3 of the Finance Act 1994 (c 9) (insurance premium tax) as received under a taxable insurance contract by an insurer on or after the day on which this Act is passed.

FINANCE ACT 2007

(2007 Chapter 11)

PART 7
MISCELLANEOUS

101 IPT: meaning of "premium"

(1) (*inserts* FA 1994 s 72(1B))

(2) The amendment made by subsection (1) has effect in relation to amounts charged on or after 22nd March 2007.

SCHEDULES

SCHEDULE 24
PENALTIES FOR ERRORS

Note—Please see *VAT Statutes* ante for the text of this Schedule.

FINANCE ACT 2008

(2008 Chapter 9)

An Act to Grant certain duties, to alter other duties, and to amend the law relating to the National Debt and the Public Revenue, and to make further provision in connection with finance.

[21 July 2008]

PART 7
ADMINISTRATION

Press releases—HMRC Guidance Note, 18 July 2008 (HMRC set-off across taxes following Finance Bill 2008).

CHAPTER 1
INFORMATION ETC

New information etc powers

114 Computer records etc

Note—Please see *VAT Statutes* ante for the text of this Section.

CHAPTER 3
PENALTIES

122 Penalties for errors

Note—Please see *VAT Statutes* ante for the text of this Section.

123 Penalties for failure to notify etc

Note—Please see *VAT Statutes* ante for the text of this Section.

IPT

CHAPTER 4
APPEALS ETC

Reviews and appeals etc: general

124 HMRC decisions etc: reviews and appeals

Note—Please see *VAT Statutes* ante for the text of this Section.

CHAPTER 5
PAYMENT AND ENFORCEMENT

Taking control of goods etc

127 Enforcement by taking control of goods: England and Wales

Note—Please see *VAT Statutes* ante for the text of this Section.

128 Summary warrant: Scotland

Note—Please see *VAT Statutes* ante for the text of this Section.

129 Consequential provision and commencement

Note—Please see *VAT Statutes* ante for the text of this Section.

Set off

130 Set-off: England and Wales and Northern Ireland

Note—Please see *VAT Statutes* ante for the text of this Section.

131 No set-off where insolvency procedure has been applied

Note—Please see *VAT Statutes* ante for the text of this Section.

133 Set-off etc where right to be paid a sum has been transferred

Note—Please see *VAT Statutes* ante for the text of this Section.

Other measures

135 Interest on unpaid tax in case of disaster etc of national significance

Note—Please see *VAT Statutes* ante for the text of this Section.

136 Fee for payment

Note—Please see *VAT Statutes* ante for the text of this Section.

Supplementary

139 Interpretation of Chapter

Note—Please see *VAT Statutes* ante for the text of this Section.

PART 8
MISCELLANEOUS

Insurance premium tax

142 Tax representatives

(1) (*amends* FA 1994 ss 57, 58, 65(1), 73(1), Sch 7 paras 18, 20).

(2) (*repeals* FA 1997 s 27(4), (5)).

143 Overseas insurers

(1) Section 65 of FA 1994 (insurance premium tax: liability of insured where insurer not established in United Kingdom) is amended as follows.

(2) (*amends* FA 1994 s 65(1)).

(3) (*inserts* FA 1994 s 65(1A), (1B))

Payments from Exchequer accounts

158 Power of Treasury to make payments

Note—Please see *VAT Statutes* ante for the text of this Section.

159 Payments from certain Exchequer accounts: mechanism

Note—Please see *VAT Statutes* ante for the text of this Section.

Other matters

160 Power to give statutory effect to concessions

Note—Please see *VAT Statutes* ante for the text of this Section.

PART 9
FINAL PROVISIONS

165 Interpretation

166 Short title

Note—Please see *VAT Statutes* ante for the text of these Sections.

SCHEDULES

SCHEDULE 36
INFORMATION AND INSPECTION POWERS

Section 113

Note—Please see *VAT Statutes* ante for the text of this Schedule.

SCHEDULE 41
PENALTIES: FAILURE TO NOTIFY AND CERTAIN VAT AND EXCISE WRONGDOING

Section 123

Note—Please see *VAT Statutes* ante for the text of this Schedule.

IPT

FINANCE ACT 2009

(2009 Chapter 10)

An Act to Grant certain duties, to alter other duties, and to amend the law relating to the National Debt and the Public Revenue, and to make further provision in connection with finance.

[21 July 2009]

PART 7
ADMINISTRATION

Standards and values

92 HMRC Charter

Note—Please see *VAT Statutes* ante for the text of this Section.

93 Duties of senior accounting officers of qualifying companies

Note—Please see *VAT Statutes* ante for the text of this Section.

94 Publishing details of deliberate tax defaulters

Note—Please see *VAT Statutes* ante for the text of this Section.

Information etc

95 Amendment of information and inspection powers

Note—Please see *VAT Statutes* ante for the text of this Section.

96 Extension of information and inspection powers to further taxes

(1) In paragraph 63(1) of Schedule 36 to FA 2008 (information and inspection powers: meaning of "tax"), for paragraph (*e*) (and the "and" before it) substitute—

"(*e*) insurance premium tax,
(*f*) inheritance tax,
(*g*) stamp duty land tax,
(*h*) stamp duty reserve tax,
(*i*) petroleum revenue tax,
(*j*) aggregates levy,
(*k*) climate change levy,
(*l*) landfill tax, and
(*m*) relevant foreign tax,".

(2) Schedule 48 contains further amendments of that Schedule.

(3) The amendments made by this section and Schedule 48 come into force on such day as the Treasury may by order appoint.

(4) An order under subsection (3) may—

(*a*) appoint different days for different purposes, and
(*b*) contain transitional provision and savings.

(5) The Treasury may by order make any incidental, supplemental, consequential, transitional or transitory provision or saving which appears appropriate in consequence of, or otherwise in connection with, this section and Schedule 48.

(6) An order under subsection (5) may—

(*a*) make different provision for different purposes, and
(*b*) make provision amending, repealing or revoking an enactment or instrument (whenever passed or made).

(7) An order under this section is to be made by statutory instrument.

(8) A statutory instrument containing an order under subsection (5) is subject to annulment in pursuance of a resolution of the House of Commons.

97 Powers to obtain contact details for debtors

Note—Please see *VAT Statutes* ante for the text of this Section.

98 Record-keeping

(1) Schedule 50 contains provision about obligations to keep records.

(2) The amendments made by that Schedule come into force on such day as the Treasury may by order made by statutory instrument appoint.

Assessments, claims etc

99 Time limits for assessments, claims etc

(1) Schedule 51 contains provision about time limits for assessments, claims etc

(2) The amendments made by that Schedule come into force on such day as the Treasury may by order made by statutory instrument appoint.

(3) An order under subsection (2)—

(*a*) may make different provision for different purposes, and
(*b*) may include transitional provision and savings.

Interest

101 Late payment interest on sums due to HMRC

Note—Please see *VAT Statutes* ante for the text of this Section.

102 Repayment interest on sums to be paid by HMRC

Note—Please see *VAT Statutes* ante for the text of this Section.

103 Rates of interest

Note—Please see *VAT Statutes* ante for the text of this Section.

104 Supplementary

Note—Please see *VAT Statutes* ante for the text of this Section.

108 Suspension of penalties during currency of agreement for deferred payment

Note—Please see *VAT Statutes* ante for the text of this Section.

109 Miscellaneous amendments

Note—Please see *VAT Statutes* ante for the text of this Section.

SCHEDULES

SCHEDULE 46

DUTIES OF SENIOR ACCOUNTING OFFICERS OF QUALIFYING COMPANIES

Section 93

Note—Please see *VAT Statutes* ante for the text of this Schedule.

SCHEDULE 47

AMENDMENT OF INFORMATION AND INSPECTION POWERS

Section 95

Note—Please see *VAT Statutes* ante for the text of this Schedule.

SCHEDULE 48

EXTENSION OF INFORMATION AND INSPECTION POWERS

Section 96

Note—Please see *VAT Statutes* ante for the text of this Schedule.

SCHEDULE 49

POWERS TO OBTAIN CONTACT DETAILS FOR DEBTORS

Section 97

Note—Please see *VAT Statutes* ante for the text of this Schedule.

SCHEDULE 50

RECORD-KEEPING

Section 98

Insurance premium tax

1 (1) Paragraph 1 of Schedule 7 to FA 1994 (insurance premium tax: records) is amended as follows.

(2) In sub-paragraph (3)—

(*a*) after "may" insert

"—

(*a*) ", and

(*b*) insert at the end—

"(*b*) authorise the Commissioners to direct that any such records need only be preserved for a shorter period than that specified in the regulations, and

(*c*) authorise a direction to be made so as to apply generally or in such cases as the Commissioners may stipulate."

(3) For sub-paragraphs (4) to (6) substitute—

"(4) A duty under the regulations to preserve records may be discharged—

(*a*) by preserving them in any form and by any means, or

(*b*) by preserving the information contained in them in any form and by any means, subject to any conditions or exceptions specified in writing by the Commissioners."

2 In consequence of the amendment made by paragraph 1(3), in the Criminal Procedure (Consequential Provisions) (Scotland) Act 1995, in Schedule 4, omit paragraph 89(4)(*a*).

SCHEDULE 51

TIME LIMITS FOR ASSESSMENTS, CLAIMS ETC

Section 99

Insurance premium tax

1 Schedule 7 to FA 1994 (insurance premium tax) is amended as follows.

2 In paragraph 8(4) (recovery of overpaid tax), for "three years" substitute "4 years".

3 In paragraph 22(9) (interest payable by Commissioners), for "three years" substitute "4 years".

IPT

4— (1) Paragraph 26 (assessments: time limits) is amended as follows.

(2) In sub-paragraph (1), for the words from "three years after" (in the first place) to the end substitute "4 years after the relevant event".

(3) After that sub-paragraph insert—

"(1A) In this paragraph "the relevant event", in relation to an assessment, means—

(*a*) the end of the accounting period concerned, or

(*b*) in the case of an assessment under paragraph 25 of an amount due by way of a penalty other than a penalty referred to in paragraph 25(2), the event giving rise to the penalty."

(4) In sub-paragraph (3), for "sub-paragraph (1)" substitute "sub-paragraph (1A)".

(5) For sub-paragraph (4) substitute—

"(4) An assessment of an amount due from a person in a case involving a loss of tax—

(*a*) brought about deliberately by the person (or by another person acting on that person's behalf), or

(*b*) attributable to a failure by the person to comply with an obligation under section 53(1) or (2) or 53AA(1) or (3), may be made at any time not more than 20 years after the relevant event.

(5) In sub-paragraph (4)(*a*) the reference to a loss brought about deliberately by the person includes a loss brought about as a result of a deliberate inaccuracy in a document given to Her Majesty's Revenue and Customs by or on behalf of that person."

SCHEDULE 53
LATE PAYMENT INTEREST

Section 101

Note—Please see *VAT Statutes* ante for the text of this Schedule.

SCHEDULE 54
REPAYMENT INTEREST

Section 102

Note—Please see *VAT Statutes* ante for the text of this Schedule.

SCHEDULE 57
AMENDMENTS RELATING TO PENALTIES

Section 109

Note—Please see *VAT Statutes* ante for the text of this Schedule.

INSURANCE PREMIUM TAX STATUTORY INSTRUMENTS

IPT

CHRONOLOGICAL LIST OF PRINTED STATUTORY INSTRUMENTS

SI Year/No	Title
SI 1994/1774	Insurance Premium Tax Regulations 1994
SI 1997/1431	The Distress for Customs and Excise Duties and Other Indirect Taxes Regulations 1997
SI 1998/1461	Air Passenger Duty and Other Indirect Taxes (Interest Rate) Regulations 1998
SI 2001/2635	Financial Services and Markets Act 2000 (Law Applicable to Contracts of Insurance) Regulations 2001

CHRONOLOGICAL LIST OF STATUTORY INSTRUMENTS

SI Year/No	Title
SI 1994/1698	*Insurance Premium Tax (Taxable Insurance Contracts) Order 1994* (amends FA 1994; see ss 69, 70, 73, Sch 7A)
SI 1994/1773	Finance Act 1994 (Appointed Day) Order 1994 (see FA 1994 ss 59, 60)
SI 1994/1774	Insurance Premium Tax Regulations 1994
SI 1994/1819	*Insurance Premium Tax (Prescribed Rates of Interest) Order 1994* (superseded)
SI 1995/1587	*Insurance Premium Tax (Amendment) Regulations 1995* (amending)
SI 1996/166	Insurance Premium Tax (Prescribed Rates of Interest) (Amendment) Order 1996 (amending)
SI 1996/2099	*Insurance Premium Tax (Amendment) Regulations 1996* (amending)
SI 1996/2955	*Insurance Premium Tax (taxable Insurance Contracts) Order 1996* (amending)
SI 1997/1015	Finance Act 1996 s 197 (Appointed Day) Order 1997 (see FA 1996 s 197)
SI 1997/1016	*Air Passenger Duty and Other Indirect Taxes (Interest Rate) Regulations 1997* (see FA 1994 Sch 7 paras 21, 22) (revoked)
SI 1997/1157	*Insurance Premium Tax (Amendment) Regulations 1997* (amending)
SI 1997/1431	The Distress for Customs and Excise Duties and Other Indirect Taxes Regulations 1997
SI 1997/1432	The Finance Act 1997, sections 52 and 53 (Appointed *Day) Order 1997* (see FA 1994 ss 52 and 53)
SI 1997/1433	*The Finance Act 1997 (Repeal of Distress and Diligence Enactments) (Appointed Day)Order 1997* (see FA 1997 Sch 7 paras 7 (7)–(12))
SI 1997/1627	*The Insurance Premium Tax (Taxable Insurance Contracts) Order 1997* (amending)
SI 1997/2781	*Transfer of Functions (Insurance) Order 1997* (amending)
SI 1998/60	*The Insurance Premium Tax (Amendment) Regulations 1998* (amending)
SI 1998/1461	Air Passenger Duty and Other Indirect Taxes (Interest Rate) Regulations 1998
SI 2000/631	*Air Passenger Duty and Other Indirect Taxes (Interest Rate) (Amendment) Regulations 2000*
SI 2001/2635	Financial Services and Markets Act 2000 (Law Applicable to Contracts of Insurance) Regulations 2001
SI 2001/3337	*Air Passenger Duty and Other Indirect Taxes (Interest Rate) (Amendment) Regulations 2001*
SI 2006/2700	*Insurance Premium Tax (Amendment) Regulations 2006*
SI 2007/2403	*Financial Services and Markets Act 2000 (Motor Insurance) Regulations 2007*
SI 2008/1945	*Insurance Premium Tax (Amendment) Regulations 2008*
SI 2008/2693	*Amusement Machine Licence Duty, etc (Amendments) Regulations 2008*
SI 2008/3234	*Taxes and Duties (Interest Rate) (Amendment) Regulations 2008*
SI 2009/56	*Transfer of Tribunal Functions and Revenue and Customs Appeals Order 2009*
SI 2009/2032	*Taxes and Duties (Interest Rate) (Amendment) Regulations 2009*

IPT

1994/1774
Insurance Premium Tax Regulations 1994

Made by the Commissioners of Customs and Excise under FA 1994 ss 53(6), 54, 55(1)–(8), 57(15), 58(2), (4), 62(1), (3)–(7), 65(1)–(3), (5), (7)–(13), 68(1)–(11), 74(2), (7), (8), and Sch 7 paras 1(1)–(3), 7(7), (8), 8(6).

Made . . . . *6th July 1994*
Laid before the House of Commons . . . . *7th July 1994*
Coming into force . . . . *1st August 1994*

ARRANGEMENT OF REGULATIONS

IPT

PART VI

TAX REPRESENTATIVES

PART VII

LIABILITY OF INSURED PERSONS

PART VIII

DISTRESS AND DILIGENCE

PART I
PRELIMINARY

Citation and commencement

1 These Regulations may be cited as the Insurance Premium Tax Regulations 1994 and shall come into force on 1st August 1994.

Interpretation

2— (1) In these Regulations—

"accounting period" means—

(*a*) in the case of a registered person, each period of three months ending on the dates notified to him by the Commissioners, whether by means of a certificate of registration issued by them or otherwise;

(*b*) in the case of a registrable person who is not registered, each quarter; or

(*c*) in the case of any registrable person, such other period in relation to which he is required by or under regulation 12 to make a return;

and, in every case, the first accounting period of a registrable person shall commence on the effective date determined in accordance with section 53 [or 53AA][1] of the Act upon which the person was or should have been registered;

"the Act" means Part III of the Finance Act 1994;

"Collector" means a Collector, Deputy Collector or Assistant Collector of Customs and Excise;

"Lloyd's" means the society incorporated by section 3 of Lloyd's Act 1871;

"managing agent" has the same meaning as in section 12(1) of Lloyd's Act 1982;

"registered person" means a person who is registered under section 53 [or 53AA][1] of the Act and, except in regulation 30, "register" and "registration" shall be construed accordingly;

"registration number" means the unique identifying number allocated to a registered person and notified to him by the Commissioners;

"return" means a return which is required to be made in accordance with regulation 12;

["taxable intermediary's fees" means fees which, to the extent of any payment in respect of them, are chargeable to tax by virtue of section 52A of the Finance Act 1994 and references in these regulations to "fee" or "fees" shall be construed accordingly;][1]

"underwriting member" has the same meaning as in section 2(1) of Lloyd's Act 1982.

(2) Any reference in these Regulations to "this Part" is a reference to the Part of these Regulations in which that reference is made.

(3) Any reference in these Regulations to a form prescribed in the Schedule to these Regulations shall include a reference to a form which the Commissioners are satisfied is a form to the like effect.

Amendments—[1] Words "or 53AA" in definitions of "accounting period" and "registered person" and definition of "taxable intermediary's fees" inserted by the Insurance Premium Tax (Amendment) Regulations, SI 1997/1157 with effect from 1 May 1997.

Requirement, direction, demand or approval

3 Any requirement, direction, demand or approval by the Commissioners under or for the purposes of these Regulations shall be made or given by a notice in writing.

PART II
REGISTRATION AND PROVISIONS FOR SPECIAL CASES

Notification of liability to register

4— (1) A person who is required by section 53(2) of the Act to notify the Commissioners of the facts there mentioned shall do so on the form numbered 1 in the Schedule to these Regulations.

(2) Where the notification referred to in this regulation is made by a partnership, it shall include the particulars set out on the form numbered 2 in the Schedule to these Regulations.

(3) The notification referred to in this regulation shall be made within thirty days of the earliest date after 31st July 1994 on which the person either forms or continues to have the intention to receive premiums in the course of a taxable business.

Commentary—*De Voil Indirect Tax Service* **V18.132**.

[Notification of liability to register—taxable intermediaries

4A— (1) A person who is required by section 53AA(3) of the Act to notify the Commissioners of the facts there mentioned shall do so on the form numbered 1 in the Schedule to these Regulations.

(2) Where the notification referred to in this regulation is made by a partnership, it shall include the particulars set out on the form numbered 2 in the Schedule to these Regulations.

(3) The notification referred to in this regulation shall be made within thirty days of the earliest date after 30th April 1997 on which the person either forms or continues to have the intention to charge taxable intermediary's fees in the course of any business of his.][1]

Amendments—[1] Reg 4A and the immediately preceding heading inserted by the Insurance Premium Tax (Amendment) Regulations, SI 1997/1157 with effect from 1 May 1997.

Changes in particulars

[5— (1) A person who has made a notification under regulation 4 [or 4A][2], whether or not it was made in accordance with paragraph (3) [of regulation 4 or 4A above][2], shall, within thirty days of—

(*a*) discovering any inaccuracy in; or
(*b*) any change occurring which causes to become inaccurate,

any information contained in or provided with the notification, notify the Commissioners in writing and furnish them with full particulars thereof.

(2) Without prejudice to paragraph (1) above, a registrable person shall, within thirty days of any change occurring in any of the circumstances referred to in paragraph (4) below, notify the Commissioners in writing and furnish them with particulars of—

(*a*) the change; and
(*b*) the date on which the change occurred.

(3) A registrable person who discovers that any information contained in or provided with a notification under paragraph (2) above is inaccurate shall, within thirty days of his discovering the inaccuracy, notify the Commissioners and furnish them with particulars of—

(*a*) the inaccuracy;
(*b*) the date on which the inaccuracy was discovered;
(*c*) why the information was inaccurate; and
(*d*) the correct information.

(4) The circumstances mentioned in paragraph (2) above are the following circumstances relating to the registrable person[, any insurance business carried on by him or any business in the course of which he charges taxable intermediary's fees][2]—

(*a*) his name, his trading name (if different) and address;
(*b*) the name, the trading name (if different) and address of his tax representative;
(*c*) his status, namely whether he carries on business as a sole proprietor, body corporate, partnership or other unincorporated body;
(*d*) in the case of a partnership, the name and address of the partners;

(e) in the case of a syndicate of underwriting members of Lloyd's which has been registered as such, the number or other identifying feature by reference to which it was registered.

(5) Where in relation to a registrable person the Commissioners are satisfied that any of the information recorded in the register kept under section 53 [or 53AA][2] of the Act is or has become inaccurate they may correct the register accordingly.

(6) For the purposes of paragraph (5) above it is immaterial whether or not the registrable person has made any notification he was required to make under this regulation.][1]

Commentary—*De Voil Indirect Tax Service* **V18.132.**

Amendments—[1] Para (5) substituted by the Insurance Premium Tax (Amendment) Regulations, SI 1995/1587 with effect from 17 July 1995.

[2] First words in para (1) and words in para (5) inserted and second words in para (1) and words in para (4) substituted by the Insurance Premium Tax (Amendment) Regulations, SI 1997/1157 with effect from 1 May 1997.

Notification of liability to be de-registered

6 A person who is required by section 53(3) of the Act to notify the Commissioners of the facts there mentioned shall, within thirty days of his having ceased to have the intention to receive premiums in the course of any taxable business, notify the Commissioners in writing and shall therein inform them of—

(a) the date on which he ceased to have the intention of receiving premiums in the course of any taxable business; and

(b) if different, the date on which the last such premium was received.

Commentary—*De Voil Indirect Tax Service* **V18.136.**

[Notification of liability to be de-registered— taxable intermediaries

6A A person who is required by section 53AA(4) of the Act to notify the Commissioners of the facts there mentioned shall, within thirty days of his having ceased to have the intention of charging taxable intermediary's fees, give notice to the Commissioners in writing—

(a) of the date on which he ceased to charge taxable intermediary's fees in the course of any business of his; and

(b) if different, the date on which the last such fee was received.][1]

Commentary—*De Voil Indirect Tax Service* **V18.187.**

Amendments—[1] Reg 6A and the immediately preceding heading inserted by the Insurance Premium Tax (Amendment) Regulations, SI 1997/1157 with effect from 1 May 1997.

Transfer of a going concern

7— (1) Where—

(a) a taxable business is transferred as a going concern;

(b) the registration of the transferor has not already been cancelled;

(c) as a result of the transfer of the business the registration of the transferor is to be cancelled and the transferee becomes liable to be registered; and

(d) an application is made on the form numbered 3 in the Schedule to these Regulations by both the transferor and the transferee,

the Commissioners may with effect from the date of the transfer cancel the registration of the transferor and register the transferee with the registration number previously allocated to the transferor.

(2) An application under paragraph (1) above shall be treated as the notification referred to in regulation 6.

(3) Where the transferee of a business has been registered under paragraph (1) above with the registration number previously allocated to the transferor—

(a) any liability of the transferor existing at the date of the transfer to make a return or account for or pay any tax under Part III of these Regulations shall become the liability of the transferee;

(b) any entitlement of the transferor, whether or not existing at the date of the transfer, to credit or payment under Part IV of these Regulations shall become the entitlement of the transferee.

(4) In addition to the provisions set out in paragraph (3) above, where the transferee of a business has been registered under paragraph (1) above with the registration number previously allocated to the transferor during an accounting period subsequent to that in which the transfer took place (but with effect from the date of the transfer) and any—

(a) return has been made;

(b) tax has been accounted for; or

(c) entitlement to credit has been claimed,

by either the transferor or the transferee, it shall be treated as having been done by the transferee.

(5) Where—

(a) a taxable business is transferred as a going concern;

(b) the transferee makes a payment to a person which represents the repayment of any premium or part of a premium received in the course of that business; and (*c*) the transferor has paid tax on that premium or part,

then, whether or not the transferee has been registered under paragraph (1) above with the registration number previously allocated to the transferor, any entitlement to credit under Part IV of these Regulations shall become the entitlement of the transferee.

Commentary—*De Voil Indirect Tax Service* **V18.133**.

Registration of Lloyd's syndicates

8— (1) Where a taxable business is carried on by persons who are underwriting members of Lloyd's who are members of a syndicate of such underwriting members the registration of those persons for the purposes of the Act may be by reference to the syndicate; and, where such a syndicate is not known by any name, the registration may be by reference to any number or other identifying feature of the syndicate.

(2) In determining whether premiums are received by any syndicate which has been registered in the manner described in paragraph (1) above no account shall be taken of any change in the members of the syndicate.

Commentary—*De Voil Indirect Tax Service* **V18.134**.

Representation of Lloyd's syndicates

9— (1) Anything required to be done by or under the Act (whether by these Regulations or otherwise) by or on behalf of a syndicate of underwriting members of Lloyd's shall be the joint and several responsibility of the persons mentioned in paragraph (2) below; but if it is done by any of those persons it shall be sufficient compliance with any such requirement.

(2) The persons are—

(*a*) the underwriting members of the syndicate;

(*b*) the managing agent of the syndicate; and

(*c*) as regards any accounting period for which it is required by paragraph (3) below to act as the syndicate's representative, Lloyd's.

(3) Where a syndicate of underwriting members of Lloyd's has made an election that Lloyd's shall act as its representative Lloyd's shall so act in relation to any accounting period as regards which—

(*a*) that election has effect;

(*b*) the syndicate is registered as described in regulation 8; and

(*c*) the scheme established by Part V of these Regulations applies to the syndicate.

(4) An election under paragraph (3) above shall be made in writing and shall specify the first accounting period of the syndicate in respect of which the election is to have effect, being an accounting period beginning on or after the date the election is made.

(5) Subject to paragraphs (6) and (7) below, an election under paragraph (3) above shall have effect for the accounting period specified in the election and all subsequent accounting periods.

(6) An election under paragraph (3) above shall not have effect unless written notification of the election is given to the Commissioners before the beginning of the accounting period specified in the election.

(7) An election under paragraph (3) above shall cease to have effect with effect from the accounting period specified in any notice in writing given by the syndicate to the Commissioners for this purpose, being an accounting period beginning after the date the notice is given.

Commentary—*De Voil Indirect Tax Service* **V18.138**.

Representation of unincorporated body

10— (1) Where anything is required to be done by or under the Act (whether by these Regulations or otherwise) by or on behalf of an unincorporated body other than a partnership, it shall be the joint and several responsibility of—

(*a*) every member holding office as president, chairman, treasurer, secretary or any similar office; or

(*b*) if there is no such office, every member holding office as a member of a committee by which the affairs of the body are managed; or

(*c*) if there is no such office or committee, every member;

but, subject to paragraph (2) below, if it is done by any of the persons referred to above that shall be sufficient compliance with any such requirement.

(2) Where an unincorporated body other than a partnership is required to make any notification such as is referred to in regulations 4 to 6, it shall not be sufficient compliance unless the notification is made by a person upon whom a responsibility for making it is imposed by paragraph (1) above.

(3) Where anything is required to be done by or under the Act (whether by these Regulations or otherwise) by or on behalf of a partnership, it shall be the joint and several responsibility of every partner; but if it is done by one partner or, in the case of a partnership whose principal place of business is in Scotland, by any other person authorised by the partnership with respect thereto that shall be sufficient compliance with any such requirement.

Death, bankruptcy or incapacity of registrable persons

11— (1) If a registrable person dies or becomes bankrupt or incapacitated, the Commissioners may, from the date on which he died or became bankrupt or incapacitated, as the case may be, treat as a registrable person any person carrying on any taxable business of his [or any business in the course of which he charged taxable intermediary's fees][1] and any legislation relating to insurance premium tax shall apply to any person so treated as though he were a registered person.

(2) Any person carrying on such business as aforesaid shall, within thirty days of commencing to do so, inform the Commissioners in writing of that fact and of the date of the death or bankruptcy or of the nature of the incapacity and the date on which it began.

(3) Where the Commissioners have treated a person carrying on a business as a registrable person under paragraph (1) above, they shall cease so to treat him if—

(*a*) the registration of the registrable person is cancelled, whether or not any other person is registered with the registration number previously allocated to him;

(*b*) the bankruptcy is discharged or the incapacity ceases; or

(*c*) he ceases carrying on the business of the registrable person.

(4) In relation to a registrable person which is a company, the references in this regulation to the registrable person becoming incapacitated shall be construed as references to its going into liquidation or receivership or to [entering administration][2]; and references to the incapacity ceasing shall be construed accordingly.

Commentary—*De Voil Indirect Tax Service* **V18.141**.

Amendments—[1] Words in para (1) inserted by the Insurance Premium Tax (Amendment) Regulations, SI 1997/1157 with effect from 1 May 1997.

[2] Words in para (4) substituted by the Enterprise Act 2002 (Insolvency) Order, SI 2003/2096 art 5, Schedule para 54 with effect from 15 September 2003. However, this amendment does not apply in any case where a petition for an administration order was presented before that date: SI 2003/2096 art 6.

PART III
ACCOUNTING, PAYMENT AND RECORDS

Making of returns

12— (1) Subject to paragraphs (2) and (4) below and save as the Commissioners may otherwise allow, a registrable person shall, in respect of each accounting period, make a return to the Controller, Central Collection Unit (IPT) on the form numbered 4 in the Schedule to these Regulations.

(2) Lloyd's may, in respect of any two or more syndicates of underwriting members of Lloyd's for which it is required by regulation 9(3) to act as representative as regards an accounting period which, as regards each such syndicate, begins on the same date and ends on the same date, make a return on the form numbered 5 in the Schedule to these Regulations; and, provided it is accompanied by a summary schedule on the form numbered 6 in the Schedule to these Regulations, the making of a return under this paragraph shall be treated as sufficient compliance with paragraph (1) above in relation to the accounting period of each of the syndicates concerned.

(3) Subject to paragraph (4) below, a registrable person shall make each return not later than the last day of the month next following the end of the period to which it relates.

(4) Where the Commissioners consider it necessary in the circumstances of any particular case, they may—

(*a*) vary the length of any accounting period or the date on which it begins or ends or by which any return must be made;

(*b*) allow or direct the registrable person to make a return in accordance with sub-paragraph (*a*) above;

(*c*) allow or direct a registrable person to make returns to a specified address;

and any person to whom the Commissioners give any direction such as is referred to in this regulation shall comply therewith.

Commentary—*De Voil Indirect Tax Service* **V18.146**.

Correction of errors

13— (1) In this regulation—

"credit" means credit to which a person is entitled under Part IV of these Regulations;

"overdeclaration" means, in relation to any return, the amount (if any) which was wrongly treated as tax due for the accounting period concerned and which caused either the amount of tax which was payable to be overstated or the entitlement to a payment under regulation 19(1) to be understated or both or would have caused such an overstatement or understatement were it not for the existence of an underdeclaration in relation to that return;

"underdeclaration" means, in relation to any return, the aggregate of—

(*a*) the amount (if any) of tax due for the accounting period concerned which was not taken into account; and (*b*) the amount (if any) which was wrongly deducted as credit,

and which caused either the amount of tax which was payable to be understated or the entitlement to a payment under regulation 19(1) to be overstated or both or would have caused such an understatement or overstatement were it not for the existence of an overdeclaration in relation to that return.

(2) This regulation applies where a registrable person has made a return which was inaccurate as the result of an overdeclaration or underdeclaration.

(3) Where, in relation to any overdeclarations or underdeclarations that are discovered by the registrable person in an accounting period—

(*a*) the total of the overdeclarations discovered does not exceed [£50,000][1], he may enter that total in [Boxes 6 to 8 (overdeclarations), as appropriate,][1] in the return for that accounting period;

(*b*) the total of the underdeclarations discovered does not exceed [£50,000][1], he may enter that total in [Boxes 3 and 4 (underdeclarations), as appropriate,][1] in the return for that accounting period;

and, where he does so, he shall calculate the tax payable by him or the payment to which he is entitled accordingly.

[But if Box 10 of the registrable person's return for the accounting period requires an entry for net value of taxable premiums (excluding tax) that is less than £5,000,000 (see regulation 12 and Forms 4 and 5 in the Schedule), the total mentioned in sub-paragraph (*a*) or (*b*) must not for these purposes exceed 1% of that net value unless the respective total is [£10,000 or less][2].][1]

(4) Where the return for the accounting period in which the overdeclaration or underdeclaration was discovered is made by Lloyd's in accordance with regulation 12(2), paragraph (3) above shall apply as if the references to the totals of the overdeclarations or underdeclarations ...[1] were references to each such total for each syndicate in respect of which the return is made ...[1].

(5) No amount shall be entered in any return in respect of any overdeclaration or underdeclaration except in accordance with this regulation.

(6) Where any amount has been entered in a return in accordance with this regulation, that return shall be regarded as correcting any earlier return to which that amount relates.

Commentary—*De Voil Indirect Tax Service* **V18.147**.

Amendments—[1] In para (3)(*a*), (*b*), words substituted and final sentence inserted, and in para (4), words revoked, by the Value Added Tax, etc (Correction of Errors, etc) Regulations, SI 2008/1482 reg 3 with effect in relation to the overdeclarations or underdeclarations in reg 13(3) which registrable persons first discover in their accounting periods that begin on 1 July 2008 or later. Paras (3), (4) previously read as follows—

"(3) Where, in relation to any overdeclarations or underdeclarations that are discovered by the registrable person in an accounting period—

(*a*) the total of the overdeclarations discovered does not exceed £2,000, he may enter that total in the box opposite the legend "Overdeclarations from previous periods" in the return for that accounting period;

(*b*) the total of the underdeclarations discovered does not exceed £2,000, he may enter that total in the box opposite the legend "Underdeclarations from previous periods" in the return for that accounting period;

and, where he does so, he shall calculate the tax payable by him or the payment to which he is entitled accordingly.

(4) Where the return for the accounting period in which the overdeclaration or underdeclaration was discovered is made by Lloyd's in accordance with regulation 12(2), paragraph (3) above shall apply as if the references to the totals of the overdeclarations or underdeclarations not exceeding £2,000 were references to each such total for each syndicate in respect of which the return is made not exceeding £2,000.".

[2] In para (3), words substituted for words "less than £10,000" by the Amusement Machine Licence Duty, etc (Amendments) Regulations, SI 2008/2693 reg 4(1)(*a*) with effect for a discovery first made on 1 November 2008 or later.

Claims for overpaid tax

14 Except where the amount to which the claim relates has been entered in a return in accordance with regulation 13 or is included in an amount so entered, any claim under paragraph 8 of Schedule 7 to the Act shall be made in writing to the Commissioners and shall, by reference to such documentary evidence as is in the possession of the claimant, state the amount of the claim and the method by which that amount was calculated.

Commentary—*De Voil Indirect Tax Service* **V18.185**.

Payment of tax

15 Save as the Commissioners may otherwise allow or direct, any person required to make a return shall pay to the Controller, Central Collection Unit (IPT) such amount of tax as is payable by him in respect of the accounting period to which the return relates no later than the last day on which he was required to make the return.

Commentary—*De Voil Indirect Tax Service* **V18.146**.

Records

16— (1) Every registrable person shall, for the purpose of accounting for tax, keep and preserve the following—

(*a*) his business and accounting records;

(*b*) policy documents, cover notes, endorsements and similar documents, and copies of such documents that are issued by him;

(*c*) copies of all invoices, renewal notices and similar documents issued by him;

IPT

(*d*) all credit or debit notes or other documents received by him which evidence an increase or decrease in the amount of any premium [or fee][1], and copies of such documents that are issued by him;

(*e*) such other records as the Commissioners may specify in a notice published by them and not withdrawn by them.

(2) Every registrable person shall keep and preserve the records specified in paragraph (1) above for a period of six years.

(3) The reference in paragraph (1)(*d*) above to any premium shall be construed for the purposes of that paragraph as it would be construed for the purposes of Part V of these Regulations.

Commentary—*De Voil Indirect Tax Service* **V18.171**.

Amendments—[1] Words in para (1)(*d*) inserted by the Insurance Premium Tax (Amendment) Regulations, SI 1997/1157 with effect from 1 May 1997.

PART IV
CLAIMS IN RESPECT OF CREDIT

Scope

[**17**— (1) This Part applies where—

(*a*) an insurer has paid tax and all or part of the premium on which the tax was charged is repaid; or

(*b*) a taxable intermediary has paid tax and all or part of the fee on which the tax was charged is repaid.

(2) Where—

(*a*) an insurer receives a premium in an accounting period and repays that premium or part of it in that accounting period; or

(*b*) a taxable intermediary receives a fee in an accounting period and repays that fee or part of it in that accounting period,

this Part shall apply as if the tax on the premium or fee (as the case may be) had already been paid by him.][1]

(3) This Part applies subject to regulation 7.

Commentary—*De Voil Indirect Tax Service* **V18.121**.

Amendments—[1] Paras (1), (2) substituted by the Insurance Premium Tax (Amendment) Regulations, SI 1997/1157 with effect from 1 May 1997.

Claims in returns

18— (1) Where this Part applies, the insurer [or, as the case may be, taxable intermediary][1] shall be entitled to credit of an amount which represents the difference between the amount of tax paid by him and the amount of tax he would have been liable to pay had the premium [or fee][1] received by him been reduced or extinguished, as the case may be, by the amount of the repayment.

(2) Subject to paragraph (3) below, an insurer [or taxable intermediary][1] who is entitled to credit under this Part may claim it by deducting its amount from any tax due from him for the accounting period in which the premium [or fee][1] was repaid or any subsequent accounting period and, where he does so, he shall make his return for that accounting period accordingly.

(3) Where the Commissioners have given a special or general direction under section 55(5) of the Act prescribing rules according to which any credit may or shall be held over to an accounting period subsequent to that in which the [premium or fee, or part of such premium or fee][1] was repaid, that credit, subject to any subsequent such direction varying or withdrawing the rules, may only be claimed in accordance with those rules.

Commentary—*De Voil Indirect Tax Service* **V18.121**.

Amendments—[1] Words in paras (1), (2) inserted and words in para (3) substituted by the Insurance Premium Tax (Amendment) Regulations, SI 1997/1157 with effect from 1 May 1997.

Payments in respect of credit

19— (1) Subject to paragraph (5) below, where the total credit claimed by the insurer [or taxable intermediary][1] in accordance with this Part exceeds the total of the tax due from him for the accounting period, the Commissioners shall pay to him an amount equal to the excess.

(2) Where the Commissioners have cancelled the registration of an insurer [or taxable intermediary][1] in accordance with section 53(5) [or 53AA(c)][1] of the Act, and he is not a registrable person, he shall make any claim in respect of credit to which this Part applies by making an application in writing.

(3) An insurer [or taxable intermediary][1] making an application under paragraph (2) above shall furnish to the Commissioners full particulars in relation to the credit claimed, including (but not restricted to)—

(*a*) the return in which the relevant tax was accounted for;

(*b*) the date and manner of payment of that tax;

(*c*) the date of the repayment of the [premium or fee, or part of such premium or fee][1]; and (*d*) the amounts of both the tax which was paid and the repayment.

(4) Subject to paragraph (5) below, where the Commissioners are satisfied that the insurer [or taxable intermediary as the case may be][1] is entitled to credit as claimed by him, and that he has not previously had the benefit of that credit, they shall pay to him an amount equal to the credit.

(5) The Commissioners shall not be liable to make any payment under this regulation unless and until the insurer [or taxable intermediary][1] has made all the returns which he was required to make.

Commentary—*De Voil Indirect Tax Service* **V18.121**.

Amendments—[1] Words in paras (1)–(5) inserted and words in para (3)(*c*) substituted by the Insurance Premium Tax (Amendment) Regulations, SI 1997/1157 with effect from 1 May 1997.

[PART IVA
REIMBURSEMENT ARRANGEMENTS][1]

Commentary—*De Voil Indirect Tax Service* **V18.185**.

Amendments—[1] Part IVA (regs 19A–19H) inserted by the Insurance Premium Tax (Amendment) Regulations, SI 1998/60 with effect from 11 February 1998.

[Interpretation of Part IVA

19A In this Part—

"claim" means a claim made (irrespective of when it was made) under paragraph 8 of Schedule 7 to the Act for repayment of an amount paid to the Commissioners by way of tax which was not tax due to them; and "claimed" and "claimant" shall be construed accordingly;

"reimbursement arrangements" means any arrangements (whether made before, on or after 30th January 1998) for the purposes of a claim which—

(*a*) are made by a claimant for the purpose of securing that he is not unjustly enriched by the repayment of any amount in pursuance of the claim; and

(*b*) provide for the reimbursement of persons (consumers) who have, for practical purposes, borne the whole or any part of the cost of the original payment of that amount to the Commissioners;

"relevant amount" means that part (which may be the whole) of the amount of a claim which the claimant has reimbursed or intends to reimburse to consumers.][1]

Amendments—[1] Part IVA (regs 19A–19H) inserted by the Insurance Premium Tax (Amendment) Regulations, SI 1998/60 with effect from 11 February 1998.

[Reimbursement arrangements—general

19B Without prejudice to regulation 19H below, for the purposes of paragraph 8(3) of Schedule 7 to the Act (defence by the Commissioners that repayment by them of an amount claimed would unjustly enrich the claimant) reimbursement arrangements made by a claimant shall be disregarded except where they—

(*a*) include the provisions described in regulation 19C below; and

(*b*) are supported by the undertakings described in regulation 19G below.][1]

Amendments—[1] Part IVA (regs 19A–19H) inserted by the Insurance Premium Tax (Amendment) Regulations, SI 1998/60 with effect from 11 February 1998.

[Reimbursement arrangements—provisions to be included

19C The provisions referred to in regulation 19B(a) above are that—

(*a*) reimbursement for which the arrangements provide will be completed by no later than 90 days after the repayment to which it relates;

(*b*) no deduction will be made from the relevant amount by way of fee or charge (howsoever expressed or effected);

(*c*) reimbursement will be made only in cash or by cheque;

(*d*) any part of the relevant amount that is not reimbursed by the time mentioned in paragraph (*a*) above will be repaid by the claimant to the Commissioners;

(*e*) any interest paid by the Commissioners on any relevant amount repaid by them will also be treated by the claimant in the same way as the relevant amount falls to be treated under paragraphs (*a*) and (*b*) above; and

(*f*) the records described in regulation 19E below will be kept by the claimant and produced by him to the Commissioners, or to an officer of theirs in accordance with regulation 19F below.][1]

Amendments—[1] Part IVA (regs 19A–19H) inserted by the Insurance Premium Tax (Amendment) Regulations, SI 1998/60 with effect from 11 February 1998.

[Repayments to the Commissioners

19D The claimant shall, without prior demand, make any repayment to the Commissioners that he is required to make by virtue of regulation 19C(*d*) and (*e*) above within 14 days of the expiration of the period of 90 days referred to in regulation 19C(*a*) above.][1]

IPT

Amendments—[1] Part IVA (regs 19A–19H) inserted by the Insurance Premium Tax (Amendment) Regulations, SI 1998/60 with effect from 11 February 1998.

[Records

19E The claimant shall keep records of the following matters—

(*a*) the names and addresses of those consumers whom he has reimbursed or whom he intends to reimburse;

(*b*) the total amount reimbursed to each such consumer;

(*c*) the amount of interest included in each total amount reimbursed to each consumer;

(*d*) the date that each reimbursement is made.][1]

Amendments—[1] Part IVA (regs 19A–19H) inserted by the Insurance Premium Tax (Amendment) Regulations, SI 1998/60 with effect from 11 February 1998.

[Production of records

19F— (1) Where a claimant is given notice in accordance with paragraph (2) below, he shall, in accordance with such notice produce to the Commissioners, or to an officer of theirs, the records that he is required to keep pursuant to regulation 19E above.

(2) A notice given for the purposes of paragraph (1) above shall—

(*a*) be in writing;

(*b*) state the place and time at which, and the date on which the records are to be produced; and

(*c*) be signed and dated by the Commissioners, or by an officer of theirs,

and may be given before or after, or both before and after the Commissioners have paid the relevant amount to the claimant.][1]

Amendments—[1] Part IVA (regs 19A–19H) inserted by the Insurance Premium Tax (Amendment) Regulations, SI 1998/60 with effect from 11 February 1998.

[Undertakings

19G— (1) Without prejudice to regulation 19H(*b*) below, the undertakings referred to in regulation 19B(*b*) above shall be given to the Commissioners by the claimant no later than the time at which he makes the claim for which the reimbursement arrangements have been made.

(2) The undertakings shall be in writing, shall be signed and dated by the claimant, and shall be to the effect that—

(*a*) at the date of the undertakings he is able to identify the names and addresses of those consumers whom he has reimbursed or whom he intends to reimburse;

(*b*) he will apply the whole of the relevant amount repaid to him, without any deduction by way of fee or charge or otherwise, to the reimbursement in cash or by cheque, of such consumers by no later than 90 days after his receipt of that amount (except insofar as he has already so reimbursed them);

(*c*) he will apply any interest paid to him on the relevant amount repaid to him wholly to the reimbursement of such consumers by no later than 90 days after his receipt of that interest;

(*d*) he will repay to the Commissioners without demand the whole or such part of the relevant amount repaid to him or of any interest paid to him as he fails to apply in accordance with the undertakings mentioned in sub-paragraphs (*b*) and (*c*) above;

(*e*) he will keep the records described in regulation 19E above; and

(*f*) he will comply with any notice given to him in accordance with regulation 19F above concerning the production of such records.][1]

Amendments—[1] Part IVA inserted (regs 19A–19H) by the Insurance Premium Tax (Amendment) Regulations, SI 1998/60 with effect from 11 February 1998.

[Reimbursement arrangements made before 11th February 1998

19H Reimbursement arrangements made by a claimant before 11th February 1998 shall not be disregarded for the purposes of paragraph 8(3) of Schedule 7 to the Act if, not later than 11th March 1998—

(*a*) he includes in those arrangements (if they are not already included) the provisions described in regulation 19C above; and

(*b*) gives the undertakings described in regulation 19G above.][1]

Amendments—[1] Part IVA inserted (regs 19A–19H) by the Insurance Premium Tax (Amendment) Regulations, SI 1998/60 with effect from 11 February 1998.

PART V
SPECIAL ACCOUNTING SCHEME

Interpretation

20— (1) In this Part—

"date of receipt", in relation to any premium, means the date on which apart from the operation of the scheme the premium is received or taken to be received by the provisions of the Act;

"initial period" means the first of the accounting periods which begin on or after the date specified in a notification made under regulation 21(1);

"premium written date", in relation to any premium, means the date as at which the insurer makes an entry in his accounts showing the premium as due to him.

(2) Any reference in this Part to the accounts of any person shall be construed as a reference to—

(*a*) the books, accounts or other similar records which he maintains in whatever form for the purpose of enabling him to show the premiums receivable by him in the revenue account he is required to prepare [in accordance with rules made under Part 10 of the Financial Services and Markets Act 2000][1]; and "premiums receivable" has the same meaning as [in those rules][1]; or

(*b*) where he is not required to prepare the revenue account referred to in sub-paragraph (*a*) above, any books, accounts or other records which would enable him to prepare one.

(3) Any reference in this Part to a premium shall be construed as including a reference to anything that, although not actually received by or on behalf of an insurer, would be a premium if it were so received.

(4) In deciding whether and (if it does) how the scheme applies to an accounting period of an insurer to whom the scheme has previously applied as regards one or more accounting periods ending before the beginning of the initial period specified in a notification he has made under regulation 21(1), the fact of such previous application of the scheme shall be ignored.

Commentary—*De Voil Indirect Tax Service* **V18.127**.

Amendments—[1] Words in para (2)(*a*) substituted by the Financial Services and Markets Act 2000 (Consequential Amendments and Repeals) Order, SI 2001/3649 art 462 with effect from 1 December 2001.

Notification by insurer that scheme to apply

21— (1) An insurer who is a registrable person and—

(*a*) is required to prepare the revenue account referred to in regulation 20(2)(*a*); or

(*b*) not being required to prepare such a revenue account, keeps accounts as described in regulation 20(2)(*b*),

may notify the Commissioners in writing that the scheme should apply to him as regards accounting periods beginning on or after a date specified in the notification, being a date falling after the date the notification is made.

(2) An insurer who has made a notification under paragraph (1) above may notify the Commissioners in writing that he wishes to withdraw the notification and, provided he makes the notification referred to in this paragraph no later than the last day by which he is required to make the return for the initial period and before he has made that return, the scheme shall not apply to him as regards any accounting period.

(3) The fact that an insurer has on a previous occasion withdrawn or been expelled from the scheme under regulation 26 or 27 or withdrawn a notification under paragraph (2) above shall not prevent him making a notification under paragraph (1) above.

Commentary—*De Voil Indirect Tax Service* **V18.127**.

Relevant accounting periods

22 Subject to regulations 21(2), 26 and 27, the scheme shall apply as regards all the accounting periods of an insurer who has made a notification under regulation 21(1) with effect from the initial period.

Premiums treated as received on premium written date

23— (1) Subject to paragraph (8) below, any premium in relation to which—

(*a*) an insurer has made an entry in his accounts showing the premium as due to him;

(*b*) the premium written date falls within a relevant accounting period; and

(*c*) the date of receipt does not fall within an accounting period which is earlier than the initial period and which is not a relevant accounting period,

shall be treated for the purposes of the Act as received by the insurer on the premium written date; and the insurer shall account for tax due in respect of the relevant accounting period concerned accordingly.

(2) Paragraph (1) above shall apply even if the premium or any part of it is never actually received by the insurer; and, where it is never actually received because the contract under which it is or would have been received is terminated or is not entered into, the premium shall nonetheless be taken for the purposes of the Act to have been received under the contract (including, where appropriate, a taxable insurance contract) under which the insurer treated it as due.

(3) Where in relation to any premium to which paragraph (1) above applies the premium written date is a date other than the date of receipt, the premium shall be treated for the purposes of the Act as not having been received by the insurer on the date of receipt; but this is subject to paragraph (4) below.

IPT

(4) Paragraph (3) above shall not apply to any excess which falls to be treated as a separate premium in accordance with regulation 24(2).

(5) An insurer to whom the scheme applies as regards an accounting period may assume that the scheme will apply as regards all subsequent accounting periods and account for tax due in respect of that period accordingly.

(6) Subject to paragraph (7) below, where in relation to a premium—

(*a*) the premium written date falls before 1st October 1994;

(*b*) the premium was actually received by the insurer on or after 1st October 1994; and

(*c*) the contract under which the premium was received is not a contract to which, if the premium had actually been received on the premium written date, section 67(3) of the Act would have applied,

the premium shall be treated for the purposes of the Act as received before 1st October 1994 and the insurer shall accordingly not account for any tax on that premium.

(7) Paragraph (6) above shall not apply to any premium where—

(*a*) the contract under which the premium was received relates to a risk the period of cover for which begins on or after 1st October 1994; and

(*b*) it is not the normal practice as regards the class of contract to which that contract belongs for an insurer to make an entry in his accounts showing the premium as due as at a date before the period of cover begins.

(8) Where the initial period begins on 1st October 1994, nothing in this regulation shall be taken as requiring a premium—

(*a*) which was actually received by the insurer before 1st October 1994;

(*b*) in respect of which the premium written date falls within a relevant accounting period;

(*c*) which is not taken by virtue of section 67 of the Act to be received on 1st October 1994; and

(*d*) which was received under a contract which relates to a risk the period of cover for which begins before 1st October 1994,

to be treated as received on a date other than the date of receipt.

(9) Where in relation to any premium—

(*a*) an insurer has made an entry in his accounts showing the premium as due to him;

(*b*) the entry was made on a date falling within a relevant accounting period; and

(*c*) the premium written date would, apart from this paragraph, fall in a relevant accounting period which is earlier than the accounting period referred to in paragraph (*b*) above,

the insurer shall be treated for the purposes of this regulation as if he had made the entry showing the premium as due to him as at the date on which the entry was made and that date (and no other date) shall be the premium written date accordingly.

Commentary—*De Voil Indirect Tax Service* **V18.127**.

Amount of premium

24— (1) Subject to any direction made under section 66 of the Act, where in relation to any premium to which regulation 23(1) applies the amount which is entered in the accounts as due (the initial amount) is not the amount which is or would be found apart from the operation of the scheme to be the amount of the premium in accordance with the provisions of the Act the amount of the premium shall be taken to be the initial amount.

(2) Where paragraph (1) above applies and the amount of the premium which is received exceeds the initial amount, the excess shall be treated as a separate premium and shall be treated as received on a date determined in accordance with paragraphs (3) and (4) below.

(3) Where an amount of premium is treated as a separate premium in accordance with paragraph (2) above and—

(*a*) the initial amount is not less than the amount which has been agreed with the insured by the insurer or his agent as the amount which, as at the date the entry is made, is due under the contract; and

(*b*) the insurer makes an entry in his accounts showing the excess as due,

it shall be treated as received on the date he makes that entry in his accounts.

(4) In any case where an amount of premium is treated as a separate premium in accordance with paragraph (2) above and paragraph (3) above does not apply, the excess shall be treated as received on the date as at which the initial amount is entered in the accounts as due.

(5) An insurer who intends to enter in his accounts as due any excess over the initial amount of any premium which, if he were to make such an entry, would be treated as received on a date determined in accordance with paragraph (3) above may assume that it will be so treated until such time as he ceases to have that intention.

(6) Where in relation to an amount of premium which is treated as a separate premium in accordance with paragraph (2) above the date of receipt is a date other than the date determined in accordance with paragraphs (3) and (4) above, it shall be treated as not having been received by the insurer on the date of receipt.

Commentary—*De Voil Indirect Tax Service* **V18.127**.

Credit

25— (1) Subject to paragraph (2) below, where tax has been paid—

(*a*) in respect of a premium to which regulation 24(1) applies and the initial amount exceeds the amount which is or would be found apart from the operation of the scheme to be the amount of the premium in accordance with the provisions of the Act; or

(*b*) in respect of a premium or part of a premium which has not been received,

then, if it is shown to the satisfaction of the Commissioners that that excess, premium or part, as the case may be, will never actually be received, the amount of that excess, premium or part shall be treated as an amount of premium which the insurer has repaid on the date upon which the Commissioners are so satisfied and he shall be entitled to credit for the amount concerned in accordance with Part IV of these Regulations.

(2) It shall be a condition of any claim being made by an insurer in reliance upon paragraph (1) above that, if the excess, premium or part (as the case may be) or any part thereof is in fact received by the insurer, he shall pay to the Commissioners an amount equal to the tax chargeable on the amount received; and any amount which the insurer is liable to pay under this paragraph shall be treated as tax due for the accounting period in which the amount of excess or premium was received.

Commentary—*De Voil Indirect Tax Service* **V18.127**.
Concession IPT3—Special accounting scheme: introductory provisions.

Withdrawal from the scheme

26— (1) An insurer may notify the Commissioners in writing that the scheme should not apply to him as regards accounting periods beginning on or after a date specified in the notification (being a date falling after the date the notification is made) and the scheme shall cease to apply to him accordingly.

(2) The scheme shall nonetheless continue to apply to an insurer who has made a notification under paragraph (1) above unless and until—

(*a*) he has made all the returns which he was required to make;

(*b*) he has paid all the tax which was payable in respect of the accounting periods for which he was required to make those returns; and

(*c*) the scheme has applied as regards such number of relevant accounting periods as is required in order for the scheme to have applied to him for a period of not less than twelve consecutive months beginning with the first day of the initial period;

and, when he has complied with sub-paragraphs (*a*) to (*c*) above and with any requirement to make returns or pay tax arising since the date the notification was made, the scheme shall cease to apply with effect from the first of his accounting periods which begin on or after the date of such compliance.

Commentary—*De Voil Indirect Tax Service* **V18.127**.

Expulsion from the scheme

27— (1) In any case where the Commissioners consider it necessary for the protection of the revenue, including (but not restricted to) a case where the revenue is prejudiced by reason of the premium written date in relation to premiums falling in accounting periods later than those in which falls the date of receipt, they may give notice to an insurer who has made the notification under regulation 21(1) that the scheme is not to apply to him; and the scheme shall accordingly not apply or cease to apply, as the case may be.

(2) Where a notice is given under paragraph (1) above before the last day of the initial period, the scheme shall not apply to any of the accounting periods of the insurer.

(3) Where a notice is given under paragraph (1) above on or after the last day of the initial period, the notice shall specify the accounting period of the insurer with effect from which the scheme is not to apply to him, being an accounting period the last day of which falls after the date the notice is given.

Commentary—*De Voil Indirect Tax Service* **V18.127**.

Tax to be accounted for on cessation

28— (1) Where the scheme has ceased to apply to an insurer by virtue of regulation 26 or 27, he shall account for and pay any tax chargeable on premiums in relation to which the date of receipt falls within a relevant accounting period and for which he has not accounted and which he has not paid in reliance upon the assumption referred to in regulation 23(5) as if the premiums were received in the accounting period with effect from which the scheme has ceased to apply to him.

(2) Where the Commissioners have cancelled the registration of an insurer and the last of his accounting periods is a relevant accounting period, paragraph (1) above shall apply as if—

(*a*) the scheme had ceased to apply to him by virtue of regulation 26 or 27; and

(*b*) the reference to the accounting period with effect from which the scheme has ceased to apply to him were a reference to the last of his accounting periods.

Commentary—*De Voil Indirect Tax Service* **V18.127**.

PART VI
TAX REPRESENTATIVES

Notification in certain cases

29— *(1) Where the Commissioners approve a person as an insurer's [or taxable intermediary's]*[1] *tax representative in a case where action has been taken as mentioned in section 57(4) of the Act or a request has been made as mentioned in section 57(10) of the Act, as the case may be, they shall be taken to have given such approval on the date they serve on the insurer [or taxable intermediary]*[1] *a notice in writing confirming their approval or on such later date as may be specified in the notice.*

(2) Where the Commissioners inform an insurer [or taxable intermediary][1] *that they have received a notification such as is referred to in section 57(8) of the Act, they shall be taken to have so informed him on the date they serve on him a notice in writing to that effect.*

(3) Where the Commissioners make a direction such as is described in section 57(11) of the Act, they shall be taken to have made the direction—

(a) on the date they serve on both the insurer [or, as the case may be, taxable intermediary][1] *and the person who is to be his tax representative a notice in writing confirming that that person shall be his tax representative;*

(b) where such notices are served on different dates, the later of them; or

(c) where such notices specify a date falling after the date on which the later of them is served, the date specified in the notices.[2]

Commentary—*De Voil Indirect Tax Service* **V18.127**.

Amendments—[1] Words in paras (1)–(3) inserted by the Insurance Premium Tax (Amendment) Regulations, SI 1997/1157 with effect from 1 May 1997.

[2] This regulation revoked by the Insurance Premium Tax (Amendment) Regulations, SI 2008/1945 regs 2, 3 with effect from 1 September 2008.

Registration

30— *(1) The Commissioners shall register alongside the name of an insurer [or taxable intermediary]*[1] *the name of any tax representative of his for the time being.*

(2) Where the Commissioners withdraw their approval of a tax representative who has been registered by them under paragraph (1) above, they shall cancel that registration.[2]

Amendments—[1] Words inserted by the Insurance Premium Tax (Amendment) Regulations, SI 1997/1157 with effect from 1 May 1997.

[2] This regulation revoked by the Insurance Premium Tax (Amendment) Regulations, SI 2008/1945 regs 2, 3 with effect from 1 September 2008.

Liability to notify

31 *A tax representative shall not—*

(a) be jointly and severally liable with the insurer [or taxable intermediary][1]*; or*

(b) be required to secure the insurer's [or taxable intermediary's][1] *compliance with or the discharge of his obligation,*

in relation to any requirement that the insurer [or taxable intermediary][1] *make a notification such as is referred to in regulation 4 or 6.*[2]

Amendments—[1] Words inserted by the Insurance Premium Tax (Amendment) Regulations, SI 1997/1157 with effect from 1 May 1997.

[2] This regulation revoked by the Insurance Premium Tax (Amendment) Regulations, SI 2008/1945 regs 2, 3 with effect from 1 September 2008.

PART VII
LIABILITY OF INSURED PERSONS

Interpretation

32 In this Part—

"contract" means a taxable insurance contract;

"liability notice" means a notice served under regulation 34;

"material date" has the same meaning as in section 65(4) of the Act;

"tax debt" means a liability to pay an amount which is tax or is deemed to be or recoverable as if it were tax which, at the time of any payment, has not been discharged.

Scope

[**33** This Part applies where an insurer who is a registrable person—

(*a*) does not have any business establishment or other fixed establishment in the United Kingdom, and

(*b*) is established in a country or territory in respect of which it appears to the Commissioners that the condition in section 65(1A) of the Act is met.][1]

Amendments—[1] This regulation substituted by the Insurance Premium Tax (Amendment) Regulations, SI 2008/1945 regs 2, 4 with effect from 1 September 2008. This regulation previously read as follows—

"**33** This Part applies where—

(*a*) an insurer who is a registrable person does not have any business establishment or other fixed establishment in the United Kingdom, and

(*b*) no person is that insurer's tax representative by virtue of section 57 of the Act.".

Liability notices

34 Where this Part applies, the Commissioners may serve a notice on the person who is insured under a contract or, where there are two or more such persons, one or more of them.

Power to assess tax due

35— (1) This regulation applies where—

(*a*) the Commissioners have served a liability notice or notices; and

(*b*) the insurer—

(i) has failed to make any return he was required to make or any such return appears to the Commissioners to be incomplete or incorrect; or

(ii) has failed to pay any tax or amount deemed to be tax, including an amount which he was liable to pay by virtue of this Part.

(2) Where this regulation applies—

(*a*) the Commissioners may assess to the best of their judgment the amount of any tax due in respect of premiums received by the insurer under the contract after the material date and before the date of the assessment; and

(*b*) the amount so assessed shall be deemed to be the amount of tax due in respect of that contract for the period by reference to which the assessment is made.

Commentary—*De Voil Indirect Tax Service* **V18.128**.

Persons liable for tax assessed

36— (1) Where the Commissioners make an assessment under regulation 35 and notify it to the insured person, or each of the insured persons, on whom a liability notice in respect of the contract has been served—

(*a*) the insurer; and

(*b*) the insured persons mentioned in this regulation,

shall be jointly and severally liable to pay the amount of tax assessed, to the extent that the assessment has not subsequently been reduced or withdrawn, and that tax shall be recoverable accordingly.

(2) An insured person who has been notified of an assessment made under regulation 35 shall be liable in accordance with this regulation to pay the tax so assessed notwithstanding that he has already paid an amount representing that tax or any part of it as part of a premium.

Commentary—*De Voil Indirect Tax Service* **V18.128**.

Adjustment of assessments

37— (1) Where—

(*a*) an amount of tax has been assessed under regulation 35; and

(*b*) the amount of that tax, or any part of it, has also been assessed under section 56 of the Act and notified to the insurer,

the assessment which has been made under regulation 35 shall be treated as reduced to the extent that the amount referred to in sub-paragraph (*b*) above has been included in the amount thereof.

(2) Where an assessment such as is referred to in paragraph (1)(*a*) or (*b*) above is subsequently withdrawn, that paragraph shall not apply; and where the assessment is reduced, it shall apply as if any reference to the amount of tax which has been assessed were a reference to the reduced amount.

Commentary—*De Voil Indirect Tax Service* **V18.128**.

Time for payment

38— Any insured person who is liable to pay an amount of tax which has been assessed under regulation 35 shall do so no later than thirty days after the date on which it was notified to him.

Commentary—*De Voil Indirect Tax Service* **V18.128**.

Interest on reimbursements

39— (1) Where an insurer is liable by virtue of section 65(9) of the Act to pay to an insured person an amount equal to the amount which has been recovered from him, then, if and to the extent that the insurer would not be liable to do so apart from this regulation, he shall pay interest to him.

(2) The interest payable under paragraph (1) above shall be paid at the rate of 8 per cent per annum for the period beginning with the date on which the amount was recovered from the insured person and ending with the date the insurer paid to him an amount equal to that amount.

Commentary—*De Voil Indirect Tax Service* **V18.128**.

Allocation of payments

40— (1) This regulation applies where an insurer pays an amount of tax to the Commissioners and—

(*a*) at the time of the payment there exists a tax debt of his by virtue of his being liable to pay tax which has been assessed under regulation 35;

(*b*) at the time of the payment there exists a tax debt of his which—

(i) is not within sub-paragraph (*a*) above; and

(ii) relates to an accounting period which corresponds to any extent with the period by reference to which the assessment referred to in sub-paragraph (*a*) above was made; and

(*c*) the amount of the payment is not sufficient to satisfy all his tax debts in full.

(2) Where this regulation applies and the payment would not otherwise be applied as described in this paragraph, the payment shall be applied to reduce or extinguish the tax debt within paragraph (1)(*a*) above before it is applied to any other tax debt.

(3) Where—

(*a*) this regulation applies;

(*b*) there are two or more tax debts within paragraph (1)(*a*) above; and

(*c*) the payment is not sufficient to satisfy those tax debts in full,

there shall be applied to each such tax debt such proportion of the payment as bears the same relationship to the whole of the payment as does the tax debt to the total of those tax debts.

Commentary—*De Voil Indirect Tax Service* **V18.128**.

Records

41— (1) Where—

(*a*) an insured person has been served with a liability notice;

(*b*) he is carrying on a business; and

(*c*) the contract provides cover for any matter associated with that business,

the insured person shall keep and preserve the records specified in paragraph (2) below.

(2) The records which an insured person shall keep and preserve are such of the following as relate to the contract—

(*a*) his business and accounting records;

(*b*) policy documents, cover notes, endorsements and similar documents;

(*c*) all invoices, renewal notices and similar documents issued to him;

(*d*) all credit or debit notes or other documents received by him which evidence an increase or decrease in the premium, and copies of such documents that are issued by him.

(3) Every insured person who is required to keep and preserve records by paragraph (1) above shall do so for a period of six years.

(4) The reference in paragraph (2)(*d*) above to any premium shall be construed for the purposes of that paragraph as it would be construed for the purposes of Part V of these Regulations.

Commentary—*De Voil Indirect Tax Service* **V18.128**.

PART VIII
DISTRESS AND DILIGENCE

[A42 In this Part—

"Job Band" followed by a number between "1" and "12" means the band for the purposes of pay and grading in which the job an officer performs is ranked in the system applicable to Customs and Excise.]

Amendments—Inserted by Insurance Premium Tax (Amendment) Regulations, SI 1996/2099, Reg 3 with effect from 2 September 1996.

42 …

Amendments—This regulation revoked by the Distress for Customs and Excise Duties and Other Indirect Taxes Regulations, SI 1997/1431 with effect from 1 July 1997. See SI 1997/1431 for the replacement provisions.

Diligence

[43 In Scotland, the following provisions have effect:

(*a*) where the Commissioners are empowered to apply to the sheriff for a warrant to authorise a sheriff officer to recover any amount of tax or sum recoverable as if it were tax remaining due and unpaid, any application, and any certificate required to accompany that application, may be made on their behalf by a Collector or an officer of rank not below that of [Job Band 7][2];

(*b*) where, during the course of [an attachment][3] the Commissioners are entitled as a creditor to do any act, then any such act, with the exception of the exercise of the power contained in [section 30(4) of the Debt Arrangement and Attachment (Scotland) Act (asp 17)][3], may be done on their behalf by a Collector or an officer of rank not below that of [Job Band 7][2].][1]

Amendments—[1] This regulation substituted by the Insurance Premium Tax (Amendment) Regulations, SI 1995/1587 with effect from 17 July 1995.

[2] Words substituted by Insurance Premium Tax (Amendments) Regulations, SI 1996/2099, Reg 4 with effect from 2 September 1996.

[3] Words in para (*b*) substituted by the Debt Arrangement and Attachment (Scotland) Act 2002 s 61, Sch 3 Pt 2 para 34 with effect from 30 December 2002.

Note—In Schedule, Forms 1, 4, 5 and 6 substituted by Insurance Premium Tax (Amendment) Regulations, SI 1997/1157, reg 15, Sch with effect from 1 May 1997. Form 1 subsequently substituted by the Insurance Premium Tax (Amendment) Regulations, SI 2006/2700 reg 2, Schedule, with effect from 1 December 2006.

SCHEDULE

Regulation 4(1)

FORM 1

HM Revenue
& Customs

Insurance Premium Tax

Application for Registration

When you have filled in this form
and signed it, please send it to:

The Controller
Central Collection Unit (IPT)
HM Revenue & Customs
Alexander House
21 Victoria Avenue
Southend-on-Sea X
SS99 1AA

For official use
Date of receipt

Insurance Premium Tax

Application for Registration

Before you start, please read the Registration sections of the notice 'Insurance Premium Tax'. Write clearly in ink and use capital letters.

1 Please give your full name and your business address.

Name

Business address

Postcode

Phone

Fax no

2 Please give your trading name if it is different from the name given at question 1.

Only complete question **3** if you do not have a business establishment in the United Kingdom (UK). Otherwise, go to question 4.

3 (a) Do you wish to appoint an agent to act on your behalf in the UK?

Please tick ☑

Yes ☐ Go to **3**(b).

No ☐ Go to **4.**

(b) If you wish to appoint an agent in the UK to act on your behalf, please complete this authority and provide the agent's details. This authority allows us to exchange and disclose information about you with your agent and to deal with them on matters within the responsibility of HM Revenue & Customs (HMRC) as specified on this form. We will hold this authority until you tell us that the details have changed.

I, *(print your name)*

of *(name of your business, company or partnership if appropriate)*

authorise HMRC to disclose information to
(agent's business name)

who is acting on my/our behalf. This authorisation is limited to IPT matters only.

Signature

Date

Give **your agent's** details here

Address

Postcode

Phone

Fax

Client reference

4 What is the legal status of your business?

If you are a partnership, please remember to complete form IPT 2 as well as this form.

Please tick ☑

Sole proprietor ☐

Partnership ☐

Limited Company ☐

Give details from your certificate of incorporation:

Certificate number

Date of certificate

Unincorporated Body ☐ (other than partnership)

Specify type of body

Lloyd's syndicate ☐

IPT

5 Do you wish to use this form to notify that you are going to use the special accounting scheme from the first of your accounting periods? (Use of the scheme is mandatory for a Lloyd's syndicate wishing to elect Lloyd's to act on its behalf.)

Please tick ☑
Yes ☐ No ☐

Only complete **6** if you are a Lloyd's syndicate. Otherwise go straight to 7.

6 (a) Please give your syndicate number.

[ ]

(b) Are you electing that Lloyd's may act for you from the first of your accounting periods?

Please tick ☑
Yes ☐ No ☐

(c) Are all your premiums processed through Lloyd's Policy Signing Office (LPSO)?

Please tick ☑
Yes ☐ Go to **6**(e).
No ☐ Go to **6**(d).

(d) What percentage (%) of your premium income is not processed through LPSO?

[ ] %

(e) Who will be responsible for submitting IPT returns?

Please tick ☑
Lloyd's ☐
Managing agent ☐

(f) Please give your managing agent's name and address.

Name
Address
Postcode
Phone Fax

(g) Are you involved in Mirror Syndicate activity?

Please tick ☑
Yes ☐ No ☐

(h) Are you reinsured to close?

Please tick ☑
Yes ☐ Give the number of the syndicate which has taken over your liability.
No ☐

7 Are you in run off?

Please tick ☑
Yes ☐ No ☐

8 Please tick the box that best describes your business.

Please tick ☑

UK Insurer	☐	Branch of non-UK Insurer	☐
Captive	☐	Representative Office	☐
Other	☐	Taxable Intermediary	☐

Please give details

[ ]

9 (a) Are you applying to register because a business has been transferred to you as a going concern?

Please tick ☑

Yes ☐ Give details below:

Date of transfer ☐ IPT registration no. of previous owner ☐

No ☐ Go to 10.

(b) Do you wish to keep the IPT number of the previous owner?

If you wish to keep the number, please remember to complete form IPT 68.

Please tick ☑

Yes ☐

No ☐

10 Please give the date you expect to receive your first taxable premium.

The term premium includes any fee, charged by an intermediary, which is subject to IPT.

11 What class(es) of insurance business do you intend to provide?

See Section 5 of the notice 'Insurance Premium Tax' which will help you to answer this question.

Please continue on a separate sheet of paper if necessary, and attach it to this form.

12 Please give the expected value of your taxable premium income for the 12 month period commencing from the date that you have given in question 10.

If you do not have completely accurate figures, please give an estimate instead.

£

13 Are you registered for VAT in the UK?

Please tick ☑

Yes ☐ Give your VAT registration no.

No ☐

14 Please indicate your preferred method of payment.

If you wish to pay by direct debit, please complete the accompanying mandate form. Mandate forms can be obtained from the Central Collection Unit.

Please tick ☑

Direct debit ☐ Credit transfer ☐

Cheque ☐ Postal order ☐

Cash ☐

15 Please complete and sign the declaration

Declaration

I,

(enter your full name in capital letters) declare that the information given on this form and contained in any accompanying document is true and complete.

Please tick ☑ Signature Date

Sole proprietor ☐ Partner ☐ Director ☐ Company Secretary ☐ Authorised Official ☐ Other ☐ Please give details below

For official use only

LVO code and reg no

Stagger ☐ Group reg ☐ Lloyd's return ☐

	Registration	Tax Rep	TOGC
Approved - Initials/date			
Refused - Initials/date			
Letter of approval issued			

IPT 1 Page 4

Amendments—Form 1 substituted by the Insurance Premium Tax (Amendment) Regulations, SI 2008/1945 regs 2, 5, Schedule, with effect from 1 September 2008.

Regulation 4(2)

FORM 2

These details form part of your application to register.

Please make sure that every partner completes and signs one of the sections below.

Please use CAPITAL LETTERS and write clearly in ink.

Full name of Partner:

Home address:

Postcode:

Home telephone:

Signature: Date:

Full name of Partner:

Home address:

Postcode:

Home telephone:

Signature: Date:

Full name of Partner:

Home address:

Postcode:

Home telephone:

Signature: Date:

CD 3679/1R/NB(05/94)

Full name of Partner:

Home address:

Postcode:

Home telephone:

Signature: Date:

Full name of Partner:

Home address:

Postcode:

Home telephone:

Signature: Date:

Full name of Partner:

Home address:

Postcode:

Home telephone:

Signature: Date:

CD 3679/2/NB(05/94)

Regulation 7(1)

FORM 3

Before you begin, please read the notes overleaf.
Remember to complete both parts of the form.

Part 1: If you are the new owner of a business, please read this form carefully and answer all the questions in Part 1.

1. Please give your full name:

2. I took over a business as a going concern on

3. I apply to use the previous owner's IPT registration number which is

4. If this application is allowed, I agree to the following conditions:
   - I will send in my first IPT return form to Customs and Excise, with all the tax owing for the period shown on the form;
   - I will send in any outstanding returns which are due from the previous owner;
   - I will pay any IPT still owing on premiums received by the previous owner before the business was transferred;
   - any IPT return made by the previous owner for a period after the transfer date will be treated as made by me; and
   - I will have no right to claim any money paid by Customs to the previous owner, before the IPT registration number is transferred.

Signature(s)

Please tick one box

- ☐ Sole Proprietor
- ☐ Partner (Remember, all partners must sign)
- ☐ Director
- ☐ Company Secretary
- ☐ Authorised Official
- ☐ Other - please give details below

Part 2: If you are the previous owner of a business, please read this form carefully and answer all the questions in Part 2.

1. Please give your full name, **and** your trading name if you have one:

2. I transferred my business / changed my legal status on

   The new owner is

3. From the above date, I wish to cancel my IPT registration because I will stop receiving taxable insurance premiums from that date. I agree to transfer my number to the new owner. The IPT registration number is

4. If this application is allowed, I agree to the following conditions:
   - the new owner will be entitled to any money or credit which Customs & Excise would normally have paid to me if the number had not been transferred; and
   - I will have no right to claim any money paid by Customs to the new owner.

5. Please give an address where we can contact you after the business has been taken over by the new owner.

Postcode Telephone number

Signature(s)

Please tick one box

☐ Sole Proprietor ☐ Partner (Remember, all partners must sign)

☐ Director ☐ Company Secretary

☐ Authorised Official ☐ Other - please give details below

IPT 68 Page 2 (01/01)

Regulation 12(1)

FORM 4

HM Revenue & Customs

Insurance Premium Tax Return

For the Period

to

For Official Use

IPT Registration Number Period

You could be liable to a financial penalty if your completed return and all IPT payable are not received by the due date.

Due Date:

For official use D O R only

Fold here

Before you fill in this form please read the notes on the back.

Fill in all boxes clearly in ink, and write 'none' where necessary. Don't put a dash or leave any box blank. If there are no pence write '**00**' in the pence column. **Do not** enter more than one amount in any box.

For Official Use

		£	p
1	Standard rate IPT due for this period		
2	Higher rate IPT due for this period		
3	Underdeclarations of standard rate IPT from previous periods		
4	Underdeclarations of higher rate IPT from previous periods		
5	Total (in the sum of boxes 1 to 4)		
6	Underdeclarations of standard rate IPT from previous periods		
7	Underdeclarations of higher rate IPT from previous periods		
8	Total overdeclarations from previous periods		
9	Net tax payable or repayable (the difference between box 5 and box 8)		
10	Net value of taxable premiums (excluding tax)		

Special accounting scheme - please tick this box if you are using the scheme

if you are enclosing a payment please tick this box.

DECLARATION: You, or someone on your behalf, must sign below:

I, ______________________ declare that the

(Full name of signatory in BLOCK LETTERS)

information given above is true and complete.

Signature Date

A false declaration can result in prosecution.

Amendments—Form 4 and Form 5 substituted by the Value Added Tax, etc (Correction of Errors, etc) Regulations, SI 2008/1482 reg 3(3) with effect in respect of or as regards accounting periods that begin on 1 July 2008 or later.

Regulation 12(2)

FORM 5

HM Revenue & Customs

Lloyd's Composite IPT return for Syndicates

For the Period

to

For Official Use

IPT Registration number | Period

You could be liable to a financial penalty if your completed return and all the IPT payable are not received by the due date.

Due Date:

For official use DOR only

Fold here

Fill in all boxes clearly in ink, and write 'none' where necessary. Don't put a dash or leave any box blank. If there are no pence write '00' in the pence column. **Do not** enter more than one amount in any box.

For Official Use

		£	p
1	Standard rate IPT due for this period		
2	Higher rate IPT due for this period		
3	Underdeclarations of standard rate IPT from previous periods		
4	Underdeclarations of higher rate IPT from previous periods		
5	Total (the sum of boxes 1 to 4)		
6	Overdeclarations of standard rate IPT from previous periods		
7	Overdeclarations of higher rate IPT from previous periods		
8	Total overdeclarations from previous periods		
9	Net tax payable or repayable (the difference between box 5 and box 8)		
10	Net value of taxable premiums (excluding tax)		

If you are enclosing a payment please tick this box.

DECLARATION by the representatives of Syndicates, as defined in Regulation 9 of the Insurance Premium Tax Regulations 1994.

I, ______________________ declare that the

(Full name of signatory in BLOCK LETTERS)

information given above is true and complete.

Signature ______________ Date ______________

A false declaration can result in prosecution.

IPT100L Page 1 HMRC 05/08

Amendments—Form 4 and Form 5 substituted by the Value Added Tax, etc (Correction of Errors, etc) Regulations, SI 2008/1482 reg 3(3) with effect in respect of or as regards accounting periods that begin on 1 July 2008 or later.

Regulation 12(2)

FORM 6

Form 6

Lloyd's Composite Return - Schedule of Participating Syndicates

Regulation 12(2)

Period

..........................to..........................

Lloyd's Syndicate number	IPT registration number	Standard rate IPT due for this period 1 £ p	Higher rate IPT due for this period 2 £ p	Underdeclarations of standard rate IPT from previous periods 3 £ p	Underdeclarations of higher rate IPT from previous periods 4 £ p	Total (the sum of boxes 1 to 4) 5 £ p	Overdeclarations of standard rate IPT from previous periods 6 £ p	Overdeclarations of higher rate IPT from previous periods 7 £ p	Total Overdeclarations from previous periods 8 £ p	Net tax payable or repayable (the difference between box 5 and box 8) 9 £ p	Net value of taxable premiums (excluding tax) 10 £ p
	Totals										

SPECIMEN

IPT 100L(S) PCU(April 1997)

Amendment—Form 6 substituted by Insurance Premium Tax (Amendment) Regulations, SI 1997/1157, reg 15, Sch with effect from 1 May 1997.

1997/1431

Distress for Customs and Excise Duties and Other Indirect Taxes Regulations 1997

Made by the Commissioners of Customs and Excise under FA 1997 ss 51(1), (2), (3)

Made . . . . *9th June 1997*
Laid before House of Commons . . . . *9th June 1997*
Coming into force . . . . *1st July 1997*

Citation and commencement

1 These Regulations may be cited as The Distress for Customs and Excise Duties and Other Indirect Taxes Regulations 1997 and shall come into force on 1st July 1997.

Interpretation

2— (1) In these Regulations—

"authorised person" means a person acting under the authority of the Commissioners;

"costs" means any costs, charges, expenses and fees;

"officer" means, subject to section 8(2) of the Customs and Excise Management Act 1979, a person commissioned by the Commissioners pursuant to section 6(3) of that Act;

"person in default" means a person who has refused or neglected to pay any relevant tax due from him;

"relevant tax" means any of the following—

. . .

(*c*) insurance premium tax;

. . .

"walking possession agreement" means an agreement under which, in consideration of any goods and chattels distrained upon being allowed to remain in the custody of the person in default and of the delaying of their sale, that person—

(*a*) acknowledges that the goods and chattels specified in the agreement are under distraint and held in walking possession; and (*b*) undertakes that, except with the consent of the Commissioners and subject to such conditions as they may impose, he will not remove or allow the removal of any of the specified goods and chattels from the place named in the agreement;

"1994 Act" means Part III of the Finance Act 1994;

"1996 Act" means Part III of the Finance Act 1996;

(2) Any reference in these Regulations to an amount of relevant tax includes a reference to any amount recoverable as if it were an amount of that relevant tax.

Note—Words omitted are not relevant for the purposes of IPT.

Revocations and transitional provisions

3— (1) The Regulations specified in Schedule 3 are hereby revoked to the extent set out there.

(2) Where a warrant is signed before the coming into force of these Regulations, these Regulations shall apply to anything done, after these Regulations come into force, in relation to that warrant or as a consequence of distress being levied.

Levying distress

4— (1) Subject to regulation 5 below, if upon written demand a person neglects or refuses to pay any relevant tax due from him an officer may levy distress on the goods and chattels of that person and by warrant signed by him direct any authorised person to levy such distress.

(2) Where a warrant has been signed, distress shall be levied by or under the direction of, and in the presence of, the authorised person.

(3) Subject to regulation 6 below, distress may be levied on any goods and chattels located at any place whatever including on a public highway.

Restrictions on levying distress

5— (1) Where—

. . .

(*b*) an amount of insurance premium tax is due and the Commissioners may be required under section 59 of the 1994 Act to review a decision which, if that decision were varied or withdrawn, would cause the amount to be reduced or extinguished; or

. . .

no distress shall be levied before expiry of the last day on which the person who is liable to pay the amount concerned is required, by rules made under paragraph 9 of Schedule 12 to the VAT Act, to serve a notice of appeal with respect to that decision.

. . .

Note—Words omitted are not relevant for the purposes of IPT.

Goods and chattels not subject to levy

6 No distress shall be levied on any goods and chattels mentioned in Schedule 1 which at the time of levy are located in a place and used for a purpose mentioned in that Schedule.

Times for levying distress

7— (1) Subject to paragraph (2) below, a levy of distress shall commence only during the period between eight o'clock in the morning and eight o'clock at night on any day of the week but it may be continued thereafter outside that period until the levy is completed.

(2) Where a person holds himself out as conducting any profession, trade or business during hours which are partly within and partly outside, or wholly outside the period mentioned in paragraph (1) above, a levy of distress may be commenced at any time during that period or during the hours of any day in which he holds himself out as conducting that profession, trade or business and it may be continued thereafter outside that period or those hours until the levy is completed.

Costs

8— (1) A person in respect of whose goods and chattels a warrant has been signed shall be liable to pay to an officer or authorised person all costs, in connection with anything done under these Regulations described in column 1 of Schedule 2, as determined in accordance with column 2 of that Schedule.

(2) An authorised person may, after deducting and accounting for the amount of relevant tax to the Commissioners, retain costs from any amount received.

Sale

9 If any person upon whose goods and chattels distress has been levied does not pay the amount of relevant tax due together with costs within 5 days of a levy, an officer or authorised person may sell the distress for payment of the amount of relevant tax and costs; and the officer or authorised person, after deducting and retaining the amount of relevant tax and costs shall restore any surplus to the owner of the goods upon which distress was levied.

Disputes as to costs

10— (1) In the case of any dispute as to costs, the amount of those costs shall be taxed by a district judge of the county court of the district where the distress was levied, and he may make such order as he thinks fit as to the costs of the taxation.

(2) In the application of this regulation to Northern Ireland, in the case of any dispute as to costs, the amount of those costs shall be taxed in the same manner as costs in equity suits or proceedings in the county court in Northern Ireland.

SCHEDULE 1
GOODS AND CHATTELS NOT SUBJECT TO LEVY

Regulation 6

1 Any of the following goods and chattels which are located in a dwelling house at which distress is being levied and are reasonably required for the domestic needs of any person residing in that dwelling house—

(*a*) beds and bedding;
(*b*) household linen;
(*c*) chairs and settees;
(*d*) tables;
(*e*) food;
(*f*) lights and light fittings;
(*g*) heating appliances;
(*h*) curtains;
(*i*) floor coverings;
(*j*) furniture, equipment and utensils used for cooking, storing or eating food;
(*k*) refrigerators;
(*l*) articles used for cleaning, mending, or pressing clothes;
(*m*) articles used for cleaning the home;
(*n*) furniture used for storing—
  (i) clothing, bedding or household linen;
  (ii) articles used for cleaning the home;
  (iii) utensils used for cooking or eating food;
(*o*) articles used for safety in the home;
(*p*) toys for the use of any child within the household;
(*q*) medical aids and medical equipment.

2 Any of the following items which are located in premises used for the purposes of any profession, trade or business—

(*a*) fire fighting equipment for use on the premises;
(*b*) medical aids and medical equipment for use on the premises.

SCHEDULE 2
SCALE OF COSTS

Regulation 8(1)

Matter (1)	Costs (2)
1 For attending to levy distress where payment is made of an amount of relevant tax due and distress is not levied:	£12.50.
2 For levying distress—	
(a) where an amount of relevant tax demanded and due does not exceed £100:	£12.50.
(b) where an amount of relevant tax demanded and due exceeds £100:	12½% on the first £100, 4% on the next £400, 2½% on the next £1,500, 1% on the next £8,000, ¼% on any additional sum.
3 For taking possession of distrained goods—	
(a) where a person remains in physical possession of goods at the place where distress was levied (the person to provide his own food and lodgings):	£4.50 per day.
(b) where possession is taken under a walking possession agreement:	£7.00.

Matter (1)	Costs (2)
4 For appraising goods upon which distress has been levied:	Reasonable costs of appraisement.
5 For arranging removal and storage of goods upon which distress has been levied:	Reasonable costs of arrangement.
6 For removing and storing goods upon which distress has been levied:	Reasonable costs of removal and storage.
7 For advertising the sale of goods upon which distress has been levied:	Reasonable costs of advertising.
8 For selling the distress—	
(a) where a sale by auction is held at the auctioneer's premises:	15% of the sum realised.
(b) where a sale by auction is held elsewhere:	7½% of the sum realised and the auctioneer's reasonable costs.
(c) where a sale by other means is undertaken:	7½% of the sum realised and reasonable costs.

9 In addition to any amount specified in this scale in respect of the supply of goods or services on which value added tax is chargeable there may be added a sum equivalent to value added tax at the appropriate rate on that amount.

SCHEDULE 3
REVOCATIONS

Regulation 3 (1)

Note—The IPT repeals made under this Schedule are already in effect and have therefore been omitted.

1998/1461

Air Passenger Duty and Other Indirect Taxes (Interest Rate) Regulations 1998

Made by the Treasury under FA 1996 s 197

Made . . . . *15th June 1998*
Laid before the House of Commons . . . . *15th June 1998*
Coming into force . . . . *6th July 1998*

Citation and commencement

1 These Regulations may be cited as the Air Passenger Duty and Other Indirect Taxes (Interest Rate) Regulations 1998 and shall come into force on 6th July 1998.

Interpretation

2— (1) In these Regulations unless the context otherwise requires—

"established rate" means—

(*a*) on the coming into force of these Regulations, [6 per cent][1] per annum; and

(*b*) in relation to any day after the first reference day after the coming into force of these Regulations, the reference rate found on the immediately preceding reference day;

"operative day" means the [[twelfth][3] working day after the reference day][2];

"reference day" means the [...[3] working day following the day on which the most recent meeting of the Monetary Policy Committee of the Bank of England took place][2];

"section 197" means section 197 of the Finance Act 1996;

the "relevant enactments" are those referred to in regulations 4(1) and 5(1) below;

"working day" means any day other than a non-business day within the meaning of section 92 of the Bills of Exchange Act 1882.

[(2) In these Regulations the reference rate found on a reference date is the official bank rate determined by the most recent meeting of the Monetary Policy Committee of the Bank of England.][3]

Amendments—[1] Words substituted by the Air Passenger Duty and Other Indirect Taxes (Interest Rate) (Amendment) Regulations, SI 2000/631 regs 2, 3 with effect from 1 April 2000.

[2] In para (1), in definition of "operative day" words substituted for words "sixth day of each month", and in definition of "reference day" words substituted for words "twelfth working day before the next operative day" by the Taxes and Duties (Interest Rate) (Amendment) Regulations, SI 2008/3234 reg 3(1), (2) with effect from 7 January 2009.

[3] In para (1), in definition of "operative day" word substituted for word "eleventh" and in definition of "reference day", word "second" revoked, and para (2) substituted, by the Taxes and Duties (Interest Rate) (Amendment) Regulations, SI 2009/2032 regs 15, 16 with effect from 12 August 2009. Para (2) previously read as follows—

"(2) In these Regulations the reference rate found on a reference day is the percentage per annum found by averaging the base lending rates at close of business on that day of—

(*a*) Bank of Scotland,

(*b*) Barclays Bank plc,
(*c*) Lloyds Bank plc,
(*d*) [HSBC Bank plc],
(*e*) National Westminster Bank plc, and
(*f*) The Royal Bank of Scotland plc,

and, if the result is not a whole number, rounding the result to the nearest such number, with any result midway between two whole numbers rounded down.".

[2A *In determining the rate of interest applicable under section 197 for the purposes of any enactments referred to in these Regulations, if the result is less than zero the rate shall be treated as zero for those purposes.]*[1]

Amendments—[1] Reg 2A inserted by the Taxes and Duties (Interest Rate) (Amendment) Regulations, SI 2008/3234 reg 3(1), (3) with effect from 7 January 2009, and revoked by the Taxes and Duties (Interest Rate) (Amendment) Regulations, SI 2009/2032 regs 15, 17 with effect from 12 August 2009.

3 The Air Passenger Duty and Other Indirect Taxes (Interest Rate) Regulations 1997 are hereby revoked.

[Applicable rate of interest payable to the Commissioners of Customs and Excise in connection with excise duties, insurance premium tax, VAT, landfill tax, and customs duty

4— (1) For the purposes of—

(*a*) [section 60(8) of, and paragraphs 7 and 8(1) of Schedule 6 to,][4] the Finance Act 1994,
(*b*) paragraph 21 of Schedule 7 to that Act,
(*c*) [sections 74 and 85A(3)][4] of the Value Added Tax Act 1994,
(*d*) [section 56(5) of and][4] paragraph 26 of Schedule 5 to the Finance Act 1996,
(*e*) paragraph 17 of Schedule 5 to the Finance Act 1997, …[2]
(*f*) section 126 of the Finance Act 1999, […[3]
(*g*) paragraphs 41(2)(*f*), 70(1)(*b*)[, 81(3) and 123(6)][4] of Schedule 6 to the Finance Act 2000 (climate change levy),][2] [and
(*h*) sections 25(2)(*f*)[, 30(3)(*f*) and 42(6)][4] of, and paragraphs 6 and 8(3)(*a*) of Schedule 5 to, the Finance Act 2001 (aggregates levy),][3]

the rate applicable under section 197 shall, subject to paragraph (2) below, be 8.5 per cent per annum.

(2) Where, on any reference day after the coming into force of these Regulations, the reference rate found on that day differs from the established rate, the rate applicable under section 197 of the Finance Act 1996 for the purposes of the enactments referred to in paragraph (1) above shall, from the next operative day, be the percentage per annum determined in accordance with the formula specified in paragraph (3) below.

(3) The formula specified in this paragraph is—

$$RR + 2.5,$$

where RR is the reference rate referred to in paragraph (2) above.][1]

[(4) With effect from 1st November 2001 the rate of interest prescribed in paragraph (1) above for the purposes of paragraph 17 of Schedule 5 to the Finance Act 1997 also applies in the application of that paragraph to assessments under paragraph 14 or 15 of that Schedule as amended by paragraph 19 of Schedule 3 to the Finance Act 2001.][2]

Amendments—[1] This regulation substituted by the Air Passenger Duty and Other Indirect Taxes (Interest Rate) (Amendment) Regulations, SI 2000/631 regs 2, 4 with effect from 1 April 2000.
[2] Word "and" in para (1)(*e*) revoked, and para (1)(*f*) and para (4) inserted, by the Air Passenger Duty and Other Indirect Taxes (Interest Rate) (Amendment) Regulations, SI 2001/3337 reg 2 with effect from 1 November 2001.
[3] Word "and" in para (1)(*f*) revoked, and para (1)(*h*) inserted, by the Air Passenger Duty and Other Indirect Taxes (Interest Rate) (Amendment) Regulations, SI 2003/230 regs 2, 3 with effect from 1 April 2003.
[4] In para (1), in sub-para (a), words substituted for words "paragraph 7 of Schedule 6 to ", in sub-para (*c*), words substituted for words "section 74", in sub-para (*d*), words inserted, in sub-para (*g*), words substituted for words "and 81(3)", and in sub-para (*h*), words substituted for words "and 30(3)(*f*)", by the Transfer of Tribunal Functions and Revenue and Customs Appeals Order, SI 2009/56 art 3, Sch 2 paras 38, 39 with effect from 1 April 2009.

[Applicable rate of interest payable by the Commissioners of Customs and Excise in connection with air passenger duty, insurance premium tax, VAT, landfill tax, and customs duty

5— (1) For the purposes of—

(*a*) [Parts 2 and 3 of Schedule 3 to the Finance Act 2001 (interest payable on repayments etc),][2]
(*b*) paragraph 22 of Schedule 7 to that Act,
[(*ba*) section 60(6) of the Finance Act 1994,][4]
(*c*) section 78 of the Value Added Tax Act 1994,
(*d*) [section 56(3) and (4) of and][4] paragraph 29 of Schedule 5 to the Finance Act 1996, …[2]
(*e*) section 127 of the Finance Act 1999, […[3]
(*f*) paragraphs 62(3)(*f*)[, 66, 123(4) and 123(5)][4] of Schedule 6 to the Finance Act 2000 (climate change levy)][2] [and
(*g*) [section 42(4) and (5) of and][4] paragraphs 2 and 6(1)(*b*) of Schedule 8 to the Finance Act 2001 (aggregates levy),][3]

the rate applicable under section 197 of the Finance Act 1996 shall be 5 per cent per annum.

IPT

(2) Where, on a reference day after the coming into force of these Regulations, the reference rate found on that date differs from the established rate, the rate applicable under section 197 for the purposes of the enactments referred to in paragraph (1) above shall, from the next operative day, be the [higher of—

(*a*) 0.5% per annum, and

(*b*) the percentage per annum found by applying the formula specified in paragraph (3).][5]

[(3) The formula specified in this paragraph is—

$$RR-1,$$

where RR is the reference rate referred to in paragraph (2).][5]

Amendments—[1] This regulation substituted by the Air Passenger Duty and Other Indirect Taxes (Interest Rate) (Amendment) Regulations, SI 2000/631 regs 2, 5 with effect from 1 April 2000.

[2] In para (1), words in sub-para (*a*) substituted, word "and" in sub-para (*d*) revoked, and sub-para (*f*) added by the Air Passenger Duty and Other Indirect Taxes (Interest Rate) (Amendment) Regulations, SI 2001/3337 regs 1, 3 with effect from 1 November 2001.

[3] Word "and" in para (1)(*e*) revoked, and para (1)(*g*) inserted, by the Air Passenger Duty and Other Indirect Taxes (Interest Rate) (Amendment) Regulations, SI 2003/230 regs 2, 4 with effect from 1 April 2003.

[4] In para (1), sub-para (*ba*) inserted, in sub-para (*c*) words substituted for words "section 78", in sub-paras (*d*), (*g*) words inserted, and in sub-para (*f*) words substituted for words "and 66", by the Transfer of Tribunal Functions and Revenue and Customs Appeals Order, SI 2009/56 art 3, Sch 2 paras 38, 40 with effect from 1 April 2009.

[5] In para (2), words substituted, and para (3) substituted, by the Taxes and Duties (Interest Rate) (Amendment) Regulations, SI 2009/2032 regs 15, 18 with effect from 12 August 2009. Words in para (2) previously read as follows—

"percentage per annum determined in accordance with the formula specified in paragraph (3) below.".

Para (3) previously read as follows—

"(3) The formula specified in this paragraph is—

RR – 1,

where RR is the reference rate referred to in paragraph (2) above.".

Effect of change in applicable rate

6 Where the rate applicable under section 197 for the purposes of any of the relevant enactments changes on an operative day by virtue of these Regulations, that change shall have effect for periods beginning on or after the operative day in relation to interest running from before that day as well as in relation to interest running from, or from after that day.

7 Where the rate applicable under section 197 for the purposes of any of the relevant enactments changes on an operative day by virtue of these Regulations, the rate in force immediately prior to any change shall continue to have effect for periods immediately prior to the change and so on in the case of any number of successive changes.

Applicable rate of interest prior to the coming into force of these Regulations

8 The rate applicable under section 197 for interest running from before the date these Regulations come into force in relation to periods prior to that date shall be specified for the relevant enactments in the following Tables—

Table 2
Paragraph 21 of Schedule 7 to the Finance Act 1994

Interest for any period	*Rate*
From 1st October 1994 and before 6th February 1996	5·5 per cent
After 5th February 1996 and before 6th July 1998	6·25 per cent

Table 6
Paragraph 22 of Schedule 7 to the Finance Act 1994

Interest for any period	*Rate*
after 1st October 1994 and before 1st April 1997	8 per cent
after 31st March 1997 and before 6th July 1998	6 per cent

9 …

Note—This regulation is not relevant for the purposes of IPT.

2001/2635
Financial Services and Markets Act 2000 (Law Applicable to Contracts of Insurance) Regulations 2001

Made by the Treasury under FSMA 2000 ss 424(3), 417(1), 428(3).

Made . . . . *19 July 2001*
Laid before Parliament . . . . *20 July 2001*
Coming into force . . . . *in accordance with regulation 1*

PART I
GENERAL

Citation and commencement

1 These Regulations may be cited as the Financial Services and Markets Act 2000 (Law Applicable to Contracts of Insurance) Regulations 2001 and come into force on the day on which section 19 of the Act comes into force.

Interpretation

2— (1) In these Regulations—

"the Act" means the Financial Services and Markets Act 2000;

"the 1990 Act" means the Contracts (Applicable Law) Act 1990;

"applicable law", in relation to a contract of insurance, means the law that is applicable to that contract;

"contract of general insurance" and "contract of long-term insurance" have the meanings given by the Regulated Activities Order;

"EEA State of the commitment" means, in relation to a contract of long-term insurance entered into on a date—

(*a*) if the policyholder is an individual, the EEA State in which he resides on that date; or

(*b*) otherwise, the EEA State in which the establishment of the policyholder to which the contract relates is situated on that date;

"establishment", in relation to a person ("A"), means—

(*a*) A's head office;

(*b*) any of A's agencies;

(*c*) any of A's branches; or

(*d*) any permanent presence of A in an EEA State, which need not take the form of a branch or agency and which may consist of an office managed by A's staff or by a person who is independent of A but has permanent authority to act for A as if he were an agency;

"large risk" has the meaning given by Article 5(d) of the first non-life insurance directive and includes risks specified by paragraph (iii) of that definition insured by professional associations, joint ventures or temporary groups;

"mandatory rules" means the rules from which the law allows no derogation by way of contract;

"the Regulated Activities Order" means the Financial Services and Markets Act 2000 (Regulated Activities) Order 2001.

(2) References to the EEA State where the risk covered by a contract of insurance is situated are to—

(*a*) if the contract relates to buildings or to buildings and their contents (in so far as the contents are covered by the same contract of insurance), the EEA State in which the property is situated;

(*b*) if the contract relates to vehicles of any type, the EEA State of registration;

(*c*) if the contract covers travel or holidays risks and has a duration of four months or less, the EEA State in which the policyholder entered into the contract;

(*d*) in any other case—

(i) if the policyholder is an individual, the EEA State in which he resides on the date the contract is entered into;

(ii) otherwise, the EEA State in which the establishment of the policyholder to which the contract relates is situated on that date.

[(2A) If the contract of insurance relates to a vehicle dispatched from one EEA State to another, in respect of the period of 30 days beginning with the day on which the purchaser accepts delivery a reference to the EEA State in which a risk is situated is a reference to the State of destination (and not, as provided by paragraph (2)(*b*), to the State of registration).][1]

(3) References to the country in which a person resides are to—

(*a*) if he is an individual, the country in which he has his habitual residence;

(*b*) in any other case, the country in which he has his central administration.

(4) Where an EEA State (including the United Kingdom) includes several territorial units, each of which has its own laws concerning contractual obligations, each unit is to be considered as a separate state for the purposes of identifying the applicable law under these Regulations.

Amendments—[1] Sub-para (2A) inserted by the Financial Services and Markets Act 2000 (Motor Insurance) Regulations, SI 2007/2403 reg 3 with effect from 5 September 2007.

3–10 …

Note—Regulations beyond the scope of this publication have been omitted.

INSURANCE PREMIUM TAX EXTRA-STATUTORY CONCESSIONS

CONTENTS

Note—These Concessions are numbered as they appear in HMRC VAT Notice 48, section 4, *IPT: Concessions designed to remove inequities or anomalies in administration.*

VAT NOTICE 48

July 2009.

This notice cancels and replaces Notice 48 (March 2002). Details of any changes to the previous version can be found in paragraph 1.1 of this notice.

SECTION 4: IPT—CONCESSIONS DESIGNED TO REMOVE INEQUITIES OR ANOMALIES IN ADMINISTRATION

4.1 IPT—Special accounting introductory provisions

4.1.1 (PART I) INCEPTION WRITTEN OPTION

1—(1) Where the special accounting scheme applies to an insurer for the accounting period beginning on 1 October 1994, he need not account for any tax due on a premium—

(a) actually received on or after 1 October 1994 and in a relevant accounting period;

(b) received under a contract that relates to a risk the period of cover for which begins before 1 October 1994; and

(c) for which the tax point applicable under the special accounting scheme falls before 1 October 1995.

(2) Where (1)(a) and (b) above apply, but the tax point adopted by the insurer under the special accounting scheme falls on or after 1 October 1995, the insurer need not account for tax where the total premium received or written relates entirely to a risk the period of cover for which began before 1 October 1994.

Note—This concession will be withdrawn with effect from 1 April 2010. See the HMRC Technical Note, 'Withdrawal of Extra-statutory Concessions', published April 2009.

4.1.2 (PART II) STRICT WRITTEN PREMIUM OPTION

2—(1) Where the special accounting scheme applies to an insurer for the accounting period beginning on 1 October 1994 and the insurer—

(a) treats as tax due one forty-first of all premiums written on or after 1 October 1994 that are received (or due) under a taxable insurance contract but on which tax is not chargeable; and

(b) does not include such amounts treated as tax in claims for overdeclarations or make a claim for refund of overpaid tax in respect of them,

then he may claim as a credit against tax due one forty-first of any refund written on or after 1 October 1994 of all or part of a premium that was originally received under a taxable insurance contract but on which tax was not due.

(2) For the purposes of this paragraph, regulation 25 of the Insurance Premium Tax Regulations 1994 shall apply to premiums written on or after 1 October 1994 that are due under taxable insurance contracts but on which tax was not chargeable.

(3) For the purposes of this paragraph, a premium is written on or after 1 October 1994 if the tax point applicable under the special accounting scheme falls on or after that date; and a refund is written on or after 1 October 1994 if it is entered in the insurer's accounts as at a date falling on or after that date.

3. Nothing in this part shall require an insurer to account for tax on the portion of a premium that is attributable to exempt matters in accordance with section 69 of the Finance Act 1994, or prevent him from taking advantage of any de minimis rules.

4.1.3 (PART III)

4. An insurer may elect to use one or both options described in Parts I and II above but, where he chooses to use both options each option must be applied to the entirety of a clearly defined sector of business.

5. The Commissioners may withdraw or restrict the application of any part of this Concession to an individual insurer if they consider it is being used to avoid tax.

Note—This concession will be withdrawn with effect from 1 April 2010. See the HMRC Technical Note, 'Withdrawal of Extra-statutory Concessions', published April 2009.

4.2 IPT—De minimis provisions

1. Where an insurer is able to demonstrate that the total premium for a taxable insurance contract which provides cover for both exempt and non-exempt matters is below the de minimis limits set out in paragraph 3 below, then—

(a) that contract may be treated as though it were exempt; and

(b) credit may be claimed in respect of any tax that has already been accounted for on premiums

IPT

received or written under that contract (subject to the normal provisions as to the manner in which an insurer is able to claim and benefit from such credit).

2. Where an insurer applies this concession to a taxable insurance contract he must monitor payments received or due in relation to that contract. If a premium written or received by an insurer takes the total premium relating to a contract over the limits set out in paragraph 3 below, the insurer must account for tax on that total premium at the tax point applicable to the additional premium which takes the total premium over the limits set out in paragraph 3.

3. A total premium for a taxable insurance contract is below the de minimis limits if it is £500,000 or less, and 10 per cent or less of it is attributable to non-exempt matters.

4. Where the only taxable contracts under which an insurer intends to provide insurance are those in respect of which, to the best of the insurer's knowledge, the total premiums will each be below the de minimis limits, then provided—

(a) application has been made in writing to the Commissioners for exemption from the requirement to make returns;
(b) any information as may reasonably be requested by the Commissioners about the number and value of taxable insurance contracts entered into by the insurer has been supplied to them; and
(c) the Commissioners approve that insurer's application

the insurer will be exempted from the requirements of registrable persons to make returns.

5. For the purposes of this concession the "total premium" for a taxable insurance contract is the total of all premiums which have been received under that contract once there can be no more premium payments (either by or to the insurer) made under it.

4.3 IPT—Insurance relating to motor cars or motor cycles

For the purposes of Finance Act 1994 Sch 6A, a premium under a taxable insurance policy relating to a motor car or motor cycle (other than a motor car or motor cycle on hire) will not be regarded as falling within paragraph 2(1) to the extent that it relates to a policy of motor vehicle insurance which provides cover of the kind generally known as—

- fully comprehensive,
- third party, fire and theft, or
- third party.

The Commissioners may withdraw or restrict the application of this concession to an individual insurer if they consider it is being used to avoid tax.

4.4 IPT—Home contents insurance

For the purposes of Schedule 6A to the Finance Act 1994 a premium under a taxable insurance contract relating to relevant goods will not fall within paragraph 3(1) to the extent that it relates to insurance of the kind generally known as household contents insurance and which principally relates to risks arising in connection with items in the private dwellings of individuals.

"Relevant goods" are as defined in FA 1994 Sch 6A para 3(6).

The Commissioners may withdraw or restrict the application of this concession to an individual insurer if they consider it is being used to avoid tax.

Note—This concession will be withdrawn with effect from 1 April 2010. See the HMRC Technical Note, 'Withdrawal of Extra-statutory Concessions', published April 2009.

4.5 IPT—Arrangements for discounted insurance

1. By concession, where—

(a) a premium under a taxable insurance contract is liable to insurance premium tax at the higher rate; and
(b) the insurance is arranged or provided by one of the persons in Finance Act 1994 Sch 6A paras 2(2) or 3(2) for less than the actual cost of providing that insurance to the insured,

the higher rate element of any premium received by the insurer will be the amount paid by the insured (or any person on his behalf).

2. For the purposes of paragraph 1 above—

(a) "higher rate element" is as defined in FA 1994 s 69(5) (as amended); and
(b) references to payments being made on behalf of the insured shall not be taken to include any sum paid to the insurer or any person acting on behalf of the insurer by a person mentioned in FA 1994 Sch 6A paras 2(2) or 3(2).

The Commissioners may withdraw or restrict the application of this concession to an individual insurer if they consider it is being used to avoid tax.

INSURANCE PREMIUM TAX
PRESS RELEASES

IPT

CONTENTS

9 December 2003. BB 25/03	Implementation of Customs' ruling on the liability of the "reinsurance" of surety bonds.
12 February 2004. BB 5/04	Revised treatment of guaranteed asset protection (gap) insurance.
5 July 2005. BB 13/05	Implementation of tribunal decision regarding the liability of the reinsurance of surety bonds.
April 2008. Notice ET1	Notice of requirement to give security for Environmental Taxes.
19 August 2008. HMRC Brief 39/08	Revised registration procedures for overseas insurers.

IPT

9 December 2003. Business Brief 25/03

Implementation of Customs' ruling on the liability of the "reinsurance" of surety bonds

Customs has recently completed a review of the insurance premium tax (IPT) liability of premiums receivable under contracts covering risks guaranteed by way of surety bonds (ie contracts for the "reinsurance" of surety bonds).

As a result of the review, Customs has concluded that these "reinsurance" contracts are in fact contracts of primary insurance for IPT purposes (the bond contracts falling outside the scope of IPT because they are contracts of guarantee and not written as contracts of insurance). Therefore, premiums receivable under these contracts are liable to UK IPT when the risk covered (ie the surety bond provider) is located in the UK.

IMPLEMENTATION

Due to the uncertainty over the treatment of these products both before and during the period of Customs' review, it was agreed at the start of the review that any ruling would take effect from a current date. To allow a reasonable period for businesses to register for IPT if necessary and make the necessary adjustments to their systems, Customs has decided to delay implementation of their ruling until 1 April 2004.

As a result, all insurers or reinsurers underwriting surety bond "reinsurance" contracts as described above will be required to register for IPT (if not already registered) and account for IPT on all premiums with a tax point that falls on or after the 1 April 2004 which are receivable in respect of contracts that incept on or after that date.

Customs are aware that many of the companies liable to account for IPT as a result of this ruling are located outside the UK and are not currently IPT registered. In such circumstances, UK bond provider companies should notify their "reinsurers" of the liability to account for IPT and advise them to contact Customs on the number shown below as soon as possible. It is important to note that, in certain instances of non-compliance, Customs are able to recover unpaid IPT from the insured parties.

Note—See now Business Brief 13/05 below for a reversal of this ruling.

IPT

12 February 2004. Business Brief 5/04

Revised treatment of guaranteed asset protection (gap) insurance

Customs have recently completed a review of the IPT treatment of credit protection and gap insurance (ie "guaranteed asset protection" insurance covering the gap between an asset's sale value and write-off value) both of which are currently excluded from the higher rate. As a result of this review, it has been decided that a certain type of gap insurance has been excluded incorrectly from the higher rate and this brief explains the revised treatment to take effect from 1 April 2004.

BACKGROUND

When the higher rate of IPT was introduced in 1997 it was decided that it did not apply to credit protection and gap insurance. This decision was published in the revised IPT Notice issued in 1997 and has been included in subsequent rewrites. The decision was taken on the understanding that gap and credit protection insurance could only be sold through motor dealers in connection with finance arrangements and therefore fell outside the higher rate because they were not taxable insurance contracts "… relating to a motor car or motor cycle …".

Since this decision was taken, however, a new type of insurance, which is also known as "gap" insurance, has come onto the market. This particular type of gap insurance (sometimes referred to as "vehicle replacement" or "return to invoice" insurance) relates to the motor vehicle itself and is not linked to any finance arrangements. Furthermore, it often allows the dealer a great deal of pricing flexibility, therefore lending itself to VAT avoidance.

REVISED TREATMENT

In view of this, it has been decided that only credit protection and financial gap insurance (ie gap insurance sold as part of finance arrangements to cover the gap between the amount owed on a loan for a vehicle and the amount paid out under the motor insurance policy if the vehicle is written off) properly fall within the exclusion.

This means that non-financial gap insurance is now liable to the higher rate of IPT when sold through suppliers of motor vehicles or persons connected to them. This revised liability applies to premiums received on or after 1 April 2004 and, for businesses using the special accounting scheme, to premiums written in respect of annual contracts incepting on or after that date (the treatment of any contracts normally written for a period other than one year will be considered on a case by case basis).

FURTHER HELP AND ADVICE

General guidance on IPT can be found in Customs' Notice IPT1 "Insurance Premium Tax".

The views expressed in this Business Brief are those of HM Customs and Excise.

5 July 2005. Business Brief 13/05

Implementation of tribunal decision regarding the liability of the reinsurance of surety bonds

This Business Brief article announces HM Revenue & Customs' (HMRC) decision not to appeal a recent Tribunal decision (*Travellers Casualty & Surety and others*), which found that the reinsurance of surety bonds is exempt from Insurance Premium Tax (IPT). It reverses the ruling given in Business Brief 25/03.

BACKGROUND

Following a lengthy review, Customs (now HMRC) concluded in 2003 that the reinsurance of surety bonds was in fact primary insurance and therefore liable to IPT (unlike reinsurance which is exempt from IPT). This conclusion was based upon the fact that the underlying bond contracts were written as contracts of guarantee rather than contracts of insurance and therefore fell outside the scope of IPT. Customs took the view that to be 'reinsurance' for IPT, the underlying risk being 'reinsured' must be written under a contract of insurance.

This ruling was announced in Business Brief 25/03 and implemented from 1 April 2004, requiring businesses writing this type of reinsurance to register and account for IPT on premiums with a tax point falling after this date.

The ruling was subsequently appealed to a Tribunal by seven of the principal UK surety bond underwriters (ie the recipients of the reinsurance). They were supported by the Association of British Insurers (ABI) who represented the industry during the period of review.

THE TRIBUNAL DECISION

The Tribunal found that the insurance of surety bonds was clearly a specialist sector of the reinsurance market and there was no case law or textbook that specifically covers its status or otherwise as 'reinsurance'. On balance, however, it decided that the insurance of surety risks did fall within the definition of reinsurance for IPT, on the basis that the wider reinsurance markets regard the transfer of an insurer's surety risk to other insurers as reinsurance, and the interpretation of terms of statute should not conflict with commercial usage without good reason.

HMRC has decided not to appeal this decision.

PRACTICAL IMPLICATIONS

As a result of this decision, the reinsurance of surety bonds and similar products is exempt from IPT, irrespective of whether the underlying contract is one of insurance or one of guarantee. Businesses that were registered for IPT solely because of the ruling contained in our earlier Business Brief may now apply to be deregistered. Businesses that have already accounted for IPT on premiums received under surety reinsurance contracts may claim a refund from HMRC as detailed below.

INFORMATION ON MAKING CLAIMS OR ADJUSTMENTS

Businesses that think this decision applies to them and have already accounted for IPT may claim any resulting repayment due to them from HMRC by using one of the following methods:

1 where, during the course of an accounting period, you discover previous errors not exceeding £2000 net, an adjustment may be made on your IPT return for the period of discovery (or, if the business is to deregister, the final return) or,

2 if, during the course of an accounting period, you discover previous errors exceeding £2000 net, a separate claim should be submitted to HMRC (in these cases, the errors must not be corrected through your IPT returns). Details of where to send your claim can be obtained from HM Revenue & Customs' National Advice Service on 0845 010 9000.

All adjustments or claims are limited to a three-year period and will be subject to the conditions set out below.

– Businesses must be able to produce suitable evidence that they accounted for IPT on the basis outlined above, and must be able to substantiate the amount claimed.

- HMRC may reject all or part of a claim if repayment would unjustly enrich the claimant. For example, if a business has passed the tax on to the customer but is unable, or does not intend, to pass on the repayment.

A notification to HMRC that a business intends making a claim in the future is not a valid claim.

April 2008. Notice ET1

Notice of requirement to give security for Environmental Taxes

1. INTRODUCTION

1.1 What is this notice about?

There is provision in the laws on Insurance Premium Tax, Landfill Tax, Aggregates Levy and Climate Change Levy for us to require you to provide an amount of security if we consider that tax is at risk of being unpaid by your business.

This Notice is our Statement of Practice on the circumstances where we may require security for Insurance Premium Tax, Landfill Tax, Aggregates Levy and Climate Change Levy. For our Statement of Practice on VAT Security see Notice 700/52 Notice of Requirement to give security to HM Revenue and Customs.

This notice and others mentioned are available both on paper and on our website.

2. WHEN WILL YOU ISSUE A NOTICE OF REQUIREMENT TO GIVE SECURITY?

We may issue a Notice of Requirement to you for example if:

- you have in your previous or current business, failed to comply with your tax obligations
- your business is run by disqualified directors or by undischarged bankrupts
- you have previously been prosecuted or penalised for a tax offence, or
- other persons concerned in the current registration of your business are connected with past failures to pay tax due.

There may also be other circumstances when we may ask you to provide security.

2.1 Will I receive any warning before you require security?

Not always. Where we have strong grounds to suspect that revenue is at risk of being unpaid by your business we may require security without warning.

3. HOW MUCH SECURITY WILL YOU REQUIRE FROM ME?

We base the amount of security on a long-standing and well-tested formula that is approved by the independent VAT & Duties Tribunals. This formula reflects the minimum time it would take us to recover the debt if, in future, you do not pay your tax. We calculate the amount of security using the most accurate information available to us at the time which may include the:

- tax declared on tax returns from your current business
- tax declared on tax returns from your previous businesses
- tax declared on tax returns from businesses of a similar size, with similar customers and in the same trade class, or
- taxable turnover/premium declared on your application to register.

We may also add any outstanding tax from your current registered business to our calculation before issuing a Notice of Requirement.

If you make quarterly returns, we will require an amount of security based on the tax we estimate you would have to pay over six months.

If you make monthly returns, we will accept a lower amount of security based on the tax we estimate you would have to pay over four months.

4. WHAT FORMS OF SECURITY WILL YOU ACCEPT?

We will normally accept security in the following forms:

- cash or bankers draft
- bank or building society guarantee, or
- a joint bank or building society account.

However, we will only accept a guarantee from a financial institution approved by us. Please contact the address shown on the Notice of Requirement and we will advise you whether the guarantor is acceptable.

IPT

4.1 When will I have to provide the security?

The security is required immediately. Please contact us if you need time to make the necessary arrangements.

5. WHAT WILL HAPPEN IF I DON'T PROVIDE THE SECURITY?

It is a **criminal offence** to continue to trade without providing the security and we may prosecute you.

A person is guilty of a criminal offence if he:

	Description
Landfill tax	Carries out taxable activities (as defined in section 69(1) of the Finance Act 1996) without giving security he has been required to give.
Aggregates levy	Is responsible for any aggregate being subjected to commercial exploitation in the United Kingdom where, at the time it is so subjected, he has been required to give security and he has not complied with that requirement.
Climate change levy	Is liable to account for the levy on a taxable supply that he makes where, at the time the supply is made, he has been required to give security and has not complied with that requirement.
Climate change levy	Is liable to account for the levy on a taxable supply that another person makes to him where, if he makes any arrangements for the making of the supply at a time when he as been required to give security and he has not complied with that requirement.
Insurance premium tax	Enters into taxable insurance contracts (as defined by section 73(1) of the Finance Act 1994) without giving security.

You may be liable to a penalty of up to **£5,000 for each taxable supply/taxable activity/taxable insurance contract** you make or enter into without providing the security.

If you do not provide the security, we may prosecute you for the whole period of trading from the date the Notice of Requirement was issued.

5.1 Can I be prosecuted as well as my company?

Yes. If you are involved in a business that continues to trade without providing the security you may be prosecuted individually. You may also be personally responsible for paying any fines and compensation awarded by the court.

6. HOW LONG WILL YOU HOLD THE SECURITY FOR?

We will regularly review the requirement and will return the security when we consider you are no longer a risk to the collection of tax. If you have any information that you feel may alter our decision to hold security, please contact us and we will reconsider the requirement.

At the very least, we will review the requirement within 12 months of you providing the security (if you make monthly returns) or 2 years (if you make quarterly returns).

6.1 When will you use the security?

If you fall behind with payments of your tax we may offset the security against the amount you owe. We may then ask you to provide a further amount of security.

7. STATUTORY REVIEW AND APPEAL

7.1 What if I disagree with the decision to require security?

If you disagree with our decision to require security as described in Section 2 of this notice you have the right to require us to review our decision. You should do this within 45 days of receiving the Notice of Requirement to give security. You should contact us as soon as possible if you:

- think there are facts that may not have been fully considered, or
- can provide further information.

It is in your interests to provide any further information as soon as possible.

You must ask for a statutory review of your case prior to lodging an appeal at independent tribunal.

7.2 Your right to appeal to tribunal

If you are not satisfied with the outcome of a review you can appeal to an independent VAT & Duties Tribunal. You have 30 days from the date of the review decision to lodge your appeal. Where your 30-days time limit has expired you must apply direct to the appropriate Tribunal Centre. For more information see Notice 990: Excise and Customs Appeals.

7.3 Can I continue to make taxable supplies/carry out taxable activities/enter into taxable insurance contracts if I appeal?

If you have been served with a Notice of Requirement for security, you continue to trade at your own risk. Your appeal does not affect your ongoing liability to prosecution should you continue to trade without providing the security.

However, in order to allow time for your appeal to be heard, we may agree to await the decision of the Tribunal before taking steps to begin or continue any proposed or ongoing prosecution of you or your business. We will write to you if we agree to await the decision of the Tribunal.

If the Tribunal dismisses your appeal, or you withdraw it, we may decide to commence or re-commence immediately our prosecution of you or your business.

Commentary—*De Voil Indirect Tax Service* **V5.186.**

19 August 2008. HMRC Brief 39/08

Revised registration procedures for overseas insurers

This Revenue & Customs brief outlines the revised procedures for non-UK based insurers to register and account for Insurance Premium Tax (IPT). It also explains the revised circumstances under which we would seek to recover tax directly from an insured person. These changes were announced in Budget 2008 and come into effect from 21 July 2008.

BACKGROUND

All insurers underwriting taxable insurance in respect of risks located in the UK are required to register and account for IPT, regardless of where the insurer is based. Prior to the changes announced in the Budget, insurers based in another EU member state or outside the EU, were required to appoint a UK tax representative to deal with their IPT affairs. The tax representative was jointly and severally liable so that, in the event of a failure by the insurer, the representative assumed legal responsibility for the insurer's IPT obligations, such as submitting returns and paying any tax due.

Following representations from the insurance industry, a review of the tax representative requirement, including a formal consultation exercise, was carried out in 2007. It was clear from this that the requirement was difficult and onerous to operate and, in extreme cases, resulted in non-compliance by overseas insurers, putting their UK counterparts at a competitive disadvantage. Furthermore, recent European Court of Justice judgments have caused us to consider its approach to the issues.

As a result, measures were announced in Budget 2008 to remove the compulsory requirement to appoint a joint and severally liable tax representative. Our power to recover IPT from the insured person was also restricted to circumstances where the insurer is based outside the EU and is not covered by a Mutual Assistance provision or similar agreement.

REVISED PROCEDURES FOR NON-UK BASED INSURERS

From 21 July 2008, non-UK based insurers will have two options for dealing with their UK IPT affairs. They can either appoint an agent to act on their behalf, or they can deal with us directly.

APPOINTING AN AGENT

Whilst it would be preferable to have an agent based in the UK, we recognise that non-UK based insurers may prefer to use an agent based elsewhere in the EU to represent its tax affairs in both the UK and in other member states. We will, therefore, allow non-UK based insurers to appoint an agent based anywhere in the EU. We cannot, however, accept an agent based outside the EU.

We will require written authorisation from the insurer to deal with an agent on their behalf and will need a new authorisation each time there is a change of agent. The authorisation must give full details of the agent and the date on which they begin to act for the insurer. Existing tax representatives can continue to act for insurers and neither they nor the insurer they act for needs to take any action in respect of the IPT registration. The tax representative continues to be jointly and severally liable for any tax due before 21 July 2008.

Where an agent is appointed all documents, such as returns etc, will be sent to the agent rather than to the insurer. While the agent will be expected to deal with the insurer's day to day IPT affairs, such as compiling and submitting returns or making payments etc, they will not be liable for any tax due. However, in the future, agents may be liable to civil penalties in respect of certain errors on returns or other documents. Insurers need to ensure that whoever they nominate to act as agent is fully capable of handling their IPT affairs. The insurer may not, for example, be able to rely on any failure by the agent as an excuse for failure to discharge their own IPT responsibilities. In particular, the insurer and their agent will need to ensure that there are suitable arrangements in place for the relevant business records to be made available in the UK, should we need to see them.

DEALING DIRECTLY WITH HMRC

As an alternative to appointing an agent, non-UK insurers may decide to deal with us directly. This option is available to newly registered insurers or insurers who are already registered and are currently using a tax representative. In the case of existing registrations, the insurer simply needs to notify us in writing of the date from which they will be dealing with their own IPT affairs. Insurers who deal with their own IPT affairs will need to ensure that, as far as possible, arrangements are in place for records to be produced in the UK should we need to see them. In most cases, this will involve the insurer posting a selection of requested records to us for examination. The records would be returned on completion of our enquiries.

REGISTRATION FORM

The IPT registration form, IPT1, will be amended to reflect these changes. There will be a space on the form for non-UK insurers, who are registering for the first time, to indicate whether they intend to appoint an agent or to deal with us directly. There will also be a space to record the agent's particulars and a declaration that we can deal with the agent in respect of the insurer's UK IPT affairs. Insurers who are already registered need take no action unless they wish to change their current arrangements, in which case they should write in to advise us at the address shown below.

RETURNS AND PAYMENTS

Where an agent is based in another member state, or where the insurer is dealing with their own IPT affairs, contact with the insurer will be via one of our offices in London. Return forms will be issued to the agent or insurer as required via the London office, but should be sent back to the normal address shown on the back of the IPT return form:

HM Revenue & Customs
Central Collection Unit (IPT)
21 Victoria Avenue
Southend on Sea X
SS99 1AS

Because of the additional time involved in posting correspondence to a non-UK address, insurers or agents will have less time in which to complete and submit the returns, but hopefully this will be kept to no more than a few days. Payments can be made in any currency. We accept payment via direct debit, from a UK bank account. We are also able to accept payments directly from a UK or overseas bank account using BACS or CHAPS. Where possible we would encourage insurers or agents to make direct electronic transfers between bank accounts using one of the methods mentioned above.

Where payment is not made by electronic means, we can accept cheques, preferably drawn on a UK bank account, which should accompany the return form. While we will also accept cheques drawn on an overseas account, insurers or agents should bear in mind that these may take longer to clear through the banking system. Insurers or agents should also note that any exchange rate fluctuations between Sterling and other currencies will be borne by the business.

LIABILITY OF INSURED PERSON TO ACCOUNT FOR IPT

Prior to the changes announced in the Budget, we were able to recover IPT directly from an insured person in instances where a non-UK based insurer, had underwritten a taxable risk in the UK but had either failed to register and/or account for tax due. This provision applied to customers of all non-UK insurers irrespective of where the insurer was based. The Mutual Assistance Directives enable us to exchange information with the fiscal authorities in other EU member states and, where necessary, ask them to recover tax on our behalf. In addition, the UK has similar agreements in place with several countries outside the EU. With effect from 21 July 2008, therefore, the power to recover tax from the insured person has been restricted to customers of insurers based in countries where no such arrangements exist.

The IPT guidance and public notice will be amended shortly to reflect these changes.

For further help or advice please contact the National Advice Service on 0845 010 9000 or 0845 000 0200 (text phone).

Commentary—*De Voil Indirect Tax Service* **V18.128**, **V18.132**.

INSURANCE PREMIUM TAX INDEX

Defined words and phrases are listed separately at the end.

ACCOUNTING FOR TAX
provision for regulations, FA 1994 s 54(a)
special accounting scheme. *See* SPECIAL ACCOUNTING SCHEME
ACCOUNTING PERIODS
meaning, FA 1994 ss 54, 73(1), SI 1994/1774 reg 2(1)
variation of, SI 1994/1774 reg 12(4)
AIRCRAFT
commercial, contract covering, FA 1994 Sch 7A para 7
APPEALS
Commissioners, to—
application for review, FA 1994 s 59(2), (3), (5)
matters subject to review, FA 1994 s 59(1)
notification by Commissioners of decisions, FA 1994 s 59(4)
powers of Commissioners on review, FA 1994 s 59(6), (8)
HMRC review, FA 1994 s 59C
nature of, FA 1994 s 59F
offer of, FA 1994 s 59A
out of time, FA 1994 s 59E
right to require, FA 1994 s 59B
time, extensions of, FA 1994 s 59D
tribunal, to—
appeal tribunal, meaning, FA 1994 s 73(1)
assessment on, FA 1994 s 60(5)
matters subject to appeal, FA 1994 s 59(1)
payment of tax, precondition of, FA 1994 s 60(4)(4A)
powers, FA 1994 s 60
settlement by agreement, FA 1994 s 60(10)
ASSESSMENT
interest on overpaid tax, to recover—
procedure for making, FA 1994 Sch 7 para 25
supplementary, FA 1994 Sch 7 para 27
time limit for, FA 1994 Sch 7 para 26
penalties, to recover—
procedure for making, FA 1994 Sch 7 para 25
supplementary, FA 1994 Sch 7 para 27
time limit for, FA 1994 Sch 7 para 26
tax, to recover—
appeal against, FA 1994 ss 59(1), (1A), (2), 60
excess credit, to recover, FA 1994 s 56(2), (3)
failure to make return, following, FA 1994 s 56
inaccurate or incomplete return, following, FA 1994 s 56
insured person, on, FA 1994 s 65(3), SI 1994/1774 regs 35, 37
interest on, FA 1994 Sch 7 para 21
liquidator, on, FA 1994 s 56(4), (8)
personal representative, on, FA 1994 s 56(4), (8)
receiver, on, FA 1994 s 56(4), (8)
recovery of tax charged under, FA 1994 s 56(7)
ASSESSMENT – *contd*
tax, to recover – *contd*
reduction by appeal tribunal, FA 1994 s 60(6)
supplementary, FA 1994 Sch 7 para 27
time limits for, FA 1994 s 56(5), Sch 7 para 26(1)
trustee in bankruptcy, on, FA 1994 s 56(4), (8)
trustee in sequestration, on, FA 1994 s 56(4), (8)

BANKRUPTCY
companies. *See* INSOLVENCY
trustee in—
assessment on, FA 1994 s 56(4), (8)
duties, FA 1994 s 62(5), SI 1994/1774 reg 11
treatment as registered person, FA 1994 s 62(5), SI 1994/1774 reg 11
BUDGET RESOLUTION
approval by House of Commons, PCTA 1968 s 5(1), (2)
repayment of tax charged under, PCTA 1968 ss 1(6), (7), 5(3), FA 1994 Sch 7 para 34
statutory effect, PCTA 1968 ss 1(1)–(6), 5(3)

CHANNEL TUNNEL
contracts relating to, FA 1994 Sch 7A paras 10, 11
CHARGEABLE AMOUNT
appeal as to, FA 1994 ss 59(1), (2), 60
contracts covering both exempt and non-exempt matters—
calculation of, FA 1994 s 69
premium below de minimis limit, ESC 4.2
different rates of tax applying, where, FA 1994 s 69
meaning, FA 1994 s 50
CIVIL OFFENCES
breach of walking possession agreement, FA 1994 Sch 7 para 19
dishonest claim for credit, FA Sch 7 para 12(1)–(4)
dishonest evasion of tax, FA 1994 Sch 7 para 12(1), (3)
failure of insured person to pay tax, FA 1994 Sch 7 para 16
failure of non-UK insurer to appoint tax representative, FA 1994 Sch 7 para 18
failure to comply with regulations generally, FA 1994 Sch 7 para 17
failure to make return, FA 1994 Sch 7 para 15
failure to notify liability to be de-registered, FA 1994 Sch 7 para 17
failure to notify liability to register, FA 1994 Sch 7 para 14
failure to pay tax by due date, FA 1994 Sch 7 para 15
failure to provide information or documents, FA 1994 Sch 7 para 17

IPT

CIVIL OFFENCES – *contd*
penalties. *See* PENALTIES
COLLECTOR
meaning, SI 1994/1774 reg 2(1)
COMMENCEMENT, FA 1994 s 49
COMMISSION
premium payments referable to, FA 1994 s 72(1)(*c*), (8), (8A)
COMMISSIONERS OF CUSTOMS AND EXCISE
disclosure of information by or to, FA 1994 Sch 7 para 28
management of tax by, FA 1994 s 48(2)
power to make orders and regulations, FA 1994 s 74(1), (2)
review of decisions by. *See* REVIEW OF COMMISSIONERS' DECISIONS
CONTRACTS
non-taxable, FA 1994 Sch 7A, SI 1994/1698 arts (1) (5), SI 1997/1627
CREDIT
adjustments for unpaid tax, FA 1994 s 55(8)
appeal as to, FA 1994 ss 59(1), (2), 60
assessment to recover, FA 1994 s 56(2), (3)
calculation of, FA 1994 s 55(3)(*a*)
carry forward of, FA 1994 s 55(3)(*e*), (5)
claim for, FA 1994 s 55(6)(*a*), (7), SI 1994/1774 reg 18, SI 1997/1157
conditions for, FA 1994 s 55(6)(*b*), (*c*)
de-registered insurer, entitlement to, FA 1994 s 55(3)(*f*), SI 1994/1774 reg 19(2), (3)
dishonest claim for—
civil offence, FA 1994 Sch 7 para 12(1), (2), (4)
penalty, FA 1994 Sch 7 para 12(1), (3)
excess, assessment to recover, FA 1994 s 56(2), (3)
fraudulent claim for—
criminal offence, FA 1994 Sch 7 para 9(2)
penalty, FA 1994 Sch 7 para 10(1), (2), (8)
interest on underclaim arising from Commissioners' error, FA 1994 Sch 7 paras 22, 23
payment of all or part of, FA 1994 s 55(3)(*c*), (*d*), (4), SI 1994/1774 reg 19
set-off against tax due, FA 1994 s 55(2)(*b*)
tax on repaid premiums for, FA 1994 s 55(1), SI 1994/1774 regs 17–19
tax on unpaid premiums, for, FA 1994 s 55(2), SI 1994/1774 regs 17–19
transfer of business as going concern, entitlement following, FA 1994 s 62(7)
CRIMINAL OFFENCES
admissibility of evidence, FA 1994 Sch 7 para 12(5), (6)
false documents, provision of, 1994 FA 1994 Sch 7 para 9(3)
false information, provision of, FA 1994 Sch 7 para 9(4)
fraudulent claim for credit, FA 1994 Sch 7 para 9(2)
fraudulent evasion of tax, FA 1994 Sch 7 para 9(1), (6)
multiple offences, FA 1994 Sch 7 para 9(5)
penalties, FA 1994 Sch 7 para 10
proceedings in respect of—
generally, FA 1994 Sch 7 para 11
interaction with civil proceedings, FA 1994 Sch 7 para 12(5)–(7)

CRIMINAL OFFENCES – *contd*
security, evasion of requirement for, FA 1994 Sch 7 para 9(7)

DEATH
registrable person, of, duties of person carrying on business, SI 1994/1774 reg 11
DE-REGISTRATION OF INSURER
appeal relating to, FA 1994 ss 59(1), (2), 60
claim for credit following, FA 1994 s 55(3)(*f*), SI 1994/1774 reg 19(2), (3)
duty to notify liability for, FA 1994 s 53(3), (5), (5A), SI 1994/1774 regs 6, 6A
failure to notify liability for, penalty, FA 1994 Sch 7 para 17
notice of, SI 1994/1774 reg 6
transfer of business as going concern, treatment as, SI 1994/1774 reg 7(2)
DE-REGISTRATION OF INTERMEDIARY
notification, SI 1994/1774 reg 6A
DILIGENCE
enforcement by, FA 1997 s 52, SI 1997/1432
recovery of tax, Scotland, FA 1994 Sch 7 para 7(8)–(12), SI 1994/1774 reg 43
DISCLOSURE OF INFORMATION
Commissioners, by, to Secretary of State, FA 1994 Sch 7 para 28
Secretary of State, by, to Commissioners, FA 1994 Sch 7 para 28
DISTRESS
enforcement by, FA 1997 s 53(5), SI 1997/1432
penalty for breach of walking possession agreement, FA 1994 Sch 7 para 19
recovery of tax, England and Wales, FA 1994 Sch 7 para 7(7), SI 1994/1774 reg 42, SI 1997/1431
walking possession agreement, FA 1994 Sch 7 para 19(1), (2)
DOCUMENTS
Commissioners' powers to inspect and remove, FA 1994 Sch 7 paras 3–6
failure to provide, civil penalty, FA 1994 Sch 7 para 17
false, fraudulent provision of—
criminal offence, FA 1994 Sch 7 para 9(3)
penalty, FA 1994 Sch 7 para 10(3), (4)
DOMESTIC APPLIANCES
insurance relating to, higher rate tax liability, FA 1994 Sch 6A para 3

EMPLOYEE
taxable insurance contract deductions under employment contract, FA 1994 s 72(7A)
EVASION OF TAX
dishonest—
civil offence, FA 1994 Sch 7 para 12(1)
penalty, FA 1994 Sch 7 para 12(1), (3)
fraudulent—
criminal offence, FA 1994 Sch 7 para 10
penalty, FA 1994 Sch 7 para 10
EXCHANGE LOSSES
contracts, FA 1994 Sch 7A para 14
EXEMPTION
contracts covering both exempt and non-exempt matters—
chargeable amount, FA 1994 s 69
de minimis limit for exemption, ESC 4.2

EXEMPTION – *contd*
exempt matters—
list of, FA 1994 Sch 7A
meaning, FA 1994 s 69(12)
EXPORT
credit on goods for, contracts covering, FA 1994 Sch 7A para 13

FEES
treatment as premiums, FA 1994 s 52A
FINANCIAL FACILITIES
overseas customers, for, contracts covering, FA 1994 Sch 7A para 15
FRAUD
criminal offences, FA 1994 Sch 7 para 9
penalties, FA 1994 Sch 7 para 10
search powers of Commissioners, FA 1994 Sch 7 para 4

GOODS IN TRANSIT
foreign or international, contracts covering, FA 1994 Sch 7A para 12
GROUPS OF COMPANIES
amendment of group registration, FA 1994 s 63(5), (6)
appeal against refusal of group application, FA 1994 ss 59(1), (2), 60
application for group treatment, FA 1994 s 63(4), (8)
consequences of group treatment, FA 1994 s 63(1)
control, meaning, FA 1994 s 63(9)
eligibility for treatment as group, FA 1994 s 63(2), (3)
representative member, FA 1994 s 63(1)
termination of group treatment, FA 1994 s 63(5), (7)
GUARANTEED ASSET PROTECTION INSURANCE
review of treatment, PR 12/2/2004

HANDICAPPED PERSONS
contracts covering motor vehicles for, FA 1994 Sch 7A para 3
HIGHER RATE CONTRACT
appeal against Commissioners' decision, FA 1994 s 59
domestic appliances etc, insurance relating to, FA 1994 para 3
fees to be treated as premiums under, FA 1994 s 52A
meaning, FA 1994 s 52A(4)
motor car or motor cycle, insurance relating to, FA 1994 Sch 6A para 2
travel insurance, FA 1994 Sch 6A para 4, FA 1998 s 146
HOUSE OF COMMONS RESOLUTION
repayment of tax charged under, PCTA 1968 ss 1(6), (7), 5(3), FA 1994 Sch 7 para 34
statutory effect, PCTA 1968 ss 1(1)–(6), 5(3)

INCAPACITY
registrable person, of, duties carrying on business, SI 1994/1774 reg 11
INFORMATION
Commissioners' powers—
inspectors and removal of documents, FA 1994 Sch 7 paras 3–6
to require information generally, FA 1994 Sch 7 paras 2, 4A
disclosure—
Commissioners, by, to Secretary of State, FA 1994 Sch 7 para 28

INFORMATION – *contd*
disclosure – *contd*
Secretary of State, by, to Commissioners, FA 1994 Sch 7 para 28
failure to provide, civil penalty, FA 1994 Sch 7 para 17
false, fraudulent provision of—
criminal offence, FA 1994 Sch 7 para 9(3), (4)
penalties, FA 1994 Sch 7 para 10(3), (4)
registration, in connection with, FA 1994 ss 53(1A), 53A, SI 1994/1774 regs 4, 5, Sch
INSOLVENCY
individuals. *See* BANKRUPTCY
INSUFFICIENCY OF FUNDS
reasonable excuse for default, whether, FA 1994 Sch 7 para 20
INSURANCE BUSINESS
meaning, FA 1994 s 73(1)
INSURANCE CONTRACT
announced increase in rate of tax, deemed date of contract, FA 1994 ss 67B, 67C, FA 1998 s 146(5)
higher-rate contract. *See* HIGHER-RATE CONTRACT
information required in connection with, FA 1994 Sch 7 paras 2, 3
non-taxable, FA 1994 Sch 7A
taxable. *See* TAXABLE INSURANCE CONTRACT
INSURANCE PREMIUMS
administration costs, referable to, FA 1994 s 72(1)(*b*)
commission referable to, FA 1994 s 72(1), (8), (8A)
deemed amount—
alteration following change in tax rate, FA 1994 Sch 7 para 35
direction by Commissioners, premiums of less than market value, FA 1994 s 66
premiums in non-monetary form, FA 1994 s 72(3)–(5)
special accounting scheme, premiums received under, FA 1994 s 68(4)–(6), (8), FA 1998 s 146(4)
deemed date of receipt—
increase in rate of tax, following announcement of, FA 1994 ss 67A, 67C, FA 1998 s 146(5)
premiums received before October 1994 but referable to later date, FA 1994 s 67
special accounting scheme, premiums received under, FA 1994 s 68(3), (5), (7), (8), (11), (14) , FA 1998 s 146(4)
divided company, insurance provided by, FA 1994 Sch 6A para 3A
employee's paid by deduction from salary, FA 1994 s 72(7A), (8A)
fees, treatment as premiums, FA 1994 s 52A
higher rate of tax, liability for, FA 1994 s 51A, Sch 6A
instalments, paid by, FA 1994 s 72(1)(*d*), (6)
intermediary, paid through, FA 1994 s 72(7)–(9)
meaning, FA 1994 s 72(1)
motor car or motor cycle, relating to, Sch 6A para 2
non-monetary form, in—
deemed value of, FA 1994 s 72(3)–(5)
generally, FA 1994 ss 66(6), 72(2)
special accounting scheme, FA 1994 s 68(14)

IPT

INSURANCE PREMIUMS – *contd*
non-receipt of, special accounting scheme, FA 1994 s 68(5)
partly attributable to exempt matters—
chargeable amount, FA 1994 s 69
de minimis limit for exemption, ESC 4.2
payroll deduction scheme, paid through, FA 1994 s 72 (7A), (8A)
taxable insurance contract, under, FA 1994 s 72(1A)
INSURANCE-RELATED SERVICE
meaning, FA 1994 s 52A(9), Sch 6A para 1(1)
INSURED PERSON
assessment on, FA 1994 s 65(3), SI 1994/1774 regs 35, 37
failure to pay tax, penalty, FA 1994 Sch 7 para 16
interest on reimbursement by insurer, SI 1994/1774 reg 39
liability for tax, FA 1994 s 65, SI 1994/1774 regs 33, 36
liability notice, SI 1994/1774 regs 32, 34
records to be kept by, SI 1994/1774 reg 41
reimbursement by insurer, SI 1994/1774 reg 39
set-off of payments made by insurer, SI 1994/1774 reg 40
time limit for payment of tax, SI 1994/1774 reg 38
INSURER
cancellation of registration, FA 1994 s 53(3), (5), (5A)
liability for tax, FA 1994 s 52
meaning, FA 1994 s 73(1)
overseas with no UK establishment—
failure to appoint tax representative—
consequences, FA 1994 s 65, SI 1994/1774 regs 32–41. *See also* INSURED PERSON
penalty for, FA 1994 Sch 7 para 18
requirement for tax representative *See* TAX REPRESENTATIVE
registration of. *See* REGISTRATION OF INSURERS
INTEREST
setting of rates of, FA 1996 s 197, SI 1997/1015–1016
INTEREST ON TAX REPAID
Commissioners' error, arising from—
amount of, appeal against, FA 1994 ss 59(1), (2), 60
appeal, following, FA 1994 s 60(6), (7)
applicable period for calculation of interest, FA 1994 Sch 7 para 22(3)–(6)
claim for, FA 1994 Sch 7 para 22(8), (9)
credit in respect of, FA 1994 Sch 7 paras 22(1), 23
eligibility for, FA 1994 Sch 7 para 22(1), (1A)
rate of, FA 1994 Sch 7 para 22(2), FA 1996 s 183, SI 1998/1461
time limit for claims, FA 1994 Sch 7 para 22(9)
INTEREST ON UNPAID TAX
appeal in respect of, FA 1994 ss 59(1), (2), 60
assessment to recover—
procedure for making, FA 1994 Sch 7 para 25
supplementary, FA 1994 Sch 7 para 27
time limit for, FA 1994 Sch 7 para 26
disallowance in computing income, profits or losses, TA 1988 s 827(1B)
rate of, FA 1994 Sch 7 para 21(5), FA 1996 s 183, SI 1998.1461

INTEREST ON UNPAID TAX – *contd*
reckonable date for, FA 1994 Sch 7 para 21(4)
INTERMEDIARY
administration order, FA 1994 s 62(5)
bankruptcy, FA 1994 s 62(5)
credit, right to, FA 1994 s 55
death, FA 1994 s 62(5)
fees, SI 1997/1157
group of companies, carrying on business as member of, FA 1994 s 63(1)
incapacity, FA 1994 s 62(5)
liquidation, FA 1994 s 62(5)
overseas with no UK establishment, requirement for tax representative, *See* TAX REPRESENTATIVE
receivership, FA 1994 s 62(5)
registration of. *See* REGISTRATION OF INTERMEDIARIES
sequestration of estate, FA 1994 s 62(5)
INVESTMENT
classes of, FSMA 2000 s 22, Sch 22 Pt II
order-making power, FSMA 2000 Sch 22 Pt III
regulated activities, classes of, FSMA 2000 s 22, Sch 2 Pt I

JOB BAND
meaning, SI 1994/1774 reg A42

LIABILITY
insured person, of, FA 1994 s 65, SI 1994/1774 regs 32–41. *See also* INSURED PERSON
insurer, of, FA 1994 s 52
notice of, FA 1994 s 65(2), SI 1994/1774 regs 32, 34
LIFEBOAT
contract covering—
lifeboat and equipment, chargeable amount, FA 1994 s 69, Sch 7A para 6
lifeboat only, non-taxable, FA 1994 Sch 7A para 5
LIQUIDATOR
assessment to recover tax from, FA 1994 s 56(4), (8)
duties, FA 1994 s 62(5), SI 1994/1774 reg 11
treatment as registered person, FA 1994 s 62(5), SI 1994/1774 reg 11
LLOYD'S UNDERWRITING SYNDICATE
election for representation by Lloyd's, SI 1994/1774 reg 9(3)–(7)
overdeclaration of tax, correction of, SI 1994/1774 reg 13(4)
persons responsible for fulfilling obligations of, SI 1994/1774 reg 9
registration of, FA 1994 s 62(3), (4), SI 1994/1774 reg 8
returns on behalf of, form of, SI 1994/1774 reg 12(2), Sch
underdeclaration of tax, correction of, SI 1994/1774 reg 13(4)
LONG TERM BUSINESS
contract constituting, FA 1994 Sch 7A para 2

MOTOR VEHICLE
insurance relating to, higher rate tax liability, FA 1994 Sch 6A para 2

NOTICE
changes in registration details, SI 1994/1774 reg 5
Commissioners' decisions on appeals, FA 1994 s 59(4)

NOTICE – *contd*
liability of insured person for tax, FA 1994 s 65(2), SI 1994/1774 regs 32, 34
liability to be de-registered, FA 1994 s 53(3), (5), (5A), SI 1994/1774 regs 6, 6A
liability to register, FA 1994 s 53(1), (2), SI 1994/1774 regs 4, 4A, Sch
service by post, FA 1994 Sch 7 para 30
special accounting scheme—
expulsion of insurer from, FA 1994 s 68(9), SI 1994/1774 reg 27
insurer joining, FA 1994 s 68(2), (9), SI 1994/1774 reg 21
insurer withdrawing from, FA 1994 s 68(9), SI 1994/1774 reg 26(1)
writing, to be given in, SI 1994/1774 reg 3

OFFENCES. *See* CIVIL OFFENCES; CRIMINAL OFFENCES; PENALTY
ORDERS
persons empowered to make, FA 1994 s 74(1)
procedure for making, FA 1994 s 74(3)–(9)
OVERDECLARATION OF TAX
correction in subsequent return, SI 1994/1774 reg 13
OVERPAID TAX
interest on. *See* INTEREST ON TAX REPAID
repayment of. *See* REPAYMENT OF TAX
OVERSEAS CUSTOMER
financial facilities for, contracts covering, FA 1994 Sch 7A para 15
goods or services supplied to, contracts covering, FA 1994 Sch 7A para 13
meaning, FA 1994 Sch 7A para 16(3)

PARTNERSHIP
persons responsible for fulfilling obligations of, SI 1994/1774 reg 10(3)
registration of, FA 1994 s 62(1), SI 1994/1774 reg 4(2), Sch
PAYMENT OF TAX
certificate by Commissioners of non-payment, treatment as evidence, FA 1994 Sch 7 para 29
deposit in Commissioners' general account or Consolidated Fund, FA 1994 Sch 7 para 31
failure to make by due date, penalty, FA 1994 Sch 7 para 15
prior to appeal hearing—
requirement for, FA 1994 s 60(4), (4A)
undue hardship, exception for, FA 1994 s 60(4A)(4B)
time limit for—
insured person, SI 1994/1774 reg 38
insurer, FA 1994 s 54(*c*), SI 1994/1774 reg 15
PENALTY
civil offences, for—
appeal against—
Commissioners, to, FA 1994 s 59, Sch 7 para 13
matters subject to appeal, FA 1994 ss 59(1), (2), (8)
tribunal, to, FA 1994 s 60, Sch 7 para 13
assessment to recover—
procedure for making, FA 1994 Sch 7 para 25
supplementary, FA 1994 Sch 7 para 27
time limit for, FA 1994 Sch 7 para 26

PENALTY – *contd*
civil offences, for – *contd*
breach of walking possession agreement, FA 1994 Sch 7 para 19
dishonest claim for credit, FA 1994 Sch 7 para 12(1)–(4)
dishonest evasion of tax, FA 1994 Sch 7 para 12(1), (3)
failure of insured person to pay tax, FA 1994 Sch 7 para 16
failure of non-UK insurer to appoint tax representative, FA 1994 Sch 7 para 18
failure to comply with regulations generally, FA 1994 Sch 7 para 17
failure to make return, FA 1994 Sch 7 para 15
failure to notify liability to be de-registered, FA 1994 Sch 7 para 17
failure to notify liability to register, FA 1994 Sch 7 para 14
failure to pay tax by due date, FA 1994 Sch 7 para 15
failure to provide information or documents, FA 1994 Sch 7 para 17
criminal offences, for, FA 1994 Sch 7 para 10
disallowance in computing income, profits or losses, TA 1988 s 827(1B)
interaction between civil and criminal proceedings, FA 1994 Sch 7 para 12(5)–(7)
mitigation, criminal penalties, FA 1994 Sch 7 para 11
PERSONAL REPRESENTATIVE
assessment to recover tax from, FA 1994 s 56(4), (8)
carrying on deceased's business, duties of, SI 1994/1774 reg 11
PREMIUMS. *See* INSURANCE PREMIUMS

RAILWAY
rolling stock, foreign or international, contract covering, FA 1994 Sch 7A para 9
RATE OF TAX
announced increase in—
deemed date for receipt of certain premiums, FA 1994 ss 67A, 67C, FA 1998 s 146(5)
deemed date of certain contracts, FA 1994 ss 67B, 67C, FA 1998 s 146(5)
change in, consequential alteration to amount or premium, FA 1994 Sch 7 para 35
current rate, FA 1994 s 51
higher rate, liability for, FA 1994 s 51A, Sch 7
REASONABLE EXCUSE
breach of walking possession agreement, FA 1994 Sch 7 para 19(4)
failure to appoint tax representative, FA 1994 Sch 7 para 18(2)
failure to comply with regulations generally, FA 1994 Sch 7 para 17(3)
failure to make return, FA 1994 Sch 7 para 15(5)
failure to notify liability to be de-registered, FA 1994 Sch 7 para 17(3)
failure to notify liability to register, FA 1994 Sch 7 para 14(3)
failure to pay tax by due date, FA 1994 Sch 7 para 15

REASONABLE EXCUSE – *contd*
failure to provide information or documents, FA 1994 Sch 7 para 17(3)
insufficiency of funds, whether, FA 1994 Sch 7 para 20
reliance on another, whether, FA 1994 Sch 7 para 20
RECEIVER
assessment to recover tax from, FA 1994 s 56(4), (8)
duties, FA 1994 s 62(5), SI 1994/1774 reg 11
treatment as registered person, FA 1994 s 62(5), SI 1994/1774 reg 11
RECORDS
Commissioners' power to require, inspect and remove, FA 1994 Sch 7 paras 2–6
insured person liable to tax, to be kept by, SI 1994/1774 reg 41
registrable person, to be kept by, FA 1994 Sch 7 para 1, SI 1994/1774 reg 16
RECOVERY OF TAX
authorisation for, FA 1994 Sch 7 para 7(1)
diligence by, Scotland, FA 1994 Sch 7 para 7(8)–(12), SI 1994/1774 reg 43
distress by, England and Wales, FA 1994 Sch 7 para 7(7), SI 1994/1774 reg 42
REGISTERED PERSON
meaning, SI 1994/1774 reg 2(1)
REGISTRABLE PERSON
meaning, FA 1994 s 73(3)
records to be kept by, FA 1994 Sch 7 para 1
REGISTRATION NUMBER
meaning, SI 1994/1774 reg 2(1)
transfer with business transferred as going concern, SI 1994/1774 reg 7(4)
REGISTRATION OF INSURERS. *See also* DE-REGISTRATION OF INSURERS
amendment of details, FA 1994 s 53A, SI 1994/1774 reg 5
appeals relating to, FA 1994 ss 59(1), (2), 60
cancellation of, FA 1994 s 53(3), (5), (5A)—
appeal relating to, FA 1994 ss 59(1), (2), 60
duty to notify liability for, FA 1994 s 53(3), SI 1994/1774 reg 6
failure to notify liability for, penalty, FA 1994 Sch 7 para 17
certificate by Commissioners as to, treatment as evidence, FA 1994 Sch 7 para 29
changes in details of, FA 1994 s 53A, SI 1994/1774 reg 5
duty to notify liability for, FA 1994 s 53(1), (2), SI 1994/1774 regs 4, 4A
effective date of, FA 1994 s 53(4)
failure to notify liability for—
penalty, FA 1994 Sch 7 para 14
reasonable excuse for, FA 1994 Sch 7 para 14(3)
groups of companies. *See* GROUPS OF COMPANIES
information required for, FA 1994 ss 53(1A), 53A
liability for, FA 1994 s 53(1), (2)
Lloyd's underwriting syndicates, FA 1994 s 62(4)
notice of, SI 1994/1774 reg 4, Sch
overseas insurers, PR 19/8/08
partnerships, FA 1994 s 62(1), SI 1994/1774 reg 4(2), Sch
penalties—
failure to notify liability for, FA 1994 Sch 7 para 14

REGISTRATION OF INSURERS – *contd*
penalties – *contd*
failure to notify liability to be de-registered, FA 1994 Sch 7 para 17
registered person, meaning, SI 1994/1774 reg 2(1)
registrable person, meaning, FA 1994 s 73(3)
time limit for notification of liability for, SI 1994/1774 reg 4(3)
unincorporated bodies, FA 1994 s 62(2)
REGISTRATION OF INTERMEDIARIES
cancellation of, FA 1994 s 53AA(4), (6), (7)
Commissioners, notification of certain facts to, FA 1994 s 53AA(3), (4)
contents of register, FA 1994 s 53AA(2)
correction of entries in register, FA 1994 s 53AA(8)
de-registration, claim for credit following, FA 1994 s 55(3)(*f*)
de-registration, notification, SI 1994/1774 reg 6A, SI 1997/1157
liability for, FA 1994 s 53AA(1)
notification, FA 1994 s 53AA(3), (4), (8), SI 1994/1774 reg 4A, SI 1997/1157
records, SI 1994/1774, SI 1997/1157
regulations, power to make, s 53AA(8)
time for registration, FA 1994 s 53AA(5)
REGULATIONS
persons empowered to make, FA 1994 s 74(2)
procedure for making, FA 1994 s 74(2)–(9)
REINSURANCE CONTRACT
non-taxable, FA 1994 Sch 7A para 1
surety bonds, relating to, PR 9/12/03, PR 5/7/05
RELIANCE ON ANOTHER PERSON
reasonable excuse, whether, FA 1994 Sch 7 para 20
REPAYMENT OF TAX
amount of, appeal, FA 1994 ss 59(1), (2), 60
appeal, following, FA 1994 s 60(6), (7)
authorisation for, FA 1994 Sch 7 para 8(1), (7)
claim for, FA 1994 Sch 7 para 8(2), (6), SI 1994/1774 reg 14
interest on. *See* INTEREST ON TAX REPAID
resolution, charged under, PCTA 1968 ss 1(6), (7), 5(3), FA 1994 Sch 7 para 34
time limit for claim, FA 1994 Sch 7 para 8(4)
transfer of business as going concern, following, FA 1994 s 62(7)
unjust enrichment, refusal on grounds of, FA 1994 Sch 7 para 8(3)
REPRESENTATIVE
personal. *See* PERSONAL REPRESENTATIVE
tax. *See* TAX REPRESENTATIVE
RESOLUTION
approval by House of Commons, PCTA 1968 s 5(1), (2)
repayment of tax charged under, PCTA 1968 ss 1(6), (7), 5(3), FA 1994 Sch 7 para 34
statutory effect, PCTA 1968 ss 1(1)–(6), 5(3)
RETURN
appeal hearing, submission required before, FA 1994 s 60(3)
claim for credit to be included in, FA 1994 s 55(7), SI 1994/1774 reg 18
correction of over- or underdeclaration in, SI 1994/1774 reg 13

RETURN – *contd*
failure to submit—
assessment in consequence of, FA 1994 s 56
certificate by Commissioners of, treatment as evidence, FA 1994 Sch 7 para 29
credit, effect on, FA 1994 s 55(4)
penalty for, FA 1994 Sch 7 para 15
form of, FA 1994 s 54(*b*), SI 1994/1774 reg 12(1), (2), Sch
meaning, SI 1994/1774 reg 2(1)
time limit for, SI 1994/1774 reg 12(3), (4)

REVIEW OF COMMISSIONERS' DECISIONS
application for, FA 1994 s 59
matters subject to review, FA 1994 s 59(1)
nature of, FA 1994 s 59F
notification by Commissioners of decisions, FA 1994 s 59(4)
offer of, FA 1994 s 59A
out of time, FA 1994 s 59E
powers of Commissioners on review, FA 1994 s 59(6), (8)
requirement, FA 1994 s 59C
right to require, FA 1994 s 59B
time, extensions of, FA 1994 s 59D

RISK
outside UK, contract covering, FA 1994 Sch 7A para 8
premium payments referable to, FA 1994 s 72(1)(*a*)

SECURITY
appeal against requirement for, FA 1994 ss 59(1), (2), 60
deposit in Commissioners' general account or Consolidated Fund, FA 1994 Sch 7 para 31
environmental taxes, for, PR April 2008
evasion of requirement for—
criminal offence, FA 1994 Sch 7 para 9(7)
penalty, FA 1994 Sch 7 para 10(7)
power to require, FA 1994 Sch 7 para 24

SERVICE OF NOTICES
form of, FA 1994 Sch 7 para 30

SHIP
commercial, contract covering, FA 1994 Sch 7A para 4

SPECIAL ACCOUNTING SCHEME
accounting periods to which applicable, SI 1994/1774 reg 22
commencement provision, ESC 4.1
credit—
entitlement to, SI 1994/1774 reg 25(1), ESC 4.1
repayment if premium subsequently received, SI 1994/1774 reg 25(2)
deemed amount of insurance premiums, FA 1994 s 68(4)–(6), (8), SI 1994/1774 reg 24
deemed date of receipt of insurance premiums, FA 1994 s 68(3), (5), (7), (8), (11), (14), FA 1998 s 146(4), SI 1994/1774 reg 23
expulsion of insurer from scheme—
notification to insurer, FA 1994 s 68(9), SI 1994/1774 reg 27
tax to be accounted for, SI 1994/1774 reg 28
inception written option, ESC 4.1
initial amount, meaning, SI 1994/1774 reg 24(1)
initial period, meaning, SI 1994/1774 reg 20(1)

SPECIAL ACCOUNTING SCHEME – *contd*
notification to be given by insurer, FA 1994 s 68(2), (9), SI 1994/1774 reg 21(1), (3)
withdrawal of notification, SI 1994/1774 reg 21(2)
premium written date, meaning, SI 1994/1774 reg 20(1)
premiums in non-monetary form, FA 1994 s 68(12)
premiums not received, FA 1994 s 68(5), SI 1994/1774 reg 25
relevant accounting period, meaning, FA 1994 s 68(1)
strict written option, ESC 4.1
transitional provisions on commencement, ESC 4.1
withdrawal from scheme—
earliest date of, SI 1994/1774 reg 26(2)
notification by insurer, FA 1994 s 68(8), SI 1994/1774 reg 26(1)
returns required from insurer, SI 1994/1774 reg 26(2)
tax to be accounted for, FA 1994 s 68(1), SI 1994/1774 reg 26(2), 28

TAX
premium payments referable to, FA 1994 ss 72(1)(*a*), 73(1)

TAX REPRESENTATIVE
application for approval of, FA 1994 s 54(3)–(7)
approval of, SI 1994/1774 reg 29(1), SI 1997/1157
direction by Commissioners as to, SI 1994/1774 reg 29(3), SI 1997/1157
failure of non-UK insurer to appoint—
consequences, FA 1994 s 65(1), SI 1994/1774 regs 32–41. *See also* INSURED PERSON
penalty for, FA 1994 Sch 7 para 18
liabilities of, SI 1994/1774 reg 31, SI 1997/1157
meaning, FA 1994 s 73(1)
penalty for failure to appoint, FA 1994 Sch 7 para 18
registration of, SI 1994/1774 reg 30
termination of appointment, SI 1994/1774 reg 29(2), SI 1997/1157
withdrawal of approval of, SI 1994/1774 reg 30(2)

TAXABLE BUSINESS
meaning, FA 1994 s 73(1)

TAXABLE INSURANCE CONTRACT
charge to tax on, FA 1994 s 49
employment contract, intermediary authorised to deduct amount under, FA 1994 s (7A)
exempt and non-exempt matters, covering—
chargeable amount, FA 1994 s 69
de minimis limit for exemption, ESC 4.1
higher rate matters, covering—
exempt matters, and, FA 1994 s 69
standard rate matters, and, FA 1994 s 69
meaning, FA 1994 ss 70, 71
payment received under, amount deemed as, FA 1994 s 72(1A)
standard rate matters, covering—
exempt matters, and, FA 1994 s 69
higher rate matters, and, FA 1994 s 69

TAXABLE INTERMEDIARY *See* INTERMEDIARY

TRANSFER OF BUSINESS AS A GOING CONCERN
application for, form of, SI 1994/1774 reg 7, Sch

IPT

TRANSFER OF BUSINESS AS A GOING CONCERN – *contd*
continuity of insurance premium tax provisions, FA 1994 s 62(6), (7)
credit, entitlement to, FA 1994 s 62(7), SI 1994/1774 reg 7(3)–(5)
liabilities, transfer with, SI 1994/1774 reg 7(3)
repayment of tax following, FA 1994 s 62(7), SI 1994/1774 reg 7(3)

TRAVEL INSURANCE
higher rate tax liability, FA 1994 Sch 6A para 4
person travelling: meaning, FA 1994 Sch 6A para 4(5)
travel risks: meaning, FA 1994 Sch 6A para 4(5)

TREASURY
power to make orders, FA 1994 s 74(1)

TRUSTEE IN BANKRUPTCY
assessment to recover tax from, FA 1994 s 56(4), (8)
duties, FA 1994 s 62(5), SI 1994/1774 reg 11
treatment as registered person, FA 1994 s 62(5), SI 1994/1774 reg 11

TRUSTEE IN SEQUESTRATION
assessment to recover from, FA 1994 s 56(4), (8)
duties, FA 1994 s 62(5), SI 1994/1774 reg 11
treatment as registered person, FA 1994 s 62(5), SI 1994/1774 reg 11

UNDERDECLARATION OF TAX
correction in subsequent return, SI 1994/1774 reg 13

UNINCORPORATED BODY
persons responsible for fulfilling obligations of, SI 1994/1774 reg 10(1)
registration, FA 1994 s 62(1), (2), SI 1994/1774 reg 10(2)

UNITED KINGDOM
contracts covering risks outside, FA 1994 Sch 7A para 8

WALKING AGREEMENT
meaning, FA 1994 Sch 7 para 19(2)
penalty for breach of, FA 1994 Sch 7 para 19

WORDS AND PHRASES

Words in brackets indicate the context in which the word or phrase is used.

accounting period, FA 1994 ss 54, 73(1), SI 1994/1774 reg 2(1)
accounts (special accounting scheme), SI 1994/1774 reg 20(2)
aircraft tribunal, FA 1994 s 73(1)
applicable period (interest on tax repaid), FA 1994 Sch 7 para 22(3)–(7)
authorised person, FA 1993 s 73(1)

buying, FSMA 2000 Sch 22 para 27

Channel tunnel equipment, FA 1994 Sch 7A para 11(4), (5)
Channel tunnel system, FA 1994 Sch 7A para 10(3)
chargeable amount, FA 1994 s 50
collector, SI 1994/1774 reg 2(1)
commercial aircraft, FA 1994 Sch 7A para 7(3)
commercial ship, FA 1994 Sch 7A para 4(3)
Commissioners, FA 1994 s 73(1)
conduct, FA 1994 s 73(1)
control (groups of companies), FA 1994 s 63(9)

disability allowance, FA 1994 Sch 7A para 3(4)(*b*)
disposing, FSMA 2000 Sch 22 para 27

established rate, SI 1998/1461, reg 2(1)
exempt matter, FA 1994 s 69(3)
export, FA 1994 Sch 7A para 13(4)

financial facility, FA 1994 Sch 7A para 15(3)
foreign or international railway rolling stock, FA 1994 Sch 7A para 9(3)

handicapped, FA 1994 Sch 7A para 3(4)(*a*)
higher rate matter, FA 1994 s 69 (12)(*a*)–(*d*)

increase (tax), FA 1994 s 67A
initial amount (special accounting scheme), SI 1994/1774 reg 24(1)
initial period (special accounting scheme), SI 1994/1774 reg 20(1)
insurance business, FA 1994 s 73(1)
insurance premium, FA 1994 s 72(1)
insurance related service, FA 1994 s 52A(9), Sch 6A para 1(1)
insurer, FA 1994 s 73(1)
investment, FSMA 2000 s 22(4)

Job Band, SI 1994/1774 reg A42

legislation relating to insurance premium tax, FA 1994 s 73(1)
lifeboat, FA 1994 Sch 7A para 5(3)
lifeboat equipment, FA 1994 Sch 7A para 6(3)
Lloyd's, SI 1994/1774 reg 2(1)

managing agent, SI 1994/1774 reg 2(1)
mobility supplement, FA 1994 Sch 7A para 3(4)(*c*)

non-exempt matter, FA 1994 s 69(4)

offering, FSMA 2000 Sch 22 para 27
overdeclaration, SI 1994/1774 reg 13(1)
overseas customer, FA 1994 Sch 7A para 16(3)

premium, FA 1994 s 72(1)
premium (special accounting scheme), SI 1994/1774 reg 20(3)
premium written date (special accounting scheme), SI 1994/1774 reg 20(1)
prescribed, FA 1994 s 73(1)
prescribed rate (interest on unpaid tax), FA 1994 Sch 7 para 21(5)
property, FSMA 2000 Sch 22 para 27

railway rolling stock, foreign or international, FA 1994 Sch 7A para 9(3)
reckonable date (interest on unpaid tax), FA 1994 Sch 7 para 21(4)
registered person, SI 1994/1774 reg 2(1)
registrable person, FA 1994 s 73(3)
registration number, SI 1994/1774 reg 2(1)
relevant accounting period (special accounting schemes), FA 1994 s 68(1)
relevant supply of goods, FA 1994 Sch 7A para 16(2)
return, SI 1994/1774 reg 2(1)

selling, FSMA 2000 Sch 22 para 27
ship, commercial, FA 1994 Sch 7A para 4(3)
supply, FA 1994 Sch 6A para 1(1)

tax, FA 1994 s 73(1)
tax representative, FA 1994 ss 57, 73(1)
taxable business, FA 1994 s 73(1)
taxable insurance contract, FA 1994 ss 70, 71
taxable intermediary, SI 1994/1774 reg 2 (1)

underdeclaration, SI 1994/1774 reg 13(1)
underwriting member, SI 1994/1774 reg 2(1)

walking possession agreement, FA 1994 Sch 7 para 19(2)

IPT

LANDFILL TAX

CONTENTS

PROVISIONAL COLLECTION OF TAXES ACT 1968

(1968 Chapter 2)

1 Temporary statutory effect of House of Commons resolutions affecting …, [landfill tax][2], …

(1) This section applies only to …, [landfill tax][2]

(2) Subject to that, and to the provisions of subsections (4) to (8) below, where the House of Commons passes a resolution which—

(*a*) provides for the renewal for a further period of any tax in force or imposed during the previous financial year (whether at the same or a different rate, and whether with or without modifications) or for the variation or abolition of any existing tax, and

(*b*) contains a declaration that it is expedient in the public interest that the resolution should have statutory effect under the provisions of this Act,

the resolution shall, for the period specified in the next following subsection, have statutory effect as if contained in an Act of Parliament and, where the resolution provides for the renewal of a tax, all enactments which were in force with reference to that tax as last imposed by Act of Parliament shall during that period have full force and effect with respect to the tax as renewed by the resolution.

In this section references to the renewal of a tax include references to its reimposition, and references to the abolition of a tax include references to its repeal.

(3) The said period is—

(*a*) in the case of a resolution passed in [November or December][3] in any year, one expiring with [5th May in the next calendar year][3];

[(*aa*) in the case of a resolution passed in February or March in any year, one expiring with 5th August in the same calendar year; and][5]

(*b*) in the case of any other resolution, one expiring at the end of four months after the date on which it is expressed to take effect or, if no such date is expressed, after the date on which it is passed.

(4) A resolution shall cease to have statutory effect under this section unless within the next [thirty][4] days on which the House of Commons sits after the day on which the resolution is passed—

(*a*) a Bill renewing, varying or, as the case may be, abolishing the tax is read a second time by the House, or

(*b*) a Bill is amended by the House [in Committee or on Report, or by any [Public Bill Committee][6] of the House][1] so as to include provision for the renewal, variation or, as the case may be, abolition of the tax.

(5) A resolution shall also cease to have statutory effect under this section if—

(*a*) the provisions giving effect to it are rejected during the passage of the Bill containing them through the House, or

(*b*) an Act comes into operation renewing, varying or, as the case may be, abolishing the tax, or

(*c*) Parliament is dissolved or prorogued.

(6) Where, in the case of a resolution providing for the renewal or variation of a tax, the resolution ceases to have statutory effect by virtue of subsection (4) or (5) above, or the period specified in subsection (3) above terminates, before an Act comes into operation renewing or varying the tax, any money paid in pursuance of the resolution shall be repaid or made good, and any deduction made in pursuance of the resolution shall be deemed to be an unauthorised deduction.

(7) Where any tax as renewed or varied by a resolution is modified by the Act renewing or varying the tax, any money paid in pursuance of the resolution which would not have been payable under the new conditions affecting the tax shall be repaid or made good, and any deduction made in pursuance of the resolution shall, so far as it would not have been authorised under the new conditions affecting the tax, be deemed to be an unauthorised deduction.

(8) When during any session a resolution has had statutory effect under this section, statutory effect shall not be again given under this section in the same session to the same resolution or to a resolution having the same effect.

Note—Words and any subsection not relevant for the purposes of landfill tax have been omitted.

Amendments—[1] Words in sub-s (4)(*b*) added by FA 1968 s 60.

[2] Words in the heading and in sub-s (1) added by virtue of FA 1998 s 148.

[3] Words in sub-s (3)(*a*) substituted by FA 1993 s 205 in relation to resolutions passed after 27 July 1993.

[4] Word in sub-s (4) substituted by FA 1993 s 205 in relation to resolutions passed after 27 July 1993.

[5] Words in sub-s (3) inserted by F(No 2)A 1997 s 50 in relation to resolutions passed after 31 July 1997.

[6] Words in sub-s (4)(*b*) substituted by FA 2007 s 112(1) with effect from 19 July 2007.

5 House of Commons resolution giving provisional effect to motions affecting taxation

(1) This section shall apply if the House of Commons resolves that provisional statutory effect shall be given to one or more motions to be moved by the Chancellor of the Exchequer, or some other Minister, and which, if agreed to by the House, would be resolutions—

(*a*) to which statutory effect could be given under section 1 of this Act, or
(*b*) …
(*c*) …

(2) Subject to subsection (3) below, on the passing of the resolution under subsection (1) above, sections 1 … of this Act, … shall apply as if each motion to which the resolution applies had then been agreed to by a resolution of the House.

(3) Subsection (2) above shall cease to apply to a motion if that motion, or a motion containing the same proposals with modifications, is not agreed to by a resolution of the House (in this section referred to as "a confirmatory resolution") within the next ten days on which the House sits after the resolution under subsection (1) above is passed, and, if it ceases to apply, all such adjustments, whether by way of discharge or repayment of tax, or discharge of security, or otherwise, shall be made as may be necessary to restore the position to what it would have been if subsection (2) above had never applied to that motion, and to make good any deductions which have become unauthorised deductions.

(4) …

Note—Sub-ss (1)(*b*), (4) and words omitted from sub-s (2) are not relevant to landfill tax; sub-s (1)(*c*) is repealed.

6 Short title, repeals and saving as respects Northern Ireland

(1) This Act may be cited as the Provisional Collection of Taxes Act 1968.

(2) …

(3) …[1]

Note—Sub-s (2) repeals enactments specified in Schedule.

Amendments—[1] Sub-s (3) repealed by Northern Ireland Constitution Act 1973 s 41(1)(*a*) and Sch 6 Pt I, with effect from 18 July 1973.

INTERPRETATION ACT 1978

(1978 Chapter 30)

Note—See VAT Statutes, *ante*.

INCOME AND CORPORATION TAXES ACT 1988

(1988 Chapter 1)

PART XIX
SUPPLEMENTAL

Miscellaneous

827 VAT penalties etc

(1), (1A), (1B) …

[(1C) Where a person is liable to make a payment by way of—

(a) penalty under Part V of Schedule 5 to the Finance Act 1996 (landfill tax), or

(b) interest under paragraph 26 or 27 of that Schedule,

the payment shall not be allowed as a deduction in computing any income, profits or losses [for any corporation tax purposes (but see also subsection (3)(a) below)][2]*.]*[1]

(1D)–(1F), (2) …

[(3) For income tax purposes—

(a) provision corresponding to that made by this section (other than subsection (2) above) is made by sections 54 and 869 of ITTOIA 2005, and

(b) provision corresponding to that made by subsection (2) above is made by section 777 of ITTOIA 2005 (as read with Chapter 10 of Part 6 of that Act).][2, 3]

Note—Words omitted are not relevant for the purposes of landfill tax.

Amendments—[1] Sub-s (1C) inserted by FA 1996 Sch 5 para 40.

[2] Words in sub-s (1C) substituted, and sub-s (3) inserted, by the Income Tax (Trading and Other Income) Act 2005, s 882(1), Sch 1, Pt 1, paras 1, 332(*a*), (*c*) with effect, for the purposes of income tax for the year 2005–06 and subsequent tax years, and for the purposes of corporation tax for accounting periods ending after 5 April 2005.

[3] This section repealed by CTA 2009 ss 1322, 1326, Sch 1 paras 1, 268, Sch 3 Part 1. CTA 2009 applies for accounting periods ending on or after 1 April 2009 (for corporation tax purposes) and for tax years 2009–10 onwards (for income and capital gains tax purposes).

FINANCE ACT 1996

(1996 Chapter 8)

ARRANGEMENT OF SECTIONS

PART III

LANDFILL TAX

The basic provisions

An Act to grant certain duties, to alter other duties, and to amend the law relating to the National Debt and the Public Revenue, and to make further provision in connection with Finance.

[29th April 1996]

PART III
LANDFILL TAX

The basic provisions

Press releases etc—C & E Business Brief 18/96 27-8-96 (guidance notes issued to help registrable landfill site operators).
IR Tax Bulletin June 1996 p 317 (Revenue views on treatment of payments of landfill tax for purposes of Schedule D Cases I and II.

39 Landfill tax

(1) A tax, to be known as landfill tax, shall be charged in accordance with this Part.

(2) The tax shall be under the care and management of the Commissioners of Customs and Excise.

40 Charge to tax

(1) Tax shall be charged on a taxable disposal.

(2) A disposal is a taxable disposal if—

(*a*) it is a disposal of material as waste,
(*b*) it is made by way of landfill,
(*c*) it is made at a landfill site, and
(*d*) it is made on or after 1st October 1996.

(3) For this purpose a disposal is made at a landfill site if the land on or under which it is made constitutes or falls within land which is a landfill site at the time of the disposal.

Commentary—*De Voil Indirect Tax Service* **V20.103**.
Simon's Tax Cases—s 40(2), *C&E Comrs v Parkwood Landfill Ltd* [2002] STC 417; *Waste Recycling Group Ltd v R&C Comrs* [2009] STC 200.

41 Liability to pay tax

(1) The person liable to pay tax charged on a taxable disposal is the landfill site operator.

(2) The reference here to the landfill site operator is to the person who is at the time of the disposal the operator of the landfill site which constitutes or contains the land on or under which the disposal is made.

42 Amount of tax

(1) The amount of tax charged on a taxable disposal shall be found by taking—

(*a*) [£40][2] for each whole tonne disposed of and a proportionately reduced sum for any additional part of a tonne, or
(*b*) a proportionately reduced sum if less than a tonne is disposed of.

(2) Where the material disposed of consists entirely of qualifying material this section applies as if the reference to [[£40][2] were to £2.50][1].

(3) Qualifying material is material for the time being listed for the purposes of this section in an order.

(4) The Treasury must have regard to the object of securing that material is listed if it is of a kind commonly described as inactive or inert.

Press releases etc—C & E News Release 48/96 18-9-96 (Foundry sand is chargeable at £2 per tonne).
Regulations—See Landfill Tax (Qualifying Material) Order, SI 1996/1528.
Amendments—[1] Words in sub-s (2) substituted by FA 2007 s 15(4) with effect in relation to disposals made, or treated as made, on or after 1 April 2008.
[2] Figures in sub-ss (1)(*a*), (2) substituted by FA 2008 s 18(1) with effect in relation to disposals made, or treated as made, on or after 1 April 2009.

Exemptions

43 Material removed from water

(1) A disposal is not a taxable disposal for the purposes of this Part if it is shown to the satisfaction of the Commissioners that the disposal is of material all of which—

(*a*) has been removed (by dredging or otherwise) from water falling within subsection (2) below, and

(*b*) formed part of or projected from the bed of the water concerned before its removal.

(2) Water falls within this subsection if it is—

(*a*) a river, canal or watercourse (whether natural or artificial), or

(*b*) a dock or harbour (whether natural or artificial).

(3) A disposal is not a taxable disposal for the purposes of this Part if it is shown to the satisfaction of the Commissioners that the disposal is of material all of which—

(*a*) has been removed (by dredging or otherwise) from water falling within the approaches to a harbour (whether natural or artificial),

(*b*) has been removed in the interests of navigation, and

(*c*) formed party of or projected from the bed of the water concerned before its removal.

(4) A disposal is not a taxable disposal for the purposes of this Part if it is shown to the satisfaction of the Commissioners that the disposal is of material all of which—

(*a*) consists of naturally occurring mineral material, and

(*b*) has been removed (by dredging or otherwise) from the sea in the course of commercial operations carried out to obtain substances such as sand or gravel from the seabed.

[(5) A disposal is not a taxable disposal for the purposes of this Part if it is shown to the satisfaction of the Commissioners that the disposal is of material all of which comprises material falling within subsection (1) or (3) and other material which has been added to that material for the purpose of securing that it is not liquid waste.][1]

Commentary—*De Voil Indirect Tax Service* **V20.122**.
Amendments—[1] Sub-s (5) inserted by the Landfill Tax (Material Removed from Water) Order, SI 2007/2909 art 2 with effect from 30 October 2007: SI 2007/2909 art 1.

[43A Contaminated land

(1) A disposal is not a taxable disposal for the purposes of this Part if it is a disposal within subsection (2) below.

(2) A disposal is within this subsection if—

(*a*) it is of material all of which has been removed from land in relation to which a certificate issued under section 43B below was in force at the time of the removal;

(*b*) none of that material has been removed from a part of the land in relation to which, as at the time of the removal, the qualifying period has expired;

(*c*) it is a disposal in relation to which any conditions to which the certificate was made subject are satisfied; and

(*d*) it is not a disposal within subsection (4) below.

(3) For the purpose of subsection (2)(*b*) above the qualifying period expires, in relation to the part of the land in question—

(*a*) in the case of a reclamation which qualified under section 43B(7)(*a*) below, where the object involves the construction of—

(i) a building; or

(ii) a civil engineering work,

when the construction commences;

(*b*) in any other case of a reclamation which qualified under section 43B(7)(*a*) below, when pollutants have been cleared to the extent that they no longer prevent the object from being fulfilled; or

(*c*) in the case of a reclamation which qualified under section 43B(7)(*b*) below, when pollutants have been cleared to the extent that the potential for harm has been removed.

(4) Subject to subsection (5) below, a disposal is within this subsection if it is of material the removal of any of which is required in order to comply with—

(*a*) a works notice served under section 46A of the Control of Pollution Act 1974;

(*b*) an enforcement notice served under section 13 of the Environmental Protection Act 1990;

(*c*) a prohibition notice served under section 14 of the Environmental Protection Act 1990;

(*d*) an order under section 26 of the Environmental Protection Act 1990;

Landfill Tax

(*e*) a remediation notice served under section 78E of the Environmental Protection Act 1990;
(*f*) an enforcement notice served under section 90B of the Water Resources Act 1991; ...[2]
(*g*) a works notice served under section 161A of the Water Resources Act 1991;
[(*h*) an enforcement notice served under regulation 36 of the Environmental Permitting (England and Wales) Regulations 2007;
(*j*) a suspension notice served under regulation 37 of those Regulations; or
(*k*) an order under regulation 44 of those Regulations.][5]
(*l*) a notice served under regulation 28(2) of the Water Environment (Controlled Activities) (Scotland) Regulations 2005.][4]

(5) A disposal shall not be regarded as falling within subsection (4) above where the removal of the material has been carried out by or on behalf of any of the following bodies:
(*a*) a local authority;
(*b*) a development corporation;
(*c*) the Environment Agency;
(*d*) the Scottish Environment Protection Agency;
(*e*) ...[6]
(*f*) Scottish Enterprise;
(*g*) Highlands and Islands Enterprise;
(*h*) ...[3]

(6) In this section—
"development corporation" means—
(*a*) in England and Wales, a corporation established under section 135 of the Local Government, Planning and Land Act 1980;
(*b*) in Scotland, a corporation established under section 2 of the New Towns (Scotland) Act 1968;
...[6]
"Highlands and Islands Enterprise" means the body established by section 1(*b*) of the Enterprise and New Towns (Scotland) Act 1990;
"land" includes land covered by water;
"Scottish Enterprise" means the corporation established by section 1(*a*) of the Enterprise and New Towns (Scotland) Act 1990;
...[3]

(7) For the purposes of this section—
(*a*) the removal of material includes its removal from one part of the land for disposal on another part of the same land;
(*b*) the clearing of pollutants includes their being cleared from one part of the land for disposal on another part of the same land.][1]

Commentary—*De Voil Indirect Tax Service* **V20.125**.

Amendments—[1] This section inserted by Landfill Tax (Contaminated Land) Order, SI 1996/1529 art 3, with effect from 1 August 1996.

[2] In sub-s (4) word in para (*f*) repealed with effect in England and Wales by the Pollution Prevention and Control (England and Wales) Regulations, SI 2000/1973 reg 39, Sch 10 para 21 with effect from 1 August 2000. With effect in Scotland, paras (*h*)–(*k*) are inserted as follows by virtue of the Pollution Prevention and Control (Scotland) Regulations, SI 2000/323 reg 36, Sch 10 para 6 with effect from 28 September 2000—
"(*h*) an enforcement notice served under regulation 19 of the Pollution Prevention and Control (Scotland) Regulations 2000;
(*j*) a suspension notice served under regulation 20 of those Regulations; or
(*k*) an order under regulation 33 of those Regulations."

[3] Words in sub-s (5)(*h*), and in sub-s (6) definition of "Welsh Development Agency", repealed by the Welsh Development Agency (Transfer of Functions to the National Assembly for Wales and Abolition) Order, SI 2005/3226 art 7(1), Sch 2 para 10 with effect from 23 November 2005.

[4] In sub-s (4) word "or" omitted from after para (*j*) repealed, and para (*l*) and preceding word "or" inserted, by the Water Environment and Water Services (Scotland) Act 2003 (Consequential Provisions and Modifications) Order, SI 2006/1054 art 2, Sch 1 para 2 with effect from 1 April 2006.

[5] Sub-s (4)(*h*)–(*k*) substituted by the Environmental Permitting (England and Wales) Regulations, SI 2007/3538 reg 73, Sch 21 para 25 with effect, in relation to England and Wales, from 6 April 2008.

[6] Sub-s (5)(*e*), and in sub-s (6) definition of "English Partnerships", repealed by the Housing and Regeneration Act 2008 ss 56, 321(1), Sch 8 para 64, Sch 16, with effect from 1 December 2008 (by virtue of SI 2008/3068 arts 1(2), 2(1)(*w*), (3)).

Prospective amendments—Sub-ss (4)(*b*)–(*d*) repealed by the Pollution Prevention and Control Act 1999 Sch 3 with effect from a day to be appointed.

Section 43A to be repealed by the Landfill Tax (Material from Contaminated Land) (Phasing out of Exemption) Order, SI 2008/2669 art 4(a) with effect from 1 April 2012.

[43B Contaminated land: certificates

(1) Subject to subsection (2) below, the Commissioners shall issue a certificate in relation to any land where—
(a) an application in writing is made by a person carrying out, or intending to carry out, a reclamation of that land (the applicant);
(b) the applicant provides to them such information as they may direct, whether generally or as regards that particular case[, within such time as they may direct][2]*;*
(c) the application is made not less than 30 days before the date from which the certificate is to take effect; and
(d) the reclamation qualifies under subsection (7) below.

(2) The Commissioners shall not refuse an application for a certificate in a case where the conditions specified in subsection (1)(a) to (d) above are satisfied unless it appears to them—

(a) necessary to do so for the protection of the revenue; or

(b) except where the applicant is one of the bodies mentioned in subsection (5) of section 43A above, that all or part of the reclamation of land to which the application relates is required in order to comply with a notice or order mentioned in subsection (4) of that section.

(3) The Commissioners may make a certificate subject to such conditions set out in the certificate as they think fit, including (but not restricted to) conditions—

(a) that the certificate is to be in force only in relation to a particular quantity of material;

(b) that the certificate is to be in force only in relation to disposals made at a particular landfill site or sites;

(c) that the certificate is to be in force in relation to part only of the land to which the application relates.[3]

(4) A certificate issued under this section—

(*a*) shall have effect from the date it is issued to the applicant or such later date as the Commissioners may specify in the certificate; and

(*b*) shall cease to have effect on such date as the Commissioners may set out in the certificate, but in any event no later than the day on which the person to whom the certificate was issued ceases to have the intention to carry out any activity involving reclamation of the land in relation to which the certificate was issued.

(5) Where a certificate has been issued to a person, the Commissioners—

(*a*) may vary it by issuing a further certificate to that person; or

(*b*) may withdraw it by giving notice in writing to that person; but this is subject to subsection (6) below.

(6) The Commissioners shall not withdraw a certificate unless it appears to them—

(*a*) necessary to do so for the protection of the revenue;

(*b*) that the reclamation did not in fact qualify under subsection (7) below or no longer so qualifies;

(*c*) that there will not be any or any more disposals within section 43A(2) above of material from the land to which the certificate relates; or

(*d*) except where the person to whom the certificate was issued is one of the bodies mentioned in subsection (5) of section 43A above, that the removal of material from the land to which the certificate relates is required in order to comply with a notice or order mentioned in subsection (4) of that section.

(7) A reclamation qualifies under this subsection if—

(*a*) it is, or is to be, carried out with the object of facilitating development, conservation, the provision of a public park or other amenity, or the use of the land for agriculture or forestry; or

(*b*) in a case other than one within paragraph (*a*) above, it is, or is to be, carried out with the object of reducing or removing the potential of pollutants to cause harm,

and, in either case, the conditions specified in subsection (8) below are satisfied.

(8) The conditions mentioned in subsection (7) above are—

(*a*) that the reclamation constitutes or includes cleaning the land of pollutants which are causing harm or have the potential for causing harm;

(*b*) that, in a case within subsection (7)(*a*) above, those pollutants would (unless cleared) prevent the object concerned being fulfilled; and

(*c*) that all relevant activities have ceased or have ceased to give rise to any pollutants in relation to that land.

(9) For the purposes of subsection (8) above the clearing of pollutants—

(*a*) need not be such that all pollutants are removed;

(*b*) need not be such that pollutants are removed from every part of the land in which they are present;

(*c*) may involve their being cleared from one part of the land and disposed of on another part of the same land.

(10) For the purposes of subsection (8)(*c*) above an activity is relevant if—

(*a*) it has at any time resulted in the presence of pollutants in, on or under the land in question otherwise than—

(i) without the consent of the person who was the occupier of the land at the time, or

(ii) by allowing pollutants to be carried onto the land by air or water, and

(*b*) at that time it was carried out—

(i) by the applicant or a person connected with him, or

(ii) by any person on the land in question.

(11) For the purposes of subsection (10) above—

(*a*) any question whether a person is connected with another shall be determined in accordance with section 839 of the Taxes Act 1988;

(*b*) the occupier of land that is not in fact occupied is the person entitled to occupy it.

Landfill Tax

(12) In this section "land" has the meaning given by section 43A(6) above.][1]

Commentary—*De Voil Indirect Tax Service* **V20.125**.
Simon's Tax Cases—43B(8)(*c*), *Augean plc v R&C Comrs* [2008] STC 2894.
Amendments—[1] This section inserted by Landfill Tax (Contaminated Land) Order, SI 1996/1529 art 3, with effect from 1 August 1996.
[2] Words in sub-s (1)(*b*) inserted by the Landfill Tax (Material from Contaminated Land) (Phasing out of Exemption) Order, SI 2008/2669 art 2(1) with effect from 15 November 2008. This amendment applies in relation to applications made before 15 November 2008 (as well as those made on or after that date) (SI 2008/2669 art 2(2).
[3] Sub-ss (1)–(3) repealed by the Landfill Tax (Material from Contaminated Land) (Phasing out of Exemption) Order, SI 2008/2669 art 3(1)(*a*) with effect from 1 December 2008. This amendment does not have effect until 1 April 2012 in relation to applications made before 1 December 2008.
Prospective amendments—Sub-ss (4)–(12) to be repealed by the Landfill Tax (Material from Contaminated Land) (Phasing out of Exemption) Order, SI 2008/2669 art 4(*b*) with effect from 1 April 2012.

[43C Site restoration

(1) A disposal is not a taxable disposal for the purposes of this Part if—

(*a*) the disposal is of material all of which is treated for the purposes of section 42 above as qualifying material,
(*b*) before the disposal the operator of the landfill site notifies the Commissioners in writing that he is commencing the restoration of all or a part of the site and provides such other written information as the Commissioners may require generally or in the particular case, and
(*c*) the material is deposited on and used in the restoration of the site or part specified in the notification under paragraph (*b*) above.

(2) In this section "restoration" means work, other than capping waste, which is required by a relevant instrument to be carried out to restore a landfill site to use on completion of waste disposal operations.

(3) The following are relevant instruments—

(*a*) a planning consent;
(*b*) …[3]
(*c*) a resolution authorising the disposal of waste on or in land.][1]
[(*d*) a permit authorising the disposal of waste on or in land.][2]

Commentary—*De Voil Indirect Tax Service* **V20.126**.
Simon's Tax Cases—43C(1)(*c*), (2), *C&E Comrs v Ebbcliff Ltd* [2004] STC 1496.
Amendments—[1] This section inserted by Landfill Tax (Site Restoration and Quarries) Order, SI 1999/2075, art 2(*a*), with effect from 1 October 1999.
[2] Sub-s (3)(*d*) inserted by Landfill Tax (Site Restoration, Quarries and Pet Cemeteries) Order, SI 2005/725 arts 2, 3 with effect from 6 April 2005.
[3] Subsection (3)(*b*) repealed by the Environmental Permitting (England and Wales) Regulations, SI 2007/3538 reg 74(2), Sch 23 with effect, in relation to England and Wales, from 6 April 2008.

44 Mining and quarrying

(1) A disposal is not a taxable disposal for the purposes of this Part if it is shown to the satisfaction of the Commissioners that the disposal is of material all of which fulfils each of the conditions set out in subsections (2) to (4) below.

(2) The material must result from commercial mining operations (whether the mining is deep or open-cast) or from commercial quarrying operations.

(3) The material must be naturally occurring material extracted from the earth in the course of the operations.

(4) The material must not have been subjected to, or result from, a non-qualifying process carried out at any stage between the extraction and the disposal.

(5) A non-qualifying process is—

(*a*) a process separate from the mining or quarrying operations, or
(*b*) a process forming part of those operations and permanently altering the material's chemical composition.

Commentary—*De Voil Indirect Tax Service* **V20.123**.

[44A Quarries

(1) A disposal is not a taxable disposal for the purposes of this Part if it is—

(*a*) of material all of which is treated for the purposes of section 42 above as qualifying material,
(*b*) made at a qualifying landfill site, and
(*c*) made, or treated as made, on or after 1st October 1999.

(2) A landfill site is a qualifying landfill site for the purposes of this section if at the time of the disposal—

(*a*) the landfill site is or was a quarry,
(*b*) subject to subsection (3) below, it is a requirement of planning consent in respect of the land in which the quarry or former quarry is situated that it be wholly or partially refilled, and
(*c*) subject to subsection (4) below, the licence[, permit][2] or, as the case may require, resolution authorising disposals on or in the land comprising the site permits only the disposal of material which comprises qualifying material.

(3) Where a quarry—

(*a*) was in existence before 1st October 1999, and

(*b*) quarrying operations ceased before that date,

the requirement referred to in subsection (2)(*b*) must have been imposed on or before that date.

(4) Where a licence [or permit][2] authorising disposals on or in the land does not (apart from the application of this subsection) meet the requirements of subsection (2)(*c*) above and an application has been made to vary the licence [or permit][2] in order to meet them, it shall be deemed to meet them for the period before—

(*a*) the application is disposed of, or

(*b*) the second anniversary of the making of the application if it occurs before the application is disposed of.

(5) For the purposes of subsection (4) an application is disposed of if—

(*a*) it is granted,

(*b*) it is withdrawn,

(*c*) it is refused and there is no right of appeal against the refusal,

(*d*) a time limit for appeal against refusal expires without an appeal having been commenced, or

(*e*) an appeal against refusal is dismissed or withdrawn and there is no further right of appeal.][1]

Commentary—*De Voil Indirect Tax Service* **V20.123**.
Simon's Tax Cases—44A(2)(*b*), *C&E Comrs v Ebbcliff Ltd* [2004] STC 391.
Amendments—[1] This section inserted by Landfill Tax (Site Restoration and Quarries) Order, SI 1999/2075, art 2(*b*), with effect from 1 October 1999.
[2] Words in sub-ss (2)(*c*), (4) inserted by Landfill Tax (Site Restoration, Quarries and Pet Cemeteries) Order, SI 2005/725 arts 2, 4 with effect from 6 April 2005.

45 Pet cemeteries

(1) A disposal is not a taxable disposal for the purposes of this Part if—

(*a*) the disposal is of material consisting entirely of the remains of dead domestic pets, and

(*b*) the landfill site at which the disposal is made fulfils the test set out in subsection (2) below.

(2) The test is that during the relevant period—

(*a*) no landfill disposal was made at the site, or

(*b*) the only landfill disposals made at the site were of material consisting entirely of the remains of dead domestic pets.

(3) For the purposes of subsection (2) above the relevant period—

(*a*) begins with 1st October 1996 or (if later) with the coming into force in relation to the site of the licence[, resolution or permit][1] mentioned in section 66 below, and

(*b*) ends immediately before the disposal mentioned in subsection (1) above.

Commentary—*De Voil Indirect Tax Service* **V20.124**.
Amendment—[1] Words in sub-s (3)(*a*) substituted by Landfill Tax (Site Restoration, Quarries and Pet Cemeteries) Order, SI 2005/725 arts 2, 5 with effect from 6 April 2005.

46 Power to vary

(1) Provision may be made by order to produce the result that—

(*a*) a disposal which would otherwise be a taxable disposal (by virtue of this Part as it applies for the time being) is not a taxable disposal;

(*b*) a disposal which would otherwise not be a taxable disposal (by virtue of this Part as it applies for the time being) is a taxable disposal.

(2) Without prejudice to the generality of subsection (1) above, an order under this section may—

(*a*) confer exemption by reference to certificates issued by the Commissioners and to conditions set out in certificates;

(*b*) allow the Commissioners to direct requirements to be met before certificates can be issued;

[(*c*) provide for reviews and appeals relating to decisions about certificates.][1]

(3) Provision may be made under this section in such way as the Treasury think fit (whether by amending this Part or otherwise).

Order—Landfill Tax (Site Restoration, Quarries and Pet Cemeteries) Order, SI 2005/725.
Amendment—[1] Sub-s (2)(*c*) substituted by the Transfer of Tribunal Functions and Revenue and Customs Appeals Order, SI 2009/56 art 3, Sch 1 para 233 with effect from 1 April 2009. Sub-s (2)(*c*) previously read as follows—

"(*c*) provide for the review of decisions about certificates and for appeals relating to decisions on review."

Administration

47 Registration

(1) The register kept under this section may contain such information as the Commissioners think is required for the purposes of the care and management of the tax.

(2) A person who—

(*a*) carries out taxable activities, and

(*b*) is not registered,

is liable to be registered.

(3) Where—

(*a*) a person at any time forms the intention of carrying out taxable activities, and

(*b*) he is not registered,

he shall notify the Commissioners of his intention.

(4) A person who at any time ceases to have the intention of carrying out taxable activities shall notify the Commissioners of that fact.

(5) Where a person is liable to be registered by virtue of subsection (2) above the Commissioners shall register him with effect from the time when he begins to carry out taxable activities; and this subsection applies whether or not he notifies the Commissioners under subsection (3) above.

(6) Where the Commissioners are satisfied that a person has ceased to carry out taxable activities they may cancel his registration with effect from the earliest practicable time after he so ceased; and this subsection applies whether or not he notifies the Commissioners under subsection (4) above.

(7) Where—

(*a*) a person notifies the Commissioners under subsection (4) above,

(*b*) they are satisfied that he will not carry out taxable activities,

(*c*) they are satisfied that no tax which he is liable to pay is unpaid,

(*d*) they are satisfied that no credit to which he is entitled under regulations made under section 51 below is outstanding, and

(*e*) subsection (8) below does not apply,

the Commissioners shall cancel his registration with effect from the earliest practicable time after he ceases to carry out taxable activities.

(8) Where—

(*a*) a person notifies the Commissioners under subsection (4) above, and

(*b*) they are satisfied that he has not carried out, and will not carry out, taxable activities,

the Commissioners shall cancel his registration with effect from the time when he ceased to have the intention to carry out taxable activities.

(9) For the purposes of this section regulations may make provision—

(*a*) as to the time within which a notification is to be made;

(*b*) as to the form and manner in which any notification is to be made and as to the information to be contained in or provided with it;

(*c*) requiring a person who has made a notification to notify the Commissioners if any information contained in or provided in connection with it is or becomes inaccurate;

(*d*) as to the correction of entries in the register.

(10) References in this Part to a registrable person are to a person who—

(*a*) is registered under this section, or

(*b*) is liable to be registered under this section.

Commentary—*De Voil Indirect Tax Service* **V20.161**.
Regulations—Land fill Tax Regulations, SI 1996/1527.
Cross references—See Landfill Tax Regulations, SI 1996/1527 reg 4 (notification of liability to be registered), SI 1996/1597 reg 5 (changes in particulars), SI 1996/1527 reg 6 (notification of cessation of taxable activities).

48 Information required to keep register up to date

(1) Regulations may make provision requiring a registrable person to notify the Commissioners of particulars which—

(*a*) are of changes in circumstances relating to the registrable person or any business carried on by him,

(*b*) appear to the Commissioners to be required for the purpose of keeping the register kept under section 47 above up to date, and

(*c*) are of a prescribed description.

(2) Regulations may make provision—

(*a*) as to the time within which a notification is to be made;

(*b*) as to the form and manner in which a notification is to be made;

(*c*) requiring a person who has made a notification to notify the Commissioners if any information contained in it is inaccurate.

Regulations—Landfill Tax Regulations, SI 1996/1527.
Cross references—See Landfill Tax Regulations, SI 1996/1527 reg 5 (changes in particulars).

49 Accounting for tax and time for payment

Regulations may provide that a registrable person shall—

(*a*) account for tax by reference to such periods (accounting periods) as may be determined by or under the regulations;

(*b*) make, in relation to accounting periods, returns in such form …[1] and at such times as may be so determined;

(*c*) pay tax at such times and in such manner as may be so determined.

Regulations—Landfill Tax Regulations, SI 1996/1527.
Cross references—See Landfill Tax Regulations, SI 1996/1527 reg 11 (making of returns), SI 1996/1527 reg 15 (payment of tax).
Amendments—[1] Words "as may be prescribed" in s 49(*b*) repealed by FA 2009 s 119, Sch 60 para 12 with effect from 21 July 2009. The omission of these words does not affect any regulation made under this provision before the passing of FA 2009, and does not prevent the powers conferred by the provision from being used after the passing of FA 2009 to revoke any regulations made under the powers before that time; FA 2009 s 119, Sch 60 para 13(3).

50 Power to assess

(1) Where—

(*a*) a person has failed to make any returns required to be made under this Part,
(*b*) a person has failed to keep any documents necessary to verify returns required to be made under this Part,
(*c*) a person has failed to afford the facilities necessary to verify returns required to be made under this Part, or
(*d*) it appears to the Commissioners that returns required to be made by a person under this Part are incomplete or incorrect,

the Commissioners may assess the amount of tax due from the person concerned to the best of their judgment and notify it to him.
(2) Where a person has for an accounting period been paid an amount to which he purports to be entitled under regulations made under section 51 below, then, to the extent that the amount ought not to have been paid or would not have been paid had the facts been known or been as they later turn out to be, the Commissioners may assess the amount as being tax due from him for that period and notify it to him accordingly.

(3) Where a person is assessed under subsections (1) and (2) above in respect of the same accounting period the assessments may be combined and notified to him as one assessment.

(4) Where the person failing to make a return, or making a return which appears to the Commissioners to be incomplete or incorrect, was required to make the return as a personal representative, trustee in bankruptcy, receiver, liquidator or person otherwise acting in a representative capacity in relation to another person, subsection (1) above shall apply as if the reference to tax due from him included a reference to tax due from that other person.

(5) An assessment under subsection (1) or (2) above of an amount of tax due for an accounting period shall not be made after the later of the following—

(*a*) two years after the end of the accounting period;
(*b*) one year after evidence of facts, sufficient in the Commissioners' opinion to justify the making of the assessment, comes to their knowledge;

but where further such evidence comes to their knowledge after the making of an assessment under subsection (1) or (2) above another assessment may be made under the subsection concerned in addition to any earlier assessment.

(6) Where—

(*a*) as a result of a person's failure to make a return in relation to an accounting period the Commissioners have made an assessment under subsection (1) above for that period,
(*b*) the tax assessed has been paid but no proper return has been made in relation to the period to which the assessment related, and
(*c*) as a result of a failure to make a return in relation to a later accounting period, being a failure by the person referred to in paragraph (*a*) above or a person acting in a representative capacity in relation to him, as mentioned in subsection (4) above, the Commissioners find it necessary to make another assessment under subsection (1) above,

then, if the Commissioners think fit, having regard to the failure referred to in paragraph (*a*) above, they may specify in the assessment referred to in paragraph (*c*) above an amount of tax greater than that which they would otherwise have considered to be appropriate.

(7) Where an amount has been assessed and notified to any person under subsection (1) or (2) above it shall be deemed to be an amount of tax due from him and may be recovered accordingly unless, or except to the extent that, the assessment has subsequently been withdrawn or reduced.

(8) For the purposes of this section notification to—

(*a*) a personal representative, trustee in bankruptcy, receiver or liquidator, or
(*b*) a person otherwise acting in a representative capacity in relation to another person,

shall be treated as notification to the person in relation to whom the person mentioned in paragraph (*a*) above, or the first person mentioned in paragraph (*b*) above, acts.

(9) Subsection (5) above has effect subject to paragraph 33 of Schedule 5 to this Act.

(10) In this section "trustee in bankruptcy" means, as respects Scotland, an interim or permanent trustee (within the meaning of the Bankruptcy (Scotland) Act 1985) or a trustee acting under a trust deed (within the meaning of that Act).

Credit

51 Credit: general

(1) Regulations may provide that where—

(*a*) a person has paid or is liable to pay tax, and
(*b*) prescribed conditions are fulfilled,

the person shall be entitled to credit of such an amount as is found in accordance with prescribed rules.

(2) Regulations may make provision as to the manner in which a person is to benefit from credit, and in particular may make provision—

(*a*) that a person shall be entitled to credit by reference to accounting periods;
(*b*) that a person shall be entitled to deduct an amount equal to his total credit for an accounting period from the total amount of tax due from him for the period;
(*c*) that if no tax is due from a person for an accounting period but he is entitled to credit for the period, the amount of the credit shall be paid to him by the Commissioners;
(*d*) that if the amount of credit to which a person is entitled for an accounting period exceeds the amount of tax due from him for the period, an amount equal to the excess shall be paid to him by the Commissioners;
(*e*) for the whole or part of any credit to be held over to be credited for a subsequent accounting period;
(*f*) as to the manner in which a person who has ceased to be registrable is to benefit from credit.

(3) Regulations under subsection (2)(*c*) or (*d*) above may provide that where at the end of an accounting period an amount is due to a person who has failed to submit returns for an earlier period as required by this Part, the Commissioners may withhold payment of the amount until he has complied with that requirement.

(4) Regulations under subsection (2)(*e*) above may provide for credit to be held over either on the person's application or in accordance with directions given by the Commissioners from time to time; and the regulations may allow directions to be given generally or with regard to particular cases.

(5) Regulations may provide that—

(*a*) no benefit shall be conferred in respect of credit except on a claim made in such manner and at such time as may be determined by or under regulations;
(*b*) payment in respect of credit shall be made subject to such conditions (if any) as the Commissioners think fit to impose, including conditions as to repayment in specified circumstances;
(*c*) deduction in respect of credit shall be made subject to such conditions (if any) as the Commissioners think fit to impose, including conditions as to the payment to the Commissioners, in specified circumstances, of an amount representing the whole or part of the amount deducted.

(6) Regulations may require a claim by a person to be made in a return required by provision made under section 49 above.

(7) Nothing in section 52 or 53 below shall be taken to derogate from the power to make regulations under this section (whether with regard to bad debts, the environment or any other matter).

Commentary—*De Voil Indirect Tax Service* **V20.145**.
Regulations—Landfill Tax Regulations, SI 1996/1527.
Cross references—See Landfill Tax Regulations, SI 1996/1527 regs 17–20 (credit: general), SI 1996/1527 reg 21 (credit permanent removals etc).

52 Bad debts

(1) Regulations may be made under section 51 above with a view to securing that a person is entitled to credit if—

(*a*) he carries out a taxable activity as a result of which he becomes entitled to a debt which turns out to be bad (in whole or in part), and
(*b*) such other conditions as may be prescribed are fulfilled.

(2) The regulations may include provision under section 51(5)(*b*) or (*c*) above requiring repayment or payment if it turns out that it was not justified to regard a debt as bad (or to regard it as bad to the extent that it was so regarded).

(3) The regulations may include provision for determining whether, and to what extent, a debt is to be taken to be bad.

Commentary—*De Voil Indirect Tax Service* **V20.146**.
Regulations—Landfill Tax Regulations, SI 1996/1527.
Cross references—See Landfill Tax Regulations, SI 1996/1527 reg 22–29 (credit: bad debts).

53 Bodies concerned with the environment

(1) Regulations may be made under section 51 above with a view to securing that a person is entitled to credit if—

(*a*) he pays a sum to a body whose objects are or include the protection of the environment, and

(*b*) such other conditions as may be prescribed are fulfilled.

(2) The regulations may in particular prescribe conditions—

(*a*) requiring bodies to which sums are paid (environmental bodies) to be approved by another body (the regulatory body);

(*b*) requiring the regulatory body to be approved by the Commissioners;

(*c*) requiring sums to be paid with the intention that they be expended on such matters connected with the protection of the environment as may be prescribed.

(3) The regulations may include provision under section 51(5)(*b*) or (*c*) above requiring repayment or payment if—

(*a*) a sum is not in fact expended on matters prescribed under subsection (2)(*c*) above, or

(*b*) a prescribed condition turns out not to have been fulfilled.

(4) The regulations may include—

(*a*) provision for determining the amount of credit (including provision for limiting it);

(*b*) provision that matters connected with the protection of the environment include such matters as overheads (including administration) of environmental bodies and the regulatory body;

(*c*) provision as to the matters by reference to which an environmental body or the regulatory body can be, and remain, approved (including matters relating to the functions and activities of any such body);

[(*ca*) provision for an environmental body to be and remain approved only if it complies with conditions imposed from time to time by the regulatory body or for the regulatory body to be and remain approved only if it complies with conditions imposed from time to time by the Commissioners (including provision for the variation or revocation of such conditions);][1]

(*d*) provision allowing [the withdrawal of approval of an environmental body by the Commissioners or by the regulatory body, and the withdrawal of approval of the regulatory body by the Commissioners,][2] (whether prospectively or retrospectively);

(*e*) provision that, if approval of the regulatory body is withdrawn, another body may be approved in its place or its functions may be performed by the Commissioners;

(*f*) provision allowing the Commissioners to disclose to the regulatory body information which relates to the tax affairs of persons carrying out taxable activities and which is relevant to the credit scheme established by the regulations.

Commentary—*De Voil Indirect Tax Service* **V20.148**.
Regulations—Landfill Tax Regulations, SI 1996/1527.
Cross references—See Landfill Tax Regulations, SI 1996/1527 regs 30–36 (credit: bodies concerned with the environment).
Amendments—[1] Sub-s (4)(*ca*) inserted by FA 2007 s 24. This amendment is deemed to have come into force on 22 March 2007.
[2] Words in sub-s (4)(*d*) substituted by FA 2008 s 151(2). This amendment is treated as having come into force on 19 March 2008.

[Appeals][4]

54 Review of Commissioners' decisions

(1) [Subject to section 55, an appeal shall lie to an appeal tribunal from any person who is or will be affected by any of the following decisions—][4]

(*a*) a decision as to the registration or cancellation of registration of any person under this Part;

(*b*) a decision as to whether tax is chargeable in respect of a disposal or as to how much tax is chargeable;

[(*ba*) a decision to [withdraw a certificate under section 43B above][3];

(*bb*) *a decision to make a certificate issued under section 43B above subject to a condition that it is to be in force in relation to part only of the land to which the application for the certificate related;*][1, 3]

(*c*) a decision as to whether a person is entitled to credit by virtue of regulations under section 51 above or as to how much credit a person is entitled to or as to the manner in which he is to benefit from credit;

[(*ca*) a decision to withdraw approval of an environmental body under any provision contained in regulations by virtue of section 53(4)(*d*) above;][2]

(*d*) a decision as to an assessment falling within subsection (2) below or as to the amount of such an assessment;

(*e*) a decision to refuse a request under section 58(3) below;

(*f*) a decision to refuse an application under section 59 below;

(*g*) a decision as to whether conditions set out in a specification under the authority of provision made under section 68(4)(*b*) below are met in relation to a disposal;

(*h*) a decision to give a direction under any provision contained in regulations by virtue of section 68(5) below;

(*i*) a decision as to a claim for the repayment of an amount under paragraph 14 of Schedule 5 to this Act;

(*j*) a decision as to liability to a penalty under Part V of that Schedule or as to the amount of such a penalty;
(*k*) a decision under paragraph 19 of that Schedule (as mentioned in paragraph 19(5));
(*l*) a decision as to any liability to pay interest under paragraph 26 or 27 of that Schedule or as to the amount of the interest payable;
(*m*) a decision as to any liability to pay interest under paragraph 29 of that Schedule or as to the amount of the interest payable;
(*n*) a decision to require any security under paragraph 31 of that Schedule or as to its amount;
(*o*) a decision as to the amount of any penalty or interest specified in an assessment under paragraph 32 of that Schedule.

(2) An assessment falls within this subsection if it is an assessment under section 50 above in respect of an accounting period in relation to which a return required to be made by virtue of regulations under section 49 above has been made.

(3)–(8) …[4]

Commentary—*De Voil Indirect Tax Service* **V20.174**.
Cross references—See FA 1997 Sch 5 para 19(3) (review of a decision contained in an assessment under FA 1997 Sch 5 para 14, 15 or 17).
Amendments—[1] Sub-paras (1)(*ba*), (*bb*) inserted by the Landfill Tax (Contaminated Land) Order, SI 1996/1529 art 4, with effect from 1 October 1996 (see s 57 below and SI 1996/1529 art 1).
[2] Sub-s (1)(*ca*) inserted by FA 2008 s 151(3). This amendment is treated as having come into force on 19 March 2008.
[3] In sub-s (1)(*ba*), words substituted for words "refuse an application for a certificate under section 43B above, or to withdraw such a certificate", and sub-s (1)(*bb*) repealed, by the Landfill Tax (Material from Contaminated Land) (Phasing out of Exemption) Order, SI 2008/2669 art 3(1)(*b*), (*c*) with effect from 1 December 2008. These amendments do not have effect until 1 April 2012 in relation to applications made before 1 December 2008.
[4] Heading substituted for previous heading "Review and appeal"; words at the beginning of sub-s (1) substituted for the words "This section applies to the following decisions of the Commissioners"; sub-ss (3)–(8) repealed, by the Transfer of Tribunal Functions and Revenue and Customs Appeals Order, SI 2009/56 art 3, Sch 1 para 234 with effect from 1 April 2009, subject to transitional and savings provisions in Sch 3 paras 2, 3. Sub-ss (3)–(8) previously read as follows—

"(3) Any person who is or will be affected by any decision to which this section applies may by notice in writing to the Commissioners require them to review the decision.

(4) The Commissioners shall not be required under this section to review any decision unless the notice requiring the review is given before the end of the period of 45 days beginning with the day on which written notification of the decision, or of the assessment containing the decision, was first given to the person requiring the review.

(5) For the purposes of subsection (4) above it shall be the duty of the Commissioners to give written notification of any decision to which this section applies to any person who—

(*a*) requests such a notification,
(*b*) has not previously been given written notification of that decision, and
(*c*) if given such a notification, will be entitled to require a review of the decision under this section.

(6) A person shall be entitled to give a notice under this section requiring a decision to be reviewed for a second or subsequent time only if—

(*a*) the grounds on which he requires the further review are that the Commissioners did not, on any previous review, have the opportunity to consider certain facts or other matters, and
(*b*) he does not, on the further review, require the Commissioners to consider any facts or matters which were considered on a previous review except in so far as they are relevant to any issue not previously considered.

(7) Where the Commissioners are required in accordance with this section to review any decision it shall be their duty to do so; and on the review they may withdraw, vary or confirm the decision.

(8) Where—

(*a*) it is the duty under this section of the Commissioners to review any decision, and
(*b*) they do not, within the period of 45 days beginning with the day on which the review was required, give notice to the person requiring it of their determination on the review,

they shall be deemed for the purposes of this Part to have confirmed the decision."

Prospective amendments—Sub-ss (1)(*ba*) to be repealed by the Landfill Tax (Material from Contaminated Land) (Phasing out of Exemption) Order, SI 2008/2669 art 4(*c*) with effect from 1 April 2012.

[54A Offer of review

(1) HMRC must offer a person (P) a review of a decision that has been notified to P if an appeal lies under section 54 in respect of the decision.

(2) The offer of the review must be made by notice given to P at the same time as the decision is notified to P.

(3) This section does not apply to the notification of the conclusions of a review.][1]

Amendment—[1] Sections 54A–54G inserted by the Transfer of Tribunal Functions and Revenue and Customs Appeals Order, SI 2009/56 art 3, Sch 1 para 235 with effect from 1 April 2009.

[54B Right to require review

(1) Any person (other than P) who has the right of appeal under section 54 against a decision may require HMRC to review that decision if that person has not appealed to the appeal tribunal under section 54G.

(2) A notification that such a person requires a review must be made within 30 days of that person becoming aware of the decision.][1]

Amendment—[1] Sections 54A–54G inserted by the Transfer of Tribunal Functions and Revenue and Customs Appeals Order, SI 2009/56 art 3, Sch 1 para 235 with effect from 1 April 2009.

[54C Review by HMRC

(1) HMRC must review a decision if—

(*a*) they have offered a review of the decision under section 54A, and (*b*) P notifies HMRC accepting the offer within 30 days from the date of the document containing the notification of the offer.

(2) But P may not notify acceptance of the offer if P has already appealed to the appeal tribunal under section 54G.

(3) HMRC must review a decision if a person other than P notifies them under section 54B.

(4) HMRC shall not be required to review a decision if P, or another person, has appealed to the appeal tribunal under section 54G in respect of the decision.][1]

Amendment—[1] Sections 54A–54G inserted by the Transfer of Tribunal Functions and Revenue and Customs Appeals Order, SI 2009/56 art 3, Sch 1 para 235 with effect from 1 April 2009.

[54D Extensions of time

(1) If under section 54A, HMRC have offered P a review of a decision, HMRC may within the relevant period notify P that the relevant period is extended.

(2) If under section 54B another person may require HMRC to review a matter, HMRC may within the relevant period notify the other person that the relevant period is extended.

(3) If notice is given the relevant period is extended to the end of 30 days from—

(*a*) the date of the notice, or

(*b*) any other date set out in the notice or a further notice.

(4) In this section "relevant period" means—

(*a*) the period of 30 days referred to in—

(i) section 54C(1)(*b*) (in a case falling within subsection (1)), or

(ii) section 54B(2) (in a case falling within subsection (2)), or

(*b*) if notice has been given under subsection (1) or (2), that period as extended (or as most recently extended) in accordance with subsection (3).][1]

Amendment—[1] Sections 54A–54G inserted by the Transfer of Tribunal Functions and Revenue and Customs Appeals Order, SI 2009/56 art 3, Sch 1 para 235 with effect from 1 April 2009.

[54E Review out of time

(1) This section applies if—

(*a*) HMRC have offered a review of a decision under section 54A and P does not accept the offer within the time allowed under section 54C(1)(*b*) or 54D(3); or

(*b*) a person who requires a review under section 54B does not notify HMRC within the time allowed under that section or section 54D(3).

(2) HMRC must review the decision under section 54C if—

(*a*) after the time allowed, P, or the other person, notifies HMRC in writing requesting a review out of time,

(*b*) HMRC are satisfied that P, or the other person, had a reasonable excuse for not accepting the offer or requiring review within the time allowed, and

(*c*) HMRC are satisfied that P, or the other person, made the request without unreasonable delay after the excuse had ceased to apply.

(3) HMRC shall not be required to review a decision if P, or another person, has appealed to the appeal tribunal under section 54G in respect of the decision.][1]

Amendment—[1] Sections 54A–54G inserted by the Transfer of Tribunal Functions and Revenue and Customs Appeals Order, SI 2009/56 art 3, Sch 1 para 235 with effect from 1 April 2009.

[54F Nature of review etc

(1) This section applies if HMRC are required to undertake a review under section 54C or 54E.

(2) The nature and extent of the review are to be such as appear appropriate to HMRC in the circumstances.

(3) For the purpose of subsection (2), HMRC must, in particular, have regard to steps taken before the beginning of the review—

(*a*) by HMRC in reaching the decision, and

(*b*) by any person in seeking to resolve disagreement about the decision.

(4) The review must take account of any representations made by P, or the other person, at a stage which gives HMRC a reasonable opportunity to consider them.

(5) The review may conclude that the decision is to be—

(*a*) upheld,

(*b*) varied, or

(*c*) cancelled.

(6) HMRC must give P, or the other person, notice of the conclusions of the review and their reasoning within—

(*a*) a period of 45 days beginning with the relevant date, or

(*b*) such other period as HMRC and P, or the other person, may agree.

(7) In subsection (6) "relevant date" means—

(*a*) the date HMRC received P's notification accepting the offer of a review (in a case falling within section 54A), or

(*b*) the date HMRC received notification from another person requiring review (in a case falling within section 54B), or

(*c*) the date on which HMRC decided to undertake the review (in a case falling within section 54E).

(8) Where HMRC are required to undertake a review but do not give notice of the conclusions within the time period specified in subsection (6), the conclusion of the review is deemed to be that the decision is upheld.

(9) HMRC must notify the appellant of any conclusion under subsection (8).][1]

Amendment—[1] Sections 54A–54G inserted by the Transfer of Tribunal Functions and Revenue and Customs Appeals Order, SI 2009/56 art 3, Sch 1 para 235 with effect from 1 April 2009.

[54G Bringing of appeals

(1) An appeal under section 54 is to be made to the appeal tribunal before—

(*a*) the end of the period of 30 days beginning with—

(i) in a case where P is the appellant, the date of the document notifying the decision to which the appeal relates, or

(ii) in a case where a person other than P is the appellant, the date that person becomes aware of the decision, or

(*b*) if later, the end of the relevant period (within the meaning of section 54D).

(2) But that is subject to subsections (3) to (5).

(3) In a case where HMRC are required to undertake a review under section 54C—

(*a*) an appeal may not be made until the conclusion date, and

(*b*) any appeal is to be made within the period of 30 days beginning with the conclusion date.

(4) In a case where HMRC are requested to undertake a review by virtue of section 54E—

(*a*) an appeal may not be made—

(i) unless HMRC have decided whether or not to undertake a review, and

(ii) if HMRC decide to undertake a review, until the conclusion date; and

(*b*) any appeal is to be made within the period of 30 days beginning with—

(i) the conclusion date (if HMRC decide to undertake a review), or

(ii) the date on which HMRC decide not to undertake a review.

(5) In a case where section 54F(8) applies, an appeal may be made at any time from the end of the period specified in section 54F(6) to the date 30 days after the conclusion date.

(6) An appeal may be made after the end of the period specified in subsection (1), (3)(*b*), (4)(*b*) or (5) if the appeal tribunal gives permission to do so.

(7) In this section "conclusion date" means the date of the document notifying the conclusions of the review.][1]

Amendment—[1] Sections 54A–54G inserted by the Transfer of Tribunal Functions and Revenue and Customs Appeals Order, SI 2009/56 art 3, Sch 1 para 235 with effect from 1 April 2009.

55 [Appeals: further provisions][1]

(1), (2) ...[1]

[(3) Subject to subsections (3A) and (3B), where an appeal under section 54 relates to a decision falling within section 54(1)(*b*) or (*d*), it shall not be entertained unless the amount which HMRC have determined to be payable as tax has been paid or deposited with them.

(3A) In a case where the amount determined to be payable as tax has not been paid or deposited an appeal may be entertained if—

(*a*) HMRC are satisfied (on the application of the appellant), or

(*b*) the appeal tribunal decides (HMRC not being so satisfied and on the application of the appellant),

that the requirement to pay or deposit the amount determined would cause the appellant to suffer hardship.

(3B) Notwithstanding the provisions of sections 11 and 13 of the Tribunals, Courts and Enforcement Act 2007, the decision of the tribunal as to the issue of hardship is final.][1]

(4) On an appeal under this section against an assessment to a penalty under paragraph 18 of Schedule 5 to this Act, the burden of proof as to the matters specified in paragraphs (*a*) and (*b*) of sub-paragraph (1) of paragraph 18 shall lie upon the Commissioners.

Cross references—See FA 1997 Sch 5 para 19(3) (appeal following decision by Commissioners contained in an assessment under FA 1997 Sch 5 para 14, 15 or 17).

Amendment—[1] Heading substituted for former heading "Appeals: general"; sub-ss (1), (2) repealed; sub-s (3) substituted, sub-ss (3A), (3B) inserted by the Transfer of Tribunal Functions and Revenue and Customs Appeals Order, SI 2009/56 art 3, Sch 1 para 236 with effect from 1 April 2009, subject to transitional and savings provisions in Sch 3 paras 2, 3. Sub-ss (1), (2), (3) previously read as follows—

"(1) Subject to the following provisions of this section, an appeal shall lie to an appeal tribunal with respect to any of the following decisions—

(*a*) any decision by the Commissioners on a review under section 54 above (including a deemed confirmation under subsection (8) of that section);

(*b*) any decision by the Commissioners on such review of a decision referred to in section 54(1) above as the Commissioners have agreed to undertake in consequence of a request made after the end of the period mentioned in section 54(4) above.

(2) Where an appeal is made under this section by a person who is required to make returns by virtue of regulations under section 49 above, the appeal shall not be entertained unless the appellant—

(*a*) has made all the returns which he is required to make by virtue of those regulations, and

(*b*) has paid the amounts shown in those returns as payable by him.

(3) Where an appeal is made under this section with respect to a decision falling within section 54(1)(*b*) or (*d*) above the appeal shall not be entertained unless—

(*a*) the amount which the Commissioners have determined to be payable as tax has been paid or deposited with them, or

(*b*) on being satisfied that the appellant would otherwise suffer hardship the Commissioners agree or the tribunal decides that it should be entertained notwithstanding that that amount has not been so paid or deposited."

56 Appeals: other provisions

(1) …[1]

(2) [Where on an appeal under section 54][1]—

(*a*) it is found that the amount specified in the assessment is less than it ought to have been, and

(*b*) the tribunal gives a direction specifying the correct amount,

the assessment shall have effect as an assessment of the amount specified the direction and that amount shall be deemed to have been notified to the appellant.

(3) Where on an appeal under section 55 above it is found that the whole or part of any amount paid or deposited in pursuance of section 55(3) above is not due, so much of that amount as is found not to be due shall be repaid with interest [at the rate applicable under section 197 of this Act][1].

(4) Where on an appeal under section 55 above it is found that the whole or part of any amount due to the appellant by virtue of regulations under section 51(2)(*c*) or (*d*) or (*f*) above has not been paid, so much of that amount as is found not to have been paid shall be paid with interest [at the rate applicable under section 197 of this Act][1].

(5) Where an appeal under section 55 above has been entertained notwithstanding that an amount determined by the Commissioners to be payable as tax has not been paid or deposited and it is found on the appeal that that amount is due [it shall be paid with interest at the rate applicable under section 197 of this Act][1].

[(5A) Interest under subsection (5) shall be paid without any deduction of income tax.][1]

(6) Without prejudice to paragraph 25 of Schedule 5 to this Act, nothing in section 55 above shall be taken to confer on a tribunal any power to vary an amount assessed by way of penalty except in so far as it is necessary to reduce it to the amount which is appropriate under paragraphs 18 to 24 of that Schedule.

(7) Without prejudice to paragraph 28 of Schedule 5 to this Act, nothing in section 55 above shall be taken to confer on a tribunal any power to vary an amount assessed by way of interest except in so far as it is necessary to reduce it to the amount which is appropriate under paragraph 26 or 27 of that Schedule.

[(8) Sections 85 and 85B of the Value Added Tax Act 1994 (settling of appeals by agreement and payment of tax where there is a further appeal) shall have effect as if—

(*a*) the references to section 83 of that Act included references to section 54 of this Act, and

(*b*) the references to value added tax included references to landfill tax.][1]

Cross references—See FA 1997 Sch 5 para 19(3) (appeal following decision by Commissioners contained in an assessment under FA 1997 Sch 5 para 14, 15 or 17).

Amendment—[1] The following amendments made by the Transfer of Tribunal Functions and Revenue and Customs Appeals Order, SI 2009/56 art 3, Sch 1 para 237 with effect from 1 April 2009, subject to transitional and savings provisions in Sch 3 paras 2, 3, 9—

- sub-s (1) repealed;
- in sub-s (2) words substituted for the words "Where on the appeal";
- in sub-ss (3), (4) words substituted for the words "at such rate as the tribunal may determine";
- in sub-s (5) words substituted for the words "the tribunal may, if it thinks fit, direct that that amount shall be paid with interest at such rate as may be specified in the direction";
- sub-s (5A) inserted;
- sub-s (8) substituted.

Sub-ss (1), (8) previously read as follows—

"(1) Subsection (2) below applies where the Commissioners make a decision falling within section 54(1)(*d*) above and on a review of it there is a further decision with respect to which an appeal is made under section 55 above; and the reference here to a further decision includes a reference to a deemed confirmation under section 54(8) above."

"(8) Sections 85 and 87 of the Value Added Tax Act 1994 (settling of appeals by agreement and enforcement of certain decisions of tribunal) shall have effect as if—

(*a*) the references to section 83 of that Act included references to section 55 above, and

(*b*) the references to value added tax included references to landfill tax.".

57 Review and appeal: commencement

Sections 54 to 56 above shall come into force on—

(*a*) 1st October 1996, or

(*b*) such earlier day as may be appointed by order.

Miscellaneous

58 Partnership, bankruptcy, transfer of business, etc

(1) As regards any case where a business is carried on in partnership or by another unincorporated body, regulations may make provision for determining by what persons anything required by this Part to be done by a person is to be done.

(2) The registration under this Part of an unincorporated body other than a partnership may be in the name of the body concerned; and in determining whether taxable activities are carried out by such a body no account shall be taken of any change in its members.

(3) The registration under this Part of a body corporate carrying on a business in several divisions may, if the body corporate so requests and the Commissioners see fit, be in the names of those divisions.

(4) As regards any case where a person carries on a business of a person who has died or become bankrupt or incapacitated or whose estate has been sequestrated, or of a person which is in liquidation or receivership or [administration][1], regulations may—

(*a*) require the first-mentioned person to inform the Commissioners of the fact that he is carrying on the business and of the event that has led to his carrying it on;

(*b*) make provision allowing the person to be treated for a limited time as if he were the other person;

(*c*) make provision for securing continuity in the application of this Part where a person is so treated.

(5) Regulations may make provision for securing continuity in the application of this Part in cases where a business carried on by a person is transferred to another person as a going concern.

(6) Regulations under subsection (5) above may in particular—

(*a*) require the transferor to inform the Commissioners of the transfer;

(*b*) provide for liabilities and duties under this Part of the transferor to become, to such extent as may be provided by the regulations, liabilities and duties of the transferee;

(*c*) provide for any right of either of them to repayment or credit in respect of tax to be satisfied by making a repayment or allowing a credit to the other;

but the regulations may provide that no such provision as is mentioned in paragraph (*b*) or (*c*) of this subsection shall have effect in relation to any transferor and transferee unless an application in that behalf has been made by them under the regulations.

Regulations—Landfill Tax Regulations, SI 1996/1527.

Cross references—See Landfill Tax Regulations, SI 1996/1527 reg 7 (transfer of a going concern), SI 1996/1527 reg 8 (representation of an unincorporated body), SI 1996/1527 reg 9 (bankruptcy or incapacity of registrable persons).

Amendments—[1] Words in sub-s (4) substituted by the Enterprise Act 2002 (Insolvency) Order, SI 2003/2096 art 4, Schedule paras 27, 28 with effect from 15 September 2003. This amendment does not apply in relation to any case where a petition for an administration order was presented before that date: SI 2003/2096, arts 1(1), 6.

59 Groups of companies

(1) Where under the following provisions of this section any bodies corporate are treated as members of a group, for the purposes of this Part—

(*a*) any liability of a member of the group to pay tax shall be taken to be a liability of the representative member;

(*b*) the representative member shall be taken to carry out any taxable activities which a member of the group would carry out (apart from this section) by virtue of section 69 below;

(*c*) all members of the group shall be jointly and severally liable for any tax due from the representative member.

(2) Two or more bodies corporate are eligible to be treated as members of a group if the condition mentioned in subsection (3) below is fulfilled and—

(*a*) one of them controls each of the others,

(*b*) one person (whether a body corporate or an individual) controls all of them, or

(*c*) two or more individuals carrying on a business in partnership control all of them.

(3) The condition is that the prospective representative member has an established place of business in the United Kingdom.

(4) Where an application to that effect is made to the Commissioners with respect to two or more bodies corporate eligible to be treated as members of a group, then—

(*a*) from the beginning of an accounting period they shall be so treated, and

(*b*) one of them shall be the representative member,

unless the Commissioners refuse the application; and the Commissioners shall not refuse the application unless it appears to them necessary to do so for the protection of the revenue.

(5) Where any bodies corporate are treated as members of a group and an application to that effect is made to the Commissioners, then, from the beginning of an accounting period—

(*a*) a further body eligible to be so treated shall be included among the bodies so treated,

(*b*) a body corporate shall be excluded from the bodies so treated,

(*c*) another member of the group shall be substituted as the representative member, or
(*d*) the bodies corporate shall no longer be treated as members of a group,

unless the application is to the effect mentioned in paragraph (*a*) or (*c*) above and the Commissioners refuse the application.

(6) The Commissioners may refuse an application under subsection (5)(*a*) or (*c*) above only if it appears to them necessary to do so for the protection of the revenue.

(7) Where a body corporate is treated as a member of a group as being controlled by any person and it appears to the Commissioners that it has ceased to be so controlled, they shall, by notice given to that person, terminate that treatment from such date as may be specified in the notice.

(8) An application under this section with respect to any bodies corporate must be made by one of those bodies or by the person controlling them and must be made not less than 90 days before the date from which it is to take effect, or at such later time as the Commissioners may allow.

(9) For the purposes of this section a body corporate shall be taken to control another body corporate if it is empowered by statute to control that body's activities or if it is that body's holding company within the meaning of section [1159 of and Schedule 6 to][1] the Companies Act [2006][1]; and an individual or individuals shall be taken to control a body corporate if he or they, were he or they a company, would be that body's holding company within the meaning of [those sections][1].

Amendments—[1] In sub-s (9), words substituted for words "736 of", "1985" and "that section", by the Companies Act 2006 (Consequential Amendments) (Taxes and National Insurance) Order, SI 2009/1890 art 4(1)(*c*) with effect from 1 October 2009.

60 Information, powers, penalties, [secondary liability,][1] etc

Schedule 5 to this Act (which contains provisions relating to information, powers, penalties[, secondary liability][1] and other matters) shall have effect.

Amendments—[1] Words inserted by FA 2000 s 142(1), (2) with effect from 28 July 2000.

61 Taxable disposals: special provisions

(1) Where—

(*a*) a taxable disposal is in fact made on a particular day,
(*b*) within the period of 14 days beginning with that day the person liable to pay tax in respect of the disposal issues a landfill invoice in respect of the disposal, and
(*c*) he has not notified the Commissioners in writing that he elects not to avail himself of this subsection,

for the purposes of this Part the disposal shall be treated as made at the time the invoice is issued.

(2) The reference in subsection (1) above to a landfill invoice is to a document containing such particulars as regulations may prescribe for the purposes of that subsection.

(3) The Commissioners may at the request of a person direct that subsection (1) above shall apply—

(*a*) in relation to disposals in respect of which he is liable to pay tax, or
(*b*) in relation to such of them as may be specified in the direction,

as if for the period of 14 days there were substituted such longer period as may be specified in the direction.

Regulations—Landfill Tax Regulations, SI 1996/1527.
Cross references—See Landfill Tax Regulations, SI 1996/1527 reg 37 (contents of a landfill invoice).

62 Taxable disposals: regulations

(1) For the purposes of this Part, regulations may make provision under this section in relation to a disposal which is a taxable disposal (or would be apart from the regulations).

(2) The regulations may provide that if particular conditions are fulfilled—

(a) the disposal shall be treated as not being a taxable disposal, or
(b) the disposal shall, to the extent found in accordance with prescribed rules, be treated as not being a taxable disposal.

(3) The regulations may provide that if particular conditions are fulfilled—

(a) the disposal shall be treated as made at a time which is found in accordance with prescribed rules and which falls after the time when it would be regarded as made apart from the regulations, or
(b) the disposal shall, to the extent found in accordance with prescribed rules, be treated as made at a time which is found in accordance with prescribed rules and which falls after the time when it would be regarded as made apart from the regulations.

(4) In finding the time when the disposal would be regarded as made apart from the regulations, section 61(1) above and any direction under section 61(3) above shall be taken into account.

(5) The regulations may be framed by reference to—

(a) conditions specified in the regulations or by the Commissioners or by an authorised person, or
(b) any combination of such conditions;

and the regulations may specify conditions, or allow conditions to be specified, generally or with regard to particular cases.

(6) The regulations may make provision under subsections (2)(b) and (3)(b) above in relation to the same disposal.

(7) The regulations may only provide that a disposal is to be treated as not being a taxable disposal if or to the extent that—

[(a) the material comprised in the disposal is held temporarily pending one or more of the following—

(i) the incineration or recycling of the material, or

(ii) the removal of the material for use elsewhere, or

(iii) the use of the material, if it is qualifying material within the meaning of section 42(3) above, for the restoration to use of the site at which the disposal takes place, or any part of that site, upon completion of waste disposal operations at the site, or as the case may be, that part of the site, or

(iv) the sorting of the material with a view to its removal elsewhere or its eventual disposal, and][1]

(b) [the material in question is held temporarily][1] *in an area designated for the purpose by an authorised person.*[2]

Regulations—Landfill Tax Regulations, SI 1996/1527.
Cross references—See Landfill Tax Regulations, SI 1996/1527 regs 38–40 (temporary disposals).
Amendments—[1] Sub-s (7)(*a*) and words in sub-s (7)(*b*) substituted by FA 2000 s 141(1)–(3), with effect from 28 July 2000.
[2] Section 62 repealed by FA 2009 s 119, Sch 60 para 4 with effect from 21 July 2009. The repeal of s 62 does not affect any regulation made under it before the passing of FA 2009, and does not prevent the powers conferred by the repealed provision from being used after the passing of FA 2009 to revoke any regulations made under the powers before that time: FA 2009 s 119, Sch 60 para 13(3).

63 Qualifying material: special provisions

(1) This section applies for the purposes of section 42 above.

(2) The Commissioners may direct that where material is disposed of it must be treated as qualifying material if it would in fact be such material but for a small quantity of non-qualifying material; and whether a quantity of non-qualifying material is small must be determined in accordance with the terms of the direction.

(3) The Commissioners may at the request of a person direct that where there is a disposal in respect of which he is liable to pay tax the material disposed of must be treated as qualifying material if it would in fact be such material but for a small quantity of non-qualifying material, and—

(*a*) a direction may apply to all disposals in respect of which a person is liable to pay tax or to such of them as are identified in the direction;

(*b*) whether a quantity of non-qualifying material is small must be determined in accordance with the terms of the direction.

(4) If a direction under subsection (3) above applies to a disposal any direction under subsection (2) above shall not apply to it.

(5) An order may provide that material must not be treated as qualifying material unless prescribed conditions are met.

(6) A condition may relate to any matter the Treasury think fit (such as the production of a document which includes a statement of the nature of the material).

Interpretation

64 Disposal of material as waste

(1) A disposal of material is a disposal of it as waste if the person making the disposal does so with the intention of discarding the material.

(2) The fact that the person making the disposal or any other person could benefit from or make use of the material is irrelevant.

(3) Where a person makes a disposal on behalf of another person, for the purposes of subsections (1) and (2) above the person on whose behalf the disposal is made shall be treated as making the disposal.

(4) The reference in subsection (3) above to a disposal on behalf of another person includes references to a disposal—

(*a*) at the request of another person;

(*b*) in pursuance of a contract with another person.

Commentary—*De Voil Indirect Tax Service* **V20.104**.
Simon's Tax Cases—*C&E Comrs v Parkwood Landfill Ltd* [2002] STC 417; Waste Recycling Group Ltd v R&C Comrs [2009] STC 200.

65 Disposal by way of landfill

(1) There is a disposal of material by way of landfill if—

(*a*) it is deposited on the surface of land or on a structure set into the surface, or (*b*) it is deposited under the surface of land.

(2) Subsection (1) above applies whether or not the material is placed in a container before it is deposited.

(3) Subsection (1)(*b*) above applies whether the material—

(*a*) is covered with earth after it is deposited, or

(*b*) is deposited in a cavity (such as a cavern or mine).

(4) If material is deposited on the surface of land (or on a structure set into the surface) with a view to it being covered with earth the disposal must be treated as made when the material is deposited and not when it is covered.

(5) An order may provide that the meaning of the disposal of material by way of landfill (as it applies for the time being) shall be varied.

(6) An order under subsection (5) above may make provision in such way as the Treasury think fit, whether by amending any of subsections (1) to (4) above or otherwise.

(7) In this section "land" includes land covered by water where the land is above the low water mark of ordinary spring tides.

(8) In this section "earth" includes similar matter (such as sand or rocks).

Commentary—*De Voil Indirect Tax Service* **V20.105**.
Simon's Tax Cases—s 65(1), *C&E Comrs v Parkwood Landfill Ltd* [2002] STC 417.

[65A Prescribed landfill site activities to be treated as disposals

(1) An order may prescribe a landfill site activity for the purposes of this section.

(2) If a prescribed landfill site activity is carried out at a landfill site, the activity is to be treated—

(*a*) as a disposal at the landfill site of the material involved in the activity,

(*b*) as a disposal of that material as waste, and

(*c*) as a disposal of that material made by way of landfill.

(3) Connected provision may be made by order.

(4) Provision may be made under this section in such way as the Treasury think fit.

(5) An order under subsection (1) may prescribe a landfill site activity by reference to conditions.

(6) Those conditions may, in particular, relate to either or both of the following—

(*a*) whether the landfill site activity is carried out in a designated area of a landfill site, and

(*b*) whether there has been compliance with a requirement to give information relating to—

(i) the landfill site activity, or

(ii) the material involved in the landfill site activity, including information relating to whether the activity is carried out in a designated area of a landfill site.

(7) An order under this section—

(*a*) may amend, or otherwise modify, this Part or any other enactment relating to landfill tax, but

(*b*) may not alter any rate at which landfill tax is charged.

(8) Subsections (5) to (7) do not limit the generality of subsection (4).

(9) In this section—

"connected provision" means provision which appears to the Treasury to be necessary or expedient in connection with provision made under subsection (1);

"designated area" means an area of a landfill site designated in accordance with—

(*a*) an order under this section, or

(*b*) regulations under Part 1 of Schedule 5;

"landfill site activity" means any of the following descriptions of activity, or an activity that falls within any of the following descriptions—

(*a*) using or otherwise dealing with material at a landfill site;

(*b*) storing or otherwise having material at a landfill site.][1]

Amendment—[1] Section 65A inserted by FA 2009 s 119, Sch 60 paras 1, 2 with effect from 21 July 2009.

66 Landfill sites

Land is a landfill site at a given time if at that time—

(*a*) a licence which is a site licence for the purposes of Part II of the Environmental Protection Act 1990 (waste on land) is in force in relation to the land and authorises disposals in or on the land,

(*b*) a resolution under section 54 of that Act (land occupied by waste disposal authorities in Scotland) is in force in relation to the land and authorises deposits or disposals in or on the land,

[(*ba*) a permit under regulations under section 2 of the Pollution Prevention and Control Act 1999 is in force in relation to the land and authorises deposits or disposals in or on the land,][1] (*c*) a disposal licence issued under Part II of the Pollution Control and Local Government (Northern Ireland) Order 1978 (waste on land) is in force in relation to the land and authorises deposits on the land,

(*d*) a resolution passed under Article 13 of that Order (land occupied by district councils in Northern Ireland) is in force in relation to the land and relates to deposits on the land, or

(*e*) a licence under any provision for the time being having effect in Northern Ireland and corresponding to section 35 of the Environmental Protection Act 1990 (waste management licences) is in force in relation to the land and authorises disposals in or on the land.

Commentary—*De Voil Indirect Tax Service* **V20.105**.

Amendment—[1] Para (*ba*) inserted by the Pollution Prevention and Control Act 1999 s 6(1) Sch 2 para 19 with effect from 21 March 2000 (by virtue of SI 2000/800).

67 Operators of landfill sites

The operator of a landfill site at a given time is—

(*a*) the person who is at the time concerned the holder of the licence, where section 66(*a*) above applies;

(*b*) the waste disposal authority which at the time concerned occupies the landfill site, where section 66(*b*) above applies;

[(*ba*) the person who is at the time concerned the holder of the permit, where section 66(*ba*) above applies;][1]

(*c*) the person who is at the time concerned the holder of the licence, where section 66(*c*) above applies;

(*d*) the district council which passed the resolution, where section 66(*d*) above applies;

(*e*) the person who is at the time concerned the holder of the licence, where section 66(*e*) above applies.

Amendments—[1] Para (*ba*) inserted with effect in England and Wales by the Pollution Prevention and Control (England and Wales) Regulations, SI 2000/1973 reg 39, Sch 10 para 22 with effect from 1 August 2000, and with effect in Scotland by the Pollution Prevention and Control (Scotland) Regulations, SI 2000/323 reg 36, Sch 10 para 6 with effect from 28 September 2000.

68 Weight of material disposed of

(1) The weight of the material disposed of on a taxable disposal shall be determined in accordance with regulations.

(2) The regulations may—

(*a*) prescribe rules for determining the weight;

(*b*) authorise rules for determining the weight to be specified by the Commissioners in a prescribed manner;

(*c*) authorise rules for determining the weight to be agreed by the person liable to pay the tax and an authorised person.

(3) The regulations may in particular prescribe, or authorise the specification or agreement of, rules about—

(*a*) the method by which the weight is to be determined;

(*b*) the time by reference to which the weight is to be determined;

(*c*) the discounting of constituents (such as water).

(4) The regulations may include provision that a specification authorised under subsection (2)(*b*) above may provide—

(*a*) that it is to have effect only in relation to disposals of such descriptions as may be set out in the specification;

(*b*) that it is not to have effect in relation to particular disposals unless the Commissioners are satisfied that such conditions as may be set out in the specification are met in relation to the disposals;

and the conditions may be framed by reference to such factors as the Commissioners think fit (such as the consent of an authorised person to the specification having effect in relation to disposals).

(5) The regulations may include provision that—

(*a*) where rules are agreed as mentioned in subsection (2)(*c*) above, and

(*b*) the Commissioners believe that they should no longer be applied because they do not give an accurate indication of the weight or they are not being fully observed or for some other reason,

the Commissioners may direct that the agreed rules shall no longer have effect.

(6) The regulations shall be so framed that where in relation to a given disposal—

(*a*) no specification of the Commissioners has effect, and

(*b*) no agreed rules have effect,

the weight shall be determined in accordance with rules prescribed in the regulations.

Commentary—*De Voil Indirect Tax Service* **V20.141, 142**.

Regulations—Landfill Tax Regulations, SI 1996/1527.

Cross references—See Landfill Tax Regulations, SI 1996/1527 regs 41–44 (determination of weight of material disposed of).

69 Taxable activities

(1) A person carries out a taxable activity if—

(*a*) he makes a taxable disposal in respect of which he is liable to pay tax, or

(*b*) he permits another person to make a taxable disposal in respect of which he (the first-mentioned person) is liable to pay tax.

(2) Where—

(*a*) a taxable disposal is made, and

(*b*) it is made without the knowledge of the person who is liable to pay tax in respect of it,

that person shall for the purposes of this section be taken to permit the disposal.

70 Interpretation: other provisions

(1) Unless the context otherwise requires—

"accounting period" shall be construed in accordance with section 49 above;

"appeal tribunal" means a [the First-tier Tribunal or, where determined by or under Tribunal Procedure Rules, the Upper Tribunal;][2];

"authorised person" means any person acting under the authority of the Commissioners;

"the Commissioners" means the Commissioners of Customs and Excise;

"conduct" includes any act, omission or statement;

["the Environment Agency" means the body established by section 1 of the Environment Act 1995;][1]

["HMRC" means Her Majesty's Revenue and Customs;][2]

"material" means material of all kinds, including objects, substances and products of all kinds;

"prescribed" means prescribed by an order or regulations under this Part;

"registrable person" has the meaning given by section 47(10) above;

["the Scottish Environment Protection Agency" means the body established by section 20 of the Environment Act 1995;][1]

"tax" means landfill tax;

"taxable disposal" has the meaning given by section 40 above.

(2) A landfill disposal is a disposal—

(*a*) of material as waste, and

(*b*) made by way of landfill.

[(2A) A local authority is—

(*a*) the council of a county, county borough, district, London borough, parish or group of parishes (or, in Wales, community or group of communities);

(*b*) the Common Council of the City of London;

(*c*) as respects the Temples, the Sub-Treasurer of the Inner Temple and the Under-Treasurer of the Middle Temple respectively;

(*d*) the council of the Isles of Scilly;

(*e*) any joint committee or joint board established by two or more of the foregoing;

(*f*) in relation to Scotland, a council constituted under section 2 of the Local Government etc (Scotland) Act 1994, any two or more such councils and any joint committee or joint board within the meaning of section 235(1) of the Local Government (Scotland) Act 1973.][1]

(3) A reference to this Part includes a reference to any order or regulations made under it and a reference to a provision of this Part includes a reference to any order or regulations made under the provision, unless otherwise required by the context or any order or regulations.

(4) This section and sections 64 to 69 above apply for the purposes of this Part.

Amendments—[1] Definitions of the "Environment Agency" and the "Scottish Environment Protection Agency" in sub-s (1), and sub-s (2A), inserted by the Landfill Tax (Contaminated Land) Order, SI 1996/1529 art 5, with effect from 1 August 1996.

[2] In sub-s (1) words in the definition of "appeal tribunal" substituted for the words "VAT and duties tribunal"; definition of "HMRC" inserted by the Transfer of Tribunal Functions and Revenue and Customs Appeals Order, SI 2009/56 art 3, Sch 1 para 238 with effect from 1 April 2009.

Supplementary

71 Orders and regulations

(1) The power to make an order under section 57 above shall be exercisable by the Commissioners, and the power to make an order under any other provision of this Part shall be exercisable by the Treasury.

(2) Any power to make regulations under this Part shall be exercisable by the Commissioners.

(3) Any power to make an order or regulations under this Part shall be exercisable by statutory instrument.

(4) An order to which this subsection applies shall be laid before the House of Commons; and unless it is approved by that House before the expiration of a period of 28 days beginning with the date on which it was made it shall cease to have effect on the expiration of that period, but without prejudice to anything previously done under the order or to the making of a new order.

(5) In reckoning any such period as is mentioned in subsection (4) above no account shall be taken of any time during which Parliament is dissolved or prorogued or during which the House of Commons is adjourned for more than four days.

(6) A statutory instrument containing an order or regulations under this Part (other than an order under section 57 above or an order to which subsection (4) above applies) shall be subject to annulment in pursuance of a resolution of the House of Commons.

(7) Subsection (4) above applies to—

(*a*) an order under section 42(3) above providing for material which would otherwise be qualifying material not to be qualifying material;

(*b*) an order under section 46 above which produces the result that a disposal which would otherwise not be a taxable disposal is a taxable disposal;

(*c*) an order under section 63(5) above other than one which provides only that an earlier order under section 63(5) is not to apply to material;

[(*ca*) an order under section 65A above which produces the result that a landfill site activity which would not otherwise be prescribed for the purposes of section 65A is so prescribed;

(*cb*) an order under section 65A above which amends this Part or any enactment contained in an Act;][1]

(*d*) an order under section 65(5) above providing for anything which would otherwise not be a disposal of material by way of landfill to be such a disposal.

(8) Any power to make an order or regulations under this Part—

(*a*) may be exercised as regards prescribed cases or descriptions of case;

(*b*) may be exercised differently in relation to different cases or descriptions of case.

(9) An order or regulations under this Part may include such supplementary, incidental, consequential or transitional provisions as appear to the Treasury or the Commissioners (as the case may be) to be necessary or expedient.

(10) No specific provision of this Part about an order or regulations shall prejudice the generality of subsections (8) and (9) above.

Amendments—[1] Sub-sections (7)(*ca*) and (*cb*) inserted by FA 2009 s 119, Sch 60 paras 1, 3 with effect from 21 July 2009.

PART VII

MISCELLANEOUS AND SUPPLEMENTAL

Miscellaneous: indirect taxation

197 Setting of rates of interest

(1) The rate of interest applicable for the purposes of an enactment to which this section applies shall be the rate which for the purposes of that enactment is provided for by regulations made by the Treasury under this section.

(2) This section applies to—

(*a*)–(*c*) …

(*d*) [sections 56(3) to (5) of and][2] paragraphs 26 and 29 of Schedule 5 to this Act (interest payable to or by the Commissioners in connection with landfill tax).

[(*e*) paragraph 17 of Schedule 5 to the Finance Act 1997 (interest on amounts repayable in respect of overpayments by the Commissioners in connection with … landfill tax).][1]

(*f*), (*g*) …

(3) Regulations under this section may—

(*a*) make different provision for different enactments or for different purposes of the same enactment,

(*b*) either themselves specify a rate of interest for the purposes of an enactment or make provision for any such rate to be determined, and to change from time to time, by reference to such rate or the average of such rates as may be referred to in the regulations,

(*c*) provide for rates to be reduced below, or increased above, what they otherwise would be by specified amounts or by reference to specified formulae,

(*d*) provide for rates arrived at by reference to averages or formulae to be rounded up or down,

(*e*) provide for circumstances in which changes of rates of interest are or are not to take place, and

(*f*) provide that changes of rates are to have effect for periods beginning on or after a day determined in accordance with the regulations in relation to interest running from before that day, as well as in relation to interest running from, or from after, that day.

(4) The power to make regulations under this section shall be exercisable by statutory instrument subject to annulment in pursuance of a resolution of the House of Commons.

(5) *Where—*

(a) regulations under this section provide, without specifying the rate determined in accordance with the regulations, for a new method of determining the rate applicable for the purposes of any enactment, or

(*b*) *the rate which, in accordance with regulations under this section, is the rate applicable for the purposes of any enactment changes otherwise than by virtue of the making of regulations specifying a new rate,*

the Commissioners of Customs and Excise shall make an order specifying the new rate and the day from which, in accordance with the regulations, it has effect.[3]

(6) …

(7) Subsections (1) and (6) above shall have effect for periods beginning on or after such day as the Treasury may by order made by statutory instrument appoint and shall have effect in relation to interest running from before that day, as well as in relation to interest running from, or from after, that day; and different days may be appointed under this subsection for different purposes.

Note—Sub-ss (2)(*a*)–(*c*), (*f*), (*g*), (6) are not relevant to landfill tax.
Sub-s (1) has effect for periods beginning on or after 1 April 1997 (see FA 1996, s 197 (Appointed Day) Order, SI 1997/1015.
Amendments—[1] Inserted by FA 1997 s 50, Sch 5 para 21.
[2] In sub-s (2)(*d*) words inserted by the Transfer of Tribunal Functions and Revenue and Customs Appeals Order, SI 2009/56 art 3, Sch 1 para 239 with effect from 1 April 2009.
[3] Sub-s (5) repealed by FA 2009 s 105(6)(*b*) with effect from 21 July 2009.

Supplemental

206 Short title

This Act may be cited as the Finance Act 1996.

SCHEDULE 5

LANDFILL TAX

Section 60

PART I

INFORMATION

[Information: general][1]

1— (1) Every person who is concerned (in whatever capacity) with any landfill disposal shall furnish to the Commissioners such information relating to the disposal as the Commissioners may reasonably require.

(2) The information mentioned in sub-paragraph (1) above shall be furnished within such time and in such form as the Commissioners may reasonably require.

Amendments—[1] Heading substituted by FA 2009 s 119, Sch 60 paras 5, 6 with effect from 21 July 2009.

[Information: material at landfill sites

1A— (1) Regulations may make provision about giving the Commissioners information relating to material at a landfill site or a part of a landfill site.

(2) Regulations under this paragraph may require a person to give information.

(3) Regulations under this paragraph may—

(*a*) require a person, or authorise an officer of Revenue and Customs to require a person, to designate a part of a landfill site (an "information area"), and

(*b*) require material, or prescribed descriptions of material, to be deposited in an information area.

(4) Regulations under this paragraph may make provision about information relating to what is done with material.

(5) Sub-paragraphs (2) to (4) do not prejudice the generality of sub- paragraph (1).][1]

Amendments—[1] Heading and para (1A) inserted by FA 2009 s 119, Sch 60 paras 5, 7 with effect from 21 July 2009.

[Information: site restoration

1B— (1) Before commencing restoration of all or part of a landfill site, the operator of the site must—

(*a*) notify the Commissioners in writing that the restoration is to commence, and

(*b*) provide such other written information as the Commissioners may require generally or in the particular case.

(2) In this paragraph "restoration" means work, other than capping waste, which is required by a relevant instrument to be carried out to restore a landfill site to use on completion of waste disposal operations.

(3) The following are relevant instruments—

(*a*) a planning consent,

(*b*) a waste management licence, and

(*c*) a permit authorising the disposal of waste on or in land.][1]

Amendments—[1] Heading and para (1B) inserted by FA 2009 s 119, Sch 60 paras 5, 7 with effect in relation to restoration of landfill sites commencing on or after 1 September 2009; FA 2009 s 119, Sch 60 para 13(2).

[Records; registrable persons][4]

2— (1) Regulations may require registrable persons to make records.

(2) Regulations under sub-paragraph (1) above may be framed by reference to such records as may be stipulated in any notice published by the Commissioners in pursuance of the regulations and not withdrawn by a further notice.

(3) Regulations may—

(*a*) require registrable persons to preserve records of a prescribed description (whether or not the records are required to be made in pursuance of regulations) for such period not exceeding six years as may be specified in the regulations;

(*b*) authorise the Commissioners to direct that any such records need only be preserved for a shorter period than that specified in the regulations;

(*c*) authorise a direction to be made so as to apply generally or in such cases as the Commissioners may stipulate.

(4) Any duty under regulations to preserve records may be discharged by the preservation of the information contained in them by such means as the Commissioners may approve; and where that information is so preserved a copy of any document forming part of the records shall (subject to the following provisions of this paragraph) be admissible in evidence in any proceedings, whether civil or criminal, to the same extent as the records themselves.

(5) The Commissioners may, as a condition of approving under sub-paragraph (4) above any means of preserving information contained in any records, impose such reasonable requirements as appear to them necessary for securing that the information will be as readily available to them as if the records themselves had been preserved.

(6) A statement contained in a document produced by a computer shall not by virtue of sub-paragraph (4) above be admissible in evidence—

(*a*) [2]

(*b*) in civil proceedings in Scotland, except in accordance with sections 5 and 6 of the Civil Evidence (Scotland) Act 1988;

(*c*) in criminal proceedings in Scotland, except in accordance with Schedule 8 to the Criminal Procedure (Scotland) Act 1995;

(*d*) …[1];

(*e*) …[3]

(7) In the case of civil proceedings in England and Wales to which sections 5 and 6 of the Civil Evidence Act 1968 apply, a statement contained in a document produced by a computer shall not be admissible in evidence by virtue of sub-paragraph (4) above except in accordance with those sections.

Regulations—Landfill Tax Regulations, SI 1996/1527.

Cross references—See Landfill Tax Regulations, SI 1996 1527 reg 12 (landfill tax account), SI 1996/1527 reg 16 (records).

Amendments—[1] Para (6)(*d*) repealed by the Civil Evidence (Northern Ireland) Order, SI 1997/2983 (NI 21) art 13(2) Sch 2, with effect from 6 September 1999 (by virtue of SR 1999/339).

[2] Sub-para (6)(*a*) repealed by the Criminal Justice Act 2003 ss 332, 336(3), Sch 37 Pt 6 with effect from 4 April 2005 (by virtue of SI 2005/950).

[3] Sub-para (6)(*e*) repealed by the Criminal Justice (Evidence) (Northern Ireland) Order, SI 2004/1501 art 46(2), Sch 2 with effect from 3 April 2006 (by virtue of the Criminal Justice (Evidence) (Northern Ireland) Order 2004 (Commencement No 3) Order, SR 2006/63, art 2).

[4] Heading substituted by FA 2009 s 119, Sch 60 paras 5, 8 with effect from 21 July 2009.

Prospective amendments—Sub-paragraphs (4)–(7) to be substituted by FA 2009 s 98, Sch 50 para 21 with effect from such day as the Treasury may by order made by statutory instrument appoint, as follows—

"(4) A duty under regulations under this paragraph to preserve records may be discharged—

(*a*) by preserving them in any form and by any means, or

(*b*) by preserving the information contained in them in any form and by any means,

subject to any conditions or exceptions specified in writing by the Commissioners."

[Records: material at landfill sites

2A— (1) Regulations may require a person to make records relating to material at a landfill site or a part of a landfill site.

(2) Regulations under this paragraph may make provision about records relating to what is done with material.

(3) Sub-paragraphs (2) to (7) of paragraph 2 apply in relation to regulations under this paragraph as they apply in relation to regulations under paragraph 2.

(4) But, in the application of paragraph 2(3)(*a*) in relation to regulations under this paragraph, the reference to registrable persons has effect as a reference to persons.][1]

Amendments—[1] Heading and paragraph (2A) inserted by FA 2009 s 119, Sch 60 paras 5, 9 with effect from 21 July 2009.

Documents

3— (1) Every person who is concerned (in whatever capacity) with any landfill disposal shall upon demand made by an authorised person produce or cause to be produced for inspection by that person any documents relating to the disposal.

(2) Where, by virtue of sub-paragraph (1) above, an authorised person has power to require the production of any documents from any person, he shall have the like power to require production of the documents concerned from any other person who appears to the authorised person to be in possession of them; but where any such other person claims a lien on any document produced by him, the production shall be without prejudice to the lien.

(3) The documents mentioned in sub-paragraphs (1) and (2) above shall be produced—

(*a*) at such place as the authorised person may reasonably require, and

(*b*) at such time as the authorised person may reasonably require.

(4) An authorised person may take copies of, or make extracts from, any document produced under sub-paragraph (1) or (2) above.

(5) If it appears to him to be necessary to do so, an authorised person may, at a reasonable time and for a reasonable period, remove any document produced under sub-paragraph (1) or (2) above and shall, on request, provide a receipt for any document so removed; and where a lien is claimed on a document produced under sub-paragraph (2) above the removal of the document under this sub-paragraph shall not be regarded as breaking the lien.

(6) Where a document removed by an authorised person under sub-paragraph (5) above is reasonably required for any purpose he shall, as soon as practicable, provide a copy of the document, free of charge, to the person by whom it was produced or caused to be produced.

(7) Where any documents removed under the powers conferred by this paragraph are lost or damaged the Commissioners shall be liable to compensate their owner for any expenses reasonably incurred by him in replacing or repairing the documents.

PART II

POWERS

Entry and inspection

4 For the purpose of exercising any powers under this Part of this Act an authorised person may at any reasonable time enter and inspect premises used in connection with the carrying on of a business.

Entry and search

5— …[1]

Cross references—Criminal Justice and Police Act 2001 s 50, Sch 1 Pt 1 (s 50 of that Act which provides additional powers of seizure from premises applies to the power of seizure conferred under sub-para (2) above; for the relevant provisions of the Criminal Justice and Police Act 2001, see the *VAT* section of this publication, ante).

Amendments—[1] This para repealed by FA 2007 ss 84, 114, Sch 22 paras 3, 10(*a*), Sch 27 Pt 5(1) with effect from 1 December 2007 (by virtue of SI 2007/3166 art 3(*a*)).

Arrest

6— …[1]

Amendments—[1] This para repealed by FA 2007 ss 84, 114, Sch 22 paras 3, 10(*b*), Sch 27 Pt 5(1) with effect from 1 December 2007 (by virtue of SI 2007/3166 art 3(*a*)).

Order for access to recorded information etc

7—(1) Where, on an application by an authorised person, a justice of the peace or, in Scotland, a justice (within the meaning of section 307 of the Criminal Procedure (Scotland) Act 1995) is satisfied that there are reasonable grounds for believing—

(*a*) that an offence in connection with tax is being, has been or is about to be committed, and

(*b*) that any recorded information (including any document of any nature whatsoever) which may be required as evidence for the purpose of any proceedings in respect of such an offence is in the possession of any person,

he may make an order under this paragraph.

(2) An order under this paragraph is an order that the person who appears to the justice to be in possession of the recorded information to which the application relates shall—

(*a*) give an authorised person access to it, and

(*b*) permit an authorised person to remove and take away any of it which he reasonably considers necessary,

not later than the end of the period of 7 days beginning with the date of the order or the end of such longer period as the order may specify.

(3) The reference in sub-paragraph (2)(*a*) above to giving an authorised person access to the recorded information to which the application relates includes a reference to permitting the authorised person to take copies of it or to make extracts from it.

(4) Where the recorded information consists of information [stored in any electronic form][1], an order under this paragraph shall have effect as an order to produce the information in a form in which it is visible and legible [or from which it can readily be produced in a visible and legible form][1] and, if the authorised person wishes to remove it, in a form in which it can be removed.

(5) This paragraph is without prejudice to paragraphs 3 to 5 above.

Amendments—[1] In sub-para (4), words substituted and words inserted by Criminal Justice and Police Act 2001 ss 70, 138, Sch 2 Pt 2 para 13 with effect from 1 April 2003 (by virtue of SI 2003/708).

Removal of documents etc

8— (1) An authorised person who removes anything in the exercise of a power conferred by or under paragraph 5 or 7 above shall, if so requested by a person showing himself—

(*a*) to be the occupier of premises from which it was removed, or

(*b*) to have had custody or control of it immediately before the removal,

provide that person with a record of what he removed.

(2) The authorised person shall provide the record within a reasonable time from the making of the request for it.

(3) Subject to sub-paragraph (7) below, if a request for permission to be allowed access to anything which—

(*a*) has been removed by an authorised person, and

(*b*) is retained by the Commissioners for the purposes of investigating an offence,

is made to the officer in overall charge of the investigation by a person who had custody or control of the thing immediately before it was so removed or by someone acting on behalf of such a person, the officer shall allow the person who made the request access to it under the supervision of an authorised person.

(4) Subject to sub-paragraph (7) below, if a request for a photograph or copy of any such thing is made to the officer in overall charge of the investigation by a person who had custody or control of the thing immediately before it was so removed, or by someone acting on behalf of such a person, the officer shall—

(*a*) allow the person who made the request access to it under the supervision of an authorised person for the purpose of photographing it or copying it, or

(*b*) photograph or copy it, or cause it to be photographed or copied.

(5) Subject to sub-paragraph (7) below, where anything is photographed or copied under sub-paragraph (4)(*b*) above the officer shall supply the photograph or copy, or cause it to be supplied, to the person who made the request.

(6) The photograph or copy shall be supplied within a reasonable time from the making of the request.

(7) There is no duty under this paragraph to allow access to, or to supply a photograph or copy of, anything if the officer in overall charge of the investigation for the purposes of which it was removed has reasonable grounds for believing that to do so would prejudice—

(*a*) that investigation,

(*b*) the investigation of an offence other than the offence for the purposes of the investigation of which the thing was removed, or

(*c*) any criminal proceedings which may be brought as a result of the investigation of which he is in charge or any such investigation as is mentioned in paragraph (*b*) above.

(8) Any reference in this paragraph to the officer in overall charge of the investigation is a reference to the person whose name and address are endorsed on the warrant concerned as being the officer so in charge.

9— (1) Where, on an application made as mentioned in sub-paragraph (2) below, the appropriate judicial authority is satisfied that a person has failed to comply with a requirement imposed by paragraph 8 above, the authority may order that person to comply with the requirement within such time and in such manner as may be specified in the order.

(2) An application under sub-paragraph (1) above shall be made—

(*a*) in the case of a failure to comply with any of the requirements imposed by sub-paragraphs (1) and (2) of paragraph 8 above, by the occupier of the premises from which the thing in question was removed or by the person who had custody or control of it immediately before it was so removed, and

(*b*) in any other case, by the person who had such custody or control.

(3) In this paragraph "the appropriate judicial authority" means—

(*a*) in England and Wales, a magistrates' court;

(*b*) in Scotland, the sheriff;

(*c*) in Northern Ireland, a court of summary jurisdiction, as defined in Article 2(2)(*a*) of the Magistrates' Court (Northern Ireland) Order 1981.

(4) In England and Wales and Northern Ireland, an application for an order under this paragraph shall be made by way of complaint; and sections 21 and 42(2) of the Interpretation Act (Northern Ireland) 1954 shall apply as if any reference in those provisions to any enactment included a reference to this paragraph.

Power to take samples

10— (1) An authorised person, if it appears to him necessary for the protection of the revenue against mistake or fraud, may at any time take, from material which he has reasonable cause to believe is intended to be, is being, or has been disposed of as waste by way of landfill, such samples as he may require with a view to determining how the material ought to be or to have been treated for the purposes of tax.

(2) Any sample taken under this paragraph shall be disposed of in such manner as the Commissioners may direct.

PART III
RECOVERY

General

11 Tax due from any person shall be recoverable as a debt due to the Crown.

Preferential and preferred debts

12— (1) …[1]

(2) …[1]

(3) (*inserts* Bankruptcy (Scotland) Act 1985 Sch 3 para 2 (1B)).

(4) (*inserts* Bankruptcy (Scotland) Act 1985 Sch 3 para 8B).

(5) (*amends* Insolvency (Northern Ireland) Order, SI 1989/2405 art 346(1) and *inserts* Insolvency (Northern Ireland) Order, SI 1989/2405 Sch 4 para 3B).

Amendments—[1] Sub-paras (1), (2) repealed by the Enterprise Act 2002 ss 278(2), 279, Sch 26 with effect 15 September 2003 (by virtue of SI 2003/2093).

Distress and diligence

13 …

Amendments—This paragraph repealed by FA 1997 Sch 18 Part V(2) with effect from 1 July 1997 (by virtue of SI 1997/1433).

Recovery of overpaid tax

14— (1) Where a person has paid an amount to the Commissioners by way of tax which was not tax due to them, they shall be liable to repay the amount to him.

(2) The Commissioners shall only be liable to repay an amount under this paragraph on a claim being made for the purpose.

(3) It shall be a defence, in relation to a claim under this paragraph, that repayment of an amount would unjustly enrich the claimant.

[(4) The Commissioners shall not be liable, on a claim made under this paragraph, to repay any amount paid to them more than three years before the making of the claim.][1]

(5) A claim under this paragraph shall be made in such form and manner and shall be supported by such documentary evidence as may be prescribed by regulations.

(6) Except as provided by this paragraph, the Commissioners shall not be liable to repay an amount paid to them by way of tax by virtue of the fact that it was not tax due to them.

Cross references—See FA 1997 Sch 5 Part I (unjust enrichment).
FA 1997 Sch 5, para 14 (assessment of excessive repayment).
Landfill Tax Regulations, SI 1996/1527 reg 13 (correction of errors), SI 1996/1527 reg 14 (claims for overpaid tax).
Amendments—[1] Sub-para (4) substituted by FA 1997 s 50, Sch 5 para 5(3) with effect from 19 March 1997.
Prospective amendments—In sub-para (4) words "4 years" to be substituted for the words "three years" by FA 2009 s 99, Sch 51 paras 37, 38 with effect from such day as the Treasury may by order made by statutory instrument appoint.

PART IV
CRIMINAL PENALTIES

Criminal offences

15— (1) A person is guilty of an offence if—

(*a*) being a registrable person, he is knowingly concerned in, or in the taking of steps with a view to, the fraudulent evasion of tax by him or another registrable person, or

(*b*) not being a registrable person, he is knowingly concerned in, or in the taking of steps with a view to, the fraudulent evasion of tax by a registrable person.

(2) Any reference in sub-paragraph (1) above to the evasion of tax includes a reference to the obtaining of a payment under regulations under section 51(2)(*c*) or (*d*) or (*f*) of this Act.

(3) A person is guilty of an offence if with the requisite intent—

(*a*) he produces, furnishes or sends, or causes to be produced, furnished or sent, for the purposes of this Part of this Act any document which is false in a material particular, or

(*b*) he otherwise makes use for those purposes of such a document;

and the requisite intent is intent to deceive or to secure that a machine will respond to the document as if it were a true document.

(4) A person is guilty of an offence if in furnishing any information for the purposes of this Part of this Act he makes a statement which he knows to be false in a material particular or recklessly makes a statement which is false in a material particular.

(5) A person is guilty of an offence by virtue of this sub-paragraph if his conduct during any specified period must have involved the commission by him of one or more offences under the preceding provisions of this paragraph; and the preceding provisions of this sub-paragraph apply whether or not the particulars of that offence or those offences are known.

(6) A person is guilty of an offence if—

(*a*) he enters into a taxable landfill contract, or

(*b*) he makes arrangements for other persons to enter into such a contract,

with reason to believe that tax in respect of the disposal concerned will be evaded.

(7) A person is guilty of an offence if he carries out taxable activities without giving security (or further security) he has been required to give under paragraph 31 below.

(8) For the purposes of this paragraph a taxable landfill contract is a contract under which there is to be a taxable disposal.

Criminal penalties

16— (1) A person guilty of an offence under paragraph 15(1) above is liable—

(*a*) on summary conviction, to a penalty of the statutory maximum or of three times the amount of the tax, whichever is the greater, or to imprisonment for a term not exceeding six months or to both;

(*b*) on conviction on indictment, to a penalty of any amount or to imprisonment for a term not exceeding seven years or to both.

(2) The reference in sub-paragraph (1) above to the amount of the tax shall be construed, in relation to tax itself or a payment falling within paragraphs 15(2) above, as a reference to the aggregate of—

(*a*) the amount (if any) falsely claimed by way of credit, and

(*b*) the amount (if any) by which the gross amount of tax was falsely understated.

(3) A person guilty of an offence under paragraph 15(3) or (4) above is liable—

(*a*) on summary conviction, to a penalty of the statutory maximum (or, where sub-paragraph (4) below applies, to the alternative penalty there specified if it is greater) or to imprisonment for a term not exceeding six months or to both;

(*b*) on conviction on indictment, to a penalty of any amount or to imprisonment for a term not exceeding seven years or to both.

(4) Where—

(*a*) the document referred to in paragraph 15(3) above is a return required under this Part of this Act, or

(*b*) the information referred to in paragraph 15(4) above is contained in or otherwise relevant to such a return,

the alternative penalty is a penalty equal to three times the aggregate of the amount (if any) falsely claimed by way of credit and the amount (if any) by which the gross amount of tax was understated.

(5) A person guilty of an offence under paragraph 15(5) above is liable—

(*a*) on summary conviction, to a penalty of the statutory maximum (or, if greater, three times the amount of any tax that was or was intended to be evaded by his conduct) or to imprisonment for a term not exceeding six months or to both;

(*b*) on conviction on indictment, to a penalty of any amount or to imprisonment for a term not exceeding seven years or to both;

and paragraph 15(2) and sub-paragraph (2) above shall apply for the purposes of this sub-paragraph as they apply respectively for the purposes of paragraph 15(1) and sub-paragraph (1) above.

(6) A person guilty of an offence under paragraph 15(6) above is liable on summary conviction to a penalty of level 5 on the standard scale or three times the amount of the tax, whichever is the greater.

(7) A person guilty of an offence under paragraph 15(7) above is liable on summary conviction to a penalty of level 5 on the standard scale.

(8) In this paragraph—

(*a*) "credit" means credit for which provision is made by regulations under section 51 of this Act;

(*b*) "the gross amount of tax" means the total amount of tax due before taking into account any deduction for which provision is made by regulations under section 51(2) of this Act.

Criminal proceedings etc

17 Sections 145 to 155 of the Customs and Excise Management Act 1979 (proceedings for offences, mitigation of penalties and certain other matters) shall apply in relation to offences under paragraph 15 above and penalties imposed under paragraph 16 above as they apply in relation to offences and penalties under the customs and excise Acts as defined in that Act.

PART V
CIVIL PENALTIES

Evasion

18— *(1) Where—*

(a) for the purpose of evading tax, a registrable person does any act or omits to take any action, and

(b) his conduct involves dishonesty (whether or not it is such as to give rise to criminal liability),

he is liable to a penalty equal to the amount of tax evaded, or (as the case may be) sought to be evaded, by his conduct; but this is subject to sub-paragraph (7) below.

(2) The reference in sub-paragraph (1)(a) above to evading tax includes a reference to obtaining a payment under regulations under section 51(2)(c) or (d) or (f) of this Act in circumstances where the person concerned is not entitled to the sum.

(3) The reference in sub-paragraph (1) above to the amount of tax evaded or sought to be evaded is a reference to the aggregate of—

(a) the amount (if any) falsely claimed by way of credit, and

(b) the amount (if any) by which the gross amount of tax was falsely understated.

(4) In this paragraph—

(a) "credit" means credit for which provision is made by regulations under section 45 of this Act;

(b) "the gross amount of tax" means the total amount of tax due before taking into account any deduction for which provision is made by regulations under section 45(2) of this Act.

(5) Statements made or documents produced by or on behalf of a person shall not be inadmissible in any such proceedings as are mentioned in sub-paragraph (6) below by reason only that it has been drawn to his attention—

(a) that, in relation to tax, the Commissioners may assess an amount due by way of a civil penalty instead of instituting criminal proceedings and, though no undertaking can be given as to whether the Commissioners will make such an assessment in the case of any person, it is their practice to be influenced by the fact that a person has made a full confession of any dishonest conduct to which he has been a party and has given full facilities for investigation, and

(b) that the Commissioners or, on appeal, an appeal tribunal have power under paragraph 25 below to reduce a penalty under this paragraph,

and that he was or may have been induced thereby to make the statements or produce the documents.

(6) The proceedings referred to in sub-paragraph (5) above are—

(a) any criminal proceedings against the person concerned in respect of any offence in connection with or in relation to tax, and

(b) any proceedings against him for the recovery of any sum due from him in connection with or in relation to tax.

(7) Where, by reason of conduct falling within sub-paragraph (1) above, a person is convicted of an offence (whether under this Part of this Act or otherwise) that conduct shall not also give rise to liability to a penalty under this paragraph.[1]

Amendments—[1] This para repealed by FA 2008 s 122, Sch 40 para 21(*e*) with effect from 1 April 2009 (by virtue of SI 2009/571 art 2).

This para repealed only in so far as it relates to conduct involving dishonesty which relates to—

(a) an inaccuracy in a document, or

(b) a failure to notify HMRC of an under-assessment by HMRC (SI 2009/571 art 6).

19— *(1) Where it appears to the Commissioners—*

(a) that a body corporate is liable to a penalty under paragraph 18 above, and

(b) that the conduct giving rise to that penalty is, in whole or in part, attributable to the dishonesty of a person who is, or at the material time was, a director or managing officer of the body corporate (a named officer),

the Commissioners may serve a notice under this paragraph on the body corporate and on the named officer.

(2) A notice under this paragraph shall state—

(a) the amount of the penalty referred to in sub-paragraph (1)(a) above (the basic penalty), and

(b) that the Commissioners propose, in accordance with this paragraph, to recover from the named officer such portion (which may be the whole) of the basic penalty as is specified in the notice.

(3) Where a notice is served under this paragraph, the portion of the basic penalty specified in the notice shall be recoverable from the named officer as if he were personally liable under paragraph 18 above to a penalty which corresponds to that portion; and the amount of that penalty may be assessed and notified to him accordingly under paragraph 32 below.

(4) Where a notice is served under this paragraph—

(a) the amount which, under paragraph 32 below, may be assessed as the amount due by way of penalty from the body corporate shall be only so much (if any) of the basic penalty as is not assessed on and notified to a named officer by virtue of sub-paragraph (3) above, and

(b) the body corporate shall be treated as discharged from liability for so much of the basic penalty as is so assessed and notified.

(5) No appeal shall lie against a notice under this paragraph as such but—

(a) where a body corporate is assessed as mentioned in sub-paragraph (4)(a) above, the body corporate may [appeal against][2] *of the Commissioners' decision as to its liability to a penalty and as to the amount of the basic penalty as if it were specified in the assessment;*

(b) where an assessment is made on a named officer by virtue of sub-paragraph (3) above, the named officer may [appeal against][2] *require a review of the Commissioners' decision that the conduct of the body corporate referred to in sub-paragraph (1)(b) above is, in whole or in part, attributable to his dishonesty and of their decision as to the portion of the penalty which the Commissioners propose to recover from him;*

[(c) sections 54 to 56 of this Act shall apply accordingly.][2]

(6) In this paragraph a "managing officer", in relation to a body corporate, means any manager, secretary or other similar officer of the body corporate or any person purporting to act in any such capacity or as a director; and where affairs of a body corporate are managed by its members, this paragraph shall apply in relation to the conduct of a member in connection with his functions of management as if he were a director of the body corporate.[1]

Amendments—[1] This para repealed by FA 2008 s 122, Sch 40 para 21(*e*) with effect from 1 April 2009 (by virtue of SI 2009/571 art 2).

This para repealed only in so far as it relates to conduct involving dishonesty which relates to—

(a) an inaccuracy in a document, or

(b) a failure to notify HMRC of an under-assessment by HMRC (SI 2009/571 art 6).

[2] In so far as this para continues to apply, words in sub-para (5)(*a*), (*b*) substituted for the words "require a review"; sub-para (5)(*c*) substituted by the Transfer of Tribunal Functions and Revenue and Customs Appeals Order, SI 2009/56 art 3, Sch 1 para 240 with effect from 1 April 2009. Sub-para (5)(*c*) previously read as follows—

"(*c*) sections 49 and 50 of this Act shall apply accordingly."

Misdeclaration or neglect

20—(1) Where, for an accounting period—

(a) a return is made which understates a persons liability to tax or overstates his entitlement to credit, or

(b) an assessment is made which understates a person's liability to tax and, at the end of the period of 30 days beginning on the date of the assessment, he has not taken all such steps as are reasonable to draw the understatement to the attention of the Commissioners,

the person concerned is liable, subject to sub-paragraphs (3) and (4) below, to a penalty equal to 5 per cent. of the amount of the understatement of liability or (as the case may be) overstatement of entitlement.

(2) Where—

(a) a return for an accounting period overstates or understates to any extent a person's liability to tax or his entitlement to credit, and

(b) that return is corrected, in such circumstances and in accordance with such conditions as may be prescribed by regulations, by a return for a later accounting period which understates or overstates, to the corresponding extent, that liability or entitlement,

it shall be assumed for the purposes of this paragraph that the statement made by each such return is a correct statement for the accounting period to which the return relates.

(3) Conduct falling within sub-paragraph (1) above shall not give rise to liability to a penalty under this paragraph if the person concerned furnishes full information with respect to the inaccuracy concerned to the Commissioners—

(a) at a time when he has no reason to believe that enquiries are being made by the Commissioners into his affairs, so far as they relate to tax, and

(b) in such form and manner as may be prescribed by regulations or specified by the Commissioners in accordance with provision made by regulations.

(4) Where, by reason of conduct falling within sub-paragraph (1) above—

(a) a person is convicted of an offence (whether under this Part of this Act or otherwise), or

(b) a person is assessed to a penalty under paragraph 18 above,

that conduct shall not also give rise to liability to a penalty under this paragraph.

(5) In this paragraph "credit" means credit for which provision is made by regulations under section 51 of this Act.[1]

Regulations—Landfill Tax Regulations, SI 1996/1527.

Cross references—See Landfill Tax Registrations, SI 1996/1527 reg 13(7) (correction of errors).

Amendments—[1] This para repealed by FA 2008 s 122, Sch 40 para 21(*e*) with effect from 1 April 2009 (by virtue of SI 2009/571 art 2)

Registration

21— (1) A person who fails to comply with section 47(3) of this Act is liable to a penalty equal to 5 per cent of the relevant tax or, if it is greater or the circumstances are such that there is no relevant tax, to a penalty of £250; but this is subject to sub-paragraph (4) below.

(2) In sub-paragraph (1) above "relevant tax" means the tax (if any) for which the person concerned is liable for the period which—

(*a*) begins on the date with effect from which he is, in accordance with section 47 of this Act, required to be registered, and

(*b*) ends on the date on which the Commissioners received notification of, or otherwise became aware of, his liability to be registered.

(3) A person who fails to comply with section 47(4) of this Act is liable to a penalty of £250.

(4) Where, by reason of conduct falling within sub-paragraph (1) above—

(*a*) a person is convicted of an offence (whether under this Part of this Act or otherwise), or

(*b*) a person is assessed to a penalty under paragraph 18 above,

that conduct shall not also give rise to liability to a penalty under this paragraph.

Prospective amendments—Para 21(1), (2), (4) to be repealed by FA 2008 s 123, Sch 41 para 25(*h*)(ii) with effect from 1 April 2010 (by virtue of SI 2009/511 art 2).

Information

22— (1) If a person—

(*a*) fails to comply with any provision of paragraph 1 or 3 above, or

(*b*) fails to make records as required by any provision of regulations made under paragraph 2 above,

he is liable to a penalty of £250; but this is subject to sub-paragraph (4) below.

(2) Where—

(*a*) a penalty (an initial penalty) is imposed on a person under sub-paragraph (1) above, and

(*b*) the failure which led to the initial penalty continues after its imposition,

he is (subject to sub-paragraph (4) below) liable to a further penalty of £20 for each day during which (or any part of which) the failure continues after the day on which the initial penalty was imposed.

(3) A person who fails to preserve records in compliance with any provision of regulations made under paragraph 2 above (read with that paragraph and any direction given under the regulations) is liable to a penalty of £250; but this is subject to sub-paragraph (4) below.

(4) Where by reason of a failure falling within sub-paragraph (1) or (3) above—

(*a*) a person is convicted of an offence (whether under this Part of this Act or otherwise), or

(*b*) a person is assessed to a penalty under paragraph 18 above [or a penalty for a deliberate inaccuracy under Schedule 24 to the Finance Act 2007 (penalties for errors)][1],

that failure shall not also give rise to liability to a penalty under this paragraph.

Amendments—[1] Words in sub-para (4)(*b*) inserted by the Finance Act 2008, Schedule 40 (Appointed Day, Transitional Provisions and Consequential Amendments) Order, SI 2009/571 art 8, Sch 1 paras 28, 29 with effect from 1 April 2009.

Breach of regulations

23— (1) Where regulations made under this Part of this Act impose a requirement on any person, they may provide that if the person fails to comply with the requirement he shall be liable to a penalty of £250; but this is subject to sub-paragraphs (2) and (3) below.

(2) Where by reason of any conduct—

(*a*) a person is convicted of an offence (whether under this Part of this Act or otherwise), or

(*b*) a person is assessed to a penalty under paragraph 18 above [or a penalty for a deliberate inaccuracy under Schedule 24 to the Finance Act 2007 (penalties for errors)][1],

that conduct shall not also give rise to liability to a penalty under the regulations.

(3) Sub-paragraph (1) above does not apply to any failure mentioned in paragraph 22 above.

Cross references—See FA 1997 Sch 5 para 4(3) (contravention of requirement to repay Commissioners).

Amendments—[1] Words in sub-para (2)(*b*) inserted by the Finance Act 2008, Schedule 40 (Appointed Day, Transitional Provisions and Consequential Amendments) Order, SI 2009/571 art 8, Sch 1 paras 28, 29 with effect from 1 April 2009.

Prospective amendments—Para 23A to be inserted by the Tribunals, Courts and Enforcement Act 2007 s 62(3), Sch 13 paras 122, 123 with effect from a date to be appointed. Para 23A to be repealed by FA 2008 s 129, Sch 43 para 5 with effect from such day as the Commissioners may by statutory instrument appoint.

Para 23A to read—

"**Controlled Goods Agreements**

23A—(1) This paragraph applies where an enforcement agent acting under the power conferred by section 51(A1) of the Finance Act 1997 (power to use the procedure in Schedule 12 to the Tribunals, Courts and Enforcement Act 2007) has entered into a controlled goods agreement with the person against whom the power is exercisable ("the person in default").

(2) In this paragraph, "controlled goods agreement" has the meaning given by paragraph 13(4) of that Schedule.

(3) If the person in default removes or disposes of goods (or permits their removal or disposal) in breach of the controlled goods agreement, he is liable to a penalty equal to half of the tax or other amount recoverable under section 51(A1) of the Finance Act 1997.

(4) The person in default shall not be liable to a penalty under subparagraph

(3) above if he satisfies the Commissioners or, on appeal, an appeal tribunal, that there is a reasonable excuse for the breach in question.
(5) This paragraph extends only to England and Wales.".

Walking possession agreements

24— (1) This paragraph applies where—

(*a*) in accordance with regulations under [section 51 of the Finance Act 1997 (enforcement by distress)][1] a distress is authorised to be levied on the goods and chattels of a person (a person in default) who has refused or neglected to pay any tax due from him or any amount recoverable as if it were tax due from him, and

(*b*) the person levying the distress and the person in default have entered into a walking possession agreement.

(2) For the purposes of this paragraph a walking possession agreement is an agreement under which, in consideration of the property distrained upon being allowed to remain in the custody of the person in default and of the delaying of its sale, the person in default—

(*a*) acknowledges that the property specified in the agreement is under distraint and held in walking possession, and

(*b*) undertakes that, except with the consent of the Commissioners and subject to such conditions as they may impose, he will not remove or allow the removal of any of the specified property from the premises named in the agreement.

(3) If the person in default is in breach of the undertaking contained in a walking possession agreement, he is liable to a penalty equal to half of the tax or other amount referred to in sub-paragraph (1)(*a*) above.

(4) This paragraph does not extend to Scotland.

Amendments—[1] Words in sub-s (1)(*a*) above substituted for words "paragraph 13(1) above" by FA 1997 s 53(8) with effect from 1 July 1997 (see SI 1997/1432).
Prospective amendments—Sub-para (4) to be substituted by the Tribunals, Courts and Enforcement Act 2007 s 62(3), Sch 13 paras 122, 124 with effect from a date to be appointed. That sub-para as substituted, to read—
"(4) This paragraph extends only to Northern Ireland.".

Mitigation of penalties

25— (1) Where a person is liable to a penalty under this Part of this Schedule the Commissioners or, on appeal, an appeal tribunal may reduce the penalty to such amount (including nil) as they think proper.

(2) Where the person concerned satisfies the Commissioners or, on appeal, an appeal tribunal that there is a reasonable excuse for any breach, failure or other conduct, that is a factor which (among other things) may be taken into account under sub-paragraph (1) above.

(3) In the case of a penalty reduced by the Commissioners under sub-paragraph (1) above an appeal tribunal, on an appeal relating to the penalty, may cancel the whole or any part of the reduction made by the Commissioners.

PART VI
INTEREST

Interest on under-declared tax

26— (1) Sub-paragraph (2) below applies where—

(*a*) under section 50(1) of this Act the Commissioners assess an amount of tax due from a registrable person for an accounting period and notify it to him, and

(*b*) the assessment is made on the basis that the amount (the additional amount) is due from him in addition to any amount shown in a return made in relation to the accounting period.

(2) The additional amount shall carry interest for the period which—

(*a*) begins with the day after that on which the person is required by provision made under section 49 of this Act to pay tax due from him for the accounting period, and

(*b*) ends with the day before the relevant day.

(3) For the purposes of sub-paragraph (2) above the relevant day is the earlier of—

(*a*) the day on which the assessment is notified to the person;

(*b*) the day on which the additional amount is paid.

(4) Sub-paragraph (5) below applies where under section 50(2) of this Act the Commissioners assess an amount as being tax due from a registrable person for an accounting period and notify it to him.

(5) The amount shall carry interest for the period which—

(*a*) begins with the day after that on which the person is required by provision made under section 49 of this Act to pay tax due from him for the accounting period, and

(*b*) ends with the day before the relevant day.

(6) For the purposes of sub-paragraph (5) above the relevant day is the earlier of—

(*a*) the day on which the assessment is notified to the person;

(*b*) the day on which the amount is paid.

(7) Interest under this paragraph shall be payable at the rate applicable under section 197 of this Act.

(8) Interest under this paragraph shall be paid without any deduction of income tax.

(9) Sub-paragraph (10) below applies where—

(*a*) an amount carries interest under this paragraph (or would do so apart from that sub-paragraph), and

(*b*) all or part of the amount turns out not to be due.

(10) In such a case—

(*a*) the amount or part (as the case may be) shall not carry interest under this paragraph and shall be treated as never having done so, and

(*b*) all such adjustments as are reasonable shall be made, including adjustments by way of repayment by the Commissioners where appropriate.

Note—The rate of interest for the purposes of this section has been prescribed as follows—

Commencement date	*Rate*	*Order No*
1 April 1997	6.25%	1997/1016
6 July 1998	9.5%	1998/1461
1 April 2000	8.5%	2000/631

Interest on unpaid tax etc

27— (1) Sub-paragraph (2) below applies where—

(*a*) a registrable person makes a return under provision made under section 49 of this Act (whether or not he makes it at the time required by such provision), and

(*b*) the return shows that an amount of tax is due from him for the accounting period in relation to which the return is made.

(2) The amount shall carry interest for the period which—

(*a*) begins with the day after that on which the person is required by provision made under section 49 of this Act to pay tax due from him for the accounting period, and

(*b*) ends with the day before that on which the amount is paid.

(3) Sub-paragraph (4) below applies where—

(*a*) under section 50(1) of this Act the Commissioners assess an amount of tax due from a registrable person for an accounting period and notify it to him, and

(*b*) the assessment is made on the basis that no return required by provision made under section 49 of this Act has been made by the person in relation to the accounting period.

(4) The amount shall carry interest for the period which—

(*a*) begins with the day after that on which the person is required by provision made under section 49 of this Act to pay tax due from him for the accounting period, and

(*b*) ends with the day before that on which the amount is paid.

(5) Sub-paragraph (6) below applies where—

(*a*) under section 50(1) of this Act the Commissioners assess an amount of tax due from a registrable person for an accounting period and notify it to him, and

(*b*) the assessment (the supplementary assessment) is made on the basis that the amount (the additional amount) is due from him in addition to any amount shown in a return, or in any previous assessment, made in relation to the accounting period.

(6) The additional amount shall carry interest for the period which—

(*a*) begins with the day on which the supplementary assessment is notified to the person, and

(*b*) ends with the day before that on which the additional amount is paid.

(7) Sub-paragraph (8) below applies where under section 50(2) of this Act the Commissioners assess an amount as being tax due from a registrable person for an accounting period and notify it to him.

(8) The amount shall carry interest for the period which—

(*a*) begins with the day on which the assessment is notified to the person, and

(*b*) ends with the day before that on which the amount is paid.

(9) Sub-paragraph (10) below applies where under paragraph 32 below the Commissioners—

(*a*) assess an amount due from a person by way of penalty under Part V of this Schedule and notify it to him, or

(*b*) assess an amount due from a person by way of interest under paragraph 26 above and notify it to him.

(10) The amount shall carry interest for the period which—

(*a*) begins with the day on which the assessment is notified to the person, and

(*b*) ends with the day before that on which the amount is paid.

(11) Interest under this paragraph shall be compound interest calculated—

(*a*) at the penalty rate, and

(*b*) with monthly rests;

and the penalty rate is the rate found by taking the rate at which interest is payable under paragraph 26 above and adding 10 percentage points to that rate.

(12) Interest under this paragraph shall be paid without any deduction of income tax.

(13) Where—

(*a*) the Commissioners assess and notify an amount as mentioned in sub-paragraph (5)(*a*) or (7) or (9)(*a*) or (*b*) above,

(*b*) they also specify a date for the purposes of this sub-paragraph, and

(*c*) the amount concerned is paid on or before that date,

the amount shall not carry interest by virtue of sub-paragraph (6) or (8) or (10) above (as the case may be).

(14) Sub-paragraph (15) below applies where—

(*a*) an amount carries interest under this paragraph (or would do so apart from that sub-paragraph), and

(*b*) all or part of the amount turns out not to be due.

(15) In such a case—

(*a*) the amount or part (as the case may be) shall not carry interest under this paragraph and shall be treated as never having done so, and

(*b*) all such adjustments as are reasonable shall be made, including adjustments by way of repayment by the Commissioners where appropriate.

Cross reference—FA 2009 s 108 (suspension of penalties during currency of agreement for deferred payment).

28— (1) Where a person is liable to pay interest under paragraph 27 above the Commissioners or, on appeal, an appeal tribunal may reduce the amount payable to such amount (including nil) as they think proper.

(2) Where the person concerned satisfies the Commissioners or, on appeal, an appeal tribunal that there is a reasonable excuse for the conduct giving rise to the liability to pay interest, that is a factor which (among other things) may be taken into account under sub-paragraph (1) above.

(3) In the case of interest reduced by the Commissioners under sub-paragraph (1) above an appeal tribunal, on an appeal relating to the interest, may cancel the whole or any part of the reduction made by the Commissioners.

Interest payable by Commissioners

29— (1) Where, due to an error on the part of the Commissioners, a person—

(*a*) has paid to them by way of tax an amount which was not tax due and which they are in consequence liable to repay to him,

(*b*) has failed to claim payment of an amount to the payment of which he was entitled in pursuance of provision made under section 51(2)(*c*) or (*d*) or (*f*) of this Act, or

(*c*) has suffered delay in receiving payment of an amount due to him from them in connection with tax,

then, if and to the extent that they would not be liable to do so apart from this paragraph, they shall (subject to the following provisions of this paragraph) pay interest to him on that amount for the applicable period.

[(1A) In sub-paragraph (1) above—

(*a*) the reference in paragraph (*a*) to an amount which the Commissioners are liable to repay in consequence of the making of a payment that was not due is a reference to only so much of that amount as is the subject of a claim that the Commissioners are required to satisfy or have satisfied; and

(*b*) the amounts referred to in paragraph (*c*) do not include any amount payable under this paragraph.][1]

(2) The applicable period, in a case falling within sub-paragraph (1)(*a*) above, is the period—

(*a*) beginning with the date on which the payment is received by the Commissioners, and

(*b*) ending with the date on which they authorise payment of the amount on which the interest is payable.

(3) The applicable period, in a case falling within sub-paragraph (1)(*b*) or (*c*) above, is the period—

(*a*) beginning with the date on which, apart from the error, the Commissioners might reasonably have been expected to authorise payment of the amount on which the interest is payable, and

(*b*) ending with the date on which they in fact authorise payment of that amount.

[(4) In determining the applicable period for the purposes of this paragraph there shall be left out of account any period by which the Commissioners' authorisation of the payment of interest is delayed by the conduct of the person who claims the interest.][3]

[(4A) The reference in sub-paragraph (4) above to a period by which the Commissioners' authorisation of the payment of interest is delayed by the conduct of the person who claims it includes, in particular, any period which is referable to—

(*a*) any unreasonable delay in the making of the claim for interest or in the making of any claim for the payment or repayment of the amount on which interest is claimed;

(*b*) any failure by that person or a person acting on his influence to provide the Commissioners—

(i) at or before the time of the making of a claim, or

(ii) subsequently in response to a request for information by the Commissioners.

with all the information required by them to enable the existence and amount of the claimant's entitlement to a payment or repayment, and to interest on that payment or repayment, to be determined; and

(*c*) the making, as part of or in association with either—

(i) the claim for interest, or

(ii) any claim for the payment or repayment of the amount on which interest is claimed,

of a claim to anything to which the claimant was not entitled.][3]

[(5) In determining for the purposes of sub-paragraph (4A) above whether any period of delay is referable to a failure by any person to provide information in response to a request by the Commissioners, there shall be taken to be so referable, except so far as may be provided for by regulations, any period which—

(*a*) begins with the date on which the Commissioners require that person to provide information which they reasonably consider relevant to the matter to be determined; and

(*b*) ends with the earliest date on which it would be reasonable for the Commissioners to conclude—

(i) that they have received a complete answer to their request for information;

(ii) that they have received all that they need in answer to that request; or

(iii) that it is unnecessary for them to be provided with any information in answer to that request.][3]

(6) …[3]

(7) The Commissioners shall only be liable to pay interest under this paragraph on a claim made in writing for that purpose.

[(8) A claim under this paragraph shall not be made more than three years after the end of the applicable period to which it relates.][2]

[(9) References in this paragraph—

(*a*) to receiving payment of any amount from the Commissioners, or

(*b*) to the authorisation by the Commissioners of the payment of any amount

include references to the discharge by way of set-off (whether in accordance with regulations under paragraph 42 or 43 below or otherwise) of the Commissioners' liability to pay that amount.][2]

(10) Interest under this paragraph shall be payable at the rate applicable under section 197 of this Act.

Note—The rate of interest for the purposes of this section has been prescribed as follows—

Commencement date	*Rate*	*Order No*
1 April 1997	6%	1997/1016 and 1998/1461

Cross references—See FA 1997 Sch 5 para 15 (assessments of overpayments of interest.)

Amendments—[1] Sub-para (1A) inserted by FA 1997 s 50, Sch 5 para 11(2) and always deemed to have had effect.

[2] Sub-paras (8) and (9) substituted by FA 1997 s 50, Sch 5 para 11(3), (4) and always deemed to have had effect.

[3] Sub-paras (4), (4A), (5) substituted for sub-paras (4)–(6) by FA 1997 s 50, Sch 5 para 12 with effect for the purposes of determining whether any period beginning or after the day of passing FA 1997 (19 March 1997) is left out of account.

Prospective amendments—In sub-para (8) words "4 years" to be substituted for "three years" by FA 2009 s 99, Sch 51 paras 37, 39 with effect from such day as the Treasury may by order made by statutory instrument appoint.

30— (1) Where—

(*a*) any interest is payable by the Commissioners to a person on a sum due to him under this Part of this Act, and

(*b*) he is a person to whom regulations under section 51 of this Act apply,

the interest shall be treated as an amount to which he is entitled by way of credit in pursuance of the regulations.

(2) Sub-paragraph (1) above shall be disregarded for the purpose of determining a person's entitlement to interest or the amount of interest to which he is entitled.

PART VII

MISCELLANEOUS

Security for tax

31 Where it appears to the Commissioners requisite to do so for the protection of the revenue they may require a registrable person, as a condition of his carrying out taxable activities, to give

Landfill Tax

security (or further security) of such amount and in such manner as they may determine for the payment of any tax which is or may become due from him.

Assessments to penalties etc

32— (1) Where a person is liable—

(*a*) to a penalty under Part V of this Schedule, or

(*b*) for interest under paragraph 26 or 27 above,

the Commissioners may, subject to sub-paragraph (2) below, assess the amount due by way of penalty or interest (as the case may be) and notify it to him accordingly; and the fact that any conduct giving rise to a penalty under Part V of this Schedule may have ceased before an assessment is made under this paragraph shall not affect the power of the Commissioners to make such an assessment.

(2) In the case of the penalties and interest referred to in the following paragraphs of this sub-paragraph, the assessment under this paragraph shall be of an amount due in respect of the accounting period which in the paragraph concerned is referred to as the relevant period—

(*a*) in the case of a penalty under paragraph 18 above relating to the evasion of tax, and in the case of interest under paragraph 27 above on an amount due by way of such a penalty, the relevant period is the accounting period for which the tax evaded was due;

(*b*) in the case of a penalty under paragraph 18 above relating to the obtaining of a payment under regulations under section 51(2)(*c*) or (*d*) or (*f*) of this Act, and in the case of interest under paragraph 27 above on an amount due by way of such a penalty, the relevant period is the accounting period in respect of which the payment was obtained;

(*c*) in the case of interest under paragraph 26 above, and in the case of interest under paragraph 27 above on an amount due by way of interest under paragraph 26 above, the relevant period is the accounting period in respect of which the tax was due;

(*d*) in the case of interest under paragraph 27 above on an amount of tax, the relevant period is the accounting period in respect of which the tax was due.

(3) In a case where the amount of any penalty or interest falls to be calculated by reference to tax which was not paid at the time it should have been and that tax cannot be readily attributed to any one or more accounting periods, it shall be treated for the purposes of this Part of this Act as tax due for such period or periods as the Commissioners may determine to the best of their judgment and notify to the person liable for the tax and penalty or interest.

(4) Where a person is assessed under this paragraph to an amount due by way of any penalty or interest falling within sub-paragraph (2) above and is also assessed under subsection (1) or (2) of section 50 of this Act for the accounting period which is the relevant period under sub-paragraph (2) above, the assessments may be combined and notified to him as one assessment, but the amount of the penalty or interest shall be separately identified in the notice.

(5) Sub-paragraph (6) below applies in the case of an amount due by way of interest under paragraph 27 above.

(6) Where this sub-paragraph applies in the case of an amount—

(*a*) a notice of assessment under this paragraph shall specify a date, being not later than the date of the notice, to which the amount of interest which is assessed is calculated, and

(*b*) if the interest continues to accrue after that date, a further assessment or further assessments may be made under this paragraph in respect of amounts which so accrue.

(7) If, within such period as may be notified by the Commissioners to the person liable for the interest under paragraph 27 above, the amount referred to in paragraph 27(2), (4), (6), (8) or (10) above (as the case may be) is paid, it shall be treated for the purposes of paragraph 27 above as paid on the date specified as mentioned in sub-paragraph (6)(*a*) above.

(8) Where an amount has been assessed and notified to any person under this paragraph it shall be recoverable as if it were tax due from him unless, or except to the extent that, the assessment has subsequently been withdrawn or reduced.

(9) Subsection (8) of section 50 of this Act shall apply for the purposes of this paragraph as it applies for the purposes of that section.

Assessments: time limits

33— (1) Subject to the following provisions of this paragraph, an assessment under—

(*a*) any provision of section 50 of this Act, or

(*b*) paragraph 32 above,

shall not be made more than [three years][1] after the end of the accounting period concerned or, in the case of an assessment under paragraph 32 above of an amount due by way of a penalty which is not a penalty referred to in sub-paragraph (2) of that paragraph, [three years][1] after the event giving rise to the penalty.

(2) Subject to sub-paragraph (5) below, an assessment under paragraph 32 above of—

(*a*) an amount due by way of any penalty referred to in sub-paragraph (2) of that paragraph, or

(*b*) an amount due by way of interest,

may be made at any time before the expiry of the period of two years beginning with the time when the amount of tax due for the accounting period concerned has been finally determined.

(3) In relation to an assessment under paragraph 32 above, any reference in sub-paragraph (1) or (2) above to the accounting period concerned is a reference to that period which, in the case of the penalty or interest concerned, is the relevant period referred to in sub-paragraph (2) of that paragraph.

(4) Subject to sub-paragraph (5) below, if tax has been lost—

(*a*) as a result of conduct falling within paragraph 18(1) above or for which a person has been convicted of fraud, or

(*b*) in circumstances giving rise to liability to a penalty under paragraph 21 above,

an assessment may be made as if, in sub-paragraph (1) above, each reference to [three years][1] were a reference to twenty years.

(5) Where after a person's death the Commissioners propose to assess an amount as due by reason of some conduct of the deceased—

(*a*) the assessment shall not be made more than three years after the death, and

(*b*) if the circumstances are as set out in sub-paragraph (4) above, the modification of sub-paragraph (1) above contained in that sub-paragraph shall not apply but any assessment which (from the point of view of time limits) could have been made immediately after the death may be made at any time within three years after it.

Amendments—[1] Words in sub-paras (1) and (4) substituted for the words "three years" by FA 1997 s 50 Sch 5 para 6 with effect from 19 March 1997.

Prospective amendments—In sub-paras (1), (5)(*a*) words "4 years" to be substituted for "three years", in sub-para (1) "the relevant event" to be substituted for "the end of" to the end, sub-para (1A) to be inserted, in sub-para (3) "sub-paragraph (1A)" to be substituted for "sub-paragraph (1)", sub-para (4) to be substituted, sub-para (5)(*b*) to be repealed, by FA 2009 s 99, Sch 51 paras 37, 40 with effect from such day as the Treasury may by order made by statutory instrument appoint. Sub-para (1A) to read as follows—

"(1A) In this paragraph "the relevant event", in relation to an assessment, means—

(*a*) the end of the accounting period concerned, or

(*b*) in the case of an assessment under paragraph 32 of an amount due by way of a penalty other than a penalty referred to in paragraph 32(2), the event giving rise to the penalty."

Sub-para (4) to be substituted by the following—

"(4) An assessment of an amount due from a person in a case involving a loss of tax—

(*a*) brought about deliberately by the person (or by another person acting on that person's behalf), or

(*b*) attributable to a failure by the person to comply with an obligation under section 47(2) or (3),

may be made at any time not more than 20 years after the relevant event (subject to sub-paragraph (5)).

(4A) In sub-paragraph (4)(*a*) the reference to a loss brought about deliberately by the person includes a loss brought about as a result of a deliberate inaccuracy in a document given to Her Majesty's Revenue and Customs by or on behalf of that person."

Supplementary assessments

34— If, otherwise than in circumstances falling within subsection (5)(*b*) of section 50 of this Act, it appears to the Commissioners that the amount which ought to have been assessed in an assessment under any provision of that section or under paragraph 32 above exceeds the amount which was so assessed, then—

(*a*) under the like provision as that assessment was made, and

(*b*) on or before the last day on which that assessment could have been made,

the Commissioners may make a supplementary assessment of the amount of the excess and shall notify the person concerned accordingly.

Disclosure of information

35— (1) Notwithstanding any obligation not to disclose information that would otherwise apply, the Commissioners may disclose information to—

(*a*) the Secretary of State,

(*b*) the Environment Agency,

(*c*) the Scottish Environment Protection Agency,

(*d*) the Department of the Environment for Northern Ireland,

(*e*) a district council in Northern Ireland, or

(*f*) an authorised officer of any person (a principal) mentioned in paragraphs (*a*) to (*e*) above,

for the purpose of assisting the principal concerned in the performance of the principal's duties.

(2) Notwithstanding any such obligation as is mentioned in sub-paragraph (1) above, any person mentioned in sub-paragraph (1)(*a*) to (*f*) above may disclose information to the Commissioners or to an authorised officer of the Commissioners for the purpose of assisting the Commissioners in the performance of duties in relation to tax.

(3) Information that has been disclosed to a person by virtue of this paragraph shall not be disclosed by him except—

(*a*) to another person to whom (instead of him) disclosure could by virtue of this paragraph have been made, or

(*b*) for the purpose of any proceedings connected with the operation of any provision of, or made under, any enactment in relation to the environment or to tax.

(4) References in the preceding provisions of this paragraph to an authorised officer of any person (the principal) are to any person who has been designated by the principal as a person to and by whom information may be disclosed by virtue of this paragraph.

(5) The Secretary of State shall notify the Commissioners in writing of the name of any person designated by the Secretary of State under sub-paragraph (4) above.

(6) No charge may be made for a disclosure made by virtue of this paragraph.

The register: publication

36— (1) The Commissioners may publish, by such means as they think fit, information which—

(*a*) is derived from the register kept under section 47 of this Act, and

(*b*) falls within any of the descriptions set out below.

(2) The descriptions are—

(*a*) the names of registered persons;

(*b*) the addresses of any sites or other premises at which they carry on business;

(*c*) the registration numbers assigned to them in the register;

(*d*) the fact (where it is the case) that the registered person is a body corporate which under section 59 of this Act is treated as a member of a group;

(*e*) the names of the other bodies corporate treated under that section as members of the group;

(*f*) the addresses of any sites or other premises at which those other bodies carry on business.

(3) Information may be published in accordance with this paragraph notwithstanding any obligation not to disclose the information that would otherwise apply.

Evidence by certificate etc

37— (1) A certificate of the Commissioners—

(*a*) that a person was or was not at any time registered under section 47 of this Act, [or][1]

(*b*) that any return required by regulations made under section 49 of this Act has not been made or had not been made at any time, …[1]

(*c*) …[1]

shall be sufficient evidence of that fact until the contrary is proved.

(2) A photograph of any document furnished to the Commissioners for the purposes of this Part of this Act and certified by them to be such a photograph shall be admissible in any proceedings, whether civil or criminal, to the same extent as the document itself.

(3) Any document purporting to be a certificate under sub-paragraph (1) or (2) above shall be taken to be such a certificate until the contrary is proved.

Amendments—[1] Words inserted and repealed by FA 2008 s 138, Sch 44 para 7 with effect from 21 July 2008. Sub-para (1)(*c*) previously read as follows—

"(*c*) that any tax shown as due in a return made in pursuance of regulations made under section 49 of this Act, or in an assessment made under section 50 of this Act, has not been paid,".

Service of notices etc

38 Any notice, notification or requirement to be served on, given to or made of any person for the purposes of this Part of this Act may be served, given or made by sending it by post in a letter addressed to that person at his last or usual residence or place of business.

39— (1) This paragraph applies to directions, specifications and conditions which the Commissioners or an authorised person may give or impose under any provision of this Part.

(2) A direction, specification or condition given or imposed by the Commissioners may be withdrawn or varied by them.

(3) A direction, specification or condition given or imposed by an authorised person may be withdrawn or varied by him or by another authorised person.

(4) No direction, specification or condition shall have effect as regards any person it is intended to affect unless—

(*a*) a notice containing it is served on him, or

(*b*) other reasonable steps are taken with a view to bringing it to his attention.

(5) No withdrawal or variation of a direction, specification or condition shall have effect as regards any person the withdrawal or variation is intended to affect unless—

(*a*) a notice containing the withdrawal or variation is served on him, or

(*b*) other reasonable steps are taken with a view to bringing the withdrawal or variation to his attention.

No deduction of penalties or interest

40 (*inserts* TA 1988 s 827(1C)).

Destination of receipts

41

Amendments—Paragraph repealed by Commissioners for Revenue and Customs Act 2005 ss 50, 52, Sch 4 para 65 and Sch 5 with effect from 18 April 2005 by virtue of the Commissioners for Revenue and Customs Act (Commencement) Order, SI 2005/1126, art 2(2).

Set-off of amounts

42— (1) Regulations may make provision in relation to any case where—

(*a*) a person is under a duty to pay to the Commissioners at any time an amount or amounts in respect of landfill tax, and

(*b*) the Commissioners are under a duty to pay to that person at the same time an amount or amounts in respect of any tax (or taxes) under their care and management.

(2) The regulations may provide that if the total of the amount or amounts mentioned in sub-paragraph (1)(*a*) above exceeds the total of the amount or amounts mentioned in sub-paragraph (1)(*b*) above, the latter shall be set off against the former.

(3) The regulations may provide that if the total of the amount or amounts mentioned in sub-paragraph (1)(*b*) above exceeds the total of the amount or amounts mentioned in sub-paragraph (1)(*a*) above, the Commissioners may set off the latter in paying the former.

(4) The regulations may provide that if the total of the amount or amounts mentioned in sub-paragraph (1)(*a*) above is the same as the total of the amount or amounts mentioned in sub-paragraph (1)(*b*) above no payment need be made in respect of the former or the latter.

[(4A) The regulations may provide for any limitation on the time within which the Commissioners are entitled to take steps for recovering any amount due to them in respect of landfill tax to be disregarded, in such cases as may be described in the regulations, in determining whether any person is under such a duty to pay as is mentioned in sub-paragraph (1)(*a*) above.][1]

(5) The regulations may include provision treating any duty to pay mentioned in sub-paragraph (1) above as discharged accordingly.

(6) References in sub-paragraph (1) above to an amount in respect of a particular tax include references not only to an amount of tax itself but also to other amounts such as interest and penalty.

(7) In this paragraph "tax" includes "duty".

Regulations—Landfill Tax Regulations, SI 1996/1527.
Cross references—See Landfill Tax Regulations, SI 1996/1527 regs 45, 47 (set-off of amounts).
Amendments—[1] Sub-para (4A) inserted by FA 1997 s 50, Sch 5 para 13(1).

43...[1]

Regulations—Landfill Tax Regulations, SI 1996/1527.
Cross references—See Landfill Tax Regulations, SI 1996/1527 regs 46, 47 (set-off of amounts).
Amendments—[1] Para 43 repealed by FA 2009 s 119, Sch 60 paras 5, 10 with effect from 1 September 2009 by virtue of FA 2009 s 119, Sch 60 para 13(1). Prior to that date, para 43 read as follows:

"43—

(1) Regulations may make provision in relation to any case where—

(*a*) a person is under a duty to pay to the Commissioners at any time an amount or amounts in respect of any tax (or taxes) under their care and management, and

(*b*) the Commissioners are under a duty to pay to that person at the same time an amount or amounts in respect of landfill tax.

(2) The regulations may provide that if the total of the amount or amounts mentioned in sub-paragraph (1)(*a*) above exceeds the total of the amount or amounts mentioned in sub-paragraph (1)(*b*) above, the latter shall be set off against the former.

(3) The regulations may provide that if the total of the amount or amounts mentioned in sub-paragraph (1)(*b*) above exceeds the total of the amount or amounts mentioned in sub-paragraph (1)(*a*) above, the Commissioners may set off the latter in paying the former.

(4) The regulations may provide that if the total of the amount or amounts mentioned in sub-paragraph (1)(*a*) above is the same as the total of the amount or amounts mentioned in sub-paragraph (1)(*b*) above no payment need be made in respect of the former or the latter.

[(4A) The regulations may provide for any limitation on the time within which the Commissioners are entitled to take steps for recovering any amount due to them in respect of any of the taxes under their care and management to be disregarded, in such cases as may be described in the regulations, in determining whether any person is under such a duty to pay as is mentioned in sub-paragraph (1)(*a*) above.]

(5) The regulations may include provision treating any duty to pay mentioned in sub-paragraph (1) above as discharged accordingly.

(6) References in sub-paragraph (1) above to an amount in respect of a particular tax include references not only to an amount of tax itself but also to other amounts such as interest and penalty.

(7) In this paragraph "tax" includes "duty"."

Amounts shown as tax on invoices

44— (1) Where—

(*a*) a registrable person issues an invoice showing an amount as tax chargeable on an event, and

(*b*) no tax is in fact chargeable on the event,

an amount equal to the amount shown as tax shall be recoverable from the person as a debt due to the Crown.

(2) Where—

(*a*) a registrable person issues an invoice showing an amount as tax chargeable on a taxable disposal, and

(*b*) the amount shown as tax exceeds the amount of tax in fact chargeable on the disposal,

an amount equal to the excess shall be recoverable from the person as a debt due to the Crown.
(3) References in this paragraph to an invoice are to any invoice, whether or not it is a landfill invoice within the meaning of section 61 of this Act.

Adjustment of contracts

45— (1) This paragraph applies where—
(*a*) material undergoes a landfill disposal,
(*b*) a payment falls to be made under a disposal contract relating to the material, and
(*c*) after the making of the contract there is a change in the tax chargeable on the landfill disposal.
(2) In such a case the amount of the payment mentioned in sub-paragraph (1)(*b*) above shall be adjusted, unless the disposal contract otherwise provides, so as to reflect the tax chargeable on the landfill disposal.
(3) For the purposes of this paragraph a disposal contract relating to material is a contract providing for the disposal of the material, and it is immaterial—
(*a*) when the contract was made;
(*b*) whether the contract also provides for other matters;
(*c*) whether the contract provides for a method of disposal and (if it does) what method it provides for.
(4) The reference in sub-paragraph (1) above to a change in the tax chargeable is a reference to a change—
(*a*) to or from no tax being chargeable, or
(*b*) in the amount of tax chargeable.

46— (1) This paragraph applies where—
(*a*) work is carried out under a construction contract,
(*b*) as a result of the work, material undergoes a landfill disposal,
(*c*) the contract makes no provision as to the disposal of such material, and
(*d*) the contract was made on or before 29th November 1994 (when the proposal to create tax was announced).
(2) In such a case the amount of any payment which falls to be made—
(*a*) under the construction contract, and
(*b*) in respect of the work,
shall be adjusted, unless the contract otherwise provides, so as to reflect the tax (if any) chargeable on the disposal.
(3) For the purposes of this paragraph a construction contract is a contract under which all or any of the following work is to be carried out—
(*a*) the preparation of a site;
(*b*) demolition;
(*c*) building;
(*d*) civil engineering.

Adjustment of rent etc

47— (1) This paragraph applies where—
(*a*) an agreement with regard to any sum payable in respect of the use of land (whether the sum is called rent or royalty or otherwise) provides that the amount of the sum is to be calculated by reference to the turnover of a business,
(*b*) the agreement was made on or before 29th November 1994 (when the proposal to create tax was announced), and
(*c*) the circumstances are such that (had the agreement been made after that date) it can reasonably be expected that it would have provided that tax be ignored in calculating the turnover.
(2) In such a case the agreement shall be taken to provide that tax be ignored in calculating the turnover.

[PART VIII

SECONDARY LIABILITY: CONTROLLERS OF LANDFILL SITES][1]

[Meaning of controller

48— (1) For the purposes of this Part of this Schedule a person is the controller of the whole, or a part, of a landfill site at a given time if he determines, or is entitled to determine, what disposals of material, if any, may be made—
(*a*) at every part of the site at that time, or
(*b*) at that part of the site at that time,
as the case may be.

(2) But a person who, because he is an employee or agent of another, determines or is entitled to determine what disposals may be made at a landfill site or any part of a landfill site is not the controller of that site or, as the case may be, that part of that site.

(3) Where a person is the controller of the whole or a part of a landfill site, that site or, as the case may be, that part of the site is referred to in this Part of this Schedule as being under his control.

(4) Any reference in this Part of this Schedule to a controller (without more) is a reference to a controller of the whole or a part of a landfill site.][1]

Amendments—[1] Pt VIII of this Schedule inserted by FA 2000 s 142(3), Sch 37, with effect for taxable disposals made after 27 July 2000.

[Secondary liability

49— (1) Where—

(*a*) a taxable disposal is made at a landfill site,

(*b*) at the time when that disposal is made a person is the operator of the landfill site by virtue of section 67(*a*), (*c*) or (*e*) of this Act, and

(*c*) at that time a person other than the operator mentioned in paragraph (*b*) above is the controller of the whole or a part of the landfill site,

the controller shall be liable to pay to the Commissioners an amount of the landfill tax chargeable on the disposal.

(2) The amount which the controller is liable to pay shall be determined in accordance with the following provisions of this paragraph.

(3) In a case where the whole of the landfill site is under the control of the controller, he shall be liable to pay the whole of the landfill tax chargeable.

(4) In a case where a part of the landfill site is under the control of the controller, he shall be liable to pay an amount of the landfill tax calculated in accordance with sub-paragraphs (5) and (6) below.

(5) The amount of landfill tax which the controller is liable to pay is the amount which would have been chargeable had a separate taxable disposal consisting of the amount of material referred to in sub-paragraph (6) below been made at the time of the disposal mentioned in sub-paragraph (1)(*a*) above.

(6) That amount of material is the amount by weight of the material comprised in the disposal mentioned in sub-paragraph (1)(*a*) above which was disposed of on the part of the landfill site under the control of the controller.

(7) If the amount mentioned in sub-paragraph (6) above is nil, the controller shall have no liability under sub paragraph (1) above in relation to landfill tax chargeable on the disposal.

(8) For the purposes of sub-paragraph (1)(*b*) and (*c*) above—

(*a*) section 61 of this Act, and

(*b*) any regulations made under section 62 of this Act,

shall not apply for determining the time when the disposal in question is made.][1]

Amendments—[1] Pt VIII of this Schedule inserted by FA 2000 s 142(3), Sch 37, with effect for taxable disposals made after 27 July 2000.

[Operator entitled to credit

50— (1) This paragraph applies where—

(*a*) the operator of a landfill site is liable to pay landfill tax on a taxable disposal by reference to a particular accounting period,

(*b*) a controller of the whole or a part of that site is (apart from this paragraph) liable under paragraph 49 above to pay an amount of that tax, and

(*c*) for the accounting period in question the operator is entitled to credit under regulations made under section 51 of this Act.

(2) The amount of the tax which the controller is (apart from this sub-paragraph) liable to pay shall be reduced by the amount calculated in accordance with the following formula—

$$\frac{A \times C}{G}$$

where—

A is the amount of tax mentioned in sub-paragraph (1)(*b*) above;
C is the amount of credit mentioned in sub-paragraph (1)(*c*) above; and
G is the operator's gross tax liability for the accounting period in question.

(3) For the purposes of sub-paragraph (2) above, the operator's gross tax liability for the accounting period in question is the gross amount of landfill tax—

(*a*) which is chargeable on disposals made at all landfill sites of which he is the operator, and

(*b*) for which he is required to account by reference to that accounting period.

(4) In sub-paragraph (3) above, the gross amount of landfill tax means the amount of tax before any credit or any other adjustment is taken into account in the period in question.

(5) If the amount calculated in accordance with the formula in sub-paragraph (2) above is greater than the amount of tax mentioned in sub-paragraph (1)(*b*) above, the amount of the tax which the controller is liable to pay shall be reduced to nil.][1]

Amendments—[1] Pt VIII of this Schedule inserted by FA 2000 s 142(3), Sch 37, with effect for taxable disposals made after 27 July 2000.

[Payment of secondary liability

51— (1) This paragraph applies where a controller is liable under paragraph 49 above (after taking account of any reduction under paragraph 50 above) to pay an amount of landfill tax ("the relevant amount").

(2) The controller is required to pay the relevant amount to the Commissioners only if—

(*a*) a notice containing the required information is served on him, or

(*b*) other reasonable steps are taken with a view to bringing the required information to his attention,

before the end of the period of two years beginning with the day immediately following the relevant accounting day.

(3) The relevant accounting day is the last day of the accounting period by reference to which the landfill site operator liable to pay the landfill tax in question is required to account for that tax.

(4) If the controller is required to pay the relevant amount by virtue of this paragraph, the amount shall be paid before the end of the period of thirty days beginning with the day immediately following the notification day.

(5) The notification day is—

(*a*) in a case where notice is served on a controller as mentioned in sub-paragraph (2)(*a*) above, the day on which the notice is served, or

(*b*) in a case where other reasonable steps are taken as mentioned in sub-paragraph (2)(*b*) above, the day on which the last of those steps is taken.

(6) For the purposes of sub-paragraph (2) above the required information is the relevant amount and, if that amount is one reduced in accordance with paragraph 50 above, also—

(*a*) the amount of the controller's liability under paragraph 49 above apart from the reduction,

(*b*) the amount of credit to which the operator is entitled, and

(*c*) the operator's gross tax liability.][1]

Amendments—[1] Pt VIII of this Schedule inserted by FA 2000 s 142(3), Sch 37, with effect for taxable disposals made after 27 July 2000.

[Assessments

52— (1) Where an amount of landfill tax is—

(*a*) assessed under section 50 of this Act, and

(*b*) notified to a licensed operator,

the Commissioners may also determine that a controller of the whole or a part of any landfill site operated by the licensed operator shall be liable to pay so much of the amount assessed as they consider just and equitable.

(2) A controller is required to pay an amount determined under sub-paragraph (1) above only if—

(*a*) a notice stating the amount is served on him, or

(*b*) other reasonable steps are taken with a view to bringing the amount of the liability to his attention,

before the expiry of the period of two years beginning with the day immediately following the assessment day.

(3) The assessment day is the day on which the assessment in question is notified to the licensed operator.

(4) If a controller is required to pay an amount by virtue of this paragraph, it shall be paid before the end of the period of thirty days beginning with the day immediately following the notification day.

(5) The notification day is—

(*a*) in a case where notice is served on a controller as mentioned in sub-paragraph (2)(*a*) above, the day on which the notice is served, or

(*b*) in a case where other reasonable steps are taken as mentioned in sub-paragraph (2)(*b*) above, the day on which the last of those steps is taken.

(6) For the purposes of this paragraph a licensed operator is a person who is the operator of a landfill site by virtue of section 67(*a*), (*c*) or (*e*) of this Act.][1]

Amendments—[1] Pt VIII of this Schedule inserted by FA 2000 s 142(3), Sch 37, with effect for taxable disposals made after 27 July 2000.

[Assessment withdrawn or reduced

53— (1) Where—

(*a*) a controller is liable to pay an amount determined under paragraph 52 above, and

(*b*) the assessment notified to the licensed operator is withdrawn or reduced,

the Commissioners may determine that the controller's liability is to be cancelled or to be reduced to such an amount as they consider just and equitable.

(2) Sub-paragraphs (3) to (5) below apply where the Commissioners make a determination under sub-paragraph (1) above that the controller's liability is to be reduced (but not cancelled).

(3) In such a case they shall—

(*a*) serve the controller with notice stating the amount of the reduced liability, or

(*b*) take other reasonable steps with a view to bringing the reduced amount to the controller's attention.

(4) If the controller has already been served with notice of the amount determined under paragraph 52 above, or if other steps have already been taken to bring that amount to his attention—

(*a*) the Commissioners shall serve the notice mentioned in sub-paragraph (3)(*a*) above, or take the steps mentioned in sub-paragraph (3)(*b*) above, before the end of the period of thirty days beginning with the day immediately following that on which they make the determination under sub-paragraph (1) above, and

(*b*) the reduced amount shall be payable, or treated as having been payable, on or before the day on which the amount referred to in sub-paragraph (1)(*a*) above would have been payable apart from this paragraph.

(5) In a case where the controller has not been served with notice of the amount determined under paragraph 52 above, or no other steps have been taken to bring that amount to his attention, he shall be liable to pay the reduced amount only if—

(*a*) the notice mentioned in sub-paragraph (3)(*a*) above is served, or

(*b*) the other steps mentioned in sub-paragraph (3)(*b*) above are taken,

before the expiry of the period of two years beginning with the day immediately following that on which the Commissioners make the determination under sub-paragraph (1) above.

(6) Sub-paragraph (7) below applies where—

(*a*) the Commissioners make a determination under sub-paragraph (1) above that the controller's liability is to be cancelled, and

(*b*) the controller has already been served with notice of the amount determined under paragraph 52 above, or other steps have already been taken to bring that amount to his attention.

(7) In such a case the Commissioners shall—

(*a*) serve the controller with notice stating that the liability has been cancelled, or

(*b*) take other reasonable steps with a view to bringing the cancellation to the controller's attention,

before the end of the period of thirty days beginning with the day immediately following that on which they make the determination that the liability is to be cancelled.][1]

Amendments—[1] Pt VIII of this Schedule inserted by FA 2000 s 142(3), Sch 37, with effect for taxable disposals made after 27 July 2000.

[Adjustments

54— (1) This paragraph applies in any case where the liability of a licensed operator to pay landfill tax is adjusted otherwise than by—

(*a*) his being entitled to credit under regulations made under section 51 of this Act,

(*b*) his being notified of an amount assessed under section 50 of this Act, or

(*c*) the withdrawal or reduction of an assessment under section 50 of this Act which was notified to him.

(2) In such a case the Commissioners may determine that a controller of the whole or any part of a landfill site operated by the licensed operator—

(*a*) shall be liable to pay to the Commissioners such an amount as they consider just and equitable, or

(*b*) shall be entitled to an allowance of such an amount as they consider just and equitable.

(3) A controller is required to pay an amount determined under sub-paragraph (2)(*a*) above only if—

(*a*) a notice stating the amount is served on him, or

(*b*) other reasonable steps are taken with a view to bringing the amount of the liability to his attention,

before the end of the period of two years beginning with the day immediately following the relevant accounting day.

(4) The relevant accounting day is the last day of the accounting period of the operator within which the adjustment in question was taken into account.

Landfill Tax

(5) If a controller is required to pay an amount by virtue of sub-paragraph (3) above, it shall be paid before the end of the period of thirty days beginning with the day immediately following the notification day.

(6) The notification day is—

(*a*) in a case where notice is served on a controller as mentioned in sub-paragraph (3)(*a*) above, the day on which the notice is served, or

(*b*) in a case where other reasonable steps are taken as mentioned in sub-paragraph (3)(*b*) above, the day on which the last of those steps is taken.

(7) The Commissioners may determine in what manner a controller is to benefit from an allowance determined under sub-paragraph (2)(*b*) above.

(8) For the purposes of this paragraph a licensed operator is a person who is the operator of a landfill site by virtue of section 67(*a*), (*c*) or (*e*) of this Act.][1]

Amendments—[1] Pt VIII of this Schedule inserted by FA 2000 s 142(3), Sch 37, with effect for taxable disposals made after 27 July 2000.

[Amounts payable to be treated as tax

55 An amount which a controller is required to pay under paragraph 52, 53 or 54(2)(*a*) above or under paragraph 58 below shall be deemed to be an amount of tax due from him and shall be recoverable accordingly.][1]

Amendments—[1] Pt VIII of this Schedule inserted by FA 2000 s 142(3), Sch 37, with effect for taxable disposals made after 27 July 2000.

[Controller not carrying out taxable activity

56 A controller is not to be treated for the purposes of this Act as carrying out a taxable activity by reason only of any liability under this Part of this Schedule.][1]

Amendments—[1] Pt VIII of this Schedule inserted by FA 2000 s 142(3), Sch 37, with effect for taxable disposals made after 27 July 2000.

[Joint and several liability

57— (1) In any case where the condition in sub-paragraph (4), (5) or (6) below is satisfied, the controller and the operator shall be jointly and severally liable for the principal liability.

(2) But the amount which may be recovered from the controller in consequence of such liability shall not exceed the amount of the secondary liability.

(3) For the purposes of this paragraph—

(*a*) the principal liability is the amount referred to in sub-paragraph (4)(*a*), (5)(*a*) or (6)(*a*) below, as the case may be, and

(*b*) the secondary liability is the amount referred to in sub-paragraph (4)(*b*), (5)(*b*) or (6)(*b*) below, as the case may be.

(4) The condition in this sub-paragraph is satisfied if—

(*a*) the operator of a landfill site is liable under section 41 of this Act for landfill tax, and

(*b*) a controller is liable under paragraph 49 above, after taking account of any reduction under paragraph 50 above, to pay an amount of that tax.

(5) The condition in this sub-paragraph is satisfied if—

(*a*) the operator of a landfill site is notified of the amount of an assessment made under section 50 of this Act, and

(*b*) in consequence of a determination made under paragraph 52 above by the Commissioners in connection with the assessment, a controller is liable to pay an amount (after taking account of any reduction under paragraph 53 above).

(6) The condition in this sub-paragraph is satisfied if—

(*a*) the liability of the operator of a landfill site to pay landfill tax is adjusted in such a way that paragraph 54 above applies, and

(*b*) in consequence of a determination made under paragraph 54(2)(*a*) above by the Commissioners in connection with the adjustment, a controller is liable to pay an amount.][1]

Amendments—[1] Pt VIII of this Schedule inserted by FA 2000 s 142(3), Sch 37, with effect for taxable disposals made after 27 July 2000.

[Interest payable by a controller

58— (1) This paragraph applies where—

(*a*) the operator of a landfill site and the controller of the whole or a part of that site are by virtue of paragraph 57 above jointly and severally liable for an amount, and

(*b*) that amount carries interest by virtue of any provision of this Schedule.

(2) The controller and the operator shall be jointly and severally liable to pay the interest.

(3) But the amount which may be recovered from the controller in consequence of such liability shall not exceed the amount calculated in accordance with the following formula—

$$\frac{(I-[A+B])\times S}{P}$$

where—

I is the total amount of interest in question;

A is the amount of interest carried for the period which—

(*a*) begins with the first day of the period for which interest is carried, and

(*b*) ends with the day on which the controller becomes liable to pay the secondary liability;

B is the amount of interest carried for any day falling after that on which the secondary liability is met in full;

S is the amount of the secondary liability;

P is the amount of the principal liability.

In this paragraph secondary liability and principal liability have the same meaning as in paragraph 57 above.

(4) The controller is liable for an amount of interest only if—

(*a*) a notice stating the amount is served on him, or

(*b*) other reasonable steps are taken with a view to bringing the amount of the liability to his attention,

before the end of the period of two years beginning with the day immediately following the final day.

(5) The final day is the last day of the period for which the interest in question is carried.

(6) If the controller is required to pay an amount in accordance with this paragraph, it shall be paid before the end of the period of thirty days beginning with the day immediately following the notification day.

(7) The notification day is—

(*a*) in a case where notice is served on a controller as mentioned in sub-paragraph (4)(*a*) above, the day on which the notice is served, or

(*b*) in a case where other reasonable steps are taken as mentioned in sub-paragraph (4)(*b*) above, the day on which the last of those steps is taken.

(8) Where by virtue of sub-paragraph (2) above a controller is liable to pay interest which arises under paragraph 27 above, paragraph 28 above shall apply in relation to that interest as it applies to interest which a person is liable under paragraph 27 above to pay.][1]

Amendments—[1] Pt VIII of this Schedule inserted by FA 2000 s 142(3), Sch 37, with effect for taxable disposals made after 27 July 2000.

[Reviews and Appeals][2]

59 [Sections 54 to 56][2] of this Act shall apply to a decision of the Commissioners under this Part of this Schedule—

(*a*) that a person is a controller,

(*b*) that a person is liable under this Part of this Schedule to pay any amount (including a penalty under paragraph 60 below),

(*c*) that a person is not entitled under this Part of this Schedule to an allowance, or

(*d*) as to the amount of any liability or any allowance under this Part of this Schedule,

[as they apply][2] to the other decisions of the Commissioners specified in [section 54(1)][2].][1]

Amendments—[1] Pt VIII of this Schedule inserted by FA 2000 s 142(3), Sch 37, with effect for taxable disposals made after 27 July 2000.

[2] Heading substituted for the previous heading "Reviews"; words at beginning substituted for the words "Section 54"; words at end substituted in the first place for the words "as it applies" and in the second place for the words "subsection (1) of that section" by the Transfer of Tribunal Functions and Revenue and Customs Appeals Order, SI 2009/56 art 3, Sch 1 para 240(3), (4) with effect from 1 April 2009.

[Notice that person is, or is no longer, a controller

60— (1) This paragraph applies where—

(*a*) on the date when this paragraph comes into force, a person is a controller of the whole or a part of a landfill site, or

(*b*) after that date, a person becomes or ceases to be a controller of the whole or a part of a landfill site.

(2) The controller, and the operator of the landfill site in question, shall be under a duty to secure that notice which complies with the requirements of sub-paragraph (3) below appropriate to the case in question is given to the Commissioners.

(3) The requirements of this sub-paragraph are that the notice—

(*a*) states that a person is, has become or has ceased to be a controller,

(*b*) identifies that person and the site under his control or formerly under his control,

(*c*) states the date when he became or ceased to be the controller, and

(*d*) is given within the period of thirty days beginning with the day immediately following—

(i) the day when this paragraph comes into force, in a case falling within sub-paragraph (1)(*a*) above, or

(ii) the day when the person in question becomes or ceases to be the controller, in a case falling within sub-paragraph (1)(*b*) above.

(4) If a person fails to comply with sub-paragraph (2) above, he is liable to a penalty of £250.

(5) Paragraph 25 above applies to a penalty under sub-paragraph (4) above as it applies to a penalty under Part V of this Schedule.][1]

Amendments—[1] Pt VIII of this Schedule inserted by FA 2000 s 142(3), Sch 37, with effect for taxable disposals made after 27 July 2000.

[Extension of time limits where notice not served

61— (1) This paragraph applies where—

(*a*) a person is liable under paragraph 49 above to pay an amount of landfill tax or liable under paragraph 58 above to pay interest, or

(*b*) the Commissioners are entitled under paragraph 52, 53 or 54 above to determine an amount which a person is liable to pay.

(2) The reference to two years in paragraph 51(2), 52(2), 53(5), 54(3) or 58(4) above (as the case may be) shall be treated as a reference to twenty years if the requirement of paragraph 60(2) above to give notice to the Commissioners in relation to the person mentioned in sub-paragraph (1) above being or becoming a controller has not been complied with.][1]

Amendments—[1] Pt VIII of this Schedule inserted by FA 2000 s 142(3), Sch 37, with effect for taxable disposals made after 27 July 2000.

FINANCE ACT 1997

(1997 Chapter 16)

An act to grant certain duties, to alter other duties, and to amend the law relating to the National Debt and the Public Revenue, and to make further provision in connection with finance.

[19 March 1997]

PART IV

PAYMENTS AND OVERPAYMENTS IN RESPECT OF INDIRECT TAXES

Excise duties and other indirect taxes

50 Overpayments, interest, assessments, etc

(1) Schedule 5 to this Act (which makes provision in relation to excise duties, insurance premium tax and landfill tax which corresponds to that made for VAT by sections 44 to 48 above) shall have effect.

(2) …

Notes—Provisions omitted not relevant to landfill tax.

Enforcement of payment

51 Enforcement by distress

(1) The Commissioners may by regulations make provision—

(*a*) for authorising distress to be levied on the goods and chattels of any person refusing or neglecting to pay—

(i) any amount of relevant tax due from him, or

(ii) any amount recoverable as if it were relevant tax due from him;

(*b*) for the disposal of any goods or chattels on which distress is levied in pursuance of the regulations; and

(*c*) for the imposition and recovery of costs, charges, expenses and fees in connection with anything done under the regulations.

(2) The provision that may be contained in regulations under this section shall include, in particular—

(*a*) provision for the levying of distress, by any person authorised to do so under the regulations, on goods or chattels located at any place whatever (including on a public highway); and

(*b*) provision authorising distress to be levied at any such time of the day or night, and on any such day of the week, as may be specified or described in the regulations.

(3) Regulations under this section may—

(*a*) make different provision for different cases, and

(*b*) contain any such incidental, supplemental, consequential or transitional provision as the Commissioners think fit;

and the transitional provision that may be contained in regulations under this section shall include transitional provision in connection with the coming into force of the repeal by this Act of any other power by regulations to make provision for or in connection with the levying of distress.

(4) The power to make regulations under this section shall be exercisable by statutory instrument subject to annulment in pursuance of a resolution of the House of Commons.

(5) The following are relevant taxes for the purposes of this section, that is to say—

(*a*)–(*c*) …
(*d*) landfill tax;
(*e*), (*f*) …

(6) In this section "the Commissioners" means the Commissioners of Customs and Excise.

(7) Regulations made under this section shall not have effect in Scotland.

Note—Provisions omitted are not relevant to landfill tax.

Prospective amendments—Sub-s (A1) to be inserted by the Tribunals, Courts and Enforcement Act 2007 s 62(3), Sch 13 para 126(1), (2) with effect from a date to be appointed. Sub-s (A1) to be repealed by FA 2008 s 129(1), Sch 43 para 6 with effect from a date to be appointed. That sub-s to read as follows—

"(A1) The Commissioners may, in England and Wales, use the procedure in Schedule 12 to the Tribunals, Courts and Enforcement Act 2007 (taking control of goods) to recover any of these that a person refuses or neglects to pay—

(*a*) any amount of relevant tax due from him;
(*b*) any amount recoverable as if it were relevant tax due from him.".

In sub-s (1), words "not having effect in England and Wales or Scotland" to be inserted after word "regulations" by the Tribunals, Courts and Enforcement Act 2007, s 62(3), Sch 13 para 126(1), (3) with effect from a date to be appointed.

Sub-s (7) to be repealed by the Tribunals, Courts and Enforcement Act 2007 ss 62(3), 146, Sch 13 para 126(1), (4), Sch 23 Pt 3 with effect from a date to be appointed.

52 Enforcement by diligence

(1) Where any amount of relevant tax or any amount recoverable as if it were relevant tax is due and has not been paid, the sheriff, on an application by the Commissioners accompanied by a certificate by them—

(*a*) stating that none of the persons specified in the application has paid the amount due from him;
(*b*) stating that payment of the amount due from each such person has been demanded from him; and
(*c*) specifying the amount due from and unpaid by each such person,

shall grant a summary warrant in a form prescribed by Act of Sederunt authorising the recovery, by any of the diligences mentioned in subsection (2) below, of the amount remaining due and unpaid.

(2) The diligences referred to in subsection (1) above are—

[(*a*) an attachment][1];
(*b*) an earnings arrestment;
(*c*) an arrestment and action of furthcoming or sale.

(3) Subject to subsection (4) below and without prejudice to [section 39(1) of the Debt Arrangement and Attachment (Scotland) Act 2002 (asp 17) (expenses of attachment)][2] the sheriff officer's fees, together with the outlays necessarily incurred by him, in connection with the execution of a summary warrant shall be chargeable against the debtor.

(4) No fees shall be chargeable by the sheriff officer against the debtor for collecting, and accounting to the Commissioners for, sums paid to him by the debtor in respect of the amount owing.

(5) The following are relevant taxes for the purposes of this section, that is to say—

(*a*)–(*c*) …
(*d*) landfill tax;
(*e*), (*f*) …

(6) In this section "the Commissioners" means the Commissioners of Customs and Excise.

(7) This section shall come into force on such day as the Commissioners of Customs and Excise may by order made by statutory instrument appoint, and different days may be appointed under this subsection for different purposes.

(8) This section extends only to Scotland.

Notes—Provisions omitted are not relevant to landfill tax. The appointed day under sub-s (7) above is 1 July 1997 (see SI 1997/1432).

Amendments—[1] Sub-s (2)(*a*) substituted by the Debt Arrangement and Attachment (Scotland) Act 2002, s 61, Sch 3, Pt 1, para 26(*a*) with effect from 30 December 2002; see the Debt Arrangement and Attachment (Scotland) Act 2002, s 64(2).

[2] Words in sub-s 3 substituted by the Debt Arrangement and Attachment (Scotland) Act 2002, s 61, Sch 3, Pt 1, para 26(*b*) with effect from 30 December 2002; see the Debt Arrangement and Attachment (Scotland) Act 2002, s 64(2).

Prospective amendments—This section to be repealed by FA 2008 s 129(2), Sch 43 para 15 with effect from a date to be appointed.

Sub-s (2)(*aa*), and words "and section 196(1) of the Bankruptcy and Diligence etc (Scotland) Act 2007 (asp 3) (expenses of money attachment)" in sub-s (3), to be inserted by the Bankruptcy and Diligence etc (Scotland) Act 2007 s 226(1), Sch 5 para 24 with effect from a date to be appointed. Sub-s (2)(*aa*) as inserted, to read—

"(*aa*) a money attachment;".

53 Amendments consequential on sections 51 and 52

…

(8) In paragraph 24(1)(*a*) of Schedule 5 to the Finance Act 1996 (walking possession agreements in connection with enforcement of landfill tax), for "paragraph 13(1) above" there shall be substituted "section 51 of the Finance Act 1997 (enforcement by distress)".

(9) This section shall come into force on such day as the Commissioners of Customs and Excise may by order made by statutory instrument appoint, and different days may be appointed under this subsection for different purposes.

Notes—Words omitted not relevant for the purposes of landfill tax. The appointed day under sub-s (9) above is 1 July 1997 (see SI 1997/1432).

SCHEDULES

SCHEDULE 5

INDIRECT TAXES: OVERPAYMENTS ETC

Section 50

PART I

UNJUST ENRICHMENT

Application of Part I

1— (1) This Part of this Schedule has effect for the purposes of the following provisions (which make it a defence to a claim for repayment that the repayment would unjustly enrich the claimant), namely—

(*a*) section 137A(3) of the Customs and Excise Management Act 1979 (excise duties);

(*b*) paragraph 8(3) of Schedule 7 to the Finance Act 1994 (insurance premium tax); and

(*c*) paragraph 14(3) of Schedule 5 to the Finance Act 1996 (landfill tax).

(2) Those provisions are referred to in this Part of this Schedule as unjust enrichment provisions.

(3) In this Part of this Schedule—

"the Commissioners" means the Commissioners of Customs and Excise;

"relevant repayment provision" means—

(*a*) section 137A of the Customs and Excise Management Act 1979 (recovery of overpaid excise duty);

(*b*) paragraph 8 of Schedule 7 to the Finance Act 1994 (recovery of overpaid insurance premium tax); or

(*c*) paragraph 14 of Schedule 5 to the Finance Act 1996 (recovery of overpaid landfill tax);

"relevant tax" means any duty of excise, insurance premium tax or landfill tax; and

"subordinate legislation" has the same meaning as in the Interpretation Act 1978.

Disregard of business losses

2— (1) This paragraph applies where—

(*a*) there is an amount paid by way of relevant tax which (apart from an unjust enrichment provision) would fall to be repaid under a relevant repayment provision to any person ("the taxpayer"), and

(*b*) the whole or a part of the cost of the payment of that amount to the Commissioners has, for practical purposes, been borne by a person other than the taxpayer.

(2) Where, in a case to which this paragraph applies, loss or damage has been or may be incurred by the taxpayer as a result of mistaken assumptions made in his case about the operation of any provisions relating to a relevant tax, that loss or damage shall be disregarded, except to the extent of the quantified amount, in the making of any determination—

(*a*) of whether or to what extent the repayment of an amount to the taxpayer would enrich him; or

(*b*) of whether or to what extent any enrichment of the taxpayer would be unjust.

(3) In sub-paragraph (2) above "the quantified amount" means the amount (if any) which is shown by the taxpayer to constitute the amount that would appropriately compensate him for loss or damage shown by him to have resulted, for any business carried on by him, from the making of the mistaken assumptions.

(4) The reference in sub-paragraph (2) above to provisions relating to a relevant tax is a reference to any provisions of—

(*a*) any enactment, subordinate legislation or Community legislation (whether or not still in force) which relates to that tax or to any matter connected with it; or (*b*) any notice published by the Commissioners under or for the purposes of any such enactment or subordinate legislation.

(5) This paragraph has effect for the purposes of making any repayment on or after the day on which this Act is passed, even if the claim for that repayment was made before that day.

Reimbursement arrangements

3— (1) The Commissioners may by regulations make provision for reimbursement arrangements made by any person to be disregarded for the purposes of any or all of the unjust enrichment provisions except where the arrangements—

(*a*) contain such provision as may be required by the regulations; and

(*b*) are supported by such undertakings to comply with the provisions of the arrangements as may be required by the regulations to be given to the Commissioners.

(2) In this paragraph "reimbursement arrangements" means any arrangements for the purposes of a claim under a relevant repayment provision which—

(*a*) are made by any person for the purpose of securing that he is not unjustly enriched by the repayment of any amount in pursuance of the claim; and

(*b*) provide for the reimbursement of persons who have for practical purposes borne the whole or any part of the cost of the original payment of that amount to the Commissioners.

(3) Without prejudice to the generality of sub-paragraph (1) above, the provision that may be required by regulations under this paragraph to be contained in reimbursement arrangements includes—

(*a*) provision requiring a reimbursement for which the arrangements provide to be made within such period after the repayment to which it relates as may be specified in the regulations;

(*b*) provision for the repayment of amounts to the Commissioners where those amounts are not reimbursed in accordance with the arrangements;

(*c*) provision requiring interest paid by the Commissioners on any amount repaid by them to be treated in the same way as that amount for the purposes of any requirement under the arrangements to make reimbursement or to repay the Commissioners;

(*d*) provision requiring such records relating to the carrying out of the arrangements as may be described in the regulations to be kept and produced to the Commissioners, or to an officer of theirs.

(4) Regulations under this paragraph may impose obligations on such persons as may be specified in the regulations—

(*a*) to make the repayments to the Commissioners that they are required to make in pursuance of any provisions contained in any reimbursement arrangements by virtue of sub-paragraph (3)(*b*) or (*c*) above;

(*b*) to comply with any requirements contained in any such arrangements by virtue of sub-paragraph (3)(*d*) above.

(5) Regulations under this paragraph may make provision for the form and manner in which, and the times at which, undertakings are to be given to the Commissioners in accordance with the regulations; and any such provision may allow for those matters to be determined by the Commissioners in accordance with the regulations.

(6) Regulations under this paragraph may—

(*a*) contain any such incidental, supplementary, consequential or transitional provision as appears to the Commissioners to be necessary or expedient; and

(*b*) make different provision for different circumstances.

(7) Regulations under this paragraph may have effect (irrespective of when the claim for repayment was made) for the purposes of the making of any repayment by the Commissioners after the time when the regulations are made; and, accordingly, such regulations may apply to arrangements made before that time.

(8) Regulations under this paragraph shall be made by statutory instrument subject to annulment in pursuance of a resolution of the House of Commons.

Contravention of requirement to repay Commissioners

4— (1) Where any obligation is imposed by regulations made by virtue of paragraph 3(4) above, a contravention or failure to comply with that obligation shall, to the extent that it relates to amounts repaid under section 137A of the Customs and Excise Management Act 1979, attract a penalty under section 9 of the Finance Act 1994 (penalties in connection with excise duties).

(2) For the purposes of Schedule 7 to the Finance Act 1994 (insurance premium tax), a contravention or failure to comply with an obligation imposed by regulations made by virtue of paragraph 3(4) above shall be deemed, to the extent that it relates to amounts repaid under paragraph 8 of that Schedule (recovery of overpaid insurance premium tax), to be a failure to comply with a requirement falling within paragraph 17(1)(*c*) of that Schedule (breach of regulations).

(3) Paragraph 23 of Schedule 5 to the Finance Act 1996 (power to provide for penalty) shall have effect as if an obligation imposed by regulations made by virtue of paragraph 3(4) above were, to

the extent that it relates to amounts repaid under paragraph 14 of that Schedule (recovery of overpaid landfill tax), a requirement imposed by regulations under Part III of that Act; and the provisions of that Schedule in relation to penalties under Part V of that Schedule shall have effect accordingly.

PART II
TIME LIMITS

Repayments

5— (1), (2) …

(3) (*substitutes* FA 1996 Sch 5 para 14(4)).

Notes—Omitted provisions not relevant to landfill tax.

Assessments

6— (1) In each of the enactments specified in sub-paragraph (2) below (which provide for the time limits applying to the making of assessments), for the words "six years", wherever they occur, there shall be substituted the words "three years".

(2) Those enactments are—

(*a*) (*amends* FA 1994, s 12(4)(*a*), (5)].

(*b*) (*amends* FA 1994 Sch 7 para 26(1), (4)).

(*c*) (*amends* FA 1996 Sch 5 para 33(1), (4)).

PART III
INTEREST

Interest on overpaid landfill tax

11— (1) Paragraph 29 of Schedule 5 to the Finance Act 1996 (interest payable by the Commissioners in connection with landfill tax) shall have effect, and be deemed always to have had effect, with the amendments for which this paragraph provides.

(2) (*inserts* FA 1996 Sch 5 para 29(1A)).

(3), (4) (*substitute* FA 1996 Sch 5 para 29(8), (9)).

12— (1) (*substitutes* FA 1996 Sch 5 para 29(4)–(6)).

(2) Sub-paragraph (1) above shall have effect for the purposes of determining whether any period beginning on or after the day on which this Act is passed is left out of account.

PART IV
SET-OFF INVOLVING LANDFILL TAX

13 (*inserts* FA 1996 Sch 5 para 42(4A), 43(4A)).

PART V
RECOVERY OF EXCESS PAYMENTS BY THE COMMISSIONERS

Assessment for excessive repayment

14— (1) Where—

(*a*) any amount has been paid at any time to any person by way of a repayment under a relevant repayment provision, and

(*b*) the amount paid exceeded the amount which the Commissioners were liable at that time to repay to that person,

the Commissioners may, to the best of their judgement, assess the excess paid to that person and notify it to him.

(2) Where any person is liable to pay any amount to the Commissioners in pursuance of an obligation imposed by virtue of paragraph 3(4)(*a*) above, the Commissioners may, to the best of their judgement, assess the amount due from that person and notify it to him.

(3) In this paragraph "relevant repayment provision" means—

(*a*) section 137A of the Customs and Excise Management Act 1979 (recovery of overpaid excise duty);

(*b*) paragraph 8 of Schedule 7 to the Finance Act 1994 (recovery of overpaid insurance premium tax);...[1]

(*c*) paragraph 14 of Schedule 5 to the Finance Act 1996 (recovery of overpaid landfill tax) [or

(*d*) Part I of Schedule 3 to the Finance Act 2001 (payments made and rebates disallowed in error)][1]

Amendments—[1] Word in sub-para (3)(*b*) repealed, and sub-para (3)(*d*) and word preceding inserted, by FA 2001 ss 15, 110, Sch 3 para 19(1), (2), Sch 33 Pt 1(4) with effect from 1 November 2001 (by virtue of SI 2001/3300).

Assessment for overpayments of interest

15— (1) Where—

(*a*) any amount has been paid to any person by way of interest under a relevant interest provision, but

(*b*) that person was not entitled to that amount under that provision,

the Commissioners may, to the best of their judgement, assess the amount so paid to which that person was not entitled and notify it to him.

(2) In this paragraph "relevant interest provision" means—

(*a*) …[1]

(*b*) paragraph 22 of Schedule 7 to that Act (interest payable by the Commissioners on overpayments etc of insurance premium tax); …[1]

(*c*) paragraph 29 of Schedule 5 to the Finance Act 1996 (interest payable by the Commissioners on overpayments etc of landfill tax) [or

(*d*) Part II of Schedule 3 to the Finance Act 2001 (interest)][1]

Amendments—[1] Sub-para (2)(*a*) repealed, word in sub-para (2)(*b*) repealed, and sub-para (2)(*d*) and word preceding inserted, by FA 2001 ss 15, 110, Sch 3 para 19(1), (3), Sch 33 Pt 1(4) with effect from 1 November 2001 (by virtue of SI 2001/3300).

Assessments under paragraphs 14 and 15

16— (1) An assessment under paragraph 14 or 15 above shall not be made more than two years after the time when evidence of facts sufficient in the opinion of the Commissioners to justify the making of the assessment comes to the knowledge of the Commissioners.

(2) Where an amount has been assessed and notified to any person under paragraph 14 or 15 above, it shall be recoverable (subject to any provision having effect in accordance with paragraph 19 below) as if it were relevant tax due from him.

(3) Sub-paragraph (2) above does not have effect if, or to the extent that, the assessment in question has been withdrawn or reduced.

Interest on amounts assessed

17— (1) Where an assessment is made under paragraph 14 or 15 above, the whole of the amount assessed shall carry interest at the rate applicable under section 197 of the Finance Act 1996 from the date on which the assessment is notified until payment.

(2) Where any person is liable to interest under sub-paragraph (1) above the Commissioners may assess the amount due by way of interest and notify it to him.

(3) Without prejudice to the power to make assessments under this paragraph for later periods, the interest to which an assessment under this paragraph may relate shall be confined to interest for a period of no more than two years ending with the time when the assessment under this paragraph is made.

(4) Interest under this paragraph shall be paid without any deduction of income tax.

(5) A notice of assessment under this paragraph shall specify a date, being not later than the date of the notice, to which the amount of interest is calculated; and, if the interest continues to accrue after that date, a further assessment or assessments may be made under this paragraph in respect of amounts which so accrue.

(6) If, within such period as may be notified by the Commissioners to the person liable for interest under sub-paragraph (1) above, the amount referred to in that sub-paragraph is paid, it shall be treated for the purposes of that sub-paragraph as paid on the date specified as mentioned in sub-paragraph (5) above.

(7) Where an amount has been assessed and notified to any person under this paragraph it shall be recoverable as if it were relevant tax due from him.

(8) Sub-paragraph (7) above does not have effect if, or to the extent that, the assessment in question has been withdrawn or reduced.

Supplementary assessments

18 If it appears to the Commissioners that the amount which ought to have been assessed in an assessment under paragraph 14, 15 or 17 above exceeds the amount which was so assessed, then—

(*a*) under the same paragraph as that assessment was made, and

(*b*) on or before the last day on which that assessment could have been made,

the Commissioners may make a supplementary assessment of the amount of the excess and shall notify the person concerned accordingly.

Review of decisions and appeals

19— (1), (2) …

(3) Sections 54 to 56 of the Finance Act 1996 (review and appeal in the case of landfill tax) shall have effect in relation to any decision which—

(*a*) is contained in an assessment under paragraph 14, 15 or 17 above,

(*b*) is a decision about whether any amount is due to the Commissioners or about how much is due, and

(*c*) is made in a case in which the relevant repayment provision is paragraph 14 of Schedule 5 to that Act or the relevant interest provision is paragraph 29 of that Schedule,

as if that decision were a decision to which section 54 of that Act applies.

Notes—Provisions omitted not relevant to landfill tax.

Interpretation of Part V

20— (1) In this Part of this Schedule "the Commissioners" means the Commissioners of Customs and Excise.

(2) In this Part of this Schedule "relevant tax", in relation to any assessment, means—

(*a*) a duty of excise if the assessment relates to—

(i) a repayment of an amount paid by way of such a duty,

(ii) an overpayment of interest under [Part II of Schedule 3 to the Finance Act 2001][1], or

(iii) interest on an amount specified in an assessment in relation to which the relevant tax is a duty of excise;

(*b*) insurance premium tax if the assessment relates to—

(i) a repayment of an amount paid by way of such tax,

(ii) an overpayment of interest under paragraph 22 of Schedule 7 to the Finance Act 1994, or

(iii) interest on an amount specified in an assessment in relation to which the relevant tax is insurance premium tax;

and

(*c*) landfill tax if the assessment relates to—

(i) a repayment of an amount paid by way of such tax,

(ii) an overpayment of interest under paragraph 29 of Schedule 5 to the Finance Act 1996, or

(iii) interest on an amount specified in an assessment in relation to which the relevant tax is landfill tax.

(3) For the purposes of this Part of this Schedule notification to a personal representative, trustee in bankruptcy, interim or permanent trustee, receiver, liquidator or person otherwise acting in a representative capacity in relation to another shall be treated as notification to the person in relation to whom he so acts.

Amendments—[1] Words in sub-para (2)(*a*)(ii) substituted by FA 2001 s 15, Sch 3 para 19(1), (5) with effect from 1 November 2001 (by virtue of SI 2001/3300).

Consequential amendment

21 (*inserts* FA 1996 s 197(2)(*e*)).

SCHEDULE 18

REPEALS

Section 113

PART V

INDIRECT TAXES

(2) (*repeals* FA 1996 Sch 5 para 13).

FINANCE ACT 1998

(1998 Chapter 36)

An Act to grant certain duties, to alter other duties, and to amend the law relating to the National Debt and the Public Revenue, and to make further provision in connection with Finance.

[31 July 1998]

PART V

OTHER TAXES

Landfill tax

148 Provisional collection of landfill tax

(1) (*amends* PCTA 1968 s 1(1)).

(2)–(4) …[1]

Amendments—[1] Sub-ss (2)–(4) repealed by FA 2001 s 110, Sch 33 Pt 3(3) with effect from 11 May 2001.

HUMAN RIGHTS ACT 1998

(1998 Chapter 42)

An Act to give further effect to rights and freedoms guaranteed under the European Convention on Human Rights; to make provision with respect to holders of certain judicial offices who become judges of the European Court of Human Rights; and for connected purposes.

[9th November 1998]

Note—Please see VAT Statutes *ante* for the text of this Act.

FINANCE ACT 2000

(2000 Chapter 17)

An act to grant certain duties, to alter other duties, and to amend the law relating to the National Debt and the Public Revenue, and to make further provision in connection with finance.

[28 July 2000]

PART V
OTHER TAXES

Landfill tax

140 Rate

(1) (*spent*).

(2) This section has effect in relation to taxable disposals made, or treated as made, on or after 1st April 2000.

141 Disposals which are not taxable

(1) In section 62 of the Finance Act 1996 (regulations about taxable disposals) amend subsection (7) (limit on power to make regulations providing that a disposal is not taxable) as follows.

(2) (substitutes FA 1996 s 62(7)(*a*)).

(3) (*amends FA 1996 s 62*(7)(*b*)).

142 Secondary liability

(1) (*amends FA 1996 s 60*).

(2) (*amends sidenote to FA 1986 s 60*).

(3) (*adds FA 1986 Sch 5 Part VIII*).

(4) Subsection (3) has effect in relation to taxable disposals made on or after the day on which this Act is passed.

SCHEDULES

SCHEDULE 37

LANDFILL TAX: NEW PART VIII OF SCHEDULE 5 TO THE FINANCE ACT 1996

Section 142

Note—This Schedule sets out FA 1996 Sch 5 Part VIII inserted by FA 2000 s 142(3).

FINANCE ACT 2001

(2001 Chapter 9)

An Act to grant certain duties, to alter other duties, and to amend the law relating to the National Debt and the Public Revenue, and to make further provision in connection with Finance.

[11 May 2001]

PART 4

OTHER TAXES

Landfill tax

104 Landfill tax: rate

(*spent*)

PART 5

MISCELLANEOUS AND SUPPLEMENTARY PROVISIONS

Supplementary

...

110 Repeals and revocations

(1) The enactments mentioned in Schedule 33 to this Act (which include provisions that are spent or of no practical utility) are repealed or revoked to the extent specified.

(2) The repeals and revocations specified in that Schedule have effect subject to the commencement provisions and savings contained or referred to in the notes set out in that Schedule.

SCHEDULES

SCHEDULE 33

REPEALS

Section 110

PART 3

OTHER TAXES

(3) LANDFILL TAX AND CLIMATE CHANGE LEVY

Note—As the repeals are already in force, this table has been omitted.

FINANCE ACT 2005

(2005 Chapter 7)

An Act to Grant certain duties, to alter other duties, and to amend the law relating to the National Debt and the Public Revenue, and to make further provision in connection with finance.

[7 April 2005]

PART 4

OTHER TAXES

Landfill tax

99 Rate of landfill tax

(1) (*spent*)

(2) The amendments made by this section have effect in relation to taxable disposals made, or treated as made, on or after 1st April 2005.

FINANCE ACT 2006

(2006 Chapter 25)

An Act to Grant certain duties, to alter other duties, and to amend the law relating to the National Debt and the Public Revenue, and to make further provision in connection with finance.

[19 July 2006]

PART 9
MISCELLANEOUS PROVISIONS

Landfill tax

170 Rate of landfill tax

(1) (*spent*)

(2) The amendments made by this section have effect in relation to taxable disposals made, or treated as made, on or after 1st April 2006.

FINANCE ACT 2007

(2007 Chapter 11)

PART 1
CHARGES, RATES, THRESHOLDS ETC

Environment

15 Rates of landfill tax

(1) Section 42 of FA 1996 (amount of landfill tax) is amended as follows.

(2) (*amends* FA 1996 s 42(1)(*a*), (2))

(3) The amendments made by subsection (2) have effect in relation to disposals made (or treated as made) on or after 1st April 2007 (but before 1st April 2008).

(4) (*amends* FA 1996 s 42(1)(*a*))

(5) The amendments made by subsection (4) come into force on 1st April 2008 and have effect in relation to disposals made (or treated as made) on or after that date.

PART 2
ENVIRONMENT

Other measures

24 Landfill tax: bodies concerned with the environment

(1) (*inserts* FA 1996 s 53(4)(*ca*))

(2) The amendment made by subsection (1) is deemed to have come into force on 22nd March 2007.

SCHEDULES

SCHEDULE 24
PENALTIES FOR ERRORS

Note—Please see *VAT Statutes* ante for the text of this Schedule.

FINANCE ACT 2008

(2008 Chapter 9)

An Act to Grant certain duties, to alter other duties, and to amend the law relating to the National Debt and the Public Revenue, and to make further provision in connection with finance.

[21 July 2008]

PART 1
CHARGES, RATES, ALLOWANCES, RELIEFS ETC

Environmental taxes and duties

18 Standard rate of landfill tax

(1) In section 42(1)(*a*) and (2) of FA 1996 (amount of landfill tax), for "£32" substitute "£40".

(2) The amendments made by subsection (1) come into force on 1 April 2009 and have effect in relation to disposals made (or treated as made) on or after that date.

PART 7
ADMINISTRATION

Press releases—HMRC Guidance Note, 18 July 2008 (HMRC set-off across taxes following Finance Bill 2008).

CHAPTER 1
INFORMATION ETC

New information etc powers

114 Computer records etc

Note—Please see *VAT Statutes* ante for the text of this Section.

CHAPTER 3
PENALTIES

122 Penalties for errors

Note—Please see *VAT Statutes* ante for the text of this Section.

123 Penalties for failure to notify etc

Note—Please see *VAT Statutes* ante for the text of this Section.

CHAPTER 4
APPEALS ETC

Reviews and appeals etc: general

124 HMRC decisions etc: reviews and appeals

Note—Please see *VAT Statutes* ante for the text of this Section.

CHAPTER 5
PAYMENT AND ENFORCEMENT

Taking control of goods etc

127 Enforcement by taking control of goods: England and Wales

Note—Please see *VAT Statutes* ante for the text of this Section.

128 Summary warrant: Scotland

Note—Please see *VAT Statutes* ante for the text of this Section.

129 Consequential provision and commencement

Note—Please see *VAT Statutes* ante for the text of this Section.

Set off

130 Set-off: England and Wales and Northern Ireland

Note—Please see *VAT Statutes* ante for the text of this Section.

131 No set-off where insolvency procedure has been applied

Note—Please see *VAT Statutes* ante for the text of this Section.

133 Set-off etc where right to be paid a sum has been transferred

Note—Please see *VAT Statutes* ante for the text of this Section.

Other measures

135 Interest on unpaid tax in case of disaster etc of national significance

Note—Please see *VAT Statutes* ante for the text of this Section.

136 Fee for payment

Note—Please see *VAT Statutes* ante for the text of this Section.

Supplementary

139 Interpretation of Chapter

Note—Please see *VAT Statutes* ante for the text of this Section.

PART 8
MISCELLANEOUS

Climate change levy and landfill tax

151 Landfill tax credit: withdrawing approval of environmental bodies

(1) Part 3 of FA 1996 (landfill tax) is amended as follows.

(2) (*amends* FA 1996 s 53(4)(*d*)).

(3) (*inserts* FA 1996 s 54(1)(*ca*)).

(4) The amendments made by this section are treated as having come into force on 19 March 2008.

PART 8
MISCELLANEOUS

Payments from Exchequer accounts

158 Power of Treasury to make payments

Note—Please see *VAT Statutes* ante for the text of this Section.

159 Payments from certain Exchequer accounts: mechanism

Note—Please see *VAT Statutes* ante for the text of this Section.

Other matters

160 Power to give statutory effect to concessions

Note—Please see *VAT Statutes* ante for the text of this Section.

PART 9
FINAL PROVISIONS

165 Interpretation

Note—Please see *VAT Statutes* ante for the text of this Section.

166 Short title

Note—Please see *VAT Statutes* ante for the text of this Section.

SCHEDULES

SCHEDULE 36
INFORMATION AND INSPECTION POWERS

Section 113

Note—Please see *VAT Statutes* ante for the text of this Section.

SCHEDULE 41

PENALTIES: FAILURE TO NOTIFY AND CERTAIN VAT AND EXCISE WRONGDOING

Section 123

Note—Please see *VAT Statutes* ante for the text of this Section.

FINANCE ACT 2009

(2009 Chapter 10)

An Act to Grant certain duties, to alter other duties, and to amend the law relating to the National Debt and the Public Revenue, and to make further provision in connection with finance.

[21 July 2009]

PART 7

ADMINISTRATION

Standards and values

92 HMRC Charter

Note—Please see *VAT Statutes* ante for the text of this Section.

93 Duties of senior accounting officers of qualifying companies

Note—Please see *VAT Statutes* ante for the text of this Section.

94 Publishing details of deliberate tax defaulters

Note—Please see *VAT Statutes* ante for the text of this Section.

Information etc

95 Amendment of information and inspection powers

Note—Please see *VAT Statutes* ante for the text of this Section.

96 Extension of information and inspection powers to further taxes

(1) In paragraph 63(1) of Schedule 36 to FA 2008 (information and inspection powers: meaning of "tax"), for paragraph (*e*) (and the "and" before it) substitute—

"(*e*) insurance premium tax,
(*f*) inheritance tax,
(*g*) stamp duty land tax,
(*h*) stamp duty reserve tax,
(*i*) petroleum revenue tax,
(*j*) aggregates levy,
(*k*) climate change levy,
(*l*) landfill tax, and
(*m*) relevant foreign tax,".

(2) Schedule 48 contains further amendments of that Schedule.

(3) The amendments made by this section and Schedule 48 come into force on such day as the Treasury may by order appoint.

(4) An order under subsection (3) may—

(*a*) appoint different days for different purposes, and
(*b*) contain transitional provision and savings.

(5) The Treasury may by order make any incidental, supplemental, consequential, transitional or transitory provision or saving which appears appropriate in consequence of, or otherwise in connection with, this section and Schedule 48.

(6) An order under subsection (5) may—

(*a*) make different provision for different purposes, and
(*b*) make provision amending, repealing or revoking an enactment or instrument (whenever passed or made).

(7) An order under this section is to be made by statutory instrument.

(8) A statutory instrument containing an order under subsection (5) is subject to annulment in pursuance of a resolution of the House of Commons.

97 Powers to obtain contact details for debtors

Note—Please see *VAT Statutes* ante for the text of this Section.

98 Record-keeping

(1) Schedule 50 contains provision about obligations to keep records.

(2) The amendments made by that Schedule come into force on such day as the Treasury may by order made by statutory instrument appoint.

Assessments, claims etc

99 Time limits for assessments, claims etc

(1) Schedule 51 contains provision about time limits for assessments, claims etc

(2) The amendments made by that Schedule come into force on such day as the Treasury may by order made by statutory instrument appoint.

(3) An order under subsection (2)—

(*a*) may make different provision for different purposes, and

(*b*) may include transitional provision and savings.

Interest

101 Late payment interest on sums due to HMRC

Note—Please see *VAT Statutes* ante for the text of this Section.

102 Repayment interest on sums to be paid by HMRC

Note—Please see *VAT Statutes* ante for the text of this Section.

103 Rates of interest

Note—Please see *VAT Statutes* ante for the text of this Section.

104 Supplementary

Note—Please see *VAT Statutes* ante for the text of this Section.

108 Suspension of penalties during currency of agreement for deferred payment

Note—Please see *VAT Statutes* ante for the text of this Section.

109 Miscellaneous amendments

Note—Please see *VAT Statutes* ante for the text of this Section.

PART 8
MISCELLANEOUS

Other environmental taxes and duties

119 Landfill tax: prescribed landfill site activities

Schedule 60 contains provision about charging landfill tax on prescribed activities at landfill sites.

SCHEDULES

SCHEDULE 46
DUTIES OF SENIOR ACCOUNTING OFFICERS OF QUALIFYING COMPANIES

Section 93

Note—Please see *VAT Statutes* ante for the text of this Schedule.

SCHEDULE 47
AMENDMENT OF INFORMATION AND INSPECTION POWERS

Section 95

Note—Please see *VAT Statutes* ante for the text of this Schedule.

SCHEDULE 48

EXTENSION OF INFORMATION AND INSPECTION POWERS

Section 96

Note—Please see *VAT Statutes* ante for the text of this Schedule.

SCHEDULE 49

POWERS TO OBTAIN CONTACT DETAILS FOR DEBTORS

Section 97

Note—Please see *VAT Statutes* ante for the text of this Schedule.

SCHEDULE 50

RECORD-KEEPING

Section 98

Landfill tax

21 In paragraph 2 of Schedule 5 to FA 1996 (landfill tax: records), for sub-paragraphs (4) to (7) substitute—

"(4) A duty under regulations under this paragraph to preserve records may be discharged—

(*a*) by preserving them in any form and by any means, or

(*b*) by preserving the information contained in them in any form and by any means, subject to any conditions or exceptions specified in writing by the Commissioners."

SCHEDULE 51

TIME LIMITS FOR ASSESSMENTS, CLAIMS ETC

Section 99

Landfill tax

37 Schedule 5 to FA 1996 (landfill tax) is amended as follows.

38 In paragraph 14(4) (recovery of overpaid tax), for "three years" substitute "4 years".

39 In paragraph 29(8) (interest payable by Commissioners), for "three years" substitute "4 years".

40— (1) Paragraph 33 (assessments: time limits) is amended as follows.

(2) In sub-paragraph (1)—

(*a*) for "three years" (in the first place) substitute "4 years", and

(*b*) for the words from "the end of" to the end substitute "the relevant event".

(3) After that sub-paragraph insert—

"(1A) In this paragraph "the relevant event", in relation to an assessment, means—

(*a*) the end of the accounting period concerned, or

(*b*) in the case of an assessment under paragraph 32 of an amount due by way of a penalty other than a penalty referred to in paragraph 32(2), the event giving rise to the penalty."

(4) In sub-paragraph (3), for "sub-paragraph (1)" substitute "sub-paragraph (1A)".

(5) For sub-paragraph (4) substitute—

"(4) An assessment of an amount due from a person in a case involving a loss of tax—

(*a*) brought about deliberately by the person (or by another person acting on that person's behalf), or

(*b*) attributable to a failure by the person to comply with an obligation under section 47(2) or (3),

may be made at any time not more than 20 years after the relevant event (subject to sub-paragraph (5)).

(4A) In sub-paragraph (4)(*a*) the reference to a loss brought about deliberately by the person includes a loss brought about as a result of a deliberate inaccuracy in a document given to Her Majesty's Revenue and Customs by or on behalf of that person."

(6) In sub-paragraph (5)—

(*a*) in paragraph (*a*), for "three years" substitute "4 years", and

(*b*) omit paragraph (*b*) (and the "and" before it).

SCHEDULE 53
LATE PAYMENT INTEREST
Section 101

Note—Please see *VAT Statutes* ante for the text of this Schedule.

SCHEDULE 54
REPAYMENT INTEREST
Section 102

Note—Please see *VAT Statutes* ante for the text of this Schedule.

SCHEDULE 57
AMENDMENTS RELATING TO PENALTIES
Section 109

Note—Please see *VAT Statutes* ante for the text of this Schedule.

SCHEDULE 60
LANDFILL TAX: PRESCRIBED LANDFILL SITE ACTIVITIES
Section 119

Introduction

1 Part 3 of FA 1996 (landfill tax) is amended as follows.

Prescribed landfill site activities to be treated as disposals

2 After section 65 insert—

"65A Prescribed landfill site activities to be treated as disposals

(1) An order may prescribe a landfill site activity for the purposes of this section.

(2) If a prescribed landfill site activity is carried out at a landfill site, the activity is to be treated—

(*a*) as a disposal at the landfill site of the material involved in the activity,
(*b*) as a disposal of that material as waste, and
(*c*) as a disposal of that material made by way of landfill.

(3) Connected provision may be made by order.

(4) Provision may be made under this section in such way as the Treasury think fit.

(5) An order under subsection (1) may prescribe a landfill site activity by reference to conditions.

(6) Those conditions may, in particular, relate to either or both of the following—

(*a*) whether the landfill site activity is carried out in a designated area of a landfill site, and
(*b*) whether there has been compliance with a requirement to give information relating to—

(i) the landfill site activity, or
(ii) the material involved in the landfill site activity, including information relating to whether the activity is carried out in a designated area of a landfill site.

(7) An order under this section—

(*a*) may amend, or otherwise modify, this Part or any other enactment relating to landfill tax, but
(*b*) may not alter any rate at which landfill tax is charged.

(8) Subsections (5) to (7) do not limit the generality of subsection (4).

(9) In this section—

"connected provision" means provision which appears to the Treasury to be necessary or expedient in connection with provision made under subsection (1);

"designated area" means an area of a landfill site designated in accordance with—

(*a*) an order under this section, or
(*b*) regulations under Part 1 of Schedule 5;

"landfill site activity" means any of the following descriptions of activity, or an activity that falls within any of the following descriptions—

(*a*) using or otherwise dealing with material at a landfill site;
(*b*) storing or otherwise having material at a landfill site."

Landfill Tax

3 In section 71(7) (orders and regulations), after paragraph (*c*) insert—

"(*ca*) an order under section 65A above which produces the result that a landfill site activity which would not otherwise be prescribed for the purposes of section 65A is so prescribed;

(*cb*) an order under section 65A above which amends this Part or any enactment contained in an Act;".

Material temporarily held

4 Omit section 62 (taxable disposals: regulations about material temporarily held at a landfill site).

Material at landfill sites

5 Part 1 of Schedule 5 (information) is amended as follows.

6 For the heading before paragraph 1 substitute—

"Information: general"

7 After paragraph 1 insert—

"Information: material at landfill sites

1A— (1) Regulations may make provision about giving the Commissioners information relating to material at a landfill site or a part of a landfill site.

(2) Regulations under this paragraph may require a person to give information.

(3) Regulations under this paragraph may—

(*a*) require a person, or authorise an officer of Revenue and Customs to require a person, to designate a part of a landfill site (an "information area"), and

(*b*) require material, or prescribed descriptions of material, to be deposited in an information area.

(4) Regulations under this paragraph may make provision about information relating to what is done with material.

(5) Sub-paragraphs (2) to (4) do not prejudice the generality of sub-paragraph (1)."

8 For the heading before paragraph 2 substitute—

"Records: registrable persons"

9 After paragraph 2 insert—

"Records: material at landfill sites

2A— (1) Regulations may require a person to make records relating to material at a landfill site or a part of a landfill site.

(2) Regulations under this paragraph may make provision about records relating to what is done with material.

(3) Sub-paragraphs (2) to (7) of paragraph 2 apply in relation to regulations under this paragraph as they apply in relation to regulations under paragraph 2.

(4) But, in the application of paragraph 2(3)(*a*) in relation to regulations under this paragraph, the reference to registrable persons has effect as a reference to persons."

Site restoration

10 Omit section 43C (site restoration).

11 In Part 1 of Schedule 5 (information), after paragraph 1A (inserted by paragraph 7) insert—

"Information: site restoration

1B— (1) Before commencing restoration of all or part of a landfill site, the operator of the site must—

(*a*) notify the Commissioners in writing that the restoration is to commence, and

(*b*) provide such other written information as the Commissioners may require generally or in the particular case.

(2) In this paragraph "restoration" means work, other than capping waste, which is required by a relevant instrument to be carried out to restore a landfill site to use on completion of waste disposal operations.

(3) The following are relevant instruments—

(*a*) a planning consent,

(*b*) a waste management licence, and

(*c*) a permit authorising the disposal of waste on or in land."

Landfill tax returns

12 In section 49(*b*) (accounting for tax and time for payment), omit "as may be prescribed".

Commencement and savings

13— (1) The repeal made by paragraph 10 comes into force on 1 September 2009.

(2) The amendment made by paragraph 11 (information about site restoration) has effect in relation to restoration of landfill sites commencing on or after 1 September 2009.

(3) The repeal of section 62 made by paragraph 4, and the repeal in section 49 made by paragraph 12—

(*a*) do not affect any regulations made under the repealed provisions before the passing of this Act, and

(*b*) do not prevent the powers conferred by the repealed provisions from being used after the passing of this Act to revoke any regulations made under the powers before that time.

LANDFILL TAX
STATUTORY INSTRUMENTS

CHRONOLOGICAL LIST OF PRINTED STATUTORY INSTRUMENTS

SI Year/No	Title
SI 1996/1527	Landfill Tax Regulations 1996
SI 1996/1528	Landfill Tax (Qualifying Material) Order 1996
SI 1997/1431	Distress for Customs and Excise Duties and Other Indirect Taxes Regulations 1997
SI 1998/1461	Air Passenger Duty and Other Indirect Taxes (Interest Rate) Regulations 1998
SI 2007/965	Landfill Tax (Amendment) Regulations 2007

CHRONOLOGICAL LIST OF STATUTORY INSTRUMENTS

SI Year/No	Title
SI 1996/1527	Landfill Tax Regulations 1996
SI 1996/1528	Landfill Tax (Qualifying Material) Order 1996
SI 1996/1529	*Landfill Tax (Contaminated Land) Order 1996* (amending)
SI 1996/2100	*Landfill Tax (Amendment) Regulations 1996* (amending)
SI 1997/1015	*Finance Act 1996 s 197 (Appointed Day) Order 1997* (see FA 1996 s 197)
SI 1997/1016	*Air Passenger Duty and Other Indirect Taxes (Interest Rates) Regulations 1997 (see FA 1996 Sch 5 paras 26, 29)* (revoked)
SI 1997/1431	The Distress for Customs and Excise Duties and Other Indirect Taxes Regulations 1997
SI 1997/1432	*The Finance Act 1997, sections 52 and 53, (Appointed Day) Order 1997* (see FA 1997 ss 52 and 53)
SI 1997/1433	*The Finance Act 1997 (Repeal of Distress and Diligence Enactments) (Appointed Day) Order 1997* (see FA 1997 Sch 5 para 13)
SI 1998/61	*Landfill Tax (Amendment) Regulations 1998* (amending)
SI 1998/1461	Air Passenger Duty and Other Indirect Taxes (Interest Rate) Regulations 1998
SI 1999/2075	*Landfill Tax (Site Restoration and Quarries) Order 1999* (amending)
SI 1999/3270	*Landfill Tax (Amendment) Regulations 1999* (amending)
SI 2000/631	*Air Passenger Duty and Other Indirect Taxes (Interest Rate) (Amendment) Regulations 2000* (amending)
SI 2000/1973	*Pollution Prevention and Control (England and Wales) Regulations 2000* (amending)
SI 2002/1	*Landfill Tax (Amendment) Regulations 2002* (amending)
SI 2003/605	*Landfill Tax (Amendment) Regulations 2003* (amending)
SI 2003/2313	*Landfill Tax (Amendment) (No 2) Regulations 2003* (amending)
SI 2004/769	*Landfill Tax (Amendment) Regulations 2004* (amending)
SI 2005/725	*Landfill Tax (Site Restoration, Quarries and Pet Cemeteries) Order 2005* (amending)
SI 2005/759	*Landfill Tax (Amendment) Regulations 2005* (amending)
SI 2006/865	*Landfill Tax (Amendment) Regulations 2006* (amending)
SI 2007/965	Landfill Tax (Amendment) Regulations 2007
SI 2007/2909	*Landfill Tax (Material Removed from Water) Order 2007*
SI 2007/3538	*Environmental Permitting (England and Wales) Regulations 2007 (amending)*
SI 2008/770	*Landfill Tax (Amendment) Regulations 2008*
SI 2008/2693	*Amusement Machine Licence Duty, etc (Amendments) Regulations 2008*
SI 2009/56	*Transfer of Tribunal Functions and Revenue and Customs Appeals Order 2009*
SI 2009/1890	*Companies Act 2006 (Consequential Amendments) (Taxes and National Insurance) Order 2009*
SI 2009/1930	*Landfill Tax (Amendment) Regulations 2009*
SI 2009/2032	*Taxes and Duties (Interest Rate) (Amendment) Regulations 2009*

1996/1527
Landfill Tax Regulations 1996

Made by the Commissioners of Customs and Excise under FA 1996 ss 47(9), 48(1), (2), 49, 51(1)–(6), 52(1)–(3), 53(1)–(4), 58(1), (4)–(6), 61(2), 62(1)–(3), (5), (6), 68(1)–(6) and Sch 5 paras 2(1)–(3), 13(1), (6), 14(5), 20(3), 23(1), 42(1)–(5), 43(1)–(5)

Made . . . . *12 June 1996*
Laid before the House of Commons . . . . . *12 June 1996*
Coming into force . . . . *1 August 1996*

ARRANGEMENT OF REGULATIONS

PART I
PRELIMINARY

Citation and commencement

1 These Regulations may be cited as the Landfill Tax Regulations 1996 and shall come into force on 1st August 1996.

Interpretation

2— (1) In these Regulations—

"accounting period" means—

(*a*) in the case of a registered person, each period of three months ending on the dates notified to him by the Commissioners, whether by means of a registration certificate issued by them or otherwise;

(*b*) in the case of a registrable person who is not registered, each quarter; or

(*c*) in the case of any registrable person, such other period in relation to which he is required by or under regulation 11 to make a return;

and, in every case, the first accounting period of a registrable person shall begin on the effective date of registration;

"the Act" means the Finance Act 1996;

"Collector" means a Collector, Deputy Collector or Assistant Collector of Customs and Excise;

"credit", except where the context otherwise requires, means credit which a person is entitled to claim under Part IV of these Regulations;

"disposal" means a landfill disposal (which expression has the meaning given in section 70(2) of the Act) made on or after 1st October 1996 and "disposed of " shall be construed accordingly;

"effective date of registration" means the date determined in accordance with section 47 of the Act upon which the person was or should have been registered;

"landfill invoice" means an invoice of the description in regulation 37;

"landfill site" has the meaning given in section 66 of the Act;

"landfill tax account" has the meaning given in regulation 12;

"landfill tax bad debt account" has the meaning given in regulation 26;

"quarter" means a period of three months ending at the end of March, June, September or December;

"registered person" means a person who is registered under section 47 of the Act and "register" and "registration" shall be construed accordingly;

"registrable person" has the meaning given in section 47(10) of the Act;

"registration number" means the identifying number allocated to a registered person and notified to him by the Commissioners;

"return" means a return which is required to be made in accordance with regulation 11;

"taxable business" means a business or part of a business in the course of which taxable activities are carried out;

["transfer note" is a transfer note within the meaning of—

(*a*) the Environmental Protection (Duty of Care) Regulations 1991; or

(*b*) the Controlled Waste (Duty of Care) Regulations (Northern Ireland) 2002;][1]

"working day" means any day of the week except Saturday and Sunday and a bank holiday or public holiday, in either case, for England.

(2) In these Regulations any question whether a person is connected with another shall be determined in accordance with section 839 of the Taxes Act 1988.

(3) Any reference in these Regulations to "this Part" is a reference to the Part of these Regulations in which that reference is made.

(4) Any reference in these Regulations to a form prescribed in the Schedule to these Regulations shall include a reference to a form which the Commissioners are satisfied is a form to the like effect.

Amendments—[1] In sub-para (1), definition of "transfer note" substituted by the Landfill Tax (Amendment) Regulations, SI 2004/769 reg 2 with effect from 1 May 2004. That definition previously read as follows—
" 'transfer note' has the same meaning as in the Environmental Protection (Duty of Care) Regulations 1991;".

Designation, direction or approval

3 Any designation, direction or approval by the Commissioners under or for the purposes of these Regulations shall be made or given by a notice in writing.

PART II
REGISTRATION AND PROVISION FOR SPECIAL CASES

Notification of liability to be registered

4— (1) A person who is required by section 47(3) of the Act to notify the Commissioners of his intention to carry out taxable activities shall do so on the form numbered 1 in the Schedule to these Regulations.

(2) Where the notification referred to in this regulation is made by a person who operates or intends to operate more than one landfill site, it shall include the particulars set out on the form numbered 2 in the Schedule to these Regulations.

(3) Where the notification referred to in this regulation is made by a partnership, it shall include the particulars set out on the form numbered 3 in the Schedule to these Regulations.

(4) The notification referred to in this regulation shall be made within 30 days of the earliest date after 1st August 1996 on which the person either forms or continues to have the intention to carry out taxable activities.

Changes in particulars

5— (1) A person who has made a notification under regulation 4, whether or not it was made in accordance with paragraph (4) of that regulation, shall, within 30 days of—

(*a*) discovering any inaccuracy in; or

(*b*) any change occurring which causes to become inaccurate,

any of the information which was contained in or provided with the notification, notify the Commissioners in writing and furnish them with full particulars.

(2) Without prejudice to paragraph (1) above, a registrable person shall, within 30 days of any change occurring in any of the circumstances referred to in paragraph (4) below, notify the Commissioners in writing and furnish them with particulars of—

(*a*) the change; and

(*b*) the date on which the change occurred.

(3) A registrable person who discovers that any information contained in or provided with a notification under paragraph (1) or (2) above was inaccurate shall, within 30 days of his discovering the inaccuracy, notify the Commissioners in writing and furnish them with particulars of—

(*a*) the inaccuracy;
(*b*) the date on which the inaccuracy was discovered;
(*c*) how the information was inaccurate; and
(*d*) the correct information.

(4) The circumstances mentioned in paragraph (2) above are the following circumstances relating to the registrable person or any taxable business carried on by him:

(*a*) his name, his trading name (if different), his address and the landfill sites he operates;
(*b*) his status, namely whether he carries on business as a sole proprietor, body corporate, partnership or other unincorporated body;
(*c*) in the case of a partnership, the name and address of any partner.

(5) Any person failing to comply with a requirement imposed in any of paragraphs (1) to (3) above shall be liable to a penalty of £250.

(6) Where in relation to a registered person the Commissioners are satisfied that any of the information recorded in the register is or has become inaccurate they may correct the register accordingly.

(7) For the purposes of paragraph (6) above, it is immaterial whether or not the registered person has notified the Commissioners of any change which has occurred in accordance with paragraphs (1) to (3) above.

Notification of cessation of taxable activities

6 A person who is required by section 47(4) of the Act to notify the Commissioners of his having ceased to have the intention to carry out taxable activities shall, within 30 days of his so having ceased, notify the Commissioners in writing and shall therein inform them of—

(*a*) the date on which he ceased to have the intention of carrying out taxable activities; and
(*b*) if different, the date on which he ceased to carry out taxable activities.

Transfer of a going concern

7— (1) Where—

(*a*) a taxable business is transferred as a going concern;
(*b*) the registration of the transferor has not already been cancelled;
(*c*) as a result of the transfer of the business the registration of the transferor is to be cancelled and the transferee has become liable to be registered; and
(*d*) an application is made on the form numbered 4 in the Schedule to these Regulations by both the transferor and the transferee,

the Commissioners may with effect from the date of the transfer cancel the registration of the transferor and register the transferee with the registration number previously allocated to the transferor.

(2) An application under paragraph (1) above shall be treated as the notification referred to in regulation 6.

(3) Where the transferee of a business has been registered under paragraph (1) above with the registration number previously allocated to the transferor—

(*a*) any liability of the transferor existing at the date of the transfer to make a return or account for or pay any tax under Part III of these Regulations shall become the liability of the transferee;
(*b*) any entitlement of the transferor, whether or not existing at the date of the transfer, to credit or payment under Part IV of these Regulations shall become the entitlement of the transferee.

(4) In addition to the provisions set out in paragraph (3) above, where the transferee of a business has been registered under paragraph (1) above with the registration number previously allocated to the transferor during an accounting period subsequent to that in which the transfer took place (but with effect from the date of the transfer) and any—

(*a*) return has been made;
(*b*) tax has been accounted for; or
(*c*) entitlement to credit has been claimed,

by either the transferor or the transferee, it shall be treated as having been done by the transferee.

(5) Where—

(*a*) a taxable business is transferred as a going concern;
(*b*) the transferee removes material as described in regulation 21(2) or (4); and
(*c*) the transferor has paid tax on the disposal concerned,

then, whether or not the transferee has been registered under paragraph (1) above with the registration number previously allocated to the transferor, any entitlement to credit arising under Part V of these Regulations shall become the entitlement of the transferee.

Representation of unincorporated body

8— (1) Where anything is required to be done by or under the Act (whether by these Regulations or otherwise) by or on behalf of an unincorporated body other than a partnership, it shall be the joint and several responsibility of—

(*a*) every member holding office as president, chairman, treasurer, secretary or any similar office; or

(*b*) if there is no such office, every member holding office as a member of a committee by which the affairs of the body are managed; or

(*c*) if there is no such office or committee, every member;

but, subject to paragraph (2) below, if it is done by any of the persons referred to above that shall be sufficient compliance with any such requirement.

(2) Where an unincorporated body other than a partnership is required to make any notification such as is referred to in regulations 4 to 6, it shall not be sufficient compliance unless the notification is made by a person upon whom a responsibility for making it is imposed by paragraph (1) above.

(3) Where anything is required to be done by or under the Act (whether by these Regulations or otherwise) by or on behalf of a partnership, it shall be the joint and several responsibility of every partner; but if it is done by one partner or, in the case of a partnership whose principal place of business is in Scotland, by any other person authorised by the partnership with respect thereto that shall be sufficient compliance with any such requirement.

Bankruptcy or incapacity of registrable persons

9— (1) If a registrable person becomes bankrupt or incapacitated, the Commissioners may, from the date on which he became bankrupt or incapacitated, as the case may be, treat as a registrable person any person carrying on any taxable business of his; and any legislation relating to landfill tax shall apply to any person so treated as though he were a registered person.

(2) Any person carrying on such business as aforesaid shall, within 30 days of commencing to do so, inform the Commissioners in writing of that fact and the date of the bankruptcy order or of the nature of the incapacity and the date on which it began.

(3) Where the Commissioners have treated a person carrying on a business as a registrable person under paragraph (1) above, they shall cease so to treat him if—

(*a*) the registration of the registrable person is cancelled, whether or not any other person is registered with the registration number previously allocated to him;

(*b*) the bankruptcy is discharged or the incapacity ceases; or

(*c*) he ceases carrying on the business of the registrable person.

(4) In relation to a registrable person which is a company, the references in this regulation to the registrable person becoming incapacitated shall be construed as references to its going into liquidation or receivership or [entering administration][1]; and references to the incapacity ceasing shall be construed accordingly.

Amendments—[1] Words in para (4) substituted by the Enterprise Act 2002 (Insolvency) Order, SI 2003/605 art 5, Schedule paras 65, 66 with effect from 15 September 2003. However, this amendment does not apply in relation to any case where a petition for an administration order was presented before that date: SI 2003/2096 at 6.

PART III
ACCOUNTING, PAYMENT[, RECORDS AND INFORMATION AREAS][1]

Amendments—[1] In heading to Part III, words substituted for words "and records" by the Landfill Tax (Amendment) Regulations, SI 2009/1930 reg 2(1), (2) with effect from 1 September 2009.

Interpretation

10 In this Part, "accounting period" has the meaning given in regulation 2(1).

Making of returns

11— (1) Subject to paragraph (3) below and save as the Commissioners may otherwise allow, a registrable person shall, in respect of each accounting period, make a return to the Controller, Central Collection Unit (LT), [in a form that is determined by the Commissioners in a public notice.][1]

(2) Subject to paragraph (3) below, a registrable person shall make each return not later than the last working day of the month next following the end of the period to which it relates.

(3) Where the Commissioners consider it necessary in the circumstances of any particular case, they may—

(*a*) vary the length of any accounting period or the date on which it begins or ends or by which any return must be made;

(*b*) allow or direct the registrable person to make a return in accordance with sub-paragraph (*a*) above;

(*c*) allow or direct a registrable person to make returns to a specified address, and any person to whom the Commissioners give any direction such as is referred to in this regulation shall comply therewith.

Amendments—[1] In para (1), words substituted for words "on the form numbered 5 in the Schedule to these Regulations" by the Landfill Tax (Amendment) Regulations, SI 2009/1930 reg 2(1), (3) with effect from 1 September 2009,

Landfill tax account

12— (1) Every registrable person shall make and maintain an account to be known as "the landfill tax account".

(2) The landfill tax account shall be in such form and contain such particulars as may be stipulated in a notice published by the Commissioners and not withdrawn by a further notice.

Correction of errors

13— (1) In this regulation—

"overdeclaration" means, in relation to any return, the amount (if any) which was wrongly treated as tax due for the accounting period concerned and which caused the amount of tax which was payable to be overstated, or the entitlement to a payment under regulation 20 to be understated (or both) or would have caused such an overstatement or understatement were it not for the existence of an underdeclaration in relation to that return;

"underdeclaration" means, in relation to any return, the aggregate of—

(*a*) the amount (if any) of tax due for the accounting period concerned which was not taken into account; and

(*b*) the amount (if any) which was wrongly deducted as credit,

and which caused the amount of tax which was payable to be understated, or the entitlement to a payment under regulation 20 to be overstated (or both) or would have caused such an understatement or overstatement were it not for the existence of an overdeclaration in relation to that return.

(2) This regulation applies where a registrable person has made a return which was inaccurate as the result of an overdeclaration or underdeclaration.

(3) …[1]

(4) Where in any accounting period—

(*a*) a registrable person discovers one or more [overdeclarations or][1] underdeclarations; and

(*b*) having treated the amount of those [overdeclarations or][1] underdeclarations as reduced by the amount [respectively of any underdeclarations or overdeclarations][1] for the same accounting periods, the total of those [overdeclarations or][1] underdeclarations does not exceed [£50,000][1],

he may enter the [overdeclarations or][1] underdeclarations in his return for the accounting period in which they were discovered by including their amount in [the boxes for underdeclarations and overdeclarations as appropriate in the form referred to in regulation 11(1)][4].

[But if the registrable person's VAT turnover is small, the total mentioned in sub-paragraph (*b*) must not for these purposes exceed 1% of that turnover unless the total is [£10,000 or less][3].

And if that person is not registered for VAT, the total mentioned in sub-paragraph (*b*) must not for these purposes exceed £10,000.][1]

[The VAT turnover is small only if Box 6 of that person's value added tax return for the prescribed accounting period in which the discovery is made must contain a total less than £5,000,000 (total value of sales and all other outputs excluding any value added tax).][2]

(5) Where a registrable person enters an amount in a return in accordance with paragraph …[1] (4) above he shall calculate the tax payable by him or the payment to which he is entitled accordingly.

(6) Where an amount has been entered in accordance with this regulation in a return which has been made—

(*a*) the return shall be regarded as correcting any earlier return to which that amount relates; and

(*b*) the registrable person shall be taken to have furnished information with respect to the inaccuracy in the prescribed form and manner for the purposes of paragraph 20 of Schedule 5 to the Act.

(7) No amount shall be entered in a return in respect of any overdeclaration or underdeclaration except in accordance with this regulation; and as regards any underdeclaration that cannot be corrected under paragraph (4) above a person shall not be taken to have furnished information with respect to an inaccuracy in the prescribed form and manner for the purposes of paragraph 20 of Schedule 5 to the Act unless he provides such information to the Commissioners in writing.

Amendments—[1] Para (3) revoked, words in para (4) inserted, and words "(3) or" in para (5) revoked, by the he Value Added Tax, etc (Correction of Errors, etc) Regulations, SI 2008/1482 reg 5 with effect in relation to overdeclarations or underdeclarations in reg 13 which registrable persons first discover in their accounting periods that begin on 1 July 2008 or later. Paras (3), (4) previously read as follows—

"(3) Where in any accounting period a registrable person has discovered one or more overdeclarations, he may enter the overdeclarations in the return for the accounting period in which they were discovered by including their amount in the box opposite the legend "Overdeclarations from previous periods (no limit)".

(4) Where in any accounting period—

(*a*) a registrable person discovers one or more underdeclarations; and

(*b*) having treated the amount of those underdeclarations as reduced by the amount of any overdeclarations for the same accounting periods, the total of those underdeclarations does not exceed £2,000,

he may enter the underdeclarations in his return for the accounting period in which they were discovered by including their amount in the box opposite the legend "Underdeclarations from previous periods (must not exceed £2,000, see general notes)".".

2 In para (4), words inserted by the Value Added Tax, etc (Correction of Errors, etc) Regulations, SI 2008/1482 reg 8(1) with effect from 1 July 2008.

3 In para (4), words substituted for words "less than £10,000" by the Amusement Machine Licence Duty, etc (Amendments) Regulations, SI 2008/2693 reg 4(1)(*b*) with effect for a discovery first made on 1 November 2008 or later.

4 In para (4), words substituted for words "Box 2 (underdeclarations) or Box 4 (overdeclarations), as appropriate (see Form 5 in the Schedule)" by the Landfill Tax (Amendment) Regulations, SI 2009/1930 reg 2(1), (4) with effect from 1 September 2009.

Claims for overpaid tax

14 Except where the amount to which the claim relates has been entered in a return in accordance with regulation 13 or is included in an amount so entered, any claim under paragraph 14 of Schedule 5 to the Act shall be made in writing to the Commissioners and shall, by reference to such documentary evidence as is in the possession of the claimant, state the amount of the claim and the method by which that amount was calculated.

[Interpretation of regulations 14A to 14H

14A In this regulation and in regulations 14B to 14H below—

"claim" means a claim made (irrespective of when it was made) under paragraph 14 of Schedule 5 to the Act for repayment of an amount paid to the Commissioners by way of tax which was not tax due to them; and "claimed" and "claimant" shall be construed accordingly;

"reimbursement arrangements" means any arrangements (whether made before, on or after 30th January 1998) for the purposes of a claim which—

(*a*) are made by a claimant for the purpose of securing that he is not unjustly enriched by the repayment of any amount in pursuance of the claim; and

(*b*) provide for the reimbursement of persons (consumers) who have, for practical purposes, borne the whole or any part of the cost of the original payment of that amount to the Commissioners;

"relevant amount" means that part (which may be the whole) of the amount of a claim which the claimant has reimbursed or intends to reimburse to consumers.][1]

Amendments—[1] This regulation inserted by the Landfill Tax (Amendment) Regulations, SI 1998/61 with effect from 11 February 1998.

[Reimbursement arrangements—general

14B Without prejudice to regulation 14H below, for the purposes of paragraph 14(3) of Schedule 5 to the Act (defence by the Commissioners that repayment by them of an amount claimed would unjustly enrich the claimant) reimbursement arrangements made by a claimant shall be disregarded except where they—

(*a*) include the provisions described in regulation 14C below; and

(*b*) are supported by the undertakings described in regulation 14G below.][1]

Amendments—[1] This regulation inserted by the Landfill Tax (Amendment) Regulations, SI 1998/61 with effect from 11 February 1998.

[Reimbursement arrangements—provisions to be included

14C The provisions referred to in regulation 14B(*a*) above are that—

(*a*) reimbursement for which the arrangements provide will be completed by no later than 90 days after the repayment to which it relates;

(*b*) no deduction will be made from the relevant amount by way of fee or charge (howsoever expressed or effected);

(*c*) reimbursement will be made only in cash or by cheque;

(*d*) any part of the relevant amount that is not reimbursed by the time mentioned in paragraph (*a*) above will be repaid by the claimant to the Commissioners;

(*e*) any interest paid by the Commissioners on any relevant amount repaid by them will also be treated by the claimant in the same way as the relevant amount falls to be treated under paragraphs (*a*) and (*b*) above; and

(*f*) the records described in regulation 14E below will be kept by the claimant and produced by him to the Commissioners, or to an officer of theirs in accordance with regulation 14F below.][1]

Amendments—[1] This regulation inserted by the Landfill Tax (Amendment) Regulations, SI 1998/61 with effect from 11 February 1998.

[Repayments to the Commissioners

14D The claimant shall, without prior demand, make any repayment to the Commissioners that he is required to make by virtue of regulation 14C(*d*) and (*e*) above within 14 days of the expiration of the period of 90 days referred to in regulation 14C(*a*) above.][1]

Amendments—[1] This regulation inserted by the Landfill Tax (Amendment) Regulations, SI 1998/61 with effect from 11 February 1998.

[Records

14E The claimant shall keep records of the following matters—

(*a*) the names and addresses of those consumers whom he has reimbursed or whom he intends to reimburse;

(*b*) the total amount reimbursed to each such consumer;

(*c*) the amount of interest included in each total amount reimbursed to each consumer;

(*d*) the date that each reimbursement is made.][1]

Amendments—[1] This regulation inserted by the Landfill Tax (Amendment) Regulations, SI 1998/61 with effect from 11 February 1998.

[Production of records

14F— (1) Where a claimant is given notice in accordance with paragraph (2) below, he shall, in accordance with such notice produce to the Commissioners, or to an officer of theirs, the records that he is required to keep pursuant to regulation 14E above.

(2) A notice given for the purposes of paragraph (1) above shall—

(*a*) be in writing;

(*b*) state the place and time at which, and the date on which the records are to be produced; and

(*c*) be signed and dated by the Commissioners, or by an officer of theirs,

and may be given before or after, or both before and after the Commissioners have paid the relevant amount to the claimant.][1]

Amendments—[1] This regulation inserted by the Landfill Tax (Amendment) Regulations, SI 1998/61 with effect from 11 February 1998.

[Undertakings

14G— (1) Without prejudice to regulation 14H(*b*) below, the undertakings referred to in regulation 14B(*b*) above shall be given to the Commissioners by the claimant no later than the time at which he makes the claim for which the reimbursement arrangements have been made.

(2) The undertakings shall be in writing, shall be signed and dated by the claimant, and shall be to the effect that—

(*a*) at the date of the undertakings he is able to identify the names and addresses of those consumers whom he has reimbursed or whom he intends to reimburse;

(*b*) he will apply the whole of the relevant amount repaid to him, without any deduction by way of fee or charge or otherwise, to the reimbursement in cash or by cheque, of such consumers by no later than 90 days after his receipt of that amount (except insofar as he has already so reimbursed them);

(*c*) he will apply any interest paid to him on the relevant amount repaid to him wholly to the reimbursement of such consumers by no later than 90 days after his receipt of that interest;

(*d*) he will repay to the Commissioners without demand the whole or such part of the relevant amount repaid to him or of any interest paid to him as he fails to apply in accordance with the undertakings mentioned in sub-paragraphs (*b*) and (*c*) above;

(*e*) he will keep the records described in regulation 14E above; and

(*f*) he will comply with any notice given to him in accordance with regulation 14F above concerning the production of such records.][1]

Amendments—[1] This regulation inserted by the Landfill Tax (Amendment) Regulations, SI 1998/61 with effect from 11 February 1998.

[Reimbursement arrangements made before 11th February 1998

14H Reimbursement arrangements made by a claimant before 11th February 1998 shall not be disregarded for the purposes of paragraph 14(3) of Schedule 5 to the Act if, not later than 11th March 1998—

(*a*) he includes in those arrangements (if they are not already included) the provisions described in regulation 14C above; and

(*b*) gives the undertakings described in regulation 14G above.][1]

Amendments—[1] This regulation inserted by the Landfill Tax (Amendment) Regulations, SI 1998/61 with effect from 11 February 1998.

Payment of tax

15 Save as the Commissioners may otherwise allow or direct, any person required to make a return shall pay to the Controller, Central Collection Unit (LT), such amount of tax as is payable by him in respect of the accounting period to which the return relates no later than the last day on which he was required to make the return.

Records

16— (1) Every registrable person shall, for the purpose of accounting for tax, preserve the following—

(*a*) his business and accounting records;
(*b*) his landfill tax account;
(*c*) transfer notes and any other original or copy records in relation to material brought onto or removed from the landfill site (including any record made [on or before 31st August 2009][1] for the purpose of Part IX of these Regulations [before that Part was revoked with effect from 1st September 2009, or for the purpose of regulation 16A(4) below][1]);
(*d*) all invoices (including landfill invoices) and similar documents issued to him and copies of such invoices and similar documents issued by him;
(*e*) all credit or debit notes or other documents received by him which evidence an increase or decrease in the amount of any consideration for a relevant transaction, and copies of such documents that are issued by him;
(*f*) such other records as the Commissioners may specify in a notice published by them and not withdrawn by a further notice.

(2) Subject to paragraphs (3) and (4) below, every registrable person shall preserve the records specified in paragraph (1) above for a period of six years.

(3) Subject to paragraph (4) below, a registrable person who has made a landfill tax bad debt account shall preserve that account for a period of five years from the date of the claim made under Part VI of these Regulations.

(4) The Commissioners may direct that registrable persons shall preserve the records specified in paragraph (1) above for a shorter period than that specified in this regulation; and such direction may be made so as to apply generally or in such cases as the Commissioners may stipulate.

(5) In paragraph (1) above—

(*a*) the reference to material being brought onto a landfill site is a reference to material that is brought onto the site for the purpose of a relevant transaction;
(*b*) the reference to material being removed from a landfill site is a reference to material being removed that has at some previous time fallen wholly or partly within paragraph (*a*) above.

(6) In this regulation "relevant transaction" means a disposal or anything that would be a disposal but for the fact that the material is not disposed of as waste.

Amendments—[1] In para (1)(*c*), words inserted by the Landfill Tax (Amendment) Regulations, SI 2009/1930 reg 2(1), (5) with effect from 1 September 2009.

[Information areas

16A— (1) An officer of Revenue and Customs is authorised to require a person to designate a part of a landfill site (an "information area"), and a person must designate an information area if so required.

(2) Where material at a landfill site is not going to be disposed of as waste and the Commissioners consider, or an officer of theirs considers, there to be a risk to the revenue—

(*a*) the material must be deposited in an information area; and
(*b*) a registrable person must give the Commissioners, or an officer of theirs, information and maintain a record in accordance with paragraph 4 below.

(3) A designation ceases to have effect if a notice in writing to that effect is given to a registrable person by the Commissioners or by an officer of Revenue and Customs.

(4) A registrable person must maintain a record in relation to the information area of the following information, and give this information to the Commissioners or an officer of theirs if requested—

(*a*) the weight and description of all material deposited there;
(*b*) the intended destination or use of all such material and, where any material has been removed or used, the actual destination or use of that material;
(*c*) the weight and description of any such material sorted or removed.][1]

Amendments—[1] This reg inserted by the Landfill Tax (Amendment) Regulations, SI 2009/1930 reg 2(1), (6) with effect from 1 September 2009.

PART IV
CREDIT: GENERAL

Interpretation

17 In this Part—

"relevant accounting period" means—

(*a*) in the case of an entitlement to credit arising under Part V of these Regulations, the accounting period in which the reuse condition or, as the case may be, the enforced removal condition was satisfied;

(*b*) in the case of an entitlement to credit arising under Part VI of these Regulations, the accounting period in which the period of one year from the date of the issue of the landfill invoice expired;

(*c*) in the case of an entitlement arising under Part VII of these Regulations, the accounting period in which the qualifying contribution was made;

"relevant amount" means the amount of the credit as determined in accordance with Part V, VI or VII of these Regulations, as the case may be;

"relevant tax" means the tax, if any, that was required to have been paid as a condition of the entitlement to credit.

Scope

18— (1) This Part applies to entitlements to credit arising under Part V, VI or VII of these Regulations.

(2) No credit arising under any provisions of these Regulations may be claimed except in accordance with this Part.

Claims in returns

19— (1) Subject to paragraphs (2) and (3) below, a person entitled to credit may claim it by deducting its amount from any tax due from him for the relevant accounting period or any subsequent accounting period and, where he does so, he shall make his return for that accounting period accordingly.

(2) Where the entitlement to credit arises under Part VII of these Regulations paragraph (1) above shall apply as if there were substituted for "or any subsequent accounting period" the words "or any subsequent accounting period in the same contribution year as determined in relation to that person under regulation 31".

(3) The Commissioners may make directions generally or with regard to particular cases prescribing rules in accordance with which credit may or shall be held over to be credited in an accounting period subsequent to the relevant accounting period; and where such a direction has been made that credit, subject to any subsequent such direction varying or withdrawing the rules, may only be claimed in accordance with those rules.

Payments in respect of credit

20— (1) Subject to paragraph (5) below, where the total credit claimed by a registrable person in accordance with this Part exceeds the total of the tax due from him for the accounting period, the Commissioners shall pay to him an amount equal to the excess.

(2) Where the Commissioners have cancelled the registration of a person in accordance with section 47(6) of the Act, and he is not a registrable person, he shall make any claim in respect of credit to which this Part applies by making an application in writing.

(3) A person making an application under paragraph (2) above shall furnish to the Commissioners full particulars in relation to the credit claimed, including (but not restricted to)—

(*a*) except in the case of an entitlement to credit arising under Part VII of these Regulations, the return in which the relevant tax was accounted for;

(*b*) except in the case of an entitlement to credit arising under Part VII of these Regulations, the amount of the tax and the date and manner of its payment;

(*c*) the events by virtue of which the entitlement to credit arose.

(4) Subject to paragraph (5) below, where the Commissioners are satisfied that a person who has made a claim in accordance with paragraphs (2) and (3) above is entitled to credit, and that he has not previously had the benefit of that credit, they shall pay to him an amount equal to the credit.

(5) The Commissioners shall not be liable to make any payment under this regulation unless and until the person has made all the returns which he was required to make.

PART V
CREDIT: PERMANENT REMOVALS ETC

Entitlement to credit

21— (1) An entitlement to credit arises under this Part where—

(*a*) a registered person has accounted for an amount of tax and, except where the removal by virtue of which sub-paragraph (*b*) below is satisfied takes place in the accounting period in which credit arising under this Part is claimed in accordance with Part IV of these Regulations, he has paid that tax; and

(*b*) in relation to the disposal on which that tax was charged, either—

(i) the reuse condition has been satisfied; or

(ii) the enforced removal condition has been satisfied.

(2) The reuse condition is satisfied where—

(*a*) the disposal has been made with the intention that the material comprised in it—

(i) would be recycled or incinerated; or

(ii) removed for use (other than by way of a further disposal) at a place other than a relevant site; [or

(iii) removed for use in restoration of a relevant site and the material involved has previously been used to create or maintain temporary hard standing, to create or maintain a temporary screening bund or to create or maintain a temporary haul road;][2]

(*b*) that material, or some of it, has been recycled, incinerated or permanently removed from the landfill site, as the case may be, in accordance with that intention;

(*c*) that recycling, incineration or removal—

(i) has taken place no later than one year after the date of the disposal; or

(ii) where water had been added to the material in order to facilitate its disposal, has taken place no later than five years after the date of the disposal; and

(*d*) the registered person has, before the disposal, notified the Commissioners in writing that he intends to make one or more removals of material in relation to which sub-paragraphs (*a*) to (*c*) above will be satisfied.

(3) For the purpose of paragraph (2)(*a*)(ii) above a relevant site is the landfill site at which the disposal was made or any other landfill site.

(4) The enforced removal condition is satisfied where—

(*a*) the disposal is in breach of the terms of the licence[, resolution or permit][1], as the case may be, by virtue of which the land constitutes a landfill site;

(*b*) the registered person has been directed to remove the material comprised in the disposal, or some of it, by a relevant authority and he has removed it, or some of it; and

(*c*) a further taxable disposal of the material has been made and, except where the registered person is the person liable for the tax chargeable on that further disposal, he has paid to the site operator an amount representing that tax.

(5) For the purpose of paragraph (4)(*b*) above the following are relevant authorities—

(*a*) the Environment Agency;

(*b*) the Scottish Environment Protection Agency;

(*c*) the Department of the Environment for Northern Ireland;

(*d*) a district council in Northern Ireland.

(6) The amount of the credit arising under this Part shall be equal to the tax that was charged on the disposal; except that where only some of the material comprised in that disposal is removed, the amount of the credit shall be such proportion of that tax as the material removed forms of the total of the material.

[(7) In this Regulation—

"disposal area" means any area of a landfill site where any disposal takes place;

"haul road" means any road within the landfill site which gives access to a disposal area;

"hard standing" means a base within a landfill site on which any landfill site activity such as sorting, treatment, processing, storage or recycling is carried out;

"screening bund" means any structure on a landfill site (whether below or above ground) put in place to protect or conceal any landfill site activity or to reduce nuisance from noise.][2]

Amendments—[1] Words substituted by the Landfill Tax (Amendment) Regulations, SI 2005/759 regs 2, 3 with effect from 6 April 2005.

[2] Para (2)(*a*)(iii) and preceding word "or", and para (7), inserted by the Landfill Tax (Amendment) Regulations, SI 2009/1930 reg 2(1), (7), (8) with effect from 1 September 2009.

PART VI
CREDIT: BAD DEBTS

Interpretation

22 In this Part—

"claim" means a claim in accordance with Part IV of these Regulations for an amount of credit arising under this Part and "claimant" shall be construed accordingly;

"customer" means a person for whom a taxable activity is carried out by the claimant;

"outstanding amount" means, in relation to any claim—

(*a*) if at the time of the claim the claimant has received no payment in respect of the amount written off in his accounts, the amount so written off; or

(*b*) if at that time he has received a payment, the amount by which the amount written off exceeds the payment (or the aggregate of the payments);

"relevant disposal" means any taxable disposal upon which a claim is based;

"security" means—

(*a*) in relation to England, Wales and Northern Ireland, any mortgage, charge, lien or other security; and (*b*) in relation to Scotland, any security (whether heritable or moveable), any floating charge and any right of lien or preference and right of retention (other than a right of compensation or set-off).

Scope

23 An entitlement to credit arises under this Part where—

(*a*) a registered person has carried out a taxable activity for a consideration in money for a customer with whom he is not connected;

(*b*) he has accounted for and paid tax on the disposal concerned;

(*c*) the whole or any part of the consideration for the disposal has been written off in his accounts as a bad debt;

(*d*) he has issued a landfill invoice in respect of the disposal which shows the amount of tax chargeable;

(*e*) that invoice was issued—

(i) within 14 days of the date of the disposal, or

(ii) within such other period as may have been specified in a direction of the Commissioners made under section 61(3) of the Act;

(*f*) a period of one year (beginning with the date of the issue of that invoice) has elapsed; and

(*g*) the following provisions of this Part have been complied with.

Amount of credit

24 The credit arising under this Part shall be of an amount equal to such proportion of the tax charged on the relevant disposal as the outstanding amount forms of the total consideration.

Evidence required in support of claim

25 The claimant, before he makes a claim, shall hold in respect of each relevant disposal—

(*a*) a copy of the landfill invoice issued by him;

(*b*) records or any other documents showing that he has accounted for and paid tax on the disposal; and

(*c*) records or any other documents showing that the consideration has been written off in his accounts as a bad debt.

Records required to be kept

26— (1) Any person who makes a claim shall make a record of that claim.

(2) The record referred to in paragraph (1) above shall contain the following information in respect of each claim made:

(*a*) in respect of each relevant disposal—

(i) the amount of tax charged;

(ii) the return in which that tax was accounted for and when it was paid;

(iii) the date and identifying number of the landfill invoice that was issued;

(iv) any consideration that has been received (whether before the claim was made or subsequently);

(v) the details of any transfer note;

(*b*) the outstanding amount;

(*c*) the amount of the claim;

(*d*) the return in which the claim was made.

(3) Any records made in pursuance of this regulation shall be kept in a single account known as "the landfill tax bad debt account".

Attribution of payments

27— (1) Where—

(*a*) the claimant has carried out a taxable activity for a customer;

(*b*) there exist one or more other matters in respect of which the claimant is entitled to a debt owed by the customer (whether they involve a taxable disposal or not and whether they are connected with waste or not); and

(*c*) a payment has been received by the claimant from the customer,

the payment shall be attributed to the taxable activity and the other matters in accordance with the rule set out in paragraphs (2) and (3) below (and the debts arising in respect of the taxable activity and the other matters are collectively referred to in those paragraphs as debts).

(2) The payment shall be attributed to the debt which arose earliest and, if not wholly attributed to that debt, thereafter to debts in the order of the dates on which they arose, except that attribution under this paragraph shall not be made if the payment was allocated to a debt by the customer at the time of payment and the debt was paid in full.

(3) Where—

(*a*) the earliest debt and the other debts to which the whole of the payment could be attributed arose on the same day; or (*b*) the debts to which the balance of the payment could be attributed in accordance with paragraph (2) above arose on the same day,

the payment shall be attributed to those debts by multiplying, for each such debt, the payment made by a fraction of which the numerator is the amount remaining unpaid in respect of that debt and the denominator is the amount remaining unpaid in respect of all those debts.

Repayment of credit

28— (1) Where a claimant—

(*a*) has benefited from an amount of credit to which he was entitled under this Part; and

(*b*) either—

(i) a payment for the relevant disposal is subsequently received; or

(ii) a payment is, by virtue of regulation 27, treated as attributed to the relevant disposal,

he shall repay to the Commissioners such amount as equals the amount of the credit, or the balance thereof, multiplied by a fraction of which the numerator is the amount so received or attributed, and the denominator is the amount of the outstanding consideration.

(2) Where the claimant—

(*a*) fails to comply with the requirements of regulation 26; or

(*b*) in relation to the documents mentioned in that regulation, fails to comply with either—

(i) regulation 16; or

(ii) any obligation arising under paragraph 3 of Schedule 5 to the Act,

he shall repay to the Commissioners the amount of the claim to which the failure to comply relates.

Writing off debts

29— (1) This regulation shall apply for the purpose of determining whether, and to what extent, the consideration is to be taken to have been written off as a bad debt.

(2) The whole or any part of the consideration for a taxable activity shall be taken to have been written off as a bad debt where—

(*a*) the claimant has written it off in his accounts as a bad debt; and

(*b*) he has made an entry in relation to that activity in the landfill tax bad debt account in accordance with regulation 26 (and this shall apply regardless of whether a claim can be made in relation to that activity at that time).

(3) Where the claimant owes an amount of money to the customer which can be set off, the consideration written off in the landfill tax bad debt account shall be reduced by the amount so owed.

(4) Where the claimant holds in relation to the customer an enforceable security, the consideration written off in the landfill tax bad debt account shall be reduced by the value of the security.

PART VII
CREDIT: BODIES CONCERNED WITH THE ENVIRONMENT

Interpretation and general provisions

30— (1) In this Part—

"approved body" means a body approved for the time being under regulation 34;

"approved object" has the meaning given in regulation 33;

["contributing third party" means a person who has made or agreed to make (whether or not under a legally binding agreement) a payment to a registered person to secure the making by him of a qualifying contribution or to reimburse him, in whole or in part, for any such contribution he has made;][1]

"income" includes interest;

"qualifying contribution" has the meaning given in regulation 32;

"the regulatory body" means such body, if any, as in relation to which an approval of the Commissioners under regulation 35 has effect for the time being;

"running costs" includes any cost incurred in connection with the management and administration of a body or its assets.

(2) A body shall only be taken to spend a qualifying contribution in the course or furtherance of its approved objects—

(*a*) in a case where the contribution is made subject to a condition that it may only be invested for the purpose of generating income, where the body so spends all of that income;

(*b*) in a case not falling within sub-paragraph (*a*) above, where the body becomes entitled to income, where it so spends both the whole of the qualifying contribution and all of that income;

(*c*) in a case not falling within either of sub-paragraphs (*a*) and (*b*) above, where the body so spends the whole of the qualifying contribution; or

(*d*) where—

(i) it transfers any qualifying contribution or income derived therefrom to another approved body, and

(ii) that transfer is subject to a condition that the sum transferred shall be spent only in the course or furtherance of that other body's approved objects.

(3) Any approval, or revocation of such approval, by the Commissioners or the regulatory body shall be given by notice in writing to the body affected and shall take effect from the date the notice is given or such later date as the Commissioners or, as the case may be, the regulatory body may specify in it.

Amendments—[1] Definition "contributing third party" inserted by the Landfill Tax (Amendment) Regulations, SI 1999/3270, regs 2, 3, with effect from 1 January 2000.

Entitlement to credit

31— (1) Subject to the following provisions of this regulation, an entitlement to credit arises under this Part in respect of qualifying contributions made by registered persons.

(2) Subject to paragraph (3) below, a person shall be entitled to credit in respect of 90 per cent of the amount of each qualifying contribution made by him in any accounting period; and for this purpose a qualifying contribution made—

[(*a*) in one accounting period;][1]

(*b*) before the return for the previous accounting period has been made; and

(*c*) before the period within which that return is required to be made has expired,

shall be treated as having been made in the accounting period mentioned in sub-paragraph (*b*) above (and not in the accounting period in which it was in fact made).

(3) In respect of the qualifying contributions made in each contribution year, a person shall not be entitled to credit of an amount greater than [6.0][3] per cent of his relevant tax liability.

[(4) For the purpose of paragraphs (2) and (3) the contribution year of a person is his first contribution year and then each period of 12 months beginning on 1st April][2].

[(5) The reference in paragraph (4) to the first contribution year of a person is a reference to the period beginning with his effective date of registration and ending on the day immediately preceding the first day of the next contribution year][2].

[(6) Where one contribution year ends and another contribution year begins in an accounting period, the amount of any qualifying contribution which, by virtue of paragraph (2) is treated as made in that period shall be apportioned, in accordance with paragraph (6A), between those contribution years][2].

[(6A) The apportionment shall be on the basis of either—

(*a*) the number of days of the accounting period that fall before 1st April and the number of days that fall on and after that day; or

(*b*) the amount of tax charged on taxable disposals made in the accounting period before 1st April and the amount of tax charged on taxable disposals made in that period on and after that day,

whichever the registered person may choose][2].

(6B)–(6E) …[2]

(7) Subject to [paragraph (10)][1] below, the reference in paragraph (3) above to the relevant tax liability of a person is a reference to the aggregate of—

(*a*) the tax payable by him, if any, in respect of the accounting period in relation to which that liability falls to be determined; and

(*b*) the tax payable by him, if any, in respect of any earlier accounting period or periods which fall within the same contribution year as that accounting period;

and where in respect of any accounting period he is entitled to a payment under regulation 20 the aggregate of the tax payable by him in respect of the accounting periods mentioned in sub-paragraphs (*a*) and (*b*) above shall be reduced by the amount of that payment.

(8), (9) … [1]

(10) For the purposes of [paragraph (7)][1] above any entitlement to credit arising under this Part shall be disregarded in determining the tax payable by a person in respect of any period.

Note—Landfill Tax (Amendment) Regulations, SI 2003/605 reg 5 (any contribution year of a person that commenced before 1 April 2003 and, but for SI 2003/605, would end after that day shall end when SI 2003/605 comes into force).

Amendments—[1] Para (2)(*a*) and words in paras (4), (7), (10) substituted, words in para (5) and paras (6A)–(6E) inserted, and paras (8), (9) revoked, by the Landfill Tax (Amendment) Regulations, SI 1999/3270, regs 2, 4, with effect from 1 January 2000.

[2] Paras (4), (5), (6), (6A) and figure in para (3) substituted, and paras (6B)–(6E) revoked, by the Landfill Tax (Amendment) Regulations, SI 2003/605 regs 2, 3, with effect from 1 April 2003. However, nothing in SI 2003/605 affects a qualifying contribution that was made, or treated as made, before the coming into force of SI 2003/605: SI 2003/605 reg 6. Note that reg 6 is revoked by the Landfill Tax (Amendment) Regulations, SI 2007/965 reg 6 with effect from 1 April 2007, save that it will continue to have effect with respect to a qualifying contribution that was made, or treated as made, before 1 April 2003 if, but only if, the condition specified in SI 2007/965 reg 6(3) is satisfied: SI 2007/965 reg 6(2).

[3] Figure in para (3) substituted by the Landfill Tax (Amendment) Regulations, SI 2008/770 reg 2 with effect from 1 April 2008.

Qualifying contributions

32— (1) A payment is a qualifying contribution if—

(*a*) it is made by a registered person to an approved body;

(*b*) it is made subject to a condition that the body shall spend the sum paid or any income derived from it or both only in the course or furtherance of its approved objects;

(*c*) the requirements of [paragraphs (2) to (2B)][1] below have been complied with in relation to that payment; and

(*d*) it is not repaid to him[, or to a contributing third party,][1] in the same accounting period as that in which it was made.

(2) A person claiming credit arising under this Part shall make a record containing the following information—

(*a*) the amount and date of each payment he has made to an approved body;

(*b*) the name and enrolment number of that body;

[(*c*) the name and address of any contributing third party; and

(*d*) the amount of the payment made or to be made by the contributing third party and the date, or as the case may require, dates on which payment of the whole or any part of that amount—

(i) was received, or

(ii) is expected to be received][1].

[(2A) A person claiming credit under this Part for a contribution in relation to which there is a contributing third party shall have provided to the regulatory body or, if they are performing the functions specified in regulation 34(1) below, to the Commissioners the following information—

(*a*) the name and address of the contributing third party;

(*b*) the amount of the payment made or to be made by the contributing third party and the date, or as the case may require, dates on which payment of the whole or any part of that amount—

(i) was received, or

(ii) is expected to be received;

(*c*) the enrolment number of the approved body to whom the contribution was made.

(2B) A person claiming credit under this Part for a contribution in relation to which there is a contributing third party shall have informed the approved body to which the contribution is made of the name and address of the contributing third party.][1]

[(3) For the purposes of this Part where any qualifying contribution or income derived therefrom is transferred to a body as described in regulation 30(2)(*d*)—

(*a*) the body to whom the sum is transferred shall be treated as having received qualifying contributions of the amount concerned; and

(*b*) that body shall be treated as having received those qualifying contributions from the registered person or persons who originally paid them (but this shall not give rise to any further entitlement to credit in respect of those contributions).][1]

Amendments—[1] Words in para (1)(*c*), and whole of para (3) substituted, words in para (1)(*d*) and whole of paras (2)(*c*), (2A), (2B) inserted, by the Landfill Tax (Amendment) Regulations, SI 1999/3270, regs 2, 5, with effect from 1 January 2000.

Bodies eligible for approval

33— (1) [A body is eligible to be approved if—][1]

(*a*) it is—

(i) a body corporate, or

(ii) a trust, partnership or other unincorporated body;

(*b*) its objects are or include any of the objects within paragraph (2) below (approved objects);

(*c*) it is precluded from distributing and does not distribute any profit it makes or other income it receives;

(*d*) it applies any profit or other income to the furtherance of its objects (whether or not approved objects);

[(*e*) it is precluded from applying any of its funds for the benefit of any of the persons—

(i) who have made qualifying contributions to it, or

(ii) who were a contributing third party in relation to such contributions,

except that such persons may benefit where they belong to a class of persons that benefits generally;][1]… [1]

[(*f*) it is not controlled by one or more of the persons and bodies listed in paragraphs (1A) and (1B) below;

(*g*) none of the persons or bodies listed in paragraph (1B) below is concerned in its management; and

(*h*) it pays to the regulatory body an application fee of £100 or such lesser sum as the regulatory body may require.][1]

[(1A) The persons and bodies mentioned in paragraph (1)(*f*) above are—

(*a*) a local authority;

(*b*) a body corporate controlled by one or more local authorities;
(*c*) a registered person;
(*d*) a person connected with any of the persons or bodies mentioned in sub-paragraphs (*a*) to (*c*) above.

(1B) The persons and bodies mentioned in paragraph (1)(*f*) and (*g*) above are—

(*a*) a person who controlled or was concerned in the management of a body the approval of which was revoked otherwise than under regulation 34(1)(*ee*);
(*b*) a person who has been convicted of an indictable offence;
(*c*) a person who is disqualified for being a charity trustee or a trustee for a charity by virtue of section 72 of the Charities Act 1993;
(*d*) a person connected with any of the persons or bodies mentioned in sub-paragraphs (*a*) to (*c*) above;
(*e*) a person who is incapable by reason of mental disorder.

(1C) For the purpose of paragraph 1(B)(*e*) above, a person shall be treated as incapable by reason of mental disorder where—

(*a*) in England and Wales, the judge has exercised any of his functions under Part VII of the Mental Health Act 1983;
(*b*) in Scotland, the court has appointed a curator bonis, tutor or judicial factor; or
(*c*) in Northern Ireland, the court has exercised any of its powers under Part VIII of the Mental Health (Northern Ireland) Order 1986 (whether or not by virtue of Article 97(2) of that Order),

but shall cease to be so treated where the judge or court concerned has made a finding that he is not or is no longer incapable of managing and administering his property and affairs.][1]

(2) The objects of a body are approved objects insofar as they are any of the following objects—

(*a*) in relation to any land the use of which for any economic, social or environmental purpose has been prevented or restricted because of the carrying on of an activity on the land which has ceased—

(i) reclamation, remediation or restoration; or
(ii) any other operation intended to facilitate economic, social or environmental use;

but this is subject to paragraph (3) below;

(*b*) in relation to any land the condition of which, by reason of the carrying on of an activity on the land which has ceased, is such that pollution (whether of that land or not) is being or may be caused—

(i) any operation intended to prevent or reduce any potential for pollution; or
(ii) any operation intended to remedy or mitigate the effects of any pollution that has been caused,

but this is subject to paragraph (3) below;

(*c*), (*cc*) …[3]

(*d*) where it is for the protection of the environment, the provision, maintenance or improvement of—

(i) a public park; or
(ii) another public amenity,

in the vicinity of a landfill site, provided the conditions in paragraph (6) below are satisfied;

[(*da*) where it is for the protection of the environment, and subject to paragraph (3A) below, the conservation or promotion of biological diversity through—

(i) the provision, conservation, restoration or enhancement of a natural habitat; or
(ii) the maintenance or recovery of a species in its natural habitat,

on land or in water situated in the vicinity of a landfill site;][4]

(*e*) where it is for the protection of the environment, the maintenance, repair or restoration of a building or other structure which—

(i) is a place of religious worship or of historic or architectural interest,
(ii) is open to the public, and
(iii) is situated in the vicinity of a landfill site,

provided the conditions in paragraph (6) below are satisfied;

(*f*) the provision of financial, administration and other similar services to bodies which are within this regulation and only such bodies.

[(2A) In paragraph (2)(*da*) above "biological diversity" has the same meaning as in the United Nations Environmental Programme Convention on Biological Diversity of 1992.][4]

(3) An object shall not be, or shall no longer be, regarded as falling within paragraph (2)(*a*) or (*b*) above if the reclamation, remediation, restoration or other operation—

(*a*) is such that any benefit from it will accrue to any person who has carried out or knowingly permitted the activity which has ceased;
(*b*) involves works which are required to be carried out by a notice or order within paragraph (4) below; or
(*c*) is wholly or partly required to be carried out by a relevant condition.

[(3A) An object shall not be, or shall no longer be, regarded as falling within paragraph (2)(*da*) above if it involves works which—

(*a*) are required to be carried out by a notice or order within paragraph (4) below;
(*b*) are required to be carried out in accordance with an agreement made under section 16 of the National Parks and Access to the Countryside Act 1949;
(*c*) are required to be carried out in accordance with an agreement made under section 15 of the Countryside Act 1968;
(*d*) give effect to any provision of a management scheme under section 28J of the Wildlife and Countryside Act 1981 or are required to be carried out by a notice served under section 28K of that Act;
(*e*) are wholly or partly required to be carried out by a relevant condition; or
(*f*) are carried out with a view to profit.][4]

(4) The notices and order mentioned in paragraph (3) above are—

(*a*) a works notice served under section 46A of the Control of Pollution Act 1974;
(*b*) an enforcement notice served under section 13 of the Environmental Protection Act 1990;
(*c*) a prohibition notice served under section 14 of the Environmental Protection Act 1990;
(*d*) an order under section 26 of the Environmental Protection Act 1990;
(*e*) a remediation notice served under section 78E of the Environmental Protection Act 1990;
(*f*) an enforcement notice served under section 90B of the Water Resources Act 1991;
(*g*) a works notice served under section 161A of the Water Resources Act 1991;
[(*h*) an enforcement notice served under regulation 24 of the Pollution Prevention and Control (England and Wales) Regulations 2000;
(*i*) a suspension notice served under regulation 25 of those Regulations;
(*j*) an order under regulation 35 of those Regulations.][2]
[(*k*) a notice served under regulation 28(2) of the Water Environment (Controlled Activities) (Scotland) Regulations 2005.][5]

(5) …[3]

(6) The conditions mentioned in sub-paragraphs (*d*) and (*e*) of paragraph (2) above are—

(*a*) in a case falling within sub-paragraph (*d*), that the provision of the park or amenity is not required by a relevant condition; and
(*b*) in a case falling within either of those sub-paragraphs, that the park, amenity, building or structure (as the case may be) is not to be operated with a view to profit.

(7) Where the objects of a body are or include any of the objects set out in paragraph (2) above, the following shall also be regarded as objects within that paragraph—

(*a*) the use of qualifying contributions in paying the running costs of the body, but this is subject to paragraph (8) below;
(*b*) …[1] the use of qualifying contributions in paying a contribution to the running costs of the regulatory body.

(8) The use of qualifying contributions in paying the running costs of the body shall only be regarded as an approved object if the body determines so to use no more than such proportion of the total of qualifying contributions, together with any income derived from them, (or, in the case of a contribution within regulation 30(2)(*a*), only that income) as the proportion of that total forms of the total funds at its disposal and does not in fact use a greater amount.

(9) For the purposes of paragraph (1) above [a body or person (in either case, for the purposes of this paragraph, "the person")][1] shall be taken to control a body where—

(*a*) in the case of a body which is a body corporate, the person is empowered by statute to control that body's activities or if he is that body's holding company within the meaning of section [1159 of and Schedule 6 to][6] the Companies Act [2006][6], and an individual shall be taken to control a body corporate if he, were he a company, would be that body's holding company within the meaning of that Act;
(*b*) in the case of a body which is a trust or a partnership, where—
 (i) the person, taken together with any nominee of his, or
 (ii) any nominee of the person, taken together with any nominee of that nominee or any other nominee of the person,

forms a majority of the total number of trustees or partners, as the case may be;

(*c*) in the case of any other body, where the person, whether directly or through any nominee, has the power—
 (i) to appoint or remove any officer of the body;
 (ii) to determine the objects of the body;
 (iii) to determine how any of the body's funds may be applied.

(10) For the purposes of paragraphs (3)[, (3A)][4] and (6) above a condition is relevant if it is—

(*a*) a condition of any planning permission or other statutory consent or approval granted on the application of any person making a qualifying contribution to the body, or
[(*b*) a term of an agreement made under—
 (i) section 106 of the Town and Country Planning Act 1990,
 (ii) section 75 of the Town and Country Planning (Scotland) Act 1997, or
 (iii) article 40 of the Planning (Northern Ireland) Order 1991,

to which such a person is a party.][1]

Note—Landfill Tax (Amendment) Regulations, SI 2003/605 reg 5 (any contribution year of a person that commenced before 1st April 2003 and, but for SI 2003/605, would end after that day shall end when SI 2003/605 comes into force).

Amendments—[1] Words in paras (1), (9) and whole of paras (1)(*e*), (*f*), (10)(*b*) substituted, words in para (1)(*e*), (7)(*b*) revoked, and whole of paras (1A)–(1C), (2)(*cc*), and words in para (5) inserted, by the Landfill Tax (Amendment) Regulations, SI 1999/3270, regs 2, 6, with effect from 1 January 2000.

[2] Sub-paras (4)(*h*)–(*k*) inserted with effect in England and Wales by the Pollution Prevention and Control (England and Wales) Regulations, SI 2000/1973 reg 39, Sch 10 para 21 with effect from 1 August 2000. With effect in Scotland, sub-paras (4)(*h*)–(*k*) inserted as follows by the Pollution Prevention and Control (Scotland) Regulations, SI 2000/323 reg 36, Sch 10 para 14 with effect from 28 September 2000:

"(*h*) an enforcement notice served under regulation 19 of the Pollution Prevention and Control (Scotland) Regulations 2000;

(*i*) a suspension notice served under regulation 20 of those Regulations;

(*j*) an order under regulation 33 of those Regulations.".

[3] Sub-paras (2)(*c*), (*cc*) and para (5) revoked, by the Landfill Tax (Amendment) Regulations, SI 2003/605 reg 2, 4, with effect from 1 April 2003. However, nothing in SI 2003/605 affects a qualifying contribution that was made, or treated as made, before the coming into force of SI 2003/605: SI 2003/605 reg 6. Note that reg 6 is revoked by the Landfill Tax (Amendment) Regulations, SI 2007/965 reg 6 with effect from 1 April 2007, save that it will continue to have effect with respect to a qualifying contribution that was made, or treated as made, before 1 April 2003 if, but only if, the condition specified in SI 2007/965 reg 6(3) is satisfied: SI 2007/965 reg 6(2).

[4] Sub-paras (2)(*da*), (2A) and (3A) inserted, and reference in sub-para (10) inserted, by the Landfill Tax (Amendment) (No 2) Regulations, SI 2003/2313 with effect from 1 October 2003.

[5] Sub-s (4)(*k*) inserted by the Water Environment and Water Services (Scotland) Act 2003 (Consequential Provisions and Modifications) Order, SI 2006/1054 art 2, Sch 1 para 3 with effect from 1 April 2006.

[6] In para (9)(*a*), words substituted for words "736 of" and "1985", by the Companies Act 2006 (Consequential Amendments) (Taxes and National Insurance) Order, SI 2009/1890 art 4(1)(*h*) with effect from 1 October 2009.

[Obligations of approved bodies

33A— (1) An approved body shall—

(*a*) continue to meet all the requirements of regulation 33 above;

[(*aa*) comply with such conditions as the regulatory body may impose from time to time under regulation 34(1)(*aa*) (including any conditions varied under regulation 34(1)(*ab*));][3]

(*b*) apply qualifying contributions and any income derived therefrom only to approved objects;

(*c*) not apply any of its funds for the benefit of any of the persons who have made qualifying contributions to it or who were contributing third parties in relation to such contributions (except to the extent that they benefit by virtue of belonging to a class of persons that benefits generally);

(*d*) make and retain records of the following—

(i) the name, address and registration number of each registered person making a qualifying contribution to the body;

(ii) the name and address of any contributing third party in relation to a qualifying contribution received by the body;

(iii) the amount and date of receipt of each qualifying contribution and the amount and date of receipt of any income derived therefrom;

(iv) in the case of a transfer of the whole or part of any qualifying contribution or income derived therefrom to or from the body, the date of the transfer, the amount transferred, the name and enrolment number of the body from or, as the case may require, to which it was transferred, the name, address and registration number of the person who made the qualifying contribution and the name and address of any contributing third party in relation to the qualifying contribution;

(v) in respect of each qualifying contribution and any income derived therefrom, including any such amount transferred to the body by another approved body, the date of and all other details relating to its expenditure;

(*e*) provide the following information to the regulatory body or, if they are performing the functions specified in regulation 34(1) below, to the Commissioners within 7 days of the receipt by it of any qualifying contribution—

(i) the amount of the contribution;

(ii) the date it was received;

(iii) the name and registration number of the person making the contribution;

(iv) the name and address of any contributing third party in relation to the contribution notified to it by virtue of regulation 32(2B) above;

(*f*) notify the regulatory body within 7 days of any [transfer by that approved body][3] of qualifying contributions or of income derived therefrom of—

(i) the date of the transfer;

(ii) the enrolment number of the approved body by …[3] which the transfer was made;

(iii) the amount transferred;

(iv) the name and registration number of the person who made the qualifying contribution;

(v) the name and address of any contributing third party in relation to the contribution; and

(vi) the approved objects to which the transferred funds are to be applied;

(*g*) provide the regulatory body or, if they are performing the functions specified in regulation 34(1) below, the Commissioners with information from or access to the records referred to in [sub-paragraph (*d*)][2] above within 14 days (or such longer period as the regulatory body or, as the case may require, the Commissioners may allow) of a request being made for such information or access;

(*h*) submit to the regulatory body or, if they are performing the functions specified in regulation 34(1) below, to the Commissioners within [28][4] days of the end of the relevant period determined in accordance with paragraph (2) below details of—

(i) qualifying contributions and any other income or profit whatsoever received by it,
(ii) any expenditure made by it during the period, and
(iii) any balances held by it at the end of the period;

[(*ha*) submit to the regulatory body at its request, not later than the day specified in paragraph (3), so many of the following details as it requires at any time during the relevant period—

(i) qualifying contributions and any other income or profit whatsoever received by it during the period,
(ii) any expenditure made by it during the period, and
(iii) any balances held during the period;

(*hb*) if the Commissioners are performing the functions specified in regulation 34(1) instead of the regulatory body, submit, at their request, not later than the day specified in paragraph (3), so many of the following details as they may require at any time during the relevant period—

(i) qualifying contributions and any other income or profit whatsoever received by it during the period,
(ii) any expenditure made by it during the period, and
(iii) any balances held during the period;][3]

[(*i*) submit to the regulatory body at its request, not later than [fourteenth day following the day on which the request is made][4], independently audited financial accounts for the approved body's last financial year; but such a request may not be made earlier than 10 months following the end of that financial year; and][3]

(*j*) pay to the regulatory body an amount equal to 5 per cent of each qualifying contribution it receives, or such lesser amount as the regulatory body may require, towards its running costs within 14 days of receipt of a demand for payment.

[(2) For the purposes of paragraphs (1)(*h*), (1)(*ha*) and (1*hb*) the relevant period in respect of an approved body is—

(*a*) in the case of the first such period, the period commencing with the date on which the body was approved and ending on the following 31st March; and
(*b*) in the case of subsequent periods, the period of 12 months commencing with the day after the end of the first or, as the case may require, a subsequent period.][3]

[(3) The day referred to in paragraphs [(1)(*ha*) and (1)(*hb*) is the twenty-eighth][4] day following the day on which a request is made.

(4) Where an approved body submits details in accordance with a request made under paragraph (1)(*ha*) or paragraph (1)(*hb*) the requirement in paragraph (1)(*h*) shall not apply in respect of those details.][3]][1]

Amendments—[1] This regulation inserted by the Landfill Tax (Amendment) Regulations, SI 1999/3270, regs 2, 7, with effect from 1 January 2000.
[2] Words substituted by the Landfill Tax (Amendment) Regulations, SI 2002/1 regs 2, 3 with effect from 1 February 2002.
[3] In para (1), sub-paras (*aa*), (*ha*), (*hb*) inserted, words in sub-para (*f*) substituted and revoked, sub-para (*i*) substituted; para (2) substituted and paras (3), (4) inserted; by the Landfill Tax (Amendment) Regulations, SI 2007/965 reg 3 with effect from 1 April 2007.
[4] Words in paras (1)(*h*), (*i*), (3) substituted, by the Landfill Tax (Amendment) Regulations, SI 2008/770 reg 3 with effect from 1 April 2008.

Functions of the regulatory body

34— (1) The regulatory body—

[(*a*) shall, on application being made to it by a body which is eligible to be approved under regulation 33 above, approve that body;][1]

[(*aa*) may—

(i) at the time a body is approved, or
(ii) subsequently, by notice delivered to that body,

impose such conditions as it sees fit;

(*ab*) may, by notice delivered to a body, vary or revoke any condition of the approval;][2]

(*b*)–(*d*) … [1]

[(*e*) …[3]

(*ee*) shall revoke the approval of any body which applies for its approval to be revoked;][1]

(*f*) shall maintain a roll of bodies which it has approved;

(*g*) shall allocate an identifying number (the enrolment number) to each such body;

(*h*) shall remove from the roll any body whose approval [has been revoked under sub-paragraph (*ee*) or regulation 35(1)(*h*)][3];

Landfill Tax

(*i*) shall satisfy itself, by reference to such records or other documents or information it thinks fit, that the qualifying contributions received by the body have been spent by it only in the course or furtherance of its approved objects; … [1]

(*j*) shall publish information regarding which bodies it has approved and which approvals [has been revoked under sub-paragraph (*ee*) or regulation 35(1)(*h*)][3][; …[2]

[(*k*) shall, when notified by an approved body of the transfer to or by it of the whole or part of a qualifying contribution or of income derived therefrom, notify the registered person who made the qualifying contribution, and any contributing third party in relation to it, of—

(i) the date of the transfer,

(ii) the name and enrolment number of the body by or, as the case may require, to whom the transfer was made;

(iii) the amount transferred; and

(iv) the approved objects to which the transferred funds are to be applied][1][; and][2]

[(*l*) shall comply with such conditions as the Commissioners may impose from time to time under regulation 35(1)(*aa*) (including any conditions varied under regulation 35(1)(*ab*)).][2]

(2) Where—

(*a*) the Commissioners revoke their approval of the regulatory body without approving another body with effect from the day after the revocation takes effect; and

(*b*) they have not given notice in writing to each body which has been enrolled (and which has not been removed from the roll), no later than the date such revocation takes effect, that they [will be] [1] performing any of the functions specified in paragraph (1) above,

the approval of all such bodies shall be deemed to have been revoked on the day the Commissioners revoked their approval.

Amendments—[1] Paras (1)(*a*), (*e*), and words in para (2)(*b*) substituted, paras (1)(*b*)–(*d*) and word in para (1)(*i*) revoked, and para (1)(*k*) and word "and" immediately preceding it inserted, by the Landfill Tax (Amendment) Regulations, SI 1999/3270, regs 2, 8, with effect from 1 January 2000.

[2] Paras (1)(*aa*), (*ab*) inserted, word "and" in para (1)(*j*) revoked, and para (1)(*l*) and preceding word "and" inserted, by the Landfill Tax (Amendment) Regulations, SI 2007/965 reg 4 with effect from 1 April 2007.

[3] Words in para (1)(*e*) revoked, and words in para (1)(*h*), (*j*) substituted, by the Landfill Tax (Amendment) Regulations, SI 2008/770 reg 4 with effect from 1 April 2008.

Functions of the Commissioners

35— (1) The Commissioners—

[(*a*) may approve a body to carry out the functions prescribed by regulation 34(1) above;][1]

[(*aa*) may—

(i) at the time the body is approved, or

(ii) subsequently, by notice delivered to that body,

impose such conditions as they see fit;

(*ab*) may, by notice delivered to the body, vary or revoke any condition of the approval;][2]

(*b*) … [1]

(*c*) may revoke the approval;

(*d*) shall not approve a body without first revoking the approval for any other body with effect from a time earlier than that for which the new approval is to take effect;

(*e*) for any time as regards which no approval has effect, may perform any of the functions specified in regulation 34(1);

(*f*) may disclose to the [relevant][1] body information which relates to the tax affairs of registered persons and which is relevant to the credit scheme established by this Part; …[3]

(*g*) having regard to any information received from the [relevant][1] body, may serve notices [under regulation 36; and][3].

[(*h*) may, with respect to the approval of a body approved under regulation 34(1)(*a*), revoke that approval if the approved body fails to comply with any requirement of regulation 33A(1).][3]

[(2) Without prejudice to the generality of paragraph (1)(*c*) above, the Commissioners may revoke their approval of the regulatory body where it appears to them necessary to do so for the proper operation of the credit scheme established by this Part.][1]

Amendments—[1] Paras (1)(*a*), (2), substituted, para (1)(*b*) revoked, and words in paras (1)(*f*), (*g*) inserted, by the Landfill Tax (Amendment) Regulations, SI 1999/3270, regs 2, 9, with effect from 1 January 2000.

[2] Paras (1)(*aa*), (*ab*) inserted by the Landfill Tax (Amendment) Regulations, SI 2007/965 reg 5 with effect from 1 April 2007.

[3] Word in para (1)(*f*) revoked, words in para (1)(*g*) substituted, and para (1)(*h*) inserted, by the Landfill Tax (Amendment) Regulations, SI 2008/770 reg 5 with effect from 1 April 2008.

Repayment of credit

36— (1) Where a person has benefited from an amount of credit to which he was entitled under this Part and the Commissioners serve upon him a notice in relation to a qualifying contribution paid to an approved body—

(*a*) specifying that—

(i) they are not satisfied that the contribution has been spent by the body only in the course or furtherance of its approved objects; or

(ii) they are not satisfied that any income derived from the contribution has been so spent by the body;

(*b*) specifying a breach of a condition to which the approval of the body was made subject and which occurred before the contribution was spent by the body; or

(*c*) specifying that—

(i) the approval of the body has been revoked; and

(ii) the contribution had not been spent by the body before that revocation took effect,

he shall repay to the Commissioners the credit claimed in respect of the qualifying contribution.

(2) For the purpose of paragraph (1) above where—

(*a*) repayment is required in relation to credit that has been claimed in respect of more than one qualifying contribution in an accounting period; and

(*b*) regulation 31(3) applied so that the amount of credit was restricted,

the person shall be deemed to have claimed credit in respect of such proportion of each contribution made in that accounting period as the total credit claimed in accordance with that regulation forms of the total of the contributions made.

[(3) Where—

(*a*) a person has benefited from an amount of credit to which he was entitled under this Part; and

(*b*) the whole or a part of the qualifying contribution in respect of which the entitlement to credit arose has been repaid to him or a person who was a contributing third party in relation to the qualifying contribution,

he shall pay to the Commissioners an amount equal to 90 per cent of the amount repaid to him or, as the case may require, to the contributing third party.][1]

(4) Paragraph (5) below applies where—

(*a*) a person has benefited from an amount of credit to which he was entitled under this Part; and

(*b*) he is entitled to a payment under regulation 20 in respect of a later accounting period in the same contribution year as the accounting period in respect of which that credit was claimed.

(5) Where this paragraph applies the person shall pay to the Commissioners an amount equal to the difference between—

(*a*) the aggregate of—

(i) the amount of the credit from which he has benefited, and

(ii) any other amounts of credit arising under this Part which he is or was entitled to claim,

in respect of that contribution year; and

(*b*) the amount of credit which he would have been entitled to claim if he had in fact claimed the aggregate amount mentioned in sub-paragraph (*a*) above in the return for the accounting period in respect of which he was entitled to the payment under regulation 20.

(6) Where—

(*a*) a person has benefited from an amount of credit to which he was entitled under this Part;

(*b*) he acquires an asset from a body to which he has made a qualifying contribution for—

(i) no consideration, or

(ii) a consideration which is less than the open market value of the asset,

he shall pay to the Commissioners an amount equal to 90 per cent of the amount by which the open market value exceeds the consideration; but this is subject to paragraph (7) below.

(7) A person required to pay an amount to the Commissioners by paragraph (6) above—

(*a*) shall not be required to pay more than the total amount of relevant credit;

(*b*) shall not be entitled to claim any further amounts of credit in respect of qualifying contributions made by him to the body in question on or after the date on which he acquired the asset.

(8) For the purposes of paragraphs (6) and (7) above—

(*a*) "asset" includes land, goods or services and any interest in any of these;

(*b*) the open market value of an asset is the amount of the consideration in money that would be payable for the asset by a person standing in no such relationship with any person as would affect that consideration;

(*c*) "relevant credit" means credit arising under this Part—

(i) from which a person has benefited, and

(ii) which has arisen in respect of qualifying contributions made by him to the body in question or treated by virtue of regulation 32(3) as having been received by that body from him.

Amendments—[1] Para (3) substituted by the Landfill Tax (Amendment) Regulations, SI 1999/3270, regs 2, 10, with effect from 1 January 2000.

PART VIII
LANDFILL INVOICES

Contents of a landfill invoice

37— (1) An invoice is a landfill invoice if it contains the following information:

(*a*) an identifying number;
(*b*) the date of its issue;
(*c*) the date of the disposal or disposals in respect of which it is issued or, where a series of disposals is made for the same person, the dates between which the disposals were made;
(*d*) the name, address and registration number of the person issuing it;
(*e*) the name and address of the person to whom it is issued;
(*f*) the weight of the material disposed of;
(*g*) a description of the material disposed of;
(*h*) the rate of tax chargeable in relation to the disposal or, if the invoice relates to more than one disposal and the rate of tax for each of them is not the same, the rate of tax chargeable for each disposal;
(*i*) the total amount payable for which the invoice is issued; and
(*j*) where the amount of tax is shown separately, a statement confirming that that tax may not be treated as the input tax of any person.

(2) In paragraph (1)(*j*) above "input tax" has the same meaning as in section 24(1) of the Value Added Tax Act 1994.

PART IX
TEMPORARY DISPOSALS

Amendments—[1] Part IX (paras 38–40) revoked by the Landfill Tax (Amendment) Regulations, SI 2009/1930 reg 2(1), (9) with effect from 1 September 2009.

Scope and effect

38— *(1) A disposal to which this Part applies—*

(a) shall not be treated as made at the time when apart from this Part it would be regarded as made; and
(b) shall be treated as having been made—
(i) when it is treated as being an exempt disposal by virtue of regulation 39, or
(ii) to the extent that it is not so treated, at the time when it is treated as having been made by virtue of regulation 40.

(2) This Part applies to a disposal where—

(a) an authorised person has designated an area (the designated area) for the purpose of this Part;
(b) material is disposed of in the designated area at a time when the designation has effect;
(c) [the material comprised in the disposal is held temporarily][1] *pending all of the material being put to a qualifying use within the relevant period; and*
(d) such other conditions as the Commissioners or an authorised person may specify for the purpose of this Part, whether generally or with regard to particular cases, are satisfied.

(3) A designation ceases to have effect if—

(a) notice to that effect is given in writing by the Commissioners or by an authorised person;
(b) any period for which the designation was to have effect by virtue of a condition specified in relation thereto expires;
(c) any disposal to which this Part does not apply (whether because [the material comprised in it is not held in accordance with paragraph (2)(c) above][1] *or for some other reason) is made in the designated area; or*
(d) a disposal is treated by virtue of regulation 40 as having been made at a certain time and all of the material comprised in that disposal is not removed from the designated area within seven days of that time.

[(4) A use is a qualifying use if, within the relevant period, the material is—

(a) re-cycled or incinerated; or
(b) used (other than by way of a further disposal)—
(i) at a place other than a relevant site; or
(ii) for site restoration purposes at the landfill site at which the disposal was made.][1]

[(4A) Sorting of material pending—

(i) its use by way of any qualifying use within paragraph (4) above, or
(ii) its disposal within the relevant period,

is also a qualifying use.][1]

(5) For the purposes of [paragraphs (4) and (4A)][1] *above—*

(a) a use is not a qualifying use if it would constitute a breach of any condition relating to the use of the material to be disposed of which has been specified in relation to that designated area or generally;

[(aa) material is used for site restoration purposes if—

(i) the material is treated for the purposes of section 42 of the Act as qualifying material;

(ii) before the material is used the operator of the landfill site notifies the Commissioners in writing that he is commencing the restoration of all or a part of the site and provides such other written information as the Commissioners may require generally or in the particular case; and

(iii) the material is used in the restoration of the site or part specified in the notification under paragraph (ii) above;][1]

[(ab) "restoration" means work, other than capping waste, which is required by a relevant instrument to be carried out to restore a landfill site to use on completion of waste disposal operations;][1]

[(ac) the following are relevant instruments—

(i) a planning consent;

(ii) a waste management licence;

(iii) a resolution authorising the disposal of waste on or in land;][1]

[(iv) a permit authorising the disposal of waste on or in land;][2]

(b) a relevant site is the landfill site at which the disposal was made or any other landfill site;

(c) …[1]

[(6) Subject to paragraph (7) below, the relevant period is the period of one year commencing with the date of the disposal or such other period as the Commissioners or an authorised person may approve or direct.][1]

[(7) In relation to site restoration which is a qualifying use falling within paragraph (4)(b)(ii) above, the relevant period is the period of three years commencing with the date of the disposal or such other period as the Commissioners or an authorised person may approve or direct.][1, 3]

Amendments—[1] Words in paras (2)(*c*), (3)(*c*), (5) substituted; paras (4), (4A) substituted for para (4); in para (5), sub-paras (*aa*)–(*ac*) inserted, and sub-para (*c*) revoked; and paras (6), (7) added, by the Landfill Tax (Amendment) Regulations, SI 2002/1 regs 2, 4 with effect from 1 February 2002.

[2] Sub-para (5)(*ac*)(iv) inserted by the Landfill Tax (Amendment) Regulations, SI 2005/759 regs 2, 5 with effect from 6 April 2005.

[3] Part IX (paras 38–40) revoked by the Landfill Tax (Amendment) Regulations, SI 2009/1930 reg 2(1), (9) with effect from 1 September 2009.

Disposals to be treated as exempt

39— (1) Where there is a disposal to which this part applies and—

(a) the material comprised in the disposal has been put to a qualifying use within the relevant period, if it would otherwise be a taxable disposal that disposal shall be treated as not being a taxable disposal (shall be treated as being an exempt disposal); but this is subject to paragraph (2) below;

(b) some of the material comprised in a disposal has been put to a qualifying use within the relevant period (and some has not), the disposal shall be treated as being an exempt disposal to the extent of the part so dealt with and the remaining part shall be treated in accordance with regulation 40.

(2) A disposal shall not be treated as being an exempt disposal unless the landfill site operator concerned has made and, in relation to that disposal, maintained the record specified in paragraph (3) below (the temporary disposal record).

(3) The temporary disposal record mentioned in paragraph (2) above is a record, in relation to the designated area, of—

(a) the weight and description of all material disposed of;

[(b) the intended destination or use of all such material and, where any material has been removed or used, the actual destination or use of that material;][1]

(c) the weight and description of any material [sorted or][1] *removed.*[2]

Amendments—[1] In para (3), sub-para (*b*) substituted, and words in sub-para (*c*) inserted, by the Landfill Tax (Amendment) Regulations, SI 2002/1 regs 2, 5 with effect from 1 February 2002.

[2] Part IX (paras 38–40) revoked by the Landfill Tax (Amendment) Regulations, SI 2009/1930 reg 2(1), (9) with effect from 1 September 2009.

Disposals to be treated as made at certain times

40— *(1) Where in the case of a disposal to which this Part applies the disposal is not wholly treated as being an exempt disposal it shall, to the extent that it is not so treated, be treated as having been made at the earliest of the following times—*

(a) when the relevant period has expired;

(b) when the designation ceases to have effect;

(c) when there has been a breach of any condition specified by the Commissioners or an authorised person;

(d) when there has been a failure to make the temporary disposal record;

(e) when there has been a failure to maintain the temporary disposal record;

(f) when any of the material concerned is used (other than by way of a further disposal) at the same or another landfill site (but not in the same designated area).

(2) The reference in paragraph (1)(e) above to a failure to maintain the temporary disposal record is a reference to an omission to enter in a record that has been made the information specified in regulation 39(3) in relation to any disposal made after the record was made.[1]

Amendments—[1] Part IX (paras 38–40) revoked by the Landfill Tax (Amendment) Regulations, SI 2009/1930 reg 2(1), (9) with effect from 1 September 2009.

PART X
DETERMINATION OF WEIGHT OF MATERIAL DISPOSED OF

Scope

41 This Part applies for the purpose of determining the weight of material comprised in a disposal; and references in this Part to weight shall be construed as references to the weight of such material.

Basic method

42— (1) Except where regulation 43 or 44 applies and subject to paragraph (2) below, a registrable person shall determine weight by weighing the material concerned.

(2) The weighing of the material shall be carried out at the time of the disposal; and for this purpose any time at which section 61 of the Act [requires][1] the disposal to be treated as made shall be disregarded.

Amendments—[1] In para (2), word substituted for words "or Part IX of these Regulations require", by the Landfill Tax (Amendment) Regulations, SI 2009/1930 reg 2(1), (10) with effect from 1 September 2009.

Specified methods

43— (1) Except where regulation 44 applies, this regulation applies where the Commissioners have specified rules for determining weight in a notice published by them and not withdrawn by a further notice.

(2) A specification made by the Commissioners as described in paragraph (1) above may make provision for—

(*a*) the method by which weight is to be determined;

(*b*) the time by reference to which weight is to be determined.

(3) A specification made by the Commissioners as described in paragraph (1) above may provide—

(*a*) that it is to have effect only in relation to disposals of such descriptions as may be set out in the specification;

(*b*) that it is not to have effect in relation to particular disposals unless the Commissioners are satisfied that such conditions as may be set out in the specification are met in relation to the disposals.

(4) Where this regulation applies the registrable person shall determine weight in accordance with the rules in the specification (and not in accordance with the rule in regulation 42).

Agreed methods

44— (1) This regulation applies where—

(*a*) the registrable person and an authorised person have agreed in writing that weight shall be determined in accordance with rules other than those described in regulation 42 or specified under regulation 43; and

(*b*) a direction under paragraph (3) below has not been made.

(2) Rules may be agreed under this regulation as regards—

(*a*) the method by which weight is to be determined;

(*b*) the time by reference to which weight is to be determined;

(*c*) the discounting of water forming a constituent of material disposed of, but this is subject to paragraph (5) below.

(3) Where rules have been agreed under this regulation and the Commissioners believe that they should no longer be applied because they do not give an accurate indication of the weight or they are not being fully observed or for some other reason they may direct that the agreed rules shall no longer have effect.

(4) Where this regulation applies the registrable person shall determine weight in accordance with the rules agreed (and not in accordance with the rule in regulation 42 or 43).

(5) Subject to paragraphs (6) to (8) below, rules may be agreed regarding the discounting of water if, and only if—

(*a*) no water is present in the material naturally and the water is present because—

(i) it has been added for the purpose of enabling the material to be transported for disposal;

(ii) it has been used for the purpose of extracting any mineral; or

(iii) it has arisen, or has been added, in the course of an industrial process; or (*b*) the material is the residue from the treatment of effluent or sewage by a water treatment works.

(6) Rules may not be agreed under paragraph (5) above where any of the material is capable of escaping from the landfill site concerned by leaching unless—

(*a*) it is likely to do so in the form of water only; or

(*b*) the leachate is to be collected on the site concerned and treated in order to eliminate any potential it has to cause harm.

(7) Where the material falls within paragraph (5)(*a*) above rules may not be agreed under paragraph (5) above unless the total water which has been added, or (in a case falling within paragraph (5)(*a*)(iii) above) has arisen or has been added or both, constitutes 25 per cent or more of the weight at the time of the disposal.

(8) Where the material falls within paragraph (5)(*b*) above rules may not be agreed under paragraph (5) above except for the discounting of water which has been added prior to disposal (and not of water which is present in the material naturally).

(9) For the purposes of paragraph (8) above any water which has been extracted prior to disposal shall be deemed to be water that has been added, except that where the water extracted exceeds the quantity of water added that excess shall be deemed to have been present naturally.

PART XI
SET-OFF OF AMOUNTS

Landfill tax amount owed to Commissioners

45— (1) Subject to regulation 47, this regulation applies where—

(*a*) a person is under a duty to pay to the Commissioners at any time an amount or amounts in respect of landfill tax; and

(*b*) the Commissioners are under a duty to pay to that person at the same time an amount or amounts in respect of any tax or taxes under their care and management.

(2) Where the total of the amount or amounts mentioned in paragraph (1)(*a*) above exceeds the total of the amount or amounts mentioned in paragraph (1)(*b*) above, the latter shall be set off against the former.

(3) Where the total of the amount or amounts mentioned in paragraph (1)(*b*) above exceeds the total of the amount or amounts mentioned in paragraph (1)(*a*) above, the Commissioners may set off the latter in paying the former.

(4) Where the total of the amount or amounts mentioned in paragraph (1)(*a*) above is the same as the total of the amount or amounts mentioned in paragraph (1)(*b*) above, no payment need be made in respect of either.

(5) Where this regulation applies and an amount has been set off in accordance with any of paragraphs (2) to (4) above, the duty of both the person and the Commissioners to pay the amount or amounts concerned shall be treated as having been discharged accordingly.

(6) References in paragraph (1) above to an amount in respect of a particular tax include references not only to an amount of tax itself but also to amounts of penalty, surcharge or interest.

(7) In this regulation "tax" includes "duty".

Landfill tax amount owed by Commissioners

46— (1) Subject to regulation 47, this regulation applies where—

(*a*) a person is under a duty to pay to the Commissioners at any time an amount or amounts in respect of any tax or taxes under their care and management; and

(*b*) the Commissioners are under a duty to pay to that person at the same time an amount or amounts in respect of landfill tax.

(2) Where the total of the amount or amounts mentioned in paragraph (1)(*a*) above exceeds the total of the amount or amounts mentioned in paragraph (1)(*b*) above, the latter shall be set off against the former.

(3) Where the total of the amount or amounts mentioned in paragraph (1)(*b*) above exceeds the total of the amount or amounts mentioned in paragraph (1)(*a*) above, the Commissioners may set off the latter in paying the former.

(4) Where the total of the amount or amounts mentioned in paragraph (1)(*a*) above is the same as the total of the amount or amounts mentioned in paragraph (1)(*b*) above, no payment need be made in respect of either.

(5) Where this regulation applies and an amount has been set off in accordance with any of paragraphs (2) to (4) above, the duty of both the person and the Commissioners to pay the amount or amounts concerned shall be treated as having been discharged accordingly.

(6) Paragraphs (6) and (7) of regulation 45 shall apply in relation to this regulation as they apply in relation to that regulation.

No set-off where insolvency procedure applied

47— (1) Neither regulation 45 nor 46 shall require any such amount as is mentioned in paragraph (1)(*b*) of those regulations (in either case, "the credit") to be set against any such sum as is mentioned in paragraph (1)(*a*) of those regulations (in either case, "the debit") in any case where—

(*a*) an insolvency procedure has been applied to the person entitled to the credit;

(*b*) the credit became due after that procedure was so applied;

(*c*) the liability to pay the debit either arose before that procedure was so applied or (having risen afterwards) relates to, or to matters occurring in the course of—

(i) the carrying on of any business; or

(ii) in the case of any sum such as is mentioned in regulation 46(1)(*b*), the carrying out of taxable activities,

at times before the procedure was so applied.

(2) Subject to paragraph (3) below, the following are the times when an insolvency procedure is to be taken, for the purposes of this regulation, to have been applied to any person, that is to say—

(*a*) when a bankruptcy order, winding-up order, …[1] or award of sequestration is made in relation to that person [or that person entering administration][1];

(*b*) when that person is put into administrative receivership;

(*c*) when that person, being a corporation, passes a resolution for voluntary winding-up;

(*d*) when any voluntary arrangement approved in accordance with Part I or Part VIII of the Insolvency Act 1986, or Part II or Chapter II of Part VIII of the Insolvency (Northern Ireland) Order 1989, comes into force in relation to that person;

(*e*) when a deed of arrangement registered in accordance with the Deeds of Arrangement Act 1914 or Chapter I of Part VIII of that Order of 1989 takes effect in relation to that person;

(*f*) when that person's estate becomes vested in any other person as that person's trustee under a trust deed.

(3) References in this regulation, in relation to any person, to the application of an insolvency procedure to that person shall not include—

(*a*) the making of a bankruptcy order, winding-up order, …[1] or award of sequestration [or that person entering administration][1] at a time when any such arrangements or deed as is mentioned in paragraph (2)(*d*) to (*f*) above is in force in relation to that person;

(*b*) the making of a winding-up order at any of the following times—

(i) immediately upon [the appointment of the administrator ceasing to have effect][1];

(ii) when that person is being wound-up voluntarily;

(iii) when that person is in administrative receivership; or

(*c*) the making of an administration order in relation to that person at any time when that person is in administrative receivership.

(4) For the purposes of this regulation a person shall be regarded as being in administrative receivership throughout any continuous period for which (disregarding any temporary vacancy in the office of receiver) there is an administrative receiver of that person, and the reference in paragraph (2) above to a person being put into administrative receivership shall be construed accordingly.

Amendments—[1] Words in para (2) revoked and inserted, and words in para (3) revoked, inserted and substituted, by the Enterprise Act 2002 (Insolvency) Order, SI 2003/605 art 5, Schedule paras 65, 67 with effect from 15 September 2003. However, these amendments do not apply in relation to any case where a petition for an administration order was presented before that date: SI 2003/2096 art 6.

PART XII
DISTRESS AND DILIGENCE

[A48 In this Part—

"Job Band" followed by a number between "1" and "12" means the band for the purposes of pay and grading in which the job an officer performs is ranked in the system applicable to Customs and Excise.]

Amendments—[1] Inserted by Landfill Tax (Amendment) Regulations, SI 1996/2100 reg 3 with effect from 2 September 1996.

48 …

Amendments—This regulation revoked by the Distress for Customs and Excise Duties and Other Indirect Taxes Regulations, SI 1997/1431 with effect from 1 July 1997. See SI 1997/1431 for the replacement provisions.

Diligence

49 In Scotland the following provisions shall have effect:

(*a*) where the Commissioners are empowered to apply to the sheriff for a warrant to authorise a sheriff officer to recover any amount of tax or sum recoverable as if it were tax remaining due and unpaid, any application, and any certificate required to accompany that application, may be made on their behalf by a Collector or an officer of rank not below that of [Job Band 7][1];

(*b*) where during the course of [an attachment][2] the Commissioners are entitled as a creditor to do any act, then any such act, with the exception of the exercise of the power contained in [section 30(4) of the Debt Arrangement and Attachment (Scotland) Act 2002 (asp 17)][2], may be done on their behalf by a Collector or an officer of rank not below that of [Job Band 7][1]

Amendments—[1] Words in paras (*a*) and (*b*) substituted by Landfill Tax (Amendment) Regulations, SI 1996/2100 reg 4 with effect from 2 September 1996.

[2] Words in para (*b*) substituted by the Debt Arrangement and Attachment (Scotland) Act 2002 s 61, Sch 3 Pt 2 para 36 with effect from 30 December 2002.

SCHEDULE

Regulation 4(1)

FORM 1

Landfill Tax

Application for Registration

The general notes, included with this form, will help you to answer the following questions.
Please write clearly in ink and use BLOCK LETTERS.

Remember you should also complete form LT 1A, or LT 50 and LT 51 if you are applying to be registered as a group.

1 Please give the full name of the business.

- *if you are a sole proprietor please give your full name*
- *if your business is a limited company please give the company's name*
- *if your business is a partnership please give its trading name.*
  The names of partners must be shown on form LT 2

....

....

....

....

2 Please give your trading name (if different from the name given at **1**)

....

....

....

....

3 Please give the address of your principal place of business

- *Your landfill tax return forms will be sent to this address, unless you specify an alternative communication address at* ***4***
- *If this address is a landfill site it should also be included on the form LT 1A, or LT 50/51 if you are applying for group registration*

....

....

....

....

Postcode: ....

Tel no:

Fax no:

4 Please specify an alternative communications address, if appropriate.

- *Return forms and other correspondence are normally sent to the principal place of business, as at* ***3*** *above.*
- *Exceptionally you may ask for correspondence to be issued to another address.*

Name:

Business address ....

....

....

....

Postcode: ....

Tel no:

Fax no:

5 Are you applying for group registration?

- *If **Yes**, please ensure that you complete forms LT 50 and LT 51*

Please tick ☑

Yes ☐ No ☐

6 Are you applying to be registered in divisions?

- *Each division of your company to be registered separately, must complete forms LT 1 and LT 1A*

Please tick ☑

Yes ☐ No ☐

7 What is the legal status of your business?

Please tick ☑

Sole proprietor ☐ Partnership ☐

Limited Company ☐

Give details from your certificate of incorporation:

Certificate no. Date of certificate

Other ☐ If other, please give details below:

8 Has your landfill activity been transferred to you as a going concern?

Only complete this box if:

- *you are taking over an existing landfill operation from someone else; or*
- *you have changed the legal status of your business*

Please tick ☑

No ☐ **Go to 10** Yes ☐ **Give details below then go to 9**

Date of transfer

Business name of previous owner

Landfill tax registration number of previous owner

9 Do you want to keep the previous owner's landfill tax registration number?

- *If you are applying to keep the number please complete form LT 68*

Please tick ☑

Yes ☐ No ☐

10 Please give your preferred method of payment.

Please tick ☑

Credit transfer ☐ Cheque ☐

Other ☐ *(please specify)*

11 How many landfill sites do you operate?

- *Please give details on the enclosed form LT 1A, or LT 50 and LT 51 if you are applying to be registered as part of a group*
- *Please see general notes for further information*

Number of sites

- This number should agree with the number shown on LT 1A, or LT 50 and LT 51 for group registrations.
- If you are applying to be registered as a group, this must be the total number of sites operated by the group as a whole as stated on forms LT 50 and LT 51.
- If the address at question 3 is a landfill site it *must* be entered on form LT 1A or LT 50 and LT 51 for group registrations.

12 Please give the date of your first expected taxable disposal:

- *Please see general notes for further information on taxable disposals*

Date:

13 Are you registered for VAT in the UK?

Please tick ☑

Yes ☐ Give your VAT registration no.

No ☐

14 Are there any other landfill business(es) you are, or have been, involved in in the last 24 months? This excludes any sites included in this application.

- *Please give the landfill tax registration numbers of any businesses you are or have been involved in. If you are a partnership or a limited company this means any businesses in which any partners or directors have been involved*
- *Please continue on a separate sheet if necessary*

Please tick ☑

Yes ☐ No ☐

Landfill tax registration numbers of other businesses:

15 Please complete and sign the declaration

Declaration

I,

(enter your full name in BLOCK LETTERS) declare that the information given on this form and contained in any accompanying document is true and complete.

Signature Date

Please tick ☑

Sole proprietor ☐ Director ☐ Trustee ☐

Partner ☐ Company secretary ☐ Authorised official ☐

Data Protection Act 1998

HM Customs and Excise collects information in order to administer the taxes for which it is responsible (such as VAT, insurance premium tax, excise duties, air passenger duty, landfill tax), and for detecting and preventing crime.

Where the law permits we may also get information about you from third parties, or give information to them, for example in order to check its accuracy, prevent or detect crime or protect public funds in other ways. These third parties may include the police, other government departments and agencies.

Regulation 4(2)

FORM 2

Landfill Tax

Application for Registration

Landfill site details

Please complete this form with the details of all the sites you operate. If you are applying to be registered as a group, you may wish to include your site details on forms LT 50 and LT 51 instead of this form. The general notes will help you. If you require a continuation sheet please photocopy this form.

Do not include any sites which will not receive further waste.

Trading name of site (if different from those entered in boxes 1 and 2 on form LT 1)

Licence No:

Name:

Site address: ....

....

....

....

Postcode: ....

Tel no:

Fax no:

Type of waste landfilled and estimated tonnes in a year (see note).

Estimated Tonnes

Standard:

Lower:

Exempt:

Is a weighbridge used to establish the weight of waste on this site?

Please tick ☑

Yes ☐ No ☐

Controller. Does a person other than the operator determine what materials are disposed of at this site, or part of this site?

Please tick ☑

Yes ☐ No ☐

Trading name of site (if different from those entered in boxes 1 and 2 on form LT 1)

Licence No:

Name:

Site address: ....

....

....

....

Postcode: ....

Tel no:

Fax no:

Type of waste landfilled and estimated tonnes in a year (see note).

Estimated Tonnes

Standard:

Lower:

Exempt:

Is a weighbridge used to establish the weight of waste on this site?

Please tick ☑

Yes ☐ No ☐

Controller. Does a person other than the operator determine what materials are disposed of at this site, or part of this site?

Please tick ☑

Yes ☐ No ☐

LT 1A Page 1 IB (December 2000)

Trading name of site (if different from those entered in boxes 1 and 2 on form LT 1)

Licence No:

Name:

Site address: ....

....

....

Postcode: ....

Tel no:

Fax no:

Is a weighbridge used to establish the weight of waste on this site?

Please tick ☑

Yes ☐ No ☐

Type of waste landfilled and estimated tonnes in a year (see note).

Estimated Tonnes

Standard:

Lower:

Exempt:

Controller. Does a person other than the operator determine what materials are disposed of at this site, or part of this site?

Please tick ☑

Yes ☐ No ☐

Trading name of site (if different from those entered in boxes 1 and 2 on form LT 1)

Licence No:

Name:

Site address: ....

....

....

Postcode: ....

Tel no:

Fax no:

Is a weighbridge used to establish the weight of waste on this site?

Please tick ☑

Yes ☐ No ☐

Type of waste landfilled and estimated tonnes in a year (see note).

Estimated Tonnes

Standard:

Lower:

Exempt:

Controller. Does a person other than the operator determine what materials are disposed of at this site, or part of this site?

Please tick ☑

Yes ☐ No ☐

LT 1A Page 2 (12/00)

Trading name of site (if different from those entered in boxes 1 and 2 on form LT 1)

Licence No:

Name:

Site address: ....
....
....
....
Postcode: ....

Tel no:

Fax no:

Is a weighbridge used to establish the weight of waste on this site?

Please tick ☑

Yes ☐ No ☐

Type of waste landfilled and estimated tonnes in a year (see note).

Estimated Tonnes

Standard:

Lower:

Exempt:

Controller. Does a person other than the operator determine what materials are disposed of at this site, or part of this site?

Please tick ☑

Yes ☐ No ☐

Trading name of site (if different from those entered in boxes 1 and 2 on form LT 1)

Licence No:

Name:

Site address: ....
....
....
....
Postcode: ....

Tel no:

Fax no:

Is a weighbridge used to establish the weight of waste on this site?

Please tick ☑

Yes ☐ No ☐

Type of waste landfilled and estimated tonnes in a year (see note).

Estimated Tonnes

Standard:

Lower:

Exempt:

Controller. Does a person other than the operator determine what materials are disposed of at this site, or part of this site?

Please tick ☑

Yes ☐ No ☐

LT 1A Page 3 (12/00)

Trading name of site (if different from those entered in boxes 1 and 2 on form LT 1)

Licence No:

Name:

Site address: ....
....
....
....
Postcode: ....

Tel no:

Fax no:

Type of waste landfilled and estimated tonnes in a year (see note).

Estimated Tonnes

Standard:

Lower:

Exempt:

Is a weighbridge used to establish the weight of waste on this site?

Please tick ☑

Yes ☐ No ☐

Controller. Does a person other than the operator determine what materials are disposed of at this site, or part of this site?

Please tick ☑

Yes ☐ No ☐

Data Protection Act 1998

HM Customs and Excise collects information in order to administer the taxes for which it is responsible (such as VAT, insurance premium tax, excise duties, air passenger duty, landfill tax), and for detecting and preventing crime.

Where the law permits we may also get information about you from third parties, or give information to them, for example in order to check its accuracy, prevent or detect crime or protect public funds in other ways. These third parties may include the police, other government departments and agencies.

Regulation 4(3)

FORM 3

These details form part of your application to be registered for landfill tax.

Trading name of Partnership:

Please make sure that **every** partner completes and signs one of the sections below. If there is insufficient space to include all partners, please photocopy this form or contact the Central Collection Unit (see page 1) for additional copies. Please use BLOCK LETTERS and write clearly in ink.

Full name of partner:

Home address: ....

....

....

....

Postcode: ....

Home telephone:

Signature: Date:

Full name of partner:

Home address: ....

....

....

....

Postcode: ....

Home telephone:

Signature: Date:

LT 2 Page 2 (09/00)

Full name of partner:

Home address: ....

....

....

....

Postcode: ....

Home telephone:

Signature: Date:

Full name of partner:

Home address: ....

....

....

....

Postcode: ....

Home telephone:

Signature: Date:

Regulation 7(1)

FORM 4

Remember that both parts of the form need to be completed

Part 1: If you are the previous owner of the landfill business, please read this form carefully and answer all the following questions.

1 Please give your full name, **and** your trading name if you have one:

2 I transferred my business/changed my legal status on:

3 The new owner is:

4 From the above date, I wish to cancel my landfill tax registration because I will cease operating a landfill business from that date. I agree to transfer my number to the new owner. The landfill tax registration number is:

5 If this application is allowed, I agree to the following conditions:

- the new owner will be entitled to any money or credit which Customs and Excise would normally have paid to me if the number had not been transferred; and
- I will have no right to claim any money paid by Customs and Excise to the new owner.

6 Please give an address where we can contact you after the business has been taken over by the new owner.

Postcode .... Telephone no. ....

Please tick one box only

- ☐ Sole Proprietor
- ☐ Company Secretary
- ☐ Director
- ☐ Executor
- ☐ Partner (All partners must sign).

If there are insufficient boxes on this form, please use a photocopy.

- ☐ Other - please give details

Signature(s)

Part 2: If you are the new owner of a landfill business, please read this form carefully and answer all the following questions.

1 Please give your full name:

2 I took over a business as a going concern on:

3 I apply to use the previous owner's landfill tax registration number which is:

4 If this application is approved, I agree to the following conditions:

- I will send my first and subsequent landfill tax return form to Customs and Excise no later than the due date, with all the tax shown on the form as due for the period which it covers;
- I will send in any outstanding returns which are due from the previous owner;
- I will pay any landfill tax, interest and penalties due (and not paid) from the previous owner before the business was transferred;
- any landfill tax return made by the previous owner for a period after the transfer date will be treated as made by me; and
- I will have no right to claim any money paid by Customs to the previous owner, before the landfill tax registration number is transferred.

Please tick one box only

- ☐ Sole Proprietor
- ☐ Company Secretary
- ☐ Director
- ☐ Executor
- ☐ Partner (All partners must sign).

If there are insufficient boxes on this form, please use a photocopy.

- ☐ Other - please give details below

Signature(s)

LT 68 page 2 (07/00)

Regulation 11(1)

FORM 5

HM Revenue & Customs

Landfill Tax Return

For the period

to

For Official Use

Landfill tax registration number | Period

Warning

You could be liable to penalty interest if all the landfill tax payable are not received by the due date

Due date:

For official use D O R only

Before you complete this form please read the enclosed general notes. Both sides should be completed.

Fill in all boxes clearly in ink, and write 'none' where necessary. Do not put a dash or leave any box blank. If there are no pence write '**00**' in the pence column. **Do not** enter more than one amount in any box.

Fold here

For Official Use

Box		£	p
1	Tax due for this period		
2	Underdeclarations from previous periods (see general notes for details on limits)		
3	**Total** (the sum of boxes 1 and 2)		
4	Overdeclarations from previous periods (see general notes for details on limits)		
5	Tax credit claimed in respect of contributions to environmental bodies		
6	Please specify the amount of bad debt relief claimed for landfill tax in this period		
7	Other credits (see general notes)		
8	**Total credits** (the sum of boxes 4, 5, 6 and 7)		
9	Net tax due or repayable box 3 minus box 8)		

If you have made any contributions to environmental bodies, please ensure that boxes 13 - 20 on the reverse of this form are completed otherwise your claim may be rejected.

If you are enclosing a payment please tick this box (✓)

Official use

LT 100 HMRC 05/08

For official use only

Please give the weight of waste in tonnes, per catergory, landfilled in this return period

		Tonnes
10	Standard rate of waste	
11	Lower rate waste	
12	Exempt waste	

Please provide information on any environmental bodies to which contributions have been made and for which a rebate is being claimed in box 5 overleaf.

	Environmental body enrolment number(s)	**Amount of contribution** £	p
13			
14			
15			
16			
17			
18			
19			
20			

Declaration:
You must sign below:

I, ______ declare that the

(Full name of signatory in BLOCK LETTERS)

information given above is true and complete.

Signature ______ Date ______

A false declaration can result in prosecution.

Complaints:
The Adjudicator reviews complaints not settled to your satisfaction by HM Revenue & Customs. The recommendations of the Adjudicator are independent and the service is free. The Adjudicator only looks at complaints not general enquires. Telephone the Adjudicator on **0207 930 2292**

Amendments—Form 5 substituted by the Value Added Tax, etc (Correction of Errors, etc) Regulations, SI 2008/1482 reg 5(6) with effect in relation to returns that relate to periods that begin on 1 July 2008 or later.
Form 5 revoked by the Landfill Tax (Amendment) Regulations, SI 2009/1930 reg 2(1), (11) with effect from 1 September 2009.

Landfill Tax

1996/1528
The Landfill Tax (Qualifying Material) Order 1996

Made . . . . *12th June 1996*
Laid before the House of Commons . . . . *12th June 1996*
Coming into force . . . . *1st October 1996*

Whereas section 42(2) of the Finance Act 1996 provides for a lower rate of landfill tax to be charged where the material disposed of consists entirely of qualifying material:

Whereas section 42(3) of that Act provides that qualifying material is material for the time being listed in an Order made by the Treasury:

Whereas section 42(4) of that Act requires the Treasury to have regard to the object of securing that material is listed in that Order if it is of a kind commonly described as inactive or inert:

Whereas the Treasury have had regard to that object:

Now the Treasury, in exercise of the powers conferred on them by sections 42(3) and 63(5) and (6) of the Finance Act 1996 and of all other powers enabling them in that behalf, hereby make the following Order:

1 This Order may be cited as the Landfill Tax (Qualifying Material) Order 1996 and shall come into force on 1st October 1996.

2 Subject to articles 3 to 5 below, the material listed in column 2 of the Schedule to this Order is qualifying material for the purpose of section 42 of the Act.

3 The Schedule to this Order shall be construed in accordance with the notes contained in it.

4 The material listed in column 2 of the Schedule to this Order must not be treated as qualifying material unless any condition set out alongside the description of the material in column 3 of that Schedule is satisfied.

5 Where the owner of the material immediately prior to the disposal and the operator of the landfill site at which the disposal is made are not the same person, material must not be treated as qualifying material unless it satisfies the relevant condition.

6 In the case of a disposal at a landfill site in Great Britain, the relevant condition is that a transfer note includes in relation to each type of material of which the disposal consists—

(*a*) a description of the material—

(i) which accords with its description in column 2 of the Schedule to this Order, or

(ii) where a note contained in that Schedule lists the material (other than by way of exclusion), which accords with that description, or

(iii) which is some other accurate description; or

(*b*) where the material is water within Group 9 of the Schedule to this Order—

(i) the description "water", and

(ii) a description of the material held in suspension which, if that material had been disposed of separately, would comply with the requirements of paragraph (*a*) above.

7 In the case of a disposal at a landfill site in Northern Ireland, the relevant condition is that any document produced to evidence the transfer of the material includes, in relation to each type of material of which the disposal consists, a description of that material as specified in paragraph (*a*) or, as the case may be, paragraph (*b*) of article 6 above.

8 In article 6 above "transfer note" has the same meaning as in the Environmental Protection (Duty of Care) Regulations 1991.

SCHEDULE

Article 2

Column 1 *Group*	*Column 2* *Description of material*	*Column 3* *Conditions*
Group 1	Rocks and soils	Naturally occurring
Group 2	Ceramic or concrete materials	
Group 3	Minerals	Process or prepared, not used
Group 4	Furnace slags	
Group 5	Ash	
Group 6	Low activity inorganic compounds	
Group 7	Calcium sulphate	Disposed of either at site not licensed to take putrescible waste or in containment cell which takes only calcium sulphate
Group 8	Calcium hydroxide and brine	Deposited in brine cavity
Group 9	Water	Containing other qualifying material in suspension

Notes:

(1) Group 1 includes clay, sand, gravel, sandstone, limestone, crushed stone, china clay, construction stone, stone from the demolition of buildings or structures, slate, topsoil, peat, silt and dredgings.

(2) Group 2 comprises only the following—

(*a*) glass;

(*b*) ceramics;
(*c*) concrete.

(3) For the purposes of Note (2) above—

(*a*) glass includes fritted enamel, but excludes glass fibre and glass-reinforced plastic;
(*b*) ceramics includes bricks, bricks and mortar, tiles, clay ware, pottery, china and refractories;
(*c*) concrete includes reinforced concrete, concrete blocks, breeze blocks and aircrete blocks, but excludes concrete plant washings.

(4) Group 3 comprises only the following—

(*a*) moulding sands;
(*b*) clays;
(*c*) mineral absorbents;
(*d*) man-made mineral fibres;
(*e*) silica;
(*f*) mica;
(*g*) mineral abrasives.

(5) For the purposes of Note (4) above—

(*a*) moulding sands excludes sands containing organic binders;
(*b*) clays includes moulding clays and clay absorbents, including Fuller's earth and bentonite;
(*c*) man-made mineral fibres includes glass fibres, but excludes glass-reinforced plastic and asbestos.

(6) Group 4 includes—

(*a*) vitrified wastes and residues from thermal processing of minerals where, in either case, the residue is both fused and insoluble;
(*b*) slag from waste incineration.

(7) Group 5—

(*a*) comprises only bottom ash and fly ash from wood, coal or waste combustion; and
(*b*) excludes fly ash from municipal, clinical and hazardous waste incinerators and sewage sludge incinerators.

(8) Group 6 comprises only titanium dioxide, calcium carbonate, magnesium carbonate, magnesium oxide, magnesium hydroxide, iron oxide, ferric hydroxide, aluminium oxide, aluminium hydroxide and zirconium dioxide.

(9) Group 7 includes gypsum and calcium sulphate based plasters, but excludes plasterboard.

1997/1431

Distress for Customs and Excise Duties and Other Indirect Taxes Regulations 1997

Made by the Commissioners of Customs and Excise under FA 1997 ss 51(1), (2), (3)

Made . . . . *9 June 1997*
Laid before House of Commons . . . . *9 June 1997*
Coming into force . . . . *1 July 1997*

Citation and commencement

1 These Regulations may be cited as The Distress for Customs and Excise Duties and Other Indirect Taxes Regulations 1997 and shall come into force on 1st July 1997.

Interpretation

2— (1) In these Regulations—

"authorised person" means a person acting under the authority of the Commissioners;
"costs" means any costs, charges, expenses and fees;
"officer" means, subject to section 8(2) of the Customs and Excise Management Act 1979, a person commissioned by the Commissioners pursuant to section 6(3) of that Act;
"person in default" means a person who has refused or neglected to pay any relevant tax due from him;
"relevant tax" means any of the following—

...
(*d*) landfill tax;
...

"walking possession agreement" means an agreement under which, in consideration of any goods and chattels distrained upon being allowed to remain in the custody of the person in default and of the delaying of their sale, that person—

(*a*) acknowledges that the goods and chattels specified in the agreement are under distraint and held in walking possession; and
(*b*) undertakes that, except with the consent of the Commissioners and subject to such conditions as they may impose, he will not remove or allow the removal of any of the specified goods and chattels from the place named in the agreement;

"1994 Act" means Part III of the Finance Act 1994;
"1996 Act" means Part III of the Finance Act 1996;

(2) Any reference in these Regulations to an amount of relevant tax includes a reference to any amount recoverable as if it were an amount of that relevant tax.

Note—Words omitted are not relevant for the purposes of landfill tax.

Revocations and transitional provisions

3— (1) The Regulations specified in Schedule 3 are hereby revoked to the extent set out there.

(2) Where a warrant is signed before the coming into force of these Regulations, these Regulations shall apply to anything done, after these Regulations come into force, in relation to that warrant or as a consequence of distress being levied.

Levying distress

4— (1) Subject to regulation 5 below, if upon written demand a person neglects or refuses to pay any relevant tax due from him an officer may levy distress on the goods and chattels of that person and by warrant signed by him direct any authorised person to levy such distress.

(2) Where a warrant has been signed, distress shall be levied by or under the direction of, and in the presence of, the authorised person.

(3) Subject to regulation 6 below, distress may be levied on any goods and chattels located at any place whatever including on a public highway.

Restrictions on levying distress

5— (1) Where—

…

(*c*) an amount of landfill tax is due and the Commissioners may be required under section 54 of the 1996 Act to review a decision which, if that decision were varied or withdrawn, would cause the amount to be reduced or extinguished,

no distress shall be levied before expiry of the last day on which the person who is liable to pay the amount concerned is required, by rules made under paragraph 9 of Schedule 12 to the VAT Act, to serve a notice of appeal with respect to that decision.

…

Note—Words omitted are not relevant for the purposes of landfill tax.

Goods and chattels not subject to levy

6 No distress shall be levied on any goods and chattels mentioned in Schedule 1 which at the time of levy are located in a place and used for a purpose mentioned in that Schedule.

Times for levying distress

7— (1) Subject to paragraph (2) below, a levy of distress shall commence only during the period between eight o'clock in the morning and eight o'clock at night on any day of the week but it may be continued thereafter outside that period until the levy is completed.

(2) Where a person holds himself out as conducting any profession, trade or business during hours which are partly within and partly outside, or wholly outside the period mentioned in paragraph (1) above, a levy of distress may be commenced at any time during that period or during the hours of any day in which he holds himself out as conducting that profession, trade or business and it may be continued thereafter outside that period or those hours until the levy is completed.

Costs

8— (1) A person in respect of whose goods and chattels a warrant has been signed shall be liable to pay to an officer or authorised person all costs, in connection with anything done under these Regulations described in column 1 of Schedule 2, as determined in accordance with column 2 of that Schedule.

(2) An authorised person may, after deducting and accounting for the amount of relevant tax to the Commissioners, retain costs from any amount received.

Sale

9 If any person upon whose goods and chattels distress has been levied does not pay the amount of relevant tax due together with costs within 5 days of a levy, an officer or authorised person may sell the distress for payment of the amount of relevant tax and costs; and the officer or authorised person, after deducting and retaining the amount of relevant tax and costs shall restore any surplus to the owner of the goods upon which distress was levied.

Disputes as to costs

10— (1) In the case of any dispute as to costs, the amount of those costs shall be taxed by a district judge of the county court of the district where the distress was levied, and he may make such order as he thinks fit as to the costs of the taxation.

(2) In the application of this regulation to Northern Ireland, in the case of any dispute as to costs, the amount of those costs shall be taxed in the same manner as costs in equity suits or proceedings in the county court in Northern Ireland.

SCHEDULE 1

GOODS AND CHATTELS NOT SUBJECT TO LEVY

Regulation 6

1 Any of the following goods and chattels which are located in a dwelling house at which distress is being levied and are reasonably required for the domestic needs of any person residing in that dwelling house—

(*a*) beds and bedding;
(*b*) household linen;
(*c*) chairs and settees;
(*d*) tables;
(*e*) food;
(*f*) lights and light fittings;
(*g*) heating appliances;
(*h*) curtains;
(*i*) floor coverings;
(*j*) furniture, equipment and utensils used for cooking, storing or eating food;
(*k*) refrigerators;
(*l*) articles used for cleaning, mending, or pressing clothes;
(*m*) articles used for cleaning the home;
(*n*) furniture used for storing—
  (i) clothing, bedding or household linen;
  (ii) articles used for cleaning the home;
  (iii) utensils used for cooking or eating food;
(*o*) articles used for safety in the home;
(*p*) toys for the use of any child within the household;
(*q*) medical aids and medical equipment.

2 Any of the following items which are located in premises used for the purposes of any profession, trade or business—

(*a*) fire fighting equipment for use on the premises;
(*b*) medical aids and medical equipment for use on the premises.

SCHEDULE 2

SCALE OF COSTS

Regulation 8(1)

Matter (*1*)	*Costs* (*2*)
1 For attending to levy distress where payment is made of an amount of relevant tax due and distress is not levied:	£12.50.
2 For levying distress—	
(a) where an amount of relevant tax demanded and due does not exceed £100:	£12.50.
(b) where an amount of relevant tax demanded and due exceeds £100:	12½% on the first £100 4% on the next £400, 2½% on the next £1,500, 1% on the next £8,000, ¼% on any additional sum.
3 For taking possession of distrained goods—	
(a) where a person remains in physical possession of goods at the place where distress was levied (the person to provide his own food and lodging):	£4.50 per day.
(b) where possession is taken under a walking possession agreement:	£7.00.

Landfill Tax

Matter	*Costs*
(*1*)	(*2*)
4 For appraising goods upon which distress has been levied:	Reasonable costs of appraisement.
5 For arranging removal and storage of goods upon which distress has been levied:	Reasonable costs of arrangement.
6 For removing and storing goods upon which distress has been levied:	Reasonable costs of removal and storage.
7 For advertising the sale of goods upon which distress has been levied:	Reasonable costs of advertising.
8 For selling the distress—	
(a) where a sale by auction is held at the auctioneer's premises:	15% of the sum realised.
(b) where a sale by auction is held elsewhere:	7½% of the sum realised and auctioneer's reasonable costs.
(c) where a sale by other means is undertaken:	7½% of the sum realised and reasonable costs.

1998/1461
Air Passenger Duty and Other Indirect Taxes (Interest Rate) Regulations 1998

Made by the Treasury under FA 1996 s 197

Made . . . . 15th June 1998
Laid before the House of Commons . . . . 15th June 1998
Coming into force . . . . 6th July 1998

Citation and commencement

1 These Regulations may be cited as the Air Passenger Duty and Other Indirect Taxes (Interest Rate) Regulations 1998 and shall come into force on 6th July 1998.

Interpretation

2— (1) In these Regulations unless the context otherwise requires—

"established rate" means—

(*a*) on the coming into force of these Regulations, [6 per cent][1] per annum; and

(*b*) in relation to any day after the first reference day after the coming into force of these Regulations, the reference rate found on the immediately preceding reference day;

"operative day" means the [[twelfth][3] working day after the reference day][2];

"reference day" means the [...[3] working day following the day on which the most recent meeting of the Monetary Policy Committee of the Bank of England took place][2] ;

"section 197" means section 197 of the Finance Act 1996;

the "relevant enactments" are those referred to in regulations 4(1) and 5(1) below;

"working day" means any day other than a non-business day within the meaning of section 92 of the Bills of Exchange Act 1882.

[(2) In these Regulations the reference rate found on a reference date is the official bank rate determined by the most recent meeting of the Monetary Policy Committee of the Bank of England.][3]

Amendments—[1] Words substituted by the Air Passenger Duty and Other Indirect Taxes (Interest Rate) (Amendment) Regulations, SI 2000/631 regs 2, 3 with effect from 1 April 2000.

[2] In para (1), in definition of "operative day" words substituted for words "sixth day of each month", and in definition of "reference day" words substituted for words "twelfth working day before the next operative day" by the Taxes and Duties (Interest Rate) (Amendment) Regulations, SI 2008/3234 reg 3(1), (2) with effect from 7 January 2009.

[3] In para (1), in definition of "operative day" word substituted for word "eleventh" and in definition of "reference day", word "second" revoked, and para (2) substituted, by the Taxes and Duties (Interest Rate) (Amendment) Regulations, SI 2009/2032 regs 15, 16 with effect from 12 August 2009. Para (2) previously read as follows—

"(2) In these Regulations the reference rate found on a reference day is the percentage per annum found by averaging the base lending rates at close of business on that day of—

(*a*) Bank of Scotland,
(*b*) Barclays Bank plc,
(*c*) Lloyds Bank plc,
(*d*) [HSBC Bank plc],
(*e*) National Westminster Bank plc, and
(*f*) The Royal Bank of Scotland plc,

and, if the result is not a whole number, rounding the result to the nearest such number, with any result midway between two whole numbers rounded down.".

[Applicable rate of interest equal to zero

***2A** In determining the rate of interest applicable under section 197 for the purposes of any enactments referred to in these Regulations, if the result is less than zero the rate shall be treated as zero for those purposes.]*[1]

Amendments—[1] Regulation 2A inserted by the Taxes and Duties (Interest Rate) (Amendment) Regulations, SI 2008/3234 reg 3(1), (3) with effect from 7 January 2009.
[2] This regulation revoked by the Taxes and Duties (Interest Rate) (Amendment) Regulations, SI 2009/2032 regs 15, 17 with effect from 12 August 2009.

3 The Air Passenger Duty and Other Indirect Taxes (Interest Rate) Regulations 1997 are hereby revoked.

[Applicable rate of interest payable to the Commissioners of Customs and Excise in connection with excise duties, insurance premium tax, VAT, landfill tax, and customs duty

4— (1) For the purposes of—

(*a*) [section 60(8) of, and paragraphs 7 and 8(1) of Schedule 6 to,][4] the Finance Act 1994,
(*b*) paragraph 21 of Schedule 7 to that Act,
(*c*) [sections 74 and 85A(3)][4] of the Value Added Tax Act 1994,
(*d*) [section 56(5) of and][4] paragraph 26 of Schedule 5 to the Finance Act 1996,
(*e*) paragraph 17 of Schedule 5 to the Finance Act 1997, …[2]
(*f*) section 126 of the Finance Act 1999, […[3],
(*g*) paragraphs 41(2)(f), 70(1)(*b*)[, 81(3) and 123(6)][4] of Schedule 6 to the Finance Act 2000 (climate change levy),][2] [and
(*h*) sections 25(2)(*f*)[, 30(3)(*f*) and 42(6)][4] of, and paragraphs 6 and 8(3)(a) of Schedule 5 to, the Finance Act 2001 (aggregates levy),][3]

the rate applicable under section 197 shall, subject to paragraph (2) below, be 8.5 per cent per annum.

(2) Where, on any reference day after the coming into force of these Regulations, the reference rate found on that day differs from the established rate, the rate applicable under section 197 of the Finance Act 1996 for the purposes of the enactments referred to in paragraph (1) above shall, from the next operative day, be the percentage per annum determined in accordance with the formula specified in paragraph (3) below.

(3) The formula specified in this paragraph is—

$$RR + 2.5,$$

where RR is the reference rate referred to in paragraph (2) above.][1]

[(4) With effect from 1st November 2001 the rate of interest prescribed in paragraph (1) above for the purposes of paragraph 17 of Schedule 5 to the Finance Act 1997 also applies in the application of that paragraph to assessments under paragraph 14 or 15 of that Schedule as amended by paragraph 19 of Schedule 3 to the Finance Act 2001.][2]

Amendments—[1] This regulation substituted by the Air Passenger Duty and Other Indirect Taxes (Interest Rate) (Amendment) Regulations, SI 2000/631 regs 2, 4 with effect from 1 April 2000.
[2] Word "and" in para (1)(*e*) revoked, and para (1)(*g*) and para (4) inserted, by the Air Passenger Duty and Other Indirect Taxes (Interest Rate) (Amendment) Regulations, SI 2001/3337 reg 2 with effect from 1 November 2001.
[3] Word "and" in para (1)(*f*) revoked, and para (1)(*h*) inserted, by the Air Passenger Duty and Other Indirect Taxes (Interest Rate) (Amendment) Regulations, SI 2003/230 regs 2, 3 with effect from 1 April 2003.
[4] In para (1), in sub-para (*a*), words substituted for words "paragraph 7 of Schedule 6 to", in sub-para (*c*), words substituted for words "section 74", in sub-para (*d*), words inserted, in sub-para (*g*), words substituted for words "and 81(3)", and in sub-para (*h*), words substituted for words "and 30(3)(*f*)", by the Transfer of Tribunal Functions and Revenue and Customs Appeals Order, SI 2009/56 art 3, Sch 2 paras 38, 39 with effect from 1 April 2009.

[Applicable rate of interest payable by the Commissioners of Customs and Excise in connection with air passenger duty, insurance premium tax, VAT, landfill tax, and customs duty

5— (1) For the purposes of—

(*a*) [Parts 2 and 3 of Schedule 3 to the Finance Act 2001 (interest payable on repayments etc)][2],
(*b*) paragraph 22 of Schedule 7 to that Act,
[(*ba*) section 60(6) of the Finance Act 1994,][4]
(*c*) section 78 of the Value Added Tax Act 1994,
(*d*) [section 56(3) and (4) of and][4] paragraph 29 of Schedule 5 to the Finance Act 1996, …[2]
(*e*) section 127 of the Finance Act 1999, […[3]
(*f*) paragraphs 62(3)(*f*)[, 66, 123(4) and 123(5)][4] of Schedule 6 to the Finance Act 2000 (climate change levy)][2] [and
(*g*) [section 42(4) and (5) of and][4] paragraphs 2 and 6(1)(*b*) of Schedule 8 to the Finance Act 2001 (aggregates levy),][3]

the rate applicable under section 197 of the Finance Act 1996 shall be 5 per cent per annum.

(2) Where, on a reference day after the coming into force of these Regulations, the reference rate found on that date differs from the established rate, the rate applicable under section 197 for the purposes of the enactments referred to in paragraph (1) above shall, from the next operative day, be the [higher of—

(*a*) 0.5% per annum, and
(*b*) the percentage per annum found by applying the formula specified in paragraph (3).][5]

[(3) The formula specified in this paragraph is—

$RR - 1,$

where RR is the reference rate referred to in paragraph (2).][1]

Landfill Tax

Amendments—[1] This regulation substituted by the Air Passenger Duty and Other Indirect Taxes (Interest Rate) (Amendment) Regulations, SI 2000/631 regs 2, 5 with effect from 1 April 2000.
[2] In para (1), words in sub-para (*a*) substituted, word "and" in sub-para (*d*) revoked, and sub-para (*f*) added by the Air Passenger Duty and Other Indirect Taxes (Interest Rate) (Amendment) Regulations, SI 2001/3337 regs 1, 3 with effect from 1 November 2001.
[3] Word "and" in para (1)(*e*) revoked, and para (1)(*g*) inserted, by the Air Passenger Duty and Other Indirect Taxes (Interest Rate) (Amendment) Regulations, SI 2003/230 regs 2, 4 with effect from 1 April 2003.
[4] In para (1), sub-para (*ba*) inserted, in sub-para (*c*) words substituted for words "section 78", in sub-paras (*d*), (*g*) words inserted, and in sub-para (*f*) words substituted for words "and 66", by the Transfer of Tribunal Functions and Revenue and Customs Appeals Order, SI 2009/56 art 3, Sch 2 paras 38, 40 with effect from 1 April 2009.
[5] In para (2), words substituted, and para (3) substituted, by the Taxes and Duties (Interest Rate) (Amendment) Regulations, SI 2009/2032 regs 15, 17 with effect from 12 August 2009. Words in para (2) previously read as follows—

"percentage per annum determined in accordance with the formula specified in paragraph (3) below.".

Para (3) previously read as follows—

"(3) The formula specified in this paragraph is—

RR – 1,

where RR is the reference rate referred to in paragraph (2) above.".

Effect of change in applicable rate

6 Where the rate applicable under section 197 for the purposes of any of the relevant enactments changes on an operative day by virtue of these Regulations, that change shall have effect for periods beginning on or after the operative day in relation to interest running from before that day as well as in relation to interest running from, or from after that day.

7 Where the rate applicable under section 197 for the purposes of any of the relevant enactments changes on an operative day by virtue of these Regulations, the rate in force immediately prior to any change shall continue to have effect for periods immediately prior to the change and so on in the case of any number of successive changes.

Applicable rate of interest prior to the coming into force of these Regulations

8 The rate applicable under section 197 for interest running from before the date these Regulations come into force in relation to periods prior to that date shall be specified for the relevant enactments in the following Tables—

Table 4
Paragraph 26 of Schedule 5 to the Finance Act 1996

Interest for any period	*Rate*
from 1st April 1997 and before 6th July 1998	6·25 per cent

Table 8
Paragraph 29 of Schedule 5 to the Finance Act 1996

Interest for any period	*Rate*
from 1st April 1997 and before 6th July 1998	6 per cent

9 ...

Note—This regulation not relevant for the purposes of landfill tax.

2007/965
Landfill Tax (Amendment) Regulations 2007

Made by the Commissioners for Her Majesty's Revenue and Customs under FA 1996 ss 51(1), 53(1), 53(4)(*a*), (*b*), (*c*) and (*ca*) and 71(9)

Made . . . . *22nd March 2007*
Laid before the House of Commons . . . . *22nd March 2007*
Coming into force . . . . *1st April 2007*

1 Citation commencement and interpretation

(1) These Regulations may be cited as the Landfill Tax (Amendment) Regulations 2007 and come into force on 1st April 2007.

(2) In these Regulations—

"the Principal Regulations" means the Landfill Tax Regulations 1996;
"the 2003 Regulations" means the Landfill Tax (Amendment) Regulations 2003.

2–5

(*amend* the Landfill Tax Regulations 1996, SI 1996/1527)

6 Revocation of regulation 6 of the 2003 Regulations with saving

(1) Omit regulation 6 of the 2003 Regulations.

(2) Regulation 6 of the 2003 Regulations (saving for contributions made before 1st April 2003) shall continue to have effect with respect to a qualifying contribution that was made, or treated as made, before 1st April 2003 if, but only if, the condition specified in paragraph (3) is satisfied.

(3) The condition referred to in paragraph (2) is that the approved body to which such a qualifying contribution was given or transferred is required to spend that contribution on one or more of the objects described in paragraph (4) pursuant to a written agreement made before the coming into force of these Regulations.

(4) The objects referred to in paragraph (3) are—

(*a*) for the purpose of encouraging the use of more sustainable waste management practices—

(i) research and development

(ii) education; or

(iii) collection and dissemination of information about waste management practices generally;

(*b*) for the purpose of encouraging the development of products from waste or the development of markets for recycled waste—

(i) research and development

(ii) education; or

(iii) collection and dissemination of information about the development of products from waste or the development of markets for recycled waste.

(5) In paragraph 4(*a*) "waste management practices" includes waste minimisation, minimisation of pollution and harm from waste, reuse of waste, waste recovery activities and the clearing of pollutants from contaminated land.

LANDFILL TAX
EXTRA-STATUTORY CONCESSIONS

CONTENTS

Note—These Concessions are numbered as they appear in VAT Notice 48.

July 2009.

This notice cancels and replaces Notice 48 (March 2002). Details of any changes to the previous version can be found in paragraph 1.1 of this notice.

SECTION 5: LANDFILL TAX—CONCESSIONS DESIGNED TO REMOVE INEQUITIES OR ANOMALIES IN ADMINISTRATION

5.1 Landfill tax—Used foundry sand

By way of concession, used foundry sand shall be treated as falling within Group 3 (Minerals) of the Landfill Tax (Qualifying Material) Order 1996. This means that used foundry sand, when disposed to landfill, shall attract the lower rate of landfill tax.

SECTION 10: CONCESSIONS OBSOLETE SINCE LAST EDITION OF UPDATE 1 TO NOTICE 48 (PUBLISHED OCTOBER 2000)

10.3 Landfill tax—Temporary disposal of material in designated areas for storage or sorting pending use in site restoration

1. For the purposes of Part IX of the Landfill Tax Regulations 1996—

(a) the following may be treated as a qualifying use—

- *storage of qualifying material for later use in restoration of the landfill site, and*
- *sorting of material into qualifying material for storage for use, or for immediate use, in restoration of the landfill site and other material for disposal; and*

(b) the relevant period as defined in regulation 38(5)(c) for the purposes of the application of regulation 38(2)(c) in respect of such use may be treated as being 3 years.

2. The concession applies only to disposals of material made on or after 1 October 1999.

3. Before applying this concession to any disposal, a site operator must apply to the Commissioners for an area to be designated under regulation 38 for, or in the case of an existing designated area for its designation to be amended to permit, the temporary disposal of material in the area pending all the material being put to the qualifying use set out in the concession.

4. Application of this concession is subject to compliance with all conditions imposed by or under Part IX of the above regulations applicable to, and to the operation of, the area designated for temporary disposals of material pending its being put to the qualifying use specified in the concession, including the record keeping requirement imposed by regulation 39.

LANDFILL TAX
PRESS RELEASES ETC

CONTENTS

PRESS RELEASES ETC

21 March 1996. News Release 18/96

Landfill tax—further amendments to meet industry concerns

The Government today tabled a number of amendments to the landfill tax provisions in the Finance Bill [see below] for debate at Report Stage on 27 and 28 March. They deal mainly with exemptions from the tax and the adjustment of contracts provisions and reflect the close and helpful dialogue that continues to take place with industry in the run up to the introduction of the tax on 1 October.

DREDGINGS

The Paymaster General announced in Committee that dredgings from inland waterways, harbours and ports will be exempt from landfill tax. The waste is naturally occurring and exists only through natural forces. Dredging also has the beneficial effect of keeping waterways clear for navigation and preventing floods. Customs & Excise have consulted with the dredging industry on the precise wording of the clause to ensure that it does not give rise to any ambiguity, and the wording of the new clause to the Finance Bill reflects the industry's concerns.

MINES AND QUARRIES WASTE

The Paymaster General also announced in committee that waste from mines and quarries would be exempt. The exemption will apply to all naturally occurring waste arising from mining and quarrying operations which has not been processed in a way which permanently alters its chemical characteristics, whether it is landfilled at the point of production or elsewhere. As with dredgings, Customs & Excise have consulted with representatives of the industry on the precise terms of the exemption to ensure their concerns are reflected.

CONTAMINATED LAND

Customs & Excise have also consulted widely about a proposed exemption from the tax for waste from historically contaminated land. The consultation took place on a draft clause linking the exemption to planning approval, in order to provide an objective criterion for eligibility to the exemption. However, following the consultation exercise, it was clear that it was not possible to proceed in this way as too many clearance projects do not require planning permission or do not have as part of the planning approval a requirement to clear polluted land.

The Government now intends to provide an exemption for waste from the clearance of contaminated land where clearance of all or part of the contamination is necessary to allow the land to be used for the intended purpose when the development or work on the land is complete. The exemption will apply to waste arising from the reclamation of the land, but current polluters will not be able to benefit from it.

The Government has not tabled a Report Stage amendment to provide for an exemption based on this alternative approach as time constraints would not have allowed for any further consultation. However, under another new clause tabled today, the Treasury will be able to make orders to add to, delete or vary the definition of waste exempt from the tax. The Government intends to use this order-making power to introduce the exemption for historically contaminated land. This will enable Customs & Excise to consult further over any difficulties with a view to putting a draft order out for consultation early in April.

ADJUSTMENT OF CONTRACTS

The Finance Bill as published allows contracts relating to material which is disposed of to landfill, or to be transported or otherwise handled before such disposal, to be adjusted to take account of the introduction of the tax or any future change in rate. Under the Bill as published, the payment under the contract could be adjusted to the amount "which can reasonably be expected the parties would have agreed". There was concern that the "reasonableness" test could have led to a great deal of litigation. Following consultation with those involved, the Government has tabled an amendment to simplify the provision so that landfill tax can be passed on automatically unless the contract specifically provides otherwise.

To meet concerns of those in the construction industry, the Government has tabled a second amendment to the adjustment of contracts provisions. This will enable constructors contracts for the redevelopment of sites, including the preparation of the site, to be adjusted in such a way that the tax can be passed on to the company on whose behalf the construction company is undertaking the work.

TECHNICAL AMENDMENTS

A number of minor amendments of a more technical nature have also been tabled—

- to extend the adjustment of rent provisions so that where a landfill site lease describes payments related to turnover as royalties or a similar term, the tax can be ignored;
- to clarify the definition of a landfill site and landfill site operator for tax purposes;
- to limit the period during which any repayment of overpaid landfill tax can be claimed to six years from the date the overpayment occurred; and
- to allow Customs & Excise to require the preservation of records which a landfill site operator has not been required to create under landfill tax regulations.

26 March 1996. News Release 21/96

Government announces outcome of consultation on scope of lower rate of landfill tax

In response to a Parliamentary Question from Matthew Banks, MP for Southport, the Paymaster General, David Heathcoat-Amory, has announced today the outcome of the Customs & Excise consultation exercise on the scope of the lower rate of landfill tax.

The Chancellor announced in the last Budget that, when the tax is introduced on 1 October, inactive or inert waste would be liable to landfill tax at a lower rate of £2 per tonne and all other taxable waste would be liable at £7 per tonne. Customs & Excise issued a consultation paper on 15 December 1995 setting out the Government's proposals for what wastes would be liable at £2 per tonne.

Customs & Excise have now analysed the replies which they received to the consultation exercise. On the basis of the information provided and representations made, the Government has concluded that the lower rate of landfill tax should apply to the wastes listed below. Mixtures consisting only of listed wastes will qualify for the lower rate, as will water with suspended solids consisting only of listed wastes.

In order to be taxable at the lower rate, listed wastes (or mixtures of such wastes) must not contain or be contaminated with any material which is not listed below. But a *de minimis* level will apply to enable wastes to qualify for the lower rate if they consist wholly of listed wastes, apart from a small quantity of material which is not listed, provided that that material does not lead to any potential for pollution. Where wastes appear on the lower rate list and are also covered by an exemption, the exemption will apply.

1 *Naturally occurring rocks and soils*—including clay, sand, gravel, sandstone, limestone, crushed stone, china clay, clean building or demolition stone such as sandstone, limestone or slate, topsoil, peat, silt and dredgings.

2 *Ceramic or cemented materials*—glass; ceramics—including bricks, tiles, clay ware, pottery, china, bricks and mortar; concrete including reinforced concrete, concrete blocks, breeze blocks and thermalite blocks.

3 *Processed or prepared mineral materials, which have not been used or contaminated*—moulding sands and clays; clay absorbents, including Fuller's earth and bentonite and other mineral absorbents; man-made mineral fibres, including glass fibre; silica; mica; abrasives.

4 *Furnace slags.*

5 *Certain ash*—bottom ash and fly ash from wood or coal combustion (including pulverised fuel ash from coal combustion).

6 *Low activity inorganic compounds*—titanium dioxide; calcium carbonate; magnesium carbonate; magnesium oxide; magnesium hydroxide; ferric oxide; ferric hydroxide; aluminium oxide.

7 *Gypsum and plaster*—these will be subject to the lower rate only if disposed of in landfill sites licensed only to take inactive or inert waste.

8 *Other wastes*—there are, in addition to the above, a few wastes on which Customs & Excise are seeking further information before a conclusion is reached as to whether the lower rate is appropriate.

27 August 1996. Business Brief 18/96

Customs & Excise publish information notes about landfill tax

Customs & Excise have published a series of information notes on the landfill tax (see below). The notes will help registrable landfill site operators who will be responsible for accounting for and paying landfill tax to Customs & Excise.

Landfill tax is introduced on 1 October 1996. From that date most waste disposed of at a registrable landfill site is liable to landfill tax. There are two rates of tax—£2 per tonne if the waste is inactive (this means it is less likely to cause pollution) and £7 per tonne for active waste.

Every business produces waste that it pays to have collected and disposed of, some of which goes to landfill. Therefore, the costs of waste disposal will probably increase after October 1996. Businesses may want to investigate the sort of waste they generate and consider whether they can do anything to reduce those costs. They may, for example, think about recycling or reuse rather than landfill. Therefore, the information notes may also be of interest to others involved in the disposal of waste, such as waste producers and waste carriers.

Some of the tax can be used to fund environmental purposes by allowing credit of landfill tax to operators of landfill sites who make contributions to approved environmental bodies. Information note 8/96 explains how this scheme works and will be of interest to those concerned about environmental issues.

The list of information notes are as follows—

Note	*Subject*
1/96 (revised)	Introduction to landfill tax
2/96	Registration
3/96	Tax liability
4/96	Calculating the weight of waste
5/96	Tax points
6/96	Records
7/96	Accounting for tax
8/96	Environmental bodies
9/96	Penalties and interest
10/96	Reviews and appeals
11/96	Contaminated land

For further information or copies of the information notes please contact the Landfill Tax Helpdesk, HM Customs & Excise, Dobson House, Regent Centre, Gosforth, Newcastle upon Tyne NE3 3PF. Telephone number 0645 128 484 or fax number 0645 129 595 (both at local call rate).

18 September 1996. News Release 48/96

Foundry sand and the landfill tax

Foundry sand will initially attract the lower rate of £2 per tonne of landfill tax, Customs & Excise announced today.

Customs & Excise's announcement follows an extensive consultation exercise with the foundry industry and will allow landfill site operators and producers to plan with certainty for the introduction of the tax on 1 October 1996. This decision will be reviewed when the results of further tests on foundry sand are available. Sand is used in the foundry industry for casting and is eventually discarded to landfill sites.

Landfill tax was first announced in the Chancellor's 1994 Budget and there has been extensive consultation with all sectors of the industry and individual producers on the basis and structure of the tax.

The standard rate of landfill tax is £7 per tonne.

30 September 1996. News Release 51/96

Introduction of landfill tax

A new and imaginative way to encourage more environmentally friendly ways of waste disposal, while helping to create more jobs, comes into place tomorrow.

The landfill tax will help motivate waste producers to reduce their use of landfill sites and find better ways of dealing with their waste. The money raised from the tax will be used to reduce employers' national insurance contributions by £500 million from next April. This will help to create and maintain existing jobs.

The Exchequer Secretary, Phillip Oppenheim, welcomed the introduction of this new initiative—

> "After extensive debate and consultation, both in Parliament and with those involved, I believe we have struck the right balance. We are helping to protect the environment while reducing the cost of employment. This shows the Government is keen to use sensible economic ways to achieve its environmental aims."

Environmental Minister James Clappison said—

> "The landfill tax represents a significant new policy. The shift from taxing employment to taxing resources has rightly been an aim of the EU but it is the UK that is setting the pace. It marks an important step in extending the use of economic instruments to achieve environmental objectives. The central purpose of the tax is to ensure that landfill costs reflect the full cost of the environmental impact of the activity. By doing this business and consumers are encouraged, in a cost effective and non-regulatory manner, to produce less waste, and to reuse or recover value from more waste."

Department of Social Security Minister Oliver Heald said—

"The 0·2% reduction in the main rate of employers' national insurance contributions proposed for April 1997 comes on top of the substantial reductions of employers' contribution rates we have made in recent years. These demonstrate the Government's determination to help businesses and jobs by driving down employers' non-wage labour costs which are already amongst the lowest in Europe."

The tax will be administered by Customs & Excise who will collect it from landfill site operators. It will be levied per tonne of waste at two rates, £2 per tonne for inactive waste such as builders rubble, and £7 per tonne for active waste such as plastic packaging. There will be an incentive for landfill site operators to fund environmental trusts set up for approved environmental purposes. Site operators making payments to these bodies will be able to claim a tax credit of 90 per cent of their contributions, up to a maximum of 20 per cent of their landfill tax bill in a 12 month period.

NOTES

Landfill tax was announced by the Chancellor in the 1994 Budget and is expected to raise £450 million. The rates and other details were announced in the 1995 Budget, following an eight month consultation by Customs & Excise with groups affected by the tax on how it should be implemented. There are two rates, £2 per tonne for inactive waste, £7 per tonne for other taxable wastes.

The Government proposes to reduce the main rate of national insurance contributions for employers from 10·2 per cent to 10 per cent on 6 April 1997, saving businesses £500 million.

This year Customs & Excise have run a series of trade seminars around the country explaining details of the tax to affected businesses.

5 June 1997. Business Brief 12/97

Clearance of contaminated land

Customs have agreed to grant extra-statutory remission of landfill tax to late applications for the contaminated land exemption, provided certain conditions are satisfied.

Exemption from landfill tax of qualifying wastes from contaminated land reclamation depends on Customs issuing an exemption certificate to the reclaimant. However, an exemption certificate cannot be back dated so that reclaimants applying too late will have had to pay landfill tax on some of their wastes which were disposed of to landfill. In a number of cases applicants have claimed they were late applying for the exemption due to unfamiliarity with, or misunderstanding of, the legal provisions relating to landfill tax.

Claims for remission of tax will only be considered for waste that clearly would have qualified for exemption and that was charged landfill tax at disposal. Such waste must have come from reclamations which have had at least some of their wastes certified to ensure that the application would have been subject to verification by a local Customs Officer.

The Extra Statutory Class Concession (ESCC) applies to exemption certificates issued before 30 June 1997 and claims for remission must be made to Customs by 30 September 1997.

Further details of the ESCC are contained in a Landfill Tax Briefing issued on 26 May 1997. Copies are available from the Landfill Tax Help Desk, HM Customs & Excise, Dobson House, Regent Centre, Gosforth, Newcastle-upon-Tyne, NE3 3PF. Telephone 0645 128484 or Fax 0645 129595.

20 December 2002. Information note.

Changes to the Landfill Tax Credit Scheme (LTCS) from 1 April 2003

PRE-BUDGET REPORT (PBR) 2002

The pre-Budget report 2002, which may be found on the HM Treasury web site at www.hm-treasury.gov.uk, announced changes to the Landfill Tax Credit Scheme (LTCS) as set out below.

The Government has reviewed the role of the scheme in consultation with key stakeholders. The Government recognises that the scheme has supported many worthwhile community and environment projects that have improved the quality of the environment at the local level. The scheme has also been successful in generating local community involvement in such projects. However, there is less evidence that the LTCS has delivered a step change towards more sustainable waste management, and it has also been criticised for its administrative complexity and for failing to deliver value for money for the tax which is forgone. Recent changes have improved the administration of the scheme, but will not deliver the strategic and coherent approach to waste management which is needed.

The Government has therefore decided to reform the LTCS from 1 April 2003. The level of funding for the replacement schemes will be capped at the value of the tax which would have been forgone in 2002–03 if all the available tax credits had been claimed by landfill operators.

Approximately one third of the funding, around £47 million, will continue to be made available through a reformed tax credit scheme for spending on local community environmental projects, ensuring that the current level of support for these types of projects is maintained. The remainder, around £100 million in 2003–04 rising to £110 million in 2004–05 and 2005–06, will be allocated to public spending to encourage sustainable waste management.

The Government will announce its final decisions on sustainable waste management spending over the coming months. Reducing the rate of growth of waste volumes and increasing recycling through kerbside recycling schemes and secondary market development will be priorities for additional investment. The Devolved Administrations will be responsible for the waste spending programmes in their regions.

The Government will also announce further decisions on the administration of the tax credit scheme for local community environmental projects over the coming months. Meanwhile, tax credits which have already been claimed by landfill operators, or which may be claimed until 31 March 2003, will need to be spent under the existing LTCS arrangements. This will ensure that projects which have been allocated tax credit funding will continue to benefit until such time as they are completed.

WHAT THIS MEANS IF YOU ARE A LANDFILL SITE OPERATOR WHO HAS DONATED MONEY THROUGH THE LTCS, OR INTEND TO DO SO IN THE FUTURE.

Up to 31 March 2003 you may continue to claim credit for contributions to environmental bodies (EBs) in the way that you do now. Your contribution can be in respect of a project falling into any of the currently approved objects, including those in categories C and CC. However, from 1 April next year you will no longer be able to claim any credit for a contribution to a project under categories C and CC. An EB that has received a contribution from you up to 31 March 2003, in respect of projects in categories C and CC, may spend that contribution after 31 March 2003.

If you are committed to making contributions to a C or CC project after 31 March 2003, you may wish to consider bringing forward your contribution subject of course to not exceeding your maximum entitlement of 20 per cent of your annual landfill tax liability.

Also from 1 April 2003, the maximum credit of 20 per cent of your annual landfill tax liability that you are entitled to claim in a contribution year will be reduced to ensure that the scheme is capped at a maximum value of around £47 million. This means that from 1 April 2003 you will need to ensure that your contributions do not exceed the revised figure for the maximum allowable credit during a contribution year. As a guide we anticipate that this figure will be around 6 per cent however a precise figure will be announced before 1 April 2003. If your landfill tax accounting period straddles 1 April you will need to pro-rata your contribution so that it reflects the different maximum entitlements. You may calculate this precisely on the basis of your actual liabilities before and after 1 April 2003 or use a simplified calculation based on the number of days in the accounting period each side of 1 April 2003.

The revised maximum entitlement may mean that you need to review commitments you have made to the future funding of projects other than those in categories C and CC.

ALTERNATIVE FUNDING FOR CATEGORY C AND CC PROJECTS AFTER 1 APRIL 2003

Projects which already have tax credits allocated, and where the tax credits are already available, will continue to be able to be funded from those tax credits until they are spent or the project is completed. Decisions on the criteria or scope of the replacement spending scheme will be made in due course. However, the Government is conscious of the need to make announcements in good time for 1 April. Depending on the scope of the replacement spending scheme, it may be possible that projects which are currently eligible for funding under the LTCS will be able to be considered for funding under it.

Commentary—*De Voil Indirect Tax Service* **V20.148.**

21 February 2003. Information Note

Changes to the landfill tax credit scheme—further information

This note gives further information on the changes to the landfill tax credit scheme that were announced at the pre-Budget report last November and should be read in conjunction with the information note issued on 20 December 2002. This information supersedes any previous agreements or previously issued information.

DETAILED CHANGES TO THE LANDFILL TAX CREDIT SCHEME

The following changes will come into effect from 1 April—

- The reduction of the maximum percentage credit of annual landfill tax liability for a landfill site operator from 20% to 6·5%. If your accounting period covers time before and after 1 April then you will need to apportion your maximum percentage credit eg if your accounting period covers March, April and May then you are entitled to a maximum percentage credit in respect of March of 20% of your liability while for April and May that entitlement is 6·5%.

– Landfill site operators will not be able to claim credit in respect of contributions made to object c & cc projects after the 31 March 2003. However there are arrangements for covering that part of an accounting period that falls before 1 April 2003 where the end of the accounting period is not until after 1 April 2003 so that any entitlement to credit can be apportioned. For example, if your accounting period covers March, April and May then when you decide on how much you wish to contribute and to which project it should go, you should be aware that you can claim credit for March at up to 20% of your landfill tax liability. (For April and May it will be at 6·5%). In addition this contribution can go to an object c & cc project if you wish. In respect of April and May it cannot go to a c & cc project. If you do not make it clear to the environmental body that you wish your contribution to go to a c & cc project then any contribution from that accounting period will be assumed to be ineligible for object c & cc projects.
– All current contribution years will end on 31 March 2003 and from that date all operators' contribution years will run from 1 April to 31 March every year.
– Environmental bodies (EBs) will need to account separately for funds that were received in respect of contributions made before and after the end of March. It may be that EBs will ask operators to provide some sort of indicator to them as to what proportion of a contribution is in respect of the period before 1 April and what proportion is in respect of the period on or after that date.

Commentary—*De Voil Indirect Tax Service* **V20.148.**

31 Mar 2003. Written Ministerial Statement (Col 38WS)

Landfill tax rate from April 2003

The Economic Secretary to the Treasury (John Healey): Legislation will be introduced in the Finance Bill 2003, to take effect from 1 April 2003, which will increase the standard rate of landfill tax from £13 per tonne to £14 per tonne. The increase is part of a series of £1 per tonne escalator increases, announced in Budget 1999. These increases have been publicised in the landfill public notice (LFT1). HM Customs and Excise is writing to all landfill operators registered for the tax to confirm the date of the change.

1 October 2003. Business Brief 19/03

Introduction of new biodiversity related object for the Landfill Tax Credit Scheme (LTCS)

In this year's Budget the Government announced changes to the Landfill Tax Credit Scheme (LTCS) including the introduction of a new object to encourage biodiversity. This refers to biodiversity in conservation on a specific habitat or species at a specific site in England, Scotland, Wales or Northern Ireland. The legal term for this change to the LTCS is the "biodiversity object".

From 1 October 2003 a new object will be introduced to the LTCS by amending Regulations. This new object allows contributions to be made by landfill site operators towards biodiversity related projects (including projects where public access to the habitat is not available). The introduction of this new object follows consultation by Customs with stakeholders in the LTCS.

The Government has also been working with Entrust, the regulator of the scheme, and other stakeholders to improve the scheme's operation. Administration of the scheme is being simplified through a reduction in the level of information required from projects and through the use of common systems wherever possible. Better information will be recorded on project funding and audit processes have been improved. The Government will also improve monitoring and evaluation of the scheme and has developed measures of value for money.

FURTHER INFORMATION

The amendment to the Landfill Tax Regulations 1996 is made by the Landfill Tax (Amendment) (No 2) Regulations, SI 2003/2313. Entrust, the LTCS regulator, is able to provide further information on the operation of the scheme and the new object. Details of the scheme and how Entrust can be contacted can be found at www.ltcs.org.uk.

Commentary—*De Voil Indirect Tax Service* **V20.148.**

19 March 2004. Business Brief 9/04

Landfill tax credit scheme

1 INCREASE IN THE MAXIMUM CREDIT CLAIMABLE

In Budget 2004 the Chancellor announced an increase in the maximum credit claimable under the Landfill Tax Credit Scheme. Landfill site operators who make contributions to bodies with objects concerned with the environment, enrolled under the landfill tax credit scheme, may claim a credit against their annual landfill tax liability. The maximum credit that they may claim currently is 6.5 per cent of that liability. With effect from the start of the new landfill tax contribution year, 1 April 2004, the percentage is to be increased from 6.5 per cent to 6.8 per cent, in line with the Government's commitment to maintain the real value of the scheme.

Landfill site operators whose accounting period covers time before and after 1 April will need to apportion their maximum percentage credit so that it reflects the different entitlements. They may calculate this precisely on the basis of their liabilities before and from 1 April 2004, or use a simplified calculation based on the number of days in the accounting period each side of 1 April 2004.

For example, if their accounting period covers March, April and May then they are entitled to a maximum percentage credit in respect of March of 6.5 per cent of their liability, while for April and May that entitlement is 6.8 per cent.

2 LANDFILL SITE OPERATORS IN NORTHERN IRELAND—WASTE TRANSFER NOTES

The Chancellor also announced changes to record-keeping requirements for landfill site operators in Northern Ireland. Since 1 October 2002, under Northern Ireland environmental law, it has been a general requirement that waste transfer notes are preserved for a period of two years. However, with effect from 1 May 2004, for Customs' purposes, landfill site operators in Northern Ireland will have to preserve waste transfer notes for six years, unless a shorter period has been agreed with Customs.

The change brings the requirements for landfill site operators in Northern Ireland, on the preservation of records and evidence to support a claim to bad debt relief, into line with those for Great Britain.

3 RATES OF LANDFILL TAX

The standard rate of landfill tax, which applies to active waste disposed of to landfill, will increase to £15 per tonne from 1 April 2004, as announced in Budget 1999. The Government announced in Budget 2003 that the rate would increase to £18 per tonne in 2005–06 and by at least £3 per tonne in the years thereafter on the way to a medium-to-long-term rate of £35 per tonne.

Budget 2004 announced that the lower rate, which applies to inactive waste disposed of to landfill, remains at £2 per tonne.

22 March 2004. Business Brief 10/04

Tax liability of materials re-used on landfill sites

Customs wish to announce a change in policy relating to material used on landfill sites.

BACKGROUND

For landfill tax purposes, material is disposed of as waste, if, when disposing of it or having it disposed of on his behalf, the producer intends to discard or throw it away. The fact that someone else uses it or intends to use it, or would have done so is irrelevant. It is the original producer's intention that determines if the material is waste. Only if the material is recycled is the original producer's intention no longer relevant.

DETAILS OF THE CHANGE

Up to now, for the purposes of landfill tax, Customs' guidance has been that material had to undergo a chemical change to be considered to have been recycled. With immediate effect, Customs will accept that if a material is processed, changing it to a useable material, the process does not have to change the material's chemical properties in order for it to be considered to have been recycled.

The tax liability will now hinge on the intention of the recycler, as evidenced by the nature of the transaction. If a landfill site operator can demonstrate to Customs' satisfaction that the material he uses in site engineering is not discarded by its producer, it will not be subject to the tax.

Currently, one of the provisions for which landfill site operators can apply in order to operate a tax-free area is if they intend to carry out recycling of waste (which includes composting). Customs' revised interpretation of what constitutes recycling widens the scope of this qualifying use with immediate effect.

8 September 2004. Business Brief 24/04

Landfill tax–court of appeal judgment in the case of *Ebbcliff Ltd* supports Customs' interpretation of the exemption for restoring landfill sites

This Business Brief article reports on the end of litigation following the Court of Appeal's decision to dismiss Ebbcliff's appeal that most of the waste deposited at its site qualified for an exemption from landfill tax.

BACKGROUND

Ebbcliff operate a landfill facility. They registered for landfill tax, and paid tax on waste material deposited at the site. In October 1999 a landfill tax exemption was introduced for inert material, such as soil, used in the restoration of landfill sites. The scheme adopted by Ebbcliff for filling and contouring the site involves the disposal of inert waste into the landfill phase, clay for the capping layer (the impermeable layer of clay or artificial membrane near the top of the site that prevents rainwater from entering and helps to capture landfill gas) and restoration soils above that.

THE LAW AND CUSTOMS' INTERPRETATION

Certain work ('restoration') at a landfill site can qualify for an exemption from landfill tax. The term 'restoration' is defined as work, other than capping waste, which is required by a waste management licence or a planning consent to be carried out to restore a landfill site to use on completion of waste disposal operations. Ebbcliff's view was the exemption applies to all of the inert waste deposited on site above and below the capping layer. Customs' view, which the High Court and the Court of Appeal agreed with, is that restoration means only that work which amounts to waste disposal above the capping layer, i e the restoration soils. The judgment makes the point that "If the exemption was designed to cover all disposals of inert waste made for the purposes of restoring a derelict site to beneficial use, it is hard to see what policy reason there would be for excluding the capping layer from the exemption while including both the waste below and the soil above in the 'exemption'.

LANDFILL SITES WITHOUT A CAP

The Court of Appeal said that in such a case 'it will be a question of fact to be determined in the light of the evidence the point at which the filling of the site ends and the restoration of the site commences.'

Simon's Tax Cases—*C&E Comrs v Ebbcliff Ltd* [2004] STC 1496.

4 April 2005. Business Brief 9/05

Landfill tax—Extension of landfill tax exemptions and a tax credit from 6 April 2005

This Business Brief article provides information on the extension of exemptions and a tax credit to those landfill site operators whose sites are covered by waste management permits. It also gives details on where to claim, for those landfill site operators who have been unable to claim the exemptions and credit in the past. This article is not relevant to those whose sites are covered by waste management licences or resolutions, as they are already entitled to claim the exemptions and tax credit. Although the majority of permits will be issued in the period 2006 to 2007, some are being issued before then. Permits will ultimately replace waste management licences and resolutions.

BACKGROUND

Section 66 of the Finance Act 1996 defines which landfill sites fall within the scope of the landfill tax. Its original scope included only sites that were covered by a waste management licence or a resolution. This section was amended by the Pollution Prevention and Control

Act 1999 and the Environment (Northern Ireland) Order 2002, which added to the list land which is covered by a permit under regulations under section 2 of that Act or Article 4 of that Order.

The above amendments did not insert all the necessary references to permits elsewhere in the Finance Act 1996 and the Landfill Tax Regulations. The changes set out below will rectify these omissions. Budget Notice CE14, paragraph 10, published on 16 March 2005, gives details of the sections of the Finance Act 1996 and the Landfill Tax Regulations 1996 to be amended.

CHANGES

The changes are contained in two Statutory Instruments that come into force on 6 April 2005. These will extend to permit holders the following exemptions and credit:

(a) The exemption for restoring a landfill site with qualifying material (see Note below);
(b) The exemption for filling quarries with qualifying material;
(c) The exemption for the disposal of the remains of dead domestic pets at pet cemeteries;
(d) The entitlement to credit when directed by a relevant authority, for example, the Environment Agency, to remove waste to another landfill site from the site where it was originally deposited; and
(e) The entitlement to temporarily dispose of qualifying material tax free for site restoration purposes.

Note: If the restoration at a) above is required under the terms of planning consent rather than the permit (as is currently the case in the majority, if not all, sites covered by licences) then the current, unamended, law already allows for the exemption.

CLAIMS

Landfill site operators who have been unable to claim the exemptions and credit in the past should send full details to:

Environmental Taxes UoE,
HM Customs & Excise,
Dobson House,
Regent Centre,
Gosforth,
Newcastle upon Tyne,
NE3 3PF.

April 2008. Notice ET1

Notice of requirement to give security for environmental taxes

Note—See under *IPT* section, ante, for the full text of this notice which is HMRC's Statement of Practice on the circumstances where they may require security for Insurance Premium Tax, Landfill Tax, Aggregates Levy and Climate Change Levy.

22 December 2008. HMRC Brief 58/08

Use of material on landfill sites—Court of Appeal judgment in *Waste Recycling Group Limited* case

1. This brief is for landfill site operators and is our response to the judgment of the Court of Appeal in *Commissioners for Her Majesty's Revenue and Customs v Waste Recycling Group Limited* [2008] All ER (D) 300 (Jul).

BACKGROUND

2. On 22 July 2008 the Court ruled in favour of Waste Recycling Group Limited in their action relating to landfill tax liability. The Court found that where material received on a landfill site is put to a use on the site (for example, for the daily coverage of sites required under environmental regulation, and construction of on-site haul roads), it is not taxable, as there is not, at the relevant time, a disposal with the intention of discarding the material.

3. We accepted the Court's decision and did not seek leave to appeal to the House of Lords.

DESCRIPTION OF USE OF MATERIAL

4. Notwithstanding any possible future changes to landfill tax legislation that the Government might decide to introduce, the judgment means that materials put to use on a landfill site are not taxable. Illustrative non-taxable uses of material include:

Cell engineering

– Mineral material (including clay) used as part of an artificially established (geological) barrier on the bottom, sides or top (cap) of a landfill. Materials used to protect from damage any geosynthetic product used for landfill containment on the base, sides or top of the landfill.

- Drainage material at the base and up the sides of the site used to collect leachate and allow its transport to a low point for collection/ extraction.
- Material used beneath the landfill cap and up the sides of the site to allow landfill gas to accumulate for extraction. Material used as a preferential drainage layer above the cap to encourage surface water run off.
- Mineral material (including clay) used to protect the cap and provide a restoration layer for planting.

Daily cover

Material used to cover waste during operations and/or at the end of the working day to reduce emissions of odour, dust etc and to reduce the risk of waste disturbance by birds, vermin or insects.

Temporary site haul roads

Material used for the construction of roads within the waste disposal area which give access to the landfill working areas.

Temporary hard-standing

Material used for the construction of bases/surfaces within the waste disposal area on which activities, for example treatment or recycling operations, take place.

Permanent site haul roads

Material used for constructing roads prior to the commencement of landfilling on the site or off the waste disposal area (characterised by construction in tarmac or concrete and incorporating drains, kerbs etc).

Permanent hard standing

Material used for constructing hard-standing areas prior to the commencement of landfilling on the site or off the waste disposal area (characterised by construction in tarmac or concrete with sealed drainage).

Cell bunds—part of the engineering structure

Mineral material including clay used to form separate cells on the base of the landfill as part of the engineered containment.

Cell bunds—not part of the engineering structure

Material used for the construction of bunds within the waste disposal area to separate individual cells, except on the base of the landfill as part of the engineered containment.

Temporary screening bunds

Material used as a temporary shield while landfill or recovery activities take place.

Permanent noise/visual screening bunds or mounds

Material used for the construction of permanent noise or visual screening structures that are intended to remain after the end of landfilling operations.

Gas and leachate pipes and boreholes

Material used to “backfill” the space between the edge of the hole drilled to extract or monitor landfill gas or leachate and the pipe inserted into that hole.

MAKING A CLAIM FOR TAX

5. We will not expect or require operators to correct past declaration errors, which were made on the basis of our prevailing interpretation of the law. Operators will, however, be required to apply the new interpretation of the law from the date of this Brief. Where a landfill site operator wishes to correct past errors and make a claim to us for a repayment of tax incorrectly paid, they may do so, subject to the conditions set out in this section of the Brief.

6. We may reject all or part of a claim if repayment would unjustly enrich the claimant. Broadly speaking, unjust enrichment means that a claimant would get a windfall profit, because the tax or duty that they are seeking to recover was, in effect, paid by the consumer or consumers (their customer or customers) and the claimant is not planning to pass the refund back to the consumer(s).

7. Landfill tax legislation sets out the rules for claiming overpaid tax. Claims can be made in two ways: by adjustment to the current landfill tax return, or by submitting a written claim to us.

8. Where the operator is registered for VAT, an adjustment may be made to their current landfill tax return, but the value of the errors must not exceed the greater of:

- £10,000
- 1 per cent of the box 6 figure on the claimant's VAT return for the VAT return period of discovery, subject to an upper limit of £50,000

9. For operators not liable to be registered for VAT there is a single error limit on the current landfill tax return of £10,000.

10. Where the errors exceed the limits set out in paragraphs 8 and 9, a written claim should be submitted to us (in these cases the errors must not be corrected through the claimant's returns). Any operator (even one eligible to do so) may opt not to seek a repayment through an adjustment to their landfill tax return. An operator that is any of the following:

- ineligible to adjust their landfill tax returns (see paragraph 8 and 9)
- currently deregistered for landfill tax
- does not wish to make a claim by adjusting their returns

should submit a written claim to us with the following information included:

- a statement of the amount being claimed
- the method of calculation in as much detail as possible

The following information should also be included to substantiate the claim:

- the reason for the claim
- the prescribed accounting periods in respect of which claims are being made, allocating amounts to periods
- the dates on which any overpayments, over-declarations or under-claims were made and, if the overpayment was made pursuant to an assessment or voluntary disclosure, the date on which the assessment or disclosure was made
- details of all documents, schedules, etc used in support of the claim

along with:

- a claim for statutory, simple interest under paragraph 29 to Schedule 5 of the Finance Act 1996 (where the claimant considers they are entitled to make one)
- the operator's bank account name, number and sort code (where the claimant wishes a repayment to be credited to their bank account)

11. We are not liable to repay any amount paid to us more than 3 years before the making of the claim and operators must be able to produce evidence that they overpaid the tax on material used on the landfill site for uses described in paragraph 4 above, and must be able to substantiate the amount claimed. Please note that notification to us that an operator intends making a claim in the future will not be treated as a valid claim for time limit purposes. Subject to the three-year limitation period, any claim should also be for all prescribed accounting periods in which the overpayment(s) occurred. Should a claim not take into account all errors or all affected accounting periods, we will seek to set-off amounts owed for these periods against amounts claimed in other periods.

12. Contributions to environmental bodies made as a result of any overpayment of tax will be taken into account and credits in respect of such contributions will not operate to reduce the amount of tax that can be claimed. Otherwise, claims will be paid or credited on a net basis, that is, those amounts paid to us. If, for instance, in a given accounting period the tax due to us was reduced, because the operator has subsequently claimed a credit in respect of bad debts or other credits, the amount of tax claimed should be reduced accordingly.

13. Claimants may be asked to supply information to verify the accuracy of their claim. Where claims have been submitted prior to the publication of this Brief, they will now be considered and information for the purposes of verification may be sought.

14. Advice on the guidance for making a claim set out in this Brief should be sought from our Environmental Taxes Unit of Expertise (address and phone number below).

WHERE TO SEND THE CLAIMS

15. All claims should be sent to:

The Environmental Taxes Unit of Expertise (UoE)
HM Revenue & Customs
Dobson House
Regent Centre
Gosforth
Newcastle upon Tyne
NE3 3PF

Enquiries in relation to the submission of claims or to claims that have already been submitted to the UoE should be made by telephone to 0191 201 1749 or by email.

Commentary—*De Voil Indirect Tax Service* **V20.104**.

LANDFILL TAX INDEX

Defined words and phrases are listed separately at the end.

ACCOUNTING FOR TAX
regulations, power to make, FA 1996 s 49
ACCOUNTING PERIOD
meaning, FA 1996 ss 49, 70(1), SI 1996/1527 reg 2(1)
ACTIVE WASTE
rate of tax, PR 27/8/96, PR 30/9/96
AMOUNT OF TAX
calculating, FA 1996 s 42
qualifying material, FA 1996 ss 38(2)–(4), 63
APPEALS
agreement, settling by, FA 1996 s 56(8)
appeal tribunal, meaning, FA 1996 s 70(1)
bringing, FA 1996 s 54G
decision on review of earlier decision, against, FA 1996 s 56(2)
generally, FA 1996 ss 55–57
HMRC review, FA 1996 ss 54, 54C
nature of, FA 1996 s 54F
offer of, FA 1996 s 54A
out of time, FA 1996 s 54E
right to require, FA 1996 s 54B
time, extensions of, FA 1996 s 54D
interest on overpaid tax, repayment of, FA 1996 s 56(3)
prerequisites for making, FA 1996 s 55(2), (3)
variation powers of tribunal, restrictions on, FA 1996 s 56(6), (7)
ARREST
fraud offences, for, FA 1996 Sch 5 para 6
ASSESSMENT
combined assessments, FA 1996 s 50(3)
credit, person receiving excess, FA 1996 s 50(2)
excessive repayment, FA 1997 Sch 5 paras 14–17
further assessment necessary, FA 1996 s 50(6)
notification to representative, FA 1996 s 50(8)
power to assess, FA 1996 s 50
recovery of deemed amounts of tax, FA 1996 s 50(7)
representative of another person, FA 1996 s 50(4), (8)
review of decision, FA 1996 s 54
supplementary assessments, FA 1996 Sch 5 para 34, FA 1997 Sch 5 para 18
time for making, FA 1996 s 50(5)
time limits, FA 1996 Sch 5 para 33
AUTHORISED PERSON
meaning, FA 1996 s 70(1)

BAD DEBTS
credit for, *See under* CREDIT
regulations as to, FA 1996 s 52
BANKRUPT
carrying on the business of, FA 1996 s 58(4)
BIODIVERSITY
Tax Credit Scheme, object of, PR 1/10/03
BODY CORPORATE
controlling another body corporate, FA 1996 s 59(9)
registration, FA 1996 s 58(3)

CHARGE TO TAX
taxable disposal, on, FA 1996 s 40
CIVIL PROCEEDINGS
admissibility of computer-generated documents, FA 1996 Sch 5 para 2(6)
COLLECTION OF TAX
provisional, FA 1998 s 148
COMMISSIONERS OF CUSTOMS AND EXCISE
appeal against decisions of. *See* APPEALS
authorised person, FA 1996 s 70(1)
designation, direction or approval by, SI 1996/1527 reg 3
responsibility for landfill tax, FA 1996 s 39(2)
review of decisions, FA 1996 ss 54, 57
CONDITIONS
service, FA 1996 Sch 5 para 39
CONDUCT
meaning, FA 1996 s 70(1)
CONTAMINATED LAND
certificate as to—
cessation, FA 1996 s 43B(4)(*b*)
clearing of pollutants, FA 1996 s 43B(9)
conditions, issued subject to, FA 1996 ss 43B(3), 54(*bb*)
effective date of, FA 1996 s 43B(4)(*a*)
issue, FA 1996 s 43B(1)
refusal of application for, FA 1996 ss 43B(2), 54(1)(*ba*)
variation, FA 1996 s 43B(5)(*a*)
withdrawal, FA 1996 s 43B(5)(*b*), (6)–(12)
clearance, PR 5/6/97
exempt disposal, FA 1996 s 43A, PR 21/3/96
removal of material from, FA 1996 s 43A
CONTRACT
adjustment of payment under, FA 1996 Sch 5 para 45, PR 21/3/96
CREDIT
bad debts, for—
amount of credit, SI 1996/1527 reg 24
attribution of payments, SI 1996/1527 reg 27
customer, meaning, SI 1996/1527 reg 22
entitlement to credit for, SI 1996/1527 reg 23
evidence required in support of claim, SI 1996/1527 reg 25
generally, FA 1996 s 52
outstanding amount, meaning, SI 1996/1527 reg 22
records to be kept, SI 1996/1527 reg 26
relevant disposal, meaning, SI 1996/1527 reg 22
repayment of credit, SI 1996/1527 reg 28
security, meaning, SI 1996/1527 reg 22

Landfill Tax

CREDIT – *contd*
bad debts, for – *contd*
writing off bad debts, SI 1996/1527 reg 29
biodiversity related object, PR 1/10/03
bodies concerned with the environment—
approved bodies, obligations of, SI 1996/1527 reg 33A
Commissioners' functions, SI 1996/1527 reg 35
eligibility for approval, SI 1996/1527 reg 33
entitlement to credit, SI 1996/1527 reg 31
generally, SI 1996/1527 reg 30
regulatory body, functions of, SI 1996/1527 reg 34
relevant credit, meaning, SI 1996/1527 reg 36(8)(*c*)
repayment of credit, SI 1996/1527 reg 36
claim in return, SI 1996/1527 reg 19
enforced removal condition, satisfaction of, SI 1996/1527 reg 21(4)
entitlement to, SI 1996/1527 reg 21
environmental bodies, for payments to, FA 1996 s 53
maximum, increase in, PR 19/3/2004
payments in respect of, SI 1996/1527 reg 20
regulations as to—
generally, FA 1996 s 51
scope, SI 1996/1527 reg 18
relevant accounting period, meaning, SI 1996/1527 reg 17
relevant amount, meaning, SI 1996/1527 reg 17
relevant tax, meaning, SI 1996/1527 reg 17
removal of waste to other site, for, PR 5/4/05
reuse condition, satisfaction of, SI 1996/1527 reg 21(2)
tax credit scheme, changes to, PR 20/12/02, PR 21/2/03
transfer of going concern, FA 1996 s 58(6)

CRIMINAL PROCEEDINGS
admissibility of computer-generated documents, FA 1996 Sch 5 para 2(6)

DECEASED PERSON
carrying on the business of, FA 1996 s 58(4)

DILIGENCE
recovery of tax, FA 1996 Sch 5 para 13(2)–(6), FA 1997 s 52, SI 1996/1527 reg 49

DIRECTIONS
service, FA 1996 Sch 5 para 39

DISPOSAL
landfill. *See* LANDFILL DISPOSAL
taxable disposal. *See* TAXABLE DISPOSAL
temporary—
disposals treated as made at certain times, SI 1996/1527 reg 40
exempt disposals, SI 1996/1527 reg 39, ESC 10.3
regulations, scope and effect, SI 1996/1527 reg 38
storage or sorting, for, ESC 10.3
waste. *See* DISPOSAL OF WASTE

DISPOSAL OF WASTE. ***See also*** **LANDFILL DISPOSAL**
benefiting from or making use of the material, FA 1996 s 64(2)
contaminated land, from restoration of, PR 21/3/96, PR 5/6/97
generally, FA 1996 s 64

DISPOSAL OF WASTE – *contd*
landfill site, at, FA 1996 s 40(3)
meaning, FA 1996 s 64(1)
mines and quarry waste, exemption for, PR 21/3/96
on behalf of another person, FA 1996 s 64(3), (4)

DISTRESS
recovery of tax, FA 1996 Sch 5 para 13(1), FA 1997 s 51, SI 1996/1527 reg A48, SI 1997/1431

DOCUMENTS
disclosure, etc, FA 1996 Sch 5 para 3
removal, FA 1996 Sch 5 paras 8–9

DREDGING
exemption from tax, PR 21/3/96

EARTH
meaning, FA 1996 s 65(8)

ENTRY AND SEARCH
arrest, powers of, FA 1996 Sch 5 para 6
documents etc, removal of, FA 1996 Sch 5 paras 8–9
power to search, entry and inspection, FA 1996 Sch 5 para 4

ENVIRONMENT AGENCY
meaning, FA 1996 s 70(1)

EVASION
penalties, FA 1996 Sch 5 paras 15(1), (2), (5), (6), 16(1), (2), (6), 18, 19

EVIDENCE
admissibility of computer-generated documents, FA 1996 Sch 5 para 2(6)
certificate of Commissioners, by, FA 1996 Sch 5 para 37

FOUNDRY SAND
tax on, PR 18/9/96, ESC 5.1

FRAUD
offence, FA 1996 Sch 5 para 15(1)–(5)
penalties, FA 1996 Sch 5 paras 15(3)–(5), 16(3), (4), 18(1)

GROUP OF COMPANIES
generally, FA 1996 s 59
liability to tax, FA 1996 s 59(1)
representative member—
liabilities of, FA 1996 s 59(1)
tax due from, liability for, FA 1996 s 59(1)
taxable activities, carrying out, FA 1996 s 59(1)
UK, having place of business in, FA 1996 s 59(3)
two or more bodies, treated as members of, FA 1996 s 59(2)–(9)

INACTIVE MATERIAL
listing, FA 1996 s 42(4)
rate of tax, PR 27/8/96, PR 30/9/96

INCAPACITATED PERSON
carrying on the business of, FA 1996 s 58(4)

INERT MATERIAL
listing, FA 1996 s 42(4)

INFORMATION
disclosure—
Commissioners, by, FA 1996 Sch 5 para 35
documents, FA 1996 Sch 5 para 3
generally, FA 1996 Sch 5 para 1
documents, disclosure etc, FA 1996 Sch 5 para 3
penalties for failure to comply with provisions, FA 1996 Sch 5 para 22
recorded, order for access to, FA 1996 Sch 5 para 7

INFORMATION – *contd*
records, making and keeping, FA 1996 Sch 5 para 2
INFORMATION NOTES
landfill tax, concerning, PR 27/8/96
INTEREST
assessment as to, FA 1996 Sch 5 para 32
Commissioners, payable by, FA 1996 s 197, Sch 5 paras 29, 30
no deduction for, TA 1988 s 827(1C)
rate of, 1998/1461
under-declared tax, on, FA 1996 s 197, Sch 5 para 26
unpaid tax etc, on, FA 1996 Sch 5 paras 27–28
INVOICES
amounts shown as tax on, FA 1996 Sch 5 para 44
contents, SI 1996/1527 reg 37

LAND
meaning, FA 1996 s 65(7)
LANDFILL CONTRACT
meaning, FA 1996 Sch 5 para 45(3)
LANDFILL DISPOSAL
generally, FA 1996 s 65
meaning, FA 1996 s 70(2)
prescribed landfill site activities treated as, FA 1996 s 65A
weight of material disposed of, calculating—
agreed methods, SI 1996/1527 reg 44
basic method, SI 1996/1527 reg 42
generally, FA 1996 s 68
regulations, scope of, SI 1996/1527 reg 41
specified methods, SI 1996/1527 reg 43
LANDFILL INVOICE
meaning, FA 1996 s 61(2)
LANDFILL SITE
activities treated as disposals, FA 1996 s 65A
controller—
meaning, FA 1996 Sch 5 para 48
secondary liability, FA 1996 Sch 5 Pt VIII
exemptions, extension of, PR 5/4/05
meaning, FA 1996 s 66
operator of. *See* LANDFILL SITE OPERATOR
quarries, FA 1996 s 44A
restoration, FA 1996 s 43C
re-used material, tax liability of, PR 22/3/2004
use of material on, PR 22/12/08
LANDFILL SITE OPERATOR
generally, FA 1996 s 67
liability to pay tax, FA 1996 s 41(1)
meaning, FA 1996 s 41(2)
LANDFILL TAX
generally, FA 1996 s 39, PR 30/9/96
information notes, PR 27/8/96
introduction, PR 30/9/96
lower rate, consultation exercise on scope of, PR 26/3/96
payment, SI 1996/1527 reg 15
rates, PR 27/8/96, PR 30/9/96, PR 19/3/2004
responsibility for, FA 1996 s 39(2)
secondary liability, FA 1996 Sch 5 Pt VIII
LANDFILL TAX ACCOUNT
duty to keep, SI 1996/1527 reg 12(1)
form etc, SI 1996/1527 reg 12(2)
LIABILITY TO TAX
landfill site operator, FA 1996 s 41
secondary, FA 1996 Sch 5 Pt VIII
LIQUIDATION
carrying on the business of a person in, FA 1996 s 58(4)

LOCAL AUTHORITY
meaning, FA 1996 s 70(2A)

MATERIAL
disposal. *See* LANDFILL DISPOSAL; TAXABLE DISPOSAL
meaning, FA 1996 s 70(1)
qualifying, FA 1996 s 42(3), SI 1996/1528 arts 1–8, Schedule
MISDECLARATION
penalties, FA 1996 Sch 5 para 20

NEGLECT
penalties, FA 1996 Sch 5 para 20
NORTHERN IRELAND
site operators, record-keeping requirements, PR 19/3/2004
NOTICES
service, FA 1996 Sch 5 para 38
NOTIFICATION
service, FA 1996 Sch 5 para 38

OFFENCES
criminal offences, FA 1996 Sch 5 para 15
penalties. *See* PENALTIES
ORDERS
defining taxable disposals, FA 1996 s 46
power to make, FA 1996 s 71
OVERPAID TAX
claims for, SI 1996/1527 reg 14
recovery, FA 1996 Sch 5 para 14
time limit for recovery, PR 21/3/96

PARTNERSHIP
registration, FA 1996 s 58(2)
regulations as to, FA 1996 s 58(1)
representation of, SI 1996/1527 reg 8
PENALTIES
assessments to, FA 1996 Sch 5 para 32
breach of regulations, for, FA 1996 Sch 5 para 23
civil penalties, FA 1996 Sch 5 paras 18–25
criminal, FA 1996 Sch 5 paras 15–17
deception, FA 1996 Sch 5 paras 15(3), (4), (5), 16(3), (4), 18(1)
evasion of tax, FA 1996 Sch 5 paras 15(1), (2), (5), (6), 16(1), (2), (6), 18, 19
failure to register, FA 1996 Sch 5 para 21
information provisions, failure to comply with, FA 1996 Sch 5 para 22
misdeclaration or neglect, FA 1996 Sch 5 para 20
mitigation, FA 1996 Sch 5 para 25
no deduction for, TA 1988 s 827(1C)
security, failure to provide, FA 1996 Sch 5 paras 15(7), 16(7), 31
walking possession agreements, breach of, FA 1996 Sch 5 para 24
PETS
disposal of remains, FA 1996 s 45
PREFERENTIAL DEBTS
recovery of tax, SI 1989/2405 art 346(1), Sch 4 para 3B

QUALIFYING MATERIAL
generally, FA 1996 s 63
meaning, FA 1996 s 42(3)
QUARRY
qualifying landfill sites, FA 1996 s 44A

RATE OF TAX
active waste, PR 27/8/96
foundry sand, for, PR 18/9/96, ESC 5.1
inactive waste, PR 27/8/96
RECEIPTS
destination, FA 1996 Sch 5 para 41

RECEIVERSHIP
carrying on the business of a person in, FA 1996 s 58(4)
RECORDS
making and keeping, FA 1996 Sch 5 para 2, SI 1996/1527 reg 16, PR 21/3/96
RECOVERY OF TAX
distress and diligence, FA 1996 Sch 5 para 13
generally, FA 1996 Sch 5 para 11
overpaid tax, FA 1996 Sch 5 para 14
preferential debts, SI 1989/2405 art 346(1), Sch 4 para 3B
REGISTER OF TAXABLE PERSONS *See also* REGISTRATION
cancellation of registration—
generally, FA 1996 s 47(6)–(8)
transfer of going concern, following, SI 1996/1527 reg 7
cessation of taxable activities, FA 1996 s 47(4), (6), SI 1996/1527 reg 6
Commissioners, matters to be notified to, FA 1996 s 47(3), (4)
contents, FA 1996 s 47(1)
information requirements, FA 1996 s 48
persons registrable, FA 1996 s 47(2)
publication of information, FA 1996 Sch 5 para 36
registrable person, FA 1996 s 47(10)
regulations in respect of, power to make, FA 1996 ss 47(9), 48
time for registration, FA 1996 s 47(5)
REGISTRATION
application forms, SI 1996/1527 Schedule
bankruptcy or incapacity of registrable person, SI 1996/1527 reg 9
liability to be registered—
change in particulars following notification of, SI 1996/1527 reg 5
generally, SI 1996/1527 reg 4
notification provisions—
cessation of taxable activities, SI 1996/1527 reg 6
change in particulars, SI 1996/1527 reg 5
liability to be registered, SI 1996/1527 reg 4
partnership, SI 1996/1527 reg 8
unincorporated body, SI 1996/1527 reg 8
penalty for failure to register, FA 1996 Sch 5 para 21
register. *See* REGISTER OF TAXABLE PERSONS
transfer of going concern, SI 1996/1527 reg 7
unincorporated body, representation of, SI 1996/1527 reg 8
REGULATIONS
accounting for tax, FA 1996 s 49
bad debts, as to, FA 1996 s 52
bankrupt's business, carrying on, FA 1996 s 58(4)
credit, provision of, FA 1996 s 51
deceased person, carrying on the business of, FA 1996 s 58(4)
distress and diligence, FA 1996 Sch 5 para 13(1), (6)
environmental bodies, as to credit for payments to, FA 1996 s 53
incapacitated person, carrying on the business of, FA 1996 s 58(4)
information provisions, FA 1996 s 48
liquidation, carrying on the business of a person in, FA 1996 s 58(4)
partnerships, FA 1996 s 58(1)
penalties for breach of, FA 1996 Sch 5 para 23
power to make, FA 1996 s 71
REGULATIONS – *contd*
receivership, carrying on the business of a person in, FA 1996 s 58(4)
records, as to making and keeping, FA 1996 Sch 5 para 2
registration etc of taxable persons, FA 1996 s 47(9)
set-off, as to, FA 1996 Sch 5 paras 42, 43
time for payment, FA 1996 s 49
transfer of business as going concern, FA 1996 s 58(5)
unincorporated body, FA 1996 s 58(1)
weight of material disposed of, determining, FA 1996 s 68
RENT
adjustment, FA 1996 Sch 5 para 46, PR 21/3/96
REPAYMENT OF TAX
transfer of going concern, FA 1996 s 58(6)
unjust enrichment, FA 1997 Sch 5 Part I
REQUIREMENT
service, FA 1996 Sch 5 para 38
RETURNS
errors, correction of, SI 1996/1527 reg 13
failure to make, assessment following, FA 1996 s 50(1)
form, SI 1996/1527 Schedule
incomplete or incorrect, FA 1996 s 50(1)
landfill tax account. *See* LANDFILL TAX ACCOUNT
making, SI 1996/1527 reg 11
overdeclaration, meaning, SI 1996/1527 reg 13(1)
underdeclaration, meaning, SI 1996/1527 reg 13(1)
verification of, failure to keep documents or afford necessary facilities, FA 1996 s 50(1)

SAMPLES
disposal, FA 1996 Sch 5 para 10(2)
power to take, FA 1996 Sch 5 para 10(1)
SCOTTISH ENVIRONMENT PROTECTION AGENCY
meaning, FA 1996 s 70(1)
SECURITY FOR TAX
notice of requirement, PR April 2008
penalty for failure to provide, FA 1996 Sch 5 paras 15(7), 16(7)
provision, FA 1996 Sch 5 para 31
SERVICE OF NOTICES
generally, FA 1996 Sch 5 para 38
SET-OFF
Commissioners—
tax owed by, SI 1996/1527 reg 46
tax owed to, SI 1996/1527 reg 45
generally, FA 1996 Sch 5 paras 42, 43
insolvency procedure applied, situation where, SI 1996/1527 reg 47
SPECIFICATIONS
service, FA 1996 Sch 5 para 39

TAXABLE ACTIVITY
carrying out, FA 1996 s 69
meaning, FA 1996 s 69(1)
TAXABLE DISPOSAL
exclusion—
contaminated land, material removed from, FA 1996 ss 43A, 43B
material removed from water, FA 1996 s 43
mining and quarrying material, FA 1996 s 44
pet cemeteries, FA 1996 s 45
quarries, FA 1996 s 44A
site restoration, FA 1996 s 43C
temporary disposals, ESC 10.3
Treasury order, by, FA 1996 s 46

WORDS AND PHRASES

Words in brackets indicate the context in which the word or phrase is used.

accounting period, FA 1996 ss 49, 70(1), SI 1996/1527 reg 2(1)
appeal tribunal, FA 1996 s 70(1)
authorised person, FA 1996 s 70(1)

claim, SI 1996/1527 reg 22
Collector, SI 1996/1527 reg 2(1)
Commissioners, the, FA 1996 s 70(1)
conduct, FA 1996 s 70(1)
contributing third party, SI 1996/1527 reg 30
controller, FA 1996 Sch 5 para 48
credit, SI 1996/1527 reg 2(1)
customer, SI 1996/1527 reg 22

development corporation, FA 1996 s 43(6)
disposal, SI 1996/1527 reg 2(1)
disposal of material as waste, FA 1996 s 64(1)
disposal of material by way of landfill, FA 1996 s 65(1)

earth, FA 1996 s 65(8)
effective date of registration, SI 1996/1527 reg 2(1)
Environment Agency, FA 1996 s 70(1)
established rate, SI 1998/1461 reg 2(1)

group of companies, FA 1996 s 59(2)

Highlands and Islands Enterprise, FA 1996 s 43(6)

Job Band, SI 1996/1527 reg A48

land, FA 1996 s 65(7)
landfill disposal, FA 1996 s 70(2)
landfill invoice, FA 1996 s 61(2), SI 1996/1527 reg 37
landfill site, FA 1996 s 66
landfill site operator, FA 1996 s 41(2)
landfill tax, FA 1996 s 39(1)
landfill tax account, SI 1996/1527 reg 12
landfill tax bad debt account, SI 1996/1527 reg 26

local authority, FA 1996 s 70(2A)

material, FA 1996 s 70(1)

non-qualifying process, FA 1996 s 44(5)

outstanding amounts, SI 1996/1527 reg 22
overdeclaration, SI 1996/1527 reg 13(1)

prescribed, FA 1996 s 70(1)

qualifying material, FA 1996 s 42(3)
quarter, SI 1996/1527 reg 2(1)

register, SI 1996/1527 reg 2(1)
registered person, SI 1996/1527 reg 2(1)
registrable person, FA 1996 ss 47(10), 70(1)
registration, SI 1996/1527 reg 2(1)
registration number, SI 1996/1527 reg 2(1)
relevant accounting period, SI 1996/1527 reg 17
relevant amount, SI 1996/1527 reg 17
relevant disposal, SI 1996/1527 reg 22
relevant tax, SI 1996/1527 reg 17
restoration, FA 1996 s 43C
return, SI 1996/1527 reg 11
running costs, SI 1996/1527 reg 30

Scottish Enterprise, FA 1996 s 43(6)
Scottish Environment Protection Agency, FA 1996 s 70(1)
security, SI 1996/1527 reg 22

tax, FA 1996 s 70(1)
taxable activity, FA 1996 s 69(1)
taxable business, SI 1996/1527 reg 2(1)
taxable disposal, FA 1996 ss 40, 70(1)
taxable landfill contract, FA 1996 Sch 5 para 15(8)
transfer note, SI 1996/1527 reg 2(1), SI 1996/1528 art 8
trustee in bankruptcy, FA 1996 s 50(10)

underdeclaration, SI 1996/1527 reg 13(1)

waste management practices, SI 1996/1527 reg 33(5)
working day, SI 1996/1527 reg 2(1)

AGGREGATES LEVY

CONTENTS

PROVISIONAL COLLECTION OF TAXES ACT 1968

(1968 Chapter 2)

1 Temporary statutory effect of House of Commons resolutions …

(1) This section applies only to … [aggregates levy][7]…

(1A) …[2]

(2) Subject to that, and to the provisions of subsections (4) to (8) below, where the House of Commons passes a resolution which—

(*a*) provides for the renewal for a further period of any tax in force or imposed during the previous financial year (whether at the same or a different rate, and whether with or without modifications) or for the variation or abolition of any existing tax, and

(*b*) contains a declaration that it is expedient in the public interest that the resolution should have statutory effect under the provisions of this Act,

the resolution shall, for the period specified in the next following subsection, have statutory effect as if contained in an Act of Parliament and, where the resolution provides for the renewal of a tax, all enactments which were in force with reference to that tax as last imposed by Act of Parliament shall during that period have full force and effect with respect to the tax as renewed by the resolution.

In this section references to the renewal of a tax include references to its reimposition, and references to the abolition of a tax include references to its repeal.

(3) The said period is—

(*a*) in the case of a resolution passed in [November or December][3] in any year, one expiring with [5th May in the next calendar year][4];

[(*aa*) in the case of a resolution passed in February or March in any year, one expiring with 5th August in the same calendar year; and][6]

(*b*) in the case of any other resolution, one expiring at the end of four months after the date on which it is expressed to take effect or, if no such date is expressed, after the date on which it is passed.

(4) A resolution shall cease to have statutory effect under this section unless within the next [thirty][5] days on which the House of Commons sits after the day on which the resolution is passed—

(*a*) a Bill renewing, varying or, as the case may be, abolishing the tax is read a second time by the House, or

(*b*) a Bill is amended by the House [in Committee or on Report, or by any [Public Bill Committee][8] of the House][1] so as to include provision for the renewal, variation or, as the case may be, abolition of the tax.

(5) a resolution shall also cease to have statutory effect under this section if—

(*a*) the provisions giving effect to it are rejected during the passage of the Bill containing them through the House, or

(*b*) an Act comes into operation renewing, varying or, as the case may be, abolishing the tax, or

(*c*) Parliament is dissolved or prorogued.

(6) Where, in the case of a resolution providing for the renewal or variation of a tax, the resolution ceases to have statutory effect by virtue of subsection (4) or (5) above, or the period specified in subsection (3) above terminates, before an Act comes into operation renewing or varying the tax, any money paid in pursuance of the resolution shall be repaid or made good, and any deduction made in pursuance of the resolution shall be deemed to be an unauthorised deduction.

(7) Where any tax as renewed or varied by a resolution is modified by the Act renewing or varying the tax, any money paid in pursuance of the resolution which would not have been payable under the new conditions affecting the tax shall be repaid or made good, and any deduction made in pursuance of the resolution shall, so far as it would not have been authorised under the new conditions affecting the tax, be deemed to be an unauthorised deduction.

(8) When during any session a resolution has had statutory effect under this section, statutory effect shall not be again given under this section in the same session to the same resolution or to a resolution having the same effect.

Note—Words omitted from the heading and sub-s (1) are not relevant for the purposes of aggregates levy.

Amendments—[1] Words in sub-s (4)(*b*) added by FA 1968 s 60.

[2] Sub-s (1A) repealed by FA 1993 ss 205(3), 213, Sch 23 Pt VI in relation to resolutions passed after 27 July 1993.

[3] Words in sub-s (3)(*a*) substituted for the words "March or April" by FA 1993 s 205 (4), (7) in relation to resolutions passed after 27 July 1993.

[4] Words in sub-s (3)(*a*) substituted for the words "5th August in the same calendar year" by FA 1993 s 205 (4), (7) in relation to resolutions passed after 27 July 1993.

[5] Word in sub-s (4) substituted for the word "twenty-five" by FA 1993 s 205(5), (7) in relation to resolutions passed after 27 July 1993.

[6] Words in sub-s (3) inserted by F(No 2)A 1997 s 50 in relation to resolutions passed after 31 July 1997.

[7] Words in sub-s (1) inserted by FA 2001 s 49(1) with effect from 11 May 2001.

[8] Words in sub-s (4)(*b*) substituted by FA 2007 s 112(1) with effect from 19 July 2007.

INCOME AND CORPORATION TAXES ACT 1988

(1988 Chapter 1)

827 VAT penalties etc

…

[(1E) Where a person is liable to make a payment by way of—

(a) any penalty under any provision of Part 2 of the Finance Act 2001 (aggregates levy),

(b) interest under any of paragraphs 5 to 9 of Schedule 5 to that Act (interest on aggregates levy due and on interest),

(c) interest under paragraph 6 of Schedule 8 to that Act (interest on recoverable overpayments etc), or

(d) interest under paragraph 5 of Schedule 10 to that Act (interest on penalties),

the payment shall not be allowed as a deduction in computing any income, profits or losses [for any corporation tax purposes (but see also subsection (3)(a) below)][2] *]* [1]

…[3]

Note—Words omitted from this section are not relevant for the purposes of aggregates levy.

Amendments—[1] Sub-s (1E) inserted by FA 2001 s 49(3) with effect from 11 May 2001.

[2] Words in sub-s (1E) substituted by the Income Tax (Trading and Other Income) Act 2005, s 882(1), Sch 1, Pt 1, paras 1, 332(*a*) with effect, for the purposes of income tax for the year 2005–06 and subsequent tax years, and for the purposes of corporation tax for accounting periods ending after 5 April 2005.

[3] This section repealed by CTA 2009 ss 1322, 1326, Sch 1 paras 1, 268, Sch 3 Pt 1. CTA 2009 has effect for corporation tax purposes for accounting periods ending on or after 1 April 2009 and for income tax and capital gains tax purposes for the tax year 2009–10 and subsequent tax years.

FINANCE ACT 1996

(1996 Chapter 8)

PART VII
MISCELLANEOUS AND SUPPLEMENTAL

Miscellaneous: indirect taxation

197 Setting of rates of interest

(1) The rate of interest applicable for the purposes of an enactment to which this section applies shall be the rate which for the purposes of that enactment is provided for by regulations made by the Treasury under this section.

(2) This section applies to—

(*a*)–(*g*) …

[(*h*) the following provisions of the Finance Act 2001 (interest payable to or by the Commissioners in connection with aggregates levy), that is to say—

(i) sections 25(2)(*f*) [, 30(3)(*f*) and 42(4) to (6)][3];

(ii) [paragraphs 6 and 8(3)(*a*)][2] of Schedule 5; and

(iii) paragraphs 2 and 6(1)(*b*) of Schedule 8.][1]

(*i*) …

(3) Regulations under this section may—

(*a*) make different provision for different enactments or for different purposes of the same enactment,

(*b*) either themselves specify a rate of interest for the purposes of an enactment or make provision for any such rate to be determined, and to change from time to time, by reference to such rate or the average of such rates as may be referred to in the regulations,

(*c*) provide for rates to be reduced below, or increased above, what they otherwise would be by specified amounts or by reference to specified formulae,

(*d*) provide for rates arrived at by reference to averages or formulae to be rounded up or down,

(*e*) provide for circumstances in which changes of rates of interest are or are not to take place, and

(*f*) provide that changes of rates are to have effect for periods beginning on or after a day determined in accordance with the regulations in relation to interest running from before that day, as well as in relation to interest running from, or from after, that day.

(4) The power to make regulations under this section shall be exercisable by statutory instrument subject to annulment in pursuance of a resolution of the House of Commons.

(5) Where—

(*a*) regulations under this section provide, without specifying the rate determined in accordance with the regulations, for a new method of determining the rate applicable for the purposes of any enactment, or

(*b*) the rate which, in accordance with regulations under this section, is the rate applicable for the purposes of any enactment changes otherwise than by virtue of the making of regulations specifying a new rate,

the Commissioners of Customs and Excise shall make an order specifying the new rate and the day from which, in accordance with the regulations, it has effect.

(6) …

(7) Subsections (1) and (6) above shall have effect for periods beginning on or after such day as the Treasury may by order made by statutory instrument appoint and shall have effect in relation to interest running from before that day, as well as in relation to interest running from, or from after, that day; and different days may be appointed under this subsection for different purposes.

Commentary—*De Voil Indirect Tax Service* **V5.196, V5.361–5.365**.
Note—Sub-ss (2)(*a*)–(*g*), (*i*), (6) are not relevant to aggregates levy.
Sub-s (1) has effect for periods beginning on or after 1 April 1997 (see FA 1996 s 197 (Appointed Day) Order, SI 1997/1015).
Amendments—[1] Sub-s (2)(*h*) inserted by FA 2001 s 49(2) with effect from 11 May 2001.
[2] Words in sub-s (2)(*h*) substituted by FA 2002 s 132(2), (3). This amendment is deemed to have come into force on 1 April 2002.
[3] In sub-s (2)(*h*)(i), words substituted for words "and 30(3)(*f*)" by the Transfer of Tribunal Functions and Revenue and Customs Appeals Order, SI 2009/56 art 3(1), Sch 1 paras 232, 239(1), (2)(*f*)) with effect from 1 April 2009.

FINANCE ACT 2001

(2001 Chapter 9)

ARRANGEMENT OF SECTIONS

PART 2
AGGREGATES LEVY

Charging provisions

Administration and enforcement

Credits and repayments

Non-resident taxpayers

Other special cases

An Act to grant certain duties, to alter other duties, and to amend the law relating to the National Debt and the Public Revenue, and to make further provision in connection with Finance.

[11 May 2001]

PART 2
AGGREGATES LEVY

Charging provisions

16 Charge to aggregates levy

(1) [A tax][1], to be known as aggregates levy, shall be charged in accordance with this Part on aggregate subjected to commercial exploitation.

(2) The charge to the levy shall arise whenever a quantity of taxable aggregate is subjected, on or after the commencement date, to commercial exploitation in the United Kingdom.

(3) The person charged with the levy arising on any occasion on a quantity of aggregate subjected to commercial exploitation shall be the person responsible for its being so subjected on that occasion.

(4) The levy shall be charged at the rate of [£2][2] per tonne of aggregate subjected to commercial exploitation; and the amount of levy charged on a part of a tonne of aggregate shall be the proportionately reduced amount.

(5) The levy shall be under the care and management of the Commissioners of Customs and Excise (in this Part referred to as "the Commissioners").

(6) In this Part "the commencement date" means such date as the Treasury may by order made by statutory instrument appoint for the purposes of this section.

Regulations—Finance Act 2001, section 16, (Appointed Day) Order, SI 2002/809 (the date appointed as the commencement date for the purposes of this section is 1 April 2002).

Simon's Tax Cases—*C&E Comrs v East Midlands Aggregates Ltd* [2004] STC 1582.

Amendments—[1] Words in sub-s (1) substituted by FA 2002 s 132(1), (3), Sch 38 para (2). These amendments are deemed to have come into force on 1 April 2002.

[2] In sub-s (4), figure substituted for previous figure "£1.95" by FA 2008 s 20 with effect in relation to aggregate subjected to commercial exploitation on or after 1 April 2009.

17 Meanings of "aggregate" and "taxable aggregate"

(1) In this Part "aggregate" means (subject to section 18 below) any rock, gravel or sand, together with whatever substances are for the time being incorporated in the rock, gravel or sand or naturally occur mixed with it.

(2) For the purposes of this Part any quantity of aggregate is, in relation to any occasion on which it is subjected to commercial exploitation, a quantity of taxable aggregate except to the extent that—

(*a*) it is exempt under this section;

(*b*) it has previously been used for construction purposes (whether before or after the commencement date);

(*c*) it is, or derives from, any aggregate that has already been subjected to a charge to aggregates levy;

[(*d*) it is aggregate that on the commencement date is on a site other than—

(i) its originating site; or

(ii) a site that is required to be registered under the name of a person who is the operator, or one of the operators, of that originating site.][4]

(3) For the purposes of this Part aggregate is exempt under this section if—

(*a*) …[3]

(*b*) it consists wholly of aggregate won by being removed from the ground on the site of any building or proposed building in the course of excavations lawfully carried out—

(i) in connection with the modification or erection of the building; and

(ii) exclusively for the purpose of laying foundations or of laying any pipe or cable;

(*c*) it consists wholly of aggregate won—

(i) by being removed from the bed of any river, canal or watercourse (whether natural or artificial) or of any channel in or approach to any port or harbour (whether natural or artificial); and

(ii) in the course of the carrying out of any dredging undertaken exclusively for the purpose of creating, restoring, improving or maintaining that river, canal, watercourse, channel or approach;

(*d*) it consists wholly of aggregate won by being removed from the ground along the line or proposed line of any highway or proposed highway and in the course of excavations carried out—

(i) for the purpose of improving or maintaining the highway or of constructing the proposed highway; and

(ii) [not][4] for the purpose of extracting that aggregate; …[5]

[(*da*) it consists wholly of aggregate won by being removed from the ground along the line or proposed line of any railway, tramway or monorail or proposed railway, tramway or monorail and in the course of excavations carried out—

(i) for the purpose of improving or maintaining the railway, tramway or monorail or of constructing the proposed railway, tramway or monorail; and

(ii) not for the purpose of extracting that aggregate;][6]

(*e*) it consists wholly of the spoil, waste or other by-products[, not including the overburden,][2] resulting from the extraction or other separation from any quantity of aggregate of any china clay or ball clay; [or][5]

[(*f*) it consists wholly of the spoil from any process by which—

(i) coal, lignite, slate or shale; or

(ii) a substance listed in section 18(3) below,

has been separated from other rock after being extracted or won with that other rock;][2]

(4) For the purposes of this Part a quantity of any aggregate shall be taken to be a quantity of aggregate that is exempt under this section if it consists wholly or mainly of any one or more of the following, or is part of anything so consisting, namely—

(*a*) coal, lignite, slate or shale;

(*b*) …[2]

(*c*) the spoil or waste from, or other by-products of—

(i) any industrial combustion process, or

(ii) the smelting or refining of metal;

(*d*) the drill-cuttings resulting from any operations carried out in accordance with a licence granted under the Petroleum Act 1998 [or the Petroleum (Production) Act (Northern Ireland) 1964][4] …[4];

(*e*) anything resulting from works carried out in exercise of powers which are required to be exercised in accordance with, or are conferred by, provision made by or under the New Roads and Street Works Act 1991, the Roads (Northern Ireland) Order 1993 or the Street Works (Northern Ireland) Order 1995;

(*f*) clay, soil or vegetable or other organic matter.

(5) For the purposes of this section aggregate subjected to exploitation in the United Kingdom is aggregate that has already been subjected to a charge to aggregates levy if, and only if—

(*a*) there has been a previous occasion on which a charge to aggregates levy on that aggregate has arisen; and
(*b*) at least some of the aggregates levy previously charged on that aggregate is either—
(i) levy in respect of which there is or was no entitlement to a tax credit; or
(ii) levy in respect of which any entitlement to a tax credit is or was an entitlement to a tax credit of an amount less than the amount of the levy charged on it.

(6) For the purposes of subsection (5)(*b*) above, any credit the entitlement to which arises in a case which—
(*a*) falls within section 30(1)(*c*) [or 30A][1] below, and
(*b*) is prescribed for the purposes of this subsection,
shall be disregarded.

(7) In this section—
"coal" has the same meaning as in the Coal Industry Act 1994; and
"highway" includes any road within the meaning of the Roads (Scotland) Act 1984 or the Road Traffic (Northern Ireland) Order 1995.

Simon's Tax Cases—*C&E Comrs v East Midlands Aggregates Ltd* [2004] STC 1582.
Amendments—[1] Words in sub-s (6)(*a*) inserted by FA 2002 s 129(2) with effect from 24 July 2002.
[2] Words in sub-s (3)(*e*) inserted, sub-s (3)(*f*) inserted, and sub-s (4)(*b*) repealed, by FA 2002 ss 130, 141, Sch 40 Pt 4(3). These amendments are deemed to have come into force on 1 April 2002.
[3] Sub-s (3)(*a*) repealed by FA 2002 ss 131(1), (4), 141, Sch 40 Pt 4(3). This amendment is deemed to have come into force on 1 April 2002.
[4] Sub-s (2)(*d*) substituted, words in sub-s (3)(*d*) substituted, and in sub-s (4)(*d*), words inserted and repealed, by FA 2002 ss 132(1), (3), 141, Sch 38 para 3, Sch 40 Pt 4(3). These amendments are deemed to have come into force on 1 April 2002.
[5] In sub-s (3) word "or" in para (*d*) repealed, and word in para (*e*) inserted, by FA 2007 ss 22(1), (2), (4), 114, Sch 27 Pt 1(1) with effect from 19 July 2007.
[6] Sub-s (3)(*da*) inserted by FA 2007 s 22(1), (3), (5) with effect from 1 August 2007 (by virtue of the Finance Act 2007 section 22(3) (Appointed Day) Order, SI 2007/2118 art 2).

18 Exempt processes

(1) In this Part references to aggregate—
(*a*) include references to the spoil, waste, off-cuts and other by-products resulting from the application of any exempt process to any aggregate; but
(*b*) do not include references to anything else resulting from the application of any such process to any aggregate.

(2) In this Part "exempt process" means—
(*a*) the cutting of any rock to produce [stone with one or more flat surfaces][1];
(*b*) any process by which a relevant substance is extracted or otherwise separated (whether as part of the process of winning it from any land or otherwise) from any aggregate;
(*c*) any process for the production of lime or cement from limestone or from limestone and [anything else][2].

(3) In this section "relevant substance" means any of the following—
(*a*) anhydrite;
(*b*) ball clay;
(*c*) barytes;
(*d*) …[2];
(*e*) china clay;
(*f*) feldspar;
(*g*) fireclay;
(*h*) …[2];
(*i*) fluorspar;
(*j*) fuller's earth;
(*k*) gems and semi-precious stones;
(*l*) gypsum;
(*m*) any metal or the ore of any metal;
(*n*) muscovite;
(*o*) perlite;
(*p*) potash;
(*q*) pumice;
(*r*) rock phosphates;
(*s*) sodium chloride;
(*t*) talc;
(*u*) vermiculite.

(4) The Treasury may by order made by statutory instrument—
(*a*) modify the list of substances in subsection (3) above by adding any substance to that list or by removing any substance from it; and
(*b*) make any such transitional provision in connection with the modification of that list under this subsection as they may think fit.

(5) The Treasury shall not make an order under subsection (4) above by virtue of which any substance ceases to be a relevant substance unless a draft of the order has been laid before Parliament and approved by resolution of the House of Commons.

(6) A statutory instrument containing an order under subsection (4) above that has not had to be approved in draft for the purposes of subsection (5) above shall be subject to annulment in pursuance of a resolution of the House of Commons.

Amendments—[1] Words in sub-s (2)(*a*) substituted by FA 2002 s 131(2), (4). This amendment is deemed to have come into force on 1 April 2002.

[2] Words in sub-s (2)(*c*) substituted, and words in sub-s (3)(*d*) and (*h*) repealed, by FA 2002 ss 132(1), (3), 141, Sch 38 para 4, Sch 40 Pt 4(3). These amendments are deemed to have come into force on 1 April 2002.

19 Commercial exploitation

(1) For the purposes of this Part a quantity of aggregate is subjected to exploitation if, and only if—

(*a*) it is removed from a site falling within subsection (2) below;
(*b*) it becomes subject to an agreement to supply it to any person;
(*c*) it is used for construction purposes; or
(*d*) it is mixed, otherwise than in permitted circumstances, with any material or substance other than water.

(2) The sites which, in relation to any quantity of aggregate, fall within this subsection are—

(*a*) the originating site of the aggregate;
(*b*) any site which is not the originating site of the aggregate but is registered under the name of a person [under whose name that originating site is also registered][1];
(*c*) any site not falling within paragraph (*a*) or (*b*) above to which the quantity of aggregate had been removed for the purpose of having an exempt process applied to it on that site but at which no such process has been applied to it.

(3) For the purposes of this Part the exploitation to which a quantity of aggregate is subjected shall be taken to be commercial exploitation if, and only if—

(*a*) it is subjected to exploitation in the course or furtherance of a business carried on by the person, or one of the persons, responsible for subjecting it to exploitation;
(*b*) the exploitation to which it is subjected does not consist in its removal from one registered site to another in a case where both sites are registered under the name of the same person;
(*c*) the exploitation to which it is subjected does not consist in or require its removal to a registered site for the purpose of having an exempt process applied to it on that site;
(*d*) the exploitation to which it is subjected does not consist in or require its removal to any premises for the purpose of having china clay or ball clay extracted or otherwise separated from it on that site; and
(*e*) the exploitation to which it is subjected is not such that, as a result and without its being subjected to any process involving its being mixed with any other substance or material (apart from water), it again becomes part of the land at the site from which it was won.

[(3A) For the purposes of subsection (3)(*a*) above "business" includes any activity of a Government department, local authority or charity.][1]

(4) Where, at the time when any aggregate is won from any site, the same person is in occupation of both—

(*a*) that site, and
(*b*) [other land][1] which is occupied, together with that site—
 (i) for the purposes of the carrying on of any agricultural business, or
 (ii) for the purposes of the carrying on of any forestry business or otherwise for the purposes of forestry,

subsection (3)(*e*) above shall have effect as if the reference to the land at the site from which the aggregate was won included the [other land][1], so long as it and that site continue to be occupied by that person for such purposes.

(5) For the purposes of this Part where a quantity of aggregate is subjected to exploitation, the exploitation shall be taken to be in the United Kingdom if, and only if, the aggregate is in the United Kingdom or United Kingdom waters when it is subjected to exploitation.

(6) For the purposes of this section a quantity of aggregate becomes subject to an agreement to supply it to any person—

(*a*) except to the extent that it is not separately identifiable at the time when the agreement is entered into, at that time; and
(*b*) to that extent, at the time when it is appropriated to the agreement;

but references in this Part to the supply of a quantity of aggregate do not include references to any supply which is effected, or is to be effected, by the transfer or creation of any interest or right in or over land.

(7) For the purposes of this section a quantity of aggregate is mixed with a material or substance in permitted circumstances if—

(*a*) the material or substance with which it is mixed consists wholly of a quantity of taxable aggregate that has not previously been subjected to commercial exploitation in the United Kingdom; and

(*b*) the mixing takes place on a site which, in a case where it falls within subsection (2) above in relation to any part of the aggregate included in the mixture, so falls in relation to every part of it.

Simon's Tax Cases—*C&E Comrs v East Midlands Aggregates Ltd* [2004] STC 1582.

Amendments—[1] Words in sub-ss (2), (4) substituted, and sub-s (3A) inserted, by FA 2002 s 132(1), (3), Sch 38 para 5. These amendments are deemed to have come into force on 1 April 2002.

20 Originating sites

(1) In this Part references, in relation to any aggregate, to its originating site are references (subject to subsection (2) below)—

(*a*) in the case of aggregate which has been won from the seabed of any area of sea in the United Kingdom or United Kingdom waters ...[1], to the site where it is first landed after being so won;

(*b*) in the case of aggregate which results from the application of an exempt process to any aggregate ...[1], to the site where that process was so applied;

(*c*) ...[1]

(*d*) in any other case, to the site from which the aggregate was won or, as the case may be, from which it was most recently won.

(2) Where any aggregate which is on its originating site on the commencement date has been mixed before that date with aggregate the originating site of which would (but for this subsection) be different, the site where the mixture is situated on that date shall be deemed for the purposes of this Part to be the originating site of all the aggregate comprised in the mixture.

Amendments—[1] Words in sub-s (1)(*a*), (*b*) repealed, and sub-s (1)(*c*) repealed, by FA 2002 ss 131(3)(*a*), (4), 141, Sch 40 Pt 4(3). These amendments are deemed to have come into force on 1 April 2002.

21 Operators of sites

(1) For the purposes of this Part the persons operating a site are each of the following—

(*a*) the person who occupies the site; and

(*b*) if a person other than the occupier exercises any right to exercise control over aggregate on that site, that other person;

and "operator", in relation to a site, shall be construed accordingly.

(2) In subsection (1) above the reference to exercising control over aggregate on a site is a reference to doing any of the following, that is to say—

(*a*) winning aggregate from land at that site;

(*b*) ...[1]

(*c*) carrying out any exempt process at that site;

(*d*) storing aggregate at that site.

Amendments—[1] Sub-s (2)(*b*) repealed by FA 2002 ss 131(3)(*b*), (4), 141, Sch 40 Pt 4(3). These amendments are deemed to have come into force on 1 April 2002.

22 Responsibility for exploitation of aggregate

(1) Subject to subsection (2) below, the persons who shall be taken for the purposes of this Part to be responsible for subjecting a quantity of aggregate to exploitation are each of the following—

(*a*) in a case of the exploitation of a quantity of aggregate by its removal from its originating site or from a connected site, the operator of that site;

(*b*) in a case of the exploitation of a quantity of aggregate by its removal from a site falling within section 19(2)(*c*) above, the operator of the site and (if different) the owner of the aggregate at the time when the removal takes place;

(*c*) in a case of the exploitation of a quantity of aggregate—

(i) by its being subjected, at a time when it is not on its originating site or a connected site, to any agreement, or

(ii) by its being used at such a time for construction purposes,

the person agreeing to supply it or using it for construction purposes;

(*d*) in a case of the exploitation of a quantity of aggregate—

(i) by its being subjected, at a time when it is on its originating site or a connected site, to any agreement, or

(ii) by its being used at such a time for construction purposes,

the person mentioned in paragraph (*c*) above and (if different) the operator of that site;

(*e*) in a case of the exploitation of a quantity of aggregate by its being mixed at premises that are not comprised in its originating site or a connected site with any material or substance, the owner of the aggregate at the time when the mixing takes place and the occupier of the premises where it takes place;

(*f*) in a case of the exploitation of a quantity of aggregate by its being mixed at its originating site or a connected site with any material or substance, the owner of the aggregate at the time when the mixing takes place and (if different) the operator of the site.

(2) A person who is responsible for subjecting a quantity of aggregate to exploitation shall not be taken for the purposes of this Part to be responsible for subjecting it to commercial exploitation unless that takes place in the course or furtherance of a business carried on by him. [For the purposes of this subsection "business" includes any activity of a Government department, local authority or charity.][1]

(3) Where by virtue of this section more than one person is charged with aggregates levy, their liabilities under this Part as persons charged with the levy shall be joint and several.

(4) In this section "connected site", in relation to any quantity of aggregate, means any site that falls in relation to that quantity of aggregate within section 19(2)(*b*).

Amendments—[1] Words in sub-s (2) inserted by FA 2002 s 132(1), (3), Sch 38 para 6. This amendment is deemed to have come into force on 1 April 2002.

23 Weight of aggregate

(1) The Commissioners may make regulations for determining the weight of any aggregate for the purposes of aggregates levy.

(2) The regulations may—

(*a*) prescribe rules for determining the weight;

(*b*) authorise rules for determining the weight to be specified by the Commissioners in a prescribed manner;

(*c*) authorise rules for determining the weight to be agreed between the person charged with the levy and a person acting under the authority of the Commissioners.

(3) The regulations may, in particular, provide for the rules prescribed or authorised under the regulations to include rules about—

(*a*) the method by which the weight is to be determined;

(*b*) the time by reference to which the weight is to be determined;

(*c*) the discounting of constituents (such as water).

(4) The regulations may include provision that rules specified by virtue of subsection (2)(*b*) above—

(*a*) are to have effect only in such cases as may be described in the rules; and

(*b*) are not to have effect in particular cases unless the Commissioners are satisfied that such conditions as may be set out in the rules are met in those cases.

(5) Conditions for which provision is made by virtue of subsection (4)(*b*) above may be framed by reference to such factors as the Commissioners think fit (such as the consent, in a particular case, of a person acting under the authority of the Commissioners).

(6) The regulations may include provision that—

(*a*) where rules are agreed as mentioned in subsection (2)(*c*) above, and

(*b*) the Commissioners believe that they should no longer be applied (whether because they do not give an accurate indication of the weight or are not being fully observed or for some other reason),

the Commissioners may direct that the agreed rules shall no longer have effect.

Administration and enforcement

24 The register

(1) It shall be the duty of the Commissioners to establish and maintain a register of persons who are required to be registered for the purposes of aggregates levy.

(2) A person is required to be registered for the purposes of aggregates levy if he—

(*a*) carries out taxable activities, and

(*b*) is not exempted from registration by regulations under subsection (4) below.

(3) For the purposes of subsection (2) above a person carries out a taxable activity if a quantity of aggregate is subjected to commercial exploitation in the United Kingdom in circumstances in which he is responsible for its being so subjected.

(4) The Commissioners may by regulations provide for persons carrying out taxable activities to be, to such extent and subject to such conditions or restrictions as may be prescribed, either—

(*a*) exempt from the requirement of registration; or

(*b*) exempt from such obligations or liabilities imposed by or under this Part on persons required to be registered for the purposes of aggregates levy as may be prescribed.

(5) The Commissioners shall keep such information in the register as they consider it appropriate so to keep for the purposes of the care and management of aggregates levy.

(6) In particular, where it appears to the Commissioners that any person is operating or using any premises, or intends to operate or use any premises—

(*a*) for winning any aggregate,

(*b*) ...[1]

(*c*) for applying an exempt process to any aggregate,
[(*ca*) for mixing, otherwise than in permitted circumstances (within the meaning given by section 19(7)), any aggregate with any material or substance other than water,][2]
(*d*) for storing any aggregate, or
(*e*) for the first landing in the United Kingdom of aggregate won from the seabed of any area of sea in the United Kingdom or United Kingdom waters,

they may, if they think fit, register those premises, in any entry relating to that person and under his name, as a registered site.

(7) Where any premises are registered in accordance with subsection (6) above as a registered site, the particulars included in the register shall set out as the boundaries of the site such boundaries as appear to the Commissioners best to secure that avoidance of levy is not facilitated by the registration of any part of any premises that is not used or operated as mentioned in subsection (6) above.

(8) Where any entry in the register at any time specifies that any premises registered under a person's name as a registered site are to be taken to be the originating site of—

(*a*) …[1]
(*b*) any aggregate resulting from the carrying out of any exempt process there, or
(*c*) any aggregate won or landed there,

any question for the purposes of this Part as to the boundaries at that time of the originating site of any such aggregate shall be conclusively determined in accordance with that entry.

(9) Schedule 4 to this Act (provisions with respect to registration for the purposes of aggregates levy) shall have effect.

(10) The preceding provisions of this section and the provisions of Schedule 4 to this Act shall come into force on such date as the Treasury may by order made by statutory instrument appoint; and different days may be appointed under this subsection for different purposes.

Regulations—Finance Act 2001, section 24 and Schedule 4, (Appointed Day) Order, SI 2001/4033 (the appointed day for entry into force of this section is 11 January 2002).
Simon's Tax Cases—*C&E Comrs v East Midlands Aggregates Ltd* [2004] STC 1582.
Amendments—[1] Sub-ss (6)(*b*) and (8)(*a*) repealed by FA 2002 ss 131(3)(*c*), (4), 141, Sch 40 Pt 4(3). These amendments are deemed to have come into force on 1 April 2002.
[2] Sub-s (6)(*ca*) inserted by FA 2002 s 132(1), (3), Sch 38 para 7. This amendment is deemed to have come into force on 1 April 2002.

25 Returns and payment of levy

(1) The Commissioners may by regulations make provision—

(*a*) for persons charged with aggregates levy to be liable to account for it by reference to such periods ("accounting periods") as may be determined by or under the regulations;
(*b*) for persons who are or are required to be registered for the purposes of aggregates levy to be subject to such obligations to make returns for those purposes for such periods, at such times and in such form as may be so determined; and
(*c*) for persons who are required to account for aggregates levy for any period to become liable to pay the amounts due from them at such times and in such manner as may be so determined.

(2) Without prejudice to the generality of the powers conferred by subsection (1) above, regulations under this section may contain provision—

(*a*) for aggregates levy falling in accordance with the regulations to be accounted for by reference to one accounting period to be treated in prescribed circumstances, and for prescribed purposes, as levy due for a different period;
(*b*) for the correction of errors made when accounting for aggregates levy by reference to any period;
(*c*) for the entries to be made in any accounts in connection with the correction of any such errors and for the financial adjustments to be made in that connection;
(*d*) for a person, for purposes connected with the making of any such entry or financial adjustment, to be required to provide to any prescribed person, or to retain, a document in the prescribed form containing prescribed particulars of the matters to which the entry or adjustment relates;
(*e*) for enabling the Commissioners, in such cases as they may think fit, to dispense with or relax a requirement imposed by regulations made by virtue of paragraph (*d*) above;
(*f*) for the amount of levy which, in accordance with the regulations, is treated as due for a later period than that by reference to which it should have been accounted for to be treated as increased by an amount representing interest at the rate applicable under section 197 of the Finance Act 1996 for such period as may be determined in accordance with the regulations.

(3) Subject to the following provisions of this section, if any person ("the taxpayer") fails—

(*a*) to comply with so much of any regulations under this section as requires him, at or before a particular time, to make a return for any accounting period, or
(*b*) to comply with so much of any regulations under this section as requires him, at or before a particular time, to pay an amount of aggregates levy due from him,

he shall be liable to a penalty of £250.

(4) Liability to a penalty under subsection (3) above shall not arise if the taxpayer satisfies the Commissioners or, on appeal, an appeal tribunal—

(*a*) that there is a reasonable excuse for the failure to make the return or to pay the levy in accordance with regulations; and

(*b*) that there is not an occasion after the last day on which the return or payment was required by the regulations to be made when there was a failure without reasonable excuse to make it.

(5) Where, by reason of any failure falling within paragraph (*a*) or (*b*) of subsection (3) above—

(*a*) a person is convicted of an offence (whether under this Act or otherwise), or

(*b*) a person is assessed to a penalty under paragraph 7 of Schedule 6 to this Act (penalty for evasion) [or a penalty for a deliberate inaccuracy under Schedule 24 to the Finance Act 2007 (penalties for errors)][1],

that person shall not, by reason of that failure, be liable also to a penalty under that subsection (3).

(6) In subsection (1)(*b*) above the reference to a person who is required to be registered for the purposes of aggregates levy includes a reference to a person who would be so required but for any exemption conferred by regulations under section 24(4) above.

Amendment—[1] Words in sub-s (5)(*b*) inserted by the Finance Act 2008, Schedule 40 (Appointed Day, Transitional Provisions and Consequential Amendments) Order, SI 2009/571 art 8, Sch 1 paras 31, 32 with effect from 1 April 2009.

26 Security for levy

(1) Where it appears to the Commissioners necessary to do so for the protection of the revenue they may require any person who is or is required to be registered to give security, or further security, for the payment of any aggregates levy which is or may become due from him.

(2) The power of the Commissioners to require any security, or further security, under this section shall be a power to require security, or further security, of such amount and in such manner as they may determine.

(3) A person who is responsible for any aggregate being subjected to commercial exploitation in the United Kingdom is guilty of an offence if, at the time it is so subjected—

(*a*) he has been required to give security under this section; and

(*b*) he has not complied with that requirement.

(4) A person guilty of an offence under this section shall be liable, on summary conviction, to a penalty of level 5 on the standard scale.

(5) Sections 145 to 155 of the Customs and Excise Management Act 1979 (proceedings for offences, mitigation of penalties and certain other matters) shall apply in relation to an offence under this section as they apply in relation to offences and penalties under the customs and excise Acts.

(6) In subsection (1) above the reference to a person who is required to be registered for the purposes of aggregates levy includes a reference to a person who would be so required but for any exemption conferred by regulations under section 24(4) above.

27 Recovery and interest

Schedule 5 to this Act (which makes provision for the recovery of amounts of aggregates levy due from any person and for the interest payable on such amounts) shall have effect.

28 Evasion, misdeclaration and neglect

Schedule 6 to this Act (which makes provision for and in connection with the imposition of criminal and civil penalties for the evasion of aggregates levy and for related misconduct) shall have effect.

29 Information and evidence

Schedule 7 to this Act (which provides for the supply of information to the Commissioners, for the powers under which the Commissioners may collect information for enforcement purposes and about evidence) shall have effect.

Credits and repayments

30 Credit for aggregates levy

(1) The Commissioners may, in accordance with the following provisions of this section, by regulations make provision in relation to cases where, after a charge to aggregates levy has arisen on any quantity of aggregate—

(*a*) any of that aggregate is exported from the United Kingdom in the form of aggregate;

(*b*) an exempt process is applied to any of that aggregate;

(*c*) any of that aggregate is used in a prescribed industrial or agricultural process;

(*d*) any of that aggregate is disposed of (by dumping or otherwise) in such manner not constituting its use for construction purposes as may be prescribed; or (*e*) the whole or any part of a debt due to a person responsible for subjecting the aggregate to commercial exploitation is written off in his accounts as a bad debt.

(2) The provision that may be made in relation to any such case as is mentioned in subsection (1) above is provision—

(*a*) for such person as may be specified in the regulations to be entitled to a tax credit in respect of any aggregates levy charged on the aggregate in question;

(*b*) for a tax credit to which any person is entitled under the regulations to be brought into account when he is accounting for aggregates levy due from him for such accounting period or periods as may be determined in accordance with the regulations; and

(*c*) for a person entitled to a tax credit to be entitled, in any prescribed case where he cannot bring the tax credit into account so as to set it against a liability to aggregates levy, to a repayment of levy of an amount so determined.

(3) Regulations under this section may contain any or all of the following provisions—

(*a*) provision making any entitlement to a tax credit conditional on the making of a claim by such person, within such period and in such manner as may be prescribed;

(*b*) provision making entitlement to bring a tax credit into account, or to receive a repayment in respect of such a credit, conditional on compliance with such requirements as may be determined in accordance with the regulations;

(*c*) provision requiring a claim for a tax credit to be evidenced and quantified by reference to such records and other documents as may be so determined;

(*d*) provision requiring a person claiming any entitlement to a tax credit to keep, for such period and in such form and manner as may be so determined, those records and documents and a record of such information relating to the claim as may be so determined;

(*e*) provision for the withdrawal of a tax credit where any requirement of the regulations is not complied with;

(*f*) provision for interest at the rate applicable under section 197 of the Finance Act 1996 to be treated as added, for such period and for such purposes as may be prescribed, to the amount of any tax credit;

(*g*) provision for anything falling to be determined in accordance with the regulations to be determined by reference to a general or specific direction given in accordance with the regulations by the Commissioners.

(4) Without prejudice to the generality of the preceding provisions of this section, regulations under this section may also contain—

(*a*) provision for ascertaining whether, when and to what extent an amount is to be taken for the purposes of any regulations under this section to have been written off in any accounts as a bad debt;

(*b*) provision requiring a person who for the purposes of any such regulations is taken to have written off any amount as a bad debt to keep, for such period and in such form and manner as may be prescribed, information relating to anything subsequently paid in respect of the amount written off;

(*c*) provision for the withdrawal of the whole or an appropriate part of any tax credit relating to an amount taken to have been written off as a bad debt where the whole or any part (or further part) of the amount written off is subsequently paid;

(*d*) provision for ascertaining whether, and to what extent, anything received by any person is to be taken as a payment of, or of a part of, an amount taken, for the purposes of any regulations under this section, to have been written off;

(*e*) provision for determining the value for the purposes of provision made by virtue of paragraph (*d*) above of things received otherwise than in the form of money.

(5) Regulations made under this section shall have effect subject to the provisions of section 32 below.

[30A Transitional tax credit in Northern Ireland

(1) The Commissioners may by regulations make provision of the kind described in section 30(2) above (entitlement to tax credit) in relation to cases within subsection (2) below.

(2) The cases are those where a charge to aggregates levy has arisen on a quantity of aggregate which has been subjected to commercial exploitation in Northern Ireland during a period—

(*a*) starting on the prescribed date, and

(*b*) ending on 31st March 2011.

(3) The date prescribed for the purposes of subsection (2)(*a*) above may be earlier than the date on which this section comes into force.

(4) The amount of a tax credit to which a person is entitled under the regulations must not be more than 80% of any aggregates levy charged on the aggregate in question.

(5) Regulations under this section may in particular make provision—

(*a*) for a person operating a site to be entitled to a tax credit under the regulations in respect of a period for which he holds an aggregates levy credit certificate which has been issued in respect of the site and which has not been withdrawn;

(*b*) for an aggregates levy credit certificate to be issued to a person in respect of a site only if an aggregates levy credit agreement is in force in respect of the site;

(*c*) for the withdrawal of an aggregates levy credit certificate where the aggregates levy credit agreement in respect of which it was issued is no longer in force;

(*d*) for the form and content of aggregates levy credit certificates and aggregates levy credit agreements.

(6) Regulations under this section which make provision such as is mentioned in subsection (5)(*d*) above may be framed by reference to any provisions of a notice published by the Commissioners in pursuance of the regulations and not withdrawn by a further notice.

(7) If regulations under this section make provision such as is mentioned in subsection (5) above, the Commissioners or the Northern Ireland Department may—

(*a*) enter into aggregates levy credit agreements;

(*b*) issue and withdraw aggregates levy credit certificates;

(*c*) take such other steps as the Commissioners or the Northern Ireland Department consider appropriate in relation to aggregates levy credit agreements and aggregates levy credit certificates.

(8) Regulations under this section which make provision such as is mentioned in subsection (5) above must include provision requiring the Northern Ireland Department to inform the Commissioners if the Northern Ireland Department issues or withdraws an aggregates levy credit certificate.

(9) Subsections (3) to (5) of section 30 above apply to regulations under this section as they apply to regulations under that section.

(10) The Treasury may by order made by statutory instrument amend subsection (4) above by substituting for the percentage for the time being specified in that subsection a percentage lower than 80%.

(11) An order under subsection (10) above shall not be made unless a draft of the order has been laid before Parliament and approved by a resolution of the House of Commons.

(12) Any expenses of the Northern Ireland Department under this section shall be charged on the Consolidated Fund of Northern Ireland.

(13) In this section—

"aggregates levy credit agreement" means an agreement entered into in respect of a site by the person operating the site and the Commissioners or the Northern Ireland Department;

"aggregates levy credit certificate" means a certificate issued to the person operating a site by the Commissioners or the Northern Ireland Department as evidence of the fact that an aggregates levy credit agreement has been entered into in respect of the site;

"the Northern Ireland Department" means the Department of the Environment in Northern Ireland.][1]

Amendments—[1] Section 30A substituted by FA 2004 s 291(1), (2), (4), (5) with effect from 23 July 2004 by virtue of Finance Act 2004, section 291, (Appointed Day) Order, SI 2004/1942 art 2. Section 30A previously read as follows—

"30A Transitional tax credit in Northern Ireland

(1) The Commissioners may by regulations make provision of the kind described in section 30(2) above (entitlement to tax credit) in relation to cases where aggregate is used in Northern Ireland for a prescribed purpose—

(*a*) on or after the commencement date, and

(*b*) before 1st April 2007.

(2) In relation to the use of aggregate in the year ending with a date shown in the first column of the following table, the amount of any tax credit to which a person would otherwise be entitled by virtue of the regulations shall be reduced by the percentage of that amount shown opposite that date in the second column.

Year ending	*Reduction in tax credit*
31st March 2004	20%
31st March 2005	40%
31st March 2006	60%
31st March 2007	80%

(3) Subsections (3) to (5) of section 30 above apply to regulations under this section as they apply to regulations under that section.

(4) The Treasury may by order made by statutory instrument amend subsection (2) above so as to—

(*a*) change the period in relation to which the amount of a tax credit is to be reduced;

(*b*) change the amount by which a tax credit is to be reduced.

(5) An order under subsection (4) above shall not be made unless a draft of the order has been laid before Parliament and approved by a resolution of the House of Commons.".

31 Repayments of overpaid levy

(1) Where a person has paid an amount to the Commissioners by way of aggregates levy which was not levy due to them, they shall be liable to repay the amount to him.

(2) The Commissioners shall not be liable to repay an amount under this section except on the making of a claim for that purpose.

(3) A claim under this section must be made in such form and manner, and must be supported by such documentary evidence, as may be required by regulations made by the Commissioners.

(4) The preceding provisions of this section are subject to the provisions of section 32 below.

(5) Except as provided by this section, the Commissioners shall not, by virtue of the fact that it was not levy due to them, be liable to repay any amount paid to them by way of aggregates levy.

32 Supplemental provisions about repayments etc

(1) The Commissioners shall not be liable, on any claim for a repayment of aggregates levy, to repay any amount paid to them more than three years before the making of the claim.

(2) In the case of any claim for a repayment of an amount of aggregates levy other than a claim to a repayment to which a person is entitled by virtue of tax credit regulations, it shall be a defence to that claim that the repayment of that amount would unjustly enrich the claimant.

(3) Subsection (4) below applies for the purposes of subsection (2) above where—

(*a*) there is an amount paid by way of aggregates levy which (apart from subsection (2) above) would fall to be the subject of a repayment of aggregates levy to any person ("the taxpayer"); and

(*b*) the whole or a part of the cost of the payment of that amount to the Commissioners has, for practical purposes, been borne by a person other than the taxpayer.

(4) Where, in a case to which this subsection applies, loss or damage has been or may be incurred by the taxpayer as a result of mistaken assumptions made in his case about the operation of any provisions relating to aggregates levy, that loss or damage shall be disregarded, except to the extent of the quantified amount, in the making of any determination as to—

(*a*) whether or to what extent the repayment of an amount to the taxpayer would enrich him; or

(*b*) whether or to what extent any enrichment of the taxpayer would be unjust.

(5) In subsection (4) above "the quantified amount" means the amount (if any) which is shown by the taxpayer to constitute the amount that would appropriately compensate him for loss or damage shown by him to have resulted, for any business carried on by him, from the making of the mistaken assumptions.

(6) The reference in subsection (4) above to provisions relating to aggregates levy is a reference to any provisions of—

(*a*) any enactment or subordinate legislation (whether or not still in force) which relates to that levy or to any matter connected with it; or

(*b*) any notice published by the Commissioners under or for the purposes of any enactment or subordinate legislation relating to aggregates levy.

(7) Schedule 8 to this Act (which contains further provision about payments and repayments by the Commissioners and about the setting off of amounts due to or from the Commissioners under this Part and the setting of other amounts against such amounts) shall have effect.

Prospective amendments—In sub-s (1) the words "4 years" to be substituted for the words "three years" by FA 2009 s 99, Sch 51 paras 27, 28 with effect from such day as the Treasury may by order made by statutory instrument appoint.

Non-resident taxpayers

33 Appointment of tax representatives

(1) The Commissioners may by regulations make provision for securing that every non-resident taxpayer has a person resident in the United Kingdom to act as his tax representative for the purposes of aggregates levy.

(2) Regulations under this section may, in particular, contain any or all of the following—

(*a*) provision requiring notification to be given to the Commissioners where a person becomes a non-resident taxpayer;

(*b*) provision requiring the appointment of tax representatives by non-resident taxpayers;

(*c*) provision for the appointment of a person as a tax representative to take effect only where the person appointed is approved by the Commissioners;

(*d*) provision authorising the Commissioners to give a direction requiring the replacement of a tax representative;

(*e*) provision authorising the Commissioners to give a direction requiring a person specified in the direction to be treated as the appointed tax representative of a non-resident taxpayer so specified;

(*f*) provision about the circumstances in which a person ceases to be a tax representative and about the withdrawal by the Commissioners of their approval of a tax representative;

(*g*) provision enabling a tax representative to act on behalf of the person for whom he is the tax representative through an agent of the representative;

(*h*) provision for the purposes of any provision made by virtue of paragraphs (*a*) to (*g*) above regulating the procedure to be followed in any case and imposing requirements as to the information and other particulars to be provided to the Commissioners;

(*i*) provision as to the time at which things done under or for the purposes of the regulations are to take effect.

(3) Subject to subsection (4) below, a person who—

(*a*) becomes subject, in accordance with any regulations under this section, to an obligation to request the Commissioners' approval for any person's appointment as his tax representative, but

(*b*) fails (with or without making the appointment) to make the request as required by the regulations,

shall be liable to a penalty of £10,000.

(4) A failure such as is mentioned in subsection (3) above shall not give rise to liability to a penalty under this section if the person concerned satisfies the Commissioners or, on appeal, an appeal tribunal that there is a reasonable excuse for the failure.

34 Effect of appointment of tax representatives

(1) The tax representative of a non-resident taxpayer shall be entitled to act on the non-resident taxpayer's behalf for the purposes of any provision made by or under this Part.

(2) The tax representative of a non-resident taxpayer shall be under a duty, except to such extent as the Commissioners by regulations otherwise provide, to secure the non-resident taxpayer's compliance with, and discharge of, the obligations and liabilities to which the non-resident taxpayer is subject by virtue of any provision made by or under this Part (including obligations and liabilities arising or incurred before he became the non-resident taxpayer's tax representative).

(3) A person who is or has been the tax representative of a non-resident taxpayer shall be personally liable—

(*a*) in respect of any failure while he is or was the non-resident taxpayer's tax representative to secure compliance with, or the discharge of, any obligation or liability to which subsection (2) above applies, and

(*b*) in respect of anything done in the course of, or for purposes connected with, acting on the non-resident taxpayer's behalf,

as if the obligations and liabilities to which subsection (2) above applies were imposed jointly and severally on the tax representative and the non-resident taxpayer.

(4) A tax representative shall not be liable by virtue of this section to be registered for the purposes of aggregates levy; but the Commissioners may by regulations—

(*a*) require the registration of the names of tax representatives against the names of the non-resident taxpayers of whom they are the representatives;

(*b*) make provision for the deletion of the names of persons who cease to be tax representatives.

(5) A tax representative shall not by virtue of this section be guilty of any offence except in so far as—

(*a*) he has consented to, or connived in, the commission of the offence by the non-resident taxpayer;

(*b*) the commission of the offence by the non-resident taxpayer is attributable to any neglect on the part of the tax representative; or

(*c*) the offence consists in a contravention by the tax representative of an obligation which, by virtue of this section, is imposed both on the tax representative and on the non-resident taxpayer.

Other special cases

35 Groups of companies etc

(1) Schedule 9 to this Act (which provides for two or more bodies corporate to be treated as members of the same group for the purposes of this Part) shall have effect.

(2) Any aggregates levy with which a body corporate is charged in respect of aggregate subjected to commercial exploitation at a time when the body is a member of a group shall be treated for the purposes of this Part as if it were the representative member for that group (instead of that body) which is charged with the levy.

(3) All the bodies corporate who are members of a group when any aggregates levy becomes due from the representative member, together with any bodies corporate who become members of the group while any such levy remains unpaid, shall be jointly and severally liable for any aggregates levy due from the representative member.

(4) Subject to subsections (2) and (3) above, the Commissioners may by regulations make such provision as they consider appropriate about—

(*a*) the person by whom any obligation or liability imposed by or under this Part is to be performed or discharged, and

(*b*) the manner in which it is to be performed or discharged,

in a case where the person who (apart from the regulations) would be subject to the obligation or liability is one of a number of bodies corporate registered in the name of the representative member for a group.

(5) References in this section to aggregates levy being or becoming due from the representative member include references to any amounts being or becoming recoverable as if they were aggregates levy due from that member.

(6) For the purposes of this Part—

(*a*) a body corporate is a member of a group at any time in relation to which it falls to be treated as such a member in accordance with Schedule 9 to this Act; and (*b*) the body corporate which is to be taken to be the representative member for a group at any time is the member of the group which in relation to that time is the representative member under that Schedule in the case of that group.

36 Partnerships and other unincorporated bodies

(1) The Commissioners may by regulations make provision for determining by what persons anything required to be done under this Part is to be done where, apart from those regulations, that requirement would fall on—

(*a*) persons carrying on business in partnership; or

(*b*) persons carrying on business together as an unincorporated body;

but any regulations under this subsection must be construed subject to the following provisions of this section.

(2) In determining for the purposes of this Part who at any time is the person chargeable with any aggregates levy where the persons responsible for subjecting any aggregate to commercial exploitation are persons carrying on any business—

(*a*) in partnership, or

(*b*) as an unincorporated body,

the firm or body shall be treated, for the purposes of that determination (and notwithstanding any changes from time to time in the members of the firm or body), as the same person and as separate from its members.

(3) Without prejudice to section 36 of the Partnership Act 1890 (rights of persons dealing with firm against apparent members of firm), where—

(*a*) persons have been carrying on in partnership any business in the course or furtherance of which any aggregate has been subjected to commercial exploitation, and

(*b*) a person ceases to be a member of the firm,

that person shall be regarded for the purposes of this Part (including subsection (7) below) as continuing to be a partner until the date on which the change in the partnership is notified to the Commissioners.

(4) Where a person ceases to be a member of a firm during an accounting period (or is treated as so ceasing by virtue of subsection (3) above) any notice, whether of assessment or otherwise, which—

(*a*) is served on the firm under or for the purposes of any provision made by or under this Part, and

(*b*) relates to, or to any matter arising in, that period or any earlier period during the whole or part of which he was a member of the firm,

shall be treated as served also on him.

(5) Without prejudice to section 16 of the Partnership Act 1890 (notice to acting partner to be notice to the firm), any notice, whether of assessment or otherwise, which—

(*a*) is addressed to a firm by the name in which it is registered, and

(*b*) is served in accordance with this Part,

shall be treated for the purposes of this Part as served on the firm and, accordingly, where subsection (4) above applies, as served also on the former partner.

(6) Subject to subsection (7) below, nothing in this section shall affect the extent to which, under section 9 of the Partnership Act 1890 (liability of partners for debts of the firm), a partner is liable for aggregates levy owed by the firm.

(7) Where a person is a partner in a firm during part only of an accounting period, his personal liability for aggregates levy incurred by the firm in respect of aggregate subjected to commercial exploitation in that period shall include, but shall not exceed, such proportion of the firm's liability as may be just and reasonable in the circumstances.

37 Insolvency etc

(1) The Commissioners may by regulations make provision in accordance with the following provisions of this section for the application of this Part in cases in which an insolvency procedure is applied to a person or to a deceased person's estate.

(2) The provision that may be contained in regulations under this section may include any or all of the following—

(*a*) provision requiring any such person as may be prescribed to give notification to the Commissioners, in the prescribed manner, of the prescribed particulars of any relevant matter;

(*b*) provision requiring a person to be treated, to the prescribed extent, as if, for the purposes of this Part or such of its provisions as may be prescribed, he were the same person as the subject of the procedure; and

(*c*) provision for securing continuity in the application of any of the provisions of this Part where, by virtue of any regulations under this section, any person is treated as if he were the same person as the subject of the procedure.

(3) In subsection (2) above "relevant matter", in relation to a case in which an insolvency procedure is applied to any person or estate, means—

(*a*) the application of that procedure to that person or estate;
(*b*) the appointment of any person for the purposes of the application of that procedure;
(*c*) any other matter relating to—
(i) the application of that procedure to the subject of the procedure or to his estate;
(ii) the holding of an appointment made for the purposes of that procedure; or
(iii) the exercise or discharge of any powers or duties conferred or imposed on any person by virtue of such an appointment.

(4) Regulations made by virtue of subsection (2)(*b*) above may include provision for a person to cease, on the occurrence of such an event as may be prescribed, to be treated as if he were the same person as the subject of the procedure.

(5) Regulations under this section prescribing the manner in which any notification is to be given to the Commissioners may require it to be given in such manner and to contain such particulars as may be specified in a general notice published by the Commissioners in accordance with the regulations.

(6) Regulations under this section may provide that the extent to which, and the purposes for which, a person is to be treated under the regulations as if he were the same person as the subject of the procedure may be determined by reference to a notice given in accordance with the regulations to the person so treated.

(7) For the purposes of this section, an insolvency procedure is applied to a person if—
(*a*) a bankruptcy order, winding-up order or administration order is made [or an administrator is appointed][2] in relation to that person or a partnership of which he is a member;
(*b*) an award of sequestration is made in relation to that person's estate or the estate of a partnership of which he is a member;
(*c*) that person is put into administrative receivership;
(*d*) that person passes a resolution for voluntary winding up;
(*e*) any voluntary arrangement approved in accordance with—
(i) Part I or VIII of the Insolvency Act 1986, or
(ii) Part II or Chapter II of Part VIII of the Insolvency (Northern Ireland) Order 1989,
comes into force in relation to that person or a partnership of which that person is a member;
(*f*) a deed of arrangement registered in accordance with—
(i) the Deeds of Arrangement Act 1914, or
(ii) Chapter I of Part VIII of that Order,
takes effect in relation to that person;
(*g*)–(*j*) …[1]
(*k*) that person's estate becomes vested in any other person as that person's trustee under a trust deed (within the meaning of the Bankruptcy (Scotland) Act 1985).

(8) For the purposes of this section, an insolvency procedure is applied to a deceased person's estate if—
(*a*) after that person's death—
(i) a bankruptcy order, or
(ii) an order with corresponding effect but a different name,
is made in relation to that person's estate under any of the provisions of the Insolvency Act 1986 or the Insolvency (Northern Ireland) Order 1989 as they are applied to the administration of the insolvent estates of deceased persons; or
(*b*) an award of sequestration is made on that person's estate after his death.

(9) In subsection (7) above—
(*a*) the reference to any administration order is a reference to an administration order under [Schedule B1 to][2] the Insolvency Act 1986 or Article 21 of the Insolvency (Northern Ireland) Order 1989;
(*b*) the reference to a person being put into administrative receivership is a reference to the appointment in relation to him of an administrative receiver, within the meaning of section 251 of that Act of 1986 or Article 5(1) of that Order of 1989; and
(*c*) references to a member of a partnership include references to any person who is liable as a partner under section 14 of the Partnership Act 1890 (persons liable by "holding out").

(10) In this section "the subject of the procedure", in relation to the application of any insolvency procedure, means the person to whom, or to whose estate, the procedure is applied.

Amendments—[1] Sub-s (7)(*g*)–(*j*) repealed by FA 2002 ss 132(1), 141, Sch 38 para 8, Sch 40 Pt 4(3). These amendments are deemed to have come into force on 1 April 2002.
[2] Words in sub-s (7)(*a*) inserted, and words in sub-s (9)(*a*) substituted, by the Enterprise Act 2002 (Insolvency) Order, SI 2003/2096 art 4, Schedule paras 35, 36 with effect from 15 September 2003, except in relation to any case where a petition for an administration order was presented before that date: SI 2003/2096, arts 1(1), 6.

38 Death and incapacity

(1) The Commissioners may, in accordance with subsection (2) below, by regulations make provision for the purposes of aggregates levy in relation to cases where a person carries on a business of an individual who has died or become incapacitated.

(2) The provisions that may be contained in regulations under this section are—

(*a*) provision requiring the person who is carrying on the business to inform the Commissioners of the fact that he is carrying on the business and of the event that has led to his carrying it on;

(*b*) provision allowing that person to be treated for a limited time as if he and the person who has died or become incapacitated were the same person; and

(*c*) such other provision as the Commissioners think fit for securing continuity in the application of this Part where a person is so treated.

39 Transfer of a business as a going concern

(1) The Commissioners may by regulations make provision for securing continuity in the application of this Part in cases where any business carried on by a person is transferred to another person as a going concern.

(2) Regulations under this section may, in particular, include any or all of the following—

(*a*) provision requiring the transferor to inform the Commissioners of the transfer;

(*b*) provision for liabilities and duties under this Part of the transferor to become, to such extent as may be provided by the regulations, liabilities and duties of the transferee;

(*c*) provision for any right of either of them to a tax credit or repayment of aggregates levy to be satisfied by allowing the credit or making the repayment to the other;

(*d*) provision as to the preservation of any records or accounts relating to the business which, by virtue of any regulations under paragraph 2 of Schedule 7 to this Act, are required to be preserved for any period after the transfer.

(3) Regulations under this section may provide that no such provision as is mentioned in paragraph (*b*) or (*c*) of subsection (2) above shall have effect in relation to any transferor and transferee unless an application for the purpose has been made by them under the regulations.

Review and appeal

40 [Appeals][1]

(1) [Subject to section 41, an appeal shall lie to an appeal tribunal from any person who is or will be affected by any decision of HMRC with respect to any of the following matters—][1]

(*a*) whether or not a person is charged in any case with an amount of aggregates levy;

(*b*) the amount of aggregates levy charged in any case and the time when the charge is to be taken as having arisen;

(*c*) the registration of any person or premises for the purposes of aggregates levy or the cancellation of any registration;

(*d*) the person liable to pay the aggregates levy charged in any case, the amount of a person's liability to aggregates levy and the time by which he is required to pay an amount of that levy;

(*e*) the imposition of a requirement on any person to give security, or further security, under section 26 above and the amount and manner of providing any security required under that section;

(*f*) whether or not liability to a penalty or to interest on any amount arises in any person's case under any provision made by or under this Part, and the amount of any such liability;

(*g*) any matter the decision as to which is [appealable][1] under this section in accordance with paragraph 8(6) or (7) of Schedule 6 to this Act;

(*h*) the extent of any person's entitlement to any tax credit or to a repayment in respect of a tax credit and the extent of any liability of the Commissioners under this Part to pay interest on any amount;

(*i*) whether or not any person is required to have a tax representative by virtue of any regulations under section 33 above;

(*j*) the giving, withdrawal or variation, for the purposes of any such regulations, of any approval or direction with respect to the person who is to act as another's tax representative;

(*k*) whether a body corporate is to be treated, or is to cease to be treated, as a member of a group, the times at which a body corporate is to be so treated and the body corporate which is, in relation to any time, to be the representative member for a group;

(*l*) any matter not falling within the preceding paragraphs the decision with respect to which is contained in

[(i) an assessment under paragraphs 2 or 3 of Schedule 5 in respect of an accounting period in relation to which any return required to be made by virtue of regulations under section 25 has been made; or

(ii) an assessment under any provision of Schedule 5 other than paragraphs 2 or 3.][1]

[(2) *Any person who is or will be affected by any decision to which this section applies may by notice in writing to the Commissioners require them to review the decision.*

(3) *The Commissioners shall not be required under this section to review any decision unless the notice requiring the review is given before the end of the period of forty-five days beginning with the day on which written notification of the decision, or of an assessment containing or giving effect to the decision, was first given to the person requiring the review.*

(4) *For the purposes of subsection (3) above it shall be the duty of the Commissioners to give written notification of any decision to which this section applies to any person who—*

(*a*) *requests such a notification;*
(*b*) *has not previously been given written notification of that decision; and*
(*c*) *if given such a notification, will be entitled to require a review of the decision under this section.*

(5) *A person shall be entitled to give a notice under this section requiring a decision to be reviewed for a second or subsequent time only if—*
(*a*) *the grounds on which he requires the further review are that the Commissioners did not, on any previous review, have the opportunity to consider certain facts or other matters; and*
(*b*) *he does not, on the further review, require the Commissioners to consider any facts or matters which were considered on a previous review except in so far as they are relevant to any issue to which the facts or matters not previously considered relate.*

(6) *Where the Commissioners are required by a notice under this section to review any decision, it shall be their duty to do so.*

(7) *On a review under this section the Commissioners may (subject to subsection (9) below) withdraw, vary or confirm the decision reviewed.*

(8) *Where—*
(*a*) *it is the duty under this section of the Commissioners to review any decision, and*
(*b*) *they do not, within the period of forty-five days beginning with the day on which the review was required, give notice to the person requiring it of their determination on the review,*

they shall be deemed to have confirmed the decision.

(9) *Where the Commissioners decide, on a review under this section, that a liability to a penalty or to an amount of interest arises, they shall not be entitled to modify the amount payable in respect of that liability except—*
(*a*) *in exercise of a power conferred by section 46(1) below (penalties) or paragraph 10(3) of Schedule 5 to this Act, paragraph 6(6) of Schedule 8 to this Act or paragraph 5(5) of Schedule 10 to this Act (penalty interest); or*
(*b*) *for the purpose of making the amount payable conform to the amount of the liability imposed by this Part.*][1]

(10) This section has effect subject to paragraph 8(5) of Schedule 6 to this Act.

Amendments—[1] Heading substituted for former heading "Review of Commissioners' decisions"; in sub-s (1) words at the beginning substituted for the words "This section applies to any decision of the Commissioners with respect to any of the following matters—"; word in sub-(1)(*g*) substituted for the word "reviewable"; sub-s (1)(*l*)(i), (ii) substituted for the words "any assessment under this Part."; sub-ss (2)–(9) repealed by the Transfer of Tribunal Functions and Revenue and Customs Appeals Order, SI 2009/56 art 3, Sch 1 para 303 with effect from 1 April 2009, subject to transitional and savings provisions in Sch 3 paras 2, 3.

[40A Offer of review

(1) HMRC must offer a person (P) a review of a decision that has been notified to P if an appeal lies under section 40 in respect of the decision.

(2) The offer of the review must be made by notice given to P at the same time as the decision is notified to P.

(3) This section does not apply to the notification of the conclusions of a review.][1]

Amendment—[1] Sections 40A–40G inserted by the Transfer of Tribunal Functions and Revenue and Customs Appeals Order, SI 2009/56 art 3, Sch 1 para 304 with effect from 1 April 2009.

[40B Right to require review

(1) Any person (other than P) who has the right of appeal under section 40 against a decision may require HMRC to review that decision if that person has not appealed to the appeal tribunal under section 40G.

(2) A notification that such a person requires a review must be made within 30 days of that person becoming aware of the decision.][1]

Amendment—[1] Sections 40A–40G inserted by the Transfer of Tribunal Functions and Revenue and Customs Appeals Order, SI 2009/56 art 3, Sch 1 para 304 with effect from 1 April 2009.

[40C Review by HMRC

(1) HMRC must review a decision if—
(*a*) they have offered a review of the decision under section 40A, and
(*b*) P notifies HMRC accepting the offer within 30 days from the date of the document containing the notification of the offer.

(2) But P may not notify acceptance of the offer if P has already appealed to the appeal tribunal under section 40G.

(3) HMRC must review a decision if a person other than P notifies them under section 40B.

(4) HMRC shall not review a decision if P, or another person, has appealed to the appeal tribunal under section 40G in respect of the decision.][1]

Amendment—[1] Sections 40A–40G inserted by the Transfer of Tribunal Functions and Revenue and Customs Appeals Order, SI 2009/56 art 3, Sch 1 para 304 with effect from 1 April 2009.

[40D Extensions of time

(1) If under section 40A, HMRC have offered P a review of a decision, HMRC may within the relevant period notify P that the relevant period is extended.

(2) If under section 40B another person may require HMRC to review a matter, HMRC may within the relevant period notify the other person that the relevant period is extended.

(3) If notice is given the relevant period is extended to the end of 30 days from—

(*a*) the date of the notice, or

(*b*) any other date set out in the notice or a further notice.

(4) In this section "relevant period" means—

(*a*) the period of 30 days referred to in—

(i) section 40C(1)(*b*) (in a case falling within subsection (1)), or

(ii) section 40B(2) (in a case falling within subsection (2)), or

(*b*) if notice has been given under subsection (1) or (2), that period as extended (or as most recently extended) in accordance with subsection (3).][1]

Amendment—[1] Sections 40A–40G inserted by the Transfer of Tribunal Functions and Revenue and Customs Appeals Order, SI 2009/56 art 3, Sch 1 para 304 with effect from 1 April 2009.

[40E Review out of time

(1) This section applies if—

(*a*) HMRC have offered a review of a decision under section 40A and P does not accept the offer within the time allowed under section 40C(1)(*b*) or 40D(3); or

(*b*) a person who requires a review under section 40B does not notify HMRC within the time allowed under that section or section 40D(3).

(2) HMRC must review the decision under section 40C if—

(*a*) after the time allowed, P, or the other person, notifies HMRC in writing requesting a review out of time,

(*b*) HMRC are satisfied that P, or the other person, had a reasonable excuse for not accepting the offer or requiring review within the time allowed, and

(*c*) HMRC are satisfied that P, or the other person, made the request without unreasonable delay after the excuse had ceased to apply.

(3) HMRC shall not review a decision if P, or another person, has appealed to the appeal tribunal under section 40G in respect of the decision.][1]

Amendment—[1] Sections 40A–40G inserted by the Transfer of Tribunal Functions and Revenue and Customs Appeals Order, SI 2009/56 art 3, Sch 1 para 304 with effect from 1 April 2009.

[40F Nature of review etc

(1) This section applies if HMRC are required to undertake a review under section 40C or 40E.

(2) The nature and extent of the review are to be such as appear appropriate to HMRC in the circumstances.

(3) For the purpose of subsection (2), HMRC must, in particular, have regard to steps taken before the beginning of the review—

(*a*) by HMRC in reaching the decision, and

(*b*) by any person in seeking to resolve disagreement about the decision.

(4) The review must take account of any representations made by P, or the other person, at a stage which gives HMRC a reasonable opportunity to consider them.

(5) The review may conclude that the decision is to be—

(*a*) upheld,

(*b*) varied, or

(*c*) cancelled.

(6) HMRC must give P, or the other person, notice of the conclusions of the review and their reasoning within—

(*a*) a period of 45 days beginning with the relevant date, or

(*b*) such other period as HMRC and P, or the other person, may agree.

(7) In subsection (6) "relevant date" means—

(*a*) the date HMRC received P's notification accepting the offer of a review (in a case falling within section 40A), or

(*b*) the date HMRC received notification from another person requiring review (in a case falling within section 40B), or

(*c*) the date on which HMRC decided to undertake the review (in a case falling within section 40E).

(8) Where HMRC are required to undertake a review but do not give notice of the conclusions within the time period specified in subsection (6), the review is to be treated as having concluded that the decision is upheld.

(9) If subsection (8) applies, HMRC must notify P or the other person of the conclusion which the review is treated as having reached.][1]

Amendment—[1] Sections 40A–40G inserted by the Transfer of Tribunal Functions and Revenue and Customs Appeals Order, SI 2009/56 art 3, Sch 1 para 304 with effect from 1 April 2009.

[40G Bringing of appeals

(1) An appeal under section 40 is to be made to the appeal tribunal before—

(*a*) the end of the period of 30 days beginning with—

(i) in a case where P is the appellant, the date of the document notifying the decision to which the appeal relates, or

(ii) in a case where a person other than P is the appellant, the date that person becomes aware of the decision, or

(*b*) if later, the end of the relevant period (within the meaning of section 40D).

(2) But that is subject to subsections (3) to (5).

(3) In a case where HMRC are required to undertake a review under section 40C—

(*a*) an appeal may not be made until the conclusion date, and

(*b*) any appeal is to be made within the period of 30 days beginning with the conclusion date.

(4) In a case where HMRC are requested to undertake a review by virtue of section 40E—

(*a*) an appeal may not be made—

(i) unless HMRC have decided whether or not to undertake a review, and

(ii) if HMRC decide to undertake a review, until the conclusion date; and

(*b*) any appeal is to be made within the period of 30 days beginning with—

(i) the conclusion date (if HMRC decide to undertake a review), or

(ii) the date on which HMRC decide not to undertake a review.

(5) In a case where section 40F(8) applies, an appeal may be made at any time from the end of the period specified in section 40F(6) to the date 30 days after the conclusion date.

(6) An appeal may be made after the end of the period specified in subsection (1), (3)(*b*), (4)(*b*) or (5) if the appeal tribunal gives permission to do so.

(7) In this section "conclusion date" means the date of the document notifying the conclusion of the review.][1]

Amendment—[1] Sections 40A–40G inserted by the Transfer of Tribunal Functions and Revenue and Customs Appeals Order, SI 2009/56 art 3, Sch 1 para 304 with effect from 1 April 2009.

41 [Appeals: further provisions][1]

(1) ...[1]

[(2) Subject to subsections (2A) and (2B), where an appeal under section 40 relates to a decision (whether or not contained in an assessment) that an amount of aggregates levy is due from any person, it shall not be entertained unless the amount which HMRC have determined to be due has been paid or deposited with them.][1]

[(2A) In a case where the amount determined to be payable as aggregates levy has not been paid or deposited an appeal shall be entertained if—

(*a*) HMRC are satisfied (on the application of the appellant), or

(*b*) the appeal tribunal decides (HMRC not being so satisfied and on the application of the appellant),

that the requirement to pay or deposit the amount determined would cause the appellant to suffer hardship.

(2B) Notwithstanding the provisions of sections 11 and 13 of the Tribunals, Courts and Enforcement Act 2007, the decision of the appeal tribunal as to the issue of hardship is final.][1]

(3) On an appeal [under section 40][1] relating to a penalty under paragraph 7 of Schedule 6 to this Act (evasion), the burden of proof as to the matters specified in paragraphs (*a*) to (*c*) of sub-paragraph (1) of that paragraph shall lie upon the Commissioners.

Amendments—[1] Heading substituted for former heading "Appeals against reviewed decisions; sub-s (1) repealed"; sub-s (2) substituted; sub-ss (2A), (2B) inserted; words in sub-s (3) substituted for the words "under this section" by the Transfer of Tribunal Functions and Revenue and Customs Appeals Order, SI 2009/56 art 3, Sch 1 para 305 with effect from 1 April 2009, subject to transitional and savings provisions in Sch 3 paras 2, 3. Sub-ss (1), (2) previously read as follows—

"(1) Subject to the following provisions of this section, an appeal shall lie to an appeal tribunal with respect to any of the following decisions—

(*a*) any decision by the Commissioners on a review under section 40 above (including a deemed confirmation under subsection (8) of that section);

(*b*) any decision by the Commissioners on any such review of a decision referred to in section 40(1) above as the Commissioners have agreed to undertake in consequence of a request made after the end of the period mentioned in section 40(3) above."

"(2) Where an appeal under this section relates to a decision (whether or not contained in an assessment) that an amount of aggregates levy is due from any person, that appeal shall not be entertained unless—

(*a*) the amount which the Commissioners have determined to be due has been paid or deposited with them; or

(*b*) on being satisfied that the appellant would otherwise suffer hardship—

(i) the Commissioners agree, or

(ii) the tribunal decide,

that it should be entertained notwithstanding that that amount has not been so paid or deposited."

42 Determinations on appeal

(1) Where, on an appeal under section [40][1] above—

(*a*) it is found that an assessment of the appellant …[1] is an assessment for an amount that is less than it ought to have been, and

(*b*) the tribunal give a direction specifying the correct amount,

the assessment shall have effect as an assessment of the amount specified in the direction and (without prejudice to any power under this Part to reduce the amount of interest payable on the amount of an assessment) as if it were an assessment notified to the appellant in that amount at the same time as the original assessment.

(2) On an appeal under section [40][1] above, the powers of the appeal tribunal in relation to any decision of the Commissioners shall include a power, where the tribunal allow an appeal on the ground that the Commissioners could not reasonably have arrived at the decision, either—

(*a*) to direct that the decision, so far as it remains in force, is to cease to have effect from such time as the tribunal may direct; or

(*b*) to require the Commissioners to conduct, in accordance with the directions of the tribunal, [a review or][1] a further review of the original decision [as appropriate][1].

(3) Where, on an appeal under section [40][1] above, the appeal tribunal find that a liability to a penalty or to an amount of interest arises, the tribunal shall not give any direction for the modification of the amount payable in respect of that liability except—

(*a*) in exercise of a power conferred on the tribunal by section 46(1) below (penalties) or paragraph 10(3) or (6) of Schedule 5 to this Act, paragraph 6(6) or (9) of Schedule 8 to this Act or paragraph 5(5) or (8) of Schedule 10 to this Act (penalty interest); or

(*b*) for the purpose of making the amount payable conform to the amount of the liability imposed by this Part.

(4) Where, on an appeal under section [40][1] above, it is found that the whole or part of any amount paid or deposited in pursuance of section 41(2) above is not due, so much of that amount as is found not to be due shall be repaid with interest [at the rate applicable under section 197 of the Finance Act 1996][1].

(5) Where, on an appeal under section [40][1] above, it is found that the whole or part of any amount due to the appellant by way of any repayment in respect of a tax credit has not been paid, so much of that amount as is found not to have been paid shall be paid with interest [at the rate applicable under section 197 of the Finance Act 1996][1].

(6) Where—

(*a*) an appeal under section [40][1] above has been entertained notwithstanding that an amount determined by the Commissioners to be payable as aggregates levy has not been paid or deposited, and

(*b*) it is found on the appeal that that amount is due,

[it shall be paid with interest at the rate applicable under section 197 of the Finance Act 1996][1].

[(6A) Interest under subsection (6) shall be paid without any deduction of income tax.][1]

[(7) Sections 85 and 85B of the Value Added Tax Act 1994 (settling of appeals by agreement and payment of tax where there is a further appeal) shall have effect as if—

(*a*) the references to section 83 of that Act included references to section 40 above, and

(*b*) the references to value added tax included references to aggregates levy.][1]

Amendment—[1] The following amendments made by the Transfer of Tribunal Functions and Revenue and Customs Appeals Order, SI 2009/56 art 3, Sch 1 para 306 with effect from 1 April 2009, subject to transitional and savings provisions in Sch 3 paras 2, 3, 9—

– in sub-ss (1)–(5), (6)(*a*) figures substituted for figures "41";

– in sub-(1)(*a*) words "made, confirmed or treated as confirmed by the Commissioners on a review under section 40 above ("the original assessment")" repealed;

– in sub-s (2)(*b*) words inserted in both places;

– in sub-ss (4), (5) words at the end substituted for the words "at such rate as the tribunal may determine";

– in sub-s (6) words at the end substituted for the words "the tribunal may, if they think fit, direct that that amount shall be paid with interest at such rate as may be specified in the direction";

– sub-s (6A) inserted;

– sub-s (7) substituted. The text previously read as follows—

"(7) Sections 85 and 87 of the Value Added Tax Act 1994 (settling of appeals by agreement and enforcement of certain decisions of tribunal) shall have effect as if—

(*a*) the references to section 83 of that Act included references to section 41 above; and

(*b*) the references to value added tax included references to aggregates levy.".

43 Adjustments of contracts

(1) Where—

(*a*) an agreement to supply a quantity of aggregate to any person has been entered into at any time before the commencement date, and

(*b*) on or after that date aggregates levy is charged on that quantity of aggregate,

so much of the agreement as requires any payment to be made to the supplier at the time when or after the charge to levy on that quantity of aggregate arises shall be adjusted so as to secure that the cost of discharging the liability to pay the levy, to the extent that it would otherwise have been borne by the supplier, is borne by the person making the payment.

(2) Where—

(*a*) an agreement with regard to any sum payable in respect of the use of land (whether the sum is called rent or royalty or otherwise) provides that the amount of the sum is to be calculated by reference to—

(i) the turnover of a business, or

(ii) the price received for minerals extracted from the land,

(*b*) the agreement was entered into before commencement date, and

(*c*) the circumstances are such that (had the agreement been made on or after that date) it might reasonably be expected that it would have provided that aggregates levy charged in particular circumstances be ignored in calculating the turnover or price,

the agreement shall be taken to provide that aggregates levy charged in those circumstances shall be ignored in calculating the turnover or, as the case may be, price.

General provisions

44 Destination of receipts

All money and securities for money collected or received for or on account of aggregates levy shall—

(*a*) if collected or received in Great Britain, be placed to the general account of the Commissioners kept at the Bank of England under section 17 of the Customs and Excise Management Act 1979; and

(*b*) if collected or received in Northern Ireland, be paid into the Consolidated Fund of the United Kingdom in such manner as the Treasury may direct.

45 Regulations and orders

(1) The powers of the Commissioners under this Part to make regulations shall be exercisable by statutory instrument subject to annulment in pursuance of a resolution of the House of Commons.

(2) Where regulations made under this Part impose a relevant requirement on any person, they may provide that if the person fails to comply with the requirement he shall be liable, subject to subsection (3) below, to a penalty of £250.

(3) Where by reason of any conduct—

(*a*) a person is convicted of an offence (whether under this Act or otherwise), or

(*b*) a person is assessed to a penalty under paragraph 7 of Schedule 6 to this Act [or a penalty for a deliberate inaccuracy under Schedule 24 to the Finance Act 2007 (penalties for errors)][1],

that person shall not by reason of that conduct be liable also to a penalty under any regulations under this Part.

(4) In subsection (2) above "relevant requirement" means any requirement other than one the penalty for a contravention of which is specified in section 25(3) or 33(3) above or in paragraph 2 of Schedule 7 to this Act.

(5) Subject to subsection (6) below, a power under this Part to make any provision by order or regulations—

(*a*) may be exercised so as to apply the provision only in such cases as may be described in the order or regulations;

(*b*) may be exercised so as to make different provision for different cases or descriptions of case; and

(*c*) shall include power by the order or regulations to make such supplementary, incidental, consequential or transitional provision as the Treasury or, as the case may be, the Commissioners may think fit.

(6) Subsection (5) above does not apply to an order under section 16(6) or 24(10) above.

Amendment—[1] Words in sub-s (3)(*b*) inserted by the Finance Act 2008, Schedule 40 (Appointed Day, Transitional Provisions and Consequential Amendments) Order, SI 2009/571 art 8, Sch 1 paras 31, 33 with effect from 1 April 2009.

46 Civil penalties

(1) Where a person is liable to a civil penalty imposed by or under this Part—

(*a*) the Commissioners or, on appeal, an appeal tribunal may reduce the penalty to such amount (including nil) as they think proper; but

(*b*) on an appeal relating to any penalty reduced by the Commissioners, an appeal tribunal may cancel the whole or any part of the Commissioners' reduction.

(2) In determining whether a civil penalty should be, or should have been, reduced under subsection (1) above, no account shall be taken of any of the following matters, that is to say—

(*a*) the insufficiency of the funds available to any person for paying any aggregates levy due or for paying the amount of the penalty;

(*b*) the fact that there has, in the case in question or in that case taken with any other cases, been no or no significant loss of aggregates levy;

(*c*) the fact that the person liable to the penalty or a person acting on his behalf has acted in good faith.

(3) For the purposes of any provision made by or under this Part under which liability to a civil penalty does not arise in respect of conduct for which there is shown to be a reasonable excuse—

(*a*) an insufficiency of funds available for paying any amount is not a reasonable excuse; and

(*b*) where reliance has been placed on any other person to perform any task, neither the fact of that reliance nor any conduct of the person relied upon is a reasonable excuse.

(4) Schedule 10 to this Act (which makes provision about the assessment of civil penalties imposed and about interest on such penalties) shall have effect.

(5) If it appears to the Treasury that there has been a change in the value of money since the time when the amount of a civil penalty provided for by this Part was fixed, they may by order made by statutory instrument substitute, for the amount for the time being specified as the amount of that penalty, such other sum as appears to them to be justified by the change.

(6) In subsection (5) above the reference to the time when the amount of a civil penalty was fixed is a reference—

(*a*) in the case of a penalty which has not previously been modified under that subsection, to the time of the passing of this Act; and

(*b*) in any other case, to the time of the making of the order under that subsection that made the most recent modification of the amount of that penalty.

(7) An order under subsection (5) above—

(*a*) shall not be made unless a draft of the order has been laid before Parliament and approved by resolution of the House of Commons; and

(*b*) shall not apply to the penalty for any conduct before the coming into force of the order.

(8) In this section "civil penalty" means any penalty liability to which arises otherwise than in consequence of a person's conviction for a criminal offence.

47 Service of notices etc

(1) Any notice, notification or requirement that is to be or may be served on, given to or imposed on any person for the purposes of any provision made by or under this Part may be served, given or imposed by sending it to that person or his tax representative by post in a letter addressed to that person or representative at the latest or usual residence or place of business of that person or representative.

(2) Any direction required or authorised by or under this Part to be given by the Commissioners may be given by sending it by post in a letter addressed to each person affected by it at his latest or usual residence or place of business.

(3) Any direction, notice or notification required or authorised by or under this Part to be given by the Commissioners may be withdrawn or varied by them by a direction, notice or notification given in the same manner as the one withdrawn or varied.

48 Interpretation of Part

(1) In this Part—

"accounting period" means a period which, in pursuance of any regulations under section 25(1) above, is an accounting period for the purposes of aggregates levy;

"aggregate" shall be construed in accordance with sections 17(1) and 18 above;

"agreement" includes any arrangement or understanding (whether or not legally enforceable), and cognate expressions shall be construed accordingly;

"agricultural" means agricultural within the meaning of the Agriculture Act 1967 or the Agriculture Act (Northern Ireland) 1949;

"appeal tribunal" means [the First-tier Tribunal or, where determined by or under Tribunal Procedure Rules, the Upper Tribunal;][2];

"the commencement date" has the meaning given by section 16(6) above;

"commercial exploitation" shall be construed in accordance with section 19 above;

"the Commissioners" means the Commissioners of Customs and Excise;

"conduct" includes acts and omissions;

"construction purposes" shall be construed in accordance with subsection (2) below;

"exempt process" shall be construed in accordance with section 18(2) above;

"forestry" includes the cultivation, maintenance and care of trees or woodland of any description;

"gravel" includes gravel comprising or containing pebbles or stones or both;

["HMRC" means Her Majesty's Revenue and Customs;][2]

"limestone" includes chalk and dolomite;

"member", in relation to a group, shall be construed in accordance with section 35(6) above;

"mixed" includes blended, and cognate expressions shall be construed accordingly;

"non-resident taxpayer" means a person who—

(*a*) is or is required to be registered for the purposes of aggregates levy, or would be so required but for an exemption by virtue of regulations under section 24(4) above; and

(*b*) is not resident in the United Kingdom;

"operate" and "operator", in relation to any site, shall be construed in accordance with section 21 above;

"originating site" shall be construed in accordance with section 20 above;
"prescribed" means prescribed by regulations made by the Commissioners under this Part;
"registered" means registered in the register maintained under section 24 above;
"representative member", in relation to a group, shall be construed in accordance with section 35(6) above;
"rock" does not include any rock contained in a quantity of aggregate consisting wholly or mainly of gravel or sand;
"structure" includes roads and paths, the way on which any railway track is or is to be laid and embankments;
"subordinate legislation" has the same meaning as in the Interpretation Act 1978;
"tax credit" means a tax credit for which provision is made by tax credit regulations;
"tax credit regulations" means regulations under section 30 [or 30A][1] above;
"tax representative", in relation to any person, means the person who, in accordance with any regulations under section 33 above, is for the time being that person's tax representative for the purposes of aggregates levy;
"taxable aggregate" shall be construed in accordance with section 17(2) to (4) above;
"United Kingdom waters" means—

(*a*) the territorial sea adjacent to the United Kingdom; or
(*b*) any area designated by Order in Council under section 1(7) of the Continental Shelf Act 1964.

(2) References in this Part to the use of anything for construction purposes are references to either of the following, except in so far as it consists in the application to it of an exempt process, that is to say—

(*a*) using it as material or support in the construction or improvement of any structure;
(*b*) mixing it with anything as part of the process of producing mortar, concrete, tarmacadam, coated roadstone or any similar construction material.

(3) References in this Part to winning any aggregate are references to winning it—

(*a*) by quarrying, dredging, mining or collecting it from any land or area of the seabed; or
(*b*) by separating it in any other manner from any land or area of the seabed in which it is comprised.

(4) References in this Part, in relation to any accounting period, to aggregates levy due from any person for that period are references (subject to any regulations made by virtue of section 25(2)(*a*) above) to the aggregates levy for which that person is required, in accordance with regulations under section 25 above, to account by reference to that period.

(5) References in this Part to a repayment of aggregates levy or of an amount of aggregates levy are references to any repayment of an amount to any person by virtue of—

(*a*) any tax credit regulations;
(*b*) section 31 above;
(*c*) paragraph 11(3) of Schedule 5 to this Act; or
(*d*) paragraph 6(3) of Schedule 10 to this Act.

(6) For the purposes of this Part a person is resident in the United Kingdom at any time if, at that time—

(*a*) that person has an established place of business in the United Kingdom;
(*b*) that person has a usual place of residence in the United Kingdom; or
(*c*) that person is a firm or unincorporated body which (without being resident in the United Kingdom by virtue of paragraph (*a*) above) has amongst its partners or members at least one individual with a usual place of residence in the United Kingdom.

Amendments—[1] In sub-s (1), in the definition of "tax credit regulations", words inserted by FA 2004 s 291(1), (3)–(5) with effect from 23 July 2004 (by virtue of SI 2004/1942).
[2] In sub-s (1), in the definition of "appeal tribunal", words substituted for the words "a VAT and duties tribunal"; definition of "HMRC" inserted by the Transfer of Tribunal Functions and Revenue and Customs Appeals Order, SI 2009/56 art 3, Sch 1 para 307 with effect from 1 April 2009.

Supplemental

49 Minor and consequential amendments

(1) (*amends* PCTA 1968 s 1(1)).
(2) (*adds* FA 1996 s 197(2)(*h*)).
(3) (*inserts* TA 1988 s 827(1E)).

SCHEDULES

SCHEDULE 4

AGGREGATES LEVY: REGISTRATION

Section 24

Notification of registrability etc

[1— (1) An unregistered person who—

(*a*) is required to be registered for the purposes of aggregates levy; or (*b*) has formed the intention of carrying out taxable activities that are registrable, shall notify the Commissioners of that fact.

(1A) An unregistered person who—

(*a*) would be required to be registered for the purposes of aggregates levy but for an exemption by virtue of regulations under section 24(4) of this Act; or

(*b*) has formed the intention of carrying out taxable activities that would be registrable but for such an exemption,

shall, in such cases or circumstances as may be prescribed in the regulations, notify the Commissioners of that fact.

(1B) For the purposes of sub-paragraphs (1) and (1A) above, taxable activities are "registrable" if a person carrying them out is, by reason of doing so, required by section 24(2) of this Act to be registered for the purposes of aggregates levy.][1]

(2) Subject to sub-paragraphs (5) and (6) below, a person who fails to comply with sub-paragraph (1) [or (1A)][1] above shall be liable to a penalty.

(3) The amount of the penalty shall be—

(*a*) the amount equal to 5 per cent of the relevant levy; or

(*b*) if it is greater or the circumstances are such that there is no relevant levy, £250.

(4) In sub-paragraph (3) above "relevant levy" means the aggregates levy (if any) to which the person in question is liable in respect of aggregate subjected to commercial exploitation in the period which—

(*a*) begins with the date with effect from which he is required to be registered for the purposes of that levy or, as the case may be, would be so required but for an exemption by virtue of regulations under section 24(4) of this Act; and

(*b*) ends with the date on which the Commissioners received notification of, or otherwise first became aware of, the fact that that person was required to be registered or is a person who would be so required but for such an exemption.

(5) A failure to comply with sub-paragraph (1) [or (1A)][1] above shall not give rise to any liability to a penalty under this paragraph if the person concerned satisfies the Commissioners or, on appeal, an appeal tribunal that there is a reasonable excuse for the failure.

(6) Where, by reason of any conduct falling within sub-paragraph (2) above—

(*a*) a person is convicted of an offence (whether under this Act or otherwise), or

(*b*) a person is assessed to a penalty under paragraph 7 of Schedule 6 to this Act (penalty for evasion) [or a penalty for a deliberate inaccuracy under Schedule 24 to the Finance Act 2007 (penalties for errors)][2],

that person shall not by reason of that conduct be liable also to a penalty under this paragraph.

Regulations—Finance Act 2001, section 24 and Schedule 4, (Appointed Day) Order, SI 2001/4033 (appointed day for entry into force of this paragraph is 11 January 2002).

Amendments—[1] Sub-paras (1), (1A) and (1B) substituted for sub-para (1), and words in sub-paras (2), and (5) inserted, by FA 2002 s 132(1), (3), Sch 38 para 9. These amendments are deemed to have come into force on 1 April 2002.

[2] Words in sub-para (6)(*b*) inserted by the Finance Act 2008, Schedule 40 (Appointed Day, Transitional Provisions and Consequential Amendments) Order, SI 2009/571 art 8, Sch 1 paras 31, 34 with effect from 1 April 2009.

Prospective amendments—Para 1(2) to (6) to be repealed by FA 2008 s 123, Sch 41 para 25(*l*) with effect from 1 April 2010 (by virtue of SI 2009/511 art 2).

Form of registration

2— (1) The Commissioners shall register a person who is required to be registered for the purposes of aggregates levy with effect from the time when the requirement arose.

(2) Where any two or more bodies corporate are members of the same group they shall be registered together as one person in the name of the representative member.

(3) The registration of a body corporate carrying on a business in several divisions may, if the body corporate so requests and the Commissioners see fit, be in the names of those divisions.

(4) The registration of—

(*a*) any two or more persons carrying on a business in partnership, or

(*b*) an unincorporated body,

may be in the name of the firm or body concerned.

Regulations—Finance Act 2001, section 24 and Schedule 4, (Appointed Day) Order, SI 2001/4033 (appointed day for entry into force of this paragraph is 11 January 2002).

Notification of loss or prospective loss of registrability

3— (1) A person who, having become liable to give a notification by virtue of paragraph 1 above, ceases (whether before or after being registered) to have the intention of carrying out taxable activities shall notify the Commissioners of that fact.

(2) A person who fails to comply with sub-paragraph (1) above shall be liable to a penalty of £250.

Regulations—Finance Act 2001, section 24 and Schedule 4, (Appointed Day) Order, SI 2001/4033 (appointed day for entry into force of this paragraph is 11 January 2002).

Cancellation of registration

4— (1) If the Commissioners are satisfied that a registered person—

(*a*) has ceased to carry out taxable activities, and

(*b*) does not have the intention of carrying out taxable activities,

they may cancel his registration with effect from such time after he last carried out such activities as appears to them to be appropriate.

(2) Sub-paragraph (1) above applies whether or not the registered person has notified the Commissioners under paragraph 3 above.

(3) Where a registered person is exempted from the requirement to be registered by virtue of regulations under section 24(4), the Commissioners may cancel his registration with effect from the time when he became so exempted or such later time as appears to them to be appropriate.

(4) The Commissioners shall be under a duty to exercise the power conferred by sub-paragraph (1) or (3) above with effect from any time if, where the power is exercisable, they are satisfied that the conditions specified in sub-paragraph (5) below are satisfied and were or will be satisfied at that time.

(5) Those conditions are—

(*a*) that the person in question—

(i) has given a notification under paragraph 3 above; or

(ii) is exempted from the requirement to be registered by virtue of regulations under section 24(4) of this Act;

(*b*) that no aggregates levy due from that person, and no amount recoverable as if it were such levy, remains unpaid;

(*c*) that no tax credit to which that person is entitled by virtue of any tax credit regulations is outstanding; and

(*d*) that that person is not subject to any outstanding liability to make a return for the purposes of aggregates levy.

(6) Where—

(*a*) a registered person notifies the Commissioners under paragraph 3 above, and

(*b*) they are satisfied that (if he had not been registered) he would not have been required to be registered at any time since the time when he was registered,

they shall cancel his registration with effect from the date of his registration.

(7) Where—

(*a*) a registered person is exempted from the requirement to be registered by virtue of regulations under section 24(4) of this Act, and

(*b*) the Commissioners are satisfied that he has been so exempted at all times since being registered,

they shall cancel his registration with effect from the date of his registration.

Regulations—Finance Act 2001, section 24 and Schedule 4, (Appointed Day) Order, SI 2001/4033 (appointed day for entry into force of this paragraph is 11 January 2002).

Correction of the register etc

5— (1) The Commissioners may by regulations make provision for and with respect to the correction of entries in the register.

(2) Regulations under this paragraph may, to such extent as appears to the Commissioners appropriate for keeping the register up to date, make provision requiring—

(*a*) registered persons, and

(*b*) persons who are required to be registered, and

(*c*) persons who would be so required but for any exemption by virtue of regulations under section 24(4) of this Act,

to notify the Commissioners of changes in circumstances relating to themselves, their businesses or any other matter with respect to which particulars are contained in the register (or would be, were the person registered).

Regulations—Finance Act 2001, section 24 and Schedule 4, (Appointed Day) Order, SI 2001/4033 (appointed day for entry into force of this paragraph is 20 December 2001).

Supplemental regulations about notifications

6— (1) For the purposes of any provision made by or under section 24 of this Act or this Schedule for any matter to be notified to the Commissioners, regulations made by the Commissioners may make provision—

(*a*) as to the time within which the notification is to be given;

(*b*) as to the form and manner in which the notification is to be given; and

(*c*) as to the information and other particulars to be contained in or provided with any notification.

(2) For those purposes the Commissioners may also by regulations impose obligations requiring a person who has given a notification to notify the Commissioners if any information contained in or provided in connection with that notification is or becomes inaccurate.

(3) The power under this paragraph to make regulations as to the time within which any notification is to be given shall include power to authorise the Commissioners to extend the time for the giving of a notification.

Regulations—Finance Act 2001, section 24 and Schedule 4, (Appointed Day) Order, SI 2001/4033 (appointed day for entry into force of this paragraph is 20 December 2001).

Publication of information on the register

7— (1) The Commissioners may publish, by such means as they think fit, any information which—

(*a*) is derived from the register; and

(*b*) falls within any of the descriptions set out below.

(2) The descriptions are—

(*a*) the names of registered persons;

(*b*) particulars of registered sites;

(*c*) the fact (where it is the case) that the registered person is a body corporate which is a member of a group;

(*d*) the names of the other bodies corporate which are members of the group.

(3) Information may be published in accordance with this paragraph notwithstanding any obligation not to disclose the information that would otherwise apply.

Regulations—Finance Act 2001, section 24 and Schedule 4, (Appointed Day) Order, SI 2001/4033 (appointed day for entry into force of this paragraph is 11 January 2002).

Interpretation of Schedule

8— (1) In this Schedule—

(*a*) references to the register are references to the register maintained under section 24 of this Act;

(*b*) references to registering a person are references to registering him in that register; and

(*c*) references to a person's registration are references to his registration in that register;

and "unregistered" shall be construed accordingly.

(2) For the purposes of this Schedule a person carries out a taxable activity if a quantity of aggregate is subjected to commercial exploitation in the United Kingdom in circumstances in which he is responsible for its being so subjected.

Regulations—Finance Act 2001, section 24 and Schedule 4, (Appointed Day) Order, SI 2001/4033 (appointed day for entry into force of this paragraph is 11 January 2002).

SCHEDULE 5

AGGREGATES LEVY: RECOVERY AND INTEREST

Section 27

Recovery of levy as debt due

1 Aggregates levy shall be recoverable as a debt due to the Crown.

Assessments of amounts of levy due

2— (1) Where it appears to the Commissioners—

(*a*) that any period is an accounting period by reference to which a person is liable to account for aggregates levy,

(*b*) that any aggregates levy for which that person is liable to account by reference to that period has become due, and

(*c*) that there has been a default by that person that falls within sub-paragraph (2) below,

they may assess the amount of the levy due from that person for that period to the best of their judgement and notify that amount to that person.

(2) The defaults falling within this sub-paragraph are—

(*a*) any failure to make a return required to be made by any provision made by or under this Part of this Act;

(*b*) any failure to keep any documents necessary to verify returns required to be made under any such provision;

(*c*) any failure to afford the facilities necessary to verify returns required to be made under any such provision;

(*d*) the making, in purported compliance with any requirement of any such provision to make a return, of an incomplete or incorrect return;

(*e*) any failure to comply with a requirement imposed by or under Schedule 4 to this Act.

(3) Where it appears to the Commissioners that a default falling within sub-paragraph (2) above is a default by a person on whom the requirement to make a return is imposed in his capacity as the representative of another person, sub-paragraph (1) above shall apply as if the reference to the amount of aggregates levy due included a reference to any aggregates levy due from that other person.

(4) In a case where—

(*a*) the Commissioners have made an assessment for any accounting period as a result of any person's failure to make a return for that period,

(*b*) the levy assessed has been paid but no proper return has been made for that period,

(*c*) as a result of a failure (whether by that person or a representative of his) to make a return for a later accounting period, the Commissioners find it necessary to make another assessment under this paragraph in relation to the later period, and

(*d*) the Commissioners think it appropriate to do so in the light of the absence of a proper return for the earlier period,

they may, in the assessment in relation to the later period, specify an amount of aggregates levy due that is greater than the amount that they would have considered to be appropriate had they had regard only to the later period.

(5) Where an amount has been assessed and notified to any person under this paragraph, it shall be recoverable on the basis that it is an amount of aggregates levy due from him.

(6) Sub-paragraph (5) above does not have effect if, or to the extent that, the assessment in question has been withdrawn or reduced.

Supplementary assessments

3— (1) If, where an assessment has been notified to any person under paragraph 2 above or this paragraph, it appears to the Commissioners that the amount which ought to have been assessed as due for any accounting period exceeds the amount that has already been assessed, the Commissioners may make a supplementary assessment of the amount of the excess and notify that person accordingly.

(2) Where an amount has been assessed and notified to any person under this paragraph it shall be recoverable on the basis that it is an amount of aggregates levy due from him.

(3) Sub-paragraph (2) above does not have effect if, or to the extent that, the assessment in question has been withdrawn or reduced.

Time limits for assessments

4— (1) An assessment under paragraph 2 or 3 above of an amount of aggregates levy due for any accounting period—

(*a*) shall not be made more than two years after the end of the accounting period unless it is made within the period mentioned in sub-paragraph (2) below; and

(*b*) subject to sub-paragraph (3) below, shall not in any event be made more than three years after the end of that accounting period.

(2) The period referred to in sub-paragraph (1)(*a*) above is the period of one year after evidence of facts sufficient in the Commissioners' opinion to justify the making of the assessment first came to their knowledge.

(3) Subject to sub-paragraph (4) below, where aggregates levy has been lost—

(*a*) as a result of any conduct for which a person has been convicted of an offence involving fraud,

(*b*) in circumstances giving rise to liability to a penalty under paragraph 1 of Schedule 4 to this Act (failure to notify of registrability etc), or

(*c*) as a result of conduct falling within paragraph 7(1) of Schedule 6 to this Act (evasion),

that levy may be assessed under paragraph 2 or 3 above as if, in sub-paragraph (1)(*b*) above, for "three years" there were substituted "twenty years".

(4) Where, after a person's death, the Commissioners propose to assess an amount of aggregates levy as due by reason of some conduct of the deceased—

(*a*) the assessment shall not be made more than three years after the death; and

(*b*) if the circumstances are as set out in sub-paragraph (3) above—

(i) the modification of sub-paragraph (1) above contained in that sub-paragraph shall not apply; but

(ii) any assessment which (applying that modification) could have been made immediately after the death may be made at any time within three years after it.

(5) Nothing in this paragraph shall prejudice the powers of the Commissioners under paragraph 2(4) above.

Prospective amendments—In sub-paras (1)(*b*), (4)(*a*) the words "4 years" to be substituted for the words "three years", sub-para (4)(*b*) and the word "and" before it to be repealed, and sub-para (3) to be substituted, by FA 2009 s 99, Sch 51 paras 27, 29, with effect from such day as the Treasury may by order made by statutory instrument appoint. Sub-para (3) to read as follows—

"(3) An assessment of an amount due from a person in a case involving a loss of aggregates levy—

(*a*) brought about deliberately by the person (or by another person acting on that person's behalf), or (*b*) attributable to a failure by the person to comply with an obligation under section 24(2) or paragraph 1 of Schedule 4,

may be made at any time not more than 20 years after the end of the accounting period to which it relates (subject to sub-paragraph (4)).

(3A) In sub-paragraph (3)(*a*) the reference to a loss brought about deliberately by the person includes a loss brought about as a result of a deliberate inaccuracy in a document given to Her Majesty's Revenue and Customs by or on behalf of that person."

Penalty interest on unpaid levy

5— (1) Where—

(*a*) a person makes a return for the purposes of any regulations made under section 25 of this Act (whether or not at the time required by the regulations), and

(*b*) the return shows that an amount of aggregates levy is due from him for the accounting period for which the return is made,

that amount shall carry penalty interest for the period specified in sub-paragraph (2) below.

(2) That period is the period which—

(*a*) begins with the day after that on which the person is required in accordance with regulations under section 25 of this Act to pay aggregates levy due from him for the accounting period in question; and

(*b*) ends with the day before that on which the amount shown in the return is paid.

Interest on overdue levy paid before assessment

6— (1) Where—

(*a*) the circumstances are such that there was a time when an assessment could have been made under paragraph 2 or 3 above of an amount of levy due from any person, but

(*b*) before the making and notification to that person of any assessment of that amount, the amount was paid,

the whole of the amount paid shall be taken to have carried interest for the period specified in sub-paragraph (2).

(2) That period is the period which—

(*a*) begins with the day after that on which the person is required in accordance with regulations under section 25 of this Act to pay aggregates levy due from him for the accounting period to which the amount in question relates; and

(*b*) ends with the day before that on which that amount was paid.

(3) The interest payable by virtue of this paragraph shall be payable at the rate applicable under section 197 of the Finance Act 1996.

Penalty interest on levy where no return made

7— (1) Where—

(*a*) the Commissioners make an assessment under paragraph 2 or 3 above of an amount of aggregates levy due from any person for any accounting period and notify it to him, and

(*b*) the assessment is made at a time after the time by which a return is required by regulations under section 25 of this Act to be made by that person for that accounting period and before any such return has been made,

that amount shall carry penalty interest for the period specified in sub-paragraph (2) below.

(2) That period is the period which—

(*a*) begins with the day after that on which the person is required in accordance with regulations under section 25 of this Act to pay aggregates levy due from him for the accounting period in question; and

(*b*) ends with the day before that on which the assessed amount is paid.

Ordinary and penalty interest on under-declared levy

8— (1) Subject to sub-paragraph (4) below, where—

(*a*) the Commissioners make an assessment under paragraph 2 or 3 above of an amount of aggregates levy due from any person for any accounting period and notify it to him,

(*b*) the assessment is made after a return for the purposes of any regulations under section 25 has been made by that person for that accounting period, and

(*c*) the assessment is made on the basis that the amount ("the additional amount") is due from him in addition to any amount shown in the return, or in a previous assessment made in relation to the accounting period,

the additional amount shall carry interest for the period specified in sub-paragraph (2) below.

(2) That period is the period which—

(*a*) begins with the day after that on which the person is required in accordance with regulations under section 25 of this Act to pay aggregates levy due from him for the accounting period in question; and

(*b*) ends with the day before the day on which the additional amount is paid.

(3) Interest under this paragraph—

(*a*) in respect of so much of the period specified in sub-paragraph (2) above as falls before the day on which the assessment is notified to the person in question, shall be payable at the rate applicable under section 197 of the Finance Act 1996; and

(*b*) in respect of the remainder (if any) of that period, shall be penalty interest.

(4) Where—

(*a*) the Commissioners make an assessment under paragraph 2 or 3 above of an amount of aggregates levy due from any person for any accounting period and notify it to him,

(*b*) they also specify a date for the purposes of this sub-paragraph, and

(*c*) the amount assessed is paid on or before that date,

the only interest carried by that amount under this paragraph shall be interest, at the rate given by sub-paragraph (3)(*a*) above, for the period before the day on which the assessment is notified.

Penalty interest on unpaid ordinary interest

9— (1) Subject to sub-paragraph (2) below, where the Commissioners make an assessment under paragraph 12 below of an amount of interest payable at the rate given by paragraph 8(3)(*a*) above, that amount shall carry penalty interest for the period which—

(*a*) begins with the day on which the assessment is notified to the person on whom the assessment is made; and

(*b*) ends with the day before the day on which the assessed interest is paid.

(2) Where—

(*a*) the Commissioners make an assessment under paragraph 12 below of an amount of interest due from any person,

(*b*) they also specify a date for the purposes of this sub-paragraph, and

(*c*) the amount of interest assessed is paid on or before that date,

the amount paid before that date shall not carry penalty interest under this paragraph.

Penalty interest

10— (1) Penalty interest under any of paragraphs 5 to 9 above shall be compound interest calculated—

(*a*) at the penalty rate; and

(*b*) with monthly rests.

(2) For this purpose the penalty rate is the rate found by—

(*a*) taking the rate applicable under section 197 of the Finance Act 1996 for the purposes of paragraph 8(3)(*a*) above; and

(*b*) adding 10 percentage points to that rate.

(3) Where a person is liable under any of paragraphs 5 to 9 above to pay any penalty interest, the Commissioners or, on appeal, an appeal tribunal may reduce the amount payable to such amount (including nil) as they think proper.

(4) Subject to sub-paragraph (5) below, where the person concerned satisfies the Commissioners or, on appeal, an appeal tribunal that there is a reasonable excuse for the conduct giving rise to the liability to pay penalty interest, that is a matter which (among other things) may be taken into account under sub-paragraph (3) above.

(5) In determining whether there is a reasonable excuse for the purposes of sub-paragraph (4) above, no account shall be taken of any of the following matters, that is to say—

(*a*) the insufficiency of the funds available to any person for paying any aggregates levy due or for paying the amount of the interest;

(*b*) the fact that there has, in the case in question or in that case taken with any other cases, been no or no significant loss of aggregates levy;

(*c*) the fact that the person liable to pay the interest or a person acting on his behalf has acted in good faith.

(6) In the case of interest reduced by the Commissioners under sub-paragraph (3) above an appeal tribunal, on an appeal relating to the interest, may cancel the whole or any part of the reduction made by the Commissioners.

Supplemental provisions about interest

11— (1) Interest under any of paragraphs 5 to 9 above shall be paid without any deduction of income tax.

(2) Sub-paragraph (3) below applies where—

(*a*) an amount carries interest under any of paragraphs 5 to 9 above (or would do so apart from that sub-paragraph); and

(*b*) all or part of the amount turns out not to be due.

(3) In such a case—

(*a*) the amount or part that turns out not to be due shall not carry interest under the applicable paragraph and shall be treated as never having done so; and

(*b*) all such adjustments as are reasonable shall be made, including (subject to section 32 of, and Schedule 8 to, this Act) adjustments by way of repayment.

Assessments to interest

12— (1) Where a person is liable for interest under any of paragraphs 5 to 9 above, the Commissioners may assess the amount due by way of interest and notify it to him accordingly.

(2) If, where an assessment has been notified to any person under sub-paragraph (1) above or this sub-paragraph, it appears to the Commissioners that the amount which ought to have been assessed exceeds the amount that has already been assessed, the Commissioners may make a supplementary assessment of the amount of the excess and notify that person accordingly.

(3) Where an amount has been assessed and notified to any person under this paragraph, it shall be recoverable as if it were aggregates levy due from him.

(4) Sub-paragraph (3) above—

(*a*) shall not apply so as to require any interest to be payable on interest except—

(i) in accordance with paragraph 9 above; or

(ii) in so far as it falls to be compounded in accordance with paragraph 10 above;

and

(*b*) shall not have effect if, or to the extent that, the assessment in question has been withdrawn or reduced.

(5) Paragraph 4 above shall apply in relation to assessments under this paragraph as if any assessment to interest were an assessment under paragraph 2 above to aggregates levy due for the period which is the relevant accounting period in relation to that interest.

(6) Subject to sub-paragraph (7) below, where a person—

(*a*) is assessed under this paragraph to an amount due by way of any interest, and

(*b*) is also assessed under paragraph 2 or 3 above for the accounting period which is the relevant accounting period in relation to that interest,

the assessments may be combined and notified to him as one assessment.

(7) A notice of a combined assessment under sub-paragraph (6) above must separately identify the interest being assessed.

(8) The relevant accounting period for the purposes of this paragraph is—

(*a*) in the case of interest on the levy due for any accounting period, that accounting period; and

(*b*) in the case of interest on interest (whether under paragraph 9 above or by virtue of any compounding under paragraph 10 above) the period which is the relevant accounting period for the interest on which the interest is payable.

(9) In a case where—

(*a*) the amount of any interest falls to be calculated by reference to aggregates levy which was not paid at the time when it should have been, and

(*b*) that levy cannot be readily attributed to any one or more accounting periods,

that levy shall be treated for the purposes of interest on any of that levy as aggregates levy due for such period or periods as the Commissioners may determine to the best of their judgement and notify to the person liable.

Further assessments to penalty interest

13— (1) Where an assessment is made under paragraph 12 above to an amount of penalty interest under any of paragraphs 5 to 9 above—

(*a*) the notice of assessment shall specify a date, not later than the date of the notice of assessment, to which the amount of interest which is assessed is calculated; and

(*b*) if the interest continues to accrue after that date, a further assessment or further assessments may be made under paragraph 12 above in respect of the amounts so accruing.

(2) Where—

(*a*) an assessment to penalty interest is made specifying a date for the purposes of sub-paragraph (1)(*a*) above, and

(*b*) within such period as may for the purposes of this sub-paragraph have been notified by the Commissioners to the person liable for the interest, the amount on which the interest is payable is paid,

that amount shall be deemed for the purposes of any further liability to interest to have been paid on the specified date.

Recovery by distress

14 In section 51(5) of the Finance Act 1997 (definition of relevant taxes for the purposes of the power to make provision by regulations for enforcement by distress of the relevant taxes), after paragraph (*d*) there shall be inserted—

"(*da*) aggregates levy;".

Prospective amendments—Para 14A to be inserted by the Tribunals, Courts and Enforcement Act 2007 s 62(3), Sch 13 paras 139, 140 with effect from a date to be appointed. Para 14A to be repealed by FA 2008 s 129, Sch 43 para 8 with effect from such day as the Commissioners may by statutory instrument appoint.

Para 14A to read—

"*Controlled goods agreements*

14A—(1) This paragraph applies where an enforcement agent acting under the power conferred, by virtue of paragraph 14 above, by section 51(A1) of the Finance Act 1997 (power to use the procedure in Schedule 12 to the Tribunals, Courts and Enforcement Act 2007) has entered into a controlled goods agreement with the person against whom the power is exercisable ("the person in default").
(2) In this paragraph, "controlled goods agreement" has the meaning given by paragraph 13(4) of that Schedule.
(3) Subject to sub-paragraph (4), if the person in default removes or disposes of goods (or permits their removal or disposal) in breach of the controlled goods agreement, he is liable to a penalty equal to half of the levy or other amount recoverable under section 51(A1) of the Finance Act 1997.
(4) The person in default shall not be liable to a penalty under subparagraph
(3) above if he satisfies the Commissioners or, on appeal, an appeal tribunal, that there is a reasonable excuse for the breach in question.
(5) This paragraph extends only to England and Wales.".

Walking possession agreements

15— (1) This paragraph applies where—

(*a*) in accordance with regulations made by virtue of paragraph 14 above a distress is authorised to be levied on the goods and chattels of a person;

(*b*) that person ("the person in default") has refused or neglected to pay an amount of aggregates levy due from him or an amount recoverable from him as if it were aggregates levy; and

(*c*) the person levying the distress and the person in default have entered into a walking possession agreement.

(2) For the purposes of this paragraph a walking possession agreement is an agreement under which, in consideration of the property distrained upon being allowed to remain in the custody of the person in default and of the delaying of its sale, the person in default—

(*a*) acknowledges that the property specified in the agreement is under distraint and held in walking possession; and

(*b*) undertakes that, except with the consent of the Commissioners and subject to such conditions as they may impose, he will not remove or allow the removal of any of the specified property from the premises named in the agreement.

(3) Subject to sub-paragraph (4) below, if the person in default is in breach of the undertaking contained in a walking possession agreement, he shall be liable to a penalty equal to one half of the levy or other amount referred to in sub-paragraph (1)(*b*) above.

(4) The person in default shall not be liable to a penalty under sub-paragraph (3) above if he satisfies the Commissioners or, on appeal, an appeal tribunal that there is a reasonable excuse for the breach in question.

(5) This paragraph does not extend to Scotland.

Prospective amendments—Sub-para (5) to be substituted by the Tribunals, Courts and Enforcement Act 2007 s 62(3), Sch 13 paras 139, 141 with effect from a date to be appointed. Sub-para (5) as substituted, to read—
"(5) This paragraph extends only to Northern Ireland.".

Recovery by diligence

16 In section 52(5) of the Finance Act 1997 (definition of relevant taxes for the purposes of the power to make provision by regulations for enforcement by diligence of the relevant taxes), after paragraph (*d*) there shall be inserted—

"(*da*) aggregates levy;".

Preferential debts in England and Wales and Northern Ireland

17 (1), (2) …[1]

(3) In the Insolvency (Northern Ireland) Order 1989—

(*a*) in Article 346(1) (preferential debts), after "climate change levy,", there shall be inserted "aggregates levy,"; and

(*b*) in Schedule 4 (categories of preferential debts), the paragraph set out in sub-paragraph (4) below shall be inserted after paragraph 3C.

(4) That paragraph is as follows—

"3D. Any aggregates levy which is referable to the period of 6 months next before the relevant date (which period is referred to below as "the 6-month period").

For the purposes of this paragraph—

(*a*) where the whole of the accounting period to which any aggregates levy is attributable falls within the 6-month period, the whole amount of that levy is referable to that period; and

(*b*) in any other case the amount of any aggregates levy which is referable to the 6-month period is the proportion of the levy which is equal to such proportion (if any) of the accounting period in question as falls within the 6-month period;

and references here to accounting periods shall be construed in accordance with Part 2 of the Finance Act 2001."

Amendments—[1] Sub-paras (1), (2) repealed by the Enterprise Act 2002 ss 278(2), 279, Sch 26 with effect 15 September 2003 (by virtue of SI 2003/3093).

Preferred debts in Scotland

18

Amendment—This paragraph repealed by the Enterprise Act 2002 ss 278(2), 279, Sch 26 with effect from 15 September 2003 (by virtue of SI 2003/3093).

Interpretation of Schedule etc

19— (1) In this Schedule "penalty interest" shall be construed in accordance with paragraph 10 above.

(2) Any notification of an assessment under any provision of this Schedule to a person's representative shall be treated for the purposes of this Part of this Act as notification to the person in relation to whom the representative acts.

(3) In this Schedule "representative", in relation to any person, means—

(*a*) any of that person's personal representatives;

(*b*) that person's trustee in bankruptcy or liquidator;

(*c*) any person holding office as a receiver in relation to that person or any of his property;

(*d*) that person's tax representative or any other person for the time being acting in a representative capacity in relation to that person.

(4) In this paragraph "trustee in bankruptcy" includes, as respects Scotland—

(*a*) an interim or permanent trustee (within the meaning of the Bankruptcy (Scotland) Act 1985); and

(*b*) a trustee acting under a trust deed (within the meaning of that Act).

SCHEDULE 6

AGGREGATES LEVY: EVASION, MISDECLARATION AND NEGLECT

Section 28

PART 1

CRIMINAL OFFENCES

Evasion

1— (1) A person is guilty of an offence if he is knowingly concerned in, or in the taking of steps with a view to—

(*a*) the fraudulent evasion by that person of any aggregates levy with which he is charged; or

(*b*) the fraudulent evasion by any other person of any aggregates levy with which that other person is charged.

(2) The references in sub-paragraph (1) above to the evasion of aggregates levy include references to obtaining, in circumstances where there is no entitlement to it, either a tax credit or a repayment of aggregates levy.

(3) A person guilty of an offence under this paragraph shall be liable (subject to sub-paragraph (4) below)—

(*a*) on summary conviction, to a penalty of the statutory maximum or to imprisonment for a term not exceeding six months, or to both;

(*b*) on conviction on indictment, to a penalty of any amount or to imprisonment for a term not exceeding seven years, or to both.

(4) In the case of any offence under this paragraph, where the statutory maximum is less than three times the sum of the amounts of aggregates levy which are shown to be amounts that were or were intended to be evaded, the penalty on summary conviction shall be the amount equal to three times that sum (instead of the statutory maximum).

(5) For the purposes of sub-paragraph (4) above the amounts of levy that were or were intended to be evaded shall be taken to include—

(*a*) the amount of any tax credit, and

(*b*) the amount of any repayment of aggregates levy,

which was, or was intended to be, obtained in circumstances where there was no entitlement to it.

(6) In determining for the purposes of sub-paragraph (4) above how much aggregates levy (in addition to any amount falling within sub-paragraph (5) above) was or was intended to be evaded, no account shall be taken of the extent (if any) to which any liability to aggregates levy of any person fell, or would have fallen, to be reduced by the amount of any tax credit or repayment of aggregates levy to which he was, or would have been, entitled.

Misstatements

2— (1) A person is guilty of an offence if, with the requisite intent and for purposes connected with aggregates levy—

(*a*) he produces or provides, or causes to be produced or provided, any document which is false in a material particular; or

(*b*) he otherwise makes use of such a document;

and in this sub-paragraph "the requisite intent" means the intent to deceive any person or to secure that a machine will respond to the document as if it were a true document.

(2) A person is guilty of an offence if, in providing any information under any provision made by or under this Part of this Act—

(*a*) he makes a statement which he knows to be false in a material particular; or

(*b*) he recklessly makes a statement which is false in a material particular.

(3) A person guilty of an offence under this paragraph shall be liable (subject to sub-paragraph (4) below)—

(*a*) on summary conviction, to a penalty of the statutory maximum or to imprisonment for a term not exceeding six months, or to both;

(*b*) on conviction on indictment, to a penalty of any amount or to imprisonment for a term not exceeding seven years, or to both.

(4) In the case of any offence under this paragraph, where—

(*a*) the document referred to in sub-paragraph (1) above is a return required under any provision made by or under this Part of this Act, or

(*b*) the information referred to in sub-paragraph (2) above is contained in or otherwise relevant to such a return,

the amount of the penalty on summary conviction shall be whichever is the greater of the statutory maximum and the amount equal to three times the sum of the amounts (if any) by which the return understates any person's liability to aggregates levy.

(5) In sub-paragraph (4) above the reference to the amount by which any person's liability to aggregates levy is understated shall be taken to be equal to the sum of—

(*a*) the amount (if any) by which his gross liability was understated; and

(*b*) the amount (if any) by which any entitlements of his to tax credits and repayments of aggregates levy were overstated.

(6) In sub-paragraph (5) above "gross liability" means liability to aggregates levy before any deduction is made in respect of any entitlement to any tax credit or repayments of aggregates levy.

Conduct involving evasions or misstatements

3— (1) A person is guilty of an offence under this paragraph if his conduct during any particular period must have involved the commission by him of one or more offences under the preceding provisions of this Schedule.

(2) For the purposes of any proceedings for an offence under this paragraph it shall be immaterial whether the particulars of the offence or offences that must have been committed are known.

(3) A person guilty of an offence under this paragraph shall be liable (subject to sub-paragraph (4) below)—

(*a*) on summary conviction, to a penalty of the statutory maximum or to imprisonment for a term not exceeding six months, or to both;

(*b*) on conviction on indictment, to a penalty of any amount or to imprisonment for a term not exceeding seven years, or to both.

(4) In the case of any offence under this paragraph, where the statutory maximum is less than three times the sum of the amounts of aggregates levy which are shown to be amounts that were or were intended to be evaded by the conduct in question, the penalty on summary conviction shall be the amount equal to three times that sum (instead of the statutory maximum).

(5) For the purposes of sub-paragraph (4) above the amounts of levy that were or were intended to be evaded by any conduct shall be taken to include—

(*a*) the amount of any tax credit, and

(*b*) the amount of any repayment of aggregates levy,

which was, or was intended to be, obtained in circumstances where there was no entitlement to it.

(6) In determining for the purposes of sub-paragraph (4) above how much aggregates levy (in addition to any amount falling within sub-paragraph (5) above) was or was intended to be evaded, no account shall be taken of the extent (if any) to which any liability to aggregates levy of any person fell, or would have fallen, to be reduced by the amount of any tax credit or repayments of aggregates levy to which he was, or would have been, entitled.

Preparations for evasion

4— (1) Where a person—

(*a*) becomes a party to any agreement under or by means of which a quantity of taxable aggregate is or is to be subjected to commercial exploitation in the United Kingdom, or

(*b*) makes arrangements for any other person to become a party to such an agreement, he is guilty of an offence if he does so in the belief that aggregates levy chargeable on the aggregate in question will be evaded.

(2) Subject to sub-paragraph (3) below, a person guilty of an offence under this paragraph shall be liable, on summary conviction, to a penalty of level 5 on the standard scale.

(3) In the case of any offence under this paragraph, where level 5 on the standard scale is less than three times the sum of the amounts of aggregates levy which are shown to be amounts that were or were intended to be evaded in respect of the aggregate in question, the penalty shall be the amount equal to three times that sum (instead of level 5 on the standard scale).

(4) For the purposes of sub-paragraph (3) above the amounts of levy that were or were intended to be evaded shall be taken to include—

(*a*) the amount of any tax credit, and

(*b*) the amount of any repayment of aggregates levy,

which was, or was intended to be, obtained in circumstances where there was no entitlement to it.

(5) In determining for the purposes of sub-paragraph (3) above how much aggregates levy (in addition to any amount falling within sub-paragraph (4) above) was or was intended to be evaded, no account shall be taken of the extent (if any) to which any liability to aggregates levy of any person fell, or would have fallen, to be reduced by the amount of any tax credit or repayments of aggregates levy to which he was, or would have been, entitled.

Criminal proceedings etc

5 Sections 145 to 155 of the Customs and Excise Management Act 1979 (proceedings for offences, mitigation of penalties and certain other matters) shall apply in relation to offences and penalties under this Part of this Schedule as they apply in relation to offences and penalties under the customs and excise Acts.

Arrest

6— (1) Where an authorised person has reasonable grounds for suspecting that a fraud offence has been committed he may arrest anyone whom he has reasonable grounds for suspecting to be guilty of the offence.

(2) In this paragraph—

"authorised person" means any person acting under the authority of the Commissioners; and "a fraud offence" means an offence under any of paragraphs 1 to 3 above.[1]

Amendments—[1] This para repealed by FA 2007 ss 84, 114, Sch 22 paras 3, 12(*a*), Sch 27 Pt 5(1) with effect from 1 December 2007 (by virtue of SI 2007/3166 art 3(*a*)).

PART 2
CIVIL PENALTIES

Evasion

7— (1) Subject to sub-paragraph (5) below, where—

(a) any person engages in any conduct for the purpose of evading aggregates levy [and][1]

(b) …[1]

(c) that conduct involves dishonesty (whether or not it is such as to give rise to criminal liability),

that person shall be liable to a penalty …[1]

[(1A) The amount of the penalty shall be—

(a) equal to the amount of the levy evaded, or (as the case may be) intended to be evaded, by the person's conduct if at the time of engaging in that conduct he was or was required to be registered;

(b) equal to twice that amount if at that time the person neither was nor was required to be registered.][1]

(2) The references in sub-paragraph (1) above to evading aggregates levy include references to obtaining, in circumstances where there is no entitlement to it, either—

(a) a tax credit; or

(b) a repayment of aggregates levy.

(3) For the purposes of [sub-paragraph (1A)][1] *above the amount of levy that was or was intended to be evaded by any conduct shall be taken to include—*

(a) the amount of any tax credit, and

(b) the amount of any repayment of aggregates levy,

which was, or was intended to be, obtained in circumstances where there was no entitlement to it.

(4) In determining for the purposes of [sub-paragraph (1A)][1] *above how much aggregates levy (in addition to any amount falling within sub-paragraph (3) above) was or was intended to be evaded, no account shall be taken of the extent (if any) to which any liability to aggregates levy of any person fell, or would have fallen, to be reduced by the amount of any tax credit or repayments of aggregates levy to which he was, or would have been, entitled.*

(5) Where, by reason of conduct falling within sub-paragraph (1) above, a person is convicted of an offence (whether under this Act or otherwise) that person shall not by reason of that conduct be liable also to a penalty under this paragraph.[2]

Amendments—[1] Word in sub-para (1) inserted, and words repealed, sub-para (1A) inserted, and words in sub-paras (3), (4) substituted, by FA 2002 ss 133(1)–(4), (6), 141, Sch 40 Pt 4(3). These amendments are deemed to have come into force on 1 May 2002.

[2] Para 7 repealed by FA 2008 s 122, Sch 40 para 21(*i*) with effect from 1 April 2009 (by virtue of SI 2009/571 art 2). This para repealed only in so far as it relates to conduct involving dishonesty which relates to—
(a) an inaccuracy in a document, or
(b) a failure to notify HMRC of an under-assessment by HMRC (SI 2009/571 art 6).

Liability of directors etc for civil penalties

8— (1) Where it appears to the Commissioners—

(a) that a body corporate is liable to a penalty under paragraph 7 above, and

(b) that the conduct giving rise to that penalty is, in whole or in part, attributable to the dishonesty of a person who is, or at the material time was, a director or managing officer of the body corporate (a "named officer"),

the Commissioners may serve a notice under this paragraph on the body corporate and on the named officer.

(2) A notice under this paragraph shall state—

(a) the amount of the penalty referred to in sub-paragraph (1)(a) above ("the basic penalty"); and

(b) that the Commissioners propose, in accordance with this paragraph, to recover from the named officer such portion of the basic penalty (which may be the whole of it) as is specified in the notice.

(3) Where a notice is served under this paragraph, the portion of the basic penalty specified in the notice shall be recoverable from the named officer as if he were personally liable under paragraph 7 above to a penalty which corresponds to that portion.

(4) Where a notice is served under this paragraph—

(a) the amount which may be assessed under Schedule 10 to this Act as the amount due by way of penalty from the body corporate shall be only so much (if any) of the basic penalty as is not assessed on and notified to a named officer; and

(b) the body corporate shall be treated as discharged from liability for so much of the basic penalty as is so assessed and notified.

(5) Subject to the following provisions of this paragraph, the giving of a notice under this paragraph as such shall not be a decision which may be [appealed under section 40][2] *of this Act.*

(6) Where a body corporate is assessed as mentioned in sub-paragraph (4)(a) above, the decisions of the Commissioners that may be [appealed under section 40][2] *of this Act shall include their decision—*

(a) as to the liability of the body corporate to a penalty; and

(b) as to the amount of the basic penalty that is specified in the assessment;

and sections [40A to 42][2] *of this Act shall apply accordingly.*

(7) Where an assessment is made on a named officer by virtue of this paragraph, the decisions which may be [appealed under section 40][2] *of this Act at the request of the named officer shall include—*

(a) the Commissioners' decisions in the case of the body corporate as to the matters mentioned in sub-paragraph (6)(a) and (b) above;

(b) their decision that the conduct of the body corporate referred to in sub-paragraph (1)(b) above is, in whole or in part, attributable to the dishonesty of the named officer; and

(c) their decision as to the portion of the penalty which the Commissioners propose to recover from him;

and sections [40A to 42][2] *of this Act shall apply accordingly.*

(8) In this paragraph a "managing officer", in relation to a body corporate, means—

(a) any manager, secretary or other similar officer of the body corporate; or

(b) any person purporting to act in any such capacity or as a director.

(9) Where the affairs of a body corporate are managed by its members, this paragraph shall apply in relation to the conduct of a member in connection with his functions of management as if he were a director of the body corporate.[1]

Amendments—[1] Para 8 repealed by FA 2008 s 122, Sch 40 para 21(*i*) with effect from 1 April 2009 (by virtue of SI 2009/571 art 2).
This para repealed only in so far as it relates to conduct involving dishonesty which relates to—
(a) an inaccuracy in a document, or
(b) a failure to notify HMRC of an under-assessment by HMRC (SI 2009/571 art 6).

[2] Insofar as it continues to apply, in sub-paras (5), (7) words substituted for the words "reviewed under section 40", in sub-para (6) words substituted for the words "reviewed in accordance with section 40"; in sub-paras (6), (7), figures substituted for the figures "41 and 42" by the Transfer of Tribunal Functions and Revenue and Customs Appeals Order, SI 2009/56 art 3, Sch 1 para 309 with effect from 1 April 2009.

Misdeclaration or neglect

9— (1) Subject to sub-paragraphs (3) to (5) below, where for an accounting period—

(a) a return is made which understates a person's liability to aggregates levy or overstates his entitlement to any tax credit or repayment of aggregates levy, or

(b) at the end of the period of 30 days beginning on the date of the making of any assessment which understates a person's liability to aggregates levy, that person has not taken all such steps as are reasonable to draw the understatement to the attention of the Commissioners,

the person concerned shall be liable to a penalty equal to 5 per cent of the amount of the understatement of liability or (as the case may be) overstatement of entitlement.

(2) Where—

(a) a return for an accounting period—

(i) overstates or understates to any extent a person's liability to aggregates levy, or

(ii) understates or overstates to any extent his entitlement to any tax credits or repayments of aggregates levy,

and

(b) that return is corrected—

(i) in such circumstances as may be prescribed by regulations made by the Commissioners, and

(ii) in accordance with such conditions as may be so prescribed,

by a return for a later accounting period which understates or overstates, to the corresponding extent, any liability or entitlement for the later period,

it shall be assumed for the purposes of this paragraph that the statement made by each such return is a correct statement for the accounting period to which the return relates.

(3) Conduct falling within sub-paragraph (1) above shall not give rise to liability to a penalty under this paragraph if the person concerned provides the Commissioners with full information with respect to the inaccuracy concerned—

(a) at a time when he has no reason to believe that enquiries are being made by the Commissioners into his affairs, so far as they relate to aggregates levy; and

(b) in such form and manner as may be prescribed by regulations made by the Commissioners or specified by them in accordance with any such regulations.

(4) Conduct falling within sub-paragraph (1) above shall not give rise to liability to a penalty under this paragraph if the person concerned satisfies the Commissioners or, on appeal, an appeal tribunal that there is a reasonable excuse for his conduct.

(5) Where, by reason of conduct falling within sub-paragraph (1) above—

(a) a person is convicted of an offence (whether under this Act or otherwise), or

(b) a person is assessed to a penalty under paragraph 7 above,

that person shall not by reason of that conduct be liable also to a penalty under this paragraph.[1]

Amendments—[1] Para 9 repealed by FA 2008 s 122, Sch 40 para 21(*i*) with effect from 1 April 2009 (by virtue of SI 2009/571 art 2).

[Incorrect records etc evidencing claim for tax credit

9A— (1) This paragraph applies where—

(*a*) a claim is made for a tax credit in such a case as is mentioned in—

(i) section 30(1)(*c*) of this Act (aggregate used in a prescribed industrial or agricultural process), or

(ii) section 30A of this Act (transitional tax credit in Northern Ireland);

(*b*) a record or other document is provided to the Commissioners as evidence for the claim; and

(*c*) the record or document is incorrect.

(2) The person who provided the document to the Commissioners, and any person who provided it to anyone else with a view to its being used as evidence for a claim for a tax credit, shall be liable to a penalty.

(3) The amount of the penalty shall be equal to 105 per cent of the difference between—

(*a*) the amount of tax credit that would have been due on the claim if the record or document had been correct, and

(*b*) the amount (if any) of tax credit actually due on the claim.

(4) The providing of a record or other document shall not give rise to a penalty under this paragraph if the person who provided it satisfies the Commissioners or, on appeal, an appeal tribunal that there is a reasonable excuse for his having provided it.

(5) Where by reason of providing a record or other document—

(*a*) a person is convicted of an offence (whether under this Act or otherwise), *or*[2]

(*b*) *a person is assessed to a penalty under paragraph 7 or 9 above,*[2]

that person shall not by reason of the providing of the record or document be liable also to a penalty under this paragraph.][1]

Amendments—[1] This paragraph inserted by FA 2002 s 133(5), (6). This amendment is deemed to have come into force on 1 May 2002.

[2] Para 9A(5)(*b*) and preceding word "or" repealed by FA 2008 s 122, Sch 40 para 21(*i*) with effect from 1 April 2009 (by virtue of SI 2009/571 art 2). Sub-para (5)(*b*) repealed only in so far as it relates to conduct involving dishonesty which relates to—
(a) an inaccuracy in a document, or
(b) a failure to notify HMRC of an under-assessment by HMRC (SI 2009/571 art 6).

PART 3
INTERPRETATION OF SCHEDULE

10— (1) References in this Schedule to obtaining a tax credit are references to bringing an amount into account as a tax credit for the purposes of aggregates levy on the basis that that amount is an amount which may be so brought into account in accordance with tax credit regulations.

(2) References in this Schedule to obtaining a repayment of aggregates levy are references to obtaining either—

(*a*) the payment or repayment of any amount, or

(*b*) the acknowledgement of a right to receive any amount,

on the basis that that amount is the amount of a repayment of aggregates levy to which there is an entitlement.

SCHEDULE 7
AGGREGATES LEVY: INFORMATION AND EVIDENCE ETC

Section 29

Provision of information

1— (1) Every person involved (in whatever capacity) in subjecting any aggregate to exploitation in the United Kingdom, or in any connected activities, shall provide the Commissioners with such information relating to the matters in which he is or has been involved as the Commissioners may reasonably require.

(2) Information required under sub-paragraph (1) above shall be provided to the Commissioners within such period after being required, and in such form, as the Commissioners may reasonably require.

(3) Subject to sub-paragraphs (4) and (5) below and to paragraph 3(5) of Schedule 10 to this Act (which relates to supplementary assessments of daily penalties), if a person fails to provide information which he is required to provide under this paragraph, he shall be liable—

(*a*) to a penalty of £250; and

(*b*) to a further penalty of £20 for every day after the last relevant date and before the day after that on which the required information is provided.

(4) Liability to a penalty specified in sub-paragraph (3) above shall not arise if the person required to provide the information satisfies the Commissioners or, on appeal, an appeal tribunal—

(*a*) in the case of the penalty under paragraph (*a*) of that sub-paragraph that there is a reasonable excuse—

(i) for the initial failure to provide the required information on or before the last relevant date; and

(ii) for every subsequent failure to provide it;

and

(*b*) in the case of any penalty under paragraph (*b*) of that sub-paragraph for any day, that there is a reasonable excuse for the failure to provide the information on or before that day.

(5) Where, by reason of any failure by any person to provide information required under this paragraph—

(*a*) that person is convicted of an offence (whether under this Act or otherwise), or

(*b*) that person is assessed to a penalty under paragraph 7 of Schedule 6 to this Act (penalty for evasion) [or a penalty for a deliberate inaccuracy under Schedule 24 to the Finance Act 2007 (penalties for errors)][1],

that person shall not by reason of that failure be liable also to a penalty under this paragraph.

(6) In this paragraph "the last relevant date" means the last day of the period within which the person in question was required to provide the information.

Amendments—[1] Words in sub-para (5)(*b*) inserted by the Finance Act 2008, Schedule 40 (Appointed Day, Transitional Provisions and Consequential Amendments) Order, SI 2009/571 art 8, Sch 1 paras 31, 35 with effect from 1 April 2009.

Records

2— (1) The Commissioners may by regulations impose obligations to keep records on persons who are or are required to be registered and on persons who would be so required but for an exemption by virtue of regulations under section 24(4) of this Act.

(2) Regulations under this paragraph may be framed by reference to such records as may be stipulated in any notice published by the Commissioners in pursuance of the regulations and not withdrawn by a further notice.

(3) Regulations under this paragraph may—

(*a*) require any records kept in pursuance of the regulations to be preserved for such period, not exceeding six years, as may be specified in the regulations;

(*b*) authorise the Commissioners to direct that any such records need only be preserved for a shorter period than that specified in the regulations;

(*c*) authorise a direction to be made so as to apply generally or in such cases as the Commissioners may stipulate.

(4) Any duty under regulations under this paragraph to preserve records may be discharged by the preservation of the information contained in them by such means as the Commissioners may approve.

(5) The Commissioners may, as a condition of approving under sub-paragraph (4) above any means of preserving information contained in any records, impose such reasonable requirements as appear to them necessary for securing that the information will be as readily available to them as if the records themselves had been preserved.

(6) Subject to sub-paragraphs (7) and (8) below, a person who fails to preserve any record in compliance with—

(*a*) any regulations under this paragraph, or

(*b*) any notice, direction or requirement given or imposed under such regulations,

shall be liable to a penalty of £250.

(7) A failure such as is mentioned in sub-paragraph (6) above shall not give rise to any penalty under that sub-paragraph if the person required to preserve the record satisfies the Commissioners or, on appeal, an appeal tribunal that there is a reasonable excuse for the failure.

(8) Where, by reason of any such failure by any person as is mentioned in sub-paragraph (6) above—

(*a*) that person is convicted of an offence (whether under this Act or otherwise), or

(*b*) that person is assessed to a penalty under paragraph 7 of Schedule 6 to this Act (penalty for evasion) [or a penalty for a deliberate inaccuracy under Schedule 24 to the Finance Act 2007 (penalties for errors)][1],

that person shall not by reason of that failure be liable also to a penalty under this paragraph.

(9) The Commissioners may if they think fit at any time modify or withdraw any approval or requirement given or imposed for the purposes of this paragraph.

Amendments—[1] Words in sub-para (8)(*b*) inserted by the Finance Act 2008, Schedule 40 (Appointed Day, Transitional Provisions and Consequential Amendments) Order, SI 2009/571 art 8, Sch 1 paras 31, 35 with effect from 1 April 2009.

Prospective amendments—In sub-para (9) the words "approval or" and "given or" to be repealed and sub-paras (4), (5) to be substituted by FA 2009 s 98, Sch 50 paras 15, 16, with effect from such day as the Treasury may by order made by statutory instrument appoint, as follows—

"(4) A duty under regulations under this paragraph to preserve records may be discharged—

(*a*) by preserving them in any form and by any means, or

(*b*) by preserving the information contained in them in any form and by any means,

subject to any conditions or exceptions specified in writing by the Commissioners."

Evidence of records that are required to be preserved

3— (1) Subject to the following provisions of this paragraph, where any obligation to preserve records is discharged in accordance with paragraph 2(4) above, a copy of any document forming part of the records shall be admissible in evidence in any proceedings, whether civil or criminal, to the same extent as the records themselves.

(2) A statement contained in a document produced by a computer shall not by virtue of this paragraph be admissible in evidence—

(*a*) …[1]

(*b*) in civil proceedings in Scotland, except in accordance with sections 5 and 6 of the Civil Evidence (Scotland) Act 1988;

(*c*) in criminal proceedings in Scotland, except in accordance with Schedule 8 to the Criminal Procedure (Scotland) Act 1995; or

(*d*) …[2]

Amendments—[1] Sub-para (2)(*a*) repealed by the Criminal Justice Act 2003 ss 332, 336(3), Sch 37 Pt 6 with effect from 4 April 2005 (by virtue of SI 2005/950).

[2] Sub-para (2)(*d*) repealed by the Criminal Justice (Evidence) (Northern Ireland) Order, SI 2004/1501 art 46(2), Sch 2 with effect from 3 April 2006 (by virtue of the Criminal Justice (Evidence) (Northern Ireland) Order 2004 (Commencement No 3) Order, SR 2006/63, art 2).

Prospective amendments—Para 3 to be repealed by FA 2009 s 98, Sch 50 paras 15, 17 with effect from such date as the Treasury may by order made by statutory instrument appoint.

Production of documents

4— (1) Every person involved (in whatever capacity) in subjecting any aggregate to exploitation in the United Kingdom, or in any connected activities, shall upon demand made by an authorised person produce or cause to be produced for inspection by that person any documents relating to the matters in which he is or has been involved.

(2) Where, by virtue of sub-paragraph (1) above, an authorised person has power to require the production of any documents from any person—

(*a*) he shall have the like power to require production of the documents concerned from any other person who appears to the authorised person to be in possession of them; and

(*b*) the production of any document by that other person in pursuance of a requirement under this sub-paragraph shall be without prejudice to any lien claimed by that other person on that document.

(3) The documents mentioned in sub-paragraphs (1) and (2) above shall be produced at such time and place as the authorised person may reasonably require.

(4) Subject to sub-paragraphs (5) and (6) below and to paragraph 3(5) of Schedule 10 to this Act (which relates to supplementary assessments of daily penalties), if a person fails to produce any document which he is required to produce under this paragraph, he shall be liable—

(*a*) to a penalty of £250; and

(*b*) to a further penalty of £20 for every day after the last relevant date and before the day after that on which the document is produced.

(5) Liability to a penalty specified in sub-paragraph (4) above shall not arise if the person required to produce the document in question satisfies the Commissioners or, on appeal, an appeal tribunal—

(*a*) in the case of the penalty under paragraph (*a*) of that sub-paragraph, that there is a reasonable excuse—

(i) for the initial failure to produce the document at the required time; and

(ii) for every subsequent failure to produce it;

and

(*b*) in the case of any penalty under paragraph (*b*) of that sub-paragraph for any day, that there is a reasonable excuse for the failure to produce the document on or before that day.

(6) Where, by reason of any failure by any person to provide information required under this paragraph—

(*a*) that person is convicted of an offence (whether under this Act or otherwise), or

(*b*) that person is assessed to a penalty under paragraph 7 of Schedule 6 to this Act (penalty for evasion) [or a penalty for a deliberate inaccuracy under Schedule 24 to the Finance Act 2007 (penalties for errors)][1],

that person shall not by reason of that failure be liable also to a penalty under this paragraph.

(7) In this paragraph "the last relevant date" means the last day of the period within which the person in question was required to produce the document.

Amendments—[1] Words in sub-para (6)(*b*) inserted by the Finance Act 2008, Schedule 40 (Appointed Day, Transitional Provisions and Consequential Amendments) Order, SI 2009/571 art 8, Sch 1 paras 31, 35 with effect from 1 April 2009.

Powers in relation to documents produced

5— (1) An authorised person may take copies of, or make extracts from, any document produced under paragraph 4 above.

(2) If it appears to him to be necessary to do so, an authorised person may, at a reasonable time and for a reasonable period, remove any document produced under paragraph 4 above.

(3) An authorised person who removes any document under sub-paragraph (2) above shall, if requested to do so, provide a receipt for the document so removed.

(4) Where a lien is claimed on a document produced under paragraph 4(2) above, the removal of the document under sub-paragraph (2) above shall not be regarded as breaking the lien.

(5) Where a document removed by an authorised person under sub-paragraph (2) above is reasonably required for any purpose he shall, as soon as practicable, provide a copy of the document, free of charge, to the person by whom it was produced or caused to be produced.

(6) Where any documents removed under the powers conferred by this paragraph are lost or damaged, the Commissioners shall be liable to compensate their owner for any expenses reasonably incurred by him in replacing or repairing the documents.

Entry and inspection

6 For the purpose of exercising any powers under this Part of this Act an authorised person may at any reasonable time enter and inspect premises used in connection with the carrying on of a business.

Entry and search

7— *(1) Where—*

(a) a justice of the peace is satisfied on information on oath that there is reasonable ground for suspecting that a fraud offence which appears to be of a serious nature is being, has been or is about to be committed on any premises or that evidence of the commission of such an offence is to be found there, or

(b) in Scotland a justice (within the meaning of section 307 of the Criminal Procedure (Scotland) Act 1995) is satisfied by evidence on oath as mentioned in paragraph (a) above,

he may issue a warrant in writing authorising any authorised person to enter those premises, if necessary by force, at any time within one month from the time of the issue of the warrant and to search them.

(2) A person who enters the premises under the authority of the warrant may—

(a) take with him such other persons as appear to him to be necessary;

(b) seize and remove any such documents or other things at all found on the premises as he has reasonable cause to believe may be required as evidence for the purposes of proceedings in respect of a fraud offence which appears to him to be of a serious nature;

(c) search, or cause to be searched, any person found on the premises whom he has reasonable cause to believe to be in possession of any documents or other things which may be so required.

(3) Sub-paragraph (2) above shall not authorise any person to be searched by a member of the opposite sex.

(4) The powers conferred by a warrant under this paragraph shall not be exercisable—

(a) by more than such number of authorised persons as may be specified in the warrant;

(b) outside such periods of the day as may be so specified; or

(c) if the warrant so provides, otherwise than in the presence of a constable in uniform.

(5) An authorised person seeking to exercise the powers conferred by a warrant under this paragraph or, if there is more than one such authorised person, such one of them as is in charge of the search shall provide a copy of the warrant endorsed with his name as follows—

(a) if the occupier of the premises concerned is present at the time the search is to begin, the copy shall be supplied to the occupier;

(b) if at that time the occupier is not present but a person who appears to the authorised person to be in charge of the premises is present, the copy shall be supplied to that person;

(c) if neither paragraph (a) nor paragraph (b) above applies, the copy shall be left in a prominent place on the premises.

(6) In this paragraph "a fraud offence" means an offence under any of paragraphs 1 to 3 of Schedule 6 to this Act.[1]

Amendments—[1] This para repealed by FA 2007 ss 84, 114, Sch 22 paras 3, 12(*b*), Sch 27 Pt 5(1) with effect from 1 December 2007 (by virtue of SI 2007/3166 art 3(*a*)).

Order for access to recorded information etc

8— (1) Where, on an application by an authorised person, a justice of the peace or, in Scotland, a justice (within the meaning of section 307 of the Criminal Procedure (Scotland) Act 1995) is satisfied that there are reasonable grounds for believing—

(*a*) that an offence in connection with aggregates levy is being, has been or is about to be committed, and

(*b*) that any recorded information (including any document of any nature at all) which may be required as evidence for the purpose of any proceedings in respect of such an offence is in the possession of any person,

he may make an order under this paragraph.

(2) An order under this paragraph is an order that the person who appears to the justice to be in possession of the recorded information to which the application relates shall—

(*a*) give an authorised person access to it, and

(*b*) permit an authorised person to remove and take away any of it which he reasonably considers necessary,

not later than the end of the period of seven days beginning with the date of the order, or the end of such longer period as the order may specify.

(3) The reference in sub-paragraph (2)(*a*) above to giving an authorised person access to the recorded information to which the application relates includes a reference to permitting the authorised person to take copies of it or to make extracts from it.

(4) Where the recorded information consists of information contained in a computer, an order under this paragraph shall have effect as an order to produce the information—

(*a*) in a form in which it is visible and legible; and

(*b*) if the authorised person wishes to remove it, in a form in which it can be removed.

(5) This paragraph is without prejudice to the preceding paragraphs of this Schedule.

Removal of documents etc

9— (1) An authorised person who removes anything in the exercise of a power conferred by or under paragraph 7 or 8 above shall, if so requested by a person showing himself—

(*a*) to be the occupier of premises from which it was removed, or

(*b*) to have had custody or control of it immediately before the removal,

provide that person with a record of what he removed.

(2) The authorised person shall provide the record within a reasonable time from the making of the request for it.

(3) Subject to sub-paragraph (7) below, if a request for permission to be allowed access to anything which—

(*a*) has been removed by an authorised person, and

(*b*) is retained by the Commissioners for the purposes of investigating an offence,

is made to the officer in overall charge of the investigation by a person who had custody or control of the thing immediately before it was so removed, or by someone acting on behalf of such a person, the officer shall allow the person who made the request access to it under the supervision of an authorised person.

(4) Subject to sub-paragraph (7) below, if a request for a photograph or copy of any such thing is made to the officer in overall charge of the investigation by a person who had custody or control of the thing immediately before it was so removed, or by someone acting on behalf of such a person, the officer shall—

(*a*) allow the person who made the request access to it under the supervision of an authorised person for the purpose of photographing it or copying it; or

(*b*) photograph or copy it, or cause it to be photographed or copied.

(5) Subject to sub-paragraph (7) below, where anything is photographed or copied under sub-paragraph (4)(*b*) above, the officer shall supply the photograph or copy, or cause it to be supplied, to the person who made the request.

(6) The photograph or copy shall be supplied within a reasonable time from the making of the request.

(7) There is no duty under this paragraph to allow access to anything, or to supply a photograph or copy of anything, if the officer in overall charge of the investigation for the purposes of which it was removed has reasonable grounds for believing that to do so would prejudice—

(*a*) that investigation;

(*b*) the investigation of an offence other than the offence for the purposes of the investigation of which the thing was removed; or

(*c*) any criminal proceedings which may be brought as a result of the investigation of which he is in charge or any such investigation as is mentioned in paragraph (*b*) above.

(8) Any reference in this paragraph to the officer in overall charge of the investigation is a reference to the person whose name and address are endorsed on the warrant concerned as being the officer so in charge.

Enforcement of paragraph 9

10— (1) Where, on an application made as mentioned in sub-paragraph (2) below, the appropriate judicial authority is satisfied that a person has failed to comply with a requirement imposed by paragraph 9 above, the authority may order that person to comply with the requirement within such time and in such manner as may be specified in the order.

(2) An application under sub-paragraph (1) above shall not be made except—

(*a*) in the case of a failure to comply with any of the requirements imposed by paragraph 9(1) and (2) above—

(i) by the occupier of the premises from which the thing in question was removed; or

(ii) by the person who had custody or control of it immediately before it was so removed;

(*b*) in any other case, by the person who had such custody or control.

(3) In this paragraph "the appropriate judicial authority" means—

(*a*) in England and Wales, a magistrates' court;

(*b*) in Scotland, the sheriff;

(*c*) in Northern Ireland, a court of summary jurisdiction, as defined in Article 2(2)(*a*) of the Magistrates' Courts (Northern Ireland) Order 1981.

(4) In England and Wales and Northern Ireland, an application for an order under this paragraph shall be made by way of complaint; and sections 21 and 42(2) of the Interpretation Act (Northern Ireland) 1954 shall apply as if any reference in those provisions to any enactment included a reference to this paragraph.

Power to take samples

11— (1) An authorised person, if it appears to him necessary for the protection of the revenue against mistake or fraud, may at any time take, from material which he has reasonable cause to believe is aggregate which is intended to be, is being, or has been subjected to exploitation in the United Kingdom, such samples as he may require with a view to determining how the material ought to be treated, or to have been treated, for the purposes of aggregates levy.

(2) Any sample taken under this paragraph shall be disposed of in such manner as the Commissioners may direct.

Evidence by certificate

12— (1) In any proceedings a certificate of the Commissioners—

(*a*) that a person was or was not at any time registered [or][1], (*b*) that any return required by regulations made under section 25 of this Act has not been made or had not been made at any time,

(*c*)

(*d*) …[1]

shall be evidence or, in Scotland, sufficient evidence of that fact.

(2) A photograph of any document provided to the Commissioners for the purposes of this Part of this Act and certified by them to be such a photograph shall be admissible in any proceedings, whether civil or criminal, to the same extent as the document itself.

(3) In any proceedings any document purporting to be a certificate under sub-paragraph (1) or (2) above shall be taken to be such a certificate unless the contrary is shown.

Amendments—[1] Words inserted and repealed by FA 2008 s 138, Sch 44 para 9 with effect from 21 July 2008. Paras (*c*), (*d*) previously read as follows—

"(*c*) that any levy shown as due in a return made in pursuance of regulations made under section 25 of this Act has not been paid, or

(*d*) that any amount shown as due in any assessment made under this Part of this Act has not been paid,".

Inducements to provide information

13— (1) This paragraph applies—

(*a*) to any criminal proceedings against a person in respect of an offence in connection with or in relation to aggregates levy; and

(*b*) to any proceedings against a person for the recovery of any sum due from him in connection with or in relation to that levy.

(2) Statements made or documents produced or provided by or on behalf of a person shall not be inadmissible in any proceedings to which this paragraph applies by reason only that—

(*a*) a matter falling within sub-paragraph (3) or (4) below has been drawn to that person's attention; and

(*b*) he was or may have been induced, as a result, to make the statements or to produce or provide the documents.

(3) The matters falling within this sub-paragraph are—

(*a*) that, in relation to aggregates levy, the Commissioners may assess an amount due by way of a civil penalty instead of instituting criminal proceedings;

(*b*) that it is the practice of the Commissioners (without giving any undertaking as to whether they will make such an assessment in any case) to be influenced by whether a person—

(i) has made a full confession of any dishonest conduct to which he has been a party; and

(ii) has otherwise co-operated to the full with any investigation.

(4) The matter falling within this sub-paragraph is the fact that the Commissioners or, on appeal, an appeal tribunal have power under any provision of this Part of this Act to reduce a penalty.

Disclosure of information

14— (1) Notwithstanding any obligation not to disclose information that would otherwise apply but subject to sub-paragraph (2) below, the Commissioners may disclose any information obtained or held by them in or in connection with the carrying out of their functions in relation to aggregates levy to any of the following—

(*a*) any Minister of the Crown;

(*b*) the Scottish Ministers;

(*c*) any Minister, within the meaning of the Northern Ireland Act 1998, or any Northern Ireland department;

(*d*) the National Assembly for Wales;

(*e*) the Environment Agency;

(*f*) the Scottish Environment Protection Agency;

(*g*) a mineral planning authority in England and Wales (within the meaning of the Town and Country Planning Act 1990);

(*h*) a planning authority in Scotland;

(*i*) a district council in Northern Ireland;

(*j*) an authorised officer of any person mentioned in paragraphs (*a*) to (i) above.

(2) Information shall not be disclosed under sub-paragraph (1) above except for the purpose of assisting a person falling within paragraphs (*a*) to (*j*) of that sub-paragraph in the performance of his duties.

(3) Notwithstanding any such obligation as is mentioned in sub-paragraph (1) above, any person mentioned in sub-paragraph (1)(*a*) to (*j*) above may disclose information—

(*a*) to the Commissioners, or

(*b*) to an authorised officer of the Commissioners,

for the purpose of assisting the Commissioners in the performance of duties in relation to aggregates levy.

(4) Information that has been disclosed to a person by virtue of this paragraph shall not be disclosed by him except—

(*a*) to another person to whom (instead of him) disclosure could by virtue of this paragraph have been made; or

(*b*) for the purpose of any proceedings connected with the operation of any provision made by or under any enactment relating to the environment or to aggregates levy.

(5) References in the preceding provisions of this paragraph to an authorised officer of any person ("the principal") are to any person who has been designated by the principal as a person to and by whom information may be disclosed by virtue of this paragraph.

(6) Where the principal is a person falling within any of paragraphs (*a*) to (*c*) above, the principal shall notify the Commissioners in writing of the name of any person designated by the principal for the purposes of this paragraph.

(7) No charge may be made for any disclosure made by virtue of this paragraph.

(8) In this paragraph "enactment" includes an enactment contained in an Act of the Scottish Parliament or in any Northern Ireland legislation.

Interpretation of Schedule

15 In this Schedule—

"authorised person" means any person acting under the authority of the Commissioners;

"connected activities", in relation to the exploitation of aggregate in the United Kingdom, means any activities carried out—

(*a*) for purposes connected with the carrying out of any such exploitation or with any transaction involving the carrying out of any such exploitation; or

(*b*) for the purposes of, in connection with or in relation to the carrying on of any business involving any such exploitation.

SCHEDULE 8
AGGREGATES LEVY: REPAYMENTS AND CREDITS

Section 32

Reimbursement arrangements

1— (1) The Commissioners may by regulations make provision for reimbursement arrangements made by any person to be disregarded for the purposes of section 32(2) of this Act except where the arrangements—

(*a*) contain such provision as may be required by the regulations; and

(*b*) are supported by such undertakings to comply with the provisions of the arrangements as may be required by the regulations to be given to the Commissioners.

(2) In this paragraph "reimbursement arrangements" means any arrangements for the purposes of a claim to a repayment of aggregates levy which—

(*a*) are made by any person for the purpose of securing that he is not unjustly enriched by the repayment of any amount in pursuance of the claim; and

(*b*) provide for the reimbursement of persons who have for practical purposes borne the whole or any part of the cost of the original payment of that amount to the Commissioners.

(3) Without prejudice to the generality of sub-paragraph (1) above, the provision that may be required by regulations under this paragraph to be contained in reimbursement arrangements includes—

(*a*) provision requiring a reimbursement for which the arrangements provide to be made within such period after the repayment to which it relates as may be specified in the regulations;

(*b*) provision for the repayment of amounts to the Commissioners where those amounts are not reimbursed in accordance with the arrangements;

(*c*) provision requiring interest paid by the Commissioners on any amount repaid by them to be treated in the same way as that amount for the purposes of any requirement under the arrangements to make reimbursement or to repay the Commissioners;

(*d*) provision requiring such records relating to the carrying out of the arrangements as may be described in the regulations to be kept and produced to the Commissioners, or to an officer of theirs.

(4) Regulations under this paragraph may impose obligations on such persons as may be specified in the regulations—

(*a*) to make the repayments to the Commissioners that they are required to make in pursuance of any provisions contained in any reimbursement arrangements by virtue of sub-paragraph (3)(*b*) or (*c*) above;

(*b*) to comply with any requirements contained in any such arrangements by virtue of sub-paragraph (3)(*d*) above.

(5) Regulations under this paragraph may make provision for the form and manner in which, and the times at which, undertakings are to be given to the Commissioners in accordance with

the regulations; and any such provision may allow for those matters to be determined by the Commissioners in accordance with the regulations.

Interest payable by the Commissioners

2— (1) Where, due to an error on the part of the Commissioners, a person—

(*a*) has paid to them by way of aggregates levy an amount which was not levy due and which they are in consequence liable to repay to him,

(*b*) has failed to claim a repayment of levy to which he was entitled, under tax credit regulations, in respect of any tax credits, or

(*c*) has suffered delay in receiving payment of an amount due to him from them in connection with aggregates levy,

then, if and to the extent that they would not be liable to do so apart from this paragraph, they shall (subject to the following provisions of this paragraph) pay interest to him on that amount for the applicable period.

(2) In sub-paragraph (1) above, the reference in paragraph (*a*) to an amount which the Commissioners are liable to repay in consequence of the making of a payment that was not due is a reference to only so much of that amount as is the subject of a claim that the Commissioners are required to satisfy or have satisfied.

(3) In that sub-paragraph the amounts referred to in paragraph (*c*)—

(*a*) do not include any amount payable under this paragraph;

(*b*) do not include the amount of any interest for which provision is made by virtue of section 30(3)(*f*) of this Act; but

(*c*) do include any amount due (in respect of an adjustment of overpaid interest) by way of a repayment under—

(i) paragraph 11(3) of Schedule 5 to this Act; or

(ii) paragraph 6(3) of Schedule 10 to this Act.

(4) The applicable period, in a case falling within sub-paragraph (1)(*a*) above, is the period—

(*a*) beginning with the date on which the payment is received by the Commissioners; and

(*b*) ending with the date on which they authorise payment of the amount on which the interest is payable.

(5) The applicable period, in a case falling within sub-paragraph (1)(*b*) or (*c*) above, is the period—

(*a*) beginning with the date on which, apart from the error, the Commissioners might reasonably have been expected to authorise payment of the amount on which the interest is payable; and

(*b*) ending with the date on which they in fact authorise payment of that amount.

(6) In determining the applicable period for the purposes of this paragraph there shall be left out of account any period by which the Commissioners' authorisation of the payment of interest is delayed by circumstances beyond their control.

(7) The reference in sub-paragraph (6) above to a period by which the Commissioners' authorisation of the payment of interest is delayed by circumstances beyond their control includes, in particular, any period which is referable to—

(*a*) any unreasonable delay in the making of any claim for the payment or repayment of the amount on which interest is claimed;

(*b*) any failure by any person to provide the Commissioners—

(i) at or before the time of the making of a claim, or

(ii) subsequently in response to a request for information by the Commissioners,

with all the information required by them to enable the existence and amount of the claimant's entitlement to a payment or repayment to be determined; and

(*c*) the making, as part of or in association with any claim for the payment or repayment of the amount on which interest is claimed, of a claim to anything to which the claimant was not entitled.

(8) In determining for the purposes of sub-paragraph (7) above whether any period of delay is referable to a failure by any person to provide information in response to a request by the Commissioners, there shall be taken to be so referable, except so far as may be provided for by regulations, any period which—

(*a*) begins with the date on which the Commissioners require that person to provide information which they reasonably consider relevant to the matter to be determined; and

(*b*) ends with the earliest date on which it would be reasonable for the Commissioners to conclude—

(i) that they have received a complete answer to their request for information;

(ii) that they have received all that they need in answer to that request; or

(iii) that it is unnecessary for them to be provided with any information in answer to that request.

(9) The Commissioners shall not be liable to pay interest under this paragraph except on the making of a claim for that purpose.

(10) A claim under this paragraph must be in writing and must be made not more than three years after the end of the applicable period to which it relates.

(11) References in this paragraph—

(*a*) to receiving payment of any amount from the Commissioners, or

(*b*) to the authorisation by the Commissioners of the payment of any amount,

include references to the discharge by way of set-off (whether in accordance with regulations under paragraph 9 or 10 below or otherwise) of the Commissioners' liability to pay that amount.

(12) Interest under this paragraph shall be payable at the rate applicable under section 197 of the Finance Act 1996.

Prospective amendments—In sub-para (10) the words "4 years" to be substituted for the words "three years" by FA 2009 s 99, Sch 51 paras 27, 30 with effect from such day as the Treasury may by order made by statutory instrument appoint.

Assessment for excessive repayment

3— (1) Where—

(*a*) any amount has been paid at any time to any person by way of a repayment of aggregates levy, and

(*b*) the amount paid exceeded the amount which the Commissioners were liable at that time to repay to that person,

the Commissioners may, to the best of their judgement, assess the excess paid to that person and notify it to him.

(2) Where—

(*a*) any amount has been paid to any person by way of repayment of levy,

(*b*) the repayment is in respect of a tax credit the entitlement to which arose in a case falling within section 30(1)(*e*) (bad debts),

(*c*) the whole or any part of the credit is withdrawn on account of the payment of the whole or any part of the debt taken as bad,

(*d*) the amount of the repayment exceeded the amount which the Commissioners would have been liable to repay had the withdrawal taken place before the determination of the amount of the repayment,

the Commissioners may, to the best of their judgement, assess the excess repaid to that person and notify it to him.

(3) Where any person is liable to pay any amount to the Commissioners in pursuance of an obligation imposed by virtue of paragraph 1(4)(*a*) above, the Commissioners may, to the best of their judgement, assess the amount due from that person and notify it to him.

(4) Subject to sub-paragraph (5) below, where—

(*a*) an assessment is made on any person under this paragraph in respect of a repayment of levy made in relation to any accounting period, and

(*b*) the Commissioners have power under Schedule 5 to this Act to make an assessment on that person to an amount of aggregates levy due from that person for that period,

the assessments may be combined and notified to him as one assessment.

(5) A notice of a combined assessment under sub-paragraph (4) above must separately identify the amount being assessed in respect of repayments of levy.

Assessment for overpayments of interest

4 Where—

(*a*) any amount has been paid to any person by way of interest under paragraph 2 above, but

(*b*) that person was not entitled to that amount under that paragraph,

the Commissioners may, to the best of their judgement, assess the amount so paid to which that person was not entitled and notify it to him.

Assessments under paragraphs 3 and 4

5— (1) An assessment under paragraph 3 or 4 above shall not be made more than two years after the time when evidence of facts sufficient in the opinion of the Commissioners to justify the making of the assessment comes to the knowledge of the Commissioners.

(2) Where an amount has been assessed and notified to any person under paragraph 3 or 4 above, it shall be recoverable as if it were aggregates levy due from him.

(3) Sub-paragraph (2) above does not have effect if, or to the extent that, the assessment in question has been withdrawn or reduced.

Interest on amounts assessed

6— (1) Where an assessment is made under paragraph 3 or 4 above, the whole of the amount assessed shall carry interest, for the period specified in sub-paragraph (2) below, as follows—

(*a*) so much of that amount as represents the amount of a tax credit claimed by a person who was not entitled to it shall carry penalty interest; and

(*b*) so much of that amount as does not carry penalty interest under paragraph (*a*) above shall carry interest at the rate applicable under section 197 of the Finance Act 1996.

(2) That period is the period which—

(*a*) begins with the day after that on which the person is notified of the assessment; and
(*b*) ends with the day before that on which payment is made of the amount assessed.

(3) Interest under this paragraph shall be paid without any deduction of income tax.

(4) Penalty interest under this paragraph shall be compound interest calculated—

(*a*) at the penalty rate; and
(*b*) with monthly rests.

(5) For this purpose the penalty rate is the rate found by—

(*a*) taking the rate applicable under section 197 of the Finance Act 1996 for the purposes of sub-paragraph (1)(*b*) above; and
(*b*) adding 10 percentage points to that rate.

(6) Where a person is liable under this paragraph to pay any penalty interest, the Commissioners or, on appeal, an appeal tribunal may reduce the amount payable to such amount (including nil) as they think proper.

(7) Subject to sub-paragraph (8) below, where the person concerned satisfies the Commissioners or, on appeal, an appeal tribunal that there is a reasonable excuse for the conduct giving rise to the liability to pay penalty interest, that is a matter which (among other things) may be taken into account under sub-paragraph (6) above.

(8) In determining whether there is a reasonable excuse for the purposes of sub-paragraph (7) above, no account shall be taken of any of the following matters, that is to say—

(*a*) the insufficiency of the funds available to any person for paying any aggregates levy due or for paying the amount of the interest;
(*b*) the fact that there has, in the case in question or in that case taken with any other cases, been no or no significant loss of aggregates levy;
(*c*) the fact that the person liable to pay the interest or a person acting on his behalf has acted in good faith.

(9) In the case of interest reduced by the Commissioners under sub-paragraph (6) above an appeal tribunal, on an appeal relating to the interest, may cancel the whole or any part of the reduction made by the Commissioners.

Assessments to interest under paragraph 6

7— (1) Where any person is liable to interest under paragraph 6 above the Commissioners may assess the amount due by way of interest and notify it to him accordingly.

(2) Without prejudice to the power to make assessments under this paragraph for later periods, the interest to which an assessment under this paragraph may relate shall be confined to interest for a period of no more than two years ending with the time when the assessment under this paragraph is made.

(3) Where an amount has been assessed and notified to any person under this paragraph it shall be recoverable as if it were aggregates levy due from him.

(4) Sub-paragraph (3) above does not have effect if, or to the extent that, the assessment in question has been withdrawn or reduced.

(5) Where an assessment is made under this paragraph to an amount of interest under paragraph 6 above—

(*a*) the notice of assessment shall specify a date, not later than the date of the notice of assessment, to which the amount of interest which is assessed is calculated; and
(*b*) if the interest continues to accrue after that date, a further assessment or further assessments may be made under this paragraph in respect of the amounts so accruing.

(6) Where—

(*a*) an assessment to interest is made specifying a date for the purposes of sub-paragraph (5)(*a*) above, and
(*b*) within such period as may for the purposes of this sub-paragraph have been notified by the Commissioners to the person liable for the interest, the amount on which the interest is payable is paid,

that amount shall be deemed for the purposes of any further liability to interest to have been paid on the specified date.

Supplementary assessments

8 If it appears to the Commissioners that the amount which ought to have been assessed in an assessment under paragraph 3, 4 or 7 above exceeds the amount which was so assessed, then—

(*a*) under the same paragraph as that assessment was made, and
(*b*) on or before the last day on which that assessment could have been made,

the Commissioners may make a supplementary assessment of the amount of the excess and notify the person concerned accordingly.

Set-off of or against amounts due under this Part of this Act

9— (1) The Commissioners may by regulations make provision in relation to any case where—

(*a*) a person is under a duty to pay to the Commissioners at any time an amount or amounts in respect of aggregates levy; and

(*b*) the Commissioners are under a duty to pay to that person at the same time an amount or amounts in respect of that levy or any of the other taxes under their care and management.

(2) Regulations under this paragraph may provide that if the total of the amount or amounts mentioned in sub-paragraph (1)(*a*) above exceeds the total of the amount or amounts mentioned in sub-paragraph (1)(*b*) above, the latter shall be set off against the former.

(3) Regulations under this paragraph may provide that if the total of the amount or amounts mentioned in sub-paragraph (1)(*b*) above exceeds the total of the amount or amounts mentioned in sub-paragraph (1)(*a*) above, the Commissioners may set off the latter in paying the former.

(4) Regulations under this paragraph may provide that if the total of the amount or amounts mentioned in sub-paragraph (1)(*a*) above is the same as the total of the amount or amounts mentioned in sub-paragraph (1)(*b*) above no payment need be made in respect of the former or the latter.

(5) Regulations under this paragraph may provide for any limitation on the time within which the Commissioners are entitled to take steps for recovering any amount due to them in respect of aggregates levy to be disregarded, in such cases as may be described in the regulations, in determining whether any person is under such a duty to pay as is mentioned in sub-paragraph (1)(*a*) above.

(6) Regulations under this paragraph may include provision treating any duty to pay mentioned in sub-paragraph (1) above as discharged accordingly.

(7) References in sub-paragraph (1) above to an amount in respect of a particular tax include references not only to an amount of tax itself but also to other amounts such as interest and penalties that are or may be recovered as if they were amounts of tax.

(8) In this paragraph "tax" includes levy or duty.

Set-off of or against other taxes and duties

10— (1) The Commissioners may by regulations make provision in relation to any case where—

(*a*) a person is under a duty to pay to the Commissioners at any time an amount or amounts in respect of any tax (or taxes) under their care and management other than aggregates levy; and

(*b*) the Commissioners are under a duty, at the same time, to make any repayment of aggregates levy to that person or to make any other payment to him of any amount or amounts in respect of aggregates levy.

(2) Regulations under this paragraph may provide that if the total of the amount or amounts mentioned in sub-paragraph (1)(*a*) above exceeds the total of the amount or amounts mentioned in sub-paragraph (1)(*b*) above, the latter shall be set off against the former.

(3) Regulations under this paragraph may provide that if the total of the amount or amounts mentioned in sub-paragraph (1)(*b*) above exceeds the total of the amount or amounts mentioned in sub-paragraph (1)(*a*) above, the Commissioners may set off the latter in paying the former.

(4) Regulations under this paragraph may provide that if the total of the amount or amounts mentioned in sub-paragraph (1)(*a*) above is the same as the total of the amount or amounts mentioned in sub-paragraph (1)(*b*) above no payment need be made in respect of the former or the latter.

(5) Regulations under this paragraph may provide for any limitation on the time within which the Commissioners are entitled to take steps for recovering any amount due to them in respect of any of the taxes under their care and management to be disregarded, in such cases as may be described in the regulations, in determining whether any person is under such a duty to pay as is mentioned in sub-paragraph (1)(*a*) above.

(6) Regulations under this paragraph may include provision treating any duty to pay mentioned in sub-paragraph (1) above as discharged accordingly.

(7) References in sub-paragraph (1) above to an amount in respect of a particular tax include references not only to an amount of tax itself but also to other amounts such as interest and penalties that are or may be recovered as if they were amounts of tax.

(8) In this paragraph "tax" includes levy or duty.

Restriction on powers to provide for set-off

11— (1) Regulations made under paragraph 9 or 10 above shall not require any such amount or amounts as are mentioned in sub-paragraph (1)(*b*) of that paragraph ("the credit") to be set against any such amount or amounts as are mentioned in sub-paragraph (1)(*a*) of that paragraph ("the debit") in any case where—

(*a*) an insolvency procedure has been applied to the person entitled to the credit;

(*b*) the credit became due after that procedure was so applied; and (*c*) the liability to pay the debit either arose before that procedure was so applied or (having arisen afterwards) relates to, or to matters occurring in the course of, the carrying on of any business at times before the procedure was so applied.

(2) For the purposes of this paragraph, an insolvency procedure is applied to a person if—

(*a*) a bankruptcy order, winding-up order or administration order is made [or an administrator is appointed][2] in relation to that person or an award of sequestration is made on that person's estate;

(*b*) that person is put into administrative receivership;

(*c*) that person passes a resolution for voluntary winding up;

(*d*) any voluntary arrangement approved in accordance with—

(i) Part I or VIII of the Insolvency Act 1986, or

(ii) Part II or Chapter II of Part VIII of the Insolvency (Northern Ireland) Order 1989,

comes into force in relation to that person;

(*e*) a deed of arrangement registered in accordance with—

(i) the Deeds of Arrangement Act 1914, or

(ii) Chapter I of Part VIII of that Order,

takes effect in relation to that person;

(*f*)–(*h*) ...[1]

(*i*) that person's estate becomes vested in any other person as that person's trustee under a trust deed (within the meaning of the Bankruptcy (Scotland) Act 1985).

(3) In this paragraph references, in relation to any person, to the application of an insolvency procedure to that person shall not include—

(*a*) the making of a bankruptcy order, winding-up order ...[2] or award of sequestration [or the appointment of an administrator][2] at a time when any such arrangement or deed as is mentioned in paragraph (*d*), (*e*) or (*i*) of sub-paragraph (2) above is in force in relation to that person;

(*b*) the making of a winding-up order at any of the following times, that is to say—

[(i) immediately upon the appointment of an administrator in respect of the person ceasing to have effect;][2]

(ii) when that person is being wound up voluntarily;

(iii) when that person is in administrative receivership;

or

(*c*) the making of an administration order in relation to that person at any time when that person is in administrative receivership.

(4) For the purposes of this paragraph a person shall be regarded as being in administrative receivership throughout any continuous period for which (disregarding any temporary vacancy in the office of receiver) there is an administrative receiver of that person.

(5) In this paragraph—

"administration order" means an administration order under [Schedule B1 to][2] the Insolvency Act 1986 or Article 21 of the Insolvency (Northern Ireland) Order 1989;

"administrative receiver" means an administrative receiver within the meaning of section 251 of that Act of 1986 or Article 5(1) of that Order of 1989.

Amendments—[1] Sub-para (2)(*f*)–(*h*) repealed by FA 2002 ss 132(1), (3), 141, Sch 38 para 10, Sch 40 Pt 4(3). These amendments are deemed to have come into force on 1 April 2002.

[2] Words in sub-paras (2)(*a*), (3)(*a*) inserted, words in sub-para (3)(*a*) repealed, and sub-para (3)(*b*)(i) and words in sub-para (5) substituted, by the Enterprise Act (Insolvency) Order, SI 2003/2096 art 4, Schedule paras 35, 37 with effect from 15 September 2003 (except in relation to any case where a petition for an administration order was presented before that date): SI 2003/2096, arts 1(1), 6.

Supplemental provisions of Schedule

12— (1) Any notification of an assessment under any provision of this Schedule to a person's representative shall be treated for the purposes of this Part of this Act as notification to the person in relation to whom the representative acts.

(2) In this paragraph "representative", in relation to any person, means—

(*a*) any of that person's personal representatives;

(*b*) that person's trustee in bankruptcy or liquidator;

(*c*) any person holding office as a receiver in relation to that person or any of his property;

(*d*) that person's tax representative or any other person for the time being acting in a representative capacity in relation to that person.

(3) In this paragraph "trustee in bankruptcy" includes, as respects Scotland—

(*a*) an interim or permanent trustee (within the meaning of the Bankruptcy (Scotland) Act 1985); and

(*b*) a trustee acting under a trust deed (within the meaning of that Act).

(4) The powers conferred by paragraphs 9 and 10 of this Schedule are without prejudice to any power of the Commissioners to provide by tax credit regulations for any amount to be set against another.

SCHEDULE 9

AGGREGATES LEVY: GROUP TREATMENT

Section 35

Eligibility for group treatment

1 Two or more bodies corporate are eligible to be treated as members of a group for the purposes of this Part of this Act if—

(*a*) each of them has an established place of business in the United Kingdom; and

(*b*) they are all under the same control.

Application for group treatment

2— (1) Subject to sub-paragraph (3) below, where an application is made to the Commissioners with respect to two or more bodies corporate and those bodies are all eligible to be treated as members of the same group, then, from the specified time—

(*a*) they shall be so treated for the purposes of this Part of this Act; and

(*b*) such one of them as is specified in the application shall be the representative member.

(2) Subject to sub-paragraph (3) below, where—

(*a*) any bodies corporate are treated as members of a group for the purposes of this Part of this Act, and

(*b*) an application is made to the Commissioners for the addition to the group of a body corporate that is eligible to be treated as a member of the group,

then, from the specified time, that body shall be included among the bodies so treated.

(3) The Commissioners may refuse an application under sub-paragraph (1) or (2) above if, and only if, it appears to them necessary to do so for the protection of the revenue; and an application that is refused under this sub-paragraph shall be, and be treated as always having been, ineffective.

(4) Where—

(*a*) it appears to the Commissioners that an application has been made for the purposes of this paragraph for a body corporate to be treated as a member of a group, but

(*b*) that body is not eligible to be treated as a member of that group,

the Commissioners shall give notice to the applicant that the application is ineffective.

(5) The Commissioners shall not refuse an application under sub-paragraph (3) above after the end of the period of ninety days beginning with the day on which the application is received by the Commissioners.

Modification of group treatment

3— (1) Subject to sub-paragraph (2) below, where any bodies corporate are treated as members of a group for the purposes of this Part of this Act and an application for the purpose is made to the Commissioners, then, from the specified time—

(*a*) a body corporate shall be excluded from the bodies so treated;

(*b*) one of those bodies corporate shall be substituted for another body corporate as the representative member; or

(*c*) the bodies corporate shall no longer be treated as members of a group.

(2) The Commissioners may refuse an application made for the purpose mentioned in sub-paragraph (1)(*a*) or (*c*) above if, and only if—

(*a*) the case is not one appearing to them to fall within paragraph 4(2)(*a*) and (*b*) below; and

(*b*) it appears to them necessary to refuse the application for the protection of the revenue.

(3) The Commissioners may refuse an application made for the purpose mentioned in sub-paragraph (1)(*b*) above if, and only if, it appears to them necessary to do so for the protection of the revenue.

(4) An application that is refused under this paragraph shall be, and be treated as always having been, ineffective.

(5) The specified time for the purposes of an application under sub-paragraph (1) above shall not be before the beginning of the accounting period which is current when the application is made.

Termination of group treatment

4— (1) If it appears to the Commissioners necessary to do so for the protection of the revenue, the Commissioners may, by notice given to any body corporate that is treated as a member of a group and to the representative member, terminate that treatment from such time as may be specified in the notice.

(2) Where—

(*a*) a body corporate is treated as a member of a group, and (*b*) it appears to the Commissioners that it is not eligible to be treated as a member of that group,

they shall, by notice given to the body corporate and the representative member, terminate that treatment from such time as may be specified in the notice.

(3) Where—

(*a*) a body corporate ceases as from any time to be treated as a member of a group,
(*b*) immediately before that time that body was the representative member,
(*c*) there are two or more other bodies corporate which will continue after that time to be treated as members of the group, and
(*d*) none of those bodies corporate is substituted from that time, or from before that time, as the representative member of the group under paragraph 3(1)(*b*) above,

the Commissioners shall, by notice given to such one of the bodies corporate mentioned in paragraph (*c*) above as they think fit, substitute that body corporate as the representative member as from that time.

(4) The time specified in a notice under sub-paragraph (1) above shall not be a time before the day on which the notice is given to the representative member.

(5) Subject to sub-paragraph (6) below, the time specified in a notice under sub-paragraph (2) or (3) above may be a time before the giving of the notice.

(6) In the case of a notice given under sub-paragraph (2) above in respect of a body corporate's having ceased to be eligible to be treated as a member of a group, the time specified in the notice shall not be before the time when it so ceased.

Applications relating to group treatment

5 An application under this Schedule with respect to any bodies corporate must be made by one of those bodies or by the person controlling them.

Notifications relating to group treatment

6— (1) Where—

(*a*) two or more bodies corporate are treated as members of a group for the purposes of this Part of this Act, and
(*b*) any of those bodies ceases to be eligible to be so treated,

the body corporate which ceases to be so eligible shall notify the Commissioners of that fact.

(2) A body corporate which is designated as representative member in relation to any other bodies corporate shall not cease to have an established place of business in the United Kingdom without first notifying the Commissioners of that fact.

(3) A body corporate which fails to comply with sub-paragraph (1) or (2) above shall be liable to a penalty of £250.

Supplemental regulations about applications and notifications

7— (1) For the purposes of any provision made by or under this Schedule for an application to be made to the Commissioners, regulations made by the Commissioners may make provision—

(*a*) as to the time within which the application is to be made;
(*b*) as to the form and manner in which the application is to be made;
(*c*) as to the information and other particulars to be contained in or provided with any application.

(2) For those purposes the Commissioners may also by regulations impose obligations requiring a person who has made an application to notify the Commissioners if any information contained in or provided in connection with that application is or becomes inaccurate.

(3) The power under this paragraph to make regulations as to the time within which any application is to be made shall include power to authorise the Commissioners to extend the time for the making of an application.

(4) Sub-paragraphs (1) to (3) above shall apply for the purposes of any provision made by or under this Schedule for any matter to be notified to the Commissioners as they apply for the purposes of any provision so made for an application to be made to them; and for this purpose references to the making of the application shall be construed as references to the giving of the notification.

Interpretation of Schedule

8— (1) For the purposes of this Schedule two or more bodies are under the same control if—

(*a*) one of them controls each of the others;
(*b*) one person (whether a body corporate or an individual) controls all of them; or
(*c*) two or more individuals carrying on a business in partnership control all of them.

(2) For the purposes of this Schedule a body corporate shall be taken to control another body corporate if, and only if—

(*a*) it is empowered by statute to control that body's activities; or (*b*) it is that body's holding company within the meaning of section [1159 of and Schedule 6 to][1] the Companies Act [2006 (c 46)][1].

(3) For the purposes of this Schedule an individual or individuals shall be taken to control a body corporate if, and only if (were he or they a company) he or they would be that body's holding company within the meaning of [those provisions][1].

(4) In this Schedule "the specified time", in relation to an application made under paragraph 2(1) or (2) or 3(1) above, means the beginning of such accounting period as may be specified in the application.

Amendments—[1] In para (2)(*b*), words substituted for words "736 of" and "1985", and in para (3), words substituted for words "section 736 of the Companies Act 1985", by the Companies Act 2006 (Consequential Amendments) (Taxes and National Insurance) Order, SI 2009/1890 art 4(1)(*e*), (2) with effect from 1 October 2009.

SCHEDULE 10

AGGREGATES LEVY: ASSESSMENT OF CIVIL PENALTIES AND INTEREST ON THEM

Section 46

Preliminary

1— (1) In this Schedule "civil penalty" means any penalty liability to which—

(*a*) is imposed by or under this Part of this Act; and

(*b*) arises otherwise than in consequence of a person's conviction for a criminal offence.

(2) In this Schedule—

(*a*) references to a person's being liable to a civil penalty include references to his being a person from whom the whole or any part of a civil penalty is recoverable by virtue of paragraph 8 of Schedule 6 to this Act; and

(*b*) references, in relation to a person from whom the whole or any part of a civil penalty is so recoverable, to the penalty to which he is liable are references to so much of the penalty as is recoverable from him.

(3) Any notification of an assessment under any provision of this Schedule to a person's representative shall be treated for the purposes of this Part of this Act as notification to the person in relation to whom the representative acts.

(4) In this paragraph "representative", in relation to any person, means—

(*a*) any of that person's personal representatives;

(*b*) that person's trustee in bankruptcy or liquidator;

(*c*) any person holding office as a receiver in relation to that person or any of his property;

(*d*) that person's tax representative or any other person for the time being acting in a representative capacity in relation to that person.

(5) In this paragraph "trustee in bankruptcy" includes, as respects Scotland—

(*a*) an interim or permanent trustee (within the meaning of the Bankruptcy (Scotland) Act 1985); and

(*b*) a trustee acting under a trust deed (within the meaning of that Act).

Assessments to penalties etc

2— (1) Where a person is liable to a civil penalty, the Commissioners may assess the amount due by way of penalty and notify it to him accordingly.

(2) If, where an assessment has been notified to any person under sub-paragraph (1) above or this sub-paragraph, it appears to the Commissioners that the amount which ought to have been assessed exceeds the amount that has already been assessed, the Commissioners may make a supplementary assessment of the amount of the excess and notify that person accordingly.

(3) The fact that any conduct giving rise to a civil penalty may have ceased before an assessment is made under this paragraph shall not affect the power of the Commissioners to make such an assessment.

(4) Where an amount has been assessed and notified to any person under this paragraph, it shall be recoverable as if it were aggregates levy due from him.

(5) Sub-paragraph (4) above—

(*a*) shall not apply so as to require any interest to be payable on a penalty otherwise than in accordance with this Schedule; and

(*b*) shall not have effect if, or to the extent that, the assessment in question has been withdrawn or reduced.

(6) Subject to sub-paragraph (7) below, where a person—

(*a*) is assessed under this paragraph to an amount due by way of a penalty, and

(*b*) is also assessed under any one or more provisions of Schedule 5 to this Act for an accounting period to which the conduct attracting the penalty is referable,

the assessments may be combined and notified to him as one assessment.

(7) A notice of a combined assessment under sub-paragraph (6) above must separately identify the penalty being assessed.

(8) The power to make an assessment under this paragraph is subject to paragraph 8(4) of Schedule 6 to this Act.

Further assessments to daily penalties

3— (1) This paragraph applies where an assessment is made under paragraph 2 above to an amount of a civil penalty to which any person is liable—

(*a*) under paragraph 1(3) of Schedule 7 to this Act (failure to provide information); or

(*b*) under paragraph 4(4) of that Schedule (failure to produce a document).

(2) The notice of assessment shall specify a time, not later than the end of the day of the giving of the notice of assessment, to which the amount of any daily penalty is calculated.

(3) For the purposes of sub-paragraph (2) above "daily penalty" means—

(*a*) in a case within sub-paragraph (1)(*a*) above, a penalty imposed by virtue of paragraph 1(3)(*b*) of Schedule 7 to this Act; and

(*b*) in a case within sub-paragraph (1)(*b*) above, a penalty imposed by virtue of paragraph 4(4)(*b*) of that Schedule.

(4) If further penalties accrue in respect of a continuing failure after that date to provide the information or, as the case may be, produce the document, a further assessment or further assessments may be made under paragraph 2 above in respect of the amounts so accruing.

(5) Where—

(*a*) an assessment to a civil penalty is made specifying a date for the purposes of sub-paragraph (2) above, and

(*b*) the failure in question is remedied within such period as may for the purposes of this sub-paragraph have been notified by the Commissioners to the person liable for the penalty,

the failure shall be deemed for the purposes of any further liability to civil penalties to have been remedied on the specified date.

Time limits on penalty assessments

4— (1) Subject to sub-paragraphs (2) and (3) below, an assessment under paragraph 2 above to a civil penalty shall not be made more than three years after the conduct to which the penalty relates.

(2) Subject to sub-paragraph (3) below, if aggregates levy has been lost—

(*a*) as a result of any conduct for which a person has been convicted of an offence involving fraud,

(*b*) in circumstances giving rise to liability to a penalty under paragraph 1 of Schedule 4 to this Act, or

(*c*) as a result of conduct falling within paragraph 7(1) of Schedule 6 to this Act (evasion),

an assessment may be made for any civil penalty relating to that conduct as if, in sub-paragraph (1) above, for "three years" there were substituted "twenty years".

(3) Where, after a person's death, the Commissioners propose to assess an amount of a civil penalty due by reason of some conduct of the deceased—

(*a*) the assessment shall not be made more than three years after the death; and

(*b*) if the circumstances are as set out in sub-paragraph (2) above—

(i) the modification of sub-paragraph (1) above contained in that sub-paragraph shall not apply; but

(ii) any assessment which (applying that modification) could have been made immediately after the death may be made at any time within three years after it.

Prospective amendments—In sub-paras (1), (3A) the words "4 years" to be substituted for the words "three years", sub-para (3)(*b*) and the word "and" preceding it, to be repealed and sub-para (2) to be substituted, by FA 2009 s 99, Sch 51 paras 27, 31, with effect from such day as the Treasury may by order made by statutory instrument appoint. Sub-para (2) to read as follows:

"(2) An assessment of a person to a civil penalty in a case involving a loss of aggregates levy—

(*a*) brought about deliberately by the person (or by another person acting on that person's behalf), or

(*b*) attributable to a failure by the person to comply with an obligation under section 24(2) or paragraph 1 of Schedule 4,

may be made at any time not more than 20 years after the conduct to which the penalty relates (subject to sub-paragraph (3)).

(2A) In sub-paragraph (2)(*a*) the reference to a loss brought about deliberately by the person includes a loss brought about as a result of a deliberate inaccuracy in a document given to Her Majesty's Revenue and Customs by or on behalf of that person."

Penalty interest on unpaid penalties

5— (1) Subject to sub-paragraph (2) below, where the Commissioners make an assessment under paragraph 2 above of any civil penalty to which a person is liable the amount of that penalty shall carry penalty interest for the period which—

(*a*) begins with the day on which the assessment is notified to the person on whom the assessment is made; and (*b*) ends with the day before the day on which the assessed penalty is paid.

(2) Where—

(*a*) the Commissioners make an assessment under paragraph 2 above of an amount of any civil penalty to which any person is liable,

(*b*) they also specify a date for the purposes of this sub-paragraph, and

(*c*) the amount of the penalty assessed is paid on or before that date,

the amount paid before that date shall not carry penalty interest under this paragraph.

(3) Penalty interest under this paragraph shall be compound interest calculated—

(*a*) at the penalty rate; and

(*b*) with monthly rests.

(4) For this purpose the penalty rate is the rate found by—

(*a*) taking the rate applicable under section 197 of the Finance Act 1996 for the purposes of paragraph 8(3)(*a*) of Schedule 5 to this Act; and

(*b*) adding 10 percentage points to that rate.

(5) Where a person is liable under this paragraph to pay any penalty interest, the Commissioners or, on appeal, an appeal tribunal may reduce the amount payable to such amount (including nil) as they think proper.

(6) Subject to sub-paragraph (7) below, where the person concerned satisfies the Commissioners or, on appeal, an appeal tribunal that there is a reasonable excuse for the conduct giving rise to the liability to pay penalty interest, that is a matter which (among other things) may be taken into account under sub-paragraph (5) above.

(7) In determining whether there is a reasonable excuse for the purposes of sub-paragraph (6) above, no account shall be taken of any of the following matters, that is to say—

(*a*) the insufficiency of the funds available to any person for paying any aggregates levy or penalty due or for paying the amount of the interest;

(*b*) the fact that there has, in the case in question or in that case taken with any other cases, been no or no significant loss of aggregates levy;

(*c*) the fact that the person liable to pay the interest or a person acting on his behalf has acted in good faith.

(8) In the case of interest reduced by the Commissioners under sub-paragraph (5) above, an appeal tribunal, on an appeal relating to the interest, may cancel the whole or any part of the reduction made by the Commissioners.

Supplemental provisions about interest

6— (1) Interest under paragraph 5 above shall be paid without any deduction of income tax.

(2) Sub-paragraph (3) below applies where—

(*a*) an amount carries interest under paragraph 5 above (or would do so apart from that sub-paragraph); and

(*b*) all or part of the amount turns out not to be due.

(3) In such a case—

(*a*) the amount or part that turns out not to be due shall not carry interest under paragraph 5 above and shall be treated as never having done so; and

(*b*) all such adjustments as are reasonable shall be made, including (subject to section 32 of, and Schedule 8 to, this Act) adjustments by way of repayment.

Assessments to penalty interest on unpaid penalties

7— (1) Where a person is liable for interest under paragraph 5 above, the Commissioners may assess the amount due by way of interest and notify it to him accordingly.

(2) If, where an assessment has been notified to any person under sub-paragraph (1) above or this sub-paragraph, it appears to the Commissioners that the amount which ought to have been assessed exceeds the amount that has already been assessed, the Commissioners may make a supplementary assessment of the amount of the excess and notify that person accordingly.

(3) Where an amount has been assessed and notified to any person under this paragraph, it shall be recoverable as if it were aggregates levy due from him.

(4) Sub-paragraph (3) above—

(*a*) shall not apply so as to require any interest to be payable on interest (except in so far as it falls to be compounded in accordance with paragraph 5(3) above); and

(*b*) shall not have effect if, or to the extent that, the assessment in question has been withdrawn or reduced.

(5) Paragraph 4 above shall apply in relation to assessments under this paragraph as if any assessment to interest on a penalty were an assessment under paragraph 2 above to the penalty in question.

(6) Subject to sub-paragraph (7) below, where a person—

(*a*) is assessed under this paragraph to an amount due by way of any interest on a penalty, and (*b*) is also assessed under any one or more provisions of Schedule 5 to this Act for the accounting period to which the conduct attracting the penalty is referable,

the assessments may be combined and notified to him as one assessment.

(7) A notice of a combined assessment under sub-paragraph (6) above must separately identify the interest being assessed.

Further assessments to interest on penalties

8— (1) Where an assessment is made under paragraph 7 above to an amount of penalty interest under paragraph 5 above—

(*a*) the notice of assessment shall specify a date, not later than the date of the notice of assessment, to which the amount of interest which is assessed is calculated; and

(*b*) if the interest continues to accrue after that date, a further assessment or further assessments may be made under paragraph 7 above in respect of the amounts so accruing.

(2) Where—

(*a*) an assessment to penalty interest is made specifying a date for the purposes of sub-paragraph (1)(*a*) above, and

(*b*) within such period as may for the purposes of this sub-paragraph have been notified by the Commissioners to the person liable for the interest, the amount on which the interest is payable is paid,

that amount shall be deemed for the purposes of any further liability to interest to have been paid on the specified date.

FINANCE ACT 2002

(2002 Chapter 23)

An Act to grant certain duties, to alter other duties, and to amend the law relating to the National Debt and the Public Revenue, and to make further provision in connection with finance.

[24 July 2002]

PART 5
OTHER TAXES

Aggregates levy

129 Aggregates levy: transitional relief for Northern Ireland

(1) (*inserts* FA 2001 s 30A).

(2) (*amends* FA 2001 s 17(6)(*a*)).

130 Aggregates levy: amendments to provisions exempting spoil etc

(1) (*amends* FA 2001 s 17(3)(*e*) and *inserts* FA 2001 s 17(3)(*f*)).

(2) (*repeals* FA 2001 s 17(4)(*b*)).

(3) This section shall be deemed to have come into force on 1st April 2002.

131 Aggregates levy: crushing and cutting rock

(1) (*repeals* FA 2001 s 17(3)(*a*)).

(2) (*amends* FA 2001 s 18(2)(*a*).

(3) (*amends* FA 2001 s 20(1), and *repeals* FA 2001 s 20(1)(*c*), 21(2)(*b*), 24(6)(*b*), and 24(8)(*a*)).

(4) This section shall be deemed to have come into force on 1st April 2002.

132 Aggregates levy: miscellaneous amendments

(1) Schedule 38 to this Act, which makes amendments to provisions in Part 2 of the Finance Act 2001 (aggregates levy), has effect.

(2) (*amends* FA 1996 s 197(2)(*h*)(ii)).

(3) This section shall be deemed to have come into force on 1st April 2002.

133 Aggregates levy: amendments to provisions about civil penalties

(1) Part 2 of Schedule 6 to the Finance Act 2001 (c 9) (aggregates levy: civil penalties) is amended as follows.

(2) (*amends FA 2001 Sch 6 para 7(1)(a) and repeals sub-para 7(1)(b)*).

(3) (*inserts FA 2001 Sch 6 para 7(1A)*).

(4) (*amends FA 2001 Sch 6 para 7(3) and (4)).*[1]

(5) (*inserts* FA 2001 Sch 6 para 9A).

(6) This section shall be deemed to have come into force on 1st May 2002.

Amendments—[1] Sub-ss (2)–(4) repealed by FA 2008 s 122, Sch 40 para 21(*j*) with effect from 1 April 2009 (by virtue of SI 2009/571 art 2). Sub-ss (2)–(4) repealed only in so far as they relate to conduct involving dishonesty which relates to—
(a) an inaccuracy in a document, or
(b) a failure to notify HMRC of an under-assessment by HMRC (SI 2009/571 art 6).

PART 6
MISCELLANEOUS AND SUPPLEMENTARY PROVISIONS

Supplementary

141 Repeals

(1) The enactments mentioned in Schedule 40 to this Act (which include provisions that are spent or of no practical utility) are repealed to the extent specified.

(2) The repeals specified in that Schedule have effect subject to the commencement provisions and savings contained or referred to in the notes set out in that Schedule.

SCHEDULES

SCHEDULE 38
AGGREGATES LEVY AMENDMENTS

Section 132

Introduction

1 This Schedule makes amendments to provisions of Part 2 of the Finance Act 2001 (c 9) (aggregates levy).

The charge

2 In section 16(1) (charge to aggregates levy), for "A levy" substitute "A tax".

Meaning of "aggregate" etc

3— (1) Section 17 (meaning of "aggregate" etc) is amended as follows.

(2) (*substitutes* FA 2001 s 17(2)(*d*)).

(3) (*amends* FA 2001 s 17(3)(*d*)(ii)).

(4) (*amends* FA 2001 s 17(4)(*d*)).

Exempt processes

4 (*amends* FA 2001 s 18(2)(*c*) and repeals s 18(3)(*d*) and (*h*)).

Commercial exploitation

5— (1) Section 19 (commercial exploitation) is amended as follows.

(2) (*amends* FA 2001 s 19(2)(*b*)).

(3) (*inserts* FA 2001 s 19(3A)).

(4) In subsection (4) (exemption in certain cases where aggregate is won from one site and incorporated into a neighbouring site), for the words "adjacent land" in both places substitute "other land".

Responsibility for commercial exploitation

6 (*amends* FA 2001 s 22(2)).

The register

7 (*inserts* FA 2001 s 24(6)(*ca*)).

Insolvency etc

8 In section 37 (regulations about cases of insolvency etc), in subsection (7) (meaning of "insolvency procedure) omit paragraphs (*g*) to (*j*) (appointment of receiver and other interim or provisional orders).

Notification of registrability etc

9— (1) Paragraph 1 of Schedule 4 (notification of registrability etc) is amended as follows.

(2) (*substitutes* FA 2001, Sch 4, para 1(1)–(1B)).

(3) In sub-paragraphs (2) and (5), after "sub-paragraph (1)" insert "or (1A)".

Restriction on powers to provide for set-off

10 In paragraph 11 of Schedule 8 (restriction on powers to provide for set-off), in sub-paragraph (2) (meaning of "insolvency procedure") omit paragraphs (*f*), (*g*) and (*h*) (appointment of receiver and other interim or provisional orders).

SCHEDULE 40
REPEALS

Section 141

PART 4
OTHER TAXES

(3) AGGREGATES LEVY

Note—All repeals relevant to aggregates levy are in effect and have therefore been omitted.

FINANCE ACT 2004

(2004 Chapter 12)

An Act to Grant certain duties, to alter other duties, and to amend the law relating to the National Debt and the Public Revenue, and to make further provision in connection with finance.

[22 July 2004]

PART 6
OTHER TAXES

Aggregates levy

290 Transitional tax credit in Northern Ireland: changes to existing scheme

(1) (*amended* FA 2001 s 30A(4))

(2) This section shall be deemed to have come into force on 1st April 2004.

291 Transitional tax credit in Northern Ireland: new scheme

(1) Part 2 of the Finance Act 2001 (c 9) (aggregates levy) is amended as set out in subsections (2) and (3).

(2) (*substitutes* FA 2001 s 30A)

(3) (*amends* FA 2001 s 48(1))

(4) The preceding provisions of this section come into force on such day as the Treasury may by order made by statutory instrument appoint.

(5) An order under subsection (4) may—

(*a*) make different provision for different purposes;

(*b*) make incidental, consequential, supplemental or transitional provision and savings.

Order—Finance Act 2004, Section 291 (Appointed Day) Order, SI 2004/1942 (appointed day is 23 July 2004).

FINANCE ACT 2007

(2007 Chapter 11)

PART 1
CHARGES, RATES, THRESHOLDS ETC

Environment

14 Rate of aggregates levy

(1) (*amends* FA 2001 s 16(4))

(2) The amendment made by subsection (1) has effect in relation to aggregate subjected to commercial exploitation on or after 1st April 2008.

PART 2
ENVIRONMENT

Other measures

22 Aggregates levy: exemption for aggregate removed from railways etc

(1) Section 17(3) of FA 2001 (exempt aggregate) is amended as follows.

(2)–(4) (*insert* FA 2001 s 17(3)(*da*))

(5) The amendment made by subsection (3) comes into force on such day as the Treasury may by order made by statutory instrument appoint.

Orders—Finance Act 2007 section 22(3) (Appointed Day) Order, SI 2007/2118 (appoints 1 August 2007 as the date on which the amendment in sub-s (3) comes into force).

SCHEDULES

SCHEDULE 24
PENALTIES FOR ERRORS

Note—Please see *VAT Statutes* ante for the text of this Schedule.

SCHEDULE 27
REPEALS

Section 114

PART 1
ENVIRONMENT

(1) EXEMPT AGGREGATES: RAILWAYS ETC

Short title and chapter	*Extent of repeal*
Finance Act 2001 (c 9)	In section 17(3), the word "or" at the end of paragraph (*d*).

FINANCE ACT 2008

(2008 Chapter 9)

An Act to Grant certain duties, to alter other duties, and to amend the law relating to the National Debt and the Public Revenue, and to make further provision in connection with finance.

[21 July 2008]

PART 1
CHARGES, RATES, ALLOWANCES, RELIEFS ETC

Environmental taxes and duties

20 Rate of aggregates levy

(1) (*amends* FA 2001 s 16(4))

(2) The amendment made by subsection (1) has effect in relation to aggregate subjected to commercial exploitation on or after 1 April 2009.

PART 7
ADMINISTRATION

Press releases—HMRC Guidance Note, 18 July 2008 (HMRC set-off across taxes following Finance Bill 2008).

CHAPTER 1
INFORMATION ETC

New information etc powers

114 Computer records etc

Note—Please see *VAT Statutes* ante for the text of this Section.

CHAPTER 3
PENALTIES

122 Penalties for errors

Note—Please see *VAT Statutes* ante for the text of this Section.

123 Penalties for failure to notify etc

Note—Please see *VAT Statutes* ante for the text of this Section.

CHAPTER 4
APPEALS ETC

Reviews and appeals etc: general

124 HMRC decisions etc: reviews and appeals

Note—Please see *VAT Statutes* ante for the text of this Section.

CHAPTER 5
PAYMENT AND ENFORCEMENT

Taking control of goods etc

127 Enforcement by taking control of goods: England and Wales

Note—Please see *VAT Statutes* ante for the text of this Section.

128 Summary warrant: Scotland

Note—Please see *VAT Statutes* ante for the text of this Section.

129 Consequential provision and commencement

Note—Please see *VAT Statutes* ante for the text of this Section.

Set off

130 Set-off: England and Wales and Northern Ireland

Note—Please see *VAT Statutes* ante for the text of this Section.

131 No set-off where insolvency procedure has been applied

Note—Please see *VAT Statutes* ante for the text of this Section.

133 Set-off etc where right to be paid a sum has been transferred

Note—Please see *VAT Statutes* ante for the text of this Section.

Other measures

135 Interest on unpaid tax in case of disaster etc of national significance

Note—Please see *VAT Statutes* ante for the text of this Section.

136 Fee for payment

Note—Please see *VAT Statutes* ante for the text of this Section.

Supplementary

139 Interpretation of Chapter

Note—Please see *VAT Statutes* ante for the text of this Section.

PART 8
MISCELLANEOUS

Payments from Exchequer accounts

158 Power of Treasury to make payments

Note—Please see *VAT Statutes* ante for the text of this Section.

159 Payments from certain Exchequer accounts: mechanism

Note—Please see *VAT Statutes* ante for the text of this Section.

Other matters

160 Power to give statutory effect to concessions

Note—Please see *VAT Statutes* ante for the text of this Section.

PART 9
FINAL PROVISIONS

165 Interpretation

Note—Please see *VAT Statutes* ante for the text of this Section.

166 Short title

This Act may be cited as the Finance Act 2008.

SCHEDULES

SCHEDULE 36
INFORMATION AND INSPECTION POWERS

Section 113

Note—Please see *VAT Statutes* ante for the text of this Section.

SCHEDULE 41
PENALTIES: FAILURE TO NOTIFY AND CERTAIN VAT AND EXCISE WRONGDOING

Section 123

Note—Please see *VAT Statutes* ante for the text of this Section.

FINANCE ACT 2009

(2009 Chapter 10)

An Act to Grant certain duties, to alter other duties, and to amend the law relating to the National Debt and the Public Revenue, and to make further provision in connection with finance.

[21 July 2009]

PART 7
ADMINISTRATION

Standards and values

92 HMRC Charter

Note—Please see *VAT Statutes* ante for the text of this Section.

93 Duties of senior accounting officers of qualifying companies

Note—Please see *VAT Statutes* ante for the text of this Section.

94 Publishing details of deliberate tax defaulters

Note—Please see *VAT Statutes* ante for the text of this Section.

Information etc

95 Amendment of information and inspection powers

Note—Please see *VAT Statutes* ante for the text of this Section.

96 Extension of information and inspection powers to further taxes

(1) In paragraph 63(1) of Schedule 36 to FA 2008 (information and inspection powers: meaning of "tax"), for paragraph (*e*) (and the "and" before it) substitute—

"(*e*) insurance premium tax,
(*f*) inheritance tax,
(*g*) stamp duty land tax,
(*h*) stamp duty reserve tax,
(*i*) petroleum revenue tax,
(*j*) aggregates levy,
(*k*) climate change levy,
(*l*) landfill tax, and
(*m*) relevant foreign tax,".

(2) Schedule 48 contains further amendments of that Schedule.

(3) The amendments made by this section and Schedule 48 come into force on such day as the Treasury may by order appoint.

(4) An order under subsection (3) may—

(*a*) appoint different days for different purposes, and
(*b*) contain transitional provision and savings.

(5) The Treasury may by order make any incidental, supplemental, consequential, transitional or transitory provision or saving which appears appropriate in consequence of, or otherwise in connection with, this section and Schedule 48.

(6) An order under subsection (5) may—

(*a*) make different provision for different purposes, and
(*b*) make provision amending, repealing or revoking an enactment or instrument (whenever passed or made).

(7) An order under this section is to be made by statutory instrument.

(8) A statutory instrument containing an order under subsection (5) is subject to annulment in pursuance of a resolution of the House of Commons.

97 Powers to obtain contact details for debtors

Note—Please see *VAT Statutes* ante for the text of this Section.

98 Record-keeping

(1) Schedule 50 contains provision about obligations to keep records.

(2) The amendments made by that Schedule come into force on such day as the Treasury may by order made by statutory instrument appoint.

Assessments, claims etc

99 Time limits for assessments, claims etc

(1) Schedule 51 contains provision about time limits for assessments, claims etc

(2) The amendments made by that Schedule come into force on such day as the Treasury may by order made by statutory instrument appoint.

(3) An order under subsection (2)—

(*a*) may make different provision for different purposes, and
(*b*) may include transitional provision and savings.

Interest

101 Late payment interest on sums due to HMRC

Note—Please see *VAT Statutes* ante for the text of this Section.

102 Repayment interest on sums to be paid by HMRC

Note—Please see *VAT Statutes* ante for the text of this Section.

103 Rates of interest

Note—Please see *VAT Statutes* ante for the text of this Section.

104 Supplementary

Note—Please see *VAT Statutes* ante for the text of this Section.

108 Suspension of penalties during currency of agreement for deferred payment

Note—Please see *VAT Statutes* ante for the text of this Section.

109 Miscellaneous amendments

Note—Please see *VAT Statutes* ante for the text of this Section.

SCHEDULES

SCHEDULE 46

DUTIES OF SENIOR ACCOUNTING OFFICERS OF QUALIFYING COMPANIES

Section 93

Note—Please see *VAT Statutes* ante for the text of this Schedule.

SCHEDULE 47

AMENDMENT OF INFORMATION AND INSPECTION POWERS

Section 95

Note—Please see *VAT Statutes* ante for the text of this Schedule.

SCHEDULE 48

EXTENSION OF INFORMATION AND INSPECTION POWERS

Section 96

Note—Please see *VAT Statutes* ante for the text of this Schedule.

SCHEDULE 49

POWERS TO OBTAIN CONTACT DETAILS FOR DEBTORS

Section 97

Note—Please see *VAT Statutes* ante for the text of this Schedule.

SCHEDULE 50

RECORD-KEEPING

Section 98

…

Aggregates levy

15 Schedule 7 to FA 2001 (aggregates levy: information and evidence etc) is amended as follows.

16— (1) Paragraph 2 (records) is amended as follows.

(2) For sub-paragraphs (4) and (5) substitute—

"(4) A duty under regulations under this paragraph to preserve records may be discharged—

(*a*) by preserving them in any form and by any means, or

(*b*) by preserving the information contained in them in any form and by any means,

subject to any conditions or exceptions specified in writing by the Commissioners."

(3) In sub-paragraph (9), omit "approval or" and "given or".

17 Omit paragraph 3 (evidence of records that are required to be preserved).

SCHEDULE 51

TIME LIMITS FOR ASSESSMENTS, CLAIMS ETC

Section 99

…

Aggregates levy

27 Part 2 of FA 2001 (aggregates levy) is amended as follows.

28 In section 32(1) (repayments of overpaid aggregates levy), for "three years" substitute "4 years".

29— (1) Paragraph 4 of Schedule 5 (time limits for assessments) is amended as follows.

(2) In sub-paragraph (1)(*b*), for "three years" substitute "4 years".

(3) For sub-paragraph (3) substitute—

"(3) An assessment of an amount due from a person in a case involving a loss of aggregates levy—

(*a*) brought about deliberately by the person (or by another person acting on that person's behalf), or

(*b*) attributable to a failure by the person to comply with an obligation under section 24(2) or paragraph 1 of Schedule 4,

may be made at any time not more than 20 years after the end of the accounting period to which it relates (subject to sub-paragraph (4)).

(3A) In sub-paragraph (3)(*a*) the reference to a loss brought about deliberately by the person includes a loss brought about as a result of a deliberate inaccuracy in a document given to Her Majesty's Revenue and Customs by or on behalf of that person."

(4) In sub-paragraph (4)—

(*a*) in paragraph (*a*), for "three years" substitute "4 years", and

(*b*) omit paragraph (*b*) (and the "and" before it).

30 In paragraph 2(10) of Schedule 8 (interest payable by Commissioners), for "three years" substitute "4 years".

31— (1) Paragraph 4 of Schedule 10 (time limits on penalty assessments) is amended as follows.

(2) In sub-paragraph (1), for "three years" substitute "4 years".

(3) For sub-paragraph (2) substitute—

"(2) An assessment of a person to a civil penalty in a case involving a loss of aggregates levy—

(*a*) brought about deliberately by the person (or by another person acting on that person's behalf), or

(*b*) attributable to a failure by the person to comply with an obligation under section 24(2) or paragraph 1 of Schedule 4,

may be made at any time not more than 20 years after the conduct to which the penalty relates (subject to sub-paragraph (3)).

(2A) In sub-paragraph (2)(*a*) the reference to a loss brought about deliberately by the person includes a loss brought about as a result of a deliberate inaccuracy in a document given to Her Majesty's Revenue and Customs by or on behalf of that person."

(4) In sub-paragraph (3)—

(*a*) in paragraph (*a*), for "three years" substitute "4 years", and

(*b*) omit paragraph (*b*) (and the "and" before it).

SCHEDULE 53

LATE PAYMENT INTEREST

Section 101

Note—Please see *VAT Statutes* ante for the text of this Schedule.

SCHEDULE 54

REPAYMENT INTEREST

Section 102

Note—Please see *VAT Statutes* ante for the text of this Schedule.

SCHEDULE 57

AMENDMENTS RELATING TO PENALTIES

Section 109

Note—Please see *VAT Statutes* ante for the text of this Schedule.

AGGREGATES LEVY
STATUTORY INSTRUMENTS

CHRONOLOGICAL LIST OF PRINTED STATUTORY INSTRUMENTS

SI Year/No	Title
SI 1997/1431	Distress for Customs and Excise Duties and Other Indirect Taxes Regulations 1997
SI 2001/4027	Aggregates Levy (Registration and Miscellaneous Provisions) Regulations 2001
SI 2001/4033	Finance Act 2001, section 24 and Schedule 4, (Appointed Day) Order 2001
SI 2002/761	Aggregates Levy (General) Regulations 2002
SI 2004/1959	Aggregates Levy (Northern Ireland Tax Credit) Regulations 2004

CHRONOLOGICAL LIST OF STATUTORY INSTRUMENTS

SI Year/No	Title
SI 1997/1431	Distress for Customs and Excise Duties and Other Indirect Taxes Regulations 1997
SI 2001/4027	Aggregates Levy (Registration and Miscellaneous Provisions) Regulations 2001
SI 2001/4033	Finance Act 2001, section 24 and Schedule 4, (Appointed Day) Order 2001
SI 2002/761	Aggregates Levy (General) Regulations 2002
SI 2003/465	*Aggregates Levy (Registration and Miscellaneous Provisions) (Amendment) Regulations 2003*
SI 2003/466	*Aggregates Levy (General) (Amendment) Regulations 2003*
SI 2007/2118	*Finance Act 2007 section 22(3) (Appointed Day) Order 2007*
SI 2007/2168	*Aggregates Levy (Registration and Miscellaneous Provisions) (Amendment) Regulations 2007*
SI 2008/2693	*Amusement Machine Licence Duty, etc (Amendments) Regulations 2008*

STATUTORY INSTRUMENTS

1997/1431

Distress for Customs and Excise Duties and Other Indirect Taxes Regulations 1997

Made by the Commissioners of Customs and Excise under FA 1997 ss 51(1), (2), (3)

Made . . . . *9th June 1997*
Laid before House of Commons . . . . *9th June 1997*
Coming into force . . . . *1st July 1997*

Citation and commencement

1 These Regulations may be cited as The Distress for Customs and Excise Duties and Other Indirect Taxes Regulations 1997 and shall come into force on 1st July 1997.

Interpretation

2— (1) In these Regulations—

"authorised person" means a person acting under the authority of the Commissioners;

"costs" means any costs, charges, expenses and fees;

"officer" means, subject to section 8(2) of the Customs and Excise Management Act 1979, a person commissioned by the Commissioners pursuant to section 6(3) of that Act;

"person in default" means a person who has refused or neglected to pay any relevant tax due from him;

"relevant tax" means any of the following—

...

[(*g*) aggregates levy;][1]

"walking possession agreement" means an agreement under which, in consideration of any goods and chattels distrained upon being allowed to remain in the custody of the person in default and of the delaying of their sale, that person—

(*a*) acknowledges that the goods and chattels specified in the agreement are under distraint and held in walking possession; and

(*b*) undertakes that, except with the consent of the Commissioners and subject to such conditions as they may impose, he will not remove or allow the removal of any of the specified goods and chattels from the place named in the agreement;

"1994 Act" means Part III of the Finance Act 1994;

"1996 Act" means Part III of the Finance Act 1996;

(2) Any reference in these Regulations to an amount of relevant tax includes a reference to any amount recoverable as if it were an amount of that relevant tax.

Note—Words omitted are not relevant for the purposes of aggregates levy.

Amendments—[1] Para (1)(*g*) added by the Aggregates Levy (General) Regulations, SI 2002/761 reg 39 with effect from 1 April 2002.

Revocations and transitional provisions

3— (1) The Regulations specified in Schedule 3 are hereby revoked to the extent set out there.

(2) Where a warrant is signed before the coming into force of these Regulations, these Regulations shall apply to anything done, after these Regulations come into force, in relation to that warrant or as a consequence of distress being levied.

Levying distress

4— (1) Subject to regulation 5 below, if upon written demand a person neglects or refuses to pay any relevant tax due from him an officer may levy distress on the goods and chattels of that person and by warrant signed by him direct any authorised person to levy such distress.

(2) Where a warrant has been signed, distress shall be levied by or under the direction of, and in the presence of, the authorised person.

(3) Subject to regulation 6 below, distress may be levied on any goods and chattels located at any place whatever including on a public highway.

Goods and chattels not subject to levy

6 No distress shall be levied on any goods and chattels mentioned in Schedule 1 which at the time of levy are located in a place and used for a purpose mentioned in that Schedule.

Times for levying distress

7— (1) Subject to paragraph (2) below, a levy of distress shall commence only during the period between eight o'clock in the morning and eight o'clock at night on any day of the week but it may be continued thereafter outside that period until the levy is completed.

(2) Where a person holds himself out as conducting any profession, trade or business during hours which are partly within and partly outside, or wholly outside the period mentioned in paragraph (1) above, a levy of distress may be commenced at any time during that period or

during the hours of any day in which he holds himself out as conducting that profession, trade or business and it may be continued thereafter outside that period or those hours until the levy is completed.

Costs

8— (1) A person in respect of whose goods and chattels a warrant has been signed shall be liable to pay to an officer or authorised person all costs, in connection with anything done under these Regulations described in column 1 of Schedule 2, as determined in accordance with column 2 of that Schedule.

(2) An authorised person may, after deducting and accounting for the amount of relevant tax to the Commissioners, retain costs from any amount received.

Sale

9 If any person upon whose goods and chattels distress has been levied does not pay the amount of relevant tax due together with costs within five days of a levy, an officer or authorised person may sell the distress for payment of the amount of relevant tax and costs; and the officer or authorised person, after deducting and retaining the amount of relevant tax and costs shall restore any surplus to the owner of the goods upon which distress was levied.

Disputes as to costs

10— (1) In the case of any dispute as to costs, the amount of those costs shall be taxed by a district judge of the county court of the district where the distress was levied, and he may make such order as he thinks fit as to the costs of the taxation.

(2) In the application of this regulation to Northern Ireland, in the case of any dispute as to costs, the amount of those costs shall be taxed in the same manner as costs in equity suits or proceedings in the county court in Northern Ireland.

SCHEDULE 1
GOODS AND CHATTELS NOT SUBJECT TO LEVY

Regulation 6

1 Any of the following goods and chattels which are located in a dwelling house at which distress is being levied and are reasonably required for the domestic needs of any person residing in that dwelling house—

(*a*) beds and bedding;
(*b*) household linen;
(*c*) chairs and settees;
(*d*) tables;
(*e*) food;
(*f*) lights and light fittings;
(*g*) heating appliances;
(*h*) curtains;
(*i*) floor coverings;
(*j*) furniture, equipment and utensils used for cooking, storing or eating food;
(*k*) refrigerators;
(*l*) articles used for cleaning, mending, or pressing clothes;
(*m*) articles used for cleaning the home;
(*n*) furniture used for storing—
  (i) clothing, bedding or household linen;
  (ii) articles used for cleaning the home;
  (iii) utensils used for cooking or eating food;
(*o*) articles used for safety in the home;
(*p*) toys for the use of any child within the household;
(*q*) medical aids and medical equipment.

2 Any of the following items which are located in premises used for the purposes of any profession, trade or business—

(*a*) fire fighting equipment for use on the premises;
(*b*) medical aids and medical equipment for use on the premises.

SCHEDULE 2
SCALE OF COSTS

Regulation 8(1)

Matter (*1*)	*Costs* (*2*)
1 For attending to levy distress where payment is made of an amount of relevant tax due and distress is not levied:	£12.50.
2 For levying distress—	
(a) where an amount of relevant tax demanded and due does not exceed £100:	£12.50.
(b) where an amount of relevant tax demanded and due exceeds £100:	12½% on the first £100 4% on the next £400, 2½% on the next £1,500, 1% on the next £8,000, ¼% on any additional sum.
3 For taking possession of distrained goods—	
(a) where a person remains in physical possession of goods at the place where distress was levied (the person to provide his own food and lodging):	£4.50 per day.
(b) where possession is taken under a walking possession agreement:	£7.00.
4 For appraising goods upon which distress has been levied:	Reasonable costs of appraisement.
5 For arranging removal and storage of goods upon which distress has been levied:	Reasonable costs of arrangement.
6 For removing and storing goods upon which distress has been levied:	Reasonable costs of removal and storage.
7 For advertising the sale of goods upon which distress has been levied:	Reasonable costs of advertising.
8 For selling the distress—	
(*a*) where a sale by auction is held at the auctioneer's premises:	15% of the sum realised.
(*b*) where a sale by auction is held elsewhere:	7½% of the sum realised and auctioneer's reasonable costs.
(*c*) where a sale by other means is undertaken:	7½% of the sum realised and reasonable costs.

2001/4027

Aggregates Levy (Registration and Miscellaneous Provisions) Regulations 2001

Made by the Commissioners of Customs and Excise under FA 2001 ss 24(4), 33(1), 33(2), 34(2), 34(4), 35(4), 36(1), 45, Sch 4 paras 5, 6, and Sch 9 para 7; and FA 1999 s 132

Made . . . . *19 December 2001*
Laid before the House of Commons . . . . . . *20 December 2001*
Coming into force . . . . *11 January 2002*

PART I
PRELIMINARY

1 These Regulations may be cited as the Aggregates Levy (Registration and Miscellaneous Provisions) Regulations 2001 and come into force on 11th January 2002.

PART II
REGISTRATION

Notification of registrability—form, manner, timing, etc

2— (1) A person who is required to notify the Commissioners under paragraph 1(1)(*a*) or (*b*) of Schedule 4 to the Act (notification of registrability for aggregates levy) shall do so on Form AL 1.

(2) But a partner so required shall do so on Form AL 1 and Form AL 2.

(3) All persons who notify their registrability under paragraph (1) or (2) above shall in addition notify the Commissioners of their site details on Form AL 1A.

(4) A person may make the notification required by paragraph (1), (2) or (3) above on either—

(*a*) a version of a relevant form completed (other than in respect of the inclusion of the requisite signature) by telephone; or

(*b*) subject to his possession of an approved digital certificate, an electronic version of a relevant form;

and, in either case, the version used shall not differ in any material respect from Form AL 1, Form AL 2 or Form AL 1A but may include relevant modifications.

(5) In all cases the required notification must contain and provide full information and particulars about every matter referred to in Form AL 1, Form AL 1A and, in the case of a partner, Form AL 2, together with such further details as the Commissioners may require.

(6) A person so required on 11th January 2002 must deliver the notification to the Commissioners no later than 1st March 2002.

(7) A person to whom paragraph (6) above does not apply, but who becomes so required after 11th January 2002, must deliver the notification to the Commissioners within 30 days starting from the day after becoming so required.

(8) A person who is required but fails to comply with this regulation remains subject to paragraph 1(1) of Schedule 4 to the Act.

(9) In this regulation—

"approved digital certificate" means a digital certificate which is accepted by the Commissioners as identifying a person for the purpose of their authorisation of his use of an electronic communication in respect of an assigned matter;

"assigned matter" has the meaning given in section 1(1) of the Customs and Excise Management Act 1979;

"electronic communication" has the same meaning as in section 15(1) of the Electronic Communications Act 2000;

"electronic version" means the version which is submitted by means of an electronic communication;

"notify" and "notification" are to be construed according to the context so as to cover notification by post, telephone and by means of an electronic communication according to the context;

"relevant form" means Form AL 1, Form AL 2 and Form AL 1A.

Exemption from registration

[**3**— (1) Where the only taxable activities that a person carries out or intends to carry out are relevant taxable activities, that person shall be exempt from the requirement of registration and all consequent obligations and liabilities.

(2) For the purposes of this regulation, a "relevant taxable activity" is the commercial exploitation of aggregate which is exempt under section 17(3)(*b*), (*c*), (*d*), [(*da*),][2] (*e*) or (*f*) or section 17(4)(*a*), (*c*), (*d*), (*e*) or (*f*) of the Act.

(3) Where at least one of the relevant taxable activities which such a person carries out is the commercial exploitation of aggregate which is exempt under section 17(3)(*e*) or (*f*) or section 17(4)(*a*) of the Act or clay (exempt under section 17(4)(*f*) of the Act), that person shall notify the Commissioners (notification under paragraph 1A of Schedule 4 to the Act) of this fact in writing in such a manner and providing such information as may be directed by the Commissioners or stipulated by them in a published notice.

(4) A person who has notified the Commissioners under paragraph (3) above shall also notify them of any change in circumstance in writing in such a manner and providing such information as may be directed by the Commissioners or stipulated by them in a published notice.

(5) In this regulation—

"aggregate" has the meaning given in section 17(1) of the Act;

"commercial exploitation" has the meaning given in section 19 of the Act;

"published notice" refers to a notice published by the Commissioners and not withdrawn or replaced by a further notice.][1]

Commentary—*De Voil Indirect Tax Service* **V22.108**.

Press releases etc—C&E Business Brief 34/02 24-12-02 (exemption from registration and other obligations).

Amendments—[1] This regulation substituted by the Aggregates Levy (Registration and Miscellaneous Provisions) (Amendment) Regulations, SI 2003/465 with effect from 1 April 2003.

[2] In para (2), reference inserted by the Aggregates Levy (Registration and Miscellaneous Provisions) (Amendment) Regulations, SI 2007/2168 reg 2(1). This amendment only has effect in relation to the commercial exploitation on or after 16 August 2007 of aggregate which is exempt under FA 2001 s 17(3)(*da*).

Changes in particulars

4—(1) A person who has made a notification (the "original notification") to the Commissioners under regulation 2(1), 2(2), 2(3) or 2(4) at any time shall also, as appropriate, notify them about the following matters.

(2) The first such matter is any inaccuracy or inadequacy in the information, particulars or details contained in or provided with the original notification.

(3) The second such matter is any change in circumstances that causes that information or those particulars or details to become inaccurate or inadequate.

(4) The third such matter is any change in circumstances relating to that person, that person's business or any other matter with respect to which particulars are contained in the register.

(5) A notification required by this regulation must—

(*a*) be given in writing;
(*b*) provide full particulars enabling the register kept by the Commissioners to be kept up to date; and
(*c*) be delivered to the Commissioners within 30 days.

(6) The first of those 30 days begin, as the case requires, on—

(*a*) the day after the person discovers that the original notification was inaccurate or is in a position to rectify the inadequacy in that notification (see paragraph (2) above); or
(*b*) the day after the change in circumstances occurred (see paragraphs (3) and (4) above).

(7) The full particulars referred to in paragraph (5)(*b*) above include (but are not limited to)—

(*a*) the nature of the relevant inaccuracy, inadequacy or change;
(*b*) the date on which the inaccuracy in the original notification was discovered or the inadequacy could be rectified;
(*c*) the date on which the change occurred;
(*d*) the nature of the inaccuracy, inadequacy or change;
(*e*) the correct information, particulars or details.

(8) A relevant change of circumstances under paragraph (3) or (4) above includes (but is not limited to)—

(*a*) the person's name, trading name, address or principal place of business;
(*b*) the person's status (namely, as sole proprietor, partner, unincorporated body, or body corporate);
(*c*) the name and address of a partner or a change in the membership of a partnership;
(*d*) the name and address of a trustee or beneficiary of a trust;
(*e*) the site details.

(9) The Commissioners may, on their own initiative or following a notification under this regulation, correct an entry in the register in a case where they are satisfied that it should be corrected or otherwise brought up to date.

(10) Where a person makes a notification under this regulation that is or becomes inaccurate, inadequate or misleading, the provisions of paragraphs (1) to (9) above shall apply to that notification as if it were the original notification.

Cessation of taxable activities

5— (1) This regulation applies to a person who has become liable to notify the Commissioners under either regulation 2 or 3.

(2) Where such a person ceases to have the intention of carrying on taxable activities (paragraph 3(1) of Schedule 4 to the Act) he shall notify the Commissioners of that fact.

(3) Such a person shall make that notification in writing setting out—

(*a*) the day on which he ceased to have the intention, and
(*b*) the day on which he carried out his final taxable activity.

(4) This notification must be delivered to the Commissioners within 30 days starting from the day after the later of the days referred to in paragraph (3) above.

PART III GROUPS

References to groups, etc

6— (1) For the purposes of this Part—

(*a*) a body corporate is a member of a group at any time in relation to which it falls to be treated as such a member in accordance with Schedule 9 to the Act; and
(*b*) the body corporate which is to be taken as the representative member for a group at any time is the member of the group which in relation to that time is the representative member under that Schedule in the case of that group.

(2) A body corporate that is a member of a group shall, under section 24 of and Schedule 4 to the Act, be registered in the name of the representative member.

Liability for returns

7 The obligation of a member of a group to make a return under regulations made under section 25 of the Act shall be discharged by the representative member making a return representing the cumulative total of what would be the individual returns for the group members were it not for the group treatment.

Group treatment

8— (1) An application for group treatment under paragraph 2(1) of Schedule 9 to the Act shall be made to the Commissioners in writing.

(2) In addition, each body corporate which is applying to be treated as a member of the group shall make an application to the Commissioners to that effect in writing.

(3) Any application under paragraphs (1) or (2) above shall include such information and declaration as the Commissioners may require.

Applications and notifications

9— (1) An application under paragraph 2(2) or 3(1) of Schedule 9 to the Act to add a body corporate to a group, exclude a body corporate from a group, change the representative member for a group or to cease group treatment shall be made in writing to the Commissioners and include such information and declaration as they may require.

(2) A notification under paragraph 6(1) or 6(2) of Schedule 9 to the Act in relation to a body corporate ceasing to be eligible to be treated as a member of a group or a body corporate which is the representative member for a group ceasing to have an established place of business in the United Kingdom shall be made in writing to the Commissioners and include such information and declaration as they may require.

(3) The notification required by paragraph (2) above shall be delivered to the Commissioners no later than the earlier of 30 days after the body corporate becomes aware that it will cease to be eligible to be treated as a member of a group or that it will cease to have an established place of business in the United Kingdom or 30 days after the body corporate ceases to be so eligible or ceases to have such an established place of business, as the case may require.

(4) The first of the 30 days referred to in paragraph (3) above is the first day after the one on which the body corporate becomes aware that it will cease to be so eligible or that it will cease to have an established place of business in the United Kingdom or the day after the one on which the body corporate ceases to be so eligible or ceases to have an established place of business in the United Kingdom, as the case may require.

Modifications etc

10 A person who has made an application or notification to the Commissioners under this Part shall notify them immediately should any information contained in or provided in connection with that application or notification be or become inaccurate.

Miscellaneous

11 In this Part, "member" and "representative member" have the same meanings as in section 48(1) of the Act.

PART IV
PARTNERSHIPS AND OTHER SPECIAL CASES

Partnerships

12— (1) This regulation applies for determining by what person anything required to be done by or under the Act is to be done where, apart from this regulation, that requirement would fall on persons carrying on business in partnership.

(2) Any such requirement shall be the joint and several responsibility of every partner.

(3) Subject to paragraphs (4) and (5) below—

(*a*) compliance with such a requirement by at least one of the partners shall suffice as compliance by all of them; and

(*b*) in the case of a partnership whose principal place of business is in Scotland, such compliance by a person duly authorised by the partnership shall suffice as compliance by the partners.

(4) Each partner shall comply with the requirement imposed by regulation 2 in relation to Form AL 2.

(5) A person joining or leaving a partnership, as the case requires, shall comply with the requirements imposed by regulation 4 so far as they apply to any change in the membership of a partnership.

Other unincorporated associations

13— (1) This regulation applies for determining by what persons anything required to be done by or under the Act is to be done where, apart from this regulation, that requirement would fall on persons carrying on business together as an unincorporated body other than a partnership.

(2) Any such requirement shall be the joint and several responsibility of—

(*a*) first, every person holding office in that body as president, chairman, treasurer, secretary or other similar office; or (*b*) secondly, if there is no such office holder, every person who is a member of a committee by which the affairs of that body are managed; or

(*c*) thirdly, if there is no such office holder or member, every person carrying on that business.

(3) Compliance with such a requirement by one or more of the persons referred to in paragraph (2) above shall suffice as compliance with that requirement by all of them.

(4) But a purported notification under regulation 2(1), 2(2), 2(3) or 2(4) shall not be treated as complying with any of those regulations unless it is made by a person required to do so under paragraph (2)(*a*), (2)(*b*) or (2)(*c*) above, as appropriate.

Non resident taxpayers—requirement and provision for tax representatives

14— (1) This regulation applies to a person (a "non-resident taxpayer") who—

(*a*) is or is required to be registered for the purposes of the levy, and

(*b*) is not resident in the United Kingdom.

(2) A person who falls within this description shall notify the Commissioners in writing of this fact.

(3) Such notification shall be delivered to the Commissioners within 30 days starting from the day after the first day on which the person falls within the description.

(4) The Commissioners may—

(*a*) require or permit such a taxpayer to appoint some person resident in the United Kingdom to act as his tax representative for the purposes of the levy with effect from a date they specify, and

(*b*) oblige the taxpayer to request them, no later than such earlier date than the date in (*a*) above as they may specify, to approve the appointment of that person as the tax representative.

(5) Any appointment of a person as a tax representative shall take effect only if, and from the date, approved by the Commissioners.

(6) A request for approval under paragraph (4)(*b*) above shall be in writing and contain such information and particulars, and corresponding declaration by the taxpayer and the proposed tax representative, as the Commissioners may require.

15— (1) A non-resident may appoint a different tax representative as a replacement for a tax representative whose appointment has taken effect.

(2) Such appointment shall take effect only if, and from the date, approved by the Commissioners.

(3) A request to the Commissioners for the purposes of paragraph (2) above shall be in writing and contain such information and particulars, and corresponding declaration by the taxpayer and the proposed replacement tax representative, as the Commissioners may require.

16— (1) The Commissioners may, with effect from a date or dates they specify, for good cause and by way of written notice served on the non-resident taxpayer—

(*a*) withdraw their approval of any person appointed as a tax representative for that non-resident taxpayer;

(*b*) require that non-resident taxpayer to replace any tax representative with a different tax representative; and

(*c*) oblige that non-resident taxpayer to request their approval for a person's appointment as a replacement tax representative.

(2) Regulations 14(5) and (6) shall apply for the purposes of this regulation in corresponding manner as they apply for the purposes of regulation 14(4).

17— (1) This regulation applies in a case where the Commissioners require the appointment of a tax representative under regulation 14(4)(*a*) and the non-resident taxpayer—

(*a*) becomes liable to a penalty under section 33(3) of the Act (penalty for failing in obligation to request the Commissioners' approval of tax representative), or

(*b*) unreasonably fails to obtain the Commissioners' approval in accordance with regulation 14(4)(*b*) (approval of tax representative).

(2) Where this regulation applies, the Commissioners may give a direction requiring a specified person to be treated as the appointed and approved tax representative of that non-resident taxpayer from a specified date.

(3) Accordingly, a person specified in a direction under paragraph (2) above shall be treated as the tax representative of the non-resident taxpayer from the specified date until such date as the Commissioners may specify in a further direction.

(4) The Commissioners may only specify a person under paragraph (2) above who—

(*a*) is eligible to act as a tax representative, and

(*b*) is suitable in all the circumstances to be the tax representative for the relevant non-resident taxpayer.

(5) The Commissioners may give a direction requiring a specified person to be treated as the appointed and approved tax representative of a non-resident taxpayer as a replacement for a person specified in a direction under paragraph (2) above.

(6) Paragraphs (3) and (4) above apply in relation to paragraph (5) above in corresponding manner as they apply to paragraph (2) above.

(7) Regulations 15 and 16 do not apply in relation to a person specified in a direction under this regulation.

18— (1) A person shall cease to be the tax representative for a non-resident taxpayer from the time when—

(*a*) the non-resident taxpayer ceases to be registered;
(*b*) the non-resident taxpayer replaces that person with a different tax representative under regulation 15 or 16;
(*c*) the Commissioners so direct under regulation 17;
(*d*) the person dies, becomes incapacitated or becomes subject to an insolvency procedure;
(*e*) the person ceases to be eligible to act as a tax representative;
(*f*) the person delivers to the Commissioners notification in writing that he withdraws as tax representative for the non-resident taxpayer; or
(*g*) the non-resident taxpayer delivers to the Commissioners notification in writing that he withdraws an appointment that they permitted but did not require.

(2) A person who is specified in a direction under regulation 17 shall not—

(*a*) cease to be (or be treated as) the tax representative except in accordance with that regulation; or
(*b*) be permitted to withdraw under paragraph (1)(*f*) above.

(3) The name of a tax representative (or a person treated as such) shall be registered against the name of the non-resident taxpayer of whom that person is (or is treated as) the representative (section 24(1) of the Act).

(4) That name shall be deleted from the register if the person ceases to be the tax representative for that non-resident taxpayer and the Commissioners consider it appropriate to do so.

19— (1) A tax representative (or a person treated as such) shall notify and provide full particulars to the Commissioners in writing about any of the following matters.

(2) Such notification must be delivered to the Commissioners no later than 30 days starting from the first day after the matter arises.

(3) The first matter is any change in the name, constitution or ownership of the tax representative's business, any change in the site details or any event that may require the register to be varied.

(4) The second matter is the tax representative lawfully ceasing to be the appointed tax representative of the relevant non-resident taxpayer.

(5) The third matter is the tax representative ceasing to be eligible to act as a tax representative.

20 In this Part "eligible to act as a tax representative" is to be construed with reference to section 33(1) of the Act which provides that a tax representative must be resident in the United Kingdom.

PART V
PENALTIES

21 A person who fails to comply with a requirement imposed on him by or under any of the following regulations shall be liable to a penalty of £250 for each such failure—

(*a*) regulation 2(1), 2(2), 2(3), 2(5), 2(6) or 2(7) (form, manner and timing of notification about registrability);
(*b*) regulation 4(1) or (5) (notification of changes in particulars);
(*c*) regulation 10 (notification of changes in relation to groups);
(*d*) regulation 14(2) or 14(3) (notification by non-resident taxpayer);
(*e*) regulation 19(1) or 19(2) (notification by tax representative).

PART VI
INTERPRETATION

22— (1) In these Regulations, except where the context requires otherwise—

"the Act" refers to sections 16 to 49 of and Schedules 4 to 10 to the Finance Act 2001 and any reference to a section of, a Schedule to or a paragraph of a Schedule to the Act refers to the appropriate section of, Schedule to or paragraph of a Schedule to that Act;
"Form AL 1", "Form AL 2" and "Form AL 1A" refer respectively to the forms numbered 1, 2 and 3 in the Schedule to these Regulations;
"levy" refers to aggregates levy;
"Part", "regulation" or "regulations" refers to the appropriate Part, regulation or regulations of these Regulations;
"partner" refers to a person carrying on a business in partnership with at least one other person;
"taxable activity" and "taxable activities" are to be construed in accordance with the provisions of section 24(3) and paragraph 8(2) of Schedule 4 to the Act.

(2) A reference in these Regulations to a form prescribed in the Schedule to these Regulations shall include a reference to a form which the Commissioners are satisfied is to like effect.

SCHEDULE

Form 1
Application for Registration

Aggregates Levy (AL)

Application for Registration

When you have completed and signed this form, please send it using the official reply envelope provided to:

HM Customs and Excise
National Registration Service
Ty Myrddin
Old Station Road
CARMARTHEN
SA31 1BT

Data Protection Act 1998

HM Customs and Excise collects information in order to administer the taxes for which it is responsible (such as VAT, insurance premium tax, excise duties, air passenger duty, landfill tax and climate change levy), and for detecting and preventing crime.

Where the law permits we may also get information about you from third parties, or give information to them, for example in order to check its accuracy, prevent or detect crime or protect public funds in other ways. These third parties may include the police, other government departments and agencies.

Complaints

If you have a complaint, please telephone your local complaints manager, the telephone number is in the telephone directory.

If you are unhappy with our response you can ask the Adjudicator to look into your complaint. The Adjudicator reviews complaints not settled to your satisfaction by Customs. The recommendations of the Adjudicator are independent and the service is free. The Adjudicator only looks at complaints, not general enquiries.
Telephone the Adjudicator on 020 7930 2292.

For Official Use Only

Registration number

EDR

Date of receipt

Initials

Keyer | Checker

AL 1 Page 1 IB (December 2001)

Aggregates Levy

Application for Registration

Please read the general notes before completing this form. Please write clearly in **black** ink and use **BLOCK LETTERS** or use typescript. Where there is a "**Yes**" or "**No**" option, please tick "✓" the appropriate box.

If you require any additional aggregates levy forms please contact the National Registration Service at the address shown on the front of this form.

Remember you must also complete Form AL 1A with your site details

1 If your business is registered for VAT please give your VAT registration number.

2 What is the legal status of your business?

Please tick boxes as appropriate.

- **If your business is a partnership -** you must complete and return Form AL 2 as well as this form.
- **If your business is a trust -** you must complete and return Form AL 6 as well as this form. Form AL 1 should be completed by a trustee if the business is run by the trustees. If the business is run by the beneficiaries all beneficiaries should complete Form AL 1.

Corporate body (eg Limited Company) ☐
Please give incorporation details

Certificate number

Date of incorporation D D M M Y Y Y Y

Sole Proprietor ☐
Partnership ☐
Local Authority ☐
Non profit making / unincorporated body ☐
Public Corporation ☐
Trust ☐

3 Are you applying for group registration as the representative member of an aggregates levy group?

Yes ☐ No ☐

If "**yes**", you must provide the additional information set out on Forms AL 50 and AL 51

4 Are you applying to be registered in divisions?

Yes ☐ No ☐

If "**yes**" you must provide the additional information set out in the Aggregates Levy Public Notice

5 Please give the full name of the business.

- **Corporate or unincorporated bodies -** please give the name of the company, association etc.
- **Groups -** please give the name of the representative member.
- **Partnerships -** please give your trading name, if you do not have a trading name give the names of all the partners.

....
....
....
....
....
....

6 Please give the trading name of your business (if different from the name given at 5).

....

....

....

....

....

....

7 Please give the address of your principal place of business. This is where the day-to-day running of your business takes place. Your aggregates levy return forms/ communications will be sent to this address unless you specify an alternative communication address at 8.

- If this address is an aggregate extraction site it should be included on Form AL 1A.
- If this address is not in the UK and you are commercially exploiting aggregate in the UK it is important that you read the completion notes that come with this form.

....

....

....

....

Postcode:

Telephone no:

Fax no:

Mobile phone no:

E-mail:

Website address:

8 Please specify an alternative communications address, if appropriate.

- Return forms and other correspondence are normally sent to the principal place of business, as at 7 above.
- Exceptionally you may ask for all your returns and correspondence to be issued to this address.

Name:

Address: ....

....

....

....

Postcode:

Telephone no:

Fax no:

E-mail:

9 Please indicate, by ticking the relevant box(es), which aggregates activities your business(es) is involved in, indicating what percentage of your total sales each activity represents.

- If you are applying as the representative member of an aggregates levy group please indicate the business activities of all group members.

		✓	%
1	Quarry extraction	☐	☐
2	Sand/gravel extraction	☐	☐
3	The importation of aggregate from outside the UK	☐	☐
4	Use of a mobile crusher to commercially extract aggregates	☐	☐

5 Other, please explain and show a percentage

....

....

10 Please give the date of your first commercial exploitation of aggregate.

- This must be on or after 1 April 2002.
- Please see general notes for further information on commercial exploitation.
- If you are applying as the representative member of an aggregates levy group, please show the date or anticipated date of the first occasion aggregate will be subjected to commercial exploitation by any group member including the representative member.

Date: D D | M M | Y Y Y Y

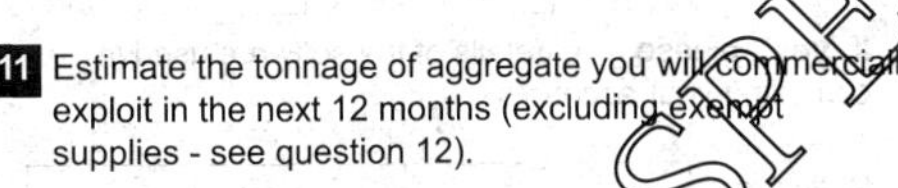

11 Estimate the tonnage of aggregate you will commercially exploit in the next 12 months (excluding exempt supplies - see question 12).

- If you are applying as the representative member of an aggregates levy group please give the estimated tonnage for all group members.

tonnes

12 Do you expect any of your commercial activity to be exempt from the levy or subject to relief?

- If you are applying as the representative member of an aggregates levy group please give the estimated tonnage for all group members.

Yes ☐ No ☐

If "**yes**", estimate the tonnage of exempt/relieved or exported supplies you expect to make in the next 12 months

Exempt tonnes

Relieved tonnes

Export tonnes

13 Please indicate the preferred stagger for your returns by ticking the appropriate box.

- If you intend to apply for non-standard tax periods tick the box provided and enter the stagger period most closely matching your non-standard periods.

Stagger 0 Monthly Returns ☐

Stagger 1 Quarters Ending Mar / Jun / Sept / Dec ☐

Stagger 2 Quarters Ending Jan / Apr / Jul / Oct ☐

Stagger 3 Quarters Ending Feb / May / Aug / Nov ☐

Do you wish to apply for non-standard tax periods?

Yes ☐ No ☐

14 Please give details of the bank or building society account that you use for the aggregates levy business.

- If you have a Girobank Account give the sort code and account number for making payments into your account - advised at the front of your cheque book.

Sort code:

Account no:

Girobank Account no:

Account title

15 Will you account for aggregates levy using a computerised system?

Yes ☐ No ☐

If "**yes**", please give details of the software used in compiling your accounts

Software

Version

16 Have you taken over a business registrable for aggregates levy as a going concern, or changed the legal entity that owns the business (*for example from a sole proprietor to a limited company*)?

Yes ☐ No ☐

If "**yes**", what date did the transfer take place? D D M M Y Y Y Y

Business name of previous owner

Aggregates Registration number of previous owner

Do you want to keep this number? If "**yes**", you and the previous owner must also complete and return Form AL68. If you do keep the registration number, remember that you will become liable for the previous owner's aggregates levy debts

Yes ☐ No ☐

17 Is your business involved in any other activities registered, approved or authorised by Customs and Excise? (*Please tick boxes as appropriate and give the registration number*).

		Registration number
☐	Landfill Tax	
☐	Excise Duties	
☐	Other (give details)	
	....	
☐	Imports / Exports	

18 Only for completion on applications made after 1 April 2002.

Are there any other aggregates business(es) you are, or have been, involved in during the last 24 months?

- Please give the Aggregates Registration Numbers of any businesses you are or have been involved in. If you are a partnership or a limited company this means any businesses in which any partners or directors have been involved.
- Please continue on a separate sheet if necessary.

Yes ☐ No ☐

Aggregates Registration numbers of other businesses

19 Please sign and complete the declaration

Declaration:

Please sign and date the declaration below (corporate bodies - a director or company secretary must sign the form)

I, ____

(insert full name in BLOCK LETTERS)

declare that the information given on this form and contained in any accompanying document is true and complete.

Signature: ______________________ *Mr, Mrs, Miss, Ms* Date: D D M M Y Y Y Y

Please tick	✓				
Sole proprietor	☐	Director	☐	Trustee	☐
Partner	☐	Beneficiary of a Trust	☐	Authorised Official	☐
Company Secretary	☐				

Form 2
Partnership Details

Aggregates Levy (AL)

Partnership Details

When you have completed and signed this form, please send it to:

HM Customs and Excise
National Registration Service
Ty Myrddin
Old Station Road
Carmarthen
SA31 1BT

SPECIMEN

Data Protection Act 1998

HM Customs and Excise collects information in order to administer the taxes for which it is responsible (such as VAT, insurance premium tax, excise duties, air passenger duty, landfill tax and climate change levy), and for detecting and preventing crime.

Where the law permits we may also get information about you from third parties, or give information to them, for example in order to check its accuracy, prevent or detect crime or protect public funds in other ways. These third parties may include the police, other government departments and agencies.

Complaints
If you have a complaint, please telephone your local complaints manager, the telephone number is in the telephone directory.

If you are unhappy with our response you can ask the Adjudicator to look into your complaint. The Adjudicator reviews complaints not settled to your satisfaction by Customs. The recommendations of the Adjudicator are independent and the service is free. The Adjudicator only looks at complaints, not general enquiries. Telephone the Adjudicator on 020 7930 2292.

For Official Use Only

Date of receipt

Reg No:

AL 2
Version 0.4

1

These details form part of your application to be registered for aggregates levy or will amend your registration details already submitted.

If you are registering your partnership details for the first time : Please make sure that **every** partner completes, signs and dates one of the sections below. If there is insufficient space to include all the partners, please photocopy this form or contact the National Registration Service (see page 1 for the address) for additional copies.

If you wish to change your partnership details : Please quote your aggregates levy registration number below. Please make sure that **every** partner joining or leaving the partnership completes and signs one of the sections below and gives the date they joined or left the partnership. They should indicate if they have left or joined the partnership by ticking the appropriate box.

If you have any problems completing this form please contact the National Registration Service on 08457-585831 or refer to the aggregates levy Public Notice. Further information on the aggregates levy is also available on the HM Customs & Excise website: www.hmce.gov.uk

Registration Number:
- *complete only if you are amending your partnership details.*

Trading name of Partnership.

Please write clearly in **black** ink and use **BLOCK LETTERS** or typescript.

Full name of partner

Home Address

Postcode

Home Telephone Number

Signature

Date (if you are registering for the first time give the date you completed this section. If you are changing your partnership details give the date you joined or left the partnership)

Joined partnership ☐ Left partnership ☐

AL 2
Version 0.4

Full name of partner

Home Address

Postcode

Home Telephone Number

Signature

Date (if you are registering for the first time give the date you completed this section. If you are changing your partnership details give the date you joined or left the partnership)

Joined partnership

Left partnership

Full name of partner

Home Address

Postcode

Home Telephone Number

Signature

Date (if you are registering for the first time give the date you completed this section. If you are changing your partnership details give the date you joined or left the partnership)

Joined partnership

Left partnership

Full name of partner

Home Address

Postcode

Home Telephone Number

Signature

Date (if you are registering for the first time give the date you completed this section. If you are changing your partnership details give the date you joined or left the partnership)

Joined partnership

Left partnership

Full name of partner

Home Address

Postcode

Home Telephone Number

Signature

Date (if you are registering for the first time give the date you completed this section. If you are changing your partnership details give the date you joined or left the partnership)

Joined partnership

Left partnership

Form 3
Site Details

Aggregates Levy (AL)

Site Details

When you have completed and signed this form, please send it to:

HM Customs and Excise
Central Collection Unit (AL)
Alexander House
21 Victoria Avenue
Southend-on-Sea
SS99 1AS

Data Protection Act 1998

HM Customs and Excise collects information in order to administer the taxes for which it is responsible (such as VAT, insurance premium tax, excise duties, air passenger duty, landfill tax and climate change levy), and for detecting and preventing crime.

Where the law permits we may also get information about you from third parties, or give information to them, for example in order to check its accuracy, prevent or detect crime or protect public funds in other ways. These third parties may include the police, other government departments and agencies.

Complaints

If you have a complaint, please telephone your local complaints manager, the telephone number is in the telephone directory.

If you are unhappy with our response you can ask the Adjudicator to look into your complaint. The Adjudicator reviews complaints not settled to your satisfaction by Customs. The recommendations of the Adjudicator are independent and the service is free. The Adjudicator only looks at complaints, not general enquiries.
Telephone the Adjudicator on 020 7930 2292.

For Official Use Only

Date of receipt:						

Reg No:									

Aggregates Levy

Application for Registration

Aggregates Levy Site Details

Please complete this form with the details of all the sites you operate, intend to operate or use for the commercial exploitation of aggregate. Where you are asked for the ordnance survey grid reference you should give the grid reference of the entrance to the site.

If you require a continuation sheet please telephone 0845 010 9000, or photocopy page 3 of this form.

You can also use this form to notify us if:

- you now operate an additional site (or sites) which have not been notified previously; or
- the site details have changed; or
- a site is now closed.

A site is any premises which you use, or intend to use, for:

- winning any aggregate;
- mixing any aggregate;
- applying an exempt process to any aggregate;
- storing any aggregate;
- the first landing in the United Kingdom of aggregate won from the sea-bed within United Kingdom waters.

Please Note: To ensure that avoidance of levy is not facilitated Customs and Excise may determine the boundaries of those sites.

For further information on sites please see the Aggregates Levy Public Notice AGL 1.

Application for Registration - Aggregates Levy Site Details

Please read the general notes above before completing this form.
Please write clearly in **Black** ink and use **BLOCK LETTERS** or use typescript
Where there is a **"Yes"** or **"No"** option, please tick "✓" the appropriate box.

❶ Are you amending site details to an existing aggregates levy registration?

Yes ☐ No ☐

If "Yes", please quote your aggregates levy registration number:

❷ complete with the site details

Site ID, for official use only: [ ]

If you are changing your site details please indicate the reason by ticking the appropriate box

New site [ ] Amend existing site [ ] Site closed [ ] Date D D M M Y Y Y Y

Trading name of site

Business Name
(This should be the same as supplied on the AL 1 or AL 51)

Site Address

Postcode

Ordnance Survey grid reference

Telephone number

Fax number

E-Mail:

Is a weighbridge used to establish the weight of aggregate at this site? Yes [ ] No [ ]

Please give the reason for site closure (if appropriate)

If you have taken over this site from another operator please give their business name and aggregates levy registration number here.

Name

Registration number

SPECIMEN

❸ Please sign and complete the declaration:

Declaration,

I,

(enter your full name in BLOCK LETTERS)

declare that the information given on this form and contained in any accompanying document is true and complete.

Signature: Date: D D M M Y Y Y Y

Mr,Mrs, Miss, Ms

Sole proprietor	[ ]	Director	[ ]	Trustee	[ ]
Partner	[ ]	Company Secretary	[ ]	Authorised Official	[ ]

2001/4033
Finance Act 2001, section 24 and Schedule 4, (Appointed Day) Order 2001

Made by the Treasury under FA 2001 s 24(10)

Made . . . . *19 December 2001*

1 This Order may be cited as the Finance Act 2001, section 24 and Schedule 4, (Appointed Day) Order 2001.

2 The date appointed as the day on which paragraphs 5 and 6 of Schedule 4 to the Finance Act 2001 come into force is 20th December 2001.

3 The date appointed as the day on which section 24 of and paragraphs 1, 2, 3, 4, 7 and 8 of Schedule 4 to the Finance Act 2001 come into force is 11th January 2002.

2002/761
Aggregates Levy (General) Regulations 2002

Made by the Commissioners of Customs and Excise under FA 2001 ss 17(6), 23, 25(1) and (2), 30, 31(3), 37, 38, 39, 45, Sch 6 paras 9(2), (3), Sch 7 para 2, Sch 8 paras 1, 9, 10 and 11, FA 1997 s 51, FA 1999 s 132

Made . . . . *21 March 2002*
Laid before the House of Commons . . . . *21 March 2002*
Coming into force . . . . *1 April 2002*

ARRANGEMENT OF REGULATIONS

PART I
PRELIMINARY

Citation and commencement

1 These Regulations may be cited as the Aggregates Levy (General) Regulations 2002 and come into force on 1st April 2002.

General interpretation

2 In these Regulations except where the context requires otherwise—

"the Act" refers to sections 16 to 49 of and Schedules 4 to 10 to the Finance Act 2001 and any reference to a section of, Schedule to or paragraph of a Schedule to the Act refers to the appropriate section of, Schedule to or paragraph of a Schedule to that Act;

"aggregate" has the meaning given in section 17(1) of the Act;

"AL" refers to aggregates levy;

"commercial exploitation" and "commercially exploited" are to be construed in accordance with section 19 of the Act;

"disposed of to landfill" is to be interpreted in accordance with sections 65 and 70(2) of the Finance Act 1996;

"exempt aggregate" means aggregate which is not taxable aggregate;

"exempt process" has the meaning given in section 18(2) of the Act;

"originating site" has the meaning given in section 20(1) of the Act;

"Part", "regulation" or "regulations" refers to the appropriate Part, regulation or regulations of these Regulations;

"published notice" refers to a notice published by the Commissioners and not withdrawn or replaced by a further notice;

"registrable person" refers to a person who is registered or required to be registered under section 24 of and Schedule 4 to the Act other than a person who is exempt from the requirement of registration under regulations made under section 24(4) of the Act;

"Schedule" refers to the Schedule to these Regulations;

"taxable aggregate" is to be construed in accordance with section 17 of the Act;

"working day" excludes Saturday, Sunday and any bank or public holiday.

PART II
WEIGHT OF AGGREGATE

Determination of the weight of aggregate

3— (1) Subject to regulation 4, the weight of any quantity of aggregate shall be determined by the use of a weighbridge at a site covered by section 19(2) of the Act.

(2) The terms and conditions attached to the use of a weighbridge shall be stipulated by the Commissioners in a published notice and shall include provisions relating to the records to be kept and the discounting of constituents (such as water).

(3) Where this regulation applies, the weight of any quantity of aggregate is to be determined at the time when it is first subjected to commercial exploitation.

4— (1) Where the use of a weighbridge is not practicable, the weight of any quantity of aggregate is to be determined in accordance with a method approved by the Commissioners ("approved method").

(2) Any such approval shall be in writing, shall be subject to such terms and conditions as the Commissioners may specify, including (but not limited to) the records to be kept, the time at which the weight of any quantity of aggregate is to be determined and the discounting of constituents (such as water).

(3) Where it appears to the Commissioners that an approved method is not being applied correctly or that it produces an inaccurate result, they may direct that it shall no longer have effect.

(4) In the absence of an approved method, the Commissioners may prescribe the method to be used.

(5) Any direction made or method prescribed under this regulation shall be in writing and shall take effect from a specified date.

PART III
ACCOUNTING, PAYMENT, RECORDS, TAX CREDITS, REPAYMENTS, SET-OFF, ETC

Accounting periods

5— (1) A registrable person shall be subject to accounting periods.

(2) In the case of a registered person, these shall be each three month period ending on the dates notified to him at any time by the Commissioners for this purpose.

(3) In the case of any other registrable person, these shall be each three month period ending on 31 March, 30 June, 30 September or 31 December.

(4) However, in such cases and subject to such conditions as may be stipulated by the Commissioners in a published notice, the Commissioners may vary the start, end and length of any accounting period.

Returns

6— (1) A registrable person is obliged to make a return to the Commissioners covering each of his accounting periods.

(2) The registrable person is obliged to make that return no later than the last working day of the month immediately following the end of the period to which it relates.

(3) In the case of an accounting period that does not end on the last day of a month, the registrable person is obliged to make that return no later than the due day directed by the Commissioners.

(4) The Commissioners may allow the registrable person extra time in which to make that return.

(5) The registrable person must make that return in a form that is prescribed by the Commissioners in a published notice ("prescribed form").

(6) Subject to his possession of an approved digital certificate, the registrable person may make that return in a prescribed form using an electronic version of the return.

(7) The registrable person must make that return by securing that it is delivered either to the address prescribed by the Commissioners in a published notice or to any other address that they may direct or allow.

(8) In this regulation—

"approved digital certificate" means a digital certificate which is accepted by the Commissioners as identifying a person for the purpose of their authorisation of his use of an electronic communication in respect of an assigned matter;

"assigned matter" has the meaning given in section 1(1) of the Customs and Excise Management Act 1979;

"delivered" is to be construed according to the context so as to cover delivery by post and by means of an electronic communication as appropriate;

"electronic communication" has the same meaning as in section 15(1) of the Electronic Communications Act 2000;

"electronic version" means the version which is submitted by means of an electronic communication.

Content of returns

7— (1) The registrable person must declare in the return the AL due from him for the relevant accounting period, taking into consideration—

(*a*) the AL due on the commercial exploitation of taxable aggregate—

(i) the time of which falls in that accounting period, and

(ii) for which he is liable to account; and,

(*b*) any authorised or required adjustment or any correction of errors (see regulations 15(4), 18(3), 28 and 29).

(2) The registrable person must provide in the return accurate information about every matter that the prescribed form requires.

(3) The registrable person must sign, date and declare on the document forming his return that the information provided in it is true and complete.

(4) The registrable person must comply with paragraphs (1), (2) and (3) above in the manner prescribed by the Commissioners in a published notice.

(5) In this regulation, "sign" is to be construed according to the context so as to cover signatures in writing and signatures in electronic form as appropriate.

Payment

8— (1) A registrable person must pay to the Commissioners the amount of AL due from him for a given accounting period no later than the due date for the return for that period (see regulations 6(2), 6(3) and 6(4)).

(2) The registrable person must make that payment by securing that it is delivered either to the address or bank account prescribed by the Commissioners in a published notice or to any other address or bank account that they may direct or allow.

(3) The Commissioners may allow a registrable person who has made arrangements with them for the payment of any amount of AL due from him by means of direct debit an extra 7 days in which the payment may be made.

(4) The Commissioners shall only act pursuant to paragraph (3) above in accordance with such conditions as they shall stipulate in a published notice.

Records

9— (1) A registrable person is obliged to keep a record to be known as the "aggregates levy account" (periodic summary of AL due).

(2) A registrable person who makes a claim under regulations 12 and 15(1) (tax credits in respect of bad debts) is obliged to keep a record to be known as the "aggregates levy bad debts account".

(3) A registrable person who makes a claim under regulations 13 and 15(1) (other tax credits) is obliged to keep a record to be known as the "aggregates levy tax credits account".

(4) A record within this regulation must be kept in the manner stipulated in a published notice.

10 A registrable person is obliged to keep the following records—

(*a*) his business and accounting records;
(*b*) his stock record;
(*c*) copies of all invoices issued by him;
(*d*) all invoices received by him;
(*e*) copies of all credit and debit notes or similar documents issued by him;
(*f*) all credit and debit notes or similar documents received by him;
(*g*) documentary evidence (including the workings and all relevant background documents) to explain and support any calculation of the weight of—
  (i) taxable aggregate which has been subject to commercial exploitation; and
  (ii) exempt aggregate;
(*h*) documentary evidence regarding the adjustment of an entry concerning the amount of AL for which he is liable to account;
(*i*) documentary evidence regarding any claim by him for a tax credit under regulation 12 (bad debts) including, as appropriate, evidence of insolvency or liquidation and, in each case, regarding any relevant surrounding circumstances;
(*j*) documentary evidence regarding any claim by him for a tax credit under regulation 13 (other tax credits) including, as appropriate, evidence of export and end use and, in each case, regarding any relevant surrounding circumstances;
(*k*) documentary evidence regarding amounts of aggregate which have been dumped or disposed of to landfill;
(*l*) a record of the information he relies on in making each return pursuant to regulation 7;
(*m*) any other record that may be directed by the Commissioners or stipulated in a published notice.

11— (1) Subject to paragraph (2) below, a registrable person is required to preserve any record required by regulation 9 or 10 for a period of six years.

(2) The Commissioners may direct that any such record need only be preserved for such lesser period as they specify.

(3) For the purposes of paragraph (1) above, a record within regulation 9 need only be preserved in relation to events taking place not more than six years earlier.

Bad debts: entitlement to tax credit

12— (1) Paragraph (3) below applies where—

(*a*) a person has commercially exploited taxable aggregate within the meaning of section 19(1)(*a*) or (*b*) of the Act ("relevant commercial exploitation") and has accounted for and paid the AL chargeable in respect of that relevant commercial exploitation;
(*b*) that person has made a charge to a third party ("the customer") in respect of that relevant commercial exploitation;
(*c*) that person and the customer are not connected;
(*d*) the whole or any part of the consideration which represents the charge for that relevant exploitation ("the consideration") has been written off in his accounts as a bad debt; and
(*e*) the customer has become insolvent or gone into liquidation.

(2) Any question whether a person is connected with another for the purposes of paragraph (1) above shall be determined in accordance with section 839 of the Income and Corporation Taxes Act 1988.

(3) Subject to paragraph (4) below, the person shall be entitled to a tax credit in respect of the amount of AL accounted for and paid by him in respect of the outstanding amount (subject to the provisions of this Part including those provisions relating to the making of a relevant claim to the Commissioners).

(4) Where the charge made for the relevant commercial exploitation in question is less than twice the amount of AL accounted for and paid by a person in respect of that relevant commercial exploitation, the amount of the tax credit which he can claim under paragraph (3) above shall be restricted to half the outstanding amount.

(5) In this regulation and regulation 18—

"claim" refers to a claim in accordance with regulation 15 or 16 and "claimant" shall be construed accordingly;

"the outstanding amount" refers to—

(*a*) if at the time of the claim no part of the consideration written off in the claimant's accounts as a bad debt has been received, an amount equal to the amount of the consideration so written off;

(*b*) if at that time any part of the consideration so written off has been received, an amount by which that part is exceeded by the amount of the consideration written off.

(6) In paragraph (5) above, "received" refers to receipt either by the claimant or by a person to whom a right to receive the whole or any part of the consideration written off has been assigned.

(7) Accordingly, subject to paragraph (4) above, the tax credit arising under this regulation shall be of an amount equal to such proportion of the AL accounted for and paid in respect of the relevant commercial exploitation as the outstanding amount forms of the total consideration.

(8) The whole or any part of the consideration shall be taken to have been written off as a bad debt when an entry is made in relation to that supply in the claimant's aggregates levy bad debts account (see regulation 9(2)).

(9) Where the claimant owes an amount of money to the customer which can be set off, the amount of the consideration written off in the accounts shall be reduced by the amount so owed.

(10) Where the claimant holds in relation to the customer an enforceable security, the amount of the consideration written off in the claimant's accounts shall be reduced by the value of that security.

(11) In paragraph (10) above, "security" refers to—

(*a*) in England, Wales or Northern Ireland, any mortgage, charge, lien or other security;

(*b*) in Scotland, any security (whether heritable or moveable), any floating charge and right of lien or preference and right of retention (other than a right of compensation or set-off).

Other tax credits: entitlement

13— (1) This regulation applies to a person who has commercially exploited taxable aggregate and who has accounted for the AL chargeable on that commercial exploitation.

(2) Such a person is entitled to a tax credit in respect of any AL accounted for in respect of that commercial exploitation where the taxable aggregate in question—

(*a*) is exported or removed from the United Kingdom without further processing;

(*b*) is used in an exempt process;

(*c*) is used in any of the industrial or agricultural processes listed in the Schedule;

(*d*) is disposed of (by dumping or otherwise) in any of the following ways:

(i) it is returned without further processing to its originating site or any site which is not its originating site but is registered under the same name;

(ii) it is disposed of to landfill;

(iii) it is gravel or sand and is used for beach restoration purposes at a site which is not its originating site.

(3) This regulation is subject to the provisions of this Part including those provisions relating to the making of a relevant claim to the Commissioners and the keeping of records including any records that are directed by the Commissioners or stipulated in a published notice.

(4) For the purposes of subsection (6) of section 17 of the Act, all the processes listed in the Schedule are prescribed for the purposes of that subsection.

Tax credits: general

14 A tax credit shall only arise under regulation 12 or 13 if a claim is made by a person so entitled acting in accordance with regulation 15 or 16, as the case requires.

15— (1) Subject to paragraph (6) below, a person shall claim any such tax credit by bringing it into account when he is accounting for AL due from him for any accounting period.

(2) Subject to paragraph (3) below, a person shall not be entitled to make such a claim unless he is in possession of the records required by paragraphs (*i*), (*j*) and (*k*) of regulation 10 as appropriate.

(3) In the case of a claim for a tax credit under regulation 13(2)(*a*) (export or removal from the United Kingdom), a person shall be entitled to make such a claim in accordance with paragraph (1) above despite the fact that he is not in possession of the records required by paragraph (*j*) of regulation 10 provided that he obtains such records within three months of his making such a claim. If not, he shall make the appropriate adjustment to cancel the tax credit claimed in his next AL return. Any further claim will be subject to paragraphs (1) and (2) above.

(4) Accordingly—

(*a*) the requirements of regulation 7 (content of returns), regulation 8 (payment) and regulation 9 (accounts) apply subject to paragraph (1) above; but

(*b*) paragraph (1) above applies subject to regulation 28 (corrections) and regulation 29 (corrections of errors not exceeding [£50,000][1]).

(5) A claim subject to paragraphs (1) to (4) above shall be regarded as a claim for repayment of AL for the purposes of section 32 of the Act (supplemental provisions about repayments, etc) (and see paragraph (7) below).

(6) Where the total tax credit claimed by a person exceeds the total of the AL due from him for the accounting period in question, the Commissioners shall repay to him an amount equal to the excess (but see regulations 30 and 31).

(7) Given the provision made by section 30(5) of the Act, this regulation has effect subject to section 32 of the Act (application of supplemental provisions about repayments: three year time limit, unjust enrichment etc).

Amendments—[1] Figure in para (4)(*b*) substituted for figure "£2,000" by the Value Added Tax, etc (Correction of Errors, etc) Regulations, SI 2008/1482 reg 7(1) with effect in relation to under-calculations or over-calculations respectively, in the Aggregates Levy (General) Regulations, SI 2002/761 reg 29(2), (3), which registrable persons first discover in their accounting periods that start on 1 July 2008 or later: SI 2008/1482 reg 7(3).

16— (1) Where the Commissioners have cancelled the registration of a person in accordance with paragraph 4 of Schedule 4 to the Act, and he is not a registrable person, the Commissioners shall repay to him the amount of any tax credit if they are satisfied that he has made a proper claim to them in writing for this purpose.

(2) A claim under paragraph (1) above may be combined with a claim under regulation 15(1) if appropriate.

(3) A person making a claim under paragraph (1) above must furnish to the Commissioners full particulars in relation to the tax credit claimed including (but not restricted to)—

(*a*) the return in which the relevant AL was accounted for;

(*b*) the amount of the AL in question and the date and manner of its payment to the Commissioners;

(*c*) the events by virtue of which the bad debt or other entitlement to a tax credit arose; and

(*d*) any supporting documentary or other evidence.

(4) Where the Commissioners are satisfied that a person who has made a claim in accordance with paragraphs (1) and (3) above is entitled to a tax credit and that he has not previously had the benefit of that credit, they shall repay to him an amount equal to the credit (but see regulations 30 and 31).

(5) The Commissioners shall not be liable to make any repayment under this regulation unless and until the person has made all the returns which he was required to make (and see regulations 30 and 31).

(6) Given the provision made by section 30(5) of the Act, this regulation has effect subject to section 32 of the Act (application of supplemental provisions about repayments: three year time limit, unjust enrichment etc).

Bad debts and other tax credits: supplementary provisions

17— (1) Where—

(*a*) a claimant in relation to regulation 12 has engaged in a relevant commercial exploitation of taxable aggregate,

(*b*) there exist one or more other matters in respect of which the claimant is entitled to a debt owed by the customer (whether or not they involve further charges in respect of the relevant commercial exploitation of taxable aggregate), and

(*c*) a payment has been received by the claimant from or on behalf of the customer,

the payment shall be attributed to the relevant commercial exploitation in respect of which the claim is made under regulation 12 ("the appropriate commercial exploitation") and the other matters in accordance with the rules set out in paragraphs (3) and (5) below.

(2) The debts arising in respect of the relevant commercial exploitation and the other matters are collectively referred to as debts in paragraphs (3) to (5) below.

(3) The payment shall be attributed to the debt that arose earliest and, if not wholly attributable to that debt, to the other debts in the order of the dates on which they arose.

(4) Attribution under paragraph (3) above shall not be made to the extent that the payment was allocated to a debt by the customer at the time of payment.

(5) Where—

(*a*) the earliest debt and the other debts to which the whole of the payment could be attributed arose on the same day, or

(*b*) the debts to which the balance of the payment could be attributed in accordance with paragraph (3) above arose on the same day,

the payment shall be attributed to each remaining debt according to the proportion that the debt in question contributes to the total remaining debt.

18— (1) Where a person—

(*a*) has received the benefit of a tax credit provided for by regulation 12 (bad debts), and

(*b*) a payment—

(i) for the relevant commercial exploitation in question is subsequently received by him (or by a person to whom a right to receive the whole or any part of the consideration written off has been assigned), or

(ii) is attributed to that relevant commercial exploitation by virtue of regulation 17,

that tax credit shall be withdrawn with effect from the time when sub-paragraph (*b*)(i) or (*b*)(ii) above is satisfied, as the case requires.

(2) Where a person—

(*a*) has received the benefit of a tax credit provided for by regulation 13 (tax credits other than bad debts), and

(*b*) it subsequently transpires that any relevant requirement of this Part is not complied with,

that tax credit shall be withdrawn with effect from the time when he received that benefit.

(3) Where a tax credit is withdrawn under this regulation—

(*a*) the requirements of regulation 7 (content of returns), regulation 8 (payment) and regulation 9 (accounts) apply subject to this regulation; but

(*b*) this regulation applies subject to regulation 28 (corrections) and regulation 29 (corrections of errors not exceeding [£50,000][1]).

(4) Paragraph (3) above applies subject to paragraph 3 of Schedule 8 to the Act (assessment for excessive repayment).

Amendments—[1] Figure in para (3)(*b*) substituted for figure "£2,000" by the Value Added Tax, etc (Correction of Errors, etc) Regulations, SI 2008/1482 reg 7(1) with effect in relation to under-calculations or over-calculations respectively, in the Aggregates Levy (General) Regulations, SI 2002/761 reg 29(2), (3), which registrable persons first discover in their accounting periods that start on 1 July 2008 or later: SI 2008/1482 reg 7(3).

Form and manner of claim for repayment of overpaid AL

19 A claim under section 31 of the Act (claim for repayment of AL which was not AL due) shall be made in writing to the Commissioners and shall, by reference to such documentary evidence as is in the possession of the claimant, state the amount of the claim and the method by which that amount was calculated.

Tax credits and other repayments: unjust enrichment—reimbursement arrangements to be disregarded

20 In this regulation and in regulations 21 to 26—

"claim" refers to a claim made under section 31 of the Act (claim for repayment of AL which was not AL due);

"reimbursement arrangements" refers to any arrangements for the purposes of the claim which—

(*a*) are made by the claimant for the purpose of securing that he is not unjustly enriched by the repayment of any amount in pursuance of the claim; and

(*b*) provide for the reimbursement of persons (recipients) who have for practical purposes borne the whole or any part of the cost of the original payment of that amount to the Commissioners;

"relevant amount" refers to that part (which may be the whole) of the amount of the claim which the claimant has reimbursed or intends to reimburse to other persons (recipients).

21 For the purposes of section 32(2) of the Act (defence by the Commissioners that repayment by them of an amount claimed would unjustly enrich the claimant) reimbursement arrangements made by a claimant shall be disregarded except where they—

(*a*) include the provisions described in regulation 22, and

(*b*) are supported by the undertakings described in regulation 26.

22 The provisions referred to in regulation 21(*a*) are that—

(*a*) reimbursement for which the arrangements provide will be completed by no later than 90 days after the repayment to which it relates;

(*b*) no deduction will be made from the relevant amount by way of fee or charge (however expressed or effected);

(*c*) reimbursement will be made only in cash or by cheque;

(*d*) any part of the relevant amount that is not reimbursed by the time mentioned in paragraph (*a*) above will be repaid by the claimant to the Commissioners;

(*e*) any interest paid by the Commissioners on any relevant amount repaid by them will also be treated by the claimant in the same way as the relevant amount falls to be treated under paragraphs (*a*) and (*b*) above; and

(*f*) the records described in regulation 24 will be kept by the claimant and produced by him to the Commissioners in accordance with regulation 25.

23 The claimant shall, without prior demand, make any repayment to the Commissioners that he is required to make by virtue of regulation 22(*d*) or 22(*e*) within 14 days of the expiry of the period of 90 days referred to in regulation 22(*a*).

24 The claimant shall keep records of the following matters—

(*a*) the names and addresses of those persons (recipients) whom he has reimbursed or whom he intends to reimburse;

(*b*) the total amount reimbursed to each such person (recipient);

(*c*) the amount of interest included in each total amount reimbursed to each person (recipient);

(*d*) the date that each reimbursement is made.

25— (1) Where a claimant is given notice in accordance with paragraph (2) below he shall, in accordance with such notice, produce to the Commissioners the records that he is required to keep pursuant to regulation 24.

(2) A notice given for the purposes of paragraph (1) above shall—

(*a*) be in writing;

(*b*) state the date on which and the place and time at which the records are to be produced; and

(*c*) be signed and dated by the Commissioners.

(3) Such a notice may be given before or after, or before and after, the Commissioners have paid the relevant amount to the claimant.

26— (1) The undertakings referred to in regulation 21(*b*) shall be given to the Commissioners by the claimant no later than the time at which he makes the claim for which the reimbursement arrangements have been made.

(2) The undertakings shall be in writing and shall be signed and dated by the claimant.

(3) The undertakings shall be to the effect that—

(*a*) at the date of the undertakings he is able to identify the names and addresses of those persons (recipients) whom he has reimbursed or whom he intends to reimburse;

(*b*) he will apply the whole of the relevant amount repaid to him (without any deduction by way of fee, charge or otherwise) to the reimbursement in cash or by cheque of such persons (recipients) no later than 90 days after he receives that amount (unless he has properly reimbursed them already);

(*c*) he will apply any interest paid to him on the relevant amount repaid to him wholly to the reimbursement of such persons (recipients) no later than 90 days after he receives that interest;

(*d*) he will repay to the Commissioners without demand the whole or such part of the relevant amount repaid to him or of any interest paid to him as he fails to apply in accordance with the undertakings mentioned in sub-paragraph (*b*) or (*c*) above;

(*e*) he will keep the records described in regulation 24; and

(*f*) he will comply with any notice given to him in accordance with regulation 25 concerning the production of such records.

Correction of errors in AL returns

27 A registrable person—

(*a*) shall only be taken as providing full information in the prescribed or specified form and manner for the purposes of paragraph 9(3) of Schedule 6 to the Act (disclosure about inaccurate AL return),

(*b*) with respect to any inaccuracy to which paragraph 9(1)(*a*) of Schedule 6 to the Act applies (civil penalty for misdeclaration or neglect in relation to inaccurate return),

if he delivers that information in writing to the Commissioners, or acts in accordance with regulation 29, at a time to which paragraph 9(3)(*a*) of Schedule 6 to the Act applies (no reason to believe enquiries being made into his AL affairs).

28— (1) A registrable person shall correct any error made by him in accounting for AL or in connection with his AL account and, as appropriate, make any adjustment required by regulation 7(1)(*b*) (adjustment of AL returns).

(2) That correction or adjustment shall be made within such time and by means of such payment, financial adjustment, entry in accounts or other method as the Commissioners may require.

(3) This regulation has effect subject to, as the case requires—

(*a*) the time limit applying to regulations 15(1), 18(1) and 18(2) (tax credits) (see regulations 15(7) and 18(4)—amounts paid more than three years before claim made and assessment subject to time limit in paragraph 5 of Schedule 8 to the Act);

(*b*) a time limit of three years after the end of the accounting period in relation to which the error was made or the adjustment became required; or

(*c*) any time limit for an assessment in relation to the error (see paragraphs 2(1), 2(2)(*d*), 3 and 4 of Schedule 5 to the Act).

29— (1) This regulation applies by way of an exception to regulation 28 but only in relation to errors.

(2) Where a registrable person discovers that any return or returns which he has previously made is or are based on an under-calculation, he must correct the error or errors by adding the appropriate amount to the AL due for the accounting period in which the discovery is made under regulation 7(1)(*b*).

(3) Where a registrable person discovers that any return or returns which he has previously made is or are based on an over-calculation, he must correct the error or errors by deducting the appropriate amount from the AL due for the accounting period in which the discovery is made under regulation 7(1)(*b*).

(4) For the purposes of paragraphs (2) and (3) above—

"under-calculation" refers to the total amount of AL due in accordance with regulation 7(1) in the accounting period or periods to which the previous return or returns related which was not properly taken into consideration for that period or those periods as appropriate ("understated AL");

"over-calculation" refers to the total amount that was wrongly taken as AL due in accordance with regulation 7(1) in the accounting period or periods to which the previous return or returns related and which was wrongly taken into consideration for that period or those periods as appropriate ("overstated AL").

(5) For the purposes of paragraph (4) above—

(*a*) in reckoning the total amount constituting the under-calculation, an allowance must be made for any overstated AL;

(*b*) in reckoning the total amount constituting the over-calculation, an allowance must be made for any understated AL.

(6) In any case, the total net amount of any under-calculation or over-calculation corrected under this regulation shall not exceed [£50,000][1].

[But if the registrable person's VAT turnover is small, this total must not for these purposes exceed 1% of that turnover unless the total is [£10,000 or less][3].

And if that person is not registered for VAT, the total net amount must not for these purposes exceed £10,000.][1]

[The VAT turnover is small only if Box 6 of that person's value added tax return for the prescribed accounting period in which the discovery is made must contain a total less than £5,000,000 (total value of sales and all other outputs excluding any value added tax).][2]

(7) A registrable person making a correction under paragraph (2) or (3) above shall make proper allowance for that correction for the purposes of complying with regulation 9(1) (AL account) or 9(3) (AL tax credits account) as appropriate.

(8) Where an error in a return has to any extent been corrected under this regulation—

(*a*) that return shall be regarded as having been corrected to that extent, and

(*b*) the registrable person shall to that extent be taken to have provided full information with respect to the inaccuracy in the prescribed form and manner for the purposes of paragraph 9(3) of Schedule 6 to the Act (disclosure about inaccurate AL return).

(9) A person shall not correct an error in a return (where that error is the result of an under-calculation or over-calculation) except in accordance with this regulation.

(10) This regulation has effect subject to, as the case requires—

(*a*) any requirement of the Commissioners under regulation 28(2), and

(*b*) any applicable time limit specified in regulation 28(3).

Amendments—[1] In para (6), figure substituted for figure "£2,000", and final two sentences inserted, by the Value Added Tax, etc (Correction of Errors, etc) Regulations, SI 2008/1482 reg 7(1), (2) with effect in relation to under-calculations or over-calculations respectively, in the Aggregates Levy (General) Regulations, SI 2002/761 reg 29(2), (3), which registrable persons first discover in their accounting periods that start on 1 July 2008 or later: SI 2008/1482 reg 7(3).

[2] In para (6), words inserted by the Value Added Tax, etc (Correction of Errors, etc) Regulations, SI 2008/1482 reg 8(1) with effect in relation to under-calculations or over-calculations respectively, in the Aggregates Levy (General) Regulations, SI 2002/761 reg 29(2), (3), which registrable persons first discover in their accounting periods that start on 1 July 2008 or later: SI 2008/1482 reg 7(3).

[3] In para (6), words substituted for words "less than £10,000" by the Amusement Machine Licence Duty, etc (Amendments) Regulations, SI 2008/2693 reg 4(1)(*d*) with effect for a discovery first made on 1 November 2008 or later.

Set-off

30— (1) This regulation applies where—

(*a*) a person is under a duty to pay to the Commissioners at any time an amount or amounts in respect of AL; and

(*b*) the Commissioners are under a duty to pay to that person at the same time an amount or amounts in respect of any AL (or other tax or duty) under their care and management.

(2) Where the total of the amount or amounts mentioned in paragraph (1)(*a*) above exceeds the total of the amount or amounts mentioned in paragraph (1)(*b*) above, the latter shall be set off against the former.

(3) Where the total of the amount or amounts mentioned in paragraph (1)(*b*) above exceeds the total of the amount or amounts mentioned in paragraph (1)(*a*) above, the Commissioners may set off the latter in paying the former.

(4) Where the total of the amount or amounts mentioned in paragraph (1)(*a*) above is the same as the total of the amount or amounts mentioned in paragraph (1)(*b*) above, no payment need be made in respect of either.

(5) Where this regulation applies and an amount has been set off in accordance with any of paragraphs (2) to (4) above, the duty of both the person in question and the Commissioners to pay the amount concerned shall be treated as having been discharged accordingly.

31— (1) This regulation applies where—

(*a*) a person is under a duty to pay to the Commissioners at any time an amount or amounts in respect of any tax or duty (other than AL) under their care and management; and

(*b*) the Commissioners are under a duty, at the same time, to make a payment or repayment to that person of an amount or amounts of or in respect of AL.

(2) Where the total of the amount or amounts mentioned in paragraph (1)(*a*) above exceeds the total of the amount or amounts mentioned in paragraph (1)(*b*) above, the latter shall be set off against the former.

(3) Where the total of the amount or amounts mentioned in paragraph (1)(*b*) above exceeds the total of the amount or amounts mentioned in paragraph (1)(*a*) above, the Commissioners may set off the latter in paying the former.

(4) Where the total of the amount or amounts mentioned in paragraph (1)(*a*) above is the same as the total of the amount or amounts mentioned in paragraph (1)(*b*) above, no payment need be made in respect of either.

(5) Where this regulation applies and an amount has been set off in accordance with any of paragraphs (2) to (4) above, the duty of both the person in question and the Commissioners to pay the amount concerned shall be treated as having been discharged accordingly.

32— (1) Neither regulation 30 or 31 shall require any such amount as is mentioned in paragraph (1)(*b*) of either regulation ("the credit") to be set off against any item mentioned in paragraph (1)(*a*) of either regulation ("the debit") where—

(*a*) an insolvency procedure has been applied to the person entitled to the credit;

(*b*) the credit became due after that procedure was applied; and

(*c*) the liability to pay the debt either arose before that procedure was so applied or (having arisen afterwards) relates to, or to matters occurring in the course of, the carrying on of any business relevant for AL purposes at times before the procedure was so applied.

(2) An insolvency procedure is applied to a person for the purposes of this regulation in the circumstances described by sub-paragraphs (2) to (5) of paragraph 11 of Schedule 8 to the Act (insolvency procedures for the purposes of this regulation).

33 A reference in regulation 30 or 31 to an amount in respect of tax or duty includes a reference to an amount of any related penalty, surcharge or interest that may be recovered as if it was an amount of tax or duty.

PART IV
DEATH, INCAPACITY, INSOLVENCY, TRANSFERS

Individuals: death or incapacity

34— (1) The Commissioners may, for AL purposes and subject to this regulation, treat a person who carries on relevant activities on behalf of an individual who has died or become temporarily incapacitated as if they were the same person.

(2) Such treatment may continue pending someone other than that individual being registered under section 24 of and Schedule 4 to the Act in relation to those activities or the incapacity ceasing.

(3) A person who carries on relevant activities in the circumstances described in paragraph (1) above must notify the Commissioners of this in writing and that notification must also include the date of death or the date and nature of the incapacity.

(4) This notification must be delivered to the Commissioners within 21 days starting with the day after the person begins carrying on the relevant activities.

(5) In this regulation, "relevant activities" refers to any activities in relation to which the individual in question is or was a registrable person.

Insolvency

35— (1) The Commissioners may, for AL purposes and subject to this regulation, treat a person who carries on relevant activities of a registrable person to whom an insolvency procedure is applied as if they were the same person.

(2) Such treatment may continue pending someone other than that registrable person being registered under section 24 of and Schedule 4 to the Act in relation to those activities or the insolvency procedure no longer being applied.

(3) A person who carries on relevant activities in the circumstances described in paragraph (1) above must notify the Commissioners of this in writing and that notification must also include the date when the insolvency procedure was first applied.

(4) This notification must be delivered to the Commissioners within 21 days starting with the day after the person begins carrying on the relevant activities.

(5) In this regulation—

"relevant activities" refers to any activities in relation to which the individual in question is or was a registrable person;

"registrable person" may include, as appropriate, the estate of a deceased individual.

(6) An insolvency procedure is applied to a person for the purposes of this regulation in the circumstances described by sub-sections (7) to (9) of section 37 of the Act (insolvency procedures for the purposes of this regulation).

Representatives: death, incapacity or insolvency

36— (1) If the Commissioners so require, a representative who controls the assets of a registrable person because of death, incapacity or the application of an insolvency procedure shall, for the purposes of AL and subject to this regulation, be treated as if he was the registrable person.

(2) Any requirement resulting from paragraph (1) above for the representative to pay AL shall only apply to the extent of the assets he controls.

(3) Any other requirement resulting from paragraph (1) above shall apply in the same way as it would have applied to the registrable person but for the death, incapacity or insolvency procedure.

(4) In this regulation "registrable person" may include, as appropriate, the estate of a deceased individual.

(5) An insolvency procedure is applied to a person for the purposes of this regulation in the circumstances described by sub-sections (7) to (9) of section 37 of the Act (insolvency procedures for the purposes of this regulation).

Transfers of going concerns

37— (1) Where—

(*a*) a business carried on by a person who is registered under section 24 of and Schedule 4 to the Act is transferred to another person as a going concern,

(*b*) the registration of the transferor has not been cancelled,

(*c*) the transfer requires that the transferor's registration be cancelled and that the transferee either be registered for AL or notify the Commissioners that he is registrable for AL, and

(*d*) a written application for this purpose is made to the Commissioners by the transferor and transferee,

the Commissioners may, with effect from the date of the transfer, cancel the registration of the transferor and register the transferee in his place with the registration number previously allocated to the transferor.

(2) Should the Commissioners cancel the registration of the transferor and register the transferee in his place under paragraph (1) above then, in order to secure continuity in the application of the Act—

(*a*) any liability of the transferor existing at the date of the transfer to make a return or account for or pay AL shall become the liability of the transferee;

(*b*) any entitlement of the transferor, whether or not existing at the date of the transfer, to a tax credit or repayment under the Act or Part III of these Regulations shall become the entitlement of the transferee;

(*c*) any other provision by or under the Act relating to AL that applied to the transferor before his registration was cancelled (or any such provision that continues to apply to the transferor after that cancellation) shall apply to the transferee; and

(*d*) any circumstances relating to the application of the Act (or any provision made under the Act) to the AL affairs of the transferor before his registration was cancelled (or any such circumstances that continue to apply to the transferor after that cancellation) shall apply to the transferee.

(3) In addition to the provisions set out in paragraph (2) above, where—

(*a*) the Commissioners cancel the registration of the transferor and register the transferee in his place under paragraph (1) above with effect from a date earlier than the accounting period in which they do so, and

(*b*) either the transferor or the transferee has, in relation to any time on or after that date but before the start of that accounting period—

(i) made a return,

(ii) accounted for AL, or

(iii) claimed a relevant tax credit,

the matters referred to in sub-paragraphs (*b*)(i) to (*b*)(iii) above shall be treated as having been done by the transferee.

PART V
PENALTIES

38— (1) A person who fails to comply with a requirement imposed on him by or under any of the following provisions of these Regulations shall be liable to a penalty of £250 for each such failure—

(*a*) regulation 7(1), 7(2), 7(3) or 7(4);
(*b*) regulation 8(2);
(*c*) regulation 9(1), 9(2), 9(3) or 9(4);
(*d*) regulation 10;
(*e*) regulation 28(1) or 28(2);
(*f*) regulation 29(7) or 29(9);
(*g*) regulation 34(3) or 34(4);
(*h*) regulation 35(3) or 35(4).

(2) A specific act or omission shall attract only one such penalty if the circumstances are such that, but for this paragraph, it would attract more than one penalty.

PART VI
CONSEQUENTIAL AMENDMENTS

39 (*amends the Distress for Customs and Excise Duties and Other Indirect Taxes Regulations, SI 1997/1431*).

SCHEDULE
INDUSTRIAL AND AGRICULTURAL PROCESSES

Regulation 13

A Industrial processes

Code	*Description*
001	Iron, steel and non-ferrous metal manufacture and smelting processing including foundry processes, investment casting, sinter plants and wire drawing.
002	Alloying.
003	Emission abatement for air, land and water.
004	[Drinking water, air and oil][1] filtration and purification.
005	Sewage treatment.
006	Production of energy.
007	Ceramic processes.
008	Refractory processes.
009	Manufacture of glass and glass products.
010	Manufacture of fibre glass.
011	Manufacture of man-made fibres.
012	[Production and processing of food and drink][1] eg sugar refining, production of gelatin.
013	Manufacture of plastics, rubber and PVC.
014	Chemical manufacturing eg soda ash, sea water magnesia, alumina.
015	Manufacture of precipitated calcium carbonate.
016	Manufacture of pharmaceuticals, bleaches, toiletries and detergents.
017	Aerating processes.
018	Manufacture of fillers for coating, sealants, adhesives, paints, grouts, mastics, putties and other binding or modifying media.
019	Manufacture of pigments, varnishes and inks.
020	Production of [growing media and][1] line markings for sports pitches [and other leisure facilities][1].
021	Incineration.
022	Manufacture of desiccant.
023	Manufacture of carpet backing, underlay and foam.
024	Resin processes.
025	Manufacture of lubricant additives.
026	Leather tanning.
027	Paper manufacture.
028	Production of art materials.
029	Production of play sand eg for children's sand pits.
030	Clay pigeon manufacture.
031	Abrasive processes: specialist sand blasting, iron free grinding (pebble mills) and sandpaper manufacture.
032	Use as [a propping agent][1] in oil exploration eg fracture sands and drilling fluids.

Code	*Description*
033	Flue gas desulphurisation and flue gas scrubbing.
034	Manufacture of mine suppressant.
035	Manufacture of fire extinguishers.
036	Manufacture of materials used for fireproofing.
037	Acid neutralisation.
038	Manufacture of friction materials eg automotive.

B Agricultural processes

Code	*Description*
039	Manufacture of additives to soil [eg agricultural lime][1].
040	Manufacture of animal feeds.
041	Production of animal bedding material.
042	Production of fertiliser.
043	Manufacture of pesticides and herbicides.
044	Production of growing media[, including compost, for agricultural and horticultural use only][1].
045	Soil treatment, including mineral enrichment and reduction of acidity.

Press releases etc—C&E Business Brief 29/02 14-11-02 (changes to industrial and agricultural reliefs).
Amendments—[1] Words in Codes 004, 012, 032 substituted, and words in Codes 020, 039 and 044 inserted, by the Aggregates Levy (General) (Amendment) Regulations, SI 2003/466 with effect from 1 April 2003.

2004/1959
Aggregates Levy (Northern Ireland Tax Credit) Regulations 2004

Made . . . . *23 July 2004*
Laid before the House of Commons . . . . *26 July 2004*
Coming into force . . . . *1 September 2004*

The Commissioners of Customs and Excise, in exercise of the powers conferred upon them by sections 17(6), 30A and 45 of, and paragraph 2 of Schedule 7 to, the Finance Act 2001 and of all other powers enabling them in that behalf, hereby make the following Regulations:

1 These Regulations may be cited as the Aggregates Levy (Northern Ireland Tax Credit) Regulations 2004 and come into force on 1st September 2004.

2 In these Regulations—

"the Act" refers to sections 16 to 49 of, and Schedules 4 to 10 to, the Finance Act 2001;
"aggregates levy credit agreement" has the meaning given in regulation 7;
"aggregates levy credit certificate" has the meaning given in regulation 5;
"AL" refers to aggregates levy;
"the AL General Regulations" means The Aggregates Levy (General) Regulations 2002;
"commercial exploitation" and "commercially exploited" are to be construed in accordance with section 19 of the Act;
"published notice" refers to a notice published by the Commissioners and not withdrawn or replaced by a further notice;
"registered site" has the meaning given in section 24 of the Act;
"regulation" refers to the appropriate regulation of these Regulations;
"site operator" is to be construed in accordance with section 21 of the Act;
"taxable aggregate" is to be construed in accordance with section 17 of the Act;
"United Kingdom" means Great Britain and Northern Ireland.

3— (1) This regulation applies to an eligible person within the meaning of paragraph (6) below who on or after 1st April 2004 and before 1st April 2011 has commercially exploited within Northern Ireland taxable aggregate which has been extracted from a registered site in Northern Ireland and has accounted for the AL chargeable on that commercial exploitation.

(2) Subject to regulation 4, such a person is entitled to a tax credit as prescribed at paragraph (3) below in respect of any AL accounted for in respect of that commercial exploitation.

(3) The amount of any tax credit to which a person is entitled under this regulation is fixed at 80% of the AL due on the aggregate in question.

(4) This regulation supplements the provisions of Part III of the AL General Regulations (accounting, payment, records, tax credits, repayments, set-off etc).

(5) The tax credit prescribed by this regulation is prescribed for the purposes of subsection (6) of section 17 of the Act.

(6) In this regulation, an "eligible person" is a person who—

(*a*) is registered for AL under section 24 of, and Schedule 4 to, the Act in relation to a registered site situated in Northern Ireland;

(*b*) has entered into an aggregates levy credit agreement with the Commissioners in respect of any of the registered sites of which he is the site operator; and

(*c*) is in possession of an aggregates levy credit certificate issued to him by the Commissioners which relates to the registered site from which the aggregate in respect of which the claim is made was extracted, covers the period of that claim and has not been withdrawn.

4— (1) Regulation 3(2) shall not apply where any aggregate in respect of which a claim for a tax credit might otherwise be made under regulation 3 is or is to be transferred from Northern Ireland to another part of the United Kingdom in any form.

(2) However, regulation 3(2) shall apply where the claimant can demonstrate to the satisfaction of the Commissioners that such a transfer is only the first stage of an onward export of that aggregate without further processing from the United Kingdom.

5— (1) In these Regulations, an "aggregates levy credit certificate" is a certificate which—

(*a*) relates to a single specified registered site in Northern Ireland;

(*b*) is issued by the Commissioners to a site operator as evidence of the existence of an aggregates levy credit agreement between the Commissioners and that site operator in respect of that registered site and of the site operator's continued compliance with the terms of that agreement; and

(*c*) is not transferable.

(2) The Commissioners may make further provision as to the form and content of an aggregates levy credit certificate in a published notice.

6— (1) An aggregates levy credit certificate may be withdrawn by the Commissioners at any time if the site operator to whom it has been issued fails to comply with any of the terms of the related aggregates levy credit agreement which he has entered into in respect of the same registered site.

(2) The withdrawal of an aggregates levy credit certificate must be notified to the site operator in writing and will take effect from the date of such notification or such later date as it may specify.

7— (1) In these Regulations an "aggregates levy credit agreement" is an agreement between a site operator in Northern Ireland and the Commissioners which relates to a specified registered site and is evidence that the site operator has agreed to comply with the Code of Practice for the Aggregates Industry in Northern Ireland (an environmental improvement scheme for quarrying) and to be monitored in respect of such compliance.

(2) An aggregates levy credit agreement shall set out the obligations of the site operator in relation to the commissioning of environmental audits and the meeting of specified targets for improvements in environmental practice for the registered site to which it relates within specified time limits.

(3) The Commissioners may make further provision as to the form and content of an aggregates levy credit agreement in a published notice.

8 Where a person is eligible to claim a tax credit under regulation 3 or a tax credit under section 30(1)(a) of the Act (export in the form of aggregate), he is entitled to make only one such claim in respect of any quantity of aggregate.

9 A person who makes a claim under these Regulations is obliged to keep the following records in addition to those required under Part III of the AL General Regulations:

(*a*) a record to be known as the "aggregates levy Northern Ireland tax credit account";

(*b*) the relevant aggregates levy credit certificate;

(*c*) documentary evidence regarding any claim by him for a tax credit under regulation 3; and

(*d*) documentary evidence relating to environmental audits and improvement works.

10— (1) A tax credit shall only arise under regulation 3 if a claim is made by a person so entitled acting in accordance with regulation 15 or 16 of the AL General Regulations as the case requires.

(2) A person shall not be entitled to make such a claim unless he is in possession of the records required by regulation 9.

11 A person who fails to comply with any requirement imposed on him by regulation 9 shall be liable to a penalty of £250.

12 The Aggregates Levy (Northern Ireland Tax Credit) Regulations 2002 are revoked.

AGGREGATES LEVY
PRESS RELEASES

CONTENTS

28 November 2001. Business Brief 17/01

Changes to primary legislation

The aggregates levy, a new tax on the commercial exploitation of aggregate in the UK, will come into effect on 1 April 2002. As a result of consultation with industry, and in addition to the changes announced in the pre-Budget report, the Government intends to make a number of technical changes to the aggregates levy provisions contained within FA 2001, subject to Parliamentary approval. These technical changes are detailed below.

The first draft of the secondary legislation for the levy will shortly be released for comment.

(I) UNCRUSHED ROCK

The current legislation exempts aggregate that has not been subjected to an industrial crushing process. However, it is now recognised that aggregate is sometimes produced without being crushed.

Given that the environmental effects of aggregate extraction are the same, regardless of whether that aggregate is crushed or not, the legislation will be amended to bring uncrushed rock within the scope of the levy. However, the current exemption for the production of dimension stone will still apply and will be amended to clarify that it also applies to building stone.

(II) TECHNICAL AMENDMENTS

(a) Aggregate, which is removed from its originating site before the commencement date

Currently, aggregate which is removed from its originating site before the commencement date will not be subject to the levy. However an amendment will be made to ensure that the levy cannot be avoided merely by removing aggregate from its originating site to a different site within the same registration before 1 April 2002.

(b) Aggregate necessarily arising from a road construction project

Aggregate, which is necessarily arising from the line of the road in a road construction project, will be exempt from the levy. However, the inclusion of the words "wholly or mainly" in s 17(3)(*d*)(ii) of the law could be interpreted as meaning that the exemption might still apply even if some of the extraction taking place was to obtain aggregate, rather than the aggregate being only a necessary by- product of this non-quarrying activity. It is therefore planned to amend the law to clarify the original policy intention and ensure that the exemption only applies to aggregate necessarily arising from within the line of the road in a road building project.

(c) Lime and cement manufacture

The current exemption for lime and cement manufacture in s 18(2)(*c*) will be amended to make clear that all inputs into lime or cement manufacture will be exempt, not just the limestone.

(d) Treatment of calcite

It is proposed that calcite is removed from the list of exempt relevant substances at s 18(3)(*d*) to ensure a level playing field between the markets for calcite and calcium carbonate, while at the same time removing the potential assurance difficulties relating to definitional issues between the two substances. The effect of this change is that while calcite will no longer have an outright exemption from the levy, both calcite and calcium carbonate used in non-aggregate, industrial applications will be eligible for a tax credit under s 30 of the law.

(e) Treatment of flint

The law will be amended to ensure that flint will be subject to the levy when it is used as an aggregate. However, flint will remain exempt if it is cut and used as a type of building stone. Also, flint used in non-aggregate applications, such as in the agriculture and animal feed sectors, will be eligible for a tax credit under s 30 of the law.

(f) Commercial exploitation of aggregate

As the law currently stands, aggregate can be moved tax free to another site owned by someone who is an operator on an originating site, but who is not necessarily a registered operator of that site. In order to maintain a clear audit trail, it is proposed that the law is amended to restrict the provision to movement of aggregate between sites that are registered under the name of the same person.

(g) Definition of "business"

The law will be amended to reflect the policy that "business", for the purposes of aggregates levy, includes local authorities and charities. This is to clarify that the levy will also apply to aggregate used by such non-profit making organisations.

(h) Registration of sites

It is proposed that the law is amended to ensure that the Commissioners have the power to register premises where mixing of aggregate takes place, given that mixing is one of the four tax points for the levy.

(i) Insolvency and set off provisions

It is proposed that the insolvency provisions contained at s 37(7)(*g*)(*h*)(*i*) and (*j*) and the set off provisions contained at Sch 8 para 11(2)(*f*)(*g*) and (*h*) will be removed. This is to reflect the fact that they are interim procedures which are not regarded as formal insolvency's by the Commissioners for VAT purposes.

If you have any questions about any of these issues, please contact our aggregate levy helpline numbers on 0161 827 0906 or 0161 827 0321. A public notice containing further technical details about the aggregates levy will be available in early January.

22 February 2002. Business Brief 4/02

Phased introduction in Northern Ireland

The Government announced in the pre-Budget report that it is minded to phase in the aggregates levy in Northern Ireland, where aggregates are used in processed products. This recognises the potential effects of the levy on this specific sector. Phasing in the levy, including 100% relief for use of aggregates in processed products in 2002–03, will be subject to EU state aid approval.

A note on the broad scope of the phased introduction was included with all registration packs issued to those businesses in Northern Ireland who might be required to register for the levy. If you did not receive a registration pack but believe you may be liable to register, because for instance your business produces aggregate or imports it from the Republic of Ireland, please call Customs & Excise on 0845 7585831.

This business brief provides further information on the manner in which the phased introduction will operate if state aid approval is granted. In particular, it provides further detail on the uses of aggregate that will be eligible for relief and the proposed mechanism by which the relief will operate. The necessary legislation is currently being prepared and Customs & Excise will consult with representatives of local industry once a draft is available.

(a) Uses of aggregate eligible for relief

Any aggregate used to make the following in Northern Ireland will be entitled to the relief—

- concrete (whether pre-cast, ready-mix or prepared on site);
- mortar;
- asphalt (whether delivered pre-mixed or mixed on site eg slurry seal);
- coated roadstone and coated chippings; and
- surface dressing (where dry aggregate chippings are rolled into bitumen on site).

Aggregate put to uses other than those listed above in Northern Ireland will not be entitled to this relief. Nor will any dry aggregate that is transported from Northern Ireland to Great Britain. There is already provision within the legislation for the relief of all exports of aggregate from the UK.

The entitlement to relief will not be affected by the origin of the aggregate (whether extracted in Northern Ireland or Great Britain or imported), nor will it be affected by the ultimate destination of products manufactured for onward sale, so long as they are manufactured in Northern Ireland.

(b) Extent of the relief

In the first year of the levy's operation there will be 100% relief from tax for aggregates used in Northern Ireland to make the products specified above. In subsequent years the amount of levy to be paid will increase according to the following timetable—

2003–04 = 20% of the levy;
2004–05 = 40% of the levy;
2005–06 = 60% of the levy;
2006–07 = 80% of the levy; and
2007–08 and subsequent years = 100% of the levy.

(c) Operation of the relief

The Northern Ireland relief will operate in the same manner as the relief for aggregate used in prescribed industrial or agricultural processes. The only extra requirement envisaged is that suppliers of aggregate must keep a separate account for the reliefs claimed under this scheme.

Full details of how this relief system operates is contained in "A general guide to the aggregates levy" section 5 which is available from Customs & Excise in Belfast. General information on the levy is available at www.hmce.gov.uk.

(d) Further guidance

We intend to issue an information note that will provide detailed guidance on the precise operation of the proposed relief when the legislation has been drafted.

If you have any questions about any of these issues or aspects of the levy, please contact Customs & Excise in Northern Ireland on 028 9056 2271/2838.

14 November 2002. Business Brief 29/02

Changes to industrial and agricultural reliefs

Aggregates Levy is a tax on the commercial exploitation of aggregate in the UK, and came into effect on 1 April 2002. Any aggregate that is used in prescribed industrial and agricultural processes is relieved from the levy. The list of relieved processes was drawn up through consultation with industry and is set out in the Aggregates Levy (General) Regulations 2002.

Continuing dialogue with industry and experience of the levy to date has identified a number of areas, which lack clarity or require amendment. Customs & Excise therefore intend to amend the Regulations to provide greater clarity and ensure that the list of prescribed processes reflects their policy objectives.

These changes are set out below and will take effect from 1 April 2003.

(a) Code 004—water filtration

Water and air filtration and purification becomes—

"Drinking water, air and oil filtration and purification"

This makes it clear that water filtration can only be relieved if it is a part of the process of providing drinking water, and also adds oil filtration to the list of relieved processes.

(b) Code 012—food processing

Production of food and food processing e g sugar refining, production of gelatin becomes—

"Production and processing of food and drink e g sugar refining, production of gelatin"

This is merely a change in wording to provide greater clarity.

(c) Code 032—oil exploration

Use of proppart in oil exploration e g fracture sands and drilling fluids becomes—

"Use as a propping agent in oil exploration e g fracture sands and drilling fluids"

This replaces "proppart" with "propping agent", as the latter is the correct technical term.

(d) Code 039—additives to soil

Manufacture of additives to soil becomes—

"Manufacture of additives to soil e g agricultural lime"

This change is to remove any confusion as to which code to use when claiming relief in respect of agricultural lime.

(e) Code 044—growing media

Production of growing media becomes—

"Production of growing media, including compost, for agricultural and horticultural use only"

This makes it clear that relief is limited to use in growing media for the agricultural sector, which includes horticulture. Relief will not be claimable where aggregate is used in growing media for non-agricultural processes such as the laying of sports pitches. This change more accurately reflects the wording of the primary legislation (FA 2001 s 30(1)(*c*)).

If you have any questions about the Aggregates Levy, please contact the National Advice Service on 0845 010 9000. A public notice will be available in April 2003 giving full technical details of all of the prescribed industrial and agricultural processes.

24 December 2002. Business Brief 34/02

Exemption from registration and other obligations

Aggregates Levy is a tax on the commercial exploitation of aggregate in the UK and came into effect on 1 April 2002. Any person responsible for commercially exploiting aggregate, including exempt aggregate, must register for the levy and carry out certain obligations of registered persons unless specifically exempted from doing so under The Aggregates Levy (Registration and Miscellaneous Provisions) Regulations 2001.

Subject to Parliamentary approval, Customs and Excise intend to amend the Regulations so that any person who exploits solely exempt aggregate will not have to register for aggregates levy nor carry out certain obligations such as submitting nil returns.

These changes are set out below and will take effect from 1 April 2003.

a) Full exemption from registration and all obligations

This will apply to any person who commercially exploits only—

- soil, vegetable matter or other organic matter; or
- spoil, waste or other by-products of any industrial combustion process, or the smelting or refining of metal; or
- drill-cuttings from licensed oil exploration; or
- arisings from roads when utilities work is carried out.

b) Exemption from registration and consequent obligations but required to notify Customs of activities

Any person who exploits only—

- coal, lignite, slate or shale; or
- spoil, waste or other by-products resulting from the separation of coal, lignite, slate or shale after extraction; or
- spoil, waste or other by-products resulting from the separation of specified minerals after extraction; or
- china clay and ball clay and spoil or waste resulting from its extraction; or
- any other clay

shall be exempt from registration and consequent obligations such as submitting returns but will be required to notify Customs of site details, activities undertaken and responsible persons. Notifications should be sent to—

HM Customs and Excise, Aggregates Levy Team, Dobson House, Regent Centre, Gosforth, Newcastle Upon Tyne, NE3 3PF.

If you have any questions about the Aggregates Levy, please contact the National Advice Service on 0845 010 9000. A public notice will be available in April 2003 and will include these changes.

10 December 2003. Business Brief 27/03

Extended relief for Northern Ireland

The Chancellor made the following announcement in today's pre-Budget Report (PBR)—

> "Since Budget 2003, the Government and the aggregates and construction industries in Northern Ireland have worked hard to improve the analysis of the operation of the levy and the aggregates market in the Province, including an independent study, *Assessment of the State of the Construction Aggregates Sector in Northern Ireland*, that the Government commissioned which is published alongside the pre-Budget Report. The Government has also examined proposals for an extension to the current five-year scheme, which provides relief from the levy for aggregate used in processed products in Northern Ireland.
>
> Following discussions with stakeholders and the evidence from the study, and subject to state aid approval, the Government intends to extend the scope and length of the current relief for aggregates in Northern Ireland, providing aggregates businesses in Northern Ireland that wish to benefit from the extended relief agree to implement environmental improvements to their operations. The relief will continue to cover aggregate in processed products and be extended to cover virgin aggregate, coming into effect during 2004 and fixed at the current level of 80 per cent of the full rate until 31 March 2012. The environmental improvements that quarry operators will need to sign up to will be regularly monitored and reviewed and enforcement activity will be stepped up."

This Business Brief article provides information on how the new relief scheme will operate if European Commission state aid approval is granted.

1 Who will be eligible to claim the new relief?

Businesses which are registered for the aggregates levy and commercially exploit virgin aggregate extracted in Northern Ireland. Eligibility will be conditional upon claimants entering into and complying with the terms of a Negotiated Agreement (see question 11 for details).

"Commercial exploitation" is defined in Notice AGL1 "Aggregates Levy" available on the Customs and Excise website www.hmce.gov.uk/forms/notices/agl1 or in hard copy from the National Advice Service on 0845 010 9000.

2 What will the new scheme apply to?

The relief will continue to cover aggregate in processed products (concrete, asphalt etc) and be extended to cover virgin aggregate.

3 What will the rate of relief be?

The relief will be 80% of the full rate of levy (as at present), which will apply for the duration of the new scheme, until 31 March 2012.

4 So how much tax will be payable per tonne?

The full rate of levy on aggregate exploited in the UK is currently £1.60 per tonne. If this remains unchanged in Budget 2004, relieved aggregate in Northern Ireland would be liable at 20% of that rate ie 32 pence per tonne.

5 When will the new scheme come into effect?

The introduction of the new scheme is still subject to state aid approval from the European Commission. The scheme will start shortly after that approval is received but in any case will not be earlier than 1 April 2004.

6 Will aggregate used outside Northern Ireland be eligible for relief?

The new scheme will not affect current arrangements for exports of virgin aggregate from the UK, which will remain eligible for 100% relief from the levy.

Aggregate used to manufacture processed products in Northern Ireland which is subsequently exported from the UK will be eligible for the 80% relief under the new scheme.

Aggregate or products made from aggregate sent from Northern Ireland to Great Britain will not be eligible for the relief and will be subject to the full rate of levy upon first commercial exploitation.

7 Will imports of aggregate into Northern Ireland be liable to relief?

This is an issue that will be explored with the European Commission but Customs expects that, under EU law, the relief will have to be extended to imports of aggregate into Northern Ireland.

8 Is this new scheme permanent?

No. The new scheme will operate until 31 March 2012.

9 What happens after 31 March 2012?

It is too early to say. The impact of the new scheme will be kept under review and this will inform what happens after 31 March 2012.

10 Will I still be able to claim relief under the current relief scheme?

No. The current scheme will be abolished and replaced by the new scheme.

11 What is a Negotiated Agreement?

The detail of the form and content of Negotiated Agreements is still being discussed by the Department of Environment Northern Ireland (DoENI) and main industry representative bodies in Northern Ireland, the Quarry Products Association Northern Ireland (QPANI) and the British Aggregates Association (BAA).

Broadly, however, these agreements will set targets for improvement in environmental performance of quarrying operations; among the areas of performance likely to be covered are air quality, blasting, dust, energy efficiency, groundwater and waste management. Each agreement will be individually tailored to the circumstances of the quarry, taking into account, for example, current standards and scope for improvement.

Once discussions between DoENI and the QPANI and BAA have been finalised, all aggregates levy registered businesses in Northern Ireland will be sent details of how to set up a Negotiated Agreement and thus claim relief under the new scheme.

12 Do I have to belong to the QPANI or BAA to be eligible for relief?

No. Eligibility to relief is based on the criteria outlined in question 1 above.

13 How can I contribute to the DoENI–trade discussions about Negotiated Agreements if I am not a member of the QPANI or the BAA?

DoENI will be launching shortly a public consultation exercise on the HELM report, which is to be used as the basis for trade discussions about the form and content of Negotiated Agreements. If you would like to take part in these discussions, please write to:

Department of the Environment, Environmental Policy Division
River House, 48 High Street,
Belfast,
BT1 2AW.

14 Who will be responsible for monitoring compliance with Negotiated Agreements?

The DoENI will be responsible for conducting the initial assessment of a quarry's environmental standards and monitoring performance against the targets set out in the agreement. Compliance will be reflected by the issue/renewal of a certificate by DoENI, which, in turn, will be used by the business to support claims to relief during the period of the certificate's validity.

15 What would happen if a business did not meet the terms of its Negotiated Agreement?

This has yet to be decided but it is likely that failure to meet agreed targets would result in punitive action, including rendering the business concerned ineligible to claim relief for a specified period.

16 What will the Government do if state aid approval is not granted?

It is too early to say but the Government will keep the industry updated of progress and work with it to try to overcome any potential obstacles.

17 Where can I obtain a copy of the Symonds' Report on the state of the quarrying industry in Northern Ireland?

It is available from the aggregates levy pages of the Customs and Excise website at www.hmce.gov.uk/business/othertaxes/agg-levy.

10 May 2004. Business Brief 13/04

Extended relief for Northern Ireland

The Government has confirmed that the scope and duration of the aggregates levy relief scheme in Northern Ireland has been extended. This follows notification from the European Commission that the Government's proposals for such an extended scheme have received state aid clearance. Further details are available in HM Treasury news release 44/04.

This Business Brief article provides information on how the new relief scheme will operate.

1. What is the aggregates levy?

Aggregates levy is an environmental tax on the commercial exploitation in the UK of virgin aggregate (rock, sand and gravel) and was introduced across the UK on 1 April 2002 at a rate of 1.60 per tonne (this rate remained unchanged in Budgets 2003 and 2004). Anybody who commercially exploits aggregate in the UK is liable to register and account for the levy to Customs and Excise. 710 traders are currently registered for the tax across the UK, 140 of which are registered in Northern Ireland.

2. Who is eligible to claim the new relief?

Relief is available to businesses which are registered for the aggregates levy with Customs and commercially exploit virgin aggregate extracted in Northern Ireland. Eligibility is conditional upon the claimant being in possession of an Aggregates Levy Credit Certificate. The certificate will be issued to an operator in Northern Ireland by the Department of the Environment (acting as Customs' agent) if he can demonstrate to the Department's satisfaction that he either holds or has applied for the relevant regulatory authorisations, and if he enters into an agreement with the Department committing the business to implementing environmental improvements to its operations. More details about these arrangements, including special arrangements for the start of the scheme, are set out in the answer to question 12 below.

"Commercial exploitation" is defined in Notice AGL1 "Aggregates Levy" available on the Customs and Excise website www.hmce.gov.uk/forms/notices/agl1 or in hard copy from the National Advice Service on 0845 010 9000.

3. What does the scheme apply to?

The relief covers aggregate in processed products (concrete, asphalt etc.) and virgin aggregate in its raw state.

4. What is the level of relief?

The relief is 80% of the full rate of levy for the duration of the new scheme—until 31 March 2011.

5. How much tax is payable per tonne?

The full rate of levy on aggregate exploited in the UK is currently 1.60 per tonne. Relieved aggregate in Northern Ireland is liable at 20% of that rate, i.e. currently 32 pence per tonne.

6. From what date is the extended scheme effective?

1 April 2004.

7. So can I claim relief from this date?

Quarry operators in Northern Ireland will be able to claim the extended relief from the date set out on their Aggregates Levy Credit Certificate issued to them by the Department of the Environment in Northern Ireland. Details about the circumstances in which such a certificate will be issued are set out in the answer to question 12 below.

Retroactive legal cover for the relief will be provided by the Finance Bill currently before Parliament and by regulations made under the Finance Bill provisions, which will be laid before Parliament once the Bill receives Royal Assent later in the year.

8. So the new scheme is not permanent. What happens after 31 March 2011?

It is too early to say. The impact of the new scheme will be kept under review and this will inform what happens after 31 March 2011.

9. Is aggregate used outside Northern Ireland eligible for relief?

The new scheme does not affect arrangements for exports of virgin aggregate from the UK, which remain eligible for 100% relief from the levy.

Aggregate used to manufacture processed products in Northern Ireland which is subsequently exported from the UK is eligible for the 80% relief.

Aggregate or products made from aggregate sent from Northern Ireland to Great Britain is not eligible for the relief and is subject to the full rate of levy upon first commercial exploitation. (NB relief may be claimed if the aggregate or processed products are merely transiting Great Britain as part of an export movement.)

10. Are imports of aggregate into Northern Ireland liable to relief?

No. Those importing such aggregate will not be subject to the cost of complying with the environmental improvements provided for under the scheme so it would not be fair on operators in Northern Ireland to extend the relief to such imports.

11. Do I have to belong to a trade association to be eligible for relief?

No. Eligibility to relief is based on the criteria outlined at question 2 above.

12. What will entitle me to relief?

To qualify for relief, a business will need to be registered with Customs and Excise for the aggregates levy. It will also need to exploit virgin aggregate extracted in Northern Ireland and be in possession of an Aggregates Levy Credit Certificate. The issue of certificates by the Department of the Environment in Northern Ireland, and therefore entitlement to relief, will be conditional on a business/operator signing and complying with an Aggregates Levy Credit Agreement with that Department. This agreement will commit the business to making improvements to the way it operates and set targets for improvement in environmental performance of quarrying operations.

It will take a few months to sort out agreements with all operators in Northern Ireland. Initially therefore a business will need to satisfy the Department of the Environment in Northern Ireland that it either holds or has applied for the relevant regulatory authorisations, and agrees to enter into an Aggregates Levy Credit Agreement with the Department, which will commit the business to compliance with the Code of Practice for the aggregates industry in Northern Ireland. The business will also have to arrange for an audit of its site to be completed by an accredited environmental consultant. Once these commitments have been made, the Department of the Environment will issue an Aggregates Levy Credit Certificate and the business will be able to claim relief from aggregates levy from the date set out on that certificate (regardless of when it is received by the operator).

The Department of the Environment will be able to enter a date on the certificate that is on or after 1 April 2004. For applications received in the first few weeks, where it is satisfied that an operator holds or has applied for relevant regulatory authorisations and has made the necessary commitments outlined above, the Department of the Environment will provide for claims to be backdated to 1 April when it completes the certificates. This provides strong incentives for operators to join the scheme as soon as possible.

The audit mentioned above will have to be returned to the Department of the Environment by a specified date. The Department will review all audits and set site-specific targets for improvement in the light of them. Continued eligibility to relief will be dependent on businesses meeting such targets, which will be regularly monitored and reviewed.

13. What will the Aggregates Levy Credit Agreements between operators and Department of the Environment do?

These agreements will set targets for improvement in environmental performance of quarrying operations; among the areas of performance that will be covered are air quality, blasting, dust, energy efficiency, groundwater and waste management. Each agreement will be individually tailored to the circumstances of the quarry, taking into account, for example, current standards and scope for improvement.

All aggregates levy registered businesses in Northern Ireland have been sent guidance on exactly how the new relief scheme will work.

14. Who will be responsible for monitoring compliance with the agreements?

The Department of the Environment in Northern Ireland will be responsible for conducting the initial assessment of a quarry's environmental standards based on information provided by applicant businesses, drawing up an agreement with each business and monitoring performance against the targets set out in the agreement. Compliance will be reflected by the issue/renewal of the Aggregates Levy Credit Certificate by the Department of the Environment, which, in turn, will be used by the business to support claims to relief during the period of the certificate's validity.

15. What happens if a business does not meet the terms of its agreement?

Failure to meet agreed targets will result in punitive action, including rendering the business concerned ineligible to claim relief.

16. Can businesses in Northern Ireland continue to claim relief under the old 5-year degressive scheme—which still had nearly 3 years left to run?

No. The old 5-year scheme has been abolished and replaced by the new scheme. Any business that does not have a valid Aggregates Levy Credit Certificate covering the period from the start of the new scheme will be liable to pay the full rate of aggregates levy on all aggregate they commercially exploit until they obtain such a certificate.

Further information

Further details are available in Treasury news release 44/04. For further information on the aggregates levy please contact the Customs National Advice Service on 0845 010 9000. For further information about the credit agreements, please contact: Department of the Environment, Environmental Policy Group, 20–21 Donegall Street, Belfast BT1 2GP; E-mail: Evelyn.Hoy@doeni.gov.uk; Phone 028 9054 4570 or 4511.

7 July 2006. Business Brief 08/06

Update to Notice AGL1 Aggregates Levy (July 2006) – change to water discount calculation

This Business Brief article provides information about an update to Notice AGL1 Aggregates Levy that makes changes to the section on added water discount.

HMRC has reviewed the standard water discounting arrangements in place since 1 July 2005 for water added to aggregates. There are a couple of areas that require clarification to ensure that the moisture content discounts are reasonable and consistent.

DUST DAMPENING OF AGGREGATE

From 1 September 2006, businesses cannot use the standard percentages for dust dampening of aggregate, where this involves no more than spraying stockpiles of aggregate. The standard percentages are not appropriate in this case, as it would, in effect, amount to a refund or reduction of the rate of the levy for businesses.

For such dust dampening, businesses (if they had changed to using standard percentages), will have to revert to the pre-July 2005 position of providing evidence and agreeing a more exact percentage of added water with their local aggregates officer.

MARINE DREDGED AGGREGATE

Aggregate extracted from the seabed, that is, marine dredged aggregate or 'ballast as dredged' has been eligible for the standard discount percentages since 1 July 2005.

After discussion with industry, including the British Marine Aggregate Producers Association, HM Revenue & Customs confirm that the standard percentage discounts, 7% for washed sand, and 3.5% for washed gravel, may be applied to marine dredged aggregate.

REVISED TEXT

The revised paragraph 11.7 to Notice AGL1 Aggregates Levy that was introduced into the notice in Update 1 dated May 2005 now reads as follows:

11.7 How do I calculate the added water discount?

From 1 July 2005 there are two options. First, you can use our standard added water percentages, which means that you do not have to weigh pre-washed and washed samples regularly to determine the weight as accurately as possible. This could save you time and expense. These percentages are:

Washed sand:	7%
Washed gravel:	3.5%
Washed rock / aggregate:	4%

Alternatively, you can agree a more exact percentage of added water, in which case you must provide evidence of the weight of the water. This second option was in fact the only one available up until 1 July 2005.

Whichever option you choose, you must first obtain written agreement to the proposed option and method from your local aggregates levy officer.

From 1 September 2006 you can only use the second option (ie agreeing with an officer a percentage allowable) for dust dampening of aggregate, as this involves no more than spraying stockpiles of aggregate and does not count as washing.

April 2008. Notice ET1

Notice of requirement to give security for environmental taxes

Note—See under *IPT* section, ante, for the full text of this notice which is HMRC's Statement of Practice on the circumstances where they may require security for Insurance Premium Tax, Landfill Tax, Aggregates Levy and Climate Change Levy.

AGGREGATES LEVY INDEX

Defined words and phrases are listed separately at the end.

WORDS AND PHRASES

Words in brackets indicate the context in which the word or phrase is used.

CLIMATE CHANGE LEVY

CONTENTS

PROVISIONAL COLLECTION OF TAXES ACT 1968

(1968 Chapter 2)

An Act to consolidate the Provisional Collection of Taxes Act 1913 and certain other enactments relating to the provisional collection of taxes or matters connected therewith.

[1st February 1968]

1 Temporary statutory effect of House of Commons resolutions affecting …, [climate change levy][5], …

(1) This section applies only to … [, climate change levy][5]…

(2) Subject to that, and to the provisions of subsections (4) to (8) below, where the House of Commons passes a resolution which—

(*a*) provides for the renewal for a further period of any tax in force or imposed during the previous financial year (whether at the same or a different rate, and whether with or without modifications) or for the variation or abolition of any existing tax, and

(*b*) contains a declaration that it is expedient in the public interest that the resolution should have statutory effect under the provisions of this Act,

the resolution shall, for the period specified in the next following subsection, have statutory effect as if contained in an Act of Parliament and, where the resolution provides for the renewal of a tax, all enactments which were in force with reference to that tax as last imposed by Act of Parliament shall during that period have full force and effect with respect to the tax as renewed by the resolution.

In this section references to the renewal of a tax include references to its reimposition, and references to the abolition of a tax include references to its repeal.

(3) The said period is—

(*a*) in the case of a resolution passed in [November or December][2] in any year, one expiring with [5th May in the next calendar year][2];

[(*aa*) in the case of a resolution passed in February or March in any year, one expiring with 5th August in the same calendar year; and][4]

(*b*) in the case of any other resolution, one expiring at the end of four months after the date on which it is expressed to take effect or, if no such date is expressed, after the date on which it is passed.

(4) A resolution shall cease to have statutory effect under this section unless within the next [thirty][3] days on which the House of Commons sits after the day on which the resolution is passed—

(*a*) a Bill renewing, varying or, as the case may be, abolishing the tax is read a second time by the House, or

(*b*) a Bill is amended by the House [in Committee or on Report, or by any [Public Bill Committee][6] of the House][1] so as to include provision for the renewal, variation or, as the case may be, abolition of the tax.

(5) A resolution shall also cease to have statutory effect under this section if—

(*a*) the provisions giving effect to it are rejected during the passage of the Bill containing them through the House, or

(*b*) an Act comes into operation renewing, varying or, as the case may be, abolishing the tax, or

(*c*) Parliament is dissolved or prorogued.

(6) Where, in the case of a resolution providing for the renewal or variation of a tax, the resolution ceases to have statutory effect by virtue of subsection (4) or (5) above, or the period specified in subsection (3) above terminates, before an Act comes into operation renewing or varying the tax, any money paid in pursuance of the resolution shall be repaid or made good, and any deduction made in pursuance of the resolution shall be deemed to be an unauthorised deduction.

(7) Where any tax as renewed or varied by a resolution is modified by the Act renewing or varying the tax, any money paid in pursuance of the resolution which would not have been payable under the new conditions affecting the tax shall be repaid or made good, and any deduction made in pursuance of the resolution shall, so far as it would not have been authorised under the new conditions affecting the tax, be deemed to be an unauthorised deduction.

(8) When during any session a resolution has had statutory effect under this section, statutory effect shall not be again given under this section in the same session to the same resolution or to a resolution having the same effect.

Commentary—*Simon's Taxes* **A1.104.**

Note—Words omitted from the heading and sub-s (1) are not relevant for the purposes of climate change levy.

Amendments—[1] Words in sub-s (4)(*b*) added by FA 1968 s 60.

[2] Words in sub-s (3)(*a*) substituted by FA 1993 s 205 in relation to resolutions passed after 27 July 1993.

[3] Words in sub-s (4) substituted by FA 1993 s 205 in relation to resolutions passed after 27 July 1993.

[4] Sub-s(3)(*aa*) inserted by F(No 2)A 1997 s 50(1), (3) in relation to resolutions passed after 31 July 1997.

[5] Words in heading and sub-s (1) inserted by FA 2000 s 30, Sch 7 para 1 with effect from 28 July 2000.
[6] Words in sub-s (4)(*b*) substituted by FA 2007 s 112(1) with effect from 19 July 2007.

5 House of Commons resolution giving provisional effect to motions affecting taxation

(1) This section shall apply if the House of Commons resolves that provisional statutory effect shall be given to one or more motions to be moved by the Chancellor of the Exchequer, or some other Minister, and which, if agreed to by the House, would be resolutions—

(*a*) to which statutory effect could be given under section 1 of this Act, or

(*b*), (*c*) ...[1]

(2) Subject to subsection (3) below, on the passing of the resolution under subsection (1) above, sections 1 ... of this Act ... shall apply as if each motion to which the resolution applies had then been agreed to by a resolution of the House.

(3) Subsection (2) above shall cease to apply to a motion if that motion, or a motion containing the same proposals with modifications, is not agreed to by a resolution of the House (in this section referred to as "a confirmatory resolution") within the next ten days on which the House sits after the resolution under subsection (1) above is passed, and, if it ceases to apply, all such adjustments, whether by way of discharge or repayment of tax, or discharge of security, or otherwise, shall be made as may be necessary to restore the position to what it would have been if subsection (2) above had never applied to that motion, and to make good any deductions which have become unauthorised deductions.

(4) ...

Commentary—*Simon's Taxes* **A1.104.**
Note—Sub-s (1)(*b*), (4) and words omitted from sub-s (2) are not relevant to climate change levy.
Amendments—[1] Words in sub-s (2) substituted and sub-s (1)(*c*), and word immediately preceding it, repealed by FA 1993 s 205(1), (6), (7) Sch 23 Pt VI in relation to resolutions passed after 27 July 1993.

6 Short title, repeals and saving as respects Northern Ireland

(1) This Act may be cited as the Provisional Collection of Taxes Act 1968.

(2), (3) ...[1]

Note—Sub-s (2) repeals enactments specified in Schedule. Effect has been given to these repeals where applicable in the relevant provisions of the earlier enactments.
Amendments—[1] Sub-s (3) repealed by Northern Ireland Constitution Act 1973 s 41(1)(*a*) and Sch 6 Pt 1, with effect from 18 July 1973.

FINANCE ACT 1996

(1996 Chapter 8)

An Act to grant certain duties, to alter other duties, and to amend the law relating to the National Debt and the Public Revenue, and to make further provision in connection with Finance.

[29th April 1996]

PART VII

MISCELLANEOUS AND SUPPLEMENTAL

Miscellaneous: indirect taxation

197 Setting of rates of interest

(1) The rate of interest applicable for the purposes of an enactment to which this section applies shall be the rate which for the purposes of that enactment is provided for by regulations made by the Treasury under this section.

(2) This section applies to—

(*a*)–(*f*) ...

[(*g*) the following provisions of Schedule 6 to the Finance Act 2000 (interest payable to or by the Commissioners in connection with climate change levy), that is to say, paragraphs 41(2)(*f*), 62(3)(*f*), 66, 70(1)(*b*)[, 81(3) and 123(4) to (6)][2].][1]

(*h*), (*i*) ...

(3) Regulations under this section may—

(*a*) make different provision for different enactments or for different purposes of the same enactment,

(*b*) either themselves specify a rate of interest for the purposes of an enactment or make provision for any such rate to be determined, and to change from time to time, by reference to such rate or the average of such rates as may be referred to in the regulations,

(*c*) provide for rates to be reduced below, or increased above, what they otherwise would be by specified amounts or by reference to specified formulae, (*d*) provide for rates arrived at by reference to averages or formulae to be rounded up or down,

(*e*) provide for circumstances in which changes of rates of interest are or are not to take place, and

(*f*) provide that changes of rates are to have effect for periods beginning on or after a day determined in accordance with the regulations in relation to interest running from before that day, as well as in relation to interest running from, or from after, that day.

(4) The power to make regulations under this section shall be exercisable by statutory instrument subject to annulment in pursuance of a resolution of the House of Commons.

(5) Where—

(*a*) regulations under this section provide, without specifying the rate determined in accordance with the regulations, for a new method of determining the rate applicable for the purposes of any enactment, or

(*b*) the rate which, in accordance with regulations under this section, is the rate applicable for the purposes of any enactment changes otherwise than by virtue of the making of regulations specifying a new rate,

the Commissioners of Customs and Excise shall make an order specifying the new rate and the day from which, in accordance with the regulations, it has effect.

(6) (*amends FA 1994 Schs 6, 7 and VATA 1994 s 74*).

(7) Subsections (1) and (6) above shall have effect for periods beginning on or after such day as the Treasury may by order made by statutory instrument appoint and shall have effect in relation to interest running from before that day, as well as in relation to interest running from, or from after, that day; and different days may be appointed under this subsection for different purposes.

Note—Sub-ss (2)(*a*)–(*f*), (*h*), (*i*), (6) are not relevant to climate change levy.
Sub-s (1) has effect for periods beginning on or after 1 April 1997 (see FA 1996 s 197 (Appointed Day) Order, SI 1997/1015).
Amendments—[1] Sub-s (2)(*g*) inserted by FA 2000 Sch 7 para 6 with effect from 28 July 2000.
[2] Words in sub-s (2)(*g*) substituted for words "and 81(3)" by the Transfer of Tribunal Functions and Revenue and Customs Appeals Order, SI 2009/56 art 3(1), Sch 1 paras 232, 239(1), (2)(*e*) with effect from 1 April 2009.

FINANCE ACT 2000

(2000 Chapter 17)

An act to grant certain duties, to alter other duties, and to amend the law relating to the National Debt and the Public Revenue, and to make further provision in connection with finance.

[28 July 2000]

30 Climate change levy

(1) Schedule 6 to this Act (which makes provision for a new tax that is to be known as climate change levy) shall have effect.

(2) Schedule 7 to this Act (climate change levy: consequential amendments) shall have effect.

(3) Part V of Schedule 6 to this Act (registration for the purposes of climate change levy) shall not come into force until such date as the Treasury may appoint by order made by statutory instrument; and different days may be appointed under this subsection for different purposes.

Regulations—Climate Change Levy (Combined Heat and Power Stations) Regulations, SI 2005/1714; Climate Change Levy (Fuel Use and Recycling Processes) Regulations, SI 2005/1715.

SCHEDULES

SCHEDULE 6
CLIMATE CHANGE LEVY

Section 30

Cross references—See the Climate Change Levy (Combined Heat and Power Stations) Exemption Certificate Regulations, SI 2001/486 (exemption certificates for combined heat and power stations).

PART I
THE LEVY

Climate change levy

1— (1) A tax to be known as climate change levy ("the levy") shall be charged in accordance with this Schedule.

(2) The levy is under the care and management of the Commissioners of Customs and Excise.

Levy charged on taxable supplies

2— (1) The levy is charged on taxable supplies.

(2) Any supply of a taxable commodity is a taxable supply, subject to the provisions of Part II of this Schedule.

Meaning of "taxable commodity"

3— (1) The following are taxable commodities for the purposes of this Schedule, subject to sub-paragraph (2) and to any regulations under sub-paragraph (3)—

(*a*) electricity;

(*b*) any gas in a gaseous state that is of a kind supplied by a gas utility;

(*c*) any petroleum gas, or other gaseous hydrocarbon, in a liquid state;

(*d*) coal and lignite;

(*e*) coke, and semi-coke, of coal or lignite;

(*f*) petroleum coke.

(2) The following are not taxable commodities—

(*a*) hydrocarbon oil or road fuel gas within the meaning of the Hydrocarbon Oil Duties Act 1979;

(*b*) waste within the meaning of Part II of the Environmental Protection Act 1990 or the meaning given by Article 2(2) of the Waste and Contaminated Land (Northern Ireland) Order 1997.

(3) The Treasury may by regulations provide that a commodity of a description specified in the regulations is, or is not, a taxable commodity for the purposes of this Schedule.

PART II

TAXABLE SUPPLIES

Introduction

4— (1) A supply of a taxable commodity (or part of such a supply) is a taxable supply for the purposes of the levy if levy is chargeable on the supply under—

paragraph 5 (supplies of electricity),
paragraph 6 (supplies of gas), or
paragraph 7 (other supplies in course or furtherance of business),

and the supply (or part) is not excluded under paragraphs 8 to 10 or exempt under paragraphs 11 to 22.

(2) In this Schedule—

(*a*) references to a supply of a taxable commodity include a supply that is deemed to be made under paragraph 23, and

(*b*) references to a taxable supply include a supply that is deemed to be made under paragraph 24 [or 45A][1],

but paragraphs 23 and 24 have effect subject to any exceptions provided for under paragraph 21.

Amendments—[1] Words in sub-para (2)(*b*) inserted by FA 2007 s 23, Sch 2 paras 1, 2 with effect from 1 November 2007: SI 2007/2902 art 2(1).

Supplies of electricity

5— (1) Levy is chargeable on a supply of electricity if—

(*a*) the supply is made by an electricity utility, and

(*b*) the person to whom the supply is made—

(i) is not an electricity utility, or

(ii) is the utility itself.

(2) Levy is chargeable on a supply made from a combined heat and power station of electricity produced in the station if—

(*a*) the station is a partly exempt combined heat and power station,

(*b*) the supply is not one that is deemed to be made under paragraph 23(3) (self-supply by producer), and

(*c*) the person to whom the supply is made is not an electricity utility.

(3) Levy is chargeable on a supply of electricity that is deemed to be made under [paragraph 20(6)(*a*), 20B(6)(*a*), 23(3)[, 24 or 45A][2]][1].

(4) Except as provided by sub-paragraphs (1) to (3), levy is not chargeable on a supply of electricity.

Amendments—[1] Words in sub-para (3) substituted by FA 2003 s 191(1), (2) with effect for supplies deemed to be made after 30 March 2003.

[2] In sub-para (3), words substituted for the words "or 24" by FA 2007 s 23, Sch 2 paras 1, 3 with effect from 1 November 2007: SI 2007/2902 art 2(1).

Supplies of gas

6— (1) Levy is chargeable on a supply of any gas if—

(*a*) the supply is made by a gas utility, and

(*b*) the person to whom the supply is made—

(i) is not a gas utility, or

(ii) is the utility itself.

(2) Levy is chargeable on a supply of gas that is deemed to be made under paragraph 23(3) (self-supply by producer) if the gas—

(*a*) is held in a gaseous state immediately prior to being released for burning, and

(*b*) is of a kind supplied by a gas utility.

[(2A) Levy is chargeable on a supply of gas that is deemed to be made under paragraph 24 [or 45A][2].][1]

(3) Except as provided by [sub-paragraph (1), (2) or (2A)][1], levy is not chargeable on a supply of any gas that is supplied in a gaseous state.

Amendments—[1] Sub-para (2A) inserted, and words in sub-para (3) substituted, by FA 2003 s 191(1), (3) with effect for supplies deemed to be made after 9 July 2003.

[2] Words in sub-para (2A) inserted by FA 2007 s 23, Sch 2 paras 1, 4 with effect from 1 November 2007: SI 2007/2902 art 2(1).

Other supplies made in course or furtherance of business

7— (1) This paragraph applies to a supply of a taxable commodity other than—

(*a*) electricity, or

(*b*) gas in a gaseous state.

(2) Levy is chargeable on any such supply if the supply is made in the course or furtherance of a business.

Excluded supplies: supply for domestic or charity use

8— (1) A supply is excluded from the levy if it is—

(*a*) for domestic use (see paragraph 9), or

(*b*) for charity use.

(2) For the purposes of this paragraph, a supply is for charity use if the commodity supplied is for use by a charity otherwise than in the course or furtherance of a business.

(3) If a supply is partly for domestic or charity use and partly not, the part of the supply that is for domestic or charity use is excluded from the levy.

(4) Where a supply of a commodity is partly for domestic or charity use and partly not—

(*a*) if at least 60 per cent of the commodity is supplied for domestic or charity use, the whole supply is treated as a supply for domestic or charity use, and

(*b*) in any other case, an apportionment shall be made to determine the extent to which the supply is for domestic or charity use.

Excluded supplies: meaning of "for domestic use"

9— (1) For the purposes of paragraph 8 the following supplies are always for domestic use—

(*a*) a supply of not more than one tonne of coal or coke held out for sale as domestic fuel;

(*b*) a supply to a person at any premises of—

(i) any gas in a gaseous state that is provided through pipes and is of a kind supplied by a gas utility, or

(ii) petroleum gas in a gaseous state provided through pipes,

where the gas or petroleum gas (together with any other gas or petroleum gas provided through pipes to him at the premises by the same supplier) was not provided at a rate exceeding 4397 kilowatt hours a month;

(*c*) a supply of petroleum gas in a liquid state where the petroleum gas is supplied in cylinders the net weight of each of which is less than 50 kilogrammes and either the number of cylinders supplied is 20 or fewer or the petroleum gas is not intended for sale by the recipient;

(*d*) a supply of petroleum gas in a liquid state, otherwise than in cylinders, to a person at any premises at which he is not able to store more than two tonnes of such petroleum gas;

(*e*) a metered supply of electricity to a person at any premises where the electricity (together with any other electricity provided to him at the premises by the same supplier) was not provided at a rate exceeding 1000 kilowatt hours a month;

(*f*) an unmetered supply of electricity to a person where the electricity (together with any other unmetered electricity provided to him by the same supplier) was not provided at a rate exceeding 1000 kilowatt hours a month.

(2) For the purposes of paragraph 8, supplies not within sub-paragraph (1) are for domestic use if and only if the commodity supplied is for use in—

(*a*) a building, or part of a building, which consists of a dwelling or number of dwellings,

(*b*) a building, or part of a building, used for a relevant residential purpose, (*c*) self-catering holiday accommodation (including any accommodation advertised or held out as such),

(*d*) a caravan,

(*e*) a houseboat (that is to say, a boat or other floating decked structure designed or adapted for use solely as a place of permanent habitation and not having means of, or capable of being readily adapted for, self-propulsion), or

(*f*) an appliance that—

(i) is not part of a combined heat and power station,

(ii) is located otherwise than in premises of a description mentioned in any of paragraphs (*a*) to (*e*), and

(iii) is used to heat air or water that, when heated, is supplied to premises of, or each of, such a description.

(3) For the purposes of this paragraph use for a relevant residential purpose means use as—

(*a*) a home or other institution providing residential accommodation for children,

(*b*) a home or other institution providing residential accommodation with personal care for persons in need of personal care by reason of old age, disablement, past or present dependence on alcohol or drugs or past or present mental disorder,

(*c*) a hospice,

(*d*) residential accommodation for students or school pupils,

(*e*) residential accommodation for members of any of the armed forces,

(*f*) a monastery, nunnery or similar establishment, or

(*g*) an institution which is the sole or main residence of at least 90 per cent of its residents,

except use as a hospital, a prison or similar institution or an hotel or inn or similar establishment.

[(4) The power to make provision by order under section 2(1C) of the Value Added Tax Act 1994 varying, or varying any provision contained in, Schedule A1 to that Act (supplies for domestic use and non-business use by a charity that attract reduced VAT rate) includes power to make provision for any appropriate corresponding variation of, or of any provision contained in, this paragraph.][2]

[(5) The power to make provision under section 29A(3) of the Value Added Tax Act 1994 varying Schedule 7A to that Act (charge at reduced rate) includes power to make provision for any appropriate corresponding variation of this paragraph.][1]

Amendments—[1] Sub-para (5) inserted by FA 2001 s 99(6), Sch 31 para 7 with effect from 11 May 2001.
[2] Sub-para (4) repealed by FA 2001 s 110, Sch 33 Pt III(1) with effect from 1 November 2001.

Excluded supplies: supply before 1st April 2001

10 Any supply made before 1st April 2001 is excluded from the levy.

Exemption: supply not for burning in the UK

11— (1) A supply of a taxable commodity to which this sub-paragraph applies is exempt from the levy if the person to whom the supply is made ...[1]—

(*a*) ...[1] intends to use the commodity in making supplies of it to any other person, or

(*b*) ...[1] intends to cause the commodity to be exported from the United Kingdom and has no intention to cause it to be thereafter brought back into the United Kingdom.

(2) Sub-paragraph (1) applies to supplies of a taxable commodity other than—

(*a*) electricity, or

(*b*) any gas in a gaseous state.

(3) A supply of electricity, or of gas in a gaseous state, is exempt from the levy if the person to whom the supply is made ...[1]—

(*a*) ...[1] intends to cause the commodity to be exported from the United Kingdom, and

(*b*) has no intention to cause it to be thereafter brought back into the United Kingdom.

(4) Regulations under paragraph 22 may, in particular, include provision as to the application of sub-paragraph (3) in cases where a person who is both an exporter and an importer of a commodity intends to be a net exporter of the commodity.

Amendment—[1] Words in sub-paras (1), (3) repealed by FA 2007 ss 23, 114, Sch 2 paras 1, 11, Sch 27 Pt 1(1) with effect from 19 July 2007.
Words repealed in sub-para (1) previously read as follows—
"has, before the supply is made, notified the supplier", and "that he" (in two places).
Words repealed in sub-para (3) previously read as follows—
"has, before the supply is made, notified the supplier that", and "he".

[Exemption: Northern Ireland gas supplies

11A A supply of gas is exempt from the levy if—

(*a*) the supply is made by a gas utility, and

(*b*) the person to whom the supply is made intends to cause the gas to be burned in Northern Ireland.][1]

Amendments—[1] This paragraph inserted by FA 2001 s 105(2), (7) with effect for supplies made after 31 March 2001.

Exemption: supply used in transport

12— (1) A supply of a taxable commodity is exempt from levy if the commodity is to be burned (or, in the case of electricity, consumed)—

(*a*) in order to propel a train,

(*b*) in order to propel a non-railway vehicle while it is being used for, or for purposes connected with, transporting passengers,

(*c*) in a railway vehicle, or a non-railway vehicle, while it is being used for, or for purposes connected with, transporting passengers,

(*d*) in a railway vehicle while it is being used for, or for purposes connected with, transporting goods, or

(*e*) in a ship while it is engaged on a journey any part of which is beyond the seaward limit of the territorial sea.

Paragraphs (*a*) to (*c*) are subject to the exception in sub-paragraph (3).

(2) In this paragraph—

"railway vehicle" and "train" have the meaning given by section 83 of the Railways Act 1993;

"non-railway vehicle" means—

(*a*) any vehicle other than a railway vehicle, or

(*b*) any ship,

that is designed or adapted to carry not less than 12 passengers.

(3) Sub-paragraph (1)(*a*) to (*c*) does not apply in relation to the transporting of passengers to, from or within—

(*a*) a place of entertainment, recreation or amusement, or

(*b*) a place of cultural, scientific, historical or similar interest,

that is a place to which rights of admission, or where rights to use facilities at it, are supplied by the person to whom the commodity is supplied or by a person connected with him within the meaning of section 839 of the Taxes Act 1988.

Exemption: supplies to producers of commodities other than electricity

13 A supply of a taxable commodity to a person is exempt from the levy if—

(*a*) the supply is not a supply of electricity that is deemed to be made under paragraph 23(3), and

(*b*) the commodity is to be used by that person—

(i) in producing taxable commodities other than electricity,

(ii)in producing hydrocarbon oil or road fuel gas,

[(ii a) in producing biodiesel for chargeable use within the meaning of section 6AA of the Hydrocarbon Oil Duties Act 1979 (excise duty on biodiesel),][1]

[(ii b) in producing bioblend for delivery for home use from any place mentioned in section 6AB(1)(*b*) of that Act (excise duty on bioblend),][1]

[(ii c) in producing bioethanol for chargeable use within the meaning of section 6AD of that Act (excise duty on bioethanol),][1]

[(ii d) in producing bioethanol blend for delivery for home use from any place mentioned in section 6AE(1)(*b*) of that Act (excise duty on bioethanol blend),][1]

(iii)in producing, for chargeable use within the meaning of section 6A of the Hydrocarbon Oil Duties Act 1979 (fuel substitutes), [liquids (within the meaning of that section) in respect of which a charge is capable of arising under that section][1], or

(iv)in producing uranium for use in an electricity generating station.

[Expressions which are used in this paragraph and the Hydrocarbon Oil Duties Act 1979 have the same meaning in this paragraph as they have in that Act][1].

Amendments—[1] Sub-paras (*b*)(iia)–(iid) inserted; in sub-para (*b*)(iii), words substituted for the words "liquids that are not hydrocarbon oil"; and the final sentence substituted, by FA 2004 s 289(2)–(4), (6) with effect—

(*a*) as regards biodiesel and bioblend, in relation to supplies made after 21 July 2004; and

(*b*) as regards bioethanol and bioethanol blend, in relation to supplies made after 31 December 2004.

The final sentence previously read as follows—

"For this purpose 'hydrocarbon oil' and 'road fuel gas' have the same meaning as in the Hydrocarbon Oil Duties Act 1979 and 'liquid' has the same meaning as in section 6A of that Act.".

[13A— (1) The Commissioners may by regulations make provision amending paragraph 13 for the purpose of—

(*a*) extending the circumstances in which a supply of a taxable commodity is exempt from the levy, or

(*b*) restricting the circumstances in which a supply of a taxable commodity is exempt from the levy.

(2) Regulations under this paragraph that include provision made for the purpose mentioned in sub-paragraph (1)(*a*) may provide for the provision to have retrospective effect.

(3) A statutory instrument that contains (whether alone or with other provisions) regulations under this paragraph made for the purpose mentioned in sub-paragraph (1)(*b*) shall not be made unless a draft of the instrument has been laid before Parliament and approved by a resolution of the House of Commons.][1]

Amendments—[1] This paragraph inserted by FA 2004 s 289(5) with effect from 22 July 2004.

Exemption: supplies (other than self-supplies) to electricity producers

14— (1) A supply of a taxable commodity to a person is exempt from the levy if—

(*a*) the commodity is to be used by that person in producing electricity in a generating station that is neither—

(i) a fully exempt combined heat and power station, nor

(ii) a partly exempt combined heat and power station,

and

(*b*) the supply is not a supply of electricity that is deemed to be made under paragraph 23(3).

(2) Sub-paragraph (1) does not exempt a supply where the person to whom the supply is made—

(*a*) is an exempt unlicensed electricity supplier of a description prescribed by regulations made by the Treasury, …[2]

(*b*) uses the commodity supplied in producing electricity[, and

(*c*) uses the electricity produced otherwise than in exemption-retaining ways.][1]

(3) Sub-paragraph (1) does not exempt a supply where the person to whom the supply is made—

(*a*) is an auto-generator,

(*b*) uses the commodity supplied in producing electricity, and

[(*c*) uses the electricity produced otherwise than in exemption-retaining ways.][1]

[(3A) For the purposes of this paragraph, electricity is used in an "exemption-retaining" way if it is used—

(*a*) in making supplies that are excluded under paragraphs 8 to 10 or exempt under any of paragraphs 11, 12 [, 18 and 18A][3], or

(*b*) in any of the ways mentioned in sub-paragraphs (i) to (iv) of paragraph 13(*b*).][1]

(4) In this paragraph "exempt unlicensed electricity supplier" means a person—

(*a*) to whom an exemption from section 4(1)(*c*) of the Electricity Act 1989 (persons supplying electricity to premises) has been granted by an order under section 5 of that Act, or

(*b*) to whom an exemption from Article 8(1)(*c*) of the Electricity Supply (Northern Ireland) Order 1992 has been granted by an order under Article 9 of that Order,

except where he is acting otherwise than for purposes connected with the carrying on of activities authorised by the exemption.

(5) Sub-paragraph (4) applies subject to—

(*a*) any direction under paragraph 151(1), and

(*b*) any regulations under paragraph 151(2).

Amendments—[1] Word "and", sub-paras (2)(*c*), and (3A) inserted, and sub-para (3)(*c*) substituted by FA 2001 s 105(3)–(5), (7) with effect for supplies made after 31 March 2001.

[2] In para (2)(*a*), the word "and" repealed by FA 2001 s 110, Sch 33 Pt 3(3) with effect from 11 May 2001.

[3] Words in sub-para (3A)(*a*) substituted by FA 2003 s 188(2)(*a*) with effect from 10 July 2003.

Exemption: supplies (other than self-supplies) to combined heat and power stations

15— (1) A supply of a taxable commodity to a person is exempt from the levy if—

(*a*) [that person intends to cause the commodity to be used][1] in—

(i) a fully exempt combined heat and power station, or

(ii) a partly exempt combined heat and power station,

in producing any outputs of the station, and

(*b*) the supply is not a supply of electricity that is deemed to be made under paragraph 23(3).

For this purpose "outputs" has the meaning given by paragraph 148(9).

(2) Where—

(*a*) a supply of a taxable commodity to a person would (apart from this sub-paragraph) be exempted in full by sub-paragraph (1), and

(*b*) at the time the supply is made, the efficiency percentage for the combined heat and power station in which the commodity is to be used …[2] is less than the threshold efficiency percentage for the station,

sub-paragraph (1) only exempts the relevant fraction of the supply.

(3) For the purposes of sub-paragraph (2), the "relevant fraction" of a supply of a taxable commodity that is to be used in a combined heat and power station is the fraction—

(*a*) whose numerator is the efficiency percentage for the station at the time the supply is made, and

(*b*) whose denominator is the threshold efficiency percentage for the station at that time.

(4) For the purposes of this paragraph—

(*a*) the "threshold efficiency percentage" for a combined heat and power station is the percentage set as the threshold efficiency percentage for the station by regulations made by the Treasury;

[(*b*) the "efficiency percentage" for a combined heat and power station shall be determined in accordance with regulations under paragraph 149.][3]

(5) ...[3]

Amendments—[1] Words in sub-para (1)(*a*) substituted by FA 2001 s 105(6), (7) with effect for supplies made after 31 March 2001.

[2] In para (2)(*b*), the words "by that person" repealed by FA 2001 s 110, Sch 33 Pt 3(3) with effect for supplies made after 31 March 2001.

[3] Sub-para (4)(*b*) substituted, and sub-para (5) repealed, by FA 2003 ss 189(1), (2), 216, Sch 43 Pt 4 with effect for supplies made on or after 22 July 2005 (by virtue of SI 2005/1713).

Exemption: supplies (other than self-supplies) of electricity from partly exempt combined heat and power stations

16— (1) This paragraph applies to a supply that—

(*a*) is a supply made from a partly exempt combined heat and power station of electricity produced in the station, and

(*b*) is not a supply that is deemed to be made under paragraph 23(3).

(2) The supply is exempt from the levy if the quantity of electricity supplied by the supply is not such as causes the exceeding of any specified limit that, by virtue of regulations made by the Treasury, applies in relation to the station for any specified period.

(3) In this paragraph "specified" means prescribed by, or determined in accordance with, regulations made by the Treasury.

Exemption: self-supplies by electricity producers

17— (1) This paragraph applies to a supply of electricity that is deemed to be made under paragraph 23(3) by a person ("the producer") to himself.

(2) If the producer is an auto-generator, the supply is exempt from the levy unless—

(*a*) it is a supply from a partly-exempt combined heat and power station of electricity produced in the station, and

(*b*) the quantity of electricity supplied by the supply is such as causes the exceeding of any such limit as is mentioned in paragraph 16(2) that applies in relation to the station.

(3) If the producer is not an auto-generator, the supply is exempt from the levy if it is a supply made from a fully exempt combined heat and power station of electricity produced in the station.

(4) If the producer is not an auto-generator, the supply is exempt from the levy if—

(*a*) it is a supply from a partly-exempt combined heat and power station of electricity produced in the station, and

(*b*) the quantity of electricity supplied by the supply is not such as causes the exceeding of any such limit as is mentioned in paragraph 16(2) that applies in relation to the station.

Exemption: supply not used as fuel

18— (1) A supply of a taxable commodity is exempt from the levy if the person to whom the supply is made intends to cause the commodity to be used otherwise than as fuel.

(2) The Treasury may by regulations specify, in relation to any commodity, uses of that commodity that, for the purposes of sub-paragraph (1), are to be taken as being, or as not being, uses of that commodity as fuel.

(3) The uses of a commodity that may be specified under sub-paragraph (2) as being uses of that commodity as, or otherwise than as, fuel include uses ("mixed uses") of the commodity that involve it being used partly as fuel and partly not; but the Treasury must have regard to the object of securing that a mixed use is not specified as being a use of the commodity otherwise than as fuel if it involves the use of the commodity otherwise than as fuel in a way that is merely incidental to its use as fuel.

Exemption: supply for use in recycling processes

[18A— (1) A supply of a taxable commodity is exempt from the levy if the person to whom the supply is made intends to cause the commodity to be used as fuel in a prescribed recycling process falling within sub-paragraph (2).

(2) A recycling process falls within this sub-paragraph if there is another process ("the competing process") that—

(*a*) is not a recycling process,

(*b*) uses taxable commodities otherwise than as fuel,

(*c*) produces a product of the same kind as one produced by the recycling process,

(*d*) uses a greater amount of energy than the recycling process to produce a given quantity of that product, and

(*e*) involves a lesser charge to levy for a given quantity of that product than would, but for this paragraph, be the case for the recycling process.

(3) For the purposes of sub-paragraph (2)(*b*) taxable commodities are used "otherwise than as fuel" only if the supplies of those commodities to the person using them are exempted from the levy by virtue of paragraph 18.

(4) Sub-paragraphs (5) and (6) apply where the recycling process or the competing process, as well as producing a product that is of the same kind as one produced by the other process ("the corresponding product"), also produces one or more products that are not ("different products").

(5) If the production of the different products is merely incidental to the production of the corresponding product, the different products shall be treated for the purposes of sub-paragraph (2)(*d*) and (*e*) as being of the same kind as the corresponding product.

(6) If the production of the different products is not merely incidental to the production of the corresponding product—

(*a*) the amounts of energy referred to in sub-paragraph (2)(*d*), and the amounts of the charge to levy referred to in sub-paragraph (2)(*e*), shall be determined on a just and reasonable apportionment;

(*b*) the exemption conferred by sub-paragraph (1) shall be restricted to the proportion of the supply that is the same as the proportion of the energy used by the recycling process to produce the corresponding product (as determined for the purposes of paragraph (*a*)).

(7) In this paragraph "prescribed" means prescribed by regulations made by the Treasury.][1]

Amendments—[1] This paragraph inserted by FA 2003 s 188(1) with effect from 10 July 2003.

Exemption: electricity from renewable sources

19— (1) A supply of electricity is exempt from the levy if—

(*a*) the supply is not one that is deemed to be made under paragraph 23(3),

(*b*) the supply is made under a contract that contains a renewable source declaration given by the supplier,

(*c*) prescribed conditions are fulfilled, and

(*d*) the supplier, and each other person (if any) who is a generator of any renewable source electricity allocated by the supplier to supplies under the contract, has in a written notice given to the Commissioners agreed that he will fulfil those conditions so far as they may apply to him.

(2) In this paragraph "renewable source declaration" means a declaration that, in each averaging period, the amount of electricity supplied by exempt renewable supplies made by the supplier in the period will not exceed the difference between—

(*a*) the total amount of renewable source electricity that during that period is either acquired or generated by the supplier, and

(*b*) so much of that total amount as is allocated by the supplier otherwise than to exempt renewable supplies made by him in the period.

In this sub-paragraph "averaging period" has the same meaning as in paragraph 20 and "exempt renewable supplies" means supplies made on the basis that they are exempt under this paragraph.

(3) For the purposes of this paragraph and paragraph 20, electricity is "renewable source electricity" if—

(*a*) it is generated in a prescribed manner, and

(*b*) prescribed conditions are fulfilled.

A manner of generating electricity may be prescribed by reference to the means by which the electricity is generated or the materials from which it is generated (or both).

(4) In prescribing a manner of generating electricity under sub-paragraph (3), the Commissioners must have regard to the object of securing that exemption under this paragraph is only available for supplies of electricity that has a renewable source.

[(4A) For the purposes of this paragraph, coal mine methane shall be regarded as a renewable source.][1, 2]

(5) The conditions that may be prescribed under sub-paragraph (1)(*c*) include, in particular, conditions in connection with—

(*a*) the giving of effect to renewable source declarations;

(*b*) the supply of information;

(*c*) the inspection of records and, for that purpose, the production of records in legible form and entry into premises;

(*d*) monitoring by the Gas and Electricity Markets Authority, or the Director General of Electricity Supply for Northern Ireland, of the application of provisions of, or made under, this paragraph;

(*e*) the doing of things to or by a person authorised by the Authority or the Director General (as well as to or by the Authority or the Director General);

(*f*) things being done at times or in ways specified by the Authority, the Director General or such an authorised person.

(6) A condition prescribed under sub-paragraph (1)(*c*) may be one that is required to be fulfilled throughout a period, including a period ending after the time when a supply whose exemption turns on the fulfilment of the condition is treated as being made.

(7) The conditions that may be prescribed under sub-paragraph (3)(*b*) include, in particular, conditions in connection with—

(*a*) the generation of the electricity;
(*b*) the materials from which the electricity is generated;
(*c*) any of the matters mentioned in paragraphs (*b*) to (*f*) of sub-paragraph (5).

(8) Each of—

(*a*) the Gas and Electricity Markets Authority, and
(*b*) the Director General of Electricity Supply for Northern Ireland,

shall supply the Commissioners with such information (whether or not obtained under this paragraph), and otherwise give the Commissioners such co-operation, as the Commissioners may require in connection with the application (whether generally or in relation to any particular case) of any relevant provisions.

(9) In sub-paragraph (8) "relevant provisions" means provisions of or made under—

(*a*) this paragraph or paragraph 20, or
(*b*) paragraph 23(3) so far as relating to electricity, or paragraph 23(4).

(10) None of—

(*a*) section 57(1) of the Electricity Act 1989,
(*b*) section 42(1) of the Gas Act 1986, and
(*c*) Article 61(1) of the Electricity (Northern Ireland) Order 1992,

(provisions restricting disclosure of information) applies to any disclosure of information made in pursuance of sub-paragraph (8).

Amendments—[1] Sub-para (4A) inserted by FA 2002 s 126 with effect for supplies of electricity made on or after 1 November 2003 (by virtue of SI 2003/2622).
[2] Sub-para (4A) repealed by FA 2008 s 149 in relation to electricity generated on or after 1 November 2008.

Exemption under paragraph 19: averaging periods

20— (1) This paragraph applies where a person ("the supplier") makes supplies of electricity on the basis that they are exempt under paragraph 19 ("exempt renewable supplies").

(2) The rules about balancing and averaging periods are—

(*a*) a balancing period is a period of 3 months;
(*b*) when a balancing period ends, a new one begins;
(*c*) the first balancing period and the first averaging period begin at the same time;
(*d*) unless the supplier specifies an earlier time, that time is the time when he is treated as making the first of the exempt renewable supplies;
(*e*) when an averaging period ends, a new one begins;
(*f*) an averaging period ends once it has run for 2 years (but may end sooner under paragraph (*g*) or sub-paragraph (4)(*a*) or (5)(*a*));
(*g*) if the supplier stops making exempt renewable supplies, the end of the balancing period in which he makes the last exempt renewable supply is also the end of the averaging period in which that balancing period falls.

(3) At the end of each balancing period calculate—

(*a*) the total of—

(i) the quantity of renewable source electricity that the supplier acquired or generated in that period, and
(ii) any balancing credit carried forward to that balancing period; and

(*b*) the total of—

(i) the quantity of electricity supplied by exempt renewable supplies made by him in that period, and
(ii) any balancing debit carried forward to that balancing period.

(4) If the total mentioned in sub-paragraph (3)(*a*) exceeds that mentioned in sub-paragraph (3)(*b*)—

(*a*) the averaging period within which the balancing period fell ends at the end of the balancing period, and
(*b*) a balancing credit equal to the difference between the two totals is carried forward to the next balancing period.

(5) If the totals mentioned in paragraphs (*a*) and (*b*) of sub-paragraph (3) are the same—

(*a*) the averaging period within which the balancing period fell ends at the end of the balancing period, and
(*b*) no balancing credit or debit is carried forward to the next balancing period.

[(6) If the total mentioned in sub-paragraph (3)(*b*) exceeds that mentioned in sub-paragraph (3)(*a*), then—

(*a*) in a case where, at the time when the balancing period ends, an averaging period also ends because of sub-paragraph (2)(*f*) or (*g*), the supplier is for the purposes of this Schedule deemed to make at that time a taxable supply of a quantity of electricity equal to the excess;
(*b*) in any other case, a balancing debit equal to the excess is carried forward to the next balancing period.][1]

Amendments—[1] Sub-para (6) substituted for sub-paras (6)–(8) by FA 2003 s 193(1), (2), (4) with effect where the end of the balancing period referred to in sub-para (6)(*a*) as substituted falls after 30 March 2003.

Sub-paras (6)–(8) previously read as follows—

"(6) Sub-paragraphs (7) and (8) apply if the total mentioned in sub-paragraph (3)(*b*) exceeds that mentioned in sub-paragraph (3)(*a*).

(7) Where the end of the balancing period is by virtue of sub-paragraph [(2)(*g*)][1] the end of an averaging period, the supplier is liable to account to the Commissioners for an amount equal to the amount that would be payable by way of levy on a taxable supply that—

(*a*) is made at the end of the balancing period, [and][1]

(*b*) is a supply of a quantity of electricity equal to the difference between the two totals, ...[1]

(*c*) ...[1]

For the purposes of this Schedule, the amount for which the supplier is liable to account shall be treated as an amount of levy for which he is liable to account for an accounting period ending at the end of the balancing period.

(8) Where sub-paragraph (7) does not apply, a balancing debit equal to the difference between the two totals is carried forward to the next balancing period.".

[Exemption: electricity produced in combined heat and power stations

20A— (1) A supply of electricity is exempt from the levy chargeable under paragraph 5(1) if—

(*a*) the supply is not one that is deemed to be made under paragraph 23(3);

(*b*) the supply is made under a contract that contains a CHP declaration given by the supplier;

(*c*) prescribed conditions are fulfilled; and

(*d*) the supplier, and each other person (if any) who is a generator of any CHP electricity allocated by the supplier to supplies under the contract, has in a written notice given to the Commissioners agreed that he will fulfil those conditions so far as they may apply to him.

(2) Sub-paragraph (1) does not apply in relation to a supply to a person of electricity produced in a wholly or partly exempt combined heat and power station where the supply is made to that person from the station.

(3) In this paragraph "CHP declaration" means a declaration that, in each averaging period, the amount of electricity supplied by exempt CHP supplies made by the supplier in the period will not exceed the difference between—

(*a*) the total amount of CHP electricity that during that period is either acquired or generated by the supplier; and

(*b*) so much of that total amount as is allocated by the supplier otherwise than to exempt CHP supplies made by him in the period.

In this sub-paragraph "averaging period" has the same meaning as in paragraph 20B; and "exempt CHP supplies" means supplies made on the basis that they are exempt under this paragraph.

(4) For the purposes of this paragraph and paragraph 20B, electricity is "CHP electricity" if—

(*a*) the electricity was—

(i) produced in a fully exempt combined heat and power station, or

(ii) produced in a partly exempt combined heat and power station and originally supplied from the station without causing the limit referred to in paragraph 16(2) to be exceeded,

(*b*) the electricity is not renewable source electricity (within the meaning of paragraph 19); and

(*c*) prescribed conditions are fulfilled.

(5) The conditions that may be prescribed under sub-paragraph (1)(*c*) include, in particular, conditions in connection with—

(*a*) the giving of effect to CHP declarations;

(*b*) the supply of information;

(*c*) the inspection of records and, for that purpose, the production of records in legible form and entry into premises;

(*d*) monitoring by the Gas and Electricity Markets Authority, or the Director General of Electricity Supply for Northern Ireland, of the application of provisions of, or made under, this paragraph;

(*e*) the doing of things to or by a person authorised by the Authority or the Director General (as well as the doing of things to or by the Authority or the Director General);

(*f*) things being done at times or in ways specified by the Authority, the Director General or such an authorised person.

(6) A condition prescribed under sub-paragraph (1)(*c*) may be one that is required to be fulfilled throughout a period, including a period ending after the time when a supply whose exemption turns on the fulfilment of the condition is treated as being made.

(7) The conditions that may be prescribed under sub-paragraph (4)(*c*) include, in particular, conditions in connection with any of the matters mentioned in paragraphs (*b*) to (*f*) of sub-paragraph (5).

(8) Each of—

(*a*) the Gas and Electricity Markets Authority, and

(*b*) the Director General of Electricity Supply for Northern Ireland, shall supply the Commissioners with such information (whether or not obtained under this paragraph), and otherwise give the Commissioners such co-operation, as the Commissioners may require in connection with the application of this paragraph (whether generally or in relation to any particular case).

(9) Paragraph 19(10) (disclosure of information) applies in relation to sub-paragraph (8) above as it applies in relation to paragraph 19(8).][1]

Amendments—[1] This paragraph inserted by FA 2002 s 123 with effect for supplies of electricity made after 31 March 2003 (by virtue of SI 2003/603).

[Exemption under paragraph 20A: averaging periods

20B— (1) This paragraph applies where a person ("the supplier") makes supplies of electricity on the basis that they are exempt under paragraph 20A ("exempt CHP supplies").

(2) The rules about balancing and averaging periods are—

(*a*) a balancing period is a period of three months;

(*b*) when a balancing period ends, a new one begins;

(*c*) the first balancing period and the first averaging period begin at the same time;

(*d*) unless the supplier specifies an earlier time, that time is the time when he is treated as making the first of the exempt CHP supplies;

(*e*) when an averaging period ends, a new one begins;

(*f*) an averaging period ends once it has run for two years (but may end sooner under paragraph (*g*) or sub-paragraph (4)(*a*) or (5)(*a*));

(*g*) if the supplier stops making exempt CHP supplies, the end of the balancing period in which he makes the last exempt CHP supply is also the end of the averaging period in which the balancing period falls.

(3) At the end of each balancing period calculate—

(*a*) the total of—

(i) the quantity of CHP electricity that the supplier acquired or generated in that period, and

(ii) any balancing credit carried forward to that balancing period; and

(*b*) the total of—

(i) the quantity of electricity supplied by exempt CHP supplies made by him in that period, and

(ii) any balancing debit carried forward to that balancing period.

(4) If the total mentioned in sub-paragraph (3)(*a*) exceeds that mentioned in sub-paragraph (3)(*b*)—

(*a*) the averaging period within which the balancing period fell ends at the end of the balancing period, and

(*b*) a balancing credit equal to the difference between the two totals is carried forward to the next balancing period.

(5) If the totals mentioned in paragraphs (*a*) and (*b*) of sub-paragraph (3) are the same—

(*a*) the averaging period within which the balancing period fell ends at the end of the balancing period, and

(*b*) no balancing credit or debit is carried forward to the next balancing period.

[(6) If the total mentioned in sub-paragraph (3)(*b*) exceeds that mentioned in sub-paragraph (3)(*a*), then—

(*a*) in a case where, at the time when the balancing period ends, an averaging period also ends because of sub-paragraph (2)(*f*) or (*g*), the supplier is for the purposes of this Schedule deemed to make at that time a taxable supply of a quantity of electricity equal to the excess;

(*b*) in any other case, a balancing debit equal to the excess is carried forward to the next balancing period.][2]][1]

Amendments—[1] This paragraph inserted by FA 2002 s 123 with effect for supplies of electricity made after 31 March 2003 (by virtue of SI 2003/603).

[2] Sub-para (6) substituted for sub-paras (6)–(8) by FA 2003 s 192(1), (3), (5) with effect where the end of the balancing period referred to in sub-para (6)(*a*) as substituted falls after 31 March 2003.

Sub-paras (6)–(8) previously read as follows—

"(6) Sub-paragraphs (7) and (8) apply if the total mentioned in sub-paragraph (3)(*b*) exceeds that mentioned in sub-paragraph (3)(*a*).

(7) Where the end of the balancing period is by virtue of sub-paragraph (2)(*g*) the end of an averaging period, the supplier is liable to account to the Commissioners for an amount equal to the amount that would be payable by way of levy on a taxable supply that—

(*a*) is made at the end of the balancing period, and

(*b*) is a supply of a quantity of electricity equal to the difference between the two totals.

For the purposes of this Schedule, the amount for which the supplier is liable to account shall be treated as an amount of levy for which he is liable to account for an accounting period ending at the end of the balancing period.

(8) Where sub-paragraph (7) does not apply, a balancing debit equal to the difference between the two totals is carried forward to the next balancing period.".

Regulations to avoid double charges to levy

21— (1) The Commissioners may by regulations make provision for avoiding, counteracting or mitigating double charges to levy.

(2) For the purposes of this paragraph there is a double charge to levy where—

(*a*) a supply of a taxable commodity ("the produced commodity") is a taxable supply, and

(*b*) a taxable commodity used directly or indirectly in producing the produced commodity has been the subject of a taxable supply.

(3) Regulations under this paragraph may, in particular, make provision for a supply of a taxable commodity to be wholly or to any extent—

(*a*) exempt from the levy, or

(*b*) deemed not a supply of the commodity.

(4) The provision mentioned in sub-paragraph (3) includes provision for exceptions to any of sub-paragraphs (1) to (3) of paragraph 23 or paragraph 24(3).

(5) The powers conferred by this paragraph are in addition to the powers to make provision by tax credit regulations in relation to any such case as is mentioned in paragraph 62(1)(*g*).

Regulations giving effect to exemptions

22— (1) The Commissioners may by regulations make provision for giving effect to the exclusions and exemptions provided for by paragraphs 8 to 21.

(2) Regulations under this paragraph may, in particular, include provision for—

(*a*) determining the extent to which a supply of a taxable commodity is, or is to be treated as being, a taxable supply;

(*b*) authorising a person making supplies of a taxable commodity to another person to treat the supplies to that other person as being taxable supplies only to an extent certified by the Commissioners.

Deemed supply: use of commodities by utilities and producers

23— (1) Where an electricity utility—

(*a*) has electricity available to it, and

(*b*) as regards a quantity of the electricity, makes no supply of that quantity to another person but causes it to be consumed in the United Kingdom,

the utility is for the purposes of this Schedule deemed to make a supply to itself of that quantity of the electricity.

(2) Where a gas utility—

(*a*) holds gas in a gaseous state, and

(*b*) as regards a quantity of the gas, makes no supply of that quantity to another person but causes it to be burned in the United Kingdom,

the utility is for the purposes of this Schedule deemed to make a supply to itself of that quantity of the gas.

(3) Where—

(*a*) a person has produced a taxable commodity,

(*b*) the commodity is either—

(i) a taxable commodity other than electricity, or

(ii) electricity that has been produced from taxable commodities, and

(*c*) as regards a quantity of the commodity, the person makes no supply of that quantity to another person but causes it to be burned (or, in the case of electricity, consumed) in the United Kingdom,

the person is for the purposes of this Schedule deemed to make a supply to himself of that quantity of the commodity.

(4) The Commissioners may by regulations make provision for electricity to be treated for the purposes of sub-paragraph (3)(*b*)(ii)—

(*a*) as produced from taxable commodities unless prescribed conditions are fulfilled, or

(*b*) as produced otherwise than from taxable commodities only where prescribed conditions are fulfilled.

(5) The conditions that may be prescribed under sub-paragraph (4) include, in particular, conditions in connection with the materials from which the electricity is produced.

Deemed supply: [change of circumstances etc][1]

24— [(1) This paragraph applies in the following cases.][1]

[(1A) The first case is where—

(*a*) a supply of a taxable commodity has been made,

(*b*) the supply was not a taxable supply, and

(*c*) there is such a change in circumstances or any person's intentions that, if the changed circumstances or intentions had existed at the time the supply was made, the supply would have been a taxable supply.][1]

[(1B) The second case is where—

(*a*) a supply of a taxable commodity has been made,

(*b*) the supply was made on the basis that it was not a taxable supply, and (*c*) it is later determined that the supply was (to any extent) a taxable supply.][1]

[(2) This paragraph does not apply where the reason that—

(*a*) the supply was not a taxable supply, or

(*b*) the supply was made on the basis that it was not a taxable supply,

is that it was, or was thought to be, exempt from the levy under paragraph 19 or 20A (exemption for supply of electricity produced from renewable sources or in combined heat and power stations) (but see paragraph 20 or 20B).][1]

(3) [Where this paragraph applies][1] the person to whom the supply was made is for the purposes of this Schedule deemed to make a taxable supply of the commodity to himself.

[(3A) Where—

(*a*) had matters been as mentioned in sub-paragraph (1A)(*c*), only part of the supply would have been a taxable supply, or

(*b*) the determination referred to in sub-paragraph (1B)(*c*) is that only part of the supply was a taxable supply,

the reference in sub-paragraph (3) to the commodity shall be read as a reference to a corresponding part of it.][1]

(4) Where—

(*a*) a supply of a taxable commodity was not a taxable supply by virtue of being supplied for use in premises of a description mentioned in any of paragraphs (*a*) to (*f*) of paragraph 9(2), and

(*b*) those premises cease to be premises of any of those descriptions,

sub-paragraph (3) only applies to so much (if any) of the commodity supplied as was not used in the premises before they ceased to be premises of any of those descriptions.

(5) The Commissioners may by regulations make provision specifying descriptions of occurrences and non-occurrences that are to be taken as being, or as not being, changes of circumstances or intentions for the purposes of [sub-paragraph (1A)(*c*)][1].

Amendments—[1] Words in Heading substituted; sub-paras (1)–(2) substituted for sub-paras (1), (2); words in sub-para (3) inserted; sub-para (3A) inserted; and words in sub-para (5) substituted, by FA 2003 s 190(1)–(6), (8) with effect for supplies made on or after 22 July 2005 (by virtue of SI 2005/1713).

PART III
TIME OF SUPPLY

Introduction

25 This Part of this Schedule applies to determine when a supply of a taxable commodity is treated as taking place.

Electricity or gas: supply when climate change levy accounting document issued

26— (1) This paragraph applies—

(*a*) to supplies of electricity, and

(*b*) to supplies of gas where the gas is supplied in a gaseous state and is of a kind supplied by a gas utility.

(2) Where this paragraph applies, a supply is treated as taking place each time a climate change levy accounting document in respect of a supply is issued by the person making the supply.

(3) A supply that is treated as taking place under this paragraph is a supply of the electricity or gas covered by the accounting document.

(4) Nothing in this paragraph applies to any electricity or gas that is covered by a special utility scheme (see paragraph 29).

Electricity or gas: duty to issue climate change levy accounting document

27— (1) This paragraph applies where on any day—

(*a*) electricity, or gas that is in a gaseous state and is of a kind supplied by a gas utility, is actually supplied to a person ("the consumer"),

(*b*) the supply by which the electricity or gas is supplied is a taxable supply, and

(*c*) the person liable to account for the levy on that supply is the person making the supply ("the supplier").

(2) A climate change levy accounting document covering the electricity or gas actually supplied on that day must be issued by the supplier no later than—

(*a*) the end of the period of 15 weeks beginning with that day, if on that day the consumer is a small-scale user of the commodity supplied;

(*b*) the end of the period of 6 weeks beginning with that day, if on that day the consumer is not a small-scale user of the commodity supplied.

(3) A climate change levy accounting document issued under this paragraph that covers the electricity, or the gas of any kind, actually supplied on any day must also cover any electricity or (as the case may be) any gas of that kind that—

(*a*) has been actually supplied by the supplier to the consumer on any earlier day, and
(*b*) has not been covered by a previous climate change levy accounting document.

(4) For the purposes of this paragraph—

(*a*) an accounting document shall be taken to cover the electricity or gas actually supplied on a day if it covers the electricity or gas actually supplied during a period that includes that day; and
(*b*) an accounting document shall be taken to cover the electricity or gas actually supplied on a day or during a period if it is an accounting document for a quantity of electricity or gas that is a reasonable estimate of the quantity actually supplied.

(5) A climate change levy accounting document issued under this paragraph must contain a statement of—

(*a*) the quantity of electricity or gas that it covers,
(*b*) the period during which, or during which it is estimated that, that quantity was actually supplied,
(*c*) the supplier's name and address,
(*d*) the customer's name and address, and
(*e*) the reference number used by the supplier for the customer.

(6) For the purposes of this paragraph a person is, on any day, a small-scale user of a commodity if the rate at which he is taken to be supplied with that commodity on that day does not exceed the prescribed rate.

(7) The Commissioners may make provision by regulations as to the rate at which a person is, for the purposes of sub-paragraph (6), taken to be supplied with a commodity on any day.

(8) Regulations under sub-paragraph (7) may, in particular, include provision for—

(*a*) rates to be determined or estimated in accordance with the regulations;
(*b*) rates to be so determined or estimated by reference to the quantity of a commodity actually supplied, or estimated to have been actually supplied, during a period ending with, or at any time before or after, the day in question;
(*c*) cases where a person is supplied with a commodity of any kind by two or more suppliers.

(9) Nothing in this paragraph applies to any electricity or gas—

(*a*) that is covered by a special utility scheme (see paragraph 29), or
(*b*) that is actually supplied before 1st April 2001.

(10) This paragraph applies subject to paragraph 36(5).

Electricity or gas: actual supply not followed by climate change levy accounting document

28— (1) This paragraph applies where on any day—

(*a*) electricity, or gas that is in a gaseous state and is of a kind supplied by a gas utility, is actually supplied to a person ("the consumer"),
(*b*) the supply by which the electricity or gas is supplied is a taxable supply,
(*c*) the person liable to account for the levy on that supply is the person making the supply ("the supplier"), and
(*d*) the supplier does not within the period applicable under sub-paragraph (2) of paragraph 27 issue a climate change levy accounting document under that paragraph covering the electricity or gas.

(2) Where this paragraph applies, a supply is treated as taking place at the end of that period.

(3) A supply that is treated as taking place under this paragraph is a supply of all the electricity or (as the case may be) gas of the same kind that—

(*a*) has been actually supplied by the supplier to the consumer before the end of that period, and
(*b*) has not been covered by a climate change levy accounting document.

(4) Sub-paragraph (4) of paragraph 27 (interpretation of "covered by an accounting document") applies for the purposes of this paragraph as for those of that paragraph.

(5) Nothing in this paragraph applies to any electricity or gas—

(*a*) that is covered by a special utility scheme (see paragraph 29),
(*b*) that is actually supplied before 1st April 2001, or
(*c*) that is treated under paragraph 36(3) as supplied on that day.

Electricity or gas: special utility schemes

29— (1) For the purposes of this Schedule a "special utility scheme" is a scheme for determining when—

(*a*) a supply of electricity, or
(*b*) a supply of gas that is in a gaseous state and is of a kind supplied by a gas utility,

is treated as taking place in cases where the electricity or gas is covered by the scheme.

(2) If in the opinion of the Commissioners it is reasonable to do so, they may in accordance with the provisions of this paragraph prepare a special utility scheme for a utility or for two or more utilities.

In this paragraph "utility" includes a person who makes supplies on which levy is chargeable by virtue of paragraph 5(2) (partly exempt combined heat and power stations).

(3) A special utility scheme shall specify the period for which it is to have effect.

(4) No special utility scheme shall be of any effect in relation to any electricity or gas supplied by a utility unless the utility elects in writing to be bound by it for the specified period.

(5) If a utility makes such an election—

(*a*) the scheme shall have effect for the specified period in relation to such electricity or gas supplied by the utility as is covered by the scheme, and

(*b*) during the specified period the scheme applies to determine when a supply of a taxable commodity is treated as taking place if the commodity is electricity or gas covered by the scheme.

(6) A special utility scheme may—

(*a*) cover all or any of the electricity or gas supplied by a utility for which the scheme is prepared;

(*b*) provide for paragraph 36 or 37 not to apply, or to apply with modifications, to electricity or gas covered by the scheme.

(7) The Commissioners may by regulations make further provision with respect to special utility schemes, including (in particular) provision amending this paragraph.

Other commodities: general rules for supply by UK residents

30— (1) This paragraph applies to supplies that are not of either of the descriptions mentioned in paragraphs (*a*) and (*b*) of paragraph 26(1) (electricity and gas in a gaseous state).

(2) The general rules as to when such supplies are taken to be made are, in cases where the supply is made by a person resident in the United Kingdom, as follows—

(*a*) if the commodity is to be removed, the supply takes place at the time of the removal;

(*b*) if the commodity is not to be removed, the supply takes place when the commodity is made available to the person to whom it is supplied;

(*c*) if the commodity (being sent or taken on approval or sale or return or similar terms) is removed before it is known whether a supply will take place, the supply takes place when it becomes certain that the supply has taken place or, if sooner, 12 months after the removal.

(3) These general rules are subject to—

paragraph 31 (earlier invoice),
paragraph 32 (later invoice),
paragraph 34 (deemed supplies), and
paragraph 36 (directions by Commissioners).

Other commodities: earlier invoice

31— (1) If before the time applicable under paragraph 30(2) the person making the supply—

(*a*) issues an invoice in respect of the supply, or

(*b*) receives a payment in respect of it,

the supply is treated, to the extent that it is covered by the invoice or payment, as taking place when the invoice is issued or the payment is received.

(2) Sub-paragraph (1) does not apply where the commodity (being sent or taken on approval or sale or return or similar terms) is removed before it is known whether a supply will take place.

(3) Sub-paragraph (1) applies subject to any direction under paragraph 35(3).

Other commodities: later invoice

32— (1) If within 14 days after the time applicable under paragraph 30(2) the person making the supply issues an invoice in respect of it, the supply is treated as taking place at the time the invoice is issued.

(2) This does not apply—

(*a*) to the extent that the supply is treated as taking place at the time mentioned in paragraph 31(1) (earlier invoice), or

(*b*) if the person liable to account for any levy charged on the supply has notified the Commissioners in writing that he elects not to avail himself of sub-paragraph (1).

(3) The Commissioners may, at the request of a person liable to account for any levy charged on any supplies, direct that sub-paragraph (1) shall apply—

(*a*) in relation to those supplies, or

(*b*) in relation to such of those supplies as may be specified in the direction,

with the substitution for the period of 14 days of such longer period as may be specified in the direction.

(4) Sub-paragraphs (1) to (3) apply subject to any direction under paragraph 35.

Other commodities: supply by non-UK residents

33— (1) This paragraph applies to supplies that—

(*a*) are not of either of the descriptions mentioned in paragraphs (*a*) and (*b*) of paragraph 26(1) (electricity and gas in a gaseous state), and

(*b*) are made by a person who is not resident in the United Kingdom.

(2) The supply is treated as taking place—

(*a*) when the commodity is delivered to the person to whom it is supplied, or

(*b*) if earlier, when it is made available in the United Kingdom to that person.

(3) Sub-paragraph (2) applies subject to—

(*a*) sub-paragraph (4),

(*b*) paragraph 34 (deemed supplies), and

(*c*) any direction under paragraph 35.

(4) If within 14 days after the time applicable under sub-paragraph (2) the person to whom the supply is made elects in writing for the supply to be treated as taking place at the time the election is made, the supply is treated as taking place at the time the election is made.

Other commodities: deemed supplies

34— (1) This paragraph applies to supplies that—

(*a*) are not of either of the descriptions mentioned in paragraphs (*a*) and (*b*) of paragraph 26(1) (electricity and gas in a gaseous state), and

(*b*) are deemed to be made under paragraph 23[, 24 or 45A][3].

(2) A supply that is deemed to be made under paragraph 23 is treated as taking place when the commodity is burned […][2].

(3) A supply that is deemed to be made under paragraph 24 is treated as taking place upon the occurrence of the change in circumstances or intentions [or, as the case may be, upon the later determination][1].

[(4) A supply that is deemed to be made under paragraph 45A is treated as taking place upon the later determination.][3]

Amendments—[1] Words in sub-para (3) inserted by FA 2003 s 190(7), (8) with effect for supplies made on or after 22 July 2005 (by virtue of SI 2005/1713).

[2] Words in sub-para (2) omitted by FA 2006 ss 172(7), 178, Sch 26 Pt 8(1) (being unnecessary because the paragraph does not apply in the case of electricity).

[3] In sub-para (1)(*b*), words substituted for the words "or 24", and sub-para (4) inserted, by FA 2007 s 23, Sch 2 paras 1, 5 with effect from 1 November 2007: SI 2007/2902 art 2(1).

Other commodities: directions by Commissioners

35— (1) This paragraph applies to supplies that are not of either of the descriptions mentioned in paragraphs (*a*) and (*b*) of paragraph 26(1) (electricity and gas in a gaseous state).

(2) The Commissioners may, at the request of the person liable to account for any levy charged on any supplies to which this paragraph applies, make a direction under sub-paragraph (3) or (4) altering the time at which those supplies (or such of those supplies as may be specified in the direction) are to be treated as taking place.

(3) The Commissioners may direct that the supplies shall be treated as taking place—

(*a*) at times or on dates determined by or by reference to the occurrence of some event described in the direction, or

(*b*) at times or on dates determined by or by reference to the time when some event so described would in the ordinary course of events occur,

provided the resulting times or dates are in every case earlier than would otherwise apply.

(4) The Commissioners may direct that the supplies shall be treated as taking place—

(*a*) at the beginning of the relevant working period (as defined in the case of the person making the request in and for the purposes of the direction), or

(*b*) at the end of the relevant working period (as so defined).

(5) A direction under sub-paragraph (4) shall not apply to the extent that the time when the supplies in question are made is determined by paragraph 31(1).

Supplies invoiced or paid for before 1st April 2001

36— (1) This paragraph applies where—

(*a*) the taxable commodities covered by an invoice issued, or payment received, before 1st April 2001 are to any extent commodities that have not been burned (or, in the case of electricity, consumed) before the invoice is issued or payment is received, and

(*b*) the advance invoicing or payment is not acceptable normal practice.

It does not matter whether the invoice mentioned in paragraph (*a*) is, or is not, a climate change levy accounting document.

(2) A fair apportionment shall be made to determine the quantity of the taxable commodities covered by the invoice or payment that will not be, or was not, burned (or consumed) before 1st April 2001.

(3) Where this paragraph applies, a supply is treated as taking place on 1st April 2001.

That supply is a supply of the quantity of the taxable commodities that is mentioned in, and determined under, sub-paragraph (2).

(4) For the purposes of this paragraph advance invoicing or payment is "acceptable normal practice" if—

(*a*) the supply is of a kind in the case of which it is normal practice for invoices to be issued, or payments made, in respect of taxable commodities not already burned (or consumed),

(*b*) that practice does not involve issuing invoices, or making payments, more than 15 weeks in advance of the burning (or consumption) of any of the taxable commodities in respect of which the invoice is issued or payment is made, and

(*c*) the advance invoicing or payment is in accordance with the practice.

(5) Nothing in paragraph 27 requires a climate change levy accounting document to be issued to cover any commodities that are supplied by a supply that, under sub-paragraph (3), is treated as made on 1st April 2001.

(6) This paragraph applies to invoices issued, and payments received, before the passing of this Act (as well as to those issued or received after its passing).

Supplies of electricity or gas spanning change of rate etc

37— (1) This paragraph applies in the case of a supply of electricity, or of gas that is in a gaseous state and is of a kind supplied by a gas utility, affected by—

(*a*) a change in the descriptions of supplies that are taxable supplies,

(*b*) a change in any rate of levy in force,

(*c*) a change consisting in the rate of levy applicable to the supply ceasing to be, or becoming, the rate that is applicable to …[1] reduced-rate supplies, or

(*d*) the change consisting in the transition from 31st March 2001 to 1st April 2001.

(2) For the purposes of this paragraph a supply is affected by a change if the electricity or gas of which it is a supply ("the supplied commodity") is actually supplied partly before the change and partly after.

However, this paragraph does not apply in the case of a supply that, under paragraph 36(3), is treated as made on 1st April 2001.

(3) If the person liable to account for any levy on the supply so elects—

(*a*) the rate at which levy is chargeable on any part of the supply, or

(*b*) any question whether, or to what extent, the supply is a taxable supply,

shall be determined in accordance with sub-paragraph (5) or (6).

(4) An election for determination in accordance with sub-paragraph (6) may be made only where—

(*a*) there is such a change as is mentioned in sub-paragraph (1)(*c*), and

(*b*) all the supplied commodity is actually supplied before the supply is treated as taking place.

(5) Where the election is for determination in accordance with this sub-paragraph, the rules are—

"A Treat the fraction of the supplied commodity actually supplied before the change ("the pre-change fraction") as supplied by a supply made before the change and treat the fraction of the supplied commodity actually supplied after the change ("the post-change fraction") as supplied by a supply made after the change.

B Where the pre-change and post-change fractions are not known (because, for example, there are no relevant meter readings available)—

"the pre-change fraction" is calculated by dividing—

(*a*) the number of days in the period over which the supply is actually made that fall before the change, by

(*b*) the number of days in that period; and

"the post-change fraction" is the difference between 1 and the pre-change fraction.

C If use of the fractions given by rule B would produce an inequitable result, the pre-change and post-change fractions may be derived from a reasonable estimate of the fractions of the supplied commodity actually supplied before and after the change.

(6) Where the election is for determination in accordance with this sub-paragraph, treat the change as taking place immediately after the time at which the last of the supplied commodity was actually supplied.

Amendment—[1] In sub-para (1)(*c*), words "half-rate supplies or" omitted by FA 2006 ss 172(9), 178, Sch 26 Pt 8(1) with effect from 1 November 2007: SI 2007/2901 art 2(1).

This amendment does not apply in relation to a half-rate supply made before 1 April 2006: SI 2007/2901 art 2(2). For this purpose, "half-rate supply" carries the meaning it has in this Schedule before 1 November 2007. FA 2006 s 172(3)–(6) applies for determining when a supply is to be regarded as made: SI 2007/2901 art 2(3).

Other supplies spanning change of rate etc

38— (1) This paragraph applies where there is—

(*a*) a change in the descriptions of supplies that are taxable supplies,

(*b*) a change in the rate of levy in force,

(*c*) a change consisting in the rate of levy applicable to any supply ceasing to be, or becoming, the rate that is applicable to ...[1] reduced-rate supplies, or

(*d*) the change consisting in the transition from 31st March 2001 to 1st April 2001.

(2) Where—

(*a*) a supply affected by the change would apart from special provisions be treated under paragraph 30(2) or 33(2) as made wholly or partly at a time when it would not have been affected by the change, or

(*b*) a supply not so affected would apart from special provisions be treated under paragraph 30(2) or 33(2) as made wholly or partly at a time when it would have been so affected,

the rate at which levy is chargeable on the supply, or any question whether it is a taxable supply, shall, if the person liable to account for any levy on the supply so elects, be determined without regard to the special provisions.

(3) In this paragraph "special provisions" means the provisions of paragraphs 31, 32, 33(4) and 35.

Amendment—[1] In sub-para (1)(*c*) words "half-rate supplies or" omitted by FA 2006 ss 172(10), 178, Sch 26 Pt 8(1) with effect from 1 November 2007.

This amendment does not apply in relation to a half-rate supply made before 1 April 2006: SI 2007/2901 art 2(2). For this purpose, "half-rate supply" carries the meaning it has in this Schedule before 1 November 2007. FA 2006 s 172(3)–(6) applies for determining when a supply is to be regarded as made: SI 2007/2901 art 2(3).

Regulations as to time of supply

39— (1) The Commissioners may make provision by regulations as to the time at which a supply is to be treated as taking place—

(*a*) in cases where the supply is for a consideration and the whole or part of the consideration—

(i) is determined or payable periodically, or from time to time, or at the end of any period, or

(ii) is determined at the time when the commodity is appropriated for any purpose;

(*b*) in the case of a supply otherwise than for consideration;

(*c*) in the case of any supply that is deemed to be made under paragraph 23[, 24 or 45A][1].

(2) In any such case as is mentioned in sub-paragraph (1) the regulations may provide that a taxable commodity shall be treated as separately and successively supplied at prescribed times or intervals.

(3) Paragraphs 26 to 36 (main rules as to time of supply) have effect subject to any regulations under this paragraph.

(4) The power to make regulations under this paragraph includes power to provide for specified provisions of the regulations to be treated as special provisions for the purposes of paragraph 38 (supplies spanning change of rate etc).

Amendments—[1] Words in sub-para (1)(*c*) substituted for the words "or 24" by FA 2007 s 23, Sch 2 paras 1, 6 with effect from 1 November 2007: SI 2007/2902 art 2(1).

PART IV

PAYMENT AND RATE OF LEVY

Persons liable to account for levy

40— (1) The person liable to account for the levy charged on a taxable supply is, except in a case where sub-paragraph (2) [or (3)][1] applies, the person making the supply.

(2) In the case of a taxable supply made by a person who—

(*a*) is not resident in the United Kingdom, and

(*b*) is not a utility,

the person liable to account for the levy charged on the supply is the person to whom the supply is made.

[(3) In the case of levy charged on a taxable supply under paragraph 45B, the person liable to account for the levy is the operator of the facility to which the supply was made.][1]

Amendments—[1] Sub-para (3) and consequential amendments inserted by FA 2009 s 118, Sch 59 paras 2, 3 with effect where the certification period begins on or after 1 April 2009.

Returns and payment of levy

41— (1) The Commissioners may by regulations make provision—

[(*a*) for persons liable to account for levy to do so—

(i) by reference to such periods ("accounting periods") as may be determined by or under the regulations, or

(ii) in such other way as may be so determined;][1]

(*b*) for persons who are or are required to be registered for the purposes of the levy to be subject to such obligations to make returns for those purposes for such periods, at such times and in such form as may be so determined; and (*c*) for persons who are required to account for levy …[1] to become liable to pay the amounts due from them at such times and in such manner as may be so determined.

(2) Without prejudice to the generality of the powers conferred by sub-paragraph (1), regulations under this paragraph may contain provision—

(*a*) for levy falling in accordance with the regulations to be accounted for by reference to one accounting period to be treated in prescribed circumstances, and for prescribed purposes, as levy due for a different period;

(*b*) for the correction of errors made when accounting for levy by reference to any period;

(*c*) for the entries to be made in any accounts in connection with the correction of any such errors and for the financial adjustments to be made in that connection;

(*d*) for a person, for purposes connected with the making of any such entry or financial adjustment, to be required to provide to any prescribed person, or to retain, a document in the prescribed form containing prescribed particulars of the matters to which the entry or adjustment relates;

(*e*) for enabling the Commissioners, in such cases as they may think fit, to dispense with or relax a requirement imposed by regulations made by virtue of paragraph (*d*);

(*f*) for the amount of levy which, in accordance with the regulations, is treated as due for a later period than that by reference to which it should have been accounted for to be treated as increased by an amount representing interest at the rate applicable under section 197 of the Finance Act 1996 for such period as may be determined in accordance with the regulations.

[(2A) Paragraph 91(5) provides for the application of Part 7 of this Schedule (recovery and interest) in relation to cases where, by virtue of regulations under sub-paragraph (1)(*a*)(ii) above [or by virtue of paragraph 45B(8)][3], a person is liable to account for levy otherwise than by reference to accounting periods.

(2B) Regulations under this paragraph may provide for the application of any provision of this Schedule in relation to such cases.][1]

(3) Subject to the following provisions of this paragraph, if any person ("the taxpayer") fails—

(*a*) to comply with so much of any regulations under this paragraph as requires him, at or before a particular time, to make a return for any accounting period, or

(*b*) to comply with so much of any regulations under this paragraph as requires him, at or before a particular time, to pay an amount of levy due from him,

he shall be liable to a penalty of £250.

(4) Liability to a penalty under sub-paragraph (3) shall not arise if the taxpayer satisfies the Commissioners or, on appeal, an appeal tribunal—

(*a*) that there is a reasonable excuse for the failure to make the return or to pay the levy in accordance with the regulations; and

(*b*) that there is not an occasion after the last day on which the return or payment was required by the regulations to be made when there was a failure without a reasonable excuse to make it.

(5) Where, by reason of any failure falling within paragraph (*a*) or (*b*) of sub-paragraph (3)—

(*a*) a person is convicted of an offence (whether under this Schedule or otherwise), or

(*b*) a person is assessed to a penalty under paragraph 98 (penalty for evasion) [or to a penalty for a deliberate inaccuracy under Schedule 24 to the Finance Act 2007 (penalties for errors)][2],

that person shall not, by reason of that failure, be liable also to a penalty under that sub-paragraph (3).

Amendments—[1] Sub-para (1)(*a*) substituted, words "for any period" in sub-para (1)(*c*) repealed, and sub-paras (2A) and (2B) inserted, by FA 2003 ss 192(1), (2), 216, Sch 43 Pt 4 with effect from 10 July 2003.

Sub-para (1)(*a*) previously read as follows—

"(*a*) for persons liable to account for levy to do so by reference to such periods ("accounting periods") as may be determined by or under the regulations;".

[2] Words in sub-para (5)(*b*) inserted by the Finance Act 2008, Schedule 40 (Appointed Day, Transitional Provisions and Consequential Amendments) Order, SI 2009/571 art 8, Sch 1 para 30(1), (2) with effect from 1 April 2009.

[3] Words in sub-para (2A) inserted by FA 2009 s 118, Sch 59 paras 2, 4 with effect where the certification period begins on or after 1 April 2009.

Amount payable by way of levy

42— (1) The amount payable by way of levy on a taxable supply is—

(*a*) if the supply is [not][2] a reduced-rate supply, the amount ascertained from the Table in accordance with sub-paragraph (2);

(b) …[2]

(*c*) if the supply is a reduced-rate supply, 20 per cent of the amount that would be payable if the supply were [not][2] a reduced-rate supply.

[(1A) Sub-paragraph (1) is subject to paragraph 45B.][3]

[TABLE

Taxable commodity supplied	*Rate at which levy payable if supply is not a reduced-rate supply*

Electricity	£0.00470 per kilowatt hour
Gas supplied by a gas utility or any gas supplied in a gaseous state that is of a kind supplied by a gas utility	£0.00164 per kilowatt hour
Any petroleum gas, or other gaseous hydrocarbon, supplied in a liquid state	£0.01050 per kilogram
Any other taxable commodity	£0.01281 per kilogram][1]

(2) The levy payable on a fraction of a quantity of a commodity is that fraction of the levy payable on that quantity of the commodity.

Amendments—[1] Table substituted by FA 2008 s 19(1), with effect in relation to supplies treated as taking place on or after 1 April 2009.

[2] In sub-paras (1)(*a*), (*c*), the words "neither a half-rate supply nor" substituted, and sub-para (1)(*b*) omitted, by FA 2006 ss 172(11), 178, Sch 26 Pt 8(1) with effect from 1 November 2007: SI 2007/2901 art 2(1). Para (1)(*b*) previously read as follows—

"(*b*) if the supply is a half-rate supply, 50 per cent of the amount that would be payable if the supply were neither a half-rate supply nor a reduced rate supply;".

These amendments do not apply in relation to a half-rate supply made before 1 April 2006: SI 2007/2901 art 2(2). For this purpose, "half-rate supply" carries the meaning it has in this Schedule before 1 November 2007. FA 2006 s 172(3)–(6) applies for determining when a supply is to be regarded as made: SI 2007/2901 art 2(3).

[3] Sub-paragraph (1A) inserted by FA 2009 s 118, Sch 59 paras 2, 5 with effect in relation to certification periods beginning on or after 1 April 2009.

Half-rate for supplies to horticultural producers

43— (1) For the purposes of this Schedule a half-rate supply is a taxable supply in respect of which the following conditions are satisfied—

(a) the first condition is that the person to whom the supply is made is a horticultural producer;

(b) the second condition is that the horticultural producer intends to use the taxable commodity supplied—

(i) in the heating, for the growth of horticultural produce primarily with a view to the production of horticultural produce for sale, of any building or structure, or of the earth or other growing medium in it,

(ii) in the lighting, for the growth of horticultural produce primarily with a view to the production of horticultural produce for sale, of any building or structure, or

(iii) in the sterilisation of the earth or other growing medium to be used for the growth of horticultural produce as mentioned in sub-paragraph (i) in any building or structure.

(2) In this paragraph "horticultural producer" means a person growing horticultural produce primarily for sale.

(3) In this paragraph "horticultural produce" means—

(a) fruit;

(b) vegetables of a kind grown for human consumption, including fungi, but not including maincrop potatoes or peas grown for seed, for harvesting dry or for vining;

(c) flowers, pot plants and decorative foliage;

(d) herbs;

(e) seeds other than pea seeds, and bulbs and other material, being seeds, bulbs or material for sowing or planting for the production of—

(i) fruit,

(ii) vegetables falling within paragraph (b),

(iii) flowers, plants or foliage falling within paragraph (c), or

(iv) herbs,

or for reproduction of the seeds, bulbs or other material planted; or

(f) trees and shrubs, other than trees grown for the purpose of afforestation;

but does not include hops.

(4) The Commissioners may by regulations make provision for facilitating the enjoyment of the reduced rate of levy payable on half-rate supplies.

(5) Regulations under sub-paragraph (4) may, in particular, include provision—

(a) for determining the extent to which a taxable supply is, or is to be treated as being, a half-rate supply;

(b) for authorising a person making taxable supplies to another person to treat the supplies to that other person as being half-rate supplies only to an extent certified by the Commissioners;

(c) for a person making half-rate supplies ("the supplier") to account for levy on those supplies as if the supplies were neither half-rate supplies nor reduced-rate supplies.

(6) Provision such as is mentioned in sub-paragraph (5)(c) may be made only where tax credit regulations provide for a horticultural producer to be entitled to a tax credit in respect of 50 per cent of the levy accounted for by the supplier on any half-rate supplies—

(a) that are made by the supplier to the horticultural producer, and

(*b*) *on which the supplier has accounted for levy on the basis mentioned in sub-paragraph* (5)(*c*).[1]

Amendment—[1] This paragraph repealed by FA 2006 ss 172(12), 178, Sch 26 Pt 8(1) with effect from 1 November 2007: SI 2007/2901 art 2(1).

This amendment does not apply in relation to a half-rate supply made before 1 April 2006: SI 2007/2901 art 2(2). For this purpose, "half-rate supply" carries the meaning it has in this Schedule before 1 November 2007. FA 2006 s 172(3)–(6) applies for determining when a supply is to be regarded as made: SI 2007/2901 art 2(3).

Regulations made under this para made before 1 November 2007 are unaffected by the repeal of this para: SI 2004/2901 art 2(4).

Reduced-rate for supplies covered by climate change agreement

[44— (1) For the purposes of this Schedule, a taxable supply is a reduced-rate supply if—

(*a*) the taxable commodity is supplied to a facility specified in a certificate given by the Secretary of State to the Commissioners as a facility which is to be taken as being covered by a climate change agreement for a period specified in the certificate, and

(*b*) the supply is made at a time falling in that period.

(2) Sub-paragraph (1) has effect subject to [sub-paragraphs (2A) to (2D) and][2] [paragraphs 45 and 45B][3].

[(2A) The Secretary of State may—

(*a*) give a certificate that includes provision specifying one or more descriptions of taxable commodity as being ineligible for reduced-rate supply,

(*b*) vary a certificate so that it includes provision (or further provision) specifying one or more descriptions of taxable commodity as being ineligible for reduced-rate supply, or

(*c*) vary a certificate so that it ceases to include the provision (or some of the provision) specifying one or more descriptions of taxable commodity as being ineligible for reduced-rate supply.

(2B) A taxable supply of a taxable commodity to a facility is not a reduced-rate supply if, at the time of the supply, the commodity falls within a description that is specified (by virtue of sub-paragraph (2A)(*a*) or (*b*)) in the certificate relating to the facility.

(2C) The Secretary of State may only include provision in a certificate by virtue of sub-paragraph (2A)(*a*) or (*b*)—

(*a*) if the Treasury consents in writing to the specification before the specification is made, and

(*b*) if, and for as long as, the result is compatible with the common market by virtue of Commission Regulation (EC) No 800/2008 of 6 August 2008 declaring certain categories of aid compatible with the common market in application of Articles 87 and 88 of the Treaty establishing the European Community (General block exemption Regulation) (OJ 2008 No L214/3).

(2D) In sub-paragraphs (2A) to (2C) "certificate" means such a certificate as is mentioned in sub-paragraph (1)(*a*).][2]

(3) The Commissioners may by regulations make provision for giving effect to sub-paragraph (1).

(4) Regulations under this paragraph may, in particular, include provision for determining whether any taxable commodity is supplied to a facility.

(5) The provision that may be made by virtue of sub-paragraph (4) includes, in particular, provision for a taxable commodity of any description specified in the regulations to be taken as supplied to a facility only if the commodity is delivered to the facility.][1]

Amendments—[1] This paragraph substituted by FA 2007 s 23, Sch 2 paras 1, 7 with effect from 1 November 2007: SI 2007/2902 art 2(1). This amendment only applies in relation to a supply actually made on or after 1 November 2007: SI 2007/2902 art 2(2).

This paragraph previously read as follows—

"44—(1) Where the Secretary of State gives a certificate to the Commissioners stating that, for a period specified in the certificate, a facility is to be taken as being covered by a climate change agreement, the Commissioners shall publish a notice in respect of the facility.

(2) Such a notice shall—

(*a*) state the day on which it is published,

(*b*) identify the facility or facilities in respect of which it is published,

(*c*) for each facility—

(i) set out the first and last days of the period specified for the facility in the Secretary of State's certificate, and

(ii) indicate the effect of sub-paragraph (3),

and

(*d*)indicate that the notice may be varied by later notices.

(3) For the purposes of this Schedule, a reduced-rate supply is a taxable supply in respect of which the following conditions are satisfied—

(*a*) the first condition is that the taxable commodity supplied by the supply is supplied to a facility identified in a notice published under sub-paragraph (1);

(*b*) the second condition is that the supply is made at a time falling in the period that begins with the later of—

(i) the first day set out for the facility under sub-paragraph (2)(*c*), and

(ii) the day on which the notice is published,

and ends with the last day set out for the facility under sub-paragraph (2)(*c*).

(4) Sub-paragraph (3) has effect subject to paragraph 45.

(5) The Commissioners may, for the purposes of sub-paragraph (3), by regulations make provision for determining whether any taxable commodity is supplied to a facility.

(6) The provision that may be made by regulations under sub-paragraph (5) includes, in particular, provision for a taxable commodity of any description specified in the regulations to be taken as supplied to a facility only if the commodity is delivered to the facility.".

[2] Sub-paras (2A)–(2D) and consequential amendment inserted by FA 2009 s 117(1), (2) with effect from 21 July 2009.
[3] Words substituted by FA 2009 s 118, Sch 59 paras 2, 6 with effect where the certification period begins on or after 1 April 2009.

[Reduced-rate supplies: variation of certificates under paragraph 44][1]

45— (1) This paragraph applies where the Secretary of State, after having given in respect of a facility such a certificate as is mentioned in paragraph 44(1) ("the original certificate"), gives a certificate (a "variation certificate") to the Commissioners stating—

(*a*) that, throughout the period ("the original period") specified for the facility in the original certificate, the facility is to be taken as not being covered by a climate change agreement; or
(*b*) that, for so much of the original period as falls on or after a day specified in the variation certificate (being a day falling within the original period), the facility is to be taken as no longer being covered by a climate change agreement.

(2)–(4) …[1]

(5) If—

(*a*) the statement in the variation certificate in respect of the facility is of the type described in sub-paragraph (1)(*a*), and
(*b*) the day on which [the variation certificate is given][1] falls before the beginning of the original period,

[the original certificate has effect as if the facility had never been specified in it][1].

(6) If—

(*a*) the statement in the variation certificate in respect of the facility is of the type described in sub-paragraph (1)(*a*), and
(*b*) the day on which [the variation certificate is given][1] falls during the original period,

[the original certificate has effect as if the last day of the period specified for the facility in the original certificate were the day on which the variation certificate is given][1].

(7) If the statement in the variation certificate in respect of the facility is of the type described in sub-paragraph (1)(*b*), [the original certificate has effect as if the last day of the period specified for the facility in the original certificate were the later of—

(*a*) the day on which the variation certificate is given, and
(*b*) the day specified in the variation certificate.][1]

Amendments—[1] Sub-paras (2)–(4) repealed; words in sub-paras (5), (6), (7) substituted; and Heading substituted, by FA 2007 ss 23, 114, Sch 2 paras 1, 8, Sch 27 Pt 1(1) with effect from 1 November 2007: SI 2007/2902 art 2(1).
Sub-paras (2)–(4) previously read as follows—
"(2) Where the Commissioners receive a variation certificate in respect of a facility before they have published a notice under paragraph 44(1) in response to the original certificate so far as relating to the facility, their obligation to publish a notice under paragraph 44(1) in respect of the facility shall have effect as an obligation to publish such a notice in response to the original certificate as varied by the variation certificate.
(3) Where the Commissioners receive a variation certificate but sub-paragraph (2) does not apply, they shall publish a notice (a "variation notice") that—
(*a*) states the day on which it is published,
(*b*) identifies the facility or facilities in respect of which it is published,
(*c*) sets out, for each facility in respect of which the statement in the variation certificate is of the type described in sub-paragraph (1)(*b*), the date specified for the facility in the variation certificate, and
(*d*) for each facility, indicates the effect of sub-paragraphs (4) to (7) as they apply in the case of the facility.
(4) Sub-paragraphs (5) to (7) set out the effect of a variation notice being published in respect of a facility.".
The words substituted in sub-para (5) previously read as follows—
"the variation notice is published", and "the notice ("the original notice") published under paragraph 44(1) in response to the original certificate has effect as if the facility had never been identified in it".
The words substituted in sub-para (6) previously read as follows—
"the variation notice is published", and "the original notice has effect as if the last day set out for the facility under paragraph 44(2)(*c*) were the day on which the variation notice is published".
The words substituted in sub-para (7) previously read as follows—
"the original notice has effect as if the last day set out for the facility under paragraph 44(2)(*c*) were the later of—
(*a*) the day on which the variation notice is published, and
(*b*) the day set out in the variation notice for the facility under sub-paragraph (3)(*c*).".
The Heading previously read as follows—
"Reduced-rate supplies: variation of notices under paragraph 44".

[Reduced-rate supplies: deemed supply

45A— (1) This paragraph applies where—

(*a*) a taxable supply has been made to any person ("the recipient"),
(*b*) the supply was made on the basis that it was a reduced-rate supply, and
(*c*) it is later determined that the supply was not a reduced-rate supply.

(2) For the purposes of this Schedule—

(*a*) the recipient is deemed to make a taxable supply to itself of the taxable commodity, and
(*b*) the amount payable by way of levy on that deemed supply is 80 per cent. of the amount that would be payable if the supply were not a reduced-rate supply.][1]

[(3) This paragraph does not apply where a supply is treated as not being a reduced-rate supply by virtue of paragraph 45B.][2]

Amendments—[1] This paragraph inserted by FA 2007 s 23, Sch 2 paras 1, 9 with effect from 1 November 2007: SI 2007/2902 art 2(1). This amendment only applies in relation to a supply actually made on or after 1 November 2007 and on the basis that it is a reduced-rate supply: SI 2007/2902 art 2(3).

[2] Sub-para (3) inserted by FA 2009 s 118, Sch 59 paras 2, 7 with effect where the certification period begins on or after 1 April 2009.

[Removal of reduced rate where targets set by climate change agreement not met

45B— (1) This paragraph applies where, by virtue of such a certificate as is mentioned in paragraph 44(1), a facility is to be taken as being covered by a climate change agreement for a period specified in that certificate ("the certification period").

(2) If it appears to the Secretary of State that the progress made in the certification period towards meeting targets set for the facility by the agreement has been such as under the provisions of the agreement is unsatisfactory, the Secretary of State may issue a certificate under this paragraph.

(3) The certificate must (in addition to specifying the facility, agreement and certification period to which it applies) specify—

(*a*) T, that is, the value (expressed in terms of a reduction in tonnes of carbon dioxide equivalent) of achieving the targets set for the facility by the agreement, and

(*b*) P, that is, the value (expressed in the same terms) of the progress made by the facility, during the certification period, towards meeting those targets.

(4) Where a certificate has been issued under this paragraph—

(*a*) each taxable supply made to the facility at any time falling within the certification period is to be treated as not being a reduced-rate supply, and

(*b*) accordingly, an amount (determined in accordance with sub-paragraph (5)) is payable by way of levy on that taxable supply.

(5) The amount payable under this paragraph on a taxable supply is—

$$\frac{T\text{-}P}{T} \times 0.8R$$

where—

T and P have the values mentioned in sub-paragraph (3);

R is the amount which would have been payable by way of levy on the supply (had it not been a reduced-rate supply) at the time that it was made, in accordance with paragraph 42(1)(*a*).

(6) The Secretary of State must send the certificate to—

(*a*) the Commissioners, and

(*b*) the person who is the operator of the facility.

(7) A certificate under this paragraph may be issued after the certification period ends.

(8) A person liable to account for levy under this paragraph—

(*a*) is liable to account for it otherwise than by reference to an accounting period, and

(*b*) must not (by virtue of regulations under paragraph 41) become liable to pay it as from a date before the date on which the certificate under this paragraph is issued.

(9) Levy due under this paragraph is payable in addition to any levy already payable on any supply made in the certification period.

(10) In this paragraph—

"certification period", in a case where the certificate referred to in sub-paragraph (1) has been varied under paragraph 45, means the period for which that certificate has effect as varied;

"tonne of carbon dioxide equivalent" has the meaning given in the Climate Change Act 2008.][1]

Amendments—[1] This paragraph inserted by FA 2009 s 118, Sch 59 para 1 with effect where the certification period begins on or after 1 April 2009.

Climate change agreements

46 In this Schedule "climate change agreement" means—

(*a*) an agreement that falls within paragraph 47, or

(*b*) a combination of agreements that falls within paragraph 48.

Climate change agreements: direct agreement with Secretary of State

47— (1) An agreement (including one entered into before the passing of this Act) falls within this paragraph if it is an agreement—

(*a*) entered into with the Secretary of State,

(*b*) expressed to be entered into for the purposes of the reduced rate of climate change levy,

(*c*) identifying the facilities to which it applies,

(*d*) to which a representative of each facility to which it applies is a party,

(*e*) setting, or providing for the setting of, targets for the facilities to which it applies,

(*f*) specifying certification periods (as to which see paragraph 49(1)) for the facilities to which it applies, and

(*g*) providing for five-yearly (or more frequent) reviews by the Secretary of State of targets set by or under the agreement for those facilities and for giving effect to outcomes of such reviews.

(2) In this paragraph and paragraph 48 "representative", in relation to a facility to which an agreement applies, means—

(*a*) the person who is the operator of the facility at—

(i) the time the agreement is entered into, or

(ii) if later, the time the facility last became a facility to which the agreement applies,

or

(*b*) a person authorised by that operator to agree to the facility being a facility to which the agreement applies.

Climate change agreement: combination of umbrella and underlying agreements

48— (1) A combination of agreements falls within this paragraph if the following conditions are satisfied.

(2) The first condition is that the combination is a combination of—

(*a*) an umbrella agreement (including one entered into before the passing of this Act), and

(*b*) an agreement (including one entered into before the passing of this Act) that, in relation to the umbrella agreement, is an underlying agreement.

(3) The second condition is that between them the two agreements—

(*a*) set, or provide for the setting of, targets for the facilities to which the underlying agreement applies,

(*b*) specify certification periods (as to which see paragraph 49(1)) for the facilities to which the underlying agreement applies, and

(*c*) provide for five-yearly (or more frequent) reviews by the Secretary of State of targets set by or under the agreements for those facilities and for giving effect to outcomes of such reviews.

(4) For the purposes of this paragraph an "umbrella agreement" is an agreement—

(*a*) entered into with the Secretary of State,

(*b*) expressed to be entered into for the purposes of the reduced rate of climate change levy,

(*c*) identifying the facilities to which it applies, and

(*d*) to which a representative of each facility to which it applies is a party.

(5) For the purposes of this paragraph an agreement is an "underlying agreement" in relation to an umbrella agreement if it is an agreement—

(*a*) expressed to be entered into for the purposes of the umbrella agreement,

(*b*) entered into—

(i) with the Secretary of State, or

(ii) with a party to the umbrella agreement other than the Secretary of State,

(*c*) approved by the Secretary of State if he is not a party to it,

(*d*) identifying which of the facilities to which the umbrella agreement applies are the facilities to which it applies, and

(*e*) to which a representative of each facility to which it applies is a party.

(6) In the case of a climate change agreement that is a combination of agreements that falls within this paragraph, references to the facilities to which the climate change agreement applies are references to the facilities to which the underlying agreement applies.

Climate change agreement: supplemental provisions

49— (1) The first certification period specified by a climate change agreement for a facility to which it applies shall begin with the later of—

(*a*) the date on which the agreement, so far as relating to the facility, is expressed to take effect, and

(*b*) 1st April 2001;

and each subsequent certification period so specified shall begin immediately after the end of a previous certification period.

(2) Where a climate change agreement (the "new agreement") applies to a facility to which another climate change agreement previously applied, the first certification period specified by the new agreement for the facility shall be—

(*a*) a period beginning as provided by sub-paragraph (1), or

(*b*) a period that—

(i) begins earlier than that, and

(ii) is a period that was a certification period specified for the facility by any climate change agreement that previously applied to the facility.

A period such as is mentioned in paragraph (*b*) includes a period beginning, or beginning and ending, before the date on which the new agreement, so far as relating to the facility, is expressed to take effect.

(3) For the purposes of giving certificates such as are mentioned in paragraphs 44(1) and 45(1), the Secretary of State may take a facility as being covered by a climate change agreement for a period if the facility is one to which the agreement applies and either—

(*a*) that period is the first certification period specified by the agreement for the facility, or

(*b*) that period is a subsequent certification period for the facility and it appears to the Secretary of State that progress made in the immediately preceding certification period towards meeting targets set for the facility by the agreement or by a climate change agreement that previously applied to the facility is, or is likely to be, such as under the provisions of the agreement in question is to be taken as being satisfactory.

(4) For the purposes of sub-paragraph (3)(*b*) a climate change agreement may (in particular) provide that progress towards meeting any targets for a facility is to be taken as being satisfactory if, in the absence (or partial absence) of any such progress required under the agreement, alternative requirements provided for by the agreement are satisfied.

(5) For the purposes of sub-paragraphs (2) and (3), the circumstances in which a facility to which a climate change agreement applies is one to which another such agreement previously applied include those where the facility is—

(*a*) a part, or a combination of parts, of a facility to which another such agreement previously applied,

(*b*) a combination of two or more such facilities,

(*c*) any combination of parts of such facilities, or

(*d*) any combination of such facilities and parts of such facilities.

(6) Paragraphs 47 and 48 and sub-paragraph (4) above are not to be taken as meaning that an agreement, or combination of agreements, containing provision in addition to any mentioned in those paragraphs and that sub-paragraph is not a climate change agreement.

(7) For the purposes of paragraphs 47 and 48 and this paragraph "target", in relation to a facility to which a climate change agreement applies, means a target relating to—

(*a*) energy, or energy derived from a source of any description, used in the facility or an identifiable group of facilities within which the facility falls, or

(*b*) emissions, or emissions of any description, from the facility or such a group of facilities;

and for this purpose "identifiable group" means a group that is identified in the agreement or that at any relevant time can be identified under the agreement.

(8) Nothing in this Schedule is to be taken as requiring the Secretary of State to—

(*a*) enter into any climate change agreement,

(*b*) enter into a climate change agreement with any particular person or persons, in respect of any particular facility or facilities or on any particular terms, or

(*c*) approve any, or any particular, proposed climate change agreement.

Facilities to which climate change agreements can apply

50— (1) This paragraph applies where, in connection with concluding or varying a climate change agreement, it falls to be determined whether a facility is to be, or is to continue to be, identified in the agreement as a facility to which the agreement applies.

(2) For the purposes of such a determination "facility" is (subject to any regulations under sub-paragraph (3) or (4)) to be taken as meaning—

(*a*) an installation covered by paragraph 51; or

(*b*) a site on which there is or are—

(i) such an installation or two or more such installations,

(ii) a part, or parts, of such an installation,

(iii) a part, or parts, of each of two or more such installations, or

(iv) any combination of such installations and parts of such installations.

(3) The Secretary of State may by regulations make provision for an installation covered by paragraph 51 to be taken to be a facility for those purposes only if—

(*a*) the taxable commodities supplied to the installation by taxable supplies are intended to be burned (or, in the case of electricity, consumed)—

(i) in the installation, or

(ii) on the site where the installation is situated but not in the installation,

and

(*b*) the amounts of taxable commodities, and of any other commodities specified in the regulations, subject to each of those intentions are such that any conditions specified in the regulations are satisfied.

(4) The Secretary of State may by regulations make provision for a site to be taken to be a facility for those purposes only if—

(*a*) the taxable commodities supplied to the site by taxable supplies are intended to be burned (or, in the case of electricity, consumed)—

(i) in installations on the site that are covered by paragraph 51 (or in parts of such installations), or

(ii) on the site but not in any such installation (or part of such an installation),

and

(*b*) the amounts of taxable commodities, and of any other commodities specified in the regulations, subject to each of those intentions are such that any conditions specified in the regulations are satisfied.

(5) Regulations under sub-paragraph (3) or (4) may make provision for deeming, for the purposes of the regulations, commodities to be intended to be burned (or, in the case of electricity, consumed) in circumstances specified in the regulations.

(6) In this paragraph and paragraph 51 "installation" means a stationary technical unit.

Energy-intensive installations

51— (1) An installation is covered by this paragraph if it falls within any one or more of the descriptions of installation set out in the Table.

[(2) Sub-paragraph (2A) applies where—

(*a*) an installation falls within any one or more of those descriptions, and

(*b*) there is, on the same site as the installation, a location at which ancillary activities are carried out.][1]

[(2A) The installation (taken alone) is not covered by this paragraph, but the combination—

(*a*) of the installation and that location, or

(*b*) where there is more than one such location, of the installation and all of those locations,

is to be taken as being an installation covered by this paragraph.][1]

[(2B) In sub-paragraph (2) "ancillary activities" means activities that—

(*a*) are directly associated with any of the primary activities carried out in the installation,

(*b*) have a technical connection with those primary activities, and

(*c*) could have an effect on environmental pollution.][1]

(3) [Sub-paragraphs (1) to (2B)][1] are subject to any regulations under paragraph 52.

(4) …[1]

(5) …[1]

(6) In [sub-paragraph (2B)][1]—

"environmental pollution" has the same meaning as in the Pollution Prevention and Control Act 1999;

"primary activity", in relation to an installation falling within any one or more of the descriptions of installation set out in the Table, means an activity the carrying out of which at the installation results in the installation falling within one or more of those descriptions.

TABLE

DESCRIPTIONS OF ENERGY-INTENSIVE INSTALLATIONS

[Installations regulated under the Environmental Permitting (England and Wales) Regulations 2007][2]

1 Part A installations.

Installations that would be so regulated but for a threshold or exception

2 Installations that would be Part A installations but for—

(*a*) a relevant numeric threshold, or

(*b*) a relevant exception.

Installations that would be so regulated if certain modifications were made to the Regulations

3 Installations that would be Part A installations if the relevant modifications were made.

Corresponding installations in Scotland and Northern Ireland

4 Installations that are situated in Scotland or Northern Ireland, but if situated in England and Wales—

(*a*) would be Part A installations,

(*b*) would be Part A installations but for—

(i) a relevant numeric threshold, or

(ii) a relevant exception, or

(*c*) would be Part A installations if the relevant modifications were made.

Interpretation of entries 1 to 4

5—(1) [In this entry "the Schedule" means Schedule 1 to the Environmental Permitting (England and Wales) Regulations 2007.][2]

(2) In entries 1 to 4—

(*a*) ["Part A installation" has the meaning given in regulation 3(2) of the Environmental Permitting (England and Wales) Regulations 2007;][2]

(*b*) "relevant exception" means—

(i) the exception in paragraph (*b*)(i) of Part A(1) of Section 2.1 of [Part 2 of the Schedule][2],
(ii) the exceptions in paragraph (*c*) of Part A(1) of Section 5.1 of [Part 2 of the Schedule][2] for activities falling within Part B of that Section and for the incineration of specified hazardous waste in an exempt incineration plant, or
(iii) the exception in paragraph (*e*) of Part A(1) of Section 5.1 of [Part 2 of the Schedule][2] for incineration as part of a Part B activity in so far as this exception relates to the activities referred to in paragraphs (*a*) and (*b*) of Part B of that Section;

(*c*) "the relevant modifications" means the omission of the following provisions of [Part 2 of the Schedule][2]:

(i) the final twelve words of paragraph (*b*) of Part A(1) of Section 4.4;
(ii) the final twelve words of paragraph (*b*) of Part A(1) of Section 4.5;
(iii) [paragraph 1 of the Interpretation and application of Part A(1) of Section 5.4;][2]
(iv) the final fourteen words of paragraph (*c*) of Part A(1) of Section 6.1;
(v) the final fourteen words of paragraph (*c*) of Part A(1) of Section 6.4; and
(vi) the final fourteen words of paragraph (*f*)(ii) of Part A(1) of Section 6.8; and

(*d*) "relevant numeric threshold" means a numeric threshold specified in any of the following provisions of [Part 2 of the Schedule][2]:

(i) paragraphs (*c*) and (*d*) of Part A(1) of Section 2.1;
(ii) Part A(2) of Section 2.1;
(iii) paragraph (*b*) of Part A(1) of Section 2.2;
(iv) Part A(1) of Section 2.3;
(v) paragraph (*b*) of Part A(1) of Section 3.1;
(vi) paragraph (*b*) of Part A(2) of Section 3.1;
(vii) paragraph (*b*) of Part A(1) of Section 3.3;
(viii) Part A(2) of Section 3.3;
(ix) paragraph (*a*) of Part A(1) of Section 3.4;
(x) Part A(2) of Section 3.6;
(xi) paragraphs (*c*) and (*d*) of Part A(1) of Section 4.1;
(xii) paragraphs (*d*) and (*e*) of Part A(1) of Section 5.1;
(xiii) Part A(1) of Section 5.2;
(xiv) Part A(1) of Section 5.3;
(xv) paragraph (c) of Part A(1) of Section 5.4;
(xvi) paragraph (b) of Part A(1) of Section 6.1;
(xvii) Part A(1) of Section 6.3;
(xviii) paragraphs (*a*) and (*b*) of Part A(1) of Section 6.4;
(xix) Part A(2) of Section 6.4;
(xx) Part A(2) of Section 6.7;
(xxi) paragraphs (*a*) to (*e*) of Part A(1) of Section 6.8;
(xxii) Part A(2) of Section 6.8; and
(xxiii) Part A(1) of Section 6.9; and

(*e*) any reference to a part of the United Kingdom includes the territorial waters adjacent to that part.][1]

Regulations—Climate Change Agreements (Energy-intensive Installations) Regulations, SI 2006/59; Climate Change Agreements (Eligible Facilities) Regulations, SI 2006/60.

Amendments—[1] Sub-paras (2), (2A), and (2B) substituted for sub-para (2), words in sub-paras (3), (6) substituted, sub-paras (4), (5) repealed, and entries in the Table substituted by the Climate Change Agreements (Energy-intensive Installations) Regulations, SI 2001/1139 with effect from 23 March 2001.

[2] Cross-heading, entries 5(1), 5(2)(*a*), 5(2)(*c*)(iii), and words in entries 5(2)(*b*)–(*d*), substituted, by the Environmental Permitting (England and Wales) Regulations, SI 2007/3538 reg 73, Sch 21 para 27 with effect from 6 April 2008 in relation to England and Wales.

Power to vary the installations covered by paragraph 51

52— (1) The Treasury may make provision by regulations for varying the installations covered by paragraph 51.

(2) The provision that may be made by regulations under this paragraph includes, in particular, provision—

(*a*) for the installations covered by paragraph 51 to include, or not to include, any installation of a description specified in the regulations;
(*b*) amending the Table in paragraph 51 by adding a description of installation to the Table, removing a description of installation from the Table or altering a description of installation set out in the Table;
(*c*) amending paragraph 51.

PART V

REGISTRATION

Note—Paragraphs 59, 60 come into force on 2 January 2001 and ss 53–58, 61 come into force on 29 January 2001 by virtue of SI 2000/3350 arts 2, 3.

Requirement to be registered

53— (1) A person is required to be registered with the Commissioners for the purposes of the levy if a taxable supply is made in respect of which he is the person liable to account for the levy charged.

(2) The Commissioners shall, for the purposes of sub-paragraph (1) and in accordance with the provisions of this Part of this Schedule, establish and maintain a register of persons liable to account for levy.

(3) The Commissioners shall keep such information in the register as they consider appropriate for the care and management of the levy.

[(4) Regulations made by the Commissioners may provide that, in such cases or circumstances and subject to such conditions or requirements as may be prescribed in the regulations, the Commissioners may exempt a person from the requirement to be registered.][1]

Amendments—[1] Sub-para (4) inserted by FA 2003 s 192(1), (3) with effect from 10 July 2003.

Interpretation of Part V

54 In this Part of this Schedule—

(*a*) references to the register are references to the register maintained under paragraph 53(2);
(*b*) references to registering a person are references to registering him in that register; and
(*c*) references to a person's registration are references to his registration in that register.

Notification of registrability etc

55— (1) A person who—

(*a*) intends to make, or have made to him, any taxable supply in respect of which (if made) he will be the person liable to account for the levy charged, or
(*b*) is required to be registered for the purposes of the levy,

shall (if he is not so registered) notify the Commissioners of that fact.

(2) Subject to sub-paragraphs (5) and (6), a person who fails to comply with sub-paragraph (1) shall be liable to a penalty.

(3) The amount of the penalty shall be—

(*a*) the amount equal to 5 per cent of the relevant levy; or
(*b*) if it is greater or the circumstances are such that there is no relevant levy, £250.

(4) In sub-paragraph (3) "relevant levy" means the levy (if any) for which the person in question is liable to account in respect of taxable supplies made in the period which—

(*a*) begins with the date with effect from which he is required to be registered for the purposes of the levy; and
(*b*) ends with the date on which the Commissioners received notification of, or otherwise first became aware of, the fact that he was required to be registered.

(5) A failure to comply with sub-paragraph (1) shall not give rise to any liability to a penalty under this paragraph if the person concerned satisfies the Commissioners or, on appeal, an appeal tribunal that there is a reasonable excuse for the failure.

(6) Where, by reason of any conduct falling within sub-paragraph (2)—

(*a*) a person is convicted of an offence (whether under this Act or otherwise), or
(*b*) a person is assessed to a penalty under paragraph 98 (penalty for evasion) [or to a penalty for a deliberate inaccuracy under Schedule 24 to the Finance Act 2007 (penalties for errors)][1],

that person shall not by reason of that conduct be liable also to a penalty under this paragraph.

Amendments—[1] Words in sub-para (6)(*b*) inserted by the Finance Act 2008, Schedule 40 (Appointed Day, Transitional Provisions and Consequential Amendments) Order, SI 2009/571 art 8, Sch 1 para 30(1), (3) with effect from 1 April 2009.
Prospective amendments—Para 55(2)–(6) to be repealed by FA 2008 s 123, Sch 41 para 25(*k*) with effect from 1 April 2010 (by virtue of SI 2009/511 art 2).

Form of registration

56— (1) The Commissioners shall register a person if—

(*a*) they receive from him a notification given in pursuance of paragraph 55, or
(*b*) although they have not received from him such a notification, it appears to them that he is required to be registered.

Where the Commissioners register a person who is required to be registered, they shall register him with effect from the time when the requirement arose.

(2) Where any two or more bodies corporate are members of the same group they shall be registered together as one person in the name of the representative member.

(3) The registration of a body corporate carrying on a business in several divisions may, if the body corporate so requests and the Commissioners see fit, be in the names of those divisions.

(4) The registration of—

(*a*) any two or more persons carrying on a business in partnership, or
(*b*) an unincorporated body,

may be in the name of the firm or body concerned.

Notification of loss or prospective loss of registrability

57— (1) Where a person who has become liable to give a notification by virtue of paragraph 55 ceases (whether before or after being registered for the purposes of the levy) to intend to make, or to intend to have made to him, taxable supplies in respect of which (if made) he would be the person liable to account for the levy charged, he shall notify the Commissioners of that fact.

(2) A person who fails to comply with sub-paragraph (1) shall be liable to a penalty of £250.

Cancellation of registration

58— (1) If the Commissioners are satisfied that a registered person—

(*a*) has ceased to make, or have made to him, taxable supplies on which he is liable to account for the levy charged, and

(*b*) does not intend to make, or have made to him, any such supplies,

they may cancel his registration with effect from such time after he last made, or had made to him, taxable supplies as appears to them to be appropriate.

(2) Sub-paragraph (1) applies whether or not the registered person has notified the Commissioners under paragraph 57.

(3) The Commissioners shall be under a duty to exercise the power conferred by sub-paragraph (1) with effect from any time if, where the power is exercisable, they are satisfied that the conditions specified in sub-paragraph (4) are satisfied and were or will be satisfied at that time.

(4) Those conditions are—

(*a*) that the person in question has given a notification under paragraph 57;

(*b*) that no levy due from that person, and no amount recoverable as if it were levy, remains unpaid;

(*c*) that no tax credit to which that person is entitled by virtue of any tax credit regulations is outstanding; and

(*d*) that that person is not subject to any outstanding liability to make a return for the purposes of the levy.

(5) Where—

(*a*) a registered person notifies the Commissioners under paragraph 57, and

(*b*) they are satisfied that (if he had not been registered) he would not have been required to be registered at any time since the time when he was registered,

they shall cancel his registration with effect from the date of his registration.

Correction of the register etc

59— (1) The Commissioners may by regulations make provision for and with respect to the correction of entries in the register.

(2) Regulations under this paragraph may, to such extent as appears to the Commissioners appropriate for keeping the register up to date, make provision requiring—

(*a*) registered persons, and

(*b*) persons who are required to be registered,

to notify the Commissioners of changes in circumstances relating to themselves, their businesses or any other matter with respect to which particulars are contained in the register (or would be, were the person registered).

Supplemental regulations about notifications

60— (1) For the purposes of any provision made by or under this Part of this Schedule for any matter to be notified to the Commissioners, regulations made by the Commissioners may make provision—

(*a*) as to the time within which the notification is to be given;

(*b*) as to the form and manner in which the notification is to be given; and

(*c*) as to the information and other particulars to be contained in or provided with any notification.

(2) For those purposes the Commissioners may also by regulations impose obligations requiring a person who has given a notification to notify the Commissioners if any information contained in or provided in connection with that notification is or becomes inaccurate.

(3) The power under this paragraph to make regulations as to the time within which any notification is to be given shall include power to authorise the Commissioners to extend the time for the giving of a notification.

Publication of information on the register

61— (1) The Commissioners may publish, by such means as they think fit, any information which—

(*a*) is derived from the register; and

(*b*) falls within any of the descriptions set out below.

(2) The descriptions are—

(*a*) the names of registered persons;
(*b*) the fact (where it is the case) that the registered person is a body corporate which is a member of a group;
(*c*) the names of the other bodies corporate which are members of the group.

(3) Information may be published in accordance with this paragraph notwithstanding any obligation not to disclose the information that would otherwise apply.

PART VI
CREDITS AND REPAYMENTS

Tax credits

62— (1) The Commissioners may, in accordance with the following provisions of this paragraph, by regulations make provision in relation to cases where—

(*a*) after a taxable supply has been made, there is such a change in circumstances or any person's intentions that, if the changed circumstances or intentions had existed at the time the supply was made, the supply would not have been a taxable supply;
(*b*) after a supply of a taxable commodity is made on the basis that it is a taxable supply, it is determined that the supply was not (to any extent) a taxable supply;
(*c*) after a taxable supply has been made on the basis that it was [not][2] a reduced-rate supply, it is determined that the supply was (to any extent) a ...[2] reduced-rate supply;
(*d*) *levy is accounted for on a half-rate supply as if the supply were neither a half-rate supply nor a reduced-rate supply;*[2]
(*e*) after a charge to levy has arisen on a supply of a taxable commodity ("the original commodity") to a person who uses the commodity supplied in producing taxable commodities primarily for his own consumption, that person makes supplies of any of the commodities in whose production he has used the original commodity;
(*f*) after a person has become entitled to a debt as a result of making a taxable supply, the debt turns out to be bad (in whole or in part);
(*g*) the making of a taxable supply gives rise to a double charge to levy within the meaning of paragraph 21.

(2) The provision that may be made in relation to any such case as is mentioned in sub-paragraph (1) is provision—

(*a*) for such person as may be specified in the regulations to be entitled to a tax credit in respect of any levy charged on the supply (or, in such a case as is mentioned in sub-paragraph (1)(*g*), one of the supplies) in question;
(*b*) for a tax credit to which any person is entitled under the regulations to be brought into account when he is accounting for [such levy due from him][1] as may be determined in accordance with the regulations; and
(*c*) for a person entitled to a tax credit to be entitled, in any prescribed case where he cannot bring the tax credit into account so as to set it against a liability to levy, to a repayment of levy of an amount so determined.

(3) Regulations under this paragraph may contain any or all of the following provisions—

(*a*) provision making any entitlement to a tax credit conditional on the making of a claim by such person, within such period and in such manner as may be prescribed;
(*b*) provision making entitlement to bring a tax credit into account, or to receive a repayment in respect of such a credit, conditional on compliance with such requirements (including the making of a claim) as may be determined in accordance with the regulations;
(*c*) provision requiring a claim for a tax credit to be evidenced and quantified by reference to such records and other documents as may be so determined;
(*d*) provision requiring a person claiming any entitlement to a tax credit to keep, for such period and in such form and manner as may be so determined, those records and documents and a record of such information relating to the claim as may be so determined;
(*e*) provision for the withdrawal of a tax credit where any requirement of the regulations is not complied with;
(*f*) provision for interest at the rate applicable under section 197 of the Finance Act 1996 to be treated as added, for such period and for such purposes as may be prescribed, to the amount of any tax credit;
(*g*) provision for determining whether, and to what extent, a debt is to be taken as bad;
(*h*) provision for the withdrawal of a tax credit to which a person has become entitled in a case within sub-paragraph (1)(*f*) where any part of the debt that has been taken to be bad falls to be regarded as not having been bad;
(*i*) provision for determining whether, and to what extent, any part of a debt that has been taken to be bad should be regarded as not having been bad;
(*j*) provision for anything falling to be determined in accordance with the regulations to be determined by reference to a general or specific direction given in accordance with the regulations by the Commissioners.

(4) Regulations made under this paragraph shall have effect subject to the provisions of paragraph 64.

Amendments—[1] Words in sub-para (2)(*b*) substituted for the words "levy due from him for such accounting period or periods" by FA 2003 s 192(1), (4) with effect from 10 July 2003.

[2] In sub-s (1)(*c*), words "neither a half-rate supply nor" substituted, words "half-rate or" repealed, and sub-s (1)(*d*) repealed, by FA 2006 ss 172(13), 178, Sch 26 Pt 8(1) with effect from 1 November 2007: SI 2007/2901 art 2(1).

These amendments do not apply in relation to a half-rate supply made before 1 April 2006: SI 2007/2901 art 2(2). For this purpose, "half-rate supply" carries the meaning it has in this Schedule before 1 November 2007. FA 2006 s 172(3)–(6) applies for determining when a supply is to be regarded as made: SI 2007/2901 art 2(3).

Regulations made under this para made before 1 November 2007 are unaffected by the above amendments: SI 2004/2901 art 2(4).

Repayments of overpaid levy

63— (1) Where a person has paid an amount to the Commissioners by way of levy which was not levy due to them, they shall be liable to repay the amount to him.

(2) The Commissioners shall not be liable to repay an amount under this paragraph if, or to the extent that, any person has become entitled to a tax credit in respect of that amount by virtue of tax credit regulations.

(3) The Commissioners shall not be liable to repay an amount under this paragraph except on the making of a claim for that purpose.

(4) A claim under this paragraph must be made in such form and manner, and must be supported by such documentary evidence, as may be required by regulations made by the Commissioners.

(5) The preceding provisions of this paragraph are subject to the provisions of paragraph 64.

(6) Except as provided by this paragraph or tax credit regulations, the Commissioners shall not, by virtue of the fact that it was not levy due to them, be liable to repay any amount paid to them by way of levy.

Supplemental provisions about repayments etc

64— (1) The Commissioners shall not be liable, on any claim for a repayment of levy, to repay any amount paid to them more than three years before the making of the claim.

(2) It shall be a defence to any claim for a repayment of an amount of levy that the repayment of that amount would unjustly enrich the claimant.

(3) Sub-paragraph (4) applies for the purposes of sub-paragraph (2) where—

(*a*) there is an amount paid by way of levy which (apart from sub-paragraph (2)) would fall to be the subject of a repayment of levy to any person ("person A"); and

(*b*) the whole or a part of the cost of the payment of that amount to the Commissioners has, for practical purposes, been borne by a person other than person A.

(4) Where, in a case to which this sub-paragraph applies, loss or damage has been or may be incurred by person A as a result of mistaken assumptions made in his case about the operation of any provisions relating to levy, that loss or damage shall be disregarded, except to the extent of the quantified amount, in the making of any determination as to—

(*a*) whether or to what extent the repayment of an amount to person A would enrich him; or

(*b*) whether or to what extent any enrichment of person A would be unjust.

(5) In sub-paragraph (4) "the quantified amount" means the amount (if any) which is shown by person A to constitute the amount that would appropriately compensate him for loss or damage shown by him to have resulted, for any business carried on by him, from the making of the mistaken assumptions.

(6) The reference in sub-paragraph (4) to provisions relating to levy is a reference to any provisions of—

(*a*) any enactment or subordinate legislation (whether or not still in force) which relates to the levy or to any matter connected with it; or

(*b*) any notice published by the Commissioners under or for the purposes of any enactment or subordinate legislation relating to the levy.

Prospective amendments—In sub-para (1), the words "4 years" to be substituted for the words "three years" by FA 2009 s 99, Sch 51 paras 32, 33 with effect from such day as the Treasury may by order made by statutory instrument appoint.

Reimbursement arrangements

65— (1) The Commissioners may by regulations make provision for reimbursement arrangements made by any person to be disregarded for the purposes of paragraph 64(2) except where the arrangements—

(*a*) contain such provision as may be required by the regulations; and

(*b*) are supported by such undertakings to comply with the provisions of the arrangements as may be required by the regulations to be given to the Commissioners.

(2) In this paragraph "reimbursement arrangements" means any arrangements for the purposes of a claim to a repayment of levy which—

(*a*) are made by any person for the purpose of securing that he is not unjustly enriched by the repayment of any amount in pursuance of the claim; and

(*b*) provide for the reimbursement of persons who have for practical purposes borne the whole or any part of the cost of the original payment of that amount to the Commissioners.

(3) Without prejudice to the generality of sub-paragraph (1), the provision that may be required by regulations under this paragraph to be contained in reimbursement arrangements includes—

(*a*) provision requiring a reimbursement for which the arrangements provide to be made within such period after the repayment to which it relates as may be specified in the regulations;

(*b*) provision for the repayment of amounts to the Commissioners where those amounts are not reimbursed in accordance with the arrangements;

(*c*) provision requiring interest paid by the Commissioners on any amount repaid by them to be treated in the same way as that amount for the purposes of any requirement under the arrangements to make reimbursement or to repay the Commissioners;

(*d*) provision requiring such records relating to the carrying out of the arrangements as may be described in the regulations to be kept and produced to the Commissioners, or to an officer of theirs.

(4) Regulations under this paragraph may impose obligations on such persons as may be specified in the regulations—

(*a*) to make the repayments to the Commissioners that they are required to make in pursuance of any provisions contained in any reimbursement arrangements by virtue of sub-paragraph (3)(*b*) or (*c*);

(*b*) to comply with any requirements contained in any such arrangements by virtue of sub-paragraph (3)(*d*).

(5) Regulations under this paragraph may make provision for the form and manner in which, and the times at which, undertakings are to be given to the Commissioners in accordance with the regulations; and any such provision may allow for those matters to be determined by the Commissioners in accordance with the regulations.

Interest payable by the Commissioners

66— (1) Where, due to an error on the part of the Commissioners, a person—

(*a*) has paid to them by way of levy an amount which was not levy due and which they are in consequence liable to repay to him,

(*b*) has failed to claim a repayment of levy to which he was entitled, under any tax credit regulations, in respect of any tax credits, or

(*c*) has suffered delay in receiving payment of an amount due to him from them in connection with levy,

then, if and to the extent that they would not be liable to do so apart from this paragraph, they shall (subject to the following provisions of this paragraph) pay interest to him on that amount for the applicable period.

(2) In sub-paragraph (1), the reference in paragraph (*a*) to an amount which the Commissioners are liable to repay in consequence of the making of a payment that was not due is a reference to only so much of that amount as is the subject of a claim that the Commissioners are required to satisfy or have satisfied.

(3) In that sub-paragraph the amounts referred to in paragraph (*c*)—

(*a*) do not include any amount payable under this paragraph;

(*b*) do not include the amount of any interest for which provision is made by virtue of paragraph 62(3)(*f*); but

(*c*) do include any amount due (in respect of an adjustment of overpaid interest) by way of a repayment under paragraph 87(3) or 110(3).

(4) The applicable period, in a case falling within sub-paragraph (1)(*a*), is the period—

(*a*) beginning with the date on which the payment is received by the Commissioners; and

(*b*) ending with the date on which they authorise payment of the amount on which the interest is payable.

(5) The applicable period, in a case falling within sub-paragraph (1)(*b*) or (*c*), is the period—

(*a*) beginning with the date on which, apart from the error, the Commissioners might reasonably have been expected to authorise payment of the amount on which the interest is payable; and

(*b*) ending with the date on which they in fact authorise payment of that amount.

(6) In determining the applicable period for the purposes of this paragraph there shall be left out of account any period by which the Commissioners' authorisation of the payment of interest is delayed by circumstances beyond their control.

(7) The reference in sub-paragraph (6) to a period by which the Commissioners' authorisation of the payment of interest is delayed by circumstances beyond their control includes, in particular, any period which is referable to—

(*a*) any unreasonable delay in the making of any claim for the payment or repayment of the amount on which interest is claimed;

(*b*) any failure by any person to provide the Commissioners—

(i) at or before the time of the making of a claim, or

(ii) subsequently in response to a request for information by the Commissioners, with all the information required by them to enable the existence and amount of the claimant's entitlement to a payment or repayment, and to interest on that payment or repayment, to be determined; and

(*c*) the making, as part of or in association with any claim for the payment or repayment of the amount on which interest is claimed, of a claim to anything to which the claimant was not entitled.

(8) In determining for the purposes of sub-paragraph (7) whether any period of delay is referable to a failure by any person to provide information in response to a request by the Commissioners, there shall be taken to be so referable, except so far as may be provided for by regulations, any period which—

(*a*) begins with the date on which the Commissioners require that person to provide information which they reasonably consider relevant to the matter to be determined; and

(*b*) ends with the earliest date on which it would be reasonable for the Commissioners to conclude—

(i) that they have received a complete answer to their request for information;

(ii) that they have received all that they need in answer to that request; or

(iii) that it is unnecessary for them to be provided with any information in answer to that request.

(9) The Commissioners shall not be liable to pay interest under this paragraph except on the making of a claim for that purpose.

(10) A claim under this paragraph must be in writing and must be made not more than three years after the end of the applicable period to which it relates.

(11) References in this paragraph—

(*a*) to receiving payment of any amount from the Commissioners, or

(*b*) to the authorisation by the Commissioners of the payment of any amount,

include references to the discharge by way of set-off (whether in accordance with regulations under paragraph 73 or 74 or otherwise) of the Commissioners' liability to pay that amount.

(12) Interest under this paragraph shall be payable at the rate applicable under section 197 of the Finance Act 1996.

Prospective amendments—In sub-s (10), the words "4 years" to be substituted for the words "three years" by FA 2009 s 99, Sch 51 paras 32, 34 with effect from such day as the Treasury may by order made by statutory instrument appoint.

Assessment for excessive repayment

67— (1) Where—

(*a*) any amount has been paid at any time to any person by way of a repayment of levy, and

(*b*) the amount paid exceeded the amount which the Commissioners were liable at that time to repay to that person,

the Commissioners may, to the best of their judgement, assess the excess paid to that person and notify it to him.

(2) Where—

(*a*) any amount has been paid to any person by way of repayment of levy,

(*b*) the repayment is in respect of a tax credit the entitlement to which arose in a case falling within paragraph 62(1)(*f*) (tax credit where all or part of a debt is bad),

(*c*) the whole or any part of the credit is withdrawn on account of any part of the debt taken as bad falling to be regarded as not having been bad, and

(*d*) the amount paid exceeded the amount which the Commissioners would have been liable to repay to that person had that withdrawal been taken into account,

the Commissioners may, to the best of their judgement, assess the excess paid to that person and notify it to him.

(3) Where any person is liable to pay any amount to the Commissioners in pursuance of an obligation imposed by virtue of paragraph 65(4)(*a*), the Commissioners may, to the best of their judgement, assess the amount due from that person and notify it to him.

(4) Subject to sub-paragraph (5), where—

(*a*) an assessment is made on any person under this paragraph in respect of a repayment of levy made in relation to any accounting period, and

(*b*) the Commissioners have power under Part VII of this Schedule to make an assessment on that person to an amount of levy due from that person for that period,

the assessments may be combined and notified to him as one assessment.

(5) A notice of a combined assessment under sub-paragraph (4) must separately identify the amount being assessed in respect of repayments of levy.

Assessment for overpayments of interest

68 Where—

(*a*) any amount has been paid to any person by way of interest under paragraph 66, but

(*b*) that person was not entitled to that amount under that paragraph, the Commissioners may, to the best of their judgement, assess the amount so paid to which that person was not entitled and notify it to him.

Assessments under paragraphs 67 and 68

69— (1) An assessment under paragraph 67 or 68 shall not be made more than two years after the time when evidence of facts sufficient in the opinion of the Commissioners to justify the making of the assessment comes to the knowledge of the Commissioners.

(2) Where an amount has been assessed and notified to any person under paragraph 67 or 68, it shall be recoverable as if it were levy due from him.

(3) Sub-paragraph (2) does not have effect if, or to the extent that, the assessment in question has been withdrawn or reduced.

Interest on amounts assessed

70— (1) Where an assessment is made under paragraph 67 or 68, the whole of the amount assessed shall carry interest, for the period specified in sub-paragraph (2), as follows—

(*a*) so much of that amount as represents the amount of a tax credit claimed by a person who was not entitled to it (but not any amount assessed under paragraph 67(2)) shall carry penalty interest;

(*b*) so much of that amount as does not carry penalty interest under paragraph (*a*) shall carry interest at the rate applicable under section 197 of the Finance Act 1996.

(2) That period is the period which—

(*a*) begins with the day after that on which the person is notified of the assessment; and

(*b*) ends with the day before that on which payment is made of the amount assessed.

(3) Interest under this paragraph shall be paid without any deduction of income tax.

(4) Penalty interest under this paragraph shall be compound interest calculated—

(*a*) at the penalty rate, and

(*b*) with monthly rests.

(5) For this purpose the penalty rate is the rate found by—

(*a*) taking the rate applicable under section 197 of the Finance Act 1996 for the purposes of sub-paragraph (1)(*b*); and

(*b*) adding 10 percentage points to that rate.

(6) Where a person is liable under this paragraph to pay any penalty interest, the Commissioners or, on appeal, an appeal tribunal may reduce the amount payable to such amount (including nil) as they think proper.

(7) Subject to sub-paragraph (8), where the person concerned satisfies the Commissioners or, on appeal, an appeal tribunal that there is a reasonable excuse for the conduct giving rise to the liability to pay penalty interest, that is a matter which (among other things) may be taken into account under sub-paragraph (6).

(8) In determining whether there is a reasonable excuse for the purposes of sub-paragraph (7), no account shall be taken of any of the following matters, that is to say—

(*a*) the insufficiency of the funds available to any person for paying any levy due or for paying the amount of the interest;

(*b*) the fact that there has, in the case in question or in that case taken with any other cases, been no or no significant loss of levy;

(*c*) the fact that the person liable to pay the interest or a person acting on his behalf has acted in good faith.

(9) In the case of interest reduced by the Commissioners under sub-paragraph (6) an appeal tribunal, on an appeal relating to the interest, may cancel the whole or any part of the reduction made by the Commissioners.

Assessments to interest under paragraph 70

71— (1) Where any person is liable to interest under paragraph 70 the Commissioners may assess the amount due by way of interest and notify it to him accordingly.

(2) Without prejudice to the power to make assessments under this paragraph for later periods, the interest to which an assessment under this paragraph may relate shall be confined to interest for a period of no more than two years ending with the time when the assessment under this paragraph is made.

(3) Where an amount has been assessed and notified to any person under this paragraph it shall be recoverable as if it were levy due from him.

(4) Sub-paragraph (3) does not have effect if, or to the extent that, the assessment in question has been withdrawn or reduced.

(5) Where an assessment is made under this paragraph to an amount of interest under paragraph 70—

(*a*) the notice of assessment shall specify a date, not later than the date of the notice of assessment, to which the amount of interest which is assessed is calculated; and (*b*) if the interest continues to accrue after that date, a further assessment or further assessments may be made under this paragraph in respect of the amounts so accruing.

(6) Where—

(*a*) an assessment to interest is made specifying a date for the purposes of sub-paragraph (5)(*a*), and

(*b*) within such period as may for the purposes of this sub-paragraph have been notified by the Commissioners to the person liable for the interest, the amount on which the interest is payable is paid,

that amount shall be deemed for the purposes of any further liability to interest to have been paid on the specified date.

Supplementary assessments

72 If it appears to the Commissioners that the amount which ought to have been assessed in an assessment under paragraph 67, 68 or 71 exceeds the amount which was so assessed, then—

(*a*) under the same paragraph as that assessment was made, and

(*b*) on or before the last day on which that assessment could have been made,

the Commissioners may make a supplementary assessment of the amount of the excess and notify the person concerned accordingly.

Set-off of or against amounts due under this Schedule

73— (1) The Commissioners may by regulations make provision in relation to any case where—

(*a*) a person is under a duty to pay to the Commissioners at any time an amount or amounts in respect of levy; and

(*b*) the Commissioners are under a duty to pay to that person at the same time an amount or amounts in respect of levy or any of the other taxes under their care and management.

(2) Regulations under this paragraph may provide that if the total of the amount or amounts mentioned in sub-paragraph (1)(*a*) exceeds the total of the amount or amounts mentioned in sub-paragraph (1)(*b*), the latter shall be set off against the former.

(3) Regulations under this paragraph may provide that if the total of the amount or amounts mentioned in sub-paragraph (1)(*b*) exceeds the total of the amount or amounts mentioned in sub-paragraph (1)(*a*), the Commissioners may set off the latter in paying the former.

(4) Regulations under this paragraph may provide that if the total of the amount or amounts mentioned in sub-paragraph (1)(*a*) is the same as the total of the amount or amounts mentioned in sub-paragraph (1)(*b*) no payment need be made in respect of the former or the latter.

(5) Regulations under this paragraph may provide for any limitation on the time within which the Commissioners are entitled to take steps for recovering any amount due to them in respect of levy to be disregarded, in such cases as may be described in the regulations, in determining whether any person is under such a duty to pay as is mentioned in sub-paragraph (1)(*a*).

(6) Regulations under this paragraph may include provision treating any duty to pay mentioned in sub-paragraph (1) as discharged accordingly.

(7) References in sub-paragraph (1) to an amount in respect of a particular tax include references not only to an amount of tax itself but also to other amounts such as interest and penalties that are or may be recovered as if they were amounts of tax.

(8) In this paragraph "tax" includes duty.

Set-off of or against other taxes and duties

74— (1) The Commissioners may by regulations make provision in relation to any case where—

(*a*) a person is under a duty to pay to the Commissioners at any time an amount or amounts in respect of any tax (or taxes) under their care and management other than levy; and

(*b*) the Commissioners are under a duty, at the same time, to make any repayment of levy to that person or to make any other payment to him of any amount or amounts in respect of levy.

(2) Regulations under this paragraph may provide that if the total of the amount or amounts mentioned in sub-paragraph (1)(*a*) exceeds the total of the amount or amounts mentioned in sub-paragraph (1)(*b*), the latter shall be set off against the former.

(3) Regulations under this paragraph may provide that if the total of the amount or amounts mentioned in sub-paragraph (1)(*b*) exceeds the total of the amount or amounts mentioned in sub-paragraph (1)(*a*), the Commissioners may set off the latter in paying the former.

(4) Regulations under this paragraph may provide that if the total of the amount or amounts mentioned in sub-paragraph (1)(*a*) is the same as the total of the amount or amounts mentioned in sub-paragraph (1)(*b*) no payment need be made in respect of the former or the latter.

(5) Regulations under this paragraph may provide for any limitation on the time within which the Commissioners are entitled to take steps for recovering any amount due to them in respect of any of the taxes under their care and management to be disregarded, in such cases as may be described in the regulations, in determining whether any person is under such a duty to pay as is mentioned in sub-paragraph (1)(*a*).

(6) Regulations under this paragraph may include provision treating any duty to pay mentioned in sub-paragraph (1) as discharged accordingly.

(7) References in sub-paragraph (1) to an amount in respect of a particular tax include references not only to an amount of tax itself but also to other amounts such as interest and penalties that are or may be recovered as if they were amounts of tax.

(8) In this paragraph "tax" includes duty.

Restriction on powers to provide for set-off

75— (1) Regulations made under paragraph 73 or 74 shall not require any such amount or amounts as are mentioned in sub-paragraph (1)(*b*) of that paragraph ("the credit") to be set against any such amount or amounts as are mentioned in sub-paragraph (1)(*a*) of that paragraph ("the debit") in any case where—

(*a*) an insolvency procedure has been applied to the person entitled to the credit;

(*b*) the credit became due after that procedure was so applied; and

(*c*) the liability to pay the debit either arose before that procedure was so applied or (having arisen afterwards) relates to, or to matters occurring in the course of, the carrying on of any business at times before the procedure was so applied.

(2) For the purposes of this paragraph, an insolvency procedure is applied to a person if—

(*a*) a bankruptcy order, winding-up order or administration order is made [or an administrator is appointed][1] in relation to that person or an award of sequestration is made on that person's estate;

(*b*) that person is put into administrative receivership;

(*c*) that person passes a resolution for voluntary winding up;

(*d*) any voluntary arrangement approved in accordance with—

(i) Part I or VIII of the Insolvency Act 1986, or

(ii) Part II or Chapter II of Part VIII of the Insolvency (Northern Ireland) Order 1989,

comes into force in relation to that person;

(*e*) a deed of arrangement registered in accordance with—

(i) the Deeds of Arrangement Act 1914, or

(ii) Chapter I of Part VIII of that Order,

takes effect in relation to that person;

(*f*) a person is appointed as the interim receiver of some or all of that person's property under section 286 of the Insolvency Act 1986 or Article 259 of the Insolvency (Northern Ireland) Order 1989;

(*g*) a person is appointed as the provisional liquidator in relation to that person under section 135 of that Act or Article 115 of that Order;

(*h*) an interim order is made under Part VIII of that Act, or Chapter II of Part VIII of that Order, in relation to that person; or

(*i*) that person's estate becomes vested in any other person as that person's trustee under a trust deed (within the meaning of the Bankruptcy (Scotland) Act 1985).

(3) In this paragraph references, in relation to any person, to the application of an insolvency procedure to that person shall not include—

(*a*) the making of a bankruptcy order, winding-up order …[1] or award of sequestration [or the appointment of an administrator][1] at a time when any such arrangement or deed as is mentioned in paragraph (*d*), (*e*) or (*i*) of sub-paragraph (2) is in force in relation to that person;

(*b*) the making of a winding-up order at any of the following times, that is to say—

[(i) immediately upon the appointment of an administrator in respect of the person ceasing to have effect;][1]

(ii) when that person is being wound up voluntarily;

(iii) when that person is in administrative receivership;

or

(*c*) the making of an administration order in relation to that person at any time when that person is in administrative receivership.

(4) For the purposes of this paragraph a person shall be regarded as being in administrative receivership throughout any continuous period for which (disregarding any temporary vacancy in the office of receiver) there is an administrative receiver of that person.

(5) In this paragraph—

"administration order" means an administration order under [Schedule B1 to][1] the Insolvency Act 1986 or Article 21 of the Insolvency (Northern Ireland) Order 1989;

"administrative receiver" means an administrative receiver within the meaning of section 251 of that Act or Article 5(1) of that Order.

Amendments—[1] Words in sub-para (2)(*a*) inserted, in sub-para (3)(*a*), words repealed and words inserted, sub-para (3)(*b*)(i) substituted, and words in sub-para (5) substituted, by the Enterprise Act 2002 (Insolvency) Order, SI 2003/2096 art 4, Schedule paras 31, 32 with effect from 15 September 2003. These amendments do not apply in relation to any case where a petition for an administration order was presented before 15 September 2003: SI 2003/2096 arts 1(1), 6.

Part VI: supplemental provisions

76— (1) Any notification of an assessment under any provision of this Part of this Schedule to a person's representative shall be treated for the purposes of this Schedule as notification to the person in relation to whom the representative acts.

(2) In this paragraph "representative", in relation to any person, means—

(*a*) any of that person's personal representatives;

(*b*) that person's trustee in bankruptcy or liquidator;

(*c*) any person holding office as a receiver in relation to that person or any of his property;

(*d*) that person's tax representative or any other person for the time being acting in a representative capacity in relation to that person.

(3) In this paragraph "trustee in bankruptcy" includes, as respects Scotland—

(*a*) an interim or permanent trustee (within the meaning of the Bankruptcy (Scotland) Act 1985); and

(*b*) a trustee acting under a trust deed (within the meaning of that Act).

(4) The powers conferred by paragraphs 73 and 74 are without prejudice to any power of the Commissioners to provide by tax credit regulations for any amount to be set against another.

PART VII
RECOVERY AND INTEREST

Recovery of levy as debt due

77 Levy shall be recoverable as a debt due to the Crown.

Assessments of amounts of levy due

78— (1) Where it appears to the Commissioners—

(*a*) that any period is an accounting period by reference to which a person is liable to account for levy,

(*b*) that any levy for which that person is liable to account by reference to that period has become due, and

(*c*) that there has been a default by that person that falls within sub-paragraph (2),

they may assess the amount of levy due from that person for that period to the best of their judgement and notify that amount to that person.

[(1A) Where it appears to the Commissioners—

(*a*) that any levy for which a person is liable to account otherwise than by reference to an accounting period has become due, and

(*b*) that there has been a default by that person that falls within sub-paragraph (2),

they may assess the amount of that levy to the best of their judgement and notify it to him.][1]

(2) The defaults falling within this sub-paragraph are—

(*a*) any failure to make a return required to be made by any provision made by or under this Schedule;

(*b*) any failure to keep any documents necessary to verify returns required to be made under any such provision;

(*c*) any failure to afford the facilities necessary to verify returns required to be made under any such provision;

(*d*) the making, in purported compliance with any requirement of any such provision to make a return, of an incomplete or incorrect return;

(*e*) any failure to comply with a requirement imposed by or under Part V of this Schedule (registration).

(3) Where it appears to the Commissioners that a default falling within sub-paragraph (2) is a default by a person on whom the requirement to make a return is imposed in his capacity as the representative of another person, sub-paragraph (1) shall apply as if the reference to the amount of levy due included a reference to any levy due from that other person.

(4) In a case where—

(*a*) the Commissioners have made an assessment for any accounting period as a result of any person's failure to make a return for that period,

(*b*) the levy assessed has been paid but no proper return has been made for that period,

(*c*) as a result of a failure (whether by that person or a representative of his) to make a return for a later accounting period, the Commissioners find it necessary to make another assessment under this paragraph in relation to the later period, and

(*d*) the Commissioners think it appropriate to do so in the light of the absence of a proper return for the earlier period,

they may, in the assessment in relation to the later period, specify an amount of levy due that is greater than the amount that they would have considered to be appropriate had they had regard only to the later period.

(5) Where an amount has been assessed and notified to any person under this paragraph, it shall be recoverable on the basis that it is an amount of levy due from him.

(6) Sub-paragraph (5) does not have effect if, or to the extent that, the assessment in question has been withdrawn or reduced.

Amendments—[1] Sub-para (1A) inserted by FA 2003 s 192(1), (5) with effect from 10 July 2003.

Supplementary assessments

79— (1) If, where an assessment has been notified to any person under paragraph 78 or this paragraph, it appears to the Commissioners that the amount which ought to have been assessed as due for any accounting period exceeds the amount that has already been assessed, the Commissioners may make a supplementary assessment of the amount of the excess and notify that person accordingly.

(2) Where an amount has been assessed and notified to any person under this paragraph it shall be recoverable on the basis that it is an amount of levy due from him.

(3) Sub-paragraph (2) does not have effect if, or to the extent that, the assessment in question has been withdrawn or reduced.

Time limits for assessments

80— (1) An assessment under paragraph 78 or 79 of an amount of levy due for any accounting period—

(*a*) shall not be made more than two years after the end of the accounting period unless it is made within the period mentioned in sub-paragraph (2); and

(*b*) subject to sub-paragraph (3), shall not in any event be made more than three years after the end of that accounting period.

(2) The period referred to in sub-paragraph (1)(*a*) is the period of one year after evidence of facts sufficient in the Commissioners' opinion to justify the making of the assessment first came to their knowledge.

(3) Subject to sub-paragraph (4), where levy has been lost—

(*a*) as a result of any conduct for which a person has been convicted of an offence involving fraud,

(*b*) in circumstances giving rise to liability to a penalty under paragraph 55 (failure to notify of registrability etc), or

(*c*) as a result of conduct falling within paragraph 98(1) (evasion),

that levy may be assessed under paragraph 78 or 79 as if, in sub-paragraph (1)(*b*) above, for "three years" there were substituted "twenty years".

(4) Where, after a person's death, the Commissioners propose to assess an amount of levy as due by reason of some conduct of the deceased—

(*a*) the assessment shall not be made more than three years after the death; and

(*b*) if the circumstances are as set out in sub-paragraph (3)—

(i) the modification of sub-paragraph (1) contained in that sub-paragraph shall not apply; but

(ii) any assessment which (applying that modification) could have been made immediately after the death may be made at any time within three years after it.

(5) Nothing in this paragraph shall prejudice the powers of the Commissioners under paragraph 78(4).

Prospective amendments—In sub-paras (1)(*b*), (4)(*a*) the words "4 years" to be substituted for the words "three years", sub-para (4)(*b*) to be repealed, sub-para (3) to be substituted and sub-para (3A) inserted by FA 2009 s 99, Sch 51 paras 32, 35(1)–(3) with effect from such day as the Treasury may by order made by statutory instrument appoint. Sub-paras (3) and (3A) to read—

"(3) An assessment of an amount due from a person in a case involving a loss of levy—

(*a*) brought about deliberately by the person (or by another person acting on that person's behalf), or

(*b*) attributable to a failure by the person to comply with an obligation under paragraph 53 or 55, may be made at any time not more than 20 years after the end of the accounting period to which it relates (subject to sub-paragraph (4)).

(3A) In sub-paragraph (3)(*a*) the reference to a loss brought about deliberately by the person includes a loss brought about as a result of a deliberate inaccuracy in a document given to Her Majesty's Revenue and Customs by or on behalf of that person."

Ordinary interest on overdue levy paid before assessment

81— (1) Where—

(*a*) the circumstances are such that an assessment could have been made under paragraph 78 or 79 of an amount of levy due from any person, but

(*b*) before such an assessment was made and notified to that person that amount was paid (so that no such assessment was necessary),

the whole of the amount paid shall carry interest for the period specified in sub-paragraph (2).

(2) That period is the period which—

(*a*) begins with the day after that on which the person is required in accordance with regulations under paragraph 41 to pay levy due from him for the accounting period to which the amount paid relates; and

(*b*) ends with the day before that on which the amount is paid.

(3) Interest under this paragraph shall be payable at the rate applicable under section 197 of the Finance Act 1996.

Penalty interest on unpaid levy

82— (1) Where—

(*a*) a person makes a return for the purposes of any regulations made under paragraph 41 (whether or not at the time required by the regulations), and

(*b*) the return shows that an amount of levy is due from him for the accounting period for which the return is made,

that amount shall carry penalty interest for the period specified in sub-paragraph (2).

(2) That period is the period which—

(*a*) begins with the day after that on which the person is required in accordance with regulations under paragraph 41 to pay levy due from him for the accounting period in question; and

(*b*) ends with the day before that on which the amount shown in the return is paid.

Penalty interest on levy where no return made

83— (1) Where—

(*a*) the Commissioners make an assessment under paragraph 78 or 79 of an amount of levy due from any person for any accounting period and notify it to him, and

(*b*) the assessment is made at a time after the time by which a return is required by regulations under paragraph 41 to be made by that person for that accounting period and before any such return has been made,

that amount shall carry penalty interest for the period specified in sub-paragraph (2).

(2) That period is the period which—

(*a*) begins with the day after that on which the person is required in accordance with regulations under paragraph 41 to pay levy due from him for the accounting period in question; and

(*b*) ends with the day before that on which the assessed amount is paid.

(3) Where the person, after the assessment is made, makes for the purposes of any regulations under paragraph 41 a return for the accounting period in question, the assessed amount shall not carry penalty interest under this paragraph to the extent that that amount is shown in the return as an amount of levy due from him for that accounting period (and, accordingly, carries penalty interest under paragraph 82).

Ordinary and penalty interest on under-declared levy

84— (1) Subject to sub-paragraph (4), where—

(*a*) the Commissioners make an assessment under paragraph 78 or 79 of an amount of levy due from any person for any accounting period and notify it to him,

(*b*) the assessment is made after a return for the purposes of any regulations under paragraph 41 has been made by that person for that accounting period, and

(*c*) the assessment is made on the basis that the amount ("the additional amount") is due from him in addition to any amount shown in the return, or in a previous assessment made in relation to the accounting period,

the additional amount shall carry interest for the period specified in sub-paragraph (2).

(2) That period is the period which—

(*a*) begins with the day after that on which the person is required in accordance with regulations under paragraph 41 to pay levy due from him for the accounting period in question; and

(*b*) ends with the day before the day on which the additional amount is paid.

(3) Interest under this paragraph—

(*a*) in respect of so much of the period specified in sub-paragraph (2) as falls before the day on which the assessment is notified to the person in question, shall be payable at the rate applicable under section 197 of the Finance Act 1996 for the purposes of paragraph 81(3); and

(*b*) in respect of the remainder (if any) of that period, shall be penalty interest.

(4) Where—

(*a*) the Commissioners make an assessment under paragraph 78 or 79 of an amount of levy due from any person for any accounting period and notify it to him,

(*b*) they also specify a date for the purposes of this sub-paragraph, and

(*c*) the amount assessed is paid on or before that date,

the only interest carried by that amount under this paragraph shall be interest, at the rate given by sub-paragraph (3)(*a*), for the period before the day on which the assessment is notified.

Penalty interest on unpaid ordinary interest

85— (1) Subject to sub-paragraph (2), where the Commissioners make an assessment under paragraph 88 of an amount of interest payable at the rate given by paragraph 81(3), that amount shall carry penalty interest for the period which—

(*a*) begins with the day on which the assessment is notified to the person on whom the assessment is made; and

(*b*) ends with the day before the day on which the assessed interest is paid.

(2) Where—

(*a*) the Commissioners make an assessment under paragraph 88 of an amount of interest due from any person,

(*b*) they also specify a date for the purposes of this sub-paragraph, and

(*c*) the amount of interest assessed is paid on or before that date,

the amount paid before that date shall not carry penalty interest under this paragraph.

Penalty interest

86— (1) Penalty interest under any of paragraphs 82 to 85 shall be compound interest calculated—

(*a*) at the penalty rate, and

(*b*) with monthly rests.

(2) For this purpose the penalty rate is the rate found by—

(*a*) taking the rate applicable under section 197 of the Finance Act 1996 for the purposes of paragraph 81(3); and

(*b*) adding 10 percentage points to that rate.

(3) Where a person is liable under any of paragraphs 82 to 85 to pay any penalty interest, the Commissioners or, on appeal, an appeal tribunal may reduce the amount payable to such amount (including nil) as they think proper.

(4) Subject to sub-paragraph (5), where the person concerned satisfies the Commissioners or, on appeal, an appeal tribunal that there is a reasonable excuse for the conduct giving rise to the liability to pay penalty interest, that is a matter which (among other things) may be taken into account under sub-paragraph (3).

(5) In determining whether there is a reasonable excuse for the purposes of sub-paragraph (4), no account shall be taken of any of the following matters, that is to say—

(*a*) the insufficiency of the funds available to any person for paying any levy due or for paying the amount of the interest;

(*b*) the fact that there has, in the case in question or in that case taken with any other cases, been no or no significant loss of levy;

(*c*) the fact that the person liable to pay the interest or a person acting on his behalf has acted in good faith.

(6) In the case of interest reduced by the Commissioners under sub-paragraph (3) an appeal tribunal, on an appeal relating to the interest, may cancel the whole or any part of the reduction made by the Commissioners.

Supplemental provisions about interest

87— (1) Interest under any of paragraphs 81 to 85 shall be paid without any deduction of income tax.

(2) Sub-paragraph (3) applies where—

(*a*) an amount carries interest under any of paragraphs 81 to 85 (or would do so apart from that sub-paragraph); and

(*b*) all or part of the amount turns out not to be due.

(3) In such a case—

(*a*) the amount or part that turns out not to be due shall not carry interest under the applicable paragraph and shall be treated as never having done so; and

(*b*) all such adjustments as are reasonable shall be made, including (subject to paragraphs 64 to 76) adjustments by way of repayment.

Assessments to interest

88— (1) Where a person is liable for interest under any of paragraphs 81 to 85, the Commissioners may assess the amount due by way of interest and notify it to him accordingly.

(2) If, where an assessment has been notified to any person under sub-paragraph (1) or this sub-paragraph, it appears to the Commissioners that the amount which ought to have been assessed exceeds the amount that has already been assessed, the Commissioners may make a supplementary assessment of the amount of the excess and shall notify that person accordingly.

(3) Where an amount has been assessed and notified to any person under this paragraph, it shall be recoverable as if it were levy due from him.

(4) Sub-paragraph (3)—

(*a*) shall not apply so as to require any interest to be payable on interest except—

(i) in accordance with paragraph 85, or

(ii) in so far as it falls to be compounded in accordance with paragraph 86;

and

(*b*) shall not have effect if, or to the extent that, the assessment in question has been withdrawn or reduced.

(5) Paragraph 80 shall apply in relation to assessments under this paragraph as if any assessment to interest were an assessment under paragraph 78 to levy due for the period which is the relevant accounting period in relation to that interest.

(6) Subject to sub-paragraph (7), where a person—

(*a*) is assessed under this paragraph to an amount due by way of any interest, and

(*b*) is also assessed under paragraph 78 or 79 for the accounting period which is the relevant accounting period in relation to that interest,

the assessments may be combined and notified to him as one assessment.

(7) A notice of a combined assessment under sub-paragraph (6) must separately identify the interest being assessed.

(8) The relevant accounting period for the purposes of this paragraph is—

(*a*) in the case of interest on levy due for any accounting period, that accounting period; and

(*b*) in the case of interest on interest (whether under paragraph 85 or by virtue of any compounding under paragraph 86), the period which is the relevant accounting period for the interest on which the interest is payable.

(9) In a case where—

(*a*) the amount of any interest falls to be calculated by reference to levy which was not paid at the time when it should have been, and

(*b*) that levy cannot be readily attributed to any one or more accounting periods,

that levy shall be treated for the purposes of interest on any of that levy as levy due for such period or periods as the Commissioners may determine to the best of their judgement and notify to the person liable.

Further assessments to penalty interest

89— (1) Where an assessment is made under paragraph 88 to an amount of penalty interest under any of paragraphs 82 to 85—

(*a*) the notice of assessment shall specify a date, not later than the date of the notice of assessment, to which the amount of interest which is assessed is calculated; and

(*b*) if the interest continues to accrue after that date, a further assessment or further assessments may be made under paragraph 88 in respect of the amounts so accruing.

(2) Where—

(*a*) an assessment to penalty interest is made specifying a date for the purposes of sub-paragraph (1)(*a*), and

(*b*) within such period as may for the purposes of this sub-paragraph have been notified by the Commissioners to the person liable for the interest, the amount on which the interest is payable is paid,

that amount shall be deemed for the purposes of any further liability to interest to have been paid on the specified date.

Prospective amendment—Para 89A to be inserted by the Tribunals, Courts and Enforcement Act 2007 s 62(3), Sch 13 paras 135, 136, with effect from a date to be appointed. Para 89A to be repealed by FA 2008 s 129, Sch 43 para 7 with effect from such day as the Commissioners may by statutory instrument appoint.

Para 89A to read—

"**Controlled goods agreements**

89A—(1) This paragraph applies where an enforcement agent acting under the power conferred by section 51(A1) of the Finance Act 1997 (power to use the procedure in Schedule 12 to the Tribunals, Courts and Enforcement Act 2007) has entered into a controlled goods agreement with the person against whom the power is exercisable ("the person in default").

(2) In this paragraph, "controlled goods agreement" has the meaning given by paragraph 13(4) of that Schedule.

(3) Subject to sub-paragraph (4), if the person in default removes or disposes of goods (or permits their removal or disposal) in breach of the controlled goods agreement, he is liable to a penalty equal to half of the levy or other amount recoverable under section 51(A1) of the Finance Act 1997.

(4) The person in default shall not be liable to a penalty under subparagraph (3) above if he satisfies the Commissioners or, on appeal, an appeal tribunal, that there is a reasonable excuse for the breach in question.

(5) This paragraph extends only to England and Wales.".

Walking possession agreements

90— (1) This paragraph applies where—

(*a*) in accordance with regulations under section 51 of the Finance Act 1997 (enforcement by distress), a distress is authorised to be levied on the goods and chattels of a person ("the person in default") who has refused or neglected to pay an amount of levy due from him or an amount recoverable from him as if it were levy; and

(*b*) the person levying the distress and the person in default have entered into a walking possession agreement.

(2) For the purposes of this paragraph a walking possession agreement is an agreement under which, in consideration of the property distrained upon being allowed to remain in the custody of the person in default and of the delaying of its sale, the person in default—

(*a*) acknowledges that the property specified in the agreement is under distraint and held in walking possession; and

(*b*) undertakes that, except with the consent of the Commissioners and subject to such conditions as they may impose, he will not remove or allow the removal of any of the specified property from the premises named in the agreement.

(3) Subject to sub-paragraph (4), if the person in default is in breach of the undertaking contained in a walking possession agreement, he shall be liable to a penalty equal to one half of the levy or other amount referred to in sub-paragraph (1)(*a*).

(4) The person in default shall not be liable to a penalty under sub-paragraph (3) if he satisfies the Commissioners or, on appeal, an appeal tribunal that there is a reasonable excuse for the breach in question.

(5) This paragraph does not extend to Scotland.

Prospective amendments—Sub-para (5) to be substituted by the Tribunals, Courts and Enforcement Act 2007 s 62(3), Sch 13 paras 135, 137, with effect from a date to be appointed. Sub-para (5) as substituted, to read—

"(5) This paragraph extends only to Northern Ireland.".

Interpretation etc of Part VII

91— (1) In this Part of this Schedule "penalty interest" shall be construed in accordance with paragraph 86.

(2) Any notification of an assessment under any provision of this Part of this Schedule to a person's representative shall be treated for the purposes of this Schedule as notification to the person in relation to whom the representative acts.

(3) In this Part of this Schedule "representative", in relation to any person, means—

(*a*) any of that person's personal representatives;

(*b*) that person's trustee in bankruptcy or liquidator;

(*c*) any person holding office as a receiver in relation to that person or any of his property;

(*d*) that person's tax representative or any other person for the time being acting in a representative capacity in relation to that person.

(4) In this paragraph "trustee in bankruptcy" includes, as respects Scotland—

(*a*) an interim or permanent trustee (within the meaning of the Bankruptcy (Scotland) Act 1985); and

(*b*) a trustee acting under a trust deed (within the meaning of that Act).

[(5) In relation to cases where, by virtue of regulations under paragraph 41(1)(*a*)(ii) [or by virtue of paragraph 45B(8)][2], a person is liable to account for levy otherwise than by reference to accounting periods, this Part of this Schedule shall have effect as if—

(*a*) references to levy due for "an" or "any" accounting period were references simply to levy due;

(*b*) references to levy due for a specified accounting period were references to the levy in question;

(*c*) references to an assessment for a specified accounting period were references to an assessment in respect of the levy in question;

(*d*) any time limit framed by reference to the end of the accounting period for which levy is due were framed by reference to the date on which payment of the levy is due;

(*e*) references to the making of a return for an accounting period were references to the payment of the levy in question;

(*f*) references to the amount shown in such a return were references to the amount of levy paid;

(*g*) paragraph 88(8) and (9) were omitted.][1]

Amendments—[1] Sub-para (5) inserted by FA 2003 s 192(1), (6) with effect from 10 July 2003.

[2] Words in sub-para (5) inserted by FA 2009 s 118, Sch 59 paras 2, 8 with effect where the certification period begins on or after 1 April 2009.

PART VIII

EVASION, MISDECLARATION AND NEGLECT

Criminal offences: Evasion

92— (1) A person is guilty of an offence if he is knowingly concerned in, or in the taking of steps with a view to—

(*a*) the fraudulent evasion by that person of any levy with which he is charged; or (*b*) the fraudulent evasion by any other person of any levy with which that other person is charged.

(2) The references in sub-paragraph (1) to the evasion of levy include references to obtaining, in circumstances where there is no entitlement to it, either a tax credit or a repayment of levy.

(3) A person guilty of an offence under this paragraph shall be liable (subject to sub-paragraph (4))—

(*a*) on summary conviction, to a penalty of the statutory maximum or to imprisonment for a term not exceeding six months, or to both;

(*b*) on conviction on indictment, to a penalty of any amount or to imprisonment for a term not exceeding seven years, or to both.

(4) In the case of any offence under this paragraph, where the statutory maximum is less than three times the sum of the amounts of levy which are shown to be amounts that were or were intended to be evaded, the penalty on summary conviction shall be the amount equal to three times that sum (instead of the statutory maximum).

(5) For the purposes of sub-paragraph (4) the amounts of levy that were or were intended to be evaded shall be taken to include—

(*a*) the amount of any tax credit, and

(*b*) the amount of any repayment of levy,

which was, or was intended to be, obtained in circumstances where there was no entitlement to it.

(6) In determining for the purposes of sub-paragraph (4) how much levy (in addition to any amount falling within sub-paragraph (5)) was or was intended to be evaded, no account shall be taken of the extent (if any) to which any liability to levy of any person fell, or would have fallen, to be reduced by the amount of any tax credit or repayment of levy to which he was, or would have been, entitled.

Criminal offences: Misstatements

93— (1) A person is guilty of an offence if, with the requisite intent and for purposes connected with the levy—

(*a*) he produces or provides, or causes to be produced or provided, any document which is false in a material particular, or

(*b*) he otherwise makes use of such a document;

and in this sub-paragraph "the requisite intent" means the intent to deceive any person or to secure that a machine will respond to the document as if it were a true document.

(2) A person is guilty of an offence if, in providing any information under any provision made by or under this Schedule—

(*a*) he makes a statement which he knows to be false in a material particular; or

(*b*) he recklessly makes a statement which is false in a material particular.

(3) A person guilty of an offence under this paragraph shall be liable (subject to sub-paragraph (4))—

(*a*) on summary conviction, to a penalty of the statutory maximum or to imprisonment for a term not exceeding six months, or to both;

(*b*) on conviction on indictment, to a penalty of any amount or to imprisonment for a term not exceeding seven years, or to both.

(4) In the case of any offence under this paragraph, where—

(*a*) the document referred to in sub-paragraph (1) is a return [or other notification][1] required under any provision made by or under this Schedule, or

(*b*) the information referred to in sub-paragraph (2) is contained in or otherwise relevant to such a return [or notification][1],

the amount of the penalty on summary conviction shall be whichever is the greater of the statutory maximum and the amount equal to three times the sum of the amounts (if any) by which the return [or notification][1] understates any person's liability to levy.

(5) In sub-paragraph (4) the reference to the amount by which any person's liability to levy is understated shall be taken to be equal to the sum of—

(*a*) the amount (if any) by which his gross liability was understated; and

(*b*) the amount (if any) by which any entitlements of his to tax credits and repayments of levy were overstated.

(6) In sub-paragraph (5) "gross liability" means liability to levy before any deduction is made in respect of any entitlement to any tax credit or repayments of levy.

Amendments—[1] Words in sub-para (4) inserted by FA 2003 s 191(1), (7) with effect from 10 July 2003.

Criminal offences: Conduct involving evasions or misstatements

94— (1) A person is guilty of an offence under this paragraph if his conduct during any particular period must have involved the commission by him of one or more offences under the preceding provisions of this Part of this Schedule.

(2) For the purposes of any proceedings for an offence under this paragraph it shall be immaterial whether the particulars of the offence or offences that must have been committed are known.

(3) A person guilty of an offence under this paragraph shall be liable (subject to sub-paragraph (4))—

(*a*) on summary conviction, to a penalty of the statutory maximum or to imprisonment for a term not exceeding six months, or to both;

(*b*) on conviction on indictment, to a penalty of any amount or to imprisonment for a term not exceeding seven years, or to both.

(4) In the case of any offence under this paragraph, where the statutory maximum is less than three times the sum of the amounts of levy which are shown to be amounts that were or were intended to be evaded by the conduct in question, the penalty on summary conviction shall be the amount equal to three times that sum (instead of the statutory maximum).

(5) For the purposes of sub-paragraph (4) the amounts of levy that were or were intended to be evaded by any conduct shall be taken to include—

(*a*) the amount of any tax credit, and

(*b*) the amount of any repayment of levy,

which was, or was intended to be, obtained in circumstances where there was no entitlement to it.

(6) In determining for the purposes of sub-paragraph (4) how much levy (in addition to any amount falling within sub-paragraph (5)) was or was intended to be evaded, no account shall be taken of the extent (if any) to which any liability to levy of any person fell, or would have fallen, to be reduced by the amount of any tax credit or repayments of levy to which he was, or would have been, entitled.

Criminal offences: Preparations for evasion

95— (1) Where a person—

(*a*) becomes a party to any agreement under or by means of which a supply of a taxable commodity is or is to be made, or

(*b*) makes arrangements for any other person to become a party to such an agreement,

he is guilty of an offence if he does so in the belief that levy chargeable on the supply will be evaded.

(2) Subject to sub-paragraph (3), a person guilty of an offence under this paragraph shall be liable, on summary conviction, to a penalty of level 5 on the standard scale.

(3) In the case of any offence under this paragraph, where level 5 on the standard scale is less than three times the sum of the amounts of levy which are shown to be amounts that were or were intended to be evaded in respect of the supply in question, the penalty shall be the amount equal to three times that sum (instead of level 5 on the standard scale).

(4) For the purposes of sub-paragraph (3) the amounts of levy that were or were intended to be evaded shall be taken to include—

(*a*) the amount of any tax credit, and

(*b*) the amount of any repayment of levy,

which was, or was intended to be, obtained in circumstances where there was no entitlement to it.

(5) In determining for the purposes of sub-paragraph (3) how much levy (in addition to any amount falling within sub-paragraph (4)) was or was intended to be evaded, no account shall be taken of the extent (if any) to which any liability to levy of any person fell, or would have fallen, to be reduced by the amount of any tax credit or repayments of levy to which he was, or would have been, entitled.

Offences under paragraphs 92 to 95: procedural matters

96 Sections 145 to 155 of the Customs and Excise Management Act 1979 (proceedings for offences, mitigation of penalties and certain other matters) shall apply in relation to offences and penalties under paragraphs 92 to 95 as they apply in relation to offences and penalties under the customs and excise Acts.

Arrest for offences under paragraphs 92 to 94

97— (1) Where an authorised person has reasonable grounds for suspecting that a fraud offence has been committed he may arrest anyone whom he has reasonable grounds for suspecting to be guilty of the offence.

(2) In this paragraph—

"authorised person" means any person acting under the authority of the Commissioners; and "a fraud offence" means an offence under any of paragraphs 92 to 94.[1]

Amendments—[1] This para repealed by FA 2007 ss 84, 114, Sch 22 paras 3, 11(*a*), Sch 27 Pt 5(1) with effect from 1 December 2007 (by virtue of SI 2007/3166 art 3(*a*)).

Civil penalties: Evasion

98— (1) Subject to sub-paragraph (5), where—

(a) any person engages in any conduct for the purpose of evading levy, and

(b) that conduct involves dishonesty (whether or not it is such as to give rise to criminal liability),

that person shall be liable to a penalty.

(2) The amount of the penalty shall be—

(a) equal to the amount of levy evaded, or (as the case may be) intended to be evaded, by the person's conduct if at the time of engaging in that conduct he was or was required to be registered for the purposes of the levy;

(b) equal to twice that amount if at that time the person neither was nor was required to be registered for those purposes.

(3) The references in sub-paragraph (1) to evading levy include references to obtaining, in circumstances where there is no entitlement to it, either—

(a) a tax credit; or

(b) a repayment of levy.

(4) For the purposes of sub-paragraph (2) the amount of levy that was or was intended to be evaded by any conduct shall be taken to include—

(a) the amount of any tax credit, and

(b) the amount of any repayment of levy,

which was, or was intended to be, obtained in circumstances where there was no entitlement to it.

(5) In determining for the purposes of sub-paragraph (2) how much levy (in addition to any amount falling within sub-paragraph (4)) was or was intended to be evaded, no account shall be taken of the extent (if any) to which any liability to levy of any person fell, or would have fallen, to be reduced by the amount of any tax credit or repayments of levy to which he was, or would have been, entitled.

(6) Where, by reason of conduct falling within sub-paragraph (1), a person is convicted of an offence (whether under this Act or otherwise) that person shall not by reason of that conduct be liable also to a penalty under this paragraph.[1]

Amendments—[1] Para 98 repealed by FA 2008 s 122, Sch 40 para 21(*h*) with effect from 1 April 2009 (by virtue of SI 2009/571 art 2).

This para repealed only in so far as it relates to conduct involving dishonesty which relates to—

(a) an inaccuracy in a document, or

(b) a failure to notify HMRC of an under-assessment by HMRC (SI 2009/571 art 6).

Liability of directors etc for penalties under paragraph 98

99— (1) Where it appears to the Commissioners—

(a) that a body corporate is liable to a penalty under paragraph 98, and

(b) that the conduct giving rise to that penalty is, in whole or in part, attributable to the dishonesty of a person who is, or at the material time was, a director or managing officer of the body corporate (a "named officer"),

the Commissioners may serve a notice under this paragraph on the body corporate and on the named officer.

(2) A notice under this paragraph shall state—

(a) the amount of the penalty referred to in sub-paragraph (1)(a) ("the basic penalty"), and

(b) that the Commissioners propose, in accordance with this paragraph, to recover from the named officer such portion of the basic penalty (which may be the whole of it) as is specified in the notice.

(3) Where a notice is served under this paragraph, the portion of the basic penalty specified in the notice shall be recoverable from the named officer as if he were personally liable under paragraph 98 to a penalty which corresponds to that portion.

(4) Where a notice is served under this paragraph—

(a) the amount which may be assessed under Part IX of this Schedule as the amount due by way of penalty from the body corporate shall be only so much (if any) of the basic penalty as is not assessed on and notified to a named officer; and

(b) the body corporate shall be treated as discharged from liability for so much of the basic penalty as is so assessed and notified.

(5) Subject to the following provisions of this paragraph, the giving of a notice under this paragraph as such shall not be a decision which may be [appealed][2] *under paragraph 121.*

(6) Where a body corporate is assessed as mentioned in sub-paragraph (4)(a), the decisions of the Commissioners that may be [appealed][2] *in accordance with paragraph 121 shall include their decision—*

(a) as to the liability of the body corporate to a penalty, and

(b) as to the amount of the basic penalty that is specified in the assessment;

and paragraphs [121A to 123][2] *shall apply accordingly.*

(7) Where an assessment is made on a named officer by virtue of this paragraph, the decisions which may be [appealed][2] *under paragraph 121 at the request of the named officer shall include—*

(a) the Commissioners' decisions in the case of the body corporate as to the matters mentioned in sub-paragraph (6)(a) and (b);

(b) their decision that the conduct of the body corporate referred to in sub-paragraph (1)(b) is, in whole or in part, attributable to the dishonesty of the named officer; and

(c) their decision as to the portion of the penalty which the Commissioners propose to recover from him;

and paragraphs [121A to 123][2] *shall apply accordingly.*

(8) In this paragraph a "managing officer", in relation to a body corporate, means—

(a) any manager, secretary or other similar officer of the body corporate; or

(b) any person purporting to act in any such capacity or as a director.

(9) Where the affairs of a body corporate are managed by its members, this paragraph shall apply in relation to the conduct of a member in connection with his functions of management as if he were a director of the body corporate.[1]

Amendments—[1] Para 99 repealed by FA 2008 s 122, Sch 40 para 21(*h*) with effect from 1 April 2009 (by virtue of SI 2009/571 art 2).

This para repealed only in so far as it relates to conduct involving dishonesty which relates to—

(a) an inaccuracy in a document, or

(b) a failure to notify HMRC of an under-assessment by HMRC (SI 2009/571 art 6).

[2] Insofar as this para continues to apply, word substituted for the word "reviewed" in sub-paras (5), (6), (7); words substituted for the words "122 and 123" in sub-paras (6), (7).

Civil penalties: Misdeclaration or neglect

100— (1) Subject to sub-paragraphs (3) to (5), where …[1]*—*

(a) a return [or other notification][1] *is made which understates a person's liability to levy or overstates his entitlement to any tax credit or repayment of levy, or*

(b) at the end of the period of 30 days beginning on the date of the making of any assessment which understates a person's liability to levy, that person has not taken all such steps as are reasonable to draw the understatement to the attention of the Commissioners,

the person concerned shall be liable to a penalty equal to 5 per cent of the amount of the understatement of liability or (as the case may be) overstatement of entitlement.

(2) Where—

(a) a return for an accounting period—

(i) overstates or understates to any extent a person's liability to levy, or

(ii) understates or overstates to any extent his entitlement to any tax credits or repayments of levy,

and

(b) that return is corrected—

(i) in such circumstances as may be prescribed, and

(ii) in accordance with such conditions as may be prescribed,

by a return for a later accounting period which understates or overstates, to the corresponding extent, any liability or entitlement for the later period,

it shall be assumed for the purposes of this paragraph that the statement made by each such return is a correct statement for the accounting period to which the return relates.

(3) Conduct falling within sub-paragraph (1) shall not give rise to liability to a penalty under this paragraph if the person concerned provides the Commissioners with full information with respect to the inaccuracy concerned—

(a) at a time when he has no reason to believe that enquiries are being made by the Commissioners into his affairs, so far as they relate to the levy; and

(b) in such form and manner as may be prescribed by regulations made by the Commissioners or specified by them in accordance with any such regulations.

(4) Conduct falling within sub-paragraph (1) shall not give rise to liability to a penalty under this paragraph if the person concerned satisfies the Commissioners or, on appeal, an appeal tribunal that there is a reasonable excuse for his conduct.

(5) Where, by reason of conduct falling within sub-paragraph (1)—

(a) a person is convicted of an offence (whether under this Act or otherwise), or

(b) a person is assessed to a penalty under paragraph 98,

that person shall not by reason of that conduct be liable also to a penalty under this paragraph.[2]

Amendments—[1] Words "for an accounting period" in sub-para (1) repealed, and words in sub-para (1)(*a*) inserted, by FA 2003 ss 192(1), (8), 216, Sch 43 Pt 4 with effect from 10 July 2003.

[2] Para 100 repealed by FA 2008 s 122, Sch 40 para 21(*h*) with effect from 1 April 2009 (by virtue of SI 2009/571 art 2).

[Civil penalties: incorrect certificates][3]

101— (1) …[3]

(2) Where—

(*a*) a person gives, in relation to any supply (or supplies) of a taxable commodity (or taxable commodities) being made to him, to the supplier a certificate that the supply (or supplies) is (or are) to any extent—

(i) for domestic or charity use,
(ii) exempt under any of paragraphs [11,][3] 12, 13, 14, [15, 18 [, 18A][2] and 21][1] [or][4]
(iii) *a half-rate supply (or half-rate supplies)[, or*[4]
(iv) a reduced-rate supply (or reduced-rate supplies),][1] and

(*b*) the certificate is [(or becomes)][3] incorrect,

the person shall be liable to a penalty.

(3) The amount of the penalty to which a person is liable under [this paragraph][3] shall be equal to 105 per cent of the difference between—

(*a*) the amount of levy (which may be nil) that would have been chargeable on the supply (or supplies) if the …[3] certificate had been correct, and

(*b*) the amount of levy actually chargeable.

(4) The giving of a [certificate (or not revoking or varying it)][3] shall not give rise to a penalty under this paragraph if [the person concerned][3] satisfies the Commissioners or, on appeal, an appeal tribunal that [the person has a reasonable excuse][3].

(5) Where by reason of giving a [certificate (or not revoking or varying it)][3]—

(*a*) a person is convicted of an offence (whether under this Act or otherwise), or

(*b*) a person is assessed to a penalty under paragraph 98,

that person shall not by reason of [that][3] be liable also to a penalty under this paragraph.

Amendments—[1] Words in sub-para (2)(*a*)(ii) substituted for the words "18 and 21, or", and words in sub-para (2)(*a*) (iii) and (iv) inserted, by FA 2002 s 127 in relation to certificates given in respect of any supplies made after 23 April 2002.

[2] Words in sub-para (2)(*a*)(ii) inserted by FA 2003 s 188(2)(*b*) with effect from 10 July 2003.

[3] Sub-para (1) repealed; words in sub-para (2) inserted; in sub-para (3), words "notification or" repealed; words in sub-paras (3), (4), (5) substituted; and Heading substituted, by FA 2007 ss 23, 114, Sch 2 paras 1, 12, Sch 27 Pt 1(1) with effect from 19 July 2007.

Sub-para (1) previously read as follows—

"Where—

(*a*) a person gives a notification for the purposes of paragraph 11 in relation to any supply (or supplies) of a taxable commodity (or taxable commodities), and

(*b*) the notification is incorrect,

the person shall be liable to a penalty."

Words substituted in sub-para (3) previously read as follows—

"sub-paragraph (1) or (2)".

Words substituted in sub-para (4) previously read as follows—

"notification or certificate", "the person who gave it", and "there is a reasonable excuse for his having given it".

Words substituted in sub-para (5) previously read as follows—

"notification or certificate", and "the giving of the notification or certificate".

Heading previously read as follows—

"Civil penalties: Incorrect notifications etc".

[4] In sub-para (2)(*a*)(ii) word inserted, and sub-para (2)(*a*)(iii) repealed, by FA 2006 ss 172(14), 178, Sch 26 Pt 8(1) with effect from 1 November 2007: SI 2007/2901 art 2(1).

These amendments do not apply in relation to a half-rate supply made before 1 April 2006: SI 2007/2901 art 2(2). For this purpose, "half-rate supply" carries the meaning it has in this Schedule before 1 November 2007. FA 2006 s 172(3) (6) applies for determining when a supply is to be regarded as made: SI 2007/2901 art 2(3).

Interpretation of Part VIII

102— (1) References in this Part of this Schedule to obtaining a tax credit are references to bringing an amount into account as a tax credit for the purposes of levy on the basis that that amount is an amount which may be so brought into account in accordance with tax credit regulations.

(2) References in this Part of this Schedule to obtaining a repayment of levy are references to obtaining either—

(*a*) the payment or repayment of any amount, or

(*b*) the acknowledgement of a right to receive any amount,

on the basis that that amount is the amount of a repayment of levy to which there is an entitlement.

PART IX

CIVIL PENALTIES

Preliminary

103— (1) In this Part of this Schedule "civil penalty" means any penalty liability to which—

(*a*) is imposed by or under this Schedule, and

(*b*) arises otherwise than in consequence of a person's conviction for a criminal offence.

(2) In this Part of this Schedule—

(*a*) references to a person's being liable to a civil penalty include references to his being a person from whom the whole or any part of a civil penalty is recoverable by virtue of paragraph 99; and

(*b*) references, in relation to a person from whom the whole or any part of a civil penalty is so recoverable, to the penalty to which he is liable are references to so much of the penalty as is recoverable from him.

(3) Any notification of an assessment under any provision of this Part of this Schedule to a person's representative shall be treated for the purposes of this Schedule as notification to the person in relation to whom the representative acts.

(4) In this paragraph "representative", in relation to any person, means—

(*a*) any of that person's personal representatives;

(*b*) that person's trustee in bankruptcy or liquidator;

(*c*) any person holding office as a receiver in relation to that person or any of his property;

(*d*) that person's tax representative or any other person for the time being acting in a representative capacity in relation to that person.

(5) In this paragraph "trustee in bankruptcy" includes, as respects Scotland—

(*a*) an interim or permanent trustee (within the meaning of the Bankruptcy (Scotland) Act 1985); and

(*b*) a trustee acting under a trust deed (within the meaning of that Act).

Reduction of penalties

104— (1) Where a person is liable to a civil penalty—

(*a*) the Commissioners or, on appeal, an appeal tribunal may reduce the penalty to such amount (including nil) as they think proper; but

(*b*) on an appeal relating to any penalty reduced by the Commissioners, an appeal tribunal may cancel the whole or any part of the Commissioners' reduction.

(2) In determining whether a civil penalty should be, or should have been, reduced under sub-paragraph (1), no account shall be taken of any of the following matters, that is to say—

(*a*) the insufficiency of the funds available to any person for paying any levy due or for paying the amount of the penalty;

(*b*) the fact that there has, in the case in question or in that case taken with any other cases, been no or no significant loss of levy;

(*c*) the fact that the person liable to the penalty or a person acting on his behalf has acted in good faith.

Matters not amounting to reasonable excuse

105 For the purposes of any provision made by or under this Schedule under which liability to a civil penalty does not arise in respect of conduct for which there is shown to be a reasonable excuse—

(*a*) an insufficiency of funds available for paying any amount is not a reasonable excuse; and

(*b*) where reliance has been placed on any other person to perform any task, neither the fact of that reliance nor any conduct of the person relied upon is a reasonable excuse.

Assessments to penalties etc

106— (1) Where a person is liable to a civil penalty, the Commissioners may assess the amount due by way of penalty and notify it to him accordingly.

(2) If, where an assessment has been notified to any person under sub-paragraph (1) or this sub-paragraph, it appears to the Commissioners that the amount which ought to have been assessed exceeds the amount that has already been assessed, the Commissioners may make a supplementary assessment of the amount of the excess and shall notify that person accordingly.

(3) The fact that any conduct giving rise to a civil penalty may have ceased before an assessment is made under this paragraph shall not affect the power of the Commissioners to make such an assessment.

(4) Where an amount has been assessed and notified to any person under this paragraph, it shall be recoverable as if it were levy due from him.

(5) Sub-paragraph (4)—

(*a*) shall not apply so as to require any interest to be payable on a penalty otherwise than in accordance with this Part of this Schedule; and

(*b*) shall not have effect if, or to the extent that, the assessment in question has been withdrawn or reduced.

(6) Subject to sub-paragraph (7), where a person—

(*a*) is assessed under this paragraph to an amount due by way of a penalty, and

(*b*) is also assessed under any one or more provisions of Part VII of this Schedule for an accounting period to which the conduct attracting the penalty is referable,

the assessments may be combined and notified to him as one assessment.

(7) A notice of a combined assessment under sub-paragraph (6) must separately identify the penalty being assessed.

(8) The power to make an assessment under this paragraph is subject to paragraph 99(4).

Further assessments to daily penalties

107— (1) This paragraph applies where an assessment is made under paragraph 106 to an amount of a civil penalty to which any person is liable—

(*a*) under paragraph 124(3) (failure to provide information); or
(*b*) under paragraph 127(4) (failure to produce a document).

(2) The notice of assessment shall specify a time, not later than the end of the day of the giving of the notice of assessment, to which the amount of any daily penalty is calculated.

(3) For the purposes of sub-paragraph (2) "daily penalty" means—

(*a*) in a case within sub-paragraph (1)(*a*), a penalty imposed by virtue of paragraph 124(3)(*b*); and
(*b*) in a case within sub-paragraph (1)(*b*), a penalty imposed by virtue of paragraph 127(4)(*b*).

(4) If further penalties accrue in respect of a continuing failure after that date to provide the information or, as the case may be, produce the document, a further assessment or further assessments may be made under paragraph 106 in respect of the amounts so accruing.

(5) Where—

(*a*) an assessment to a civil penalty is made specifying a date for the purposes of sub-paragraph (2), and
(*b*) the failure in question is remedied within such period as may for the purposes of this sub-paragraph have been notified by the Commissioners to the person liable for the penalty,

the failure shall be deemed for the purposes of any further liability to civil penalties to have been remedied on the specified date.

Time limits on penalty assessments

108— (1) Subject to sub-paragraphs (2) and (3), an assessment under paragraph 106 to a penalty shall not be made more than three years after the conduct to which the penalty relates.

(2) Subject to sub-paragraph (3), if levy has been lost—

(*a*) as a result of any conduct for which a person has been convicted of an offence involving fraud,
(*b*) in circumstances giving rise to liability to a penalty under paragraph 55 (failure to notify of registrability etc), or
(*c*) as a result of conduct falling within paragraph 98(1) (evasion),

an assessment may be made for any civil penalty relating to that conduct as if, in sub-paragraph (1), for "three years" there were substituted "twenty years".

(3) Where, after a person's death, the Commissioners propose to assess an amount of a civil penalty due by reason of some conduct of the deceased—

(*a*) the assessment shall not be made more than three years after the death; and
(*b*) if the circumstances are as set out in sub-paragraph (2)—

(i) the modification of sub-paragraph (1) contained in that sub-paragraph shall not apply; but
(ii) any assessment which (applying that modification) could have been made immediately after the death may be made at any time within three years after it.

Prospective amendments—In sub-paras (1), (2) the words "4 years" to be substituted for the words "three years", sub-para (2) to be substituted and sub-para (2A) to be inserted, by FA 2009 s 99, Sch 51 para 36(1)–(4), with effect from such day as the Treasury may by order made by statutory instrument appoint. Sub-paras (2) and (2A) to read as follows:

"(2) An assessment of a person to a penalty in a case involving a loss of levy—

(*a*) brought about deliberately by the person (or by another person acting on that person's behalf), or
(*b*) attributable to a failure by the person to comply with an obligation under paragraph 53 or 55,may be made at any time not more than 20 years after the conduct to which the penalty relates (subject to sub-paragraph (3)).

(2A) In sub-paragraph (2)(*a*) the reference to a loss brought about deliberately by the person includes a loss brought about as a result of a deliberate inaccuracy in a document given to Her Majesty's Revenue and Customs by or on behalf of that person."

Penalty interest on unpaid penalties

109— (1) Subject to sub-paragraph (2), where the Commissioners make an assessment under paragraph 106 of any civil penalty to which a person is liable the amount of that penalty shall carry penalty interest for the period which—

(*a*) begins with the day on which the assessment is notified to the person on whom the assessment is made; and
(*b*) ends with the day before the day on which the assessed penalty is paid.

(2) Where—

(*a*) the Commissioners make an assessment under paragraph 106 of an amount of any civil penalty to which any person is liable,
(*b*) they also specify a date for the purposes of this sub-paragraph, and
(*c*) the amount of the penalty assessed is paid on or before that date,

the amount paid before that date shall not carry penalty interest under this paragraph.

(3) Penalty interest under this paragraph shall be compound interest calculated—

(*a*) at the penalty rate, and
(*b*) with monthly rests.

(4) For this purpose the penalty rate is the rate found by—

(*a*) taking the rate applicable under section 197 of the Finance Act 1996 for the purposes of paragraph 81(3); and

(*b*) adding 10 percentage points to that rate.

(5) Where a person is liable under this paragraph to pay any penalty interest, the Commissioners or, on appeal, an appeal tribunal may reduce the amount payable to such amount (including nil) as they think proper.

(6) Subject to sub-paragraph (7), where the person concerned satisfies the Commissioners or, on appeal, an appeal tribunal that there is a reasonable excuse for the conduct giving rise to the liability to pay penalty interest, that is a matter which (among other things) may be taken into account under sub-paragraph (5).

(7) In determining whether there is a reasonable excuse for the purposes of sub-paragraph (6), no account shall be taken of any of the following matters, that is to say—

(*a*) the insufficiency of the funds available to any person for paying any levy or penalty due or for paying the amount of the interest;

(*b*) the fact that there has, in the case in question or in that case taken with any other cases, been no or no significant loss of levy;

(*c*) the fact that the person liable to pay the interest or a person acting on his behalf has acted in good faith.

(8) In the case of interest reduced by the Commissioners under sub-paragraph (5), an appeal tribunal, on an appeal relating to the interest, may cancel the whole or any part of the reduction made by the Commissioners.

Supplemental provisions about interest

110— (1) Interest under paragraph 109 shall be paid without any deduction of income tax.

(2) Sub-paragraph (3) applies where—

(*a*) an amount carries interest under paragraph 109 (or would do so apart from that sub-paragraph); and

(*b*) all or part of the amount turns out not to be due.

(3) In such a case—

(*a*) the amount or part that turns out not to be due shall not carry interest under paragraph 109 and shall be treated as never having done so; and

(*b*) all such adjustments as are reasonable shall be made, including (subject to paragraphs 64 to 76) adjustments by way of repayment.

Assessments to penalty interest on unpaid penalties

111— (1) Where a person is liable for interest under paragraph 109, the Commissioners may assess the amount due by way of interest and notify it to him accordingly.

(2) If, where an assessment has been notified to any person under sub-paragraph (1) or this sub-paragraph, it appears to the Commissioners that the amount which ought to have been assessed exceeds the amount that has already been assessed, the Commissioners may make a supplementary assessment of the amount of the excess and notify that person accordingly.

(3) Where an amount has been assessed and notified to any person under this paragraph, it shall be recoverable as if it were levy due from him.

(4) Sub-paragraph (3)—

(*a*) shall not apply so as to require any interest to be payable on interest (except in so far as it falls to be compounded in accordance with paragraph 109(3)); and

(*b*) shall not have effect if, or to the extent that, the assessment in question has been withdrawn or reduced.

(5) Paragraph 108 shall apply in relation to assessments under this paragraph as if any assessment to interest on a penalty were an assessment under paragraph 106 to the penalty in question.

(6) Subject to sub-paragraph (7), where a person—

(*a*) is assessed under this paragraph to an amount due by way of any interest on a penalty, and

(*b*) is also assessed under any one or more provisions of Part VII of this Schedule for the accounting period to which the conduct attracting the penalty is referable,

the assessments may be combined and notified to him as one assessment.

(7) A notice of a combined assessment under sub-paragraph (6) must separately identify the interest being assessed.

Further assessments to interest on penalties

112— (1) Where an assessment is made under paragraph 111 to an amount of penalty interest under paragraph 109—

(*a*) the notice of assessment shall specify a date, not later than the date of the notice of assessment, to which the amount of interest which is assessed is calculated; and (*b*) if the interest continues to accrue after that date, a further assessment or further assessments may be made under paragraph 111 in respect of the amounts so accruing.

(2) Where—

(*a*) an assessment to penalty interest is made specifying a date for the purposes of sub-paragraph (1)(*a*), and

(*b*) within such period as may for the purposes of this sub-paragraph have been notified by the Commissioners to the person liable for the interest, the amount on which the interest is payable is paid,

that amount shall be deemed for the purposes of any further liability to interest to have been paid on the specified date.

Up-rating of amounts of penalties

113— (1) If it appears to the Treasury that there has been a change in the value of money since the time when the amount of a civil penalty provided for by this Schedule was fixed, they may by regulations substitute, for the amount for the time being specified as the amount of that penalty, such other sum as appears to them to be justified by the change.

(2) In sub-paragraph (1) the reference to the time when the amount of a civil penalty was fixed is a reference—

(*a*) in the case of a penalty which has not previously been modified under that sub-paragraph, to the time of the passing of this Act; and

(*b*) in any other case, to the time of the making of the regulations under that sub-paragraph that made the most recent modification of the amount of that penalty.

(3) Regulations under sub-paragraph (1) shall not apply to the penalty for any conduct before the coming into force of the regulations.

PART X

NON-RESIDENTS, GROUPS AND OTHER SPECIAL CASES

Non-resident taxpayers: appointment of tax representatives

114— (1) The Commissioners may by regulations make provision for securing that every non-resident taxpayer has a person resident in the United Kingdom to act as his tax representative for the purposes of the levy.

(2) Regulations under this paragraph may, in particular, contain any or all of the following—

(*a*) provision requiring notification to be given to the Commissioners where a person becomes a non-resident taxpayer;

(*b*) provision requiring the appointment of tax representatives by non-resident taxpayers;

(*c*) provision for the appointment of a person as a tax representative to take effect only where the person appointed is approved by the Commissioners;

(*d*) provision authorising the Commissioners to give a direction requiring the replacement of a tax representative;

(*e*) provision authorising the Commissioners to give a direction requiring a person specified in the direction to be treated as the appointed tax representative of a non-resident taxpayer so specified;

(*f*) provision about the circumstances in which a person ceases to be a tax representative and about the withdrawal by the Commissioners of their approval of a tax representative;

(*g*) provision enabling a tax representative to act on behalf of the person for whom he is the tax representative through an agent of the representative;

(*h*) provision for the purposes of any provision made by virtue of paragraphs (*a*) to (*g*) regulating the procedure to be followed in any case and imposing requirements as to the information and other particulars to be provided to the Commissioners;

(*i*) provision as to the time at which things done under or for the purposes of the regulations are to take effect.

(3) Subject to sub-paragraph (4), a person who—

(*a*) becomes subject, in accordance with any regulations under this paragraph, to an obligation to request the Commissioners' approval for any person's appointment as his tax representative, but

(*b*) fails (with or without making the appointment) to make the request as required by the regulations,

shall be liable to a penalty of £10,000.

(4) A failure such as is mentioned in sub-paragraph (3) shall not give rise to liability to a penalty under this paragraph if the person concerned satisfies the Commissioners or, on appeal, an appeal tribunal that there is a reasonable excuse for the failure.

Effect of appointment of tax representatives

115— (1) The tax representative of a non-resident taxpayer shall be entitled to act on the non-resident taxpayer's behalf for the purposes of any provision made by or under this Schedule.

(2) The tax representative of a non-resident taxpayer shall be under a duty, except to such extent as the Commissioners by regulations otherwise provide, to secure the non-resident taxpayer's compliance with, and discharge of, the obligations and liabilities to which the non-resident taxpayer is subject by virtue of any provision made by or under this Schedule (including obligations and liabilities arising or incurred before he became the non-resident taxpayer's tax representative).

(3) A person who is or has been the tax representative of a non-resident taxpayer shall be personally liable—

(*a*) in respect of any failure while he is or was the non-resident taxpayer's tax representative to secure compliance with, or the discharge of, any obligation or liability to which sub-paragraph (2) applies, and

(*b*) in respect of anything done in the course of, or for purposes connected with, acting on the non-resident taxpayer's behalf,

as if the obligations and liabilities to which sub-paragraph (2) applies were imposed jointly and severally on the tax representative and the non-resident taxpayer.

(4) A tax representative shall not be liable by virtue of this paragraph to be registered for the purposes of the levy; but the Commissioners may by regulations—

(*a*) require the names of tax representatives to be registered against the names of the non-resident taxpayers of whom they are the representatives;

(*b*) make provision for the deletion of the names so registered of persons who cease to be tax representatives.

(5) A tax representative shall not by virtue of this paragraph be guilty of any offence except in so far as—

(*a*) he has consented to, or connived in, the commission of the offence by the non-resident taxpayer;

(*b*) the commission of the offence by the non-resident taxpayer is attributable to any neglect on the part of the tax representative; or

(*c*) the offence consists in a contravention by the tax representative of an obligation which, by virtue of this paragraph, is imposed both on the tax representative and on the non-resident taxpayer.

Groups of companies etc

116— (1) The Commissioners may make provision by regulations for two or more bodies corporate to be treated as members of a group for the purposes of the Schedule.

(2) Regulations under sub-paragraph (1) may, in particular, make provision for or about—

(*a*) eligibility for group treatment;

(*b*) representative members of groups;

(*c*) applications for, or the variation or ending of, group treatment;

(*d*) the decisions to be made on applications;

(*e*) the variation or ending of group treatment by notice given by the Commissioners otherwise than on an application;

(*f*) treating a member of a group as charged with levy that would otherwise be levy with which another member of the group would be charged;

(*g*) the members of a group liable for levy, or amounts recoverable as levy, due from a member of a group.

(3) The provision mentioned in sub-paragraph (2)(*c*) includes provision—

(*a*) about the time within which applications are to be made,

(*b*) for authorising the Commissioners to extend such time, and

(*c*) for applications that seek group treatment, or its variation or ending, with effect from a time before they are made.

(4) The provision mentioned in sub-paragraph (2)(*e*) includes provision for a notice to have effect from a time before it is given.

(5) Regulations under sub-paragraph (1) may make provision for imposing requirements on a body corporate to notify the Commissioners of prescribed matters relating to group treatment.

(6) A body corporate which fails to comply with any such requirement imposed by such regulations shall be liable to a penalty of £250.

Partnerships and other unincorporated bodies

117— (1) The Commissioners may by regulations make provision for determining by what persons anything required to be done under this Schedule is to be done where, apart from those regulations, that requirement would fall on—

(*a*) persons carrying on business in partnership; or

(*b*) persons carrying on business together as an unincorporated body;

but any regulations under this sub-paragraph must be construed subject to the following provisions of this paragraph.

(2) In determining for the purposes of this Schedule who at any time is the person accountable for any levy in a case where, apart from this sub-paragraph, the persons accountable are persons carrying on any business—

(*a*) in partnership, or

(*b*) as an unincorporated body,

the firm or body shall be treated, for the purposes of that determination (and notwithstanding any changes from time to time in the members of the firm or body), as the same person and as separate from its members.

(3) Without prejudice to section 36 of the Partnership Act 1890 (rights of persons dealing with firm against apparent members of firm), where—

(*a*) persons have been carrying on in partnership any business in the course or furtherance of which there has been done any thing that resulted in the firm becoming liable to account for any levy, and

(*b*) a person ceases to be a member of the firm,

that person shall be regarded for the purposes of this Schedule (including sub-paragraph (7) below) as continuing to be a partner until the date on which the change in the partnership is notified to the Commissioners.

(4) Where a person ceases to be a member of a firm during an accounting period (or is treated as so ceasing by virtue of sub-paragraph (3)) any notice, whether of assessment or otherwise, which—

(*a*) is served on the firm under or for the purposes of any provision made by or under this Schedule, and

(*b*) relates to, or to any matter arising in, that period or any earlier period during the whole or part of which he was a member of the firm,

shall be treated as served also on him.

(5) Without prejudice to section 16 of the Partnership Act 1890 (notice to acting partner to be notice to the firm), any notice, whether of assessment or otherwise, which—

(*a*) is addressed to a firm by the name in which it is registered, and

(*b*) is served in accordance with this Schedule,

shall be treated for the purposes of this Schedule as served on the firm and, accordingly, where sub-paragraph (4) applies, as served also on the former partner.

(6) Subject to sub-paragraph (7), nothing in this paragraph shall affect the extent to which, under section 9 of the Partnership Act 1890 (liability of partners for debts of the firm), a partner is liable for levy owed by the firm.

(7) Where a person is a partner in a firm during part only of an accounting period, his personal liability for levy incurred by the firm in respect of taxable supplies made in that period shall include, but shall not exceed, such proportion of the firm's liability as may be just and reasonable in the circumstances.

Death and incapacity

118— (1) The Commissioners may, in accordance with sub-paragraph (2), by regulations make provision for the purposes of the levy in relation to cases where a person carries on a business of an individual who has died or become incapacitated.

(2) The provisions that may be contained in regulations under this paragraph are—

(*a*) provision requiring the person who is carrying on the business to inform the Commissioners of the fact that he is carrying on the business and of the event that has led to his carrying it on;

(*b*) provision allowing that person to be treated for a limited time as if he and the person who has died or become incapacitated were the same person; and

(*c*) such other provision as the Commissioners think fit for securing continuity in the application of this Schedule where a person is so treated.

Transfer of a business as a going concern

119— (1) The Commissioners may by regulations make provision for securing continuity in the application of this Schedule in cases where any business carried on by a person is transferred to another person as a going concern.

(2) Regulations under this paragraph may, in particular, include any or all of the following—

(*a*) provision requiring the transferor to inform the Commissioners of the transfer;

(*b*) provision for liabilities and duties under this Schedule of the transferor to become, to such extent as may be provided by the regulations, liabilities and duties of the transferee;

(*c*) provision for any right of either of them to a tax credit or repayment of levy to be satisfied by allowing the credit or making the repayment to the other;

(*d*) provision as to the preservation of any records or accounts relating to the business which, by virtue of any regulations under paragraph 125, are required to be preserved for any period after the transfer.

(3) Regulations under this paragraph may provide that no such provision as is mentioned in paragraph (*b*) or (*c*) of sub-paragraph (2) shall have effect in relation to any transferor and transferee unless an application for the purpose has been made by them under the regulations.

Insolvency etc

120— (1) The Commissioners may by regulations make provision in accordance with the following provisions of this paragraph for the application of this Schedule in cases in which an insolvency procedure is applied to a person or to a deceased individual's estate.

In this paragraph "the relevant person" means the person to whom, or the deceased individual to whose estate, the insolvency procedure is applied.

(2) The provision that may be contained in regulations under this paragraph may include any or all of the following—

(*a*) provision requiring any such person as may be prescribed to give notification to the Commissioners, in the prescribed manner, of the prescribed particulars of any relevant matter;

(*b*) provision requiring a person to be treated, to the prescribed extent, as if he were the same person as the relevant person for the purposes of this Schedule or such of its provisions as may be prescribed; and

(*c*) provision for securing continuity in the application of any of the provisions of this Schedule where, by virtue of any regulations under this paragraph, any person is treated as if he were the same person as the relevant person.

(3) In sub-paragraph (2) "relevant matter", in relation to a case in which an insolvency procedure is applied to any person or to any deceased individual's estate, means—

(*a*) the application of that procedure to that person or estate;

(*b*) the appointment of any person for the purposes of the application of that procedure;

(*c*) any other matter relating to—

(i) the application of that procedure to the person to whom, or the estate to which, it is applied;

(ii) the holding of an appointment made for the purposes of that procedure; or

(iii) the exercise or discharge of any powers or duties conferred or imposed on any person by virtue of such an appointment.

(4) Regulations made by virtue of sub-paragraph (2)(*b*) may include provision for a person to cease to be treated as if he were the same person as the relevant person on the occurrence of such an event as may be prescribed.

(5) Regulations under this paragraph prescribing the manner in which any notification is to be given to the Commissioners may require it to be given in such manner and to contain such particulars as may be specified in a general notice published by the Commissioners in accordance with the regulations.

(6) Regulations under this paragraph may provide that the extent to which, and the purposes for which, a person is to be treated under the regulations as if he were the same person as the relevant person may be determined by reference to a notice given in accordance with the regulations to the person so treated.

(7) For the purposes of this paragraph, an insolvency procedure is applied to a person if—

(*a*) a bankruptcy order, winding-up order or administration order is made [or an administrator is appointed][1] in relation to that person or a partnership of which he is a member;

(*b*) an award of sequestration is made on that person's estate or on the estate of a partnership of which he is a member;

(*c*) that person is put into administrative receivership;

(*d*) that person passes a resolution for voluntary winding up;

(*e*) any voluntary arrangement approved in accordance with—

(i) Part I or VIII of the Insolvency Act 1986, or

(ii) Part II or Chapter II of Part VIII of the Insolvency (Northern Ireland) Order 1989,

comes into force in relation to that person or a partnership of which that person is a member;

(*f*) a deed of arrangement registered in accordance with—

(i) the Deeds of Arrangement Act 1914, or

(ii) Chapter I of Part VIII of that Order,

takes effect in relation to that person;

(*g*) a person is appointed as the receiver or manager of some or all of that person's property, or of income arising from some or all of his property;

(*h*) a person is appointed as the interim receiver of some or all of that person's property under section 286 of the Insolvency Act 1986 or Article 259 of the Insolvency (Northern Ireland) Order 1989;

(*i*) a person is appointed as the provisional liquidator in relation to that person under section 135 of that Act or Article 115 of that Order;

(*j*) an interim order is made under Part VIII of that Act, or Chapter II of Part VIII of that Order, in relation to that person; or (*k*) that person's estate, or the estate of a partnership of which that person is a member, becomes vested in any other person as that person's, or the partnership's, trustee under a trust deed (within the meaning of the Bankruptcy (Scotland) Act 1985).

(8) For the purposes of this paragraph, an insolvency procedure is applied to a deceased individual's estate if—

(*a*) a bankruptcy order, or an order by some other name but corresponding to a bankruptcy order, is made after the individual's death in relation to his estate under provisions of—

(i) the Insolvency Act 1986, or
(ii) the Insolvency (Northern Ireland) Order 1989,

as applied to the administration of the insolvent estates of deceased individuals; or

(*b*) an award of sequestration is made on the individual's estate after the individual's death.

(9) In sub-paragraph (7)—

(*a*) "administration order" means an administration order under [Schedule B1 to][1] the Insolvency Act 1986 or Article 21 of the Insolvency (Northern Ireland) Order 1989;

(*b*) references to a member of a partnership include references to any person who is liable as a partner under section 14 of the Partnership Act 1890 (persons liable by "holding out").

Amendments—[1] Words in sub-para (7)(*a*) inserted, and words in sub-para (9)(*a*) substituted, by the Enterprise Act 2002 (Insolvency) Order, SI 2003/2096 art 4, Schedule paras 31, 33 with effect from 15 September 2003. These amendments do not apply in relation to any case where a petition for an administration order was presented before 15 September 2003: SI 2003/2096 arts 1(1), 6.

PART XI

REVIEW AND APPEAL

[Appeals][1]

121— [(1) Subject to paragraph 122, an appeal shall lie to an appeal tribunal from any person who is or will be affected by any decision of HMRC with respect to any of the following matters—][1]

(*a*) whether or not a person is charged in any case with an amount of levy;

(*b*) the amount of levy charged in any case and the time when the charge is to be taken as having arisen;

(*c*) the registration of any person for the purposes of the levy or the cancellation of any registration;

(*d*) the person liable to pay the levy charged in any case, the amount of a person's liability to levy and the time by which he is required to pay an amount of levy;

(*e*) whether to prepare a special utility scheme for a utility;

(*f*) the imposition of a requirement on any person to give security, or further security, under paragraph 139 and the amount and manner of providing any security required under that paragraph;

(*g*) whether or not liability to a penalty or to interest on any amount arises in any person's case under any provision made by or under this Schedule, and the amount of any such liability;

(*h*) any matter the decision as to which is [appealable][1] under this paragraph of this Part of this Schedule in accordance with paragraph 99(6) or (7);

(*i*) the extent of any person's entitlement to any tax credit or to a repayment in respect of a tax credit and the extent of any liability of the Commissioners under this Schedule to pay interest on any amount;

(*j*) whether or not any person is required to have a tax representative by virtue of any regulations under paragraph 114;

(*k*) the giving, withdrawal or variation, for the purposes of any such regulations, of any approval or direction with respect to the person who is to act as another's tax representative;

(*l*) the giving, withdrawal or variation of a utility direction under paragraph 151(1);

(*m*) whether a body corporate is to be treated, or is to cease to be treated, as a member of a group, the times at which a body corporate is to be so treated and the body corporate which is, in relation to any time, to be the representative member for a group;

(*n*) any matter not falling within the preceding paragraphs the decision with respect to which is contained in—

(i) an assessment under paragraph 78 or 79 in respect of an accounting period in relation to which any return required to be made by virtue of regulations under paragraph 41 has been made, or

(ii) an assessment under any provision of this Schedule other than paragraph 78 or 79.

[(2) *Any person who is or will be affected by any decision to which this paragraph applies may by notice in writing to the Commissioners require them to review the decision.*

(3) *The Commissioners shall not be required under this paragraph to review any decision unless the notice requiring the review is given before the end of the period of forty-five days beginning with the day on which written notification of the decision, or of an assessment containing or giving effect to the decision, was first given to the person requiring the review.*

(4) For the purposes of sub-paragraph (3) it shall be the duty of the Commissioners to give written notification of any decision to which this paragraph applies to any person who—

(a) requests such a notification;

(b) has not previously been given written notification of that decision; and

(c) if given such a notification, will be entitled to require a review of the decision under this paragraph.

(5) A person shall be entitled to give a notice under this paragraph requiring a decision to be reviewed for a second or subsequent time only if—

(a) the grounds on which he requires the further review are that the Commissioners did not, on any previous review, have the opportunity to consider certain facts or other matters; and

(b) he does not, on the further review, require the Commissioners to consider any facts or matters which were considered on a previous review except in so far as they are relevant to any issue to which the facts or matters not previously considered relate.

(6) Where the Commissioners are required by a notice under this paragraph to review any decision, it shall be their duty to do so.

(7) On a review under this paragraph the Commissioners may (subject to sub-paragraph (9)) withdraw, vary or confirm the decision reviewed.

(8) Where—

(a) it is the duty under this paragraph of the Commissioners to review any decision, and

(b) they do not, within the period of forty-five days beginning with the day on which the review was required, give notice to the person requiring it of their determination on the review,

they shall be deemed to have confirmed the decision.

(9) Where the Commissioners decide, on a review under this paragraph, that a liability to a penalty or to an amount of interest arises, they shall not be entitled to modify the amount payable in respect of that liability except—

(a) in exercise of a power conferred by paragraph 104(1) (penalties) or paragraph 70(6), 86(3) or 109(5) (penalty interest); or

(b) for the purpose of making the amount payable conform to the amount of the liability imposed by this Schedule.][1]

(10) This paragraph has effect subject to paragraph 99(5).

Amendments—[1] Heading substituted for former heading "Review of Commissioners' decisions"; words at the beginning in sub-para (1) substituted for the words "This paragraph applies to a decision of the Commissioners with respect to any of the following matters—"; word in sub-para (1)(*h*) substituted for the word "reviewable"; sub-paras (2)–(9) repealed by the Transfer of Tribunal Functions and Revenue and Customs Appeals Order, SI 2009/56 art 3, Sch 1 para 288 with effect from 1 April 2009, subject to transitional and savings provisions in Sch 3 paras 2, 3.

[121A Offer of review

(1) HMRC must offer a person (P) a review of a decision that has been notified to P if an appeal lies under paragraph 121 in respect of the decision.

(2) The offer of the review must be made by notice given to P at the same time as the decision is notified to P.

(3) This paragraph does not apply to the notification of the conclusions of a review.][1]

Amendment—[1] Paras 121A–121G inserted by the Transfer of Tribunal Functions and Revenue and Customs Appeals Order, SI 2009/56 art 3, Sch 1 para 289 with effect from 1 April 2009.

[121B Right to require review

(1) Any person (other than P) who has the right of appeal under paragraph 121 against a decision may require HMRC to review that decision if that person has not appealed to the appeal tribunal under paragraph 121G.

(2) A notification that such a person requires a review must be made within 30 days of that person becoming aware of the decision.][1]

Amendment—[1] Paras 121A–121G inserted by the Transfer of Tribunal Functions and Revenue and Customs Appeals Order, SI 2009/56 art 3, Sch 1 para 289 with effect from 1 April 2009.

[121C Review by HMRC

(1) HMRC must review a decision if—

(*a*) they have offered a review of the decision under paragraph 121A, and

(*b*) P notifies HMRC accepting the offer within 30 days from the date of the document containing the notification of the offer.

(2) But P may not notify acceptance of the offer if P has already appealed to the appeal tribunal under paragraph 121G.

(3) HMRC must review a decision if a person other than P notifies them under paragraph 121B.

(4) HMRC shall not review a decision if P, or another person, has appealed to the appeal tribunal under paragraph 121G in respect of the decision.][1]

Amendment—[1] Paras 121A–121G inserted by the Transfer of Tribunal Functions and Revenue and Customs Appeals Order, SI 2009/56 art 3, Sch 1 para 289 with effect from 1 April 2009.

[121D Extensions of time

(1) If under paragraph 121A, HMRC have offered P a review of a decision, HMRC may within the relevant period notify P that the relevant period is extended.

(2) If under paragraph 121B another person may require HMRC to review a matter, HMRC may within the relevant period notify the other person that the relevant period is extended.

(3) If notice is given the relevant period is extended to the end of 30 days from—

(*a*) the date of the notice, or

(*b*) any other date set out in the notice or a further notice.

(4) In this paragraph "relevant period" means—

(*a*) the period of 30 days referred to in—

(i) paragraph 121C(1)(*b*) (in a case falling within sub-paragraph (1)), or

(ii) paragraph 121B(2) (in a case falling within sub-paragraph (2)), or

(*b*) if notice has been given under sub-paragraph (1) or (2), that period as extended (or as most recently extended) in accordance with sub-paragraph (3).][1]

Amendment—[1] Paras 121A–121G inserted by the Transfer of Tribunal Functions and Revenue and Customs Appeals Order, SI 2009/56 art 3, Sch 1 para 289 with effect from 1 April 2009.

[121E Review out of time

(1) This paragraph applies if—

(*a*) HMRC have offered a review of a decision under paragraph 121A and P does not accept the offer within the time allowed under paragraph 121C(1)(*b*) or 121D(3); or

(*b*) a person who requires a review under paragraph 121B does not notify HMRC within the time allowed under that paragraph or paragraph 121D(3).

(2) HMRC must review the decision under paragraph 121C if—

(*a*) after the time allowed, P, or the other person, notifies HMRC in writing requesting a review out of time,

(*b*) HMRC are satisfied that P, or the other person, had a reasonable excuse for not accepting the offer or requiring review within the time allowed, and

(*c*) HMRC are satisfied that P, or the other person, made the request without unreasonable delay after the excuse had ceased to apply.

(3) HMRC shall not review a decision if P, or another person, has appealed to the appeal tribunal under paragraph 121G in respect of the decision.][1]

Amendment—[1] Paras 121A–121G inserted by the Transfer of Tribunal Functions and Revenue and Customs Appeals Order, SI 2009/56 art 3, Sch 1 para 289 with effect from 1 April 2009.

[121F Nature of review etc

(1) This paragraph applies if HMRC are required to undertake a review under paragraph 121C or 121E.

(2) The nature and extent of the review are to be such as appear appropriate to HMRC in the circumstances.

(3) For the purpose of sub-paragraph (2), HMRC must, in particular, have regard to steps taken before the beginning of the review—

(*a*) by HMRC in reaching the decision, and

(*b*) by any person in seeking to resolve disagreement about the decision.

(4) The review must take account of any representations made by P, or the other person, at a stage which gives HMRC a reasonable opportunity to consider them.

(5) The review may conclude that the decision is to be—

(*a*) upheld,

(*b*) varied, or

(*c*) cancelled.

(6) HMRC must give P, or the other person, notice of the conclusions of the review and their reasoning within—

(*a*) a period of 45 days beginning with the relevant date, or

(*b*) such other period as HMRC and P, or the other person, may agree.

(7) In sub-paragraph (6) "relevant date" means—

(*a*) the date HMRC received P's notification accepting the offer of a review (in a case falling within paragraph 121A), or

(*b*) the date HMRC received notification from another person requiring review (in a case falling within paragraph 121B), or

(*c*) the date on which HMRC decided to undertake the review (in a case falling within paragraph 121E).

(8) Where HMRC are required to undertake a review but do not give notice of the conclusions within the time period specified in sub-paragraph (6), the review is to be treated as having concluded that the decision is upheld.

(9) If sub-paragraph (8) applies, HMRC must notify the appellant of the conclusion which the review is treated as having reached.][1]

Amendment—[1] Paras 121A–121G inserted by the Transfer of Tribunal Functions and Revenue and Customs Appeals Order, SI 2009/56 art 3, Sch 1 para 289 with effect from 1 April 2009.

[121G Bringing of appeals

(1) An appeal under paragraph 121 is to be made to the appeal tribunal before—

(*a*) the end of the period of 30 days beginning with—

(i) in a case where P is the appellant, the date of the document notifying the decision to which the appeal relates, or

(ii) in a case where a person other than P is the appellant, the date that person becomes aware of the decision, or

(*b*) if later, the end of the relevant period (within the meaning of paragraph 121D).

(2) But that is subject to sub-paragraphs (3) to (5).

(3) In a case where HMRC are required to undertake a review under paragraph 121C—

(*a*) an appeal may not be made until the conclusion date, and

(*b*) any appeal is to be made within the period of 30 days beginning with the conclusion date.

(4) In a case where HMRC are requested to undertake a review by virtue of paragraph 121E—

(*a*) an appeal may not be made—

(i) unless HMRC have decided whether or not to undertake a review, and

(ii) if HMRC decide to undertake a review, until the conclusion date; and

(*b*) any appeal is to be made within the period of 30 days beginning with—

(i) the conclusion date (if HMRC decide to undertake a review), or

(ii) the date on which HMRC decide not to undertake a review.

(5) In a case where paragraph 121F(8) applies, an appeal may be made at any time from the end of the period specified in paragraph 121F(6) to the date 30 days after the conclusion date.

(6) An appeal may be made after the end of the period specified in sub-paragraph (1), (3)(*b*), (4)(*b*) or (5) if the appeal tribunal gives permission to do so.

(7) In this paragraph "conclusion date" means the date of the document notifying the conclusions of the review.][1]

Amendment—[1] Paras 121A–121G inserted by the Transfer of Tribunal Functions and Revenue and Customs Appeals Order, SI 2009/56 art 3, Sch 1 para 289 with effect from 1 April 2009.

[Appeals: further provisions][1]

122— (1) …[1]

[(2) Subject to sub-paragraphs (2A) and (2B), where an appeal relates to a decision (whether or not contained in an assessment) that an amount of levy is due from any person, it shall not be entertained unless the amount which HMRC have determined to be due has been paid or deposited with them.][1]

[(2A) In a case where the amount determined to be payable as levy has not been paid or deposited an appeal shall be entertained if—

(*a*) HMRC are satisfied (on the application of the appellant), or

(*b*) the appeal tribunal decides (HMRC not being so satisfied and on the application of the appellant),

that the requirement to pay or deposit the amount determined would cause the appellant to suffer hardship.

(2B) Notwithstanding the provisions of sections 11 and 13 of the Tribunals, Courts and Enforcement Act 2007, the decision of the appeal tribunal as to the issue of hardship is final.][1]

(3) On an appeal under this paragraph relating to a penalty under paragraph 98 (evasion), the burden of proof as to the matters specified in paragraphs (*a*) and (*b*) of sub-paragraph (1) of that paragraph shall lie upon the Commissioners.

Amendments—[1] Heading substituted for former heading "Appeals against reviewed decisions"; sub-para (1) repealed; sub-para (2) substituted; sub-paras (2A), (2B) inserted by the Transfer of Tribunal Functions and Revenue and Customs Appeals Order, SI 2009/56 art 3, Sch 1 para 290 with effect from 1 April 2009, subject to transitional and savings provisions in Sch 3 paras 2, 3. Sub-paras (1), (2) previously read as follows—

"(1) Subject to the following provisions of this paragraph, an appeal shall lie to an appeal tribunal with respect to any of the following decisions—

(*a*) any decision by the Commissioners on a review under paragraph 121 (including a deemed confirmation under paragraph 121(8));

(*b*) any decision by the Commissioners on any such review of a decision referred to in paragraph 121(1) as the Commissioners have agreed to undertake in consequence of a request made after the end of the period mentioned in paragraph 121(3).

(2) Where an appeal under this paragraph relates to a decision (whether or not contained in an assessment) that an amount of levy is due from any person, that appeal shall not be entertained unless—

(*a*) the amount which the Commissioners have determined to be due has been paid or deposited with them; or

(*b*) on being satisfied that the appellant would otherwise suffer hardship—

(i) the Commissioners agree, or

(ii) the appeal tribunal decide,

that it should be entertained notwithstanding that that amount has not been so paid or deposited."

Determinations on appeal

123— (1) Where, on an appeal under paragraph [121][1]—

(*a*) it is found that an assessment of the appellant ...[1] is an assessment for an amount that is less than it ought to have been, and

(*b*) the appeal tribunal give a direction specifying the correct amount,

the assessment shall have effect as an assessment of the amount specified in the direction and (without prejudice to any power under this Schedule to reduce the amount of interest payable on the amount of an assessment) as if it were an assessment notified to the appellant in that amount at the same time as the original assessment.

(2) On an appeal under paragraph [121][1], the powers of the appeal tribunal in relation to any decision of the Commissioners shall include a power, where the tribunal allow an appeal on the ground that the Commissioners could not reasonably have arrived at the decision, either—

(*a*) to direct that the decision, so far as it remains in force, is to cease to have effect from such time as the tribunal may direct; or

(*b*) to require the Commissioners to conduct, in accordance with the directions of the tribunal, [a review or][1] a further review of the original decision [as appropriate][1].

(3) Where, on an appeal under paragraph [121][1], the appeal tribunal find that a liability to a penalty or to an amount of interest arises, the tribunal shall not give any direction for the modification of the amount payable in respect of that liability except—

(*a*) in exercise of a power conferred on the tribunal by paragraph 104(1) (penalties) or paragraph 70(6) or (9), 86(3) or (6) or 109(5) or (8) (penalty interest); or

(*b*) for the purpose of making the amount payable conform to the amount of the liability imposed by this Schedule.

(4) Where, on an appeal under paragraph [121][1], it is found that the whole or part of any amount paid or deposited in pursuance of paragraph 122(2) is not due, so much of that amount as is found not to be due shall be repaid with interest [at the rate applicable under section 197 of the Finance Act 1996][1].

(5) Where, on an appeal under paragraph [121][1], it is found that the whole or part of any amount due to the appellant by way of any repayment in respect of a tax credit has not been paid, so much of that amount as is found not to have been paid shall be paid with interest [at the rate applicable under section 197 of the Finance Act 1996][1].

(6) Where—

(*a*) an appeal under paragraph [121][1] has been entertained notwithstanding that an amount determined by the Commissioners to be payable as levy has not been paid or deposited, and

(*b*) it is found on the appeal that that amount is due,

[it shall be paid with interest at the rate applicable under section 197 of the Finance Act 1996][1]

[(6A) Interest under sub-paragraph (6) shall be paid without any deduction of income tax.][1]

[(7) Sections 85 and 85B of the Value Added Tax Act 1994 (settling of appeals by agreement and payment of tax where there is a further appeal) shall have effect as if—

(*a*) the references to section 83 of that Act included references to paragraph 121 above, and

(*b*) the references to value added tax included references to climate change levy.][1]

Amendments—[1] The following amendments made by the Transfer of Tribunal Functions and Revenue and Customs Appeals Order, SI 2009/56 art 3, Sch 1 para 291 with effect from 1 April 2009, subject to transitional and savings provisions in Sch 3 paras 2, 3, 9—

- in sub-paras (1)–(5), (6)(*a*), figure substituted for figure "122";
- in sub-para (1)(a) words "made, confirmed or treated as confirmed by the Commissioners on a review under paragraph 121 ("the original assessment")" repealed;
- in sub-para (2)(*b*) words inserted in both places;
- in sub-paras (4), (5), words at the end substituted for the words "at such rate as the appeal tribunal may determine";
- in sub-para (6), words at the end substituted for the words "the appeal tribunal may, if they think fit, direct that that amount shall be paid with interest at such rate as may be specified in the direction.";
- sub-para (6A) inserted;
- sub-para (7) substituted. Text previously read as follows—

"(7) Sections 85 and 87 of the Value Added Tax Act 1994 (settling of appeals by agreement and enforcement of certain decisions of tribunal) shall have effect as if—

(*a*) the references to section 83 of that Act included references to paragraph [121]; and

(*b*) the references to value added tax included references to levy."

PART XII

INFORMATION AND EVIDENCE

Provision of information

124— (1) Every person involved (in whatever capacity) in making or receiving supplies of taxable commodities, or in any connected activities, shall provide the Commissioners with such information relating to the matters in which he is or has been involved as the Commissioners may reasonably require.

(2) Information required under sub-paragraph (1) shall be provided to the Commissioners within such period after being required, and in such form, as the Commissioners may reasonably require.

(3) Subject to sub-paragraphs (4) and (5) and to paragraph 107(5) (which relates to supplementary assessments of daily penalties), if a person fails to provide information which he is required to provide under this paragraph, he shall be liable—

(*a*) to a penalty of £250; and

(*b*) to a further penalty of £20 for every day after the last relevant date and before the day after that on which the required information is provided.

(4) Liability to a penalty specified in sub-paragraph (3) shall not arise if the person required to provide the information satisfies the Commissioners or, on appeal, an appeal tribunal—

(*a*) in the case of the penalty under paragraph (*a*) of that sub-paragraph that there is a reasonable excuse—

(i) for the initial failure to provide the required information on or before the last relevant date; and

(ii) for every subsequent failure to provide it;

and

(*b*) in the case of any penalty under paragraph (*b*) of that sub-paragraph for any day, that there is a reasonable excuse for the failure to provide the information on or before that day.

(5) Where, by reason of any failure by any person to provide information required under this paragraph—

(*a*) that person is convicted of an offence (whether under this Act or otherwise), or

(*b*) that person is assessed to a penalty under paragraph 98 (penalty for evasion) [or to a penalty for a deliberate inaccuracy under Schedule 24 to the Finance Act 2007 (penalties for errors)][1],

that person shall not by reason of that failure be liable also to a penalty under this paragraph.

(6) In this paragraph "the last relevant date" means the last day of the period within which the person in question was required to provide the information.

Amendments—[1] Words in sub-para (5)(*b*) inserted by the Finance Act 2008, Schedule 40 (Appointed Day, Transitional Provisions and Consequential Amendments) Order, SI 2009/571 art 8, Sch 1 para 30(1), (4) with effect from 1 April 2009.

Records

125— (1) The Commissioners may by regulations impose obligations to keep records on [persons who—

(*a*) are registered,

(*b*) are required to be registered, or

(*c*) are exempted from the requirement to be registered by regulations under paragraph 53(4).][1]

(2) Regulations under this paragraph may be framed by reference to such records as may be stipulated in any notice published by the Commissioners in pursuance of the regulations and not withdrawn by a further notice.

(3) Regulations under this paragraph may—

(*a*) require any records kept in pursuance of the regulations to be preserved for such period, not exceeding six years, as may be specified in the regulations;

(*b*) authorise the Commissioners to direct that any such records need only be preserved for a shorter period than that specified in the regulations;

(*c*) authorise a direction to be made so as to apply generally or in such cases as the Commissioners may stipulate.

(4) Any duty under regulations under this paragraph to preserve records may be discharged by the preservation of the information contained in them by such means as the Commissioners may approve.

(5) The Commissioners may, as a condition of approving under sub-paragraph (4) any means of preserving information contained in any records, impose such reasonable requirements as appear to them necessary for securing that the information will be as readily available to them as if the records themselves had been preserved.

(6) Subject to sub-paragraphs (7) and (8), a person who fails to preserve any record in compliance with—

(*a*) any regulations under this paragraph, or

(*b*) any notice, direction or requirement given or imposed under such regulations,

shall be liable to a penalty of £250.

(7) A failure such as is mentioned in sub-paragraph (6) shall not give rise to any penalty under that sub-paragraph if the person required to preserve the record satisfies the Commissioners or, on appeal, an appeal tribunal that there is a reasonable excuse for the failure.

(8) Where, by reason of any such failure by any person as is mentioned in sub-paragraph (6)—

(*a*) that person is convicted of an offence (whether under this Act or otherwise), or (*b*) that person is assessed to a penalty under paragraph 98 (penalty for evasion) [or to a penalty for a deliberate inaccuracy under Schedule 24 to the Finance Act 2007 (penalties for errors)][2],

that person shall not by reason of that failure be liable also to a penalty under this paragraph.

(9) The Commissioners may if they think fit at any time modify or withdraw any approval or requirement given or imposed for the purposes of this paragraph.

Amendments—[1] In sub-para (1), words substituted for the words "persons who are, or are required to be, registered" by FA 2003 s 192(1), (9) with effect from 10 July 2003.

[2] Words in sub-para (8)(*b*) inserted by the Finance Act 2008, Schedule 40 (Appointed Day, Transitional Provisions and Consequential Amendments) Order, SI 2009/571 art 8, Sch 1 para 30(1), (5) with effect from 1 April 2009.

Prospective amendments—In sub-para (9), the words "approval or" and "given or" to be repealed, sub-paras (4) and (5) to be substituted, by FA 2009 s 98, Sch 50 paras 18, 19(1)–(3), with effect from such day as the Treasury may by order made by statutory instrument appoint. Sub-paragraph (4) to read as follows:

"(4) A duty under regulations under this paragraph to preserve records may be discharged—

(*a*) by preserving them in any form and by any means, or

(*b*) by preserving the information contained in them in any form and by any means,

subject to any conditions or exceptions specified in writing by the Commissioners.".

Evidence of records that are required to be preserved

126— (1) Subject to the following provisions of this paragraph, where any obligation to preserve records is discharged in accordance with paragraph 125(4), a copy of any document forming part of the records shall be admissible in evidence in any proceedings, whether civil or criminal, to the same extent as the records themselves.

(2) A statement contained in a document produced by a computer shall not by virtue of this paragraph be admissible in evidence—

(*a*) …[1]

(*b*) in civil proceedings in Scotland, except in accordance with sections 5 and 6 of the Civil Evidence (Scotland) Act 1988;

(*c*) in criminal proceedings in Scotland, except in accordance with Schedule 8 to the Criminal Procedure (Scotland) Act 1995;

(*d*) …[2]

Amendments[1] Sub-para (2)(*a*) repealed by the Criminal Justice Act 2003 s 332, Sch 37 Pt 6 with effect from 4 April 2005 (by virtue of SI 2005/950).

[2] Sub-para (2)(*d*) repealed by the Criminal Justice (Evidence) (Northern Ireland) Order, SI 2004/1501, s 46(2), Sch 2, with effect from 3 April 2006 (by virtue of 3 April 2006: see the Criminal Justice (Evidence) (Northern Ireland) Order 2004 (Commencement No 3) Order, SR 2006/63, art 2).

Prospective amendments—Paragraph 126 to be omitted by FA 2009 s 98, Sch 50 paras 18, 20, with effect from such day as the Treasury may by order made by statutory instrument appoint.

Production of documents

127— (1) Every person involved (in whatever capacity) in making or receiving supplies of taxable commodities, or in any connected activities, shall upon demand made by an authorised person produce or cause to be produced for inspection by that person any documents relating to the matters in which he is or has been involved.

(2) Where, by virtue of sub-paragraph (1), an authorised person has power to require the production of any documents from any person—

(*a*) he shall have the like power to require production of the documents concerned from any other person who appears to the authorised person to be in possession of them; and

(*b*) the production of any document by that other person in pursuance of a requirement under this sub-paragraph shall be without prejudice to any lien claimed by that other person on that document.

(3) The documents mentioned in sub-paragraphs (1) and (2) shall be produced at such time and place as the authorised person may reasonably require.

(4) Subject to sub-paragraphs (5) and (6) and to paragraph 107(5) (which relates to supplementary assessments of daily penalties), if a person fails to produce any document which he is required to produce under this paragraph, he shall be liable—

(*a*) to a penalty of £250; and

(*b*) to a further penalty of £20 for every day after the last relevant date and before the day after that on which the document is produced.

(5) Liability to a penalty specified in sub-paragraph (4) shall not arise if the person required to produce the document in question satisfies the Commissioners or, on appeal, an appeal tribunal—

(*a*) in the case of the penalty under paragraph (*a*) of that sub-paragraph, that there is a reasonable excuse—

(i) for the initial failure to produce the document at the required time; and

(ii) for every subsequent failure to produce it;

and

(*b*) in the case of any penalty under paragraph (*b*) of that sub-paragraph for any day, that there is a reasonable excuse for the failure to produce the document on or before that day.

(6) Where, by reason of any failure by any person to provide information required under this paragraph—

(*a*) that person is convicted of an offence (whether under this Act or otherwise), or

(*b*) that person is assessed to a penalty under paragraph 98 (penalty for evasion) [or to a penalty for a deliberate inaccuracy under Schedule 24 to the Finance Act 2007 (penalties for errors)][1],

that person shall not by reason of that failure be liable also to a penalty under this paragraph.

(7) In this paragraph "the last relevant date" means the last day of the period within which the person in question was required to produce the document.

Amendments—[1] Words in sub-para (6)(*b*) inserted by the Finance Act 2008, Schedule 40 (Appointed Day, Transitional Provisions and Consequential Amendments) Order, SI 2009/571 art 8, Sch 1 para 30(1), (6) with effect from 1 April 2009.

Powers in relation to documents produced

128— (1) An authorised person may take copies of, or make extracts from, any document produced under paragraph 127.

(2) If it appears to him to be necessary to do so, an authorised person may, at a reasonable time and for a reasonable period, remove any document produced under paragraph 127.

(3) An authorised person who removes any document under sub-paragraph (2) shall, if requested to do so, provide a receipt for the document so removed.

(4) Where a lien is claimed on a document produced under paragraph 127(2), the removal of the document under sub-paragraph (2) shall not be regarded as breaking the lien.

(5) Where a document removed by an authorised person under sub-paragraph (2) is reasonably required for any purpose he shall, as soon as practicable, provide a copy of the document, free of charge, to the person by whom it was produced or caused to be produced.

(6) Where any documents removed under the powers conferred by this paragraph are lost or damaged, the Commissioners shall be liable to compensate their owner for any expenses reasonably incurred by him in replacing or repairing the documents.

Entry and inspection

129 For the purpose of exercising any powers under this Schedule, an authorised person may at any reasonable time enter and inspect premises used in connection with the carrying on of a business.

Entry and search

130— (1) Where—

(a) a justice of the peace is satisfied on information on oath that there is reasonable ground for suspecting that a fraud offence which appears to be of a serious nature is being, has been or is about to be committed on any premises or that evidence of the commission of such an offence is to be found there, or

(b) in Scotland a justice (within the meaning of section 307 of the Criminal Procedure (Scotland) Act 1995) is satisfied by evidence on oath as mentioned in paragraph (a),

he may issue a warrant in writing authorising any authorised person to enter those premises, if necessary by force, at any time within one month from the time of the issue of the warrant and to search them.

(2) A person who enters the premises under the authority of the warrant may—

(a) take with him such other persons as appear to him to be necessary;

(b) seize and remove any such documents or other things at all found on the premises as he has reasonable cause to believe may be required as evidence for the purposes of proceedings in respect of a fraud offence which appears to him to be of a serious nature;

(c) search, or cause to be searched, any person found on the premises whom he has reasonable cause to believe to be in possession of any documents or other things which may be so required.

(3) Sub-paragraph (2) shall not authorise any person to be searched by a member of the opposite sex.

(4) The powers conferred by a warrant under this paragraph shall not be exercisable—

(a) by more than such number of authorised persons as may be specified in the warrant;

(b) outside such periods of the day as may be so specified; or

(c) if the warrant so provides, otherwise than in the presence of a constable in uniform.

(5) An authorised person seeking to exercise the powers conferred by a warrant under this paragraph or, if there is more than one such authorised person, such one of them as is in charge of the search shall provide a copy of the warrant endorsed with his name as follows—

(a) if the occupier of the premises concerned is present at the time the search is to begin, the copy shall be supplied to the occupier;

(b) if at that time the occupier is not present but a person who appears to the authorised person to be in charge of the premises is present, the copy shall be supplied to that person;

(c) if neither paragraph (a) nor paragraph (b) applies, the copy shall be left in a prominent place on the premises.

(6) In this paragraph "a fraud offence" means an offence under any of paragraphs 92 to 94.[1]

Cross references—Criminal Justice and Police Act 2001 s 50, Sch 1 Pt 1 (s 50 of that Act which provides additional powers of seizure from premises applies to the power of seizure conferred under sub-para (2) above; for the relevant provisions of the Criminal Justice and Police Act 2001, see the *VAT* section of this publication).

Amendments—[1] This para repealed by FA 2007 ss 84, 114, Sch 22 paras 3, 11(*b*), Sch 27 Pt 5(1) with effect from 1 December 2007 (by virtue of SI 2007/3166 art 3(*a*)).

Order for access to recorded information etc

131— (1) Where, on an application by an authorised person, a justice of the peace or, in Scotland, a justice (within the meaning of section 307 of the Criminal Procedure (Scotland) Act 1995) is satisfied that there are reasonable grounds for believing—

(*a*) that an offence in connection with levy is being, has been or is about to be committed, and

(*b*) that any recorded information (including any document of any nature at all) which may be required as evidence for the purpose of any proceedings in respect of such an offence is in the possession of any person,

he may make an order under this paragraph.

(2) An order under this paragraph is an order that the person who appears to the justice to be in possession of the recorded information to which the application relates shall—

(*a*) give an authorised person access to it, and

(*b*) permit an authorised person to remove and take away any of it which he reasonably considers necessary,

not later than the end of the period of seven days beginning with the date of the order or the end of such longer period as the order may specify.

(3) The reference in sub-paragraph (2)(*a*) to giving an authorised person access to the recorded information to which the application relates includes a reference to permitting the authorised person to take copies of it or to make extracts from it.

(4) Where the recorded information consists of information [stored in any electronic form][1], an order under this paragraph shall have effect as an order to produce the information—

(*a*) in a form in which it is visible and legible [or from which it can readily be produced in a visible and legible form][1]; and

(*b*) if the authorised person wishes to remove it, in a form in which it can be removed.

(5) This paragraph is without prejudice to the preceding paragraphs of this Part of this Schedule.

Amendments—[1] In sub-para (4), words substituted, and words inserted, by the Criminal Justice and Police Act 2001 ss 70, 138, Sch 2 Pt 2 para 13 with effect from 1 April 2003 (by virtue of SI 2003/708); for the relevant provisions of that Act, see the *VAT* section of this publication.

Removal of documents etc

132— (1) An authorised person who removes anything in the exercise of a power conferred by or under paragraph 130 or 131 shall, if so requested by a person showing himself—

(*a*) to be the occupier of premises from which it was removed, or

(*b*) to have had custody or control of it immediately before the removal,

provide that person with a record of what he removed.

(2) The authorised person shall provide the record within a reasonable time from the making of the request for it.

(3) Subject to sub-paragraph (7), if a request for permission to be allowed access to anything which—

(*a*) has been removed by an authorised person, and

(*b*) is retained by the Commissioners for the purposes of investigating an offence,

is made to the officer in overall charge of the investigation by a person who had custody or control of the thing immediately before it was so removed, or by someone acting on behalf of such a person, the officer shall allow the person who made the request access to it under the supervision of an authorised person.

(4) Subject to sub-paragraph (7), if a request for a photograph or copy of any such thing is made to the officer in overall charge of the investigation by a person who had custody or control of the thing immediately before it was so removed, or by someone acting on behalf of such a person, the officer shall—

(*a*) allow the person who made the request access to it under the supervision of an authorised person for the purpose of photographing it or copying it; or

(*b*) photograph or copy it, or cause it to be photographed or copied.

(5) Subject to sub-paragraph (7), where anything is photographed or copied under sub-paragraph (4)(*b*), the officer shall supply the photograph or copy, or cause it to be supplied, to the person who made the request.

(6) The photograph or copy shall be supplied within a reasonable time from the making of the request.

(7) There is no duty under this paragraph to allow access to anything, or to supply a photograph or copy of anything, if the officer in overall charge of the investigation for the purposes of which it was removed has reasonable grounds for believing that to do so would prejudice—

(*a*) that investigation;

(*b*) the investigation of an offence other than the offence for the purposes of the investigation of which the thing was removed; or

(*c*) any criminal proceedings which may be brought as a result of the investigation of which he is in charge or any such investigation as is mentioned in paragraph (*b*).

(8) Any reference in this paragraph to the officer in overall charge of the investigation is a reference to the person whose name and address are endorsed on the warrant concerned as being the officer so in charge.

Enforcement of paragraph 132

133— (1) Where, on an application made as mentioned in sub-paragraph (2), the appropriate judicial authority is satisfied that a person has failed to comply with a requirement imposed by paragraph 132, the authority may order that person to comply with the requirement within such time and in such manner as may be specified in the order.

(2) An application under sub-paragraph (1) shall not be made except—

(*a*) in the case of a failure to comply with any of the requirements imposed by paragraph 132(1) and (2)—

(i) by the occupier of the premises from which the thing in question was removed, or

(ii) by the person who had custody or control of it immediately before it was so removed;

(*b*) in any other case, by the person who had such custody or control.

(3) In this paragraph "the appropriate judicial authority" means—

(*a*) in England and Wales, a magistrates' court;

(*b*) in Scotland, the sheriff;

(*c*) in Northern Ireland, a court of summary jurisdiction, as defined in Article 2(2)(*a*) of the Magistrates' Courts (Northern Ireland) Order 1981.

(4) In England and Wales and Northern Ireland, an application for an order under this paragraph shall be made by way of complaint; and sections 21 and 42(2) of the Interpretation Act (Northern Ireland) 1954 shall apply as if any reference in those provisions to any enactment included a reference to this paragraph.

Power to take samples and examine meters

134— (1) An authorised person, if it appears to him necessary for the protection of the revenue against mistake or fraud, may at any time take, from material which he has reasonable cause to believe is—

(*a*) a taxable commodity which is intended to be, is being or has been the subject of a taxable supply, or

(*b*) a product of the burning of a taxable commodity (other than electricity) which is being or has been the subject of a taxable supply,

such samples as he may require with a view to determining how the material ought to be treated, or to have been treated, for the purposes of the levy.

(2) An authorised person, if it appears to him necessary for the protection of the revenue against mistake or fraud, may at any time examine any meter which he has reasonable cause to believe is intended to be, is being or has been used for ascertaining the quantity of any taxable commodity supplied by a taxable supply.

(3) Any sample taken under sub-paragraph (1) shall be disposed of in such manner as the Commissioners may direct.

Evidence by certificate

135— (1) In any proceedings a certificate of the Commissioners—

(*a*) that a person was or was not at any time registered for the purposes of the levy [or][1],

(*b*) that any return required by regulations made under paragraph 41 has not been made or had not been made at any time,

(*c*), (*d*) ...[1]

shall be evidence or, in Scotland, sufficient evidence of that fact.

(2) A photograph of any document provided to the Commissioners for the purposes of this Schedule and certified by them to be such a photograph shall be admissible in any proceedings, whether civil or criminal, to the same extent as the document itself.

(3) In any proceedings any document purporting to be a certificate under sub-paragraph (1) or (2) shall be taken to be such a certificate unless the contrary is shown.

Amendments—[1] Words inserted and repealed by FA 2008 s 138, Sch 44 para 8 with effect from 21 July 2008. Sub-para (1)(*c*), (*d*) previously read as follows—

"(*c*) that any levy shown as due in a return or other notification made in pursuance of regulations made under paragraph 41 has not been paid, or

(*d*) that any amount shown as due in any assessment made under this Schedule has not been paid,".

Inducements to provide information

136— (1) This paragraph applies—

(*a*) to any criminal proceedings against a person in respect of an offence in connection with or in relation to levy; and

(*b*) to any proceedings against a person for the recovery of any sum due from him in connection with or in relation to levy.

(2) Statements made or documents produced or provided by or on behalf of a person shall not be inadmissible in any proceedings to which this paragraph applies by reason only that—

(*a*) a matter falling within sub-paragraph (3) or (4) has been drawn to that person's attention; and

(*b*) he was or may have been induced, as a result, to make the statements or to produce or provide the documents.

(3) The matters falling within this sub-paragraph are—

(*a*) that, in relation to levy, the Commissioners may assess an amount due by way of a civil penalty instead of instituting criminal proceedings;

(*b*) that it is the practice of the Commissioners (without giving any undertaking as to whether they will make such an assessment in any case) to be influenced by whether a person—

(i) has made a full confession of any dishonest conduct to which he has been a party; and

(ii) has otherwise co-operated to the full with any investigation.

(4) The matter falling within this sub-paragraph is the fact that the Commissioners or, on appeal, an appeal tribunal have power under any provision of this Schedule to reduce a penalty.

Disclosure of information

137— (1) Notwithstanding any obligation not to disclose information that would otherwise apply, but subject to sub-paragraph (2), the Commissioners may disclose any information obtained or held by them in or in connection with the carrying out of their functions in relation to the levy to any of the following—

(*a*) any Minister of the Crown;

(*b*) the Scottish Ministers;

(*c*) any Minister, within the meaning of the Northern Ireland Act 1998, or any Northern Ireland department;

(*d*) the National Assembly for Wales;

(*e*) the Environment Agency;

(*f*) the Scottish Environment Protection Agency;

(*g*) the Gas and Electricity Markets Authority;

(*h*) the Director General of Electricity Supply for Northern Ireland;

(*i*) the Director General of Gas for Northern Ireland;

(*j*) an authorised officer of any person mentioned in paragraphs (*a*) to (*i*).

(2) Information shall not be disclosed under sub-paragraph (1) except for the purpose of assisting a person falling within paragraphs (*a*) to (*j*) of that sub-paragraph in the performance of his duties.

(3) Notwithstanding any such obligation as is mentioned in sub-paragraph (1), any person mentioned in sub-paragraph (1)(*a*) to (*j*) may disclose information—

(*a*) to the Commissioners, or

(*b*) to an authorised officer of the Commissioners,

for the purpose of assisting the Commissioners in the performance of duties in relation to the levy.

(4) Information that has been disclosed to a person by virtue of this paragraph shall not be disclosed by him except—

(*a*) to another person to whom (instead of him) disclosure could by virtue of this paragraph have been made; or

(*b*) for the purpose of any proceedings connected with the operation of any provision made by or under any enactment relating to the environment or to levy.

(5) References in the preceding provisions of this paragraph to an authorised officer of any person ("the principal") are to any person who has been designated by the principal as a person to and by whom information may be disclosed by virtue of this paragraph.

(6) Where the principal is a person falling within any of paragraphs (*a*) to (*c*) of sub-paragraph (1), the principal shall notify the Commissioners in writing of the name of any person designated by the principal for the purposes of this paragraph.

(7) No charge may be made for any disclosure made by virtue of this paragraph.

(8) In this paragraph "enactment" includes an enactment contained in an Act of the Scottish Parliament or in any Northern Ireland legislation.

Meaning of "authorised person"

138 In this Part of this Schedule "authorised person" means any person acting under the authority of the Commissioners.

PART XIII
MISCELLANEOUS AND SUPPLEMENTARY

Security for levy

139— (1) Where it appears to the Commissioners necessary to do so for the protection of the revenue they may require any person who is or is required to be registered for the purposes of the levy to give security, or further security, for the payment of any levy which is or may become due from him.

(2) The power of the Commissioners to require any security, or further security, under this paragraph shall be a power to require security, or further security, of such amount and in such manner as they may determine.

(3) A person who is liable to account for the levy on a taxable supply that he makes is guilty of an offence if, at the time the supply is made—

(*a*) he has been required to give security under this paragraph, and
(*b*) he has not complied with that requirement.

(4) A person who is liable to account for the levy on a taxable supply that another person makes to him is guilty of an offence if he makes any arrangements for the making of the supply at a time when—

(*a*) he has been required to give security under this paragraph, and
(*b*) he has not complied with that requirement.

(5) A person guilty of an offence under this paragraph shall be liable, on summary conviction, to a penalty of level 5 on the standard scale.

(6) Sections 145 to 155 of the Customs and Excise Management Act 1979 (proceedings for offences, mitigation of penalties and certain other matters) shall apply in relation to an offence under this paragraph as they apply in relation to offences and penalties under the customs and excise Acts.

Destination of receipts

140

Amendment—Paragraph repealed by the Commissioners for Revenue and Customs Act 2005 ss 50, 52, Sch 4 para 81 and Sch 5 with effect from 18 April 2005 by virtue of the Commissioners for Revenue and Customs Act (Commencement) Order, SI 2005/1126, art 2(2).

Provisional collection of levy

141

Amendment—This paragraph repealed by FA 2001 s 110, Sch 33 Pt 3(3) with effect from 11 May 2001.

[Invoices incorrectly showing levy due

141A— (1) This paragraph applies where—

(*a*) a person issues an invoice showing an amount as levy chargeable on a supply, and
(*b*) no levy is chargeable on the supply, or the amount chargeable is less than the amount shown.

(2) The person shall be liable to a penalty unless he satisfies the Commissioners or, on appeal, a tribunal that there is a reasonable excuse for the inclusion in the invoice of the false information.

(3) The amount of the penalty is £50 or, if more, the following amount—

(*a*) where no levy is chargeable, the amount shown as chargeable;
(*b*) where an amount of levy is chargeable, the difference between that amount and the amount shown as chargeable.

(4) It is irrelevant for the purposes of sub-paragraph (1) whether or not the supply shown on the invoice actually takes place or has taken place.

(5) A reference in this paragraph to an invoice is a reference to any kind of invoice (and not just a climate change levy accounting document).][1]

Amendment—[1] This paragraph inserted by FA 2002 s 128 with effect for invoices issued on or after 24 July 2002.

Adjustment of contracts

142— (1) Sub-paragraph (2) applies in the case of a contract for the supply of a taxable commodity if—

(*a*) the contract is entered into before 1st April 2001 (whether before or after the passing of this Act) or at a time when supplies such as are provided for by the contract are not taxable supplies, but
(*b*) supplies falling to be made under the contract will be, or become or will become, taxable supplies.

(2) The supplier of the commodity may unilaterally vary the contract by adjusting the price chargeable for any supply made under the contract if he does so for the purpose of passing on,

to the person liable to pay for the supply, the burden (or any part of the burden) of the levy for which the supplier is liable to account on the supply.

(3) Sub-paragraph (4) applies in the case of a contract for the supply of a taxable commodity if it provides (whether as a result of a variation under sub-paragraph (2) or otherwise) for the passing on, to the person liable to pay for the supply, of the burden (or any part of the burden) of any levy for which the supplier is liable to account on the supply.

(4) The supplier of the commodity may unilaterally vary the contract by adjusting the price chargeable for any supply made under the contract if he does so for the purpose of giving effect (to any extent) to—

(*a*) any change in the rate at which levy is charged on the supply;

(*b*) levy ceasing to be chargeable on the supply.

(5) The powers conferred by this paragraph are in addition to any contractual powers.

Climate change levy accounting documents

143— (1) Provision may be made by regulations requiring registered persons who make taxable supplies—

(*a*) in prescribed cases, or

(*b*) to persons of prescribed descriptions,

to provide the persons supplied with climate change levy accounting documents.

(2) For the purposes of this Schedule a "climate change levy accounting document" for a taxable supply is an invoice—

(*a*) …[1]

(*b*) stating the date on which it is issued, and

(*c*) containing the required statements.

(3) For the purposes of sub-paragraph (2)(*c*) "the required statements" means—

(*a*) in the case of a climate change levy accounting document issued under paragraph 27, the statements required by paragraph 27(5);

(*b*) in the case of a climate change levy accounting document whose provision is required by regulations, statements of prescribed particulars of or relating to—

(i) the supply,

(ii) the persons by and to whom the supply is made, and

(iii) the levy chargeable.

(4) Where regulations make provision requiring a climate change levy accounting document to be provided in connection with any description of supply, regulations may make provision for—

(*a*) requiring the accounting document to be provided within a prescribed time after, or at a prescribed time before, the supply is treated as taking place;

(*b*) allowing an accounting document to be provided later than required by the regulations where it is provided in accordance with general or special directions given by the Commissioners.

(5) Regulations may make provision conferring power on the Commissioners to allow the requirements of any regulations as to the statements to be contained in a climate change levy accounting document to be relaxed or dispensed with.

(6) Regulations may make provision for allowing a climate change levy accounting document required to be issued under paragraph 27 to be issued later than the time applicable under paragraph 27(2) where it is issued in accordance with general or special directions given by the Commissioners.

(7) In this paragraph "regulations" means regulations made by the Commissioners.

Amendments—[1] Sub-para (2)(*a*) repealed by FA 2008 s 150 with effect from 21 July 2008. Para (*a*) previously read as follows—

"(*a*) stating that it is a climate change levy accounting document (for which purpose the inclusion of the phrase "climate change levy accounting document" or the phrase "CCL accounting document", whether as shown here or with any of the letters shown here as small letters appearing as capitals, shall be sufficient),".

Service of notices etc

144— (1) Any notice, notification or requirement that is to be or may be served on, given to or imposed on any person for the purposes of any provision made by or under this Schedule may be served, given or imposed by sending it to that person or his tax representative by post in a letter addressed to that person or his representative at the latest or usual residence or place of business of that person or representative.

(2) Any direction required or authorised by or under this Schedule to be given by the Commissioners may be given by sending it by post in a letter addressed to each person affected by it at his latest or usual residence or place of business.

Variation and withdrawal of directions etc

145 Any direction, notice or notification required or authorised by or under this Schedule to be given by the Commissioners may be withdrawn or varied by them by a direction, notice or notification given in the same manner as the one withdrawn or varied.

Regulations and orders

146— (1) Any power under this Schedule to make regulations shall be exercisable by statutory instrument.

(2) A statutory instrument that—

(*a*) contains regulations made under this Schedule, and

(*b*) is not subject to a requirement that a draft of the instrument be laid before Parliament and approved by a resolution of the House of Commons,

shall be subject to annulment in pursuance of a resolution of the House of Commons.

(3) A statutory instrument that contains (whether alone or with other provisions) regulations under paragraph 3(3), 14(3), 15(4)(*a*), 16, 18(2), [18A,][1] 52, 113(1), 148(4), 149 or 151(2) (regulations made by the Treasury) shall not be made unless a draft of the statutory instrument containing the regulations has been laid before Parliament and approved by a resolution of the House of Commons.

(4) Where regulations under this Schedule made by the Commissioners impose a relevant requirement on any person, they may provide that if the person fails to comply with the requirement he shall be liable, subject to sub-paragraph (5), to a penalty of £250.

(5) Where by reason of any conduct—

(*a*) a person is convicted of an offence (whether under this Act or otherwise), or

(*b*) a person is assessed to a penalty under paragraph 98 [or to a penalty for a deliberate inaccuracy under Schedule 24 to the Finance Act 2007 (penalties for errors)][2],

that person shall not by reason of that conduct be liable also to a penalty under any regulations under this Schedule.

(6) In sub-paragraph (4) "relevant requirement" means any requirement other than one the penalty for a contravention of which is specified in paragraph 41(3), 114(3) or 125(6).

(7) A power under this Schedule to make any provision by regulations—

(*a*) may be exercised so as to apply the provision only in such cases as may be described in the regulations;

(*b*) may be exercised so as to make different provision for different cases or descriptions of case; and

(*c*) shall include power by the regulations to make such supplementary, incidental, consequential or transitional provision as the authority making the regulations may think fit.

Amendment—[1] Words in sub-para (3) inserted by FA 2003 s 188(2)(*c*) with effect from 10 July 2003.

[2] Words in sub-para (5)(*b*) inserted by the Finance Act 2008, Schedule 40 (Appointed Day, Transitional Provisions and Consequential Amendments) Order, SI 2009/571 art 8, Sch 1 para 30(1), (7) with effect from 1 April 2009.

PART XIV
INTERPRETATION

General

147 In this Schedule—

"accounting period" means a period which, in pursuance of any regulations under paragraph 41, is an accounting period for the purposes of the levy;

"agreement" includes any arrangement or understanding (whether or not legally enforceable), and cognate expressions shall be construed accordingly;

"appeal tribunal" means a [the First-tier Tribunal or, where determined by or under Tribunal Procedure Rules, the Upper Tribunal;][4];

"auto-generator" has the meaning given by paragraph 152;

"climate change agreement" has the meaning given by paragraph 46;

"climate change levy accounting document" has the meaning given by paragraph 143(2);

"combined heat and power station" has the meaning given by paragraph 148(1);

"the Commissioners" means the Commissioners of Customs and Excise;

"conduct" includes acts and omissions;

"electricity utility" has the meaning given by paragraph 150(2) (but see paragraph 150(4));

"fully exempt combined heat and power station" has the meaning given by paragraph 148(2);

"gas utility" has the meaning given by paragraph 150(3) (but see paragraph 150(4));

["HMRC" means Her Majesty's Revenue and Customs;[4]

"half-rate supply" has the meaning given by paragraph 43(1);[3]

"member", in relation to a group, shall be construed in accordance with regulations under paragraph 116;

"non-resident taxpayer" means a person who—

(*a*) is or is required to be registered for the purposes of the levy, and

(*b*) is not resident in the United Kingdom;

"partly exempt combined heat and power station" has the meaning given by paragraph 148(3);

"prescribed" (except in paragraphs 14(3), 16(3) [, 18A][1] and 148(4)) means prescribed by regulations made by the Commissioners under this Schedule;

"produced"—

(*a*) in relation to electricity, means generated, and
(*b*) in relation to any other commodity, includes extracted;

"reduced-rate supply" has the meaning given by paragraph [44(1)][2] (which, by virtue of paragraph [44(2)][2], has effect subject to [paragraph 44(2A) to (2D) and][5] [paragraphs 45 and 45B][6]);

"registered" means registered in the register maintained under paragraph 53(2);

"representative member", in relation to a group, shall be construed in accordance with regulations under paragraph 116;

"resident in the United Kingdom" has the meaning given by paragraph 156;

"ship" includes hovercraft;

"special utility scheme" has the meaning given by paragraph 29(1);

"subordinate legislation" has the same meaning as in the Interpretation Act 1978;

"supply for charity use" shall be construed in accordance with paragraph 8;

"supply for domestic use" shall be construed in accordance with paragraphs 8 and 9;

"tax credit" means a tax credit for which provision is made by tax credit regulations;

"tax credit regulations" means regulations under paragraph 62;

"tax representative", in relation to any person, means the person who, in accordance with any regulations under paragraph 114, is for the time being that person's tax representative for the purposes of the levy;

"taxable commodity" shall be construed in accordance with paragraph 3;

"taxable supply" shall be construed in accordance with paragraphs 2(2) and 4;

"the United Kingdom" includes the territorial waters adjacent to any part of the United Kingdom;

"utility" has the meaning given by paragraph 150(1).

Amendment—[1] Words in definition of "prescribed" inserted by FA 2003 s 188(2) with effect from 10 July 2003.
[2] In the definition of "reduced-rate supply", figures substituted for "44(3)" and "44(4)" by FA 2007 s 23, Sch 2 paras 1, 10 with effect from 1 November 2007: SI 2007/2902 art 2(1). These amendments only apply in relation to a supply actually made on or after 1 November 2007: SI 2007/2902 art 2(2).
[3] The definition of "half-rate supply" repealed by FA 2006 ss 172(15), 178, Sch 26 Pt 8(1) with effect from 1 November 2007: SI 2007/2901, art 2(1). This amendment does not apply in relation to a half-rate supply made before 1 April 2006.
[4] In definition of "appeal tribunal" words substituted for the words "VAT and duties tribunal"; definition of "HMRC" inserted by the Transfer of Tribunal Functions and Revenue and Customs Appeals Order, SI 2009/56 art 3, Sch 1 para 292 with effect from 1 April 2009.
[5] Words inserted by FA 2009 s 117(1), (3) with effect from 21 July 2009.
[6] Words substituted by FA 2009 s 118, Sch 59 paras 2, 9 with effect where the certification period begins on or after 1 April 2009.

Meaning of "combined heat and power station" etc

148— (1) In this Schedule "combined heat and power station" means a station producing electricity or motive power that is (or may be) operated for purposes including the supply to any premises of—

(*a*) heat produced in association with electricity or motive power, or
(*b*) steam produced from, or air or water heated by, such heat.

(2) In this Schedule "fully exempt combined heat and power station" means a combined heat and power station in respect of which there is in force a certificate (a "full-exemption certificate")—

(*a*) given by the Secretary of State,
(*b*) stating that the station is a fully exempt combined heat and power station for the purposes of the levy, and
(*c*) [complying (so far as applicable) with][1] any provision made by regulations under sub-paragraph (10).

(3) In this Schedule "partly exempt combined heat and power station" means a combined heat and power station in respect of which there is in force a certificate (a "part-exemption certificate")—

(*a*) given by the Secretary of State,
(*b*) stating that the station is a partly exempt combined heat and power station for the purposes of the levy, and
(*c*) [complying (so far as applicable) with][1] any provision made by regulations under sub-paragraph (10).

(4) The Secretary of State shall give a full-exemption certificate in respect of a combined heat and power station where—

(*a*) an application is made for a certificate under this paragraph in respect of the station, and
(*b*) it appears to him that such conditions as may be prescribed are satisfied in relation to the station.

For this purpose "prescribed" means prescribed by regulations made by the Treasury.

(5) The Secretary of State shall give a part-exemption certificate in respect of a combined heat and power station where—

(*a*) an application is made for a certificate under this paragraph in respect of the station, and
(*b*) his decision on the application is to refuse to give a full-exemption certificate.

(6) …[1]

(7) In prescribing conditions under sub-paragraph (4), the Treasury must have regard to the object of securing that a combined heat and power station will only be a fully exempt combined heat and power station for the purposes of this Schedule if it is one in which electricity or motive power is produced concurrently with heat in a manner that makes efficient use of the commodities used in their production.

(8) A condition prescribed under sub-paragraph (4) may, in particular, relate to any of the following—

(*a*) a station's outputs;
(*b*) the commodities used in the production of such outputs;
(*c*) the methods of producing such outputs;
(*d*) the efficiency with which such outputs are produced.

(9) For the purposes of sub-paragraph (8), a station's "outputs" are any electricity or motive power produced in the station and any of the following supplied from the station, namely—

(*a*) heat or steam, or
(*b*) air, or water, that has been heated or cooled.

(10) The Secretary of State may by regulations make provision for or about—

(*a*) certificates under this paragraph;
(*b*) applications for such certificates;
(*c*) the information that is to accompany such applications.

(11) The provision that may be made by virtue of sub-paragraph (10)(*a*) includes in particular—

(*a*) provision in respect of the periods for which certificates under this paragraph are to be in force;
(*b*) provision for the (non-retrospective) variation or revocation of such certificates.

Amendments—[1] Words in sub-paras (2)(*c*) and (3)(*c*) substituted, and sub-para (6) repealed, by FA 2003 ss 189(1), (3), 216, Sch 43 Pt 4 with effect for supplies made on or after 22 July 2005 (by virtue of SI 2005/1713).

Determination of efficiency percentages for combined heat and power stations

149— (1) The Treasury may by regulations make provision for determining …[1] the efficiency percentage for a combined heat and power station.

(2) Regulations under this paragraph may, in particular, include—

(*a*) provision in respect of methods of calculating efficiency percentages;
(*b*) provision in respect of the measurements and data to be used in calculating such percentages;
(*c*) provision in respect of the procedures for determining such percentages;
(*d*) provision in respect of verifying—
 (i) calculations by which such percentages are produced, and
 (ii) measurements and data used in such calculations;
(*e*) provision that, so far as framed by reference to any document, is framed by reference to that document as from time to time in force.

(3) In making provision under this paragraph, the Treasury must have regard to the object of securing that the efficiency percentage for a combined heat and power station is (save for any appropriate adjustments) a percentage that reflects a fair assessment of the efficiency with which commodities are transformed in the station into electricity or motive power.

Amendments—[1] Words in sub-para (1) repealed by FA 2003 ss 189(1), (4), 216, Sch 43 Pt 4 with effect for supplies made on or after 22 July 2005 (by virtue of SI 2005/1713).

[Certification of electricity from fully or partly exempt combined heat and power station

149A— (1) The Commissioners may by regulations make provision for the Gas and Electricity Markets Authority, or the Director General of Electricity Supply for Northern Ireland, to certify as respects any quantity of electricity that—

(*a*) the electricity has been produced in a fully exempt combined heat and power station;
(*b*) the electricity has been produced in a partly exempt combined heat and power station and supplied from the station without causing the limit referred to in paragraph 16(2) to be exceeded.

(2) Regulations under this paragraph may provide that for any purposes of this Schedule (or any regulations made under it)—

(*a*) electricity is not to be regarded as having been produced as specified in sub-paragraph (1)(*a*) unless it has been certified under that provision;
(*b*) electricity is not to be regarded as having been produced and supplied as specified in sub-paragraph (1)(*b*) unless it has been certified under that provision.

(3) Regulations under this paragraph may in particular provide that the supply of any electricity does not qualify for the exemption under paragraph 16(2) unless the electricity is certified as specified in sub-paragraph (1)(*b*).

(4) Regulations under this paragraph may also make provision for determining whether electricity is produced and supplied as specified in sub-paragraph (1)(*b*).][1]

Amendment—[1] This paragraph inserted by FA 2002 s 124 with effect from 24 July 2002.

Meaning of "utility"

150— (1) In this Schedule "utility" means an electricity utility or a gas utility.

(2) In this Schedule "electricity utility" means the holder of—

(*a*) a licence under section 6(1)(*d*) of the Electricity Act 1989 (supply licences), or

(*b*) a licence under Article 10(1)(*c*) or (2) of the Electricity Supply (Northern Ireland) Order 1992,

except where the holder is acting otherwise than for purposes connected with the carrying on of activities authorised by the licence.

Until the coming into force of the substitution for section 6 of the Electricity Act 1989 provided for by the Utilities Act 2000, paragraph (*a*) above shall have effect as if the reference to section 6(1)(*d*) were to section 6(1)(*c*) or (2).

(3) In this Schedule "gas utility" means the holder of—

(*a*) a licence under section 7A(1) of the Gas Act 1986 (supply licences), or

(*b*) a licence under Article 8(1)(*c*) of the Gas (Northern Ireland) Order 1996,

except where the holder is acting otherwise than for purposes connected with the carrying on of activities authorised by the licence.

(4) Sub-paragraphs (1) to (3) have effect subject to—

(*a*) any direction under paragraph 151(1), and

(*b*) any regulations under paragraph 151(2).

Person treated as, or as not being, a utility

151— (1) The Commissioners may by direction (a "utility direction") make, in respect of a person (or persons) specified in the direction, provision authorised by sub-paragraph (3).

(2) The Treasury may by regulations ("utility regulations") make, in respect of any person of a description specified in the regulations, provision authorised by sub-paragraph (3).

(3) The provision authorised by this sub-paragraph is provision for—

(*a*) a person who is an unregulated electricity supplier to be treated for levy purposes as being an electricity utility;

(*b*) a person who is an unregulated gas supplier to be treated for levy purposes as being a gas utility;

(*c*) a person who is an electricity utility to be treated for levy purposes as not being an electricity utility;

(*d*) a person who is a gas utility to be treated for levy purposes as not being a gas utility.

(4) References in sub-paragraph (3) to provision for a person to be treated in a particular way for "levy purposes" are to provision for him to be treated in that way for—

(*a*) the purposes of this Schedule, or

(*b*) such of those purposes as are specified in the direction or regulations by which the provision is made.

(5) The power to make any provision by a utility direction or utility regulations may be exercised so that the provision applies in relation to a person only to an extent specified in, or determined under, the direction or regulations.

(6) A utility direction cannot take effect until it has been—

(*a*) given by the Commissioners to each person in respect of whom it makes provision, and

(*b*) published by the Commissioners.

(7) Paragraph 146(7)(*b*) and (*c*) applies to the power to make provision by a utility direction as to a power to make provision by regulations.

(8) In this paragraph—

"unregulated electricity supplier" means a person who—

(*a*) makes supplies of electricity, and

(*b*) is not an electricity utility;

"unregulated gas supplier" means a person who—

(*a*) makes supplies of gas that is in a gaseous state and is of a kind supplied by a gas utility, and

(*b*) is not a gas utility.

Meaning of "auto-generator"

152— (1) In this Schedule "auto-generator" means a person who produces electricity if the electricity that he produces is primarily for his own consumption.

(2) The Commissioners may by regulations specify requirements to be fulfilled before the electricity that a person produces is, for the purposes of sub-paragraph (1), to be taken as produced primarily for his own consumption.

(3) For the purposes of this paragraph, electricity is for a person's own consumption if it is for consumption by him or a person connected with him within the meaning of section 839 of the Taxes Act 1988.

Meaning of "levy due for an accounting period"

153 References in this Schedule, in relation to any accounting period, to levy due from any person for that period are references (subject to any regulations made by virtue of paragraph 41(2)(*a*)) to the levy for which that person is required, in accordance with regulations under paragraph 41, to account by reference to that period.

Meaning of "repayment of levy"

154 References in this Schedule to a repayment of levy or of an amount of levy are references to any repayment of an amount to any person by virtue of—

(*a*) any tax credit regulations; or
(*b*) paragraph 63, 87(3) or 110(3).

Interpretation of "in the course or furtherance of a business"

155— (1) Anything done in connection with the termination or intended termination of a business shall, for the purposes of this Schedule, be treated as being done in the course or furtherance of the business.

(2) Where in a disposition of a business as a going concern, or of its assets (whether or not in connection with its reorganisation or winding up), there is a supply of a taxable commodity, that supply shall for the purposes of this Schedule be taken to be made in the course or furtherance of the business.

Meaning of "resident in the United Kingdom"

156 For the purposes of this Schedule a person is resident in the United Kingdom at any time if, at that time—

(*a*) that person has an established place of business in the United Kingdom;
(*b*) that person has a usual place of residence in the United Kingdom; or
(*c*) that person is a firm or unincorporated body which (without having a relevant connection with the United Kingdom by virtue of paragraph (*a*)) has amongst its partners or members at least one individual with a usual place of residence in the United Kingdom.

References to the Gas and Electricity Markets Authority: transitional provision

157— (1) Until such time as a transfer of functions from the Director General of Electricity Supply to the Gas and Electricity Markets Authority ("the Authority") has taken effect, references in paragraph 19 to the Authority shall be taken to be references to the Director General.

(2) Until such time as all the functions of the Director General of Electricity Supply have been transferred in accordance with the Utilities Act 2000 (transfer to the Authority) or abolished, references to the Authority in paragraph 137 shall be taken to include the Director General.

(3) Until such time as all the functions of the Director General of Gas Supply have been transferred in accordance with the Utilities Act 2000 (transfer to the Authority) or abolished, references to the Authority in paragraph 137 shall be taken to include the Director General.

(4) The power conferred by paragraph 146(7) includes, in particular, power for regulations under paragraph 19 to make transitional provision in connection with the transfer of functions from the Director General of Electricity Supply to the Authority."

SCHEDULE 7

CLIMATE CHANGE LEVY: CONSEQUENTIAL AMENDMENTS

Section 30

Provisional Collection of Taxes Act 1968 (*c 2*)

1 (*amends* PCTA 1968 s 1(1)).

Bankruptcy (*Scotland*) *Act 1985* (*c 66*)

2 …[1]

Insolvency Act 1986 (*c 45*)

3 …[1]

Income and Corporation Taxes Act 1988 (*c 1*)

4 (*inserts* TA 1988 s 827(1D)).

Insolvency (*Northern Ireland*) *Order 1989* (*NI 19*)

5 …[2]

Finance Act 1996 (c 8)

6 (*inserts* FA 1996 s 197(2)(*g*)).

Finance Act 1997 (c 16)

7— (1) The Finance Act 1997 is amended as follows.

(2), (3) (*amend* FA 1997 ss 51(5), 52(5)).

(4) Sub-paragraph (3) extends only to Scotland.

Amendments—[1] Paras 2, 3: repealed by the Enterprise Act 2002 s 278(2), Sch 26 with effect from 15 September 2003 (by virtue of SI 2003/2093, art 2(1), Sch 1; for transitional provisions see art 4(1), (1A)–(1D), (2), (3), (4)(*b*) thereof (as amended by SI 2003/2332, art 2)).

[2] Para 5 repealed by the Insolvency (Northern Ireland) Order 2005, SI 2005/1455 art 31, Sch 9 with effect from 27 March 2006 (by virtue of the Insolvency (2005 Order) (Commencement No 1) Order (Northern Ireland) 2006, SR 2006/21, art 2; for transitional provisions in relation to preferential status for Crown debts in cases started before that date see the Insolvency (2005 Order) (Transitional Provisions and Savings) Order (Northern Ireland) 2006, SR 2006/22, art 3).

FINANCE ACT 2001

An Act to grant certain duties, to alter other duties, and to amend the law relating to the National Debt and the Public Revenue, and to make further provision in connection with Finance.

[11 May 2001]

PART IV
OTHER TAXES

Value added tax

…

99 VAT: re-enactment of reduced-rate provisions

…

(6) The consequential amendments in Part II of Schedule 31 to this Act have effect.

…

Climate change levy

105 Climate change levy

(1) Schedule 6 to the Finance Act 2000 (climate change levy) is amended as follows.

(2) (*inserts* FA 2000 Sch 6 para 11A).

(3) (*inserts* FA 2000 Sch 6 para 14(2)(*c*)).

(4) (*substitutes* FA 2000 Sch 6 para 14(3)(*c*)).

(5) (*inserts* FA 2000 Sch 6 para 14(3A)).

(6) In paragraph 15(1)(*a*) (exemption for supplies to combined heat and power stations), for "the commodity is to be used by that person" there is substituted "that person intends to cause the commodity to be used".

(7) The amendments made by this section have effect in relation to supplies made on or after 1st April 2001.

PART V
MISCELLANEOUS AND SUPPLEMENTARY PROVISIONS

Supplementary

110 Repeals and revocations

(1) The enactments mentioned in Schedule 33 to this Act (which include provisions that are spent or of no practical utility) are repealed or revoked to the extent specified.

(2) The repeals and revocations specified in that Schedule have effect subject to the commencement provisions and savings contained or referred to in the notes set out in that Schedule.

SCHEDULE 33
REPEALS

Section 110

PART III
OTHER TAXES

Note—The repeals under this Part relating to climate change levy are already in force and have therefore been omitted.

FINANCE ACT 2002

(2002 Chapter 23)

An Act to grant certain duties, to alter other duties, and to amend the law relating to the National Debt and the Public Revenue, and to make further provision in connection with finance.

[24 July 2002]

PART 5
OTHER TAXES

Climate change levy

123 Climate change levy: electricity produced in combined heat and power station

(1) (*inserts* FA 2000 Sch 6 paras 20A, 20B).

(2) Subsection (1) has effect in relation to supplies of electricity made on or after such day as the Treasury may by order made by statutory instrument appoint.

Commentary—*De Voil Indirect Tax Service* **V21.127.**
Orders—FA 2002, section 123, (Appointed Day) Order, SI 2003/603 (the day appointed under sub-s (2) above is 1 April 2003).

124 Climate change levy: certification requirement

(*inserts* FA 2000 Sch 6 para 149A).

125 Climate change levy: exemption for renewable sources

(1) In Schedule 6 to the Finance Act 2000 (c 17) (climate change levy), in paragraph 20(7), (exemption under paragraph 19: liability to account)—

(*a*) for the words from "(2)(*c*)" to "2 years)" substitute "(2)(*g*)",
(*b*) after paragraph (*a*) insert "and", and
(*c*) omit paragraph (*c*) and the preceding "and".

(2) This section has effect in relation to averaging periods under paragraph 20 of that Schedule which end on or after the day on which this Act is passed.

Commentary—*De Voil Indirect Tax Service* **V21.129.**

[*126 Climate change levy: electricity produced from coal mine methane*

(1) (inserts FA 2000 Sch 6 para 19(4A))

(2) This section has effect in relation to supplies of electricity made on or after such day as the Treasury may by order made by statutory instrument appoint.][1]

Commentary—*De Voil Indirect Tax Service* **V21.129.**
Orders—Finance Act 2002, section 126, (Appointment Day) Order, SI 2003/2622 (1 November 2003 appointed for the purposes of sub-s (2)).
Amendments—[1] This section repealed by FA 2008 s 149 in relation to electricity generated on or after 1 November 2008.

127 Climate change levy: incorrect certificates

(1) In Schedule 6 to the Finance Act 2000 (climate change levy), in sub-paragraph (2)(*a*) of paragraph 101 (civil penalties: incorrect notifications etc)—

(*a*) in sub-paragraph (ii) for "18 and 21, or" substitute "15, 18 and 21,";
(*b*) (*inserts* FA 2000 Sch 6 para 101(2)(*a*)(iv)).

(2) This section applies in relation to certificates given in respect of any supplies made on or after 24th April 2002.

Commentary—*De Voil Indirect Tax Service* **V21.161.**

128 Climate change levy: invoices incorrectly showing levy due

(1) (*inserts* FA 2000 Sch 6 para 141A).

(2) This section applies only in relation to invoices issued on or after the day on which this Act is passed.

Commentary—*De Voil Indirect Tax Service* **V21.161.**

PART 6

MISCELLANEOUS AND SUPPLEMENTARY PROVISIONS

Supplementary

141 Repeals

(1) The enactments mentioned in Schedule 40 to this Act (which include provisions that are spent or of no practical utility) are repealed to the extent specified.

(2) The repeals specified in that Schedule have effect subject to the commencement provisions and savings contained or referred to in the notes set out in that Schedule.

SCHEDULES

SCHEDULE 40

REPEALS

Section 141

PART 4

OTHER TAXES

(2) CLIMATE CHANGE LEVY

Note—The repeal made under this heading is already in force and has therefore been omitted.

FINANCE ACT 2003

(2003 Chapter 14)

An Act to grant certain duties, to alter other duties, and to amend the law relating to the National Debt and the Public Revenue, and to make further provision in connection with finance.

[10 July 2003]

PART 8

OTHER TAXES

Climate change levy

188 Exemption for fuel used in recycling processes

(1) (*inserts* FA 2000 Sch 6 para 18A)

(2) (*amends* FA 2000 Sch 6 paras 14, 101, 146, 147)

189 CHP exemption to be based on current efficiency

(1) Schedule 6 to the Finance Act 2000 (c 17) (climate change levy) is amended as follows.

(2) In paragraph 15 (exemption for supplies to combined heat and power stations)—

(*a*) (*substitutes* FA 2000 Sch 6 para 15(4)(*b*))

(*b*) omit sub-paragraph (5).

(3) In paragraph 148 (meaning of "combined heat and power station" etc)—

(*a*) (*amends* FA 2000 Sch 6 para 148(2)(*c*) and (3)(*c*))

(*b*) (*repeals* FA 2000 Sch 6 para 148(6))

(4) (*amends* FA 2000 Sch 6 para 149(1))

(5) This section has effect in relation to supplies made on or after such day as the Treasury may by order made by statutory instrument appoint.

190 Supplies not known to be taxable when made, etc

(1) In Schedule 6 to the Finance Act 2000 (c 17) (climate change levy), paragraph 24 (deemed supply: change of circumstances or intentions) is amended as follows.

(2) In the heading, for "*change of circumstances or intentions*" substitute "*change of circumstances etc*".

(3) (*substitutes* FA 2000 Sch 6 para 24(1)–(2))

(4) In sub-paragraph (3), at the beginning insert "Where this paragraph applies,".

(5) (*inserts* FA 2000 Sch 6 para 24(3A))

(6) In sub-paragraph (5) for "sub-paragraph (1)(*c*)" substitute "sub-paragraph (1A)(*c*)".

(7) (*amends* FA 2000 Sch 6 para 34(3))

(8) This section has effect in relation to supplies made on or after such day as the Treasury may by order made by statutory instrument appoint.

191 Deemed supplies

(1) Schedule 6 to the Finance Act 2000 (c 17) (climate change levy) is amended as follows.

(2), (3) (*amend* paras 5(3), 6(3), and *insert* para 6(2A))

(4) Subsection (2) has effect in relation to supplies deemed to be made on or after 31st March 2003, and subsection (3) in relation to supplies deemed to be made on or after the day on which this Act is passed.

192 Amendments about registration, payment etc

(1) Schedule 6 to the Finance Act 2000 (climate change levy) is amended as follows.

(2)–(10) (*amend* paras 41, 53, 62, 78, 91, 93, 100, 125, 135)

Amendments—Sub-s (8) repealed by FA 2008 s 122, Sch 40 para 21(*k*) with effect from 1 April 2009 (by virtue of SI 2009/571 art 2).

193 Electricity from renewable sources etc

(1) Schedule 6 to the Finance Act 2000 (climate change levy) is amended as follows.

(2) (*amends* para 20)

(3) (*amends* para 20B)

(4) The amendment made by subsection (2) has effect where the end of the balancing period referred to in paragraph (*a*) of the sub-paragraph (6) substituted by that subsection falls on or after 31st March 2003.

(5) The amendment made by subsection (3) has effect where the end of the balancing period referred to in paragraph (*a*) of the sub-paragraph (6) substituted by that subsection falls on or after 1st April 2003.

PART 9
MISCELLANEOUS AND SUPPLEMENTARY PROVISIONS

Supplementary

215 Interpretation

In this Act "the Taxes Act 1988" means the Income and Corporation Taxes Act 1988 (c 1).

216 Repeals

(1) The enactments mentioned in Schedule 43 to this Act (which include provisions that are spent or of no practical utility) are repealed to the extent specified.

(2) The repeals specified in that Schedule have effect subject to the commencement provisions and savings contained or referred to in the notes set out in that Schedule.

SCHEDULES

SCHEDULE 43
REPEALS

Section 216

The effect of the repeals set out in this Schedule, so far as relevant to climate change levy, has been noted in the relevant legislation.

FINANCE ACT 2004

(2004 Chapter 12)

An Act to Grant certain duties, to alter other duties, and to amend the law relating to the National Debt and the Public Revenue, and to make further provision in connection with finance.

[22 July 2004]

PART 6

OTHER TAXES

Climate change levy

289 Supplies to producers of commodities

(1) Schedule 6 to the Finance Act 2000 (c 17) (climate change levy) is amended as set out in subsections (2) to (5).

(2) (*inserts* FA 2000 Sch 6 para 13(*b*)(iia)–(iid))

(3) (*amends* FA 2000 Sch 6 para 13(*b*)(iii))

(4) (*amends* FA 2000 Sch 6 para 13, last sentence)

(5) (*inserts* FA 2000 Sch 6 para 13A)

(6) The amendments made by subsections (2) to (4) have effect—

(*a*) as regards biodiesel and bioblend, in relation to supplies made on or after the day on which this Act is passed;

(*b*) as regards bioethanol and bioethanol blend, in relation to supplies made on or after 1st January 2005.

FINANCE ACT 2006

(2006 Chapter 25)

An Act to Grant certain duties, to alter other duties, and to amend the law relating to the National Debt and the Public Revenue, and to make further provision in connection with finance.

[19 July 2006]

PART 9

MISCELLANEOUS PROVISIONS

Climate change levy

171 Climate change levy: rates

(1) (*substitutes* FA 2000 Sch 6 para 42(1) Table)

(2) This section has effect in relation to supplies treated as taking place on or after 1st April 2007.

172 Abolition of half-rate supplies etc

(1) For the purposes of climate change levy, no supply made on or after 1st April 2006 is a half-rate supply.

(2) Subsections (3) to (6) have effect for determining when a supply is to be regarded as made for the purposes of subsection (1).

(3) A supply—

(*a*) of electricity, or

(*b*) of gas that is in a gaseous state and is of a kind supplied by a gas utility,

is to be regarded as made at the time when the electricity or gas is actually supplied.

(4) In the case of a supply of a taxable commodity not falling within subsection (3) by a person who is resident in the United Kingdom—

(*a*) if the commodity is to be removed, the supply is to be regarded as made at the time of the removal,

(*b*) if the commodity is not to be removed, the supply is to be regarded as made when the commodity is made available to the person to whom it is supplied.

This subsection does not apply if subsection (6) (deemed self-supply) applies in the case of the supply.

(5) In the case of a supply of a taxable commodity not falling within subsection (3) by a person who is not resident in the United Kingdom, the supply is to be regarded as made—

(*a*) when the commodity is delivered to the person to whom it is supplied, or
(*b*) if earlier, when it is made available in the United Kingdom to that person.

This subsection does not apply if subsection (6) (deemed self-supply) applies in the case of the supply.

(6) In any case where, by virtue of paragraph 23(3) of Schedule 6 to FA 2000, a person is, for the purposes of that Schedule, deemed to make a supply to himself of a quantity of a taxable commodity—

(*a*) which he has produced, and
(*b*) which does not fall within subsection (3),

the supply is to be regarded as made at the time when he produced that particular quantity of the taxable commodity.

(7) (*amends* FA 2000 Sch 6 para 34(2))

(8) In consequence of subsection (1), Schedule 6 to FA 2000 (climate change levy) is amended as follows.

(9) In paragraph 37 (supplies of electricity or gas spanning change of rate etc) in sub-paragraph (1)(*c*) omit "half-rate supplies or".

(10) In paragraph 38 (other supplies spanning change of rate etc) in sub-paragraph (1)(*c*) omit "half-rate supplies or".

(11) In paragraph 42(1) (amount payable by way of levy)—

(*a*) in paragraph (*a*), for "neither a half-rate supply nor" substitute "not";
(*b*) omit paragraph (*b*);
(*c*) in paragraph (*c*), for "neither a half-rate supply nor" substitute "not";
(*d*) in the Table (and in the Table substituted for it by section 171 of this Act), in the heading to column (2), for "neither a half-rate supply nor" substitute "not".

(12) Paragraph 43 (half-rate for supplies to horticultural producers) shall cease to have effect.

(13) In paragraph 62 (tax credits) in subsection (1)—

(*a*) in paragraph (*c*)—
  (i) for "neither a half-rate supply nor" substitute "not";
  (ii) omit "half-rate or";
(*b*) omit paragraph (*d*).

(14) In paragraph 101 (civil penalties: incorrect notifications) in sub-paragraph (2)(*a*)—

(*a*) at the end of sub-paragraph (ii) insert "or";
(*b*) omit sub-paragraph (iii).

(15) In paragraph 147 (interpretation: general) omit the definition of "half-rate supply".

(16) Subsections (8) to (15) come into force on such day as the Treasury may by order made by statutory instrument appoint.

(17) The power to make an order under subsection (16)—

(*a*) may be exercised so as to bring a provision into force only in such cases as may be described in the order,
(*b*) may be exercised so as to make different provision for different cases or descriptions of case,
(*c*) includes power to make incidental, consequential, supplemental or transitional provision or savings.

Order—Finance Act 2006 (Climate Change Levy: Amendments and Transitional Savings in Consequence of Abolition of Half-Rate Supplies) (Appointed Day) Order, SI 2007/2901 (1 November 2007 is appointed as the day on which sub-ss (8)–(15) come into force; amendments made by sub-ss (8)–(15) do not apply in relation to half-rate supplies made before 1 April 2006: SI 2007/2901 art 2(2)).

PART 10
SUPPLEMENTARY PROVISIONS

178 Repeals

(1) The enactments mentioned in Schedule 26 (which include provisions that are spent or of no practical utility) are repealed to the extent specified.

(2) The repeals specified in that Schedule have effect subject to the commencement provisions and savings contained or referred to in the notes set out in that Schedule.

SCHEDULES

SCHEDULE 26
REPEALS

Section 178

PART 8

MISCELLANEOUS PROVISIONS

(1) CLIMATE CHANGE LEVY: ABOLITION OF HALF-RATE SUPPLIES ETC

Short title and chapter	*Extent of repeal*
Finance Act 2000 (c 17)	In Schedule 6— (a) in paragraph 34(2), the words "(or, in the case of electricity, consumed)"; (b) in paragraph 37(1)(*c*), the words "half-rate supplies or"; (c) in paragraph 38(1)(*c*), the words "half-rate supplies or"; (d) paragraph 42(1)(*b*); (e) paragraph 43; (f) in paragraph 62(1), in paragraph (*c*), the words "half-rate or" and paragraph (*d*); (g) paragraph 101(2)(*a*)(iii); (h) in paragraph 147, the definition of "half-rate supply".

These repeals have effect in accordance with section 172 of this Act.

FINANCE ACT 2007

(2007 Chapter 11)

PART 1

CHARGES, RATES, THRESHOLDS ETC

Environment

13 Rates of climate change levy

(1) (*substitutes* Table in FA 2000 Sch 6 para 42(1))

(2) The amendment made by subsection (1) has effect in relation to supplies treated as taking place on or after 1st April 2008.

16 Emissions trading: charges for allocations

(1) The Treasury may impose charges by providing for Community tradeable emissions allowances to be allocated in return for payment.

(2) The Treasury must by regulations make provision for and in connection with allocations of allowances in return for payment.

(3) The regulations must provide for allocations to be overseen by an independent person appointed by the Treasury.

(4) The regulations may make any other provision about allocations which the Treasury consider appropriate, including (in particular)—

(*a*) provision as to the imposition of fees, and as to the making and forfeiting of deposits, in connection with participation in allocations,

(*b*) provision as to the persons by whom allocations are to be conducted,

(*c*) provision for the [creation of criminal offences, or for the imposition and recovery of civil penalties,][1] for failure to comply with the terms of a scheme made under subsection (5), (*d*) provision for and in connection with the recovery of payments due in respect of allowances allocated (including provision as to the imposition and recovery of interest and penalties), and

(*e*) provision conferring rights of appeal against decisions made in allocations, the forfeiting of deposits and the imposition of penalties (including provision specifying the person, court or tribunal to hear and determine appeals).

(5) The Treasury may make schemes about the conduct and terms of allocations (to have effect subject to any regulations under this section); and schemes may in particular include provision about—

(*a*) who may participate in allocations,

(*b*) the allowances to be allocated, and

(*c*) where and when allocations are to take place.

(6) "Community tradeable emissions allowances" are transferable allowances which—

(*a*) relate to the making of emissions of greenhouse gases, and

(*b*) are allocated as part of a system made for the purpose of implementing any Community obligation of the United Kingdom relating to such emissions;

and "greenhouse gases" means carbon dioxide, methane, nitrous oxide, hydrofluorocarbons, perfluorocarbons and sulphur hexafluoride.

[(6A) Subsection (4)(*c*) does not permit the creation of a criminal offence with maximum penalties in excess of the maximum penalties which an instrument under section 2(2) of the European Communities Act 1972 may provide in respect of an offence created by such an instrument.][1]

(7) Regulations under this section are to be made by statutory instrument.

(8) A statutory instrument containing regulations under this section is subject to annulment in pursuance of a resolution of the House of Commons unless a draft of the regulations has been laid before, and approved by a resolution of, that House.

Amendments—[1] Sub-s (6A) inserted, and in sub-s (4)(*c*) words substituted for words "imposition and recovery of penalties", by FA 2008 s 164 with effect from 21 July 2008.

PART 2

ENVIRONMENT

Other measures

23 Climate change levy: reduced-rate supplies etc

Schedule 2 contains amendments of Schedule 6 to FA 2000 in relation to reduced-rate supplies and other matters.

97 Penalties for errors

Note—Please see *VAT Statutes* ante for the text of this Section.

SCHEDULES

SCHEDULE 2

CLIMATE CHANGE LEVY: REDUCED-RATE SUPPLIES ETC

Section 23

Introductory

1 Schedule 6 to FA 2000 (climate change levy) is amended as follows.

Reduced-rate supplies

2 (*amends* FA 2000 Sch 6 para 4(2)(*b*))

Order—Finance Act 2007 (Climate Change Levy: Reduced-rate Supplies etc) (Appointed Day) Order, SI 2007/2902 (1 November 2007 appointed as the day on which paras 2–10 come into force).

3 (*amends* FA 2000 Sch 6 para 5(3))

Order—Finance Act 2007 (Climate Change Levy: Reduced-rate Supplies etc) (Appointed Day) Order, SI 2007/2902 (1 November 2007 appointed as the day on which paras 2–10 come into force).

4 (*amends* FA 2000 Sch 6 para 6(2A))

Order—Finance Act 2007 (Climate Change Levy: Reduced-rate Supplies etc) (Appointed Day) Order, SI 2007/2902 (1 November 2007 appointed as the day on which paras 2–10 come into force).

5— (1) Paragraph 34 (other commodities: deemed supplies) is amended as follows.

(2) (*amends* FA 2000 Sch 6 para 34(1)(*b*))

(3) (*inserts* FA 2000 Sch 6 para 34(4))

Order—Finance Act 2007 (Climate Change Levy: Reduced-rate Supplies etc) (Appointed Day) Order, SI 2007/2902 (1 November 2007 appointed as the day on which paras 2–10 come into force).

6 (*amends* FA 2000 Sch 6 para 39(1)(*c*))

Order—Finance Act 2007 (Climate Change Levy: Reduced-rate Supplies etc) (Appointed Day) Order, SI 2007/2902 (1 November 2007 appointed as the day on which paras 2–10 come into force).

7 (*substitutes* FA 2000 Sch 6 para 44)

Order—Finance Act 2007 (Climate Change Levy: Reduced-rate Supplies etc) (Appointed Day) Order, SI 2007/2902 (1 November 2007 appointed as the day on which paras 2–10 come into force). The amendments made by this para only apply in relation to a supply actually made on or after 1 November 2007: SI 2007/2902 art 2(2).

8— (1) Paragraph 45 (reduced-rate supplies: variation of notices under paragraph 44) is amended as follows.

(2) (*repeals* FA 2000 Sch 6 para 45(2)–(4))

(3) (*amends* FA 2000 Sch 6 para 45(5))

(4) (*amends* FA 2000 Sch 6 para 45(6))

(5) (*amends* FA 2000 Sch 6 para 45(7))

(6) (*amends* FA 2000 Sch 6 para 45 heading)

Order—Finance Act 2007 (Climate Change Levy: Reduced-rate Supplies etc) (Appointed Day) Order, SI 2007/2902 (1 November 2007 appointed as the day on which paras 2–10 come into force).

9 (*inserts* FA 2000 Sch 6 para 45A)

Order—Finance Act 2007 (Climate Change Levy: Reduced-rate Supplies etc) (Appointed Day) Order, SI 2007/2902 (1 November 2007 appointed as the day on which paras 2–10 come into force). This amendment only applies in relation to a supply actually made on or after 1 November 2007 and on the basis that it is a reduced-rate supply: SI 2007/2902 art 2(3).

10 (*amends* FA 2000 Sch 6 para 147)

Order—Finance Act 2007 (Climate Change Levy: Reduced-rate Supplies etc) (Appointed Day) Order, SI 2007/2902 (1 November 2007 appointed as the day on which paras 2–10 come into force). The amendments made by this para only apply in relation to a supply actually made on or after 1 November 2007: SI 2007/2902 art 2(2).

Notifications and certificates

11 (*amends* FA 2000 Sch 6 para 11(1), (3))

12— (1) Paragraph 101 (civil penalties: incorrect notifications etc) is amended as follows.

(2) (*repeals* FA 2000 Sch 6 para 101(1))

(3) (*amends* FA 2000 Sch 6 para 101(2))

(4) (*amends* FA 2000 Sch 6 para 101(3))

(5) (*amends* FA 2000 Sch 6 para 101(4))

(6) (*amends* FA 2000 Sch 6 para 101(5))

(7) (*amends* FA 2000 Sch 6 para 101 heading)

Commencement

13— (1) Paragraphs 2 to 10 come into force on such day as the Treasury may by order made by statutory instrument appoint.

(2) But any power to make regulations under any provision inserted or amended by any of those paragraphs may be exercised at any time after this Act is passed.

(3) The power to make an order under sub-paragraph (1)—

(*a*) may be exercised so as to bring a provision into force only in such cases as may be described in the order,

(*b*) may be exercised so as to make different provision for different cases or descriptions of case,

(*c*) includes power to make incidental, consequential, supplemental or transitional provision or savings.

SCHEDULE 24

PENALTIES FOR ERRORS

Note—Please see *VAT Statutes* ante for the text of this Schedule.

SCHEDULE 27
REPEALS

Section 114

PART 1
ENVIRONMENT

(2) Climate Change Levy: Reduced-rate Supplies etc

Short title and chapter	*Extent of repeal*
Finance Act 2000 (c 17)	In Schedule 6— (*a*) in paragraph 11, in sub-paragraph (1) the words "has, before the supply is made, notified the supplier" and "that he" (in both places), and, in sub-paragraph (3), the words "has, before the supply is made, notified the supplier that" and "he", (*b*) paragraph 45(2) to (4), and (*c*) in paragraph 101, sub-paragraph (1), and, in sub-paragraph (3), the words "notification or"

The repeal of paragraph 45(2) to (4) of Schedule 6 to FA 2000 has effect in accordance with Schedule 2 to this Act.

FINANCE ACT 2008

(2008 Chapter 9)

An Act to Grant certain duties, to alter other duties, and to amend the law relating to the National Debt and the Public Revenue, and to make further provision in connection with finance.

[21 July 2008]

PART 1
CHARGES, RATES, ALLOWANCES, RELIEFS ETC

Environmental taxes and duties

19 Rates of climate change levy

(1) (*amends* FA 2000 Sch 6 para 42(1)).

(2) The amendment made by subsection (1) has effect in relation to supplies treated as taking place on or after 1 April 2009.

21 Carbon reduction trading scheme: charges for allocations

(1) The Treasury may impose charges by providing for carbon reduction trading scheme allowances to be allocated in return for payment.

(2) The charges may only be imposed by regulations.

(3) The regulations may make any other provision about allocations of allowances which the Treasury consider appropriate, including (in particular)—

(*a*) provision as to the imposition of fees, and as to the making and forfeiting of deposits, in connection with participation in the allocations,

(*b*) provision as to the persons by whom allocations are to be conducted,

(*c*) provision for allocations to be overseen by an independent person appointed by the Treasury,

(*d*) provision for the imposition and recovery of penalties for failure to comply with the terms of a scheme made under subsection (4),

(*e*) provision for and in connection with the recovery of payments due in respect of allowances allocated (including provision as to the imposition and recovery of interest and penalties), and

(*f*) provision conferring rights of appeal against decisions made in allocations, the forfeiting of deposits and the imposition of penalties (including provision specifying the person, court or tribunal to hear and determine appeals).

(4) The Treasury may make schemes about the conduct and terms of allocations (to have effect subject to any regulations under this section); and schemes may in particular include provision about—

(*a*) who may participate in allocations,
(*b*) the allowances to be allocated, and
(*c*) where and when allocations are to take place.

(5) In this section—

"carbon reduction trading scheme allowances" means tradeable allowances that—

(*a*) are provided for in a relevant trading scheme, and
(*b*) represent the right to carry on a specified amount of activities that consist of the emission of greenhouse gas or that cause or contribute, directly or indirectly, to such emissions;

"relevant trading scheme" means a trading scheme that—

(*a*) is made under Part 3 of the Climate Change Act 2008,
(*b*) applies to persons by reference to their consumption of electricity (whether or not by reference to other matters as well), and
(*c*) applies only to persons who consume electricity—

(i) for business or charitable purposes, or
(ii) for the performance of functions of a public nature,

(whether or not they also consume electricity for other purposes);

"specified" means specified in the relevant trading scheme.

(6) Regulations under this section are to be made by statutory instrument.

(7) A statutory instrument containing the first regulations under this section may not be made unless a draft of the regulations has been laid before, and approved by a resolution of, the House of Commons.

(8) Any other statutory instrument containing regulations under this section is subject to annulment in pursuance of a resolution of the House of Commons unless a draft of the regulations has been laid before, and approved by a resolution of, that House.

PART 7

ADMINISTRATION

Press releases—HMRC Guidance Note, 18 July 2008 (HMRC set-off across taxes following Finance Bill 2008).

CHAPTER 1

INFORMATION ETC

New information etc powers

114 Computer records etc

Note—Please see *VAT Statutes* ante for the text of this Section.

CHAPTER 3

PENALTIES

122 Penalties for errors

Note—Please see *VAT Statutes* ante for the text of this Section.

123 Penalties for failure to notify etc

Note—Please see *VAT Statutes* ante for the text of this Section.

CHAPTER 4

APPEALS ETC

Reviews and appeals etc: general

124 HMRC decisions etc: reviews and appeals

Note—Please see *VAT Statutes* ante for the text of this Section.

CHAPTER 5

PAYMENT AND ENFORCEMENT

Taking control of goods etc

127 Enforcement by taking control of goods: England and Wales

Note—Please see *VAT Statutes* ante for the text of this Section.

128 Summary warrant: Scotland

Note—Please see *VAT Statutes* ante for the text of this Section.

129 Consequential provision and commencement

Note—Please see *VAT Statutes* ante for the text of this Section.

Set off

130 Set-off: England and Wales and Northern Ireland

Note—Please see *VAT Statutes* ante for the text of this Section.

131 No set-off where insolvency procedure has been applied

Note—Please see *VAT Statutes* ante for the text of this Section.

133 Set-off etc where right to be paid a sum has been transferred

Note—Please see *VAT Statutes* ante for the text of this Section.

Other measures

135 Interest on unpaid tax in case of disaster etc of national significance

Note—Please see *VAT Statutes* ante for the text of this Section.

136 Fee for payment

Note—Please see *VAT Statutes* ante for the text of this Section.

Supplementary

139 Interpretation of Chapter

Note—Please see *VAT Statutes* ante for the text of this Section.

PART 8
MISCELLANEOUS

Climate change levy and landfill tax

149 Climate change levy: coal mine methane no longer to be renewable source

(1) (*repeals* FA 2000 Sch 6 para 19(4A)).

(2) Accordingly, omit—

(*a*) (*repeals* FA 2002 s 126).

(*b*) (*repeals* the CCL (General) Regulations, SI 2001/838 reg 47(2A)).

(3) The repeals and revocation made by this section have effect in relation to electricity generated on or after 1 November 2008.

150 Climate change levy accounting documents: abolition of self-identification

(*repeals* FA 2000 Sch 6 para 143(2)(*a*)).

Other matters

164 EU emissions trading: criminal offences

(1) Section 16 of FA 2007 (EU emissions trading: charges for allocations) is amended as follows.

(2) (*amends* FA 2007 s 16(4)(*c*)).

(3) (*inserts* FA 2007 s 16(6A)).

PART 9
FINAL PROVISIONS

165 Interpretation

166 Short title

Note—Please see *VAT Statutes* ante for the text of these Sections.

SCHEDULES

SCHEDULE 36

INFORMATION AND INSPECTION POWERS

Section 113

Commencement—Finance Act 2008, Schedule 36 (Appointed Day and Savings) Order, SI 2009/404 art 2 (appointed day for the coming into force of Sch 36 is 1 April 2009).

Note—Please see *VAT Statutes* ante for the text of this Section.

SCHEDULE 41

PENALTIES: FAILURE TO NOTIFY AND CERTAIN VAT AND EXCISE WRONGDOING

Section 123

Note—Please see *VAT Statutes* ante for the text of this Section.

FINANCE ACT 2009

(2009 Chapter 10)

An Act to Grant certain duties, to alter other duties, and to amend the law relating to the National Debt and the Public Revenue, and to make further provision in connection with finance.

[21 July 2009]

PART 7

ADMINISTRATION

Standards and values

92 HMRC Charter

Note—Please see *VAT Statutes* ante for the text of this Section.

93 Duties of senior accounting officers of qualifying companies

Note—Please see *VAT Statutes* ante for the text of this Section.

94 Publishing details of deliberate tax defaulters

Note—Please see *VAT Statutes* ante for the text of this Section.

Information etc

95 Amendment of information and inspection powers

Note—Please see *VAT Statutes* ante for the text of this Section.

96 Extension of information and inspection powers to further taxes

(1) In paragraph 63(1) of Schedule 36 to FA 2008 (information and inspection powers: meaning of "tax"), for paragraph (*e*) (and the "and" before it) substitute—

"(*e*) insurance premium tax,
(*f*) inheritance tax,
(*g*) stamp duty land tax,
(*h*) stamp duty reserve tax,
(*i*) petroleum revenue tax,
(*j*) aggregates levy,
(*k*) climate change levy,
(*l*) landfill tax, and
(*m*) relevant foreign tax,".

(2) Schedule 48 contains further amendments of that Schedule.

(3) The amendments made by this section and Schedule 48 come into force on such day as the Treasury may by order appoint.

(4) An order under subsection (3) may—

(*a*) appoint different days for different purposes, and
(*b*) contain transitional provision and savings.

(5) The Treasury may by order make any incidental, supplemental, consequential, transitional or transitory provision or saving which appears appropriate in consequence of, or otherwise in connection with, this section and Schedule 48.

(6) An order under subsection (5) may—

(*a*) make different provision for different purposes, and

(*b*) make provision amending, repealing or revoking an enactment or instrument (whenever passed or made).

(7) An order under this section is to be made by statutory instrument.

(8) A statutory instrument containing an order under subsection (5) is subject to annulment in pursuance of a resolution of the House of Commons.

97 Powers to obtain contact details for debtors

Note—Please see *VAT Statutes* ante for the text of this Section.

98 Record-keeping

(1) Schedule 50 contains provision about obligations to keep records.

(2) The amendments made by that Schedule come into force on such day as the Treasury may by order made by statutory instrument appoint.

Assessments, claims etc

99 Time limits for assessments, claims etc

(1) Schedule 51 contains provision about time limits for assessments, claims etc

(2) The amendments made by that Schedule come into force on such day as the Treasury may by order made by statutory instrument appoint.

(3) An order under subsection (2)—

(*a*) may make different provision for different purposes, and

(*b*) may include transitional provision and savings.

Interest

101 Late payment interest on sums due to HMRC

Note—Please see *VAT Statutes* ante for the text of this Section.

102 Repayment interest on sums to be paid by HMRC

Note—Please see *VAT Statutes* ante for the text of this Section.

103 Rates of interest

Note—Please see *VAT Statutes* ante for the text of this Section.

104 Supplementary

Note—Please see *VAT Statutes* ante for the text of this Section.

108 Suspension of penalties during currency of agreement for deferred payment

Note—Please see *VAT Statutes* ante for the text of this Section.

109 Miscellaneous amendments

Note—Please see *VAT Statutes* ante for the text of this Section.

PART 8

MISCELLANEOUS

Climate change levy

117 Taxable commodities ineligible for reduced-rate supply

(1) Schedule 6 to FA 2000 (climate change levy) is amended as follows.

(2) In paragraph 44 (reduced rate for supplies covered by climate change agreement), after sub-paragraph (2) insert—

"(2A) The Secretary of State may—

(*a*) give a certificate that includes provision specifying one or more descriptions of taxable commodity as being ineligible for reduced-rate supply,

(*b*) vary a certificate so that it includes provision (or further provision) specifying one or more descriptions of taxable commodity as being ineligible for reduced-rate supply, or (*c*) vary a certificate so that it ceases to include the provision (or some of the provision) specifying one or more descriptions of taxable commodity as being ineligible for reduced-rate supply.

(2B) A taxable supply of a taxable commodity to a facility is not a reduced-rate supply if, at the time of the supply, the commodity falls within a description that is specified (by virtue of sub-paragraph (2A)(*a*) or (*b*)) in the certificate relating to the facility.

(2C) The Secretary of State may only include provision in a certificate by virtue of sub-paragraph (2A)(*a*) or (*b*)—

(*a*) if the Treasury consents in writing to the specification before the specification is made, and

(*b*) if, and for as long as, the result is compatible with the common market by virtue of Commission Regulation (EC) No. 800/2008 of 6 August 2008 declaring certain categories of aid compatible with the common market in application of Articles 87 and 88 of the Treaty establishing the European Community (General block exemption Regulation) (O.J. 2008 No. L214/3).

(2D) In sub-paragraphs (2A) to (2C) "certificate" means such a certificate as is mentioned in sub-paragraph (1)(*a*)."

(3) In consequence of subsection (2)—

(*a*) in paragraph 44(2), after "subject to" insert "sub-paragraphs (2A) to (2D) and", and

(*b*) in paragraph 147 (general interpretation), in the definition of "reduced- rate supply", after "subject to" insert "paragraph 44(2A) to (2D) and".

118 Removal of reduced rate where targets not met

(1) Schedule 59 contains provision for removing the reduced rate of climate change levy where the targets set by a climate change agreement have not been met.

(2) The amendments made by that Schedule have effect where the certification period begins on or after 1 April 2009.

SCHEDULES

SCHEDULE 46

DUTIES OF SENIOR ACCOUNTING OFFICERS OF QUALIFYING COMPANIES

Section 93

Note—Please see *VAT Statutes* ante for the text of this Schedule.

SCHEDULE 47

AMENDMENT OF INFORMATION AND INSPECTION POWERS

Section 94

Note—Please see *VAT Statutes* ante for the text of this Schedule.

SCHEDULE 48

EXTENSION OF INFORMATION AND INSPECTION POWERS

Section 95

Note—Please see *VAT Statutes* ante for the text of this Schedule.

SCHEDULE 49

POWERS TO OBTAIN CONTACT DETAILS FOR DEBTORS

Section 97

Note—Please see *VAT Statutes* ante for the text of this Schedule.

SCHEDULE 50

RECORD-KEEPING

Section 98

Climate change levy

18 Schedule 6 to FA 2000 (climate change levy) is amended as follows.

19— (1) Paragraph 125 (records) is amended as follows.

(2) For sub-paragraphs (4) and (5) substitute—

"(4) A duty under regulations under this paragraph to preserve records may be discharged—

(*a*) by preserving them in any form and by any means, or

(*b*) by preserving the information contained in them in any form and by any means, subject to any conditions or exceptions specified in writing by the Commissioners."

(3) In sub-paragraph (9), omit "approval or" and "given or".

20 Omit paragraph 126 (evidence of records that are required to be preserved).

SCHEDULE 51
TIME LIMITS FOR ASSESSMENTS, CLAIMS ETC

Section 99

Climate change levy

32 Schedule 6 to FA 2000 (climate change levy) is amended as follows.

33 In paragraph 64(1) (repayments of overpaid climate change levy), for "three years" substitute "4 years".

34 In paragraph 66(10) (interest payable by the Commissioners), for "three years" substitute "4 years".

35— (1) Paragraph 80 (time limits for assessments) is amended as follows.

(2) In sub-paragraph (1)(*b*), for "three years" substitute "4 years".

(3) For sub-paragraph (3) substitute—

"(3) An assessment of an amount due from a person in a case involving a loss of levy—

(*a*) brought about deliberately by the person (or by another person acting on that person's behalf), or

(*b*) attributable to a failure by the person to comply with an obligation under paragraph 53 or 55,

may be made at any time not more than 20 years after the end of the accounting period to which it relates (subject to sub-paragraph (4)).

(3A) In sub-paragraph (3)(*a*) the reference to a loss brought about deliberately by the person includes a loss brought about as a result of a deliberate inaccuracy in a document given to Her Majesty's Revenue and Customs by or on behalf of that person."

(4) In sub-paragraph (4)—

(*a*) in paragraph (*a*), for "three years" substitute "4 years", and

(*b*) omit paragraph (*b*) (and the "and" before it).

36— (1) Paragraph 108 (time limits on penalty assessments) is amended as follows.

(2) In sub-paragraph (1), for "three years" substitute "4 years".

(3) For sub-paragraph (2) substitute—

"(2) An assessment of a person to a penalty in a case involving a loss of levy—

(*a*) brought about deliberately by the person (or by another person acting on that person's behalf), or

(*b*) attributable to a failure by the person to comply with an obligation under paragraph 53 or 55,

may be made at any time not more than 20 years after the conduct to which the penalty relates (subject to sub-paragraph (3)).

(2A) In sub-paragraph (2)(*a*) the reference to a loss brought about deliberately by the person includes a loss brought about as a result of a deliberate inaccuracy in a document given to Her Majesty's Revenue and Customs by or on behalf of that person."

(4) In sub-paragraph (3)—

(*a*) in paragraph (*a*), for "three years" substitute "4 years", and

(*b*) omit paragraph (*b*) (and the "and" before it).

SCHEDULE 53
LATE PAYMENT INTEREST

Section 101

Note—Please see *VAT Statutes* ante for the text of this Schedule.

SCHEDULE 54

REPAYMENT INTEREST

Section 102

SCHEDULE 57

AMENDMENTS RELATING TO PENALTIES

Section 109

Note—Please see *VAT Statutes* ante for the text of this Schedule.

SCHEDULE 59

CLIMATE CHANGE LEVY: REMOVAL OF REDUCED RATE

Section 118

PART 1

NEW PROVISION FOR REMOVAL OF REDUCED RATE

1 In Schedule 6 to FA 2000 (climate change levy), after paragraph 45A insert—

"*Removal of reduced rate where targets set by climate change agreement not met*

45B— (1) This paragraph applies where, by virtue of such a certificate as is mentioned in paragraph 44(1), a facility is to be taken as being covered by a climate change agreement for a period specified in that certificate ("the certification period").

(2) If it appears to the Secretary of State that the progress made in the certification period towards meeting targets set for the facility by the agreement has been such as under the provisions of the agreement is unsatisfactory, the Secretary of State may issue a certificate under this paragraph.

(3) The certificate must (in addition to specifying the facility, agreement and certification period to which it applies) specify—

(*a*) T, that is, the value (expressed in terms of a reduction in tonnes of carbon dioxide equivalent) of achieving the targets set for the facility by the agreement, and

(*b*) P, that is, the value (expressed in the same terms) of the progress made by the facility, during the certification period, towards meeting those targets.

(4) Where a certificate has been issued under this paragraph—

(*a*) each taxable supply made to the facility at any time falling within the certification period is to be treated as not being a reduced-rate supply, and

(*b*) accordingly, an amount (determined in accordance with sub-paragraph (5)) is payable by way of levy on that taxable supply.

(5) The amount payable under this paragraph on a taxable supply is—

$$\frac{T\text{-}P}{T} \times 0.8R$$

where—

T and P have the values mentioned in sub-paragraph (3);

R is the amount which would have been payable by way of levy on the supply (had it not been a reduced-rate supply) at the time that it was made, in accordance with paragraph 42(1)(*a*).

(6) The Secretary of State must send the certificate to—

(*a*) the Commissioners, and

(*b*) the person who is the operator of the facility.

(7) A certificate under this paragraph may be issued after the certification period ends.

(8) A person liable to account for levy under this paragraph—

(*a*) is liable to account for it otherwise than by reference to an accounting period, and

(*b*) must not (by virtue of regulations under paragraph 41) become liable to pay it as from a date before the date on which the certificate under this paragraph is issued.

(9) Levy due under this paragraph is payable in addition to any levy already payable on any supply made in the certification period.

(10) In this paragraph—

"certification period", in a case where the certificate referred to in sub-paragraph (1) has been varied under paragraph 45, means the period for which that certificate has effect as varied;

"tonne of carbon dioxide equivalent" has the meaning given in the Climate Change Act 2008."

PART 2

CONSEQUENTIAL AMENDMENTS

2 Schedule 6 to FA 2000 is amended as follows.

3— (1) Paragraph 40 (persons liable to account for levy) is amended as follows.

(2) In sub-paragraph (1), after "sub-paragraph (2)" insert "or (3)".

(3) After sub-paragraph (2) insert—

"(3) In the case of levy charged on a taxable supply under paragraph 45B, the person liable to account for the levy is the operator of the facility to which the supply was made."

4 In paragraph 41(2A) (application of Part 7 where person liable to account otherwise than by reference to accounting period), after "regulations under sub-paragraph (1)(*a*)(ii) above" insert "or by virtue of paragraph 45B(8)".

5 In paragraph 42 (amount payable by way of levy), after sub-paragraph (1) insert—

"(1A) Sub-paragraph (1) is subject to paragraph 45B."

6 In paragraph 44(2) (definition of "reduced-rate supply" to have effect subject to paragraph 45), for "paragraph 45" substitute "paragraphs 45 and 45B".

7 In paragraph 45A (deemed supplies), after sub-paragraph (2) insert—

"(3) This paragraph does not apply where a supply is treated as not being a reduced-rate supply by virtue of paragraph 45B."

8— (1) Paragraph 91 (interpretation etc of Part 7 of the Schedule) is amended as follows.

(2) In sub-paragraph (5) (modification of references to accounting periods in case of levy due otherwise than by reference to such periods), after "regulations under paragraph 41(1)(*a*)(ii)" insert "or by virtue of paragraph 45B(8)".

9 In paragraph 147 (interpretation), in the definition of "reduced-rate supply", for "paragraph 45" substitute "paragraphs 45 and 45B".

CLIMATE CHANGE LEVY STATUTORY INSTRUMENTS

CHRONOLOGICAL LIST OF PRINTED STATUTORY INSTRUMENTS

SI Year/No	Title
SI 1997/1431	The Distress for Customs and Excise Duties and other Indirect Taxes Regulations 1997
SI 2000/1973	*Pollution Prevention and Control (England and Wales) Regulations 2000* (revoked)
SI 2000/3350	Finance Act 2000, Schedule 6 Part V, (Appointed Day) Order 2000
SI 2001/7	Climate Change Levy (Registration and Miscellaneous Provisions) Regulations 2001
SI 2001/486	Climate Change Levy (Combined Heat and Power Stations) Exemption Certificate Regulations 2001
SI 2001/838	Climate Change Levy (General) Regulations 2001
SI 2001/1136	Climate Change Levy (Electricity and Gas) Regulations 2001
SI 2001/1137	Climate Change Levy (Solid Fuel) Regulations 2001
SI 2001/1138	*Climate Change Levy (Use as Fuel) Regulations 2001* (revoked)
SI 2001/1139	Climate Change Agreements (Energy-intensive Installations) Regulations 2001
SI 2001/1140	*Climate Change Levy (Combined Heat and Power Stations) Prescribed Conditions and Efficiency Percentages Regulations 2001* (revoked)
SI 2005/1714	Climate Change Levy (Combined Heat and Power Stations) Regulations 2005
SI 2005/1715	Climate Change Levy (Fuel Use and Recycling Processes) Regulations 2005
SI 2006/59	Climate Change Agreements (Energy-intensive Installations) Regulations 2006
SI 2006/60	Climate Change Agreements (Eligible Facilities) Regulations 2006
SI 2007/2901	Finance Act 2006 (Climate Change Levy: Amendments and Transitional Savings in Consequence of Abolition of Half-rate Supplies) (Appointed Day) Order 2007
SI 2007/2902	Finance Act 2007 (Climate Change Levy: Reduced-rate Supplies etc) (Appointed Day) Order 2007
SI 2007/3538	Pollution Prevention and Control (England and Wales) Regulations 2007

1997/1431

Distress for Customs and Excise Duties and Other Indirect Taxes Regulations 1997

Made by the Commissioners of Customs and Excise under FA 1997 ss 51(1)–(3)

Made . . . . *9th June 1997*
Laid before House of Commons . . . . *9th June 1997*
Coming into force . . . . *1st July 1997*

Citation and Commencement

1 These Regulations may be cited as The Distress for Customs and Excise Duties and Other Indirect Taxes Regulations 1997 and shall come into force on 1st July 1997.

Interpretation

2— (1) In these Regulations—

"authorised person" means a person acting under the authority of the Commissioners;

"costs" means any costs, charges, expenses and fees;

"officer" means, subject to section 8(2) of the Customs and Excise Management Act 1979, a person commissioned by the Commissioners pursuant to section 6(3) of that Act;

"person in default" means a person who has refused or neglected to pay any relevant tax due from him;

"relevant tax" means any of the following—

. . .

(*f*) climate change levy;

. . .

"VAT Act" means the Value Added Tax Act 1994;

"walking possession agreement" means an agreement under which, in consideration of any goods and chattels distrained upon being allowed to remain in the custody of the person in default and of the delaying of their sale, that person—

(*a*) acknowledges that the goods and chattels specified in the agreement are under distraint and held in walking possession; and

(*b*) undertakes that, except with the consent of the Commissioners and subject to such conditions as they may impose, he will not remove or allow the removal of any of the specified goods and chattels from the place named in the agreement;

"1994 Act" means Part III of the Finance Act 1994;

"1996 Act" means Part III of the Finance Act 1996;

(2) Any reference in these Regulations to an amount of relevant tax includes a reference to any amount recoverable as if it were an amount of that relevant tax.

Note—Words omitted are not relevant for the purposes of the climate change levy.

Revocations and transitional provisions

3— (1) The Regulations specified in Schedule 3 are hereby revoked to the extent set out there.

(2) Where a warrant is signed before the coming into force of these Regulations, these Regulations shall apply to anything done, after these Regulations come into force, in relation to that warrant or as a consequence of distress being levied.

Levying distress

4— (1) Subject to regulation 5 below, if upon written demand a person neglects or refuses to pay any relevant tax due from him an officer may levy distress on the goods and chattels of that person and by warrant signed by him direct any authorised person to levy such distress.

(2) Where a warrant has been signed, distress shall be levied by or under the direction of, and in the presence of, the authorised person.

(3) Subject to regulation 6 below, distress may be levied on any goods and chattels located at any place whatever including on a public highway.

Restrictions on levying distress

5— (1) Where—

(*a*) an amount of any duty of customs or excise (other than vehicle excise duty) or any agricultural levy of the European Community is due and the Commissioners may be required under section 14 of the 1994 Act to review a decision which, if that decision were varied or withdrawn would cause the amount to be reduced or extinguished;

. . .

no distress shall be levied before expiry of the last day on which the person who is liable to pay the amount concerned is required, by rules made under paragraph 9 of Schedule 12 to the VAT Act, to serve a notice of appeal with respect to that decision.

(2) . . .

Note—Words omitted are not relevant for the purposes of the climate change levy.

Goods and chattels not subject to levy

6 No distress shall be levied on any goods and chattels mentioned in Schedule 1 which at the time of levy are located in a place and used for a purpose mentioned in that Schedule.

Times for levying distress

7— (1) Subject to paragraph (2) below, a levy of distress shall commence only during the period between eight o'clock in the morning and eight o'clock at night on any day of the week but it may be continued thereafter outside that period until the levy is completed.

(2) Where a person holds himself out as conducting any profession, trade or business during hours which are partly within and partly outside, or wholly outside the period mentioned in paragraph (1) above, a levy of distress may be commenced at any time during that period or during the hours of any day in which he holds himself out as conducting that profession, trade or business and it may be continued thereafter outside that period or those hours until the levy is completed.

Costs

8— (1) A person in respect of whose goods and chattels a warrant has been signed shall be liable to pay to an officer or authorised person all costs, in connection with anything done under these Regulations described in column 1 of Schedule 2, as determined in accordance with column 2 of that Schedule.

(2) An authorised person may, after deducting and accounting for the amount of relevant tax to the Commissioners, retain costs from any amount received.

Sale

9 If any person upon whose goods and chattels distress has been levied does not pay the amount of relevant tax due together with costs within 5 days of a levy, an officer or authorised person may sell the distress for payment of the amount of relevant tax and costs; and the officer or authorised person, after deducting and retaining the amount of relevant tax and costs shall restore any surplus to the owner of the goods upon which distress was levied.

Disputes as to costs

10— (1) In the case of any dispute as to costs, the amount of those costs shall be taxed by a district judge of the county court of the district where the distress was levied, and he may make such order as he thinks fit as to the costs of the taxation.

(2) In the application of this regulation to Northern Ireland, in the case of any dispute as to costs, the amount of those costs shall be taxed in the same manner as costs in equity suits or proceedings in the county court in Northern Ireland.

SCHEDULE 1

GOODS AND CHATTELS NOT SUBJECT TO LEVY

Regulation 6

1 Any of the following goods and chattels which are located in a dwelling house at which distress is being levied and are reasonably required for the domestic needs of any person residing in that dwelling house—

(*a*) beds and bedding;
(*b*) household linen;
(*c*) chairs and settees;
(*d*) tables;
(*e*) food;
(*f*) lights and light fittings;
(*g*) heating appliances;
(*h*) curtains;
(*i*) floor coverings;
(*j*) furniture, equipment and utensils used for cooking, storing or eating food;
(*k*) refrigerators;
(*l*) articles used for cleaning, mending, or pressing clothes;
(*m*) articles used for cleaning the home;
(*n*) furniture used for storing—
  (i) clothing, bedding or household linen;
  (ii) articles used for cleaning the home;
  (iii) utensils used for cooking or eating food;
(*o*) articles used for safety in the home;
(*p*) toys for the use of any child within the household;
(*q*) medical aids and medical equipment.

2 Any of the following items which are located in premises used for the purposes of any profession, trade or business—

(*a*) fire fighting equipment for use on the premises;
(*b*) medical aids and medical equipment for use on the premises.

SCHEDULE 2
SCALE OF COSTS

Regulation 8(1)

Matter	*Costs*
(*1*)	(*2*)
1 For attending to levy distress where payment is made of an amount of relevant tax due and distress is not levied:	£12·50.
2 For levying distress—	
(*a*) where an amount of relevant tax demanded and due does not exceed £100:	£12·50.
(*b*) where an amount of relevant tax demanded and due exceeds £100:	12½% on the first £100, 4% on the next £400, 2½% on the next £1,500, 1% on the next £8,000, ¼% on any additional sum.
3 For taking possession of distrained goods—	
(*a*) where a person remains in physical possession of goods at the place where distress was levied (the person to provide his own food and lodgings):	£4·50 per day.
(*b*) where possession is taken under a walking possession agreement:	£7·00.
4 For appraising goods upon which distress has been levied:	Reasonable costs of appraisement.
5 For arranging removal and storage of goods upon which distress has been levied:	Reasonable costs of arrangement.
6 For removing and storing goods upon which distress has been levied:	Reasonable costs of removal and storage.
7 For advertising the sale of goods upon which distress has been levied:	Reasonable costs of advertising.
8 For selling the distress—	
(*a*) where a sale by auction is held at the auctioneer's premises:	15% of the sum realised.
(*b*) where a sale by auction is held elsewhere:	7½% of the sum realised and auctioneer's reasonable costs.
(*c*) where a sale by other means is undertaken:	7½% of the sum realised and reasonable costs.

9 In addition to any amount specified in this scale in respect of the supply of goods or services on which value added tax is chargeable there may be added a sum equivalent to value added tax at the appropriate rate on that amount.

2000/1973
Pollution Prevention and Control (England and Wales) Regulations 2000

Made . . . . 21 July 2000
Coming into force . . . . 1 August 2000

Revocation—These Regulations revoked by the Environmental Permitting (England and Wales) Regulations, SI 2007/3538 reg 74(1), Sch 22 with effect from 6 April 2008.

2000/3350
Finance Act 2000, Schedule 6 Part V, (Appointed Day) Order 2000

Made by the Treasury under the Finance Act 2000 s 30(3)

Made . . . . 21 December 2000

1 This Order may be cited as the Finance Act 2000, Schedule 6 Part V, (Appointed Day) Order 2000.

2 The date appointed as the day on which paragraphs 59 and 60 of Part V of Schedule 6 to the Finance Act 2000 come into force is 2 January 2001.

3 The date appointed as the day on which paragraphs 53, 54, 55, 56, 57, 58 and 61 of Part V of Schedule 6 to the Finance Act 2000 come into force is 29 January 2001.

2001/7
Climate Change Levy (Registration and Miscellaneous Provisions) Regulations 2001

Made by the Commissioners of Customs and Excise under FA 2000 s 30, Sch 6 paras 59, 60, 114, 115(4), 116, 117(1), 146(1), 146(4) and 146(7)

Made . . . . *4th January 2001*
Laid before the House of Commons . . . . *5th January 2001*
Coming into force . . . . *29th January 2001*

PART I
PRELIMINARY

Citation and commencement

1 These Regulations may be cited as the Climate Change Levy (Registration and Miscellaneous Provisions) Regulations 2001 and shall come into force on 29th January 2001.

PART II
REGISTRATION

Notification of registrability: form, manner, timing, etc

2— (1) A person who is required to notify the Commissioners under paragraph 55(1) of the Act (notification of registrability for climate change levy) must do so on Form CCL 1.

(2) But a partner so required must do so on Form CCL 1 and Form CCL 2.

(3) Such notification must contain and provide full information and particulars about every matter referred to on Form CCL 1 and, in the case of a partner, Form CCL 2 together with such further details as the Commissioners may require.

(4) A person so required on 29th January 2001 must deliver the notification to the Commissioners no later than 28th February 2001.

(5) A person to whom paragraph (4) does not apply, but who becomes so required after 29th January 2001, must deliver the notification to the Commissioners within 30 days starting from the day after becoming so required.

(6) A person who is required but fails to comply with this regulation remains subject to paragraph 55(1) of the Act.

Changes in particulars

3— (1) A person who has made a notification (the "original notification") to the Commissioners under regulation 2(1), 2(2) or 2(3) at any time must also, as appropriate, notify them about the following items.

(2) The first such item is any inaccuracy or inadequacy in the information, particulars or details contained in or provided with the original notification.

(3) The second such item is any change in circumstances that causes that information or those particulars or details to become inaccurate or inadequate.

(4) The third such item is any change in circumstances relating to that person, that person's business or any other matter with respect to which particulars are contained in the register (or would, were the person registered).

(5) A notification required by this regulation must—

(*a*) be given in writing,
(*b*) provide full particulars enabling the register to be kept up to date, and
(*c*) be delivered to the Commissioners within 30 days.

(6) The first of those 30 days begins, as the case requires, on—

(*a*) the day after the person discovers that the original notification was inaccurate or is in a position to rectify the inadequacy in that notification (see paragraph (2)), or
(*b*) the day after the change in circumstances occurred (see paragraphs (3) and (4)).

(7) The full particulars referred to in paragraph (5)(*b*) include (but are not limited to)—

(*a*) the nature of the relevant inaccuracy, inadequacy or change;
(*b*) the date on which the inaccuracy in the original notification was discovered or the inadequacy could be rectified;
(*c*) the date on which the change occurred;
(*d*) the nature of the inaccuracy, inadequacy or change;
(*e*) the correct information, particulars or details.

(8) A relevant change of circumstances under paragraph (3) or (4) above includes (but is not limited to)—

(*a*) the person's name, trading name, address or principal place of business;
(*b*) the person's status (namely, as sole proprietor, partner, unincorporated body, or body corporate);
(*c*) the name and address of a partner or a change in the membership of a partnership;

(*d*) the name and address of a trustee or beneficiary of a trust.

(9) The Commissioners may, on their own initiative or following a notification under this regulation, correct an entry in the register in a case where they are satisfied that it should be corrected or otherwise brought up to date.

(10) Where a person makes a notification under this regulation that itself is or becomes inaccurate, inadequate or misleading, that notification must be treated in the same way as an original notification for the purposes of paragraphs (1) to (9).

Finishing taxable activities

4— (1) This regulation applies to a person who is required to notify the Commissioners that he ceases to intend making, or having made to him, taxable supplies in respect of which he would be the person liable to account for levy (paragraph 57(1) of the Act).

(2) Such a person must make that notification in writing setting out—

(*a*) the day on which the intention ceased, and

(*b*) the day on which he made or received the final taxable supply.

(3) This notification must be delivered to the Commissioners within 30 days starting from the day after the intention ceased, or the final taxable supply was made or received, whichever is the later.

PART III
GROUPS

References to groups, etc

5— (1) This Part makes provision about two or more bodies corporate being treated as members of the same group for the purposes of the Act ("group treatment").

(2) For those purposes, or any regulation or direction made by or under the Act—

(*a*) a body corporate is a member of a group at any time in relation to which it falls to be treated as such a member in accordance with this Part; and

(*b*) the body corporate which is to be taken to be the representative member for a group at any time is the member of the group which in relation to that time is the representative member under this Part in the case of that group.

(3) A body corporate that is a member of a group shall, under Part V of the Act, be registered in the name of the representative member.

Eligibility for group treatment

6— (1) Subject to the provisions of this Part, two or more bodies corporate are eligible to be treated as members of a group if—

(*a*) at least one of them is resident in the United Kingdom,

(*b*) they are all under the same control, and

(*c*) each of them—

(i) is registered, or is required to notify or has notified the Commissioners under paragraph 55(1) of the Act (notification of registrability), and

(ii) is not a person to whom paragraph 57(1) of the Act applies (loss of registrability).

(2) For the purposes of this regulation, two or more bodies are under the same control if—

(*a*) one of them controls each of the others;

(*b*) one person (whether a body corporate or an individual) controls all of them; or

(*c*) two or more individuals carrying on a business in partnership control all of them.

(3) For the purposes of this regulation, a body corporate shall be taken to control another body corporate only if—

(*a*) it is empowered by statute to control that body's activities, or

(*b*) it is that body's holding company within the meaning of [1159 of and Schedule 6 to][1] the Companies Act [2006][1];

and an individual or individuals shall be taken to control a body corporate only if (were he or they a company) he or they would be that body corporate's holding company within the meaning of [those provisions][1].

(4) A body corporate shall not be the representative member for a group at any time when it does not have an established place of business in the United Kingdom.

Amendments—[1] In para (3), words substituted for words "736 of", "1985" and "that section", by the Companies Act 2006 (Consequential Amendments) (Taxes and National Insurance) Order, SI 2009/1890 art 4(1)(*a*) with effect from 1 October 2009.

Liability for levy due from members of a group

7— (1) Group treatment shall not affect a body corporate being charged with levy in respect of a taxable supply whether to or from another member of the group or otherwise.

(2) However any levy with which a body corporate is charged in respect of a taxable supply treated as made while that body corporate is a member of a group shall be treated for the purposes of the Act as if it were the representative member for that group (instead of that body) which is charged with the levy.

(3) Accordingly the obligation on a member of a group to make a return pursuant to regulations made under paragraph 41 of the Act shall be discharged by the representative member making a return representing the aggregate of what would be the individual returns for the group members were it not for the group treatment.

(4) All bodies corporate who are members of a group when any levy becomes due from the representative member, together with any bodies corporate who become members of the group while any levy remains unpaid, shall be jointly and severally liable for any levy due from the representative member.

(5) References in this regulation to levy being or becoming due from the representative member include references to any amounts being or becoming recoverable as if they were levy due from that member.

Group treatment

8— (1) A body corporate shall be treated as a member of a group only—

(*a*) if a written application by that body corporate for such treatment is approved by the Commissioners, and

(*b*) from a date specified by the Commissioners for such treatment.

(2) A body corporate shall be the representative member for a group only—

(*a*) if a written application by that body corporate for this purpose is approved by the Commissioners, and

(*b*) from a date specified by the Commissioners for this purpose.

(3) The Commissioners need not approve an application by a body corporate to be a member of a group if they are not satisfied that every other proposed member agrees to the body corporate in question being a member of that proposed group.

(4) The Commissioners need not approve an application by a body corporate to be a representative member for a group if they are not satisfied that every proposed member agrees to the body corporate in question being the representative member for that proposed group.

(5) Any application under paragraph (1) or (2) must—

(*a*) be made in writing by the body corporate in question, and

(*b*) include such information and declaration as the Commissioners require.

(6) A body corporate that is a member of a group—

(*a*) shall no longer be a member of that group from the time it ceases to be eligible for group treatment; and

(*b*) shall notify the Commissioners in writing that it will cease or has ceased to be eligible for group treatment.

(7) The notification required by paragraph (6)(*b*) shall be delivered to the Commissioners no later than the earlier of 30 days after the body corporate becomes aware that it will cease to be eligible or 30 days after the body corporate ceases to be eligible.

(8) A body corporate that is the representative member for a group—

(*a*) shall no longer be the representative member for that group from the time it ceases to be eligible to be a representative member; and

(*b*) shall notify the Commissioners in writing that it will cease to be eligible to be a representative member.

(9) The notification required by paragraph (8)(*b*) shall be delivered to the Commissioners no later than the earlier of 30 days after the body corporate becomes aware that it will cease to be eligible or 30 days after the body corporate ceases to be eligible.

(10) The bodies corporate that are treated as members of a group shall take all reasonable steps to ensure that one of their number is the representative member for the group.

(11) If it appears to the Commissioners that there is no representative member for a group they may specify one of the eligible bodies corporate in that group as being the representative member and shall then notify each of the members in writing accordingly.

(12) Any body corporate specified by the Commissioners under paragraph (11), and remaining eligible, shall be taken to be the representative member of the group in question until a lawful substitution takes effect.

(13) A specification made or notice served under paragraph (11) may have effect from a time earlier than when it is made or served.

(14) The first of the 30 days referred to in paragraphs (7) and (9) is the first day after the one on which the body corporate becomes aware that it will cease to be eligible or the day after the one on which the body corporate ceases to be eligible, as the case may require.

Modifications, etc

9— (1) Where—

(*a*) any bodies corporate are treated as members of a group, and

(*b*) a written application for membership from a further eligible body corporate, that includes such information and declaration as they may require, is approved by the Commissioners,

then, from a time specified by the Commissioners, that further body corporate shall be included as a member of that group.

(2) The Commissioners need not approve an application by a body corporate under paragraph (1) if they are not satisfied that every existing member agrees to the further body corporate being a member of the group.

(3) The Commissioners need not specify a time under paragraph (1)(*b*) above that—

(*a*) is sooner than 30 days after the day they receive the relevant application, or

(*b*) is not the first day of an accounting period applying to the group by or under regulations made under paragraph 41 of the Act.

(4) Where any bodies corporate are treated as members of a group and a written application for the purpose, that includes such information and declaration as they may require, is made to the Commissioners, then, from a time specified by the Commissioners—

(*a*) a body corporate shall be excluded from the bodies so treated;

(*b*) one of those bodies corporate shall be substituted for another body corporate as the representative member; or

(*c*) the bodies corporate shall no longer be treated as members of a group.

(5) The Commissioners need not approve an application under paragraph (4) if they are not satisfied that every existing member agrees to the application in question.

(6) The Commissioners need not specify a time under paragraph (4)(*a*), 4(*b*) or 4(*c*) that is

(*a*) sooner than 30 days after the one on which they receive the relevant application, or

(*b*) is not the first day of an accounting period applying to the group by or under regulations made under paragraph 41 of the Act.

(7) Where a body corporate ceases at any time to be treated as a member of a group, and—

(*a*) there is only one other body corporate which was treated as a member of that group immediately before that time, or

(*b*) none of the other bodies corporate which were so treated immediately before that time has an established place of business in the United Kingdom,

the other body corporate or, as the case may be, each of the other bodies corporate shall also cease as from that time to be treated as a member of the group.

Miscellaneous

10— (1) The Commissioners may refuse in full or in part an application under regulation 8(1), 8(2), 9(1) or 9(4) if it appears to them necessary to do so for the protection of the revenue.

(2) A person who has made an application or notification to the Commissioners under this Part must notify them immediately should any information contained in or provided in connection with that application or notification be or become inaccurate.

11— (1) The Commissioners may, by written notice served on each member of a group, exclude a body from group treatment if it appears to them necessary to do so for the protection of the revenue or that the body in question is unable to comply with the requirements of group treatment.

(2) Such exclusion may take effect from a time earlier than when the written notice is served.

PART IV
PARTNERSHIPS AND OTHER SPECIAL CASES

Partnerships

12— (1) This regulation applies for determining by what person anything required to be done by or under the Act is to be done where, apart from this regulation, that requirement would fall on persons carrying on business in partnership.

(2) Any such requirement shall be the joint and several responsibility of every partner.

(3) Subject to paragraphs (4) and (5):

(*a*) compliance with such a requirement by at least one of the partners shall be sufficient compliance by all of them; and

(*b*) in the case of a partnership whose principal place of business is in Scotland, such compliance by a person duly authorised by the partnership shall be sufficient compliance by the partners.

(4) Each partner must comply with the requirement imposed by regulation 2 in relation to the Form CCL 2.

(5) A person joining or leaving a partnership, as the case requires, must comply with the requirements imposed by regulation 3 so far as they apply to any change in the membership of a partnership.

Other unincorporated associations

13— (1) This regulation applies for determining by what persons anything required to be done by or under the Act is to be done where, apart from this regulation, that requirement would fall on persons carrying on business together as an unincorporated body other than a partnership.

(2) Any such requirement shall be the joint and several responsibility of—

(*a*) first, every person holding office in that body as president, chairman, treasurer, secretary or other similar office; or

(*b*) secondly, if there is no such office holder, every person who is a member of a committee by which the affairs of that body are managed; or

(*c*) thirdly, if there is no such office holder or member, every person carrying on that business.

(3) Compliance with such a requirement by one or more of the persons referred to in paragraph (2) shall be sufficient compliance with that requirement by all of them.

(4) But a purported notification under regulation 2(1), 2(2) or 2(3) shall not be treated as complying with any of those regulations unless it is made by a person required to do so under paragraph (2)(*a*), (2)(*b*) or (2)(*c*) of this regulation, as appropriate.

Non resident taxpayers: requirement and provision for tax representatives

14— (1) This regulation applies to a person (a "non-resident taxpayer") who—

(*a*) is or is required to be registered for the purposes of the levy, and

(*b*) is not resident in the United Kingdom.

(2) A person who meets this description must notify the Commissioners in writing of this fact.

(3) Such notification must be delivered to the Commissioners within 30 days starting from the day after the first day on which the person meets the description.

(4) The Commissioners may—

(*a*) require or permit such a taxpayer to appoint some person resident in the United Kingdom to act as his tax representative for the purposes of the levy with effect from a date they specify [(for such residence, see paragraph 156 of the Act)][1], and

(*b*) oblige the taxpayer to request them, no later than such earlier date as they may specify, to approve the appointment of that person as the tax representative.

[In regulations 17(4)(*a*), 18(1)(*e*) and 19(5), "eligible" only refers to a person's being so resident in the United Kingdom.][1]

(5) Any appointment of a person as a tax representative shall take effect only if and from the date approved by the Commissioners.

(6) A request for approval under paragraph (4)(*b*) must be in writing and contain such information and particulars, and corresponding declaration by the taxpayer and the proposed tax representative, as the Commissioners may require.

Amendments—[1] Words in para (4) inserted by the Climate Change Levy (Miscellaneous Amendments) Regulations, SI 2005/1716 reg 8 with effect from 22 July 2005.

15— (1) A non-resident taxpayer may appoint a different tax representative as a replacement for a tax representative whose appointment has taken effect.

(2) Such appointment shall take effect only if and from a date approved by the Commissioners.

(3) A request to the Commissioners for the purposes of paragraph (2) must be in writing and contain such information and particulars, and corresponding declaration by the taxpayer and the proposed replacement tax representative, as the Commissioners may require.

16— (1) The Commissioners may, with effect from a date or dates they specify, for good cause and by way of written notice served on the non-resident taxpayer—

(*a*) withdraw their approval of any person appointed as a tax representative for that non-resident taxpayer,

(*b*) require that non-resident taxpayer to replace any tax representative with a different tax representative, and

(*c*) oblige that non-resident taxpayer to request their approval for a person's appointment as a replacement tax representative.

(2) Regulations 14(5) and (6) shall apply for the purposes of this regulation in corresponding manner as they apply for the purposes of regulation 14(4).

17— (1) This regulation applies in a case where the Commissioners require the appointment of a tax representative under regulation 14(4)(*a*) and the non-resident taxpayer—

(*a*) becomes liable to a penalty under paragraph 114(3) of the Act (penalty for failing in obligation to request Commissioners' approval of tax representative), or

(*b*) unreasonably fails to obtain the Commissioners' approval in accordance with regulation 14(4)(*b*) (approval of tax representative).

(2) Where this regulation applies, the Commissioners may give a direction requiring a specified person to be treated as the appointed and approved tax representative of that non-resident taxpayer from a specified date.

(3) Accordingly a person specified in a direction under paragraph (2) shall be treated as the tax representative of the non-resident taxpayer from the specified date until such date as the Commissioners may specify in a further direction.

(4) The Commissioners may only specify a person under paragraph (3) who—

(*a*) is eligible to act as a tax representative, and
(*b*) is suitable in all the circumstances to be the tax representative for the relevant non-resident taxpayer.

(5) The Commissioners may give a direction requiring a specified person to be treated as the appointed and approved tax representative of a non-resident taxpayer as a replacement for a person specified in a direction under paragraph (2) of this regulation.

(6) Paragraphs (3) and (4) apply in relation to paragraph (5) in corresponding manner as they apply to paragraph (2).

(7) Regulations 15 and 16 do not apply in relation to a person specified in a direction under this regulation.

18— (1) A person shall cease to be the tax representative for a non-resident taxpayer from when—

(*a*) the non-resident taxpayer ceases to be registered;
(*b*) the non-resident taxpayer replaces that person with a different tax representative under regulation 15 or 16;
(*c*) the Commissioners so direct under regulation 17;
(*d*) the person dies or becomes incapacitated or subject to an insolvency procedure;
(*e*) the person ceases to be eligible to be a tax representative;
(*f*) the person delivers to the Commissioners notification in writing that he withdraws as tax representative for the non-resident taxpayer; or
(*g*) the non-resident taxpayer delivers to the Commissioners notification in writing that he withdraws an appointment that they permitted but did not require.

(2) A person who is specified in a direction under regulation 17 shall not—

(*a*) cease to be (or be treated as) the tax representative except in accordance with that regulation; or
(*b*) be permitted to withdraw under paragraph (1)(*f*) of this regulation.

(3) The name of a tax representative (or a person treated as such) shall be registered against the name of the non-resident taxpayer of whom that person is (or is treated as) the representative (paragraph 53(2) of the Act).

(4) That name shall be deleted from the register if the person ceases to be the tax representative for that non-resident taxable person and the Commissioners consider it appropriate to do so.

19— (1) A tax representative (or a person treated as such) shall notify and provide full particulars to the Commissioners in writing about any of the following matters.

(2) Such notification must be delivered to the Commissioners no later than 30 days starting from the first day after the matter arises.

(3) The first matter is any change in the name, constitution or ownership of the tax representative's business or of any event that may require the register to be varied.

(4) The second matter is the tax representative lawfully ceasing to be the appointed tax representative of the relevant non-resident taxpayer.

(5) The third matter is the tax representative ceasing to be eligible to act as a tax representative.

PART V
PENALTIES

Penalties to be provided for by regulations

20 A person who fails to comply with a requirement imposed on him by or under any of the following regulations shall be liable to a penalty of £250 for each such failure—

(*a*) regulation 2(1), 2(2), 2(3), 2(4) or 2(5) (form, manner, etc of notification about registrability);
(*b*) regulation 3(1), 3(5) or 3(10) (changes in particulars of notification about registrability);
(*c*) regulation 4(2) (notification of ceasing taxable activities);
(*d*) regulation 14(2) or 14(3) (notification by non resident taxpayer);
(*e*) regulation 19(1) or 19(2) (notification by tax representative).

PART VI
INTERPRETATION

Interpretation

21 In these regulations, except where the context requires otherwise—

"the Act" refers to Schedule 6 to the Finance Act 2000 and any reference to a paragraph or Part of the Act refers to the appropriate paragraph or Part of that Schedule;

"Form CCL 1" and "Form CCL 2" refer respectively to the forms numbered 1 and 2 in the Schedule to these Regulations (or to such forms as the Commissioners are satisfied are to like effect);

"levy" refers to climate change levy;

"Part", "regulation" or "regulations" refers to the appropriate Part, regulation or regulations of these Regulations;

"partner" refers to a person carrying on a business in partnership with at least one other person.

SCHEDULE

Form 1 Climate Change Levy (CCL)
Application for Registration

SCHEDULE

Form 1 **Regulation 2(1)**

HM Customs and Excise

Climate Change Levy (CCL)

Application for Registration

Data Protection Act 1998

HM Customs and Excise collects information in order to administer the taxes for which it is responsible (such as VAT, insurance premium tax, excise duties, air passenger duty, landfill tax, climate change levy), and for detecting and preventing crime.

Where the law permits we may also get information about you from third parties, or give information to them, for example in order to check its accuracy, prevent or detect crime or protect public funds in other ways. These third parties may include the police, other government departments and agencies.

When you have completed and signed this form, please send it using the official reply envelope provided to:

The Controller
Central Collection Unit (CCL)
HM Customs and Excise
Alexander House
21 Victoria Avenue
Southend-on-Sea
SS99 1AY

For official use only:

DTRN

EDR

CCL ID completed/attached

Initials	
Keyer	Checker

Date of receipt

Climate Change Levy (CCL)

Version 0.5

Application for Registration

Please read the general notes before completing this form. Please write clearly in black ink and use BLOCK LETTERS or use typescript.

Applicants for Divisional Registration must complete Form CCL 1D and for Group Registration Forms CCL 50 and CCL 51.

1. Please show your Departmental Trader Registration Number;

This is the number under which registered traders account for all their business with Customs and Excise.

2. Please give the name of the business.

3. Do you have a trading name? *Please tick* ✓ Yes No

If yes, please give the trading name of the business.

4. What is the legal status of your business?

Please insert appropriate numbers from list below.

1. Incorporated company.
2. Sole proprietor.
3. Partnership.
4. Public corporation.
5. Local authority.
6. Non profit making body/unincorporated body.

If your business is a partnership Form CCL 2 must be completed giving details of the partners.

Please insert (if applicable) details from your certificate of incorporation:

- Company registration number:
- Date of incorporation:

5. Is your business a Trust? *Please tick* ✓ Yes No

If yes, you must supply the names of all Trustees and beneficiaries.

If your business is a Trust form CCL 2T and CCL2TB should be completed giving details of all Trustees and beneficiaries of the Trust.

Version 0.5

6. Please give the address of your principal place of business.

Address:	
Country:	
Postcode:	
Tel. no: (Include dialling code)	
Fax no: (include dialling code)	
E-mail address:	
Website address:	

7. Please give the anticipated or actual date of your first taxable supply of an energy product subject to CCL.

D D M M Y Y Y Y

- This date must be no earlier than 1 April 2001.
- Please see general notes for further information on taxable supplies.

Please note: If you are applying as the representative member of a CCL group, please show the date or anticipated date of the first taxable supply to be made by any group member including the representative member.

8. Please indicate your main and subsidiary business activities by inserting the appropriate codes in the boxes:

Main Subsidiary/ies

1. Energy supplier.
2. Energy imports.
3. Energy exports.
4. Self supply of energy.

Please see Box 7 of the general notes for details of taxable energy supplies.

Do you use a combined heat and power (CHP) plant to generate energy? *Please tick* ✓ Yes No

If no, go to Box 9

If yes, are you participating in the CHP Quality Assurance (CHPQA) Programme run by the Department of the Environment, Transport and the Regions (DETR)? *Please tick* ✓ Yes No

If yes, what is your CHPQA certificate number?

If you have more than one CHPQA number please give details in a separate letter.

Has the DETR issued a certificate confirming that you have a fully exempt CHP plant for CCL purposes? *Please tick* ✓ Yes No

If yes, you are not registrable for CCL in respect of your fully exempt CHP plant(s) for the period covered by the certificate. If the only supplies you are making are from fully exempt CHP plants certificated by the DETR you do not need to complete this form.

If no, you are registrable in respect of supplies made or supplies you intend to make by any of your partially exempt CHP plants if those supplies exceed the limit advised to you on the DETR certificate. Please see the CCL Notice for more details of the registration requirements for partially exempt CHP plants.

If you are applying as the representative member of a CCL group please complete the boxes including CHP plants for all group members.

Version 0.5

9. Has your energy supply business been transferred to you as a going concern.

Please tick ✓

Yes No

Only complete this box if:

- you are taking over an existing energy supply business from some one else; or
- you have changed the legal status of your business

Please give the Departmental Trader Registration Number of the person who transferred the business to you:

Date of transfer: D D M M Y Y Y Y

Do you wish to keep the previous owner's Departmental Trader Registration Number

Please tick ✓

Yes No

10. Please indicate which energy products you supply and, where appropriate, those generated from renewable sources. Please also show the number of units supplied each year to business and domestic customers. If you are applying as the representative member of a CCL group please estimate the energy products supplied for all group companies in the table.

	Energy Supplied (Y/N)	Renewable source (Y/N/partly)	Business units supplied per year	Domestic/non-business charity units supplied per year
Electricity			kWh	kWh
Gas			kWh	kWh
Liquefied Petroleum Gas (LPG)			kg	kg
Solid and other fuels (coal and lignite, coke and semi-coke of coal and lignite and petroleum coke).			kg	kg

SPECIMEN

11. Please indicate preferred period and date for your returns by entering the appropriate stagger code in the box:

Stagger 0 Monthly Returns

Stagger 1 Quarters ending 31 March
30 June
30 September
31 December

Stagger 2 Quarters ending 31 January
30 April
31 July
31 October

Stagger 3 Quarters ending 28/29 February
31 May
31 August
30 November

NB: If you wish to apply for non-standard tax periods please enter the stagger period most closely matching your non-standard tax periods.

Version 0.5

Please tick ✓

12. Do you wish to apply for non-standard tax periods? Yes ☐ No ☐

Do you intend to use the annual return scheme for CCL? Yes ☐ No ☐

Please send me further information about the annual return scheme for CCL. Yes ☐ No ☐

13. Do you wish to apply to register as the representative member of a Climate Change Levy Group? Yes ☐ No ☐

If yes, please ensure that you complete Forms CCL 50 and CCL 51.

14. Do you wish to apply for divisional registration? If yes, each division of your company to be registered separately must complete Form CCL 1D. Please note: you cannot apply for both group registration and divisional registration for your company. Yes ☐ No ☐

15. Have you been involved with any other business registered for CCL or VAT in the last 5 years? Yes ☐ No ☐

- Please give the Departmental Trader Registration Number or VAT number of any businesses you are or have been involved in. If you are a partnership or a limited company this means any businesses in which any partners or directors in the business you are seeking to register have been involved in as a sole proprietor, partner or director.
- Please continue on a separate sheet if necessary.

16. Bank Details

Please give your Bank or Building Society Account details.

Sort Code: ☐☐☐☐☐☐ Account Number: ☐☐☐☐☐☐☐☐

Girobank Account Number: ☐☐☐☐☐☐☐☐☐

Bank Account Title:

Please tick ✓

17. Are you resident in the United Kingdom? Yes ☐ No ☐

If yes, please go to Box 20.

If no, please go to Box 18a.

Version 0.5

18a. Do you make taxable supplies as a gas or electricity utility in the United Kingdom? *Please tick* ☑ Yes ☐ No ☐

If yes, you will be liable to register for CCL, please go to Boxes 19a and 19b.

If no, please go to Box 18b.

18b. Do you receive or intend to receive taxable supplies of liquefied petroleum gas or solid fuel from a supplier outside the United Kingdom? *Please tick* ☑ Yes ☐ No ☐

If yes, you will be liable to register for CCL, please go to boxes 19a and 19b.

If no, you are not liable to register for CCL and you are not required to complete this form.

19a. Please show your country of residence: ☐

19b. Will you wish to appoint a tax representative? *Please tick* ☑ Yes ☐ No ☐

If your answer to question 19b is yes Form CCL 1TR must be completed.

20. Computer Accounts

Is your accounting system computerised? *Please tick* ☑ Yes ☐ No ☐

If yes, please give details below:

Accounting Software: ☐ Version: ☐

21. Declaration

Declaration

I, ☐

(enter your FULL NAME (no initials) in BLOCK LETTERS) declare that the information given on this form and contained in any accompanying documentation is true and complete.

Signature ☐

Please tick ☑ Mr ☐ Mrs ☐ Miss ☐ Ms ☐

Sole proprietor ☐ Director ☐

Trustee ☐ Partner ☐

Beneficiary of a Trust ☐ Authorised official ☐

Company Secretary ☐

Date D D M M Y Y Y Y

Form 2
Climate Change Levy (CCL)
Partnership Details

Form 2 **Regulation 2(2)**

Climate Change Levy (CCL)

Partnership Details

When you have completed and signed this form, please send it together with Form CCL 1 (Application for Registration) using the official envelope provided to:

The Controller
Central Collection Unit (CCL)
HM Customs and Excise
Alexander House
21 Victoria Avenue
Southend-on-Sea
SS99 1AY

Data Protection Act 1998

HM Customs and Excise collects information in order to administer the taxes for which it is responsible (such as VAT, insurance premium tax, excise duties, air passenger duty, landfill tax, climate change levy), and for detecting and preventing crime.

Where the law permits we may also get information about you from third parties, or give information to them, for example in order to check its accuracy, prevent or detect crime or protect public funds in other ways. These third parties may include the police, other government departments and agencies.

Complaints

If you have a complaint please telephone the National Customs and Excise Advice Service, the telephone number is in the telephone directory.

If you are unhappy with our response you can ask the Adjudicator to look into your complaint. The Adjudicator reviews complaints not settled to your satisfaction by Customs. The recommendations of the Adjudicator are independent and the service is free. The Adjudicator only looks at complaints, not general enquiries. Telephone the Adjudicator on 020 7930 2292.

For official use only

Date of receipt:

DTR No:

These details form part of your application to be registered for Climate Change Levy

Trading name of partnership:

Please make sure that every partner completes and signs one of the sections below. If there is insufficient space to include all partners, please photocopy this form or contact the Central Collection Unit (page 1) for additional copies.

Please use BLOCK LETTERS and write clearly in black ink or use typescript.

Full name of partner:

Home Address:

Postcode:

Home Telephone:

Signature:

Date:

Full name of partner:

Home Address:

Postcode:

Home Telephone:

Signature:

Date:

Full name of partner:

Home Address:

Postcode:

Home Telephone:

Signature:

Date:

Full name of partner:

Home Address:

Postcode:

Home Telephone:

Signature: Date:

Full name of partner:

Home Address:

Postcode:

Home Telephone:

Signature: Date:

Full name of partner:

Home Address:

Postcode:

Home Telephone:

Signature: Date:

2001/486
Climate Change Levy (Combined Heat and Power Stations) Exemption Certificate Regulations 2001

Made by the Secretary of State for the Environment, Transport and the Regions under FA 2000 Sch 6 para 148(10), (11)

Made . . . . *21 February 2001*
Laid before Parliament . . . . *26 February 2001*
Coming into force . . . . *19 March 2001*

Citation and commencement

1 These Regulations may be cited as the Climate Change Levy (Combined Heat and Power Stations) Exemption Certificate Regulations 2001 and shall come into force on 19th March 2001.

Interpretation

2 In these Regulations,

"CHPQA" means the Combined Heat and Power Quality Assurance Standard, Issue 1, November 2000 published by the Department of the Environment, Transport and the Regions;

"CHPQA certificate" means a certificate issued in respect of a combined heat and power station following assessment of the station against criteria set out in CHPQA, and "CHPQA scheme reference number" means the number stated as the scheme reference number in that certificate;

"efficiency percentage" has the same meaning as in paragraph 15(4)(*b*) of Schedule 6;

"exemption certificate" means a certificate given by the Secretary of State under paragraph 148(4) or (5) of Schedule 6 (full-exemption and part-exemption certificates in respect of combined heat and power stations for the purposes of climate change levy);

"operator" means the person by whom a combined heat and power station is operated;

"prescribed conditions" means any conditions prescribed by regulations made by the Treasury under paragraph 148(4) of Schedule 6;

"Schedule 6" means Schedule 6 to the Finance Act 2000; and

"threshold efficiency percentage" has the same meaning as in paragraph 15(4)(*a*) of Schedule 6.

Applications for, and content of, exemption certificates

3— (1) An application for an exemption certificate in respect of a combined heat and power station shall be made by the operator in writing and shall be accompanied by a copy of the current CHPQA certificate relating to the station.

(2) The operator shall send a copy of the current CHPQA certificate relating to the station to the Secretary of State by 30th June in each year after the year in which an application is made in accordance with paragraph (1).

(3) An exemption certificate shall remain in force until revoked in accordance with regulation 4(2).

(4) An exemption certificate shall state—

(*a*) the date on which it comes into force (which shall not be earlier than the date on which it is issued);

(*b*) the CHPQA scheme reference number of the combined heat and power station to which it relates;

(*c*) whether the station is fully or partly exempt; and

(*d*) (as required by paragraph 148(6) of Schedule 6) its efficiency percentage.

Variation and revocation of exemption certificates

4— (1) If it appears to the Secretary of State that there has been a material change in the circumstances of a combined heat and power station such that—

(*a*) it no longer satisfies the prescribed conditions as being fully exempt; or

(*b*) in the case of a partly exempt station, it now satisfies the prescribed conditions as being fully exempt; or

(*c*) its efficiency percentage has fallen below, or, as the case may be, risen to equal or exceed the threshold efficiency percentage,

he shall vary its exemption certificate by revising the particulars mentioned in regulation 3(4)(*c*) or (*d*), as appropriate.

(2) If—

(*a*) a combined heat and power station ceases to operate;

(*b*) the operator fails to comply with regulation 3(2); or

(*c*) the operator makes a written request to that effect to the Secretary of State,

the Secretary of State shall revoke the exemption certificate.

2001/838

Climate Change Levy (General) Regulations 2001

Made by the Commissioners of Customs and Excise under FA 2000 s 30 and Sch 6 paras 19(1), 19(3), 21, 22, 23(4), 27(7), 27(8), 29(7), 41(1), 41(2), 43(4), 43(5), 44(5), 62, 63(4), 65, 73, 74, 100(2), 100(3), 118, 119, 120, 125, 146(1), 146(4) and 146(7)

Made . . . . *9 March 2001*
Laid before the House of Commons . . . . *12 March 2001*
Coming into force . . . . *1 April 2001*

PART I
PRELIMINARY

1 These Regulations may be cited as the Climate Change Levy (General) Regulations 2001 and shall come into force on 1st April 2001.

General interpretation

2— (1) In these Regulations and [the Schedules][1], except where the context requires otherwise—

"the Act" refers to Schedule 6 to the Finance Act 2000;

"CCL" refers to climate change levy;

"excluded part", "exempt part"...[3] and "reduced-rate part" refer, respectively, to that part of a supply of a taxable commodity that would, by itself, be excluded or exempt from CCL or would be ...[3] a reduced-rate supply for CCL purposes;

"gas" refers to gas described by paragraph 3(1)(*b*) of the Act;

"Part", "regulation" or "regulations" refers to the appropriate Part, regulation or regulations of these Regulations;

"non-registrable electricity producer" refers to an electricity producer to whom a supply of a taxable commodity is not exempt under paragraph 14(1) of the Act (except in relation to uses of the electricity he produces for which that exemption is retained);

"published notice" refers to a notice published by the Commissioners and not withdrawn by a further notice;

"recipient" refers to the person to whom a supply of a taxable commodity is made;

"registrable person" refers to a person who is registered or required to be registered under Part V of the Act [(including, but for regulations 8 and 9 only (records), a person whom the Commissioners exempt from that requirement under Schedule 1 paragraph 5(9))][2];

...[1]

"supplier" refers to a person making a supply of a taxable commodity (but, in the case of regulations 11, 13 and 14, it only refers to the person who is liable to account for the CCL charged on the taxable supply in question (see paragraph 40(1) of the Act—suppliers, and paragraph 40(2) of the Act—supplies made by persons who are neither residents of the United Kingdom nor utilities));

"time of supply" refers to when a supply of a taxable commodity is treated as taking place by or under paragraphs 25 to 39 of the Act;

"working day" excludes Saturday, Sunday and any bank or public holiday.

(2) Where a provision of these Regulations requires the delivery of something to the Commissioners, it must be taken to include a requirement that delivery must be made to any address specified for the purpose in question by the Commissioners in a published notice.

Amendments—[1] In para (1), words substituted, and definition of "Schedule" revoked, by the CCL (General) (Amendment) Regulations, SI 2003/604 regs 2, 3 with effect from 1 April 2003.

[2] Words in definition of "registrable person" inserted by the Climate Change Levy (Miscellaneous Amendments) Regulations, SI 2005/1716 regs 2, 6 with effect from 22 July 2005. However, arrangements initiated or made before 22 July 2005 on the basis of SI 2001/838 Sch 1 para 5(5) or 5(6) as then in force remain subject to the provisions applicable when they were initiated or made (tax credit claims and corrections to over-estimated relief).

[3] In para (1), words ',"half-rate part" ' and 'a half-rate supply or' revoked by the Climate Change Levy (General) (Amendment) Regulations, SI 2007/2903 reg 2, Sch 1 para 1 with effect from 1 November 2007: SI 2007/2903 reg 1. These amendments do not apply in relation to a half-rate supply made before 1 April 2006: SI 2007/2903 reg 2, Sch 1 Note (*a*).

PART II
ACCOUNTING, PAYMENT, RECORDS, TAX CREDITS, REPAYMENTS, SET-OFF, ETC

Accounting periods

3— (1) A registrable person shall be subject to accounting periods.

(2) In the case of a registered person, these shall be each three month period ending on the dates notified to him at any time by the Commissioners for this purpose.

(3) In the case of any other registrable person, these shall be each three month period ending on 31st March, 30th June, 30th September or 31st December.

(4) However, in a particular case, the Commissioners may vary the start, end and length of any accounting period.

Returns

4— (1) A registrable person is obliged to make a return to the Commissioners covering each of his accounting periods.

(2) The registrable person is obliged to make that return no later than the last working day of the month immediately following the end of the period to which it relates.

(3) In the case of an accounting period that does not end on the last day of a month, the registrable person is obliged to make that return no later than the due day directed by the Commissioners.

(4) The Commissioners may allow the registrable person extra time in which to make that return.

(5) The registrable person must make that return in a form that is prescribed by the Commissioners in a published notice ("prescribed form").

(6) The registrable person must make that return by securing that it is delivered either to the address prescribed by the Commissioners in a published notice or to any other address that they may direct or allow.

Content of returns

5— (1) The registrable person must declare in the return the CCL due from him for the relevant accounting period, taking into consideration—

(*a*) the CCL due on taxable supplies—

(i) the time of supply of which is in that accounting period, and
(ii) for which he is liable to account;

and,

(*b*) any authorised or required adjustment or any correction of errors (see regulations 14(2), 17(3), 27 and 28 and, [Schedule 1 paragraph 8(1)(*b*)][1]).

(2) The registrable person must provide in the return accurate information about every matter that the prescribed form requires.

(3) The registrable person must sign, date and declare on the document forming his return that the information provided in it is true and complete.

(4) The registrable person must comply with paragraphs (1), (2) and (3) in the manner prescribed by the Commissioners in a published notice.

Amendments—[1] In para (1), words "in Schedule 1, paragraphs 5(9G) and 8(1)(*b*)" substituted by the Climate Change Levy (General) (Amendment) Regulations, SI 2007/2903 reg 2, Sch 1 para 2 with effect from 1 November 2007: SI 2007/2903 reg 1. This amendment does not apply in relation to a half-rate supply made before 1 April 2006: SI 2007/2903 reg 2, Sch 1 Note (*a*).

Payment

6— (1) A registrable person must pay to the Commissioners the amount of CCL due from him for a given accounting period no later than the due date for the return for that period (see regulations 4(2), 4(3) and 4(4)).

(2) The registrable person must make that payment by securing that it is delivered either to the address or bank account prescribed for this purpose by the Commissioners in a published notice or to any other address or bank account that they may direct or allow.

(3) The Commissioners may allow a registrable person who has made arrangements with them for the payment of any amount of CCL due from him by means of direct debit an extra 7 days in which the payment may be made.

(4) The Commissioners shall only act pursuant to paragraph (3) in accordance with conditions they shall stipulate in a published notice.

[Interpretation of Regulations 6B to 6G

6A In regulations 6B to 6G—

"authorised person" means a person who has been authorised by the Commissioners under regulation 6B(1), and "authorised" and "authorisation" shall be construed accordingly;

"current accounting year" means the period of 12 months commencing on a date indicated by the Commissioners in their notification of authorisation of a person, or while a person remains authorised, the most recent anniversary thereof, and is an accounting period within the meaning of regulation 3;

"the scheme" means the annual accounting scheme established by regulations 6B to 6G;

"transitional accounting period" means the period commencing on the first day of a person's accounting period in which the Commissioners authorise him to use the scheme, and ending on the day immediately preceding the first day of that person's [first current accounting year][2], and is an accounting period within the meaning of regulation 3.][1]

Amendments—[1] Regulation inserted by the CCL (General) (Amendment) Regulations, SI 2002/1152 with effect from 1 June 2002.

[2] Words in definition of "transitional accounting period" substituted by the CCL (General) (Amendment) Regulations, SI 2003/604 regs 2, 5 with effect from 1 April 2003.

[Annual accounting scheme

6B— (1) The Commissioners may, subject to the requirements in paragraph (2) below and in regulations 6C to 6G, authorise a registered person to pay and account for CCL by reference to any transitional accounting period, and any subsequent current accounting year, at such times, and for such amounts, as may be determined in accordance with the scheme.

(2) The Commissioners shall not be required to authorise a person under regulation 6B(1) unless an application is made to the Commissioners in such form and in such manner as the Commissioners may prescribe in a published notice.][1]

Amendments—[1] Regulation inserted by the Climate Change Levy (General) (Amendment) Regulations, SI 2002/1152 with effect from 1 June 2002.

[Admission to the scheme

6C— (1) A person shall be eligible to apply for authorisation if—

(*a*) he has been registered for at least 12 months at the date of his application for authorisation;

(*b*) he has reasonable grounds for believing that the amount of CCL on taxable supplies made or to be made by him in the period of 12 months beginning on the date of his application for authorisation will not exceed £2,000;

(*c*) his registration is not in the name of a representative member of a group of two or more bodies corporate under paragraph 56(2) of Schedule 6 to the Act;

(*d*) his registration is not in the name of a division under paragraph 56(3) of Schedule 6 to the Act; and

(*e*) he has not in the 12 months preceding the date of his application for authorisation ceased to operate the scheme.

(2) The Commissioners may refuse to authorise a person where they consider it necessary to do so for the protection of the revenue.][1]

Amendments—[1] Regulation inserted by the Climate Change Levy (General) (Amendment) Regulations, SI 2002/1152 with effect from 1 June 2002.

[Cessation of authorisation

6D— (1) An authorised person shall continue to account for CCL in accordance with the scheme until he ceases to be authorised.

(2) An authorised person ceases to be authorised when—

(*a*) at the end of any [transitional accounting period][2] or current accounting year the amount of CCL on taxable supplies made by him during that period or year has exceeded £2,000;

(*b*) his authorisation is terminated in accordance with regulation 6E;

(*c*) he—

(i) becomes insolvent and ceases to trade, other than for the purpose of disposing of stocks and assets,

(ii) ceases business or ceases to be registered,

(iii) dies, becomes bankrupt or incapacitated;

(*d*) he ceases to operate the scheme of his own volition.][1]

Amendments—[1] Regulation inserted by the CCL (General) (Amendment) Regulations, SI 2002/1152 with effect from 1 June 2002.

[2] Words in para (2)(*a*) substituted by the CCL (General) (Amendment) Regulations, SI 2003/604 regs 2, 6 with effect from 1 April 2003.

[6E— (1) The Commissioners may terminate an authorisation in any case where—

(*a*) a false statement has been made by or on behalf of an authorised person in relation to his application for authorisation;

(*b*) an authorised person fails to make by the due date a return for his transitional accounting period or current accounting year;

(*c*) an authorised person fails to make by the due date any payment shown as due on any return for his transitional accounting period or current accounting year;

(*d*) the Commissioners receive notification that the amount of CCL on taxable supplies in a transitional [accounting period][3] or current accounting year will exceed £2,000;

(*e*) at any time during an authorised person's [transitional accounting period][2] or current accounting year they have reason to believe that the amount of CCL on taxable supplies during the period or, as the case may be, year will exceed £2,000;

(*f*) it is necessary to do so for the protection of the revenue;

(*g*) an authorised person has not, in relation to a return made by him prior to authorisation, paid to the Commissioners all such sums shown as due thereon; or

(*h*) an authorised person has not, in relation to any assessment made under Schedule 6 to the Act, paid to the Commissioners all such sums due as shown thereon.

(2) Where an authorised person has reason to believe that the amount of CCL on taxable supplies made by him during a transitional accounting period or current accounting year will exceed £2,000, he shall within 30 days notify the Commissioners in writing.][1]

Amendments—[1] Regulation inserted by the Climate Change Levy (General) (Amendment) Regulations, SI 2002/1152 with effect from 1 June 2002.
[2] Words in para (1)(*e*) substituted by the CCL (General) (Amendment) Regulations, SI 2003/604 regs 2, 6 with effect from 1 April 2003.
[3] Words in para (1)(*d*) inserted by the CCL (General) (Amendment) Regulations, SI 2003/604 regs 2, 7 with effect from 1 April 2003.

[6F— (1) The date from which an authorised person ceases to be authorised shall be—

(*a*) where regulation 6D(2)(*a*) applies, the day following the last day of the relevant transitional accounting period or current accounting year;

(*b*) where regulation 6D(2)(*b*) applies, the day on which the Commissioners terminate his authorisation;

(*c*) where regulation 6D(2)(*c*) applies, the day on which any one of the events mentioned in that paragraph occurs; or

(*d*) where regulation 6D(2)(*d*) applies, the date on which the Commissioners are notified in writing of the authorised person's decision to cease using the scheme.

(2) Where an authorised person ceases to be authorised, he or as the case may be, his representative, shall—

(*a*) if his authorisation ceases before the end of his transitional accounting period or current accounting year, make a return within one month of the date specified in paragraph (1)(*b*), (1)(*c*) or (1)(*d*) above, together with any payment due to the Commissioners in respect of his liability for CCL for that part of the period or year arising before the date he ceased to be authorised; or

(*b*) if his authorisation ceases at the end of his transitional accounting period or current accounting year, make a return together with any payment due to the Commissioners in respect of his liability for CCL in accordance with regulations 4, 5 and 6;

and, in either case, from the day following the day on which he ceases to be authorised, account for and pay CCL as provided for otherwise than by the scheme.][1]

Amendments—[1] Regulation inserted by the Climate Change Levy (General) (Amendment) Regulations, SI 2002/1152 with effect from 1 June 2002.

[6G The Commissioners may vary any one of the amounts specified in regulations 6C(1)(*b*), 6D(2)(*a*) and 6E(1)(*d*) and (*e*) and (2) by prescribing a new amount in a published notice.][1]

Amendments—[1] Regulation inserted by the Climate Change Levy (General) (Amendment) Regulations, SI 2002/1152 with effect from 1 June 2002.

Records

7— (1) A registrable person is obliged to keep a record to be known as the "climate change levy account" (periodic summary of CCL due).

(2) A registrable person who makes a claim under regulations 10 and 14(1) (tax credits in respect of bad debts) is obliged to keep a record to be known as the "climate change levy bad debts account".

(3) A registrable person who makes a claim under regulations 11 and 14(1) (other tax credits) is obliged to keep a record to be known as the "climate change levy tax credits account".

(4) A record within this regulation must be kept in the manner stipulated in a published notice.

8 A registrable person is obliged to keep the following records—

(*a*) his business and accounting records;

(*b*) a copy of each CCL accounting document issued by him;

(*c*) each supplier certificate and supporting analysis document received, issued or prepared by or for him to evidence that a taxable supply (or part of such a supply) by or to him was—

(i) excluded or exempt from CCL, or

(ii) a …[3] reduced-rate supply;

[(*ca*) any record required by or under Part IV(*a*) (combined heat and power stations);][2]

(*d*) documentary evidence (including any relevant invoice) detailing each taxable supply made by him;

(*e*) documentary evidence (including any relevant invoice) received by him in connection with his receipt of any taxable commodity;

(*f*) documentary evidence regarding the adjustment of an entry concerning the amount of CCL charged for which he is liable to account;

(*g*) documentary evidence regarding any claim by him for a tax credit under regulation 10 (bad debts), regulation 11 (other tax credits) or [Schedule 1][1] (tax credit for recipient) and, in each case, regarding any relevant surrounding circumstances;

(*h*) the documents relevant to any special utility scheme binding him;

(*i*) a record of the information he relies on in making each return pursuant to regulation 5;

(*j*) any other record that may be stipulated in a published notice.

Amendments—[1] Words substituted by the CCL (General) (Amendment) Regulations, SI 2003/604 regs 2, 4 with effect from 1 April 2003.
[2] Para (*ca*) inserted by the CCL (General) (Amendment) Regulations, SI 2003/604 regs 2, 8 with effect from 1 April 2003.

[3] In para (*c*)(ii), words "half-rate or " revoked by the Climate Change Levy (General) (Amendment) Regulations, SI 2007/2903 reg 2, Sch 1 para 3 with effect from 1 November 2007: SI 2007/2903 reg 1. This amendment does not apply in relation to a half-rate supply made before 1 April 2006: SI 2007/2903 reg 2, Sch 1 Note (*a*).

9— (1) A registrable person is required to preserve any record required by regulation 7 or 8 for a period of at least six years.

(2) For the purposes of paragraph (1), a record within regulation 7 need only be preserved in relation to events taking place not more than six years earlier.

(3) For the purposes of paragraph (1), a record within regulation 8(*c*) must be preserved by the registrable person for a period of six years from the time of supply of the final supply to which it relates.

(4) For the purposes of paragraph (1), a record within regulation 8(*d*) or 8(*e*) must be preserved by the registrable person for a period of six years from the relevant time of supply or, if there is no such time, from the time of delivery.

(5) The Commissioners may direct that any such record need only be preserved for such period as they specify shorter than six years.

Bad debts: entitlement to tax credit

10— (1) Paragraph (3) applies where—

(*a*) a person has supplied a taxable commodity and has accounted for and paid the CCL chargeable on the supply,

(*b*) that person and the recipient of the supply are not connected or are not the same person,

(*c*) that person has issued to the recipient a climate change levy accounting document (or, if the issue of such a document is not required by or under the Act, other invoice) relating to the supply showing the CCL chargeable,

(*d*) the whole or any part of the price for the supply has been written off in his accounts as a bad debt, and

(*e*) the period of 6 months referred to in paragraph (8) has elapsed.

(2) Any question whether a person is connected with another for the purposes of paragraph (1) shall be determined in accordance with section 839 of the Income and Corporation Taxes Act 1988.

(3) The person shall be entitled to a tax credit in respect of the amount of CCL chargeable calculated by reference to the outstanding amount (subject to the provisions of this Part including those provisions relating to the making of a relevant claim to the Commissioners).

(4) In this regulation and regulation 16—

"claim" refers to a claim in accordance with regulation 14 or 15, and "claimant" shall be construed accordingly;

"the outstanding amount" refers to—

(*a*) if at the time of the claim no part of the price written off in the claimant's accounts as a bad debt has been received, an amount equal to the amount of the price so written off;

(*b*) if at that time any part of the price so written off has been received, an amount by which that part is exceeded by the amount of the price written off.

(5) In paragraph (4), "received" refers to receipt either by the claimant or by a person to whom has been assigned a right to receive the whole or any part of the price written off.

(6) Accordingly, the tax credit arising under this regulation shall be of an amount equal to such proportion of the CCL charged on the supply as the outstanding amount forms of the total price.

(7) For the purposes of this regulation, where the whole or any part of the price for the supply does not consist of money, the amount in money that shall be taken to represent any non-monetary part of the price shall be so much of the amount made up of—

(*a*) the price excluding the CCL chargeable, and

(*b*) the CCL charged on the supply,

as is attributable to the non-monetary consideration in question.

(8) Neither the whole nor any part of the price for a supply shall be taken to have been written off in accounts as a bad debt until a period of not less than six months has elapsed from the time when such whole or part became due and payable to, or to the order of, the person who made the relevant supply.

(9) Subject to paragraph (8), the whole or any part of the price for a relevant supply shall be taken to have been written off as a bad debt when an entry is made in relation to that supply in the claimant's climate change levy bad debts account (see regulation 7(2)).

(10) Where the claimant owes an amount of money to the recipient of the relevant supply which can be set off, the price written off in the accounts shall be reduced by the amount so owed.

(11) Where the claimant holds in relation to the recipient of the relevant supply an enforceable security, the consideration written off in the account of the claimant shall be reduced by the value of that security.

(12) In paragraphs (8) to (11), "relevant supply" refers to any taxable supply on which a claim is based.

(13) In paragraph (11), "security" refers to—

(*a*) in England, Wales or Northern Ireland, any mortgage, charge, lien or other security;

(*b*) in Scotland, any security (whether heritable or moveable), any floating charge and right of lien or preference and right of retention (other than a right of compensation or set-off).

Other tax credits: entitlement

11— (1) The supplier in each of the following cases is entitled to a tax credit in respect of any relevant amount of CCL charged on the supply in question (subject to the provisions of this Part including those provisions relating to the making of a relevant claim to the Commissioners)—

(*a*) after a taxable supply has been made, there is such a change in circumstances or any person's intentions that, if the changed circumstances or intentions had existed at the time of supply, the supply would not have been a taxable supply;

(*b*) after a supply of a taxable commodity is made on the basis that it is a taxable supply, it is determined that the supply was not (to any extent) a taxable supply;

(*c*) after a taxable supply has been made on the basis that it was …[1] a reduced-rate supply, it is determined that the supply was (to any extent) a half-rate or reduced-rate supply;

(*d*) *CCL is accounted for on a half-rate supply as if the supply were neither a half-rate supply nor a reduced-rate supply;*[1]

(*e*) after a charge to CCL has arisen on a supply of a taxable commodity ("the original commodity") to a person who uses the commodity supplied in producing taxable commodities primarily for his own consumption, that person makes supplies of any of the commodities in whose production he has used the original commodity;

(*f*) the making of a taxable supply gives rise to a double charge to CCL within the meaning of paragraph 21 of the Act.

(2) In paragraph (1), "relevant amount of CCL" refers to—

(*a*) in relation to a case described by sub-paragraph (*a*), (*b*), (*c*), ()(*d*)[1] or (*e*) of paragraph (1), the difference between the amount of CCL that ought to have been charged by or under the Act at the time of supply and the amount of CCL that was actually accounted for and paid by the supplier; and

(*b*) in relation to a case described by sub-paragraph (*f*) of paragraph (1), the amount of CCL actually charged and paid on the later supply having regard to the relative times of supply.

Amendments—[1] In para (1)(*c*), words "neither a half-rate supply nor" substituted, para (1)(*d*) and words ", (*d*)" in para (2)(*a*) revoked, by the Climate Change Levy (General) (Amendment) Regulations, SI 2007/2903 reg 2, Sch 1 paras 4–6 with effect from 1 November 2007: SI 2007/2903 reg 1. These amendments do not apply in relation to a half-rate supply made before 1 April 2006: SI 2007/2903 reg 2, Sch 1 Note (*a*).

Tax credits: general

12— (1) The provisions of this Part have effect subject to the requirements of Part III and [Schedule 1][1] (certification scheme for excluded, exempt …[2] and reduced-rate supplies).

(2) Accordingly, no tax credit shall arise by virtue of regulation 11 where the circumstances are such that provision is made by [Schedule 1][1] for a tax credit, for the benefit of the recipient, relating to the amount in question.

Amendments—[1] Words substituted by the CCL (General) (Amendment) Regulations, SI 2003/604 regs 2, 4 with effect from 1 April 2003.

[2] In para (1) words ", half-rate" revoked, by the Climate Change Levy (General) (Amendment) Regulations, SI 2007/2903 reg 2, Sch 1 para 7 with effect from 1 November 2007: SI 2007/2903 reg 1. This amendment does not apply in relation to a half-rate supply made before 1 April 2006: SI 2007/2903 reg 2, Sch 1 Note (*a*).

13 A tax credit shall only arise under regulation 10 or 11 if a claim is made by the supplier acting in accordance with regulation 14 or 15, as the case requires.

14— (1) Subject to paragraph (4), the supplier shall claim any such tax credit by bringing it into account when he is accounting for CCL due from him for any accounting period.

(2) Accordingly—

(*a*) the requirements of regulation 5 (content of returns), regulation 6 (payment of CCL) and regulation 7 (CCL accounts) apply subject to paragraph (1); but

(*b*) paragraph (1) applies subject to regulation 27 (corrections) and regulation 28 (corrections not exceeding [£50,000][1]).

(3) A claim subject to paragraphs (1) and (2) shall be regarded as a claim for repayment of CCL for the purposes of paragraph 64 of the Act (supplemental provisions about repayments, etc) (and see paragraph (5)).

(4) Where the total tax credit claimed by a supplier exceeds the total of the CCL due from him for the accounting period in question, the Commissioners shall repay to him an amount equal to the excess (but see regulations 29 and 30).

(5) Given the provision made by paragraph 62(4) of the Act, this regulation has effect subject to paragraph 64 of the Act (application of supplemental provisions about repayments: three year time limit, unjust enrichment, etc).

Amendments—[1] In para (2)(*b*) figure substituted for figure "£2,000" by the Value Added Tax, etc (Correction of Errors, etc) Regulations, SI 2008/1482 reg 6(1) with effect in relation to under-calculations or over-calculations respectively in the CCL Regulations, SI 2001/838 regs 28(2), (3) which registrable persons first discover in their accounting periods that start on 1 July 2008 or later.

15— (1) Where the Commissioners have cancelled the registration of a person in accordance with Part V of the Act, and he is not a registrable person, the Commissioners shall repay to him the amount of the tax credit if they are satisfied that he has made a proper claim to them in writing for this purpose.

(2) A claim under paragraph (1) may be combined with a claim under regulation 14(1) if appropriate.

(3) A person making a claim under paragraph (1) must furnish to the Commissioners full particulars in relation to the tax credit claimed including (but not restricted to)—

(*a*) the return in which the relevant CCL was accounted for;

(*b*) the amount of the CCL in question and the date and manner of its payment to the Commissioners;

(*c*) the events by virtue of which the bad debt or entitlement to a tax credit arose; and

(*d*) any supporting documentary or other evidence.

(4) Where the Commissioners are satisfied that a person who has made a claim in accordance with paragraphs (1) and (3) is entitled to a tax credit and that he has not previously had the benefit of that credit, they shall repay to him an amount equal to the credit (but see regulations 29 and 30).

(5) The Commissioners shall not be liable to make any repayment under this regulation unless and until the person has made all the returns which he was required to make (and see regulation 29 and 30).

(6) Given the provision made by paragraph 62(4) of the Act, this regulation has effect subject to paragraph 64 of the Act (application of supplemental provisions about repayments: three year time limit, unjust enrichment, etc).

Bad debts: supplementary provisions

16— (1) Where—

(*a*) a claimant in relation to regulation 10 has made a taxable supply,

(*b*) there exist one or more other matters in respect of which the claimant is entitled to a debt owed by the recipient (whether or not they involve a taxable supply), and

(*c*) a payment has been received by the claimant from or on behalf of the recipient,

the payment shall be attributed to the taxable supply and the other matters in accordance with the rules set out in paragraphs (3) and (5).

(2) The debts arising in respect of the taxable supply and the other matters are collectively referred to as debts in paragraphs (3) to (5).

(3) The payment shall be attributed to the debt that arose earliest and, if not wholly attributable to that debt, to the other debts in the order of the dates on which they arose.

(4) Attribution under paragraph (3) shall not be made to the extent that the payment was allocated to a debt by the recipient (customer) at the time of payment.

(5) Where—

(*a*) the earliest debt and the other debts to which the whole of the payment could be attributed arose on the same day, or

(*b*) the debts to which the balance of the payment could be attributed in accordance with paragraph (3) arose on the same day,

the payment shall be attributed to each remaining debt according to the proportion that the debt in question contributes to the total remaining debt.

17— (1) Where a supplier—

(*a*) has received the benefit from a tax credit provided for by regulation 10 (bad debts), and

(*b*) a payment—

(i) for the taxable supply in question is subsequently received by him (or by a person to whom has been assigned a right to receive the whole or any part of the price written off), or

(ii) is attributed to that taxable supply by virtue of regulation 16,

that tax credit shall be withdrawn with effect from when sub-paragraph (*b*)(i) or (*b*)(ii) is satisfied, as the case requires.

(2) Where a supplier—

(*a*) has received the benefit from a tax credit provided for by regulation 11 (tax credits other than bad debts), and

(*b*) it subsequently transpires that any relevant requirement of this Part is not complied with,

that tax credit shall be withdrawn with effect from when he received that benefit.

(3) Where a tax credit is withdrawn under this regulation—

(*a*) the requirements of regulation 5 (content of returns), regulation 6 (payment of CCL) and regulation 7 (CCL accounts) apply subject to this regulation; but (*b*) this regulation applies subject to regulation 27 (corrections) and regulation 28 (corrections not exceeding [£50,000][1]).

(4) Paragraph (3) applies subject to paragraph 67 of the Act (assessment for excessive repayment).

Amendments—[1] In para (3)(*b*) figure substituted for figure "£2,000" by the Value Added Tax, etc (Correction of Errors, etc) Regulations, SI 2008/1482 reg 6(1) with effect in relation to under-calculations or over-calculations respectively in the CCL Regulations, SI 2001/838 regs 28(2), (3) which registrable persons first discover in their accounting periods that start on 1 July 2008 or later.

Form and manner of claim for repayment of overpaid CCL if no person entitled to tax credit

18 A claim under paragraph 63 of the Act (claim for repayment of CCL which was not CCL due if no entitlement to tax credit) shall be made in writing to the Commissioners and shall, by reference to such documentary evidence as is in the possession of the claimant, state the amount of the claim and the method by which that amount was calculated.

Tax credits and other repayments: unjust enrichment—reimbursement arrangements to be disregarded

19 In this regulation and in regulations 20 to 25—

"claim" refers to a claim made under regulation 14 or 15 or under paragraph 63 of the Act (claim for repayment of CCL which was not CCL due if no person entitled to tax credit) and "claimed" and "claimant" must be construed accordingly;

"reimbursement arrangements" refers to any arrangements for the purposes of the claim which—

(*a*) are made by the claimant for the purpose of securing that he is not unjustly enriched by the repayment of any amount in pursuance of the claim; and

(*b*) provide for the reimbursement of persons (recipients) who have for practical purposes borne the whole or any part of the cost of the original payment of that amount to the Commissioners;

"relevant amount" refers to that part (which may be the whole) of the amount of the claim which the claimant has reimbursed or intends to reimburse to other persons (recipients).

20 For the purposes of paragraph 64(2) of the Act (defence by the Commissioners that repayment by them of an amount claimed would unjustly enrich the claimant) reimbursement arrangements made by a claimant shall be disregarded except where they—

(*a*) include the provisions described in regulation 21, and

(*b*) are supported by the undertakings described in regulation 25.

21 The provisions referred to in regulation 20(*a*) are that—

(*a*) reimbursement for which the arrangements provide will be completed by no later than 90 days after the repayment to which it relates;

(*b*) no deduction will be made from the relevant amount by way of fee or charge (however expressed or effected);

(*c*) reimbursement will be made only in cash or by cheque;

(*d*) any part of the relevant amount that is not reimbursed by the time mentioned in paragraph (*a*) will be repaid by the claimant to the Commissioners;

(*e*) any interest paid by the Commissioners on any relevant amount repaid by them will also be treated by the claimant in the same way as the relevant amount falls to be treated under paragraphs (*a*) and (*b*); and

(*f*) the records described in regulation 23 will be kept by the claimant and produced by him to the Commissioners in accordance with regulation 24.

22 The claimant shall, without prior demand, make any repayment to the Commissioners that he is required to make by virtue of regulation 21(*d*) or 21(*e*) within 14 days of the expiry of the period of 90 days referred to in regulation 21(*a*).

23 The claimant shall keep records of the following matters—

(*a*) the names and addresses of those persons (recipients) whom he has reimbursed or whom he intends to reimburse;

(*b*) the total amount reimbursed to each such person (recipient);

(*c*) the amount of interest included in each total amount reimbursed to each person (recipient);

(*d*) the date that each reimbursement is made.

24— (1) Where a claimant is given notice in accordance with paragraph (2) he shall, in accordance with such notice, produce to the Commissioners the records that he is required to keep pursuant to regulation 23.

(2) A notice given for the purposes of paragraph (1) shall—

(*a*) be in writing;

(*b*) state the date on which and the place and time at which the records are to be produced; and

(*c*) be signed and dated by the Commissioners.

(3) Such a notice may be given before or after, or before and after, the Commissioners have paid the relevant amount to the claimant.

25— (1) The undertakings referred to in regulation 20(*b*) shall be given to the Commissioners by the claimant no later than the time at which he makes the claim for which the reimbursement arrangements have been made.

(2) The undertakings shall be in writing and shall be signed and dated by the claimant.

(3) The undertakings shall be to the effect that—

(*a*) at the date of the undertakings he is able to identify the names and addresses of those persons (recipients) whom he has reimbursed or whom he intends to reimburse;

(*b*) he will apply the whole of the relevant amount repaid to him (without any deduction by way of fee, charge or otherwise) to the reimbursement in cash or by cheque of such persons (recipients) no later than 90 days after he receives that amount (unless he has properly reimbursed them already);

(*c*) he will apply any interest paid to him on the relevant amount repaid to him wholly to the reimbursement of such persons (recipients) no later than 90 days after he receives that interest;

(*d*) he will repay to the Commissioners without demand the whole or such part of the relevant amount repaid to him or of any interest paid to him as he fails to apply in accordance with the undertakings mentioned in sub-paragraph (*b*) or (*c*);

(*e*) he will keep the records described in regulation 23; and

(*f*) he will comply with any notice given to him in accordance with regulation 24 concerning the production of such records.

Corrections to CCL returns

26 A registrable person—

(*a*) shall only be taken as providing full information in the prescribed or specified form and manner for the purposes of paragraph 100(3) of the Act (disclosure about inaccurate CCL return),

(*b*) with respect to any inaccuracy to which paragraph 100(1)(*a*) of the Act applies (civil penalty for misdeclaration or neglect in relation to inaccurate return),

if he delivers that information in writing to the Commissioners, or acts in accordance with regulation 28, at a time to which paragraph 100(3)(*a*) of the Act applies (no reason to believe enquiries being made into CCL affairs).

27— (1) A registrable person shall correct any error made by him in accounting for CCL or in connection with his CCL account and, as appropriate, make any adjustment required by regulation (5)(1)(*b*) (adjustments to CCL returns).

(2) That correction or adjustment shall be made within such time and by means of such payment, financial adjustment, entry in accounts or other method as the Commissioners may require.

(3) This regulation has effect subject to, as the case requires—

(*a*) the time limit applying to regulations 14(1), 17(1) and 17(2) (tax credits) (see regulations 14(5) and 17(4)—amounts paid more than three years before claim made and assessment subject to time limit in paragraph 69 of Act);

(*b*) the time limit applying to paragraph 8(1) of [Schedule 1][1] (recipient's tax credit) (see paragraph 8(5) of [Schedule 1][1]—amounts paid more than three years before claim made);

(*c*) a time limit of three years after the end of the accounting period in relation to which the error was made or the adjustment became required; or

(*d*) any time limit for an assessment in relation to the error in question (see paragraphs 78(1), 78(2)(*d*), 79 and 80 of the Act).

Amendments—[1] Words substituted by the CCL (General) (Amendment) Regulations, SI 2003/604 regs 2, 4 with effect from 1 April 2003.

28— (1) This regulation applies by way of an exception to regulation 27 but only in relation to errors.

(2) Where a registrable person discovers that a return he has previously made is based on an under-calculation he must correct the error by adding an appropriate amount to the CCL due for the accounting period in which the discovery is made under regulation 5(1)(*b*) (CCL due).

(3) Where a registrable person discovers that a return he has previously made is based on an over-calculation he must correct the error by deducting an appropriate amount from the CCL due for the accounting period in which the discovery is made under regulation 5(1)(*b*) (CCL due).

(4) For the purposes of paragraphs (2) and (3)—

"under-calculation" refers to the aggregate, which must not exceed [£50,000][1], of—

(*a*) the CCL due on taxable supplies—

(i) the times of supply of which were in the accounting period to which the previous return related, and

(ii) for which the registrable person in question was liable to account;

(*b*) but which was not properly taken into consideration for that period (see regulation 5(1)) ("understated CCL");

"over-calculation" refers to the aggregate, which must not exceed [£50,000][1], of—

(*a*) amounts that were wrongly taken as CCL due on taxable supplies—

(i) the times of supply of which were in the accounting period to which the previous return related, and

(ii) for which the registrable person in question was liable to account;

(*b*) and which were wrongly taken into consideration for that period (see regulation 5(1)) ("overstated CCL").

[(4A) But if the registrable person's VAT turnover is small, each aggregate in paragraph (4) must not for those purposes exceed 1% of that turnover unless the aggregate is [£10,000 or less][3]. And if that person is not registered for VAT, each aggregate must not for those purposes exceed £10,000.][1]

[The VAT turnover is small only if Box 6 of that person's value added tax return for the prescribed accounting period in which the discovery is made must contain a total less than £5,000,000 (total value of sales and all other outputs excluding any value added tax).][2]

(5) For the purposes of [paragraphs (4) and (4A)][1]—

(*a*) in reckoning the aggregate constituting the under-calculation no allowance shall be made for any overstated CCL; and

(*b*) in reckoning the aggregate constituting the over-calculation no allowance shall be made for any understated CCL.

(6) A registrable person making a correction under paragraph (2) or (3) shall make proper allowance for that correction for the purposes of complying with regulation 7(1) (CCL account) or 7(3) (tax credits account), as appropriate.

(7) Where an error in a return has to any extent been corrected under this regulation—

(*a*) that return shall be regarded as having been corrected to that extent, and

(*b*) the registrable person shall to that extent be taken to have provided full information with respect to the inaccuracy in the prescribed form and manner for the purposes of paragraph 100(3) of the Act (disclosure about inaccurate CCL return).

(8) A person shall not correct an error in a return (where that error is the result of an under-calculation or over-calculation) except in accordance with this regulation.

(9) This regulation has effect subject to, as the case requires—

(*a*) any requirement of the Commissioners under regulation 27(2), and

(*b*) any applicable time limit specified in regulation 27(3).

Amendments—[1] In para (4) figure substituted in each place for figure "£2,000", para (4A) inserted, and words in para (5) substituted for words "paragraph (4)", by the Value Added Tax, etc (Correction of Errors, etc) Regulations, SI 2008/1482 reg 6(1), (2) with effect in relation to under-calculations or over-calculations respectively in the CCL Regulations, SI 2001/838 reg 28(2), (3) which registrable persons first discover in their accounting periods that start on 1 July 2008 or later.

[2] In para (4A), words inserted by the Value Added Tax, etc (Correction of Errors, etc) Regulations, SI 2008/1482 reg 8(1) with effect from 1 July 2008.

[3] In para (4A), words substituted for words "less than £10,000" by the Amusement Machine Licence Duty, etc (Amendments) Regulations, SI 2008/2693 reg 4(1)(*c*) with effect for a discovery first made on 1 November 2008 or later.

Set-off

29— (1) This regulation applies where—

(*a*) a person is under a duty to pay to the Commissioners at any time an amount or amounts in respect of CCL; and

(*b*) the Commissioners are under a duty to pay to that person at the same time an amount or amounts in respect of any CCL (or other tax or duty) under their care and management.

(2) Where the total of the amount or amounts mentioned in paragraph (1)(*a*) exceeds the total of the amount or amounts mentioned in paragraph (1)(*b*), the latter shall be set-off against the former.

(3) Where the total of the amount or amounts mentioned in paragraph (1)(*b*) exceeds the total of the amount or amounts mentioned in paragraph (1)(*a*), the Commissioners may set off the latter in paying the former.

(4) Where the total of the amount or amounts mentioned in paragraph (1)(*a*) is the same as the total of the amount or amounts mentioned in paragraph (1)(*b*), no payment need be made in respect of either.

(5) Where this regulation applies and an amount has been set off in accordance with any of paragraphs (2) to (4), the duty of both the person in question and the Commissioners to pay the amount concerned shall be treated as having been discharged accordingly.

30— (1) This regulation applies where—

(*a*) a person is under a duty to pay to the Commissioners at any time an amount or amounts in respect of any tax or duty (other than CCL) under their care and management; and

(*b*) the Commissioners are under a duty, at the same time, to make a payment or repayment to that person of an amount or amounts of or in respect of CCL.

(2) Where the total of the amount or amounts mentioned in paragraph (1)(*a*) exceeds the total of the amount or amounts mentioned in paragraph (1)(*b*), the latter shall be set-off against the former.

(3) Where the total of the amount or amounts mentioned in paragraph (1)(*b*) exceeds the total of the amount or amounts mentioned in paragraph (1)(*a*), the Commissioners may set off the latter in paying the former.

(4) Where the total of the amount or amounts mentioned in paragraph (1)(*a*) is the same as the total of the amount or amounts mentioned in paragraph (1)(*b*), no payment need be made in respect of either.

(5) Where this regulation applies and an amount has been set off in accordance with any of paragraphs (2) to (4), the duty of both the person in question and the Commissioners to pay the amount concerned shall be treated as having been discharged accordingly.

31— (1) Regulation 29 or 30 shall not require any such amount as is mentioned in paragraph (1)(*b*) of either regulation ("the credit") to be set against any item mentioned in paragraph (1)(*a*) of either regulation ("the debit") where—

(*a*) an insolvency procedure has been applied to the person entitled to the credit;

(*b*) the credit became due after that procedure was applied; and

(*c*) the liability to pay the debt either arose before that procedure was so applied or (having arisen afterwards) relates to, or to matters occurring in the course of, the carrying on of any business relevant for CCL purposes at times before the procedure was so applied.

(2) An insolvency procedure is applied to a person for the purposes of this regulation in the circumstances described by paragraphs 75(2) to 75(5) of the Act (insolvency procedures for purposes of this regulation).

32 A reference in regulation 29 or 30 to an amount in respect of tax or duty includes a reference to an amount of any related penalty, surcharge or interest that may be recovered as if it was an amount of tax or duty.

Special rules for excluded, exempt …[2] and reduced-rate supplies

33 The provisions of this Part have effect subject to Part III of and [Schedule 1][1] to these Regulations (accounting and payment in the case of excluded, exempt …[2] and reduced-rate supplies).

Amendments—[1] Words substituted by the CCL (General) (Amendment) Regulations, SI 2003/604 regs 2, 4 with effect from 1 April 2003.

[2] In para 33 and in preceding heading, words ", half-rate" revoked, by the Climate Change Levy (General) (Amendment) Regulations, SI 2007/2903 reg 2, Sch 1 para 8 with effect from 1 November 2007: SI 2007/2903 reg 1. These amendments do not apply in relation to a half-rate supply made before 1 April 2006: SI 2007/2903 reg 2, Sch 1 Note (*a*).

PART III
EXCLUDED, EXEMPT …[1] AND REDUCED-RATE SUPPLIES

Amendments—[1] In heading to Part III, words ", half-rate" revoked, by the Climate Change Levy (General) (Amendment) Regulations, SI 2007/2903 reg 2, Sch 1 para 9 with effect from 1 November 2007: SI 2007/2903 reg 1. This amendment does not apply in relation to a half-rate supply made before 1 April 2006: SI 2007/2903 reg 2, Sch 1 Note (*a*).

Supplier certificates: basic rules

34— (1) Any exclusion or exemption provided for by, under or by virtue of—

(*a*) paragraph 9(2)(*f*) (community heating arrangements), 11 (onward supplies and exports), 12 (transport), 13 (commodity producers), 14 (electricity producers), 15 (combined heat and power stations)[, 18 (non fuel use) or 18A (recycling processes)][2] of the Act, or

(*b*) regulation 41 (or any other relevant regulation made under paragraph 21 of the Act to avoid a double charge to CCL),

shall only be given effect if and to the extent that …[3] the recipient [delivers][3] to the supplier a certificate that accords with paragraph (2).

(2) Any such certificate shall—

(*a*) represent that the supply (or a quantified part of the supply) meets the requirements for each such exclusion or exemption,

(*b*) comply, as necessary, with regulations 37(2), 37(3), 37(4) and 38(2), and

(*c*) be supported, if necessary, in accordance with paragraph (3).

(3) Where the certificate represents that a quantified part of the supply meets the requirements for an exclusion or exemption referred to in paragraph (1), the recipient must support that certificate with an analysis document demonstrating that the part is calculated in a manner consistent with regulation 38 and [Schedule 1][1].

Amendments—[1] Words substituted by the CCL (General) (Amendment) Regulations, SI 2003/604 regs 2, 4 with effect from 1 April 2003.

[2] Words in sub-para (1)(*a*) substituted by the Climate Change Levy (Miscellaneous Amendments) Regulations, SI 2005/1716 regs 4, 6 with effect from 22 July 2005. However, arrangements initiated or made before 22 July 2005 on the basis of SI 2001/838 Sch 1 para 5(5) or 5(6) as then in force remain subject to the provisions applicable when they were initiated or made (tax credit claims and corrections to over-estimated relief).

[3] In para (1), words ", before the time of supply," revoked and words substituted for words "has delivered", by the Climate Change Levy (General) (Amendment) Regulations, SI 2007/2903 reg 2, Sch 1 para 10 with effect from 1 November 2007: SI 2007/2903 reg 1. This amendment applies only to a supply that is treated as taking place on or after 1 November 2007: SI 2007/2903 reg 2, Sch 1 Note (*c*).

35— (1) A taxable supply is to be treated as being a [reduced-rate][3] supply only if and to the extent that …[3] the recipient [delivers][3] to the supplier a certificate that accords with paragraph (2).

(2) Any such certificate shall—

(*a*) represent that the supply (or a quantified part of the supply) meets the requirements for a [reduced-rate][3] supply in paragraph [44(1)][3] of the Act [(reduced-rate for supplies covered by climate change agreements)][3],

(*b*) comply, as necessary, with regulations 37(2), 37(3), 37(4) and 38(2), and

(*c*) be supported, if necessary, in accordance with paragraph (3).

(3) Where the certificate represents that a quantified part of the supply meets the requirements for a [reduced-rate][3] supply, the recipient must support that certificate with an analysis document demonstrating that the part is calculated in a manner consistent with regulation 38 and [Schedule 1][1].

[(4) This regulation does not apply to a supply made after 31st March 2006.][2]

[(5) Paragraphs (6) to (9) have effect for determining when a supply is to be regarded as made for the purposes of paragraph (4).][2]

[(6) A supply—

()(a) of electricity, or

()(b) of gas that is in a gaseous state and is of a kind supplied by a gas utility,

is to be regarded as made at the time when the electricity or gas is actually supplied.][2]

[(7) In the case of a supply of a taxable commodity not falling within paragraph (6) by a person who is resident in the United Kingdom—

()(a) if the commodity is to be removed, the supply is to be regarded as made at the time of the removal,

()(b) if the commodity is not to be removed, the supply is to be regarded as made when the commodity is made available to the person to whom it is supplied.

This paragraph does not apply if paragraph (9) (deemed self-supply) applies in the case of the supply.][2]

[(8) In the case of a supply of a taxable commodity not falling within paragraph (6) by a person who is not resident in the United Kingdom, the supply is to be regarded as made—

()(a) when the commodity is delivered to the person to whom it is supplied, or

()(b) if earlier, when it is made available in the United Kingdom to that person.

This paragraph does not apply if paragraph (9) (deemed self-supply) applies in the case of the supply.][2]

[(9) In any case where, by virtue of paragraph 23(3) of the Act, a person is, for the purposes of the Act, deemed to make a supply to himself of a quantity of a taxable commodity—

()(a) which he has produced, and

()(b) which does not fall within paragraph (6),

the supply is to be regarded as made at the time when he produced that particular quantity of the taxable commodity.][2, 3]

Amendments—[1] Words substituted by the CCL (General) (Amendment) Regulations, SI 2003/604 regs 2, 4 with effect from 1 April 2003.

[2] Paras (4)–(9) inserted by the CCL (General) (Amendment) Regulations, SI 2006/954 regs 1(2), 2 with effect from 1 April 2006.

[3] In para (1), words substituted for words "half-rate" and "has delivered", and words ", before the time of supply," revoked, in para (2) words substituted for words "half-rate", "43", and (horticultural producers), in para (3) words substituted for words "half-rate", and paras (4)–(9) revoked, by the Climate Change Levy (General) (Amendment) Regulations, SI 2007/2903 reg 2, Sch 1 paras 11–15 with effect from 1 November 2007: SI 2007/2903 reg 1.

The amendments made to paras (1)–(3) do not apply in relation to a half-rate supply made before 1 April 2006: SI 2007/2903 reg 2, Sch 1 Note (*a*).

In relation to a reduced-rate supply or a supply made on that basis, the substitution of words "reduced-rate" for words "half-rate" in para (1), and the amendments made to paras (2), (3), only apply if the supply is made on or after 1 November 2007: SI 2007/2903 reg 2, Sch 1 Note (*b*).

The revocation of words ", before the time of supply", and substitution of words "reduced-rate" for "half-rate" in para (1), only apply to a supply that is treated as taking place on or after 1 November 2007: SI 2007/2903 reg2, Sch 1 Note (*c*).

36— (1) For the purposes of regulation 45(2) (certain supplies to a facility covered by climate change agreement), a taxable commodity shall be regarded for CCL purposes as supplied to a facility that is certified as being covered by a climate change agreement only if and to the extent that …[2] the recipient [delivers][2] to the supplier a certificate that accords with paragraph (2).

(2) Any such certificate shall—

(*a*) represent that the supply (or a quantified part of the supply) meets the requirements for a reduced-rate supply in paragraph 44 of the Act (facilities covered by climate change agreements),

(*b*) comply, as necessary, with regulation 37(2), 37(3), 37(4) and 38(2), and
(*c*) be supported, if necessary, in accordance with paragraph (3).

(3) Where the certificate represents that a quantified part of the supply meets the requirements for a reduced-rate supply for the purposes of regulation 45(2), the recipient must support that certificate with an analysis document demonstrating that the part is calculated in a manner consistent with regulation 38 and [Schedule 1][1].

Amendments—[1] Words substituted by the CCL (General) (Amendment) Regulations, SI 2003/604 regs 2, 4 with effect from 1 April 2003.

[2] Words ", before the time of supply," revoked, and words substituted for words "has delivered" by the Climate Change Levy (General) (Amendment) Regulations, SI 2007/2903 reg 2, Sch 1 paras 16 with effect from 1 November 2007: SI 2007/2903 reg 1. This amendment only applies to a supply that is treated as taking place on or after 1 November 2007: SI 2007/2903 reg 2, Sch 1 Note (*c*).

37— (1) A certificate delivered under regulation 34, 35 or 36 (a "supplier certificate") only has effect …[1] on or after the certificate's implementation date.

(2) A supplier certificate and an analysis document shall—

(*a*) be in a form prescribed by the Commissioners for this purpose in a published notice, and
(*b*) in the case of the supplier certificate, be signed and dated by a person duly authorised for this purpose by the recipient.

(3) Where regulation 34, 35 or 36 applies to part of a supply and at least one other of them applies to another part of that supply, any supplier certificate the recipient delivers under one of those regulations shall be combined by him with a supplier certificate under any other applicable regulation such that the resulting composite certificate satisfies paragraph (2) of every applicable regulation.

(4) A recipient shall not combine—

(*a*) a supplier certificate relating to the supply of one taxable commodity with a supplier certificate relating to the supply of any other such commodity;
(*b*) a supplier certificate delivered to one supplier with a supplier certificate delivered to another supplier;
(*c*) a supplier certificate relating to a reference number the supplier uses for him with a supplier certificate relating to another reference number the supplier uses for him; or
(*d*) supplier certificates combined contrary to sub-paragraph (*a*) with supplier certificates combined contrary to sub-paragraph (*b*).

(5) A recipient who delivers a supplier certificate to a supplier must deliver a copy to the Commissioners within 30 days of doing so (together with any supporting analysis document).

(6) In this regulation, "implementation date" refers to the earlier of—

(*a*) the fifth working day after the one on which the certificate is delivered to the supplier at any address the supplier designates for this purpose, and
(*b*) the day on which (or any day after which) the certificate is so delivered if, on that day, the supplier first applies the information contained in that certificate to the relevant supplies he makes to the recipient.

(7) To the extent that a person does anything before 1st April 2001 in purported compliance or conformity with or purported pursuit of regulation 34, 35, 36, 38, 43 or this regulation it shall, to that extent, be regarded as having been done on 1st April 2001.

Amendments—[1] In para (1), words "in relation to a supply the time of supply of which is" revoked by the Climate Change Levy (General) (Amendment) Regulations, SI 2007/2903 reg 2, Sch 1 para 17 with effect from 1 November 2007: SI 2007/2903 reg 1. This amendment only applies to a supply that is treated as taking place on or after 1 November 2007: SI 2007/2903 reg 2, Sch 1 Note (*c*).

Supplier certificates: accounting for and payment of CCL

38— (1) [Schedule 1][1] to these Regulations has effect for the purpose of—

(*a*) supplementing the provisions of regulations 34 to 37 (which, accordingly, have effect subject to that Schedule), and
(*b*) determining the manner in which a person who is required to account for CCL does so in the case of a supply of a quantity of a taxable commodity [to which regulation 34, 35 or 36 applies.][2]

(2) A recipient shall include in a supplier certificate the percentage of the supply or supplies on which CCL is not due calculated in accordance with that Schedule (recipient's relief percentage).

(3) This Part and [Schedule 1][1] must be read as one.

Amendments—[1] Words substituted by the CCL (General) (Amendment) Regulations, SI 2003/604 regs 2, 4 with effect from 1 April 2003.

[2] In para (1)(*b*), words substituted for sub-paras (i), (ii) by the Climate Change Levy (General) (Amendment) Regulations, SI 2007/2903 reg 2, Sch 1 para 18 with effect from 1 November 2007: SI 2007/2903 reg 1. In relation to a reduced-rate supply or a supply made on that basis, this amendment only applies if the supply is made on or after 1 November 2007: SI 2007/2903 reg 2, Sch 1 Note (*c*).

Sub-paras (i), (ii) previously read as follows—
"(i) to which regulation 34, 35 or 36 applies, or
(ii) that otherwise includes a reduced-rate part.".

Special cases

39— (1) Regulations 34 to 38 apply, as appropriate, even if the supplier and the recipient are the same person (deemed self-supplies and the case provided for by paragraph (2)).

(2) A recipient who is liable to account for the CCL charged on a taxable supply shall be regarded as the same person as the supplier for the purposes of this Part and [Schedule 1][1] (see paragraph 40(2) of the Act—taxable supplies made by persons who are neither resident in the United Kingdom nor utilities).

Amendments—[1] Words substituted by the CCL (General) (Amendment) Regulations, SI 2003/604 regs 2, 4 with effect from 1 April 2003.

Suppliers to producers of commodities

40— (1) An exemption provided for by paragraph 13 or 14(1) of the Act (supplies to producers of commodities other than electricity and certain supplies to electricity producers) has effect subject to paragraph (2).

(2) The supply of the taxable commodity in question shall be a taxable supply (and not an exempt supply) to the extent that it is to be used by the recipient for the purposes of—

(*a*) headquarters administration facilities;
(*b*) telephone call centres;
(*c*) dedicated visitor centres;
(*d*) any commercial matters (including power for computers and ancillary equipment, and legal, contractual or taxation matters);
(*e*) road tanker deliveries otherwise than at the production site.

(3) This regulation has effect without prejudice to the generality of paragraph 13 or 14(1) of the Act.

Non-registrable electricity producers

41— (1) Paragraph (2) applies if and to the extent that a non-registrable electricity producer produces electricity and makes a supply of it to an electricity utility (or a person treated as such for CCL purposes).

(2) If and to the extent that this paragraph applies, that supply of electricity shall be treated for the purposes of paragraph 14(1) of the Act as a use of that electricity in relation to which the exemption provided for by that paragraph is retained.

42— (1) A supply of a taxable commodity to a non-registrable electricity producer shall be treated as being a half-rate supply to the extent that he both—

()(a) uses that commodity to produce electricity, and
()(b) uses that electricity in making a supply meeting the description of a half-rate supply in paragraph 43(1) of the Act (horticultural producers).

(2) Paragraph (1) has effect subject to regulations 35, 37, 38 and 39.

[(3) This regulation does not apply to a supply made after 31st March 2006.][1]

[(4) Regulations 35(6) to 35(9) (cessation of certification following abolition of half-rate supplies) have effect for determining when a supply is to be regarded as made for the purposes of paragraph (3).][1, 2]

Amendments—[1] Paras (3), (4) inserted by the CCL (General) (Amendment) Regulations, SI 2006/954 regs 1(2), 3 with effect from 1 April 2006.

[2] Reg 42 revoked by the Climate Change Levy (General) (Amendment) Regulations, SI 2007/2903 reg 2, Sch 1 para 19 with effect from 1 November 2007: SI 2007/2903 reg 1. This amendment does not apply in relation to a half-rate supply made before 1 April 2006: SI 2007/2903 reg 2, Sch 1 Note (*a*).

43— (1) A non-registrable electricity producer who delivers a supplier certificate that is required to be supported by an analysis document shall annex to that analysis document details of—

(*a*) the quantity of electricity that is attributable to self supplies,
(*b*) the individual quantities of electricity supplied by him to other persons, and
(*c*) the identity and address of each other person to whom he supplies electricity.

(2) This regulation has effect by way of supplement to the requirements of regulations 34(3), 35(3) and 36(3) and, to that extent, is subject to regulation 38.

(3) In this regulation—

"electricity" refers to electricity to which the supplier certificate in question relates;
"self supplies" refers to any supplies of electricity that are deemed by paragraph 23(3) of the Act (use of commodities by producers) to be made to himself by the relevant non-registrable electricity producer (own use).

(4) In these Regulations and [Schedule 1][1] a reference to an analysis document includes a reference to any annexe required by paragraph (1).

Amendments—[1] Words substituted by the CCL (General) (Amendment) Regulations, SI 2003/604 regs 2, 4 with effect from 1 April 2003.

Facilities covered by climate change agreements

44— (1) For the purposes of paragraph 44 of the Act (reduced-rate for supplies covered by climate change agreement), a taxable commodity shall not be regarded as being supplied otherwise than to a facility covered by a climate change agreement solely because it is delivered and stored elsewhere prior to being burned within that facility.

(2) Paragraph (1) does not apply in a case where the taxable commodity in question is electricity or gas.

45— (1) This regulation applies where a taxable commodity is supplied to a non-registrable electricity producer otherwise than at a facility that is certified as being covered by a climate change agreement in accordance with paragraph 44(1) of the Act.

(2) That taxable commodity shall be regarded as supplied to a facility certified as being covered by a climate change agreement to the extent that it is used to produce electricity that is in fact supplied to such a facility by that non-registrable electricity producer.

(3) This regulation has effect subject to regulations 36, 37, 38 and 39.

PART IV
RENEWABLE SOURCE ELECTRICITY

Interpretation of Part IV

46. ..[1] In this Part—

"exempt renewable supplies" refers to that expression in paragraph 19(2) of the Act;

["MWh" is an abbreviation for megawatt-hour;][1]

["relevant Authority" refers to the Gas and Electricity Markets Authority or, in relation to electricity produced or supplied in Northern Ireland or produced in the Republic of Ireland, the Director General of Electricity Supply for Northern Ireland;][1]

"renewable source contract" refers to the contract mentioned in paragraph 19(1)(*b*) of the Act (contract containing renewable source declaration).

(2)–(4) …[1]

Amendments—[1] Para (1) renumbered as regulation 46, and paras (2)–(4) revoked, by the CCL (General) (Amendment) Regulations, SI 2003/604 regs 2, 9, 10 with effect from 1 April 2003.

Generation and certification of renewable source electricity

47— (1) Subject to paragraphs (3) to (15) and regulation 48, electricity is "renewable source electricity" for the purposes of the Act to the extent that it has been generated from renewable sources provided that it is not electricity generated from a large hydro generating station.

(2) In this regulation—

["biomass" means fuel used in a generating station of which at least 98 per cent of the energy content is derived from plant or animal matter, or substances derived directly or indirectly therefrom (whether or not such matter or substances are waste) and includes agricultural, forestry or wood wastes or residues, sewage and energy crops (provided that such plant or animal matter is not or is not derived directly from or indirectly from fossil fuel);][1]

"declared net capacity" means the highest generation of electricity (at the main alternator terminals) which, on the assumption that the source of power is available without interruption, can be maintained indefinitely without causing damage to the plant less so much of that capacity as is consumed by the plant;

"distribution system" and "transmission system" in relation to Great Britain have the meanings given in section 4 of the Electricity Act 1989 as it will have effect once it has been amended by section 28 of the Utilities Act 2000; in relation to Northern Ireland "transmission system" system has the meaning given in article 3 of the Electricity (Northern Ireland) Order 1992;[3]

"fossil fuel" means coal, substances produced directly or indirectly from coal, lignite, natural gas, crude liquid petroleum, or petroleum products (and "natural gas" and "petroleum products" have the same meanings as in the Energy Act 1976);

"generator", except in the definition of "hydro generating station" below, means the operator of a generating station;

"hydro generating station" means a generating station which is wholly or mainly driven by water other than stations driven by tidal flows, waves, ocean currents or geothermal sources and the "station" extends to all structures and works for holding or channelling water for a purpose directly related to the generation of electricity together with any turbines and associated generators directly connected to or fed by such common structures or works;

"large hydro generating station" means a hydro generating station with a declared net capacity of more than 10 megawatts;

"renewable sources" means sources of energy other than [peat,][1] fossil fuel or nuclear fuel and includes—

[(*a*) biomass, and

(*b*)][1] waste

provided that it is not waste with an energy content 90 per cent. or more of which is derived from fossil fuel;

"waste" has the meaning given in section 75(2) of the Environmental Protection Act 1990 as that subsection will have effect once it has been amended by paragraph 88 of Schedule 22 to the Environment Act 1995, but does not include gas derived from landfill sites or gas produced from the treatment of sewage.

[(2A) For the purposes of this Part and paragraphs 19 and 20 of the Act, coal mine methane shall be regarded as a renewable source and not a fossil fuel (see paragraph 19(4A) of the Act).][2]

(3) In the following paragraphs, except in relation to paragraphs (7), (8) and (12), references to fossil fuel do not include references to any fossil fuel content of [biomass or][1] waste.

(4) Paragraph (11) is to apply where a generating station is fuelled by renewable sources and fossil fuel in order to calculate the respective proportions of electricity generated by that station from renewable sources and from fossil fuel in any period specified by the relevant Authority, but paragraph (11) does not apply to generating stations to which paragraph (10) applies.

(5) Where the renewable sources used to fuel a generating station includes waste (whether or not the generating station is fuelled by waste in combination with other renewable sources or fossil fuel) paragraphs (7), (8) and (9) apply in order to calculate the amount of renewable source electricity which is to be regarded as generated from that waste in any period specified by the relevant Authority.

[(5A) Where the renewable sources used to fuel a generating station includes biomass (whether or not the generating station is fuelled by biomass in combination with other renewable sources or fossil fuel) paragraph (9) applies in order to calculate the amount of renewable source electricity which is to be regarded as generated from that biomass in any period specified by the relevant Authority.][1]

(6) Paragraph 10 applies where fossil fuel is used only for the purposes specified in that paragraph.

(7) Subject to paragraphs (8) and (9), where a generating station is fuelled by waste, the proportion of electricity generated from waste which is to be regarded as renewable source electricity is 50 per cent. of the proportion of electricity which has been generated by that station from waste provided that the relevant Authority determines that the generator has no reasonable grounds to believe that more than 50 per cent. of the energy content of the waste used is derived from fossil fuel.

(8) On request by a generator who considers that more than 50 per cent. of the electricity generated from waste by that station has been generated from waste which is not or has not been derived from fossil fuel, the relevant Authority shall determine in accordance with paragraph (12) the proportion of electricity so generated from such waste and that proportion shall be regarded as renewable source electricity.

(9) Where the relevant Authority determines that a generating station is fuelled by waste at least 98 per cent. of the energy content of which is derived from plant or animal substances (including agricultural, forestry, wood and human wastes or residues), the amount of electricity generated from such waste which is to be regarded as renewable source electricity is 100 per cent. of the electricity which is generated from such [biomass or][1] waste.

(10) Where a generating station uses fossil fuel only for one or more of the following purposes—

(*a*) the ignition of gases of low or variable calorific value;

(*b*) the heating of the combustion system to its normal operating temperature or the maintenance of that temperature;

(*c*) emission control;

provided that the relevant Authority determines that in any year the energy content of the fossil fuel used for the above purposes in the generating station does not exceed 10 per cent. of the energy content of the renewable sources used, that fossil fuel shall be treated as if it were the renewable source used as the remainder of the fuel in the generating station.

(11) Where a generating station is fuelled partly by renewable sources and partly by fossil fuel, (with the exception of generating stations to which paragraph (10) applies) the respective proportions of electricity which have been generated from fossil fuel and any one or more renewable sources shall be determined by the relevant Authority in the manner described in paragraph (12), and the proportion of electricity generated from renewable sources other than waste (to which paragraphs (7), (8) and (9) apply) shall be regarded as renewable source electricity.

(12) In any case where the relevant Authority is required or requires to determine the proportions of electricity generated from either fossil fuel or any one or more renewable sources, it shall do so by reference to the energy content of the relevant fuels.

(13) Where the amount of electricity generated by a hydro generating station has been increased due to the flow rate, height or pressure of water being artificially increased as a result of pumping, the amount of renewable source electricity generated by that station shall be calculated by deducting from the amount of electricity generated by the station any electricity which has not been generated from renewable sources which is used for such pumping.

(14) …[1]

(15) Where the relevant Authority is required to make any determination under this regulation it shall only be so required once it has been provided with adequate information on which to base its decision.

Amendments—[1] In para (2), definition of "biomass" inserted, and words in definition of "renewable sources" inserted; words in paras (3), (9) inserted; para (5A) inserted; and para (14) revoked; by the CCL (General) (Amendment) Regulations, SI 2003/604 regs 2, 11–14 with effect from 1 April 2003.

[2] Para (2A) inserted by the Climate Change Levy (General) (Amendment) (No 2) Regulations, SI 2003/2633 with effect from 1 November 2003. Para (2A) revoked by FA 2008 s 149 in relation to electricity generated on or after 1 November 2008.

[3] In para (2) definition of "distribution system and transmission system" revoked by the Climate Change Levy (General) (Amendment) Regulations, SI 2007/2903 reg 2, Sch 1 para 20 with effect from 1 November 2007: SI 2007/2903 reg 1.

48— (1) A quantity of electricity constitutes "renewable source electricity" for the purposes of paragraphs 19 and 20 of the Act only if and to the extent that it complies with regulation 47 and is the subject of a certificate (a "levy exemption certificate") issued by the relevant Authority to confirm that the requirements of regulation 47 are satisfied in relation to that quantity.

[(1A) The relevant Authority must only issue a levy exemption certificate on the basis of the most accurate figures for electricity produced in a generating station that the person who generates that electricity makes known to the Authority.][1]

[(1B) The relevant Authority must disregard any figures that are made known to it or of which it becomes aware after the end of the second month following the end of the month in which the electricity is produced.][1, 3]

(2) Each levy exemption certificate ("[Renewables LEC][2]") shall carry a unique identifying reference ("identifier").

(3) The relevant Authority need not issue a [Renewables LEC][2] in relation to any quantity of electricity under paragraph (1) if—

(*a*) the person who generates that electricity does not provide the relevant Authority with such information, particulars, records and declarations as it may require for the purposes of that paragraph or regulation 47;

(*b*) the person who generates that electricity does not, if so required, provide the relevant Authority with updated readings from any relevant electricity meter;

(*c*) any person authorised by the relevant Authority has not, on request, been granted access at any reasonable time to the premises from where that electricity is generated;

(*d*) any person authorised by the relevant Authority has not, on request and having been granted access to premises in accordance with sub-paragraph (*c*), been permitted—

(i) to inspect or test anything that is on those premises, and

(ii) to inspect any records that are on those premises,

connected with the generation or supply of that electricity;

(*e*) any person authorised by the relevant Authority has not, on request, been granted access to any premises at any reasonable time to take updated readings from any relevant electricity meters;

(*f*) any one or more of sub-paragraphs (*a*) to (*e*) have not been satisfied within such time as the relevant Authority considers reasonable for the purpose in question; or

(*g*) the relevant Authority is for any reason not satisfied that the electricity in question should be regarded as renewable source electricity.

[(4) The relevant Authority need not issue a Renewables LEC as respects a quantity of electricity less than 1 MWh.

However the relevant Authority may aggregate or disaggregate such quantities relating to the same generating station, certifying each complete MWh as appropriate.][1]

[(5) The relevant Authority need not issue a Renewables LEC unless it is satisfied that the Renewables LEC, if issued, would represent electricity consumed or to be consumed in the United Kingdom.

For this purpose, the relevant Authority may have regard in particular to whether any part of that electricity is or may be allocated by the operator of the generating station or a supplier for consumption outside the United Kingdom.][1]

[(6) A Renewables LEC must be regarded for all purposes of this Part as only relating to the actual electricity in relation to which it was issued.][1]

Amendments—[1] Paras (1A), (1B), and paras (4)–(6) inserted by the CCL (General) (Amendment) Regulations, SI 2003/604 regs 2, 15, 16 with effect from 1 April 2003.

[2] Words in paras (2), (3) substituted by the CCL (General) (Amendment) Regulations, SI 2003/604 regs 2, 18 with effect from 1 April 2003.

[3] Para (1B) revoked by the Climate Change Levy (General) (Amendment) Regulations, SI 2007/2903 reg 2, Sch 1 para 21 with effect from 1 November 2007: SI 2007/2903 reg 1. This amendment only applies in relation to figures that have not been disregarded before 1 November 2007 under SI 2001/838 reg 48(1B) or 51B(3): SI 2007/2903 reg 2, Sch 1 Note (*d*).

Conditions for exemption from CCL

49— (1) Any part of a quantity of electricity that is the subject of a [Renewables LEC][2] shall be regarded as never having been renewable source electricity capable of being the subject of exempt renewable supplies for the purposes of paragraph 19 of the Act if one or more of the conditions prescribed in paragraphs (2), (3), (4) and (5) are not fulfilled.

(2) The electricity must not be allocated to a supply to a person who—

(*a*) intends to cause the electricity to be exported from the United Kingdom, and

(*b*) has no intention to cause it to be brought back into the United Kingdom afterwards.

(3) Should the electricity be allocated to some supply pursuant to some renewable source contract, the supplier must inform the relevant Authority of this fact and of the relevant [Renewables LEC][2] identifier.

(4) At any time up to 6 years after the day the electricity is generated—

(*a*) the person who generated it must provide the relevant Authority on request with readily legible records relating to and detailing—

(i) the generation process,

(ii) the supplies made of that electricity and the relevant recipients,

(iii) [any relevant Renewables LEC (and, if different from the relevant recipient, the identity of any person to whom entitlement to that Renewables LEC is transferred)][1], and

(iv) any relevant information, particulars or records referred to in regulation 48(3)(*a*);

and

(*b*) any supplier of that electricity must provide the relevant Authority on request with readily legible records relating to and detailing—

(i) the supplies he received or made of that electricity,

(ii) the relevant recipients of any supplies he made of that electricity, and

(iii) [any relevant Renewables LEC (and, if different from the relevant recipient, the identity of any person to whom entitlement to that Renewables LEC is transferred)][1].

(5) The following time limits apply as part of the conditions described in this regulation—

(*a*) paragraph (3)—the supplier must comply within such reasonable time as the relevant Authority allows for this purpose;

(*b*) paragraph (4)—the generator and the supplier, as appropriate, must comply within such reasonable time as the relevant Authority allows for this purpose.

Amendments—[1] Words in para (4) substituted by the CCL (General) (Amendment) Regulations, SI 2003/604 regs 2, 17 with effect from 1 April 2003.

[2] Words in paras (1), (3) substituted by the CCL (General) (Amendment) Regulations, SI 2003/604 regs 2, 18 with effect from 1 April 2003.

50 Supplies shall not be regarded as exempt renewable supplies for the purposes of paragraph 19 of the Act unless—

(*a*) the supplier provides the recipient with a written notice for the duration of the renewable source contract, updated as necessary, setting out how to identify those supplies of electricity that—

(i) are or will be made under the renewable source contract, and

(ii) are or will be referred to on a climate change levy accounting document (or an invoice) issued in respect of those supplies;

(*b*) the supplier retains a copy of each such notice for 6 years starting from the day after it is provided to the recipient;

(*c*) the supplier supplies a copy of any such notice to the Commissioners no later than the fourteenth day after the Commissioners so request.

51— (1) The exemption provided for by paragraph 19(1) of the Act (exemption: supply of electricity from renewable sources) shall only be given effect if the supplier, and each other person (if any) who is a generator of any renewable source electricity allocated by the supplier to supplies under the renewable source contract in question, has delivered a copy of the relevant notice to the relevant Authority.

(2) In paragraph (1), "relevant notice" refers to the written notice mentioned in paragraph 19(1)(*d*) of the Act relating to the supply of electricity and contract in question (notice to Commissioners agreeing to fulfil conditions of exemption).

[PART IV(*A*)
COMBINED HEAT AND POWER STATIONS][1]

Amendments—[1] This Part inserted by the CCL (General) (Amendment) Regulations, SI 2003/604 regs 2, 19 with effect from 1 April 2003.

[Interpretation of Part IV(A)

51A— [(1)][2] For the purposes of this Part and [Schedules 1 and 2][2]—

"authorised person" (except for the purposes of Schedule 2, paragraph 7(*a*)) refers to a person authorised by the relevant Authority;

"CHP declaration contract" refers to the contract mentioned in paragraph 20A(1)(*b*) of the Act;

["CHPQA" refers to the Combined Heat and Power Quality Assurance Standard, Issue 1, November 2000 originally published by the Department for the Environment, Transport and the Regions (including the later of version Final 1.0 or 2.0 of CHPQA Guidance Notes 0 to 4 (including 2(S), 3(S) and 4(S)), 10 to 28 and 30);][2]

"CHP Relief Condition" refers to paragraphs 2 to 7 and paragraph 12 of Schedule 2;

"exemption certificate" refers to a full-exemption certificate or a part-exemption certificate (see paragraphs 148(2) and 148(3) of the Act and the Climate Change Levy (Combined Heat and Power Stations) Exemption Certificate Regulations 2001);

"fully exempt CHP" refers to a fully exempt combined heat and power station (see paragraph 148(2) of the Act);

"indirect supplies" refers to supplies in relation to which provision is made by paragraph 20A(1) of the Act (exemption for supply made by electricity utility of CHP electricity);

"MWh" is an abbreviation for megawatt-hour;

"operator" refers to the person who operates a station or who generates or produces electricity in that station;

"outputs" or "output" refers to the meaning given by paragraph 148(9) of the Act (electricity or motive power produced in a station, and (*a*) heat or steam, or (*b*) air, or water, that has been heated or cooled);

"partly exempt CHP" refers to a partly exempt combined heat and power station (see paragraph 148(3) of the Act);

"QPO" means qualifying power output;

"QPO electricity" refers to electricity that—

(*a*) has been produced in a fully exempt CHP;

(*b*) has been produced in a partly exempt CHP and supplied from it without causing the limit referred to in paragraph 16(2) of the Act to be exceeded;

"station" refers to a fully or partly exempt CHP;

"relevant Authority" refers to the Gas and Electricity Markets Authority or, in relation to electricity produced or supplied in Northern Ireland or produced in the Republic of Ireland, the Director General of Electricity Supply for Northern Ireland.][1]

[(2) In the case of electricity produced in a given station after 21st July 2005, this Part and Schedule 2 (and the related penalties provided for by regulation 60(1)(*ha*) and regulation 60(1)(*hb*)) only apply if at least some of that electricity is supplied otherwise than from that station (indirect supplies, see paragraph 20A(2) of the Act).][2]

Amendments—[1] This regulation inserted by the CCL (General) (Amendment) Regulations, SI 2003/604 regs 2, 19 with effect from 1 April 2003.

[2] Para (1) numbered as such, words therein substituted, definition of "CHPQA" inserted, and para (2) inserted, by the Climate Change Levy (Miscellaneous Amendments) Regulations, SI 2005/1716 regs 6, 7(1), (2) with effect from 22 July 2005. However, arrangements initiated or made before 22 July 2005 on the basis of SI 2001/838 Sch 1 para 5(5) or 5(6) as then in force remain subject to the provisions applicable when they were initiated or made (tax credit claims and corrections to over-estimated relief).

[Certification of electricity produced in a combined heat and power station

51B— [(1) The relevant Authority must certify QPO electricity in accordance with this Part and Schedule 2.][2]

(2) The relevant Authority must only certify on the basis of the most accurate figures for electricity produced in an individual station that the station's operator makes known to the Authority.

(3) *The relevant Authority must disregard any figures that are made known to it or of which it becomes aware after the end of the second month following the end of the month in which the electricity is produced.*[3]

(4) *Paragraph* (3) *does not apply to regulation 51D, regulation 51E or Schedule 2 paragraph 11 (wrongly certified electricity and periodic reconciliation).*[3]

(5) The station's operator must only make known figures for the purposes of paragraph (2) that are made in accordance with the metering requirements of [the CHPQA][2]

[(6) The relevant Authority must only certify for the purposes of paragraphs (1) and (2) on the basis that—

(*a*) each quantity of electricity produced by an individual station is referable to the Annual Operation in which it is produced, and

(*b*) every such quantity in a given Annual Operation comprises the same relative proportions of QPO electricity and non-QPO electricity.

This requirement is subject to the other provisions of this Part and Schedule 2 (non-certification, restricting validity to indirect supplies, reconciliation).

"Annual Operation" has the same meaning as in regulations 2(3), 3(2), 4 and 6(1) of the Climate Change Levy (Combined Heat and Power Stations) Regulations 2005 (namely, 1st January to 31st December).][2]

(7) The relevant Authority must not certify any electricity produced in a station when no exemption certificate is in force for that station.

(8) Where the relevant Authority certifies under paragraph (1), it must issue a levy exemption certificate ("CHP LEC") as respects that electricity.

[The relevant Authority must both certify QPO electricity in accordance with paragraphs (1), (2), (3),[3] (6) and (7) and issue the relevant CHP LEC no later than the end of the third month following the end of the month in which the electricity is produced.

Whilst the relative proportions mentioned in paragraph (6)(*b*) are unknown, the relevant Authority must use a reasonable estimate of what those relative proportions will be.

If the relevant Authority must investigate further whether the electricity in question is "QPO electricity", it must certify the QPO electricity and issue the relevant CHP LEC no later than the end of the month following the month in which that investigation ought reasonably to have been concluded.][2]

(9) A CHP LEC must be regarded for all purposes of this Part and Schedule 2 as only relating to the actual electricity in relation to which it was issued.

(10) Each CHP LEC must carry a unique identifying reference.][1]

Amendments—[1] This regulation inserted by the CCL (General) (Amendment) Regulations, SI 2003/604 regs 2, 19 with effect from 1 April 2003.

[2] Paras (1), (6) and words in para (5) substituted, and words in para (8) inserted, by the Climate Change Levy (Miscellaneous Amendments) Regulations, SI 2005/1716 regs 6, 7(3)–(6) with effect from 22 July 2005. However, arrangements initiated or made before 22 July 2005 on the basis of SI 2001/838 Sch 1 para 5(5) or 5(6) as then in force remain subject to the provisions applicable when they were initiated or made (tax credit claims and corrections to over-estimated relief).

[3] Paras (3), (4), and reference "(3)," in para (8), revoked by the Climate Change Levy (General) (Amendment) Regulations, SI 2007/2903 reg 2, Sch 1 paras 22, 23 with effect from 1 November 2007: SI 2007/2903 reg 1. These amendments only apply in relation to figures that have not been disregarded before 1 November 2007 under SI 2001/838 reg 48(1B) or 51B(3): SI 2007/2903 reg 2, Sch 1 Note (*d*).

[51C— (1) The relevant Authority must neither certify electricity nor issue a CHP LEC as respects any electricity under any of the following circumstances.

(2) The first circumstance is where the quantity of electricity in question is less than 1 MWh.

However the relevant Authority may aggregate or disaggregate such quantities relating to the same station, certifying each complete MWh as appropriate.

(3) The second circumstance is where the relevant Authority is not satisfied that the CHP LEC, if issued, would represent electricity consumed or to be consumed in the United Kingdom.

For this purpose, the relevant Authority may have regard in particular to whether any part of that electricity is or may be allocated by the operator or a supplier for consumption outside the United Kingdom.

(4) The third circumstance is any one or more of the following—

(*a*) the operator not providing the relevant Authority with such information, particulars, records and declarations as the relevant Authority may require for the purposes of this Part or Schedule 2;

(*b*) the operator not providing the relevant Authority with any updated readings the relevant Authority may require from any relevant electricity meter;

(*c*) any authorised person not being granted, on request, access at any reasonable time to the station in question;

(*d*) any authorised person not being permitted, on request and having been granted access to the station—

(i) to inspect or test anything that is at the station and connected with the production or supply of any relevant electricity, and

(ii) to inspect any records that are at that station and so connected;

(*e*) any authorised person not, on request, being granted access to any premises at any reasonable time to take updated readings from any relevant electricity meter;

(*f*) the operator having been notified of an assessment to a civil penalty or to penalty interest in relation to an event subject to this Part or Schedule 2 and, irrespective of any relevant review or appeal, that amount being unrecovered (for assessments, see paragraphs 106 and 111 of the Act; for review and appeal, see Part XI of the Act);

(*g*) any one or more of sub-paragraphs (*a*) to (*e*) not being satisfied within such time as the relevant Authority considers reasonable for the purpose in question;

(*h*) …[2]][1]

Amendments—[1] This regulation inserted by the CCL (General) (Amendment) Regulations, SI 2003/604 regs 2, 19 with effect from 1 April 2003.

[2] Para (4)(*h*) revoked by the Climate Change Levy (Miscellaneous Amendments) Regulations, SI 2005/1716 regs 6, 7(7) with effect from 22 July 2005. However, arrangements initiated or made before 22 July 2005 on the basis of SI 2001/838 Sch 1 para 5(5) or 5(6) as then in force remain subject to the provisions applicable when they were initiated or made (tax credit claims and corrections to over-estimated relief).

[51D— (1) If the relevant Authority becomes aware that it has issued a CHP LEC in relation to—

(*a*) production when no exemption certificate was in force for the relevant station, or

(*b*) production in relation to which there is a breach of regulation 51B(5) (metering standards), it shall as soon as practicable both restrict the validity of that CHP LEC to indirect supplies (see regulations 51I to 51M) and notify that restriction to the person to whom it was issued (see regulation 51B(8)).

(2) A CHP LEC so restricted is referred to in the remainder of this Part and in Schedule 2 as a "restricted CHP LEC" and any other CHP LEC is referred to as an "unrestricted CHP LEC" (but see also Schedule 2 paragraphs 8(3), 11(5) and 13(2)).][1]

Amendments—[1] This regulation inserted by the CCL (General) (Amendment) Regulations, SI 2003/604 regs 2, 19 with effect from 1 April 2003.

[51E— (1) The relevant Authority shall, in carrying out its functions under this Part, have regard to the proper administration of CCL.

(2) The relevant Authority shall in particular, and as appropriate, act in accordance with and have regard to Schedule 2 paragraphs 8, 10 and 11.

(3) The relevant Authority must keep a record of each CHP LEC for 6 years from the date of issue.

The record must show the person to whom it was issued, whether the CHP LEC is unrestricted or restricted, and any indirect supply of the electricity to which the CHP LEC is relevant (see regulation 51J(3)).][1]

Amendments—[1] This regulation inserted by the CCL (General) (Amendment) Regulations, SI 2003/604 regs 2, 19 with effect from 1 April 2003.

[CCL treatment dependent on certification

51F Electricity shall not be regarded as QPO electricity for the purposes of regulation 4(1)(*a*) of the Climate Change Levy (Electricity and Gas) Regulations 2001 (direct supplies of electricity by utility from fully exempt CHP) unless it remains the subject of an unrestricted CHP LEC.][1]

Amendments—[1] This regulation inserted by the CCL (General) (Amendment) Regulations, SI 2003/604 regs 2, 19 with effect from 1 April 2003.

[51G— (1) Electricity shall not be regarded as QPO electricity for any of the following purposes unless it remains the subject of an unrestricted CHP LEC—

(*a*) the outputs of a station referred to in paragraph 15(1) of the Act (supplies to CHP exempt if to be used in producing station's outputs);

(*b*) the electricity referred to in paragraphs 16(1)(*a*), 17(3) and 17(4) of the Act (supplies from partly exempt CHP are exempt from CCL if specified limit not exceeded; self-supplies from station exempt if producer not auto-generator).

(2) Each of the following exemptions shall only be given effect subject to the CHP Relief Condition (see regulation 51H(1)) being fulfilled as follows—

(*a*) for paragraph 15(1) of the Act, the Condition must be fulfilled in relation to any QPO electricity that is a relevant output for the purposes of that paragraph (supplies to CHP exempt if for use in producing station's outputs);

(*b*) for paragraph 16(2) of the Act, the Condition must be fulfilled in relation to any QPO electricity referred to in that paragraph (supplies from partly exempt CHP are exempt from CCL if specified limit not exceeded);

(*c*) for paragraph 17(2) of the Act, the Condition must be fulfilled in relation to any QPO electricity that is the subject of the supply referred to in that paragraph (self-supply by auto-generator exempt);

(*d*) for paragraph 17(3) or 17(4) of the Act, the Condition must be fulfilled in relation to any QPO electricity that is electricity for the purposes of that paragraph (self-supplies from fully or partly exempt CHP exempt from CCL if producer not auto-generator).][1]

Amendments—[1] This regulation inserted by the CCL (General) (Amendment) Regulations, SI 2003/604 regs 2, 19 with effect from 1 April 2003.

[51H— (1) Schedule 2 has effect and, accordingly, the CHP Relief Condition binds any person who—

(*a*) represents to a supplier entitlement to the exemption from CCL provided for by paragraph 15(1) of the Act (supplies of taxable commodities to stations, and see also paragraph (4));

(*b*) does not account for CCL on a supply because an exemption is provided for by paragraph 16(2), 17(3) or 17(4) of the Act (supplies from partly exempt CHP and self-supplies from fully or partly exempt CHP);

(*c*) does not account for CCL on a supply because an exemption is provided for by paragraph 17(2) of the Act (self-supply by autogenerator) (but only if the electricity in question is QPO electricity).

(2) Paragraph 1 and regulations 51F and 51G only apply in relation to supplies that are treated as taking place on or after 1 April 2003 (see paragraphs 25 to 39 of the Act, time of supply).

(3) Regulations 51F and 51G apply in addition to regulation 60(1)(*hb*) (penalties relating to CHP Relief Condition)).

(4) Part III and Schedule 1 apply independently of this Part (certification, etc in relation to excluded, exempt …[2] and reduced-rate supplies).][1]

Amendments—[1] This regulation inserted by the CCL (General) (Amendment) Regulations, SI 2003/604 regs 2, 19 with effect from 1 April 2003.
[2] In para (4), words ", half-rate" revoked by the Climate Change Levy (General) (Amendment) Regulations, SI 2007/2903 reg 2, Sch 1 para 24 with effect from 1 November 2007: SI 2007/2903 reg 1. This amendment does not apply in relation to a half-rate supply made before 1 April 2006: SI 2007/2903 reg 2, Sch 1 Note (*a*).

[Supplies pursuant to CHP declaration contract

51I Electricity is only "CHP electricity" for the purposes of paragraphs 20A and 20B of the Act (exemption for indirect supplies) if it remains the subject of an unrestricted CHP LEC or a restricted CHP LEC.][1]

Amendments—[1] This regulation inserted by the CCL (General) (Amendment) Regulations, SI 2003/604 regs 2, 19 with effect from 1 April 2003.

[51J— (1) Any electricity that is the subject of a CHP LEC shall be regarded as never having been CHP electricity capable of being the subject of exempt CHP supplies for the purposes of paragraph 20A of the Act (indirect supplies) if one or more of the conditions prescribed in the following paragraphs are not fulfilled.

(2) The electricity must only be allocated to a supply to a person who intends it to be consumed in the United Kingdom.

(3) Should the electricity be allocated to some supply pursuant to some CHP declaration contract, the supplier must inform the relevant Authority of this fact and of the relevant CHP LEC's unique identifying reference (see regulation 51B(10)).

(4) At any time up to 6 years after the day the electricity is produced, any supplier of that electricity must on request and within such time as the relevant Authority considers reasonable provide that Authority with readily legible records relating to and detailing—

(*a*) the supplies that supplier received or made of that electricity,

(*b*) the relevant suppliers or recipients of any supplies that supplier received or made of that electricity,

(*c*) the relevant CHP LECs and, if different from the relevant supplier or recipient, the identity of any person from or to whom entitlement to the CHP LEC was obtained or transferred.][1]

Amendments—[1] This regulation inserted by the CCL (General) (Amendment) Regulations, SI 2003/604 regs 2, 19 with effect from 1 April 2003.

[51K Supplies shall not be regarded as exempt CHP supplies for the purposes of paragraph 20A of the Act unless—

(*a*) the supplier provides the recipient with a written notice for the duration of the CHP declaration contract, updated as necessary, setting out how to identify those supplies of electricity that—

(i) are or will be made under the CHP declaration contract, and

(ii) are or will be referred to on a climate change levy accounting document (or an invoice) issued in respect of those supplies;

(*b*) the supplier retains a copy of each such notice for 6 years starting from the day after it is provided to the recipient;

(*c*) the supplier provides a copy of any such notice to the Commissioners no later than 14 days after the Commissioners request one.][1]

Amendments—[1] This regulation inserted by the CCL (General) (Amendment) Regulations, SI 2003/604 regs 2, 19 with effect from 1 April 2003.

[51L The exemption provided for by paragraph 20A(1) of the Act (indirect supplies) shall only be given effect if the supplier, and each other person (if any) who is an operator in relation to any CHP electricity allocated by the supplier to supplies under the CHP declaration contract in question, has delivered a copy of the notice referred to in paragraph 20A(1)(*d*) of the Act (agreement to fulfil conditions) to the relevant Authority.][1]

Amendments—[1] This regulation inserted by the CCL (General) (Amendment) Regulations, SI 2003/604 regs 2, 19 with effect from 1 April 2003.

[51M— (1) A supply of electricity is exempt from the levy chargeable under paragraph 5(1) of the Act, and electricity is "CHP electricity" for the purposes of paragraphs 20A and 20B of the Act, only if paragraph (2) is satisfied in relation to that electricity.

(2) The electricity must not have been produced when the station that produced it has received State aid exceeding any relevant limit in the "Community guidelines on State aid for environmental protection (2001/C 37/03).][1]

Amendments—[1] This regulation inserted by the CCL (General) (Amendment) Regulations, SI 2003/604 regs 2, 19 with effect from 1 April 2003.

PART V
ELECTRICITY AND GAS

Self-supply of electricity by producer

52— (1) For the purposes of paragraph 23(3)(*b*)(ii) of the Act (self-supply by producer of electricity from taxable commodities), electricity shall be treated as produced from taxable commodities except to the extent that—

(*a*) it is produced from material that is not a taxable commodity for the purposes of the Act (see paragraph 3 of the Act); or

(*b*) it constitutes renewable source electricity as prescribed by regulation 47 (excluding, for this purpose, regulation 48).

(2) Electricity shall not be regarded as falling within paragraph (1)(*a*) to the extent that it is produced by or in—

(*a*) a large hydro generating station within the meaning of regulation 47(2), or

(*b*) a nuclear power station.

(3) Accordingly electricity produced by or in a large hydro station or a nuclear power station shall be treated as produced from taxable commodities for the purposes of paragraph 23(3)(*b*)(ii) of the Act.

Small-scale users of electricity and gas

53— (1) Paragraphs (2) and (4) prescribe the rates for the purposes of paragraph 27(6) of the Act (maximum rates of supply for small-scale electricity and gas users).

(2) In the case of electricity, the prescribed rate—

(*a*) is any rate at which the supplier supplies electricity to a person provided that the supplier issues an invoice or statement of account (however termed or styled) to that person in respect of those supplies no more than once in each period of six weeks, or

(*b*) is the rate at which the supplier supplies electricity to the person in question provided that in any period of one year that includes the Reference Day the maximum demand from that person is less than 100 kilowatts.

(3) The "maximum demand" for the purposes of paragraph (2)(*b*) shall be determined by the supplier as follows—

(*a*) establish the three highest demands for that person in a period of one year including the Reference Day;

(*b*) the mean of those three demands is the relevant "maximum demand";

(*c*) disregard any supplies of electricity made to the person by a different supplier.

(4) In the case of gas, the prescribed rate—

(*a*) is any rate at which the supplier supplies gas to a person provided that the supplier issues an invoice or statement of account (however termed or styled) to that person in respect of those supplies no more than once in each period of six weeks, or

(*b*) in any other case, is 750 megawatt hours in a period of one year.

(5) The rate at which a person must be taken to be supplied with gas for the purposes of paragraph (4)(*b*) shall be determined by the supplier as follows—

(*a*) estimate, for each individual reference number used or to be used by the supplier in question for that person, the quantity of gas to be supplied in the period starting on the Reference Day and ending 1 year later;

(*b*) the relevant gas rate shall be taken to be—

(i) if there is only one such quantity, that quantity; or

(ii) the highest of those individual quantities;

(*c*) disregard—

(i) the aggregate of those individual quantities (if there is more than one);

(ii) any supplies of gas that may be made to the person by a different supplier.

(6) The supplier need not make a further determination under paragraph (3) or (5) if he has reasonable grounds to believe that the further determination would result in the person—

(*a*) remaining a small-scale user; or

(*b*) remaining a person who is not a small-scale user.

(7) In this regulation—

"Reference Day" refers to the day mentioned in paragraph 27(6) of the Act;

"reference number" refers to that expression in paragraph 27(5)(*e*) of the Act;

"estimate" requires the use of any reasonable and accurate method.

Special utility schemes

54— (1) This regulation applies at any time after a special utility scheme has taken effect under paragraphs 29(4) and 29(5) of the Act but before the end of the period specified for which it is to have effect under paragraph 29(3) of the Act.

(2) If the Commissioners are satisfied that there will be no risk to the revenue, they may agree with the utility in question to amend the scheme or terminate it early.

(3) The Commissioners may terminate the scheme early if the utility in question—

(*a*) fails to abide by the scheme despite having elected in writing to be bound by it under paragraph 29(4) of the Act, or

(*b*) becomes, for any reason, incapable of abiding by the scheme.

(4) Termination under paragraph (3) shall take effect from such time as the Commissioners shall state in a written notice served by them for the purposes of that paragraph on the utility in question or on any relevant representative referred to in regulation 57 (representatives: incapacity, insolvency, etc).

(5) The Commissioners shall not state a time in that written notice that is earlier than when it is served under paragraph (4).

(6) Paragraph (5) shall not preclude the Commissioners from recovering by or under the Act any CCL that would have been due at any time up to the time so stated but for the special utility scheme having effect up to that time.

(7) A special utility scheme shall not be either amended or terminated early except in accordance with this regulation.

PART VI
DEATH, INCAPACITY, INSOLVENCY, TRANSFERS

Individuals: death or incapacity

55— (1) The Commissioners may, for CCL purposes and subject to this regulation, treat a person who carries on relevant activities on behalf of an individual who has died or become temporarily incapacitated as if they were the same person.

(2) Such treatment may continue pending someone other than that individual being registered under Part V of the Act in relation to those activities or the incapacity ceasing.

(3) A person who carries on relevant activities in the circumstances described in paragraph (1) must notify the Commissioners of this in writing and that notification must also include the date of death or the date and nature of the incapacity.

(4) This notification must be delivered to the Commissioners within 21 days starting with the day after the person begins carrying on the relevant activities.

(5) In this regulation, "relevant activities" refers to any activities in relation to which the individual in question is or was a registrable person.

Insolvency

56— (1) The Commissioners may, for CCL purposes and subject to this regulation, treat a person who carries on relevant activities of a registrable person to whom an insolvency procedure is applied as if they were the same person.

(2) Such treatment may continue pending someone other than that registrable person being registered under Part V of the Act in relation to those activities or the insolvency procedure no longer being applied.

(3) A person who carries on relevant activities in the circumstances described in paragraph (1) must notify the Commissioners of this in writing and that notification must also include the date the insolvency procedure was first applied.

(4) This notification must be delivered to the Commissioners within 21 days starting with the day after the person begins carrying on the relevant activities.

(5) In this regulation—

"relevant activities" refers to any activities in relation to which the individual in question is or was a registrable person;

"registrable person" may include, as appropriate, the estate of a deceased individual.

(6) An insolvency procedure is applied to a person for the purposes of this regulation in the circumstances described by paragraphs 120(7) to 120(9) of the Act (insolvency procedures for the purposes of this regulation).

Representatives: death, incapacity or insolvency

57— (1) If the Commissioners so require, a representative who controls the assets of a registrable person because of death, incapacity or the application of an insolvency procedure shall, for the purposes of CCL and subject to this regulation, be treated as if he was the registrable person.

(2) Any requirement resulting from paragraph (1) for the representative to pay CCL shall only apply to the extent of the assets he controls.

(3) Any other requirement resulting from paragraph (1) shall apply in the same way as it would have applied to the registrable person but for the death, incapacity or insolvency procedure.

(4) In this regulation—

"relevant activities" refers to any activities in relation to which the registrable person in question is or was registrable;

"registrable person" may include, as appropriate, the estate of a deceased individual.

(5) An insolvency procedure is applied to a person for the purposes of this regulation in the circumstances described by paragraphs 120(7) to 120(9) of the Act (insolvency procedures for the purposes of this regulation).

Insolvency: consumers liable to penalty or interest

58— (1) This regulation applies where, in relation to a person ("the consumer")—

(*a*) the Commissioners assess and notify an amount due by way of penalty from the consumer for conduct falling within paragraph 98 (evasion) or 101 (incorrect notification for exclusion or exemption) of the Act;

(*b*) that amount or any penalty interest it carries remains unpaid; and

(*c*) an insolvency procedure applies to the consumer.

(2) The person appointed for the purposes of the application of the insolvency procedure ("the appointee") must notify the Commissioners of this in writing and that notification must also include the date the insolvency procedure first applied.

(3) This notification must be delivered to the Commissioners within 21 days starting with the day after the appointment takes effect or notice of the penalty or interest reaches the appointee, whichever is the later.

(4) Subject to this regulation, the appointee shall be treated to the extent and for the duration of the appointment as the same person as the consumer for the purposes of Part IX of the Act (civil penalties).

(5) An insolvency procedure is applied to a person for the purposes of this regulation in the circumstances described by paragraphs 120(7) to 120(9) of the Act (insolvency procedures for the purposes of this regulation).

Transfers of going concerns

59— (1) Where—

(*a*) a business carried on by a person who is registered under Part V of the Act is transferred to another person as a going concern,

(*b*) the registration of the transferor has not been cancelled,

(*c*) the transfer requires that the transferor's registration be cancelled and that the transferee either be registered for CCL or notify the Commissioners that he is registrable for CCL, and

(*d*) a written application for this purpose is made to the Commissioners by the transferor and transferee,

the Commissioners may, with effect from the date of the transfer, cancel the registration of the transferor and register the transferee in his place with the registration number previously allocated to the transferor.

(2) Should the Commissioners cancel the registration of the transferor and register the transferee in his place under paragraph (1) then, in order to secure continuity in the application of the Act—

(*a*) any liability of the transferor existing at the date of the transfer to make a return or account for or pay CCL shall become the liability of the transferee;

(*b*) any entitlement of the transferor, whether or not existing at the date of the transfer, to a tax credit or repayment under the Act, Part II of these Regulations or [Schedule 1][1] to these Regulations shall become the entitlement of the transferee;

(*c*) any other provision by or under the Act relating to CCL that applied to the transferor before his registration was cancelled (or any such provision that continues to apply to the transferor after that cancellation) shall apply to the transferee; and

(*d*) any circumstances relating to the application of the Act (or any provision made under the Act) to the CCL affairs of the transferor before his registration was cancelled (or any such circumstances that continue to apply to the transferor after that cancellation) shall apply to the transferee.

(3) In addition to the provisions set out in paragraph (2), where—

(*a*) the Commissioners cancel the registration of the transferor and register the transferee in his place under paragraph (1) with effect from a date earlier than the accounting period in which they do so, and

(*b*) either the transferor or the transferee has, in relation to any time on or after that date but before the start of that accounting period—

(i) made a return,

(ii) accounted for CCL, or

(iii) claimed a relevant tax credit,

the matters referred to in sub-paragraphs (*b*)(i) to (*b*)(iii) shall be treated as having been done by the transferee.

Amendments—[1] Words substituted by the CCL (General) (Amendment) Regulations, SI 2003/604 regs 2, 4 with effect from 1 April 2003.

PART VII
PENALTIES

60— (1) A person who fails to comply with a requirement imposed on him by or under any of the following provisions of these Regulations shall be liable to a penalty of £250 for each such failure—

(*a*) regulation 5(1), 5(2), 5(3) or 5(4);
(*b*) regulation 6(2);
(*c*) regulation 7(1), 7(2), 7(3) or 7(4);
(*d*) regulation 8;
(*e*) regulation 27(1) or 27(2);
(*f*) regulation 28(6) or 28(8);
(*g*) regulation 37(5);
(*h*) regulation 38 and paragraph 4, 12(3), 14(1), 14(2), 15(*a*) or 15(*b*) of [Schedule 1][1];
[(*ha*) regulation 51B(5);][2]
[(*hb*) regulation 51H(1) and paragraph 2, 3(1), 3(3), 3(4), 3(5), 4, 5, 6, 7, 11(2) or 12(1) of Schedule 2;][2]
(*i*) regulation 55(3) or 55(4);
(*j*) regulation 56(3) or 56(4);
(*k*) regulation 58(2) or 58(3).

(2) A specific act or omission shall attract only one such penalty if the circumstances are such that, but for this paragraph, it would attract more than one penalty.

Amendments—[1] Words substituted by the CCL (General) (Amendment) Regulations, SI 2003/604 regs 2, 4 with effect from 1 April 2003.
[2] Paras (1)(*ha*), (*hb*) inserted by the CCL (General) (Amendment) Regulations, SI 2003/604 regs 2, 20 with effect from 1 April 2003.

PART VIII
CONSEQUENTIAL AMENDMENTS

61 In regulation 2(1) of the Distress for Customs and Excise Duties and Other Indirect Taxes Regulations 1997 under the meaning given for "relevant tax" insert—

"(*f*) climate change levy;"

[SCHEDULE 1][1]
CERTIFICATION AND MANNER OF PAYMENT OF CCL DUE IN THE CASE OF EXCLUDED, EXEMPT …[2] OR REDUCED-RATE SUPPLIES

Regulation 38

Amendments—[1] Schedule renumbered by the CCL (General) (Amendment) Regulations, SI 2003/604 regs 2, 21 with effect from 1 April 2003.
[2] Words ", half-rate" revoked by the Climate Change Levy (General) (Amendment) Regulations, SI 2007/2903 reg 2, Sch 1 para 25 with effect from 1 November 2007: SI 2007/2903 reg 1. This amendment does not apply in relation to a half-rate supply made before 1 April 2006: SI 2007/2903 reg 2, Sch 1 Note (*a*).

Amendments—[1] Entries substituted by the Climate Change Levy (Miscellaneous Amendments) Regulations, SI 2005/1716 regs 5(*a*), 6 with effect from 22 July 2005. However, arrangements initiated or made before 22 July 2005 on the basis of SI 2001/838 Sch 1 para 5(5) or 5(6) as then in force remain subject to the provisions applicable when they were initiated or made (tax credit claims and corrections to over-estimated relief).

Basic rules

1 This Schedule applies in relation to a supply to which regulation 34, 35 or 36 applies …[1].

Amendments—[1] Words "or that otherwise includes a reduced-rate part" revoked by the Climate Change Levy (General) (Amendment) Regulations, SI 2007/2903 reg 2, Sch 1 para 26 with effect from 1 November 2007: SI 2007/2903 reg 1. In relation to a reduced-rate supply or a supply made on that basis, this amendment only applies if the supply is made on or after 1 November 2007: SI 2007/2903 reg 2, Sch 1 Note (*b*).

2 CCL shall not be due on the percentage of the supply properly determined in accordance with the following formula (the "CCL relief formula"):

$$P = \frac{(C + M \ldots\ + 0.8R)}{Q} \times 100$$

Notes

P = the percentage of the supply on which CCL is not due (the "CCL relief percentage") which must not be less than 0 per cent. nor more than 100 per cent.

Q = the quantity of the taxable commodity supplied.

In the case of electricity:

(*a*) Q includes any of that quantity that falls within the exclusion from CCL provided for by paragraph 9(2)(*f*)—community heating arrangements;

(*b*) Q does not include any of that quantity, apart from as described in (*a*) above, that falls within the exclusion from CCL provided for by paragraph 8—domestic or charity use;

[(*c*) Q does not include any of that quantity that falls within the exemption from CCL provided for by or under paragraph 16, 19 or 20A—electricity supplied exempt directly or indirectly from combined heat and power stations, or electricity supplied from renewable source.][1]

In all cases, Q does not include any quantity referable to exclusions under paragraph 8 (domestic or charity use) but does include any such quantity referable to the exclusion provided for by paragraphs 8 and 9(2)(*f*) (community heating arrangements).

C = the quantity of the taxable commodity referable to the sum of every relevant excluded part (paragraphs 8 and 9(2)(*f*)—community heating arrangements).

M = the quantity of the taxable commodity referable to the sum of every exempt part:

(*a*) paragraph 11—onward supplies and exports;
(*b*) paragraph 12—transport;
(*c*) paragraph 13—commodity producers;
(*d*) paragraph 14—electricity producers;
(*e*) paragraph 15—combined heat and power stations;
(*f*) paragraph 18—non-fuel use;
[(*fa*) paragraph 18A—recycling processes;][1]
(*g*) paragraph 21—regulation 41 of these Regulations (or other relevant regulations made under that paragraph of the Act to avoid double charges to CCL).

...[2]

0.8R = 80% of the quantity of the taxable commodity referable to the sum of every reduced-rate part (paragraph 44—climate change agreement).

The paragraph numbers referred to in these notes refer to the relevant paragraphs in Schedule 6 to the Finance Act 2000.

Amendments—[1] Words substituted and inserted by the Climate Change Levy (Miscellaneous Amendments) Regulations, SI 2005/1716 regs 5(*b*), 6 with effect from 22 July 2005. However, arrangements initiated or made before 22 July 2005 on the basis of SI 2001/838 Sch 1 para 5(5) or 5(6) as then in force remain subject to the provisions applicable when they were initiated or made (tax credit claims and corrections to over-estimated relief).

[2] Words "+ 0.5H" in climate change levy relief formula, and words "0.5H = 50% of the quantity of the taxable commodity referable to the sum of every half-rate part (paragraph 43—horticultural producers)." revoked, by the Climate Change Levy (General) (Amendment) Regulations, SI 2007/2903 reg 2, Sch 1 para 27 with effect from 1 November 2007: SI 2007/2903 reg 1. This amendment does not apply in relation to a half-rate supply made before 1 April 2006: SI 2007/2903 reg 2, Sch 1 Note (*a*).

[2A (1) For a supply made after 31st March 2006, the CCL relief formula in paragraph 2 is as follows (and the notes there, except the one about "0.5H", apply accordingly).

$$P = \frac{C + M + 0.8R}{Q} \times 100$$

(2) Regulations 35(6) to 35(9) (cessation of certification following abolition of half-rate supplies) have effect for determining when a supply is to be regarded as made for the purposes of sub-paragraph (1).][1, 2]

Amendments—[1] Paragraph 2A inserted by the CCL (General) (Amendment) Regulations, SI 2006/954 regs 1(2), 4 with effect from 1 April 2006.

[2] Para 2A revoked, by the Climate Change Levy (General) (Amendment) Regulations, SI 2007/2903 reg 2, Sch 1 para 28 with effect from 1 November 2007: SI 2007/2903 reg 1.

3— (1) Any supplier certificate delivered by the recipient shall represent to the best of the recipient's judgment any information required by regulation 34(2) (exclusions and exemptions), [regulation 35(2) or 36(2) (reduced-rates),][1] or regulation 37(3) (combinations).

(2) A supplier certificate may relate to more than one supply (subject to Part III of these Regulations and the other provisions of this Schedule).

(3) Accordingly, if it relates to more than one supply, a supplier certificate shall provide a recipient's relief percentage based on—

(*a*) the likely number of supplies to which it will relate,
(*b*) the likely quantity of the taxable commodity in question that will be supplied to him by the supplier if those supplies are made, and
(*c*) any other relevant circumstances.

Amendments—[1] In para (1), words substituted for words "regulation 35(2) (half-rates), regulation 36(2) (certain reduced-rates)" by the Climate Change Levy (General) (Amendment) Regulations, SI 2007/2903 reg 2, Sch 1 para 28 with effect from 1 November 2007: SI 2007/2903 reg 1. This amendment does not apply in relation to a half-rate supply made before 1 April 2006: SI 2007/2903 reg 2, Sch 1 Note (a). In relation to a reduced-rate supply or a supply made on that basis, these amendments only apply if the supply is made on or after 1 November 2007: SI 2007/2903 reg 2, Sch 1 Note (b).

4 The supplier shall apply the CCL relief percentage to any supply he makes to which the supplier certificate relates and may, for this purpose, rely on the percentage (the "recipient's relief percentage") provided by the recipient in accordance with regulation 38(2).

[Compulsory updates, corrections and payment of CCL due, exemption from CCL registration][1]

5— (1) The recipient shall review the correctness of the supplier certificate no later than the earlier of—

(*a*) the sixtieth day after the expiry of one year starting from its implementation date, or

(*b*) the sixtieth day after the recipient has burned (or, in the case of electricity, consumed) the last of the taxable commodity supplied to which the supplier certificate relates.

(2) That correctness shall be reviewed in relation to—

(*a*) (if sub-paragraph (1)(*a*) applies), the elapsed period of one year starting with the implementation date (and this period is referred to in sub-paragraph (3) as the "review period"), or

(*b*) (if sub-paragraph (1)(*b*) applies), the CCL relief percentage calculated on the basis of actual events.

(3) If—

(*a*) the review demonstrates that the supplier certificate was correct, and

(*b*) that certificate also relates to supplies made or to be made by the supplier after the end of the review period,

that supplier certificate shall be regarded for the purposes of Part III of these Regulations and this Schedule as having as its implementation date the anniversary of its original implementation date (and sub-paragraphs (1) and (2) shall apply accordingly).

[This sub-paragraph is subject to paragraph 16 (5 year renewal limit).][1]

(4) Sub-paragraphs (5) to (10) apply if the review demonstrates that the supplier certificate was incorrect.

(5) If the supplier certificate was incorrect because the CCL relief percentage applied was too low, the recipient may act in accordance with paragraphs 6 to 10 (provision for tax credits) (subject to paragraph 11).

[(6) For the purposes of sub-paragraph (5), the benefit and extent of any relevant tax credit must be allocated to supplies in reverse chronological order (see paragraphs 6 to 10, tax credits for recipients, etc).

This means that supplies treated as taking place later have priority over supplies treated as taking place earlier.][1]

[(7) Sub-paragraphs (8) to (9F) apply if (*a*) the supplier certificate was incorrect because the CCL relief percentage was too high, and (*b*) paragraphs 24(1B) and 24(3)[, or paragraph 45A,][2] of the Act (Deemed supply: change of circumstances etc [or Reduced-rate supplies: deemed supply][2]) apply accordingly in relation to supplies made on the basis of that certificate in that review period.][1]

[(8) For the purposes of sub-paragraph (7), the extent to which the supplier certificate was incorrect must be allocated to supplies in reverse chronological order (about which see sub-paragraph (6)). Any supplies then deemed to be made under paragraph 24(3) [or 45A(2)][2] of the Act are treated as taking place at the time of the review in question under sub-paragraph (1).][1]

[(9) But the Commissioners may exempt the recipient from any consequential requirement to be registered if the following conditions and requirements are satisfied (for registration, see paragraphs 24(3), 40[, 45A(2)(*a*)][2] and 53(1) of the Act).][1]

[(9A) First, the recipient must not otherwise be a registrable person (for registrable, see regulation 2(1)).][1]

[(9B) Secondly, the recipient must deliver a relevant written application to the Commissioners within 30 days starting from the day after compliance with sub-paragraph (1).][1]

[(9C) That application must include notification of the following—

(*a*) the type and quantity of taxable commodity so deemed to be supplied by the recipient under paragraph 24(3) [or 45A(2)][2] of the Act,

(*b*) the amount of CCL payable by the recipient as a result, and

(*c*) the number of such payments the recipient anticipates having to make annually.][1]

[(9D) Thirdly, the recipient must pay the CCL due on those supplies to the Commissioners no later than the 30th day after the one on which the approval decision is delivered.][1]

[(9E) If the Commissioners do not exempt the recipient but sub-paragraphs (9A), (9B) and (9C) are satisfied, the 30 days for notifying registrability starts on the day the refusal decision is delivered (for notifying registrability, see regulations 2(5) and 20(*a*) of the Climate Change Levy (Registration and Miscellaneous Provisions) Regulations 2001).][1]

[(9F) Exemption from registration under sub-paragraph (9) applies only in relation to the consequential requirement mentioned there in relation to sub-paragraphs (7) and (8). Such exemption may be of limited duration and revoked by the Commissioners at any time.][1]

[(9G) This sub-paragraph applies instead of sub-paragraphs (7) to (9F) to the extent that the supplier certificate was incorrect because the CCL relief percentage was too high in relation to half-rate supplies (see paragraph 43(1) of the Act).

The recipient must pay to the Commissioners, no later than the 30th day after the last one for that person's compliance with sub-paragraph (1), the balance of the CCL due for those supplies.

If the recipient is a registrable person, the error may be corrected by the making of an appropriate adjustment under regulation 5(1)(b) (adjustment in CCL return) in relation to an accounting period ending no later than six months after the last day for that person's compliance with sub-paragraph (1).][1, 2]

(10) If the recipient does not review the accuracy of the supplier certificate in accordance with sub-paragraph (1), and the certificate was (or remains) incorrect, paragraph 101 of the Act shall apply accordingly (civil penalty for incorrect certification, etc subject to reasonable excuse).

(11) This paragraph only applies in relation to a supply or supplies to which regulation 34 or 35 applies (supplier certificates for exclusions, exemptions and half-rates).[2]

Amendments—[1] Heading substituted, words inserted in para (3), and paras (6)–(9G) substituted for paras (6)–(9), by the Climate Change Levy (Miscellaneous Amendments) Regulations, SI 2005/1716 regs 5(*c*)–(*e*), 6 with effect from 22 July 2005. However, arrangements initiated or made before 22 July 2005 on the basis of SI 2001/838 Sch 1 para 5(5) or 5(6) as then in force remain subject to the provisions applicable when they were initiated or made (tax credit claims and corrections to over-estimated relief).

[2] In paras (7)–(9), (9C) words inserted, and paras (9G), (11) revoked, by the Climate Change Levy (General) (Amendment) Regulations, SI 2007/2903 reg 2, Sch 1 paras 31–35 with effect from 1 November 2007: SI 2007/2903 reg 1.

The amendment to para (9G) does not apply in relation to a half-rate supply made before 1 April 2006: SI 2007/2903 reg 2, Sch 1 Note (a).

In relation to a reduced-rate supply or a supply made on that basis, the amendments to paras (8), (9), (9C), (11) only apply if the supply is made on or after 1 November 2007: SI 2007/2903 reg 2, Sch 1 Note (b).

[Tax credit for recipient and reconciliation for input fuel to combined heat and power stations][1]

6— (1) The recipient in each of the following cases is entitled to a tax credit in respect of any relevant amount of CCL charged on the supply in question (subject to paragraph 5(5) and the other provisions of this Schedule including those provisions relating to the making of a relevant claim to the Commissioners)—

(*a*) after a taxable supply has been made, there is such a change in circumstances or any person's intentions that, if the changed circumstances or intentions had existed at the time the supply was made, the supply would not have been a taxable supply;

(*b*) after a supply of a taxable commodity is made on the basis that it is a taxable supply, it is determined that the supply was not (to any extent) a taxable supply;

(*c*) after a taxable supply has been made on the basis that it was [not][2] a reduced-rate supply, it is determined that the supply was (to any extent) a …[2] reduced-rate supply;

(d) CCL is accounted for on a half-rate supply as if the supply were neither a half-rate supply nor a reduced-rate supply;[2]

(*e*) after a charge to CCL has arisen on a supply of a taxable commodity ("the original commodity") to a person who uses the commodity supplied in producing taxable commodities primarily for his own consumption, that person makes supplies of any of the commodities in whose production he has used the original commodity.

(2) In sub-paragraph (1), "relevant amount of CCL" refers to the difference between—

(*a*) the amount of CCL that ought to have been charged by or under the Act at the time of supply had the supplier certificate been correct, and

(*b*) the amount of CCL that the supplier accounted for (or ought to have accounted for) on the basis of the incorrect supplier certificate.

Amendments—[1] Heading substituted by the Climate Change Levy (Miscellaneous Amendments) Regulations, SI 2005/1716 regs 5(*f*), 6 with effect from 22 July 2005. However, arrangements initiated or made before 22 July 2005 on the basis of SI 2001/838 Sch 1 para 5(5) or 5(6) as then in force remain subject to the provisions applicable when they were initiated or made (tax credit claims and corrections to over-estimated relief).

[2] In para (1)(*c*) word substituted for words "neither a half-rate supply nor", words "half-rate or" revoked, and para (1)(*d*) revoked, by the Climate Change Levy (General) (Amendment) Regulations, SI 2007/2903 reg 2, Sch 1 paras 36, 37 with effect from 1 November 2007: SI 2007/2903 reg 1. These amendments do not apply in relation to a half-rate supply made before 1 April 2006: SI 2007/2903 reg 2, Sch 1 Note (a).

7 A tax credit shall only arise under paragraph 6 if a claim is made by the recipient acting in accordance with paragraph 8 or 9, as the case requires.

8— (1) Subject to sub-paragraph (4), the recipient shall claim any such tax credit—

(*a*) …[1]

(*b*) by bringing it into account when he is accounting for CCL due from him for any accounting period …[1].

(2) Accordingly, in the case of a claim under sub-paragraph (1)(*b*)—

(*a*) the requirements of regulation 5 (content of returns), regulation 6 (payment of CCL) and regulation 7 (CCL accounts) apply subject to sub-paragraph (1)(*b*); but (*b*) sub-paragraph (1)(*b*) applies subject to regulation 27 (corrections) and regulation 28 (corrections not exceeding [£50,000][2]).

(3) A claim subject to sub-paragraphs (1) and (2) shall be regarded as a claim for repayment of CCL for the purposes of paragraph 64 of the Act (supplemental provisions about repayments, etc) (and see sub-paragraph (4)).

(4) Where the total tax credit claimed by a recipient exceeds the total of any CCL due from him for the accounting period …[1] the Commissioners shall repay to him an amount equal to the excess (but see regulations 29 and 30).

(5) Given the provision made by paragraph 62(4) of the Act, this paragraph has effect subject to paragraph 64 of the Act (application of supplemental provisions about repayments: three year time limit, unjust enrichment, etc).

(6) …[1]

Amendments—[1] Paras (1)(*a*), (6) and words in paras (1)(*b*), (4) revoked by the Climate Change Levy (Miscellaneous Amendments) Regulations, SI 2005/1716 regs 5(*g*)–(*j*), 6 with effect from 22 July 2005. However, arrangements initiated or made before 22 July 2005 on the basis of SI 2001/838 Sch 1 para 5(5) or 5(6) as then in force remain subject to the provisions applicable when they were initiated or made (tax credit claims and corrections to over-estimated relief).

[2] In para (2)(*b*) figure substituted for figure "£2,000" by the Value Added Tax, etc (Correction of Errors, etc) Regulations, SI 2008/1482 reg 6(1) with effect in relation to under-calculations or over-calculations respectively in the CCL Regulations, SI 2001/838 reg 28(2), (3) which registrable persons first discover in their accounting periods that start on 1 July 2008 or later.

9— (1) Where the recipient is [not registrable or is exempt from registration (see paragraph 5(9)),][1] the Commissioners shall repay to him the amount of the tax credit if they are satisfied that he has made a proper claim to them in writing for this purpose.

(2) A recipient making a claim under sub-paragraph (1) must furnish to the Commissioners full particulars in relation to the tax credit claimed, including (but not limited to)—

(*a*) any relevant supplier certificate on the basis of which the relevant CCL was accounted for by the supplier;

(*b*) any relevant analysis document supporting any such supplier certificate;

(*c*) the amount of the CCL in question and the date and manner of its payment to the Commissioners whether by the recipient, the supplier or otherwise;

(*d*) the circumstances, events, records and documentary or other evidence by virtue of which the recipient claims that any relevant entitlement to a tax credit arises;

(*e*) the period of time by reference to which the recipient consumed the relevant taxable commodity or was supplied with the relevant taxable commodity by the supplier to whom he delivered the relevant supplier certificate; and

(*f*) any matter, item or particular in any way relevant to the question whether or not a tax credit arises under this Schedule in favour of the recipient.

(3) Where the Commissioners are satisfied that a person who has made a claim in accordance with sub-paragraphs (1) and (2) is entitled to a tax credit and that he has not previously had the benefit of that credit, they shall repay to him an amount equal to the credit (but see regulations 29 and 30).

(4) …[1]

(5) Given the provision made by paragraph 62(4) of the Act, this regulation has effect subject to paragraph 64 of the Act (application of supplemental provisions about repayments: three year time limit, unjust enrichment, etc).

(6) …[1]

Amendments—[1] Words in para (1) substituted, and paras (4), (6) revoked, by the Climate Change Levy (Miscellaneous Amendments) Regulations, SI 2005/1716 regs 5(*k*), (*l*), 6 with effect from 22 July 2005. However, arrangements initiated or made before 22 July 2005 on the basis of SI 2001/838 Sch 1 para 5(5) or 5(6) as then in force remain subject to the provisions applicable when they were initiated or made (tax credit claims and corrections to over-estimated relief).

[**9A** Paragraphs 5 to 9 apply subject to the modifications in paragraph 9C, but those modifications are only relevant to the extent that the recipient's relief percentage is determined on the basis of a quantity of taxable commodity referable to paragraph 15 of the Act (supplies to combined heat and power stations).][1]

Amendments—[1] Paragraphs 9A–9C inserted by the Climate Change Levy (Miscellaneous Amendments) Regulations, SI 2005/1716 regs 5(*m*), 6 with effect from 22 July 2005. However, arrangements initiated or made before 22 July 2005 on the basis of SI 2001/838 Sch 1 para 5(5) or 5(6) as then in force remain subject to the provisions applicable when they were initiated or made (tax credit claims and corrections to over-estimated relief).

[**9B**— (1) For the purposes of the following sub-paragraphs, regard a completed calendar year as one for which 31st December is passed and an incompleted calendar year as one for which 31st December is not passed.

(2) The reconciliation day for a completed calendar year is the earlier of—

(*a*) the first day of the month in the subsequent calendar year in which regulation 3(2) of the Climate Change Levy (Combined Heat and Power Stations) Exemption Certificate Regulations 2001 is met in relation to the station in question (current CHPQA certificate sent to Secretary of State by 30th June);

(*b*) the 60th day after any day in the subsequent calendar year on which the station's exemption certificate is revoked pursuant to regulation 4(2) of those Regulations (station ceases to operate, current CHPQA certificate not sent to Secretary of State by 30th June, or relevant written request to Secretary of State).

The "reconciliation span" relating to this reconciliation day is the completed calendar year.

(3) A reconciliation day for an incompleted calendar year is the 60th day after any day in that incompleted calendar year on which the station's exemption certificate is revoked pursuant to regulation 4(2) of those Regulations.

The "reconciliation span" relating to any such reconciliation day spans 1st January in that calendar year to the day before that reconciliation day, inclusive.][1]

Amendments—[1] Paragraphs 9A–9C inserted by the Climate Change Levy (Miscellaneous Amendments) Regulations, SI 2005/1716 regs 5(*m*), 6 with effect from 22 July 2005. However, arrangements initiated or made before 22 July 2005 on the basis of SI 2001/838 Sch 1 para 5(5) or 5(6) as then in force remain subject to the provisions applicable when they were initiated or made (tax credit claims and corrections to over-estimated relief).

[9C— (1) The recipient must review the correctness of the supplier certificate no later than a reconciliation day in paragraph 9B.

This review is only in relation to that part of the recipient's relief percentage that is determined on the basis mentioned in paragraph 9A (taxable commodities supplied to combined heat and power stations).

(2) That correctness must be reviewed in relation to the efficiency percentage determined for the relevant reconciliation span (for determination of efficiency percentage, see regulations 3(2) and 6(2) of the Climate Change Levy (Combined Heat and Power Stations) Regulations 2005).

In the case of a reconciliation span for an incompleted calendar year, treat the actual efficiency percentage as one determined for the 12 month period preceding the relevant reconciliation day and as if that period was an Annual Operation (for Annual Operation, see regulation 51B(6)), but as zero for any time the exemption certificate stands revoked.

(3) The review must properly take into account—

(*a*) each quantity of taxable commodity supplied on the basis of the supplier certificate or certificates in question and not previously the subject of a review under this paragraph, and

(*b*) the actual efficiency percentage for the station in question at the time or times when that taxable commodity is supplied.

(4) Sub-paragraph (5) or (6) applies if the review demonstrates that the supplier certificate was incorrect as respects the taxable commodity referable to paragraph 15 of the Act (supplies to combined heat and power stations).

(5) If the CCL relief percentage applied was too low, the recipient may act in accordance with paragraphs 6 to 9 (recipient's tax credit for supply incorrectly made on basis of its being a taxable supply) (but only in relation to the taxable commodity referable to paragraph 15 of the Act—supplies to combined heat and power stations).

After 21st July 2005, and irrespective of when the supplies in question were made or other relevant events occurred, paragraph 5(5) does not apply where this paragraph applies.

(6) If the CCL relief percentage applied was too high, paragraphs 5(7) to [5(9F)][2] apply accordingly (deemed taxable self supplies, exemption from registration, payment of CCL due, etc).

(7) This paragraph only applies to supplies made after 31st December 2004, but not to those supplies in relation to which corresponding arrangements have been initiated or made before 22nd July 2005.

Corresponding arrangements are only—

(*a*) claims by the recipient for tax credits or similar repayments, or

(*b*) steps taken by the recipient to correct the position following a review demonstrating that a CCL relief percentage was too high (delivery of updated supplier certificate such that error corrected in one year, adjustment in CCL return, payment to Commissioners—see paragraph 5(6) as in force before 22nd July 2005).][1]

Amendments—[1] Paragraphs 9A–9C inserted by the Climate Change Levy (Miscellaneous Amendments) Regulations, SI 2005/1716 regs 5(*m*), 6 with effect from 22 July 2005. However, arrangements initiated or made before 22 July 2005 on the basis of SI 2001/838 Sch 1 para 5(5) or 5(6) as then in force remain subject to the provisions applicable when they were initiated or made (tax credit claims and corrections to over-estimated relief).

[2] In para (6) reference substituted for reference "5(9G)" by the Climate Change Levy (General) (Amendment) Regulations, SI 2007/2903 reg 2, Sch 1 para 38 with effect from 1 November 2007: SI 2007/2903 reg 1. These amendments do not apply in relation to a half-rate supply made before 1 April 2006: SI 2007/2903 reg 2, Sch 1 Note (a).

10 If and to the extent that they may be relevant for the purposes of this Schedule, regulations 19 to 25 (unjust enrichment: reimbursement arrangements to be disregarded) shall apply in relation to a tax credit provided for by this Schedule as if—

(*a*) the reference in regulation 19 to "claim" included a claim made under this Schedule; and

(*b*) the references in those regulations to "(recipient)" or "(recipients)" were not present.

11 No tax credit shall arise under Part II of these Regulations where provision for a tax credit is made in this Schedule.

Miscellaneous

12— (1) The recipient may deliver to the supplier a further certificate updating the information in the original supplier certificate in the light of actual or anticipated [events.][1]

(2) …[1]

(3) The supplier shall then apply the CCL relief percentage to any supplies he makes to which the updated supplier certificate relates and may, for this purpose, rely on the relevant recipient's relief percentage as updated.

(4) Paragraphs 5 (compulsory updates) and 6 (recipient's tax credits) have effect subject to any updates made by the recipient under this paragraph.

(5) Any provision of these Regulations, including this Schedule, that applies to or in relation to a supplier certificate shall apply to or in relation to such a supplier certificate as updated under this paragraph.

Amendments—[1] Words in para (1) substituted, and para (2) revoked, by the Climate Change Levy (Miscellaneous Amendments) Regulations, SI 2005/1716 regs 5(*n*), (*o*), 6 with effect from 22 July 2005. However, arrangements initiated or made before 22 July 2005 on the basis of SI 2001/838 Sch 1 para 5(5) or 5(6) as then in force remain subject to the provisions applicable when they were initiated or made (tax credit claims and corrections to over-estimated relief).

13— (1) Where a recipient changes supplier, any supplier certificate delivered to any earlier supplier (and any supporting analysis document) shall not have effect in relation to supplies from the later supplier.

[(1A) Where a supplier changes under paragraph (1) without the recipient's active participation and the supplier certificate and supporting analysis document are transferred to the later supplier—

(*a*) continuity is preserved for all CCL purposes in relation to the change, and

(*b*) the certificate and document are deemed to have been originally given by the recipient to that later supplier.

If there is no such transfer, the supplier certificate and supporting analysis document shall not have effect in relation to supplies from the later supplier.][1]

(2) [In the case of sub-paragraph (1) or if continuity is not preserved in the case of sub-paragraph (1A),][1] paragraphs 5 to 11 shall apply in relation to the combined effect of the supplier certificate the recipient delivered to the earlier supplier and the supplier certificate he delivers to the later supplier.

Amendments—[1] Sub-para (1A) inserted, and words in sub-para (2) substituted, by the Climate Change Levy (Miscellaneous Amendments) Regulations, SI 2005/1716 regs 5(*p*), (*q*), 6 with effect from 22 July 2005. However, arrangements initiated or made before 22 July 2005 on the basis of SI 2001/838 Sch 1 para 5(5) or 5(6) as then in force remain subject to the provisions applicable when they were initiated or made (tax credit claims and corrections to over-estimated relief).

14— (1) A supplier to whom a supplier certificate is delivered shall, within 90 days starting with the day after it is delivered, deliver to the Commissioners in writing a summary of the information contained in that certificate.

(2) The supplier shall include in that summary—

(*a*) such information as is necessary to identify the recipient in question,

(*b*) such information as is necessary to identify each address to which the supplies in question are supplied, and

(*c*) the relevant recipient's relief percentage and, if different, the CCL relief percentage actually applied by the supplier to the supplies in question.

15 A recipient who delivers a supplier certificate shall—

(*a*) retain a copy for a period of six years starting with the time of supply of the final supply to which it relates,

(*b*) retain any relevant analysis document for a period of six years starting with the time of supply of the final supply to which it relates, and

(*c*) make a copy of any such certificate and analysis document available to the Commissioners on request.

[**16** A supplier certificate ceases to be valid for the purposes of regulation 34, 35 or 36 on the 5th anniversary of its implementation date (about which, see regulation 37(6)).][1]

Amendments—[1] Paragraph 16 inserted by the Climate Change Levy (Miscellaneous Amendments) Regulations, SI 2005/1716 regs 5(*r*), 6 with effect from 22 July 2005. However, arrangements initiated or made before 22 July 2005 on the basis of SI 2001/838 Sch 1 para 5(5) or 5(6) as then in force remain subject to the provisions applicable when they were initiated or made (tax credit claims and corrections to over-estimated relief).

[SCHEDULE 2

THE CHP RELIEF CONDITION

Regulation 51H(1)]

Amendments—This Schedule inserted by the CCL (General) (Amendment) Regulations, SI 2003/604 regs 2, 22 with effect from 1 April 2003.

[Introduction

1 These obligations are for the purpose of ensuring the correct application of CCL to the outputs of a fully exempt or a partly exempt combined heat and power station.][1]

Amendments—[1] This paragraph inserted by the CCL (General) (Amendment) Regulations, SI 2003/604 regs 2, 22 with effect from 1 April 2003.

[CHP LEC and outputs record

2 A person to whom regulation 51H(1) applies must for the purposes of that regulation keep and maintain a discrete, proper, accurate and true record (the "CHP outputs record") of—

(*a*) any relevant supply of electricity constituting an output of the station in question for the purposes of paragraph 15(1) of the Act (supplies to stations);

(*b*) any relevant supply in relation to which CCL is not accounted for because of an exemption provided for by paragraph 16(2), 17(3) or 17(4) of the Act (supplies from partly exempt CHP and self-supplies);

(*c*) any relevant supply in relation to which CCL is not accounted for because of an exemption provided for by paragraph 17(2) of the Act (self-supply by autogenerator) (but only if the electricity in question is QPO electricity).][1]

Amendments—[1] This paragraph inserted by the CCL (General) (Amendment) Regulations, SI 2003/604 regs 2, 22 with effect from 1 April 2003.

[**3**— (1) That record must also identify separately, according to the following categories, each MWh of QPO electricity that is an output of the station in question and allocate to each such MWh a CHP LEC issued in respect of QPO electricity.

(2) The categories are—

(*a*) self-supplies of the electricity;

(*b*) supplies made to the person who consumes the electricity;

(*c*) supplies made to a person who makes a supply of the electricity.

(3) A CHP LEC (or any part of it) that remains allocated to a supply must not be allocated to any other supply.

(4) The allocation must be made no later than the [end of the second month following the one in which the CHP LEC is issued][2].

(5) Any restricted CHP LEC must be identified as such in the record no later than the 30th day after the one on which the notification that the relevant Authority has restricted its validity to indirect supplies is received (see regulation 51D and paragraph 11(5)).][1]

Amendments—[1] This paragraph inserted by the CCL (General) (Amendment) Regulations, SI 2003/604 regs 2, 22 with effect from 1 April 2003.

[2] Words in sub-para (4) substituted by the Climate Change Levy (Miscellaneous Amendments) Regulations, SI 2005/1716 regs 6, 7(8) with effect from 22 July 2005. However, arrangements initiated or made before 22 July 2005 on the basis of SI 2001/838 Sch 1 para 5(5) or 5(6) as then in force remain subject to the provisions applicable when they were initiated or made (tax credit claims and corrections to over-estimated relief).

[**4** That record must also show the quantity of all electricity that is an output of the station in question but in relation to which no CHP LEC is issued (including for this purpose, and discretely identified, any renewable source electricity (see Part IV) or electricity produced when no exemption certificate is in force for the station).][1]

Amendments—[1] This paragraph inserted by the CCL (General) (Amendment) Regulations, SI 2003/604 regs 2, 22 with effect from 1 April 2003.

[**5** That record must show—

(*a*) when each relevant supply of electricity is treated as taking place and the recipient of each such supply;

(*b*) the CHP LEC (if any) relating to that electricity and, if different from the recipient, the identity of any person to whom entitlement to the CHP LEC is transferred;

(*c*) the date (or dates) on which each other event to which it relates occurs;

(*d*) the date on which each entry to the record is made.][1]

Amendments—[1] This paragraph inserted by the CCL (General) (Amendment) Regulations, SI 2003/604 regs 2, 22 with effect from 1 April 2003.

[**6** That record must be kept for 6 years starting from each reconciliation day to which it is relevant (see paragraphs 10 and 13(3)).][1]

Amendments—[1] This paragraph inserted by the CCL (General) (Amendment) Regulations, SI 2003/604 regs 2, 22 with effect from 1 April 2003.

[**7** Subject to paragraph 6, that record must be made available on request and at any reasonable time to a person authorised by—

(*a*) the Secretary of State, or

(*b*) the relevant Authority.][1]

Amendments—[1] This paragraph inserted by the CCL (General) (Amendment) Regulations, SI 2003/604 regs 2, 22 with effect from 1 April 2003.

[8— [(1) This paragraph only applies whilst the relevant Authority has information on the basis of which it reasonably believes that the person mentioned in paragraph 2 is not fully complying with the CHP outputs record requirements in paragraphs 2 to 7.][2]

(2) The relevant Authority [must][2] refuse to certify or issue any CHP LEC in relation to electricity produced in the station (see regulations 51B(1) and 51B(8)).

(3) The relevant Authority [must][2] also restrict the validity of any relevant and as yet unrestricted CHP LEC to indirect supplies, in which case the relevant Authority must as soon as practicable notify that restriction to the person to whom it was issued (see regulation 51B(8)).

A CHP LEC is relevant for this purpose if it has not been reconciled in accordance with this Schedule (see paragraph 13(1)).][1]

Amendments—[1] This paragraph inserted by the CCL (General) (Amendment) Regulations, SI 2003/604 regs 2, 22 with effect from 1 April 2003.

[2] Sub-para (1) and word in sub-paras (2), (3) substituted by the Climate Change Levy (Miscellaneous Amendments) Regulations, SI 2005/1716 regs 6, 7(9), (10) with effect from 22 July 2005. However, arrangements initiated or made before 22 July 2005 on the basis of SI 2001/838 Sch 1 para 5(5) or 5(6) as then in force remain subject to the provisions applicable when they were initiated or made (tax credit claims and corrections to over-estimated relief).

[Reconciliation of outputs

9 For the purposes of the following paragraphs, regard a completed calendar year as one for which 31 December is passed and an incompleted calendar year as one for which 31 December is not passed.][1]

Amendments—[1] This paragraph inserted by the CCL (General) (Amendment) Regulations, SI 2003/604 regs 2, 22 with effect from 1 April 2003.

[10— (1) The reconciliation day for a completed calendar year is the earlier of—

(*a*) the first day of the month in the subsequent calendar year in which regulation 3(2) of the Climate Change Levy (Combined Heat and Power Stations) Exemption Certificate Regulations 2001 is met in relation to the station (current CHPQA certificate sent to Secretary of State by 30 June);

(*b*) the day in the subsequent calendar year on which revocation of the current exemption certificate takes effect pursuant to regulation 4(2) of those Regulations (station ceases to operate, current CHPQA certificate not sent to Secretary of State by 30 June, or relevant written request to Secretary of State).

The "reconciliation span" relating to this reconciliation day spans 1 January in the completed calendar year to the day before the reconciliation day, inclusive.

(2) A reconciliation day for an incompleted calendar year is any day in that incompleted calendar year on which revocation of the current exemption certificate takes effect pursuant to regulation 4(2) of those Regulations.

The "reconciliation span" relating to any such reconciliation day spans 1 January in that calendar year to the day before that reconciliation day, inclusive.

(3) The relevant Authority shall act in accordance with paragraph 11 no later than the 90th day following a reconciliation day, subject as appropriate to regulations 51C and 51D (relevant Authority neither certifying electricity nor issuing CHP LEC, or relevant Authority dealing with incorrect certification).

(4) A reconciliation day in paragraph (2) may arise irrespective of any overlap between the reconciliation span in that paragraph with the reconciliation span in paragraph (1).][1]

Amendments—[1] This paragraph inserted by the CCL (General) (Amendment) Regulations, SI 2003/604 regs 2, 22 with effect from 1 April 2003.

[11— (1) The relevant Authority shall determine whether insufficient or excessive CHP LECs have been issued and remain unrestricted as respects each reconciliation span, having proper regard to the difference between—

(*a*) the quantity of QPO electricity actually produced in the station during that reconciliation span, and

(*b*) the quantity of QPO electricity represented by the CHP LECs issued as respects electricity produced in the station during that reconciliation span and remaining unrestricted.

(2) If the relevant Authority determines that insufficient CHP LECs have been issued and remain unrestricted as respects a reconciliation span, it must—

(*a*) to the extent of that insufficiency, and

(*b*) as respects that reconciliation span,

issue additional CHP LECs (see regulation 51B(8)) as respects the QPO electricity outputs of the station.

Any such CHP LEC must, within 60 days of issue, be allocated by the person referred to in paragraph 2 to relevant and appropriate supplies identified in the record as taking place in that reconciliation span.

(3) If the relevant Authority determines that excessive CHP LECs have been issued and remain unrestricted as respects a reconciliation span, it must act in accordance with paragraphs (4) and (5), as appropriate.

(4) If the reconciliation day arises because regulation 3(2) of the Climate Change Levy (Combined Heat and Power Stations) Exemption Certificate Regulations 2001 is met (see paragraph 10(1)(*a*)), the relevant Authority must treat the excess CHP LECs as being prospectively referable to figures made known to it by the operator for the purposes of regulation 51B(2) as respects production in the station after the relevant reconciliation day.

(5) If the relevant reconciliation day arises because the exemption certificate is revoked (see paragraph 10(1)(*b*)), the relevant Authority must restrict the validity of any excess CHP LECs to indirect supplies, in which case it must as soon as practicable notify that restriction to the person to whom the CHP LEC in question was issued or to any person appearing to control the station (see regulation 51B(8)).

The relevant Authority must ensure that those CHP LECs remaining unrestricted afterwards (and not yet reconciled, see paragraph 13(1)) collectively represent QPO electricity produced in the station during the reconciliation span.

(6) For the purposes of this paragraph, the relevant Authority must regard calendar year 2003 as beginning on 1 April 2003.

(7) For the purposes of regulation 51B(6) (QPO electricity referable to calendar year), the relevant Authority must not regard electricity referable to before 1 April 2003 as QPO electricity.][1]

[(8) In the case of electricity and a station to which this paragraph applied before 22nd July 2005 but not after 21st July 2005 (see regulation 51A(2)), the relevant Authority must treat 22nd July 2005 as a reconciliation day for an incompleted calendar year running from 1st January to 21st July 2005 inclusive (the "reconciliation span").

The determination in sub-paragraph (1) must be made on the basis that a partly exempt station's annual limit for that incompleted calendar year is the former limit multiplied by the fraction with a numerator of 202 and a denominator of 365.

For these purposes, the "former limit" is the one in force on 1st January 2005 under regulation 5(2) of the Climate Change Levy (Combined Heat and Power Stations) Prescribed Conditions and Efficiency Percentages Regulations 2001.][2]

Amendments—[1] This paragraph inserted by the CCL (General) (Amendment) Regulations, SI 2003/604 regs 2, 22 with effect from 1 April 2003.

[2] Sub-para (8) inserted by the Climate Change Levy (Miscellaneous Amendments) Regulations, SI 2005/1716 regs 6, 7(11) with effect from 22 July 2005. However, arrangements initiated or made before 22 July 2005 on the basis of SI 2001/838 Sch 1 para 5(5) or 5(6) as then in force remain subject to the provisions applicable when they were initiated or made (tax credit claims and corrections to over-estimated relief).

[Monitoring and balancing obligation

12— (1) The CHP outputs record must never show or indicate as respects a reconciliation span—

(*a*) a deficit of unrestricted CHP LECs in relation to the total quantity of QPO electricity identified in the record pursuant to paragraph 3(2)(*a*) and 3(2)(*b*) (self-supplies and supplies to consumers);

(*b*) a deficit of unrestricted plus restricted CHP LECs in relation to the total quantity of QPO electricity identified pursuant to paragraph 3(2)(*a*), 3(2)(*b*) and 3(2)(*c*) (self-supplies, supplies to consumers and supplies to others).

(2) Each deficit representing 1 MWh shall be regarded as a separate breach of this paragraph for the purposes of regulation 60(1)(*hb*) (penalties).

(3) Paragraph (1) has effect subject to paragraphs 3(4), 3(5), 11(2) and 11(5).

(4) Paragraph (1) continues to apply after a CHP LEC is reconciled (see paragraph 13(1)).][1]

Amendments—[1] This paragraph inserted by the CCL (General) (Amendment) Regulations, SI 2003/604 regs 2, 22 with effect from 1 April 2003.

[Interpretation

13— (1) A CHP LEC is "reconciled" for the purposes of this Schedule only if—

(*a*) it is the subject of a reconciliation span in relation to which the relevant Authority has performed its functions under paragraph 10(3), and

(*b*) it is allocated, if required, in accordance with paragraph 11(2).

(2) A CHP LEC the validity of which is restricted under paragraph 8(3) or 11(5) may be regarded as a restricted CHP LEC for the purposes of regulations 51I to 51M.

(3) The CHP outputs record is relevant to a reconciliation day to the extent that it records (or is required to record) events taking place during the reconciliation span relating to that reconciliation day (see paragraphs 6, 10(1) and 10(2)).

(4) See also regulation 51A.][1]

Amendments—[1] This paragraph inserted by the CCL (General) (Amendment) Regulations, SI 2003/604 regs 2, 22 with effect from 1 April 2003.

2001/1136
Climate Change Levy (Electricity and Gas) Regulations 2001

Made by the Treasury and the Commissioners of Customs and Excise under FA 2000 s 30 and Sch 6 paras 14(2), 146(1), 146(7), 151(2) and 152(2)

Made . . . . 22 *March 2001*
Coming into force . . . . 1 *April 2001*

Citation and commencement

1 These Regulations may be cited as the Climate Change Levy (Electricity and Gas) Regulations 2001 and shall come into force on 1st April 2001.

Interpretation

2 In these Regulations—

"the Act" refers to Schedule 6 to the Finance Act 2000;
"CCL" refers to climate change levy;
"electricity supply licence" refers to a licence mentioned in paragraph 150(2)(*a*) or 150(2)(*b*) of the Act;
"gas" refers to gas described by paragraph 3(1)(*b*) of the Act;
"gas supply licence" refers to a licence mentioned in paragraph 150(3)(*a*) or 150(3)(*b*) of the Act.

Certain supplies by and to unregulated electricity suppliers and electricity utilities

3— (1) An unregulated electricity supplier (within the meaning of paragraph 151(8) of the Act) shall be treated for all CCL purposes as being an electricity utility to the extent of any supplies he makes in relation to which he is in breach of a requirement to hold an electricity supply licence.

(2) A holder of an electricity supply licence, who receives supplies of electricity in the course of acting otherwise than for purposes connected with the carrying on of activities authorised by that licence, shall be treated as being an electricity utility for the purposes of the CCL treatment under paragraph 5 of the Act of the supplies of electricity so received.

(3) In paragraph (1), "unregulated electricity supplier" includes the holder of an electricity supply licence acting otherwise than for the purposes connected with the carrying on of activities authorised by that licence.

Certain supplies of electricity by electricity utilities

4— (1) A person who is an electricity utility shall be treated for the purposes of the CCL chargeable under paragraph 5(1) of the Act (CCL on supplies of electricity) as not being an electricity utility to the extent of any part of a supply he makes of electricity—

(*a*) produced in a fully exempt combined heat and power station, and
(*b*) not supplied to him at any time by another person.

(2) Where an electricity utility makes a supply of electricity on which CCL would be chargeable, but for this paragraph, under both paragraph 5(1) and either paragraph 5(2) or 5(3) of the Act—

(*a*) that electricity utility shall be treated, for the purposes of the CCL chargeable under paragraph 5(1), as not being an electricity utility to the extent of that supply, and
(*b*) CCL shall, accordingly, only be chargeable on that supply under paragraph 5(2) or 5(3).

Supplies to exempt unlicensed electricity suppliers

5— (1) The description of exempt unlicensed electricity supplier prescribed for the purposes of paragraph 14(2) of the Act (exemption: certain supplies to electricity producers) is that given in paragraph (2) of this regulation.

(2) The description referred to in paragraph (1) of this regulation is any exempt unlicensed electricity supplier who—

(*a*) meets the description in paragraph 14(4) of the Act, and
(*b*) is not an auto-generator.

Autogenerators: requirements for electricity produced to be taken as for own consumption

6 Electricity shall only be taken as produced primarily for a person's own consumption for the purposes of paragraph 152(1) of the Act (autogenerators) if it fulfils both of the following requirements at the time it is produced—

(*a*) it must not be produced by an electricity utility or by a person treated as such for the purposes of any supplies of electricity he makes;
(*b*) it must not be produced by a person who has consumed, in the preceding 3 months, less than 75 per cent of the electricity produced by him in that period.

Certain supplies by and to unregulated gas suppliers and gas utilities

7— (1) An unregulated gas supplier (within the meaning of paragraph 151(8) of the Act) shall be treated for all CCL purposes as being a gas utility to the extent of any supplies he makes in relation to which he is in breach of a requirement to hold a gas supply licence.

(2) An unregulated gas supplier (within the meaning of paragraph 151(8) of the Act) shall be treated for all CCL purposes as being a gas utility to the extent that any part of his supplies of gas fall within the exception provided for by paragraph 5 of Schedule 2A to the Gas Act 1986 (exception to prohibition on unlicensed activities for supplies to very large consumers).

(3) A holder of a gas supply licence, who receives supplies of gas in the course of acting otherwise than for purposes connected with the carrying on of activities authorised by that licence, shall be treated as being a gas utility for the purposes of the CCL treatment under paragraph 6 of the Act of the supplies of gas so received.

(4) A holder of a gas supply licence who is not an electricity utility, and who receives supplies of gas and uses that gas to produce electricity, shall be treated as being an electricity utility for the purposes of the CCL treatment under paragraph 5 of the Act of any supplies he makes of the electricity so produced.

(5) In this regulation, "unregulated gas supplier" includes the holder of a gas supply licence acting otherwise than for purposes connected with the carrying on of activities authorised by that licence.

2001/1137
Climate Change Levy (Solid Fuel) Regulations 2001

Made by the Treasury under FA 2000 s 30, Sch 6 paras 3(3), 146(1) and 146(7)

Made . . . . *22 March 2001*
Coming into force . . . . *1 April 2001*

1 These Regulations may be cited as the Climate Change Levy (Solid Fuel) Regulations 2001 and shall come into force on 1st April 2001.

2— (1) Solid fuel is not a taxable commodity for the purposes of Schedule 6 to the Finance Act 2000 if—

(*a*) a supply of that solid fuel would otherwise be chargeable with CCL, but
(*b*) at the time when that supply would be treated as taking place the solid fuel in question has an open market value not exceeding £15 per tonne.

(2) In this regulation—

"CCL" refers to climate change levy;
"solid fuel" refers only to coal and lignite; coke, and semi-coke, of coal or lignite; petroleum coke;
"time when the supply would be treated as taking place" refers to the time of supply determined by or under paragraphs 25 to 39 of Schedule 6 to the Finance Act 2000;
"open market value" refers to the amount that would, by virtue of sections 19(2) and 19(5) of the Value Added Tax Act 1994 and on the basis that no CCL is chargeable, fall to be taken as the value of a supply of that solid fuel for the purposes of value added tax if the supply were for such consideration in money as would be payable by a person standing in no such relationship with any person as would affect that consideration.

2001/1138
Climate Change Levy (Use as Fuel) Regulations 2001

Made by the Treasury under FA 2000 s 30 and Sch 6 paras 18(2), 18(3), 146(1) and 146(7) of Schedule 6 to the Finance Act 2000

Made . . . . *22 March 2001*
Coming into force . . . . *1 April 2001*

Amendment—These regulations are revoked by the Climate Change Levy (Fuel Use and Recycling Processes) Regulations, SI 2005/1715 reg 5 with effect from 22 July 2005.

2001/1139
Climate Change Agreements (Energy-intensive Installations) Regulations 2001

Made by the Treasury under FA 2000 Sch 6 para 52

Made . . . . *22 March 2001*
Coming into force in accordance with regulation 1

Citation and commencement

1 These Regulations may be cited as the Climate Change Agreements (Energy-intensive Installations) Regulations 2001 and shall come into force on the day after the day on which they are made.

Amendment of paragraph 51 of Schedule 6 to the Finance Act 2000

2— (1) Paragraph 51 of Schedule 6 to the Finance Act 2000 (Energy-intensive installations) has effect subject to the following amendments.

(2) For sub-paragraph (2) substitute—

"(2) Sub-paragraph (2A) applies where—

(*a*) an installation falls within any one or more of those descriptions, and

(*b*) there is, on the same site as the installation, a location at which ancillary activities are carried out.

(2A) The installation (taken alone) is not covered by this paragraph, but the combination—

(*a*) of the installation and that location, or

(*b*) where there is more than one such location, of the installation and all of those locations,

is to be taken as being an installation covered by this paragraph.

(2B) In sub-paragraph (2) "ancillary activities" means activities that—

(*a*) are directly associated with any of the primary activities carried out in the installation,

(*b*) have a technical connection with those primary activities, and

(*c*) could have an effect on environmental pollution."

(3) In sub-paragraph (3), for "sub-paragraphs (1) and (2)" substitute "sub-paragraphs (1) to (2B)".

(4) Omit sub-paragraphs (4) and (5).

(5) In sub-paragraph (6), for "sub-paragraph (4)" substitute "sub-paragraph (2B)".

(6) In the Table, for entries 1 to 33 (and the italic cross-headings) there is substituted—

"Installations regulated under the Pollution Prevention and Control (England and Wales) Regulations 2000 (SI 2000/1973)

1 Part A installations.

Installations that would be so regulated but for a threshold or exception

2 Installations that would be Part A installations but for—

(*a*) a relevant numeric threshold, or

(*b*) a relevant exception.

Installations that would be so regulated if certain modifications were made to the Regulations

3 Installations that would be Part A installations if the relevant modifications were made.

Corresponding installations in Scotland and Northern Ireland

4 Installations that are situated in Scotland or Northern Ireland, but if situated in England and Wales—

(*a*) would be Part A installations,

(*b*) would be Part A installations but for—

(i) a relevant numeric threshold, or

(ii) a relevant exception, or

(*c*) would be Part A installations if the relevant modifications were made.

Interpretation of entries 1 to 4

5— (1) In this entry "the Schedule" means Schedule 1 to the Pollution Prevention and Control (England and Wales) Regulations 2000.

(2) In entries 1 to 4—

(*a*) "Part A installation" has the meaning given in Part 3 of the Schedule;

(*b*) "relevant exception" means—

(i) the exception in paragraph (*b*)(i) of Part A(1) of Section 2.1 of Part 1 of the Schedule,

(ii) the exceptions in paragraph (*c*) of Part A(1) of Section 5.1 of Part 1 of the Schedule for activities falling within Part B of that Section and for the incineration of specified hazardous waste in an exempt incineration plant, or

(iii) the exception in paragraph (*e*) of Part A(1) of Section 5.1 of Part 1 of the Schedule for incineration as part of a Part B activity in so far as this exception relates to the activities referred to in paragraphs (*a*) and (*b*) of Part B of that Section;

(*c*) "the relevant modifications" means the omission of the following provisions of Part 1 of the Schedule:

(i) the final twelve words of paragraph (*b*) of Part A(1) of Section 4.4;

(ii) the final twelve words of paragraph (*b*) of Part A(1) of Section 4.5;

(iii) paragraph 1 of the Interpretation of Part A(1) of Section 5.4;

(iv) the final fourteen words of paragraph (*c*) of Part A(1) of Section 6.1;

(v) the final fourteen words of paragraph (*c*) of Part A(1) of Section 6.4; and

(vi) the final fourteen words of paragraph (*f*)(ii) of Part A(1) of Section 6.8; and

(*d*) "relevant numeric threshold" means a numeric threshold specified in any of the following provisions of Part 1 of the Schedule:

(i) paragraphs (*c*) and (*d*) of Part A(1) of Section 2.1;
(ii) Part A(2) of Section 2.1;
(iii) paragraph (*b*) of Part A(1) of Section 2.2;
(iv) Part A(1) of Section 2.3;
(v) paragraph (*b*) of Part A(1) of Section 3.1;
(vi) paragraph (*b*) of Part A(2) of Section 3.1;
(vii) paragraph (*b*) of Part A(1) of Section 3.3;
(viii) Part A(2) of Section 3.3;
(ix) paragraph (*a*) of Part A(1) of Section 3.4;
(x) Part A(2) of Section 3.6;
(xi) paragraphs (*c*) and (*d*) of Part A(1) of Section 4.1;
(xii) paragraphs (*d*) and (*e*) of Part A(1) of Section 5.1;
(xiii) Part A(1) of Section 5.2;
(xiv) Part A(1) of Section 5.3;
(xv) paragraph (*c*) of Part A(1) of Section 5.4;
(xvi) paragraph (*b*) of Part A(1) of Section 6.1;
(xvii) Part A(1) of Section 6.3;
(xviii) paragraphs (*a*) and (*b*) of Part A(1) of Section 6.4;
(xix) Part A(2) of Section 6.4;
(xx) Part A(2) of Section 6.7;
(xxi) paragraphs (*a*) to (*e*) of Part A(1) of Section 6.8;
(xxii) Part A(2) of Section 6.8; and
(xxiii) Part A(1) of Section 6.9; and

(*e*) any reference to a part of the United Kingdom includes the territorial waters adjacent to that part."

2001/1140
Climate Change Levy (Combined Heat and Power Stations) Prescribed Conditions and Efficiency Percentages Regulations 2001

Amendment—These regulations revoked by the Climate Change Levy (Combined Heat and Power Stations) Regulations, SI 2005/1714 reg 8 with effect from 22 July 2005.

2005/1714
Climate Change Levy (Combined Heat and Power Stations) Regulations 2005

Made by the Treasury under FA 2000 s 30, Sch 6 paras 15(4), 16(2), 16(3), 146(7), 147, 148(4), 148(7), 148(8), 148(9), 149(1), 149(2) and 149(3)

Made . . . . *21 July 2005*
Coming into force in accordance with regulation 1

Preliminary

1 These Regulations may be cited as the Climate Change Levy (Combined Heat and Power Stations) Regulations 2005 and shall come into force on the day after the day on which they are made.

2— (1) In these Regulations—

"the Act" refers to Schedule 6 to the Finance Act 2000;
"CCL" refers to climate change levy;
"CHPQA" refers to the Combined Heat and Power Quality Assurance Standard, Issue 1, November 2000 originally published by the Department for the Environment, Transport and the Regions (the "Standard") (including the later of version Final 1.0 or 2.0 of CHPQA Guidance Notes 0 to 4 (including 2(S), 3(S) and 4(S)), 10 to 28 and 30);
"station" refers to a combined heat and power station or, in appropriate circumstances, to combined heat and power stations forming at least part of a single CHP Scheme.

(2) But, for the purposes of regulation 3(2), "CHPQA" refers to the current issue of that Standard and current versions of those and any subsequent Guidance Notes.

An issue or version is current for these purposes to the extent that it is neither varied, replaced nor revoked by another issue or version.

(3) These Regulations must be applied in a way consistent with the CHPQA and paragraph (2).

But, for the purposes of regulations 3(2) and 4, any reference in the CHPQA to any relevant "registered" quantity (whether or not mentioned in either regulation) must be treated as a reference to the actual quantity of that name for determination and calculation in accordance with the CHPQA.

That determination and calculation must be on the basis of events in relation to the given station during the given Annual Operation (for "Annual Operation", see CHPQA Section 4—1st January to 31st December).

Supplies to combined heat and power stations: exemption for inputs

3— (1) A station's threshold efficiency percentage is set as 20 per cent (see paragraphs 15(2)(*b*), 15(3)(*b*) and 15(4)(*a*) of the Act).

(2) A station's efficiency percentage for a given Annual Operation is its Power Efficiency in relation to that Operation (see paragraphs 15(4)(*b*), 149(1) and 149(2)(*e*) of the Act and Section 5.6 of the Standard).

Supplies from partly exempt combined heat and power stations: exemption for outputs

4 The limit (see paragraph 16(2) of the Act) on the quantity of electricity that may be produced in and supplied from a partly exempt station exempt from CCL for a given Annual Operation is its CHP Qualifying Power Output in relation to that Operation (see Section 5.8 of the Standard).

Fully exempt combined heat and power stations: conditions to be satisfied for full-exemption certificate

5— (1) The condition to be satisfied in relation to a station for the purpose of the Secretary of State giving a full-exemption certificate is as follows (see paragraph 148(4) of the Act).

(2) The station's Quality Index as determined and calculated in accordance with the CHPQA must at least meet the Threshold Quality Index Criterion specified for that station in the CHPQA (see Sections 5.5 and 4 of the Standard).

Transitional provisions: inputs efficiency percentage and outputs partly exempt limit

6— (1) Paragraph (2) applies only if regulations 2(2) and 2(3) result in more than one issue of the Standard or version of a Guidance Note being current during the Annual Operation in question and, if they are treated as separately current for the whole Annual Operation, this yields different efficiency percentages for the purposes of regulation 3(2).

(2) The efficiency percentage in regulation 3(2) is then the weighted mean of those different efficiency percentages.

The weighting must reflect the proportion of fuel input to the station during the period in relation to which the relevant issue or version is current.

That proportion must be calculated relative to the station's actual total fuel input for the Annual Operation in question.

7— (1) Paragraph (2) applies only if regulation 4 results in a limit ("A") for calendar year 2005 that is less than the limit ("B") that would have applied for that year under regulation 5(2) of the Climate Change Levy (Combined Heat and Power Stations) Prescribed Conditions and Efficiency Percentages Regulations 2001.

(2) The limit in regulation 4 for 2005 is then the following sum.

$$\left[\frac{X \times A}{365}\right] + \left[\frac{Y \times B}{365}\right]$$

X = 365 −Y

Y = the number of days elapsed for 2005 up to and including the day these Regulations are made.

Revocations

8 The Climate Change Levy (Combined Heat and Power Stations) Prescribed Conditions and Efficiency Percentages Regulations 2001 and the Climate Change Levy (Combined Heat and Power Stations) Prescribed Conditions and Efficiency Percentages (Amendment) Regulations 2003 are revoked.

2005/1715

Climate Change Levy (Fuel Use and Recycling Processes) Regulations 2005

Made . . . . 21st July 2005

Coming into force in accordance with regulation 1

Made by the Treasury under FA 2000 s 30 and Sch 6 paras 18(2), 18(3), 18A(1), 18A(7), 146(7) and 147 to the Finance Act 2000

Citation and commencement

1 These Regulations may be cited as the Climate Change Levy (Fuel Use and Recycling Processes) Regulations 2005 and shall come into force on the day after the day on which they are made.

Interpretation

2 In these Regulations—

"the Act" refers to Schedule 6 to the Finance Act 2000;
"CCL" refers to climate change levy.

Use as fuel or otherwise

3 For the purposes of paragraph 18(1) of the Act (CCL exemption if commodity supplied for non-fuel use)—

(*a*) the uses of a taxable commodity that are specified in Schedule 1 to these Regulations are not to be taken as being uses of that commodity as fuel; and
(*b*) any uses of a taxable commodity that are not specified in Schedule 1 are specified by this paragraph as uses that are to be taken as being uses of that commodity as fuel.

Recycling processes

4 The recycling processes described in Schedule 2 to these Regulations are prescribed for the purposes of paragraph 18A(1) of the Act (CCL exemption if commodity supplied for use in recycling process for which there is a relevant competing process, see paragraph 18A(2) of the Act).

Revocations

5 The Climate Change Levy (Use as Fuel) Regulations 2001 and the Climate Change Levy (Use as Fuel) (Amendment) Regulations 2003 are revoked.

SCHEDULE 1

USES OTHERWISE THAN AS FUEL

Regulation 3(*a*)

A WHOLLY NON-FUEL USES

1 Electricity in electrolysis for the production of:

Fluorine
Chloroalkali (chlorine, caustic soda and caustic potash)
Hydrogen peroxide, persulphates, chlorates and peroxyorganic acids by electro-oxidation
Aluminium
Copper
Basic materials directly from an ore or other compound (electrowinning)
Advanced chemicals from other more basic chemicals

2 Electricity in the following types of electrolysis:

Electro-organic synthesis of fine organics and intermediates such as adiponitrile
Gold and silver electrolysis, and the electrolytic dissolution of platinum group metal alloys and alkali earth metals such as sodium, potassium, lithium and calcium
Electrolysis to purify materials (as distinct from electrowinning)
Electrolysis in refining tin or copper from impure metals or ingots
Electrolysis involving sodium chlorate, potassium permanganate, potassium dichromate, managanese dioxide, cuprous oxide, sorbitol, fatty alcohols

3 Electricity in battery formation

4 Natural gas as feedstock to produce hydrogen and for hydrogenation reactions

5 Natural gas in the production of hydrogen and carbon monoxide for the reduction and subsequent purification of nickel

6 Natural gas as a feedstock in producing acetic acid and acetic anhydride by a partial oxidation process

7 Natural gas to provide carbon in producing carbon-carbon composites

8 Natural gas in manufacturing sodium cyanide

9 Natural gas and propane in steam reformers to produce a mixture of hydrogen and carbon monoxide in the production of:

Fertilisers
OXO (Oxonation) chemicals—detergent and plasticiser alcohols
Phosgene
Ammonia
Higher alcohols, synthetic fuels, plastics precursors
Methanol, methyl tertiary butyl ether, formaldehyde, formic acid, acetic acid, methyl amines, single cell proteins

10 Methane as a feedstock in producing higher paraffins and their derivatives

11 Liquefied petroleum gas as a propellant in aerosols

12 Liquefied petroleum gas as feedstock in the cracking process to produce lower olefins

13 Lower olefins as feedstock for conversion by chemical processes

14 Propylene as feedstock in the manufacture of propan-2-ol (iso-propyl alcohol), polypropylene and cumene

15 Petroleum coke in the manufacture of carbon and graphite electrodes

16 Coke as a resistor in electro-thermal furnaces

17 Coke in the manufacture of titanium dioxide by the chloride process

B MIXED USES

These mixed uses are the only ones that involve relevant commodities being used partly as fuel and partly not, but which are specified as being uses that are not to be taken as being uses of those commodities as fuel (see paragraph 18(3) of the Act).

18 Coal, coke and natural gas as chemical reductants for ironmaking, for example, in blast furnaces

19 Coal, coke and natural gas as chemical reductants in the blast furnace production of zinc and other non-ferrous metals

20 Coal and coke in the recarburising of iron and steel

21 Coke breeze in a sinter plant to assist in the agglomeration of iron ore and its subsequent chemical reduction in blast furnaces

22 Coke injected into electric arc furnaces to control the chemistry of the steel and the steelmaking slag

23 Coke charged to electric arc furnaces to control the oxygen activity of the steel melt

24 Coke as a carburiser in iron casting

25 Coke as a source of carbon dioxide in the Ammonia Soda process for producing soda ash

26 Anthracite as a reductant in the smelting of precious metals

27 Gas for vacuum reduction in metal powder production and to maintain carbon content in metal during the sintering process

28 Gas to maintain or increase the carbon content of metals during heat treatment

29 Natural gas as a reductant in emission control systems, for example, in the reduction of oxides of nitrogen

30 Natural gas in the manufacture of methocrylate monomers and polymers including that natural gas used for emission control which is an integral and essential part of the manufacturing process

31 Natural gas as feedstock in the production of carbon black

32 Natural gas as feedstock in a gas generator supplying a reducing atmosphere for the treatment or annealing of metal products

33 Liquid propane in the production of ethylene where heat is provided either by combustion of the waste products or from another source

34 Commodities in reduction furnaces for the production of lead

35 Commodities in the reduction of chlorine

36 Commodities to form reducing atmospheres, for example, in the refining and manipulation of molten copper to control oxygen levels

37 Commodities in ASARCO (American Smelting and Refining Company) shaft furnaces, the deoxidisation of copper swarf and the annealing of copper and copper alloys to provide a reducing atmosphere

SCHEDULE 2
RECYCLING PROCESSES

Regulation 4

Description

The preparation of scrap metal for recycling.

"Preparation" is only shredding, fragmentation, pre-treatment and melting of scrap.

"Scrap" is only—

(*a*) post–consumer scrap, namely, goods that have performed the function for which they were designed and have been discarded (for example, end of life road vehicles, discarded food cans, steel girders or rods from demolished buildings, worn out battery electrodes, discarded lead roofing);

(*b*) scrap generated from the process of which that preparation forms part or from a different process (for example, off–cuts from metal stampings, unmarketable goods).

"Metal" is only aluminium, lead or steel.

"Melting" is only—

(*a*) the pre-heating and first melting of scrap before casting into intermediates; or

(*b*) the heating of scrap as part of the recycling process before any solidification and re-melting.

It excludes melting of any type of non-scrap metal added to the recycling process to improve the quality or adjust the composition of the recycled metal or intermediates.

"Intermediates" are only items for further processing or re-melting, such as rolling slabs or ingots.

2006/59
Climate Change Agreements (Energy-intensive Installations) Regulations 2006

Made by the Treasury under FA 2000 s 30 and Sch 6 paras 52(1), 52(2)(*a*) and 146(7) and approved by a resolution of the House of Commons in accordance with para 146(3) of that Schedule

Made . . . . 18th January 2006

Coming into force in accordance with regulation 1

1 These Regulations may be cited as the Climate Change Agreements (Energy-intensive Installations) Regulations 2006 and come into force on the third day after the one on which they are made.

2— (1) The energy-intensive installations covered by the Finance Act 2000 Schedule 6 paragraph 51 ("paragraph 51") include any installation falling within any one or more of the descriptions of installation specified in the Schedule to these Regulations.

(2) But paragraph (3) applies where—

(*a*) an installation falls within any one or more of those descriptions, and

(*b*) there is, on the same site as that installation, at least one location at which ancillary activities are carried out.

(3) That installation (taken alone) is not covered by paragraph 51, but the combination of that installation and every such location is to be taken as an installation so covered.

(4) In paragraph (2), "ancillary activities" are only—

(*a*) those that are directly associated with any of the primary activities carried out in the installation,

(*b*) have a technical connection with those primary activities, and

(*c*) could have an effect on environmental pollution.

(5) In paragraph (4)—

"primary activities", in relation to an installation falling within any one or more of the descriptions of installation set out in the Schedule to these Regulations, refers to an activity the carrying out of which at the installation results in the installation falling within one or more of those descriptions;

"environmental pollution" bears the same meaning as in the Pollution Prevention and Control Act 1999.

Commentary—*De Voil Indirect Tax Service* **V21.142**.

SCHEDULE

DESCRIPTIONS OF ENERGY-INTENSIVE INSTALLATIONS INCLUDED AS COVERED BY THE FINANCE ACT 2000 SCHEDULE 6 PARAGRAPH 51

Regulation 2(1)

Each of the following descriptions includes a stipulation that the installation is a stationary technical unit (see the Finance Act 2000 Schedule 6 paragraph 50(6)) that does not fall within any one or more of the descriptions of installation set out in the Table in paragraph 51 of that Schedule.

1 An installation where—

(*a*) nitrogen, oxygen or argon is separated from air, and then compressed or liquefied;

(*b*) nitrogen, oxygen and argon are separated from air, and then made into a compressed or liquefied mixture of at least two of the former.

2 An installation where kaolinitic clay in combination with any of its accessory minerals are extracted and processed.

3 An installation where calcium carbonate based minerals are processed for use as filler or whitener for paper, plastics, pharmaceuticals, ceramics, food, paint or other products.

4 An installation where pre-formed or manufactured metal components are heat-treated to facilitate their efficient formability or to enhance their service performance.

5 An installation where (in controlled, environment-protected structures) horticultural crops are grown, harvested and receive primary preparation for market.

6 An installation where textiles are manufactured.

7 An installation where plastic film is produced using extrusion to convert melted polymer into blown or cast film.

[8 An installation not otherwise covered by paragraph 51 of Schedule 6 to the Finance Act 2000.][1]

Commentary—*De Voil Indirect Tax Service* **V21.142**.
Amendments—[1] Paragraph 8 inserted by Climate Change Agreements (Miscellaneous Amendments) Regulations, SI 2006/1848 reg 3, with effect from 12 July 2006.

2006/60
Climate Change Agreements (Eligible Facilities) Regulations 2006

Made . . . . *18th January 2006*
Laid before the House of Commons . . . . *20th January 2006*
Coming into force . . . . *21st January 2006*

The Secretary of State makes the following Regulations in exercise of the powers conferred by paragraphs 50(3), 50(4) and 146(7) of Schedule 6 to the Finance Act 2000—

Citation and Commencement

1 These Regulations may be cited as the Climate Change Agreements (Eligible Facilities) Regulations 2006 and shall come into force on 21st January 2006.

Interpretation

2 In these Regulations—

"eligible process" means a relevant process or activity or a combination of relevant processes or activities as described in the Schedule to these Regulations carried out at an installation or site which, when taken alone or together within the business sector to which the installation or site belongs, meets the energy intensity criteria specified in regulation 3;
"energy costs" means the actual cost of energy, including all taxes except deductible VAT, purchased or generated by the operator of the installation or site or by a business sector;
"import penetration ratio" means the value of imports as a percentage of the value of total sales in the United Kingdom (the latter to include the value of exports);
"installation" means any installation that is covered by paragraph 51 of Schedule 6 to the Finance Act 2000 by virtue of the Climate Change Agreements (Energy-intensive Installations) Regulations 2006;
"production value" means turnover, including subsidies, directly linked to the price of the product, plus or minus the changes in stock of finished products, work in progress and goods and services purchased for resale, minus the purchases of goods and services for resale;
"site" means a site on which there is an installation or part of an installation.

Eligible Facilities

3 (1) This regulation specifies the circumstances in which, for the purposes of determining in connection with concluding or varying a climate change agreement, an installation or site is to be or is to continue to be identified in a climate change agreement as a facility to which the agreement applies.

(2) An installation or a site shall be taken to be a facility for the purposes specified in paragraph (1) only if, at the time of entering into or last varying that climate change agreement—

(*a*) it is an "eligible facility" under the Climate Change Agreements (Eligible Facilities) Regulations 2001, and
(*b*) the installation or site where taxable commodities supplied by taxable supplies are intended to be burned (or in the case of electricity, consumed) over the following 12 month period satisfies the conditions set out in paragraph (3).

(3) The conditions referred to in paragraph (2)(*b*) are that—

(*a*) the installation or site meets the energy intensity criteria, or
(*b*) the installation or site belongs to a business sector that meets the energy intensity criteria, and

the taxable commodities referred to in paragraph (2)(*b*) will be used at the installation or site for the purpose of carrying out an eligible process.

(4) For the purpose of paragraph (3)(*a*) and (*b*) the energy intensity criteria will be met where, for the period referred to in paragraph (2)(*b*), the predicted energy costs—

(*a*) amount to 10% or more of the production value of the installation or site or business sector, or
(*b*) amount to 3% or more but less than 10% of the production value of the installation or site or business sector so long as there is an import penetration ratio of at least 50%.

(5) For the purpose of paragraph (4), the predicted energy costs for the period referred to in paragraph (2)(*b*) shall be determined by the energy costs and production value and import penetration data for the installation or site or business sector during the 12 month period immediately prior to entering into or last varying a climate change agreement.

Commentary—*De Voil Indirect Tax Service* **V21.142.**

[SCHEDULE
LIST OF RELEVANT PROCESSES AND ACTIVITIES

Regulation 2

1 At an installation or site where—

(*a*) nitrogen, oxygen or argon is separated from air, and then compressed or liquefied; or

(*b*) nitrogen, oxygen and argon are separated from air, and then made into a compressed or liquefied mixture of at least two of the former:

separating the above substances from air using one or more of the following air separation technologies: cryogenic distillation, pressure swing adsorption, vacuum swing absorption or membrane separation, compressing and liquefying the separated substances, pumping them (in a compressed or liquefied form) from within the installation for further use within or outside the installation.

2 At an installation or site where kaolinitic clay in combination with any of its accessory minerals is extracted and processed: blasting and crushing, dry mining or hydraulic mining, refining, blending, drying and packaging, classifying, hydrocloning, pumping, centrifuging, grinding, shredding, magnetic separating, bleaching, pressing, pugging, milling, micro-separating.

3 At an installation or site where calcium carbonate based minerals are processed for use as filler or whitener for paper, plastics, pharmaceuticals, ceramics, food, paint or other products: crushing, drying, milling, classifying, screening, packaging.

4 At an installation or site where pre-formed or manufactured metal components are heat-treated to facilitate their efficient formability or to enhance their service performance: all processes and activities involved in the heat treatment of pre-formed or manufactured metal components to facilitate their efficient formability or to enhance their service performance.

5 At an installation or site where (in controlled, environment-protected structures) horticultural crops are grown, harvested and receive primary preparation for market: planting, seeding, heating, lighting, ventilating, irrigating, fertilising, cooling, preparing and sterilising growing media, grading and conveying.

6 At an installation or site where textiles are manufactured: spinning, weaving, knitting, finishing but not printing or dyeing.

7 At an installation or site where plastic film is produced using extrusion to convert melted polymer into blown or cast film: all processes and activities involved in the production of plastic film using extrusion to convert melted polymer into blown or cast film.

8 At an installation or site where geosynthetic materials comprising at least one component made from a synthetic or natural polymer in the form of a sheet, strip or other three-dimensional structure are manufactured for use in geotechnical or civil engineering applications: all processes and activities involved in the manufacture of such materials.

9 At an installation or site where silica sand in combination with any associated minerals is extracted, processed and packaged: blasting, quarrying, crushing, classifying, milling, pumping, grinding, acid leaching, drying and packaging.

10 At an installation or site where potassium chloride is extracted, separated, and purified to produce potash and high-grade soluble potassium chloride: sub-surface mining of sylvinite and other halite minerals, separating potassium chloride from those minerals and purifying it including crushing, grinding, froth flotation, drying, compacting, grading and, where relevant, recrystallising it from supersaturated brine.

11 At an installation or site where glass products or chemicals using glass as a base material are produced from raw materials, pre-formed glass or cullet for use as reflective additives in road markings or as toughened glass for the automotive market: partial melting, fusing, bending, toughening, cutting, grinding, etching, polishing (both mechanical and chemical), surface treating and drying.

12 At an installation (which must be a building where the predominant business activity is commercial temperature controlled storage or product freezing) or site upon which there is such an installation where—

(*a*) products are cooled or frozen for the purposes of—

(i) storing them under controlled temperatures below ambient levels; or

(ii) producing ice; or

(*b*) products are stored under controlled temperatures below ambient levels:

cooling and freezing products and all processes and activities involved in controlling temperatures below ambient levels.][1]

Commentary—*De Voil Indirect Tax Service* **V21.142.**

Amendments—[1] Schedule substituted by the Climate Change Agreements (Eligible Facilities) (Amendment) Regulations, SI 2006/1931 art 2 with effect from 15 August 2006. Former Schedule previously read as follows—

"The relevant processes and activities are—

(1) at an installation or site where—

(*a*) nitrogen, oxygen or argon is separated from air, and then compressed or liquefied; or
(*b*) nitrogen, oxygen and argon are separated from air, and then made into a compressed or liquefied mixture of at least two of the former,

separating the above substances from air using one or more of the following air separation technologies: cryogenic distillation, pressure swing adsorption, vacuum swing absorption or membrane separation, compressing and liquefying the separated substances, pumping them (in a compressed or liquefied form) from within the installation for further use within or outside the installation;

(2) at an installation or site where kaolinitic clay in combination with any of its accessory minerals is extracted and processed, blasting and crushing, dry mining or hydraulic mining, refining, blending, drying and packaging, classifying, hydrocloning, pumping, centrifuging, grinding, shredding, magnetic separating, bleaching, pressing, pugging, milling, micro separating;

(3) at an installation or site where calcium carbonate based minerals are processed for use as filler or whitener for paper, plastics, pharmaceuticals, ceramics, food, paint or other products, crushing, drying, milling, classifying, screening, packaging;

(4) at an installation or site where pre-formed or manufactured metal components are heat-treated to facilitate their efficient formability or to enhance their service performance, all processes and activities involved in the heat treatment of pre-formed or manufactured metal components to facilitate their efficient formability or to enhance their service performance;

(5) at an installation or site where (in controlled, environment–protected structures) horticultural crops are grown, harvested and receive primary preparation for market, planting, seeding, heating, lighting, ventilating, irrigating, fertilising, cooling, preparing and sterilising growing media, grading and conveying;

(6) at an installation or site where textiles are manufactured, spinning, weaving, knitting, finishing but not printing or dyeing;

(7) at an installation or site where plastic film is produced using extrusion to convert melted polymer into blown or cast film, all processes and activities involved in the production of plastic film using extrusion to convert melted polymer into blown or cast film."

2007/2901

Finance Act 2006 (Climate Change Levy: Amendments and Transitional Savings in Consequence of Abolition of Half-rate Supplies) (Appointed Day) Order 2007

Made by the Treasury under FA 2006 ss 172(16) and 172(17)

Made . . . . 8th October 2007

1 This Order may be cited as the Finance Act 2006 (Climate Change Levy: Amendments and Transitional Savings in Consequence of Abolition of Half-rate Supplies) (Appointed Day) Order 2007.

2— (1) 1st November 2007 is appointed as the day on which sections 172(8) to 172(15) of the Finance Act 2006 come into force.

(2) The amendments to the Finance Act 2000 Schedule 6 (climate change levy) made by those sections do not apply in relation to a half-rate supply made before 1st April 2006.

(3) In or for the purposes of paragraph (2)—

(*a*) "half-rate supply" carries the meaning it has in that Schedule before 1st November 2007;
(*b*) sections 172(3) to 172(6) of the Finance Act 2006 (abolition of half-rate supplies etc) apply for determining when a supply is to be regarded as made.

(4) Regulations under paragraph 43 or 62 of that Schedule (half-rate for supplies to horticultural producers, and related tax credits) made before 1st November 2007 are unaffected by paragraph (1).

2007/2902

Finance Act 2007 (Climate Change Levy: Reduced-rate Supplies etc) (Appointed Day) Order 2007

Made by the Treasury under FA 2007 Schedule 2 paragraphs 13(1) and 13(3)

Made . . . . 8th October 2007

1 This Order may be cited as the Finance Act 2007 (Climate Change Levy: Reduced-rate Supplies etc) (Appointed Day) Order 2007.

2— (1) 1st November 2007 is appointed as the day on which Schedule 2 paragraphs 2 to 10 to the Finance Act 2007 come into force (climate change levy: reduced-rate supplies).

(2) The amendments made by paragraphs 7 and 10 of that Schedule only apply in relation to a supply actually made on or after that day.

(3) The amendment made by paragraph 9 of that Schedule only applies in relation to a supply actually made on or after that day and on the basis that it is a reduced-rate supply.

(4) In this article, "supply" and "reduced-rate supply" carry the respective meaning each has in the Finance Act 2000 Schedule 6 (climate change levy) on or after 1st November 2007.

2007/3538

Environmental Permitting (England and Wales) Regulations 2007

Made by the Secretary of State, in relation to England, and the Welsh Ministers, in relation to Wales, under the Pollution Prevention and Control Act 1999 s 2, Sch 1

Made . . . . 13 December 2007
Coming into force . . . . 6 April 2008

2 Interpretation: general

(1) Except where otherwise provided, in these Regulations—

"the 1990 Act" means the Environmental Protection Act 1990;

"the 1995 Act" means the Environment Act 1995;
"the 1994 Regulations" means the Waste Management Licensing Regulations 1994;
"the 2000 Regulations" means the Pollution Prevention and Control (England and Wales) Regulations 2000;
"activity" means, subject to Part 1 of Schedule 1, an activity listed in Part 2 of that Schedule;
"the Agency" means the Environment Agency;
"agricultural waste" means waste from premises used for agriculture within the meaning of the Agriculture Act 1947;
"appropriate authority" means—

(*a*) in relation to England, the Secretary of State, and
(*b*) in relation to Wales, the Welsh Ministers;

["the Batteries Directive" means Directive 2006/66/EC of the European Parliament and of the Council on batteries and accumulators and waste batteries and accumulators and repealing Directive 91/157/EEC;][1]
"directly associated activity" means—

(*a*) in relation to a SED activity, an operation which—

(i) has a technical connection with the SED activity,
(ii) is carried on on the same site as the SED activity, and
(iii) could have an effect on a discharge of volatile organic compounds into the environment;

(*b*) in relation to any other activity, an operation which—

(i) has a technical connection with the activity,
(ii) is carried on on the same site as the activity, and
(iii) could have an effect on pollution;

"disposal" has the same meaning as in the Waste Framework Directive and related terms must be construed accordingly;
"emission" means—

(*a*) in relation to a Part A installation, the direct or indirect release of substances, vibrations, heat or noise from individual or diffuse sources in the installation into the air, water or land,
(*b*) in relation to a Part B installation, the direct release of substances or heat from individual or diffuse sources in the installation into the air,
(*c*) in relation to Part A mobile plant, the direct or indirect release of substances, vibrations, heat or noise from the mobile plant into the air, water or land,
(*d*) in relation to Part B mobile plant, the direct release of substances or heat from the mobile plant into the air, and
(*e*) in relation to a waste operation not falling within paragraph (a) to (d), the direct or indirect release of substances, vibrations, heat or noise from individual or diffuse sources related to the operation into the air, water or land;

"the End-of-Life Vehicles Directive" means Directive 2000/53/EC of the European Parliament and of the Council on end-of life vehicles;
"enforcement notice" has the meaning given in regulation 36(1);
"environmental permit" has the meaning given in regulation 13(1);
"establishment" has the same meaning as in the Waste Framework Directive;
"excluded waste operation" has the meaning given in regulation 4;
"exempt waste operation" has the meaning given in regulation 5;
"exemption registration authority" has the meaning given in paragraph 2 of Schedule 2;
"hazardous waste", except in Section 5.1 of Part 2 of Schedule 1, has the meaning given by—

(*a*) in England, regulation 6 of the Hazardous Waste (England and Wales) Regulations 2005,
(*b*) in Wales, regulation 6 of the Hazardous Waste (Wales) Regulations 2005;

"installation" means (except where used in the definition of "excluded plant" in Section 5.1 of Part 2 of Schedule 1)—

(*a*) a stationary technical unit where one or more activities are carried on, and
(*b*) any other location on the same site where any other directly associated activities are carried on, and references to an installation include references to part of an installation;

"the IPPC Directive" means Council Directive 96/61/EC concerning integrated pollution prevention and control;
"landfill" has the meaning given in Article 2(g) of the Landfill Directive;
"landfill closure notice" means a closure notice served under paragraph 10 of Schedule 10;
"the Landfill Directive" means Council Directive 1999/31/EC on the landfill of waste, as read with Council Decision 2003/33/EC establishing criteria and procedures for the acceptance of waste at landfills pursuant to Article 16 of and Annex II to Directive 1999/31/EC;
"local authority" has the meaning given in regulation 6;
"mobile plant" means plant which—

(*a*) is not an installation,
(*b*) is used to carry on an activity or waste operation, and

(*c*) where not used to carry on a Part A activity, is designed to move or be moved whether on roads or other land;

"non-hazardous waste", except in Section 5.1 of Part 2 of Schedule 1, means waste which is not hazardous waste;

"operator" has the meaning given in regulation 7;

"Part A installation", "Part A(1) installation", "Part A(2) installation" and "Part B installation" have the meanings given in regulation 3(2);

"Part A mobile plant", "Part A(1) mobile plant", "Part A(2) mobile plant" and "Part B mobile plant" have the meanings given in regulation 3(3);

"pollution" means any emission as a result of human activity which may—

(*a*) be harmful to human health or the quality of the environment,
(*b*) cause offence to a human sense,
(*c*) result in damage to material property, or
(*d*) impair or interfere with amenities and other legitimate uses of the environment;

"public register" has the meaning given by regulation 46(1);

"recovery" has the same meaning as in the Waste Framework Directive and related terms must be construed accordingly;

"regulated facility" has the meaning given by regulation 8;

"regulator" means the authority on whom functions are conferred by regulation 32, or by a direction under regulation 33;

"relevant function" has the meaning given by regulation 9;

"revocation notice" means a notice served under regulation 22(3);

"rule-making authority" means—

(*a*) in relation to a regulated facility for which a local authority is the regulator, the appropriate authority, and
(*b*) in relation to any other regulated facility, the Agency;

"standard facility" means a regulated facility described in standard rules published under regulation 26(5);

"SED activity" means an activity falling within section 7 of Part 2 of Schedule 1;

"SED installation" means—

(*a*) a stationary technical unit where one or more SED activities are carried on, and
(*b*) any other location on the same site where any other directly associated activities are carried on;

"suspension notice" has the meaning given in regulation 37(1);

"undertaking" has the same meaning as in the Waste Framework Directive;

"waste", except where otherwise defined, means anything that—

(*a*) is waste for the purposes of the Waste Framework Directive, and
(*b*) is not excluded from the scope of that Directive by Article 2(1) of that Directive;

["waste battery or accumulator" has the meaning given by Article 3(7) of the Batteries Directive, but does not include any waste which is excluded from the scope of that Directive by Article 2(2);][1]

"the Waste Framework Directive" means Directive 2006/12/EC of the European Parliament and of the Council on waste;

"the Waste Incineration Directive" means Directive 2000/76/EC of the European Parliament and of the Council on the incineration of waste;

"waste oil" means mineral-based lubricating or industrial oil which has become unfit for the use for which it was originally intended and, in particular, used combustion engine oil, gearbox oil, mineral lubricating oil, oil for turbines and hydraulic oil;

"waste operation" means recovery or disposal of waste;

"WEEE" has the meaning given by Article 3(*b*) of the WEEE Directive;

"WEEE Directive" means Directive 2002/96/EC of the European Parliament and of the Council on waste electrical and electronic equipment; and

"working day" means a day other than—

(*a*) a Saturday or a Sunday,
(*b*) Good Friday or Christmas Day, or
(*c*) a day which is a bank holiday under the Banking and Financial Dealings Act 1971.

(2) Where the duration of a period of time is expressed as being from one event to another event, that period—

(*a*) starts on the day on which the first event occurs, and
(*b*) ends on the day on which the second event occurs.

(3) In these Regulations, a power to give a direction includes a power to vary or revoke it.

Amendments—[1] Definitions of "the Batteries Directive" and "waste battery or accumulator" inserted by the Waste Batteries and Accumulators Regulations, SI 2009/890 reg 92, Sch 8 para 2(1), (2) with effect from 5 May 2009.

3 Interpretation: activities, installations and mobile plant

(1) In these Regulations—

"Part A activity" means a Part A(1) activity or a Part A(2) activity;

"Part A(1) activity" means an activity falling within Part A(1) of any Section in Part 2 of Schedule 1;

"Part A(2) activity" means an activity falling within Part A(2) of any Section in Part 2 of Schedule 1; and

"Part B activity" means an activity falling within Part B of any Section in Part 2 of Schedule 1.

(2) In these Regulations—

"Part A installation" means a Part A(1) installation or a Part A(2) installation;

"Part A(1) installation" means an installation where a Part A(1) activity is carried on, including an installation also carrying on a Part A(2) activity or a Part B activity;

"Part A(2) installation" means an installation where a Part A(2) activity is carried on, not being a Part A(1) installation but including an installation also carrying on a Part B activity; and

"Part B installation" means, subject to Sections 2.2, 5.1 and 6.4 of Part 2 of Schedule 1, an installation where a Part B activity is carried on, not being a Part A installation.

(3) In these Regulations—

"Part A mobile plant" means Part A(1) mobile plant or Part A(2) mobile plant;

"Part A(1) mobile plant" means mobile plant used to carry on a Part A(1) activity, including plant also carrying on a Part A(2) activity or a Part B activity;

"Part A(2) mobile plant" means mobile plant used to carry on a Part A(2) activity, not being Part A(1) mobile plant but including plant also carrying on a Part B activity; and

"Part B mobile plant" means mobile plant used to carry out a Part B activity, not being Part A mobile plant.

SCHEDULE 1
ACTIVITIES

Regulations 2(1) and 3

PART 2
ACTIVITIES

CHAPTER 1
ENERGY ACTIVITIES

SECTION 1.1
COMBUSTION ACTIVITIES

Interpretation of Section 1.1

1 In this Section "recovered oil" means waste oil which has been processed before being used.

Part A(1)

(*a*) Burning any fuel in an appliance with a rated thermal input of 50 or more megawatts.

(*b*) Unless carried on as part of a Part A(2) or Part B activity, burning any—

(i) waste oil;

(ii) recovered oil; or

(iii) fuel manufactured from, or comprising, any other waste,

in an appliance with a rated thermal input of 3 or more megawatts, but less than 50 megawatts.

Interpretation and application of Part A(1)

1 For the purpose of paragraph (*a*), where two or more appliances with an aggregate rated thermal input of 50 megawatts or more are operated on the same site by the same operator those appliances must be treated as a single appliance with a rated thermal input of 50 megawatts or more.

2 Nothing in this Part of this Section applies to burning fuels in an appliance installed on an offshore platform situated on, above or below those parts of the sea adjacent to England and Wales from the low water mark to the seaward baseline of the United Kingdom territorial sea.

3 In paragraph 2, "offshore platform" means any fixed or floating structure which—

(*a*) is used for the purposes of or in connection with the production of petroleum; and

(*b*) in the case of a floating structure, is maintained on a station during the course of production,

but does not include any structure where the principal purpose of the use of the structure is the establishment of the existence of petroleum or the appraisal of its characteristics, quality or quantity or the extent of any reservoir in which it occurs.

4 In paragraph 3, "petroleum" includes any mineral oil or relative hydrocarbon and natural gas existing in its natural condition in strata but does not include coal or bituminous shales or other stratified deposits from which oil can be extracted by destructive distillation.

5 In paragraph (*b*)(iii), "fuel" does not include gas produced by biological degradation of waste in a landfill that does not require a permit under these Regulations.

Part B

Unless falling within Part A(1)(*a*) of this Section—

(*a*) Burning any fuel (other than a fuel mentioned in Part A(1)(*b*)) in—

(i) a boiler;
(ii) a furnace;
(iii) a gas turbine; or
(iv) a compression ignition engine,

with a net rated thermal input of 20 or more megawatts, but a rated thermal input of less than 50 megawatts.

(*b*) Burning any—

(i) waste oil;
(ii) recovered oil;
(iii) solid fuel which has been manufactured from waste by an activity involving the application of heat,

in an appliance with a rated thermal input of less than 3 megawatts.

(*c*) Burning fuel manufactured from or including waste (other than a fuel mentioned in paragraph (*b*)) in any appliance with a net rated thermal input of 0.4 or more megawatts, but a rated thermal input of less than 3 megawatts—

(i) which is used together with other appliances which each have a rated thermal input of less than 3 megawatts; and
(ii) where the aggregate net rated thermal input of all the appliances is at least 0.4 megawatts.

Interpretation and application of Part B

1 This Part does not apply to any activity falling within Part A(1) or Part A(2) of Section 5.1.

2 In this Part, "net rated thermal input" is the rate at which fuel can be burned at the maximum continuous rating of the appliance multiplied by the net calorific value of the fuel and expressed as megawatts thermal.

3 In paragraph (*c*), "fuel" does not include gas produced by biological degradation of waste.

SECTION 1.2
GASIFICATION, LIQUEFACTION AND REFINING ACTIVITIES

Part A(1)

(*a*) Refining gas where this is likely to involve the use of 1,000 or more tonnes of gas in any period of 12 months.

(*b*) Reforming natural gas.

(*c*) Operating coke ovens.

(*d*) Coal or lignite gasification.

(*e*) Producing gas from oil or other carbonaceous material or from mixtures thereof, other than from sewage, unless the production is carried out as part of an activity which is a combustion activity (whether or not that combustion activity is described in Section 1.1).

(*f*) Purifying or refining any product of any of the activities falling within paragraphs (*a*) to (*e*) or converting it into a different product.

(*g*) Refining mineral oils.

(*h*) The loading, unloading, handling or storage of, or the physical, chemical or thermal treatment of—

(i) crude oil;
(ii) stabilised crude petroleum;
(iii) crude shale oil;
(iv) where related to another activity described in this paragraph, any associated gas or condensate; or
(v) emulsified hydrocarbons intended for use as a fuel.

(*i*) The further refining, conversion or use (otherwise than as a fuel or solvent) of the product of any activity falling within paragraphs (*g*) or (*h*) in the manufacture of a chemical.

(*j*) Activities involving the pyrolysis, carbonisation, distillation, liquefaction, gasification, partial oxidation, or other heat treatment of—

(i) coal (other than the drying of coal);
(ii) lignite;
(iii) oil;
(iv) other carbonaceous material; or
(v) mixtures thereof, otherwise than with a view to making charcoal.

(*k*) Odorising natural gas or liquefied petroleum gas where that activity is related to a Part A activity.

Interpretation and application of Part A(1)

1 Paragraph (*j*) does not include—

(*a*) the use of any substance as a fuel;
(*b*) the incineration of any substance as a waste;
(*c*) any activity for the treatment of sewage or sewage sludge.

2 In paragraph (*j*), the heat treatment of oil, other than distillation, does not include the heat treatment of waste oil or waste emulsions containing oil in order to recover the oil from aqueous emulsions.

3 In this Part, "carbonaceous material" includes such materials as charcoal, coke, peat, rubber and wood, but does not include wood which has not been chemically treated.

Part A(2)

(*a*) Refining gas where this activity does not fall within Part A(1)(*a*) of this Section.

Part B

(*a*) Odorising natural gas or liquefied petroleum gas, except where that activity is related to a Part A activity.
(*b*) Blending odorant for use with natural gas or liquefied petroleum gas.
(*c*) The storage of petrol in stationary storage tanks at a terminal, or the loading or unloading at a terminal of petrol into or from road tankers, rail tankers or inland waterway vessels.
(*d*) The unloading of petrol into stationary storage tanks at a service station, if the total quantity of petrol unloaded into such tanks at the service station in any period of 12 months is likely to be 500m3 or more.
(*e*) Motor vehicle refuelling activities at an existing service station after the prescribed date, if the petrol refuelling throughput at the existing service station in any period of 12 months is, or is likely to be, 3500m3 or more.
(*f*) Motor vehicle refuelling activities at new service stations, if the petrol refuelling throughput at the service station in any period of 12 months is likely to be 500m3 or more.

Interpretation of Part B

1 In this Part—

"existing service station" means a service station—

(*a*) which is put into operation; or
(*b*) for which planning permission under the Town and Country Planning Act 1990 was granted,

before 31st December 2009;

"inland waterway vessel" means a vessel, other than a sea-going vessel, having a total dead weight of 15 or more tonnes;

"new service station" means a service station which is put into operation on or after 31st December 2009, other than an existing service station;

"petrol" means any petroleum derivative (other than liquefied petroleum gas), with or without additives, having a Reid vapour pressure of 27.6 or more kilopascals, which is intended for use as a fuel for motor vehicles;

"prescribed date" means—

(*a*) if an application for the grant or variation of an environmental permit is made on or before 1st January 2010—

(i) if the application is granted, the date of grant,
(ii) if the application is refused and the applicant appeals against the refusal, the date of the appeal determination or the date the appeal is withdrawn, or
(iii) if the application is refused, and the applicant does not appeal against the refusal, the day after the last day on which an appeal could have been brought; or

(*b*) if no such application is made, 1st January 2010;

"service station" means any premises where petrol is dispensed to motor vehicle fuel tanks from stationary storage tanks;

"terminal" means any premises which are used for the storage and loading of petrol into road tankers, rail tankers or inland waterway vessels.

2 Any other expressions used in this Part which are also used in Directive 94/63/EC on the control of volatile organic compound (VOC) emissions resulting from the storage of petrol and its distribution from terminals to service stations have the same meaning as in that Directive.

CHAPTER 2

PRODUCTION AND PROCESSING OF METALS

SECTION 2.1
FERROUS METALS

Interpretation of Section 2.1

1 In this Section, "ferrous alloy" means an alloy of which iron is the largest constituent, or equal to the largest constituent, by weight, whether or not that alloy also has a non-ferrous metal content greater than any percentage specified in Section 2.2.

Part A(1)

(*a*) Roasting or sintering metal ore, including sulphide ore, or any mixture of iron ore with or without other materials.

(*b*) Producing, melting or refining iron or steel or any ferrous alloy, including continuous casting, except where the only furnaces used are—

(i) electric arc furnaces with a designed holding capacity of less than 7 tonnes, or

(ii) cupola, crucible, reverbatory, rotary, induction, vacuum, electro-slag or resistance furnaces.

(*c*) Processing ferrous metals and their alloys by using hot-rolling mills with a production capacity of more than 20 tonnes of crude steel per hour.

(*d*) Loading, unloading or otherwise handling or storing more than 500,000 tonnes in total in any period of 12 months of iron ore, except in the course of mining operations, or burnt pyrites.

Part A(2)

(*a*) Unless falling within Part A(1)(*b*) of this Section producing pig iron or steel, including continuous casting, in a plant with a production capacity of more than 2.5 tonnes per hour.

(*b*) Operating hammers in a forge, the energy of which is more than 50 kilojoules per hammer, where the calorific power used is more than 20 megawatts.

(*c*) Applying protective fused metal coatings with an input of more than 2 tonnes of crude steel per hour.

(*d*) Casting ferrous metal at a foundry with a production capacity of more than 20 tonnes per day.

Part B

(*a*) Unless falling within Part A(1)(*b*) of this Section, producing pig iron or steel, including continuous casting, in a plant with a production capacity of 2.5 or less tonnes per hour.

(*b*) Unless falling within Part A(2)(*a*) or (*d*) of this Section, producing, melting or refining iron or steel or any ferrous alloy (other than producing pig iron or steel, including continuous casting) using—

(i) one or more electric arc furnaces, none of which has a designed holding capacity of 7 or more tonnes; or

(ii) a cupola, crucible, reverberatory, rotary, induction, electro-slag or resistance furnace.

(*c*) Desulphurising iron, steel or any ferrous alloy.

(*d*) Heating iron, steel or any ferrous alloy (whether in a furnace or other appliance) to remove grease, oil or any other non-metallic contaminant (including such operations as the removal by heat of plastic or rubber covering from scrap cable) unless—

(i) it is carried on in one or more furnaces or other appliances the primary combustion chambers of which have in aggregate a rated thermal input of less than 0.2 megawatts;

(ii) it does not involve the removal by heat of plastic or rubber covering from scrap cable or of any asbestos contaminant; and

(iii) it is not related to any other activity falling within this Part of this Section.

(*e*) Unless falling within Part A(1) or Part A(2) of this Section, casting iron, steel or any ferrous alloy from deliveries of 50 or more tonnes of molten metal.

Section 2.2
Non-Ferrous Metals

Interpretation and application of Section 2.2

1 In this Section "non-ferrous metal alloy" means an alloy which is not a ferrous alloy, as defined in Section 2.1.

2 Part A(1)(*c*) to (*h*) and Part B do not apply to hand soldering, flow soldering or wave soldering.

Part A(1)

(*a*) Unless falling within Part A(2) of this Section, producing non-ferrous metals from ore, concentrates or secondary raw materials by metallurgical, chemical or electrolytic activities.

(*b*) Melting, including making alloys, of non-ferrous metals, including recovered products (refining, foundry casting etc) where—

(i) the plant has a melting capacity of more than 4 tonnes per day for lead or cadmium or 20 tonnes per day for all other metals; and

(ii) any furnace (other than a vacuum furnace), bath or other holding vessel used in the plant for the melting has a design holding capacity of 5 or more tonnes.

(*c*) Except where the activity is related to an activity described in Part A(2)(*a*), or Part B(*a*), (*d*) or (*e*) of this Section, refining any non-ferrous metal or alloy, other than the electrolytic refining of copper.

(*d*) Producing, melting or recovering by chemical means or by the use of heat, lead or any lead alloy, if—

(i) the activity may result in the release into the air of lead; and

(ii) in the case of lead alloy, the percentage by weight of lead in the alloy in molten form is more than 23 per cent if the alloy contains copper and 2 per cent in other cases.

(*e*) Recovering any gallium, indium, palladium, tellurium, or thallium if the activity may result in their release into the air.

(*f*) Producing, melting or recovering (whether by chemical means or by electrolysis or by the use of heat) cadmium or mercury or any alloy containing more than 0.05 per cent by weight of either of those metals or both in aggregate.

(*g*) Mining zinc or tin bearing ores where the activity may result in the release into water of cadmium or any compound of cadmium in a concentration which is greater than the background concentration.

(*h*) Manufacturing or repairing involving the use of beryllium or selenium or an alloy containing one or both of those metals, if the activity may result in the release into the air of any substance in paragraph 6(3) of Part 1; but an activity does not fall within this paragraph by reason of it involving an alloy that contains beryllium if that alloy in molten form contains less than 0.1 per cent by weight of beryllium and the activity falls within Part B(*a*) or (*d*) of this Section.

(i) Pelletising, calcining, roasting or sintering any non-ferrous metal ore or any mixture of such ore and other materials.

Interpretation of Part A(1)

1 In paragraph (*g*), "background concentration" means any concentration of cadmium or any compound of cadmium which would be present in the release irrespective of any effect the activity may have had on the composition of the release and, without prejudice to the generality of the foregoing, includes such concentration of those substances as is present in—

(*a*) water supplied to the site where the activity is carried on;
(*b*) water abstracted for use in the activity; and
(*c*) precipitation onto the site on which the activity is carried on.

Part A(2)

(*a*) Melting, including making alloys, of non-ferrous metals, including recovered products (refining, foundry casting, etc) where—

(i) the plant has a melting capacity of more than 4 tonnes per day for lead or cadmium or 20 tonnes per day for all other metals, and no furnace (other than a vacuum furnace), bath or other holding vessel used in the plant for the melting has a design holding capacity of 5 or more tonnes; or

(ii) the plant uses a vacuum furnace of any design holding capacity.

Part B

(*a*) Melting, including making alloys, of non-ferrous metals (other than tin or any alloy which in molten form contains 50 per cent or more by weight of tin), including recovered products (refining, foundry casting, etc) in plant with a melting capacity of 4 tonnes or less per day for lead or cadmium or 20 tonnes or less per day for all other metals.

(*b*) The heating in a furnace or any other appliance of any non-ferrous metal or non-ferrous metal alloy for the purpose of removing grease, oil or any other non-metallic contaminant, including such operations as the removal by heat of plastic or rubber covering from scrap cable, if not related to another activity described in this Part of this Section; but an activity does not fall within this paragraph if—

(i) it involves the use of one or more furnaces or other appliances the primary combustion chambers of which have in aggregate a net rated thermal input of less than 0.2 megawatts; and

(ii) it does not involve the removal by heat of plastic or rubber covering from scrap cable or of any asbestos contaminant.

(*c*) Melting zinc or a zinc alloy in conjunction with a galvanising activity at a rate of 20 or less tonnes per day.

(*d*) Melting zinc, aluminium or magnesium or an alloy of one or more of these metals in conjunction with a die-casting activity at a rate of 20 or less tonnes per day.

(*e*) Unless falling within Part A(1) or Part A(2) of this Section, the separation of copper, aluminium, magnesium or zinc from mixed scrap by differential melting.

Interpretation and application of Part B

1 In this Part "net rated thermal input" is the rate at which fuel can be burned at the maximum continuous rating of the appliance multiplied by the net calorific value of the fuel and expressed as megawatts thermal.

2 When determining the extent of an installation carrying on an activity within paragraph (*e*), any location where the associated storage or handling of scrap which is to be heated as part of that activity is carried on, other than a location where scrap is loaded into a furnace, must be ignored.

SECTION 2.3
SURFACE TREATING METALS AND PLASTIC MATERIALS

Part A(1)

(*a*) Unless falling within Part A(2) of this Section, surface treating metals and plastic materials using an electrolytic or chemical process where the aggregated volume of the treatment vats is more than 30m³.

Part A(2)

(*a*) Surface treating metals and plastic materials using an electrolytic or chemical process where the aggregated volume of the treatment vats is more than 30m³ and where the activity is carried on at the same installation as one or more activities falling within—

(i) Part A(2) or Part B of Section 2.1;

(ii) Part A(2) or Part B of Section 2.2; or

(iii) Part A(2) or Part B of Section 6.4.

Part B

(*a*) Any process for the surface treatment of metal which is likely to result in the release into air of any acid-forming oxide of nitrogen and which does not fall within Part A(1) or Part A(2) of this Section.

CHAPTER 3
MINERAL INDUSTRIES

SECTION 3.1
PRODUCTION OF CEMENT AND LIME

Part A(1)

(*a*) Producing cement clinker or producing and grinding cement clinker.

(*b*) Producing lime—

(i) in kilns or other furnaces with a production capacity of more than 50 tonnes per day; or

(ii) if the activity is likely to involve the heating in any period of 12 months of 5,000 or more tonnes of calcium carbonate or calcium magnesium carbonate or both in aggregate.

Part A(2)

(*a*) Unless falling with Part A(1) of this Section, grinding cement clinker.

(*b*) Unless falling within Part A(1) of Section 2.1 or 2.2, grinding metallurgical slag in plant with a grinding capacity of more than 250,000 tonnes in any period of 12 months.

Part B

(*a*) Storing, loading or unloading cement or cement clinker in bulk prior to further transportation in bulk.

(*b*) Blending cement in bulk or using cement in bulk other than at a construction site, including the bagging of cement and cement mixtures, the batching of ready-mixed concrete and the manufacture of concrete blocks and other cement products.

(*c*) Slaking lime for the purpose of making calcium hydroxide or calcium magnesium hydroxide.

(*d*) Producing lime where the activity is not likely to involve the heating in any period of 12 months of 5,000 or more tonnes of calcium carbonate or calcium magnesium carbonate or both in aggregate.

SECTION 3.2
ACTIVITIES INVOLVING ASBESTOS

Interpretation of Section 3.2

1 In this Section "asbestos" means any of the following fibrous silicates: actinolite, amosite, anthophyllite, chrysotile, crocidolite and tremolite.

Part A(1)

(*a*) Producing asbestos or manufacturing products based on or containing asbestos.

(*b*) Stripping asbestos from railway vehicles except—

(i) in the course of the repair or maintenance of the vehicle;

(ii) in the course of recovery operations following an accident; or

(iii) where the asbestos is permanently bonded in cement or in any other material (including plastic, rubber or resin).

(*c*) Destroying a railway vehicle by burning if asbestos has been incorporated in, or sprayed on to, its structure.

Part B

(*a*) Unless related to an activity falling within Part A(1) of this Section, the industrial finishing of—

(i) asbestos cement;

(ii) asbestos cement products;
(iii) asbestos fillers;
(iv) asbestos filters;
(v) asbestos floor coverings;
(vi) asbestos friction products;
(vii) asbestos insulating board;
(viii) asbestos jointing, packaging and reinforcement material;
(ix) asbestos packing;
(x) asbestos paper or card; or
(xi) asbestos textiles.

SECTION 3.3
MANUFACTURING GLASS AND GLASS FIBRE

Part A(1)

(*a*) Manufacturing glass fibre.

(*b*) Manufacturing glass frit or enamel frit and its use in any activity where that activity is related to its manufacture and the aggregate quantity of such substances manufactured in any period of 12 months is likely to be 100 or more tonnes.

Part A(2)

(*a*) Manufacturing glass, unless falling within Part A(1) of this Section, where the melting capacity of the plant is more than 20 tonnes per day.

Part B

Unless falling within Part A(1) or Part A(2) of this Section—

(*a*) Manufacturing glass at any location with the capacity to make 5,000 or more tonnes of glass in any period of 12 months, and any activity involving the use of glass which is carried on at any such location in conjunction with its manufacture.

(*b*) Manufacturing glass where the use of lead or any lead compound is involved.

(*c*) Manufacturing any glass product where lead or any lead compound has been used in the manufacture of the glass except—

(i) making products from lead glass blanks; or
(ii) melting, or mixing with another substance, glass manufactured elsewhere to produce articles such as ornaments or road paint.

(*d*) Polishing or etching glass or glass products in the course of any manufacturing activity if—

(i) hydrofluoric acid is used; or
(ii) hydrogen fluoride may be released into the air.

(*e*) Manufacturing glass frit or enamel frit and its use in any activity where that activity is related to its manufacture.

SECTION 3.4
PRODUCTION OF OTHER MINERAL FIBRES

Part A(1)

(*a*) Unless falling within Part A(1) or Part A(2) of Section 3.3, melting mineral substances in plant with a melting capacity of more than 20 tonnes per day.

(*b*) Unless falling within Part A(1) of Section 3.3, producing any fibre from any mineral.

SECTION 3.5
OTHER MINERAL ACTIVITIES

Part A(2)

(*a*) Manufacturing cellulose fibre reinforced calcium silicate board using unbleached pulp.

Part B

(*a*) Unless falling within Part A(1) or Part A(2) of any Section, the crushing, grinding or other size reduction, other than the cutting of stone, or the grading, screening or heating of any designated mineral or mineral product except where the operation of the activity is unlikely to result in the release into the air of particulate matter.

(*b*) Any of the following activities unless carried on at an exempt location—

(i) crushing, grinding or otherwise breaking up coal, coke or any other coal product;
(ii) screening, grading or mixing coal, coke or any other coal product;
(iii) loading or unloading petroleum coke, coal, coke or any other coal product except unloading on retail sale.

(*c*) The crushing, grinding or other size reduction, with machinery designed for that purpose, of bricks, tiles or concrete.

(*d*) Screening the product of any activity described in paragraph (*c*).

(*e*) Coating road stone with tar or bitumen.

(*f*) Loading, unloading, or storing pulverised fuel ash in bulk prior to further transportation in bulk.

(*g*) The fusion of calcined bauxite for the production of artificial corundum.

Interpretation and application of Part B

1 In this Part—

"coal" includes lignite;

"designated mineral or mineral product" means—

(*a*) clay, sand and any other naturally occurring mineral other than coal;
(*b*) metallurgical slag;
(*c*) boiler or furnace ash produced from the burning of coal, coke or any other coal product;
(*d*) gypsum which is a by-product of any activity;

"exempt location" means—

(*a*) any premises used for the sale of petroleum coke, coal, coke or any coal product where the throughput of such substances at those premises in any period of 12 months is in aggregate likely to be less than 10,000 tonnes; or
(*b*) any premises to which petroleum coke, coal, coke or any coal product is supplied only for use there;

"retail sale" means sale to the final customer.

2 This Part does not apply to any activity carried on underground.

SECTION 3.6
CERAMIC PRODUCTION

Part A(1)

(*a*) Manufacturing ceramic products (including roofing tiles, bricks, refractory bricks, tiles, stoneware or porcelain) by firing in kilns, where—

(i) the kiln production capacity is more than 75 tonnes per day; or
(ii) the kiln capacity is more than 4m3 and the setting density is more than 300 kg/m3,

and a reducing atmosphere is used other than for the purposes of colouration.

Part A(2)

(*a*) Unless falling within Part A(1) of this Section, manufacturing ceramic products (including roofing tiles, bricks, refractory bricks, tiles, stoneware or porcelain) by firing in kilns, where—

(i) the kiln production capacity is more than 75 tonnes per day; or
(ii) the kiln capacity is more than 4m3 and the setting density is more than 300 kg/m3.

Part B

(*a*) Unless falling within Part A(1) or A(2) of this Section, firing heavy clay goods or refractory materials (other than heavy clay goods) in a kiln.
(*b*) Vapour glazing earthenware or clay with salts.

Interpretation of Part B

1 In this Part—

"clay" includes a blend of clay with ash, sand or other materials;

"refractory material" means material (such as fireclay, silica, magnesite, chrome-magnesite, sillimanite, sintered alumina, beryllia and boron nitride) which is able to withstand high temperatures and to function as a furnace lining or in other similar high temperature applications.

CHAPTER 4

THE CHEMICAL INDUSTRY

Interpretation of Chapter 4

1 In Part A(1) of the Sections of this Chapter, "producing" means producing in a chemical plant by chemical processing for commercial purposes substances or groups of substances listed in the relevant Sections.

SECTION 4.1
ORGANIC CHEMICALS

Interpretation of Section 4.1

1 In this Section, "pre-formulated resin or pre-formulated gel coat" means any resin or gel coat which has been formulated before being introduced into polymerisation or co-polymerisation activity, whether or not the resin or gel coat contains a colour pigment, activator or catalyst.

Part A(1)

(*a*) Producing organic chemicals such as—

(i) hydrocarbons (linear or cyclic, saturated or unsaturated, aliphatic or aromatic);

(ii) organic compounds containing oxygen, such as alcohols, aldehydes, ketones, carboxylic acids, esters, ethers, peroxides, phenols, epoxy resins;

(iii) organic compounds containing sulphur, such as sulphides, mercaptans, sulphonic acids, sulphonates, sulphates and sulphones and sulphur heterocyclics;

(iv) organic compounds containing nitrogen, such as amines, amides, nitrous-, nitro- or azo-compounds, nitrates, nitriles, nitrogen heterocyclics, cyanates, isocyanates, di-isocyanates and di-isocyanate prepolymers;

(v) organic compounds containing phosphorus, such as substituted phosphines and phosphate esters;

(vi) organic compounds containing halogens, such as halocarbons, halogenated aromatic compounds and acid halides;

(vii) organometallic compounds, such as lead alkyls, Grignard reagents and lithium alkyls;

(viii) plastic materials, such as polymers, synthetic fibres and cellulose-based fibres;

(ix) synthetic rubbers;

(x) dyes and pigments;

(xi) surface-active agents.

(*b*) Producing any other organic compounds not described in paragraph (*a*).

(*c*) Polymerising or co-polymerising any unsaturated hydrocarbon or vinyl chloride (other than a pre-formulated resin or pre-formulated gel coat which contains any unsaturated hydrocarbon) which is likely to involve, in any period of 12 months, the polymerisation or co-polymerisation of 50 or more tonnes of any of those materials, or any combination of those materials in aggregate.

(*d*) Any activity involving the use in any period of 12 months of 1 or more tonnes of toluene di-isocyanate or other di-isocyanate of comparable volatility or, where partly polymerised, the use of partly polymerised di-isocyanates or prepolymers containing 1 or more tonnes of those monomers, if the activity may result in a release into the air which contains such a di-isocyanate monomer.

(*e*) The flame bonding of polyurethane foams or polyurethane elastomers.

(*f*) Recovering—

(i) carbon disulphide;

(ii) pyridine or any substituted pyridine.

(*g*) Recovering or purifying acrylic acid, substituted acrylic acid or any ester of acrylic acid or of substituted acrylic acid.

Part B

(*a*) Unless falling within Part A(1) of this Section, any activity where the carrying on of the activity by the person concerned at the location in question is likely to involve the use in any 12 month period of 5 tonnes or more of any di-isocyanate or of any partly polymerised di-isocyanate or, in aggregate, of both.

(*b*) Cutting polyurethane foams or polyurethane elastomers with heated wires.

(*c*) Any activity for the polymerisation or co-polymerisation of any pre-formulated resin or pre-formulated gel coat which contains any unsaturated hydrocarbon, where the activity is likely to involve, in any period of 12 months, the polymerisation or co-polymerisation of 100 or more tonnes of unsaturated hydrocarbon.

(*d*) Unless falling within Part A(1) of this Section, any activity involving the use of toluene di-isocyanate or partly polymerised di-isocyanate if—

(i) less than 1 tonne of toluene di-isocyanate monomer is likely to be used in any 12 month period; and

(ii) the activity may result in a release into the air which contains toluene di-isocyanate.

SECTION 4.2
INORGANIC CHEMICALS

Part A(1)

(*a*) Producing inorganic chemicals such as—

(i) gases, such as ammonia, hydrogen chloride, hydrogen fluoride, hydrogen cyanide, hydrogen sulphide, oxides of carbon, sulphur compounds, oxides of nitrogen, hydrogen, oxides of sulphur, phosgene;

(ii) acids, such as chromic acid, hydrofluoric acid, hydrochloric acid, hydrobromic acid, hydroiodic acid, phosphoric acid, nitric acid, sulphuric acid, oleum and chlorosulphonic acid;

(iii) bases, such as ammonium hydroxide, potassium hydroxide, sodium hydroxide;

(iv) salts, such as ammonium chloride, potassium chlorate, potassium carbonate, sodium carbonate, perborate, silver nitrate, cupric acetate, ammonium phosphomolybdate;

(v) non-metals, metal oxides, metal carbonyls or other inorganic compounds such as calcium carbide, silicon, silicon carbide, titanium dioxide;

(vi) halogens or interhalogen compound comprising two or more of halogens, or any compound comprising one or more of those halogens and oxygen.

(*b*) Unless falling within any other Section, any manufacturing activity which is likely to result in the release into the air of any hydrogen halide (other than the manufacture of glass or the coating, plating or surface treatment of metal) or which is likely to result in the release into the air or water of any halogen or any of the compounds mentioned in paragraph (*a*)(vi) (other than the treatment of water).

(*c*) Unless falling within any other Section, any manufacturing activity involving the use of hydrogen cyanide or hydrogen sulphide.

(*d*) Unless falling within any other Section, any manufacturing activity (other than the application of a glaze or vitreous enamel) involving the use of, or the use or recovery of, any compound of any of the following elements—

(i) antimony;
(ii) arsenic;
(iii) beryllium;
(iv) gallium;
(v) indium;
(vi) lead;
(vii) palladium;
(viii) platinum;
(ix) selenium;
(x) tellurium;
(xi) thallium,

where the activity may result in the release into the air of any of those elements or compounds or the release into water of any substance listed in paragraph 7 of Part 1.

(*e*) Recovering any compound of cadmium or mercury.

(*f*) Unless falling within any other Section, any manufacturing activity involving the use of mercury or cadmium or any compound of either element or which may result in the release into air of either of those elements or their compounds.

(*g*) Unless carried on as part of any other activity within this Schedule—

(i) recovering, concentrating or distilling sulphuric acid or oleum;
(ii) recovering nitric acid;
(iii) purifying phosphoric acid.

(*h*) Unless falling within any other Section, any activity (other than the combustion or incineration of carbonaceous material as defined in the Interpretation of Part A(1) of Section 1.2) which is likely to result in the release into the air of any acid-forming oxide of nitrogen.

(*i*) Unless carried on as part of any other activity within this Schedule, recovering ammonia.

(*j*) Extracting any magnesium compound from sea water.

SECTION 4.3
CHEMICAL FERTILISER PRODUCTION

Part A(1)

(*a*) Producing (including any blending which is related to their production) phosphorus, nitrogen or potassium based fertilisers (simple or compound fertilisers).

(*b*) Converting chemical fertilisers into granules.

SECTION 4.4
PLANT HEALTH PRODUCTS AND BIOCIDES

Part A(1)

(*a*) Producing plant health products or biocides.

(*b*) Formulating such products if this may result in the release into water of any substance listed in paragraph 7 of Part 1 in a quantity which, in any period of 12 months, is greater than the background quantity by more than the amount specified in that paragraph for that substance.

SECTION 4.5
PHARMACEUTICAL PRODUCTION

Part A(1)

(*a*) Producing pharmaceutical products using a chemical or biological process.

(*b*) Formulating such products if this may result in the release into water of any substance listed in paragraph 7 of Part 1 in a quantity which, in any period of 12 months, is greater than the background quantity by more than the amount specified in that paragraph for that substance.

SECTION 4.6
EXPLOSIVES PRODUCTION

Part A(1)

(*a*) Producing explosives.

SECTION 4.7
MANUFACTURING ACTIVITIES INVOLVING CARBON DISULPHIDE OR AMMONIA

Part A(1)

(*a*) Unless falling within Part A(2) of Section 6.7, any manufacturing activity which may result in the release of carbon disulphide into the air.

(*b*) Any activity for the manufacture of a chemical which may result in the release of ammonia into the air other than an activity in which ammonia is only used as a refrigerant.

SECTION 4.8
THE STORAGE OF CHEMICALS IN BULK

Part B

(*a*) The storage in tanks, other than in tanks for the time being forming part of a powered vehicle, of any of the substances listed below except where the total storage capacity of the tanks installed at the location in question in which the relevant substance may be stored is less than the figure specified below in relation to that substance—

(i) one or more acrylates, 20 tonnes (in aggregate);
(ii) acrylonitrile, 20 tonnes;
(iii) anhydrous ammonia, 100 tonnes;
(iv) anhydrous hydrogen fluoride, 1 tonne;
(v) toluene di-isocyanate, 20 tonnes;
(vi) vinyl chloride monomer, 20 tonnes;
(vii) ethylene, 8,000 tonnes.

CHAPTER 5
WASTE MANAGEMENT

SECTION 5.1
INCINERATION AND CO-INCINERATION OF WASTE

Interpretation of Section 5.1

1 In this Section—

"co-incineration" means the use of wastes as a regular or additional fuel in a co-incineration plant or the thermal treatment of waste for the purpose of disposal in a co-incineration plant;

"co-incineration plant" means any stationary or mobile plant whose main purpose is the generation of energy or production of material products, and—

(*a*) which uses wastes as a regular or additional fuel; or
(*b*) in which waste is thermally treated for the purpose of disposal.

If co-incineration takes place in such a way that the main purpose of the plant is not the generation of energy or production of material products but rather the thermal treatment of waste, the plant must be regarded as an incineration plant.

This definition covers the site and the entire plant including all co-incineration lines, waste reception, storage, on site pre-treatment facilities, waste-, fuel- and air-supply systems, boiler, facilities for the treatment of exhaust gases, on-site facilities for treatment or storage of residues and waste water, stack devices and systems for controlling incineration operations, recording and monitoring incineration conditions, but does not cover co-incineration in an excluded plant;

"excluded plant" means—

(*a*) a plant treating only the following wastes—

(i) vegetable waste from agriculture and forestry,
(ii) vegetable waste from the food processing industry, if the heat generated is recovered,
(iii) fibrous vegetable waste from virgin pulp production and from production of paper from pulp, if it is co-incinerated at the place of production and the heat generated is recovered,
(iv) wood waste with the exception of wood waste which may contain halogenated organic compounds or heavy metals as a result of treatment with wood-preservatives or coating, and which includes in particular such wood waste originating from construction and demolition waste,
(v) cork waste,
(vi) radioactive waste,
(vii) animal carcasses as regulated by Regulation (EC) No 1774/2002 of the European Parliament and of the Council of 3 October 2002 laying down health rules concerning animal by-products not intended for human consumption, or
(viii) waste resulting from the exploration for, and the exploitation of, oil and gas resources from off-shore installations and incinerated on board the installation; and

(*b*) an experimental plant used for research, development and testing in order to improve the incineration process and which treats less than 50 tonnes of waste per year;

"hazardous waste" means any solid or liquid waste as defined in regulation 6 of (in relation to England) the Hazardous Waste (England and Wales) Regulations 2005 or (in relation to Wales) the Hazardous Waste (Wales) Regulations 2005 except for—

(*a*) combustible liquid wastes including waste oils provided that they meet the following criteria—

(i) the mass content of polychlorinated aromatic hydrocarbons, for example polychlorinated biphenyls or pentachlorinated phenol, amounts to concentrations not higher than those set out in the relevant Community legislation,

(ii) these wastes are not rendered hazardous by virtue of containing other constituents listed in Schedule 2 to (in relation to England) the Hazardous Waste (England and Wales) Regulations 2005, or (in relation to Wales) the Hazardous Waste (Wales) Regulations 2005 in quantities or in concentrations which are inconsistent with the achievement of the objectives set out in Article 4 of the Waste Framework Directive, and

(iii) the net calorific value amounts to at least 30 MJ per kilogramme;

(*b*) any combustible liquid wastes which cannot cause, in the flue gas directly resulting from their combustion, emissions other than those from gasoil as defined in Article 1(1) of Council Directive 93/12/EEC relating to the sulphur content of certain liquid fuels or a higher concentration of emissions than those resulting from the combustion of gasoil as so defined;

"incineration plant" means any stationary or mobile technical unit and equipment dedicated to the thermal treatment of wastes with or without recovery of the combustion heat generated, including—

(*a*) the incineration by oxidation of waste; and

(*b*) other thermal treatment processes such as pyrolysis, gasification or plasma processes in so far as the substances resulting from the treatment are subsequently incinerated.

This definition covers the site and the entire incineration plant including all incineration lines, waste reception, storage, on site pre-treatment facilities, waste-fuel and air-supply systems, boiler, facilities for the treatment of exhaust gases, on-site facilities for treatment or storage of residues and waste water, stack, devices and systems for controlling incineration operations recording and monitoring incineration conditions, but does not cover incineration in an excluded plant;

"non-hazardous waste" means waste which is not hazardous waste;

"waste" means any solid or liquid waste as defined in Article 1(*a*) of the Waste Framework Directive.

Part A(1)

(*a*) The incineration of hazardous waste in an incineration plant.

(*b*) Unless carried on as part of any other Part A(1) activity, the incineration of hazardous waste in a co-incineration plant.

(*c*) The incineration of non-hazardous waste in an incineration plant with a capacity of 1 tonne or more per hour.

(*d*) Unless carried on as part of any other activity in this Part, the incineration of hazardous waste in a plant which is not an incineration plant or a co-incineration plant.

(*e*) Unless carried on as part of any other activity in this Part, the incineration of non-hazardous waste in a plant which is not an incineration plant or a co-incineration plant but which has a capacity of 1 tonne or more per hour.

(*f*) The incineration, other than incidentally in the course of burning landfill gas or solid or liquid waste, of any gaseous compound containing halogens in a plant which is not an incineration plant or a co-incineration plant.

Part A(2)

(*a*) The incineration of non-hazardous waste in an incineration plant with a capacity of less than 1 tonne per hour.

(*b*) Unless carried on as part of any other Part A activity, the incineration of non-hazardous waste in a co-incineration plant.

(*c*) The incineration of animal carcasses in a plant, which is not an incineration plant or a co-incineration plant, with a capacity of more than 10 tonnes per day but less than 1 tonne per hour.

Part B

(*a*) The incineration of non-hazardous waste in a plant which is—

(i) not an incineration plant or a co-incineration plant, and

(ii) on premises where there is plant, other than incineration plant or co-incineration plant, which has an aggregate capacity of 50 kilogrammes or more per hour but less than 1 tonne per hour.

(*b*) The cremation of human remains.

Application of Part B

1 When determining the extent of an installation carrying on an activity within Part B, any location of the following description must be ignored: any location where the associated storage or handling of wastes and residues which are to be incinerated as part of that activity is carried on, other than a location where the associated storage or handling of animal remains intended for burning in an incinerator used wholly or mainly for the incineration of such remains or residues from the burning of such remains in such an incinerator is carried on.

SECTION 5.2
DISPOSAL OF WASTE BY LANDFILL

Part A(1)

(*a*) The disposal of waste in a landfill—

(i) receiving more than 10 tonnes of waste in any day, or

(ii) with a total capacity of more than 25,000 tonnes,

but excluding disposals in a landfill taking only inert waste.

SECTION 5.3
DISPOSAL OF WASTE OTHER THAN BY INCINERATION OR LANDFILL

Part A(1)

(*a*) The disposal of hazardous waste (other than by incineration or landfill) in a facility with a capacity of more than 10 tonnes per day.

(*b*) The disposal of waste oils (other than by incineration or landfill) in a facility with a capacity of more than 10 tonnes per day.

(*c*) Disposal of non-hazardous waste in a facility with a capacity of more than 50 tonnes per day by—

(i) biological treatment, not being treatment specified in any paragraph other than paragraph D8 of Annex IIA to the Waste Framework Directive, which results in final compounds or mixtures which are discarded by means of any of the operations numbered D1 to D12 in that Annex (D8), or

(ii) physico-chemical treatment, not being treatment specified in any paragraph other than paragraph D9 in Annex IIA to the Waste Framework Directive, which results in final compounds or mixtures which are discarded by means of any of the operations numbered D1 to D12 in that Annex (for example, evaporation, drying, calcination, etc) (D9).

Interpretation and application of Part A(1)

1 In paragraph (*b*) "disposal" means the processing or destruction of waste oil as well as its storage and tipping above ground.

2 This Part does not apply to the treatment of—

(*a*) waste soil; or

(*b*) contaminated material, substances or products, for the purpose of remedial action with respect to land or controlled waters, as defined in section 104 of the Water Resources Act 1991,

by means of mobile plant.

3 The reference to a D paragraph number in brackets at the end of paragraphs (*c*)(i) and (ii) is to the number of the corresponding paragraph in Annex IIA of the Waste Framework Directive (disposal operations).

SECTION 5.4
RECOVERY OF WASTE

Part A(1)

(*a*) Recovering by distillation of any oil or organic solvent.

(*b*) Cleaning or regenerating carbon, charcoal or ion exchange resins by removing matter which is, or includes, any substance listed in paragraphs 6 to 8 of Part 1.

(*c*) Unless carried on as part of any other Part A activity, recovering hazardous waste in a plant with a capacity of more than 10 tonnes per day by means of the following operations—

(i) the use principally as a fuel or other means to generate energy (R1),

(ii) solvent reclamation/regeneration (R2),

(iii) recycling/reclamation of inorganic materials other than metals and metal compounds (R5),

(iv) regeneration of acids or bases (R6),

(v) recovering components used for pollution abatement (R7),

(vi) recovery of components from catalysts (R8),

(vii) oil re-refining or other reuses of oil (R9).

Interpretation and application of Part A(1)

1 Paragraphs (*a*) and (*b*) of this Part do not apply to—

(*a*) distilling oil for the production or cleaning of vacuum pump oil; or (*b*) an activity which is ancillary to and related to another activity, whether described in this Schedule or not, which involves the production or use of the substance which is recovered, cleaned or regenerated,

except where the activity involves distilling more than 100 tonnes per day.

2 This Part does not apply to the treatment of—

(*a*) waste soil; or

(*b*) contaminated material, substances or products, for the purpose of remedial action with respect to land or controlled waters, as defined in section 104 of the Water Resources Act 1991,

by means of mobile plant.

3 The reference to an R paragraph number in brackets at the end of paragraphs (*c*)(i) to (vii) is to the number of the corresponding paragraph in Annex IIB of the Waste Framework Directive (recovery operations).

Section 5.5
The Production of Fuel From Waste

Part A(1)

(*a*) Making solid fuel (other than charcoal) from waste by any process involving the use of heat.

CHAPTER 6
OTHER ACTIVITIES

Section 6.1
Paper, Pulp and Board Manufacturing Activities

Part A(1)

(*a*) Producing, in industrial plant, pulp from timber or other fibrous materials.

(*b*) Producing, in industrial plant, paper and board where the plant has a production capacity of more than 20 tonnes per day.

(*c*) Any activity associated with making paper pulp or paper, including activities connected with the recycling of paper such as de-inking, if the activity may result in the release into water of any substance in paragraph 7 of Part 1 in a quantity which, in any period of 12 months, is greater than the background quantity by more than the amount specified in that paragraph in relation to that substance.

Interpretation of Part A(1)

1 In paragraph (*c*), "paper pulp" includes pulp made from wood, grass, straw and similar materials and references to the making of paper are to the making of any product using paper pulp.

Part A(2)

(*a*) Manufacturing wood particleboard, oriented strand board, wood fibreboard, plywood, cement-bonded particleboard or any other composite wood-based board.

Section 6.2
Carbon Activities

Part A(1)

(*a*) Producing carbon or hard-burnt coal or electro graphite by means of incineration or graphitisation.

Section 6.3
Tar and Bitumen Activities

Part A(1)

(*a*) The following activities—

(i) distilling tar or bitumen in connection with any process of manufacture, or

(ii) heating tar for the manufacture of electrodes or carbon-based refractory materials,

where the activity is likely to involve the use in any period of 12 months of 5 or more tonnes of tar or of bitumen or both in aggregate.

Part B

(*a*) Any activity not falling within Part A(1) of this Section or of Section 6.2 involving—

(i) heating, but not distilling, tar or bitumen in connection with any manufacturing activity, or

(ii) oxidising bitumen by blowing air through it, at plant where no other activities described in any Section in this Schedule are carried on,

where the carrying on of the activity is likely to involve the use in any period of 12 months of 5 or more tonnes of tar or bitumen or both in aggregate.

Interpretation of Part B

1 In this Part "tar" and "bitumen" include pitch.

SECTION 6.4
COATING ACTIVITIES, PRINTING AND TEXTILE TREATMENTS

Part A(1)

(*a*) Applying or removing a coating material containing any tributyltin compound or triphenyltin compound, if carried on at a shipyard or boatyard where vessels of a length of 25 metres or more can be built, maintained or repaired.

(*b*) Pre-treating (by operations such as washing, bleaching or mercerization) or dyeing fibres or textiles in plant with a treatment capacity of more than 10 tonnes per day.

(*c*) Treating textiles if the activity may result in the release into water of any substance in paragraph 7 of Part 1 in a quantity which, in any period of 12 months, is greater than the background quantity by more than the amount specified in that paragraph in relation to that substance.

Part A(2)

(*a*) Unless falling within Part A(1) of this Section, surface treating substances, objects or products using organic solvents, in particular for dressing, printing, coating, degreasing, waterproofing, sizing, painting, cleaning or impregnating, in plant with a consumption capacity of more than 150 kg per hour or more than 200 tonnes per year.

Part B

(*a*) Unless falling within Part A(1) or Part A(2) of this Section or Part A(2)(*c*) of Section 2.1, any process (other than for the repainting or re-spraying of or of parts of aircraft or road or railway vehicles) for applying to a substrate, or drying or curing after such application, printing ink or paint or any other coating material as, or in the course of, a manufacturing activity, where the process may result in the release into the air of particulate matter or of any volatile organic compound and is likely to involve the use in any period of 12 months of—

(i) 20 or more tonnes of printing ink, paint or other coating material which is applied in solid form,
(ii) 20 or more tonnes of any metal coating which is sprayed on in molten form,
(iii) 25 or more tonnes of organic solvents in respect of any cold set web offset printing activity or any sheet fed offset litho printing activity, or
(iv) 5 or more tonnes of organic solvents in respect of any activity not mentioned in sub-paragraph (iii).

(*b*) Unless falling within Part A(2) of this Section, repainting or re-spraying road vehicles or parts of them if the activity may result in the release into the air of particulate matter or of any volatile organic compound and the carrying on of the activity is likely to involve the use of 1 or more tonne of organic solvents in any period of 12 months.

(*c*) Repainting or re-spraying aircraft or railway vehicles or parts of them if the activity may result in the release into the air of particulate matter or of any volatile organic compound and the carrying on of the activity is likely to involve the use in any period of 12 months of—

(i) 20 or more tonnes of any paint or other coating material which is applied in solid form,
(ii) 20 or more tonnes of any metal coatings which are sprayed on in molten form, or
(iii) 5 or more tonnes of organic solvents.

Interpretation and application of Part B

1 In this Part—

"aircraft" includes gliders and missiles;

"coating material" means paint, printing ink, varnish, lacquer, dye, any metal oxide coating, any adhesive coating, any elastomer coating, any metal or plastic coating and any other coating material.

2 The amount of organic solvents used in an activity must be calculated as—

(*a*) the total input of organic solvents into the process, including both solvents contained in coating materials and solvents used for cleaning or other purposes; less

(*b*) any organic solvents that are removed from the process for re-use or for recovery for re-use.

3 When determining the extent of an installation carrying on an activity within Part B any location where the associated cleaning of used storage drums prior to painting or their incidental handling in connection with such cleaning is carried on must be ignored, unless that location forms part of an SED installation.

SECTION 6.5
THE MANUFACTURE OF DYESTUFFS, PRINTING INK AND COATING MATERIALS

Part B

(*a*) Unless falling within Part A(1) or Part A(2) of any other Section—

(i) manufacturing or formulating printing ink or any other coating material containing, or involving the use of, an organic solvent, where the carrying on of the activity is likely to involve the use of 100 or more tonnes of organic solvents in any period of 12 months,

(ii) manufacturing any powder for use as a coating material where there is the capacity to produce 200 tonnes or more of such powder in any period of 12 months.

Interpretation of Part B

1 In this Part, "coating material" has the same meaning as in Section 6.4.

2 The amount of organic solvents used in an activity must be calculated as—

(*a*) the total input of organic solvents into the process, including both solvents contained in coating materials and solvents for cleaning or other purposes; less

(*b*) any organic solvents, not contained in coating materials, that are removed from the process for re-use or for recovery for re-use.

SECTION 6.6
TIMBER ACTIVITIES

Part A(1)

(*a*) Curing, or chemically treating, as part of a manufacturing process, timber or products wholly or mainly made of wood if any substance in paragraph 7 of Part 1 is used.

Part B

(*a*) Unless falling within Part A(2) of Section 6.1, manufacturing products wholly or mainly of wood at any works if the activity involves a relevant activity and the throughput of the works in any period of 12 months is likely to be more than—

(i) 10,000 cubic metres in the case of works at which wood is only sawed, or wood is sawed and subjected to excluded activities, or

(ii) 1,000 cubic metres in any other case.

Interpretation of Part B

1 In this Part—

"excluded activity" means any relevant activity (other than sawing) which, ignoring any sawing carried on at the works, would be unlikely to result in the release into the air of any substance in paragraph 6(3) of Part 1 in a quantity capable of causing significant harm;

"relevant activity" means the sawing, drilling, sanding, shaping, turning, planing, curing or chemical treatment of wood;

"throughput" means the amount of wood which is subjected to a relevant activity, but where wood is subject to two or more relevant activities at the same works, the second and any subsequent activity must be ignored;

"wood" includes any product consisting wholly or mainly of wood; and

"works" includes a sawmill or any other premises where relevant activities are carried on.

SECTION 6.7
ACTIVITIES INVOLVING RUBBER

Part A(2)

(*a*) Manufacturing new tyres (but not remoulds or retreads) if this involves the use in any period of 12 months of 50,000 or more tonnes of one or more of the following—

(i) natural rubber,

(ii) synthetic organic elastomers,

(iii) other substances mixed with them.

Part B

(*a*) Unless falling within Part A(1) or Part A(2) of any Section, the mixing, milling or blending of—

(i) natural rubber, or

(ii) synthetic organic elastomers,

if carbon black is used.

(*b*) Any activity which converts the product of an activity falling within paragraph (*a*) into a finished product if related to an activity falling within that paragraph.

SECTION 6.8
THE TREATMENT OF ANIMAL AND VEGETABLE MATTER AND FOOD INDUSTRIES

Interpretation of Section 6.8

1 In this Section—

"animal" includes a bird or a fish;

"excluded activity" means—

(*a*) any activity carried on in a farm or agricultural holding other than the manufacture of goods for sale, (*b*) the manufacture or preparation of food or drink for human consumption but excluding—

(i) the extraction, distillation or purification of animal or vegetable oil or fat otherwise than as an activity incidental to the cooking of food for human consumption,

(ii) any activity involving the use of green offal or the boiling of blood except the cooking of food (other than tripe) for human consumption,

(iii) the cooking of tripe for human consumption elsewhere than on premises on which it is to be consumed,

(*c*) the fleshing, cleaning and drying of pelts of fur-bearing mammals,
(*d*) any activity carried on in connection with the operation of a knacker's yard,
(*e*) any activity for the manufacture of soap not falling within Part A(1) of Section 4.1,
(*f*) the storage of vegetable matter not falling within any other Section,
(*g*) the cleaning of shellfish shells,
(*h*) the manufacture of starch,
(*i*) the processing of animal or vegetable matter at premises for feeding a recognised pack of hounds which have been granted an authorisation under the Animal By-Products Regulations 2005 or the Animal By-Products (Wales) Regulations 2006,
(*j*) the salting of hides or skins, unless related to any other activity listed in this Schedule,
(*k*) any activity for composting animal or vegetable matter or a combination of both, except where that activity is carried on for the purposes of cultivating mushrooms,
(*l*) any activity for cleaning, and any related activity for drying or dressing, seeds, bulbs, corms or tubers (and "related activity" means an activity being carried on by the same person at the same site),
(*m*) the drying of grain or pulses,
(*n*) any activity for the production of cotton yarn from raw cotton or for the conversion of cotton yarn into cloth;

"food" includes—

(*a*) drink,
(*b*) articles and substances of no nutritional value which are used for human consumption, and
(*c*) articles and substances used as ingredients in the preparation of food;

"green offal" means the stomach and intestines of any animal, other than poultry or fish, and their contents.

Part A(1)

(*a*) Tanning hides and skins at a plant with a treatment capacity of more than 12 tonnes of finished products per day.
(*b*) Slaughtering animals at a plant with a carcass production capacity of more than 50 tonnes per day.
(*c*) Disposing of or recycling animal carcasses or animal waste, other than by rendering or by incineration falling within Section 5.1, at a plant with a treatment capacity exceeding 10 tonnes per day of animal carcasses or animal waste or both in aggregate.
(*d*) Treating and processing materials intended for the production of food products from—

(i) animal raw materials (other than milk) at a plant with a finished product production capacity of more than 75 tonnes per day; or

(ii) vegetable raw materials at a plant with a finished product production capacity of more than 300 tonnes per day (average value on a quarterly basis).

(*e*) Treating and processing milk, the quantity of milk received being more than 200 tonnes per day (average value on an annual basis).
(*f*) Processing, storing or drying by the application of heat the whole or part of any dead animal or any vegetable matter (other than the treatment of effluent so as to permit its discharge into controlled waters or into a sewer unless the treatment involves the drying of any material with a view to its use as animal feedstuff) if the processing, storing or drying—

(i) does not fall within any other Section, or Part A(2) of this Section and is not an excluded activity; and

(ii) may result in the release into water of any substance in paragraph 7 of Part 1 in a quantity which, in any period of 12 months, is greater than the background quantity by more than the amount specified in relation to the substance in that paragraph.

Part A(2)

(*a*) Disposing of or recycling animal carcasses or animal waste by rendering at plant with a treatment capacity exceeding 10 tonnes per day of animal carcasses or animal waste or both in aggregate.

Part B

(*a*) Processing, storing or drying by the application of heat the whole or part of any dead animal or any vegetable matter (other than the treatment of effluent so as to permit its discharge into controlled waters or into a sewer unless the treatment involves the drying of any material with a view to its use as animal feedstuff) if the processing, storing or drying—

(i) does not fall within another Section, or Part A(1) or Part A(2) of this Section;

(ii) is not an excluded activity; and

(iii) may result in the release into the air of—

(*aa*) any substance in paragraph 6(3) of Part 1, or

(*bb*) any offensive smell noticeable outside the premises on which the activity is carried on.

(*b*) Breeding maggots in any case where 5 or more kg of animal matter, vegetable matter or both in aggregate, are introduced into the process in any week.

SECTION 6.9
INTENSIVE FARMING

Part A(1)

(*a*) Rearing poultry or pigs intensively in an installation with more than—

(i) 40,000 places for poultry;

(ii) 2,000 places for production pigs (over 30 kg); or

(iii) 750 places for sows.

SECTION 7
SED ACTIVITIES

Part B

(*a*) The activities listed in the table below if they are operated above the solvent consumption threshold for the activity.

Activity	*Solvent consumption threshold in tonnes/year*
Heatset web offset printing	15
Publication rotogravure	25
Other rotogravure, flexography, rotary screen printing, laminating or varnishing units	15
Rotary screen printing on textile/cardboard	30
Surface cleaning using substances or preparations which because of their content of volatile organic compounds classified as carcinogens, mutagens or toxic to reproduction under Directive 67/548/EEC on the approximation of laws, regulations and administrative provisions relating to the classification, packaging and labelling of dangerous substances are assigned or need to carry one or more of the risk phrases R45, R46, R49, R60 or R61, or halogenated VOC's which are assigned or need to carry the risk phrase R40	1
Other surface cleaning	2
Vehicle coating and vehicle refinishing	0.5
Coil coating	25
Other coating activities, including metal, plastic, textile (except rotary screen printing on textile), fabric, film and paper coating	5
Winding wire coating	5
Coating activity applied to wooden surfaces	15
Dry cleaning	0
Wood impregnation	25
Coating activity applied to leather	10
Footwear manufacture	5
Wood and plastic lamination	5
Adhesive coating	5
Manufacture of coating preparations, varnishes, inks and adhesives	100
Rubber conversion	15

Vegetable oil and animal fat extraction and vegetable oil refining activities	10
Manufacturing of pharmaceutical products	50

Interpretation and application of Part B

1 For the purposes of this Part—

"adhesive" means any preparation, including all the organic solvents or preparations containing organic solvents necessary for its proper application, which is used to adhere separate parts of a product;

"adhesive coating" means any activity in which an adhesive is applied to a surface, excluding the application of adhesive and laminating associated with printing activities;

"coating" means any preparation, including all the organic solvents or preparations containing organic solvents necessary for its proper application, which is used to provide a decorative, protective or other functional effect on a surface;

"coating activity" means any activity in which a single or a multiple application of a continuous film of a coating is applied (including a step in which the same article is printed using any technique) but does not include the coating of substrate with metals by electrophoretic and chemical spraying techniques;

"coil coating" means any activity where coiled steel, stainless steel, coated steel copper alloys or aluminium strip is coated with either a film forming or laminate coating in a continuous process;

"consumption" means the total input of organic solvents into an installation per calendar year, or any other twelve month period, less any volatile organic compounds that are recovered for reuse;

"dry cleaning" means any industrial or commercial activity using volatile organic compounds to clean garments, furnishing and similar consumer goods excluding the manual removal of stains and spots in the textile and clothing industry;

"flexography" means a printing activity using an image carrier of rubber or elastic photopolymers on which the printing areas are above the non-printing areas, and liquid inks which dry through evaporation;

"footwear manufacture" means any activity of producing complete footwear or parts of footwear;

"heat web offset printing" means a web-fed printing activity using an image carrier in which the printing and non-printing area are in the same plane, where—

(*a*) the non-printing area is treated to attract water and reject ink,
(*b*) the printing area is treated to receive and transmit ink to the surface to be printed, and
(*c*) evaporation takes place in the oven where hot air is used to heat the printed material;

"ink" means a preparation, including all the organic solvents or preparations containing organic solvents necessary for its proper application which is used in a printing activity to impress text or images on to a surface;

"laminating associated to a printing activity" means the adhering together of two or more flexible materials to produce laminates;

"manufacturing of coating preparations, varnishes, inks and adhesives" means the manufacture of coating preparations, varnishes, inks and adhesives as final products and where carried on at the same site, the manufacture of intermediates by the mixing of pigments, resins and adhesive materials with organic solvent or other carrier, including—

(*a*) dispersion and predispersion activities,
(*b*) viscosity and tint adjustments, and
(*c*) operations for filling the final product into its container;

"manufacturing of pharmaceutical products" means one or more of the following activities—

(*a*) chemical synthesis,
(*b*) fermentation,
(*c*) extraction, or
(*d*) formulation and finishing,

of pharmaceutical products and, where carried on at the same site, the manufacture of intermediate products;

"the Motor Vehicle Directive" means Council Directive 70/156/EEC on the approximation of the laws of the Member States relating to the type-approval of motor vehicles and their trailers;

"organic compound" means any compound containing at least the element carbon and one or more of hydrogen, halogens, oxygen, sulphur, phosphorus, silicon or nitrogen, with the exception of carbon oxides and inorganic carbonates and bicarbonates;

"organic solvents" means any volatile organic compound which is used alone or in combination with other agents, and without undergoing a chemical change to dissolve raw materials, products or waste materials, as a—

(*a*) cleaning agent to dissolve contaminants,
(*b*) dissolver,

(*c*) dispersion medium,
(*d*) viscosity adjuster,
(*e*) surface tension adjuster,
(*f*) plasticiser, or
(*g*) preservative;

"other coating activities" means a coating activity applied to—

(*a*) trailers, defined in categories O1, O2, O3, and O4 in the Motor Vehicle Directive,
(*b*) metallic and plastic surfaces including surfaces of airplanes, ships, trains, or
(*c*) textile, fabric, film and paper surfaces;

"printing activity" means any activity (not being a step in a coating activity) for reproducing text and/or images in which, with the use of an image carrier, ink is transferred onto any type of surface, including the use of associated varnishing, coating and laminating techniques;

"publication rotogravure" means a rotogravure printing activity used for printing paper for magazines, brochures, catalogues or similar products, using toluene-based inks;

"reuse" means the use of organic solvents recovered from an installation for any technical or commercial purpose and including use as a fuel but excluding the final disposal of such recovered organic solvent as waste;

"rotary screen printing" means a web-fed printing activity in which liquid ink which dries only through evaporation is passed onto the surface to be printed by forcing it through a porous image carrier, in which the printing area is open and the non-printing area is sealed off;

"rotogravure" means a printing activity, using a cylindrical image carrier in which the printing area is below the non-printing area and liquid inks which dry through evaporation, and in which the recesses are filled with ink and the surplus is cleaned off the non-printing area before the surface to be printed contacts the cylinder and lifts the ink from the recesses;

"rubber conversion" means—

(*a*) any activity of mixing, milling, blending, calendering, extrusion and vulcanisation of natural or synthetic rubber, and
(*b*) any ancillary operations for converting natural or synthetic rubber into a finished product;

"surface cleaning" means any activity, except dry cleaning, using organic solvents to remove contamination from the surface of material including degreasing but excluding the cleaning of equipment; and a cleaning activity consisting of more than one step before or after any other activity must be considered as one surface cleaning activity;

"varnish" means a transparent coating;

"varnishing" means an activity by which varnish or an adhesive coating for the purpose of sealing the packaging material is applied to a flexible material;

"vegetable oil and animal fat extraction and vegetable oil refining activities" means any activity to extract vegetable oil from seeds and other vegetable matter, the processing of dry residues to produce animal feed, the purification of fats and vegetable oils derived from seeds, vegetable matter or animal matter;

"vehicle coating" means a coating activity applied to the following vehicles—

(*a*) new cars, defined as vehicles of category M1 in the Motor Vehicle Directive, and of category N1 in so far as they are coated at the same installation as M1 vehicles,
(*b*) truck cabins, defined as the housing for the driver, and all integrated housing for the technical equipment, of vehicles of categories N2 and N3 in the Motor Vehicle Directive,
(*c*) vans and trucks, defined as vehicles of categories N1, N2 and N3 in the Motor Vehicle Directive, but not including truck cabins, or
(*d*) buses, defined as vehicles in categories M2 and M3 in the Motor Vehicle Directive;

"vehicle refinishing" means any industrial or commercial coating activity and associated degreasing activities performing—

(*a*) the original coating of road vehicles as defined in the Motor Vehicle Directive or part of them with refinishing-type materials, where this is carried on away from the original manufacturing line, or
(*b*) the coating of trailers (including semi-trailers) (category O in the Motor Vehicle Directive);

"volatile organic compound" or "VOC" means—

(*c*) any organic compound having a vapour pressure of 0.01 or more kPa at 293.15K or having a corresponding volatility under the particular conditions of use, or
(*d*) the fraction of creosote which exceeds a vapour pressure of 0.01 kPA at 293.15K;

"web-fed" means that the material to be printed is fed to the machine from a reel as distinct from separate sheets;

"winding wire coating" means any coating activity of metallic conductors used for winding the coils in transformers and motors, etc;

"wood and plastic lamination" means any activity to adhere together wood or plastic to produce laminated products;

"wood impregnation" means any activity giving a loading of preservative in timber.

2 An activity must be deemed to be operated above the solvent consumption threshold specified for that activity under this Part if the activity is likely to be operated above that threshold in any period of 12 months.

3 An activity listed in this Part includes the cleaning of equipment but, except for a surface cleaning activity, not the cleaning of products.

CLIMATE CHANGE LEVY
EXTRA-STATUTORY CONCESSIONS

CONTENTS

Note—These Concessions are numbered as they appear in VAT Notice 48.

7.1 Climate Change Levy: salt sector entitlement to a levy negotiated agreement

Certain provisions for relief from CCL have created the potential for acute distortion of competition within the sector producing refined salt. The sector has now signed with Government an agreement to deliver specific energy-saving targets, and Treasury intend in due course to amend the appropriate Regulations to entitle the sector to the 80 per cent rebate scheme for CCL. Pending such amendment, this ESC allows the discount to the sector with effect from 24 September 2001.

7.2 Climate Change Levy: exemption for certain recycling processes

This concession permits taxable commodities used in certain processes to be treated as being exempt from Climate Change Levy.

Customs reserve the right to refuse to apply the concession, or to withdraw it, if the Commissioners consider it is being used for avoidance of the levy.

THE ARRANGEMENTS

The concession will apply only to taxable commodities used in a recycling process where taxable commodities used in a directly competing primary process are eligible for exemption from CCL under FA 2000 Sch 6 para 18 and the Climate Change Levy (Use as Fuel) Regulations 2001, because they are not used as fuel or treated as not so used (including dual use).

For taxable commodities to be eligible for exemption all of the following criteria must be met—

- the recycling process in which they are used must be less energy intensive than the primary process;
- the recycling process must be liable to a higher CCL charge per tonne of output than the primary process; and
- the objective of the recycling process must be to produce the same output as the primary process.

"Recycling process" means a process by which a substance is manufactured primarily from materials that have been previously used.

"Primary process" means a process by which a substance is manufactured primarily from raw materials.

"Less energy intensive" means using less energy to manufacture an equal quantity of the same output.

The Commissioners must have confirmed that the relevant process is eligible before any claims for relief can be made.

7.4 Climate Change Levy: simplified bad debt relief arrangements

This concession permits gas and electricity suppliers to enter into arrangements for the administration of Climate Change Levy bad debt relief ("BDR") in a simplified manner.

Customs reserve the right to refuse to apply the concession if the Commissioners consider it is being used to avoidance of the levy.

THE ARRANGEMENTS:

Any gas or electricity supplier who wishes to use these simplified arrangements must notify the Commissioners in writing of their intention prior to making the first claim. The notification must specify the first month in which the arrangements will be utilised, and the billing systems that will be affected.

From that time all subsequent bad debt relief claims originating in the specified billing systems must be included in the arrangements.

(a) *All qualifying criteria within Climate Change Levy legislation must be met before a claim may be made.*

(b) *Each month for commercial accounts only, the supplier must calculate the total values billed to customers and the levy element of these totals. From this, a percentage of levy to total billing will be derived. All supplies liable to levy in a billing system must be included in this calculation; a random sample is not acceptable. Calculations must also be on a system-by-system basis, as combining billing systems may change the result.*

(c) *To make a claim for bad debt relief under these arrangements the supplier will apply to the debt written-off, the percentage calculated in (b) for the most recent six months prior to that in which the claim is actually being made. The percentage to be applied is the percentage that was calculated for the same taxable commodity and from the same energy billing system as that in which the debt arose.*

(d) *Should the application of the above calculations produce an inequitable result in the opinion of either party, then an equitable percentage based on best information should be agreed with*

Customs and Excise. This agreed percentage would be applied in the accounting period that the inequity is discovered. If an equitable percentage is not agreed with Customs and Excise then the normal bad debt relief rules apply.

(e) *Suppliers who opt to use these arrangements must pay back the levy element of any payments that are received after levy bad debt relief has been claimed. This must be paid back by applying the same percentage that was used to claim the original relief. Such amounts will be due in the same accounting period in which the payments was received.*

(f) *Should the arrangements prove to be unsatisfactory in that either party considers that it provides an inequitable result, it is a source of dispute or that it proves difficult or time consuming to operate or audit, then the scheme shall be withdrawn at either party's written notification. This notification will not be retrospective without prejudice to the Commissioners' right to refuse to apply the scheme on the grounds of avoidance.*

This concession will be withdrawn on 1 June 2003.

CLIMATE CHANGE LEVY
PRESS RELEASES ETC

CONTENTS

13 December 2000. Commons written answer (Hansard, 13 December 2000, Col 175)

Climate change levy: agreements with business

Mr Clappison: To ask the Chancellor of the Exchequer when he will publish agreements with business, including agreements with individual companies, groups of companies and sectors, relating to the climate change levy. [141467]

Mr Timms: Energy intensive sectors exposed to international competition—as defined by the Pollution Prevention and Control Regulations—will be entitled to 80 per cent rebate on the climate change levy in return for entering into Negotiated Agreements which will deliver demanding reductions in their energy use. These agreements are entered into with the Secretary of State for the Environment, Transport and the Regions.

8 July 2002. Business Brief 18/02

New exemption for certain recycling processes

Customs & Excise have published a new Concession, exempting certain recycling processes from Climate change levy (CCL) [see ESC 7.2 in the *Extra-statutory Concessions* section, ante]. Production processes are exempt from CCL where there is a "dual fuel" or "non-fuel" use of energy, putting recycling processes making the same products at a competitive disadvantage. The new concession exempts those environmentally friendly recycling processes as well.

SCOPE OF THE EXEMPTION

The exemption applies only to recycling processes which produce the same output as processes eligible for exemption from CCL under FA 2000 Sch 6 para 18 and the Climate change levy (Use as Fuel) Regulations 2001, because they are not used as fuel or treated as not so used (including dual uses). The relevant recycling processes must also be less energy intensive and liable to a higher CCL charge per tonne of output than the competing primary process. The full text of the concession is available from the Climate change levy team and has also been published on the Customs & Excise website.

APPLYING FOR THE EXEMPTION

Businesses and trade organisations that consider their processes are eligible for the exemption should apply in writing by means of a pro-forma. This document forms an annex to "CCL technical brief 16", which is available from Customs at the address below and on www.hmce.go-v.uk.

Businesses will not be able to claim the exemption until approval for the particular process has been confirmed by Customs & Excise, but on approval the relief can be backdated to the implementation of the levy on 1 April 2001. As Customs approve particular processes, they will confirm their eligibility on the Department's website and by means of further CCL technical briefs.

If you have any questions about the Climate change levy please contact the National Advice Service on 0845 010 9000. Further technical details about eligibility for the new exemption and a copy of the pro-forma is available from—Climate change levy team, HM Customs & Excise, Ralli Quays, 3 Stanley Street, Manchester, M60 9LA, telephone—0161 827 0924.

6 February 2003. Business Brief 02/03

New exemptions for certain non-fuel use of taxable commodities

Customs and Excise have published an extra statutory concession (ESC) exempting further non-fuel uses of taxable commodities from Climate Change Levy (CCL) [see ESC 7.5, ante]. These new exemptions are in addition to those already contained in the Climate Change Levy (Use as Fuel) Regulations 2001 (SI 2001/1138).

The new Regulations necessary will not come into force until later in year. However, from 29 January 2003 Customs and Excise will, by concession, treat those further non-fuel uses (specified below) as if they were already specified under the non-fuel use exemption.

Customs invites applications reclaiming levy already paid in respect of the new exemptions.

NEW EXEMPTIONS

The newly exempt non-fuel uses are—

- Coal, coke and natural gas used as chemical reductants in the blast furnace production of zinc and other non-ferrous metals.
- Liquid propane used in the production of ethylene where heat is provided either by combustion of the waste products or from another source.
- Coal and coke used in the recarburising of iron and steel.

- Natural gas used purely as a feedstock in the production of carbon black.
- Liquefied Petroleum Gas used as feedstock in the cracking process to produce lower olefins.
- Lower olefins used as a feedstock for conversion by chemical processes.
- Coke used in the manufacture of titanium dioxide by the chloride process.

The full text of the concession will be available from the following page on the Customs and Excise website: http://www.hmce.gov.uk/business/othertaxes/ccl.htm

APPLYING FOR A REFUND

Where a supply of a taxable commodity has already been made in respect of one of the newly exempt non-fuel uses, and the levy has been accounted for, a refund of the amount paid by the consumer can be claimed by application to Customs and Excise.

Consumers of taxable commodities can apply for a refund of levy already paid in respect of the new exemptions by completing form CCL 200X, available from the Customs and Excise National Advice Service (0845 010 9000). Claims should be submitted with the supporting evidence required in accordance with the instructions on the application form. Any claim can be backdated to the introduction of the tax on 1 April 2001.

DEADLINE FOR REFUNDS

The ESC will be withdrawn on 30 June 2003. After this date claims for refunds of levy will not be considered.

FURTHER INFORMATION

If you have any questions about the Climate Change Levy please contact the National Advice Service on 0845 010 9000. Further technical detail about the new exemptions is available from the Climate Change Levy Team, HM Customs and Excise, Ralli Quays, 3 Stanley Street, Manchester, M60 9LA. Tel: 0161– 827–0924.

Commentary—*De Voil Indirect Tax Service* **V21.124**.

10 December 2003. Business Brief 27/03

CCL: Pre-Budget Report

There were two announcements relating to climate change levy (CCL) in today's pre-Budget Report.

(I) INTERACTION WITH THE EU EMISSIONS TRADING SCHEME

An EU-wide emissions trading scheme is due to be introduced in 2005. The arrangements for the scheme are set out in the EU Emissions Trading Directive. A UK inter-departmental Government group is considering what changes may be needed to climate change policy instruments such as the CCL and the associated climate change agreements (CCAs), once the European Union's Emissions Trading Scheme (EU ETS) is introduced. This work is continuing and aims to ensure that the introduction of the EU ETS—

- is consistent with the UK's long-term emissions policy goals expressed in the Energy White Paper published in February 2003;
- is coherent with complementary measures which give equivalent incentives across sectors to reduce emissions;
- is as simple as possible to operate for business. Administration, compliance and transition costs should be kept to a minimum; and
- minimises impacts on international competitiveness and on fuel poverty.

The Government has identified the first change that will be needed to help ensure the successful introduction of the EU ETS. The EU ETS will operate alongside a number of existing climate change policy instruments. One of the main tools of climate change abatement has been the use of CCAs, which tie reductions in the CCL to negotiated agreements, and which have already delivered substantial carbon savings. Taking account of this, the Government has decided to create a level playing field between CCAs and the EU ETS, and will introduce the equivalent CCL discount for those sectors in CCAs who would like their direct emissions to be covered by the EU ETS instead of the CCA, once the scheme is up and running.

(II) CLIMATE CHANGE AGREEMENTS WITH ENERGY INTENSIVE SECTORS

The Government announced in Budget 2003 that it was reviewing the current eligibility criteria for climate change agreements, under which energy-intensive sectors can obtain 80 per cent discounts from the CCL if they agree to increase energy-efficiency or meet targets for emissions reductions. Eligibility to such agreements is currently related to the Pollution Prevention Control Regulations 2000, with the aim of protecting the competitiveness of UK industry, particularly those which are energy intensive. The Government believes that, in keeping with this original principle, there is scope to widen this eligibility while still providing strong incentives to encourage energy efficiency.

Following consultation with industry, the Government has decided that, subject to State aid approval, it will extend the eligibility criteria for CCAs during 2004. Therefore, in addition to the existing criteria, the Government will consider CCAs for sectors which meet a specific energy-intensity threshold, and will look to take account of any competitive distortions in those sectors. Further consultation with industry will take place between Pre-Budget Report 2003 and Budget 2004 on what level the energy intensity threshold should be set, on competition issues and the practicalities (including the administrative burden) of such a system.

FURTHER INFORMATION

Further information on the EU ETS can be found at the Department for Environment Food and Rural Affairs website, at www.defra.gov.uk/environment/climatechange/trading/

Further information on CCAs can be found in Notice CCL1/3 "Reliefs and special treatments for taxable supplies" available on the Customs website at www.hmce.gov.uk/forms/notices/ccl1–3 and from the Customs National Advice Service on 0845 010 9000.

23 July 2003. Business Brief 19/04

Climate change agreements with energy intensive sectors

The Government has written to trade associations setting out details of the application process for climate change agreements (CCAs) under the new extended eligibility criteria announced in Budget 2004. Having announced in Budget 2004 its intention to extend the criteria, it is now seeking information from sectors to establish which processes will qualify for agreements under the new criteria. Sectors are being invited to submit an application for any processes in their sector they believe to be eligible for a CCA under the extended arrangements.

BACKGROUND

The Government announced in Budget 2003 that it was reviewing the eligibility criteria for CCAs, under which energy-intensive sectors can obtain 80% discounts from the climate change levy if they agree to increase energy-efficiency or meet targets for emissions reductions. Eligibility to such agreements is currently related to the Pollution Prevention Control Regulations 2000, with the aim of protecting the competitiveness of UK industry, particularly for those sectors which are energy intensive. It was announced in Budget 2004 that, subject to European Commission state aid approval, the Government would extend the eligibility criteria for CCAs. In addition to the existing criteria, the Government will consider CCAs for sectors which meet a specific energy-intensity threshold, and will look to take account of any competitive distortions in those sectors.

DETAIL

To qualify under the new eligibility criteria, businesses will have to be in sectors above a threshold of energy intensity (using the definition of energy intensity set out in the Energy Products Directive relating to purchases of energy products and electricity against production value). All businesses in sectors that meet or exceed a 12% threshold of energy-intensity will be eligible to enter a CCA. Businesses in sectors that meet or exceed a 3% threshold, but are below the 12% threshold, will be eligible to enter an agreement only if they meet or exceed one of the following two international competitiveness tests—

- an import penetration ratio of 50%. This is the percentage ratio of imports to home demand (where home demand is defined as total manufacturers' sales plus imports minus exports); or
- an export to production ratio of 30%. This is the percentage ratio of exports to total manufacturers' sales.

APPLICATION PROCESS

Although any new agreements cannot start until after state aid approval has been given, the Department for Environment, Food and Rural Affairs (DEFRA), who administer CCAs, have now issued instructions and application forms for energy-intensive sectors that believe they should be entitled to eligibility under the new criteria. Sectors that have not been sent details but who wish to consider applying can obtain them from the web at www.defra.gov.uk/environment/ccl/extension.htm.

The application form is in the form of a spreadsheet that automatically makes the calculations needed to determine eligibility. If you have difficulty accessing these forms, please contact James Craig at Future Energy Solutions on 0870 190 6083.

TIMING

It is hoped that agreements made under the new arrangements will be agreed in the autumn and, subject to state aid approval being received in time, come into effect on 1 January 2005 to coincide with the introduction of the EU Emissions Trading Scheme. DEFRA are therefore requesting that applications are returned to them by 31 August 2004 (applications will, of course, be accepted after that date, but a late response will make it more difficult to draw up any agreement in time for the proposed 1 January 2005 start date).

FURTHER INFORMATION

Guidance on the CCA agreement process can be found on the DEFRA website at www.defra.gov.uk/environment/ccl/extension.htm.

Further information on CCAs can be found in Notice "CCL1/3 Reliefs and special treatments for taxable supplies" available on the Customs' website at www.hmce.gov.uk/forms/notices/ccl1–3 and from Customs National Advice Service on 0845 010 9000.

5 December 2005. Business Brief 23/05.

Extended eligibility for climate change agreements with energy intensive sectors

State aid approval has been secured from the European Commission to extend the eligibility criteria that allow sectors to enter into climate change agreements (CCAs) with the Secretary of State for the Department for Environment, Food and Rural Affairs (Defra). Under these agreements, businesses make commitments to reduce their emissions and/or improve their energy efficiency in exchange for an 80% reduction in the rates of climate change levy.

DETAIL

At present, only installations carrying out energy intensive processes in, or similar to those in, Part A of the Pollution Prevention and Control (England and Wales) Regulations, SI 2000/1973 can qualify for CCAs and benefit from the 80% tax reduction.

Providing Parliament approves the regulations needed before the changes can be brought into force, a larger number of energy intensive sectors will be eligible to enter a CCA.

The draft regulations set out the industrial processes that will be eligible for Climate Change Agreements under the new eligibility criteria. To qualify for inclusion in the draft regulations under the new criteria, businesses will have to be in sectors above a threshold of energy intensity (using a definition of energy intensity set out in the EU Taxation of Energy Products Directive which came into force on 1 January 2004). This definition states that—"An energy-intensive business shall mean a business entity ... where ...the purchases of energy products and electricity amount to at least 3% of the production value ...". There will be a one-off test of energy intensity, based on measuring a four year period of data (the lowest year's data will be discounted). The eligibility thresholds are as follows—

- all businesses in sectors that meet or exceed a 10% threshold of energy intensity; and
- businesses in sectors that meet or exceed a 3% threshold of energy intensity, but fall below the 10% threshold will be eligible to benefit if they meet or exceed the international competitiveness test of having an import penetration ratio of 50% (this is the percentage ratio of imports to home demand, where home demand is defined as total manufacturers' sales plus imports minus exports).

Defra issued instructions and application forms for energy-intensive sectors in summer 2004. The following sectors have so far concluded draft agreements under the extended arrangements, which can be signed formally once the House of Commons has approved the draft regulations and they enter into force—British Calcium Carbonate Federation, covering the production of calcium carbonate based mineral products; Contract Heating Treatment Association, covering the heat treatment of metals; British Compressed Gases Association, covering the production of industrial gases; Kaolin and Ball Clay Association, covering the production or processing of kaolinitic clay. Defra are continuing to negotiate agreements with other sectors.

Those already eligible for CCAs under the current arrangements will continue to benefit and will be unaffected by these changes.

FURTHER INFORMATION

Guidance on the CCA agreement process can be found on the Defra website at http://www.defra.gov.uk/environment/ccl/extension.htm.

Further information on CCAs can be found in Notice 'CCL1/3 Reliefs and special treatments for taxable supplies' available on HM Revenue & Customs' website at www.hmrc.gov.uk and from HM Revenue & Customs' National Advice Service on 0845 010 9000.

Commentary—*De Voil Indirect Tax Service* **V21.141**.

April 2008. Notice ET1

Notice of requirement to give security for environmental taxes

Note—See under *IPT* section, ante, for the full text of this notice which is HMRC's Statement of Practice on the circumstances where they may require security for Insurance Premium Tax, Landfill Tax, Aggregates Levy and Climate Change Levy.

CLIMATE CHANGE LEVY INDEX

Defined words and phrases are listed separately at the end.

WORDS AND PHRASES

Words in brackets indicate the context in which the word or phrase is used.

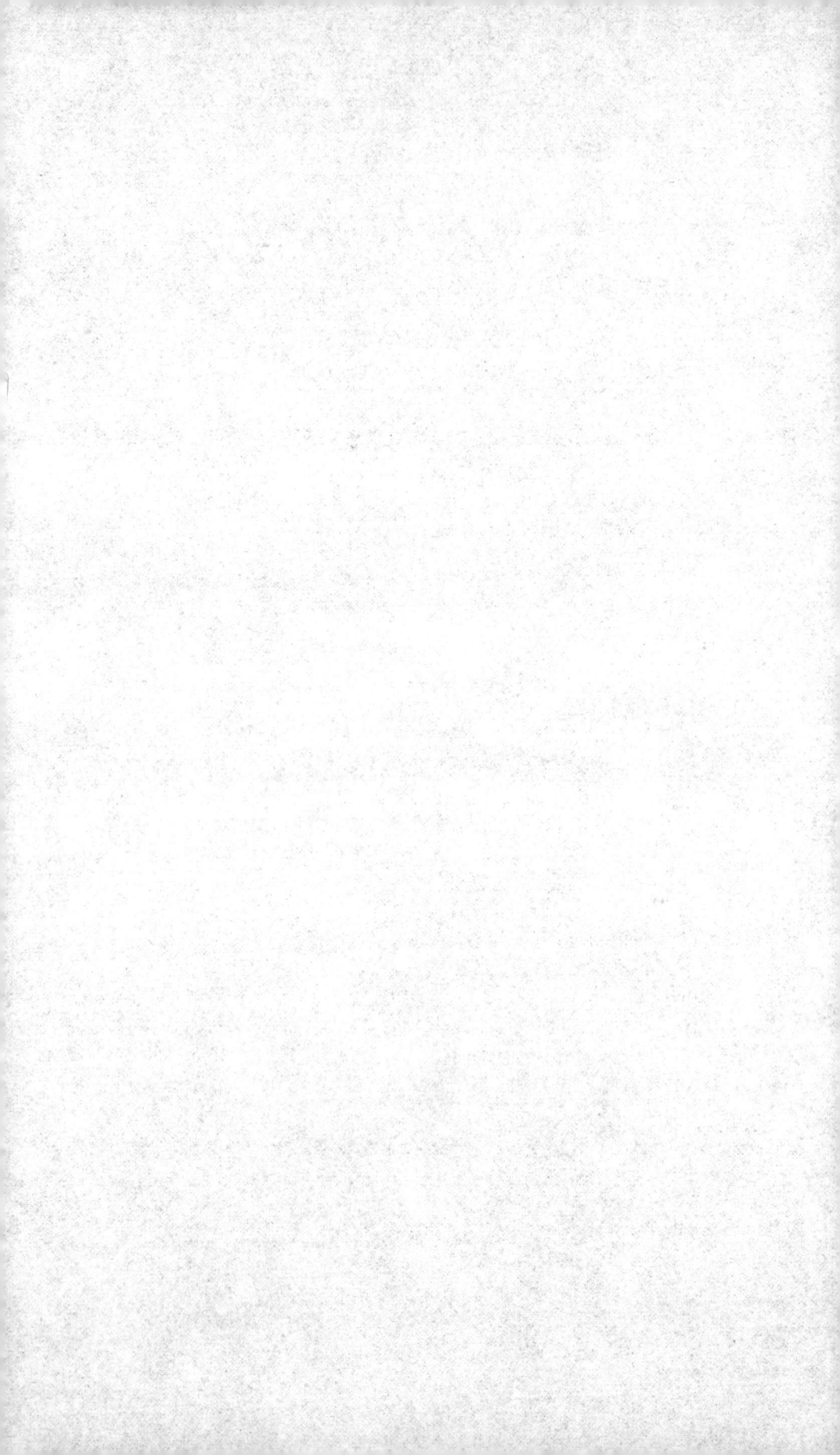